PRIBALTIYSK... HOTEL

★ ★ ★ ★

The «Pribaltiyskaya» - the largest hotel in St.Petersburg - is located on the edge of the Gulf of Finland and can accommodate 2400 guests in its fully conditioned 1200 guest rooms including suites with 1-3 bedrooms and rooms for the disabled.

The hotel offers a comprehensive variety of services both for business people and just for travellers. To ensure your comfort the Service Bureau will help you with sightseeing tours, guides, rent-a-car service, train and air plane tickets.

The «Pribaltiyskaya» has created the perfect venue for business meetings with a congress hall for 900 persons, a conference room with 250 seating capacity, fully equipped Business Center with the latest technology.

The «Pribaltiyskaya» chefs offer a good choice of international and Russian dishes and home-made pastries in the numerous in-house restaurants and banquet rooms where guests are entertained by live piano, folk music and jazz band.

Besides, there are comfortable bars and cosy cafes on each floor which are ideal for light snacks, drinks and delightful conversation.

Among the numerous facilities there is a health club including sauna with a swimming pool, massage room, bowling alleys, Ford car service, bank, dry-cleaning and laundry, Beauty Parlour, cobbler and tailor, «Baltic Star» shop. Room service is 24 hours.

You are always a welcome guest in the «Pribaltiyskaya» hotel.

PRIBALTIYSKAYA HOTEL
14, KORABLESTROITELEY ST., SAINT-PETERSBURG, 199226, RUSSIA.   TEL. 7 (812) 356-02-63 FAX 7 (812) 356-00-94

British Library Cataloguing in Publication Data
The World Travel Guide: Incorporating the ABTA/ANTOR Factfinder – 14th Edition
1. World Visitors' Guides
910'. 2'02

ISBN: 0 946393 478
ISSN: 0267 8738

Typesetting and Colour Reproduction by Alphabet Sct, London SW10; Target Litho, London EC2; Tower Litho, London EC2; Concept Bureau, London EC1; Kingswood, London N1. Paper supplied by William Guppys. Printed by Nuffield Web, Basildon. Cover Design by Warren Evans.

Editor	Sally McFall
Assistant Editors	Nonke Beyer, Huw Jones
Editorial Assistants	Sophie Howard, Daniel White
Contributors	Richard Cawthorne, Patrick Fitzgerald, Karl Herrington, Laura Le Cornu, Stephen Mulvey, Rob Parsons, Mike Taylor, Dr Glyn Williams
Production Manager	Gavin Crosswell
Advertisement Design	Warren Evans, Reid Savage
Art Editor	Karen Harkness
Cartographer	David Burles
Technical Director	Tim Smith
Technical Assistant	Mike Curtis
Group Operations Manager	David Barham
Group Operations Manager's Assistant	Ashleigh Baldwin
Customer Liaison Officers	Dean Dokubo, Waltraud Meints, Lisa Nesbit
Customer Services Administration	Dee Britton, May Chen
Chief Credit Controller	Mavis Thomas
Book Sales Director	Steve Collins
Book Sales Manager	Martin Newman
International Circulation Controllers	Peter Korniczky, Jullian Manning
Sales Director	George Armstrong
Sales Manager	Edward Thomas
Senior Key Account Manager	John Lewisohn
Features Manager	Steve Godwin Austen
USA Consultants:	
SF Communications: Director	David Frank
Sales Manager	John White
Compass (The Americas): Director	Colin Jackson
Financial Director	Bruce Law
Production Director	Brian Quinn
Publisher	Philip Barklem
Chairman	Nigel Barklem

The Publishers would like to thank all the tourist offices, embassies, high commmissions, consulates, airlines and other organisations and individuals who assisted in the preparation of this edition. Most of the photographs used in this publication were supplied by the respective tourist office, embassy or high commission. The Publishers would also like to thank other organisations and individuals whose photographs appear. Reg Prince of Visionshield Ltd, 54 Farringdon Road, London EC1R 3BL (tel/fax: +44 (171) 490 2285) supplied the airport front cover photograph.

IMPORTANT NOTICE

Columbus Press Limited is part of the Columbus Holdings Group.
Directors: Nigel Barklem; Philip Barklem; Sir Michael Grylls MP; Jeremy Isaac; Bruce Law; Brian Quinn; Nigel Wray.

World Travel Guide

COLUMBUS
PRESS

The Association of British Travel Agents (ABTA), formed in 1950, is a company limited by guarantee. It is a self-regulatory body representing over 2400 travel agents and approximately 610 tour operator Member companies throughout Britain. With many Members having branch offices, there are nearly 7000 ABTA outlets overall, accounting for over 90% of the travel trade in Britain.

ABTA, as the representative of the travel industry, maintains dialogue with governments and other authoritative bodies, both in the UK and abroad. ABTA administers a comprehensive system of financial protection in the event of a financial failure of a Member. All Members must also adhere to a strict Code of Practice in order to create a favourable trading environment for its Members and to encourage the best possible standards for consumers.

1995 ABTA CONVENTION

In 1995, the ABTA Convention will be taking place in Sun City, South Africa on October 1-6 and some 2000 delegates are expected to attend this vital travel trade event.

Commenting on the choice of location, ABTA's President, Colin Trigger, said "We have tried to match an obvious demand for ABTA to return to its well-tried formula of autumn overseas conventions while producing a cost-effective delegate package. It enables ABTA Members not just to experience the benefits of the Convention itself, but also to judge the business opportunities for a large and attractive destination country. There is no doubt that ABTA '95 will be one of the most memorable of our many overseas conventions – of which this will be the 25th."

SATOUR's General Manager for UK, Republic of Ireland and Scandinavia, Russel Barlow-Jones, said "We are very honoured in being able to host the ABTA Convention in our Explore South Africa '95 Promotional Year. This Convention will also confirm South Africa's growing conference market by highlighting the country's superb conference and incentive facilities."

'Reviewing this, the 14th edition, does raise a question: 'How did we ever manage without it?' A mature publication for a maturing industry; I commend it.'
Colin Trigger F. Inst. TT
President, ABTA

ACCESS

Johannesburg's *Jan Smuts International Airport (JNB)* is the nearest international gateway to the Convention site.

Negotiations with ABTA partner airlines have secured special return fares for Members and non-Members. Further information regarding prices will be available in May 1995.

LOCATION

Sun City is one of the premier holiday resorts in southern Africa.

The complex comprises luxury hotels, casinos, superb sporting facilities and is a well-equipped conference venue. It is located on the edge of Pilanesberg National Park, in the North-West Province of South Africa.

Sun City offers the largest and most comprehensive conference facilities in the southern hemisphere. These range from boardrooms to the 6000-seater

Superbowl. The latest addition is the new Royal Ballroom in the Entertainment Centre. A wide range of venues, plus resident stage designers, lighting and sound engineers and the full range of auxiliary equipment including audio-visual facilities, fax, telex, photocopying, secretarial and translation services are all available.

ACCOMMODATION

The resort offers four hotels. The Palace Hotel in the 'Lost City' will be the convention headquarters; however, most delegates will stay at the Cascades, Sun City and Cabanas hotels, plus the nearby park lodges. Nearly three-quarters of available on-site accommodation has been reserved for ABTA Members.

PROGRAMME

The 1995 ABTA Convention offers six days of exciting and informative events. Social activities alternate with business forums and plenary business sessions. New to this year's Convention is *Solutions,* building on the success of the *ABTA Showcase.* This business-to-business exhibition is scheduled to run for two days and will form an integral part of the 1995 Convention, serving as an ideal point to forge new business links and an opportunity to come face-to-face with the prime decision-makers in the industry.

FURTHER CONTACTS

Africa Ecology Tourism – page A27

National Parks Board – page A30

Pilanesberg National Parks – page A32

Spoornet – pages A27, A30

Sun City– page A28, A29

United Touring Company – page A38

Wilton Valley Game Ranch – page A34

For further information, please contact:

ABTA, 55-57 Newman Street, London W1P 4AH

Tel: (0171) 637 2444. Fax: (0171) 637 0713.

ALLIANCE OF CANADIAN TRAVEL ASSOCIATIONS

The Alliance of Canadian Travel Associations, also known as ACTA, is a national non-profit trade association which was established in 1977.

ACTA's mission is to represent the interests of its members, primarily retail and wholesale to the public, to governments, to suppliers and other bodies to further develop high professional standards among members, and to support and assist them in maximising their economic objectives.

ACTA's executive board of directors consists of 20 travel industry professionals working to improve the industry and assist ACTA members in reaching their professional objectives. ACTA's seven provincial associations are a powerful source for its strength as a national association. Each association is represented by a provincial president who is a full voting member on the national body's executive board of directors.

In addition to the services provided by the provincial associations, ACTA also provides the following national level programs and services:

Membership

Membership fees support the efforts and activities of the executive board and working committees of both the national and provincial associations.

Canadian Travel Industry Identification Card

This card provides photo-identification proof that the bearer is a bona-fide travel industry professional.

Conferences and international travelmarts

Another of ACTA's objectives is to raise industry professional standards by continually developing and implementing educational programs to improve the skills of agency managers and travel consultants.

'Informative and valuable commodity. The World Travel Guide certainly contains a wealth of travel-related information of importance to the industry.'
Tom Reilly, Executive Director.

ACTA Marketing Services

ACTA Marketing Services is another benefit exclusive to ACTA members. Through AMS, ACTA members receive substantial savings on many products and services.

Industry and government relations

ACTA maintains continuous and effective representation and dialogue with industry and government bodies on those issues and matters of concern and of relevance to its members.

International industry representation

ACTA keeps abreast of international developments in the travel industry and represents the views of its members worldwide through its alliance with affiliated associations in other countries.

Committees and Research

ACTA conducts constant review and research to further streamline and maximise membership benefits.

For further information, please contact:
ACTA Suite 201, 1729 Bank Street, Ottawa, Ontario, Canada KIV 7Z5
Tel: (613) 521 0474. Fax: (613) 521 0805.

AUSTRALIAN FEDERATION OF TRAVEL AGENTS

The Australian Federation of Travel Agents was founded in 1957 to establish and maintain a code of ethics for travel agents, to stimulate and promote the desire to travel, to weld into one organisation those persons involved in the sale of travel to the public and to establish a friendly relationship between principals, agents and the public.

AFTA has over 2000 members who are responsible for over 80% of the retail travel business in Australia. The Australian Council of Tour Wholesalers with 43 members has a permanent seat on the AFTA Board.

Major Activities

• Annual Conventions • AFTA Travel Insurance for consumer protection • Australian Travel Agents Qualifications Program for Managers and Consultants • AFTA travel industry identification card • Industry and Government relations • Annual Industry Research Projects • Consumer grievance and ethics service • Conciliation process for industry disputes • Visa/medical/travel administration service

'An essential reference book for every travel consultant in the world.'
John R Dart, Chief Executive

For further information, please contact:
AFTA, 3rd Floor, 309 Pitt Street, Sydney, N.S.W. 2000, Australia
Tel: (02) 264 3299. Fax: (02) 264 1085.

ASSOCATION OF NATIONAL TOURIST OFFICE REPRESENTATIVES

ANTOR, the Association of National Tourist Office Representatives in the United Kingdom, has a membership of over 80 National Tourist Offices representing countries from all over the world, with vastly different attractions, resources, geographical features and cultural heritages. This voluntary non-political organisation has been established since the early 1950s. It serves the dual role of a forum for the exchange of views and experiences of its members, and of a driving force for joint promotional activities aimed at both the trade and the consumer.

Drawing on broad knowledge and experience, ANTOR brings a fully-international approach to problems affecting all aspects of the travel industry, with which ANTOR works in close partnership. It maintains contact with the media and other organisations in the travel industry, such as ABTA, and is frequently called on for its views on matters relating to the industry as a whole.

'Most informative source of destination information.'
Pierre Claus, Executive Secretary

ANTOR thus aims, through mutual cooperation, to coordinate and improve services that government tourist offices offer to the British travel industry and to the consumer. ANTOR's regular business meetings for its members are also often addressed by leading tourism experts.

For further information, please contact:
ANTOR, 4 Bouverie Street, London EC4Y 8AX
Tel/Fax: (0171) 353 4550.

AMERICAN SOCIETY OF TRAVEL AGENTS

Integrity in Travel

The American Society of Travel Agents (ASTA) is recognized as the world's most prestigious travel trade association. The ASTA logo represents a symbol of professionalism and is recognized by travel industry professionals and travelers worldwide. When you join ASTA, you become a partner with more than 25,000 members including travel agents, tour operators, airlines, cruise lines, hoteliers, car rental companies, tourism bureaus and other travel suppliers from around the world.

ASTA has the strongest connections in the travel industry. ASTA has 92 chapters around the world in 135 countries creating a communications network that will enhance your bottom-line and enable you to expand your operations globally. If your company offers inbound services, ASTA can help you network with US and International members who are sending clients to your country. If your company sends clients to the United States, you will have professional contacts throughout the US.

'The World Travel Guide is a comprehensive worldwide reference book for all segments of the travel and tourism industry'.
**Jeanne Epping,
ASTA President and CEO**

ASTA gives you many opportunities to promote your services worldwide. You can meet thousands of travel agents, suppliers and other industry professionals or promote your company by exhibiting at the annual World Congress, the annual International Convention and four regional domestic conferences.

When you join ASTA, you will be served by a staff of 90 top-calibre individuals, trained to consider your complete satisfaction as their number one priority.

For membership details contact:
American Society of Travel Agents – World Headquarters, Suite 200, 1101 King Street, Alexandria, VA 22314 USA
Tel: (703) 739 2782. Fax: (703) 684 8319. Telex: 440203.

INSTITUTE OF AMERICAN TRAVEL & TOURISM

The Institute of Travel & Tourism was inaugurated in 1956 to set, maintain and improve standards within the travel and tourism industry and to establish a body which would recognise those attaining high standards. It aims to help managers and potential managers develop and maintain their professional knowledge by awarding a recognised professional qualification, which entitles members to use designatory letters after their names.

The Institute runs a series of one-day seminars. In 1995 some of the subjects to be covered include Brochure Production and Printing, Package Travel

Regulations Law, Technology, Financial Management and Business Strategies.

The Institute holds an Annual Conference. The 1995 Conference will be held in Nashville, USA and looks to be the most exciting conference to date. The theme will be "Y'all come back".

'The World Travel Guide would be the choice for professional travel agents to give their customers the very best service.'
Linda Gibson, Chief Executive

For further information, please contact:
ITT, 113 Victoria Street, St Albans, Hertfordshire AL1 3TJ
Tel: (01727) 854 395. Fax: (01727) 847 415.

WORLD ASSOCIATION OF TRAVEL & TOURISM

WATA, the **World Association of Travel Agencies**, is a non-profit making organisation created by independent travel agents for the benefit of all travel agencies around the world. It helps locally respected agencies combine their personal touch with the influence gained by global recognition. Since its foundation in 1949, WATA has become a truly well-respected name in the travel industry worldwide. With over 200 members from 189 cities in 84 countries, WATA today has established an international network of travel agents who enjoy some unique privileges and benefits.

WATA's basic idea is to bring local (preferably privately owned) travel agencies into an international network, so that every member is offered all the facilities and advantages of being associated with an international body – in addition to enjoying local prominence. As a consequence, a substantial volume of business to the agency's turnover can be expected.

'The World Travel Guide is the most complete source of information for a Travel Agent. It's always on my desk.'
Marco Agustoni
WATA Secretary General

WATA maintains a permanent secretariat at its headquarters in Geneva to cover the Association's administrative needs. WATA headquarters also provides information, assistance and a number of services to individual members. These include the offices of an Ombudsman between members and other sections of the travel trade, plus assistance in the recovery of outstanding payments anywhere in the world.

• The General Assembly: for unparalleled opportunities
Held every year, the WATA General Assembly provides a forum for discussion of the Association's business and an unparalleled opportunity to 'talk travel' with fellow members from the four corners of the globe.

• Regional Assemblies: for local discussions

Held every year, these shorter meetings provide the chance to discuss regional travel problems and technical difficulties.

• Senior Employees Assembly: another perspective

This new Assembly aims to familiarise employees who are actually involved in the day-to-day running of WATA agencies to become acquainted with the advantages and possibilities WATA offers.

Membership of WATA is open to any travel agency, preferably privately owned, which can prove a sound financial structure, adheres to the highest professional standards expected in the industry and enjoys a prominent standing in the local community.

All WATA members have the same rights, privileges and obligations within the association.
• Members must adhere strictly to the WATA ethics.
• Members must favour the WATA organisation.
• The collaboration between member agencies must be genuine.
• Members must assist at the general and regional assemblies.

Please apply for an application form and a copy of the Articles of Association.

For further information, please contact:
The Secretary General, WATA, PO Box 2317, CH-1211 Geneva 1, Switzerland
Tel: (022) 731 4760. Fax: (022) 732 8161.

Contents

Countries marked in green appear in colour, the section having been sponsored by the tourist board or tourism authority to help promotion of the destination for business and leisure travel. The presence of such sponsorship should not be taken to imply a different editorial approach.

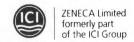

A2 **Contents**

THE PERSONAL TOUCH

FROM YOUR GLOBAL HOST

An Interactive Hospitality Service providing Professional Personnel for:

Travel • Leisure • Trade • Promotions • Special Events • Incentive Programs • Social Affairs. All customized to your individual needs

AT YOUR SERVICE

⇥ Corporate Hosts d'Affaires

Charismatic and exuberant hosts and hostesses. Designated courtesy corps for corporate hospitality, V.I.Ps., trade shows, conventions, etc.

⇥ International Escorts (Hourly, Daily, Weekly)

Multilingual and exceptional social companions, the perfect complement for all celebratory and convivial pursuits. Get-away companions - vacations, sailing, sports, leisure and adventure. For the arts, culture, sights, or whatever. These escorts are well informed and cognizant of all interesting sights and sounds of the city. They know what's happening - where and when.

"GIVE AN ESCORT". A unique gift idea for visiting business associates, clients, relatives and friends.

⇥ Business/Social intermediaries

Bilingual secretarial/travel companions - domestic and international. Executive assistants - function according to need. Independent tour guides, fashion coordinators/shopping consultants or any other special interest itinerary.

⇥ Beautiful People Unlimited

Models, entertainers, spokespersons and other creative talents available to enhance and project your company's image graciously, adding glamour, sparkle and pizzazz to any occasion, eg., publicity, presentations, special events, etc.

⇥ International Promotions

Marketing activities, public relations, global related service alliances. At your request, we will search, select and introduce any other related professional personnel or service.

⇥ Concierge Service

In addition to our comprehensive and personalized services, we also offer complementary reservation service, as a courtesy to our clients, saving them time, trouble and uncertainty by arranging entré to the city's select restaurants, nightclubs, theatres, sports events, art exhibits and other places of interest.

We are the business traveler's friends away from home

ATTENTION:
TRAVEL ORGANIZERS • HOTEL CONCIERGES
BUSINESS CONSULTANTS
Consider us your USA and International partner.
Please Note:
10% Commission fee paid for all referrals.
All major credit cards accepted

© 1995 Promtact Int'l Inc. All Rights Reserved

MEMBER
ASTA ®
American Society of Travel Agents
Integrity in Travel ®

PROMTACT
INTERNATIONAL, INC.
YOUR GLOBAL HOST

Headquarters:
1841 Broadway, Suite 1000, New York, NY 10023-7603
Phone: (212) 765-7793 • Fax: (212)765-8158
Service available Worldwide

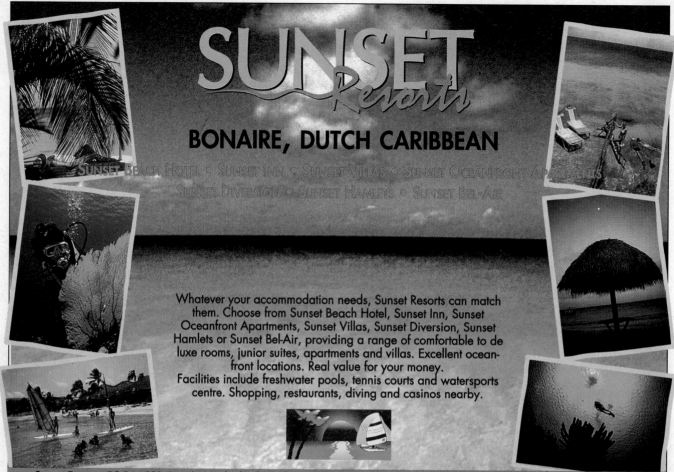

SUNSET *Resorts*

BONAIRE, DUTCH CARIBBEAN

SUNSET BEACH HOTEL • SUNSET INN • SUNSET VILLAS • SUNSET OCEANFRONT APARTMENTS
SUNSET DIVERSION • SUNSET HAMLETS • SUNSET BEL-AIR

Whatever your accommodation needs, Sunset Resorts can match them. Choose from Sunset Beach Hotel, Sunset Inn, Sunset Oceanfront Apartments, Sunset Villas, Sunset Diversion, Sunset Hamlets or Sunset Bel-Air, providing a range of comfortable to de luxe rooms, junior suites, apartments and villas. Excellent ocean-front locations. Real value for your money.
Facilities include freshwater pools, tennis courts and watersports centre. Shopping, restaurants, diving and casinos nearby.

Sunset Resorts, PO Box 333, Bonaire, Netherlands Antilles (Dutch West Indies) Tel: (5997) 8291 or 8448 • Fax: (5997) 8865 or 8118
Tel/Fax: Holland (31) 5720 610 85. Germany (49) 30 36 10718. France (33) 1 46 22 54 11. USA (305) 225 0527 Fax: (305) 225 0572

A6   **Contents**

*Each of
our luxurious rooms
or suites is individually
furnished, according to
its historic period or
flavor of location.*

*Nowhere else can
you better experience
local character and
history than in a
Grand Heritage Hotel.
Each is a unique
masterpiece featuring
architectural detail
restored to its
original splendor.*

*Experience traditional
delicacies from our hotels'
given regions suitable
to today's tastes.*

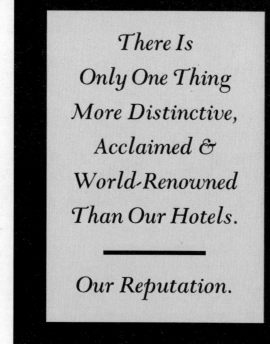

There Is
Only One Thing
More Distinctive,
Acclaimed &
World-Renowned
Than Our Hotels.

—————

Our Reputation.

*The business traveller also
can expect the extras that
make Grand Heritage Hotels
the corporate choice - from
the exclusive Heritage Club
Level to outstanding
conference facilities.*

*For travellers
accustomed to
the highest standards
of excellence
Grand Heritage Hotels
offer uncompromising
service.*

*There's a distinction to our hotels that spans centuries
and speaks to our guests from a rich and glorious past.
It is immediately discernible in each of our unique landmark hotels and is found in their classic decor brimming
with historic character. You can also experience it in the
extraordinary service that exemplifies the spirit of the
old-world and that lives on in each member of our international staff. ¶ The discriminating traveller will find
the proper mix of historic accommodations and modern
amenities that makes each Grand Heritage Hotel as
unique in service and as varied as our guests. ¶ Seek
out Grand Heritage Hotels and discover a journey
through time and a reputation that is generations in
the making.*

Accessible in all airline systems under
Grand Heritage Hotel's code GH.
Commissions paid within 48 hours.

For individual reservations call:

North America	1-800 HERITAGE
Austria	49 (06103) 55013/14
London	44 (081) 941 8276
England	44 (0800) 28 28 11
Germany	49 (06103) 55013/14
Italy	39 (02) 33 15 312
Brazil	55 (11) 251-4775
Japan	81 (33) 215-5141
Paris	33 (1) 53 76 1730
Northern Ireland	44 (0800) 28 28 11
Rep. of Ireland	44 (81) 941-8276

GrandHeritageHotels
INTERNATIONAL

USA: *410 Severn Avenue Suite 406 Annapolis Maryland 21403*
410-267-0070 Fax: 410-268-3809
LONDON: *The Pride Gallery 24A Radley Mews London England W8 6JP*
44-071-376-1777 Fax: 44-071-376-2004

For group inquiries:

USA   800-854-0070
Europe   071-376-1777

In the USA: Birmingham, Alabama • San Diego, California • Mount Dora, Florida • Chicago, Illinois • New Orleans, Louisiana • Detroit, Michigan • Aiken,
South Carolina • Nashville, Tennessee   In France: Mougins • Paris   In Italy: Sorrento   In The United Kingdom: Avon • Cheshire • County Durham •
Cumbria • Edinburgh • Glasgow • Gloucestershire • London • Northumberland • Staffordshire • Surrey • West Sussex • Wiltshire

Introducing the most important components of your CRS

Forget 'bits', 'bytes' and 'floppy disks'. It's the people behind the technology that make the difference to the service you receive.

The AMADEUS terminal that sits on your desk is your gateway into the minds of the world's most experienced travel industry professionals. This unique group of experts not only provides the pricing and booking information that you need to serve your clients better, but is also there to help you build an increasingly efficient and competitive business. Twenty-four hours a day, 365 days a year.

At AMADEUS we are not slaves to technology but we do believe in continuous development and innovation. We offer dynamic products which are increasingly powerful yet easy-to-use. What's more, your link with service providers is in 'real-time', which ensures the accuracy of information so you can have guaranteed booking confirmation within seconds. With the highest commitment to quality, it's little wonder that AMADEUS is installed in more than 22,000 travel agency offices in Europe, South America, Africa and Asia, as well as the worldwide sales offices of 90 airlines.

With AMADEUS you'll always be in the very best of company for the very best in service.

AMADEUS
GLOBAL TRAVEL DISTRIBUTION

AMADEUS spells service in any language

c/ Salvador de Madariaga, 1. 28027 Madrid. Tel. 34 1 582 01 60. Fax 34 1 582 01 88

euro ★ air aviation
YOUR FLYING PARTNER IN GREECE

FLY SMARTER. THINK CHARTER.

If your business can't afford to wait, you need to know about air charter.

Because if you're flying to more than one destination, or if your destination isn't a major hub, or if more than one of you is going, or if you hate standing in airport lines, charter can save you time and might just save you money.

So, who should you call before your next trip?
CALL NOW: (301) 725 3828.

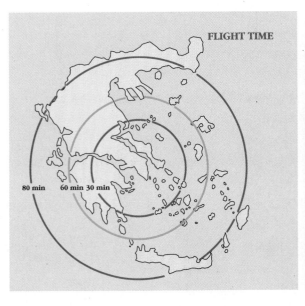

FLIGHT TIME

80 min   60 min 30 min

TO GET THERE FAST, CALL US FIRST.

EURO AIR AVIATION
Charter flight to the Greek Islands
Air taxi
Air Ambulance

Information: Tel: (301) 725 3827
(301) 725 3828
Fax: (301) 721 7519

EUR0 AIR AVIATION
65, VAS. SOFIAS AVE.
ATHENS 115 21
GREECE

The champagne of holiday destinations, France offers visitors unrivalled diversity and choice.

From the cultural and romantic delights of Paris to the quiet of its medieval villages; from the sophistication of the Côte d'Azur to the family beaches of Brittany.

Quite literally there's something for everyone in France. And the standard is consistently excellent.

France respects the good things in life, not just wine and food for which it is justly famous, but its hotels, beaches, ski resorts and unspoilt countryside have an enviable reputation worldwide.

The French also love to celebrate.

From Alsace in the north to Provence way down south, fêtes, carnivals and concerts are frequent events.

With all this, is it any surprise that France is the favourite tourist destination of the French themselves? Especially when everything is excellent value for money and there are holidays to suit every pocket.

France. For a holiday that's pure joie de vivre, there's nowhere in the world quite like it.

For more information please contact The French Government Tourist Office, 178 Piccadilly, London W1V 0AL Fax: 0171 493 6594.

FRANCE

France

FROM SORRENTO TO THE SEYCHELLES...
WE'RE TAKING THEM THERE

travel **is Europe's first TV channel** dedicated entirely to travel programmes.

travel **offers unbiased information** and quality entertainment, featuring worldwide travel programmes that fire the imagination and broaden the knowledge and understanding of holidaymakers and business travellers alike. And Travel Text offers viewers a dedicated teletext service with constantly updated travel facts and availability.

travel **broadcasts seven days a week,** twelve hours a day across Europe to a TV audience of regular travellers looking for advice, information and the latest holiday offers.

For further information call Harvey Cazaly or Louise Cottrell on +44 (0) 171 636 5401 or Fax +44 (0) 171 636 6424.

TV THAT TAKES YOU THERE

Landmark Travel Channel Ltd., 66 Newman Street, London W1P 3LA.

Barbados Plus

The Designer Caribbean

We're not just talking Barbados.

With Barbados Plus you can design Caribbean holidays just the way your clients want them. Tailor-made to suit their wishes and just one company with which you need to deal.

We don't just provide the usual services you expect: flight, meet-and-greet, ground transfers, a range of accommodation and tour representative services. With Barbados as our starting point, we offer the Greater Caribbean from Antigua in the north to Guyana in the south, a region as culturally diverse as Europe itself.

Would your client like to do more than soak up the sun on a beach in Barbados? Would they like to visit the Devil's Bridge in Antigua? Experience the mystery of Dominica's unspoilt rainforest? Or spend the day shopping and sightseeing in St Lucia? Then Barbados Plus are the people to call.

We also offer incentive group programmes, undertake conference arrangements, organise a full range of island tours and innovative activity programmes – such as our Dine-Around package: a chance to spend some special evenings at the best of Barbados' restaurants and entertainment night spots.

Whether your clients want a holiday in Barbados alone or would like a Caribbean cocktail they can mix themselves, call Barbados Plus:

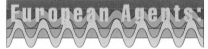

European Agents:

AIREKA Reisorganisatie bv
Singel 302, 1016 AD Amsterdam, Holland.
Tel: +31 (20) 625 0909.
Fax: +31 (20) 620 2551.

UK Agents:

Calibre Travel 67-71 Oxford Street,
London W1R 1RB, England
Tel: +44 (0) 71 287 1971.
Fax: +44 (0) 71 437 3757.

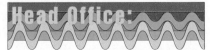

Head Office:

Remac Tours Chapel Street,
Speightstown, St Peter, Barbados WI
Tel/Fax (24 hours):+(1 809) 422 0546.

Remac Tours

Barbados Plus© is a Division of Remac Tours.

If you intend visiting Russia, take our advice:

DON'T LIMIT YOURSELF to Moscow and St. Petersburg. Discover the heart of Russia and visit Siberia! The state-owned company "Intourist" Tyumen is proud to present several of its itineraries.

The Ancient Capital of Siberia

ANCIENT TOBOLS was founded on a high hill, at the confluence of the Irtysh and Tobol rivers. At the decree of Peter the Great, Tobolsk became the capital of Siberia. The famous Tobolsk Kremlin built during his reign evokes many memories, such as the poetry of Ershov and the music of Alyabyev, both sons of Tobolsk, and tragically the fate of the last Russian Tsar, who found himself in Tobolsk against his will. Modern-day Tobolsk has particular interest for business people: the gigantic oil refinery, the fur and fishing industries, and the unique bone carvings made by master craftsmen.

Tobolsk is linked with Tyumen and neighbouring Yekaterinburg by road and rail. In summer it is accessible by river.

Hunting and Fishing Tours

"THE WHITE BIRCH under my window is covered with snow, shining like silver," wrote Sergei Yesenin. The birch tree and the birch grove are poetical symbols of Russia.

In the north of the Tyumen region is the settlement of Berezovo ('Birchville'). The opal knight Menshikov was exiled here. The settlement spread along the shores of the river Ob, amidst the taiga, where mighty cedars, white-trunked birch and majestic juniper trees grow. The berries from nature's plantations are an elixir of strength, beauty and health.

The natural wealth of the Berezovo area is legendary. The river boasts a great variety of fish, including sturgeon and salmon, and in the woods, game, squirrel, elk, reindeer, bear and hare abound. It is important to note that Berezovo is an ecologically clean region of Siberia.

There are 17 routes for fishermen and hunters available, including the "Bear Hunt", "Wolf Hunt", "Elk Hunt", "Spring and Autumn Waterfowl Hunt", "Winter Fishing", "Ice Fishing" etc.

Transport: AIRCRAFT, helicopter, land-rover, launch.

Connections: Scheduled and chartered flights. Comprehensive provision of hunting and fishing equipment. Parties are accompanied by huntsmen, doctors and guides.

You can travel from Tyumen to Berezovo on the 'Moskva' boat. The season of 'White Nights' from late May to mid-July is unforgettable.

We've told you about Tobolsk and Berezovo. In this vast region there are many such historical, well-preserved sites and modern towns and settlements. American and European specialists work in numerous oil and gas fields and refineries.

Come and visit us too!

INTOURIST TYUMEN

For further information, contact:
625000 Tyumen, Gerzena Street 74, Russia.
Tel: 242 371 or 268 042. Fax: 244 961. Telex:
735843 INTUR SU.

A22   **Contents**

A24 **Contents**

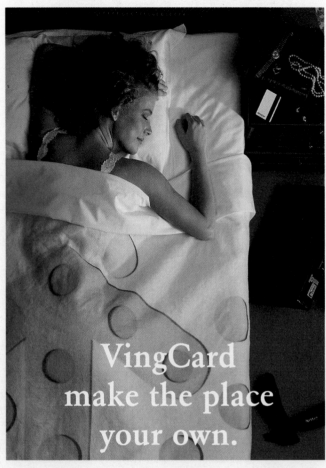

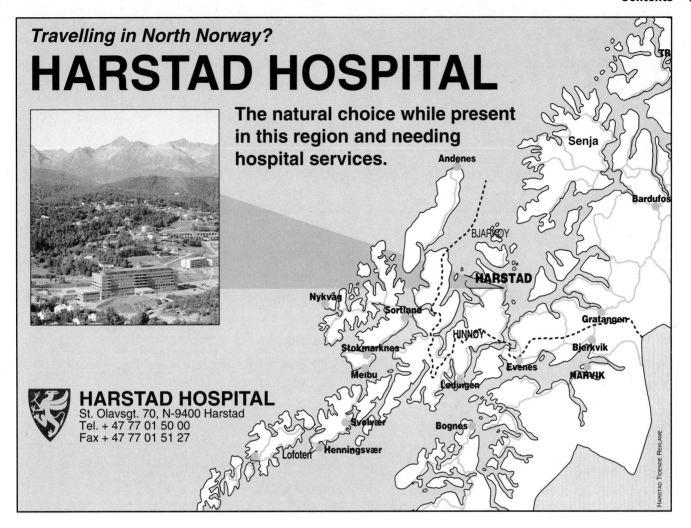

Travelling in North Norway?

HARSTAD HOSPITAL

The natural choice while present in this region and needing hospital services.

HARSTAD HOSPITAL
St. Olavsgt. 70, N-9400 Harstad
Tel. + 47 77 01 50 00
Fax + 47 77 01 51 27

A26 **Contents**

UNCONVENTIONAL

CONVENTION.

Whether for a conference or as an incentive, you won't find a more inspiring setting than the world's most famous African experience.

The incomparable Palace of the Lost City at Sun City.

Located in the heart of Southern Africa, this extraordinary hotel and the Sun City complex provide some of the most sophisticated and comprehensive conference facilities. Our experienced staff will assist in the arrangement of innovative and imaginative ground programmes including themed events.

This spectacular resort offers every form of leisure you can imagine. Unparalleled entertainment, watersports, the famous Gary Player million dollar golf course, and the breathtaking beauty and wildlife of the Pilanesberg National Game Park.

The Palace of the Lost City will leave a lasting impression on the minds of your delegates or staff, and ensure that their experience is the most memorable ever.

THE PALACE
OF THE LOST CITY AT SUN CITY

THE MOST EXTRAORDINARY HOTEL IN THE WORLD.

FOR RESERVATIONS CONTACT YOUR LOCAL TRAVEL AGENT
OR YOUR NEAREST SUN INTERNATIONAL OFFICE:
SOUTH AFRICA (HEAD OFFICE): TELEPHONE (27 11) 780-7444 FACSIMILE: 27 11) 780-7701
GERMANY: TELEPHONE: (6171) 57071 FACSIMILE: (6171) 54149
FRANCE: TELEPHONE (1) 42-61-2266 FACSIMILE: (1) 42-86-8985
UNITED KINGDOM: TELEPHONE (1491) 411-222 FACSIMILE: (1491) 576-194
JAPAN: TELEPHONE: (3) 326-01571 FACSIMILE: (3) 326-01570
ITALY: TELEPHONE: (392) 481-94271 FACSIMILE: (392) 480-13233
UNITED STATES OF AMERICA: TELEPHONE: (203) 622-1330 FACSIMILE: (203) 6221331

OGILVY & MATHER RIGHTFORD SEARLE-TRIPP & MAKIN 646991/R1

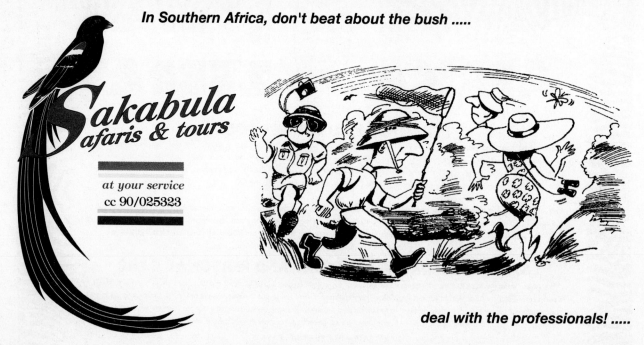

Some seek gems of knowledge...

...for those who seek jewels of another kind.

The high art of shopping

You will marvel at the mountain, ogle the ocean and be awed by the wildlife. But nothing will prepare you for Hyde Park Corner – South Africa's best dressed centre.

Hyde Park is not your average shopping mall. It's an island of style, amidst the hustle and bustle of the city.

Nestled in the exclusive suburb of Hyde Park, it offers a unique, cosmopolitan shopping experience for those with more than just groceries in mind.

At Hyde Park, indulgence is the mother of necessity. Here the *chic*, the sophisticated and the drop-dead gorgeous rub designer shopping bags, and browsing is transformed into high art.

Hyde Park is customised to suit your every whim, from *haute couture* and *haute* culture to *haute cuisine*. It provides a total shopping experience for the discerning buyer in

search of exclusive fashions, *objet d'art*, gourmet treats, international literature and music, or a place to simply sip an espresso and watch the world go by.

Hyde Park is not solely about shop, shop, shopping till you swoon. In this cosmopolitan centre you can have your cake, eat it and still come back for more.

At Hyde Park, we haven't simply elevated shopping to a class of its own. We've reinvented it.

Exclusively Yours

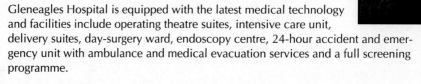

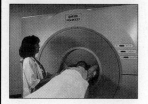

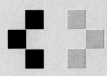

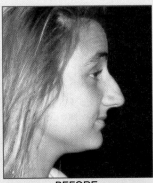
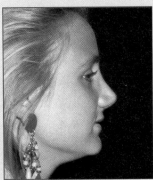

A Successful Travel Business.

we make the connection

A Satisfied Customer.

FASTRAK   **FASTLINK**   **CHAMELEON** LINKMASTER

Successful business is all about good communications.

At IMMINUS, we understand that better than anyone. For ten years we've worked alongside the travel industry, providing fully managed links to some of the biggest names in the business.

It's an approach that has made us one of Europe's fastest growing and most successful network service providers.

More than 1,200 customers use our Fastlink service and over 7,000 travel agents use Fastrak, every day. Also our Chameleon Linkmaster service continues to develop, and supports our existing portfolio of highly adaptable value added services. These include EDI ticket printing and access to the Worldspan CRS.

At a global level, our close ties with network provider Sprint International provide quick, cost effective connections to major holiday and business

destinations in over 120 countries world-wide.

So whatever your travel requirement, you can be sure that IMMINUS has the communications solution to connect business success with customer satisfaction.

For more information on IMMINUS and its range of products and services, please contact our Sales Department on 0733 230666.

I M M I N U S
local access · global solutions

IMMINUS Limited, Ashurst, Southgate Park, Bakewell Road, Orton Southgate, Peterborough, PE2 6YS

CRUISE THE WORLD
of
MARCO POLO

Southeast Asia
China & Japan - Africa & India
Antarctica - New Zealand & Australia

From Cape Town to Cairns, Bali to Beijing, the Marco Polo offers a new dimension in the world of destinational cruising. From 12 days to 26 days, your clients can cruise to some of the world's most exotic ports of call while enjoying the elegant comforts of a luxury liner.

And with the added bonus of early booking discounts of up to 20%, low single cabin supplements and free regional air connections, Marco Polo represents the best value in the world of cruise holidays. Send for your brochures today. You'll be surprised!

ORIENT LINES

For immediate reservations, call our specialist reservations consultants on 0171-409 2500.
Orient Lines (Europe) Ltd. 38 Park Street, London W1Y 3PF.

Additional brochures are obtainable through ABC Stock-Check
ATOL 3133

Cedarberg Travel

THE FREEDOM TO EXPLORE

Offices in London & South Africa

For all your FIT requirements in South Africa & Nambia contact:

Cedarberg Travel Ltd. (UK)
Tel: [+44] 0181 783 1545
Fax: [+44] 0181 979 3893

Cedarberg Travel CC. (RSA)
Tel: [+27] 27 482 2444
Fax: [+27] 27 482 1420

South Africa & Namibia

TOUR OPERATOR & SELF - DRIVE SPECIALISTS

- Tailor-made and special interest holidays
- Golfing, hot-air ballooning, water sports
- Steam train journeys
- Game-viewing and wilderness safaris
- Country house hotels and lodges
- Luxury self-contained chalets and cottages
- Car and 4x4 rental

Travel World NEWS
The Monthly Review for Travel Agents

All The Travel News At Your Fingertips!

Presented In A Concise And

Standard Format Every Month.

Each Issue Includes The Following Sections:

INDUSTRY NEWS ...	LATIN AMERICA	MIDDLE EAST	FLIGHTS ....
NORTH AMERICA ...	AFRICA	EUROPE	CRUISES ....
CARIBBEAN	ASIA/PACIFIC	FAM TRIPS	SPECIAL INTEREST

Travel World News
50 Washington Street
South Norwalk, CT 06854-2710

For subscription and/or advertising information:
Call   203/853-4955
Write 50 Washington St., S. Norwalk, CT 06854-2710
Fax   203/866-1153

SECOND-CLASS POSTAGE

At the beginning of each entry in the World Travel Guide is a black-and-white map showing the main towns, rivers and geographical features of the country. In addition, more detailed information is contained in the following regional, city and expanded colour maps. All maps were compiled by David Burles, and all are in black and white unless otherwise specified.

Calendar of Events

Event	Country	Location	Starts	Ends

MARCH 1995

Event	Country	Location	Starts	Ends
SMTV – Salon Mondial du Tourisme	France	Paris	Mar 22	Mar 27
Reisemarkt Ruhr Tourism Holiday & Leisure Fair	Germany	Essen	Mar 22	Mar 26
Boat Show	Ireland	Dublin	Mar 22	Mar 26
British Travel Fair '95	UK	Birmingham – NEC	Mar 22	Mar 23
TUR '95	Sweden	Gothenburg	Mar 23	Mar 26
ASTA Eastern Regional Conference	USA	The Greenbrier Resort, WVA	Mar 23	Mar 26
Holiday and Travel Show	New Zealand	Auckland	Mar 31	Apr 2

APRIL 1995

Event	Country	Location	Starts	Ends
EuroBahama Mart	Bahamas, The		Apr 1	
Cayman Marketplace	Cayman Islands	Grand Cayman	Apr 1	
Travel Trade Fair	UK	Birmingham – NEC	Apr 13	Apr 14
Hiiumaa Tourism Days '95	Estonia	Hiiumaa	Apr 20	Apr 22
German Travel Market	Germany	Hannover	Apr 20	Apr 22
World Holiday and Travel Fair	South Africa	Johannesburg	Apr 20	Apr 23
Pacific Asia Travel Association (PATA) Convention	New Zealand	Wellington	Apr 23	Apr 27
Scotland Travel Fair	UK – Scotland	Glasgow	Apr 26	Apr 27
AH&MA Annual Convention	USA	Atlanta, GA	Apr 26	Apr 30
Tourism & Commercial Exhibition – Bahrain Fair	Bahrain		Apr 27	May 5
The 21st International Trade Fair	Japan	Tokyo	Apr 27	Apr 30
ASTA Travel Industry March on Washington	USA	Washington, DC	Apr 27	

MAY 1995

Event	Country	Location	Starts	Ends
Denmark Workshop	Denmark	Copenhagen	May 1	
INDABA (South African Inbound Tourism Exhibition)	South Africa	Durban	May 1	May 5
ANTOR Meets the Press	UK	London	May 1	
Zimbabwe Trade Fair	Zimbabwe	Bulawayo	May 1	
National Tourism Week	USA	Nationwide	May 7	May 13
ASTA Western Regional Conference	USA	Beaver Creek, CO	May 11	May 14
IACVB Annual Convention	USA	Phoenix, AZ	May 15	May 19
Made in Bahrain	Bahrain	Manama	May 15	May 19
EIBTM	Switzerland	Geneva	May 16	May 18
Cruise & Ferry	UK	London	May 16	May 18
European Incentive & Bus. Travel & Meetings Exhibn	UK	York	May 16	May 18
Australian Tourism Exchange	Australia	Sydney	May 22	May 26

JUNE 1995

Event	Country	Location	Starts	Ends
C.H.I.C.	Bahamas, The		Jun 1	
TRENZ (Tourism Rendezvous New Zealand)	New Zealand	Auckland	Jun 1	
ANTOR Meets the Tour Operators	UK	London	Jun 1	
ITT Ivor Elms Lecture	UK	London	Jun 7	

HOTEL
METROPOL
MOSCOW

**Uniquely
Inter·Continental**

* Central Moscow location
* 403 luxury guest rooms including more than 70 suites
* 3 gourmet restaurants
* 2 bars, 1 café
* business centre
* fitness centre, swimming pool, sauna
* beauty parlour
* 16 banquet/function rooms
* Satellite communication services
* Conference centre for 300 people equipped for simultaneous translation

---

Hotel Metropol Moscow
1/4 Teatralny Proezd, Moscow 103012, Russia
Telephone: (7501 or 7095) 927 6000
Facsimile: (7501 or 7095) 927 6010

Metropol restaurant

Guest rooms

Boyarsky restaurant

Evropeisky restaurant

Swimming pool

Business centre

BARC Ltd. Co.

RUSSIA
Address: 199397
Bering St. 38
St Petersburg

Welcome to the Russian Arctic!

BARC – THE <u>FIRST</u> COMPANY IN RUSSIA TO ORGANIZE EXOTIC TOURS TO THE NORTH POLE

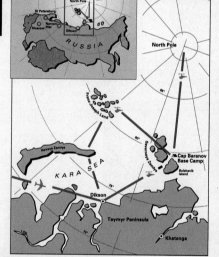

We Specialize in:

Exotic Tours • Scientific Expeditions • Active Tourism (Skiing) • City Tours

EXCLUSIVE TOURS:

• Flights to the North Pole • Voyages in Severnaya Zemlya archipelago and Franz Josef Land, Novaya Zemlya, Taimyr peninsula • Adventure with polar bears • Arkhangelsk – White Sea • Norilsk – pearl of Siberia

Our Tours are original and unique:
Precision & Care · 10 Years' Experience in the Russian Arctic · Good Value!!

Programmes 1995
North Pole
Severnaya Zemlya archipelago

Days	Itinerary	Code	Dates
		NP1	05/03 – 16/03
1	Arrival in St Petersburg	NP2	12/03 – 23/03
2	St Petersburg – Dikson	NP3	19/03 – 30/03
3	Dikson –Polar Station 'Prima'	NP4	26/03 – 06/04
4	'Prima' – North Pole – 'Prima'	NP5	02/04 – 13/04
5	Rest	NP6	09/04 – 20/04
6	October Revolution, Komsomoletz	NP7	16/04 – 27/04
7	Bolshevik Island	NP8	23/04 – 04/05
8	Polar Station 'Prima'	NP9	30/04 – 11/05
9	'Prima' – Dikson	NP10	07/05 – 18/05
10	Dikson – St Petersburg	NP11	14/05 – 25/05
11	St Petersburg excursion	NP12	21/05 – 01/06
12	Departure from St Petersburg	NP13	28/05 – 08/06
		NP14	04/06 – 15/06

Programmes 1995
Severnaya Zemlya archipelago
and Franz Josef Land

Days	Itinerary	Code	Dates
		SZ1	11/06 – 22/06
		SZ2	18/06 – 29/06
		SZ3	25/06 – 06/06
		SZ4	02/07 – 13/07
1	Arrival in St Petersburg	SZ5	09/07 – 20/07
2	St Petersburg – Dikson	SZ6	16/07 – 27/07
3	Dikson –Polar Station 'Prima'	SZ7	23/07 – 03/08
4	October Revolution, Komsomoletz	SZ8	30/07 – 10/08
5	Franz Joseph Land	SZ9	06/08 – 17/08
6	Franz Joseph Land – Severnaya Zemlya	SZ10	13/08 – 24/08
7	Polar Station 'Prima'	SZ11	20/08 – 31/08
8	Bolshevik Island	SZ12	27/08 – 07/09
9	'Prima' – Dikson	SZ13	03/09 – 14/09
10	Dikson – St Petersburg	SZ14	10/09 – 21/09
11	St Petersburg excursion	SZ15	17/09 – 28/09
12	Departure from St Petersburg	SZ16	24/09 – 15/10

 Sincerely Yours   Tel: (812) 352-24-39, 352-20-77. Fax: (812) 352-24-70, 352-26-88. Telex: 121423 NILAS SU.

Event	Country	Location	Starts	Ends
International Air Show	France	Paris	Jun 9	Jun 18
Travel Education Forum	USA	Chicago, IL	Jun 22	Jun 25
Tourism & Commercial Exhibition	Bahrain		Jun 27	Jul 5

JULY 1995

International Trade Fair	Tanzania	Dar Es Salaam	Jul 1	
National Tourism '95	Estonia	Haapsalu	Jul 8	Jul 9
Boat Show	Saudi Arabia	Jeddah	Jul 9	Jul 14
IACVB Annual Convention	USA	Phoenix, AZ	Jul 15	Jul 19

AUGUST 1995

Ship to Shore Cruise Conference	Canada	Vancouver, BC	Aug 23	Aug 27

SEPTEMBER 1995

LatinBahama Mart	Bahamas, The		Sep 1	
BTC Conference and Baltic Travel Mart	Lithuania	Vilnius	Sep 1	
ITS (International Travel Show)	Thailand	Bangkok	Sep 1	
SITE and ITME Show	USA	Chicago, IL	Sep 12	Sep 14
Incentive Travel & Meeting Executives Show	USA	Chicago, IL	Sep 19	Sep 21
Inwetex	Russian Federation	St Petersburg	Sep 23	Sep 25

OCTOBER 1995

Dive Show	UK	Birmingham – NEC	Oct 7	Oct 8
Coach & Bus '95	UK	Birmingham – NEC	Oct 12	Oct 14
Daily Mail British Ski Show	UK	Birmingham – NEC	Oct 12	Oct 15
ACTA Thunder Bay Trade Show	Canada	Thunder Bay, ON	Oct 21	Oct 22
Tourism – TOUR SALON	Poland	Poznan	Oct 24	May 27
TTW (Travel Trade Workshop)	Switzerland	Montreux	Oct 24	Oct 26

NOVEMBER 1995

ARTA 15th Annual Cruise Conference	USA	Miami, FL	Nov 2	Nov 5
65th ASTA World Travel Congress	USA	Philadelphia, PA	Nov 5	Nov 10
AH&MA Fall Conference	USA	New York City, NY	Nov 11	Nov 14
NTA Annual Convention	USA	Orlando, FL	Nov 12	Nov 17
World Travel Market	UK	London	Nov 13	Nov 16
Travel Trade Cruise-a-long	USA	Miami, FL	Nov 18	Nov 21
Telecommunications & Network	Israel	Tel Aviv	Nov 21	Nov 23
Boat Show	Germany	Berlin	Nov 22	Nov 26
Salon Nautico Boat Show	Spain	Barcelona	Nov 25	Dec 3
Sports and Recreation	Slovenia	Ljubljana	Nov 28	Dec 3

DECEMBER 1995

ITM – International Travel Market	Germany	Cologne	Dec 1	Dec 3
ITM – International SPATE	UK – Scotland	Glasgow	Dec 6	Dec 7

How To Use This Book

Welcome to the 1995 14th edition of the *World Travel Guide*. Now at over 1100 pages, it is even more comprehensive.

The beginning of 1995 saw Austria, Finland and Sweden joining the European Union, increasing the number of member states to 15. Another development was the resumption of civilian air links with the Federal Republic of Yugoslavia (Serbia and Montenegro) – the UN lifted sanctions regarding the suspension of passenger air links and flights restarted in January 1995. Unfortunately, the civil war in the area is still continuing.

Every attempt has been made to give the most accurate and up-to-date information in each country's entry at the time of going to press, although travellers should check with the respective Embassy or High Commission as certain regulations are likely to change. The CIS republics in particular, as well as the Baltic States of Estonia, Latvia and Lithuania and Eastern European countries, are undergoing changes at such an accelerated rate that information is likely to have changed somewhat between the time of preparing the book and the date of publication. Therefore, travellers are particularly advised to check all important regulations regarding these countries before travelling.

In other circumstances, certain information has been retained (for example, in sections on the former republics of Yugoslavia and other countries currently experiencing civil unrest, such as Somalia and Rwanda, or international detachment, such as Iraq) that may not be useful in the present circumstances, but may prove so again if the situations are resolved in the near future.

Below is a brief description of all the sections contained in this book. In addition to the country-by-country entries, which occupy the vast majority of the text, attention is also drawn to the various sections at the front and the back of the book, all of which are a source of much useful additional information. These will be referred to in the text where necessary.

CONTENTS

Every country in this book is listed in alphabetical order in the Contents at the beginning of the book, along with the page number on which each country's entry begins. Alternative names of countries are also listed to avoid confusion, eg French Polynesia – see Tahiti; Kampuchea – see Cambodia; or Ivory Coast – see Côte d'Ivoire. Readers may also discover that smaller destinations may be found within a larger area, eg Bali – see Indonesia; Isle of Man – see United Kingdom; Crete – see Greece; or Dubai – see United Arab Emirates.

MAP INDEX

This is an index of all the special maps included in the *World Travel Guide,* apart from the black-and-white country maps at the beginning of every country's entry. Maps included range from more detailed coloured maps of the country to city maps, area maps, maps indicating states, counties or provinces within a country and subway/metro maps. The Map Index indicates the type of map and the page number on which it can be found.

CALENDAR OF EVENTS

This section gives major travel trade and sports events, as well as important festivals, trade fairs and business conferences, around the world. Information included consists of the name of the event, the date, the venue and the country and city in which the event takes place.

INTERNATIONAL ORGANISATIONS

This is a list of organisations concerned with world trade, which can be used as a supplement to the Business Profile section in each country entry. Some of these organisations, such as the Commonwealth, though not primarily trade organisations, nevertheless make decisions and form political alliances of economic significance.

COUNTRY-BY-COUNTRY GUIDE

Every country in the world is included, listed alphabetically and dealt with under various headings which are described in greater detail below. For some countries, not all headed sections would be relevant, in which case they have been omitted. In others, the amount of information which it is necessary to convey has resulted in the extension and subdivision of some of the sections. Despite the problems which are caused by attempting to describe both very large and very small countries within a common framework, every effort has been made to standardise the way in which the information is presented. The only significant exception to this is the entry for the United States of America, which is divided into detailed sections on each gateway State.

Certain islands, states and territories do not have their own entry in the *World Travel Guide,* but are instead grouped together; this applies particularly to island groups. Examples include Svålbard, which can be found under Norway; the Galapagos Islands, which can be found under Ecuador; and Easter Island, which can be found under Chile. In other cases, countries may, correctly or not, be known popularly by more than one name: Sri Lanka/Ceylon, Myanmar/Burma, Belarus/Byelorussia, Cambodia/Kampuchea, Côte d'Ivoire/Ivory Coast, for instance. A further complication is caused by areas which are politically an integral part of a country with its own entry; thus the Canary and Balearic Islands have their own sub-sections at the end of Spain, while information on Madeira and the Azores may be found at the end of the entry on Portugal. If in doubt as to where information may be found, refer to the *Contents* pages. The entries for countries which appear in colour have been sponsored by the National Tourism Office or Tourism Representative in the UK. They are designed to assist the travel trade in the presentation and marketing of these countries as destinations for both business and holiday travel. The use of colour for a particular country does not imply a different editorial approach.

MAPS

Each country section is headed by a map of the country, showing its location within a more general region. Over the years, we have introduced more maps of major cities of the world and, for certain countries, more detailed regional maps showing areas of particular interest to the tourist or business traveller – these are now listed in the separate *Map Index* (see above). Comments and suggestions from users of the book concerning cities and areas which could also be covered in this way will be gratefully received.

More detailed maps of the Middle East, Europe, the Caribbean and the South Pacific countries as well as southern Africa and Asia may be found in the regional maps section at the front of the book. Attention is also drawn to the two world maps, one of which shows time zones. All maps in the book are for reference purposes only, and have no political significance.

Time Zones: The World Time Zones map at the front of the book shows the time in each part of the world. All time zones are based on the Greenwich Meridian, zero degrees longitude. Note that in many countries some form of Daylight Saving Time/Summertime is observed, during which clocks will be altered to make maximum use of daylight. This will be specified under each country's entry. It is noteworthy that many parts of the world are moving towards standard regional Daylight Saving Times (a process associated with the formation of regional trade blocs, similar to the EU); some countries in the Tropics have adopted Daylight Saving Time/Summertime only for commercial reasons. (Although the EU has requested that all clock changes should be standardised, the UK only comes into line with the rest of Europe for the start of daylight saving and finishes daylight saving later in the year than most of the other European countries.)

CONTACT ADDRESSES

Addresses are given in the following order: the name and address of the national Tourist Board within the particular country; the Ministry of Tourism if applicable and/or the Ministry of Foreign Affairs; the diplomatic representation of the particular country in either the UK or mainland Europe; the name and address of the country's Tourist Board in the UK, where applicable; the British Embassy or High Commission in the particular country; the country's diplomatic representation and Tourist Board in the USA; the US Embassy in the country in question; the country's diplomatic representation and Tourist Board in Canada; and the Canadian Embassy or High Commission in the country. Addresses of Consulates or sections specifically handling visa applications can also be found here. In a few cases it has not been possible to follow this format and alternative addresses have been given.

GENERAL DETAILS

POPULATION: Figures given are taken from the most reliable statistics available.

GEOGRAPHY: The country's location is given, followed by a list of the main geographical features.

LANGUAGE: Information is given about the principal official, spoken and understood languages.

RELIGION: The main religious denominations are given.

TIME: Information on national and regional time-zones is given, together with details of Daylight Saving Time/Summertime where appropriate. This supplements the information in the time-zone map (see above).

ELECTRICITY: Information is included on voltages and, where available, on cycles (in Hertz) and the types of plugs used. These can vary within a country. Various travel plugs enable visitors to use their appliances without changing to the locally-used plug.

COMMUNICATIONS: Information is given on the **Telephone**, **Fax**, **Telex/telegram** and **Postal** services available. If a country is available through the IDD (International Direct Dialling) system, the country code is given; dialling this code from any other country will connect it with the country in question. Also included is the outgoing international code from the country, where available. The **Press** section lists the main English-language papers published in that country and, where none exist, the most important papers published in the national language(s).

International Radio Services: The chart shows a selection of frequencies for receiving the **BBC World Service** (except in the UK) and **Voice of America** in each country (except Canada and the USA) in MHz. Reception quality can vary; as a general rule, lower frequencies give better results early in the morning and late at night, higher ones in the middle of the day. Variations in sunspot activity may also adversely affect reception and, from time to time, the BBC makes further changes in broadcasting frequencies to counter this. The most up-to-date information is available in the World Service magazine *Worldwide*.

TIMATIC INFORMATION: To access TIMATIC country information on HEALTH and VISA regulations through the Computer Reservation System (CRS), type the appropriate command line listed in the TIMATIC box. For example, to find the Health Regulations for visitors to Singapore, type TIDFT/SIN/HE at the appropriate place on the SABRE system. To find the Visa Regulations, type TIDFT/SIN/VI at the appropriate place on the system.

PASSPORT/VISA

Information is presented by means of a quick-glance table on the passport and visa requirements for British and other EU nationals, as well as Australian, Canadian, American and Japanese nationals. Due to practical reasons, the information given in the chart on passport/visa requirements for EU nationals does not, as yet, include the new member states of Austria, Finland and Sweden. Nationals of these three countries should contact the relevant diplomatic representations regarding any changes to requirements specific to them.

Information, where available, is also given on types and prices of visas and their duration, where to apply for visas, application requirements, the length of time an application takes to process and the procedures to be followed when renewing visas. There is also some information for visitors seeking temporary residence. Other relevant information is included where necessary.

In many cases, the same regulations for passports and visas (or other identity documents) apply equally to all countries who are members of a particular international organisation (such as the Commonwealth or the EU). Occasionally, in the notes following the charts, the organisation only, rather than the often lengthy list of member states, will be referred to. For this reason, lists giving the membership of the EU, British Dependent Territories, the Commonwealth, the CFA (French Community in Africa), the Arab League, ECOWAS (Economic Community of West African States) and other organisations may be found in the *International Organisations* section.

In the interests of clarity and brevity, various groups of people who are often exempt from passport and visa requirements have generally not been referred to in the charts or notes. These include holders of seamen's books, UN travel passes, service or diplomatic passports and stateless persons. Information may be obtained from the relevant Embassy or High Commission.

Unless otherwise stated in the chart, all travellers should be in possession of a return ticket and/or sufficient funds for the duration of their stay. In many cases they will be required to prove this on arrival in the country, or when they apply for their visa prior to departure.

The Visa sections of Embassies or High Commissions are normally open Monday to Friday with varying opening hours. During peak holiday times visas can often take longer to issue.

Note: *Although every effort has been made to ensure the accuracy of the information included in this section, entry requirements may be subject to change at short notice. If in doubt, check with the Embassy or High Commission concerned, being sure to state the nature of* the visit (ie business, touristic, transit) and the intended length of stay, and to confirm exactly what documentation will be required for the application. Remember that Transit visas may be required for stopovers.

Entry and other restrictions: Nationals of Taiwan (China) and Israel especially (though not exclusively) may be subject to restrictions when visiting other countries. These range from limiting the categories of persons who may visit to a total ban on entering a country, even for transit purposes. Travellers whose passports indicate that they have entered these countries may also be subject to restrictions. Some countries enforce stricter regulations for those crossing land borders. Travellers from Commonwealth countries who have passports conferring less than full British citizenship may also be subject to additional requirements (this affects nationals of up to 20% of the countries listed in this guide). In such cases it is advisable to check with the relevant Embassy or with the Foreign Office well in advance. Brief details follow.

British passports: Under the terms of the British Nationality Act 1981, which came into force on January 1, 1983, 'Citizenship of the United Kingdom and Colonies' has been divided into three categories:
British Citizen, for those closely connected with the UK. The holder has automatic right of abode in the UK.
British Dependent Territories Citizen, for those with certain specific ties with one or more of the dependent territories.
British Overseas Citizen, for those citizens of the UK and Colonies who have not acquired either of the above citizenship.
Since January 1, 1983, no endorsement about immigration status has been necessary on passports issued to *British Citizens* as they will automatically be exempt from UK immigration control and have the right to take up employment or to establish themselves in business in another member state of the EU.
Visitors should check with the relevant Embassy or High Commission if they have any queries regarding what level of citizenship is necessary to qualify for entry to any country destination without possession of a visa.
All applications and enquiries should be made to the Passport Office, Clive House, Petty France, London SW1 (who also handle visa requirements relating to **British Dependent Territories**), or to its regional offices in Belfast, Glasgow, Liverpool, Newport and Peterborough.
Note: The one-year **British Visitors Passport (BVP)** is being phased out as of January 1, 1995. BVPs issued before this date will remain valid for the full one-year period. However, nationals of the UK should note that Spain has not renewed its acceptance agreement and will therefore not accept BVPs after September 30, 1995. After this date a full British passport will be needed.

MONEY

The entries for each country provide information on currency denominations, currency restrictions, recent exchange rates for Sterling and the US Dollar and banking hours. Where necessary, information is also included on matters relating to currency exchange and the use of travellers cheques and credit cards. The following sections are intended as a general guide; details are given in the individual country entries.
Currency: The denominations of notes and coins given are correct at the time of going to press, but new ones may be introduced or old ones withdrawn, particularly in countries with high rates of inflation. In some countries, certain foreign currencies may be accepted instead of or in addition to the local currency.
In most cases, UK Sterling and US Dollar bank notes and travellers cheques can be exchanged at banks and bureaux de change. Sometimes, however, a **Currency exchange** section is included, giving additional information and local regulations. In certain countries of the world, some foreign currencies are more readily accepted than others, and details are included where this is likely to affect a visitor carrying Sterling notes or travellers cheques. The French Franc, for instance, is advisable for countries of the French Monetary Area (for a list of countries in the French Monetary Area, see below under *International Organisations),* and the US Dollar is more readily accepted throughout much of South America and the Caribbean. In general, the Pound Sterling and US Dollar are almost universally negotiable. Banks may recommend one in preference to the other, depending on the exchange rates, and will also be able to offer up-to-date information as to the acceptability of Sterling in a particular country. It is worth remembering that certain currencies can be reconverted into Sterling only at very disadvantageous

rates; others cannot be reconverted at all. In some cases, banknotes of a very low value will not be negotiable in the UK, whilst denominations which are considered too high may attract a less favourable rate of exchange. However, US travellers can expect to get a better rate for US$100 notes than for US$5, but please note that many banks will refuse to exchange US$1 notes. Coins should not be brought back, as UK banks will not be able to exchange them, or may do so only at a very disadvantageous rate. Some countries prohibit reconversion except at airports or borders, and then only up to a certain limit. It is often advisable only to change the amount necessary.
Currency restrictions permitting, it may be advisable to change enough money in the UK to cover immediate expenses such as taxi fares from the airport, in the event of the airport bank not being open (these banks do not always keep normal banking hours, see individual country entries under **Travel – International**). Visitors should also note that each country has specific Bank Holidays (see **Public Holidays**).
Credit cards: Information has been given on the acceptability of credit cards, although space clearly does not permit a list of organisations which will accept any particular card. Most of the major credit card companies produce booklets providing information.
Travellers cheques: These are widely accepted as shown. In some places there are preferences, usually for either US Dollar or French Franc travellers cheques.
Exchange rate indicators: A selection of exchange rates, spanning the past four years, have been included in each country entry. These figures are usually middle rates, ie the average of buying and selling prices. Some countries operate a 2- or 3-tiered exchange rate, in which case the rates quoted are the most advantageous, and are the ones which would apply to a foreign visitor. In other countries, there is an official rate of exchange, but visitors may often find the unofficial rates to be more to their advantage. It must be stressed that these figures are only a guide, enabling the visitor to judge the approximate value of each currency over the period. Exchange rates will vary from bank to bank, both in the UK and in the country itself. The figures are based on rates supplied by the *Financial Times*.
Subject to availability, permitted currencies can usually be bought in UK banks before departure. It is not, however, possible to indicate whether it is more profitable to buy foreign currency in the UK or in the country being visited. Exchange rates fluctuate from day to day and a British bank would not know what rates were being offered in a foreign country at any given time, nor what commission rates were likely to be charged. In almost all cases it is best to obtain travellers cheques, either in Sterling or, for countries where Sterling is not easily negotiable, in US Dollars. The advantages of these being both widely accepted and easily refundable more than offset the small profits that may be made by buying foreign currency in the UK.
Currency restrictions: Most countries permit the unlimited import of foreign currency, although it is often subject to declaration on arrival. In such cases the export of foreign currency will usually be limited to the amount imported and declared. Some countries insist on the exchange of a certain quantity of foreign currency for each day of the visit and this may need to be done in advance. In some cases, receipts must be kept in order to reconvert surplus local currency on departure; in others, special forms or permits may be required.
The import and export of local currency is sometimes prohibited, or limited to certain amounts or denominations of coins or banknotes.
Travellers should note that black market transactions are not necessarily favourable, in some cases illegal, and are always unaccountable (which may cause problems when leaving a country) and often result in severe punishment (including, in some places, a possible death sentence).
Further details and up-to-date information may be obtained from UK banks, or from the relevant Embassy, High Commission or Tourist Office. For addresses, see the section at the start of each country entry.

DUTY FREE

All duty-free allowances, including differentials for EU and non-EU travellers, are given where applicable, as well as information on prohibited items and any other relevant details.
The import or export of animals, plants, meat or meat

products, commercial samples and certain other goods may involve complicated regulations or restrictions, and details given in the text are not necessarily exhaustive and should only be used as a general guide. Further information may be obtained from the appropriate High Commission, Embassy or Tourist Board, HM Customs and Excise *or* the British Overseas Trade Board.
On January 1, 1993, the Single European Market was introduced. Although there are now no legal limits imposed on importing duty-paid tobacco and alcoholic products from one EU country to another, travellers may be questioned at customs if they exceed amounts recommended in this book and may be asked to prove that the goods are for personal use only. A separate paragraph within the duty-free section for EU member countries gives exact quantities of the goods affected.

PUBLIC HOLIDAYS

This section lists all public, statutory holidays which will affect the traveller during the period January 1995 to April 1996. The holidays given are usually those when businesses and banks will close. Note that the dates for Islamic holidays are approximate, since they must accord with sightings of the moon. The dates given are correct within one or two days. For further information relating to the Islamic way of life, see the *World of Islam* section at the back of the book. (Similar variations of dating occur for Hindu, Buddhist and Chinese holidays.)
In some cases, official dates for public holidays had not been fixed at the time of going to press. Check with the respective Tourist Office, Embassy or High Commission for further details.

HEALTH

Vaccination requirement and/or recommendations are presented in a quick-glance chart. Wherever an immunisation is considered 'advisable', we strongly advise that precautions are taken, even though they may not be strictly necessary. Occasionally this advice may conflict with advice given by the relevant Tourist Board or Embassy, but we feel that the recommendations of the Department of Health and the WHO are worth heeding, on the principle of safeguarding against even a minimal risk. It is important to note that general standards of hygiene and sanitation may be higher in tourist areas and city centres. Where immunisation is required, vaccination should be taken well in advance so that adequate intervals between doses can be maintained: rapid courses do not guarantee the same level of immunisation. Children and pregnant women may require special vaccination procedures. (See the immunisation chart in the *Health* section, to be found at the back of this book.)
The information contained in the *Health* section of the book and in the individual country entries has been compiled from several sources including the Department of Health, the World Health Organisation, the London School of Hygiene and Tropical Medicine and the *British Medical Journal* (official publication of the British Medical Association).
We would particularly like to thank: Dr G R Williams, MRCP, DTMH, Consultant Physician in Infectious Diseases at the Ayrshire General Hospital, for his help in updating the *Health* section and, in particular, the chart of vaccination and prophylaxis requirements and programmes; and Dr Paul Clarke of MASTA and the London School of Hygiene and Tropical Medicine in London.

TRAVEL

This information is divided into sections for **International** and **Internal** travel for the country. As the information on **AIR** and **ROAD** sub-sections tends to be different, depending on whether international or internal travel is being discussed, they are therefore dealt with twice, once as *international* and once as *internal*. Information within the sub-sections for **SEA (or SEA/RIVER/LAKE)** and **RAIL** will be included, where applicable, in the relevant section. The **URBAN** sub-section only occurs in the **Internal** section.

–International

AIR: The name and code of the major *airline* serving the country is given (usually the national airline). In almost all cases the **Approximate flight time** from London and other major cities to the main airport is also given; it must be stressed that these figures *are* approximate, and depend on a number of factors

including the airline taken, the number and duration of stopovers and the route. Information is also supplied on the major **International airports**, including the distance from the city centre. Where available, a list of airport facilities and additional details of available modes of transport are also included. Also included is a **Departure tax,** where applicable, giving the amount payable when leaving the country.
SEA: Where applicable, ferry and cruise ports will be mentioned and details, where available, will be given of international ferry services.
RIVER: In cases where a river, such as the Danube or the Nile, runs through more than one country, services available from one country to the other will be specified.
RAIL: Where applicable, the main international rail routes are described. The section also covers special fares and reductions available, for example, the *Inter-Rail* ticket scheme. The respective Tourist Board or national Railway Office can be contacted for details.
ROAD: The main links between countries are described with details of ferry crossings where appropriate. Where crossing borders by road is likely to cause difficulties or inconvenience, this is noted.

–Internal

AIR: Where appropriate, further information is given on internal air services and domestic airports.
SEA/RIVER/LAKE: Where applicable, ferry ports will be mentioned and details, where available, will be given of internal ferry services. Main river and lake services will also be mentioned.
RAIL: The main internal rail routes are described. The section also covers special fares and reductions available. Prices have normally not been included, as these are subject to change, often at short notice. Contact the respective Tourist Board or national Railway Office for details.
ROAD: The main road routes are described, as are the quality and extent of the major coach, bus, taxi and car hire services. Driving regulations and documentation required are also referred to.
URBAN: Where appropriate, many countries also have a section giving details of travel facilities in and around the main cities.
For some countries, a **Journey time chart** has also been included, giving the approximate journey times between the capital and major towns/cities/islands in the country. These figures are based on the fastest and most direct services, and are intended only as a guide.

ACCOMMODATION

Details are given in this section on the range of available **Hotel** accommodation including government classifications, regulations, etc, according to the latest information available at the time of going to press. The *World Travel Guide* provides details of the national hotel association where possible, together with specific information on the national **Grading** system. The national grading system should not be confused with local award schemes such as the AA or Michelin star systems. Information is also included on other forms of accommodation, including **SELF-CATERING, GUEST-HOUSES, CAMPING/CARAVANNING** and **YOUTH HOSTELS**.

RESORTS & EXCURSIONS

This section offers a description of the country's main tourist regions, most popular resorts and the facilities provided in and around them. Any recommended places of interest and excursions are also included. Some countries may be extremely difficult to visit at the present time for political reasons. However, some description of those areas which would normally be of interest to travellers is given for future reference in the event of them becoming accessible again. Where information is available, advice is given on the current political and travel situation and whether special permission is needed for travel within the country.

Subdivisions

The *Resorts & Excursions* sections of many countries have been subdivided using the heading style shown above. **Note:** In some cases, the divisions in the *Resorts & Excursions* section will not correspond exactly with administrative boundaries. These divisions have been made in an attempt to group towns or regions together for touristic purposes, and have no political significance.

Popular Itineraries

This section, where appropriate, gives a selection of 5- and 7-day itineraries covering major cities, towns, sights and places of interest in the country and listed within a logical touring sequence.

SOCIAL PROFILE

This section describes the range of leisure activities and facilities available, especially those with a national or regional flavour.
FOOD & DRINK: Information is included on the national cuisine and recommended dishes, as well as general information on bars, restaurants, national drinks and licensing hours.
NIGHTLIFE: Information on the extent and range of the main forms of evening entertainment within the main centres of the country.
SPORT: Descriptions of sporting facilities and spectator sports are included.
SPECIAL EVENTS: Special events including festivals, ceremonies, celebrations, exhibitions and sporting occasions which might be of interest to a foreign visitor.
SOCIAL CONVENTIONS: Includes information on customs or expected modes of behaviour, the required style of dress and acceptable or unacceptable gifts.
Photography: Any general restrictions on photography, such as the photographing of military installations etc, are indicated. **Tipping:** Where to tip, roughly how much to tip and where not to tip at all. In a few cases other categories have also been included where necessary.

BUSINESS PROFILE

Information is presented under the following headings:
ECONOMY: There is a brief description of the economy of each country. The section also identifies the country's principal exports and imports and its major trading partners. Important recent economic developments and future prospects are also mentioned. The section is largely descriptive and does not provide detailed trade or other economic statistics.
BUSINESS: This section includes the best times to visit, the necessity or otherwise for visiting cards, prior appointments, translation/interpreter services and punctuality, the required style of dress for business meetings, as well as business/office hours.
COMMERCIAL INFORMATION: The national chamber of commerce in each country is in a position to be able to offer detailed commercial advice and information to any prospective business traveller. For this reason the address, telephone number and fax number of the chamber of commerce and/or other relevant organisation(s) has been included in this section.
CONFERENCES/CONVENTIONS: A brief description of the conference/convention scene within the country is included here along with the name, address, telephone and fax number of the national conference organisation. Where appropriate, a description of the organisation itself and the facilities it can provide is also included.

CLIMATE

This section includes a brief description of the country's climate, including recommendations on clothing. The information is supplemented by at least one climate graph per country, giving average maximum and minimum monthly temperatures, precipitation, humidity and sunshine hours.
Attention is also drawn to the *Weather* section at the back of the book.

APPENDICES

DIVING
This section discusses vital information on scuba diving which will be of particular use to travel agents booking their customers into diving holidays.
EDUCATION
This section covers such topics as the development of education in tourism, partly due to the growth of employment in the tourism industry, and some of the different types of courses and qualifications available in tourism training.
INTERNATIONAL TRAVEL TRADE MEDIA
This section gives an overview of major travel trade publications worldwide. Information is included on each publication's contents, markets, country of origin, circulation, frequency of publication, language, methods of distribution, year established and publisher.
HEALTH
This section contains essential information for anyone travelling abroad, particularly to tropical countries, and supplements the information contained in the *Health* section of each country's entry. Information is included on special and rare diseases, malaria prophylaxis, accidents and bites, pregnancy, contraception, immunisation, sources of advice and specialist associations. There are maps showing yellow fever endemic areas, areas of malaria risk and where chloroquine-resistance of *plasmodium falciparum* has been reported. It is vital for travellers to obtain up-to-date information on countries they intend to visit as local circumstances are liable to change rapidly.
COUNTRY CURRENCY CODES
This section lists the country currency codes assigned by the International Standards Organisation.
THE DISABLED TRAVELLER
This section is designed to provide the travel trade with information relevant to the booking of holidays for people with disabilities. A selection of sources of further information is also given. Note that certain tour operators cater exclusively for the special needs of people with disabilities, while many others draw attention to suitable destinations and accommodation in their brochures.
THE WORLD OF ISLAM
This section is intended to give an introduction to the religious and cultural attitudes of Muslims, and supplements information contained in the *Public Holidays*, *Social Profile* and *Business Profile* sections of countries where Islam is practised. Information is included on the basic religious tenets, social customs and conventions, women and Islam and the Islamic calendar.
THE WORLD OF CHRISTIANITY
This section is intended to give a brief introduction to the religious and cultural attitudes of Christians, and supplements information contained in the *Public Holidays*, *Social Profile* and *Business Profile* sections of countries where Christianity is practised. Information is included on basic religious tenets, social customs and conventions.
THE WORLD OF BUDDHISM
This section is intended to give a brief introduction to the religious and cultural attitudes of Buddhism, and supplements information contained in the *Public Holidays*, *Social Profile* and *Business Profile* sections of countries where Buddhism is practised. Information is included on basic religious tenets, social customs and conventions.
WEATHER
This section is intended as a general introduction to the way in which weather conditions can affect individuals, and supplements the information contained in the *Climate* section of each country's entry. Information is included on humidity, wind and wind-chill factor, temperature range, precipitation and precautions. There is also an example of a climate chart, giving conversions between Fahrenheit and Centigrade, and millimetres and inches.
TRAVEL CONTACTS
This section provides a selective list of ground operators in most countries of the world. These companies are approved by *Travel Contacts* whose directory (established 1980) is available free to anyone needing reliable ground-handling services. Listed companies are chosen because they have been proved to offer professional, honest and efficient service. Nevertheless, neither *Columbus Press* nor *Travel Contacts Ltd* can accept any liability for any information contained within this section, nor for any business dealings which may be entered into with any company listed in the text. A copy of the directory is available from: Travel Contacts Ltd, 45 Idmiston Road, London SE27 9HL. Tel: (0181) 766 7868. Fax: (0181) 766 6123.
FINAL NOTE
If there is anything which you would like to see expanded, clarified or included for the first time, or if you come across any information which is no longer accurate, we would be very grateful if you could let us know. Such suggestions will be considered for future editions of the *World Travel Guide*. Address your suggestions to:
The Editor
World Travel Guide
Columbus Press
Columbus House
28 Charles Square
London N1 6HT
Tel: (0171) 417 0700. Fax: (0171) 417 0701.

International Organisations

Listed below are major international organisations concerned with economics and trade.

ASOCIACION LATINOAMERICANA DE INTEGRACION – ALADI

(Latin American Integration Association – LAIA)
Cebollatí 1461, Casilla 577, Montevideo, Uruguay.
Tel: (2) 401 121. Fax: (2) 490 649. Telex: 26944.
Members: Argentina, Bolivia, Brazil, Chile, Colombia, Ecuador, Mexico, Paraguay, Peru, Uruguay, Venezuela.

ASSOCIATION OF SOUTH EAST ASIAN NATIONS – ASEAN

Jalan Sisingamangaraja, PO Box 2072, Jakarta, Indonesia.
Tel: (21) 712 272. Fax: (21) 739 8234. Telex: 47214.
Members: Brunei, Indonesia, Malaysia, Philippines, Singapore, Thailand.

CARIBBEAN COMMUNITY & COMMON MARKET – CARICOM

Bank of Guyana Building, PO Box 10827, Georgetown, Guyana.
Tel: (2) 69281. Fax: (2) 66091. Telex: 2263.
Members: Antigua & Barbuda, Bahamas, Barbados, Belize, British Virgin Islands, Dominica, Grenada, Guyana, Jamaica, Montserrat, St Kitts & Nevis, St Lucia, St Vincent & the Grenadines, Trinidad & Tobago, US Virgin Islands. **Observers:** Dominican Republic, Haiti, Mexico, Netherlands Antilles, Puerto Rico, Suriname, Venezuela.

CENTRAL AMERICAN COMMON MARKET – CACM

(Mercado Común Centroamericano)
4a Avenida 10-25, Zona 14, Apartado Postal 1237, 01901 Guatemala City, Guatemala.
Tel: (2) 682 151. Fax: (2) 681 071. Telex: 5676.
Members: Costa Rica, Guatemala, El Salvador, Honduras, Nicaragua.

THE COLOMBO PLAN FOR CO-OPERATIVE ECONOMIC AND SOCIAL DEVELOPMENT IN ASIA AND THE PACIFIC

12 Melbourne Avenue, PO Box 596, Colombo 4, Sri Lanka.
Tel: (1) 581 813. Fax: (1) 581 754. Telex: 21537.
Members: Afghanistan, Australia, Bangladesh, Bhutan, Cambodia, Canada, Fiji, India, Indonesia, Iran, Japan, Laos, Malaysia, Maldives, Myanmar, Nepal, New Zealand, Pakistan, Papua New Guinea, Philippines, Singapore, Sri Lanka, South Korea, Thailand, United Kingdom, United States of America.

COMMONWEALTH

Commonwealth Secretariat, Marlborough House, Pall Mall, London SW1Y 5HX, England.
Tel: (0171) 839 3411. Fax: (0171) 930 0827. Telex: 27678.
Members: Antigua & Barbuda, Australia, Bahamas, Bangladesh, Barbados, Belize, Botswana, Brunei, Canada, Cyprus, Dominica, The Gambia, Ghana, Grenada, Guyana, India, Jamaica, Kenya, Kiribati,

Lesotho, Malawi, Malaysia, Maldives, Malta, Mauritius, Namibia, Nauru, New Zealand, Nigeria, Pakistan, Papua New Guinea, St Kitts & Nevis, St Lucia, St Vincent & the Grenadines, Seychelles, Sierra Leone, Singapore, Solomon Islands, South Africa, Sri Lanka, Swaziland, Tanzania, Tonga, Trinidad & Tobago, Tuvalu, Uganda, United Kingdom, Vanuatu, Western Samoa, Zambia, Zimbabwe.
Dependencies & Associated States: *Australia:* Australian Antarctic Territory, Christmas Island (Pacific), Cocos Islands, Coral Sea Islands Territory, Heard & McDonald Islands, Norfolk Island; *New Zealand:* Cook Islands, Niue, Ross Dependency, Tokelau; *United Kingdom:* Anguilla, Ascension Island, Bermuda, British Antarctic Territory, British Indian Ocean Territory, British Virgin Islands, Cayman Islands, Channel Islands, Falkland Islands, Gibraltar, Hong Kong, Isle of Man, Montserrat, Pitcairn Islands, St Helena, South Georgia, South Sandwich Islands, Tristan da Cunha, Turks & Caicos Islands.

COMMONWEALTH OF INDEPENDENT STATES – CIS

Minsk, Belarus.
Members: Armenia, Azerbaijan, Belarus, Georgia, Kazakhstan, Kyrgyzstan, Moldova, Russian Federation, Tajikistan, Turkmenistan, Ukraine, Uzbekistan.

CO-OPERATION COUNCIL FOR THE ARAB STATES OF THE GULF

PO Box 7153, Riyadh 11462, Saudi Arabia.
Tel: (1) 482 7777. Fax: (1) 482 9089. Telex: 403635.
Members: Bahrain, Kuwait, Oman, Qatar, Saudi Arabia, United Arab Emirates.

COUNCIL OF ARAB ECONOMIC UNITY

PO Box (1), Mohammed Fareed, Cairo, Egypt.
Tel: 755 321. Fax: 754 090.
Members: Egypt, Iraq, Jordan, Kuwait, Libya, Mauritania, Palestine Liberation Organisation, Somalia, Sudan, Syria, United Arab Emirates, Yemen (Republic of).

ECONOMIC COMMUNITY OF WEST AFRICAN STATES – ECOWAS

Abuja, Nigeria.
Members: Benin, Burkina Faso, Cape Verde, Côte d'Ivoire, The Gambia, Ghana, Guinea, Guinea-Bissau, Liberia, Mali, Mauritania, Niger, Nigeria, Senegal, Sierra Leone, Togo.

THE EUROPEAN UNION – EU

No final decision has been made on a headquarters for the Union. Meetings of the principal organs take place in *Brussels, Luxembourg* and *Strasbourg.*
Members: Austria, Belgium, Denmark, Finland, France, Federal Republic of Germany, Greece, Ireland, Italy, Luxembourg, The Netherlands, Portugal, Spain, Sweden, United Kingdom.

EUROPEAN FREE TRADE ASSOCIATION – EFTA

9-11 rue de Varembé, 1211 Geneva 20, Switzerland.
Tel: (22) 749 1111. Fax: (22) 733 9291. Telex: 414102.
Members: Iceland, Liechtenstein, Norway, Switzerland.

THE FRANC ZONE

Direction Générale des Services Etrangers (Service de la Zone Franc), Banque de France, 39 rue Croix-des-Petits-Champs, BP 140-01, Paris Cedex 01, France.
Tel: (1) 42 92 31 26. Fax: (1) 42 92 39 88. Telex: 220932.
Members: Benin, Burkina Faso, Cameroon, Central African Republic, Chad, Comoro Islands, Congo, Côte d'Ivoire, Equatorial Guinea, Gabon, Mali, Niger, Senegal, Togo.

GENERAL AGREEMENT ON TARIFFS AND TRADE – GATT

Centre William Rappard, 154 rue de Lausanne, 1211 Geneva 21, Switzerland.
Tel: (22) 739 5007. Fax: (22) 7339 5458. Telex: 412324.

LEAGUE OF ARAB STATES

Arab League Building, Tahrir Square, Cairo, Egypt.
Tel: (2) 750 511. Fax: (2) 775 626. Telex: 92111.
Members: Algeria, Bahrain, Comoros, Djibouti, Egypt, Iraq, Jordan, Kuwait, Lebanon, Libya, Mauritania, Morocco, Oman, Palestine Liberation Organisation, Qatar, Saudi Arabia, Somalia, Sudan, Syria, Tunisia, United Arab Emirates, Yemen (Republic of).

NORDIC COUNCIL

Tyrgatan 7, Box 19506, 10432 Stockholm, Sweden.
Tel: (8) 143 420. Fax: (8) 117 536. Telex: 12867.
Members: Denmark (with the autonomous territories of the Faroe Islands and Greenland), Finland (with the autonomous territory of the Åland Islands), Iceland, Norway, Sweden.

ORGANISATION FOR ECONOMIC CO-OPERATION AND DEVELOPMENT – OECD

2 rue André-Pascal, 75775 Paris Cedex 16, France.
Tel: (1) 45 24 82 00. Fax: (1) 45 24 85 00. Telex: 640048.
Members: Australia, Austria, Belgium, Canada, Denmark, Finland, France, Federal Republic of Germany, Greece, Iceland, Ireland, Italy, Japan, Luxembourg, The Netherlands, New Zealand, Norway, Portugal, Spain, Sweden, Switzerland, Turkey, United Kingdom, United States of America.

ORGANISATION OF AFRICAN UNITY – OAU

PO Box 3243, Addis Ababa, Ethiopia.
Tel: (1) 517 700. Fax: (1) 513 036. Telex: 21046.
Members: Algeria, Angola, Benin, Botswana, Burkina Faso, Burundi, Cameroon, Cape Verde, Central African Republic, Chad, Comoro Islands, Congo, Côte d'Ivoire, Djibouti, Egypt, Equatorial Guinea, Eritrea, Ethiopia, Gabon, The Gambia, Ghana, Guinea, Guinea-Bissau, Kenya, Lesotho, Liberia, Libya, Madagascar, Malawi, Mali, Mauritania, Mauritius, Mozambique, Namibia, Niger, Nigeria, Rwanda, São Tomé & Príncipe, Senegal, Seychelles, Sierra Leone, Somalia, Sudan, Swaziland, Tanzania, Togo, Tunisia, Uganda, Zaïre, Zambia, Zimbabwe.

ORGANISATION OF AMERICAN STATES – OAS

1889 F Street, NW, Washington, DC 20006, USA.
Tel: (202) 458 3000. Fax: (202) 458 3967. Telex: 440118.
Members: Antigua & Barbuda, Argentina, Bahamas, Barbados, Belize, Bolivia, Brazil, Canada, Chile, Colombia, Costa Rica, Cuba*, Dominica, Dominican Republic, Ecuador, El Salvador, Grenada, Guatemala, Guyana, Haiti, Honduras, Jamaica, Mexico, Nicaragua, Panama, Paraguay, Peru, St Kitts & Nevis, St Lucia, St Vincent & the Grenadines, Suriname, Trinidad & Tobago, United States of America, Uruguay, Venezuela.
* The Cuban government was suspended fom OAS activities in 1962.

ORGANISATION OF THE PETROLEUM EXPORTING COUNTRIES – OPEC

Obere Donaustrasse 93, 1020 Vienna, Austria.
Tel: (1) 211 120. Fax: (1) 264 320. Telex: 134474.
Members: Algeria, Gabon, Indonesia, Iran, Iraq, Kuwait, Libya, Nigeria, Qatar, Saudi Arabia, United Arab Emirates, Venezuela.

SOUTH PACIFIC FORUM

(c/o South Pacific Forum Secretariat), GPO Box 856, Suva, Fiji.
Tel: 312 600. Fax: 302 204. Telex: 2229.
Members: Australia, Cook Islands, Fiji, Kiribati, Marshall Islands, Federated States of Micronesia, Nauru, New Zealand, Niue, Papua New Guinea, Solomon Islands, Tonga, Tuvalu, Vanuatu, Western Samoa.

SOUTHERN AFRICAN DEVELOPMENT COMMUNITY – SADC

Private Bag 0095, Gaborone, Botswana.
Tel: 351 863. Fax: 372 848. Telex: 2555.
Members: Angola, Botswana, Lesotho, Malawi, Mozambique, Namibia, South Africa, Swaziland, Tanzania, Zambia, Zimbabwe.

UNION OF THE ARAB MAGHREB

c/o Office du Président, Tunis, Tunisia.
The location of the Union's Secretariat rotates with the chairmanship.
Members: Algeria, Libya, Mauritania, Morocco, Tunisia.

UNITED NATIONS

United Nations Plaza, New York, NY 10017, USA.
Tel: (212) 963 1234. Fax: (212) 758 2718.
Members: All sovereign countries except: Taiwan (China) Kiribati, Nauru, Switzerland, Tonga, Tuvalu, Vatican City.

UNITED NATIONS CONFERENCE ON TRADE AND DEVELOPMENT – UNCTAD

Palais des Nations, 1211 Geneva 10, Switzerland.
Tel: (22) 907 1234. Fax: (22) 907 0057. Telex: 412962.

UN INTERNATIONAL BANK FOR RECONSTRUCTION AND DEVELOPMENT – IBRD (WORLD BANK)

1818 H Street, NW, Washington, DC 20433, USA.
Tel: (202) 477 1234. Fax: (202) 477 6391. Telex: 248423.

UN INTERNATIONAL MONETARY FUND (IMF)

700 19th Street, NW, Washington, DC 20431, USA.
Tel: (202) 623 7430. Fax: (202) 623 6772. Telex: 440040.

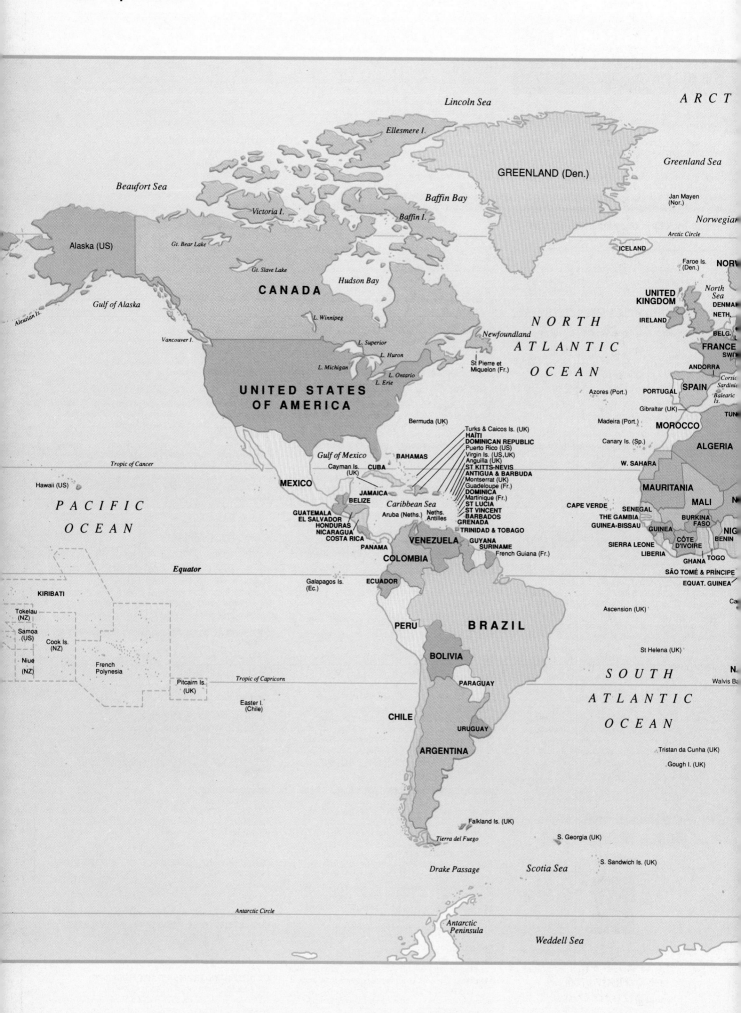

Lincoln Sea

ARCT

Ellesmere I.

GREENLAND (Den.)

Greenland Sea

Baffin Bay

Jan Mayen (Nor.)

Beaufort Sea

Norwegian

Victoria I.

Arctic Circle

Baffin I.

ICELAND

Faroe Is. (Den.) **NOR**

Alaska (US)

Gt. Bear Lake

Gt. Slave Lake

Hudson Bay

UNITED KINGDOM

North Sea

DENMA

NETH.

Gulf of Alaska

CANADA

IRELAND

BELG.

Aleutian Is.

N O R T H

FRANCE

SWI

Vancouver I.

L. Winnipeg

A T L A N T I C

ANDORRA

Corsic Sardinic

L. Superior

Newfoundland

O C E A N

SPAIN

PORTUGAL

Balearic Is.

L. Huron

St Pierre et Miquelon (Fr.)

L. Michigan

L. Ontario

UNITED STATES OF AMERICA

L. Erie

Azores (Port.)

Gibraltar (UK)

Madeira (Port.)

MOROCCO

TUN

Bermuda (UK)

Tropic of Cancer

Turks & Caicos Is. (UK)

HAÏTI

Canary Is. (Sp.)

ALGERIA

Gulf of Mexico

DOMINICAN REPUBLIC

Puerto Rico (US)

W. SAHARA

Hawaii (US)

Cayman Is. (UK)

CUBA

BAHAMAS

Virgin Is. (US,UK)

Anguilla (UK)

ST KITTS-NEVIS

ANTIGUA & BARBUDA

MEXICO

MAURITANIA

P A C I F I C

JAMAICA

Montserrat (UK)

Guadeloupe (Fr.)

DOMINICA

MALI

N

BELIZE

Martinique (Fr.)

ST LUCIA

CAPE VERDE

O C E A N

GUATEMALA

EL SALVADOR

Aruba (Neths.)

Caribbean Sea

Neths. Antilles

ST VINCENT

BARBADOS

GRENADA

SENEGAL

THE GAMBIA

BURKINA FASO

NIG

HONDURAS

NICARAGUA

TRINIDAD & TOBAGO

GUINEA-BISSAU

GUINEA

BENIN

COSTA RICA

PANAMA

VENEZUELA

GUYANA

SURINAME

SIERRA LEONE

CÔTE D'IVOIRE

COLOMBIA

French Guiana (Fr.)

LIBERIA

GHANA **TOGO**

Equator

SÃO TOMÉ & PRÍNCIPE

Galapagos Is. (Ec.)

ECUADOR

EQUAT. GUINEA

KIRIBATI

Ascension (UK)

Ca

Tokelau (NZ)

PERU

B R A Z I L

Samoa (US)

Cook Is. (NZ)

BOLIVIA

St Helena (UK)

N.

Niue (NZ)

French Polynesia

Tropic of Capricorn

PARAGUAY

S O U T H

Walvis Ba

Pitcairn Is. (UK)

Easter I. (Chile)

CHILE

URUGUAY

A T L A N T I C

O C E A N

Tristan da Cunha (UK)

Gough I. (UK)

ARGENTINA

Falkland Is. (UK)

Tierra del Fuego

S. Georgia (UK)

S. Sandwich Is. (UK)

Drake Passage

Scotia Sea

Antarctic Circle

Antarctic Peninsula

Weddell Sea

CEAN

Franz Josef Land

Severnaya Zemlya

Nor.)

Kara Sea

Laptev Sea

New Siberian Is.

Novaya
Zemlya

East Siberian Sea

Barents Sea

Wrangel I.

Chukchi Sea

FINLAND

L. Ladoga

RUSSIAN FEDERATION

Bering Sea

ESTONIA

LATVIA

LITHUANIA

BELARUS

C O M M O N W E A L T H   O F   I N D E P E N D E N T   S T A T E S

L. Baikal

Sea of
Okhotsk

Kamchatka

EP. UKRAINE

AK REP.

KAZAKHSTAN

Caspian
Sea

Aral Sea

L. Balkhash

MONGOLIA

Sakhalin

Aleutian Is.

RY

MOLDOVA

MANIA

OSL

BULG.

CEDONIA

ECE

Black Sea

GEORGIA

ARMENIA

AZER-
BAIJAN

UZBEKISTAN

KIRGHIZIA

Hokkaido

DEMOCRATIC
PEOPLE'S REP.
OF KOREA

Kurile Is.

TURKMENISTAN

TAJIKISTAN

REP. OF
KOREA

JAPAN

TURKEY

CYPRUS

Crete

anean Sea

SYRIA

LEB.

AFGHANISTAN

CHINA

Honshu

Kyushu

Shikoku

ISRAEL

IRAQ

IRAN

JORDAN

NEPAL

BHUTAN

East
China
Sea

Ryukyu Is.

EGYPT

BAHRAIN

QATAR

KUWAIT

The
Gulf

PAKISTAN

PACIFIC

SAUDI
ARABIA

U.A.E.

OMAN

Arabian
Sea

BANGLADESH

MYANMAR

Hong Kong (UK)
Macau (Port.)

TAIWAN

INDIA

LAOS

Hainan I.

Philippine Sea

Northern
Mariana Is.

_O C E A N_

SUDAN

Red Sea

YEMEN

Bay of
Bengal

THAILAND

VIETNAM

CAMBODIA

South
China
Sea

PHILIPPINES

Guam (US)

Marshall Is.

DJIBOUTI

Socotra (Yem.)

SRI
LANKA

BRUNEI

ETHIOPIA

MALDIVES

MALAYSIA

Belau (US)

Federated States
of Micronesia

W. SAMOA

UGANDA

SOMALIA

SINGAPORE

Borneo

KENYA

L. Victoria

Sumatra

Irian
Jaya

PAPUA
NEW GUINEA

NAURU

KIRIBATI

RWANDA

URUNDI

ÏRE

TANZANIA

COMOROS

SEYCHELLES

British Indian
Ocean Territory (UK)

INDONESIA

Java

SOLOMON IS.

TUVALU

Tokelau
(NZ)

ZAMBIA

MALAWI

MADAGASCAR

MAURITIUS

Réunion (Fr.)

_I N D I A N_

Coral Sea

VANUATU

FIJI

TONGA

Samoa
(US)

ZIMBABWE

MOZAM-
BIQUE

_O C E A N_

New
Caledonia (Fr.)

Wallis &
Futuna (Fr.)

Niue
(NZ)

SWANA

AUSTRALIA

SWAZILAND

UTH

RICA

LESOTHO

Tasman Sea

North I.

Crozet Is. (Fr.)

Tasmania

NEW ZEALAND

Prince Edward Is.
(S. Af.)

South I.

Kerguelen Is. (Fr.)

_S O U T H E R N   O C E A N_

A N T A R C T I C A

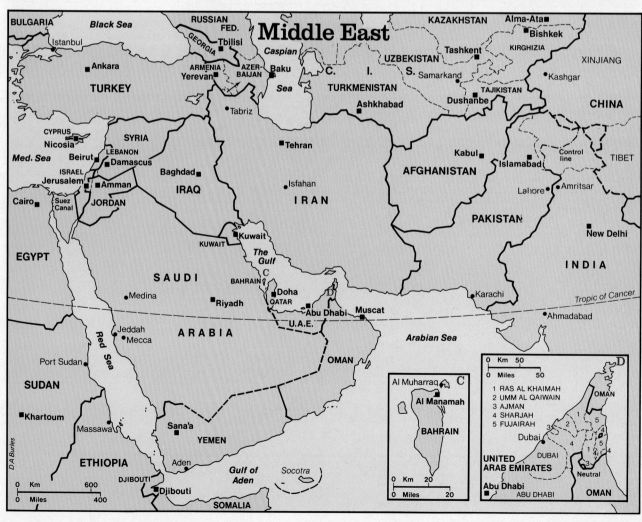

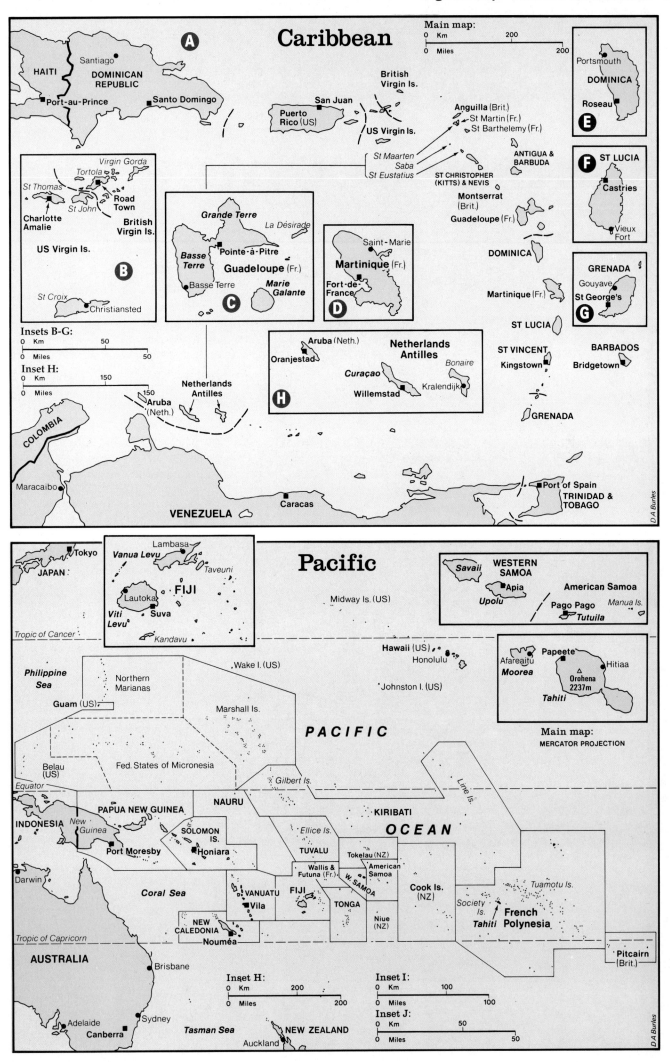

Caribbean

Main map:
0 Km 200
0 Miles 200

A

HAITI
Santiago
DOMINICAN REPUBLIC
Port-au-Prince
Santo Domingo

British Virgin Is.
San Juan
Puerto Rico (US)
US Virgin Is.
Anguilla (Brit.)
St Martin (Fr.)
St Barthelemy (Fr.)
St Maarten
Saba
St Eustatius
ANTIGUA & BARBUDA
ST CHRISTOPHER (KITTS) & NEVIS
Montserrat (Brit.)
Guadeloupe (Fr.)
DOMINICA
Martinique (Fr.)
ST LUCIA
ST VINCENT
Kingstown
GRENADA
BARBADOS
Bridgetown

Portsmouth
DOMINICA
Roseau
E

F ST LUCIA
Castries
Vieux Fort

GRENADA
Gouyave
St George's
G

B
Virgin Gorda
Tortola
St Thomas
Charlotte Amalie
St John
Road Town
British Virgin Is.
US Virgin Is.
St Croix
Christiansted

Insets B-G:
0 Km 50
0 Miles 50

Inset H:
0 Km 150
0 Miles 150

C
Grande Terre
La Désirade
Basse Terre
Pointe-à-Pitre
Guadeloupe (Fr.)
Basse Terre
Marie Galante

D
Saint-Marie
Martinique (Fr.)
Fort-de-France

Netherlands Antilles
Aruba (Neth.)
Oranjestad
Curaçao
Willemstad
Bonaire
Kralendijk
H

Netherlands Antilles
Aruba (Neth.)

COLOMBIA
Maracaibo
VENEZUELA
Caracas
Port of Spain
TRINIDAD & TOBAGO
GRENADA

D A Burles

Pacific

Tokyo
JAPAN

Lambasa
Vanua Levu
Taveuni
Lautoka
FIJI
Viti Levu
Suva
Kandavu

Midway Is. (US)

WESTERN SAMOA
Savaii
Apia
Upolu
American Samoa
Pago Pago
Tutuila
Manua Is.

Tropic of Cancer

Hawaii (US)
Honolulu

Papeete
Afareaitu
Moorea
Hitiaa
Orohena 2237m
Tahiti

Johnston I. (US)

Philippine Sea
Northern Marianas
Wake I. (US)
Guam (US)
Marshall Is.

PACIFIC

Main map:
MERCATOR PROJECTION

Belau (US)
Fed. States of Micronesia
Gilbert Is.
Equator

INDONESIA
New Guinea
PAPUA NEW GUINEA
NAURU
KIRIBATI
Line Is.

OCEAN

Port Moresby
SOLOMON IS.
Honiara
Ellice Is.
TUVALU
Tokelau (NZ)
American Samoa
Wallis & Futuna (Fr.)
W. SAMOA
Tuamotu Is.

Darwin
Coral Sea
VANUATU
Vila
FIJI
TONGA
Niue (NZ)
Cook Is. (NZ)
Society Is.
Tahiti
French Polynesia

NEW CALEDONIA
Nouméa
Tropic of Capricorn

AUSTRALIA
Brisbane
Pitcairn (Brit.)

Adelaide
Sydney
Canberra

Tasman Sea
NEW ZEALAND
Auckland

Inset H:
0 Km 200
0 Miles 200

Inset I:
0 Km 100
0 Miles 100

Inset J:
0 Km 50
0 Miles 50

D A Burles

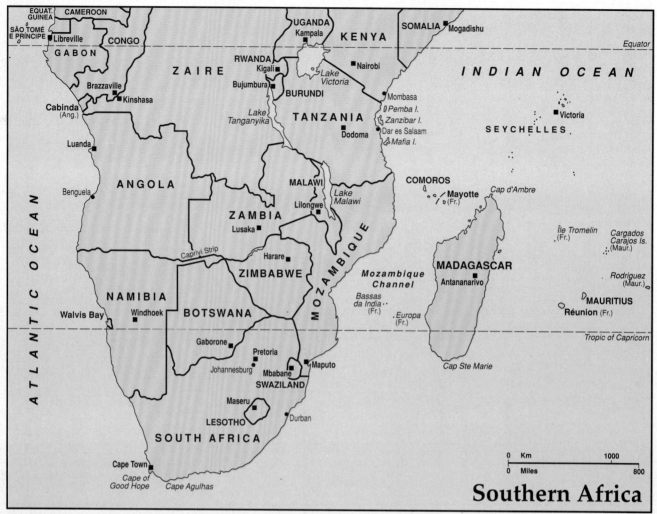

Southern Africa

EQUAT.
GUINEA
CAMEROON
SÃO TOMÉ
E PRÍNCIPE
Libreville
CONGO
GABON
Brazzaville
Kinshasa
Cabinda
(Ang.)
Luanda
ZAIRE
UGANDA
Kampala
RWANDA
Kigali
Bujumbura
BURUNDI
Lake
Victoria
KENYA
Nairobi
SOMALIA   Mogadishu
Equator
INDIAN   OCEAN
Mombasa
Pemba I.
Zanzibar I.
Dar es Salaam
Mafia I.
TANZANIA
Dodoma
Lake
Tanganyika
SEYCHELLES
Victoria
Benguela
ANGOLA
ATLANTIC OCEAN
MALAWI
Lilongwe
Lake
Malawi
ZAMBIA
Lusaka
Caprivi Strip
Harare
ZIMBABWE
MOZAMBIQUE
COMOROS
Mayotte
(Fr.)
Cap d'Ambre
Île Tromelin
(Fr.)
Cargados
Carajos Is.
(Maur.)
Mozambique
Channel
MADAGASCAR
Antananarivo
Rodriguez
(Maur.)
Bassas
da India
(Fr.)
Europa
(Fr.)
MAURITIUS
Réunion (Fr.)
NAMIBIA
Walvis Bay
Windhoek
BOTSWANA
Gaborone
Pretoria
Johannesburg
Mbabane
Maputo
SWAZILAND
Tropic of Capricorn
Cap Ste Marie
Maseru
LESOTHO
Durban
SOUTH AFRICA
Cape Town
Cape of
Good Hope   Cape Agulhas

| 0 | Km | 1000 |
| 0 | Miles | 800 |

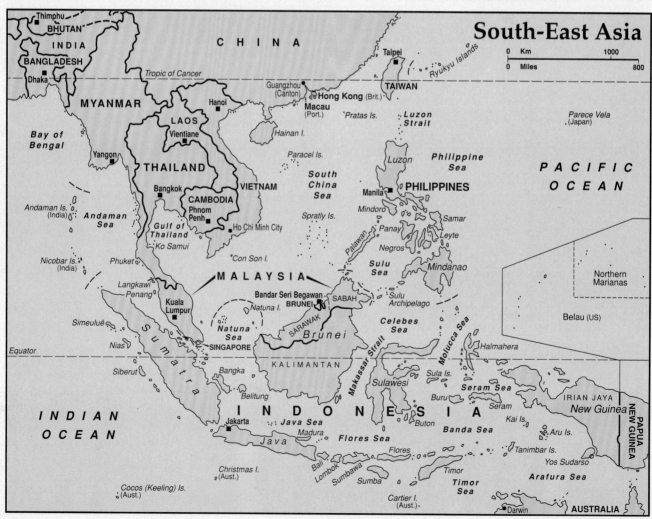

South-East Asia

Thimphu
BHUTAN
INDIA
BANGLADESH
Dhaka
CHINA
Taipei
Ryukyu Islands
Tropic of Cancer
MYANMAR
Hanoi
LAOS
Vientiane
Guangzhou
(Canton)
Hong Kong (Brit.)
Macau
(Port.)
TAIWAN
Bay of
Bengal
Yangon
THAILAND
Bangkok
CAMBODIA
Phnom
Penh
VIETNAM
Hainan I.
Pratas Is.
Paracel Is.
South
China
Sea
Luzon
Strait
Luzon
Manila
PHILIPPINES
Philippine
Sea
Parece Vela
(Japan)
PACIFIC
OCEAN
Andaman Is.
(India)
Andaman
Sea
Gulf of
Thailand
Ko Samui
Ho Chi Minh City
Con Son I.
Spratly Is.
Mindoro
Samar
Palawan
Panay
Leyte
Nicobar Is.
(India)
Phuke t
MALAYSIA
Negros
Sulu
Sea
Mindanao
Langkawi
Penang
Kuala
Lumpur
Bandar Seri Begawan
BRUNEI
SABAH
Sulu
Archipelago
Northern
Marianas
Simeuluë
Natuna I.
Natuna
Sea
SARAWAK
Brunei
Celebes
Sea
Belau (US)
Nias
SINGAPORE
KALIMANTAN
Makassar Strait
Molucca
Sea
Halmahera
Siberut
Bangka
Sulawesi
Sula Is.
Seram Sea
IRIAN JAYA
New Guinea
PAPUA
NEW
GUINEA
INDIAN
OCEAN
Belitung
Jakarta
INDONESIA
Java Sea
Madura
Buton
Buru
Seram
Kai Is.
Aru Is.
Yos Sudarso
Java
Flores Sea
Banda Sea
Christmas I.
(Aust.)
Bali
Lombok
Sumbawa
Flores
Sumba
Timor
Tanimbar Is.
Arafura
Sea
Cocos (Keeling) Is.
(Aust.)
Cartier I.
(Aust.)
Timor
Sea
Darwin
AUSTRALIA

| 0 | Km | 1000 |
| 0 | Miles | 800 |

Afghanistan

Location: Southwest Asia; northwest part of Indian subcontinent.

Note: At present, visitors are advised against travel to Afghanistan. Fighting continues between opposing factions in the civil war and indiscriminate rocket attacks, aerial bombardments and other violence can occur without warning in Kabul and elsewhere in the country. Land mines are prevalent throughout the countryside. Westerners are vulnerable to politically and criminally motivated attacks, including robbery, kidnapping and hostage-taking. Both the British and US Embassies in Kabul are closed. Those needing to visit Afghanistan should check with the appropriate government office (Foreign Office for British citizens or the State Department for US citizens) for up-to-date information. Certain information is included below in case of future change.
Source: US State Department – January 19, 1994.

Afghan Tourist Organisation (ATO)
Ansari Wat, Shar-i-Nau, Kabul, Afghanistan
Tel: (93) 30323.
Embassy of the Islamic State of Afghanistan
31 Prince's Gate, London SW7 1QQ
Tel: (0171) 589 8891. Fax: (0171) 581 3452. Telex: 916641. Opening hours (visa applications): 1000-1300 Monday to Friday.
Afghanaid
292 Pentonville Road, London N1 9NR
Tel: (0171) 278 2832. Fax: (0171) 837 8155.
British Embassy
Karte Parwan, Kabul, Afghanistan
Tel: (93) 30511.
The Embassy is presently closed.
Embassy of the Islamic State of Afghanistan
2341 Wyoming Avenue, NW, Washington, DC 20008
Tel: (202) 234 3770/1. Fax: (202) 328 3516. Telex: 248206.
Consulate in: San Francisco.
Embassy of the United States of America
Wazir Akbar Khan Mena, Kabul, Afghanistan
Tel: (93) 62230.
The Embassy is presently closed.

AREA: 652,225 sq km (251,773 sq miles).
POPULATION: 18,052,000 (1992). The United Nations estimate that there are approximately 5.5 million refugees as a result of the fighting, of whom 3.15 million live in camps in Pakistan and about 2.35 million in Iran; their estimate of the population within the country was 14,709,000 (1987).
POPULATION DENSITY: 27.7 per sq km.
CAPITAL: Kabul. **Population:** 1,036,407 (1982).
GEOGRAPHY: Afghanistan is a landlocked country, sharing its borders with the CIS to the north, China to the northeast, Pakistan to the east and south and Iran to the west. On the eastern tip of the Iranian plateau, central Afghanistan is made up of a tangled mass of mountain chains. The Hindu Kush is the highest range, rising to

more than 7500m (24,600ft). The Bamian Valley separates the Hindu Kush from Koh-i-Baba, the central mountain range and source of the Helmand River. To the north and southwest of these mountains alluvial plains provide fertile agricultural soil. To the northeast is Kabul, the capital. The other major cities are Jalalabad, Kandahar, Mazar-i-Sharif and Herat.
LANGUAGE: The official languages are Pashtu and Dari Persian. The more educated Afghans speak English. Some French, German and Russian is also spoken.
RELIGION: Islamic majority (mostly Sunni), with Hindu, Jewish and Christian minorities.
TIME: GMT + 4.5.
ELECTRICITY: 220 volts AC, 50Hz.
COMMUNICATIONS: Telephone/Fax: No IDD. At the time of writing, there are no telephone services operating. In general, there is a severe shortage of lines for operator-connected international calls.
Telex/telegram: May be sent from the Central Post Office, Kabul (closes at 2100). **Post:** At the time of writing, there are no postal services available. Normally, airmail takes about a week to Europe. **Press:** *The Kabul Times* is the main English-language newspaper.
BBC World Service and Voice of America frequencies: From time to time these change. See the section *How to Use this Book* for more information.
BBC:

| MHz | 15.31 | 14.13 | 11.95 | 9.740 |

A service is also available on 1413kHz.
Voice of America:

| MHz | 15.43 | 9.760 | 6.110 | 9.645 |

PASSPORT/VISA

Regulations and requirements may be subject to change at short notice, and you are advised to contact the appropriate diplomatic or consular authority before finalising travel arrangements. Details of these may be found at the head of this country's entry. Any numbers in the chart refer to the footnotes below.

	Passport Required?	Visa Required?	Return Ticket Required?
Full British	Yes	Yes	Yes
BVP	Not valid	-	-
Australian	Yes	Yes	Yes
Canadian	Yes	Yes	Yes
USA	Yes	Yes	Yes
Other EU (As of 31/12/94)	Yes	Yes	Yes
Japanese	Yes	Yes	Yes

Entry restrictions: Nationals of Israel may be refused entry.
PASSPORTS: Valid passports are required by all.
British Visitors Passport: Not accepted.
VISAS: Required by all except those holding confirmed onward tickets and continuing their journey to another country by the same aircraft within two hours.
Types of visa: Enquiries should be made at Embassy or Grazandoy office (Kabul) for details about visiting Afghanistan. At the time of writing, tourist visas and transit visas are not being issued. When a Business visa is required, it is necessary to write first to the Export Promotion Department, Ministry of Commerce, Darulaman Wat, Kabul, describing the purpose of the visit. Two to three weeks should be allowed for authorisation to be granted.
Application to: Consulate (or Consular Section at Embassy). For addresses, see top of entry.
Application requirements: (a) Authorisation. (b) Valid passport. (c) 3 passport-size photos. (d) Fee (£20 for UK citizens).
Note: Exit and re-entry permits must be obtained before attempting to leave Afghanistan.

MONEY

Currency: Afghani (Af) = 100 puls. Notes are in denominations of Af1000, 500, 100, 50, 20 and 10. Coins are in denominations of Af5, 2 and 1, and 50 and 25 puls.
Credit cards: Not accepted.
Exchange rate indicators: The following figures are included as a guide to the movements of the Afghani

against Sterling and the US Dollar:

Date:	Oct '92	Sep '93	Jan '94	Jan '95
£1.00=	99.25	2115.75	2500.00	5414.45
$1.00=	62.54	1385.56	1689.76	3460.82

Currency restrictions: The import and export of local currency is unrestricted. The import of foreign currency is unlimited if declared; the declared sum is the maximum allowed for export.
Banking hours: Generally 0800-1200 and 1300-1630 Saturday to Wednesday; 0800-1300 Thursday. Some banks are closed Wednesday. At the time of writing, most banks are closed.

DUTY FREE

The following goods can be taken into Afghanistan without incurring customs duty:
A reasonable amount of tobacco products; any amount of perfume.
Prohibited items: Alcohol. The export of antiques, carpets and furs is prohibited without licence. All valuable goods (radios, cameras, etc) must be registered on arrival.

PUBLIC HOLIDAYS

Feb 1 '95 Leilat al-Meiraj. **Mar 3** Start of Eid al-Fitr. **Mar 21** Nauroz (New Year's Day, Iranian Calendar). **Apr 28** Islamic Revolution Day. **May 1** Workers' Day. **May 10** Start of Eid al-Adha. **Jun 9** Ashura. **Aug 9** Mouloud (Prophet's Birthday). **Aug 19** Independence Day. **Dec 20** Leilat al-Meiraj. **Feb 22 '96** Start of Eid al-Fitr. **Mar 21** Nauroz (New Year's Day, Iranian Calendar). **Apr 28** Islamic Revolution Day. **Apr 29** Eid al-Adha.
Note: Muslim festivals are timed according to local sightings of various phases of the Moon and the dates given above are approximations. During the lunar month of Ramadan that precedes Eid al-Fitr, Muslims fast during the day and feast at night and normal business patterns may be interrupted. Some disruption may continue into Eid al-Fitr itself. Eid al-Fitr and Eid al-Adha may last anything from two to ten days, depending on the region. For more information see the section *World of Islam* at the back of the book.

HEALTH

Regulations and requirements may be subject to change at short notice, and you are advised to contact your doctor well in advance of your intended date of departure. Any numbers in the chart refer to the footnotes below.

	Special Precautions?	Certificate Required?
Yellow Fever	Yes	1
Cholera	Yes	2
Typhoid & Polio	Yes	-
Malaria	3	-
Food & Drink	4	-

[1]: Certificate required if arriving from endemic or infected areas. Travellers arriving from non-endemic zones shold note that vaccination is strongly recommended for travel outside the urban areas, even if an outbreak of the disease has not been reported and they would normally not require a vaccination certificate to enter the country.
[2]: Following WHO guidelines issued in 1973, a cholera vaccination certificate is no longer a condition of entry to Afghanistan. However, cholera is a serious risk in this country and precautions are essential. Up-to-date advice should be sought before deciding whether these precautions should include vaccination as medical opinion is divided over its effectiveness. See the *Health* section at the back of the book.
[3]: Malarial risk, primarily in the benign *vivax* form, exists from May to November below 2000m (6562 ft). The *falciparum* strain occurs in the south of the country. Chloroquine-resistant *falciparum* has been reported.
[4]: All water should be regarded as being potentially contaminated. Milk is unpasteurised and should be boiled. Powdered or tinned milk is available and is advised, but make sure that it is reconstituted with pure water. Avoid dairy products which are likely to have been made from unboiled milk. Only eat well-cooked meat and fish, preferably served hot. Pork, salad and mayonnaise may carry increased risk. Vegetables should be cooked and fruit peeled.
Rabies is present. For those at high risk, vaccination before arrival should be considered. If you are bitten abroad seek medical advice without delay. For more information consult the *Health* section at the back of the book.
Bilharzia (schistosomiasis) is present. Avoid swimming and paddling in fresh water. Swimming pools which are well-chlorinated and maintained are safe.

Health

| GALILEO/WORLDSPAN: | **TI-DFT/KBL/HE** |
| SABRE: | **TIDFT/KBL/HE** |

Visa

| GALILEO/WORLDSPAN: | **TI-DFT/KBL/VI** |
| SABRE: | **TIDFT/KBL/VI** |

For more information on Timatic codes refer to Contents.

Timatic

Health care: Medical care is very limited and doctors and hospitals demand immediate cash payment for most services. Medical insurance is strongly recommended.

TRAVEL - International

AIR: Afghanistan's national airline is *Ariana Afghan Airlines.*
Approximate flight times: From Kabul to *London* is 10-11 hours including a 2-hour stopover in Moscow; to *Moscow* is 6 hours and to *Tashkent* is 1 hour 30 minutes.
International airport: *Kabul Airport (KBL)* is 16km (10 miles) from the city. Airport facilities include banking, buffet-bar, car park, post office and restaurant (opening hours: 0700-2400). Taxis are available to the city centre (travel time – 30 minutes). Airport facilities in Kabul have been expanded and new airports have been built near the border.
RAIL: Afghanistan's rail network consists of a short spur from the CIS, crossing the Amu Darya at Hairatan, where it stops. There are plans to extend it to Kabul.
ROAD: Overland travel is currently very risky in some parts of the country. Buses operate along the Asia Highway, which links Afghanistan to Iran and Pakistan. There are good road links from Mazar-i-Sharif and Herat to the CIS.

TRAVEL - Internal

AIR: Internal flights connect Kabul with Herat, Kandahar and Mazar-i-Sharif.
ROAD: There are over 18,000km (11,000 miles) of roads, of which 2800km (1700 miles) are paved. An arc of all-weather roads runs from Mazar-i-Sharif through Kabul and Kandahar to Herat. Bus services operate from Kabul to the provinces. Traffic drives on the right.
Documentation: An International Driving Permit is required.
URBAN: Buses, trolleybuses and taxis operate in Kabul. It is essential to check these services with relevant airline offices.

ACCOMMODATION

HOTELS: The only top-class hotel in the country is the Intercontinental in Kabul. There is a 5% government tax, but no service charge. Elsewhere in the city there is limited moderate and low-class accommodation; prices are often very inexpensive and include service charges. Only basic accommodation is available elsewhere. In some rural areas there are hotels run by the provincial authority, but these are of a low standard. The Afghan Tourist Organisation in Kabul deals with all bookings (for address, see top of entry).
CAMPSITES/LODGES: There are campsites along the Central Route, including Bande Amir and various tourist lodges for visitors to Nuristan.

RESORTS & EXCURSIONS

Kabul: The capital has little remaining from its historic past. The *Garden of Babur* and a well-presented museum are amongst the few conventional attractions for tourists. Travel outside Kabul is not generally permitted to tourists but, if allowed, it is worth trying to visit the *Valley of Paghman,* 90 minutes by road west of the capital, where the rich have second houses; and, to the north, **Karez-i-Amir, Charikar** and the *Valley of Chakardara.*
Jalalabad: The capital of Nangarhar Province is an attractive winter resort, with many cypress trees and flowering shrubs.
Hindu Kush: Consisting of two huge mountain ranges, the region is wild and remote, and although one can travel by car the steepness of the routes makes vehicles prone to breakdowns. The Hindu Kush is best left for travellers prepared to rough it. For those who make the journey, the mountain, valley and lake scenery is stupendous. **Bamian** is the main centre.

SOCIAL PROFILE

FOOD & DRINK: Indian-style cuisine. Most modern restaurants in Kabul offer international cuisine as well as Afghan specialities such as *pilaus, kebabs, bolani* and *ashak.* Traditional foods and tea from *chaikhanas* are found in all areas at cheap prices including service. Afghan dishes can be very good, but very spicy, so visitors with a weak stomach should take care when ordering. There are few bars outside luxury hotels and restaurants and alcohol is available only for non-Muslims.
NIGHTLIFE: Traditional music and dance is performed in hotels and restaurants.
SHOPPING: Special purchases include Turkman hats,

Kandahar embroidery, Istaff pottery, local glassware from Herat, nomad jewellery, handmade carpets and rugs, Nuristani woodcarving, silkware, brass, copper and silver work. **Note:** Many craft items may only be exported under licence. **Shopping hours:** Generally 0800-1200 and 1300-1800 Saturday to Wednesday; 0800-1300 Thursday. Some shops close all day Wednesday.
SPORT: The national sport is the **Buzkashi,** a fiercely competitive equestrian event dating from the time of Alexander the Great. It resembles a rather lawless version of polo, with the ball being replaced by the headless body of a goat. Played in Kabul at the Ghazi Stadium (late October) and at Kunduz during the Afghan New Year.
SOCIAL CONVENTIONS: Outside Kabul, Afghanistan is still very much a tribal society. Religion and traditional customs have a strong influence within the family, and there are strict male and female roles in society. It is considered insulting to show the soles of the feet. Guests may have to share a room as specific accommodation is rarely set aside. Women are advised to wear trousers or long skirts and avoid revealing dress. Handshaking is acceptable as a form of greeting although nose-rubbing and embracing are traditional. Smoking is a common social habit and cheap by European standards. It is a compliment to accept an offered cigarette from your host. **Photography:** Care should be taken when using cameras. Military installations should not be photographed.

BUSINESS PROFILE

ECONOMY: Agriculture accounts for over 60% of Gross Domestic Product and the majority of the population exist at subsistence level. Their position has been exacerbated by the almost continuous war for the last 14 years: since 1979 it is estimated that one-third of the country's farms have been abandoned. This has led to recurring food shortages, with the result that the Government has been obliged to import large quantities of foodstuffs. Afghanistan has significant deposits of natural gas, coal, salt, barite and other ores. Hydroelectricity accounts for 80% of energy production. There is some manufacturing industry, principally textiles, chemical fertilisers, leather and plastics. The former Soviet Union was Afghanistan's largest trading partner by a considerable margin, but there are also important trade links with India and Pakistan. Although the country has appreciable economic potential, the dislocation wrought by years of occupation and civil war will take years to repair.
BUSINESS: Price bargaining is expected and oral agreements are honoured. Formal wear is expected and meetings should be pre-arranged. **Office hours:** Generally 0800-1200 and 1300-1630 Saturday to Wednesday; 0830-1300 Thursday, but some offices are closed all day Wednesday.
COMMERCIAL INFORMATION: The following organisations can offer advice: Afghan Chambers of Commerce and Industry, Mohd Jan Khan Watt, Kabul. Tel: (93) 26796 *or* 25201; *or* Federation of Afghan Chambers of Commerce and Industry, Daraulaman Watt, Kabul.

CLIMATE

Although occupying the same latitudes as South-Central USA, the mountainous nature of much of Afghanistan produces a far colder climate. Winter may be considered permanent in regions above 2500m (8200ft); regions above 4000m (13,000ft) are uninhabitable. Being landlocked, there are considerable differences in temperature between summer and winter and between day and night in lowland regions and in the valleys. The southern lowlands have intensely hot summers and harsh winters.

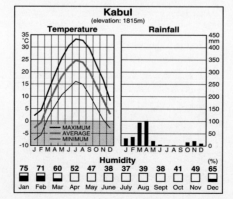

Kabul
(elevation: 1815m)

Temperature   Rainfall

	Jan	Feb	Mar	Apr	May	June	July	Aug	Sept	Oct	Nov	Dec
Humidity (%)	75	71	60	52	47	38	37	39	38	41	49	65

MAXIMUM / AVERAGE / MINIMUM

Albania

Location: Easterh Europe, Adriatic and Ionian Coast.

Albanian Ministry of Tourism
Marketing and Promotion Department, Deshmoret e Kombit Bulevardi, Tirana, Albania
Tel: (42) 28254. Fax: (42) 27931.
Albturist
c/o Hotel Dajti, 6 Deshmoret e Kombit Bulevardi, Tirana, Albania
Tel: (42) 34572. Fax: (42) 34359. Telex: 2148 *or* 2113.
Embassy of the Republic of Albania
6 Wilton Court, 59 Eccleston Square, London SW1V 1PH
Tel: (0171) 834 2508 *or* 976 5295. Fax: (0171) 834 2508. Opening hours: 0930-1500 Monday to Friday.
Albturist (Travel Agency)
c/o Regent Holidays (UK) Limited, 15 John Street, Bristol BS1 2HR
Tel: (0117) 921 1711. Fax: (0117) 925 4866. Telex: 444606 (a/b REGENT R). Opening hours: 0900-1730 Monday to Friday.
British Embassy
Office of the British Chargé d'Affaires, c/o French Embassy, Rruga Skenderbeg 14, Tirana, Albania
Tel: (42) 34250. Telex: 2150.
Embassy of the Republic of Albania
Suite 1010, 1511 K Street, NW, Washington, DC 20005
Tel: (202) 223 4942 *or* 223 8187. Fax: (202) 628 7342. *The Embassy also deals with enquiries from Canada.*
Embassy of the United States of America
PO Box 100, Rruga Labinoti 103, Tirana, Albania
Tel: (42) 32875 *or* 33520. Fax: (42) 32222.
The Canadian Embassy in Budapest deals with enquiries relating to Albania (see *Hungary* later in the book).

AREA: 28,748 sq km (11,100 sq miles).
POPULATION: 3,300,000 (1991 estimate).
POPULATION DENSITY: 114.8 per sq km.
CAPITAL: Tirana. **Population:** 243,000 (1990).
GEOGRAPHY: Albania shares borders with Montenegro and Serbia to the north, with the Former Yugoslav Republic of Macedonia to the northeast, and with Greece to the south; to the west are the Adriatic and Ionian Seas. Most of the country is wild and mountainous, with extensive forests. There are fine sandy beaches and, inland, many beautiful lakes.
LANGUAGE: The official language is Albanian. Greek is widely spoken in the south. Many Albanians also speak Italian and English.
RELIGION: Three religions coexist in Albania: Muslim, Catholic and Orthodox. The majority of the population is Muslim. The Government closed all

mosques and churches in 1967 and declared atheism as part of the constitution in 1976. After the overthrow of the communist regime, the existing religious institutions were reopened and are now widely in use.
TIME: GMT + 1 (GMT + 2 from last Sunday in March to Saturday before last Sunday in September).
ELECTRICITY: 220 volts AC, 50Hz.
COMMUNICATIONS: Telephone: IDD is available to major towns. Country code: 355. Outgoing international code: 00. City codes: Tirana 42, Durresi 52, Elbasan 545, Shkodra 224, Gjirokastra 726, Korça 824, Vlora 63, Berati 62. For other regions, international connections are made through the nearest city. **Telegram/telex/fax:** These services are offered in post offices. **Post:** All mail to and from Albania is subject to long delays, sometimes up to 2 months. Letters should be sent recorded delivery to avoid loss. There are DHL offices in Tirana and Durres, offering services between Albania and other countries. The postal and telecommunication sytems are to undergo extensive modernisation in the near future. Services include letter and parcel post, telephone booths and video information. Post office hours: 0800-1700 Monday to Friday and 0800-1300 Saturday. **Press:** Publications that diverge from the Party line have only been permitted since 1990. There are about 400 national and regional newspapers, many of which are independent. The main newspapers are published daily. The *Rilindja Demokratike*, the organ of the ruling Democratic Party, sells 15-20,000 copies. The only daily, the *Zëri i Popullit* (Voice of the People), is the Socialist Party (formerly the Communist Party) newspaper, the daily circulation of which has been reduced from 180,000 in 1990 to 15,000 in 1992. English-language newspapers available include the *International Herald Tribune, The Sunday Times, The Independent, Balkan News* and *The Observer*. Over 30 magazines are published in Albania.
BBC World Service and Voice of America frequencies: From time to time these change. See the section *How to Use this Book* for more information.

BBC:				
MHz	**17.64**	**15.07**	**9.410**	**6.180**
Voice of America:				
MHz	**1.260**	**6.040**	**9.760**	**15.20**

PASSPORT/VISA

Regulations and requirements may be subject to change at short notice, and you are advised to contact the appropriate diplomatic or consular authority before finalising travel arrangements. Details of these may be found at the head of this country's entry. Any numbers in the chart refer to the footnotes below.

	Passport Required?	Visa Required?	Return Ticket Required?
Full British	Yes	No	Yes
BVP	Not valid	-	-
Australian	Yes	Yes	Yes
Canadian	Yes	No	Yes
USA	Yes	No	Yes
Other EU (As of 31/12/94)	Yes	No	Yes
Japanese	Yes	Yes	Yes

Note: Regulations and requirements may be subject to change. It is advisable to contact appropriate diplomatic or consular authority before finalising travel arrangements.
PASSPORTS: A valid passport is required by all.
British Visitors Passport: Not acceptable.
VISAS: Required by all except nationals of:
(a) countries referred to in the chart above;
(b) Austria, Bulgaria, Finland, Iceland, Liechtenstein, Norway, Sweden, Switzerland and Turkey;
(c) those continuing their journey to a third country by the same aircraft or the next available one.
Note: Nationals of these countries pay an entry fee of US$5 at Tirana airport or at the border point. In some cases proof of sufficient funds to cover stay is required. Nationals of Saudi Arabia, Egypt, United Arab Emirates, Kuwait, Oman, Israel, Qatar, Malta and Bahrain can obtain visas at the point of entry. Albanians residing abroad and having another nationality need not pay any entry or visa fee.
Types of visa: Business and Tourist. Tourist visas cost US$5 each. Business visas are given for single or multiple entry.
Validity: Duration of visas is individually specified for each visit.
Application to: Consulate (or Consular Section at Embassy) or Tourist Board. For addresses, see top of entry.
Application requirements: (a) Application form(s). (b) Valid passport. (c) Sufficient funds to cover duration of stay. (d) For business, letters from company and from sponsor etc.
Working days required: Minimum 1 week.
Temporary residence: Application to be made to the Embassy of the Republic of Albania.

MONEY

Currency: Lek (Lk) = 100 qindarka. Notes are in denominations of Lk1000, 500, 200, 100, 50, 10, 5, 3 and 1. Coins are in denominations of Lk2 and 1, and 50, 20, 10 and 5 qindarkas.
Currency exchange: All bills are normally settled in cash or cheque. Many bureaux de change can exchange unlimited amounts in cash. Banks offer the best rate of exchange.
Credit cards: American Express is accepted by banks and several tourist hotels.
Travellers cheques are cashed by some banks on presentation of own passport. Some hotels also accept Eurocheques.
Exchange rate indicators: The following figures are included as a guide to the movements of the Lek against Sterling and the US Dollar:

Date:	**Oct '92**	**Sep '93**	**Jan '94**	**Jan '95**
£1.00=	**173.97**	**168.35**	**162.47**	**157.12**
$1.00=	***109.62**	***110.25**	***109.81**	**100.43**

Note [*]: Since the middle of 1992 exchange rates have been tied to the US Dollar.
Currency restrictions: The import and export of local currency is prohibited. Foreign currency must be declared on arrival. The export of foreign currency is limited to the amount declared.
Banking hours: 0800-1400 Monday to Friday.

DUTY FREE

The following items may be taken into Albania without incurring customs duty:
A reasonable quantity of tobacco products; alcoholic beverages and perfumes for personal use.
Prohibited items: Firearms, ammunition, narcotics, drugs and goods jeopardizing the protection of public order and social security. Special export permits are required for precious metals, antique coins and scrolls, antiques, national costumes of artistic or folkloristic value, books and works of art which form part of the national heritage and culture.
Note: Passage through Customs can be difficult.

PUBLIC HOLIDAYS

Jan 1-2 '95 New Year. **Mar 3** Lesser Bairam (End of Ramadan). **Mar 8** International Women's Day. **Apr 14** Good Friday. **Apr 17** Easter Monday. **Apr 23** Orthodox Easter. **May 1** May Day. **May 10** Greater Bairam (Feast of the Sacrifice). **Nov 28** Independence and Liberation Day. **Dec 25** Christmas Day. **Jan 1-2 '96** New Year. **Feb 22** Lesser Bairam (End of Ramadan). **Mar 8** International Women's Day. **Apr 5** Good Friday. **Apr 8** Easter Monday. **Apr 15** Orthodox Easter. **Apr 29** Greater Bairam (Feast of the Sacrifice).
Note: Muslim festivals are timed according to local sightings of various phases of the Moon and the dates given above are approximations. During the lunar month of Ramadan that preceedes Lesser Bairam (Eid al-Fitr), Muslims fast during the day and feast at night and normal business patterns may be interrupted. Some disruption may continue into Lesser Bairam itself. Lesser Bairam and Greater Bairam (Eid al-Adha) may last anything from two to ten days, depending on the region. For more information see the section *World of Islam* at the back of the book.

HEALTH

Regulations and requirements may be subject to change at short notice, and you are advised to contact your doctor well in advance of your intended date of departure. Any numbers in the chart refer to the footnotes below.

	Special Precautions?	Certificate Required?
Yellow Fever	No	1
Cholera	Yes	No
Typhoid & Polio	Yes	No
Malaria	No	-
Food & Drink	2	-

[1]: A yellow fever vaccination certificate is required from travellers over one year of age if arriving from infected or endemic areas.
[2]: Mains water is normally chlorinated, and whilst relatively safe may cause mild abdominal upsets. Bottled water is available and is advised. Drinking water outside main cities and towns is likely to be contaminated and sterilisation is considered essential. Milk is pasteurised and dairy products are safe for consumption. Local meat, poultry, seafood, fruit and vegetables are under the control of sanitary/hygiene authorities and are generally considered safe to eat.
Hepatitis A and *B* are both present in Albania.
Rabies is present. For those at high risk, vaccination before arrival should be considered. If you are bitten abroad seek medical advice without delay. For more information consult the *Health* section at the back of the book.
Health care: Medical insurance is advisable. In cases of emergency all foreign tourists get medical aid free of charge. If, however, there is no reciprocal health agreement between Albania and the visitor's country of origin, the visitor will be liable for any hospital or consultation fees incurred.

TRAVEL - International

AIR: The national carrier is *Albanian Airlines*. Established in August 1992 in cooperation with *Tyrolean Airways*, the airline operates services to major European cities. Other airlines offering services to Tirana are *Ada Air, Adria Airways, Alitalia, Arberia Airlines, Austrian Airlines, Croatia Airways, ICP Air, Hemus Air, Malev, Olympic Airways* and *Swissair.*
Approximate flight time: From London to Tirana is 4 to 5 hours (including stopover times, the best being via Zurich, 45 minutes, and via Rome, 1 hour 30 minutes). Other connections are slow. Passengers may travel via Zurich, Athens, Rome, Vienna, Istanbul, Sofia, Paris or Budapest.
International airport: *Tirana Rinas (TIA)* is 25km (18 miles) from the capital. There is a small duty-free shop. An *Albanian Airlines* shuttle runs to the city centre where its offices are based (travel time – 30 minutes). Taxis are also available from and to the airport.
Departure tax: Lk1000 is levied on all foreign nationals. Nationals of Albania pay Lk500.
SEA: The main ports are Durres, Vlora and Saranda. Durres has ferry connections to Italy (to Bari is 3.5 hours, to Brindisi and to Trieste is 23 hours) and to Slovenia (to Koper is 22 hours); Vlora has ferry connections to Bari (travel time – 11 hours), Otranto and Brindisi; and Saranda has a connection from Corfu for day trippers. Other ports in southern Albania can be reached from Bari, Brindisi and Ortona (all in Italy) as well as Corfu and Igoumenitsa (Greece).
RAIL: There is an international freight link from Shkodra in Albania to Podgorica (formerly Titograd) in Montenegro.
ROAD: There are road links to all neighbouring countries with border crossings at Hani i Hotit (Podgorica in Montenegro), Qafe Prush (Kosovo), Morina (Prizren in Kosovo), Bllata (Diber in the Former Yugoslav Republic of Macedonia), Qafa e Thaës (Struga and Ohrid in the Former Yugoslav Republic of Macedonia), Tushemisht (Ohrid in the Former Yugoslav Republic of Macedonia), Gorica (Resnja in the Former Yugoslav Republic of Macedonia), Kapshtica (Florina in Greece) and Kakavija (Ioanina in Greece). There is an international private bus service between Tirana and Istanbul, Sofia, Shkup and Athens. It is now permitted to travel in a private car. Parking places are generally available near hotels or at other designated areas. A fully comprehensive insurance policy is absolutely essential.

TRAVEL - Internal

RAIL: The total rail network runs to approximately 720km (450 miles) and is single-track and unelectrified along the whole of its length. Trains are diesel, dilapidated and mostly overcrowded.
ROAD: There are around 18,000km (11,250 miles) of roads in Albania, but only 7450km (4656 miles) are considered main roads. Maintained by the State, they are more or less suitable for motor vehicles, although only

Timatic

Health
GALILEO/WORLDSPAN: **TI-DFT/TIA/HE**
SABRE: **TIDFT/TIA/HE**

Visa
GALILEO/WORLDSPAN: **TI-DFT/TIA/VI**
SABRE: **TIDFT/TIA/VI**

For more information on Timatic codes refer to Contents.

2850km (1781 miles) are paved and, of those, three-quarters are in a very poor condition. Motorways and the widening of existing road are planned for the future. All roads are used by pedestrians, cyclists, ox- and horse-drawn wagons, agricultural vehicles and herds of cattle and poultry, although the number of cars has increased considerably during the last three years. There are strict speed limits according to type of vehicle and type of road as well as within towns. Normal rules and international road signs apply. Traffic drives on the right. **Bus:** The major form of transportation within Albania. The main routes from Shkodra, Korça, Saranda, Gjirokastra, Peshkopia and Durres to Tirana are operated by private bus companies.

URBAN: A cheap, flat-fare urban **bus** service operates in the main cities, although the buses are extremely overcrowded and pickpocketing is rife. **Taxis** can be found in Tirana in front of the main hotels housing foreigners.

JOURNEY TIMES: The following chart gives approximate journey times from Tirana (in hours and minutes) to other major cities/towns in Albania.

	Road
Durres	1.00
Elbasan	1.00
Shkodra	2.30
Berat	3.00
Vlora	3.00
Korça	4.00

ACCOMMODATION

Albtourist Enterprise runs all state-owned tourist hotels. According to the facilities offered, hotels are classified in two categories. The rooms in first-category hotels have shower and WC. There are bars and restaurants in every tourist hotel. Telecommunication services are also available. The bed capacity is expected to continue increasing.

RESORTS & EXCURSIONS

During the Communist reign, foreign visitors were few and far between and were only allowed to travel in groups to a limited number of destinations within Albania. Having recognised the scenic beauty and cultural heritage of Albania, the Government has drafted ambitious plans in the field of tourism. The Ministry of Tourism was set up and a strategy on tourism development has been compiled, which has identified priority tourism development zones. This has been done in cooperation with the European Bank for Reconstruction and Development. In this context, the Government is working towards compiling new liberal legislation in order to attract foreign investment in the construction of new tourist facilities. There are plans for the construction of new hotels, tourist villages, camping areas, which will be followed by the development of infrastructure. These will be situated in mountainous areas, near lakes and along the coastline.

For the tourist there is much to discover: extensive beaches, mountain scenery such as Mount Dêja with numerous valleys, rivers, lakes such as Lake Préspa, outstanding flora and fauna and sites of great archaeological and historical interest.

In Roman times, **Apolonia,** located 12km (7.5 miles) from the city of **Fier,** was a large, prosperous city at the mouth of the Vjosë where there is still much left to be excavated. The amphitheatre, a colonnade of shops and several other parts of the Roman city centre are open to the public. There are monuments of Agonothetes and Odeon, as well as an ancient portico and the Mosaic House with a fountain. Unfortunately, some of the statues and other portable objects were removed before 1946 and sent to other countries. Those remaining have been placed in the well-organised museum which is to be found on the site of a 13th-century monastery. In the courtyard of the monastery is a Byzantine-style church, the *Church of St Mary,* believed to have been built in the 14th century. Not far from Apolonia, on the route to Durres, is the *Monastery of Ardenica.*

Known as the 'city of a thousand windows', **Berat** has been declared a 'Museum City'. Built on the slopes of a mountain, the old Turkish part of the town is very picturesque, being largely encompassed by the medieval fortress. To house the increasing population, a new town has been built further down the valley beside the largest textile combine in the country. The *Onufri Museum,* dedicated to the 16th-century painter and his contemporaries, houses restored icons in an orthodox church and there is a magnificent castle.

The ancient town of **Butrint** was once an important centre for the Illyrian tribes. It has been known as a settlement since 1000BC and has belonged to both the Greek and Roman empires during its long history which have left a rich legacy. Several excavations dating from

the 1st and 4th centuries AD can now be visited, among them a theatre, the *Temple of Aesculapius,* the *Nypheum,* the ancient gate with tow, the *Dionysos Altar,* Roman houses and baths. The *Baptistery,* with a floor of colourful mosaics, is not to be missed. The nearby tourist site of **Ksamil** offers magnificent views of the lake of Butrint, the islands and citrus- and olive-tree plantations. The important port of **Durres** is the second-largest city in Albania with the second-largest concentration of industry. The city was colonised by the Greeks in 627BC and was named *Epidamnos,* which later became *Dyrrachium* under the Romans. From the *Venetian Tower* at the harbour, the medieval *Town Wall* leads to the *amphitheatre* dating back to the 2nd century BC and containing an early Christian crypt with a rare wall mosaic. There is also an excellent *Archaeological Museum.* Between the 1st and 3rd centuries Durres was an important port and trading centre on the *Via Egnatia* trading route between Rome and Byzantium (Istanbul). Following a number of earthquakes, much of ancient Durres sank into the sea or collapsed and was subsequently built over. Today the city is best known for the nearby beach resort of *Durres Plazh.*

Gjirokastra has also been designated a 'Museum City' as so many of the houses retained their traditional wood- and stone-work. The narrow and winding cobbled streets ensure the virtual exclusion of motor traffic. The town is dominated by the 13th-century *Fortress* which was extended by Ali Pasha in 1811. It now contains the *National Museum of Weapons;* the collection ranges from medieval armour to a shot-down US reconnaissance aircraft. The view is not to be missed. The surrounding area is renowned for its many mineral springs.

Visible for miles around, **Kruja** is an attractive medieval town perched on top of a mountain. It was the centre of Albanian resistance to the Ottoman Turks under Skanderbeg, the national hero, and the *Skanderbeg Museum* is to be found inside the recently restored castle. The street leading up to the castle is built in the style of a medieval Turkish bazaar.

Korça was the seat of government during the Turkish reign. In the 18th century, the city was able to exploit its location at the crossroads of several caravan routes and became a major trading point during the 18th century. Standing at the foot of the dramatic Morava mountain near the Greek border, Korça is home to the *Mirahor Mosque,* dating back to 1466, the *Museum for Medieval Art,* the *Museum of Education* (where the first Albanian school was opened in 1887) and a listed, though decaying, bazaar quarter.

The charming resort of **Pogradecii** near the Macedonian border stands beside *Lake Ohrid,* renowned for its clear water and rich in trout, carp and sardines. About 5km (3 miles) to the east is the tourist centre of **Drilon,** surrounded by extensive ornamental gardens.

Albania's southern coastline remains completely unspoilt. Situated opposite Corfu, **Saranda** is now much visited by day trippers who come to enjoy this previously inaccessible resort.

Situated on the lake of the same name that divides Albania from Montenegro, **Shkodra** is dominated by the ruins of the *Fortress of Rozafa,* one of the ancient Ilyrian castles, built on a rock hill from where a spectacular panorama of the surrounding countryside, Lake Shkodra and the *Lead Mosque* can be enjoyed. A museum is dedicated to one of the greatest Albanian writers, Migjeni. The *Mesi Bridge,* 8km (5 miles) from Shkodra, is also well worth a visit, as is the *Monument to Gjergj Kastrioti Skanderbeg,* famous national hero, at his burial grounds in **Lezha.**

Created in 1614 by Sulejman Bargjini, **Tirana** has only been the capital of Albania since 1920. The city has examples of early 19th-century architecture such as the *Ethem-Bey Mosque* (built 1789-1823) and the 35m-high (117ft) clocktower (1830). The old bazaar quarter was demolished in 1961 to make way for the *Palace of Culture,* which houses the Opera and Ballet Theatre and the National Library. The city centre and the government buildings on *Skanderbeg Square* date back to the Italian era, creating the impression of a provincial Italian town, while the *Pyramid,* which was built as a museum for Enver Hoxha, is to be turned into an international Cultural Centre. Today, Tirana is not only the most populous city in Albania, but also the political, economic, cultural and spiritual centre of the country with national museums of archaeology, history and art. The *National Historical Museum* and the *National Art Gallery* are highly recommended, along with the *Exhibition of Folk Culture.* The best view over the city is to be had from the *Martyrs' Cemetery* which contains the *Mother Albania Monument.*

Vlora is not only a major port, but of great historical importance, for it was here in 1912 that the Assembly was convened which first proclaimed Albania as an independent state and set up the first national government, headed by Ismail Qemali. In recognition of

this, it was proclaimed a 'Hero City' in 1962. The *Muradite Mosque* (1538-42) was designed by the famous architect Mimar Sinan whose family originate in Albania. On a hill above the city is the tourist centre **Liria** which offers panoramic views of the beach and town.

SOCIAL PROFILE

FOOD & DRINK: Private restaurants are appearing overnight in Albania and usually offer better food than the hotels. In the more popular places, it is necessary to reserve a table and to be punctual. Food is typically Balkan with Turkish influences evident on any menu – *byrek, kofte, shish kebab.* Albanian specialities include *fërgesë tiranë,* a hot fried dish of meat, liver, eggs and tomatoes, and *tavllë kosi* or *tavllë elbanasi,* a mutton and yoghurt dish. Fish specialities include the *koran,* a trout from Lake Ohrid and the *Shkodra carp.* In summer *tarator,* a cold yoghurt and cucumber soup, is particularly refreshing. Popular Albanian desserts include *oshaf,* a fig and sheep's milk pudding, cakes soaked in honey and candied fruits or *reçel.* Guests of honour are quite often presented with baked sheep's head. A favourite in the south is *kukurec* (stuffed sheep's intestines). Continental breakfasts are usually served in hotels, but in the country the Albanian breakfast of *pilaf* (rice) or *paça* (a wholesome soup made from animals' innards) may not be to everyone's taste. **Drink:** All bars and restaurants serve Albanian drinks such as *Raki,* local red and white wines and different liquors. The Albanian cognac, with its distinctive aroma, is also popular. Many imported drinks can also be found, including Austrian canned beer, Macedonian wine, Cola imitations and ouzo from Greece. Turkish coffee (*kafe Turke*) is popular with Albanians, but many bars also serve Italian expresso (*ekspres*).

NIGHTLIFE: The most popular form of nightlife is the *xhiro,* the evening stroll along the main boulevards and squares of each town and village. Cultural life takes the form of theatre, opera and concerts. Discos and games arcades are beginning to appear. Some hotels have taverns with music and dancing.

SHOPPING: Special purchases include carpets, filigree silver and copper, woodcarvings, ceramic and any kind of needlework. Old markets are often worth exploring. Bartering is very much the order of the day for foreigners as well as for locals. Some of the tourist hotels also have shops. **Shopping hours:** Generally 0700-1200 and 1600-1900 Monday to Saturday (although regional variations are possible). Many shops are also open Sunday.

SOCIAL CONVENTIONS: One-third of the population live in urban areas, with the rest pursuing a relatively quiet rural existence. Many Albanian characteristics and mannerisms resemble those of the mainland Greeks, most notably in the more rural areas; for instance, a nod of the head means 'no' and shaking one's head means 'yes'. Handshaking is the accepted form of greeting. Albanians should be addressed with *Zoti* (Mr) and *Zonja* (Mrs). The former widespread greeting of *Shoku* (Comrade) has all but disappeared. Small gifts are customary when visiting someone's house, although flowers are not usually given. Any attempt to speak Albanian is greatly appreciated. Visitors should accept offers of raki, coffee or sweets. Dress is generally informal. Bikinis are acceptable on the beach; elsewhere women are expected to dress modestly although attitudes are becoming increasingly relaxed. Offices and restaurants are often unheated. Visitors should be aware that foreigners tend to be charged a lot more than locals, with this applying to entry fees as well as general merchandise. Smoking is permitted except where the sign *Ndalohet pirja duhanit* is displayed. It is also worth noting that the crime rate has risen, especially theft, and visitors should be careful not to overtly display valuables. Passports which allow entry to EU countries without a visa, foreign currency and cameras are mostly at risk, although all possessions should be kept close at hand at all times. Avoid remote areas and streets, especially at night. **Tipping:** Previously frowned upon by the authorities, tips are gratefully received in restaurants or for any service provided.

BUSINESS PROFILE

ECONOMY: Albania is Europe's poorest country and faces a very difficult period trying to adjust to its new status after years of isolation. However, it is blessed with considerable natural resources; it is one of the world's largest producers of chromium, and also has considerable reserves of copper, nickel, pyrites and coal. There are also substantial oil deposits, both on- and off-shore. Agriculture, which still provides for 30% of the GNP and employs half the workforce, is undergoing upheaval following decollectivisation. The Parliament has approved legislation to enable the transition to a market economy with complete privatisation of some sectors. Small and medium-sized enterprises have been

privatised, while the privatisation of larger ones will take place in the future. Albania is gradually taking its place within the international community. Membership of the IMF, the World Bank and the European Bank for Reconstruction and Development was secured in 1991. Thanks to economic reform and encouragement by international bodies, the economic indices have begun to make an increase in comparison with the early stage of the transition period. The Government is concentrating on the creation of favourable legislation for foreign investment in Albania. Besides joint ventures with foreign companies, the first investment in different sectors has begun. One of the fields opening up prospects is the field of tourism and this is due to existing potential. Foreign investors have expressed their interest in investing in this field and the first results have begun to be seen. There are plans for the construction of some tourist hotels, to be followed by other projects along the coast and in the interior of the country.
BUSINESS: Punctuality is expected. Business cards are common and European practices are observed. **Office hours:** 0700-1500 Monday to Friday. All offices are closed Saturday and Sunday.
COMMERCIAL INFORMATION: The following organisation can offer advice: Dhoma e Tregtisë dhe Industrise e Republikës së Shqiperisë (Chamber of Commerce & Industry of the Republic of Albania), Rruga Kavajes 6, Tirana. Tel: (42) 24246 or 22934 or 27997. Fax: (42) 27997. Telex: 2179 (a/b DHOMA AB).

CLIMATE

Temperate climate with warm and dry periods from June to September, cool and wet from October to May. April/May/June and mid-September to mid-October are the best months for visits.
Required clothing: Warm clothing and rainwear is advisable for winter. Lightweight for summer.

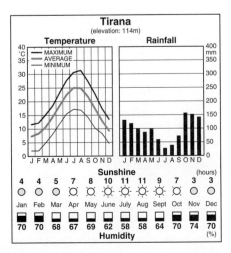

Algeria

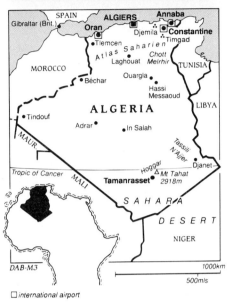

□ international airport

Location: North Africa, Mediterranean Coast.

Note: At the time of writing, land borders with Morocco have been closed. There have recently been a number of attacks on tourists, from robbing and car jacking to kidnapping and murder, perpetrated by militant Islamists and terrorists have threatened to kill foreigners who do not leave Algeria. The Foreign Office advises against all but essential visits. For up-to-date information, contact the FCO Travel Advice Unit. Tel: (0171) 270 4129.
Sources: US State Department – July 21, 1994; and FCO Travel Advice Unit – November 30, 1994.

Office National du Tourisme (ONT)
8 avenue de Pékin, Alger-Gare, Algiers, Algeria
Tel: (2) 605 960. Fax: (2) 591 315. Telex: 66590.
Embassy of the Democratic and Popular Republic of Algeria
54 Holland Park, London W11 3RS
Tel: (0171) 221 7800. Fax: (0171) 221 0448. Opening hours: 0930-1700 Monday to Friday.
Algerian Consulate
6 Hyde Park Gate, London SW7 5EW
Tel: (0171) 221 7800. Fax: (0171) 221 0448. Opening hours (for visa applications): 0930-1130 Monday to Friday.
British Embassy
BP 43, Résidence Cassiopée, Bâtiment B, 7 chemin des Glycines, 16000 Alger-Gare, Algiers, Algeria
Tel: (2) 605 601 or 605 411 or 605 038. Fax: (2) 604 410. Telex: 66151 (a/b PRDRM DZ) or 66266 (a/b VISA DZ) (Consular section).
Embassy of the Republic of Algeria
2118 Kalorama Road, NW, Washington, DC 20008
Tel: (202) 265 2800. Fax: (202) 667 2174. Telex: 892443.
Algerian Embassy Consular Section and Cultural Affairs Office
2137 Wyoming Avenue, NW, Washington, DC 20008
Tel: (202) 265 2800. Fax: (202) 667 2174.
Embassy of the United States of America
BP 549, 4 chemin Cheikh Bachir El-Ibrahimi, 16000 Alger-Gare, Algiers, Algeria
Tel: (2) 691 186 or 691 425 or 691 255 or 691 854 or 693 875. Fax: (2) 693 979. Telex: 66047.
Algerian Embassy
435 Daly Avenue, Ottawa, Ontario K1N 6H3
Tel: (613) 232 9453/4 or 232 5823 (Consular section). Fax: (613) 232 9099.
Canadian Embassy
PO Box 225, 27 bis rue Ali Massoudi, Alger-Gare, Algiers, Algeria
Tel: (2) 606 611. Fax: (2) 605 920. Telex: 66043 (a/b CANAD DZ).

AREA: 2,381,741 sq km (919,595 sq miles).
POPULATION: 25,324,000 (1991).

POPULATION DENSITY: 10.6 per sq km.
CAPITAL: Algiers (El Djezaïr). **Population:** 1,687,579 (1987).
GEOGRAPHY: Algeria is situated along the North African coast, bordered to the east by Tunisia and Libya, to the southeast by Niger, to the southwest by Mali, and to the west by Mauritania and Morocco. It is Africa's second-largest country, with 1000km (600 miles) of coastline. Along the coastal strip are the main towns, fertile land, beach resorts and 90% of the population. Further south lies the area of the *Hauts Plateaux*, mountains of to 2000m (6600ft) covered in cedar, pine and cypress forests with broad arable plains dividing the plateaux. The remaining 85% of the country is the Sahara Desert in its various forms, sustaining only 500,000 people, many of whom are nomadic tribes with goat and camel herds. The oil and minerals boom has created new industrial centres like Hassi Messaoud, which have grown up within previously barely inhabited regions of the northern Sahara. The plains of gravel and sand in the deep south are interrupted by two mountain ranges: the dramatic *Hoggar* massif, rising to almost 3000m (9800ft), and the *Tassili N'Ajjer* or 'Plateau of Chasms'. Both have long been important centres of Tuareg culture.
LANGUAGE: The official language is Arabic, but French is still used for most official and business transactions. Berber dialects are still spoken in the south. In general, English is spoken only in major business or tourist centres.
RELIGION: Over 90% of the population adhere to Islam, the majority being Sunni.
TIME: GMT + 1.
ELECTRICITY: 127/220 volts AC, 50Hz. The European 2-pin plug is standard.
COMMUNICATIONS: Telephone: IDD is available. Country code: 213. Outgoing international code: 00. There are public telephones in all post offices, leading hotels and on many main streets. **Telex/telegram:** Telex facilities are available at the main post office in Algiers (address below) and also at the El-Aurassi hotel. Telegrams can be sent from any post office from 0800-1900. The main post office in Algiers has a 24-hour service. **Post:** Mail posted in any of the main cities along the coast takes three to four days to reach Europe; posted elsewhere, it could take very much longer. A letter delivery service operates Saturday to Thursday. Parcels sent by surface mail may take up to two months to reach Algeria. All parcels sent by air or surface mail are subject to long delays in customs. Post office hours: generally 0800-1700 Saturday to Wednesday; 0800-1200 Thursday, but the main post office in Algiers (at 5 boulevard Mohamed Khémisti) is open around the clock.
Press: Daily newspapers are printed in Arabic or French. *El Moudjahid* has the highest circulation and is printed in French. Other main dailies printed in French are *L'Opinion, Alger Républicain* and *Le Matin. Al Chaab* and *El Massaa* are the leading Arabic-language dailies. Another daily, *Horizons,* has an English section.
BBC World Service and Voice of America frequencies: From time to time these change. See the section *How to Use this Book* for more information.

BBC:			
MHz	17.70	15.07	12.09	9.410
Voice of America:			
MHz	15.21	9.760	6.040	5.995

PASSPORT/VISA

Regulations and requirements may be subject to change at short notice, and you are advised to contact the appropriate diplomatic or consular authority before finalising travel arrangements. Details of these may be found at the head of this country's entry. Any numbers in the chart refer to the footnotes below.

	Passport Required?	Visa Required?	Return Ticket Required?
Full British	Yes	Yes	Yes
BVP	Not valid	-	-
Australian	Yes	Yes	Yes
Canadian	Yes	Yes	Yes
USA	Yes	Yes	Yes
Other EU (As of 31/12/94)	Yes	Yes	Yes
Japanese	Yes	Yes	Yes

Restricted entry: Those with Israeli stamps on their passports will have great difficulty entering Algeria. Nationals of Israel will automatically be refused entry.
Note: Currently, the government of Algeria requires all foreigners entering the country to exchange the equivalent of US$200 into local currency and documentary proof of legal exchange of currency is demanded on departure.
PASSPORTS: Valid passport required by all.
British Visitors Passport: Not acceptable.

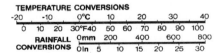

TEMPERATURE CONVERSIONS

Tirana (elevation: 114m)

VISAS: Required by all except:
(a) nationals of Argentina, Benin, Bosnia-Hercegovina, Croatia, Guinea-Bissau, Guinea Republic, Libya, Mali, Malta, Mauritania, Senegal, Seychelles, Slovenia, Syria, Tunisia, Yemen and Yugoslavia (Serbia and Montenegro);
(b) children under 15 years of age travelling alone.
Types of visa: Transit, Tourist and Business. Cost depends on visa type.
Validity: *Tourist:* approximately 30 days. *Transit:* approximately 48 hours. *Business:* approximately 15 days.
Application to: Consulate (or Consular Section at Embassy). For addresses, see top of entry.
Application requirements: (a) Completed application form. (b) 2 passport-size photos. (c) Applicants for Business visas need a letter from their sponsoring company.
Working days required: Generally 2 or 3 days but less in urgent cases. Nationals of The Netherlands and Portugal who are not resident in the UK must expect a delay of 3 or 4 weeks.
Temporary residence: Apply at Consulate.
Note: Exit permits are required for alien residents and those who have stayed in Algeria for more than 3 months.

MONEY

Currency: Dinar (AD) = 100 centimes. Notes are in denominations of AD200, 100, 50, 20 and 10. Coins are in denominations of AD5 and 1, and 50, 20, 10, 5, 2 and 1 centimes.
Currency exchange: In the past, difficulties have arisen when trying to exchange currency in Algeria, with only one national bank *(La Banque d'Extérieure d'Algérie)* able to exchange foreign currency at branches in major business centres. Difficulties are now decreasing and it is possible, for example, to exchange currency at some of the larger hotels. However, the facilities for currency exchange remain limited. Passengers arriving by plane during daylight hours are strongly advised to exchange a good deal of the money they intend to spend, during their stay, at the bank in the airport.
Credit cards: Very limited acceptance of Visa, American Express, Diners Club and Access/Mastercard and only in urban areas. Check with your credit card company for details of merchant acceptability and other services which may be available.
Travellers cheques: Only top-class (4-star and above) hotels and government-run craft (souvenir) shops accept these, and only in certain establishments.
Exchange rate indicators: The following figures are included as a guide to the movements of the Dinar against Sterling and the US Dollar:

Date:	**Oct '92**	**Sep '93**	**Jan '94**	**Jan '95**
£1.00=	**33.95**	**30.15**	**35.24**	**67.35**
$1.00=	**21.39**	**19.74**	**23.82**	**43.05**

Currency restrictions: Unlimited amounts of foreign currency (except for gold coins) may be imported, but it must all be declared. Visitors must fill in the currency declaration form at the same time as they complete their disembarkation card and have the form stamped by customs on arrival (even if the customs officer does not ask to see the form). At Algiers airport this should be done at the special customs desk situated after Passport Control but before baggage claim and customs. Every time visitors exchange currency they will be given a receipt and the amount exchanged will be entered onto this form. This form and the receipts *must* be surrendered on departure from Algeria. Visitors are required to produce their currency declaration forms when paying hotel bills to ensure that the Dinars being used to pay the bill have been legally changed from foreign currency. Visitors must change the equivalent of at least AD1000 *on entry* (AD500 for minors) and only amounts larger than AD1000 can be reconverted into foreign currency on departure. Visitors wishing to purchase tickets in Algeria for international transportation (air/rail/bus/sea) must exchange foreign currency specifically for this purpose *in excess of the AD1000 minimum obligatory exchange* and produce the exchange receipt and currency declaration form when purchasing their tickets. The import and export of local currency is limited to AD50.
Note: Because of the very strict adherence of the authorities to these regulations, visitors are strongly advised not to be associated with the black market, which tends to concentrate on the French Franc and portable electronics.
Banking hours: 0900-1630 Sunday to Thursday.

DUTY FREE

The following goods may be taken into Algeria by persons over 17 years of age without incurring customs duty:
200 cigarettes or 50 cigars or 250g of tobacco; 1 bottle of spirits (opened).
Prohibited items: Gold, firearms and drugs may not be imported. Gold, firearms and jewellery may not be exported.
Note: Personal jewellery weighing in excess of 100g is subject to a temporary importation permit which will ensure its re-exportation. Alternatively it can be left with customs on arrival. It is compulsory to declare all gold, pearls and precious stones on arrival in the country.

PUBLIC HOLIDAYS

Jan 1 '95 New Year's Day. **Feb 1** Start of Ramadan. **Mar 3** Eid al-Fitr (End of Ramadan). **May 1** Labour Day. **May 10** Eid al-Adha (Feast of the Sacrifice). **May 31** Islamic New Year. **Jun 9** Ashoura. **Jun 19** Ben Bella's Overthrow. **Jul 5** Independence Day. **Aug 9** Mouloud (Prophet's Birthday). **Nov 1** Anniversary of the Revolution. **Dec 20** Leilat al-Meiraj. **Jan 1 '96** New Year's Day. **Jan 22** Start of Ramadan. **Feb 22** Eid al-Fitr (End of Ramadan). **Apr 29** Eid al-Adha (Feast of the Sacrifice).
Note: Muslim festivals are timed according to local sightings of various phases of the Moon and the dates given above are approximations. The Algerian observance of Ramadan (lasting one lunar month and culminating in the feast days of Eid al-Fitr) has recently relaxed, and restaurants in Algiers and other business centres will be open during the day. However, in the towns and oases of the south where religious observance tends to be more orthodox, some difficulty might be had in finding eating places and getting transport during the daylight hours. For a more detailed description of Ramadan and its meaning see *World of Islam* at the back of this book.

HEALTH

Regulations and requirements may be subject to change at short notice, and you are advised to contact your doctor well in advance of your intended date of departure. Any numbers in the chart refer to the footnotes below.

	Special Precautions?	**Certificate Required?**
Yellow Fever	Yes	1
Cholera	No	No
Typhoid & Polio	Yes	-
Malaria	2	-
Food & Drink	3	-

[1]: A certificate is required by travellers over one year of age arriving from endemic or infected areas.
[2]: Malaria risk is limited. The benign *vivax* strain occurs in two small foci in Arib (Aïn-Defla Department) and Ihrir (Illizi Department).
[3]: Mains water is normally chlorinated, and whilst relatively safe may cause mild abdominal upsets. Bottled water is available and is advised for the first few weeks of the stay. Drinking water outside main cities and towns is likely to be contaminated and sterilisation is considered essential. Milk is unpasteurised and should be boiled. Powdered or tinned milk is available and is advised, but make sure that it is reconstituted with pure water. Local meat, poultry, seafood, fruit and vegetables are generally considered safe to eat.
Bilharzia (schistosomiasis) is present. Avoid swimming and paddling in fresh water. Swimming pools which are well-chlorinated and maintained are safe.
Health care: Medical insurance is not always valid in this country and a medical insurance supplement with specific overseas coverage is recommended. Health care facilities are generally of a high standard in the north but more limited in the south. Doctors and hospitals usually ask for immediate cash payment for their services. Emergency cases will be dealt with free of charge.

TRAVEL - International

AIR: Algeria's national airline is *Air Algérie (AH).*
Approximate flight time: From London to Algiers is 2 hours 30 minutes.

Timatic

Health
GALILEO/WORLDSPAN: **TI-DFT/ALG/HE**
SABRE: **TIDFT/ALG/HE**

Visa
GALILEO/WORLDSPAN: **TI-DFT/ALG/VI**
SABRE: **TIDFT/ALG/VI**

For more information on Timatic codes refer to Contents.

International airports: *Algiers (ALG)* (Houari Boumediène) is 20km (12 miles) east of Algiers. Coaches depart every 30 minutes to the city, fare about AD10. Taxi fare to the city is approximately AD100 (travel time – 30 minutes). Airport facilities include banking and exchange (0600-2400), a state-run duty-free and craft shop (0600-2400), car park, garage, left luggage *(consigne)*, post office, car hire (ONAT) and 24-hour restaurant and bar.
Oran (ORN) (Es Senia) is 10km (6 miles) from the city, linked by taxis and a regular bus service. The taxi fare is approximately AD100. Airport facilities include banking, limited catering and car hire (ONAT).
Annaba (AAE) (El Mellah) is 12km (7.5 miles) from the city. Bus service departs to the city every 30 minutes. Coach service is available on request and taxis are also available; maximum taxi fare to the city is AD100. There are no duty-free shops but there are restaurant, banking and car hire facilities (ONAT).
Constantine (Ain El Bey) is 9km (6 miles) from the city. There are bus and taxi links with the city and limited airport facilities.
SEA: The main ports are Algiers, Annaba, Arzew, Béjaia and Oran. Regular shipping lines serve Algiers from Mediterranean ports. The two major shipping lines are *Entreprise Nationale de Transport Maritime de Voyageurs-Algérie Ferries (ENTMV)* and *Compagnie de Navigation Mixte.*
RAIL: There is one daily train connecting Algiers with Tunis via Constantine and Annaba. A reservation is required for this route. First-class carriages are air-conditioned, the train also carries a buffet car and couchettes. Another daily train runs between Algiers and Marrakech. Stops en route are Oran, Fès, Mèknes, Rabat and Casablanca. Reservations are required and a supplement is charged. Air-conditioned coaches and light refreshments/buffet car are available. At present services are interrupted due to the closure of the border between Algeria and Morocco and through trains are not operating.
ROAD: Due to border closures, land crossings between Morocco and Algiera are not possible at present. The main road entry points are Maghnia (Morocco), Souk-Ahras, Tebessa and El Kala (Tunisia), Fort Thiriet (Libya), In Guezzam (Niger) and Bordj Mokhtar (Mali). There is a good network of paved roads in the coastal regions and paved roads connect the major towns in the northern Sahara. Further south, the only substantial stretches of paved roads are on the two trans-Saharan 'highways', one of which runs to the west through Reggane and up through Morocco to the coast, while the other runs through Tamanrasset and Djanet on its way to Ghardaia and Algiers. The precise route taken by trans-Saharan travellers often depends on the season. Please note that many desert 'roads' are up to 10km-wide (6-mile) ribbons of unimproved desert and are suitable only for well-maintained 4-wheel-drive vehicles. **Coach:** Services run by *SNTV (National Travel and Transport Company)* with four international routes from Libya, Tunisia, Morocco and Niger.

TRAVEL - Internal

AIR: *Air Algérie* operates frequent services from Algiers domestic airport (adjacent to Algiers International) to the major business centres of Annaba, Constantine and Oran. Less frequent services run from Algiers, Oran, Constantine and Annaba to the other less important commercial centres and gateway oases such as Ghardaia (six hours from Algiers) and Ouargla, as well as important oil towns such as In Amenas and Hassi Messaoud. Services are generally reliable, but air travel to the far south may be subject to delay during the dry summer months because of sand storms. Despite this, air is by far the most practical means of transport to the far south for the visitor with limited resources of time; Djanet and Tamanrasset are the oasis gateways to the *Tassili N'Ajjer* and the *Hoggar* respectively.
Note: The London office of *Air Algérie* can provide a timetable of services and prices, make reservations and issue tickets. There is an *Air Algérie* office in every town which is served by *Air Algérie*. Reservations and itineraries can be arranged from these offices, but as some of the more isolated offices are not connected by computer or telex, reservations should be confirmed well in advance. Offices are *very* busy in the major towns.
SEA: Government ferries service the main coastal ports: Algiers, Annaba, Arzew, Béjaia, Djidjelli, Ghazaouet, Mostaganem, Oran and Skikda.
RAIL: There are 4000km (2500 miles) of railway in Algeria. Daily but fairly slow services operate in the northern part of the country between Algiers and Oran, Béjaia, Skikda, Annaba and Constantine. The southern routes connect once a day from Annaba to Tebessa via Souk Ahras, Constantine with Touggout via Biskra (twice a day) and Mohammadia with Bechar. Trains on

the southern routes only carry second-class coaches.
ROAD: Road surfaces are reasonably good. All vehicles travelling in the desert should be in good mechanical condition, as breakdown facilities are virtually non-existent. Travellers *must* carry full supplies of water and petrol. Traffic drives on the right. **Coach:** Relatively inexpensive coaches link major towns. Services are regular but this mode of travel is not recommended for long journeys, such as travel to the south from the coastal strip. Services leave from the coach stations close to the centres of Algiers and Oran. **Car hire:** Can be arranged through the state-run travel agency ONAT at the airport on arrival or in most towns. Many hotels can also arrange car hire. **Documentation:** An International Driving Permit is required. A *carnet de passage* may be required if one's own car is to be used. Cars are allowed entry for three months without duty. Insurance must be purchased at the border. Proof of ownership is essential. Enquire at ONAT for details.
URBAN: Municipal **bus** services operate in Algiers, its suburbs and the coastal area. 10-journey carnets and daily, weekly or longer duration passes are available. There are also two public elevators and a funicular which leads up to the hill overlooking the old *souk* in Algiers. A metro is planned. **Taxi:** All taxis are metered and are plentiful in most cities and major towns, though busy during the early evening in the main cities as many people use them to return home after work. The habit of taxi sharing is extensive. The amount on the meter is the correct fare, but there are surcharges after dark. Travellers are advised not to use unlicensed taxis, as these are likely to be uninsured.
JOURNEY TIMES: The following chart gives approximate journey times (in hours and minutes) from Algiers to other major cities/towns in Algeria.

	Air	Road
Constantine	0.45	4.00
Ghardaia	0.55	6.00
Oran	0.50	4.00
Tlemcen	1.00	6.00
Béjaia	0.45	3.00
Biskra	1.15	5.00
El Oued	1.25	6.00
Annaba	0.55	6.00
H. Messaoud	1.05	8.00

ACCOMMODATION

The government department ONAT *(Office National Algérien de l'Animation de la Promotion et de l'Information Touristique)* produces a brochure listing hotels, hotel tariffs, car hire prices, transfer (hotel/airport) charges and specially arranged tours. This brochure is available from *Air Algérie* offices.
HOTELS: In general, good hotel accommodation in Algeria is limited. The business centres, and in particular Algiers, tend to have either extremely expensive luxury hotels or cheaper hotels primarily suited to the local population visiting on business or for social purposes. Oran or Algiers are full of cheaper hotels, but they tend to be crowded and difficult to get into, even with a confirmed booking. For assurance on business, reserve rooms only at the best hotels. **Grading:** All hotels are subject to government regulations and are classified by a star rating: deluxe (**5-star**), second class (**4/3-star**) and tourist class (**2/1-star**).
The Coast: The hotels in the resorts along the Mediterranean coast are increasing in number, and many are of a reasonably high standard. Often the good hotels in these resorts run their own nightclubs. The government travel agency, ONAT, which has offices all over the country, owns the majority of the best hotels, and its network of higher standard accommodation is growing year by year. ONAT offices will make reservations, but only in their own hotels. Winter rates for coastal resorts apply from October 1 to May 31, and summer rates for the remainder of the year.
The Oases: Good hotels in the gateway oases of the mid-south such as Ghardaia and Ouargla are few and far between, and during the season (any time other than high summer, which runs from late June to early September) it is vital to book well in advance. Once again ONAT can help, especially during high season when room availability is limited. It is generally wiser in season to book through ONAT for the first night or so, and look around once there if not satisfied.
The Far South: Hotels in the very far south are extremely limited; for instance the only hotel in Djanet, a favourite stopping place for trans-Saharan expeditions and gateway oasis for trips to the *Tassili N'Ajjer*, is the Hotel Zeribas, a *campement* of 20 straw huts. In Tamanrasset, better-class hotels have been built since the oasis became a fashionable winter resort. Room availability is, however, still limited.
CAMPING/CARAVANNING: Camping is free on common land or on the beaches but permission from the local authorities is necessary. Campsites with good facilities are found in Larhat, Ain el-Turk and Annaba.
YOUTH HOSTELS: There is a good network of youth hostels throughout the country, costing approximately AD10 per night.

RESORTS & EXCURSIONS

For the purposes of this section the country has been divided into three regions: The Coastal Strip, The Hauts Plateaux and The Sahara.

The Coastal Strip

The capital city, **Algiers**, has been a port since Roman times and many impressive ruins can be seen, such as those at Djemila, Timgad and especially Tipaza (see below), which are all in good condition because of the dry desert climate. The city was commercialised by the French in the mid-19th century and much of the fabric of the city dates from this time. However, it still has a Maghreb feel to it, with many zig-zag alleyways, mosques, a *casbah*, *medersas* (study houses) and the beautiful Turkish houses and palaces much admired by Le Corbusier. The *Bardo Ethnographic and Local Art Museum* and the *National Museum of Fine Arts* are amongst the finest in North Africa. Despite these attractions, it is not likely that anyone but the business traveller will want to spend much time in the capital; it is an unavoidable stop en route to either the coast or the far south, the place to arrange itineraries and accommodation for onward internal travel.
Within easy reach of Algiers along the coast lie some fine resorts. **Zeralda** is a beach resort with a holiday village and a replica nomad village. **Tipaza** has exceptional Roman, Punic and Christian ruins, and a Numidian mausoleum. The **Chiffa Gorges** and **Kabylia** in the mountains provide more rural scenery. Fig and olive groves in summer become ski resorts in the winter. To the east of Algiers, the **Turquoise Coast** offers rocky coves and long beaches within easy reach of the city, equipped with sports, cruise and watersports facilities. The **Sidi Fredj** peninsula has a marina, an open-air theatre and complete amenities including sporting facilities.
The western coast around Algeria's second city, **Oran**, has a similar range of beaches, historic remains and mosques. Along the coast from the city, which is primarily a business centre and an oil depot, there are a number of resorts, many with well-equipped hotels. Notable beaches include *Ain El Turk, Les Andalouses, Canastel, Kristel, Monastagem* and *Sablettes*. Les Andalouses is the most developed and offers all types of watersports facilities and nightclub entertainment as well as first-class accommodation.

The Hauts Plateaux

Tlemcen was an important imperial city from the 12th to 16th centuries, when Morocco ruled the whole of the Maghreb. It stands in the wooded foothills of the Tellein Atlas and is a pleasant retreat from the stifling heat of high summer. Sights include the *Grand Mosque*, the *Mansourah Fortress* and the *Almohad ramparts*.
Constantine, to the east, is a natural citadel lying across the River Rhumnel. Founded by the Carthaginians, who called it Cirta, it is the oldest continuously inhabited city in Algeria. Sights include the *Ahmed Bey Palace* (one of the most picturesque in the Maghreb) and the *Djamma el-Kebir Mosque*.

The Sahara

The Sahara is the most striking and also most forbidding feature of the country. Relatively uninhabited, the area is drawing increasing numbers of winter tourists. Accommodation, though generally good value, is often scarce in oasis regions, and during the season it is advisable to book in advance through ONAT or a hotel representative. *Air Algérie* operates frequent flights from Algiers to Ghardaia, Djanet and Tamanrasset, as well as to several smaller towns, oases and oil settlements, but services can be delayed in high summer due to adverse weather conditions. Roads are much improved, although summer sand storms and winter rains can make all but the major routes hazardous.
The best way to enter the south is to cross the El Kautara Gorges in the south of Constantine. The sudden glimpse of the Sahara through the El Kautara Gorges is breathtaking. These gorges are said to separate the winter areas from the land of everlasting summer and are called *Fouur Es Sahra* (the Sahara's mouth) by the inhabitants. Further down, most Algerian oases generally defy the European cliché of a small patch of palms forever threatened by encroaching dunes: they are often fairly large towns with highly organised, walled-in gardens for the date palms, and mosques, shops and monuments. Favourite starting places for exploring the Sahara are **Laghouat**, a town with a geometric plan, or the **M'Zab Valley**, which has seven typical holy towns and is inhabited by a Muslim fundamentalist sect called the Mozabites. Each town is distinguished by a minaret with four spires, a striking characteristic of all Mozabite towns. The most famous among them is **Ghardaia,** coiled within a group of bare, ochre rocks. The streets, made of clay or paving stones, curl up through the blue and beige buildings towards the white obelisk of the minaret. Not far from Ghardaia, situated on a hill, is the holy town of **Beni-Isgheu**, the four gates of which are constantly guarded. The special feature of this town is its permanent auction market. In the east of the M'Zab region is **Ouargla**, referred to as 'the golden key to the desert'. This town is well worth visiting for its malekite (another Islamic sect) minaret overlooking an expansive landscape. At the foot of the minaret lies the market square, the porticos of the *souks* and the terraced house roofs of the inhabitants. Further on is an oasis surrounded by palm trees and beyond that lie the beaches of the Sebkha. Deeper into the south lies the town of **El Goléa**, referred to as 'the pearl of the desert' or 'the enchanted oasis' because of its luxuriant vegetation and abundant water. The town is dominated by an old *ksar* (fort) whose ruins are well-preserved. Moving ever further south one comes to the **Hoggar Mountains**, an impressive, jagged range reaching as far as Libya and surrounded by desert on all sides. It consists of a plateau made of volcanic rock and consists of eroded cliffs and granite needles forming fascinating shapes in pink, blue or black basalt. At the top of the *Assekreu* nestles the famous refuge of Charles de Foucault at 2800m (9259ft). *Mount Tahat*, which belongs to the *Atakor Massif*, can be seen in the distance, reaching 3000m (9921ft) at its highest point. The picturesque capital, **Tamanrasset**, situated at the heart of the Hoggar Mountains, is full of life and character and an important stopping place for commercial traffic travelling to and from West Africa. Being a large town with many hotels and restaurants, tourists often stay in 'Tam' (as it is sometimes called) and use it as a base for touring the Hoggar Mountains (the Assekreu and Charles de Foucault's hermitage) or hiking in the open desert to the south and west in the company of camel drivers who carry their luggage. It is also a popular winter holiday resort and a centre for oil exploration and exploitation. It is visited regularly by the camel caravans of *Les hommes Al*, blue-robed Touaregs, who are the ancient nomadic inhabitants of this wide region. They make their way around the inscrutable desert through an ancient knowledge of landmarks passed on from father to son. These nomads have a fair complexion, a blue veil over their faces and are often very tall. The tiny oasis of **Djanet**, another watering hole for commercial traffic and trans-Saharan expeditions, can be found in the *Tassili N'Ajjer*, or 'Plateau of Chasms'. This is a vast volcanic plateau crossed by massive gorges gouged out by rivers which have long since dried out or gone underground. The Tassili conceals a whole group of entirely unique rupestrian paintings (rock paintings) which go back at least as far as the neolithic age. The paintings, depicting daily life, hunting scenes and herds of animals, have a striking beauty and reveal ways of life several thousand years old. They spread out over a 130,000 sq km surface (50,000 sq miles) and form an extraordinary open-air museum which has been miraculously conserved due to the pure quality of the air. Tours are available, lasting from one day to up to two weeks, of the Tassili Plateau and the rupestrian paintings, as well as long-distance car treks in the Ténéré. These visits are organised by private agencies run by the Touaregs and most of them offer a high-quality service. Tourists are collected at the airport (either Djanet or Tamanrasset) and the agency provides them with transportation (usually in 4-wheel-drive vehicles), mattresses and food, but travellers must bring their own sleeping bags.

SOCIAL PROFILE

FOOD & DRINK: Algiers and popular coastal towns have a fair selection of good restaurants, serving mainly French and Italian-style food, though the spicy nature of the sauces sets the cuisine apart from its European counterparts. Even classic dishes will have an unmistakeable Algerian quality. Fish dishes are exceptionally good. Menus generally feature a soup or salad to start, roast meat (lamb or beef) or fish as a main course and fresh fruit to finish. In the towns you will find stalls selling *brochettes* (kebabs) in French bread and covered in a spicy sauce (if desired). The range of foodstuffs in the south is limited, and it can be more a question of doing something with whatever is available. Local cooking, which you might be served as a guest of a household, will often consist of roast meat (generally lamb), *cous-cous* with a vegetable sauce (excellent if fresh) and fresh fruit to finish. Food is no longer expensive because of the devaluation of Algerian money and, therefore, good quality food is very reasonably priced. **Drink:** The sale of alcohol is not encouraged, it is available only in the more expensive restaurants and hotels and is generally not cheap. There are no licensing hours and hotel bars tend to stay open for as long as there is custom. Algeria produces some good wines but very few of them seem to be served in the country itself. If available try Medea, Mansourah and Mascara red wines and Medea, Mascara and Lismara rosés. The major hotels may have a reasonable cellar of European wines. All visitors are advised to respect Muslim attitudes to alcohol.

NIGHTLIFE: The main towns offer reasonable entertainment facilities, including hotel restaurants, nightclubs, discotheques, folk dancing and traditional music. In Oran and Algiers, some cinemas show French and English films.

SHOPPING: Possible souvenirs include leatherware, rugs, copper and brassware, local dresses and jewellery. Berber carpets are beautifully decorated and from the Sahara comes finely-dyed basketwork and primitive-style pottery. Bargaining is customary in street markets and smaller shops. The rue Didouche Mourad is the best shopping street in Algiers. There are two state-run craft centres with fixed prices. One is located at Algiers airport. **Shopping hours:** *Winter:* 0800-1800 Saturday to Thursday. *Summer:* 0800-1830 Saturday to Thursday.

SPORT: Horseracing is popular. The northern coastline offers **fishing**, **swimming** and **sailing**, mainly in Algiers and Annaba. **Football** is also popular.

SOCIAL CONVENTIONS: French-style courtesy should be adopted with new acquaintances. The provision and acceptance of hospitality are as important a part of Algerian culture as elsewhere in the Arab world. In the main cities the urban population lives at a frantic pace much akin to European urban dwellers, but in the south and in rural areas people are much more open and friendly. Algerian women have strict social and dress codes (only one eye is allowed to be revealed in public) and Western women should respect Muslim tradition and cover themselves as much as possible or they may incite hostility. For more information see the section *World of Islam* at the back of the book. **Photography:** Military installations and personnel should not be photographed and visitors are advised to make sure there is nothing that could be of a governmental or military nature around their prospective photographic subject. **Tipping:** 10% is usual.

BUSINESS PROFILE

ECONOMY: Petroleum and natural gas resources have overtaken agriculture in importance. Algeria has the fourth-highest GNP per capita in Africa. Most of the country consists of the Sahara desert, and despite investments in the agricultural sector (the main crops being grapes, cereals and citrus fruits), Algeria is far from self-sufficent in foodstuffs. The largest export sector is that of petroleum products, although Algeria is somewhat constrained in its earnings from this source by the requirements of OPEC, to which it belongs. Other exports are fruit and minerals, principally iron ore and phosphates. The country's major trading partners are France, Germany, Italy and Spain. From these it imports most industrial equipment and consumer goods. From 1972, all international trading has been carried out by a number of state trading organisations, although this is likely to change in the near future with the liberalisation of commerce proposed by the Algerian government. Management decisions and financial control are being devolved to individual enterprises. Previous tight restrictions on foreign investment have been relaxed since the passage of new legislation in March 1990. **BUSINESS:** Suits should always be worn in winter months, shirt sleeves during the summer. Prior appointments are necessary for larger business firms. Businessmen generally speak Arabic and French and, as a great deal of bargaining is necessary, it is rarely convenient to carry out transactions through an interpreter. Patience is always important. Visitors are usually entertained in hotels or restaurants, where Algerian businessmen are seldom accompanied by their wives. Only rarely are visitors entertained at home. If visiting during Ramadan (and this should be avoided if possible) care should be taken to observe local custom in public places. (For a more detailed description see *World of Islam* at the back of this book.) The climate is best between October and May. **Office hours:** Generally 0800-1200 and 1300-1700 Saturday to Wednesday.

COMMERCIAL INFORMATION: The following organisation can offer advice: Chambre Nationale de Commerce (CNC), BP 100, Palais Consulaire, rue Amilcar Cabral, Algiers. Tel: (2) 575 555. Fax: (2) 629 991. Telex: 61345.

CLIMATE

Summer temperatures are high throughout the country, particularly in the south where it is both very dry and very hot. During this time road travel is difficult and air travel prone to delay due to sandstorms. Northern cities have high humidity, while those along the coast are cooled by sea breezes. In the winter the oases of the far south are pleasant and attract many visitors. The desert temperature drops dramatically at night. North of the Sahara temperatures are very mild from September to May and vary very little between day and night. South of the Sahara, temperatures are pleasant from October to April, but there are great variations between day and night. Coastal towns are prone to storms from the sea. Rainfall is relatively low throughout the country and in the far south it is virtually unknown.

Required clothing: Cotton and linen lightweights for winter months and evenings in desert areas. Woollens and light rainwear are advised for the winter along the coastal strip and the *Hauts Plateaux*. South of the Sahara, from mid-December to mid-January, temperatures drop and warm clothes are necessary both in the morning and the evening. A mountain sleeping bag is also required when camping.

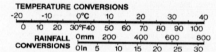

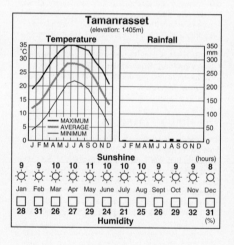

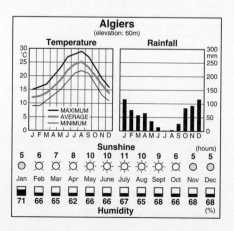

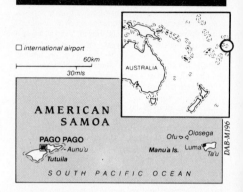

American Samoa

☐ international airport

Location: South Pacific.

Office of Tourism
PO Box 1147, Pago Pago, AS 96799
Tel: 633 1091. Fax: 633 1094.
Embassy of the United States of America
24-31 Grosvenor Square, London W1A 1AE
Tel: (0171) 499 9000. Fax: (0171) 629 9124.
Embassy of the United States of America
100 Wellington Street, Ottawa, Ontario K1P 5T1
Tel: (613) 238 5335 *or* 238 4470. Fax: (613) 238 5720.

AREA: 194.8 sq km (76.1 sq miles).
POPULATION: 46,800 (1990 estimate).
POPULATION DENSITY: 240.2 per sq km.
CAPITAL: Pago Pago. **Population:** 3075 (1980).
GEOGRAPHY: American Samoa comprises seven islands: Tutuila, the largest with an area of 53 sq miles; Ta'u, Olosega and Ofu, known as the Manu'a group; and Aunu'u, Rose and Swain's. The Manu'a group is volcanic in origin and dominated by high peaks. Rose and Swain's Islands are uninhabited coral atolls located to the east and north respectively of the other two island groups.
LANGUAGE: Samoan, but many islanders speak English.
RELIGION: Half of the population are Christian Congregational; also Roman Catholics, Latter Day Saints and Protestants.
TIME: GMT - 11.
ELECTRICITY: 110V. US-style 2-pin plugs are in use.
COMMUNICATIONS: Telephone: IDD is available. Country code: 684. **Fax:** Several hotels have facilities. **Telex/telegram:** Facilities are available at main towns and hotels. **Post:** The Main Post Office in the Lumana'i Building in Fagatogo is open 24 hours. There are also branches in Leone and Faguita villages, open 0800-1600 Monday to Friday and 0830-1200 Saturday. **Press:** The main international newspapers available on the islands are *The Herald Tribune, The New York Times, The Washington Post* and *USA Today*. The island's own English-language newspaper is the *News Bulletin*, published from Monday to Friday. The *Samoa Journal and Advertiser* and *Samoa News* are also published in English.
BBC World Service and Voice of America frequencies: From time to time these change. See the section *How to Use this Book* for more information.
BBC:

MHz	17.83	15.34	9.740	11.95

Voice of America:

MHz	5.985	11.72	9.525	5.18

PASSPORT/VISA

Regulations and requirements may be subject to change at short notice, and you are advised to contact the appropriate diplomatic or consular authority before finalising travel arrangements. Details of these may be found at the head of this country's entry. Any numbers in the chart refer to the footnotes below.

	Passport Required?	Visa Required?	Return Ticket Required?
Full British	Yes	No	· Yes
BVP	Not valid	-	-
Australian	Yes	No	Yes
Canadian	Yes	No	Yes
USA	No	No	Yes
Other EU (As of 31/12/94)	Yes	No	Yes
Japanese	Yes	No	Yes

PASSPORTS: Passport required by all except nationals of the USA with other proof of identity with a valid onward or return ticket for stays of up to 30 days. Passports must be valid for at least 60 days beyond period of stay.
British Visitors Passport: Not accepted.
VISAS: Not required for either tourist or business visits of up to 30 days, provided a confirmed reservation and documentation for onward travel is held. Travellers wishing to stay for more than 30 days should obtain special permission from the Immigration Department in Pago Pago. Approval to remain on the islands is given in 30-day periods only.
Application to: Consular Section at any US Embassy. For addresses, see top of entry.
Working days required: At least 2 weeks before departure.
Temporary residence: Apply to Immigration Department in Pago Pago.

MONEY

Currency: US Dollar (US$) = 100 cents. See the *USA* section further on in the book for information on denominations, exchange rates, etc.
Currency exchange: Exchange facilities are available at the airport and through trade banks.
Credit cards: American Express is widely accepted whereas Access/Mastercard has more limited use. Check with your credit card company for details of merchant acceptability and other services which may be available.
Currency restrictions: Free import and export of both local and foreign currency.
Banking hours: 0900-1500 Monday to Friday.

DUTY FREE

The following items may be imported into American Samoa without incurring customs duty:
200 cigarettes or 50 cigars; 2 bottles of alcohol; a reasonable amount of perfume.

PUBLIC HOLIDAYS

Jan 1 '95 New Year's Day. **Jan 16** Martin Luther King Day. **Feb 20** Presidents' Day. **Apr 17** Flag Day. **May 29** Memorial Day. **Jul 4** Independence Day. **Sep 4** Labour Day. **Oct 9** Columbus Day. **Nov 11** Veterans' Day. **Nov 23** Thanksgiving Day. **Dec 25** Christmas Day. **Jan 1 '96** New Year's Day. **Jan 15** Martin Luther King Day. **Feb 19** Presidents' Day. **Apr 17** Flag Day.

HEALTH

Regulations and requirements may be subject to change at short notice, and you are advised to contact your doctor well in advance of your intended date of departure. Any numbers in the chart refer to the footnotes below.

	Special Precautions?	Certificate Required?
Yellow Fever	No	1
Cholera	No	No
Typhoid & Polio	Yes	-
Malaria	No	-
Food & Drink	2	-

[1]: A yellow fever vaccination certificate is required from travellers over one year of age arriving from infected areas.
[2]: Mains water is normally chlorinated, and whilst relatively safe, may cause mild abdominal upsets. Bottled water is available and is advised for the first few weeks of the stay. Drinking water outside main cities and towns may be contaminated and sterilisation is advisable. Milk is pasteurised and dairy products are safe for consumption. Local meat, poultry, seafood, fruit and vegetables are generally considered safe to eat.
Health care: There are good medical facilities at the *LBJ Tropical Medical Centre.* The *Fag'alu Institution* offers 24-hour medical and dental treatment. Health insurance is recommended.

TRAVEL - International

AIR: The international airline is *Samoa Air.*
Approximate flight time: From Pago Pago to London is 25 hours, depending on route taken and stopover times. A typical journey would probably involve stopovers in Los Angeles and Honolulu.
International airport: *Pago Pago (PPG)* is 11.5km (7 miles) from the city. Buses, taxis and limousines are available. There are duty-free facilities and a restaurant at the airport. Regular scheduled trips are available plus charters and sightseeing.
SEA: The international port is Pago Pago (Tutuila), which is served by the following passenger/cruise lines: *Chandris, Pacific Far East Line, P&O Cruises, Princess Cruises* and *Sitmar.* The port is also served by the following cargo/passenger lines: *China Navigation, Daiwa Line, Farrell Line, Polynesian Shipping* and *Union Steamship.*

TRAVEL - Internal

SEA: There is a weekly ferry service from Pago Pago to the Manu'a Islands. A government-run excursion boat sails regularly around Tutuila, calling at the north coast villages of Afono, Vatia and Fagasa. Contact local authorities for details.
ROAD: There are 80km (50 miles) of asphalt road on Tutuila Island and many more miles of paved or unpaved roads throughout the islands. Traffic drives on the right. **Bus:** A local service operates between the airport and the centre of Pago Pago. The *aiga bus* operates an inexpensive but unscheduled service between Fagatogo and outlying villages. **Taxi:** Plentiful; the government-fixed fares are displayed in all taxis. **Car hire:** Both *Hertz* and *Avis* have agents on the islands; drivers must be at least 25 years old. There are also local companies; they impose a minimum age of 21. **Documentation:** An International Driving Permit or valid national driving licence will be accepted.

ACCOMMODATION

HOTELS: There is a wide range of accommodation available in American Samoa, from international-standard hotels to simple guest-houses. For further information, contact the American Hotel & Motel Association, Suite 600, 1201 New York Avenue, NW, Washington DC 20005-3931. Tel: (202) 289 3100. Fax: (202) 289 3199.
Fale, ma Ti (Samoan home): The Tourism Office will help to make arrangements for visitors who wish to stay in a Samoan household. This will be of particular interest to those who wish to learn more of Samoan customs.

RESORTS & EXCURSIONS

The harbour of **Pago Pago**, made famous by Somerset Maugham's short story *Rain*, is actually the crater of an extinct volcano. A spectacular cable-car ride above the harbour offers breathtaking views; Upolu in neighbouring Western Samoa is sometimes visible.
Tula Village is a traditional Samoan settlement. Situated at the far end of the eastern district of Tutuila, it overlooks a coastline of white sandy beaches and reefs that are exposed at low tide.
Amanave Village is in an area renowned for the rugged beauty of its volcanic coastline.
On the north coast of the island, a mountain-pass ride from **Fagasa**, is the *Forbidden Bay*, claimed to be one of the most beautiful in the South Pacific.
The traditional *'turtle and shark'* legend is performed in **Vaitogi**. Mountain excursions are available at nearby Aoloau.
Cruises: A 2-day cruise around the islands (or one day to Western Samoa) includes an overnight stay in a local *Fale* (Samoan home) on the unspoiled island of **Savaii.**

SOCIAL PROFILE

FOOD & DRINK: Restaurants offer a variety of cuisines, including American, Chinese, Japanese, Italian and Polynesian. There are also various drive-in restaurants. The Samoan feast, *fia fia,* consists of suckling pig, chicken, fish, *palusami* (coconut cream wrapped in *taro* leaves and cooked in the *umu,* or pit oven), breadfruit, coconut, bananas, lime and mango. **Drink:** The national drink is *kava,* which is drunk in solemn and sacred ceremonies. If you become intimate with Samoans, you may be invited to a *kava* ceremony – a genuine one, as distinct from those laid on for tourists. If you attend a genuine *kava* ceremony, do not sip until you tip a little *kava* from its coconut shell cup onto the ground immediately in front of you while saying *manuia* (mah-noo-ee-ah), meaning good luck. Do not drain your cup. Leave a little and tip it out before handing the cup back to the server. Remember that drinking *kava* is a solemn, sacred ceremony and should never be confused with a casual round of drinks in Western society. The taste may take a while to acquire. Most places have a 'happy hour' serving cheaper drinks 1630-1830.
NIGHTLIFE: There are many nightspots with music and dancing. Samoan *fia fias* – feasting and traditional dancing – are organised regularly by several establishments. Samoan village *fia fias* can be arranged through local tour operators. Visitors are usually welcome at any event in the villages and churches.
SHOPPING: Special purchases include handmade *tapa* cloth, the *puletasi* (women's dress) or *lavalava* (men's costume) made by local dressmakers, shell beads and purses, woodcarvings, woven *laufala* table and floor mats, carved *kava* bowls, Samoan records and duty-free goods. **Shopping hours:** 0800-1700 Monday to Friday, 0800-1300 Saturday.
SPORT: Fishing: The surrounding waters offer spear-fishing and game-fishing for marlin, yellowfin tuna, wahoo and skipjack. Fully equipped fishing boats are available for hire through hotels or tour agents.
Watersports: Skindiving, snorkelling and surfing facilities are excellent. Surfing is good at Carter Beach, Alofay Bay and Leone Bay. There are many safe beaches and many hotels have swimming pools. **Tennis:** Several hotels have tennis courts that are open to non-residents. **Golf:** There is a 9-hole course on Tutuila. **Hiking:** Trails lead into the interior of the islands.
SPECIAL EVENTS: During the celebrations around *Flag Day*, April 17, there are many sporting and singing competitions with events taking place for up to a week. The *Inter-island Tennis Championship* takes place around Good Friday. *Tourism Week* is at the beginning of May and hosts tourism awareness programmes and related activities. *Palolo Day*, in October/November, marks the annual emergence of the reefworm for mating. The reefworm is a local delicacy and Samoans celebrate this day with parties and music. Mother's Day *(Aso o Tina)* takes place on the Monday after Mothering Sunday, when the women of the islands parade and congregate in Apia to hear an address by the Prime Minister. *Manu'a Cession Day* includes many singing and dancing festivities.
SOCIAL CONVENTIONS: Traditional Samoan society is still bound by very strict customs; and despite the younger generation's dissatisfaction with the old values, they are very much adhered to. The Government issues an official list of behaviour codes for both Western and American Samoa. Skimpy shorts or other revealing clothes should be avoided except when swimming or climbing coconut palms, although disapproval of shorts, if they are not *too* short, is on the wane. Samoan social behaviour conforms to strict and rather complicated rituals, to which the visitor will probably be introduced on arrival, and which should be respectfully observed. In the early evening hours, even if swimming offshore, be sure to avoid making any noise that could interrupt the Samoans' prayer period. Usually three gongs are sounded. The first is the signal to return to the house, the second is for prayer and the third sounds the all-clear. In some villages, swimming and fishing are forbidden on Sunday. A visitor who happens to be invited to stay in a Samoan household should be mindful of these customs. On leaving, making a gift, a *mea alofa* (literally a 'thing of love') of shirts, belts or dress-length fabrics is most appreciated. Samoans are extremely hospitable and visitors may receive more than one invitation to stay with neighbours. However, it is inappropriate to leave your first hosts before a pre-arranged date. **Tipping:** It is not customary to tip.

BUSINESS PROFILE

ECONOMY: The economy is based mainly on agriculture and fishing, with two tuna canneries providing employment for almost a quarter of the population. Recently industrial estates have been built in an effort to encourage light industrial development. Tourism is a growing industry.
BUSINESS: Shirt and smart trousers will suffice for business visits. Ties need only be worn for formal occasions. The best time to visit is May to October.
COMMERCIAL INFORMATION: The following organisations can offer advice: American Samoa Development Corporation, Pago Pago, AS 96799. Tel: 633 4241. Telex: 782511; *or*
Office of Economic Development Planning, Territorial Planning Commission, Pago Pago, AS 96799. Tel: 633 5155. Fax: 633 4195.

CLIMATE

Very warm, tropical climate. The heaviest rainfalls are usually between December and April. The climate is best during the winter months, May to September, when there are moderate southeast trade winds.
Required clothing: Lightweight cottons and linens throughout the year with warm wrap for cooler winter evenings. Rainwear is advised for the wet season.

Location: Western Europe; border of France and Spain.

Sindicat d'Initiativa de las Valls d'Andorra
Carrer Dr Vilanova, Andorra la Vella, Andorra
Tel: 820 214. Fax: 825 823.
Ministeri de Turisme i Esports
Carrer Prat de la Creu, 62-64 Andorra la Vella, Andorra
Tel: 829 345. Fax: 860 184. Telex: 469.
Andorran Delegation
63 Westover Road, London SW18 2RF
Tel: (0181) 874 4806.
Embassy of Spain
39 Chesham Place, London SW1X 8SB
Tel: (0171) 235 5555. Fax: (0171) 259 5392. Telex:
21110 (a/b SPAMB G).
British Consulate (in Barcelona)
13th Floor, Edificio Torre de Barcelona, Avenida
Diagonal 477, 08036 Barcelona, Spain
Tel: (3) 419 9044. Fax: (3) 405 2411. Telex: 52799 (a/b
BRBAR E).
Embassy of Spain
2375 Pennsylvania Avenue, NW, Washington, DC 20037
Tel: (202) 452 0100 *or* 728 2340. Fax: (202) 728 2317.
Embassy of Spain
Suite 802, 350 Sparks Street, Ottawa, Ontario K1R 7S8
Tel: (613) 237 2193/4. Fax: (613) 236 1502.

AREA: 467.8 sq km (180.6 sq miles).
POPULATION: 54,507 (1990).
POPULATION DENSITY: 116.5 per sq km.
CAPITAL: Andorra la Vella. **Population:** 20,437
(1990).
GEOGRAPHY: Andorra is situated in the Pyrénées,
bordered by France to the north and east and Spain to the
south and west. The landscape consists of gorges and
narrow valleys surrounded by mountains. Much of the
landscape is forested, but there are several areas of rich
pastureland in the valleys. There are four rivers and
several mountain lakes. Ski resorts and the spa town of
Les Escaldes are Andorra's main attractions.
LANGUAGE: The official language is Catalan. Spanish
and French are also spoken.
RELIGION: Roman Catholic.
TIME: GMT + 1 (GMT + 2 from last Sunday in March
to Saturday before last Sunday in September).
ELECTRICITY: Sockets: 240 volts AC, 50Hz.
Lighting: 125 volts AC.

COMMUNICATIONS: Telephone: Full IDD is
available. Country code: 376. Outgoing international
code: 0. **Telex:** Some telex services are available; enquire
at hotels. **Post:** Internal mail services are free;
international mail takes about a week within Europe. A
Poste Restante service is available in Andorra la Vella.
Post office hours: 0900-1300 and 1500-1700 in Andorra
la Vella, otherwise variable. **Press:** Andorra has two
weekly publications, *Andorra 7* and *Poble Andorra*.
**BBC World Service and Voice of America
frequencies:** From time to time these change. See the
section *How to Use this Book* for more information.
BBC:

MHz	17.64	11.70	12.09	9.760

Voice of America:

MHz	15.21	9.760	6.040	5.995

PASSPORT/VISA

*Regulations and requirements may be subject to change at short notice, and you
are advised to contact the appropriate diplomatic or consular authority before
finalising travel arrangements. Details of these may be found at the head of this
country's entry. Any numbers in the chart refer to the footnotes below.*

	Passport Required?	Visa Required?	Return Ticket Required?
Full British	1	2	No
BVP	Valid	2	No
Australian	Yes	2	Yes
Canadian	Yes	2	Yes
USA	Yes	2	Yes
Other EU (As of 31/12/94)	1	2	No
Japanese	Yes	2	Yes

PASSPORTS: [1] Valid passport required by all except
for nationals of France and Spain, providing they hold a
valid ID card; and nationals of the UK holding a BVP.
British Visitors Passport: Acceptable. A BVP can be
used for holidays or unpaid business trips of up to 3
months.
VISAS: [2] There are no visa requirements for entry into
Andorra. However, as Andorra is bordered by France and
Spain the relevant regulations for these countries should
be studied. Visitors wishing to have their passport
stamped with the Andorran coat of arms should apply to
the Sindicat d'Initiativa in the capital.
Validity: Stays of up to 3 months are allowed without a
visa.
Temporary residence: Apply in person at the
Immigration Office, Edifici Rebés, C/ Joan Maragall,
Andorra la Vella, Andorra.

MONEY

Currency: Although most currencies are accepted, the
main currencies in circulation are Spanish Pesetas and, to
a lesser extent, French Francs. Please consult the entries
for *Spain* and *France* later in this book.
Currency exchange: Andorran banks and bureaux de
change will exchange foreign currency.
Credit cards: Diners Club, Visa, American Express and
Access/Mastercard are accepted. Check with your credit
card company for details of merchant acceptability and
other services which may be available.
Currency restrictions: There are no frontier formalities
when entering the country, but French and Spanish
authorities may carry out formalities on departure.
Banking hours: 0900-1300 and 1500-1700 Monday to
Friday; 0900-1200 Saturday.

DUTY FREE

Andorra is a duty-free zone and there is little point
buying duty-free items to take in. See also under *Food &
Drink* below.
Prohibited/restricted items: Controlled drugs, firearms,
ammunition, explosives (including fireworks), flick
knives, pornography, radio transmitters, certain
foodstuffs, plants, flowers, animals and birds and items
made from endangered species are prohibited. No works
of art and certain other items can be exported without
permission.

PUBLIC HOLIDAYS

Jan 1 '95 New Year's Day. **Jan 6** Epiphany. **Feb 26**
Carnival. **Mar 14** Constitution Day. **Apr 14** Good
Friday. **Apr 17** Easter Monday. **May 1** Labour Day. **Jun
5** Whit Monday. **Jun 24** Day of the Capital/St John. **Aug
5** Fiesta of the Capital. **Aug 15** Assumption. **Sep 8**
National Day. **Nov 1** All Saints' Day. **Dec 8** Immaculate
Conception. **Dec 21** St Thomas. **Dec 24-26** Christmas.
Dec 31 New Year's Eve. **Jan 1 '96** New Year's Day. **Jan
6** Epiphany. **Feb/Mar** Carnival. **Mar 14** Constitution

Day. **Apr 5** Good Friday. **Apr 8** Easter Monday.
Note: In July, August and September, parishes have their
own public holidays during which festivals are held.

HEALTH

*Regulations and requirements may be subject to change at short notice, and
you are advised to contact your doctor well in advance of your intended date of
departure. Any numbers in the chart refer to the footnotes below.*

	Special Precautions?	Certificate Required?
Yellow Fever	No	No
Cholera	No	No
Typhoid & Polio	No	-
Malaria	No	-
Food & Drink	No	-

Rabies is present. For those at high risk, vaccination
before arrival should be considered. If you are bitten
abroad, seek medical help without delay. For more
information, consult the *Health* section at the back of the
book.
Health care: Most health costs are covered by UK health
agreements but additional insurance is advised. Please
note that as entry to Andorra is usually through France or
Spain, their health regulations should also be complied
with.

TRAVEL - International

AIR: Andorra's nearest international airport is *Barcelona
(BCN)* in Spain, 225km (140 miles) from Andorra. For
more information on the airport and its facilities, please
consult the entry for *Spain* later in the book. Shared taxis
and buses are available.
Toulouse (TLS), in France, is 180km (112 miles) from
Andorra.
The nearest airport is *Seo de Urgel*, which is served by
three flights a day from Barcelona. It is 20km (12 miles)
from Andorra.
RAIL: Routes from Perpignan, Villefranche, Toulouse
and Barcelona go to La Tour de Carol, 20km (12 miles)
from Andorra. The nearest station is L'Hospitalet, but
buses run from both L'Hospitalet and La Tour de Carol.
ROAD: Mountainous roads exist over the Envalita pass
to Perpignan, Tarbes and Toulouse (France); and
southwards to Barcelona and Lérida (Spain). Buses run
regularly from Barcelona. Taxis may also be taken and
sharing is commonly practised to cut costs.

TRAVEL - Internal

ROAD: A good road runs from the Spanish to the French
frontiers through Saint Julià, Andorra la Vella, Les
Escaldes, Encamp, Canillo and Soldeu. There is one
major east–west route and a minor road to El Serrat,
which are closed in winter. The bus journey from La
Tour de Carol takes 2 hours 20 minutes and runs once
daily at 1330. From L'Hospitalet the service takes 2
hours 40 minutes and runs early enough to permit a day
return trip from France. A seasonal service runs from Ax-
les-Thermes and services may be available from Seo de
Urgel in Spain. There are also internal buses and
minibuses linking the villages on the 186km (115 miles)
of road. Traffic drives on the right. **Documentation:** A
national driving licence is sufficient.

ACCOMMODATION

HOTELS: There are over 200 hotels and inns (9000
beds in total), principally catering for the summer
months, although some stay open all year round. Rooms
during the summer months (July to August) should be
booked well in advance. Hotels (and restaurants) are
registered with the Sindicat d'Initiativa and are bound to
keep to the registered prices and services.
MOUNTAIN REFUGES: These offer cheap and basic
accommodation; normally they will have one room
available for visitors, and may or may not have a hearth
and bunk beds. Enquire locally concerning locations and
prices.
CAMPING: There are 25 campsites in Andorra, most of
which are close to the main towns and well-signposted.
Several have shops and other facilities. There are also
facilities for caravans.

RESORTS & EXCURSIONS

The country is mountainous, traversed by a main road
which runs roughly northeast to southwest, along which
most of the settlements are to be found. Many of these
are villages or hamlets with Romanesque churches and
houses built in the local style; others, off the main road,
are even more unspoilt, and provide spectacular views

across the rugged countryside. For the visitor, however, Andorra's two greatest attractions are the fact that it is both a duty-free state and a centre for winter sports, a combination which has led to a great deal of overt commercialism, particularly in the main towns of Andorra la Vella and Les Escaldes.

Andorra la Vella, the country's capital, lies at the junction of two mountain streams. Sights there include a fine 12th-century church and the 'Casa de la Val', the ancient seat of government.

Adjoining the capital is the spa town of **Les Escaldes** which also has examples of Romanesque architecture. These towns are also the centre of the colourful Andorran local festival in early September, in honour of La Vierge de Meritxell. 18km (11 miles) from Les Escaldes, off the main road, is the hamlet of **El Serrat**, which commands a breathtaking view across the mountains. The town of **Encamp**, between the capital and the French frontier, is also worth a visit.

Ski resorts: There are several ski resorts in the country, most of which offer good facilities. The main ski resort in Andorra is **Soldeu**, the first major settlement on the road after the French frontier at Port d'Envarlira. Both nursery slopes and skiing for intermediates are available with a good ski school offering tuition at reasonable prices. There are also ski centres at **Pas de la Casa/Grau Roig**, on the French frontier, and at **Arcalis, Arinsal, and Pal**, all north of Andorra la Vella.

The Sindicat d'Initiativa can provide details on prices, snow conditions, as well as other information about tourist opportunities in the country; address at top of entry.

SOCIAL PROFILE

FOOD & DRINK: Cuisine is mainly Catalan, and generally expensive. Quality and prices in the 250 or so restaurants are similar to those in small French and Spanish resort towns. Local dishes include *coques* (flavoured flat cakes), *trinxat* (a potato and cabbage dish), *truites de carreroles* (a type of mushroom omelette), local sausages and cheeses, and a variety of dishes of pork and ham. **Drink:** Alcoholic drinks bought in shops and supermarkets are cheap (Andorra being a duty-free zone), but prices in bars can be expensive. They do, however, stay open late.

NIGHTLIFE: There are centres around the bars and hotels. Discotheques can be found during both summer and winter.

SHOPPING: There is duty-free shopping for all goods. Petrol, alcohol, cameras and watches, etc can be purchased at low prices. Electrical goods are very good value. **Shopping hours:** 0900-2000 Monday to Saturday, 0900-1900 Sunday.

SPORT: There is excellent **skiing**, mainly around Soldeu (for further information, see *Resorts & Excursions* above). A bus service picks up skiers from hotels and inns, and takes them to the slopes, returning in the evening. There are many good nursery slopes. Other available activities include **horseriding, tennis, swimming, trout fishing, clay-pigeon shooting, hiking** and **rock climbing. Football, rugby, basketball** and **motorbike** and **car rallies** are the most popular spectator sports.

SPECIAL EVENTS: Regional festivals take place annually in the following locations:
Andorra la Vella: From the first Saturday in August for three days.
Canillo: From the third Saturday in June for three days.
Encamp: 3-day festival in August.
Escaldes-Engordany: 3-day *International Jazz Festival* in July.
La Massana: 3-day festival in August.
Ordino: The *International Music Festival* in June and July and a 2-day festival in September.
Meritxell: Concerts by famous musicians and singers in September.
Sant Julià-de-Loria: From the last Sunday in July for three days.
SOCIAL CONVENTIONS: Normal social courtesies should be extended when visiting someone's home. Handshaking is the accepted form of greeting. Dress is informal and smoking is very common; customs are similar to those of Spain. **Tipping:** Service charges are usually included in the bill. Porters and waiters expect a further 10%.

BUSINESS PROFILE

ECONOMY: Andorra is principally an agricultural country with some mineral resources. Potatoes and tobacco are the main products, although there is some livestock farming. The principal raw materials are lead, iron and alum. The country's energy requirements are met by the government-owned electricity company which can supply around 60% of Andorran requirements. As a

Romanesque statue of the Virgin at St Julià

duty-free zone the economy has expanded rapidly in recent years, trading in both European and foreign goods. The main sources of government revenue are taxes on petrol, tourism and consumer goods. There is some concern about the long-term implications of Spanish membership of the EU and the likely resulting fall in tax revenues. Andorra's main trading partners are neighbouring France and Spain.

BUSINESS: Suits are recommended at all times with white shirt and black shoes. Prior appointments are necessary and meetings tend to be formal. Lunch is usually after 1430 and can extend through the afternoon until 2100-2200. Although English is widely spoken, a knowledge of Spanish or French is appreciated. **Office hours** vary considerably. It is advisable to arrange business appointments in advance.

CONFERENCES/CONVENTIONS: For information on conference and convention facilities, contact the Centre de Congressos i Exposicions, Plaça Poble, Andorra la Vella. Tel: 861 131 *or* 826 000.

CLIMATE

Temperate climate with warm summers and cold winters. Rain falls throughout the year.
Required clothing: Lightweights for the summer and warm mediumweights during winter. Waterproofing is advisable throughout the year.

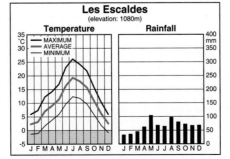

Les Escaldes
(elevation: 1080m)
Temperature — Rainfall
MAXIMUM / AVERAGE / MINIMUM
J F M A M J J A S O N D

Angola

□ *international airport*
600km
300mls

Location: Southwest Africa.

Note: Angola has been riven by civil war for nearly 20 years and visitors are warned against travel to Angola. Travel within Angola is unsafe because of the presence of armed troops, roadside bandits, unexploded land mines and hostile actions against aircraft. Although elections were recently held, there is a probability that fighting may once again resume, particularly in the interior of the country and around the capital. Travel in many areas of the capital is considered unsafe at night because of the increased incidence of armed robberies and car-jacking, as well as the presence of police checkpoints after dark manned by armed and poorly trained personnel. Visitors should also be aware that rapidly changing military activity may hinder their ability to depart from areas which they enter. Check with the appropriate government office (Foreign Office for British citizens and the State Department for US citizens) for up-to-date information.
Sources: US State Department – August 1, 1994; and FCO Travel Advice Unit – November 30, 1994..

National Tourist Agency
CP 1240, Palácio de Vidro, Luanda, Angola
Tel: (2) 372 750.
Ministry of Trade and Tourism
Largo Kinaxixi 14, Luanda, Angola
Tel: (2) 344 525. Telex: 3282.
Embassy of the People's Republic of Angola
98 Park Lane, London W1Y 3TA
Tel: (0171) 495 1752. Fax: (0171) 495 1635. Telex: 8813285 (a/b EMBAUK G). Opening hours: 0900-1200 and 1330-1600 Monday to Friday (closed Wednesday).
British Embassy
CP 1244, Rua Diogo Cão 4, Luanda, Angola
Tel: (2) 334 582/3 *or* 392 991. Fax: (2) 333 331. Telex: 3130 (a/b PRODLDA AN). *Commercial Section:* Tel: (2) 392 998.
Embassy of the Republic of Angola
Suite 400, 1819 L Street, NW, Washington, DC 20036
Tel: (202) 785 1156. Fax: (202) 785 1258.
Embassy of the United States of America
PO Box 6484, Rua Houari Boumedienne, Luanda, Angola
Tel: (2) 345 481. Fax: (2) 390 515.
The Canadian High Commission in Zimbabwe deals with enquiries relating to Angola (see *Zimbabwe* later in the book).

AREA: 1,246,700 sq km (481,354 sq miles).
POPULATION: 10,020,000 (1990 estimate).
POPULATION DENSITY: 8 per sq km.

CAPITAL: Luanda. **Population:** 1,200,000 (1982 est.).
GEOGRAPHY: Angola is bordered by Zaïre to the north, Zambia to the east, Namibia to the south and the Atlantic Ocean to the west. Mountains rise from the coast, levelling to a plateau which makes up most of the country. The country is increasingly arid towards the south; the far south is on the edge of the Namib Desert. The northern plateau is thickly vegetated. Cabinda is a small enclave to the north of Angola proper, surrounded by the territories of Zaïre and Congo. The discovery of large oil deposits off the coast of the enclave has led to it becoming the centre of Angola's foreign business interests. The oil industry, based primarily at Malongo, is run jointly by Gulf Oil and Sonangol, the Angolan state oil producers.
LANGUAGE: The official language is Portuguese. African languages (Ovimbundu, Kimbundu, Bakongo and Chokwe) are spoken by the majority of the population.
RELIGION: Mainly Roman Catholic; there are also Anglican minorities. Local Animist beliefs are held by a significant minority.
TIME: GMT + 1.
ELECTRICITY: 220 volts AC, 60Hz. Plugs are of the European-style round 2-pin type.
COMMUNICATIONS: **Telephone:** Until recently all calls had to be made through the international operator, booking at least six hours in advance. Direct calls to Luanda (but not to the rest of the country) are becoming increasingly available. Country code: 244.
Telex/telegram: Telegram services are fairly reliable, but are occasionally subject to delay. Telex facilities are available in main hotels. **Post:** Airmail between Europe and Angola takes five to ten days. Surface mail between Europe and Angola takes at least two months. There is a fairly reliable internal service. Most correspondence is by telex. **Press:** The daily newspaper is *O Jornal de Angola*; *Diario da República* is an official government news-sheet. There are no English-language newspapers.
BBC World Service and Voice of America frequencies: From time to time these change. See the section *How to Use this Book* for more information.

BBC:				
MHz	**21.66**	**17.88**	**15.40**	**9.600**
Voice of America:				
MHz	**21.49**	**15.60**	**9.525**	**6.035**

PASSPORT/VISA

Regulations and requirements may be subject to change at short notice, and you are advised to contact the appropriate diplomatic or consular authority before finalising travel arrangements. Details of these may be found at the head of this country's entry. Any numbers in the chart refer to the footnotes below.

	Passport Required?	Visa Required?	Return Ticket Required?
Full British	Yes	Yes	Yes
BVP	Not valid	-	-
Australian	Yes	Yes	Yes
Canadian	Yes	Yes	Yes
USA	Yes	Yes	Yes
Other EU (As of 31/12/94)	Yes	Yes	Yes
Japanese	Yes	Yes	Yes

PASSPORTS: Passports valid for 3 months after intended period of stay required by all.
British Visitors Passport: Not accepted.
VISAS: Required by all except those continuing their journey to a third country without leaving the airport. Some business travellers are allowed entry, but only as guests of an accepted business firm; tourist travel is not allowed in Angola at this time.
Types of visa: Business. Single-entry costs £63.
Exit permits: Required by all visitors; must be issued by the same consulate that issued the visa.
Application to: Consulate (or Consular Section at Embassy). For addresses, see top of entry.
Application requirements: (a) Valid passport. (b) 1 application form. (c) 1 passport-size photograph. (d) Covering letter from company wishing to send person to Angola. (e) Letter of invitation from company in Angola being visited or the Angolan Government Department.
Working days required: Applications should be made well in advance.

Timatic

Health
GALILEO/WORLDSPAN: **TI-DFT/LAD/HE**
SABRE: **TIDFT/LAD/HE**

Visa
GALILEO/WORLDSPAN: **TI-DFT/LAD/VI**
SABRE: **TIDFT/LAD/VI**

For more information on Timatic codes refer to Contents.

MONEY

Currency: New Kwanza (NKZ) = 100 lwei (LW). Notes are in denominations of NKZ5000, 1000, 500, 100, 50 and 20. Coins are in denominations of NKZ20, 10, 5, 2 and 1, and LW50.
Note: The old Kwanza was replaced by the New Kwanza in 1990. It has subsequently undergone several official exchange rate devaluations. In October 1993, a basic rate of US$1 = NKZ6550 was established, a devaluation of 38.5%.
Credit cards: Credit cards are generally not accepted. American Express and Diners Club enjoy limited acceptance. Amex is accepted at the Le Méridien Presidente Hotel in Luanda; otherwise check with your credit card company for details of merchant acceptability and other services which may be available.
Exchange rate indicators: The following figures are included as a guide to the movements of the New Kwanza against Sterling and the US Dollar:

Date:	**Oct '92**	**Sep '93**	**Jan '94**	**Jan '95**
£1.00=	**950.40**	**5996.70**	**9781.30**	**793011**
$1.00=	**598.87**	**3927.11**	**6611.22**	**506879**

Currency restrictions: All imported currency should be declared on arrival. The local currency import limit is NKZ15,000; there is no limit on the import of foreign currency, subject to declaration on arrival. Export of local currency is prohibited; up to NKZ5000 equivalent of foreign currency may be exported by those leaving on a return ticket purchased in Angola.
Banking hours: 0845-1600 Monday to Friday.

DUTY FREE

The following items may be imported into Angola without payment of duty:
A reasonable amount of tobacco and perfume (opened).
Prohibited items: Firearms, ammunition and alcohol.

PUBLIC HOLIDAYS

Jan 1 '95 New Year's Day. **Feb 4** Anniversary of the Outbreak of Armed Struggle against Portuguese Colonialism. **Mar 27** Victory Day. **Apr 14** Youth Day. **May 1** Workers' Day. **Aug 1** Armed Forces Day. **Sep 17** National Heroes' Day, Birthday of Dr Agostinho Neto. **Nov 11** Independence Day. **Dec 1** Pioneers' Day. **Dec 10** Anniversary of the Foundation of the MPLA. **Dec 25** Family Day. **Jan 1 '96** New Year's Day. **Feb 4** Anniversary of the Outbreak of Armed Struggle against Portuguese Colonialism. **Mar 27** Victory Day. **Apr 14** Youth Day.

HEALTH

Regulations and requirements may be subject to change at short notice, and you are advised to contact your doctor well in advance of your intended date of departure. Any numbers in the chart refer to the footnotes below.

	Special Precautions?	Certificate Required?
Yellow Fever	Yes	1
Cholera	Yes	2
Typhoid & Polio	Yes	-
Malaria	Yes/3	-
Food & Drink	4	-

[1]: A Yellow Fever vaccination certificate is required from travellers over one year of age coming from infected areas. Pregnant women and infants under nine months should not be vaccinated and therefore should avoid exposure to infection. Travellers arriving from non-endemic zones should note that vaccination is strongly recommended for travel outside the urban areas, even if an outbreak of the disease has not been reported and they would normally not require a vaccination certificate to enter the country.
[2]: Following WHO guidelines issued in 1973, a cholera vaccination certificate is no longer a condition of entry to Angola. However, cholera is a serious risk in this country and precautions are essential. Up-to-date advice should be sought before deciding whether these precautions should include vaccination as medical opinion is divided over its effectiveness. See the *Health* section at the back of the book.
[3]: Malaria risk, predominantly in the malignant *falciparum* form, exists all year throughout the country, even in urban areas, and is reported to be resistant to chloroquine and sulfadoxine-pyrimethamine. Mefloquine (MEF) is the recommended prophylaxis, at a weekly dose of 250mg.
[4]: All water should be regarded as being potentially contaminated. Water used for drinking, brushing teeth or making ice should have first been boiled or otherwise sterilised. Milk is unpasteurised and should be boiled. Powdered or tinned milk is available and is advised, but make sure that it is reconstituted with pure water. Avoid dairy products which are likely to have been made from unboiled milk. Only eat well-cooked meat and fish, preferably served hot. Pork, salad and mayonnaise may carry increased risk. Vegetables should be cooked and fruit peeled.
Many insect-borne diseases, such as *onchocerciasis* (river blindness) and *trypanosomiasis* (sleeping sickness), exist all year throughout the country, including urban areas.
Rabies is present. For those at high risk, vaccination before arrival should be considered. If you are bitten abroad seek medical advice without delay. For more information consult the *Health* section at the back of the book.
Bilharzia (schistosomiasis) is present. Avoid swimming and paddling in fresh water. Swimming pools which are well-chlorinated and maintained are safe.
Meningitis outbreaks occur. Vaccination is advisable.
Health care: Full health insurance is essential and should include medical evacuation insurance. There are three main hospitals in Luanda: the Hospital Americo Boavida, the Hospital Josefina Machel and the Hospital do Prenda. There are some hospital facilities in the other main towns, but at the moment adequate medical facilities are virtually non-existent. Medical treatment is free although often inadequate, and visitors should travel with their own supply of remedies for simple ailments such as stomach upsets, as pharmaceutical supplies are usually extremely difficult to obtain.

TRAVEL - International

AIR: Angola's national airline is *TAAG Angola Airlines (DT)*.
Approximate flight time: From London to Luanda is 19 hours 30 minutes (this includes a stopover of 5 hours in Lisbon).
International airport: *Luanda (LAD)* is 4km (2.5 miles) from the city. There are no taxis: visitors must be met by their sponsors. Airport facilities include restaurant, bar, post office, currency exchange (0800-1230 and 1430-1800) and 24-hour medical facilities with cholera and yellow fever vaccination available.
Note: Most British and American visitors with business interests in the Cabinda enclave bypass Luanda by flying to Gabon by *UTA*, then on by private jet. On arrival, they are taken immediately by helicopter to the Malongo Base. This is only possible by special arrangement with the Gabonese and Angolan governments as no visas are available at present.
SEA: The main ports are Cabinda, Lobito, Luanda and Namibe.
RAIL/ROAD: All land frontiers are currently closed. Plans to re-open the Benguela railway seem unlikely to achieve fruition until a greater degree of peace is achieved.

TRAVEL - Internal

Note: All travel in the country is very strictly controlled and limited. Tourist travel is not allowed in Angola at this time, but some business travel is permitted. Most of the country is only accessible by air.
AIR: *TAAG Angola Airlines* operate flights within Angola. There are scheduled services between major towns. Also, private jets are operated by some Portuguese, French and Italian business interests (trading most notably in oil and diamonds) in the north of the country, particularly to and from the Cabinda enclave, which is only accessible by air (see above for information on travelling directly to Cabinda from Gabon). Helicopter access to Cabinda is possible as well. Passengers on internal flights must carry official authorisation *(guia de marcha)*.
Approximate flight times: From Luanda to *Benguela* and *Cabinda* is 50 minutes, to *Huambo* is 1 hour, to *Namibe* is 1 hour 45 minutes and to *Lubango* is 1 hour 10 minutes.
RAIL: Due to the instability of the political situation, rail services are erratic. Trains run on three separate routes inland from Luanda: to Malanje (daily) with short branches to Dondo and Golungo Alta, Lobito to Dilolo

(the Benguela Railway, daily), and Mocamedes to Menongue (daily). There are no sleeping cars and no air-conditioned services, though food and drink are available on some journeys. Children under three travel free and children 3-11 pay half fare.

ROAD: Traffic drives on the right. There were once nearly 8000km (5000 miles) of tarred roads but much of the infrastructure was destroyed in the conflict after 1975. Many roads are unsuitable for travel at the present time, and local advice should be sought and followed carefully. Identity papers must be carried.

Documentation: An International Driving Permit is required.

URBAN: Local buses run in Luanda. A flat fare is charged.

ACCOMMODATION

Many hotels in Angola had recently undergone refurbishment, and have air-conditioning, a private bath or shower, a phone, radio and TV. However, there is a general shortage of accommodation, and it is advisable to book well in advance (at least one month prior to departure); accommodation cannot be booked at the airport. For further information, contact the National Tourist Agency (for address, see top of entry). Most bookings must be made by the person, company or organisation being visited through the state hotel organisation, ANGHOTEL. Tel: (2) 92648 *or* 334 241. Telex: 3492 (a/b ANGOTE AN). There is also accommodation in Kissama National Park (see *Resorts & Excursions* below).

RESORTS & EXCURSIONS

In **Luanda** the main places to visit are the fortress (containing the *Museum of Armed Forces),* the *National Museum of Anthropology* and the *Museum of Slavery,* 25km (16 miles) along the coast from Luanda.
The **Kissama National Park** lies 70km (45 miles) south of Luanda, and is home to a great variety of wild animals. Accommodation is available in bungalows located in the middle of the park, but visitors must bring their own food. The park is closed during the rainy season.
The **Kalandula Waterfalls,** located in the Malange area, make an impressive spectacle, particularly at the end of the rainy season.
There are plenty of beaches: Luanda itself is built around a bay and there are bathing beaches (the *Ilha* beaches) five minutes from the centre of the city. Watersports are possible on the *Mussolo Peninsula.* 45km (28 miles) south of Luanda is *Palmeirinhas*, a long, deserted beach. The scenery is magnificent, but bathing here is hazardous. Fishing is possible both here and at *Santiago* beach, 45km (28 miles) north of Luanda.

SOCIAL PROFILE

FOOD & DRINK: There are severe food and drink shortages at present. Tables should be booked well in advance in the few restaurants and hotels, although only the Le Méridien Presidente Hotel can really offer high-class service. Notice needs to be given for extra guests.
NIGHTLIFE: There are some nightclubs and cinemas in Luanda. Cinema seats should be booked in advance.
SHOPPING: Traditional handicrafts are sold in the city; shopping is not easy outside the main cities.
SPORT: Watersports are available on Mussolo Peninsula, **swimming** is available on Ilha beaches and Palmeirinhas. Santiago has **fishing.**
SOCIAL CONVENTIONS: Normal social courtesies should be observed. **Photography:** It is inadvisable to photograph public places, public buildings or public events. Copies of photography permits should be deposited with the British Embassy; permits should be carried at all times. **Tipping:** Where service charge is not added to the bill, 10% is acceptable, although tipping is not officially encouraged. Tipping can be in kind (eg cigarettes).

BUSINESS PROFILE

ECONOMY: Angola is rich in natural resources, including oil, coffee and diamonds. Agriculture employs over 50% of the population. Gulf Oil and Texaco have developed major oilfields off the shore of Cabinda (an enclave in the north of the country) but the country has only one refinery and so exports most of its oil in the crude form; plans to develop the country's refining capacity have been shelved since the collapse of oil prices in the late 1980s (Angola is not a member of

OPEC). The economy was adversely affected by the departure of 700,000 Portuguese after independence and the consequences of civil strife and the South African incursions. Since then, the economy has for the most part been centrally planned with a dominant state sector. Import controls and austerity measures forced on the authorities by the civil war have further inhibited economic growth. Capital and technical expertise are being sought from the West to help further development of resources. Angola's largest trading partners are Portugal, Brazil, France and the USA, from whom it imports much of its food and almost all its manufactured equipment.

BUSINESS: Lightweight suits are recommended. Many Angolan business people dress casually, wearing safari suits and open-neck shirts. Any dark colours can be worn for social occasions. As Portuguese is the official language, a knowledge of this is an advantage in business transactions; French and Spanish are also useful. There are limited translation services. Avoid June to September as Angolans tend to take their holidays at this time.
Office hours: 0730-1200 and 1430-1800 Monday to Thursday, 0730-1230 and 1430-1730 Friday.
COMMERCIAL INFORMATION: The following organisation can offer advice: Associação Comercial de Luanda (Chamber of Commerce), CP 1275, 1° andar, Edifício Palácio de Comércio, Luanda. Tel: (2) 322 453.

CLIMATE

The north of the country is hot and wet during the summer months (November to April); winters are slightly cooler and mainly dry. The south is hot throughout much of the year with a slight decrease in temperature in winter (May to October).
Required clothing: Lightweight cottons and linens throughout the year in the south. Tropical clothing for summers in the north. Nights can be cold, so warm clothing should be taken. Waterproofing is advisable for the rainy season throughout the country.

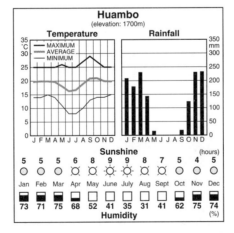

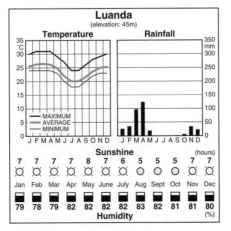

Anguilla

Location: Caribbean; Leeward Islands.

Department of Tourism
The Secretariat, The Valley, Anguilla
Tel: 497 2759 *or* 497 2451. Fax: 497 3389. Telex: 9313 (a/b ANG GOVT LA).
Anguilla Tourist Office
3 Epirus Road, London SW6 7UJ
Tel: (0171) 937 7725. Fax: (0171) 938 4793. Opening hours: 0930-1700 Monday to Friday.
Anguilla Tourist Information Office
c/o Medhurst Associates Inc, 271 Main Street, Northport, NY 11768
Tel: (516) 261 1234 *or* (800) 553 4939. Fax: (516) 261 9606.

AREA: Anguilla: 91 sq km (35 sq miles). **Sombrero:** 5 sq km (3 sq miles). **Total:** 96 sq km (38 sq miles).
POPULATION: 8960 (1992).
POPULATION DENSITY: 93.3 per sq km.
CAPITAL: The Valley. **Population:** 595 (1992).
GEOGRAPHY: Anguilla, the northernmost of the Leeward Islands, also comprises the island of Sombrero, lying 48km (30 miles) north of Anguilla, and several small islets or cays. The nearest islands are St Maarten, 8km (5 miles) south of Anguilla, and St Kitts and Nevis, 112km (70 miles) to the southeast. The islands are mainly flat – the highest point, Crocus Hill, is only 60m (214ft) above sea level – with arguably some of the best beaches in the world.
LANGUAGE: English is the official and commercial language.
RELIGION: Roman Catholic, Anglican, Baptist, Methodist and Moravian with Hindu, Jewish and Muslim minorities.
TIME: GMT - 4.
ELECTRICITY: 110/220 volts AC, 60Hz.
COMMUNICATIONS: Telephone: Full IDD is available. Country code: 1 809. Outgoing international code: 011. **Fax:** Cable and Wireless operate fax services.
Telex/telegram: Cable and Wireless (West Indies) Ltd have telex facilities available to the public at their office. Cables may be sent from Cable and Wireless (West Indies) Ltd Public Booth, The Valley, which controls all British-owned cables in the area. **Post:** The General Post Office is in The Valley, open 0800-1530 Monday to Friday and 0800-1200 Saturday. There is a 'travelling service' to other districts on Anguilla. Airmail to Europe takes from four days to two weeks. **Press:** The government of Anguilla publishes two monthly papers: *The Government Information Service Bulletin* and *The Official Gazette*, both English-language. *The Vantage* is published weekly.
BBC World Service and Voice of America frequencies: From time to time these change. See the section *How to Use this Book* for more information.

BBC:			
MHz	17.84	15.26	9.915	6.195
Voice of America:			
MHz	15.12	11.58	9.775	5.995

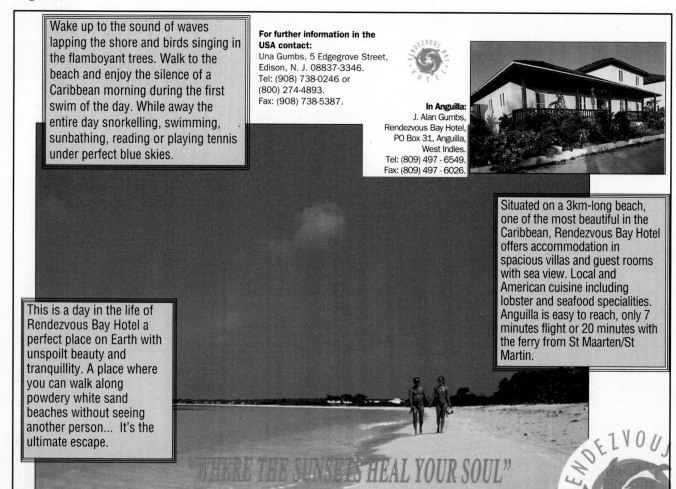

Wake up to the sound of waves lapping the shore and birds singing in the flamboyant trees. Walk to the beach and enjoy the silence of a Caribbean morning during the first swim of the day. While away the entire day snorkelling, swimming, sunbathing, reading or playing tennis under perfect blue skies.

Situated on a 3km-long beach, one of the most beautiful in the Caribbean, Rendezvous Bay Hotel offers accommodation in spacious villas and guest rooms with sea view. Local and American cuisine including lobster and seafood specialities. Anguilla is easy to reach, only 7 minutes flight or 20 minutes with the ferry from St Maarten/St Martin.

This is a day in the life of Rendezvous Bay Hotel a perfect place on Earth with unspoilt beauty and tranquillity. A place where you can walk along powdery white sand beaches without seeing another person... It's the ultimate escape.

"WHERE THE SUNSETS HEAL YOUR SOUL"

PASSPORT/VISA

Regulations and requirements may be subject to change at short notice, and you are advised to contact the appropriate diplomatic or consular authority before finalising travel arrangements. Details of these may be found at the head of this country's entry. Any numbers in the chart refer to the footnotes below.

	Passport Required?	Visa Required?	Return Ticket Required?
Full British	Yes	No	Yes
BVP	Not valid	-	-
Australian	Yes	No	Yes
Canadian	Yes	No	Yes
USA	Yes	No	Yes
Other EU (As of 31/12/94)	Yes	No	Yes
Japanese	Yes	No	Yes

PASSPORTS: Valid passport required by all.
British Visitors Passport: Not accepted.
VISAS: May be required by some nationals; check with the Passport Office, Clive House, Petty France, London SW7.

MONEY

Currency: Eastern Caribbean Dollar (EC$) = 100 cents. Notes are in denominations of EC$100, 20, 10, 5 and 1. Coins are in denominations of EC$1, and 50, 25, 10, 5, 2 and 1 cents.
Currency exchange: Currency may be exchanged in the capital.
Credit cards: American Express is most widely used, although Visa has limited acceptance. Check with your

credit card company for details of merchant acceptability and other services which may be available.
Travellers cheques: US currency cheques are the easist.
Exchange rate indicators: The following are included as a guide to the movements of the EC Dollar against Sterling and the US Dollar:

Date:	Oct '92	Sep '93	Jan '94	Jan '95
£1.00=	4.27	4.13	3.99	2.80
$1.00=	2.70	2.70	2.70	1.79

Note: The EC Dollar is tied to the US Dollar.
Currency restrictions: Free import and export of both local and foreign currency if declared.
Banking hours: 0800-1500 Monday to Thursday, 0800-1700 Friday.

DUTY FREE

The following goods can be taken into Anguilla without incurring customs duty:
200 cigarettes or 50 cigars or 250g of tobacco; 1 quart of wine or spirits.
Prohibited items: Weapons and non-prescribed drugs.

PUBLIC HOLIDAYS

Jan 1 '95 New Year's Day. **Apr 14** Good Friday. **Apr 17** Easter Monday. **May 1** Labour Day. **Jun 1** Anguilla Day. **Jun 5** Whit Monday. **Jun 9** Queen's Official Birthday. **Aug 6** Constitution Day. **Aug 7** August Monday. **Aug 10** August Thursday. **Dec 15** Separation Day. **Dec 25-26** Christmas Day. **Jan 1 '96** New Year's Day. **Apr 5** Good Friday. **Apr 8** Easter Monday.

HEALTH

Regulations and requirements may be subject to change at short notice, and you are advised to contact your doctor well in advance of your intended date of departure. Any numbers in the chart refer to the footnotes below.

	Special Precautions?	Certificate Required?
Yellow Fever	No	No
Cholera	No	No
Typhoid & Polio	Yes	-
Malaria	No	-
Food & Drink	1	-

[1]: Water precautions recommended except in major hotels and restaurants.
Health care: There are three government-appointed medical practitioners on Anguilla, two private practitioners and a 24-bed hospital located in The Valley. There are also health centres at The Valley, East End, South Hill and West End. Minor emergency treatment is usually free for UK citizens with proof of UK residence. Health insurance is recommended as costs for other categories of treatment are high.

TRAVEL - International

AIR: Anguilla is served by *LIAT (LI)* (Leeward Islands Air Transport) based in Antigua.
Approximate flight times: From Anguilla to *London* is 12 hours (including a stopover time in Antigua of 2 hours 30 minutes), to *Los Angeles* is 10 hours and to *New York* 6 hours.
International airport: *Wallblake Airport (AXA)* is 3km (2 miles) from The Valley. *Air Anguilla, Carib Aviation* and *Tyden Air* offer air taxi services, with several daily flights to and from St Maarten, St Thomas, Tortola and St Kitts.
Departure tax: EC$13 for international departures.
SEA: The main port is Road Bay where there is a jetty capable of handling ships of up to 1000 tonnes. Ferries operate between Blowing Point, Anguilla and Marigot on St Maarten at regular intervals between 0800-1700.

TRAVEL - Internal

ROAD: The road network is good but basic and the main road is of asphalt, stretching throughout the 25km (16-mile) length of Anguilla. Unpaved roads lead to beaches. Traffic drives on the left. **Taxis** are available at the airport and seaports with fixed prices to the various hotels. Island tours can be arranged on an individual basis. In addition, there are numerous **car hire** agencies available, including *Apex* and *Budget*. Bicycles and mopeds can also be hired.
Documentation: A temporary licence, valid for three months, can be issued at the police headquarters in The Valley on presentation of a national driving licence.

ACCOMMODATION

Accommodation on Anguilla ranges from luxury-class hotels to guest-houses, apartments, villas and cottages. Many establishments are situated on the beach and offer boating, snorkelling, fishing and scuba diving equipment. There are new resorts at Cap Juluca, Coccoloba and The Great House. For further details contact the Tourist Office. Twelve hotels are currently members of the Anguilla Hotel and Tourism Association, PO Box 321, The Valley. Tel: 497 2944. Fax: 497 3091. **Grading:** International standards apply. There are four hotels in the deluxe class, six in first class and two in second class.

RESORTS & EXCURSIONS

Anguilla is small and secluded; the main resorts are based around the hotels, many of which are situated off the islands' white coral beaches. Most excursions will be a leisurely exploration of other equally idyllic beaches. The visitor should see, however, *Wallblake House,* an impressively restored plantation house whose foundations date back to 1787. Other historical landmarks include *The Fountain,* a huge underground cave with a constant supply of fresh water at *Shoal Bay.* The ruins of the *Dutch Fort,* built in the 1700s, are located at **Sandy Hill,** famous as the scene of fierce fighting during the second French invasion of Anguilla in 1796. The *Tomb of Governor Richardson* (1679-1742) at Sandy Hill is well preserved. Also of interest are the *Salt Ponds* at **Sandy Ground** and **West End.** There are over 30 beaches on Anguilla, some of which stretch for miles, dotted with hidden coves and grotto-like rock areas. Boats are available for charter. Some of the best beaches are *Rendezvous, Shoal Bay, Road Bay, Maundays Bay, Cove Bay, Meads Bay* and *Crocus Bay.* Visitors who enjoy solitude and privacy should charter a boat to **Sandy Island,** fringed with coconut palms, 15 minutes from Sandy Ground Harbour; or **Sombrero Island,** 48km (30 miles) northwest of Anguilla, which has a picturesque lighthouse. The even smaller sandy cays of **Scrub, Dog** and **Prickly Pear Islands** are within reach of Anguilla by power boat.

SOCIAL PROFILE

FOOD & DRINK: Restaurants offer a mixture of Continental, American and Anguillan dishes. Seafoods include lobster, whelk and a variety of fish.
NIGHTLIFE: Anguilla's nightlife is centred on the hotels.
SHOPPING: The Department of Tourism sponsors handicrafts and the island-built racing boats are world-famous. Souvenirs will also include shells and small models of island sloops. There are a few small boutiques with limited stocks of swimwear, and a gift shop offering international name brands in bone china, crystals and jewellery. **Shopping hours:** 0800-1200 and 1300-1700 Monday to Friday; 0800-1600 Saturday.
SPORT: Boat racing is the national sport. For the visitor, all watersports including **snorkelling, scuba diving** and **fishing** are available.
SPECIAL EVENTS: Aug '95 *Carnival* (beginning Friday preceding August Monday lasting a week; Calypso competitions, house parties and pageants). Boat races are held almost every holiday; the most impressive on Anguilla Day, August Monday, August Thursday and New Year's Day. Athletics competitions are held on Anguilla Day.
SOCIAL CONVENTIONS: The Government is anxious to set limits to the commercialisation of the island and visitors will find that social life is centred on the tourist areas. The atmosphere is relaxed and English customs prevail. Beachwear should be confined to resorts. **Tipping:** 10% should be left in restaurants.

BUSINESS PROFILE

ECONOMY: Anguilla's economy is based on agriculture and fisheries. Lobster fishing is the most productive activity; livestock and crop growing (solely for internal consumption) are also important. Anguilla produces salt, the bulk of which is sold to Trinidad for use in its petroleum industry. Boatbuilding is the island's other major employer. The expanding tourist industry has ensured steady economic growth since the 1980s, although the pace has been restrained by the Government's concern to avoid the excesses of development experienced in resorts elsewhere. Nonetheless, unemployment is high; estimated at 40% of the population. The residents pay no income tax and the Anguillan government receives development aid from Britain.
BUSINESS: Anguilla is a small island with few business opportunities as such; lightweight suits or shirt and tie should be adequate for meetings. **Office hours:** 0800-1200 and 1300-1600 Monday to Friday.
COMMERCIAL INFORMATION: The following organisation can offer advice: Anguilla Chamber of Commerce, PO Box 321, The Valley. Tel: 497 2701. Fax: 497 5858.

CLIMATE

Hot throughout the year tempered by trade winds in local areas. The main rainy season is between October and December. The hurricane season is July to October.
Required clothing: Lightweight cottons throughout the year. Waterproofing is advisable during the rainy season.

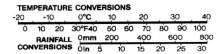

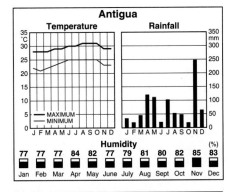

Antarctica

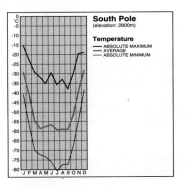

Location: South Pole.
British Antarctic Survey
High Cross, Madingley Road, Cambridge CB3 0ET
Tel: (01223) 61188 *or* 251400. Fax: (01223) 62616.
Antarctica covers an area of 36 million sq km (14 million sq miles) around the South Pole and is covered with an ice sheet 2km (3 miles) deep on average. It has no permanent human population other than personnel at a number of research stations run by different nations, including Argentina, Australia, Brazil, Chile, People's Republic of China, France, Germany, India, Japan, Republic of Korea (South), New Zealand, Pakistan, Poland, the Russian Federation, South Africa, the UK, the USA and Uruguay. The constitutional position of Antarctica is governed by the terms of the Antarctic Treaty of 1959 (which came into effect in 1961) and signed initially by Argentina, Australia, Chile, France, New Zealand, Norway, the UK, Belgium, Japan, South Africa, the former USSR and the USA. The first seven of these have historic claims to the ice-bound continent (none of which were or are generally recognised) and the Treaty preserves the *status quo,* neither recognising nor repudiating the old claims, but forbidding their expansion in any way. The terms of the Treaty also forbid, absolutely, the assertion of new claims.
The discovery in 1987 by the British Antarctic Survey of a 'hole' in the ozone layer of the Earth's atmosphere did more than perhaps any other event, bar nuclear accidents, to bring ecology to prominence in the international political agenda.
The Antarctic Treaty made no provision for mineral exploitation and in November 1988 an Antarctic Minerals Convention was finally opened for signing. This was intended to regulate but not prevent the extraction of minerals and caused much protest from environmental lobbyists. The preservation of Antarctica as perhaps the last great wilderness on earth seemed to get a step nearer at the 15th Consultative Conference of parties to the Treaty in October 1989. Some areas of the continent were designated worthy of special protection, with regulations covering sea pollution.
At the Antarctic Treaty Consultative Meetings in 1991, provisional agreement was reached on a new Environmental Protocol to the Antarctic Treaty, which guarantees a further ban on mining for 50 years and provides for a fully comprehensive regime of environmental protection.
Expedition cruises are now available to Antarctica and other polar regions and there is a new tour escorted by the famous explorer and travel writer, Sir Ranulph Fiennes. For further information, contact Abercrombie & Kent. Tel: (0171) 730 9600.

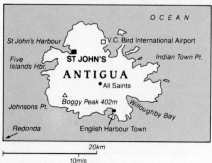

Scale: 20km / 10mls

Location: Caribbean, Leeward Islands.

Antigua Department of Tourism
PO Box 363, Long and Thames Streets, St John's, Antigua
Tel: 462 0480 *or* 462 0029. Fax: 462 2483.
Ministry of Economic Development, Industry and Tourism
Queen Elizabeth Highway, St John's, Antigua
Tel: 462 0092. Telex: 2122.
Antigua & Barbuda High Commission
15 Thayer Street, London W1M 5LD
Tel: (0171) 486 7073/4/5. Fax: (0171) 486 9970. Telex: 814503 (a/b AK ANTEGA G). Opening hours: 0900-1730 Monday to Friday.
Antigua & Barbuda Tourist Office
Address, contact numbers and opening hours as above.
British High Commission
PO Box 483, Price Waterhouse Centre, 11 Old Parham Road, St John's, Antigua
Tel: 462 0008/9. Fax: 462 2806 *or* 482 271. Telex: 2113 (a/b UKREP ANT AK).
Embassy of Antigua & Barbuda
Suite 4M, 3400 International Drive, NW, Washington, DC 20008
Tel: (202) 362 5122 *or* 362 5211 *or* 362 5166. Fax: (202) 362 5225.
Antigua Department of Tourism
Suite 311, 610 Fifth Avenue, New York, NY 10020
Tel: (212) 541 4117. Fax: (212) 757 1607.
United States Embassy
PO Box 664, Queen Elizabeth Highway, St John's, Antigua
Tel: 462 3505/6. Fax: 462 3516. Telex: 2140 (a/b USEMB).
Antigua Department of Tourism & Trade
Suite 304, 60 St Clair Avenue East, Toronto, Ontario M4T 1N5
Tel: (416) 961 3085. Fax: (416) 961 7218.
The Canadian High Commission in Barbados deals with enquiries relating to Antigua & Barbuda (see *Barbados* **later in the book).**

Timatic

Health
GALILEO/WORLDSPAN: TI-DFT/ANU/HE
SABRE: TIDFT/ANU/HE

Visa
GALILEO/WORLDSPAN: TI-DFT/ANU/VI
SABRE: TIDFT/ANU/VI

For more information on Timatic codes refer to Contents.

AREA: Antigua: 280 sq km (110 sq miles); **Barbuda:** 160 sq km (60 sq miles); **Redonda:** 1.6 sq km (0.6 sq miles). **Total:** 441.6 sq km (170.5 sq miles).
POPULATION: 66,000 (1991 estimate).
POPULATION DENSITY: 144.7 per sq km (1991).
CAPITAL: St John's. **Population:** 36,000 (1986 estimate).
GEOGRAPHY: Antigua & Barbuda comprises three islands, Antigua, Barbuda and Redonda. Low-lying and volcanic in origin, they are part of the Leeward Islands group in the northeast Caribbean. **Antigua's** coastline curves into a multitude of coves and harbours (they were once volcanic craters) and there are more than 365 beaches of fine white sand, fringed with palms. The island's highest point is Boggy Peak (402m, 1319ft); its capital is St John's. **Barbuda** lies 40km (25 miles) north of Antigua and is an unspoiled natural haven for wild deer and exotic birds. Its 8km-long (5-mile) beach is reputed to be amongst the most beautiful in the world. The island's village capital, Codrington, was named after the Gloucestershire family that once leased Barbuda from the British Crown for the price of 'one fat pig per year if asked for'. There are excellent beaches and the ruins of some of the earliest plantations in the West Indies. The coastal waters are rich with all types of crustaceans and tropical fish. **Redonda,** smallest in the group, is little more than an uninhabited rocky islet. It lies 40km (25 miles) southwest of Antigua.
LANGUAGE: English is the official language. English *patois* is widely spoken.
RELIGION: Anglican, Methodist, Moravian, Roman Catholic, Pentecostal, Baptist and Seventh Day Adventists.
TIME: GMT - 4.
ELECTRICITY: 220/110 volts AC, 60Hz. American-style 2-pin plugs. Some hotels have also outlets for 240 volts AC, in this case European-style 2-pin plugs are used.
COMMUNICATIONS: Telephone: IDD is available to all numbers. Country code: 1 809. No area codes. Outgoing international code: 011. **Fax:** Services are available from Cable & Wireless. Many hotels have fax facilities. **Telex/telegram:** These facilities are offered by Cable & Wireless (West Indies). **Post:** A *Poste Restante* service is available at the post office in St John's. Post office hours: 0800-1200 and 1300-1600 Monday to Friday. **Press:** All newspapers printed on the islands are weekly, many with political or governmental associations. All are in English. The main newspapers are *The Nation, The Worker's Voice, The Outlet* and *The Sentinel.*
BBC World Service and Voice of America frequencies: From time to time these change. See the section *How to Use this Book* for more information.
BBC:

MHz	17.84	15.26	9.915	5.975

Voice of America:

MHz	15.20	11.70	6.130	9.455

PASSPORT/VISA

Regulations and requirements may be subject to change at short notice, and you are advised to contact the appropriate diplomatic or consular authority before finalising travel arrangements. Details of these may be found at the head of this country's entry. Any numbers in the chart refer to the footnotes below.

	Passport Required?	Visa Required?	Return Ticket Required?
Full British	1/2	No	Yes
BVP	2	–	–
Australian	Yes	No	Yes
Canadian	1	No	Yes
USA	1	No	Yes
Other EU (As of 31/12/94)	Yes	No	Yes
Japanese	Yes	No	Yes

PASSPORTS: [1] Nationals of Canada, the USA and the UK (see note 2 below) do not require a passport, providing that they have other documents with proof of identity, such as a birth certificate, a citizenship card/naturalisation certificate, or a voter's registration card. A valid passport is required by all other nationals. Passports have to be valid for at least 6 months beyond period of stay.
British Visitors Passport: [2] Although the immigration authorities of Antigua and Barbuda may accept a British Visitors Passport for persons arriving for holidays or unpaid business trips of up to 3 months, no formal agreement exists to this effect, and the situation may, therefore, change at short notice. The lack of a formal agreement may also cause delays for passengers, with a BVP only, when arriving back in the UK.
VISAS: Required by all except:
(a) nationals of countries referred to on the chart above;
(b) citizens of Commonwealth countries;

(c) nationals of Argentina, Austria, Brazil, Finland, Liechtenstein, Malta, Mexico, Monaco, Norway, Peru, San Marino, Suriname, Sweden, Switzerland, Turkey and Venezuela.
These exemptions are valid for up to 6 months. Nationals of all other countries require a visa.
Types of visa: *Single-entry visa* – cost £24; *Multiple-entry visa* – cost £28. Transit visas are not required by persons continuing their journey within 24 hours.
Validity: The Single-entry visa is valid for 3 months, the Multiple-entry visa for 6 months.
Application to: Consulate (or Consular Section at Embassy or High Commission). For addresses, see top of entry.
Application requirements: (a) Completed form. (b) 2 identical passport-size photos. (c) Valid passport. (d) Fee (by postal order or cash only). (e) Onward or return ticket. (f) Evidence of sufficient funds to cover duration of stay.
Working days required: 2-4 days.
Temporary residence: Applications should be sent to the Prime Minister's Office, Factory Road, St John's, Antigua. Tel: 462 4956. Fax: 462 3225, but it is advisable to enquire first at the Embassy or High Commission.

MONEY

Currency: Eastern Caribbean Dollar (EC$) = 100 cents. Notes are in denominations of EC$100, 20, 10 and 5. Coins are in denominations of EC$1, and 50, 25, 10, 5, 2 and 1 cents. US currency is accepted almost everywhere.
Currency exchange: Although the EC Dollar is tied to the US Dollar, exchange rates will vary at different exchange establishments. There are international banks in St John's and US Dollars and Sterling can be exchanged at hotels and in the larger shops.
Credit cards: Diners Club, Visa, Mastercard and American Express are accepted. Check with your credit card company for details of merchant acceptability and other services which may be available.
Travellers cheques: Can be exchanged at international banks, hotels and the larger stores.
Exchange rate indicators: The following figures are included as a guide to the movements of the EC Dollar against Sterling and the US Dollar:

Date:	Oct '92	Sep '93	Jan '94	Jan '95
£1.00=	4.27	4.13	3.99	4.22
$1.00=	2.70	2.70	2.70	2.70

Note: The EC Dollar is tied to the US Dollar.
Currency restrictions: Free import and export of both local and foreign currency if declared.
Banking hours: 0800-1400 Monday to Thursday (*Barclays* 0800-1400 Monday, Tuesday and Wednesday); 0800-1700 Friday.

DUTY FREE

The following items may be taken into Antigua & Barbuda without payment of customs duty:
200 cigarettes or 50 cigars or 250g (8oz) of tobacco; 1 litre of wine or spirits; 6oz of perfume.
Prohibited items: Weapons and non-prescribed drugs (list available from Tourist Office).

PUBLIC HOLIDAYS

Jan 2 '95 For New Year's Day. **Apr 14** Good Friday. **Apr 17** Easter Monday. **May 1** Labour Day. **Jun 5** Whit Monday. **Jul 3** CARICOM Day. **Aug 7-8** Carnival. **Nov 1** Independence Day. **Dec 25-26** Christmas. **Jan 1 '96** New Year's Day. **Apr 5** Good Friday. **Apr 8** Easter Monday.

HEALTH

Regulations and requirements may be subject to change at short notice, and you are advised to contact your doctor well in advance of your intended date of departure. Any numbers in the chart refer to the footnotes below.

	Special Precautions?	Certificate Required?
Yellow Fever	No	1
Cholera	No	No
Typhoid & Polio	Yes	-
Malaria	No	-
Food & Drink	2	-

[1]: A yellow fever certificate is required of travellers aged one year or over arriving from infected areas.
[2]: Mains water is normally chlorinated, and whilst relatively safe may cause mild abdominal upsets. Bottled water is available and is advised for the first few weeks

of the stay. Milk is pasteurised and dairy products are safe for consumption. Local meat, poultry, seafood, fruit and vegetables are generally considered safe to eat.
Health care: Health insurance is recommended as medical treatment is expensive.

TRAVEL - International

AIR: Antigua & Barbuda is served by several international airlines, including *British Airways. LIAT (Leeward Islands Air Transport), BWIA* and *Lufthansa* provide scheduled passenger flights from Antigua to over 20 islands in the West Indies. Subsidiary companies *(Four Island Air Services Ltd* and *Inter Island Air Services Ltd)* of *LIAT* run flights within the Leeward Islands.
Approximate flight times: St John's to *London* is 8 hours, to *Los Angeles* is 9 hours and to *New York* is 3.5 hours.
International airport: *VC Bird International (ANU)*, formerly Coolidge International, is 10km (6 miles) northeast of St John's. The airport provides access to major international centres, such as London, New York, Miami, Frankfurt/M, Toronto and Montréal, with feeder services to all the Eastern Caribbean islands, the US Virgin Islands and Puerto Rico. Taxi service to city and hotels. Facilities include full outgoing duty-free shopping (liquor, perfume, straw items, T-shirts, souvenirs and handicrafts), restaurant (0730-2000), bar (0730-2400) and currency exchange (0900-1500).
Departure tax: US$10.
SEA: St John's has a deep-sea harbour served by cruise liners from the USA, Puerto Rico, the UK, Europe and South America. Fly-cruises from London are available with *Holland America, Royal Caribbean, Cunard, Costa, Sunline, Sitmar* and *Princess* Cruises. Many smaller ships sail to other Caribbean islands.

TRAVEL - Internal

AIR: A small airstrip at Codrington on Barbuda is equipped to handle light aircraft.
SEA: Local boats are available for excursions.
ROAD: There are nearly 1000km (600 miles) of roads in the country, about 140km (90 miles) of which are all-weather. Driving is on the left. The speed limit outside towns is 88kmph (55mph). **Bus:** The bus network is small, the buses infrequent. **Taxi:** Available everywhere with standardised rates. US Dollars are more readily accepted by taxi drivers. **Car hire:** This can be organised from your home country but is almost as easy to do on arrival. There are several reputable car hire companies on Antigua (some of which also hire out mopeds and bicycles). Rental rates are for the day and there is no mileage charge. **Documentation:** A national licence is accepted but a local driver's permit must be obtained. This is a simple formality and does not require a test. The permit is issued from a police station on presentation of a valid driver's licence plus a small fee.
JOURNEY TIMES: The following chart gives approximate journey times (in hours and minutes) from St John's to other major towns/resorts/centres in Antigua.

	Road
VC Bird (airport)	0.10
Dickenson Bay	0.10
English Harbour	0.35
St James's	0.35
Royal Antiguan	0.15
Half Moon Bay	0.30
Long Bay	0.35
Jolly Beach	0.20
Shirley Heights	0.35

ACCOMMODATION

Accommodation must be booked well in advance during Tennis Weeks, International Sailing Week and Carnival Week (see *Special Events* in the *Social Profile* section). No special accommodation facilities exist for students and young travellers and there are no official campsites in Antigua or Barbuda. Sleeping and living on the beaches is not permitted.
HOTELS: Hotel rates are considerably cheaper in the summer months (May to November). A government tax of 7% is added to hotel bills. 90% of hotels belong to the Antigua Hotels & Tourist Association, PO Box 454, Lower Redcliffe Street, St John's. Tel: 462 0374 *or* 462 3702 *or* 462 4928. Fax: 462 3702. **Grading:** There are three grades of hotel: *Deluxe* (20% of all graded hotels), *Superior* (60% of all graded hotels) and *Standard* (20% of all graded hotels). A full list of hotels and guest-houses, with rates, is available from the tourist office, and at *VC Bird International Airport* in Antigua.
Antigua: Most of the larger hotels have rooms with either full air-conditioning or with fans and provide a choice of meal plans. The more luxurious establishments offer a large variety of watersports, tennis and evening entertainments. Guest-houses, much cheaper than the hotels, provide basic, but clean accommodation, sometimes with meals. Self-catering accommodation is available for the budget vacationer.
Barbuda: Currently there are four hotels, two villas and a couple of guest-houses.

RESORTS & EXCURSIONS

ANTIGUA: Antiguans claim to have a different beach for every day of the year and their island's many beautiful soft, sandy beaches and coves certainly constitute its main attraction. The most popular resorts have hotels located either on beaches or close by, many of them taking their names from the beaches. But for the energetic, there's plenty to see and do away from the beaches. The island is rich in colourful bird and insect life; off-shore, beneath the waters of the Caribbean, are splendid tropical fish and coral; and there are several sites of historic interest.
An excursion to **Bird Island** can be made from Dickenson Bay. Many hotels offer excursions in glass-bottomed boats for a leisurely view of the reef. A restored pirate ship sails around the island and takes passengers for day or evening trips; food, unlimited drink and entertainment are included.
Nelson's Dockyard in English Harbour is one of the safest landlocked harbours in the world. It was used by Admirals Nelson, Rodney and Hood as a safe base for the British navy during the Napoleonic wars. *Clarence House,* overlooking Nelson's dockyard, was once the home of the Duke of Clarence, later King William IV. It is now the Governor General's summer residence, and is periodically open to visitors.
Shirley Heights and **Fort James** are two examples of the efforts made by the British to fortify the colony during the 18th century. Shirley Heights was named after General Shirley, later Governor of the Leeward Islands in 1781. One of the main buildings, known as the *Block House,* was erected as a stronghold in the event of a siege by General Mathew in 1787. Close by is the cemetery, containing an obelisk commemorating the soldiers of the 54th Regiment.
St John's Cathedral appears on postcards and in almost all visitors' photographs. The church was originally built in 1683, but was replaced by a stone building in 1745. An earthquake destroyed it almost a century later, and in 1845 the cornerstone of the present Anglican cathedral was laid. The figures of St John the Baptist and St John the Divine erected at the south gate were supposedly taken from one of Napoleon's ships and brought to the island by a British man-of-war.
The Market is in the west of St John's, and makes a lively and colourful excursion, especially on the busy Saturday mornings.
Indian Town, one of Antigua's national parks, is at the northeastern point of the island. Breakers roaring in with the full force of the Atlantic behind them have carved *Devil's Bridge* and have created blow-holes with fuming surf.
A newer sight is the lake that now monopolises the countryside in the centre of Antigua. The result of the **Potworks Dam**, it is Antigua's largest man-made lake, with a capacity of one thousand million gallons.
Fig Tree Drive is a scenic route through the lush tropical hills and picturesque fishing villages along the southwest coast. Taxis will take visitors on a round-trip.
At **Greencastle Hill** there are megaliths said to have been erected for the worship of the Sun God and Moon Goddess.
Parham, in the east of the island, is notable for its octagonal church, built in the mid-18th century, which still retains some Stucco work.
BARBUDA: Less developed than Antigua, Barbuda has a wilder, more spontaneous beauty. Deserted beaches and a heavily wooded interior abounding in birdlife, wild pigs and fallow deer are the main attractions of this unspoilt island. A visit to **Codrington**, the main village, makes an interesting excursion: the settlement is on the edge of a lagoon and the inhabitants rely largely on the sea for their existence.
REDONDA: This uninhabited rocky islet, lying about 56km (35 miles) northeast of Antigua, was once an important source of phosphates and guano (the remains of some of the mining buildings can still be seen) but for more than a century its chief claim to fame has been its association with a fairly harmless brand of English eccentricity. In 1865, Redonda was 'claimed' by Matthew Shiell as a kingdom for his son, Philippe. King Philippe I's 'successor', the poet John Gawsworth, appointed many leading literary figures of his day as dukes and duchesses of his kingdom; the lucky peers included JB Priestley, Dylan Thomas and Rebecca West. The current king lives in Sussex, but his subjects are not likely to produce any great works of fiction as they are all either goats, lizards or seabirds. The island is also well known amongst birdwatchers for its small population of burrowing owls, a bird now extinct on Antigua.

SOCIAL PROFILE

FOOD & DRINK: Casual wear is accepted in all bars and restaurants. There are no licensing restrictions, but excessive consumption of alcohol is frowned upon and further service will be refused. Antigua's gastronomic speciality is lobster, with red snapper and occasionally other fish running a close second when available. Larger hotels offer a wide selection of imported meats, vegetables, fruits and cheeses. Local specialities include barbecued free-range chicken, roast suckling pig, pilaffs, curries, goat water, fungi and saltfish. **Drink:** Imported wines and spirits are available as well as imported sodas and local fruit drinks. Local drinks include ice-cold fruit juice, coconut milk, Antiguan-produced red and white rums *(Cavalier)*, rum punches, and beer from Barbados *(Banks)* and Jamaica *(Red Stripe)*. There is a 7% government tax on most restaurant bills.
NIGHTLIFE: There is a wide choice of restaurants and bars around main tourist areas. Steel bands, combos and limbo dancers travel round hotels, performing nightly during the winter season (November to April). There are three casinos on the island and two nightclubs/discotheques. Some hotels have their own discotheques.
SHOPPING: Uniquely Antiguan purchases include straw goods, pottery, *batik* and silk-screen printed fabrics, and jewellery incorporating semi-precious Antiguan stones. English bone china and crystal, and French perfumes, watches and table linens are all available at very attractive prices. The *Heritage Quay Tourist Complex* is a shopping and entertainment complex with 40 duty-free shops, a theatre, restaurants and a casino and supper club. It forms part of the newest development in downtown St John's. **Shopping hours:** 0800-1200 and 1300-1600 Monday to Saturday, although some shops and chemists do not close for lunch. Early closing on Thursday.
SPORT: Cricket: This, the national game, is played to the highest international standard. In Viv Richards, Antigua produced one of the finest cricketers the game has ever seen. **Tennis:** Antigua has many lawn tennis courts. Professionals descend for the International Tennis Weeks in January (Men) and April (Women), both for competition and to train for the international tennis circuit. **Horseriding:** This can be organised through hotels. On public holidays, there is horseracing at Cassada Gardens. **Squash:** The Bucket Club and Temo Sports Club allow temporary membership for visitors. **Golf:** There are two first-class golf courses: the spectacular 18-hole golf course at Cedar Valley; and the 9-hole course at Half Moon Bay. Daily, weekly and monthly memberships at Cedar Valley include tennis privileges as well as golf. **Watersports:** Most resort hotels offer some facilities for most watersports. **Windsurfing** is popular and boards are easy to find. **Water-skiing** and sunfish **sailboating** are also available from most of the larger resorts' hotels. Deep-sea fishing (see below) and **scuba diving** are easily arranged and **snorkelling** equipment is cheap and easy to hire from hotels. There are very fine coral reefs in Antiguan and Barbudan coastal waters. **Swimming:** There are more than 365 beaches, all of them open to the public. **Sailing:** Antigua offers spectacular sailing and is famous for its international sailing regatta held once a year during April or May. The less adventurous may wish to hire a dinghy and find their own secluded cove or sheltered beach and anchor for a day of peace and quiet. **Deep-sea fishing:** There is excellent year-round fishing for wahoo, kingfish, mackerel, dorado, tuna and barracuda. Small to very large yachts can be chartered. There is an annual Sportfishing Tournament at the end of April to early May. The tournament record is a 56lb kingfish. **Crab-racing:** A sport for the very, very lazy, crab-racing is staged in certain bars once or twice a week. A punter may win enough to pay for his next round of drinks, but stakes are moderate and the crabs are unlikely to make anyone a millionaire.
SPECIAL EVENTS: The following is a selection of events in Antigua celebrated annually:
Apr 30-May 6 '95 *Antigua Sailing Week.* **Jul 31-Aug 8** *Carnival.*
SOCIAL CONVENTIONS: Dress is informal unless formal dress is specifically requested. As a gesture towards the islanders themselves, it is preferable not to

wear scanty clothing or beachwear in towns or villages. Relatives and good friends generally embrace. Friends tend to drop by unannounced, but an invitation is necessary for acquaintances or business associates. Although gifts will generally be well received, they are normally only given on celebratory occasions. Flowers are appropriate for dinner parties; bring a bottle only when specifically requested. Smoking is accepted in most public places. **Tipping:** 10% is included on hotel bills for staff gratuities, plus a 7% government tax. Taxi drivers expect 10% of the fare, and dockside and airport porters expect EC$1 per bag.

BUSINESS PROFILE

ECONOMY: Antigua was one of the first Caribbean islands to actively encourage tourism, beginning in the late 1960s. The late 1980s have seen another phase of major development and tourism is today the main source of revenue. There are more than 30 luxury hotels and over 50 guest-houses and apartments, and further expansions of the facilities are planned. Fears of over-reliance on tourism have, however, led the Government into attempts to diversify the economy towards manufacturing, agriculture and fisheries. Local agriculture has been promoted to reduce dependency on imported food, although the lack of water resources is proving to be a major handicap. There are a number of light industries producing rum, clothing, furniture and household appliances; there is also an electronic assembly plant producing goods for export. Offshore banking and other financial services are the newest addition to the economy. On top of these, Antigua receives rent for two American military bases and significant overseas aid. Even so, the island has a large trade and balance-of-payments deficit. Antigua and Barbuda's main trading partners are the USA, the UK and Canada, and countries within the CARICOM Caribbean trading bloc, of which Antigua & Barbuda is a member. Puerto Rico is an important export market.
BUSINESS: A lightweight or safari suit, a long- or short-sleeved shirt and a tie are suitable for most business visits. Handshaking is the normal greeting for acquaintances and for formal introductions. Calling cards are expected from people who do not live on the islands. **Office hours:** 0800-1200 and 1300-1600 Monday to Friday. **Government office hours:** 0800-1630 Monday to Thursday; 0800-1500 Friday.
COMMERCIAL INFORMATION: The following organisation can offer advice: Antigua and Barbuda Chamber of Commerce and Industry Ltd, PO Box 774, Redcliffe Street, St John's. Tel: 462 0743. Fax: 462 4575.
CONFERENCES/CONVENTIONS: 10% of the membership of the Antigua Hotels & Tourist Association (see *Accommodation* for details) offer meeting facilities. Information is available direct from the Tourist Office.

CLIMATE

The islands enjoy a very pleasant tropical climate which remains warm and relatively dry throughout the year.
Required clothing: Lightweight cottons or linen, with rainwear needed from September to December.

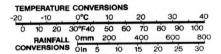

TEMPERATURE CONVERSIONS
-20   -10   0°C   10   20   30   40
0 10 20 30°F40 50 60 70 80 90 100
RAINFALL 0mm 200 400 600 800
CONVERSIONS 0In 5 10 15 20 25 30

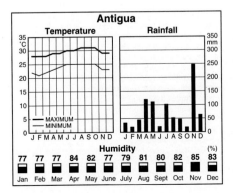

Antigua

Temperature / Rainfall

Humidity (%)

Jan	Feb	Mar	Apr	May	June	July	Aug	Sept	Oct	Nov	Dec
77	77	77	84	82	77	79	81	80	82	85	83

Argentina

International airport □

Location: Southeastern South America.

Secretaría de Turismo de la Nación
Calle Suipacha 1111, 21°, 1368 Buenos Aires, Argentina
Tel: (1) 312 5621. Fax: (1) 313 6834. Telex: 24882.
Asociación Argentina de Agencias de Viajes y Turismo
Viamonte 640, 10°, 1053 Buenos Aires, Argentina
Tel: (1) 322 2804. Telex: 25449.
Embassy of the Argentine Republic
53 Hans Place, London SW1X 0LA
Tel: (0171) 584 6494. Fax: (0171) 589 3106. Opening hours: 0900-1700 Monday to Friday.
Argentine Consulate
Fifth Floor, Trevor House, 100 Brompton Road, London SW3 1ER
Tel: (0171) 589 3104. Fax: (0171) 584 7863. Opening hours: 1000-1300 Monday to Friday.
British Embassy
Casilla de Correo 2050, Dr Luis Agote 2412/52, 1425 Buenos Aires, Argentina
Tel: (1) 803 7070/1. Fax: (1) 803 1731.
Embassy of the Argentine Republic
1600 New Hampshire Avenue, NW, Washington, DC 20009
Tel: (202) 939 6400/1/2/3. Fax: (202) 332 3171. *Consulate address:* 2136 R Street, NW, Washington, DC 20009.
Consulate General of the Argentine Republic
12 West 56th Street, New York, NY 10019
Tel: (212) 603 0400. Fax: (212) 397 3523.
Argentina Government Tourist Office
12 West 56th Street, New York, NY 10019
Tel: (212) 603 0443. Fax: (212) 397 3523.
Embassy of the United States of America
Unit 4334, Avenida Colombia 4300, 1425 Buenos Aires, Argentina
Tel: (1) 774 7611 *or* 777 4533/4 *or* 777 8842. Fax: (1) 775 4205 *or* 777 0197. Telex: 18156.
Embassy of the Argentine Republic
Suite 620, Royal Bank Center, 90 Sparks Street, Ottawa, Ontario K1P 5B4
Tel: (613) 236 2351/4. Fax: (613) 235 2659.
Canadian Embassy
Casilla de Correo 1598, 2828 Tagle, 1425 Buenos Aires, Argentina
Tel: (1) 805 3032 *or* 806 1212 (immigration). Fax: (1) 806 1209. Telex: 21383 (a/b CANAD AR).

AREA: 2,766,889 sq km (1,068,302 sq miles).
POPULATION: 32,370,298 (1991).
POPULATION DENSITY: 11.7 per sq km.
CAPITAL: Buenos Aires. **Population:** 11,382,002

(1990 estimate).
GEOGRAPHY: Argentina is situated in South America, east of the Andes, and is bordered by Chile to the west, the Atlantic Ocean to the east and Uruguay, Bolivia, Paraguay and Brazil to the north and northeast. There are four main geographical areas: the Andes, the North and Mesopotamia, the Pampas and Patagonia. The climate and geography of Argentina vary considerably, ranging from the great heat of the Chaco, through the pleasant climate of the central Pampas to the sub-Antarctic cold of the Patagonian Sea. Mount Aconcagua soars almost 7000m (23,000ft) and waterfalls at Iguazú stretch around a massive semi-circle, thundering 70m (230ft) to the bed of the Paraná River. In the southwest is a small 'Switzerland' with a string of beautiful icy lakes framed by mountains.
LANGUAGE: Spanish is the official language. English, German, French and Italian are sometimes spoken.
RELIGION: 90% Roman Catholic, 2% Protestant.
TIME: GMT - 3.
ELECTRICITY: 220 volts AC, 50Hz. Lamp fittings are of the screw-type. Plug fittings in older buildings are of the 2-pin round type, but some new buildings use the 3-pin flat type.
COMMUNICATIONS: Telephone: IDD is available (but not generally in use). Country code: 54. Outgoing international code: 00. The system is often overburdened and international calls are expensive. Local calls can be made from public call-boxes which are located in shops and restaurants and are identifiable by a blue sign outside. **Fax:** Most large hotels have facilities. **Telex/telegram:** Telex service from ENTEL (state-owned) in Buenos Aires. A cable service to other Latin American countries exists, run by All America Cables Limited. International telexes can be sent from public booths at Las Heras, Peru, Sarmiento, Corrientes, San Martin and Ezeiza Airport. **Post:** Airmail to Europe takes between five to ten days. Surface mail to Europe can take as long as 50 days, so it is advisable to send everything airmail. Internal postal services are subject to delay. Post office hours: 0800-2000 Monday to Friday, 0800-1400 Saturday. **Press:** The *Buenos Aires Herald* is the leading English-language newspaper in Latin America. Argentina's principal dailies include *Clarín, Crónica, El Cronista Comercial, La Nación, La Razón* and *Ambito, Financiero.*
BBC World Service and Voice of America frequencies: From time to time these change. See the section *How to Use this Book* for more information.

BBC:				
MHz	15.26	15.19	11.75	9.915
Voice of America:				
MHz	15.12	11.91	9.590	6.130

PASSPORT/VISA

Regulations and requirements may be subject to change at short notice, and you are advised to contact the appropriate diplomatic or consular authority before finalising travel arrangements. Details of these may be found at the head of this country's entry. Any numbers in the chart refer to the footnotes below.

	Passport Required?	Visa Required?	Return Ticket Required?
Full British	Yes	No/1	2
BVP	Not valid	-	-
Australian	Yes	Yes	Yes
Canadian	Yes	No/1	2
USA	Yes	No/1	2
Other EU (As of 31/12/94)	Yes	No/1	2
Japanese	Yes	No/1	Yes

PASSPORTS: Valid passport required by all except nationals of Argentina, Bolivia, Brazil, Chile, Paraguay and Uruguay who, for journeys that do not go beyond Argentina and these 5 countries, may use their national ID cards.
British Visitors Passport: Not accepted.
VISAS: [1] Required by all for business purposes. For tourist visits, visas are required by all except the following countries who may visit for a maximum period of 90 days:

(a) nationals of the countries shown in the chart above; (b) nationals of Algeria, Austria, Barbados, Bolivia, Brazil, Chile, Colombia, Costa Rica, Dominica, Dominican Republic, Ecuador, El Salvador, Finland, Guatemala, Honduras, Hungary, Israel, *Jamaica, Liechtenstein, Mexico, Monaco, Nicaragua, Norway, Paraguay, Peru, Poland, Sweden, Switzerland, Turkey, Uruguay, Vatican City and Yugoslavia (Serbia and Montenegro).
Note: [2] Return tickets are not required by bona fide tourists from countries referred to in the chart above. [*] For a maximum of 30 days only.
Types of visa: Tourist, Business, Resident and Transit. Transit visas are not needed for the nationals listed above or those holding confirmed onward or return tickets for travel within the following 48 hours and who do not leave the airport (nationals of South Korea (Republic) and holders of Taiwan (China) passports must leave within six hours).
Application to: Consulate (or Consular Section at Embassy). For addresses, see top of entry.
Application requirements: (a) Passport. (b) Application forms. (c) Fee (approx. £18.27). (d) Letter of introduction from employer if on business or from embassy if a tourist.
Working days: 1.
Note: Minors travelling to or from Argentina, if unaccompanied by their fathers, must carry the father's or other legal guardian's authorisation to travel, which must be certified by an Argentine Consul if issued abroad. Fines of up to US$600 are levied if passengers do not comply with immigration requirements. Passengers will be deported.

MONEY

Currency: Neuvo Peso (P) = 100 centavos. Introduced in 1992, it replaced the Austral. Neuvo Peso notes are in denominations of P100, 50, 20, 10, 5, 2 and 1. Coins are in denominations of 50, 25, 10 and 5 centavos.
Currency exchange: Banks and *cambios* are available in all the major cities.
Credit cards: Diners Club, American Express and Access/Mastercard are accepted. Check with your credit card company for details of merchant acceptability and other services which may be available.
Travellers cheques: It is often difficult to exchange these in the smaller towns, except at branches of the Bank of London and South America. Citibank will exchange travellers cheques for US Dollars in cash at 1% commission.
Exchange rate indicators: The following figures are included as a guide to the movements of the Peso against Sterling and the US Dollar:

Date:	Oct '92	Sep '93	Jan '94	Jan '95
£1.00=	1.57	1.53	1.48	1.56
$1.00=	0.99	1.00	1.00	1.00

Currency restrictions: The import and export of both local and foreign currency is unlimited.
Banking hours: 1000-1500 Monday to Friday.

DUTY FREE

The following goods may be imported into Argentina without incurring customs duty:
400 cigarettes; 50 cigars; 2 litres of alcohol; 5kg of foodstuffs; goods to the value of US$200 (inclusive of any duty-free items listed above).
For those arriving from Bolivia, Brazil, Chile, Paraguay or Uruguay:
200 cigarettes; 20 cigars; 1 litre of alcohol; 2kg of foodstuffs; goods to the value of US$100 (inclusive of any duty-free items listed above).
Prohibited items: Animals and birds from Africa or Asia (except Japan), parrots, and fresh foodstuffs such as meat, dairy products and fruit. Hunting guns may only be imported with a licence which must be procured before arrival from the nearest Argentine Consulate. The hunter must submit personal documents, a certificate of good conduct issued by the local police of the district where the hunter lives, together with the serial number, calibre, type and brand of each gun (a maximum of two guns are allowed per hunter). Explosives, inflammable items, narcotics and pornographic material are also forbidden.
Note: All gold must be declared. It is wise to arrange Customs clearance for expensive consumer items (cameras, typewriters, etc) to forestall any problems.

PUBLIC HOLIDAYS

Jan 1 '95 New Year's Day. **Apr 13** Maundy Thursday. **Apr 14** Good Friday. **May 1** Labour Day. **May 25** Anniversary of the 1810 Revolution. **Jun 10** Occupation of the Islas Malvinas. **Jun 21** For Flag Day. **Jul 9** Independence Day. **Aug 17** Death of General José de San Martín. **Oct 12** Discovery of America. **Dec 8** Immaculate Conception. **Dec 25** Christmas. **Jan 1 '96** New Year's Day. **Apr 4** Maundy Thursday. **Apr 5** Good Friday.

HEALTH

Regulations and requirements may be subject to change at short notice, and you are advised to contact your doctor well in advance of your intended date of departure. Any numbers in the chart refer to the footnotes below.

	Special Precautions?	Certificate Required?
Yellow Fever	No	No
Cholera	Yes/1	No
Typhoid & Polio	Yes/2	-
Malaria	Yes/3	-
Food & Drink	4	-

[1]: A few cases of cholera have occurred in the northern provinces of Argentina, especially in suburban areas and among children below the age of 5 years.
[2]: Protection is advised for both polio and typhoid in the form of vaccinations.
[3]: Malaria risk, primarily in the benign *vivax* form, exists from October through May below 1200m (3937 ft) in rural areas of Iruya, Orán, San Martín, Santa Victoria Dep. (Salta Prov.) and Ledesma, San Pedro and Santa Barbara Dep. (Jujuy Prov.). Protection in the form of 300mg of chloroquine prophylaxis administered weekly is advised.
[4]: Tap water is considered safe to drink. Drinking water outside main cities and towns may be contaminated and sterilisation is advisable. Milk is pasteurised and dairy products are safe for consumption. Local meat, poultry, seafood, fruit and vegetables are generally considered safe to eat.
Rabies is present. For those at high risk, vaccination before arrival should be considered. If bitten abroad seek medical advice without delay. For more information consult the *Health* section at the back of the book.
Other diseases of which there is a noteworthy level of risk are hepatitis A, trypanosomiasis, gastroenteritis, viral hepatitis, intestinal parasitosis and anthrax.
Health care: Medical insurance is recommended. Medical facilities are generally of a high standard.

TRAVEL - International

AIR: Argentina's national airline is *Aerolíneas Argentinas (AR)*.
Approximate flight times: From Buenos Aires to *London* is 18 hours (including a good connection in Madrid), to *Los Angeles* is 16 hours and 5 minutes, to *New York* is 14 hours and 15 minutes, to *Singapore* is 29 hours and 30 minutes and to *Sydney* is 16 hours.
International airport: *Buenos Aires (BUE)* (Ezeiza), 50km (31.5 miles) from the city. There is an hourly coach service to the city as well as taxis. The airport has a bank, restaurant, *cambio*, duty-free shop and a car rental facility. There is also a coach connection to *Jorge Newbery* airport (locally called *Aeroparque*) hourly for domestic flight connections. A taxi service is available. There are frequent flights from Buenos Aires to all neighbouring republics.
Departure tax: US$13. For flights to Montevideo (Uruguay), the departure tax is US$5. Passengers in transit and children under two years of age are exempt.
SEA: The main ports are Buenos Aires, La Plata (Ensenada), Rosario and Bahía Blanca. Two Italian ocean lines (*Italmar* and *Costa*) run services from Spanish and Italian ports. There are ferry connections down the Paraná River from Paraguay and ferries and hydrofoils link Buenos Aires with Montevideo in Uruguay.
RAIL: The major direct international route is from Buenos Aires to Asunción in Paraguay. There is also a part-rail service from Buenos Aires to Colonia (by hydrofoil boat), then to Montevideo (by bus), at which point rail service resumes on to Brazil. The timetables and journey times are often disrupted and delays must be expected.
ROAD: There are well-maintained road routes from Uruguay, Brazil, Paraguay, Bolivia and Chile. **Coach:** Direct daily services between Buenos Aires, Puerto Alegre, São Paulo and Rio de Janeiro.

TRAVEL - Internal

AIR: Domestic flights from *Jorge Newbery* (Aeroparque) and *Córdoba* (Pajas Blancas) to destinations throughout Argentina are run by *Aerolíneas Argentinas, Austral* and the army airline *LADE*. Air travel is the most efficient way to get around, but the services are very busy and subject to delay. You are advised to book in advance for all flights. It is possible to buy a 30-day unlimited travel ticket from *Aerolíneas* or *Austral*.
Departure tax: US$3 for domestic flights.
RAIL: The domestic rail network extends over 43,000km (27,000 miles), which makes it one of the largest in the world. Children under three travel free and children 3-11 pay half fare. There are three classes: air-conditioned, first class and second class. There are restaurant and sleeping facilities for first-class passengers and most long-distance trains run several times a week. Low-class rail travel is also good value. There are six main rail routes from Buenos Aires: Buenos Aires–Rosario (where one branch goes to Tucumán and Jujuy via Córdoba and the second branch goes to Tucumán and Jujuy via La Banda), Buenos Aires–Mendoza, Buenos Aires–Santa Rosa, Buenos Aires–Mar del Plata, Buenos Aires–Posadas and Buenos Aires–Bahia Blanca (where one branch goes to Zapala and a second branch to San Carlos de Bariloche). Rail travellers are warned that once out of Buenos Aires information is very hard to come by.
Special fares: The *Argempass* entitles visitors to unlimited first-class train travel, but is only sold in Argentina at railway booking offices. 30-day, 60-day and 90-day passes are available. A supplement is charged for sleeping car accommodation. The passes must be used within 30 days of purchase and are valid from the first day of use to the last day at 2400. Other discount tickets include: *Group Pass* – 10-25% discount for a group of 10-25 persons; *Family Pass* – 25% discount for a mother, father and up to 2 children; *Youth Pass* – 25% discount for persons under 30 years of age; *Senior Pass* – 25% discount for women 55 years of age and older and men 60 years of age and older; and *Student Pass* – 25% discount for students.
ROAD: Cross-country highways are well built and equipped, but road conditions off the main routes can be unreliable. Nonetheless, buses are considered to be a more reliable form of long-distance transport than trains. Traffic drives on the right. **Car hire:** There are a number of agencies in Buenos Aires. **Documentation:** International Driving Permit is required and this must be stamped at the offices of the *Automóvil Club Argentino*.
URBAN: The metro *(subte)* service in Buenos Aires operates from early morning to late at night on a fixed fare basis; tokens can be purchased at booking offices. **Bus** services are provided by *colectivo* minibuses operating 24 hours a day on a flat fare; however, these are often crowded. There are extensive bus services in other towns, including trolleybuses in Rosario. **Taxi:** Available in most cities and large towns and can either be hailed on the street or found at taxi ranks. They are usually recognisable by their yellow roofs.
JOURNEY TIMES: The following chart gives approximate journey times (in hours and minutes) from Buenos Aires to other major cities/towns in Argentina.

	Air	Road	Rail
Córdoba	1.10	9.00	12.00
Bariloche	2.10	22.00	36.00
Cataratas	1.30	17.00	24.00
Iguazú	1.40	20.00	-
Mendoza	1.50	17.00	30.00
Mar del Plata	0.40	4.00	4.00
Rio Gallegos	4.15	36.00	-
Rosario	0.50	4.00	4.00
Salta	2.00	15.00	20.00
Ushuaia	3.00	30.00	-

ACCOMMODATION

HOTELS: Hotels range in standard from the most luxurious in Buenos Aires to the lowest class in the rural areas. In Buenos Aires, the cheaper hotels can mostly be found around Avenida de Mayo. Generally service is excellent. All hotels add 3% tourism tax, 24% service charge for food and drink and 15% room tax. Most are air-conditioned, many have fine restaurants. For further information contact the Secretaría de Turismo de la Nacíon (for address, see top of entry). **Grading:** Maximum and minimum rates are fixed for 1-, 2- and 3-star hotels, guest-houses and inns; 4- and 5-star hotels are free to charge any rate they choose. All hotels, guest-houses and inns, as well as campsites, are graded according to the number of beds available and the services supplied.
SELF-CATERING: It is possible to rent cheap self-catering apartments and flats, with or without maid service, either by the day or week. Some can provide meals. Most apartments are in Buenos Aires.
CAMPING/CARAVANNING: Most resort cities welcome campers, and there are motels, campsites and caravan sites throughout Argentina. Campsites can be found virtually in every major region. Dormobiles are for hire.

RESORTS & EXCURSIONS

BUENOS AIRES: The capital city, which dominates the commercial life of the country, is also an elegant shoppers' paradise and a cosmopolitan cultural centre, and takes pride in *The National Art Museum*, the *Folk Art Museum* and the *Teatro*. There are now few reminders of the city's past, although the immense *cathedral,* which contains the remains of San Martín, Argentina's liberator, is one exception. The district of *La Boca,* one of the older areas and the home of the tango, is well worth a night-time visit. The city has numerous parks and squares and is well served by public transport.
THE NORTH: To the northwest of the capital lie the most ancient cities in the country. **Córdoba** is interesting for its architecture and scenery, and **Salta** for its colonial cathedral containing a gold altar. **Tucumán,** the 'Garden of Argentina', is set in a landscape of great natural beauty. The squares of the city are planted with palm and orange trees, and it has some of the finest colonial churches in the country. One of the most famous sights in the whole of Argentina is the **Iguazú Falls** in the northeast of the country, on the border with Brazil and Paraguay, around which a vast tourist industry has been built up.
COASTAL RESORTS: One of the most popular resorts on the Atlantic coast, with several kilometres of fine beaches, is **Mar del Plata.** Others include **Villa Gezell, Pinamar, Miramar** and **Necochea** (which has, reputedly, the largest casino in the world). New resorts are constantly springing up along this developing area of coastline. Most can offer deep-sea fishing and other watersports. **Bahía Blanca,** the largest southern city, is mainly commercial but it is also the gateway to the fascinating lakeland around **Bariloche.**
THE ANDES: This region has many national parks with abundant wildlife, as well as opportunities for shooting and fishing. Skiing is available at **Cerro Chapelco Tronador** and **San Martín de los Andes.** The foothills of the Andes, west of the capital, are noted for their vineyards. The Andes proper contain many spectacular natural features, including **Mount Aconcagua**, one of the highest in the Western hemisphere.

SOCIAL PROFILE

FOOD & DRINK: North American, Continental and Middle Eastern cuisine is generally available, whilst local food is largely a mixture of Basque, Spanish and Italian. Beef is of a particularly high quality, and meat-eaters should not miss out on the chance to dine at a *parillada,* or grill room, where a large variety of barbecue-style dishes can be sampled. Popular local dishes include *empanadas* (minced meat and other ingredients covered with puff pastry) and *locro* (pork and maize stew). In general, restaurants are good value, and are classified by a fork sign with three forks implying a good evening out. Hotel residents are usually asked to sign a charge slip. **Drink:** Argentine wines are very good and inexpensive. Local distilleries produce name brands of most well-known spirits. Whiskies and gins are excellent, as are classic and local wines. Caribbean and South American rum add flavour to cocktails. There are no licensing laws.
NIGHTLIFE: Buenos Aires' nightlife is vibrant. There are many theatres and concert halls featuring foreign artists. Economic instability has meant a contraction of some of the more extravagant nightclubs for which Buenos Aires was famous, though there are still a large number of smaller intimate *boîtes* (clubs) and many stage shows. There are casinos throughout Argentina.
SHOPPING: Special purchases from Argentina include leather goods of all descriptions (gloves, coats, jackets and purses, etc), hand-embroidered blouses and vicuña woollen goods. Argentina practices a 18% VAT tax-back shopping system for Argentine products of over US$200 in certain shops. Visitors should look for a 'tax free' sticker displayed at all stores which take part. On making purchases at these stores, visitors must show both their passport (or identity card if national of a bordering country) and the migration card. The refund must be noted down at the back of the invoice by the shop assistant, which will be given to the purchaser with stamps on the back and a triplicate. The price of the stamps is equivalent to the money you will receive on leaving the country when you show the invoice at the Banco de la Nación Argentina at either the Ezeiza International Airport, Jorge Newbery Airport or the Buenos Aires Port. These branches are open 24 hours a day. The money back will be presented in pesos, which can be changed into foreign currency at the bank. **Shopping hours:** 0900-1930 Monday to Friday and 0900-1300 Saturday.
SPORT: Football, tennis, golf, polo, horse-racing and motor racing are all very popular. **Football** is obsessively followed; the national team were world champions in 1978 and 1986, and runners-up in the World Cup of 1990. Palermo Park has a **golf** course, public **tennis** courts and professional **polo** grounds. The polo season is from October to December. **Swimming** is enjoyed in rivers, lakes and small resorts along the Atlantic coast; **water-skiing** along the San Antonio River in the Tigre Delta Region; **scuba diving** in Patagonia; yachting and **boating** along the River Plate; and **fishing** on the Atlantic coast off the piers. There is very fine freshwater fishing along the Paraná River and in Argentina's many artificial lakes with fine trout and salmon. **Skiing:** There is excellent skiing on the eastern slopes of the Andes, with an increasing number of ski resorts and runs. The season is generally May to September. An all-season resort is being built on the slopes of Mount Tronador, an extinct volcano. *Bariloche* is the oldest, most established, and best-equipped ski resort. The runs at *San Antonio, San Bernado, La Canaleta, Puente del Inca* and *Las Cuevas* on the border of Argentina and Chile, offer the most exciting skiing. There are also skiing facilities and resort hotels at *Chapelco, Vallecitos, Las Leñas* and *Esquel.* One note of caution: there is a chronic shortage of accommodation at these resorts, though the situation is being rectified as quickly as possible. It is vital to book early.
SPECIAL EVENTS: The following is a selection of the special events occurring annually in Argentina:
Jan *Sea Festival,* Mar del Plata; *Jineteada* (breaking in horses) and *Folklore Festival,* Diamante, Prov. Entre Ríos; *Chaya* (a musical instrument) *Festival,* La Rioja; *Doma* (breaking in horses) and *Folklore Festival,* Intendente Alvear, Prov. La Pampa; *Folklore Festival,* Cosquín, Prov. Córdoba.
Feb *Carnival,* Esquina, Prov. Corrientes; *Pachamama* (Mother Earth) *Festival,* Amaicha del Valle, Prov. Tucumán; *Trout Fishing Festival,* Río Grande.
Mar *Grape Harvest Festival,* Mendoza.
Apr *Holy Week,* Salta; *Festival of Our Lady Del Valle,* Catamarca.
Jul *Poncho Week,* Catamarca; *Simoca Fair,* Simoca, Prov. Tucumán; *Santiago Week,* Santiago del Estero; *Dorado Fishing Competition,* Formosa.
Aug *Snow Festival,* Río Turbio, Prov. Santa Cruz; *Jujuy Week,* Jujuy; *Dorado Festival,* Posadas, Prov. Misiones; *Snow Festival,* Bariloche.
Sep *Chamamé Music Festival,* Corrientes; *Agriculture Festival,* Esperanza, Prov. Santa Fé.
Oct *Fiesta de la Cerveza,* Villa General Belgrano.
Nov *Sea Salmon Fishing Contest,* Comodoro Rivadavia; *Tradition Week* (gaucho shows), San Antonio de Areco.
Dec *Gaucho Festival,* Gral. Madaria, Prov. Buenos Aires; *Trout Festival,* San Junín de los Andes, Prov. Neuquén.
SOCIAL CONVENTIONS: The custom of shaking hands on greeting is practised more in Argentina than in the UK. Entertaining often takes place in the home and it is customary to send flowers to the hostess the following day. Dinner is usually served between 2100-2200. Avoid casual discussion of the Falklands/Malvinas war. Dress is not usually formal, though clothes should be conservative away from the beach. Formal wear is worn for official functions and dinners, particularly in exclusive restaurants. Smoking is prohibited on public transport, in cinemas and theatres. **Tipping:** Tips are theoretically outlawed but some hotels or restaurants will add 25% service charge, plus an 18% tax charge. In these cases, a minimal tip is still expected. Otherwise, 10% on top of the bill will suffice. The same applies in bars. Taxi drivers tend to expect tips from visitors.

BUSINESS PROFILE

ECONOMY: Argentina is rich in natural resources and also has a large and profitable agricultural sector; the country is one of the world's major exporters of wheat and also produces maize, oilseeds, sorghum, soya beans and sugar. Beef is no longer the dominant trading commodity that it once was. Agriculture accounts for 70% of export earnings, and although it has been affected by Argentina's economic crisis, it has not suffered as badly as the inefficient industrial sector. Steel and petrochemicals are two key industries which have recently been released from state control and are looking for new business. The state telephone company is expected to join the private sector soon. Farming products aside, Argentina exports textiles and some metal and chemical products. Brazil is the largest of the country's South American trading partners. There is comparatively little trade with neighbouring Chile with whom political relations are very bad. Further afield, Argentina has important trading relationships with both superpowers: the United States is the main source of manufactured products while the CIS buys large quantities of grain from the Argentinian surplus. The fastest-growing aspects of the country's foreign trade are, however, Japan and the EU, especially Germany and The Netherlands. Trade relations with the UK have improved sharply in the last few years in line with the diplomatic rapprochement: insurance cover has been made available by the British government to exporters since June 1993. Throughout the 1980s, the Argentinian economy has been stricken by the twin scourges of hyper-inflation and a massive foreign debt. Austerity measures introduced by President Alfonsín – in particular the 1988 'Primavera' plan – were well received by international financiers but sparked major civil disorder inside Argentina, with serious clashes between demonstrators and the army. Within a year, Alfonsín was voted out of office. Carlos Menem's administration retained some of the policies of his predecessor, but attempted to accelerate the privatisation programme and liberalise other parts of Argentina's vast public sector. The Government has also embarked on a comprehensive overhaul of the country's financial system.
BUSINESS: Business cards are usually given and businessmen expect to deal with someone of equal status. Punctuality is expected by visitors. Literature is in Spanish although many Argentinian business people speak English or Italian as a second language. **Office hours:** 0900-1900 Monday to Friday.
COMMERCIAL INFORMATION: The following organisation can offer advice: Cámara Argentina de Comercio (Chamber of Commerce), Avenida Leandro N. Alem 36, 1003 Buenos Aires. Tel: (1) 331 8051. Fax: (1) 331 8055. Telex: 18542.
CONFERENCES/CONVENTIONS: For more information contact the Secretaría de Turismo de la Nación (for address, see top of entry).

CLIMATE

The north is subtropical with rain throughout the year, while Tierra del Fuego in the south has a sub-arctic climate. The main central area is temperate, but can be hot and humid during summer (December to February) and cool in winter.
Required clothing: European clothes for the main central area. Lightweight cottons and linens in the north. Warm clothes are necessary in the south and during cool winter months in the central area. Waterproofing is advisable for all areas.

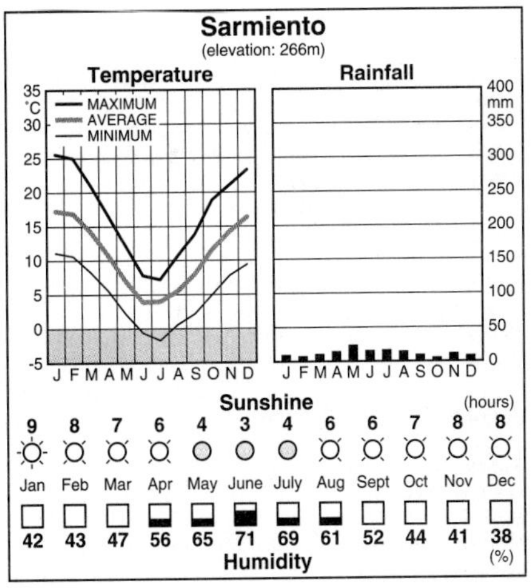

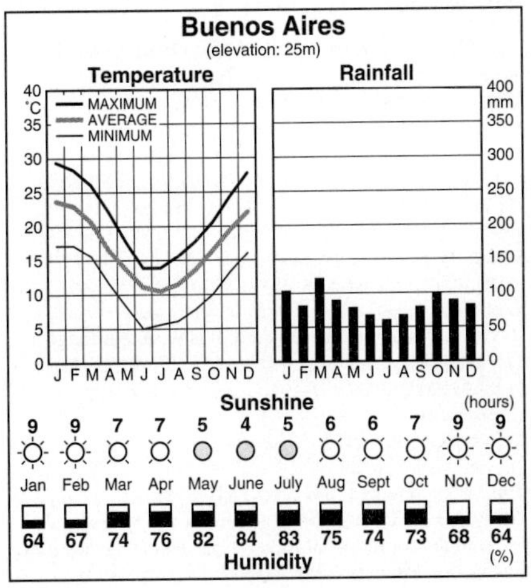

□ *international airport*

Location: Caucasus, east of Turkey.

Note: Political unrest and ethnic conflict in the Trans-Caucasian republics has made much of the region unsafe for tourists; those intending to visit Armenia should seek up-to-date advice from the Foreign Office or State Department (or other diplomatic and travel information service). Common street crime is increasing in Armenia, particularly at night. Street demonstrations and other disturbances may occur without warning. Armed conflict is taking place along the Armenian–Azerbaijani border and in and around the Armenian-populated region of Nagorno Karabakh in Azerbaijan. Fighting continues on a daily basis and front lines change frequently. Visitors should be aware of the volatility of the situation. The economic, transportation and energy blockade currently imposed on the republic by neighbouring Azerbaijan has a direct bearing on every sphere of activity in Armenia, from health care and economic reorganisation to social life, tourist infrastructure and food supplies.
Sources: US State Department – September 23, 1993; and BBC correspondent Stephen Mulvey – November 30, 1994.

Ministry of Foreign Affairs
10 Marshal Baghramian Street, Yerevan 375019, Armenia
Tel: (8852) 523 531. Fax: (8852) 565 616. Telex: 243313.
Embassy of the Republic of Armenia
25A Cheniston Gardens, London W8 6TG
Tel: (0171) 938 2595. Fax: (0171) 938 5435. Opening hours: 1000-1700 Monday to Friday; *Visa section*: 1000-1300 and 1400-1600 Monday to Friday.
Intourist
219 Marsh Wall, Isle of Dogs, London E14 9PD
Tel: (0171) 538 8600. Fax: (0171) 538 5967. Opening hours: 0900-1700 Monday to Friday.
Embassy of the Republic of Armenia
Suite 210, 1660 L Street, NW, Washington, DC 20036
Tel: (202) 628 5766. Fax: (202) 628 5769.
Consular section: Tel: (202) 393 5983. Fax: (202) 393 5962.
Intourist USA Inc
Suite 603, 610 Fifth Avenue, New York, NY 10020
Tel: (212) 757 3884. Fax: (212) 459 0031.
Embassy of the United States of America
18 General Baghramian Street, Yerevan, Armenia
Tel: (8852) 524 661. Fax: (8852) 151 138. Telex: 243137 (a/b AMEMY).
Intourist
Suite 630, 1801 McGill College Avenue, Montréal, Québec H3A 2N4
Tel: (514) 849 6394. Fax: (514) 849 6743.
The Canadian Embassy in the Russian Federation deals with enquiries relating to Armenia (see *Russian Federation* later in the book).

AREA: 29,800 sq km (11,500 sq miles).
POPULATION: 3,742,000 (1994 estimate; the actual population figure is likely to be lower as large numbers have left in search of work elsewhere, without officially emigrating).
POPULATION DENSITY: 112.6 per sq km.
CAPITAL: Yerevan. **Population:** 1,202,000 (1990 estimate).
GEOGRAPHY: Armenia lies on the southern slope of the Armenian Mountains in the Lesser Caucasus and is bordered by Georgia, Turkey, Azerbaijan and Iran. Its highest peak is Mount Aragats, 4009m (13,153ft), and even its deepest valleys lie 450-700m (1200-1870ft) above sea level. Its biggest lake is Lake Sevan in the east.
LANGUAGE: Armenian. Russian is usually understood, but rarely used.
RELIGION: Armenia is the oldest Christian nation in the world, its conversion dating from the year 310AD. The Armenian Apostolic Church developed separately from both the Catholic and Orthodox branches of Christianity. It remains the dominant church, although there are Catholic and Protestant communities and a Russian Orthodox minority. Ethnic Azerbaijanis, who once formed a sizeable Muslim minority, left Armenia in 1990-91 as ethnic tensions ran out of control.
TIME: GMT + 4.
ELECTRICITY: Powercuts are frequent.
COMMUNICATIONS: Telephone: IDD is available to Yerevan. Country code: 7. Yerevan city code: 8852. Outgoing calls to other CIS countries can be made by dialling with the appropriate codes, but only with difficulty. Outgoing international calls to other countries must be made through the operator and long waits are inevitable. Some hotels and many businessmen now have satellite links. **Post:** International postal services are severely disrupted, with erratic and extremely infrequent deliveries made via Moscow. The Armenian Ministry of Communications has reached a reciprocal agreement with its French counterpart, but as only two sacks of mail per week are handled according to this agreement, letters routed via Paris may still be subject to considerable delay. **Press:** The main dailies are *Hayastan, Hayastan Hanrapetutyun, Azg, Yerkir* and *Yerekoyan Yerevan,* all of which are now published only in Armenian (Russian editions have been discontinued since the Russian minority in the republic has dropped from 8% to less than 2% in recent years). *Golos Armenii* (The Voice of Armenia) survives as the only Russian-language daily. *Yerevan News,* an English-language weekly circulated primarily among the foreign missions and small foreign business community, is published by Noyan Topan, an independent information news agency based in Yerevan.
Media: The state information news agency, *Armenpress,* can be contacted in Yerevan on tel: (8852) 526 702 *or* 528 390; fax: (8852) 529 262. **Radio/TV:** The *State Committee for Television and Radio Broadcasting of the Armenian Republic* is located at ul. Mravyana 5, 375025 Yerevan. *Radio Yerevan* broadcasts in Armenian and Russian within Armenia, as well English, French, Spanish, Turkish, Arabic, Farsi (Persian) and Kurdish outside the country. *Armenian Television* now broadcasts exclusively in Armenian, but the Russian Ostankino television channel can usually be received (power cuts permitting).
BBC World Service frequencies: From time to time these change. See the section *How to Use This Book* for more information.
BBC:

| MHz | 17.64 | 12.09 | 9.410 | 6.195 |

Voice of America also broadcasts in Armenia.

PASSPORT/VISA

Regulations and requirements may be subject to change at short notice, and you are advised to contact the appropriate diplomatic or consular authority before finalising travel arrangements. Details of these may be found at the head of this country's entry. Any numbers in the chart refer to the footnotes below.

	Passport Required?	Visa Required?	Return Ticket Required?
Full British	Yes	Yes	Yes
BVP	Not valid	-	-
Australian	Yes	Yes	Yes
Canadian	Yes	Yes	Yes
USA	Yes	Yes	Yes
Other EU (As of 31/12/94)	Yes	Yes	Yes
Japanese	Yes	Yes	Yes

PASSPORTS: Valid passport required by all.
British Visitors Passport: Not accepted.
VISAS: Required by all except:
(a) nationals of Bulgaria, China, Cuba, Czech Republic, Hungary, North Korea, Poland, Romania and Vietnam;
(b) nationals of Bosnia-Hercegovina, Croatia, Former

Yugoslav Republic of Macedonia and Slovenia if travelling on business (authorisation from Foreign Ministry in Yerevan is essential).
Types of visa: Single-entry and Multiple-entry visas. Visas must be used within one month from date of issue.
Cost: *Single-entry* – £35 or US$50 (£50 or US$75 if issued within 5 days). *Single-entry with invitation* – £20 or US$35. **Multiple-entry* – £135 (US$200).
Note [*]: *Multiple-entry* visas are only obtainable with an official invitation.
Validity: *Single-entry* – 21 days; *Multiple-entry* – 1 year.
Application to: Consular Section at Embassy. For addresses, see top of entry.
Application requirements: (a) Completed application form. (b) 1 recent passport-size photo. (c) Photocopy of the first 5 pages of a valid passport, trimmed to actual size (if British visitors hold a new EC-format passport, pages 32 and 33 must also be photocopied). (d) Visa fee in banker's draft, postal order or travellers cheque made payable to The Armenian Government. (e) Postal applications should be send by Registered mail including return mailing cost of £5 for nationals of the UK and Ireland, US$10 for other European nationals and US$45 if requesting return by courier. (f) Official invitation letter, duly authorised in Armenia, for Single-entry visa with invitation or for Multiple-entry visa.
Working days required: Applications for visas may not be made earlier than 3 months before departure, and in no case later than 10 working days before departure, whether by post or personal visit.

MONEY

Currency: The official currency is the Armenian Dram, introduced to replace the Rouble in 1993. Dram notes are printed in denominations of 500, 200, 100, 50, 25, 20 and 10 Drams. The exchange rate stabilised in the second half of 1994, to stand at roughly 400 Drams to the US Dollar, but further inflation is possible. At present the Dram is not convertible and cannot be used to settle accounts outside Armenia, not even within the CIS. US Dollars and Russian Roubles are sometimes used in unofficial transactions.
Credit cards: Not accepted.
Travellers cheques: Not accepted.
Currency restrictions: The import and export of local currency is prohibited for non-residents. The import and export of foreign currency is unlimited for non-residents, if declared on arrival. Residents may import the amount declared on departure if no more than Rub500,000, which must be declared on arrival. Residents may export up to Rub500,000 and up to US$500 in foreign currency, if declared on departure and accompanied by permission from an authorised foreign exchange bank or a custom declaration form TC-28 confirming the amount of currency originally imported.

DUTY FREE

The following goods may be imported into Armenia by persons of 18 years of age or older without incurring customs duty:
A reasonable amounts of goods and duty-free items for personal use.
Note: On entering the country, tourists must complete a customs declaration form which must be retained until departure. This allows the import of articles intended for personal use, including currency and valuables which must be registered on the declaration form. Customs inspection can be long and detailed.
Prohibited imports: Military weapons and ammunition, narcotics and drug paraphernalia, pornography, loose pearls and anything owned by a third party that is to be carried in for that third party. An information sheet is available on request from Intourist.
Prohibited exports: As prohibited imports, as well as annulled securities, state loan certificates, lottery tickets, works of art and antiques (unless permission has been granted by the Ministry of Culture), saiga horns, punctuate and red deer antlers (unless on organised hunting trip), and punctuate deer skins.

Timatic	Health
	GALILEO/WORLDSPAN: **TI-DFT/EVN/HE**
	SABRE: **TIDFT/EVN/HE**
	Visa
	GALILEO/WORLDSPAN: **TI-DFT/EVN/VI**
	SABRE: **TIDFT/EVN/VI**

For more information on Timatic codes refer to Contents.

PHOTO CREDIT: INTOURIST

An Armenian welcome. Stone relief work shows influence of antique Greece, Hellenistic Syria and Asia Minor on Armenian architecture.

PUBLIC HOLIDAYS

Jan 1-2 '95 New Year. **Jan 6** Armenian Christmas. **Apr 14-17** Easter. **Apr 24** Day of Remembrance of the Victims of the Genocide. **May 9** Peace Day. **May 28** Anniversary of Declaration of First Armenian Republic, 1918. **Sep 21** Public Holiday. **Dec 7** Day of Remembrance of the Victims of the Earthquake. **Dec 31-Jan 2 '96** New Year. **Jan 6** Armenian Christmas. **Apr 5-8** Easter. **Apr 24** Day of Remembrance of the Victims of the Genocide.

HEALTH

Regulations and requirements may be subject to change at short notice, and you are advised to contact your doctor well in advance of your intended date of departure. Any numbers in the chart refer to the footnotes below.

	Special Precautions?	Certificate Required?
Yellow Fever	No	No
Cholera	No	No
Typhoid & Polio	Yes	-
Malaria	No	-
Food & Drink	1	-

[1]: All water should be regarded as being a potential health risk. Water used for drinking, brushing teeth or making ice should have first been boiled or otherwise sterilised. Only eat well-cooked meat and fish, preferably served hot. Pork, salad and mayonnaise may carry increased risk. Vegetables should be cooked and fruit peeled. Milk is pasteurised and dairy products should be safe for consumption, however, the incidence of communicable diseases among livestock is increasing because of a breakdown in vaccination programmes. *Rabies* is present. For those at high risk, vaccination before arrival should be considered. If you are bitten abroad, seek medical advice without delay. For more information consult the *Health* section at the back of the book.

Health care: Power shortages and disrupted medical supplies have undermined normal health services to such a degree that travellers would be well advised to consider a health insurance policy guaranteeing emergency evacuation in case of serious accident or illness, as medical insurance is not often valid within the country. Doctors and hospitals often expect immediate cash payment for health services. Travellers are also advised to take a supply of those medicines that they are likely to require (but check first that they may be legally imported) as there is a severe shortage of even the most basic medical supplies, such as disposable needles, anaesthetics and antibiotics and elderly travellers and those with existing health problems may be at risk due to inadequate medical facilities.

TRAVEL - International

AIR: The *Armenian Airlines Company* (under the umbrella of the then USSR Ministry of Civil Aviation) was restructured as the *State Airlines Company of Armenia (SACA)* in 1991. There are weekly flights linking Yerevan with Paris, Amsterdam, Athens, Beirut and Tehran and twice-weekly flights to Fujairah, UAE. Lack of demand, unreliable fuel supplies and an uneconomic fare structure has resulted in greatly reduced services to other CIS republics. Daily flights to Moscow are often subject to delays and cancellations. In 1994 there was a once-weekly commercial charter flight linking Yerevan with Kiev. For political reasons there are no international transport links between Armenia and Azerbaijan; Georgia is sometimes used as a stopover point. Travel agents specialising in flights to Armenia, and hotel bookings, include Sabera Tours in Paris (tel: (1) 42 61 51 13 *or* 42 28 04 13) or Yerevan (tel: (8852) 525 448 *or* 528 548), Sunvil Travel in London (tel:

(0181) 568 4499) and Levon Travel in Los Angeles and Yerevan (tel: (8852) 525 210).

International airport: *Zvartnots*, 14km (9 miles) from Yerevan. Buses and taxis that once existed to ferry passengers from the airport to the city centre are now extremely scarce, due to petrol shortages. Passengers arriving in Yerevan by air should, if possible, arrange to be collected from the airport.

RAIL: Armenia's rail links to Azerbaijan and Turkey have been closed indefinitely, as has the route into Iran via Nakhichevan. The track running into Georgia is currently the only functioning international rail link; traffic on this line has, in the past, been disrupted by power failures, sabotage and unrest in Georgia and the Northern Caucasus. Passengers travelling to Georgia should be aware of the possibility of theft or robbery.

ROAD: A road link between Armenia and Iran is being used increasingly for freight transport. A road linking Yerevan to the Georgian capital, Tbilisi, has a bad reputation for highway robbery, although efforts by the Georgian authorities to enforce law and order are reported to be paying off. There are no road crossings into Turkey. It is possible to travel by road, across occupied Azerbaijani territory, to the enclave of Nagorno Karabakh, however, it is essential to obtain a visa from the permanent representative of Nagorno Karabakh in Yerevan.

TRAVEL - Internal

Note: Internal travel, especially by air, may be disrupted by fuel shortages and other problems.

AIR: Yerevan has a small domestic airport, as well as an international airport, which offers flights to other destinations in Armenia.

ROAD: The road network comprises 10,200km (6375 miles), of which 9500km (5938 miles) are paved. Road surfaces can be very poor, even in the case of major highways. Supplies of petrol, diesel and oil are at present limited, and more expensive than anywhere else in the CIS. Fuel purchases are typically made from small tanker trucks parked at the side of the road. The fuel shortage has disrupted urban transport services which were previously cheap and efficient. It is common practice to flag down private cars as well as official taxis. **Coaches:** These run between the major centres of population. **URBAN:** There is a small metro system in Yerevan. Buses and trolleybuses still run in the city, but are very unreliable. Taxis are available in the city centre. Chauffeur-driven cars are available through official or unofficial channels, but these are expensive. There is no street lighting after dark.

ACCOMMODATION

Hotels previously run by Intourist are now mostly being privatised. In Yerevan the new Armenia Hotel is an Armenian/German joint venture, functioning exclusively in foreign currency and supplied with power from its own generators. In 1993, rooms cost approximately US$80 per day. The Hotel Hrazdan, mainly occupied by foreign missions, also has its own generator, but is state-owned and functions primarily as a guest-house for official visitors. Private individuals may occasionally be allowed to stay there by special arrangement. The Hotel Dvin, opposite the Hrazdan, is less comfortable but has privileged supplies of electricity and running water. It also has a satellite telephone service for guests.

RESORTS & EXCURSIONS

Note: While petrol shortages have made travel around Armenia extremely difficult, in terms of security, the war with Azerbaijan has affected only the extreme eastern part of the republic. None of the sites mentioned below are in areas likely to become involved in the fighting. At the time of writing (December 1994), a ceasefire has been in operation for six months.

Armenia is an ancient country that was once counted as a great power, if only for a short period. The realm of King Tigranes II, in the 1st century BC, stretched from the Caspian Sea to Syria and the Mediterranean, before it was conquered by the Romans.

Yerevan, the present capital of Armenia, is one of the oldest cities in the world, founded nearly 2800 years ago in the time of ancient Babylon. Sadly, little remains to remind the visitor of the city's ancient heritage. Most of the old town was demolished in the 1930s, ostensibly to upgrade standards of public health but, according to locals, more crucially with a view to facilitating the policing of the city. Yerevan was rebuilt using the attractive pinkish-brown volcanic tufa stone seen throughout the republic, in so-called 'Armenian national style' architecture – solid, sometimes imposing and essentially Soviet in character. Mount Ararat lies across the border in Turkey, although it is claimed as part of the territory of greater Armenia, and is where Noah's Ark is said to have settled after the Flood. Yerevan's *History and Art Museum* includes a section tracing the development of Armenian art from the 7th century to the present day. The history section features models and artefacts informing visitors about life in Armenia and the pre-Armenian state of Urartu. The Yerevan library of ancient manuscripts *(Materadaran)* houses over 12,000 texts, many beautifully illuminated and some dating as far back as the 9th century. The contents of the library testify to Armenia's long history of culture and education.

In the year AD301, Armenia became the first country to adopt Christianity as the official state religion (with the exception of the now vanished kingdom of King Abgar of Edessa). Many of the most interesting sights in the republic are associated with the heritage of the Armenian apostolic church. **Echmiadzin,** 20km (12 miles) west of Yerevan, was the capital of Armenia from AD180-340 and remains the site of the country's most important cathedral, and home of the church's Supreme Catholicos. The *Cathedral of St Gregory the Illuminator* is believed to stand on the site of a much older church, itself predated by a pagan shrine. The existing 17th-century cathedral is a fine example of Armenian ecclesiastical architecture, with its squat belltower and elaborately carved dome. In addition to chalices, vestments and other religious artefacts, the cathedral's treasury contains a spearhead believed to have been used to pierce the side of the crucified Christ, and a chunk of wood from Mount Ararat, claimed to be part of a plank from Noah's Ark. There are a number of other churches at Echmiadzin, including the excavated remains of the 7th-century *Church of St Gregory at Zvartnots.* The building, reputed to have been of extraordinary beauty, was largely destroyed by an earthquake in the 10th century. The *Geghard Monastery,* located 35km (22 miles) east of Yerevan in a steep, rocky valley, is one of Armenia's most dramatic sights. The monks who still inhabit the monastery occasionally sacrifice sheep on an open-air stone altar. 'Wishing trees' by the road approaching the site are decorated with coloured scraps of cloth, tied on by pilgrims and picnickers hoping their prayers will be answered. A monastery has occupied this site since the 4th century AD, and the existing churches, all magnificently carved, date from the 13th century. Leading from the vaulted chambers of the main church and adjoining *jamatoun,* or meeting room, are two chapels hewn into the rock of the mountain itself. One of these contains a holy spring, the other a burial vault decorated with an ornate coat of arms. Higher up the slope, a passage leads into the mountainside to the 13th-century tomb of Prince Papak and his wife Rouzakan, a structure noted for its extraordinary acoustics.

Garni, on the road between Geghard and Yerevan, is the site of a temple to the Roman god Mithras. In the 1st century AD Nero sent money and slaves to build the temple, as a tribute to the Armenian King Tiridates for his support in fighting off the Parthians. During the centuries following the conversion of the kings of Armenia to Christianity, the temple served as a royal summer palace. Repeated earthquakes have destroyed most of the original structure, but the temple's vertiginous position dominating the valley from a plateau 300m (984ft) above the Azat River is breathtakingly beautiful. A ruined 9th-century church stands near the restored temple, and a Roman bath house has recently been excavated, revealing a well-preserved mosaic floor.

Lake Sevan, 70km (43 miles) east of Yerevan, is the largest lake in the Caucasus, and much vaunted for its pure waters, stunning setting and delicious salmon trout. The principal lakeside resort is **Sevan** on the northern shore, once popular with Soviet tourists, now optimistically awaiting development to attract wealthy foreigners. Tragically, ill-considered irrigation and hydroelectric projects implemented during the 1970s have triggered an ecological crisis. The water level of the lake has dropped by as much as 16m (41ft). It is now feared that the ecology of Lake Sevan may be irreversibly damaged if radical action is not taken.

North of Sevan, further into the mountains, is **Dilizhan,** a resort much favoured during the Soviet period for the medicinal powers attributed to its mineral water. The authorities aspire in the long term to develop ski and spa resorts in this region, but at present tourist infrastructure remains at a primitive level. A few kilometres east of Dilizhan, in a wooded gorge, is the *Agartsin Monastery,* believed to have been the major cultural centre in medieval Armenia, and one of the very few perfectly preserved examples of the architecture of its period (10th-13th centuries). The refectory building is particularly prized. 25km (16 miles) from Dilizhan, the 12th-century *Goshavank Monastery* features some of the finest examples of the delicate, lacey style of stone carving developed by medieval craftsmen in the region.

In the northwest of the republic, **Gumri,** Armenia's second-largest city, and **Vanatsor** (known during the Soviet period as Leninakan and Kirovaken respectively) suffered badly in the 1988 earthquake and have yet to be rebuilt.

POPULAR ITINERARIES: 5-day: Yerevan–Garni–Geghard–Lake Sevan–Dilizhan–Yerevan. **7-day:** Yerevan–Zvartnots–Echmiadzin–Sardarapat–Astarak–Lake Sevan–Yerevan.

SOCIAL PROFILE

FOOD & DRINK: Until the economic blockade began to bite, a restaurant and cafe culture was starting to flourish in Armenia, with street stalls and privately-run establishments competing with the colourless state restaurants typical of the Soviet era. The dishes mentioned here are served in private homes, but hotels and restaurants are more likely to serve the greasy, less interesting cuisine which is the culinary heritage of the Soviet era. Much Armenian cooking is based on lamb, either grilled and served as shashlik with flat bread, or prepared as soup (the most popular being *bozbash,* a dish which exists in infinite variations) or stew, often in combination with fruit or nuts. The newly butchered sheep carcasses hanging from trees near most *shashlik* stalls, although perhaps appearing somewhat gruesome to foreign visitors, testify to the freshness of the meat sizzling on the grill. A meal usually starts with a large spread of hors d'oeuvres, which may include peppers and vine leaves stuffed with rice and meat, pickled and fresh vegetables, salty white sheep's cheese eaten with fresh green herbs and flat bread, and various kinds of cured meat *(basturma).* Almost magical, health-giving properties are ascribed to dried apricots from the Caucasus. Another dessert speciality is made from grape juice, dried into thin sheets of a deep, reddish brown colour, and then rolled up into long cylinders around walnuts or other nuts. The 'ishkan' salmon trout from Lake Sevan is proclaimed as a great delicacy, but it is now seldom available. **Drink:** Armenian brandies are excellent. Production of Armenian wines and brandies suffered during Mikhail Gorbachev's anti-alcohol drive in the 1980s, but locals are still proud to inform visitors that Winston Churchill always insisted on Armenian in preference to French brandy, after first tasting it at the Yalta conference. During the season following the grape harvest, locals sell effervescent, mildly fermented grape juice from roadside stands. Coffee is served Turkish-style – strong and black in tiny cups – although in view of national sensibilities visitors would be ill-advised to refer to this cultural similarity.

NIGHTLIFE: Power shortages and economic chaos have all but extinguished nightlife in the republic. Nightclubs have ceased to function, and concerts of classical music are now a rare occurrence.

SHOPPING: Art salons in Yerevan sell a range of locally produced crafts including lace, ceramics, ornately carved wooden crosses and paintings. Antiques such as rugs and icons are far more expensive, and will only be licensed for export if bought from an official shop, rather than a market or private individual.

SPECIAL EVENTS: May-Sep '95 *We and the World (Music Festival),* Yerevan.

SOCIAL CONVENTIONS: Almost all entertaining takes place in private homes, and guests may find themselves subjected to overwhelming hospitality and generosity, as well as being expected to eat enormously and participate in endless toasts. Visitors invited to an Armenian's home should arrive bearing some kind of small gift, such as flowers and alcohol (preferably imported) or chocolates. Handshaking is the normal form of greeting. Business cards are invariably exchanged at any kind of official meeting and not infrequently on first meeting people socially as well. Conversation tends to be highly politicised, and guests may be well advised to avoid expressing strong opinions. Women tend to be less retiring than in nearby Muslim countries. **Tipping:** Expected by waiters and doormen in restaurants – sometimes in advance to ensure service. Taxi fares should always be negotiated before starting a journey, and visitors should be aware that rates proposed initially are likely to be unreasonably high, in the expectation that foreigners will have unlimited cash and little idea of how much they ought to be paying. It is therefore advisable to make enquiries about 'going rates' per kilometre of travel before entering into negotiations with taxi drivers. The same applies to market stall holders etc.

BUSINESS PROFILE

ECONOMY: The economic blockade of Armenia by its neighbour Azerbaijan since 1989 has thrown the Armenian economy into crisis. Extreme shortages of fuels, foodstuffs and other important goods forced the Government to declare a state of emergency in 1992. Armenia is now heavily dependent on foreign aid for basic food supplies, including grain. Bread is rationed. The reason for this boycott is the ongoing struggle for control of Nagorno Karabakh, an Armenian-populated enclave with Azerbaijan. Although a ceasefire which began in May 1994 appears to have some chance of becoming permanent, there are still many obstacles in the way of a resolution of the conflict. Civil strife and economic chaos in Georgia has further exacerbated the situation in Armenia. The railway linking Yerevan with Tbilisi, on which Armenia is now totally dependent for supplies, has been frequently attacked by saboteurs and a gas pipeline repeatedly blown up. Gas is too scarce for domestic central heating, so Armenians are obliged to gather wood to heat their homes. Most areas of Yerevan receive electricity for only two hours a day, and this is typical for the country as a whole. The water supply can also be erratic. Armenian industry receives less than one third of its electricity requirements. The Government hopes to improve the power supply in 1995 by re-opening a nuclear power station that was closed after the earthquake of 1988. The effect on the economy has been very severe. Hundreds of thousands – possibly one quarter of the population – have gone abroad in search of work. Of those remaining, many are unemployed, and large numbers are Armenian refugees from Azerbaijan. The growing private sector, seen for example in the large numbers of kiosks, roadside stalls and private shops sprouting up in most towns, may go some way towards offsetting the decline in the rest of the economy. Mineral deposits bringing foreign revenue into Armenia include copper, zinc, gold, marble, bauxite and molybdenum. The textile and chemical industry, as well as aluminium production, are also important, while the manufacturing industry is mostly concentrated on mechanical engineering. Armenia has taken initial steps to bring its banking systems into line with international standards. The privatisation of agriculture has resulted in thousands of smallholders practising subsistence farming. Privatisation of industry should resume in 1995 as part of a programme of economic reforms being coordinated with the International Monetary Fund. The Government's handling of the economy is likely to be one of the main issues influencing the result of parliamentary elections in 1995, if these take place as planned. In the long term, if and when relations with Azerbaijan, and consequently with Turkey, are normalised, Armenia hopes to benefit from closer regional cooperation with other members of the Black Sea Economic Cooperation organisation. Armenia may also benefit from investment by members of the large Armenian diaspora, many of whom still feel a strong sense of commitment to their ancestral homeland, and have the financial wherewithal and business experience to contribute substantially to the revitalisation of the economy.

COMMERCIAL INFORMATION: The following organisations can offer advice: Armenintorg – Armenian State Foreign Economic and Trade Association, H Kochar St, 375012 Yerevan. Tel: (8852) 224 310. Fax: (8852) 220 034. Telex: 243323; *or*

Ministry of Foreign Economic Relations, pl. Respubliki 2, 373010 Yerevan. Tel: (8852) 562 157 *or* 520 579; *or*

Ministry of Trade, ul. V. Teryana 69, 375009 Yerevan. Tel: (8852) 562 591; *or*

Chamber of Commerce and Industry of the Republic of Armenia, ul. Alevardyan 39, 375010 Yerevan. Tel: (8852) 565 438. Fax: (8852) 565 071. Telex: 243322 (a/b AFAZU).

CLIMATE

Continental, mountain climate (over 90% of the territory of the republic is over 900m/2286ft above sea level). During the summer, days may be hot and dry with temperatures falling sharply at night. Winters are extremely cold with heavy snow.

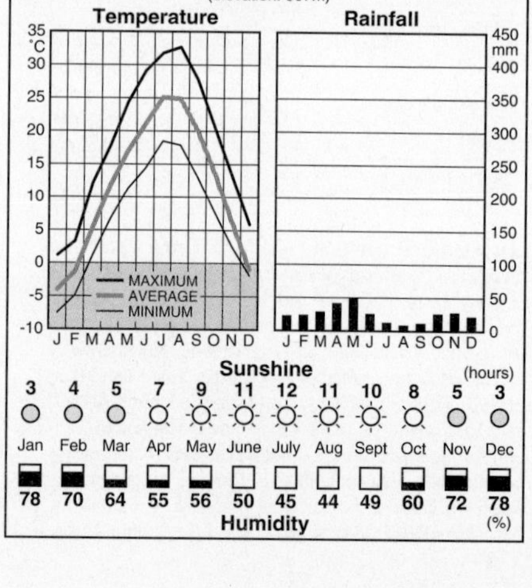
Yerevan
(elevation: 907m)
Temperature
Rainfall
35 °C 30 25 20 15 10 5 0 -5 -10
450 mm 400 350 300 250 200 150 100 50 0
MAXIMUM
AVERAGE
MINIMUM
J F M A M J J A S O N D
J F M A M J J A S O N D
Sunshine
(hours)
3 4 5 7 9 11 12 11 10 8 5 3
Jan Feb Mar Apr May June July Aug Sept Oct Nov Dec
78 70 64 55 56 50 45 44 49 60 72 78
Humidity
(%)

Aruba

Location: South Caribbean.

Aruba Tourism Authority
PO Box 1019, L. G. Smith Boulevard 172, Oranjestad, Aruba
Tel: (8) 23777 *or* 21019. Fax: (8) 34702.
Aruba Tourism Authority – PR Department
PO Box 1019, A. Schuttestraat 2, Oranjestad, Aruba
Tel: (8) 23778/9. Fax: (8) 30075 *or* 34702.
Cabinet of the Plenipotentiary Minister of Aruba
Schimmelpennincklaan 1, 2517 JN The Hague, The Netherlands
Tel: (70) 356 6233. Fax: (70) 345 1446.
Aruba Tourism Authority
Schimmelpennincklaan 1, 2517 JN The Hague, The Netherlands
Tel: (70) 356 6220. Fax: (70) 360 4877.
Aruba Tourism Authority
Ground Level, 1000 Harbor Boulevard, Weehawken, NJ 07087
Tel: (201) 330 0800. Fax: (201) 330 8757.
Aruba Tourism Authority
2344 Salzedo Street, Miami, FL 33134-5033
Tel: (305) 567 2720. Fax: (305) 567 2721.
Aruba Tourism Authority
Suite 1506, 199 Fourteenth Street, Atlanta, GA 30309-3686
Tel: (404) 892 7822. Fax: (404) 873 2193.
Aruba Tourism Authority
Suite 204, 86 Bloor Street West, Toronto, Ontario M5S 1M5
Tel: (416) 975 1950. Fax: (416) 975 1947.

AREA: 184 sq km (70 sq miles).
POPULATION: 70,000 (1994).
POPULATION DENSITY: 380.4 per sq km.
CAPITAL: Oranjestad.
GEOGRAPHY: Aruba is the smallest island in the Leeward group of the Dutch Caribbean islands, which also include Bonaire and Curaçao. They are popularly known as the ABCs. As the westernmost island of the group, Aruba is the final link in the long Antillean chain, lying 29km (18 miles) off the Venezuelan coast. The island is 30km (19.6 miles) long and 9km (6 miles) across at its widest and has a flat landscape dominated by Jamanota Mountain 188m (617ft). The west and southwest coast, known as Palm Beach, boasts 11km (7 miles) of palm-fringed powder-white sands, while in complete contrast the east coast has a desolate, windswept shoreline of jagged rocks carved into weird shapes by the pounding surf.
LANGUAGE: The official language is Dutch. English and Spanish are also spoken. The islanders also speak a local language called Papiamento, which is a combination of Dutch, Spanish, Portuguese, English and Indian languages.
RELIGION: 80% of the population are Roman Catholic.

TIME: GMT - 4.
ELECTRICITY: 110 volts AC, 60Hz.
COMMUNICATIONS: Telephone: IDD available. Country code: 297. Outgoing international code: 00. **Telex/telegram:** Facilities exist at the Telegraph and Radio Office in the Post Office Building in Oranjestad and at Lands Radio Dienst. Most hotels offer telex, fax and telegram service to residents. **Post:** Post office hours: 0730-1200 and 1300-1630. **Press:** The oldest established newspaper (in Dutch) is *Amigoe di Aruba* and the English-language papers are *The News* and *Aruba Today*.
BBC World Service and Voice of America frequencies: From time to time these change. See the section *How to Use this Book* for more information.
BBC:

MHz	17.84	15.22	9.915	5.975

Voice of America:

MHz	15.12	11.58	9.590	6.130

PASSPORT/VISA

Regulations and requirements may be subject to change at short notice, and you are advised to contact the appropriate diplomatic or consular authority before finalising travel arrangements. Details of these may be found at the head of this country's entry. Any numbers in the chart refer to the footnotes below.

	Passport Required?	Visa Required?	Return Ticket Required?
Full British	Yes	No/4	Yes
BVP	Not valid/2	-	-
Australian	Yes	No/4	Yes
Canadian	1	No/4	Yes
USA	1	No/4	Yes
Other EU (As of 31/12/94)	Yes	No/3/4	Yes
Japanese	Yes	No/4	Yes

PASSPORTS: Valid passport required by all except: **[1]** nationals of Canada and the USA holding a voter's registration card, naturalisation card, alien registration card (green card), birth certificate or affidavit of birth, or a passport which has expired within the last 5 years.
British Visitors Passport: [2] Should be considered as unacceptable. Although the immigration authorities of this country may in certain circumstances accept British Visitors Passports for persons arriving for holidays or

Annual Carnival time in Aruba

International airport
Main road
Historical site

6km
3mls

Kudarabi
California Lighthouse
California Point
Arashi Beach
GOLF COURSE
Hadikurari
Westpunt
Wreck of WW2 German freighter
Alto Vista Chapel
Boca di Pos di Noord
Palm Beach
Santa Anna Church
Noord
Wariruri
Boca Mahos
Eagle Beach
Bushiribana
Natural Bridge
Andicouri Beach
Noordkaap
Manshebu
Paradera
Druif Baai
Ayo Boulders
Punta Brabu
Fort Zoutman
Hooiberg (Mt Haystack) △165m
Boca Ketu
Paarden Baai
Reina Beatrix Airport
Santa Cruz
ARIKOK CAVES
ORANJESTAD
A R U B A
Boca Prins Beach
Jamanota △188m
Barcadera
FONTEIN CAVES
Spaans Lagoen
GUADIRIKIRI CAVES
Rincon
Savaneta
Brasil
San Nicolas
Savaneta Beach
Boca Grandi
C A R I B B E A N   S E A
Commandeurs Baai
Seroe California
St Nicolas Baai
Baby Beach
Colorado Point

unpaid business trips of up to 3 months, travellers are reminded that no formal agreement exists to this effect and the situation may, therefore, change at short notice. In addition, UK nationals using a BVP and returning to the UK from a country with which no such formal agreement exists may be subject to delays and interrogation by UK immigration.
VISAS: Visas *are* required by nationals of Afghanistan, Bahrain, China, Cambodia, Cuba, Dominican Republic, Egypt, Ethiopia, Haiti, Iraq, Iran, Jordan, North Korea, Kuwait, Libya, Mauritius, Mongolia, Morocco, Myanmar, Oman, Pakistan, Peru, Qatar, Saudi Arabia, Sudan, Syria, Tunisia, UAE, Vietnam and Yemen. Nationals of these countries are exempt if they are legal residents of a country whose nationals do not need a visa or have been living in such a country for more than five years. In these cases a stay of a maximum of 14 days is granted.
All other nationals may enter Aruba without a visa for a period of 14 days as tourists only, provided they have a return or onward ticket and proof of sufficient funds for the length of stay. For stays of over 14 days the traveller will be issued with a Temporary Certificate of Admission by the Immigration authorities on arrival in Aruba.
Notes: [3] Nationals of Belgium, Luxembourg and The Netherlands can stay for up to 3 months as tourists. [4] All visitors wishing to work or to do any business whatsoever in Aruba must have a written permit from the Ministry of Justice at the Department for Public Order and Security (D.O.O.V.). Further information and application forms for Written Permits can be obtained free of charge from the Directie Openbare Ordeen Veiligheid (D.O.O.V.), Torenstraat, San Nicolas, Aruba. Tel: (8) 43322.

MONEY

Currency: Aruba Florin (AFL) = 100 cents. Notes are in denominations of AFL100, 50, 25, 10 and 5. Coins are in denominations of AFL1, and 50, 25, 10 and 5 cents.
Currency exchange: The US Dollar is widely accepted in Aruba.
Exchange rate indicators: The following figures are included as a guide to the movements of the Aruba Florin against Sterling and the US Dollar:

Date:	Oct '92	Sep '93	Jan '94	Jan '95
£1.00=	2.83	2.74	2.64	2.77
$1.00=	1.78	1.79	1.79	1.79

Currency restrictions: No limit on import or export of foreign currency. The Aruba Florin cannot be exchanged out of Aruba.
Banking hours: 0800-1200 and 1300-1600 Monday to Friday.

DUTY FREE

The following items may be taken into Aruba without payment of duty:
200 cigarettes or 100 cigars or 250g of tobacco; 1 litre of alcoholic beverages; 250ml of perfume (if more is taken the whole is dutiable); gifts to a value of AFL100.
Note: A duty-free allowance is only available to persons over 21 years of age.

PUBLIC HOLIDAYS

Jan 1 '95 New Year's Day. **Jan 25** Commemoration of G F (Betico) Croes. **Feb 26** Lenten Carnival. **Mar 18** Aruba Flag Day. **Apr 14** Good Friday. **Apr 17** Easter Monday. **Apr 30** Queen's Day. **May 1** Labour Day. **May 20** Ascension Day. **Dec 25-26** Christmas. **Jan 1 '96** New Year's Day. **Jan 25** Commemoration of G F (Betico) Croes. **Feb 18** Lenten Carnival. **Mar 18** Aruba Flag Day. **Apr 5** Good Friday. **Apr 8** Easter Monday. **Apr 30** Queen's Day.

HEALTH

Regulations and requirements may be subject to change at short notice, and you are advised to contact your doctor well in advance of your intended date of departure. Any numbers in the chart refer to the footnotes below.

	Special Precautions?	Certificate Required?
Yellow Fever	No	No
Cholera	No	No
Typhoid & Polio	No	-
Malaria	No	-
Food & Drink	1	-

[1]: Tap water is considered safe to drink. Milk is pasteurised and dairy products are safe for consumption. Local meat, poultry, seafood, fruit and vegetables are generally considered safe to eat.
Health care: There are excellent medical facilities at the Horacio Oduber Hospital. The new Posada Clinic offers a complete hemodialysis treatment in a vacation atmosphere. Many hotels also have doctors on call. Full medical insurance is advised. There is no Reciprocal Health Agreement with the UK.

TRAVEL - International

AIR: Aruba's national airline is *Air Aruba (FQ)*.
Approximate flight times: From Oranjestad to *London* is 11 hours 40 minutes (including a good connection,

normally in Amsterdam), to *Los Angeles* is 10 hours and to *New York* is 4 hours.
International airport: *Reina Beatrix (AUA)* is 5km (3 miles) southeast of Oranjestad. Airport facilities include a duty-free shop, bank (0800-1600 Monday to Sunday), restaurants (1100-2230) and tourist information (0730-2200, tel: (8) 29041 *or* 24800 ext 164). Taxi service is available between the airport and the city. The limited airport bus service must be paid for with pre-paid travel coupons issued by travel agents.
Departure tax: Approximately US$12.50 per person for all travellers over two years of age.
SEA: Aruba has extensive virtually duty-free shopping facilities and many cruise ships call in on their Caribbean itineraries.

TRAVEL - Internal

AIR: *Air Aruba* offers several daily flights between Aruba, Bonaire and Curaçao. Flights to other Caribbean islands and South America can also be arranged through *Air Aruba* (tel: (8) 22467) as well as *Avia Air* (tel: (8) 34600) or *Oduber Aviation* (tel: (8) 26975).
ROAD: The road system throughout the island is very good. Driving is on the right and international signs are used. **Bus:** Public bus service runs between the towns and hotels on Eagle Beach and Palm Beach about every half hour and hourly on Sundays and public holidays. Check with the tourist office or hotels for schedule. **Taxi:** The main taxi office is at Pos Abao 41. Tel: (8) 22116. Fax: (8) 36988. Taxis are not metered. Rates are fixed and should be checked before getting into the cab. There is no need to tip drivers except for help with unusually heavy luggage. **Car hire:** There are plenty of cars available for hire and renting a car is one of the most pleasant ways to explore the island. Most major companies have offices in Aruba (*Hertz, National, Budget* and *Avis*); there are also many well-established local car rental firms. It is also possible to rent scooters, motorcycles and cycles. Minimum age for renting a car is 23. Hotels can assist with bookings. **Documentation:** A valid foreign licence or an International Driving Permit are both acceptable.
JOURNEY TIMES: The following chart gives approximate journey times (in hours and minutes) from Aruba to other major centres.

	Air
Amsterdam	9.00
Bonaire	0.30
Caracas	0.40
Curaçao	0.20
Las Piedras	0.20
Miami	2.30
New York	4.00

ACCOMMODATION

HOTELS: The majority of hotels are in the Palm Beach and Eagle Beach resort area on the southwest coast, offering accommodation of a very high standard. Many of these luxury hotels have beach frontage and their own swimming pools, plus extensive sport, entertainment and shopping facilities. Rates are much lower in the summer, which is the island's low season. Some tour operators offer out-of-season accommodation packages. Rooms are subject to 6% government room tax and hotels also add 16.55% service charge. **Grading:** All hotels are graded into first class and deluxe. About 40% of all hotels are of the deluxe standard (high-rise hotels with good facilities) and about 60% are first-class hotels. For more information, contact the Aruba Tourism Authority (see top of entry for address) *or* the Aruba Hotel and Tourism Association (A.H.A.T.A.), PO Box 542, Oranjestad. Tel: (8) 22607 *or* 33188 *or* 28570. Fax: (8) 24202.
GUEST-HOUSES: There is limited scope for this kind of accommodation. Many guest-houses are in the Noord area not far from the main hotel area. Contact the tourism authority for details.
SELF-CATERING: There are apartment complexes and a list is available through the Aruba Tourism Authority offices (for addresses, see above).

EVERYTHING YOU COULD POSSIBLY IMAGINE
IN A CARIBBEAN VACATION...

...PLUS A DESERT, A DUTCH WINDMILL,
SOME CASINOS AND A SUBMARINE.

Close your eyes and picture yourself

on an island where it hardly ever rains. 4-wheeling down

a rugged coast where divi divi trees bend to

a constant tropical breeze, catching a big wind on a sleek, new

windsurfer, galloping through a barren desert,

cruising in a submarine to the bottom of the ocean or —

maybe just enjoying an easy afternoon

snorkel in an idyllically quiet lagoon alone.

ARUBA

AN ISLAND ALL YOUR OWN

RESORTS & EXCURSIONS

Aruba's principal attraction is its beaches; these include *Arashi Beach* (near California Point on the northwest tip, particularly good for snorkelling), *Spaans Lagoen* and *Commandeurs Baai, Bachelor's Beach* (good for windsurfing), and the particularly shallow areas of *Baby Beach* and the 'Grapefield' (all on the south coast). Near Baby Beach, at Seroe Colorado, is *Rodger's Beach,* where the surf is a little stronger. Beaches on the north coast include *Boca Prins, Dos Playa* and *Andicouri.* One of the attractions on this shore is the **Natural Bridge,** an arch carved from coral cliffs by the crashing ocean surf. The bridge is the biggest and highest in the Caribbean and is Aruba's most famous natural wonder. So too is the surf on this coast, but visitors are warned that it can be very rough. Local advice concerning conditions for surfing on the island at any particular time should be followed carefully, but there will usually be one beach somewhere to suit all levels of skill and courage. Another favourite pastime is exploring the surrounding shallow water with specially equipped sub-marine vessels. *Atlantis Submarines* offer tours over one of the most spectacular reefs on the south side of the island. There are hourly departures; for information and reservations, telephone (8) 36090. The *Seaworld Explorer,* by means of a moving underwater observatory, offers the opportunity to see a sunken German freighter. For further information, phone (8) 6031. Not all of the coast is completely deserted; for instance, much of **Palm Beach,** the seven or so miles of sand and palm trees on the west and southwest shores of the island, has now been developed into a unique hotel resort. Low-rise resort hotels are more common on **Eagle Beach,** located between the point to the west of Druif Bay and south of Palm Beach. Visitors after more isolated relaxation will need to seek out some of the more remote sunbathing and swimming spots (of which there are plenty) or turn their attention to the **Cunucu,** the interior, a land of cactus, windswept divi-divi trees, old villages and hamlets and unsignposted dirt roads stretching across the often mysterious landscape. The distinctive shape of the divi-divi trees (also known as *watapanas)* has become Aruba's unofficial trademark; blown by the northeasterly trade winds, the trees are forced to grow at alarming angles. The island can easily be driven round in a day, and cars can be hired without difficulty; see the *Travel – Internal* section above for further information.

Aruba's Dutch heritage is always present, and nowhere more so than in the capital of **Oranjestad,** characterised by pastel-coloured gabled buildings, and a windmill brought piece by piece from Holland, now used as a restaurant. There are four museums here open to the public: the *Historical Museum,* the *Geological Museum,* the *Archaeological Museum* and the *Numismatic Museum.* The first is housed in the *Fort Zoutman,* the oldest building on Aruba (1796) with the *Willem III-Tower* having been added in 1868. The *Bonbini Festival* is held every Tuesday from 1830-2030 throughout the year in the courtyard of the Historical Museum and offers the opportunity to get an insight into local customs, music and cuisine as well as a chance to get to know the islanders. Oranjestad has a daily market in the *Paardenbaai* (Schooner Harbour) where traders sell fresh fish straight from the boat and fruit and vegetables from the mainland. The capital is also famous for its shopping district, centred on Caya Gilberto François (Betico) Croes. One of the roads north from the capital runs inland, passing the **Bubali Bird Sanctuary.** Birdwatching and natural wildlife tours as well as archaeological and geological trips can be arranged by contacting Mr E Boestra of Marlin Booster Tracking Inc (tel: (8) 45086; fax: (8) 41513) or Mr Ferdi Maduro of Corvalou Tours (tel: (8) 35742 *or* 30487). These guided tours are available in various languages. On the northern tip of the island is the **California Lighthouse** set in an area of desolate sand dunes. Off this coast is the wreck of a German freighter from the Second World War which is now the home of countless exotic fish and a very popular spot for scuba divers. The *Chapel of Alto Vista* at **Alto Vista** is another popular site on the north coast. There are several systems of caves on Aruba. **Fontein** was once used by the Arawak Indians who were the original inhabitants of the island. On the walls of the caves are ancient drawings thought to be part of the Indian sacrificial rite. Nearby, the caves at **Guadirikiri** are a haven for bats. **Arikok,** which has been designated a national park, has by far the best preserved Indian drawings on the island. Interesting is also a visit to *Frenchman's Pass* where Arawak Indians defended Aruba against the French in 1700.

Inland – in fact almost in the geographical centre of the island – is the old settlement of **Santa Cruz,** named after what is allegedly the place where the first cross was raised on Aruba. **Hooiberg** (Mount Haystack) looms out of the flat landscape of the interior to the northwest of Santa Cruz. A series of several hundred steps leads up to the

Top picture: Windsurfer's paradise – with a competition every June. Above: Palm Beach. Right: Marina Centre of Oranjestad.

165m (541ft) peak, from where it is possible to see across to Venezuela. Northwest of Hooiberg is the old town of Seroe Patrishi with historical graves dating as far back as the early 18th century. Further north is the town of **Noord**, noted for its *Church of Santa Anna,* the oldest church of Aruba, with its beautiful 100-year-old hand-carved oak altar. The road from Noord turns north to the California Lighthouse (see above). North from Santa Cruz, turning back towards the coast, the road to **Casibari** and **Ayo** passes spectacular boulders, the result of some unexplained geological catastrophe. The road continues to the coast at **Bushiribana**, centre of the island's former gold-mining industry. Gold was discovered here in 1824 and actively mined until the beginning of World War I. Kettles and ovens used in the smelting process have been preserved; nearby are the ruins of a pirate's castle. Gold was also mined at **Balashi** in the south.

In the southeastern part of the island is Aruba's second-largest town, **San Nicolas**, which owed its prosperity to the oil refinery, once one of the largest in the world. To the east is the area known as **Seroe Colorado**, notable not only for several fine beaches but also for being the home of the local iguana community.

SOCIAL PROFILE

FOOD & DRINK: Not much food is grown locally, but the variety in the local cuisine is extensive. Aruban specialities include *stobà* (lamb or goat stew), *cala* (bean fritters), *pastechi* (meat-stuffed turnovers), *ayacas* (leaf-wrapped meat roll) and *sopito* (fish chowder). There is a very wide range of international cuisine and several of the more famous fast-food chains have premises on the island.
NIGHTLIFE: There is one drive-in cinema screening current American, European and Latin American films. The highlight of Aruba's nightlife, however, is the casinos, of which there are 10, open from 1100 until the early morning. There are several discotheques in Oranjestad, as well as nightclubs offering revues and live music.
SHOPPING: As a 'free zone', duty on most items in Aruba is so low that shopping here can have obvious advantages. Stores carry goods from all parts of the world and there are some excellent buys, including perfume, linens, jewellery, watches, cameras, crystal, china and other luxury items plus a range of locally made handicrafts. **Shopping hours:** 0800-1200 and 1400-1800 Monday to Saturday.
SPORT: The island's clear warm waters and excellent facilities make it a haven for all kinds of watersports. There is **surfing** on the north coast, at Dos Playa and Andicouri beaches, but surfers are warned to pay attention to the strong currents in the area. Some of the best **windsurfing** sites can be found around Aruba. Equipment for hire is available from Divi Winds (tel: (8) 21450), Pelican Watersports (tel: (8) 63600), Red Sail Sports (tel: (8) 61603), Roger's Windsurfing Place (tel: (8) 61918) or Sailboard Vacations (tel: (8) 62527). The clear waters of Aruba offer visibilities of as much as 30m (90ft), and, with the coral reef, offer good **snorkelling** and **scuba diving.** Diving tours include wall dives and reef or wreck dives. There are several companies able to hire out equipment for either sport. Details can be obtained from most hotels, De Palm Watersports (tel: (8) 24545), Pelican Watersports (tel: (8) 31228) and Red Sail Sports (tel: (8) 61603). Diving excursions can be arranged through Aruba Acqua (tel: (8) 23380), Aruba Pro Dive (tel: (8) 25520), Charlie's Buddies (tel: (8) 34877), Dax Divers (tel: (8) 36000), Mermaid Sport Divers (tel: (8) 35546), Native Divers (tel: (8) 34742), Scuba Aruba (tel: (8) 34142), Aruba Scuba Center (tel: (8) 25216) or Unique Watersports of Aruba (tel: (8) 25885). Snorkelling equipment can be hired from Mi Dushi/Tattoo (tel: (8) 26034) or Wave Dancer (tel: (8) 25520). There are various companies offering **parasailing** on the beaches. Further information is available from Aqua Excotic Parasail, Caribbean Parasail or Aruba Parasail. **Sailing** is at its best in Aruba. There is a variety of options to choose from such as day cruises with snorkelling, or moonlight and sunset dinner or dancing cruises. Cruises can be arranged through Aruba Pirate's (tel: (8) 254450), De Palm Tours (tel: (8) 24545), Mi Dushi/Tattoo (tel: (8) 28919), Red Sail Sports (tel: (8) 61603), Wave Dancer (tel: (8) 25520), Andante (tel: (8) 47718) or Pelican Watersports (tel: (8) 31228). There is good **deep-sea fishing** in the area (sailfish, wahoo, blue and white marlin, tuna and bonito) with a choice of half- or full-day trips. For information, enquire at hotel, De Palm Tours or at the waterfront in Oranjestad. Especially deep-sea fishing is recommended as Aruba boasts one of the world's best fishing grounds. The principal hotels have extensive sporting facilities including **water-skiing** and **tennis.** The island also has a **bowling** rink, the Eagle Bowling Palace, located at Pos Abao z/n. Tel: (8) 35058. Fax: (8) 36310. This is a modern 12-lane facility which includes a cocktail lounge and snackbar (opening hours: 1000-0200). Aruba claims one of the most professional

An inheritance from Holland, the Olde Molen

and challenging 18-hole **golf** courses in the Caribbean. Tierra del Sol's par 71 championship course was designed by the Robert Trent Jones II Group, renowned for protecting the natural ecology of their sites. The course is located on the northern tip of the island, near the California Lighthouse, with magnificent views of the Caribbean. This is the first green course on the island which so far has had only natural desert courses. **Minigolf** can be played at the Joe Mendez Adventure Golf course, uniquely elevated and surrounded by water. Paddle and bumper boats for hire, as well as a gameroom and bar, are available here. **Volleyball, soccer** and **baseball** are played at the Complejo Deportivo Guillermo Prospero Trinidad. **Horseriding** is another popular pastime on the island. Rancho El Paso (tel: (8) 63310) offers riding trips of one or two hours duration in the *Cunucu* (countryside) or along the coast. Rancho del Campo (tel: (8) 50290) specialises in rides across the countryside to the Natural Pool, one of Aruba's most beautiful sites. Arrangements for trips through the countryside and to the old gold mine can also be made at the Ponderosa Ranch (tel: (8) 25027). **SPECIAL EVENTS:** The following list is a selection of some of the events celebrated in Aruba in 1995/96. For further information contact the Aruba Tourism Authority. **Mar 19 '95** *Aruba International Half-Marathon.* **Apr** *Aruba Culinary Exhibition.* **Apr 24-30** *International Bowling Tournament.* **Apr 30-May 1** *National Drag Races.* **May 11-14** *ATEX 1995.* **Jun** *Aruba Hi-winds Windsurfing Tournament.* **Jun 24** *St John's Day.* **Oct 19-31** *Aruba International Dance Festival.* **End of Oct-beginning of Nov** *International Deep-sea Fishing Tournament.* **Nov** *Caribbean Shootout International Drag Race; Catamaran Regatta.* **Dec 5** *Sint Nicolaas Day celebrations.* **Feb 18 '96** *Carnival.*
SOCIAL CONVENTIONS: Much of the social activity will take place in hotels where the atmosphere will be informal, often American in feel. The islanders do not wear shorts in town though it is acceptable for visitors to do so. Bathing suits are strictly for beach or the poolside only. In the evenings people tend to dress up, especially when visiting the casinos. Jackets are not required for men, except for official government functions. **Tipping:** Hotels add a 15% service charge to any food or beverage bill. Restaurants may add 15% service to the bill; if not, 10-15% is normal. Taxi fares do not include tips, but there may be charges for luggage and tips are well appreciated.

BUSINESS PROFILE

ECONOMY: In 1824 gold was discovered in Balashi, bolstering Aruba's economy until 1916 when gold yields became so poor the mines were left to fall into ruin. In 1929 Aruba's industry was rekindled with the opening of the Lago oil refinery in San Nicolas, Aruba's second city, which for many years was the largest refinery in the world. This closed in 1985, however, and brought an end to the industry, a large increase in unemployment and a dramatic drop in government revenue. Since then tourism has become the island's major industry. Exploration for oil and gas has already begun in Aruban waters; the oil refinery was re-opened in 1990 and agreement has been reached with an American operator to establish a transhipment and storage facility. For the present, revenue other than tourism is derived from Aruba's freeport status, ship bunkering and repair facilities, and transhipment of oil products (mainly between Venezuela and the USA). Light industry is limited to the production of some tobacco products, drinks and consumer goods.
BUSINESS: Office hours: 0800-1700 Monday to Friday. **COMMERCIAL INFORMATION:** The following organisation can offer advice: Aruba Chamber of Commerce and Industry, PO Box 140, Zoutmanstraat 21, Oranjestad. Tel: (8) 21566. Fax: (8) 33962. Telex: 5174.

CLIMATE

With a mean temperature of 28°C (83°F), this dry and sunny island is made pleasantly cool throughout the year by constant trade winds. Showers of short duration occur during the months of October, November and December.

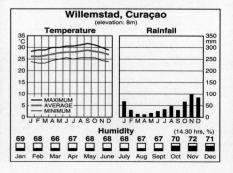

Willemstad, Curaçao
(elevation: 8m)

	Jan	Feb	Mar	Apr	May	June	July	Aug	Sept	Oct	Nov	Dec
Humidity (14.30 hrs, %)	69	68	66	67	68	68	68	67	67	70	72	71

Australia

Location: Indian/Pacific Oceans.

Australian Tourist Commission
PO Box 2721, Level 3, 80 William Street,
Woolloomooloo, Sydney, NSW 2001, Australia
Tel: (2) 360 1111. Fax: (2) 331 6469.
High Commission of the Commonwealth of Australia
Australia House, The Strand, London WC2B 4LA
Tel: (0171) 379 4334 *or* (0891) 600 333 (visa enquiries
and immigration; calls are charged at the higher rate of
39/49p per minute). Fax: (0171) 240 5333 *or* 465 8218
(visas). Opening hours: 0930-1530 Monday to Friday.
Australian Consulate
Chatsworth House, Lever Street, Manchester M1 2DL
Tel: (0161) 228 1344. Fax: (0161) 236 4074. Opening
hours: 0930-1530 Monday to Friday.
Australian Tourist Commission
Gemini House, 10-18 Putney Hill, London SW15 6AA
Tel: (0181) 780 2227. Fax: (0181) 780 1496.
British High Commission
Commonwealth Avenue, Yarralumla, Canberra, ACT
2600, Australia
Tel: (6) 270 6666. Fax: (6) 273 3236. Telex: 7162222
(a/b UKREP).
Consulates in: Adelaide, Brisbane, Melbourne, Perth,
Sydney and Darwin.
Embassy of the Commonwealth of Australia
1601 Massachusetts Avenue, NW, Washington, DC 20036
Tel: (202) 797 3000. Fax: (202) 797 3168.
Australian Consulate General
Suite 420, International Building, Rockefeller Centre,
630 Fifth Avenue, New York, NY 10011
Tel: (212) 245 4000. Fax: (212) 265 4197.
Australian Tourist Commission
31st Floor, 489 Fifth Avenue, New York, NY 10017
Tel: (212) 687 6300. Fax: (212) 552 1315.
Also dealing with enquiries from Canada.
Australian Tourist Commission
Suite 1200, 2121 Avenue of the Stars, Los Angeles, CA
90067
Tel: (310) 552 1988. Fax: (310) 552 1215.
Embassy of the United States of America
Moonah Place, Canberra, ACT 2600, Australia
Tel: (6) 270 5000. Fax: (6) 270 5970. Telex: 62104 (a/b
USAEMB).
Consulates in: Melbourne, Sydney, Perth and Brisbane.
Australian High Commission
Suite 710, 50 O'Connor Street, Ottawa, Ontario K1P 6L2
Tel: (613) 236 0841. Fax: (613) 236 4376.
Consulates in: Toronto and Vancouver.
Canadian High Commission
Commonwealth Avenue, Canberra, ACT 2600, Australia
Tel: (6) 273 3844. Fax: (6) 273 3285.
Consulates in: Sydney and Perth.
Note: Addresses of Tourist Representatives for
individual States can be found at the head of each State
entry.

AREA: 7,682,300 sq km (2,966,151 sq miles).
POPULATION: 17,292,000 (1991 estimate).
POPULATION DENSITY: 2.3 per sq km.
CAPITAL: Canberra. **Population:** 310,100 (1990
estimate).
GEOGRAPHY: Australia is bounded by the Arafura
Sea and Timor Seas to the north, the Coral and Tasman
Seas of the South Pacific to the east, the Southern Ocean
to the south, and the Indian Ocean to the west. Its
coastline covers 36,738km (22,814 miles). Most of the
population has settled along the eastern and southeastern
coastal strip. Australia is the smallest continent (or the
largest island) in the world. About 40% of the continent
is within the Tropics and Australia is almost the same

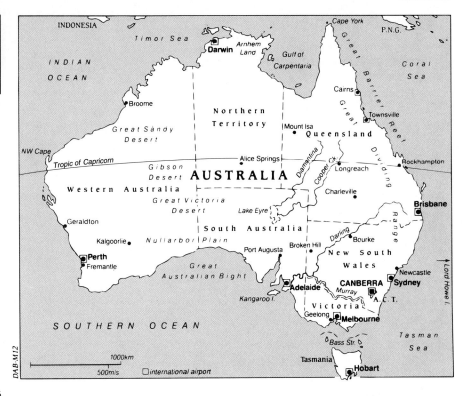

size as the mainland of the United States of America. The
terrain is extremely varied, ranging from tortured red
desert to lush green rainforest. Australia's beaches and
surfing are world-renowned, while the country is also
rich in reminders of its long, if often mysterious, past.
These range from prehistoric Aboriginal art to Victorian
colonial architecture. The landscape consists mainly of a
low plateau mottled with lakes and rivers and skirted
with coastal mountain ranges, highest in the east with the
Great Dividing Range. There are jungles in the far
northeast (Cape York Peninsula). The southeast is a huge
fertile plain. Further to the north lies the enormous Great
Barrier Reef, a 2012km (1250-mile) strip of coral that
covers a total area of 350,000 sq km. Although Australia
is the driest land on Earth it, nevertheless, has enormous
snowfields the size of Switzerland. It is a country with a
sense of space. There are vast mineral deposits. More
detailed geographical descriptions of each State can be
found under the individual State entries below.
LANGUAGE: The official language is English. Many
other languages are retained by minorities, including
Italian, German, Greek and Chinese dialects and
Aboriginal languages.
RELIGION: Mainly Protestant, with a large Roman
Catholic minority and smaller minorities of all other
major religions.
TIME: Australia spans three time zones:
Northeast/southeast: GMT + 10 (GMT + 9 October to
March).
Central: GMT + 9.5 (GMT + 8.5 October to March).
West: GMT + 8 (GMT + 7 October to March).
Some States operate daylight saving time during the
Australian summer. Clocks in these States are put
forward by one hour in October and put back again in
March.
ELECTRICITY: 240/250 volts AC, 50Hz. 3-pin plugs
are in use, however, sockets are different than those
found in most countries and an adaptor socket may be
needed. Outlets for 110 volts for small appliances are
found in most hotels.
COMMUNICATIONS: Telephone: There are full
facilities for national and international
telecommunications. Full IDD is available. Country
code: 61. Outgoing international code: 0011. Payphones
are red, green, gold or blue. Only local calls can be made
from red phones. Green, gold and blue phones also have
International Direct Dialling (IDD) and Subscriber Trunk
Dial (STD). The minimum cost of a local phone call is
30c. Phonecards are available at newsagents,
supermarkets and chemists and can be bought in
denominations of A$5, 10 and 20 and used for local,
STD or international calls. Creditphones, which take
most major credit cards, can be found at airports, city
centre locations and many hotels. **Fax:** The Overseas
Telecommunications Commission accepts documents
over the counter for transmission. Free collection by
courier is available in Brisbane, Sydney, Melbourne,
Perth and Adelaide. Fax number guides are available at

post offices, and prices vary. **Telex/telegram:** Services
are run by the Overseas Telecommunications
Commission and local offices. There are telex facilities at
central post offices in Brisbane, Canberra, Sydney,
Melbourne, Perth, Adelaide, Newcastle and Hobart. The
OTC also operates a 24-hour public telex at Sydney,
Brisbane, Canberra and Melbourne. Cables can be sent
Urgent (2-4 hours delivery), Ordinary (4-6 hours) or
Letter rate (24 hours). Telegrams may be sent through the
telephone operator. Hotels usually add a surcharge. **Post:**
There are post offices in all the main towns of every
State. Opening hours are 0900-1700 Monday to Friday.
Stamps are often available at hotel and motel reception
areas and selected newsagents. *Poste Restante* facilities
are available throughout the country; mail should be
addressed to the nearest post office. **Press:** The main
daily newspapers are *The Australian* and the *Australian
Financial Review*. The weekly newspapers with the
largest circulation are *The Morning Bulletin*, the *Sunday
Telegraph* and the *Sunday Mail*. Newspapers have a
generally high circulation throughout the continent.
**BBC World Service and Voice of America
frequencies:** From time to time these change. See the
section *How to Use this Book* for more information.

BBC:

MHz	17.83	15.34	11.95	9.740

Voice of America:

MHz	15.12	11.91	9.590	7.405

PASSPORT/VISA

*Regulations and requirements may be subject to change at short notice, and you
are advised to contact the appropriate diplomatic or consular authority before
finalising travel arrangements. Details of these may be found at the head of this
country's entry. Any numbers in the chart refer to the footnotes below.*

	Passport Required?	Visa Required?	Return Ticket Required?
Full British	Yes	Yes	Yes
BVP	Not valid	-	-
Australian	-	-	-
Canadian	Yes	Yes	Yes
USA	Yes	Yes	Yes
Other EU (As of 31/12/94)	Yes	Yes	Yes
Japanese	Yes	Yes	Yes

PASSPORTS: Valid passport required by all.
British Visitors Passport: Not acceptable.
VISAS: Required by all except New Zealand citizens
travelling on New Zealand passports.
Types of visa: *Visitor* (less than 3 months); *Visitor* (3
months and over); *Working Holiday; Business.*
Cost: *Working Holiday:* £71; *Visitor* (over 3 months):
£16; *Visitor* (less than 3 months): free of charge.
Validity: Varies according to type of visa, purpose of
trip and validity of passport. Visitor visa (to be used

within 1 year or life of passport whichever is shorter) valid for 3 months and over; Visitor visa (to be used within 1 year) valid for up to 3 months; Working Holiday visa is valid for 12 months.

Application to: Consulate (or Consular Section at Embassy or High Commission). For addresses, see top of entry.

Application requirements: (a) Completed application form. (b) Valid passport. (c) Separate passport-size photo. (d) Proof of sufficient funds for duration of stay. (e) If applying by mail, send the passport by recorded delivery and enclose a stamped, self-addressed envelope large enough for return of passport. (f) Business visitors must provide details of purpose of visit on company notepaper.

Note: Embassy representatives must submit applications to the office closest to the client's house. Delays will otherwise occur.

Working days required: Normally 1-5 days if applying in person; 21 days if applying by post.

Note: The Australian High Commission has asked that ABTA members should not sign visitor application forms on behalf of their clients. Travellers should also take particular note of the declarations relating to health, drugs and criminal convictions, as difficulties will arise if incorrect information is given.

Temporary residence: Applicants for temporary residence in Australia should consult the Embassy or High Commission and complete the relevant forms.

MONEY

Currency: Australian Dollar (A$) = 100 cents. Notes are in denominations of A$100, 50, 20, 10 and 5. Coins are in denominations of A$2 and 1, and 50, 20, 10 and 5 cents.

Currency exchange: Exchange facilities are available for all incoming and outgoing flights at all international airports in Australia. International-class hotels will exchange major currencies for guests. It is recommended that visitors change money at the airport or at city banks.

Credit cards: Visa, Diners Club, Access/Mastercard, Carte Blanche and American Express are accepted. Use may be restricted in small towns and Outback areas. Check with your credit card company for details of merchant acceptability and other services which may be available.

Travellers cheques: These are accepted in major currencies at banks or large hotels. However, some banks may charge a small fee for cashing travellers cheques.

Exchange rate indicators: The following figures are included as a guide to the movements of the Australian Dollar against Sterling and the US Dollar:

Date:	Oct '92	Sep '93	Jan '94	Jan '95
£1.00=	2.22	2.36	2.18	1.99
$1.00=	1.39	1.55	1.47	1.29

Currency restrictions: Export and import of coins/notes in Australian or foreign currency above A$5000 must be reported to customs at the port of entry or departure.

Banking hours: 0930-1600 Monday to Thursday; 0930-1700 Friday. These hours vary throughout the country.

DUTY FREE

The following items may be taken into Australia without payment of duty:

250 cigarettes or 250g of tobacco or cigars; 1 litre of any alcoholic liquor; other goods to a value of A$400.

Prohibited items: There are very strict regulations against the import of non-prescribed drugs, weapons, firearms and certain foodstuffs and other potential sources of disease and pestilence. For more information, read the Australian Customs information leaflets and *Australia, A Protected Place.* They are available from the Australian High Commission.

There are severe penalties for drug trafficking.

PUBLIC HOLIDAYS

Jan 1 '95 New Year's Day. **Jan 2** For New Year's Day. **Jan 26** Australia Day. **Apr 14** Good Friday. **Apr 17**

Easter Monday. **Apr 25** Anzac Day. **Dec 25** Christmas Day. **Jan 1 '96** New Year's Day. **Jan 26** Australia Day. **Apr 5** Good Friday. **Apr 8** Easter Monday. **Apr 25** Anzac Day.

HEALTH

Regulations and requirements may be subject to change at short notice, and you are advised to contact your doctor well in advance of your intended date of departure. Any numbers in the chart refer to the footnotes below.

	Special Precautions?	Certificate Required?
Yellow Fever	No	1
Cholera	No	No
Typhoid & Polio	No	-
Malaria	No	-
Food & Drink	No	-

[1]: A yellow fever certificate is required from travellers over 1 year of age arriving within 6 days of a visit to any region in any country that has had an instance of yellow fever in the previous 10 years as listed in the *Weekly Epidemiological Record.* See the *Health* section at the back of this book.

Health care: There are strict Customs and Health controls on entering and leaving the country, and Australian law can inflict severe penalties on health infringements. Australia reserves the right to isolate any person who arrives without the required certificates. Carriers are responsible for expenses of isolation of all travellers arriving by air who are not in possession of the required vaccination certificates. All arriving aircraft are sprayed before disembarkation to prevent the spread of disease-carrying insects. Standards of hygiene are high in Australia, especially in food preparation. Doctors and dentists are highly trained and hospitals are well equipped. There is a Reciprocal Health Agreement with the UK, New Zealand, Italy, Malta and Sweden in emergencies only, which allows residents from these five countries free hospital treatment. Proof of UK residence, such as an NHS medical card or a UK driving licence, must be shown. Prescribed medicines, ambulances and treatment at some doctor's surgeries must be paid for. Personal insurance for illness and accidents is highly recommended for all visitors. Those wishing to benefit from the Agreement should enrol at a *Medicare* office; this can be done *after* treatment.

TRAVEL - International

AIR: The national airline is *Qantas (QF).*

For free advice on air travel, call the *Air Travel Advisory Bureau* in the UK on (0171) 636 5000 (London) *or* (0161) 832 2000 (Manchester).

Approximate flight times: From *London* to Adelaide is 23 hours 55 minutes, to Brisbane is 23 hours 55 minutes, to Cairns is 25 hours 45 minutes, to Darwin is 21 hours 50 minutes, to Melbourne is 24 hours 25 minutes, to Perth is 21 hours 40 minutes, to Sydney is 21 hours 45 minutes and to Townsville is 26 hours 5 minutes.

From *Los Angeles* to Perth is 21 hours and to Sydney is 17 hours 55 minutes.

From *New York* to Perth is 27 hours 35 minutes and to Sydney 21 hours and 5 minutes.

From *Singapore* to Sydney is 9 hours 15 minutes and to Perth is 5 hours.

Approximately 30 international airlines fly to Australia.

International airports: Canberra, Sydney, Adelaide, Melbourne, Perth, Darwin, Brisbane, Hobart, Townsville and Cairns. All airports have a duty-free shop, bank/bureau de change and car hire; these will almost always be available on arrival and departure of international flights.

Canberra Airport is 10km (6 miles) east of the city. Transport into the city is available by taxi or rental car (travel time – 20 minutes). **Note:** Until recently *Canberra Airport* served domestic flights exclusively. However, *Britannia Airways* now fly to Canberra from *Luton Airport,* north of London.

Sydney Airport (Kingsford Smith) is 12km (7 miles) south of the city (travel time – 35 minutes). Coaches meet all incoming international and domestic flights. The international terminal is separate to the domestic terminal. Passengers may be set down at city airline terminals and city hotels, motels and guest-houses on request. There are also buses and taxis. Airport facilities include a duty-free shop, banks, restaurant (open one hour before and after every flight), car hire, car park and a travellers' information desk (open 0530 to one hour after last flight).

Adelaide Airport is 6km (4 miles) south of the city (travel time – 25 minutes). Coaches meet all international and domestic flights. Buses and taxis are available to the city and hotels. Airport facilities include a duty-free shop,

restaurant, bar (two hours before and one hour after flights) and car hire.

Melbourne Airport is 22km (14 miles) northwest of the city (travel time – 35 minutes). Skybus Coach or taxis are available to the city centre. Airport facilities include a buffet (open 0630), restaurant, bar (open 90 minutes before first departure), public bar (1000-2200), banks, post office, car park and duty-free shop.

Perth Airport is 10km (6 miles) northeast of the city (travel time – 35 minutes). There are separate international and domestic terminals. Airporter bus runs 0500-2100 and meets both international and domestic flights. Taxis are also available. Airport facilities include banks, duty-free shop, 24-hour restaurant, buffet, bar (0900-0100; 0100-0900, open one hour before and after arrival of international aircraft), car park, garage and gift shop (access from public area 0500-2400; access from transit/departure lounge 2400-0500).

Brisbane Airport is 13km (8 miles) northeast of the city (travel time – 35 minutes). Coach services are available to the city, Gold Coast, Sunshine Coast and major hotels. Coaches meet all international flights. Taxis are also available. Airport facilities include a car park, duty-free shop and a bar-buffet.

Darwin Airport is 8km (5 miles) from the city (travel time – 15 minutes). Coaches and taxis meet all incoming international daytime flights and all flights operated by *Ansett Australia Airlines, Ansett WA* and *Australian Airlines.* Airport facilities include a general goods kiosk (open 0700 to last departure) and bar (open 1100 to last departure).

Hobart Airport is 22km (14 miles) east of the city (travel time – 35 minutes). Coaches meet all incoming flights. Buses and taxis are available to the city. Airport facilities include a restaurant and bar (0630-2100).

Cairns Airport (Queensland) is 6km (4 miles) from the city (travel time – 15 minutes). Coaches meet all incoming flights, plus airport bus, limousines, car rental, taxis to city and other areas by arrangement. Airport facilities include a duty-free shop, restaurant (open 0600), bar (open 30 minutes before first flight to 30 minutes after last flight).

Townsville Airport (Queensland) is 5km (3 miles) from the city (travel time – 10 minutes). Coaches meet all incoming flights operated by *Qantas* and *Ansett.* The first coach leaves at 0735 and the last at 1949. Buses and taxis are available to city and hotels.

All other State capital cities are served by connections from the above international airports.

Departure tax: This is being phased out as of January 1995. The tax will be incorporated in the ticket price.

SEA: Cruise liners dock at Sydney, Melbourne, Hobart, Perth (Port of Fremantle), Adelaide and Brisbane.

TRAVEL - Internal

AIR: Australians rely on aviation to get from place to place as inhabitants of smaller countries rely on trains and buses. The network of scheduled services extends to more than 150,000km (95,000 miles) and covers the whole continent. Both first-class and second-class service is available, with meals and hostess service on many routes. Recent deregulation of Australia's domestic airlines means that flight services are more competitively priced. Aircraft can be chartered by pilots who pass a written examination on Australian air regulations and have their licences validated for private operations within Australia.

The major **domestic airlines** are: *Ansett Australia Airlines (AN), Qantas Domestic (TN)* and *East West (EW),* and these serve the major resorts and cities throughout Australia.

In addition, *Ansett Express (WX), Hazelton Airlines (ZL)* and *Eastern Australia Airlines (UN)* operate throughout New South Wales; *Ansett WA (MV)* operates throughout Western Australia; *Air North (HS)* operates throughout the Northern Territory; *Lloyd Aviation (UD)* operates throughout South Australia; *Kendell Airlines (KD)* operates throughout Victoria and South Australia; *Sunstate Airlines* operates throughout Victoria and Queensland; *Australian Regional Airlines (TN)* operates throughout Queensland; and *Airlines of Tasmania (IP)* operates throughout Tasmania.

Nearly all the domestic airlines operate special deals or air-passes at greatly reduced prices. Contact *Qantas* for telephone numbers.

SEA: There are 36,738km (22,600 miles) of coastline and many lakes, inland waterways and inlets, all of which can be used for touring by boat. From paddle steamers along the Murray River to deep-sea fishing cruisers along the vast Barrier Reef, all are available for charter or passenger booking. Most tour operators also handle shipping cruises. There is a regular car ferry service linking Victoria with Tasmania.

RAIL: Over 40,000km (24,850 miles) of track cover the country, but only one service spans the continent from

Diving Courses

Learn to Dive Starts every day except Sundays
Advanced, Rescue, Divemaster and **Instructor** courses
run regularly

—— Available in English, German and Japanese ——

Live-aboard Dive Trips

Overnight departs daily (except Tuesday & Wednesday)
3-day, 2-night (or longer) departs every day except
Tuesdays

PADI 5-Star Instructor Development Centre

Three comfortable catamarans
A wide selection of exclusive dive sites on
the Outer Barrier Reef
Diving gear sales and maintenance
Snorkellers welcome • **P**rivate charters available

Deep Sea Divers Den

319 Draper Street, Cairns, Queensland 4870, Australia
Tel: +61-70 312223 Fax: +61-70 311210

coast to coast – the twice-weekly *Indian Pacific*, running 4000km (2480 miles) on standard 1435mm (56.5-inch) gauge from Sydney on the east coast to Perth on the west coast, a journey time of three days (68 hours), including a 500km (300-mile) stretch of straight track, the longest in the world. The *Indian Pacific* is fully air-conditioned and soundproofed, with first- and second-class sleeping cars and a lounge car with a piano, bar and videotapes for first-class passengers. It is also well-known for its sumptuous breakfasts and all food during the journey is prepared on board the train. For most of the year, a twice-weekly service is provided by the *Trans-Australian* running from Adelaide to Perth (two days). Other express service links (not always daily) from the state capitals are as follows:

The *Melbourne Sydney Express* links Sydney and Melbourne overnight, and the *Intercapital Daylight Express* provides a daytime service. The *Ghan* links Adelaide to Alice Springs (overnight). The *Overland* links Melbourne with Adelaide (overnight). The *Brisbane Limited Express* links Brisbane with Sydney twice a day, one connection is overnight. The *Canberra Monaro Express* and the fast *XPT Express* link Canberra with Sydney in four or five hours. The *Sunlander* and the *Queenslander* link Brisbane with Cairns (one and a half days). The *Queenslander* underwent extensive renovation in 1992. The *Prospector* links Perth with Kalgoorlie and this is one of Australia's fastest trains (6-7 hours). The *Vinelander* links Melbourne with Meldura (overnight); the *Sunraysia* provides a daytime service on the same route. The *Spirit of Capricorn* links Brisbane with Rockhampton (overnight). The *Spirit of the Outback* runs the same route but connects further to Longreach. The *Pacific Coast Motorail* links Sydney with Murwillumbah (overnight).

Both first- and second-class tickets are available, with sleeping accommodation on longhauls. Several routes have motorail facilities. Long-distance trains are air-conditioned and have excellent catering facilities and showers. Reservations for seats and sleeping berths are essential on all long-distance trains and are accepted up to six months in advance. For reservations, write to the Australian National Travel Centre, 132 North Terrace, Adelaide, SA 5000, or telephone (8) 231 7699.

Luggage allowance: All interstate rail passengers are allowed 80kg (176lb). Medium-sized suitcases and hand luggage can be placed in the passengers' compartments. Large suitcases must be carried in the guard's van and checked in 30 minutes prior to departure.

Sleeping berths: Single and twin apartments are available for a surcharge on most inter-capital overnight services. All 'Twinettes' have two sleeping berths and wash basin. Twinettes are available either first-class or holiday-class; the first also offer individual showers. 'Roomette' (single compartment) cars have showers at the end of each car. These are first-class only.

Cheap fares: Unlimited travel, valid from 14 to 60 days, is available with an *Austrailpass*, which must be purchased outside Australia, and can only be used by non-Australian passport holders. First- and second-class passes are available. Each State operator offers its own *Austrailpass* scheme. The *Austrail Flexi-Pass* is valid for eight days although it cannot be used on the 'Ghan' or the 'Indian Pacific'. The *Kangaroo Road 'n Rail Pass* is also available, offering unlimited travel on both the rail and *Australian Coachlines* bus networks throughout the country. It is also possible to obtain discounts on certain rental car schemes. **Note:** An *Austrailpass* or *Kangaroo Road 'n Rail Pass* does not include meal or sleeping berth charges. A surcharge must be paid on the *XPT Express* service in New South Wales. The passes must be used within 12 months of issue.

Representative in the UK: Railways of Australia, c/o *Longhaul Leisurail*, PO Box 113, Peterborough PE3 8HY. Tel: (01733) 335 599. Fax: (01733) 505 451. Most major tourist attractions can be reached by train; tickets for multiple destinations can be purchased from travel agents outside Australia. **Note:** Booking domestic travel for Australia outside the country can result in discounts of up to 30%. Contact the respective Tourist Boards.

ROAD: Traffic drives on the left. Road signs are international. The speed limit is 60kmph (35mph) per hour in cities and towns and 100kmph (62mph) per hour on country roads and highways unless signs indicate otherwise. Seatbelts must be worn at all times and driving licences must be in the driver's possession when driving. Driving off major highways in the Outback becomes more difficult between November and February because of summer rain, as many roads are little more than dirt tracks. Road travel is best between April and October. Distances between towns can be considerable, and apart from ensuring that all vehicles are in peak condition, it is advisable to carry spare water, petrol and equipment. Travellers are advised to check with local Automobile Associations before departure in order to obtain up-to-date information on road and weather conditions.

Coach: Major cities are linked by an excellent national coach system, run by *Australian Coachlines* (combining *Pioneer Express* and *Greyhound Australia)* and *Bus Australia*. Tasmania also has its own coach service, *Tasmanian Redline Coaches.* There are numerous other companies operating state and interstate services. The main coach express routes are: Sydney to Adelaide, Melbourne (inland) and Canberra; Canberra to Melbourne; Melbourne to Adelaide and Broken Hill; Adelaide to Alice Springs, Perth and Brisbane; Darwin to Alice Springs and Kakadu; Alice Springs to Ayers Rock; Cairns to Brisbane; Brisbane to Sydney (inland and coastal) and Melbourne. Coach passes are available for travel on the express services for between 7 and 90 days, eg the *Aussie Discoverer,* the *Eastern Discoverer,* the *Aussiepass,* the *Bus Australia Pass,* the *Down Under Pass,* etc. These normally give unlimited travel throughout the country. The *Kangaroo Road 'n Rail Pass* offers unrestricted rail and coach travel throughout mainland Australia on *Railways of Australia* and *Australian Coachlines* coaches. It is advisable to purchase all these passes before departure from country of origin. Coaches are one of the cheapest ways to travel around Australia, as well as one of the most comfortable, with air-conditioning, big adjustable seats and on-board bathrooms; some also have television and the latest videos.

Representation in the UK: *Australian Coachlines (Greyhound International* and *Pioneer Express),* c/o *Greyhound International*, Sussex House, London Road, East Grinstead, West Sussex RH19 1LD. Tel: (01342) 317 317. Fax: (01342) 328 519. For *all Australian ground transportation:* c/o Australian Destination Centre, PO Box 528, Slough SL1 8QH. Tel/Fax: (01628) 669 212.

Car hire: Available at all major airports and major hotels to those over 21 years old. **Documentation:** International, foreign or national Driving Permits, translated into English, are generally valid for three months. These must be carried on the person while driving.

URBAN: Comprehensive public transport systems are provided in all the main towns. The State capitals have suburban rail networks, those in Sydney and Melbourne being particularly extensive, and trams run in Melbourne and Adelaide. Meter-operated **taxis** can be found in all major cities and towns. There is a minimum 'flagfall charge' and then a charge for the distance travelled. Taxi drivers do not expect to be tipped. A small additional payment may be required for luggage and telephone bookings. Some taxis accept payment by credit card. For further details, see individual State entries.

JOURNEY TIMES: The following chart gives approximate journey times (in hours and minutes) from Sydney to other major cities in Australia.

	Air	Rail	Coach	Sea
Canberra	0.40	5.00	4.00	-
Adelaide	1.55	28.40	23.40	-
Brisbane	1.15	16.00	16.30	-
Darwin	5.00	-	92.50	-
Melbourne	1.15	13.00	14.30	-
Perth	4.35	65.45	60.00	-
Hobart	2.05	-	-	14.00

ACCOMMODATION

HOTEL/MOTEL: Every State has a selection of hotels run by international chains such as the Hilton and Intercontinental. More authentic accommodation for the tourist can be found outside the cities. The smaller hotels are more relaxed, and offer more of the flavour of their location. The highways out of the State cities are lined with good quality motels offering self-contained family units, and often an in-house restaurant service.

Most hotels and motels provide rooms with telephones, private shower and/or bath, toilet, small fridge and tea- and coffee-making facilities. Check-out time is 1000 or 1100. Hotel/motels and motor inns have licensed restaurant and a residents' bar; some may provide a public bar (see below). Motels in rural areas will normally only be able to offer breakfast. Motor inns in rural areas will probably have a licensed restaurant, and possibly a residents' bar as well. Private hotels are not permitted to provide bars. The principal difference between a hotel and a motel in Australia is that a hotel must, by law, provide a public bar among its facilities. For this reason there are many motels which are hotels in all but name, offering an excellent standard of comfort and service but preferring to reserve their bar exclusively for the use of their guests, rather than for the public at large.

Grading: Hotels and motels in Australia are graded in a star rating system by the Australian Automobile Clubs. In most cases, different rooms will be offered at different rates depending on their size, aspect or facilities; this is particularly true of seafront hotels. In general, hotels in cities cost more than their rural counterparts. The fact that an establishment is unclassified does not imply that it is inferior. It may still be in the process of being classified. The following grading definitions are intended as a guide only and are subject to change:

5-star accommodation: International-style establishments offering a superior standard of appointments, furnishings and decor with an extensive range of first-class guest services. A variety of room styles and/or suites available. Choice of dining facilities, 24-hour room service and additional shopping or recreational facilities available.

4-star accommodation: Exceptionally well-appointed establishments with high-quality furnishings and a high degree of comfort. Fully air-conditioned. High standards of presentation and guest services provided. Restaurant and meals available on premises.

3-star accommodation: Well-appointed establishments offering a comfortable standard of accommodation with above average floor coverings, furnishings, lighting and ample heating/cooling facilities.

2-star accommodation: Well-maintained establishments offering an average standard of accommodation with average furnishings, bedding, floor coverings, lighting and heating/cooling facilities.

1-star accommodation: Establishments offering a basic standard of accommodation. Simply furnished, adequate lighting. Motel units all have private facilities. Resident manager.

Note: Some hotels are graded with an additional *open* or *hollow* star. This indicates a slightly higher grade of facilities than the normal facilities for its classification. For more information on accommodation classification contact the Australian Hotels Association, Level 3, Tourism House, 40 Blackall Street, Barton, ACT 2600. Tel: (6) 273 4007. Fax: (6) 273 4011.

Information is also available from the Australian Hotels Association, Level 5, 8 Quay Street, Sydney, NSW 2000. Tel: (2) 281 6944 *or* 281 6922. Fax: (2) 290 1737; *or* the Motor Inn, Motel and Accommodation Association, Level 12, 309 Pitt Street, Sydney, NSW 2000. Tel: (2) 261 3793.

GUEST-HOUSES, HOMESTAY, SELF-CATERING AND FARMSTAY HOLIDAYS: Service apartments and self-contained flats are available at main tourist resorts, especially along the east coast. Many of the less accessible areas have accommodation on farmsteads, from guest-houses on the huge sheep stations to basic staff quarters on smaller arable farms, giving an insight into an alternative aspect of Australian life. There are many homes and farms which open their doors to foreign visitors and offer splendid hospitality. Bed & breakfast private home accommodation is available throughout Australia. For information on bed & breakfast accommodation, contact Bed & Breakfast Australia, PO Box 408, 5 Yarabah Avenue, Gordon, NSW 2072. Tel: (2) 498 5344. Fax: (2) 498 6438. Some hotels have self-catering apartments. For more information contact the Australian Tourist Commission. Guest-houses are not allowed to serve alcohol. **Grading:** Holiday units and apartments are classified according to a 5-star system with criteria comparable to those for hotels and motels above.

COUNTRY PUB ACCOMMODATION: These offer cold beer, meals and simple but comfortable accommodation for travellers from A$30 a night. Pubs tend to be easy to find and advance reservations are not always necessary. However, standards may vary according to the type of pub and its location. For further information, contact Australian Pub Stays, Suite 1, 27-33 Raglan Street, South Melbourne, VIC 3205. Tel: (3) 696 0433. Fax: (3) 696 0329.

YOUTH HOSTELS: Found throughout the country, but there are greater concentrations near cities and densely populated areas. Associations responsible are affiliated to most other international organisations. Further details may be obtained from the Australian Youth Hostel Association, National Office, 10 Mallett Street, Camperdown, NSW 2050. Tel: (2) 565 1699. Fax: (2) 565 1325.

ON-CAMPUS ACCOMMODATION: University colleges and halls of residence offer inexpensive accommodation for both students and non-students during the vacation periods (May, August and late November to late February).

CAMPING/CARAVANNING: Camping tours cover most of the country, especially the wilder areas. Participants generally join a group under an experienced guide team and everyone helps with cooking, washing, etc. All equipment and transport is supplied; some also provide portable showers. More rugged tours with Land-Rovers are available, offering limited facilities, although company equipment is again provided with a driver/guide and cook. This can be one of the best ways to explore the Australian Outback. Camping site information is available from all major tourist centres. It is inadvisable to camp on undesignated sites.

A number of companies can arrange **motor camper**

rentals, with a range of fully-equipped vehicles. Full details can be obtained from the Australian Tourist Commission. **Grading:** Caravan parks are classified according to a 5-star system with criteria similar to those for hotels and motels above.

RESORTS & EXCURSIONS

Australia's main tourist attractions are Sydney, the Great Barrier Reef, the Gold Coast of Queensland, and Ayers Rock, in the rugged Outback of the Northern Territory. Other attractions in the continent range from the wild flowers of Western Australia to the wines of the Barossa Valley, and from Western Australia's ghost towns to the remarkable wildlife on the island of Tasmania. It is possible to visit the relatively undisturbed Aboriginal communities on Bathurst and Melville Islands, about 80km (50 miles) north of Darwin, providing valuable insights into the continent's ancient indigenous culture. The Australian coastline has thousands of miles of beautiful beaches. Information on resorts, excursions and places of interest within Australia is given under each individual State entry below.
The range of adventure and special interest holidays is almost limitless. Many of the safari tours include luxury transport, and comfortable accommodation is available at many of the sheep stations. Further details may be obtained from the many brochures and leaflets published by the Australian Tourist Commission.
POPULAR ITINERARIES: 5-day: (a) Adelaide–Barossa Valley–River Murray–Adelaide. (b) Hobart–Cradle Mountain–Launceston. (c) Adelaide–Adelaide Hills–Flinders Ranges–Kangaroo Island. (d) Melbourne–Great Ocean Road–Adelaide. (e) Sydney–Hunter Valley–Blue Mountains–Snowy Mountains. **7-day:** (a) Sydney–Canberra–Khancoban–Melbourne. (b) Darwin–Kakadu–Katherine–Alice Springs–Ayers Rock–Darwin. (c) Brisbane–Hamilton Island–Townsville–Cairns. (d) Alice Springs–Katherine–Kakadu–Bungle Bungles–Broome. (e) Sydney–Jarris Bay–Narooma–Merimbuta–Eden–Melbourne.

SOCIAL PROFILE

FOOD & DRINK: There are numerous speciality dishes and foods including Sydney rock oysters, *barramundi* (freshwater fish), tiger prawns, macadamia nuts and *yabbies* (small freshwater lobsters). Beef is the most popular meat and lamb is also of a high quality. There is a wide variety of excellent fruits and vegetables. Service is European style and varies from waitress and waiter service to self-service. Bistros, cafés, family-style restaurants and 'pub' lunches at the counter offer good food at reasonable prices. Some restaurants will allow guests to bring their own alcohol and are called 'BYO' restaurants. Being a country of immigrants, Australia also offers an enormous variety of cuisines, eg Italian, French, Greek, Spanish, Chinese, Vietnamese, Malaysian, Thai, Japanese, Indian, African, Lebanese and Korean. **Drink:** The major vineyards (wineries) are outside Perth, Sydney, Melbourne, Hobart, Canberra and Adelaide. The largest single wine-making region is in the Barossa Valley, South Australia, two hours drive from Adelaide, where high-quality red and white wines are produced. Most restaurants and all hotels are licensed to serve alcohol; private hotels and guest-houses cannot be licensed by law. Australian wines are good and inexpensive. Beer is served chilled. Licensing hours in public bars are 1000-2200 Monday to Saturday, however most pubs are open until 2400; Sunday varies. Restaurants, clubs and hotel lounges have more flexible hours. Drinking age is 18 years or over.
SHOPPING: Special purchases include excellent local wines; wool, clothing, leather and sheepskin products; opal and other precious or semi-precious stones; and modern art sculpture and paintings. Exhibitions of bark paintings, boomerangs and other tribal objects are on view and for sale in Darwin, Alice Springs and the State capitals; many depict stories from the Dreamtime. A brochure titled *Shopping Guide to Australian Crafts* gives crafts outlets in all major cities, their opening hours and the type of goods they offer, and is available free of charge from Crafts Australia, 414 Elizabeth Street, Surrey Hills, NSW 2010. Tel: (2) 211 1445. Fax: (2) 211 1443. Many cities and towns have small shops devoted to the sale of 'Australiana', where Australian souvenirs, ranging from T-shirts to boomerangs, can be bought. **Shopping hours:** Opening hours for most stores in the cities are 0900-1700 Monday to Thursday, 0900-2100 Friday and 0900-1700 Saturday, except in South Australia and Western Australia where shops are open all day Saturday. Late-night shopping is available on Friday to 2100 in Melbourne, Adelaide, Brisbane, Hobart and Darwin. Late-night shopping is available Thursday at the same time in Sydney, Canberra and Perth. Corner stores, restaurants and snack bars are open in most cities until well into the night.
SPORT: The national sports are **cricket** and **rugby**, both played successfully at international level. **Australian-rules football** and **European football** are also very popular. **Tennis:** The *Australian Open* is played at the National Tennis Centre in Melbourne early in the year, attracting top tennis players from all over the world. There are also many other tournaments throughout the country and tennis courts are available in most areas for the tennis enthusiast. **Golf:** Some of the world's finest courses can be found in Australia, with spectacular settings and excellent facilities. **Racing:** The main event in the Australian horseracing calendar is the annual *Melbourne Cup*, run on the first Tuesday in November. **Skiing:** Possible during June to August in the mountainous areas of the southeast. One of the best locations is Mount Kosciusko, south of Sydney, at 2126m (7300ft). **Watersports:** Water-skiing, deep-sea fishing, sailing, windsurfing, swimming, surfing and skindiving predominate, especially along the 2500km (1500 miles) of the Great Barrier Reef, where there are numerous tiny islands much used by snorkellers, scuba divers and wildlife enthusiasts. **Special interest holidays:** A huge range of these are available – farming, flying and gliding, ballooning, cycling, rafting, golfing, pony trekking, bushwalking, visiting national parks, gemstone fossicking, etc. For further details, see under the individual State entries below or contact the Australian Tourist Board.
SPECIAL EVENTS: For a selection of festivals and special events occurring in each State and territory throughout Australia during 1995 consult the regional sections below.
SOCIAL CONVENTIONS: A largely informal atmosphere prevails; shaking hands is the customary greeting. Casual wear is worn everywhere except in the most exclusive restaurants, social gatherings and important business meetings. Some restaurants may have 'no smoking' areas. **Tipping:** Not as common as it is in Europe and America nor is a service charge added to the bill in restaurants. 10% for food and drink waiters is usual in top-quality restaurants, but is optional elsewhere. However, with taxis it is not usual to tip but round up the cost to the next dollar.

BUSINESS PROFILE

ECONOMY: Australia has a highly diverse economy and a standard of living comparable with Western industrialised countries. Manufacturing contributes approximately one-sixth of GDP, principally from iron, steel and engineering. There is a strong agricultural base which contributes 40% of export earnings, although the relative importance of this sector has diminished in recent years due to exceptional growth in exploitation of mineral deposits. Australia has vast reserves of coal, oil, natural gas, nickel, zircon, iron ore, bauxite and diamonds (in the Kimberley Mountains). In 1986 Australia overtook the USA as the world's leading exporter of coal which now accounts for 15% of export earnings. Uranium is another key export product: Australian ore fuels many of the Western nations' nuclear power plants. Minerals now contribute the largest slice, and petroleum products and agricultural goods contribute roughly equal amounts to the balance of payments. The main agricultural industry, sheep, has suffered a downturn in recent years as textile manufacturers have turned to man-made fibres instead of wool. This has been further exacerbated by the reduced demand from Arab countries, traditionally major importers of live sheep. Australia's largest trading partner is Japan – both for imports and exports – followed by the United States (a key export market), New Zealand, China and the European Union nations (principally the UK and Germany). Japanese investment in Australia, particularly in property and tourist ventures, accelerated during the late 1980s to the point where large swathes of the eastern seaboard are Japanese-owned. During the 1980s there was a marked shift in Australian trading patterns towards the fast-growing economies of the Pacific Rim, a trend which seems likely to continue. The recession of the late 1980s and early 1990s has hit the Australian economy hard, exemplified by the financial demise of several of Australia's internationally-known entrepreneurs. But the effects go much wider; unemployment is at its highest since the 1930s and several key industries, such as wool, are facing possibly terminal decline. Despite this, Australia's relative proximity to the fast-growing Pacific Rim region and its economic compatibility (abundant raw materials in a region where they are, China apart, relatively scarce) should be of great benefit. The large and increasing proportion of Australian trade is now carried out with East Asia and ethnic Asians now account for more than half the recent immigrants into Australia.
BUSINESS: Suits are necessary in Sydney and Melbourne. Brisbane business people may wear shirts, ties and shorts; visiting business people should wear lightweight suits for initial meeting. Prior appointments necessary. A great deal of business is conducted over drinks. Best months for business travel are March to November. **Office hours:** 0900-1730 Monday to Friday.
COMMERCIAL INFORMATION: The following organisations can offer advice: Australian-British Chamber of Commerce, Suite 10-16, 3rd Floor, Morley House, 314-322 Regent Street, London W1R 5AE. Tel: (0171) 636 4525. Fax: (0171) 636 4511; *or* Australian Chamber of Commerce and Industry (ACCI), PO Box E14, Queen Victoria Terrace, Canberra, ACT 2600. Tel: (6) 273 2311. Fax: (6) 273 3196; *or* International Chamber of Commerce, PO Box E118, Queen Victoria Terrace, Canberra, ACT 2600. Tel: (6) 295 1961. Fax: (6) 295 0170.
Note: Routine commercial enquiries should be directed to the Consulate General. The federal chambers of commerce are able to provide further information. Consult regional entries below.
CONFERENCES/CONVENTIONS: The Australian Tourist Commission (addresses at the beginning of entry) is the first point of contact for information about conferences and conventions in Australia. It publishes a *Meeting Planners' Guide to Australia* which gives extensive information on meeting facilities in all major cities and their surrounding areas, as well as details on the cities themselves and various activities outside the boardroom. There is also a nationwide organisation overseeing conference and convention activity throughout the country: Association of Australian Convention Bureaux (AACB), Level 2, 80 William Street, Woolloomooloo, NSW 2011. Tel: (2) 360 3500. Fax: (2) 331 7767. Over 5000 conference and convention establishments belong to this association. More detailed information about specific venues is available from the regional Convention and Visitors' Bureaux in each State and territory (see regional entries below). These can also provide details of the many private companies throughout Australia offering conference and convention services.

CLIMATE

Australia is in the southern hemisphere and the seasons are opposite to those in Europe and North America. There are two climatic zones: the tropical zone (in the north above the Tropic of Capricorn) and the temperate zone. The tropical zone (consisting of 40% of Australia) has two seasons, summer ('wet') and winter ('dry') while the temperate zone has all four seasons.
November/March (spring-summer): Warm or hot everywhere, tropical in the north, and warm to hot with mild nights in the south.
April/September (autumn-winter): Northern and central Australia have clear warm days, cool nights; the south has cool days with occasional rain but still plenty of sun. Snow is totally confined to mountainous regions of the southeast.
Note: For further details, including climate statistics, see under individual State entries.
Required clothing: Lightweights during summer months with warmer clothes needed during the cooler winter period throughout most of the southern States. Lightweight cottons and linens all year in the central/northern States with warm clothes only for cooler winter evenings and early mornings. Sunglasses, sunhats and sunblock lotion are recommended year round in the north and during the summer months in the south.

Australian Capital Territory

Canberra Tourist Bureau
Level 8, CBS Towers, Cnr Akuna and Bunda Streets, Canberra, ACT 2600, Australia
Tel: (6) 205 0666. Fax: (6) 205 0629.

AREA: 2400 sq km (1511 sq miles).
POPULATION: 289,700 (1991).
POPULATION DENSITY: 120.7 per sq km.
CAPITAL: Canberra (also national capital).
Population: 310,100 (1990 estimate).
GEOGRAPHY: Canberra is located in New South Wales on the western slopes of the Great Dividing Range, and was conceived in the early 1900s in order to create a capital city in a federal State separate from any

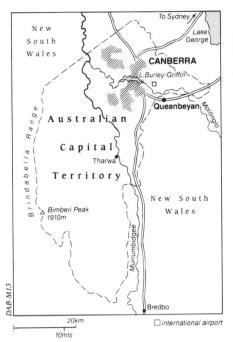

of the uniting States. Roughly half the population is under 26. Spectacular green countryside is ringed by mountains nearly 600m (2000ft) above sea level. Lake Burley-Griffin, a man-made lake, is now the main feature of this constantly expanding modern capital. Hills, trees and greenery remain prominent among the architecture of a city that is attractive, tidy, spacious and efficient as befits the national capital city, although it lacks the charm of slow historical development.

TIME: GMT + 10 (GMT + 11 from last Sunday in October to first Saturday in March).

PUBLIC HOLIDAYS

The Australian Capital Territory observes all the public holidays observed nationwide (see the main entry for Australia above) and, in addition, the following are observed:

Mar 20 '95 Canberra Day. **Apr 15** Easter Saturday. **Jun 12** Queen's Birthday. **Oct 2** Labour Day. **Dec 26** Boxing Day. **Mar 18 '96** Canberra Day. **Apr 6** Easter Saturday.

TRAVEL

AIR: Until recently there were no direct international flights to Canberra. However, *Britannia Airways* have introduced direct flights to the city from Luton Airport, north of London. These are charter flights, running approximately twice a month (November-March) via Cairns or Adelaide. Travel by air to Canberra is also possible via direct flights from Sydney and Melbourne. The city centre is 8km (5 miles) from Canberra Airport. Canberra is part of a national network of internal flights.
RAIL: Through trains run from Canberra to Sydney and Melbourne, with connections to other States. Economy *Aussiepass* tickets apply on both local and interstate systems.
ROAD: Main road links, which are used by coach services, connect Canberra to Sydney (travel time – 4 hrs, 15 mins) and to Melbourne (travel time – 14 hrs, 30 mins), thereby allowing access to all other parts of the country. *Aussiepass* and *Eaglepass* tickets apply.
URBAN: Bus: An internal bus network operates for the city of Canberra. Pre-purchase day tickets and 10-journey multi-tickets are available. There is a *Canberra Explorer Bus* linking major attractions in the city that visitors can board or depart from at any point. **Taxi:** Radio-controlled, metered taxis are available at all hours.

ACCOMMODATION

Note: More detailed coverage of the range of accommodation available in Australia may be found by consulting the *Accommodation* section in the general entry for Australia above.
HOTELS: Accommodation includes international chain hotels such as those run by Trusthouse Forte and Hilton. There are also small private hotels and it is possible to stay at several of the Territory's sheep stations.
CAMPING/CARAVANNING: A number of companies can arrange **motor camper** rentals, with a range of fully equipped vehicles. Full details can be obtained from the Tourist Board.

RESORTS & EXCURSIONS

Canberra is an elegant city of wide streets, gardens and parkland. The old *Parliament House* is impressive enough, but has been surpassed by its replacement, a grand modern edifice completed in 1988, Australia's bicentennial year. The *War Memorial*, Byzantine in style, constructed from cream-coloured sandstone with a copper dome, is deservedly the city's most popular attraction, and is the scene of the annual Anzac Parade. *Lake Burley-Griffin*, a vast man-made waterway named after Canberra's architect, features prominently throughout the city area. Cruises and boating are popular. Near *Tidbinbilla Deep Space Tracking Station*, 70km (40 miles) southeast of the city, is *Tidbinbilla Nature Reserve* where visitors have the opportunity to hand-feed kangaroos. The *Canberra Space Centre* contains model spacecraft and space photographs. *Blundell's Cottage*, which pre-dates the lake, is a stone-slab construction calling to mind the location's earlier incarnation as a sheep station.
The new *Museum of Australia*, north of the lake, will be a further cultural addition to the present *Australian National Gallery*, *National Library* and *National Science and Technology Centre*.
There are several hills in the immediate area of Canberra; from the 195m (650ft) *Telecom Telecommunications Tower*, topping the 825m-high (2750ft) *Black Mountain*, there is an excellent view of the area for those who don't feel dizzy in revolving restaurants (meal optional). Helicopter and ballooning trips provide other ways of taking in the view.
The *Snowy Mountains* are to the south of Canberra, in New South Wales, and provide excellent opportunities for winter skiing and summertime pursuits such as bushwalking, horseriding and watersports. Trips from Canberra can be arranged.

SOCIAL PROFILE

FOOD: Restaurants and hotels serve trout from the streams and lakes of the Snowy Mountains. Beef and lamb come from the farmlands surrounding Canberra. *ACT Barbecue and Picnic Facilities* is a brochure giving details of 60 picnic locations in Canberra.
NIGHTLIFE: Despite the daytime orderliness, nightlife is actively promoted by the large range of pubs, restaurants and nightclubs. There are many film shows.
SHOPPING: A wide range of goods, including Australian arts and crafts, is available from department stores and specialist shops. Galleries and museums are often open outside normal trading hours. **Shopping hours:** Opening hours for most stores in the city are 0900-1730 Monday to Thursday; 0900-2100 Friday and 0900-1600 Saturday.
SPORT: The State follows the national passion for **football**, **cricket** and **rugby**, and Lake Burley-Griffin provides facilities for all aspects of **watersports**. **Skiing** is possible during the winter months at high altitudes in the mountains. Tours from Canberra provide the tourist with the opportunity to visit working sheep properties with demonstrations of **sheep-mustering, sheep-shearing** and even **boomerang** throwing.
SPECIAL EVENTS: The following is a selection of events and festivals taking place in the Australian Capital Territory:
Apr 9 '95 *Mobil Canberra Marathon.* **Apr 25** *Anzac Day Commemoration March.* **Apr 29-May 7** *Autumnfest,* Canberra. **Sep 16-Oct 15** *Floriade 1995,* Canberra. **Sep 16-17** *Spring Bulb and Camellia Show,* Yarralumla. **Sep 8** *Qantas Canberra Cup* (horseracing). **Oct 9-26** *National Festival of Australian Theatre,* Canberra. **Nov 6-17** *ACI National Wine Show 1995,* Canberra. **Nov 24-26** *Canberra International Rally; Osibi National African Culture Festival,* Canberra. **Jan 20 '96** *Multicultural Festival,* Canberra. **Jan 26** *Australia Day* ceremonies, Canberra and surrounding areas. **Jan 27-28** *World Cup Showjumping,* Canberra. **Feb 23-25** *Royal Canberra Show.* **Apr 5-8** *National Folk Festival.* **Apr 14** *Mobil Canberra Marathon,* Canberra. **Mar 9-18** *Canberra Festival.*
For a full list of special events contact the Canberra Tourist Bureau.

BUSINESS PROFILE

COMMERCIAL INFORMATION: The following organisation can offer advice: ACT Chamber of Commerce & Industry, PO Box E14, Queen Victoria Terrace, Canberra, ACT 2600. Tel: (6) 273 2311. Fax: (6) 273 3196. Telex: 62733.
CONFERENCES/CONVENTIONS: Canberra has recently completed its National Convention Centre with seating facilities for 2500. Other major convention centres include Australian Institute of Sport, Park Hyatt Pavilion and Capital Parkroyal. For more information on

conferences and conventions in Australian Capital Territory contact the Australian Tourist Commission *or* the Canberra Visitors & Convention Bureau, Unit 1, JAA House, 19 Napier Close, Deakin, ACT 2600. Tel: (6) 285 3900. Fax: (6) 282 2725.

CLIMATE

Very warm with little rainfall during summer months. Winters can be cold and snow may fall occasionally. Rainfall can be heavy in winter.
Required clothing: Lightweights during summer months with warmer mediumweight clothes necessary in winter. Waterproofing advisable throughout the year, especially in winter.

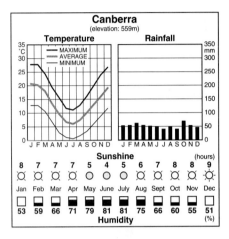

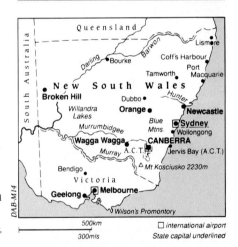

New South Wales Travel Centre
19 Castlereagh Street, Sydney, NSW 2001, Australia
Tel: (2) 231 4444. Fax: (2) 232 6080.
Tourism New South Wales
GPO Box 7050, 5th & 6th Floors, 140 George Street, Sydney, NSW 2001, Australia
Tel: (2) 931 1111. Fax: (2) 931 1424.
Tourism New South Wales
Gemini House, 10-18 Putney Hill, London SW15 6AA
Tel: (0181) 789 1020. Fax: (0181) 789 4577.
Sydney Convention & Visitors Bureau
421A Finchley Road, London NW3 6HJ.
Tel: (0171) 431 4045. Fax: (0171) 431 7920.

AREA: 801,600 sq km (309,417 sq miles).
POPULATION: 5,902,400 (1991 estimate).
POPULATION DENSITY: 7.4 per sq km.
CAPITAL: Sydney. **Population:** 3,698,500 (1991).
GEOGRAPHY: The landscape ranges from the subtropical north to the Snowy Mountains in the south. There are over 1300km (800 miles) of coastline with golden beaches, and picturesque waterways and rivers include the 1900km (1200-mile) Murray River.
TIME: GMT + 10 (GMT + 11 from last Sunday in October to first Saturday in March) except in the Broken Hill Area which keeps GMT + 9.5.

PUBLIC HOLIDAYS

New South Wales observes all the public holidays observed nationwide (see the main entry for Australia above) and, in addition, the following are observed: **Apr 15 '95** Easter Saturday. **Jun 12** Queen's Birthday. **Oct 2** Labour Day. **Dec 26** Boxing Day. **Apr 6 '96** Easter Saturday.

TRAVEL

AIR: Sydney is an international gateway to Australia, and international flights from Europe, New Zealand, Asia, Africa and the Americas all serve the city. Flights to and from Europe take about 24 hours. The main domestic airlines operating in New South Wales are: *Aeropelican (PO), Aquatic Air (Seaplane), Crane Air (FD), Eastern Airlines (UN), Hazelton Air Services (ZL), Kendall Airlines (KD), Macknight Airlines (MT), Norfolk Airlines (UG), Oxley Airlines (VQ), Yanda Air Services (ST), Sunstate Airlines (OF), Western NSW Airlines (FO), Ansett NSW (WX)* and *Ansett Australia Airlines (AN).*

Airports: *Kingsford Smith* is Sydney's international airport; it is 11km (7 miles) from the city centre (travel time – 35 minutes). For more information, see general introduction to Australia above.

SEA: Sydney is a major international port, and cruise lines call from Europe, the Far East and the USA. There are also many day- and half-day cruises from Sydney Harbour, offering everything from sightseeing tours to nearby attractions such as wildlife and aboriginal communities, the Blue Mountains and the Hunter Valley wine region, to night-time cabaret showboats.

RAIL: Sydney has through trains to all other State capitals. An internal system of railways runs throughout the State, connecting all the most important towns, tourist resorts and running through to Canberra in the south. Fast *XPT* trains run on some routes.

ROAD: Sydney is the focal point of a network that connects every major city. Road distances from many places, however, are enormous, and a journey by even the fastest coach to Darwin, on the northern coast, takes over 92 hours. The State is well served with an excellent road system, as required by the most heavily populated region of the country. Main highways are the *Barrier Highway*, running west to Adelaide, the *Hume Highway* running south to Canberra and Melbourne, the *New England Highway* running north to Brisbane, the *Pacific Highway* running along the coast to Brisbane and Melbourne, and the *Mitchell Highway* running northeast to Charleville and connecting to the routes to Mount Isa and Darwin in the north. The State is well served by national coach operators and regional bus lines.

URBAN: Sydney's extensive electrified suburban **rail** network includes a city centre underground link and a monorail link. There are also **bus** and **ferry** services. Weekly and other period passes are available, as are multi-journey tickets. The Sydney Explorer Bus stops at over 20 attractions on its route and visitors can join or leave it at any point. A special *Sydney Pass,* valid for three days, offers unlimited travel in Sydney on buses, ferries, harbour cruises, the Sydney Explorer Bus and the Airport Express Bus for A$35.

ACCOMMODATION

HOTELS: Sydney offers excellent hotels run by all the international chains, and many medium to small houses. Further outside the city you can stay on one of the sheep stations to the west of the capital amongst some of the best sheep country in the world. The State is well travelled by the native Australians, and so offers an excellent network of accommodation outside the larger cities, mostly of motel or similar class.

CAMPING/CARAVANNING: A number of companies can arrange **motor camper** rentals, with a range of fully equipped vehicles. Full details can be obtained from the Tourist Board.

Note: For more detailed coverage of the range of accommodation available in Australia, see the *Accommodation* section in the general entry for Australia above.

RESORTS & EXCURSIONS

New South Wales is perhaps the most varied of all the States; the landscape ranges from snow-capped mountains with excellent skiing facilities to long, golden sandy beaches, and from the utter emptiness of the Outback to the cosmopolitan vitality of the State capital.

Sydney: The State capital is perhaps best known abroad for the *Opera House,* a building whose distinctive shape is echoed by the sails of the boats in the almost equally famous harbour. Tours of the Opera House are available every day (0900-1600), except Christmas Day and Good Friday. Sydney is also a major commercial and business centre with first-class conference and exhibition facilities. The city centre skyline rivals that of Manhattan, with the added attraction that Sydney is far more likely to be seen under a clear blue sky. There is a spectacular view of the city and its surroundings from the 305m-high (1000ft) *Sydney Tower* above the Centrepoint Shopping Complex (opening times: 0930-2130 Monday to Friday; 0900-1130 Saturday). The city itself is also the home of more than enough concert halls, museums, art galleries and theatres to lay the ghost forever of Australia as a cultural wasteland. Among the many other interesting sights Sydney has to offer are the *Taronga Zoo,* the *Royal Botanic Gardens,* the *Harbour Bridge*, the *Art Gallery of New South Wales*, the *Australian Museum* and *The Rocks* area (the birthplace of the country) now restored to its original state – cobbled streets, gas lamps, craft shops and tiny restaurants. Apart from exploring the various quarters on foot, such as *Chinatown, Paddington, Kings Cross,* all bustling with life 24 hours a day, and *Darling Harbour*, Sydney's premier urban development project featuring exhibition halls, museums, gardens, an aquarium, restaurants and a shopping complex, the city can also be enjoyed from the water with numerous harbour cruises departing from Circular Quay. Other ways of seeing the city are from the bright red *Sydney Explorer* Bus which stops at 20 popular tourist spots on its 18km (11-mile) loop around the city or from the monorail train. Sydney is also justly famous for its many excellent beaches in and around the city, such as *Manly*, to the north (15 minutes by hydrofoil), or *Watson's Bay*, to the south. Most beaches are within reach of public transport. For reasons of safety, swim in the areas marked with flags only.

Nearby *Botany Bay*, the first foothold of British settlers, is still a botanist's delight with mangrove swamps and native wildlife.

Outside Sydney: New South Wales caters for all kinds of holiday, whatever the time of year. The region of *Mount Kosciusko* and the *Snowy Mountains* in the southeast of the State is popular during the skiing season (June to September). In summer bushwalking is a popular activity in this region; cruises are offered to *Grace Lea Island* on *Lake Eucumbene*. Resorts in the Snowy Mountain region include *Charlotte Pass, Guthega, Perisher Valley, Thredbo* and *Smiggin Holes*. For those in search of sun, the beaches in the State are excellent – Sydney's famous surf beaches of *Bondi*, *Avalon* and *Palm Beach* are matched by the resorts to the south and to the north above Port Jackson. Visits to the *Hunter Valley* wine district and the **Kuring-gai Chase National Park** with its Koala Sanctuary are also recommended. To the west of Sydney are the *Blue Mountains* and the **Warrumbungle National Park** with its bizarre rock outcrops. *Lightning Ridge*, to the northwest, is a frontier town where the world's only source of black opal is to be found. *Broken Hill*, close to the State frontier with South Australia, is another mining town, now with golf courses, swimming pools and bowling clubs. 113km (70 miles) from the town, by a good road, are the *Menindee Lakes,* an area of water eight times the size of Sydney Harbour and a major attraction for motor boat and sailing craft owners.

SYDNEY

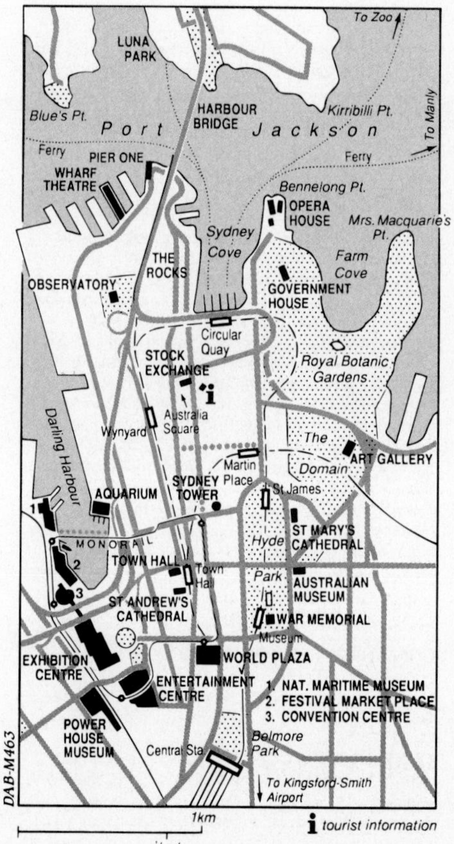

To Zoo
LUNA PARK
HARBOUR BRIDGE
Kirribilli Pt.
To Manly
Blue's Pt.
Port Jackson
Ferry
PIER ONE
Ferry
WHARF THEATRE
Bennelong Pt.
OPERA HOUSE
Mrs. Macquarie's Pt.
Sydney Cove
Farm Cove
THE ROCKS
OBSERVATORY
GOVERNMENT HOUSE
Circular Quay
STOCK EXCHANGE
Royal Botanic Gardens
Darling Harbour
Australia Square
Wynyard
The Domain
ART GALLERY
Martin Place
SYDNEY TOWER
St James
AQUARIUM
ST MARY'S CATHEDRAL
MONORAIL
Hyde Park
TOWN HALL
Town Hall
AUSTRALIAN MUSEUM
ST ANDREW'S CATHEDRAL
WAR MEMORIAL
Museum
WORLD PLAZA
EXHIBITION CENTRE
ENTERTAINMENT CENTRE
1. NAT. MARITIME MUSEUM
2. FESTIVAL MARKET PLACE
3. CONVENTION CENTRE
POWER HOUSE MUSEUM
Central Sta
Belmore Park
To Kingsford-Smith Airport
DAB-M463
1km
½ml
i tourist information

Norfolk Island: Situated 1400km (870 miles) off the east coast of Australia, Norfolk Island is best reached by plane from Sydney. Its history as a penal colony has left the island with some of Australia's finest Georgian colonial architecture. Many of the island's small population are directly related to the mutineers of *HMS Bounty* who settled in the area. A variety of accommodation is available. **Note:** Norfolk Island comes under the control of the Australian government not New South Wales.

Lord Howe Island: Situated 700km (400 miles) northeast of Sydney, Lord Howe Island is made up of 1300 sq hectares of both rich lowland and mountains covered with lush vegetation, surrounded by white sandy beaches. It also has the southernmost coral reef in the world and boasts some of the rarest flora, bird and marine life.

SOCIAL PROFILE

FOOD & DRINK: International cuisine, with local speciality seafood. Fine red and white wines from the Hunter Valley.

NIGHTLIFE: The Kings Cross area of Sydney is an exciting nightlife area. There are also some night-time cruises offering dinner and dancing. Sydney is known as a city that never sleeps.

SHOPPING: Best buys are Australian opals and gemstones, Aboriginal arts and crafts, and woollen and sheepskin goods. In Sydney, shops are open 0830-1730 Monday to Friday and 0830-1600 Saturday, and many shops also stay open until 2100 Thursday and 1000-1600 Sunday.

SPORT: The coastline of New South Wales has some of the best **surfing** conditions in the world, stretching for over 2000km (1250 miles) to the north and south of Sydney, and the port itself has facilities for all kinds of **maritime sports.** Of note is the annual **boat race** from Sydney to Hobart in Tasmania in December, covering over 2000km (1250 miles). South of Sydney are the mountains of the Great Dividing Range, with Australia's highest mountain, Mount Kosciusko, at 2139m (7314ft), offering **skiing** from June to September.

SPECIAL EVENTS: The following is a selection of festivals and special events taking place in New South Wales:

Mar 11-12 '95 *Myall Prawn Festival.* **Apr 7-18** *Royal Easter Show,* Sydney. **Apr 13-17** *Griffith Food & Wine Festival.* **Apr 14** *Sydney Garden Festival.* **Jun 8** *Bounty Day,* Norfolk Island. **Aug 12-20** *Australian Safari Race,* Sydney to Darwin. **Aug 27** *Sydney Marathon.* **Sep 1-30** *Hunter Valley Wine and Food Fair.* **Sep** *Mudgee Wine Festival.* **Sep 29-Oct 2** *Manly Jazz Festival.* **Nov 4-10** *Snowy Mountains Trout Festival,* Cooma. **Nov 16-19** *Australian PGA 1995,* Sydney. **Nov 19** *Glebe Street Fair,* Sydney. **Nov 24-26** *Australian Bush Music Festival,* Glen Innes. **Nov 26** *Sydney Christmas Parade.* **Nov 30-Dec 3** *Greg Norman's Golf Classic,* Hornsby. **Dec 31 '95-Feb 6 '96** *Sydney Festival and Carnivale,* Sydney. **Jan 20-28** *Australian Flat Land Hang Gliding Championships,* Forbes. **Mar 29-Apr 9** *Royal Easter Show,* Sydney. **Apr 5-8** *Griffith Food and Wine Festival,* Griffith.

For a full list of special events, contact Tourism New South Wales.

BUSINESS PROFILE

COMMERCIAL INFORMATION: The following organisation can offer advice: State Chamber of Commerce, PO Box 4280, 83 Clarence Street, GPO Sydney, NSW 2001. Tel: (2) 350 8100. Fax: (2) 350 8199. Telex: 127113.

CONFERENCES/CONVENTIONS: Sydney has launched a major initiative to become an important convention and meeting destination. The Sydney Convention and Exhibition Centre at Darling Harbour has facilities for up to 5000 people. Other major convention centres include Centrepoint Exhibition and Convention Centre, University of NSW, RAS Exhibition Centre, Sydney Opera House, Powerhouse Museum, Sydney Town Hall, University of Sydney, YWCA, Queen Victoria Building, Bankstown Town Hall, Bondi Surf Bathers' Life Saving Club, Curzon Hall, Film Australia, Hills Centre, Taronga Centre and the NSW Harness Racing Club. For more information on conferences and conventions in NSW contact the

Australian Tourist Commission *or* the Sydney Convention & Visitors Bureau in London (see address above) *or* the Sydney Convention & Visitors Bureau in New South Wales, Level 5, 80 William Street, Woolloomooloo, NSW 2011. Tel: (2) 331 4045. Fax: (2) 360 1223.

CLIMATE

Warm semi-tropical summers particularly in lower central area. Mountain areas in the west are cooler, particularly in winter. Rainfall is heaviest from March to June.

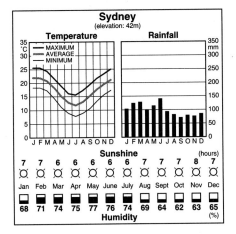

Sydney (elevation: 42m)

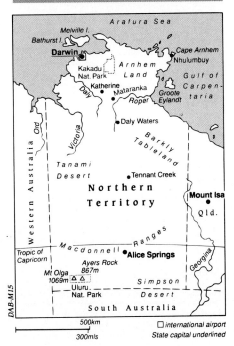

Northern Territory

Northern Territory Tourist Commission
PO Box 1155, 3rd and 4th Floors, Tourism House, 43 Mitchell Street, Darwin, NT 0801, Australia
Tel: (89) 893 900. Fax: (89) 893 888.
Northern Territory Tourist Commission
612 Kingston Road, London SW20 8DN
Tel: (0181) 544 9845. Fax: (0181) 544 9843.
Northern Territory Tourist Commission
Suite 204, 5855 Greenvalley Circle, Culver City, CA 90230
Tel: (310) 645 9875. Fax: (310) 645 9876.

AREA: 1,346,200 sq km (836,659 sq miles).
POPULATION: 166,700 (1991 estimate).
POPULATION DENSITY: 0.1 per sq km.
CAPITAL: Darwin. **Population:** 73,300 (1990 estimate).
GEOGRAPHY: A wilderness roughly 1670km (1038

miles) north–south and 1000km (620 miles) east–west, the Northern Territory comprises nearly one-sixth of Australia. The geography of the Northern Territory is the closest to the popular image of the Great Australian Outback.
The northern area centred on the capital, **Darwin**, is tropical with rich vegetation and a varied coastline. Beyond Darwin, 200km (125 miles) east, is World Heritage-listed **Kakadu National Park,** which is part of the 12,600 sq km (4500 sq-mile) area of Arnhem Land. It is an area of vast flood plains and rocky escarpments steeped in natural and cultural heritage. Aboriginal peoples have lived here for at least 40,000 years. Katherine township is 350km (220 miles) from Darwin and a further 30km (20 miles) northeast is **Katherine Gorge National Park** with 13 gorges towering up to 60m (200ft) high.
The southern part of the Northern Territory is centred on the town of **Alice Springs**, which is almost at the geographical centre of Australia and the starting point of many of the Red Centre's unique and natural wonders, including Ayers Rock and the Uluru National Park. Other notable features of the Red Centre are King's Canyon, Ross River, Trephina, Ormiston and Glen Helen Gorge, the Olgas near Ayers Rock and the Devil's Marbles at Tennant Creek. There are also other parks and reserves with abundant bird and animal life.
TIME: GMT + 9.5.

PUBLIC HOLIDAYS

The Northern Territory observes all the public holidays observed nationwide (see the main entry for Australia above) and, in addition, the following are observed:
Apr 15 '95 Easter Saturday. **May 1** May Day. **Jun 12** Queen's Birthday. **Aug 7** Picnic Day. **Dec 26** Boxing Day. **Apr 6 '96** Easter Saturday.

TRAVEL

AIR: The Northern Territory can be reached by international flights to Darwin from the UK, Singapore, Bangkok, Bali, Brunei and Timor. At present there are six international carriers operating to the Northern Territory. Flying time from the United Kingdom is approximately 22 hours, from Singapore approximately 3 hours, from Bangkok approximately 5 hours, from Bali approximately 90 minutes, from Brunei approximately 4 hours and from Timor approximately 2 hours. Connections are available from most Asian ports. *Darwin Airport* is 8km (5 miles) from the city centre (travel time – approximately 15 minutes).
Alice Springs Airport is 12km (7.5 miles) from the city centre (travel time – approximately 20 minutes).
There are three domestic airlines (*Australian Airlines, Ansett* and *East-West*) that cover the Territory from all capital cities within Australia with connections from most other towns. Smaller commuter airlines connect some of the remoter areas within the Territory.
SEA: International cruise lines call at Darwin, the Northern Territory's only large port.
RAIL: The main rail service to the Territory is by the *Ghan* from Adelaide which reaches only as far as Alice Springs. There is no internal network.
ROAD: There are three main highways serving the Northern Territory: the *Stuart Highway*, south to Adelaide, Canberra, Melbourne and Sydney; the *Barkly Highway*, east to Mount Isa and Queensland; and the *Victoria Highway*, west to join an unsealed road running across the top of the Western Desert which runs on to Perth. Off these roads there are many uncharted rough tracks often only suitable for 4-wheel-drive vehicles, and often ending in impassable desert. The dangers of travelling off main roads in the Northern Territory without a qualified guide cannot be stressed too strongly. **Coach:** The national coach services are run by *Ansett Pioneer, Greyhound* and *Bus Australia,* all of which serve the main townships within the Territory with direct services to all capital cities. Well-equipped coaches take over 92 hours to cover the distance from Darwin to Sydney; from Darwin, coaches depart daily to Kakadu National Park (travel time – 4 hours and 50 minutes) and to Alice Springs (travel time – 19 hours).
URBAN: There are local bus services in Darwin and Alice Springs Monday to Saturday. Darwin Harbour ferries operate Monday to Friday.

ACCOMMODATION

The *Northern Territory Holiday Planner,* published by the Northern Territory Tourist Commission, gives details of tours, holidays and accommodation in the Territory.

HOTEL: International standard hotels are found in Darwin, Alice Springs and Ayers Rock, and a good standard of hotel and motel accommodation can be found in all the major tourist areas and centres of population.
LODGE/MOTEL: Lodges and budget motels are available in some of the remote areas.
CAMPING/CARAVANNING: The Northern Territory contains some of the most inhospitable country in the world. From Alice Springs the nearest major town, in any direction, is 1000km (620 miles) away; clearly, any car or caravan must be in prime mechanical condition. During the wet season from November to April, travel in the Outback is advisable only in suitable cross-country vehicles, as many conventional roads become impassable for ordinary cars. The *Stuart Highway* between Darwin and Alice Springs and through to Adelaide in South Australia is a fully sealed road accessible all year. A number of companies can arrange **motor camper** rentals, with a range of fully equipped vehicles. Full details can be obtained from the Tourist Commission.

RESORTS & EXCURSIONS

The Northern Territory is a huge and diverse region. The north, the 'Top End' of Australia, is subtropical, with such high rainfall in the rainy season that much of it is accessible only by air. The south of the Territory is an arid desert, known as the 'Red Centre'.
Aboriginal lands and sacred sites: There are many places and objects in the Territory that are of special significance to the Aboriginal people and laws protecting these sacred sites carry heavy penalties for entering, damaging or defacing them. It is necessary to obtain a permit before entering Aboriginal lands. These permits are not issued lightly, nor are they generally issued for touristic purposes. Some areas that have historic significance to the Aborigines *are* open to the public (for example, Ayers Rock and Corroboree Rock near Alice Springs, and Ubirr Rock in Kakadu National Park – see below). Visitors are welcome at these places, but due respect should be shown for the site and its historical significance. For further information, maps and permit applications advice, contact the Tourist Commission at their London office.

The Top End

The territorial capital, **Darwin**, which was savaged by Cyclone Tracy on Christmas Eve 1974, has been rebuilt as a modern provincial city. Darwin and the rest of the Top End have two distinct seasons. In the summer or 'Wet' season, from November to April, monsoon conditions mean late afternoon thunderstorms, high humidity and heavy downpours. This is the green season when the waterfalls flow and the wildlife abounds. From May through to October is the 'Dry' season, with unlimited sunshine and balmy evenings. The wetlands begin to dry out, confining the bird and animal life to ever smaller areas.
The Top End is the area to see lush tropical vegetation, either in Darwin's *Botanical Gardens,* the *Crocodile Farm* just outside Darwin, the Territory's various National Parks, or at **Katherine Gorge** on the road south (see below). Also south of Darwin are the **Howard Springs** and **Berry Springs Nature Parks, Territory Wild Life Park** and the **Fogg Dam Bird Sanctuary**. There are many good opportunities for swimming and fishing near the city, for example at Mindil Beach, Mandorah Beach or Fannre Bay.
KAKADU NATIONAL PARK: This may be found about a 2-hour drive to the east of Darwin down the Arnhem Highway. The park includes the flood plains between the Wildman and the Alligator rivers which empty into Van Diemen Gulf to the north. It is bordered by the **Arnhem Land escarpment**, where the spectacular waterfalls of *Jim Jim* and *Twin Falls* cascade hundreds of feet into crystal clear rock pools below. At **Ubirr** (Obiri Rock) and **Nourlangie Rock** are fascinating galleries of Aboriginal rock painting, many dating back over 20,000 years. These paintings show mythical and spiritual figures and an ancient lifestyle which still holds great significance for the Aboriginal people today.
Within the park there are three resort-style hotels and a number of camping and caravan sites from which to explore this beautiful area. Numerous creeks, rivers and *billabongs* provide excellent fishing, particularly for the much prized *barramundi*, which is found in abundance here. Thousands of birds inhabit the wetlands – over 260 species – and wildlife abounds throughout the year. Aerial tours over the Arnhem Land escarpment depart daily and local fishing trips can be easily arranged. A popular way to explore the waterways is on a boat cruise on the *South Alligator River* or scenic *Yellow Waters,* giving access to nature at its best. It is possible to spot

crocodiles basking on the riverbanks, buffaloes wallowing in the mud, and the graceful *jabiru* (Australia's only stork) wading amongst the water lilies. Kakadu National Park is the habitat for all wildlife common to Northern Australia and as such provides a diverse and exciting experience in the tropical Top End. Tours and safaris from 2 to 21 days are available by air, coach or 4-wheel-drive from Darwin.

KATHERINE GORGE/NITMILUK NATIONAL PARK: The township of Katherine is in the area known as the 'Never Never' about 350km (220 miles) southeast of Darwin. This is pioneer territory, made famous by Mrs Aeneas Gunn in her book *We of the Never Never*. This is the centre of a thriving beef cattle industry and the *Old Elsey* and *Springvale Homesteads* are monuments to the Outback settlers who founded the original township.

Katherine Gorge, some 30km (20 miles) northeast of the town, is one of Australia's great natural wonders and the famous boat cruises through the spectacular gorges, towering up to 60m (200ft) high, are a highlight of any visit to the region. There are in fact 13 gorges and each has its own glowing colours and fascinating outcrops, steep canyon walls above cool, blue waters. Marked walking tracks are well maintained for easy access to features of interest in the park. Canoeing, swimming and boat tours are all available along with scenic helicopter rides over the gorges. There is a good range of accommodation both in the town and Nitmiluk National Park and campers and caravanners are also well catered for.

The Red Centre

Alice Springs is located in what is almost the geographic centre of the continent. A pleasant solid town, set in red desert country, it is a popular tourist resort and a base for exploring the wonders of the Outback. There are many excellent hotels and motels, a casino, a variety of restaurants and varied sporting facilities ranging from golf and tennis to hot-air ballooning and tandem parachuting.

The *Royal Flying Doctor Base* is open most days to the public (excluding Sundays and public holidays) and the *School of the Air* is operational during the school term; visiting hours are 1330-1530 Monday to Friday. There are also museums and preserved buildings which help the visitor to appreciate the history of this remote town. Not least among these are the *Dreamtime Gallery* and the *Centre for Aboriginal Artists and Craftsmen*. The *Old Telegraph Station,* 3km (2 miles) north of the town, is an historical reserve featuring original buildings, restored equipment and an illustrated display including early photographs, papers and documents.

The region around Alice Springs is pitted with colourful gorges, canyons, valley pools and awe-inspiring chasms. These include **Stanley Chasm**, 50km (30 miles) west of Alice, **Glen Helen Gorge**, 140km (9 miles) west, **Ormiston Gorge**, 130km (80 miles) west, **Kings Canyon**, 310km (186 miles) and **N'Dhala Gorge**, 90km (5.5 miles) east, which is also notable for its ancient rock engravings. **Palm Valley** lies around an hour's drive to the southwest and **Rainbow Valley** to the southeast on the edge of the **Simpson Desert**.

Anzac Hill lies just behind Alice Springs and provides a panoramic view of the town and surrounding ranges. **Château Hornsby**, the Northern Territory's only vineyard, is situated approximately 15km (9 miles) from the town centre and is an unusual venue for barbecues, Outback evenings, Aboriginal Corroborees and even camel safaris.

AYERS ROCK: Alice Springs is also the base for tours to **Ayers Rock** (about 450km (280 miles) or five hours drive away) and the East and Western **MacDonnell Ranges.** Ayers Rock is the world's largest monolith and plays an important part in Aboriginal mythology in which it is known as 'Uluru' and is believed to have been created by ancestors of the Aborigines. Visitors may climb the rock or explore some of the fascinating caves at its base. Sunset and sunrise must be seen as the sun's rays change the rock's colour from blazing orange to red and even deep purple, depending on the atmospheric conditions.

14km (9 miles) from Ayers Rock is the **Ayers Rock Resort** – a village built to cater for the rapidly growing number of visitors to the area. The resort contains two top-class hotels, lodges, self-catering maisonettes, shops, bank, post office, caravan park and campsites and caters for all the needs of the traveller. Tours depart throughout the day for the Rock and the nearby **Olgas**, as well as other points of interest.

Ayers Rock has its own airport with five daily flights to Alice Springs and direct connections to Sydney and other Australian cities. Car hire is available and all major coach companies service Ayers Rock on a daily basis.

Other points of interest in the Red Centre include Aboriginal tours to **Ipolera** and **Pitjantjatjara** country; and the **Ross River Homestead** for horseriding, log cabins and Outback ambience.

SOCIAL PROFILE

FOOD: *Barramundi* is the local speciality.
NIGHTLIFE: There is plenty of exciting nightlife in Darwin, which also offers the *Diamond Beach Casino,* built in an extraordinary modern architectural style. This 30-million-dollar casino complex also encompasses luxury accommodation, restaurants, discos and sporting and convention facilities and is surrounded by lush gardens perched along the shores of Mindil Beach. Alice Springs also has a casino.
SHOPPING: Darwin specialties include Aboriginal artefacts and Outback clothing. Aboriginal items, bush clothing and opals are available in Alice Springs.
SPECIAL EVENTS: The following is a selection of festivals and special events taking place in the Northern Territory:
Mar 24-25 '95 *Central Australia Expo '95,* Alice Springs. **Apr 23-30** *Heritage Week,* Alice Springs. **Apr 29-May 6** *National Dance Week,* Alice Springs, Darwin, Katherine, Tennant Creek and Nhulunbuy. **May 6-13** *Arafura Sports Festival,* Darwin. **Jun 10-11** *Red Cross Canoe Marathon,* Katherine. **Jun 30-Jul 2** *NT Expo,* Darwin. **Jul 1-Aug 7** *Darwin Cup Carnival 1995* (horseracing). **Jul 7-8** *Alice Springs Show,* Adelaide River. **Jul 15** *Lions Camel Cup,* Alice Springs. **Jul 19-22** *Katherine Show.* **Jul 27-29** *Royal Darwin Show.* **Aug 6** *Darwin Beer Can Regatta.* **Aug 19-Sep 10** *Northern Territory Art Award,* Alice Springs. **Sep 2** *Spring Flower Show,* Tennant Creek. **Sep 24-30** *Schweppes Australian Universities Games,* Darwin. **Oct 17** *Henley-on-Todd,* Alice Springs. **Oct 25-Nov 12** *World Solar Challenge,* Darwin.
For a full list of special events contact the Northern Territory Tourist Commission.

BUSINESS PROFILE

COMMERCIAL INFORMATION: The following organisation can offer advice: Northern Territory Government Department of Industry and Development Central Offiice, Development House, PO Box 4160, Darwin, Northern Territory. Tel: (89) 895 755. Fax: (89) 894 382.
CONFERENCES/CONVENTIONS: Major convention centres in Darwin are The Beaufort Hotel, Darwin Performing Arts Centre, Diamond Beach Hotel Casino, Marrara International Indoor Sports Stadium and the Sheraton Darwin. In Alice Springs, the major convention centres are Arulen Arts Centre and Sheraton Alice Springs. There are also a number of resort convention facilities outside the cities, such as the Sheraton Ayers Rock and Yulara Resort. For more information on conferences and conventions in the Northern Territory contact the Australian Tourist Commission *or* the Northern Territory Convention Bureau, 67 Stuart Highway North, Alice Springs, NT. Tel: (89) 518 555. Fax: (89) 518 550.

CLIMATE

Hot most of the year; the coastal areas have heavy monsoonal rain November to March.
Required clothing: Lightweight cottons and linens most of the year. Waterproofing is necessary in the northern areas during the wet season. A warm sweater or jacket is advised for the Centre during winter months, as evenings can be quite cool.

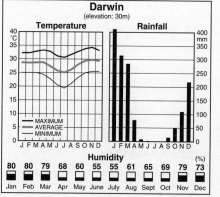

Darwin
(elevation: 30m)

Temperature	Rainfall

— MAXIMUM
— AVERAGE
— MINIMUM

Humidity

Jan	Feb	Mar	Apr	May	June	July	Aug	Sept	Oct	Nov	Dec	(%)
80	80	79	68	60	55	55	61	65	69	79	73	

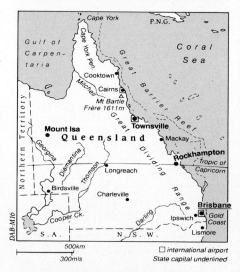

Queensland

International airport
State capital underlined

500km
300mls

Queensland Tourist and Travel Corporation
36th Floor, Riverside Centre, 123 Eagle Street, Brisbane, QLD 4000, Australia
Tel: (7) 833 5400. Fax: (7) 833 5479.
Queensland Tourist and Travel Corporation
Queensland House, 392 The Strand, London WC2R 0LZ
Tel: (0171) 240 0525. Fax: (0171) 836 5881.
Queensland Tourist and Travel Corporation
Suite 330, 3rd Floor, Northrop Plaza, 1800 Century Park East, Los Angeles, CA 90067
Tel: (310) 788 0997. Fax: (310) 788 0128.

AREA: 1,727,000 sq km (107,334 sq miles).
POPULATION: 2,996,100 (1991 estimate).
POPULATION DENSITY: 1.7 per sq km.
CAPITAL: Brisbane. **Population:** 1,327,000 (1991).
GEOGRAPHY: Two and a half times the size of Texas or six times the size of the United Kingdom, more than half of Queensland lies above the Tropic of Capricorn, and it is known as the 'Sunshine State'. Within its borders are the Great Barrier Reef, numerous resort islands, endless kilometres of golden sandy beaches, national park forests, vast plains, lush rainforests, forested mountains and massive wilderness areas for safari touring.
TIME: GMT + 10.

PUBLIC HOLIDAYS

Queensland observes all the public holidays observed nationwide (see the main entry for Australia above) and, in addition, the following are observed:
Apr 15 '95 Easter Saturday. **May 1** Labour Day. **Jun 12** Queen's Birthday. **Dec 26** Boxing Day. **Apr 6 '96** Easter Saturday.

TRAVEL

AIR: The international airport at *Brisbane* is Eagle Farm. Approximate flying time from London is 24 hours. The airport is 13km (8 miles) northeast of the city centre (travel time – approximately 35 minutes). Flights from Europe, Asia, the Far East, New Zealand, Canada and the USA all land at Eagle Farm. International travellers can land directly at *Townsville* – 5km (3 miles) from the city – on flights from Europe, Asia, New Zealand and the Far East. Queensland's third international airport is *Cairns,* 6km (4 miles) from the city. It is an excellent gateway both to the Great Barrier Reef and the tropical north, also hosting flights from Europe, Asia, the Far East, New Zealand, Canada and the USA.
For more flight details see the *Travel* section in the general introduction for Australia above.
The extensive internal airline system means that Queensland is connected with nearly all major Australian gateways. Brisbane is connected directly to Sydney, Melbourne, Adelaide, Alice Springs and Darwin, as well as having interstate connections with Cairns, Mount Isa, Townsville and other smaller airstrips. Cairns and Townsville also offer easy connections to the rest of Australia. The two major domestic airlines are *Australian Airlines* and *Sunstate Airlines*. Airlines such as *Lloyd Air, Seair Pacific* and *Sunstate* offer charter flights and feeder

services to Queensland's main towns and Barrier Reef island resorts.

RAIL: Queensland has its own railway system, the main route being the *Sunlander* and the *Queenslander* which connects the coast from Brisbane to Cairns. In addition, other services, such as the *Inlander, Westlander, Midlander* and *Capricornian* open up the Outback to travellers. The 'Sunshine Railpass' allows unlimited travel on Queensland's rail routes. Passes are valid for 14, 21 and 31 days in first- or economy-class, offering excellent travel facilities for those intending extensive travel throughout the State.

ROAD: There is a high standard of highways and road networks offering easy connections between towns and cities. The *Bruce Highway* runs down the whole east coast from Cairns to Brisbane and continues into New South Wales. An extensive coach network offers an easy and cheap way of getting around. The tropical inland areas can be explored with 4-wheel-drive vehicles, many of the interior roads being unsealed. Four-wheel-drive vehicles and guided self-drive tours are available. The other main highways running into the interior are the *Capricorn Highway* (Rockhampton–Winton), the *Flinders Highway* (Townsville–Mount Isa, connecting with the network in the Northern Territory) and the *Warrego Highway* (Brisbane–Charleville). The *Mitchell* and *Landsborough Highways,* which in places have unsealed road surfaces, run roughly north–south, connecting the main east–west highways and terminating at Sydney. The *Newell Highway* runs inland between Brisbane and Melbourne.

URBAN: Brisbane's electrified **rail** system is easy to use for suburban services, particularly cross-river. There are also cross-river **ferries**, and a comprehensive **bus** network with zonal fares and 10-journey pre-purchase fares obtainable through newsagents. Day and other period tickets are also available. The *City Sights Bus* stops at 20 places of interest around the city for A$9 (adult) and A$5 (children). In Cairns, bus services operate Monday to Saturday and there is a touring bus, *Cairns Red Explorer,* that departs from the Transit Centre. **Taxis** are also available.

ACCOMMODATION

HOTELS: International standard hotels are available in Brisbane, Cairns and the Gold Coast together with a high standard of hotel/motel accommodation throughout the State. Information about prices and location of accommodation can be obtained through the Queensland Tourist and Travel Corporation office.

MOTELS: Motels are usually in or on the outskirts of towns and cities and normally offer self-contained rooms at reasonable rates.

SELF-CONTAINED APARTMENTS: These are available throughout the larger resort areas and offer a variety of facilities.

FARMSTAYS/HOMESTAYS: 'Holiday Host' services operate throughout Australia, matching hosts with visitors, in stations, family homes and farm properties.

YOUTH HOSTELS: Budget dormitory-style accommodation is available throughout Queensland.

CAMPING/CARAVANNING: Parks are located in tourist areas around Queensland, and offer facilities of varying standards. Camping is permitted in parks, but permission must be sought from the National Parks Association of Queensland, PO Box 1040, Fortune House, 10/45 Black Street, Milton, QLD 4064. Tel: (7) 367 0878. Fax: (7) 367 0890. A number of companies can arrange **motor camper** rentals, with a range of fully equipped vehicles. Full details can be obtained from the Tourist Board.

Note: More detailed coverage of the range of accommodation available in Australia may be found by consulting the *Accommodation* section in the general entry for Australia above.

RESORTS & EXCURSIONS

Brisbane is the economic hub and State capital of Queensland, with a year-round warm subtropical climate. It is Australia's fastest growing city, a fact which is due almost entirely to the 'discovery' of the region as a holiday paradise, providing easy access to adjacent coastal resorts. In addition to being a gateway to sun, sand, surf and coral, Brisbane itself offers many attractions. Probably the most famous of these is the *Lone Pine Koala Sanctuary,* situated on the slopes above the River Brisbane. The *Botanic Gardens* and *Bunya Park* are also splendid wildlife areas. *Queensland Maritime Museum,* located on Stanley Street in the city's 19th-century dry dock area, offers historic boats and nautical relics. *The City Hall* in King George Square houses an art gallery, museum and library. Other buildings of note include the *State Parliament House* with its glittering copper roof, *St John's Cathedral, The Mansions* and the

Old Windmill, the city's oldest surviving building and once a treadmill worked by convicts. Brisbane is also the cultural centre of the State, attracting major artists and exhibitions to its galleries, museums and entertainment centres. Visits to the *Queensland Museum* in Bowen Bridge Road, and to the art gallery at the *Department of Aboriginal and Islanders Advancement* are recommended for those wishing to learn about the cultural, artistic and scientific history of the State. Brisbane's newest attraction is *South Bank Park,* on the site of the 1988 World Expo and now a leisure entertainment centre with an interesting Butterfly House, Rainforest Display and an enormous outdoor swimming lake. Outdoor festivals are another major attraction, with themes such as *Ekka* (Royal National Exhibition) and *Warana* (Fun in the Sun). The city now boasts 7-day shopping.

The Gold Coast, probably the best beach area in the country, comprises 42km (26 miles) of white surfing beaches, theme parks *(Sea World, Movie World* and *Dream World),* a casino, hotels and restaurants. It has year-round sunshine and lively tourist facilities. Surfing and swimming are popular at *Surfers Paradise* beach. Inland are lush green mountains, rainforests, walking trails and scenic villages.

An hour's drive northwards from Brisbane, the **Sunshine Coast** offers miles of unspoilt beaches, untouched wilderness, lakes and mountains.

A visit to the **Glasshouse Mountains** is recommended, particularly for the artist or photographer. Nature-lovers will also appreciate the **Lamington National Park** in the McPherson Mountains, and the **Currumbin Bird Sanctuary,** 80km (50 miles) south of Brisbane.

Charters Towers is 135km (85 miles) west of Townsville, with restored old buildings dating back to the town's gold-mining heyday in the 1870s.

Cairns is the major gateway to the far north. As well as the Barrier Reef (see below), there are rainforests in the **Atherton Tableland** to the west and to the south is **Mission Beach** with 14km (9 miles) of white sandy beaches, looking out to **Dunk Island.** To the north, there is the charming old town of **Port Douglas** which attracts many visitors, as well as **Daintree,** and its daily barge service to **Cape Tribulation National Park,** and **Cooktown,** close to **Endeavour National Park** where excellent examples of Aboriginal rock art can be found, and beyond that is the wilderness of **Cape York Peninsula** to be explored. **Townsville** is North Queensland's largest tropical city, boasting an international airport and a casino. Cruises are available to nearby islands and trips to the Barrier Reef (see below) for diving, walking or white-water rafting. This pleasant city, its streets lined with palm trees and tropical flora, has a number of interesting attractions on offer, such as *Great Barrier Reef Wonderland,* the largest coral aquarium in the world, with a transparent walk-in tunnel, and *Magnetic Island,* a resort island with superb beaches, an aquarium, bushwalking trackings and a koala sanctuary only 13km (7 miles) offshore and a 25-minute ferry ride from the city centre.

GREAT BARRIER REEF: This playground and beauty spot is also one of the world's great natural wonders. It stretches for 2000km (1240 miles) along the Queensland coast, its width varying from 25km (15 miles) to 50km (30 miles). There is unique plant and animal life to be found with visibility often as deep as 60m (200ft). Dotted along the coast are 25 island resorts, lying on or between the Barrier Reef and the mainland. For the serious reef enthusiast, Heron or Lady Elliot Islands at **Coral Cays** are renowned as the best diving spots on the reef. **Lizard, Bedarra** and **Orpheus Islands** are quiet, secluded and luxurious hideaways. **Hayman Island** is an international resort, with 5-star luxury facilities. **Radisson Resort, Great Keppel Islands, South Molle, Hamilton** and **Lindeman Island** are all-year round resorts with facilities for families. **Quoin Island** in Gladstone Harbour also caters for families. Tropical **Dunk Island** and **Brampton Island** are popular with honeymooners. **Fitzroy, Newry** and **Hinchinbrook Islands** offer unspoilt beauty, and **Hook, Palm Bay, Wapparaburra Haven** and **Great Keppel Island** have camping facilities. Outside the main reef areas, the islands of **Fraser, Moreton, Bribie, North and South Stradbroke** offer some of the best unpopulated surfing beaches and national parks in Australia.

SOCIAL PROFILE

FOOD & DRINK: The food of the area relies to a large extent on the sea and the subtropical climate for specialities in cuisine. Local delicacies include mud crabs, king and tiger prawns, mackerel and fresh *barramundi,* as well as avocados, mangoes, pawpaws, pineapples, strawberries, bananas and the highly recommended local speciality, the *macadamia nut.* In Fortitude Valley, just out of Brisbane city centre, there are a number of European, Asian and Chinese

restaurants. Brisbane is supplied with local wines from vineyards at Stanthorpe to the southwest, producing both red and white wines, and from other Australian vineyards. All beers on sale are brewed locally.

NIGHTLIFE: Although much of the tourist activity is centred on the beaches and the Barrier Reef, Brisbane offers a wide selection of entertainment. Most of the large hotels have dinner and dancing facilities and there are several nightclubs in the city, especially in Southbank Parklands where discos and restaurants abound. The Gold Coast has many nightclubs, as well as Jupiter's Casino. Townsville has the spectacular Sheraton Breakwater Casino on Sir Leslie Thiess Drive, offering a full range of gaming facilities and high-quality entertainment.

SPORT: The geographic proximity to the Barrier Reef and the long stretches of golden beaches in Queensland mean predominant leisure pursuits are associated with the sea. The range is wide, from **surfing** off the beaches to **scuba diving** on the corals of the Reef; **deep-sea fishing** for black marlin and **sailing** round the islands. There are many **golf** courses throughout the State. **Squash** and **tennis** are both popular sports, as is **bushwalking;** the Brisbane Bushwalking Club, PO Box 4051, 2 Alderley Avenue, Brisbane, QLD, tel: (7) 856 4050, can supply details.

SPECIAL EVENTS: The following is a selection of festivals and special events taking place in Queensland: **May 25-Jun 2 '95** *Brisbane Biennial International Music Festival.* **Jun 9-12** *Marlin Cup '95,* Gold Coast. **Jun 10-11** *Working Draught Horse Expo '95,* Toowoomba. **Jul 16** *Gold Coast International Marathon,* Southport. **Aug 10-19** *Brisbane Royal National Show.* **Aug 19-26** *XXXX Ansett Race Week,* Hamilton Island. **Aug 26-Sep 3** *Annual Australian Heritage Festival,* Toowoomba. **Sep 10-17** *The Dunk Island Billfish Classic,* Dunk Island. **Sep 23-30** *Carnival of Flowers,* Toowoomba. **Oct 26-29** *Queensland Golf Open,* Windaroo. **Dec 14-17** *Coolum Golf Classic.* **Feb 23-Mar 3 '96** *Apple and Grape Harvest Festival,* Stanthorpe.

BUSINESS PROFILE

COMMERCIAL INFORMATION: The following organisation can offer advice: State Chamber of Commerce and Industry, GPO Box 1390, Brisbane, QLD 4001. Tel: (7) 221 1766. Fax: (7) 221 6872.

CONFERENCES/CONVENTIONS: Brisbane's major convention centres are Brisbane Entertainment Centre, Brisbane City Hall, Queensland Cultural Centre, RNA Exhibition Grounds, Sheraton Brisbane Hotel, Hilton International Hotel and the Mayfair Crest International Hotel. Cairns' major convention centres are Cairns International, Cairns Civic Centre, Cairns Show Grounds, the Botanical Gardens, Sheraton Mirage Resort and Cairns Hilton. The Gold Coast also has some excellent convention facilities, especially the Hotel Conrad and Jupiter's Casino with seating for 2300 . Smaller centres can be found elsewhere along the Gold Coast at Royal Pines Resort and Sheraton Mirage Gold Coast. For more information on conferences and conventions in Queensland contact the Australian Tourist Commission *or* Brisbane Visitor & Convention Bureau, PO Box 12260, Brisbane City Hall, King George Square, Brisbane, QLD 4002. Tel: (7) 221 8411. Fax: (7) 229 5126; *or* Far North Queensland Promotion Bureau Ltd, PO Box 865, 36-38 Aplin Street, Cairns, QLD 4870. Tel: (70) 513 588. Fax: (70) 510 127.

CLIMATE

Queensland straddles the Tropic of Capricorn and this accounts for the pleasant climate throughout most of the region. Exceptions are the far north and the dry arid western Outback. Brisbane enjoys an average of 7.1 hours of sunshine daily in the winter. July to August is generally humid but sea breezes temper the humidity and make for perfect holiday conditions.

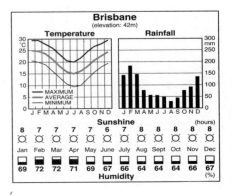

Brisbane
(elevation: 42m)

South Australia

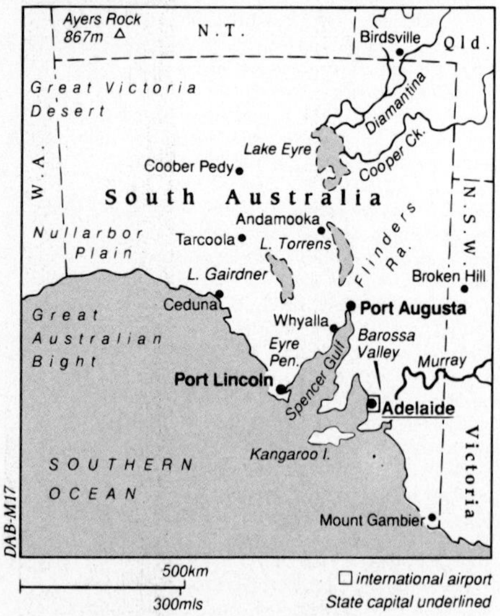

South Australian Tourism Commission
170-178 North Terrace, Adelaide, SA 5000, Australia
Tel: (8) 303 2222. Fax: (8) 303 2269.
South Australian Tourism Commission
612 Kingston Road, London SW20 8DN
Tel: (0181) 545 0450. Fax: (0181) 545 0122.
Australian Travel Headquarters (Representing South Australia)
Suite 160, 1700E Dyer Road, Santa Ana, CA 92705
Tel: (714) 852 2270. Fax: (714) 852 2277.

AREA: 984,000 sq km (380,070 sq miles).
POPULATION: 1,447,200 (1991 estimate).
POPULATION DENSITY: 1.5 per sq km.
CAPITAL: Adelaide. **Population:** 1,049,900 (1990 estimate).
GEOGRAPHY: Except for the State capital of Adelaide, South Australia is sparsely inhabited – it is four times the area of the UK. It is the country's driest State, a region of rocky plains and desert landscape broken by the fertile wine-growing area of the Barossa Valley. South Australia stretches upwards to the Northern Territory, and eastwards to Queensland, New South Wales and Victoria. The countryside ranges from the beach resorts of the Adelaide suburbs to the vast expanses of isolated, semi-desert Outback, from the craggy mountains of Flinders Ranges to the meandering Murray River. Offshore is the popular resort of Kangaroo Island. Adelaide is an attractive European-style coastal city nestling in the foothills of Mount Lofty Ranges.
TIME: GMT + 9.5 (GMT + 10.5 from last Sunday in October to third Saturday in March).

PUBLIC HOLIDAYS

South Australia observes all the public holidays observed nationwide (see the main entry for Australia above) and, in addition, the following are also observed:
Apr 15 '95 Easter Saturday. **May 15** Adelaide Cup Day. **Jun 12** Queen's Birthday. **Oct 2** Labour Day. **Dec 26** Proclamation Day. **Apr 6 '96** Easter Saturday.

TRAVEL

AIR: Adelaide receives international flights and direct flights from Europe via Singapore. Approximate flying time from London is 24 hours. The city is already linked to every State capital city. Connecting flights available through Darwin, Alice Springs, Perth, Brisbane, Canberra, Melbourne and Sydney. For more flight details see general introduction above.
There is an excellent system of internal airways, serving all regional towns, and the majority of flights are run by *Ansett Australia Airlines, Australian Airlines* and *Compass Airlines*. There are nine Government and 20 private airfields in the region.
International airport: *Adelaide Airport* is 6km (4 miles) from the city centre, a drive of ten minutes.
SEA: Adelaide is an international port, with passenger services from Europe and the Far East.
RAIL: Adelaide, where the popular *Ghan* train departs for Alice Springs, is a major terminal on the national rail network. (See also under general section on internal rail connections above.)
ROAD: The southern territories are fully connected to the national system of coach lines that cross Australia from all the State capitals. Typical coach journey times are: Melbourne to Adelaide – 9.5 hours; Alice Springs to Adelaide – 20 hours; Sydney to Adelaide – 24 hours; Brisbane to Adelaide – 33.5 hours; Perth to Adelaide – 35 hours; Darwin to Adelaide – 46 hours. There are 10,180km (6330 miles) of roads within the State. The main highways north are the *Stuart Highway* to Darwin via Coober Pedy and Alice Springs and the *Birdsville Track* to Queensland. The other main State highways are: the *Eyre Highway* west to Perth, the *Princes Highway* along the coast to Melbourne and the *Sturt Highway* east to Canberra and Sydney. **Car hire** services are available at all the main hotels, the railway station and the airport.
URBAN: There is a fully integrated public transport system in Adelaide with **bus**, **tram** and **local rail** lines plus the *O-Bahn* bus system. Pre-purchase booklets of cash-fare tickets and weekly and other passes are all available. A free bus, known as the Bee-line, number 99B, operates Monday to Saturday in the city. The *Adelaide Explorer Bus* leaves the South Australian Travel Centre at 10 King William Street and stops at eight major attractions for a charge of A$18 (adult) and A$12 (children).

ACCOMMODATION

HOTELS: South Australia has 372 hotels and guest-houses, and Adelaide itself contains 126, ranging from budget hostels to 5-star international hotels. Bed & Breakfast, Farmstay and Cottage accommodation is available throughout South Australia, mostly in the Adelaide and Adelaide Hills area. Further information is available from the Hotel and Hospitality Industry Association, 60 Hindmarsh Square, Adelaide, SA 5000. Tel: (8) 232 4525. Fax: (8) 232 4979.
CAMPING/CARAVANNING: South Australia has almost 200 caravan parks. Typical examples near Adelaide are as follows: Adelaide Caravan Park, West Beach, Marineland Village and Port Glanville Caravan Park. They all offer sites with full amenities and power. A number of companies can arrange **motor camper** rentals, with a range of fully equipped vehicles. Full details can be obtained from the South Australian Tourism Commission and Travel Centres. In addition, there are a wide variety of holiday flats and apartments for rent in the State.
Note: More detailed coverage of the range of accommodation available in Australia may be found by consulting the *Accommodation* section in the general entry for Australia above.

RESORTS & EXCURSIONS

Adelaide is the State's capital and by a long way its most populous town. It has to the west a long stretch of attractive coastline with excellent white sandy beaches. The best view of Adelaide and the surrounding countryside can be had from *Mount Lofty*, to the east of the city. The city itself has a European air, primarily because of the large German and southern European minorities. The streets are filled with cafés, European-style churches, art galleries and antique shops. One of the key attractions is the *Festival Theatre* complex in the parkland overlooking the Torrens River. It houses an excellent theatre company, and boasts a concert hall, two theatres, many restaurants and an outdoor amphitheatre. In March every two years (next in 1996), an *International Festival* is held, featuring everything from jazz to classical theatre and ballet. The *South Australian Museum* has the largest collection of Aboriginal artefacts in the world as well as a huge exhibition of Melanesian art and New Guinean wildlife. Adelaide is a spacious city surrounded by parklands, golf courses and the botanical and zoological gardens. The city in recent years has assumed a more youthful appearance, in contrast to its reputation as the 'City of Churches'. It has a wide range of vibrant nightlife and an array of cosmopolitan restaurants. From Adelaide it is easy to travel the 55km (34 miles) to the wine centre of the country, the **Barossa Valley,** originally settled by German refugees in the 1830s and still indelibly marked by their influence on its wineries, restaurants and shops. The main towns are *Tanunda, Angaston* and *Nuriootpa,* all notable for Lutheran churches and the vineyards – tours and tastings can be arranged. The other wine regions in South Australia are the Mid-North, Riverland, McLaren Vale and the Coonawarra in the southeast.
Taking a **Murray River** steamer will afford the visitor a view of lush pastureland, limestone cliffs and also the wine country. The Murray–Darling–Murrumbidgee river network is one of the largest in the world – 2600km (1615 miles) from source to sea – and brings irrigation to a wide area. The vegetation and wildlife evoke images of the Deep South and Mississippi in the United States. Opposite Adelaide in the St Vincent Gulf lies Australia's third-largest island, **Kangaroo Island** – a natural wildlife sanctuary with a rugged coastline noted for fine fishing and its large sea lion colony at *Seal Bay.* South Australia's best slice of the Outback is to be found in the ancient Aboriginal heritage area of **Flinders Ranges,** a region of granite peaks and spectacular and colourful gorges, dotted with eucalyptus trees. In the centre of the Flinders area is *Wilpena Pound,* a popular resort area; accommodation is also available at *Arkaroola,* at the northern peak of the Flinders. The opal town of **Coober Pedy** is so hot that 45% of the inhabitants live underground; even the church is underground, and the name of the town in Aboriginal means 'white man lives in a hole.' The area produces 90% of the world's supply of opals and those who wish to dig for the semi-precious stones can obtain a miner's permit. **Andamooka** is another mining town and conditions are better here for 'noodlers' (amateur prospectors). Accommodation is limited in the towns.

SOCIAL PROFILE

FOOD & DRINK: The local delicacies are mainly German food in the Barossa region and, on the coast, crabs, whiting, crayfish and other seafood. Kangaroo steak is a speciality of the region and can be ordered in many Australian restaurants. Adelaide has a variety of international cuisine available, including American, Chinese, French, Greek, Italian, Indian, Indonesian, Japanese, Lebanese, Malaysian, Mexican, Mongolian and Vietnamese. There are many excellent seafood restaurants. **Drink:** The local wines and beers are strongly recommended and can be tasted at the Vintage Festival, reminiscent in many ways of German beer festivals in Europe. South Australia contains one of the most important valley regions producing Australian wines, both red and white, and naturally Adelaide and the city environs offer the best selection. There is also a brewery in Adelaide supplying stout and lagers.
NIGHTLIFE: Adelaide has an extraordinary nightlife scene, despite its once conservative image. Another conversion was Adelaide Casino, once a grand Victorian railway station and now a haven for baccarat and roulette players amid its magnificent Corinthian columns (open 1000-0400 Monday to Thursday and continuously from Friday to Sunday). There is also a concentration of nightclubs and discotheques on Hindley Street in the heart of the city, opposite Rundle Mall.
SHOPPING: Excellent quality wines from the Barossa Valley, producing over 60% of the national supply. Adelaide is a city that concentrates on culture, and is full of antique shops and art galleries. Opening hours are the same as for the rest of Australia, except for Saturday when Adelaide's shops are open all day. There are also some street markets in Adelaide which are open on Sunday.
SPORT: The third-largest river in the world, the River Murray, winds its way through South Australia providing **cruises, houseboat hire, sailing** and **water-skiing**. One of the sporting specialities is **deep-sea fishing** and **scuba diving** centred on Kangaroo Island. **Ballooning** and **gliding** is popular in the Barossa Valley. Adelaide is the home of the *Australian Formula One Grand Prix.*
SPECIAL EVENTS: South Australia lives up to its name of the *Festival State* with a huge variety of festivals and special events taking place throughout the State all year round. The following is just a selection:
Apr 15-17 '95 *Oakbank Easter Racing Carnival.* **Apr 17-23** *Barossa Valley Vintage Festival.* **May 12-15** *Kernewek Lowender Cornish Festival.* **May 13-14** *Clare Gourmet Weekend.* **Jun 2-12** *South Australian Music Awards,* Barmera. **Jun 10-12** *Gawler Three Day Equestrian Event,* Gauler. **Aug 19-20** *Barossa Classic Gourmet Weekend.* **Sep 1-9** *Royal Adelaide Show.* **Nov 9-12** *Australia Formula One Grand Prix,* Adelaide. **Feb 25-Mar 6 '96** *Adelaide Festival Fringe.* **Mar 1-7** *Adelaide Festival of Arts.*
For a full list of special events contact the South Australian Tourism Commission.

BUSINESS PROFILE

COMMERCIAL INFORMATION: The following organisation can offer advice: Chamber of Commerce and Industry SA Inc, 136 Greenhill Road, Unley, SA 5061. Tel: (8) 373 1422. Fax: (8) 272 9662.
CONFERENCES/CONVENTIONS: Adelaide's major convention centres are Adelaide Convention Centre and Exhibition Hall, Adelaide Festival Centre, Hilton International Adelaide, Royal Showground and Exhibition Centre and the new seaside hotel, the Ramada Grand. For more information on conferences and conventions in South Australia contact the Australian

Tourist Commission *or* Adelaide Convention & Tourism Authority, GPO Box 1972, Level 3, 60 Waymouth Street, Adelaide, SA 5000. Tel: (8) 212 4794. Fax: (8) 231 9224.

CLIMATE

Warm and temperate with long hot summers and short mild winters, with low rainfall. One of the hottest places in the area in summer is Coober Pedy, 1000km (540 miles) northwest of Adelaide, reaching a temperature of up to 45°C.
Required clothing: Lightweight cottons and linens in summer, warmer mediumweights in winter. Waterproofing is advisable throughout most of the year, particularly in winter.

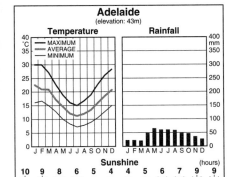

Tasmania

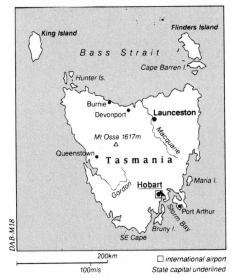

Tourism Tasmania
GPO Box 399, 1 Franklin Wharf, Hobart, TAS 7001, Australia
Tel: (02) 308 100. Fax: (02) 312 175.

AREA: 68,800 sq km (42,467 sq miles).
POPULATION: 466,900 (1991 estimate).
POPULATION DENSITY: 6.9 per sq km.
CAPITAL: Hobart. **Population:** 183,500 (1990 estimate).
GEOGRAPHY: A separate island located 240km (149 miles) south of Melbourne across Bass Strait. Roughly heart-shaped, Tasmania is 296km (184 miles) long, ranging from 315km (196 miles) wide in the north to 70km (44 miles) in the south. The island has a diverse landscape comprising rugged mountains (snowcapped in winter), dense bushland (including the Horizontal Forest, so-called because the tree trunks are bent over parallel to the ground), tranquil countryside and farmland. Bruny

Island, south of Hobart across the D'Entrecasteaux Channel, has superb beaches. The two parts of the island are joined by a narrow isthmus of sand-dunes, the home of fairy penguins from August to April.
TIME: GMT + 10 (GMT + 11 from first Sunday in October to last Saturday in March).

PUBLIC HOLIDAYS

Tasmania observes all the public holidays observed nationwide (see the main entry for Australia above) and, in addition, the following are also observed:
Mar 6 '95 Eight Hour Day. **Apr 15** Easter Saturday. **Jun 12** Queen's Birthday. **Oct 26** Hobart Show Day (regional observance only). **Nov 6** Recreation Day (regional observance only). **Dec 26** Boxing Day. **Mar 4 '96** Eight Hour Day. **Apr 6** Easter Saturday.

TRAVEL

AIR: Direct international flights to Tasmania run from Christchurch in New Zealand. The airport is 22km (14 miles) from Hobart city centre, a drive of about 35 minutes. *Qantas* and *Ansett* operate direct links with international flights every day. Tasmania is connected to the mainland by internal flights from Sydney and Melbourne, and from there to all the other mainland cities.
SEA: There is a direct ferry, the *Spirit of Tasmania*, which runs thrice-weekly from Melbourne to Devonport on the north coast of the island.
RAIL: There are no passenger train services.
ROAD: All settlements on the island are linked by a road system running for 22,000km (13,670 miles) over which there are bus services connecting the main towns. The main routes are: the *Lyell Highway* from Hobart to Queenstown, the *Huon Highway* from Hobart to Southport, the *Midland Highway* from Hobart to Launceston, the *Tasman Highway* from Hobart along the east coast and the *Bass Highway* linking the ports of the north coast. **Coach:** Tasmania has its own coach services, *Tasmanian Redline Coaches,* which offers a *Super Tassie Bus Pass* to out-of-state visitors as does *Hobart Coaches.*
URBAN: Local bus networks are operated in Hobart, Launceston and Burnie.

ACCOMMODATION

The Tasmanian Department of Tourism publishes a booklet giving details of 8- to 16-day rates; available from the Australian Tourist Commission.
HOTELS, MOTELS & GUEST-HOUSES: There are international hotels in Hobart and Launceston and a wide range of tourist hotels, motels and guest-houses in all the major centres. Hotels tend to be slightly more expensive in Hobart and Launceston, and in the main tourist areas.
SELF-CATERING: Available in the main centres. For further details, see the main Australia entry.
FARMSTAY/HOMESTAY: See *Accommodation* in the general introduction above.
CAMPING & CARAVANNING: A number of companies can arrange **motor camper** rentals, with a range of fully equipped vehicles. Full details can be obtained from Tourism Tasmania. There are a large number of camping and caravan sites in Tasmania. It should be noted that camping is not permitted in any roadside picnic or rest areas.
Note: More detailed coverage of the range of accommodation available in Australia may be found by consulting the *Accommodation* section in the general entry for Australia above.

RESORTS & EXCURSIONS

Hobart, the capital, is Australia's second-oldest city after Sydney and is situated on the south side of the island. The city is characterised by strong links with the sea, typified by the wharves, jetties and warehouses – some dating back to the last century – which cluster around the waterfront. Examples of the island's history can be seen in the *Van Diemen's Land Memorial Folk Museum*, the *Tasmanian Maritime Museum* and the *Allport Library and Museum of Fine Arts*. **Mt Wellington**, towering 1270m (4170ft) to the west of the city, provides the backdrop to Hobart. From the lookout at the top (about 20km (12 miles) by road) the clear air offers a spectacular view of Hobart, its suburbs, the Derwent Estuary and Storm Bay. Apart from the view the area offers picnic facilities and walking trails. *The Royal Tasmanian Botanical Gardens* provides a long walk through beautiful scenery, free of charge.
Launceston, the second city, still maintains much of its

colonial Georgian flavour. It is the natural gateway for the rural beauty of the island, including the Cataract Gorge and the **Launceston Wildlife Sanctuary**. Nearby is the historic town of Evandale.
Port Arthur, 100km (82 miles) from Hobart, is the site of an old penal colony built in the early 19th century. Guided tours are available. Not far away is *Eaglehawk Neck*, noted for its bizarre rock formations.
There are many National Parks in Tasmania, most of which are within easy reach of Hobart. These include *South West, Ben Lomond, Cradle Mountain-Lake St Clair* and *Frenchman's Cap*, all of which contain examples of the island's unique plant and wildlife.

SOCIAL PROFILE

FOOD & DRINK: Some of the best seafood in the world is available in Tasmania, including Angazie oysters, Atlantic salmon and ocean trout. Freshwater wild brown trout is harvested in the Tasmanian highlands. Goat, quail and venison are the area's speciality meats and other specialities include cheeses, apples, apricots and liqueur honey.
NIGHTLIFE: There are casinos in Hobart and Launceston. Hobart's waterfront area, Salamanca Place, is the home of many night-time haunts in its old stone warehouses, as well as the Wrest Point Hotel casino.
SPORT: The coastline offers all maritime sports and some of the best **sailing** facilities in the world, with crystal clear waters teeming with marine life. Port Arthur offers a base for superb deep-sea and trout **fishing**. A wide range of adventure holidays are also available; these include **canoeing, hiking** tours, **pony trekking, bushwalking, gliding** and **rock-climbing**.
SPECIAL EVENTS: The following is a selection of festivals and special events taking place in Tasmania:
Mar '95 *Wooden Boat Festival.* **Apr** *Australian Masters Games.* **Apr 25-30** *Targa Tasmania.* **May** *Circular Head Poetry and Music Festival.* **Jun** *Sun Coast Jazz Festival.* **Aug** *Tasmania Run.* **Sep 15-17** *Launceston Garden Festival.* **Oct** *Hobart Show.* **Nov** *Great Oyster Bay Festival.* **Nov 12-17** *Australian Veteran Golf.* **Dec** *Sydney to Hobart Yacht Race; Melbourne to Hobart Yacht Race; Hobart Summer Festival.* **Jan 26 '96** *Australia Day celebrations,* state-wide.
For a full list of special events contact Tourism Tasmania or the Australian Tourist Commission.

BUSINESS PROFILE

COMMERCIAL INFORMATION: The following organisation can offer advice: Tasmanian Chamber of Commerce and Industry, GPO Box 793H, Hobart, TAS 7001. Tel: (02) 345 933. Fax: (02) 311 278.
CONFERENCES/CONVENTIONS: The major convention centres in Hobart are Wrest Point Federal Hotel, Casino and Convention Centre and Sheraton Hobart Hotel. Launceston's major convention centres are Launceston Convention Centre/Albert Hall, Federal Launceston Country Club and Casino, and Launceston Novotel. For more information on conferences and conventions in Tasmania, contact the Australian Tourist Commission *or* the Tasmanian Convention Bureau, 16 Davey Street, Hobart, TAS 7000. Tel: (02) 310 055. Fax: (02) 348 492.

CLIMATE

Similar climate to southern Australia, with warm, dry summers and cold, wet winters. There is often snow above 1000m (3280ft) in July and August.
Required clothing: Cottons and linens in summer, warmer mediumweights in winter. Waterproofing advisable throughout the year particularly in winter.

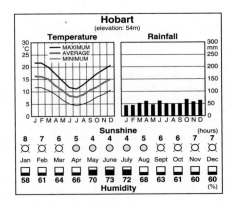

Victoria

New South Wales

Mildura

Murrumbidgee

Riverina

Murray

Wagga Wagga

CANBERRA

A.C.T.

Echuca

Albury

Horsham

Snowy

Mtns.

Bendigo

Victoria

Ballarat

Melbourne

Geelong

Sale

Gippsland

Cape Otway

Port Philip Bay

Wilson's Promontory

400km

200mls

☐ *international airport*

State capital underlined

DAB-M19

Tourism Victoria
GPO Box 2219T, 55 Swanston Street, Melbourne, VIC
3001, Australia
Tel: (3) 653 9777. Fax: (3) 653 9755.
Melbourne Tourism Authority
7 Puers Lane, Jordans, Beaconsfield, Bucks HP9 2TE
Tel: (01494) 871 677. Fax: (01494) 875 775.

AREA: 227,600 sq km (141,454 sq miles).
POPULATION: 4,244,282 (1992).
POPULATION DENSITY: 19.4 per sq km.
CAPITAL: Melbourne. **Population:** 3,022,533 (1992).
GEOGRAPHY: Victoria, Australia's second-smallest
State, is also the most densely populated and the
continent's major agricultural and industrial producer.
Located in southeastern Australia, bordered by South
Australia and New South Wales, the landscape consists
of mountains, rainforests, deserts, snowfields, vineyards,
wheatlands and market gardens. It is possible to drive
from a cold, wet Melbourne winter to the dry desert
sunshine of Mildura in one day or to be in snowfields in
three hours. The mountain coolness of the alpine region
is an easy escape from summer heat.
TIME: GMT + 10 (GMT + 11 from last Sunday in
October to first Saturday in March).

PUBLIC HOLIDAYS

Victoria observes all the public holidays observed
nationwide (see the main entry for Australia above) and,
in addition, the following are also observed:
Mar 13 '95 Labour Day. **Jun 12** Queen's Birthday. **Nov
7** Melbourne Cup Day (regional observance only). **Dec
26** Boxing Day. **Mar 11 '96** Labour Day.

TRAVEL

AIR: The international airport at *Melbourne*
(Tullamarine) receives flights from the UK (approximate
flying time from London – 24 hours), Europe, Asia and
USA. *Tullamarine Airport* is 22km (14 miles) from the
city (travel time – 35 minutes). For more flight details see
the general Australia entry above. Internal flights are
available from all State capitals.
SEA: Passenger/vehicle ferry from Tasmania to
Melbourne.
RAIL: Overnight trains link Melbourne and Sydney (13
hours), and an overnight train runs to Adelaide (12
hours). Trains run to other main centres including
Canberra (8.5 hours), Brisbane (48 hours) and Perth (72
hours).
ROAD: Connected to all States by coach services. Main
coach routes and travelling times are: Melbourne to
Canberra – 9.5 hours; Melbourne to Adelaide – 9.5
hours; Melbourne to Sydney – 14.5 hours; Melbourne to
Broken Hill – 19 hours; Melbourne to Brisbane – 25
hours. There is a well-developed road system covering
156,700km (97,400 miles) on which local buses operate.
URBAN: Melbourne has an extensive network of electric
railways, linked in the city centre by an **underground**
loop-line. There is also a **tram** network which has an
integrated ticket structure with the **bus** and **rail** systems.
Fares are zonal, with travel cards for daily or weekly
travel and multi-journey tickets. The *Melbourne Explorer
Bus* goes to major attractions in the city and the visitor
may join or leave the bus at any stopping point in its
journey.

ACCOMMODATION

HOTELS: A full range of accommodation is available in
Victoria, ranging from international-standard hotels in
Melbourne to farm stay, home stay and self-catering
holidays.
CAMPING/CARAVANNING: A number of companies
can arrange **motor camper** rentals, with a range of fully
equipped vehicles. Full details can be obtained from the
Tourist Board.
Note: More detailed information on the range of
accommodation available in Australia may be found by
consulting the *Accommodation* section in the general
entry for Australia above.

RESORTS & EXCURSIONS

Melbourne is a highly cosmopolitan city of almost three
million people with sizeable Italian, Greek and Chinese
minorities, each with their own quarter. The architecture
is often fascinating, a blend in the suburbs of ornate
stucco and cast iron and in the city centre a skyline which
mixes graceful spires with modern skyscrapers. The
Victorian Arts Centre consists of the *National Gallery*,
which houses Australia's greatest collection of fine art,
and the magnificent concert hall and theatre complex, the
country's premier venue for the performing arts. Other
places to visit include the various gardens, *Parliament
House, Captain Cook's Cottage* and other National Trust
properties. Also recommended is a trip to the races, a ride
in one of Melbourne's trams, a river cruise down the
River Yarra, or a visit to the *Royal Melbourne Zoo*, one
of the finest open-air zoos in the world with no cages,
only natural enclosures.
Outside Melbourne: 35km (22 miles) from the State
capital are the **Dandenong Ranges,** which provide
excellent views of the city over the peaks from the
Summit Lookout. At Mount Dandenong itself is the
sanctuary named after William Ricketts, one of the early
champions of Aboriginal rights; his haunting carvings of
Aboriginal faces still stare out over the forested
landscape. Victoria was also the home of the outlaw Ned
Kelly, often regarded as a national hero in Australia, and
was the scene of the eventful days of bushranging during
the gold rush of the 1850s and 1860s. **Sovereign Hill,**
120km (75 miles) northwest of Melbourne, is an old
gold-rush town from this period, now restored to its
original condition. Other towns of this era are **Ballarat**
and **Bendigo,** respectively 115km (71 miles) and 150km
(93 miles) from Melbourne. Nostalgia is also available in
the shape of *Puffing Billy*, a train of bright red carriages
which runs along the short line from Belgrave to Emerald
through the Dandenong Ranges. **Phillip Island Nature
Reserve,** 112km from Melbourne, is home to Fairy
Penguins and other examples of Antipodean wildlife.
In the east of the State is **Gippsland,** a lush fertile region
dotted with lakes and parkland. The west is drier, with
huge sheep-grazing lands. Towards the centre are the
Grampian Mountains, famous for wild flowers and
birdlife. Another famous wildlife sanctuary is in the
Wilson's Promontory National Park, southeast of
Melbourne and the southernmost tip of the Australian
mainland. The **Port Campbell National Park,** southwest
of Melbourne, contains some of the most beautiful – and
dangerous – coastlines in Victoria. East of Melbourne are
the **Gippsland Lakes,** the largest network of inland
waterways in Australia.
Victoria, like the rest of Australia, has many fine beaches
with opportunities for watersports. These include *Port
Phillip Bay, Westernport Bay, Ninety Mile Beach* (in the
Gippsland Lakes area) and those of the *Bellarine
Peninsula* near Geelong.

SOCIAL PROFILE

FOOD & DRINK: There is an enormous variety of
cuisines available in Melbourne and restaurants offering
specific types can be found in sectionalised districts:
Lygon Street for Italian, Little Bourke Street for Chinese,
Lonsdale Street for Greek, Victoria Street for
Vietnamese, Sydney Road for Turkish and Spanish, and
Acland Street for Central European. Other cuisines that
are well represented in the city's restaurants include
French, American, Mexican, Lebanese, African,
Malaysian, Afghan, Swiss and Mongolian.
SPORT: Horseracing: The *Melbourne Cup* is the most
important event. **Football:** Australian Rules football is a
very popular sport, and Melbourne is its focal point
during the winter months. **Cricket:** The Melbourne
Cricket Ground (MCG) plays host to the highest standard
of international and national matches, and is ranked
amongst cricket's most sacred pitches.
SPECIAL EVENTS: The following is a selection of
festivals and special events taking place in Victoria:
Aug 12-Dec 10 '95 *Spring Floral Festival,* Olinda. **Sep
4-16** *World Masters Squash Championships,* Melbourne.

Sep 9 *Autumn Moon Lantern Festival,* Melbourne. **Oct
17-22** *Melbourne Writers Festival.* **Oct 19-Nov 4**
Melbourne International Festival of Arts. **Nov 7**
Melbourne Cup (horseracing). **Nov 19** *Melbourne
Christmas Parade.* **Nov 23-26** *Heineken Australian Golf
Open 1995,* Melbourne. **Dec 27-31** *Red Cross Murray
Marathon,* Murray River. **Jan 15-28 '96** *Ford Australian
Tennis Open,* Melbourne. **Feb 9-18** *Melbourne Music
Festival.* **Mar 30-Apr 7** *Bendigo Easter Fair,* Bendigo.
Apr 1-22 *Melbourne International Comedy Festival.*

BUSINESS PROFILE

COMMERCIAL INFORMATION: The following
organisation can offer advice: Victoria Employers'
Chamber of Commerce and Industry, Employers' House,
50 Burwood Road, Hawthorn, VIC 3122. Tel: (3) 810
6333. Fax: (3) 819 3676.
CONFERENCES/CONVENTIONS: Melbourne,
Australia's second-largest city and gateway to the southern
region, has convention facilities to match international
standards – the World Congress Centre opened in 1990,
offering 28 meeting areas for up to 3500 delegates. A new
exhibition complex linked by walkway to World Congress
Centre, Melbourne, is planned for 1996. Also, a casino-
leisure complex will open in 1995. Major convention
facilities include Dallas Brooks Conference Centre,
Melbourne Hilton on the Park, Hyatt on Collins, the
Radisson President Hotel and Convention Centre, Regent
of Melbourne, Royal Exhibition Building and Convention
Centre, Southern Cross Hotel, Flinders Park Tennis Centre
and Victorian Arts Centre. For more information on
conferences and conventions in Victoria, contact the
Australian Tourist Commission *or* the Melbourne Tourism
Authority, Level 5, 114 Flinders Street, Melbourne, VIC
3000. Tel: (3) 654 2288. Fax: (3) 654 8195.

CLIMATE

Hot summers and relatively cold winters. Rainfall is
distributed throughout the year. Southern areas can have
changeable weather even in summer, often with four
seasons' weather in one day.

Western Australia

Timor Sea

INDIAN
OCEAN

Wyndham

Kimberley
Plateau

Broome

Fitzroy

Wolf Creek Crater

Port Hedland

Great Sandy
Desert

N.T.

NW Cape

Fortescue

Tropic of Capricorn

Carnarvon

Gascoyne

Gibson
Desert

Western   Australia

• Meekatharra

Great
Victoria
Desert

S.A.

• Geraldton

☐ **Kalgoorlie**

Nullarbor Plain

Perth

Fremantle

• Norseman

Busselton

Esperance

Cape Leeuwin

Albany

500km

300mls

☐ *international airport*
State capital underlined

DAB-M20

Western Australia Tourism Commission
6th Floor, 16 St George's Terrace, Perth, WA 6000,
Australia
Tel: (9) 220 1700. Fax: (9) 220 1702.
Western Australia Tourist Centre
Forrest Place, Cnr of Wellington Street, Perth, WA 6000,
Australia
Tel: (9) 483 1111. Fax: (9) 481 0190.
Western Australia Tourism Commission
Western Australia House, 115 The Strand, London
WC2R 0AJ
Tel: (0171) 240 2881. Fax: (0171) 379 9826.

AREA: 2,525,500 sq km (1,569,422 sq miles).
POPULATION: 1,636,800 (1991 estimate).
POPULATION DENSITY: 0.7 per sq km.

CAPITAL: Perth. **Population:** 1,193,100 (1990 estimate).
GEOGRAPHY: Western Australia covers one-third of
Australia; it is larger than Western Europe, but has a
population only one-sixth of that of London. It is bordered
in the east by South Australia and the Northern Territory
and surrounded by the Indian Ocean and in the north by
the Timor Sea. On the west coast one is nearer to Bali and
Indonesia than to Sydney, making Perth a viable stopover
destination en route to the rest of Australia. To the south,
the nearest land mass is Antarctica, 2600km (1600 miles)
away. It has mineral wealth in iron, bauxite, nickel,
natural gas, oil, diamonds and gold. There are vast
wheatlands, forests and deserts, and several national
parks. A popular resort is Rottnest Island; there are also
many excellent mainland beaches, particularly around
Perth. The Kimberleys, in the far north, is one of the
oldest geological areas on earth, a region where time and
weather have formed deep gorges and impressive
mountains, arid red plains and coastal sandstone rich in
fossils. In the northwest there are two notable features:
Wolf Creek Crater, an immense hole left in the desert by a
giant meteorite 50,000 years ago, and the Bungle
Bungles, an ancient sandstone massif covering 450 sq km
(175 sq miles). Southeast of Perth, near Hyden, there is
the 2700-million-year-old Wave Rock.
TIME: GMT + 8.

PUBLIC HOLIDAYS

Western Australia observes all the public holidays
observed nationwide (see the main entry for Australia
above) and, in addition, the following are also observed:
Mar 6 '95 Labour Day. **Jun 5** Foundation Day. **Oct 2**
Queen's Birthday. **Dec 26** Boxing Day. **Mar 4 '96**
Labour Day.

TRAVEL

AIR: There are international flights to Perth from Europe
and Asia. Flying time from London is 22 hours. There
are internal flights from all State capitals. *Perth Airport*
is 10km (6 miles) from the city (travel time – 35
minutes). *Ansett WA (MV)* is Western Australia's
regional airline.
SEA: Port of Fremantle serves Perth. The port is 19km
(11 miles) from the city of Perth.
RAIL: The *Indian Pacific* service runs across Australia
from Sydney, and the *Trans-Australian* runs from Port
Pirie, Adelaide and Melbourne. There is a daily service
from Kalgoorlie and Bunbury.
ROAD: The highway network in Western Australia is
almost entirely concentrated in the coastal areas. The
main exception to this is the *Great Northern Highway*
which runs from Perth to Port Headland on the northwest
coast. Along the south coast is the *Eyre Highway,* which
runs into South Australia. The *Brand/Northwest Coastal
Highway* runs from Perth around the west coast to
Kimberley. There is only one express coach route from
Perth and it goes to Adelaide (travel time – 35 hours).
URBAN: Local *trains* run from Perth to Armadale,
Midland and Fremantle. There are **bus** and **ferry** services
in Perth itself. A zonal fares structure covers all transport
modes; tickets issued on one mode are valid for transfer
to either of the others (bus, rail and ferry). A free Clipper
Bus service circles the city centre Monday to Friday.

ACCOMMODATION

The Western Australia Tourism Commission provides
information to consumers and travel agents, which can be
obtained from their offices (addresses above).
HOTELS: There is a wide range of hotels and motels in
Western Australia, including 5-star (luxury), 4-star
(deluxe), 3-star (standard) and 2-star (economy).
HOLIDAY FLATS: A wide range of holiday flats are
available, both in Perth and the rest of the State.
CAMPING/CARAVANNING: There are many caravan
parks and campsites in the State, most of which are
located off the main highways. Further information can
be obtained from the Western Australia Tourism
Commission. A number of companies arrange **motor
camper** rentals, with a range of vehicles. Full details can
be obtained from the Tourism Commission.

RESORTS & EXCURSIONS

'**Perth** has the climate that California thinks it has' is a
popular saying in Western Australia; the city is sunny all
year round but made pleasant due to the temperate
breezes. It is a boom city and modern skyscrapers
overshadow the colonial buildings such as the *Court
House,* the *Town Hall* and the *Old Mill.* The *Swan River*
winds through the city, and a cruise up river to the
vineyards and wine-tasting is a top tourist attraction. The
Omni Theatre Planetarium in West Perth simulates the
experience of space flight for the visitor. *Kings Park,* a

beautiful parkland in the midst of town, the *West
Australian Art Gallery* in James Street and the vast
Entertainment Centre are also worth seeing. The most
popular beach destinations are *Port, Cottesloe, City,
Scarborough* and the nude bathing beach at *Swanbourne.*
The Swan River also provides safe swimming.
Fremantle, just 19km (12 miles) from Perth, is a port
city full of charming terraced houses and historic
buildings. The *Western Australian Maritime Museum* and
Fishing Boat Harbour, with its many superb outdoor
seafood restaurants, are the main attractions.
Outside Perth: Just 17km (11 miles) north of Perth is
the new *Underwater World* at **Hillarys Boat Harbour**
showing over 4000 sea creatures in their natural
environments. *Atlantis Marine Park* in *Yanchep,* an
hour's drive north, has performing dolphins. South of
Perth is *Cable Ski Park* with thrilling water rides and
Adventure World, a favourite family entertainment
complex on **Bibra Lake** with thrill rides, native animals,
parkland and waterways in beautiful surroundings. Set in
bushland an hour's drive inland from Perth is **El Caballo
Blanco,** where Spanish Andalusian dancing stallions
perform. Also nearby is **Pioneer World,** a re-creation of
a pioneer town and **Cohunu Wildlife Park,** with
abundant wildlife. Further east there is the thriving gold-
mining town of **Kalgoorlie** and towns which were once
the centre of Western Australia's gold rush, such as
Coolgardie. The **Darling Ranges,** behind Perth, are
popular among visitors and contain several national
parks. The **Avon Valley,** a 90-minute drive from Perth, is
an agricultural area. In this region can be found the town
of **York** where the *York Motor Museum* and *The
Residency Museum* are worth seeing. The southwest
region is well known for its coastline, wineries and
vineyards. Further north, there are long stretches of
undeveloped coastline and rust-coloured landscape.
Wildflowers abound in this region during September-
October. **Nambung National Park** is well-known for its
amazing limestone formations known as *The Pinnacles.*
At **Monkey Mia,** on the coast, there are wild dolphins
that come into the shallows to greet visitors. Also in the
north of the State lie **The Kimberleys,** a wild region rich
in Aboriginal legends, which in recent years has become
a thriving diamond-mining centre. It is one of the oldest
geological areas on earth. The city of **Broome,** on the
north coast, is the pearl capital of the world. At the
opposite end of the State is **Albany,** the first European
settlement in Western Australia, which has many restored
buildings and some extraordinary natural wonders.

SOCIAL PROFILE

FOOD & DRINK: Excellent seafood from the coast
around Perth – king prawns, rock lobster (locals call this
crayfish, jewfish barramundi), Westralian *dhufish* and
special freshwater lobster called *marron*. There are
excellent local wines in Western Australia and vineyards
at Swan Valley, Mount Barker and Margaret River.
NIGHTLIFE: There are many nightclubs in the
Northbridge area of Perth and the Burswood Resort and
Casino complex is only minutes from Perth city centre.
SHOPPING: Best buys are Argyle diamonds, opals,
emu leather products and Aboriginal art. Shops are open
all day Saturday and late night Thursday.
SPECIAL EVENTS: Jun 3-4 '95 *Carnarfin 1995,*
Carnarvon. **Sep 30-Oct 7** *Perth Royal Show 1995.* **Nov
10-19** *Festival Fremantle.* **Feb 9-11 '96** *Western
Australia Foodfest,* Perth. **Feb 16-18** *Great Southern
Wine Festival,* Albany. **Mar 1-15** *Inter Dominian
Harness Racing Championships,* Perth. **Apr 2-10**
Australian Mens Softball Championships, Mirramooka.

BUSINESS PROFILE

COMMERCIAL INFORMATION: The following
organisation can offer advice: Chamber of Commerce and
Industry of Western Australia (CCIWA), PO Box 6209,
Confederation House, 190 Hay Street, East Perth, WA
6892. Tel: (9) 421 7555. Fax: (9) 325 6550. Telex: 93609.
CONFERENCES/CONVENTIONS: The major
convention centres are the Hilton Hotel, Hyatt Regency
Hotel, Observation City Resort Hotel, Perth International
Hotel, Sheraton Hotel, the Superdrome and also
Burswood Resort and Convention and Exhibition Centre,
only 3km (2 miles) from the city centre with seating
available for 2000 for conventions or 21,000 for
exhibitions. For more information on conferences and
conventions contact the Australian Tourist Commission
or the Perth Convention Bureau, 4th Floor, 16 St
George's Terrace, Perth, WA 6000. Tel: (9) 220 1737.
Fax: (9) 220 1702.

CLIMATE

North is tropical. South is subtropical to temperate.
Rainfall varies from area to area.

□ *international airport*

Location: Western Europe.

Note: Austria became a full member of the European
Union as of January 1, 1995.

Österreich Werbung (ANTO)
Margaretenstrasse 1, A-1040 Vienna, Austria
Tel: (1) 588 660. Fax: (1) 588 6620.
Embassy of the Republic of Austria
18 Belgrave Mews West, London SW1X 8HU
Tel: (0171) 235 3731. Fax: (0171) 235 8025. Telex:
28327 (a/b OBELO G). Opening hours: 0900-1130
Monday to Friday.
Austrian National Tourist Office
30 St George Street, London W1R 0AL
Tel: (0171) 629 0461. Fax: (0171) 499 6038.
Enquiries by mail, telephone or fax only.
British Embassy
Jaurèsgasse 12, A-1030 Vienna, Austria
Tel: (1) 713 1575/9. Fax: (1) 714 7824. Telex: 132810
(a/b BRITEM B).
Consular Section: Jaurèsgasse 10, A-1030 Vienna,
Austria
Tel: (1) 714 6117/8. Fax: (1) 712 7316. Telex: 133410
(a/b BRITEM A) *or* 132810 (a/b BRITEM B).
Embassy of the Republic of Austria
3524 International Court, NW, Washington, DC 20008
Tel: (202) 895 6700 *or* 895 6767 (Consular section). Fax:
(202) 895 6750.
Austrian Consulate-General
50 Third Avenue, New York, NY 10022
Tel: (212) 688 0091 *or* 737 6400. Fax: (212) 772 8926.
Austrian National Tourist Office
PO Box 1142, Times Square, New York, NY 10108-
1142
Tel: (212) 944 6880. Fax: (212) 730 4568.
Embassy of the United States of America
Unit 27937, Boltzmanngasse 16, A-1091 Vienna, Austria
Tel: (1) 31339. Fax: (1) 310 0682. Telex: 114634.
US Consulate
4th Floor, Gartenbaupromenade 2, A-1010 Vienna,
Austria
Tel: (1) 31339. Fax: (1) 513 4351.
Austrian Embassy
445 Wilbrod Street, Ottawa, Ontario K1N 6M7
Tel: (613) 789 1444. Fax: (613) 789 3431. Telex: 053-
3290.
Austrian National Tourist Office
Suite 3330, 2 Bloor Street East, Toronto, Ontario M4W 1A8
Tel: (416) 967 3381. Fax: (416) 967 4101.

Canadian Embassy
Schubertring 10, A-1010 Vienna, Austria
Tel: (1) 533 3691/5 or 533 6626/8. Fax: (1) 535 4473.

AREA: 83,859 sq km (32,378 sq miles).
POPULATION: 7,812,100 (1991).
POPULATION DENSITY: 93.2 per sq km.
CAPITAL: Vienna (Wien). **Population:** 1,533,176 (1991).
GEOGRAPHY: Austria is a landlocked country, bordered by Switzerland, Liechtenstein, Germany, the Czech Republic, the Slovak Republic, Hungary, Slovenia and Italy. It is predominantly Alpine. The imposing Dachstein region of Upper Austria, the massive Tyrolean peaks, the lakes of Carinthia and the Salzkammergut, the River Danube and the forests of Styria are amongst the many outstanding features of the country.
LANGUAGE: German is the official language. Regional dialects are pronounced and within the different regions of the country one will encounter marked variations from *Hochdeutsch*, ie 'standard' German. There are Croatian and Slovene-speaking minorities in the Burgenland and southern Corinthia respectively.
RELIGION: 89% Roman Catholic, 6% Protestant.
TIME: GMT + 1 (GMT + 2 from last Sunday in March to Saturday before last Sunday in September).
ELECTRICITY: 220 volts AC, 50Hz. Round 2-pin European plugs are standard.
COMMUNICATIONS: Telephone: Full IDD facilities available. Country code: 43. Outgoing international code: 00. Call boxes are grey and found in all areas. International calls can be made from pay-phones with four coin slots. Trunk calls within Austria are approximately 33% cheaper between 1800-2000 Monday to Friday and at the weekend (from 1800 Friday to 0800 Monday). **Telex/telegram:** Telex services are available in several main hotels (for guests only) or at the main telecommunications centre in Vienna. Country code: 47. Telegram facilities are available from any post office.
Post: Letters up to 20g and postcards within Europe are sent by airmail. Letters within Europe take two to four days, and to the USA four to six days. Stamps may be purchased in post offices or tobacco shops. Post boxes are painted yellow. A *Poste Restante* service is available at most post offices. Address mail to 'Postlagernd' ('Hauptpostlagernd' if a main post office), followed by the person's name, town, and post code. Post office hours: generally 0800-1200 and 1400-1700/1800 Monday to Friday, but main post offices and those at major railway stations are open for 24 hours, seven days a week, including public holidays. **Press:** Newspapers are in German. The *Wiener Zeitung*, established in 1703, is the oldest newspaper in the world. The national daily with the largest circulation is the *Neue Kronen-Zeitung*.
BBC World Service and Voice of America frequencies: From time to time these change. See the section *How to Use this Book* for more information.
BBC:

MHz	11.78	9.750	9.195	3.955
Voice of America:				
MHz	15.20	9.760	6.040	5.995

PASSPORT/VISA

Regulations and requirements may be subject to change at short notice, and you are advised to contact the appropriate diplomatic or consular authority before finalising travel arrangements. Details of these may be found at the head of this country's entry. Any numbers in the chart refer to the footnotes below.

	Passport Required?	Visa Required?	Return Ticket Required?
Full British	1	No/2	No
BVP	Valid	No	No
Australian	Yes	No	Yes
Canadian	Yes	No	Yes
USA	Yes	No	Yes
Other EU (As of 31/12/94)	1	No	No
Japanese	Yes	No/2	No

PASSPORTS: [1] Valid passports required by all except for nationals of EU countries and nationals of Andorra, Finland, Liechtenstein, Malta, Monaco, Norway, San Marino, Sweden and Switzerland who may enter with a valid national ID card (or BVP for UK nationals).
British Visitors Passport: Acceptable. A BVP can be used for holidays or unpaid business trips to Austria. For further information on BVPs, see the *Passport/Visa* section of *How to Use this Book* at the beginning of the book.
VISAS: Required by all except:
(a) nationals of the countries referred to in the chart above for stays of up to 90 days ([2] except citizens of the UK and Japan who can stay for a period of up to six months and nationals of Liechtenstein, Luxembourg and

Switzerland who can stay for an unlimited period);
(b) nationals of countries referred to above under passport exemptions;
(c) nationals of Argentina, Bahamas, Barbados, Bolivia, Brazil, Chile, Colombia, Costa Rica, Croatia, Cyprus, Czech Republic, Ecuador, El Salvador, Guatemala, Hong Kong (British citizens only), Iceland, Israel, Jamaica, South Korea, Malaysia, Mexico, New Zealand, Panama, Paraguay, Poland, Seychelles, Singapore, Slovak Republic, Slovenia, Trinidad & Tobago, Tunisia, Uruguay and Venezuela for stays of up to 90 days;
(d) nationals of Hungary for stays of up to 30 days;
(e) nationals of *Bosnia-Hercegovina and the *Former Yugoslav Republic of Macedonia (FYROM) as tourists only holding proof of tourist status (ie return or onward ticket, booked accommodation and sufficient funds to cover length of stay).
Note [*]: As of October 1994, nationals of Bosnia-Hercegovina and the Former Yugoslav Republic of Macedonia must have new passports issued by the individual republics of Bosnia-Hercegovina or FYROM. Nationals of these countries with passports issued by the former country of Yugoslavia will not be allowed to enter Austria.
Types of visa: Only one type of Entry visa is issued, and it is not specified in the visa whether the purpose of the trip is tourism, business or transit. Transit visas are required by all except those noted under Passport and Visa exemptions above and those continuing their journey on the same day, holding confirmed onward tickets and other documentation for their destination and who do not leave the airport.
Cost: Multiple entry: approx £23.20 payable in postal orders or certified bank drafts.
Validity: Up to 1 month. Visas are never extended, but applications for a new visa can be made.
Application to: Consulate (or Consular Section at Embassy). For addresses, see top of entry.
Application requirements: (a) Completed application form. (b) Valid passport. (c) Consular fee. (d) For transit, the visa from the destination country must be obtained first. (e) Postal applicants should enclose a self-addressed, pre-paid envelope for the return of the passport.
Note: Nationals of the following countries must complete the application form *in duplicate* and in addition submit one passport photograph: Albania, Algeria, Bahrain, Cambodia, Cuba, Egypt, Ethiopia, Iran, Iraq, Jordan, North Korea, Kuwait, Lebanon, Libya, Mongolia, Morocco, Oman, Saudi Arabia, Syria, United Arab Emirates, Vietnam, Western Samoa, Yemen and Palestinians. In certain cases flight tickets, bank statements or other items must also be produced.
Working days required: Visa applications are usually dealt with within 24 hours. If processing takes longer the applicant is informed accordingly. A self-addressed envelope (preferably registered or recorded delivery) is required.
Temporary residence: Seek advice from the Austrian Embassy.

MONEY

Currency: Austrian Schilling (ASch) = 100 Groschen. Bank notes are in denominations of ASch5000, 1000, 500, 100, 50 and 20. Coins are in denominations of ASch1000, 500, 100, 50, 25, 20, 10, 5 and 1, and 50, 10 and 5 Groschen. The ASch1000, 500, 100, 50 and 25 coins are for collection purposes only.
Currency exchange: Foreign currencies and travellers cheques are exchanged at all banks, savings banks and exchange counters at airports and railway stations at the official exchange rates. In general, shops, travel agents and hotels also accept foreign currency.
Credit cards: Most major credit cards and Eurocheque cards are accepted in large cities and tourist areas, as are travellers cheques. However, credit cards are less widely accepted in Austria than they are in the USA or the United Kingdom.
Exchange rate indicators: The following figures are included as a guide to the movements of the Austrian Schilling against Sterling and the US Dollar:

Date:	Oct '92	Sep '93	Jan '94	Jan '95
£1.00=	47.12	17.28	18.04	17.16
$1.00=	10.78	11.31	12.19	11.09

Currency restrictions: No restrictions except for export of more than ASch100,000 in Austrian currency, for which a permit is required. Gold coins to a limit of 200g per person per trip may be exported, providing the coins do not have legal tender status.
Banking hours: Banks in Vienna are open 0800-1230 and 1330-1500 Monday, Tuesday, Wednesday and Friday. Thursday hours are 0800-1230 and 1330-1730 (head offices do not close for the break). Different opening hours may be kept in the various Federal

Provinces. The exchange counters at airports and at railway stations are generally open from the first to the last plane or train, which usually means from 0800-2200 including weekends.

DUTY FREE

The following goods can be taken into Austria without incurring any customs duty by:
(a) Travellers over 17 years of age arriving from EU countries:
200 cigarettes or 50 cigars or 250g tobacco; 2.25 litres (3 bottles) of wine or 2.1 litres champagne or fortified wine or spirits up to 22%; 1 litre of spirits; other goods of up to ASch2500 (including foodstuffs and non-alcoholic beverages of up to ASch200).
(b) Travellers arriving from EU countries with duty-paid goods:
800 cigarettes and 400 cigarillos and 200 cigars and 1kg of tobacco; 90 litres of wine (including up to 60 litres of sparkling wine); 10 litres of spirits; 20 litres of intermediate products (such as fortified wine); 110 litres of beer.
(c) Travellers from non-EU countries:
200 cigarettes or 100 cigarillos or 50 cigars or 250g of tobacco; 2 litres of wine or sparkling wine and 1 litre of spirits; 1 bottle of eau de cologne (up to 300g); 50g of perfume; souvenirs up to a value of ASch400 for non-residents (ASch1000 for Austrian residents).
Note: Arrivals from outside Europe are allowed double the above allowances; to qualify, the visitor must not have stopped for more than 24 hours in another European country en route to Austria.

PUBLIC HOLIDAYS

Jan 1 '95 New Year's Day. **Jan 6** Epiphany. **Apr 17** Easter Monday. **May 1** Labour Day. **May 25** Ascension Day. **Jun 5** Whit Monday. **Jun 15** Corpus Christi. **Aug 15** Assumption. **Oct 26** National Holiday. **Nov 1** All Saints' Day. **Dec 8** Immaculate Conception. **Dec 25** Christmas Day. **Dec 26** St Stephen's Day. **Jan 1** '96 New Year's Day. **Jan 6** Epiphany. **Apr 8** Easter Monday.

HEALTH

Regulations and requirements may be subject to change at short notice, and you are advised to contact your doctor well in advance of your intended date of departure. Any numbers in the chart refer to the footnotes below.

	Special Precautions?	Certificate Required?
Yellow Fever	No	No
Cholera	No	No
Typhoid & Polio	No	-
Malaria	No	-
Food & Drink	1	-

[1]: Milk is pasteurised and dairy products are safe for consumption. Local meat, poultry, seafood, fruit and vegetables are generally considered safe to eat.
Rabies is present in Austria, although there have been no incidents reported in recent years. For those at high risk, vaccination before arrival should be considered. If you are bitten abroad seek medical advice without delay. For more information consult the *Health* section.
Ticks often live in heavily afforested areas during the summer months in some of the more eastern parts of Austria and can create discomfort and, in very rare cases, serious infection to people who are bitten by them. Immunisation is available and travellers likely to find themselves in those woods should take a course of

---

IMPORTANT NOTE

As of 1 January, Austria, Finland and Sweden are due to join the EU.

However, for the purposes of the passport and visa information, these three countries have been treated as separate from the EU; it will take some time for other countries to decide how they want to change their regulations towards nationals of these countries.

For up-to-the-minute information on nationals of Austria, Finland and Sweden, please contact the relevant embassies before travelling.

injections. The immunisation consists either of three different shots, which travellers should have injected one year before leaving their country of origin, or of an injection after a tick bite, which is available from every doctor in Austria. For more information contact Immuno Ltd, Arctic House, Rye Lane, Dunton Green, nr. Sevenoaks, Kent TN14 5HB, UK. Tel: (01732) 458 101. Fax: (01732) 455 175.

Health care: Costs of medical treatment are high and medical insurance is, therefore, strongly advised. There is a Reciprocal Health Agreement with the UK but it is of a limited nature, only allowing UK citizens free emergency in-patient treatment at public hospitals. Everything else (including ambulances, prescribed medicines and consultations with general practitioners) must be paid for. However, the reciprocal health care agreement between Austria and the UK may change due to the entrance of Austria into the EU in 1995 and, before travelling, visitors are advised to check with the International Relations Unit, Department of Health, Room 518, Richmond House, 79 Whitehall, London SW1A 2NS.

TRAVEL - International

AIR: Austria's national airline is *Austrian Airlines (OS)*.

For free advice on air travel, call the *Air Travel Advisory Bureau* in the UK on (0171) 636 5000 (London) *or* (0161) 832 2000 (Manchester).

Approximate flight times: From *London* to Innsbruck is 2 hours, to Salzburg is 1 hour 50 minutes and to Vienna is 2 hours 10 minutes.

From *Los Angeles* to Vienna is 15 hours.
From *New York* to Vienna is 9 hours.
From *Singapore* to Vienna is 14 hours.
From *Sydney* to Vienna is 25 hours.

International airports: *Vienna* (Wien-Schwechat), *Graz* (Thalerhof), *Innsbruck* (Kranebitten), *Klagenfurt* (Wörther See), *Linz* (Hörsching) and *Salzburg* (Maxglan).

Vienna (VIE) (Wien-Schwechat) is 18km (11 miles) east of the city. Airport facilities include duty-free shops (0900-1900), banks (0800-1230 and 1330-1500), bureaux de change (0800-2300), post office (0730-2000), 3 restaurants (two open 1000-2200 and the other 1100-1500 and 1800-2400), self-service restaurant (24-hour), four cafés (0600-2100), 2 bars (one open 0600-2200 and the other 0900-1900), left luggage (24-hours), conference facilities (0700-2230), medical facilities, car hire *(ARAC/Austrian Rent-a-Car, Avis, Budget, Hertz, Denzel Europcar Inter-rent and Intercity Car Rental)*, car park and nursery. The airport bus goes between the airport and the city centre every 20-30 minutes from 0500-2330 (travel time – 20 minutes). Rail service is available every hour (and every half hour from 0511-0905) to and from Wien Nord Station (travel time – 35 minutes). A rail service is also available from the airport to the Vienna railway stations of Südbahnhof (travel time – 20 minutes) and Westbahnhof (travel time – 35 minutes) every hour. Taxis are available to the city and can be found north of the Arrivals Hall, costing approximately ASch320. A chaffeur-driven car service is also available from the Arrivals Hall.

Innsbruck (INN) (Kranebitten) is 5.5km (3.5 miles) from the city. Airport facilities include duty-free shop (0630-1800), currency exchange, restaurant (0900-2100), medical facilities and car hire *(Avis, Budget, Hertz* and *Inter-rent)*. Bus services are available every 20-30 minutes to the city centre (travel time – 20 minutes). Taxi services are also available.

Salzburg (SZG) (Maxglan) is 5km (3 miles) west of the city. Airport facilities include duty-free shopping (0700-2200), currency exchange (0600-1800), post office (0900-1200 and 1400-1800), two restaurants and three snack bars (0800-2200), bar, left luggage, conference rooms (within the Airest Restaurant, 0700-2300) and car hire *(Avis, ARAC/Interauto, Budget, Europcar* and *Hertz)*. Bus no. 77 departs to the city centre every 15 minutes weekdays and every 30 minutes weekends (travel time – 17 minutes). Taxis are available from the front of the main building for approx. ASch180 (travel time – 20 minutes). Some hotels have courtesy coaches.

Klagenfurt (KLU) (Wörther See) is 3km (2 miles) from the city. Bus and taxi services are available.

Note: Airports have fixed charges for portering.

SEA/RIVER: The quickest and most practical international sea route from London to Vienna is via the Dover–Ostend ferry (3 hours 30 minutes). The distance by road is approximately 1600km (1000 miles). It is a day's drive in summer, but can take longer in winter. Munich is four to five hours from Vienna; Milan and Zurich are a good day's drive. *DDSG* operates a passenger service on the Danube from Passau all the way to Vienna. For information and reservations,

telephone (851) 33035. *Wurm und Kock* offers both passenger service and cruises to Linz. Overnight cruise packages from Passau to Linz include hotel accommodation for only slightly more than the regular one-way passenger fare. Evening and music cruises are available in the summer. For further information, telephone *Wurm und Kock* on (851) 2066. *DDSG* also operate a hydrofoil service from the Praterlände hydrofoil dock in Vienna to Budapest (travel time – 6 hours). A regular hydrofoil service also runs three times daily during the summer months from Vienna to Bratislava (travel time – 1 hour); for further information contact the Czech Danube Shipping Line, Fajnorovo Nabr. 2, Bratislava 81102, Slovak Republic. Tel: (427) 759 518. Fax: (427) 759 516. The Eurailpass includes travel on DDSG river boats.

RAIL: There are daily international services from London to Austrian destinations. The through trains are as follows:

Calais–Basle–Innsbruck *(Arlberg Express)*.
Ostend–Aachen–Cologne–Munich–Salzburg (Note: In winter there is no direct service on this route: change trains at Munich).
Ostend–Brussels–Cologne–Frankfurt/M–Vienna *(Austria Nachtexpress)*.

Fare reductions are indicated in the international railway fare catalogue (TCV), and Austria is included in the *Eurailpass* and *Eurail Youthpass* scheme. Other major international train routes include Innsbruck–Munich, Vienna–Salzburg–Munich, Vienna–Prague–Berlin, Vienna–Warsaw (or Kiev)–Minsk–Moscow, Vienna–Budapest–Bucharest, Vienna–Belgrade–Athens, Vienna–Belgrade–Istanbul, Innsbruck–Verona–Venice (or Milan), Innsbruck–Verona–Bologna–Florence–Rome, Vienna–Nuremberg–Frankfurt/M–Cologne, Vienna–Salzburg–Munich–Paris, Vienna–Venice, Innsbruck–Zurich.

ROAD: Some tour operators offer package holidays to Austria by coach from the UK. A full list is available from the Tourist Office. See above under *Sea/River* for information on roads into Austria from foreign ports.

TRAVEL - Internal

AIR: Vienna is connected to Graz, Klagenfurt, Linz and Salzburg by both *Austrian Airlines (OS)* and *Austrian Air Services (SO)*. Tyrolean Airlines run services from Vienna to Innsbruck. **Charter:** A number of companies offer chartering services for single- and twin-engined aircraft and executive jets.

RIVER/LAKE: A number of operators run cruises along the Danube to the Black Sea, and from Bregenz across Lake Constance. On some cruises a passport is needed; they last from one to eight days depending on the itinerary. These services run between spring and autumn. **Ferries:** There are regular passenger boat services from mid-May to mid-September along the Danube and on Austria's lakes. The Danube steamer services are run by the *DDSG* and other boat trips by private or state-owned companies. International rail tickets are valid on Danube River boats. More information on these services, including connections with Bratislava, Budapest, Belgrade, Istanbul and Yalta, can be obtained from: DDSG-Reisedienst, Handelskai 265, A-1021 Vienna. Tel: (1) 217 100.

RAIL: *Austrian Federal Railways (ÖBB)* run an efficient internal service throughout Austria. There is a frequent intercity service from Vienna to Salzburg, Innsbruck, Graz and Klagenfurt, and regular motorrail services through the Tauern Tunnel. Information and booking can be obtained from train stations, the Austrian Travel Agency *(Austropa)* and its ticket distribution offices. The most scenic routes are Innsbruck–Brennero, Innsbruck–Buchs, Innsbruck–Bruck an der Mur–Vienna, Innsbruck–Feldkirch–Innsbruck, Innsbruck–Garmisch–Zugspitze, Innsbruck–Salzburg–Innsbruck, Linz–Selzthal–Amstetten–Linz, Salzburg–Zell am See–Innsbruck, Salzburg–Gmunden–Stainach–Salzburg, Salzburg–Vienna, Salzburg–Villach–Salzburg, Vienna–Puchberg am Schneeberg–Hochschneeberg–Vienna, Vienna–Bruch an der Mur–Innsbruck, Vienna–Klagenfurt–Udine–Trieste. Railways have fixed charges for portering. Tickets can be obtained from any station ticket office or from most Austrian travel agents. Second-class couchette cars on most Austrian internal routes have four berths per compartment instead of six and a supplement of 33% over the price of a 6-berth compartment is charged. For further information consult the Tourist Office. **Discount fares:** Throughout Austria, children under six travel free and children 6-14 pay half fare. Senior Citizens (women 60 and over and men 65 and over) may buy train and bus tickets at half price after purchasing a Senior Citizen's ID card for approx.

ASch240. This ID can be purchased at all Austrian railway stations and major post offices or through the post by sending a cheque for US$25, a photocopy of the passport page showing photograph and holder's age, plus one passport-size photo to OeBB Verkehrs-einnahmen und Reklamationsstelle, Mariannengasse 20, A-1090 Vienna (discounts are not valid on subway, trolley or bus lines). Austria offers a number of discount rail passes. The *Rabbit Card,* sold worldwide by travel agencies, Rail Europe and DER Tours/GermanRail offices and at Austrian travel agencies and railway stations, is valid for unlimited travel on all Austrian Federal Railway lines and on any four days within a period of ten days on state and private rail lines in Austria. There is also a *Junior Rabbit Card* for persons under 26 years of age. The *Bundesnetzkarte* (National Network Pass) is only sold in Austria and offers unlimited train travel in all of Austria for either one month or one year. There is also a *Regional-Netzkarte* (Regional Network Pass) offering unlimited train travel in any one of the country's 18 provinces for any four days within ten days. Other domestic fare reductions include short-distance return tickets and school excursions (with up to 70% reductions).

ROAD: Austria has an excellent internal network of roads. Traffic drives on the right. Free help is readily given by the Austrian Motoring Association (OAMTC). Some of the roads are toll roads (a charge is made before entry onto these roads, mainly to help pay for their upkeep). Seat belts must be worn and children under the age of 12 may not sit in the front seat unless a special child's seat has been fitted. Both driver and passenger on a motorbike must wear helmets, and the bike must have lights on at all times. Speed limits are 50kmph (31mph) in built-up areas, 100kmph (62mph) outside built-up areas and 130kmph (81mph) on motorways. **Bus** and **coach** services are run by federal and local authorities, as well as private companies. There are over 1800 services in operation. Some 70 international coach services travel to or through Austria and 22 routes with timetables and prices can be found in the Austrian bus guide which can be consulted via the Tourist Office. Coach excursions and sightseeing tours run from most major cities. **Car hire:** There are car hire firms with offices in most cities, as well as at airports and major railway stations. **Documentation:** British driving licences are generally recognised in Austria and enable the holder to drive in Austria for up to a year. Minimum age is 18. Car registration papers issued in the UK are also valid in Austria, and Third Party insurance is law. A Green Card is *strongly recommended*.

URBAN: Vienna has an extensive system of **metro, bus, light rail** and **tramway** services. Most routes have a flat fare, and there are pre-purchase multi-journey tickets and passes. Those trams marked *Schaffnerlos* on the outside of the carriage do not have conductors, but tickets can be bought from machines on board. Tickets are available from newspaper shops or tobacconists called *Trafik*. The classic way to travel round the capital is by horse-drawn carriage *(Fiaker);* fares should be agreed in advance. There are bus systems in all the other main towns, and also tramways in Linz, Innsbruck and Graz, and trolleybuses in Linz, Innsbruck and Salzburg.

JOURNEY TIMES: The following chart gives approximate journey times (in hours and minutes) from Vienna to other major cities/towns in Austria.

	Air	Road	Rail
Salzburg	0.45	3.00	3.00
Linz	0.45	2.00	2.00
Innsbruck	1.20	5.00	5.30
Bregenz	-	7.00	10.00
Klagenfurt	0.55	4.00	4.20
Graz	0.40	2.40	2.30

ACCOMMODATION

It is advisable to make inquiries and reservations well in advance (especially for July, August, Christmas and Easter). Room reservations are binding for the hotel-keeper and for the guest or travel agency. Compensation may be claimed if reserved rooms are not occupied. Hotels, *pensions* and other forms of tourist accommodation are classified by the Federal Chamber of Commerce and Industry. See the *Grading* section below for details. For further information contact: Österreichische Hoteliervereinigung, Michaelertrakt, Schatzkammerstiege, Hofburg, A-1010 Vienna. Tel: (1) 533 0952. Fax: (1) 533 707 121.

HOTELS: 95% of 5-star hotels, 80% of 4-star hotels and 10% of 3-star hotels in Austria belong to the Bundeskammer der Gewerblichen Wirtschaft, Sektion Fremdenverkehr, Wiedner Hauptstrasse 63, A-1040 Vienna. Tel: (1) 501 050. Fax: (1) 50 20 62 74.

Grading: Classifications are according to the guidelines established by the International Hotel Association and relate to the facilities provided; 5-star for deluxe, 4-star for first class, 3-star for standard, 2-star for economy and 1-star for budget. The facilities offered are as follows:
5-star hotels: Private bathrooms with shower or bath, hand basin and WC with all bedrooms. Telephone, alarm bell, TV on request in all bedrooms. Room service, day and night reception and foreign languages spoken. Restaurant, bars, lifts and garage space (in the cities) in all hotels.
4-star hotels: At least 80% of bedrooms with private bathroom with bath or shower, hand basin and WC. There is a telephone and alarm bell in all rooms, and TV or radio on request in most. Room service and day and night reception, dining rooms, foreign languages spoken, lifts in all hotels.
3-star hotels: All rooms with alarm bell, all with a hand basin and 50% with private bathroom with bath or shower, hand basin and WC. Foreign languages spoken at reception. Lifts and dining room.
2-star hotels: All rooms with hand basin. Toilet facilities may be shared. The dining room may serve as another public room. Some with reception and foreign language capability.
1-star hotels: All rooms have hand basins. Toilet facilities may be shared. The dining room may double as a general public room.
Note: Some hotels may still be under the old grades of A, B, C, etc. Full information and hotel list is available from the Austrian National Tourist Office.
SELF-CATERING: Holiday apartments and chalets are available for rent throughout Austria. For full details contact your local travel agent or the following individual agencies:
Vienna: Ruefa Reisen GesmbH, Mariahilferstrasse 95, A-1060 Vienna. Tel: (1) 59902. Fax: (1) 59902-80. Telex: 115405.
Burgenland: Blaguss Reisen GmbH, Untere Hauptstrasse 12, A-7100 Neusiedl am See. Tel: (2167) 8141. Fax: (2167) 8872. Telex: 18160.
Carinthia: Kärntner Reisebüro, Neuer Platz 2, A-9020 Klagenfurt. Tel: (463) 56400. Fax: (463) 54450. Telex: 422118.
Lower Austria: Niederösterreich Reservierungs-zentrale, Heidenschusse 2, A-1010 Vienna. Tel: (1) 533 3114-34. Fax: (1) 535 0319. Telex: 115220.
Salzburg Province: Interhome, Johann Wolfstrasse 7, A-5020 Salzburg. Tel: (662) 845 586. Fax: (662) 845 5895. Telex: 632994.
Ruefa Reisen GesmbH, Rainerstrasse 7, A-5020 Salzburg. Tel: (662) 874 561-0. Fax: (662) 874 561-20. Telex: 631186.
Dr Degener GmbH, Linzer Gasse 4, A-5024 Salzburg. Tel: (662) 889 110. Fax: (662) 889 11213. Telex: 633596.
Styria: Steiermärkisches Landesreisebüro, Hauptplatz 14, Graz. Tel: (316) 826 456. Fax: (316) 817 261. Telex: 311113.
Tyrol: Tiroler Landesreisebüro, Bozner Platz 7, A-6020 Innsbruck. Tel: (512) 598 850. Fax: (512) 575 407. Telex: 533825.
Upper Austria: Oberösterreich Touristik, Buchungsstelle, Schillerstrasse 50, A-4020 Linz. Tel: (732) 663 024. Fax: (732) 600 229.
Oberösterreichisches Landesreisebüro, Hauptplatz 9, A-4010 Linz. Tel: (732) 771 061-49. Fax: (732) 771 061-49. Telex: 21493.
Vorarlberg: Pego, rental of holiday apartments and chalets all over Austria. Peter Godula, Sägeweg 1, A-6700 Bludenz. Tel: (5552) 65666. Fax: (5552) 63801. Telex: 52169.
FARM HOLIDAYS: Lists of farmhouse accommodation taking paying guests for most provinces in Austria are available at the Austrian National Tourist Office. Listings include farms as well as pensions and inns with an attached farming operation.
CAMPING/CARAVANNING: There are 489 camping sites in Austria, all of which can be entered without any major formalities. One hundred and fifty of these are equipped for winter camping. Reductions for children are available, and for members of FICC, AIT and FIA. It is advisable to take along the camping carnet. Fees are charged on the usual international scale for parking caravans, motorbikes and cars. The parking of caravans without traction vehicle on or beside the public highways (including motorway parking areas) is prohibited. One can park caravans with traction vehicle beside public highways, if the parking regulations are observed. Some mountain roads are closed for caravans. For detailed information, contact the automobile clubs or the Austrian National Tourist Office. The address of the Camping & Caravanning Club is Mariahilferstrasse 180, A-1150 Vienna. Tel: (1) 729 912.
Note: When camping in private grounds, permission of landowner, police and municipal council is needed.
YOUTH HOSTELS: Youth hostels can be found throughout Austria and are at the disposal of anyone carrying a membership card of the International Youth Hostel Association. It is advisable to book in advance, especially during peak periods. For more details contact the Österreichischer Jugendherbergsverband, Gonzagagasse 22, A-1010 Vienna. Tel: (1) 533 53530.
DISABLED TRAVELLERS: A hotel guide for disabled travellers is available from ANTO or from: Verband der Querschnittsgelähmten Österreichs, A-8144 Tobelbad, Styria. Tel: (3136) 2571. For Vienna a special hotel guide for disabled persons has been published. This guide is available from Verband der Querschnittsgelähmten Österreichs, Liechtensteinstrasse 57, A-1090 Vienna. Tel: (1) 340 121. There are also hotels with special facilities for disabled persons in towns all over Austria.

RESORTS & EXCURSIONS

Austria is not only famous for the world's premier skiing regions, but also for breathtaking scenery, magnificent mountains and established hiking trails. The western Federal Provinces **Vorarlberg, Tyrol** and **Salzburg Province** are the most popular tourist regions, though the southern **Carinthia** (bordering Italy and Slovenia) is now taking a larger share of the trade due to its mild climate and attractive lakes.
Austria lends itself to walking and climbing as well as skiing, with an extensive network of hiking and mountain routes carefully signposted and cross-referenced to detailed maps. Alpine huts between 915m and 2744m, with resident wardens in the summer, are for rent. Further information can be obtained from the Austrian Alpine Club (*Österreichischer Alpenverein)*, Wilhelm-Greil-Strasse 15, A-6010 Innsbruck. Tel: (512) 59547.
Skiing facilities can be found in over 600 winter sport resorts between Brand in the west and Semmering in the east. Skiing enthusiasts of all ages and levels have the choice of more than 400 schools and top ski-instructors. **St Anton** is probably the most cosmopolitan with a lively après-ski nightlife. A cable ride to the Vallugagrat offers an ascent with typically stunning Alpine views.

Vienna

The Austrian capital and one of the federal provinces is an important nexus for East–West trade and a frequent host to major congresses either in the *Vienna International Centre* (UNO City) or at the *Austria Center Vienna*. Vienna is situated in the northeast of the country with the Danube running through the northern suburbs of the city. The Ringstrasse is the boundary of the Inner City or Innenstadt, with its fine examples of the city's architecture, shops and hotels. An atmosphere of elegance and style of bygone eras very much prevails in this area, which should be experienced on foot. Art Nouveau buildings line the streets of some suburbs, as Vienna was the birthplace of this then controversial style. The *Austrian National Library* at the Josefsplatz is regarded as an outstanding example of Baroque architecture. The *Schloss Schönbrunn,* home to the Vienna Zoo with its landscaped park, can be compared with the sumptuous palace at Versailles. Many fine art collections like the *Kunsthistorisches Museum,* with the works of Breughel, Dürer and the *Akademie der Bildenden Künste* (Hieronymus Bosch) are internationally renowned. Opulent balls run from New Year's Eve to *Mardi Gras*, the most famous being the *Opernball.* Spring sees the *Festival of Vienna* with concerts, operas and theatre performances. The *Wiener Oper* itself offers a well-selected programme between September and June. Guided tours of the opera and the stage are held regularly during July and August, and at other times when the performance schedule permits it. Right behind the opera is the *Hotel Sacher,* famous the world over for its chocaholic's dream *Sacher Torte* and other Viennese specialities. There are more than 50 museums open to the public, grand palaces, shops, antique markets, international choirs and orchestras, as well as fine restaurants and cosy coffee-houses, which are very much part of the Austrian culture. The Habsburgs who ruled the country for six centuries resided in the *Hofburg* which has the *Kaiser-Appartements* and the *Crown Jewels*. Essential for any tourist is a visit to the *Spanish Riding School* in the Hofburg, where the famous white Lippizaner stallions perform finely executed dressage manoeuvres to the music of Mozart and the Strauss family (closed during July and August). Vienna was the centre of the cultural Renaissance during the 18th and 19th centuries, and home not only to Mozart and the Strauss' but also to Haydn, Beethoven, Schubert, Bruckner, Brahms and Mahler.
Excursions/sightseeing: Vienna is ideal for art and music enthusiasts. The *Viennese Boys' Choir* and the *Viennese Philharmonic* are internationally renowned. Well worth a visit is the art collection at the *Belvedere,* the *Chapel of the Hofburg,* the *Burgtheater* (known as Die Burg), the *Parliament,* the *Old Town Hall,* the University and the Votive church along the Ringstrasse; as well as *St Stephen's Cathedral* and the churches of *St Charles* and *St Rupert.* Not to be missed is the Augustinian Friars and the Capuchin church with the Imperial crypt of the Habsburg family. Vienna's abundance of museums include the *Natural History Museum,* the *Austrian Museum of Applied Arts,* the *Museum of the 20th Century,* the *Museum of Modern Art,* the *Künstlerhaus,* the *Clock and Watch Museum* and the *Technology Museum.* The are also memorial sites for Mozart, Haydn, Beethoven, Schubert, Strauss and Freud.

Burgenland

Austria's youngest Federal Province in the easternmost part of the country is a popular tourist destination. The wooded hills in the south of the region turn into the foothills of the Alps. The northeast largely consists of expanses of the Central European Plain. The mild climate is especially well suited for the cultivation of wine.
Resorts: Eisenstadt, Mogersdorf, Mörbisch, Neusiedl am See, Podersdorf, Raiding Rust, St Margarethen, Bad Tatzmannsdorf and Illmitz.
Excursions/sightseeing: The *Esterhazy Palace*, the *Cathedral* and the *Haydengasse,* as well as the *Bergkirche* and the Franciscan church are well worth a visit in **Eisenstadt**. A thoughtful atmosphere lies over the *Jewish Cemetery* and the former *Jewish Ghetto*. The region is dotted with interesting palaces and fortresses. In July and August **Mörbisch** hosts an operetta festival against the backdrop of the Neusiedler Lake. Not to be missed is the *Local History Museum* in **Neusiedl am See**. **Raiding** is the birthplace of Franz Liszt. Passion plays are staged every five years in **St Margarethen**. The nature reserve of **Illmitz** is ideal for hiking and walks. **Bad Tatzmannsdorf** is a noted spa.

Carinthia

Surrounded by Austria's highest mountain, the Grossglockner (3797m/9644ft), and the Karawanken in the south, the lifestyle here is friendlier and the summers are warmer. The famous lakes reach water temperatures of 28°C, which earned Carinthia the European Environment Award for their superb water quality.
From the **Wörther See** to the *National Park* of **Hohe Tauern,** from the Carinthian summer to the bicycle path on the banks of the Drau, Carinthia offers a variety of excursions even in winter. At this time the lakes become skating rinks and the 10 ski-resorts with 1000km (625 miles) pistes open their doors.
The Provincial capital, **Klagenfurt,** is full of tradition, with more than 50 arcades and the Lindwurm, a medieval dragon, part of the layout. **Villach** combines its flair with a hot spring.
Resorts: Friesach, Heiligenblut, Millstatt, Obervellach, Ossiach, St Veit an der Glan, Villach, Klagenfurt, Veldem and Pörtschach.
Excursions/sightseeing: In **Klagenfurt** the Cathedral, the theatre, the concert hall, the zoo with the reptile house, the birthplace of Robert Musil, the planetarium and several museums are worth visiting. The **Wörther See** has good beaches. The churches and monasteries of **Gurk, Maria Gail, Maria Saal** and **Viktring** are popular, as is the *City Museum* of **Friesach.** Carinthia has a rich legacy of churches, fortresses, palaces and museums – history is always close at hand.

Lower Austria

Lower Austria is the largest Federal Province, encompassing stark mountain scenery, the Alpine foothills, the Danube Valley with its vineyards and the hilly country north of the Danube with its meadows, lakes and ponds.
Resorts: Baden bei Wien, Semmering (spa and ski-resort), Bad Deutsch-Altenburg, Dürnstein, Krems an der Donau, Retz, Rohrau, St Pölten, Wiener Neustadt and Zwettl.
Excursions/sightseeing: The spa of **Baden** has a casino, a summer theatre and a trotting course, whereas **Bad Deutsch-Altenburg** boasts a museum and the Roman archaeological park *Carnuntum.* In **Dürnstein**, the castle ruins, the medieval town centre and church of

the same epoch are part of every tour. The sights of **Retz** include subterranean wine-cellars, well-restored medieval city walls, windmills and a Dominican church. **Rohrau,** Joseph Haydn's birthplace is also worth a visit. The Provincial capital, **St Pölten** is home to a Cathedral, the bishop's residence, a Franciscan church, a church of the Carmelite Nuns, a museum and several Baroque patrician houses. The *Austrian Military Academy* (an old castle), the Cathedral, a Capuchin church and a former Jesuit church (now the city's museum) can be visited in **Wiener Neustadt**. Well worth a visit is the abbey, the library, the state rooms and the chapter house of **Zwettl**. **Burg Rosenau** hosts a *Museum of Free Masonry*. All over Lower Austria are beautiful and interesting churches, abbeys, castles and palaces.

Salzburg Province

Salzburg is an elegant and spacious town, set against a backdrop of breathtaking mountain scenery. The snow-capped mountains of the Hohen Tauern rise in the south whereas the north offers the hills and lakes of the Salzkammergut. All sights are within walking distance of the old city centre, overlooked by the fortress *Hohensalzburg*. The city is probably best known for Wolfgang Amadeus Mozart who gets commemorated in the yearly *Salzburger Festspiele* which take place in the *Grossen* and *Kleinen Festspielhaus,* as well as on the Cathedral square or in the University church. Mozart's birthplace in the Getreidegasse and his house at the Marktplatz are museums. Like Vienna, Salzburg is a fine example of Baroque architecture which stands second only to music in the country's cultural history.
Resorts: Badgastein (spa and winter resort), Bad Hofgastein, Grossgmain, Hallein, St Gilgen, Kaprun (glacier skiing in summer), Oberndorf and Zell-am-See.
Excursions/sightseeing: Salzburg: The *Abbey Church of St Peter* with cemetery and catacombs, the Franciscan church, the *Nonnberg Convent,* the *Trinity Church, St Sebastian's Cemetery,* the *Church of Parsch,* the *Palace of the Prince-Archbishops,* the carillon, the *Town Hall,* the *Pferdeschwemme* (a fountain), the festival halls, the *Mirabell Palace* with its landscaped gardens, the *Mönchsbert* and the *Kapuzinerberg,* several museums, the theatre, *Hellbrunn Palace* with the fountains, *Leopoldskron* and *Klessheim Palaces, Maria Pein Pilgrimage Church,* the Gaisberg and the Untersberg are ideal for tours and walks. **Salzburg Province:** The salt mines and the *Celtic Museum* of **Hallein** are well worth a visit. **Irrsdorf** near Strasswalchen boasts a wonderful carved gate. Further sights include the *Castle Hohenwerfen,* the open-air museum of **Grossgmain** and the *Liechtensteinklamm* as well as the *Krimmler Waterfalls* in the *National Park Hohe Tauern,* the oldest in Austria.

Styria

Styria is a popular and especially attractive holiday destination. In the Dachstein Gebirge overshadowing the Enns Valley skiing is possible all year round. The south of the province is dominated by large vineyards. Styria also has a wealth of green pine forests suitable for rambles and hikes during the summer. In the Provincial capital **Graz**, one should plan a visit to the university and to one of the oldest museums in the world. The *Styrian Armoury*, housing a fine collection of ancient armour, and the *Schloss Eggenberg*, a 17th-century palace, are also not to be missed.
Resorts: Graz, Bruck an der Mur, Eisenerz, Leoben, Murau, Oberzeiring, Piber, Schladming, Stübing/Gratwein, Bad Aussee and Ramsau.
Excursions/sightseeing: The sights of **Graz** include several museums, the Herrengasse, Liberation Square, the *Cathedral,* the *Mausoleum of Emperor Ferdinand II,* the *Leech Church,* the pedestrian zone of the old quarter, numerous patrician houses, a 17th-century castle, *Palais Attems, Castle Hill* with the clocktower, the opera, the theatre and the *Maria Trost Pilgrimage Church.* **Eisenerz** boasts a fortified church. Part of any itinerary should be a visit to the museum and the Convent of **Leoben** and to the silver mine in **Oberzeiring**. The studfarm of the famous Lipizzaner breed of horse can be found in **Piber**. Old farm buildings and representative houses of all Austrian provinces are exhibited in the open-air museum of **Stübing/Gratwein**. The whole Province is scattered with churches, convents, palaces and castles.

Tyrol

Situated in the heart of the Alpine region, it is the most mountainous region of all, with forests, hamlets and alpine pastures, beautiful valleys and mountain lakes. In summer it is a popular destination for hikes; in winter, all winter sports are on offer. Traditional Tyrolean architecture is reflected in the villages, churches and castles.
Innsbruck, the Tyrolean capital and twice home of the Winter Olympics, is the centre of another internationally renowned ski complex comprising six major resorts. An 800-year-old university town, it has numerous fine buildings dating from Austria's cultural Renaissance in the 16th-18th centuries, and a 12th-century castle. For spectacular views over the town and southern Alps, take the funicular to Hungerburg and then the cable car to Hafelekar at 2334m (5928ft).
Resorts: Innsbruck, Erl, Steinach am Brenner, Hall in Tirol, Kitzbühel, Kramsach, Landeck, Lienz and Matrei in East Tyrol, Rattenberg, Seefeld in Tirol and Thiersee.
Excursions/sightseeing: Do not miss the *Golden Roof,* the Herzog-Friedrich-Strasse, *Helbling House,* the *City Tower,* the *Court Church,* the *Hofburg,* the parish *Church of St Jakob,* the Maria-Theresien-Strasse, the *Palace of the Diet,* the *Triumphal Arch,* the *Wilten Basilica, Mount Isel,* the *Ambras Palace,* the *Tyrolean Museum,* the *Landestheater,* a conference centre and the *Seegrube* at **Innsbruck**. Passion plays take place every five years in **Erl**. A sight not to be missed is the Mint Tower at the Hasegg Castle in **Hall in Tirol**. In **Rattenberg,** a medieval atmosphere prevails. A visit to the *Cathedral Chapter of Stams* and the basilica is recommended.

Upper Austria

The south of this Federal Province is dominated by the Salzkammergut lake district. The north offers a relaxed holiday in the many quiet villages and farms – the Mühlviertel. Rolling plains, densely wooded highlands and lush meadows are interspersed with rocks of natural granite. The Pyhrn-Eisenwurzen region is more mountainous, while Innviertel-Hausruckwald (in the west of Upper Austria) is an area of endless farmlands, rivers and forests. The many spas and convalescence centres of this region offer treatment for a wide range of illnesses.
Resorts: Bad Ischl, Hallstatt, St Wolfgang, Mondsee, Gmunden, Braunau, Schärding, Freistadt, Grein, Windischgarsten and Steyr.
Excursions/sightseeing: A tour of the Province's capital **Linz** is not complete without the *Cathedral,* the old quarter, the *Palace Museum, Bruckner House, den Pöstlingberg* and a visit to the many churches and monasteries, for example *St Florian.* The summer villa of Emperor Franz Josef can be found in **Bad Ischl**, as well as a salt mine and several museums. **Hallstatt** lent its name to a whole era; the **Mondsee** is one of the warmest lakes in the Salzkammergut. **St Wolfgang** does not only offer an impressive altar, but a rack-railway as well. **Gmunden**, the Nice of Upper Austria, is known for its many cultural festivals. **Braunau's** and **Schärding's** old city centres are not to be missed. **Freistadt** has medieval forts, while **Grein** offers a navigation museum, *Clam Castle* and the old theatre. **Steyr** fascinates with the old inner city, the *Working-World Museum* and the pilgrimage church *Christkindl.*
Resorts: Bad Goisern, Gosau, Obertraun and Grünau in the Salzkammergut and Hinterstoder, Windischgarsten and Spital am Pyhrn (region Pyhrn-Eisenwurzen).

Vorarlberg

Situated at the far western tip of Austria, the scenery of the Vorarlberg is dramatically diverse. The glaciers of the Silvretta mountain ranges drop dramatically to the shores of Lake Constance with its lush vegetation. Bregenz in the summer lends itself to bicycle tours, swimming, sailing or just sightseeing, whereas the winter season populates the numerous slopes and hiking trails of the Vorarlberg.
Excursions/sightseeing: Bregenz is noted for its Upper City with the *Martin's Tower,* the largest floating stage worldwide, the *Congress Centre,* the *Mehrerau Abbey Church,* the *Vorarlberg Country Museum* and the viewing platform on Mount Pfänder, where one can watch the flight of several birds of prey.
Feldkirch: The historical old quarter of which the *Cathedral St Nicholas* is a part, the *Schattenburg* housing the *Local History Museum,* and the *National Conservatoire* can be found here. In **Levis,** near Feldkirch, the *Castle Amberg* and the Hospital should not be missed. **Tosters**' sights include the castle ruin and the *St Corneli Church* with a 1000-year-old yew. Visitors should pay a visit to the famous Renaissance palace of **Hohenems**. The city is also known for the *Jewish Museum* and the only *Jewish Cemetery* in the Vorarlberg.
Schwarzenberg im Bregenzerwald: A picturesque, completely restored farming village, hometown of the painter Angelika Kaufmann. *The Country Museum* and the church are worth a visit.

Winter Sports Resorts

Austria is one of the major countries for winter sports in Europe and offers the most up-to-date facilities. The most popular areas for skiing are the provinces of Tyrol, Salzburg and Vorarlberg, with some well-known resorts in Carinthia, Styria and Upper and Lower Austria. Besides skiing, all types of other winter sports can be enjoyed, particularly tobogganing, sleigh rides, skating, curling and bowling. The country has a lively après-ski scene. Contact the ANTO for full details of ski resorts in the country. The following is a list, in alphabetical order, of basic information on popular ski regions and resorts in Austria.
Alpbach: Picture postcard village. Skiing from Christmas to mid-March.
Arlberg: *St Anton*: Quiet nightlife. Popular with younger people. Skiing from beginning of December to mid-April. *St Christoph*: Family resort though no nursery slopes. *Holzgau*: 3 nursery slopes. *Lech:* Skiing from beginning of December to end of April. Fashionable and large. *Zürs*: Skiing from beginning of December to end of April. Small, expensive town. Lift-pass sharing with *Lech, St Anton im Tirol, St Christoph im Tirol, Stuben* and *Dalaas im Klostertal,* with more than 100 lifts.
Axamer Lizum: Snow guaranteed. A few nursery slopes. Evening entertainment in the hotel bars. *Mutters*: Picturesque village with breathtaking views. Good for families, skiers of all levels and non-skiers. *Seefeld*: Comparatively expensive. Skiing from end of December to mid-March. Good après-ski, impressive sports centre.
Badgastein Area: *Badgastein*: Numerous downhill and cross-country ski runs. Spa and casino. Skiing from end of December to beginning of April. *Bad Hofgastein*: Quiet village, good school. Beginners and intermediates. *Dorfgastein*: Small and friendly. Well-equipped Alpine huts. Beginners and intermediates. *Sportgastein:* This new resort can be reached by car or bus from Badgastein. Joint ski-pass **Gastein Super Ski**.
Brandnertal: *Bürserberg*: Small village. Beginners and intermediates. *Brand*: Family resort. Selection of leisure activities (paragliding, horseriding, tennis).
Bregenzerwald: *Warth:* Skiing from mid-December to end of April. Relatively unknown and secluded near Lech. Intermediates, good après-ski. Lift-pass sharing with *Schröcken, Damüls, Au* and the *Großen Walsertal.*
Innsbruck Area: *Igls:* Picturesque village. Perfect for intermediates. Bobsleigh events. Ice skating, curling and sleigh rides. Olympic course nearby. Good après-ski. Skiing from mid-December to mid-March. *Innsbruck*: Beautiful town with Baroque architecture. Music, theatre, discos, bars. Skiing from mid-December to mid-March. Free ski bus. **Innsbruck Super Ski Pass** offers skiing in Arlberg, Kitzbühel and Stubai glacier areas.
Ischgl Area: *Ischgl*: Easy-going atmosphere, unsophisticated Tyrolean village. Skiing from mid-December to mid-April. *Galtür*: Ideal for families and intermediates. Sports centre.
Kaiserwinkel Area: *Kossen:* Small village. Wonderful scenery and dramatic views. Excellent cross-country skiing. *Walchsee:* Good cross-country skiing. Ice-skating, tobogganing, horse-drawn sleigh rides, swimming, tennis, horseriding. *Schwendt:* Horse-drawn sleigh rides.
Kitzbühel Area: *Kitzbühel*: International resort. Olde Worlde atmosphere. Tea rooms and cafés. Good selection of après ski. Skiing from mid-December to mid-March. *Kirchberg:* Something for everyone. Skiing from mid-December to mid-March. *Kirchdorf*: Relaxed village atmosphere. Ideal for beginners and intermediates. Cross-country skiing. Tobogganing. Lively après-ski. **Kitzbüheler Ski Pass** gives access to 64 lifts in the region. **Kirchdorf Super Skipass** covers St Johann, Steinplatte, Kitzbühel and Fieberbrunn.
Kleinwalsertal: *Hirschegg*: Intermediates. *Riezlern:* Beginners and intermediates.
Montafon: *Schruns:* Skiing from December to end of April. Large skiing-regions, active nightlife. *Gargellen:* Skiing fom mid-December to end of April. Relaxed, friendly and reasonable. *Gaschurn:* Skiing from mid-December to end of April. Friendly, family atmosphere. *Partenen:* Ideal for intermediates.
Nauders: Small with vigorous nightlife. Skiing from mid-December to beginning of April.
Obergurgl Area: *Hochgurgl*: Small purpose-built resort for all skiers. *Obergurgl*: Skiing from beginning of December to end of April. Friendly and traditional.
Obertauern: Snow guaranteed. Excellent nightlife. Ski to hotels. Skiing from beginning of December to end of April.
Pongau: *Flachau*: Beginners and intermediates. A few

difficult runs. *St Johann in Pongau*: Runs of all difficulties. Large school. *Wagrain:* Beginners and intermediates. Quiet though good nightlife. *Filzmoos:* Tranquil, friendly atmosphere. Beginners and intermediates. *Altenmarkt*: Several runs. Joint ski-pass **Salzburger Sportwelt Amadé**.
Saalbach/Hinterglemm: *Hinterglemm:* Spacious new resort. Intermediates. *Saalbach*: Larger and more expensive, though established. Artificial snow-making and Austria's largest cable car. Good entertainment for non-skiers.
Schladming: Unpretentious and friendly. Good shopping. Good though restricted nightlife.
Schneewinkel Area: *St Johann in Tirol:* Old market town. Beginners and intermediates. Good nightlife. Tennis, health centre, ice-skating, night tobagganing, cross-country skiing. *Fieberbrunn*: Quiet family resort. *Oberndorf:* Good cross-country skiing. Tobaganning and horse-drawn sleigh rides. *Waidring:* Ideal for beginners and intermediates. Good ski school. Excellent for children. Cross-country skiing, skating, toboganning, curling. *St Ulrich:* Lakeside town. *Hochfilzen:* Ice-skating and tobagganing. **Schneewinkel Pass** gives access to 54 lifts.
Serfaus: Quiet après-ski. Reasonable prices. Easy slopes. Skiing from mid-December to mid-April.
Sölden Area: *Sölden*: Skiing from beginning of December to end of April. South-facing sunny resort. *Hochsölden*: Secluded. South-facing slopes.
Stubaital: *Fulpmes*: Good après-ski. *Neustift*: Pretty village, ideal for non-skiers. Skiing from mid-December to mid-March.
Tux Glacier Area: *Hintertux:* All-year-round skiing. All levels. *Madseit:* Small village surrounded by woods. *Juns:* Old comfortable houses. *Lanersbach:* Social and cultural centre of area. Intermediate and advanced with nursery slopes. *Vorderlanersbach:* Tyrolean village. Magnificent views. **Super Ski Pass** covers the entire Tux and Ziller valley.
Wilden Kaiser Area: *Söll*: Skiing from mid-December to mid-March. Nightlife informal and lively. *Ellmau*: Ideal for intermediates. Downhill and cross-country runs for beginners and intermediates, sledging. *Going:* Small village. *Hopfgarten:* Rustic hamlet. *Itter*: Good school. Picturesque surroundings, cosy nightlife. *Westendorf*: Very good après-ski. Skiing from mid-December to mid-March. The **Wilder Kaiser Brixental Ski Pass** covers the largest ski circuit in Tyrol, including Ellmau, Scheffau, Söll, Itter, Hopfgarten, Westendorf, Going and Brixen.
Wildschönau: *Niederau:* Modern resort. Skiing from mid-December to beginning of April. Night skiing. Very popular, vigorous nightlife. *Auffach*: Perfect for intermediates. School. Friendly and professional. *Oberau*: Baroque church. Night skiing. Ideal for beginners, a favourite for school trips. *Thierbach:* Idyllic hamlet.
Zell-am-See Area: Skiing from mid-December to mid-March. Active nightlife. *Kaprun:* Skiing from Christmas to end of March. Good glacier-skiing. Guaranteed snow. Joint ski-pass **Europa Sportregion**.
Zillertal: *Mayrhofen*: Popular. Skiing from mid-December to mid-March. *Zell am Ziller*: Small resort. Skiing from mid-December to mid-March. Restricted après-ski. *Finkenberg*: 3 nursery slopes, 19 for intermediates. Ice-skating, curling, bowling, tobagganing. Good après-ski. Good ski school, especially for children. *Fügen and Hochfügen*: Well laid-out, though few slopes. *Gerlos*: Suitable for skiers of all levels. Very good school. Cross-country runs of high standard.
Zugspitzarea: *Ehrwald*: Easy nursery slopes, ideal for family-skiing. *Lermoos*: Skiing from Christmas to beginning of April. Good après-ski and leisure activities.

SOCIAL PROFILE

FOOD & DRINK: Traditional Viennese dishes are *Wiener Schnitzel*, boiled beef *(Tafelspitz)*, calf's liver with herbs in butter *(geröstete Leber)*, *goulash*, and various types of smoked and cured pork. Viennese cuisine is strongly influenced by southeast European cuisine, notably that of Hungary, Serbia, Romania and Dalmatia. Many of the simpler meals are often made with rice, potatoes and dumplings *(Knödel)*, with liquid sauces. The main meal of the day is lunch. *Mehlspeisen* is the national term for cakes and puddings, all of which are wonderfully appetising. There are more than 57 varieties of *Torte*, which are often consumed with coffee at around 1500. Open all day, the Austrian coffee shop *(Kaffeehaus)* is little short of a national institution and often provides the social focus of a town or neighbourhood.
Drink: Spirits such as whisky and gin, together with imported beers, tend to be on the expensive side, but local wines (often served in open carafes) are excellent and cheap. Most of the wines are white *(Riesling, Veltliner)* but there are also some good red wines from Baden and Burgenland, as well as imported wines from other European countries. Generally the strict registration laws mean that the quality of the wine will be fully reflected in its price. *Obstler* is a drink found in most German-speaking countries, and is made by distilling various fruits. It is usually very strong, and widely drunk as it is cheap and well flavoured. Most bars or coffee houses have waiter service and bills are settled with the arrival of drinks. All restaurants have waiter service.
Note: There are no national licensing laws in Austria, but each region has local police closing hours. Most coffee houses and bars serve wine as well as soft drinks and beers.
SHOPPING: High-quality goods such as handbags, glassware, chinaware and winter sports equipment represent the cream of specialist items found in Austria. A 20% to 32% value-added-tax (called MwSt) is included in the list price of items sold, and tourists can claim a partial refund on this tax on unused goods which are taken with them when they leave Austria.
Shopping hours: Shops and stores are generally open Monday to Friday from 0800-1830 with a 1- or 2-hour lunch break. Most shops close at noon Saturday. For information on cashback on duty free, contact Austria Tax-free Shopping, Biberstrasse 10, A-1010 Vienna.
NIGHTLIFE: The Austrians believe in 'early to bed and early to rise' and consequently nightlife in Vienna is relatively quiet and civilised. One of the best ways to spend an evening is in one of the wine gardens *(Heurigen)* found outside the towns. There are casinos and nightclubs in most of the major cities, which depend largely on the tourist trade, as the native Austrians prefer the theatre and opera.
SPORT: Cycling: Bicycles can be rented in most areas. **Fishing:** Excellent facilities, but permits required. **Gliding:** Facilities available in most areas. **Riding:** Available in most areas. **Hang-gliding:** A growing sport in the mountains. **Swimming, sailing, mountaineering, rambling:** All popular, especially during the summer months. **Skiing**: See *Winter Sports Resorts* section in *Resorts & Excursions* above.
SPECIAL EVENTS: In 1995, Austria celebrates '1000 years Austria', its millenium anniversary, and its 50-year anniversary as the Second Republic. There will therefore be many special events throughout the country in celebration. The following is a selection of other major events and festivals, many of which occur annually:
Mar 19-26 '95 *Ski Festival*, Gaschurn. **Apr 6-May 15** *Spring Festival*, Bregenz. **Apr 8-17** *Easter Festival*, Salzburg. **Apr 18-May 16** *4th Vienna Spring Festival.* **May 5-Jun 11** *Vienna Festival*. **Mid-May to end-Jun** *Spring Festival,* Millstatt. **May 25-28** *Narzissen Festival,* Bad Aussee. **Jun 3-5** *Whitsun Festival,* Salzburg. **Jul 1-Aug 31** *Summer Concert Season*, Vienna. **Jun 12-24** *Schubertiade*, Feldkirch. **Jun 24-Jul 16** *Styriarte*, Graz. **End-Jun to mid-Sep** *Summer Operetta Days*, Baden. **Beginning to mid-Jul** *Chamber Music Festival,* Lockenhaus. **Jul 2-7** *9th Chambermusic Festival,* Pertisau. **Jul 14-Aug 27** *Lake Performances*, Mörbisch. **Jul 20-Aug 22** *Bregenz Festival*. **Jul 20-Aug 30** *Attergauer Cultural Summer,* St Georgen. **Jul 25-Aug 31** *Salzburg Festival*. **Aug 13-26** *Festival of Early Music*, Innsbruck. **Aug 13-Sep 10** *International Chamber Music Festival,* Waldviertel. **Aug 15** *Kaiserfestival,* Bad Ischl. **Aug 25-27** *International Country, Folk and Blues Festival,* Mayrhofen. **Beginning Sep-beginning Oct** *Musical Autumn,* Millstatt. **Sep 2-9** *Musical Days,* Mondsee. **Sep 8-17** *Haydn Festival*, Eisenstadt. **Sep 10-Oct 1** *International Bruckner Festival,* Linz. **Mid-Sep** *Oldtimer Grand Prix*, Salzburgring. **Nov 12-19** *13th Vienna Schubert Days.* **Dec** *10th Vienna Mozart Festival.* **Dec 5-6** *St Nicholas and Krampus Procession,* countrywide. **Dec 31-Jan 1 '96** *New Year's Eve and Day Concerts by the Vienna Philharmonic Orchestra.*
For details of other events celebrated in Austria in 1995-96, consult the Austrian National Tourist Office.
SOCIAL CONVENTIONS: Austrians tend to be quite formal in both their social and business dealings. They do not use first names when being introduced, but after the initial meeting first names are often used. Handshaking is normal when saying hello and goodbye. It is considered impolite to enter a restaurant or shop without saying *Guten Tag* or, more usually, *Grüss Gott;* similarly, to leave without saying *Auf Wiedersehen* can cause offence. Social pleasantries and some exchange of small-talk is appreciated. If invited out to dinner, flowers should be brought for the hostess. The Church enjoys a high and respected position in Austrian society, which should be kept in mind by the visitor. It is customary to dress up for the opera or the theatre.
Tipping is widespread but large amounts are not expected. On restaurant bills a service charge of 10-15% is included, but it is usual to leave a further 5%. Attendants at theatres, cloakrooms, petrol pumps, etc expect to be tipped ASch2-3. Railway and airports have fixed charges for portering. Taxi drivers expect ASch3-4 for a short trip and 10% for a longer one.

BUSINESS PROFILE

ECONOMY: Austria has enjoyed steady and stable growth with fairly low inflation and unemployment since 1955. It is one of the most prosperous countries in the world. Manufacturing accounts for over 30% of GNP. Since the Second World War, much of the country's industrial capacity has been in State hands and is only gradually being relinquished: given the relative success of those enterprises under the wing of the state holding company, OIAG, this is not surprising. Iron and steel, chemicals, metal working and engineering all fall into this category. Agriculture has proved equally successful with domestic products meeting 90% of the country's food needs. Crops include sugarbeet, potatoes, grain, grapes, tobacco, flax, hemp and wine. Austria has moderate deposits of iron, lignite, magnesium, lead, copper, salt, zinc and silver. Although there are some oil reserves, Austria must import the bulk of its energy requirements; much of it comes from Eastern Europe. Austria was a member of the European Free Trade Association (EFTA) and is now a full member of the EU as of January 1, 1995. This may be seen as a natural development from Austria's recent export patterns: EU members account for 68% of imports and 63% of exports. Germany is Austria's largest trading partner by a considerable margin, followed by Italy, France and the UK and, outside the EU, Switzerland. The previously substantial trade with both the USA and the former USSR has been falling in recent years.
BUSINESS: Austrians are quite formal in their business dealings. A working knowledge of German will be very advantageous. Best times to visit are the spring and autumn months. **Office hours:** 0800-1600 Monday to Friday.
COMMERCIAL INFORMATION: The following organisation can offer advice: Wirtschaftskammer Österreich (Federal Economic Chamber), Wiedner Hauptstrasse 63, A-1045 Vienna. Tel: (1) 50105. Fax: (1) 50206. Telex: 111871.
CONFERENCES/CONVENTIONS: Austria has 31 conference venues, including over 20 in Vienna and a floating conference centre, the *MS Mozart,* on the river Danube. The provincial capitals of Salzburg, Innsbruck, Graz, Linz, Bregenz, Klagenfurt and Eisenstadt also offer convention venues, as do several health and spa resorts. Furthermore there are 71 hotels in Austria which specialise in the conference/convention field. For more detailed information, contact the Austrian Convention Bureau, Margaretenstrasse 1, A-1040 Vienna. Tel: (1) 581 2161. Fax: (1) 581 2162.

CLIMATE

Austria enjoys a moderate continental climate: summers are warm and pleasant with cool nights, and winters are sunny, with snow levels high enough for widespread winter sports.
Required clothing: European clothes according to season. Alpine wear for mountain resorts.

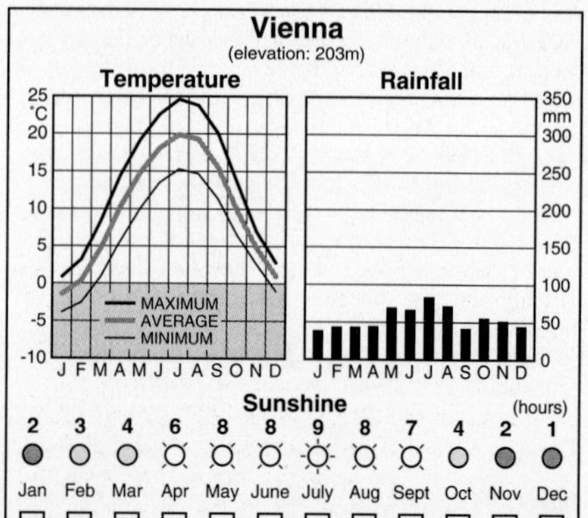

□ *international airport*

Location: Caucasus, western Caspian Sea region.

Note: Extreme internal instability, war with neighbouring Armenia and foreign occupation of 15-20% of the territory of the country means that much of Azerbaijan is unsafe for tourists. Public disturbances may occur without warning. The situation in the capital of Baku remains unsettled and government tanks and armed troops continue to patrol certain areas of the city, in particular around the parliament and presidency buildings. Armed conflict is taking place in and around the Armenian-populated area of Nagorno Karabakh located inside Azerbaijan and along the borders with Armenia and Iran. Furthermore, in recent years the crime rate in the republic has soared. Street robbery is commonplace, and many locals carry guns as a matter of course. Visitors should be wary of venturing out alone after dark. Those intending to visit the region should seek up-to-date advice from the appropriate government office (Foreign Office for British citizens). Readers should also bear in mind that the accuracy of information supplied below concerning accommodation, economic activity, tourist facilities and food supplies may be affected by the volatility of the situation.
Source: US State Department – October 24, 1994.

Ministry of Foreign Affairs
Ghanjlar meydani 3, 370004 Baku, Azerbaijan
Tel: (12) 933 012.
Embassy of the Republic of Azerbaijan
Kensington Office Centre, Room 208, London House, 19 Old Court Place, London W8 4PL
Tel: (0171) 938 2222. Fax: (0171) 937 8335.
Embassy of the Republic of Azerbaijan
Ulitsa Stanislavskogo 16, Moscow, Russian Federation
Tel: (095) 229 1649.
Azerbaijan also has embassies or consulates in Ankara, Beijing, Bonn, Cairo, Istanbul, Riyadh and Tehran.
Intourist
219 Marsh Wall, Isle of Dogs, London E14 9PD
Tel: (0171) 538 8600. Fax: (0171) 538 5967.

Health	
GALILEO/WORLDSPAN: **TI-DFT/BAK/HE**	
SABRE: **TIDFT/BAK/HE**	
Visa	
GALILEO/WORLDSPAN: **TI-DFT/BAK/VI**	
SABRE: **TIDFT/BAK/VI**	

For more information on Timatic codes refer to Contents.

British Embassy
c/o Stary Hotel Intourist, Room 215, Baku, Azerbaijan
Tel: (12) 926 306/7 *or* 924 813 *or* INMARSAT (873) 144 6455.
Embassy of the Republic of Azerbaijan
Suite 700, 927 15th Street, NW, Washington DC 20005
Tel: (202) 842 0001. Fax: (202) 842 0004.
Intourist USA Inc
Suite 603, 610 Fifth Avenue, New York, NY 10020
Tel: (212) 757 3884. Fax: (212) 459 0031.
Embassy of the United States of America
Prospect Azadlyg 83, Baku, Azerbaijan
Tel: (12) 960 019 *or* 926 306/7/8/9, exts. 441, 442, 446, 447, 448 and 450; *or* 926 306 (after hours) *or* 963 621 *or* 960 895 *or* INMARSAT (873) 151 2713. Telex: 142110 (a/b AMEMB SU).
Intourist
Suite 630, 1801 McGill College Avenue, Montréal, Québec H3A 2N4
Tel: (514) 849 6394. Fax: (514) 849 6743.
The Canadian Embassy in Moscow deals with enquiries relating to Azerbaijan (see *Russian Federation* **later in the book).**

AREA: 86,600 sq km (33,400 sq miles).
POPULATION: 7,174,000 (1991 estimate).
POPULATION DENSITY: 83 per sq km.
CAPITAL: Baku. **Population:** 1,149,000 (1990 estimate).
GEOGRAPHY: Azerbaijan is bordered by the Russian Federation, Georgia and Iran, and is divided by the Republic of Armenia into a smaller western part in the Lesser Caucasus and a larger eastern part, stretching from the Greater Caucasus to the Mugan, Mili and Shirvan Steppes and bordered by the Caspian Sea in the east. Its highest peaks are Mount Bazar-Dyuzi (4114m/13497ft) and Sag-Dag (3886m/12749ft).
LANGUAGE: Azerbaijani.
RELIGION: 70% Shia Muslim; the remainder are mostly Sunni Muslim.
TIME: GMT + 4.
COMMUNICATIONS: Telephone: International direct dialling is available to Baku. Country code: 994. Other parts of the republic may only be contacted using operator-connected calls. All outgoing international calls from Azerbaijan, including calls to CIS republics, must be made through the operator. The limited number and dubious reliability of international phone lines from the republic makes telephone communication very difficult.
Post: International postal services are severely disrupted. Long delays are inevitable – letters may take weeks if not months to arrive and parcels are unlikely to arrive intact. Registering post may increase its chances of arriving at its destination, but will not necessarily accelerate the process. **Press:** The principal daily newspaper is *Khalg Gazeti* (state-owned). The media remain subject to strict censorship and state control. A measure of freedom and a fledgling opposition press developed during the period of Elchibey's Popular Front administration, but since Heidar Aliyev became President the press has reverted to its role as mouthpiece of the Government. **Media:** *Azerinform* is the Azerbaijani information news agency. The *State Committee for Television and Radio* can be contacted at ul. Mekhti Huseina 1, 370011 Baku. Tel: (12) 927 155. *Radio Baku* broadcasts in Azerbaijani, Russian, Turkish, Arabic and Farsi (Persian), while *Baku Television* broadcasts in Azerbaijani and Russian only. English-language news services include *Sharg* (tel: (12) 929 161 *or* 925 506) and *Azeri News Service* (tel: (12) 989 603) and *Turan* (tel: (12) 938 931 *or* 984 027).
BBC World Service frequencies: From time to time these change. See the section *How to Use This Book* for more information.
BBC:

MHz	17.64	12.09	9.410	6.195

PASSPORT/VISA

Regulations and requirements may be subject to change at short notice, and you are advised to contact the appropriate diplomatic or consular authority before finalising travel arrangements. Details of these may be found at the head of this country's entry. Any numbers in the chart refer to the footnotes below.

	Passport Required?	Visa Required?	Return Ticket Required?
Full British	Yes	Yes	Yes
BVP	Not valid	-	-
Australian	Yes	Yes	Yes
Canadian	Yes	Yes	Yes
USA	Yes	Yes	Yes
Other EU (As of 31/12/94)	Yes	Yes	Yes
Japanese	Yes	Yes	Yes

Note: Visas may be obtained through Azerbaijani embassies or consulates in Ankara or Istanbul, Turkey and Bonn, Germany. Georgian visas are valid for transit through Azerbaijan for a period of up to 5 days.
PASSPORTS: Required by all. Passports must be valid for at least the length of the visa.
British Visitors Passport: Not accepted.
VISAS: Required by all except resident nationals of the CIS republics.
Types of visa: *Individual; Tourist; Business* (for business or educational visits, trade fairs and exhibitions); and *Transit* (see below). Generally, *Business* and *Individual* visas need a letter of invitation, although this can be waived in some cases if application is made to and approved by the Ministry of the Interior. *Transit visas:* Travellers with Transit visas are allowed a maximum of 48 hours to transit provided they are in possession of confirmed onward travel documentation and valid entry requirement for the onward destination. Passengers may leave the airport under certain conditions on a Transit visa, but anyone intending independent excursions must obtain a full visa.
Cost: Regular visas are free of charge. However, at the time of writing, *Express visas* (those processed within a period of 1-4 days) for UK nationals cost £27 for single-entry and £47 for multiple-entry; for US nationals, US$20 for single-entry and US$75 for multiple-entry; and for Canadian nationals, the equivalent of £34 for single-entry and £47 for multiple-entry. Nationals of Pakistan may receive their *Express visas* free of charge. Other nationals should check with the Consulate (or Consular Section at the Embassy) for the cost of their visas. Tour operators charge a fee for obtaining visas for their clients.
Application to: Consulate (or Consular Section at Embassy). For addresses, see top of entry.
Application requirements: *Tourist/Individual visa:* (a) Completed application form. (b) 1 recent passport-size photo. (c) Valid passport. (d) For Tourist visa, a copy of a voucher (exchange order) issued by an authorised travel company with indication of reference number, names, dates of entry and exit, itinerary, means of transportation, class of services and amount of money paid by a client. (e) For Individual visa, a letter of invitation from a person resident in Azerbaijan. (f) Fee.
Business visa: (a) Completed application form. (b) 1 recent passport-size photo. (c) Valid passport. (d) An introductory letter from company or firm indicating the purpose, itinerary, organisation to be visited, period of stay and exact departure dates of flights. (e) An invitation from the organisation, department or institution to be visited in Azerbaijan. (f) Fee.
Applications may be sent in by post, but must be retrieved from the Embassy in person.
Working days required: Applications for visas may not be made earlier than 3 months before departure, and in no case later than 15 working days before departure, whether by post or personal visit. Regular visas usually take between 5-15 days and Express visas from 1-4 days.

MONEY

Currency: On August 15, 1992, Azerbaijan introduced a new currency, the Manat. 1 Manat = Rub10. Each Manat is subdivided into 100 gyapik (in coins). In September 1993 the Manat entered fully into circulation. However, at the time of writing, the Russian Rouble (but not the old Soviet Rouble) remains legal tender, although market traders and shopkeepers in certain parts of the republic are now unwilling to accept Roubles.
Credit cards: Not accepted. Generally, Azerbaijan is a cash-only economy.
Travellers cheques: Not accepted.
Currency exchange: The US Dollar is the most preferred currency and is required in many hotels and preferred in many restaurants. However, many local hotels, exchange bureaux and restaurants will not accept dollar bills dated before 1992 or those which are torn or in any way disfigured. The Deutschmark is widely accepted, whereas Sterling is less widely recognised. Travellers are advised to take banknotes in small denominations. Visitors should refer to Rouble exchange rates to establish a reasonable exchange rate for the Manat. In theory, money changed into Manats or Roubles can be reconverted on leaving the country, but only on payment of a substantial commission and production of proof of the original exchange transaction. In view of this, and the constant fluctuations in the exchange rate, visitors are advised to change relatively small amounts of money as it is required. Rates offered by banks, bureaux de change and illegal street traders are unlikely to vary significantly.
Currency restrictions: The import and export of local currency is prohibited. Foreign currency must be declared on arrival. The export of foreign currency is limited to the amount declared on arrival. Residents may only import or export up to Rub500,000, if declared on

departure and arrival.
Banking hours: 1000-1700 Monday to Friday. Midday closing hours vary.

DUTY FREE

The following goods may be imported into Azerbaijan without incurring customs duty:
250 cigarettes or 250g of tobacco products; 1 litre of spirits; 2 litres of wine; a reasonable quantity of perfume for personal use; gifts up to a value of Rub1000.
Note: On entering the country, tourists must complete a customs declaration form which must be retained until departure. This allows the import of articles intended for personal use, including currency and valuables which must be registered on the declaration form. Customs inspections can be long and detailed.
Prohibited imports: Military weapons and ammunition, narcotics and drug paraphernalia, pornography, loose pearls and anything owned by a third party that is to be carried in for that third party. If you have any query regarding items that may be imported, an information sheet is available on request from Intourist.
Prohibited exports: As prohibited imports, as well as annulled securities, state loan certificates, lottery tickets, works of art and antiques (unless permission has been granted by the Ministry of Culture), saiga horns, punctuate and red deer antlers (unless on organised hunting trip), and punctuate deer skins.

PUBLIC HOLIDAYS

Jan 1 '95 New Year's Day. **Mar 8** International Women's Day. **May 28** Republic Day. **Oct 9** Day of the Armed Services. **Oct 18** Day of Statehood. **Nov 17** Day of National Survival. **Dec 31** Day of Azerbaijani Solidarity Worldwide. **Jan 1 '96** New Year's Day. **Mar 8** International Women's Day.

HEALTH

Regulations and requirements may be subject to change at short notice, and you are advised to contact your doctor well in advance of your intended date of departure. Any numbers in the chart refer to the footnotes below.

	Special Precautions?	Certificate Required?
Yellow Fever	No	No
Cholera	No	No
Typhoid & Polio	No	-
Malaria	1	-
Food & Drink	2	-

[1]: Malaria risk, exclusively in the benign *vivax* form, exists throughout the year in southern areas of Azerbaijan. A weekly dose of 300mg of chloroquine is the recommended prophylaxis.
[2]: All water should be regarded as being a potential health risk. Water used for drinking, brushing teeth or making ice should have first been boiled or otherwise sterilised. Milk is pasteurised and dairy products are safe for consumption. Only eat well-cooked meat and fish, preferably served hot. Pork, salad and mayonnaise may carry increased risk. Vegetables should be cooked and fruit peeled.
Rabies is present. For those at high risk, vaccination before arrival should be considered. If you are bitten abroad, seek medical advice without delay. For more information consult the *Health* section at the back of the book.
Health care: The health service provides free medical treatment for all citizens. However, medical care in Azerbaijan is limited. If a traveller becomes ill during a booked tour in Azerbaijan, emergency treatment is free, with small sums to be paid for medicines and hospital treatment. If a longer stay than originally planned becomes necessary because of the illness, the visitor has to pay for all further treatment – a travel insurance is therefore recommended. It is advisable to take a supply of those medicines that are likely to be required (but check first that they may be legally imported) as medicines can prove difficult to get hold of. Bearing in mind the shortage of medical supplies and relatively primitive standard of health care in the republic, travellers may be well advised to take out an insurance policy which includes emergency repatriation in case of serious illness or accident. Also, medical insurance is not always valid within the country.

TRAVEL - International

AIR: Since independence, *Azerbaijan Airlines* (a state-owned company) has taken over from *Aeroflot* in the republic. Flights into Baku from Moscow and St Petersburg are subject to frequent delays and

cancellations. Travelling to Baku via Moscow inevitably involves at least one night's stopover in Moscow, and transfer from Sheremetevo international airport to Vnukovo airport, over an hour's drive from the city. *Transaero,* a new Russian private airline which flies throughout the CIS is a more comfortable alternative. For further information, telephone *Transaero* offices in Baku (tel: (12) 986 166) or Moscow (tel: (095) 292 7513 *or* 292 7526). *Azerbaijan Airlines* has weekly flights to Cologne, Tehran, Dubai and Karachi. There are also daily flights on *Azerbaijan Airlines* and *Turkish Airlines* on alternating days from Istanbul. International carriers travelling via Turkey are generally the most reliable.
International airport: *Bina* is approximately 15km (9 miles) from Baku (travel time – 40 minutes).
SEA: Passenger ferries from Baku across the Caspian Sea sail regularly to Krasnovodsk in Turkmenistan and to Bandar Anzali and Bandar Nowshar in Iran. Winter storms may disrupt these services.
RAIL: Azerbaijan is connected with Tbilisi in Georgia and Makhachkala in Dagestan (Russian Federation), as well as Moscow and major cities in the CIS. The line running to Yerevan in Armenia through the autonomous republic of Nakhichevan is closed indefinitely. As a result of this, the line to Tabriz in Iran has also closed. There is a railway running from Baku to Tehran, and an Iranian-Azerbaijani government-sponsored joint venture is to undertake the construction of an additional track to Nakhichevan through Iran, bypassing Armenia. Visitors should be aware that all rail travel is dangerous. Bandits frequently attack and rob travellers and there is little evidence that the police or railway authorities are willing or able to intervene usefully should such an eventuality arise.

TRAVEL - Internal

Note: Internal travel to several regions is restricted; travellers must obtain special permission from the Ministry of the Interior to visit these areas.
ROAD: Azerbaijan's road network totals 30,400km (19,000 miles) of which 28,600km (17,875 miles) are paved. Military operations and mass migrations of refugees in many parts of the republic may affect travel by both road and rail. Traffic drives on the right.
URBAN: It is common practice to flag down private cars as well as official taxis. Taxi fares should always be negotiated before starting a journey, and visitors should be aware that rates proposed initially are likely to be unreasonably high, in the expectation that foreigners will have unlimited cash and little idea of how much they ought to be paying.

ACCOMMODATION

Soviet Intourist hotels have been taken over by the new Azerbaijani tourist authority, but all hotels are still state-run and standards of hygiene, service and catering remain primitive at best. Security in hotels is often a problem. The Hotel Anba in Baku (formerly the Moskva) is now run by an Azerbaijani-Turkish joint venture and is in the process of being renovated. At US$120 per night, and offering mediocre food and modest accommodation, it cannot be described as good value for money, but it may be the safest place for foreigners to stay. It is one of the few hotels in the capital served with reliable satellite phones and regularly supplied with Western newspapers. Other hotels with satellite connections from hotel rooms in Baku are the Old Intourist Hotel in the centre of the old city, which is relatively pleasant but difficult to get into, many of the rooms being occupied semi-permanently by foreign oil companies, and the Azerbaijan or New Intourist Hotel, considerably less safe and comfortable than the Anba, but with a telephone satellite service available in hotel rooms and a telephone and fax service available on the ground floor.

RESORTS & EXCURSIONS

During the Soviet period, the small numbers of foreigners who visited Azerbaijan tended to be whisked past the republic's principal tourist attractions during a brief interlude in a longer tour of the Trans-Caucasus republics. Soviet tourists headed mainly for resorts on the Caspian Sea. Although the present conditions of economic and political stability do not make Azerbaijan an obvious holiday destination, the republic has a number of sights of great historic, architectural and natural interest.
Baku: The medieval walled city – *Icheri Shekher* – within Baku has been restored, and retains a distinctly Middle-Eastern and relaxed atmosphere, with its tea-houses and busy street-life. Its attractive narrow streets and stone buildings spread up from the waterfront, where the 12th-century Maiden's Tower (*Kyz-Kalasy*) looks out over the bay. Locals claim that the view from the top of

the tower rivals the beauty of the Bay of Naples. Nearby are two *caravanserais* (inns), one dating from the 14th century, the other from the 16th century, originally built to accommodate travelling merchants from northern India and central Asia. The *caravanserais,* with their courtyards and vaulted roofs, have been restored and now function as restaurants. There are also a number of mosques located in the medieval city, one of which, the *Dzhuma Mosque,* houses the *Museum of Carpets and Applied Arts,* with a fine display of Azerbaijani carpets, as well as jewellery, embroidery, woodcarving and filigree metalwork. The *Synyk Kalah Minaret* dates from 1093 and is the oldest building still standing in the city. Beyond the minaret is the 15th-century royal court complex, the *Palace of the Shirvan Shahs.* The palace, mausoleum and law courts are all open to the public. Equally distinctive are the opulent houses and public buildings built during the Baku oil boom at the turn of the century. Millionaire oil merchants indulged themselves with neo-gothic, mock oriental and pseudo-renaissance fantasies in stone, developing a local architectural confidence which spilled over into the Soviet period: the Sabuchinsky railway station for example, dating from 1926, is designed to resemble an enormous *madrassah* (Islamic religious academy). A number of tourist sights are located near enough to Baku for one-day excursions to be feasible.
The village of **Kobustan,** about 70km (43 miles) south of Baku, has a unique array of rock paintings, some of them 10,000 years old and spread over 100 sq km (39 sq miles) of caves and rocky outcrops. The subject matter includes hunting scenes, ritual dances, religious ceremonies, ships, animals and constellations, and many of the rocks are further adorned with signatures and remarks added by visiting Roman soldiers in the 1st century AD, suggesting that the area has a long history as a tourist attraction.
The Apsheron Peninsula, stretching out into the Caspian Sea beyond Baku, has several 14th-century fortresses, built by the Shirvan shahs fearing attack from the sea. Best preserved are those at **Ramana, Nardaran** and **Mardkyany.** Ramana also features the remains of ancient oil fields where Zoroastrian fire-worshippers still occasionally stage ritual dances, leaping over the flames which rise from the oil-soaked ground over natural gas vents. The tip of the peninsula is a nature reserve. Some 20km (12 miles) northeast of Baku is the *Surakhany Temple,* established by Parsee fire-worshippers living in Baku in the 18th century. The temple was predated by a much older Zoroastrian shrine on the same site. Surakhany remained a popular destination for Indian pilgrims until the revolution. Some of the pilgrims' cells now house a wax museum, intended to introduce the rudiments of fire worship to the uninitiated.
The city of **Shumakha,** 130km (80 miles) west of Baku in the foothills of the Caucasus, predated Baku as the principal trading centre and capital of the Shirvan shahs. Repeated earthquakes, most recently in 1902, and the ravages of invading armies, have destroyed most of the ancient city which was founded in the 2nd century AD. A 10th-century mosque and a ruined fortress dating from the same period, the *Seven Domes Royal Mausoleum* and a modern carpet-weaving centre where traditional techniques are demonstrated provide the main focus of tourist interest in the city.
Shekhi is located 380km (236 miles) west of Baku close to the Georgian border. Archaeological evidence suggests that the city may be one of the oldest settlements in the Caucasus, dating back 2500 years. Tourists can still visit the 18th-century frescoed summer palace and the fortress built by a local warlord who declared Shekhi the capital of an independent khanate. Shekhi was famed for its silk, which is still produced locally, and the bazaars and *caravanserais* testify to its importance as a trading town. Some of the *caravanserais* have been restored and now function as hotels and restaurants,

SOCIAL PROFILE

FOOD & DRINK: Azerbaijani food combines Turkish, Georgian and central Asian elements, as well as, more regrettably, frequent traces of an uninspiring Soviet culinary heritage. The much celebrated *plov* can range from the disappointing (greasy, with overboiled rice and fatty mutton) to delicious (fragrant and spicy with pine nuts, vegetables and dried fruit, in addition to the obligatory rice and meat). Certain types of *plov* use chicken instead of mutton, and include chestnuts. Grilled kebabs of various kinds are popular, including *lyulya kebab* made from spiced, minced lamb pressed onto skewers. These are often sold from roadside stalls. Meals often start with rich, heavy soups: *piti* is a mutton soup bulked out with chickpeas and slowly cooked in individual earthenware pots in the oven, and served in the same pots. Also popular is *dogva* – a sharp, yoghurt and spinach-based soup containing rice and meatballs.

Typical lakeside view

Sturgeon, served both smoked and fresh, and caviar have traditionally been fished from the Caspian Sea. Rising pollution levels have given rise to alarm about falling fish stocks, but sturgeon is still widely available at a price. *Kutab* pastries stuffed with spinach or pumpkin and similar to Turkish *birekas* are another local speciality. Foreigners should be aware that, as in most of the former Soviet Union, going to restaurants is treated less as an opportunity to eat and talk than as an occasion for competitive toasting and dancing to loud disco music.
Drink: In the *chai khanas* (tea houses), men linger for hours drinking sweet black tea out of tiny glasses. Foreign women who are bold enough to take their chance in this exclusively male preserve will not be refused entry, but may feel themselves the subject of unwelcome scrutiny. Although the majority of Azeris are nominally Shia Muslims, alcohol is widely available. Wines and brandies are produced locally, Russian vodka is popular, and imported spirits represent a form of conspicuous consumption.
NIGHTLIFE: A few restaurants, late-night bars and nightclubs are beginning to open in Baku, catering largely for the foreign business community and wealthy local businessmen. Concerts, theatre, opera and ballet are not in general of a sufficiently high standard to make a visit to these events a necessary proposition.
SHOPPING: If visitors are intent on acquiring an Azerbaijani carpet it may be worth taking the trouble to travel to the carpet-weaving centre at Nardaran. Locally produced silk, ceramics and other craftwork is also sold at the Sharg Bazary (a modern, covered market) in Baku. Prices here are likely to be negotiable. Any carpet or other artefact made before 1960 is subject to an export tax and must be certified for export by the Ministry of Culture. Items purchased at official art salons or tourist shops will already be duly certified. This is not true of goods sold at markets or by private individuals.
SPECIAL EVENTS: Mar '95 *Novrus Bairam* (a celebration of national culture, with staged and street performances of folk music and dance).
SOCIAL CONVENTIONS: Visitors to Azerbaijan may find themselves the recipients of an unexpected bounty in the form of gifts of flowers, food and souvenirs. It is therefore advisable to travel equipped with suitable items – consumables or souvenirs – with which to reciprocate. Local women, particularly in rural areas, tend to be extremely retiring. They will serve a meal, but seldom eat with foreign guests. Visitors may present women with flowers, but overenthusiastic attempts to engage them in

conversation may cause offence and embarrassment. Foreign women are treated initially with elaborate courtesy which can often develop into excessive and unwelcome attention. It is therefore advisable for women to dress modestly and cultivate a certain coolness of manner. Handshaking is the normal form of greeting. Business cards are invariably exchanged at any kind of official meeting, and not infrequently on first meeting people socially as well. **Tipping:** Expected by waiters and doormen in restaurants – sometimes in advance to ensure service. It is advisable to make enquiries about 'going rates' before entering into negotiations with taxi drivers, market stall holders, etc.

BUSINESS PROFILE

ECONOMY: Political upheaval and disruption of trading links within the former Soviet Union have resulted in dramatically falling production levels in Azerbaijan, as in all the republics. Wine and brandy production and the associated agricultural sector, previously an important element in the Azerbaijani economy, has never recovered from Mikhail Gorbachev's anti-alcohol drive in the mid-1980s. Politically conservative and distracted by the war with Armenia, and more recently by civil strife within the republic, successive post-independence governments have made relatively little progress with economic reform programmes. The vast majority of housing, agriculture, industry and commerce remains state-controlled. Unemployment has risen sharply and the majority of the population lives below the poverty line. The republic relies mainly on revenue from cotton, grapes and livestock breeding. Industry is dominated by food-processing, textiles and steel; other sectors are radio and telecommunications. However, the republic's substantial oil deposits, both offshore and on land, represent a long-term economic advantage and bait for foreign investment, an advantage not enjoyed by either neighbouring Georgia or Armenia. Collapsing production in the oil sector due to lack of investment is now bringing the Government under pressure to involve foreign capital. At present, Azerbaijan is producing barely enough oil to satisfy its own domestic needs, yet it is exporting oil on the international market. It is estimated that with capital investment, oil production could increase five-fold to 40 million tonnes per year. Major deals with Western companies have been repeatedly

postponed. However, in September 1994, Azerbaijan signed a US$8-billion deal with a Western consortium of eight companies to develop three Caspian Sea oil fields. Rival Islamic powers are vying for economic and ideological influence in Azerbaijan. The Gulf States have provided aid packages and released loans on favourable terms, as well as investing in oil exploration and capitalisation; Iran is attempting to regain the religious heart of a largely secular population; and the influence of Turkey, presenting itself as a power bridging the gap between Europe and the Islamic world, is evident in training programmes and large numbers of joint ventures, particularly in the construction industry. Azerbaijan is a signatory of the Black Sea conference treaty.
COMMERCIAL INFORMATION: The following organisation can offer advice: Chamber of Commerce and Industry of the Republic of Azerbaijan, ul. Istiglaliyat 31/33, 370601 Baku. Tel: (12) 398 503.

CLIMATE

Generally warm, but low temperatures can occur, particularly in the mountains and valleys. Most of the rainfall is in the west.

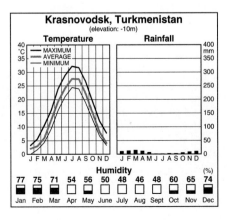

Krasnovodsk, Turkmenistan
(elevation: -10m)

	Temperature	Rainfall	

Humidity												(%)
77	75	71	54	56	50	48	46	48	60	65	74
Jan	Feb	Mar	Apr	May	June	July	Aug	Sept	Oct	Nov	Dec

The Islands of The Bahamas

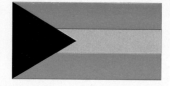

□ international airport

200km
100mls

Grand Bahama
Gt. Abaco
Freeport
Bimini
Berry Is.
Eleuthera
NASSAU
Governor's Harbour
Andros Town
New Providence I.
ATLANTIC OCEAN
Andros
Cat Island
San Salvador
Rum Cay
Gt. Exuma
Tropic of Cancer
BAHAMAS
Long I.
Samana Cay
Crooked I.
Acklins I.
Mayaguana
Little Inagua
CUBA
Gt. Inagua
Matthew Town

Atlantic Ocean
Caribbean Sea
S. AMERICA

DAB-M23

Location: Caribbean; southeast of Florida.

Bahamas Ministry of Tourism
PO Box N-3701, Bay Street, Nassau, The Bahamas
Tel: 322 7500. Fax: 328 0945. Telex: 20164.

High Commission of the Commonwealth of The Bahamas
10 Chesterfield Street, London W1X 8AH
Tel: (0171) 408 4488. Fax: (0171) 499 9937. Opening hours: 0930-1730 Monday to Friday.

Bahamas Tourist Office
3 The Billings, Walnut Tree Close, Guildford, Surrey GU1 4UL
Tel: (01483) 448 900. Fax: (01483) 448 990. Opening hours: 0930-1730 Monday to Friday.

British High Commission
PO Box N-7516, 3rd Floor, Bitco Building, East Street, Nassau, The Bahamas
Tel: 325 7471/2/3. Fax: 323 3871.

Embassy of the Commonwealth of The Bahamas
2220 Massachussetts Avenue, NW, Washington, DC 20008
Tel: (202) 319 2660. Fax: (202) 319 2668.

Bahamas Consulate General
231 East 46th Street, New York, NY 10017
Tel: (212) 421 6420. Fax: (212) 688 5926. Opening hours: 1000-1600 Monday to Friday.

Bahamas Tourist Office
28th Floor North, 150 East 52nd Street, New York, NY 10022
Tel: (212) 758 2777. Fax: (212) 753 6531.

Embassy of the United States of America
PO Box N-8197, Mosmar Building, Queen Street, Nassau, The Bahamas
Tel: 322 1181 or 328 2206 or 328 3496 (Visa Section). Fax: 328 7838. Telex: 20138 (a/b AMEMB).

High Commission for the Commonwealth of The Bahamas
Suite 1020, 360 Albert Street, Ottawa, Ontario K1R 7X7
Tel: (613) 232 1724. Fax: (613) 232 0097.

Bahamas Tourist Office
Suite 1101, 121 Bloor Street East, Toronto, Ontario M4W 3M5
Tel: (416) 968 2999. Fax: (416) 968 6711.

Canadian Consulate
PO Box SS-6371, 21 Out Island Traders Building, Ernest Street, Nassau, The Bahamas
Tel: 393 2124 or 393 4271. Fax: 393 1305.

AREA: 13,939 sq km (5382 sq miles).
POPULATION: 260,000 (1994 estimate).
POPULATION DENSITY: 18.3 per sq km.
CAPITAL: Nassau. **Population:** 171,502 (1990 estimate).
GEOGRAPHY: The Bahamas consist of 700 low-lying islands, mostly islets (cays or keys) and rocks. The whole archipelago extends 970km (600 miles) southeastward from the coast of Florida, surrounded by clear, colourful waters. The soil is thin, but on the more developed islands, cultivation has produced exotic flowers. On other islands are large areas of pine forest, rocky and barren land, swamp and unspoilt beaches. The Bahamas are divided into two oceanic features, the Little Bahama Bank and the Great Bahama Bank.
LANGUAGE: The official and national language is English.
RELIGION: The three main Christian denominations are Baptist, Anglican and Roman Catholic.
TIME: GMT - 5 (GMT - 4 from first Sunday in April to Saturday before last Sunday in October).
ELECTRICITY: 120 volts AC, 60Hz.
COMMUNICATIONS: Telephone: IDD is available. Country code: 1 809. International outgoing code: 011. New Providence and all islands have automatic telephone systems. The state telephone company, *BaTelCo*, offers both manual- and automatic-dial mobile radio telephones for use on New Providence Island. **Fax:** This service is available to the public at the Centralised Telephone Office in East Street, Nassau. Machines can also be rented. **Telex/telegram:** 24-hour international telex and telegraph facilities are available in Nassau and Freeport; efficient telegram service to all parts of the world. **Post:** Postal service to Europe takes up to five days. Post office hours: 0900-1700 Monday to Friday and 0900-1200 Saturday. **Press:** The three daily newspapers include the *Tribune*, the *Nassau Guardian* and the *Freeport News*. Weekly newspapers include *The Bahama Journal, The Punch* and *The Freeport Times*. International newspapers available in the Bahamas are: *The Times, The Miami Herald, Wall Street Journal, The Daily Telegraph* and *USA Today*.
BBC World Service and Voice of America frequencies: From time to time these change. See the section *How to Use this Book* for more information.

BBC:

| MHz | 17.84 | 15.22 | 9.915 | 6.195 |

Voice of America:

| MHz | 15.21 | 11.70 | 6.130 | 0.930 |

PASSPORT/VISA

Regulations and requirements may be subject to change at short notice, and you are advised to contact the appropriate diplomatic or consular authority before finalising travel arrangements. Details of these may be found at the head of this country's entry. Any numbers in the chart refer to the footnotes below.

	Passport Required?	Visa Required?	Return Ticket Required?
Full British	Yes	2	Yes
BVP	Not valid	-	-
Australian	Yes	No	Yes
Canadian	1	No	Yes
USA	1	No	Yes
Other EU (As of 31/12/94)	Yes	2	Yes
Japanese	Yes	No	Yes

PASSPORTS: Valid passport required by all except **[1]** nationals of Canada (for 3 weeks providing they hold a birth certificate, a citizenship card or a landed resident card and a photo ID) and the USA (for 8 months

700 times more inviting.

The 700 Islands of The Bahamas.

From cosmopolitan to secluded … holiday programmes from active to purely relaxing … a comprehensive range of tour operators … 2 direct British Airways flights per week … endless choices for you and your clients … all supported by our stunning national press and 48 sheet poster campaign.

Call our friendly Bahamas experts for brochures and more information, at The Bahamas Tourist Office on 0990 777-700 or Fax 01483 448-990.

2 FLIGHTS DIRECT PER WEEK

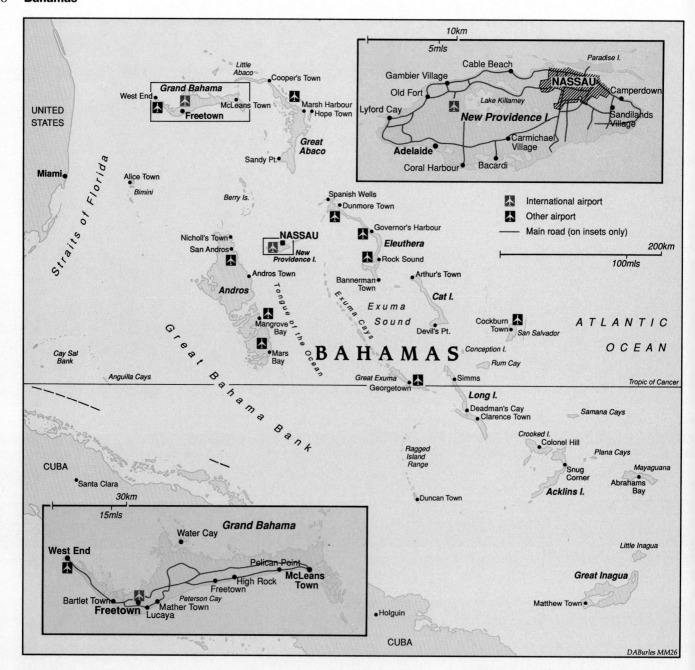

DABurles MM26

providing they hold an original or certified birth certificate accompanied by a police clearance record and a driving licence or a voter's registration card along with an official photo ID).
Note: Expired passports are not considered proper ID, even if they are endorsed with unexpired visas.
British Visitors Passport: Not accepted.
VISAS: Required by all except nationals of:
(a) **[2]** EU countries for visits of less than 8 months (3 months for nationals of Denmark, France, Germany, Ireland and Portugal);
(b) Argentina, Bolivia, Brazil, Chile, Colombia (if travelling via USA and holding multiple US entry visas), Costa Rica, Ecuador, El Salvador, Guatemala, Honduras, Nicaragua, Panama, Paraguay, Peru, Uruguay and Venezuela, for visits of less than 2 weeks;
(c) Commonwealth countries (with the exception of nationals of the Maldives, Namibia, Pakistan and Nauru, who *do* require a visa), Djibouti, Fiji and São Tomé & Príncipe for visits of less than 3 months;

(d) Austria, Finland, Israel, Japan, Mexico and Sweden for visits of less than 3 months;
(e) Iceland, Liechtenstein, Norway, San Marino, Switzerland, Turkey and the USA for visits of less than 8 months.
Types of visa: *Single-entry:* £15; *Multiple-entry:* £30.
Validity: Dependent on length of stay and nationality. Applications for extension should be made to the Immigration Department.
Application to: Consulate (or Consular Section at Embassy or High Commission). For addresses, see top of entry.
Application requirements: (a) Application form from Embassy or High Commission. (b) Valid passport. (c) Sufficient funds to cover stay. (d) 2 passport photos. (e) Return or onward ticket or itinerary.
Working days required: Dependent on nationality of applicant.
Temporary residence: Apply at the Immigration Department, PO Box N-831, Nassau, New Providence.

MONEY

Currency: Bahamian Dollar (Ba$) = 100 cents. Notes are in denominations of Ba$100, 50, 20, 10, 5, 3 and 1, and 50 cents. Coins are in denominations of Ba$5, 2 and 1, and 50, 25, 15, 10, 5 and 1 cents. The Bahamian Dollar has parity with the US Dollar and the latter is also accepted as legal tender.
Credit cards: Diners Club, Access/Mastercard, Visa and American Express are accepted. Check with your credit card company for details of merchant acceptability and other services which may be available.
Exchange rate indicators: The following figures are

included as a guide to the movements of the Bahamian Dollar against Sterling and the US Dollar:

Date:	Oct '92	Sep '93	Jan '94	Jan '95
£1.00=	1.59	1.53	1.48	1.55
$1.00=	1.00	1.00	1.00	1.00

Currency restrictions: There is no restriction on the import of foreign currency. Prior permission from the Central Bank of Bahamas is required for the export of local currency in excess of Ba$70 per person. Foreign currency in excess of a value equivalent to US$5000 must be declared on leaving.
Banking hours: 0930-1500 Monday to Thursday, 0930-1700 Friday.

DUTY FREE

The following goods may be taken into The Bahamas without incurring customs duty:
200 cigarettes or 100 cigarillos or 50 cigars or 250g of tobacco; 1 litre of spirits; 50g of perfume; goods up to the value of £36.
Note: A duty-free allowance is only available to persons over 21 years of age.
Prohibited items: Firearms, weapons, radio transmitters and drugs.

PUBLIC HOLIDAYS

Jan 2 '95 For New Year's Day. **Apr 14** Good Friday.
Apr 17 Easter Monday. **Jun 2** Labour Day. **Jun 5** Whit Monday. **Jul 10** Independence Day. **Aug 17** Emancipation Day. **Oct 12** Discovery Day. **Dec 25** Christmas Day. **Dec 26** Boxing Day. **Jan 1 '96** New

Health	
GALILEO/WORLDSPAN: **TI-DFT/NAS/HE**	
SABRE: **TIDFT/NAS/HE**	

Visa	
GALILEO/WORLDSPAN: **TI-DFT/NAS/VI**	
SABRE: **TIDFT/NAS/VI**	

For more information on Timatic codes refer to Contents.

Abaco boat

Year's Day. **Apr 5** Good Friday. **Apr 8** Easter Monday.
Note: Holidays which fall on Saturday or Sunday are
usually observed on the following Monday.

HEALTH

*Regulations and requirements may be subject to change at short notice, and
you are advised to contact your doctor well in advance of your intended date of
departure. Any numbers in the chart refer to the footnotes below.*

	Special Precautions?	Certificate Required?
Yellow Fever	No	1
Cholera	No	No
Typhoid & Polio	Yes	-
Malaria	No	-
Food & Drink	2	-

[1]: A yellow fever vaccination certificate is required
from travellers aged over one year arriving within six
months of visiting an infected area.
[2]: Tap water is safe to drink although it can often be
salty in taste. Milk is pasteurised and dairy products are
safe for consumption. Local meat, poultry, seafood, fruit
and vegetables are generally considered safe to eat.
Health care: There are General Hospitals and two
private hospitals on New Providence and Grand Bahama.
There are health clinics on the Family Islands. Medical
insurance is recommended.

TRAVEL - International

AIR: The Bahamas' national airline is *Bahamasair (UP)*.
Other airlines with regular flights to the Bahamas are
*Chalk's International, Delta, British Airways,
Caledonian Airways, Paradise Island Airways, American
Eagle, USAir* and *Gulfstream International*.
For free advice on air travel, call the *Air Travel Advisory
Bureau* in the UK on (0171) 636 5000 (London) or
(0161) 832 2000 (Manchester).
Approximate flight times: From *Los Angeles* to Nassau
is 7 hours, from *New York* is 3 hours and from *Singapore*
is 33 hours.
The number of airlines planning to make direct flights
from Europe is increasing.
International airports: *Nassau International (NAS)* is
16km (10 miles) west of the city. Taxi services are
available, but no buses. Airport facilities include banking
(0930-1500 Monday to Thursday, 0930-1700 Friday), car
parking, car hire (0900-1800), post office, bar/restaurant
(0700-2200) and an outgoing duty-free shop (0930-1700).
Freeport International (FPO) is 5km (3 miles) from the
city. Only taxis are available. Airport facilities include
banking, car hire, car parking, bar/restaurant and a duty-
free shop (opening times are as for *Nassau International*
above).
There are scheduled turbo-prop services between several
airports in Florida and *Treasure Cay (TCB)*, Abaco
Island, *Rock Sound (RSD)*, Eleuthera and *Georgetown
(GCT)*.
The new international airport at Moss Town, Exuma has
been completed.
Departure tax: Ba\$15 (Freeport – Ba\$18). Children
under three years of age and passengers for immediate
transit are exempt.
SEA: A large number of international passenger ships
from New York and Miami call at Nassau. In addition,
the following cruise ships call there: *Carnavale, Crown
Princess, Dawn Princess, Noordam, Nordic Prince,
Regal Princess, Sky Princess, Oceanic, Mardi Gras,
Fantasy* and *Nordic Empress*. Nassau has direct
passenger-cargo connections with the United States, the
UK, the West Indies and South America. Facilities for
cruisers in Nassau and some harbours of the Out Islands
(Eleuthera, Andros and Exuma) are being improved.
Contact Bahamas Tourist Office for an up-to-date list of
cruise operators to The Bahamas, with all relevant
contact numbers.

TRAVEL - Internal

AIR: *Bahamasair* links Nassau and Freeport to the
Family Islands. Charter services are available from
*Bahamasair Charter, Pinder's Charter Service, Lucaya
Beach Air Service* and *Congo Air*.
Approximate flight times: From Nassau, New
Providence Island to *Freeport* is 30 minutes, to *Marsh
Harbour* or *Treasure Cay*, Abaco is 35 minutes, to
Governor's Harbour is 30 minutes, and to *Georgetown*
on Exuma is 40 minutes.
SEA: The Out Islands are served by a mail boat which
leaves Nassau several times a week carrying mail and
provisions to the islands. Passengers share facilities

Sunset island

with the crew. Arrangements should be made through
boat captains at Potters Cay.
ROAD: Traffic drives on the left. **Bus:** The *jitney* (bus)
provides inexpensive touring. Paradise Island is served
by a bus service which stops at every hotel. A horse-
drawn surrey ride which takes three passengers is
available along the streets of Nassau. **Taxis** in New
Providence are metered. The rates are government
controlled. **Car hire:** *Avis, Budget* and *Hertz* are
represented at the airports and in Nassau. Motor
scooter hire is also available. **Cycles** can be rented by
the day or by the week. **Documentation:** A British
driving licence is valid for up to three months.
Motorcycle riders and passengers are required to wear
crash helmets.
JOURNEY TIMES: The following chart gives
approximate journey times (in hours and minutes) from
Nassau to other major centres.

	Air	Sea
Central Andros, Andros	0.15	3.00
Governor's Harbour, Eleuthera	0.30	5.30
Freeport, Grand Bahama	0.30/0.45	12.00
Marsh Harbour, Abaco	0.45	11.00
George Town, Exuma	0.45	13.00

ACCOMMODATION

The Bahamas offer a wide selection of accommodation,
ranging from small, private guest-houses where only
lodging is available, to large luxury resorts, complete
with swimming pools, private beaches, sailboats,
skindiving equipment, full dining facilities and
nightclub entertainment. Information can also be

obtained from The Bahamas' Hotel Association, PO
Box N-7799, West Bay Street, sub Dean's Lane,
Nassau. Tel: 322 8381. Fax: 326 5346. Telex: 20392.
Classifications: Many of the larger resorts offer
accommodation on either a Modified American Plan
(MAP) which consists of room, breakfast and dinner
or European Plan (EP) which consists of room only.
Accommodation is classified as *Hotels, Colonies,
Guest-Houses, Apartment Hotels* or
Apartment/Cottage Units.
HOTELS: Hotels vary in size and facilities. There are
luxury hotels offering full porter, bell and room
service, planned activities, sports, shops and beauty
salon, swimming pool and entertainment; some have a
private beach, golf course and tennis courts. Double
and single rooms are often the same price. The small
hotels are more informal and while activities are less
extensive, they usually offer a dining room and bar.
There are new resorts situated on New Providence
Island, which has sporting facilities and luxury
accommodation. The Crystal Palace Casino on Cable
Beach has a casino, health spa, luxury accommodation
and gourmet restaurants. Some hotels include service
charge on the bill.
COTTAGE COLONIES: Separate cottages or villas,
with maid service, surrounding a main clubhouse with
a bar and dining room – these are 'Cottage Colonies'.
They are not equipped with kitchenette and
housekeeping facilities for the preparation of meals,
although some have facilities for preparing beverages
and light snacks. They offer the facilities of a hotel,
such as a private beach/swimming pool, and are
designed to offer maximum privacy.
GUEST-HOUSES: Often less expensive than hotels

Bahamas signs

and located near downtown Nassau. Many offer European Plan only, but restaurants are plentiful. Rooms may be with or without a bath. In the Out Islands hotels are small with a casual atmosphere.

APARTMENT HOTELS: These consist of apartment units with complete kitchen and maid service. Other hotel facilities (ie swimming pool, sporting activities, restaurant and bar, etc) are normally available on the premises.

APARTMENT/COTTAGE UNITS: These have complete kitchen facilities and some have maid service. Generally, there are no restaurant facilities and tenants are required to prepare their own meals. A few are situated in landscaped estates with their own beach, much like the cottage colonies but without the main clubhouse. Others offer inexpensive accommodation in less spacious but comfortable surroundings. Restaurant and bar facilities are not available.

CAMPING: Camping is not permitted in any of the islands of The Bahamas.

RESORTS & EXCURSIONS

There are over 700 islands in The Bahamas, many of which have escaped the notice of tourists. The islands offer clear warm water and sandy beaches. Several are relatively large – see below for a description of some of these – but others are tiny and uninhabited. All the larger islands offer a high standard of accommodation and leisure facilities.

Nassau, Cable Beach and Paradise Island: The capital of The Bahamas, Nassau, stands on **New Providence Island.** In the capital, tourists can shop in the 'straw market', a kind of bazaar, or more sophisticated shops in *Bay Street.* The 18th-century *Fort Charlotte,* on West

Bay Street has a moat, open battlements, dungeons and a magnificent view of the harbour. The nearby *Ardastra Gardens* have tropical flowers and pink flamingoes. There are two casinos. The *Queen's Staircase,* at the top of Elizabeth Avenue, is a 40m (102ft) climb up steps carved into the limestone leading to *Fort Fincastle* and the *Water Tower.* Built in 1793, Fort Fincastle is in the shape of a ship's bow. The Water Tower is the highest point in the island, 85m (216ft) above sea level. An elevator takes visitors to an observation deck for panoramic views. Sunbathing, diving, fishing and boating are the main daytime amusements on these islands. An underwater observatory and marine park, *Coral World,* has recently opened a few minutes' away from downtown Nassau.

Grand Bahama Island: The main towns are **Freeport/Lucaya** and **West End,** which both have airports. The island offers wide white sandy beaches, two casinos and good shopping facilities, entertainment and restaurants at the *International Bazaar* and *Port Lucaya.* The *Rand Memorial Nature Centre* offers an excellent nature walk and the *Garden of the Groves* has exotic flowers, waterfalls and colourful birds. The history of the Lucayan Indians can be learned at the *Grand Bahama Museum,* along with its exhibitions of historic coins and Junkanoo costumes.

Andros: The largest and probably the least well known of the bigger islands. Laced with creeks and densely forested inland, the interior is still largely untouched and natural. Off the eastern shore is the world's largest coral reef outside Australia. Beyond the reef, the ocean floor drops away steeply to a depth of 8km (5 miles), called the Tongue of the Ocean, and deep-water fishing here is a major attraction.

The Abacos: A crescent-shaped chain of islands to the north of New Providence. Many of the towns here have the atmosphere of New England fishing villages. The islands are particularly noted for their tradition of shipbuilding, the original 200-year-old practice of which can still be observed in *Man-O-War Cay. Treasure Cay* has an excellent golf course and here, as in the other major islands, there are excellent leisure facilities. Other attractions include *Alton Lowe's Museum* in **New Plymouth,** *Elbow Cay, Green Turtle Cay* and *Marsh Harbour,* the bare-boat charter centre of the northern Bahamas. Scuba divers are drawn to **Pelican Cay National Park**, an underwater preserve where night dives can be arranged.

Eleuthera: A narrow island 177km (110 miles) long but seldom more than 3km (2 miles) wide. Attractions include the *Ocean Hole, Glass Window Bridge, Harbour Island* (with *Dunmore Town,* one of the oldest settlements in The Bahamas), *Spanish Wells,* off the northern tip of the island, *Preacher's Cave* and the underwater caves at *Hatchet Bay.* The scuba diving from Eleuthera is particularly superb.

The Exumas: The waters surrounding this 160km-long (100-mile) chain of islands have been described by yachtsmen as being the finest cruising region in the world. There are also spectacular reefs protected by the **National Land and Sea Park**. Inland, several once-great plantation houses now stand ruined and deserted, although the names of their owners still live on in many local family surnames. In April, *Elizabeth Harbour* is the setting for the *Family Island Regatta.*

Cat Island: One of the eastern bulwarks of The Bahamas, Cat Island has 60m (200ft) cliffs (a rare height for The Bahamas), dense natural forest and pre-

Columbian Arawak Indian caves. On *Mount Alvernia* is the Hermitage built by Father Jerome. The *Cat Island Regatta* takes place here during the August bank holiday.

Bimini: Lying between Andros and Florida, Bimini is widely regarded as one of the best fishing centres in the world. Hemingway used to live in *Alice Town* in Blue Marlin Cottage, and mementoes of his life can be seen in the local museum.

Berry Island: Popular with fishing enthusiasts and also noted for its serene landscapes and white sand beaches. *Great Harbour Cay* has a championship golf course and a marina. Scuba divers can admire the underwater rock formations and 5m (15ft) staghorn coral reefs off *Mamma Rhoda Rock*.

Long Island: This island certainly lives up to its name, being almost 100km (60 miles) long but rarely more than 5km (3 miles) wide. The landscape consists of rugged headlands dropping sharply down to the sea, fertile pastureland, rolling hills and sandy beaches washed by surf. At *Conception Island* divers can explore over 30 shipwrecks and tours are arranged from the Stella Maris resort complex at the north end of the island. The *Long Island Regatta* at Salt Pond takes place here in May.

San Salvador: This was Columbus' first landing place in the New World. *Cockburn Town* is the main settlement, which is not far from the spot where Columbus is said to have landed, although other sites also claim this distinction. Game fishing and diving are the most popular pastimes.

The Out Islands: These stretch across a huge area of clear ocean and are fringed with hundreds of kilometres of white sandy beaches. The islands have resort facilities for groups of up to 200 people and are ideal for a relaxing, secluded holiday. Though secluded, the islands are not isolated. They are served by the national flag carrier, *Bahamasair*, from Nassau and Freeport.

SOCIAL PROFILE

FOOD & DRINK: There is a wide choice of restaurants and bars. Specialities include conch, grouper cutlets, baked crab and red snapper fillets in anchovy sauce. Fresh fruit is available from the Out Islands, including sweet pineapple, mango, breadfruit and papaya. Table service is usual in restaurants.

Drink: Local drinks are based on rum. The local liqueur is *Nassau Royal,* served alone or in coffee. Bars may have counter and/or waiter service.

NIGHTLIFE: Hotels have bars and nightclubs. Beach parties and discotheques are organised regularly. Live entertainment includes calypso, goombay music and limbo dancing. Nightclubs are found in Nassau and Freeport.

SHOPPING: Special purchases include china, cutlery, leather, fabrics, spirits from Britain, Scandinavian glass and silver, Swiss watches, German and Japanese cameras and French perfume. Local products include all types of straw artefacts, sea-shell jewellery and woodcarvings.

SPORT: Tennis, squash, baseball, softball, basketball, volleyball, soccer, rugby, golf, American football and **cricket** are all popular. Excellent facilities exist for tennis and squash. **Golf:** Ten 18-hole courses are available and the islands are hosts to major tournaments. **Watersports** are exceptionally well catered for in The Bahamas; **sailing, parasailing, powerboat racing, diving, swimming, snorkelling** and **water-skiing** are all widely available. The temperature of the sea rarely drops below 21°C even in midwinter. Equipment is available from shops, hotels and marinas.

SPECIAL EVENTS: The following is a selection of special events occurring in The Bahamas during 1995-96:

Mar 22-25 '95 *Snipe Winter Sailing Championships,* Montagu Bay, Nassau. **Apr 2-9** *Bonefishing/Flyfishing School,* Georgetown, Exuma. **Apr 5** *Supreme Court Opening,* Nassau. **Apr 8** *Annual Red Cross Fair,* Nassau. **Apr 27-30** *42nd Annual Family Island Regatta,* Exuma. **May 17-20** *Bimini Festival,* North Bimini. **May 17-20** *Annual Green Turtle Club Fishing Tournament,* Green Turtle Cay, Abaco. **Late May/early Jun** *Caribbean Music Festival,* Nassau. **Jun 2-4** *Pineapple Festival,* Gregory Town, Eleuthera. **Jun 2-5** *28th Annual Long Island Regatta,* Salt Pond, Long Island. **Jul 1** *Bahama Sailing Cup,* Green Turtle Cay, Abaco. **Jul 2** *28th Annual Miss Commonwealth Beauty Pageant.* **Jul 4-11** *Regatta Time in Abaco.* **Jul 8-12** *Annual Staniel Cay Bonefish Tournament,* Exuma. **Jul 8-15** *The Bahamas Games.* **Aug 6-9** *Family Tournament,* North Bimini. **Aug 15** *Fox Hill Day*

Main picture: Fascinatin' Bitch Bar. Above: Palm beach

Celebration. **Sep 6-9 & 13-16** *Small B.O.A.T. Fishing Tournament,* North Bimini. **Nov 15-18** *The Wahoo,* North Bimini. **Dec 1-3** *Annual New Plymouth Historical Cultural Weekend,* Green Turtle Cay, Abaco. **Dec 2** *Annual Beaux Arts Masked Ball,* Paradise Island. **Dec 4-10** *Sun International Bahamas Open,* Paradise Island. **Dec 11-15** *Annual Renaissance Singers Concert.* **Dec 14 and Dec 26 '96** *Junkanoo* (a brilliantly colourful parade, originating in Africa, which takes place in Nassau during the early hours of Boxing Day and New Year's Day, accompanied by a cacaphony of cowbells, horns and whistles, goat-skin drums and other home-made instruments. Throughout the year visitors can have a sampling of Junkanoo at special shows and during other celebrations).

SOCIAL CONVENTIONS: The pace of life is generally leisurely. Informal wear is acceptable in the resorts with some degree of dressing up in the evenings, particularly for dining, dancing and casinos in Nassau or Freeport. Further from the main towns dress is more casual, although there is still a tendency to dress up at night. Small outposts like Green Turtle Cay, for example, will not require more than a shirt and long trousers. It is not acceptable to wear beachwear in towns. **Tipping:** 15% is usual for most services including taxis. Some hotels and restaurants, however, include service charge on the bill.

BUSINESS PROFILE

ECONOMY: One of the wealthiest countries in the Caribbean, tourism is the main industry. Agriculture and fishing, which account for 50% of GNP, have been targeted for development. The Bahamas are also an important offshore banking centre. Most foodstuffs and virtually all other products must be imported, mainly from the USA, although oil is purchased firstly from Indonesia and Saudi Arabia. The Government is trying to diversify the economy and offers formal incentives to foreign investors. Tax concessions are available in Freeport on Grand Bahama. Other than the USA, the UK and Puerto Rico are The Bahamas' major trading partners.

BUSINESS: Normal courtesies are observed, ie appointments and exchanging calling cards. **Office**

hours: 0900-1700 Monday to Friday.

COMMERCIAL INFORMATION: The following organisation can offer advice: Bahamas Chamber of Commerce, PO Box N-665, Shirley Street, Nassau. Tel: 322 2145. Fax: 322 4649.

CONFERENCES/CONVENTIONS: Conference venues can seat up to 2000 people. Information may be obtained from the Bahamas Tourist Office or the Bahamas Ministry of Tourism in Nassau (see top of entry for addresses).

CLIMATE

Apart from Grand Turk in the extreme southeast, The Bahamas are slightly cooler than other Caribbean island groups due to their proximity to the continental North American cold air systems.

Required clothing: Lightweight or tropical, washable cottons all year round. Light raincoats are useful during the wet season.

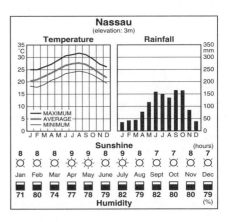

Nassau (elevation: 3m)

	Jan	Feb	Mar	Apr	May	June	July	Aug	Sept	Oct	Nov	Dec
Sunshine (hours)	8	8	8	9	9	9	9	9	7	7	7	7
Humidity (%)	71	80	74	77	78	79	82	79	82	80	80	79

Location: Middle East, Gulf Coast.

Bahrain Tourism Company (BTC)
PO Box 5831, Manama, Bahrain
Tel: 530 530. Fax: 530 867. Telex: 8929.
Embassy of the State of Bahrain
98 Gloucester Road, London SW7 4AU
Tel: (0171) 370 5132/3. Fax: (0171) 370 7773. Telex:
917829. Opening hours: 0900-1500 Monday to Friday
(0900-1300 for visa enquiries, 1430-1500 for visa
collection).
British Embassy
PO Box 114, 21 Government Avenue, Manama, 306,
Bahrain
Tel: 534 404 *or* 534 865/6. Fax: 531 273. Telex: 8213
(a/b PRODRO BN).
Embassy of the State of Bahrain
3502 International Drive, NW, Washington, DC 20008
Tel: (202) 342 0741/42/43/44. Fax: (202) 362 2192.
Also deals with enquiries from Canada.
Embassy of the United States of America
PO Box 26431, Building No. 979, Road 3119, Block
331, Zinj, Manama, Bahrain
Tel: 273 300. Fax: 272 594.
Consulate of the State of Bahrain
1869 René Léveque Boulevard West, Montréal, Québec
H3H 1R4
Tel: (514) 931 7444. Fax: (514) 931 5988.
**The Canadian High Commission in Kuwait deals with
enquiries relating to Bahrain (see** *Kuwait* **later in the
book).**

AREA: 693.15 sq km (267.63 sq miles).
POPULATION: 503,022 (1990 estimate).
POPULATION DENSITY: 725.7 per sq km.
CAPITAL: Manama. Population: 138,784 (1990
estimate).
GEOGRAPHY: Bahrain is composed of a group of 33
islands (3 large and 30 small ones), lying halfway down
the Arabian Gulf, 25km (15 miles) from the east coast of
Saudi Arabia, slightly under 30km (20 miles) off the
Qatar peninsula. The islands are low-lying, the highest
ground being a hill in the centre of Bahrain. The main
island has the valuable asset of an adequate supply of
fresh water both on land and offshore. In the north are
extensive date gardens with irrigated fruit and vegetable
gardens. A causeway between Bahrain and the east coast
of Saudi Arabia recently opened to traffic.
LANGUAGE: The official language is Arabic. English
is widely spoken in business and trade circles. Farsi
(Persian), Hindi and Urdu are also used.
RELIGION: Muslim, both Shia and Sunnis. There are
also Christian, Bahai, Hindu and Parsee minorities.
TIME: GMT + 3.
ELECTRICITY: Manama and other towns: 230 volts
AC, single-phase and 400 volts, 3-phase; 50Hz. (Awali,
120 volts AC, 60Hz.) Lamp fittings are of both the
bayonet and screw types. Plug fittings are normally of the
13-amp pin type.

COMMUNICATIONS: Telephone: Full IDD service is
available. Country code: 973. Outgoing international
code: 0. **Fax:** Bahrain Telecommunications Company
(*BATELCO*) operates a service from the Sh Mubarak
Building on Government Avenue. **Telex/telegram:**
Bahrain possesses one of the most modern international
communications networks in the Gulf. A 24-hour service
is run by Cable and Wireless, Mercury House, Al-Khalifa
Avenue, Manama, as well as at the airport. **Post:** Airmail
service to Europe takes three to four days. The main post
office is at Manama. Efficient 1-day international courier
services operate out of Bahrain. **Press:** The main Arabic
dailies include *Al-Ayyam* and *Akhbar Al Khaleej.* The
English-language daily is the *Gulf Daily News.*
**BBC World Service and Voice of America
frequencies:** From time to time these change. See the
section *How to Use this Book* for more information.
BBC:

MHz	11.76	6.150	1.323	0.639
Voice of America:				
MHz	15.44	11.90	9.700	7.205

PASSPORT/VISA

*Regulations and requirements may be subject to change at short notice, and you
are advised to contact the appropriate diplomatic or consular authority before
finalising travel arrangements. Details of these may be found at the head of this
country's entry. Any numbers in the chart refer to the footnotes below.*

	Passport Required?	Visa Required?	Return Ticket Required?
Full British	Yes	No	Yes
BVP	Not valid	-	-
Australian	Yes	Yes	Yes
Canadian	Yes	Yes	Yes
USA	Yes	Yes	Yes
Other EU (As of 31/12/94)	Yes	Yes	Yes
Japanese	Yes	Yes	Yes

Prohibited entry: Holders of Israeli passports. Holders
of passports with visas or endorsements for Israel (valid
or expired) are permitted to transit Bahrain provided they
do so by the same through aircraft.
PASSPORTS: Valid passport required by all.
British Visitors Passport: Not accepted.
VISAS: Required by all except:
(a) nationals of Kuwait, Oman, Qatar, Saudi Arabia and
the United Arab Emirates;
(b) citizens of the UK for a maximum of 4 weeks
(providing they hold a full passport with at least 6
months' validity and that it is indicated on page 2 of their
passports that they were born in the UK).
A long-term 1-2 year visa for working in Bahrain will be
supplied if the employing company in Bahrain obtains a
'No Objection Certificate' on behalf of the individual.
Types of visa: Business/Tourist. Cost: £10. There is also
a 72-hour Transit visa.
Application to: Consulate (or Consular Section at
Embassy). For addresses, see top of entry.
Application requirements: (a) Letter from company and
a 'No Objection Certificate' from the Immigration
Office, Bahrain. (b) Passport. (c) 1 passport-size photo.
(d) 1 completed application form. (e) 1 stamped, self-
addressed envelope for return of passport if applying by
post. (f) Fee.
Working days required: 1.

MONEY

Currency: Dinar (BD) = 1000 fils. Notes appear in
denominations of BD20, 10, 5, and 1, and 500 fils. Coins
are in denominations of 100, 50, 25, 10, 5 and 1 fils.
Credit cards: Diners Club, Access/Mastercard,
American Express and Visa are accepted. Check with
your credit card company for details of merchant
acceptability and other services which may be available.
Exchange rate indicators: The following figures are
included as a guide to the movements of the Dinar
against Sterling and the US Dollar:

Date:	Oct '92	Sep '93	Jan '94	Jan '95
£1.00=	0.61	0.58	0.56	0.58
$1.00=	0.38	0.38	0.38	0.38

Currency restrictions: There are no restrictions on the
import or export of either local or foreign currency.
Banking hours: 0800-1200 and usually 1600-1800
Saturday to Wednesday; 0800-1100 Thursday. Many
banks are open on both Saturday and Sunday.
Government offices, businesses and most offices are
closed on Friday, which is a weekly holiday.

DUTY FREE

The following goods may be imported into Bahrain
without incurring customs duty:
*400 cigarettes or 50 cigars or 225g of tobacco for
personal use; a reasonable amount of perfume for
personal use; 2 bottles of wine or spirits (non-Muslim
passengers only).*
Prohibited items: Firearms, ammunition, drugs,
jewellery and all items originating in Israel may only be
imported under licence. All uncut, bleached or undrilled
pearls produced outside the Gulf are under strict import
regulations.

PUBLIC HOLIDAYS

Jan 1 '95 New Year's Day. **Feb 1** Beginning of
Ramadan. **Mar 3** Eid al-Fitr. **May 10** Eid al-Adha (Feast
of the Sacrifice). **May 31** Muharram (Islamic New Year).
Jun 9 Ashoura. **Aug 9** Mouloud (Prophet's Birthday).
Dec 16 National Day. **Dec 20** Leilat al-Meiraj (Ascension
of the Prophet). **Jan 1 '96** New Year's Day. **Jan 20**
Beginning of Ramadan. **Feb 22** Eid al-Fitr. **Apr 29** Eid
al-Adhar (Feast of the Sacrifice).
Note: Muslim festivals are timed according to local
sightings of various phases of the Moon and the dates
given above are approximations. During the lunar month
of Ramadan that precedes Eid al-Fitr, Muslims fast during
the day and feast at night and normal business patterns
may be interrupted. Many restaurants are closed during the
day and there are restrictions on smoking and drinking.
Some disruption may continue into Eid al-Fitr itself. Eid
al-Fitr and Eid al-Adha may last anything from two to ten
days, depending on the region. For more information see
the section *World of Islam* at the back of the book.

HEALTH

*Regulations and requirements may be subject to change at short notice, and
you are advised to contact your doctor well in advance of your intended date of
departure. Any numbers in the chart refer to the footnotes below.*

	Special Precautions?	Certificate Required?
Yellow Fever	No	1
Cholera	No	No
Typhoid & Polio	Yes	-
Malaria	No	-
Food & Drink	2	-

[1]: A yellow fever vaccination certificate is required
from travellers over one year old coming from infected
areas.
[2]: Water may be contaminated, and that used for
drinking, brushing teeth or making ice should have first
been boiled or otherwise sterilised. All modern hotels
have their own filtration plants. Milk is unpasteurised and
should be boiled. Powdered or tinned milk is available
and is advised, but make sure that it is reconstituted with
pure water. Avoid dairy products which are likely to have
been made from unboiled milk. Only eat well-cooked
meat and fish, preferably served hot. Salad and
mayonnaise may carry increased risk. Vegetables should
be cooked and fruit peeled.
Health care: There is a comprehensive medical service,
with general and specialised hospitals in the main towns.
Medical insurance is essential. Pharmacies are well
equipped with supplies.

TRAVEL - International

AIR: Approximate flight times: From Bahrain to
London is 6 hours, to *Los Angeles* is 21 hours and to *New
York* is 14 hours.
International airport: *Bahrain International (BAH)*
(Muharraq) is 6.5km (4 miles) northeast of Manama.
Taxi services run across the causeway to the main island.
Airport facilities include a 24-hour bank, 24-hour duty-
free shop, 24-hour first aid, 24-hour bar, 24-hour snack
bar, 24-hour restaurant, 24-hour nursery, 24-hour tourist
information, post office (open 0700-1415), car rental and
car parking.
Departure tax: BD3 for international departures.
SEA: The main international port is Mina Sulman on the

Timatic

Health
GALILEO/WORLDSPAN: **TI-DFT/BAH/HE**
SABRE: **TIDFT/BAH/HE**

Visa
GALILEO/WORLDSPAN: **TI-DFT/BAH/VI**
SABRE: **TIDFT/BAH/VI**

For more information on Timatic codes refer to Contents.

Famous red clay pottery is available from the village of
A'ali. There are weavers at Bani Jamra village and
basket-makers at Jasra village. **Shopping hours:** 0800-
1200 and 1530-1830 Saturday to Thursday. Some shops
are open for a few hours on Fridays in the Souk.
SPORT: Football is the national game. There are plans
for the construction of an Olympic-sized stadium. The
golf clubs at Awali also accept temporary membership.
Horse- and camel-**racing** are held on Fridays at Rifaa.
Skindiving, fishing and **sailing** are popular, particularly
at Awali, Zallaq and Nabih Salih. Zallaq has a sailing
club and there is a yacht club at Sitra. There are
swimming pools at the main hotels.
SOCIAL CONVENTIONS: Traditional beliefs and
customs are strong influences and people are generally
more formal than Westerners. Attitudes to women are
more liberal than in most Gulf States. It is acceptable to
sit cross-legged on cushions or sofas in people's homes
but it is still insulting to display the soles of the feet or to
accept food or anything else with the left hand. It is polite
to drink two small cups of coffee or tea when offered.
Guests will generally be expected to share a bedroom
since guest bedrooms and privacy are almost unknown.
Sports clothes may be worn in the street and short dresses
are acceptable. Smoking is very common and cheap by
European standards. Women should avoid wearing
revealing clothing. **Tipping:** 10% is expected by taxi
drivers and waiters, particularly when service is not
included, and is normal practice. Airport porters expect
100 fils for each piece of luggage.

BUSINESS PROFILE

ECONOMY: Oil dominates Bahrain's economy,
providing almost 85% of export earnings: aluminium
accounts for most of the rest. However, the country's oil
reserves are dwindling rapidly and the Government is
attempting to diversify the economy. As well as
aluminium, an iron-ore processing facility and an
ammonia-methanol plant have been built. Financial
services have experienced rapid growth in recent years as
companies trading in the region have set up their regional
centres in Bahrain, where the relatively relaxed
environment is an important factor in a region where
rigorous social mores are often the norm. Japan is
Bahrain's main export market, taking around 50% of the
total; Britain, the USA, Switzerland and France are the
other important purchasers. The majority of Bahrainian
imports, which cover a wide range of products, come
from four countries: Germany, the UK, the USA and
Japan.
BUSINESS: Businessmen are expected to wear suits and
ties. Business must be done on a personal introduction
basis. Normal social courtesies should be observed.
Bargaining is common practice: Arabs regard their word
as their bond and expect others to do the same. The best
time to visit is October to April. **Office hours:** Usually
0730-1200 and 1430-1800 Saturday to Thursday.
Government office hours: 0700-1300 Saturday to
Thursday.
COMMERCIAL INFORMATION: The following
organisation can offer advice: Bahrain Chamber of
Commerce and Industry, PO Box 248, Manama. Tel: 233
913. Fax: 241 294. Telex: 8691.

CLIMATE

Summer months (June to September) are very hot. The
weather is far cooler from December to March,
particularly in the evenings. Rainfall is slight and only
likely in winter. Spring and autumn are the most pleasant
seasons.
Required clothing: Lightweight cottons and linens from
spring to autumn, mediumweight clothes from November
to March. Warmer clothes are necessary in winter and on
cool evenings.

main island. The deep-water oil tanker terminals are on
the northeast of the island. There are few regular
passenger sailings as it is more usual to travel to Bahrain
by air.
ROAD: The King Fahad Causeway between Bahrain and
Saudi Arabia opened in 1986. There are bus and taxi
services available to cross from one to the other.
However, it must be noted that normal Saudi Arabian
visa regulations apply.

TRAVEL - Internal

SEA: Transport between the smaller islands is by
motorboat or dhow. For details, contact local travel
agents.
ROAD: Manama is served by an excellent road system,
largely created during the last few years. Traffic drives
on the right. **Bus:** Routes now serve most of the towns
and villages, with a standard fare of 50 fils. **Taxi:** Taxis
are identifiable by orange and red colouring on their
wings. Fares increase by 50% between midnight and
0500 hours. Taxis waiting outside hotels may charge
more. Fares should always be agreed beforehand.
Documentation: An International Driving Permit is
necessary and must be endorsed by the Traffic
Department before it can be used. All applications must
be in person. Holders of licences for the UK, the USA
and Australia are not required to take a driving test, but
must apply for a licence and take an eyesight test. All
others must take a test.

ACCOMMODATION

Bahrain has many first-class hotels catering for the
business community, but there is little in the way of
cheaper accommodation. Advanced booking is advised.
For details contact the Bahrain Embassy.

RESORTS & EXCURSIONS

Bahrain is the largest island in an archipelago off the east
coast of Saudi Arabia, accessible by a causeway
adjoining the two countries. An adequate freshwater
supply, unique in the region, and the benefits of having
one of the largest oil refineries in the Gulf, have given
the country great prosperity. Watersports, golf, tennis,
and horseracing are enjoyed throughout the country.
Manama, Bahrain's capital, is modern, dominated by a
Manhattan-style skyline. The souk lies in the centre of

the old town, near the archway of *Bab al-Bahrain* and,
although much of the surrounding area is modern, the
street layout and division of occupations still follows
traditional lines: the gold souk, for instance, is to be
found to the southeast of the market area and is
particularly impressive during the hours of darkness.
Much land, including the diplomatic area, has been
reclaimed from the sea. The ancient city capital of **Bilas
Al Qadir,** which dates from AD900, is just outside the
new city.
Excursions: The *Suk-al-Khamis Mosque,* which was built
in the 7th century, is one of the oldest in the Gulf. Bahrain
also has one of the newest: the *Al Fateh Mosque,*
completed in 1988 which includes a library and conference
hall. Other buildings of note are *Siyadi House,* a typical
wood-carved pearl merchant's house from the turn of the
century, and the 19th-century house of Shaikh Isa which is
a good illustration of the local Islamic architectural style.
Visitors can also see the 16th-century Portuguese fort near
Budaiya, the basket-makers at **Khabadad,** the potteries at
A'ali and the **Al Areen Wildlife Park**. *Jebel Dukhan* is
the highest point in Bahrain, from where the whole south
side of the island can be seen. The area around the ruler's
country residence at *Shaikhs Beach* has many sandy
beaches and apartments. **Zallaq** on the west coast has a
sailing club. Near the roundabout on the *King Faisal
Highway* Gold Suq dhow builders and fishtrap-makers
continue their traditional crafts. Ancient burial mounds can
be seen in many places.

SOCIAL PROFILE

FOOD & DRINK: There is a good selection of
restaurants serving all kinds of food including Arabic,
European, Indian, Chinese, Japanese, Lebanese and
American. Arab food is mainly spicy and strongly
flavoured. Lamb is the principal meat with chicken,
turkey and duck. Salad and dips are common. **Drink:**
Water, *arak* (grape spirit flavoured with aniseed) or beer
are the most common drinks; the sale of alcohol is not
encouraged although it is available to non-Muslims in
nightclubs, good restaurants and luxury hotels, except
during Ramadan. Strong Arabic coffee and tea is also
widely available.
NIGHTLIFE: Restaurants, nightclubs and cinemas
showing English and Arabic films can be found in the
main towns.
SHOPPING: There is a wide range of shops with
imported goods. Pearls are the main local product.

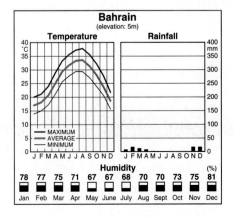

Bangladesh

□ *international airport*

Location: Northeast of Indian sub-continent.

Bangladesh Parjatan Corporation (National Tourism Organization)
233 Airport Road, Tejgaon, Dhaka 1215, Bangladesh
Tel: (2) 817 855-9. Fax: (2) 817 235. Telex: 642206 (a/b TOUR BJ).

High Commission for the People's Republic of Bangladesh
28 Queen's Gate, London SW7 5JA
Tel: (0171) 584 0081/4. Fax: (0171) 225 2130. Telex: 918016 (a/b BDTIDN G).

Assistant High Commission
31-33 Guildhall Buildings, 12 Navigation Street, Birmingham B2 4BT
Tel: (0121) 643 2386. Fax: (0121) 643 9004. Opening hours: 0930-1630 Monday to Friday;
and

Assistant High Commission
28-32 Princess Street, Manchester M1 4LB
Tel: (0161) 236 4853. Fax: (0161) 236 1064.

British High Commission
PO Box 6079, United Nations Road, Baridhara, Dhaka 12, Bangladesh
Tel: (2) 882 705. Fax: (2) 883 437. Telex: 671066.
Consular & Immigration section: Tel: (2) 883 666.

Embassy of the People's Republic of Bangladesh
Suite 300-325, 2201 Wisconsin Avenue, NW, Washington, DC 20007
Tel: (202) 342 8372. Fax: (202) 333 4971. Telex: 248519 (a/b BANGLA UR).

Embassy of the United States of America
PO Box 323, Diplomatic Enclave, Madani Avenue, Baridhara Model Town, Dhaka 1212, Bangladesh
Tel: (2) 884 700/22. Fax: (2) 883 744. Telex: 642319 (a/b AEDKA BJ).

High Commission for the People's Republic of Bangladesh
Suite 402, 85 Range Road, Ottawa, Ontario K1N 8J6
Tel: (613) 236 0138/9. Fax: (613) 567 3213. Telex: 053-2834283 (a/b BANGLADOOT).

Canadian High Commission
PO Box 569, House 16A, Road 48, Gulshan Model Town, Dhaka 12, Bangladesh
Tel: (2) 883 639 *or* 607 071. Fax: (2) 883 043. Telex: 642328 (a/b BMCN BJ).

AREA: 144,000 sq km (55,598 sq miles).
POPULATION: 110,000,000 (1994 estimate).
POPULATION DENSITY: 764 per sq km.

CAPITAL: Dhaka. **Population:** 7,000,000 (1991).
GEOGRAPHY: The People's Republic of Bangladesh, formerly East Pakistan, is bounded to the west and northwest by West Bengal (India), to the north by Assam and Meghalaya (India), to the east by Assam and Tripura (India) and by Myanmar (Burma) to the southeast. The landscape is mainly flat with many bamboo, mango and palm-covered plains. A large part of Bangladesh is made up of alluvial plain, caused by the effects of the two great river systems of the Ganges (Padma) and the Brahmaputra (Jamuna) and their innumerable tributaries. In the northeast and east of the country the landscape rises to form forested hills. To the southeast, along the Burmese and Indian borders, the land is hilly and wooded. About a seventh of the country's area is underwater and flooding occurs regularly.
LANGUAGE: The official language is Bengali (Bangla). English is widely spoken especially in government and commercial circles.
RELIGION: 86.6% Muslim, 12.1% Hindu, and small Buddhist and Christian minorities. Religion is the main influence on attitudes and behaviour. Since 1988 Islam has been the official state religion.
TIME: GMT + 6.
ELECTRICITY: 220/240 volts AC, 60Hz. Plugs are of the British 5- and 15-amp, 2- or 3-pin (round) type.
COMMUNICATIONS: Telephone: Limited IDD available. Country code: 880. Outgoing international code: 00. **Fax:** There are facilities at the Sheraton and Sonargaon hotels in Dhaka and services are now widely available in all the large towns. **Telex/telegram:** There are public telex facilities in the larger towns and at the Sheraton and Sonargaon hotels in Dhaka. Telegrams may be sent from main post offices and there are three rates of charge. **Post:** Airmail takes three to four days to Europe; surface mail can take several months. Post boxes are blue for airmail and red for surface mail. **Press:** There are six daily English-language papers, the most popular being the *Bangladesh Observer,* followed by the *Bangladesh Times,* the *Daily Star,* the *Morning Sun* and the *New Nation.* The main English-language weeklies are *Holiday, Dialogue,* the *Dhaka Courier* and *Friday.* The main Bengali dailies are *Ittefaq, Inquilab, Banglar Bani, Sangbad, Dainik Bangla, Meillat, Khabar, Bangla Bazar* and *Jankantha.* Almost all these newspapers are published in Dhaka and circulated throughout the country. **Media:** CNN and BBC World Service TV programmes are broadcast on Bangladesh Television between 0700-1130 and 1400-1630.
BBC World Service and Voice of America frequencies: From time to time these change. See the

PHOTO CREDIT: DANIEL WHITE

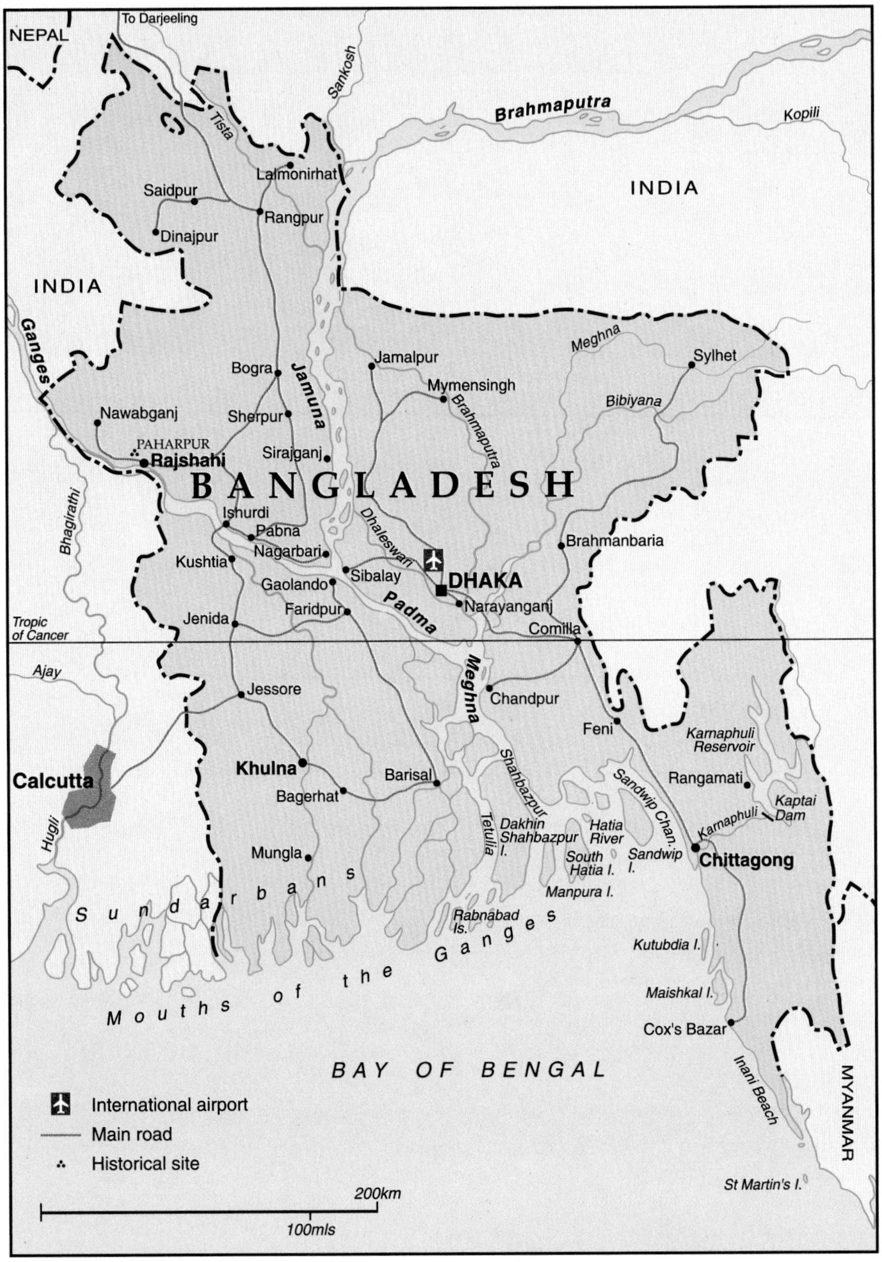

Map

NEPAL
To Darjeeling
Brahmaputra
Kopili
INDIA
Saidpur
Lalmonirhat
Tista
Sankosh
Rangpur
Dinajpur
INDIA
Ganges
Bogra
Jamalpur
Meghna
Sylhet
Nawabganj
Mymensingh
Bibiyana
Sherpur
Jamuna
Brahmaputra
PAHARPUR
Rajshahi
Sirajganj
Bhagirathi
B A N G L A D E S H
Ishurdi
Pabna
Brahmanbaria
Kushtia
Nagarbari
DHAKA
Gaolando
Sibalay
Narayanganj
Jenida
Faridpur
Padma
Comilla
Tropic of Cancer
Ajay
Jessore
Chandpur
Meghna
Feni
Karnaphuli Reservoir
Calcutta
Khulna
Barisal
Rangamati
Shahbazpur
Karnaphuli
Kaptai Dam
Bagerhat
Dakhin Shahbazpur
Hatia River
Tetulia
Hugli
Mungla
South Hatia I.
Sandwip
Chittagong
Manpura I.
S u n d a r b a n s
Rabnabad Is.
M o u t h s o f t h e G a n g e s
Kutubdia I.
Maishkal I.
Cox's Bazar
BAY OF BENGAL
Inani Beach
MYANMAR
St Martin's I.

✈ International airport
— Main road
⚲ Historical site

200km
100mls

---

section *How to Use this Book* for more information.

BBC:

| MHz | 17.79 | 15.31 | 11.75 | 9.740 |

Voice of America:

| MHz | 17.74 | 15.40 | 11.71 | 9.760 |

PASSPORT/VISA

Regulations and requirements may be subject to change at short notice, and you are advised to contact the appropriate diplomatic or consular authority before finalising travel arrangements. Details of these may be found at the head of this country's entry. Any numbers in the chart refer to the footnotes below.

	Passport Required?	Visa Required?	Return Ticket Required?
Full British	Yes	Yes	Yes
BVP	Not valid	-	-
Australian	Yes	1	Yes
Canadian	Yes	2	Yes
USA	Yes	3	Yes
Other EU (As of 31/12/94)	Yes	4	Yes
Japanese	Yes	Yes	Yes

PASSPORTS: Valid passport required by all.
British Visitors Passport: Not accepted.
VISAS: Required by all except nationals of:
(a) **[1]** Australia for a period not exceeding 15 days;
(b) **[2]** Canada for a period not exceeding 15 days;
(c) **[3]** the USA for a period not exceeding 14 days;
(d) **[4]** Belgium, Denmark, France, Germany, Greece, Italy, Luxembourg, The Netherlands, Portugal, Spain for a stay of up to 15 days (all other EU nationals *do* need visas);

(e) Bahamas, Barbados, Bhutan, Botswana, Fiji, Gabon, Gambia, Grenada, Guyana, Jamaica, Lesotho, Malawi, Mauritius, Nauru, Papua New Guinea, Seychelles, Sierra Leone, Vatican City and Western Samoa;
(f) Congo, Guatemala, Guinea-Bissau and South Korea for a stay of up to three months;
(g) Malaysia and Singapore for a stay of up to 30 days;
(h) Austria, Finland, Indonesia, Maldives, Norway, Nepal, the Philippines, Sweden, Switzerland and Thailand for a stay of up to 15 days.
Note: Visas are not required by former Bangladesh nationals holding British passports provided they have Bangladeshi passports as well as documentary evidence to prove they are of Bangladeshi origin. Please also note any foreign visitor overstaying the allotted period may be charged a fine for each day of overstay.
Types of visa: Tourist and Business. As regulations are liable to change at short notice it is advisable to check details with the Embassy or High Commission (or Consular Section at Embassy).
Cost: Check with the High Commission or Embassy (or Consular Section at Embassy) to find the cost of particular visas.
Validity: *Tourist:* 3 months; *Business:* 3 months.
Application to: Consular Section at Embassy or High Commission. For addresses, see top of entry.
Application requirements: (a) 3 passport-size photos. (b) 3 forms. (c) Letter from company for Business visa.
Working days required: 1-5.

MONEY

Currency: Bangladeshi Taka (Tk) = 100 poishas. Notes are in denominations of Tk500, 100, 50, 20, 10, 5, 2 and

1. Coins are in denominations of Tk1, and 50, 25, 10 and 5 poisha.
Currency exchange: All foreign currency exchanged must be entered on a currency declaration form. Hotel bills must be paid in a major convertible currency or with travellers cheques. Many shops in the cities will offer better rates of exchange than the banks.
Credit cards: Access/Mastercard (limited), Diners Club and American Express are accepted. Check with your credit card company for details of merchant acceptability and other services which may be available.
Travellers cheques: Can be exchanged on arrival at Dhaka Airport.
Exchange rate indicators: The following figures are included as a guide to the movements of the Taka against Sterling and the US Dollar:

Date:	Oct '92	Sep '93	Jan '94	Jan '95
£1.00=	63.42	60.15	57.70	61.56
$1.00=	39.96	39.39	39.00	39.80

Currency restrictions: Import and export of local currency is limited to Tk800. Free import of foreign currency is allowed, subject to declaration. Export of foreign currency is limited to the amount declared on import. On departure, up to Tk500 may be reconverted. Banks are allowed to cash travellers cheques up to a value of US$50.
Banking hours: 0900-1500 Saturday to Wednesday, 0900-1100 Thursday.

DUTY FREE

The following goods may be imported into Bangladesh without incurring customs duty:
200 cigarettes or 50 cigars or 250g of tobacco; 2 open bottles of alcohol, total of 0.35 gallon (non-Muslims only); a reasonable amount of perfume; gifts up to value of Tk500.
Note: Duty-free items may be bought at the duty free shop at Dhaka Airport on arrival.
Prohibited items: Firearms and animals.

PUBLIC HOLIDAYS

Jan 28 '95 Shab-i-Barat. **Feb 21** National Mourning Day. **Mar 10** Jamatul Wida. **Mar 13** Eid al-Fitr (End of Ramadan). **Mar 26** Independence and National Day. **Apr 15** Bangla New Year's Day. **May 1** May Day. **May 4** Buddha Purinama. **May 24** Eid al-Adha (Feast of the Sacrifice). **Aug 13** Prophet's Birthday. **Sep 8** Janmashtami. **Oct 24** Durga Puja. **Nov 7** National Revolution Day. **Dec 16** Victory Day. **Dec 25** Christmas Day. **Jan '96** Shab-i-Barat. **Feb 21** National Mourning Day. **Feb 22** Eid al-Fitr (End of Ramadan). **Mar** Jamatul Wida. **Mar 26** Independence Day. **Apr 29** Eid al-Adha (Feast of the Sacrifice).
Note: (a) Muslim festivals are timed according to local sightings of various phases of the Moon and the dates given above are approximations. During the lunar month of Ramadan that precedes Eid al-Fitr, Muslims fast during the day and feast at night and normal business patterns may be interrupted. Many restaurants are closed during the day and there may be restrictions on smoking and drinking. Some disruption may continue into Eid al-Fitr itself. Eid al-Fitr and Eid al-Adha may last anything from two to ten days, depending on the region. For more information see the section *World of Islam* at the back of the book. (b) Buddhist festivals are declared according to local astronomical observations and it is only possible to forecast the month of their occurrence.

HEALTH

Regulations and requirements may be subject to change at short notice, and you are advised to contact your doctor well in advance of your intended date of departure. Any numbers in the chart refer to the footnotes below.

	Special Precautions?	Certificate Required?
Yellow Fever	No	1
Cholera	Yes	2
Typhoid & Polio	Yes	-
Malaria	Yes/3	-
Food & Drink	4	-

Timatic

Health	
GALILEO/WORLDSPAN: **TI-DFT/DAC/HE**	
SABRE: **TIDFT/DAC/HE**	

Visa	
GALILEO/WORLDSPAN: **TI-DFT/DAC/VI**	
SABRE: **TIDFT/DAC/VI**	

For more information on Timatic codes refer to Contents.

Visit BANGLADESH

Bangladesh Parjatan Corporation National Tourism Organization offers you a range of package tours. Be our guest and discover this country.

Tour-1: DHAKA CITY & ENVIRONS

3-day tour covering *Dhaka City*, *Sonargaon,* the ancient capital of Bengal, and *Savar*. The capital Dhaka is a city both of the past and the present, famous for its exciting history and culture. Sonargaon is famous for its Folk Art Museum and atmosphere of past glory. Savar attracts many visitors to its memorial dedicated to the sacred memory of the martyrs of the liberation war of 1971.

Tour-2: DHAKA–CHITTAGONG–COX'S BAZAR–RANGAMATI–DHAKA

6-day tour including a visit to *Chittagong* – the second-largest city of Bangladesh and busy international seaport, the picturesque lake district of the *Rangamati Hill Tracts*, known for its rare scenic beauty and unspoiled tribal life, and *Cox's Bazar* with its 120km-long unbroken sandy beach.

Tour-3: DHAKA–KHULNA–SUNDARBANS–DHAKA

Visit the home of the Royal Bengal Tiger and enjoy the fascinating beauty of the jungle. This 5-day tour also takes you to the ancient 60-dome mosque and the shrine of Hazrat Khan Jahan Ali, the great saint of Islam of the mid-15th century.

Tour-4: DHAKA–MAHASTHANGARH–NATORE–PAHARPUR–BOGRA–DHAKA

6-day tour of the archaeological sites of Bangladesh, enabling you to see the ancient city of *Pundranagar*, *Paharpur* (the biggest Buddhist monastery south of the Himalayas) and the old palace of Dighapatiya at *Natore*.

Tour-5: DHAKA–SYLHET–ZAFLONG– JAINTIAPUR–SRIMANGAL– MADHABKUNDA–SYLHET–DHAKA

5-day tour taking you to the tea plantations of Bangladesh covering the immortal shrine of Hazrat Shahjalal, the panaromic beauty of *Zaflong* and Madhabkunda Waterfall, with a night halt at *Srimangal*.

In addition to the above packages, the NTO offers tailor-made package tours to cater to tourists' personal requirements.

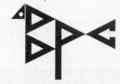

BANGLADESH PARJATAN CORPORATION

National Tourism Organization
233 Airport Road, Dhaka-1215, Bangladesh.
Tel: 817855-9. Telex: 642206 TOUR BJ. Fax: 880-2-817235.

[1]: A yellow fever certificate is required of all persons (including infants) arriving by air or sea within six days of departure from an infected area, or a country with infection in any part, or a country where the WHO judge yellow fever to be endemic or infected; or has been in such an area in transit; or has come by an aircraft which has come from such an area and has not been properly disinfected. Those arriving without a required certificate will be detained in quarantine for six days. For further information, see the *Health* section at the back of the book.

[2]: Following WHO guidelines issued in 1973, a cholera vaccination certificate is no longer a condition of entry to Bangladesh. However, cholera is a serious risk in this country and precautions are essential. Up-to-date advice should be sought before deciding whether these precautions should include vaccination as medical opinion is divided over its effectiveness. See the *Health* section at the back of the book.

[3]: Malaria risks exist throughout the year in the whole country with the exception of Dhaka City. High levels of resistance to chloroquine have been reported in the malignant *falciparum* form.

[4]: All water should be regarded as being potentially contaminated. Water used for drinking, brushing teeth or making ice should have first been boiled or otherwise sterilised. Milk is unpasteurised and should be boiled. Powdered or tinned milk is available and is advised, but make sure that it is reconstituted with pure water. Avoid all dairy products. Only eat well-cooked meat and fish, preferably served hot. Pork, salad and mayonnaise may carry increased risk. Vegetables should be cooked and fruit peeled.

Rabies is present. For those at high risk, vaccination before arrival should be considered. If bitten abroad seek medical advice without delay. For more information consult the *Health* section at the back of the book.

Health care: There are 890 government hospitals and over 200 private hospitals in the country. Visitors can also be treated at military hospitals. Health insurance is essential.

TRAVEL - International

AIR: Bangladesh's national airline is *Biman Bangladesh Airlines (BG)*.

Approximate flight times: From Dhaka to *London* (direct) is 10 hours 20 minutes, to *Los Angeles* is 22 hours and to *New York* is 23 hours.

International airport: *Dhaka International (DAC)* (Zia International). The airport is 19km (12 miles) north of the city (travel time – 45 minutes). *Biman Bangladesh* coaches run every hour from 0800-2200. To return, pick up the coach from the Tejgaon old airport building, the Golden Gate or Zakaria hotels. Parjatan Coaches are also available. Taxi and limousine services are available to the city. Car hire is also possible. Airport facilities include a restaurant, post office, bank, duty-free shops and car parking.

Departure tax: Tk300. Passengers in immediate transit are exempt.

SEA: Ferries from Myanmar and India run to the southern coastal ports. For details contact the Embassy or High Commission of the People's Republic of Bangladesh. The main seaports are Chittagong and Mongla.

RAIL: Rail connections (there are no through trains) link Bangladesh with India (West Bengal and Assam). Cycle-rickshaw, bus or porter services provide the cross-border connections.

ROAD: Only two road frontier posts are currently open between Bangladesh and India, at Benapol (for Calcutta) and Chilihatti (for Darjeeling). The crossing at Benapol is the easiest and most used. It is advisable to check when the frontier posts will be open. Conditions are likely to be difficult during the monsoon season. All other frontier posts between the two countries are currently closed. Overland travel is not currently possible between Bangladesh and Myanmar.

TRAVEL - Internal

AIR: Internal services are operated by *Biman Bangladesh Airlines*. Regular flights are run between Dhaka and several other main towns. These are cheap, and most routes are served at least two or three times a week. Airline buses connect with downtown terminals.

SEA/RIVER: Ferries operate between southern coastal ports and the Ganges River delta, where there are five major river ports: Dhaka, Narayanganj, Chandpur, Barisal and Khulna. Passages should be booked well in advance; for details contact local port authorities. The country has about 8433km (5240 miles) of navigable waterways. River services are operated by the Bangladesh Inland Waterway Transport Corporation, who run 'Rocket' ferries and launches on a number of

Terracotta work, Kantajee temple, Dinajpur

routes. The 'Rocket' services have three classes of fare; the waterways are the least expensive method of getting around Bangladesh.

RAIL: A rail system of about 2818km (1751 miles) connects major towns, with broad gauge in the west of the country and narrow gauge in the east. The network, which is slow but efficient, is limited by the geography of the country, but river ferries (see above) provide through links. Services are being upgraded. The main line is Dhaka–Chittagong, with several daily trains, some of which have air-conditioned cars. For details contact the Embassy or High Commission of the People's Republic of Bangladesh (for addresses, see top of entry).

ROAD: There are about 10,407km (6467 miles) of paved roads. It is possible to reach virtually everywhere by road, but given the geography of the country, with frequent ferry crossings a necessity, together with the poor quality of many of the roads, road travel can be very slow. Traffic drives on the left. **Bus:** Services serve all major towns; fares are generally low. **Taxi:** Generally available at airports and major hotels. Fares should always be agreed upon before travelling. **Car hire:** Cars may be hired at Dhaka airport, the Bangladesh Tourism Corporation Office or from the major hotels.

Documentation: National driving licence or International Driving Permit accepted. A temporary licence is available on presentation of a valid British or Northern Ireland driving licence.

URBAN: There are **bus** services, which are usually very crowded, in Dhaka provided by the Bangladesh Road Transport Corporation. The Central Bus Station is on Station Road (Fulbaria); there are also several other terminals which are, in general, for long-distance services. Buses and bus stations do not generally have signs in English. There are also an estimated 10,000 independent 'auto-rickshaw' 3-wheeler taxis (avoid night-time use). Conventional taxis are also available.

JOURNEY TIMES: The following chart gives approximate journey times (in hours and minutes) from Dhaka to other major cities/towns in Bangladesh.

	Air	Road	Rail
Chittagong	0.35	6.00	6.00
Sylhet	0.30	7.00	7.00
Rajshahi	0.45	12.00	13.00
Khulna	-	10.00	-
Rangpur	-	11.30	11.30
Dinajpur	-	12.00	13.00
Jessore	0.30	9.00	-

ACCOMMODATION

There are a few good hotels, mainly in Dhaka; these include the 5-star Sheraton, the Sundarban, the Purbani International and the 5-star Sonargaon. All rates are for European Plan. The Bangladesh Parjatan Corporation manages several modern hotels throughout the country.

Fishermen mending nets

Fishermen in Chittagong

Bills must be paid in hard currency or with travellers cheques.

RESORTS & EXCURSIONS

The country is divided into five administrative areas: Dhaka (North Central); Rajshahi (Northwest); Khulna (Southwest); Barisal (South); and Chittagong (Southeast). Formerly, 'Dhaka' was spelt 'Dacca'.

Dhaka (North Central)

Dhaka, the historic city and capital of Bangladesh, lies on the Buriganga River. The river connects the city with all major inland ports in the country, contributing to its trade and commerce, as it has done for centuries.
The old part of the city, to the south of centre and on the banks of the river, is dominated both by the commercial bustle of the waterfront and several old buildings. These include the uncompleted 17th-century *Lalbagh Fort,* the spectacular *Ahsan Manzil* palace museum, the *Chotta Katra* and a large number of mosques. To the north of this region is the European quarter (also known as British City), which contains the *Banga Bhavan,* the presidential palace, several parks, the *Dhakeswari Temple* and the *National Museum.* To the north and the east are to be found the commercial and diplomatic regions of Dhaka. The *Zoo and Botanical Gardens* are a bus or taxi ride into the suburbs. The waterfront has two main water transport terminals at Sadarghat and Badam Tali, located on the Buckland Road Bund. The famous 'Rocket' ferries dock here and boats can also be hired.

There are many buildings of interest along the river and in the old part of the city generally. The *Khan Mohammed Mirdha Mosque* and the *Mausoleum of Pari Bibi* are worth a visit, as are the *Baldha Gardens* with their collection of rare plants. There are dozens of mosques and bazaars to visit – the *Kashaitully Mosque* is especially beautiful.
The modern part of the city comprises the diplomatic and commercial regions and is to be found further north in areas such as Motijheel and Gulshan. Buildings of interest include the *Banga Bhavan,* the President's residence and the *National Assembly Building.*
City tours of Dhaka and its environs are available: contact the Parjatan Tourist Information Centre for further information.
Outside Dhaka: Sonargaon, about 30km (20 miles) east of Dhaka, was the capital of the region between the 13th and early 17th centuries and retains a number of historical relics of interest, although many of these are now in ruins. The **Rajendrapur National Park,** about 50km (30 miles) north of the capital, is noted for its varied birdlife. Northwest of Dhaka is **Dhamrai** which contains several Hindu temples. Further north still is **Mymensingh,** centre of a region famous for its supply of high-quality jute. The **Madhupur National Park and Game Sanctuary** is situated about 160km (99 miles) from Dhaka.

Rajshahi (Northwest)

Rajshahi Division, in the northwest of the country, is often ignored by tourists, but it contains a large number of archaeological sites. The most important of these are

at **Paharpur,** where are to be found the vast Buddhist monastery of *Somapuri Vihara* and the *Satyapir Vita* temple; there is also a museum. Other places of interest in the region include the ancient Hindu settlement of **Sherpur,** near Bogra; **Mahastanagar,** also near Bogra, which dates back to the 3rd century BC; **Vasu Vihara,** 14km (9 miles) to the northwest, the site of an ancient but now ruined monastery; **Rajshahi,** on the Ganges, which has a museum displaying many of the archaeological relics of the area; and **Gaur,** very close to the border with the Indian state of West Bengal, which contains a number of old mosques. **Bogra** is a useful base for visiting the archaeological sites of Paharpur, Mahastanagar and Sherpur, although not intrinsically interesting itself. Bangladesh Parjatan Corporation (NTO) offers package tours to these archaeological sites.

Khulna (Southwest)

Khulna Division is principally marshland and jungle. The city of the same name is the administrative capital of the division and is mainly a commercial centre, particularly for river traffic. The principal place of interest in this area of the country is the **Sundarbans National Park,** a supreme example of lush coastal vegetation and the variety of wildlife which it can support. The most famous inhabitants of this region are the Royal Bengal Tigers, but spotted deer, monkeys and a great variety of birds are also to be found here. Tours (usually for ten people or more) are organised by Parjatan Corporation during the winter; otherwise boats can be hired from **Khulna** or **Mongla,** which is the main port for the Khulna region. Accommodation is available at Heron Point. Other places of interest include the mosque of **Sat Gombud,** and the town of **Bagerhat** (home of Khan Jahan Ali, a well-known Sufi mystic).

Chittagong (Southeast)

Chittagong, the second-largest city in the country, is the principal city of the southeastern administrative division of Bangladesh. It is a thriving port set amid lovely natural surroundings studded with green-clad knolls, coconut palms, mosques and minarets, against the background of the blue waters of the Bay of Bengal.
The Old City retains many echoes of past European settlement, mainly by the Portuguese, as well as many mosques. These include the 17th-century *Shahi Jama-e-Masjid* – which closely resembles a fort – set astride a hilltop, and the earlier *Qadam Mubarek Mosque.* The *Chilla of Bada Shah* stands to the west of Bakshirhat in the old city. The higher ground to the northwest was, in due course, settled by the British, and this is now where most of the city's commercial activity is conducted. The *Dargah of Sah Amanat* is a holy shrine located in the heart of the town. About 8km (5 miles) from Chittagong is the picturesque *Foy's Lake* in the railway township of **Pahartali.** The *Tomb of Sultan Bayazid Bostami,* a holy shrine situated on a hillock in **Nasirabad,** is situated 6km (4 miles) to the northwest of the town. At its base is a large tank with several hundred tortoises, supposedly the descendants of evil spirits. In the northern corner of the Chittagong Division is **Sylhet,** known as 'the land of two leaves and a bud' because of its long renown as a tea-growing area. **Srimangal** is the main centre of the Sylhet tea gardens. Nearby **Madhabkundu** is noted for panoramic scenery and enchanting waterfalls. 43km (27 miles) from Sylhet are the ruins of **Jaintiapur,** once the capital of an ancient kingdom. Northeast of Chittagong is **Rangamati,** a place of scenic beauty and unspoiled tribal life. It is perched on the bank of the man-made Kaptai Lake. In the extreme south of Bangladesh is **Cox's Bazar,** a thriving regional tourist centre and beach resort, with a mixed population of Bengali and Burmese origin. The town has many thriving cottage industries for weaving and making cigars. This is also where the world's longest and broadest beach, *Inani Beach,* can be found; it is 120km (75 miles) long and 55m (180ft) to 90m (300ft) broad (depending on the tide). It has not, however, been fully developed for tourism. The main tourist beach is *Patenga,* which is also broad and long. Bangladesh Parjatan Corporation offers excellent accommodation and catering facilities.

Barisal (South)

Barisal is the administrative centre of the division of the same name. Situated in an area dissected by rivers, it is the most important river port in the south of the country. Just 10km (6 miles) outside Barisal at **Madubashah** is a lake and bird sanctuary. **Kuakata** is the most outstanding tourist attraction. It is a scenic beauty spot on the southernmost tip of Bangladesh in the district of

Patuakhali and has a wide sandy beach which is an ideal vantage point to watch the sun rise and set.
Other attractions include two pre-Moghul mosques: one, which boasts nine domes, is situated at the village of **Qasba Guarnadi** and the other, built in 1464, is near **Patuakhali**.
POPULAR ITINERARIES: 5-day: (a) Dhaka–Sylhet–Jaintiapur–Srimangal–Madhabkundu–Sylhet–Dhaka. (b) Dhaka–Chittagong–Rangamati–Cox's Bazar–Chittagong–Dhaka. (c) Dhaka–Mongla–Sundarbans–Bagerhat–Dhaka.

SOCIAL PROFILE

FOOD & DRINK: Limited availability of Western food, although the best hotels and restaurants have continental dishes and Dhaka has many good Chinese restaurants. There are many local specialities, usually served with rice and based on chicken and lamb. Seafood is also recommended, particularly prawns. Kebabs are widely available. Sweets include *keora*, *zorda* and *sandesh*. Table service is usual. **Drink:** Alcoholic drink is expensive and strict Muslim customs severely limit availability and drinking times, although leading hotels have bars which will serve drink; soft drinks and tea *(chai)* are freely available.
NIGHTLIFE: Leading hotels have bars, but Western-style nightclubs do not exist. Displays of local dance and music are occasionally to be seen, particularly during religious festivals.
SHOPPING: Hand-loom fabrics, silks, printed saris, coconut masks, bamboo products, mother-of-pearl jewellery, pink pearl, leather crafts, wood and cane handicrafts, folk dolls and horn items are popular purchases. **Shopping hours:** Generally 0900-2000 Saturday to Thursday, 0900-1230 Friday (shops in tourist districts often stay open later).
SPORT: Cricket and **football** are popular. Dhaka Metropolitan Soccer League begins its season in April. Games are held in the city stadium and playgrounds. **Volleyball, kabadi, badminton, hockey, basketball, tennis** and **rowing** are also popular sports. **Swimming** is available at the Intercontinental Hotel and Dhaka club, the Sonargaon Sheraton and at Cox's Bazar on the coast. All other **watersports** are at Kaptai Lake and **sailing** is also popular on the coast.
SOCIAL CONVENTIONS: In someone's home it is acceptable to sit crossed-legged on cushions or the sofa, although it is considered an insult to display the soles of the feet. If a visitor wishes to bring a gift, money must not be given as it may cause offence. Religious customs should be respected by guests. For instance, women should not be photographed unless it is certain that there will be no objection. Women should wear trousers or long skirts; revealing clothes should be avoided, particularly when visiting religious places. Dress is generally informal for men. **Photography:** In rural areas people are unused to tourists, who should ask permission before photographs are taken of individuals. Do not photograph military installations. **Tipping:** Most services expect a tip in hotels; give 10% for restaurant staff and 5% for taxi drivers.

BUSINESS PROFILE

ECONOMY: Bangladesh is one of the most under-developed and most overcrowded countries in the world. With few mineral resources, the country depends mainly on an agricultural industry which is frequently hampered by cyclones and flooding. Subsistence crops (wheat, grain and rice) take up the bulk of productive capacity. Tea and jute are the main cash crops – Bangladesh supplies about 90% of the world's raw jute. Production of both has suffered in recent years, largely due to the weather. Recent attempts to improve the quality of the local tea have been introduced to arrest the drastic decline in export earnings. There are large reserves of natural gas and some deposits of low-grade coal. Most of the manufacturing workforce is based in jute-related industries; the remainder works in textiles, chemicals and sugar. The cotton textile industry did particularly well during the 1980s and has now become a major export earner. Economic policy under the Begum Zia government has involved tentative market reforms, reduction of the bloated state sector, lowering of import barriers and some privatisation. However, Bangladeshi trade patterns have never properly recovered from the split with Pakistan, which used to take much of the country's tea crop: even though direct trade links were re-established in 1976, they have never reached previous levels. Bangladesh relies heavily on foreign aid, which accounts for around 7% of GDP and comes from a variety of sources, notably the World Bank and, increasingly, in the form of bilateral aid from Japan. The USA is substantially the largest export market followed by Italy, Japan, Singapore and the UK. Japan, Canada and Singapore are the country's main suppliers of imports, which are mostly manufactured goods. The hurricane of May 1991 caused irrevocable damage to the economy. The port of Chittagong, through which the bulk of Bangladeshi trade passes, was devastated. The country has now become more reliant than ever on the provision of foreign aid.
BUSINESS: Tropical-weight suits or shirt and tie are recommended. Suits or lounge suits are necessary when calling on Bengali officials. Cards are given and usual courtesies are observed. Visitors should not be misled by the high illiteracy rate and low educational level of most of the population. Given the opportunity, Bangladeshis prove to be good business people and tough negotiators. The best time to visit is October to March. **Office hours:** 0800-1430 Saturday to Thursday.
COMMERCIAL INFORMATION: The following organisation can offer advice: Foreign Investors Chamber of Commerce and Industry, Mahbub Castle, 35/1 Purana Paltan, Dhaka 1212. Tel: (2) 863 704. Fax: (2) 883 771. Telex: 632444.

CLIMATE

Very hot, tropical climate with a monsoon season from April to October when temperatures are highest; rainfall averages over 2540mm (100 inches). The cool season is between November and March.
Required clothing: Lightweight cottons and linens throughout the year. Warmer clothes are needed in the evenings during the cool season. Waterproofs are necessary during the monsoon season.

Sylhet, northern Chittagong, known as 'the land of two leaves and a bud'

PHOTO CREDIT: DANIEL WHITE

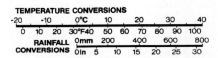

TEMPERATURE CONVERSIONS

-20	-10	0°C	10	20	30	40

0	10	20	30°F40	50	60	70	80	90	100

RAINFALL CONVERSIONS

0mm	200	400	600	800

0in	5	10	15	20	25	30

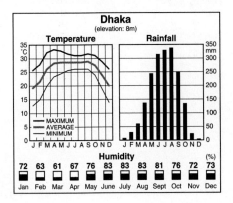

Dhaka (elevation: 8m)

Humidity (%)

72	63	61	67	76	83	83	83	81	76	72	73
Jan	Feb	Mar	Apr	May	June	July	Aug	Sept	Oct	Nov	Dec

Barbados

Location: Caribbean, Windward Islands.

Barbados Tourism Authority
PO Box 242, Harbour Road, Bridgetown, Barbados
Tel: 427 2623/4. Fax: 426 4080. Telex: 2420.

Ministry of Tourism, International Transport and the Environment
Barbados Port Authority Building, Harbour Road, St Michael, Barbados
Tel: 429 4813. Fax: 428 0925.

Barbados High Commission
1 Great Russell Street, London WC1B 3JY
Tel: (0171) 631 4975. Fax: (0171) 323 6872. Opening hours: 1000-1300 and 1415-1530 Monday to Friday (Visa section); 0930-1730 Monday to Friday (general enquiries).

Barbados Tourism Authority
263 Tottenham Court Road, London W1P 9AA
Tel: (0171) 636 9448. Fax: (0171) 637 1496. Opening hours: 0930-1730 Monday to Friday.

British High Commission
PO Box 676, Lower Collymore Rock, St Michael, Barbados
Tel: 436 6694. Fax: 436 5398 *or* 426 7916. Telex: 2219 (a/b UKREP BRI).

Embassy of Barbados
2144 Wyoming Avenue, NW, Washington, DC 20008
Tel: (202) 939 9200/1/2. Fax: (202) 332 7467. Telex: 64343.

Barbados Tourism Authority
800 Second Avenue, New York, NY 10017
Tel: (212) 986 6516 *or* (800) 221 9831. Fax: (212) 573 9850. Telex: 023666387.

Embassy of the United States of America
PO Box 302, Canadian Imperial Bank of Commerce Building, Broad Street, Bridgetown, Barbados
Tel: 436 4950. Fax: 429 5246. Telex: 2259.

High Commission for Barbados
Suite 500, 124 O'Connor Street, Ottawa, Ontario K1P 5M9
Tel: (613) 236 9517/8. Fax: (613) 230 4362.

Barbados Tourism Authority
Suite 1800, 5160 Yonge Street, North York, Ontario M2N GL19
Tel: (416) 512 6569. Fax: (416) 512 6581.

Canadian High Commission
PO Box 404, Bishop's Court Hill, Pine Road, St Michael, Barbados
Tel: 429 3550. Fax: 429 3780. Telex: 2247.

AREA: 430 sq km (166 sq miles).
POPULATION: 257,082 (1990).
POPULATION DENSITY: 597.9 per sq km.
CAPITAL: Bridgetown. **Population:** 7466 (1980).
GEOGRAPHY: Barbados is the most easterly of the Caribbean chain of islands. It lies well to the east of the West Indies, making it the most windward of the Windward Islands. To the west, coral beaches are made of fine white sand and the sea endlessly shifts from brilliant blue to emerald green over the natural coral reefs. Along the east coast there is a lively surf as the sea pounds the more rocky shoreline. Trade winds give Barbados a mild subtropical climate. This fertile and well-cultivated land (sugar cane is the main crop) is predominantly flat with only a few gently rolling hills to the north. The coral structure of the island acts as a natural filter and the water of Barbados is amongst the purest in the world.
LANGUAGE: The official language is English. Local Bajan dialect is also spoken.
RELIGION: Mainly Christian, with a Protestant majority, Roman Catholic minority, plus small Jewish, Hindu and Muslim communities.
TIME: GMT - 4.
ELECTRICITY: 110/120 volts AC, 50Hz. American-style 2-pin plugs are in use.
COMMUNICATIONS: Telephone: Inward IDD service is available to some towns. Country code: 1 809. Outgoing international code: 011. Hotels have telephones available to both residents and non-residents. **Fax:** Available at the largest hotels. Barbados External Telecommunications provides services for members of the public. **Telex/telegram:** Services are provided by Barbados External Telecommunications Ltd. The Bridgetown office has extensive telephone, telex and telegraph facilities. The Cable and Wireless office is at Lower Broad Street, open 0700-1900 Monday to Friday, 0700-1300 Saturday. There is a 24-hour service at Wildey, St Michael. Telex equipment can be rented.
Post: Deliveries are made twice a day in Bridgetown and once a day in rural areas. Post boxes, which are red, are plentiful. Post office hours: 0730-1700 Monday to Friday at Bridgetown main office; other branches are open 0730-1200 and 1300-1500 Monday, 0800-1200 and 1300-1515 Tuesday to Friday. **Press:** The main dailies are *The Barbados Advocate* and *The Nation*. The *Miami Herald, USA Today* and *The New York Times* are also available.
BBC World Service and Voice of America frequencies: From time to time these change. See the section *How to Use this Book* for more information.

BBC:

MHz	17.84	15.22	9.915	5.975

Voice of America:

MHz	15.21	11.70	6.130	0.930

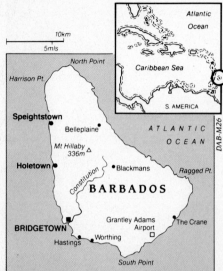

PHOTO CREDIT: ST JAMES BEACH HOTELS

Colony Beach Club

Timatic

Health	
GALILEO/WORLDSPAN:	**TI-DFT/BGI/HE**
SABRE:	**TIDFT/BGI/HE**
Visa	
GALILEO/WORLDSPAN:	**TI-DFT/BGI/VI**
SABRE:	**TIDFT/BGI/VI**

For more information on Timatic codes refer to Contents.

THE
COLOUR
OF
LUXURY

The rich and the famous have always looked with great affection on Barbados and have discovered a richer, kinder and more colourful world.

Which is why - quite apart from an abundance of natural beauty - you'll find Barbados is ideally equipped for all the sports of kings and champions. Racing, yachting, golf, tennis, cricket, polo, surfing and scuba diving in the deep, myriad-colours of our warm sea.

Barbados

Barbados Tourism Authority
263 Tottenham Court Road, London W1P 9AA
Tel: 071 636 9448

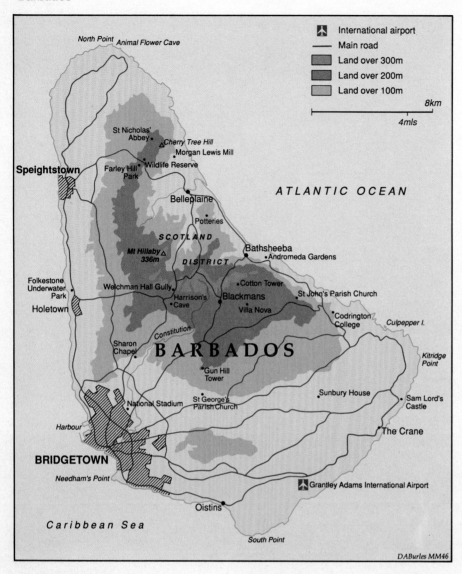

North Point — Animal Flower Cave

🛬 International airport
── Main road
▨ Land over 300m
▨ Land over 200m
▨ Land over 100m

8km
4mls

St Nicholas' Abbey
△ Cherry Tree Hill
• Morgan Lewis Mill
Speightstown
Farley Hill Park — • Wildlife Reserve

ATLANTIC OCEAN

• Belleplaine
• Potteries
SCOTLAND
Mt Hillaby △ 336m *DISTRICT*
• Bathsheeba
• Andromeda Gardens

Folkestone Underwater Park
Welchman Hall Gully
• Cotton Tower
Harrison's • Cave Blackmans
Villa Nova St John's Parish Church
Holetown
• Codrington College *Culpepper I.*

Constitution
Sharon Chapel **B A R B A D O S**

Kitridge Point

• Gun Hill Tower

• Sunbury House
• National Stadium St George's Parish Church
• Sam Lord's Castle

Harbour

BRIDGETOWN
• The Crane
Needham's Point
🛬 Grantley Adams International Airport

• Oistins

Caribbean Sea

South Point

DABurles MM46

PASSPORT/VISA

Regulations and requirements may be subject to change at short notice, and you are advised to contact the appropriate diplomatic or consular authority before finalising travel arrangements. Details of these may be found at the head of this country's entry. Any numbers in the chart refer to the footnotes below.

	Passport Required?	Visa Required?	Return Ticket Required?
Full British	Yes	No/2/3	Yes
BVP	Valid	-	-
Australian	Yes	No/3	Yes
Canadian	1	No/3	Yes
USA	1	No/3	Yes
Other EU (As of 31/12/94)	Yes	2/3	No
Japanese	Yes	No/3	Yes

PASSPORTS: Valid passport with 3 months remaining validity after departure required by all except:
[1] nationals of the USA and Canada, who hold a valid return ticket, who have embarked from their home country for stays not exceeding 3 months and who have a Naturalisation Certificate or original birth certificate accompanied by one of the following: (a) Driver's Licence with photograph. (b) Senior Citizen's Card with photograph. (c) University or college acceptance identification with photograph. (d) Employment Identification with photograph. Children under 12 years of age accompanied by their parents are exempt.
British Visitors Passport: Acceptable.
VISAS: Tourist visas are required by all except:
(a) [2] nationals of most EU countries for a stay of up to 6 months (except nationals of Spain who stay for more than 27 days, and nationals of Portugal who *do*

need a visa);
(b) nationals of the USA for a stay of up to 6 months;
(c) nationals of Commonwealth countries for a stay of up to 6 months (except nationals of India and Pakistan who *do* need visas, and nationals of South Africa who stay for less than 30 days);
(d) nationals of Argentina, Austria, Colombia, Dominican Republic, Fiji, Finland, Hong Kong, Iceland, Israel, Japan, South Korea, Liechtenstein, Norway, Peru, Sweden, Switzerland, Tunisia, Turkey and Venezuela for a stay of up to 6 months;
(e) nationals of Albania, Armenia, Azerbaijan, Belarus, Brazil, Bulgaria, Chile, Croatia, Cuba, Czech Republic, Estonia, Georgia, Hungary, Kazakhstan, Kyrgyzstan, Latvia, Lithuania, Mexico, Moldova, Nicaragua, Panama, Poland, Romania, Russian Federation, Slovak Republic, Slovenia, Suriname, Tajikistan, Turkmenistan, Ukraine and Uzbekistan who stay for less than 28 days, provided they hold return tickets;
(f) nationals of Costa Rica who stay for less than 30 days.
Note [3]: Some business visitors will require a Business visa; British passport holders should apply for an entry permit for a Business visa on arrival in Barbados at the Immigration Office; this is valid for 6 months. Entry permits held by passport holders of other nationalities are valid for 90 days. If a longer stay is required, apply for renewal at the discretion of the Immigration Office, Barbados.
Types of visa: Tourist and Business; cost: £18.
Application to: Consulate (or Consular Section at Embassy or High Commission). For addresses, see top of entry.
Application requirements: (a) 1 application form. (b) 1 passport-size photo. (c) Valid passport. (d) Company letter where required. (e) Return ticket may be required in some cases.
Working days required: 24 hours (in person); 48 hours (by post).
Temporary residence: Enquire at the Immigration Office in Barbados.

MONEY

Currency: Barbados Dollar (Bds$) = 100 cents. Notes are in denominations of Bds$100, 50, 20, 10, 5, and 2. Coins are in denominations of Bds$1, and 25, 10, 5 and 1 cents.
Currency exchange: The best exchange rates are available at commercial banks. The island is served by the Barbados National Bank and a range of at least six international banks, each with a main office in Bridgetown and further branches in Hastings, Worthing, Holetown and Speightstown.
Credit cards: Diners Club, Visa, American Express and Access/Mastercard are accepted in the resorts. Check with your credit card company for details of merchant acceptability and other services which may be available.
Travellers cheques: Accepted by all banks and most hotels.
Exchange rate indicators: The following figures are included as a guide to the movements of the Barbados Dollar against Sterling and the US Dollar:

Date:	Oct '92	Sep '93	Jan '94	Jan '95
£1.00=	3.18	3.07	2.97	3.11
$1.00=	2.00	2.01	2.01	2.01

Currency restrictions: Free import of local currency subject to declaration. Export limited to amount declared on import. No restrictions on the import or export of foreign currency.
Banking hours: Generally 0900-1500 Monday to Thursday, 0930-1300 and 1500-1700 Friday.

PHOTO CREDIT: ST JAMES BEACH HOTEL

DUTY FREE

The following items may be taken into Barbados without incurring customs duty:
*200 cigarettes or 50 cigars; *1 litre of spirits and 2 litres of wine; 50g of perfume; gifts up to a value of Bds$100.*
Note: For certain items it is now possible, on presentation of airline tickets and travel documents, to obtain duty-free goods any time from the day of arrival in the country. However, tobacco, alcohol and electronic goods must still be bought under the old system immediately prior to embarkation. [*] Only for passengers over 18 years of age.
Prohibited items: Restricted import of foreign rum, firearms and ammunition. Permits are needed for plants and animals.

PUBLIC HOLIDAYS

Jan 2 '95 For New Year's Day. **Jan 23** For Errol Barrow Day. **Apr 14** Good Friday. **Apr 17** Easter Monday. **May 1** Labour Day. **Jun 5** Whit Monday. **Aug 8** Kadooment Day. **Oct 7** United Nations Day. **Nov 30** Independence Day. **Dec 27-28** Christmas. **Jan 1 '96** New Year's Day. **Jan 21** Errol Barrow Day. **Apr 5** Good Friday. **Apr 8** Easter Monday.

HEALTH

Regulations and requirements may be subject to change at short notice, and you are advised to contact your doctor well in advance of your intended date of departure. Any numbers in the chart refer to the footnotes below.

	Special Precautions?	Certificate Required?
Yellow Fever	No	1
Cholera	No	No
Typhoid & Polio	Yes	-
Malaria	No	-
Food & Drink	2	-

[1]: A yellow fever vaccination certificate is required from travellers over one year of age coming from countries with infected areas.
[2]: The water in Barbados is considered by some to be the purest in the world; it is filtered naturally by limestone and coral and pumped from underground rivers. Milk is pasteurised and dairy products are safe for consumption. Local meat, poultry, seafood, fruit and vegetables are generally considered safe to eat.
Health care: Excellent medical facilities are available in Barbados, with both private and general wards. There are two large hospitals staffed by highly trained personnel. Barbados has a Reciprocal Health Care Agreement with the UK which entitles UK nationals to free hospital and polyclinic treatment, ambulance travel and prescribed medicines for children and elderly patients. However prescribed medicines for those other than children or the elderly and all dental treatment must be paid for. To receive treatment, UK nationals must show their UK passport or NHS medical card, as well as their temporary entry permit. Medical insurance is recommended for all other nationals.

TRAVEL - International

AIR: Barbados is served by *British West Indian Airlines (BWIA)* and *British Airways (BA)*.
Approximate flight times: From Barbados to *Miami* is 3 hours 30 minutes, to *New York* is 5 hours, to *London* is 7 hours 30 minutes and to *Los Angeles* is 9 hours.
International airport: *Barbados (BGI)* (Grantley Adams), 19km (12 miles) east of Bridgetown, near Christchurch. Airport porters are ubiquitous and charge Bds$1 for transporting luggage between the luggage claim area and the street. Facilities include a bank, bar, shops and restaurant. The outgoing duty-free shop carries a range of items including jewellery, perfumes, china, crystal, cameras, shoes and clothing. There is a regular bus service, costing Bds$1.50, to the city which departs every 10 minutes and a 24-hour taxi service.
Departure tax: Bds$25 for all departures. Passengers in transit who will be remaining in Barbados for less than 24 hours and children under 12 are exempt.
SEA: Barbados, which has a new deep-sea harbour at Bridgetown, is a port of call for a number of British, European and American cruise lines. Cruises call at the Bridgetown Cruise Ship Terminal which is a multi-purpose marketplace showcasing duty-free shops, local goods market, restaurant and bar, customs, immigration, health services and police facilities. Other services include a bureau de change, car rental, automated teller

Watersports. Top picture: Tamarind Cove Hotel.

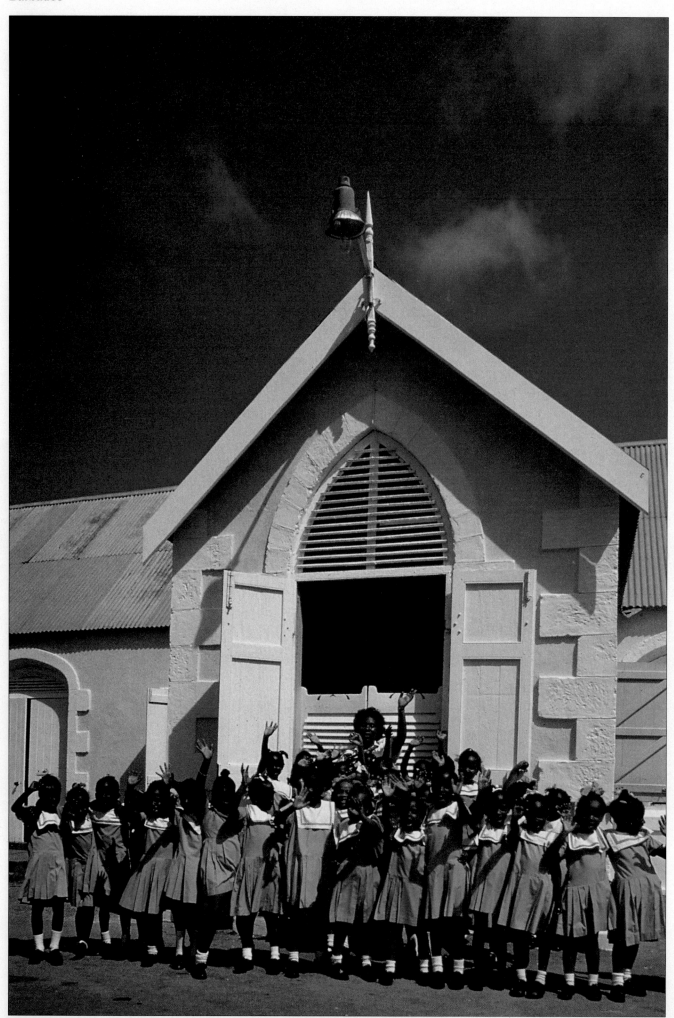

Primary school pupils

machine and a communications centre accessing telephone and facisimile machines. For details contact the Tourist Office. There is a small departure tax.

TRAVEL - Internal

AIR: *LIAT* and *BWIA* run inter-Caribbean flights to most of the neighbouring islands. *Tropicair* and *Aero Services* also have chartering facilities.
ROAD: Barbados has a good network of roads which covers the entire island. Driving time to the east coast from Bridgetown has been greatly reduced following the completion of the trans-insular highway. Traffic drives on the left. There is a speed limit of 60kmph (37mph per hour). The road journey from Bridgetown to Speightstown takes about 30 minutes and to Holetown or Oistins about 20 minutes. **Bus:** Frequent, comprehensive coverage of the island, flat rate of approx. Bds$1.50 for all journeys. Although cheap, buses are crowded during the rush hours. All buses terminate at Bridgetown. **Taxi:** Taxis do not have meters but fares are regulated by the Government. Listings are available from the Tourist Office. **Car hire:** Anything from a mini-moke to a limousine may be hired at the airport, at offices in Bridgetown and at main hotels. Petrol is comparatively cheap. Cars may be hired by the hour, day or week.
Documentation: A Barbados driving permit is required. This can be obtained from car hire companies, the Ministry of Transport (0830-1430 Monday to Friday), the airport (0800-2200 every day) or police stations in Hastings, Worthing and Holetown. There is a registration fee of Bds$10. A valid national licence or an International Driving Permit should also be held.
URBAN: Bridgetown has a local bus network and taxis are available.

ACCOMMODATION

Hotels, apartments, cottages and guest-houses are situated all the way down the coast from Speightstown to Oistins.
HOTELS: Accommodation includes uncompromising luxury and many first-class hotels. Hotel prices range to suit all budgets. Generally the luxury hotels are in the west, while the medium-priced can be found along the southwest coast. The east coast, due to its exposure to the trade winds and wild Atlantic Ocean, has only a small number of hotels and guest-houses. However, it is this area that is chosen by the Bajans for their own holidays. Hotel prices are more expensive in the winter than in the summer. High season is between December 16 to April 15, the low season runs for the remainder of the year. Rates are subject to a 5% government tax; a service charge of 10% is also applicable at most hotels. Most hotels have air-conditioning, many have swimming pools and housekeeping apartments. Most rates are for room only.
Grading: There is a hotel inspection and grading system, as well as standard services, the main ones being European Plan (EP), which is room only, and Modified American Plan (MAP), where breakfast and dinner are included with the price of the room. In addition, the Tourist Authority information gives full details on facilities. Further information is available from the Barbados Tourism Authority; address at top of entry, or from the Barbados Hotel Association, PO Box 711C, 4th Avenue, Belleville, St Michael. Tel: 426 5041 *or* 429 7113. Fax: 429 2845.
GUEST-HOUSES: There are small guest-houses throughout Barbados, particularly in Christchurch. Some offer self-catering facilities.
SELF-CATERING: There are a large number of apartments, cottages and villas available for rent, and a number of modern complexes are being built on the northwest coast. Older buildings, with a more local character, are available on the less popular east coast. There are also smaller, family-run apartment hotels such as Margate Gardens, Shangri-La and Oasis and many apartment-style hotels which leave the visitor with a choice of self-catering or restaurant eating. Almost all provide a wide range of facilities. All rates are subject to a 5% government tax; a service charge of 10% is also payable at most establishments.
CAMPING: Camping is not permitted in Barbados.

RESORTS & EXCURSIONS

The dramatic differences between the east and west coast must not be missed. The east (Atlantic side) is less developed and ruggedly beautiful. The west coast is the Caribbean side, where there is more hotel development, but the coastline remains elegant and attractive. The sea is calm and clear and this is the coast where watersports

come into their own.
Barbados is presently promoting ecotourism. The Barbados National Trust has implemented programmes to support this venture. Various hiking, bicycling and walking events are available and information can be obtained from the Barbados National Trust, 10th Avenue, Belleville, St Michael, Barbados. Tel: 436 9033.
Bridgetown: The island was discovered by the Portuguese in 1536, but throughout its colonial history, which ended with the Declaration of Independence in 1966, Barbados was under British sovereignty. This is strongly reflected in the old capital of Bridgetown which has a decidedly English character; so much so that there is even a miniature of London's Trafalgar Square, complete with a statue of Lord Nelson. The city is small and there are many excellent walking tours. Places worth a visit include the *Fairchild Market, St Michael's Cathedral* (built in 1831), *Belleville, Government House, the Barbados Museum, the Old Synagogue* and the *Garrison Savannah. Temple Yard* has a Rastafarian street market.
St John: There is a breathtaking view of the east coast from *St John's Parish Church.* The church's cemetery contains the grave of Ferdinando Paleologus, a possible descendant of the Byzantine Emperors.
Codrington College: Situated near Consett Bay, and one of the oldest schools in the Western hemisphere, built in 1745.
Sunbury House and Museum (St Philips): Contains one of the finest collections of antique furniture and household articles.
Morgan Lewis Mill: Also in the east, this is a splendid example of a Dutch windmill from the days of the sugar-cane planters. It has been completely restored and is open to the public.
Newcastle Coral Stone Gates: Situated in St Joseph, these gates were erected by 20th Century Fox for the film *Island in the Sun,* and the area affords a commanding view of the magnificent east coast beaches.
The East Coast Road: One of the most exciting drives on the island, with the Atlantic crashing over treacherous reefs onto the ragged and beautiful coast.
Andromeda Gardens: The array of exotic plants grown along terraced gardens make this the prettiest area of St Joseph.
Welchman Hall Gully: Owned by the National Trust, this botanic garden in St Thomas is home to many rare fruit and spice trees.
Holetown (St James): The monument in the town gives the date of the founding of Barbados' first settlement by the English as being 1605, although this event in fact took place in 1627. There are still a few structures dating from that time. *St James,* the first church, still retains a 17th-century font, and a bell inscribed 'God bless King William, 1696'.
Harrison's Cave (St Thomas): This eerie, luminous cavern makes a spectacular excursion. Completely lit, one can see every part from a special train which brings the visitor on a mile-long ride underground. It is open 0900-1600 every day.
Ashford Bird Park: Exotic birds and animals (particularly the lory and Barbados monkeys) are to be found here.
Bathsheba: Small pastel-coloured houses cling to the chalky cliffs that rise above the Atlantic.
Potteries: This village is famous for its ceramic artworks.
Gun Hill: Notable both for its splendid view of St George's Valley and for the lion carved out of a rock by a British soldier in the days when Gun Hill was an army lookout point.
St George's Church: 18th-century, and worth a visit for its wonderful altarpiece.
Platinum Coast: This beautiful stretch of coast is also known as Millionaires Row. There are fine beaches of white sand and clear, turquoise waters.
Speightstown: Typical West Indian village, small with attractive wooden houses and shops, old churches and an easygoing populace.
Animal Flower Cave: A cavern carved out by the sea with coral rock tinted almost every imaginable colour.
Farley Hill: Once a fine plantation house, now in ruins, still covered in hibiscus and poinsettias.
Nicholas Abbey: Another plantation house, in better condition than Farley Hill, graced with Persian arches and well-kept gardens.
The Atlantic Coast: Take the inland road through sugar-cane country with little churches and tiny towns with gingerbread houses. See the dramatic view from Crane Beach.
Sam Lord's Castle: Once an old plantation house, but now a hotel, beautifully decorated with furniture of Barbados mahogany.
Barbados Wildlife Reserve: Wildlife, some indigenous and some introduced to the island, roams free in a mahogany forest. Animals which visitors may expect to see during their visit include green monkeys, tortoises,

deer, wallabies, pelicans and otters. There is also a screened aviary where peacocks, turkeys, toucans, macaws, lovebirds, parrots and an iguana may be viewed.

SOCIAL PROFILE

FOOD & DRINK: There are a great many restaurants offering both international and traditional Bajan cuisine at a variety of prices. Local specialities include flying fish, lobster, and crane chubb. The sea urchin (oursin or sea egg) is a particular speciality. Other local foods include sweet potatoes, plantains, breadfruit, yams, and such fruits as avocado, pears, sour sop, pawpaws, bananas, figs and coconuts. An exchange system is operated between some hotels of the same class and guests can eat at other hotels for no extra cost. **Drink:** Local drink specialities include all types of rum-based cocktails, rum punch, planters punch, pina coladas and sangria. The local beer is *Banks.* The two most famous rums are *Mount Gay* and, for the connoisseur, *Cockspur's Five Star.* There are a number of bars which emulate the British pub, and serve genuine British bitter and stout.
NIGHTLIFE: Nightclubs, discos and bars provide entertainment including limbo dancing, fire-eaters, steel bands and dance bands. Entrance is often free or fairly cheap. As in all Caribbean countries, swinging nightspots tend to come and go with seasons. Coastal boat trips with live entertainment, such as the *Jolly Roger* and the *Tiami,* are very popular; most sail twice daily, and run buffets, bars and live music. **Tourist information:** All details are published in *Barbados News* and a weekly tourist sheet is available at most hotels. In addition, the Barbados Tourism Authority produces its own *What's On* guide monthly and two newspapers publish guides weekly.
SHOPPING: Shopping is a delight and there is a wide range of goods with visitors being able take all their purchases home duty-free on production of their passport and air ticket. Prices tend to be on the high side, though for such things as jewellery, clothing and ceramics the high quality often makes the expense worthwhile. Special purchases: rum, straw goods, coral and shell jewellery, prints *(batik)* and woodcraft. **Food shopping hours:** 0800-1800 Monday to Wednesday, 0800-2000 Thursday to Friday, 0800-1300 Saturday.
General shopping hours: 0800-1600 Monday to Friday, 0800-1200 Saturday.
SPORT: Cricket: Cricket is the national obsession and can be enjoyed during the dry season (January to June), both at national and club level. Test matches and the Inter-Caribbean Shield competition are played at the Kensington Oval in Bridgetown. Many of the great names of West Indian cricket are from Barbados, notably Greenidge and Marshall. **Golf:** There is one 18-hole golf course and two 9-hole golf courses at Rockley, Heywoods and Sandy Lane. Reservations are required.
Horseriding: Stables and horses are available and rides along the beach at sunset can be arranged. **Tennis** is also popular. **Horseracing:** There are three big meetings on the Garrison Savannah in spring, summer and autumn.
Watersports: Swimming, snorkelling, scuba diving, windsurfing, jet-skiing, parasailing and water-skiing are all very popular on the south and west coasts. Most hotels can arrange facilities. Independent jet-ski and parasailing operators often approach tourists, offering them rides for a price, depending on the length of time wanted. Average prices for parasailing are US$50 for a half-hour and for jet-skiing US$20 for 20 minutes. Boat chartering is available for game fishing. **Golf:** The Royal Westmoreland Golf Resort is under construction at present. The first 9 holes of the 27-hole course will be available in December 1994. The next 9 holes are projected to be available by mid-1995, and the entire 27-hole golf resort will be complete by December 1995.
SPECIAL EVENTS: The following is a selection of the major festivals and other special events celebrated annually in Barbados. For a complete list and exact dates, contact the Barbados Tourism Authority (address at beginning of entry).
Mar '95 *Cockspur Gold Cup.* **Mar-Apr** *Opera Festival.* **Apr** *Oistins Fish Festival.* **Jul** *Sir Garfield Sobers International Schools Cricket Tour.* **Jul-Aug** *Crop Over Festival.* **Nov** *National Independence Festival of Creative Arts.* **Dec** *Run Barbados* (10km (6-mile) marathon). **Jan '96** *International Windsurfing,* Silver Sands. **Feb** *Holetown Festival.* **Mar** *Cockspur Gold Cup.*
SOCIAL CONVENTIONS: Social attitudes, like administration and architecture, tend to echo the British provincial market town. However, the optimistic attitude, laid-back manner and wonderful sense of humour of the Bajans is well appreciated by many tourists. Casual wear is acceptable in most places. Dressing for dinner in hotels and restaurants is suggested. Smoking is generally unrestricted. **Tipping:**

Porters expect Bds$1 per piece. In restaurants or nightclubs, the Bajans prefer to leave it to the customer's discretion. Service is usually included in hotels. If not, 10% is the accepted tip.

BUSINESS PROFILE

ECONOMY: The Barbadian economy has traditionally relied on sugar production, but as the commodity's world market price remained so low throughout the 1980s, considerable efforts have been made since then to diversify into tourism and light industry. Tourism is now the largest employer on the island and continues to show steady growth. There is also a sizeable trade in high-quality British-manufactured china and glassware and in souvenirs for tourists. Cotton, flowers and plants are being developed as export industries. Light industries, such as electronic components, have fared less well, mainly as a result of falling demand in the United States who are the principal export market for these products. Oil has recently been discovered offshore, but the operations are small-scale. Barbados receives some overseas aid from British and American sources and is a member of the Caribbean economic community, CARICOM. The island is attempting to develop an 'offshore' financial services sector. Barbados has a good transport and communications infrastructure which should do much to assist future economic development. The main trading partners are the United States – the source of 30% of all imports – the UK and the other CARICOM nations.
BUSINESS: Lightweight tropical suits and shirt and tie are recommended. European courtesies should be observed. **Office hours:** 0800/0830-1600/1630 Monday to Friday.
COMMERCIAL INFORMATION: The following organisation can offer advice: Barbados Chamber of Commerce and Industry, PO Box 189, First Floor, Nemwil House, Lower Collymore Rock, St Michael. Tel: 426 2056. Fax: 429 2907.
CONFERENCES/CONVENTIONS: For the business traveller, conference organiser or incentive group there are a number of hotels with conference and meeting facilities. There are also a selection of conference centres, the newest being the Sherbourne Conference Centre. Located 3km (2 miles) from Bridgetown, it is adjacent to the main highway linking the south and west coast. The centre is fully air-conditioned and equipped to handle seminars, meetings, international conferences, trade shows and exhibitions. Restaurants and cafeteria facilities are available to seat 120 and 300 persons respectively. Contact Barbados Tourism Authority for more information.

CLIMATE

The balmy, subtropical climate is cooled by constant sea breezes, but it is sunnier and drier than the other islands. The dry season is from December to June; during the so-called wet season (July to November) some brief rain showers are likely. Average sunshine hours per day: 9-10 from November to March, 7-8 from April to October.
Required clothing: Lightweight cottons are advised; beachwear is not worn in towns.

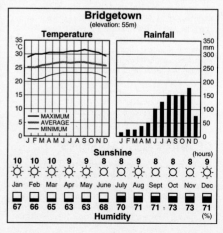

Top picture: The rugged, eastern coast of Barbados. Above: Local craft shop, Bridgetown.

Belarus

☐ international airport

300km
150mls

EUROPE
LITHUANIA
LATVIA
Zap. Dvina
Polotsk
RUSSIA
Vitebsk
Orsha
MINSK ■
Mogilev.
Grodno
B E L A R U S
• Baranovichi
Gomel
Pripyat Marshes
Dnieper
Brest
Pinsk
Mozyr
Pripyat
UKRAINE
POLAND

Location: Eastern Europe.

Ministry of Foreign Affairs
vul. Kirova 17, Minsk, Belarus
Tel: (0172) 272 922. Fax: (0172) 274 521. Telex:
252285.
Belintourist
pr. Masherava 19, 220078 Minsk, Belarus
Tel: (0172) 269 840. Fax: (0172) 231 143. Telex:
252270.
Embassy of the Republic of Belarus
1 St Stephen's Crescent, Bayswater, London W2 5QT
Tel: (0171) 221 3941. Fax: (0171) 221 3946. Opening
hours: 0900-1700 Monday to Friday.
Intourist
219 Marsh Wall, Isle of Dogs, London E14 9FJ
Tel: (0171) 538 8600. Fax: (0171) 538 5967. Opening
hours: 0900-1700 Monday to Friday.
British Embassy
vul. Sakharova 26, 220034 Minsk, Belarus
Tel: (0172) 368 687 or 368 916.
Embassy of the Republic of Belarus
1619 New Hampshire Avenue, NW, Washington, DC
20009
Tel: (202) 986 1604. Fax: (202) 986 1805.
Intourist USA Inc
Suite 603, 610 Fifth Avenue, New York, NY 10020
Tel: (212) 757 3884/5. Fax: (212) 459 0031.
Embassy of the United States of America
Starovilenskaya 46, Minsk, Belarus
Tel: (0172) 346 537.
Intourist
Suite 630, 1801 McGill College Avenue, Montréal,
Québec H3A 2N4
Tel: (514) 849 6394. Fax: (514) 849 6743.
**The Canadian Embassy in Moscow deals with
enquiries relating to Belarus (see** *Russian Federation*
later in this book).

AREA: 207,595 sq km (80,153 sq miles).
POPULATION: 10,300,000 (1992).
POPULATION DENSITY: 49.6 per sq km.
CAPITAL: Minsk. **Population:** 1,617,000 (1992).
GEOGRAPHY: Belarus is bordered by Latvia,
Lithuania, Poland, Ukraine and the Russian Federation. It
is covered largely by forests and lakes which are rich in

wildlife and is crossed by major rivers such as the
Dnieper. Agriculture and industry are well developed.
LANGUAGE: The official language is Belarussian, but
Russian is also spoken by 13% of the population.
RELIGION: Christian, mainly Eastern Orthodox and
Roman Catholic, with small Jewish and Muslim
minorities.
TIME: GMT + 2 (GMT + 3 from last Sunday in March
to Saturday before last Sunday in September).
ELECTRICITY: 220V, 50Hz. Adaptors are
recommended.
COMMUNICATIONS: Telephone: IDD is available to
all major cities, including Minsk 0172 and Brest 0162.
Country code: 7. When dialling from abroad the 0 of the
area code must not be omitted. International calls from
Belarus must go through the operator. **Fax/telex:**
Services are available in some larger hotels in Minsk
such as the Yubileynaya and the Planeta. There are also
public fax offices at vul. Opanskogo 5, Minsk (0900-
2200) and at vul. Chkalova 1, Minsk (0900-2100).
Telegrams can be sent from hotels. **Post:** Airmail to
Western Europe takes a minimum of ten days. Larger
hotels offer *Poste Restante* services. **Press:** There are
three daily newspapers in Belarus: *Narodnaya Gazeta,
Respublika* and *Zvyazda,* all printed in Belarussian. The
English-language newspaper is the *Minsk News.* **Media:**
Belarus has a news agency, *BelTA,* whose headquarters
are at vul. Kirava 26, Minsk. Tel: (0172) 271 992. Fax:
(0172) 271 346. **TV/Radio:** The radio station, *Radio
Minsk,* can be contacted at vul. Krasnaya 4, 220807
Minsk. Tel: (0172) 338 875. Fax: (0172) 366 643. The
television station, *Belarussian Television,* is located in
Minsk at vul. A. Makayenka 9, 220807 Minsk. Tel:
(0172) 334 501. Fax: (0172) 648 182. Telex: 152267.
**BBC World Service and Voice of America
frequencies:** From time to time these change. See the
section *How to Use this Book* for more information.

BBC:				
MHz	17.64	15.07	9.410	6.195
Voice of America:				
MHz	15.20	9.760	6.040	5.995

PASSPORT/VISA

*Regulations and requirements may be subject to change at short notice, and you
are advised to contact the appropriate diplomatic or consular authority before
finalising travel arrangements. Details of these may be found at the head of this
country's entry. Any numbers in the chart refer to the footnotes below.*

	Passport Required?	Visa Required?	Return Ticket Required?
Full British	Yes	Yes	No
BVP	Not valid	-	-
Australian	Yes	Yes	Yes
Canadian	Yes	Yes	Yes
USA	Yes	Yes	Yes
Other EU (As of 31/12/94)	Yes	Yes	No
Japanese	Yes	Yes	Yes

PASSPORTS: Required by all. The passport has to
remain valid for 6 months after departure.
British Visitors Passport: Not accepted.
VISAS: Required by all except nationals of Bosnia-
Herzegovina, Bulgaria, China, CIS republics, Croatia,
Cuba, Czech Republic, Hungary, North Korea, Former
Yugoslav Republic of Macedonia, Mongolia, Poland,
Romania, Slovak Republic, Slovenia, Vietnam and
Yugoslavia. Transit visas are required if crossing Belarus
to reach Ukraine or the Baltic States, but not if crossing
Belarus to reach the Russian Federation.
Types of visa: *Multiple-entry* (cost: US$300/£200),
Ordinary (cost: US$60/£40), *Tourist* (cost: US$20/£15)
or *Transit* (cost: US$30/£20). Express visas cost double
the usual amount. Tourist visas are only available to
those booking through Intourist or a travel agency in
Belarus. Children under 16 years of age do not have to
pay a visa fee.
Validity: From 30 days to 1 year. Length of visa depends
on reasons for visit and expiry date of passport (ie visas
can not be given for longer than the validity of the
passport).
Application to: Diplomatic or Consular branches of
Belarus in London, Paris, Bern, Bonn, Vienna, Washington
DC, New York, Warsaw, Beijing, Kiev, Vilnius, The
Hague, Rome, Moscow, Tel Aviv and Sofia. For nationals
of countries where Belarus has as yet no diplomatic
representation, a visa can be obtained at the point of entry
in Brest, Grodno or at Minsk airport, although this is not
encouraged and it is therefore significantly more expensive
(US$200/£100). Visas for Belarus are not valid for any
other member states of the CIS.
Application requirements: (a) Valid passport. (b) 2
application forms. (c) 2 passport-size photos. (d)
Invitation from Belarus company for Business visas or

from a Belarussian national for Ordinary visas is
recommended. (e) Stamped, self-addressed envelope for
return of passport if applying by post.
Note: Nationals of Austria and Switzerland do not need
return tickets.
Working days required: 5 for personal visits, 2-3 if
applying by post.

MONEY

Currency: The Belarussian Rubel was introduced in June
1993. 1 Belarussian Rubel = Rub10. Belarus and the
Russian Federation have entered a customs union in 1994.
Belarus has not yet officially announced when it will
leave the Rouble Zone. For information on the Russian
Rouble, see under *Money* in the *Russian Federation* entry
later in the book.
Currency exchange: Foreign currency should only be
exchanged at official bureaux and all transactions must be
recorded on the currency declaration form which is issued
on arrival. It is wise to retain all exchange receipts. Most
aspects of a tour, including accommodation, transport and
meals, are paid before departure (through Intourist or a
recognised tour operator), so large amounts of spending
money are not necessary.
Credit cards: Major European and international credit
cards, including American Express, Visa and Diners Club,
are accepted in the larger hotels and at foreign currency
shops and restaurants. Check with your credit card
company for details of merchant acceptability and other
services which may be available.
Eurocheques up to Rub300 can be cashed in banks and
major hotels.
Travellers cheques are preferable to cash, but visitors
should take some hard currency for cash purchases.
Currency restrictions: The import and export of local
currency is prohibited. All remaining local currency must
be reconverted at the point of departure. The import of
foreign currency is unlimited, subject to declaration. The
export of foreign currency is limited to the amount
declared on arrival.
Banking hours: 0900-1200 and 1400-1600 Monday to
Friday.

DUTY FREE

The following goods may be imported into Belarus
without incurring customs duty:
*250 cigarettes or 250g of tobacco products; 1 litre of
spirits; 2 litres of wine; a reasonable quantity of perfume
for personal use; gifts up to a value of Rub1000.*
Note: On entering the country, tourists must complete a
customs declaration form which must be retained until
departure. This records the import of articles intended for
personal use, including currency and valuables. Customs
inspection can be long and detailed.
Prohibited imports: Military weapons and ammunition,
narcotics and drug paraphernalia, pornography, loose
pearls and anything owned by a third party that is to be
carried in for that third party. An information sheet on
import restrictions is available on request from Intourist.
Prohibited exports: As for prohibited imports also
annulled securities, state loan certificates, lottery tickets,
works of art and antiques (unless permission has been
granted by the Ministry of Culture), saiga horns,
punctuate and red deer antlers (unless on organised
hunting trip), and punctuate deer skins.

PUBLIC HOLIDAYS

Jan 1 '95 New Year's Day. **Jan 7** Russian Orthodox
Christmas. **Mar 8** International Women's Day. **Mar 15**
Constitution Day. **Apr 14-17** Easter. **Apr 23-24** Russian
Orthodox Easter. **May** Radauniza. **May 1** Labour Day.
May 9 Victory Day. **Jul 27** Independence Day. **Nov**
Dsiady (Remembrance Day). **Dec 25** Christmas. **Jan 1
'96** New Year's Day. **Jan 7** Russian Orthodox
Christmas. **Mar 8** International Women's Day. **Mar 15**
Constitution Day. **Apr 5-8** Easter. **Apr 24-25** Russian
Orthodox Easter.

HEALTH

*Regulations and requirements may be subject to change at short notice, and
you are advised to contact your doctor well in advance of your intended date of
departure. Any numbers in the chart refer to the footnotes below.*

	Special Precautions?	Certificate Required?
Yellow Fever	No	No
Cholera	No	No
Typhoid & Polio	No	-
Malaria	No	-
Food & Drink	No	-

Rabies is present. For those at high risk, vaccination before arrival should be considered. If you are bitten abroad, seek medical advice without delay. For more information consult the *Health* section at the back of the book.
Health care: Emergency medical treatment is provided free of charge. Visitors will, however, be liable for any hospital or consultation fees incurred. It is, therefore, advisable to take out adequate health insurance. It is also advisable to carry an adequate supply of prescription medicines that may be unobtainable in Belarus.

TRAVEL - International

AIR: The national airline is *Belavia* and serves a large number of major European cities. *Lufthansa, Aeroflot Russian International Airlines (RIA), Swissair* and *Austrian Airlines* all provide a regular service to and from Minsk and most European capitals.
Approximate flight times: From Minsk to *Frankfurt/M* or *Vienna* is 2 hours 25 minutes, to *Moscow* is 1 hour 30 minutes and to *Zurich* is 2 hours 50 minutes.
International airport: *Minsk 2*, 50km (31 miles) from the city centre.
RAIL: There are several lines from Berlin via Warsaw and Brest with connections to Minsk. Another line runs from Vienna via Warsaw and Brest. Further direct trains are available from other Western and Eastern European cities.
ROAD: Foreign tourists may drive their own cars or may hire cars from Intourist (see *Travel – Internal* below). Road crossing points are as follows: Poland/Belarus: Terespol–Brest. The crossings are open 0700-2100 during the summer and 0700-1800 in winter. Those entering by car should have their visas registered at the hotel, motel or campsite where they stay for the first night and are advised to insure their vehicle with *Ingosstrakh*, which has offices at all crossing points and in most major cities. They should also purchase Intourist service and petrol coupons at the border (payment in hard currency). The petrol supply is restricted and only 4-star and diesel are available. Petrol stations accept cash. Up to one tank of petrol in canisters can be imported duty free. The Green Card is not accepted and insurance companies issue special policies for Belarus. It should be noted that, once in the CIS, foreigners may only drive on routes agreed beforehand with Intourist (see below). The supply of petrol and service stations is best on the major routes (Europa highways/motorways) through the country, such as Brest–Minsk–Smolensk–Moscow–Tver–St Petersburg–Vyborg and Brest–Minsk–Vilnius–Riga–Tallinn–St Petersburg–Vyborg. Contact Intourist for information on the temporary documentation required to import a car.
Sample distances: Minsk to Moscow: 690km (429 miles); Minsk to St Petersburg: 900km (563 miles); Minsk to Kiev: 650km (407 miles). A motoring guide is available from Intourist.

TRAVEL - Internal

RAIL: There are 5590km (3494 miles) of track in use.
ROAD: Belarus has a road network of 265,600km (166,000 miles) of which 227,000km (141,875 miles) are paved. Motoring holidays should be arranged through Intourist and foreigners may only drive on approved routes. The following documentation should be carried at all times: valid passport with valid visa; International Driving Permit; customs form guaranteeing the visitor will take the car out of the country again; insurance certificate; Intourist documentation with the approved route with overnight stays and car log book; Intourist motoring guide; and petrol coupons from Intourist. Traffic drives on the right. **Regulations:** International traffic signs and regulations are in use. Driving under the influence of alcohol is strictly forbidden. Speed limits are 60kmph (37mph) in towns and cities and 90kmph (55mph) on country lanes.
Documentation: International Driving Permit.
URBAN: Public transport is cheap and efficient. The city of Minsk has a metro system which is in the process of being expanded. Trains run between 0600 and 2400, buses, trams and trolleybuses between 0530 and 0100. Metro tickets are available at stations and bus tickets are also accepted on trams and trolleybuses. They can be purchased at stations or from the driver. Taxis have a green light on the righthand side of the windscreen.

ACCOMMODATION

HOTELS: Minsk, Brest, Grodno, Mogilev and Vitebsk have 3- and 2-star hotels. There is a 1-star hotel in Pinsk. The 3-star hotel Yubileynaya in the city centre of Minsk offers satellite TV, postal services, bureau de change, newsagent, hairdresser, beauty salon, sauna, supervised car park, casino, restaurant with regional and international cuisine, bar, snack bar and conference facilities. Business visitors can use the telex and fax services. Also situated in the city centre is the Hotel Planeta (2 stars) which offers similar services. The following organisations provide information on accommodation in Belarus: Minsk Hotel Association, Minsk Skaryny Avenue 11, Minsk. Tel: (0172) 200 804; *or*
Minsktourist Association, Tankavaya Street 30, Minsk. Tel: (0172) 237 360.
MOTELS: The motel Minsky is situated in the outskirts of the city and also has a campsite. There are tennis courts, saunas and good cross-country skiing in the nearby Prilusky nature reserve. There are hardly any other campsites in the country.

RESORTS & EXCURSIONS

Wide plains, picturesque villages, ancient castles and monasteries, deep forests, 3000 rivers, 10,000 lakes and scenic landscapes await the visitor. Belintourist offers several 1- and 2-week itineraries with different themes catering for nature-lovers, culture fans and sport enthusiasts.
Minsk: The capital of Belarus, situated 340km (213 miles) northeast of Warsaw and 120km (75 miles) southeast of Vilnius, was first mentioned in 1067, but little of the old city now survives except a ruined 12th-century Cathedral and a few 17th-century buildings. The city grew to be an important axis of communication and suffered badly during World War II. Modern Minsk is symmetrically designed with wide embankments flanking the Svisloch River. The cultural scene is very diverse with the Belarussian Ballet and good museums such as the *Museum for Architecture and Modern Life,* the *World War II Museum* and the *Museum for History and Culture*. Three other interesting museums deal with the major Belarussian writers Kolas, Kupala and Brovka. Icons form a large part of the *National Gallery*. Museums generally open 1000-1900 Tuesday to Sunday. The suburb of *Troitskoye Predmestye* should not be missed. It gives an insight into the way Minsk once looked. 19th-century houses with colourful façades line the streets. There are also excellent examples of the Baroque era such as the *Holy Trinity Cathedral* and *St Catherine's Church*. Many of the larger hotels are situated on Masherov Prospekt, which also features classical buildings, particularly the *Palace of Culture*. About 22km (14 miles) from the capital is the picturesque village of **Raubichi** with an interesting ethnographic museum housed in a disused church. Not far from Raubichi (10km/6 miles) is the idyllic *Minsk Lake* dotted with numerous islets and surrounded by dense pines. The onion-shaped domes of Russian Orthodox churches dominate the landscape throughout the country, but especially around **Logoysk** (40km/25 miles from Minsk), **Krasnoe** (60km/38 miles from Minsk) and **Molodechno** (80km/50 miles from Minsk). The memorial at **Khatyn** commemorates its destruction by the German army during World War II.
The village of **Zhirovitsa**, 190km (119 miles) from Minsk, is renowned for the beautiful 15th-century *Monastery of the Assumption*. Part of the monastery complex is a convent and a theological seminary (17th-18th century).
120km (75 miles) from Minsk is the small town of **Mir** where one can see the *Jewish Cemetery* and the 15th-century *Mir Castle*.
Historic **Nesvizh** still retains its old buildings. The former residence of the Radzivill family is one of the most attractive palaces in the country. It is surrounded by a large park with numerous lakes and elaborate gardens. Only a short walk away is the imposing Catholic Church designed by the 16th-century Italian architect Bernardoni.
270km (169 miles) from Minsk is **Vitebsk**, the birthplace of the painter Mark Chagall. There is a cultural centre named after him and his family house has been turned into a museum.
The centre of Christianity during the time of Rus (the first Russian state) lay in the Slavic town of **Polotsk**. An excellent example of architecture of the period is the *Church of St Sophia.* Also worth a visit are the two nearby castles.
The highlight of any visit to **Brest** is a tour of the *Brest Fortress* which was used to repell the German forces during World War II. Inside the Fortress is a museum which chronicles its history back to the 13th century. This history is further illustrated by a fascinating selection of exhibits in the *Museum of History and Archaeology*. In the surrounding countryside time appears to have stood still for centuries. 500-year-old trees can be found in the nature reserve *Balvezhskaya Pushcha*. Wild European bison roam the area.
In **Grodno**, the fifth-largest city of Belarus, major sites are the Old Town centre, the *Kalozh-Church* and the *Old Castle* (both 11th century).
The north and northwest, near the borders of Lithuania and Latvia, is dominated by the *Braslav Lake District*. It is a good area for watersports with a total of 30 lakes situated in atmospheric forest. Accommodation in the area is usually in small dachas along the lakeshore.
Belavezha Wood is one of the last sites where rare animals such as bisons, bears and wolves can still be seen living in their natural habitat. Long scenic hiking trails are scattered throughout the **Nature Reserve of Berezinsky**, stretching from the source of the Berezina to Palik Lake. Primeval forests, marshland, deep rivers and a rich fauna and flora dominate this unique region, hence its UNESCO listing as a protected biosphere.

SOCIAL PROFILE

FOOD & DRINK: Belarussian *borshch*, a soup made with beetroot, is served hot with sour cream. Other excellent specialities are *filet à la Minsk* and Minsk cutlet. Regional cooking is often based on potatoes with mushrooms and berries as favourite side dishes. Local dishes well worth trying are *dracheny*, a tasty potato dish with mushrooms, and *draniki* which is served with pickled berries. *Mochanka* is a thick soup mixed with lard accompanied by hot pancakes. There is also a good selection of international and Russian specialities available. Intourist meal vouchers are widely acceptable and an increasing number of hotels and restaurants in Moscow accept foreign currency, as do some bars.
Drink: *Beloveszhskaya Bitters* are made from over 100 different herbs and have an interesting taste. A favourite drink is *chai* (black tea). Coffee is generally available with meals and in cafés, although standards vary. Soft drinks, fruit juices and mineral waters are widely available. Drinks are ordered by grams or by the bottle. Former Soviet regulations forbid the serving of more than 100g of vodka per person per meal. Bars and cafés usually close by 2200.
NIGHTLIFE: A thriving cultural scene with opera, ballet, theatre, circus and puppet theatre can be found in Minsk. Excellent performances of the various folk dances are presented in the Cultural Centre. Brest also has a renowned puppet theatre and theatre.
SHOPPING: Wooden caskets, trinket boxes, straw items, decorative plates and other handicraft items are good buys. A wide range of goods such as watches, cameras, wines and spirits, furs, ceramics and glass, jewellery and toys may be bought for foreign currency only (cash or travellers cheques) at favourable prices. Typical Russian souvenirs like the wooden *matreshka* dolls and original samovars are also available. All other shops accept local currency only. Scarina Avenue is the main street with antique shops and two department stores. Most shops are closed on Sunday, but tourist shops are usually open every day. Antiquities, valuables, works of art and manuscripts other than those offered for sale in souvenir shops require an export licence.
Shopping hours: 0800/0900-2000/2100 Monday to Saturday (food shops); 1000/1100-1900/2000 Monday to Saturday (all others).
SPORT: Minsk was one of the venues of the 1980 Olympic games and has excellent sport facilities. **Tennis, gymnastics, athletics, swimming, football** and **ice-hockey** are just some of the sports which are on offer. Excellent **cross-country skiing** is available in the nature reserve near the Minsk campsite. **Skating** is also

UK STD CODES

As of 16 April 1995, the UK STD codes will change. Insert a 1 after the first zero in the old STD code, eg. 071 becomes 0171.

There are five exceptions:

CITY	NEW CODE	+ PREFIX
Bristol	0117	9
Leicester	0116	2
Leeds	0113	2
Nottingham	0115	9
Sheffield	0114	2

popular. **Hiking** is possible throughout Belarus. The Braslav Lake District situated in the north and northeast of the country is ideal for **boating** holidays. Several of the 30 lakes are connected through canals.
SPECIAL EVENTS: Jul '95 *Lyric Festival* (in honour of the birthday of the most famous Belarussian poet Yanka Kupala), Vyashinka. **Nov** *Belarussian Culture Weeks in Autumn*, Minsk.
SOCIAL CONVENTIONS: Handshaking is the usual greeting. Hospitality is part of the tradition and the people are welcoming and friendly. Company or business gifts are well received. Smoking is acceptable unless stated otherwise. **Tipping:** 10% are usual. In some hotels in Minsk and other cities a 10-15% service charge is added to the bill.

BUSINESS PROFILE

ECONOMY: In comparison to other members of the CIS, Belarus has few natural resources but has a higher level of economic development. Agriculture is mainly grain and potatoes. Livestock breeding also plays an important part. The manufacturing industry is largely based on the manufacture of agricultural machines and cars which, together with the chemical industry, forms the major mainstay of the Belarussian economy. Most industrial production has historically been geared towards export – 90% of manufactured goods are shipped outside the republic. The Government has introduced an economic reform programme, at the heart of which is a gradual transition to a market economy. Collaboration with Western businesses is a key part of this strategy.
BUSINESS: For business meetings, visitors should dress smartly. English is widely used in management circles and knowledge of German might also be useful. Appointments should be made well in advance and should be confirmed nearer the time. Cards should have a Russian translation on the back. Business transactions are likely to take quite a long time. **Office hours:** 0900-1800 Monday to Friday.
COMMERCIAL INFORMATION: The following organisation can offer advice: Chamber of Commerce and Industry of the Republic of Belarus, pr. Masherava 14, 220600 Minsk. Tel: (0172) 269 937. Fax: (0172) 269 936. Telex: 252190.
CONFERENCES/CONVENTIONS: The 3-star Hotel Yubileynaya offers conference facilities for up to 250 persons, including simultaneous translation services. The following organisation can give information regarding conferences and conventions in Belarus: State Committee of Foreign Economic Relations, Government House, 220010 Minsk. Tel: (0172) 211 758 *or* 296 278. Fax: (0172) 273 924. Telex: 252292.

CLIMATE

Temperate continental climate.
Required clothing: Medium- to heavy-weights in winter. Waterproofs are advisable throughout the year.

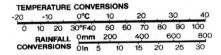

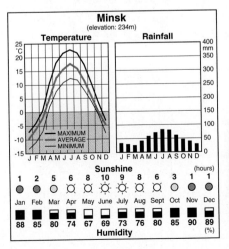

Minsk (elevation: 234m)

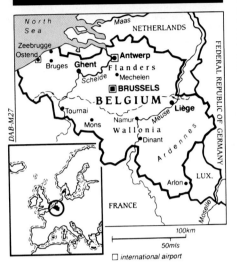

Location: Western Europe.

Office de Promotion du Tourisme de la Communauté Française
61 rue Marché-aux-Herbes, B-1000 Brussels, Belgium
Tel: (2) 504 0200. Fax: (2) 513 6950.
Tourist Office for Flanders
Grasmarkt 61, B-1000 Brussels, Belgium
Tel: (2) 504 0300. Fax: (2) 513 8803.
Embassy of the Kingdom of Belgium
103-105 Eaton Square, London SW1W 9AB
Tel: (0171) 235 5422 (general enquiries) *or* 235 5144 (Visa section). Fax: (0171) 259 6213. Telex: 22823 (a/b BELAM G). Opening hours: 0900-1200 Monday to Friday (visas); 0900-1300 and 1400-1700 (enquiries desk); 0900-1300 (telephone desk).
Belgian Tourist Office
5th Floor, 29 Princes Street, London W1R 7RG
Tel: (0171) 629 0230. Fax: (0171) 629 0454. Opening hours: 0900-1700 Monday to Friday.
British Embassy
85 rue d'Arlon, B-1040 Brussels, Belgium
Tel: (2) 287 6211. Fax: (2) 287 6360.
Consulates in: Antwerp and Liège.
Embassy of the Kingdom of Belgium
3330 Garfield Street, NW, Washington, DC 20008
Tel: (202) 333 6900. Fax: (202) 333 3079.
Belgian Consulate General
26th Floor, 1330 Avenue of the Americas, New York, NY 10019
Tel: (212) 586 5110. Fax: (212) 582 9657. Telex: 6491312 (a/b BELCG UR).
Belgian National Tourist Office
Suite 1501, 780 Third Avenue, New York, NY 10017-7076
Tel: (212) 758 8130. Fax: (212) 355 7675.
Embassy of the United States of America
27 boulevard du Régent, B-1000 Brussels, Belgium
Tel: (2) 513 3830. Fax: (2) 502 1490. Telex: 84621336.
Embassy of Belgium
4th Floor, 80 Elgin Street, Ottawa, Ontario K1P 1B7
Tel: (613) 236 7267. Fax: (613) 236 7882. Telex: 0533568.
Consulates in: Calgary, Edmonton, Halifax, London (Ontario), Montréal, Toronto, Vancouver and Winnipeg.
Belgian Tourist Office
PO Box 760, N.D.G., Montréal, Québec H4A 3S2
Tel: (514) 484 3594.

Timatic	**Health**
	GALILEO/WORLDSPAN: **TI-DFT/BRU/HE**
	SABRE: **TIDFT/BRU/HE**
	Visa
	GALILEO/WORLDSPAN: **TI-DFT/BRU/VI**
	SABRE: **TIDFT/BRU/VI**
	For more information on Timatic codes refer to Contents.

Canadian Embassy
2 avenue de Tervuren, B-1040 Brussels, Belgium
Tel: (2) 735 6040. Fax: (2) 735 3383.

AREA: 30,519 sq km (11,783 sq miles).
POPULATION: 9,978,681 (1991).
POPULATION DENSITY: 328.4 per sq km.
CAPITAL: Brussels (Bruxelles, Brussel). **Population:** 951,217 (1990).
GEOGRAPHY: Belgium is situated in Europe and bordered by France, Germany, Luxembourg and The Netherlands. The landscape is varied, the rivers and gorges of the Ardennes contrasting sharply with the rolling plains which make up much of the countryside. Notable features are the great forest of Ardennes near the frontier with Germany and Luxembourg and the wide, sandy beaches of the northern coast, which run for over 60km (37 miles). The countryside is rich in historic cities, castles and churches.
LANGUAGE: The official languages are Flemish, French and German; Flemish is slightly more widely spoken than French. German is spoken by fewer than 1% of the population, in areas around the eastern border.
RELIGION: Mainly Roman Catholic, with small minorities of Protestants and Jews.
TIME: GMT + 1 (GMT + 2 last Sunday in March to Saturday before last Sunday in September).
ELECTRICITY: 220 volts AC, 50Hz. Plugs are of the 2-pin round type.
COMMUNICATIONS: Belgium is a major historical European crossroads for communications and possesses a fully integrated service for all aspects of telecommunications. **Telephone:** Fully automatic IDD. For operator services, dial 1207. Country code: 32. Outgoing international code: 00. There are call boxes in all major towns and country districts. The cost of local calls is BFr10. Some coinless cardphones are also available. Telecards are available from newsagents, railway stations and post offices. Price: BFr100 and 500. **Telex:** Most major hotels provide this service. **Post:** Airmail takes two to three days to other West European destinations. A letter sent to Belgium from another country should have a 'B' as a prefix to the Belgian postal district concerned. *Poste Restante* facilities are available in main cities. Post office hours: 0900-1700 Monday to Friday. **Press:** Principal daily newspapers are *Le Soir, La Meuse, La Lanterne* (French) and *Het Laatste Nieuws, De Standaard, Het Nieuwsblad, De Gentenaar* (Flemish). There is a Dutch-language newspaper, *De Nieuwe Gids,* and one English-language newspaper, *The Bulletin,* printed in Belgium.
BBC World Service and Voice of America frequencies: From time to time these change. See the section *How to Use this Book* for more information.
BBC:

MHz	9.760	9.410	6.195	0.648

A service is also available on 648kHz.
Voice of America:

MHz	11.97	9.670	6.040	5.995

PASSPORT/VISA

Regulations and requirements may be subject to change at short notice, and you are advised to contact the appropriate diplomatic or consular authority before finalising travel arrangements. Details of these may be found at the head of this country's entry. Any numbers in the chart refer to the footnotes below.

	Passport Required?	Visa Required?	Return Ticket Required?
Full British	1	No	No
BVP	Valid	No	No
Australian	Yes	No	Yes
Canadian	Yes	No	Yes
USA	Yes	No	Yes
Other EU (As of 31/12/94)	1	No	No
Japanese	Yes	No	Yes

PASSPORTS: A valid passport is required by all except [1] nationals of EU countries and nationals of Andorra, Austria, Liechtenstein, Malta, Monaco, San Marino and Switzerland providing they carry a national ID card or, for UK citizens, a BVP.
Note: Where full national passports are required they must be valid for at least 3 months *after* the last day of the intended visit.
British Visitors Passport: A BVP can be used for holidays or unpaid business trips of up to 3 months to Belgium. Please note that children under 16 cannot travel on their brother's or sister's passport.
VISAS: Required by all except:
(a) nationals of countries referred to in the chart above;
(b) nationals of Andorra, Argentina, Austria, Brazil, Brunei, Chile, Costa Rica, Cyprus, Czech Republic,

Ecuador, El Salvador, Finland, Guatemala, Honduras, Hungary, Iceland, Israel, Jamaica, South Korea, Liechtenstein, Malawi, Malaysia, Malta, Mexico, Monaco, New Zealand, Nicaragua, Norway, Panama, Paraguay, Poland, San Marino, Singapore, Slovak Republic, Slovenia, Sweden, Switzerland, Turkey (if resident in an EU country and holding a residence permit valid for a further four months), Uruguay, Vatican City and Venezuela.

In all cases, this visa-free facility lasts for 3 months within any 6-month period, and is conditional on the length of stay itself being no longer than 3 months.

Types of visa: *Transit* – cost £9.20. *Visitor's visa (Tourist and Business)* – cost £20.70 for up to one month, £27.60 for a visa lasting for 3 months and £34.50 for a visa lasting up to a year. Visas are issued free of charge to:

(a) nationals of Iran, Iraq, Turkey and the Philippines for visits up to 59 days;

(b) spouses and children under 18 of EU nationals if original passport and marriage/birth certificate is shown.

Validity: *Transit:* 24 hours. *Visitor's visa:* Up to 3 months. For renewal, apply to Embassy.

Application to: Consulate (or Consular Section at Embassy). For addresses, see top of entry.

Application requirements: (a) Application form. (b) Passport-size photograph. (The required number of each of these varies according to nationality of applicant.) (c) Letter from company/bank/school/college. (d) Proof of sufficient funds to cover stay. (e) Return ticket. (f) References in Belgium. (g) Signed Belgian sponsor's letter. (h) Invitation from organisation. (i) Introduction letter from travel agency/tour operator. (j) Hotel bookings. (k) Self-addressed stamped registered envelope. (l) Fee (payable by postal order only).

Working days required: 24 hours to 6 weeks, depending on nationality, for postal or personal visits.

Temporary residence: Persons wishing to take up temporary residence should make a special application to the Belgian Embassy.

MONEY

Currency: Belgian Franc (BFr) = 100 centimes (Flemish *centiemen*). Notes are in denominations of BFr10,000, 2000, 1000, 500 and 100. Coins are in denominations of BFr50, 20, 5 and 1, and 50 centimes.

Credit cards: Access/Mastercard, American Express, Diners Club and Visa are accepted. Check with your credit card company for details of merchant acceptability and other services which may be available.

Travellers cheques: Widely accepted.

Exchange rate indicators: The following figures are included as a guide to the movements of the Belgian Franc against Sterling and the US Dollar:

Date:	Oct '92	Sep '93	Jan '94	Jan '95
£1.00=	50.20	53.25	53.49	50.10
$1.00=	31.63	34.87	36.15	32.39

Currency restrictions: There are no restrictions on the import and export of either local or foreign currency.

Banking hours: 0900-1200 and 1400-1600 Monday to Friday. Some banks open 0900-1200 Saturday.

DUTY FREE

The following goods may be taken into Belgium without incurring customs duty:

(a) Travellers arriving from EU countries:
300 cigarettes or 75 cigars or 400g of tobacco; 5 litres of still wine; 1.5 litres of spirits or 3 litres of sparkling or fortified wine; 8 litres of Luxembourg wines (if imported via the Luxembourg border); 75g of perfume and 375ml of eau de toilette; other goods up to BFr25,500.

(b) Travellers arriving from EU countries with duty-paid goods:
800 cigarettes and 400 cigarillos and 200 cigars and 1kg of tobacco; 90 litres of wine (including up to 60 litres of sparkling wine); 10 litres of spirits; 20 litres of intermediate products (such as fortified wine); 110 litres of beer.

(c) Travellers from non-EU countries:
200 cigarettes or 100 cigarillos or 50 cigars or 250g of tobacco; 2 litres of still wine; 1 litre of spirits; 8 litres of Luxembourg wines (if imported via the Luxembourg border); 50g of perfume and 250ml of eau de toilette; other goods up to BFr2000.

Prohibited items: Unpreserved meat products. Other unpreserved foodstuffs must be declared.

PUBLIC HOLIDAYS

Jan 1 '95 New Year's Day. **Apr 17** Easter Monday. **May 1** Labour Day. **May 25** Ascension Day. **Jun 5** Whit Monday. **Jul 21** National Day. **Aug 15** Assumption. **Nov 1** All Saints' Day. **Nov 11** Armistice Day. **Nov 15*** King's Birthday. **Dec 25** Christmas Day. **Dec 26*** Boxing

Day. **Jan 1 '96** New Year's Day. **Apr 8** Easter Monday. **Note [*]:** Holidays for administrative or public office only.

HEALTH

Regulations and requirements may be subject to change at short notice, and you are advised to contact your doctor well in advance of your intended date of departure. Any numbers in the chart refer to the footnotes below.

	Special Precautions?	Certificate Required?
Yellow Fever	No	No
Cholera	No	No
Typhoid & Polio	No	-
Malaria	No	-
Food & Drink	No	-

Rabies is present. For those at high risk, vaccination before arrival should be considered. If you are bitten abroad, seek medical advice without delay. For more information consult the *Health* section at the back of the book.

Health care: Medical care is expensive but of a high standard. There is a Reciprocal Health Agreement with the UK. It allows UK citizens a refund of up to 75% of medical costs. To take advantage of the Agreement, UK citizens should obtain form E111 from the post office *before* departure.

TRAVEL - International

AIR: The national airline is *Sabena (SN)*.
For free advice on air travel, call the *Air Travel Advisory Bureau* in the UK on (0171) 636 5000 (London) *or* (0161) 832 2000 (Manchester).

Approximate flight times: From *London* to Brussels is 55 minutes and to Antwerp is 50 minutes. From *Los Angeles* to Brussels is 16 hours. From *New York* to Brussels is 10 hours.

International airports: *Brussels Zaventem (BRU)* is 13km (8 miles) northeast of the city (travel time – 35 minutes). Trains to the city (travel time – approximately 23 minutes) depart every 20 minutes 0524-2346. Return is from Gare Centrale/Gare du Nord 0539-2314. Buses run to and from the city every 45 minutes 0620-2305. Taxi to the city costs approximately BFr1000. Hotel courtesy coaches go to Holiday Inn, Novotel and Sofitel. Airport facilities include car parking, car hire (0900-1800), post office, banks (0700-2300), bars, a 24-hour restaurant, incoming and outgoing duty-free shops selling a wide range of goods (including mini-computers), places of worship and conference and business facilities.
Antwerp (ANR) (Deurne) is 5.5km (3.4 miles) from the city. There is a regular bus service (no. 16) to Central Station (travel time – 20 minutes). Taxis cost approximately BFr300. Airport facilities include an outgoing duty-free shop, car hire (0900-1800), bank (0900-1200 and 1400-1600) and bar/restaurant (0800-2300). There is also a regular bus service from Antwerp to *Brussels Airport*, which is free to *Sabena* passengers flying Business class or on a Eurobudget fare.
Ostend (OST), 5km (3 miles) from the city, has car parking facilities, car hire, foreign exchange, a restaurant, a bar and a duty-free shop.
Liège (LGG). There are taxis and a regular bus service to the centre, 8km (5 miles) away.

Departure tax: £4.80 (Antwerp Deurne); £9 (Brussels Zaventem).

SEA: Antwerp is one of Europe's busiest commercial ports, but cross-Channel services generally operate out of Ostend or Zeebrugge. *Sally Lines:* Ramsgate–Ostend (travel time – 4 hours); *P&O European Ferries (RTM):* Felixstowe–Zeebrugge (travel time – 5 hours). *Jetfoil (Sally Lines):* Ramsgate–Ostend (travel time – 1 hour 40 minutes). *North Sea Ferries:* Hull–Zeebrugge.

RAIL: There are good rail links with the rest of Europe. See below under *Travel – Internal* for information on budget travel.

ROAD: Excellent road links of all categories with neighbouring countries. See below under *Travel – Internal* for information on documentation and traffic regulations.

TRAVEL - Internal

AIR: There are no internal domestic flights. *Sabena* does, however, provide non-stop buses from *Brussels Airport* to Antwerp. There is a bus service between Antwerp Town and *Brussels Airport;* this is free to certain passengers.

RAIL: Belgium has a dense railway network with hourly trains on most lines. On the main lines there are more frequent trains. **Fares:** First- and second-class, single and return tickets are available. However, a return ticket is

double the* single fare and is only valid on the day of issue. Children from 6-11 years pay half price.

Tickets at reduced fares: Weekend return fares are available from Friday noon to Sunday noon for the outward journey and from Sunday noon to Monday noon for the return journey (on long holiday weekends these periods are extended). A 50% reduction card, valid for one month, is for sale. It entitles the holder to buy an unlimited number of half-price single tickets.

Runabout tickets: These enable a visitor to travel freely across the whole of the Belgian rail network without any distance limit. They can also be used to and from neighbouring countries, where they are valid as far as, or from, the border. Principal stations in Belgium (and throughout Europe) are able to issue single and return tickets valid from the border to principal foreign stations (in conjunction with a *runabout* ticket). There are five kinds of *runabout* tickets:

(1) *Half-Fare Card:* one month's unlimited travel at half-fare.

(2) *5-day B-Tourrail ticket:* five days of unlimited travel within a period of 17 days on Belgian Rail.

(3) *5-day TTB (Train, Tram, Bus) ticket:* five days of unlimited travel within a period of 17 days on Belgian Rail, as well as on all buses, trams and underground within Belgium. These tickets are sold in all Belgian Rail stations.

(4) *Benelux 5-day Tourrail ticket:* five days of unlimited travel within a period of 17 days by rail in Belgium, The Netherlands and Luxembourg. Benelux Tourrail tickets are for sale at Benelux Railway stations.

(5) *Go Pass:* 10 second-class trips for persons aged between 6 and 26.

Rail Europ Senior Card (RES): The RES card is available to men over 65 and women over 60 and entitles the buyer to reductions of up to 30% and 50% on international tickets in 19 European countries. Enquire at Belgian Railways for further information.

ROAD: There are many different brands of petrol available, and prices vary. Traffic drives on the right. Main towns (except in the Ardennes) are connected by toll-free motorways. It is compulsory for seat belts to be worn in the front and back of vehicles. Children under 12 are not permitted to travel in the front seat of a car when there is space in the back. A warning triangle must be displayed at the scene of a breakdown or accident. The speed limit on motorways and dual carriageways is 120kmph (74mph), on single carriageways outside built-up areas is 90kmph (56mph) and in built-up areas is 50kmph (31mph). **Bus:** Extensive regional bus services are operated by the bus companies which publish regional timetables. There are long distance stopping services between towns, but no express coach services apart from the Sabena airport services (see above under *Air*). **Taxi:** Plentiful in all towns. The tip is included in the final meter price. **Car hire:** Both self-drive and chauffeur-driven cars are available. **Documentation:** A national driving licence is acceptable. EU nationals taking their own cars to Belgium are strongly advised to obtain a Green Card. Without it, insurance cover is limited to the minimum legal cover in Belgium (Third Party cover is compulsory). The Green Card tops this up to the level of cover provided by the car owner's domestic policy.

URBAN: There is a good public transport system in all the major towns and cities, with metro, tram and bus services in Brussels and Antwerp, bus and tramways in Charleroi, Ghent and Ostend and bus systems elsewhere. There is a standard flat-fare system, with discounts for 5- and 10-journey multi-ride tickets. One-day tickets and multi-mode tourist travelcards are also available.

JOURNEY TIMES: The following chart gives approximate journey times from Brussels (in hours and minutes) to other major cities/towns in Belgium and neighbouring countries.

	Air	Road	Rail
Paris	0.50	-	2.30
Amsterdam	0.40	-	3.00
Rome	2.00	-	20.00
Cologne	-	-	3.00
London	0.55	-	*8.30
Arlon	-	3.00	2.20
Antwerp	-	0.40	0.41
Bruges	-	1.00	0.53
Ghent	-	0.50	0.28
Liège	-	1.10	1.22
Ostend	-	1.20	1.10
Namur	-	1.00	0.56

Note [*]: Time taken by train and boat; time by rail and jetfoil is 5 hours and 30 minutes.

ACCOMMODATION

HOTELS: Belgium has a large range of hotels from luxury to small family pensions and inns. The best international-class hotels are found in the cities.

Grading: The Belgian Tourist Board issues a shield to all approved hotels by which they can be recognised. This must be affixed to the front of the hotel in a conspicuous position. Hotels which display this sign conform to the official standards set by Belgian law on hotels which protects the tourist and guarantees certain standards of quality. Some hotels are also graded according to the *Benelux* system in which standard is indicated by a row of 3-pointed stars from the highest (5-star) to the minimum (1-star). However, membership of this scheme is voluntary, and there may be first-class hotels which are not classified in this way. If an establishment providing accommodation facilities is classified under category H or above (1, 2, 3, 4 or 5 stars), it may call itself hotel, hostelry, inn, guest-house, motel or other similar names. *Benelux* star ratings comply with the following criteria:

5-star: Luxury hotel, meeting the highest standards of comfort, amenities and service, 24-hour room service, à la carte restaurant, gift shop, parking and baggage service, travel and theatre booking service.

4-star: First-class hotel, with lift, facilities for breakfast in the room, day and night reception, telephone in every room, radio, bar.

3-star: Very good hotel, with lift (if more than 2 floors), day reception, guest wing (food and drink optional).

2-star: Average-class hotel, with private bath and WC in at least 25% of rooms, baggage handling facilities, food and drink available.

1-star: Plain hotel, washstand with hot and cold water in every room, breakfast facilities available.

Cat H: Very plain hotel, meets all the fire safety requirements and provides moderate standards of comfort, at least one bathroom for every 10 rooms and accessible to guests at night.

Cat O: Establishments providing accommodation only, with guaranteed safety and hygiene standards only.

For more information on hotels in Belgium, contact the Belgian Tourist Board or one of the three regional hotel associations, as follows:

Flanders: Horeca Vlaanderen, BP 4, Anspachlaan 111, B-1000 Brussels. Tel: (2) 513 6484. Fax: (2) 513 8954.

Wallonia: Horeca Wallonie, Chausée de Charleroi 83, B-5000 Namur. Tel: (81) 736 367. Fax: (81) 737 689.

Brussels: Horeca Brussels, BP 4, 111 boulevard Anspach, B-1000 Brussels. Tel: (2) 513 7814. Fax: (2) 513 9277.

FARM HOLIDAYS: In some regions of the country, farm holidays are now available. In the Polders and the Ardennes visitors can (for a small cost) participate in the daily work of the farm. For addresses, the Belgian Tourist Board publishes a brochure called *Budget Holidays.*

SELF-CATERING: There are ample opportunities to rent furnished villas, flats, rooms, or bungalows for a holiday period. There is a particularly wide choice in the Ardennes and on the coast. These holiday houses and flats are comfortable and well equipped. Rentals are determined by the number of bedrooms, the amenities, the location and the season. On the coast, many apartments, studios, villas and bungalows are classified into five categories according to the standard of comfort they offer. Estate agents will supply full details. For the Ardennes region, enquiries should be made to the local tourist office. Addresses of local tourist offices and lists of coastal estate agents can be obtained from the Belgian Tourist Office.

YOUTH HOSTELS: There are two youth hostel associations: the Vlaamse Jeugdherbergcentrale (VJHC) which operates in Flanders, and the Centrale Wallonne (CWAJ) operating in the French-speaking area. The hostels of the former are large, highly organised and much frequented by schools and youth groups; the hostels of the CWAJ are smaller and more informal, similar in some ways to those in France. A complete list of youth hostels and other holiday homes for young people can be obtained from the Belgian Tourist Office, or by writing direct to 'Info-Jeunes', 27 rue Marché-aux-Herbes, B-1000 Brussels (tel: (2) 512 3274; fax: (2) 514 4111), or to 'Info-Jeugd', Gretrystraat 28, B-1000 Brussels.

CAMPING/CARAVANNING: The majority of campsites are in the Ardennes and on the coast; many of these are excellent. A list of addresses, rates and other information can be obtained from the Belgian Tourist Office. The local 'Verblijftaks' ('Taxe de Sejour') is usually included in the rates charged. On the coast during the summer season a supplement of about 25% is charged on the majority of tariffs. Camping out in places other than the recognised sites is permitted, provided the agreement of the land-owner or tenant has been obtained.

RESORTS & EXCURSIONS

The two main tourist regions in Belgium are the coast and the Ardennes. There are also many historic cities to visit with famous museums, art collections and galleries.

The Coast and West Flanders

The north coast of Belgium stretches for 69km (43 miles) from Knokke near the Dutch border to De Panne on the French border with an unbroken chain of resorts and sandy beaches. Beach cabins and windbreaks have been installed by hotels, agencies and private owners and in some resorts the beach huts are open to the public. Bathing in the sea is free on all beaches and there are facilities for sailing, sand yachting, riding, fishing, rowing, golf and tennis. The promenade is closed to all traffic and the beaches shelve gently and are safe for children.

Resorts: De Panne, Koksijde and Sint Idesbald, Oostduinkerke, Nieuwpoort, Westende and Lombardsijde, Middelkerke, Ostend, Bredene, De Haan, Wenduine, Blankenberge, Zeebrugge and Knokke-Heist.

For nightlife: Ostend, Knokke, Blankenberge and Middelkerke.

For quieter beaches: Zeebrugge, Nieuwpoort, Oostduinkerke, Westende and Lombardsijde and Wenduine.

Places of historical interest: Bruges, Damme, Veurne and Ypres (see also below).

The Ardennes

This area is famous for its cuisine, forests, lakes, streams and grottos. The River Meuse makes its way through many important tourist centres: **Dinant, Annevoie** with its castle, **Yvoir Godinne** and **Profondeville** (well known for watersports), **Namur** with its cathedral, citadel and many museums, and **Houyet** offering kayaking and other assorted outdoor activities. The River Semois passes through **Arlon** and **Florenville**; nearby are the ruins of *Orval Abbey,* **Bouillon** and its castle, **Botassart, Rochehaut** and **Bohan.** The Amblève Valley is one of the wildest in the Ardennes and the grottos in the *Fond de Quarreux* are one of the great attractions of the region. Among these is the Merveilleuse grotto at **Dinant** and the cavern at **Remouchamps.** There are prehistoric caverns at **Spy, Rochefort, Hotton** and **Han-sur-Lesse** (with an underground lake).

Art treasures from Belgium's history can be seen in the towns of Antwerp, Bruges, Brussels, Ghent, Liège and Tournai (see below). Many castles and abbeys are open to the public. The First World War battlefield and cemeteries of Ypres can also be visited.

Historic Cities

Some of the more popular historic cities in the country are as follows:

Antwerp: A busy city on the banks of the River Scheldt and once one of the most powerful urban centres in Europe. Today Antwerp is characterised by its thriving diamond industry and its successes in the field of petrochemicals. The inhabitants, or *Sinjoors* as they are known, like to perpetuate the city's Baroque image, largely created by the wealth of buildings from the time of Rubens. Well worth a visit is the *Cathedral Of Our Lady* (14th-16th century), both for its architecture – in the Brabant gothic style – and for the Rubens' masterpieces which it houses. Other attractions include the *Grote Markt,* or Main Square, containing the *Town Hall* built by Cornelius de Vriendt in the 1560s and the Brabo fountain commemorating the legend of the city's origin; the *Steen,* a 12th-century fortress now housing the *National Maritime Museum;* the *Royal Museum of Fine Arts,* home to what is arguably the world's finest collection of works by Peter Paul Rubens, as well as 1000 works by other old masters and 1500 more recent works; the *Plantin-Moretus Museum,* where Plantin's printing works were founded in the 16th century, with one of the few remaining copies of the Gutenberg Bible; and many other museums and churches.

Bruges: Like Antwerp, another city whose fortunes in the Middle Ages were built on the cloth trade. The city is close to some excellent beaches and the fertile Polder region, dotted with abbeys and parks. Best visited on foot, Bruges offers a variety of attractions including boat trips or walks along the canals and the *Lake of Love,* which in the Middle Ages was the city's internal port; the 14th-century *Town Hall* featuring a façade decorated with bas-reliefs and statues of a Biblical nature; the *Cathedral of the Holy Saviour,* a fine example of 13th-century Gothic architecture and home to many treasures; the *Grote Markt* which was formerly the commercial hub of the city, overlooked by the 83m (272ft) octagonal *Belfry* with its carillon; and several museums.

Brussels: The capital of Belgium and the centre of the European Union and NATO. The main sights in Brussels include *St Michael's Cathedral* (13th-16th century) and the famous *Grand-Place* in the heart of the city. It is here that the early 15th-century Gothic-style *Town Hall* and the *Maison du Roi,* containing the *Municipal Museum,* are located. Other attractions include *Mont des Arts,* the park which links the upper and lower parts of the city; the elegant *Place Royale* built between 1774 and 1780 in the style of Louis XVI; the *Manneken-Pis* statue which dates from 1619 and symbolises the irreverence of the 'Bruxellois'; and dozens of museums of interest, including the *Museum of Ancient Art* and the *Museum of Modern Art,* opened in 1984. Among other areas worth exploring are the *Ilot Sacré,* the picturesque area of narrow streets to the northeast of the Grand-Place; the fashionable boulevard de Waterloo; the administrative quarter, a completely symmetrical park area commanding a splendid view of the surrounding streets; the *Grand Sablon,* the area containing both the flamboyant Gothic structure of the *Church of Our Lady of Sablon* and the Sunday antique market and lastly the *Petit Sablon,* a square surrounded by Gothic columns, which support 48 small bronze statues commemorating medieval Brussels guilds.

Attractions on the outskirts of the city include the *Royal Castle* at Laeken, the town residence of the Royal Family; the *State Botanical Gardens;* the site of *the Battle of Waterloo,* 18km (11 miles) to the south of Brussels; the *Forest of Soignes* and the *Tervuren Royal Museum* which houses a large collection of Central African art.

Ghent: This former cloth town was once the capital of the Counts of Flanders and was the birthplace of the Emperor Charles V. Although an industrial city, Ghent boasts many historic buildings, including three abbeys. Attractions include *St Bavo's Cathedral,* place of Charles V's baptism and home to *The Adoration of the Mystical Lamb,* the Van Eyck brothers' masterpiece; the *Town Hall,* where the Treaty of Ghent was signed in 1576; the *Castle of the Counts,* a medieval castle surrounded by the Lieve canal, the medieval town centre; the *Museum of Fine Arts,* and the newly renovated *Museum of Industrial Archaeology.*

Liège: An industrial city, situated on the banks of the Meuse, but one with many reminders of a colourful and affluent past. Attractions include the *Church of St James,* an old abbey church of mixed architecture, including an example of the Meuse Romanesque style, with fine Renaissance stained glass; the *Cathedral of St Paul,* founded in the 10th century and boasting a priceless treasury; the 18th-century *Town Hall;* the *Curtius Museum* housing a large collection of coins, Liège furniture and porcelaine; *St Lambert Square,* with the *Perron* fountain of the city's symbol; the *Museum of Modern Art,* displaying the works of Corot, Monet, Picasso, Gauguin and Chagall to name but a few; and the *Romanesque Church of St Bartholemew,* particularly notable for its copper baptismal fonts.

Tournai: One of the oldest cities in the region, the city dates back to the Frankish period in the early Middle Ages. In common with many other Belgian cities, much was destroyed during the two World Wars, although several important buildings have survived while others have been restored. Attractions include the *Cathedral of*

BRUSSELS

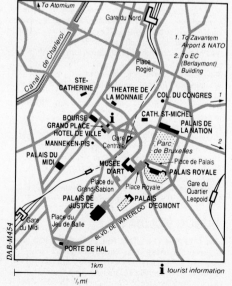

Notre Dame (12th century); the *Belfry*, which is the oldest in Belgium; the *Bridge of Holes*, a relic of the old fortified rampart which spanned the Scheldt; the *Museum of Fine Arts*, with works by Rubens and Bruegel; the imposing castle of *Antoing*, parts of which date back to the 5th century; and most recently, *Minibel*, 28km (17 miles) outside the city at the *Château of Beloeil*, a display of scaled-down reproductions of many of Belgium's most interesting treasures and curiosities (including the Brussels Town Hall and Grand Palace, the Bruges Belfry, the Castle of Counts and the Coo Falls). For more information on these and other cities of historic and cultural interest, consult the *Belgium Historic Cities* booklet available from the Belgian Tourist Office.

SOCIAL PROFILE

FOOD & DRINK: Belgian cuisine is similar to French, based on game and seafood. Each region in Belgium has its own special dish. Butter, cream and wine are generously used in cooking. Most restaurants have waiter service, although self-service cafés are becoming quite numerous. Restaurant bills always include drinks, unless they have been taken at the bar separately. In the latter case this is settled over the counter. **Drink:** Local beers are very good. Two of the most popular are *Lambic*, made from wheat and barley, and *Trappist*. Under a new law, the majority of cafés now have licenses to serve spirits. Beers and wines are freely obtainable everywhere and there are no licensing hours.

NIGHTLIFE: As well as being one of the best cities in the world for eating out (both for its high quality and range), Brussels has a very active and varied nightlife. It has ten theatres producing plays in both Flemish and French. These include the *Théâtre National* and *Théâtre Royal des Galeries*. The more avant-garde theatres include the *Théâtre Cinq-Quarante* and the *Théâtre de Poche*. Brussels' 35 cinemas, numerous discotheques and many night-time cafés are centred on two main areas: the uptown Porte Louise area and the downtown area between Place Roger and Place de la Bourse. Nightclubs include the famous *Le Crazy*, *Chez Paul*, *Maxim* and *Le Grand Escalier*; jazz clubs include *The Brussels Jazz Club* and *Bloomdido Jazz Café*. Programmes and weekly listings of events can be found in the *BBB Agenda* on sale at tourist offices. This also covers information on the many festivals that take place in Brussels itself. The Belgian Tourist Office should be consulted for folk music or drama festivals elsewhere in Belgium – the most famous of which is the *Festival of Flanders*. The other large cities of Belgium, such as Antwerp, Leuven, Mons, Ghent, Kortrijk and Namur, all have similar (though less extensive) nightlife facilities. Liège is noted for its Walloon opera and for having several theatrical troops; Ghent for its 'illuminations'; while Namur has a large casino complex.

SHOPPING: Special purchases include ceramics and hand-beaten copperware from Dinant; Belgian chocolates; crystal from Val Saint Lambert; diamonds; jewellery from Antwerp; lace from Bruges, Brussels and Mechelen (Malines), woodcarvings from Spa and *bandes dessinées* (comic-strip books) by a number of talented Belgian cartoon artists from Brussels. Main shopping centres are: Brussels, Antwerp, Bruges, Ostend, Namur, Mons, Liège, Ghent and Mechelen. **Shopping hours:** 0900-1800 Monday to Saturday (Friday 0900-2100 in main cities).

SPORT: Golf, tennis, cycling, motor-racing (including the Belgian Grand Prix), football, basketball, wrestling, horseriding, horseracing, skiing and water-skiing. The Belgian Alpine Club has a climbing school at Freyr. Bathing, fishing, boating and yachting are also available.

SPECIAL EVENTS: The following is a selection of the major festivals and other special events celebrated in Belgium in 1994:
Mar 25-Apr 23 '95 *17th International Photography Festival 1995*, Knokke-Heist. **Apr 22-May 1** *Floralies of Ghent*. **Jun 17-18** *Re-enactment of the Battle of Waterloo*, Waterloo. **Aug 17-26** *Festival on the Canals*, Bruges. **Aug 16-20** *Sail Zeebrugge*, Zeebrugge. **Mid-Sep to Mid-Dec** *Europalia '95 – Turkey*, Brussels. A full calendar of events is available from the Belgian Tourist Board.

SOCIAL CONVENTIONS: Flemings will often prefer to answer visitors in English rather than French, even if the visitor's French is good. It is customary to bring flowers or a small present for the hostess, especially if invited for a meal. Dress is similar to other Western nations, depending on the formality of the occasion. If black tie/evening dress is to be worn, this is always mentioned on the invitation. Smoking is generally unrestricted. **Tipping:** A 14% service charge

is usually included in hotel or restaurant bills. Cloakroom attendants expect BFr5-10, porters approximately BFr30 per piece of luggage. A tip is generally included in taxi fares.

BUSINESS PROFILE

ECONOMY: The traditional industries of steel, motor vehicles and textiles have suffered from the recession of the 1980s, although the governments of Belgium and Luxembourg (who formed a Convention of Economic Union in 1921, as distinct from the Benelux Union or the EU, of which both are members) reached agreement in 1984 on a 10-year joint restructuring plan for their steel industries. Coal mining has also experienced severe difficulties. Belgium relies particularly heavily on export earnings – 70% of GDP is exported, one of the highest proportions in the world – which leaves the country particularly vulnerable to fluctuating patterns of world trade. Equally, Belgium has few natural resources and must import almost all its fuel and raw materials. Manufactured goods and machinery are the largest export sectors, with the major markets inside the European Union, including France, Germany, The Netherlands and the UK. These are also Belgium's main sources of imported goods.

BUSINESS: Suits should always be worn and business is conducted on a formal basis, with punctuality valued and business cards exchanged. Transactions are usually made in French or English. **Office hours:** 0830-1730 Monday to Friday.

COMMERCIAL INFORMATION: The following organisations can offer advice: Chambre de Commerce et d'Industrie de Bruxelles, 500 avenue Louise, B-1050 Brussels. Tel: (2) 648 5002. Fax: (2) 640 9228. Telex: 22082; *or* Kamer van Koophandel en Nijverheid van Antwerpen (Antwerp Chamber of Commerce), Markgravestraat 12, B-2000 Antwerp. Tel: (3) 232 2219. Fax: (3) 233 6442. Telex: 71536.

CONFERENCES/CONVENTIONS: There is an extensive range of meeting venues throughout the country. In 1993 Belgium was the sixth-most popular conference destination, whilst Brussels was the second-most popular city. For more information or assistance in organising a conference or convention in Belgium, contact the Belgium Convention and Incentive Bureau *(BECIB)*, Grasmarkt 61, B-1000 Brussels. Tel: (2) 513 2721. Fax: (2) 513 8803 or 513 6950.

CLIMATE

Seasonal and similar to neighbouring countries, with warm weather from May to September and snow likely during winter months.
Required clothing: Waterproofs are advisable at all times of the year.

TEMPERATURE CONVERSIONS

-20	-10	0°C	10	20	30	40
0	10 20	30°F40	50 60	70 80	90	100

RAINFALL CONVERSIONS

0mm	200	400	600	800
0in 5	10	15	20	25	30

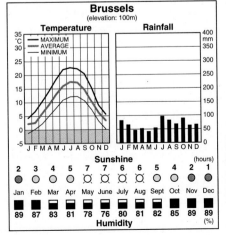

Brussels
(elevation: 100m)

Temperature — MAXIMUM — AVERAGE — MINIMUM

Rainfall

Sunshine (hours)

Jan	Feb	Mar	Apr	May	June	July	Aug	Sept	Oct	Nov	Dec
2	3	4	5	7	7	6	6	5	4	2	1
89	87	83	81	78	76	80	81	82	85	89	89

Humidity (%)

Belize

□ *international airport*

Location: Central America, Caribbean coast.

Belize Tourist Board
PO Box 325, 83 North Front Street, Belize City, Belize, CA
Tel: (2) 77213 *or* 73255. Fax: (2) 77490.
Belize Tourism Industry Association (BTIA)
PO Box 62, 99 Albert Street West, Belize City, Belize, CA
Tel: (2) 75717 *or* 78709 *or* 78710. Fax: (2) 78710.
Belize High Commission
22 Harcourt House, 19A Cavendish Square, London W1M 9AD
Tel: (0171) 499 9728. Fax: (0171) 491 4139. Opening hours: 1000-1800 Monday to Friday; 1430-1700 Tuesday, Wednesday and Thursday (visas only); 1300-1600 Friday (passport collection only).
Caribbean Tourism
Vigilant House, 120 Wilton Road, London SW1V 1JZ
Tel: (0171) 233 8382. Fax: (0171) 873 8551. Opening hours: 0930-1730 Monday to Friday.
British High Commission
PO Box 91, Embassy Square, Belmopan, Belize, CA
Tel: (8) 22146/7. Fax: (8) 22761. Telex: 284 (a/b UKREP BZE).
Embassy of Belize
2535 Massachusetts Avenue, NW, Washington, DC 20008
Tel: (202) 332 9636. Fax: (202) 332 6888.
The Embassy also deals with enquiries from Canada.
Embassy of the United States of America
PO Box 286, Gabourel Lane and Hutson Street, Belize City, Belize, CA
Tel: (2) 77161/2/3. Fax: (2) 35321.
Canadian Consulate
PO Box 610, 85 North Front Street, Belize City, Belize, CA
Tel: (2) 33722. Fax: (2) 30060.

AREA: 22,965 sq km (8867 sq miles).
POPULATION: 190,792 (1991 estimate).

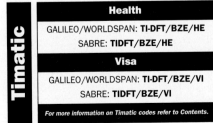

Timatic	Health		
	GALILEO/WORLDSPAN: **TI-DFT/BZE/HE**		
	SABRE: **TIDFT/BZE/HE**		
	Visa		
	GALILEO/WORLDSPAN: **TI-DFT/BZE/VI**		
	SABRE: **TIDFT/BZE/VI**		
	For more information on Timatic codes refer to Contents.		

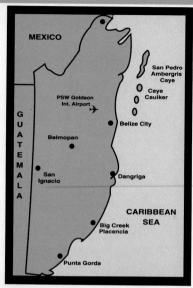

POPULATION DENSITY: 8.3 per sq km.
CAPITAL: Belmopan. **Population:** 3687 (1992 estimate). Belize City has a population of 49,671.
GEOGRAPHY: Belize is situated at the base of the Yucatán Peninsula in Central America and borders Mexico and Guatemala, with the Gulf of Honduras to the east. The country's area includes numerous small islands (cays) off the coast. The coastal strip is low and swampy, particularly in the north, with mangroves, many salt and freshwater lagoons and some sandy beaches crossed by a number of rivers. To the south and west rises the heavily forested Maya mountain range, with the Cockscomb range to the east and the Mountain Pine Ridge in the west. Over 65% of the area of the country is forested. The land to the west along the borders with Guatemala is open and relatively scenic compared to much of the interior. The shallow offshore cays straddle a coral reef second only in size to the Barrier Reef of Australia.
LANGUAGE: English is the official language, but Spanish is spoken by over half the population.
RELIGION: The people of Belize are mainly Roman Catholic (roughly 60% of the population). Other denominations include Anglican, Methodist, Mennonite, Seventh Day Adventist and Pentecostal.
TIME: GMT - 6.
ELECTRICITY: 110/220 volts AC, 60Hz. American-style 2-pin plugs.
COMMUNICATIONS: Telephone: IDD is available. Country code: 501. Outgoing international code: 00. **Fax:** Limited facilities, but Belize Telecommunications Ltd (BTL) Public Booth in Belize City and some government and company offices have facilities available. **Telex/telegram:** Full services are available from BTL Public Booth and post offices and major hotels in Belize City, Belmopan and San Ignacio. **Post:** Mail to Europe takes up to five days. **Press:** The major weeklies include *Amandala, Belize Information Service, The Belize Times, Government Gazette, The People's Pulse* and *The Reporter*.
BBC World Service and Voice of America frequencies: From time to time these change. See the section *How to Use this Book* for more information.

BBC:				
MHz	17.84	15.22	9.590	7.325
Voice of America:				
MHz	15.21	11.74	9.815	6.030

PASSPORT/VISA

Regulations and requirements may be subject to change at short notice, and you are advised to contact the appropriate diplomatic or consular authority before finalising travel arrangements. Details of these may be found at the head of this country's entry. Any numbers in the chart refer to the footnotes below.

	Passport Required?	Visa Required?	Return Ticket Required?
Full British	Yes	No	Yes
BVP	Not valid	-	-
Australian	Yes	No	Yes
Canadian	Yes	No	Yes
USA	Yes	No	Yes
Other EU (As of 31/12/94)	Yes	No	Yes
Japanese	Yes	Yes	Yes

Note: Regulations are liable to change at short notice. Contact the Consulate (or Consular Section at Embassy or High Commission) for up-to-date information. For addresses, see top of entry.
PASSPORTS: Passport valid for six months beyond the intended length of stay required by all.
British Visitors Passport: Not accepted.
VISAS: Required by all, for stays of up to 1 month, except:
(a) nationals referred to in the chart above;
(b) nationals of Commonwealth countries (except nationals of *Bangladesh, India, Nauru and Pakistan who do require a visa);
(c) nationals of Andorra, Faroe Islands, Finland, Greenland, Iceland, Macau, Marshall Islands, Federated States of Micronesia, Norway, Sweden and Tunisia;
(d) nationals of Chile, Costa Rica, Guatemala, Mexico and Uruguay;
(e) nationals of US dependent territories: American Samoa, Guam, Northern Mariana Islands, Palau, Puerto Rico and US Virgin Islands;
(f) nationals of New Zealand dependent territories: Cook Islands, Niue and Tokelau;
(g) nationals of French dependent territories: French Guiana, French Polynesia, Guadeloupe, Martinique, Mayotte, New Caledonia, Réunion, St Pierre & Miquelon and Wallis & Futuna Islands;
(h) nationals of The Netherlands dependent territories: Aruba, Bonaire, Curaçao, Saba, St Eustatius and St Maarten;
(i) nationals of Australian dependent territories:

Christmas Island, Cocos (Keeling) Island and Norfolk Island.
Note [*]: Nationals of Bangladesh need to have their visa approved by the Belize authorities in Belize.
Types of visa: Tourist (single or multiple) and Business (single or multiple).
Cost: *Single entry* – £20; *Multiple entry* – £30.
Validity: Visas are valid for a period of 30 days within 6 months of date of issue. Extentions to the period of stay must be applied for at the nearest Immigration Office in Belize.
Application to: Consulate (or Consular Section at Embassy or High Commission). For addresses, see top of entry.
Application requirements: (a) Application form. (b) Passport-size photo. (c) Sufficient funds to cover stay. (d) Valid passport.
Working days required: 24 hours in person, 2 to 3 days by post. Allow 2 to 4 weeks if clearance is needed from Belize.
Temporary residence: Apply to Immigration and Nationality Department, Belmopan. Enquire at the High Commission or Embassy.

MONEY

Currency: Belizean Dollar (Bz$) = 100 cents. Notes are in denominations of Bz$100, 50, 20, 10, 5, 2 and 1. Coins are in denominations of Bz$1, and 50, 25, 10, 5 and 1 cents.
Currency exchange: The Belize currency is tied to the US Dollar at US$1 = Bz$2. Barclays Bank International has a branch in the capital, as well as a few in the country, available for foreign exchange.
Credit cards: American Express, Visa and Access/Mastercard (limited) are accepted. Check with your credit card company for details of merchant acceptability and other services which may be available.
Travellers cheques: These can be changed. There is a charge of Bz$1 for cashing travellers cheques.
Exchange rate indicators: The following figures are included as a guide to the movements of the Belize Dollar against the Pound Sterling and the US Dollar:

Date:	Oct '92	Sep '93	Jan '94	Jan '95
£1.00=	3.16	3.06	2.95	3.09
$1.00=	2.00	2.00	2.00	2.00

Currency restrictions: The import and export of local currency is limited to Bz$100. There are no limits on the import of foreign currency; for current export limits, contact the Bank of Belize. Visitors are advised to carry a minimum of Bz$75 for each day they intend to stay.
Banking hours: 0800-1300 Monday to Thursday; 0800-1800 Friday.

DUTY FREE

The following goods may be taken into Belize without incurring customs duty:
200 cigarettes or 0.25kg tobacco; 20 fl oz of alcoholic beverages; 1 bottle of perfume for personal use.

PUBLIC HOLIDAYS

Jan 1 '95 New Year's Day. **Mar 9** Baron Bliss Day. **Apr 14** Good Friday. **Apr 17** Easter. **May 1** Labour Day. **May 24** Commonwealth Day. **Sep 10** St George's Caye Day. **Sep 21** Independence Day. **Oct 12** Pan American Day. **Nov 19** Garifuna Settlement Day. **Dec 25-26** Christmas. **Jan 1 '96** New Year's Day. **Mar 9** Baron Bliss Day. **Apr 5** Good Friday. **Apr 8** Easter.

HEALTH

Regulations and requirements may be subject to change at short notice, and you are advised to contact your doctor well in advance of your intended date of departure. Any numbers in the chart refer to the footnotes below.

	Special Precautions?	Certificate Required?
Yellow Fever	No	1
Cholera	No	No
Typhoid & Polio	Yes	-
Malaria	Yes/2	-
Food & Drink	3	-

[1]: A yellow fever vaccination certificate is required from all travellers coming from infected areas. Pregnant woment and children under nine months should not normally be vaccinated.
[2]: Malaria risk exists throughout the year, excluding Belize district and urban areas, predominantly in the benign *vivax* form. A weekly dose of 300mg of chloroquine is the recommended prophylaxis.
[3]: All water should be regarded as being potentially contaminated. Water used for drinking, brushing teeth or

making ice should have first been boiled or otherwise sterilised. Milk is unpasteurised and should be boiled. Powdered or tinned milk is available and is advised, but make sure that it is reconstituted with pure water. Avoid all dairy products. Only eat well-cooked meat and fish, preferably served hot. Pork, salad and mayonnaise may carry increased risk. Vegetables should be cooked and fruit peeled.
Rabies is present. For those at high risk, vaccination before arrival should be considered. If you are bitten abroad seek medical advice without delay. For more information consult the *Health* section at the back of the book.
Health care: There is a 174-bed hospital in Belmopan and six other general hospitals. Medical insurance is essential.

TRAVEL - International

AIR: International services, mainly of a regional nature, are provided by *Tropic Air, American Airways, Continental, Taca International* and *Tan/Sahsa*.
Approximate flight times: To Belize from *London* (via *Miami*) is 11 hours; from *Los Angeles* is 8 hours; from *Miami* is 2 hours; from *Guatemala City* is 2 hours; from *Cancun* is 3 hours and from *New York* is 5 hours.
International airport: The *Philip S W Goldson International Airport (BZE)* is 16km (10 miles) northwest of Belize City. Facilities include duty-free shop, bank, post office, shops, restaurant, buffet and bar. There is an airport bus to the city centre (travel time – 30 minutes). Unmetered taxis are available to the city and cost approx. US$15 (travel time – 15 minutes); prices should be agreed with the driver beforehand.
Note: Belmopan, the capital, is 100km (62 miles) from Belize City by road.
Departure tax: Bz$22.50, including a Bz$2.50 Security Tax, is levied on all passengers from the airport, apart from transit passengers and children under 12.
SEA: Over the past ten years Belize has greatly improved its port facilities, but these cater for cargo vessels and no cruise lines call there. There is a motor-yacht link between Punta Gorda and Puerto Barrios in Guatemala.
ROAD: There are road links with Chetumal on the Mexican border, and Melchor de Mencos in Guatemala.

TRAVEL - Internal

AIR: Local services link the main towns. *Maya Airways Ltd* and *Tropic Air* fly three times daily from the municipal airstrip at Belize City to Ambergris Caye. There are also scheduled flights daily to each of the main towns, and charter rates are offered to all local airstrips, of which there are 25. *Island Air* offers scheduled flights between the mainland and San Pedro. Five companies have charters from Belize City to the outlying districts.
SEA: The sugar industry runs motorboat links along the coast. There is a scheduled boat service from Belize City to Ambergris Caye and Caye Caulker. Small boats irregularly ply between the small cays off the coast. This transport used to be the only means of travel to the interior, along the Belize, Hondo and New rivers, but services have dwindled since the advent of all-weather roads.
ROAD: 1600km (1000 miles) of all-weather roads link the eight towns in the country, though torrential rain seasonally severs these links, particularly at ferry points. Belize has a less developed network of roads than the rest of Central America but it is steadily being improved, especially in the north. The Belize stretch of the road to Mexico is currently being improved, while the Belize–Belmopan road is in generally good condition. Traffic drives on the right. **Bus:** There are good and inexpensive daily bus services between the large towns, and to both the Mexican and Guatemalan borders. Many of the buses are modern and air-conditioned. Buses from Belize City to Punta Gorda cost approx. US$10. **Car hire:** *Avis, Budget* and *Hertz* exist in Belize City. Four-wheel-drive vehicles are recommended for excursions south of Belize City. **Documentation:** A national driving licence is acceptable.
JOURNEY TIMES: The following chart gives approximate journey times (in hours and minutes) from Belize City to other major cities/towns in the country.

	Air	Road	Sea
Northern Border	2.20	-	-
Corozal Town	-	2.00	-
Orange Walk Town	1.15	-	-
Belmopan	0.20	1.00	-
Benque Viejo	-	1.45	-
San Ignacio	-	1.30	-
Dangriga	0.30	3.30	-
Punta Gorda	0.45	8.00	-
San Pedro, Ambergris	0.15	-	1.30
Cay Caulker	-	0.45	-
Placencia	0.30	4.00	7.00

ACCOMMODATION

HOTELS: Belize has few first-class hotels, but smaller establishments give good value. There are mountain lodges in the interior and resort hotels on the Caribbean coast. Only limited accommodation is available on some of the larger cays and resort villages are being built. All approved accommodation is listed by the Belize Tourism Industry Association (see address and contact numbers above). The BTIA represents 65% of all establishments. **Grading:** Hotels have been divided into three categories according to price and standard. Rates are subject to change without notice. It is advisable to confirm reservations and rates in advance. Classes of hotels are as follows:

Upper: All hotels provide a private bath/shower and have a restaurant and bar. There is air-conditioning in all rooms.

Middle: All hotels provide a private bath/shower and air-conditioning in all rooms.

Lower: Nearly all provide a private bath/shower.

On the Barrier Reef Cays, there are a number of resort hotels of roughly the same standard as those given above.

APARTMENTS: Long-stay visitors can rent apartments on a monthly basis, while in Chaacreek, palm-thatched cottages can be rented on a daily basis.

CAMPING/CARAVANNING: Limited campsites are available. There is a caravan site in Corozal Town, and also outside San Ignacio. Camping on the beach is forbidden. Camping on private beach yards in Caye Caulker and in Tobacco Cay is available.

RESORTS & EXCURSIONS

For the purposes of this section Belize has been divided into **Mainland Belize, Coastal Belize** and **The Belize Cays**. There is no administrative or political significance in this division which has been made for convenience only.

Mainland Belize

Belmopan is the country's new capital city, carved out of the tropical jungle in the geographic centre of Belize, near the foothills of the *Maya Mountains.* It has a population of only about 4000, most of whom are civil servants, and is in the first phase of a 20-year development period. The most imposing building is the *National Assembly* on *Independence Hill,* patterned in an ancient Maya motif.

Corozal was settled around 1850 by Mestizo refugees from Mexico; now it is a well-planned community and the centre of Belize's thriving sugar industry. Just outside Corozal are two interesting Mayan ruins: *Santa Rita,* just one mile north of the Corozal with a fine view of the town and its waterfront; and *Cerros,* once a coastal trading centre which can be reached by a 20-minute boat ride across Corozal Bay.

South of Corozal is the agricultural centre of **Orange Walk,** where fresh fruit and vegetables can be bought at the markets. South of the town is the *Crooked Tree Wildlife Sanctuary* where the jabiru stork (the largest bird in the western hemisphere) can be seen, along with howler monkeys, crocodiles and many indigenous birds. Day cruises of the *New River,* south of Orange Walk, are available with stops at the spectacular Mayan citadel ruin of *Lamanai* and the *Temple of the Masks,* where visitors may see the tremendous head of the sun god, Kinich Ahau, carved into the limestone. One of the most famous Mayan ruins in Belize is *Altun Ha,* located 50km (31 miles) north of Belize City on the Northern Highway. The site was a major ceremonial centre and trading centre in the Classic period (250-900 AD) and an extraordinary head of the sun god, ornately carved in jade, was found here and is now a national symbol of Belize. *Mountain Pine Ridge Forest Reserve* is located south of the Western Highway about 115km (70 miles) from Belize City. It is an area of fine views and secluded bustling streams, and contains the *Hidden Valley Falls* which plunge 500m (1600ft) into the valley. Another popular site, inland from Belize City on the Belize River, is the *Community Baboon Sanctuary* with one of the few robust black howler monkey populations in Central America.

San Ignacio is a quaint, bustling town with a robust, pioneering atmosphere. It is surrounded by hills, and is the administrative centre for the Cayo district. Not far from San Ignacio are several Maya sites including *El Pilar* and the magnificent *Xunantunich* with its 1500-year-old *El Castillo,* the second-tallest building in Belize. Near the town of **San Antonio,** located in the Toledo District inland from Punta Gorda, is the Mayan site of *Lubaantum,* where the famous perfectly carved crystal skull was found in an ancient temple vault.

Coastal Belize

Belize City is over 300 years old and serves as the main commercial area and seaport. It is the country's biggest city, and has charming colonial architecture, functional wooden buildings and historic cathedrals. Sights include the oldest *Anglican cathedral* in Latin America *(St John's)* and *Government House,* the Belize City residence of the British Governor, built in 1814. 32km (20 miles) south of the city is the *Belize Zoo* on the Western Highway, with more than 100 species of indigenous animals including monkeys, jaguars and tapirs.

Cerros is located on the fringe of a beautiful expanse of blue-green water which is ideal for watersports. Across the bay is an interesting archaeological site.

Dangriga (Stann Creek) provides a good base for excursions to the offshore islands and nearby forests. These include *Cay Chapel,* a private island with white sand beaches, coral, and its own airstrip and marina.

Placencia is a quiet village situated at the tip of the 20km-long (12-mile) Placencia peninsula. Its protected lagoon and sandy beaches make it an ideal place for fishing, swimming and sunbathing.

The fishing village of **Punta Gorda** is the southernmost outpost of Belize. 40km (25 miles) north of here off the Southern Highway is the Mayan ruin of *Nim Li Punit,* with the tallest carved *stele* in Belize.

The Belize Cays

Ambergris Cay is the most popular tourist destination in Belize, especially the bustling fishing village of **San Pedro.** 58km (36 miles) north of Belize City, it is accessible by daily scheduled air flights. It has a number of beaches.

Cay Caulker has become increasingly popular in recent years. Its extensive underwater cave system has made it popular with divers, whilst those who wish to explore the reef without getting wet can see photographs of reef fish at the museum (school parties free).

On **Half Moon Cay** at **Lighthouse Reef** is the *Red-Footed Booby Bird Sanctuary,* founded in 1982 to protect the booby and other birds and animals. Scuba divers at Lighthouse Reef can explore walls which have spectacular sheer drops of thousands of feet and the *Blue Hole* (a deep sinkhole), following the webbed feet of Jacques Cousteau in 1984. Boats to both can be hired. There are many other cays with facilities for those interested in fishing, diving and seeing wildlife. Visitors should know restrictions on the removal of coral, orchids and turtles, and on spearfishing in certain areas. Wrecks and treasures are also government-protected.

POPULAR ITINERARIES: 5-day: (a) Corozal–Santa Rita–Cerros–Orange Walk–Lamanai–Crooked Tree Wildlife Sanctuary–Altun Ha–Community Baboon Sanctuary–Belize City. (b) Belize City–Belize Zoo–Belmopan–San Ignacio–Xunantunich–El Pilar–Dangriga. (c) Dangriga–Placencia–Nim Li Punit–Punta Gorda–San Antonio–Lubaantum. **7-day:** (a) Corozal–Orange Walk–Belize City–Lighthouse Reef–Half Moon Cay–Cay Caulker–Ambergris Cay (b) Belize City–Belmopan–San Ignacio–Dangriga–Placencia–Punta Gorda–San Antonio.

SOCIAL PROFILE

FOOD & DRINK: There is a selection of restaurants which serve American, Chinese, Latin American and Creole food. Service and quality vary but the food is generally cheap. Service is not always very good in some of the more modest places. Bars are plentiful and local drinks include anise and peppermint, known as *A & P,* and the strong *Old Belizero* rum. The local *Belikin* beer is worth sampling.

NIGHTLIFE: There is live dancing late in the evenings at Bellevue Hotel and quiet music at Fort George Bar overlooking the harbour. The native nightspots include the bar on R Front Street and Copa Cabana on New Road complete with flashing lights, tinsel, bamboo, jukebox and live bands at weekends. Other places include the Hard Rock Café and Legends Disco.

SHOPPING: Handicrafts, woodcarvings and straw items are on sale. Jewellery in pink and black coral, and tortoiseshell (not to be imported to the USA) used to be good buys; since 1982 there have been severe restrictions on the export of these and some other goods in the interests of wildlife conservation. 'In-Bond' stores carry watches, perfumes and other duty-free purchases, but Belize is not comparable in size to other free ports in the Caribbean. **Shopping hours:** 0800-1200 and 1300-1700 Monday to Saturday; some shops stay open 1900-2100 some evenings.

SPORTS: Attractions include coastal and river **fishing, scuba diving** and **snorkelling** around the reef. **Swimming** is good off the cays and on the southeast coast where many places are developing as **diving** and **watersport** resorts (see *Resorts & Excursions* above). **Soccer, basketball, softball, boxing** and occasional **horseracing** are available. Those not accompanied by a guide holding a government concession require a licence to hunt.

SPECIAL EVENTS: Mar 9 '95 *Baron Bliss Day River Regatta,* Belize City. **Apr** *San Jose Succotz Fiesta.* **Apr 15** *Holy Saturday Cross Country Classic Cycling Race,* Belize City to San Ignacio. **May** *Children's Festival of Arts; Cashew Festival,* Crooked Tree Village; *Cayo Expo,* San Ignacio; *Coconut Festival,* Cay Caulker; *Commonwealth Day Horse and Cycle Races,* Belize City, Cayo and Belmopan; *Toledo Festival of Arts,* Punta Gorda. **May 1** *Labour Day Parades.* **Jun** *Feast Day of St Peter,* San Pedro. **Jul** *Benque Viejo del Carmen Fiesta.* **Aug** *International Sea and Air Festival.* **Aug-Sep** *Annual Dance Recital.* **Sep** *Mexican National Day,* Orange Walk and Corozal; *St George's Cay Day celebrations.* **Sep 21** *Independence Day celebrations.* **Oct** *Hike and Bike for the Rain Forest,* Cayo. **Oct 12** *Pan American Day Fiesta,* Orange Walk and Corozal; *Columbus Day Regatta,* Belize City. **Nov 19** *Garifuna Settlement Day* (dancing and all-day event), Dangriga. **Dec 26** *Boxing Day Horseraces and Dances.* **Feb '96** *Fiesta De Carnaval; San Pedro Carnaval,* Ambergris Cay.

SOCIAL CONVENTIONS: British influence can still be seen in many social situations. Flowers or confectionery are acceptable gifts to give to hosts if invited to their home for a meal. Dress is casual although beachwear should not be worn in towns. It may be inadvisable to discuss politics particularly if of a partisan nature. Smoking is acceptable everywhere. **Tipping:** Few places add service charges, and 10% is normal. Taxi drivers are not tipped.

BUSINESS PROFILE

ECONOMY: Agriculture is the most important economic sector: the main products are citrus fruit, bananas and sugar cane. Timber is also important, especially mahogany and other tropical hardwoods. Fishing and livestock are being developed. The fastest growing area of the Belizean economy is tourism, fuelled by substantial foreign investment, particularly from Canadian sources, although it seems likely to remain somewhat limited. There is very little industry and few prospects of future industrial development. Given the low living standards in Belize, markets are limited, although there are some opportunities for the sale of agricultural, construction and consumer goods. The USA is the largest single trading partner, providing half of all imports and taking about 60% of Belizean exports. The UK and the EU are other important trading partners. Belize is a member of CARICOM, the Caribbean economic community, and provides some transit facilities for trade to and from other countries in the region. Belize is a significant recipient of overseas aid, most recently from the USA under the Bush administration programme to eliminate drug trafficking.

BUSINESS: Most businessmen do not wear a jacket or tie, though bush jackets (shirtjacs) are often worn. Appointments should be made and calling cards are acceptable. October to March are the best months for visits. **Office hours:** 0800-1200 and 1300-1700 Monday to Thursday; 0830-1200 and 1300-1645 Friday.

COMMERCIAL INFORMATION: The following organisation (with which 80% of all businesses are associated) can offer advice: Belize Chamber of Commerce and Industry, PO Box 291, 63 Regent Street, Belize City. Tel: (2) 75108. Fax: (2) 74984.

CONFERENCES/CONVENTIONS: Facilities are available at a number of venues, and information can be obtained from the Minister of Tourism and the Environment, The Hon. Henry Young, Belmopan. Tel: (8) 23393. Fax: (8) 22862.

CLIMATE

Subtropical with a brisk prevailing wind from the Caribbean Sea. High annual temperatures and humidity. Dry and hot climate from January to April with monsoon season from June to September.

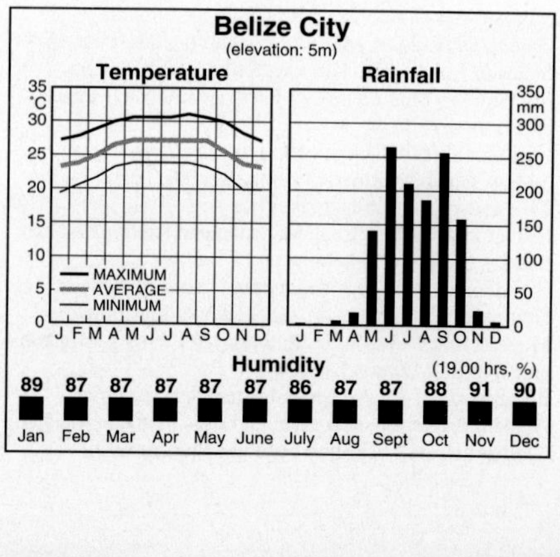
Belize City
(elevation: 5m)
Temperature
Rainfall
°C
mm
MAXIMUM
AVERAGE
MINIMUM
J F M A M J J A S O N D
J F M A M J J A S O N D
Humidity
(19.00 hrs, %)
89 87 87 87 87 87 86 87 87 88 91 90
Jan Feb Mar Apr May June July Aug Sept Oct Nov Dec

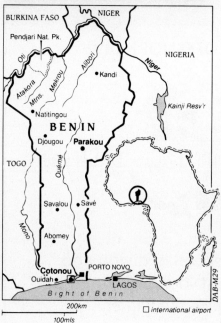

□ *international airport*

200km
100mls

Location: West Africa.

Note: Because of security concerns in remote areas, especially in the northern region of Atacora, travel can be dangerous, particularly at night. Crime rates are rising, particularly in the city of Cotonou.
Source: US State Department – April 22, 1994.

Office National du Tourisme et de l'Hôtellerie (ONATHO)
BP 89, Cotonou, Benin
Tel: 312 687. Telex: 5032.
Republic of Benin Consulate
Dolphin House, 16 The Broadway, Stanmore, Middlesex HA7 4DW
Tel: (0181) 954 8800. Fax: (0181) 954 8844. Telex: 24620. Opening hours: 1000-1230 and 1400-1630 Monday to Friday.
Embassy of the Republic of Benin
87 avenue Victor Hugo, 75116 Paris, France
Tel: (1) 45 00 98 40. Telex: 610110.
British Consulate
Lot 24, Patte d'oie, Cotonou, Benin
Tel: 301 120. Telex: 9725047 (a/b STIN CTNOU).
Embassy of the Republic of Benin
2737 Cathedral Avenue, NW, Washington, DC 20008
Tel: (202) 232 6656/7/8. Fax: (202) 265 1996. Telex: 64155.
Embassy of the United States of America
BP 2012, rue Caporal Bernard Anani, Cotonou, Benin
Tel: 300 650 *or* 300 513 *or* 301 792. Fax: 301 439 *or* 301 974.
Embassy of the Republic of Benin
58 Glebe Avenue, Ottawa, Ontario K1S 2C3
Tel: (613) 233 4429 *or* 233 4868 *or* 233 5273. Fax: (613) 233 8952.
Consulates in: Montréal and Calgary.
The Canadian Embassy in Accra deals with enquiries relating to Benin (see *Ghana* later in this book).

AREA: 112,622 sq km (43,484 sq miles).
POPULATION: 4,736,000 (1990 estimate).
POPULATION DENSITY: 42.1 per sq km.
CAPITAL: Porto Novo. **Population:** 164,000 (1984 estimate).
GEOGRAPHY: Benin is situated in West Africa and is bounded to the east by Nigeria, to the north by Niger and Burkina Faso, and to the west by Togo. Benin stretches 700km (435 miles) from the Bight of Benin to the Niger River. The coastal strip is sandy with coconut palms. Beyond the lagoons of Porto Novo, Nokoue, Ouidah and Grand Popo is a plateau rising gradually to the heights of the Atakora Mountains. From the highlands run two tributaries of Niger, while southwards the Ouémé flows down to Nokoue lagoon. Mono River flows into the sea at Grand Popo and forms a frontier with Togo.
LANGUAGE: The official language is French. However, many indigenous ethnic groups have their own languages: Bariba and Fulani are spoken in the north, Fon and Yoruba in the south. Some English is also spoken.
RELIGION: 80% Animist/traditional, 13% Muslim, 15% Christian (mainly Roman Catholic). (See *Social Conventions* in the *Social Profile* section below.)
TIME: GMT + 1.
ELECTRICITY: 220 volts AC, 50Hz.
COMMUNICATIONS: Telephone: IDD is available. Country code: 229. Outgoing international code: 00. There is an additional charge for calls made from a coin box. **Telex:** Public telex facilities are available in Cotonou at post offices and some hotels. **Post:** Airmail takes three to five days to reach Europe. Surface mail letters or parcels take from six to eight weeks. There are good *poste restante* facilities at most main post offices. Post office hours: 0800-1400 Monday to Saturday.
Press: Exclusively in French. The fortnightly *Journal Officiel de la République* is issued by the government information bureau. *La Nation* replaced the daily *Ehuzu* as the official newspaper in 1990.
BBC World Service and Voice of America frequencies: From time to time these change. See the section *How to Use this Book* for more information.
BBC:

MHz	17.79	15.40	15.07	9.410

Voice of America:

MHz	21.49	15.60	9.525	6.035

PASSPORT/VISA

Regulations and requirements may be subject to change at short notice, and you are advised to contact the appropriate diplomatic or consular authority before finalising travel arrangements. Details of these may be found at the head of this country's entry. Any numbers in the chart refer to the footnotes below.

	Passport Required?	Visa Required?	Return Ticket Required?
Full British	Yes	Yes	Yes
BVP	Not valid	-	-
Australian	Yes	Yes	Yes
Canadian	Yes	Yes	Yes
USA	Yes	Yes	Yes
Other EU (As of 31/12/94)	Yes	1	Yes
Japanese	Yes	Yes	Yes

Restricted entry: No visitor over one year of age is allowed to enter the country without a yellow fever certificate.
PASSPORTS: Valid passport required by all except nationals of the following countries in possession of a national identity card or expired passport less than 5 years old: Burkina Faso, Cameroon, Central African Republic, Chad, Congo, Côte d'Ivoire, Gabon, Ghana, Madagascar, Mali, Mauritania, Niger, Rwanda, Senegal and Togo.
British Visitors Passport: Not accepted.
VISAS: Required by all except:
(a) nationals of countries listed under Passports above;
(b) **[1]** nationals of Denmark, Germany and Italy (all other EU nationals *do* require visas);
(c) nationals of Algeria, Bulgaria, Cape Verde, Gambia, Guinea Republic, Guinea-Bissau, Liberia, Nigeria, Romania and Sierra Leone.
Types of visa: Tourist and Business. Cost: £25.
Validity: Visas are now valid for a period of 15 days only within 3 months of date of issue.
Application to: Consulate (or Consular Section at Embassy). For addresses, see top of entry.
Application requirements: (a) Valid passport. (b) Application form completed in duplicate. (c) 2 passport-size photos. (d) Prepaid registered envelope large enough to fit passport, if applying by post. (e) Letter from company, if visit is for business purposes. (f) Fee.
Working days required: Callers at Consulate are

usually able to obtain visas without delay, but where authorisation from Benin is required it may take up to 30 days.
Temporary residence: Enquire at Consulate.

MONEY

Currency: CFA Franc = 100 centimes. Notes are in denominations of CFA Fr10,000, 5000, 2500, 1000 and 500. Coins are in denominations of CFA Fr500, 250, 100, 50, 25, 10, 5, 2 and 1. Benin is part of the French Monetary Area. Only currency issued by the 'Banque des Etats de l'Afrique Centrale' is valid; currency issued by the 'Banque des Etats de l'Afrique de l'Ouest' is not.
Note: At the beginning of 1994, the CFA Franc was devalued against the French Franc.
Credit cards: Access/Mastercard, American Express, Diners Club and Visa are accepted on a limited basis. Check with your credit card company for details of merchant acceptability and other services which may be available.
Exchange rate indicators: The following figures are included as a guide to the movements of the CFA Franc against Sterling and the US Dollar:

Date:	Oct '92	Sep '93	Jan '94	Jan '95
£1.00=	413.75	433.88	436.78	843.1
$1.00=	260.71	284.14	295.22	545.06

Currency restrictions: Free import of local and foreign currency, subject to declaration. Export of local currency is limited to CFA Fr75,000 for Benin residents travelling to countries outside the French Monetary Area. Non-residents are limited to the amount declared on arrival. EU residents can export an unlimited amount. Export of foreign currency is limited to CFA Fr150,000 for Benin residents; CFA Fr100,000 for non-residents.
Banking hours: 0800-1100 and 1500-1600 Monday to Friday.

DUTY FREE

The following items may be imported into Benin without incurring customs duty:
*200 cigarettes or 100 cigarillos or 25 cigars or 250g of tobacco; *1 bottle of wine and 1 bottle of spirits; 500ml of eau de toilette and 250ml of perfume.*
Note [*]: Only available to persons of 15 years of age or older.

PUBLIC HOLIDAYS

Jan 1 '95 New Year's Day. **Jan 16** Martyrs' Day. **Mar 3** Eid al-Fitr (End of Ramadan). **Apr 1** Youth Day. **Apr 14** Good Friday. **Apr 17** Easter. **May 1** Workers' Day. **May 10** Eid al-Adha (Feast of the Sacrifice). **May 25** Ascension Day. **Jun 5** Whit Monday. **Aug 1** Independence Day. **Aug 15** Assumption. **Oct 26** Armed Forces Day. **Nov 1** All Saints' Day. **Nov 30** National Day. **Dec 25** Christmas Day. **Dec 31** Harvest Day. **Jan 1 '96** New Year's Day. **Jan 16** Martyrs' Day. **Feb 18** Eid al-Fitr (End of Ramadan). **Apr 1** Youth Day. **Apr 4** Good Friday. **Apr 7** Easter Monday. **Apr 29** Eid al-Adha (Feast of the Sacrifice).
Note: Muslim festivals are timed according to local sightings of various phases of the Moon and the dates given above are approximations. During the lunar month of Ramadan that precedes Eid al-Fitr, Muslims fast during the day and feast at night and normal business patterns may be interrupted. Many restaurants are closed during the day and there may be restrictions on smoking and drinking. Some disruption may continue into Eid al-Fitr itself. Eid al-Fitr and Eid al-Adha may last anything from two to ten days, depending on the region. For more information see the section *World of Islam* at the back of the book.

HEALTH

Regulations and requirements may be subject to change at short notice, and you are advised to contact your doctor well in advance of your intended date of departure. Any numbers in the chart refer to the footnotes below.

	Special Precautions?	Certificate Required?
Yellow Fever	Yes	1
Cholera	Yes	2
Typhoid & Polio	Yes	-
Malaria	Yes/3	-
Food & Drink	4	-

[1]: A yellow fever vaccination certificate is required by all travellers over one year of age.

[2]: Following WHO guidelines issued in 1973, a cholera vaccination certificate is no longer a condition of entry to Benin. However, cholera is a serious risk in this country and precautions are essential. Up-to-date advice should be sought before deciding whether these precautions should include vaccination as medical opinion is divided over its effectiveness. See the *Health* section at the back of the book.

[3]: Malaria is a risk all year throughout the country. It occurs predominantly in the malignant *falciparum* form. Resistance to chloroquine has been reported. A weekly dose of 250mg of mefloquine is recommended.

[4]: All water should be regarded as being potentially contaminated. Water used for drinking, brushing teeth or making ice should have first been boiled or otherwise sterilised. Milk is unpasteurised and should be boiled. Powdered or tinned milk is available and is advised, but make sure that it is reconstituted with pure water. Avoid all dairy products. Only eat well-cooked meat and fish, preferably served hot. Pork, salad and mayonnaise may carry increased risk. Vegetables should be cooked and fruit peeled.

Rabies is present. For those at high risk, vaccination before arrival should be considered. If you are bitten abroad seek medical advice without delay. For more information consult the *Health* section at the back of the book.

Bilharzia (schistosomiasis) is present. Avoid swimming and paddling in fresh water. Swimming pools which are well-chlorinated and maintained are safe.

Onchocerciasis (river blindness) exists and *trypanosomiasis* (sleeping sickness) is present and precautions are recommended.

Meningitis is a risk, depending on the area visited and the time of year.

Health care: Medical facilities are limited and not all medicines are available. Doctors and hospitals often expect immediate cash payment for health services. Medical insurance is essential, however it is not always valid within the country without a special overseas coverage supplement.

TRAVEL - International

AIR: Benin's national airline is *Transports Aériens du Bénin TAB (TS)*. Benin also has a shareholding in *Air Afrique*.

Approximate flight times: Not available, but *UTA* operates direct flights to Cotonou from Paris.

International airport: *Cotonou Cadjehoun (COO)*, 5km (3 miles) northwest of the city. Airport facilities include 24-hour left luggage, duty-free shop, restaurant, snack bar, bar, post office (0800-1600 Mon-Fri, 0800-1200 Sat-Sun and holidays), business centre, 24-hour medical facilities, bank and car rental *(Europcar, LAB* and *Socirel)*. Taxis are available to the city (travel time – 30 minutes).

Departure tax: CFA Fr2500 for all passengers leaving Benin.

SEA: Several shipping lines run regular cargo services from Marseille to Cotonou. Local shipping from Lagos arrives in Porto Novo.

RAIL: The railway line from Parakou (via Gaya) to Niamey in Niger, currently under construction, will provide the first rail link into Niger.

ROAD: There are two good main roads, one connecting Cotonou with Niamey in Niger and the other connecting Lagos with Porto Novo, Cotonou, Lomé and Accra; at present, the Nigerian border is closed. Buses and taxis are available. In 1991 work started on a road to link Benin with Togo and Burkina Faso. The first stretch will run from Djougou to Natitingou via Parakou.

TRAVEL - Internal

Note: Foreigners travelling outside Cotonou are subject to restrictions. Visitors are advised to check their position before travelling.

AIR: Government planes run services between Cotonou, Parakou, Natitingou, Djougou and Kandi. It is also possible to charter 2-seater planes.

RAIL: Benin has about 600km (400 miles) of rail track. Trains run from Cotonou to Pobé, Ouidah, Segboroué and Parakou. Food is available on some services. Upholstered seats are only available in first-class cars and these exist only on the route to Parakou. Children under four travel free and children four to nine pay half fare.

Approximate journey times: From Cotonou to *Parakou* is 7-8 hours, to *Segboroué* is 2 hours 30 minutes and to *Pobé* is 4 hours.

ROAD: The roads are in reasonably good condition and many of those which run from Cotonou to Bohicon, and Parakou to Malanville, are paved. Tracks are passable during the dry season but often impassable during the rainy season. Traffic drives on the right. Coach services

WORLD TRAVEL ATLAS

As well as a complete set of conventional plates, the World Travel Atlas contains a wealth of specialist maps and charts designed specifically for use by the travel trade and students of travel and tourism.
The only atlas of its kind, the World Travel Atlas has quickly established itself as an essential reference work for all those connected with the world of travel.

Caribbean Resorts ● World Cruise Routes ● Spanish Resorts ● World Climate ●
World Natural and Cultural Heritage Maps ● World Health ● World Driving ● Italian
Resorts ● International Tourism Statistics ● Main Airports of the World ● Greek Islands
● UK & Mediterranean clean beaches

COLUMBUS PRESS

Call Columbus Press for further details on (0171) 417 0700 or fax (0171) 417 0710.

run along major road routes. **Car hire:** A number of local firms are available in Cotonou. **Documentation:** International Driving Licence required.

URBAN: Taxis are widely available in the main towns. Settle taxi fares in advance.

ACCOMMODATION

Main hotels in Cotonou are pleasant but elsewhere there is very little accommodation for visitors. Abomey has only a small hotel and motel. Porto Novo has one hotel and Parakou two small hotels. There are two establishments *(campements)* for **game viewing** at Porga near Pendjari National Park.

RESORTS & EXCURSIONS

Abomey, situated about 100km (60 miles) northeast of the capital, was once capital of a Fon kingdom and contains an excellent museum covering the history of the Abomey kingdoms (with a throne made of human skulls) and the *Fetish Temple*. Nearby is the *Centre des Artisanants* where local craft products are sold at reasonable prices.

Cotonou has a market, the *Dan Tokpa*, which is normally open every four days. The museum here is well worth a visit. The lake village of **Ganvie**, 18km (11 miles) northwest of Cotonou, has houses built on stilts and a water-market. About 32km (20 miles) to the east is the town of **Ouidah**, notable for its old Portuguese fort and the *Temple of the Sacred Python*.

Porto Novo, the capital, is the administrative centre of the country, containing many examples of colonial and pre-colonial art and architecture. The *Ethnological Museum* is probably the most notable place of interest for a visitor.

The northwest of the country is the home of the Somba people, whose goods can be bought at the weekly market at **Boukombe**.

Benin has two national parks. **Pendjari** is normally only open between December and June and has a wide range of wildlife including cheetahs, hippos and crocodiles. Accommodation is available. The **'W' National Park** straddles the frontier region between Niger, Benin and Burkina Faso and is less well-developed.

SOCIAL PROFILE

FOOD & DRINK: There is a selection of restaurants and hotels in Cotonou, serving French food with table service, although some also serve local African specialities, particularly seafood. There are no restaurants of any note in Porto Novo.

NIGHTLIFE: Cotonou offers five nightclubs, but elsewhere there is little nightlife except during festivals.

SHOPPING: In Cotonou along the marina there are many stalls selling handicrafts and souvenirs. The Dan Tokpa market borders the Cotonou Lagoon and is stocked with many goods from Nigeria and elsewhere as well as traditional medicines and artifacts. Crafts and local goods can be purchased in many towns and villages elsewhere, particularly in markets. Good buys include ritual masks, tapestries, elongated statues and pottery. **Shopping hours:** 0900-1300 and 1600-1900 Monday to Saturday. Some shops are open 0800-1200 Sunday.

SPORT: There are limited facilities for **watersports** on the coast, but note that tides and currents render the sea very dangerous and only the strongest swimmers should venture in. In Cotonou, several hotels have **swimming** pools, and there is **tennis** at the Club du Benin and **sailing** at the Yacht Club. A dug-out canoe or motorboat can be hired on Nakoue Lagoon.

SOCIAL CONVENTIONS: Normal courtesies are

appreciated; it is customary to shake hands on arrival and departure. However, religious beliefs play a large part in society and these should be respected. Voodoo is perhaps the most striking and best-known religion, and has acquired considerable social and political power. Only priests can communicate with voodoos and spirits of the dead. If travelling, it is advisable to clear itineraries with district or provincial authorities. Casual wear is acceptable in most places. **Tipping:** It is normal to tip 10% of the bill in hotels and restaurants.

BUSINESS PROFILE

ECONOMY: One of the poorest countries in the world, Benin's economy is principally agricultural. The main commodities are cotton, peanuts, coffee and palm oil. Benin suffered severely from the global recession of the 1980s and the low level of commodity prices. The most promising development of recent years has been the discovery of offshore oil deposits, so that petroleum products are now the country's biggest export earner. There is some light industry, but almost all manufactured and consumer goods have to be imported and the balance of payments shows a large deficit. Membership of the CFA Franc Zone provides a partial cushion but ultimately the country relies heavily on large injections of French aid. As well as the CFA Franc Zone, Benin is a member of the West African economic community ECOWAS. Benin sells its products mainly to France and, in smaller quantities, to The Netherlands, Korea, Japan and India. The country's leading suppliers are Germany and France.

BUSINESS: It is essential to be able to conduct conversations in French. Normal courtesies should be observed and punctuality is especially important. Lightweight tropical suits should be worn. **Office hours:** 0830-1230 and 1500-1830 Monday to Friday.

COMMERCIAL INFORMATION: The following organisation can offer advice: Chambre de Commerce, d'Agriculture et d'Industrie de la République du Bénin (CCIB), BP 31, avenue du Général de Gaulle, Cotonou. Tel: 313 299.

CLIMATE

The south has an equatorial climate with four seasons. It is hot and dry from January to April and during August, with rainy seasons through May to July and September to December. The north has more extreme temperatures, hot and dry between November and June, cooler and very wet between July and October.

Required clothing: Lightweight cottons and linens. Avoid synthetics. A light raincoat or an umbrella is necessary in rainy seasons and warmer clothes are advised for cool evenings.

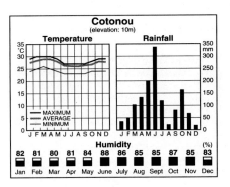

Cotonou
(elevation: 10m)

	Temperature		Rainfall	

MAXIMUM / AVERAGE / MINIMUM

Humidity (%)

Jan	Feb	Mar	Apr	May	June	July	Aug	Sept	Oct	Nov	Dec
82	81	80	81	84	88	86	85	85	87	85	83

Bermuda

Location: Western Atlantic Ocean.

Bermuda Department of Tourism
Global House, 43 Church Street, Hamilton HM 12, Bermuda
Tel: (292) 0023. Fax: (292) 7537.
British Dependent Territories Visa Section
The Passport Office, Clive House, 70-78 Petty France, London SW1H 9HD
Tel: (0171) 271 8552. Fax: (0171) 271 8645. Opening hours: 0900-1700 Monday to Friday.
Bermuda Tourism
1 Battersea Church Road, London SW11 3LY
Tel: (0171) 734 8813. Fax: (0171) 352 6501. Opening hours: 0900-1700 Monday to Friday.
Bermuda Department of Tourism
Suite 201, 310 Madison Avenue, New York, NY 10017
Tel: (212) 818 9800. Fax: (212) 983 5289.
US Consulate General
PO Box HM 325, Crown Hill, 16 Middle Road, Devonshire, Hamilton, Bermuda
Tel: (295) 1342. Fax: (295) 1592.
Bermuda Department of Tourism
Suite 1004, 1200 Bay Street, Toronto, Ontario M5R 2A5
Tel: (416) 923 9600. Fax: (416) 923 4840.

AREA: 53 sq km (20.59 sq miles).
POPULATION: 58,433 (1991 estimate).
POPULATION DENSITY: 1102.5 per sq km.
CAPITAL: Hamilton. **Population:** 6000 (1990).
GEOGRAPHY: Bermuda consists of a chain of some 150 coral islands and islets lying 917km (570 miles) off the coast of South Carolina, in the Atlantic Ocean. Ten of the islands are linked by bridges and causeways to form the principal mainland. There are no rivers or streams and the islands are entirely dependent on rainfall for fresh water. Coastlines are characterised by a succession of small bays with beaches of fine pale sand. The surrounding waters are a vivid blue-green. Inland there is an abundance of subtropical plants and flowers.
LANGUAGE: English is the official language. There is a small community of Portuguese speakers.
RELIGION: Anglican, Episcopal, Roman Catholic and other Christian denominations. There are two cathedrals in Bermuda, one Anglican and the other Roman Catholic.
TIME: GMT - 4 (GMT - 3 from first Sunday in April to Saturday before last Sunday in October).

	Health
GALILEO/WORLDSPAN: **TI-DFT/SJJ/HE**	
SABRE: **TIDFT/SJJ/HE**	
	Visa
GALILEO/WORLDSPAN: **TI-DFT/SJJ/VI**	
SABRE: **TIDFT/SJJ/VI**	

For more information on Timatic codes refer to Contents.

Timatic

ELECTRICITY: 110 volts AC, 60Hz. American (flat) 2-pin plugs.
COMMUNICATIONS: Telephone: IDD is available. Country code: 1 809. Outgoing international code: 011. The internal telephone system is operated by the Bermuda Telephone Company. Bermuda numbers dialled from within Bermuda should be prefixed with the last two digits of the country code (29 or 23) but there are no conventional area codes. **Fax:** This service is available from many hotels and offices. **Telex/telegram:** Cable & Wireless Ltd operate Bermuda's international telecommunications system. Cablegrams may be sent from the C & W office in Hamilton. **Post:** Most letters will automatically travel airmail even if surface rates are paid, although paid-for airmail will be given priority. Airmail letters to Europe take five to seven days. *Poste Restante* facilities are available. Post offices are open from 0800-1700 Monday to Friday. In addition, the General Post Office in Hamilton is open on Saturday mornings until 1200. **Press:** The main newspapers are *The Bermuda Sun* (weekly), *The Mid-Ocean News* (weekly) and *The Royal Gazette* (daily).
BBC World Service and Voice of America frequencies: From time to time these change. See the section *How to Use this Book* for more information.
BBC:

MHz	17.84	15.22	9.915	5.975
Voice of America:				
MHz	15.21	11.70	6.130	5.995

PASSPORT/VISA

Regulations and requirements may be subject to change at short notice, and you are advised to contact the appropriate diplomatic or consular authority before finalising travel arrangements. Details of these may be found at the head of this country's entry. Any numbers in the chart refer to the footnotes below.

	Passport Required?	Visa Required?	Return Ticket Required?
Full British	1	No	Yes
BVP	Valid	No	Yes
Australian	Yes	No	Yes
Canadian	1	No	Yes
USA	1	No	Yes
Other EU (As of 31/12/94)	Yes	No	Yes
Japanese	Yes	No	Yes

Note: Before entering Bermuda, it is *essential* to be in possession of either a return ticket or an onward ticket to the country to which one has a legal right of entry. Anyone arriving in Bermuda and intending to return to their own country via another one which requires a visa *must* obtain such a visa before arrival in Bermuda.
PASSPORTS: A valid passport is required by all except [1] nationals of Canada and the USA who have other documents with proof of identity, such as a birth certificate, a citizenship card/naturalization certificate, or a voters registration card. British citizens may travel on a BVP (see below).
British Visitors Passport: Acceptable. A BVP may be used for holidays or unpaid business trips of up to 3 months providing the user does not travel via the USA.
VISAS: Visas are *not* required for stays of up to 3 weeks *except* for nationals of Albania, Algeria, Bosnia-Hercegovina, Bulgaria, Cambodia, China, CIS, Croatia, Cuba, Czech Republic, Haiti, Hungary, Iran, Iraq, Jordan, Laos, Lebanon, Libya, Former Yugoslav Republic of Macedonia, Mongolia, Morocco, Nigeria, North Korea, Poland, Philippines, Romania, Slovak Republic, Slovenia, Sri Lanka, South Africa, Syria, Tunisia, Vietnam and Yugoslavia (Serbia and Montenegro) who *must* obtain a visa.
Types of visa: Tourist and Transit.
Validity: Valid for 3 months from the date of issue.
Application and enquiries to: British Dependent Territories Visas Section. For address, see top of entry.
Application requirements: Completed application forms and, for business trips, letters from a host. An onward or return ticket is a condition of entry (see note above).
Working days required: 6 to 8 weeks.
Temporary residence: Persons intending to take up residence and/or employment will require prior authorisation from the Department of Immigration, 30 Parliament Street, Hamilton HM 12, Bermuda. Tel: (29) 55151.

MONEY

Currency: Bermuda Dollar (Bda$) = 100 cents. The Bermuda Dollar is tied to the US Dollar. Notes are in denominations of Bda$100, 50, 20, 10, 5 and 1. Coins are in denominations of Bda$1, and 50, 25, 10, 5 and 1 cents.

Currency exchange: US Dollars are generally accepted at par. It is illegal to exchange money other than at authorised banks or bureaux de change.
Credit cards: Access/Mastercard, American Express, Barclaycard and Diners Club are accepted at most large hotels, shops and restaurants. Check with your credit card company for details of merchant acceptability and other services which may be available.
Travellers cheques: US Dollar cheques are widely accepted. There is no bureau de change at the airport, but the bank there is open 1100-1230 and 1300-1600 Monday to Friday.
Exchange rate indicators: The following figures are included as a guide to the movements of the Bermuda Dollar against Sterling and the US Dollar:

Date:	Oct '92	Sep '93	Jan '94	Jan '95
£1.00=	1.59	1.53	1.48	1.5468
$1.00=	1.00	1.00	1.00	1.00

Currency restrictions: There is no limit to the import of foreign currency, subject to declaration. The export of foreign currency is limited to the amount declared on import, plus the equivalent of Bda$2000 in foreign currency. There is no limit to the import of local currency. The export of local currency is limited to Bda$250.
Banking hours: 0930-1500 Monday to Thursday; 0930-1600 Friday.

DUTY FREE

The following goods may be taken into Bermuda without incurring customs duty:
200 cigarettes and 50 cigars and 454g of tobacco; 1.136 litres (1 qt) of spirits and wines.
Prohibited items: Spear guns for fishing, firearms and non-prescribed drugs (including marijuana). All visitors should declare any prescribed drugs on arrival as regulations are strictly observed. Clearance of merchandise and sales materials for use at trade conventions must be arranged in advance with the hotel concerned.

PUBLIC HOLIDAYS

Jan 2 '95 For New Year's Day. **Apr 14** Good Friday. **May 24** Bermuda Day. **Jun 19** Queen's Birthday. **Aug 3** Cup Match. **Aug 4** Somers Day. **Sep 4** Labour Day. **Nov 13** For Remembrance Day. **Dec 25** Christmas Day. **Dec 26** Boxing Day. **Jan 1 '96** New Year's Day. **Apr 5** Good Friday.
Note: Holidays falling on a weekend are usually observed the following Monday, when businesses and most restaurants are closed.

HEALTH

Regulations and requirements may be subject to change at short notice, and you are advised to contact your doctor well in advance of your intended date of departure. Any numbers in the chart refer to the footnotes below.

	Special Precautions?	Certificate Required?
Yellow Fever	No	No
Cholera	No	No
Typhoid & Polio	No	-
Malaria	No	-
Food & Drink	No	-

Health care: Health insurance is essential as medical costs are very high. There is no state-run health service. There is a fully-equipped 237-bed hospital near Hamilton.

TRAVEL - International

AIR: Bermuda has no national airline, but *British Airways (BA)* operates regular weekly flights to and from London and Bermuda.
Approximate flight times: To Bermuda from *London* is 7 hours; and from *New York* is 2 hours.
International airport: *Kindley Field (BDA)*, 15km (9.3 miles) from Hamilton. Bermuda Air Services limousines meet all arrivals. Taxis are also available. The journey to Hamilton takes 20-30 minutes. There are no duty-free shops or bureaux de change at the airport. Duty-free goods may, however, be purchased in town shops for collection at the airport on departure. The airport bank is open 1100-1230 and 1300-1600 Monday to Friday and the bar from 1100 until the departure of the last flight.
Departure tax: A tax of Bda$15 is levied on passengers over 12 years old. Children aged 2-11 pay Bda$5. Children under two years and passengers in immediate transit are exempt.
SEA: UK cruise ships of the *P&O Line* and *Cunard* occasionally call en route from Australia, New Zealand

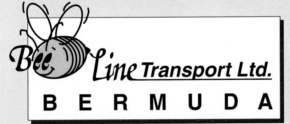

and Southampton, UK. *Royal Caribbean Cruise Lines, Chandris* and *Kloster Cruise* operate a fly-cruise programme from the UK, via New York, to Bermuda (April to September).

TRAVEL - Internal

SEA: Ferries cross Hamilton Harbour. A reduced service runs on Sundays. Ferry tokens are sold at selected hotels at a discount.
ROAD: The main island has an extensive road network but foreign visitors may not drive cars in Bermuda. Motorcycles may be hired (see below) at more or less standard rates. The speed limit is 32kmph (20mph) and traffic drives on the left. **Bus:** Buses are modern and punctual. Bermuda's state-run buses (painted pink) are a pleasant and inexpensive way to visit points of interest. The trip from Hamilton to the town of St George's, the northeastern tip of Bermuda, takes about half an hour, with the ride from Hamilton to Somerset, Bermuda's westernmost point, taking around 45 minutes. It is essential to have the correct fare in coins. A route and schedule map is available free, and books of tickets are available at sub-post offices. **Taxi:** All taxis are metered, with a surcharge after midnight; there is a maximum of four passengers per taxi. Taxis displaying small blue flags are driven by qualified guides approved by the Department of Tourism. A 25% surcharge operates between 2400 and 0600. **Carriages:** Horse-drawn carriages are available in Hamilton. **Motorcycle/bicycle hire:** Lightweight motor-assisted bicycles ('livery cycles') may be hired throughout the island. Crash helmets must be worn. Third Party insurance must be arranged. Bicycles can also be hired. The Department of Tourism produces a comprehensive sheet giving details of prices and supplies. Minimum age limit is 16 years. **Documentation:** A driving licence is not required for moped or bicycle hire. Again, note that visitors are not allowed to drive cars in Bermuda.
JOURNEY TIMES: The following chart gives approximate journey times from Hamilton (in hours and minutes) to other major towns and the airport on Bermuda.

	Air	Road	Sea
Airport	-	0.30	-
St George's	-	0.30	-
Somerset	-	0.45	0.30
Naval Dockyard	0.45	0.45	-

ACCOMMODATION

The Bermuda Department of Tourism issues a booklet *Where to stay in Bermuda* listing all accommodation. Another leaflet gives rates and added taxes. Reduced rates are available during the *Rendezvous*, or 'low' season, which runs from November to March, and there are many special package tours for speciality holidays. **HOTELS:** Hotels are all of a high standard. The top hotels offer dancing and entertainment. Hotels usually offer a choice between two meal plans. Information is available from the Bermuda Hotel Association, Carmel Buildings, corner of King Street and Reid Street, Hamilton 5-23. Tel: (29) 52127. Fax: (29) 26671. Telex: 3243. **Grading:** There is no formal grading system in Bermuda, only MAP and BP. MAP is Modified American Plan; breakfast and dinner included with the price of the room, plus in some places British-style afternoon tea. BP is Bermuda Plan; room and full breakfast only. Large hotels with many facilities make up about 7% of accommodation in Bermuda. Smaller hotels (around 16%) have less than 150 rooms. Normally less expensive than the self-contained resorts, they have limited on-site facilities for shopping and entertainment and are less formal.
GUEST-HOUSES: Guest-houses generally taking less than 12 guests are usually small private homes. Some incorporate several housekeeping units (see below) while others provide shared kitchen facilities. Most of the larger establishments are old Bermudian residences with spacious gardens which have been converted and modernised. A few have their own waterfront and/or pool. Guest-houses make up 50% of accommodation in Bermuda. **Grading:** Larger guest-houses may offer the Bermuda Plan or a slightly stripped-down version of the CP (Continental Plan) – room and light breakfast. Smaller places are casual, offering breakfast only. EP (European Plan) consists of room only. All guest-houses offer an informal life-style.
COTTAGE COLONIES: These are typically Bermudian and feature a main club-house with dining room, lounge and bar. The cottage units are spread throughout landscaped grounds and offer privacy and luxury. Though most have kitchenettes for beverages or light snacks they are not self-catering units. All have

their own beach and/or pool.
CLUB RESORTS: These are noted for privacy and luxury and are for members or by invitation only. There are two club resorts on the main island.
SELF-CATERING: Housekeeping cottages are large properties situated in landscaped estates with their own beach and pool, much like cottage colonies, but without a main club-house. They are considered to be luxury units. All have kitchen facilities but BP or a reduced CP is available at some establishments. **Apartments:** Apartments can be booked through Simply Caribbean, 3 Victoria Avenue, Harrogate HG1 1EQ. Tel: (01423) 526 887. Smaller, less expensive and with fewer amenities than the housekeeping cottages, most holiday apartments are nonetheless comfortable. Some have a pool. All have kitchen and a minimal daily maid service.
CAMPING/CARAVANNING: There are no camping facilities for visitors in Bermuda.

RESORTS & EXCURSIONS

Hamilton is the colony's capital city, situated at the end of Bermuda's *Great Sound* on the inner curve of the 'fish hook'. Here, between Parliament Street and Court Street, is the *Cabinet Building* where the Senate – the Upper House of Bermuda's Parliament – meets. The Lower Chamber of Parliament is housed in the *Sessions House* in Hamilton and is open to the public. Front Street is Hamilton's main street which runs along the water's edge from *Albouy's Point*, site of the Ferrydock and the Royal Bermuda Yacht Club to King Street in the east. Located on Queen Street in Hamilton is *Perot's Post Office*. The Perot stamp, Bermuda's first postage stamp, was printed by Bermuda's Postmaster from 1818 to 1862. Bermuda's stamps make fine gifts for friends who are collectors. In the summer months there are usually up to three cruise ships moored at the city's piers. Ferry trips are available round Hamilton Harbour, and also longer cruises to Great Sound and the rural village of Somerset. The recently restored 19th-century *Fort Hamilton* welcomes visitors to its formidable ramparts, bristling cannon, underground web of limestone tunnels and spectacular view of Hamilton. In **Hamilton parish** is the *Blue Grotto Dolphin Show*, with dolphins, sharks, eels and sea horses, and the popular *Bermuda Aquarium and Zoo*, based at *Flatts Bridge*.
In **Somerset**, on the western end of the island, *Fort Scaur* is a good place to picnic, fish, swim and enjoy the panoramic view of picturesque *Ely's Harbour*.
At the far eastern end of the chain of islands is the 17th-century town of **St George**, Bermuda's first capital, founded in 1612. It has been the focus of considerable recent restoration; today, the town's narrow winding lanes and historic landmarks appear much as they did more than three centuries ago. At the corner of Duke of Clarence Street and Featherbed Alley is a working model of a 17th-century printing press. Also to be seen are *The Confederate Museum,* a hotel for Confederate officers during America's Civil War; the *Stocks & Pillory*; and the replica of the *Deliverance,* one of Bermuda's first ships. St George also has many excellent pubs, restaurants and shops. *Gates Fort,* which dates back to 1620, is built on a promontory overlooking the sea and offers a spectacular view of the ocean and harbour. Nearby is *Fort St Catherine,* built in 1622, the largest and one of the most fascinating of the island's fortifications.
At the very tip of Bermuda, on the western side, is **Ireland Island**, with a *Maritime Museum* which displays relics of sunken wrecks and the neo-classical buildings of the Royal Naval dockyard.
Two of the best known caves are *Crystal Caves* and *Leamington Caves,* made up of sprawling underground systems and crystalline tidal pools. They are open daily in season.
The best view of the island is from **Gibb's Hill Lighthouse**, in Southampton parish.
Two notable **churches** on the island include *Old Devonshire Church* and *St Peter's Church,* on Duke of York Street in old St George.
Everywhere on the island there are circles of stone, called *Moongates*, a design brought to Bermuda in the 1800s by a sea captain who had seen them on a voyage to China. Oriental legend has it that honeymooners should walk through them and make a wish.

SOCIAL PROFILE

FOOD & DRINK: Hotel cooking is usually international with some Bermudian specialities such as Bermuda lobster (in season, September to mid-April), mussel pie, conch stew, fish chowder laced with sherry,

peppers and rum, and shark. Other seafoods include Rockfish, Red Snapper and Yellowtail. Peculiar to Bermuda is the Bermuda onion; other fine home-grown products include pawpaw and strawberries in January and February, and a variety of local citrus fruit. Traditional Sunday breakfast is codfish and bananas while desserts include sweet potato pudding, bay grape jelly and a syllabub of guava jelly, cream and sherry. There is a vast variety of restaurants, cafés, bars and taverns to suit all pockets. Service will vary although generally table service can be expected. **Drink:** Local drinks and cocktails have Caribbean rum as a base, and have colourful names such as *Dark and Stormy* and the famous *Rum Swizzle*. British, European and American beer is available. It is normal in bars to pay for each drink and to tip the barman. In restaurants, drinks are added to the bill.
NIGHTLIFE: Most hotels offer a variety of entertainment. Dancing, barbecues, nightclubs and discotheques are all available. Local music is a mixture of calypso and Latin American, and steelband music is very popular.
SHOPPING: The best buys are imported merchandise such as French perfumes, English bone china, Swiss watches, Danish silver, American costume jewellery, German cameras, Scottish tweeds, and various spirits and liqueurs. Bermuda-made articles include handicrafts, pottery, cedar ware, fashions, records and paintings by local artists. Antique shops may have the odd good bargain and shops in the countryside offer many souvenirs. Bathing suits, sports clothes and sun straws are other good buys. There is no sales tax or VAT. **Shopping hours:** 0900-1700 Monday to Saturday, with some closing early on Thursdays.
SPORT: Golf: There are eight 18-hole courses, including the *Mid-Ocean Club*, which is world-renowned for its challenge and beauty, and *Port Royal*, situated in beautiful oceanside terrain. There is also one 9-hole layout. For information on Amateur, Professional and Pro-Am tournaments, write to the Bermuda Golf Association, PO Box 433, Hamilton. **Tennis:** There are almost 100 courts on the island, with a variety of surfaces. Most of the larger Bermuda hotels have their own courts, many of them floodlit for night play. Tournaments are held all year round and several are open to visitors. For information, write to the Bermuda Lawn Tennis Association, PO Box 341, Hamilton. **Swimming:** Bermuda's most famous beaches lie along the island's southern edge. Some of the most beautiful are at Warwick Long Bay, Stonehole, Chaplin and Horseshoe Bay. **Snorkelling and scuba:** Visibility underwater is often as much as 61m (200ft) in any direction. Experienced scuba divers can go below for a historic 'tour' of old wrecks, cannons and other remnants of past disasters on the reefs. All equipment necessary is easy to hire – note, however, that spear guns are not allowed. **Fishing:** Bermuda is one of the world's finest fishing centres, especially for light-tackle fishing. Equipment may be rented for shore fishing and there are charter boats for reef and deep-sea fishing. For deep-sea aficionados, wahoo, amberjack, marlin and allison tuna abound. On the reefs, there are amberjack, great barracuda, grey snapper and yellowtail. Shore fishermen can test their skills on bonefish and pompano. The best fishing is during the months from May to November, when trophies are awarded. **Sailing:** The Blue Water Cruising Race, from Marion Massachusetts to Bermuda, takes place in June bi-annually, in odd-numbered years. The Newport to Bermuda Ocean Yacht Race is also held bi-annually, in even-numbered years. This world-famous June Blue-Water Classic (fondly referred to as the 'Thrash to the Onion Patch') attracts scores of the finest racing craft afloat. The week-long festivities which follow the arrival of the boats are held at the Royal Bermuda Yacht Club. In August the 'Non-Mariners Race' is held. Sailboats and skippers are available for hire from 'Sail Yourself' charter agencies. **Cricket:** The annual Cup Match, an island-wide, 2-day public holiday, is held once a year, when the St George's and Somerset Cricket Clubs vie for the Championship Cup.
SPECIAL EVENTS: Mar '95 *Annual Street Event*, Hamilton. **Apr** *Easter Rugby Classic; Peppercorn Ceremony,* St George; *Agricultural Show.* **May** *Invitational International Race Week; Bermuda Heritage Month.* **Jun 19** *Queen's Birthday Parade.* **Jul/Aug** *Cup Match Cricket Festival.* **Aug/Sep** *Bermuda Hockey Festival.* **Sep/Oct** *Annual Bermuda Triathlon.*
For full details of special events in 1995/96, contact Bermuda Tourism.
SOCIAL CONVENTIONS: Many of these are British influenced, and there is a very English 'feel' to the islands. It is quite customary to politely greet people on the street, even if they are strangers. Casual wear is acceptable in most places during the day, but beachwear

should be confined to the beach. Almost all hotels and restaurants require a jacket and tie in the evenings; check dress requirements in advance. Non-smoking areas will be marked. **Tipping:** When not included in the bill, 15% generally for most services. Hotels and guest-houses add a set amount per person in lieu of tips to the bill.

BUSINESS PROFILE

ECONOMY: Bermuda's economy is dominated by two industries: tourism and international financial services, which account for approximately 55% and 40% of GDP respectively. A US Naval Air station accounts for most of the remainder. Offshore banking and related services have been the mainstay of the financial sector, although in recent years insurance has assumed a prominent position. Tax receipts from the 4500 offshore companies registered in Bermuda – which is by no means a tax haven despite the absence of an income tax – and customs duties, go some way to offset the island's large balance of payments deficit: imports at $500 million per annum are approximately five times the size of exports. The small manufacturing base in Bermuda is engaged in boat-building, ship repair, perfume and pharmaceuticals. There is some agriculture, concentrated in the growing of fruit and vegetables, but most of Bermuda's food is imported along with all its oil, machinery and most manufactured goods. Bermuda has recently established an important diamond market. The United States is the largest trading partner followed by Japan, Germany and the UK.
BUSINESS: Lightweight suits or shirt and tie are acceptable, as are Bermuda shorts. Visiting cards and occasionally letters of introduction are used. Codes of practice are similar to those in the UK. **Office hours:** 0900-1700 Monday to Friday.
COMMERCIAL INFORMATION: The following organisation can offer advice: Bermuda Chamber of Commerce, Front Street, PO Box HM 655, Hamilton HM CX. Tel: (29) 54201. Fax: (29) 25779.
CONFERENCES/CONVENTIONS: The Bermuda Department of Tourism (address at top of entry) can give information, including advice on customs arrangements for the speedy handling of materials. The Chamber of Commerce can also offer assistance; *Special Groups and Incentive Services* (published by the Department of Tourism) is a list of members' services available to organisers.

CLIMATE

Semi-tropical, with no wet season. The Gulf Stream which flows between Bermuda and the North American continent keeps the climate temperate. A change of seasons comes during mid-November to mid-December and from late March through April. Either spring or summer weather may occur and visitors should be prepared for both. Showers may be heavy at times but occur mainly at night. Summer temperatures prevail from May to mid-November with the warmest weather in July, August and September – this period is occasionally followed by high winds.
Required clothing: Lightweight cottons and linens. Light waterproofs or umbrella are advisable and warmer clothes for cooler months.

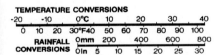

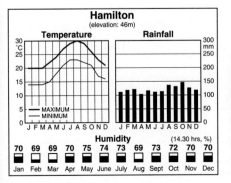

Hamilton
(elevation: 46m)

Humidity											(14.30 hrs, %)
70	69	69	70	75	74	73	69	73	72	70	70
Jan	Feb	Mar	Apr	May	June	July	Aug	Sept	Oct	Nov	Dec

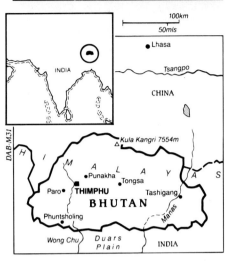

Bhutan

Location: Indian sub-continent; on border between Assam (northeast India) and China.

Bhutan Tourism Corporation Ltd (BTCL)
PO Box 159, Thimphu, Bhutan
Tel: 24045 or 23252. Fax: 22479 or 23695. Telex: 890217.
Travels in the Bhutan Himalayas (Yod Sel Tours & Treks)
PO Box 574, Thimphu, Bhutan
Tel: (2) 23912. Fax: (2) 23589.
Royal Bhutanese Embassy
Chandragupta Marg, Chanakyapuri, New Delhi 110 021, India
Tel: (11) 609 217. Fax: (11) 687 610. Telex: 3162263.
Embassy of India
India House Estate, Lungtenzampa, Thimphu, Bhutan
Tel: 22162. Fax: 23195. Telex: 890211.
The Permanent Mission of the Kingdom of Bhutan to the United Nations
27th Floor, 2 United Nations Plaza, 44th Street, New York, NY 10017
Tel: (212) 826 1919 or 826 1990/1. Fax: (212) 926 2998.

AREA: 46,500 sq km (17,954 sq miles).
POPULATION: 1,375,400 (1988 estimate).
POPULATION DENSITY: 29.6 per sq km.
CAPITAL: Thimphu. **Population:** 27,000 (1990 estimate).
GEOGRAPHY: Bhutan is located in the eastern Himalayas, bordered to the north by China and to the south, east and west by India. The altitude varies from 300m (1000ft) in the narrow lowland region to 7000m (22,000ft) in the Himalayan plateau in the north, and there are three distinct climatic regions. The foothills are tropical and home to deer, lion, leopards and the rare golden monkey as well as much tropical vegetation including many species of wild orchids. The Inner Himalaya region is temperate; wildlife includes bear, boar and sambar and the area is rich in deciduous forests. The High Himalaya region is very thinly populated, but the steep mountain slopes are the home of many species of animals including snow leopards and musk deer.
LANGUAGE: Dzongkha is the official language. A large number of dialects are spoken, due to the physical

	Health
GALILEO/WORLDSPAN:	**TI-DFT/PBH/HE**
SABRE:	**TIDFT/PBH/HE**
	Visa
GALILEO/WORLDSPAN:	**TI-DFT/PBH/VI**
SABRE:	**TIDFT/PBH/VI**

For more information on Timatic codes refer to Contents.

isolation of many villages. Sharchop Kha, from eastern Bhutan, is the most widely spoken. Nepalese is common in the south of the country. English has been the language of educational instruction since 1964 and is widely spoken.
RELIGION: Mahayana Buddhism is the state religion; the majority of Bhutanese people follow the Drukpa school of the Kagyupa sect. Nepalis, who make up about 25% of the population, are Hindu.
TIME: GMT + 6.
ELECTRICITY: 220 volts AC, 50Hz.
COMMUNICATIONS: Telephone: Services are restricted to the main centres. Country code: 975. All other calls must go through the international operator. Outgoing international code: 00. **Telex:** Services are available in main centres, but are liable to disruption.
Post: Airmail letters to Bhutan can take up to two weeks. Mail from Bhutan is liable to disruption, although this is due not to the inefficiency of the service but rather to the highly-prized nature of Bhutanese stamps which often results in their being steamed off the envelopes en route.
Press: There are very few papers, but *Kuensel*, a government news bulletin, is published weekly in English.
BBC World Service and Voice of America frequencies:
From time to time these change. See the section *How to Use this Book* for more information.
BBC:

MHz	17.79	15.31	11.75	9.740

Voice of America:

MHz	17.74	15.42	11.70	7.125

PASSPORT/VISA

Regulations and requirements may be subject to change at short notice, and you are advised to contact the appropriate diplomatic or consular authority before finalising travel arrangements. Details of these may be found at the head of this country's entry. Any numbers in the chart refer to the footnotes below.

	Passport Required?	Visa Required?	Return Ticket Required?
Full British	Yes	Yes	Yes
BVP	Not valid	-	-
Australian	Yes	Yes	Yes
Canadian	Yes	Yes	Yes
USA	Yes	Yes	Yes
Other EU (As of 31/12/94)	Yes	Yes	Yes
Japanese	Yes	Yes	Yes

Note: All tours are organised by Bhutan Tourism Corporation Ltd (BTCL).
PASSPORTS: Valid passport required by all.
British Visitors Passport: Not accepted.
VISAS: Required by all.
Note: As the only way to enter the country is via India, all travellers must ensure that they have the correct documentation for transiting that country. This will include a Double-entry visa; a special permit if travelling on the Bagdora–Phuntsholing route; and a special permit if a visit to the Manas Game Sanctuary is planned. Consult the *Passport/Visa* section for the entry on *India* later in this book. Visitors are also advised to contact the Government of India Tourist Office to check exactly what special permits or other documents may be necessary as these regulations are subject to change at short notice. In recent years access to Bhutan has become more difficult, so the Bhutan Tourism Corporation Ltd (BTCL) should also be contacted.
Application to: Visas must be obtained by postal application to the Bhutan Tourism Corporation in Thimphu. Visas will be issued on arrival in Bhutan where the visitor will be met.
Application requirements: (a) Application forms, which may be obtained from the BTCL who should be contacted direct (for address, see top of entry). (b) All necessary documents for transiting India (see **Note** above). (c) Confirmed onward or return ticket. (d) Sufficient funds for length of stay. (e) Hotel voucher. (f) Fee (usually US$20) payable in any hard currency.
Working days required: Applications should be made at least ten weeks in advance of the intended date of departure.

MONEY

Currency: 1 Ngultrum (Nu) = 100 chetrum (Ch). The Ngultrum is pegged to the Indian Rupee (which is also accepted as legal tender). Notes are in denominations Nu100, 50, 20, 10, 5, 2 and 1. Coins are in denominations of Nu1, and 50, 25, 10 and 5 chetrum.
Credit cards: American Express and Diners Club have

very limited acceptability. Check with credit card company for details of merchant acceptability and other services which may be available.
Currency exchange: Leading foreign currencies and travellers cheques can be exchanged in any branch of the Bank of Bhutan, but travellers cheques are preferred and receive a better exchange rate. Major hotels in Thimphu and Phuntsholing, and the Olathang hotel in Paro, will also exchange foreign currency.
Exchange rate indicators: The following figures are included as a guide to the movements of the Ngultrum/ Indian Rupee against Sterling and the US Dollar:

Date:	Oct '92	Sep '93	Jan '94	Jan '95
£1.00=	45.00	48.00	46.41	48.55
$1.00=	28.35	31.44	31.37	31.39

Currency restrictions: None, but foreign currency must be declared on arrival.

DUTY FREE

The following goods may be taken into Bhutan by travellers aged 17 years or over without incurring customs duty:
200 cigarettes or 50 cigars or 250g of tobacco; 1 litre of spirits; 250ml of eau de toilette.
Prohibited goods: Narcotics, plants, gold and silver bullion, and obsolete currency. The export of antiques, religious objects, manuscripts, images and anthropological materials is strictly prohibited.

PUBLIC HOLIDAYS

Jan 2 '95 Winter Solstice. **Jan 8** The Meeting of Nine Evils. **Jan 31** Traditional Day of Offering. **Nov 11** Birthday of HM Jigme Singye Wangchuck. **Dec 17** National Day of Bhutan.
Note: The traditional Buddhist holidays are observed, including Losar, Shabdung Kuchoe, Birthday of Drukgyal Sumpa, Lord Buddha's Parinirvana, Coronation Day, Birthday of Guru Rinpoche, First Sermon of Lord Buddha, Death of Drukgyal Sumpa, Thimphu Dromche, Thimphu Tshechu, The Blessed Rainy Day, Dasain and the Descending Day of Lord Buddha. Buddhist festivals are declared according to local astronomical observations and it is not possible to forecast the date of their occurrence.

HEALTH

Regulations and requirements may be subject to change at short notice, and you are advised to contact your doctor well in advance of your intended date of departure. Any numbers in the chart refer to the footnotes below.

	Special Precautions?	Certificate Required?
Yellow Fever	Yes	1
Cholera	Yes	2
Typhoid & Polio	Yes	-
Malaria	Yes/3	-
Food & Drink	4	-

[1]: Vaccination certificate required if coming from an infected area.
[2]: Following WHO guidelines issued in 1973, a cholera vaccination certificate is no longer a condition of entry to Bhutan. However, cholera is a serious risk in this country and precautions are essential. Up-to-date advice should be sought before deciding whether these precautions should include vaccination as medical opinion is divided over its effectiveness. See the *Health* section at the back of this book.
[3]: Malaria risk exists throughout the year in the southern belt of the following five districts: Chirang, Gaylegphug, Samchi, Samdrupjongkhar and Shemgang. Resistance to chloroquine and sulfadoxine/pyrimethane has been reported in the malignant *falciparum* form of the disease. A weekly dosage of 300mg of chloroquine and a daily dosage of 200mg of proguanil is the recommended prophylaxis.
[4]: All water should be regarded as being potentially contaminated. Water used for drinking, brushing teeth or making ice should have first been boiled or otherwise sterilised. Milk is unpasteurised and should be boiled. Powdered or tinned milk is available and is advised, but make sure that it is reconstituted with pure water. Avoid all dairy products. Only eat well-cooked meat and fish, preferably served hot. Pork, salad and mayonnaise may carry increased risk. Vegetables should be cooked and fruit peeled.
Rabies is present. For those at high risk, vaccination should be considered. If you are bitten abroad seek medical advice without delay. For more information consult the *Health* section at the back of the book.
Meningitis is a sporadic risk and vaccination is advised.
Health care: Full medical insurance is advised. Medical facilities are good but scarce.

TRAVEL - International

AIR: The national airline is *Druk-Air Corporation (Royal Bhutan Airlines)*. There are two ways of travelling to Bhutan: By air to Delhi (see the *Travel* section in the entry for *India* later in this book) and then by *Indian Airlines* to Bagdogra – from here it is a 3-hour drive to the border town of Phuntsholing; *or*
By air to Calcutta (see the *Travel* section in the entry for *India* later in this book) and then by *Druk-Air* to Paro, a small town near Thimphu in western Bhutan.
Departure tax: Nu300.
RAIL: The nearest railhead is Siliguri (India).

TRAVEL - Internal

RAIL: There are no internal services.
ROAD: Traffic drives on the left. The country has a fairly good internal road network with 2280km (1417 miles) of surfaced road. The main routes run north from Phuntsholing to the western and central regions of Paro and Thimphu, and east–west across the Pele La Pass linking the valleys of the eastern region. The northern regions of the High Himalayas have no roads. **Bus:** Those services which were formerly government-owned are now privately run, though yaks, ponies and mules are the chief forms of transportation. The main routes are from Phuntsholing to Thimphu, Thimphu to Bumthang, Bumthang to Tashigang, Tashigang to Samdrup Jongkar and from Tongsa to Gaylegphug.
Documentation: International Driving Permit is required.
JOURNEY TIMES: The following chart gives approximate journey times (in hours and minutes) from Thimphu to other major towns in the country.

	Road
Paro	1.30
P'sholing	6.00
W'phodrang	2.15
Punakha	2.30
Bumthang	8.45
Tongsa	6.45

ACCOMMODATION

There are comfortable hotels, cottages and guest-houses (many constructed to accommodate foreign guests during the coronation of the present King in 1974). Hotels have hot and cold running water, electricity and room telephones.

RESORTS & EXCURSIONS

Note: Many areas have now been closed to tourists. Visitors should check with the Bhutan Tourism Corporation (for address, see top of entry).
Thimphu, the capital of Bhutan, lies at a height of over 2400m (8000ft) in the fertile valley transversed by the *Wangchuk River.* In many ways it resembles a large, widely dispersed village rather than a capital. The *Tashichhodzong* is the main administrative and religious centre of the country. It was rebuilt in 1961 after being damaged by fire and earthquake, its hundred-odd spacious rooms house all the government departments and ministries, the *National Assembly Hall*, the *Throne Room of the King* and the country's largest monastery, the summer headquarters of the Je Khempo and 2000 of his monks. The yearly *Thimphu Festival* is held in the courtyard directly in front of the National Assembly Hall. The *Handicraft Emporium* displays a wide assortment of beautifully hand-woven and crafted products which make unique souvenirs. **Simtokha,** 8km (5 miles) from Thimphu, has Bhutan's most ancient *Dzong.*
The small town of **Phuntsholing** is a commercial and industrial centre as well as the gateway to Bhutan. A short walk from the hotel is the *Kharbandi Monastery.* Bhutan is well known for its stamps, and the best place to buy them is in Phuntsholing where the *Philatelic Office of Bhutan* has its headquarters. The first and only department store of Bhutan is also in Phuntsholing.
Punakha is the former capital of the country; situated at a lower altitude, it enjoys a comparatively benign climate. The valley contains many sacred temples, including *Machin Lhakhag* where the remains of Ngawang Namgyal, the unifier of Bhutan, are entombed.
Tongsa is the ancestral home of the Royal family. The *Dzong* (a fortified monastery) here commands a superb view of the river valley and contains a magnificent collection of rhino horn sculptures. The district of **Wangdiphodrang** is known for its slate carving and bamboo weaving.
A visit to the **Paro Valley** where the *Taktsang* (Tiger's Nest) *Monastery* clings dizzily to the face of a 900m (2952ft) precipice, is highly recommended. Other attractions in the area include the *Drukgyul Dzong,* further up the Paro Valley (now in ruins after the earthquake in 1954), which once protected Bhutan against numerous Tibetan invasions; and the *Paro Watchtower,* which now houses the *National Museum of Bhutan.* The temperate *Punakha Valley* houses many sacred temples including the *Machin Lhakhag* in the *Punakaha Dzong*. The 3100m-high (10,170ft) *Dochu La Pass* commands a breathtaking view of the eastern Himalayan chain.
Bumthang is the starting point for 4- and 7-day cultural tours through the rural villages including the **Mongar** and **Lhuntsi** Dzongs. **Tashigang,** a silk-spinning district, has an interesting Dzong. The **Manas Game Sanctuary** in southeast Bhutan is the home of a wide variety of wildlife and should not be missed.
POPULAR ITINERARIES: 7-day: (a) Phuntsholing–Paro–Simtokha–Thimphu.(b) Thimphu–Punakha–Wangdiphodrang–Tongsa. (c) Bumthang–Mongar–Lhuntsi–Tashigang–Manas Game Sanctuary.

SOCIAL PROFILE

FOOD & DRINK: Restaurants are relatively scarce and most tourists eat in their hotels. Meals are often buffet-style and mostly vegetarian. Cheese is a very popular ingredient in dishes and the most popular cheeses are *dartsi* (cow milk's cheese), sometimes served in a dish with red chillies *(ema dartsi),* and yak cheese. Rice is ubiquitous, sometimes flavoured with saffron. The most popular drink is *souza* (Bhutanese tea).
SHOPPING: Markets are held regularly, generally on a Sunday, and are a rich source of local clothing and jewellery, as well as foodstuffs. The handicraft emporium on the main street in the capital is open daily except Sunday and offers a magnificent assortment of handwoven and handcrafted goods. The Motithang Hotel in Thimphu recently opened a souvenir shop. Silversmiths and goldsmiths in the Thimphu Valley are able to make handicrafted articles to order. **Shopping hours:** 0900-2100 Monday to Sunday.
SPORT: Archery competitions are held frequently, and provide an opportunity for the visitor to appreciate the skills of the Bhutanese in their national sport. **Trekking:** Much of the pleasure of visiting Bhutan is enjoying the breathtaking scenery by trekking around the valleys and the mountain gorges. **Fishing:** The rivers offer superb trout fishing. **Wildlife viewing:** The country boasts over 320 varieties of birds, including the rare black-necked crane. The Manas Game Sanctuary has a wide variety of wildlife (a special permit is necessary). Other sports include **squash**, **golf**, **badminton**, **football**, **basketball** and **volleyball**.
SPECIAL EVENTS: Buddhist festivals, full of masks, dancing and ritual, generally centre on *Dzongs* (fortified monasteries) in cobbled courtyards, the most famous of which is at Paro. More than 40 religious or folk dances are performed by the monks recounting tales of Buddhist history and myth. As the dates for these festivals are based on the Bhutanese lunar calendar, it is difficult to predict them precisely. They are, however, numerous, and visitors should be able to witness and enjoy at least one of these extremely colourful events during their stay. Formal dress is required for all festivals. The following special events have been designated for 1995:
Apr 8-10 '95 *Gomkora Tshechu.* **Apr 11-14** *Paro Tshechu.* **Apr 15** *Paro Thongdrol.* **Apr 8-17** *Chorten Kora.* **Jul 8** *Kurje Lhakhang Tshechu,* Bumthang. **Oct 1-3** *Wangdi Thechu.* **Oct 3-5** *Thimphu Tshechu,* Thimphu; *Tamshing Phala Choepa,* Bumthang. **Oct 7-9** *Tangbi Mani,* Bumthang. **Nov 7-10** *Jampel Lhakang Drub,* Bumthang. **Nov 28-Dec 1** *Mongar Tshechu.* **Nov 30-Dec 2** *Tashigang Tshechu.* **Dec 29-Jan 1 '96** *Tongsa Tshechu; Luntsi Tshechu.*
SOCIAL CONVENTIONS: The lifestyle, manners and customs of the Bhutanese are in many respects unique to the area. The strongest influence on social conventions is the country's state religion, and everywhere one can see the reminders of Buddhism and the original religion of Tibet, Bonism. There are no rigid clan systems, and equal rights exist between men and women. The majority of the Bhutanese live an agrarian lifestyle. The political leaders of the country have historically also been religious leaders. For years

the country has deliberately isolated itself from visitors, and has only recently opened up to the outside world, a policy which is now to some extent being reversed.
Tipping: Not widely practised.

BUSINESS PROFILE

ECONOMY: Despite being one of the very poorest countries in the world, there is no unemployment and no starvation. Almost all the working population is involved with agriculture, forestry or fishing. The economy is therefore mainly one of subsistence and dependent on clement conditions. The failure of the 1983 rains, for example, caused a serious decline in production. Since then it has recovered and steadily increased annually, as has the production of cereals and timber – over 70% of the land area is afforested. There is some small-scale industry, contributing no more than 5% of gross domestic product, which produces textiles, soap, matches, candles and carpets. Recent economic policy has concentrated on export industries and areas such as power generation which will help these to develop. Tourism and stamps are the main sources of foreign exchange. India accounts for around 90% of both imports and exports.
BUSINESS: Lightweight or tropical suit or a shirt and tie for the south. In the capital, a full business suit and tie are recommended. The best time to visit is October and November.
COMMERCIAL INFORMATION: The following organisation can offer advice: Bhutan Chamber of Commerce and Industry, PO Box 147, Thimphu. Tel: 23140. Telex: 890229.

CLIMATE

There are four distinct seasons similiar in their divisions to those of Western Europe. The Monsoon occurs between June and August when the temperature is normally between 8°-21°C (46°-69°F). Temperatures drop dramatically with increases in altitude. Days are usually very pleasant (average about 10°C/50°F) with clear skies and sunshine. Nights are cold and require heavy woollen clothing, particularly in winter. Generally October, November and April to mid-June are the best times to visit – rainfall is at a minimum and temperatures are conducive to active days of sightseeing. The foothills are also very pleasant during the winter.
Required clothing: Lightweight cottons in the foothills, also linens and waterproof gear, light sweaters and jackets for the evenings. Upland areas: woollens for evenings, particularly during the winter months.

TEMPERATURE CONVERSIONS

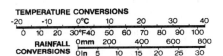

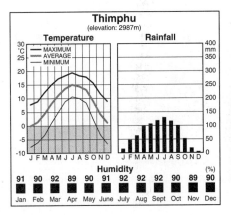

Thimphu
(elevation: 2987m)

□ *international airport*

Location: South America.

Dirección Nacional de Turismo
Calle Mercado 1328, Casilla 1868, La Paz, Bolivia
Tel: (2) 367 463. Fax: (2) 374 630. Telex: 2534.
Embassy and Consulate of the Republic of Bolivia
106 Eaton Square, London SW1W 9AD
Tel: (0171) 235 4248 *or* 235 2257 *or* 235 4255 (visa enquiries). Fax: (0171) 235 1286. Telex: 918885.
Embassy opening hours (enquiries): 1000-1300 and 1500-1700 Monday to Friday. Consulate opening hours (visa enquiries): 1000-1300 Monday to Thursday.
British Embassy
Avenida Arce 2732, Casilla 694, La Paz, Bolivia
Tel: (2) 357 424. Fax: (2) 391 063. Telex: 355-2341 (a/b PDRMELP BV).
Embassy of the Republic of Bolivia
3014 Massachusetts Avenue, NW, Washington, DC 20008
Tel: (202) 483 4410/1/2. Fax: (202) 328 3712. Telex: 440049.
Embassy of the United States of America
Casilla 425, Edificio Banco Popular del Perú, Calle Colón 112, La Paz, Bolivia
Tel: (2) 350 120. Fax: (2) 359 875. Telex: 3268.
Bolivian Embassy
Suite 504, 130 Albert Street, Ottawa, Ontario K1P 5G4
Tel: (613) 236 8237. Fax: (613) 230 9937.
Bolivian Consulate and Instituto Boliviano de Turismo
11231 Jasper Avenue, Edmonton, Alberta T5K 0L5
Tel: (403) 488 1525. Fax: (403) 488 0350.

AREA: 1,084,391 sq km (424,164 sq miles).
POPULATION: 7,612,000 (1991 estimate).
POPULATION DENSITY: 6.9 per sq km.
CAPITAL: Administrative: La Paz. **Population:** 1,049,800 (1988). **Legal:** Sucre. **Population:** 95,635 (1988).
GEOGRAPHY: Bolivia is a landlocked country

bordered by Peru to the northwest, Brazil to the north and east, Paraguay to the southeast, Argentina to the south, and Chile to the west. There are three main areas: The first is a high plateau known as the 'Altiplano', a largely barren region lying about 4000m (13,000ft) above sea level. It comprises 10% of the country's area and 70% of the population, nearly one-third of whom are urban dwellers. The second area is a fertile valley situated 1800m (5900ft) to 2700m (8850ft) above sea level. The third area comprises the lowland tropics which stretch down to the frontiers with Brazil, Argentina and Paraguay, taking up some 70% of the land area. Rainfall in this region is high, and the climate is hot.
LANGUAGE: The official language is Spanish. However, the Indians of the Altiplano speak Aymará and elsewhere, Quechua, the Inca tongue, is spoken. English is also spoken by a small number of officials and businessmen in commercial centres.
RELIGION: Roman Catholic with a Protestant minority.
TIME: GMT - 4.
ELECTRICITY: 110/220 volts AC in La Paz, 220 volts AC in the rest of the country, 50Hz. Most houses and hotels have 2-pin sockets for both electrical currents. Variations from this occur in some places.
COMMUNICATIONS: Telephone: IDD is available. Country code: 591. Outgoing international code: 011.
Fax: Services available. **Telex/telegram:** Telex facilities are available at La Paz telecommunications centre and some hotels. Telegram facilities are available from the West Coast of America Telegraph Company; head office at Edificio Electra, Calle Mercado 1150, La Paz. **Post:** Airmail to Europe takes three to four days. A *Poste Restante* service is available. **Press:** Spanish language only. The main papers published in La Paz are *Presencia, Hoy, El Diario* and *Ultima Hora.*
BBC World Service and Voice of America frequencies: From time to time these change. See the section *How to Use this Book* for more information.

BBC:				
MHz	17.84	15.26	15.22	9.915
Voice of America:				
MHz	15.12	11.58	9.775	5.995

PASSPORT/VISA

Regulations and requirements may be subject to change at short notice, and you are advised to contact the appropriate diplomatic or consular authority before finalising travel arrangements. Details of these may be found at the head of this country's entry. Any numbers in the chart refer to the footnotes below.

	Passport Required?	Visa Required?	Return Ticket Required?
Full British	Yes	No/1	Yes
BVP	Not valid	-	-
Australian	Yes	Yes	Yes
Canadian	Yes	Yes	Yes
USA	Yes	No/2	Yes
Other EU (As of 31/12/94)	Yes	1/2	Yes
Japanese	Yes	Yes	Yes

PASSPORTS: Valid passport required by all except holders of a 'Cedula de Identidad' issued to nationals of Argentina and Uruguay.
British Visitors Passport: Not acceptable.
VISAS: Required by all for touristic purposes except:
(a) **[1]** nationals of EU countries for a stay of 90 days (with the exception of nationals of France whose visas are valid for 30 days only);
(b) nationals of Austria and Switzerland for a period of 90 days;
(c) travellers in transit do not need a visa provided they are continuing their journey within 24 hours, do not leave the airport or stay overnight.
Notes: [2] Regulations regarding nationals of Argentina, Ecuador, Finland, Iceland, Ireland, Israel, Norway, Sweden, Uruguay, USA and Vatican City are currently under review. **[3]** All nationals travelling on business *do* need a Business visa.
Types of visa: Tourist, Business and Transit (not required for passengers in transit with onward tickets who do not leave the airport or stay overnight). Prices are available on application.
Validity: Tourist visas are valid for 30 or 90 days (depending on nationality) from the date of entry, Business visas are valid for one year.
Application to: Consulate (or Consular Section at Embassy). For addresses, see top of entry.
Application requirements: (a) 1 passport-size photograph (for Business visas a letter from subject's company should accompany application for visa). (b) Completed application form. (c) Passport with remaining validity of at least six months. (d) Fee.

Timatic

Health	
GALILEO/WORLDSPAN:	**TI-DFT/LPB/HE**
SABRE:	**TIDFT/LPB/HE**

Visa	
GALILEO/WORLDSPAN:	**TI-DFT/LPB/VI**
SABRE:	**TIDFT/LPB/VI**

For more information on Timatic codes refer to Contents.

Working days required: Tourist visas are issued immediately; for Business visas allow 7 days.
Temporary residence: Enquire at Bolivian Consulate.

MONEY

Currency: 1 Boliviano (B) = 100 centavos. The Boliviano is tied to the US Dollar. Notes are in denominations of B200, 100, 50, 20, 10, 5 and 2. Coins are in denominations of B2 and 1, and 50, 20, 10 and 5 centavos.
Note: The Bolivian peso ceased to be legal tender in 1990.
Currency exchange: Money is usually changed in hotels and *cambios*. Sterling *cannot* be changed. The decline in inflation over the past few years has been so dramatic that black market transactions have virtually ceased to exist.
Credit cards: Access/Mastercard, Diners Club, Visa and American Express have very limited acceptance. Check with your credit card company for details of merchant acceptability and other services which may be available.
Travellers cheques: US Dollar travellers cheques are probably the best form of currency to take to Bolivia at the present time. Sterling cheques *cannot* be exchanged.
Exchange rate indicators: The following figures are included as a guide to the movements of the Boliviano against Sterling and the US Dollar:

Date:	Oct '92	Sep '93	Jan '94	Jan '95
£1.00=	6.36	6.61	6.61	7.29
$1.00=	4.01	4.33	4.47	4.71

Currency restrictions: There are no restrictions on the import or the export of either local or foreign currency.
Banking hours: 0830-1130 and 1430-1830 Monday to Friday.

DUTY FREE

The following goods may be taken into Bolivia without incurring customs duty by persons aged 18 and over:
200 cigarettes and 50 cigars and 0.5kg of tobacco; 1 opened bottle of alcohol.
Note: Cameras must be declared.

PUBLIC HOLIDAYS

Jan 1 '95 New Year's Day. **Apr 14** Good Friday. **May 1** Labour Day. **Jun 15** Corpus Christi. **Aug 6** Independence Day. **Nov 1** All Saints' Day. **Dec 25** Christmas Day. **Jan 1 '96** New Year's Day. **Apr 5** Good Friday.
Note: There are other additional holidays celebrated in individual provinces and towns. For further details contact the Embassy or Tourist Board.

HEALTH

Regulations and requirements may be subject to change at short notice, and you are advised to contact your doctor well in advance of your intended date of departure. Any numbers in the chart refer to the footnotes below.

	Special Precautions?	Certificate Required?
Yellow Fever	Yes	1
Cholera	No	No
Typhoid & Polio	Yes	-
Malaria	2	-
Food & Drink	3	-

[1]: A yellow fever vaccination certificate is required from persons travelling to countries with infected local areas and from persons coming from such countries. All travellers going to Beni, Chuquisaca, Cochabamba, Pando, Tarija, part of the La Paz Department or Santa Cruz de la Sierra, Bolivia, must be in possession of a valid yellow fever certificate.
[2]: Malaria risk exists throughout the year below 2500m, excluding urban areas, Oruro Department, the provinces of Ingavi, Los Andes, Omasuyos, Pacajes (La Paz Dept), and Southern and Central Potosí Department. Resistance to chloroquine has been reported. The disease occurs predominantly in the benign *vivax* form.
[3]: Water used for drinking, brushing teeth or making ice should have first been boiled or otherwise sterilised. Milk is unpasteurised and should be boiled. Powdered or tinned milk is available and is advised, but make sure that it is reconstituted with pure water. Avoid all dairy products which are likely to have been made from unboiled milk. Only eat well-cooked meat and fish,

preferably served hot. Pork, salad and mayonnaise may carry increased risk. Vegetables should be cooked and fruit peeled.
Health care: Medical insurance is strongly recommended. All travellers, but especially those with heart conditions, should allow time to acclimatise to the high altitude of La Paz. In case of a medical emergency, La Paz has a good American clinic.

TRAVEL - International

AIR: The national airline is *Lloyd Aéreo Boliviano (LAB)*.
Approximate flight times: From London to *La Paz* is 17 hours and to *Santa Cruz* is 17 hours.
International airports: *La Paz (LPB)* (El Alto) is 14km (8.5 miles) from La Paz; and *Santa Cruz* (Viru-Viru) is 16km (10 miles) from the centre of Santa Cruz. For passengers arriving at La Paz, *LAB* provides a 24-hour coach service to the city every five minutes. The journey takes 20 minutes. Bus Z also goes to the city from 0600 to 2200, but the journey takes one hour. Taxis are also available to the city. Equivalent services exist for Santa Cruz. Restaurant and duty-free facilities are available at both airports.
Departure tax: US$20 is levied on all international departures (*this cannot be paid in Bolivian currency*).
SEA: Although it recently joined the International Maritime Organisation, Bolivia is wholly landlocked. However, European and US steamship companies serve the Atlantic and Pacific Coasts, navigating the Panama Canal, from which it is possible to reach ports in Peru, Chile, Brazil, Paraguay and Argentina and from there rail connections to La Paz or Santa Cruz. The nearest seaport is Arica in the extreme north of Chile.
LAKE: Steamers cross the lake to the Peruvian port of Puno from Guaqui, the most important port on Lake Titicaca. Situated 90km (56 miles) from La Paz, it is accessible both by road and rail, though generally services are slow.
RAIL: There is a twice-weekly connection from La Paz to Buenos Aires, and a twice-monthly connection to Arica (Chile). There is no service to Brazil via the line to Corumba. There is also a weekly train to Calama (Chile) with bus connections to Antofagasta.
ROAD: The Pan-American Highway which links the Argentine Republic with Peru crosses Bolivian territory from the south to the northwest. Driving in the rainy season may be hazardous. During recent years, much attention has been given to new roads, and the principal highways are now well maintained.

TRAVEL - Internal

AIR: Airlines operating internal flights are *LAB, TAM* (the army airline) and *Aero Xpress (AX)*. Because of the country's topography and tropical regions, air travel is the best method of transport. *La Paz (El Alto)*, which is the highest airport in the world, and *Santa Cruz (Viru-Viru)* are the chief internal airports.
Departure tax: Airport taxes for internal flights vary but are usually no more than US$3; it is advisable to check locally.
RIVER/LAKE: Passenger boats are operated between the various small islands on Lake Titicaca; most of them leave from Copacabana.
RAIL: Bolivia has 3538km (2199 miles) of track which goes to make up separate and unconnected networks in the eastern and western parts of the country. A daily through train or connection links La Paz and Cochabamba, with trains at least twice-weekly on other lines. Some trains have restaurant cars, but there are no sleeping-car services. The railways have recently renewed their rolling stock with Fiat railway carriages from Argentina. There are joint plans with the Brazilians to link Santa Cruz and Cochabamba.
ROAD: The internal road system covers 37,300km (23,178 miles). Work is in progress to improve the condition of major highways. Traffic drives on the right.
Bus: Long bus trips off the main routes can be erratic.
Taxi: All have fixed rates and sharing taxis is a common practice. Tipping is not necessary. **Car hire:** *Hertz* and local companies exist in La Paz. **Documentation:** An International Driving Permit is required. This can be issued by *Federación Inter-Americana de Touring y Automovil* on production of a national licence, but it is wiser to obtain the International Permit before departure.
URBAN: Bus services in La Paz are operated by a confederation of owner-operators. There are also some fixed route taxi 'Trufi' and 'Trufibus' systems which show coloured flags for particular routes. Fares are regulated.
JOURNEY TIMES: The following chart gives approximate journey times from La Paz (in hours and

minutes) to other major cities/towns in Bolivia.

	Air	Road	Rail
Cochabamba	0.25	6.00	7.00
Santa Cruz	0.50	24.00	-
Tarija	1.00	18.00	-
Sucre	0.35	11.00	13.00
Potosí	0.40	12.00	12.00
Beni	0.35	-	-

ACCOMMODATION

It is important to arrive in La Paz as early as possible in the day as accommodation, particularly at the cheaper end of the market, can be hard to find.
HOTELS: Bolivia has several deluxe and first-class hotels. Service charges and taxes amounting to 25-27% are added to bills. Rates are for room only, except where otherwise indicated. There is a wide range of cheap hotel accommodation available, generally of good value. Bolivia's hotel association is the Cámera Boliviana de Hotelería, PO Box 12827, Oficina 1705, Piso 17, Edificio Mcal. Ballivián, Calle Mercado, La Paz. Tel: (2) 353 733 *or* 350 129. Fax: (2) 350 129.
GUEST-HOUSES: Several pensions in La Paz, Cochabamba and Santa Cruz provide the tourist with reasonable comfort at a reasonable price.
CAMPING/CARAVANNING: There are few camping areas anywhere in South America. However, the adventurous traveller may often find adequate lodging for the small fee usually charged at most American or European camping grounds. Despite no formal organisation or marked zones, camping is possible in Bolivia. Mallasa, Valencia and Palca in the river gorge below the suburb of La Florida are recommended, also Chinguihue, 10km (6 miles) from the city. Club Andino Boliviano (tel: (7) 940 160) hires equipment. For details contact the Dirección Nacional de Turismo (for address, see top of entry).

RESORTS & EXCURSIONS

La Paz, the seat of national government, is situated 3632m (11,910ft) above sea level and is the world's highest capital city. Mount Illimani stands in the background. The city contains many museums and is well provided with modern and comfortable hotels. Nearby attractions include *Lake Titicaca*, the *Yungas valleys*, the *Chacaltaya* skiing resort and the exceptional rock formations in the Moon Valley.
Cochabamba, known as the garden city, is 2558m (8390ft) above sea level and boasts a long tradition of local culture and folklore.
The state of **Santa Cruz** is rich in natural resources; the city itself, despite considerable modernisation, still retains much of its colonial past. This region is also rich in tradition and folklore. There are abundant opportunities for fishing and hunting, and many natural bathing places. The area's rich cuisine is also to be sampled.
Potosí is known as the imperial city and is situated at the foot of the famous *Rich Mountain*, characteristic for its mineral wealth. In early colonial times, Potosí was the most important and highly populated city on the continent, and is now one of its greatest historical memorials. The *House of Coins* is just one example of this.
Oruro is a traditional mining centre, and preserver of many relics of a colonial past. Every year one can witness one of the most extraordinary and faithful expressions of folklore in South America during the famous carnival (February/March).
Sucre, in the state of Chuquisaca, played an important part in the struggle for independence, and is rich in museums, libraries and historical archives. Among the most important are the *Cathedral Museum*, the *National Library*, the *Colonial Museum*, the *Anthropological Museum*, the *Natural History Museum* and the *Recoleta Convent*.
Tarija stands 1957m (6480ft) above sea level. The area enjoys an excellent climate, and is festive and hospitable. Graced with beautiful flowers and magnificent wines, Tarija is the ideal place for finding peace and quiet.
The states of **Beni** and **Pando**, situated in the heart of the Bolivian jungle, occupy a region which offers the visitor landscapes of warmth and colour. The 'Golden' Pantiti with many navigable rivers is a popular place for excursions by both land and water. Good hunting and fishing are also possible in the region. The major towns in the area are **Trinidad** and **Cobija**.

SOCIAL PROFILE

FOOD & DRINK: Bolivian food is distinctive and is generally good. National dishes include *empanada saltena* (a mixture of diced meat, chicken, chives,

WORLD TRAVEL ATLAS

As well as a complete set of conventional plates, the World Travel Atlas contains a wealth of specialist maps and charts designed specifically for use by the travel trade and students of travel and tourism.

The only atlas of its kind, the World Travel Atlas has quickly established itself as an essential reference work for all those connected with the world of travel.

Caribbean Resorts • World Cruise Routes • Spanish Resorts • World Climate • World Natural and Cultural Heritage Maps • World Health • World Driving • Italian Resorts • International Tourism Statistics • Main Airports of the World • Greek Islands • UK & Mediterranean clean beaches

Call Columbus Press for further details on (0171) 417 0700 or fax (0171) 417 0710.

COLUMBUS PRESS

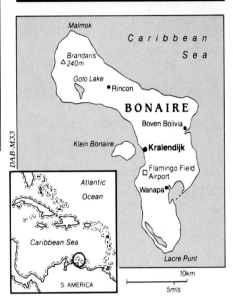

Bonaire

raisins, diced potatoes, hot sauce and pepper baked in dough), *lomo montado* (fried tenderloin steak with two fried eggs on top, rice and fried banana), *picante de pollo* (southern fried chicken, fried potatoes, rice, tossed salad with hot peppers), *chuno* (naturally freeze-dried potato used in soup called *chairo*) and *lechon al homo* (young roast pig served with sweet potato and fried plantains). International- and local-style restaurants are available in La Paz and other main towns. **Drink:** Bolivian beer, especially *cruzena,* is one of the best on the continent. *Chica,* made from fermented cereals and corn, is very strong. Mineral water and bottled drinks are available. Local bars are increasing in numbers and are unrestricted with no licensing hours.

NIGHTLIFE: La Paz has many nightclubs, which generally open around midnight. There are also numerous *whiskeria,* local bars. On Fridays and Saturdays there are folk music and dancing shows, which start late evening. Cochabamba and Santa Cruz have several discotheques.

SHOPPING: Special purchases include woodcarvings, jewellery, llama and alpaca blankets, Indian handicrafts and gold and silver costume jewellery. **Shopping hours:** 0900-1200 and 1400-1800 Monday to Friday; 0900-1200 some Saturdays.

SPORT: Football is the most popular spectator sport. **Golf, hunting, mountain climbing** and **safaris** are available. The best months for **skiing** are April, May, September and October. Bolivia has the highest ski run in the world at 5486m (18,000ft) on Mount Chacaltaya. Bolivia also boasts some of the best **lake fishing** in the world, especially for trout.

SPECIAL EVENTS: The following list is a selection of some of the events celebrated in Bolivia in 1995/96. In many places a festival is associated with a local holiday. For further details consult the Embassy or Tourist Board. **Mar '95** *Pujllay Carnival,* Tarabuco. **May** *Fiesta de la Cruz* (Feast of the Cross), Achocalla and Copacabana. **May/Jun** *Gran Poder Festival,* La Paz. **Jun 24** *San Juan Carnival,* La Paz and many other cities and communities. **Jun 28-29** *San Pedro,* Achacachi, Curva, Carabuco, Tiquina and many other villages. **Jul 25** *The Feast of Santiago.* **Sep** *Festival of Madonna of Urkupina,* Cochabamba. **Late Jan '96** *The Alasitas Fair of Miniatures,* La Paz. **Feb 17** *Carnival,* Oruro. **Mar** *Pujllay Carnival,* Tarabuco.

SOCIAL CONVENTIONS: Normal social courtesies in most Bolivian families and respect for traditions should be observed. Remember to refer to rural Bolivians as *campesinos* rather than Indians, which is considered an insult. Western dress and diet are gradually being adopted by the *campesinos* (although further to the north great poverty remains); a suit and tie for men and dress for women should be worn for smart social occasions. Casual wear is otherwise suitable. Smoking is accepted except where indicated. **Tipping:** It is customary to add 10% as a tip to the 13% service charge added to hotel and restaurant bills. Porters also expect tips of B4 for each piece of luggage.

BUSINESS PROFILE

ECONOMY: Bolivia has the second lowest per capita income in Latin America, despite having large mineral deposits of natural gas, petroleum, lead, antimony, tungsten, gold and silver. The most important mineral, however, is tin, of which Bolivia is one of the world's leading producers. Falling world prices and inherent economic difficulties throughout the 1980s resulted in a net fall in real incomes for most Bolivians. Agriculture is

the other major employer, but suffers from relatively low productivity. During the early 1980s, Bolivia suffered extremely high inflation, vastly fluctuating exchange rates and an ever-worsening overseas debt. The mid-1980s brought a marked improvement in national economic performance and the country has since consistently returned healthy growth rates. However, political uncertainty and Bolivia's poor international image have restricted foreign investment which is essential for significant economic progress. Poor communications also continue to hamper trade. Oil and gas account for 60% of export earnings; minerals and coffee account for the majority of the rest. There is a substantial unregistered and illegal trade in coca, the plant source for cocaine, which provides a livelihood for many peasants, although the Government has officially cooperated with the United States in a major continent-wide campaign to eradicate it. Bolivia is a member of the Latin American Integration Association, the River Plate Basin Alliance and, most importantly, of the Andean Pact. Joint ventures through these various organisations, such as the gas pipeline to Brazil, seem to offer the best prospects for Bolivia's future economic development. The country's largest trading partners are neighbouring Brazil, Argentina and Chile along with the USA, and then Japan and the EU countries. Of the latter, Britain has one of smallest volumes of trade. To reverse this trend, the UK and Bolivia have signed a bilateral investment promotion and protection agreement.

BUSINESS: Suit or a shirt and tie should be worn. Prior appointments are not essential. **Office hours:** 0800-1200 and 1400-1800 Monday to Friday; 0900-1200 some Saturdays.

COMMERCIAL INFORMATION: The following organisation can offer advice: Cámara Nacional de Comercio, Casilla 7, Avenida Mariscal Santa Cruz 1392, La Paz. Tel: (2) 354 255. Fax: (2) 391 004. Telex: 2305.

CLIMATE

Temperate climate but with wide differences between day and night. Wettest period is November to February. The northeast slopes of the Andes are semi-tropical. Visitors often find La Paz uncomfortable because of the thin air due to high altitude. The mountain areas can become very cold at night.

Required clothing: Lightweight linens with a raincoat. A light overcoat is necessary at night, particularly in the Altiplano and the Puna.

Location: Caribbean, 80km (50 miles) north of Venezuela.

Bonaire Government Tourist Board
Kaya Simon Bolivar 12, Kralendijk, Bonaire, Netherlands Antilles
Tel: 8322. Fax: 8408. Telex: 1292.
Office of the Minister Plenipotentiary of the Netherlands Antilles
Badhuisweg 173-175, 2597 JP The Hague, The Netherlands
Tel: (70) 351 2811. Fax: (70) 351 2722. Telex: 31161.
Promotion Corporation Bonaire
Visseringlaan 24, 2288 ER Rijswijk, The Netherlands
Tel: (70) 395 4444. Fax: (70) 336 8333.
The British Consulate in Curaçao deals with enquiries relating to Bonaire (see *Curaçao* later in this book).
Tourism Corporation Bonaire
Suite 900, 10 Rockefeller Plaza, New York, NY 10020
Tel: (212) 956 5911. Fax: (212) 956 5913.

AREA: 288 sq km (111 sq miles).
POPULATION: 11,139 (1991 estimate).
POPULATION DENSITY: 38.7 per sq km.
CAPITAL: Kralendijk. **Population:** 1700.
GEOGRAPHY: Bonaire is the second-largest island of the Antilles in the Dutch Caribbean. The landscape is flat and rocky and, due to low annual rainfall, fairly barren. The island has beautiful beaches and safe waters.
LANGUAGE: Dutch is the official language. Papiamento (a mixture of Portuguese, African, Spanish, Dutch and English) is the commonly used *lingua franca.* English and Spanish are also widely spoken.
RELIGION: Predominantly Roman Catholic with a Protestant minority. There are many evangelical churches of different denominations.
TIME: GMT - 4.
ELECTRICITY: 110-130volts AC, 50Hz.
COMMUNICATIONS: Telephone: IDD is available.

La Paz
(elevation: 3632m)

Temperature | **Rainfall**

MAXIMUM / MINIMUM

Humidity (%)

	Jan	Feb	Mar	Apr	May	June	July	Aug	Sept	Oct	Nov	Dec
	68	71	65	56	49	42	40	47	56	53	55	65

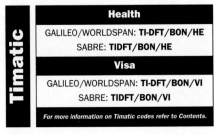

Health
GALILEO/WORLDSPAN: **TI-DFT/BON/HE**
SABRE: **TIDFT/BON/HE**

Visa
GALILEO/WORLDSPAN: **TI-DFT/BON/VI**
SABRE: **TIDFT/BON/VI**

For more information on Timatic codes refer to Contents.

Timatic

Country code: 5997. Outgoing international code: 00.
Telex/telegram: Facilities are available in the post office in Kralendijk and main hotels. **Post:** Airmail to and from Europe takes four to six days. Surface mail takes up to six weeks. **Press:** The *Beurs en Nieuwsberichten* is published in Dutch.
BBC World Service and Voice of America frequencies: From time to time these change. See the section *How to Use this Book* for more information.
BBC:

MHz	15.26	11.75	9.915	5.975

Voice of America:

MHz	15.20	11.91	9.590	5.995

PASSPORT/VISA

Regulations and requirements may be subject to change at short notice, and you are advised to contact the appropriate diplomatic or consular authority before finalising travel arrangements. Details of these may be found at the head of this country's entry. Any numbers in the chart refer to the footnotes below.

	Passport Required?	Visa Required?	Return Ticket Required?
Full British	1	No/4/5	Yes
BVP	Valid/1	-	-
Australian	Yes	4	Yes
Canadian	3	4	Yes
USA	2	4	Yes
Other EU (As of 31/12/94)	1	4/5	Yes
Japanese	Yes	4	Yes

PASSPORTS: Valid passport required by all except:
(a) **[1]** nationals of Belgium, Luxembourg and The Netherlands holding a tourist card, nationals of Germany holding an identity card and UK nationals holding a British Visitors Passport;
(b) **[2]** nationals of the USA holding voters' registration cards or birth certificate, and alien residents of the USA with acceptable documentation;
(c) **[3]** nationals of Canada with birth certificates or proof of citizenship;
(d) nationals of San Marino holding a national ID card.
(e) nationals and alien residents of Venezuela and travellers in Venezuela visiting the Netherlands Antilles holding an identity card.
VISAS: **[4]** Visas are only required for nationals of the Dominican Republic resident there. All other nationals are allowed to stay in Bonaire for 14 days without a visa (but might need a Certificate of Admission, see below) provided they have a return or onward ticket. All visitors staying more than 90 days require a visa. Transit passengers staying no longer than 24 hours holding confirmed tickets and valid passports do not require visas or Certificates of Admission.
For stays of between 14 and 28 days a **Temporary Certificate of Admission** is required, which in the case of the following countries will be issued by the Immigration authorities on arrival in Bonaire:
(a) **[5]** nationals of Belgium, Germany, Luxembourg, The Netherlands, Spain and the UK;
(b) nationals of Bolivia, Burkina Faso, Chile, Colombia, Costa Rica, Czech Republic, Ecuador, Hungary, Israel, Jamaica, South Korea, Malawi, Mauritius, Niger, The Philippines, Poland, San Marino, Slovak Republic, Swaziland and Togo.
The following must apply in writing, *before* entering the country even for tourist purposes, for a Certificate of Admission: nationals of Albania, Bosnia-Hercegovina, Bulgaria, Cambodia, China, CIS, Croatia, Cuba, Estonia, Georgia, North Korea, Latvia, Libya, Lithuania, Former Yugoslav Republic of Macedonia, Romania, Vietnam, Yugoslavia (Serbia and Montenegro) and holders of Zimbabwe passports issued on or after November 11, 1965. All other nationals have to apply for the Certificate after 14 days of stay. Further information about visa requirements may be obtained from the Office of the Minister Plenipotentiary of the Netherlands Antilles; and whilst Royal Netherlands Embassies do not formally represent the Netherlands Antilles in any way, they might also be able to offer limited advice and information. For addresses, see top of this entry and top of *The Netherlands* entry.
Temporary residence: Enquire at the Office of the Minister Plenipotentiary of the Netherlands Antilles.

MONEY

Currency: Netherlands Antilles Guilder or Florin (NAG) = 100 cents. Notes are in the denominations of NAG500, 250, 100, 50, 25, 10 and 5. Coins are in the denominations of NAG2.5 and 1; and 50, 25, 10, 5 and 1 cents. The currency is tied to the US Dollar.
Credit cards: Access/Mastercard, American Express, Diners and Visa are accepted in large establishments. Check with your credit card company for details of merchant acceptability and other available services.
Travellers cheques: US-currency cheques are the most welcome at points of exchange.
Exchange rate indicators: The following figures are included as a guide to the movement of the Netherlands Antilles Florin against Sterling and the US Dollar:

Date:	Oct '92	Sep '93	Jan '94	Jan '95
£1.00=	2.83	2.73	2.64	2.77
$1.00=	1.78	1.79	1.79	1.79

Currency restrictions: The import and export of local currency is limited to NAG200; foreign currency is unlimited. The import of Dutch or Suriname silver coins is forbidden.
Banking hours: 0830-1200 and 1330-1630 Monday to Friday.

DUTY FREE

The following items may be imported into Bonaire without incurring customs duty:
400 cigarettes or 50 cigars or 250g of tobacco; 2 litres of alcoholic beverages; 250 ml of perfume; gifts to a value of NAG100.

PUBLIC HOLIDAYS

Jan 1 '95 New Year's Day. **Feb 27** Lenten Carnival. **Apr 14** Good Friday. **Apr 17** Easter Monday. **Apr 30** Queen's Day. **May 1** Labour Day. **May 25** Ascension Day. **Sep 6** Bonaire Day. **Dec 25-26** Christmas. **Jan 1 '96** New Year's Day. **Feb 19** Lenten Carnival. **Apr 5** Good Friday. **Apr 8** Easter Monday. **Apr 30** Queen's Day.

HEALTH

Regulations and requirements may be subject to change at short notice, and you are advised to contact your doctor well in advance of your intended date of departure. Any numbers in the chart refer to the footnotes below.

	Special Precautions?	Certificate Required?
Yellow Fever	No	1
Cholera	No	No
Typhoid & Polio	2	-
Malaria	No	-
Food & Drink	3	-

[1]: A yellow fever certificate is required from travellers over six months of age coming from infected areas.
[2]: Polio and Typhoid are not endemic in Bonaire; however, precautions are advised as a few areas of risk exist within the general region of the Caribbean.
[3]: All mains water on the island is distilled from seawater, and is thus safe to drink. Bottled mineral water is widely available. Milk is pasteurised and dairy products are safe for consumption. Local meat, poultry, seafood, fruit and vegetables are generally considered safe to eat.
Mosquitoes may be a nuisance at certain times of year (mainly early to mid-summer and early to mid-winter) but present no serious hazard. Insect repellant will be useful.
Health care: The St Francis Hospital has 60 beds.

TRAVEL - International

AIR: The national airline of the Netherlands Antilles is *ALM (LM)*. KLM also offers daily flights from Amsterdam to Curaçao with connections to Bonaire.
Approximate flight times: From Bonaire to *London* is 11 hours, to *Los Angeles* is 10 hours and to *New York* is 4 hours. Times vary considerably depending on connections.
International airport: *Flamingo Field (BON)* is 6km (3.5 miles) from Kralendijk.
Departure tax: Approximately NAG20 (US$10) for passengers over two years of age on international flights; US$6 for inter-Caribbean flights.
SEA: Some good connections to Venezuela and other islands, including the boat to Curaçao and other frequent connections to Aruba.

TRAVEL - Internal

ROAD: A good **taxi** service exists on the island. Rates are government-controlled. There are numerous **car hire** firms located at hotels, the airport and the capital city. Bikes and motorbikes can also be hired without any difficulty. Traffic drives on the right. Roads are reasonably good, although jeeps may be needed for extensive touring of the island. **Documentation:** A national driving licence is acceptable, but drivers must be over 18 years of age.

ACCOMMODATION

HOTELS: There are some large, international-standard hotels on the island with good facilities for the holidaymaker, particularly in the provision of watersports equipment etc. Advanced booking is essential. For further information, contact the Bonaire Hotel and Tourism Association in Kralendijk.
GUEST-HOUSES: The visitor can opt for accommodation in beach villas or private bungalows. Various property companies can be contacted – enquire at the Government Tourist Board (address above).
Note: Rates for accommodation will be cheaper in the off-peak season (April 15-December 20).

RESORTS & EXCURSIONS

Bonaire is a place of rest and privacy. The island is ideal for those who want to enjoy a beautiful coastline and the full range of watersports facilities but don't demand too much by way of sophisticated restaurants and nightspots. Bonaire's *Marine Park* is centred on a spectacular coral reef, which is maintained and protected throughout the year by marine experts. There are frequent slide shows on underwater sports and conservation in the hotels and at watersports centres in Kralendijk.
The salt flats change colour according to fluctuations in the resident algae population, from a breathtaking fuchsia to subtle pink. Slave huts nearby were inhabited by the salt workers until the abolition of slavery in 1863. The beautiful lagoon of *Goto Meer* is a haven for flocks of flamingoes. Bonaire has its own 13,500-acre game reserve, the *Washington/Slagbaai National Park*, including *Mount Brandaris*, the island's highest point at 308m (784ft). There are two routes through the park, each enabling the visitor to see the interesting flora and fauna the island has to offer, in particular the birdlife. In **Kralendijk** itself there are several sites worth visiting, including the lively and architecturally interesting *Fish Market*, or the fruit and vegetable market. There are some handsome buildings along the waterfront, such as *Fort Oranje*.

SOCIAL PROFILE

FOOD & DRINK: The restaurants serve predominantly Creole cooking, particularly seafood dishes, including pickled conch shell meat, grilled spicy fish and lobster. Island specialities include Iguana soup and turtle dishes. A wider variety of Chinese, Indonesian, French, Italian and international cooking can also be found. There are many hotels, restaurants and bars in Kralendijk to choose from. Restaurants and bars are usually closed by midnight.
NIGHTLIFE: This is centred on both the main hotels and restaurants. Having eaten, evening entertainment includes dancing or listening to reggae groups or calypso steel bands. The island has two discos and a casino.
SHOPPING: The reductions on duty-free imports make the purchase of some perfume, jewellery or alcohol well worthwhile. **Shopping hours:** 0800-1200 and 1400-1800 Monday to Saturday.
SPORT: **Watersports** predominate, and for almost every visitor will form the central part of any holiday. **Scuba diving, snorkelling, windsurfing** and **water-skiing** are all available with facilities and tuition as necessary. The waters round the island are clear, safe and teeming with fish of every size and hue. **Fishing** and **sailing** charters are popular; half- or full-day cruises can be arranged round the bay or Klein Bonaire, the isle's tiny uninhabited sister island. Every October there is a sailing regatta during which there is a carnival atmosphere on the island. The focus of the regatta is the new marina, just a few minutes out of Kralendijk: berthing facilities for various types of vessel, a shipyard, and a drydock make Bonaire a pleasure boater's retreat. The main hotels and sporting centres on

the island also have **tennis**, **squash** and **golf** facilities.
SPECIAL EVENTS: Feb '95 *Carnival.* **Apr 23-30**
Great Underwater Video Challenge. **Sep 6** *Bonaire Day
Celebrations.* **Oct 10-15** *Sailing Regatta.*
For further details consult the Tourist Board (address
above).
SOCIAL CONVENTIONS: Dutch customs are still
prevalent throughout the islands, although they are
increasingly subject to an American influence. Dress is
casual and lightweight cottons are advised. Bathing
suits should be confined to beach and poolside areas
only. It is common to dress up in the evening. **Tipping:**
Hotels add a 5-10% government tax and 10% service
charge. Tipping is not usually required. There is
normally a 10% service charge in restaurants.

BUSINESS PROFILE

ECONOMY: During the 1950s, Bonaire began a gradual
climb out of chronic economic depression, aided by
investment in tourism and the reactivation of a long-
dormant salt industry. The economy gained a further
boost in the mid-1970s when the Bonaire Petroleum
Corporation (BOPEC) set up an oil transfer depot, a
deep-water port with facilities for transferring oil from
ocean-going to coastal tankers. Falling oil prices in
recent years have badly affected all islands in the
Netherlands Antilles, once regarded as among the most
affluent in the Caribbean. Oil-related industries have not
turned in a profit since 1979 and plans to build a refinery
in Bonaire have been indefinitely shelved. The growing
practice of transhipping oil whilst still at sea has crippled
its land-based transfer industry. All the islands have
responded by investing further in tourism, legislating to
create tax advantages for overseas investors, and by
encouraging agriculture.
BUSINESS: General business practices prevail. **Office
hours:** 0800-1200 and 1400-1830 Monday to Friday.
COMMERCIAL INFORMATION: The following
organisation can offer advice: Bonaire Chamber of
Commerce and Industry, PO Box 52, Kaya Princesa
Marie, 8 Kralendijk. Tel: 5595. Fax: 8995.

CLIMATE

Hot throughout the year, but tempered by cooling trade
winds. The main rainy season is from October to
December.
Required clothing: Lightweights with warmer top layers
for evenings; showerproofs are advisable throughout the
year.

TEMPERATURE CONVERSIONS

-20	-10	0°C	10	20	30	40

| 0 | 10 | 20 | 30°F40 | 50 | 60 | 70 | 80 | 90 | 100 |

RAINFALL 0mm 200 400 600 800
CONVERSIONS 0In 5 10 15 20 25 30

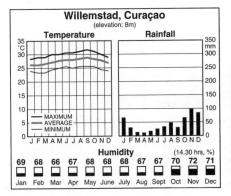

Willemstad, Curaçao
(elevation: 8m)

Humidity (14.30 hrs, %)

Jan	Feb	Mar	Apr	May	June	July	Aug	Sept	Oct	Nov	Dec
69	68	66	67	68	68	68	67	67	70	72	71

Bosnia-Hercegovina

Location: Ex-Yugoslav republic, southeastern Europe.

Note: The EU, Canada and the USA recognised Bosnia-
Hercegovina in April 1992. However, there is no UK or
Canadian diplomatic presence in Sarajevo. The nearest
embassies are in Belgrade, whose authorities do not
recognise the Republic of Bosnia-Hercegovina. The
latter's foreign ministry does not have any official
diplomatic presence in London or Canada. The US State
Department and the Foreign Office both advise against
all travel to Bosnia-Hercegovina.
*Source: US State Department – August 10, 1994;
Foreign Office – November 29, 1994.*

Ministry of Foreign Affairs
Vojvode Putnika 3, 71000 Sarajevo, Bosnia-Hercegovina
Tel: (71) 213 777. Fax: (71) 653 592.
Foreign & Commonwealth Office (Yugoslav Desk)
Tel: (0171) 270 4125/9 or 270 3000 (switchboard). Fax:
(0171) 270 4134.
**Exports Credit Guarantee Department (Country
Policy Desk)**
Tel: (0171) 512 7000. Fax: (0171) 512 7649.
Note: All the former Yugoslav republics, including
Bosnia-Hercegovina, are off cover for medium- and
long-term insurance according to ECGD policy. Short-
term cover is now only available from private sector
insurers, who will not involve themselves in so risky an
area as Bosnia-Hercegovina.
Embassy of the Republic of Bosnia-Hercegovina
Suite 760, 1707 L Street, NW, Washington, DC 20036
Tel: (212) 833 3612/3 or 833 3615. Fax: (212) 833 2061.
Embassy of the United States of America
Djure Djakovica 43, Sarajevo, Bosnia-Hercegovina
Tel: (71) 659 992.
This Embassy may not be staffed at all times.
**The US Embassy in Vienna deals with enquiries
relating to Bosnia-Hercegovina (see** *Austria* **earlier in
the book).**

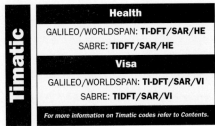

Health
GALILEO/WORLDSPAN: **TI-DFT/SAR/HE**
SABRE: **TIDFT/SAR/HE**

Visa
GALILEO/WORLDSPAN: **TI-DFT/SAR/VI**
SABRE: **TIDFT/SAR/VI**

For more information on Timatic codes refer to Contents.

AREA: 51,129 sq km (19,736 sq miles), 20% of the
territory of the former Yugoslav federation (its third-
largest republic).
POPULATION: 4,364,574 (1991), 19% of the total
population of the former Yugoslav federation (its third-
most populous republic).
POPULATION DENSITY: 85.4 per sq km.
CAPITAL: Sarajevo. **Population:** 415,631 (1991).
GEOGRAPHY: Roughly triangular in shape, and the
geopolitical centre of the former Yugoslav federation,
Bosnia-Hercegovina shares borders with Serbia and
Montenegro in the east and southeast, and Croatia to the
north and west, with a short Adriatic coastline of 20km
(12 miles) in the southeast, but no ports.
LANGUAGE: Serbo-Croat (Serbs) and Croato-Serb
(Croats). The Croats and Slavic Muslims use the Latin
alphabet, whereas the Serbs use the Cyrillic.
RELIGION: 44% Slavic Muslims, 33% Serbian
Orthodox and 17% Roman Catholic Croats.
TIME: GMT + 1 (GMT + 2 from last Sunday in March
to Saturday before last Sunday in September).
ELECTRICITY: 220 volts AC, 50Hz.
COMMUNICATIONS: Telephone: Formally
internationally IDD-connected as part of the former
Yugoslav federation. Country code: 387. Outgoing
international code: 99.
Note: All telecommunications services, including
facsimile and telex, are now intermittent and uncertain
due to the civil war and the related partition of the
republic. This is also true of postal services, internal and
international, although Bosnia-Hercegovina is outside the
remit of the UN economic sanctions imposed against
Serbia and Montenegro in June 1992. **Press/Media:** The
main newspaper, *Oslobodjenje,* is still published in
Sarajevo. *RTV* is the only TV-radio station operating
locally on an intermittent basis. *CNN* is also available via
satellite in a number of Sarajevo hotels, notably the
Holiday Inn.
**BBC World Service and Voice of America
frequencies:** From time to time these change. See the
section *How to use this Book* for more information.
BBC:

MHz	15.07	12.09	9.410	6.195

Voice of America:

MHz	15.20	9.760	6.040	5.995

PASSPORT/VISA

*Regulations and requirements may be subject to change at short notice, and you
are advised to contact the appropriate diplomatic or consular authority before
finalising travel arrangements. Details of these may be found at the head of this
country's entry. Any numbers in the chart refer to the footnotes below.*

	Passport Required?	Visa Required?	Return Ticket Required?
Full British	1	1	1
BVP	1	1	1
Australian	1	1	1
Canadian	1	1	1
USA	1	1	1
Other EU (As of 31/12/94)	1	1	1
Japanese	1	1	1

[1] The civil war and the related partition of the republic
make legal border crossing and airport (Sarajevo) entry
impossible for all foreign nationals and should thus not
be attempted given the considerable dangers involved.

MONEY

Currency: Yugoslav Dinar (Yu D) = 100 paras; Croatian
Dinar (Cr D) = 100 paras. In the Serb-controlled areas,
only the Yugoslav Dinar is legal tender, while in Croat-
controlled areas only the Croatian Dinar is accepted. The
official Sarajevo government does not have the resources
to issue its own currency, having previously relied on old
Yugoslav Dinars prior to Belgrade's suspension of the
issuing of new Yugoslav Dinars in 1991. Due to
hyperinflation in all the former Yugoslav republics, the
only true repository of value and means of exchange
locally is the German Deutschmark. Pound Sterling is of
relatively little value in the republic and rarely used.
Normal banking services in the republic have broken
down.
Exchange rate indicators: The following figures are
included as a guide to the movements of the Yugoslav
Dinar and the Croatian Dinar against Sterling and the US
Dollar:

Date:	Sep '93	Jan '94
£1.00=	Yu D161/Cr D7357	*Yu D1.00/Cr D9727.90
$1.00=	Yu D105/Cr D4818	*Yu D0.68/Cr D6575.13

Note [*]: Due to extreme hyperinflation, the Yu D has
depreciated considerably.

HEALTH

Regulations and requirements may be subject to change at short notice, and you are advised to contact your doctor well in advance of your intended date of departure. Any numbers in the chart refer to the footnotes below.		
	Special Precautions?	**Certificate Required?**
Yellow Fever	No	No
Cholera	No	No
Typhoid & Polio	No	No
Malaria	No	-
Food & Drink	1	-

[1]: All water should be regarded as being potentially contaminated. Milk is unpasteurised and should be boiled. Avoid dairy products which are likely to have been made from unboiled milk. Only eat well-cooked meat and fish, preferably served hot. Pork, salad and mayonnaise may carry increased risk. Vegetables should be cooked and fruit peeled.
Rabies is present. For those at high risk, vaccination before arrival should be considered. If you are bitten abroad seek medical advice without delay. For more information consult the *Health* section at the back of the book.
Health care: Due to the ongoing fighting, medical services are extremely stretched and limited. Medical insurance with emergency repatriation is strongly advised.

TRAVEL - International

AIR: There is no national carrier, and no foreign carriers, including *JAT* (the Yugoslav national airline, itself grounded at Belgrade by UN economic sanctions since June 1992), providing services to Sarajevo.
Note: Present Foreign & Commonwealth Office advice is that all foreign nationals avoid Bosnia-Hercegovina.

TRAVEL - Internal

RAIL/ROAD: Roadblocks manned by local militias are numerous and relief goods and trucks are frequently confiscated at these points. As the entire republic is effectively a partitioned war zone at present, all internal routes are now off-limits to foreign nationals. Sarajevo is the nodal point for all the republic's main communications routes, which go west to Banja Luka, and then to Zagreb, capital of Croatia; north to Doboj, and then to Osijek in Croatia; east to Zvornik, and then to Belgrade; south to Mostar, and then the Adriatic Sea; and southeast to Foca, and then to Podgorica (formerly Titograd), capital of Montenegro.

ACCOMMODATION

With the notable exception of a few city centre hotels used by journalists in Sarajevo (notably the Holiday Inn), no services are presently available to foreign nationals throughout the republic.

SOCIAL PROFILE

FOOD & DRINK: The traditional cuisine of the region includes obvious Turkish influences. Specialities are *bosanski nonac* (Bosnian meat and vegetable stew) and *lokum* (Turkish delight) as well as *alva* (crushed nuts in honey).
SPORT: The well-known health spa Jahorina is also renowned for good **skiing**. The Adriatic Coast offers unrestricted **fishing**, although a special permit is needed for fishing in rivers and lakes with nets or traps. Sometimes visitors can go fishing with regional fishermen. Hotels and regional authorities issue fishing permits. The regulations differ in the individual regions; contact the authorities direct. **Football** is a national favourite.
SOCIAL CONVENTIONS: Previously one of the more traditional and stable areas of the former Yugoslav federation, Bosnia-Hercegovina is now its most dangerous territory where even foreign nationality or recognised neutral status can not guarantee safety.

BUSINESS PROFILE

ECONOMY: The third poorest and least economically developed of the former Yugoslav republics, Bosnia-Hercegovina accounted for only 12.7% of Yugoslavia's GDP in 1990-91 (approximately US$7 billion), with a GDP per capita of around US$1600 in the same year, on average US$1000 less than across the Federation. Now a predominantly agricultural economy, Bosnia-Hercegovina's traditional industrial base, concentrated on mining and capital goods, largely collapsed in 1991 as a direct result of the demise of the Yugoslav market. Apart from the latter, Bosnia-Hercegovina has always been marginal, accounting for only 10% of Yugoslav foreign trade in 1990-91. In the same year, as the Slavic Muslims and Croats moved to secede from Yugoslavia, the Belgrade government subjected the area to an economic blockade and renounced all responsibility for the republic's share of the former federation's foreign debt at about 15% of the total (US$2.5 billion), which meant that the official government in Sarajevo was internationally bankrupt even before civil war and partition in 1992 completely finished off the area economically. Consequently, despite being rich in certain natural resources, mainly coal and iron ore, plus immense hydroelectrical potential, the republic is now of no interest to foreign investors, creditors and traders as long as the present chaos continues. UK economic links with Bosnia-Hercegovina are reportedly virtually non-existent.
COMMERCIAL INFORMATION: It is presently unclear as to whether these institutions in Bosnia-Hercegovina are in fact functioning in any normal manner: Chamber of Economy of Bosnia-Hercegovina, Mis. Irbina 13, 71000 Sarajevo. Tel: (71) 211 777; *or* National Bank of Bosnia-Hercegovina, Marsala Tita 25, 71000 Sarajevo. Tel: (71) 33326.

CLIMATE

Dominated by mountainous and hilly terrain, and drained by major rivers to the north (Sava) and east (Drina), Bosnia-Hercegovina has a climate that is as variable as the rest of the former Yugoslav federation, with moderate continental climatic conditions generally the norm (very cold winters and hot summers).
Required clothing: In winter, heavyweight clothing and overcoat. In summer, lightweight clothing and raincoat required, with mediumweight clothing at times in the colder and wetter north, and at higher altitudes elsewhere.

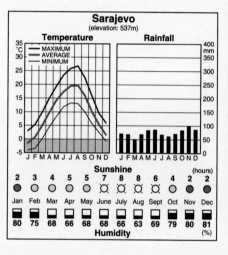

Botswana

Location: Central southern Africa.

Department of Tourism
Ministry of Commerce and Industry, Private Bag 0047, Gaborone, Botswana
Tel: 353 024 *or* 313 314. Fax: 308 675. Telex: 2674 (a/b BD).

Botswana High Commission
6 Stratford Place, London W1N 9AE
Tel: (0171) 499 0031. Fax: (0171) 495 8595. Telex: 262897 (a/b BOHICO). Opening hours: 0900-1700 Monday to Friday.

Botswana Embassy and Mission to the European Communities
169 avenue de Tervueren, B-1150 Brussels, Belgium
Tel: (2) 735 2070 *or* 735 6110. Fax: (2) 735 6318. Telex: 22849 (a/b BOTEUR).

British High Commission
Private Bag 0023, Gaborone, Botswana
Tel: 352 841/2/3. Fax: 356 105. Telex: 2370 (a/b UKREP GABORONE).

Embassy of the Republic of Botswana
Suite 7M, Intelsat Building, 3400 International Drive, NW, Washington, DC 20008
Tel: (202) 244 4990/1. Fax: (202) 244 4164.
Also deals with enquiries from Canada.

Embassy of the United States of America
PO Box 90, Gaborone, Botswana
Tel: 353 982. Fax: 356 947. Telex: 2554.

The Canadian High Commission in Harare deals with enquiries relating to Botswana (see *Zimbabwe* later in this book).

AREA: 582,000 sq km (224,711 sq miles).
POPULATION: 1,326,796 (1991).

POPULATION DENSITY: 2.3 per sq km.
CAPITAL: Gaborone. **Population:** 133,468 (1991).
GEOGRAPHY: Botswana is bordered by South Africa, Namibia, Zimbabwe and touches Zambia just west of the Victoria Falls. The tableland of the Kalahari Desert covers most of Botswana. National parks cover 17% of the country. To the northwest is the Okavango Basin, where the Moremi Wildlife Reserve and the Chobe National Park support abundant wildlife. To the far southwest is the Kalahari Gemsbok National Park. The majority of the population lives in the southeast around Gaborone, Serowe and Kanye along the South African border. The vast arid sandveld of the Kalahari occupies much of north, central and western Botswana. The seasonal rains bring a considerable difference to the vegetation, especially in the Makgadikgadi Pans and the Okavango Basin in the north. The latter, after the winter floods, provides one of the wildest and most beautiful nature reserves in Africa.
LANGUAGE: English is the official language. Setswana is the national language.
RELIGION: 85% Christian, 15% other religions.
TIME: GMT + 2.
ELECTRICITY: 220-240 volts AC, 50Hz. 15- and 13-amp plug sockets are in use.
COMMUNICATIONS: Telephone: IDD is available to over 80 countries. Country code: 267. Outgoing international code: 00. There are very few public phone boxes. **Fax:** Use of this service is increasing.
Telex/telegram: There are facilities in Gaborone and other major centres (usually in major hotels and main post offices). **Post:** Airmail service to Europe takes from one to three weeks. There are post offices in all the main towns, although there are no deliveries and post must be collected from boxes. **Press:** The daily newspaper is *The Dikgang Tsa Gompieno (Botswana Daily News),* published in Setswana and English. Periodical newspapers include *The Midweek Sun, Botswana Guardian, Mmegi Wa Dikgang, The Voice, Okavango Observer* and the *Botswana Gazette*.
BBC World Service and Voice of America frequencies: From time to time these change. See the section *How to Use this Book* for more information.

Okavango Delta scene

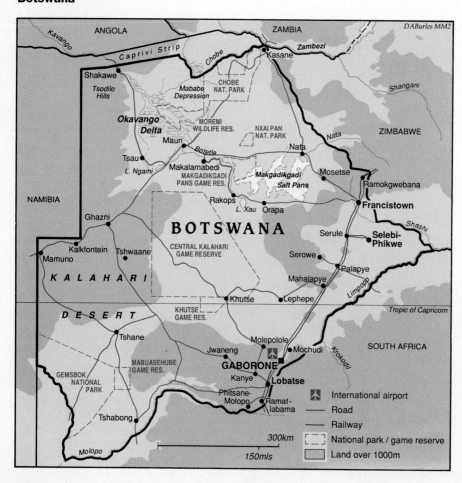

BBC:

| MHz | 21.66 | 11.94 | 6.190 | 3.255 |

Voice of America:

| MHz | 21.49 | 15.60 | 9.525 | 6.035 |

PASSPORT/VISA

Regulations and requirements may be subject to change at short notice, and you are advised to contact the appropriate diplomatic or consular authority before finalising travel arrangements. Details of these may be found at the head of this country's entry. Any numbers in the chart refer to the footnotes below.

	Passport Required?	Visa Required?	Return Ticket Required?
Full British	Yes	No	Yes
BVP	Not valid	-	-
Australian	Yes	No	No
Canadian	Yes	No	No
USA	Yes	No	No
Other EU (As of 31/12/94)	Yes	1	No
Japanese	Yes	No	Yes

PASSPORTS: Valid passport required by all. All passports must be valid for over 6 months.
British Visitors Passport: Not accepted.
VISAS: Required by all except nationals of the following countries:
(a) nationals referred to in the chart above;
(b) **[1]** nationals of EU countries (except nationals of Spain and Portugal who *do* require visas);
(c) nationals of Commonwealth countries (except nationals of Ghana, India, Mauritius, Nigeria, Pakistan and Sri Lanka who *do* require visas);
(d) nationals of Austria, Finland, Iceland, Liechtenstein, Norway, San Marino, South Africa, Sweden, Switzerland, Uruguay and Western Samoa.

Types of visa: General Entry visa; multiple or single.
Validity: Maximum of 90 days from the date of arrival.
Application to: Consulate (or Consular Section at Embassy or High Commission). For addresses, see top of entry.
Application requirements: (a) 2 completed application forms. (b) 2 passport-size photos. (c) £5 fee. (d) Passport valid for 6 months beyond length of stay.
Temporary residence: Anyone wishing to stay for more than 90 days should seek permission prior to travelling; contact The Chief Immigration Officer, PO Box 942, Gaborone, Botswana.

MONEY

Currency: Pula (P) = 100 thebe. Notes are in denominations of P100, 50, 20, 10 and 5. Coins are in denominations of P2 and P1, and 50, 25, 10, 5 and 1 thebe. Various gold and silver coins were issued to mark the country's 10th anniversary of independence, and are still legal tender.
Credit cards: Access/Mastercard, American Express, Diners Club and Visa are all accepted on a limited basis. Check with your credit card company for details of merchant acceptability and other services which may be available.
Exchange rate indicators: The following figures are included as a guide to the movements of the Pula against Sterling and the US Dollar:

Date:	Oct '91	Sep '93	Jan '94	Jan '95
£1.00=	3.70	3.79	3.79	4.19
$1.00=	2.13	2.48	2.57	2.71

Currency restrictions: Visitors may import local currency but export is limited to P500. There is no restriction on the import of foreign currency, but it should be registered with an authorised dealer if it is to be re-exported.
Banking hours: 0900-1430 Monday, Tuesday, Thursday and Friday; 0815-1200 Wednesday and 0815-1045 Saturday.

DUTY FREE

The following goods may be taken into Botswana without incurring any duty:
200 cigarettes and 50 cigars or 250g of tobacco; 2 litres of wine; 1 litre of alcoholic beverages; 50ml of perfume and 250ml of eau de toilette.

PUBLIC HOLIDAYS

Jan 1-2 '95 New Year. **Apr 14** Good Friday. **Apr 15** Easter Saturday. **Apr 17** Easter Monday. **May 25**
Ascension Day. **Jul 1** Sir Seretse Khama Day. **Jul 17** President's Day. **Jul 18** Public Holiday. **Sep 30** Botswana Day. **Oct 1** Public Holiday. **Dec 25** Christmas Day. **Dec 26** Boxing Day. **Dec 27** Public Holiday. **Jan 1-2 '96** New Year. **Apr 5** Good Friday. **Apr 6** Easter Saturday. **Apr 8** Easter Monday.

HEALTH

Regulations and requirements may be subject to change at short notice, and you are advised to contact your doctor well in advance of your intended date of departure. Any numbers in the chart refer to the footnotes below.

	Special Precautions?	Certificate Required?
Yellow Fever	No	-
Cholera	Yes	No
Typhoid & Polio	Yes	-
Malaria	Yes/1	-
Food & Drink	2	-

[1]: Malaria risk exists from November to May/June in the northern part of the country (Boteti, Chobe, Ngamiland, Okavango and Tutume districts/subdistricts), predominantly in the malignant *falciparum* form. A weekly dose of 300mg chloroquine plus a daily dose of 200mg proguanil is the recommended phrophylaxis.
[2]: Tap water is considered safe to drink, although drinking water outside main cities and towns may be contaminated and sterilisation is advisable. Milk is pasteurised and dairy products are safe for consumption. Local meat, poultry, seafood, fruit and vegetables are generally considered safe to eat.
Rabies is present. For those at high risk, vaccination before arrival should be considered. If you are bitten abroad seek medical advice without delay. For more information consult the *Health* section at the back of the book.
Bilharzia (schistosomiasis) is present. Avoid swimming and paddling in fresh water. Swimming pools which are well-chlorinated and maintained are safe.
Trypanosomiasis (sleeping sickness) is transmitted by tsetse flies in the Moremi Wildlife Reserve, Ngamiland and western parts of the Chobe National Park. Protective clothing and insect repellant are recommended.
Tick-bite fever can be a problem when walking in the bush. It is advisable to wear loose-fitting clothes and to search the body for ticks. The disease may be treated with tetracycline, though pregnant women and children under eight years of age should not take this medicine.
Health care: The dust and heat may cause a problem for asthmatics and people with allergies to dust. Those with sensitive skin should take precautions. Botswana's altitude, 1000m (3300ft) above sea level, reduces the filtering effect of the atmosphere. Hats and sunscreen are advised.
There are hospitals in Gaborone, Francistown, Kanye, Molepolole, Mochudi, Maun, Serowe, Mahalapye, Lobatse, Selebi-Phikwe, Ramotswa, Jwaneng and Orapa, but only poorly-equipped clinics in the remote villages. There are chemists in all main towns and pharmaceutical supplies are readily available.
Health insurance is essential. There is a government medical scheme and medicines supplied by government hospitals are free.

TRAVEL - International

AIR: The national airline is *Air Botswana (BP)* which only operates within Africa. *British Airways* flies direct to Gaborone twice-weekly from London.
Approximate flight time: From London to Gaborone is 15 hours (including stopovers).
International airport: *Seretse Khama International (GBE)*, 15km (9.5 miles) northwest of Gaborone. There are no regular bus services to and from the airport but the President Hotel, Oasis Motel and Gaborone Sun Hotel run minibuses (combis). Taxis are sometimes available to the city centre for approximately P20 (travel time – 45 minutes). Airport facilities include left luggage (0530-1800), bank, bar (0800-1830), snack bar (0800-1830), restaurant (0800-1830), post office (0800-1700), shops and car rental (*Avis* and *Hertz*).
A major new airport at *Kasane* (north Botswana) came into operation during 1991. A connecting flight, via an overnight stay in Gaborone, is available from *British Airways* twice a week.
See below for information on private charters to neighbouring countries.
RAIL: There are good connections between South Africa and Botswana (Johannesburg–Mafikeng–Ramatlhabama–Gaborone) and Botswana and Zimbabwe (Gaborone–Plumtree–Bulawayo–Harare). From Gaborone to Bulawayo takes 20 hours; passengers are advised to take their own food and drink as the buffet

THE OKAVANGO DELTA

is one of the largest inland deltas in the world, and also one of the world's greatest wildernesses – with some of the richest wildlife. A trip through the Moremi Game Reserve, in the eastern reaches of the Delta, takes you through a maze of waterways, lagoons and islands, where crocodiles, hippos, water monitors, elephants, lions, leopards, hyenas, giraffes, rare antelope and around 400 bird species live. Travel between the Reserve's comfortable camps and lodges is by boat, plane, four-wheel-drive or on horseback. Come on a perfect safari. Come to

BOTSWANA

DEPARTMENT OF TOURISM

Department of Tourism, Private Bag 0047, Gaborone. Tel: (+267) 353024. Fax: (+267) 308675. Telex: 2674 BD.

supply has a very limited range (mainly alcoholic). There are four classes, and sleeping compartments are available. First-class cars have comfortable reclining seats. Complicated formalities may be necessary for crossing the border from Zimbabwe and to or from South Africa, where the South African Customs Union agreement is in operation.

Botswana has assisted in the construction of the Limpopo line from Zimbabwe to Mozambique, an act which will speed up the availability of alternative routes into Botswana. Other plans include extending the network into Namibia.

ROAD: There are reasonable roads running roughly along the same routes as the railway, linking Botswana with South Africa and Zimbabwe.

TRAVEL - Internal

AIR: Major areas of the country are linked by air. There are airports in Francistown, Maun, Selebi-Phikwe, Ghanzi, Pont Drift and Kasane. There are two charter companies in Gaborone: *Kalahari Air Services* (PO Box 10102, Gaborone. Tel: 351 804, offering charters to Namibia, South Africa, Lesotho, Swaziland, Zimbabwe and Zambia; and *Okavango Air Services* (PO Box 1966, Gaborone. Tel: 313 308).

RAIL: There are rail links between Ramatlhabama, Lobatse, Gaborone, Palapye and Francistown. Work on upgrading and extending the rail network continues. In Botswana, children under seven travel free and children 7-11 pay half fare.

ROAD: Botswana has tarmac roads on the following routes: running from south to north from Lobatse to Francistown up to Ramokgwebana and from Lobatse to Kanye; running from Francistown to Kazungula via Nata; and running from Kanye to Jwaneng. There are over 2000km (1200 miles) of bitumised roads in the country. Others are either gravel or sand tracks. There are plans to construct a road network with more major highways. Reserve fuel and at least 20 litres of water should always be carried on journeys into more remote areas, and visitors are advised to make careful enquiries before setting out. **Bus:** There are bus services between Gaborone and Francistown, and from Francistown to Nata and Maun. The bus from Francistown to Maun runs three times a week leaving at around 1100. The journey takes 12-18 hours. There are no published timetables; further details can be obtained locally. Travel within major towns is by taxi. **Car hire:** Hire cars are available in Gaborone, Francistown or Maun. Four-wheel-drive vehicles are necessary in many areas. Traffic drives on the left and seat belts must be worn. It is advisable to keep the petrol tank at least half full as distances between towns can be long. There is a speed limit of 120kmph (75mph) outside built-up areas, and about 60kmph (37mph) in built-up areas. Speed limits are strongly enforced with high fines. **Documentation:** International Driving Permit is not legally required, but recommended for stays of up to six months; thereafter, a Botswana driving licence must be obtained, which will be issued without a test if a valid British licence is produced.

URBAN: There is no public transport within towns except shared taxi or minibus services operating at controlled flat fares. Exclusive use of taxis is sometimes available at a higher charge although fares should always be agreed on before setting off.

JOURNEY TIMES: The following chart gives approximate journey times from Gaborone (in hours and minutes) to other major cities and towns in Botswana.

	Air	Road	Rail
Francistown	0.50	5.00	6.35
Selebi-Phikwe	1.00	4.30	-
Jwaneng	-	1.30	-
Orapa	-	5.00	-
Lobatse	0.20	0.45	1.50
Maun	1.30	12.00	-
Kasane	2.50	13.30	-
Tshabong	2.00	15.00	-
Ghanzi	1.25	11.00	-

ACCOMMODATION

HOTELS: Although there is no grading system, all hotels generally maintain a reasonable standard, particularly those in main centres in the east of the country. The largest number of hotels and motels are in or near Gaborone (the President and the Sun Hotel being of international standard) and Francistown, some with air-conditioning, swimming pools and facilities for films, bands and discotheques. Most other hotels have fairly basic amenities, although there is a programme for improving facilities. Other towns with hotels and motels are Ghanzi, Kanye, Lobatse, Mahalapye, Maun, Molepolole, Palapye, Selebi-Phikwe, Serowe and Tuli Block.

Giraffe, Savuti

SAFARI LODGES & CAMPS: Varying standards and facilities are to be found in all the main centres and game reserves. These include Francistown, Kasane, Maun, the Okavango Delta, the western Chobe National Park, the Moremi Wildlife Reserve and Tuli Block. Facilities vary greatly; some are merely campsites with ablution blocks, and can be very reasonably priced, while others consist of luxury groups of chalets or cottages complete with swimming pools, cinemas, conference rooms and shops. Some, such as the Tsaro and Xugana Lodges in the Okavango Delta, are hired out as one unit to groups of six. Others, such as Lloyd's Camp in western Chobe and Nxamaseri Camp in the Okavango Delta, provide accommodation in luxury safari tents. Many of these camps are able to hire out equipment and boats, and offer experienced guides.

CAMPING: There are organised campsites at some hotels in the Okavango and Chobe areas. Visitors may camp beside the road. Permission should be sought before camping on private land. Grass fires should not be started, and all litter should be buried or removed. The presence of lions in some of the more remote areas makes it advisable to exercise extreme care.

A booklet entitled *Where To Stay In Botswana*, giving details of prices and facilities, may be obtained from the Department of Tourism (see top of entry for address). The following is an umbrella organisation comprising hotels and lodges, travel agents and tour operators, airlines, and hunters: The Hotel and Tourism Association of Botswana (HATAB), Private Bag 00423, Gaborone. Tel: 357 144. Fax: 303 201.

RESORTS & EXCURSIONS
Gaborone

The capital is situated in the southeast of the country. There is an excellent *National Museum* open from 0900-1800 Monday to Friday and 0900-1700 weekends, with natural history and ethnological exhibitions. As well as permanent displays, there are also temporary exhibitions

Lilac-breasted roller

and various symposia and conferences. The visitor will find *Sites of Historic and Natural Interest In and Around Gaborone* a useful pamphlet. Gaborone has several good bookshops and libraries, including the University of Botswana Library which has a 'Botswana Room' devoted solely to publications on the country. There are good craft shops and markets in the town, where pottery, basketwork, leatherwork and handwoven objects may be bought.

Excursions: Nearby is the *Gaborone Dam*, a centre for watersports, and day trips can be made to see local crafts at *Oodi, Thamaga* and *Pilane*. A trip to the weaving centre at **Lentswe-La-Odi**, just north of Gaborone, is especially recommended. Local craftwork can be bought here at a fraction of its cost in the big cities. The centre is a non-profitmaking organisation, with proceeds going back to the craftspeople. **Mochudi**, also north of Gaborone, is the regional capital of the Kgableng tribe and has an interesting museum (the *Phuthadikobo Museum*) which chronicles the history of the Kgableng people in fascinating detail. **Serowe,** located even further north of Gaborone on the way to Francistown, is one of the largest villages in Botswana and seat of the Bangwato tribe. The *Khama III Memorial Museum,* located in the Red House at the base of a hill in the village, has memorabilia of the Khama Family, the family from which Botswana's first President, Sir Seretse Khama, emerged. On his grave is a bronze duiker sculpted by the famous South African artist Anton van Wouw.

Francistown, a 19th-century goldrush town, is a stopping-off point for visitors on the way to the Okavango, Moremi and Chobe Game Reserves and is also served by *Air Botswana* from Gaborone. A new museum, the *Supa-Ngwao Museum,* has opened in Francistown with an information centre and a craft shop with books and maps.

National Parks

Botswana is a vast dry land with over 80% of the country being semi-desert (sand with thorn and scrub bush), so

Botswana Railways as one

Cecil John Rhodes had a dream of an African rail link from Cape Town in the south to Cairo in the north. An integral part of this dream was linking Mafikeng, South Africa's most northern railway terminal in 1894, to Bulawayo in Zimbabwe.

As chairman of the then Bechuanaland Railway and deputy commissioner for Bechuanaland (known as Botswana since this country's independence in 1966), Rhodes' aim was to complete 460 miles (740 kilometres) from Mafikeng, through Botswana to Bulawayo in 460 days. Funds were raised in England and construction started during 1896 with the aim to reach Bulawayo in October of the following year. An amazing achievement, even in today's terms, was accomplished when the new line was opened to rail traffic on 4 November 1897.

From 1899 to 1959, the railway operated under the name of Rhodesia Railways Ltd, but was in fact operated by the Cape Government Railway (later known as South African Railways). Cecil Rhodes' dream was never realised - he died in 1902, when there was just not enough British territory on the African map to build the railway line all the way to Cairo.

At Bechuanaland's independence on 30 September 1966, Rhodesia Railways had been operating the whole of this country's railway system for nearly seven years. The newly independent democracy of Botswana was not totally satisfied with having its main means of internal transport governed from outside its borders, however, at the time Botswana was one of the poorest African countries and had more important priorities to contend with.

It was not until 1974, when diamonds were discovered and an upswing in the country's economic situation experienced, that the first state president, Sir Seretse Khama, announced his government's intention of taking over control of its railway system. The turbulent political situation in Rhodesia, however, and the subsequent emergence of an independent Zimbabwe, saw another 13 years for this ambition to come to fruition. Nearly 20 years had elapsed from Botswana's national independence to railway independence, on 1 January 1987.

Botswana Railways introduced a new fleet of passenger coaches in the second half of 1991. Built by Union Carriage, builders of South Africa's famous Blue Train, this modern coaching fleet is the only one in Southern Africa (and one of few worldwide) that is air-conditioned. These bright blue coaches consist of two standards of seating accommodation, club class and economy, sleeping coaches with shower compartments as well as fully equipped catering vehicles. Generator vans provide air-conditioning throughout the trains - a welcome relief during the very hot summer months.

Regularly scheduled passenger services afford tourists access to all major towns and places of interest over a distance of more than 800 kilometres. In addition, large freight volumes are carried annually and during the recent drought, more than 500 000 tonnes of grain alone was transported. Botswana Railways will also introduce container freight to its range of services in the near future to facilitate ease of imports and exports.

Rail travel in Botswana is comfortable, convenient and one of the most cost effective ways to explore the true beauty of Africa.

SIR SERETSE KHAMA AIRPORT

GATEWAY TO SOUTHERN AFRICA

Department of Civil Aviation
P.O. Box 250, Gaborone, Botswana
Tel: 267-371397 or 267-351191
Fax: 267-353709

General Data:

Location:	Gaborone, Capital City
Reference Point:	Lat. 24"33'21"S Long. 025"55'08"E
Elevation:	3299ft above mean sea level
Distance from city:	11km
Airport Development Area:	1300 hectares
Runway:	The 08-26 runway is 3000 metres long and 45 metres wide with 7.5 metres shoulders and turning pads for wide body aircraft at each threshold.
Taxiway and Apron:	Dual low speed taxiway links are provided at 1900 and 2200 metres from the main landing threshold on the first stage apron which provides self manoeuvring stands for two large B747 aircraft and three medium aircraft of B737 size. General aviation, which constitutes a large proportion of the movements, is accommodated at separate apron where 20 aircraft can be parked.
Road:	A first class bitumen road connects the airport with the city of Gaborone.
Airport Buildings:	The master planning chosen is standard for an airport of this type. The single storey passenger terminal has overall dimensions of 120m x 30m. A freight centre and aircraft maintenance facilities are available. There are plans to construct a new cargo terminal and to extend the passenger terminal.

Hippo in the Boro River, Okavango

there are many remote areas to visit, with abundant wildlife.

Undoubtedly the most striking region is the **Okavango Delta** area in the north of the country in the *Kgalagadi (or Kalahari) Desert* and easily accessible from **Maun** between June and September. Home to about 36 species of mammals, 200 species of birds, 80 species of fish and a wealth of flora, the Delta was created by shifts of the earth's surface forcing a river system away from its natural path (to the Indian Ocean), to form the greatest inland delta system in the world. The region is extremely beautiful, covering an area of about 15,000 sq km (6000 sq miles) and composed of vast grass flats, low tree-covered ridges and a widespread network of narrow waterways opening into lagoons. The thick papyrus reeds which thrive in these waters make much of the northern section impenetrable except by dug-out canoe (*mokoro*). The waters, however, are often a clear blue, and crocodiles, hippos and hundreds of fabulous birds can be seen, as well as elephants, zebras and giraffes. There are three lodges in the swamps; Island Safaris, Crocodile Camp and Okavango River Lodge. At Island Safaris there is a swimming pool, and films are shown. *Chef's Island* may be reached by air or by *mokoro* and there is a tented camp at *Xaxaba*. The whole area is a designated national park. Leaving Maun by boat or canoe, with an experienced guide, it is possible to wind one's way through the intricate network of waterways to emerge 640km (400 miles) northwest at **Shakawe** near the Angolan border. These trips can also be made at night, when many of the animals are awake.

One of the most beautiful and perhaps the most spectacular game reserve in southern Africa is the **Moremi Wildlife Reserve**, covering 1812 sq km (700 sq miles) in the northeast corner of the Okavango Delta. Small boats travel along the delta, visiting lagoons like *Xakanaxa*, *Gcobega* and *Gcodikwe* with their abundance of birdlife. The roads are, however, particularly bad in this region. There is a risk from both tsetse fly and malaria. South of here, the *Gcwihaba Caverns*, about 240km (150 miles) from **Tsau**, contain beautiful stalactites. The name means 'Hyena's Hole' in the Quing language of the Bushmen.

The **Tsodilo Hills** are situated north of the Okavango Delta close to the border with the Caprivi Strip (Namibia), and are the site of over 1700 rock paintings, painted between approximately AD1000 and 1800, and mostly portraying animal life. They are thought to be the work of ancestors of the Basarwa and Bantu groups still living in the region (who have labelled the hills Male, Female and Child). There are strong similarities between these paintings and those found on sites in Zimbabwe, Tanzania, South Africa and Lesotho. The hills are reached by air or road but there are no camping facilities or water supplies so visitors should allow for water, food and petrol needs. The **Chobe National Park** with an area of approximately 11,700 sq km (4517 sq miles) is the home of a splendid variety of wildlife, including the white rhinoceros and the elephants who move in their thousands along the well-worn paths of the Chobe River every afternoon to drink. There are also herds of buffalo to be seen at the river's edge, as well as hippo, lechwe, kudu, impala, roan and puku. With the exception of certain sections, which are closed in the rainy season during November to April, the park is open throughout the year. The best time to visit it is

between May and September when it is possible to see several thousand animals in a day. An exclusive lodge has recently been completed within the National Park, 12km (8 miles) from **Kasane**, which is situated 69km (42 miles) west of the *Victoria Falls* on a good tarmac road. Although the most developed of Botswana's parks and reserves, many of the roads in the area are passable only by 4-wheel-drive vehicles.

The **Nxai Pan National Park**, situated only 32km (20 miles) north of the main Francistown to Maun road, is completely flat and covered with grass cropped short by the large quantity of wildlife that visits during the rainy season. The area is famous for the **Makgadikgade Pans**, once a huge prehistoric lake, and now a flat salt sheet which floods in the rainy season and becomes populated by thousands of brilliant pink flamingoes. Herds of zebra and wildebeest also come to drink here. When the Makgadikgade loses its water the animals move on to the *Boteti River* where they remain until the following rainy season, which heralds their movement northwards again to the Nxai Pan. There are basic camping facilities in the area, but essentials such as water, food and petrol should be brought.

Central Kalahari Game Reserve is the second-largest game reserve in the world. Howeverer, the area is closed to the general public and access is only allowed to visitors by special permit from the Department of Wildlife and National Parks, PO Box 131, Gaborone. **Khutse Game Reserve** is an expanse of dry savannah land in the centre of the Kalahari which, when filled with water, attracts hundreds of bird species. It is located about 240km (150 miles) northwest of Gaborone. Camping facilities are basic, and water, petrol and food should be brought. There are still a few small bands of Bushmen living in this region, one of the last Stone Age races on earth, some of whom guide visitors around the reserve and teach them about edible and moisture-bearing plants and how many of the animals survive despite the lack of water. **Kalahari Gemsbok National Park,** in the southwest of this region, has deep fossil river beds and high sand dunes. The park can be reached by a paved road from Gaborone to **Tsabong**, after which a 4-wheel-drive vehicle is necessary. Many herds of gemsbok and springbok (as well as other species of antelope), cheetah and lion can be seen here and the best time to visit is from March to May. On the eastern edge of the Kalahari Gemsbok is the smaller Mabuasehube Game Reserve. The area is known for its salt pans which reflect amazing colour changes during the day. Antelope, foxes and over 170 bird species (including buzzards, vultures and eagles) can be viewed here, particularly during the months from July to September.

SOCIAL PROFILE

FOOD & DRINK: Restaurants and bars can be found in main towns, often within hotels. Most lodges and safari camps also have restaurants and licensed bars, though food is generally basic outside major hotels and restaurants. **Drink:** There is local beer and in general no restrictions on alcohol.

SHOPPING: Woodcarvings, handcrafted jewellery, woven goods and attractive basketry are recommended. **Shopping hours:** 0830-1300 and 1400-1700 Monday to Friday, 0830-1300 Saturday.

SPORT: Safari companies run photographic and

sightseeing tours to the magnificent national parks and wildlife reserves in Botswana. For details contact the Tourism Division. Outside protected areas there is limited scope for **hunting**. **Fishing** trips, **water-skiing**, **motorboat** and **canoe** hire are available to varying degrees. Near to Gaborone is an artificial lake with a yacht club offering **sailing**, water-skiing and fishing; use of facilities is available to visitors at the invitation of a club member.

SPECIAL EVENTS: End of Mar '95 *Botswana Defence Force Sporting Day.* **End of Apr** *Botswana Defence Force Day.* **Third Week of Jul** *President's Day Barclays Cup* (soccer). **Mid-Aug** *Botswana Police Day.* **End of Aug** *Botswana International Trade Day; Coca-Cola Cup* (soccer). **Sep 30** *Botswana Day; Independence Cup* (soccer).

The *Botswana Defence Force Day* and *President's Day* festivities are celebrated with traditional dancing, musical events (including performances by the Defence Force Band) and karate shows.

SOCIAL CONVENTIONS: As most people in Botswana follow their traditional pattern of life, visitors should be sensitive to customs which will inevitably be unfamiliar to them. Outside urban areas, people may well be unused to visitors. Casual clothing is acceptable and in urban centres, normal courtesies should be observed. **Photography:** Airports, official residences and defence establishments should not be photographed. Permission should be obtained to photograph local people. **Tipping:** 10% in urban centres. It is obligatory to tip servants.

BUSINESS PROFILE

ECONOMY: The economy is based on nomadic agriculture, mainly livestock, and cultivation of subsistence crops – maize, sorghum and millet – which have been severely affected by drought in recent years. Cattle produces a large proportion of the country's foreign exchange earnings. The remainder comes from mineral extracts: diamond, nickel, copper and coal are well-established, while soda ash has recently come into production on an industrial scale. Platinum, gold and petroleum deposits have been located in the south and are expected in go into production during the 1990s. Botswana is closely connected to South Africa economically and is also linked, along with Lesotho and Swaziland, to the Southern African Customs Union (SACU), although Botswana has broken its former dependence on the Rand currency. The bulk of the country's imports come from within SACU, with other African countries and the EU providing most of the rest. Europe is the key export market. **BUSINESS:** Lightweight or tropical suits, or safari suits, should be worn. **Office hours:** 0800-1700 April-October; 0730-1630 October-April. **Government office hours:** 0730-1630 all year round.

COMMERCIAL INFORMATION: The Department of Trade and Investment Promotion (TIPA) assists potential investors and publishes a useful brochure: *Botswana – a strategic investment opportunity.* It is available from TIPA (address below). The following organisations can also offer advice: Botswana Chamber of Commerce and Industry, PO Box 1402, Gaborone. Tel: 352 677. Fax: 322 683; *or* Department of Trade and Investment Promotion (TIPA), Ministry of Commerce and Industry, Private Bag 00367, Gaborone. Tel: 351 790. Fax: 305 375. Telex: 2674; *or* Gaborone Convention and Exhibition Centre. Tel: 375 555. Fax: 304 264.

CLIMATE

Mainly temperate climate. Summer is between October and April and is very hot combined with the rainy season. Dry and cooler exists weather between May-September. Early mornings and evenings may be cold and frosty in winter. Annual rainfall decreases westwards and southwards.

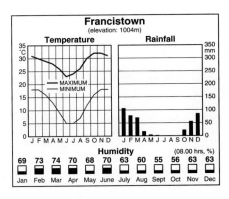

Francistown
(elevation: 1004m)

	Jan	Feb	Mar	Apr	May	June	July	Aug	Sept	Oct	Nov	Dec
Humidity (08.00 hrs, %)	69	73	74	70	68	70	63	60	55	56	63	63

Location: South America.

Centro Brasileiro de Informação Turística (CEBITUR) (Brazilian Tourist Office)
Rua Mariz e Barros 13, 6° andar, Praça de Bandeira, 20.270 Rio de Janeiro, Brazil
Tel: (21) 293 1313. Fax: (21) 273 9290. Telex: 21066.
Embassy of the Federative Republic of Brazil and **Brazilian Tourist Office**
32 Green Street, London W1Y 4AT
Tel: (0171) 499 0877. Fax: (0171) 493 5105 or 493 4621 (Commercial & Tourist Office). Telex: 261157. Opening hours: 1000-1200 and 1500-1800 Monday to Friday.
Brazilian Consulate-General
6 St Albans Street, London SW1Y 4SG
Tel: (0171) 930 9055. Fax: (0171) 839 8958. Opening hours: 1000-1600 Monday to Friday.
British Embassy
Caixa Postal 07-0586, Setor de Embaixadas Sul, Quadra 801, Conjunto K, 70.408 Brasília DF, Brazil
Tel: (61) 225 2710. Fax: (61) 225 1777. Telex: 2370-1360 (a/b EING BR).
British Consulate-General
Caixa Postal 669, CEP 20001-970, 2nd Floor, Praia do Flamengo 284, Rio de Janeiro, Brazil
Tel: (21) 552 1422 or 533 3409 (visas). Fax: (21) 552 5796. Telex: 2121577 (a/b EING BR).
Consulates also in: Belém, Manaus, Recife, Salvador, Belo Horizonte, São Paulo, Pôrto Alegre, Rio Grande, Santos and Curitiba.
Embassy of the Federative Republic of Brazil and **Brazilian Tourist Department**
3006 Massachusetts Avenue, NW, Washington, DC 20008
Tel: (202) 745 2700. Fax: (202) 745 2827.
Brazilian Consulate
27th Floor, 630 Fifth Avenue, New York, NY 10111
Tel: (212) 757 3080/7.
Embassy of the United States of America
Lote 3, Unit 3500, Avenida das Nações, 70.403 Brasília DF, Brazil
Tel: (61) 321 7272. Fax: (61) 225 9136. Telex: 611091 or 612318.
Embassies also in: Rio de Janeiro, São Paulo, Pôrto Alegre and Recife.
Embassy of the Federative Republic of Brazil
450 Wilbrod Street, Ottawa, Ontario K1N 6M8
Tel: (613) 237 1090. Fax: (613) 237 6144. Telex: 0533176 (a/b BRASEMBOTT).
Canadian Embassy
Caixa Postal 00961, 70.359-900, Setor de Embaixadas

Sul, Avenida das Nações, lote 16, Brasília DF, Brazil
Tel: (61) 321 2171. Fax: (61) 321 4529. Telex: 611296 (a/b ECANBR).

AREA: 8,511,996 sq km (3,286,500 sq miles).
POPULATION: 153,322,000 (1991 estimate).
POPULATION DENSITY: 18 per sq km.
CAPITAL: Brasília. **Population:** 1,841,028 (1991 estimate).
GEOGRAPHY: Brazil covers almost half of the South American continent and it is bordered to the north, west and south by all South American countries except Chile and Ecuador; to the east is the Atlantic. Brazil is topographically relatively flat and at no point do the highlands exceed 3000m (10,000ft). Over 60% of the country is a plateau; the remainder consists of plains. The River Plate Basin (the confluence of the Paraná and Uruguay rivers, both of which have their sources in Brazil) in the far south is more varied, higher and less heavily forested. North of the Amazon are the Guiana Highlands, partly forested, partly stony desert. The Brazilian Highlands of the interior, between the Amazon and the rivers of the south, form a vast tableland, the Mato Grosso, from which rise mountains in the southwest that form a steep protective barrier from the coast called the Great Escarpment, breached by deeply cut river beds. The population is concentrated in the southeastern states of Minas Gerais, São Paulo and Paraná. São Paulo has a population of over 10 million, while over 5 million people live in Rio de Janeiro.
LANGUAGE: The official language is Portuguese. French, German and Italian are widely spoken; English to a lesser extent.
RELIGION: Over 90% Roman Catholic.
TIME: Brazil spans several time zones:
Eastern Standard Time: GMT - 3 (GMT - 2 from third Sunday in October to third Saturday in March).
North East States and East Parà Time: GMT - 3.
Western Standard Time: GMT - 4 (GMT - 3 from third Sunday in October to third Saturday in March).
Amapa and West Para Time: GMT - 4.
Acre State: GMT - 5.
Fernando de Noronha Archipelago: GMT - 2.
ELECTRICITY: Bahia (Salvador) 127 volts AC; Brasília 220 volts AC, 60Hz; Rio de Janeiro and São Paulo 110 volts AC, 60Hz. Plugs are of the 2-pin type. Most hotels provide 110-volt and 220-volt outlets.
COMMUNICATIONS: Telephone: The telecommunications systems are state-owned. Full IDD services are available for the whole country and abroad. Country code: 55. Outgoing international code: 00. Public telephones require metal discs called 'fichas', which can be obtained from cash desks or newspaper kiosks. All calls are liable to a 20% tax. **Fax:** Facilities are available in the main post offices of major cities and some 5-star hotels; because this technology is only just being introduced, it is advisable to check that this facility is offered at your destination. **Telex/telegram:** International telegram and telex facilities exist in many cities. Offices of Embratel are in Rio de Janerio (Praca Mauá 7) and São Paulo. Rio's airport provides 24-hour telecommunication services. The domestic telex service now covers the whole of the country. **Post:** Services are reasonably reliable. Sending mail registered or franked will eliminate the risk of having the stamps steamed off. Airmail service to Europe takes four to six days. Surface mail takes at least four weeks. Post offices are open 0900-1300 Monday to Friday and 0900-1300 Saturday. **Press:** The only English newspaper is The Brazil Herald in Rio. Also in Rio there is an English-language publication, the Rio Visitor, which gives tourist information.
BBC World Service and Voice of America frequencies: From time to time these change. See the section How to Use this Book for more information.

BBC:				
MHz	17.55	15.26	11.75	9.915
Voice of America:				
MHz	15.12	11.58	9.775	5.995

PASSPORT/VISA

Regulations and requirements may be subject to change at short notice, and you are advised to contact the appropriate diplomatic or consular authority before finalising travel arrangements. Details of these may be found at the head of this country's entry. Any numbers in the chart refer to the footnotes below.

	Passport Required?	Visa Required?	Return Ticket Required?
Full British	Yes	No/3	2
BVP	Not valid	-	-
Australian	Yes	Yes	2
Canadian	Yes	Yes	2
USA	Yes	Yes	2
Other EU (As of 31/12/94)	Yes	1/3	2
Japanese	Yes	Yes	2

Restricted entry: Holders of Taiwan (China) passports will not be allowed entry to Brazil unless they are holding a Laissez-Passer issued by the Brazilian authorities.
PASSPORTS: Passport valid for at least six months from date of entry required by all except nationals of Argentina and Uruguay arriving in Brazil directly from their own countries holding a national identity card.
British Visitors Passport: Not acceptable.
Note: Persons under 18 years of age travelling with only one parent, alone, or with a guardian must hold a special authorisation.
VISAS: Required by all except:
(a) **[1]** nationals of EU countries (except nationals of France who do require a visa) for tourist purposes only;
(b) nationals of Andorra, Argentina, Austria, Bahamas, Barbados, Chile, Colombia, Ecuador, Finland, Iceland, Liechtenstein, Monaco, Morocco, Namibia, Norway, Paraguay, Peru, Philippines, San Marino, Suriname, Sweden, Switzerland, Trinidad & Tobago, Uruguay and Vatican City for tourist purposes only;
(c) nationals of Venezuela for a stay of up to 60 days for tourist purposes only.
Notes: [2] All travellers must be in possession of onward or return tickets. **[3]** All those travelling on business do need a visa.
Types of visa: Tourist, Business and Transit (required by all passengers in transit). A fee is charged if visa is not applied for personally.
Validity: Tourist visas are valid up to 90 days; however, it is up to the authorities on entry how long each visitor is allowed to stay. For an extension of this period apply in Brazil. Tourists are not allowed to work in Brazil.
Application to: Consulate. For addresses, see top of entry.
Application requirements: (a) Valid passport. (b) Application form. (c) Sufficient funds to cover duration of stay. (d) 1 passport-size photo. (e) Return or onward tickets. (f) For Business visa, letter from firm giving full details and confirming financial responsibility for the applicant (visas will not be granted if the validity of the passport expires within 6 months).
Working days required: 2 full days.
Temporary residence: Apply to Consulate.

MONEY

Currency: Real (RI) = 100 centavos. Notes are in denominations of RI100, 50, 10, 5 and 1. Coins are in denominations of RI1 and 50, 10, 5 and 1 centavos.
Note: The Real replaced the Cruzeiro in July 1994, which replaced the Cruzado in March 1990.
Currency exchange: All banks and cambios exchange recognised travellers cheques and foreign currency.
Credit cards: Access/Mastercard, American Express, Diners Club and Visa are accepted. Check with your credit card company for details of merchant acceptability and other services which may be available.
Travellers cheques: Tourists cannot exchange US travellers cheques for US banknotes but they can, however, benefit from a 15% discount when paying hotel or restaurant bills in foreign currency or travellers cheques.
Exchange rate indicators: There are frequent currency changes and no stable exchange rate indicators can be given at present. In **January 1994 and January 1995** the value of the Cruzado and the Real respectively, against Sterling and the US Dollar was as follows:

	Jan '94	Jan '95
£1.00=	Cr474.79	RI1.33
$1.00=	Cr320.91	RI0.86

Currency restrictions: Free import and export of local currency. Free import of foreign currency, subject to declaration. Free export of foreign currency up to the amount declared.
Banking hours: 1000-1630 Monday to Friday.

DUTY FREE

The following goods may be taken into Brazil without incurring any duty:
400 cigarettes or 250g of tobacco or 25 cigars; 2 litres of alcohol; up to US$500 worth of goods bought duty free in Brazil.
Prohibited goods: Meat and cheese products from various countries; contact the Consulate for details. Other varieties of animal origin transported from Africa, Asia, Italy, Portugal and Spain. The total value of imported goods may not exceed US$500.

PUBLIC HOLIDAYS

Jan 1 '95 New Year's Day. **Feb 25** Carnival. **Apr 14** Good Friday. **Apr 17** Easter Monday. **Apr 21** Tiradentes Day (Discovery of Brazil). **May 1** Labour Day. **May 25** Ascension Day. **Jun 15** Corpus Christi. **Sep 7**

Independence Day. **Oct 12** Our Lady Aparecida, Patron Saint of Brazil. **Nov 2** All Souls' Day. **Nov 15** Proclamation of the Republic. **Dec 25** Christmas Day. **Jan 1 '96** New Year's Day. **Feb 17** Carnival. **Apr 5** Good Friday. **Apr 8** Easter Monday.

Note: It is Government policy in Brazil for certain holidays to be taken on Monday if those holidays fall during the week; however, the church wishes to continue holding festivals on the traditional days. If plans are likely to be affected by such a holiday it is advisable to check the situation with the Information Office before travelling. Note also that as four of the traditional holidays are fixed by municipalities there may be some variation from region to region.

HEALTH

Regulations and requirements may be subject to change at short notice, and you are advised to contact your doctor well in advance of your intended date of departure. Any numbers in the chart refer to the footnotes below.

	Special Precautions?	Certificate Required?
Yellow Fever	1	1
Cholera	Yes/2	No
Typhoid & Polio	Yes	-
Malaria	3	-
Food & Drink	4	-

[1]: A yellow fever vaccination certificate is required from travellers over nine months of age arriving from infected regions. The following areas are regarded as infected: Angola, Bolivia, Cameroon, Colombia, Ecuador, Gambia, Guinea Republic, Mali, Nigeria, Peru, Sudan and Zaïre. Vaccination is strongly recommended for those intending to visit rural areas in Acre, Amazonas, Goiás, Maranhão, Mato Grosso, Matto Grosso do Sul, Pará and Rondônia States and the Territories of Amapá and Roraima.

[2]: Brazil continues to be seriously affected by the epidemic wave which originated in Peru in 1991 and precaution is highly recommended.

[3]: Malaria risk exists throughout the year below 900m in some rural areas of Acre, Amazonas, Goiás, Maranhão, Mato Grosso, Pará, Rondônia and Tocantins States, and in the Territories of Amapá and Roraima, as well as the outskirts of Manaus and Pôrto Velho. The malignant *falciparum* form of the disease is reportedly highly resistant to both chloroquine and sulfadoxine/pyrimethane. A weekly dose of 250mg of mefloquine is the recommended prophylaxis.

[4]: All water should be regarded as being potentially contaminated. Water used for drinking, brushing teeth or making ice should have first been boiled or otherwise sterilised. Pasteurised milk and cheese is available in towns and is generally considered safe to consume. Milk outside of urban areas is unpasteurised and should be boiled; powdered or tinned milk is available and is advised in rural areas, but make sure that it is reconstituted with pure water. Avoid dairy products which are likely to have been made from unboiled milk. Only eat well-cooked meat and fish, preferably served hot. Pork, salad and mayonnaise may carry increased risk. Vegetables should be cooked and fruit peeled. *Rabies* is present. For those at high risk, vaccination before arrival should be considered. If you are bitten abroad seek medical advice without delay. For more information consult the *Health* section at the back of the book.

Bilharzia (schistosomiasis) is present. Avoid swimming and paddling in fresh water. Swimming pools which are well-chlorinated and maintained are safe.

Other infectious diseases prevalent in Brazil include *trypanosomiasis* (Chagas disease), *mucocutaneous leishmaniasis* (on the increase in Brazil), *visceral leishmaniasis* (especially in the northeast), *onchocerciasis* (especially northern Brazil), *Bancroftian filariasis, hepatitis B and D, meningitis* and the plague.

Health care: English-speaking medical staff are found mainly in São Paulo and Rio de Janeiro. The main hospital in São Paulo is the Hospital Samaritano. Full insurance is recommended as medical costs are high.

TRAVEL - International

AIR: Brazil's main international airline is *Varig (RG)*. For free advice on air travel, call the *Air Travel Advisory Bureau* in the UK on (0171) 636 5000 (London) *or* (0161) 832 2000 (Manchester).

Approximate flight times: From *London* to Rio de Janeiro is 10 hours 50 minutes and to São Paulo is 11 hours.

From *Los Angeles* to Rio de Janeiro is 13 hours 55 minutes.

From *New York* to Rio de Janeiro is 10 hours 10 minutes.

From *Sydney* to Rio de Janeiro is 19 hours 55 minutes.

International airports: *Rio de Janeiro* (Galeão) *(GIG)*, 20km (12.5 miles) northwest of the city. There are regular bus services between the International and Santa Dumont airports, and into the city. The airport provides the following 24-hour facilities: left luggage and lockers, medical facilities, bank, bureau de change, duty-free shops, restaurant, snack bar, car parking and post office. There is also a nursery open from 0600-2330 and car hire companies *(Budget, Hertz, Interlocadora, Localiza, Locar, Locarauto, Lokarbras (Avis), Nobre* and *Unidas)*. *São Paulo* (Guarulhos) *(GRU)*, 25km (16 miles) northeast of the city. An airport bus costing approx. US$6 runs every 25 mins. during the day and every hour during the evening (travel time – 30-50 mins.). There are also taxi services. The airport provides the following 24-hour facilites: left luggage and lockers, medical facilities, duty-free shops, snack bar and post office. There are also restaurants (0600-0200), business centre (0800-1700), banks, bureau de change, bars (0600-0200), restaurant (0600-0200) and car rental *(Avis, Hertz, Interlocadora, Localiza, Locar Auto, Nobre* and *Unidas)*. *São Paulo* (Viracopos) *(VCP)*, 96km (60 miles) southwest of the city. Airport facilities include banking, a duty-free shop and a restaurant. *São Paulo* (Congonhas) *(CGH)*, 14km (8 miles) from the city. *Manaus* (Internacional Eduardo Gomes) *(MAO)*, 14km (9 miles) from the city. There are coach services into the city and to other destinations. *Salvador* (Dois de Julho) *(SSA)*, 36km (22 miles) from the city. 24-hour taxi facilities are available. Airport facilities include banking, a duty-free shop and a restaurant.

Note: *Brasília* does not have an international airport. All connections are made via Rio de Janeiro. Bus and taxi services are available to all cities.

Departure tax: US$17 is levied on international departures, payable in Real.

SEA: Passenger cruises from Europe are run by *Lamport* and *Holt* lines. Other cruise lines, some of which also organise cruises down the Amazon, are *Lindblad Travel, Delta, Costa* and *Society Expeditions*.

RAIL: Limited rail services link Brazil with Bolivia, Chile and Uruguay. The main international routes include Rio de Janeiro–Buenos Aires, Rio de Janeiro–Santiago, Rio de Janeiro–São Paulo–Montevideo, São Paulo–Bauru–Corumba–Santa Cruz–La Paz, São Paulo–Antofagasta.

ROAD: It is possible to drive or take a bus to Brazil from the USA, but it is wise to check any changes in political status or requirements in Central America before travelling. For further information, contact the Brazilian Tourist Office.

TRAVEL - Internal

AIR: There is a shuttle service between São Paulo and Rio de Janeiro, a regular service from São Paulo to Brasília, and a shuttle service from Brasília to Belo Horizonte. There are air services between all Brazilian cities, Brazil having one of the largest internal air networks in the world. At weekends it is advisable to book seats as the services are much used. The monthly magazine *Aeronautico* gives all timetables and fares for internal air travel. Air taxis are available between all major centres.

SEA/RIVER: Ferries serve all coastal ports. River transport is the most efficient method for the Amazon Delta.

RAIL: Limited rail connections exist to most major cities and towns, but there has been a substantial decline in the provision of long-distance services. Most (91%) of Brazil's 36,800km (23,000 miles) of rail lines are located within 480km (300 miles) of its Atlantic coastline. Because of the great distances and the climate, some of these journeys can be uncomfortable. Daytime and overnight trains with restaurant and sleeping-cars link São Paulo and Rio de Janeiro. Brazil's most scenic rail routes are from Curitiba to Paranagua (originating in São

Paulo) and from São Paulo to Santos. Other major rail routes include Belo Horizonte–Itabira–Vitoria (with buffet car), Campo Grande–Ponte Porta (with restaurant car), Porto Santana–Serra do Navio (second-class only), Santos Ana Costa–Juquia (second-class only), São Luis A Guarda–Parauapebas (with buffet car), São Paulo–Panorama (second-class only), São Paulo–Presidente Prudente (first-class, air-conditioned, buffet and sleeping cars available), Araguari–Campinas (restaurant or buffet car) and Santa Maria–Pôrto Alegre (with restaurant car). Children under three travel free. Children from three to nine pay half fare.

ROAD: Brazil has over 1,600,000km (approximately 1 million miles) of roads. Traffic drives on the right. **Bus:** Inter-urban transport is very much road-based (accounting for 97% of travellers) compared with air (2.2%) and rail (less than 1%). High-quality coaches have been increasingly introduced on the main routes, which are well served. Operators include: *Cometa*, which operates between São Paulo and Belo Horizonte; *Penha* (São Paulo–Pôrto Alegre); *Reunidas* (São Paulo–Aracatuba); *Motta* (São Paulo–Campo Grande); *Garcia* (São Paulo–Londrina); *Real-Expresso* (São Paulo–Rio–Brasília); *TransBrasíliana* (Rio–Belém); *Sulamericana* (Curitiba–Foz do Iguaçú); and *Expresso Brasileiro* (São Paulo–Rio). Services connect all inhabited parts of the country. Standards and timetables vary, and the visitor must be prepared for overnight stops and long waits between connecting stages. **Car hire:** Available in all major centres. Traffic drives on the right. Parking in cities is very difficult and it is best to avoid driving through the often congested city areas if at all possible. **Documentation:** International Driving Licence required.

URBAN: There are extensive bus services in all the main centres, often with express 'executivo' at premium fares run by air-conditioned coaches. Rio and São Paulo both have two-line metros and local rail lines, and there are trolleybuses in São Paulo and a number of other cities. Trolleybuses are increasingly being introduced as an energy-saving measure. Fares are generally regulated with interchange possible between some bus and metro/rail lines, for instance on the feeder bus linking the Rio metro with Copacabana. **Taxi:** In most cities these are identified by red number plates and are fitted with meters. Willingness to immediately accept a taxi-driver's advice on where to go or where to stay should be tempered by the knowledge that places to which he takes a visitor are more than likely to give him a commission – and the highest commissions will usually come from the most expensive places.

JOURNEY TIMES: The following chart gives approximate journey times (in hours and minutes) from Brasília to other major cities/towns in Brazil.

	Air
Belo Horizonte	1.00
São Paulo	1.20
Rio de Janeiro	1.25
Pôrto Alegre	2.20
Manaus	2.30
Foz do Iguaçú	3.25

ACCOMMODATION

HOTELS: Accommodation varies according to region. First-class accommodation is, by and large, restricted to the cities of the south. For further information contact the Associacão Brasileira da Industria de Hoteis, Avenida Nilo Pecanha 12, 10-1004/5/6 Rio de Janeiro. Tel: (21) 242 3768. Fax: (21) 33890.

Note: Accommodation for Carnival time should be booked well in advance.

Rio de Janeiro/São Paulo: Many modern hotels, ranging from the very expensive deluxe hotels to moderately priced hotels. It is vital to pre-book well in advance for the Carnival.

Brasília: Small number of good hotels. Most tourists visit Brasília by air from Rio or São Paulo for a day trip, or make a single-night stopover. The city is used only for national administration.

Bahia (Salvador): Small number of good hotels, some moderately priced hotels, several demi-pensions.

Amazon Basin: This region is being developed in part as a tourist attraction.

Grading: In 1979 the Federal Tourist Authority began introducing a star-range system for hotels. It is now used by most establishments in towns. The classification is not, however, the standard used in Europe and North America. **5-star** is the grade for deluxe hotels. **3-star** hotels are good value for money and offer well-kept accommodation, whilst a **1-star** hotel can only offer basic amenities.

Visitors are reminded that hotel tariffs are subject to alteration at any time, and are liable to fluctuate according to changes in the exchange rate.

Note: The best guide to hotels in Brazil is the *Guia do*

Brasil Quatro Rodas, which includes maps.
CAMPING/CARAVANNING: Cars may be hired, and camping arranged on safari tours or group 'exploration' trips in the Amazon region. The road network in Brazil is good and is being expanded, but since many parts of Brazil are wild, or semi-explored, it is wise to drive on main roads, to camp with organised groups under supervision and with official permits, or otherwise to stay in recognised hotels. The country is peaceful, but because it is so large there is a real danger of getting lost, or being injured or killed by natural accident or lack of local knowledge of survival.
Those with an 'international camper's card' pay only half the rate of a non-member (about US$4 per person). The *Camping Clube do Brasil* has 43 sites in 13 states. For those on a low budget, service stations can be used as campsites. These are equipped with shower facilities and can supply food. For further information, contact Camping Clube do Brazil, Divisao de Campings, Rua Senador Dantas, 75-29 andar, 20000 Rio de Janeiro. Tel: (21) 262 7127.
YOUTH HOSTELS: For information, contact Federaçao Brasileira de Albergues da Juventude, CP 22271, Rua General Dionisio 63, Rio de Janeiro. Tel: (21) 286 0303. Fax: (21) 221 8753.

RESORTS & EXCURSIONS

For the purposes of this section, the country has been divided into five regions: the northern, the northeastern, the west central, the southeastern and the southern.

The Northern Region

The states of Amazonas, Pará, Acre and Rondônia cover an area of more than 3,400,000 sq km (1,300,000 sq miles) but have a combined population of little more than 6,000,000. Almost entirely covered with thick rainforest, the north of Brazil is known as the 'exotic Amazon' and is an area where nature prevails over all else (except, perhaps, the slash-and-burn agriculturalists and road-builders).
Manaus is the capital of the state of Amazonas. It contains the Amazonas theatre, with a majestic neo-classical façade, a number of fine restaurants and hotels and a free-trade zone which is excellent for cheap shopping. The Amazon River and its tributaries are ideal for boat excursions, and also offer excellent angling.
Belém has a splendid park and market as well as many fine churches. The *Goeldi Museum* contains the largest collection of tropical plants in the world. **Maray's Island** is the cradle of the Marajoara civilisation. **Pôrto Velho,** the capital of the state of Rondônia, has a fascinating railway museum and the beautiful *Teotonio* and *Santo Antônio Falls.* **Rio Branco,** a city of architectural contrasts, is an important handicrafts centre.

The Northeastern Region

Known as the 'Golden Coast', this region contains the states of Bahia, Sergipe, Alagoas, Pernambuco, Paraíba, Rio Grande do Norte, Ceará, Piaui and Maranhão. It covers nearly 1,600,000 sq km (600,000 sq miles) and has a population of 35 million. The area is distinctive for its historical and folkloric traditions, as well as for its many beautiful beaches.
Salvador, the capital of Bahia, contains the beautiful arts and crafts market of the *Mercado Modelo.* The number and variety of churches in Salvador is staggering; some of the best include the *Convent of São Francisco de Assis* and the *Church of Nosso Senhor do Bonfim.* Salvador is also renowned for its museums, some of which are converted churches. The area around the city also has many excellent beaches. The towns of **Ilhéus, Pôrto Seguro** and **Aracaju** all have fine churches and colonial architecture worth visiting. **Maceiô,** capital of the state of Alagoas, has beaches reputed to be some of the finest in Brazil. **Recife,** known as the 'Venice of Brazil' on account of the canals and waterways which crisscross the city, is also well endowed with churches. **Olinda, Caruaru, Natal, Fortaleza, Teresina** and **São Luis** are also notable for their architecture, craftworkers and fine beaches.

The West Central Region

An area of huge marshes traversed by the Araguaia River, it consists of the states of Goiás, Mato Grosso and Mato Grosso do Sul. It covers an area of 1,900,000 million sq km (730,000 sq miles) and has a population of nearly eight million. The region is best known for its pleasant climate, and for its huge cattle ranches and plantations.
Brasília (which was built miles from anywhere on specially flattened Amazonian rainforest) is known worldwide for its futuristic architecture, which is most notable in the *Praça dos Três Poderes, Palácio do Planalto* and *The National Congress.*
Goiás, 200km (120 miles) to the west, serves as a jumping-off point for tourists visiting the *Araguaia River, Bananal Island* and the thermal springs of *Caldas Novas.* **Mato Grosso** is the gateway to the Pantanal, which is Brazil's largest ecological reserve where farm-hotels house tourists and organise fishing trips and photographic excursions.

The Southeastern Region

This comprises the states of São Paulo, Rio de Janeiro, Minas Gerais and Espirito Santo. It covers an area of more than 900,000 sq km (350,000 sq miles) and has a population of nearly 53 million. It is the country's most developed region and offers the best tourist facilities, including a wide variety of scenic and historic resorts.
Rio de Janeiro has one of the most beautiful settings in the world. Renowned for its excellent beaches, such as *Copacabana* and *Ipanema,* the city is chiefly known for its world-famous carnival. **São Paulo** is famed throughout the continent for its nightlife and its shopping facilities. **Belo Horizonte,** capital of the state of Minas Gerais, was originally modelled on Washington DC and is the gateway to all the colonial towns. The gold boom in Minas Gerais during the 18th century produced a number of historic towns, the most famous being **Ouro Preto.** The southeast region has a number of spas, known for their marvellous climate and mineral water; all are well equipped to accommodate the traveller, *Petrópolis, Teresópolis* and *Nova Friburgo* are but a few of these.

The Southern Region

This consists of three states, Rio Grande do Sul, Santa Catarina and Paraná, covering an area of over 570,000 sq km (220,000 sq miles). The ideal climate has made this region the most popular among European immigrants. Rio Grande do Sul is one of the richest states in Brazil, and is equipped with good tourist facilities. **Pôrto Alegre,** its capital, offers the visitor fine museums and art centres as well as delightful surrounding countryside. The most popular beaches in this area are the *Tramandai* and *Torres,* respectively 126km (78 miles) and 209km (130 miles) from Pôrto Alegre. The Gramado and Canela mountains are also popular with tourists. The state of Santa Catarina, with its island capital of **Florianópolis,** also has fine beaches at *Laguna, Itapena* and *Camburu.* Paraná is a prime coffee-producing state. The train journey between its capital **Curitiba** and **Paranaguá** is a sightseeing must, as is **Vila Velha** (the City of Stone) and – most famous of all – the *Foz do Iguaçu* (Iguacú Falls), the massive waterfalls on the border with Argentina and Paraguay.
POPULAR ITINERARIES: 7-day: (a) Northern Region: Manaus–Pôrto Velho–Rio Branco. (b) Northeastern Region: Recife–Maceiô–Aracaju–Salvador. (c) West Central Region: Brasília–Goiânia–Caldas Novas–Araguaia River–Brasília. (d) Southeastern Region: Rio de Janeiro–São Paulo–Belo Horizonte–Rio de Janeiro. (e) Southern Region: Pôrto Alegre–Florianópolis–Iguacú Falls–Pôrto Alegre.

SOCIAL PROFILE

FOOD & DRINK: Many regional variations are very different from North American and European food. One example is Bahian cookery, derived from days when slaves had to cook scraps and anything that could be caught locally, together with coconut milk and palm oil. Specialities include *vatapá* (shrimps, fish oil and coconut milk, bread and rice), *sarapatel* (liver, heart, tomatoes, peppers, onion and gravy), *caruru* (shrimps, okra, onions and peppers). From Rio Grande do Sul comes *churrasco* (barbecued beef, tomato and onion sauce), *galleto al primo canto* (pieces of cockerel cooked on the spit with white wine and oil). From Amazon comes *pato no tucupi* (duck in rich wild green herb sauce), *tacacá* (thick yellow soup with shrimps and garlic). In the northeast dried salted meat and beans are the staple diet. In Rio de Janeiro a favourite dish is *feijoada* (thick stew of black beans, chunks of beef, pork, sausage, chops, pigs' ears and tails on white rice, boiled green vegetables and orange slices). Types of establishments vary. Table service is usual in most restaurants and cafés. If resident in a hotel, drinks and meals can often be charged to account. **Drink:** All kinds of alcoholic drink are manufactured and available and there are no licensing hours or restrictions on drinking. Beer is particularly good and draught beer is called *chopp.* The local liqueur is *cachaça,* a local equivalent of whisky popular with locals, but not so much with visitors. This phenomenally strong spirit is often mixed with sugar, crushed ice and limes to make *caiparinha,* a refreshing if intoxicating cocktail. Southern Brazilian wine is of a high quality. Some bars have waiters and table service.
NIGHTLIFE: The best entertainment occurs in Rio de Janeiro and São Paulo. In Rio the major clubs do not present their main acts until after midnight and the daily paper gives current information; small clubs *(boites)* provide nightly entertainment throughout the city. São Paulo nightlife is more sophisticated, with greater choice; the shows tend to start earlier.
SHOPPING: In Rio and São Paulo major shops and markets stay open quite late in the evening. Rio and Bahia specialise in antiques and jewellery. Special purchases include gems (particularly emeralds), jewellery (particularly silver), souvenirs and permissible antiques, leather or snakeskin goods. Fashions and antiques, crystal and pottery is a speciality of São Paulo. Belém, the city of the Amazon valley, specialises in jungle items, but be careful that you are not purchasing objects that have been plundered from the jungle, contributing to the general destruction. Check for restrictions on import to your home country of goods made from skins of protected species. **Shopping hours:** 0900-1830 Monday to Friday, 0900-1300 Saturday. Most department stores close at 2200. All the above times are subject to local variations and many shops open until late in the evenings.
SPORT: Association **football** is the national obsession, the national team having won the World Cup on three occasions. **Ball games** and **athletics** are also popular. ***Capoeira,*** a martial art, was developed by black slaves in colonial times disguised as a dance to an African musical rhythm. **Mountain climbing, hang-gliding** and **racing** are popular, and safari trips are available to the Mato Grosso or the Amazon jungle; big-game **hunting** is, however, now illegal. **Waterskiing** and underwater **diving** clubs exist all along the coastline. Both deep-sea and river **fishing** are available.
SPECIAL EVENTS: There are a number of lavish festivals throughout the year in Brazil, the two most notable being Bahia's carnival just after Christmas (from December to March) and the carnival in Rio de Janeiro (February), widely regarded as the most spectacular and extravagant in the world. For details of exact dates, contact the Tourist Information Office.
Feb 25-28 '96 *Carnival.* **May-Jun** *Feast of the Holy Ghost,* Maranho. **Jun 11-26** *Amazon Folklore Festival,* Manaus. **Jul** *Winter Festival* (classical music), Campo do Jordao. **Aug** *Marathon,* Rio de Janeiro. **Dec 31** *New Year's Eve Festival,* Rio de Janeiro.
SOCIAL CONVENTIONS: Handshaking is customary on meeting and taking one's leave, and normal European courtesies are observed. Frequent offers of coffee and tea are customary. Flowers are acceptable as a gift on arrival or following a visit for a meal. A souvenir from the visitor's home country will be well-received as a gift of appreciation. Casual wear is normal particularly during hot weather. In nightclubs casual-smart (eg blazer, no tie) is acceptable. For more formal occasions the mode of dress will be indicated on invitations. Smoking is acceptable unless notified. The Catholic Church is highly respected in the community, something which should be kept in mind by the visitor. **Tipping:** 10% is usual for most services not included on the bill.

BUSINESS PROFILE

ECONOMY: Brazil is the world's fifth-largest country, whilst her economy has the tenth-highest aggregate output in the world. Although agriculture remains the largest sector in terms of employment, there are well-developed mineral and manufacturing industries. Brazil is the world's second-largest exporter of agricultural products, principally coffee, sugar, soya beans, orange juice, beef, poultry and cocoa. Sisal, tobacco, maize and cotton are also produced. Orange juice and coffee are key export earners. Industrial production is concentrated in machinery, electrical goods, construction materials, rubber and chemicals, and vehicle production. The large steel industry has experienced bad times due to the fall in world demand and objections by foreign governments to Brazil's protectionist policies (which have nonetheless been relaxed appreciably since 1988). Vast mineral reserves include iron ore, of which Brazil is the world's largest exporter, bauxite (the ore from which aluminium is produced), gold, titanium, manganese, copper and tin, which is rapidly assuming considerable economic importance. Oil discoveries have also grown rapidly, although Brazil still imports most of its oil. Natural resources are the basis of Brazil's substantial trade surplus of US$9 billion (on total exports of US$33 billion – 1988 figures): the USA, Japan and the EU are the main destinations for Brazilian exports. Yet despite its healthy trade surplus, the Brazilian economy experienced considerable difficulty during the 1980s through the familiar South American problems of hyper-inflation and enormous overseas debts. On several occasions the Government seemed to have brought inflation under control, albeit at the cost of slowing economic growth, but each time their efforts were frustrated as the pressures which built up within the system burst out into a new spiral of price and wage increases. In 1989, President Fernando Collor de Mello adopted a novel and unique method of economic management. His aim was, quite literally, to remove inflation from the financial system – by removing a large proportion of the money in the economy. Personal bank deposits were frozen. The population was, for the most part, too stunned to object too strenuously. Collor de Mello's strategy – the 'Novo Plan' – also included more orthodox measures such as a reduction in public spending, privatisation of state-owned industries and an overhaul of the tax system. By the autumn of 1990, the economy was showing signs of genuine recovery. By the time of Collor's departure from office in 1992, however, it had become clear that the structural problems persisted as much as before. In the longer term, most Brazilians feel that the best prospects for economic development lie in the exploitation of the interior and in particular the rainforests. However, unrestrained development is no longer politically possible given the strength of opposition both within the country and internationally. Of interest here is a novel agreement signed between the British and Brazilian governments to create a more ecologically sensitive approach to rainforest development, involving aid and technical assistance. (This may become a pattern for future aid packages to the Third World.) Despite its problems, many observers are optimistic about Brazil's economic prospects once improved industrial efficiency, careful fiscal management and a sound relationship with overseas creditors have taken root. Brazil's principal trading partners are the United States, Japan, Germany and its fellow members of the newly-formed southern Latin American trading bloc, Mercosur. Brazil also has important trading links with a number of Arab countries, notably Saudi Arabia and, until UN-imposed economic sanctions took effect, Iraq.

BUSINESS: Business suits are worn when meeting senior officials and local heads of business, for semi-formal social functions and in exclusive restaurants and clubs. Exchange of calling cards is usual as is the expectation of dealing with someone of equal business status. **Office hours:** 0900-1800 Monday to Friday.
COMMERCIAL INFORMATION: The following organisation can offer advice: Confederacão Nacional do Comércio (CNC) (Chamber of Commerce), SCS, Edif. Presidente Dutra, 4° andar, Quadra 11, 70.327 Brasília DF. Tel: (61) 223 0578.

CLIMATE

Varies from arid scrubland in the interior to the impassable tropical rainforests of the northerly Amazon jungle and the tropical eastern coastal beaches. The south is more temperate. Rainy seasons occur from January to April in the north, April to July in the northeast and November to March in the Rio/São Paulo area.
Required clothing: Lightweight cottons and linens with waterproofing for the rainy season (November-March). Warm clothing is needed in the south during winter (June-July). Specialist clothing is needed for the Amazon region. Warm clothing is advised if visiting the southern regions in winter time.

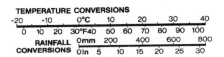

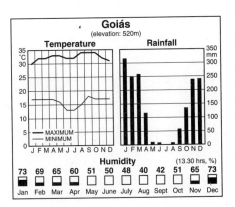

Goiás (elevation: 520m)

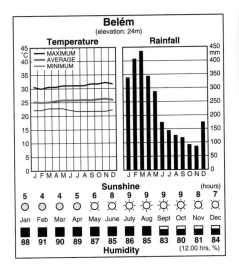

Belém (elevation: 24m)

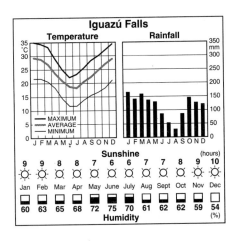

Iguazú Falls

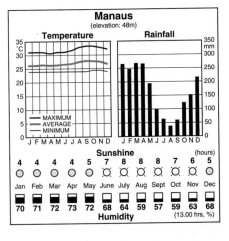

Manaus (elevation: 48m)

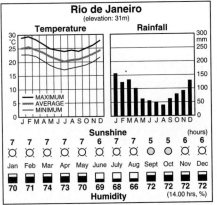

Rio de Janeiro (elevation: 31m)

British Dependent Territories

Note: The following is a list of the British Dependent Territories; many of these have their own entries in the *World Travel Guide*. For more information on these islands contact: the **Passport Office (London)**, tel: (0171) 279 3434 *or* 799 2728 (for entry requirements); the **Royal Commonwealth Society**, tel: (0171) 930 6733, fax: (0171) 930 9705; or the **Foreign Office, South Atlantic and Antarctic Department**, tel: (0171) 270 2716, fax: (0171) 270 2086.

ANGUILLA: See the section earlier in the *World Travel Guide*.

ASCENSION ISLAND: Location: South Atlantic, 1131km (703 miles) northwest of St Helena. **Area:** 88 sq km (34 sq miles). **Population:** 1192 (1993 estimate, excluding British military personnel). **Religion:** Anglican and Roman Catholic. **Time:** GMT.
A dependency of St Helena, the main importance of the island is as a communications centre and a military base. Relay stations (radio and subterranean cable) are operated by the BBC, RCA and a subsidiary of Cable & Wireless. There is a small US military presence.

BERMUDA: See the section earlier in the *World Travel Guide*.

BRITISH INDIAN OCEAN TERRITORY: Location: Consists of the Chagos Archipelago, 1930km (1199 miles) northeast of Mauritius, and the coral atoll of Diego Garcia. **Area:** 60 sq km (23 sq miles) of land and over 54,400 sq km (21,100 sq miles) of sea. **Population:** There are no permanent inhabitants. **Time: Chagos Archipelago:** GMT + 5. **Diego Garcia:** GMT + 6.
Under the terms of the 1966 agreement the islands are used jointly by the US and UK governments for military purposes. Following Iraq's invasion of Kuwait in August 1990, Diego Garcia was the base used by the US B-52 bombers taking part in the Allied action in the Gulf. In 1991, there were about 1200 US and British military personnel and 1700 civilian contractors in the Territory, giving a total population of 2900. A Fisheries Commission was formed between the UK and Mauritius in January 1994 for the promotion and organisation of scientific research and conservation within the territory's waters.

BRITISH VIRGIN ISLANDS: See the section later in the *World Travel Guide*.

CAYMAN ISLANDS: See the section later in the *World Travel Guide*.

FALKLAND ISLANDS: See the section later in the *World Travel Guide*.

GIBRALTAR: See the section later in the *World Travel Guide*.

HONG KONG: See the section later in the *World Travel Guide*.

MONTSERRAT: See the section later in the *World Travel Guide*.

PITCAIRN ISLANDS: Location: Central South Pacific, equidistant from Panama and New Zealand. The group includes the uninhabited islands of Oeno, Henderson and Ducie. **Area:** 35.5 sq km (13.7 sq miles). **Population:** 55 in Pitcairn (1993). **Population Density:** 12 per sq km (Pitcairn only). **Religion:** Seventh Day Adventist. **Time:** GMT - 8.5. **Money:** The Pitcairn Dollar is equivalent to the New Zealand Dollar and New Zealand money is also in use on the island.
Health: A yellow fever vaccination certificate is required of all travellers over one year of age coming from infected areas; see the *Health* section at back of book.
Since 1989, Henderson has been included in the United Nations 'World Heritage List' as a bird sanctuary. An exclusive economic zone (EEZ) was declared in 1992 including 370km (200 nautical miles) of the islands' waters. For further information, contact the New Zealand High Commission or Embassy. For official information on the islands, contact the Office of the Governor of Pitcairn, Henderson, Ducie and Oeno Islands, c/o the British High Commission, PO Box

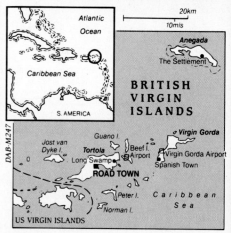

British Virgin Islands

1812, Wellington, New Zealand. Tel: (4) 472 6049. Fax: (4) 471 1974. Telex: 3325 (a/b UKREP NZ).

ST HELENA: Location: South Atlantic, about 1930km (1200 miles) west of the Angolan coast. **Area:** 122 sq km (47 sq miles). **Population:** 5644 (1987). **Population Density:** 46.3 per sq km. **Capital:** Jamestown, where about 1413 people live. **Religion:** Mostly Anglican. **Time:** GMT. **Money:** The St Helena Pound is equivalent to the UK Pound sterling. **Health:** No vaccinations are required for any international traveller. There is a reciprocal health agreement with the UK which entitles all those with proof of UK residence (ie NHS medical card or UK passport) to free hospital treatment in out-patient clinics during normal clinic times. **Travel:** There are no railways or airfields, but the *St Helena Shipping Company Limited* operates services to and from the UK six times a year, also stopping at the Canary Islands, Ascension Island and South Africa. St Helena depends on aid from Britain, although fishing, livestock, handicrafts and timber are important to the economy. There is a chamber of commerce in Jamestown. The *St Helena News* is published weekly. For official information on the islands, contact the Office of the Governor, Plantation House', St Helena. Tel: 2555. Fax: 2598. Telex: 202.

SOUTH GEORGIA AND THE SOUTH SANDWICH ISLANDS: Location: South Atlantic. South Georgia lies about 1300km (800 miles) east-southeast of the Falkland Islands, and the South Sandwich Islands lie about 750km (470 miles) southeast of South Georgia. **Area:** South Georgia: 3592 sq km (1387 sq miles); South Sandwich Islands: 311 sq km (120 sq miles). **Population:** There are no permanent inhabitants. **Time:** GMT - 2.
Dependencies of the Falkland Islands up until 1985, the islands now fall under the jurisdiction of the Commissioner for the territory, the Governor of the Falkland Islands. The islands are used for scientific purposes, and are watched over by a small British garrison. In May 1993, the British government announced an extension of its territorial jurisdiction of the waters surrounding the islands from 12 to 200 nautical miles, in response to the Argentine government's decision to sell fishing licenses for the region's waters.

TRISTAN DA CUNHA: Location: South Atlantic, 2400km (1500 miles) west of Cape Town, South Africa. The group also includes Inaccessible Island, the three Nightingale Islands and Gough Island. **Area:** 98 sq km (38 sq miles). **Population:** 300 (1993). **Religion:** Anglican with small Roman Catholic minority. **Time:** GMT.
A dependency of St Helena, Tristan da Cunha's economy is based on fishing and fish processing (mainly rock lobster), handicrafts and stamps. The island no longer receives British aid. The Government and the South Atlantic Islands Development Corporation (through its subsidiary Tristan Investments Ltd) are the only employers. For official information on the islands, contact the Administrator Philip H Johnson, The Residency, Tristan da Cunha. Tel: 5424. Fax: 5435. Telex: 5434.

TURKS AND CAICOS ISLANDS: See the section later in the *World Travel Guide.*

BRITISH ANTARCTIC TERRITORY: Location: Within the Antarctic Treaty area. **Area:** About 1,710,000 sq km (660,000 sq miles) of land. The territory also includes the South Shetlands and the South Orkneys.

Population: There are no permanent inhabitants, and the territory is used only for scientific purposes.
Since April 1967, these have been administered by the Department of Education and Science and are no longer a British Dependent Territory. See also the *Antarctica* entry earlier in the *World Travel Guide.*

UNITED KINGDOM CROWN DEPENDENCIES: The **Isle of Man** and the **Channel Islands** are not integral parts of the United Kingdom but are dependencies of the Crown and enjoy a high degree of internal self-government. For convenience, information on these islands has been placed at the end of the entry for the *United Kingdom* below.

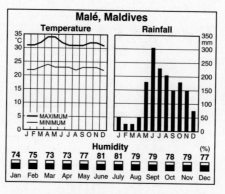

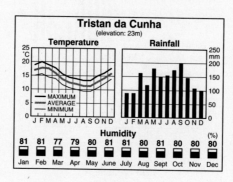

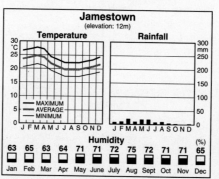

Location: Eastern Caribbean.

Diplomatic representation: The British Virgin Islands are a British Dependent Territory and are represented abroad by British Embassies. Information and advice may be obtained from the addresses below.

British Virgin Islands Tourist Board
PO Box 134, Waterfront Drive, Road Town, Tortola, British Virgin Islands
Tel: 43134. Fax: 43866.
British Dependent Territories Visa Section
The Passport Office, Clive House, 70-78 Petty France, London SW1H 9HD
Tel: (0171) 271 8552. Fax: (0171) 271 8645. Opening hours: 0900-1700 Monday to Friday.
British Virgin Islands Tourist Board
110 St Martin's Lane, London WC2N 4DY
Tel: (0171) 240 4259. Fax: (0171) 240 4270. Opening hours: 0930-1730 Monday to Friday.
British Virgin Islands Tourist Board
Suite 313, 370 Lexington Avenue, New York, NY 10017
Tel: (212) 696 0400. Fax: (212) 949 8254.
Also in: San Francisco.
The Tourist Board also deals with enquiries from Canada.

AREA: 153 sq km (59 sq miles).
POPULATION: 19,000 (1993).
POPULATION DENSITY: 108.8 per sq km.
CAPITAL: Road Town, Tortola. **Population:** 11,000 (1993).
GEOGRAPHY: The British Virgin Islands are an archipelago of more than 40 islands, only 15 of which are inhabited, forming the northern extremity of the Leeward Islands in the eastern Caribbean. The islands are volcanic in origin, with the exception of Anegada, which is formed of coral and limestone and is the lowest lying. The topography is otherwise mountainous, the highest point being Tortola's Sage Mountain, which rises to 550m (1800ft). There are remnants of a primeval rainforest on Tortola.
LANGUAGE: English.
RELIGION: Mainly Methodist and Church of God, but also Anglican, Adventist, Baptist and Roman Catholic

congregations.

TIME: GMT - 4.

ELECTRICITY: 110/60 volts AC, 60Hz. American 2-pin plugs are used.

COMMUNICATIONS: Telephone: IDD is available. Country code: 1 809 49. There are no area codes. Outgoing international code: 011. **Fax:** Cable & Wireless provides a service. **Telex/telegram:** Operated by Cable & Wireless. There are limited facilities outside main towns. **Post:** Airmail to Europe takes up to a week. **Press:** *The BVI Beacon* is published weekly. **BBC World Service and Voice of America frequencies:** From time to time these change. See the section *How to Use this Book* for more information.

BBC:

| MHz | 17.84 | 15.22 | 9.915 | 5.975 |

Voice of America:

| MHz | 15.21 | 11.70 | 6.130 | 5.995 |

PASSPORT/VISA

Regulations and requirements may be subject to change at short notice, and you are advised to contact the appropriate diplomatic or consular authority before finalising travel arrangements. Details of these may be found at the head of this country's entry. Any numbers in the chart refer to the footnotes below.

	Passport Required?	Visa Required?	Return Ticket Required?
Full British	Yes	No	Yes
BVP	Not valid	-	-
Australian	Yes	No	Yes
Canadian	No	No	Yes
USA	No	No	Yes
Other EU (As of 31/12/94)	Yes	1	Yes
Japanese	Yes	Yes	Yes

PASSPORTS: Valid passport required by all except nationals of the USA and Canada in possession of recognised form of identity.

British Visitors Passport: Not acceptable.

VISAS: Required by all except:

(a) nationals of countries referred to in the chart above;

(b) [1] nationals of EU countries (except nationals of Ireland and Portugal who *do* require visas) and nationals of Germany for stays of up to 1 month;

(c) nationals of Venezuela for stays of up to 1 month;

(d) nationals of Commonwealth countries;

(e) nationals of Finland, Iceland, Liechtenstein, Norway, San Marino, Sweden, Switzerland, Tunisia, Turkey and Uruguay, providing they are in possession of a confirmed return or onward travel document, have sufficient funds for support and pre-arranged accommodation.

Types of visa: Tourist, Business and Transit; fees vary according to nationality. Transit visas are not required by those with confirmed tickets for onward travel within 14 days of arrival; this facility is not available to nationals of Eastern European countries, who *do* require Transit visas for stays of less than 14 days (and Business/Tourist visas for longer stays).

Application to: The Home Office (address at top of entry) or the nearest British Consulate or Embassy.

Application requirements: (a) Application form. (b) Passport-size photo. (c) Valid passport. (d) Proof of sufficient funds to cover stay.

Working days required: Varies according to nationality of applicant.

Temporary residence: Work permit and residence permit required.

MONEY

Currency: US Dollar (US$) = 100 cents. Notes are in denominations of US$1000, 500, 100, 50, 20, 10, 5, 2 and 1. Coins are in denominations of US$1, and 50, 25, 10, 5 and 1 cents.

Credit cards: American Express, Mastercard and Visa are accepted. Check with your credit card company for details of merchant acceptability and other services which may be available.

Travellers cheques: Accepted in some places, particularly US Dollar cheques. All cheques are liable to a 10% stamp duty. Personal cheques are not accepted.

Exchange rate indicators: The following figures are included as a guide to the movements of the US Dollar against Sterling:

Date:	Oct '92	Sep '93	Jan '94	Jan '95
£1.00=	1.59	1.53	1.48	1.55

Currency restrictions: The import of local and foreign currency is unlimited, subject to declaration. The export of foreign and local currency is restricted to the amount declared on import.

Banking hours: 0900-1400 Monday to Thursday, 0900-1400 and 1600-1800 Friday.

DUTY FREE

Import licences are required for a small number of goods, mostly foodstuffs.

PUBLIC HOLIDAYS

Jan 1 '95 New Year's Day. **Mar 6** Commonwealth Day. **Apr 14-17** Easter. **Jun 5** Whit Monday. **Jun 6** Queen's Official Birthday. **Jul 1** Territory Day. **Aug 7-9** August Monday, Tuesday and Wednesday. **Oct 21** St Ursula's Day. **Nov 14** Prince of Wales' Birthday. **Dec 25-26** Christmas. **Jan 1 '96** New Year's Day. **Mar 6** Commonwealth Day. **Apr 5-8** Easter.

HEALTH

Regulations and requirements may be subject to change at short notice, and you are advised to contact your doctor well in advance of your intended date of departure. Any numbers in the chart refer to the footnotes below.

	Special Precautions?	Certificate Required?
Yellow Fever	No	No
Cholera	No	No
Typhoid & Polio	Yes	-
Malaria	No	-
Food & Drink	1	-

[1]: Mains water is normally chlorinated, and whilst relatively safe may cause mild abdominal upsets. Bottled water is available and is advised for the first few weeks of the stay. Milk is pasteurised and dairy products are safe for consumption. Local meat, poultry, seafood, fruit and vegetables are generally considered safe to eat.

Health care: Health insurance is recommended. There are good medical facilities on Tortola and six clinics on the other islands.

TRAVEL - International

AIR: *American Airlines* and *LIAT* run services to the islands.

Approximate flight times: From London to *Beef Island* or *Virgin Gorda* is 10 hours, including stopover time in Antigua or San Juan.

International airports: *Beef Island (EIS)* is 14.5km (9 miles) from Road Town on Tortola (travel time – 30 minutes). Taxis are available and there is a bar/restaurant. *Virgin Gorda (VIJ)* is 5km (3 miles) from Spanish Town on Virgin Gorda. Taxis are available.

There is also an airport on the island of *Anegada*.

Departure tax: US$7 for all international departures.

SEA: The British Virgin Islands' four main ports of entry are Bellamy Cay, Beef Island and Spanish Town on Tortola, as well as the Yacht Harbour on Virgin Gorda. *Commodore Cruises* and *Charger Inc* sail regularly from both Tortola and Virgin Gorda to all the US Virgin Islands.

Departure tax: US$4 for all international departures.

TRAVEL - Internal

AIR: *LIAT, American Eagle* and *Fly BVI* offer shuttle services to other islands including Virgin Gorda, Tortola and Anegada. It is also possible to charter planes for island hopping.

SEA: Yacht charter is one of the major industries and bareboats can be hired for all cruises. A permit is required for all charter boat passengers. Local boats can be hired for special tours and ferry services can be arranged, given adequate notice. The high season is from December to April. For current prices and a full list of boats for charter and hire, contact the Tourist Board.

ROAD: There is a good network. Driving is on the left and there is a maximum speed limit of 30mph (48kmph) throughout all the islands. **Taxi:** The BVI Taxi Association operates a wide range of vehicles on a range of standard journeys at fixed rates. All drivers are capable tour guides. Taxis can also be hired on an hourly or daily basis. **Car hire:** There are nine car hire companies in the British Virgin Islands. **Documentation:** A temporary British Virgin Islands licence is required; this will be issued on production of a current foreign licence for US$10. Insurance and British Virgin Islands licences are available from rental companies.

JOURNEY TIMES: The following chart gives approximate journey times (in hours and minutes) from Beef Island, Tortola to other major destinations in the

British Virgin Islands and the surrounding area.

	Air	Road	Sea
Virgin Gorda	0.05	0.30	-
Peter Is.	-	-	0.35
Guano Is.	-	-	0.20
Jost van Dyke	0.55	-	-
St Thomas (USVI)	0.15	0.55	-
San Juan (PR)	0.45	-	-

Note: PR = Puerto Rico; USVI = US Virgin Islands.

ACCOMMODATION

HOTELS: A wide range of hotel accommodation is available; a full list can be obtained from the Tourist Board (addresses at beginning of entry). There is a 7% hotel accommodation tax added to all hotel bills. For further information contact the British Virgin Islands Hotel and Commerce Association, PO Box 376, Wickham's Cay, Road Town, Tortola. Tel: 43514. Fax: 46179. **Grading:** Though there is no grading structure, many hotels in the Caribbean offer accommodation according to one of a number of plans: **FAP** is **Full American Plan**; room with all meals (including afternoon tea, supper, etc). **AP** is **American Plan**; room with three meals. **MAP** is **Modified American Plan**; breakfast and dinner included in the price of the room and, in some places, British-style afternoon tea. **CP** is **Continental Plan**; room and breakfast only. **EP** is **European Plan**; room only.

SELF-CATERING: Villas, houses and cottages can be hired on a weekly or longer basis. Information on properties is available from the Tourist Board. **CAMPING:** Only permitted on authorised sites. Details of sites and facilities are available from the Tourist Board. Backpacking is actively discouraged.

RESORTS & EXCURSIONS

There are more than 40 islands in the archipelago but only 15 are inhabited. All of them, apart from Anegada, are volcanic in origin. In general the atmosphere is quiet and uncommercialised, with miles of beautiful unspoilt beaches and concealed bays offering privacy and peace. The islands are situated in one of the finest sailing areas in the world. The scenery ranges from jagged mountain peaks covered with frangipani to banana and mango groves and palm trees.

Tortola, with a population of about 11,000, is the largest island of the group. It is linked by a bridge to **Beef Island**, site of the international airport. **Road Town,** on the south coast of Tortola, is the capital of the British Virgin Islands. It has a colourful market and delightful West Indian-style houses. Other attractions on the island are the **Mount Sage National Park** and the *J R O'Neal Botanic Gardens.*

Take the hydrofoil between Tortola and Virgin Gorda or St Thomas (US Virgin Islands). Tortola is a major yachting centre.

Many of the best beaches are on the northern part of the island, with names such as *Smugglers' Cove, Long Bay, Cane Garden Bay* and *Brewer's Bay.* There is an excellent view of the island and its coast from *Mount Sage,* 550m (1800ft) above sea level.

Other islands worth visiting are the coral island of **Anegada; Salt Island**, where salt is harvested each year and a bag sent to HM Queen Elizabeth II; **Norman Island**, with caves and a wealth of local sea-shanties and tales of treasure; and **Virgin Gorda**. Here may be found the famous *Baths,* a unique rock formation of dimly-lit grottoes and caves. Most of its attractions can be reached only by foot or boat. The smaller islands have strange names that are often the result of a historical connection with smuggling and piracy – for example, *Fallen Jerusalem, Necker Island* (owned by Richard Branson), *Great Camanoe, Great Dogs* and *Ginger Island.*

SOCIAL PROFILE

FOOD & DRINK: There is no shortage of excellent restaurants and inns serving local and international dishes. Food is imported but local island specialities are often available. These include lobster and fish chowder, mussel pie, conch stew, shark and other fish delicacies. In addition to the hotels, eateries can be found on Tortola, Virgin Gorda and Jost van Dyke. All kinds of rum punch and cocktails are served, plus a wide selection of imported beers, wines and spirits.

NIGHTLIFE: Many hotels have special nights with live music or dancing. There is one cinema (on Tortola) and several low-key nightclubs and discotheques. The Tourist Board publishes details of all forthcoming events.

SHOPPING: Special purchases include carved wooden items, straw-work, jewellery made from conch (pronounced 'konk') shell, seeds and very attractive *batik* material, designed and made locally.

SPORT: Sailing: Amongst the best in the Caribbean.

There are numerous modern marinas and the Yacht Club in Road Town, Tortola organises races and regattas and offers instruction in sailing and navigation. **Fishing:** Charters can be arranged for offshore fishing trips.
Diving: The clear waters provide ideal diving conditions and qualified instructors are available. The wreck of *HMS Rhone* off Salt Island is a favourite diving location.
Tennis: There are numerous courts on Tortola; those on Virgin Gorda are for hotel guests only.
SPECIAL EVENTS: Events likely to be of interest to the visitor include the *Spring Regatta* in Sir Francis Drake's Channel and the *Carnival* at the beginning of August. For further details, contact the Tourist Board.
SOCIAL CONVENTIONS: The British Virgin Islands remain linked to the British Commonwealth and the islanders reflect many British traditions and customs. The development of tourism proceeds with great caution; hence the unspoilt charm of these islands and cays remains the chief attraction. The pace of life is very easy-going and the visitor can expect good manners and old-fashioned British courtesies everywhere. Shaking hands is the customary form of greeting. Dress is informal for most occasions apart from the formal requirements of some hotels. Beachwear should be confined to the beach or poolside. **Tipping:** All hotels add a 10-12% service charge.

BUSINESS PROFILE

ECONOMY: Tourism is the islands' main economic activity. The number of visitors rose steadily throughout the mid- and late 1980s, mostly coming from the USA. Agricultural production is limited by poor soils, but some fruit and vegetables are produced for export, along with fish, livestock, gravel and sand. The largest export, however, is rum. The largest market for all these products is the USA. The British Virgin Islands import most of their foodstuffs and consumer goods from the US Virgin Islands, the USA itself, Puerto Rico, the UK and Europe. The whole economy suffered a dip at the end of 1989 following damage caused by Hurricane Hugo but the islands recovered with remarkable speed; production, exports and growth have all now returned to their previous levels. A burgeoning offshore financial sector has been operating since the mid-1980s and has proved to be a spectacular success by virtue of the British connection and a benign piece of customised legislation (the 1984 International Business Companies Ordinance) designed to assist offshore activities. Many companies

formerly registered in Panama have moved to the islands since the US invasion of that country in 1990. Annual GDP growth reached 15% during the late 1980s.
BUSINESS PROTOCOL: A shirt and tie are required for the summer months, with lightweight suits being acceptable at all other times. Best time to visit is December to April. **Office hours:** 0830-1700 Monday to Friday. **Government office hours:** 0830-1630 Monday to Friday.
COMMERCIAL INFORMATION: The following organisation can offer advice: Development Bank of the British Virgin Islands, PO Box 275, 1 Wickham's Cay, Road Town, Tortola. Tel: 43737. Fax: 43119.
CONFERENCES/CONVENTIONS: The British Virgin Islands Tourist Board can offer advice (see addresses listed at the beginning of the entry).

CLIMATE

The climate is tropical and tempered by trade winds. There is little variation between summer and winter. Rainfall is low, varying slightly from island to island. Night-time temperatures drop to a comfortable level.
Required clothing: Tropical lightweights. Dress is generally informal but beachwear is confined to beaches.

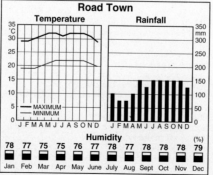

Road Town

| | Temperature | Rainfall | |
| | MAXIMUM / MINIMUM | | |

| | Jan | Feb | Mar | Apr | May | June | July | Aug | Sept | Oct | Nov | Dec |
|Humidity (%)| 78 | 77 | 75 | 75 | 76 | 77 | 77 | 78 | 77 | 78 | 78 | 79 |

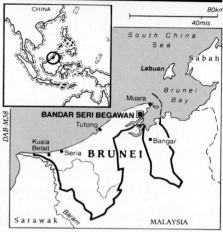

Brunei

☐ *international airport*

Location: South-East Asia; island of Borneo.

Information Bureau Section
Information Department, Prime Minister's Office, Bandar Seri Begawan 2041, Brunei
Tel: (2) 240 400. Fax: (2) 244 104. Telex: 2614.
High Commission of Brunei Darussalam
19/20 Belgrave Square, London SW1X 8PG
Tel: (0171) 581 0521. Fax: (0171) 235 9717. Opening hours: 0930-1300 and 1400-1630 Monday to Friday.
Consular Section:
19A Belgrave Mews West, London SW1X 8PG
Tel: (0171) 581 0521.
British High Commission
PO Box 2197, 3rd Floor, Hong Kong Bank Chambers, Jalan Pemancha, Bandar Seri Begawan, Brunei
Tel: (2) 222 231 *or* 226 001 (Consular section). Fax: (2) 226 002. Telex: 2211 (a/b UKREP BU).
Embassy of Negara Brunei Darussalam
Suite 300, 3rd Floor, 2600 Virginia Avenue, NW, Washington, DC 20037
Tel: (202) 342 0159. Fax: (202) 342 0158. Telex: 904081.
High Commission of Negara Brunei Darussalam
Suite 248, 866 United Nations Plaza, New York, NY 10017
Tel: (212) 838 1600. Fax: (212) 980 6478.
Also deals with enquiries from Canada.
Embassy of the United States of America
3rd Floor, Teck Guan Plaza, Jalan Sultan and Jalan McArthur, Bandar Seri Begawan, Brunei
Tel: (2) 229 670. Fax: (2) 225 293. Telex: 2609 (a/b AMEMB).

AREA: 5765 sq km (2226 sq miles).
POPULATION: 276,300 (1993).
POPULATION DENSITY: 48 per sq km.
CAPITAL: Bandar Seri Begawan. **Population:** 50,500 (1986).
GEOGRAPHY: Brunei is a small coastal state just 443km (277 miles) north of the equator in the northwest corner of Borneo, bounded on all landward sides by Sarawak (Malaysia), which splits Brunei into two parts. The landscape is mainly equatorial jungle cut by rivers. Most settlements are situated at estuaries.
LANGUAGE: Malay is the official language. English is widely used and Chinese dialects are also spoken.
RELIGION: Most of the Malay population are Sunni Muslims. There are also significant Buddhist, Confucian, Daoist and Christian minorities.

TIME: GMT + 8.
ELECTRICITY: 230 volts AC, 50Hz. Plugs are either round or square 3-pin.
COMMUNICATIONS: Telephone: Full IDD is available. Country code: 673. Outgoing international code: 00. Public telephones are available in most post office branches and main shopping areas and there is a private internal service. There are both coin- and card-operated public telephones in Brunei. Telephone cards can be obtained at post offices or at the Telecom office.
Telex/telegram: There are no public telex facilities, but they are available at government, large business offices and major hotels. Telegram facilities are available from the government telecommunications office in Bandar Seri Begawan. **Post:** Airmail letters to Europe take two to five days. Registered, recorded and express postal services ('Speedpost') are all available. Post office opening hours: 0745-1630 Monday to Thursday. **Press:** The only English-language newspaper is the daily *Borneo Bulletin*.
BBC World Service and Voice of America frequencies: From time to time these change. See the section *How to Use this Book* for more information.

BBC:				
MHz	17.83	15.31	11.95	6.195
Voice of America:				
MHz	15.42	11.76	9.770	7.120

PASSPORT/VISA

Regulations and requirements may be subject to change at short notice, and you are advised to contact the appropriate diplomatic or consular authority before finalising travel arrangements. Details of these may be found at the head of this country's entry. Any numbers in the chart refer to the footnotes below.

	Passport Required?	Visa Required?	Return Ticket Required?
Full British	Yes	1	Yes
BVP	Not valid	-	-
Australian	Yes	Yes	Yes
Canadian	Yes	2	Yes
USA	Yes	2	Yes
Other EU (As of 31/12/94)	Yes	1	Yes
Japanese	Yes	2	Yes

PASSPORTS: A passport valid for travel to Brunei with assured re-entry facilities to country of origin or domicile required by all.
British Visitors Passport: Not accepted.
VISAS: Required by all except:
(a) **[1]** nationals of the United Kingdom for up to 30 days and nationals of Belgium, Denmark, France, Germany, Luxembourg and the Netherlands for up to 14 days (nationals of other EU countries *do* require a visa);
(b) **[2]** nationals of Canada and Japan for up to 14 days;
(c) nationals of South Korea, Maldives, New Zealand, Norway, Philippines, Sweden, Switzerland and Thailand for up to 14 days;
(d) nationals of Malaysia and Singapore for up to 30 days;
(e) nationals of the USA for up to 90 days;
(f) those in transit to a third country by the same or next connecting aircraft and not leaving the airport (except for nationals of Afghanistan, Albania, Bulgaria, China, CIS, Cuba, Czech Republic, Hungary, Israel, North Korea, Mongolia, Poland, Romania, Slovak Republic, Taiwan (China), Vietnam and Yugoslavia).
Note: Return ticket is necessary for visa-free trips. All visitors must possess sufficient funds to support themselves whilst in the country.
Types of visa: Short Visit and Transit. Cost: £5 (Single-entry), £10 (Multiple-entry). Payment in cash or by postal order only.
Validity: 3 months (Single-entry). The validity of Multiple-entry visas is at the discretion of the Consulate.
Application and enquiries to: Consulate (or Consular section at Embassy or High Commission). For addresses, see top of entry.
Application requirements: (a) Passport. (b) Passport-size photo. (c) Application form. (d) Fee. (e) Letter of introduction or invitation if on business trip. (f) Copy of onward or return ticket. (g) Stamped self-addressed envelope for postal applications.
Working days required: 1 day if applying in person; 2-3 days by post.

MONEY

Currency: Brunei Dollar (Br$) = 100 sen. Notes are in the denominations Br$10,000, 1000, 500, 100, 50, 10, 5 and 1. Coins are in the denominations 50, 20, 10, 5 and 1 sen. The Brunei Dollar is officially at a par with the Singapore Dollar.
Currency exchange: Foreign currencies and travellers cheques can be exchanged at any bank. Hotels and many

department stores will also cash travellers cheques.
Credit cards: American Express, Diners Club, Access/Mastercard and Visa are generally accepted by hotels, department stores and major establishments. Check with your credit card company for details of merchant acceptability and other services which may be available.
Exchange rate indicators: The following figures are included as a guide to the movements of the Brunei Dollar against Sterling and the US Dollar:

Date:	Oct '92	Sep '93	Jan '94	Jan '95
£1.00=	2.57	2.45	2.38	2.26
$1.00=	1.62	1.60	1.61	1.46

Currency restrictions: The import of local currency is unlimited. The export of local currency is limited to Br$1000 in notes. The Singapore Dollar can be imported and exported up to a limit of Sing$1000. Indian and Indonesian banknotes are not exchangeable. Free import and export of other foreign currencies.
Banking hours: 0900-1200 and 1400-1500 Monday to Friday; 0900-1100 Saturday.

DUTY FREE

The following goods may be imported into Brunei without incurring Customs duty:
200 cigarettes or 250g tobacco products; 60ml of perfume and 250ml toilet water; 2 bottles of liquor and 12 cans of beer for personal consumption only, provided declared at customs upon arrival (persons over 17 years of age).
Prohibited items: Firearms, non-prescribed drugs and all pornography. The penalty for carrying non-prescribed drugs is death.

PUBLIC HOLIDAYS

Jan 1 '95 New Year's Day. **Jan 31-Feb 2** Chinese New Year. **Feb 1** Beginning of Ramadan. **Feb 23** National Day. **Feb 19** Memperingati Nuzul Al-Quran (Anniversary of the Revelation of the Koran). **Mar 2** Hari Raya Puasa (End of Ramadan). **May 10** Hari Raya Haji (Feast of the Sacrifice). **May 31** Hizrah (Islamic New Year). **Jun 1** Royal Brunei Armed Forces Day. **Jul 15** Sultan's Birthday. **Aug 9** Mouloud (Prophet's Birthday). **Dec 20** Isra Meraj (Ascension of the Prophet). **Dec 25** Christmas. **Jan 1 '96** New Year's Day. **Jan 20** Beginning of Ramadan. **Feb 19-21** Chinese New Year. **Feb 22** Hari Raya Puasa (End of Ramadan). **Feb/Mar** Memperingati Nuzul Al-Quran (Anniversary of the Revelation of the Koran).
Note: Muslim festivals are timed according to local sightings of various phases of the Moon and the dates given above are approximations. During the lunar month of Ramadan that precedes Hari Raya Puasa, Muslims fast during the day and feast at night and normal business patterns may be interrupted. Restaurants are closed during the day and Muslims are prohibited from smoking and drinking. Some disruption may continue into Hari Raya Puasa itself. Hari Raya Puasa and Hari Raya Haji may last anything from two to ten days. For more information see the section *World of Islam* at the back of the book.

HEALTH

Regulations and requirements may be subject to change at short notice, and you are advised to contact your doctor well in advance of your intended date of departure. Any numbers in the chart refer to the footnotes below.

	Special Precautions?	Certificate Required?
Yellow Fever	No	1
Cholera	Yes	2
Typhoid & Polio	Yes	-
Malaria	No	-
Food & Drink	3	-

[1]: A yellow fever vaccination certificate is required from travellers aged one year and over who have visited infected or endemic areas within the previous six days.
[2]: Following WHO guidelines issued in 1973, a cholera vaccination certificate is no longer a condition of entry to Brunei.
[3]: All water should be regarded as a possible health risk. Water used for drinking, brushing teeth or making ice should have first been boiled or sterilised. Milk is unpasteurised and should be boiled. Powdered or tinned milk is available and advised, but make sure it is reconstituted with pure water. Avoid all dairy products. Only eat well-cooked meat and fish, preferably served hot. Pork, salad and mayonnaise may carry increased risk. Vegetables should be cooked and fruit peeled.
Health care: Medical insurance is advised. Medical facilities are of a high standard. The health administration of Brunei reserves the right to vaccinate arrivals not in possession of required certificates and to

take any other action deemed necessary to ensure arrivals present no health risk.

TRAVEL - International

AIR: Brunei's national airline is *Royal Brunei Airline (RBA) (BI)*. Air carriers to Brunei include *Singapore Airlines, Malaysian Airlines System, Thai International* and *Philippines Airlines*. *RBA* flies to Singapore, Kuching, Kota Kinabalu, Kuala Lumpur, Manila, Bangkok, Taipei, Hong Kong, Perth, Darwin, Dubai, Frankfurt/M and London.
Approximate flight times: From Brunei to *London* is 17 hours, to *Los Angeles* is 19 hours, to *New York* is 22 hours, to *Singapore* is 2 hours and to *Sydney* is 11 hours.
International airport: *Bandar Seri Begawan (BWN)* is 10km (6 miles) northeast of the city. Taxi services are available to the city with surcharges after 2200. There are two restaurants.
Departure tax: Br$5 for flights to Singapore or Malaysia; Br$12 for all other destinations.
SEA: The port at Muara is the entry point for sea cargo. Ships and water taxis run a service between Bandar Seri Begawan and the Malay cities of Labuan (Sabah), Lawas, Limbang and Sundar (Sarawak).
ROAD: There are access roads into Brunei from Sarawak at various locations, although some are unpaved.

TRAVEL - Internal

AIR: There are no internal air services.
SEA/RIVER: There are water taxi services to Kampong Ayer, with stations at Jalan Kianggeh and Jalan McArthur. Water taxis are the most common form of transport in Kampong Ayer, Brunei's renowned water village. Regular water taxi and boat services also ply between Bandar Seri Begawan and Bangar (in Temburong), Limbang (in Sarawak), Labuan and some towns in the Malaysian state of Sabah.
ROAD: There are about 750km (450 miles) of roads in the country. Traffic drives on the left. **Bus:** Services operate to Seria (91km/57 miles from Bandar Seri Begawan), Kuala Belait (16km/10 miles from Seria), Tutong (48km/30 miles from Bandar Seri Begawan) and Muara (27km/17 miles from Bandar Seri Begawan). There is a bus station in the town centre. **Car hire:** Self-drive or chauffeur-driven cars are available at the airport and major hotels. It is important to specify whether an air-conditioned car is required. **Documentation:** International Driving Permit legally required. A temporary licence to drive in Brunei is available on presentation of a valid driving licence from the visitor's country of origin.
URBAN: Taxis are available in Bandar Seri Begawan. Fares are usually metered. If not they should be agreed before the journey. There is a 50% surcharge after 2300. Tipping is not necessary.

ACCOMMODATION

Outside the main towns, accommodation is not available. The one hotel of international standard is in Bandar Seri Begawan – the Sheraton. Other hotels in Bandar Seri Begawan include Angs Hotel, River Views Inn, National Inn and the Brunei Hotel. Hotels in Kuala Belait are the Seaview Hotel and Sentosa Hotel.

RESORTS & EXCURSIONS

There are beaches with facilities at Kuala Belait, Lumut Beach near Tutong and at Muara. Brunei is a heavily forested state, and most activity is either on the coast or at the river mouths.
The principal tourist sights in **Bandar Seri Begawan**, the capital, are: the minaret crowning the golden-domed *Sultan Omar Ali Saifuddien Mosque*, which stands in the middle of its own artificial lagoon, affording a fine view over the town and stilt village; the *Churchill Memorial*, incorporating the *Churchill Museum* and *Aquarium*; the ancient *Tomb of Sultan Bolkiah*, the fifth sultan and known as the 'singing admiral' for his love of both music and conquest; the *Brunei Museum*; and the new *Malay Technology Museum* showing traditional crafts.
Outside the capital, it is possible to travel up river to visit village settlements, such as **Kampong Parit Resort**, which have largely survived the rapid industrialisation of recent years, following the discovery of oil. **Kampong Ayer**, the water village, is reputed to be the largest collection of stilt habitations in the world. There are splendid traditional longhouses in the Temburong district, at **Rampayoh** in the Belait district and in more heavily forested areas of jungle that are accessible only by boat. Waterfalls and lakes can also be seen around Rampayoh (beware of leeches); at *Luagan Lalak* there is a picnic area. There is a hill resort at **Tasek Merimbun** where two small lakes flow into a single river.

SOCIAL PROFILE

FOOD & DRINK: European food is served in hotel restaurants, along with Malaysian, Chinese and Indian dishes. Local food is like Malay cuisine with fresh fish and rice, often quite spicy. **Drink:** Alcohol is prohibited.
SHOPPING: Special purchases include handworked silverware, brassware and bronzeware such as jugs, trays, gongs, boxes, napkin rings, spoons and bracelets; and fine handwoven sarongs, baskets and mats of pandan leaves. Shopping centres at Bandar Seri Begawan, Seria and Kuala Belait offer local products and imported items. The 'Tamu' Night Market in Bandar Seri Begawan is open from early morning to late at night and sells many fruits, spices, poultry and vegetables, as well as antiques. Food is available there at the lowest prices in town. **Shopping hours:** 0800-2130 Monday to Saturday.
SPORT: There are facilities for watching or participating in **tennis, golf, polo, football** and **hockey; swimming, sailing** and **skindiving** are also popular. Hotels will have details.
SOCIAL CONVENTIONS: Shoes should be removed when entering Muslim homes and institutions and visitors should not pass in front of a person at prayers or touch the Al-Quran, the famous Muslim holy book. Traditionally, a Bruneian shakes hands lightly, bringing his hands to his chest. However, women are not expected to shake hands. There are many honorific titles in Brunei: *Awang* (abbreviated to Awg), for instance, is generally used in the same way as the English 'Mr'; *Dayang* (Dyg) is equivalent to 'Ms' or 'Mrs'. Avoid giving or receiving with the left hand or pointing the soles of the feet towards companions. It is also considered impolite to point with the index finger (the right thumb should be used instead) or to beckon someone with your fingers (the whole hand should be waved instead, with the palm facing downwards). Also, the right fist should never be smacked into the left palm. It is widely regarded as discourteous to refuse refreshment when it is offered by a host. Dress is informal except for special occasions. Women should ensure that their head, knees and arms are covered. **Tipping:** Most hotels and restaurants add 10% to the bill.

BUSINESS PROFILE

ECONOMY: Brunei's economy depends on its oil and natural gas deposits, which are mostly offshore, and its investments. Although these are not extensive by world standards, Brunei's small population allows a very high standard of living. The Government has made recent efforts to diversify the economy, mainly by providing tax concessions on foreign investment: timber, paper, fertilisers, petrochemicals and glass are the most promising candidates for development in the growing industrial sector. Some 15% of the land is under cultivation, with rice, cassava and fruit as the main crops. Japan, which takes half of Brunei's oil production, is the country's largest single trading partner, followed by Korea, Singapore, Thailand and Australia.
BUSINESS: Suits are recommended. Business visits are best made outside the monsoon season (between April and November). The services of a translator will not normally be required as English is widely spoken. **Office hours:** 0800-1200 and 1300-1700 Monday to Thursday, 0900-1200 Saturday. **Government office hours:** 0745-1215 and 1330-1630 Monday to Thursday and Saturday.
COMMERCIAL INFORMATION: The following organisations can offer advice: High Commission of Brunei Darussalam (Commercial Section), 49 Cromwell Road, London SW7. Tel: (0171) 581 0521. Fax: (0171) 235 9717; *or* Brunei Darussalam International Chamber of Commerce and Industry, PO Box 2246, Bandar Seri Begawan 1922. Tel: (2) 236 601. Fax: (2) 228 389.

CLIMATE

Very hot tropical climate most of the year. Heavy rainfall in the monsoon season, October to March. Average temperature is 28°C.

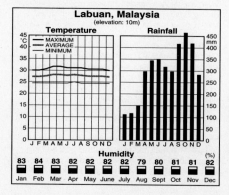

Labuan, Malaysia
(elevation: 10m)

Bulgaria

Location: Eastern Europe.

Balkantourist
Boulevard Vitosha 1, 1040 Sofia, Bulgaria
Tel: (2) 43331. Fax: (2) 800 134. Telex: 22583.
Committee for Tourism
1 Sveta Nedelja Square, 1040 Sofia, Bulgaria
Tel: (2) 874 946. Fax: (2) 882 066. Telex: 23101.
Embassy of the Republic of Bulgaria
186-188 Queen's Gate, London SW7 5HL
Tel: (0171) 584 9400 *or* 584 9433. Fax: (0171) 584 4948. Telex: 25465. Opening hours: 0930-1700 Monday to Friday (0930-1230 visa enquiries).
Bulgarian National Tourist Office
18 Princes Street, London W1R 7RE
Tel: (0171) 499 6988. Fax: (0171) 499 1905. Telex: 296467. Opening hours: 0900-1700 Monday to Friday.
British Embassy
Boulevard Vassil Levski 65-67, 1000 Sofia, Bulgaria
Tel: (2) 879 575 *or* 885 361/2. Fax: (2) 462 065. Telex: 22363 (a/b PRODROME) *or* 24212 (a/b BRITCO BG).
Embassy of the Republic of Bulgaria
1621 22nd Street, NW, Washington, DC 20008
Tel: (202) 387 7969 *or* 483 5885 (Consular section). Fax: (202) 234 7973.
Balkan Holidays (USA) Ltd
Suite 508, 41 East 42nd Street, New York, NY 10017
Tel: (212) 573 5530. Fax: (212) 573 5538.
Also deals with enquiries from Canada.
Embassy of the United States of America
Unit 1335, Saborna Street 1, Sofia, Bulgaria
Tel: (2) 884 801/2/3/4/5. Fax: (2) 801 977.
US Consulate
1 Kapitan Andreev Street, Sofia, Bulgaria
Tel: (2) 659 459.
Embassy of the Republic of Bulgaria
325 Stewart Street, Ottawa, Ontario K1N 6K5
Tel: (613) 789 3215. Fax: (613) 789 3524.
The Canadian Embassy in Budapest deals with enquiries relating to Bulgaria (see *Hungary* later in the book).

Timatic

Health	
GALILEO/WORLDSPAN:	**TI-DFT/SOF/HE**
SABRE:	**TIDFT/SOF/HE**
Visa	
GALILEO/WORLDSPAN:	**TI-DFT/SOF/VI**
SABRE:	**TIDFT/SOF/VI**

For more information on Timatic codes refer to Contents.

AREA: 110,994 sq km (42,855 sq miles).
POPULATION: 8,989,165 (1990 estimate).
POPULATION DENSITY: 81 per sq km.
CAPITAL: Sofia. **Population:** 1,220,914 (1990 estimate).
GEOGRAPHY: Bulgaria is situated in Eastern Europe and bounded to the north by the River Danube and Romania, to the east by the Black Sea, to the south by Turkey and Greece and to the west by Serbia and the Former Yugoslav Republic of Macedonia. The Balkan Mountains cross the country reaching to the edge of the Black Sea and its golden beaches. The land is heavily cultivated, covered with forests and crossed by rivers. Although Bulgaria lies in the very southeast corner of Europe the climate is never extreme in summer, even on the red-earthed plains of Southern Thrace. The Black Sea resorts have some of the largest beaches in Europe and offer sunbathing from May until October, while in winter heavy falls of snow are virtually guaranteed in the mountain skiing resorts.
LANGUAGE: Bulgarian is the official language. English is spoken by many in the cities and resorts. Turkish, Russian, German and French are also spoken.
RELIGION: Eastern Orthodox Church; Muslim and Roman Catholic minorities.
TIME: GMT + 2 (GMT + 3 from last Sunday in March to Saturday before last Sunday in September).
ELECTRICITY: 220 volts AC, 50Hz. Plugs are 2-pin.
COMMUNICATIONS: Telephone: IDD is available to mainly cities. Country code: 359. Outgoing international code: 00. Calls from some parts of the country must be placed through the international operator. There are many public telephones in the main towns. **Fax:** Facilities are available at BTA (Bulgarina Telegraph Agency) offices. **Telex/telegram:** International communications via telex and telegrams are available from Bulgaria. Public telex booths are available at general post offices and major hotels in Sofia. The General Post Office in Sofia, at 4 Gurko Street, is open 24 hours, with facilities for both telex and telegram. **Post:** Airmail to Western Europe takes from four days to two weeks. **Press:** The BTA publishes books, brochures and other literature in 21 languages and the weekly newspaper, *Sofia News,* is available in five languages (including English); the monthly magazine, *Bulgaria,* is available in ten languages. Since 1990 the press laws have been liberalised and formerly banned publications are freely available again.The most important dailies include *Demokratsiya, Duma* and *Trud.*
BBC World Service and Voice of America frequencies: From time to time these change. See the section *How to Use this Book* for more information.
BBC:

MHz	17.64	15.07	9.410	6.180

Voice of America:

MHz	9.760	6.040	5.995	15.21

Radio Varna and BTV broadcast holiday magazine programmes in English.

PASSPORT/VISA

Regulations and requirements may be subject to change at short notice, and you are advised to contact the appropriate diplomatic or consular authority before finalising travel arrangements. Details of these may be found at the head of this country's entry. Any numbers in the chart refer to the footnotes below.

	Passport Required?	Visa Required?	Return Ticket Required?
Full British	Yes	Yes/2	No
BVP	Not valid	-	-
Australian	Yes	Yes/3	No
Canadian	Yes	Yes/3	No
USA	Yes	1	No
Other EU (As of 31/12/94)	Yes	Yes/2	No
Japanese	Yes	Yes/3	No

Note: All visitors to Bulgaria must register with the police, a hotel or a guesthouse within 48 hours of arrival.
PASSPORTS: A valid passport with at least 6 months remaining validity after day of departure is required by all.
British Visitors Passport: Not acceptable.
VISAS: Required by all except:
(a) nationals of Austria, Bosnia-Hercegovina, CIS*, Croatia, Cuba, Czech Republic, Estonia*, Hungary, Latvia*, Lithuania*, South Korea, Former Yugoslav Republic of Macedonia, Mongolia, Poland, Romania, Slovak Republic, Slovenia, Tunisia and Yugoslavia (Serbia and Montenegro);
(b) **[1]** nationals of the USA as tourists for up to 30 days;
(c) **[2]** nationals of EU countries on any holiday pre-arranged through *Balkantourist* or an authorised agent/operator if it is booked for at least 3 days. In all other cases EU nationals can obtain visas at the border if

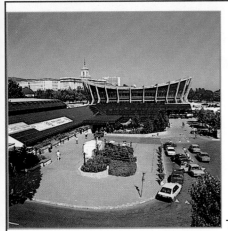
travelling by road or air. If travelling by rail, however, a visa is required in advance;
(d) **[3]** nationals of Australia, Canada and Japan on any holiday pre-arranged through *Balkantourist* or an authorised agent/operator if it is booked for at least 3 days;
(e) nationals of Bahrain, Cyprus, Finland, Hong Kong, Israel, Liechtenstein, New Zealand, Norway, Qatar, Saudi Arabia, Singapore, South Africa, Switzerland†, Sweden, Taiwan (China), United Arab Emirates and Zimbabwe on any holiday pre-arranged through *Balkantourist* or an authorised agent/operator if it is booked for at least 3 days.
Note: [*] A legalised invitation from Bulgaria is required. **[†]** If travelling by rail a visa is required in advance.
Types of visa: Tourist (£20 in cash or by postal order); Business (single-entry: £20; multiple-entry: £26 for 3 months validity, £46 for 6 months validity); Single-transit (£20); Double-transit (£26). Express visas have been introduced for visits of less than 7 working days; these will be issued immediately if applying in person, or by return if applying by post. The cost of an Express visa is £40 (in cash if applying in person, or by postal order if applying by post). Tourist visas are single-entry only and are valid for 3 months for a stay of a maximum of 30 days. Business visas are available single- and multiple-entry. Visas are issued free of charge to nationals of the following countries: China, Cyprus, North Korea and Zimbabwe.
Validity: For tourist and business trips, visas are normally valid for 3 months. Transit visas allow one to stay for up to 30 hours. Enquire at the Embassy for further details.
Application to: Consulate (or Consular section at Embassy). For addresses, see top of entry.
Application requirements: (a) Application form. (b) 1 passport-size photo. (c) Valid passport. (d) If applying for a Business visa, the application must also be accompanied by a letter of invitation from a Bulgarian company and a letter from the applicant's company (for a multiple-entry visa an additional letter/fax from the Bulgarian company certifying regular business relations). (e) If applying by post, a registered, stamped, self-addressed envelope large enough for return of passport. (f) For visitors staying with friends or relatives, an official invitation from their hosts, legalised by the respective Bulgarian local authorities, is required. (g) An Aids test may be required by certain visitors staying more than one month. (h) Fee payable in cash or by postal order.
Working days required: 7 for single-entry; 14-30 days for multiple-entry.
Temporary residence: Enquire at the Bulgarian Embassy.

MONEY

Currency: Lev (Lv) = 100 stotinki. The plural of Lev is Leva. Notes are in denominations of Lv100, 50, 20, 10, 5, 2 and 1. Coins are in denominations of Lv5, 2 and 1, and 50, 20, 10, 5, 2 and 1 stotinki.
Currency exchange: A *bordereau* receipt will be given and must be kept until departure. Visitors are advised to exchange money at bureaux de change and not on the black market.
Credit cards: Diners Club, American Express, Carte Blanche, Eurocard and Visa have a limited acceptance. Check with your credit card company for details of merchant acceptability and other services which may be available.

Exchange rate indicators: The following figures are included as a guide to the movements of the Lev against Sterling and the US Dollar:

Date:	Oct '92	Sep '93	Jan '94	Jan '95
£1.00=	43.00	39.55	39.65	102.49
$1.00=	27.10	25.90	26.80	66.26

Currency restrictions: The import and export of local currency is limited to Lv10,000. There are no restrictions on the amount of foreign currency though amounts over US$5000 have to be declared. The export of foreign currency is limited to the amount declared on import. Local currency can be exchanged at the airport on production of a *bordereau*.
Banking hours: 0800-1130 and 1400-1800 Monday to Friday; 0830-1130 Saturday.

DUTY FREE

The following goods may be taken into Bulgaria by persons over 18 years of age without paying customs duty:
200 cigarettes or 50 cigars or 250g of tobacco; 1 litre spirits and 2 litres of wine; 100g of perfume; objects and foodstuffs intended for personal use during the stay in the holiday; gifts to the value of Lv100.
The following goods must be declared:
Objects worth more than Lv60; objects intended for other persons; antiques, works of art, commercial samples, typewriters, cameras, printed matter and manuscripts, plants, fruits, seeds, firearms and ammunition for hunting purposes; currency, securities and precious stones or metals.
Note: (a) The indicated values in local currency are calculated according to the unified state prices for retail sale. (b) Luggage carried by transit passengers may be sealed at customs to avoid another check-up at the exit customs.
Prohibited items: Arms, ammunition, narcotics and pornography.
Export allowance: Articles worth more than Lv50 may be exported duty free if they have been bought with legally exchanged currency, in which case a statement of account must be presented.

PUBLIC HOLIDAYS

Jan 1 '95 New Year's Day. **Mar 3** National Day. **Apr 17** Easter Monday. **May 1** Labour Day. **May 24** Education Day. **Dec 24-25** Christmas. **Jan 1 '96** New Year's Day. **Mar 3** National Day. **Apr 8** Easter Monday.

HEALTH

Regulations and requirements may be subject to change at short notice, and you are advised to contact your doctor well in advance of your intended date of departure. Any numbers in the chart refer to the footnotes below.

	Special Precautions?	Certificate Required?
Yellow Fever	No	No
Cholera	No	No
Typhoid & Polio	No	-
Malaria	No	-
Food & Drink	1	-

Note: An Aids test may be required for visitors staying more than one month.
[1] Mains water is normally chlorinated, and whilst relatively safe may cause mild abdominal upsets. Bottled water is available and is advised for the first few weeks

of the stay. Milk is pasteurised and dairy products are safe for consumption. Local meat, poultry, seafood, fruit and vegetables are considered safe to eat.
Health care: There is a Reciprocal Health Agreement with the UK. On the production of a UK passport, hospital and other medical care will be provided free of charge; prescribed medicines must be paid for. Bulgarian physicians are trained to a very high standard, although hospitals and clinics are not usually equipped to the standard of US or West European levels. Basic medical supplies are widely available, but specialised treatments may not be.

TRAVEL - International

AIR: Bulgaria's national airline is *Balkan-Bulgarian Airlines (LZ)*.
For free advice on air travel, call the *Air Travel Advisory Bureau* in the UK on (0171) 636 5000 (London) or (0161) 832 2000 (Manchester).
Approximate flight times: From Sofia to *London* is 3 hours and to *New York* is 9 hours.
International airports: *Sofia (SOF)*, 10km (6 miles) east of the city (travel time – 20 minutes). Buses run about every ten minutes to the city centre during the day and about every 20 minutes 2100-0030. Coach by arrangement with *Balkantourist*. Taxis are also available, although many taxi drivers refuse to run their meters and travellers are advised to agree the fare beforehand. Airport facilities include banks and currency exchange (24 hours), post office, duty-free shop (stocking spirits, wines, perfume, traditional souvenirs, etc), nursery, restaurant (1100-2230), 24-hour bar, car hire (*Hertz, Avis, Budget* and *Inter-Balkan*) and car park.
Varna (VAR) is 9km (5.5 miles) from the city. Bus service to Varna city centre departs every 20 minutes. Coach service is available by arrangement with *Balkantourist*. Taxi service is also available. Airport facilities include outgoing duty-free shop, banking and currency exchange (24 hours), restaurant (0600-2230), 24-hour bar and car hire (by prior arrangement with *Balkantourist* in Varna).
Bourgas (BOJ) is 13km (8 miles) from the city. Bus service departs every 20 minutes to the city centre. Coach service is available by prior arrangement with *Balkantourist*. Taxi service is also available. Airport facilities include outgoing duty-free shop, banking and currency exchange (24 hours), restaurant (0600-2230), 24-hour bar and car hire (by prior arrangement in Bourgas).
SEA: The main international ports are Varna and Bourgas.
RAIL: There are no direct rail services between Bulgaria and Western Europe although there are frequent services between Sofia and Belgrade, Bucharest, Thessaloniki and Istanbul. Dining car facilities are available on all routes. First-class travel is recommended.
ROAD: Approach via Koulata on the border of Greece; via Ruse, Kardom and Durankulak on the border of Romania; via Svilengrad and Kapitan Andrikeevo on the border of Turkey; via Kalotina, Zlatarevo, Vrashkachuka on the border of Yugoslavia, and Guyeshevo on the border of the Former Yugoslav Republic of Macedonia.

TRAVEL - Internal

AIR: *Balkan-Bulgarian Airlines* operates eight domestic services connecting Sofia with the coast and main towns. The journeys from Sofia to Varna and Bourgas can be made in under an hour. Air travel is comparatively cheap, and is only slightly more expensive than rail travel.

A FAIRY TALE IN WHITE, BLUE AND GREEN

LOCATION: 1650 metres above sea level, some 80 kilometres away from Plovdiv (Bulgaria's second largest city) and 260 kilometres from the capital Sofia.

CLIMATE: Mountainous with Mediterranean influence, average annual temperature 8.5°C.

HOTELS: 9 hotels and 30 chalets with a total of 1650 beds, all rooms with bathrooms and WC.

RESORT AMENITIES: Restaurants, folk nights, nightclubs, cafes, indoor swimming pool, sauna, fitness centre, physiotherapy, bowling alley, souvenir shops, barber's and hairdresser's, archery, mountain bikes, fishing, guided walking tours and excursions round Bulgaria, to Istanbul and Greece.

SKI FACTS: 17.5 kilometres downhill ski-runs; 25 kilometres cross-country trails; 1 triple chairlift; 4 single chairlifts; 3 stationary draglifts and a number of baby draglifts providing total capacity of 8,500 skiers per hour; 14 ski-rooms supplying 3,200 sets of ski-equipment of world famous trademarks; ski-school with 100 English- and German-speaking instructors, running classes from the A-class beginner to the most experienced and sophisticated skiers' E-class; paragliding school; ski kindergarten for children up to 8 years old.

NEW POINTS: Aesthetic dental surgery with the latest modern equipment and high-quality dental services at affordable prices; longevity centre – prophyilaxis of ageing and premature senile symptoms and changes. Discover the secret of still active Rhodopean centinarians!

PAMPOROVO

Information and Sales: Telephone: +359 3021 438,
Marketing Department: Fax: +359 3021 263. Telex: 48511.

RIVER: Regular boat and hydrofoil services along the Bulgarian bank of the Danube link many centres, including Vidin, Lom, Kozloduj; Orjahovo, Nikopol; Svishtov, Tutrakan and Silistra. The official crossing points into Romania are by ferry from Vidin to Calafat and by road bridge from Ruse to Giurgiu.

RAIL: There are over 6500km (4040 miles) of railways in the country. Bulgarian State Railways connect Sofia with main towns. Reservations are essential and first-class travel is advised. For details contact the State Railway Office.

ROAD: There are over 13,000km (8000 miles) of roads linking the major centres and in general the quality is good. Traffic drives on the right. International road signs are used. Speed limits are strictly adhered to: 50kmph (31mph) in built-up areas, 80kmph (50mph) outside built-up areas and 120kmph (75mph) on motorways. Alcohol is strictly forbidden; on-the-spot fines are imposed for offences. Spare parts are easily available. There are a reasonable number of petrol stations (they are marked on a free map supplied by *Balkantourist*). Car theft is a serious problem in Bulgaria, particularly 4-wheel-drive vehicles and recent European sedan-style models and few vehicles are ever recovered. **Taxi:** Available in all towns and also for intercity journeys. Vehicles are metered, unless they are privately owned. A 5-10% tip is appreciated. **Car hire:** Self-drive cars can be hired through hotel reception desks and through *Hertz-Balkantourist Joint Venture Company*. There are no fly-drive arrangements through the airlines. Most transactions are in hard currency. **Documentation:** An International Driving Licence should be obtained, although foreign driving licences are accepted for short visits. A Green Card is compulsory.

URBAN: Bus, tramway and trolleybus services operate in Sofia; in addition, a metro is under construction. Flat fares are charged and tickets must be pre-purchased. Buses and taxis are provided in all the main towns. There are also trolleybuses in Plovdiv and Varna.

JOURNEY TIMES: The following chart gives approximate journey times from Sofia (in hours and minutes) to other major cities/towns in Bulgaria.

	Air	Road	Rail
Varna	1.00	8.00	7.00
Bourgas	1.00	7.00	6.00
Plovdiv	0.40	2.00	2.00
Ruse	-	9.00	8.00
Turnovo	-	3.30	-
Vitosha	-	0.30	-
Borovets	-	1.30	-
Pamporovo	-	3.30	-
Golden Sands	*0.45	*7.00	-
Albena	*0.45	*7.00	-
Sunny Beach	**0.35	**6.30	-

Notes: [*] From Varna Airport. [**] From Bourgas Airport.

ACCOMMODATION

HOTELS: Most of the hotels used by Western visitors are owned by *Balkantourist*. Advanced booking is advisable. **Grading:** Hotels are classified as deluxe, first- and second-class. Special care has been taken in some hotels to conform to international standards for these categories.
GUEST-HOUSES: Accommodation is available in small villas with private rooms, particularly near the coast.
CAMPING/CARAVANNING: Campsites are classified from 'Special' to I and II, and the top two categories have hot and cold water, showers, electricity, grocery stores, restaurants, telephones and sports grounds. The camping areas are located in main tourist areas.
YOUTH HOSTELS: These are situated in 30 main towns. For information contact: Orbita, Boulevard A. Stamboliska 45A, Sofia. Tel: (2) 879 552.

RESORTS & EXCURSIONS

Many tourists will travel in organised groups, but it is possible for tourists to make their own way by train or hired car.

Sofia

Dating back to the 4th century BC, the ancient capital of Sofia has a wealth of different architectural styles including Greek, Roman, Byzantine, Bulgarian and Turkish. The city boasts many theatres and museums (including those of archaeology and ethnography), opera houses and art galleries (including the *National Gallery of Painting and Sculpture* housed in the former Royal Palace of the King) as well as a universities, open-air markets, parks (over 300 of them, including the *Borisova Park*) and sports stadia. Visitors should see the extraordinary *Alexander Nevsky Memorial Church*

(which dominates the city with its gold-leaf dome), built to celebrate Bulgaria's liberation from the Turks in the Russo-Turkish war at the end of the last century. The crypt hosts an exhibition of beautiful icons, and the choir is excellent and well worth hearing. Other churches in Sofia include *St Sophia,* which is Byzantine and dates from the 6th century; *St George,* which dates back to the 5th century and contains 14th-century frescoes; and *Sveta Petka Samardshijska,* which is 14th century. There is an archaeological museum housed in the nine cupolas of the *Bouyouk Mosque* (the largest in Sofia). The *Banya Bashi Mosque* is also worth a visit.
An example of modern architecture is the *Battemberg Square,* which contains the *Government Buildings* and some Roman remains nearby (discovered when an underpass was being dug) with a reconstruction of the city as it was in Roman times.
EXCURSIONS & SIGHTSEEING: 121km (75 miles) from Sofia is *Rila Monastery,* perched high up on the side of a mountain in the middle of thick pine forests. Rila has a fascinating collection of murals, woodcarvings, old weapons and coins, and manuals and Bibles written on sheepskin. The monastery itself is notable for its delicate and unusual architectural features. Originally founded in the 10th century by the hermit and holy man, Ivan Rilsky, the monastery acted as a repository and sanctuary for Bulgarian culture during the 500-year Turkish occupation from 1396. Fire has destroyed most of the early architecture and the present buildings date from the 19th century, with the exception of the 14th-century *Hrelio's Tower.* There is good accommodation in the monastery and a nearby hotel. Rila is an excellent place from which to start climbs and hikes in the surrounding countryside.
The mountain of **Vitosha** on the outskirts of Sofia is a National Park with chairlifts and cable cars to help with the ascent as it is about 2000m (7000ft) high (see also below). Here, the medieval church of **Boyana** can be seen, with its beautiful and ancient frescoes, painted in about 1200 and thought to be some of the oldest in Bulgaria.
South of Sofia is **Blagoevgrad,** home of the Pirin State Ensemble (the world-renowned folkloric group); **Sandansky,** an ancient spa town and birthplace of the Roman gladiator, Spartacus; and **Melnik,** known for its wine cellars, 18th-19th century architecture and its proximity to *Rozhen Monastery* with its beautifully carved altar, stained glass windows, murals and icons.

Plovdiv

Founded in 342BC and the country's second-largest city, Plovdiv is divided by the Maritsa River and contains both an old quarter and a new commercial section. The old part contains many buildings dating from the 18th and 19th centuries (and earlier) in typical National Revival style. It is possible to wander along the narrow cobbled streets and see Roman ruins (including an amphitheatre), picturesque medieval houses and buildings from the 17th century with their upper sections hanging out into the street and almost touching those opposite. The *Archaeological Museum* has collections of gold Thracian artefacts, including cooking utensils, and the *Ethnographic Museum* is also worth seeing, as are the churches of *St Marina* and *St Nedelya.*
EXCURSIONS & SIGHTSEEING: 8km (5 miles) from Plovdiv is **Batchkovo Monastery,** founded in the 11th century, with some rare frescoes, icons, manuscripts and coins. Batchkovo lies within the area known in ancient times as Thrace (partly occupied by the Rhodope Mountains) and many items of archaeological interest have been discovered, including wonderful gold Thracian objects.
The town of **Kazanluk** has a *Museum of Rose Production* and is the centre of Bulgaria's major export: attar of roses. The valley of Kazanluk itself has countless archaeological/historical treasures – Greek, Roman, Thracian and Ottoman.
Turnovo, ancient capital of Bulgaria in the 13th and 14th centuries, contains extraordinary collections of historic works of art, including church relics. The **Preobrazhenski Monastery** is quite close, as is the open-air folk museum at **Etur.**

The Black Sea Coast

The Bulgarian Black Sea Riviera resorts are ideal for the traditional seaside family holiday. Thickly wooded mountains sweep down into wide bays and long golden beaches stretch four or five miles in length. Some of the resorts along the coast have been called a 'children's playground' as swimming is generally safe, even at 150m (500ft) away from the shore the water is only shoulder-high. Areas where currents are a problem are clearly marked. The Black Sea is one of the cleanest and clearest seas in the world and has half the salt content of the

Mediterranean. Some of the sand is pulled by currents from as far away as the Mediterranean, flowing through the Bosphorus and Dardenelles. Bulgaria offers sunny weather and good, clean air, particularly along the coast; the coast itself has a breeze which blows gently inshore, taking the edge off the heat.
Special children's pools have been installed on many of the beaches: swings, slides, playdomes and donkey rides are also available and a wide range of watersports are available at most resorts.
RESORTS: There are dozens of attractive resorts on the Black Sea Riviera. **Drouzhba** is Bulgaria's oldest Black Sea spa centred on the Grand Hotel Varna, the largest and most luxurious hotel on the Riviera and the pearl of the *Balkantourist* achievements to date. **Albena,** named after a famous local beauty, is situated on the edge of a lovely forest, and is Bulgaria's newest resort (a showcase and vivid monument to contemporary Bulgarian design), with good food and lively nightlife. **Golden Sands,** Bulgaria's second-largest resort, has good facilities and probably the best nightlife on the Black Sea Riviera and is only 15km (9 miles) from **Varna,** the Black Sea capital founded in the 6th century BC and still housing many Roman and Byzantine remains. **Sunny Beach** is a large purpose-built family resort with beautiful and safe beaches. Close to Sunny Beach can be found the 7th-century fishing village of **Nessebar** with its wooden fishermen's houses and its famous four dozen Byzantine churches. The Black Sea port town of **Burgas** has a *Maritime Park* and an extensive beach.
Everywhere in Bulgaria there is a good choice of restaurants and *mehana* (folk taverns), which are full of Bulgarian colour, vigour and friendliness with exceptional cooking and wine. There are discos, cabarets and bars suitable for every pocket and taste. The *Khan's Tent* at Sunny Beach is a must as is the *Gorski Tsar* (Forest King) at Albena.

Winter Holidays

Bulgaria is a fast-growing destination for Western skiers, for adults and children alike. There have been some dramatic improvements in all three major resorts in recent years.
RESORTS: **Borovets** is a World Cup venue. It is only 70km (45 miles) from Sofia, the capital, at 1300m (4300ft) in the Rila Mountains. There the 2400m (8000ft) *Yastrebets* (Hawk's Nest) is a steep, twisting red trail for the advanced skier, in operation from November until April. Seven comfortable, friendly and well-run hotels provide most of the accommodation and there is a village of timber-framed houses (each sleeping six) nearby. In Bulgarian resorts, hotels usually provide most of the nightlife. There is a disco in the Mousalla and live groups play at the Hotel Bor. There is also a wine bar and folk taverns (*mehana*); sleigh rides through the snow are also available.
At **Pamporovo,** 1600m (5315ft) in the Rhodope Mountains near Plovdiv, there is one of the finest ski schools in Europe. The resort has 1440 beds between seven hotels, the main one being the new Perelik (480 beds) which is a mini-resort in itself with shopping arcades, 25m (80ft) swimming pool, solarium, bars and lots more besides. Pamporovo is also the most southerly ski resort in Europe.
The third resort is **Vitosha,** 1800m (6000ft) high and overlooking Sofia, the home of the National Ski School based on the FIS methods. All the resorts have been purpose-built to blend in with the magnificent natural scenery of mountains and forest. Equipment on hire is all modern and well maintained.
Bulgaria has consistently heavy falls of snow from December until April. Some tour operators actually guarantee snow despite these resorts being so far south under sunny, vivid blue skies. From the restaurant on top of the Pamporovo TV tower you can see as far as Greece and the Aegean. The ski areas may not be quite as extensive as the Alps, but certainly novice and intermediate skiing throughout Bulgaria is considered to be some of the finest in Europe. Off-piste skiing is excellent, and cross-country skiing is becoming more and more popular with trails laid out through towering pines to rival any to be found in the Alps or elsewhere.

Special Interest Tours

These include luxury cruises along the Danube, sailing through seven countries in two brand-new Dutch-built air-conditioned river liners each accommodating 236 passengers. The fascinating tour includes transit to Passau in Germany or Vienna, to begin either a 2- or 3-week cruise to Ruse in eastern Bulgaria, with excursions at all points of call. Afterwards there is a choice of touring Bulgaria by coach, or staying on the Black Sea Riviera, or at a mountain resort inland. The return trip home is by plane.

Magic combination of sea breeze and forest freshness

Sunny Day Resort is situated 9km northeast of the summer capital of the Bulgarian Black Sea Coast – Varna.

The four comfortable hotels – the Palace, Marina, Mirage and Veronica are of different categories and offer 340 rooms and 110 suites at sea level. The beautiful beach in a quiet gulf has an air of magic, with a combination of sea breezes and forest freshness.

Hotel guests have at their disposal: café, cocktail bar, lobby bars and restaurants.

There are balneological centres for treatment and rehabilitation in the Palace and Marina hotels with a selection of cures and treatments, based on special mineral profiles and programmes, manual and underwater massages, physiotherapy and sauna.

Sports facilities include a fitness centre, indoor and outdoor mineral swimming pools and tennis courts.

The Palace and Marina hotels also have the best possibilities for congress tourism. There are spacious halls for congress and conference meetings, with capacity from 20 to 250 seats.

Varna 9006, **Bulgaria**, Resort 'St Konstantin'.

Tel: +359-52-861 971 / 5. **Fax:** +359-52-861 315.

Telex: 77615.

Grand Hotel VARNA
BULGARIA

LUXURY AND STYLE

For reservations please contact the hotel directly:

St. Constantine and Helena Resort, 9006 Varna, Bulgaria. Tel: (+359 52) 861491/98, Fax: 891920, Telex: 77324/25.

GRAND HOTEL VARNA

LOCATION – A five-star, full-service, four-season hotel located on the beautiful Bulgarian Black Sea coast, 20 min. from the airport and only 10 min. from the city of Varna.

TRANSPORT – The hotel has its own fleet of Mercedes taxi cabs, mini buses and coaches.

ACCOMMODATION – 292 luxury rooms, Presidential suite, 33 extra-large suites, excellent view over the bay or park, satellite TV and video channels, telephone, radio, mini-bar.

DINING/ENTERTAINMENT – three restaurants offering Bulgarian and international cuisine, five bars, Café, Night Club, Casino.

CONVENTION/BANQUETING – Multifunctional air-conditioned meeting rooms and halls for up to 260, full technical equipment with audio-visual aids and simultaneous translation.

HEALTH/LEISURE – Balneological Centre offering a wide range of health treatments and beauty programmes, sauna, solarium, massage room and mud treatment facilities. Sport Centre with indoor and outdoor swimming pools, four outdoor clay tennis courts, six-track bowling, gym, squash, basketball and volleyball halls, football ground.

EXECUTIVE FACILITIES – Business Centre providing full-range office support, Bank Office.

SERVICES – Free parking, car rental, flight information and ticket office, beauty salon, art gallery, shopping area.

Walking holidays have become extremely popular along special routes through the wild mountains and forests. It is possible to travel the country by horse and cart or by narrow gauge railway. There are courses in painting and photography at Plovdiv and the preserved museum town of **Koprivshtitsa** in the beautiful scenery east of Sofia. There is also the opportunity, once in Bulgaria, of taking special excursions to Moscow or Prague, Istanbul and Warsaw. As well as the more obvious tourist attractions, Bulgaria is a country of world-famous mineral water spas and increasing interest is being shown in spa holidays. There are over 500 springs. Many medical authorities accept that spa treatments are very effective in dealing with heart conditions, rheumatism, asthma and liver and kidney complaints.

The Bulgarian National Tourist Office will provide more details about *Balkantourist's* full range of amenities on request.

POPULAR ITINERARIES: 5-day: (a) Sofia–Rila Monastery–Blagoevgrad–Sandansky–Melnik–Rozhen Monastery. (b) Sofia–Plovdiv–Bachkovo Monastery–Pamporovo. (c) Plovdiv–Burgas–Nessebar–Varna.

SOCIAL PROFILE

FOOD & DRINK: The main meal is eaten in the middle of the day. Dinner is a social occasion, with dancing in all restaurants. Food is spicy, hearty and good. National dishes include cold yoghurt soup with cucumbers, peppers or aubergines stuffed with meat, *kebapcheta* (small, strongly spiced, minced meat rolls). Fruit is particularly good and cheap throughout the year. *Banitsa* is a pastry stuffed with fruit or cheese. There is a wide variety of national dishes, as well as West European standard dishes, which can be chosen on the spot at any restaurant. All good hotels have restaurants and there are many attractive folk-style restaurants and cafés throughout the country.
Drink: Coffee, heavily sweetened, is particularly popular. Drinks are also made from infusions of mountain herbs and dried leaves, particularly lime. White wines include *Karlouski Misket, Tamianka* and *Evksinograde.* Heavy red wines include *Trakia* and *Mavroud.*
NIGHTLIFE: Some restaurants have folk dancing and music. Opera is performed at the State Opera House in Sofia; other classical concerts include the National Folk Ensemble. There are nightclubs with floor shows and dancing in Sofia, as well as most major towns and all of the resorts.
SHOPPING: The main shopping area of Sofia is the Vitosha Boulevard. Bulgarian products, handicrafts, wines, spirits and confectionery can all be purchased.
Shopping hours: Shops and stores are generally open 1000-2000 Monday to Friday; 0800-1400 Saturday. Many shops open late until 1900.
SPORT: There are facilities for **tennis, mini-golf, horseriding** and **cycling.** *Balkantourist* organises **fishing** tours, and makes all the necessary arrangements for permits, guides, equipment and accommodation. **Winter sports:** See *Winter Holidays* in *Resorts & Excursions* section above. **Watersports:** Water-skiing, sailing, surfing and scuba diving are all available on the Black Sea coast.
SPECIAL EVENTS: The following is a selection of the major festivals and other special events celebrated annually in Bulgaria. For a complete list, contact the Bulgarian National Tourist Office.
Last two weeks in Mar *March Musical Days*, Ruse.
Mid-May to mid-Jun *Sofia Musical Weeks.* **Jun** *Sunny Beach Golden Orpheus Pop Festival.* **First week of Jun** *Kazanluk Rose Festival.* **Aug** *Burgas International Folklore Festival.* **Sep** *Art, Crafts and Chamber Music,* Plovdiv.
SOCIAL CONVENTIONS: Normal courtesies should be observed and handshaking is the normal form of greeting. Dress should be conservative but casual. If invited to the home, a small souvenir from one's homeland is an acceptable gift. Do not give money. Remember that a nod of the head means 'No' and a shake means 'Yes'. **Tipping:** Until recently not applicable, but 10-12% is appreciated.

BUSINESS PROFILE

ECONOMY: Bulgaria has a strong agricultural sector, in which the main products are wheat, maize, barley, sugar beet, grapes and tobacco, although its relative importance has declined in recent years. Agriculture is mainly organised around large agro-industrial complexes and is relatively efficient; current plans are looking towards further mechanisation of food-processing and packaging. Industry is concentrated in engineering, metals, chemicals and petrochemicals and, recently, electronics and biotechnology. Bulgaria is a major producer of bulk carriers and of fork-lift trucks. Tourism and road transport are both important foreign exchange earners. The external debt is low by Eastern European

standards, although Bulgaria has recently arranged large loans from the West to finance the development of its new industries. Bulgaria's largest trading partner is the CIS (50% of Bulgarian imports; 61% of exports, according to 1987 figures). Elsewhere, Libya and Iraq are important trading partners. The demise of COMECON has eliminated, at a stroke, the major market for Bulgarian goods. At first, this precipitated a major economic collapse for the fledgling Zhelev government, from which it is only now starting to recover. Power cuts and food shortages are now commonplace. The main task facing the Government was to create conditions to attract investment and generate capital internally: without these, the economy could not recover. In 1992, with its political position reasonably secure, the Government embarked on a rapid privatisation programme. The legal framework is now in place and the first sell-off of industrial concerns began in the second half of 1992. Foreign investors, who initially steered clear of Bulgaria, are showing an increasing interest in the country. Tourism and agro-industry are thought especially attractive. The Government is also devoting some effort to improving the country's antiquated infrastructure. Trade with the UK is low although political reforms are likely to encourage improved opportunities in the future. The country has few energy reserves of its own and has, until now, relied heavily on subsidised Soviet oil and gas, for which they will now have to pay market prices – in scarce hard currency. Oil from Iraq, moreover, is no longer available following UN-imposed sanctions and the destruction of the Iraqi oil industry during the Gulf War.
BUSINESS: Suits and prior appointments are necessary. Interpreters can be organised through tourist agencies. If arranged in advance through foreign trading organisations, services are free. It is common for the visiting business person to offer hospitality to the contact in Bulgaria. **Office hours:** 0800-1800 Monday to Friday. Shops in Sofia are often open longer hours.
COMMERCIAL INFORMATION: The following organisation can offer advice: Bulgarian Chamber of Commerce and Industry, Suborna Street 11A, 1040 Sofia. Tel: (2) 872 631. Fax: (2) 873 209. Telex: 22374.

CLIMATE

Varies according to altitude. Summers are warmest with some rainfall. Winters are cold with snow. It rains frequently during spring and autumn.
Required clothing: Mediumweights most of the year, warmer outdoor wear necessary in winter.

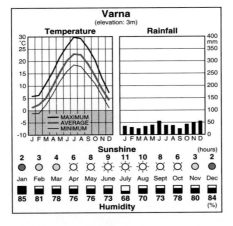
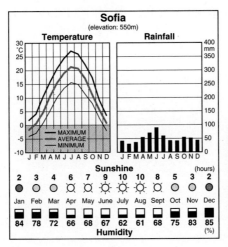

Burkina Faso

□ *international airport*

Location: West Africa.

Direction de l'Administration Touristique et Hôtelière
BP 624, Ouagadougou, Burkina Faso
Tel: 306 396. Telex: 5555 (a/b BF SEGEGOUV).
Honorary Consulate of Burkina Faso
5 Cinnamon Row, Plantation Wharf, London SW11 3TW
Tel: (0171) 738 1800. Fax: (0171) 738 2820. Telex: 296420 (a/b AFRO G). Opening hours: 1000-1230 and 1430-1630 Monday to Friday.
British Consulate
BP 1918, Ouagadougou, Burkina Faso
Tel: 336 363.
Embassy of Burkina Faso
2340 Massachusetts Avenue, NW, Washington, DC 20008
Tel: (202) 332 5577 *or* 332 6895.
Embassy of the United States of America
01 BP 35, rue Raoul Folereau, Ouagadougou 01, Burkina Faso
Tel: 306 723/4/5 *or* 312 660 *or* 312 707 (after hours). Fax: 312 368. Telex: 5290.
Embassy of Burkina Faso
48 Range Road, Ottawa, Ontario K1N 8J4
Tel: (613) 238 4796. Fax: (613) 238 3812. Telex: 0534413.
Canadian Embassy
BP 548, Canadian Development Centre, Ouagadougou 01, Burkina Faso
Tel: 311 894/5/6/7 *or* 312 585/6/7/8. Fax: 311 900. Telex: 5264 (a/b DOMCAN BF).

AREA: 274,200 sq km (105,870 sq miles).
POPULATION: 9,001,000 (1990 estimate).
POPULATION DENSITY: 32.8 per sq km.
CAPITAL: Ouagadougou. **Population:** 441,514 (1985).
GEOGRAPHY: Burkina Faso is situated in West Africa and bordered to the north and west by Mali, to the east by Niger, to the southeast by Benin and to the south by Togo, Ghana and Côte d'Ivoire. The southern part of the country, less arid than the north, is wooded savannah, gradually drying out into sand and desert in the north. The Sahara desert is relentlessly moving south, however, stripping the savannah lands of trees and slowly turning the thin layer of cultivatable soil into sun-blackened

Health	
GALILEO/WORLDSPAN: **TI-DFT/OUA/HE**	
SABRE: **TIDFT/OUA/HE**	
Visa	
GALILEO/WORLDSPAN: **TI-DFT/OUA/VI**	
SABRE: **TIDFT/OUA/VI**	

For more information on Timatic codes refer to Contents.

Timatic

rock-hard *lakenite*. Three great rivers, the Mouhoun, Nazinon and Nakambé (Black, Red and White Volta), water the great plains. The population does not live in the valleys along the river banks due to the diseases prevalent there.
LANGUAGE: The official language is French. Several indigenous languages such as Mossi, More, Dioula and Goumantche are also spoken.
RELIGION: Mainly Animist. 30% are Muslim and fewer than 10% Christians (mostly Roman Catholics).
TIME: GMT.
ELECTRICITY: 220/380 volts AC, 50Hz. 2-pin plugs are standard.
COMMUNICATIONS: Telephone: IDD is available. Country code: 226. Outgoing international code: 00. **Telex/telegram:** There are limited facilities outside Ouagadougou. Main hotels have facilities. **Post:** There are few post offices, but stamps can often be bought at hotels. *Poste Restante* facilities are available but a charge is made for letters collected. There is no local delivery, and all other mail must be addressed to a box number. Airmail to Europe takes up to two weeks. Post office hours are 0700-1230 and 1500-1730 Monday to Friday. The Main Post Office in the capital is open 0830-1200 and 1500-1830 Monday to Saturday. **Press:** French-language only.
BBC World Service and Voice of America frequencies: From time to time these change. See the section *How to Use this Book* for more information.
BBC:

MHz	17.79	15.40	15.07	12.09
Voice of America:				
MHz	21.49	15.60	9.525	6.035

PASSPORT/VISA

Regulations and requirements may be subject to change at short notice, and you are advised to contact the appropriate diplomatic or consular authority before finalising travel arrangements. Details of these may be found at the head of this country's entry. Any numbers in the chart refer to the footnotes below.

	Passport Required?	Visa Required?	Return Ticket Required?
Full British	Yes	Yes	Yes
BVP	Not valid	-	-
Australian	Yes	Yes	Yes
Canadian	Yes	Yes	Yes
USA	Yes	Yes	Yes
Other EU (As of 31/12/94)	Yes	Yes	Yes
Japanese	Yes	Yes	Yes

PASSPORTS: Valid passport required by all.
British Visitors Passport: Not accepted.
VISAS: Required by all.
Types of visa: Tourist, Business and Transit. All cost £17.50.
Validity: Multiple-entry: 3 months, with applications for extension to be made to Immigration in Burkina Faso. However, visitors may only stay for 1 month at a time.
Application to: Consulate (or Consular section at Embassy). For addresses, see top of entry.
Application requirements: (a) Valid passport. (b) 2 application forms. (c) 2 passport-size photos. (d) Sufficient funds to cover duration of stay. (e) Registered, stamped, self-addressed envelope for postal applications. (f) Company letter if on business.
Working days required: Visas can be granted immediately if papers are in order; it takes a few days if the application is made by post.
Temporary residence: Application to be made to Central Government of Burkina Faso. Enquire at Consulate.

MONEY

Currency: CFA Franc (CFA Fr). Notes are in denominations of CFA Fr10,000, 5000, 1000 and 500. Coins are in denominations of CFA Fr500, 100, 50, 25, 10, 5, 2 and 1. These notes and coins are legal tender in all the Republics which formerly comprised French West Africa (Benin, Côte d'Ivoire, Mali, Niger, Senegal, Togo and Burkina Faso).
Note: At the beginning of 1994, the CFA Franc was devalued against the French Franc.
Credit cards: Access/Mastercard (limited) and Diners Club are accepted. Check with your credit card company for details of merchant acceptability and other services which may be available.
Exchange rate indicators: The following figures are included as a guide to the movements of the CFA Franc against Sterling and the US Dollar:

Date:	Oct '92	Sep '93	Jan '94	Jan '95
£1.00=	413.75	433.87	436.78	843.10
$1.00=	260.71	284.13	295.22	545.06

Currency restrictions: No restrictions on import/export of local currency or foreign currency.
Banking hours: 0800-1200 Monday to Friday.

DUTY FREE

The following items may be imported into Burkina Faso by persons over 18 years of age without incurring customs duty:
200 cigarettes or 25 cigars or 100 cigarillos or 250g of tobacco; 1 litre of spirits and 1 litre of wine; 500ml of eau de toilette and 250ml of perfume.
Note: Sporting guns may only be imported under licence.

PUBLIC HOLIDAYS

Jan 1 '95 New Year's Day. **Jan 3** Anniversary of the 1966 *coup d'etat*. **Mar 3** Eid al-Fitr (End of Ramadan). **Mar 8** International Women's Day. **Apr 17** Easter Monday. **May 1** Labour Day. **May 10** Eid al-Adha (Feast of the Sacrifice). **May 25** Ascension Day. **Aug 4** National Day. **Aug 9** Mouloud (Prophet's Birthday). **Aug 15** Assumption. **Oct 15** Anniversary of the 1987 *coup d'etat*. **Nov 1** All Saints' Day (Toussaint). **Dec 25** Christmas. **Jan 1 '96** New Year's Day. **Jan 3** Anniversary of the 1966 *coup d'etat*. **Feb 22** Eid al-Fitr (End of Ramadan). **Mar 8** International Women's Day. **Apr 8** Easter Monday. **Apr 29** Eid al-Adha (Feast of the Sacrifice).
Note: (a) **May 17** and **Oct 20** are also usually declared holidays by the Government. (b) Muslim festivals are timed according to local sightings of various phases of the Moon and the dates given above are approximations. During the lunar month of Ramadan that precedes Eid al-Fitr, Muslims fast during the day and feast at night and normal business patterns may be interrupted. Many restaurants are closed during the day and there may be restrictions on smoking and drinking. Some disruption may continue into Eid al-Fitr itself. Eid al-Fitr and Eid al-Adha may last anything from two to ten days, depending on the region. For more information, refer to the section *World of Islam* at the back of the book.

HEALTH

Regulations and requirements may be subject to change at short notice, and you are advised to contact your doctor well in advance of your intended date of departure. Any numbers in the chart refer to the footnotes below.

	Special Precautions?	Certificate Required?
Yellow Fever	Yes	1
Cholera	Yes	2
Typhoid & Polio	Yes	-
Malaria	Yes/3	-
Food & Drink	4	

[1]: A yellow fever vaccination certificate is required from all travellers over one year of age coming from all countries.
[2]: Following WHO guidelines issued in 1973, a cholera vaccination certificate is no longer a condition of entry to Burkina Faso. However, cholera is a serious risk in this country and precautions are essential. Up-to-date advice should be sought before deciding whether these precautions should include vaccination as medical opinion is divided over its effectiveness. See the *Health* section at the back of the book.
[3]: Malaria risk exists all year throughout the country, predominantly in the malignant *falciparum* form. Resistance to chloroquine has been reported. A weekly dose of 250mg of mefloquine is the recommended prophylaxis.
[4]: All water should be regarded as being potentially contaminated. Drinking water outside main cities and towns is likely to be contaminated and sterilisation is considered essential. Milk is unpasteurised and should be boiled. Powdered or tinned milk is available and is advised, but make sure that it is reconstituted with pure water. Avoid all dairy products. Only eat well-cooked meat and fish, preferably served hot. Pork, salad and mayonnaise may carry increased risk. Vegetables should be cooked and fruit peeled.
Rabies is present. For those at high risk, vaccination before arrival should be considered. If you are bitten abroad seek medical advice without delay. For more information consult the *Health* section at the back of the book.
Bilharzia (schistosomiasis) is present. Avoid swimming and paddling in fresh water. Swimming pools which are well-chlorinated and maintained are safe.
Other prevalent diseases include *onchoerciasis* (river blindness), *trypanosomiasis* (sleeping sickness) and hepatitis A and E.
Health care: Health insurance is strongly recommended.

TRAVEL - International

AIR: Burkina Faso's national airline is *Air Burkina (VH)*. Burkina Faso has a minority shareholding in *Air Afrique*. Other airlines include *Aeroflot, Air Afrique, Air Algérie, Air Ivoire, Ethiopian* and *UTA*. There are regular and cheap flights between Paris and Belgium to Ouagadougou.
International airports: *Ouagadougou (OUA)*, 8km (5 miles) from the city, with restaurant and car hire facilities. Taxi service is available to the city. *Borgo* is 16km (10 miles) from Bobo Dioulasso (see below).
RAIL: The only route is the international line from Côte d'Ivoire running through to Ouagadougou. Four trains a day run from Ouagadougou to Bobo Dioulasso, of which two are through services to Abidjan in Côte d'Ivoire. Other trains from Bobo cross the border to serve Côte d'Ivoire destinations. Abidjan trains have sleeping and dining cars. Work is under way to extend the line from Ouagadougou to Tambao on the Mali border, but this project may have to be cancelled to meet foreign debt requirements. The existing line is also under threat of closure.
ROAD: Routes are from Ghana, Mali, Côte d'Ivoire, Togo, Benin and Niger, although these are often barely adequate. Regular bus services run during the dry season, from Bobo to Bamako in Mali, and from Ouagadougou to Niamey in Niger. The road from Ghana is being improved.

TRAVEL - Internal

AIR: *Borgo,* 16km (10 miles) from Bobo Dioulasso, is the principal domestic airport. Flights run to Bouake, Bamako and Tambao on *Air Volta (VH)*. Air taxis are available.
RAIL: A daily service runs from Ouagadougou to Bobo Dioulasso. There are two classes, with some restaurant cars, sleeping facilities and air-conditioning. This service can become overcrowded.
ROAD: In general roads are impassable during the rainy season (July-September). Police checkpoints are a common cause of delays. Traffic drives on the right. **Bus:** Regular bus services are operated in the dry season to all major towns and it is necessary to book well in advance. **Taxi:** Shared taxis are available in major centres; fares are negotiable. **Car hire:** Rented from *Burkina Faso Auto Location*, Hotel Independence, Ouagadougou; chauffeur-driven cars are also available.
Documentation: A temporary licence to drive is available from local authorities on presentation of a valid national driving licence, but an International Driving Permit is recommended.

ACCOMMODATION

There are hotels in Ouagadougou and Bobo Dioulasso with some air-conditioned rooms and additional facilities. Elsewhere there are small lodges. There is also a group of tourist-class bungalows at Arly National Park. Information can be obtained from the Division de l'Administration Touristique et Hotelière (address and contact numbers above). **Grading:** Hotels are rated by the Government in stars.

RESORTS & EXCURSIONS

The capital, **Ouagadougou**, has an interesting *Ethnography Museum* containing a substantial collection of Mossi artefacts, the town being the centre of one of the many ancient Mossi kingdoms. There is also a tourist office in the town. The Moro-Naba ceremony, with traditional costumes and drums, takes place outside the *Moro-Naba Palace* every morning around 0715.
Excursions from Ouagadougou include a wildlife-viewing trip to a small artificial lake 18km (11 miles) to the north. **Pabre,** an ancient Mossi village, is a short distance from another large reservoir north of the city. At **Sabou,** crocodiles can be seen at close quarters. However, as far as looking at wildlife is concerned, the three national parks – at *Po*, at *'W'* near the Benin and Niger border, and at *Arly* – are the most important. South of Ougadougou, near *Po*, the *Ranch de Nazinga* is a game reserve with a large population of elephants, antelopes, monkeys, baboons and wart hogs.
Bobo Dioulasso is the largest town inhabited by the Bobo people in Burkina Faso, with attractive streets and a bustling market, the *Grand Marché*. Other city attractions are the *Musée Provincial du Houët* with regional relics, arts and crafts, and the *Grand Mosquée* in the Kibidwé district. Excursions outside the city include the scenic sacred fish pond of *La Mare aux Poissons Sacrés de Dafra,* 8km (5 miles) southeast of the city; the excellent bathing pond of *La Guinguette*, located in *La Fôret de Kou*, 18km (11 miles) from the city; and the *Mare aux Hippopotames*, 66km (41 miles) northeast of the city, where visitors may be taken out in a pirogue to view the hippos for a small fee.
Southwest of Bobo Dioulasso is the town of **Banfora**, from where the impressive *Karfiguéla Waterfalls* can be seen, located 12km (3 miles) northwest of the town. 50km (31 miles) west of Banfora is the town of **Sindou,** the area where the extraordinary *Sindou Rock Formations* can be seen.

SOCIAL PROFILE

FOOD & DRINK: Outside hotels there are a few restaurants in Ouagadougou and in Bobo. Staple foods include sorghum, millet, rice, maize, nuts, potatoes and yams. Local vegetables and strawberries are available in season. Specialities include *brochettes* (meat cooked on a skewer) and chicken dishes. Beer is very reasonably priced.
NIGHTLIFE: Nightlife is particularly good in Ouagadougou and Bobo Dioulasso. There are several nightclubs in Ouagadougou with music and dancing, open-air cinemas and one covered air-conditioned one. Bobo Dioulasso has a lively street café scene, good open-air bars and restaurants and a number of open-air and air-conditioned discos.
SHOPPING: Good markets exist in Ouagadougou, Bobo Dioulasso, Oahigouya, Dori and Gorom-Gorom. Bargaining in the traditional market place is recommended. Purchases include wooden statuettes, bronze models, masks, worked skins from the tannery in Ouagadougou, jewellery, fabrics, hand-woven blankets and leather goods and crafts ranging from chess sets to ash trays. **Shopping hours:** 0800-1200 and 1500-1800 Monday to Saturday. Some shops may be open Sunday and there are daily markets in the main towns.
SPORT: Swimming: There are a couple of hotels with swimming pools in Ouagadougou open to non-residents for a small fee. Due to endemic bilharzia it is not safe to swim in most rivers, lakes or standing water. **Tennis:** Courts are in Ouagadougou and visitors can play at the Burkina Faso Club on invitation of a member. **Fishing:** There are no fishing restrictions on any of the water courses except for the use of poison, explosives, nets with mesh smaller than 3cm (1.2 inches) and electrical equipment. **Horseriding:** Horses are available for hire at the Club Hippique in Ouagadougou.
SPECIAL EVENTS: At 0715 Friday, *Nabayius Gou* ('the Emperor goes to war') is a traditional 'drama' performed at the Moro-Naba Palace in Ouagadougou depicting the magnificently bedecked emperor being restrained by his wife and subjects as he sets off to make war with his brother. The end of *Ramadan* is accompanied by festivals of singing and dancing. Traditional music and dancing can also be seen on festivals and holidays especially in the southwest region which is rich in folklore.
SOCIAL CONVENTIONS: Within the urban areas many French customs prevail. Dress should be casual and appropriate for hot weather. Lounge suits for men and formal wear for women are required for evening entertainment. Outside the cities little has changed for centuries and visitors should respect local customs and

traditions. **Tipping:** Service is generally included in the bill (about 10-15%) although it is customary to tip taxi drivers, porters and hotel staff.

BUSINESS PROFILE

ECONOMY: According to World Bank assessments, Burkina Faso is the sixth-poorest country in the world. Its economy is predominantly agricultural, employing 80% of the population and contributing 45% of GNP (1986 figures). The sector has recovered from the devastating droughts of the mid-1980s and maintains subsistence agriculture (sorghum, millet, maize and rice) plus cash crops of cotton, groundnuts, sesame and shea-nuts which are a valuable export earner. There is considerable mineral wealth, including gold and manganese, but doubts prevail as to whether exploitation is economically viable. Burkina Faso has a small manufacturing sector producing textiles, sugar and flour. The country depends heavily on overseas aid, particularly from France and the European Union, which is likely to remain the mainstay of the economy for the foreseeable future. Burkina Faso belongs to the CFA Franc Zone. Imports outweigh exports in value by a factor of four. Over one-third of exports are bought by France, which provides a similar quantity of Burkina Faso's imports. Outside the European Union, neighbouring Côte d'Ivoire is Burkina's main trading partner.
BUSINESS: Suits should be worn for government and official business, otherwise a shirt and tie should suffice. Most officials prefer to wear national dress. French is the main language spoken in business circles and if the visitor does not have command of French, interpreter services should be sought from the British Embassy.
Office hours: 0800-1230 and 1500-1730 Monday to Friday.
COMMERCIAL INFORMATION: The following organisation can offer advice: Chambre de Commerce, d'Industrie et d'Artisanat du Burkina, BP 502, avenue Nelson Mandela, Ouagadougou 01. Tel: 306 114. Fax: 306 116. Telex: 5268.

CLIMATE

Tropical. The best months are December to March. *Harmattan* wind blows from the east (November to February) with dry and cool weather. Short rains (March and April) are followed by a dry season (February to May) and long rains (June to October). Rainfall is highest in the southwest and lowest in the northeast.
Required clothing: Lightweights and rainwear for the rainy season. Plenty of scarves and handkerchiefs are recommended during the months when *Harmattan* blows.

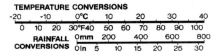

TEMPERATURE CONVERSIONS

-20	-10	0°C	10	20	30	40

0	10	20	30°F40	50	60	70	80	90	100

RAINFALL 0mm 200 400 600 800
CONVERSIONS 0In 5 10 15 20 25 30

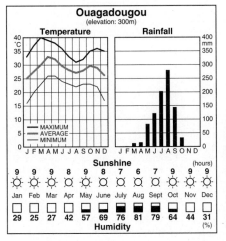

Ouagadougou
(elevation: 300m)

	Jan	Feb	Mar	Apr	May	June	July	Aug	Sept	Oct	Nov	Dec
Sunshine (hours)	9	9	9	8	9	8	7	6	7	9	9	9
Humidity (%)	29	25	27	42	57	69	76	81	79	64	44	31

Burundi

□ *international airport*

Location: Central Africa.

Note: In light of the October 1993 coup attempt and subsequent ethnic and political tensions, all areas of the country are potentially unstable. There have been reports of sporadic shootings and violence in Bujumbura, as well as in the interior where large numbers of displaced persons are encamped or hiding. Local authorities cannot guarantee a level of safety conducive to casual travel to or within the country. Burundi has periodically closed its land borders without notice and suspended air travel and telephone service in response to political distrubances. Difficulties are expected to continue and all but essential visits are advised. For up-to-date information, contact the FCO Travel Advice Unit. Tel: (0171) 270 4129.
Source: US State Department – October 7, 1994; FCO Travel Advice Unit – November 18, 1994.

Office National du Tourisme
BP 902, Bujumbura, Burundi
Tel: (2) 22202. Telex: 5010.
Embassy of the Republic of Burundi
46 square Marie-Louise, B-1040 Brussels, Belgium
Tel: (2) 230 4535. Fax: (2) 230 7883. Telex: 23572.
British Consulate
BP 1344, 43 avenue Bubanza, Bujumbura, Burundi
Tel: (2) 23711. Telex: 5126 (a/b INTAC BDI).
Embassy of the Republic of Burundi
Suite 212, 2233 Wisconsin Avenue, NW, Washington, DC 20007
Tel: (202) 342 2574.
Embassy of the United States of America
BP 34, 1720 avenue des Etats-Unis, Bujumbura, Burundi
Tel: (2) 23454. Fax: (2) 22926.
Embassy of the Republic of Burundi
Suite 800, 151 Slater Street, Ottawa, Ontario K1P 5H3
Tel: (613) 236 8483. Fax: (613) 563 1827. Telex: 0533393.

Timatic

Health	
GALILEO/WORLDSPAN:	TI-DFT/BJM/HE
SABRE:	TIDFT/BJM/HE

Visa	
GALILEO/WORLDSPAN:	TI-DFT/BJM/VI
SABRE:	TIDFT/BJM/VI

For more information on Timatic codes refer to Contents.

Canadian Consulate
CP 5, boulevard 28 novembre, Bujumbura, Burundi
Tel: (2) 21632. Fax: (2) 22816.

AREA: 27,834 sq km (10,747 sq miles).
POPULATION: 5,620,000 (1991 estimate).
POPULATION DENSITY: 196.1 per sq km.
CAPITAL: Bujumbura. **Population:** 235,440 (1991).
GEOGRAPHY: Burundi is situated in the heart of Africa and lies across the main Nile–Congo dividing range, bounded to the west by the narrow plain of the Ruzizi River and Lake Tanganyika. The interior is a broken plateau sloping east to Tanzania and the valley of the Malagarasi River. The southern tributary of the Nile system rises in the south of the country. The landscape is characterised by hills and valleys which are covered with eucalyptus trees, banana groves, cultivated fields and pasture. In the east, the fertile area gives way to savannah grassland, and tea and coffee are now grown on mountainsides.
LANGUAGE: The languages are French and Kirundi, a Bantu language. Kiswahili is also widely spoken.
RELIGION: Mainly Roman Catholic; there are Anglican and Pentecostalist minorities. Local animist beliefs are held by a significant minority.
TIME: GMT + 2.
ELECTRICITY: 220 volts AC, 50Hz.
COMMUNICATIONS: Telephone: IDD is available. Country code: 257. Outgoing international code: 90. **Telex/telegram:** Facilities are available from *Direction des Télécommunications* in Bujumbura. **Post:** The main post office in Bujumbura is open 0800-1200 and 1400-1600 Monday to Friday and 0800-1100 Saturday. **Press:** No English-language newspapers are published. Most publications are in French (such as *Le Renouveau du Burundi*) or local languages (such as *Ubumwe* in Kirundi). The two main newspapers are government-controlled.
BBC World Service and Voice of America frequencies: From time to time these change. See the section *How to Use this Book* for more information.

BBC:				
MHz	**21.47**	**17.88**	**15.42**	**9.630**
Voice of America:				
MHz	**21.49**	**15.60**	**9.525**	**6.035**

PASSPORT/VISA

Regulations and requirements may be subject to change at short notice, and you are advised to contact the appropriate diplomatic or consular authority before finalising travel arrangements. Details of these may be found at the head of this country's entry. Any numbers in the chart refer to the footnotes below.

	Passport Required?	Visa Required?	Return Ticket Required?
Full British	Yes	Yes	Yes
BVP	Not valid	-	-
Australian	Yes	Yes	Yes
Canadian	Yes	Yes	Yes
USA	Yes	Yes	Yes
Other EU (As of 31/12/94)	Yes	Yes	Yes
Japanese	Yes	Yes	Yes

PASSPORTS: Valid passport required by all.
British Visitors Passport: Not accepted.
VISAS: Required by all. Passengers arriving at Bujumbura airport from countries where Burundi does not have diplomatic representation will be issued with entry stamps providing they have previously informed their travel agency of their passport number and identity. These stamps will entitle the holder to a visa which must be obtained at the Immigration Service within 24 hours of arrival.
Types of visa: *Tourist:* a 1-month visa costs BFr800 (*Belgian* Francs). *Business:* price available on application. Visas costs can vary from US$30-60. Multiple-entry: A 3-month multiple-entry visa is available from Burundian embassies for approximately US$11. A Transit visa is not required for passengers continuing their journey to a third country and not leaving the airport. A Re-entry Permit is required for all alien residents.
Application to: Consulate (or Consular Section at Embassy). For addresses, see top of entry.
Application requirements: (a) Valid passport. (b) 3 application forms (requests for applications forms should be accompanied by a stamped, addressed envelope). (c) 3 passport-size photos. (d) Return ticket. (e) Fee (payable by postal order only). (f) Stamped, addressed envelope for recorded delivery.
Working days required: Applications should be made as far as possible in advance of the intended date of departure.

MONEY

Currency: Burundi Franc (Bufr) = 100 centimes. Notes are in denominations of Bufr5000, 1000, 500, 100, 50, 20 and 10. Coins are in denominations of Bufr10, 5 and 1.
Currency exchange: All exchange transactions must be conducted through one of the main banks in Bujumbura.
Credit cards: Diners Club and Access/Mastercard both have limited acceptance. Check with your credit card company for details of merchant acceptability and other services which may be available.
Exchange rate indicators: The following figures are included as a guide to the movements of the Burundi Franc against Sterling and the US Dollar:

Date:	Oct '92	Sep '93	Jan '94	Jan '95
£1.00=	362.52	362.10	393.60	388.24
$1.00=	228.43	237.13	266.04	250.10

Currency restrictions: Unlimited import of foreign currency, subject to declaration; export limited to amount declared on import. Import and export of local currency is limited to Bufr2000.
Banking hours: 0800-1130 Monday to Friday. There are banks in Bujumbura and Gitega.

DUTY FREE

The following goods may be taken into Burundi without incurring customs duty:
1000 cigarettes or 1kg of tobacco; 1 litre of alcohol; a reasonable amount of perfume.
Note: All baggage must be declared and duty may be required for cameras, radios, typewriters, etc.

PUBLIC HOLIDAYS

Jan 1 '95 New Year's Day. **Apr 17** Easter Monday. **May 1** Labour Day. **May 25** Ascension Day. **Jul 1** Independence Day. **Aug 15** Assumption. **Sep 18** Victory of UPRONA Party. **Nov 1** All Saints' Day. **Dec 25** Christmas Day. **Jan 1 '96** New Year's Day. **Apr 8** Easter Monday.

HEALTH

Regulations and requirements may be subject to change at short notice, and you are advised to contact your doctor well in advance of your intended date of departure. Any numbers in the chart refer to the footnotes below.

	Special Precautions?	Certificate Required?
Yellow Fever	Yes	1
Cholera	Yes	2
Typhoid & Polio	Yes	-
Malaria	Yes/3	-
Food & Drink	4	-

Note: Visitors may be asked to show proof of vaccination against meningococcal meningitis.
[1]: Yellow fever vaccination certificate is required from travellers over one year of age arriving from infected areas. Travellers arriving from non-endemic zones should note that vaccination is strongly recommended for travel outside the urban areas, even if an outbreak of the disease has not been reported and they would normally not require a vaccination certificate to enter the country.
[2]: Following WHO guidelines issued in 1973, a cholera vaccination certificate is no longer a condition of entry to Burundi. However, cholera is a serious risk in this country and precautions are essential. Up-to-date advice should be sought before deciding whether these precautions should include vaccination as medical opinion is divided over its effectiveness. See the *Health* section.
[3]: Malaria risk throughout the year, predominantly in the malignant *falciparum* form, in the whole country. Resistance to chloroquine has been reported.
[4]: All water should be regarded as being potentially contaminated. Water used for drinking, brushing teeth or making ice should have first been boiled or otherwise sterilised. Milk is unpasteurised and should be boiled. Powdered or tinned milk is available and is advised, but make sure that it is reconstituted with pure water. Avoid dairy products which are likely to have been made from unboiled milk. Only eat well-cooked meat and fish, preferably served hot. Pork, salad and mayonnaise may carry increased risk. Vegetables should be cooked and fruit peeled.
Rabies is present. For those at high risk, vaccination before arrival should be considered. If you are bitten abroad seek medical advice without delay. For more information, consult the *Health* section at the back of the book.
Bilharzia (schistosomiasis) is present. Avoid swimming and paddling in fresh water. Swimming pools which are well-chlorinated and maintained are safe.
Health care: Medical insurance is strongly recommended.

TRAVEL - International

AIR: Burundi's national airline is *Air Burundi (PB).*
International airport: *Bujumbura (BJM)* is 11km (7 miles) north of the city. Taxis are available to and from the city.
Departure tax: Bufr2420; US$20 or equivalent for alien residents. Transit passengers are exempt.
LAKE: Cargo/passenger steamers ply Lake Tanganyika between Kigoma (Tanzania) and Bujumbura, and less frequently between Kalemi (Zaïre) and Bujumbura. There is also a service to Mpulungu (Zambia). There are three classes. Steamers can often be held up depending on the cargo being loaded or unloaded.
ROAD: It is possible to drive into Burundi from Zaïre, either from the north or south. Road travel from Rwanda is reasonable, but from Tanzania, poor.

TRAVEL - Internal

AIR: There are no regular internal flights.
ROAD: Most roads are sealed. There are main roads east from Bujumbura to Muramvya (once the royal city of Burundi) and south to Gitega. Both journeys can be completed without too much strain during the dry season, but any road travel is very difficult in the rainy season. Traffic drives on the right. **Bus:** There are services around Bujumbura and main towns only. Japanese-style minibuses operate within towns and are normally cheaper and less crowded than shared taxis; departures (when the vehicle is full) are normally from bus stands. **Taxi:** *Tanus-tanus* (truck taxis) are usually available but they are often crowded. **Car hire:** *Avis* is represented in Bujumbura, and it may also be possible to arrange some form of car hire via a local garage. **Documentation:** International Driving Permit required.
JOURNEY TIMES: The following chart gives approximate journey times from Bujumbura (in hours and minutes) to other major cities/towns in Burundi.

	Air	Road	Sea
Gitega	-	1.30	-
Resha Gumonge	-	0.45	13.00
Nyanza Lake	-	-	5.00
Kirundo	0.25	4.00	-
Muyinga	-	5.00	-
Ngozi	-	3.00	-

ACCOMMODATION

HOTELS: Almost all the hotels in the country are situated in the capital, Bujumbura, although there are a few in Gitega, Ngozi, Muyinga and Kirundo. Elsewhere in the country there is virtually no accommodation for visitors.
CAMPING: Generally frowned upon, particularly near towns. Permission should always be obtained from the local authority.

RESORTS & EXCURSIONS

The capital port-city of **Bujumbura**, situated on the shore of Lake Tanganyika, is a bustling town with a population of some 215,000 inhabitants. The area was colonised by the Germans at the end of the 19th century, and there is still architecture dating from that period of Burundi's history, including the *Postmaster's House.* Other attractions include three museums and the *Islamic Cultural Centre*. On the lake there are many opportunities for watersports, including sailing, water-skiing and fishing. There is an excellent market.
Other points of interest in the country include the former royal cities of **Muramvya** and **Gitega** (with its *National Museum*), and the monument near **Rutana** which marks the source of the White Nile.

SOCIAL PROFILE

FOOD & DRINK: The choice is limited. Meals in Bujumbura's hotels are reasonable, but expensive and fairly basic. The French and Greek restaurants in the town are good. There are few restaurants outside the capital and Gitega.
NIGHTLIFE: There are several nightclubs, restaurants and bars in Bujumbura.
SPORTS: Bujumbura, on the shores of Lake Tanganyika, offers **watersports** including **sailing**, **water-skiing** and **fishing**. The public beach lies 5km (3 miles) west of the city. The Entente Sportive Club offers tourist membership for **swimming**, **tennis**,

volleyball, **basketball** and **golf**. For information on watersports contact the Cercle Nautique. The absence of motor vehicles and the lushness of the subtropical flora makes Burundi a superb place for **walking** and **hiking**.

SHOPPING: Local crafts, particularly basketwork make excellent buys. **Shopping hours:** 0800-1200 and 1400-1800 Monday to Friday; 0800-1230 Saturday.

SOCIAL CONVENTIONS: Normal social courtesies apply. However, outside the cities people may not be used to visitors and care and tact must be used in respect of local customs. Inhabitants in major towns generally have a more modern and established way of life. Dress should be reasonably conservative.

Tipping: As a rule no service charge is levied automatically; 10% is the recommended tip.

BUSINESS PROFILE

ECONOMY: Burundi is one of the world's poorest countries with an economy almost entirely based on agriculture. Cassava and sweet potatoes are the main subsistence crops while the important cash crops are coffee – the country's leading export – tea and cotton. A high dependence on coffee has left Burundi very vulnerable to fluctuations in the world market price; this has been very low throughout most of the 1980s and Burundi's earnings have suffered accordingly. The country's small mining industry produces gold, cassiterite, tungsten and tantalum. Important deposits of vanadium, nickel and uranium have been located and are currently being surveyed. An indigenous textiles industry has recently been developed. For the foreseeable future Burundi will remain a major recipient of foreign aid, principally from France, Belgium, Germany – who are also, along with Japan, the main source of Burundi's imports – and from the European Development Fund and the World Bank. Burundi's major export markets are the countries of the CFA Franc Zone, taking approximately one-third of the total, followed by Belgium-Luxembourg, the USA, the UK, France and The Netherlands.

BUSINESS: Lightweight suits are necessary. April to October and December to January are the best times to visit.

COMMERCIAL INFORMATION: The following organisation can offer advice: Chambre de Commerce et de l'Industrie du Burundi, BP 313, Bujumbura. Tel: (2) 22280.

CLIMATE

A hot equatorial climate is found near Lake Tanganyika and in the Ruzizi River plain. It is often windy on the lake. The rest of the country is mild and pleasant. The rainy season is between October and May and there is a long dry season from June to September.

Required clothing: Lightweight cottons and linens with waterproofs for the rainy season. Warm clothes for evenings.

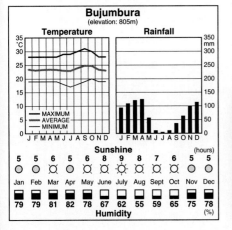

Kingdom of Cambodia

□ international airport

Location: South-East Asia.

Note: On October 23, 1991, a peace settlement was officially signed in Paris by all warring factions. Diplomatic missions, however, have not yet been set up in Western capitals, although they exist in Bangkok, Hanoi, Ho Chi Minh City, Vientiane (Laos), Beijing, Moscow and Delhi. Following the 1993 elections and the establishment of a universally recognised government, the country was renamed Kingdom of Cambodia. Parts of southern Cambodia have seen an upsurge in banditry and military activity since 1994. Some Westerners have been taken hostage by the Khmer Rouge and some have been murdered. Certain other areas in Cambodia, including some along the Thai border, are also insecure. In August 1994, Khmer Rouge radio commentaries threatened physical harm to foreign nationals. The town of Siem Reap and the ruins of Angkor Wat remain safe to tourists. The safety of road travel varies greatly from region to region. It is safer to travel in convoy and only during daylight hours in order to minimise the risk. Land mines are also still a major threat so travellers should not stray from established roads or paths. Train travel is considered unsafe.
Source: US State Department – November 8, 1994.

Ministry of Tourism
3 Monivong Boulevard, Phnom Penh, Cambodia
Tel: (23) 22669 or 24169 or 24670. Fax: (23) 24607.
Diethelm Travel (Cambodia) Ltd
8 Saigon Boulevard, Phnom Penh, Cambodia
Tel: (23) 26648. Fax: (23) 26676.
Royal Cambodian Embassy
185 Rajdamvi Road, Bangkok, Thailand
Tel: (2) 254 6630 or 294 3528.
British Mission to the Supreme National Council of Cambodia
29 Street 75, Phnom Penh, Cambodia
Tel: (23) 27124. Fax: (23) 27125.
Embassy of the United States of America
Box P, 27 Street Angphanouvong, Phnom Penh, Cambodia
Tel: (23) 26436 or 26438. Fax: (23) 26437.
Consulate of the United States of America
16 Street 228, Phnom Penh, Cambodia
Telephone and fax numbers as for the Embassy.
Canadian Embassy
c/o Australian Embassy, Villa II, Street 254, Chartaumuk, Daun Penh District, Phnom Penh, Cambodia

Tel: (23) 26000 or 26001. Fax: (23) 26003.
AREA: 181,035 sq km (69,898 sq miles).
POPULATION: 8,246,000 (1990 estimate).
POPULATION DENSITY: 45.5 per sq km.
CAPITAL: Phnom Penh. **Population:** 900,000 (1991).
GEOGRAPHY: Cambodia shares borders in the north with Laos and Thailand, in the east with Vietnam and in the southwest with the Gulf of Thailand. The landscape comprises tropical rainforest and fertile cultivated land traversed by many rivers. In the northeast area rise highlands. The capital is located at the junction of the Mekong and Tonle Sap rivers. The latter flows from a large inland lake, also called Tonle Sap, situated in the centre of the country. There are numerous offshore islands along the southwest coast.
LANGUAGE: Khmer. Chinese and Vietnamese are also spoken. French was widely spoken until the arrival of the Pol Pot regime and is spoken by those of the older generation. English is now a more popular language to learn among the younger generation.
RELIGION: 95% Buddhist, the remainder Muslim and Christian. Buddhism was reinstated as the national religion in the late 1980s after a ban on religious activity in 1975.
TIME: GMT + 7.
ELECTRICITY: 220 volts AC, 50Hz. Power cuts are frequent. Outside Phnom Penh, electrical power is available only in the evenings from around 1830-2130.
COMMUNICATIONS: Telephone: IDD communications have now been restored. Country code: 855. Phnom Penh code: 23. International calls from Cambodia have to go through the operator. **Fax** is now available. **Telex/telegram:** International telex code is 807. **Post:** Airmail to Europe takes four to five days, and to the USA one week to ten days. The Post & Telephone Office (PTT) in Phnom Penh is located across from the Hotel Monorom at the corner of Achar Mean Boulevard and 126 Street and is open from 0700-1200 and 1300-2300. The main post office in Phnom Penh is located on the western side of 13 Street between 98 Street and 102 Street, open from 0630-2100. General post office hours: 0730-1200 and 1430-1700 Monday to Friday in Phnom Penh. **Press:** The *Phnom Penh Post, Cambodian Daily* and *Cambodia Times* are printed in English.
BBC World Service and Voice of America frequencies: From time to time these change. See the section *How to Use this Book* for more information.

BBC:				
MHz	17.83	9.740	6.195	3.915
Voice of America:				
MHz	17.73	15.42	11.76	6.110

PASSPORT/VISA

Regulations and requirements may be subject to change at short notice, and you are advised to contact the appropriate diplomatic or consular authority before finalising travel arrangements. Details of these may be found at the head of this country's entry. Any numbers in the chart refer to the footnotes below.

	Passport Required?	Visa Required?	Return Ticket Required?
Full British	Yes	Yes	No
BVP	Not valid	-	-
Australian	Yes	Yes	No
Canadian	Yes	Yes	No
USA	Yes	Yes	No
Other EU (As of 31/12/94)	Yes	Yes	No
Japanese	Yes	Yes	No

PASSPORTS: Valid passport required by all.
British Visitors Passport: Not accepted.
VISAS: Required by all.
Types of visa: Tourist and Business.
Validity and cost: Generally around US$40. Validity is usually for 1 month although extensions may be granted by the Foreign Ministry in Phnom Penh.
Application to: Consulates (or Consular section of Embassy) in Bangkok, Hanoi, Ho Chi Minh City, Vientiane (Laos) and Moscow. Business visas are obtainable through the Ministry of Foreign Affairs in Phnom Penh or an official invitation. Tourists on package tours will normally have their visas arranged by the tour operator.
Application requirements: (a) Completed application form. (b) 2 passport-size photos. (c) Photocopy of passport. (d) Tour itinerary and fee. (e) Business card, if applying for Business visa.
Working days required: Minimum 3 days. Once approved it may be collected either at a Cambodian Mission or issued on arrival at Pochentong (Phnom Penh) airport. Visas valid for one month only may also be issued at Pochentong airport without pre-arrangement, although this must be checked before travel. The fee is US$20.

MONEY

Currency: Riel (CRl) = 100 sen. Notes are in denominations of CRl500 and 100.
Currency exchange: US Dollars are widely accepted and exchanged, but other currencies are little recognised.
Credit cards: Very limited acceptance.
Travellers cheques: Limited acceptance.
Exchange rate indicators: The following figures are included as a guide to the movements of the Riel against Sterling and the US Dollar:

Date:	**Oct '92**	**Sep '93**	**Jan '94**	**Jan '95**
£1.00=	**3163.0**	**5356.75**	**5169.50**	**4033.27**
$1.00=	**1993.1**	**3508.02**	**3494.09**	**2607.49**

Currency restrictions: Import and export of local currency is prohibited. Foreign currency may be exported up to the limit declared at customs on arrival. Amounts over US$2000 have to be declared.
Banking hours: 0730-1200 and 1430-1700 Monday to Friday.

DUTY FREE

The following goods may be taken into Cambodia without incurring customs duty:
200 cigarettes or an equivalent quantity of cigars or tobacco; 1 bottle of spirits; a reasonable amount of perfume.

PUBLIC HOLIDAYS

Jan 1 '95 New Year. **Apr** Cambodian New Year. **May 1** May Day. **Sep 22** Feast of the Ancestors. **Nov** Full Moon Water Festival. **Jan 1 '96** New Year. **Apr** Cambodian New Year.

HEALTH

Regulations and requirements may be subject to change at short notice, and you are advised to contact your doctor well in advance of your intended date of departure. Any numbers in the chart refer to the footnotes below.

	Special Precautions?	**Certificate Required?**
Yellow Fever	No	1
Cholera	Yes	2
Typhoid & Polio	Yes	-
Malaria	3	-
Food & Drink	4	-

[1]: A yellow fever vaccination certificate is required by travellers arriving from infected areas.
[2]: Following WHO guidelines issued in 1973, a cholera vaccination certificate is no longer a condition of entry to Cambodia. However, cholera is a serious risk in this country and precautions are essential. Up-to-date advice should be sought before deciding whether these precautions should include vaccination as medical opinion is divided over its effectiveness. See the *Health* section at the back of the book.
[3]: Malaria risk exists all year throughout the country. The malignant *falciparum* strain predominates and is reported to be highly resistant to chloroquine and resistant to sulfadoxine/pyrimethane. Resistance to mefloquine has been reported from the western provinces.
[4]: All water should be regarded as being potentially contaminated. Water for drinking, brushing teeth or making ice should first be boiled or otherwise sterilised. Milk is unpasteurised and should be boiled. Powdered or tinned milk is available and is advised, but make sure that it is reconstituted with pure water. Avoid dairy products which are likely to have been made from unboiled milk. Only eat well-cooked meat and fish, preferably served hot. Pork, salad and mayonnaise may carry increased risk. Vegetables should be cooked and fruit peeled.
Plague is present and vaccination is advised. For more information, consult the *Health* section at the back of the book.
Rabies is present. For those at high risk, vaccination before arrival should be considered. If you are bitten abroad seek medical advice without delay. For more information consult the *Health* section at the back of the book.
Bilharzia (schistosomiasis) is present. Avoid swimming and paddling in fresh water. Swimming pools which are well-chlorinated and maintained are safe.
Health care: Health insurance is absolutely essential. In 1984 there were 22 hospitals, about 1300 commune infirmaries and about 100 medical posts in the country. Doctors and hospitals expect cash payments for any medical treatment.

TRAVEL - International

AIR: Cambodia's new international carrier, *Cambodia International Airlines,* operates to Bangkok and Hong Kong. *Thai International* and *Bangkok Airways* fly to Phnom Penh from Bangkok. *Malaysia Airlines* fly from Kuala Lumpur, *Hang Khong Vietnam (VN)* from Hanoi, *Aeroflot Russian International Airlines (SU)* from Moscow, *Lao International Aviation* from Vientiane and *Kampuchean Airlines (VJ)* from Hanoi, Ho Chi Minh City and Bangkok.
International airport: *Pochentong (PNH)* is 10km (6 miles) from Phnom Penh.
Departure tax: US$8 levied on all international departures.
SEA: The port of Phnom Penh can be reached via the Mekong delta through Vietnam. A new ocean port has been built at Kompong Som (formerly Sihanoukville).
RAIL/ROAD: The Thai border is closed for all overland access. The main highway links the capital with the Vietnam border.

TRAVEL - Internal

AIR: Internal flights operate between Phnom Penh and Siem Reap (travel time – 45 minutes), Battambang, Koh Kong, Kompong Som and Stung Treng.
SEA: Government-run ferries depart from the Psar Cha Ministry of Transport Ferry Landing between 102 and 104 streets and go to Kompong Cham, Kratie, Stung Treng, Kompong Chhnang and Phnom Krom. Due to the present rise in crime, inter-city boat travel should be restricted to the fast boats to Kompong Cham and Kratie.
RAIL: Some rail services operate, but foreigners are advised not to use them at present. There are plans to restore the international service to Bangkok, but a great deal of repair work is needed.
ROAD: Traffic drives on the right. Most roads are in poor condition, although the highway to Vietnam is open. Care should be taken while driving as Cambodian drivers are prone to recklessness and accidents are relatively frequent. The safety of road travel outside urban areas varies greatly from region to region. If travel is undertaken in vehicle convoy during daylight hours only, potential risks can be reduced. Reliable information about security should be obtained before considering extensive road journeys. **Bus:** Buses to Phnom Penh suburbs are available from 182 Street and the bus station is open from 0530-1730. **Taxi:** Cruising taxis are non-existent in Cambodia. However, service taxis can be hired at Psar Chbam Pao Shared-Taxi Station between 367 Street and 369 Street. *Samlors,* however, are a slow but inexpensive way to see the city and some of the drivers, especially those found outside main hotels, speak a little French or English. **Car hire:** Official visitors can arrange to hire a government car and driver. Cars, with or without air-conditioning, are available from the General Directorate of Tourism for about US$30-50.
Documentation: An International Driving Permit is required.

ACCOMMODATION

Many hotels of various standards are available in Phnom Penh. Small and simple hotels can be found in most provincial capitals. Camping is not permitted. For further information, contact Diethelm Travel (for address, see top of entry).

RESORTS & EXCURSIONS

Since the ousting of the Pol Pot regime, many aspects of Khmer cultural life have revived. The famed *National Ballet* has been reconstituted by the surviving dancers and performs classical dances for visiting groups. *Buddhist temples* have re-opened and are the sites of various celebrations, especially at Cambodian New Year. The interrogation centre of the Pol Pot regime in **Phnom Penh** is now the chilling *Toul Sleng Museum of Genocide.* Other attractions in the capital are the *Royal Palace,* with its famous *Silver Pavilion,* and the *National Museum of Khmer Art.* River cruises operate on the Mekong and Tonle Sap rivers near the capital. The famous and magnificent temples at **Angkor,** in the country's northwest, are hard and dangerous to reach by road, but may be reached by regular charter flights. This ancient and astounding temple complex is what remains of the capital of the once mighty Khmer civilisation. *Angor Wat* itself, built to honour the Hindu god Vishnu, is often hailed as one of the most extraordinary architectural creations ever built, with its intricate bas reliefs, strange acoustics and magnificent soaring towers. **Oudong,** 30km (19 miles) from Phnom Penh, is located on a hill overlooking vast plains and is famous for the burial *chedis* of the Khmer kings. **Tonle Bati** has interesting ruins and makes an excellent picnic spot.
POPULAR ITINERARIES: 7-day: Phnom Penh–Oudong–Tonle Bati–Angkor–Phnom Penh.

SOCIAL PROFILE

FOOD & DRINK: Restaurants and other businesses abound in Phnom Penh, although the city remains poor. Food stalls are also common in Phnom Penh and can usually be found in and around the Central Market, O Ressei Market and Tuol Tom Market.
NIGHTLIFE: The *Municipal Theatre* in Phnom Penh stages performances, and classical Cambodian music and dance, performed by students, can be seen at the *Fine Arts School* in Phnom Penh.
SHOPPING: Antiques, woodcarvings, *papier mâché* masks, brass figurines, *kramas* (checked scarves), material for *sarongs* and *hols,* and items and jewellery made of gold, silver and precious stones are Cambodia's best buys. The Central Market, Tuol Tom Pong Market, Old Market and the Bijouterie d'Etat (State Jewellery Shop) are the best places for buying jewellery and the Fine Arts School sells many of the above goods in its shop. Clothing and materials are available at the Central Market.
SPECIAL EVENTS: The following events and festivals occur annually:
Mid-Apr *Chaul Chhnam,* 3-day celebration of the Cambodian New Year. **May 25** *Visak Bauchea,* Anniversary of Buddha's Birthday. **May** *Chrat Prea Angkal,* ceremonial beginning of the sowing season. **Late Sep** *Prachum Ben,* offerings made to dead ancestors. **Late Oct/early Nov** *Festival of the Reversing Current,* The Water Festival (Pirogue canoe races are held in Phnom Penh). **Late Jan/early Feb** *Têt,* Vietnamese and Chinese New Year.
SOCIAL CONVENTIONS: Sensitivity to politically related subjects in conversation is advisable. **Photography:** Permitted, with certain (obvious) restrictions. It is polite to ask permission before photographing Cambodian people, especially monks. Do not allow any type of film to pass through the old-fashioned x-ray machines at the airport.
Tipping: Modest tips are appreciated in hotels and restaurants and by tour guides.

BUSINESS PROFILE

ECONOMY: The Cambodian economy has been all but destroyed by the war in South-East Asia and the rule of the Khmer Rouge. The country has now recovered from the severe food shortages which followed the ousting of the Khmer Rouge from power by the Vietnamese. The transportation infrastructure has suffered greatly from the fighting and restoration of agriculture has been slow. Rice is the staple product in this essentially agricultural economy. The largest export is rubber, most of which goes to the CIS. There are limited mineral resources, mostly of phosphates, iron ore, bauxite, silicon and manganese but these, like the forests which are a valuable potential source of timber, have not been exploited because of the political situation and an inadequate infrastructure. The state agency KAMPEXIM handles some of Cambodia's imports and exports as well as deliveries of foreign aid. The former USSR was until recently, the country's largest trading partner. Japan and Australia are the only other trading partners of any consequence. The removal of US sanctions against Cambodia in January 1992, though relatively insignificant in itself, has made foreign companies less reluctant to do business in the country although the continuing political instability, despite the recent elections, is still serving as a deterrant to potential investors.
BUSINESS: Shirt and tie should be worn. Some knowledge of French would be useful. **Business hours:** 0730-1200 and 1430-1700 Monday to Friday.
COMMERCIAL INFORMATION: The following organisation can offer advice: Chambre de Commerce et d'Agriculture, Vither Preah Baksei Cham Krong, Phnom Penh. Tel: (23) 23775.

CLIMATE

Tropical monsoon climate. Monsoon season is from May to October. In the north, winters can be colder, while throughout most of the country temperatures remain fairly constant.

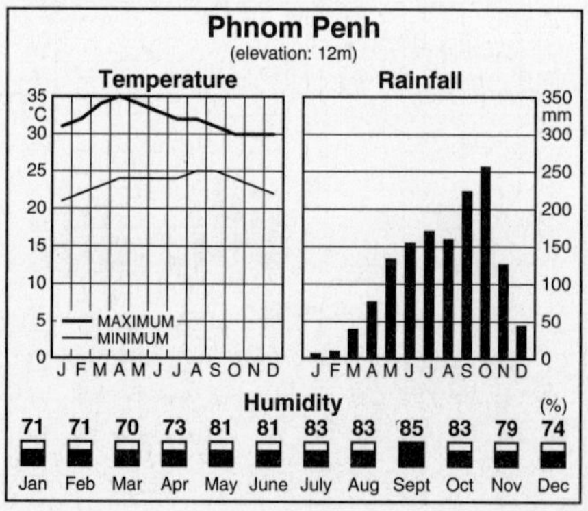

Phnom Penh
(elevation: 12m)
Temperature
Rainfall
35 °C 30 25 20 15 10 5 0
350 mm 300 250 200 150 100 50 0
MAXIMUM
MINIMUM
J F M A M J J A S O N D
J F M A M J J A S O N D
Humidity
(%)
71 71 70 73 81 81 83 83 85 83 79 74
Jan Feb Mar Apr May June July Aug Sept Oct Nov Dec

Cameroon

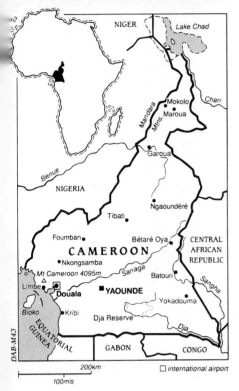

Location: Central Africa.

Société Camerounaise de Tourisme (SOCATOUR)
BP 7138, Yaoundé, Cameroon
Tel: 233 219. Telex: 8766.

Embassy of the Republic of Cameroon
84 Holland Park, London W11 3SB
Tel: (0171) 727 0771. Fax: (0171) 792 9353. Opening
hours: 0930-1230 for application *and* 1430-1630 for
collection, Monday to Friday.

British Embassy
BP 547, avenue Winston Churchill, Yaoundé, Cameroon
Tel: 220 545 *or* 220 796. Fax: 220 148. Telex: 8200 (a/b
PRODROM KN).

British Consulate
BP 1016, rue de l'Hôtel de Ville, Douala, Cameroon
Tel: 422 177 *or* 428 145. Fax: 428 896. Telex: 5353 (a/b
BRITAIN KN).

Embassy of the Republic of Cameroon
2349 Massachusetts Avenue, NW, Washington, DC
20008
Tel: (202) 265 8790/4.

Embassy of the United States of America
BP 817, rue Nachtigal, Yaoundé, Cameroon
Tel: 234 014. Fax: 230 753. Telex: 8223.

Embassy of the Republic of Cameroon
170 Clemow Avenue, Ottawa, Ontario K1S 2B4
Tel: (613) 238 2964. Fax: (613) 238 2967. Telex: 053 3736.

Canadian Embassy
BP 572, Immeuble Stamatiades, Yaoundé, Cameroon
Tel: 230 203 *or* 221 936. Fax: 221 090. Telex: 8209.

AREA: 475,442 sq km (183,569 sq miles).
POPULATION: 11,540,000 (1989 estimate).
POPULATION DENSITY: 24.3 per sq km.
CAPITAL: Yaoundé (constitutional). **Population:**
649,000 (1991 estimate). Douala (economic).

Health	
GALILEO/WORLDSPAN: **TI-DFT/DLA/HE**	
SABRE: **TIDFT/DLA/HE**	
Visa	
GALILEO/WORLDSPAN: **TI-DFT/DLA/VI**	
SABRE: **TIDFT/DLA/VI**	
For more information on Timatic codes refer to Contents.	

Population: 810,000 (1991 estimate).
GEOGRAPHY: Situated on the west coast of Africa,
Cameroon is bounded to the west by the Gulf of Guinea,
to the northwest by Nigeria, to the northeast by Chad
(with Lake Chad at its northern tip), to the east by the
Central African Republic and to the south by Congo,
Gabon and Equatorial Guinea. The far north of the
country is a semi-desert broadening into the vast Maroua
Plain, with game reserves and mineral deposits. This is
bordered to the west by the lush Mandara Mountains.
The Benue River rises here and flows westwards into the
Niger. The country to the northwest is very beautiful;
volcanic peaks covered by bamboo forest rise to over
2000m (6500ft), with waterfalls and villages scattered
over the lower slopes. Further to the south and west are
savannah uplands, while dense forest covers the east and
south. The coastal strip is tropical and cultivated.
Cameroon derives its name from the 15th-century
Portuguese sailor Fernando Po's description of the River
Wouri: *Rio dos Cameroes* ('river of shrimps').
LANGUAGE: The official languages are French and
English. They are given equal importance in the
Constitution but French is the more commonly spoken.
There are many local African languages.
RELIGION: 40% traditional animist beliefs, 40%
Christian, 20% Muslim.
TIME: GMT + 1.
ELECTRICITY: 110/220 volts AC, 50Hz. Plugs are
round 2-pin; bayonet light-fittings are used.
COMMUNICATIONS: Telephone: IDD is available to
and from Cameroon. Country code: 237. There are no
city or area codes. Outgoing international code: 00.
Telephones can usually be found in post offices and
restaurants. The main towns in Cameroon are linked by
automatic dialling, but this service is often unreliable.
Fax: Available at Intelcom offices. **Telex/telegram:**
Facilities are available at Yaoundé and Douala post
offices and at larger hotels but service is slow. Excellent
international telex facilities are available at Intelcom.
Post: Stamps can only be obtained from post offices.
Mail takes about a week to reach addresses in Europe.
Post office hours: 0730-1800 Monday to Friday. **Press:**
The main (official) newspaper is the *Cameroon Tribune*,
published daily in French and twice-weekly in English.
Other available English-language newspapers include the
Cameroon Post, The Herald, The Messenger and the
International Herald Tribune.
BBC World Service and Voice of America
frequencies: From time to time these change. See the
section *How to Use this Book* for more information.
BBC:

MHz	17.79	15.40	9.600	7.105

Voice of America:

MHz	21.48	15.58	9.575	6.035

PASSPORT/VISA

*Regulations and requirements may be subject to change at short notice, and you
are advised to contact the appropriate diplomatic or consular authority before
finalising travel arrangements. Details of these may be found at the head of this
country's entry. Any numbers in the chart refer to the footnotes below.*

	Passport Required?	Visa Required?	Return Ticket Required?
Full British	Yes	Yes	Yes
BVP	Not valid	-	-
Australian	Yes	Yes	Yes
Canadian	Yes	Yes	Yes
USA	Yes	Yes	Yes
Other EU (As of 31/12/94)	Yes	Yes	Yes
Japanese	Yes	Yes	Yes

PASSPORTS: Valid passport required by all.
British Visitors Passport: Not acceptable.
VISAS: Required by all except nationals of Central
African Republic, Congo, Gabon and Nigeria for a stay
not exceeding 90 days.
Types of visa: Two types of both Tourist and Business
visas: Transit and Short-stay, £34.65; Long-stay,
£138.57.
Validity: Short-stay visas are valid for up to 3 months,
Long-stay visas for up to 1 year. Both types of visa
should be used within 3 months of issue. Applications or
extensions should be made to the Embassy.
Application to: Consulate (or Consular section at
Embassy). For addresses, see top of entry.
Application requirements: (a) Valid passport. (b) 2
completed application forms. (c) 2 passport-size photos.
(d) Sufficient funds to cover duration of stay.
Working days required: 48 hours if application is
delivered by hand, a few days more if by mail.
Temporary residence: Applicants must have Residence
and Work Permits. Immigration authorities in Cameroon
must be contacted.

MONEY

Currency: CFA Franc (CFA Fr) = 100 centimes. Notes
are in denominations of CFA Fr10,000, 5000, 2000, 1000
and 500. Coins are in denominations of CFA Fr500, 100,
50, 25, 10 and 5. Only notes issued by the 'Banque des
Etats de l'Afrique Centrale' are valid; those issued by the
'Banque des Etats de l'Afrique de l'Ouest' are not.
Note: At the beginning of 1994, the CFA Franc was
devalued against the French Franc.
Currency exchange: It is advisable to bring French
Francs or US Dollars into the country rather than
Sterling.
Credit cards: Access/Mastercard, American Express,
Diners Club and Visa are accepted on a limited basis
(most major hotels and some restaurants will take them).
Check with your credit card company for details of
merchant acceptability and other services which may be
available.
Travellers cheques: It is easier to convert French Franc
cheques; however, it is possible to exchange Sterling
travellers cheques.
Exchange rate indicators: The following figures are
included as a guide to the movements of the CFA Franc
against Sterling and the US Dollar:

Date:	Oct '92	Sep '93	Jan '94	Jan '95
£1.00=	413.75	433.87	436.78	843.10
$1.00=	260.71	284.14	295.22	545.06

Currency restrictions: Import of both local and foreign
currency is unlimited, subject to declaration. Export of
local currency is limited to CFA Fr20,000. There is no
limit on export of foreign currency.
Banking hours: 0730-1130 and 1430-1630 Monday to
Friday.

DUTY FREE

The following goods may be taken into Cameroon
without incurring any customs duty:
*400 cigarettes or 125 cigars or 500g of tobacco; 1 litre
of spirits and 3 litres of wine; a reasonable quantity of
perfume.*
Note: Items such as radios, cameras and alcoholic
beverages must be declared on arrival, and are
usually admitted free of duty if there is only one of
each item.

PUBLIC HOLIDAYS

Jan 1 '95 New Year's Day. **Feb 11** Youth Day. **Mar 3**
Djoulde Soumae (End of Ramadan). **Apr 14** Good
Friday. **Apr 17** Easter Monday. **May 1** Labour Day. **May
10** Festival of Sheep. **May 20** National Day. **May 25**
Ascension Day. **Dec 10** Reunification Day. **Dec 25**
Christmas. **Jan 1 '96** New Year's Day. **Feb 11** Youth
Day. **Feb 22** Djoulde Soumae (End of Ramadan).
Note: Muslim festivals are timed according to local
sightings of various phases of the moon and the dates
given above are approximations. During the lunar month
of Ramadan that precedes Djoulde Soumae (Eid al-Fitr),
Muslims fast during the day and feast at night and normal
business patterns may be interrupted. Many restaurants
are closed during the day and there may be restrictions on
smoking and drinking. Some disruption may continue
into Djoulde Soumae itself. Djoulde Soumae may last
anything from two to ten days, depending on the region.
For more information, see the section *World of Islam* at
the back of the book.

HEALTH

*Regulations and requirements may be subject to change at short notice, and
you are advised to contact your doctor well in advance of your intended date of
departure. Any numbers in the chart refer to the footnotes below.*

	Special Precautions?	Certificate Required?
Yellow Fever	Yes	1
Cholera	Yes	2
Typhoid & Polio	Yes	-
Malaria	Yes	-
Food & Drink	3	-

[1]: A yellow fever vaccination certificate is required of
all travellers over one year of age.
[2]: Following WHO guidelines issued in 1973, a cholera
vaccination certificate is no longer a condition of entry to
Cameroon. However, cholera is a serious risk in this
country and precautions are essential. Up-to-date advice
should be sought before deciding whether these
precautions should include vaccination as medical
opinion is divided over its effectiveness. See the *Health*

section at the back of the book.
[3]: Water precautions are recommended outside of main hotels, but all water should be regarded as being potentially contaminated. Water used for drinking, brushing teeth or making ice should have first been boiled or otherwise sterilised. Bottled water is readily available. Milk is unpasteurised and should be boiled. Powdered or tinned milk is available and is advised, but make sure that it is reconstituted with pure water. Avoid dairy products which are likely to have been made from unboiled milk. Only eat well-cooked meat and fish, preferably served hot. Pork, salad and mayonnaise may carry increased risk. Vegetables should be cooked and fruit peeled.
Malaria risk exists all year throughout the country, predominantly in the malignant *falciparum* form. Resistance to chloroquine has been reported.
Rabies is present. For those at high risk, vaccination before arrival should be considered. If you are bitten abroad seek medical advice without delay. For more information consult the *Health* section.
Bilharzia (schistosomiasis) is present. Avoid swimming and paddling in fresh water. Swimming pools which are well-chlorinated and maintained are safe.
Meningitis risk exists, depending on area and time of year.
Health care: Health insurance is strongly advised. There are hospitals in most main towns, with 251 hospitals and health centres throughout the country. There are three hospitals in Yaoundé: the General, Reference and Jamot Hospital. Douala has one large hospital, the Laquintinie Hospital. In addition, there are several medical centres, clinics and private nursing homes located throughout the country. Medical care is competent but expensive, as are medicines. A campaign aiming at 'Health for all by the year 2000' is underway, with the emphasis on the development of preventative medicine.

TRAVEL - International

AIR: Cameroon's national airline is *Cameroon Airlines (UY)*. There are regular flights from Cameroon to Fernando Poo, Nigeria, Côte d'Ivoire, Benin and Togo.
Approximate flight time: From Paris to Douala is 6 hours.
International airport: *Douala (DLA)* is 10km (6 miles) southeast of the city. Facilities include a duty-free shop, bar, post office, bank, shops and buffet/restaurant. A bus goes to the city every 15 minutes 0600-2100. Taxis are also available; a surcharge is payable after 2200. International airports are being constructed at Yaoundé and Bafoussam.
Departure Tax: CFA Fr5000 for international flights, CFA Fr500 for domestic flights.
SEA: Irregular sailings from European ports to Douala take up to three weeks, with stops in the Canary Islands and West African ports. There are also berths on some cargo boats for six to 12 passengers.
RAIL: There are plans to extend the rail network from Mbalmayo to Bangui in the Central African Republic.
ROAD: There are road connections to Chad, Equatorial Guinea, the Central African Republic, Nigeria and Gabon. Travel on these routes is rough, and should not be attempted in the rainy season. Four-wheel-drive vehicles are recommended. The Trans-Africa Highway from Kenya to Nigeria is under construction.

TRAVEL - Internal

AIR: This is the most efficient means of national transport. There are daily flights between Douala and Yaoundé; less regular flights to other interior towns.
RAIL: Rail travel within Cameroon is slow but cheap. Daily trains run from Douala to Yaoundé, with onward connections to Ngaoundéré, and from Douala to Nkongsamba. Couchettes are available on some trains, and a few have air-conditioning and restaurant cars. Children aged 5-9 pay half-fare. There is no charge for children under 5. The final section of the Transcameroon railway was completed in 1987. It runs from Yaoundé to Ngaoundéré covering a distance of 930km (580 miles).
ROAD: There are paved roads from Douala to Yaoundé, Limbé, Buéa, Bafoussam and Bamenda and between main centres. Other roads are generally poorly maintained and become almost impassable during the rainy season. Traffic drives on the right. **Bus:** Modern coach services are available between Yaoundé and Ngaoundéré. Bus services also exist between other main centres and more rural areas, but tend to be unreliable and are often suspended during the rainy season. **Car hire:** This is limited and expensive and is available in Douala, Yaoundé and Limbé, with or without a driver.
Documentation: An International Driving Permit is required.
URBAN: Bus services operate in Douala and Yaoundé at flat fares. Taxis are available at reasonable fixed rates (none are metered). A 10% tip is optional.
JOURNEY TIMES: The following gives approximate journey times (in hours and minutes) from Yaoundé.

	Air	Road	Rail
Bafoussam	0.50	3.30	-
Bamenda	1.10	4.30	-
Douala	0.30	3.00	4.00
Dschang	0.50	-	-
Garoua	2.30	18.00	-
Koutaba	1.25	-	-
Kribi	0.45	-	-
Mamfe	1.00	-	-
Maroua	3.45	24.00	-
Ngaoundéré	2.40	12.00	10.00

ACCOMMODATION

HOTELS: Good accommodation of international standard is available in Douala, Yaoundé, Bamenda, Garoua and Maroua. The good hotels (government-rated 2-star and above) have air-conditioning, sports facilities and swimming pools; most rooms have showers. Most large hotels will accept major credit cards. Rates are for the room only. Cheaper accommodation is also available. The Hotel de Waza, just outside Waza National Park, north of Maroua in the far north of the country, is essentially a *campement* with two pavilions and individual rooms comprised of straw huts. Hotel facilities are in heavy demand: it is advisable to book in advance, and to obtain confirmation of your booking in writing. For more information on hotels in Cameroon, contact the Ministry of Tourism, BP 266, Yaoundé. Tel: 224 411. Telex: 8318; *or* Hotel Sofitel, BP 711, Mont Fébé, Yaoundé. Tel: 234 002.
CAMPING: Permitted in Boubandjidah National Park, on the banks of Mayo Lidi River.

RESORTS & EXCURSIONS

The Centre & East

Yaoundé, the capital city, stands on seven hills. There are 13 modern hotels and many markets, museums, shops and cinemas. To the northwest, jungle-clad mountains rise to an altitude of 1000m (3280ft). *Mont Fébé,* which overlooks the city, has been developed as a resort, with a luxury hotel, nightclub, casino, gardens and golf course. Its high altitude ensures a pleasant climate.
Luna Park, a permanent fun-fair and weekend holiday resort 40km (25 miles) north of the capital, can be found on the road to Obala. Further on, one can view the **Nachtigal Falls** on the River Sanga and continue to **Bertoua**, **Yokadouma** and **Moloundou** with its abundant wildlife, most notably a small population of lowland gorillas.

The West

Douala, Cameroon's economic capital, is 24km (15 miles) from the sea, on the left bank of the Wouri and dominated by Mount Cameroon. Worth visiting are the cathedral, the shopping avenues, the *Artisanat National* (a craft/souvenir market), *Deido market*, the harbour, the museum, *Wouri Bridge* and the electric coffee-grading plant.
Buéa is a charming town situated on the slopes of Mount Cameroon. For those interested in climbing the mountain (the highest in West Africa, but relatively easy), a permit from the local tourist office is necessary (these are not issued during the rainy season from March to November).
Limbé (formerly Victoria) is a pleasant port with a botanical garden and 'jungle village'. There are beautiful white sandy beaches a short drive out of town. The tourist season runs between November and February.
Dschang is a mountain resort at an altitude of 1400m (4600ft) where the temperature is pleasantly cool. The road southwards to Nkongsamba and Douala passes through some splendid scenery – spectacular valleys and waterfalls.
Bamenda, in the highlands north of Dschang, has a museum and a craft market.
Foumban, northeast of Dschang, has many traditional buildings dating from its period of German colonisation, including *Fon's Palace* which includes a craft centre. There is also a museum and a market. The town serves as an excellent base for experiencing the Bamileke region's colourful Bamoun festivals and feast days.
Kribi, a small port and beach resort south of Douala, has perhaps the finest beach in Cameroon, *Londji Beach*. It is also a convenient starting point for tours to pygmy villages and the **Campo Game Reserve** region. Buffaloes, lions and elephants roam the virgin forests inland.

The North

North Cameroon presents unexpected natural landscapes, with an average altitude of 1500m (4900ft) and plains, reaching an altitude of 300m (1000ft), covered by savannah.
Maroua is located in the foothills of the Mandara Mountains, along the Mayo River. Places worth visiting include the market, the *Diamare Museum* (mainly an ethnographic museum where local craftwares are on sale: jewellery, tooled leather articles, etc), the various African quarters and the banks of the Mayo Kaliao. There is a National Park nearby (see below).
Mokolo is a picturesque town in a rugged rocky landscape. 55km (34 miles) away is the village of **Rhumsiki,** which features a maze of paths linking the small farms known as the Kapsiki; here live the Kirdi, whose customs and folklore have changed little for centuries.
Going further north, there is a very typical village called **Koza** located at an altitude of 1100m (3600ft). From here the road continues to the village of **Mabas** which gives a panoramic view on the large Bornou plain of Nigeria and where one can still see primitive blast furnaces.

National Parks

The **Kalamaloue Reserve** is small but offers opportunities for viewing several species of antelopes, monkeys and warthogs; some elephants cross the reserve.
Waza National Park covers 170,000 hectares. There is a forest area (open from November to March) and a vast expanse of grassy and wet plains, called *Yaeres* (open from February to June). Elephants, giraffes, antelopes, hartebeest, cobs, lions, cheetahs and warthogs are numerous. There is also a rich variety of birds: eagles, crested cranes, maribous, pelicans, ducks, geese and numerous guinea-fowl. Accommodation and other facilities are available. There are no vehicles for hire at the park, but buses run from Maroua.
The **Boubandjidah National Park** is on the banks of Mayo Lidi River in the very far north of the country. There are several other parks and reserves which are not open to the public.
POPULAR ITINERARIES: 7-day: (a) Yaoundé–Luna Park–Nachtigal Falls–Bertoua–Yokadouma–Moloundou–Yaoundé. (b) Yaoundé–Douala–Dschang–Bamenda–Foumban–Yaoundé.

SOCIAL PROFILE

FOOD & DRINK: Cooking is often French or Lebanese, while local food can also be very tasty. Luxury items can be extremely expensive. The country abounds in avocado pears, citrus fruits, pineapples and mangoes. Prawns are in plentiful supply in the south. There are many restaurants in big towns and cities, with good service. **Drink:** Most international hotels have bars. There are no licensing hours, and hotel bars stay open as long as there is custom.
NIGHTLIFE: In Douala and Yaoundé particularly, nightclubs and casinos can be found independently or within most good hotels. There are also some cinemas.
SHOPPING: Local handicrafts include highly decorated pots, drinking horns, jugs, bottles and cups, great earthenware bowls and delicate pottery, dishes and trays, mats and rugs woven from grass, raffia, jewellery and camel hair or cotton and beadwork garments.
SPORT: Fishing is good in many rivers and coastal areas. **Hunting** licences are limited. **Swimming** in the sea and swimming pools of luxury hotels, which generally also have **tennis** courts, are both available. A **golf** course is available to hotel residents in Yaoundé. **Football** is a popular spectator sport.
SPECIAL EVENTS: Local entertainment troupes may be seen in most regional towns, particularly during festivals.
SOCIAL CONVENTIONS: Handshaking is the customary form of greeting. In the north, where the population is largely Muslim, Islamic traditions should be respected. Visitors should never step inside a Muslim prayer circle of rocks. In other rural areas, where traditional beliefs predominate, it is essential to use tact. **Photography:** Cameras should be used with discretion, particularly in rural areas. Always ask permission before taking a photograph. Do not photograph airports, military establishments, official buildings, or military personnel in uniform. **Tipping:**

(omitted)

The average tip for porters and hotel staff should be about 10%, otherwise service charges are usually inclusive.

BUSINESS PROFILE

ECONOMY: Cameroon enjoys one of the most successful economies in Africa by virtue of consistent agricultural performance and the rapid growth of its oil industry. The main agricultural products are cocoa (of which Cameroon is one of the world's largest producers), coffee, bananas, cotton, palm oil, wood and rubber. The country is self-sufficient in oil and has enough surplus to export both crude and refined oil. Natural gas deposits have been located but the currently low world market price inhibits the degree of exploitation. In addition, feasibility studies have been conducted in various parts of the country into the possible extraction of deposits of iron ore, bauxite, copper, chromium, uranium and other metals. Light industries such as food-processing, building materials and batteries have helped to further diversify the economy. The Government's economic strategy aims to create a market economy with a substantial level of government participation, although a liberal investment code seeks to attract foreign investment. This, coupled with the country's political stability and the continued flow of aid and other foreign capital, makes for generally bright economic prospects. The country has all but recovered from a bad patch during the late 1980s, which was largely the result of a sharp decline in oil revenues. France and The Netherlands are the major export markets followed by Germany, the USA and fellow members of the Central African customs and economic union (known by its French acronym of UDEAC).

COMMERCIAL INFORMATION: The following organisation can offer advice: Chambre de Commerce, d'Industrie et des Mines du Cameroun, BP 4011, Place du Gouvernement, Douala. Tel: 422 888. Telex: 5616.

CONFERENCES/CONVENTIONS: For information contact the Ministry of External Relations, BP 9999, Yaoundé.

CLIMATE

The south is hot and dry between November and February. The main rainy season is from July to October. Temperatures in the north vary. On the Adamaoua Plateau temperatures drop sharply at night; the rainy season is from May to October. Grassland areas inland are much cooler than the coast with regular rainfall.

Required clothing: Lightweight cotton clothes, canvas or light leather shoes or sandals. Raincoats are necessary for coastal areas.

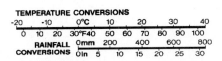

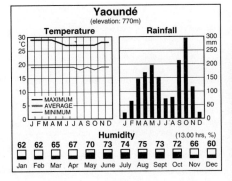

Canada

Location: North America.

Tourism Canada
Industry Canada, 4th Floor East, 235 Queen Street, Ottawa, Ontario K1A 0H6
Tel: (613) 954 3858. Fax: (613) 954 3964.

Canadian High Commission
Macdonald House, 1 Grosvenor Square, London W1X 0AB
Tel: (0171) 258 6600. Fax: (0171) 258 6302. Opening hours: 0900-1700 Monday to Friday.

Immigration Department (Visa Section)
38 Grosvenor Street, London W1X 0AA
Tel: (0891) 616 644. Fax: (0171) 258 6506. Opening hours: 0800-1100 Monday to Friday.

Canadian Tourist Office (Marketing Department)
Macdonald House, 1 Grosvenor Square, London W1X 0AB
Tel: (0171) 258 6582. Fax: (0171) 258 6322. Opening hours: 0900-1730 Monday to Friday.

Canada Centre (Consumer & Trade Information)
62-65 Trafalgar Square, London WC2N 5DT
Tel: (0171) 839 2299 (public) or 930 8540 (trade). Fax: (0171) 798 9839. Opening hours: 0930-1700 Monday to Friday.

British High Commission
80 Elgin Street, Ottawa, Ontario K1P 5K7
Tel: (613) 237 1530. Fax: (613) 237 7980. Telex: 0533318 (a/b UKREP OTT).
Consulates in: Halifax, St John's, Montréal, Toronto, Vancouver and Winnipeg.

Canadian Embassy
501 Pennsylvania Avenue, NW, Washington, DC 20001
Tel: (202) 682 1740. Fax: (202) 682 7726.

Canadian Consulate General
1251 Avenue of the Americas, New York, NY 10020-1175
Tel: (212) 596 1600 or 596 1700. Fax: (212) 596 1790.
Consulates in: Atlanta, Boston, Buffalo, Chicago, Dallas, Detroit, Los Angeles, Minneapolis, Princeton and Seattle.

Embassy of the United States of America
100 Wellington Street, Ottawa, Ontario K1P 5T1
Tel: (613) 238 5335 or 238 4470. Fax: (613) 238 5720 or 238 8750.
Consulates in: Calgary, Halifax, Montréal, Québec, Toronto and Vancouver.

Note: For major regional Tourist Information Offices, see under Provincial/Territorial entries below.

AREA: 9,970,610 sq km (3,849,674 sq miles).
POPULATION: 27,408,900 (1992 estimate).
POPULATION DENSITY: 2.8 per sq km.
CAPITAL: Ottawa. **Population:** 920,85, (1991, including Hull).
GEOGRAPHY: Canada is bounded to the west by the Pacific Ocean and Alaska, to the east by the Atlantic Ocean, to the northeast by Greenland, and to the south by the 'Lower 48' of the USA. The polar ice-cap lies to the north. The landscape is diverse, ranging from the Arctic tundra of the north to the great wheatlands of the central area. Westward are the Rocky Mountains, and in the southeast are the Great Lakes, the St Lawrence River and Niagara Falls. The country is divided into ten provinces and two territories. A more detailed description of each province can be found under the separate provincial entries below.
LANGUAGE: Bilingual: French and English. The use of the two languages reflects the mixed colonial history – Canada has been under both British and French rule.
RELIGION: 46.2% Roman Catholic, 17.5% United Church of Canada, 11.8% Anglican, 24.5% other Christian denominations and other religions.
TIME: Canada spans six time zones. Information on

which applies where may be found in the regional entries following this general introduction. The time zones are:
Pacific Standard Time: GMT - 8.
Mountain Standard Time: GMT - 7.
Central Standard Time: GMT - 6.
Eastern Standard Time: GMT - 5.
Atlantic Standard Time: GMT - 4.
Newfoundland Standard Time: GMT - 3.5.
Note: From the first Sunday in April to the last Sunday in October, one hour is added for Daylight Saving Time (except in Saskatchewan).
ELECTRICITY: 110 volts AC, 60Hz. American-style (flat) 2-pin plugs are standard.
COMMUNICATIONS: Telephone: Most public telephones operate on 25-cent coins. There is a reduced rate 1800-0800 Monday to Friday, and 1200 Saturday to 0800 Monday. Full IDD is available. Country code: 1. Outgoing international code: 011. **Fax:** Services are available in commercial bureaux and most hotels all day at locally agreed rates. **Telex/telegram:** Telegrams are handled by Canadian National Telecommunications or Canadian Pacific, and any telegrams must be telephoned or handed in to the nearest Canadian Pacific or Canadian National office (address in local phone book). Services available include *Teleport*, providing first-class door-to-door delivery, and *Intelpost*, which offers satellite communications for documents/photographs to London, Washington DC, New York, Berne and Amsterdam. In Newfoundland & Labrador telegrams are sent through *Terra Nova Tel.* **Post:** All mail from Canada to outside North America is by air. Stamps are available in hotels, chemists and railway stations, or in vending machines outside post offices and shopping centres. *Poste Restante* facilities are available. *Intelpost* is offered at main postal offices for satellite transmission of documents and photographs. Post office hours: generally 0930-1700 Monday to Friday and 0900-1200 Saturday, but times vary according to province and location; city offices will have longer hours. **Press:** There is no national daily newspaper as such, but Toronto's *The Globe & Mail* has national distribution. Daily newspapers published in the larger population centres have a wide local and regional circulation. French-language dailies are published in seven cities, including Montréal, Québec and Ottawa. In Alberta, the main English-language newspapers are the *Calgary Herald, The Edmonton Journal, The Calgary Sun* and *The Edmonton Sun;* in British Columbia, the *Vancouver Sun;* in Manitoba, the *Winnipeg Free Press* and *The Winnipeg Sun;* in New Brunswick, the *Daily Gleaner* and *The Telegraph-Journal;* in Newfoundland & Labrador, the *Telegram* and *The Western Star;* in Nova Scotia, *The Chronicle-Herald, The Mail-Star* and *The Daily News;* in Ontario, *The Globe & Mail* (the main national newspaper), *The Financial Post, The Toronto Star, The Toronto Sun, The Ottawa Citizen* and the *Ottawa Sun;* in Québec, *The Gazette* (daily); in Prince Edward Island, the *Guardian* and the *Patriot;* in Saskatchewan, the *Leader Post, Star-Phoenix, Times-Herald* and the *Daily Herald;* and in Yukon, *The Whitehorse Star.*
BBC World Service frequencies: From time to time these change. See the section *How to Use this Book* for more information.

Central, Mountain and Pacific Canada:

MHz	17.84	15.26	9.515	7.325

Atlantic and Eastern Canada:

MHz	17.84	15.26	9.740	5.975

PASSPORT/VISA

Regulations and requirements may be subject to change at short notice, and you are advised to contact the appropriate diplomatic or consular authority before finalising travel arrangements. Details of these may be found at the head of this country's entry. Any numbers in the chart refer to the footnotes below.

	Passport Required?	Visa Required?	Return Ticket Required?
Full British	Yes	No	Yes
BVP	Not valid	-	-
Australian	Yes	No	Yes
Canadian	No	No	No
USA	No	No	No
Other EU (As of 31/12/94)	Yes	1	Yes
Japanese	Yes	No	Yes

Note: Visitors to Canada must satisfy an examining officer at the Port of Entry that they are genuine visitors and have sufficient funds to maintain themselves during their stay in Canada and to return to their country of origin, as well as evidence of confirmed onward reservations out of Canada. Persons under 18 years of age who are unaccompanied by an adult should bring with them a letter from a parent or guardian giving them permission to travel to Canada.

TEMPERATURE CONVERSIONS

-20	-10	0°C	10	20	30	40

0	10	20	30°F40	50	60	70	80	90	100

RAINFALL CONVERSIONS

0mm	200		400		600		800

0in	5	10	15	20	25	30

Yaoundé
(elevation: 770m)

Humidity (13.00 hrs, %)

Jan	Feb	Mar	Apr	May	June	July	Aug	Sept	Oct	Nov	Dec
62	62	65	67	70	73	74	75	73	72	66	60

Health
GALILEO/WORLDSPAN: **TI-DFT/YOW/HE**
SABRE: **TIDFT/YOW/HE**

Visa
GALILEO/WORLDSPAN: **TI-DFT/YOW/VI**
SABRE: **TIDFT/YOW/VI**

For more information on Timatic codes refer to Contents.

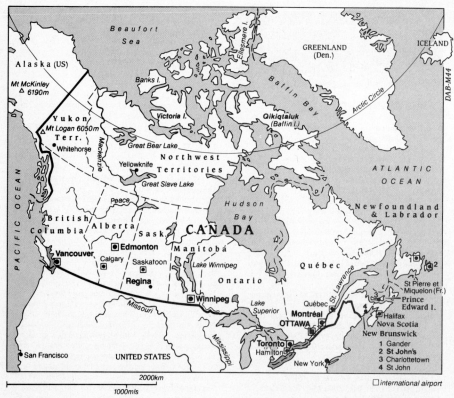

Date:	Oct '92	Sep '93	Jan '94	Jan '95
£1.00=	1.99	2.04	1.96	2.19
$1.00=	1.25	1.33	1.32	1.40

Currency restrictions: There are no restrictions on the import or export of either local or foreign currency if declared.

Banking hours: 1000-1500 Monday to Friday. Business accounts can only be set up on presentation of a letter of credit from a home bank. Some banks in major centres have extended hours – check locally.

DUTY FREE

The following goods may be taken into Canada without incurring customs duty:

200 cigarettes and 50 cigars and 400g of manufactured tobacco and 400g of tobacco sticks per person over 18 years of age; 1 bottle (1.1 litres) of spirits or wine or 24 bottles or cans (355ml) of beer or ale per person over 18 years of age if entering Alberta, Manitoba and Québec and over 19 years if entering British Columbia, Ontario, Prince Edward Island, Saskatchewan, Northwest Territories, Yukon, New Brunswick, Newfoundland & Labrador and Nova Scotia; gifts free of duties to the value of Can$60 per gift (not being advertising matter, tobacco or alcoholic beverages).

Prohibited items: The importation of firearms, explosives, endangered species of animals and plants, animal products, meat, food and plant material is subject to certain restrictions and formalities. Dogs and domestic cats may be imported from certain rabies-free countries (including the United Kingdom and the Republic of Ireland) subject to certain restrictions and formalities (but note that rabies is present in Canada and pets will generally face quarantine on returning home). Enquire at the Canadian High Commission or Embassy for further details.

Note: There is a General Sales Tax (GST) in Canada of 7% on all goods and services. Visitors may reclaim this tax on accommodation and any goods purchased and taken out of the country if over Can$100. However, GST is not reclaimable on food, drink, tobacco or any form of transport. To claim a rebate, a GST form must be completed, with all original receipts attached, and mailed to the address on the form. Forms are available in hotels and tourist offices. GST must be claimed before applying for provincial tax, with the exception of Québec and Manitoba, where the provincial sales tax can be reclaimed at the same time as GST on the GST form. GST forms should be sent to Revenue Canada, Customs and Excise, Visitors Rebate Programme, Ottawa, Ontario K1A 1J5.

PUBLIC HOLIDAYS

Jan 1-2 '95 New Year. **Apr 14** Good Friday. **Apr 17** Easter Monday. **May 22** Victoria Day. **Jul 3** For Canada Day. **Sep 4** Labour Day. **Oct 9** Thanksgiving. **Nov 11** Remembrance Day. **Dec 25** Christmas Day. **Dec 26** Boxing Day. **Jan 1 '96** New Year's Day. **Apr 5** Good Friday. **Apr 8** Easter Monday.

Note: In addition, every Province and Territory has its own local holidays; consult the regional entries below.

HEALTH

Regulations and requirements may be subject to change at short notice, and you are advised to contact your doctor well in advance of your intended date of departure. Any numbers in the chart refer to the footnotes below.

	Special Precautions?	Certificate Required?
Yellow Fever	No	No
Cholera	No	No
Typhoid & Polio	No	-
Malaria	No	-
Food & Drink	1	

[1]: Tap water is considered safe to drink. Milk is pasteurised and dairy products are safe for consumption. Local meat, poultry, seafood, fruit and vegetables are generally considered safe to eat.

Rabies is present. For those at high risk, vaccination before arrival should be considered. If you are bitten abroad, seek medical advice without delay. For more information, consult the *Health* section at the back of the book.

Health care: There are excellent health facilities (similar to the USA). Personal first-aid kits should be carried by travellers to more remote northern areas. Private health insurance up to Can$50,000 is absolutely essential as hospital charges are very expensive (from US$650 a day

PASSPORTS: Passport valid for at least one day beyond the intended departure date from Canada is required by all except:

(a) Canadian citizens holding expired Canadian passport or Canadian birth certificate or certificate of Canadian citizenship along with Canadian driver's licence with photo;

(b) permanent residents of Canada with proof of status, ie Permanent Residents Card, Record of Landing, Canadian Certificate of Identity, Returning Resident Permit (IMM 1288) or Refugee Travel Document issued by the Government of Canada to refugees who have been resettled in Canada;

(c) Convention Refugees and Members of Designated Classes who have been accepted for resettlement in Canada and in possession of valid and subsisting Canadian Immigrant Visas (IMM 1000) where the immigrant category is coded CR or DC;

(d) citizens of the USA holding proof of citizenship;

(e) persons entering from St Pierre & Miquelon or the USA who have been lawfully admitted to the USA for permanent residence;

(f) citizens of France entering from and who are residents of St Pierre & Miquelon;

(g) nationals entering from Greenland who are residents there.

British Visitors Passport: Not acceptable.

VISAS: Required by all except:

(a) nationals of countries shown in the chart above;

(b) **[1]** nationals of EU countries (with the exception of nationals of Portugal who *do* require visas);

(c) nationals of Andorra, Antigua & Barbuda, Austria, Bahamas, Barbados, Botswana, Brunei, Costa Rica, Cyprus, Dominica, Finland, Grenada, Hungary, Iceland, *Israel, South Korea, Kiribati, Liechtenstein, Malaysia, Malta, Mexico, Monaco, Namibia, Nauru, New Zealand, Norway, Papua New Guinea, St Kitts & Nevis, St Lucia, St Vincent & the Grenadines, San Marino, Saudi Arabia, Singapore, Solomon Islands, Swaziland, Sweden, Switzerland, Tuvalu, Vanuatu, Vatican City, Venezuela, Western Samoa and Zimbabwe;

(d) nationals of British Dependent Territories: Anguilla, Bermuda, British Virgin Islands, Cayman Islands, Falkland Islands, Gibraltar, Hong Kong, Montserrat, Pitcairn Islands, St Helena and Turks & Caicos Islands;

(e) those visiting Canada who, during that visit, also visit the USA or St Pierre & Miquelon (a French Overseas Territory) and return to Canada therefrom as visitors within the period authorised on their initial entry (or any extension thereto).

Notes: These visa regulations are subject to change at any time; it is advisable to check with the nearest Canadian Consulate, Embassy or High Commission prior to travel. [*] Nationals of Israel must be in possession of a valid and subsisting national Israeli passport and *not* an Israeli Orange 'Travel Document in lieu of National Passport'.

Types of visa: Tourists will be issued a Visitor's visa. Transit visas are necessary for all nationals who require a Visitor's visa. Although Transit visas are not required by British citizens, they may be required by foreign nationals with British passports; check with the Embassy or High Commission for details (addresses above).

Validity: Up to 6 months depending on circumstances of individual applicant. The determination regarding length of stay in Canada can only be decided by the examining officer at the port of entry. If no actual departure date is indicated within the visitor's passport, then the visitor will be required to depart within three months from the date of entry. Visitors must effect their departure from Canada on or before the date authorised by the examining officer on arrival. If an extension of stay is desired, an application must be made in writing to the nearest Canada Immigration Centre well before the expiry of the visitor's visa.

Cost: *Single-entry:* Can$55 (approx. UK£25). *Multiple-entry:* Can$85 (approx. UK£40).

Application to: Consulate (or Consular section at Embassy or High Commission). For addresses, see top of entry.

Application requirements: (a) Valid passport. (b) Application form. (c) 2 passport-size photos. (d) Proof of sufficient funds for length of stay (this may entail providing a letter from one's employer, mortgage statements or bank statements or letter of invitation from a Canadian resident). (e) *Fee. (f) For those applying by post, a stamped, self-addressed envelope with CVV written in the top lefthand corner.

Note [*]: If submitting application by post, payment must be in the form of Canadian Dollars or a cheque or postal order in Canadian Dollars.

Temporary residence: A work permit is required for temporary residence in Canada. Persons who wish to proceed to Canada for the purposes of study or temporary employment should contact the nearest Canadian High Commission, Embassy or Consulate, as authorisation is normally required prior to arrival. Those who will be taking up temporary employment will require an Employment Authorization, for which a fee is charged. Persons going for study purposes must obtain a Student Authorization; a charge is made for this.

MONEY

Currency: Canadian Dollar (Can$) = 100 cents. Notes are in denominations of Can$1000, 100, 50, 20, 10 and 5. Coins are in denominations of Can$1, and 50, 25, 10, 5 and 1 cents.

Credit cards: Most international credit cards are accepted.

Travellers cheques are best bought in Canadian Dollars; these are widely negotiable.

Exchange rate indicators: The following figures are included as a guide to the movements of the Canadian Dollar against Sterling and the US Dollar:

I thought you said we weren't sitting in First Class.

NO OTHER AIRLINE CAN MATCH ALL THE AMENITIES OF AIR CANADA'S NEW EXECUTIVE FIRST

Air Canada's new Executive First. Whatever it takes to get your clients where they're going on overseas flights, comfortably. Even better, now they can get all the comforts of First Class for the price of business class. This includes • Choice of window or aisle seat • Priority check-in, baggage handling, boarding • Worldwide airport Maple Leaf Lounge privileges • Nearly 50% more personal space • 21" wide reclining electronic sleeper and more leg room • Global access telephone • Personal Entertainment System • Individual armrest video screen • 6 video channels • 10 audio channels • Hot hors d'oeuvres • New 4 course meal service and premium selection of beverages • And coming soon, global fax service.

Air Canada's Executive First. Your clients can have it all. And for a lot less than they thought.

AIR CANADA
EXECUTIVE FIRST

often with 30% surcharge for non-residents imposed in some provinces). Dial '0' for emergencies.

There is no Reciprocal Health Agreement with the UK, but doctors will continue medication for prescriptions issued in Europe.

Note: Visitors intending to stay in Canada for more than six months, either as tourists, students or employees, may be required to take a medical examination. Visitors working in an occupation in which protection of public health is essential may be required to undergo a medical examination even if employment is only temporary. Check with the Canadian Consulate or High Commission for further information.

TRAVEL - International

AIR: Canada's principal national airline is *Air Canada (AC)*. The other national airline is *Canadian Airlines International (CP)*.

For free advice on air travel, call the *Air Travel Advisory Bureau* in the UK on (0171) 636 5000 (London) *or* (0161) 832 2000 (Manchester).

Approximate flight times: From *London* to Calgary is 9 hours, to Halifax is 6 hours 30 minutes, to Montréal is 7 hours, to Toronto is 7 hours 30 minutes and to Vancouver is 10 hours.

From *Los Angeles* to Montréal is 7 hours 5 minutes, to Toronto is 5 hours 25 minutes and to Vancouver is 3 hours 10 minutes.

From *New York* to Montréal is 1 hour 15 minutes, to Toronto is 1 hour 20 minutes and to Vancouver is 8 hours.

From *Singapore* to Montréal is 25 hours, to Toronto is 24 hours and to Vancouver is 16 hours 30 minutes.

From *Sydney* to Montréal is 22 hours 20 minutes, to Toronto is 22 hours 35 minutes and to Vancouver is 18 hours 45 minutes.

International airports: Canada has 13 international airports. All have full banking and catering facilities, duty-free shops and car hire. Airport-to-city bus and taxi services and, in some cases, rail links, are available.

Calgary (YYC) is 19km (11 miles) from the city (travel time – 30 minutes).

Edmonton (YEG) is 28km (19 miles) from the city

(travel time – 45 minutes).

Gander (YQX) is 3km (2 miles) from the city (travel time – 10 minutes).

Halifax (YHZ) is 42km (26 miles) from the city (travel time – 30 minutes).

Hamilton (YHM) is 10km (6 miles) from the city (travel time – 20 minutes).

Montréal (YUL) (Dorval) is 21km (14 miles) from the city (travel time – 25 minutes).

Montréal (YMX) (Mirabel) is 55km (34 miles) from the city (travel time – 60 minutes).

Ottawa (YOW) (Uplands) is 17.5km (11 miles) from the city (travel time – 25 minutes).

St John's (YYT) is 8km (5 miles) from the city (travel time – 10-15 minutes).

Saskatoon (YXE) is 7km (4.5 miles) from the city (travel time – 10 minutes).

Toronto (YYZ) (Lester B Pearson) is 28km (18 miles) from the city (travel time – 20 minutes).

Vancouver (YVR) is 15km (11 miles) from the city (travel time – 20 minutes).

Winnipeg (YWG) is 6.5km (4 miles) from the city (travel time – 20 minutes).

Departure tax: Vancouver has a departure tax which is Can$15 for international departures and Can$10 for departures to other North American destinations, including Hawaii and Mexico.

SEA: The principal ports of Canada are Montréal, Québec and Toronto on the east coast and Vancouver on the west coast. All are served by international shipping lines, but Montréal is the only port for passenger liners from Europe.

RAIL: The Canadian rail system connects to the USA at several points. Major routes are: New York–Montréal, New York–Buffalo–Niagara Falls–Toronto, Chicago–Sarnia–London–Toronto, Cleveland–Buffalo–Niagara Falls–Toronto and Detroit–Windsor–Toronto.

ROAD: The only road access to Canada is through the southern border with the USA or from the west through Alaska. Apart from private motoring, the most popular way of travelling by road is by bus. The biggest coach company in the world is the *Greyhound Bus Company* (see below under *Bus*) and this is one of the most common routes to Canada from the United States. There are many crossing points from the United States

to Canada, but some of the most common are: New York to Montréal/Ottawa; Detroit to Toronto/Hamilton; Minneapolis to Winnipeg; Seattle to Vancouver/ Edmonton/Calgary.

TRAVEL - Internal

AIR: There are a number of regional airlines, the principal ones being:

Atlantic Coast: *Air Nova; Air Atlantic.*
Western Canada: *Time Air; Air BC.*
Central Canada: *Nordair Ltd; Québecair (QB).*

There are also about 75 airlines operating local services. There are reductions for those aged 13-21; and substantial reductions for those under 12. Internal air passes are available on *Air BC* and *Air Ontario* for periods of 7-21 days. The *Air Ontario* pass covers Ontario, Québec and certain destinations in the USA and prices at the time of writing are £99 for 7 days, £149 for 14 days and £198 for 21 days. The *Air BC* pass covers Manitoba, Saskatchewan, Alberta and British Columbia and prices at the time of writing are £119 for 7 days, £169 for 14 days and £219 for 21 days. Both passes are available in the UK through the *Airpass Sales Office for Air BC* and *Air Ontario* (tel/fax: (01737) 555 300) and may only be purchased outside of Canada.

SEA/RIVER/LAKE/CANAL: Canada has many thousands of miles of navigable rivers and canals, a vast number of lakes and an extensive coastline. The whole country is well served by all manners of boats and ships, particularly the east and west coasts, where the ferries are fast, frequent and good value. The St Lawrence Seaway provides passage from the Atlantic Ocean to the Great Lakes. For further details, see below under regional entries or contact Tourism Canada.

RAIL: *Via Rail Canada* (tel: (514) 871 1331; fax: (514) 871 6704, attn: Mr John Lauber), the only passenger rail carrier in the country, still operates extensive services across Canada. The regional railways are *Ontario Northland, Algoma Central, British Columbia Railway, Great Canadian Railtour Company, Quebec North Shore & Labrador, Toronto Hamilton, Buffalo Railway, White Pass* and *Yukon Route*. Children under two years of age not occupying a separate seat may travel free (one per adult) and children 2-11 years of age pay half fare. Persons over 60 years of age and students carrying student proof will receive a 10% discount. A transcontinental service runs between Toronto and Vancouver, operating three times weekly east and west, transiting Winnipeg, Saskatoon, Edmonton and Jasper. Passengers are drawn to this route by the spectacular scenery of the three mountain ranges which are passed en route – the Rockies, the Selkirks and the Coast. The route also features views of ancient glaciers, large lakes and waterfalls. In 1992, all trains operating between Vancouver and Toronto were entirely refurbished and now include showers on all sleeping cars. The transcontinental service can be accessed by regular services from the Atlantic provinces and from Québec City and Montréal. Rapid intercity services are available between Québec, Montréal, Halifax, Toronto, Windsor and Ottawa. On these journeys the fare price includes a meal, snacks and drinks. Long-distance trains are extremely comfortable, with full restaurant services, air-conditioning, spacious reclining seats, etc. The *Rocky Mountaineer* service offers the opportunity to travel between Calgary, Banff, Jasper and Vancouver during daylight hours, enabling passengers to view the extraordinary passing scenery. Customers can purchase either a one-way or round-trip fare. A one-way trip takes two days and covers approximately 443km (275 miles) each day. Included in the price is a one-night stopover in Kamloops, bus transfer from train to Kamloops hotel, two continental breakfasts, two light lunches and complimentary beverages (coffee, tea, fruit juices, soft drinks). Alcoholic beverages, films and souvenirs are available on board at an additional cost. For visitors seeking a route into the Canadian wilderness, the *Polar Bear Express* (Toronto–North Bay–Cochrane–Moosonee) runs daily (except Friday) from late June to early September. Passengers are advised to make hotel reservations in Moosonee in advance. Other main inter-Canadian routes are Halifax–Truro–Moncton–Montréal, Moncton–St John, Montréal–Ottawa, Toronto–Brantford, Toronto–Montréal, Toronto–Ottawa, Sept Iles–Schefferville, Montréal–Quebec City, Montréal–Hervey–Jonquiere, Montréal–Hervey–Senneterre–Taschereau–Cochrane, Saskatoon–Winnipeg and Winnipeg–Hudson Bay–The Pas–Lynn Lake. Particularly scenic routes include Sault Ste. Marie–Eton–Hearst (with superb views of the Montréal River and hundreds of lakes), Winnipeg–Hudson Bay–Churchill, Edmonton–Jasper–Prince George–Prince Rupert (with exceptional scenery between Burns Lake and Prince Rupert), North Vancouver–Squamish (a one-day 87km (54-mile) round-trip tour of the Howe Sound on a steam locomotive to the logging town of Squamish where there are many Indian arts and crafts and the 374m/1000ft Shannon Falls), Victoria–Courtenay (along sheer cliffs to Malahat Summit with good views of Vancouver Island) and Vancouver–Whistler–Lillooet–Prince George (along the fjord-like coast of Howe Sound, then the craggy cliffs and rushing white-water streams in the heavily forested Cheakamus Canyon to Alta Lake, then the snow-covered mountains looming over the verdant forests and farmlands of the Pemberton Valley, before the final descent into Fraser River Canyon). For further information on other rail journeys in Canada, contact the Canadian Tourist Office (for address, see top of entry).

Discount Rail Passes: The *Canrailpass* must be purchased outside Canada and a valid passport presented at time of purchase; it allows up to 12 journeys on the Canadian railway system for a period of 30 days and is only valid on *Via Rail* trains. At the time of writing, prices are Can$550 (high season). This pass is also available, at a slightly higher cost, with a 3-day car hire option. There is also a *Youth Canrailpass* available to persons up to 24 years of age and a *Senior Canrailpasss* available to persons aged 60 and over. Prices on these passes are lower during off seasons. The *Alaska Pass* offers 8-day (Can$499), 15-day (Can$629), 22-day (Can$749) and 30-day (Can$879) travel within Alaska and British Columbia, including travel on *BC Ferries and Rail, Greyhound Lines of Canada, Alaskon Express, Norline Coaches, White Pass & Yukon Railroad* and *Alaska Railroad.* For more information on discounts available, contact the Canadian Tourist Office. In the UK, *Via Rail* representatives can be reached through *Long Haul Leisurail* (tel: (01733) 335 599) or *Airsavers Vacations* (tel: (0141) 303 0100).

ROAD: The road network covers vast distances as the country is over 7600km (4800 miles) from west to east and 4800km (3000 miles) from north to south. The longest road is the Trans-Canada Highway, running west to east for 8000km (5000 miles). Petrol and oil are sold by the litre, and costs per litre should be obtained at time of travel. The *Canadian Automobile Association* is affiliated to most European organisations, giving full use of facilities to members. Road signs are international.

Coach: One of the cheapest and most convenient ways of travelling the country apart from private motoring is by coach. Each region is well served by a large network of coach lines, the most extensive being the *Greyhound Bus Company,* which extends over 193,000km (120,000 miles) of North America. *Greyhound's Canada Travel Pass* ticket must be purchased outside of North America and entitles the holder to unlimited travel over periods of 7 (£87), 15 (£115), 30 (£160) and 60 (£205) days in Alberta, British Columbia, Manitoba, Northwest Territories, Ontario, Saskatchewan and Yukon and as far east as Montréal. The *Greyhound Canada Travel Pass PLUS* offers unlimited travel for 15 days (£145), 30 days (£190) and 60 days (£240) throughout all of Canada, including the area east of Montréal to the Maritimes. Daily extensions are available. Further information may be obtained in the UK from *Greyhound World Travel Ltd.* Tel: (01342) 317 317 (reservations). Fax: (01342) 328 519.

Grayline Coaches is another bus company that offers excursions to major Canadian resorts.

Canada also has regional bus services, the most important of which are as follows:

Atlantic Canada: Acadian Lines, Terra Nova Transport, SMT Eastern and CN Roadcruiser.

Central Canada: Canada Coach Lines, Gray Coach Lines, Voyageur and Voyageur Colonial, Grey Goose Bus Lines Limited, Saskatchewan Transportation and Orleans Express.

West Canada: Brewster Transport, Greyhound Lines of Canada and Vancouver Island Coach Lines.

Besides long-distance travel, all these companies operate a range of services, such as regional tours and escorted sightseeing for groups. *Voyageur* offers 14-day (Can$195) and 20-day (Can$259) passes for travel in eastern Canada. Children are not charged if under five years old; half the adult fare is charged for children aged 5-11 years old. *Greyhound Lines of Canada* offers unlimited travel passes for periods of 7, 15 and 30 days. The *Greyhound Canada Pass* includes all scheduled routes on *Greyhound* plus Toronto to New York and Montréal to New York. Other coach companies operating in Canada include *Voyageur Colonial:* Toronto to Montréal, Ottawa and North Bay, as well as Ottawa to Montréal; *Gray Coach:* Toronto to Niagara Falls and Buffalo; *Brewsters:* Banff to Jasper only; *Arctic Frontier Carriers:* Hay River to Yellowknife; and *Adirondack Trailways:* New York to Toronto. The *All Canada Pass,* available for periods of 15 and 30 days, includes all these previous routes plus *Orleans Express:* serving Montréal, Québec City and Rivière du Loup; *Acadian Lines:* Amherst to Truro and Halifax; and *SMT Lines:* routes through New Brunswick. These passes must be purchased outside Canada and are available through Greyhound World Travel Ltd *or* NAR (UK) Ltd in the UK (tel: (01753) 840 917). Persons aged over 65 are eligible for reductions on fares in some provinces.

Bus: Metropolitan buses operate on a flat-fare system (standard fares, irrespective of distance travelled). Fares must be paid exactly, which means that drivers do not carry change or issue tickets. Transfers should be requested when boarding a bus.

Car hire: Available in all cities and from airports to full licence holders over 21 years old. Major companies from which cars can be booked in the UK for use in Canada are *Avis, Budget, Dollar, Hertz, Thrifty, Tilden* and *Bricar.*

Traffic regulations: Traffic drives on the right. Road speeds are in kilometres per hour and are: 100kmph (60mph) on motorways, 80kmph (50mph) on rural highways and 50kmph (30mph) in cities. Distances are measured in kilometres. All road signs throughout the country are bilingual (English and French). Seatbelts are compulsory for all passengers. Radar detection devices are strictly prohibited and may not be carried in automobiles. Studded tyres are illegal in Ontario, but are permitted without seasonal limitations in the Northwest Territories, Saskatchewan and Yukon, and are allowed only in winter in other provinces. **Note:** The official date on which winter begins, for this and other purposes, will vary from province to province. **Documentation:** An International Driving Licence is recommended though it is not legally required. Visitors may drive on their national driving licences for up to three months in all provinces (six months for holders of UK licences).

JOURNEY TIMES: The following chart gives approximate journey times from Ottawa (in hours and minutes) to other major cities/towns in Canada.

	Air	Road	Rail
Toronto	1.00	5.30	5.30
Montréal	0.30	2.00	2.00
Edmonton	4.30	50.00	50.00
Québec	1.00	6.00	6.00
Halifax	2.00	24.00	24.00
Winnipeg	2.30	32.00	32.00
Calgary	4.00	50.00	-
Vancouver	5.00	62.00	110.00
Regina	5.00	40.00	-

ACCOMMODATION

There is a wide range of accommodation from hotels to hostels. Standards are high, with full facilities. International hotel chains are represented in major cities, but advance booking is essential. Guest-houses, farm vacations, bed & breakfast establishments and self-catering lodges are available throughout the country. Hunting and fishing trips to the wilderness areas of the north are often best arranged through *Outfitters.* These are guides (often licensed by the local tourist office) who can arrange supplies, tackle, transport and accommodation. For further information, contact the Canadian Tourist Office *or* the Hotel Association of Canada, Suite 1016, 130 Albert Street, Ottawa, Ontario K1P 5G4. Tel: (613) 237 7149. Fax: (613) 238 3878.

Grading: There is no national system of accommodation grading. Some provinces operate their own voluntary grading programmes; see regional entries below for details.

CAMPING/CARAVANNING: Mobile trailers and caravans are extremely popular ways of traversing the enormous expanse of the Canadian landscape. There are two different types of vehicle available: a 'motorhome' is a vehicle with connected driving cab and living space, equipped for up to five adults; whilst a 'camper' is a vehicle with a separate driving cab, more like a truck with a caravan on the back, equipped for up to three adults. There are various different models according to the size of the accommodation and facilities required, but most have a fridge, cooker, sink, heater, fitted WC and showers. All vehicles are fitted with power steering and automatic transmission. Petrol consumption is about 24km (15 miles) per imperial gallon (but petrol costs half as much as it does in Europe). Hiring is available to those who hold full licences and are over 25. The cost of hire can vary according to the season. High season runs from June to the end of September, and low season is the rest of the year. Full details can be obtained from the Canadian Tourist Office.

Camping facilities in the National Parks are generally open only from mid-May until the end of September. For further information, contact Environment Canada, Parks Service, Communications Directorate, Hull, Québec K1A 0H3. Tel: (819) 997 2800 *or* 997 3776. Fax: (819) 953 2225.

Further details on accommodation can be found in the regional entries below.

RESORTS & EXCURSIONS

Canada offers a huge range of attractions, from large cosmopolitan cities such as Montréal and Toronto in the south to isolated Inuit (Eskimo) settlements dotted around the frozen shores of Hudson Bay. The contrasting Pacific and Atlantic seaboards and the thousands of lakes and rivers of the interior provide suberb watersports and fishing. The Rocky Mountains and other ranges offer breathtaking scenery on a grand scale. Some of the best resorts are in the series of great National Parks which preserve the wildlife and forests of Canada in their virgin state. Those in the north provide basic amenities for tours of the beautiful northern wilderness. A taste of the pioneering west can be had in the rich farming and grain regions of central Canada. Further north is the New Frontier of Yukon and the Northwest Territories. A more detailed description of the historic sites and natural attractions of each province can be found in the *Resorts & Excursions* sections in the regional entries below.

POPULAR ITINERARIES: 5-day: Vancouver-Pemberton-Lillooet-Lytton-Hope.

7-day: (a) Calgary–Banff–Columbia Icefield–JasperLake Louise. (b) Vancouver–Victoria–Nanaimo–Whistler–Kamloops–Banff National Park–Banff–Calgary. (c) Toronto–Niagara Falls–Kitchener–Midhurst–Algonquin Provincial Park–Ottawa–Kingston–Lake Ontario. (d) Toronto–Niagara Falls–Kingston–1000 Islands–Ottawa–Ste-Adèle–Laurentian Mountains–Québec City–Montréal. (e) Halifax–Moncton–Charlottetown–Sydney.

SOCIAL PROFILE

FOOD & DRINK: Canadian cuisine is as varied as the country. The hundreds of miles of coastline offer varied seafood, and the central plains provide first-class beef and agricultural produce. The colonial influence is still strong, with European menus available in all major cities. The French influence in Québec is easily discernible in the many restaurants which specialise in French cuisine. Waiter service in restaurants is more common. Dress requirements and billing procedures vary.

Drink: Spirits may only be purchased from specially licensed liquor stores or restaurants displaying the sign 'Licensed Premises' if alcohol is served on the premises.

Many allow customers to bring their own beer or wine. A wide variety of alcohol is sold in most hotels, restaurants and bars. A selection of European/American wines and spirits are also imported, although the Canadians prefer their own, such as rye whisky. Bars may have table or counter service and payment is generally made after each drink. Opening hours vary from province to province. The legal age for drinking in bars is 18 or 19 depending on local regulations.

See also the *Social Profile* sections in the regional entries below.

NIGHTLIFE: Every major provincial capital in the more populated areas has nightclubs, and hotel dinner/dancing. Ottawa, Toronto, Montréal, Winnipeg and Vancouver are centres for ballet, opera and classical music, with visits from leading orchestras and internationally renowned performers. Entertainment in the more remote towns is scarce.

SHOPPING: Fine examples of Canadian craftware are available, such as artwood carvings, pottery, cottons and native artefacts. Some countries have restrictions against the import of endangered animal species products, such as polar bear, seal, walrus, etc, so visitors should check entry regulations in their home country before departure. Most provinces, except Alberta, the Northwest Territories and Yukon, levy a sales tax which varies from 4% to 11% in shops, restaurants and some hotels. Tax can be refunded when leaving Canada (see the special note above under *Duty Free*). In addition to the provincial tax a general sales tax of 7% was introduced in January 1991. **Shopping hours:** 0900-1800 Monday to Friday, with late-night shopping in some stores up to 2100 Thursday and Friday. Most shops and stores are also open Saturday and some local stores Sunday. Some shops open 24 hours a day.

SPORT: Facilities for **golf** and **tennis** are excellent throughout the country. Most large hotels have some sports facilities. A number of tour operators offer all-in golfing packages. **Canadian football**, which is similar to American football, is played everywhere, but European football (**soccer**) is becoming increasingly popular. Professional baseball is enjoyed in both Toronto and Montréal in the summer months. **Hunting, fishing** and **shooting** can be enjoyed in the many wilderness areas; all require licences, which can be obtained locally (Tourism Canada can supply detailed information on this). **Wintersports:** Ice hockey is played at the highest level and top-class competition can be enjoyed as a spectator sport in all the cities throughout Canada. Skiing can be enjoyed in innumerable resorts throughout Canada. The Canadian Tourist Office can supply details. **Watersports:** Sailing and other facilities are available throughout the country. For more information, see the regional entries below.

SPECIAL EVENTS: A list of some of the major festivals and special events may be found in the regional entries below.

SOCIAL CONVENTIONS: Handshaking predominates as the normal mode of greeting. Close friends often exchange kisses on the cheeks, particularly in French areas. Codes of practice for visiting homes are the same as in other Western countries: flowers, chocolates or a bottle of wine are common gifts for hosts and dress is generally informal and practical according to climate. It is common for black tie and other required dress to be indicated on invitations. Exclusive clubs and restaurants often require more formal dress. Smoking has been banned in most public areas. Most restaurants, theatres and cinemas, if they permit smoking, have large 'no smoking' areas. **Tipping:** Normal practice, usually 15% of the bill, more if service is exceptional. Waiters and taxi drivers should be tipped this amount. Barbers and hairdressers should receive about 10% of the bill. Porters at airports and railway stations, cloakroom attendants, bellhops, doormen and hotel porters generally expect Can$1 per item of luggage.

BUSINESS PROFILE

ECONOMY: Canada is one of the world's major trading nations and the seventh-largest exporter and importer, thus qualifying for membership of the so-called G7 group of major industrial economies. The country has immense natural resources and a high standard of living. Agriculture and fisheries are particularly important: Canada exports over half of its agricultural produce – principally grains and oil seeds – and is the world's leading exporter of fish. Timber is another important sector, given that over 40% of the land area is forest. As a mineral producer, Canada exports crude oil and natural gas, copper, nickel, zinc, iron ore, asbestos, cement, coal and potash. Energy requirements are met by a mixture of hydroelectric, nuclear and oil-fired generating stations. The largest economic sector is manufacturing, covering the whole range of activities from heavy engineering and

chemicals through vehicle production and agro-business to office automation and commercial printing. Canada has a declining, though nonetheless substantial, trade surplus of Can$5 billion per annum on a net export income of US$121 billion (1987 figures). Slightly over 75% of the country's trade is with the USA, making this the world's largest single bilateral trade route. A free-trade agreement signed with the USA in 1989 has, on provisional figures, already boosted trade still further. This also provided the basis for the North American Free Trade Agreement (NAFTA) which was signed on August 12, 1992, by the Presidents of Canada, the USA and Mexico. After the USA, Canada's trade partners are, in order of descending volume: Japan, the UK, Germany, Taiwan and France. UK exporters are well established in Canada and continue to be well placed to exploit new market opportunities.

BUSINESS: Usual courtesies observed including exchange of business cards, making appointments, etc.
Office hours: 0900-1700 Monday to Friday.
COMMERCIAL INFORMATION: The following organisations can offer advice: Canada-United Kingdom Chamber of Commerce, 3 Lower Regent Street, London SW1Y 4NZ. Tel: (0171) 930 7711. Fax: (0171) 930 9703; *or*
Canadian Chamber of Commerce, Suite 1160, 55 Metcalfe Street, Ottawa, Ontario K1P 6N4. Tel: (613) 238 4000. Fax: (613) 238 7643. Telex: 0533360; *or*
Canadian Chamber of Commerce, 1080 Beaver Hall Hill, Montréal, Québec H2A 1T2. Tel: (514) 866 4334 *or* 871 4000.

In addition each province has its own regional chamber of commerce. Consult regional entries below for more information.

CONFERENCES/CONVENTIONS: All the major business centres, ie Toronto, Calgary, Edmonton, Montréal, Ottawa and Vancouver, offer extensive convention and conference facilities. For general information on conferences and conventions in Canada, contact the Commercial Department of the Canadian Tourist Office in London. Tel: (0171) 258 6478. Fax: (0171) 258 6322. Consult the regional entries below for more information.

CLIMATE

Climate graphs for the various provinces and territories may be found in the relevant entries below.
Required clothing: *March:* Moderate temperatures. Winter clothing with some mediumweight clothing.
April: Milder days but the evenings are cool. Mediumweight clothing including a topcoat is recommended.
May: Warm days but cool at night. Mediumweight and summer clothing recommended.
June: Warm, summer clothing with some mediumweight clothing for cool evenings. The weather in June is ideal for travel and all outdoor activities.
July/August: These are the warmest months of the year. Lightweight summer clothing is recommended.
September: Warm days and cool evenings. Light- to medium-weight clothing recommended.
October: Cool, with the first frost in the air.
November: Cool to frosty. Medium- to heavy-weight clothing is recommended. First signs of snow. Motorists should have cars prepared for winter and snow tyres are recommended.
December/January/February: Winter temperatures. Winter clothing is necessary (eg overcoat, hat, boots and gloves). Heavy snowfall in most provinces.

Alberta

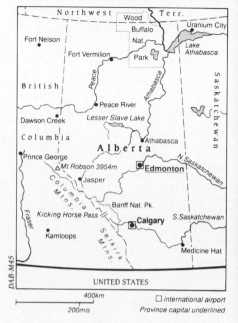

international airport
Province capital underlined

Location: Western Canada.

Alberta Economic Development & Tourism
4th Floor, City Centre Building, 10155-102 Street, Edmonton, Alberta T5J 4L5
Tel: (403) 427 4321 *or* 422 9494. Fax: (403) 427 0867.
Alberta Tourism
Alberta House, 1 Mount Street, London W1Y 5AA
Tel: (0171) 491 3430. Fax: (0171) 499 1779 *or* 629 2296.
Opening hours: 0900-1700 Monday to Friday.

AREA: 661,185 sq km (248,799 sq miles).
POPULATION: 2,545,553 (1991).
POPULATION DENSITY: 3.8 per sq km.
CAPITAL: Edmonton. **Population:** 839,924 (1991).
GEOGRAPHY: Alberta is the most westerly of the 'prairie and plains' provinces, bordered to the west by British Columbia and the Rockies, to the southeast by the badlands and prairie, while in the north, along the border with the Northwest Territories, there is a wilderness of forests, lakes and rivers. The western, Rocky Mountain border rises to 3650m (11,975ft), has permanent icefields covering 340 sq km (122 sq miles) and releases meltwaters which supply the Mackenzie River flowing to the Arctic, the Saskatchewan River flowing into Hudson Bay and the Columbia River flowing through the Rockies into Idaho and out into the Pacific.
LANGUAGE: Although Canada is officially bilingual (English and French), English is more commonly spoken in Alberta.
TIME: GMT - 7 (GMT - 6 in summer).
Note: Summer officially lasts from the first Sunday in April to the Saturday before the last Sunday in October.

PUBLIC HOLIDAYS

Public holidays as for the rest of Canada (see the general section) with the following dates also observed:
Feb 20 '95 Family Day. **Aug 7** Heritage Day. **Feb 19 '96** Family Day.

TRAVEL

AIR: The province is served by *Air Canada (AC)* and *Canadian Airlines International (CP)*. For fares and schedules, contact airlines.
International airports: *Edmonton (YEG)* is 30km (19 miles) from the city (travel time – 40 minutes).
Calgary (YYC) is 17.6km (11 miles) from the city (travel time – 30 minutes).
Both Edmonton and Calgary also receive domestic services; and both have duty-free shops, banks, restaurants and car parking.
LAKES/RIVERS: Boats can be hired privately for recreational purposes.
RAIL: *Via Rail* operates two services connecting

Edmonton with nationwide points. The *Canadian,* the transcontinental train, crosses the province thrice-weekly originating from Toronto, Ontario in the east through Edmonton and Jasper, to Vancouver in the west and vice versa. This train connects with the *SKEENA* service at Jasper with a thrice-weekly service to Prince Rupert, British Columbia. The *Rocky Mountaineer* is the only other rail service operating into the province. This is an all-daylight tour from either Calgary/Banff or Jasper to and from Vancouver in the summer months.

ROAD: Coach: *Greyhound Lines* run coach services into Alberta, thereby connecting Edmonton with all other major capitals. The main *Greyhound* terminals are at Edmonton, Banff and Calgary. Coaches are also operated in Alberta by *Brewster Transport* (Banff) and *Gray Lines of Canada* (Calgary), which also organise coach tours in the area. A coach is operated between the two city train stations of Calgary and Edmonton by *Red Arrow* (on behalf of *Via Rail)* four times a day. **Car hire:** Available in all large towns and at Edmonton and Calgary airports.

URBAN: Buses and the light rail system in Calgary are operated on a flat-fare system. Exact fares are required if tickets are purchased on boarding; pre-purchased single- and multi-journey tickets are available. Edmonton, where there is a similar fares system, has buses, trolleybuses and a light rail route. Local buses operate in all other major towns.

JOURNEY TIMES: The following chart give approximate journey times from Edmonton (in hours and minutes) to other major cities/towns in Alberta.

	Air	Road	Rail
Calgary	0.45	3.00	-
Banff	-	4.30	-
Jasper	-	4.00	4.30

ACCOMMODATION

Accommodation ranges from top-quality hotels to motorway motels, lodge estates and hostels. Banff National Park is famous for its two baronial-quality hotels, offering approximately 2000 rooms. Many lodges offer various levels of self-catering, often in conjunction with fishing and hiking trips. Several agencies offer bed & breakfast and ranch vacations throughout Alberta. For information on bed & breakfast accommodation, contact Alberta's Gem B & B Agency, 11216 48th Avenue, Edmonton, Alberta T6H 0C7. Tel/fax: (403) 434 6098. Alberta Economic Development and Tourism publishes a comprehensive guide to the province's accommodation.

Grading: A grading system is being introduced. However, much of Alberta's accommodation is at present already supervised by the provincial government under a voluntary scheme to ensure high standards of cleanliness, comfort, construction and maintenance of furnishings and facilities. Look for the 'Approved Accommodation' sign which means that the establishment conforms to these standards. For more information on accommodation in Alberta, contact Alberta Economic Development and Tourism *or* the Alberta Hotel Association, Suite 401, Centre 104, 5241 Calgary Trail South, Edmonton, Alberta T6H 5G8. Tel: (403) 436 6112. Fax: (403) 436 5404.

CAMPING/CARAVANNING: The northern area of Alberta contains hundreds of lakes and forests, with abundant game such as deer, moose, bears and the rare trumpeter swan. There are numerous campsites in the National Parks. The permanent facilities tend to be more basic in the north. A number of companies can arrange **motor camper** rentals, with a range of fully equipped vehicles. Full details can be obtained from Alberta Economic Development and Tourism; see also the *Camping/Caravanning* section in the general introduction above.

RESORTS & EXCURSIONS

EDMONTON: The provincial capital is the product of two events: the Klondike Gold Rush of 1898 and the oil boom of the late 1960s. This spacious well-planned city is famed for its huge parks on the banks of the *North Saskatchewan River*. Edmonton's love affair with its past is reflected in the *Fort Edmonton Park,* a complex of replicas of the city's frontier days; and reaches its apogee in the annual 'Klondike Days' extravaganza, held each July, when Edmontonians relive the days of the Gold Rush. *West Edmonton Mall* is reputedly the largest shopping mall in the world, with theatres, restaurants, nightclubs, amusement areas (including a miniature golf course, ice rink and swimming pool), aviaries, aquariums and museums. Edmonton also boasts *Fantasyland,* the world's largest indoor amusement park, and Canada's largest planetarium, the *Space Sciences Centre*. There are several theatres and art galleries. On a clear day, an estimated 6500 sq km (2500 sq miles) of Alberta can be seen from *Vista 33* at the *Alberta Telephone Tower. The Ukrainian Cultural Heritage Village* and *Elk Island National Park* are just outside the city.

CALGARY: The province's second city is situated at the western end of the Great Plains in the foothills of the Rocky Mountains. It is probably the fastest growing city in Canada, and hosted the 1988 Winter Olympics. The heart of the city is a pedestrian mall with excellent shopping and restaurants; the *Glenbow Museum,* art galleries and theatres are nearby. The *Calgary Zoo and Prehistoric Park* is one of the best in North America. *Heritage Park* offers a chance to explore an authentic Alberta frontier town as it was 80 years ago. There are panoramic views of the Rocky Mountains from the *Calgary Tower.*

ELSEWHERE: Calgary is the major stopping-off point en route to **Banff National Park,** 130km (80 miles) to the west in the heart of the Canadian Rockies. Banff, the first of the country's national parks, is a spectacular wilderness area with mountain, river and lake scenery – notably *Lake Louise*. Along with **Jasper National Park** to the north, it offers a huge range of activities, including boating, canoeing, raft tours, fishing and hiking. The major ski resort in the Rockies, it hosts the annual *Banff Festival of the Arts*. The small town of **Jasper** is mainly used as a stocking up point for the numerous hikers on their way into the mountains. Set in magnificent mountain scenery it is an ideal starting point for trips to *Pyramid Lake,* the *Miette Hotsprings* and *Maligne Canyon* as well as *Maligne Lake*. The local Rangers Station opposite the train station can supply maps and other information. Visitors have to buy a permit to be able to drive within the national parks. These cost Can$5 for one day or Can$10 for four days. The *Icefields Parkway* (Highway 93), runs the length of the two parks affording magnificent views of the lakes, forests and the glaciers of the *Columbia Icefield*. This includes the McKinley Glacier and the Columbia Glacier. Visitors can take a bus trip to the top of the latter or take a hiking path to the bottom edge of it. Note, though, that the temperature drops noticeably when approaching the glacier and that the hiking path can be difficult in parts. The Parkway provides the best access to the wilderness trails in the area. On Alberta's southwestern border with the USA is **Waterton Lakes National Park,** joined to Glacier National Park in Montana to form the world's first international Peace Park. Scenic views of the stunning lakeland scenery can be experienced on a cruise boat tour around the lake.

In central Alberta, the remains of dinosaurs, first discovered in 1874 in the banks of the Red Deer River, can be seen on the 48km (30-mile) *Dinosaur Trail* near **Drumheller**. Five minutes from the downtown area is the *Royal Tyrrell Museum of Palaeontology,* with hands-on exhibitions, ongoing site work and one of the world's largest collections of dinosaur remains. Southwest of Drumheller, the *Dinosaur Provincial Park* continues this theme with reconstructed skeletons of duck-billed dinosaurs. To the south of Calgary, 50km (36 miles) south of Lethbridge, **Head-Smashed-In Buffalo Jump,** designated a UNESCO World Heritage Site in 1981, is among the largest and best-preserved jump sites in the world; it was used by the native people for more than 5600 years to drive thousands of buffalo to their deaths, thus providing them with food, shelter and clothing. The top of the cliff provides an unparalleled view of the surrounding prairie.

SOCIAL PROFILE

FOOD & DRINK: Alberta's prairie is ideal for cattle rearing and its Western beef is world-famous. Beef is barbecued, braised, grilled, minced and skewered with different complements such as onions, mushrooms, green peppers, rice, sauces and beans. Unusual beef dishes are *stew* (combination of diced steak, garden vegetables and biscuits cooked in rich gravy) and *beef mincemeat* (combines chopped suet, fruits and spices) used in pies and tarts and as a traditional Christmas dish served with ice-cream, cream or rum sauce. Wild berries and nuts are used in desserts. During the season, try the blueberry muffins which are on offer in local bakeries. Honey is made from alfalfa and clover nectar and is a widely used sweetener and breakfast food. Apart from traditional foods, Alberta's towns and cities offer an excellent range of international cuisine. **Drink:** Alcohol is sold in 'liquor stores', although beer may be obtained in the majority of hotels. Liquor stores are closed on Sunday, major holidays and election days. There are no standard opening hours; some are open until 2330, many only until 1800. The minimum legal drinking age is 18.

NIGHTLIFE: Edmonton is famous for its night-time entertainment. Nightclubs, cabarets, taverns, lounges and that infamous Alberta watering hole, the beer parlour, combine to provide constant local and international entertainment. Both Calgary and Edmonton enjoy full-scale orchestras.

SHOPPING: Alberta is the only province (apart from the sparsely populated Northwest Territories and Yukon) that does not apply an extra sales tax on all purchases over and above the general sales tax of 7%. Popular purchases are Hudson's Bay blankets, furs and fur products. The Inuit (Eskimos) produce clothing and tools of a high standard. Artwork includes pottery, ceramics, sculptures and paintings. For shopping hours, see the general entry above.

SPORT: Edmonton is home to three professional sports franchises: **football, baseball** and **hockey.** Two of the largest **rodeos** in Canada are held in the summer. Many of the rivers running out from the Rocky Mountains provide superb white-water **canoeing**. The large numbers of lakes provide excellent **fishing** and **sailing** facilities. **Skiing** in the Rocky Mountains is fast becoming an international attraction. In winter, **ice hockey** is played at the highest level.

SPECIAL EVENTS: Jun 23-Jul 2 '95 *Jazz City International,* Edmonton. **Jul 6-8** *Canadian Showcase of Ukraine Culture,* Vegreville. **Jul 7-16** *Calgary Exhibition, Rodeo & Stampede.* **Jul 20-27** *Klondike Days,* Edmonton. **Aug 5-7** *Heritage Festival*, Edmonton. **Aug 12-18** *International Native Art Festival,* Calgary. **Aug 18-27** *Fringe Theatre Event,* Edmonton. **Sep 5-9** *Spruce Meadows Masters' Tournament,* Calgary.

BUSINESS PROFILE

COMMERCIAL INFORMATION: The following organisation can offer advice: Alberta Chamber of Commerce, Suite 2105, TD Tower, Edmonton Centre, Edmonton, Alberta T5J 2Z1. Tel: (403) 425 4180. Fax: (403) 429 1061.

CONFERENCES/CONVENTIONS: Calgary, Banff, Edmonton and Jasper offer conference and convention venues. Information can be obtained from the Canadian Tourist Office, Alberta Tourism or the following organisations for assistance or advice:

Calgary Conventions & Visitors Bureau, 237-8th Avenue SE, Calgary, Alberta T2G 0K8. Tel: (403) 263 8510. Fax: (403) 262 3809; *or*

Banff/Lake Louise Tourism Bureau, PO Box 1298, Banff, Alberta T0L 0C0. Tel: (403) 762 3777. Fax: (403) 762 8545; *or*

Edmonton Conventions & Tourism Authority, Suite 104, 9797 Jasper Avenue, Edmonton, Alberta T5J 1N9. Tel: (403) 426 4715. Fax: (403) 425 5283; *or*

Jasper Tourism and Commerce, PO Box 98, 632 Connaught Drive, Jasper, Alberta T0E 1E0. Tel: (403) 852 3858. Fax: (403) 852 4932.

CLIMATE

Summer, between May and September, is warm, while winters are cold, with particularly heavy snowfalls in the Rockies.

Required clothing: Light- to medium-weights during warmer months. Heavyweights are worn in winter, with alpine wear in mountains. Waterproof wear is advisable throughout the year.

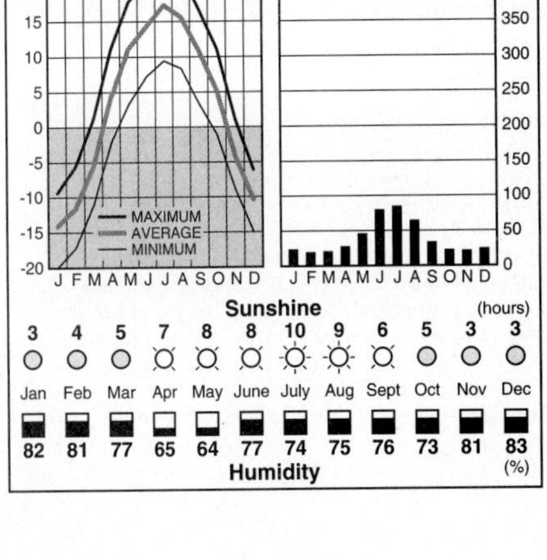

British Columbia

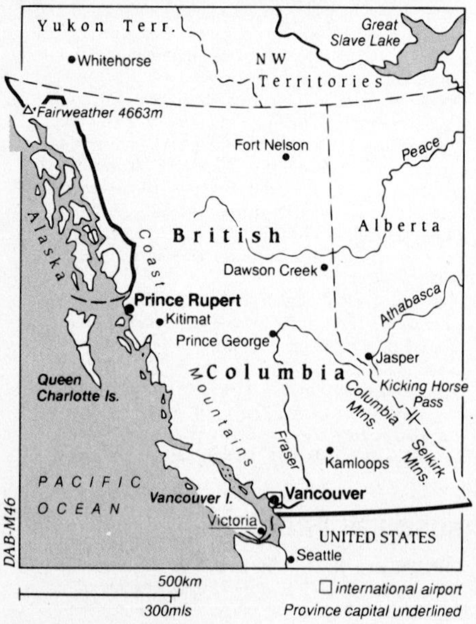

Location: Western Canada.

Discover British Columbia
First Floor, 1117 Wharf Street, Victoria, British Columbia V8W 2Z2
Tel: (604) 663 6000. Fax: (604) 356 8246.
Tourism British Columbia
British Columbia House, 1 Regent Street, London SW1Y 4NS
Tel: (0171) 930 6857. Fax: (0171) 930 2012. Opening hours: 0900-1700 Monday to Friday.

AREA: 929,730 sq km (358,969 sq miles).
POPULATION: 3,282,061 (1991).
POPULATION DENSITY: 3.5 per sq km.
CAPITAL: Victoria. **Population:** 287,897 (1991).
GEOGRAPHY: British Columbia is Canada's most westerly province, bordered to the south by the USA (Washington and Montana states), to the east by Alberta, to the north by the Northwest and Yukon Territories, and to the west by the Pacific Ocean and the 'Alaskan Panhandle'. It is mainly covered by virgin forests, and encompasses the towering Rocky Mountains, vast expanses of semi-arid sagebrush, lush pastures on Vancouver Island's east coast, farmland in the Fraser River delta, and fruitland in Okanagan Valley. The highest mountain is Fairweather at 4663m (15,298ft). Between the eastern and coastal mountains is a lower central range. The coastal range sinks into the Pacific, with larger peaks emerging at Vancouver and Queen Charlotte islands.
LANGUAGE: Although Canada is officially bilingual (English and French), English is more commonly spoken in British Columbia.
TIME: GMT - 8 (GMT - 7 in summer).
Note: Summer officially lasts from the first Sunday in April to the Saturday before the last Sunday in October.

PUBLIC HOLIDAYS

Public holidays as for the rest of Canada (see general section above) with the following date also observed:
Aug 7 '95 British Columbia Day.

TRAVEL

AIR: The following airlines operate in British Columbia: *Air Canada, Air BC, Chilcotin Cariboo Aviation, Canadian Airlines International, North Coast Air Services, Northern Thunderbird Air, Trans-Provincial Airlines, Wilderness Airlines* and *British Airways.*
International airport: *Vancouver (YVR),* 15km (11 miles) southwest of the city. It is served by airlines from the USA, Europe and the Far East. The journey to the city centre takes about 20 minutes. Airport facilities include a 24-hour restaurant, car parking, garage, car rental, nursery and duty-free shop.
The other major airports are *Victoria, Prince Rupert* and *Quesnel.*
SEA: Vancouver is an international passenger port, with regular sailings to the Far East and ports on the USA's northeastern coast.
Ferry services to and from all coastal ports and inland waters in British Columbia are available from the following shipping lines: *British Columbia Ferry Corporation, Ministry of Transportation* and *Highways Ferries.* Two ferry services link Vancouver Island with the mainland. The most spectacular route is the 15-hour one-way daylight voyage from Port Hardy on the northern tip of Vancouver Island along the Inside Passage to Prince Rupert. *British Columbia Ferry* offers a spectacular car and passenger service from Tsawwassen outside Vancouver to Swartz Bay on the tip of Vancouver Island. Foot passengers can take coaches which travel from Vancouver city centre to Victoria city centre. The *Royal Sealink* is a passenger-only service which connects Victoria and Vancouver from harbours in the city centres. There are two ferry connections from Victoria to Seattle (USA). One is the *Victoria Clipper*, a high-speed catamaran, that leaves five times a day. The crossing takes 2 hours 30 minutes. Another service is a car ferry and leaves once a day. This crossing takes 5 hours.
RAIL: *Via Rail* train routes to and within British Columbia are: Edmonton to Prince Rupert via Jasper (Alberta); Victoria to Courtenay; Vancouver to Edmonton via Jasper, and on to Toronto three times a week *(Western Transcontinental). British Columbia Railways* operate trains from north Vancouver to Lilloet (daily) and on to Prince George (thrice-weekly). A half-day service from north Vancouver follows the Pacific coast before moving inland to Whistler.
ROAD: The Trans-Canada Highway reaches British Columbia via Calgary (Alberta) and continues through the south of the province to Vancouver. The other main highways are numbers 3, 5, 6, 16, 95 and 97. Apart from Highway 97, which runs northwards to the Yukon Territory, the province's road network is concentrated in the south. Road signs are international. There are good roads south to Seattle in the USA. **Bus:** There are a number of regional services. The bus station is in the central rail station.
URBAN: Bus, LRT and ferry services are provided in Vancouver and by a provincial government corporation (which also serves Victoria). *Metro Transit* operates 'seabuses' on cross-inlet ferry services.
JOURNEY TIMES: The following chart gives approximate journey times from Vancouver (in hours and minutes) to other major cities/towns in British Columbia.

	Air	Road	Rail
Victoria	0.35	2.30	-
Kamloops	0.55	4.00	9.00
Whistler	0.30	2.00	2.30
Prince George	1.20	8.00	12.00

ACCOMMODATION

Accommodation on offer ranges from top-class hotels in Victoria and Vancouver through motels beside the main southern highways to simple cabins high up in the Rockies. Cottages and cabins are widely available on Vancouver Island. 'Ranch Holidays' are popular in the Cariboo Chilcotin region of central British Columbia. Bed & breakfast accommodation can be found by contacting the British Columbia B & B Association, Box 593, 810 West Broadway, Vancouver, British Columbia V5Z 4E2; tel: (604) 276 8616; *or* Old English B & B Registry, 1226 Silverwood Crescent, North Vancouver, British Columbia V7P 1J3; tel: (604) 986 5069; *or* All Seasons B & B Agency, Box 5511, Station B, Victoria, British Columbia V8R 6S4; tel: (604) 655 7173; fax: (604) 655 1422. Tourism British Columbia has an annual guide listing all the agencies providing accommodation in the province.
Grading: Standards are overseen by the Ministry of Tourism and approved hotels display a bright blue 'Approved Accommodation' sign to indicate that the Ministry's standards of courtesy, comfort and cleanliness have been met. For more information, contact Tourism British Columbia *or* British Columbia & Yukon Hotels Association, 2nd Floor, 948 Howe Street, Vancouver, British Columbia V6Z 1N9. Tel: (604) 681 7164. Fax: (604) 681 7649.
CAMPING/CARAVANNING: There are nearly 10,000 campsites situated in over 150 parks and recreation areas. Most campsites do not have power-supply link-ups for caravans. Several of the parks are designated as 'Nature Conservancy Areas', where all motor vehicles are banned and transport must be on foot. The type of parkland available varies from sandy beaches with vehicle access, to lakes and glaciers reached only by aircraft or boat. All campsites have a time limit of 14 days and reservations are not accepted. A number of companies can arrange **motor camper** rentals, with a range of fully equipped vehicles. Full details can be obtained from Tourism British Columbia *or* British Columbia Motels, Campgrounds and Resorts Association, Suite 209, 3003 St John's Street, Port Moody, British Columbia V3H 2C4. Tel: (604) 945 7676. Fax: (604) 945 7606. See also the *Camping/Caravanning* section in the general introduction above.

RESORTS & EXCURSIONS

VANCOUVER: Canada's third largest city is situated in the southwest of the province, overlooking the Burrard Inlet on the Pacific and backed by the Coastal Range of mountains. It is a major port. All beaches are public, the most famous being *Shipwreck Beach* near the university. Downtown Vancouver has the second largest Chinese quarter in North America and a large German and Ukrainian population. Both traditions are reflected in the proliferation of ethnic shops and restaurants. *Gastown,* the reconstructed old centre of Vancouver, is a pleasant array of cobblestone streets, cafés and shops. Of the several museums and galleries, most notable are the *Centennial Museum, H R MacMillan Planetarium, University of British Columbia's Museum of Anthropology* (housing excellent examples of northwest Indian art and artefacts), *Vancouver Art Gallery, Science World* (including four galleries of hands-on exhibits) and the *Maritime Museum.* Main points of interest in the suburbs are *Stanley Park, Vancouver Aquarium* and the *Grouse Mountain Skyride.* The latter offers views of the city and the fjords of the Pacific coast from 1211m (3974ft). It is also a comparatively young city with the large University of British Columbia campus. A visit to the extensive Botanical Gardens of the university is recommended. During the summer **Whistler,** just north of Vancouver, is a delight for naturalists but, in the winter, it is the most popular ski resort on the west coast offering an award-winning design with first-class hotels and restaurants. In addition to 180 varied ski runs covering two enormous mountains, it has facilities for golf, windsurfing, tennis, mountain biking, river rafting, horseriding, hiking, gondola and chairlift rides, as well as shopping and cultural entertainment. Ferries to Vancouver Island pass through the spectacular **Gulf Islands.** A variety of tours and charter boats are available for island-hopping excursions.
VICTORIA: The provincial capital lies at the southern tip of the heavily forested and mountainous Vancouver Island. This most English of Canadian towns is distinguished by Victorian and neo-classical architecture and well-appointed residential areas. In the harbour area are the impressive *Parliament Buildings* and the *Provincial Museum,* which gives an overview of the region's history. During summer evenings a marching band finishes up at the Parliament Buildings. Also worth visiting are *Maltwood Art Gallery, Thunderbird Park* (where visitors may see modern-day Indian carvers at work) and *Craigdarroch Castle* (an impressive 19th-century landmark mansion home). City life is enhanced by more than 60 recreational parks. The *Undersea Gardens* offer a fish's-eye view of harbour life. Some 20km (12 miles) to the north, the **Butchart Gardens** have delightful English, Japanese and Italian gardens set in a former limestone quarry. **Nanaimo,** the island's major commercial port, is on the coastal route to the north, where there are opportunities for sailing and fishing.
ELSEWHERE: Pacific Rim National Park, 306km (192 miles) north of Vancouver on the west coast, is a popular resort, with sandy beaches offering good surfing and swimming, and wilderness trails through deep, hilly forests. To the east of the province, high in the Rocky Mountains, the huge wilderness areas of **Yoho, Kootenay** and **Glacier National Parks** offer hiking, angling and rafting trips as well as excellent winter sports facilities. Nearby are the hot-spring resorts of **Radium** and **Fairmount** and the **Fort Steel Heritage Park,** which celebrates pioneer days. North of the rich angling and ranching country of the *Cariboo Chilcotin* lie vast tracts of untamed lakeland, forest and wilderness stretching to the border with the Yukon and Northwest Territories. Some sporting resorts in this area are accessible only by air. Many outfitters offer guided hunting and fishing expeditions to this area. **Queen Charlotte Island,** reached by ferry from **Prince Rupert** in the far northwest, is an adventurous side-trip with good hunting opportunities. Another good wilderness route is the **Alaska Highway,** running through **Prince George, Dawson Creek** and **Fort St John** in the northeast. This former fur-trading trail gives good access to the provincial parks of **Stone Mountain** and **Muncho Lake,** which provide basic amenities for striking out into this rugged terrain. Both the scenery and the sporting opportunities en route are excellent.

SOCIAL PROFILE

FOOD & DRINK: The cuisine of the province is enhanced by English traditions. The Pacific Ocean yields a great variety of seafood, including King Crab, oysters, shrimp and other shellfish, as well as cod, haddock and salmon (coho, spring, chum, sockeye and pink) which are smoked, pan-fried, breaded, baked, caned and barbecued, and complemented by local vegetables. Fruits grown in

the province include apples, peaches, pears, plums, apricots, strawberries, blackberries, the famous Bing cherries, and loganberries. *Victoria creams,* a famous chocolate delicacy derived from a recipe dating back to 1885, are exported worldwide from British Columbia. The original confectioners shop is situated in Victoria on Vancouver Island.
Drink: Sparkling wines are produced in Okanagan Valley and all the usual alcoholic beverages are widely available. Spirits, beer and wine can be served in licensed restaurants, dining rooms, pubs and bars. Taverns (pubs) are open until 0100, bars and cabarets until 0200. The minimum drinking age is 19.
NIGHTLIFE: Major cities and towns have top-class restaurants, nightclubs and bars, sometimes in pub style. Vancouver has an active theatre life. Better nightspots are often to be found in hotels.
SPORT: The hundreds of watersheds among the Rocky Mountains have provided British Columbia with countless rivers and lakes in every park area. **Watersports** ranging from **sailing**, **canoeing** and even specialist white-water **river rafting** are all available. Campbell River on Vancouver Island is world-famous for salmon **fishing**. The Rocky Mountains are the national centre for snow **skiing**, and attract visitors from the USA and Europe.
SPECIAL EVENTS: Apr 21-25 '95 *TerriVic Jazz Party,* Victoria. **May 1-31** *Country Living Days,* Sardis. **May 19-22** *Cloverdale Rodeo,* Surrey. **May 20-22** *Falkland Stampede,* Falkland. **May 20-28** *Hyack Festival,* New Westminster. **May 20-Oct 9** *Whistler Summer Festival,* Whistler. **May 27-28** *Swiftsure Lightship Classic Yacht Race,* Victoria. **May 29-Jun 4** *Children's Festival,* Vancouver. **Jun 22-24** *International Dragonboat Festival,* Vancouver. **Jun 23-Jul 2** *International Jazz Festival,* Vancouver. **Jun 26-Aug 6** *International Comedy Festival,* Vancouver. **Jul 14-16** *Folk Music Festival,* Vancouver. **Jul 15-23** *Marine Festival,* Nanaimo. **Jul 20-23** *Vancouver Sea Festival,* Vancouver. **Jul 23** *World Championship Bathtub Race,* Nanaimo. **Jul 29-Aug 9** *Benson & Hedges Symphony of Fire,* Vancouver. **Aug 9-13** *Peach Festival,* Penticton. **Aug 11-13** *Abbotsford Air Show,* Abbotsford. **Aug 19-Sep 4** *Pacific National Exhibition,* Vancouver. **Sep 7-17** *Fringe Theatre Festival,* Vancouver. **Sep 15-17** *Cloverdale Exhibition,* Surrey. **Oct 1-10** *Okanagan Wine Festival,* Okanagan.

BUSINESS PROFILE

COMMERCIAL INFORMATION: The following organisation can offer advice: Vancouver Chamber of Commerce, Suite 400, 999 Canada Place, Vancouver, British Columbia V6C 3E1. Tel: (604) 681 2111. Fax: (604) 681 0437.
CONFERENCES/CONVENTIONS: There are conference/convention centres in Penticton, Vancouver, Victoria and Whistler as well as over 200 hotels throughout the province which can offer meeting facilities. For more information on conferences and conventions in British Columbia, contact the Canadian Tourist Office, Tourism British Columbia *or* Tourism Vancouver, 2nd Floor, Waterfront Centre, 200 Burrard Street, Vancouver, British Columbia V7X 1M8. Tel: (604) 683 2000. Fax: (604) 682 1717.

CLIMATE

One of the mildest regions with very warm summers and relatively mild winters. Heavy snowfalls in the Rockies.
Required clothing: Lightweights for most of the summer with warmer clothes sometimes necessary in the evenings. Mediumweights are worn during winter, with Alpine wear in the mountains. Waterproof clothing is advisable throughout the year.

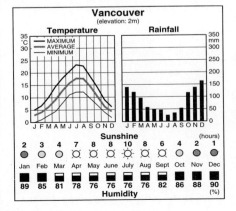

Vancouver
(elevation: 2m)

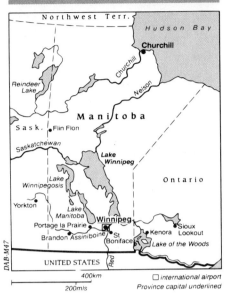

Manitoba

Location: Eastern Central Canada.

Travel Manitoba
Department 147, 7th Floor, 155 Carlton Street, Winnipeg, Manitoba R3C 3H8
Tel: (204) 945 3796. Fax: (204) 945 2302.

AREA: 548,360 sq km (211,722 sq miles).
POPULATION: 1,091,942 (1991).
POPULATION DENSITY: 2 per sq km.
CAPITAL: Winnipeg. **Population:** 652,354 (1991).
GEOGRAPHY: Manitoba is bordered by the USA state of North Dakota to the south, Saskatchewan to the west, Ontario to the east, and the Northwest Territories to the north. The landscape is diverse, ranging from rolling farmland to sandy beaches on the shores of Lake Winnipeg, and from the desert landscape of the south to northern parkland covered by lakes and forests.
LANGUAGE: Although Canada is officially bilingual (English and French), English is commonly spoken in Manitoba.
TIME: GMT - 6 (GMT - 5 in summer).
Note: Summer officially lasts from the first Sunday in April to the Saturday before the last Sunday in October.

PUBLIC HOLIDAYS

Public holidays are as for the rest of Canada (see general section above) with the following date also observed:
Aug 7 '95 Civic Day.

TRAVEL

AIR: The following airlines run inter-provincial flights: *Air Canada (AC), Canadian Airlines International (CP), Frontier Airlines* and *Nordair.* For timetables and fares, contact the airline offices.
International airport: *Winnipeg International Airport (YWG)* is 6km (4 miles) northwest of the city (travel time – 15 minutes). Airport facilities include duty-free shop, post office, 24-hour restaurant, banks, car rental and car parking.
SEA: The only major coastal port is Churchill on Hudson Bay, which is frozen for much of the year. In summer, there are services to the Northwest Territories and Ontario.
RAIL: *Via Rail* links Saskatchewan and Ontario with Winnipeg and southern Manitoba. A thrice-weekly train runs north from Winnipeg to Hudson Bay, The Pas, Lynn Lake, Thompson and Churchill. For timetables and fares, contact a local *Via Rail* office.
ROAD: Excellent road services connect Manitoba with Ontario (through Kenora), Saskatchewan (Regina) and the USA (Fargo, Minnesota and Bismarck, North Dakota). The road system within Manitoba is also excellent and covers over 19,794km (12,300 miles). **Bus:** Services are run by local authorities and interstate services are run by *Greyhound Bus Lines* and *Grey Goose Bus Lines.* For timetables and fares, contact local offices. **Taxi:** Available in all larger towns. Taxi drivers

expect a 15% tip. **Documentation:** National driving licences are accepted in Manitoba.
URBAN: There are comprehensive bus services in Winnipeg. A flat fare is charged. There are good bus services in other towns.

ACCOMMODATION

Manitoba has a wide selection of accommodation, ranging from first-class hotels in Winnipeg to guest-houses and farm holiday camps among the parklands of the north. Farm vacations are controlled by their own association, ensuring high standards. Bed & breakfast is available at a reasonable price. For information on bed & breakfast accommodation, contact B & B Association of Manitoba, 533 Sprague Street, Winnipeg, Manitoba R3G 2R9. Tel: (204) 783 9797. For all accommodation details, contact Travel Manitoba *or* the Manitoba Hotel Association, Suite 1505, 155 Carlton Street, Winnipeg, Manitoba R3C 3H8. Tel: (204) 942 0671. Fax: (204) 942 6719.
CAMPING/CARAVANNING: The parklands and the enormous spread of lakes and forests in northern Manitoba are major attractions. Camping facilities are widespread. A number of companies can arrange **motor camper** rentals, with a range of fully equipped vehicles. Full details can be obtained from Travel Manitoba.

RESORTS & EXCURSIONS

WINNIPEG: Almost equidistant from the Pacific and Atlantic Oceans, the provincial capital stands in the heart of the vast prairie which covers much of the southern part of the province. This 'Gateway to the North' at the confluence of the Red and Assiniboine rivers is one of the most culturally and racially varied of Canada's cities. Winnipeg is the fourth largest Canadian city with theatres, galleries, a ballet and an opera. Places of note include the *Legislative Building* with Manitoba's symbol, the *Golden Boy,* balancing triumphantly on its dome; the *Centennial Centre* which features the *Museum of Man and Nature,* re-creating past and present life on the prairies; and the *Commodity Exchange,* the world's largest grain market. *St Boniface,* formerly a separate city, is the French Quarter of Winnipeg. In the suburbs, the *Royal Canadian Mint,* with its high-tech building, and *Lower Fort Garry,* an old fur-trading post, are both worth visiting.
ELSEWHERE: Paddle-steamers offer excursions through the rich farmland of the **Red** and **Assiniboine** rivers. The *Prairie Dog Central* steam train runs from the city to **Grosse Isle.**
East of the capital along the Trans-Canada Highway is the German-speaking Mennonite town of **Steinbach;** and **Whiteshell Provincial Park,** with over 2500 sq km (1000 sq miles) of wilderness offering fishing, hunting and canoeing. The more developed resorts of **Falcon Lake** and **West Hawk Lake** have good facilities for swimming and sailing.
West of Winnipeg the highway cuts through the wheat belt. *Fort la Reine Museum* and the *Pioneer Village* at **Portage la Prairie** reconstruct the town's days as an 18th-century trading post. The **International Peace Garden** on the border with North Dakota has a huge complex of formal gardens and waterways.
Lake Winnipeg has good sandy beaches and boats for hire. The western shore of the lake was once New Iceland, a self-governing area settled by thousands of Icelanders fleeing volcanic eruptions in their homeland. **Gimli,** the major town, still has a large Icelandic population, which stages an annual Icelandic festival. **Hecla Provincial Park,** a group of wooded islands on the lake, offers a resort and conference centre as well as good hiking and camping facilities.
En route to the great northern wilderness, **Riding Mountain National Park** is a vast recreational area providing cross-country skiing, riding and 300km (190 miles) of hiking trails. Ukrainian immigrants colonised the farming area around **Dauphin** in the 1890s and their influence is still felt in the cuisine and costume of the area notably during the annual *Ukrainian Festival.* **The Pas** is the jumping-off point for trips to the lakes and rivers of the northern interior. Near the border with Saskatchewan is the mining and lumbering town of **Flin Flon** (a noted trout-fishing centre) and **Grass River Park,** a huge granite wilderness. **Churchill,** a sub-arctic seaport in the far northeast, is best reached by air across the vast flatlands running into **Hudson Bay.** The area has an abundance of game and wildlife, as well as the world's heaviest concentration of Northern Lights.

SOCIAL PROFILE

FOOD & DRINK: Winnipeg offers opportunities to experience cuisine of the many and diverse cultures that typify the city. Rural Manitoba also offers a wide choice of restaurants from the very expensive to the moderately

priced with good home cooking. The best restaurants are usually found in hotels and motels outside the city. It is customary to tip waiters 15% of the bill. **Drink:** The minimum age for drinking is 18, but those under 18 can drink with a meal if it is purchased by a parent or guardian. Off-licence alcohol is available only from government outlets. Opening hours are generally 1100-1400.
NIGHTLIFE: Winnipeg's nightlife is vibrant. The National Film Board of Canada screens top films once a month in the Planetarium Auditorium; admittance is free. Many other cinemas, theatres, clubs, restaurants and bars also provide entertainment. Winnipeg is home to a mixture of performing arts: the Royal Winnipeg Ballet, the Winnipeg Symphony Orchestra, Manitoba Opera and several theatre, dance and music companies. The city also offers romantic dining and moonlit dancing cruises aboard riverboats on its scenic Red and Assiniboine rivers. The elegant Crystal Casino, Canada's first full-time casino, is located here in the Fort Garry Hotel, offering blackjack, roulette and baccarat.
SHOPPING: There are several nationally known department stores in Winnipeg, with branches throughout Manitoba. City and provincial centres have a variety of unusual shops and boutiques. North of The Pas is an Indian handicraft shop where visitors can watch Indian women making moccasins, mukluks, jackets and jewellery. At the Rock Shop in Fouris, costume jewellery can be bought made from rock from a local quarry and the visitor may obtain a permit to collect his own rock.
Shopping hours: 1000-1800 Monday to Wednesday and Saturday, 1000-2130 Thursday and Friday (closed Sunday).
SPORT: There are 111 golf courses in Manitoba, six of these in Winnipeg. The lakes and parklands of Manitoba mean that **watersports** predominate. **Fishing** for trout, pike, Arctic grayling and walleye is especially popular. Several of the northern lakes are only accessible by air, and charter flights with guides are available from Winnipeg. **Swimming, diving, windsurfing** and **sailing** are also popular. The great outdoors offers excellent opportunities for **canoeing, hiking** and **horseriding**. **Skiing** is available throughout the winter months at the provincial and national parks such as *Mount Agassiz* in *Riding Mountain National Park*.
SPECIAL EVENTS: Mar 27-Apr 1 '95 *Royal Manitoba Winter Fair*, Brandon. **Jun 14-18** *Provincial Exhibition*, Brandon. **Jun 22-Jul 1** *Red River Exhibition*, Winnipeg. **Jul 6-9** *Centennial Folk Festival*, Winnipeg. **Jul 13-16** *A Taste of Manitoba*, Winnipeg. **Jul 15-23** *Fringe Festival*, Winnipeg. **Jul 20-23** *Manitoba Stampede & Exhibition*, Morris. **Aug 4-6** *Canada's National Ukraine Festival*, Dauphin. **Aug 6-19** *Folklorama*, Winnipeg.

BUSINESS PROFILE

COMMERCIAL INFORMATION: The following organisation can offer advice: Manitoba Chamber of Commerce, Suite 167, 167 Lombard Avenue, Winnipeg, Manitoba R3B 0V6. Tel: (204) 942 2561. Fax: (204) 942 2227.
CONFERENCES/CONVENTIONS: For information on conferences and conventions in Winnipeg, contact the Canadian Tourist Office *or* The Director of Convention Development, Tourism Winnipeg, Suite 232, 25 Forks Market Road, Winnipeg, Manitoba R3C 3S3. Tel: (204) 943 1970. Fax: (204) 942 4043.

CLIMATE

Summers are warm and sunny. Winters are cold, particularly in the north. Rainfall is highest in May and July.

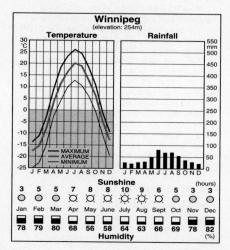

Winnipeg
(elevation: 254m)

	Jan	Feb	Mar	Apr	May	June	July	Aug	Sept	Oct	Nov	Dec
Sunshine (hours)	3	5	5	7	8	8	10	9	6	5	3	3
Humidity (%)	78	79	80	68	56	58	64	63	66	69	78	82

New Brunswick

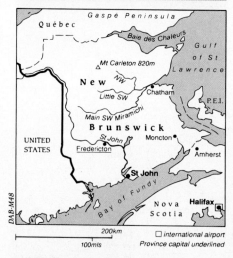

Location: East coast of Canada.

Economic Development and Tourism
PO Box 6000, 5th Floor, Centennial Building, 670 King Street, Fredericton, New Brunswick E3B 5H1
Tel: (506) 453 3984. Fax: (506) 453 5428.

AREA: 74,437 sq km (28,354 sq miles).
POPULATION: 726,800 (1992).
POPULATION DENSITY: 9.8 per sq km.
CAPITAL: Fredericton. **Population:** 46,500 (1992).
GEOGRAPHY: New Brunswick, which is below the Gaspé Peninsula, shares its western border with Maine and has 2250km (1400 miles) of coast on the Gulf of St Lawrence and the Bay of Fundy. Its landscape comprises forested hills with rivers cutting through them. The main feature is St John River Valley in the south. Northern and eastern coastal regions give way to the extensive drainage basin of the Miramichi River in the central area.
LANGUAGE: New Brunswick is officially bilingual (English and French) with approximately 35% of the population French-speaking.
TIME: GMT - 4 (GMT - 3 in summer).
Note: Daylight Saving Time officially lasts from the first Sunday in April to the Saturday before the last Sunday in October.

PUBLIC HOLIDAYS

Public holidays are as for the rest of Canada (see general section above) with the following date also observed:
Aug 7 '95 New Brunswick Day.

TRAVEL

AIR: New Brunswick is without an international airport but Fredericton, St John and Moncton are connected to Montréal and Québec by inter-provincial flights operated by *Air Canada (AC), Canadian Airlines International (CP)* and *Air Atlantic.* There are airports offering local services at *St John, Fredericton, St Leonard, Edmundston, Campbelton* and *Moncton.*
SEA: Ferries run from Nova Scotia, Maine, Prince Edward Island and Québec to New Brunswick via St John and Cape Tormentine.
There is a full coastal ferry service between all ports in the province. For timetables, contact the local tourist office.
RAIL: *Via Rail* runs six times a week from Montréal to Halifax, three times via Mont Joli and via St John.
ROAD: The Trans-Canada Highway follows the St John River Valley from Edmundston in the north to St John in the south, with the majority of the highways branching off it. There are over 16,000km (10,000 miles) of roads in the province.

ACCOMMODATION

There are 73 hotels/motels, 64 bed & breakfast inns and seven coast resorts. The main centres of population are on the coast, and these offer the best choice of hotel or motel accommodation. There are also numerous guest-houses, bed & breakfast establishments and youth hostels. For information on bed & breakfast accommodation, contact the New Brunswick B & B Association, Route 3, St Stephen's, St John, New Brunswick E3L 2Y1. Tel: (506)

---

466 5401.
Grading: Accommodation is graded by the New Brunswick Grading Authority on a voluntary basis according to the *Atlantic Canada Accommodations Grading Program* as follows:
1-star: Basic, clean, comfortable accommodation.
2-star: Basic, clean, comfortable accommodation with extra amenities.
3-star: Better quality accommodation with a greater range of services.
4-star: High-quality accommodation with extended range of facilities, amenities and guest services.
5-star: Deluxe accommodation with the greatest range of facilities, amenities and guest services.
CAMPING/CARAVANNING: The province's four major parks have extensive campsites and youth hostels. More than a hundred privately-owned campsites operate in the area. A number of companies can arrange **motor camper** rentals, with a range of fully equipped vehicles. Details can be obtained from Tourism New Brunswick.

RESORTS & EXCURSIONS

ST JOHN: New Brunswick's largest city has been a shipbuilding centre since the last century. Replicas of sailing ships can be seen in the *New Brunswick Museum.* Other historic sites include the *Loyalist Houses* and the *Country Courthouse.* The city was also a bastion for the British Loyalists, who flocked there in May 1783 to escape from the victorious American rebels after the War of Independence, and their historic landing is re-enacted every year in a 5-day celebration. The **St John River Valley** provides a scenic route to the capital, with the uncluttered resort of **Grand Lake** on the way.
FREDERICTON: 110km (70 miles) upriver from St John and the Bay of Fundy, Fredericton is the capital of Acadia. It is the legislative and academic centre of New Brunswick and possesses some fine neo-classical and Victorian architecture such as the *Legislative Building, Christchurch Cathedral* and *Government House.* The *Beaverbrook Art Gallery* is one of the finest in Canada with an extensive collection of Canadian, British and Renaissance paintings and a good group of Salvador Dali's work. Paddle-boats offer cruises and entertainment on the *St John River.* On Saturdays, the Farmer's Market is the focus for Frederictonians and visitors alike.
North of the city the highly developed resort of **Mactaquac Park** offers a huge range of outdoor activities. Nearby **King's Landing**, a reconstructed loyalist village, is also worth visiting.
ELSEWHERE: New Brunswick is a maritime province with two coastlines – on the **Gulf of St Lawrence** and the **Bay of Fundy.** Routes along these two coasts provide the best introduction to the area. The eastern shoreline, once a French stronghold, has a temperate climate and some excellent beaches, particularly near **Kouchibouguac Provincial Park.** In the south, **Shediac** hosts an annual lobster festival; at **Parlee**, nearby, is the largest and best beach in the province. Trout-fishing and canoeing on the **Miramichi River**, running into picturesque Miramichi Bay at **Chatham**, are recommended. North of this the area around **Tracadie** is still a French-speaking enclave; deep-sea fishing charters are available here. Nearby, a 500-acre *Acadian Village* re-creates the lifestyle of the 18th-century Breton settlers whose descendants still dominate the northeast corner of the province.
Most of the shipbuilding and fishing towns of the south were founded by British Loyalists fleeing the American War of Independence. The coastline is battered by the tempestuous 15m (50ft) tides of the Bay of Fundy, resulting in dramatic scenery such as **Hopewell Cape's** sandstone 'flowerpots'. **St Andrews** has some well-preserved 18th-century houses and *The Blockhouse,* built in 1812 to defend the town from American incursions. **St George** has a ferry to the little-known and unspoilt **Fundy Islands,** of which *Grand Manan,* the largest, boasts beautiful rare flora and fauna. Whales and dolphins can often be spotted from the shoreline. It is also a centre for collecting *dulse,* an edible seaweed, which is a speciality of the province. **Deer Island** and **Campobello Island** are reached by ferry from **Letete.**
To the east of St John is **Fundy National Park,** the area's most popular resort. Much of it is set on a plateau 300m (985ft) above sea level with 800km (500 miles) of hiking trails. The huge range of organised activities there include an *Arts and Crafts School.* Rowboats and canoes can be rented to navigate the tidal flats where tides can rise by 16m (50ft) a day. The Fundy tides cause an impressive tidal bore at **Moncton**, the province's second-largest city.

SOCIAL PROFILE

FOOD & DRINK: The province is famous for seafood, particularly Atlantic salmon with its delicate flavour, served with butter, new potatoes and *fiddleheads* (young

fronds of ostrich fern served with butter and seasoned, or used cold in salads). Apples, blueberries and cranberries are common dessert ingredients. Home-made baked beans and steamed brown bread are served as traditional Saturday-night supper. *Rapée pie,* made with chicken, is an Acadian speciality for Sundays or festivals. Shediac is reputed to be the lobster capital of the world. Fredericton, St John and Moncton offer international cuisine as well as local specialities, like New Brunswick *dulse,* an edible seaweed. **Drink:** The minimum drinking age is 19.
NIGHTLIFE: Music is very much a part of the lives of New Brunswick citizens. Many bars and clubs throughout the province, especially in Fredericton, St John and Moncton, feature live music, much of it with a French, Scottish and Irish flavour.
SHOPPING: Special purchases include local and provincial handicrafts which are especially worthwhile in New Brunswick. The best markets in St John are between Charlotte and Germain streets, forming the *Old City Market.* This is open all week, with farmers taking over on Friday and Saturday. Moncton has three large shopping areas: Champlain Place, Moncton Mall and Highfield Square. **Shopping hours:** 0900-1730 Monday to Saturday; 1000-2200 in malls.
SPORT: One of the best centres for **golf** is the picturesque resort town of St Andrews. **Harness racing** is held at St John during late August to early September. Harness racing meetings are also held twice a week at Fredericton Raceway. **Skiing** and **skating** are popular winter activities in New Brunswick. New Brunswick is also a maritime sporting province. **Sailing** and **skindiving** are popular, and the annual *Renforth* and *Cocagne Regattas* attract **sculling** crews from all over the world. The best beach in the province for **swimming** is found at Parlee Beach Provincial Park. Salmon and brook trout **fishing** is popular throughout the province but nowhere better than on the Mirimachi River. Deep-sea fishing boats are open for charter from all the coastal ports. Grand Manan Island is a **birdwatching** paradise and was the favourite haunt of the famous ornithologist, James Audubon.
SPECIAL EVENTS: Jul 14-22 '95 *International Festival of Baroque Music,* Lameque. **Jul 15-24** *Festival Marin du Nouveau Brunswick,* Bas-Caraquet. **Aug 6-11** *Mirimachi Folksong Festival,* Newcastle. **Aug 11-20** *Festival By The Sea,* St John.

BUSINESS PROFILE

COMMERCIAL INFORMATION: The following organisations can offer advice: Atlantic Provinces Chamber of Commerce, Suite 110, 236 St George Street, Moncton, New Brunswick E1C 1W1. Tel: (506) 857 3980. Fax: (506) 859 6131; *or*
Greater Moncton Chamber of Commerce, Suite 100, 910 Main Street, Moncton, New Brunswick E1C 1G6. Tel: (506) 857 2883. Fax: (506) 857 7209.
CONFERENCES/CONVENTIONS: For information on conferences and conventions in New Brunswick contact the Canadian Tourist Office *or* Fredericton Visitors & Convention Bureau, PO Box 130, City Hall, Queen Street, Fredericton, New Brunswick E3B 4Y7. Tel: (506) 452 9508. Fax: (506) 452 9509; *or* St John Visitors & Convention Bureau, PO Box 1971, 15 Market Square, St John, New Brunswick E2L 4L1. Tel: (506) 658 2990. Fax: (506) 632 6118.

CLIMATE

Summer is warm with cooler evenings. Autumn is relatively mild. Winters are cold with heavy snows. **Required clothing:** Light- to medium-weights during summer months, heavyweights in winter. Waterproofing is advisable all year.

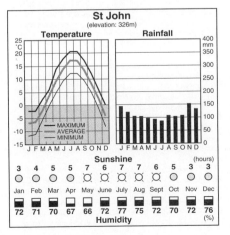

St John
(elevation: 326m)

	Jan	Feb	Mar	Apr	May	June	July	Aug	Sept	Oct	Nov	Dec
Sunshine (hours)	3	4	5	5	7	7	7	7	6	5	3	3
Humidity (%)	72	71	70	67	66	72	77	75	72	70	72	76

Newfoundland & Labrador

□ *international airport*
Province capital underlined

Location: Eastern Canada.

Department of Tourism, Culture and Recreation
PO Box 8730, St John's, Newfoundland A1B 4K2
Tel: (709) 729 2830. Fax: (709) 729 1965.

AREA: 405,720 sq km (156,185 sq miles).
POPULATION: 575,000 (1992 estimate).
POPULATION DENSITY: 1.4 per sq km.
CAPITAL: St John's. **Population:** 103,000 (1991).
GEOGRAPHY: Newfoundland & Labrador is the most easterly province. It consists of the mainland territory of the Island of Newfoundland at the mouth of the St Lawrence River and the eastern half of the Ungava Peninsula, known as Labrador, which borders on the Canadian Province of Québec. The province stretches about 1700km (1063 miles) north to south, and has about 17,000km (10,625 miles) of coastline, much of it rugged and heavily indented with bays and fjords. The interior of Newfoundland is a combination of forest, heath, lakes and rivers spread over a terrain that ranges from mountainous in the west to rolling hills in the centre and east. Labrador is also mountainous in the west, although its rivers are larger and wilder.
LANGUAGE: Although Canada is officially bilingual (English and French), 95% of this province speaks English as a first language.
TIME: Newfoundland: GMT - 3.5 (GMT - 2.5 in summer).
Labrador: GMT - 4 (GMT - 3 in summer).
Note: Daylight Saving Time officially lasts from the first Sunday in April to the Saturday before the last Sunday in October.
COMMUNICATIONS: Post: Post offices are open 0830-1700 Monday to Friday; 0900-1245 Saturday.

PUBLIC HOLIDAYS

Public holidays as for the rest of Canada (see general section above) with the following dates also observed:
Mar 13 '95 Commonwealth Day. **Mar 20** St Patrick's Day. **Apr 24** St George's Day. **Jun 26** Discovery Day. **Jul 7** Memorial Day. **Jul 10** Orangeman's Day. **Mar 11 '96** Commonwealth Day. **Mar 18** St Patrick's Day.
Note: Holidays are usually observed on the nearest Monday to the anniversary date.

TRAVEL

AIR: *Air Canada (AC)* and *Canadian Airlines International* provide services within Canada and to destinations outside the country. *Air Atlantic* and *Air Nova* operate services within the province and to the Maritime Provinces.
International airports: *Gander (YQX)* is 3km (2 miles) from the city centre. Airport facilities include car parking, restaurant, duty-free shop and banks.
St John's (YYT) is 15km (9 miles) from the city. The travel time is about 15 minutes.
Other major airports are at *Stephenville, Deer Lake, Happy Valley-Goose Bay, Wabush* and *Churchill Falls.*
SEA: Year-round, daily passenger and automobile service runs between North Sydney, Nova Scotia and Port aux Basques on Newfoundland's southwest coast. Crossing time: 6 hours. Summer services run twice a week between North Sydney and Argentia on Newfoundland Avalon Peninsula, mid-June to mid-September. Crossing time: 12 hours. There is also a summer ferry to the French islands of St Pierre & Miquelon from Fortune on Newfoundland's Burin Peninsula. Crossing time: 90 minutes. Intraprovincial ferries connect island communities with larger towns. A seasonal summer ferry connects southern Labrador and St Barbe on Newfoundland Great Northern Peninsula. Summer coastal boat service is provided by *Marine Atlantic* between Lewisporte on Newfoundland's northeast coast and Happy Valley-Goose Bay in Hamilton Sound, Labrador. Remote communities on the Labrador coast and Newfoundland's south coast are also served by coastal boats.
RAIL: A passenger service is provided by *The Québec North Shore and Labrador Railway* operates between Seven Islands in Québec and Labrador City in western Labrador.
ROAD: A modern paved highway (Route 1, the Trans-Canada Highway) crosses Newfoundland from Port aux Basques in the southwest to the capital of St John's in the east. Distance is 905km (565 miles). Paved secondary roads connect most communities to the main highway. *TerraTransport* operates a cross-island bus service along Route 1. Visitors can reach western Labrador along a partially paved highway from Baie Comeau, Québec. A seasonal gravel highway, dubbed the 'Freedom Road' by residents, connects Labrador City and Wabush with the interior town of Churchill Falls and Happy Valley-Goose Bay in east-central Labrador. There are no services along this latter stretch of road. **Coach:** Long-distance buses connect Port aux Basques, Corner Brook, Gander, St John's and Argentia.

ACCOMMODATION

There are almost 300 establishments in the province with a total of more than 5400 rooms. Most towns offer hotel or bed & breakfast accommodation, although the pre-eminence of the fishing industry means that many of the facilities are seasonal. Most of the settlements in the province are on the coast rather than the wild interior (where some cabins and lodges are, however, available). The *Hospitality Homes Scheme* offers accommodation with families in small coastal communities off the beaten track. As St John's is now an 'oil boom town', accommodation there can be hard to come by, and advance reservations are recommended. For information on hotels, contact Hospitality Newfoundland & Labrador, PO Box 13516, St John's, Newfoundland A1B 4B8. Tel: (709) 722 2000. Fax: (709) 722 8104. For information on bed & breakfast accommodation, contact the Department of Tourism and Culture (for address, see above). **Grading:** Accommodation is graded on a voluntary basis according to the *Atlantic Canada Accommodations Grading Program* as follows:
1-star: Basic, clean, comfortable accommodation.
2-star: Basic, clean, comfortable accommodation with extra amenities.
3-star: Better quality accommodation with a greater range of services.
4-star: High-quality accommodation with extended range of facilities, amenities and guest services.
5-star: Deluxe accommodation with the greatest range of facilities, amenities and guest services.
Note: A new Canadian Select Grading Program is due to start operating during 1994.
CAMPING/CARAVANNING: The wildness of the province offers superb camping facilities, both for motorhomes and tents. Both national parks (Gros Morne in western Newfoundland and Terra Nova in eastern) as well as more than 50 provincial and 25 private campgrounds provide camping services. Facilities on campsites are basic rather than luxurious, the emphasis being on seclusion and privacy. Full details can be obtained from the Department of Tourism and Culture (see address above).

RESORTS & EXCURSIONS

NEWFOUNDLAND ISLAND: Most of the island's activity and population is based on the Avalon Peninsula to the east. The peninsula is full of old settlements such as **Placentia** where the French once challenged the English for supremacy and **Trinity** which dates from the 16th century. *St John's*, the provincial capital, is a busy fishing port with a good natural harbour bounded by hills. *Signal Hill*, site of Marconi's first transatlantic radio transmission and Canada's second largest National Historic Park, offers a good overview of the town and harbour to the west. The *Newfoundland Museum* and *Quidi Vidi Battery* are both worth visiting. The coast of Newfoundland offers an exciting range of boating excursions in the summer months. There are over 60 major seabird colonies along the south and east coast representing over 300 species of birds including puffins, gannets and bald-headed eagles. Hump-backed, fin and minke whales can be seen off the coasts, often approaching the boats out of curiosity. This is combined with icebergs which slowly float in the Labrador straits on a trail southwards. The main route off the peninsula leads north and then east through **Terra Nova National Park**, an area of scenic rugged coastline adjoining Bonavista Bay. Fishing trips to the remote and barely accessible interior can be arranged at **Gander** and **Grand Falls**. The **Burin Peninsula** in the south has some beautiful coastal villages. At **Fortune** a ferry runs to the French island of St Pierre. The **Long Range Mountains** dominate the western seaboard, along which runs a 715km (444-mile) coastal road affording good views of the fjords, mountains and beaches. **Corner Brook**, the island's second city, set in a deep inlet halfway up the coast, is an outfitting centre for expeditions to the many lakes and rivers of the interior, many of which are accessible only by air.

The **Great Northern Peninsula** is a wilderness area of outstanding scenic beauty. It is best seen from **Gros Morne National Park**, a blend of rugged mountains, deep fjords and bays on the Gulf of St Lawrence. Local fishing boats can be chartered here. At the northernmost tip of the peninsula at **L'Anse aux Meadows** (which, like Gros Morne, is a UNESCO World Heritage Site) lie the restored remains of the earliest European settlement in the New World, a group of six sod houses built by Norsemen around the year 1000AD.

LABRADOR: The largely undisturbed wilderness of **Labrador** which has only 30,000 inhabitants may be reached by air or by ferry from **St Barbe** on Newfoundland Island; day trips along its coastline are also available from here. Longer trips to the mainland interior should be arranged through the many tour operators and outfitters. Labrador is desolate and, except in the few isolated towns, uninhabited. It can be bitterly cold in winter. Both downhill and cross-country skiing is possible near **Labrador City**, a mining town near the Québec border. **Goose Bay**, a US airbase settlement dating from the Second World War, is the main jumping-off point for hunting and fishing trips to the interior; it can only be reached by air or sea. The main sports fish are salmon, Arctic char, trout and northern pike. The oldest industrial complex in the New World is the 16th-century Basque whaling station at **Red Bay** on the southern coast.

SOCIAL PROFILE

FOOD & DRINK: A hearty cuisine making full use of fat pork, molasses, salt fish, salt meat, boiled vegetables and soups. Fish is a staple food, predominantly cod made into stews, fish cakes, fried, salted, dried and fresh. Salmon, trout, halibut and hake are also available. *Brewis* is a hard water biscuit that needs soaking in water to soften, then gently cooked; often salt or fresh cod is served with *scrunchions*, which are bits of fat pork, fried and crunchy. Another speciality is *damper dog* (a type of fried bread dough), *cod sound pie* (made from tough meat near the cod's backbone), *crubeens* (Irish pickled pigs' feet) and *fat back and molasses dip* (rich mixture of pork fat and molasses for dipping bread). Pies, jams, jellies and puddings are made from wild berries. **Drink:** The minimum drinking age is 19.
NIGHTLIFE: A St John's pub crawl is a real cultural experience, with a particularly strong Irish influence. Water Street and Duckworth Street offer fine restaurants and nightclubs. Newfoundland also has its own music, mostly Scottish and Irish, which can be found everywhere in local festivals, nightclubs, bars, taverns and concerts. George Street in St John's has become a club and restaurant zone and holds a variety of seasonal festivals. However, on the whole, night entertainment in many regions is scarce.
SHOPPING: Water Street in downtown St John's is a must for any shopper – it is the oldest shopping street in North America and European merchants, sailors and privateers have bartered here since 1500. Handicrafts,

Grenfell parkas and Labradorite jewellery are the most well-known products of the Newfoundland & Labrador area. **Shopping hours:** 1000-1700 Monday to Wednesday, 1000-2200 Thursday to Friday and 1000-1800 Saturday. (Malls generally open 1000-2200 Monday to Saturday.)
SPORT: Skiing is popular at Newfoundland Island's Marble Mountain, 8km (5 miles) east of Corner Brook, the second city of the province. There are also resorts at Smokey Mountain near Labrador City on the mainland and White Hills at Clarenville and **cross-country skiing** at the Menihek Nordic Club in Labrador. **Canoeing, hiking** and **mountain climbing** are popular in the interior, and **sailing, windsurfing** and **scuba diving** are available on the coast. Salmon **fishing** takes place between May 24 and September 15. Fishing in licensed rivers in Newfoundland and in all waters in Labrador needs a qualified guide.
SPECIAL EVENTS: Jul 9-Aug 20 '95 *Signal Hill Tattoo*, St John's. **Jul 13-17** *Exploits Valley Salmon Festival*, Grand Falls/Windsor. **Aug 2** *The Royal St John's Regatta*, St John's. **Aug 10-13** *Labrador Straits Bakeapple Festival*, Forteau.

BUSINESS PROFILE

COMMERCIAL INFORMATION: The following organisations can offer advice: Atlantic Provinces Chamber of Commerce, Suite 110, 236 St George Street, Moncton, New Brunswick E1C 1W1. Tel: (506) 857 3980. Fax: (506) 859 6131; *or*
St John's Board of Trade, PO Box 5127, 10 Fort William Place, St John's, Newfoundland A1C 5V5. Tel: (709) 726 2961. Fax: (709) 726 2003; *or*
Enterprise Newfoundland & Labrador Corporation, Viking Building, 136 Crosbie Road, St John's, Newfoundland A1B 3K3. Tel: (709) 729 7000. Fax: (709) 729 7135.
CONFERENCES/CONVENTIONS: For information on conferences and conventions in Newfoundland, contact the Canadian Tourist office *or* Meetings and Conventions Co-ordinator, St John's Economic Development & Tourism, Department of Tourism and Culture, PO Box 908, St John's, Newfoundland A1C 5M2. Tel: (709) 576 8455. Fax: (709) 576 8246.

CLIMATE

Very cold winters and mild summers.
Required clothing: Light- to medium-weights in warmer months, heavyweights in winter. Waterproofing is advisable throughout the year.

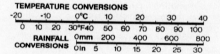

TEMPERATURE CONVERSIONS

-20	-10	0°C	10	20	30	40	
0	10	20	30°F40	50	60	70	80	90	100

RAINFALL CONVERSIONS	0mm	200		400		600		800
	0In	5	10	15	20	25	30

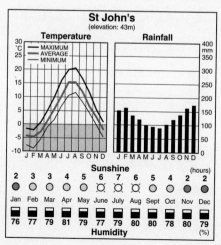

St John's
(elevation: 43m)

Temperature — MAXIMUM, AVERAGE, MINIMUM

Rainfall

Sunshine (hours)

Jan	Feb	Mar	Apr	May	June	July	Aug	Sept	Oct	Nov	Dec
2	3	3	4	5	7	6	5	4	2	2
76	77	79	81	79	77	79	80	80	78	80	79

Humidity (%)

Territory capital underlined
1000km / 500mls

Location: Northern Canada.

TravelArctic
The North Group, PO Box 2107, Yellowknife, Northwest Territories X1A 2P6
Tel: (403) 873 7200. Fax: (403) 920 2801.

AREA: 3,293,020 sq km (1,271,436 sq miles).
POPULATION: 57,649 (1991).
POPULATION DENSITY: 0.2 per sq km.
CAPITAL: Yellowknife. **Population:** 13,568 (1990).
GEOGRAPHY: The Northwest Territories cover one-third of Canada, stretching from Ellesmere Island off Greenland's north coast to the Mackenzie Mountain Range at the Yukon border. It is a huge expanse of untouched wilderness, the landscape ranging from lush forests and great rivers to stark northern tundra and Arctic island glaciers. The land rises to over 2000m (7000ft) in the west, where Canada's longest river, the Mackenzie (1800km/1125 miles), is fed by two of the country's largest lakes, the Great Bear and the Great Slave. In the east, towards the northeastern shores of Baffin Bay, there is fjord country.
LANGUAGE: Although Canada is officially bilingual (English and French), English is more commonly spoken in the Northwest Territories.
TIME: East of 68°W: GMT - 5 (GMT - 4 in summer).
68°W to 85°W: GMT - 6 (GMT - 5 in summer).
85°W to 102°W: GMT - 7 (GMT - 6 in summer).
West of 102°W: GMT - 8 (GMT - 7 in summer).
Note: Daylight Saving Time officially lasts from the first Sunday in April to the Saturday before the last Sunday in October.

PUBLIC HOLIDAYS

Public holidays are as for the rest of Canada (see general section above) with the following date also observed:
Aug 7 '95 Civic Day.

TRAVEL

AIR: The best way to reach the more remote areas within the Territory is by air. Float planes are commonly used to reach the northern lakes. The largest operators into the region are *Canadian Airlines International* and *First Air*. Other operators providing flights into the Northwest Territories include *Air Canada, Air Inuit, Alkan Air Ltd, Calm Air International Ltd, Delta Air Charter Ltd* and *NWT Air*.
Scheduled services to connections within the Northwest Territories are run by *Air Providence Ltd, Air Sahtu Ltd, Aklak Air, Buffalo Airways (1986) Ltd, Kenn Borek Air, Northwestern Air Lease Ltd, North-Wright Air Ltd, Ptarmigan Airways Ltd* and *Simpson Air (1981) Ltd*.
International airport: *Yellowknife Airport (YZF)* is less than a kilometre from the town centre (travel time – 10 minutes).
SEA/LAKES: The Mackenzie River is crossed at Fort Providence and at Arctic Red River. The Liard River is crossed at Fort Simpson. Cruises are available from Fort Simpson to the Virginia Falls, as well as cruises on the Great Slave during the summer, with an approximate cost of Can$1000 per person per week. Other local ferries are

operated by the provincial government.
ROAD: The major routes are along the Dempster Highway from the Yukon to the Mackenzie Delta, and the Mackenzie Highway from Alberta to the Great Slave Lake region. There are three bus companies that serve the region: *Dempster Highway Bus Service* operates a weekly service Tuesday and Thursday from the beginning of June to September 7 annually and is represented by the *Arctic Tour Company* (Box 2021-UK, Inuvik, Northwest Territories X0E 0T0. Tel: (403) 979 4100. Fax: (403) 979 2259), *Frontier Coachlines* (tel: (403) 873 4892; fax: (403) 873 6423) and *Greyhound Lines of Canada Ltd* (tel: (403) 874 6966).

ACCOMMODATION

Although most of the towns have hotels and bed & breakfast establishments open all year, accommodation can be scarce and often quite basic. Bear in mind the vast area of the region and the long distances between settlements of any size, especially in the Arctic zone. 'Lodges' designed for outdoor activity holidays can be found in many settlements. For details contact the local authorities. *TravelArctic* publishes an annual travel trade manual detailing accommodation in the region. For address, see top of entry.
CAMPING/CARAVANNING: Camping is only advised in summer as the winter temperatures drop below safety levels. Campsites are run by both government and private organisations. Also 'outposts' (semi-permanent camps) offer tented shelters with beds and meals, often combined with organised trips. A number of companies can arrange **motor camper** rentals, with a range of fully equipped vehicles. Full details can be obtained from *TravelArctic*.

RESORTS & EXCURSIONS

Most of the province's population and commercial activity is based in Yellowknife and around the Great Slave Lake. In the northern expanse, there are only small settlements of Inuit (Eskimos), living by age-old methods of fishing, hunting and trapping. Inuit peoples and Indians comprise 66% of the Territories' population. **Yellowknife** is a busy town perched on the pre-cambrian shield which adjoins the Great Slave Lake. The town's main industries are government/service industries and, to a certain extent, mining. Two major gold finds were made here in the 1930s. Boats and canoes can be hired for trips on the **Mackenzie River** and the **Great Slave** and **Great Bear Lakes**. These tours often follow old trapping and fur-trading routes. An experienced guide is often essential.
Near the capital are the lakeside Dene and Dogrib (Indian) tribal settlements of **Detah**, **Rae Edzo** and **Snare Lakes**, where a largely traditional way of life is still maintained. **Wood Buffalo National Park**, south of the Great Slave Lake, is home to the world's largest free-roaming bison herd and a noted paradise for naturalists and birdwatchers. Two highways serve the Big River Country to the west and visitors may view this area from the road or fly deep into the interior. In the far southwestern corner of this territory lies **Nahanni National Park**, a UNESCO World Heritage Site in the Mackenzie Mountains. Access to the park itself is by air from **Fort Simpson**, **Fort Liard** or **Watson Lake** as there are no roads in the wilderness area. **South Nahanni River** offers excellent white-water canoeing. Several operators offer boat and raft tours on the river taking in the magnificent 100m-high (312ft) **Virginia Falls** (twice the height of Niagara). The Arctic coastline and islands of the territory have a spectacular landscape of tundra, glaciated mountains and deep fjords. **Baffin Island** has some of the best of the area's rugged beauty; it is most accessible in **Auyuittuq National Park**, a haven for experienced hikers, skiers and climbers with its frozen peaks and glaciers. Much of this rough and forbidding terrain is best visited as part of a package tour or in the company of an outfitter. From **Frobisher**, trips across the tundra with the native Inuit and overnight accommodation in an igloo can be arranged. **Inuvik**, in the far northwest, sits on the majestic **Mackenzie River Delta** and is accessible by road from Dawson in the Yukon. Cruises on the Delta and Inuit settlements such as **Aklavik** are the main attractions.

SOCIAL PROFILE

FOOD & DRINK: Arctic grayling, char and caribou are specialities. Local *bannick* (a mixture of flour and water mixed with dough when required) dates from the old prospecting rations which kept for weeks in an easily transportable form. Other unusual specialities include *mutuk* (whale fat dipped in whale oil). **Drink:** Most alcohol is imported and supplies vary from town to town. Hotels and restaurants in main towns normally have a

good selection, including Canadian whiskies.
SHOPPING: There are over 40 cooperatives in the Territories specialising in handicrafts, furs, fisheries, print shops and retailing. Indian handicrafts and footwear are made locally for sale. The often higher cost of goods (an increase of up to 20% on the rest of Canada) is due to the supply and distribution charges caused by the large distances involved.
SPORT: Fishing on the thousands of clear, unpolluted lakes is the most popular sport. Chief catches are trout, great northern pike and grayling. Numerous outfitters offer inclusive packages often combining boat and air travel to remote regions. **Hunting** for caribou, musk ox and polar bear is available. The many lakes and rivers offer excellent **canoeing** and **rafting.**
SPECIAL EVENTS: Mar 31-Apr 2 '95 *Caribou Carnival*, Yellowknife. **Apr 7-10** *Beluga Jamboree*, Tuktayuktuk. **Apr 22-29** *Toonik Tyme*, Iqualuit. **Jun 16-17** *Canadian North Yellowknife Midnight Classic.* **Jun 23** *Raven Mad Daze*, Yellowknife. **Jul 7-9** *Fort McPherson Music Festival*, Fort McPherson. **Jul 15-16** *Folk on the Rock*, Yellowknife. **Oct 6-9** *Delta Daze*, Inuvik.

BUSINESS PROFILE

COMMERCIAL INFORMATION: The following organisation can offer advice: Atlantic Provinces Chamber of Commerce, Suite 110, 236 St George Street, Moncton, New Brunswick E1C 1W1. Tel: (506) 857 3980. Fax: (506) 859 6131.

CLIMATE

The region experiences a diverse climate. The north has Arctic and sub-Arctic winters whereas the south is more temperate with mild summers and cold winters.

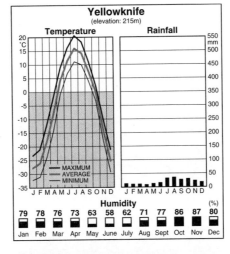

Yellowknife
(elevation: 215m)

Temperature — Rainfall

MAXIMUM / AVERAGE / MINIMUM

Humidity (%)
	Jan	Feb	Mar	Apr	May	June	July	Aug	Sept	Oct	Nov	Dec
	79	78	76	73	63	58	62	71	77	86	87	80

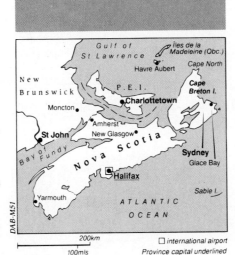

Nova Scotia

Gulf of St Lawrence — Îles de la Madeleine (Qbc.) — Havre Aubert — Cape North — Cape Breton I. — New Brunswick — P.E.I. — Charlottetown — Moncton — Amherst — New Glasgow — Nova Scotia — St John — Bay of Fundy — Sydney — Glace Bay — Halifax — Sable I. — Yarmouth — ATLANTIC OCEAN — DAB-M51

200km / 100mls

□ international airport
Province capital underlined

Location: East coast of Canada.

Tourism Nova Scotia
PO Box 456, World Trade and Convention Centre,

Halifax, Nova Scotia B3J 2R5
Tel: (902) 424 5000 *or* 424 4247. Fax: (902) 424 0629 *or* 424 2668.

AREA: 52,840 sq km (20,402 sq miles).
POPULATION: 889,942 (1991).
POPULATION DENSITY: 16.8 per sq km.
CAPITAL: Halifax. **Population:** 320,501 (1991).
GEOGRAPHY: Nova Scotia comprises the peninsula of Nova Scotia, connected to the mainland by a narrow isthmus, and Cape Breton Island in the northern part of the province, linked by a mile-long causeway. The Atlantic batters the eastern shore. The Bay of Fundy separates the southern part of the peninsula from the mainland, with the Gulf of St Lawrence to the north. The northeast is rural and rocky, while the south and southwest are lush and fertile. Much of the province is covered by rivers. The land rises to 540m (1770ft) on the northeast islands.
LANGUAGE: Although Canada is officially bilingual (English and French), English is more commonly spoken in Nova Scotia.
TIME: GMT - 4 (GMT - 3 in summer).
Note: Daylight Saving Time officially lasts from the first Sunday in April to the Saturday before the last Sunday in October.

PUBLIC HOLIDAYS

Public holidays as for the rest of Canada; see general introduction above.

TRAVEL

AIR: *Air Canada* offers direct flights from London. *Air Canada (AC)*, *Canadian Airlines International (CP)* and *Air Atlantic* fly to Halifax from Ottawa, Montréal and Toronto. *Air Atlantic* also offers local flights between Halifax and Sydney.
International airport: *Halifax (YHZ)*, 42km (26 miles) from the city. Airport facilities include a duty-free shop, car hire, banks and a restaurant.
SEA: There are regular sailings to Nova Scotia from Portland, Maine (USA), New Brunswick, Prince Edward Island and Newfoundland. Several ferries and shipping lines offer local services in and around the province. Enquire locally for further details.
RAIL: *Via Rail* trains run from Montréal to Halifax *(Ocean)* and from Halifax to Montréal *(Atlantic)* via St John three times a week with bus connections to Sydney and Yarmouth.
ROAD: The Trans-Canada Highway enters the province from New Brunswick and ends at North Sydney on the northeast coast. Smaller provincial highways branch off it and circumnavigate the coastline. Ferry services or causeways connect most islands with the mainland. **Car hire:** There are agencies at Halifax and Sydney airports and throughout the province.
URBAN: Comprehensive bus services are provided in the Halifax-Dartmouth area by *Metro Transit,* which operates a zonal fare system. There are connections with the harbour ferry on both sides.

ACCOMMODATION

Nova Scotia offers a wide range of hotels, motels, tourist homes (guest-houses), lodges and campsites. Advance reservations are recommended, especially during the summer. Many establishments are inspected or licensed by the Department of Tourism. Farmhouse holidays are possible and many Nova Scotians provide 'bed and breakfast' for visitors in the tourist season. The following organisation can help with bed & breakfast accommodation in Nova Scotia: Cape Breton Bed & Breakfast Association, c/o Enterprise Cape Breton Corporation, 15 Dorchester Street, Sydney, Nova Scotia B1P 6T7. Tel: (902) 564 3600. Fax: (902) 564 3825.
Grading: Accommodation is graded on a voluntary basis according to the *Atlantic Canada Accommodations Grading Program* as follows:
1-star: Basic, clean, comfortable accommodation.
2-star: Basic, clean, comfortable accommodation with extra amenities.
3-star: Better quality accommodation with a greater range of services.
4-star: High-quality accommodation with extended range of facilities, amenities and guest services.
5-star: Deluxe accommodation with the greatest range of facilities, amenities and guest services.
For more information about accommodation in the province, contact the Tourism Industry Association of Nova Scotia, World Trade and Convention Centre, Suite 402, 1800 Argyle Street, Halifax, Nova Scotia B3J 3N8. Tel: (902) 423 4480. Fax: (902) 422 0184.
CAMPING/CARAVANNING: Much of Nova Scotia is luxurious parkland, and one of the best ways to see the

province is by hiring a motorhome or camper; a number of companies can arrange rentals, with a range of fully equipped vehicles. Full details can be obtained from Nova Scotia Tourism and Culture, which also publishes a comprehensive guide to accommodation in Nova Scotia.

RESORTS & EXCURSIONS

HALIFAX: The provincial capital is also the commercial, administrative and maritime centre for the whole of Atlantic Canada. Situated at the mouth of the *Bedford Basin*, it is one of the finest natural harbours in the world and has a long and distinguished history as a naval and military base. Harbour tours, deep-sea fishing charters and voyages aboard the schooner *Bluenose II* are available. Despite the town's boom over the past 15 years, the historic 'Waterfront Area', comprising important 18th- and 19th-century buildings, has been kept intact. Excellent shopping, nightlife and restaurants are to be found in both the old and new sections of the town. Worth seeing are the *Province House*, a Georgian building praised by Dickens in 1842; *St Pauls*, the oldest Protestant church in Canada; the *Nova Scotia Museum;* the *Maritime Museum of the Atlantic*; and *York Redoubt*, a 200-year-old fort overlooking the harbour. Halifax itself is dominated by the *Citadel*, a star-shaped granite fort, which has defended the city since 1749. A good view of the city and bay can be had from its ramparts.
ELSEWHERE: Touring Nova Scotia is easy. The 560km-long (350-mile) peninsula features a series of interconnecting scenic routes, each one with a different view of a celebrated shore. The *Cabot Trail* is a long loop around the northern highlands of the province and passes through Cape Breton Highlands National Park. The *Lighthouse Route* travels the southern shore where seafaring traditions are especially strong. The *Evangeline Trail* is a rural road that goes through the beautiful Annapolis Valley, known for its orchards, forts and Victorian mansions. The *Sunrise Trail* follows the Northumberland Strait which features 35 sandy beaches and the warmest waters north of the Carolinas.
Dartmouth, across the mouth of the harbour from Halifax, is a modern industrial town. West of Halifax, a coastal road skirts around the fishing villages set in the deep bays and inlets of the southern shore. En route to the ferry port of **Yarmouth** are: **Peggy's Cove**, known for its rugged and beautiful coastal scenery and Canada's most photographed lighthouse; **Mahone Bay**; and **Lunenberg**, a German settlement with a maritime museum housed in two ships. North of **Liverpool** on this route is **Kejumjukic National Park** which offers wilderness trails, canoeing and winter sports.
After Yarmouth the coastal road runs northeast by French-speaking Acadian villages such as **Metaghan** and **Church Point,** which are dotted along the Bay of Fundy. Nearby, **Port Royal** and **Fort Anne** are the sites of some of the earliest French settlements in Canada. **Grand Pré National Park** commemorates the expulsion of 2000 Acadians from Nova Scotia in 1755.
From **Amherst**, the gateway town to the province, a coastal road on the north shore leads to Cape Breton Island (see below) across a mile-long causeway. The north shore displays strong Scottish influences. Street signs in **Pugwash** are in English and Gaelic and highland games are held annually in **Antigonish.**
Cape Breton Island attracts many fishermen and birdwatchers. Some of the island's most spectacular scenery can be found at the **Cape Breton Highlands National Park.** There is superb inland sailing at *Lake Bras D'Or.* **Sydney**, a centre of shipping and industry, is the island's main town. Southeast of this is the **Fortress of Louisburgh,** a restored fort and chateau; once the headquarters of the French Fleet in North America, it was demolished by General Wolfe in 1760. **Baddeck** on Cape Breton Island is home to the *Alexander Graham Bell Museum.* Bell made Baddeck his home in the latter part of his life.

SOCIAL PROFILE

FOOD & DRINK: Seafood features strongly on most menus; popular local dishes include scallops, fried, baked or grilled and usually served with tartar sauce. Fish and clam chowders and *soloman grundy* (a herring dish) are also popular. *Lunenberg sausage* exemplifies the German influence, as do *hugger in buff, fish and scrunchions, Dutch mess* and *house bunkin,* all names for tasty combinations of fish and potatoes covered in cream sauce with onions and salt pork. Desserts make use of plentiful fruit and berries and include a stewed fruit and dumplings dish called *slump* or *fungy,* and baked apple dumplings wrapped in pastry and served with cream, sugar or lemon sauce. **Drink:** Beer and alcoholic beverages are sold by the glass in licensed restaurants (food must also be ordered) and in licensed lounges (opening hours generally 1100-1400). Beer by the bottle and draught beer are sold by the glass in taverns and beverage rooms (opening hours generally 1000-2400), which often offer surprisingly good snacks and light meals. The minimum drinking age is 19.
NIGHTLIFE: Nightclubs are mostly centred on Halifax. Scottish bagpipe music and Gaelic songs can be heard all over the territory in concerts, bars, hotels and restaurants. Professional and amateur theatre is very popular; details of forthcoming attractions are available from Nova Scotia Tourism and Culture.
SPORT: Angling is one of the most popular pastimes with a variety of urban, rural and fly-in lodges available. Summer recreations include **golf, harness racing, tennis, horseriding** and **walking** tours of the acres of parkland covering the province. **Skiing** is available in winter near Halifax. Nova Scotia's boundaries enclose more than 2500 sq km (1000 sq miles) of salt and fresh water, and **watersports** predominate. **Sailing, swimming** and deep-sea **fishing** are all popular.
SPECIAL EVENTS: May 25-29 '95 *Annapolis Valley Apple Blossom Festival,* Kentville. **Jul 14-16** *Antigonish Highland Games*, Antigonish. **Sep 16-17** *International Air Show,* Shearwater.

BUSINESS PROFILE

COMMERCIAL INFORMATION: The following organisation can offer advice: Atlantic Provinces Chamber of Commerce, Suite 110, 236 St George Street, Moncton, New Brunswick E1C 1W1. Tel: (506) 857 3980. Fax: (506) 859 6131.
CONFERENCES/CONVENTIONS: Nova Scotia has a wide range of conference and convention venues. The Halifax Metro Centre arena in downtown Halifax has facilities for 10,000 people. Connected to this is the World Trade and Convention Centre, a striking landmark building made of brick and glass with a sumptuous interior. It has three convention floors, all with excellent catering and audio-visual facilities, and enough room for 2600 people at a stand-up reception or 1700 for a banquet. Certain hotels, such as Chateau Halifax and the Halifax Hilton in Halifax and the Holiday Inn in Dartmouth, also offer good meeting facilities. Also in Dartmouth is another excellent large group facility, the Dartmouth Sportsplex arena. The city of Sydney offers Centre 2000, an arena and convention complex built in celebration of Sydney's bicentennial in 1985, with various flexible meeting rooms for trade shows, receptions and banquets for up to 800. There are also some meeting facilities in more rural settings: The Pines resort, overlooking the Annapolis Basin and the Bay of Fundy; Tales and Trails lodge, placed along the scenic Fleur-de-Lis Trail; Keltic Lodge, overlooking Cape Smoky and the Atlantic Ocean; Liscombe Lodge, tucked into the evergreens where the Liscomb River meets the sea; and Lansdowne Lodge, east of Truro along the Glooscap Trail and near the beautiful Upper Stewiacke Valley. For more information, contact the Canadian Tourist Office *or* Tourism Industry Association of Nova Scotia, World Trade and Convention Centre, Suite 402, 1800 Argyle Street, Halifax, Nova Scotia B3J 3N8. Tel: (902) 423 4480. Fax: (902) 422 0184; *or*
Tourism Halifax, PO Box 1749, Halifax, Nova Scotia B3J 3A5. Tel: (902) 421 8736. Fax: (902) 421 2842.

CLIMATE

Very cold winters and mild summers.
Required clothing: Light- to medium-weights in summer months. Heavyweights in winter. Waterproofing is advisable all year.

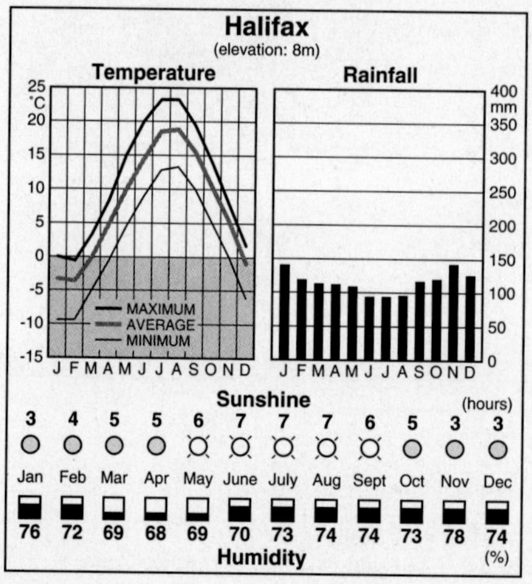
Halifax
(elevation: 8m)
Temperature
Rainfall
MAXIMUM
AVERAGE
MINIMUM
J F M A M J J A S O N D
Sunshine
(hours)
3 4 5 5 6 7 7 7 6 5 3 3
Jan Feb Mar Apr May June July Aug Sept Oct Nov Dec
76 72 69 68 69 70 73 74 74 73 78 74
Humidity
(%)

Ontario

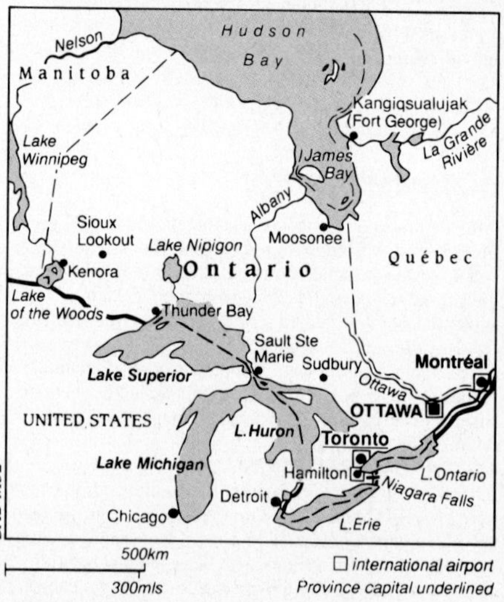
Hudson Bay
Nelson
Manitoba
Kangiqsualujak (Fort George)
La Grande Rivière
Lake Winnipeg
James Bay
Albany
Sioux Lookout
Moosonee
Lake Nipigon
Québec
Kenora
Ontario
Lake of the Woods
Thunder Bay
Sault Ste Marie
Sudbury
Montréal
Lake Superior
Ottawa
OTTAWA
UNITED STATES
L.Huron
Toronto
Lake Michigan
Hamilton
L.Ontario
Niagara Falls
Detroit
Chicago
L.Erie
DAB-M52
500km
300mls
international airport
Province capital underlined

Location: Eastern central Canada.

Ontario Ministry of Tourism and Recreation
9th Floor, 77 Bloor Street West, Toronto, Ontario M7A 2R9.
Tel: (416) 314 7568 *or* 314 0944. Fax: (416) 214 7563.

AREA: 1,068,582 sq km (412,582 sq miles)
POPULATION: 10,097,774 (1991).
POPULATION DENSITY: 9.4 per sq km.
CAPITAL: Toronto (provincial). **Population:** 3,893,046 (1991). Ottawa (federal). **Population:** 920,857 (1991, including Hull).
GEOGRAPHY: Ontario is an eastern-central province bordered by Manitoba and Québec, with a northern coastline on the James Bay and Hudson Bay; it also shares the shores of the Great Lakes with the USA. The two main populated areas, around Toronto and Ottawa, are in the southern spur, and the north remains a landscape of forests and lakes. The province contains the Niagara Falls, one of the most spectacular sights in the world.
LANGUAGE: Although Canada is officially bilingual (English and French), English is more commonly spoken in Ontario.
TIME: East of 90°W: GMT - 5 (GMT - 4 in summer).
West of 90°W: GMT - 5.
Note: Summer officially lasts from the first Sunday in April to the Saturday before the last Sunday in October.

PUBLIC HOLIDAYS

Public holidays as for the rest of Canada (see general section above) with the following date also observed: **Aug 7 '95** Civic Day.

TRAVEL

AIR: International air services are available through *Air Canada* and *Canadian Airlines International* from Toronto and by *Air Canada* from Ottawa. Many other international airlines offer direct services into Toronto. Charter airlines often offer an economical alternative to the scheduled airlines. Local air services are operated by a number of operators, including *Norontair, Bearskin Lake Air Services, Air Ontario* and *Canadian Partner,* as well as by *Air Canada* and *Canadian Airlines International.* These connect all the large towns. For rates and routes contact local offices.
International airports: *Ottawa (YOW)* (Uplands) is 13km (8 miles) southwest of the city (travel time – 25 minutes).
Toronto (YYZ) (Lester B Pearson) is 35km (22 miles) northwest of the city (travel time – 40 minutes).
SEA: The only port on the James Bay with rail links to the south is Moosonee, which is also the base for a limited local air service. The principal ports receiving sailings from the USA are Windsor (to Detroit/Lake St Clair); Sarnia (to Port Huron/St Clair River); Leamington (to Sandusky/Lake Eire); Kingston, Brockville, Cornwall and Ogdensburg (to the USA across the St Lawrence Seaway); and Wolfe Island to New York.

The principal ferry operators in the province are *Toronto Islands Ferries, Pelee Island Transportation Services, Owen Sound Transportation Company* and *Ontario Ministry of Transportation* and local river authorities. For timetables and rates, contact local offices.

RAIL: *Via Rail* connects Toronto to western Canada with services three times a week. Several corridor services connect Toronto, Windsor and Ottawa with Montréal and Québec City in Québec. Links to the USA are with *Via Rail* and *Amtrak*. Services run from Toronto to New York via Niagara Falls, and to Chicago via Windsor and Sarnia. *Via Rail* also serves all the major cities of the province, concentrating in the southern region, which holds most of the population. *Ontario Northland Rail* runs services from Toronto via North Bay to Moosonee on the James Bay. For details, contact local offices.

ROAD: There are several bridges connecting Canadian and US territories, notably at Cornwall, Fort Erie, Sarnia, Windsor, Sault Ste Marie, Fort Frances, Rainy River and Niagara Falls. A tunnel also connects Windsor to Detroit. The domestic highway network is excellent around the Great Lakes, but does not extend to the north of the province. Good trunk roads run throughout. See also under *Camping/Caravanning*. **Bus:** Services linking most towns are operated by *Greyhound Lines, Gray Coach Lines, Canada Coach Lines, Voyageur Colonial, Canada Coach, Ontario Northland, Chatham Coach* and *Go-Transit*. **Car hire:** Facilities are available from all hotels, at *Ottawa* and *Toronto Airports*, and at main railway stations. Drivers must be over 21 years old and the wearing of seatbelts is strictly enforced.

URBAN: Bus, trolleybus, metro and tramway services are provided by the *Toronto Transit Commission*. Flat fares are charged and there are free transfers. Pre-purchase tokens and multi-tickets may be obtained. Services are integrated with those of the regional *Go-Transit* bus and rail system. Bus services in Ottawa, Carleton and surrounding areas are provided by *OC Transpo*. A flat fare operates with a premium on express routes. There are free transfers, and pre-purchase multi-journey tickets and passes are sold. A one-day pass (cost: Can$5 off-peak) is available for use on all forms of transport within the Toronto Metropolitan area.

JOURNEY TIMES: The following chart gives approximate journey times from Toronto (in hours and minutes) to other major cities/towns and tourist destinations in the surrounding area.

	Air	Road	Rail
Niagara Falls	-	1.45	2.00
Ottawa	1.00	5.00	4.00
Windsor	1.10	5.00	4.30
London	0.40	2.30	2.15
Sudbury	1.05	6.00	8.00
Sault Ste Marie	1.25	10.00	-
Thunder Bay	1.45	20.00	-

ACCOMMODATION

Most of the accommodation is in the southern spur of the province where the majority of the population is located.
HOTELS: Hotel costs vary according to class. Both Ottawa and Toronto have international-standard hotels. For further information, contact Ontario Hotel & Motel Association, 2600 Skymark Avenue, Mississauga, Ontario L4W 1V2. Tel: (905) 602 9650. Fax: (905) 672 9654. **Grading:** Accommodation is graded on an entirely voluntary basis by Ontario Tourism, a private non-profitmaking federation of food service, accommodation, recreation and travel associations and businesses. There are over 1000 participating members. (There are also several other associations of a less general nature.) Ontario Tourism grades hotels in Ontario according to a 5-star system as follows:
1-star: Provides basic furnishings and very limited or no facilities, amenities and guest services.
2-star: Provides more furnishings and some facilities, amenities and guest services.
3-star: Provides better quality furnishings and a more extensive range of facilities, amenities and guest services.
4-star: Provides superior quality furnishings and a complete range of facilities, amenities and guest services.
5-star: Provides deluxe accommodation. Marked superiority in extent and quality of facilities, amenities and guest services.
Just over 75% of participating hotels are in the 3- or 4-star category.
BED & BREAKFAST: There are a number of organisations which can help with bed & breakfast accommodation, including the Federation of Ontario Bed & Breakfast Association, PO Box 437, 253 College Street, Toronto, Ontario, M5T 1R5; or Metropolitan Bed and Breakfast Registry of Toronto, Suite 269, 615 Mount Pleasant Road, Toronto, Ontario M4S 3C5. Tel: (416) 964 2566. Fax: (416) 537 0233; or Niagara Region Bed

& Breakfast Service, 4917 River Road, Niagara Falls, Ontario L2E 3G5. Tel: (905) 358 8988.
SELF-CATERING: Furnished cottages are available throughout the region.
CAMPING/CARAVANNING: The best way to explore the wilderness of the north with its lakes and forestry is to hire a **motorhome** or **camper**. A number of companies can arrange rentals of fully equipped vehicles. Full details can be obtained from Ontario Tourism.

RESORTS & EXCURSIONS

OTTAWA: The federal capital is situated on the south bank of the Ottawa River facing the French-speaking city of Hull in Québec. The imposing Gothic-style *Parliament Buildings* overlook the confluence of the Ottawa, Rideau and Gatineau Rivers and are surmounted by the 92m (302ft) *Peace Tower,* affording a panoramic view of the city and its surroundings. Guided tours are available. The colourful *Changing of the Guard* ceremony takes place here daily in July and August. *Confederation Square,* site of the *National War Memorial,* is the focal point of downtown Ottawa. The *National Arts Centre,* a hexagonal complex on the banks of the Rideau Canal, houses an opera company, theatres, studios and restaurants. The *Rideau Canal* and the *Rideau-Trent-Severn Waterway* are part of a complex of recreational lakes and canals linking Ottawa to Lake Ontario and Georgian Bay. Outstanding among the city's many museums are the *National Art Gallery*, the *National Museum of Science and Technology* and the *Museum of Civilisation*.
Gatineau Park, an 88,000-acre wilderness area, is only a 15-minute drive north of Parliament Hill. Southeast of the city, **Upper Canada Village** is a reconstructed 19th-century town consisting of historic buildings salvaged from threatened sites on the St Lawrence Seaway.
TORONTO: The provincial capital is Canada's largest city. Its accelerated growth in recent years, with a huge influx of immigrants, has resulted in one of the most vibrant and cosmopolitan cities on the continent. The city is laid out on a rectangular grid broken only by the *Rivers Don* and *Humber,* the banks of which provide a host of recreational amenities. The *CN Tower,* the world's tallest free-standing structure, has glass-fronted elevators rising 553m (1815ft) to indoor and outdoor observation decks which afford a 120km (75mile) panoramic view on a clear day. The twin gold towers of the *Royal Plaza* make it the most eye-catching of the many avant-garde commercial buildings in the city. Toronto's latest attraction, *SkyDome,* at the foot of the CN Tower, is a multi-purpose entertainment complex and sports stadium – baseball's *World Series* has been played here for the past two years – and is the world's first to have a retractable roof. It is home to the *Toronto Blue Jays* baseball team and the *Argonauts* football team. It hosts a multitude of events including rock concerts, opera, exhibitions, cricket, wrestling and motorshows. Tours of the SkyDome are available. Together with modern developments the city has seen the renovation of old neighbourhoods, particularly the tree-lined streets of Victorian houses characteristic of the city. In the eastern suburbs the spectacular *Ontario Science Centre* and the *Metro Toronto Zoo* are both worth seeing. The *Art Gallery of Ontario* and the *Royal Ontario Museum* are also noteworthy. *Casa Loma,* in the north of the city, was originally the home of Lord and Lady Pellatt. This castle was shipped over from Scotland and rebuilt on this site. It offers fantastic views of downtown Toronto from the landscaped gardens. Ferries to the **Toronto Islands** depart from *Harbourfront,* one of a group of recreational, shopping and arts complexes, including the artificial island of *Ontario Place. Canada's Wonderland* is a huge theme park to the northwest of the city.
Nearby **Niagara Falls** provide a spectacular day's outing from Toronto. **Yonge Street,** reputedly the world's longest street, links Toronto with the vast wilderness of the north and west of the province.
ELSEWHERE: The north shore of Lake Erie is dotted with resorts and good beaches; **St Thomas** and **Port Stanley** are particularly popular. North of this, between *Lakes Erie, Ontario* and *Huron,* are **London** and **Stratford,** home of Canada's annual Shakespeare festival. **Windsor,** a beautifully appointed city at the conjunction of *Lakes Erie* and *St Clair,* is at the heart of Canada's English culture.
Further north, **Midland** commands a spectacular view of the **Georgian Bay Lake District.**
At the eastern end of *Lake Superior,* **Sault Ste Marie** straddles the US border and is an important commercial centre. It is also a good starting point for trips to the northern and western wildernesses. A railway (Algoma) and the Trans-Canada Highway head westwards around the north shore of Lake Superior. The principal attraction here is the **Lake Superior Provincial Park,** a region with many beautiful ravines, lakes and waterfalls but

chiefly famed for the *Agawa Rock Pictographs*. Nearby is the hunting and fishing resort of **White River.**
The Highway continues to **Thunder Bay,** the western terminus of the St Lawrence Seaway and a noted ski resort, boasting the world's largest ski jump. Fantastic canyons and rock formations can be seen between Thunder Bay and **Lake Nipigon**; the lake itself and the town of the same name are popular resorts in the heart of historic Indian country.
The far north and west of the province is a largely uninhabited wilderness of lakes, swamps and forests. The main trans-Canadian railway crosses Ontario at about 50°N; north of that, there are very few roads and only one railway line, which follows the *Moose River* to **Moose Factory,** one of several small settlements on the shores of *James* and *Hudson Bays.*

SOCIAL PROFILE

FOOD & DRINK: Chinese, English, French, Greek, Indian, Italian, Israeli, Scandinavian, Spanish and Latin American restaurants and US-style steak houses can all be found in Toronto and Ottawa at varying prices. Toronto is rated as one of the best cities for dining out on the continent. **Drink:** Bars and restaurants offer an international selection of alcohol. Ontario has extensive vineyards providing much of Canada's wine. Each autumn, the *Niagara Grape and Wine Festival* is held. The minimum drinking age is 19. Alcohol is sold in Provincial Liquor Control Board outlets. Domestic beer is available at Brewer's Retail. Domestic wines are sold through company stores. Licensing hours are from 1200-0100. On Sunday drink is served only with meals.
NIGHTLIFE: Both main cities have establishments offering all forms of entertainment, from quiet clubs featuring a lone pianist, through Latin American combos to dance and rock bands and big-name international entertainers. Toronto is recognised as the third most important theatre centre after London and New York and cabaret/dinner theatres are also especially popular in Toronto. Toronto is also known as a good jazz and blues town. Theatres with classical entertainment are also found in Ottawa.
SHOPPING: Toronto offers everything from antiques to luxury lingerie, if the visitor has the money and time to spend. There are large suburban shopping centres and the *Eaton Centre,* a glass-domed galleria in the heart of the city, is linked to three miles of interconnecting underground shopping with 1000 retail outlets. Toronto's villages are full of colourful streets of renovated Victoriana, with garment shops, art galleries, antique stores and open-air cafés in summer. Yorkville has bath boutiques, expensive toy shops and secondhand and new women's clothes shops. The run-down Queen Street Strip has been taken over by collector's comic-book shops, punk day-glo leather emporiums, sci-fi bookstores, junk and antique shops. Ottawa also has a wide choice of shops and handicraft centres.
SPORT: Toronto has a professional **baseball** team. Both Toronto and Ottawa have professional **hockey** and **football** teams. Toronto offers **horse-racing** at Greenwood and Woodbine racetracks, **golf** courses, **tennis** courts, **swimming** in pools and in Lake Ontario, **boating,** and cross-country **skiing, riding, cycling** routes and **fishing**. Ottawa offers **boating, cycling,** winter downhill and cross-country **skiing, golf** courses, **tennis** courts and two racetracks.

SPECIAL EVENTS: Apr-Oct '95 *Shaw Festival,* Niagara-on-the-Lake. **Apr 15** *Supercross,* Toronto. **Apr 28-May 14** *Spring Festival,* Guelph. **Jun 2-4** *International Air Show,* London. **Jun 18-19** *Hamilton International Air Show,* Hamilton. **Jun 16-25** *Franco Festival des Francophone Monde,* Ottawa. **Jun 22-Jul 5** *International Freedom Festival,* Windsor. **Jun 23-Jul 2** *Du Maurier Ltd. Downtown Jazz,* Toronto. **Jun 23-Jul 11** *Benson & Hedges Symphony of Fire,* Don Mills. **Jun 23-Aug 27** *Changing of the Guards,* Ottawa. **Jun 29-Sep 1** *Muskoko Festival Theatre,* Gravenhurst. **Jul 7-9** *Northern Lights Festival Boreal,* Sudbury. **Jul 18-Aug 1** *Caribana,* Toronto. **Aug 4-5** *Glengarry Highland Games,* Maxville. **Aug 5-7** *Festival of Friends,* Hamilton. **Aug 11-12** *Canadian Championship Old Time Fiddler,* Shelburne. **Aug 18-20** *Sarnia Highland Games,* Sarnia. **Sep 2-4** *Canadian National Airshow,* Toronto. **Sep 7-16** *Toronto International Film Festival,* Toronto. **Sep 8-17** *Festival of Festivals,* Toronto; *Western Fair,* London. **Sep 15-24** *Niagara Grape and Wine Festival,* St Catherines. **Sep 20-24** *Cinefest,* Sudbury. **Sep 21-24** *Applefest,* Brighton. **Oct 6-14** *Oktoberfest,* Kitchener/Waterloo. **Nov 7-18** *Royal Agricultural Winter Fair,* Toronto. **Nov 18-Jan 13 '96** *Winter Festival of Lights,* Niagara Falls. **Nov 23-26 '95** *Winter Festival of Friends,* Hamilton. **Dec 8-9** *Dickens Victorian Christmas,* Cobourg. **Dec 8-10** *Earthsong,* Hamilton.

BUSINESS PROFILE

COMMERCIAL INFORMATION: The following organisation can offer advice: Ontario Chamber of Commerce, Suite 808, 2345 Yonge Street, Toronto, Ontario M4P 2E5. Tel: (416) 482 5222.

CONFERENCES/CONVENTIONS: Ontario offers a wide range of conference venues. Ottawa usually hosts between 35-40 major international conferences per year. Some of the organisations which have met in Ottawa recently include Interpol, International Standards Organisation, Human Life International, Lions Club International and the World Tourism Conference. The following organisations can provide assistance and information:

For conferences in Toronto: Metropolitan Toronto Convention & Visitors Association, PO Box 126, Suite 590, Queen's Quai Terminal at Harbourfront, 207 Queen's Quay West, Toronto, Ontario M5J 1A7. Tel: (416) 203 2600. Fax: (416) 867 3995; *or* Metropolitan Toronto Convention & Visitors Association, 375 Upper Richmond Road West, London SW14 7NX. Tel: (0181) 876 2946. Fax: (0181) 392 1318.

For conferences in Niagara Falls: Niagara Falls Visitor & Convention Bureau, 5433 Victoria Avenue, Niagara Falls, Ontario L2G 3L1. Tel: (905) 356 6061. Fax: (905) 356 5567.

For conferences in Hamilton: Greater Hamilton Tourism & Convention Services, 3rd Floor, 1 James Street South, Hamilton, Ontario L8P 4R5. Tel: (905) 546 4222. Fax: (905) 546 4107.

For conferences in Ottawa: Ottawa Tourism and Convention Authority, 2nd Floor, 111 Lisgar Street, Ottawa, Ontario K2P 2L7. Tel: (613) 237 5158 (tourism information) *or* 237 5150 (administration). Fax: (613) 237 7339.

CLIMATE

Summers can be very warm, while spring and autumn are cooler. Winters are cold with snowfall.

Required clothing: Light- to medium-weights during warmer months, heavyweights in winter. Waterproofing is advisable throughout the year.

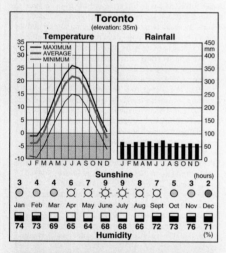

Location: East coast of Canada.

Tourism Prince Edward Island

PO Box 940, Charlottetown, Prince Edward Island C1A 7M5
Tel: (902) 368 4444. Fax: (902) 368 4438.

AREA: 5660 sq km (2185 sq miles).
POPULATION: 129,765 (1991).
POPULATION DENSITY: 23 per sq km.
CAPITAL: Charlottetown. **Population:** 15,776 (1989).
GEOGRAPHY: Prince Edward Island is a crescent-shaped island in the Gulf of the St Lawrence comprising red farm fields, northern evergreen forests, and white sand beaches. It is 224km (139 miles) long and between 6km (4 miles) and 65km (40 miles) wide.
LANGUAGE: English and some French are spoken in the province.
TIME: GMT - 4 (GMT - 3 in summer).
Note: Daylight Saving Time officially lasts from the first Sunday in April to the Saturday before the last Sunday in October.

PUBLIC HOLIDAYS

Public holidays as for the rest of Canada; see general introduction above.

TRAVEL

AIR: *Charlottetown (YYG)* airport is 3km (2 miles) from the city. *Air Atlantic* and *Air Nova* fly in here. There are no local flights within Prince Edward Island.
SEA: *Northumberland Ferries* sail from Wood Islands on the southeast coast to Caribou in Nova Scotia from late April to mid-December (travel time – 75 minutes). Advance reservations are not accepted. *Marine Atlantic* sails from Borden on the south coast to Cape Tormentine in New Brunswick all year round (travel time – 45 minutes). Advance reservations are not accepted (tel: (902) 566 7059 for further information). *CTMA Ferry* sails to Souris on the east coast from the Magdalen Islands in Québec from early April to the end of January (travel time – 5 hours). Advance reservations are recommended during the summer schedule from mid-June to early September (tel: (902) 687 2181 (travel information) *or* (418) 986 3278 (reservations)).
RAIL: There are no passenger services on the Island.
ROAD: There are three scenic drives following the coast of the Island: Lady Slipper Drive (west), Blue Heron Drive (central) and King's Byway (east). Seatbelts for adults and children are mandatory on Prince Edward Island.

ACCOMMODATION

HOTELS: Prince Edward Island offers a wide range of quality accommodation, from conventional hotels to tourist homes, lodges and family farms. Most of the towns have excellent hotels and one is never far from the sea.
BED & BREAKFAST: The *Bed and Breakfast and Country Inns Association* oversees standards of 'Farm Vacations'. For further information, contact Bed & Breakfast, Visitor Services, PO Box 940, Charlottetown, Prince Edward Island C1A 7M5. Tel: (902) 368 4444. Fax: (902) 368 4438. Cottages and apartments can also be rented.
Grading: In 1993, owners of accommodations in Prince Edward Island were invited to participate in the Canada Select Rating Program. This programme is considered to be more stringent than last year's Atlantic Canada Grading Program, so some ratings may have changed. Even some operators who improved their amenities over last year may have received a lower grade under the new national system. Participation in the grading system is voluntary. For further information, contact Canada Select Rating Program, Tourism Industry Association of Prince Edward Island, PO Box 2050, Charlottetown, Prince Edward Island C1A 7N7. Tel: (902) 566 5008. Fax: (902) 368 3605. The new star ratings are based on the extent of facilities, quality of facilities, extent of services and amenities.
1 star – Basic, clean, comfortable accommodation.
2 stars – Basic, clean and comfortable with some amenities.
3 stars – Better quality accommodation; greater range of facilities and services.
4 stars – High-quality accommodation; extended range of facilities, amenities and guest services.
CAMPING/CARAVANNING: There are over 65 travel parks for camping near sandy beaches or in the interior. Camping fees vary, depending on the facilities offered. Most private sites accept reservations but the National Park does not. For rates, reservations and other information on provincial parks, contact Department of Economic Development & Tourism, Parks and Recreation, R.R. 1, Belmont, Colchester City, Prince

Edward Island C1A 7N8 (tel: (902) 368 5540; fax: (902) 368 5737). For rates and information on the National Parks, contact Environment Canada, Canadian Parks Service, PO Box 487, Charlottetown, Prince Edward Island C1A 7L1. For general information, telephone Parks Canada on (902) 566 7050. A number of companies can arrange **motor camper** rentals, with a range of fully-equipped vehicles. Full details can be obtained from the Visitor Services Division.

RESORTS & EXCURSIONS

Charlottetown, the provincial capital, is a well-planned colonial seaport with tree-lined streets and rows of woodframe houses. Main places of interest are *Province House*, a fine Georgian building of Nova Scotia sandstone, the site of the 1864 discussions which led to the Canadian Confederation; and the *Confederation Centre of the Arts,* which houses art galleries, theatres, a restaurant and a museum.

A tourist route known as the *Blue Heron Drive* heads westwards from Charlottetown to **Fort Amherst,** the original French settlement on the Island, and on to **Prince Edward Island National Park,** 45km (25 miles) of fine white-sand beaches and red sandstone capes on the north coast. *Green Gables House*, the farmhouse immortalised in the book *Anne of Green Gables* by Lucy Maud Montgomery, is now a museum in **Cavendish,** located within the park. Further along the route, through **Stanley Bridge** where there is a large marine aquarium, is **New London,** where the author was born and wrote and there is now a museum in the house where she lived. **Dunstaffnage,** halfway between Charlottetown and Prince Edward Island National Park has a car museum worth visiting.

A second tourist route, the *Lady Slipper Drive,* circles Prince County, home to most of the province's French-speaking residents. The route passes through **Miscouche,** which has an *Acadian Museum,* and **Mont Carmel,** which has an *Acadian Pioneer Village.* **West Point,** on the western tip of Prince Edward Island, has *Cedar Dunes Provincial Park,* with a century-old wooden lighthouse and a connecting complex housing a museum, restaurant, handicraft shop and guest-rooms.

A third route, the *King's Byway,* traverses the hilly tobacco-growing region of the eastern interior. It passes through **Souris,** where ferries depart regularly for the Québecois **Isles de la Madeleine;** and **North Lake,** where boats can be chartered for what is claimed to be some of the best tuna-fishing in the world. Seal-watching tours have become very popular in the King's Byway region. **Point Prim,** located on a long promontory in the southeast of the Island, has the oldest lighthouse on the Island, built in 1846 and still in use. In the interior of the Island, accessible by this route, is **Milltown Cross,** offering the *Buffaloland Provincial Park,* home of bison and white-tailed deer, and the *Harvey Moore Migratory Bird Sanctuary,* home to many varieties of duck and geese.

SOCIAL PROFILE

FOOD & DRINK: Shellfish, lobster in particular, is a mainstay of the dinner table. Lobsters are steamed or boiled and included in casseroles and salads. Lobster suppers are a tradition on Prince Edward Island and they are often held in church basements or community halls where fresh lobster is served, along with home-made chowder, rolls, cakes and pies. Seconds are available of everything except lobster. Oysters are also popular; they may be served with tangy sauce, deep-fried, in pies, scalloped, in soufflés, soups and stews. Prince Edward Island is famous for its new potatoes – small, round early potatoes – and a favourite with locals is the new potatoes boiled with their skins, then mashed and served with lots of butter, salt and pepper. The Island offers plenty of plain, wholesome, home-cooked food in restaurants. Service is informal and friendly. There are also many seafood outlets where fresh fish and shellfish can be bought in season and taken away for cooking on barbecues or campfires. Waiters expect a 10-15% tip. **Drink:** Most dining rooms are licensed to sell alcohol. Licensed premises are open until 0200 from May to October. Off-licences (liquor stores) are open six days a week from 1000-2200. Only persons over 19 years may buy alcohol.
NIGHTLIFE: Lounges on the Island usually have some live entertainment during part or all of the week. Theatres, located mainly in Charlottetown, Victoria, Georgetown, Mont Carmel and Summerside, offer cultural, musical or light entertainment.
SHOPPING: The Island's crafts include highly original pottery, weaving, leatherwork, woodwork, quilting,

---

Toronto
(elevation: 35m)

Temperature	Rainfall
MAXIMUM	
AVERAGE	
MINIMUM	

J F M A M J J A S O N D

Sunshine (hours)

Jan	Feb	Mar	Apr	May	June	July	Aug	Sept	Oct	Nov	Dec
3	4	4	6	7	9	9	8	7	5	3	2
74	73	69	65	64	68	68	66	72	73	76	71

Humidity (%)

Prince Edward Island

Province capital underlined
100km / 50mls

hand-painted silk and jewellery. Various guilds preserve the standards of production. There are also several antique dealers, secondhand stores, auctions, yard sales and flea markets. Main shopping centres can be found in Charlottetown, Summerside, Montague and Cavendish.
Shopping hours: 0900-1700 Monday to Thursday and Saturday; 0900-2100 Friday.
SPORT: Deep-sea **fishing** is the principal sport. A record catch of bluefin tuna caught by rod and reel was landed in 1978 weighing 572kg (1021lbs). **Harness racing** is popular, and there are also opportunities for **hiking, horseriding, canoeing, diving, sailing, windsurfing** and **water-skiing**. There are excellent facilities for both **skiing** and **golfing** in some of the area's Provincial Parks, such as Mill River in Woodstock and Brudenell River in Georgetown. Brookvale Provincial Ski Park has the most outstanding facilities for cross-country skiing and was host to the 1991 Canada Winter Games. **Swimming** is also featured in most Provincial Parks, where many of the Island's finest beaches can be found.
SPECIAL EVENTS: Jul 16-22 '95 *Lobster Festival,* Summerside. **Aug 11** *Gold Cup Parade,* Charlottetown. **Aug 16-23** *Community Harvest Festival,* Kensington.

BUSINESS PROFILE

COMMERCIAL INFORMATION: The following organisation can offer advice: Atlantic Provinces Chamber of Commerce, Suite 110, 236 St George Street, Moncton, New Brunswick E1C 1W1. Tel: (506) 857 3980. Fax: (506) 859 6131.
CONFERENCES/CONVENTIONS: For information on conferences and conventions on Prince Edward Island, contact the Canadian Tourist Office *or* Prince Edward Island Convention Bureau, 36 Pownal Street, Charlottetown, Prince Edward Island C1A 3V6. Tel: (902) 368 3688. Fax: (902) 368 3108.

CLIMATE

Temperate climate with cold winters and warm summers.
Required clothing: Light- to medium-weights in warmer months, heavyweights in winter. Waterproof wear is advisable all year.

Québec

500km
300mls
□ *international airport*
Province capital underlined

Location: Eastern Canada.

Maison du Tourisme de Québec
12 Ste Anne Street (in front of the Chateau Frontenac), Québec City, Québec
Maison du Tourisme de Montréal
PO Box 979, Centre Infotouriste 1001, Square Dorchester, Montréal, Québec H3C 2W3
Tel: (514) 873 2015 *or* (0800) 363 7777 (USA and Canada). Fax: (514) 864 3838.

Québec Tourism
59 Pall Mall, London SW1Y 5JH
Tel: (0171) 930 8314 *or* 930 9742 (24-hour brochures request line). Fax: (0171) 930 7938. Opening hours: 0900-1700 Monday to Friday.
Québec Tourism
Rockefeller Center, 26th Floor, 17 West 50th Street, New York, NY 10020-2201
Tel: (212) 397 0200. Fax: (212) 757 4753. Telex: 12-6405.

AREA: 1,667,926 sq km (643,990 sq miles).
POPULATION: 6,898,963 (1991).
POPULATION DENSITY: 4.1 per sq km.
CAPITAL: Québec City. **Population:** 645,550 (1991).
GEOGRAPHY: The Province of Québec is in the east of Canada, with coasts on the North Atlantic and Hudson and James Bays; the St Lawrence Seaway, the major shipping channel of the Canadian east coast, cuts through the populous south; the cities of Québec and Montréal (Canada's second largest) stand beside it. In the north, the Laurentians resort area has snow-covered mountains in winter and scenic lakes. The far north is a spread of forest and lakes forming one of the largest areas of wilderness in Canada.
LANGUAGE: French is the official language and 82% of the population speak it as a first language; 35% can speak English.
TIME: GMT - 5 (GMT - 4 in summer).
Note: Daylight Saving Time lasts officially from the first Sunday in April to the Saturday before the last Sunday in October.

PUBLIC HOLIDAYS

Public holidays are as for the rest of Canada (except the first Monday in August – see general section above) with the following date also observed:
Jun 24 '95 Saint Jean Baptiste.

TRAVEL

AIR: *Air Canada* and other international carriers fly into Montréal. Commuter services between Montréal and Toronto, Québec City and New York also exist. The airlines offering domestic services from Montréal and Québec City to other Canadian business centres are *Air Canada* and *Canadian Airlines International.* Local air services are operated between the cities in the south and float planes serve the lakes and parkland of the north. The main airlines are *Air Alliance, Air Alma, Air Atlantic, Air Canada, Air Creebec, Air Inuit, Air Nova, Air Ontario, American Airlines, Business Express, Canadian International, Delta Airlines, First Air, Inter-Canadian, Northwest Airlines, Canadian Regional, Skycraft* and *US Air.*
International airports: Montréal has two international airports, *Mirabel (YMX)* and *Dorval (YUL).*
Mirabel lies 55km (34 miles) northwest of Montréal and offers the majority of international services from Europe and Asia. *Dorval,* 22km (15 miles) west of Montréal is primarily a domestic airport, but several trans-border US services are operated daily. A regular shuttle service connects the two airports. Buses leaves *Dorval* every 20 minutes and *Mirabel* every 30 minutes to Montréal and its major hotels. Taxi and limousine services are also available for a fixed flat fee.
SEA: Québec City and Montréal are the most important Canadian ports on the St Lawrence Seaway, which links the Atlantic Ocean with the Great Lakes and the industrial heartland of Canada and the USA. Several international passenger carriers sail to both ports; European carriers dock only at Montréal. Most of the province's lakes and rivers are served by local ferries, some of which are able to take heavy lorries. For schedules and fares contact the local shipper.
RAIL: *Via Rail* connects Montréal and Québec City to Toronto with fast regular services. It also features services to Halifax from Montréal and Québec City. Links to the USA are with *Via Rail* and *Amtrak. Via Rail* connects all major provincial towns, and *Amtrak* operates two daily trains to the USA. *Via Rail* services also connect the major cities in the south of the province, with thrice-daily mainline services from Montréal to Québec.
ROAD: The best way of travelling into and around Québec by road is by long-distance coach, especially *Orleans Express.* The services in the southern region are especially frequent. **Motorhomes** and **campers** are best for seeing the northern parklands, and the area is connected to the south by several good highways, although the most extensive network is around the populous areas in the south.
URBAN: Bus and metro services are provided in Montréal at flat fares with free transfers between metro

and bus obtainable from machines. Passes and multi-ticket books are sold and metro fares are the lowest in North America. Québec's bus services operate on a flat-fare system. No change is carried on board. Pre-purchase passes are available. There are good bus services in other towns.

ACCOMMODATION

HOTELS: The majority of the population live in the south of the province, where all the large cities offer a large choice of hotel accommodation. Some of the best hotels in the country are in Montréal and Québec City. Outside the cities, accommodation takes on a more rural flavour; lakeside lodges and cabins are very popular. Accommodation is often possible in private homes. For further information on hotels in Québec, contact the Association des Hoteliers de la Province de Québec, Suite 004, 425 Sherbrooke Street West, Montréal, Québec H2L 1J9. Tel: (514) 282 5135. Fax: (514) 849 1157.
BED & BREAKFAST: There are a number of organisations in Québec that provide information regarding bed & breakfast accommodation, including Québec Bed & Breakfast, 3729 avenue Le Corbusier, Ste-Foy, Québec City, Québec G1W 4P5. Tel: (418) 651 1860; *or* Montréal Bed & Breakfast, PO Box 575, Montréal, Québec H3X 3T8. Tel: (514) 738 9410. Fax: (514) 735 7493; *or* the Fédération des Agricotours du Québec, 4545 avenue Pierre de Coubertin, PO Box 1000, Succ. M., Montréal H1V 3R2. Tel: (514) 252 3138.
CAMPING/CARAVANNING: Northern Québec is a vast area of forest and lakes and one of the best areas for wilderness camping in Canada. A number of companies can arrange **motor camper** rentals, with a range of fully equipped vehicles. Full details can be obtained from the Fédération québecoise de camping et de caravaning, 4545 avenue Pierre de Coubertin, PO Box 1000, Succ. M. Montréal H1V 3R2. Tel: (514) 252 3003; *or* Tourisme Québec.

RESORTS & EXCURSIONS

Outside the major centres of population in the southeast, Canada's largest province consists of hilly agricultural land along the banks of the **St Lawrence** and vast tracks of barren mountains in the north. The one-hour drive along the St Lawrence from Québec to the outskirts of **Charlevoix** is along a breathtaking route of towering rock faces, looming canyons and craggy fjords. More than 100,000 lakes provide excellent fishing (chiefly for trout and salmon) whilst in the northern tundra of *Nouveau Québec,* caribou and other game are hunted. La Fédération des pourvoyeurs du Québec Inc (tel: (418) 527 5191; fax (418) 527 8326) can give information on itineraries, equipment, transport and accommodation in this region.
MONTREAL: Canada's second-largest city, on a 43km-long (27-mile) island, is a sophisticated cosmopolitan metropolis with an 65% francophone population. Careful central planning for Expo '67 and the 1976 Olympic Games have produced a spacious and beautiful modern city. A series of underground shopping and recreation complexes, linked by walkways and metro, is centred on *Place de Ville Marie.* The *Place des Arts* is the home of the Montréal Symphony Orchestra and several theatres offering year-round drama, music, ballet and opera. Both the *Montréal Museum of Fine Arts* and the *Museum of Contemporary Arts* have good collections. *Vieux Montréal,* the historic waterfront section, has been carefully restored. Main places of note here are: *Place Jacques Cartier,* the former French governor's residence; *Chateau Ramzay;* and the city's oldest church, *Notre Dame de Bonsecour. Mont Royal Park* is the city's highest point, offering an excellent vista from the centre of Montréal. Behind-the-scenes tours of the *Olympic Park,* site of the '76 games, are available. The area around *Rue Crescent* is renowned for its many jazz cafés and small restaurants.
QUÉBEC CITY: With its old city walls, the characteristic green copper roofs and fortified *Citadel,* the provincial capital is one of the most European cities in North America; indeed, in 1985, UNESCO declared it a *World Heritage Treasure.* It is the cradle of French culture in Canada with a 95% French-speaking population. The city is split into two levels, connected by stone stairways and a municipal lift. Surrounded by the old city walls is the 'Upper Town' with some fine 18th-and 19th-century architecture, notably the *Place D'Armes* and the *Chateau Frontenac.* The latter is a first-class hotel. In front of the Chateau Frontenac is a wide promenade with 310 wooden steps leading up to the Citadel from where there are incredible views across the St Lawrence River. Small street cafés, cobblestoned streets and shaded squares emphasise the European air of the 'Upper Town'. In the 'Lower Town', the network of 17th-century streets centred on *Place Royale* has recently

been restored.

ELSEWHERE: Ste Agathe des Monts, 100km (60 miles) north of Montréal, is the hub of a resort area providing some of the best skiing in North America. Further north, the **Mont Tremblant Park** provides boating, hunting and camping as well as winter sports. Northwest of this is **La Verendrye National Park**, a protected lakeland wilderness; and further on, the mining territory centred on **Rouyn-Noranda**.

L'Ile d'Orléans, east of Québec City, is a region of picturesque Québecois villages. In front of the Ile d'Orléans are the *Montmorency Falls* and further east the *Shrine of Ste Anne de Beaupré* and **Mont Ste Anne** The latter is the main ski resort in the famous **Laurentians** (or Laurentides) skiing region, which is also a provincial park.

Heading northeast from Québec along the southern bank of the St Lawrence, the main route leads first through the farming region of **Bas Saint Laurent** and thence to the **Gaspé Peninsula**. The major attraction here is the *Rocher Percé* in the **Gaspé National Park.**

Across the mouth of the river is the **Duplessis Peninsula**, site of some of the earliest landfalls in the New World. Remains left by these Viking sailors can be seen in the museum at **Sept-Iles**, the largest city in the area. The bizarre geological formations of the nearby **Mingan Archipelago** are best explored by boat.

The **Iles de la Madeleine**, 290km (180 miles) east of Gaspé in the Gulf of St Lawrence, offer miles of white sandy beaches and a host of unspoilt fishing villages.

SOCIAL PROFILE

FOOD & DRINK: Québec proudly reflects a tradition of French culture, never more so than in the restaurants and cuisine of the province. French food here is as excellent as anywhere in Europe. Immigrants from many countries, however, provide a vast selection. Italian, Greek, Japanese, Spanish and English cuisine are all available in Montréal and Québec. International menus are found at all the larger hotels, but the best food is found by wandering around the small backstreets of the cities and sampling the small but excellent restaurants scattered throughout both cities. Specialist dishes include *ragout de boulettes* (pork meatballs with seasoning) and *cretons du Québec* (chilled minced pork). The Ile d'Orleans is an island northeast of Québec City that provides abundant fruit and vegetables for the city. **Drink:** Québec follows French tradition in having excellent standards of wine and spirits to complement the high standard of cuisine. Some spirits and the rarer wines are imported from Europe. Taverns and brasseries serve alcoholic beverages from 0800-0300 every day. Cocktail lounges and cabarets stay open until 0200 and 0300 respectively in Montréal. The minimum drinking age is 18.

NIGHTLIFE: Québec City and Montréal offer some of the best nightclubs and cabarets to be found anywhere in Canada. In Montréal the action seldom begins before 2200 and usually continues until 0300 the next morning. Nightlife is concentrated in the western part of the downtown area along Crescent and Bishop Streets and around Ste-Catherine Street, where there are many bars, restaurants and clubs of all kinds. For a particularly French flavour, try the many clubs, bars, restaurants, cafés and bistros further east around St Denis and St Laurent.

SHOPPING: Québec City and Montréal have excellent shopping facilities, both in large department stores and small street markets. Specialities include furs, Indian crafts, *haute couture*, antiques, specialist fashion boutiques and discount retail outlets. **Shopping hours:** 0900-2100 Monday to Saturday. Most shops are open on Sunday.

SPORT: Sport in Québec is of an international standard, as illustrated by Montreal's hosting of the Olympic Games in 1976. Québec City and Montréal are both on the banks of the St Lawrence River and **watersports** facilities are extensive, especially **sailing, swimming** and **water-skiing**. International downhill **skiing** competitions are held to the north of Montréal at Mont Tremblant and at Mont Sainte-Anne, east of Québec City. Winter sports in general culminate with the Québec Winter Carnival in February of each year, drawing entries from all over North America. **Ice hockey:** Both Québec and Montréal have professional ice hockey teams. Montréal also has professional **baseball** and **football** (soccer) teams.

SPECIAL EVENTS: End May to End Jul '95
Benson & Hedges International Fireworks Competition, Montréal. **Jun 8-18** *International Festival of New Cinema and Video*, Montréal. **Jun 9-11** *Molson Canada Grand Prix*, Montréal. **Jun 23-25** *Mountain Bike World Cup*, Mont Ste Anne. **Jun 23-Jul 1** *Matane Shrimp Festival*, Matane. **Jun 29-Jul 9** *Jazz Festival*, Montréal. **Jul 6-16** *International Summer Festival*, Québec City. **Jul 7-16** *World Folklore Festival*, Drummondville and Québec City.

Jul 14-23 *Traversee International du Lac Memphremagog*, Magon. **Jul 20-30** *Just for Laughs Festival*, Montréal. **Aug 9-13** *Les Médiévales de Québec*. **Aug 12-20** *St-Jean Hot Air Balloon Festival*, St-Jean-sur-Richelieu. **Aug 24-Sep 4** *World Film Festival*, Montréal. **Sep 1-4** *Gatineau Hot Air Balloon Festival*, Gatineau. **Sep 17** *Montréal Island Marathon.*

BUSINESS PROFILE

COMMERCIAL INFORMATION: The following organisation can offer advice: Montréal Chamber of Commerce, Plaza Level, 5 Place Ville Marie, Montréal, Québec H3B 4Y2. Tel: (514) 871 4000 *or* 844 9571 *or* 288 9090.

CONFERENCES/CONVENTIONS: Montréal is a major meeting and convention centre and an extensive information booklet is available from the Greater Montréal Convention & Tourism Bureau, Suite 600, 1555 Peel Street, Montréal, Québec H3A 1X6. Tel: (514) 844 5400. Fax: (514) 844 5757.

For information about conferences and conventions in Québec City contact Québec Tourism *or* Greater Québec Area Tourism & Convention Bureau, Second Floor, 399 St Joseph Street East, Québec City, Québec G1K 8E2. Tel: (418) 692 2471 *or* 522 3511. Fax: (418) 529 3121.

CLIMATE

Summer months (June to August) are hot with cooler evenings. Autumn and Spring are cooler and winters are very cold and snowy.

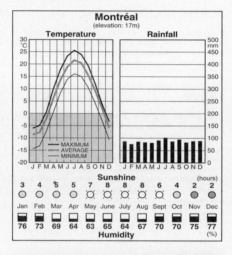

Montréal (elevation: 17m)

Saskatchewan

Location: Central Canada.

Tourism Saskatchewan
Saskatchewan Trade & Convention Centre, 500-1919 Saskatchewan Drive, Regina, Saskatchewan S4P 4L9 Tel: (306) 787 2300. Fax: (306) 787 5744.
Tourism Saskatoon
PO Box 369, 6-305 Idylwyld Drive North, Saskatoon, Saskatchewan S7K 3L3 Tel: (306) 242 1206. Fax: (306) 242 1955.
Also deals with convention enquiries.

AREA: 651,900 sq km (251,700 sq miles).
POPULATION: 1,016,944 (1992).
POPULATION DENSITY: 1.8 per sq km.
CAPITAL: Regina. **Population:** 177,577 (1991).
GEOGRAPHY: Saskatchewan is bordered by Manitoba to the east, the Northwest Territories to the north, Alberta to the west and the US States of North Dakota and Montana to the south. Its landscape is mainly prairie, parkland, forests and lakes. Prince Albert National Park is the gateway to Saskatchewan's wilderness. The highest elevation is the Cypress Hills in the southwest, 1392m (4566ft) above sea level.
LANGUAGE: Although Canada is officially bilingual (English and French), English is more commonly spoken in Saskatchewan.
TIME: East of 106°W: GMT - 6.
Note: Most of Saskatchewan does not observe Daylight Saving Time in summer.

PUBLIC HOLIDAYS

Public holidays are as for the rest of Canada (see general section above) with the following date also observed: **Aug 7 '95** Civic Day.

TRAVEL

AIR: *Air Canada* (national airline), *Canadian Airlines* (national airline) and *Time Air* (international/regional airline) provides daily scheduled service connecting Saskatoon and Regina to the rest of the world. The principal regional services are operated by *Time Air*, *Athabasca Airways* and *Prairie Flying Service*, connecting major Canadian centres as well as serving the northern communities.
International airports: *Saskatoon (YXE)* is 8km (4.5 miles) from the city (travel time – 15 minutes). Airport facilities include left luggage, car hire, car parking and restaurant (0700-2300).
Regina is 5km (3 miles) from the city.
RIVER: Saskatchewan has no coastline. Ferry services on the Saskatchewan River connect the province to Manitoba and Alberta; ferries also link it with Manitoba on the Churchill River. Houseboats may be chartered.
RAIL: *Via Rail*, Canada's national passenger train service, operates the Winnipeg–Saskatoon–Edmonton link.
ROAD: Saskatchewan has six travel corridors, namely the Northern Woods and Water Route (9 and 55) east–west, Yellowhead Highway (16) east–west, the Trans-Canada Highway (1) east–west, Red Coat Trail (13) east–west, CanAm International Highway north–south and the Saskota International Highway (9) north–south. Saskatchewan has more road surface than any other province in Canada – a total of 250,000km (150,000 miles). **Bus:** Scheduled motorcoach service is provided by *Saskatchewan Transportation Company*, *Greyhound Bus Lines* and *Moose Mountain Bus Lines*. Charter motorcoach services are also available from a number of cities and operators. **Car hire:** Car rentals are available in most Saskatchewan cities. Saskatchewan law requires that anyone driving or riding in a motor vehicle must wear available seatbelts at all times.

ACCOMMODATION

The majority of accommodation suitable for travellers is found in the south of the province, especially in Regina, Saskatoon, Moose Jaw and Weyburn. The parklands in the northern part of the province have mainly camping-style accommodation. 'Houseboat charters' on the lakes are a special feature of Saskatchewan. For further information on hotels in Saskatchewan, contact the Hotel Association of Saskatchewan, 1054 Winnipeg Street, Regina, Saskatchewan S4R 8P8. Tel: (306) 522 1664. Fax: (306) 525 1944. The *Saskatchewan Accommodation Guide* is available through Tourism Saskatchewan and is a comprehensive directory of hotels/motels, parks, campgrounds, lakeside accommodations and vacation farms that are available throughout the province.
Grading: Tourism Saskatchewan's annual guide uses the following definitions when describing

accommodation:

Mod: Modern room. Includes private bathroom facilities with wash basin, bathtub and/or shower and flush toilet.

Smod: Semi-modern room. Includes wash basin only and a pressurized hot and cold water supply.

Nmod: Non-modern room. Has no plumbing facilities.

Lhk: Light housekeeping unit. Includes kitchen facilities as well as living and sleeping quarters.

CAMPING/CARAVANNING: The parklands offer some of the best camping landscapes in Canada. There are 17 parks, all offering different rates of service and accommodation for those without mobile homes or tents. For details contact the local park authorities. A number of companies can arrange **motor camper** rentals, with a range of fully equipped vehicles. Full details can be obtained from Tourism Saskatchewan.

RESORTS & EXCURSIONS

Half of this vast province comprises provincial forest. There are 80 million acres of it north of the 54th parallel, offering unequalled opportunities for 'outdoors' enthusiasts. The south and centre enjoy a more mellow landscape, much of it given over to grain cultivation.

REGINA: The provincial capital was once called 'Pile of Bones' but was renamed in honour of Queen Victoria. Its centrepiece is the *Wascana Centre,* a huge water-park with the *McKenzie Art Gallery* and *Centre of the Arts.* The park also provides an impressive setting for the *Legislative Buildings* and the *Museum of Natural History.* Regina has long been the base of the Royal Canadian Mounted Police ('The Mounties') and the *RCMP Centennial Museum* offers a quirky insight into the development of Canada's Wild West.

SASKATOON: Built on both banks of the South Saskatchewan River, Saskatoon is one of Canada's fastest growing urban centres. The *Western Development Museum, Wanuskewin Heritage Park, Forestry Farm Park* and the *Ukrainian Arts and Crafts Museum* are its main attractions.

ELSEWHERE: The Trans-Canada Highway provides the best means of touring the far south, connecting the cities of Swift Current, Moose Jaw and Regina. It follows the cavernous **Qu'Appelle Valley,** a sunken garden studded with lakes that runs two-thirds of the way across the province. East of Regina, **Fort Qu'Appelle** and the lakeside recreation parks of **Katepwa Point, Buffalo Pound** and **Echo Valley** are worth visiting. To the west is **Swift Current,** which hosts an annual *Frontier Festival*; and, further west across low-scrub prairie, the afforested oasis of **Cypress Hills Park.**

The Yellowhead Highway, running eastwards from Saskatoon to **Yorkton,** near the border with Manitoba, is a good way to tour Saskatchewan's grain belt. This region was once settled by Ukrainians, as testified by the many silver-domed Orthodox churches, such as that at **Verigin.** Other attractions en route include the **Duck Mountain** and **Good Spirit Provincial Parks.** There is a pioneer village at **Fort Battleford National Historic Park,** northwest of Saskatoon. **Manitou Beach** has the *Manitou Beach Mineral Spa,* where visitors may relax and float effortlessly in the very salty, warm, mineral-rich waters which are pumped from *Little Manitou Lake* into pools in the spa and are supposed to provide relief from a variety of ailments. But Saskatchewan's main attractions are the endless forests and thousands of lakes of the north, accessible by the Northern Woods and Water Route. There are few permanent settlements and many regions are accessible only by air. **Prince Albert** is the main gateway. The closest park is **Prince Albert National Park,** a hilly, forested area with hundreds of lakes, ponds and rivers. Its most developed area is at **Waskesiu Lake,** which has good facilities for camping, organised sports and recreation. Further off to the northwest is **Meadow Lake Park,** which has good accommodation and facilities for hunting and winter sports. The small airport at **Lac la Ronge,** about 300km (200 miles) north of Prince Albert, is the main base for flights to the very remote northern lakes, such as **Wollaston** and **Athabasca.** Excellent fishing and white-water canoeing are available on the lake and on the **Churchill River,** which passes nearby.

SOCIAL PROFILE

FOOD & DRINK: Whitefish and pickerel are marketed by Indian cooperatives. Wild rice harvested by Indians is an excellent accompaniment to the abundant wild fowl which includes partridge, prairie chicken, wild duck and goose. 'Saskatoons', berries similar to blueberries, are used for jams, jellies and 'Saskatoon pie', eaten with fresh country cream. Other wild berries include pinchberries and cranberries which make a tart and tangy jelly, ideal with wild fowl meals. A good selection of restaurants can be found in all the province's cities and

major towns catering to all tastes and pockets. **Drink:** The minimum drinking age is 19 (sometimes older). Alcohol is sold only in licensed stores, licensed restaurants, cocktail lounges, dining and beverage rooms. Retail outlets operate throughout the province.

NIGHTLIFE: There are some nightclubs; bars and restaurants in most main towns have live entertainment as well as music and dancing. The best times for nightlife are during the 'period' historical festivals held regularly in all the major towns. The days of the settlers and cowboys are re-created with everyone dressing in costumes and eating traditional foods. The emphasis changes in each town and according to the time of year, but the largest is in the capital, Regina, a festival lasting several days – the *Buffalo Days.*

SHOPPING: There are many small craft stores that offer pottery, silkscreens, rock jewellery, potash clocks, embroidered leather, denim, purses, gloves and hats.

SPORT: When the snow melts, parklands are used for **horseriding, camping, canoeing, cycling, white-water rafting** and **cross-country walking.** The majority of the parks provide ancillary services from May to September. Saskatchewan's parks contain over 100,000 lakes and the province is named after the Indian name for the river systems (Kis-is-ska-tche-wan). **Sailing, water-skiing, golf, tennis, swimming** and **fishing** are especially popular in summer months. The fishing season is from May to April; fishing licences are required by everyone. **Shooting,** mainly for duck and grouse, is particularly good in the grain region of the southwest. **Wintersports** are the most popular in the region, including **skiing, skating** and **ice fishing.** There are 16 downhill and 39 cross-country ski areas.

SPECIAL EVENTS: May 24-28 '95 *Yorkton Short Film & Video Festival,* Yorkton. **May 25-28** *Regina Lyric Light Opera Society,* Regina. **Jun 1-3** *Mosaic – Festival of Culture,* Regina. **Jun 9-11** *Folk Festival,* Regina. **Jun 23-Jul 2** *Saskatchewan Jazz Festival,* Saskatoon. **Jul 1-Aug 31** *RCMP Retreat Ceremony,* Regina. **Jul 6-Aug 20** *Shakespeare on the Saskatchewan,* Saskatoon. **Jul 8-9** *Saskatchewan Air Show,* Bushell Park. **Jul 9** *Louise Riel Day,* Saskatoon. **Aug 3-7** *Big Valley Jamboree,* Regina. **Aug 18-20** *Moose Jaw Chautauqua,* Moose Jaw. **Nov 25-Dec 1** *Canadian Western Agribition,* Regina.

There are also about 50 amateur and professional rodeos held annually in various locations.

BUSINESS PROFILE

COMMERCIAL INFORMATION: The following organisation can offer advice: Saskatchewan Chamber of Commerce, 1630 Chateau Tower, 1920 Broad Street, Regina, Saskatchewan S4P 3V2. Tel: (306) 352 2671. Fax: (306) 781 7084.

CONFERENCES/CONVENTIONS: For information or assistance, contact the Canadian Tourist Office or Tourism Saskatoon at the address above; *or* Saskatchewan Economic Development and Tourism, 1919 Saskatchewan Drive, Regina, Saskatchewan S4P 3V7. Tel: (306) 787 2232 (general enquiries) *or* 787 2300 (tourism information). Fax: (306) 787 0715 *or* 787 1620; *or* Regina Visitors & Convention Bureau, Tourism Regina, PO Box 3355, Regina, Saskatchewan S4T 3H1. Tel: (306) 789 5099 *or* 787 9600. Fax: (306) 789 3171.

CLIMATE

Temperate in the south with cold winters in the north. The highest rainfall occurs between April and June. Summers are hot and dry with long hours of sunshine, but winter temperatures are generally cold and snowy until early March, but sunny.

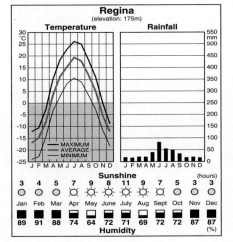

Regina
(elevation: 175m)

	Temperature	Rainfall

MAXIMUM
AVERAGE
MINIMUM

Sunshine (hours)

	Jan	Feb	Mar	Apr	May	June	July	Aug	Sept	Oct	Nov	Dec
	3	4	5	7	9	11	9	7	5	3	3	

Humidity (%)

	Jan	Feb	Mar	Apr	May	June	July	Aug	Sept	Oct	Nov	Dec
	89	91	88	74	64	72	71	69	72	72	87	87

Yukon

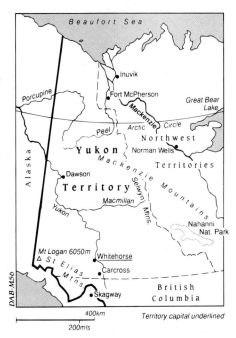

Territory capital underlined

400km
200mls

Location: Northwest Canada.

Tourism Yukon
PO Box 2703, Whitehorse, Yukon Territory Y1A 2C6
Tel: (403) 667 5340. Fax: (403) 667 2634.

AREA: 478,970 sq km (186,299 sq miles).
POPULATION: 29,961 (1991).
POPULATION DENSITY: 0.1 per sq km.
CAPITAL: Whitehorse. **Population:** 21,322 (1991).
GEOGRAPHY: Yukon Territory, Canada's 'last frontier', is largely a mountainous and forested wilderness. It is bisected by the valley of the Yukon River, which passes to the west of the Mackenzie Mountains. Mount Logan, in the St Elias Range on the border with Alaska, is the second highest peak in North America at 5959m (19,550ft).
LANGUAGE: Although Canada is officially bilingual (English and French), English is more commonly spoken in the territory.
TIME: GMT - 8 (GMT - 7 in summer).
Note: Daylight Saving Time time officially lasts from the first Sunday in April to the Saturday before the last Sunday in October.

PUBLIC HOLIDAYS

Public holidays are as for the rest of Canada (see general section above) with the following dates also observed:
Aug 21 '95 Discovery Day.

TRAVEL

AIR: The main international services are run by *Canadian Airlines International. Canadian Airlines* operates a daily service between Whitehorse and Vancouver. *Time Air* offers flights to Watson Lake. The main local carriers are *Alkan Air* (tel: (403) 668 2107; fax: (403) 667 6117), providing services across the Yukon to Inuvik in the Northwest Territories; and *Air North* (tel: (403) 668 2228), providing services from Whitehorse to Dawson City, Old Crow, Juneau and Fairbanks, with connecting flights to Anchorage in Alaska.
SEA: Cruise ships and ferries operate from Bellingham in Washington (USA) and Prince Rupert in British Columbia, arriving at Skagway in Alaska and connecting to Whitehorse by bus.
ROAD: The major road in the region is the Alaska Highway, running from Alaska to British Columbia through Whitehorse. The Dempster Highway connects Whitehorse with Inuvik in the north. **Coach:** *Gold City*

Tours offer a scheduled service from Dawson City to Inuvik in the Northwest Territory. *North West Stage Lines* offer scheduled services to Haines Junction, Destruction Bay, Faro, Ross River and Beaver Creek. **Bus:** There is a bus service between Whitehorse and Dawson; daily in summer, thrice weekly in winter. *Norline* operates to Dawson City; *Greyhound Lines of Canada* operate a 6-times-a-week service in summer from Edmonton to Whitehorse.

ACCOMMODATION

HOTELS: There are 81 hotel/motels with a total of 2483 rooms in the Yukon Territory. There are plans to construct a new 150-room hotel complex with convention facilities and a new 40-room hotel in Whitehorse. Because of the heavy tourist flow through the region in summer, bookings must be made well in advance. Apart from the main settlements with hotels, lodges and motels, accommodation is scarce in wilder areas. Many hotels are closed for the winter. Yukon Territory accommodations are not graded at the present time. For further information, contact the Yukon Hotel Association, Regina Hotel, Whitehorse, Yukon Territory. Tel: (403) 667 7801.
BED & BREAKFAST: There are many bed & breakfast properties in the Yukon Territory. For further information, contact Tourism Yukon at the address above *or* the Northern Network of B & B, PO Box 954, 451 Craig Street, Dawson City, Yukon Y0B 1G0. Tel: (403) 993 5644. Fax: (403) 993 5648.
CAMPING/CARAVANNING: Camping is only advised in summer and on government or private campsites. A number of companies can arrange **motor camper** rentals, with a range of fully equipped vehicles. Full details can be obtained from Tourism Yukon.

RESORTS & EXCURSIONS

WHITEHORSE: Yukon's capital (since 1953) lies on the west bank of the Yukon River, the water route taken by thousands of eager prospectors during the Klondike Gold Rush of 1898. More than half of the territory's population is concentrated here. The *McBride Museum* houses many of the artefacts of the gold rush era, including *Sam McGee's Cabin*. On the river itself, the *SS Klondike*, a restored sternwheeler vessel, is open for viewing. The *MV Schwatka* offers a 2-hour cruise of the *Miles Canyon* and the *Whitehorse Rapids*.
ELSEWHERE: Carcross, an hour's drive south of Whitehorse, lies between the Nares and Bennett Lakes at the foot of Nares Mountain; the *Caribou*, Yukon's oldest hotel, can be found here. Carcross connects to Skagway in Alaska via the *Klondike Highway*. **Kluane National Park**, in the southwest corner of the territory, has the tallest mountains in Canada and the largest non-polar icefields in the world. Special flightseeing tours of this park can be arranged from Whitehorse and a variety of other Yukon Territory communities.
Near Skagway (Alaska) is **Dyea**, the starting point of the famous *Chilkoot Trail*, where hikers can retrace the footsteps of the gold rush stampeders. **Dawson City**, at the heart of the Klondike, can be reached by road or by the Yukon River. In its brief heyday Dawson was hailed as the 'Paris of the North', having then some 30,000 inhabitants; at the last census there were only 1747. The city is now a designated national historic site, with buildings such as the *Commissioner's Residence* and the *Palace Grand Theatre* bearing witness to its former glories. The latter was built in 1899 from two dismantled steamboats and each summer produces an authentic 1898 vaudeville show – the 'Gaslight Follies'. Tours on the Yukon River on the miniature stern-wheeler *Yukon Lou* visit the *Sternwheelers Graveyard* and *Pleasure Island*. Visitors can pan gold at *Guggieville* or *Claim 33* on Bonanza Creek, the site of the original claim which sparked off the 1898 goldrush.
Expeditions to the wild back-country of the Yukon Territory are best conducted in the company of a licensed outfitter or guide.

SOCIAL PROFILE

FOOD & DRINK: Some of the Yukon's food is very distinctive but difficult to produce commercially. Moose meat is cooked in several ways from steaming to smoked or pot roast, and accompanied by *sourdough* and vegetables. Dall sheep, mountain goat, caribou and porcupine are also eaten. Wild fowl and fish feature in most menus. There are restaurants throughout the area, but the best selection is in Whitehorse, Dawson City and Watson Lake. **Drink:** Most alcohol is imported from

other areas of Canada and the USA. A local speciality is *hooch* (a blend of imported and Canadian rum); it is only available in the Yukon Territory.
NIGHTLIFE: Nightlife is best during the historical festivals and carnivals reflecting the pioneer spirit that explored the region (see *Special Events* below). However, Dawson City has legalised gambling, live vaudeville theatre and a floor show at Gertie's featuring cancan girls and honky tonk piano.
SHOPPING: Special items include Indian boots, gold nuggets and the original *parka* coat with a wool lining and waterproof outer cover, dating from prospecting days. Native Indian bone-carving and jewellery are popular souvenirs. Cashback on items purchased can be claimed back in Revenue Canada, Customs and Excise and Government of Canada offices.
SPORT: The most important sport in the Yukon Territory is **skiing. Canoeing, hiking, mountain climbing, horseriding, dog sledding** and **fishing** are also available in many wilderness areas.
SPECIAL EVENTS: Mar 4 '95 *Yukon Gold Loppet*, Whitehorse. **Jun 23-25** *Yukon International Festival of Story Telling*, Whitehorse. **Jul 1** *Yukon Gold Panning Championships*, Dawson City. **Aug 18-21** *Dawson City Discovery Days*, Dawson City. **Sep 3** *Great Klondike International Outhouse Race*, Dawson City. **Sep 9-10** *Klondike Trail of '98 Road Relay*, Whitehorse.

BUSINESS PROFILE

COMMERCIAL INFORMATION: The following organisation can offer advice: Yukon Chamber of Commerce, 101-302 Steele Street, Whitehorse, Yukon Territory Y1A 2C5. Tel: (403) 667 2000.
CONFERENCES/CONVENTIONS: For information on conferences and conventions in the Yukon Territory, contact the Canadian Tourist Office *or* Tourism Industry Association, Meetings and Convention Bureau, Suite 200, 1109 First Avenue, Whitehorse, Yukon Territory Y1A 5G4. Tel: (403) 668 3331. Fax: (403) 667 7379.

CLIMATE

Summers are warm with almost continuous daylight during June. Winters are bitterly cold.
Required clothing: *Summer* – days can be hot, but sweaters and light jackets are advised for the evenings. *Spring and Autumn* – coats and gloves are required for outdoor activities. *Winter* – thermal underwear, wool sweaters, parkas, wool gloves or mittens and mukluks or felt-lined boots are advised for the winter.

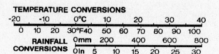

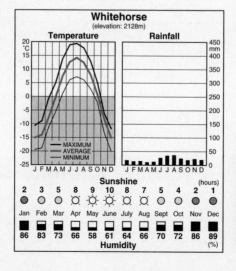

Cape Verde

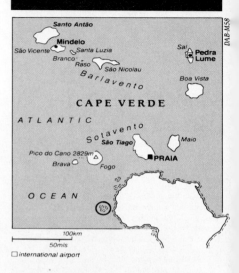

□ *international airport*

Location: Atlantic Ocean, off coast of West Africa.

Ministry of Tourism, Industry and Commerce
Palácio do Governo, Praia, São Tiago, Cape Verde
Tel: 613 210. Telex: 6035.
Instituto Nacional do Turismo – INATUR
CP294, Praia, São Tiago, Cape Verde
Tel: 614 473. Fax: 613 210.
Embassy of the Republic of Cape Verde
Koninginnegracht 44, 2514 AD The Hague, The Netherlands
Tel: (70) 346 9623. Fax: (70) 346 7702. Telex: 34321 (a/b ARCV NL).
Consulate of the Republic of Cape Verde
Mathenesserlaan 326, 3021 HX Rotterdam, The Netherlands
Tel: (10) 477 8977 *or* 477 8760. Fax: (10) 477 4553.
British Consulate
c/o Shell Cabo Verde, CP 4, Sal Avenue, Sal Vincente, Cape Verde
Tel: 314 132 *or* 314 605 *or* 314 232. Fax: 314 755. Telex: 3082 (a/b V).
Embassy of the Republic of Cape Verde
3415 Massachusetts Avenue, NW, Washington, DC 20007
Tel: (202) 965 6820. Fax: (202) 965 1207.
Also deals with enquiries from Canada.
Embassy of the United States of America
CP 201, Rua Abilio Macedo 81, Praia, São Tiago, Cape Verde
Tel: 615 616. Fax: 611 355.
The Canadian Embassy in Dakar deals with enquiries relating to Cape Verde (see *Senegal* later in the book).

AREA: 4033 sq km (1557 sq miles).
POPULATION: 341,491 (1990).
POPULATION DENSITY: 84.7 per sq km.
CAPITAL: Cidade de Praia. **Population:** 57,748 (1980).
GEOGRAPHY: Cape Verde is situated in the Atlantic Ocean, 600km (450 miles) west-northwest of Senegal, and comprises ten volcanic islands and five islets, in two groups: *Balavento* (Windwards) and *Sotavento* (Leewards). In the former group are the islands of São Vicente, Santo Antão, São Nicolau, Santa Luzia, Sal and Boa Vista, along with the smaller islands of Branco and Raso; the Sotavento group comprises the islands of São Tiago, Maio, Fogo and Brava, along with the smaller islands of Rei and Rombo. Most have mountain peaks; the highest being Pico do Cano, an active volcano, which is on Fogo. The islands are generally rocky and eroded, and have never been able to support more than

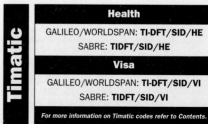

TEMPERATURE CONVERSIONS

-20	-10	0°C	10	20	30	40
0	10 20	30°F40	50 60	70 80	90	100

RAINFALL CONVERSIONS

0mm	200	400	600	800
0In	5	10	15	20	25	30

Whitehorse
(elevation: 2128m)

Temperature — Rainfall

— MAXIMUM
— AVERAGE
— MINIMUM

	Jan	Feb	Mar	Apr	May	June	July	Aug	Sept	Oct	Nov	Dec
Sunshine (hours)	2	3	5	8	9	10	8	7	5	4	2	1
Humidity (%)	86	83	73	66	58	61	64	66	70	72	86	89

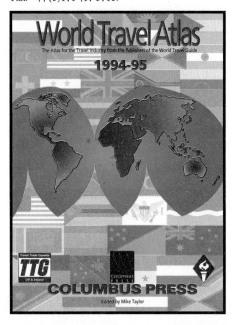

subsistence agriculture (maize, bananas, sugar cane and coffee are the main crops); low rainfall over the last ten years has crippled food production and forced the islands to depend on international aid.

LANGUAGE: The official language is Portuguese. Crioulo is spoken by most of the inhabitants. Some English and French is spoken.

RELIGION: Almost entirely Roman Catholic with a Protestant minority.

TIME: GMT - 1.

ELECTRICITY: 220 volts AC, 50Hz.

COMMUNICATIONS: Telephone: IDD is possible to main cities. Country code: 238. Improvements to rural areas are in progress and the islands have over 12,000 telephones. Some calls to and from Cape Verde must still go through the international operator. **Telex:** This is available in some hotels. **Post:** Postal facilities are not very efficient, deliveries to Europe take over a week. **Press:** Newspapers are in Portuguese. There are two weekly papers with a total circulation of 3000, two quarterly cultural magazines and one monthly newspaper. **BBC World Service and Voice of America frequencies:** From time to time these change. See the section *How to Use this Book* for more information.

BBC:

MHz	17.79	15.40	15.07	9.410

Voice of America:

MHz	21.49	15.60	9.525	6.035

PASSPORT/VISA

Regulations and requirements may be subject to change at short notice, and you are advised to contact the appropriate diplomatic or consular authority before finalising travel arrangements. Details of these may be found at the head of this country's entry. Any numbers in the chart refer to the footnotes below.

	Passport Required?	Visa Required?	Return Ticket Required?
Full British	Yes	Yes	Yes
BVP	Not valid	-	-
Australian	Yes	Yes	Yes
Canadian	Yes	Yes	Yes
USA	Yes	Yes	Yes
Other EU (As of 31/12/94)	Yes	Yes	Yes
Japanese	Yes	Yes	Yes

PASSPORTS: A passport with a minimum validity of 6 months is required by all.

British Visitors Passport: Not accepted.

VISAS: Required by all except nationals of Benin, Burkina Faso, Côte d'Ivoire, Gambia, Ghana, Guinea, Guinea-Bissau, Liberia, Mali, Mauritania, Niger, Nigeria, Senegal, Sierra Leone and Togo.

Types of visa: Transit, Re-entry permit, Exit permit.

Application to: Consulate (or Consular Section at Embassy). For addresses, see top of entry. Visitors from countries where there is no Cape Verdian Embassy or Consulate can obtain visas at Cape Verdian Border Services offices at the airports on Sal and Praia. A fee will be charged.

Application requirements: (a) 2 passport-size photographs. (b) 2 application forms.

Working days required: Where there are no complications, visas may be issued immediately; however, it is advisable to anticipate some delay.

MONEY

Currency: Cape Verde Escudo (CVEsc) = 100 centavos. Notes are in denominations of CVEsc2500, 1000, 500, 200 and 100. Coins are in denominations of CVEsc100, 50, 20, 10, 2.5 and 1, and 50 and 20 centavos.

Credit cards: These are not normally accepted but check with the relevant credit card company in case there is now some merchant acceptability.

Exchange rate indicators: The following figures are included as a guide to the movements of the Cape Verde Escudo against Sterling and the US Dollar:

Date:	Oct '92	Sep '93	Jan '94	Jan '95
£1.00=	99.05	113.55	109.60	129.72
$1.00=	62.41	74.36	74.08	82.92

Currency restrictions: The import and export of local currency is prohibited. Import of foreign currency is unlimited; currency declaration is màndatory at entry and departure. The maximum allowable export of foreign currencies is the equivalent of CVEsc25,000 or the amount declared on arrival, whichever is the larger.

Banking hours: 0800-1400 Monday to Friday.

DUTY FREE

The following goods may be taken into Cape Verde free of duty:

A reasonable amount of perfume.
Note: Duty-free alcohol and tobacco can be obtained at the international airport on Sal when leaving.

PUBLIC HOLIDAYS

Jan 1 '95 New Year's Day. **Jan 20** Nationality Day. **May 1** Labour Day. **Jul 5** Independence Day. **Aug 15** Assumption. **Nov 1** All Saints' Day. **Dec 25** Christmas Day. **Jan 1 '96** New Year's Day. **Jan 20** Nationality Day.

HEALTH

Regulations and requirements may be subject to change at short notice, and you are advised to contact your doctor well in advance of your intended date of departure. Any numbers in the chart refer to the footnotes below.

	Special Precautions?	Certificate Required?
Yellow Fever	Yes	1
Cholera	Yes	2
Typhoid & Polio	Yes	-
Malaria	3	-
Food & Drink	4	

[1]: A yellow fever vaccination certificate is required from travellers over one year of age if arriving from countries who reported cases in the last six years.

[2]: Following WHO guidelines issued in 1973, a cholera vaccination certificate is not a condition of entry to Cape Verde. However, cholera is a serious risk in this country and precautions are essential. Up-to-date advice should be sought before deciding whether these precautions should include vaccination as medical opinion is divided over its effectiveness. See the *Health* section at the back of the book.

[3]: There is a limited risk of malaria from September to November on São Tiago Island.

[4]: All water should be regarded as being potentially contaminated. Water used for drinking, brushing teeth or making ice should have first been boiled or otherwise sterilised. Milk is unpasteurised and should be boiled. Powdered or tinned milk is available and is advised, but

make sure that it is reconstituted with pure water. Avoid all dairy products. Only eat well-cooked meat and fish, preferably served hot. Pork, salad and mayonnaise may carry increased risk. Vegetables should be cooked and fruit peeled.
Health care: Health insurance is strongly advised, although in-patient treatment is free in general wards on presentation of a passport. Treatment is private and expensive on small islands.

TRAVEL - International

AIR: The national airline is *Transportes Aéreos de Cabo Verde (TACV).*
Approximate flight time: From London to Lisbon (Portugal) is 3 hours and from Lisbon to Sal is 4 hours. Note that the stopover in Lisbon will usually be overnight if flying by *TAP Air Portugal.*
International airports: *Amílcar Cabral (SID)* on Sal, 2km (1 mile) south of Espargos, is the only airport with a runway long enough to take jets; there are eight others throughout the islands. Since 1987 work has been in progress to expand facilities at *Amílcar Cabral* airport.
SEA: Mindelo is the principal port. São Vicente is served by passenger and cargo ships. There is also a port at Praia.

TRAVEL - Internal

AIR: There are internal flights to all inhabited islands except Brava.
SEA: There are regular boat and ferry services between all the islands.
ROAD: There are over 3050km (1895 miles) of roads on the islands, of which one-third are paved. Taxi fares should be agreed in advance. Buses are satisfactory. There is a road improvement programme. Traffic drives on the right. **Documentation:** An International Driving Permit is recommended, although not legally required.
JOURNEY TIMES: The following chart gives the approximate journey times (in hours and minutes) from Cidade de Praia to other major cities/towns in Cape Verde.

	Air	Sea
Saõ Vicente	0.45	-
Sal	0.45	-
Maio	0.15	-
Boa Vista	0.30	-
Fogo	0.40	-
Brava	-	12.00
São Nicolau	0.50	-

ACCOMMODATION

Hotel accommodation is currently scarce. There are international hotels on Sal Island and a tourist complex at Praia. Otherwise there are small hotels at Mindelo and on Ilha Do Sal (Sal), Fogo and Praia. In total, there are two 4-star, two 3-star and two 2-star hotels on Cape Verde. For further information, contact the Instituto Nacional do Turismo (for address, see top of entry).

RESORTS & EXCURSIONS

Tourism is not currently an important part of Cape Verde's economy, although there are several promotional schemes aimed at changing this. There are many superb diving sites around the islands, several of which have wrecks of ships dating back to the 16th century. Windsurfing opportunities are also excellent. Many of the islands have spectacular mountain scenery and beautiful deserted beaches, such as *Tarrafal* on **São Tiago**. **San Filipe** has a spectacular volcano as well as fine beaches. There are good markets on some of the islands, and a number of colourful festivals. **Mindelo** on São Vicente, with its Portuguese-style buildings, is worth a visit.

SOCIAL PROFILE

FOOD & DRINK: Restaurants are mainly in hotels. The main local culinary speciality is *cachupa*, a mess of maize and beans. Fruits include mangoes, bananas, papayas, goiabas (guavas), zimbrão, tamarinas, marmelos, azedinhas, tamaras and cocos. **Drink:** Beer, wine and local spirits are commonly available; punch is also popular. Soft drinks are expensive.
NIGHTLIFE: There are discos in hotels and several nightclubs.
SHOPPING: Some hotels have boutiques. There are

daily markets. The Santa Catarina market is held Wednesday and Saturday. Coconut shells are carved by local craftsmen; there is also pottery, lacework and basketry.
SPORT: Watersports include **sailing, swimming, surfing, diving** and **fishing**. **Tennis, archery, bodybuilding, snooker** and **ping-pong** are also available. Many facilities are provided by hotels as part of the expanding tourist trade.
SPECIAL EVENTS: There are several annual festivals, the precise dates of which change from year to year. *Todo o Mundo Canta* (a song festival) and *Todo o Mundo Danca* (a dance festival) are held annually in the 5 de Julho amusement park. There is also the *Baía das Gatas* music festival (around August) and *Carnaval* in Mindelo City (around February).
SOCIAL CONVENTIONS: The usual European social courtesies should be observed. **Tipping:** It is normal to give 10%.

BUSINESS PROFILE

ECONOMY: Although most of the population have traditionally been engaged in subsistence agriculture – producing maize and fruit – many years of drought have seen this dwindle to the point where Cape Verde needs large amounts of food aid. Remittances from emigré communities – some 300,000 Cape Verdeans live abroad, mainly in the USA – enable the islands to balance their external payments, even though exports, principally fish and fish products, cover less than 5% of imports. Apart from a few fish processing and canning factories, there has been virtually no industry on the islands, and diversification into other industries has continued as part of a 4-year development plan; salt and pozzolana are mined and various manufacturing industries have been introduced. There are hopes that the tourist trade can be developed without disrupting local lifestyles by directing visitors to less populated islands. Portugal and The Netherlands supply half of Cape Verde's import requirements.
BUSINESS: All correspondence should be in English or French. Most of Cape Verde's business links are with Portugal. **Office hours:** 0800-1230 and 1430-1800 Monday to Friday.
COMMERCIAL INFORMATION: The following organisations can offer advice: Associação Comercial Barlavento (Chamber of Commerce), CP 62, Mindelo, São Vicente. Tel: 313 281; *or* Associação Comercial de Sotavento (Chamber of Commerce), CP 78, Rua Guerra Mendes 23, 1°, Praia, São Tiago. Tel: 612 991. Fax: 612 964. Telex: 6005.
CONFERENCES/CONVENTIONS: The following organisation can offer advice: Ministry for Education and Sports, Palácio do Governo, São Tiago, Praia. Tel: 610 507. Fax: 612 764 *or* 613 490.

CLIMATE

Generally temperate, but rainfall is very low.
Required clothing: Lightweight throughout the year, tropical for midsummer.

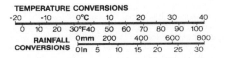

TEMPERATURE CONVERSIONS

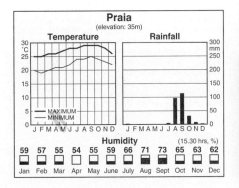

Praia
(elevation: 35m)

Cayman Islands

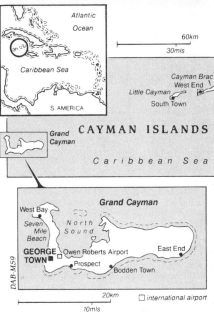

Location: Caribbean; south of Cuba, 720km (480 miles) southwest of Miami.

Cayman Islands Department of Tourism
PO Box 67, 2nd Floor, Harbour Centre, George Town, Grand Cayman
Tel: (94) 90623. Fax: (94) 94053.
Cayman Islands Government Office *and* **Department of Tourism** *and* **Cayman Airways**
Trevor House, 100 Brompton Road, London SW3 1EX
Tel: (0171) 581 9418 (Government Office) *or* 581 9960 (Department of Tourism *and* Cayman Airways). Fax: (0171) 584 4463. Opening hours: 0900-1700 Monday to Friday (Government Office), 0930-1730 Monday to Thursday, 0900-1700 Friday (Department of Tourism *and* Cayman Airways).
UK Passport Agency
Clive House, Petty France, London SW1H 9HD
Tel: (0171) 279 3434. Opening hours: 0900-1600 Monday to Friday.
Cayman Islands Department of Tourism
Suite 2733, 420 Lexington Avenue, New York, NY 10170
Tel: (212) 682 5582. Fax: (212) 986 5123.
Also in: Chicago, Houston, Los Angeles and Miami.
Cayman Islands Department of Tourism
Travel Marketing Consultants, Suite 306, 234 Eglinton Avenue East, Toronto, Ontario M4P 1K5
Tel: (416) 485 1550. Fax: (416) 485 7578.

AREA: 259 sq km (100 sq miles).
POPULATION: 29,700 (1992 estimate).
POPULATION DENSITY: 114.7 per sq km.
CAPITAL: George Town. **Population:** 15,000 (1992 estimate).
GEOGRAPHY: The Cayman Islands are situated in the Caribbean, 290km (180 miles) northwest of Jamaica, and comprise Grand Cayman, Little Cayman and Cayman Brac. The islands are peaks of a subterranean mountain range extending from Cuba towards the Gulf of Honduras. The beaches are said to be the best in the Caribbean, the most notable being Seven Mile Beach on

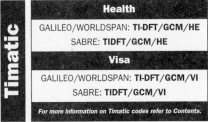

Health		
GALILEO/WORLDSPAN: **TI-DFT/GCM/HE**		
SABRE: **TIDFT/GCM/HE**		
Visa		
GALILEO/WORLDSPAN: **TI-DFT/GCM/VI**		
SABRE: **TIDFT/GCM/VI**		

For more information on Timatic codes refer to Contents.

Grand Cayman. Tall pines line many of the beaches; those located on the east and west coasts are equally well protected offshore by the Barrier Reef.

LANGUAGE: English is the official language, with minority local dialects also spoken.

RELIGION: Mainly Presbyterian with Anglican, Roman Catholic, Seventh Day Adventists, Pilgrims, Pilgrim Holiness Church of God, Jehovah's Witnesses and Bahai minorities on Grand Cayman. Baptists on Cayman Brac.

TIME: GMT - 5.

ELECTRICITY: 110 volts, 60Hz. American-style (flat) 2-pin plugs are standard.

COMMUNICATIONS: Telephone: A modern telephone system links the Cayman Islands to the world by submarine cable and satellite; IDD is now possible to North America and Europe. Country code: 1 809. Outgoing international code: 0. **Fax:** This is available at most hotels and banks. Some businesses also have public facilities. **Telex/telegram:** Telecommunications are provided by Cable and Wireless (West Indies) Limited under government franchise. Telex is available from a public booth at the Cable and Wireless office. Many hotels and apartments have their own telex facilities. Public telegraph operates daily 0730-1800, accepting cables from any country. **Post:** Mail is not delivered to private addresses in the Cayman Islands, but collected from numbered PO boxes. *Poste Restante* mail should be addressed 'General Delivery' at the post office. Post office hours: 0830-1530 Monday to Friday; 0830-1200 Saturday. **Press:** *Caymanian Compass* is published five times a week and *The New Caymanian*, once a week.

BBC World Service and Voice of America frequencies: From time to time these change. See the section *How to Use this Book* for more information.

BBC:

MHz	17.84	15.22	9.740	3.915

Voice of America:

MHz	15.21	11.70	6.130	0.930

PASSPORT/VISA

Regulations and requirements may be subject to change at short notice, and you are advised to contact the appropriate diplomatic or consular authority before finalising travel arrangements. Details of these may be found at the head of this country's entry. Any numbers in the chart refer to the footnotes below.

	Passport Required?	Visa Required?	Return Ticket Required?
Full British	1	No/2	Yes
BVP	Valid	No/2	Yes
Australian	Yes	No/2	Yes
Canadian	1	No/2	Yes
USA	1	No/2	Yes
Other EU (As of 31/12/94)	Yes	No/2	Yes
Japanese	Yes	No/2	Yes

PASSPORTS: [1] Valid passports required by all except nationals of Canada, UK and USA, if proof of nationality is provided and return or onward ticket shows that the visitor will leave the Cayman Islands within 6 months. The passport has to remain valid for the period of stay.

British Visitors Passport: Valid.

VISAS: A US visa is required for visitors travelling via the USA, with the exception of participants in the Visa Waiver Scheme (application forms and details available from international carriers). A Cayman Islands visa is required by all except:

(a) nationals of countries referred to in the chart above;
(b) nationals of Andorra, Antigua & Barbuda, Argentina, Austria, Bahamas, Bahrain, Bangladesh, Barbados, Belize, Botswana, Brazil, Chile, Costa Rica, Cyprus, Dominica, Ecuador, El Salvador, Fiji, Finland, Gambia, Ghana, Grenada, Guatemala, Guyana, Iceland, India, Israel, Jamaica, Kenya, Kiribati, Kuwait, Lesotho, Liechtenstein, Malawi, Malaysia, Malta, Mauritius, Mexico, Monaco, Nauru, New Zealand, Nigeria, Norway, Oman, Pakistan, Panama, Papua New Guinea, Peru, St Lucia, St Vincent & the Grenadines, San Marino, Saudi Arabia, Seychelles, Sierra Leone, Singapore, Solomon Islands, South Africa, Sri Lanka, Swaziland, Sweden, Switzerland, Tanzania, Tonga, Trinidad & Tobago, Tuvalu, Uganda, Vanuatu, Venezuela, Western Samoa, Zambia and Zimbabwe. Visitors who wish to conduct business should see the section *Business visits* below.

Types of visa: Tourist, Transit and Business. Cost: fee £33; telex charge £8; referral fee £3.

Validity: 1 to 6 months.

Application to: The UK Passport Agency. Enquiries may be directed to any Cayman Islands Government or Department of Tourism office (addresses at top of entry).

Application requirements: (a) 2 application forms. (b) Valid passport. (c) 2 passport-size photos. (d) Sufficient

funds to cover duration of stay.

Working days required: Dependent upon nature of application. Allow 28 days.

Business visits: [2] For visitors intending to conduct business in the Cayman Islands, a Temporary Work Permit must be obtained before arrival, which is issued by the Cayman Islands Department of Immigration. Visas, if required, should be obtained from the UK Passport Agency.

MONEY

Currency: Cayman Islands Dollar (CI$) = 100 cents. Notes are in denominations of CI$100, 50, 25, 10, 5 and 1. Coins are in denominations of 25, 10, 5 and 1 cents.

Currency exchange: US currency circulates freely. Credit cards and US Dollar travellers cheques are preferable to personal cheques.

Credit cards: All accepted. Check with your credit card company for details of merchant acceptability and other services which may be available.

Travellers cheques: In some places these are preferred to credit cards.

Exchange rate indicators: The following figures are included as a guide to the movement of the Cayman Islands Dollar against Sterling and the US Dollar:

Date:	Oct '92	Sep '93	Jan '94	Jan '95
£1.00=	1.34	1.30	1.26	1.29
$1.00=	0.85	0.85	0.85	0.83

Currency restrictions: No restriction on import or export of foreign or local currency.

Banking hours: 0930-1430 Monday to Thursday; 0930-1630 Friday.

DUTY FREE

The following goods may be taken into the Cayman Islands without incurring any customs duty:

200 cigarettes or 50 cigars or 250g of tobacco; 1 litre of spirits or 4 litres of wine or 1 case of beer.

Note: Pets require a permit from Cayman Islands Department of Agriculture.

PUBLIC HOLIDAYS

Jan 1 '95 New Year's Day. **Mar 3** Ash Wednesday. **Apr 14** Good Friday. **Apr 17** Easter Monday. **May 15** Discovery Day. **Jun 12** Queen's Official Birthday. **Jul 3** Constitution Day. **Nov 13** Remembrance Day. **Dec 25** Christmas Day. **Dec 26** Boxing Day. **Jan 1 '96** New Year's Day. **Feb 21** Ash Wednesday. **Apr 5** Good Friday. **Apr 8** Easter Monday.

HEALTH

Regulations and requirements may be subject to change at short notice, and you are advised to contact your doctor well in advance of your intended date of departure. Any numbers in the chart refer to the footnotes below.

	Special Precautions?	Certificate Required?
Yellow Fever	No	No
Cholera	No	No
Typhoid & Polio	1	No
Malaria	No	No
Food & Drink	No	-

[1]: Vaccinations are recommended.

Health care: Insect repellent is useful to counter mosquitoes and sandflies. There is a well-equipped 52-bed hospital in Grand Cayman, as well as private doctors, dentists and opticians. There is a small hospital in Cayman Brac. Health costs are similar to the UK. Private insurance is recommended.

TRAVEL - International

AIR: The Cayman Islands national airline is *Cayman Airways (KX)*. *Cayman Airways* fly to the Cayman Islands from Miami, Tampa, Atlanta, Houston and Jamaica. The most convenient gateway from UK/Europe is Miami with same-day onward connections. *Cayman Airways, American Airlines, United Airlines* and *Northwest* have flights from Miami to Grand Cayman.

Approximate flight times: From London to Miami is 8 hours and from Miami to Grand Cayman is 1 hour 5 minutes; connection times vary.

International airports: *Grand Cayman (GCM)* (Owen Roberts Airport) is 3.5km (2 miles) northeast of the city, and *Cayman Brac (CYB)* (Gerard Smith Airport) is 8km (5 miles) from the town. Taxis meet all flights (travel time – 10 minutes). Airport facilities in Grand Cayman include an outgoing duty-free shop for all international departures, car hire, and a bar/restaurant (open for all arrivals and departures) in Grand Cayman.

Departure tax: CI$8 or US$10 payable by all travellers over 12 years of age.

SEA: The main port of George Town on Grand Cayman is an important port of call for leading international cruise lines. Passenger lines operate from North America, Mexico and Europe.

TRAVEL - Internal

AIR: The main island of Grand Cayman is connected to Little Cayman and Cayman Brac by internal flights run by *Cayman Airways*. There is also a service between Cayman Brac and Little Cayman (see below under *Journey Times*).

ROAD: A good road network connects the coastal towns of all three main islands. **Bus:** A cheap but infrequent bus service runs between George Town and the West Bay residential area, connecting most of the hotels along Seven Mile Beach and also to Bodden Town and East End from George Town. **Taxi:** There are large fleets of taxis. **Car hire:** This is by far the best way to get around. All the major car hire companies are represented in George Town. Driving is on the left and drivers must be over 21. Speed limits are strictly enforced. Full insurance is required and must be arranged with the rental company. There are also two moped and motorbike hire companies. Bicycles are also available for CI$10 per day. **Documentation:** An International Driving Permit or Tourist Driving Licence (Visitor's Driving Permit) is required, which will be issued on presentation of a valid licence from the traveller's country of origin.

JOURNEY TIMES: The following chart gives approximate journey times (in hours and minutes) from George Town, Grand Cayman, to other major centres in the islands.

	Air	Road	Sea
Cayman Brac	0.40	-	-
Little Cayman	0.45	-	-
Rum Point	-	0.45	1.15
Cayman Kai	-	0.45	

Cayman Brac to Little Cayman is 20 minutes by air.

ACCOMMODATION

There is a wide variety of accommodation, ranging from luxury hotels and self-catering condominiums to more economical hotels and dive lodges. Most of Grand Cayman's condominiums are superbly situated on beaches and coastal areas and guests can walk out of the apartments onto superb beaches with crystal clear water. Many condominiums have been built in the last few years and are equipped with the latest fittings and furnishings, as well as central facilities such as swimming pools and tennis courts.

HOTELS: The leading hotels are located on the coast. Some of the best known overlook Grand Cayman's renowned *Seven Mile Beach*, a dazzling stretch of fine powdery sand said to be one of the world's most beautiful beaches. There is also a fine selection of diving resort hotels. Hotels providing accommodation with 100 rooms are considered large in the Cayman Islands. Hotels of this size are only found on Grand Cayman. Prices are seasonal, being more expensive in the winter than in the summer (when some hotels offer free accommodation for children under 12). A 6% room tax is payable to the hotel on departure. Most also add a service charge. For more information, contact Cayman Islands Reservations in London on (0171) 581 9960 *or* the Cayman Islands Hotel and Condominium Association, PO Box 1367, West Bay Road, George Town, Grand Cayman. Tel: (94) 74057. Fax: (94) 74143. **Grading:** Hotels vary in standard from *luxury* (very comfortable, with some outstanding features) to *tourist class* (budget hotel).

SELF-CATERING: There is a wide variety of apartments and villas available, from the most luxurious to the relatively austere. The Department of Tourism can give full details of these, and also of beach cottages for families, and dive lodges. The following organisation can also be of assistance: Cayman Islands Hotel & Condominium Association (CIHCA), PO Box 1367, West Bay Road, George Town, Grand Cayman. Tel: (94) 74057. Fax: (94) 74143.

RESORTS & EXCURSIONS

There are three islands in this British Dependent Territory, which has long been associated with buccaneers and pirates.

Grand Cayman: Most of the population lives on this island, surrounded by water rich in colourful marine life and spectacular coral reefs. There is a 6km (4-mile) stone wall at Bodden Town, known as the Grand Cayman's Wall of China, built to protect residents from pirate attacks. **Seven Mile Beach** is the main tourist centre. Although highly developed, it retains its charm; unlike many elsewhere, the new developments do not

overwhelm the visitor. The post office at **Hell** nearby has a lively trade postmarking cards and letters. Close by Seven Mile Beach is the unique *Cayman Turtle Farm* though, owing to conservation pressures, the meat is usually only consumed locally (for more information, see *Shopping* in the *Social Profile* section below). The capital of Grand Cayman is **George Town**. Along the harbour front are traditional Caymanian gingerbread-style buildings and, close by, modern banks and finance houses. *The Cayman Islands National Museum*, based in the centre of George Town, offers a complete history of the islands. Opening hours: 0930-1730 Monday to Friday, 1000-1600 Saturday.

Cayman Brac, where fewer than 2500 people live, gets its name 'Brac' (Gaelic for 'bluff') from the huge bluff which rises 42m (140ft) from the sea. The Brac, which is 143km (89 miles) northeast of Grand Cayman, is about 19km (12 miles) long, and not much more than a mile wide. The rocky cliffs are excellent for exploring and hiking. The area is riddled with caves and some are barely explored. There are dozens of wrecks for divers to explore. It also has a rare bird sanctuary. The island provided the basis for Robert Louis Stevenson's *Treasure Island*.

Little Cayman, the home of 41 people, and many more wild birds and iguanas, is 11km (7 miles) southeast of Cayman Brac. This tiny island is just 16km (10 miles) long, and at no point more than 3km (2 miles) wide. Expert anglers consider that its flats provide the best bone fishing in the world.

SOCIAL PROFILE

FOOD & DRINK: Restaurants are excellent, with several outstanding gourmet establishments, such as The Grand Old House, Hemingways, The Wharf and Pappagallo's. Specialities are turtle steaks, turtle soup, conch chowder and conch salad, red snapper, sea bass and lobster. There are various standards of restaurants with good service, most of which accept credit cards.
Drink: Bars and restaurants are well stocked with all beverages normally consumed in America and Europe. Draught beer is available in a few bars.
NIGHTLIFE: Grand Cayman has limited nightclubs featuring international live entertainment and dancing, and weekend dances are held at hotels on Cayman Brac.

The islands also have two indoor theatres, two outdoor theatres, while some hotels provide film and slide screenings for guests.
SHOPPING: As a shopping centre, George Town, with its fascinating boutiques and duty-free shops, is now one of the leading centres in the Caribbean region. Half a dozen modern and sophisticated shopping centres have recently been established offering prestigious North American and European lines in fashion, furnishings and household goods. Special purchases include china, crystal, silver, woollens and linen, French perfume and local crafts of black coral, sculptures, tortoise and turtle shell jewellery (turtles are bred at Cayman Turtle Farm, which also undertakes conservation measures). *US citizens, and travellers via the USA, should note that turtle products cannot be imported into that country, even by persons in transit.* Many luxury goods and essential foodstuffs are duty-free but duty of up to 20% is charged on other items.
Shopping hours: 0900-1700 Monday to Friday; 0830-1230 Saturday.
SPORT: Tennis, cricket, football, rugby, squash and **golf** are popular. The Brittania Golf Course, designed by Jack Nicklaus, may be played either as a 9-hole championship course or as an 18-hole course with the unique Cayman Ball which is half the weight of the standard ball and travels half as far. There is a new 18-hole championship golf course, The Links at Safehaven.
Watersports: The Cayman Islands have a vast range of watersports, including **swimming, sailing, parasailing, windsurfing** and, especially, **scuba diving** and **fishing**. Divers think of the Cayman Islands as the 'Divers' Islands'. There are over 20 dive operations in the Cayman Islands. There are few other islands where divers can enjoy such accessible diving sites; on Seven Mile Beach excellent diving begins 200 yards from the shore. Diving shops and boats are to be found at most hotels. Some diving resorts feature underwater photographic sales, service and training, including camera rentals and repairs, along with overnight processing of slides. The Islands' main hospital in George Town, capital of Grand Cayman, even has its own recompression chamber – the Cayman 'Unbender'. The variety of diving sites ranges from shallow dives near offshore reefs to the famous virgin sites off Cayman Brac, and the famous North Wall dive off Grand Cayman – a sheer drop to the bed of the ocean

recognised as the 'Mount Everest' of diving sites and Stingray City, known as the 'best 12ft dive in the world'. The abundance of fish, marine and coral life which can be found in the turquoise waters off the islands is protected by some of the most advanced conservation measures in the region. Scuba divers must be certified by an internationally recognised course. Courses are readily available at all levels, PADI, NAUI and BSAC. Those who do not make the grade can enjoy the reefs in the air-conditioned comfort of the *Atlantis Submarine*, which offers hour-long dives for up to 46 passengers – highly recommended. **Fishing:** The Cayman Islands established themselves as a leading international game-fishing resort in spectacular fashion by holding the first annual *Million Dollar Month Fishing Festival*, in June 1984. Prizes total over one million dollars. Grand Cayman occupies a unique location in the migratory path of the big fish – marlin, tuna, dolphin, swordfish and wahoo – which swim through the deep troughs surrounding the island. Due to the abundance of fish and dependable weather, the Cayman Islands are probably the only place in the Caribbean where the visitor can fish all year round. In 1980, some 200 blue marlin were boated in the Cayman Islands; an average catch of marlin for any Caribbean destination is 25 per year. In one 10-month period, one of the Cayman Islands' leading professional fishermen boated 78, including one of 420lb caught after a five-and-a-half hour battle. The best fishing is between Grand Cayman's west coast and the banks, 7.5km (12 miles) offshore; the Trench, 6-13km (4-8 miles) off the west coast, is particularly good. There is also outstanding fishing for tarpon and bonefish in the inshore lakes of Little Cayman, the smallest of the three islands which make up the Cayman Islands.
SPECIAL EVENTS: The following is a selection of the major festivals and other special events celebrated annually in the Cayman Islands during 1995. For a complete list, contact the Cayman Islands Department of Tourism.
Apr 15 '95 *Easter Regatta.* **Apr 16** *Cayman Cup Schooner Race.* **Apr 21-24** *Grand Cayman Film Festival.* **Apr 28-29** *12th Batabano Carnival*, Grand Cayman. **Jun 1-30** *12th Annual Million Dollar Month Fishing Tournament.* **Jun 6-12** *9th Annual Cayman Islands International Aviation Week.* **Jun 12** *Queen's Birthday Celebration.* **Jul 1-3** *Taste of Cayman; 8th*

Annual Britannia Golf Classic. **Oct 20-29** *19th Pirates Week Festival.* **Oct 31** *Hallowe'en.*
SOCIAL CONVENTIONS: The mode of life on the Cayman Islands is a blend of local traditions and of American and British patterns of behaviour. Handshaking is the usual greeting. Because of the large number of people with a similar surname (such as Ebanks and Bodden), a person may be introduced by his Christian name (such as Mr Tom or Mr Jim). Flowers are acceptable as a gift on arrival or following a visit for a meal. Dinner jackets are seldom worn. Short or long dresses are appropriate for women in the evenings. It is normal to prescribe mode of dress on invitation cards. Casual wear is acceptable in most places, but beachwear is best confined to the beach to avoid offence. Topless bathing is prohibited. **Tipping:** 10-15% is normal for most services. Hotels and apartments state the specific amount. Restaurant bills usually include 10-15% in lieu of tipping.

BUSINESS PROFILE

ECONOMY: The Cayman Islands have no direct taxation and have become important as an offshore financial centre and a tax haven. Tourism is the other main source of revenue for the Caymans. There is little agriculture, and most of the foodstuffs for the islands are imported. The standard of living on the islands is generally high, and the per capita income is the highest in the region. The healthy state of the economy has attracted immigrant workers from Jamaica, Europe and North America who now make up 30% of the working population.
BUSINESS: Business suits are recommended when calling on senior officials and local heads of business and also for semi-formal or formal functions. Exchange of calling cards is usual and letters of introduction are sometimes used. It is generally easy to gain access to offices of senior government officials, politicians and business executives. Civil servants are precluded from accepting gifts except for diaries or calendars at Christmas. Monetary gifts or expensive presents are not encouraged in the private sector. **Office hours:** 0830-1700 Monday to Friday.
COMMERCIAL INFORMATION: The following organisation can offer advice: Cayman Islands Chamber of Commerce, PO Box 1000, Commerce House, George Town, Grand Cayman. Tel: (94) 98090. Fax: (94) 90220.
CONFERENCES/CONVENTIONS: Many hotels have conference facilities. Contact the Cayman Islands Department of Tourism for details (see top of entry for address).

CLIMATE

Very warm, tropical climate throughout the year. High temperatures are moderated by trade winds. Rainy season from May to October but showers are generally brief.
Required clothing: Lightweight cottons and linens and a light raincoat or umbrella for the rainy season. Warmer clothes may be needed on cooler evenings.

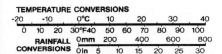

TEMPERATURE CONVERSIONS

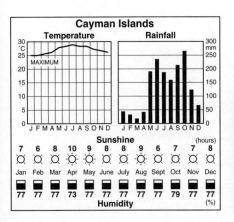

Central African Republic

☐ *international airport*

Location: Central Africa.

Note: Armed robbery is prevalent in Bangui and in the north of the country. Walking in the capital at any time of day or night is unsafe; motorised transportation is recommended. Visitors are advised to exercise caution throughout the country. For up-to-date information, contact the FCO Travel Advice Unit. Tel: (0171) 270 4129.
Source: FCO Travel Advice Unit – November 30, 1994.

Office National Centrafricain du Tourisme (OCATOUR)
BP 655, Bangui, Central African Republic
Tel: 614 566.
Embassy of the Central African Republic
30 rue des Perchamps, 75116 Paris, France
Tel: (1) 42 24 42 56. Fax: (1) 42 88 98 95. Telex: 611908.
British Consulate
c/o SOCACIG, BP 728, Bangui, Central African Republic
Tel: 610 300 *or* 611 045. Fax: 615 130. Telex: (a/b 5258 RG).
Embassy of the Central African Republic
1618 22nd Street, NW, Washington, DC 20008
Tel: (202) 483 7800/1. Fax: (202) 332 9893.
Embassy of the United States of America
BP 924, avenue David Dacko, Bangui, Central African Republic
Tel: 610 200 *or* 610 210 *or* 612 578. Fax: 614 494. Telex: 5287 (a/b RC).
The Canadian Embassy in Yaoundé deals with enquiries relating to the Central African Republic (see *Cameroon* **earlier in this book).**
Honorary Consulate General of the Central African Republic
3rd Floor, 225 St Jacques Street West, Montréal, Québec H2Y 1M6
Tel: (514) 849 8381. Fax: (514) 849 8383.

AREA: 622,984 sq km (240,535 sq miles).
POPULATION: 2,688,426 (1988).
POPULATION DENSITY: 4.3 per sq km.
CAPITAL: Bangui. **Population:** 427,435 (1988).

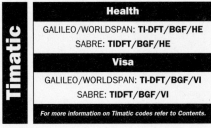

GEOGRAPHY: The Central African Republic is bordered to the north by Chad, to the east by Sudan, to the south by Zaïre and the Congo and to the west by Cameroon. It is a large, landlocked territory of mostly uninhabited forest, bush and game reserves. The Chari River cuts through the centre from east to west; towards the Cameroon border the landscape rises to 2000m (6560ft) west of Bocaranga in the northwest corner, while the southwest has dense tropical rainforest. Most of the country is rolling or flat plateau covered with dry deciduous forest, except where it has been reduced to grass savannah or destroyed by bush fire. The northeast becomes desert scrubland and mountainous in parts.
LANGUAGE: French is the official administrative language and is essential for business. The native language is Sango.
RELIGION: Animist. One-third of the population is Christian. There is a small Islamic minority.
TIME: GMT + 1.
ELECTRICITY: 220/380 volts AC, 50Hz.
COMMUNICATIONS: Telephone: IDD is available. Country code: 236, although many calls are still directed through the operator. **Telex/telegram:** Telex facilities are available at post offices in Bangui and good hotels. Telegrams may be sent from 1430-1830 Saturday and from 0800-1830 Sunday. **Post:** There is a post office in each prefecture. Local postal services are unreliable. Both postal and telecommunications services are in the course of development. Airmail services to Europe take about one week, although it is often much longer; surface mail can take up to three months. *Poste Restante* facilities are available in Bangui. Post office hours: 0730-1130 and 1430-1630 Monday to Friday; open for stamps and telegrams only 1430-1830 Saturday and 0800-1100 Sunday. **Press:** There is one daily newspaper, *E Le Songo.* The weekly publications have limited distribution and are in French.
BBC World Service and Voice of America frequencies: From time to time these change. See the section *How to Use this Book* for more information.
BBC:

MHz	21.66	21.47	17.79	17.88

Voice of America:

MHz	21.49	15.60	9.525	6.035

PASSPORT/VISA

Regulations and requirements may be subject to change at short notice, and you are advised to contact the appropriate diplomatic or consular authority before finalising travel arrangements. Details of these may be found at the head of this country's entry. Any numbers in the chart refer to the footnotes below.

	Passport Required?	Visa Required?	Return Ticket Required?
Full British	Yes	Yes	Yes
BVP	Not valid	-	-
Australian	Yes	Yes	Yes
Canadian	Yes	Yes	Yes
USA	Yes	Yes	Yes
Other EU (As of 31/12/94)	1	2	Yes
Japanese	Yes	Yes	Yes

PASSPORTS: Valid passport required by all except:
(a) [1] nationals of France holding a national ID card or passport expired for no more than 5 years;
(b) nationals of Benin, Burkina Faso, Cameroon, Chad, Congo, Côte d'Ivoire, Gabon, Monaco, Niger, Senegal, Togo and Zaïre holding a national ID card or passport expired for no more than 5 years.
British Visitors Passport: Not accepted.
VISAS: Required by all except:
(a) [2] nationals of France; also nationals of Greece provided they are carrying written proof of travelling on business (all other EU nationals *do* require a visa);
(b) nationals of Benin, Burkina Faso, Cameroon, Chad, Congo, Côte d'Ivoire, Equatorial Guinea, Gabon, Israel, Liechtenstein, Madagascar, Monaco, Niger, Romania, Rwanda, Senegal, Sudan, Switzerland, Togo and Zaïre;
(c) nationals of Lebanon provided carrying written proof of purpose of visit.
Types of visa: *Transit:* Visa not required by passengers proceeding by the same aircraft to a third country. *Entry and Exit permits:* It is necessary to obtain entry and exit permits from Bangui Immigration office. Cost: £2-4.
Validity: Check with Embassy for details.
Applications to: Consulate (or Consular section at Embassy). For addresses, see top of entry.
Application requirements: (a) 4 application forms. (b) 2 passport-size photos. (c) Full travel ticket/proof of sufficient funds. (d) Fee. (e) Yellow fever and cholera certificates.
Working days required: Applications are normally processed within 2 working days.

MONEY

Currency: CFA Franc (CFA Fr) = 100 centimes. Notes are in denominations of CFA Fr10,000, 5000, 1000, 500 and 100. Coins are in denominations of CFA Fr100, 50, 25, 10, 5, 2 and 1. These notes are legal tender in the republics which formerly comprised French Equatorial Africa (Chad, Cameroon, Central African Republic, Congo and Gabon). The CFA Fr100 note is not negotiable in the UK. The Central African Republic is part of the French monetary area.
Note: At the beginning of 1994, the CFA Franc was devalued against the French Franc.
Credit cards: Some major credit cards are accepted. Check with your credit card company for details of merchant acceptability and other services which may be available.
Exchange rate indicators: The following figures are included as a guide to the movements of the CFA Franc against Sterling and the US Dollar:

Date:	Oct '92	Sep '93	Jan '94	Jan '95
£1.00=	413.75	433.87	436.78	834.94
$1.00=	260.71	284.13	295.22	533.68

Currency restrictions: Unlimited import of foreign currency is allowed with export up to the amount declared on arrival. Free import of local currency is allowed; export of local currency is unlimited to residents of countries in the French Monetary Zone, but for all others it is CFA Fr75,000.
Banking hours: 0730-1130 Monday to Friday.

DUTY FREE

The following goods may be imported by visitors over 18 years of age into the Central African Republic without incurring customs duty:
1000 cigarettes or cigarillos or 250 cigars or 2kg of tobacco (females may only import cigarettes); a reasonable quantity of alcoholic beverage and perfume.
Prohibited items: Firearms.
Note: When leaving the Central African Republic any animal skins and diamonds must be declared.

PUBLIC HOLIDAYS

Jan 1 '95 New Year's Day. **Mar 29** Anniversary of the Death of Barthélemy Boganda. **May 1** May Day. **May 25** Ascension Day. **Jun 5** Whit Monday. **Jun 30** National Day of Prayer. **Aug 13** Independence Day. **Aug 15** Assumption. **Nov 1** All Saints' Day. **Dec 1** National Day. **Dec 25** Christmas. **Jan 1 '96** New Year's Day. **Mar 29** Anniversary of the Death of Barthélemy Boganda. **Apr 8** Easter Monday.

HEALTH

Regulations and requirements may be subject to change at short notice, and you are advised to contact your doctor well in advance of your intended date of departure. Any numbers in the chart refer to the footnotes below.		
	Special Precautions?	**Certificate Required?**
Yellow Fever	Yes	1
Cholera	Yes	2
Typhoid & Polio	Yes	-
Malaria	3	-
Food & Drink	4	-

[1]: A yellow fever vaccination certificate is required from travellers over one year of age.
[2]: A cholera vaccination certificate is required from all travellers. Cholera is a serious risk in this country and precautions are essential. See the *Health* section at the back of the book.
[3]: Risk of malaria (and of other insect-borne diseases) exists all year throughout the country. The malignant *falciparum* form is prevalent. Resistance to chloroquine has been reported.
[4]: All water should be regarded as being potentially contaminated. Water used for drinking, brushing teeth or making ice should have first been boiled or otherwise sterilised. Milk is unpasteurised and should be boiled. Powdered or tinned milk is available and is advised, but make sure that it is reconstituted with pure water. Avoid dairy products which are likely to have been made from unboiled milk. Only eat well-cooked meat and fish, preferably served hot. Pork, salad and mayonnaise may carry increased risk. Vegetables should be cooked and fruit peeled.
Rabies is present. For those at high risk, vaccination before arrival should be considered. If you are bitten abroad seek medical advice without delay. For more information consult the *Health* section at the back of the book.
Bilharzia (schistosomiasis) is present. Avoid swimming

and paddling in fresh water. Swimming pools which are well-chlorinated and maintained are safe.
Health care: Full health insurance is essential, and should include air evacuation to Europe in case of serious accident or illness. Medical facilities are severely limited outside the major centres and visitors should travel with their own supply of remedies for simple ailments such as stomach upsets; pharmaceutical supplies are usually very difficult to obtain.

TRAVEL - International

AIR: The main airline to serve the Central African Republic is *Air France (AF)*. The Central African Republic is a shareholder in *Air Afrique*.
Approximate flight time: From London to Bangui is 9 hours 40 minutes (including approximately 1 hour stopover in Paris). There are also connections between Bangui and Douala (Cameroon), Kinshasa (Zaïre), Lagos (Nigeria) and West Africa.
International airport: *Bangui M'Poko (BGF)*, 4km (2.5 miles) northwest of the city (travel time – 30 minutes). Taxis are available to Bangui and cost CFA Fr10,000-15,000 by day, CFA Fr2000-2500 by night. A bus service to the city meets all flights. Airport facilities include restaurant, post office, shops and car hire.
Departure tax: CFA Fr2000 is levied on all passengers.
RIVER: The Central African Republic has no coastline. The water route by ferry along the Ubangi to Bangui from the Congo or Zaïre is run by the Zaïre government-owned *ONATRA* company. There is a car/passenger ferry between Bangui and Zongo and between Bangassou and Ndu across the Ubangi. Fares are very cheap, although the service breaks down frequently. It is still possible to hire a boat. The price for this may be high. Do not cross the river to Zaïre on Saturday or Sunday, as the customs posts in that country do not work at the weekend.
ROAD: Road access is from Zaïre, Chad and Cameroon. There are good all-weather roads from Yaoundé (Cameroon) and Ndjaména (Chad). From Zaïre it is necessary to get a ferry across Ubangi River from Zongo to Bangui or from Ndu to Bangassou (see above).

TRAVEL - Internal

AIR: *Inter-RCA* operates regular flights to various Central African cities from Bangui, including Libreville and Ndjaména.
RIVER: River ferries sail from Bangui to several towns further up the Ubangi. Some of them are quite luxurious and the journey can be a marvellous way to travel between the Congo and Central African Republic, although the service may be intermittent and the going slow. Little information on tariffs is available, but the service *officially* operates every two weeks. Information may possibly be obtained from the Embassy in France, but arrangements are best made in Brazzaville, Congo.
ROAD: Good roads connect the few main towns, but the majority are often impassable during the rainy season and one should expect delays. Outside the urban areas, motor vehicles are rare and spare parts virtually impossible to find. Traffic drives on the right. Travellers must carry as large a petrol supply as possible as deliveries to stations outside the towns are infrequent. **Bus:** Local services run between towns; they are a cheap but sometimes a gruelling way to travel. It is also possible to pay for a lift on the numerous goods trucks which drive between the main towns. **Car hire:** Self-drive or chauffeur-driven cars are available from the local *Hertz* agent (*Location Solo Hertz*) and other local companies. **Documentation:** International Driving Permit required.

URBAN: Limited bus services run in Bangui on a 2-zone tariff. Taxis are only available in the urban areas; they do not have meters and fares must be negotiated.

ACCOMMODATION

HOTELS: There are good hotels in Bangui, some of which are very exclusive and expensive. The better hotels have air-conditioning and swimming pools. Pre-booking is essential, ideally several weeks in advance. Outside Bangui, accommodation of any standard is very difficult to find, although guest-houses exist in smaller towns.
CAMPING/CARAVANNING: Camping is available at the Centre d'Accueil des Tourists at 'Kilometre Cinq'. Since most of the country is unpopulated or traversed by nomadic herdsmen, travelling by vehicle and camping on the landscape is the normal way of life rather than a speciality. There are few organised facilities, so all provisions and requirements should be carried with the vehicles.

RESORTS & EXCURSIONS

At the beginning of the century, **Bangui** was a modest village beside the **River Ubangi**; it now extends over nearly 15 sq km (5 sq miles). Built on a rock, it is shaded by tropical greenery and features many modern buildings and avenues lined with mango trees.
Places of interest include the colourful *Central Market* (renowned for its malachite necklaces), the *Boganda Museum*, the *Arts and Crafts School*, the cathedral and the *Saint Paul Mission*, whose small brick church overlooks the river, and the Hausa quarter. The *Grande Corniche* leads to the banks of the Ubangi and provides a picturesque view of the fishermen's round huts and canoes.
Outside Bangui: The *Lobaye Region*, 100km (60 miles) from the capital, is the home of pygmies who live in unspoiled forest in encampments of small, low huts made of lianas and roofed with leaves. There are coffee plantations on the fringe of the forest. There are also pygmy villages in the *M'Baiki Region*, 100km (60 miles) southwest of Bangui. The *Boali Waterfalls* are 90km (55 miles) northwest of Bangui, near the charming and picturesque village of **Boali**. The nearby hydroelectric power plant can also be visited. The Boali Waterfalls are 250m (820ft) wide and 50m (165ft) high; the view from the restaurant at the top is stunning.
At **Bouar**, in the east of the country, there is an area of burial mounds with many upright megaliths (*tanjunu*) thought to be thousands of years old. In **Bangassou**, near the Oubangui River on the border with Zaïre, are the extraordinary *Kembe Falls* on the Kotto River.
WILDLIFE SAFARIS: There are a number of National Parks in the Central African Republic, most of which are accessible by 4-wheel-drive cars from **Birao**, in the far north of the country between the Chad and Sudanese borders, during the dry season only. The game population of these National Parks is impressive, although the activities of poachers have led to a considerable decrease in the animal population in recent years – elephants and rhinos being the species worst affected. There is no accommodation available: all supplies, including bedding, must be taken. All arrangements are best made on arrival in the country, although time should be allowed for finalising plans.

SOCIAL PROFILE

FOOD & DRINK: Western food is only available in the capital of Bangui. Most of the top-class hotels have good restaurants. The standard of these restaurants is high, but

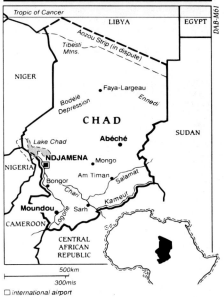

Chad

□ *international airport*

Location: North/Central Africa.

Note: There are reports of areas of lawlessness where sporadic violence occurs. It is advisable not to travel after dark, and to respect army road blocks.
Source: FCO Travel Advice Unit – December 3 1994.

Direction du Tourisme, des Parcs Nationaux et Réserves de Faune
BP 86, Ndjaména, Chad
Tel: 512 303. Fax: 572 261. Telex: 5358.
Embassy of the Republic of Chad
65 rue des Belles Feuilles, 75116 Paris, France
Tel: (1) 45 53 36 75. Fax: (1) 45 53 16 09. Telex: 610629.
Consulates in: Bonn and Brussels.
British Consulate
BP 877, avenue Charles de Gaulle (opposite Air Tchad office), Ndjaména, Chad
Tel: 513 064. Telex: 5235 (a/b ACT KD).
UK Representation:
Worldwide Visas Limited
9 Adelaide Street, London WC2
Tel: (0171) 379 0419. Fax: (0171) 497 2590.
Embassy of the Republic of Chad
2002 R Street, NW, Washington, DC 20009
Tel: (202) 462 4009. Fax: (202) 265 1937.
Also deals with enquiries from Canada.
Embassy of the United States of America
BP 413, avenue Félix Eboué, Ndjaména, Chad
Tel: 514 009 *or* 514 759 *or* 516 218. Fax: 513 372.
Telex: 5203.

AREA: 1,284,000 sq km (495,800 sq miles).
POPULATION: 5,428,000 (1988 estimate).
POPULATION DENSITY: 4.2 per sq km.
CAPITAL: Ndjaména. **Population:** 594,000 (1988 estimate).
GEOGRAPHY: Chad is situated in Africa, bounded by Libya to the north, Niger, Nigeria and Cameroon to the west, the Central African Republic to the south, and Sudan to the east. The topography ranges from equatorial forests to the driest of deserts. Lake Chad extends to an area of 25,000 sq km (9652 sq miles), reducing seasonally to 10,000 sq km (3861 sq miles); it is choked

---

they do tend to be expensive. Otherwise travellers must call at local villages and barter for provisions. Local food is basic. **Drink:** Bars are numerous in Bangui with both table and counter service. Drinking and smoking are not encouraged in Muslim society; in Muslim areas drinking is best done in private.
NIGHTLIFE: The few hotels in Bangui have expensive clubs catering for tourists and businessmen; local nightlife is centred on the district known as 'Kilometre Cinq'.
SHOPPING: Bangui has reasonable shopping facilities, notably for ebony, gold jewellery, butterfly collections and objets d'arts made from butterfly wings. However, one of the best methods of finding bargain souvenirs is by bartering with villagers outside the urban areas for their handmade goods. **Shopping hours:** 0800-1200 and 1600-1900 Monday to Saturday. Some shops close on Monday. The market in Bangui is open from 0730 until dusk.
SOCIAL CONVENTIONS: Dress is informal. Care should be taken to dress modestly in Muslim areas, and Muslim customs should be respected and observed; do not, for instance, show the soles of the feet when sitting. It is customary to shake hands. Women are strictly segregated, especially in towns. In Muslim areas do not smoke or drink in public during Ramadan. **Photography:** Film is expensive and should be sent to Europe for developing. Show caution and discretion when photographing local people, ask for prior permission. Do not photograph military installations or government buildings. **Tipping:** 10% is appropriate for most services.

BUSINESS PROFILE

ECONOMY: Agriculture, on which most of the population depends, is concentrated on subsistence crops, and coffee, cotton and wood as cash crops for export. Diamonds are the main export commodity, accounting for over 50% of foreign earnings. Other mineral deposits, including uranium and iron, have yet to be exploited. Manufacturing industry is insignificant. The Central African Republic is a member of the CFA Franc Zone and of the Central African customs and economic union, UDEAC. France, which supplies extensive development

aid, is the main trading partner for both imports and exports, while Belgium and Luxembourg are the largest single export markets.
BUSINESS: A knowledge of French is essential. Interpreter and translation services may be available at large hotels. Business cards should be in French and English. Formal wear is expected (suits and ties for men). The best months for business visits are between November and May. **Office hours:** 0630-1330 Monday to Friday; 0700-1200 Saturday.
COMMERCIAL INFORMATION: The following organisation can offer advice: Chambre de Commerce, d'Industrie, des Mines et de l'Artisanat (CCIMA), BP 813, Bangui. Tel: 614 255. Telex: 5261.

CLIMATE

Hot all year with a defined dry season. Especially hot in the northeast. Monsoon in the south (May to October).
Required clothing: Tropical with waterproofing.

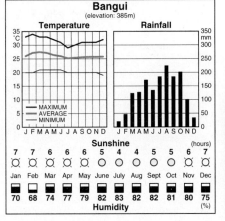

Bangui
(elevation: 385m)

— MAXIMUM
— AVERAGE
— MINIMUM

	Jan	Feb	Mar	Apr	May	June	July	Aug	Sept	Oct	Nov	Dec
Sunshine (hours)	7	7	6	6	6	5	4	4	5	5	6	7
Humidity (%)	70	68	74	77	79	82	83	82	82	81	80	75

with papyrus and covered with islands of floating vegetation. The Chari, Logone, Salamat and Aouk rivers and tributaries run south but are often just dry beds. The Chad basin is bounded by mountains and the Central African Plateau. In the east, the crystalline Ovaddai Range rises 1500m (5000ft). In the northeast lie the pink sandstone heights of Ennedi, and to the north the volcanic Tibesti range, largely sheer cliffs, ravines and canyons set among Saharan sand dunes.

LANGUAGE: French is the official language. Other widely spoken languages include Chadian Arabic (north) and Sara (south). The territory's boundaries enclose a small but highly diverse population; not surprisingly, there are over 50 local languages. The principal northern (and mainly Muslim) tribal groups are the Nare Arabs, Toubou, Fulani, Hausa, Kanembou, Boulala and Wadai. The principal southern (and mainly Christian) groups are the Baguirmi, Kotoko, Sara, Massa and Moundang.

RELIGION: 50% Muslim, 45% Animist, 5% Christian.

TIME: GMT + 1.

ELECTRICITY: 220/380 volts AC, 50Hz.

COMMUNICATIONS: Telephone: Country code: 235. It may be necessary to go through the operator. **Telex/telegram:** Available in major post offices in Ndjaména, Sarh, Moundou and Abéché. **Post:** Airmail takes about one week. Post office hours: 0730-1200 Monday to Friday; 1430-1830 Saturday; 0800-1100 Sunday (for the purchase of stamps). **Press:** Newspapers are printed in French and generally have low circulations. **BBC World Service and Voice of America frequencies:** From time to time these change. See the section *How to Use this Book* for more information.

BBC:

MHz	21.47	17.88	12.09	9.410

Voice of America:

MHz	21.49	15.60	9.525	6.035

PASSPORT/VISA

Regulations and requirements may be subject to change at short notice, and you are advised to contact the appropriate diplomatic or consular authority before finalising travel arrangements. Details of these may be found at the head of this country's entry. Any numbers in the chart refer to the footnotes below.

	Passport Required?	Visa Required?	Return Ticket Required?
Full British	Yes	Yes	Yes
BVP	Not valid	-	-
Australian	Yes	Yes	Yes
Canadian	Yes	Yes	Yes
USA	Yes	Yes	Yes
Other EU (As of 31/12/94)	Yes	Yes	Yes
Japanese	Yes	Yes	Yes

PASSPORTS: Valid passport required by all except nationals of the countries listed below under *Visas.* British Visitors Passport: Not accepted.

VISAS: Required by all except nationals of Benin, Burkina Faso, Cameroon, Central African Republic, Congo, Côte d'Ivoire, Equatorial Guinea, Mauritania, Niger, Nigeria, Senegal and Togo.

Types of visa: Validity varies from three days to three months. Visitors continuing their journey within 48 hours to a third country by the same or first connecting aircraft do not require Transit visas provided they hold tickets with reserved seats and valid documents for their destination. **Note:** Travel outside the capital requires a special authorisation from the Minister of the Interior which must be obtained on arrival. There may be difficulty obtaining it. **Application and enquiries to:** Consulate (or Consular section at Embassy). For addresses, see top of entry. Allow three working days for the application to be processed. **Application requirements:** (a) Valid passport. (b) 2 passport-size photos. (c) 2 application forms. (d) Letters of recommendation. (e) Full travel ticket. (f) Proof of sufficient funds. (g) Application fee (FFr200).

MONEY

Currency: CFA Franc (CFA Fr) = 100 centimes. Notes are in denominations of CFA Fr10,000, 5000, 1000 and 500. Coins are in denominations of CFA Fr500, 100, 50, 25, 10, 5 and 1. These notes are legal tender in the republics which formerly comprised French Equatorial Africa (Chad, Cameroon, Central African Republic, Congo and Gabon). Chad is part of the French Monetary Area. **Note:** At the beginning of 1994, the CFA Franc was devalued against the French Franc. **Currency exchange:** It is advisable to bring Dollars rather than Sterling into the country. CFA Francs can be difficult to exchange outside the French Monetary Area. **Credit cards:** Diners Club and Access/Mastercard (limited use) are accepted. Check with your credit card company for details of merchant acceptability and other

services which may be available.

Exchange rate indicators: The following figures are included as a guide to the movements of the CFA Franc against Sterling and the US Dollar:

Date:	Oct '92	Sep '93	Jan '94	Jan '95
£1.00=	413.75	433.87	436.78	843.10
$1.00=	260.71	284.14	295.22	545.06

Currency restrictions: Unlimited import of foreign currency is allowed, subject to declaration; export is allowed up to the amount declared on import. There is free import of local currency, subject to declaration. Export of local currency is limited to the amount declared on entry. **Banking hours:** 0700-1100 Monday to Saturday; 0700-1030 Friday.

DUTY FREE

The following goods may be imported into Chad without incurring customs duty for passengers over 18 years of age: *400 cigarettes or 125 cigars or 500g of tobacco (women – cigarettes only); 3 bottles of wine; 1 bottle of spirits.*

PUBLIC HOLIDAYS

Jan 1 '95 New Year's Day. **Mar 3** Eid al-Fitr (End of Ramadan). **Apr 17** Easter Monday. **May 1** Labour Day. **May 10** Eid al-Adha (Feast of the Sacrifice). **May 25** OAU Foundation Day. **Jun 5** Whit Monday. **Aug 9** Mouloud (Prophet's Birthday). **Aug 11** Independence Day. **Aug 15** Assumption. **Nov 1** All Saints' Day. **Nov 28** Proclamation of the Republic. **Dec 25** Christmas Day. **Jan 1 '96** New Year's Day. **Feb 22** Eid al-Fitr (End of Ramadan). **Apr 8** Easter Monday. **Apr 29** Eid al-Adha (Feast of the Sacrifice). **Note:** Muslim festivals are timed according to local sightings of various phases of the Moon and the dates given above are approximations. During the lunar month of Ramadan that precedes Eid al-Fitr, Muslims fast during the day and feast at night and normal business patterns may be interrupted. Many restaurants are closed during the day and there may be restrictions on smoking and drinking. Some disruption may continue into Eid al-Fitr itself. Eid al-Fitr and Eid al-Adha may last anything from two to ten days, depending on the region. For more information see the section *World of Islam* at the back of the book.

HEALTH

Regulations and requirements may be subject to change at short notice, and you are advised to contact your doctor well in advance of your intended date of departure. Any numbers in the chart refer to the footnotes below.

	Special Precautions?	Certificate Required?
Yellow Fever	Yes	1
Cholera	Yes	2
Typhoid & Polio	Yes	-
Malaria	Yes	-
Food & Drink	3	

[1]: A yellow fever certificate is required from travellers over one year of age. Risk of infection is highest south of 15°N.
[2]: Following WHO guidelines issued in 1973, a cholera vaccination certificate is no longer a condition of entry to Chad. However, cholera is a serious risk in this country and precautions are essential. Up-to-date advice should be sought before deciding whether these precautions should include vaccination as medical opinion is divided over its effectiveness. See the *Health* section at the back of the book.
[3]: All water should be regarded as being potentially contaminated. Water used for drinking, brushing teeth or making ice should have first been boiled or otherwise sterilised. Milk is unpasteurised and should be boiled. Powdered or tinned milk is available and is advised, but make sure that it is reconstituted with pure water. Avoid all dairy products. Only eat well-cooked meat and fish, preferably served hot. Pork, salad and mayonnaise may carry increased risk. Vegetables should be cooked and fruit peeled.
Malaria risk, predominantly in the malignant *falciparum* form, exists all year throughout the country. For more information consult the *Health* section at the back of the book.
Bilharzia (schistosomiasis) is present. Avoid swimming and paddling in fresh water. Swimming pools which are well-chlorinated and maintained are safe.
Meningitis risk is present depending on area visited and time of year.
Health care: Medical facilities are poor, particularly in the north, and health insurance (to include emergency repatriation cover) is essential.

TRAVEL - International

AIR: Within Chad the national airline is *Air Tchad (HT)*. Chad is a shareholder in *Air Afrique*, which operates two

flights a week from Paris to Ndjaména. *Air France* operates one flight a week on this route.
Approximate flight time: *Paris* to Ndjaména is 5 hours 30 minutes. There are no direct flights or good connections for those travelling from London. Overnight transit costs may be covered by some airlines.
International airport: *Ndjaména (NDJ)* is 4km (2.5 miles) northwest of the city. Taxis are available. There is no duty-free shop.
Departure tax: There is a tourist tax of CFA Fr2500.
RAIL: There is no railway network in Chad. There have been long-standing plans for a rail link with Cameroon but nothing has yet come of these.
ROAD: There are routes from the Central African Republic, Cameroon and Nigeria. Presently the best route from Ndjaména to Bangui (car) goes via Bongor, Lai, Doba, Gore (border) and Bossangoa rather than through Sarh. It is possible to enter Chad either by this route or from Maiduguri in Nigeria via a sliver of northern Cameroon. The border between Cameroon and Chad is the River Logone, which flows into Lake Chad. Boats ply across the river (there is no bridge). Roads can be inaccessible during the rainy season.

TRAVEL - Internal

AIR: Air services are run by *Air Tchad* when not occupied in military activities. A cotton company, *Coton-Tchad*, runs its own limited flights, and may be able to offer a seat or two, but reports are that there is a considerable demand for this.
ROAD: Travel by road outside Ndjaména is only possible in a vehicle with 4-wheel-drive and permits are usually needed: certain security conditions and a lack of housing, food, petrol and vehicle repair facilities have resulted in the Government prohibiting travel, especially in the central and northern areas of the country. This applies even to convoys of vehicles and covers the routes from Libya via Zouar and Faya-Largeau to Ndjaména and the road from Ndjaména via Ati and Abéché to the Sudanese border. Petrol is expensive. There is an unpaved road running from Maiduguri in Nigeria through Cameroon to Ndjaména; this is a major trucking route into Chad. However, its condition varies according to the maintenance it receives and the weather. The rains often render it impassable, the worst season being from the last week of July to the first week of September (when even a Land-Rover will not get through). The Cameroon road from Ngaoundéré through Garoua, Maroua and the Wazza Game Reserve to Ndjaména has paved, all-weather sections but the unimproved sections make this road difficult in the rainy season. Many other roads urgently need repair and international aid is being given for this; it is, however, a huge task. Traffic drives on the right.
Documentation: The motorist needs a *Carnet de Passage* issued by the Tourist Association in the country of origin, an International Driving Permit and either a Green Card for insurance or an all-risk insurance obtained in Chad.
URBAN: The city of Ndjaména has an adequate road system and there are limited self-drive and chauffeured car hire facilities. Minibuses and taxis operate in Ndjaména, with a flat fare charged. A 10% tip is expected by taxi drivers.

ACCOMMODATION

There are three good hotels in Ndjaména, but accommodation elsewhere is very limited. There are two small hotels at Sarh, a modern hotel complex in Zakouma National Park, and various small hunting hotels in the southwest. It is advisable to book in advance and prospective travellers should contact the Chad Embassy in Paris for latest information. For more information, contact: Société Hôtelière et Touristique, BP 478, Ndjaména.

RESORTS & EXCURSIONS

Note: Political problems have prevented Chad from developing its considerable tourist potential. Travel outside Ndjaména remains dangerous, especially in the north of the country which has yet to recover from the recent war with Libya. Permits are required to travel outside the capital (see *Passport/Visa* and *Travel* above).
Ndjaména: The historic quarter and the colourful daily market are both worth a visit, as well as the museum which has collections of the Sarh culture dating back to the 9th century.
Zakouma National Park: Located on an immense plain across which the *Bahr Salamat* and its tributaries flow from north to south, here visitors may view rhinos, herds of elephants and a wide range of other species.
Lake Chad: This was once the centre of Africa's lucrative salt trade, but is now shrinking (literally) and sparsely populated.
Tibesti Mountains: An astonishing region of chasms

and crags which has seldom been seen by non-Muslims. It remained closed to outsiders during the great era of exploration in the last century and is closed once more as it lies within territory claimed by Libya. The range is said to be home to the best racing camels in the world. The inhabitants, distantly related to the Tuareg of the Western Sahara, were made famous by Herodotus as the *Troglodytes*, stocky but immensely agile cave-dwellers who squeaked like bats and climbed like monkeys.

SOCIAL PROFILE

FOOD & DRINK: There are very few restaurants and those remaining in operation are generally found in hotels in the capital; it is not wise to eat anywhere else. Standard European-style service is normal. There is an acute shortage of some foodstuffs. There is a limited number of bars due to Muslim beliefs. Drinking and smoking are not encouraged and alcohol is generally only available in the main hotels in Ndjaména.

NIGHTLIFE: This is limited and centred in the main towns.

SHOPPING: Chad has an excellent crafts industry. Items include camel-hair carpets, all kinds of leatherware, embroidered cotton cloths, decorated calabashes, knives, weapons, pottery and brass animals. **Shopping hours:** 0900-1230 and 1600-1930 Tuesday to Saturday, being mainly closed Mondays. Food shops open Sunday mornings. The market in the capital is open from 0730 until dusk.

SOCIAL CONVENTIONS: Respect for traditional beliefs and customs is expected. Dress is informal but conservative in respect of Muslim laws. There is strict segregation of women, especially in the towns. It is customary to shake hands. The left hand should never be used for offering or accepting food, nor should the sole of the foot be exposed in the presence of a Muslim.

Tipping: 10% is normal for most services. US Dollars are a good currency to use.

BUSINESS PROFILE

ECONOMY: Civil war, poor infrastructure, few natural resources and recent droughts have hampered any real development of the economy. Subsistence level farming occupies 80% of the population. The south is the most populous region, particularly around Sarh, where the agricultural Sara people are dominant. Kotoko fishermen and the Massa people live in the southwest. The Boudama and Kouri peoples, who earn their livelihood from fishing and cattle rearing, live on islands in Lake Chad. The central *Sahel* region is the home of traditional pastoral nomads, including the Maba, Dadjo, Barma and many Arab clans. The north is mainly populated by nomadic and highly ethnocentric Toubou, Tuaregs and Arab clans. Food shortage is a problem and many areas of the country rely on international food aid. France is by far the largest trading partner, followed by Nigeria, The Netherlands, Italy, the USA, the UK, Cameroon and Germany.

BUSINESS: A knowledge of French is essential as there are no professional translators available. Best months for business visits are between November and May. **Office hours:** 0730-1400 Monday to Saturday; 0700-1200 Friday.

COMMERCIAL INFORMATION: The following organisation can offer advice: Chambre de Commerce, Chambre Consulaire, BP 458, Ndjaména. Tel: 515 264.

CLIMATE

Hot, tropical climate, though temperatures vary in different areas. The southern rainy season lasts from May to October and the central rains from June to September. The north has little rain all year. The dry season is often windy and cooler during evenings.

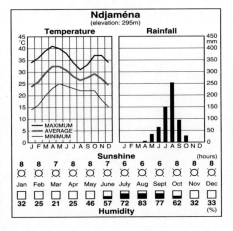

Ndjaména
(elevation: 295m)

□ *international airport*

Location: West coast of South America.

Servicio Nacional de Turismo (SERNATUR) (Tourist Office)
Casilla 14082, Avenida Providencia 1550, Santiago, Chile
Tel: (2) 236 0531 *or* 236 1416 *or* 236 1418. Fax: (2) 236 1417.

Embassy of the Republic of Chile
12 Devonshire Street, London W1N 2DS
Tel: (0171) 580 6392 *or* 580 1023 (visa enquiries and tourist office). Fax: (0171) 436 5204. Telex: 25970.

Chilean Consulate General
Address as above
Tel: (0171) 580 1023. Opening hours: 0930-1230 Monday to Wednesday and Friday.

British Embassy
Casilla 72-D *or* Casilla 16552, Avenida El Bosque Norte 0125, Santiago 9, Chile
Tel: (2) 223 9166. Fax: (2) 223 1917 *or* 235 7375 (British Council). Telex: 340483 (a/b BRITEMB CK).
Consulates in: Antofagasta, Arica, Concepción, Punta Arenas and Valparaíso.

Embassy of the Republic of Chile
1732 Massachusetts Avenue, NW, Washington, DC 20036
Tel: (202) 785 1746. Fax: (202) 887 5579.

Chilean Consulate General
Suite 302, 3rd Floor, 866 United Nations Plaza, New York, NY 10017
Tel: (212) 980 3366. Fax: (212) 888 5288.

Embassy of the United States of America
Unit 4127, Codina Building, Agustinas 1343, Santiago, Chile
Tel: (2) 671 0133. Fax: (2) 699 1141.

Embassy of the Republic of Chile
Suite 605, 151 Slater Street, Ottawa, Ontario K1P 5H3

Tel: (613) 235 4402 *or* 235 9940. Fax: (613) 235 1176.

Chilean Consulate General
Suite 710, 1010 Sherbrooke Street West, Montréal, Québec H3A 2R7
Tel: (514) 499 0405. Fax: (514) 499 8914.

Canadian Embassy
Casilla 427, 10th Floor, Ahumada 11, Santiago, Chile
Tel: (2) 696 2256/7/8/9. Fax: (2) 696 2424. Telex: 240341 (a/b DMCAN CL).

AREA: 756,626 sq km (292,135 sq miles).
POPULATION: 13,599,441 (1992 estimate).
POPULATION DENSITY: 18 per sq km.
CAPITAL: Santiago (de Chile). **Population:** 4,545,784 (1992).
GEOGRAPHY: Chile is situated in South America, bounded to the north by Peru, to the east by Bolivia and Argentina, to the west by the Pacific and to the south by the Antarctic. The country exercises sovereignty over a number of islands off the coast, including the Juan Fernández Islands, where Alexander Selkirk (the inspiration for Robinson Crusoe) was shipwrecked, and Easter Island. Chile is one of the most remarkably shaped countries in the world; a ribbon of land, 4200km (2610 miles) long and nowhere more than 180km (115 miles) wide. The Andes and a coastal highland range take up one-third or half of the width in parts, and run parallel with each other from north to south. The coastal range forms high, sloped cliffs into the sea from the northern to the central area. Between the ranges runs a fertile valley, except in the north where transverse ranges join the two major ones, and in the far south where the sea has broken through the coastal range to form an assortment of archipelagos and channels. The country contains wide variations of soil and vast differences of climate. This is reflected in the distribution of the population, and in the wide range of occupations from area to area. The northern part of the country consists mainly of the Atacama Desert, the driest in the world. It is also the main mining area. The central zone is predominantly agricultural. The south is forested and contains some agriculture; further south, the forests on the Atlantic side give way to rolling grassland on which sheep and cattle are raised.
LANGUAGE: The official language is Spanish, but English is widely spoken.
RELIGION: 89% Roman Catholic, 11% Protestant.
TIME: Mainland and Juan Fernández Islands: GMT - 4 (GMT - 3 from second Sunday in October to second Saturday in March).
Easter Island: GMT - 6 (GMT - 5 from second Sunday in October to second Saturday in March).
ELECTRICITY: 220 volts AC, 50Hz. Three-pin plugs and screw-type bulbs are used.
COMMUNICATIONS: Telephone: Full IDD available. Country code: 56. Outgoing international code: 00. Compañía de Teléfonos de Chile provides most services though there are a few independent companies. Cheap rate is applicable 1800-0500 Monday to Friday and all day Saturday, Sunday and public holidays. **Fax:** Telex Chile, Transradio Chilena and ITT Communicaciones provide services in main towns.
Telex/telegram: Telex Chile, Transradio Chilena and ITT Communicaciones Mundiales provide services in main towns. **Post:** Daily airmail services to Europe take approximately three to four days. Post office hours in Santiago: 0900-1800 Monday to Friday; 0900-1230 Saturday. **Press:** Spanish dailies include *El Mercurio, La Nación, Las Ultimas Noticias, La Epoca* and *La Tercera*. Foreign newspapers are available.
BBC World Service and Voice of America frequencies: From time to time these change. See the section *How to Use this Book* for more information.

BBC:

MHz	17.79	15.19	11.75	9.915

Voice of America:

MHz	15.21	11.58	9.775	5.995

PASSPORT/VISA

Regulations and requirements may be subject to change at short notice, and you are advised to contact the appropriate diplomatic or consular authority before finalising travel arrangements. Details of these may be found at the head of this country's entry. Any numbers in the chart refer to the footnotes below.

	Passport Required?	Visa Required?	Return Ticket Required?
Full British	Yes	No	Yes
BVP	Not valid	-	-
Australian	Yes	No	Yes
Canadian	Yes	No	Yes
USA	Yes	No	Yes
Other EU (As of 31/12/94)	Yes	1	Yes
Japanese	Yes	No	Yes

PASSPORTS: Valid passport required by all except nationals of Argentina, Brazil, Paraguay and Uruguay, who can enter with a special identity card (Cedula de Identitad) for short-term visits (except foreign residents of these countries who *do* need a passport); and nationals of Taiwan, Mexico and Peru who have an official travel document issued by the Organisation of American States. Passports have to remain valid for 6 months after departure.

Note: Passports issued to children must contain a photo and state the nationality.

British Visitors Passport: Not accepted.

VISAS: As the regulations are always subject to change at short notice it is advisable to check with the Chilean Consulate for the latest information. At present, a visa is not required by:
(a) **[1]** nationals of Belgium, Denmark, Germany, Greece, Ireland, Italy, Luxembourg, The Netherlands, Portugal, Spain and the UK (nationals of France *do* require a visa) for a stay of up to 90 days;
(b) nationals of Antigua & Barbuda, Argentina, Australia, Austria, Belize, Bolivia, Brazil, Canada, Colombia, Costa Rica, Croatia, Ecuador, El Salvador, Fiji, Finland, Guatemala, Honduras, Hungary, Iceland, Indonesia, Israel, Jamaica, Japan, Liechtenstein, Malaysia, Malta, Mexico, Monaco, Morocco, Nicaragua, Norway, Panama, Paraguay, San Marino, St Kitts & Nevis, Singapore, South Africa, Suriname, Sweden, Switzerland, Tonga, Tunisia, Turkey, Tuvalu, USA, Uruguay and Yugoslavia (Serbia and Montenegro) for a stay of up to 90 days;
(c) nationals of Peru and Slovenia for 60 days.

Types of visa: Residence visa required if intending to carry out paid employment or study in Chile. Visitor's visa required for nationals of countries with no diplomatic relations with Chile. Transit visa required by all, except nationals noted above and those continuing their journey on the same day provided they do not leave the airport transit lounge.

Validity: *Tourist:* up to 3 months depending on nationality; *Business:* 1 year.

Application to: Consulate (or Consular section at Embassy). For addresses, see top of entry.

Application requirements: Valid passport. A return ticket may also be required.

Working days: Visas are issued within 24 hours. In some cases it might take 1 week.

Temporary residence: Not easy to obtain. Enquire at Embassy.

MONEY

Currency: Peso (Ch$) = 100 centavos. Notes are in denominations of Ch$10,000, 5000, 1000 and 500. Coins are in denominations of Ch$100, 50, 10, 5 and 1.

Currency exchange: Foreign exchange transactions can be conducted through commercial banks, *cambios*, or authorised shops, restaurants, hotels and clubs. Visitors should not be tempted by the premiums of 10-15% over the official rate offered by black marketeers. *Cambios* are open 0900-1900 all week.

Credit cards: Diners Club, Visa, American Express and Access/Mastercard are accepted. Check with your credit card company for details of merchant acceptability and other services which may be available.

Travellers cheques: Must be changed before 1200 except in *cambios* (which in any case tend to offer better rates than banks). There may be some difficulty exchanging travellers cheques outside of major towns.

Exchange rate indicators: The following figures are included as a guide to the movements of the Chilean Peso against Sterling and the US Dollar:

Date:	Oct '92	Sep '93	Jan '94	Jan '95
£1.00=	593.58	625.45	633.97	625.27
$1.00=	374.03	409.59	428.50	404.24

Currency restrictions: There are no restrictions on the import and export of either local or foreign currency.

Banking hours: 0900-1400 Monday to Friday.

DUTY FREE

The following goods may be imported into Chile without incurring customs duty:
400 cigarettes and 500g of tobacco and 50 cigars or 50 cigarillos; 2.5 litres of alcohol (only for visitors over 18 years of age); a reasonable quantity of perfume.

Prohibited items: Meat products, flowers, fruit and vegetables unless permission is sought prior to travelling. Prohibited items without permission are liable to be confiscated at the airport.

PUBLIC HOLIDAYS

Jan 1 '95 New Year's Day. **Apr 14-15** Easter. **May 1** Labour Day. **May 21** Battle of Iquique. **Aug 15** Assumption. **Sep 11** Anniversary of 1973 coup. **Sep 18**

Independence Day. **Oct 12** Day of the Race. **Nov 1** All Saints' Day. **Dec 8** Immaculate Conception. **Dec 25** Christmas. **Jan 1 '96** New Year's Day. **Apr 5-6** Easter.

HEALTH

Regulations and requirements may be subject to change at short notice, and you are advised to contact your doctor well in advance of your intended date of departure. Any numbers in the chart refer to the footnotes below.

	Special Precautions?	Certificate Required?
Yellow Fever	No	No
Cholera	No	No
Typhoid & Polio	1	-
Malaria	No	-
Food & Drink	2	-

[1]: Immunisation is recommended.
[2]: All water should be regarded as being potentially contaminated. Water used for drinking, brushing teeth or making ice should have first been boiled or otherwise sterilised. Milk is pasteurised and is safe to drink without boiling, except in very remote areas of the countryside. Only eat well-cooked meat and fish, preferably served hot. Pork, salad and mayonnaise may carry increased risk. Vegetables should be cooked and fruit peeled.

Health care: Health insurance is essential.

TRAVEL - International

AIR: Chile has two national airlines, both privately owned: *LAN-Chile (LA)* and *LADECO (UC)*.

Approximate flight times: From Santiago to London is 18 hours 45 minutes.

International airports: *Santiago (SCL)* (Comodoro Arturo Merino Benitez). The airport is 16km (10 miles) from Santiago (travel time – 30 minutes). Bus services to the city centre depart every 20 minutes from 0600-2130; a nightservice is in operation after 2130. Return is from the metro stations Los Héroes, Estación Central and Las Rejas or Moneda/corner of San Martín. Small shuttle buses offer a door-to-door service. Taxis to the city are also available. Airport facilities include bar, bureau de change, car rental, post office and tourist office.
Chacalluta Airport (ARI), 14km (8 miles) northeast of the northern city of Arica, is linked by direct scheduled flights with Miami and several South American capitals.

Departure tax: US$12.50 or the Peso equivalent.

SEA: The principal port is Empremar in Valparaíso. Important shipping lines are *Compañía Chilena de Navegación Interoceánica* (CCNI), *Compañía Argentina de Navegacion Dodero* (CADND) from Buenos Aires; *Compañía Sud Americana de Vapores* (CSAV) from New York and European ports; *Delta Line Cruises* from the United States via the Panama Canal and *Royal Netherlands Company* from Rotterdam and Le Havre.

RAIL: Some rail connections with neighbouring countries use buses in part of the journey. The main service is from Santiago to Puerto Montt. From La Paz, Bolivia, there are trains running twice a week to Arica (on the northern border with Peru). Antofagasta can now only be reached by bus. Connections from Argentina are made by train as far as San Carlos de Bariloche and then on by bus to Puerto Montt.

ROAD: The Pan American Highway enters Chile through Arica. *TEPSA* buses come to Chile from as far north as Ecuador. There are also services from Brazil to Santiago.

TRAVEL - Internal

AIR: There are frequent services to main towns. The southern part of the country relies heavily on air links. Reservations are essential. Internal passenger air services are operated by the main Chilean airlines *LAN, LADECO* and *Aeronorte*, as well as by a number of air taxi companies. Services connecting the main towns are frequent during weekdays, and are fairly regular. There are four 21-day 'Visit Chile' tickets priced from US$250-500 which cover internal travel. They must be obtained abroad with reservations made well in advance. Once bought, tickets cannot be changed, though reservations can. A coupon ticket on the Santiago–Antofagasta–Arica–Santiago route may suit some travellers better. There are regular flights by *LAN* from Santiago to **Easter Island**, which stop at the island en route to Tahiti. The flights are twice-weekly from November to February, once-weekly at other times; it is essential to book in advance throughout the year. The flight takes five hours. An air-taxi runs a daily service during the summer months to the **Juan Fernández Islands** from Valparaíso and Santiago.

Departure tax: US$12.50 (or Peso equivalent) per passenger is levied on all flights leaving from Santiago.

SEA: Coastal passenger shipping lines are unreliable and infrequent. Boat services run from Valparaíso to **Easter Island** and **Robinson Crusoe Island** (part of the Juan Fernández Islands) once a month. Contact local travel agents on arrival for details.

RAIL: The State railway runs for 8000km (4971 miles) throughout Chile, beginning in Santiago and ending in Puerto Montt in the south. Services are limited by the geography of the country, but the backbone route (from Santiago to Puerto Montt) has two daily trains with sleeping and restaurant cars, and some air-conditioned accommodation. Principal trains also carry motor cars. Children under 1.20m in height travel free. For details contact the Chilean Tourist Office.

ROAD: Chile has about 78,000km (48,468 miles) of good roads. The Pan American Highway crosses the country from north to south (a total of 3600km or 2236 miles) from the Peruvian border to Puerto Montt. It is advisable in remoter areas to carry spare petrol and an additional spare tyre. Tyres should be hard-wearing. Traffic drives on the right. **Bus:** Intercity buses are cheap and reliable. There is a luxury north–south service running most of the length of the country. Most long-distance coaches have toilets and serve food and drink. Sometimes a lower fare can be negotiated. For details, contact the Chilean Tourist Office. **Taxi:** Most have meters, but for long journeys fares should be agreed beforehand. A surcharge of 50% applies on Sundays after 2100. Taxis in Santiago are black and yellow. Tipping is not expected. **Car hire:** Self-drive cars are available at the airport and in major city centres. They are rented on a daily basis plus a mileage charge and 20% tax. A large guarantee deposit is often required. The Automóvil Club de Chile, Avenida Vitacura 8620, Santiago (tel: (2) 212 5702), can supply road maps. **Documentation:** An International Driving Permit is necessary.

URBAN: Santiago has two metro lines, bus, minibus and shared 'Taxibus' services. A third metro line is under construction. Flat fares are charged on the metro, although there are plans to introduce distance-related fares. 10-journey tickets *(carnets)* are available. Taxis are plentiful, the number approaching one per 100 inhabitants, an extremely high figure. They can be flagged down in the streets. The different tariffs are displayed in the taxis. Taxi drivers do not expect tips. The buses and minibuses have flat fares. There is a higher rate for shared taxis. There are bus and taxi services in most other towns.

JOURNEY TIMES: The following chart gives approximate journey times from Santiago (in hours and minutes) to other major cities/towns in Chile.

	Air	Road	Rail
Arica	2.40	28.00	84.00
Concepción	1.30	9.00	7.00
Portillo	2.30	-	-
Puerto Montt	1.45	11.00	17.00
Punta Arenas	3.25	120.00	-
Viña del Mar	-	2.00	-
Easter Island	5.00		

ACCOMMODATION

HOTELS: Chile offers excellent accommodation. Several new luxury hotels have recently opened in Santiago and throughout the country. In all regions of Chile, whatever hotels lack in facilities is made up for by a comfortable homely atmosphere; Chile's famous hospitality is very apparent in provinces where it is common to see the owner or manager sit down to dinner with guests. Advance bookings are essential in resort areas during the high season.
The cost of accommodation in Santiago is rather higher than in the provinces. Rates in Valparaíso, Viña del Mar and other holiday resorts may be increased during the summer holiday from January to March. Members of foreign motoring organisations can obtain discounts at hotels by joining the Automóvil Club de Chile, Avenida Vitacura 8620, Santiago. Tel: (2) 212 5702. The address of the Chilean national hotel association is HOTELGA, PO Box 3410, Correo Central, Santiago. Tel: (2) 698 8765 *or* 671 1937. Fax: (2) 698 8850.

Grading: Hotels in Chile are graded from **5 to 2 stars**. There are 11 5-star hotels, 58 4-star hotels, 94 3-star hotels and 32 2-star hotels in the country. A description of the facilities included in the Chilean hotel system is as follows:
5-star: Luxurious rooms with air-conditioning, private bathroom and 24-hour room service; garden; restaurant; bar; swimming pool; laundry services; shops; conference rooms; recreational and medical facilities.
4-star: Rooms with air-conditioning and private bathroom; restaurant; bar; laundry services; tourist information; conference rooms; medical and

recreational facilities.

3-star: Rooms with private bathrooms; laundry services; first aid and continental breakfast.

2-star: 30% of rooms with private bathroom.

Government tax: VAT of 18% is levied on all hotel bills, except those paid in foreign currencies by foreign visitors for which an export bill is required.

CAMPING/CARAVANNING: Camping facilities exist throughout Chile. A list of campsites may be obtained from Chilean Embassies. Official sites are expensive.

YOUTH HOSTELS: Membership of the Asociación Chilena de Albergues Turísticos Juveniles is required; a card costs US$3.50. For US$7.50 a card including Argentina, Uruguay and Brazil is obtainable. Many hostels are extremely crowded.

RESORTS & EXCURSIONS

In Santiago there are four tourist information centres, including one at the airport. This caters particularly for foreigners just arriving in the country. There are also regional tourist offices throughout the country. Visitors to Chile are faced with a wide variety of excursions from which to choose; for the purposes of this guide, the country has been divided into three geographical areas, ranging from north to south. The *Turistel* series of guide books, sponsored by the telephone company, is published annually. A combined volume of all three parts is also available.

Northern Region

Arica, near the northern border with Peru, is an excellent tourist centre. It has good beaches and the famous *San Marcos Cathedral.* Conditions in the area are ideal for deep-sea fishing. Travelling south through the Atacama Desert, excursions can be made to the hot springs of Mamina and to the oasis of the *Pica Valley.* The port of **Antofagasta** is the stopping point for air services and for most shipping lines. From here, a visit can be made to *Chuquicamata,* the world's largest open cast copper mine. Visits can also be made from the port at Antofagasta to the archaeological oasis town of **San Pedro de Atacama** and to the geysers at *El Tatio.* Further south is **Coquimbo,** situated in one of the best harbours on the coast. Nearby is the beautiful bathing

resort of **Los Vilos.** Nine miles north of Coquimbo is **La Serena,** the provincial capital. This charming and well laid-out town is graced with fine buildings and streets, and good reproductions of the attractive Spanish colonial style of architecture. The town is at the mouth of the *Elqui River* and excursions can be made from here to the rich fruit-growing region of the *Elqui Valley,* which is also full of reminiscences of the Chilean Nobel Prize Winner Gabriela Mistral. Tours can also be arranged to the *Tololo Observatory,* the largest in the southern hemisphere.

Central Region and the Islands

This is the most temperate and pastoral region of the country, where the snowcapped peaks of the Andes provide a backdrop for rolling green fields, vineyards and orange groves. **Valparaíso,** the principal port, has many attractions. Only 8km (5 miles) to the north is **Viña del Mar,** Chile's principal and most fashionable seaside resort with casinos, clubs and modern hotels. The *Valparaíso Sporting Club* offers a race course, polo grounds and playing fields.

From Valparaíso there are excellent road and rail services to **Santiago,** where a visitor will find all the conveniences of a modern capital city, including good hotels to suit all tastes. In the northeast of the city is the *San Cristobal Hill* where a zoo, gardens, restaurants and fine views of the city can be found; the *Club Hippico* and the *Prince of Wales Country Club* provide sporting facilities. From Santiago it is also possible to visit ski resorts such as **Portillo, Farellones** and the newest and most fashionable, **Valle Nevado.** Immediately south of Santiago, in the heartland of Chile, one can visit many vineyards where the reputable Chilean wine is produced. Travelling south through the heartland of Chile one reaches **Talca** with its fine parks and museums. 650km (403 miles) west of Valparaíso are the **Juan Fernández Islands,** which can be reached either by plane or boat from the Chilean mainland. Alexander Selkirk was shipwrecked here in the early eighteenth century, and Defoe based his 'Robinson Crusoe' on Selkirk's adventures.

Easter Island is another Pacific Chilean possession, situated 3800km (2361 miles) west of the mainland. It is most famous for the *Moai,* gigantic stone figures up to 9m (30ft) tall which are found all over the island. Other

sites include the crater of the volcano *Rano Kao,* the rock carvings at **Oronco** and the museum in the main town of **Hanga Roa.** The best method of travel to the island is by air. Tour guides and guest-house keepers tend to meet every plane, so although it is possible to book good hotel accommodation from Santiago or Valparaíso, it is not essential. Many of the hotels specialise in catering for groups and will arrange tours if asked. Tours can also be arranged with a tour guide. Jeeps, trucks, motorbikes and horses can all be hired.

Southern Region

A visit to the impressive waterfalls at **Laguna de Laja** is recommended. **Termuco** marks the beginning of the Lake District, where Lake Villarica and the Trancura and Cincira rivers combine to create beautiful scenery, and an angler's paradise. **Lake Todos** is also well worth a visit. At the southernmost end of the railway line and the Pan American Highway, there is the picturesque town of

Araucanian woman in Temuco

Chile has a large surplus of fruit and vegetables available for export to North America and Europe but is not entirely self-sufficient in agricultural produce. The industrial base has grown considerably over the last 30 years and now includes steel manufacturing, oil production, shipbuilding, cement and consumer goods. The mainstay of the export economy for the time being is metals and ores: Chile is the world's leading exporter of copper and also produces zinc, iron ore, molybdenum, manganese, iodine and lithium. The United States is the largest trading partner, followed by Japan, Brazil and Germany. Chile has made vigorous efforts in the last few years to open negotiations for a free trade agreement with the United States but has so far been met with indifference in Washington.

BUSINESS: Business people should wear formal clothes in dark colours for official functions, dinners, smart restaurants and hotels. Dress is usually stipulated on invitations. There is a tendency to formality with many Old World courtesies. Best months for business visits are April to December.

COMMERCIAL INFORMATION: The following organisation can offer advice: Cámara de Comercio de Santiago de Chile AG, Casilla 1297, Santa Lucía 302, 3°, Santiago. Tel: (2) 632 1232. Fax: (2) 698 4820. Telex: 240868.

CONFERENCES/CONVENTIONS: Information on conferences and conventions can be obtained from the Organización de Profesionales de Congresos y Eventos (OPCE), Toledo 1991, Providencia, Santiago. Tel: (2) 225 6888. Fax: (2) 274 2789.

CLIMATE

Ranges from hot and arid in the north to very cold in the far south. The central areas have a mild Mediterranean climate with a wet season (May to August). Beyond Puerto Montt in the south is one of the wettest and stormiest areas in the world.

Required clothing: Lightweight cottons and linens in northern and central areas. Rainwear is advised during rainy seasons. Mediumweights and waterproofing are needed in the south.

Puerto Montt and, nearby, the colourful small fishing port of **Angelmo**. Inveterate travellers will wish to go on to visit **Chiloe Island** and possibly also the southernmost part of the country, the fjords, spectacular glaciers and harsh landscape of Chilean Patagonia. The whole area of **Magellanes** and **Tierra del Fuego** is worth exploring during the summer season.

SOCIAL PROFILE

FOOD & DRINK: Santiago has many international restaurants; waiter service is normal. The evening will often include floorshows and dancing. Examples of typical national dishes are *empañada* (combination of meat, chicken or fish, with onions, eggs, raisins and olives inside a flour pastry), *humitas* (seasoned corn paste, wrapped in corn husks and boiled), *cazuela de ave* (soup with rice, vegetables, chicken and herbs), *bife a lo pobre* (steak with french fries, onions and eggs) and *parrillada* (selection of meat grilled over hot coals). Seafood is good. Best known are the huge lobsters from Juan Fernández Islands. Abalone, sea urchins, clams, prawns and giant *choros* (mussels) are also common. **Drink:** Chile is famous for its wine. *Pisco* is a powerful liqueur distilled from grapes after wine pressing. Grapes are also used to make the sweet brown *chicha* as well as *aguardiente*, similar to brandy. Beer is drunk throughout the country.

NIGHTLIFE: While many restaurants and hotels offer entertainment there are also a number of independent discotheques and nightclubs. **Casinos:** The Municipal Casino in Viña del Mar offers large gambling salons, full cabaret and *boite* with Chile's best dance bands. A casino operates in Gran Hotel in Puerto Varas between September and March. Arica also has a casino operating throughout the year with baccarat, roulette, Black Jack, a restaurant and late-night cabaret.

SHOPPING: Special purchases include textiles such as colourful handwoven ponchos, vicuna rugs and copper work. Chilean stones such as lapis lazuli, jade, amethyst, agate and onyx are all good buys. **Shopping hours:** 1000-2000 Monday to Friday; 0900-1400 Saturday. The large shopping centres in Santiago are also open 1000-

2100 on Sunday.

SPORT: Baseball, tennis, volleyball, hockey, polo, rugby and **football**. The national **golf** championship and the International Horsemanship Championship are held in Viña del Mar in January. The two main **horseraces** of the year are the Derby (Viña del Mar, January) and *El Ensayo* (Santiago, October). The Rod and Gun Club (*Club de Pesca y Caza*) in any city can arrange for licences to **fish** and to **hunt** small game. **Watersports:** Skindiving, water-skiing and boating are available. In the central valley brown trout are found and there is rainbow trout fishing in the south. **Winter sports:** The skiing season runs from June to September with the best resort at Portillo. Ski-championships are held in Portillo, Farellones and in Valle Nevado in July.

SPECIAL EVENTS: Mar '95 *Los Andes International Fair.* **Mar-Apr** *Talca International Fair.* **Apr** *19th National Tourist Industry Congress* (location to be announced). **Jul** *Skiing Championships,* Portillo, Farellones and Valle Nevado. **Oct** *El Ensayo* (horse-races), Santiago de Chile. **Jan '96** *National Golf Tournament; Derby; International Equestrian Tournament,* all in Viña del Mar.

SOCIAL CONVENTIONS: Handshaking is the customary form of greeting. Most Chileans use a double surname and only the paternal name should be used in addressing them. Normal courtesies should be observed when visiting local people. It is very common to entertain at home and it is acceptable for invitees to give small presents as a token of thanks. Informal, conservative clothes are acceptable in most places but women should not wear shorts outside resort areas. **Tipping:** Restaurants and bars add 10% to bill. However, waiters will expect a 10% cash tip in addition.

BUSINESS PROFILE

ECONOMY: With a well-developed industrial and service sector, Chile has one of Latin America's strongest economies. However, it still depends on export of primary commodities – metals and ores, fruit, fish and wood – for a large proportion of its export earnings.

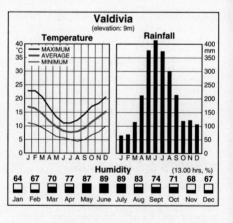

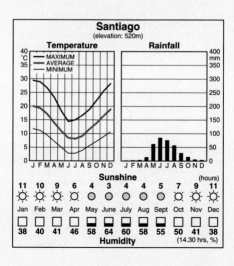

China (The People's Republic of)

Location: Far East.

China National Tourism Administration
Department of Marketing and Promotion, 9-A Jian Guo
Men Nei Avenue, Beijing 100740, People's Republic of
China
Tel: (1) 513 8866. Fax: (1) 512 2851.

China International Travel Service (CITS)
Head Office, 103 Fuxingmennei Avenue, Beijing
100800, People's Republic of China
Tel: (1) 601 1122. Fax: (1) 512 2068 *or* 601 2013.
Telex: 22350 (a/b CITSH CN).

Embassy of the People's Republic of China
49-51 Portland Place, London W1N 3AH
Tel: (0171) 636 9375. Fax: (0171) 636 2981. Opening
hours: 0900-1200 and 1500-1800 Monday to Friday.
Commercial Section:
Cleveland Court, 1/3 Leinster Gardens, London W2 6EP
Tel: (0171) 262 3911. Fax: (071) 706 2777.
Consular Section:
31 Portland Place, London W1N 3AG
Tel: (0171) 631 1430 *or* 636 5637 (telephone enquiries:
1400-1600 only). Fax: (0171) 636 9756. Telex: 23851
(a/b CHINA G). Opening hours: 0900-1200 Monday to
Friday.
Visa and General Information Service:
Tel: (0891) 880 808 (calls are charged at the higher rate
of 39p/49p per minute).

Consulate General of the People's Republic of China
Denison House, Denison Road, Victoria Park,
Manchester M14 5RX
Tel: (0161) 224 7480. Fax: (0161) 257 2672. Opening
hours: 1430-1700 Monday to Friday.

China National Tourist Office
4 Glentworth Street, London NW1 5PG
Tel: (0171) 935 9427. Fax: (0171) 487 5842.

British Embassy
11 Guang Hua Lu, Jian Guo Men Wai, Beijing 100600,
People's Republic of China
Tel: (1) 532 1961/5 *or* 532 1930/1938-9. Fax: (1) 532
1939. *Answerphone*: (1) 532 2011. Telex: 22191 (a/b
PRDRM CN).

British Consulate General
244 Yong Fu Lu, Shanghai 20031, People's Republic of
China
Tel: (21) 433 0508 (4 lines) *or* 437 4569 (1 line). Fax:
(21) 433 0498. Telex: 33476 (a/b BRIT CN).

Fishing lights in Yangshuo

Main Travel Agents in China

China International Travel Service
Head Office (CITS), 103 Fuxingmennei Ave.,
Beijing 100800, People's Republic of China
Tel: (1) 601 1122 *or* 601 2055. Fax: (1) 601
2013 *or* 512 2068. Telex: 22350 (a/b CITSH
CN).

China Travel Service
Head office (CTS), 8 Dongjiaomingxiang,
Beijing 100005, People's Republic of China
Tel: (1) 512 9933. Fax: (1) 512 9008. Telex:
22487 (a/b CTSHO CN).

China Youth Travel Service
Head Office (CYTS), 23-B
Dongjiaomingxiang, Beijing 100006,
People's Republic of China
Tel: (1) 512 7770. Fax: (1) 512 0571. Telex:
20024 (a/b CYTS CN).

China International Travel Service Beijing
28 Jianguomenwai Street, Beijing 100022,
People's Republic of China
Tel: (1) 515 8562. Fax: (1) 515 8602.

China International Sports Travel Co.
4 Tiyuguan Road, Chongwen District, Beijing
100061, People's Republic of China
Tel: (1) 701 7364. Fax: (1) 701 7370.

China Comfort Travel
Head Office, 57 Di An Men Xi Dajie, Beijing
100009, People's Republic of China
Tel: (1) 601 6288. Fax: (1) 601 6336. Telex:
222862 (a/b KHT CN).

China Women Travel Service
103 Dongsi Nan Street, Beijing 100010,
People's Republic of China
Tel: (1) 553 307 *or* 513 6311. Fax: (1) 512
9021. Telex: 21160 (a/b CWTS CN).

**China International Travel Service
Shaanxi**
32 North Changan Road, Xian 710061,
People's Republic of China
Tel: (29) 751 2066. Fax: (29) 751 1453.
Telex: 70115 (a/b CITSX CN).

China Travel Service Shaanxi
272 Jiefang Road, Xian 710004, People's
Republic of China
Tel: (29) 712 557. Fax: (29) 714 152. Telex:
70148 (a/b CTSS CN).

**China International Travel Service
Shanghai**
33 Zhongshan Road E.1, Shanghai 200002,
People's Republic of China
Tel: (21) 321 7200. Fax: (21) 329 1788.
Telex: 33277 (a/b SCITS CN).

Shanghai Jinjiang Tours Ltd.
27/F Union Building, 100 Yanan Road, E.,
Shanghai 200002, People's Republic of China
Tel: (21) 329 0690. Fax: (21) 320 0595.
Telex: 33429 (a/b SJJTC CN).

Shanghai CYTS Tours Corp.
2 Hengshan Road, Shanghai 200031, People's
Republic of China
Tel: (21) 433 1826. Fax: (21) 433 0507.
Telex: 30241 (a/b CYTS CN).

China International Travel Service Guilin
14 Ronghu Road, Guilin 541002, People's
Republic of China
Tel: (773) 223 518. Fax: (773) 222 936.

Guilin Overseas Tourist Corp.
8 Zhishan Road, Guilin 541002, People's
Republic of China
Tel: (773) 334 026. Fax: (773) 335 391.
Telex: 48463 (a/b GLTRA CN).

China Guangxi Tourist Corp.
40 Xinmin Road, Nanning 530212, People's
Republic of China
Tel: (771) 202 042. Fax: (771) 204 105.
Telex: 48142 (a/b CITSN CN).

**China International Travel Service
Guangdong**
179 Huanshi Road, Guangzhou 510010,
People's Republic of China
Tel: (20) 666 6271 *or* 666 7715. Fax: (20)
667 8048. Telex: 44450 (a/b CITS CN).

China Travel Service Guangdong
10 Qiaoguang Road, Guangzhou 510115,
People's Republic of China
Tel: (20) 333 6888. Fax: (20) 333 6625.
Telex: 44217 (a/b CTS CN).

**Guangdong Railway China Youth Travel
Service**
69 Dadao Road, Dongshan, Guangzhou
510600, People's Republic of China
Tel: (20) 775 2401 *or* 775 2407. Fax: (20)
776 2509.

Xinjiang Nature Travel Service
64 Dongfeng Road, Urumqi 830002, People's
Republic of China
Tel: (991) 227 791. Fax: (991) 217 174.
Telex: 79049 (a/b XJTCA).

**The Kunming Scenery-Custom
International Tourist Service**
2/F Yunnan Hotel, Yongan Road, Kunming
650041, People's Republic of China
Tel: (871) 313 9042 *or* 313 6594 *or* 313
5860. Fax: (871) 313 5851.

Overseas Tourist Offices

China National Tourist Office, London
4 Glentworth Street, London NW1 5PG, UK
Tel: (0171) 935 9427.
Fax: (0171) 487 5842.

China National Tourist Office, New York
Suite 6413, 350 Fifth Avenue, New York, NY
10118, USA
Tel: (212) 760 9700 (information) *or* 760
8218 (business). Fax: (212) 760 8809.

China National Tourist Office, Los Angeles
Suite 201, 333 West Broadway, Glendale,
CA 91204, USA
Tel: (818) 545 7504/5. Fax: (818) 545 7506.

Office du Tourisme de Chine, Paris
116 avenue des Champs-Elysées, 75008
Paris, France
Tel: (1) 44 21 82 82. Fax: (1) 44 21 81 00.

China National Tourist Office, Sydney
19th Floor, 44 Market Street, Sydney, NSW
2000, Australia
Tel: (2) 299 4057. Fax: (2) 290 1958.

**China National Tourism Administration,
Tokyo Office**
6F Hamamatsu Cho Building, 1-27-13
Hamamatsu Cho, Minato-Ku, Tokyo, Japan
Tel: (3) 34 33 14 61. Fax: (3) 34 33 86 53.

China National Tourist Office, Tel Aviv
PO Box 3281, Tel Aviv 61030, Israel
Tel: (3) 522 6272/3 *or* 524 0891. Fax: (3) 522 6281.

China National Tourist Office, Singapore
1 Shenton Way, No. 17-05, Ribina House,
Singapore 0106
Tel: 221 8681/2. Fax: 221 9267.

Fremdenverkehrsamt der VR China
Ilkenhansstrasse 6, 60433 Frankfurt/M,
Federal Republic of Germany
Tel: (69) 520 135. Fax: (69) 528 490.

China National Tourist Office, Madrid
Gran Via 88, Grupo 2, Planta 16, 28013
Madrid, Spain
Tel: (1) 548 0011. Fax: (1) 548 0597.

**China International Travel Service, Hong
Kong**
6th Floor, Tower 2, South Seas Centre, 75
Mody Road, Tsim Sha Tsui, Kowloon, Hong
Kong
Tel: 732 5888. Fax: 721 7154.

Airlines

Air China
Capital International Airport, Beijing,
People's Republic of China
Tel: (1) 456 3220 *or* 456 3221. Telex: 210327
(a/b BJKLH CN).

China Eastern Airlines
Hongqiao Airport, Shanghai, People's
Republic of China
Tel: (21) 255 8899. Fax: (21) 255 8668.

China Southern Airlines
Baiyun Airport, Guangzhou, People's
Republic of China
Tel: (20) 666 1381. Fax: (20) 666 7637.

China Northern Airlines
Dongta Airport, Shenyang, People's Republic
of China
Tel: (24) 822 563. Fax: (24) 829 4432.

Shanghai Airlines
Hongqiao Airport, Shanghai, People's
Republic of China
Tel: (21) 255 8558. Fax: (21) 255 8107.

Xiamen Airlines Ltd
Xiamen, People's Republic of China
Tel: (592) 622 961. Fax: (592) 628 263.

China Southwest Airlines
Shuangliu Airport, Chengdu, People's
Republic of China
Tel: (28) 558 1466. Fax: (28) 558 2630.

China Northwest Airlines
Xiguan Airport, Xian, People's Republic of
China
Tel: (29) 423 892. Fax: (29) 724 2022.

China General Aviation Corporation
Wusu Airport, Taiyuan, Shanxi Province,
People's Republic of China
Tel: (351) 707 5600. Fax: (351) 704 0094.

Xinjiang Airlines
Diwopu Airport, Urumqi, People's Republic
of China
Tel: (991) 335 688. Fax: (991) 335 688-294.

Sichuan Airlines
9 Third Section, Yihuan Road South,
Chengdu, People's Republic of China
Tel: (28) 555 1161. Fax: (28) 558 2641.

Come to China...
...The Natural Choice

China – a majestic country of fascinating perspectives. Its history extends over 5000 years, and its countless treasures are priceless. They range from the magnificence of the Great Wall and the grandeur of the imperial regalia to the vast reservoir of goodwill.

Today China is one of the most fascinating tourist destinations in the world.

In order to extend the success of *Visit China Year 1992* and to fully display China's tourist products to the world, China is launching a series of promotional activities. Between 1993 and 1996 every year will be characterised by a particular theme: *China Landscape '93, China Heritage '94, China Folklore '95,* and *China Resort '96.* Our programme will eventually lead to a second more influential *Visit China Year* in 1997.

Terracotta soldiers and horses near Xi'an

For further information, please contact our office at the address below. We can offer you free brochures, maps and posters. Slides and videos are also available on a loan basis. You are welcome to call in.

China National Tourist Office, 4 Glentworth Street, London NW1 5PG
Tel:+44 171 935 9427   Fax: +44 171 487 5842

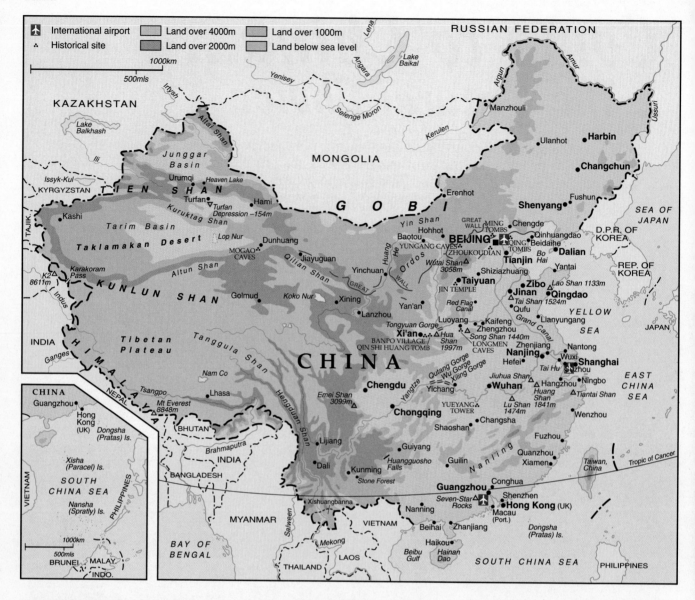

Embassy of the People's Republic of China
2300 Connecticut Avenue, NW, Washington, DC 20008
Tel: (202) 328 2500/1/2. Fax: (202) 232 7855.
Consulate General of the People's Republic of China
520 12th Avenue, New York, NY 10036
Tel: (212) 330 7409. Opening hours: 1000-1500 Monday
to Friday.
China National Tourist Office
Suite 6413, 350 Fifth Avenue, New York, NY 10118
Tel: (212) 760 9700 (information) or 760 8218
(business). Fax: (212) 760 8809.
Embassy of the United States of America
3 Xiu Shui Bei Jie, Beijing 100600, People's Republic of
China
Tel: (1) 532 3831. Fax: (1) 532 3178. Telex: 22701.
Embassy of the People's Republic of China
515 St Patrick Street, Ottawa, Ontario K1N 5H3
Tel: (613) 789 3434. Fax: (613) 789 1911.
Visa section:
Tel: (613) 789 9608. Fax: (613) 789 1414. Opening
hours: 0900-1200 and 1400-1530 Monday to Friday.
Canadian Embassy
19 Dong Zhi Men Wai Da Jie, Beijing 100600, People's
Republic of China
Tel: (1) 532 3536. Fax: (1) 532 4072. Telex: 22717 (a/b
CANAD CN).

AREA: 9,571,300 sq km (3,695,500 sq miles).
POPULATION: 1,171,710,000 (1992 estimate).
Roughly a quarter of the world's population live in
China.
POPULATION DENSITY: 122.4 per sq km.
CAPITAL: Beijing (Peking). **Population:** 7,000,000
(1990 estimate). The largest city in the country,
Shanghai, has a population of over seven million and
39 other cities have a population of over one million.
GEOGRAPHY: China is bounded to the north by the
CIS and Mongolia; to the east by North Korea, the

Yellow Sea and the South China Sea; to the south by
Vietnam, Laos, Myanmar, India, Bhutan and Nepal;
and to the west by India, Pakistan, Afghanistan and the
CIS. Hong Kong and Macau form enclaves on the
southeast coast. China comprises 23 Provinces, 5
Autonomous Regions and 3 Municipalities directly
under Central Government. It has a varied terrain
ranging from high plateaux in the west to flatlands in
the east; mountains take up almost one-third of the
land. The most notable high mountain ranges are the
Himalayas, the Altai Mountains, the Tianshan
Mountains and the Kunlun Mountains. On the border
with Nepal is the 8848m-high (29,198ft) Mount Jolmo
Lungma (Mount Everest). In the west is the
Qinghai/Tibet Plateau, with an average elevation of
4000m (13,200ft), known as 'the Roof of the World'.
At the base of the Tianshan Mountains is the Turfan
Depression or Basin, China's lowest area, 154m
(508ft) below sea level at the lowest point. China has
many great river systems, notably the Yellow (Huang
He) and Yangtse Kiang (Chang Jiang). Only 10% of
all China is suitable for agriculture.
LANGUAGE: The official language is Mandarin
Chinese. Among the enormous number of local
dialects, in the south, large groups speak Cantonese,
Fukienese, Xiamenhua and Hakka. Mongolia, Tibet
and Xinjiang, which are autonomous regions, have

their own languages. Translation and interpreter
services are good. English is spoken by many guides.
RELIGION: The principal religions and philosophies
are Buddhism, Daoism and Confucianism. There are
100 million Buddhists. Also about 20 million Muslims,
five million Protestants (including large numbers of
Evangelists) and four million Roman Catholics, largely
independent of Vatican control.
TIME: GMT + 8. Despite the vast size of the country,
Beijing time is standard throughout China.
ELECTRICITY: 220/240 volts AC, 50Hz. Two-pin
sockets (a few have three-pin sockets) are in use.
COMMUNICATIONS: Telephone: IDD is available.
Country code: 86. Outgoing international code: 00.
Antiquated internal service with public telephones in
hotels and shops displaying telephone unit sign. It is
often easier to make international phone calls from
China than it is to make calls internally.
Telex/telegram: Beijing now has an automatic telex
service to the UK. Country code: 85. Facilities are
available at main and branch post offices in larger
towns and cities. A growing number of hotels offer
telex and fax facilities but often only incoming.
Rates are generally expensive. **Post:** Service to
Europe takes about a week. All postal
communications to China should be addressed
'People's Republic of China'. **Press:** The main
English-language daily is the *China Daily*. There is
also the *Beijing Review*, with weekly editions in
English, French, Spanish, Japanese and German.
National newspapers include *The People's Daily* and
The Guangming Daily, with many provinces having
their own local dailies as well.
**BBC World Service and Voice of America
frequencies:** From time to time these change. See the
section *How to Use this Book* for more information.
BBC:

MHz	21.71	15.28	11.82	7.180

Voice of America:

MHz	17.73	15.42	11.76	6.110

Timatic

Health		
GALILEO/WORLDSPAN: **TI-DFT/PEK/HE**		
SABRE: **TIDFT/PEK/HE**		

Visa		
GALILEO/WORLDSPAN: **TI-DFT/PEK/VI**		
SABRE: **TIDFT/PEK/VI**		

For more information on Timatic codes refer to Contents.

CHINA: Provinces

Autonomous Regions:
Xinjiang Uygur

Municipalities:
B Beijing
T Tianjin
S Shanghai

Special Economic Zones:
1 Bohai
2 Xiamen
3 Shantou
4 Shenzhen
5 Zhuhai

2000km
1000mls

DAB-M274

Tang Music Dance

PASSPORT/VISA

Regulations and requirements may be subject to change at short notice, and you are advised to contact the appropriate diplomatic or consular authority before finalising travel arrangements. Details of these may be found at the head of this country's entry. Any numbers in the chart refer to the footnotes below.

	Passport Required?	Visa Required?	Return Ticket Required?
Full British	Yes	Yes	Yes
BVP	Not valid	-	-
Australian	Yes	Yes	Yes
Canadian	Yes	Yes	Yes
USA	Yes	Yes	Yes
Other EU (As of 31/12/94)	Yes	Yes	Yes
Japanese	Yes	Yes	Yes

PASSPORTS: Valid passport required by all.
British Visitors Passport: Not acceptable.
VISAS: Required by all.
Types of visa: *Tourist/UK* – Cost: £25 single-entry, £50 Double-entry, £75 Multiple-entry (6 months), £150 Multiple-entry (12 months). Cash or postal order payable to the Chinese Embassy is preferable, as cheques are not accepted; *Tourist/Other nationals* – Cost: will vary according to nationality; contact the Embassy for further information; *Group; Business* – see below for further information; *Transit* – generally required for people in transit through China for a period of no more than 10 days; these cannot be extended when in China; contact the Embassy for further information. For the cost of the last three kinds of visa, apply to the Embassy. It should be noted that it is considerably cheaper to buy visas in Hong Kong, where they cost less than half the price.
Validity: Tourist and Group visas are normally issued to individuals or groups on package tours, although they are also issued to individuals as well. Visa validity is therefore dependent upon duration of package tour or individual stay. Validity of Business visas varies. Transit

visas are valid for up to 10 days.
Application to: Consulate (or Consular section at Embassy). For addresses, see top of entry. Applications by post require an additional £10 for postage and handling charges, and a strong self-addressed envelope must be included. Recorded delivery or registered post is recommended.
Application requirements: For a Group visa, applications should be accompanied by a confirmation letter or fax from the Chinese travel company concerned. For Tourist and Business visas: (a) Completed application form. (b) 1 passport-size photograph. (c) Valid passport with at least 6 months' validity and one blank visa page left. (d) Sufficient funds for duration of stay. Travellers applying for a Transit visa may also be required to show a visa for the country of destination or an airline ticket. Business visitors can obtain a visa from the Embassy or Consulate only if they have received an invitation from either a Ministry, Corporation, Foreign Trade Corporation or an official Chinese organisation. Visas can also be issued in Hong Kong on application to the China International Travel Service Hong Kong Ltd, 6F Tower Two, South Seas Centre, 75 Mody Road, Tsimshatsui, Kowloon, Hong Kong. Tel: 732 5888. Fax: 33 67 67 85 *or* 721 7154. This normally takes 3 working days and costs HK$80. Visas can be issued the same day on payment of HK$200.
Working days required: As all visas are granted by the Authorities of China, some time will elapse depending upon the merits of application. Apply as far in advance as possible.
Temporary residence: Enquiries should be made to the Chinese Embassy.
Note: (a) The majority, but not all, visits to China tend to be organised through the official state travel agency *CITS* (China International Travel Service). This liaison with *CITS* is generally handled by the tour operator organising the inclusive holiday chosen by the visitor, though it is possible for individuals to organise affairs in their own right. Once the tour itinerary details have been confirmed

to the visitor or visiting group, finances to cover accommodation and the cost of the tour must be deposited with *CITS* through a home bank. Evidence of the payment of funds for the tour must be presented to *CITS* officials on arrival in China. Once again, for package trips, all the necessary formalities for a visit to China can be handled by the tour operator concerned. (b) Under new immigration procedures, it may now be possible for nationals of certain countries (including the UK) to obtain visas on arrival at Beijing Airport. Contact the Embassy or Tourist Office for further details. (c) Those wishing to visit Tibet are strongly advised to join a travel group. Individuals should obtain permission to visit Tibet from the following organisation before applying for a visa: Tibet Tourism Administration of China, 208 Beijing West Avenue, Lhasa 850001. Tel: (891) 34632. Fax: (891) 26793.

MONEY

Currency: 1 Yuan (Renminbi RMB) (¥) = 10 chiao/jiao or 100 fen. Notes are in the denominations of ¥100, 50, 10, 5, 2 and 1, and 5, 2 and 1 chiao/jiao. Coins are in denominations of ¥1, 5, 2 and 1 fen and 5 and 1 chiao/jiao.
Note: From January 1, 1994, China reverted to the single currency system. The *Foreign Exchange Certificates (FEC)* issued by the Bank of China as a RMB version for the exchange of foreign currencies were abolished on that date.
Currency exchange: RMB (People's money) is not traded outside China. There is only one national bank, the People's Bank, which has over 30,000 branches. In hotels and *Friendship Stores* for tourists, imported luxury items such as spirits may be bought with Western currency.
Credit cards: Access/Mastercard, Visa, Diners Club, Federal Card, East-American Visa, Million Card, JCB Card and American Express are valid in major provincial cities in designated establishments.
Exchange rate indicators: The following figures are included as a guide to the movements of the Yuan against Sterling and the US Dollar:

Date:	Oct '92	Sep '93	Jan '94	Jan '95
£1.00=	9.02	8.85	8.58	13.09
$1.00=	5.68	5.80	5.80	8.46

Currency restrictions: Export of local currency is prohibited. Unlimited foreign currency may be imported but must be declared. The unused amount of foreign currency may be exported.
Banking hours: 0930-1200 and 1400-1700 Monday to Friday; 0900-1700 Saturday.

DUTY FREE

The following items may be imported into China by passengers staying less than six months without incurring customs duty:
400 cigarettes (600 cigarettes for stays of over six months); 2 litres of alcoholic beverage; a reasonable amount of perfume for personal use.
Prohibited items: Arms, ammunition, radio transmitters/receivers, exposed but undeveloped film.
Note: Baggage declaration forms must be completed upon arrival noting all valuables (cameras, watches, jewellery, etc), a copy of which must be presented to customs upon leaving the country for checking.

PUBLIC HOLIDAYS

Jan 1 '95 New Year's Day. **Jan 31-Feb 2** Chinese New Year. **Mar 8** International Women's Day. **May 1** Labour Day. **May 4** Chinese Youth Day. **Jun 1** International Children's Day. **Jul 1** Founding of the Communist Party of China. **Aug 1** Army Day. **Sep 9** Teachers' Day. **Oct 1-2** National Days. **Jan 1 '96** New Year's Day. **Feb 19-21** Chinese New Year. **Mar 8** International Women's Day.

HEALTH

Regulations and requirements may be subject to change at short notice, and you are advised to contact your doctor well in advance of your intended date of departure. Any numbers in the chart refer to the footnotes below.

	Special Precautions?	Certificate Required?
Yellow Fever	Yes	1
Cholera	2	2
Typhoid & Polio	Yes	-
Malaria	3	-
Food & Drink	4	-

[1]: A yellow fever vaccination certificate is required from travellers if arriving from infected areas.
[2]: Cholera epidemics are very rare, but occasional

outbreaks are reported in Southern China. Following WHO guidelines issued in 1973, a cholera vaccination certificate is no longer a condition of entry to China. Up-to-date advice should be sought before deciding whether precautions should include vaccination as medical opinion is divided over its effectiveness. See the *Health* section at the back of the book.

[3]: Malaria risk exists throughout the country below 1500m except in Heilongjiang, Jilin, Inner Mongolia, Gansu, Beijing, Shanxi, Ningxia, Qinghai, Xinjiang (except in the Yili Valley) and Tibet (Xizang, except in the Zangbo Valley in the extreme southeast). North of 33°N, the risk lasts from July to November, between 33°N and 25°N from May to December, and south of 25°N throughout the year. The disease occurs primarily in the benign *vivax* form but the malignant *falciparum* form is also present and has been reported to be 'highly resistant' to chloroquine.

[4]: Outside main centres all water used for drinking, brushing teeth or freezing should have first been boiled or otherwise sterilised. Only eat well-cooked meat and fish, preferably served hot. Pork, salad and mayonnaise may carry increased risk. Vegetables should be cooked and fruit peeled.

Rabies is present, although the Government policy which bans dogs and cats from main cities makes this less of a risk in these areas. For those at high risk, vaccination before arrival should be considered. If you are bitten abroad seek medical advice without delay. For more information, consult the *Health* section at the back of the book.

Bilharzia (schistosomiasis) is present in southeastern and eastern China. Avoid swimming and paddling in fresh water. Swimming pools which are well-chlorinated and maintained are safe.

Health care: Medical costs are low. Many medicines common to Western countries are unavailable in China. The hospital system is excellent. There are many traditional forms of medicine still used in China, the most notable being acupuncture. Medical insurance is advised.

TRAVEL - International

AIR: The national airline is *CAAC (CA) (Air China)*.
Approximate flight time: From *London* to Beijing is approximately 10 hours by direct flight (*Air China* and *British Airways*). From *New York* to Beijing is 22 hours. From *Los Angeles* to Beijing is 12 hours.
International airports: *Beijing/Peking (BJS/PEK)* airport (Capital International Central) is 26km (16 miles) northeast of the city (travel time – 45 minutes by bus, 30 minutes by taxi).
Guangzhou/Canton airport (Baiyun) is 7km (4 miles) from the city (travel time – 20 minutes).
Shanghai (SHA) airport (Hongqiao) is 12km (7.5 miles) southwest of the city (travel time – 20 minutes).
Facilities at the above airports include taxis, duty-free shops, banks/cambios, bars and restaurants.
There are also airports at other major cities throughout the country.
Departure tax: Levy varies from city to city, eg: Beijing/Peking: Domestic ¥25, International ¥90. Shanghai: Domestic ¥25, International ¥90. Guangzhou/Canton: Domestic ¥50, International ¥115. Xian: ¥65, International ¥100. Guilin: Domestic Domestic ¥75, International ¥145. Children under 12 are exempt.
SEA: Principal seaports are Qingdao (Tsingtao), Shanghai, Fuzhou (Foochow), Guangzhou (Canton) and Hong Kong/Kowloon. *Pearl Cruises* operate over 20 cruises a year to China. Other cruise lines are *Royal Viking, Sitmar* and *CTC*. There is a regular (once or twice weekly) ferry service linking Tianjin with Kobe in Japan and the west coast of South Korea.
RAIL: International services run twice a week from Beijing to Moscow (Russian Federation) and Pyongyang (Democratic People's Republic of Korea). A regular train service runs from Hong Kong to Guangzhou (Canton), which is of a higher standard than internal trains in China. There are several trains daily.
ROAD: The principal road routes into China follow the historical trade routes through Myanmar, India, the CIS and Mongolia.

TRAVEL - Internal

Note: All travel destinations and routes are normally organised through CITS, who ensure that the arrangements for individual itineraries are practical and who provide guides for each party. Independent travel, however, is becoming increasingly possible, and full details of this are available from the China National Tourist Office at the address above. The CITS guides are generally very helpful and amenable.

Main picture: The Great Wall. Above: Cantonese Morning tea, Guangzhou. Right: Foshan Ancestral Temple, Guangzhou.

AIR: Most long-distance internal travel is by air. The *Civil Aviation Administration of China (CAAC)* operates along routes linking Beijing to over 80 other cities. Tickets will normally be purchased by guides and the price will be included in any tour costs. Independent travellers can also book through the local *Chinese International Travel Service*, which charges a small commission, or they can buy tickets in booking offices. It is advisable to purchase internal air tickets well in advance if the time of travel is to be during May, September or October. The tourist price for a ticket is 70% on a train ticket and 100% on an air ticket. There are many connections to Hong Kong from Beijing/Guangzhou (Peking/Canton) as well as other cities.

SEA/RIVER: All major rivers are served by river ferries. Coastal ferries operate between Dalian, Tianjin (Tientsin), Qingdao (Tsingtao) and Shanghai.

RAIL: Railways provide the principal means of transport for goods and people throughout China. The major routes are from Beijing to Guangzhou, Shanghai, Harbin, Chengdu and Urumqi. There are four types of fare: hard seat, soft seat (only on short-distance trains such as the Hong Kong to Guangzhou (Canton) line), hard sleeper and soft sleeper. Children under 1m tall travel free and those under 1.3m pay a quarter of the fare.

ROAD: 80% of settlements can be reached by road. Roads are not always of the highest quality. Distances should not be underestimated and vehicles should be in prime mechanical condition as China is still very much an agricultural nation without the mechanical expertise or services found in the West. From Beijing to Shanghai is 1461km (908 miles), and from Beijing to Nanjing (Nanking) is 1139km (718 miles). Traffic drives on the right. **Bus:** Reasonable services are operated between the main cities. Buses are normally crowded. **Car hire:** Available.

URBAN: There are limited metro services in Beijing and Tianjin, and tramways and trolleybuses in a number of other cities. New lines are under construction in Beijing. Most cities have extensive bus services. Guides who accompany every visitor or group will ensure that internal travel within the cities is as trouble-free as possible. **Taxi:** Taxis are available in large cities but can be hard to find. It is best to check if the taxi is metered. If not, then it is important to agree a fare beforehand, especially at railway stations where it is best to bargain before getting into the taxi. Visitors should write down their destination before starting any journey. Taxis can be hired by the day. Most people travel by bicycle or public transport. In most cities bicycles or other types of rickshaws are available for short rides.

JOURNEY TIMES: The following chart gives approximate journey times (in hours and minutes) from Beijing to other major cities/towns in China.

	Air	Rail
Tianjin	0.50	1.40
Wuhan	1.45	16.00
Xian	1.55	22.00
Nanjing	1.40	15.30
Shanghai	1.50	20.00
Chengdu	2.25	60.00
Kunming	3.20	80.00
Guangzhou	3.00	37.00
Urumqi	4.00	95.00

ACCOMMODATION

HOTELS: China has 2552 tourist hotels with 386,000 rooms, among which 1028 hotels have been star-graded according to international standards. Most of the hotels have comforable and convenient facilities including air-conditioning and private bathrooms, Chinese and Western restaurants, coffee shops, bars, banqueting halls, conference rooms, multi-function halls, ballrooms, swimming pools, bowling alleys, beauty parlours, massage rooms, saunas, clinics and ticket booking offices. Some even include shopping and business malls, banks and post offices.

For further information, contact the China National Hotel Association, 9-A Jian Guo Men Nei Avenue, Beijing 100740. Tel: (1) 513 8866. Fax: (1) 512 2096.

DORMITORIES: These are found in most tourist centres and provide cheaper accommodation for budget travellers. Standards range from poor to adequate.

RESORTS & EXCURSIONS

China is a vast country, requiring visitors to travel for much of their time in order to see at least a selection of the cultural, historical and natural wonders of the land. Altogether there are 26 provinces, each with their own

A waiting bamboo-raft

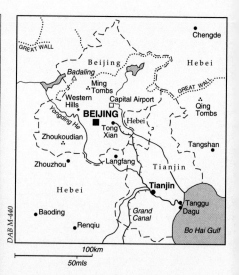

Temple of Heaven, an excellent example of 15th-century Chinese architecture; the *Summer Palace,* the former court resort for the emperors of the Qing Dynasty, looking out over the *Kunming Lake;* the *Great Wall* (see below), the section at Badaling being easily accessible from Beijing; and the *Ming Tombs,* where 13 Ming emperors chose to be buried. Two magnificent tombs here have been excavated, one of which is open to the public.

The Great Wall, said to be the only man-made structure visible from the moon, is a spectacular sight which should not be missed. Stretching for a distance of 5400km (3375 miles), it starts at the Shanhaiguan Pass in the east and ends at the Jiayuguan Pass in the west. The section at **Badaling,** which most tourists visit, is roughly 8m (26ft) high and 6m (20ft) wide. Constructed of large granite blocks and bricks some 2600 years ago, the wall is one of the universally acknowledged wonders of the world.

Beidaihe, a small sea-coast resort with beaches, temples and parks, is a popular vacation area 277km (172 miles) from Beijing. Attractions include the *Yansai Lake* and *Shan Hai Guan,* a massive gateway at the very start of the Great Wall.

Chengde is a mountain escape from the summer heat of Beijing and a former retreat of the Qing emperors. There are many temples and parks, including the remains of the *Qing Summer Palace* with its impressive Imperial Garden. The *Eight Outer Temples,* lying at the foot of the hills to the northeast of the Palace, incorporate, amongst others, the architectural styles of the Han, Mongolian and Tibetan peoples. At over 22m (72ft) tall, the colossal wooden image of Buddha in the

dialect and regional characteristics. The western provinces of Xinjiang, Tibet, Qinghai, Sichuan and Yunnan occupy an enormous area of land, and Sichuan alone is about the size of France. The state travel agency *CITS* tends to organise a good deal of the tours in China, although more and more specialist operators are running packages so visitors are now presented with a considerable choice of excursions.

Beijing and the Northeast

The entire area of **Beijing** within the city limits is in many ways one great historical museum. The city is symmetrical and built as three rectangles, one within the other. The innermost rectangle is the *Forbidden City,* now a museum and public park, but formerly the residence of the Ming and Qing emperors. The second rectangle forms the boundaries of the *Imperial City* where there are several parks and the homes of high government officials. The outer rectangle forms the outer city with its markets and old residential districts. The *Imperial Palace,* lying inside the Forbidden City and surrounded by a high wall and broad moat, is well worth a visit. Dating from the 15th century, the Palace was home to a total of 24 emperors, and today its fabulous halls, palaces and gardens house a huge collection of priceless relics from various dynasties. Other points of interest are the *Coal Hill* (Mei Shan), a beautiful elevated park with breathtaking views; *Beihai Park,* the loveliest in Beijing; *Tiananmen Square,* the largest public square in the world, surrounded by museums, parks, the Zoo and Beijing University; the

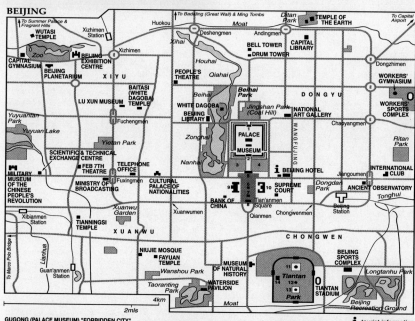

BEIJING

GUGONG (PALACE MUSEUM) "FORBIDDEN CITY"
& TIAN'ANMEN SQUARE:
1. SHENWUMEN (GATE OF SPIRITUAL VALOUR)
2. WUMEN (MERIDIAN GATE)
3. *Zongshan Park*
4. *Working People's Palace of Culture*
5. TIAN'ANMEN (GATE OF HEAVENLY PEACE)

6. MONUMENT TO THE PEOPLE'S HEROES
7. CHAIRMAN MAO MEMORIAL HALL
8. ZHENGYANG GATE
9. GREAT HALL OF THE PEOPLE
10. MUSEUM OF THE CHINESE PEOPLE'S
    REVOLUTION & CHINESE HISTORY

TIANTAN PARK (TEMPLE OF HEAVEN):
11. QINIAN DIAN (HALL OF PRAYER FOR GOOD HARVESTS)
12. HUANG DIONG YU (IMPERIAL VAULT OF HEAVEN)
13. HUAN QIU TAN (CIRCULAR MOUND ALTAR)
14. ZHAI GONG (HALL OF FASTING)

i tourist information

Temple of General Peace is recognised as the largest in the world.

Dalian is China's third port. Formerly occupied by the Soviets, it is an interesting bi-cultural city. There are guided tours of the port, residential areas, parks and the excellent beaches to the south. *Xinghai Park* combines a park with beach and restaurant facilities, while the *Tiger Beach Park* boasts of tiger-shaped rock formations. Shell mosaics and glassware are famous products of Dalian.

Harbin, the capital of Heilongjiang Province, is a Russian-style city and is the industrial centre of the northeast. Attractions include the *Provincial Museum* with its large collection of artefacts, including what are arguably the best-preserved mammoth skeletons in China; *Tai Yang Dao*, or Sun Island; the *Songhau River*, offering boat trips through the very centre of the city; and the *Arts and Crafts Factory*, known for its good selection of jadework. Harbin is host to the annual Harbin Summer Music Festival.

Hohhot (meaning 'green city' in Mongolian) is the capital of the Inner Mongolia Autonomous Region, and probably the most colourful city in China. Traditional Mongolian rodeos are performed for tourists under oriental domes and there are also tours of the grasslands, further displays of horsemanship, and visits to local communes and villages, where it is possible to stay overnight in a Mongolian *yurt*. Hohhot is famous for its woollen products. A visit to nearby **Kweihua** is also recommended: the monastery's *Five-Pagoda Temple* dates from around 1000BC.

Shenyang is now a large industrial centre, but was once an imperial capital. Remains from this period include the *Imperial Palace* – not unlike the Imperial Palace in Beijing – and two interesting tombs. The *North Imperial Tomb*, about 20km (13 miles) from the city, is the burial place of the founding father of the Qing (Ch'ing) Dynasty.

The Eastern Provinces

Fuzhou, in Fujian Province on the southeast coast, is a beautiful city on the banks of the *Min River*. Dating back some 2000 years (to the Tang Dynasty), the city has numerous parks and temples, as well as bustling shipbuilding and repair centres. Fuzhou also has hot springs dotted throughout the city. Local products include lacquerware, Shoushan stone carvings, paper umbrellas, cork carvings and Fukien black tea.

Hangzhou, about 190km (120 miles) south of Shanghai, is one of China's seven ancient capital cities. Known as 'Paradise on Earth', Hangzhou was also described by Marco Polo as "the most beautiful and magnificent city in the world". Although today's city is a prosperous industrial and agricultural centre, it is nevertheless a beauty spot still visited by Chinese and foreign tourists in great numbers. Attractions include the silk factories and the recently completed zoo. By far the most attractive excursion, however, is to the *West Lake* area, dotted with weeping willows and peach trees, stone bridges, rockeries and painted pavilions. Here can be found the *Pagoda of Six Harmonies*, various tombs and sacred hills, monasteries and temples, not least the *Linyin Temple*.

Nanjing, meaning 'southern capital', has a beautiful setting on the Chang Jiang (Yangtse) River at the foot of Zijinshan (Purple Mountain). Another former capital of China, Nanjing is now capital of Jiangsu Province. It abounds with temples, tombs, parks and lakes,

Nanjing Road in Shanghai

museums, hot springs and other places of interest, foremost amongst them being the *Tomb of the Ming Emperor*, where lies the body of Zhu Yuanzhang, founding father of the Ming Dynasty and the only Ming emperor to be buried outside Beijing. The mausoleum of China's first president, Dr Sun Yat-sen, is also here. Other places of interest are the *Yangtse River Bridge* with its observation deck, the *Purple Mountain Observatory* and the *Tombs of the Southern Tang Dynasty*, known as the 'Underground Palace'.

Shanghai is one of the world's largest cities, and is in some ways more like New York than Beijing. Lying at the estuary of the Chang Jiang (Yangtse) River, it is the centre of China's trade and industry. Squares and historical avenues, the old town and magnificent gardens, splendid parks and museums, busy harbours, palaces, pagodas and temples all co-exist in this bustling metropolis. *Yu Yuan Garden* dates back over 400 years: although relatively small, it is impressive thanks to its intricate design, with pavilions, rockeries and ponds recalling an ancient architectural style. The garden is reached via the *Town God Temple Bazaar*, where a variety of small odds and ends can be bought. One of the most well-known Bhuddist temples in Shanghai is the *Temple of the Jade Bhudda*, a replica of a palace of the Song Dynasty, and home to the famous 2m (6ft) tall statue of Sakyamuni, carved out of a single piece of white jade. Worth a visit are the *Art and History Museum* (artefacts from all dynasties); the *Carpet Factory*, where a range of carpets can be bought and shipment arranged; the *Jade Carving Factory*, with works of all sizes on show; and the *Children's Palace*

– once belonging to a rich businessman, this large house is now at the disposal of the city's children.

Suzhou is one of China's oldest cities, dating back some 2500 years, and is certainly one of her most beautiful. An old proverb says that 'in Heaven there is Paradise; on earth, Suzhou': there are indeed many beautiful gardens in this city, and its moderate climate and fertile land make it rich in agricultural produce. There are over 400 historical sites and relics under the protection of the Government, such as the *Gentle Waves Pavilion* and the *Humble Administrator's Garden* and the *Lingering Garden* (both fine classical gardens). The *Grand Canal* and *Tiger Hill* are also worth a visit. There are numerous silk mills producing exquisite fabrics, and the local embroidery is an unparalleled art form.

Wuxi is an industrial and resort city on the north bank of Lake Tai, some 125km (75 miles) west of Shanghai. The gardens, parks and sanatoriums around the lake are the main attractions, as is the *Hui Shan Clay Figure Factory*. Wuxi is virtually encircled by the Chang Jiang (Yangtse) River, and so there are plenty of boat trips to be had.

Jinan, the capital of Shandong Province, is known as the 'City of Springs'; these provide the main tourist attraction. The city also has Buddhist relics, parks and lakes. Of particular interest is the *Square Four Gate Pagoda*, the oldest stone pagoda in China.

Qingdao is one of China's most popular coastal resorts and home of the famous brewery making Tsingdao beer. The *Qingdao Aquarium* has hundreds of rare and protected fish on show.

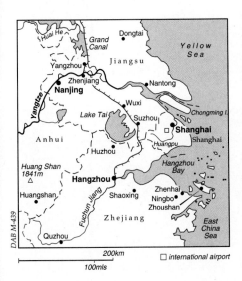

DAB M-439

200km
100mls

□ *international airport*

The Southern Provinces

Changsha, as well as being the capital of Hunan Province, is a cultural and educational centre. It is close to the birthplace of Mao Zedong at **Shaoshan**. Most attractions revolve around Mao's early life and there are museums and schools dedicated to him. One notable exception is the Han Tomb whose contents – including the 2000-year-old remains of a woman – are now in the *Hunan Provincial Museum*.

Guangzhou (Canton), sometimes known as the 'City of Flowers', is a subtropical metropolis on the south coast and the most important foreign trade centre in China, being only 182km (113 miles) from Hong Kong. Parks, museums, temples, hot springs and trips to nearby mountains (for splendid views) are the main attractions, as are the *Chenhai Tower*, a 15th-century observation tower overlooking the Pearl River, and the *Ancestral Temple* in Hunin, an ancient Taoist temple some 16km (10 miles) southwest of Guangzhou. Cantonese cuisine (the one most familiar to the majority of Westerners) is regarded as being particularly excellent, although it is often too exotic for Western tastes.

Guilin is famous for its spectacular landscape, echoed so evocatively in the paintings and wall hangings well-known in the West. Steep monolithic mountains rise dramatically from a flat landscape of meandering rivers and paddy fields. Visitors can climb the hills, take river trips and visit the parks, lakes and caves.

Kunming is a newer, showcase city with some temples and very pretty lakeside parks. It is known as the 'City of Eternal Spring' because of the pleasant climate throughout the year. Outside of Kunming are the major attractions of *Xi Shan*, the holy mountain, and the petrified limestone forest called *Shilin,* 120km (75 miles) southeast of Kunming.

Hainan Island is a tropical island off the south coast of Guangdong Province with unspoilt beaches, palm groves, fresh seafood and coconuts. In 1989 Hainan Island became a separate province in its own right, and is now one of several Special Economic Zones, a part of China's 'open door' policy.

The Central Provinces

Chengdu is the capital of Sichuan Province and a great agricultural centre. The attractions include the Tang Dynasty shrines, ancient parks and bamboo forests, Buddhist temples and an ancient Buddhist monastery. Chengdu is a base for visiting *Emei Shan*, a famous mountain to which Buddhist pilgrims flock every year, and the holy mountains of *Gongga* and *Siguniang*. There is also the spectacular giant *Stone Buddha*, in **Leshan**, which is an enormous sculpture, carved out of a cliff, on which 100 people can fit on its instep. In Sichuan Province, there is a vast nature reserve where giant pandas can be seen in their natural habitat.

Wuhan spans the Chang Jiang (Yangtse) River. As the capital of Hubei Province, it is an industrial centre. There are, however, Buddhist temples, lakes and parks, as well as the *Yellow Crane Tower* and the *Provincial Museum*, home to the famous *Chime Bells* manufactured over 2400 years ago.

Xi'an, the capital of Shaanxi Province, was once amongst the largest cities in the world and was also, from the 11th century BC onwards, the capital of 11 dynasties. It was the starting point of the *Silk Road* and is now, with the exception of Beijing, the most popular tourist attraction in China. The city is most famous for the *Tomb of Emperor Qin Shi Huangdi* and its terracotta figures, over 6000 lifesize warriors and horses buried along with the Qin Dynasty emperor responsible for the unification of China in 200BC. The *Bronze Chariot and Horse Figures* should not be missed: weighing over 1000 tons and made up of over 3000 parts, the figures are the earliest and largest of their kind ever unearthed. Although much of the city was destroyed during the Cultural Revolution, there is still a great number of tombs, pavilions, museums and pagodas, such as the *Big Wild Goose Pagoda* with its spiral staircase and the *Small Wild Goose Pagoda.*

Close to the industrial city and communications centre of **Zhengzhou** are the cities of **Luoyang** and **Kaifeng**; both were once capitals of dynasties, and both are consequently of historical interest. Near Luoyang are the *Longmen (Dragon Gate) Caves*, over 1300 in all, and they contain over 2100 grottoes and niches, several pagodas, countless inscriptions and about 100,000 images and statues of the Buddha and a marvellous Buddhist shrine dating from the 5th century.

The Northwest Provinces

Lanzhou is an oasis on the ancient trade route known as the Silk Road. The capital of Gansu Province, the

Folk dress of one of the various nationalities from the Guilin area

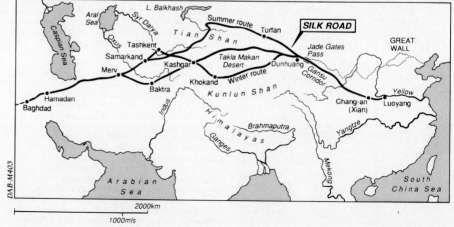

town is relatively unspoilt. There is a park and museum, and river trips can be made along the upper reaches of the *Yellow River* to the site of early Buddhist caves.

Dunhuang is a 2000-year-old town on the edge of the desert, once an important Silk Road caravan stop, famous for the *Magao Caves,* the oldest Buddhist shrines in China. These ancient hand-carved shrines are a national treasure and represent a thousand years of devotion to Buddha between the 2nd and 12th centuries. Some 500 exist today, and large areas of frescoes can still be seen. Also worth a visit when in Dunhuang are the *Yang Guan Pass* and the *Mingsha Hill.*

Turfan and **Urumqi** are situated in the far northwest, cities on the edge of the vast deserts of Xinjiang Province. These Muslim cities, lying on the Silk Road, are well known for the distinctive appearance, dress and lifestyle of the inhabitants. Urumqi is the capital of the Xinjiang Uygur Autonomous Region. The city is inhabited by 13 different nationalities, including Mongolian, Kazak, Russian, Tartar and Uzbek. The main inhabitants are the Muslim Uygurs who speak a Turkic language completely unrelated to Chinese. Northwest of Urumqi, a few hours bus ride away, is the beautiful *Lake of Heaven,* a clear turquoise-coloured lake set in the midst of the Tianshan range of mountains. It is possible to go horseriding with the local Kazaks in this spectacular scenery. Turfan is the hottest place in China, being the second-lowest point on earth next only to the Dead Sea. Nearby are the *Flaming Mountains*, which have the appearance of fire. Museums in both cities trace their fascinating histories.

Tibet (Xizang)

Tibet, known as 'the Roof of the World', has only been open to tourists since 1980. The area was closed to independent travellers in 1988, and it is now only open to tour groups on organised itineraries. About 1000 visas are allocated yearly to visit this remote area. The scenery is spectacular, and the Tibetan culture is one which has a unique fascination.

Lhasa is at an altitude of 3700m (12,000ft). The name means the 'City of Sun', due to the wonderful light and clear skies, which are peculiar to such high mountainous terrain. Despite this, for six months of the year it is bitterly cold. The attraction of Tibet is its isolation from the rest of the world and the preservation of its own way of life and religious traditions, despite efforts, particularly during the Cultural Revolution, to bring Tibet into the fold of the rest of China. The main highlights for tourists lie in the *Potala* or *Red Palace,* home to successive Dalai Lamas, which dominates Lhasa and the valley. This 17th-century edifice, built on a far more ancient site, is now a museum, the likes of which a visitor will be unlikely to see anywhere else: labyrinths of dungeons and torture chambers beneath the Palace, gigantic bejewelled Buddhas and vast treasure hoards, 10,000 chapels with human skull and thigh-bone wall decorations and wonderful Buddhist frescoes, with influences from India and Nepal. Other buildings of interest include the *Drepung Monastery* and the *Jokhang Temple,* with its golden Buddhas. Some travellers may experience health problems as a result of the altitude, so it is wise to consult your doctor prior to departure.

POPULAR ITINERARIES: 7-day: (a) Beijing–Xian–Shanghai–Suzhou–Wuxi. (b) Beijing–Shanghai–Guangzhou–Guilin. (c) Beijing–Hangzhou–Shanghai. (d) Beijing–Chengde–Xian–Beijing.
Note: Independent travel within China is by aircraft or train only.

SOCIAL PROFILE

FOOD & DRINK: Chinese cuisine has a very long history and is renowned all over the world. Cantonese (the style the majority of Westerners are most familiar with) is only one regional style of Chinese cooking. There are eight major schools of Chinese cuisine, named after the places where they were conceived: Shandong, Sichuan, Jiangsu, Zhejian, Guangdong, Hunan, Fujian and Anhui. For a brief appreciation of the cuisine, it is possible to break it down into four major regional categories:
Northern Cuisine: Beijing, which has developed from the Shandong school, is famous for *Peking Duck*, which is roasted in a special way, and eaten in a thin pancake with cucumber and a sweet plum sauce. Another speciality of the North of China is *Mongolian Hotpot*, which is a Chinese version of fondu. It is eaten in a communal style and consists of a central simmering soup

Hill of piled brocade, Guilin

The finger bone relics of Buddha unearthed at Famen Temple

Top picture: The Qin's Emperor Palace. Above: The Shangxi's folk craft: Clay tiger.

in a special large round pot into which is dipped a variety of uncooked meats and vegetables, which are cooked on the spot. A cheap and delicious local dish is *shuijiao*, which is pasta-like dough wrapped round pork meat, chives and onions, similar in idea to Italian ravioli. These can be bought by the jin (pound) in street markets and small eating houses, and are a good filler if you are out all day and do not feel like a large restaurant dinner. It should, however, be noted that in the interests of hygiene, it is best to take one's own chopsticks.

Southern Cuisine: Guangdong (Cantonese) food is famous for being the most exotic in China. The food markets in Guangzhou are a testimony to this, and the Western visitor is often shocked by the enormous variety of rare and exotic animals which are used in the cuisine, including snake, dog, turtle and wildcat.

Eastern Cuisine: Shanghai and Zhejiang cooking is rich and sweet, often pickled. Noted for seafood, hot and sour soup, noodles and vegetables.

Western Cuisine: Sichuan and Hunan food is spicy, often sour and peppery, with specialities such as diced chicken stirred with soy sauce and peanuts, and spicey *doufu* (beancurd).

Drink: One of the best-known national drinks is *maotai*, a fiery spirit which is distilled rice wine. Local beers are of good quality, notably *Qingdao*, which is similar to German lager. There are now some decent wines, which are produced mainly for tourists and export.

NIGHTLIFE: Virtually all visitors follow itineraries drawn up in advance when sampling the nightlife of the larger cities, though this is in no way a drawback. Guides will be helpful and discreet, and generally their assistance will be more than welcome. Most tours include a selection of pre-arranged restaurant meals and visits to Chinese opera, ballet and theatre.

SHOPPING: All consumer prices are set by the Government, and there is no price bargaining in shops and department stores, although it is possible to bargain fiercely in small outdoor markets, of which there are many, for items such as jade, antique ceramics and also silk garments. All antiques over 100 years old are marked with a red wax seal by the authorities, and require an export customs certificate. Access to normal shops is available, offering inexpensive souvenirs, work clothes, posters and books; this will prove much easier if accompanied by an interpreter, although it is possible to point or get the help of a nearby English-speaker. Items are sometimes in short supply, but prices will not vary much from place to place. In large cities such as Beijing and Shanghai, there are big department stores with four or five floors, selling a wide range of products. The best shopping is in local factories, shops and hotels specialising in the sale of handicrafts. Arts and crafts department stores offer local handicrafts. Special purchases include jade jewellery, embroidery, calligraphy, paintings and carvings in wood, stone and bamboo. It is advisable to keep receipts, as visitors may be asked to produce them at Customs prior to departure.

Shopping hours: 0900-1900 Monday to Sunday.

SPECIAL EVENTS: The following is a selection of the major festivals and other special events celebrated annually in China. For a complete list of events in all areas, contact the National Tourist Office.

Jan 31-Feb 2 '95 *Spring/New Year Festival,* from the 1st to the 3rd day of of the first month in the lunar calendar. **Feb 14** *Lantern Festival,* on the 15th day of the first month in the lunar calendar. **Jun 2** *Dragon Boat Festival,* on the 5th day of the fifth lunar month. **Sep 9** *Mid-Autumn Festival,* on the 15th day of the eighth lunar month.

The *Spring Festival* is the most important festival in the year for the Chinese, when families get together and share a sumptuous meal on the eve of the Chinese new year. After dinner, all the members of the family play games and chat, staying up until dawn. At midnight, people let off firecrackers to celebrate the new year. Homes are festooned with banners and pictures to bring good fortune. Other activities associated with the festival include the lion dance, the dragon-lantern dance and stilt walking.

Minority nationalities have retained their own traditional festivals, including the *Water Splashing Festival* of the Dai nationality, the *Third Month Fair* of the Bai nationality, the *Antiphonal Singing Day* of the Zhuang nationality, and the *Tibetan New Year* and *Onghor (Harvest) Festival* of the Tibetan nationality.

SOCIAL CONVENTIONS: Cultural differences may create misunderstandings between local people and visitors. The Chinese do not usually volunteer information and the visitor is advised to ask questions. Hotels, train dining cars and restaurants often ask for criticisms and suggestions which are considered seriously. Do not be offended by being followed by crowds, this is merely an open interest in visitors who are rare in the remoter provinces. The Chinese are generally reserved in manner, courtesy rather than familiarity being preferred. The full title of the country is 'The People's Republic of China', and this should be used in all formal communications. 'China' can be used informally, but there should never be any implication that another China exists. Although handshaking may be sufficient, a visitor will frequently be greeted by applause as a sign of welcome. The usual response is to applaud back. In China the family name is always mentioned first. It is customary to arrive a little early if invited out socially. Toasting at a meal is very common, as is the custom of taking a treat when visiting someone's home, such as fruit, confectionery or a souvenir from a home country. If it is the home of friends or relatives, money might be left for the children. If visiting a school or a factory, a gift from the visitor's home country, particularly something which would be unavailable in China (a text book if visiting a school for example), would be much appreciated. Stamps are also very popular as gifts, as stamp-collecting is a popular hobby in China. A good gift for an official guide is a Western reference book on China. Conservative casual wear is generally acceptable everywhere, but revealing clothes should be avoided since they may cause offence. **Photography:** Not allowed in airports. Places of historic and scenic interest may be photographed, but permission should be sought before photographing military installations, government buildings or other possibly sensitive subjects. **Tipping:** Officially not allowed and sometimes considered insulting.

BUSINESS PROFILE

ECONOMY: The vast Chinese economy has developed in fits and starts since the founding of the People's Republic in 1949. The 1980s proved to be one of the most successful, with an average growth of 9% – the world's highest. Despite some advanced manufacturing and technological enterprises – including a space programme – China's economy is essentially that of a developing country, with the majority of the population employed on the land. China is the world's largest producer of rice and a major producer of cereals and grain. Large mineral deposits, particularly coal and iron ore, provide the raw material for an extensive steel industry. Other important minerals include tungsten, molybdenum, tin, lead, bauxite (aluminium), phosphates and manganese. The 1980s saw a shift in emphasis from heavy to light industry, which now contributes roughly the same proportion to the GNP. Chemicals and high technology industries are receiving much attention at present. China is self-sufficient in oil and developing a petrochemical industry. Trade has been hampered somewhat in recent years by a shortage of foreign exchange, but China has benefited from the availability of soft loans from Western banks. The country's major imports are energy-related products, telecommuni-cations, electronics and transport. Minerals and manufactured goods are the principal imports. In the early 1990s, China had been one of a select band of countries enjoying double-digit economic growth. The major trading partners are Japan, Hong Kong, the USA and Germany. In economic terms, China has benefited considerably from its 'open door' policy – introduced in the mid-1980s – which abandoned the tight restrictions on foreign trade and encouraged foreign companies both to sell products in China and to establish joint ventures with Chinese commercial organisations. A number of Special Economic Zones (SEZ), effectively operating market economies, have been established in China's southern provinces. Advanced technology enterprises were directed to these new Zones. The China Trade Unit, based in Hong Kong, is responsible for providing British exporters with advice on trade with Southern Chinese provinces, including the SEZs.
BUSINESS: Weights and measures are mainly metric, but several old Chinese weights and measures are still used. Liquids and eggs are often sold by weight. The Chinese foot is 1.0936 of an English foot (0.33m). Suits should be worn for business visits. Appointments should be made in advance and punctuality is expected. Visiting cards should be printed with a Chinese translation on the reverse. Business visitors are usually entertained in restaurants where it is customary to arrive a little early and the host will toast the visitor. It is customary to invite the host or hostess to a return dinner. Business travellers in particular should bear in mind that the Government of the United Kingdom recognises the Government of the People's Republic of China as being the only Government of China, as do the United Nations. Best months for business visits are April to June and September to October. **Office hours:** 0800-1200 and 1400-1800 Monday to Saturday.
COMMERCIAL INFORMATION: The following organisations can offer advice: All-China Federation of Industry and Commerce, 93 Beiheyan Dajie, Beijing 100006. Tel: (1) 513 6677. Fax: (1) 512 2631; *or* China Council for the Promotion of International Trade

(CCPIT), PO Box 4509, 1 Fu Xing Men Wai Jie, Beijing 100860. Tel: (1) 801 3344. Fax: (1) 801 1370. Telex: 22315.
CONFERENCES/CONVENTIONS: The following organisations can offer advice: China International Travel Service, Head Office, Department of Conferences and Conventions, 103 Fuxingmennei Avenue, Beijing 100800. Tel: (1) 601 1122. Fax: (1) 601 2013; *or*
China National Tourist Adminstration, Department of Marketing & Promotions, 9A Jian Guo Men Nei Avenue, Beijing 100740. Tel: (1) 513 8866. Fax: (1) 512 2851.

CLIMATE

China has a great diversity of climates. The northeast experiences hot and dry summers and bitterly cold winters. The north and central region has almost continual rainfall, hot summers and cold winters. The southeast region has substantial rainfall, with semi-tropical summers and cool winters.
Required clothing: *North* – heavyweight clothing with boots and for the harsh northern winters. Lightweight clothing for summer. *South* – mediumweight clothing for winter and lightweight for summer.

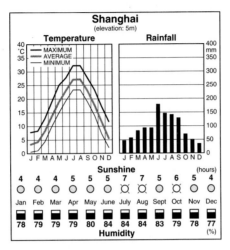

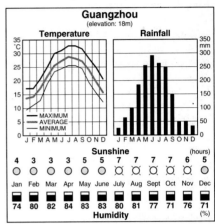

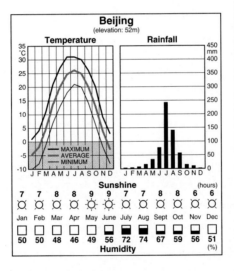

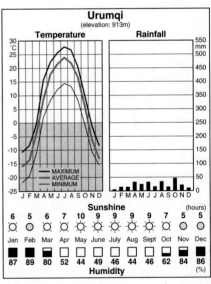

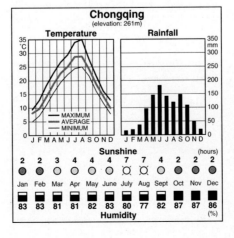

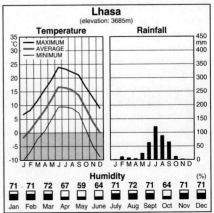

Colombia

□ *international airport*

Location: Northwest South America.

Note: Outbreaks of sporadic violence have been reported, particularly in rural areas. Terrorist attacks and kidnappings have taken place. Travellers are advised to contact their embassy and the local authorities if travelling away from the main tourist centres. There have been instances of bogus 'plain clothes policemen' asking to inspect wallets and handbags before making off with the contents.

Source: FTO Travel Advice Unit – December 3, 1994.
Corporación Nacional de Turismo
Apdo Aéreo 8400, Calle 28, No 13A-15, 16°-18°, Santa Fe de Bogotá DC, Colombia
Tel: (1) 283 9466. Fax: (1) 284 3818. Telex: 41350.
Embassy of the Republic of Colombia
Flat 3A, 3 Hans Crescent, London SW1X 0LR
Tel: (0171) 589 9177. Fax: (0171) 581 1829.
Colombian Consulate
Suite 14, 140 Park Lane, London W1Y 3AA
Tel: (0171) 495 4233 *or* 493 4565. Fax: (0171) 495 4441.
Opening hours: 1000-1400 Monday to Friday. Tourism Information Line: (0891) 880 890 (calls are charged at the higher rate of 39/49p per minute).
British Embassy
Apdo Aéreo 4508, Torre Propaganda Sancho, Calle 98, No 9-03, Piso 4, Santa Fe de Bogotá DC, Colombia
Tel: (1) 218 5111. Fax: (1) 218 2460. Telex: 44503 (a/b BRIT CO).
Consulates in: Barranquilla, Cali and Medellín.
Embassy of the Republic of Colombia
2118 Leroy Place, NW, Washington, DC 20008
Tel: (202) 387 8338. Fax: (202) 232 8643.
Colombian Consulate
10 East 46th Street, New York, NY 10017
Tel: (212) 949 9898. Fax: (212) 972 1725. Opening hours: 0900-1345 Monday to Friday.
Embassy of the United States of America
PO Box 3831, Calle 38, No 8-61, Santa Fe de Bogotá

Health

DC, Colombia
Tel: (1) 320 1300. Fax: (1) 288 5687.
Embassy of the Republic of Colombia
Suite 1002, 360 Albert Street, Ottawa, Ontario K1R 7X7
Tel: (613) 230 3760/1. Fax: (613) 230 4416. Opening hours: 0900-1600 Monday to Friday.
Canadian Embassy
Apdo Aéreo 53531, Calle 76, No 11-52 Santa Fe de Bogotá DC, Colombia
Tel: (1) 217 5555. Fax: (1) 310 4509. Telex: 037620 (a/b DMCA CO).
Consulate in: Cartagena.

AREA: 1,141,748 sq km (440,831 sq miles).
POPULATION: 33,951,171 (1993 estimate).
POPULATION DENSITY: 29.7 per sq km.
CAPITAL: Santa Fe de Bogotá. **Population:** 5,025,989 (1993 estimate).
GEOGRAPHY: Colombia is situated in South America, bounded to the north by the Caribbean, to the northwest by Panama, to the west by the Pacific Ocean, to the southwest by Ecuador and Peru, to the northeast by Venezuela and to the southeast by Brazil. The Andes Mountains extend into the country in three ranges running north to south, dipping finally into the lowlands of the Caribbean coast. Along the southern part of the Pacific coast run wide, marshy lowlands rising to a relatively low but rugged mountain chain. East of this range, the southwestern coastal lowlands extend in a low trough running from the port of Buenaventura on the Pacific coast to the Caribbean. East of this, rise the slopes of the Western Cordillera which, with the Central Cordillera range, runs north to the Caribbean lowlands from Ecuador, separated by a valley, filled in the south by volcanic ash to a height of 2500m (8202ft). Further north lies the fertile Cauca Valley, which extends to Cartago where it becomes a deep gorge running between the Cordilleras to the Caribbean lowlands. The Eastern Cordillera, the longest range, rises north of the Ecuadorean border and runs north then northeast towards Venezuela. Flat grassy prairies in the east along with the jungles and towering rainforests of the Amazon make up over half the country's area. There are also two small islands, San Andrés and Providencia, located 480km (298 miles) north of the Colombian coast, that have belonged to Colombia since 1822.
LANGUAGE: Spanish is the official language. Local Indian dialects and some English are also spoken.
RELIGION: 95% Roman Catholic; small Protestant and Jewish minorities.
TIME: GMT - 5.
ELECTRICITY: Mostly 110/120 volts (some 150-volt supplies still exist) AC, 60Hz. American-style 2-pin plugs are common.
COMMUNICATIONS: Telephone: IDD service to most areas; calls to smaller centres must be made through the international operator. Country code: 57. Outgoing international code: 90. **Fax:** Only the largest hotels have fax services. **Telex/telegram:** Facilities are available at the Tequendama and Hilton hotels in Bogotá or through national ENDT telecommunications offices. Telex facilities also exist at most of the major hotels. **Post:** Post offices are marked *Correos*. Opening hours are 0900-1700 Monday to Friday; 0800-1200 Saturday. There are two types of service: urban post (green letter boxes) and inter-urban and international (yellow boxes). Letters and packets sent by airmail normally take between five and seven days to reach their destination. **Press:** Newspapers are in Spanish. Dailies include *El Espacio, El Espectador, El Siglo* and *El Tiempo*.
BBC World Service and Voice of America frequencies: From time to time these change. See the section *How to Use this Book* for more information.
BBC:

MHz	17.84	15.22	9.915	7.325

Voice of America:

MHz	15.21	11.58	9.775	5.995

PASSPORT/VISA

	Passport Required?	Visa Required?	Return Ticket Required?
Full British	Yes	No/1	Yes
BVP	Not valid	-	-
Australian	Yes	No/1	Yes
Canadian	Yes	No/1	Yes
USA	Yes	No/1	Yes
Other EU (As of 31/12/94)	Yes	No/1	Yes
Japanese	Yes	No/1	Yes

Security of documents: For about US$20 it is possible to have passports and other important documents photocopied and witnessed by the security police; they can then be kept secure as the photocopy will generally be accepted.
PASSPORTS: Valid passport required by all (6 months minimum validity) except nationals of Chile and Ecuador, travelling direct from their respective countries and holding national identity cards.
British Visitors Passport: Not accepted.
VISAS: [1] Tourists whose stay does not exceed 90 days do not require a visa.
A 15-day extension to this period may usually be granted. All visitors must provide proof on arrival of sufficient funds to cover their stay. Business visitors do not need a Business visa if their visit does not involve the signing of documents, the receipt or payment of fees, nor visits to sites in rural areas.
Note: Nationals of the Republic of China, Taiwan (China) and Haiti *do* require visas, whatever the purpose of their visit.
Types of visa: Tourist, Business, Working and Student.
Exit visas: All travellers must obtain an exit stamp from the DAS (security police) before leaving. This is best obtained at the airport or in main cities.
Application to: Consulate (or Consular section at Embassy). For addresses, see top of entry.
Application requirements: (a) Recent passport-size photo. (b) Completed application form (c) Proof of onward journey. (d) Valid passport.
Working days required: 2 days to 3 months, depending on visa.

MONEY

Currency: Peso (Col$). Notes are in denominations of Col$10,000, 5000, 2000, 1000, 500, 200, 100 and 50. Coins are in denominations of Col$50, 20, 10, 5, 2 and 1.
Currency exchange: The exchange rate tends to be lower on the Caribbean coast than in Bogotá, Medellín and Cali. The US Dollar is the easiest currency to exchange at hotels, banks, shops and travel agencies; but establishments all charge an exchange fee.
Credit cards: All major cards are accepted, but check with your credit card company for details of merchant acceptability and other services which may be available.
Travellers cheques: These are not always easy to change in the smaller towns, except at branches of the Banco de la República. A photocopied travellers cheque is not of course negotiable but the photocopy will help if they are lost or stolen (see *Security of documents* in the *Passport/Visa* section above).
Exchange rate indicators: The following figures are included as a guide to the movements of the Colombian Peso against Sterling and the US Dollar:

Date:	Oct '92	Sep '93	Jan '94	Jan '95
£1.00=	936.19	1234.85	1187.61	1301.04
$1.00=	589.91	808.68	802.71	831.60

Currency restrictions: The import of local currency is unlimited; the export is restricted to Col$500 (depending on exchange rate). When leaving Colombia, Col$60 may be reconverted. Foreign currency may be imported up to the equivalent of US$25,000 and exported up to the amount declared on arrival.
Banking hours: 0900-1500 Monday to Friday.

DUTY FREE

The following goods may be taken into Colombia without incurring customs duty:
200 cigarettes and 50 cigars and 500g of tobacco; 6 bottles of wine or spirits; a reasonable quantity of perfume.
Note: Emeralds and articles made of gold or platinum need a receipt from the place of purchase which must be presented to customs on departure.

PUBLIC HOLIDAYS

Jan 1 '95 New Year's Day. **Jan 9** *For Epiphany. **Mar 20** *For St Joseph's Day. **Apr 13** Maundy Thursday. **Apr 14** Good Friday. **May 1** Labour Day. **May 29** *For Ascension Day. **Jun 19** *For Corpus Christi. **Jul 3** *For Saint Peter and Saint Paul. **Jul 20** Independence Day. **Aug 7** Battle of Boyacá. **Aug 21** *For Assumption. **Oct 16** *For Discovery of America. **Nov 6** *For All Saints' Day. **Nov 13** *For Independence of Cartagena. **Dec 8** Immaculate Conception. **Dec 25** Christmas Day. **Jan 1 '96** New Year's Day. **Jan 6** *Epiphany. **Mar 19** *St Joseph's Day. **Apr 4** Maundy Thursday. **Apr 5** Good Friday.
Note*: These holidays may be held on the following Monday, when they fall on any other day of the week.

HEALTH

Regulations and requirements may be subject to change at short notice, and you are advised to contact your doctor well in advance of your intended date of departure. Any numbers in the chart refer to the footnotes below.		
	Special Precautions?	**Certificate Required?**
Yellow Fever	1	Yes
Cholera	Yes	2
Typhoid & Polio	Yes	-
Malaria	3	-
Food & Drink	4	-

[1]: It is recommended that travellers arriving from an affected area or who may visit the following areas considered to be endemic for yellow fever should be vaccinated: middle valley of the Magdalena River, eastern foothills of the frontier with Ecuador to that with Venezuela, Uraba, the southeastern part of the Sierra Nevada de Santa Marta, the forest along the river Guaviare and in the Llanos Orientales or Amazones regions.
[2]: Following WHO guidelines issued in 1973, a cholera vaccination certificate is not a condition of entry to Colombia. However, cholera is a serious risk in this country and precautions are essential. Up-to-date advice should be sought before deciding whether these precautions should include vaccination as medical opinion is divided over its effectiveness. See the *Health* section at the back of the book.
[3]: Malaria risk exists throughout the year in rural areas below 800m of the Pacific coast, Uraba (Antioquia and Chocó Dep.), Bajo Cauca-Nechi (Córdoba and Antioquia Dep.), Magdalena Medio, Catatumbo (Norte de Santander Dep.), Llanos Orientales and Amazonas. The malignant *falciparum* form of the disease is reported to be 'highly resistant' to chloroquine and 'resistant' to sulfadoxine/pyrimethane.
[4]: All water should be regarded as being potentially contaminated. Water used for drinking, brushing teeth or making ice should have first been boiled or otherwise sterilised. Milk is unpasteurised and should be boiled. Powdered or tinned milk is available and is advised, but make sure that it is reconstituted with pure water. Avoid dairy products which are likely to have been made from unboiled milk. Only eat well-cooked meat and fish, preferably served hot. Pork, salad and mayonnaise may carry increased risk. Vegetables should be cooked and fruit peeled.
Rabies is present. For those at high risk, vaccination before arrival should be considered. If you are bitten abroad seek medical advice without delay. For more information consult the *Health* section at the back of the book.
Hepatitis is a risk. For precautions see the section on *Health* at the back of this book.
Health care: Visitors to Bogotá should take a couple of days to acclimatise themselves to the altitude, which may induce drowsiness. Avoid excessive intake of alcohol. Health facilities in the main cities are good. Medical insurance is essential.

TRAVEL - International

AIR: Colombia's national airline is *Avianca (AV)*.
Approximate flight times: From Bogotá to *London* is 13 hours 45 minutes, to *Los Angeles* is 10 hours 30 minutes, to *New York* is 6 hours 30 minutes, to *Singapore* is 35 hours 15 minutes and to *Sydney* is 29 hours.
International airports: *Bogotá* (El Dorado) *(BOG)* is situated 12km (7.5 miles) east of the city. Airport facilities include bank (0700-2200), duty-free shop, bar, restaurant (0700-2200), tourist information and car hire (*Avis, Hertz* and *Dollar*). Bus ('Consul') to the city (travel time – 30 minutes) departs every 20 minutes from 0600-1900. Taxis are available.
Barranquilla (Ernesto Cortissoz) *(BAQ)* is 10km (6 miles) from the city. Car rental is available.
Cali (Palmaseca) *(CLO)* is 19km (10 miles) from the city.
Cartagena (Crespo) *(CTG)* is 2km (1 mile) from the city.
Departure tax: US$17 (or the equivalent in Pesos) is charged for all international departures (children under 5 years and passengers for transit within 24 hours are exempt). This tax is doubled for stays of more than 60 days.
Note: All air tickets purchased in Colombia for destinations outside the country are liable to a total tax of 15% on one-way tickets and 7.5% on return tickets.
SEA: Shipping companies serve Colombian ports with both passenger and combination passenger/freight vessels. The following ports and lines serve the major routes: US Gulf ports – *Delta Line* cruises; from Europe – *French Line, Italian Line, Pacific Steam Navigation, Royal Netherlands SS Co.* and *Linea 'C'*. Cartagena is an important port of call for the following cruise lines: *Sun Line, Princess Cruises, Delta, Norwegian American, Holland America, Westours, Sitmar* and *Costa.*
RAIL: There are no international rail connections.
ROAD: The Pan Americana Highway, when completed, should make it possible to drive into Colombia from Panama. Vehicles can also be freighted from Panama to one of Colombia's Caribbean or Pacific ports. There are also road links with Ecuador and Venezuela. **Coach/bus:** *TEPSA* buses connect with Venezuela. Coaches are comfortable and services good. There are second-class buses from Maracaibo to Santa Marta and Cartagena, but this method of travelling can be uncomfortable.

TRAVEL - Internal

AIR: Services are offered by *Avianca (SAM)* and 15 smaller companies. There is an excellent internal air network connecting major cities, including those in the Caribbean coastal area. There are also local helicopter flights. There are flights between the mainland and the islands of San Andrés and Providencia operating from most major Colombian cities. San Andrés is a regular stop for *Avianca, Lacsa* and *Sahsa* airlines.
SEA: There is a ferry service between the mainland and the islands of San Andrés and Providencia, leaving from the Mulle de Pegasos. The journey is long (72 hours), but cheap. Information about other sailings to San Andrés can be obtained from the Maritima San Andrés office. Once on the islands, there are boat trips available to Johnny Cay and the Aquarium.
RIVER: The Magdalena River is the main artery of Colombia. Some cargo boats take passengers, though this is a slow way to travel. It is possible to hire boats for particular trips. Paddle steamers no longer run services up and down the river and hiring can be expensive. From Leticia, on the Peruvian border, a number of operators run sightseeing tours and jungle expeditions up the Amazon. It is necessary to make enquiries *in situ*, and wise to shop around before booking on any one trip (see also *Resorts & Excursions*).
RAIL: Although trains still carry freight, inter-city passenger services are virtually non-existent. Services have been frequently suspended during recent years due to operators' financial difficulties. The main route is between Bogotá and Santa Marta on the Caribbean coast, east of Barranquilla. Because of the distances, it is easier to take a plane if speed is important.
ROAD: A good highway links Santa Marta in the east with Cartagena, and passes Barranquilla en route. The brand-new Trans-Caribbean Highway has now placed Barranquilla only five hours away from Venezuela. Northeast of Santa Marta, in the Guajira Peninsula, roads are usually passable except during rainy periods. There is highway transportation between the coastal cities and the capital and other cities of the interior, but much of the highway is rutted. **Bus:** The large distances make air travel advisable. However, the best bus lines are said to be the *Flota Magdalena, Expresso Boliviano* and, especially, the *Expresso Palmita.* About 42 companies with modern buses and minibuses provide transportation between coastal towns and cities.
Car hire: *Avis, Hertz, Budget* and *National* have car rental offices, but driving in cities is *not recommended.* Traffic drives on the right. **Documentation:** An International Driving Permit is recommended, although it is not legally required.
URBAN: Bogotá has extensive trolleybus, bus and minibus services, and a funicular railway; flat fares are charged. There are also shared taxis (*buseta)* which are not expensive and stop on demand. Drivers are authorised to add a supplement for out-of-town trips and to airports. At hotels, the green and cream coloured taxis are available for tourists. They are more expensive than the others. Passengers should insist that meters are used. For those without a meter the fare should be agreed before starting a journey.
JOURNEY TIMES: The following chart gives approximate journey times from Bogotá (in hours and minutes) to other major towns/cities in Colombia.

	Air
Cartagena	1.15
Barranquilla	1.15
Medellín	1.15
Manizales	1.00
Cali	1.00
Bucaramanga	0.45
Cúcuta	1.00
Pereira	1.00
Leticia	2.00

ACCOMMODATION

HOTELS: It is advisable to choose hotels recommended by the Corporación Nacional de Turismo (for address, see top of entry). The corporation has offices in most towns, on Floor 2 of *El Dorado Airport* and at other main airports. Two tariffs are levied: 'European tariff' from May to November, and 'American tariff' from December to April, which is much higher. It is advisable to make reservations well in advance. There are several hotels and *residencias* on the island of San Andrés, and one on Providencia.
Prices rise on average 10% a year; visitors are advised to check current prices when making reservations.
Grading: There is a star grading system similar to that operating in Europe.
Note: A 5% tax is added to all hotel bills throughout the country.
CAMPING/CARAVANNING: Camping is possible in Colombia, although there are very few official camping areas. Two of the better campsites in the country are Camping del Sol and Camping de Covenas.

RESORTS & EXCURSIONS

The four major cities in Colombia are Bogotá, Medellín, Cali and Barranquilla.
Bogotá: The capital and largest city, which is situated almost in the centre of the country at an altitude of 2600m (8600ft). The city reflects a blend of Colombian tradition and Spanish colonial influences. Many historical landmarks have been preserved, such as the *Capitol Municipal Palace* and the cathedral on the main square, the *Plaza Bolivar.* Bogotá also contains the *Gold Museum,* with its unique collection of over 100,000 pre-Colombian artworks.
Medellín: Colombia's second city, with over 2 million inhabitants, lies 3300m (5500ft) above sea level in a narrow valley of the central mountain range. It is primarily industrial, and is the centre of the coffee and textile trades. The region has recently acquired a reputation for violence due to the war between the Government and the drug barons.
Cali: The centre of the principal sugar-producing region of the country, where modern technology blends with colonial tradition. Deposits of coal and precious metals are found in this area.
Barranquilla: A busy port and Colombia's fourth city, Barranquilla is located towards the mouth of the Magdalena River. It is one of the nation's main commercial centres. There is a colourful market in the so-called *Zona Negra* on a side channel of the Magdalena.
Other places of interest: Colombia has much to offer those interested in archaeology. *San Augustin Archaeological Park* contains a great number of relics and massive stone statues. The traditional city of **Popayan** is the birthplace of many of Colombia's most illustrious statesmen. As well as containing many fine colonial houses and churches, it is also noted for its Holy Week procession.
Santa Marta was one of the first major cities founded by the Spanish in South America, and its modern hotels and sparkling white beaches now make it just as popular among tourists. **Cartagena**, an ancient walled fortress city on the north coast, is also worth a visit.
Easily reached from Cartagena, by plane or boat, are the islands of **San Andrés** and **Providencia**, nearly 500km (300 miles) north of the Colombian coast. San Andrés was once the headquarters of the English pirate Captain Henry Morgan, the scourge of the Caribbean. The islands are duty free, and consequently often crowded, but there are still several less spoilt parts. Popular excursions include visits by boat to *Johnny Cay* and the *Aquarium.*
Tierradentro, in the southwest of the country, has beautiful man-made burial caves painted with pre-Colombian geometric patterns. In the same region, **Silva** is a beautiful Indian town.
The country also contains much unspoilt countryside; the **Guajura Peninsula** is home to over 100,000 nomadic Indians.

SOCIAL PROFILE

FOOD & DRINK: Restaurants offer international cuisine and table service is the norm. Local dishes are varied and tasty, with a touch of Spanish influence. Recommended dishes are *ajiaco* (chicken stew with potatoes, served with cream, corn on the cob and capers); *arepas* (corn pancakes made without salt, eaten in place of bread); *bandeja* (paisa – meat dish accompanied by cassava), rice, fried plantain (variety of bananas) and red beans, served in the area of Medellín. Seafood, known as *mariscos,* is plentiful on the Caribbean coast. Lobsters in particular are renowned for their flavour. **Drink:** It is safest to drink bottled water. Colombians rarely drink alcohol with meals. *Gaseosa* is the name given to non-alcoholic, carbonated drinks. For a small black coffee, you should ask for a *tinto,* but this term is also used to describe red wine or *vino tinto.* Colombian wines are of poor quality. Chilean and Argentinian wines are available in restaurants at reasonable prices. Colombia produces many different types of rum (ron). Cañalazo, a rum-based cocktail taken hot or cold, can be recommended. There are no licensing hours.

NIGHTLIFE: Bogotá's Colon Theatre presents ballet, opera, drama and music, with international and local groups. There are many nightclubs and discotheques in the major towns of Colombia.

SHOPPING: Special purchases include local handicrafts, cotton, wool and leather goods, woollen blankets, ruana, and travelling bags. Hotel shops carry excellent gold reproductions of ancient Colombian jewellery. Colombia produces first-grade stones and the emeralds are amongst the most perfect in the world.
Shopping hours: 0900-1230 and 1430-1830 Monday to Saturday.

SPORT: Football is Colombia's main sport, with major league games played throughout the year. **Tennis** is popular; most hotels have facilities. **Mountain climbing** begins 48km (30 miles) east of Santa Marta, with peaks of up to nearly 6000m (19,000ft). A major **cycle** race, the Tour of Colombia, takes place every March and April. **Boxing** and **bullfighting** (the latter at Bogotá, Cali, Medellín, Manizales and Cartagena) are popular sports. **Golf** clubs allow visitors to use their facilities. Good **skiing** can be found on the slopes of Nevado del Ruiz (5400m/17,700ft), 48km (30 miles) from Manizales. **Fishing** is excellent all year round; a licence is required. **Watersports: Water-skiing, boating, sailing** and **skindiving** (check with authorities before diving, as sharks and barracudas have caused fatalities).

SPECIAL EVENTS: The following is a selection of the major festivals and other special events celebrated in Colombia during 1995/96. For a complete list, contact the Colombian Consulate.
Mar '95 The International Caribbean Music Festival, Cartagena. **Apr** Festival of the Vallenato Legend. **Jun** The Cumbia Festival, El Banco; International Film Festival, Cartagena; The Porro Festival, San Pelayo. **Aug** The Sea Festival, Santa Marta; Parade of the Flower Vendors, Medellín; The Guabina and Tiple Festival, Vélez. **Sep** The National Band Contest, Paipa. **Nov** The Plains National Folk and Tourist Festival, San Martín. **Dec** The Sugar-Cane Fair, Cali. **Jan '96** The Manizales Fair, Festival of Whites and Blacks, Pasto. **Feb** The Barranquilla Carnival. **Mar** The International Caribbean Music Festival, Cartagena.
In Bogotá, the open-air Media Torta presents music, plays and folk dances on Sunday afternoons and holidays. An amateur theatre group gives frequent performances in English.

SOCIAL CONVENTIONS: Normal courtesies should be observed. It is customary to offer guests black Colombian coffee, well sugared, called tinto. Spanish style and culture can still be seen in parts of the country, although in Bogotá, North American attitudes and clothes are becoming prevalent. Casual clothes can be worn in most places; formal attire will be necessary for exclusive dining rooms and social functions. Smoking is allowed except where indicated. The visitor is advised that many of the main cities in Colombia are notorious for street crime, particularly at night. Drug-related crimes are a serious problem throughout the country and the visitor should be wary of the unsolicited attention of strangers (see Security of documents in the Passport/Visa section above). **Tipping:** Taxi drivers do not expect tips. Porters at airports and hotels are usually given a few pesos per item. Many restaurants, bars and cafés add 10% service charge to bill or suggest a 10% tip. Maids and clerks in hotels are rarely tipped. Bogotá's shoeshine boys live on their tips and expect about 50 pesos.

BUSINESS PROFILE

ECONOMY: Colombia is one of South America's stronger economies. Agriculture is extensive and varied, and accounts for 75% of export earnings. Coffee has traditionally been the principal crop (Colombia is the world's second largest producer), but as production has declined and the price fallen, other products have replaced it, including sugar, bananas, cut flowers and cotton. The cattle business may be set for significant expansion in the next few years. The country is self-sufficient in consumer goods and exports of manufactured goods – textiles, leather goods, metal products, chemicals, pharmaceuticals and cement – have been steadily increasing. Colombia has sizeable oil reserves which are now starting to come on stream: British Petroleum has a 40% stake in a huge, recently discovered field at Cusiana in the Andean foothills. Coal deposits are the largest in Latin America but again, development has also been slow due to the financial problems of the state coal company. The country has shown healthy GDP growth throughout the 1980s, averaging at 3.5% and has matched this trend so far in

the 1990s. Colombia is a member of the Andean Pact and of the Asociación Latinoamericano de Integración (ALADI) which is seeking to regularise tariffs throughout South America. The organisation is based in Montevideo, Uruguay. The United States is Colombia's largest trading partner. Germany, Japan and Venezuela follow.

BUSINESS: Business people are expected to dress smartly. English is widely understood in many business circles; the Colombian Ministry of Foreign Affairs has an official translation service, and there are a number of commercial interpreter services. A command of Spanish is always appreciated. Business visitors will sometimes be invited out to dinner, which may be preceded by a long cocktail party, with a meal starting around 2300. The best months for business visits are March to November. The business community generally takes holidays from September to February, the driest months. It is advisable to avoid Barranquilla in June and July.
Office hours: 0800-1200 and 1400-1730 Monday to Friday.

COMMERCIAL INFORMATION: The following organisations can offer advice: Confederación Columbiana de Cámaras de Comercio (CONFECAMARAS) (National Chamber of Commerce), Apdo Aéreo 29750, Carrera 13, No 27-47, Of. 502, Santa Fe de Bogotá DC. Tel: (1) 288 1200. Fax: (1) 288 4228. Telex: 44416; or
Instituto Colombiana de Comercio Exterior (INCOMEX) (Institute of Foreign Trade), Apdo Aéreo 240193, Calle 28, No 13A-15, Sante Fe de Bogotá DC. Tel: (1) 283 3284. Telex: 44860.
CONFERENCES/CONVENTIONS: For advice and assistance with conferences and conventions in Colombia, contact the Colombia Convention Center and Exhibit Corporation, Calle 26A, No 13A-10, Santa Fe de Bogotá DC. Tel: (1) 281 1099. Fax: (1) 282 5842. Telex: 45311/2.

CLIMATE

The climate is very warm and tropical on the coast and in the north, with a rainy season from May to November. This varies according to altitude. It is cooler in the upland areas and cold in the mountains. Bogotá is always spring-like, with cool days and crisp nights.
Required clothing: Lightweight cottons and linens with waterproofing during rainy season in coastal and northern areas. Medium- to heavy-weights are needed in upland and mountainous areas.

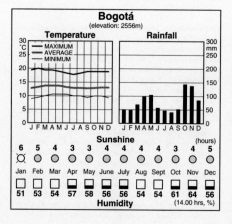

Bogotá
(elevation: 2556m)

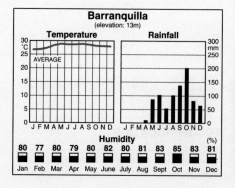

Barranquilla
(elevation: 13m)

Comoro Islands

□ international airport

Location: Indian Ocean, between East African coast and Madagascar.

Société Comorienne de Tourisme et d'Hôtellerie (COMOTEL)
Itsandra Hotel, Njazidja, Comoros
Tel: 732 365 or 611 132.
Embassy of the Federal Islamic Republic of the Comoros
20 rue Marbeau, 75016 Paris, France
Tel: (1) 40 67 90 54. Fax: (1) 40 67 72 96.
The British Embassy in Antananarivo deals with enquiries relating to the Comoro Islands (see Madagascar **later in the book).**
Permanent Mission of the Federal Islamic Republic of the Comoros to the United Nations
2nd Floor, 336 East 45th Street, New York, NY 10017
Tel: (212) 972 8010. Fax: (212) 983 4712.
The Canadian High Commission in Nairobi deals with enquiries relating to the Comoros Islands (see Kenya **later in the book).**

AREA: 1862 sq km (719 sq miles).
POPULATION: 475,000 (1990 estimate).
POPULATION DENSITY: 255.1 per sq km.
CAPITAL: Moroni. **Population:** 17,267 (1980).
GEOGRAPHY: The Comoro archipelago is situated in the Indian ocean northeast of Madagascar and consists of four main islands of volcanic origin, surrounded by coral reefs: Njazidja (formerly Grande Comore), Nzwani (formerly Anjouan), Mwali (formerly Mohéli) and Mahore (Mayotte). The latter is administered by France but is claimed by the Federal Islamic Republic of the Comoros. Land can only support subsistence agriculture but the surrounding seas are rich in marine life.
LANGUAGE: The official languages are French and Arabic. However, the majority speak Comoran, a blend of Arabic and Swahili.
RELIGION: Muslim with Roman Catholic minority.
TIME: GMT + 3.
ELECTRICITY: 220 volts AC, 50Hz.
COMMUNICATIONS: Telephone: Outgoing international calls must be made through the international operator. Country code: 269. **Post:** Mail to Western Europe takes at least a week. **Press:** There are no English-language newspapers. The two main weekly papers are Al Watwany (state-owned) and L'Archipel

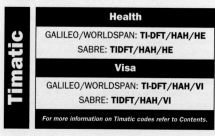

Health
GALILEO/WORLDSPAN: **TI-DFT/HAH/HE**
SABRE: **TIDFT/HAH/HE**
Visa
GALILEO/WORLDSPAN: **TI-DFT/HAH/VI**
SABRE: **TIDFT/HAH/VI**
For more information on Timatic codes refer to Contents.

(independent).
BBC World Service and Voice of America frequencies: From time to time these change. See the section *How to Use this Book* for more information.

BBC:				
MHz	**21.47**	**11.94**	**6.190**	**6.005**
Voice of America:				
MHz	**21.49**	**15.60**	**9.525**	**6.035**

PASSPORT/VISA

Regulations and requirements may be subject to change at short notice, and you are advised to contact the appropriate diplomatic or consular authority before finalising travel arrangements. Details of these may be found at the head of this country's entry. Any numbers in the chart refer to the footnotes below.

	Passport Required?	Visa Required?	Return Ticket Required?
Full British	Yes	Yes	Yes
BVP	Not valid	-	-
Australian	Yes	Yes	Yes
Canadian	Yes	Yes	Yes
USA	Yes	Yes	Yes
Other EU (As of 31/12/94)	Yes	Yes	Yes
Japanese	Yes	Yes	Yes

PASSPORTS: Valid passport required by all.
British Visitors Passport: Not accepted.
VISAS: Required by all. Issued on arrival by the Immigration Officer to all nationalities.
Types of visa: Transit (valid for 5 days), Tourist, Exit Permit.
Cost: *Transit visas:* free; not required by those continuing their journey by the same or first connecting aircraft from the same or nearest airport. *Tourist visas:* for a stay of up to 45 days, CFA Fr2000; for a stay of up to 90 days, CFA Fr4000. For a stay of 12 months, those without a resident card are charged CFA Fr10,000, and those with a resident card are charged CFA Fr25,000. *Exit permits* cost CFA Fr1500 and are required by all.
Note: All passengers must hold onward or return tickets.
Application to: Consulate (or Consular section at Embassy). For address, see top of entry.

MONEY

Currency: Comoros Franc (CFA Fr) = 100 centimes. Notes are in denominations of CFA Fr5000, 1000, 500, 100 and 50. Coins are in denominations of CFA Fr20, 10, 5, 2 and 1. The Comoros Franc is on a par with the French Franc and French Francs may also be in circulation; enquire at Embassy.
Note: At the beginning of 1994, the Comoros Franc was devalued against the French Franc.
Credit cards: There is limited acceptance of most international credit cards (mainly in hotels), but check with your credit card company for details of merchant acceptability and other services which may be available.
Travellers cheques: French Franc cheques are recommended. The Banque Internationale des Comores (BIC) is the only bank which will change travellers cheques.
Exchange rate indicators: The following figures are included as a guide to the movements of the Comoros Franc against Sterling and the US Dollar:

Date:	**Oct '92**	**Sep '93**	**Jan '94**	**Jan '95**
£1.00=	**413.75**	**433.88**	**436.79**	**628.63**
$1.00=	**260.71**	**284.14**	**295.23**	**401.81**

Currency restrictions: No restrictions on import and export of local and foreign currency.
Banking hours: 0730-1300 Monday to Thursday; 0730-1100 Friday.

DUTY FREE

The following goods may be imported into the Comoros by persons over 18 years of age without incurring any customs duty:
400 cigarettes or 100 cigars or 500g of tobacco; 1 litre of alcoholic beverage; 75cl of perfume.
Prohibited items: Plants or soil.

PUBLIC HOLIDAYS

Feb 1 '95 Beginning of Ramadan. **Mar 3** Eid al-Fitr (End of Ramadan). **May 10** Eid al-Adha (Feast of the Sacrifice). **May 31** Muharram (Islamic New Year). **Jun 9** Ashoura. **Jul 6** Independence Day. **Aug 9** Mouloud (Prophet's Birthday). **Nov 27** Anniversary of President Abdallah's Assassination. **Dec 20** Leilat al-Meiraj (Ascension of the Prophet). **Jan 21 '96** Beginning of Ramadan. **Feb 22** Eid al-Fitr (End of Ramadan). **Apr 29** Eid al-Adha (Feast of the Sacrifice).
Note: Muslim festivals are timed according to local sightings of various phases of the Moon and the dates given above are approximations. During the lunar month of Ramadan that precedes Eid al-Fitr, Muslims fast during the day and feast at night and normal business patterns may be interrupted. Many restaurants are closed during the day and there may be restrictions on smoking and drinking. Some disruption may continue into Eid al-Fitr itself. Eid al-Fitr and Eid al-Adha may last anything from two to ten days, depending on the region. For more information see the section *World of Islam* at the back of the book.

HEALTH

Regulations and requirements may be subject to change at short notice, and you are advised to contact your doctor well in advance of your intended date of departure. Any numbers in the chart refer to the footnotes below.

	Special Precautions?	Certificate Required?
Yellow Fever	No	No/1
Cholera	No	No
Typhoid & Polio	Yes	-
Malaria	2	-
Food & Drink	3	-

[1]: Some travellers from areas infected with yellow fever have been asked to provide vaccination certificates.
[2]: Malaria risk exists all year throughout the archipelago, predominantly in the malignant *falciparum* form. Resistance to chloroquine has been reported.
[3]: All water should be regarded as being potentially contaminated. Water used for drinking, brushing teeth or making ice should have first been boiled or otherwise sterilised. Milk is unpasteurised and should be boiled. Powdered or tinned milk is available and is advised, but make sure that it is reconstituted with pure water. Avoid dairy products which are likely to have been made from unboiled milk. Only eat well-cooked meat and fish, preferably served hot. Pork, salad and mayonnaise may carry increased risk. Vegetables should be cooked and fruit peeled.
Health care: Health insurance is strongly advised.

TRAVEL - International

AIR: The national airline is *Air Comores (OR).*
Approximate flight time: From London to Moroni is 18 hours; this includes a stopover (usually in Paris) of 2 hours 15 minutes.
International airport: *Moroni Hahaya (HAH),* 20km (12.5 miles) from the city. A bus runs to the town, costing about CFA Fr150. There are also taxis.
Departure tax: CFA Fr500 or FFr100.
SEA: There are irregular sailings via Madagascar, Reunion, Mauritius or East Africa (Mombasa, Kenya) to Moroni or Mutsamudu. The *Baraka–Belinga* line sails from the Comoros to France. *Norwegian American* run Arabian Sea cruises from Genoa to Mutsamudu.

TRAVEL - Internal

AIR: Each island has an airfield. *Air Comores* has four weekly connections between Moroni, Mwali (Mohéli) and Nzwani (Anjouan) and twice weekly between Moroni and Dzaoudzi.
SEA: Mahore (Mayotte), Pamanzi and Dzaoudzi islands are linked by a regular ferry service. Travellers can hire motorboats, sailing craft and canoes in port villages and towns, and a boat can be especially useful for Mwali (Mohéli) where the road system is rudimentary.
ROAD: Bush taxis *(taxis-brousse),* hired vehicles or private cars are the only forms of transport on the islands. Traffic drives on the right. All the islands have tarred roads. Four-wheel-drive vehicles are advisable for the outlying islands and in the interior, especially in the rainy season. Roads are narrow and domestic animals often roam free, so drive slowly. *Tourism Services Comoros* operates minibuses.
Documentation: An International Driving Permit is required.

ACCOMMODATION

Accommodation on the Comoro Islands is being upgraded, but currently there are only a few hotels, located mostly in Moroni, which handle the needs of travelling business people, government officials and other visitors. Room sharing is quite common. There are simple shelters *(gîtes)* on Mahore (Mayotte) and on the slopes of Karthala (an active volcano).

RESORTS & EXCURSIONS

The islands' vegetation is rich and varied: 65% of the world's perfume essence comes from the islands, being processed from the blossoms of ylang-ylang, jasmine and orange. Spices, including nutmeg, cloves, pepper, basil and vanilla, are another mainstay of the economy. Ylang-ylang base has uses in hairdressing, treatment of rheumatism and, mixed with coconut oil, as sun cream. In common with a few other places, such as the wine-growing areas of France, one of the main attractions of the Comoros is also its main non-tourist commercial activity. See *Economy* in the *Business Profile* section for more information.
Njazidja (Grand Comore): The capital **Moroni** is a charming, peaceful town containing a few broad squares and modern government buildings, as well as old, narrow, winding streets and a market place. There are a number of fine mosques including the *Vendredi Mosque,* the top of which provides an attractive view.
Mt Karthala: The more energetic may climb to the top and then descend into the crater of this active volcano. The crater is claimed to be the largest still active anywhere in the world. It is usual to make one overnight stop at the shelter provided.
Itsandra: This fishing village, 6km (4 miles) from Moroni, has a fine beach and there are opportunities to see dances performed by the local men. The town was once the ancient capital of the island, complete with royal tombs and a fortress.
Excursions: There are hot sulphur springs at *Lac Sale* and a 14th-century village at **Iconi. Mitsamiouli,** a town in the north of the island, is known both for its good diving facilities and for having the best Comoran dancers. There are many bats and spiders on the island, the former often appearing in broad daylight.
Mwali (Mohéli): Dhows (Arab sail boats) are built on the beach at **Fomboni.** There is a fine waterfall at **Miringoni.** Giant turtles may be seen at *Niumashuwa Bay.*
Nzwani (Anjouan): This island is notable for its waterfalls and abundant vegetation. The main town of **Mutsamudu** is built in Swahili-Shirazi style, complete with 17th-century houses with carved doors, twisting alleyways, mosques and a citadel. The ancient capital of **Domoni** is also worth a visit. The best beaches are in the **Bimbini** area. There are perfume distilleries at **Bambao.**
Mahore (Mayotte): This French-administered island is surrounded by a coral reef and has good beaches and excellent skindiving facilities. Tourists may explore the lagoon (claimed to be the largest in the world) by dugout canoe. The town of **Dzaoudzi** contains some old fortifications worthy of a visit. **Pamanzi** is a forested islet 5km (3 miles) offshore, fragrant with a wealth of vegetation. At **Sulu,** a waterfall plunges straight into the sea. There are the remains of an old mosque at **Tsingoni**. Elsewhere, there are 19th-century sugar refineries.

SOCIAL PROFILE

FOOD & DRINK: Restaurants serve good food with spiced sauces, rice-based dishes, cassava, plantain, couscous, barbecued goat meat, plentiful seafood and tropical fruits. There may be restrictions on drink within Muslim circles.
SHOPPING: Comoran products can be purchased at Moroni on Njazidja (Grand Comore). These include gold, pearl and shell jewellery, woven cloth, embroidered skull-caps *(koffia)* and slippers, carved chests, panels and *portes-Cran* (lecterns), pottery and basketry. Most items can be bought in the villages where they are made. **Shopping hours:** 0800-1200 and 1500-1800 Monday to Saturday.
SPORT: There is a sports centre on one of the beaches on Mahore. **Watersports:** There are many excellent **diving** sites in the archipelago. The Trou du Prophète in Misamiouli on Njazidja, Niumashuwa Bay on Mwali and Pamanzi islet off Mahore are particularly fine. There are many excellent beaches on all the islands. *Pirogue* (canoe) **races** are occasionally staged in the lagoon that surrounds Mahore. **Sailing** boats and **canoes** are available for hire in many ports.
SOCIAL CONVENTIONS: Religious customs should be respected, particularly during Ramadan. Dress should be modest although the French residents and tourists tend to be fairly relaxed about what they wear. **Tipping:** This should be 10%.

For additional copies of the
WORLD TRAVEL GUIDE
contact:

COLUMBUS
PRESS

Columbus Press, 28 Charles Square,
London N1 6HT.
Tel: (0171) 417 0700.
Fax: (0171) 417 0710.

BUSINESS PROFILE

ECONOMY: The Comoros' economy is severely
underdeveloped and depends largely on French aid.
The main economic activity is agriculture, which
produces vanilla and cloves (the main exports), ylang-
ylang (an essence extracted from trees) and copra.
There is a small fishing industry, a minimal industrial
base devoted mainly to processing vanilla, and a
developing tourist industry. Sharp declines in world
prices for its principal products have wrought yet
further damage to the Comoros' already poor balance
of payments. France is the country's major trading
partner, providing 42% of Comoros' imports and
taking 65% of exports. China, Kenya, Tanzania and
Madagascar are the other major importers into the
islands.
BUSINESS: Lightweight suit or shirt and tie required.
Business is conducted in French or Arabic; English is
seldom spoken. **Office hours:** 0730-1730 Monday to
Thursday; 0730-1100 Friday.
COMMERCIAL INFORMATION: The following
organisation can offer advice: Chambre de Commerce,
d'Industrie et d'Agriculture, BP 763, Moroni. Tel: 610
426.

CLIMATE

The climate is tropical and very warm. Coastal areas are
hot and very humid (December to March), interspaced
with rains and seasonal cyclones. The upland areas are
cooler, particularly at night, and have higher rainfall.
Required clothing: Lightweight cottons and linens with
waterproofing during the rainy season. Warmer garments
and rainwear are needed for the mountains.

TEMPERATURE CONVERSIONS

-20	-10	0°C	10	20	30	40

0	10	20	30°F	40	50	60	70	80	90	100

RAINFALL **0mm** 200 400 600 800
CONVERSIONS **0In** 5 10 15 20 25 30

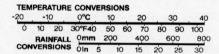

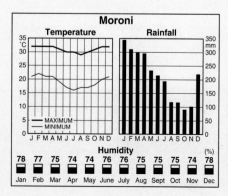

Moroni

Temperature / Rainfall

Humidity

78	77	75	74	74	74	76	76	75	75	75	78
Jan	Feb	Mar	Apr	May	June	July	Aug	Sept	Oct	Nov	Dec

Congo

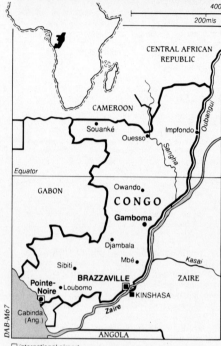

□ *international airport*

Location: West coast of Central Africa.

Note: Acts of armed violence by armed militia have
occurred in Brazzaville, although Pointe-Noire is
reported to be calm. The US State Department urges
visitors to Brazzaville not to travel outside the city centre
after dark and warns that street crime is common.
Registration at the local consulate is recommended. For
up-to-date information, contact the FCO Travel Advice
Unit. Tel: (0171) 270 4129.
*Sources: US State Department – April 20, 1994; and
FCO Travel Advice Unit – December 6, 1994.*

Direction Générale du Tourisme et des Loisirs
BP 456, Brazzaville, Congo
Tel: 830 953. Telex: 5210.
Honorary Consulate of the Republic of the Congo
Livingstone House, 11 Carteret Street, London SW1H
9DJ
Tel: (0171) 222 7575. Fax: (0171) 233 2087. Telex:
267526. Opening hours: 0930-1300 and 1400-1630
Monday to Thursday; 0930-1530 Friday.
Embassy of the Republic of the Congo *and* **Tourist
Office**
37 bis rue Paul Valéry, 75016 Paris, France
Tel: (1) 45 00 60 57. Fax: (1) 40 67 70 86. Telex:
645424. Opening hours: 0900-1230 and 1400-1800
Monday to Friday.
British Consulate
c/o British Petroleum Development Ltd, ave Marien
Ngouabi, Boîte Postale, 1181 Pointe-Noire, Congo
Tel: 943 988. Fax: 943 990. Telex: 8443 (a/b KG).
Embassy of the Republic of the Congo
4891 Colorado Avenue, NW, Washington, DC 20011
Tel: (202) 726 0825. Fax: (202) 726 1860. Telex:
197370.
Also deals with enquiries from Canada.
Embassy of the United States of America
BP 1015, avenue Amílcar Cabral, Brazzaville, Congo
Tel: 832 070. Fax: 836 338. Telex: 5367.

Timatic

Health
GALILEO/WORLDSPAN: **TI-DFT/BZV/HE**
SABRE: **TIDFT/BZV/HE**

Visa
GALILEO/WORLDSPAN: **TI-DFT/BZV/VI**
SABRE: **TIDFT/BZV/VI**

For more information on Timatic codes refer to Contents.

Honorary Consulate of the Republic of Congo
2 Cedar Avenue, Pointe Claire, Montréal, Québec H9S
4Y1
Tel: (514) 697 3781. Fax: (514) 697 9860.
**The Embassy of the United States of America in
Kinshasa deals with enquiries relating to the Congo
(see the entry for** *Zaïre* **later in the book).**

AREA: 342,000 sq km (132,047 sq miles).
POPULATION: 1,843,421 (1984).
POPULATION DENSITY: 5.4 per sq km.
CAPITAL: Brazzaville. **Population:** 596,200 (1984).
GEOGRAPHY: The Congo is situated in Africa,
bounded to the north by Cameroon and the Central
African Republic, to the east by Zaïre, to the southwest
by the Atlantic and to the west by Gabon. Vast areas are
swamps, grassland or thick forests with rivers being
virtually the only means of internal travel. The vast River
Congo and its major tributaries forms most of the
country's border with Zaïre, drawing much of its water
from the swamplands in the north of the country. The
narrow sandy coastal plain is broken by lagoons behind
which rise the Mayombe Mountains. Most of the
population lives in the south of the country.
LANGUAGE: The official language is French. Other
languages are Likala and Kikongo. English is spoken
very little.
RELIGION: The majority is Animist, with 40% Roman
Catholic. There are also Protestant and Muslim
minorities.
TIME: GMT + 1.
ELECTRICITY: 220/230 volts AC, 50Hz.
COMMUNICATIONS: Telephone: IDD service is
available. Country code: 242. Outgoing international
code: 00. Links with Western Europe are, in general,
good. **Telex/telegram:** These services are available in
cities at the main post offices and some hotels. **Post:**
There is an unreliable internal service. Post office hours:
0730/0800-1200 and 1430-1730 Monday to Friday; and
(for stamps and telegrams) 0800-2000 Monday to
Saturday; 0800-1200 Sundays and public holidays.
Press: There are several dailies which are subject to
censorship.
**BBC World Service and Voice of America
frequencies:** From time to time these change. See the
section *How to Use this Book* for more information.
BBC:

MHz	21.66	17.88	17.79	15.40

Voice of America:

MHz	21.49	15.60	9.525	6.035

PASSPORT/VISA

*Regulations and requirements may be subject to change at short notice, and you
are advised to contact the appropriate diplomatic or consular authority before
finalising travel arrangements. Details of these may be found at the head of this
country's entry. Any numbers in the chart refer to the footnotes below.*

	Passport Required?	Visa Required?	Return Ticket Required?
Full British	Yes	Yes	Yes
BVP	Not valid	-	-
Australian	Yes	Yes	Yes
Canadian	Yes	Yes	Yes
USA	Yes	Yes	Yes
Other EU (As of 31/12/94)	Yes	1	Yes
Japanese	Yes	Yes	Yes

PASSPORTS: Valid passport required by all.
British Visitors Passport: Not accepted.
VISAS: Required by all except:
(a) **[1]** nationals of France (for a stay not exceeding 3
months) and Germany (for a stay not exceeding 15 days)
for tourist purposes only (other EU nationals *do* require a
visa);
(b) nationals of the following countries, providing
onward or return tickets and documents for their next
destination are held: Benin, Burkina Faso, Cameroon,
Central African Republic, Chad, Côte d'Ivoire,
Equatorial Guinea, Gabon, Madagascar, Mauritania,
Niger, Senegal, Togo and Zaïre.
Types of visa: Tourist, Business and Transit. *Tourist and
Business visas:* Multiple-entry for 15 days costs £35, £50
for 30 days and £100 for 90 days. Single-entry visas are
available for tourists travelling only to Brazzaville for
stays of less than 15 days; cost – £25. Legalisation of
documents costs £10.
Validity: Transit visas are available on arrival for a
maximum of 72 hours. For Tourist and Business visas,
enquire at offices listed at top of entry.
Application to: Consulate (or Consular section at
Embassy). For addresses, see top of entry. Visa
applications from Luxembourg and the Netherlands must
be made via the Congo Consulate in Brussels, Belgium.

Application requirements: (a) 1 completed application form. (b) 1 passport-size photo. (c) Valid passport. (d) If on business, letter from company on headed paper explaining nature of business. (e) If passports are to be returned to the holders by post, £3.50 must be included to cover postal charges.
Working days required: 24 hours.

MONEY

Currency: CFA Franc (CFA Fr) = 100 centimes. Notes are in denominations of CFA Fr10,000, 5000, 1000 and 500. Coins are in denominations of CFA Fr500, 100, 50, 25, 10, 5, 2 and 1. The Congo is part of the French Monetary Area. The notes are legal tender in all the republics which formerly comprised French Equatorial Africa (Chad, Congo, Central African Republic, Cameroon and Gabon).
Note: At the beginning of 1994, the CFA Franc was devalued against the French Franc.
Credit cards: Access/Mastercard and Diners Club are accepted but have limited use. Check with your credit card company for details of merchant acceptability and other services which may be available.
Exchange rate indicators: The following figures are included as a guide to the movements of the CFA Franc against Sterling and the US Dollar:

Date:	Oct '92	Sep '93	Jan '94	Jan '95
£1.00=	413.75	433.87	436.79	834.94
$1.00=	260.71	284.14	295.23	533.67

Currency restrictions: There are no import or export restrictions for foreign currency, but declaration must be made on arrival. Import of local currency is unlimited, export is up to CFA Fr25,000.
Banking hours: 0630-1300 Monday to Saturday (counters close at 1130).

DUTY FREE

The following items may be imported into the Congo by visitors of 18 years of age or older without incurring customs duty:
200 cigarettes or 1 box of cigars or tobacco (women are permitted to import cigarettes only); 1 bottle of spirits; a reasonable quantity of perfume in opened bottles.
Note: A licence is required for sporting guns.

PUBLIC HOLIDAYS

Jan 1 '95 New Year's Day. **Apr 14** Good Friday. **Apr 17** Easter Monday. **May 1** Labour Day. **Aug 15** Independence Day. **Dec 25** Christmas Day. **Jan 1 '96** New Year's Day. **Apr 5** Good Friday. **Apr 8** Easter Monday.
Note: Due to political change these dates may alter. Check with Tourist Office before travelling.

HEALTH

Regulations and requirements may be subject to change at short notice, and you are advised to contact your doctor well in advance of your intended date of departure. Any numbers in the chart refer to the footnotes below.

	Special Precautions?	Certificate Required?
Yellow Fever	Yes	1
Cholera	Yes	2
Typhoid & Polio	Yes	-
Malaria	Yes/3	-
Food & Drink	4	-

[1]: A yellow fever vaccination certificate is required for all travellers over one year of age.
[2]: Following WHO guidelines issued in 1973, a cholera vaccination certificate is no longer a condition of entry to the Congo. However, cholera is not a serious risk in this country and precautions are essential. Up-to-date advice should be sought before deciding whether these precautions should include vaccination as medical opinion is divided over its effectiveness. See the *Health* section at the back of the book.
[3]: Malaria risk exists all year throughout the country, predominantly in the malignant *falciparum* form. Resistance to chloroquine has been reported. A weekly dose of 250mg of Mefloquine is the recommended prophylaxis.
[4]: All water should be regarded as being potentially contaminated. Water used for drinking, brushing teeth or making ice should have first been boiled or otherwise sterilised. Milk is unpasteurised and should be boiled. Powdered or tinned milk is available and is advised, but make sure that it is reconstituted with pure water. Avoid dairy products which are likely to have been made from unboiled milk. Only eat well-cooked meat and fish,

preferably served hot. Pork, salad and mayonnaise may carry increased risk. Vegetables should be cooked and fruit peeled.
Rabies is present. For those at high risk, vaccination before arrival should be considered. If you are bitten abroad seek medical advice without delay. For more information, consult the *Health* section at the back of the book.
Bilharzia (schistosomiasis) is present. Avoid swimming and paddling in fresh water. Swimming pools which are well-chlorinated and maintained are safe. *River blindness* (onchocerciasis) and *sleeping sickness* (trypanosomiasis) are also prevalent.
Health care: Medical and dental facilities are generally very limited outside Brazzaville. Health insurance is essential.

TRAVEL - International

AIR: *Air France* and *Air Afrique* (of which the Congo is a minority shareholder) operate international services to the Congo.
Approximate flight time: From London to Brazzaville is 11 hours (including up to 3 hours for stopover in Paris).
International airports: *Brazzaville (BZV)* (Maya Maya) is 4km (2 miles) northwest of the city. Airport facilities include a restaurant and car hire (*Europcar* and *Hertz* are both represented at the airport). Buses and taxis are available to the city.
Pointe-Noire (PNR) is 5.5km (3.5 miles) from the city. Taxis are available to the city.
Departure tax: CFA Fr500.
SEA/RIVER: Cargo ships dock at Pointe-Noire. An hourly car ferry operates between Kinshasa (Zaïre) and Brazzaville across the Congo River (journey time – 20 minutes). Ferries operate to and from the Central African Republic on the Ubangi.
ROAD: There is a road connection from Lambaréné in Gabon to Loubomo and Brazzaville. The road from Cameroon is usable only during the dry season. Entry can also be made via Zaïre and Angola.

TRAVEL - Internal

AIR: The national airline is *Lina Congo (GC)*. It runs regular services from Brazzaville to Pointe-Noire, Boundji, Djambala, Epena, Impfondo, Kindamba, Loubomo, Makoua, Ouesso, Owando, Sibiti, Souanké and Zanaga, as well as to Banjul and Libreville.
Departure tax: CFA Fr500 is levied on all passengers travelling within the Congo.
RIVER: Inland steamers ply from Brazzaville up the Congo and Ubangi. Rivers are vital to internal transport.
RAIL: *Congo-Océan* railway company runs two trains daily (with restaurant car, and with couchettes thrice-weekly) between Brazzaville and Pointe-Noire (journey time – 11-15 hours), and a train daily from Mbinda to Point Noire. Services can be erratic. Advance booking is recommended. Children under 5 travel free. Half-fare is charged for children aged 5-9.
ROAD: Roads are mostly earth tracks, sandy in dry season and impassable in the wet, suitable for Land-Rovers only. There are 243km (151 miles) of tarred roads. Traffic drives on the right. **Car hire:** There are several car hire firms represented in Brazzaville, lists of which can be obtained from main hotels.
Documentation: An International Driving Permit is

required.
URBAN: Brazzaville has a minibus and taxi service. Taxis are also available in Pointe-Noire and Loubomo. Taxi fares have a flat rate and fares should be agreed beforehand; tipping is not expected.

ACCOMMODATION

There are an adequate number of hotels in Brazzaville, Loubomo and Pointe-Noire. Prices and advance bookings can be obtained via *Air France.* Outside the towns mentioned above, there is little accommodation for visitors.

RESORTS & EXCURSIONS

The capital city of **Brazzaville** is situated on the west side of *Malebo Pool* on the **River Congo**. Sights to see include the old *Cathedral of St Firmin, Poto Poto* suburb, the *Temple Mosque*, the markets at *Oluendze* and *Moungali*, the *National Museum*, the *Municipal Gardens* and the house constructed for de Gaulle when Brazzaville was the capital of Free France.
150km (90 miles) north of the capital is the historic village of **M'Bé,** the capital of King Makoko. Also in this region is *Lake Bleu* and the *Valley of Butterflies*.
To the south of Brazzaville are the *Congo Rapids* (11km/7 miles away by tarred road), the *Foulakari Falls* and the *Trou de Dieu*, above which there is a panoramic view of the surrounding countryside.
The main town on the coast is **Pointe-Noire** (with its lively evening market), and there are several good beaches close by in the region known as the **Côte Sauvage.** There are opportunities for fishing all along the coast, as well as inland in the rivers and lakes, such as Lakes *Nango* and *Kayo*. Wildlife and spectacular scenery may both be found at **Mayombé** (150km/90 miles inland) and the *Lagoons of Gounkouati.*

SOCIAL PROFILE

FOOD & DRINK: Restaurants provide mostly French cuisine and the coast has excellent fish, giant oysters and shrimps. In Brazzaville, the main hotels have good restaurants serving French cuisine, but there are also restaurants specialising in Italian, Lebanese and Vietnamese dishes. Some restaurants, such as those at Nanga Lake and Grand Hotel in Loubomo, specialise in African dishes such as *piri piri chicken* (with pepper), *Mohambe chicken* in palm oil, palm cabbage salad and cassava leaves or *paka paka* in palm oil. Pointe-Noire and Loubomo also have restaurants and bars, usually in hotels, with table service. Some bars also have counter service.
NIGHTLIFE: Local groups are popular in the main towns. Brazzaville has several nightclubs, as does Pointe-Noire.
SHOPPING: In Brazzaville there are shops, colourful markets and an arts and crafts centre at Poto Poto which displays and sells, amongst other things, local paintings and carved wooden masks and figures. The two main markets are Moungali and Ouendze. Avenue Foch is crowded with street vendors. Basketwork can be bought at the villages of Makana and M'Pila (3km/2 miles from Brazzaville), with pottery and an open-air market.
Shopping hours: 0800-1200 and 1500-1800 Monday to Saturday. Some shops close on Monday afternoon and a few will open on Sunday morning.

SPORT: Brazzaville has facilities for **sailing**, **horseriding** and **golf**. **Angling** along the coast from Pointe-Noire is very popular and the Plage Mondaine is a protected beach resort, with **water-skiing** and **yachting**. Lagoons of Gounkouati offer excellent **fishing**.
SPECIAL EVENTS: Details of events for 1995/96 are available from the Republic of the Congo Tourist Office.
SOCIAL CONVENTIONS: Normal European courtesies should be observed when visiting people's homes. Gifts are acceptable as a token of thanks, especially if invited for a meal. Dress should be casual, and informal wear is acceptable in most places. Artistic carving, both traditional and modern dance, as well as folk songs play an important part in Congolese culture, which is strongly based on tradition. There are large numbers of foreigners resident in the Congo, working as technical assistants, businessmen and traders.
Photography: Do not photograph public buildings.
Tipping: Normally 10% in hotels and restaurants. Porters do not expect tips.

BUSINESS PROFILE

ECONOMY: There are 14 distinct ethnic groups (the majority of which are Bantu) including Kongos (45%), Tékés and Boubanguis. Nearly half the population live in towns. Subsistence living in forest villages has been increasingly abandoned by each new generation in favour of employment in towns. The Congo relies primarily on its reserves of oil and timber. Roughly 60% of the country is covered by forests, about half of which are exploitable. Forestry is thus an important economic activity and a major employer. This, together with crop farming of both staples (cassava, plantains) and cash crops (sugar, palm oil, cocoa, coffee), means 60% of the labour force work on the land. Even so, the country continues to depend on a large quantity of imported food. A further 20% of workers are employed in various industries, of which the most important is oil. The first oilfield came on stream in 1960 and the industry now accounts for nearly 90% of export earnings, affording the Congo a healthy trade surplus in recent years, even though its contribution to GDP dropped from 40% in 1985 to 15% in 1987 due to the collapse in the world oil price. The strength of the agricultural sector has saved the Congo from severe economic difficulty. The bulk of the oil exports are bought by the United States (60%), with Spain and France taking the remainder. France supplies over 60% of the Congo's imports, which largely comprise machinery, transport equipment, iron and steel, as well as foodstuffs. Italy, Spain and Japan provide the majority of the rest. Congo is a member of the CFA Franc Zone and the Central African economic and customs union, UDEAC. The country has followed socialist economic policies throughout most of its independence, but at the end of 1989 started to introduce a market economy.
BUSINESS: Jackets and ties are not usually worn by men on business visits but are expected when visiting government officials. A knowledge of French is essential as there are no professional translators available. Normal courtesies should be observed and best months for business visits are January to March and June to September. **Office hours:** Usually 0800-1200 and 1500-1800 Monday to Friday; 0700-1200 Saturday.
COMMERCIAL INFORMATION: The following organisation can offer advice: Chambre de Commerce, d'Agriculture et d'Industrie de Brazzaville, BP 92, Brazzaville. Tel: 832 115.

CLIMATE

Equatorial climate with short rains from October to December and long rains between mid-January and mid-May. The main dry season is from May to September.
Required clothing: Practical lightweight cottons and linens with a light raincoat or umbrella in the rainy season.

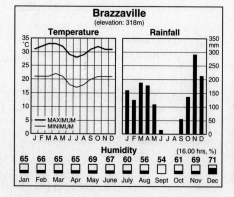

Brazzaville
(elevation: 318m)
Temperature   Rainfall

Humidity   (16.00 hrs, %)
65 66 65 65 69 67 60 56 54 61 69 71
Jan Feb Mar Apr May June July Aug Sept Oct Nov Dec

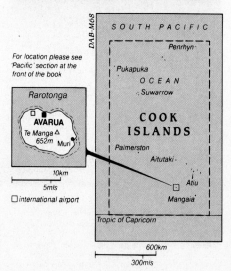

Cook Islands

For location please see 'Pacific' section at the front of the book

SOUTH PACIFIC
Penrhyn
Pukapuka
OCEAN
Suwarrow
COOK ISLANDS
Palmerston
Aitutaki
Atiu
Mangaia
Tropic of Capricorn

Rarotonga
AVARUA
Te Manga △ 652m
Muri

10km
5mls
□ international airport

600km
300mls

Location: South Pacific, Polynesia.

Cook Islands Tourist Authority
PO Box 14, Rarotonga, Cook Islands
Tel: 29435. Fax: 21435.
Cook Islands High Commission
PO Box 12242, 56 Mulgrave Street, Wellington, New Zealand
Tel: (4) 472 5126. Fax: (4) 472 5121.
Cook Islands Tourist Authority
PO Box 37391, Parnell Road, Auckland, New Zealand
Tel: (9) 379 4140. Fax: (9) 309 1876.
The British High Commission in Wellington deals with enquiries relating to the Cook Islands (see New Zealand later in the book).
Cook Islands Consulate
1/177 Pacific Highway, North Sydney, NSW 2060, Australia
Tel: (2) 955 0444. Fax: (2) 955 0447.
The Embassy of the United States of America in Wellington deals with enquiries relating to the Cook Islands (see New Zealand later in the book).
Cook Islands Tourist Authority
Suite 690, 6033 West Century Boulevard, Los Angeles, CA 90045
Tel: (310) 216 2872. Fax: (310) 216 2868.
The Canadian High Commission in Wellington deals with enquiries relating to the Cook Islands (see New Zealand later in the book).

AREA: 237 sq km (91.5 sq miles).
POPULATION: 18,552 (1992).
POPULATION DENSITY: 78 per sq km.
CAPITAL: Avarua (on Rarotonga). **Population:** 10,913 (1991, the whole island of Rarotonga).
GEOGRAPHY: The Cook Islands are situated 3500km (2200 miles) northeast of New Zealand and 1000km (600 miles) southwest of Tahiti in the South Pacific, forming part of Polynesia. The islands fall into two groups: the scattered Northern Group are all coral atolls except Aitutaki, and the Southern Group is of volcanic origin. The islands are self-governing overseas territories of New Zealand. Rarotonga is the largest and highest island with a rugged volcanic interior, its

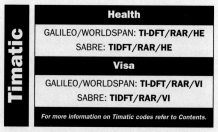

Health
GALILEO/WORLDSPAN: TI-DFT/RAR/HE
SABRE: TIDFT/RAR/HE
Visa
GALILEO/WORLDSPAN: TI-DFT/RAR/VI
SABRE: TIDFT/RAR/VI
For more information on Timatic codes refer to Contents.

Timatic

highest peak being Te Manga, at 652m (2140ft). Coral reef surrounds the island and the population lives between reef and hills where rich soil supports both tropical and subtropical vegetation. Most of the island is covered by thick evergreen bush. Most of the larger islands include lagoons surrounded by small areas of fertile land above which rise volcanic hills. The best beaches found on Aitutaki are also part of the 8-island Southern Group. The Northern Group comprises seven islands, the largest being Penrhyn, Manihiki and Pukapuka. The Cook Islands have been used as the setting for several films, the best known being *Merry Christmas Mr Lawrence*.
LANGUAGE: Maori is the national language. English is widely spoken.
RELIGION: Mainly Cook Islands Christian Church, also Roman Catholic, Latter Day Saints, Seventh Day Adventists and Assembly of God.
TIME: GMT - 10.
ELECTRICITY: 240 volts AC, 50Hz.
COMMUNICATIONS: The telecommunications system on the islands is presently being upgraded.
Telephone: IDD is available. Country code: 682. Outgoing international code: 00 (operator assistance may be required). **Fax:** Many Cook Island organisations have facilities. **Telex/telegram:** Services are provided by Cook Islands Telecom in Rarotonga; the most convenient way to use them is via one's hotel. **Post:** Post office hours: 0800-1600 Monday to Friday. **Press:** The daily *Cook Islands News* is published in Maori and English. The *New Zealand Herald* is also available.
BBC World Service and Voice of America frequencies: From time to time these change. See the section *How to Use this Book* for more information.
BBC:

MHz	17.10	15.36	9.740	7.150

Voice of America:

MHz	18.82	15.18	9.525	1.735

PASSPORT/VISA

Regulations and requirements may be subject to change at short notice, and you are advised to contact the appropriate diplomatic or consular authority before finalising travel arrangements. Details of these may be found at the head of this country's entry. Any numbers in the chart refer to the footnotes below.

	Passport Required?	Visa Required?	Return Ticket Required?
Full British	Yes	1/2	Yes
BVP	Not valid	-	-
Australian	Yes	1/2	Yes
Canadian	Yes	1/2	Yes
USA	Yes	1/2	Yes
Other EU (As of 31/12/94)	Yes	1/2	Yes
Japanese	Yes	1/2	Yes

PASSPORTS: Valid passport required by all including nationals of New Zealand. Passports should be valid for a further 12 months after intended date of departure.
British Visitors Passport: Not acceptable.
VISAS: [1] Not required by visitors for tourist visits staying a maximum of 31 days who hold confirmed onward/return tickets and documentation required by the next country to be visited as well as confirmed accommodation arrangements and proof of adequate means of financial support for term of stay. Those not satisfying these conditions require an entry permit costing NZ$30 per month (3-month maximum) of stay.
Note [2]: All nationals arriving in the Cook Islands for business purposes *do* require a visa. Visa application forms can be obtained at the following address: Cook Islands Consulate-General's Office, 127 Symmonds Street, Auckland, New Zealand. Fax: (9) 309 1876.
Validity: Visitors can extend length of stay on a monthly basis up to an additional 3 months.
Application to: Cook Islands Representative (for address, see above).
Temporary residence: Applicants should refer to the Principal Immigration Officer, PO Box 473, Rarotonga. Tel: 29363 *or* 29364.

MONEY

Currency: New Zealand Dollar (NZ$) = 100 cents, supplemented by notes and coins minted for local use which are not negotiable outside the Cook Islands. Notes are in denominations of NZ$100, 50, 20, 10 and 5. Coins are in denominations of NZ$2 and 1, and 50, 20, 10 and 5 cents.
Currency exchange: Exchange facilities are available at the airport and with trade banks.

Credit cards: Visa, Diners Club, Access/Mastercard and American Express are accepted. Check with your credit card company for details of merchant acceptability and other services which may be available.

Travellers cheques: Accepted in hotels and most shops.

Exchange rate indicators: The following figures are included as a guide to the movements of the New Zealand Dollar against Sterling and the US Dollar:

Date:	Oct '92	Sep '93	Jan '94	Jan '95
£1.00=	2.94	2.80	2.645	2.44
$1.00=	1.85	1.84	1.788	1.56

Currency restrictions: There are no currency restrictions.

Banking hours: 0900-1500 Monday to Friday.

DUTY FREE

The following goods may be imported into the Cook Islands by travellers over the age of 18 without incurring customs duty:

200 cigarettes or 50 cigars or 250g of tobacco; 2 litres of spirits or wine or 4.5 litres of beer; goods to the value of NZ$250.

Prohibited items: Fruit, meat, livestock, fireworks, firearms, gunpowder and ammunition.

PUBLIC HOLIDAYS

Jan 1 '95 New Year's Day. **Apr 14-17** Easter. **Apr 25** Anzac Day. **Jun 10** Queen's Official Birthday. **Jul 26** Rarotonga Gospel Day. **Aug 4** Constitution Day. **Oct 26** Cook Islands Gospel Day. **Dec 25** Christmas Day. **Dec 26** Boxing Day. **Jan 1 '96** New Year's Day. **Apr 5-8** Easter.

HEALTH

Regulations and requirements may be subject to change at short notice, and you are advised to contact your doctor well in advance of your intended date of departure. Any numbers in the chart refer to the footnotes below.

	Special Precautions?	Certificate Required?
Yellow Fever	No	No
Cholera	No	No
Typhoid & Polio	Yes	-
Malaria	No	-
Food & Drink	1	-

[1]: Water from taps is acceptable to most visitors, and whilst relatively safe may cause mild abdominal upsets. Bottled water is available and is advised for the first few weeks of the stay. Milk is pasteurised and dairy products are safe for consumption. Local meat, poultry, seafood, fruit and vegetables are generally considered safe to eat. *Coral reefs* are a hazard. Feet should always be covered, as cuts and grazes are liable to turn septic. Hands should be kept out of holes and cracks in the reef, as they might contain unpleasant and lethal occupants.

Health care: There is no direct Reciprocal Health Agreement with the UK, but such an agreement exists with New Zealand which may in some circumstances also apply to the Cook Islands; enquire at the Cook Islands Representative (for address, see top of entry). There is one government hospital (on Rarotonga) with a total of 151 beds.

TRAVEL - International

AIR: The Cook Islands are served by *Air New Zealand (NZ)* and *Polynesian Airlines (PH)*. The latter offers a 'Polypass' which allows flights anywhere on the airline's network: Sydney (Australia), Auckland (New Zealand), Western Samoa, American Samoa, Cook Islands, Vanuatu, New Caledonia, Fiji and, on payment of a supplement, Tahiti. The pass is valid for 30 days.

Approximate flight time: From London to Rarotonga is 24 hours (including stopover of one hour in Paris).

International airport: *Rarotonga (RAR)* is 3km (2 miles) west of Avarua (travel time – 10 minutes). The airport facilities are open according to flight arrivals and departures and include duty-free shops, bank/bureau de change, bars, shops and car rental (*Avis* and *Budget*). Hotel coaches meet each flight. Taxis and buses are also available.

Departure tax: NZ$20 for passengers over 12 years of age; NZ$10 for passengers aged 2-12 years.

SEA: Cargo/passenger lines operating to the Cook Islands are run by the *Cook Islands Shipping Company* and *New Zealand Motor Vessel Company*.

Note: Passengers who embarked in Fiji, Samoa, Tonga and Tahiti are required to have their baggage fumigated on arrival. It is advisable to carry personal articles for immediate need (as fumigation can take up to three hours), and to remove bottles from luggage as they are likely to break during fumigation.

TRAVEL - Internal

AIR: *Air Rarotonga* runs regular inter-island services to Aitutaki, Atiu, Mangaia, Mauke, Mitiaro, Penrhyn and Rakahanga.

Inter-island flight times: From Rarotonga to *Aitutaki* is 1 hour, to *Atiu* is 50 minutes, to *Mauke* is 50 minutes and to *Mitiaro* is 1 hour 25 minutes.

ROAD: Traffic drives on the left. **Bus:** There are several companies which operate services around Rarotonga on weekdays as well as Saturdays. Buses are available from a number of hotels on the Islands (0700-2230 Monday to Saturday; 0700-0130 Friday). **Taxi:** Available on Rarotonga. **Car hire:** Several companies offer cars for hire from a number of shops and hotels. Motor scooter and bicycle hire is also popular.

Documentation: Drivers of all vehicles are required to have a current Cook Islands driver's licence, which costs NZ$10 and is obtainable from the Police Station in Avarua on presentation of an international or commonwealth licence.

ACCOMMODATION

Good class accommodation is still limited, but is increasing yearly. There are now a reasonable number of New Zealand-style motels of international standard. Hotels tend to be quite small and most are situated close to, if not on, a beach. Advance booking is absolutely essential, and it is probably wiser to book via an inclusive tour operator specialising in Pacific destinations. For more information on hotels, contact the Accommodation Council, PO Box 45, Rarotonga.

RESORTS & EXCURSIONS

The developed resorts are situated on **Rarotonga** and **Aitutaki**, and provide various amenities (see *Sport* below). The best swimming beaches are at *Muri Lagoon* and *Titikaveka*. A variety of tours are available, including guided walking trips, sightseeing by air, horse-drawn and motorised drives around the islands and cruises on schooners or yachts to the outer islands. A scenic drive into the *Takuvaine/Avatiu Valleys* offers a panorama of lush tropical scenery. *Papua (Wigmore's) Waterfall,* the only waterfall on the island, is located at *Vaimaanga*. The museum at **Takamoa** has excellent examples of Cook Islands handicrafts.

During the year various festivals take place. These are generally celebrated with singing and dancing, often with a strange mixture of traditional ritual grafted on to the somewhat later Christian music and ceremony. The choirs of the Cook Islands are renowned. Places of historical interest include: the *Takamoa Mission House,* built in 1842, and believed to be the second oldest building in the South Pacific; the old *Palace of Makea* at **Taputapuatea;** *Pa's Palace,* built of coral and lime, in **Takitumu;** and *Arai-Te-Tonga (Marae),* consisting of stone structures which, in the islands' pre-European history, formed a *kouto,* or royal court, where the investiture of chiefs took place. This spot is still regarded as sacred.

SOCIAL PROFILE

FOOD: There are restaurants in hotels, and a variety of independent eating places as well, as a result of the increasing tourist trade. Local produce includes citrus and tropical fruits in large varieties, island chestnuts and garden vegetables. Seafood features on many restaurant menus. Local meat and poultry are available.

NIGHTLIFE: Island feast and dance groups feature at various hotels and details are available from local tourist information offices or hotel receptionists.

SHOPPING: Best buys are woodcarvings, handmade ukuleles, pearls, shells, woven products, embroidery, Panama hats and baskets. Coins and stamps are considered to be valuable collectors' items. *Island Craft* has factories in Avarua and Avatiu where handcarved items can be purchased. The art of carving may be observed in Punanganui Market Place. There is also a wide range of duty-free items. **Shopping hours:** 0800-1600 Monday to Friday; 0800-1200 Saturday.

Some stores near tourist areas remain open for longer.

SPORT: Fishing is available at the Deep Sea Fishing Club, and visitors can watch flying fish being netted at night in outrigger canoes equipped with bright lights. The Rarotonga Golf Club has a 9-hole **golf** course. In addition, lawn **bowls** has an enthusiastic following and is a long established sport in Rarotonga. Visitors are also welcome at Rarotonga Sailing Club, where **sailing** races are held on Saturday afternoons from October to May. **Watersports:** There is excellent **scuba diving** and **snorkelling** in the clear waters of the islands' many lagoons. It is often possible to hire equipment.

SPECIAL EVENTS: Some of the festivals and special events celebrated in the Cook Islands during 1995/96 are listed below. For further details, contact the Tourist Authority.

Apr/May '95 *Dancer of the Year*. **Aug (first week)** *Constitutional Celebrations*. **Nov** *Food Festival*. **Nov** *Tiare* (floral) *Week*. **Feb '96 (third week)** *Cultural Festival Week* (arts, crafts and canoe races).

SOCIAL CONVENTIONS: Casual wear is acceptable everywhere. Women are expected to wear dresses for church services and social functions.

Tipping: Tradition says that all gifts require something in return and tipping is therefore not practised.

BUSINESS PROFILE

ECONOMY: Tourism is the leading industry. The islands depend on extensive aid from New Zealand and are economically underdeveloped through their isolation. The islands produce fresh fruit which is the main export product. The Government is seeking to build up the islands' infrastructure as a precursor to further development.

BUSINESS: Tropical or lightweight suits are necessary. **Office hours:** 0800-1600 Monday to Friday.

COMMERCIAL INFORMATION: The following organisation can offer advice: Chamber of Commerce, PO Box 242, Rarotonga. Tel: 20295. Fax: 20969. Telex: 62067.

CLIMATE

Varies throughout the islands, but generally hot throughout the year, although the trade winds provide some moderating influence. Rainfall is heaviest in Rarotonga, while the northern atolls tend to be drier. The coolest months are May to October. Most rain falls in the warmest period.

Required clothing: Lightweight cottons and linens throughout the year. Warm clothes are advised for cooler evenings. Rainwear advised in the rainy season.

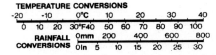

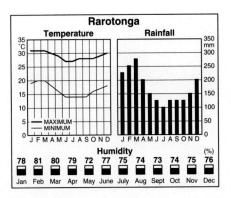

Costa Rica

☐ *international airport*

Location: Central America.

Instituto Costarricense de Turismo
Apartado 777, Edificio Genaro Valverde, Calles 5 y 7, Avenida 4A, 1000 San José, Costa Rica
Tel: 223 1733. Fax: 255 4997.
Camara Nacional de Turismo (CANATUR)
(National Tourism Chamber)
Apartado 828, San José, Costa Rica
Tel: 233 8817. Fax: 255 4513.
Embassy of the Republic of Costa Rica
2nd Floor, 36 Upper Brook Street, London W1Y 1PE
Tel: (0171) 495 3985. Fax: (0171) 495 3992. Opening hours: 0900-1300 Monday to Friday.
Consulate of the Republic of Costa Rica
Flat 2, 38 Redcliffe Square, London SW10 9JY
Tel: (0171) 373 7973. Fax: (0171) 373 7973. Opening hours: 1000-1300 Monday to Friday.
British Embassy
Apartado 815, 11th Floor, Edificio Centro Colón 1007, San José, Costa Rica
Tel: 221 5566 *or* 221 5716 *or* 221 5816. Fax: 233 9938.
Telex: 2169 (a/b PRODROM CR).
Embassy of the Republic of Costa Rica *and* **Costa Rican Tourism Bureau Information Centre**
2114 S Street, NW, Washington, DC 20008
Tel: (202) 234 2945 *or* 328 6628 (Consular section). Fax: (202) 265 4795.
Embassy of the United States of America
Pavas, San José, Costa Rica
Tel: 220 3939. Fax: 220 2305.
Costa Rican Embassy
Suite 208, 135 York Street, Ottawa, Ontario K1N 5T4
Tel: (613) 562 2855 *or* 562 2956. Fax: (613) 562 2582.
Consular Section:
Suite 301, 151 Slater Street, Ottawa, Ontario K1P 5H3
Tel: (613) 234 4604. Fax: (613) 563 8823.
Consulates in: Montréal, Toronto and Vancouver.
Canadian Embassy
Apartado 10303, Edificio Cronos, Calle 3 y Avenida Central, San José, Costa Rica
Tel: 255 3522. Fax: 223 2395. Telex: 2179 (a/b DOMCAN CR).

AREA: 51,060 sq km (19,720 sq miles).
POPULATION: 2,993,676 (1990 estimate).
POPULATION DENSITY: 58.6 per sq km.
CAPITAL: San José. **Population:** 296,625 (1991).
GEOGRAPHY: Costa Rica, lying between Nicaragua and Panama, is a complete coast-to-coast segment of the

Central American isthmus. Its width ranges from 119-282km (74-176 miles). A low thin line of hills that rises between Lake Nicaragua and the Pacific Ocean in Nicaragua, broadens and rises as it enters northern Costa Rica, eventually forming the high, rugged, mountains of volcanic origin in the centre and south. The highest peak is Chirripó Grande which reaches 3820m (12,530ft). More than half the population live on the Meseta Central, a plateau with an equitable climate. It is rimmed to the southwest by the Cordillera range, and provides the setting for the country's capital, San José. There are lowlands on both coastlines, mainly swampy on the Caribbean coast, with grassland savannah on the Pacific side merging into swamps towards the south. Rivers cut through the mountains, flowing down to both the Caribbean and the Pacific.
LANGUAGE: Spanish is the official language. English is also widely spoken.
RELIGION: Roman Catholic.
TIME: GMT - 6.
ELECTRICITY: 110/220 volts, 60Hz. 2-pin plugs are standard.
COMMUNICATIONS: Telephone: IDD is available. Country code: 506. Outgoing international code: 00. **Fax:** Facilities are available in San José at the Radiografica Costarricense SA (opening hours: 0700-2200).
Telex/telegram: International telex facilities are also available in San José at the Radiografica Costarricense SA, corner of Calle 1, Avenida 5 (opening hours: 0700-2200). Since the abolition of the inland telegram service in the UK, the Costa Rican government Telegram Company will not accept telegrams destined for the UK.
Post: Airmail letters to Western Europe usually take between six and ten days. **Press:** Daily newspapers printed in Spanish include *La Nación*, *La República* and *La Prensa Libre*. One weekly paper is printed in English, *The Tico Times*.
BBC World Service and Voice of America frequencies: From time to time these change. See the section *How to Use this Book* for more information.
BBC:

MHz	17.84	15.22	95.90	73.25

Voice of America:

MHz	15.21	11.74	9.815	6.030

PASSPORT/VISA

Regulations and requirements may be subject to change at short notice, and you are advised to contact the appropriate diplomatic or consular authority before finalising travel arrangements. Details of these may be found at the head of this country's entry. Any numbers in the chart refer to the footnotes below.

	Passport Required?	Visa Required?	Return Ticket Required?
Full British	Yes	No	Yes
BVP	Not valid	-	-
Australian	Yes	No	Yes
Canadian	1	No	Yes
USA	1	No	Yes
Other EU (As of 31/12/94)	Yes	2	Yes
Japanese	Yes	No	Yes

Note: Gypsies, hippies and persons of 'unkempt' appearance will be deported.
PASSPORTS: Valid passport required by all, with a minimum validity of six months at the date of entrance, except **[1]** Canadian and US citizens with proof of identity, eg an *original* birth certificate *and* ID containing a photograph, for visits not exceeding 90 days. A Tourist Card will be issued to them on arrival for a fee of US$25. However, for US and Canadian citizens using their passports as travel ID for visits not exceeding 90 days, a visa will be issued free of charge on arrival.
British Visitors Passport: Not acceptable.
VISAS: Required by all except:
(a) **[2]** nationals of EU countries for a period of 90 days (except nationals of France who may stay for up to 30 days and nationals of Greece and Ireland who *do* need a 30-day visa);
(b) nationals of Anguilla, Argentina, Aruba, Austria, *Bermuda, Bonaire, Canada, *Cayman Islands, Curaçao, Falkland Islands, Finland, Gibraltar, *Hong Kong, Hungary, Israel, Japan, South Korea, Liechtenstein, Montserrat, Norway, Panama, Paraguay, Pitcairn Islands, Poland, Puerto Rico, Romania, Saba, St Eustatius, St Maarten, Sweden, Switzerland, Turks & Caicos Islands, UK Virgin Islands, USA and Uruguay for a stay of up to 90 days;
(c) nationals of Albania, Antigua & Barbuda, Australia, Bahamas, Bahrain, Barbados, Belize, Bolivia, Brazil, Bulgaria, Colombia, Chile, Czech Republic, Dominica, El Salvador, French Guiana, Greenland, Grenada, Guadeloupe, Guatemala, Guyana, Honduras, Iceland, Jamaica, Kenya, Kuwait, Martinique, Mexico, Monaco, New Caledonia, New Zealand, Oman, Philippines, Qatar,

Réunion, St Kitts & Nevis, St Lucia, St Vincent & The Grenadines, San Marino, Saudi Arabia, Singapore, Slovak Republic, † South Africa, Suriname, Taiwan (China), Trinidad & Tobago, UAE, Vatican City and Venezuela for a period of 30 days.
All other nationals require a visa. In some cases an authorisation from the Migration Department in San José is also necessary.
Note: **[*]** Only applicable if holding a UK passport. **[†]** Persons holding passports issued by the former homelands of Transkei and Venda *do* need a visa which has to be authorised by the Migration Department in San José.
Types of visa: Tourist; cost – £15. Transit passengers do not require a visa if they continue their journey within 48 hours.
Validity: Visas are valid for 90 days or 1 month. Contact the Immigration Department in Costa Rica for renewal or extension procedure.
Application to: Consulate (or Consular section of Embassy). For addresses, see top of entry.
Application requirements: (a) Completed application form. (b) 1 passport-size photo. (c) Sufficient funds to cover duration of stay.
Working days required: One day to several weeks, depending on nationality of applicant. (Some visas need the authorisation of the Immigration Department in Costa Rica.)
Temporary residence: A signed contract with the prospective employer is needed. For residence as a senior citizen, only those with a minimum monthly income of US$600 will be considered.

MONEY

Currency: Costa Rican Colón (CRC) = 100 céntimos. Notes are in denominations of CRC5000, 1000, 500, 100 and 50. Coins are in denominations of CRC20, 10, 5, 2 and 1, and 50 and 25 céntimos.
Currency exchange: Visitors should consult their banks for the current rate of exchange (there is no direct local quotation for sterling; the cross rate with the US$ is used). *Casas de Cambio* give better rates of exchange than banks.
Credit cards: Mastercard, American Express, Visa and Diners Club are accepted, but check with your credit card company for details of merchant acceptability and other services which may be available.
Travellers cheques: Should always be in US Dollars.
Exchange rate indicators: The following figures are included as a guide to the movements of the Costa Rican Colón against Sterling and the US Dollar:

Date:	Oct '92	Sep '93	Jan '94	Jan '95
£1.00=	215.67	220.70	238.10	256.86
$1.00=	139.89	144.53	160.93	164.18

Currency restrictions: There are no restrictions on the import and export of either local or foreign currency.
Banking hours: 0900-1500 Monday to Friday.

DUTY FREE

The following goods may be imported into Costa Rica without incurring customs duty:
500g of tobacco produce; 3 litres of alcoholic beverage; a reasonable quantity of perfume for personal use.

PUBLIC HOLIDAYS

Jan 1 '95 New Year's Day. **Mar 19** Feast of San José (St Joseph). **Apr 11** Anniversary of the Battle of Rivas. **Apr 13** Maundy Thursday. **Apr 14** Good Friday. **May 1** Labour Day. **Jun 15** Corpus Christi. **Jun 29** St Peter and Paul. **Jul 25** Guanacaste Annexation. **Aug 2** Our Lady of Los Angeles. **Aug 15** Mother's Day. **Sept 15** Independence Day. **Oct 12** Columbus Day. **Dec 8** Immaculate Conception. **Dec 25** Christmas Day. **Jan 1 '96** New Year's Day. **Mar 19** Feast of San José (St Joseph). **Apr 4** Maundy Thursday. **Apr 5** Good Friday. **Apr 11** Anniversary of the Battle of Rivas.
Note: Most businesses close for the whole of Holy Week and between Christmas and New Year.

HEALTH

Regulations and requirements may be subject to change at short notice, and you are advised to contact your doctor well in advance of your intended date of departure. Any numbers in the chart refer to the footnotes below.

	Special Precautions?	Certificate Required?
Yellow Fever	No	No
Cholera	No	No
Typhoid & Polio	1	-
Malaria	2	-
Food & Drink	3	-

Timatic

Health
GALILEO/WORLDSPAN: **TI-DFT/SJO/HE**
SABRE: **TIDFT/SJO/HE**

Visa
GALILEO/WORLDSPAN: **TI-DFT/SJO/VI**
SABRE: **TIDFT/SJO/VI**

For more information on Timatic codes refer to Contents.

[1]: Vaccination is recommended for both polio and typhoid.
[2]: Malaria risk exists throughout the year, mostly in the benign *vivax* form, in the rural areas below 500m, of Alajuela, Guanacaste, Limón and Puntarenas.
[3]: Mains water is normally heavily chlorinated, and whilst relatively safe may cause mild abdominal upsets. Drinking water outside main cities and towns may be contaminated and sterilisation is advisable. Bottled water is available and is advised for the first few weeks of the stay. Milk is pasteurised and dairy products are safe for consumption. Local meat, poultry, seafood, fruit and vegetables are generally considered safe to eat.
Health care: Health insurance is recommended. Reliable medical services are available in Costa Rica. Standards of health and hygiene are among the best in Latin America.

TRAVEL - International

AIR: The Costa Rican national airline is *Lacsa (LR)*. *Lacsa* flies direct to Costa Rica from Miami, New Orleans, Los Angeles, New York, Mexico, Colombia, Venezuela and Panama. For routes via the USA a change of plane is necessary. Flights with one or two stops which do not go via the USA are available from *Iberia* in Madrid and *KLM* in Amsterdam. They take longer but the need to change planes is eliminated.
Approximate flight times: From San José to *London* is 12 hours (including stopover time), to *Los Angeles* is 11 hours and to *New York* is 7 hours.
International airport: *San José (SJO)* (Juan Santamaria) 18km (11 miles) northwest of the city. Coaches depart every 20 minutes 0500-2400; return pickups stop at various hotels. Buses depart to the city every 15 minutes 0600-2200; return is from Afajuefa Station 14th Street, 1/3 Avenue, every 20 minutes (travel time – 35 minutes). Taxis are also available to the city.
Departure tax: US$31 (or CRC equivalent) payable if staying more than 48 hours by all passengers leaving Costa Rica.
SEA: *Lauro Lines* run regular services to Puerto Limón from the Mediterranean (Genoa, Barcelona). *Costa Lines* run cruises which call at Puntarenas.
ROAD: The Inter-American Highway runs through Costa Rica from La Cruz on the Nicaraguan border through San José to Progreso on the Panamanian border.

TRAVEL - Internal

AIR: *SANSA,* a national airline, operates cargo and passenger services between San José and provincial towns and villages. A bus is provided from the airline offices in San José to the airport. A number of smaller airlines also provide internal flights. Reservations cannot be made outside Costa Rica.
RAIL: A train service within Costa Rica links San José to Puntarenas on the Pacific coast (two trains daily) and Puerto Limón on the Caribbean coast (once daily).
ROAD: Roads are generally very good. There are 29,586km (18,384 miles) of all-weather highways including 653km (405 miles) of the Inter-American Highway and highways linking San José with the other principal towns. Traffic drives on the right. **Bus:** Regular services to most towns, but buses are often crowded so pre-booking is advisable. Costa Rica offers a wide variety of sightseeing tours. Most tour companies feature bilingual guides and round-trip transportation from hotels. For full details, contact the Costa Rica National Tourist Institute. **Taxi:** Numerous and inexpensive in San José. Taxis are coloured red (except those serving the Juan Santamaria International Airport which are orange). Fares should be negotiated before starting the journey.
Car hire: *Hertz, Rentacar SA* and local firms have offices in San José. Distances are measured in kilometres. A speed limit of 88kmph (55mph) is enforced on most highways. **Documentation:** Drivers must have a national driving licence.
URBAN: San José has privately-run bus services, charging fares on a 2-zone system.
JOURNEY TIMES: The following chart gives approximate journey times (in hours and minutes) from San José to other major cities/towns.

	Air	Road	Rail
Alajuela	-	0.30	-
Cartago	-	0.30	-
Heredia	-	0.20	-
Puntarenas	-	2.00	4.00
Liberia	0.25	3.00	-
Quepos	0.30	3.30	-
Limón	0.25	2.00	6.00

ACCOMMODATION

HOTELS: There is a good range of reasonably priced hotel accommodation. Most proprietors speak English. San José has many hotels, from the extravagant to the smaller, family-run hotels in the less fashionable districts. There are several good hotels out of town near the airport. Larger hotels have swimming pools and other sports facilities. The majority of the hotels have their own restaurants which are generally good and reasonably priced. Hotel tariffs are liable to alteration at any time. A 13% sales tax plus 3% tourism tax is added to hotel prices. Outside the capital, charges and the standard of comfort are lower. **Grading:** These are graded from A to D according to price range. The A-grade category accounts for 20% of all hotels and costs from the equivalent of US$100. About 20% of hotels are in the B-range and cost US$50-70. C-grade hotels cost US$30-50 and D-range hotels, about 30%, cost US$10-30. For further information, contact Camara Costarricense de Hoteles y Afines (National Chamber of Hotels and Related Organisations), PO Box 8422, 1000 San José. Tel: 224 6572 *or* 234 6572.
CAMPING/CARAVANNING: Facilities exist at San Antonio de Belen, 8km (5 miles) from San José. There is also a small campsite in San Pedro district and south of the city on the Inter-American highway. There is a camping and caravan site close to Aureola. Most, but not all, national parks (see below) allow camping at designated sites.

RESORTS & EXCURSIONS

One of the Central American states forming the land-bridge between North and South America, Costa Rica has a surprising diversity of terrain (see *Geography* above). In the cities and towns the country's Spanish heritage provides the main features of interest. Elsewhere, Costa Rica's national parks are its greatest glory.

San José

The capital was founded in 1737 and is a pleasant mixture of traditional and modern Spanish architecture. Places of interest include the *Teatro Nacional*, the *Palacio Nacional* (where the legislative assembly meets), and the *Parque Central*, east of which is the Cathedral. There are a number of parks in the city, including the *Parque Nacional*, the *Parque Bolivar* and the *Parque Morazan.*
San José is a good centre for excursions into the beautiful **Meseta Central** region.

Cartago

This town was founded in 1563, but there are no old buildings as earthquakes destroyed the town in 1841 and 1910. However, some of the reconstruction was in the colonial style, the most interesting example being the *Basilica*. Excursions can be made from here to the crater of *Irazu* and to the beautiful valley of *Orosi.*

Carribbean Coast

There are a number of beaches, ports and towns worth visiting. The biggest is **Puerto Limón;** others include *Los Chiles, Guapiles, Tortuguero, Barro Del Colorado, Cahuta* and *Puerto Viejo.*

Pacific Coast

Puntarenas is Costa Rica's principal Pacific port for freight and the beaches around it are rather poor, although **San Lucas Island,** just off the port, has the magnificent beach of *El Coco*. Another island worth a visit is **Isla Del Coco** where a great hoard of treasure is supposed to have been buried by pirates. **Puerto Caldera,** a few miles south of Puntarenas, has recently become the country's premier port of call for cruise liners. **Puerto Quepos, Nicova, Liberia** and **Samara** are the region's other major towns. There are beautiful beaches in the **Guanacaste** area and near **Quepos** in the south.

National Parks

Well-kept and well-guarded national parks and nature reserves cover 11.23% of the country's territory. Information and permits can be obtained from: Servicio de Parques Nacionales, Ministerio de Recursos Naturales, Energia y Minas, San José. Tel: 233 4070; *or* Fundación de Parques Nacionales, Fundación Neotropica, Apartado 326, Paseo de los Estuciantes, 1002 San José. Tel: 233 0003. Fax: 255 2984.
Braulio Carrillo National Park is in the central region of the country just 23km (14 miles) north of San José. It has five kinds of forest, some with characteristic rainforest vegetation. Orchids and ferns, jaguars, ocelots and the Baird tapir may be seen here. There are trails through the park and many lookouts.
The **National Park of Poas** contains a smouldering volcano of the same name. It contains the only dwarf cloudforest in Costa Rica. The crater of the volcano is 1.5km (1 mile) wide and contains a hot-water lake which changes colour from turquoise to green to grey. Access is possible by road.
Tortuguero National Park protects the Atlantic green turtle egg-laying grounds; it is in an area of great ecological diversity. Its network of canals and lagoons serve as waterways for transportation and exploration. There are camping facilities and lodges.
Santa Rosen National Park is in the Dry Pacific climatic zone. There are extensive savannahs and non-deciduous forests. In addition to its abundant wildlife, recreational facilities are provided on some of the beaches.
Corcovado National Park is virgin rainforest containing many endangered species. It has the largest tree in Costa Rica, a ceibo which is 70m (230ft) high. Additionally there is *Cano Island Biological Reserve,* a bird sanctuary.
Cahuita National Park protects the only coral reef in the country. Its other attractions include howler and white-faced monkeys and 500 species of fish.
Chirripó National Park contains Costa Rica's highest mountain. Most notably it contains the quetzal, said to be South America's most beautiful bird.
Other parks are the **Manuel Antonio National Park**, the **Barra de Colorado National Wildlife Refuge** and the **Rafael L Rodriguez National Wildlife Refuge**.
In addition, many of the tiny islands in the **Gulf of Nicoya,** near Puntarenas, are 'biological protection areas'.

SOCIAL PROFILE

FOOD & DRINK: Restaurants in towns and cities serve a variety of foods including French, Italian, Mexican, North American and Chinese. Food is good, from the most expensive to the cheapest eating places (which are generally found west of the city centre). Food *sodas* (small restaurants) serve local food. Common dishes include *casado* (rice, beans, stewed beef, fried plantain and cabbage), *olla de came* (soup of beef, plantain, com, yuca, nampi and chayote), *sopa negra* (black beans with a poached egg) and *picadillo* (meat and vegetable stew). Snacks are popular and include *gallos* (filled tortillas), *tortas* (containing meat and vegetables), *arreglados* (bread filled with same and *pan de yuca* (speciality from stalls in San José). There are many types of cold drink made from fresh fruit, milk or cereal flour, for example, *cebada* (barley flour), *pinolillo* (roasted corn) and *horchata* (rice flour with cinnamon). Imported alcoholic and soft drinks are widely available. Coffee is good value and has an excellent flavour.
NIGHTLIFE: San José especially has many nightclubs and venues with folk music and dance, theatres and cinemas.
SHOPPING: Special purchases include wood and leather rocking chairs (which dismantle for export) as well as a range of local crafts available in major cities and towns. Local markets are also well worth visiting. Prices are slightly higher than many other Latin American countries. Best buys are wooden items, ceramics, jewellery and leather handicrafts. **Shopping hours:** 0850-1200 and 1400-1800 Monday to Saturday.
SPORT: Besides **swimming** in the Carribean Sea and the Pacific, most major towns and resorts have swimming pools open to the public. Horses can be hired for **riding** anywhere. The Barra de Colorado area is world famous for **fishing.** There is good **sea fishing** off Puntarenas, and in the mouth of Rio Chirripó on the Caribbean side near the Nicaraguan border. San José and Puerto Limón have **golf** courses. Association **football** is the national sport, played every Sunday morning between May and October. In San José matches can be seen at the Saprissa Stadium.
SPECIAL EVENTS: The following is a selection of the major festivals and special events celebrated in Costa Rica in 1995/96. For a complete list, contact the Tourist Office.
Mid Mar '95 *National Handicraft Fair,* San José; *Día del Boyero* (Day of the Oxcart Driver), San Antonio de Escazú. **Apr 14** *Religious Processions,* San Joaquín de Flores. **Apr 21** *Romeria* (Pilgrimage of the Virgin). **End of Apr** *International Auto Racing,* La Guacima de Alajuela; *Feria del Libro,* San José. **Aug 1** *Arrival of Pilgrims,* Cartago. **Oct 12** *Carnival Week,* Puerto Limón. **Dec 25-Jan 2 '96** *Fiestas del Fin del Año* (week-long festivities). **Mid-Jan** *Copa del Cafe International Tennis Tournament.* **Feb/Mar** *Annual Orchid Show,* Cartago.
SOCIAL CONVENTIONS: Handshaking is common and forms of address are important. Christian names are preceded by Don for a man and Donna for a woman. Normal courtesies should be observed when visiting someone's home and gifts are appreciated as a token of

thanks, especially if invited for a meal. For most occasions casual wear is acceptable, but beachwear should be confined to the beach; strapless dresses and shorts are not acceptable for women in San José.
Tipping: It is not necessary to tip taxi drivers. All hotels add 13% service tax plus 3% tourist tax to the bill by law. Restaurants add a 10% service charge. Tipping is expected by hotel staff, porters and waiters.

BUSINESS PROFILE

ECONOMY: Costa Rica's export earnings are derived partly from agriculture (coffee, bananas, meat, sugar and cocos) and from new non-traditional exports, which amounted to 50% of total exports in 1990. Staple crops are also grown for domestic consumption.
Manufacturing industry consists of food-processing, textiles, chemicals and plastics and is steadily expanding with government encouragement; new industries include aluminium, following the discovery of a large bauxite deposit. Costa Rica relies heavily on foreign loans and aid, not least because of its considerable overseas debt. Most of this comes through international bodies such as the IMF and from the United States, which is Costa Rica's main trading partner: the USA supplies 43% of imports and takes 44% of the country's exports. Costa Rica has a small net trade surplus with both the USA and the world as a whole.
BUSINESS: Customs tend to be conservative. Advance appointments, courtesy and punctuality are appreciated. It is necessary to have some knowledge of Spanish, although many locals speak English. Best months for business visits are November and December; avoid the last week of September, which is the end of the financial year. **Office hours:** 0800-1130 and 1330-1730 Monday to Friday.
COMMERCIAL INFORMATION: The following organisations can offer advice: Cámara de Comercio de Costa Rica (Chamber of Commerce), Apartado 1.114, Urbanización Tournón, 1000 San José. Tel: 221 0005. Fax: 233 7091. Telex: 2646; *or*
Cámara de Industrias de Costa Rica (Chamber of Industry), Apartado 10.003, Calles 13-15, Avenida 6, 1000 San José. Tel: 223 2411. Fax: 222 1007. Telex: 2474.

CLIMATE

In the Central Valley, where the main centres of population are located, the average temperature is 23°C. In the coastal areas the temperature is much hotter. The rainy season starts in May and finishes in November. The 'warm' dry season is December to May, though temperature differences between summer and winter are slight.
Required clothing: Lightweight cottons and linens most of the year, warmer clothes for cooler evenings. Waterproofing is necessary during the rainy season.

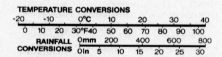

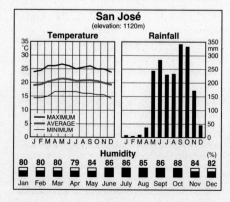

San José
(elevation: 1120m)

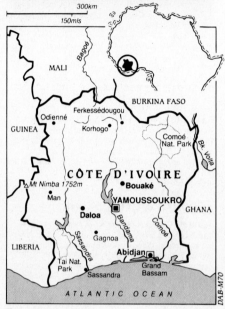

□ *international airport*

Location: West African coast.

Note: Although the country has not officially changed its name, a speech made by the President in October 1985 requested that the country's name should not be translated from the French, and the Foreign and Commonwealth Office was officially notified of this on December 12, 1986.

Direction de la Promotion Touristique
BP V184, Abidjan, Côte d'Ivoire
Tel: 214 970. Fax: 217 306. Telex: 22108.
Embassy of the Republic of Côte d'Ivoire
2 Upper Belgrave Street, London SW1X 8BJ
Tel: (0171) 235 6991. Fax: (0171) 259 5439. Opening hours: 0900-1200 and 1300-1600 Monday to Friday.
British Embassy
01 BP 2581, Third Floor, Immeuble 'Les Harmonies', angle boulevard Carde et avenue Dr Jamot, Plateau, Abidjan 01, Côte d'Ivoire
Tel: 226 850/1/2 *or* 328 209. Fax: 223 221. Telex: 23706 (a/b PRDRME CI).
Embassy of the Republic of Côte d'Ivoire
2424 Massachusetts Avenue, NW, Washington, DC 20008
Tel: (202) 797 0300. Fax: (202) 387 6381.
Embassy of the United States of America
01 BP 1712, 5 rue Jesse Owens, Abidjan, Côte d'Ivoire
Tel: 210 979 *or* 214 672. Fax: 223 259. Telex: 23660.
Embassy of the Republic of Côte d'Ivoire
9 Marlborough Avenue, Ottawa, Ontario K1N 8E6
Tel: (613) 236 9919. Fax: (613) 563 8287.
Consulates in Montréal, Toronto and Vancouver
Canadian Embassy
01 BP 4104, Immeuble Trade Centre, 23 Nogues Avenue, Le Plateau, Abidjan 01, Côte d'Ivoire
Tel: 212 009. Fax: 217 728. Telex: 23593.

AREA: 322,462 sq km (124,503 sq miles).
POPULATION: 12,600,000 (1990).

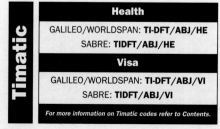

POPULATION DENSITY: 39.1 per sq km.
CAPITAL: Yamoussoukro (administrative & political). **Population:** 200,000 (1986). Abidjan (commercial). **Population:** 1,900,000 (1986).
GEOGRAPHY: Côte d'Ivoire shares borders with Liberia, Guinea, Mali, Burkina Faso and Ghana. There are 600km (370 miles) of coast on the Gulf of Guinea (Atlantic Ocean). The southern and western parts of the country are forested, and the savannah plains of the north and the mountainous western border. Three rivers, the Sassandra, the Bandama and the Comoé, run directly north–south and, on their approach to the coast, flow into a series of lagoons. Birdlife is plentiful throughout the country, but particularly so near the coast.
LANGUAGE: The official language is French. Local dialects include Dioula and Baoulé, which tribes use as trading languages.
RELIGION: 60% traditional beliefs, 25% Muslim, 15% Christian.
TIME: GMT.
ELECTRICITY: 220/230 volts AC, 50Hz. Round 2-pin plugs are standard.
COMMUNICATIONS: International telecommunications are only available in major towns/centres. **Telephone:** IDD is available. Country code: 225. Outgoing international code: 00. **Telex:** There are telex facilities at most hotels and the Central Post Office. **Post:** Airmail to Europe takes up to two weeks. Post office opening hours: 0730-1200 and 1430-1800 Monday to Friday. **Press:** All newspapers are in French. *Abidjan 7 Jours,* published weekly, gives local information, including events of interest.
BBC World Service and Voice of America frequencies: From time to time these change. See the section *How to Use this Book* for more information.
BBC:

MHz	17.79	15.40	15.07	6.005

Voice of America:

MHz	21.485	15.580	9.527	6.035

PASSPORT/VISA

Regulations and requirements may be subject to change at short notice, and you are advised to contact the appropriate diplomatic or consular authority before finalising travel arrangements. Details of these may be found at the head of this country's entry. Any numbers in the chart refer to the footnotes below.

	Passport Required?	Visa Required?	Return Ticket Required?
Full British	Yes	No	Yes
BVP	Not valid	-	-
Australian	Yes	Yes	Yes
Canadian	Yes	Yes	Yes
USA	Yes	1	Yes
Other EU (As of 31/12/94)	Yes	2	Yes
Japanese	Yes	Yes	Yes

PASSPORTS: Valid passport required by all except nationals of Benin, Burkina Faso, Mali, Mauritania, Niger, Senegal and Togo holding ID cards or a passport not expired for longer than 5 years.
British Visitors Passport: Not acceptable.
VISAS: Required by all except nationals of:
(a) **[1]** the USA for a period not exceeding 3 months;
(b) **[2]** Denmark, Germany, Republic of Ireland and the United Kingdom (all other EU countries *do* need visas);
(c) Andorra, Benin, Burkina Faso, Cape Verde, Central African Republic, Chad, Congo, Finland, Gabon, Gambia, Ghana, Guinea, Guinea-Bissau, Liberia, Mali, Mauritania, Monaco, Morocco, Niger, Nigeria, Norway, Senegal, Seychelles, Sierra Leone, South Africa, Sweden, Togo and Tunisia for a period not exceeding 3 months.
Types of visa: Tourist, Business and Transit. Single-entry: £15. Multiple-entry: £20. Business visas are only available as Multiple-entry and cost £24. Higher fees may apply to French nationals, who should consult the Embassy for details. Transit visas are not required by air travellers who do not intend to leave the airport and who have confirmed bookings on the first plane departing for their destination or on one that leaves on the same day they arrived.
Validity: Generally up to 3 months.
Application to: Consulate (or Consular section at Embassy). For addresses, see top of entry.
Application requirements: (a) Valid passport. (b) 2 application forms. (c) 2 passport-size photos. (d) Business letters if appropriate.
Working days required: 2.

MONEY

Currency: CFA Franc (CFA Fr) = 100 centimes. Notes are in denominations of CFA Fr10,000, 5000, 1000 and 500. Coins are in denominations of CFA Fr500, 100, 50, 25, 10, 5 and 1. Côte d'Ivoire is part of the French Monetary Area.
Note: At the beginning of 1994, the CFA Franc was devalued against the French Franc.
Currency exchange: Currency can be exchanged at the airport as well as at banks and hotels.
Credit cards: American Express and Access/Mastercard are widely accepted; Visa and Diners Club have more limited use. Check with your credit card company for details of merchant acceptability and other facilities which may be available.
Travellers cheques: These are accepted in hotels, restaurants and some shops.
Exchange rate indicators: The following figures are included as a guide to the movements of the CFA Franc against Sterling and the US Dollar:

Date=	Oct '92	Sep '93	Jan '94	Jan '95
£1.00=	413.75	433.87	436.79	834.94
$1.00=	260.71	284.14	295.23	533.68

Currency restrictions: The import of both foreign and local currencies is unlimited but all currencies other than the French Franc and the CFA Franc must be declared on arrival. The export of foreign currency is up to the amount declared and that of local currency is up to CFA Fr10,000. There is no restriction on the re-export of unused travellers cheques and letters of credit. Residents and business travellers should enquire at the Consulate.
Banking hours: 0745-1130 and 1430-1630 Monday to Friday.

DUTY FREE

The following goods may be imported into Côte d'Ivoire by passengers over 15 years of age without incurring customs duty:
200 cigarettes or 25 cigars or 250g of tobacco; 1 bottle of wine; 1 bottle of spirits; 1/2 litre of toilet water; 1/4 litre of perfume.
Prohibited items: Sporting guns may only be imported under licence. Limits are placed on certain personal effects; contact the Consulate prior to departure.

PUBLIC HOLIDAYS

Jan 1 '95 New Year's Day. **Mar 3** Eid al-Fitr (End of Ramadan). **Apr 14** Good Friday. **Apr 17** Easter Monday. **May 1** Labour Day. **May 10** Eid al-Adha (Feast of the Sacrifice). **May 25** Ascension Day. **Jun 5** Whit Monday. **Aug 15** Assumption. **Nov 1** All Saints' Day. **Dec 7** Independence Day. **Dec 25** Christmas. **Jan 1 '96** New Year's Day. **Feb 22** Eid al-Fitr (End of Ramadan). **Apr 5** Good Friday. **Apr 8** Easter Monday.
Note: (a) Holidays that fall on a Sunday are often observed on the following day. (b) Muslim festivals are timed according to local sightings of various phases of the Moon and the dates given above are approximations. During the lunar month of Ramadan that precedes Eid al-Fitr, Muslims fast during the day and feast at night and normal business patterns may be interrupted. Some disruption may continue into Eid al-Fitr itself. Eid al-Fitr and Eid al-Adha may last anything from two to ten days, depending on the region. For more information see the section *World of Islam* at the back of the book.

HEALTH

Regulations and requirements may be subject to change at short notice, and you are advised to contact your doctor well in advance of your intended date of departure. Any numbers in the chart refer to the footnotes below.

	Special Precautions?	Certificate Required?
Yellow Fever	Yes	1
Cholera	Yes	2
Typhoid & Polio	Yes	-
Malaria	Yes	-
Food & Drink	3	-

[1]: A yellow fever vaccination certificate is required from travellers over one year of age coming from all countries.
[2]: Following WHO guidelines issued in 1973, a cholera vaccination certificate is no longer a condition of entry to Côte d'Ivoire. However, cholera is a serious risk in this country and precautions are essential. Up-to-date advice should be sought before deciding whether these precautions should include vaccination as medical opinion is divided over its effectiveness. See the *Health* section at the back of the book.
[3]: All water should be regarded as being potentially contaminated. Water used for drinking, brushing teeth or making ice should have first been boiled or otherwise sterilised. Milk is unpasteurised and should be boiled. Powdered or tinned milk is available and is advised, but make sure that it is reconstituted with pure water. Avoid dairy products which are likely to have been made from unboiled milk. Only eat well-cooked meat and fish, preferably served hot. Pork, salad and mayonnaise may carry increased risk. Vegetables should be cooked and fruit peeled.
Malaria risk (and of other insect-borne diseases) exists all year throughout the country, including urban areas. The malignant *falciparum* form is prevalent. Resistance to chloroquine has been reported.
Rabies is present. For those at high risk, vaccination before arrival should be considered. If you are bitten abroad seek medical advice without delay. For more information consult the *Health* section at the back of the book.
Bilharzia (schistosomiasis) is present. Avoid swimming and paddling in fresh water. Swimming pools which are well-chlorinated and maintained are safe.
Meningitis risk is present depending on area visited and time of year.
Health care: Health facilities are limited; medical insurance is vital.

TRAVEL - International

AIR: The main airline to serve Côte d'Ivoire is *Air Afrique (RK),* in which Côte d'Ivoire has a shareholding.
Approximate flight time: From London to Abidjan is 6 hours.
International airports: *Abidjan (ABJ)* (Port Bouet Airport) is 16km (10 miles) southeast of Abidjan (travel time – 25 minutes). Airport facilities include duty-free shop (24 hours), restaurant, shops and car hire. A bus runs every 10 minutes to the city 0510-2300. Taxi service is available.
Yamoussoukro (San Pedro Airport) has recently been upgraded to international standard.
Departure tax: CFA Fr 5000 for most international departures and CFA 3000 for departures to other destinations within Africa. Transit passengers are exempt.
SEA: There are no regular passenger sailings but cargo liners provide limited accommodation for passengers travelling from Europe. The *Royal Viking* line operates a cruise to Abidjan.
RAIL: There are two through trains with sleeping and restaurant cars from Abidjan to Ouagadougou (Burkina Faso) daily. Those intending to travel should be aware that the Burkina Faso rail network is under constant threat of closure because of financial difficulties; check with the appropriate authorities before finalising arrangements.
ROAD: There are road links of varying quality from Kumasi (Ghana) and from Burkina Faso, Guinea and Liberia.

TRAVEL - Internal

AIR: *Air Ivoire (VU)* operates regular internal flights from Abidjan to all major towns.
Approximate flight times: From Abidjan to *Abengourou* is 35 minutes; to *Bondoukou* is 1 hour 20 minutes; to *Bouaké* is 1 hour 20 minutes; to *Bouna* is 1 hour 20 minutes; to *Boundiali* is 2 hours 35 minutes; to *Daloa* is 1 hour; to *Gagnoa* is 50 minutes; to *Guiglo* is 2 hours 15 minutes; to *Korhogo* is 1 hour 30 minutes; to *Man* is 50 minutes; to *Odienne* is 2 hours 20 minutes; to *San Pedro* is 1 hour; to *Sassandra* is 45 minutes; to *Seguela* is 1 hour 20 minutes; to *Tabou* is 1 hour 25 minutes; to *Touba* is 1 hour and to *Yamoussoukro* is 30 minutes.
Departure tax: CFA Fr800 for domestic departures.
RAIL: The Abidjan–Niger railway is one of the most advanced in Africa and runs fast trains several times daily from Abidjan to Bouaké and Ferkessédougou. Children under 4 travel free. Children aged 4-9 pay half-fare.
ROAD: Côte d'Ivoire has a good road system by West African standards, with over 2000km (1200 miles) of asphalted roads. Petrol stations are frequent except in the north. Traffic drives on the right. **Bus:** Small private buses operate throughout the country; they are comfortable and efficient. There are also luxury-class coaches for the longer journeys. **Taxi:** These are available in main cities. **Car hire:** Cars may be hired in Abidjan, main towns and at the airport.
Documentation: Insurance is compulsory for the driver, as is an International Driving Permit. The motorist must have a customs pass-sheet issued by the Automobile Club of the country of the vehicle's registration.
URBAN: Extensive bus and boat services are operated in Abidjan by *SOTRA* on a 2-tiered fare structure. Taxis are usually red and metered; rates are doubled from 2400-0600.
JOURNEY TIMES: The following chart gives approximate journey times (in hours and minutes) from Abidjan to other major towns in the Côte d'Ivoire.

	Air	Rail
Agboville	-	2.00
Dimbokro	-	4.00
Bouaké	1.20	6.00
Touba	1.00	-
Tabou	1.20	-
Man	0.50	-
Daloa	1.00	-

ACCOMMODATION

Hotels and restaurants are expensive in the larger towns. There are several hotels of international standard in Abidjan. In general, there is a choice between luxury, medium-range and cheaper accommodation in the larger towns. In all cases it is advisable to book in advance. For further information, contact the Société Ivoirienne d'Expansion Touristique et Hôtelière (SIETHO), 04 BP 375, avenue Lamblin, Plateau, Abidjan 04. Tel: 322 807 *or* 332 382. **Grading:** Hotels are graded from **1** to **5 stars.**

RESORTS & EXCURSIONS

Abidjan, the commercial capital and largest city, is dominated by the *Plateau,* the central commercial district. The older, more traditional heart of the city is *Treichville,* home of many bars, restaurants and nightclubs as well as the colourful central market. The city is one of the most expensive in the world. There is a very good museum, the *Ifon Museum.* Suburbs have grown up along the banks of the lagoon; these include **Cocody** (with the large Hotel Ivoire complex), **Marcory** and **Adjamé**. About 100km (60 miles) east of the capital is the beach resort of **Assouinde**; other places being developed as tourist attractions include **Tiagba**, a stilt-town; **Grand Bassam,** whose sandy beaches make the place a favourite weekend retreat for the inhabitants of Abidjan; and **Bondoukouo,** one of the oldest settlements in the country. In the west of the country is the attractive town of **Man**, situated in a region of thickly forested mountains and plateaux. The nearby waterfalls are a popular attraction, as are climbs to the peak of *Mount Tonkoui* and visits to the villages of **Biankouma** and **Gouessesso,** 55km (34 miles) away.
The new administrative and political capital is **Yamoussoukro**, about 230km (143 miles) north of Abidjan. The town has a lively market, an international-standard golf course and several buildings of architectural interest, including the *Palace and Plantations of the President* and the *Mosque.* Also of architectural interest but, above all, of statistical interest, is the recently completed *Cathedral Notre Dame de la Paix.* Fractionally smaller than St Peter's in Rome, it incorporates a greater area of stained glass than the total area of stained glass in France. Roman Catholicism is a minority religion in Côte d'Ivoire (some say that the Cathedral could accommodate every Roman Catholic in the country several times over). Yamoussoukro was the birthplace of Félix Houphouët-Boigny, who was Côte d'Ivoire's President for 33 years. The Cathedral was paid for almost entirely out of his own pocket.
Other towns of interest include **Korhogo**, the main city of the north and centre of a good fishing and hunting district; the former capital of **Bingerville**; and the town of **Bouaké** in the centre of the country.
There is a choice of locally organised package tours; enquire locally for details. Many of these will include visits to one of the country's national parks, including the **Comoé** in the northeast and the **Banco National Park,** 3000 hectares of equatorial forest.

SOCIAL PROFILE

FOOD & DRINK: Table service is usual in restaurants; in bars table and/or counter service is available. Abidjan and other centres have restaurants serving French, Italian, Caribbean, Lebanese and Vietnamese food. There is a growing number of African restaurants catering for foreigners. Traditional dishes are *kedjenou*

Danse Dida

(chicken cooked with different vegetables and sealed in banana leaves), *n'voufou* (mashed bananas or yam mixed with palm oil and served with aubergine sauce) and *attiéké* (cassava dish). The best area for spicy African food is the Treichville district of Abidjan. The blue pages of the Abidjan telephone book have a special restaurant section. There are no restrictions on drinking.
NIGHTLIFE: There are nightclubs in most major centres. Abidjan is the most lively area with its hotels and lagoon-side tourist resorts. There are also theatres, casinos and bars. Traditional entertainment is offered in some hotels.
SHOPPING: In the markets, hard bargaining is often necessary to get prices down to reasonable levels. Special purchases include wax prints, Ghanaian *kente* cloth, indigo fabric and woven cloth, wooden statuettes and masks, bead necklaces, pottery and basketware. **Shopping hours:** 0800-1200 and 1600-1900 Monday to Saturday.
SPORT: There are many **swimming** pools in main centres and hotels, particularly in Abidjan and the surrounding coastal resorts. All along this stretch of coast there is a dangerous deep current and all but the strongest swimmers should stay near the shore. There is good coastal and river **fishing**. Red carp, barracuda, mullet and sole can all be caught from the shores of the lagoons. Sea trips can be organised through travel agencies to catch sharks, swordfish, bonito and marlin. Most major centres have a **golf** course. In Abidjan there is a course at the Hotel Ivoire on the Riviera. Many hotels have **tennis** courts. Boats and instructors are available in Abidjan at the Marina, Hotel Ivoire, where **water-skiing** facilities are also available.
SPECIAL EVENTS: For a full list of festivals and other special events to be held in Côte d'Ivoire in 1995/96, and for the exact dates of the selection listed below, contact the Embassy, Consulate or the Direction de la Promotion Touristique (see addresses at head of entry).
Mar '95 *Carnival*, Bouaké. **Apr** *Masks Festival, Popo Carnival* and *Dripi Festival.* **Jun** *Tabaski, Sheep Festival.* **Jul** *Karité.* **Sep/Oct** *Vam Festival*, Agni, Abron and Koulango districts. **Nov** *Carnival de Bassam*, Abissa. **Dec** *Fête des Ignames*, Agni. **Jan '96 (second week)** *Katana Festival.* **Feb** *Seke Festival* and *Houphouët-Boigny Golf Trophy*, Yamoussoukro. **Mar** *Carnival*, Bouaké.
SOCIAL CONVENTIONS: One of the most striking features of Côte d'Ivoire, distinguishing it from many other African countries, is the extreme ethnic and

linguistic variety. The size of each of the 60 groups – which include the Akar, Kron, Nzima, Hone, Voltaic and Malinke peoples – varies widely and the area they occupy may cover a whole region. With very few exceptions every Ivorian has a mother tongue which is that of the village, along with traditions, family and social relations within their ethnic group. French has become the official language of schools, cities and government and therefore has an influence on lifestyle even at a modest level. Handshaking is normal. Tropical lightweight clothes are essential, a light raincoat in the rainy season and a hat for the sun. Casual wear is widely acceptable but beachwear should be confined to the beach or poolside. Ties need only be worn for formal occasions. Small tokens of appreciation, a souvenir from home or a business gift with the company logo are always welcome. Normal courtesies should be observed and it is considered polite to arrive punctually for social occasions. There are no restrictions on smoking. Snakes are regarded as sacred by some ethnic groups. **Tipping:** Most hotels and restaurants include a service charge in the bill; if not, tip 15%.

BUSINESS PROFILE

ECONOMY: Côte d'Ivoire is the world's largest producer of cocoa and the second largest of coffee and cotton. Timber and fruit are the other main commodities while the Government has successfully encouraged diversification into rice, rubber, sugar and other source materials. Agriculture and forestry thus employ the majority of the population as well as providing the country's major export earners. Côte d'Ivoire has also developed a light industrial sector producing textiles, chemicals and sugar refining and geared towards export markets. There are also assembly plants for cars and other manufactured goods. Significant offshore oil deposits were discovered in the late 1970s but have been developed slowly due to financial and technical problems. France is Côte d'Ivoire's main trading partner and The Netherlands are a key export market. Côte d'Ivoire has comprehensive trading links throughout the EU and with Nigeria, the CIS and elsewhere.
BUSINESS: French is predominantly used in business circles, although executives in larger businesses may speak English. Translators are generally available. Punctuality is expected, although the host may be late. Visiting cards are essential and given to each person met. It is usual for business visitors to be entertained by local hosts in a hotel or restaurant. Businessmen need only wear cotton safari suits. **Office hours:** 0730-1200 and 1430-1730 Monday to Friday; 0800-1200 Saturday.
COMMERCIAL INFORMATION: The following organisation can offer advice: Chambre de Commerce et d'Industrie de Côte d'Ivoire, 01 BP 1399, Abidjan 01. Tel: 324 679. Fax: 323 946. Telex: 23224.
CONFERENCES/CONVENTIONS: In Abidjan, the Palais de Congrès which is part of the Inter-Continental hotel can host conferences for more than 3000 persons. The political capital Yamoussoukro has a capacity for over 5000. The following organisation can offer advice: Centre de Commerce International d'Abidjan (CCIA), BP 468, Abidjan. Tel: 224 070/72/73. Fax: 227 112. Telex: 23460.

CLIMATE

Four seasons: Dry from December to April, long rains from May to July, a short dry season from August to September, short rains in October and November. In the north the climate is more extreme – rains (May to October) and dry (November to April).
Required clothing: Tropical lightweights; warmer clothing for evenings.

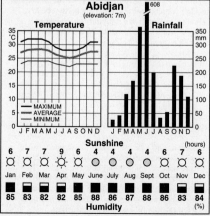

Croatia

Location: Former Yugoslav republic, southeastern Europe.

Note: At the time of writing, travel to Zagreb, the areas north of Zagreb towards the Slovenian and Hungarian borders, the Istrian Peninsula, the North Dalmatian coast, Split and the coast south to Dubrovnik and the Adriatic Islands (and travel to them via the port and airport of Split) is now considered trouble free.
Elsewhere, the military situation has been calm for some months though tensions remain. Travel to and through other areas bordering Bosnia and Hercegovina, which are under United Nations protection or close to these areas, is inadvisable. For up-to-date information, contact the FCO Travel Advice Unit. Tel: (0171) 270 4129.
Source: FCO Travel Advice Unit – November 14, 1994.

Ministry of Tourism
Avenija Vukovar 78, 41000 Zagreb, Croatia
Tel: (41) 613 347. Fax: (41) 613 216.
Embassy of the Republic of Croatia
18-21 Jermyn Street, London SW1Y 6HP
Tel: (0171) 434 2946. Fax: (0171) 434 2953.
British Embassy
PO Box 454 Ilica 12/II, 41000, Zagreb, Croatia
Tel: (41) 424 888 *or* 426 200. Fax: (41) 420 100. Telex: 21309 (a/b BRZAG CRO).
Embassy of the Republic of Croatia
2343 Massachusetts Avenue, NW, Washington, DC 20008
Tel: (202) 588 5899. Fax: (202) 588 8936.
Embassy of the United States of America
Unit 1345, Andrije Hebranga 2, 09213-1345 Zagreb
Tel: (41) 444 800 or 445 535 (after hours). Fax: (41) 458 585.
Canadian Embassy
Hotel Esplanade, Mihanovicva 1, 41000 Zagreb
Tel: (41) 450 785 (Ext. 624) *or* 435 666 *or* 428 783 (Ext. 623). Fax: (41) 450 913.

AREA: 56,538 sq km (21,829 sq miles) or 22% of the territory of the former Yugoslav federation (its second largest republic).
POPULATION: 4.8 million (1991).
POPULATION DENSITY: 84.6 per sq km.
CAPITAL: Zagreb. **Population:** 706,770 (1991).

Abidjan
(elevation: 7m)

	Jan	Feb	Mar	Apr	May	June	July	Aug	Sept	Oct	Nov	Dec
Sunshine (hours)	6	7	7	9	6	4	3	4	4	6	7	6
Humidity (%)	85	83	82	82	85	88	86	87	88	86	83	84

GEOGRAPHY: A long coastal Adriatic region (narrowing as it goes north–south; the major ports being Rijeka, Pula, Zadar, Sibenik, Split and Dubrovnik) and a larger inland area (running west–east from Zagreb to the Danubian border with Serbia). Croatia has borders with Slovenia and Hungary (north), Serbia and Montenegro (east), and Bosnia-Hercegovina (southeast from Zagreb; northeast from the Adriatic coastline).

LANGUAGE: Croatian, with the Latinate alphabet, which is identical in all essential matters to Serbo-Croat (Cyrillic alphabet).

RELIGION: Roman Catholic Croats (75% of the total population) and Eastern Orthodox Serbs (officially 11%; in actuality up to 20%, given that most of the 9% of the population who declared themselves to be 'Yugoslav' in the 1991 census were thought to be Serbs).

TIME: GMT + 1 (GMT + 2 from last Sunday in March to Saturday before last Sunday in September).

COMMUNICATIONS: Telephone/fax/telex: IDD is available. Country code: 385. Outgoing international code: 99. All such services, including facsimile and telex, are generally available for communications to and from Western Europe. Apart from a limited telex service, all telephone communications between Zagreb and Belgrade have been indefinitely cut. Internal communications are generally satisfactory, but non-existent in relation to the republic's war zones. **Press:** The main local newspapers, in decreasing order of circulation, are *Vecernji List* (Zagreb), *Slobodna Dalmacija* (Split) and *Novi List* (Rijeka). The state news agency, HINA (Croatian Information and News Agency, Zagreb), produces material in English for international distribution on a daily basis. The state TV-radio station, HTV, also produces a daily (1700-2300) unscrambled programme, including news in English, for a worldwide audience via Eutelsat 1 F5 (21.5DE).

BBC World Service and Voice of America frequencies: From time to time these change. See the section *How to use this Book* for more information.

BBC:

| MHz | 15.07 | 12.09 | 9.410 | 6.195 |

Voice of America:

| MHz | 9.670 | 6.040 | 5.995 | 1.260 |

Note: CNN is also available via satellite (Astra) in some Zagreb, Rijeka, Split and other Adriatic coast hotels.

PASSPORT/VISA

Regulations and requirements may be subject to change at short notice, and you are advised to contact the appropriate diplomatic or consular authority before finalising travel arrangements. Details of these may be found at the head of this country's entry. Any numbers in the chart refer to the footnotes below.

	Passport Required?	Visa Required?	Return Ticket Required?
Full British	Yes	No	Yes
BVP	1	No	Yes
Australian	Yes	Yes	Yes
Canadian	Yes	Yes	Yes
USA	Yes	Yes	Yes
Other EU (As of 31/12/94)	Yes	2	Yes
Japanese	Yes	No	Yes

PASSPORTS: Valid passports required by all except **[1]** UK nationals holding a British Visitors Passport.

VISAS: Required by all except:
(a) nationals of countries shown in the chart above;
(b) **[2]** nationals of EU countries (except nationals of Greece who *do* require a visa);
(c) nationals of Algeria, Austria, Bosnia-Hercegovina, Bulgaria, Chile, Czech Republic, Ecuador, Finland, Hungary, Liechtenstein, Former Yugoslav Republic of Macedonia, Malta, Monaco, Norway, Poland, Romania, San Marino, Slovak Republic, Slovenia, Switzerland, Sweden, Turkey and Vatican City.

Note: The following nationals may obtain visas on arrival in Croatia: Australia, Canada, South Africa, New Zealand and the USA.

Types of visa: *Tourist* and *Business* (single-entry) – £7. Multiple-entry visas are not being issued at present.

Validity: Up to 3 months.

Application to: Consulate (or Consular section at Embassy). For address, see top of entry.

Application requirements: (a) Valid passport. (b) Completed application forms. (c) Fee payable by cash or postal order. (d) Letter of invitation from contact in Croatia for Business visas.

Working days required: 24 hours for Tourist visas and up to 3 weeks for Business visas.

MONEY

Currency: The Kuna was introduced in May 1994. 1 Kuna (Kn) = 100 Lipa (Lp). Notes are in denominations of Kn1000, 500, 200, 100, 50, 20, 10 and 5. Coins are in denominations of Kn5, 2 and 1, and 50, 20, 10, 5, 2, and 1 lipa.

Currency exchange: Inflation has been gradually reduced during 1994 following the Government's stabilisation programme. As a result the Kuna has become convertible currency in the countries of central Europe. As elsewhere in the ex-Yugoslav republics, however, the only true repositories of value and real mediums of exchange locally are the German DM and the US Dollar (Sterling is rarely used in the republic). More foreign exchange is reportedly in circulation in private hands in the republic than ever enters the banking system, which people are extremely wary of following earlier government seizures of domestic foreign currency accounts for the financing of the war effort. Currency should only be exchanged in banks and authorised dealers.

Exchange rate indicator: The following figures are included as a guide to the movements of the Croatian Dinar against Sterling and the US Dollar:

Date:	Sep '93	Jan '94	Jan '95
£1.00=	7357.0	9727.9	8.80
$1.00=	44818.0	6575.1	5.62

Note: The unofficial, or black market, rate can run up to 400% of the official exchange rate.

Currency restrictions: The import and export of local currency is limited to Kn2000. The import and export of foreign currency is unrestricted.

Banking hours: 0700-1500 Monday to Friday, 0800-1400 Saturday.

DUTY FREE

The following goods may be taken into Croatia without incurring customs duty:
200 cigarettes or 25 cigars or 220g of tobacco; 1 litre of spirits; 250ml of perfume.

PUBLIC HOLIDAYS

Jan 1 '95 New Year's Day. **Jan 6-7** Epiphany. **Apr 17** Easter Monday. **May 1** Labour Day. **May 30** Statehood Day. **Jun 22** Anti-fascist Day. **Aug 15** Assumption. **Nov 1** All Saints' Day. **Dec 25-26** Christmas. **Jan 1 '96** New Year's Day. **Jan 6-7** Epiphany. **Apr 8** Easter Monday.

HEALTH

Regulations and requirements may be subject to change at short notice, and you are advised to contact your doctor well in advance of your intended date of departure. Any numbers in the chart refer to the footnotes below.

	Special Precautions?	Certificate Required?
Yellow Fever	No	No
Cholera	No	No
Typhoid & Polio	Yes	No
Malaria	No	No
Food & Drink	1	-

[1] Mains water is normally chlorinated, and whilst relatively safe, may cause mild abdominal upsets. Bottled water is available and is advised for the first few weeks of the stay. Milk is pasteurised and dairy products are safe for consumption. Local meat, poultry, seafood, fruit and vegetables are generally considered safe to eat.
Rabies is present. For those at high risk, vaccination before arrival should be considered. If you are bitten abroad seek medical advice without delay. For more information consult the *Health* section at the back of the book.

Health care: Prescribed medicines must be paid for. Insurance with emergency repatriation is recommended.

TRAVEL - International

AIR: Croatia's national airline is *Croatian Airlines*. It offers services from several European cities and domestic services. Only a few foreign carriers now have regular services to Zagreb (ZAG) airport.

Approximate flight times: From *London* to Zagreb is 2 hours 5 minutes. From *New York* to Zagreb is 10 hours 35 minutes.

International airports: *Pleso International Airport* (ZAG) (Zagreb) is 17km (10 miles) southwest of the city. An airport bus runs to the city centre (travel time – 25 minutes) and taxis are also available (travel time – 20 minutes). Airport facilities include 24-hour left luggage, banks/bureaux de change, restaurants, snack bars, bars, duty-free shops, post office (0700-1900), tourist information, 24-hour first aid and car rental (*Avis* and *Hertz*).
Dubrovnik (DBV) is 22km (13 miles) southeast of the city (travel time – 30 minutes). An airport bus runs to the city. Airport facilities include banks/bureaux de change (0600-2400 in summer, 0700-2200 in winter), bar, restaurant, duty-free shop (0600-2400 in summer, 0700-220 in winter), shops and car rental (*Avis, Hertz* and

InterRent).
Departure tax: US$8 on international flights from Zagreb. **Note:** Due to the war, Croatia does not as yet fully control all its airspace.

SEA: There are regular passenger and car-ferry services between Italian, Greek and Croatian ports.

RAIL: International rail routes run from Zagreb to Munich, Vienna, Venice, Budapest and Graz.

ROAD: Buses connect Zagreb to many European cities.

TRAVEL - Internal

AIR: Services are functioning regularly as regards Zagreb–Rijeka, Zagreb–Split and Zagreb–Ljubljana (Slovenia), but at present there are no services to Osijek, nor to Belgrade, Sarajevo (Bosnia-Hercegovina) and Podgorica (Montenegro) due to the war.

ROAD/RAIL: The main road/rail route to and from Western Europe now effectively stops at Zagreb (coming from Ljubljana) on account of the war in eastern Slavonia, with extensive detours via Hungary for international traffic going south to and from Serbia, Former Yugoslav Republic of Macedonia and Greece. Otherwise, the routes Zagreb–Rijeka, and Zagreb–Varazdin are open, but the Zagreb–Split route involves lengthy diversions from Knin, the centre of Serbian rebellion to Croatian rule from Zagreb, and a major war zone. **Regulations:** Traffic drives on the right. Speed limits are 60kmph (38mph) in built-up areas, 120kmph (75mph) on motorways, 80kmph (50mph) on other roads and outside built-up areas. **Documentation:** National or International Driving Permit. A Green Card should be carried by visitors taking their own car into Croatia. Without it, insurance cover is limited to the minimum legal cover; the Green Card augments this to the level of cover provided by the car owner's domestic policy.

ACCOMMODATION

Formerly a major European tourism destination, Croatia has the best of its hotels on its Adriatic coast, although the war has effectively closed all but those on the Istrian peninsula (Rijeka–Pula). Elsewhere, deluxe A-class hotels are only to be found in Zagreb, plus the Plitvice Lakes tourist area on the border with Bosnia-Hercegovina near Bihac (also closed by the war). For further information, contact the Croatian Association of Hoteliers, Hotel Kvarner, Park 1, Svibnja 4, 51410 Opatija. Tel: (51) 213 820. Fax: (51) 211 312.

RESORTS & EXCURSIONS

Note: The following information reflects the situation before the present conflict and is included in the hope that it will be useful again in the future.
The landscape ranges from small villages in the interior to the dramatic Dalmatian coastline. Formerly popular resorts are **Porec, Pula, Opatija** and **Rovinj**. Moving further south are the Split and Makarska regions.
Split was founded in the 4th century AD by the Roman Emperor Diocletian. The enormous palace he built and the walled town now form part of the old quarter. Concerts, opera and dance all take place within the palace. **Dubrovnik** was once considered to be the most beautiful city in Croatia with its medieval walls and palaces. **Zagreb**, the capital of Croatia, is the site of many 13th-century buildings. There are museums and art galleries, the *Croatian National Theatre* and interesting churches, the *Cathedrals of St Mark* and *St Stephen* in particular. **Pula** dates from the 5th century BC, and its Roman amphitheatre is still in use. **Opatija** was popular with the Austro-Hungarian nobility and some of its former elegance remains. **Rijeka** is the largest Croatian port; there are museums, art galleries, theatres and a medieval Croatian fortress. In addition there are quieter offshore islands, including **Brac, Hvar** and **Korcula**. In *Kvarner Bay* are numerous islands: **Krk, Rab** and **Pag** are the best known.

SOCIAL PROFILE

FOOD & DRINK: The Adriatic coast is renowned for the variety of seafood dishes, including scampi, *prstaci* (shellfish) and *brodet* (mixed fish stewed with rice) all cooked in olive oil and served with vegetables. In the interior visitors should sample *manistra od bobica* (beans and fresh maize soup). **Drink:** The regional wines are good. Italian expresso is also popular and cheap.

SHOPPING: Traditional handicrafts like embroidery, woodcarvings and ceramics make good souvenirs.
Shopping hours: 0800-2000 Monday to Friday; 0800-1500 Saturday.

SPORT: Skiing and **spa** resorts exist at Delnice and Platak. **Fishing** permits are available from hotels or local authorities. Local information is necessary. Freshwater angling and fishing with equipment needs a permit. 'Fish-linking' with a local small craft owner is popular. **Sailing** is popular along the coast. Berths and boats can be hired at all ports. Permits are needed for boats brought into the country. **Spectator sports:** Football is one of the more popular. **SPECIAL EVENTS:** Jul '95 *International Festival of Traditional Folklore*, Zagreb; *Film Festival*, Pula; *Arts Festival*, Split; *Moreska* (a richly costumed tournament commemorating an 11th-century victory over the Moors), Korcula; *Arts Festival*, Opatija. **Jul-Aug** *Summer Festival*, Dubrovnik; *Summer Festival*, Zagreb. **Aug** *SLUK* (The International Puppet Festival). **Oct** *Jazz Festival*, Zagreb. **SOCIAL CONVENTIONS:** People normally shake hands upon meeting and leaving. Smoking is generally acceptable but there are restrictions in public buildings and on public transport. **Photography**: Certain restrictions exist. **Tipping:** 10% is expected in hotels, restaurants and taxis.

BUSINESS PROFILE

ECONOMY: The second richest and most economically developed of the former Yugoslav republics, Croatia accounted for 25% of Yugoslavia's GDP (around US$15 billion), 22% of its agricultural and industrial output, and 20% of its exports in 1990-91, with a GDP per capita of around US$3000 in the same year (just above the all-Yugoslav average, but only 60% of that then prevailing in Slovenia). Due to damages caused by the war (estimated at US$23 billion), the loss of markets and adjustments in relation to international competition and transition to a market economy, Croatian GDP, per capita, decreased from US$3351 in 1990 to US$2505 in 1994. The Government has had some success in reviving the economy with a programme of restructuring and privatisation, which has precipitated an increase in trade and investment and the growth of foreign currency reserves which in September 1994 amounted to US$2.1 billion. Tourism, previously a mainstay of the Croatian economy, has seen a considerable revival, in 1994 showing a 50% increase in registered income from the previous year. Inflation has been reduced, allowing for the introduction of a new, more stable currency in 1994 – the Kuna. The recent granting of membership of the IMF has helped to solidify international confidence in Croatia's economic progress. **BUSINESS:** In many ways one of the more conservative areas of the former Yugoslav federation, Croatia tends towards formal business protocol, but this image of Western-style efficiency is often belied by the fact that things go very slowly on account of the cumbersome bureaucracy. Communication, however, is no problem, as English and German are widely used as second languages. Business cards including professional or academic titles should be exchanged just after formal introductions. There are also a large number of local agents, advisers, consultants and, to a lesser extent, lawyers, willing to act for foreign companies, but none should be engaged before being thoroughly checked in advance. Croatia has created a more liberal framework for foreign investments so that foreign investors are guaranteed special rights and incentives for investing in Croatia. **Office hours:** 0800-1600 Monday to Friday.
COMMERCIAL INFORMATION: The following organisations can offer advice: Chamber of Economy of Croatia, Rooseveltov Trg. 2, 41000 Zagreb. Tel: (41) 453 422 *or* 461 555. Fax: (41) 448 618 *or* 415 801; *or* Croatian Privatization Fund, Gajeva 30a, 41000 Zagreb. Tel: (41) 469 111. Fax: (41) 469 133; *or* National Bank of Croatia, Trg. Burze 5, 41000 Zagreb. Tel: (41) 464 555. Fax: (41) 441 684. Telex: 22569.
CONFERENCES/CONVENTIONS: The following organisation can offer advice: Croatian Convention Bureau, Ilica 1, 41000 Zagreb. Tel: (41) 456 455. Fax: (41) 428 674.

CLIMATE

Croatia has a varied climate, with continental climate conditions in the north and Mediterranean ones on the Adriatic coast.

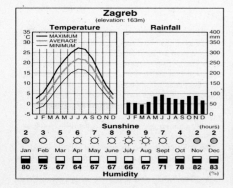

Zagreb
(elevation: 163m)

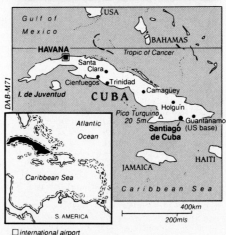

□ *international airport*

Location: Northwest Caribbean.

Empresa de Turismo Internacional (Cubatur)
Calle 23, No 156, entre N y O, Apartado 6560, Vedado, Havana, Cuba
Tel: (7) 324 521. Fax: (7) 333 104. Telex: 511212.
Embassy of the Republic of Cuba
167 High Holborn, London WC1V 6PA
Tel: (0171) 240 2488 *or* (0891) 880 820 (recorded message). Fax: (0171) 836 2602. Telex: 261094. Opening hours: 0900-1800 Monday to Friday.
Cuban Consulate
15 Grape Street, London WC2 8DR
Tel: (0171) 240 2488 *or* (0891) 880 820 (recorded information. Calls are charged at the higher rate of 39/49p per minute). Fax: (0171) 836 2602. Opening hours: 0930-1230 Monday to Friday.
Cuba Tourist Office
167 High Holborn, London WC1V 6PA
Tel: (0171) 379 1706. Fax: (0171) 240 6656. Opening hours: 0900-1700 Monday to Friday (telephone enquiries only).
Cubanacan UK Ltd
Unit 49, Skylines, Limeharbour, London E14 9TS
Tel: (0171) 537 7909. Fax: (0171) 537 7747. Opening hours: 0900-1700 Monday to Friday.
British Embassy
Calle 34, 708 Miramar, Havana, Cuba
Tel: (7) 331 771. Fax: (7) 338 104. Telex: 511656 (a/b UKEMB CU).
Cuban Interests Section
c/o Swiss Embassy, 2630 16th Street, NW, Washington, DC 20009
Tel: (202) 797 8518/19/20. Fax: (202) 797 8521.
US Interests Section
c/o Swiss Embassy, Calzada entre L y M, Vedado, Havana, Cuba
Tel: (7) 320 551/9 *or* 333 543/7. Telex: 512206.
Embassy of the Republic of Cuba
388 Main Street, Ottawa, Ontario K1S 1E3
Tel: (613) 563 0141. Fax: (613) 563 0068.
Consulates in: Montréal and Toronto.
Cuba Tourist Board
Suite 705, 55 Queen Street East, Toronto, Ontario M5C 1R5
Tel: (416) 362 0700/1/2. Fax: (416) 362 6799.
Office also in: Montréal.
Canadian Embassy
Calle 30, No 518, esq. a 7a, Miramar, Havana, Cuba
Tel: (7) 332 516/7 *or* 332 382. Fax: (7) 332 044 *or* 331 069 (Visa section). Telex: 511586 (a/b CANCU).

	Health
GALILEO/WORLDSPAN: **TI-DFT/HAV/HE**	
SABRE: **TIDFT/HAV/HE**	
	Visa
GALILEO/WORLDSPAN: **TI-DFT/HAV/VI**	
SABRE: **TIDFT/HAV/VI**	

For more information on Timatic codes refer to Contents.

AREA: 110,860 sq km (42,803 sq miles).
POPULATION: 10,736,000 (1991 estimate).
POPULATION DENSITY: 96.8 per sq km.
CAPITAL: Havana. **Population:** 2,096,054 (1989).
GEOGRAPHY: Cuba is the largest Caribbean island and the most westerly of the Greater Antilles group, lying 145km (90 miles) south of Florida. A quarter of the country is fairly mountainous. West of Havana is the narrow Sierra de los Organos, rising to 750m (2461ft) and containing the Guaniguanicos hills in the west. South of the Sierra is a narrow strip of 2320 sq km (860 sq miles) where the finest Cuban tobacco is grown. The Trinidad Mountains, starting in the centre, rise to 1100m (3609ft) in the east. Encircling the port of Santiago are the rugged mountains of the Sierra Maestra. A quarter of the island is covered with mountain forests of pine and mahogany.
LANGUAGE: The official language is Spanish. Some English and French are spoken.
RELIGION: Roman Catholic majority.
TIME: GMT - 5 (GMT - 4 from first Sunday in April to Saturday before second Sunday in October).
ELECTRICITY: 110/120 volts AC, 60Hz. American-style flat 2-pin plugs are generally used, except in certain large hotels where the European round 2-pin plug is standard.
COMMUNICATIONS: Telephone: IDD to Havana only. Country code: 53. Outgoing international code: 00 (from Havana only – all other calls must be made through the international operator, and may be subject to long delays). **Telegram:** These may be sent from all post offices in Havana and from RCA offices in major hotels in large towns. **Post:** Letters to Western Europe can take several weeks. It is advisable to use the airmail service. **Press:** Papers are in Spanish, although the Communist Party daily newspaper, *Gramma*, publishes a weekly edition, called *Gramma International*, in English and French. All media is government-controlled.
BBC World Service frequencies: From time to time these change. See the section *How to Use this Book* for more information.
BBC:

MHz	17.84	15.22	9.915	5.975

PASSPORT/VISA

Regulations and requirements may be subject to change at short notice, and you are advised to contact the appropriate diplomatic or consular authority before finalising travel arrangements. Details of these may be found at the head of this country's entry. Any numbers in the chart refer to the footnotes below.

	Passport Required?	Visa Required?	Return Ticket Required?
Full British	Yes	Yes	Yes
BVP	Not valid	-	-
Australian	Yes	Yes	Yes
Canadian	Yes	Yes	Yes
USA	Yes	Yes	Yes
Other EU (As of 31/12/94)	Yes	Yes	Yes
Japanese	Yes	Yes	Yes

PASSPORTS: Valid passport required by all. Passports must be valid for at least 6 months beyond length of stay.
British Visitors Passport: Not acceptable.
VISAS: Required by all except:
(a) holders of a Tourist Card (see below);
(b) nationals of certain countries travelling on certain kinds of official business – enquire at Consulate.
Tourist Cards: Some specialist tour operators can issue a Tourist Card valid for one single trip. Stipulations are that the traveller pre-books and pre-pays hotel accommodation in Cuba through a tour operator officially recognised by Cuba. All passengers must hold tickets and other documentation required for their onward or return journey unless holding special annotation issued by a Cuban Consulate. Tourist Cards can be used within 6 months of issue and are valid for 30 days from date of entry; extensions are possible. The cost is £10.
Types of visa: Tourist (cost – £10); Business (cost – £25); Transit. Transit visas are not required by those exempt from visas (above) or passengers continuing their journey within 72 hours and holding onward tickets and enough funds for duration of stay (at least US$50 per day or the equivalent in other currency).
Validity: Tourist Cards for up to 6 months. Business visas for 3 months, depending on requirements. Enquire at Consulate.
Application to: Consulate (or Consular section at Embassy). For addresses, see top of entry.
Application requirements: *Tourist Cards:* (a) 1 completed application form. (b) Valid passport. (c)

Return ticket or travel agent voucher for pre-paid package tour. (d) Fee (payable in cash, by postal order or cheque).
Business visa: (a) Valid passport with one blank page. (b) 2 completed application forms. (c) 2 passport-size photos. (d) Details of business contact in Cuba. (e) Fee (payable in cash, by postal order or cheque).
Working days required: Tourist visa, 1 day. Business visa, 2 weeks.
Temporary residence: Enquire at Embassy.

MONEY

Currency: Cuban Peso (Cub$) = 100 centavos. Notes are in denominations of Cub$50, 20, 10, 5, 3 and 1. Coins are in denominations of Cub$1, and 40, 20, 5, 2 and 1 centavos.
Currency exchange: Money should be exchanged at official foreign exchange bureaux, banks or international air and sea ports, who issue receipts for transactions. At official tourist shops purchases are made only in US Dollars and in Tourism tokens (see below). Black marketeers may offer as much as 35 times the official rate for US Dollars, but tourists are advised to have nothing to do with them as severe penalties for black marketeering are imposed.
Credit cards: Visa and Access/Mastercard are accepted, but check with your credit card company for details of merchant acceptability and other services which may be available.
Travellers cheques: US Dollar, Sterling and other major currencies are accepted, but US Dollar cheques drawn on a US bank are not acceptable. Do not enter the place and date details on any travellers cheque or it will be refused. The white exchange paper received when a cheque is cashed must be kept with money and shown when money is spent.
Tourism tokens: Issued by the National Bank, these are in denominations equivalent to the US Dollar. They are intended to simplify the tourist's exchange transactions.
Exchange rate indicators: The following figures are included as a guide to the movements of the Cuban Peso against Sterling and the US Dollar:

Date:	Oct '92	Sep '93	Jan '94	Jan '95
£1.00=	1.19	1.16	1.12	1.56
$1.00=	0.75	0.76	0.76	1.00

Currency restrictions: The import and export of local currency is prohibited. There is no limit on the import of foreign currency but it must all be declared on arrival. Generally, a maximum of Cub$10 may be reconverted to foreign currency for re-export at the end of the stay but it may only be reconverted on presentation of a correctly filled out official exchange record.
Banking hours: 0830-1200 and 1330-1500 Monday to Friday; 0830-1030 Saturday.

DUTY FREE

The following goods may be taken into Cuba without incurring customs duty:
200 cigarettes or 50 cigars or 220g of tobacco; 2 litres of spirits; 5 bottles of perfume; gifts up to a value of US$100.
Prohibited items: Natural fruits or vegetables, meat and dairy products, weapons and ammunition, all pornographic material and drugs, jewellery. Certain animal and plant products, including shoes and items made from straw, may be disinfected on entry to Cuba.

PUBLIC HOLIDAYS

Since 1959 there have been no religious or ethnic festivals in Cuba.
Jan 1 '95 Liberation Day. **May 1** Labour Day. **Jul 25-27** Anniversary of the Attack on Moncada Barracks. **Oct 10** Commencement of the Independence Wars. **Jan 1 '96** Liberation Day.

HEALTH

Regulations and requirements may be subject to change at short notice, and you are advised to contact your doctor well in advance of your intended date of departure. Any numbers in the chart refer to the footnotes below.

	Special Precautions?	Certificate Required?
Yellow Fever	No	No
Cholera	No	No
Typhoid & Polio	1	-
Malaria	No	-
Food & Drink	2	-

[1]: There may be an occasional risk of polio; the level of typhoid risk is unknown but assumed to be low.
[2]: Mains water is chlorinated and, whilst relatively safe, may cause mild abdominal upsets. Bottled water is available and is advised for the first few weeks of stay. Milk is pasteurised and dairy products are safe for consumption. Local meat, poultry, seafoods and fruit are generally considered safe to eat.
Health care: Cuba's medical services are very good and first aid is available free to visitors. However, health insurance is advisable in case emergency repatriation is necessary.

TRAVEL - International

AIR: Cuba's national airline is *Cubana, Empresa Consolidada de Aviación (CU).*
Approximate flight times: From *London* to Havana is 10 hours, from *Los Angeles* is 9 hours and from *New York* is 5 hours.
International airport: *Havana (HAV)* (International José Martí) is 18km (11 miles) south of the city. Bus and taxi services to the city are available. Airport facilities include duty-free shops, bank, tourist information/hotel reservation and car rental. Visitors on package tours will be met by a *Cubatur* (the government tourist company) hostess. There are also international airports at Santiago de Cuba, Camagüey, Holguin and Varadero. Facilities at Havana and Santiago de Cuba have recently been upgraded.

TRAVEL - Internal

AIR: *Cubana* operates scheduled services between most main towns, but advance booking is essential as flights are limited.
RAIL: The principal rail route is from Havana to Santiago de Cuba, with two daily trains. Some trains on this route have air-conditioning and refreshments. There are also through trains from Havana to other big towns.
ROAD: Most sightseeing is pre-arranged and even when it is not, all internal travel arrangements are made through *Cubatur*. Traffic drives on the right. **Bus:** Most tours will include travel by air-conditioned buses. The Cubans themselves use the long-distance buses that link most towns; fares are cheap, services are reliable, but the buses can be very crowded, especially during the rush hour. **Taxi:** Taxis and chauffeur-driven cars are cheap but can be scarce. It is usual to order them through the hotel. Most new taxis have meters but fares should be pre-arranged in those that do not. There are both state-run and private taxi services. **Car hire:** *Havanautos* is the main national car rental agency. **Bicycles** can be hired.
Documentation: National driving licence or International Driving Permit required.
URBAN: Buses, minibuses and plentiful shared taxis operate in Havana at low, flat fares. Buses are frequent but often very crowded.
JOURNEY TIMES: The following chart gives approximate journey times (in hours and minutes) from Havana to other major towns in Cuba.

	Air	Road
Varadero	0.15	2.00
Trinidad	0.20	4.00
Santiago de Cuba	1.15	17.00
Playas del Este	-	0.20
Pinar del Rio	0.15	1.30

ACCOMMODATION

The range of accommodation available is expanding. The best hotels are in Havana or at Varadero Beach. Since many visitors to Cuba go as part of a package holiday the hotel will have been selected in advance. The hotels are clean, functional and adequate. The following organisation can offer further information: The Cuban Hotel Association, Plaza Hotel, Agramonte Street, Old Havana. Tel: (7) 338 583. Fax: (7) 338 592.

RESORTS & EXCURSIONS

Since the fifties, **Havana** has transformed itself from the notorious gambling centre of the Caribbean to the respectable capital of the Republic of Cuba. Apart from seeing the city on organised tours, the visitor can take a bus ride from one end of the town to the other, beginning in the former brothel quarter and ending in the beautiful suburbs of **Vedado** and **Miramar.** *Revolution Square* is an awe-inspiring sight with large tableaux of revolutionary heroes surrounding it. By way of contrast, the *Cathedral Square* in Old Havana has many ancient houses and cobbled streets.
Santa Clara, 288km (179 miles) east of Havana, is a busy city at the centre of the agricultural region.
Trinidad, 444km (276 miles) east of Havana, is an ancient city with the atmosphere of an old colonial town.
Camagüey, 563km (350 miles) east of Havana, is in the centre of a fertile plain and has long been the centre of Cuba's sugar industry. In 1666, it joined the long list of Caribbean ports sacked by Captain Henry Morgan, the notorious English pirate.
Santiago de Cuba, 933km (580 miles) east of Havana, is situated around a large natural harbour and was until 1549 the capital of Cuba. Santiago witnessed the start of the Cuban revolution when, in July 1953, Fidel Castro's troops stormed the Moncada Barracks.
Guama, 179km (111 miles) southeast of Havana in Matanzas Province, is a reconstructed Indian village. Set beside a broad lagoon, the vanished culture of Cuba's first inhabitants, who were wiped out by the early colonisers, is commemorated with sculptures showing Indians taking part in everyday activities. A holiday resort has also been constructed here; palm-wood cabins are linked by bridges that cross the lagoon.
Cienfuegos, 325km (202 miles) southeast of Havana, is a prosperous modern city built around a fine harbour.
Varadero, 130km (80 miles) northeast of Havana, situated along a sheltered peninsula, is one of the most famous resorts in Cuba. Villas, parks and hotels line a beach ideal for year-round swimming.

SOCIAL PROFILE

FOOD & DRINK: Restaurants (both table- and self-service) are generally inexpensive although the choice of food can be restricted due to shortages. Cuisine is continental or Cuban with a strong emphasis on seafood. Favourite dishes are omelettes, often stuffed with meat and/or cheese; a thick soup made of chicken or black beans; roast suckling pig; chicken and rice; *plantains* (green bananas) baked or fried; and local Cuban ice cream. Tour food served in hotels is not always exciting but it is adequate and will include chicken, fish, ham and cheese, fresh papaya, melon, pineapple, mangoes, bananas, fresh vegetables and green salads. Desserts are sweet and include pastries, flans, caramel custard, guava paste and cheese. **Drink:** Bars generally have waiter and counter service. Cuban coffee is very strong, but weaker British coffee is available. Cuban beer is tasty but weak. Spirits are reasonably priced, and rum is good and plentiful and used in excellent cocktails such as *daiquiris* and *mojitos* (pronounced 'meh-hee-to').
NIGHTLIFE: Nightlife is concentrated in Havana, Varadero Beach and in the major tourist resorts. Much entertainment may be planned by the visitor's guide or tour operator, and it is common to attend in organised groups. There is a choice of floor-show entertainments, nightclubs and theatres. The *Tropicana* nightclub stages spectacular open-air shows. Theatre, opera and ballet are staged all year round in Havana and seats are very cheap. Cinemas show films in Spanish, but some have subtitles.
SHOPPING: Special purchases include cigars, rum and local handicrafts. The main hotels have a few luxury shops stocked with East European items, especially radios and crystal. There are duty-free shops at the airport and in the centre of Havana. **Shopping hours:** 0900-1900 Monday to Friday.
SPORT: All sporting events are free in Cuba. Cuba participates in many sports in the Olympic Games. **Baseball** is the national sport; **soccer** and a variety of **ball games** are also played. There are many stadiums and sport, both playing and watching, is one of the national pastimes. **Watersports:** The best diving and fishing are to be had off the more remote beaches, which are difficult to get to without one's own transport.
SPECIAL EVENTS: Mar '95 *Jazz Festival.* **Dec** *Latin American Film Festival.* **Jan/Feb '96** *Carnival,* Varadero. For further details of festivals and special events in 1995/96, contact the Cuban Tourist Board.
SOCIAL CONVENTIONS: Handshaking is the normal form of greeting. Cubans generally address each other as *compañero,* but visitors should use *señor* or *señora.* Some Cubans have two surnames after their Christian name and the first surname is the correct one to use. Normal courtesies should be observed when visiting someone's home and a small gift may be given if invited for a meal. Dress is much less formal since the revolution. Cuban men wear *guayabera* (a light pleated shirt worn outside the trousers). Formal wear is not often needed and hats are rarely worn. Men should not wear shorts except on or near the beach. Women wear light cotton dresses or trousers during the day and cocktail dresses for formal evenings. **Tipping:** Moderate tipping is expected.

BUSINESS PROFILE

ECONOMY: The economy, which is entirely state-controlled, is primarily agricultural. The main crop is sugar, of which Cuba is the world's largest exporter. With the prevailing low world price throughout the 1980s, and the continuing US embargo, the Government has attempted to diversify into other crops. Tobacco and citrus fruits are of increasing importance. Cuban industry is largely devoted to food-processing but also produces cement, fertilisers, textiles, prefabricated buildings, agricultural machinery and domestic consumer goods. Tourism is a projected growth industry and Cuba has invested heavily in developing infrastructure for that purpose. Cuba's largest trading partner is the CIS by a considerable margin: the CIS buys much of the sugar produced on the island and supplies Cuba's oil requirements in exchange. The CIS' decision to reduce the built-in subsidy which covers this barter trade and demand hard currency payment will cause serious difficulties for the Cubans. The US embargo, through which Cuba was previously able to survive, is now biting much harder. Since the collapse of the Soviet economic bloc, COMECON, Cuba's main trading partners are now Argentina, Canada, China and Spain. These latter will now assume increasing importance in Cuba's trading relations, but the withdrawal of CIS support, particularly the provision of cheap oil, threatens to force Cuba back to the pre-industrial era. A challenging period of adjustment undoubtedly lies ahead.

BUSINESS: Courtesy is expected and hospitality should not be lavish, being offered to groups rather than individuals. Best months for business visits are November to April. **Office hours:** 0830-1230 and 1330-1630 Monday to Friday; some offices also open on alternate Saturdays from 0800-1700.

COMMERCIAL INFORMATION: The following organisation can offer advice: Cámara de Comercio de la República de Cuba, Calle 21, No 661/701, esq Calle A, Apartado 4237, Vedado, Havana. Tel: (7) 303 356. Fax: (7) 333 042. Telex: 511752.

CONFERENCES/CONVENTIONS: Further information can be obtained from Cubanacan Corporation, Calle 148, entre 11 y 13, Playa, Apartado 16046, Havana. Tel: (7) 202 578. Fax: (7) 336 046. Telex: 511316; *or* Cubatur Travel Agency, Havana. Fax: (7) 333 529.

CLIMATE

Hot, subtropical climate all year. Most rain falls between May and October and hurricanes can occur in autumn (August to November). Cooler months are January to April when the least rain falls.
Required clothing: Lightweight cottons and linens most of the year; the high humidity makes it unwise to wear synthetics close to the skin. Light waterproofs are advisable all year round.

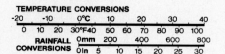

TEMPERATURE CONVERSIONS					
-20	-10	0°C	10	20	30	40

RAINFALL CONVERSIONS

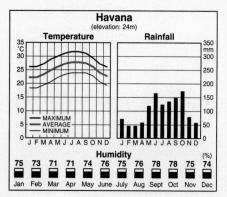

Havana
(elevation: 24m)

Humidity												(%)
75	73	71	71	74	76	75	76	78	78	75	74
Jan	Feb	Mar	Apr	May	June	July	Aug	Sept	Oct	Nov	Dec

Curaçao

Location: Caribbean, 56km (35 miles) north of Venezuela.

Curaçao Tourism Development Foundation (Tourism Development Bureau)
Pietermaai 19, Willemstad, Curaçao, NA
Tel: (9) 616 000. Fax: (9) 612 305. Telex: 1450.
Office of the Minister Plenipotentiary of the Netherlands Antilles
Antillenhuis, Badhuisweg 173-175, 2597 JP The Hague, The Netherlands
Tel: (70) 351 2811. Fax: (70) 351 2722. Telex: 31161.
Curaçao Tourism Development Bureau (UK Representative)
Axis Sales & Marketing Ltd, 421A Finchley Road, London NW3 6HJ
Tel: (0171) 431 4045. Fax: (0171) 431 7920.
Caribbean Tourism
Vigilant House, 120 Wilton Road, London SW1V 1JZ
Tel: (0171) 233 8382. Fax: (0171) 873 8551. Opening hours: 0900-1730 Monday to Friday.
British Consulate
PO Box 3803, Bombadiersweg Z/N, Willemstad, Curaçao, NA
Tel: (9) 369 533. Fax: (9) 369 533. Telex: 3372 (a/b EQIPNA).
Curaçao Tourist Board
Suite 2000, 475 Park Avenue South, New York, NY 10016
Tel: (212) 683 7660. Fax: (212) 683 9337.
Also deals with enquiries from Canada.
Consulate General of the United States of America
PO Box 158, St Anna Boulevard, Willemstad, Curaçao, NA
Tel: (9) 613 066. Fax: (9) 616 489. Telex: 1062 (a/b AMCON NA).
Canadian Consulate
PO Box 305, Maduro and Curiels Bank NV, Plaza Jojo Correa 2-4, Willemstad, Curaçao, NA
Tel: (9) 661 115. Fax: (9) 661 122 *or* 661 130. Telex: 1127 (a/b MCBNK/NA)

AREA: 444 sq km (171 sq miles).
POPULATION: 143,816 (1991 estimate).
POPULATION DENSITY: 323.9 per sq km.
CAPITAL: Willemstad. **Population:** 70,000 (1990).
GEOGRAPHY: Curaçao, the largest island in the Netherlands Antilles, is geographically part of the Dutch Leeward Islands, also known as the Dutch Antilles. It is flat, rocky and fairly barren due to its low rainfall. There are a large number of excellent beaches.
LANGUAGE: Dutch is the official language. Papiamento (a mixture of Portuguese, African, Spanish, Dutch and English) is the commonly used *lingua franca*; English and Spanish are also widely spoken.
RELIGION: The majority of the population is Roman Catholic, with Protestant minorities, both evangelical and other low-church denominations. There is also a Baha'i temple and a synagogue.
TIME: GMT - 4.
ELECTRICITY: 110/220 volts AC, 50Hz.
COMMUNICATIONS: Telephone: Good IDD service to Europe. Country code: 599. Outgoing international code: 00. Radio-telephone and operator services are available. **Telex/telegram:** Facilities available in most large hotels and in the post office in Willemstad. **Post:** Airmail to Western Europe takes four to six days. **Press:** The English-language daily is called *The Guardian*.

BBC World Service and Voice of America frequencies: From time to time these change. See the section *How to Use this Book* for more information.
BBC:

MHz	15.26	11.75	9.915	5.975

Voice of America:

MHz	15.20	11.91	9.590	5.995

PASSPORT/VISA

Regulations and requirements may be subject to change at short notice, and you are advised to contact the appropriate diplomatic or consular authority before finalising travel arrangements. Details of these may be found at the head of this country's entry. Any numbers in the chart refer to the footnotes below.

	Passport Required?	Visa Required?	Return Ticket Required?
Full British	Yes	No	Yes
BVP	Valid/1	-	-
Australian	Yes	4	Yes
Canadian	3	4	Yes
USA	2	4	Yes
Other EU (As of 31/12/94)	1	4/5	Yes
Japanese	Yes	4	Yes

PASSPORTS: Valid passport required by all except:
(a) [1] nationals of Belgium, Luxembourg and The Netherlands holding a tourist card, nationals of Germany holding a national identity card and UK nationals holding a British Visitors Passport;
(b) [2] nationals of the USA holding voters' registration cards or birth certificate, and alien residents of the USA with a certificate of US citizenship;
(c) [3] nationals of Canada with birth or baptism certificate or proof of citizenship, and alien residents of Canada holding a Canadian 'Certificate of Identity';
(d) nationals of San Marino holding a national ID card;
(e) nationals and alien residents of Venezuela, and travellers in Venezuela visiting the Netherlands Antilles, holding an identity card;
(f) nationals from Brazil, Mexico and Trinidad & Tobago visiting as bona fide tourists holding a valid identity card.
British Visitors Passport: Acceptable.
VISAS: [4] Visas are only required for nationals of the Dominican Republic resident there. All other nationals are allowed to stay in Curaçao for 14 days without a visa (but might need a Certificate of Admission, see below) provided they have a return or onward ticket and sufficient funds for length of stay. All visitors staying more than 90 days require a visa. Transit passengers staying no longer than 24 hours holding confirmed tickets and valid passports do not require visas or Certificates of Admission.
For stays of between 14 and 28 days a **Temporary Certificate of Admission** is required, which in the case of nationals of the following countries will be issued by the Immigration authorities on arrival in Curaçao:
(a) [5] Belgium, Germany, Luxembourg, The Netherlands, Spain and the UK;
(b) Bolivia, Burkina Faso, Chile, Colombia, Costa Rica, Czech Republic, Ecuador, Hungary, Israel, Jamaica, South Korea, Malawi, Mauritius, Niger, Philippines, Poland, San Marino, Slovak Republic, Swaziland and Togo.
The following must apply in writing at least one month *before* entering the country even for tourist purposes for a Certificate of Admission: nationals of Albania, Cambodia, China, CIS, Cuba, North Korea, Libya, Vietnam and holders of Zimbabwean passports issued on or after November 11, 1965.
All other nationals have to apply for the Certificate after 14 days of stay.
Further information about visa requirements may be obtained from the Office of the Minister Plenipotentiary of the Netherlands Antilles; and whilst Royal Netherlands Embassies do not formally represent the Netherlands Antilles in any way, they might also be able to offer limited advice and information. For addresses, see top of this entry and top of *The Netherlands* entry later in the book.
Temporary residence: Enquire at the Office of the Minister Plenipotentiary of the Netherlands Antilles.

MONEY

Currency: Netherlands Antilles Guilder or Florin (NAG) = 100 cents. Notes are in denominations of NAG500, 250, 100, 50, 25, 10 and 5. Coins are in denominations of NAG2.5 and 1, and 50, 25, 10, 5 and 1 cents. The currency is tied to the US Dollar.
Credit cards: Access/Mastercard, Diners Club, American Express and Visa are accepted in large establishments. Check with your credit card company for details of merchant acceptability and other services which may be available.

Travellers cheques: US currency cheques are the most welcome at points of exchange.
Exchange rate indicators: The following figures are included as a guide to the movement of the Netherlands Antilles Guilder against Sterling and the US Dollar:

Date:	Oct '92	Sep '93	Jan '94	Jan '95
£1.00=	2.83	2.74	2.64	2.80
$1.00=	1.78	1.79	1.79	1.79

Currency restrictions: The import and export of local currency is limited to NAG200; foreign currency is unrestricted. The import of Dutch or Suriname silver coins is forbidden.
Banking hours: 0830-1200 and 1330-1630 Monday to Friday.

DUTY FREE

The following items may be taken into Curaçao by those over 15 years of age without payment of duty:
400 cigarettes or 50 cigars or 250g of tobacco; 2 litres of alcoholic beverages; 250ml of perfume; gifts up to the value of NAG100.

PUBLIC HOLIDAYS

Jan 1 '95 New Year's Day. **Feb 27** Lenten Carnival. **Apr 14** Good Friday. **Apr 17** Easter Monday. **Apr 30** Queen's Day. **May 1** Labour Day. **May 25** Ascension Day. **Jul 2** Curaçao Day. **Dec 25-26** Christmas. **Jan 1 '96** New Year's Day. **Feb 19** Lenten Carnival. **Apr 5** Good Friday. **Apr 8** Easter Monday.
Note: Check with the tourist board for full details.

HEALTH

Regulations and requirements may be subject to change at short notice, and you are advised to contact your doctor well in advance of your intended date of departure. Any numbers in the chart refer to the footnotes below.

	Special Precautions?	Certificate Required?
Yellow Fever	No	1
Cholera	No	No
Typhoid & Polio	Yes	-
Malaria	No	-
Food & Drink	2	-

[1]: A yellow fever certificate is required from travellers over six months of age coming from infected areas.
[2]: All mains water on the island is distilled from seawater, and is thus safe to drink. Bottled mineral water is widely available. Milk is pasteurised and dairy products are safe for consumption. Local meat, poultry, seafood, fruit and vegetables are generally considered safe to eat.
Health care: There is a large and well-equipped modern hospital in Willemstad. Health insurance is recommended.

TRAVEL - International

AIR: The national airline of the Netherlands Antilles is *ALM (LM)*.
Approximate flight times: From Curaçao to *London* is 11 hours (depending on connection time), to *Los Angeles* is 12 hours and to *New York* is 6 hours.
International airport: *Curaçao (CUR)* (Hato) is 12km (7 miles) from Willemstad. Airport facilities include duty-free shop, bar, restaurant, buffet, bank, post office, hotel reservation facilities and car hire. Taxis are available to Willemstad.
Departure tax: Approximately NAG18 (US$10) per person; children under two years of age and passengers transiting within 24 hours are exempt.
SEA: Over 200 cruises arrive in Curaçao from America and Europe. A ferry sails regularly between Venezuela and Curaçao.

TRAVEL - Internal

AIR: *Windward Islands Air International (SXM)* operates to Saba (SAB) and St Eustatius (EUX).

Departure tax: NAG10 for all internal flights.
ROAD: Traffic drives on the right. A good public **bus** service runs throughout the island and many of the main hotels provide their own **minibus** services to Willemstad.
Taxi: These are plentiful as are **car hire** firms (both international and local), which are located at the airport and in the main hotels, as well as in the capital.
Documentation: An International Driving Licence is required.

ACCOMMODATION

HOTELS: There are a dozen or so luxury hotels on Curaçao, all offering air-conditioning, restaurants, swimming pools and/or beach access, and a choice between European Plan (room only) and Modified American Plan (half-board). Most also offer some sort of in-house entertainment, a baby-sitting service and cable TV. Some have their own casinos. Out-of-town hotels provide their guests with free transport to and from Willemstad. A 5-10% government tax and 10% service charge are levied on all hotel bills. For more information, contact the Curaçao Hotel and Tourism Association, PO Box 6115, International Trade Centre, Willemstad. Tel: (9) 636 260 *or* 636 385. Fax: (9) 636 445.
GUEST-HOUSES: For details of more modest accommodation – guest-houses, commercial hotels and self-catering – contact any of the organisations listed at the top of this entry.

RESORTS & EXCURSIONS

Willemstad, the capital, is noted for its very brightly coloured, Dutch-style houses and range of other interesting and complementary architectural styles, including *Cunucu* houses (based on African-style mud and wattle huts), thatched cottages and country houses. It is one of the finest shopping centres in the Caribbean. Monuments of interest in the city include the *Statue of Manuel Piar,* a famous freedom fighter, and two statues associated with the Second World War: one given by the Dutch royal family to the people of Curaçao (in recognition of their support), and one in commemoration of those who lost their lives. The mustard-coloured *Fort Amsterdam,* now the seat of government of the Netherlands Antilles, stands at the centre of historic Willemstad, which from 1648-1861 was a fortified town of some strategic importance. The fort's church, still standing,

doubled as a storehouse for provisions put by in case of siege; specially designed storerooms for food, sails and other essentials may still be seen. A cannonball is still embedded in the church's southwest wall. Nearby is the present Governor's Residence, dating back to the Dutch colonial days. Also worth seeing are the *Queen Emma Pontoon* bridge and the *Queen Juliana Bridge*. The latter spans the harbour at a height of 490m (1600ft). The harbour itself has a floating market where colourful barges full of agricultural produce can be seen. Nearby is the new market building, the design of which is very striking. The market comes to life after 0600 on a Saturday morning. The architecture of the **Scharloo** area, reached by crossing the *Wilhelmina drawbridge*, is fascinating, dating from as early as 1700. The *Mikvé Israel Synagogue* is the oldest in the Americas and, like the Jewish *Beth Heim Cemetery*, is worth a visit. Its courtyard museum has a fine collection of historical artefacts.

Excursions: Besides the excellent beaches and hotel resorts, the island itself has a number of other points of interest, which the visitor with only a couple of days on the island can easily see. Just outside Willemstad is the modern site of the Netherlands Antilles University, and further along the western road is the *Landhuis Papaya* (a country house), the *Ceru Grandis* (a 3-storey plantation house) and the driftwood beach of **Boca San Pedro**. Also of note is *Boca Tabla*, the thundering underwater cave of the north coast and the picturesque fishing village of **Westpoint**. **St Christoffel National Park,** occupying the most northwestern part of the island, is a nature reserve dominated by the *St Christoffel Mountain*. There are several caves decorated with Arawak Indian paintings, some unusual rock formations and many fine views across the countryside – the ruins of the *Zorguliet Plantation* and the privately owned *Savonet Plantation* and the *Savonet Museum* may be seen at the base of the mountain; the latter dates back to the 18th century and is still in use today. The indigenous flora includes orchids and some very interesting evergreens. As well as the interesting birdlife, the visitor to St Christoffel Park might see iguanas and the shy Curaçao deer. Well worth a visit are the interesting **Caves of Hato**. Magnificent stalactite formations, wall paintings and underground streams with cascading waterfalls can be seen within the 4900m (16,076ft) labyrinth.

SOCIAL PROFILE

FOOD & DRINK: Traditional Dutch food (particularly using fresh seafood and cheeses) is popular, as well as the exciting flavours of Creole food, *criollo*, which also makes good use of the great variety of fresh fish. French, Italian and other international cuisines are also on offer. Restaurant styles vary from informal bistro to the very expensive. **Drink:** A wide variety of alcohol is available.

NIGHTLIFE: There are several discos run by hotels on the island and some hotels have a casino. Performances of drama and music can be found at the *Centro Pro Arte*.

SHOPPING: Curaçao (and other Netherlands Antilles islands) is a thriving centre for duty-free shopping. An enormous range of imported goods is on sale at considerably reduced prices. Locally made curios are available for the tourist, a particularly popular souvenir being 'Curaçao' liqueur, which is made from sun-dried peel of a bitter orange and a mixture of spices. **Shopping hours:** 0800-1200 and 1400-1800 Monday to Saturday.

SPORT: Like the other islands of the Caribbean, **watersports** are widely promoted and facilities on Curaçao itself are well developed. There are excellent beaches for **swimming** (some charge an entrance fee). **Windsurfing, sailing** and **water-skiing** are popular on the island and the hotels and watersports centres are well-equipped. **Snorkelling, scuba diving** and **deep-sea fishing** are also popular with the visitor and there are plenty of opportunities to participate in these sports, as well as the chance of lessons for the amateur. Other sports provided on the island include **tennis, squash** and **golf** (at the Shell 9-hole golf course). **Horseriding** is also possible.

SPECIAL EVENTS: Apr 14-22 '95 *Curaçao International Sailing Regatta.* **Apr 17** *Easter Folkloric Parade* (Seu). **Apr 30** *Inter-island Drag Races.* **Apr 30-May 2** *International Food Festival* (Rust en Burg). **May** *KLM Jazz Festival* (Rust en Burg); *Merengue Festival.* **Jul** *Inter-island Drag Races.* **Aug** *Curaçao Salsa Festival.* **Sep** *Tourism Week; Golden Artists Music Festival.* **Oct 30** *Oktoberfest; Miss Hawaiian Tropic.* **Nov** *8th Curaçao Jazz Festival; 'Sint Nicolaas' arrives at St Anna Bay.* Carnivals are staged throughout the island every year during the week preceding Lent.

SOCIAL CONVENTIONS: The social influences are predominantly Dutch, combined with Indian and African traditions. Dress for men should include tropical lightweight suits for business appointments and formal wear for evening engagements. Similarly, women should take some evening wear, but dress for daytime is casual. Swimwear should be confined to the beach and poolside only. **Tipping:** Hotels add a 5-10% government tax and a 10% service charge. Barmen, waiters and doormen expect a 10% tip.

BUSINESS PROFILE

ECONOMY: Curaçao is the most prosperous of the Netherlands Antilles island group. It depends less on oil refining and transhipment – a business which has experienced a marked decline in recent years – than, say, Aruba. The capital Willemstad is the centre of a network of 'offshore' banking facilities and other financial services. Curaçao also houses one of the largest dry docks in the Western Caribbean although, far from being lucrative, the Curaçao Dry Dock Company turned in regular losses during the 1980s – a situation since rectified. Import substitution has been successfully pursued, so that a wide range of consumer goods from beer and paint to toilet paper are now produced locally. Venezuela, which supplies the crude oil for refinement, and the United States, which buys most of the finished product, are the largest trading partners.

BUSINESS: Suits should be worn and punctuality is essential. **Office hours:** 0800-1200 and 1330-1630 Monday to Friday.

COMMERCIAL INFORMATION: The following organisation can offer advice: Curaçao Chamber of Commerce and Industry, PO Box 10, Kaya Junior Salas 1, Willemstad. Tel: (9) 611 455. Fax: (9) 615 652.

CLIMATE

Hot throughout the year, but tempered by cooling trade winds. The main rainy season is from October to December. The annual mean temperature is 26°C, rainfall is 515mm and humidity is 75.9%. The island lies outside the Caribbean 'hurricane belt'.

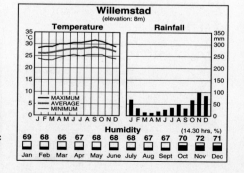

Willemstad
(elevation: 8m)

Temperature / Rainfall / Humidity

	Jan	Feb	Mar	Apr	May	June	July	Aug	Sept	Oct	Nov	Dec
Humidity (14.30 hrs, %)	69	68	66	67	68	68	68	67	67	70	72	71

Cyprus

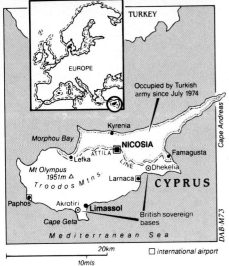

TURKEY

EUROPE

Occupied by Turkish army since July 1974

Kyrenia

Morphou Bay

NICOSIA

Lefka

Famagusta

ATTILA LINE

Mt Olympus 1951m △

Dhekelia

Troodos Mtns

Larnaca

CYPRUS

Paphos

Akrotiri

Limassol

Cape Geta

British sovereign bases

Cape Andreas

Mediterranean Sea

20km

10mls

□ *international airport*

Location: Europe, eastern Mediterranean.

Note: Since the summer of 1974, the part of the island north of a line drawn roughly between Morphou Bay and Famagusta has been occupied by Turkish troops. All the information given in this section refers to the southern part of the island, the Republic of Cyprus.

Cyprus Tourism Organisation
PO Box 4535, 19 Limassol Avenue, Melkonian Building, Nicosia, Cyprus
Tel: (2) 315 715. Fax: (2) 313 022. Telex: 2165.
High Commission of the Republic of Cyprus
93 Park Street, London W1Y 4ET
Tel: (0171) 499 8272. Fax: (0171) 491 0691. Telex: 263343. Opening hours: 0930-1645 Monday to Friday.
Consular section: Tel: (0171) 629 5350. Fax: (0171) 491 0691. Opening hours: 0930-1300 Monday to Friday.
Honorary High Commission
University Precinct, Oxford Road, Manchester M13 9RN
Tel: (0161) 273 4321. Fax: (0161) 274 3555. Opening hours: 0900-1730 Monday to Friday.
Cyprus Tourism Organisation
213 Regent Street, London W1R 8DA
Tel: (0171) 734 9822 *or* 734 2593. Fax: (0171) 287 6534. Telex: 263068. Opening hours: 1000-1800 Monday to Friday.
British High Commission
PO Box 1978, Alexander Pallis Street, Nicosia, Cyprus
Tel: (2) 473 131/7. Fax: (2) 367 198. Telex: 2208 (a/b UKREPNIC CY).
Embassy of the Republic of Cyprus
2211 R Street, NW, Washington, DC 20008
Tel: (202) 462 5772. Fax: (202) 483 6710.
Consulate General of the Republic of Cyprus
13 East 40th Street, New York, NY 10018
Tel: (212) 686 6016/7/8.
Cyprus Tourism Organisation
13 East 40th Street, New York, NY 10016
Tel: (212) 683 5280. Fax: (212) 683 5282.
Also deals with enquiries from Canada.
Embassy of the United States of America
PO Box 4536, Metochiou and Ploutarchou Street, Engomi, Nicosia, Cyprus
Tel: (2) 476 100. Fax: (2) 465 944. Telex: 4160 (a/b AMEMY CY).

Honorary Consulate of the Republic of Cyprus
Suite PH2, 2930 Edouard Montpetit Street, Montréal, Québec H3T 1J7
Tel: (514) 398 6294.
Consulate also in: Calgary.
Canadian Consulate
PO Box 2125, Suite 403, Margarita House, 15 Themistocles Dervis Street, Nicosia, Cyprus
Tel: (2) 451 630. Fax: (2) 459 096. Telex: 2110 (a/b MACRO CY).

AREA: 9251 sq km (3572 sq miles).
POPULATION: 706,900 (1991 estimate, including population of Turkish-occupied region).
POPULATION DENSITY: 75.1 per sq km.
CAPITAL: Nicosia. **Population:** 171,000 (1991).
GEOGRAPHY: Cyprus is an island in the eastern Mediterranean. The landscape varies between rugged coastlines, sandy beaches, rocky hills and forest-covered mountains. The Troodos Mountains in the centre of the island rise to almost 1950m (6400ft) and provide excellent skiing during the winter. Between these and the range of hills which runs eastward along the north coast and the 'panhandle' is the fertile Messaoria Plain. The Morphou Basin runs around the coast of Morphou Bay in the west.
LANGUAGE: The majority speak Greek and about 25% speak Turkish. The Greek Cypriot dialect is different from mainland Greek. Turkish is spoken by Turkish Cypriots. English, German and French are spoken in tourist centres.
RELIGION: Greek Orthodox, with Muslim minority.
TIME: GMT + 2 (GMT + 3 from last Sunday in March to Saturday before last Sunday in September).
ELECTRICITY: 240 volts AC, 50Hz. There are two types of plug in use, 5-amp round 3-pin and 13-amp square 3-pin (UK-type).
COMMUNICATIONS: Telephone: Full IDD is available. Country code: 357. Outgoing international code: 00. **Fax:** This is available at district post offices in Nicosia, Larnaca, Limassol and Paphos. **Telex/telegram:** There are no public telex facilities at present but most hotels will allow guests use of their facilities. A 24-hour service is available via Nicosia. There are telegraph links to the international network through major hotels and the Central Telegraph Office, Egypt Avenue, Nicosia. A 24-hour service is provided with three charge rates. **Post:** There are daily airmail services to all developed countries. Service to Europe takes three days. *Poste Restante* facilities are available in main cities and resorts. Post office opening hours: 0730-1330 Monday to Friday; 1500-1800 Thursday. **Press:** Newspapers published in English are the *Cyprus Mail* (daily) and the *Cyprus Weekly*. All others are in Greek and Turkish.
BBC World Service and Voice of America frequencies: From time to time these change. See the section *How to Use this Book* for more information.
BBC:

MHz	17.64	12.09	9.410	6.180

Voice of America:

MHz	9.67	6.04	6.18	1.32

In addition, the CTO sponsors programmes for tourists on 603kHz (498m) and FM94.8 Monday to Saturday. The times are as follows: German 0800; English 0830; French 0900; Swedish 0930; Arabic 1000.

PASSPORT/VISA

Regulations and requirements may be subject to change at short notice, and you are advised to contact the appropriate diplomatic or consular authority before finalising travel arrangements. Details of these may be found at the head of this country's entry. Any numbers in the chart refer to the footnotes below.

	Passport Required?	Visa Required?	Return Ticket Required?
Full British	Yes	No	Yes
BVP	Not valid	-	-
Australian	Yes	No	Yes
Canadian	Yes	No	Yes
USA	Yes	No	Yes
Other EU (As of 31/12/94)	Yes	No	Yes
Japanese	Yes	No	Yes

PASSPORTS: Valid passport required by all.
Note: Passports must be valid for up to 3 months after day of departure for visitors not requiring visas. Those requiring visas must have passports valid for up to 6 months beyond length of stay.
British Visitors Passport: Not accepted.
VISAS: Required by all except the following, who can stay for up to 3 months without a visa:
(a) nationals of countries referred to in the chart above;
(b) nationals of Commonwealth countries (except

nationals of Bangladesh, Bermuda and Pakistan who *do* require visas);
(c) nationals of Austria, Bahrain, Fiji, Finland, Iceland, Kuwait, Liechtenstein, Norway, Oman, Poland, Qatar, Romania, San Marino, Saudi Arabia, South Africa, Sweden, Switzerland, United Arab Emirates and Yugoslavia*;
(d) nationals of Hungary for up to 30 days.
Note [*]: This applies to nationals of Yugoslavia with passports issued *before* the outbreak of the country's current internal conflict (1990). It is advisable to check with the Consular section of the High Commission or Embassy. For addresses, see top of entry.
Types of visa: Ordinary: £6.90; Transit: free. Payable by cash or postal order only. Nationals of Bulgaria, Estonia, former Czechoslovakia*, Egypt, Israel, CIS, Latvia, Lithuania, Syria and the Vatican City are exempted from visa payment provided they have onward or return tickets and sufficient funds to cover the duration of their stay.
Note [*]: This only applies to visitors holding passports issued prior to January 1, 1992. Those with separate Czech or Slovak passports should check with the Consular section of the Embassy.
Validity: Maximum of 3 months from date of issue.
Transit: Transit visas are valid for travel through Cyprus, providing the traveller does not stay on the island for a period exceeding 5 days, and is in possession of visas and through tickets for the destination country.
Application to: Consulate (or Consular section at Embassy or High Commission). For addresses, see top of entry.
Application requirements: (a) Passport must be valid for at least 6 months for applicants requiring visas. (b) 2 completed application forms. (c) 3 passport-size photos. (d) Proof of sufficient funds to cover duration of stay. (e) Onward or return ticket. (f) For business trips, an introductory letter from the applicant's company giving details and nature of business to be conducted.
Working days required: Same day, or up to 6 weeks if application needs to be referred to Cyprus.
Temporary residence: Enquire at Embassy or High Commission, addresses above.

MONEY

Currency: Cyprus Pound (C£) = 100 cents. Notes are in denominations of C£10, 5 and 1, and 50 cents. Coins are in denominations of 50, 20, 10, 5, 2, 1 and 0.5 cents. Cents are informally known as 'shillings'.
Currency exchange: Visitors wishing to obtain non-Cypriot currency at Cypriot banks for business purposes are advised that this is only possible by prior arrangement.
Credit cards: Access/Mastercard, American Express, Visa and Diners Club are accepted. Check with your credit card company for details of merchant acceptability and other services which may be available.
Travellers cheques: May be cashed in all banks.
Exchange rate indicators: The following figures are included as a guide to the movements of the Cyprus Pound against Sterling and the US Dollar:

Date:	Oct '92	Sep '93	Jan '94	Jan '95
£1.00=	0.73	0.76	0.77	0.74
$1.00=	0.46	0.50	0.52	0.48

Currency restrictions: Foreign currency of more than the equivalent of US$1000 must be declared. The import and export of local currency is limited to a maximum of C£50.
Banking hours: Generally 0815-1230 Monday to Friday; certain banks may also open on weekday afternoons, except Tuesday, in tourist areas 1530-1730 (winter) and 1630-1830 (summer).

DUTY FREE

The following goods may be imported into Cyprus without incurring customs duty:
*200 cigarettes or 50 cigars or 250g of tobacco; 1 litre of spirits; 1 litre of wine; *300ml of perfume and eau de toilette; goods (excluding jewellery) up to C£50.*
Note [*]: To include no more than 150ml of perfume in one bottle.

PUBLIC HOLIDAYS

Jan 1 '95 New Year's Day. **Jan 6** Epiphany. **Mar 6** Green Monday. **Mar 25** Greek National Day. **Apr 1** Greek Cypriot National Day. **Apr 21** Good Friday. **Apr 24** Easter Monday. **May 1** Labour Day. **May 19** Youth and Sports Day. **Jun 12** Pentecost-Kataklysmos. **Aug 15** Assumption. **Oct 1** Cyprus Independence Day. **Oct 28** Greek National Day. **Dec 25-26** Christmas. **Jan 1 '96** New Year's Day. **Feb 2** Green Monday. **Apr 4** Good Friday. **Apr 14** Easter Sunday. **Apr 15** Easter Monday.

HEALTH

Regulations and requirements may be subject to change at short notice, and you are advised to contact your doctor well in advance of your intended date of departure. Any numbers in the chart refer to the footnotes below.

	Special Precautions?	Certificate Required?
Yellow Fever	No	No
Cholera	No	No
Typhoid & Polio	No	No
Malaria	No	No
Food & Drink	1	-

[1]: Milk is pasteurised and tap water is generally safe to drink. Powdered and tinned milk is available. Only eat well-cooked meat and fish, preferably served hot. Pork, salad and mayonnaise may carry increased risk. Vegetables should be cooked and fruit peeled.

Health care: No health agreement exists with the UK but benefits are available if arranged with the Department of Health before departure (see *Health* section at the back of the book).

TRAVEL - International

Note: Since October 1974 the Cyprus Government has declared the ports of Famagusta and Kyrenia, and the airport of Ercan, as illegal 'ports of entry' to Cyprus. Tourists entering through these illegal ports of entry will be refused entry to the government-controlled areas. Further details can be obtained from the Cyprus Tourism Organisation (for addresses, see top of entry).

AIR: Cyprus's national airline is *Cyprus Airways (CY).* For free advice on air travel, call the Air Travel Advisory Bureau in the UK on (0171) 636 5000 (London) *or* (0161) 832 2000 (Manchester).

Approximate flight times: From *London* to both Paphos and Larnaca is 4 hours 30 minutes, from *Paris* is 3 hours 30 minutes, from *Zurich* is 3 hours, from *Frankfurt/M* is 3 hours 30 minutes, from *Athens* to Cyprus is 1 hour 40 minutes and from *Stockholm* to Cyprus is 5 hours.

International airports: *Larnaca (LCA)* is 8km (5 miles) south of the city (travel time – 10 minutes). Airport facilities include outgoing duty-free shop, tourist information, car hire, bank/bureau de change (available 24 hours), bar, restaurant and a Cyprus Hotel Information and Reservation Office.

Paphos (PFO) is 11km (7 miles) east of the city (travel time – 25 minutes). Airport facilities include outgoing duty-free shop, car hire, bank/bureau de change, bar and restaurant.

SEA: Shipping lines connect the island with Greece, Israel, Egypt and Italy. For details, contact the Cyprus Tourism Organisation (for addresses, see top of entry).

TRAVEL - Internal

ROAD: Bus: Services connect all towns and villages on the island. Service is efficient and cheap. Although the local buses are slow, they are a good way of seeing the more remote villages. **Taxi:** These run between all the main towns on the island. Fares are regulated by the Government and all taxis have meters. *Service Taxis* offer an excellent, cheap service using 7-seat taxis running fixed routes between main points. Taxis run to a timetable and delivery is door to door. Fares under this system are often one-tenth of the usual rate. **Car hire:** Cars are one of the best ways to explore the island. They may be hired at airports and commercial centres, but should be reserved well in advance during the summer season. Reduced tariffs are offered if cars are hired for more than a week. Road signs are in both Greek and English. Traffic drives on the left. **Documentation:** An International Driving Permit or national driving licence is accepted for one year.

URBAN: Nicosia has its own privately-run bus company operating efficient services at flat fares. Taxis are widely available; a 15% surcharge is in operation from 2300-0600. Tipping is expected.

JOURNEY TIMES: The following chart gives approximate journey times (in hours and minutes) from Nicosia to other main towns and tourist centres in Cyprus.

	Road
Limassol	1.00
Paphos	2.15
Larnaca	0.30
Ayia Napa	1.10
Platres	1.30
Protaras	2.00
Polis	2.30

ACCOMMODATION

Types of accommodation include hotel apartments, tourist apartments, furnished apartments and tourist houses, tourist villas, hotels without a star, guest-houses, camping and youth hostels.

HOTELS: There are over 500 hotels and hotel apartments scattered throughout the island. There are also simple hotels that are ungraded. A service charge of 10% and a 3% tax are added to bills. Most hotels and hotel apartments offer discounts during the low season, which for seaside resorts is from November 1 to March 31 (excluding the period December 20 to January 6) and for hill resorts from October 1 to June 30. There are discounts for children occupying the same room as their parents: *under 1 year,* by private arrangement; *1-6 years,* 50% discount; *6-10 years,* 25% discount. **Grading:** Hotels range from deluxe **5-** to **1-star**. Hotel apartments are classified A, B or C. The range of accommodation in Cyprus is classified by the Cyprus Tourism Organisation as consisting of hotels with a star-classification system; this indicates facilities offered, physical criteria, room size and the cost, according to the class chosen.

For further information, contact the Cyprus Tourism Organisation, which controls and regulates hotels (for contact numbers, see top of entry) *or* the Cyprus Hotel Association, PO Box 4772, Nicosia. Tel: (2) 366 435. Fax: (2) 467 593. Telex: 2077 (a/b CHAMBER CY).

GUEST-HOUSES: Located mainly in Nicosia and Limassol.

CAMPING/CARAVANNING: There are four organised camping sites: Polis (open March-October, tel: (6) 321 526), Troodos (open May-October, tel: (5) 421 624), Forest Beach (east of Larnaca, tel: (4) 622 414) and Ayia Napa (open March-October, tel: (3) 721 946).

YOUTH HOSTELS: These are only open to members of the International Youth Hostels Association: apply either to the Nicosia or Limassol Youth Hostels for membership. There are hostels at 5 Hadjidaki Street, **Nicosia** (off Themistoklis Dervis Street, tel: (2) 444 808 *or* 442 027); at 37 Eleftherios Venizelos Avenue, **Paphos** (tel: (6) 232 588); **Troodos Mountains** (open April-October, tel: (5) 421 669); and at 27 Nicolaou Rossou Street, **Larnaca** (near St Lazarus Church, tel: (4) 442 027).

RESORTS & EXCURSIONS

NICOSIA: Nicosia, the capital of Cyprus since the 12th century, is situated at the heart of the *Messaoria Plain.* It is currently divided by the UN buffer zone that separates the Turkish-occupied north of the island and the government-controlled south. The old city, which has many quaint and ancient shops, is defined by walls built by the Venetians. Other attractions in Nicosia include the *Cyprus Museum, the Folk Art Museum*, the old and new *Arch-episcopal palaces, St John's Cathedral*, the *Makarios Foundation Art Gallery* and the Byzantine churches. At the end of May the annual *International State Fair* and the *Nicosia Art Festival* are held in Nicosia.

Outside Nicosia, near **Deftera**, there is a new riding school and sports centre.

Excursions: Nicosia District extends westwards into the vine-covered **Troodos Mountains**, where there are magnificent forests and valleys, and hill resorts such as **Kakopetria**, and the Byzantine churches in **Galata**. The area offers some interesting excursions including: the *Royal Tombs and Ayios Heraklidios Monastery* at **Tamassos**; the 5-dome church and the mosque in **Peristerona** village; the 12th-century church of *Assinou*, one of the finest examples of Byzantine art in the Middle East, in **Nikitari**; the church of *Stavros tou Ayiasmati* in **Platanistassa**; *St John Lampadistis Monastery* in **Kalopanayotis;** the *Panayia tou Araka Monastery* in **Lagoudera**; and the *Macheras Monastery*, about an hour's drive into the hills southwest of Nicosia. The area has countless other old churches and monasteries, including *Kykkos* (see *Hill Resorts* below) and *Araka*, containing impressive and well-preserved Byzantine frescoes and shrines, and also a few pagan shrines where the ancients worshipped their gods. **Pitsilia District** produces most of the grapes for the Commandaria wine. There are many attractive villages, such as **Zoopygi**, where almond and walnut trees grow, **Kalokhorio** and, further up, **Agros,** a village with a small hotel and a few holiday homes.

LIMASSOL: Limassol is the second-largest town in Cyprus and the island's main port. Its modern harbour is constantly being expanded to meet the demands of trade and passenger traffic. Limassol is also the centre of the wine industry in Cyprus; most of the vines used grow on the slopes of the **Troodos Mountains**. In September the town has a wine festival, during which wine and food are served free. At Carnival, held at the start of Lent, the town bursts into celebration with bands, gaily decorated floats and dancing. Limassol is rapidly becoming Cyprus' main tourist centre, with facilities such as the public tourist beach at **Dhassoudi**, backed by cafés and changing rooms. There is also a museum and public gardens with a small zoo and the castle.

Excursions: There are many places of historic and archaeological interest in and around Limassol. **Amathus,** 11km (7 miles) east of Limassol, was once the capital of a city-kingdom, but is now in ruins, partly covered by the sea. The *Acropolis*, *Necropolis* and the remains of an early Christian basilica can still be seen, as well as the new excavations in the lower part of the town. Further east lies the *Ayios Georgios Nunnery*, and to the west is *Kolossi Castle*, headquarters of the Knights of St John of Jerusalem. **Curium** has a superb Graeco-Roman theatre where concerts and Shakespeare's plays are performed in summer. The town has many sites of interest including the *House of Eustolios*, in which there are some beautiful mosaics; the *Sanctuary of Apollo Hylates;* the *Stadium;* the *Acropolis* with the ruins of the *Forum;* the *Christian Basilica* and many public buildings. To the south is the *Lady's Mile Beach* and *Akrotiri Salt Lake*, winter home of thousands of flamingoes. Limassol is also a good starting point for an excursion into the Troodos Mountains (see *Excur-sions* in *Nicosia* above).

PAPHOS: Built on a rocky escarpment, **Upper Paphos** commands a superb view of the coastline and the harbour of **Lower Paphos** is ringed by tavernas famous for their fish dishes. It is a place of historic and archaeological interest, including the remains of the *House of Dionysus*, a Roman villa with some fine mosaics, and the nearby *Villa of Theseus.* Other attractions include the *District Museum*, the castle overlooking the harbour, the *Tombs of the Kings*, the remains of the Byzantine castle of *Saranda Kolones* and the *Chrysopolitissa Basilica*, the biggest early Christian basilica on the island.

Excursions: Paphos is an excellent centre for exploration; eastwards the land rises through the vineyards, the forests and the Cedar Valley; northwards, the road leads over the foothills, passing close to the monastery of *Ayios Neophytos* (founded in AD1220), and down to the little town of **Polis** on the north coast. Polis is an unexploited and virtually undeveloped beach area with one tourist hotel, a campsite and a few self-catering establishments; accommodation is also possible in private homes. Nearby is the fishing harbour of **Latchi,** which offers a variety of fish dishes including grilled swordfish steak. Westwards from Latchi is an unspoilt beach; beyond is the little grotto known as *Fontana Amorosa.* North of Paphos is *Coral Bay* which has a bathing beach and several good restaurants. Further on is the fishing village of **Ayios Yeorgios tis Peyias** which has an early Christian basilica; and nearby is *Lara Beach* where a turtle hatchery has been established. In the opposite direction, towards Limassol, is the village of **Yeroskipos,** home of 'Turkish Delight', with a small but interesting folk museum.

LARNACA: Southeast Cyprus provides a complete contrast to the rest of the country. The one-time sleepy little town of Larnaca has now been brought to life by the nearby new international airport. There is also a new harbour with a number of deep-water berths, and a marina which accommodates up to 200 yachts. New hotels and apartment blocks have been built to keep pace with the town's growing popularity as a winter resort. The seafront is fringed by palm trees and cafés and tavernas. Other places of interest include *Ayia Phaneromeni Church,* dating from the 8th century BC and built over a rock cave; *Larnaca Fort,* the *District Museum* and the *Museum of the Pierides Family,* and the ruins of the ancient city of **Kition**. The feast of Kataklysmos (the Greek Orthodox Whitsun) is celebrated throughout Cyprus, but with special enthusiasm in Larnaca. Crowds from all over the district and from Nicosia arrive at the shore for watersports, singing, dancing, eating and drinking.

Excursions: Near the airport is the *Tekke* of **Hala Sultan**, standing in beautiful gardens on the edge of the *Salt Lake*, the winter home of migratory flamingoes. Nearby is the *Church of Panayia Angeloktisti* (meaning 'built by the angels'), containing a fine piece of Byzantine art – a 6th-century life-size mosaic of the Virgin Mary and Child.

Westwards is the village of **Lefkara**, famous for its lace, and the *Nunnery of Ayios Minas*; off the Limassol–Nicosia road stands *Stavrovouni Monastery*, the *Royal Chapel in Pyrga* and **Kornos** village, famous for its pottery. Further west is **Khirokitia**, which has the remains of one of the earliest settlements in Cyprus dating from 5800BC (neolithic period). To the east, *Larnaca Bay* has a public bathing beach with facilities comparable to those of Limassol, and several newly-built hotels.

ROYAL ARTEMIS MEDICAL CENTRE AND HEALTH CLUB

PAPHOS, CYPRUS
TEL: 236300. FAX: 243670.

GOOD PRICES ARRANGED FOR ELDERLY PEOPLE STAYING AT THE ARTEMIS HEALTH CLUB ON A MEDIUM TO LONG-TERM BASIS

A private medical, surgical, accident and emergency centre on 24 hour call. We provide specialist health care, first class private rooms, using the most up-to-date equipment and techniques. The clinic offers a team of well-established specialists, all experienced in the latest medical, surgical and health care techniques. Experienced emergency teams with our equipped private ambulance are on call 24 hours a day to visit patients in their hotel room, house or apartment.

The Royal Artemis Medical Centre and Health Club offers a friendly, pleasant environment with luxury single and double rooms which are tastefully decorated, fully air-conditioned with large glass doors leading to the balcony. All rooms include mini refrigerator, bathroom with whirlpool/spa, electrical supply for electric razors, emergency nurse call and maid service button, telephone, satellite and local television, radio and all the required modern medical equipment.

The Medical centre includes fully equipped intensive care vascular monitoring, ultrasound, radiology, biochemistry and other facilities necessary for the most up-to-date treatment of urgent conditions. Dental unit available for any problems you may have with your teeth. Consulting rooms, operating theatres, recovery and x-ray units. Full medical check up unit including cardiography, radiology, biochemical investigation, ultrasound and smear tests for women. Physiotherapy unit including indoor therapeutic salt-water heated swimming pool, spa bath. An experienced acupuncturist is available to help in special conditions.

The Health Club offers accommodation with 24-hour room service and the above mentioned facilities available for your use, as well as the pool bar and cafeteria, restaurant, sunbathing and garden area, pool table and table games.

You will automatically become a member of the Royal Artemis Health Club with the use of the swimming pool and spa free of charge.

The Medical Consultant will advise and hold talks on health related matters free of charge.

The Royal Artemis Medical Centre and Health Club is undoubtedly the international centre that can be trusted with your health and well-being. With experienced, friendly, and welcoming multi-lingual staff who are always available to give you any information you may require, you will feel with the Cypriot hospitality and the beautiful healthy weather that it is a home away from home.

Directors: Ch. Charalambous and Dr. Th. Theophilou.

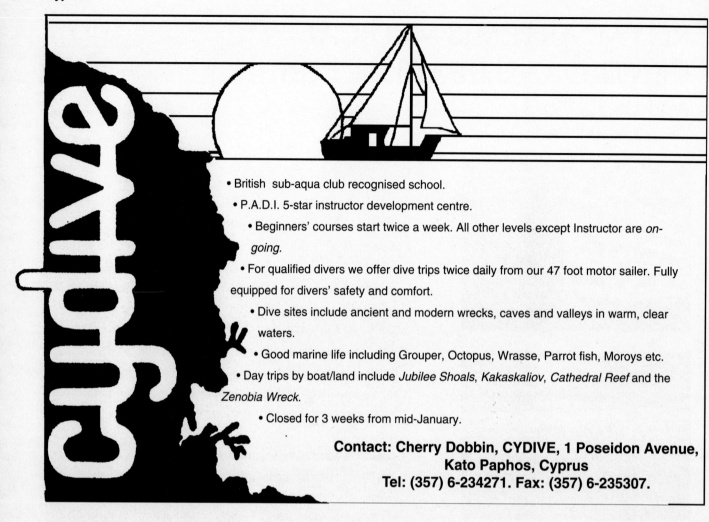

FAMAGUSTA DISTRICT: The town of Famagusta is in the zone occupied by the Turks, but much of what was once Famagusta District lies across the divide. There are excellent and comfortable hotels and hotel apartments of all categories. The whole of this area is very fertile, with many of the vegetable crops grown for export. To the southeast of Famagusta is an area famous for silvery beaches ideal for children. The village of **Ayia Napa** has a 16th-century Venetian Monastery, looking down on the fishing harbour. The village caters for the visitor with cafés, restaurants, *bouzouki* and Cypriot dancing shows, but still retains its local atmosphere. Around **Cape Greco** the coastline becomes indented with rocky coves and small sandy beaches, ideal for snorkelling, explorations by boat and picnics. *Fig Tree Bay*, *Flamingo Bay*, *Protaras* and *Pernera* beaches are among the most popular, each with cafés and beach bars. Inland, the little town of **Paralimni** also provides entertainment for the tourist with restaurants, discotheques and cafés.

HILL RESORTS: Platres, 1128m (3790ft) above sea level on the southern approaches to *Mount Olympus*, has many hotels to choose from. It is the ideal base for picnics and excursions through the forests and villages; many mountain villages offer accommodation of different categories with around 1958 beds between them. The scenery in this region is truly spectacular. Places of interest include *Phedoulas*, famous for its cherries (and their blossoms in spring) and other fruits; *Kalopanayiotis*, known for its variety of fruit; **Moutoullas**, the source of mineral water which is bottled and exported to the Middle East; **Stavros tis Psokas** where there is a controlled enclosure for the preservation of the *moufflon*, the wild sheep of Cyprus; **Prodromos,** the highest village in the island, 1400m (4600ft) above sea level, and claimed to grow the best apples; *Kykkos Monastery*, which houses a golden icon of the Virgin Mary; *Throni tis Panayias*, the tomb of the late Archbishop Makarios III in a setting so superb that it is worth a visit for this reason alone; the villages of **Moniatis, Saittas** and **Phini**, centres of a local pottery industry; *Mesapotamos Monastery* and the *Caledonian Falls*; **Omodhos** village and *Monastery of the Holy Cross* with its small *Folk Art Museum*; and the *Trooditssa Monastery*.

Kakopetria, 670m (2200ft) above sea level on the northeastern slopes of *Mount Olympus* and less than an hour's drive from Nicosia, is popular among those not suited to the higher altitudes. It is a village with a delightful central square shaded by plane trees where apples, pears and peaches grow. Like Platres, it is a centre for excursions into the surrounding landscape of forested mountains, deep gorges and fertile valleys.

WINTER SPORTS: Cyprus is becoming established as a winter destination with some hoteliers and tour operators offering off-peak incentives. Both **Platres** and **Kakopetria** are conveniently placed for the skiing season on Mount Olympus, which usually lasts from January to mid-March, but **Troodos** is actually the nearest resort to the skiing area; it has hotels and cafés. Although Cyprus is not well-known for its skiing, the *Troodos Mountains* offer excellent winter sports facilities and there are three ski-lifts on Mount Olympus. The Ski-Club, which is based in Troodos, has its own shelter and accepts tourists as temporary members. Ski equipment can be hired there.

SOCIAL PROFILE

FOOD & DRINK: Major resorts have bars and restaurants of every category. At larger hotels, the indigenous cuisine tends to have an 'international flavour' although authentic local dishes may also be available. All over the island there are restaurants offering genuine Cypriot food. Charcoal-grilled meat is very popular, as is fresh seafood. Dishes include *kebabs* (pieces of lamb or other meat skewered and roasted over a charcoal fire), *dolmas* (vine leaves stuffed with minced meat and rice), and *tava* (a tasty stew of meat, herbs and onions). One of the best ways of enjoying Cypriot food is by ordering *mezze* (snacks), a large selection of a number of different local dishes. Fresh fruit is plentiful and cheap, and very sweet desserts such as *baklava* are widely available. **Drink:** Waiter service is normal and in bars counter service is common. There are no licensing hours. Cyprus produces excellent wines, spirits and beer which can only be bought in the south. Coffee is Greek-style (short, strong and unfiltered), though cappuccino is available in most restaurants and bars. Traditional English tea can be bought everywhere. The highlight of the wine year is the annual wine festival, usually held in September, when free wine flows and local food is on offer. The festival is just one of many celebrated throughout the year in Limassol.

SHOPPING: Uniquely Cypriot purchases include handmade lace, woven curtains and table cloths, silks, basket work, pottery, silverware and leather goods. Jewellery is an art which has been practised on the island since the Mycenean period; craftsmen working in contemporary and traditional styles produce some very fine pieces. Silver spoons and forks are a traditional symbol of Cypriot hospitality. *Lefkaritika lace* is famous throughout the world as one of the products most closely associated with Cypriot workmanship (the name originates from the village Lefkara, situated on a hill on the the Nicosia–Limassol road). Other products include the simple baskets which have been made on the island for years, leather goods and pottery. The local wines and brandy also make good purchases. Imported goods sell at competitive prices, including cameras, perfume, porcelain, crystal, and of course the finest English fabrics. Shirts made to measure or ready to wear can be found at very low prices. **Shopping hours:** Shops are closed Wednesday and Saturday afternoons and all day Sunday, but otherwise opening hours are 0800-1300 and 1600-1900 (summer); 0800-1300 and 1430-1730 (winter).

SPORT: Horseriding, tennis, climbing, windsurfing, paragliding, swimming, fishing, sailing, diving, water-skiing, skindiving and, increasingly, **skiing** (see *Resorts & Excursions* above).

SPECIAL EVENTS: For a detailed list of festivals and other special events in Cyprus, contact the Cyprus Tourism Organisation. The following is a selection: **May '95** *Anthestiria Flower Festival,* throughout the country. **May 12-14** *7th International Classic Car Rally.* **May/Jun** *Makaria* (international sports festival), Nicosia. **May 25-Jun 4** *20th International Cyprus Trade Fair,* Nicosia. **Jun 12** *Kataklysmos,* throughout the country. **Jun 22-24** *Shakespeare Nights,* Kourion. **Jun-Aug** *Festival of Greek Plays.* **Aug 30-Sept 10** *Wine Festival,* Limassol. **Sep 15-Oct 15** *European Month of Culture,* Nicosia. **Sep 22-24** *23rd Rothman Cyprus Rally.*

SOCIAL CONVENTIONS: Respect should be shown for religious beliefs. Those visitors who leave the confines of their hotel and beach to explore Cyprus will find a warm reception waiting for them in the many

Soloi Theatre

villages. It is customary to shake hands and other normal courtesies should be observed. It is viewed as impolite to refuse an offer of Greek coffee or a cold drink. It is acceptable to bring a small gift of wine or confectionery, particularly when invited for a meal. For most occasions casual attire is acceptable. Beachwear should be confined to the beach or poolside. More formal wear is required for business and in more exclusive dining rooms, social functions, etc. **Tipping:** A service charge is added to all bills, but tipping is still acceptable and remains at the discretion of the individual.

BUSINESS PROFILE

ECONOMY: Cyprus has recovered well from the trauma of 1974, when almost the entire economy was destroyed or severely disrupted by the Turkish invasion and the ensuing fighting. Despite the lack of a political settlement, the economy in both sectors of the island has recovered well. The southern, Greek-Cypriot sector is predominantly agricultural, producing fruit and vegetables, potatoes, barley, citrus fruit and grapes for export. Tourism is the fastest growing sector, having now recovered to well beyond pre-invasion levels and light manufacturing producing clothing and footwear is showing steady improvement after major reorganisation during the 1980s. Clothing, in particular, makes an important contribution to exports. The UK is the largest single trading partner, while the

EU as a whole has now superseded Arab countries (Lebanon, Egypt, the Gulf States and Libya) in trading importance. Britain's sovereign military bases on the southern coast and near the partition boundary are a major source of revenue for the Government. Under a customs union agreement with the then EC, all trade barriers will be abolished by the end of a 15-year transition period ending in 2003. The southern Government made a formal application to join the Community in 1990. This was rejected by Brussels and Cyprus is likely to face continued exclusion until a political settlement is achieved.
BUSINESS: Cypriot businessmen have a tradition of hospitality and courtesy, and similar behaviour is expected from visitors. Avoid business visits in July and August. **Office hours:** All offices are closed half-day Wednesday, otherwise 0800-1300 and 1600-1900 Monday to Friday (summer); 0800-1300 and 1500-1800 Monday to Friday (winter).
COMMERCIAL INFORMATION: The following organisation can offer advice: Cyprus Chamber of Commerce and Industry, PO Box 1455, 38 Grivas Dhigenis Avenue, Nicosia. Tel: (2) 449 500 *or* 462 312. Fax: (2) 449 048. Telex: 2077 (a/b CHAMBER CY).
CONFERENCES/CONVENTIONS: Many hotels have facilities; seating for up to 1200 people is possible. Nicosia is a popular destination for budget-priced conferences and has a number of modern facilities. Advice can be obtained from the Cyprus Tourism Organisation in London (for address, see above).

CLIMATE

Warm Mediterranean climate. Hot, dry summers with mild winters during which rainfall is most likely.
Required clothing: Lightweight cottons and linens during summer months; warmer mediumweights and rainwear during the winter.

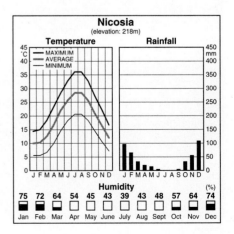

Czech Republic

Location: Central Europe.

Czech Tourist Authority
Staromestske namesti 6, 110 01 Prague 1, Czech Republic
Tel: (2) 24 89 71 11. Fax: (2) 231 4227.

Embassy of the Czech Republic
26-30 Kensington Palace Gardens, London W8 4QY
Tel: (0171) 243 1115. Fax: (0171) 727 9654. Opening hours: 0900-1300 and 1400-1700 Monday to Thursday; 0900-1300 and 1400-1600 Friday. *Consular section:* 1000-1230 Monday to Friday (except national public holidays – see below).

Czech Centre
30 Kensington Palace Gardens, London W8 4QY
Tel: (0171) 243 7981 *or* 243 7982. Fax: (0171) 727 9589. Opening hours: 0930-1300 Monday to Friday.

British Embassy
Thunovská 14, 125 50 Prague, Czech Republic
Tel: (2) 533 340 *or* 533 347/8/9 *or* 533 370 *or* 536 737 (visa enquiries). Fax: (2) 539 927. Telex: 121011 (a/b PRDM C).

Embassy of the Czech Republic
3900 Spring of Freedom Street, NW, Washington, DC 20008
Tel: (202) 363 6315/6. Fax: (202) 966 8540.

Czech Centre
1109-1111 Madison Avenue, New York, NY 10028
Opened February 1995.

Embassy of the United States of America
Trziste 15, 118 01 Prague 1, Czech Republic
Tel: (2) 24 51 08 47. Fax: (2) 532 457 *or* 24 51 10 01. Telex: 212196 (a/b AMEMBC).

Embassy of the Czech Republic
541 Sussex Drive, Ottawa, Ontario K1N 6Z6
Tel: (613) 562 3875. Fax: (613) 562 3878.

Canadian Embassy
Mickiewiczova 6, 125 33 Prague 6, Czech Republic
Tel: (2) 24 31 11 08/09/10/11/12. Fax: (2) 24 31 02 94. Telex: 121061.

AREA: 78,864 sq km (30,450 sq miles).
POPULATION: 10,302,215 (1991 estimate).
POPULATION DENSITY: 131 per sq km.
CAPITAL: Prague. **Population:** 1,215,076 (1990 estimate).
GEOGRAPHY: The Czech Republic is situated in Central Europe, sharing frontiers with Germany, Poland, the Slovak Republic and Austria. Only about one-quarter of the size of the British Isles, the republic is hilly and picturesque, with historic castles, romantic valleys and lakes, as well as excellent facilities to 'take the waters' at one of the famous spas or to ski and hike in the mountains. Among the most beautiful areas are the river valleys of the Vltava and Labe, and the Alpine-style mountains. There are two main regions. One is Bohemia, to the west. Besides Prague, the Czech capital, tourists are drawn to the spa towns of Karlovy Vary and Marianske Lazne, and to the very beautiful region of South Cechy. The Elbe flows through eastern Bohemia from the Giant Mountains, one of the most popular skiing regions. The second region, the rich agricultural area of Moravia, stretches through the centre, offering a variety of wooded highlands, vineyards, folk art and castles. There are many historical towns such as Olomouc, Kromeríz and Telc. Brno is Moravia's administrative and cultural centre.
LANGUAGE: The official language is Czech (spoken in both Bohemia and Moravia). German and English are also spoken.
RELIGION: Approximately 46% Roman Catholic and 15% Protestant, including churches such as the Reformed, Lutheran, Methodist, Moravian, Unity of Czech Brethren and Baptist. There is a community of approximately 15,000 Jews, mainly in Prague.

Prague

The Country of History

CESKÝ KRUMLOV CASTLE

PRAGUE - CHARLES BRIDGE

The Czech Tourist Authority promotes Czech tourism abroad and carries out research into domestic and foreign tourism with the emphasis on the processing and evaluation of statistical data. It then passes this information on to entrepreneurs for their exploitation.

The Czech Tourist Authority aids directly the development of entrepreneurial activities in Czech regions aimed at investing in tourism.

It cooperates with professional organisations of entrepreneurs and helps their members to participate in exhibitions and other marketing and promotional activities abroad.

Czech Tourism Authority
Staromestske nam. 6, 110 15 Prague 1,
Czech Republic
Tel: +42 2 248 97111.
Fax: +42 2 231 42 27.

KARLOVY VARY SPA

VIEW OF DRÁBSKÉ SVÉTNIČKY

Czech
Tourist Authority

Hluboka Castle

TIME: GMT + 1 (GMT + 2 from last Sunday in March to Saturday before last Sunday in September).
ELECTRICITY: Generally 220 volts AC, 50Hz. Most major hotels have standard international 2-pin razor plugs. Lamp fittings are normally of the screw type.
COMMUNICATIONS: Telephone: IDD available. Country code: 42. Outgoing international code: 00. There are public telephone booths, including special kiosks for international calls. Surcharges can be quite high on long-distance calls from hotels. Most of the public telephone boxes take phonecards. **Telex/telegram:** Facilities are available at all main towns and hotels. **Post:** There is a 24-hour service at the main post office in Prague at Jindrisska Street, Prague 1. *Poste Restante* services are available throughout the country. Post office hours: 0800-1800 Monday to Friday. **Press:** The *Bohemia Daily Standard*, the *Prague Post* and *Prognosis* are published in English.
BBC World Service and Voice of America frequencies: From time to time these change. See the section *How to Use this Book* for more information.

BBC:

MHz	15.57	12.09	6.195	3.955

Voice of America:

MHz	15.20	59.76	6.040	5.995

PASSPORT/VISA

Regulations and requirements may be subject to change at short notice, and you are advised to contact the appropriate diplomatic or consular authority before finalising travel arrangements. Details of these may be found at the head of this country's entry. Any numbers in the chart refer to the footnotes below.

	Passport Required?	Visa Required?	Return Ticket Required?
Full British	Yes	No	No
BVP	Not valid	-	-
Australian	Yes	Yes	No
Canadian	Yes	Yes	No
USA	Yes	No	No
Other EU (As of 31/12/94)	Yes/1	No	No
Japanese	Yes	Yes	No

PASSPORTS: Valid passport required by all except **[1]** nationals of Germany who can enter with a valid national ID card. Passports must be valid for at least 8 months at the time of application.
British Visitors Passport: Not accepted.
VISAS: Required by all except:
(a) nationals of EU countries (except nationals with the endorsement 'British Overseas Citizen' in their passports who *do* need visas);
(b) nationals of Austria, Bulgaria, Croatia, Estonia, Finland, Hungary, Iceland, Latvia, Lithuania, Former Yugoslav Republic of Macedonia, Malta, Monaco, Norway, Poland, San Marino, Slovak Republic, Slovenia, Sweden, Switzerland and Vatican City;
(c) nationals of Cuba, South Korea and Malaysia;
(d) nationals of the USA;
(e) nationals of the CIS (except nationals of Armenia, Azerbaijan, Georgia, Tajikistan and Uzbekistan who *do* need visas);
(f) nationals of Romania with an invitation from a Czech national which has been stamped by the respective Aliens' Police and Immigration Service office.
Types of visa: Tourist, Double Entry, Transit, Double Transit. Costs depend on nationality and cover the range £2-£60. Children aged 15 or under do not have to pay for a visa.
Validity: *Transit:* 48 hours. *Tourist:* 6 months from date of issue for 30-day visit.
Application to: Consulate (or Consular section at Embassy). For addresses, see top of entry.
Application requirements: (a) 1 application form (2 for Double Entry or Double Transit). (b) 2 recent passport-size photos. (c) Passport valid for at least 8 months, with one blank page. (d) Visa fee in the form of cash or postal order. (e) Postal applications should be accompanied by a self-addressed envelope stamped for Recorded Delivery.
Working days required: Same day in most cases. Visas

Health	
GALILEO/WORLDSPAN: **TI-DFT/PRG/HE**	
SABRE: **TIDFT/PRG/HE**	
Visa	
GALILEO/WORLDSPAN: **TI-DFT/PRG/VI**	
SABRE: **TIDFT/PRG/VI**	

For more information on Timatic codes refer to Contents.

Timatic

WITH US YOU WILL GROW NEW WINGS

ČSA – THE AIRLINE, WHICH PROVIDES ALL SERVICES ON AN INTERNATIONAL LEVEL

TELEPHONE CONNECTION:

Abu Dhabi, United Arab Emirates - 760 439; **Addis Ababa**, Ethiopia - 182222; **Algiers**, Algeria - 637408; **Amman**, Jordan - 622275, 624363, 628175; **Amsterdam**, Netherlands - 0206200839, 6200719; **Athens**, Greece - 3230173, 3230174, 3232303; **Auckland**, New Zealand -797515; **Bamako**, Mali - 2741; **Bangkok**, Thailand - 2543921-5; **Banská Bystrica**, Slovak Republic - 41975, 41976; **Barcelona**, Spain - 2178574; **Beirut**, Lebanon - 368950; **Belgrade**, Yugoslavia - 686270; **Berlin**, Germany - 5893323, 5894828; **Bombay**, India - 220736, 220765; **Bratislava**, Slovak Republic - 361042, 361045; **Brno**, Czech Republic - 42210739, 42210741; **Brussels**, Belgium - 2174285, 2171792; **Bucharest**, Romania - 6153205; **Buenos Aires**, Argentina - 308551; **Budapest**, Hungary - 1183175, 1183045; **Chicago**, U.S.A. - 312/201-1781; **Cairo**, Egypt - 3930416, 3930395; **Colombo**, Srí Lanka - 448409, 440283, 440284; **Copenhagen**, Denmark - 33120444, 33120056; **Damascus**, Syria - 2238814, 2225804; **Delhi**, India - 3311833; **Dubai**, United Arab Emirates - 213199, 216995; **Dublin**, Ireland - 370011; **Frankfurt**, Germany - 069/9200350, 069/92003516; **Geneva**, Switzerland - 022/7983330; **Hanoi**, Vietnam - 4256512; **Helsinki**, Finland - 647786, 647858; **Hong Kong** - 8683231; **Istanbul**, Turkey - 212/2303852, 212/2304832; **Jakarta**, Indonesia - 230408 ext. 136, 3255530, 334499; **Johannesburg**, South Africa - 011297011; **Karachi**, Pakistan - 5300086; **Karlovy Vary**, Czech Republic - 25760, 27855; **Kiev**, Ukraine - 2967449; **Košice**, Slovak Republic - 6222578, 6222577; **Kuala Lumpur**, Malaysia - 03/2380176, 2386323; **Kuwait**, Kuwait - 2417901, 2424662; **Larnaca**, Cyprus - 04-655892; **St. Peterburg**, Russia - 3155259, 3155264; **Limassol**, Cyprus - 05-375100; **Lisbon**, Portugal - 7265939; **London**, Great Britain - 071-2551898 Res., 071-25511366 Ad.; **Los Angeles**, U.S.A. - 310/417-8879; **Luxembourg**, Luxembourg - 491138-9; **Madrid**, Spain - 2486166, 2486128; **Manama**, Bahrain - 254081, 249349; **Manila**, Philippines - 8121114; **Mexico City**, Mexico - 5359877, 5461981; **Miami**, U.S.A. - 305/4487000; **Milan**, Italy - 86461714, 8690246; **Montreal**, Canada - 514/844-4200, 514/844-6376; **Moscow**, Russia - 2504571, 2500240; **Muscat**, Sultanate of Oman - 701488, 708457; **New York**, U.S.A.212/7656545 Exec., 212/7656022 Res.; **Nicosia**, Cyprus - 02/442082; **Ostrava**, Czech Republic - 233164, 233765; **Paris**, France - 47421811; **Piešťany**, Slovak Republik - 26184, 222950; **Poprad/Tatry**, Slovak Republic - 62587, 62755; **Praha**, Czech Republic - 24806111 series; **Prešov**, Slovak Republic - 33235; **Reykjavik**, Iceland - 690100; **Riyadh**, Saudi Arabia - 4066006; **Rome**, Italy - 4827522, 4871196; **Sao Paulo**, Brazil - 2313688; **Singapore**, Singapore - 7379844, 7379545; **Sofia**, Bulgaria - 885558, 885568; **Stockholm**, Sweden - 6605010, 6606001; **Sydney**, Australia - 2476196; **Taipei**, Taiwan - 7725214; **Teheran**, Iran - 829930; **Tel Aviv**, Israel - 5238825, 5238834; **Tokyo**, Japan - 03/3409-7414; **Toronto**, Canada - 416/3633174/5/6; **Tripoli**, Libya - 32392; **Tunis**, Tunisia - 788254; **Valetta**, Malta - 238483, 223427; **Vienna**, Austria - 5123805; **Warsaw**, Poland - 263802, 265051 ext.; **Zagreb**, Croatia - 434355; **Zlín**, Czech Republic - 24391; **Zurich**, Switzerland - 01/3638000, 3638009.

AT HOME
IN THE SKIES

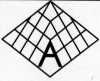

cannot be granted the same day if the application was received after 1230.
Temporary residence: Special application form required. Enquire at Embassy.

MONEY

Currency: Koruna (Kc) or Crown = 100 hellers. New notes are in denominations of Kc5000, 2000, 1000, 500, 200, 100, 50 and 20. New coins are in denominations of Kc50, 20, 10, 5, 2 and 1, and 50, 20 and 10 hellers.
Currency exchange: Foreign currency (including travellers cheques) can be exchanged at all bank branches and at authorised exchange offices, main hotels and road border crossings.
Credit cards: Major cards such as American Express, Diners Club, Visa, Access/Mastercard and others may be used to exchange currency and are also accepted in better hotels, restaurants and shops. Check with your credit card company for details of merchant acceptability and other services which may be available.
Travellers cheques: These are widely accepted (see listing in *Currency exchange* above).
Eurocheques are also accepted by certain restaurants and shops bearing the EC sign.
Exchange rate indicators: The following figures are included as a guide to the movements of the Koruna against Sterling and the US Dollar:

Date:	Sep '93	Jan '94	Sep '94	Jan '95
£1.00=	43.65	44.33	42.13	43.61
$1.00=	28.58	29.96	27.12	27.88

Currency restrictions: The import and export of local currency is not permitted. It is advisable to keep exchange transaction slips to facilitate re-conversion of local currency before departure. There is no restriction on foreign currency.
Banking hours: Generally 0800-1800 Monday to Friday.

DUTY FREE

The following goods may be imported into the Czech Republic without incurring customs duty by persons over 18 years of age:
250 cigarettes (or corresponding quantity of tobacco products); 1 litre of spirits; 2 litres of wine; gifts up to Kc3000.
Note: All forms of pornographic literature are forbidden. All items of value, such as cameras and tents, must be declared at Customs on entry to enable export clearance on departure. The export of antiques is prohibited. Firearms can be imported if accompanied by a Firearms Permit issued by a Czech diplomatic mission abroad. In this case up to 1000 shot cartridges and 50 bullets can be imported free of duty.

PUBLIC HOLIDAYS

Jan 1 '95 New Year's Day. **Apr 17** Easter Monday. **May 1** Labour Day. **May 8** Liberation from Fascism. **Jul 5** Day of the Apostles St Cyril and St Methodius. **Jul 6** Anniversary of the Martydom of Jan Hus. **Oct 28** Independence Day. **Dec 25** Christmas Day. **Dec 26** Boxing Day. **Jan 1 '96** New Year's Day. **Apr 8** Easter Monday.

HEALTH

Regulations and requirements may be subject to change at short notice, and you are advised to contact your doctor well in advance of your intended date of departure. Any numbers in the chart refer to the footnotes below.

	Special Precautions?	Certificate Required?
Yellow Fever	No	No
Cholera	No	No
Typhoid & Polio	No	-
Malaria	No	-
Food & Drink	1	-

[1]: Mains water is normally chlorinated, and whilst relatively safe may cause mild abdominal upsets. Bottled water is available and is advised for the first few weeks of the stay. Milk is pasteurised and dairy products are safe for consumption. Local meat, poultry, seafood, fruit and vegetables are generally considered safe to eat.
Health care: No vaccinations are required. There is a Reciprocal Health Agreement with the UK. On the production of a UK passport, hospital and other medical care will be provided free of charge in case of illness or accident. Prescribed medicine will be charged for. Other international agreements exist for free health care and visitors are advised to check with their national health authorities. Medical insurance is advised in all other cases.

TRAVEL - International

AIR: The national airline is *Czechoslovak Airlines (OK).* There are also some private airlines.
For free advice on air travel, call the Air Travel Advisory Bureau in the UK on (0171) 636 5000 (London) *or* (0161) 832 2000 (Manchester).
Approximate flight time: From London to Prague is 1 hour 45 minutes.
International airports: *Prague (PRG)* (Ruzyne) is 18km (11 miles) from the city (travel time – 30 minutes). Transport to/from city: *CSA Coach* every 30 minutes after flight arrivals 0530-1930 (travel time – 30 minutes); 119 bus approximately every 10 minutes (travel time – 35 minutes); taxis (24-hour service, surcharge at night). Big hotels operate frequent shuttle-bus services during the summer months to the major hotels in the city. Airport facilities include incoming and outgoing duty-free shops selling food, tobacco products, glass, china, small industrial goods and souvenirs; post office; bank/bureau de change (24-hour service); restaurant (1000-2000); bar (24 hours); car parking and car hire.
RAIL: The Czech Republic forms part of the European

Karlstejn

Hotel Palace Praha
Panská 12
11121 Praha 1
Czech Republic
Tel: +42 2 24093111
Fax: +42 2 24221240

Dear Judy and Tom,   May 1994

Greetings from Prague! Frank is again spoiling me at the Hotel Palace Praha – and both Prague and Palace are even more beautiful this spring than last.

You wouldn't believe your eyes if you could see our gorgeous suite. Frank got us the Presidential Grand de Luxe Suite – with two bedrooms, conference room, sauna, Italian marble bath! And the hotel's restaurants are incredible. Perhaps the best food I've had in any 5-star hotel I know.

Listen to this:

We wake up to breakfast in the Art Noveau-styled Café Restaurant. Fresh orange juice, flaky croissants and a heavenly omelette of French cheese, fresh mushrooms and tender ham. And the espresso was as good as the espresso I had in Rome last winter. I had two!

After some downtown shopping (which is just a minute's walk from the Palace) Frank took a break from his meetings in the conference room of the suite and we lunched in the Café Restaurant. Wow! How can seafood be so fresh? They must fly it in every day. The tortes and cake almost ruined my diet. (I resisted, barely, by sharing Frank's mousse, but then we ordered banana mousse, I couldn't help myself.)

As you know, our anniversary was on Saturday and we reserved a fantastic table in the Club Restaurant right by the piano and fountain. The waiters were exceptionally attentive, bringing me roses and champagne.

My steak was really nothing short of the best. And the wine, a domestic vintage red which the waiter recommended, was complex and fine and perfectly complemented the meal. By the time we left the Club Restaurant, it was close to midnight, so we didn't have time to visit the Piano bar – oh well, something to save for next time. I hear the Delicatesse Buffet (which takes tickets) has some surprises, too. I can't wait to come back.

A wonderful weekend. I hope you can come here sometime soon. Prague is a unique experience at the Hotel Palace Praha.

Bye for now – all the best!

Yours,

Helen

Café Restaurant

HOTEL PALACE PRAHA

**HOTEL
PALACE
PRAHA**
★ ★ ★ ★ ★

Panská 12, Praha 1,
Czech Republic.
Tel: +42 2 240 93111.
Fax: +42 2 24221240.
Telex: 123337 ihppc

**PREFERRED
HOTELS & RESORTS
WORLDWIDE**

Club Restaurant

Go to GO, one of the best travel trade fairs in Europe!

GO 96

GO International Travel Fair is organized by BVV (Brno Trade Fairs and Exhibitions) one of the most experienced fair organizers in Europe

Brno fair history goes back almost one thousand years and is older than the history of the Frankfurt fairs. Many travel industry professionals classify GO International Travel Fair as one of the most important travel fairs in Europe, a fair which they cannot afford to miss. And more and more tour operators from many countries are visiting it exactly for this reason - they can find there exhibitors who do not exhibit at any other travel fair.

There are several reasons for the international success of the GO Travel Fair. Credibility and experience of the fair organizers, geographical location in the middle of Europe, easy access from most European countries and proximity to the developing markets of former East Europe, with millions of potential travellers.

For more information or to register contact GO International Travel Fair, BVV, Výstaviště 1, 647 00 Brno, Czech Republic, tel.: (42-5) 4115-2970; fax: (42-5) 4115-3062.
In North and South America contact ABC International Ltd., 117 Westmoreland Rd., Kingston, Ontario K7M 1J6, tel.: (613) 545-3885; fax: (613) 545-9458.

1996, January 11-14

CZECH RAILWAYS

Travel through magical history !

Picturesque countryside interwoven with historical monuments from the middle ages to the present day - that is the Czech Republic now.

Travelling in comfort and reliably between natural and historic attractions means using Czech Railways. We will see to your comfort and provide all services to your complete satisfaction with our partners, Dining and Sleeping Cars (Jídelní a lůžkové vozy).

Special trips by Czech Railways´ historic steam trains are historic technology in motion in an exquisite landscape.

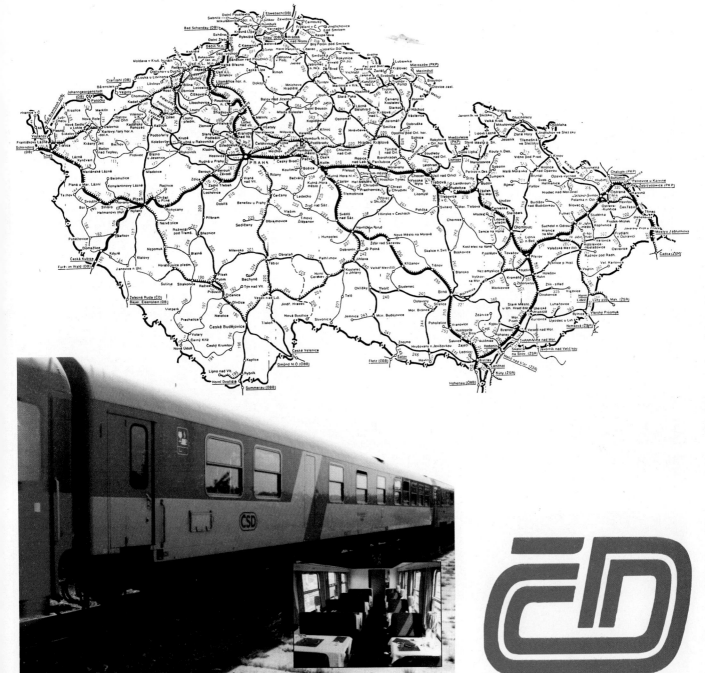

InterCity network. The most convenient routes to the Czech Republic from Western Europe are via Nuremberg or Vienna. The *Vindobona Express* is a once-daily through train that travels from Vienna to Prague (main station) and on to Berlin. It leaves Vienna at 0930 and reaches Prague at approximately 1515; a dining car is available all the way. There are also daily trains connecting with Switzerland and Germany on the routes Prague–Mnichov–Zurich–Bern and Prague–Dortmund respectively.
ROAD: The Czech Republic can be entered via Germany, Poland, the Slovak Republic or Austria.

TRAVEL - Internal

AIR: *Czechoslovak Airlines* operate an extensive domestic service. There are regular domestic flights from Prague to Ostrava.
RIVER: Navigable waterways can be found in the country and the main river ports are located at Prague, Usti nad Labem and Decin.
RAIL: The rail network is operated by *Czech State Railways*. There are several daily express trains between Prague and main cities and resorts. Reservations should be made in advance on major routes. Fares are low, but supplements are payable for travel by express trains.
ROAD: Traffic drives on the right. There is a motorway from Prague via Brno to Bratislava (Slovak Republic). **Bus:** The extensive bus network mostly covers areas not accessible by rail and is efficient and comfortable. **Car hire:** Self-drive cars may be hired through *Pragocar, Avis, Hertz* and other companies. Seat belts are compulsory and drinking is absolutely prohibited. Filling stations are quite often closed in the evenings. Another useful address is the Central Automoto Club, Na Rybnicku 16, Prague 2. Tel: (2) 24 91 18 30. There is non-stop telephone information for drivers on all Czech Republic territory on tel: (0) 123.
Documentation: A valid national driving licence is sufficient for car hire.
URBAN: Public transport is excellent. There is a metro service that runs from 0500-2400 and three flat fares are charged. There are also tramway and bus services in Prague (for which tickets must be purchased in advance from tobacconist shops or any shop displaying the sign

Predprodej Jizdenek). Buses, trolleybuses and tramways also exist in Brno, Ostrava, Plzen and several other towns. Most services run from 0430-2400. All the cities operate flat-fare systems and pre-purchased passes are available. Tickets should be punched in the appropriate machine on entering the tram or bus. Except on the Prague metro, a separate ticket is required when changing routes. There is a fine for fare evasion. Blue badges on tram and bus stops indicate an all-night service. Taxis are available in all the main towns, and are metered and cheap; higher fares are charged at night.
JOURNEY TIMES: The following chart gives approximate journey times (in hours and minutes) from Prague to other major towns/cities in the Czech Republic.

	Air	Road	Rail
Brno	-	2.15	4.45
Karlovy Vary	-	2.00	4.45
Ostrava	1.00	6.45	6.00

ACCOMMODATION

The Czech Republic is able to offer a full range of accommodation to suit every pocket. There is a wide range of hotels, graded from one to five stars, boarding hostels and private apartments. Many campsites are also open during the summer. For further information on the range of accommodation available, consult the contact addresses at the head of this entry.

RESORTS & EXCURSIONS

Travellers should make advance hotel bookings when intending to visit the Czech Republic through travel agencies. Visitors may travel alone, but usually they take a package holiday. Travel agencies offer a large selection.
Prague: Picturesquely sited on the banks of the *Moldau River,* the city of Prague has played an important part in the history of Europe. It is noted for some magnificent Gothic, Baroque and Romanesque architecture and a cultural scene of elegance. There is the annual *Spring Music Festival*, the excellent Czech Philharmonic Orchestra and the *National Theatre*. The centre is the *Hradcany* complex of the *Castle*, the *St*

Vitus Cathedral and all the Palace rooms including the *Vladislav Hall*, which were once used by Bohemian kings for jousting. The views over the Moldau (or Vltava), spanned by the medieval *Charles Bridge,* contribute to making Prague one of the loveliest cities in Europe. Worth visiting are the *St Nicholas Cupola*, the Town Hall of the Old City, where you can also see the *Gothic Tyn Church*, and the beautiful 15th-century clock in the *Old Town Square*. The *Little Town* is a quarter of winding narrow streets of small artisan houses and palaces from the 17th and 18th centuries. Quite near Prague is a grim reminder of the horrors of the Second World War – the site of the concentration camp at **Terezin***,* where there is a museum. Also in the area are the castles of *Karlstejn, Krivoklat* and *Konopiste*, the historic town of **Kutna Hora** and the dominating cathedral of *St Barbara.*
Brno dates from the 13th century and has a fine museum and the Gothic *Spilberk* castle. There is also an international music festival from September to October. A large number of international trade fairs take place in the *Brno Exhibition Centre.*
Bohemia: Southern Bohemia, with its lakes and woods, has for a long time been a favourite holiday place for families, since it has many recreation facilities and points of historic interest, such as the medieval town of **Cesky Krumlov** and *Hluboka Castle*, one of the many atmospheric Gothic castles in Bohemia, perched on wooded hillsides and adorned with the round towers and pointed caps so loved by producers of Hammer horror films. With imagination, the visitor can easily picture the lives led by the nobles who once lived here and hunted in the woods. Other outstanding examples of Czech architectural achievements can be found in Cheb, Slavonice, Telc, Olomouc and there are over 3000 castles, chateaux and other historical sights and monuments throughout the country. Less well-known but equally characteristic are Bohemia's churches. The small town of **Telc** is a perfect example of a 16th-century town with rows of pastel coloured houses. Gables and pediments adorn the houses and cover various styles. The Main Square is surrounded by Renaissance arcades with the *Chateau* at its western end. It boasts beautiful painted ceilings, a small art gallery and cloistered gardens. The country is also famed for its caves: the rock formation of the mountain ranges form underground

© RDF PRESS & VR ATELIER Praha 1992

P r a ž k á
i n f o r m a č n
s l u ž b a

BUSINESS SERVICE:

INFORMATION
 tel.: 42/2/54 44 44
INTERPRETERS
 Za Poříčskou branou 7,
 Praha 8
 tel.: 42/2/26 58 23-4, 26 58 35-6
 fax: 42/2/2422 8557
TRANSLATIONS
 Za Poříčskou branou 7,
 Praha 8
 tel.: 42/2/26 58 23-4, 26 58 35-6
 fax: 42/2/2422 8557
HOSTESSES
 Za Poříčskou branou 7,
 Praha 8
 tel.: 42/2/26 58 27
 fax: 42/2/26 58 27
PRESS CUTTINGS
 K rotundě 8, Praha 2
 tel.: 42/2/29 73 78
 fax: 42/2/24 49 49

PRAGUE INFORMATION SERVICE-
YOUR PARTNER IN PRAGUE

Pražská
informační
služba

TOURIST SERVICE:

- INFORMATION
- GUIDES
- CITY TOURS
- TICKETS
- SPECIAL PROGRAMMES
- ACCOMMODATION
- MONEY EXCHANGE

OFFICES:

OLD TOWN HALL
   tel.: 42/2/2448 2202
Staroměstské nám. 22
   tel.: 42/2/2421 2844-5
Na příkopě 20
   tel.: 42/2/26 40 18-20
Main station

PRAGUE INFORMATION SERVICE-
JUST OPPOSITE THE OLD TOWN HORLOGE

rivers and chambers decorated above and below with stalactites and stalagmites.

The health resorts or spas of Bohemia remain one of the primary attractions, as they have been for centuries. Beethoven, Edward VII and Goethe all admired the resort of **Marianske Lazne**, formerly **Marienbad**, whilst the town of **Karlovy Vary (Karlsbad)** has attracted the crowned heads of Europe for many years to bathe in the sulphurous waters; there is also a biannual *International Film Festival* at Karlovy Vary. **Frantiskovy Lazne** has delightful parks and 24 springs used to cure rheumatism, heart disease and infertility. There is also a nature reserve near the town.

Winter sports: The mountains, forests and lakes are enchanting and ideal for outdoor holidaying as well as winter sports. There are popular winter sports centres of which the *Giant Mountains* are the most popular. There are also numerous lakes and rivers amidst the glacial landscape, offering excellent fishing, canoeing, boating and freshwater swimming.

National Parks: The *Giant Mountains* of northeast Bohemia and the *Eagle Mountains* towards the Polish border and Podyjí in South Moravia are protected as National Parks and thus have an untouched quality rare in Europe.

SOCIAL PROFILE

FOOD & DRINK: Food is often based on Austro-Hungarian dishes; *Wiener schnitzel* and pork are very popular. Specialities include *bramborak,* a delicacy of a potato pancake filled with garlic and herbs, and Prague ham. Meat dishes are mostly served with *knedliky,* a type of large dough dumpling, and *zeli* (sauerkraut). Western-style fresh vegetables are often missing in lower-class restaurants. There is a wide selection of restaurants, beer taverns and wine cellars. **Drink:** Popular beverages include beers, fresh fruit juices and liqueurs. A particular speciality is *slivovice* (a plum brandy) and *merunkovice* (an apricot brandy). Pilsner beers, *borovicka* (strong gin), *becherovka* (herb brandy) and sparkling wine from Moravia are also famous. There are no rigid licensing hours.

NIGHTLIFE: Theatre and opera are of a high standard all over Eastern Europe. Much of the nightlife takes place in hotels, although nightclubs and casinos are to be found in major cities.

SHOPPING: Souvenirs include Bohemian glass and crystal, pottery, porcelain, wooden folk carvings, hand-embroidered clothing, and food items. There are a number of excellent shops specialising in glass and crystal, while various associations of regional artists and craftsmen run their own retail outlets (pay in local currency). Other special purchases include pottery (particularly from Kolovec and Straznice); china ornaments and geyserstone carvings from Karlovy Vary; delicate lace and needle embroidery from many Moravian towns; and blood-red garnets and semi-precious stones from Bohemia. **Shopping hours:** 0900-1200 and 1400-1800 Monday to Friday; 0900-1200 Saturday. In the centre of Prague, some shops will stay open through lunch and until late in the evening.

SPORT: Football, tennis and **ice hockey** are popular. There is a very good network of marked trails in all mountain areas, and it is possible to plan a **walking** tour in advance.

Winter sports tours can be arranged by many travel agents; check for details. The many and varied rivers and lakes provide excellent opportunities for **watersports – canoeing, sailing, water-skiing, fishing,** etc (see *Resorts & Excursions* above).

SPECIAL EVENTS: Most towns have their own folk festivals, with dancing, local costumes and food. These tend to be in the summer months leading up to the harvest festivals in September. The most important festival in 1995 is the *Prague Spring Music Festival* from May-June. There are also folk festivals at Straznice, Vlcnov, Hluk, Roznov and Domazlice. The following is a selection of events celebrated throughout 1995:

May/Jun '95 *Papal Visit,* Olomouc. **May 12-Jun 2** *Prague Spring – International Music Festival.* **Jun 8-17** *European Women's Basketball Championships,* Brno. **Jun 23-25** *International Folklore Festival,* Stráznice. **Jul 31-Aug 6** *Skoda Czech Men's Open* (tennis), Prague. **Aug 19-26** *Chopin Festival,* Mariánské Lazné. **Sep** *Musical Festival of Ema Destinová,* Ceské Budejovice. **Sep 27-29** *International Tourist Festival,* Karlovy Vary. **Oct 8** *Steeplechase,* Pardubice. **Jan '96** *GO '96 – International Tourist and Travel Fair,* Brno. **Feb** *Holiday World,* Prague. For further details of special events, check with travel agencies who can also arrange music festival tours.

Main picture: Telc. **Above:** Marianské Lazné.

privatisation. There has also been extensive fiscal and budgetary reform, with the aim of creating a fully-fledged capitalist financial system with strong safeguards against inflation. In 1993 the proportion of the non-state sector in the GDP reached 56.9%. Limited currency convertibility has also been introduced as a necessary step towards promoting foreign investment. This is being keenly sought, with joint ventures the favoured method of entering the market. Priority areas are the aircraft and automobile industries, electronics, nuclear energy, textiles, leather and glass, gasification of coal and transport and communications. Agriculture is particularly important as an export sector (beer and timber are much in demand). For the time being, the trade is focused on developing links with Western Europe. The country negotiated associate membership with the then European Community. However, this has been rendered void by the Czech-Slovak split. Future trade patterns are likely to see the Czech Republic improve its links with Austria and Germany.

BUSINESS: Businessmen wear suits. A knowledge of German is useful as English is not widely spoken among the older generation. Long business lunches are usual. Avoid visits during July and August as many businesses close for holidays. **Office hours:** 0800-1600 Monday to Friday.

COMMERCIAL INFORMATION: The following organisation can offer advice: Obchodní a prumyslová komora (Czech Chamber of Commerce and Industry), Argentinská 38, 170 05 Prague 7. Tel: (2) 66 79 41 11. Fax: (2) 66 71 08 05.

CONFERENCES/CONVENTIONS: The Prague International Congress Centre can seat up to 5000 people. There are also facilities in many hotels throughout the country. Trade fairs are held in Brno. Information can be obtained from BVV, PO Box 491, Vystaviste 1, 660 91 Brno. Tel: (5) 41 15 11 11. Fax: (5) 41 15 91 71.

Further information can also be obtained from the following: Palace of Culture Prague, Convention and Culture Centre, Prague. Tel: (2) 61 17 11 11. Fax: (2) 422 568 *or* 422 328 *or* 424 180; *or*
Prague Convention Bureau, Rytírská 26, 110 00 Prague 1.

CLIMATE

Cold winters, mild summers.
Required clothing: Mediumweights, heavy topcoat and overshoes for winter; lightweights for summer.

TEMPERATURE CONVERSIONS

-20	-10	0°C	10	20	30	40

0	10	20	30°F40	50	60	70	80	90	100

RAINFALL CONVERSIONS

0mm	200	400	600	800
0in	5	10	15	20	25	30

SOCIAL CONVENTIONS: Dress should be casual, but conservative, except at formal dinners and at quality hotels or restaurants. **Photography:** Areas where there are military installations should not be photographed. **Tipping:** A 5-10% tip will be discreetly accepted; some alteration in customs is to be expected in the wake of political and social changes.

BUSINESS PROFILE

ECONOMY: Of all the Soviet bloc economies, the former Czechoslovakia experienced the highest degree of state control, without even the small-scale private enterprise that existed to some extent in all Eastern European economies. Under central planning, and particularly in the aftermath of the 'Prague Spring', economic development concentrated on heavy industry at the expense of traditional strengths in light and craft-based industries, such as textiles, clothing, glass and ceramics (though these remain significant). These inefficient and, in some cases, redundant industrial monoliths are now a considerable impediment to the growth of the economy. The other problem is a dearth of natural resources – the country has, hitherto, relied

heavily on the former Soviet Union for most of its raw materials, particularly oil, supplies of which have been cut to one-third and payment required in hard currency. The oil shortage reached crisis proportions at the end of 1990 and was resolved satisfactorily only after urgent personal discussions between Presidents Havel and Gorbachev. The following year, the Czech government embarked on an ambitious programme of privatisation as the cornerstone of its declared policy of introducing a market economy. This has happened at breakneck speed despite the misgivings of observers from across the political spectrum who have raised questions about the lack of financial infrastructure, possible consequences of extensive foreign ownership, and the use of an untried 'voucher' scheme which gives equity stakes in industrial enterprises to any individuals who apply. The autumn of 1991 saw 1700 enterprises denationalised in the space of just two weeks. This was the first part of a 2-phase plan which saw most of the national industry and agriculture in private hands. However, since the division of the country agreed in June 1992, this is now likely to go ahead only in the Czech Republic. The voucher scheme was not initially popular, but steadily gained credence: 8.5 million people took part in the 1992

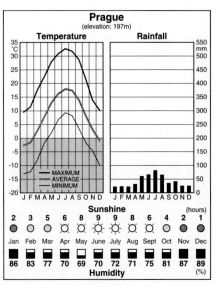

200km
100mls

NORWAY

Skagerrak

Grenen

Göteborg

Frederikshavn

Læsø

Ålborg

EUROPE

SWEDEN

Viborg **DENMARK**

Stavning Århus Samsø Helsingør
JUTLAND
Billund Legoland
Esbjerg **COPENHAGEN** Malmö
Odense Zealand
Fünen
Møn Bornholm
Lolland Falster

FEDERAL REP. OF GERMANY

DAB-M75

☐ international airport

Location: Western Europe.

Danmarks Turistråd (Tourist Office)
Vesterbrogade 6D, DK-1620 Copenhagen V, Denmark
Tel: 33 11 14 15. Fax: 33 93 14 16.
Tourist Office Information Department
Bernstorffsgade 1, DK-1577 Copenhagen V, Denmark
Tel: 33 11 13 25. Fax: 33 93 49 69.
Royal Danish Embassy
55 Sloane Street, London SW1X 9SR
Tel: (0171) 333 0200 or 333 0265 (visa enquiries by
telephone, 0900-1000 and 1500-1600 only). Fax: (0171)
333 0270 or 333 0266 or 333 0243 (trade only). Opening
hours: 0930-1300 Monday to Friday.
Danish Tourist Board
55 Sloane Street, London SW1X 9SY
Tel: (0171) 259 5958/9. Fax: (0171) 259 5955. Opening
hours: 1100-1600 Monday to Friday.
British Embassy
Kastelsvej 36-40, DK-2100 Copenhagen Ø, Denmark
Tel: 35 26 46 00. Fax: 35 43 14 00.
Consulates in: Åbenrå, Ålborg, Århus, Esbjerg,
Fredericia, Herning, Odense, Rønne (Bornholm) and
Tórshavn (Faroe Islands).
Royal Danish Embassy
3200 Whitehaven Street, NW, Washington, DC 20008
Tel: (202) 234 4300. Fax: (202) 328 1470.
Royal Danish Consulate General
One Dag Hammarskjøld Plaza, 885 Second Avenue,
New York, NY 10017
Tel: (212) 223 4545. Fax: (212) 754 1904. Telex:
0125505 (a/b GKLDK NYK).
Danish Tourist Board
18th Floor, 655 Third Avenue, New York, NY 10017
Tel: (212) 949 2333 or 949 2322. Fax: (212) 286 0896 or
983 5260.
Embassy of the United States of America
Dag Hammarskjølds Allé 24, DK-2100 Copenhagen Ø,
Denmark
Tel: 31 42 31 44. Fax: 35 43 02 23. Telex: 22216 (a/b
AMEMB DK).
Royal Danish Embassy
Suite 702, 85 Range Road, Ottawa, Ontario K1N 8J6
Tel: (613) 234 0704 or 234 0116 or 234 0204. Fax: (613)
234 7368.
Consulates in: Calgary, Edmonton, Halifax, Montréal,
Regina, St John, St John's, Toronto, Vancouver and

	Health
	GALILEO/WORLDSPAN: **TI-DFT/CPH/HE**
	SABRE: **TIDFT/CPH/HE**
	Visa
	GALILEO/WORLDSPAN: **TI-DFT/CPH/VI**
	SABRE: **TIDFT/CPH/VI**

Timatic

For more information on Timatic codes refer to Contents.

Winnipeg.
Danish Tourist Board
PO Box 636, Streetsville, Mississauga, Ontario L5M 2C2
Tel: (905) 820 8984 (information) or (519) 576 6213
(sales & marketing). Fax: (519) 576 7115.
Canadian Embassy
Kr. Bernikowsgade 1, DK-1105 Copenhagen K,
Denmark
Tel: 33 12 22 99. Fax: 33 14 05 85.

AREA: 43,093 sq km (16,638 sq miles).
POPULATION: 5,162,126 (1992 estimate).
POPULATION DENSITY: 119.8 per sq km.
CAPITAL: Copenhagen. **Population:** 464,556.
GEOGRAPHY: Denmark is the smallest Scandinavian
country, consisting of the Jutland peninsula, north of
Germany, and over 500 islands of various sizes, some
inhabited and linked to the mainland by ferry or bridge.
The landscape consists mainly of low-lying, fertile
countryside broken by beech woods, small lakes and
fjords. Greenland and the Faroe Islands are also under the
sovereignty of the Kingdom of Denmark, although both
have home rule. The Faroe Islands are a group of 18
islands in the north Atlantic inhabited by a population of
47,449 whose history dates back to the Viking period.
Fishing and sheep farming are the two most important
occupations. Tórshavn (population 16,189), the capital of
the Faroes, is served by direct flights from Copenhagen.
Further information on Greenland may be found by
consulting its individual entry.
LANGUAGE: The official language is Danish. Many
Danes also speak English, German and French.
RELIGION: Predominantly Evangelical Lutheran with a
small Roman Catholic minority.
TIME: GMT + 1 (GMT + 2 from last Sunday in March
to Saturday before last Sunday in September).
ELECTRICITY: 220 volts AC, 50Hz. Continental 2-pin
plugs are standard. On many campsites, 110-volt power
plugs are also available.
COMMUNICATIONS: Telephone: Full IDD is
available. Country code: 45. Outgoing international code:
009. There are no area codes. **Fax:** This service is
available from many main post offices and from major
hotels. **Telex/telegram:** The public telex booth at the
Copenhagen Central Telegraph Office is open 24 hours a
day. Telegrams can also be sent by phone; dial 122. **Post:**
All telephone and postal rates are printed at the post
offices. All post offices offer *Poste Restante* facilities.
Post offices are open 0900-1730 Monday to Friday, and
several are open Saturday 0900-1200. **Press:** Newspapers
are largely regional, the main papers in the capital
include *Berlingske Tidende, Ekstrabladet, Politiken* and
Aktuelt. There are also English-language newspapers
available.
**BBC World Service and Voice of America
frequencies:** From time to time these change. See the
section *How to Use this Book* for more information.
BBC:
| MHz | 12.095 | 9.410 | 6.195 | 1.296 |
A service is also available on 648kHz and 198kHz (0100-
0500 GMT).
Voice of America:
| MHz | 15.205 | 9.760 | 6.044 | 5.995 |

PASSPORT/VISA

*Regulations and requirements may be subject to change at short notice, and you
are advised to contact the appropriate diplomatic or consular authority before
finalising travel arrangements. Details of these may be found at the head of this
country's entry. Any numbers in the chart refer to the footnotes below.*

	Passport Required?	Visa Required?	Return Ticket Required?
Full British	1	2	No
BVP	Valid	No	No
Australian	Yes	No	Yes
Canadian	Yes	No	Yes
USA	Yes	No	Yes
Other EU (As of 31/12/94)	1	No	No
Japanese	Yes	No	Yes

PASSPORTS: Valid passport required by all except:
(a) **[1]** nationals of Belgium, France, Germany, Greece,
Italy, Luxembourg, The Netherlands, Portugal and Spain
in possession of a national identity card, and nationals of
the United Kingdom in possession of a BVP (nationals of
Ireland *do* require a passport);
(b) nationals of Austria, Liechtenstein and Switzerland in
possession of a national identity card;
(c) nationals of Finland, Iceland, Norway and Sweden in
possession of identification papers if travelling entirely
within Scandinavia;
(d) nationals of Bosnia-Hercegovina in possession of a
national idenity card valid for at least 6 months beyond

length of stay endorsed with a valid visa.
British Visitors Passport: Valid for nationals of the UK
who are citizens of the UK or colonies. BVPs can be
used for holidays or unpaid business trips to Denmark for
up to 3 months. Visits to Denmark, Finland, Iceland,
Norway and Sweden as a group must add up to less than
3 months in any 6-month period.
VISAS: Required by all except:
(a) **[2]** nationals of the UK, with the exception of holders of
passports described as 'British Protected Person' or with
endorsement 'holder is subject to control under the
Immigration Act 1971' or 'the Commonwealth
Immigration Act' (holders of these types of British passport
will need visas). Note that nationals whose country of
origin is Bangladesh, Ghana, India, Nigeria, Pakistan or Sri
Lanka will need an 'exempt' stamp from UK immigration
authorities, in addition to an 'indefinite stay' stamp;
(b) nationals of other countries referred to in the chart
above;
(c) nationals of Andorra, Argentina, Austria, Bahamas,
Barbados, Belize, Benin, Bolivia, Botswana, Brazil,
Brunei, Chile, Colombia, Costa Rica, Côte d'Ivoire,
Croatia, Cyprus, Czech Republic, Dominica, Dominican
Republic, Ecuador, El Salvador, Estonia, Fiji, Finland,
Grenada, Guatemala, Guyana, Honduras, Hungary,
Iceland, Israel, Jamaica, Kenya, Kiribati, South Korea,
Lesotho, Liechtenstein, Lithuania, Malawi, Malaysia,
Malta, Mauritius, Mexico, Monaco, Namibia, New
Zealand, Nicaragua, Niger, Norway, Panama, Paraguay,
Peru, Poland, St Lucia, St Vincent & the Grenadines, San
Marino, Seychelles, Singapore, Slovak Republic,
Slovenia, Solomon Islands, Suriname, Swaziland,
Sweden, Switzerland, Tanzania, Thailand, Togo,
Trinidad & Tobago, Tuvalu, Uganda, Uruguay, Vatican
City, Venezuela, Zambia and Zimbabwe.
Types of visa: Tourist, Business and Transit. Cost: £16
for Tourist; £11 for Transit, but some free reciprocal
arrangements exist. Transit visas are not required by
those continuing their journey to a third country on the
same day without leaving the airport. Visas are issued
free of charge to: nationals of Albania, Bulgaria, China,
CIS, Hong Kong (British passport holders only), India,
Iraq, Pakistan, Philippines, Syria, Turkey and
Yugoslavia; spouses and children (under 21 years of age)
of EU nationals irrespective of nationality, upon
presentation of documentary evidence.
Validity: Variable. Tourist and Business visas are
normally valid for up to 3 months from date of arrival.
Application to: Consulate (or Consular section at
Embassy). For addresses, see top of entry.
Application requirements: (a) Valid passport. (b) 2
application forms. (c) 2 passport-size photographs.
Personal applications should be made to the visa office
0930-1300 Monday to Friday. Postal applicants should
enclose a stamped, self-addressed and registered
envelope and payment by crossed postal order.
Telephone enquiries should be made between 0900-1000
and 1500-1600 only. There are special facilities for
business travellers, who should phone for details.
Working days required: 6-8 weeks.
Temporary residence: Persons wishing to stay in
Denmark for more than 3 months should make their
application *in their home country* well in advance of their
intended date of departure.

MONEY

Currency: Danish Krone (DKr) = 100 øre. Notes are in
denominations of DKr1000, 500, 100 and 50. Coins are in
denominations of DKr20, 10, 5 and 1, and 50 and 25 øre.
Currency exchange: Eurocheques are cashed by banks
and hotels; they may also be used at most restaurants and
shops. Personal cheques cannot be used by foreigners in
Denmark. Some banks may refuse to exchange large
foreign bank notes.
Credit cards: Access/Mastercard, American Express,
Diners Club and Visa are accepted. Check with your

credit card company for details of merchant acceptability and other services which may be available.

Travellers cheques: Can be cashed by banks and hotels, and can be used at most restaurants and shops.

Exchange rate indicators: The following figures are included as a guide to the movements of the Danish Krone against Sterling and the US Dollar:

Date:	Oct '92	Sep '93	Jan '94	Jan '95
£1.00=	9.36	10.14	10.05	9.52
$1.00=	5.89	6.64	6.80	6.09

Currency restrictions: No limitations on the import of either local or foreign currencies, although declarations should be made for large amounts. The export of local currency is limited to the amount declared on import, plus any amount acquired by the conversion of foreign currency. There is no limit on the export of foreign currency.

Banking hours: 0930-1600 Monday, Tuesday, Wednesday and Friday; and 0930-1800 Thursday. Several exchange bureaux are open until midnight.

DUTY FREE

The following goods may be imported into Denmark without incurring customs duty by:
(a) Non-Danish residents arriving from an EU country:
1.5 litres of spirits or 3 litres of sparkling wine (under 22%); 5 litres of table wine; 12 litres of beer (if declared also up to DKr4700 for other articles); 300 cigarettes or 150 cigarillos or 75 cigars or 400g of tobacco; 1kg of coffee or 400g of coffee extracts; 200g of tea or 80g tea-extracts; 75g of perfume; 375ml of eau de toilette; other articles: DKr4700 (single articles up to DKr2725).
(b) Residents of non-EU countries entering from outside the EU (excluding Greenland):
1 litre of spirits or 2 litres of sparkling wine (maximum 22%); 2 litres of table wine; 10 litres of beer; 200 cigarettes or 100 cigarillos or 50 cigars or 250g of tobacco; 500g of coffee or 200g of coffee-extracts; 100g of tea or 40g of tea-extracts; 50g of perfume; 250ml of eau de toilette; other articles: DKr350.
(c) Travellers over 17 years of age entering from an EU country with duty-paid goods:
800 cigarettes and 400 cigarillos and 200 cigars and 1kg of tobacco; 90 litres of wine (including up to 60 litres of sparkling wine); 10 litres of spirits; 20 litres of intermediate products (such as fortified wine); 110 litres of beer.

Note: Alcohol and tobacco allowances are for those aged 17 or over only. It is forbidden to import meat or meat products into Denmark.

PUBLIC HOLIDAYS

Jan 1 '95 New Year. **Apr 13** Maundy Thursday. **Apr 14** Good Friday. **Apr 17** Easter Monday. **May 12** Common Prayer's Day. **May 25** Ascension Day. **Jun 5** Whit Monday *and* Constitution Day. **Dec 24** Christmas Eve. **Dec 25** Christmas Day. **Dec 26** Boxing Day. **Dec 31-Jan 1 '96** New Year. **Apr 4** Maundy Thursday. **Apr 5** Good Friday. **Apr 8** Easter Monday.

HEALTH

Regulations and requirements may be subject to change at short notice, and you are advised to contact your doctor well in advance of your intended date of departure. Any numbers in the chart refer to the footnotes below.		
	Special Precautions?	**Certificate Required?**
Yellow Fever	No	No
Cholera	No	No
Typhoid & Polio	No	-
Malaria	No	-
Food & Drink	No	-

Note: *Diabetic diets* are catered for at many restaurants. See *Food & Drink* in the *Social Profile* section.

Health care: Medical facilities in Denmark are excellent. The telephone number for emergencies is 112. Doctors on call in Copenhagen can be reached by dialling 32 84 00 41, 24 hours a day. Doctors' fees for a night call are always paid in cash. Local tourist offices will tell you where to contact a dentist, and Copenhagen has an emergency dental service outside office hours; again, fees are paid in cash.

Medicine can only be bought at a chemist ('Apotek'), open 24 hours in large towns. Only medicine prescribed by Danish or other Scandinavian doctors can be dispensed. Many medicines that can be bought over the counter in the UK can only be obtained with prescriptions in Denmark.

There is a Reciprocal Health Agreement with the UK. In addition to the free emergency treatment at hospitals and casualty departments allowed to all foreign visitors, this allows UK citizens on presentation of a UK passport (form E111 is not strictly necessary) free hospital treatment if referred by a doctor, and free medical treatment given by a doctor registered with the Danish Public Health Service. It may occasionally be necessary to pay at the time of treatment; if this is so, receipts should be kept to facilitate refunds (see below). The Agreement does not cover the full costs of dental treatment or prescribed medicines, but a partial refund may be allowed, so again, keep receipts. Discounts are sometimes allowed on prescribed medicines at the time of purchase on presentation of a UK passport. The Agreement does not apply in the Faroe Islands. To obtain refunds, UK citizens should apply (with receipts) to the Kommunens Social og Sundhedsforvaltning before leaving Denmark.

TRAVEL - International

AIR: The national airlines are *SAS (SK)* and *Mærsk Air (DM)*. The major carriers are *SAS* and *British Airways*. For free advice on air travel, call the Air Travel Advisory Bureau in the UK on (0171) 636 5000 (London) *or* (0161) 832 2000 (Manchester).

Approximate flight times: From *London* to Copenhagen is 1 hour 50 minutes and to Århus is 1 hour 40 minutes. From *Los Angeles* to Copenhagen is 11 hours 15 minutes. From *New York* to Copenhagen is 8 hours 50 minutes. From *Singapore* to Copenhagen is 15 hours 5 minutes. From *Sydney* to Copenhagen is 22 hours 50 minutes.

International airports: *Copenhagen (CPH)* (Kastrup) is 10km (6 miles) southeast of the city (travel time – 30 minutes). Coach departs every 10 minutes and bus every 15 minutes from 0600-2230. Airport facilities include an outgoing duty-free shop (0600-2300), a wide range of car hire firms (0730-2200 weekdays, 0700-1800 Saturday and 1400-2200 Sunday), bank/bureau de change (0630-2200), and several restaurants and bars (at least one of which will be open between 0600 and 2400).

Århus (AAR) (Tirstrup) is 44km (27 miles) from the city. Buses connect with flight arrivals; taxis are also available. Airport facilities include a duty-free shop (open when flights depart), a wide range of car hire firms (0830-1500 weekdays, except Thursday until 1800), bank/bureau de change (0800-1500), a post office and a restaurant (open for arrival and departures of flights). There are direct scheduled services between *Billund*

(BLL) and Gatwick (UK); between *Esbjerg (EBJ)* and both Humberside (UK) and Stavanger (Norway); and between *Stauning (STA)* and Aberdeen (UK).
SEA: Denmark's major ports are Copenhagen, Esbjerg, Frederikshavn, Hirtshals and Hanstholm. There are regular ferries to and from the UK, Norway, Sweden, Poland, Iceland, the Faroe Islands and Germany. *Scandinavian Seaways* sail from Newcastle to Esbjerg from May to September, and from Harwich to Esbjerg three to seven times a week all year round. The major ferry operators from Norway, Sweden and Germany are *Scandinavian Ferry Lines, Flyvebådene, Color Line, Da-No Line, DSB* and *Stena Line*. North Jutland is connected to Iceland, the Faroes, Scotland and Norway during the summer by ferries sailing once a week.
Cruise lines calling at Copenhagen are as follows: *Scandinavian Seaways, Royal Viking, TVI Lines, Lindblad Travel, Lauro, CTC, Norwegian Cruises/Union Lloyd* and *Norwegian American*.
RAIL: Copenhagen is connected by rail to all the other capital cities of Europe, and typical express journey times from Copenhagen are: to London 26 hours; to Hamburg 5 hours; to Berlin 9 hours. All international trains connect with ferries where applicable.
ROAD: All the major road networks of Europe connect with ferry services to Copenhagen; it is advisable to book ferries in advance. For many years the possibility of constructing a bridge or tunnel between Denmark and Sweden has been discussed; nothing has come of this so far.
See below under *Travel – Internal* for information on **documentation** and **traffic regulations**.

TRAVEL - Internal

AIR: The network of scheduled services radiates from *Copenhagen* (Kastrup). Other airports well-served by domestic airlines include Rønne, Odense, Billund, Esbjerg, Karup, Skrydstrup, Sønderborg, Thisted, Ålborg and Århus. Domestic airports are generally situated between two or more cities which are within easy reach of each other. Limousines are often available. Discounts are available on certain tickets bought inside Denmark. Family, children and young person's discounts are also available.
SEA: There are frequent ferry sailings from Sjælland to Fyn, Kalundborg to Århus, Ebeltoft to Sjællands Odde and Rønne to Copenhagen. The larger ferries may have TV, video and cinema lounges, shops, play areas for children and sleeping rooms. Local car ferries link most islands to the road network.
RAIL: The main cities on all islands are connected to the rail network: Copenhagen, Odense, Esbjerg, Horsens, Randers, Herning and Ålborg. The *Danish State Railways (DSB)* operate a number of express trains called *Lyntogs* which provide long-distance, non-stop travel; it is often possible to purchase newspapers, magazines and snacks on board these trains. Payphones are also available. There is also a new type of intercity train called the *IC3* which is even faster and more direct. Seat reservations are compulsory. Children under four years old travel free, and between 4-12 at half price. There are also price reductions for persons over 65 and groups of three people or more. The *Englænderen* boat-train runs between Esbjerg and Copenhagen and connects with ships from the UK. DSB passenger fares are based on a zonal system. The cost depends on the distance travelled; the cost per kilometre is reduced the longer the journey. Cheap day tickets are available for travel on Tuesday, Wednesday, Thursday and Saturday. There are fare reductions for adults travelling in groups of three or more. The *Nord-Tourist Pass* allows unlimited travel within Denmark, Sweden, Norway and Finland. As elsewhere in Europe, *Interail* (for travellers under 26 years) and *Interail Senior* passes are valid in Denmark. Bus and ferry and, of course, rail tickets may be purchased at all railway stations.
ROAD: The road system in the Danish archipelago makes frequent use of ferries. The crossing time from Sjælland Island (Copenhagen) to Fyn Island (Odense) is about one hour. A combined bridge and tunnel link from Sjælland to Fyn has been under construction since 1987; completion of the bridge is expected in 1995 and completion of the tunnel is expected in 1997. This project will result in road connections being available between all the main centres in Denmark. Country buses operate where there are no railways, but there are few private long-distance coaches. Motorways are not subject to toll duty. Emergency telephones are available on motorways and there is a national breakdown network similar to the AA in Britain called *Falck*, which can be called out 24 hours a day. There are no petrol stations on motorways. Many petrol stations are automatic. A maximum of ten litres of petrol is allowed to be kept as a reserve in suitably safe containers. The Danish Motoring Organisation is *Forenede Danske Motorejere (FDM)*, PO Box 500, Firskovvej 32, DK-2800 Lyngby. Tel: 45 93 08 00. **Cycling:** There are cycle lanes along many roads and, in the countryside, many miles of scenic cycle track. Bikes can easily be taken on ferries, trains, buses and domestic air services. **Car hire:** Available to drivers over the age of 20, and can be reserved through travel agents or airlines. **Regulations:** Traffic drives on the right. The wearing of seat belts is compulsory. Motorcyclists must wear helmets and drive with dipped headlights at all times. Headlamps on all vehicles should be adjusted for righthand driving. Speed laws are strictly enforced, and heavy fines are levied on the spot; the car is impounded if payment is not made. Speed limits are 110kmph (60mph) on motorways, 50kmph (30mph) in built-up areas (signified by white plates with town silhouettes) and 80kmph (50mph) on other roads. All driving signs are international.
Documentation: A national driving licence is acceptable. EU nationals taking their own cars to Denmark are strongly advised to obtain a Green Card. Without it, insurance cover is limited to the minimum legal cover in Denmark; the Green Card tops this up to the level of cover provided by the car owner's domestic policy.
URBAN: Car repair is often available at petrol stations; costs include 22% VAT on labour and materials, which is not refunded when you leave the country. **Parking discs:** Parking in cities is largely governed by parking discs, available from petrol stations, post offices, tourist offices, banks and some police stations. These allow up to three hours parking in car parks. Kerbside parking is allowed for one hour 0900-1700 Monday to Friday; 0900-1300 Saturday unless stated otherwise. The hand of the disc should point to the quarter hour following time of arrival. The disc is to be placed on the side of the screen nearest the kerb. **Parking meters:** Where discs do not apply, parking meters regulate parking. Parking on a metered space is limited to three hours 0900-1800 Monday to Friday; 0900-1300 Saturday. Meter charges differ according to the area of the city.
JOURNEY TIMES: The following chart gives approximate journey times from Copenhagen (in hours and minutes) to other major cities/towns in Denmark.

	Air	Road	Rail
Ålborg	0.45	6.00	6.45
Århus	0.30	4.30	5.00
Billund	0.50	5.00	5.00
Esbjerg	1.00	5.00	5.00
Odense	0.35	3.00	3.00
Sønderborg	0.30	5.30	5.10

ACCOMMODATION

Contact the Danish Tourist Board for information on booking hotels and for details of the savings from the use of a *Scandinavian Bonus Pass* (which must be applied for in advance) or *Inn Cheques*. The Scandinavian Railpass *Nordtourist* is also valid as a *Scandinavian Bonus Pass*.
HOTELS: Travellers without reservations can book at Danmarks Turistråd in Copenhagen (address above) or at one of the provincial tourist offices. Denmark's fine beaches attract many visitors, and there are hotels and pensions in all major seaside resorts. For more information, contact HOREFA (National Hotel Association), Vodroffsvej 46, DK-1900 Frederiksberg C. Tel: 31 35 60 88. Fax: 31 35 93 76. **Grading:** There is no hotel grading system in Denmark, the standard is set by price and facilities offered. The Danish Tourist Board publishes an annual list of about 1000 establishments, describing facilities and tariffs; quoted prices are inclusive of *MOMS* (VAT).
INNS: Excellent inns are to be found all over the country. Some are small and only cater for local custom, but others are tailored for the tourist and have established high culinary reputations for both international dishes and local specialities. For further details, contact the Danish Tourist Board *or* Danish Inn Holidays. Tel: 75 62 35 44.
BED & BREAKFAST: There are private rooms to let, usually for one night, all over Denmark. Prices are in the range DKr150-250 (single/double room) with breakfast extra, but there may be variations from this. A further charge will be made if more beds are required. Signs along the highway with *Zimmer frei* or *Vårelse* on them indicate availability of accommodation; those who call in and enquire will find that arrangements are easily made. In Copenhagen rooms can be booked in person through the Tourist Information Department for a fee of DKr13. Local tourist offices may be contacted, either by writing or in person. The reservation fee is DKr10.
SELF-CATERING: Chalets are available in various parts of the country.
CAMPING/CARAVANNING: Campers must purchase a camping pass, available at campsites. Over 500 campsites are officially recognised and graded for facilities and shelter. Prices vary greatly; half price for children under four years. **Grading:** *3-star sites:* Fulfil the highest requirements. *2-star sites:* Showers, razor points, shops, laundry facilities. *1-star sites:* Fulfil minimum requirements for sanitary installations, drinking water, etc.
YOUTH AND FAMILY HOSTELS: There are 100 Youth and Family Hostels scattered around the country, all of which take members of affiliated organisations. A membership card from the National Youth Hostel Association is required.
FARMHOUSE HOLIDAYS: Rooms are often available for rent in farmhouses. Visitors stay as paying guests of the family and, although it is not expected, are welcome to help with the daily chores of the farm. Alternatively, in some cases separate apartments are available close to the main farmhouse. Many farms have their own fishing streams. All holiday homes and farmhouses are inspected and approved by the local tourist office. Prices are approximately DKr150 for bed & breakfast and DKr220 for half-board.
HOME EXCHANGE: The organisations listed below can arrange introductions between families interested in home exchange for short periods. The major expense for participants is travel plus a fee of DKr500. The best period (because of school holidays) is from late June to early August. The following organisation can provide further information; Dansk Bolig Bytte, Hesselvang 20, DK-2900 Hellerup. Tel: 31 61 04 05.

RESORTS & EXCURSIONS

Denmark has an abundance of picturesque villages and towns, historical castles and monuments, and a coastline which varies delightfully from broad sandy beaches to small coves and gentle fjords. Throughout the country rolling hills and gentle valleys provide a constant succession of attractive views; there are cool and shady forests of beech trees, extensive areas of heathland, a beautiful lake district, sand dunes and white cliffs resembling those of Dover; nor should one forget the Danish islands, each of which has its own unique attractions. Though there are few holiday resorts of the kind found in, say, France or Spain (the nearest equivalent being the *'Holiday Centre'* (HC), a purpose-built coastal resort), the Danes, who are taking strong measures to keep their coastline clean and tidy, are keen for visitors to sample the many unspoilt beaches. Incentives offered by the Tourist Board to encourage families to visit the country include discounted passes for children to a large number of parks, museums, zoos, etc. There are now nine *Sommerlands* in various locations in Denmark; these are activity parks where a flat entrance fee covers the visitor for use of all the many and varied facilities inside. At *Fårup Sommerland* in Saltum, for example, a fee of about £5.50 covers all activities including the use of the vast *Aquapark* which was recently completed. The Tourist Board has produced a 15-minute VHS video, *Family Holidays in Denmark*, which is available free on request.

Jutland

This area comprises the greater part of Denmark, extending 400km (250 miles) from the German border to its northernmost tip. Jutland's west coast has superb sandy beaches but bathing there is, however, often unsafe, due to the changing winds and tides. Care should be exercised, and any advice or notices issued by local authorities should be heeded. Also in Jutland is the major port of **Esbjerg**, which receives daily ferries from the UK.
Main towns & resorts: Ålborg, Holstebro, Århus, Vejle, Esbjerg, Frederikshavn, Randers, Viborg, Kolding, Silkeborg, Søndervig (HC), Aggertange (HC), Tranum Klitgård (HC).
Excursions & sightseeing: Ålborg contains the largest Viking burial ground, as well as a cathedral, monastery and castle. The largest Renaissance buildings in Denmark are in Ålborg. **Århus** has a collection of over 60 17th- and 18th-century buildings – houses, shops, workshops and so on from all over the country re-erected on a spacious landscaped site; as well as *Marselisborg Castle* and a museum of prehistory. **Esbjerg** and **Fanø** are also historically interesting and have a number of fine beaches. *Rosenholm, Clausholm* and *Værgard* castles are all worth a visit, while *Tivoliland* (Ålborg) and *Legoland* (Billund), which are open from April to September, provide good entertainment for children. *Søhøjlandet* is a new recreational park open to visitors which has chalet accommodation as well.

Fyn

Known as the 'Garden of Denmark', Fyn has some of Denmark's most picturesque and historic castles and manor houses, set in age-old parks and gardens. Odense is famous as the birthplace of the great fairytale writer Hans Christian Andersen. Fyn is connected to Jutland by bridges.

Main towns & resorts: Odense, Nyborg, Svendborg, Middelfart, Bogense, Klinten (HC).
Excursions & sightseeing: Castles and churches are the main attraction in **Fyn**. *Egeskov Castle* is a superb moated Renaissance castle which is fairytale in every detail. Other castles in the area include *Nyborg* (seat of the former National Assembly) and *Valdemar,* which houses a naval museum. There are also a number of beautiful beaches, particularly on the southern islands of **Langeland, Tåsinge** and **Ærø. Odense** has a festival every July and August celebrating the life and works of Hans Christian Andersen. Visitors can see the *Hans Christian Andersen Museum* and his childhood home. Other museums include a major railway museum and *Fyn Village*, a major cultural centre. Also in Odense is the recently completed *Brandts Klaedefabrik*, a major cultural centre.

Lolland, Falster, Møn & Bornholm

Lolland is generally flat, **Falster** less so, while **Møn** is a haven of small hills and valleys, with the *Møn Klint* chalk cliffs a breathtaking sight. **Bornholm** is set apart from the rest, 150km (90 miles) east of the Danish mainland, and is made up of fertile farmland, white beaches and rocky coastlines.
Main towns & resorts: Nysted, Nykobing, Nakskov, Stege, Sakskøbing, Rønne, Svaneke.
Sightseeing & excursions: *Knuthenborg Park* on **Lolland** is Denmark's largest, with 500 species of trees, flowers and plants; it also contains a safari park. *Ålholm Castle* contains the *Automobile Museum*, with Europe's biggest veteran and vintage car collection. *Corselitse* and the *Pederstrup Museum* are also worth a visit. **Bornholm** contains *Hammershus,* Denmark's largest castle ruin (built in 1260), as well as many fine churches. The small town of **Svaneke** was awarded the European Gold Medal in Architectural Heritage Year (1975).

Sjælland

Denmark's capital, **Copenhagen**, is on Sjælland and thus there is much commercial activity on the island. But there are also fine beaches, lakes, forests and royal palaces.
Main towns & resorts: Copenhagen (see below), Helsingør, Slagelse, Nastved, Roskilde, Hillerød, Frederikssund, Vedbæk (HC), Karlslunde (HC).
Sightseeing & excursions: At **Helsingør** can be found the old fortress of *Kronborg,* famed not only as the most imposing edifice in Scandinavia, but also as the setting for Shakespeare's *Hamlet. Frederiksborg Castle,* equally as impressive, is to be seen at **Hillerød**, which houses the *National History Museum.* The 12th-century cathedral at **Roskilde** and the *Viking Museum* are both worth a visit, while at **Skjoldenasholm** there is a fine *Tram Museum.* Excellent beaches can be found in Sjælland, particularly in the north of the island.

Copenhagen

The largest urban centre in Scandinavia, Copenhagen is a city of copper roofs and spires, founded in 1167. It has many old buildings, fountains, statues and squares, as well as the singular attraction of the *Little Mermaid* at the harbour entrance. The *Copenhagen Card* gives unlimited travel on buses and trains and free entry to a large number of museums and places of interest.
Excursions & sightseeing: A number of organised tours are available, taking in most of the famous sights. These include the Vikingland tour to the *Viking Ship Museum;* a Royal tour to the *Christianborg Palace* (the seat of Parliament), *Rosenborg Castle* and *Amalienborg Palace;* a coach tour to old-world *Bondebyen* and its open-air museum; and even a brewery tour, which takes in the famous *Carlsberg* and *Tuborg* breweries. *Tivoli,* Copenhagen's world-famous amusement park, is open from late April to mid-September. *Bakken* (in the deer park north of Copenhagen) and the *Charlottenlund Aquarium* are both worth a visit. In 1989 the biggest planetarium in northern Europe opened its doors.
POPULAR ITINERARIES: 5 day: Copenhagen–Odense–Århus–Ålborg–Billund (Legoland)–Copenhagen.

SOCIAL PROFILE

FOOD & DRINK: Most Danes have *smørrebrød* for their lunch. This is a slice of dark bread with butter and topped with slices of meat, fish or cheese and generously garnished. It bears no resemblance to traditional sandwiches and needs to be eaten sitting down with a knife and fork. Buffet-style lunch (the *koldt bord*) is also popular with a variety of fish, meats, hot dishes, cheese and sweets, usually on a self-service basis. Danes do not mix the various dishes on their plates but have them in strict order. A normal Danish breakfast or *morgen-complet* consists of coffee or tea and an assortment of breads, rolls, jam and cheese, often also sliced meats, boiled eggs and warm Danish pastries. Given its geographical position it is not surprising that shellfish also form an important part of Danish cuisine. Apart from traditional dishes, French or international cuisine is the order of the day. In Copenhagen, superb gourmet restaurants can be found, whilst Ålborg is noted for its impressive number of restaurants. Most towns have 'fast food' outlets for hamburgers and pizzas, and the sausage stalls on most street corners, selling hot sausages, hamburgers, soft drinks and beer, are popular. **Drink:** Danish coffee is delicious and if you like it very strong, ask for *mokka*. Denmark also has many varieties of beer, famous breweries being Carlsberg and Tuborg. Most popular is *pilsner* (a lager), but there is also *lager* (a darker beer). The other national drink is *akvavit,* popularly known as *snaps,* which is neither an aperitif, cocktail nor liqueur and is meant to be drunk with food, preferably with a beer chaser. It is served ice cold and only accompanies cold food. There are no licensing hours.
Note: The Danish Hotel and Restaurant Association is introducing a new sign to indicate restaurants where the needs of **diabetics** are given special attention. It consists of the words *'Diabetes mad – sund mad for alle'* ('Food for Diabetics – healthy food for everyone') encircling a chef's head.
NIGHTLIFE: There is a wide selection of nightlife, particularly in Copenhagen, where the first morning restaurants open to coincide with closing time at 0500. Jazz and dance clubs in the capital city are top quality and world-famous performers appear regularly. Beer gardens are numerous.
SHOPPING: Copenhagen has excellent shopping facilities. Special purchases include Bing & Grøndal and Royal Copenhagen porcelain, Holmegård glass, Georg Jensen silver, furs from AC Bang and Birger Christensen, Bornholm ceramics, handmade woollens from the Faroe Islands and Lego toys. Visitors from outside the EU can often claim back on some of the *MOMS* (VAT) on goods purchased that are sent straight to their home country from the shop in Denmark. **Shopping hours:** 0900-1730 Monday to Thursday, 0900-1900 Friday and 0900-1300 Saturday. Opening hours vary from town to town since shops can regulate their own hours. At some holiday resorts, shops are open Sunday and public holidays.
SPORT: Swimming, sailing, windsurfing and **skindiving** may be found at coastal resorts such as Bornholm and on the Jutland Coast; there are 600 harbours and many marinas where boats can be hired. There are also possibilities for freshwater **fishing** on Denmark's numerous lakes and rivers; coastal areas offer sea fishing. **Football** and **badminton** are played at international level: the national team are the current European football champions. There are about 60 **golf** courses in Denmark of which about half are 18-hole courses. **Horseriding** schools can be found throughout the country. Enquire at local tourist offices for sports facilities.
SPECIAL EVENTS: The following is only a selection of the major festivals and other special events celebrated annually in Denmark. For a complete list (published in several languages) contact the Danish Tourist Board.
'95 *Changing of the Guard Ceremony,* Amalienborg Palace, Copenhagen (all year); *550th Town Anniversary of Grenaa* (all year); *500th Town Anniversary of Kalundborg* (all year); *75th Anniversary of the Reunion,* South Jutland. **Mar 30-Aug 28** *Dyrehavsbakken,* Copenhagen. **Apr-Sep** *Tivoliland,* Aalborg. **May 27-Jun 10** *Fyrkat Play,* Hobro. **Jun** *Central Funen Festival,* Ringe. **Jun 10** *Rock under the Bridge,* Middelfart. **Jun 22-25** *Skagen Festival.* **Jun 23-25** *Riverboat Jazz Festival,* Silkeborg; *Danish Accordion and Fiddlers Meet,* Ringe. **Jun 23-Jul 9** *Viking Festival,* Frederikssund. **Jun 25-Aug 27** *Summer Matinees at Egeskov Castle,* Kværndrup. **Jun 29-Jul 2** *Roskilde Festival.* **Jun 30-Jul 16** *Jels Viking Play,* Rødding. **Jul 7-16** *Copenhagen Jazz Festival.* **Jul 12-Aug 6** *Hans Christian Andersen Festival*, Odense. **Jul 24-Aug 11** *Copenhagen Summer Festival.* **Aug 1-6** *13th Odense Film Festival.* **Mid-Aug** *Copenhagen Water Festival,* Copenhagen Harbour. **Aug 25-31** *Wagner Festival,* Århus. **Sep** *Copenhagen Film Festival.* **Sep 2-10** *Århus Festival 1995.* **Sep 10-Oct 2** *Amager Music Festival,* Copenhagen. **Nov** *Nordic Puppet Theatre Festival,* Silkeborg. **Nov 15-19** *Musical Autumn,* Odense.
SOCIAL CONVENTIONS: Normal courtesies should be observed. Guests should refrain from drinking until the host toasts his or her health. Casual dress is suitable for most places but formal wear is required at more exclusive dining rooms and social functions. Smoking is restricted on public transport and in some public buildings. **Tipping:** Hotels and restaurants quote fully inclusive prices and tipping is not necessary. Taxi fares include tip. Railway porters and washroom attendants receive tips.

BUSINESS PROFILE

ECONOMY: The standard of living is generally high. Since the war, industry has rapidly expanded in importance, although by the standards of most industrialised countries, Denmark retains an important agricultural industry. Two-thirds of Danish produce is exported, principally cheese, beef and bacon. Danish manufacturing industry, the largest economic sector, depends on imports of raw materials and components. Iron, steel and other metal industries are the most important, followed by electronics (which is growing especially quickly), chemicals and bio-technology, paper and printing, textiles, furniture and cement. Food-processing and drinks also make a significant contribution. The weakest aspect of the Danish economy is its lack of raw materials, particularly oil and other fuels. However, the discovery of offshore deposits has improved the balance of payments in this area, leaving Denmark with a small net trade surplus towards the end of the 1980s. Most of Denmark's trade is conducted within the European Union, of which it is a member. The Maastricht treaty was accepted by the Danish government in 1991 but failed to be adopted following a negative result in the first of two popular referenda; it was endorsed on the second. Germany is the largest single trading partner, providing 23% of Denmark's imports and taking 17% of exports. The comparable figures for the UK are 7.5% and 11% respectively. Sweden and the USA are the most important markets outside the Union. According to the Department of Trade and Industry, there are especially good opportunities for British exporters in the following sectors: electrical components, food and drinks, clothing, computer hardware and software, textiles and car components.
BUSINESS: English is widely used for all aspects of business. Local business people expect visitors to be punctual and the approach to business is often direct and straightforward. Avoid business visits from mid-June to mid-August which are prime holiday periods. **Office hours:** 0900-1700 Monday to Friday.
COMMERCIAL INFORMATION: The following organisations can offer advice: Det Danske Handels-kammer (Danish Chamber of Commerce), Børsen, DK-1217 Copenhagen K. Tel: 33 95 05 00 *or* 33 33 04 64. Fax: 33 32 52 16 *or* 33 91 23 23 *or* 33 15 22 66. Telex: 19520.
CONFERENCES/CONVENTIONS: The Danish Convention Bureau, a non-profitmaking organisation, was established in 1988 by the Danish Tourist Board, the Danish Council of Tourist Trade, Scandinavian Airlines, Danish State Railways, the Danish Hotel and Restaurant Association, Danish Incoming Travel Bureaus and the Danish Association of Multipurpose Halls. The Bureau's aim is to assist decision-makers and planners of meetings, congresses and incentive travel. There are over 100 affiliated companies. For further general inform-ation, brochures, or to initiate plans for a conference/ convention, contact the Danish Tourist Board in Copenhagen or London (for addresses, see above).

CLIMATE

Summer extends from June to August. Winter is from December to March, wet with long periods of frost. February is the coldest month. Spring and autumn are generally mild.
The *Faroe Islands* are under the influence of the warm current of the Gulf Stream, and they enjoy a very mild climate for the latitude. Winters are warm, but the islands are cloudy, windy and wet throughout the year. Summers are cool, but with little sunshine.
Required clothing: Lightweight for summer and heavyweight for winter snows.

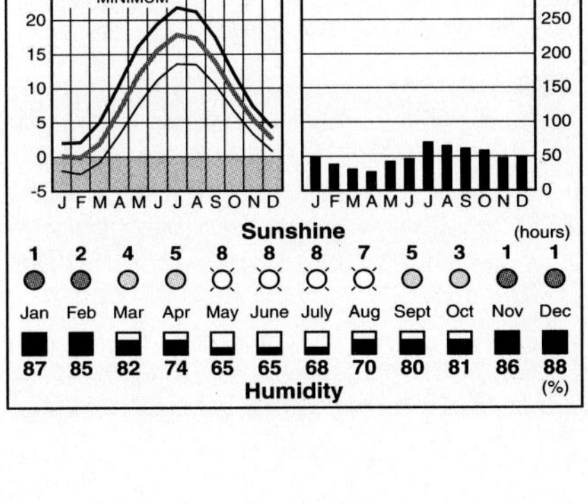

Djibouti

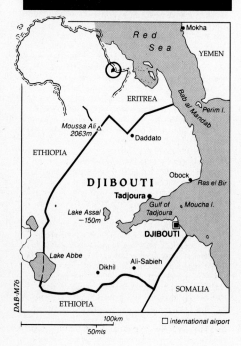

Location: Northeast Africa; Gulf of Aden.

Office de Developpement du Tourisme
BP 1938, Djibouti, Djibouti
Tel: 353 790 or 352 800. Telex: 5808.
Embassy of the Republic of Djibouti
26 rue Emile Ménier, 75116 Paris, France
Tel: (1) 47 27 49 22. Fax: (1) 45 53 50 53. Telex:
614970.
British Consulate
BP 81, Gellatly Hankey et Cie, Djibouti, Djibouti
Tel: 353 844. Fax: 353 294. Telex: 5843 (a/b
GELLATLY DJ).
Embassy of the Republic of Djibouti
Suite 515, 1156 15th Street, NW, Washington, DC 20005
Tel (202) 331 0270 or 331 0202. Fax: (202) 331 0302.
Telex: 4490085 (a/b AMDJUS).
Also deals with enquiries from Canada.
Embassy of the United States of America
BP 185, Plateau du Serpent, boulevard Maréchal Joffré,
Djibouti, Djibouti
Tel: 353 995. Fax: 353 940.
**The Canadian Embassy in Addis Ababa deals with
enquiries relating to Djibouti (see *Ethiopia* later in the
book).**

AREA: 23,200 sq km (8958 sq miles).
POPULATION: 519,900 (1990 estimate).
POPULATION DENSITY: 22.4 per sq km.
CAPITAL: Djibouti. **Population:** 200,000 (1981).
GEOGRAPHY: Djibouti is part of the African continent
bounded to the northeast and east by the Red Sea, the
southeast by Somalia, the southwest by Ethiopia and to
the north by Eritrea. The country is a barren strip of land
around the Gulf of Tadjoura, varying in width from 20km
(12 miles) to 90km (56 miles), with a coastline of 800km
(497 miles), much of it white sandy beaches. Inland is
semi-desert and desert, with thorn bushes, steppes and
volcanic mountain ranges.
LANGUAGE: The official languages are Arabic and

French. Afar and Somali are spoken locally. English is
spoken by hoteliers, taxi drivers and traders.
RELIGION: Muslim with Roman Catholic, Protestant
and Greek Orthodox minorities.
TIME: GMT + 3.
ELECTRICITY: 220 volts AC, 50Hz.
COMMUNICATIONS: Telephone: IDD available.
Country code: 253. Outgoing international code: 00. **Fax:**
There are no facilities for the public. **Telex/telegram:**
Telexes and telegrams can be sent from the main post
office from 0700-2000. Telegram services are also
available at the Telegraph office. **Post:** Letters and
parcels to western Europe can take about a week by
airmail or up to three weeks by surface mail. **Press:**
Djibouti has no daily papers. A weekly newspaper, *La
Nation de Djibouti*, is published in French.
**BBC World Service and Voice of America
frequencies:** From time to time these change. See the
section *How to Use this Book* for more information.
BBC:

MHz	21.47	17.64	15.42	6.005
Voice of America:				
MHz	21.49	15.60	9.525	6.035

PASSPORT/VISA

Regulations and requirements may be subject to change at short notice, and you are advised to contact the appropriate diplomatic or consular authority before finalising travel arrangements. Details of these may be found at the head of this country's entry. Any numbers in the chart refer to the footnotes below.

	Passport Required?	Visa Required?	Return Ticket Required?
Full British	Yes	Yes	Yes
BVP	Not valid	-	-
Australian	Yes	Yes	Yes
Canadian	Yes	Yes	Yes
USA	Yes	Yes	Yes
Other EU (As of 31/12/94)	Yes	1	Yes
Japanese	Yes	Yes	Yes

Prohibited entry and transit: The Government of the
Republic of Djibouti refuses admission and transit to
nationals of Israel.
PASSPORTS: Valid passport required by all.
British Visitors Passport: Not accepted.
VISAS: Required by all **[1]** except nationals of France
for a maximum stay of 3 months, provided a return ticket
is held.
Types of visa: Entry visa; Transit visa (Visa d'Escale).
Prices are identical (see *Application requirements*
below). 10-day Transit visas can be issued at the point of
entry to visitors holding confirmed return air tickets. A
fee will be charged. This facility is available to certain
nationals only. Contact the Embassy in Paris for further
information.
Validity: From 1 to 3 months. An extension may be
granted in Djibouti on request to the Headquarters of the
Police Nationale.
Application to: The Embassy in Paris. For address, see
top of entry. Nationals of the UK visiting Djibouti for a
short stay may apply to the French Consulate (Visa
section) in London.
Application requirements: (a) Valid passport. (b)
Application form completed in French. (c) 2 passport-size
photos. (d) Travel documents, including a photocopy of
the return ticket *or* written confirmation from a travel
agent certifying the issue of a ticket. (e) The equivalent of
FFr69 plus FFr30 to cover postage within France or FFr35
to cover postage from abroad; the amount should be sent
in the form of a postal or money order, *not* a cheque.
Working days required: Application normally takes 48
hours to process.
Note: It is obligatory for foreign nationals resident in
Djibouti to hold an exit visa.

MONEY

Currency: Djibouti Franc (Dfr) = 100 centimes. Notes
are in denominations of Dfr5000, 1000 and 500. Coins
are in denominations of Dfr100, 50, 20, 10, 5, 2 and 1.
Credit cards: These are only accepted by airlines and
some of the larger hotels.
Travellers cheques: French Franc and Sterling cheques
are not accepted unless marked as 'External Account' or
'Pour Compte Etranger'. The majority of banks are in the
place du 27 juin area.
Exchange rate indicators: The following figures are
included as a guide to the movements of the Djibouti
Franc against Sterling and the US Dollar:

Date:	Oct '92	Sep '93	Jan '94	Jan '95
£1.00=	85.00	269.25	263.00	277.87
$1.00=	79.58	76.33	177.76	177.60

Currency restrictions: No restrictions on import or
export of either foreign or local currency.
Banking hours: 0715-1145 Sunday to Thursday.

DUTY FREE

As for France; see the *France* entry later in the book.
Firearms must be declared on entry and exit.

PUBLIC HOLIDAYS

Jan 1 '95 New Year's Day. **Mar 3** Eid al-Fitr (End of
Ramadan). **May 1** Workers' Day. **May 10** Eid al-Adha
(Feast of the Sacrifice). **May 31** Muharram (Islamic New
Year). **Jun 27** Independence Day. **Aug 9** Mouloud
(Prophet's Birthday). **Dec 25** Christmas Day. **Jan 1 '96**
New Year's Day. **Feb 22** Eid al-Fitr (End of Ramadan).
Apr 29 Eid al-Adha (Feast of the Sacrifice).
Note: Muslim festivals are timed according to local
sightings of various phases of the Moon and the dates
given above are approximations. During the lunar month
of Ramadan that precedes Eid al-Fitr, Muslims fast
during the day and feast at night and normal business
patterns may be interrupted. Many restaurants are closed
during the day and there may be restrictions on smoking
and drinking. Some disruption may continue into Eid al-
Fitr itself. Eid al-Fitr and Eid al-Adha may last anything
from two to ten days, depending on the region. For
further information see the section *World of Islam* at the
back of the book.

HEALTH

Regulations and requirements may be subject to change at short notice, and you are advised to contact your doctor well in advance of your intended date of departure. Any numbers in the chart refer to the footnotes below.

	Special Precautions?	Certificate Required?
Yellow Fever	Yes	1
Cholera	Yes	2
Typhoid & Polio	Yes	-
Malaria	Yes/3	-
Food & Drink	4	-

[1]: A yellow fever vaccination certificate is required from
travellers over one year of age coming from infected areas.
[2]: Following WHO guidelines issued in 1973, a cholera
vaccination certificate is no longer a condition of entry to
Djibouti. However, cholera is a serious risk in this country and
precautions are essential. Up-to-date advice should be sought
before deciding if these precautions should include vaccination
as medical opinion is divided over its effectiveness. See the
Health section at the back of the book.
[3]: Malaria risk, predominantly in the malignant
falciparum form, exists throughout the year in the whole
country. Resistance to chloroquine has been reported.
[4]: Mains water is normally heavily chlorinated, and
whilst relatively safe may cause mild abdominal upsets.
Bottled water is available and is advised for the first few
weeks of the stay. Drinking water outside main cities and
towns is likely to be contaminated and sterilisation is
considered essential. Milk is unpasteurised and should be
boiled. Powdered or tinned milk is available and is
advised, but make sure that it is reconstituted with pure
water. Avoid dairy products which are likely to have
been made from unboiled milk. Only eat well-cooked
meat and fish, preferably served hot. Pork, salad and
mayonnaise may carry increased risk. Vegetables should
be cooked and fruit peeled.
Health care: Health insurance is advisable. Doctors and
hospitals may expect immediate cash payment for any
form of medical treatment.

TRAVEL - International

AIR: Djibouti does not have a national airline. Services
are offered by *Aeroflot (SU)*, *Air France (AF)*, *Air
Madagascar (MD)* and *Air Tanzania*.
Approximate flight time: From London to Djibouti is
11 hours (including stopovers).
International airport: *Djibouti (JIB)* is 5km (3 miles)
south of the city. Taxis are available. There are four or
five flights a week from Paris.
Departure tax: Dfr2000, except for *Air France* tickets
(tax included in ticket price).
RAIL: The *Djibouti–Ethiopian Railway* operates regular
trains from Addis Ababa and Dire Dawa with one train
daily connecting with Djibouti; tourists and business
people are prohibited from using the service.
ROAD: There are good roads from Djibouti to Assab

(Eritrea) and going west into Ethiopia via Dikhil. Most other roads are rough but passable throughout the year and there is now a road link with Addis Ababa. Check transit regulations as political conditions in Ethiopia and Eritrea are changeable. There is a bus up to the Somalian border at Loyoda (see below under *Travel – Internal* for information on documentation).

TRAVEL - Internal

AIR: Private charters may be available.
SEA: Ferry services sail to Tadjoura and Obock from Djibouti (three hours).
RAIL: The only service is provided by daily train to the border with Ethiopia (see above) which tourists and business people are prohibited from using.
ROAD: Four-wheel-drive vehicles are recommended for the interior. There is a new highway from Djibouti to Tadjoura. Traffic drives on the right. **Car hire:** Available in Djibouti and at the airport. Contact *Red Sea Cars* (tel: 354 646). Four-wheel-drive vehicles are available from *Stophi* (tel: 352 494). It is advisable to carry water and petrol on any expedition off main routes.
Documentation: An International Driving Permit is recommended, although it is not legally required. A temporary licence to drive is available from local authorities on presentation of a valid British or Northern Ireland driving licence. Insurance is not required.
URBAN: A minibus service operates in Djibouti, stopping on demand. A flat-fare system is used. **Taxi:** These are available in Djibouti and from the airport to the town; also in Ali-Sabieh, Dikhil, Dorale and Arta. Fares increase by 50% after dark.

ACCOMMODATION

Hotels in Djibouti tend to be expensive and the few cheap hotels are somewhat seedy. The major hotels are the Sheraton, the Hotel Plein Ciel, the Menelik and the Résidence de l'Europe.
Outside Djibouti, accommodation is limited, although attention is being given to upgrading and adding to the accommodation available in the hinterland. The rest shelter at Ali-Sabieh, a provincial town in the hills, has already been enlarged from two rooms to nine, and a large shaded terrace and simple cooking facilities have also been added. Countrywide, however, much remains to be done. The Government would like to establish a network of rest houses similar to the one at Ali-Sabieh throughout the country. In addition, it hopes to build several bush shelters.
Note: *Air France* can book accommodation in advance in the Sheraton and Le Plein Ciel (first-class) hotels through their London office at the same time as issuing the air ticket.

RESORTS & EXCURSIONS

Djibouti is a late 19th-century city with a market near the Mosque, and several good restaurants. Nearby are beaches at *Dorale,* 11km (7 miles), and *Kor Ambad,* 14km (9 miles). Djibouti lies within a geological feature known as the *Afar Triangle,* one of the hottest and most desolate places on Earth. Part of the Great Rift Valley system, it is a wedge of flat desert pushing into the Ethiopian Massif. Much of it is below sea level, indeed *Lake Assal,* 100km (60 miles) to the southwest of Djibouti city, is one of the lowest surface areas anywhere on the planet; and is reachable only by 4-wheel-drive vehicle. Straddling the Ethiopian frontier is another lake, *Lake Abbe,* the home of thousands of flamingoes and pelicans. A large market can be found at **Ali-Sabieh,** a major stop for the main-line train between Djibouti and Addis Ababa. On the opposite side of the **Gulf of Tadjoura,** an excellent place for skindiving, fishing and underwater photography, are the towns of

Obock and **Tadjoura,** a town with seven mosques. In the hinterland is the *Goda Mountains National Park.*

SOCIAL PROFILE

FOOD & DRINK: There are restaurants to suit all tastes, serving French, Vietnamese, Chinese, Arab and local specialities. Drink will only be limited in Muslim areas (particularly during Ramadan).
SHOPPING: Lively and colourful local markets are well worth visiting and local crafts and artefacts can be bought. **Shopping hours:** 0800-1200 and 1600-1900 Saturday to Thursday (closed Wednesday).
SPORT: There are beaches at Dorale and Kor Ambade several kilometres from Djibouti with safe **swimming**. The Gulf of Tadjoura (especially Obock) offers many species of fish and coral and is ideal for **diving**, **spearfishing** and **underwater photography**. The best time for these activities is from September to May when the waters of the Red Sea are clear.
Note: Hunting is forbidden throughout the country.
SOCIAL CONVENTIONS: Casual wear is widely acceptable, but visitors are reminded that Djibouti is a Muslim country and certain codes of behaviour should be observed. **Tipping:** A 10% service charge is usually added to bills. Tipping is rare and never requested. Not usual for taxi drivers. A tariff is normally set but visitors will be charged at a higher rate.

BUSINESS PROFILE

ECONOMY: There is little arable farming and most of the land is desert used by nomads for livestock. There is a small industrial sector. The deep-water port on the Bab-El-Mandeb Straits is vitally important to the country, as it is on the major oil route between the Gulf of Aden and the Red Sea. Djibouti's economic potential lies in the development of its service sector. Transport facilities and banking are the most productive sectors, although Djibouti's economy has suffered throughout the last decade from the political upheaval in the Horn of Africa. The Government hopes to develop Djibouti as a trading centre between Africa and the Middle East and an important telecommunications hub for the region. At present the country is dependent on foreign aid, which it obtains from France and the Middle East. Exports – mostly of food and live animals – barely reach 10% of imports at present: most of the latter originate from France, with Ethiopia, the Benelux countries, Italy and the UK supplying the rest.
BUSINESS: Suits should be worn. French and Arabic are the main languages used in business. As there are few, if any, interpreter services of note, a knowledge of either of these languages is essential. Business entertainment will often take place in hotels or restaurants. **Office hours:** 0620-1300 Saturday to Thursday.
COMMERCIAL INFORMATION: The following organisation can offer advice: Chambre Internationale de Commerce et d'Industrie, BP 84, place de l'Independence, Djibouti. Tel: 350 826 *or* 350 673. Fax: 350 096. Telex: 5957.
CONFERENCES/CONVENTIONS: Information can be obtained from the Chambre Internationale de Commerce et d'Industrie (for address, see above).

CLIMATE

Extremely hot and particulary arid between June and August when the dusty *Khamsin* blows from the desert. Between October and April it is slightly cooler with occasional light rain.

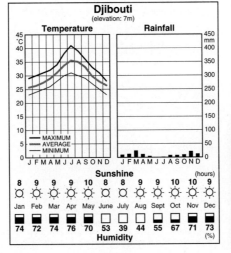

Djibouti
(elevation: 7m)

Temperature	Rainfall

MAXIMUM
AVERAGE
MINIMUM

Sunshine (hours)

	Jan	Feb	Mar	Apr	May	June	July	Aug	Sept	Oct	Nov	Dec
	8	9	9	9	10	8	8	9	9	10	10	9

	Jan	Feb	Mar	Apr	May	June	July	Aug	Sept	Oct	Nov	Dec
	74	72	74	76	70	53	39	44	55	67	71	73
Humidity (%)

Dominica
(Commonwealth of)

Location: Caribbean, Windward Islands.

National Development Corporation (NDC) – Division of Tourism
PO Box 293, Valley Road, Roseau, Dominica
Tel: 82351. Fax: 85840. Telex: 8642.
Dominica High Commission
1 Collingham Gardens, South Kensington, London SW5 0HW
Tel: (0171) 370 5194/5. Fax: (0171) 373 8743. Telex: 8813931 (a/b DACOM G).
Caribbean Tourism
Vigilant House, 120 Wilton Road, London SW1V 1JZ
Tel: (0171) 233 8382. Fax: (0171) 873 8551. Opening hours: 0900-1730 Monday to Friday.
The British High Commission in Bridgetown deals with enquiries relating to Dominica (see *Barbados* **earlier in the book).**
Caribbean Tourism Organization
20 East 46th Street, New York, NY 10017
Tel: (212) 682 0435. Fax: (212) 697 4258.
Also deals with enquiries from Canada.
High Commission for the Countries of the Organisation of Eastern Caribbean States
Suite 1610, Tower B, 112 Kent Street, Place de Ville, Ottawa, Ontario K1P 5P2
Tel: (613) 236 8952. Fax: (613) 236 3042. Telex: 0534476.
The Canadian High Commission in Bridgetown deals with enquiries relating to Dominica (see *Barbados* **earlier in the book).**

AREA: 749.8 sq km (289.5 sq miles).
POPULATION: 71,183 (1991).
POPULATION DENSITY: 94.9 per sq km.
CAPITAL: Roseau. **Population:** 20,755 (1991).
GEOGRAPHY: Dominica is the largest and most mountainous of the Windward Islands with volcanic peaks, mountain streams and rivers, dense forests, quiet

Health	
GALILEO/WORLDSPAN:	**TI-DFT/DOM/HE**
SABRE:	**TIDFT/DOM/HE**

Visa	
GALILEO/WORLDSPAN:	**TI-DFT/DOM/VI**
SABRE:	**TIDFT/DOM/VI**

For more information on Timatic codes refer to Contents.

lakes, waterfalls, geysers and boiling volcanic pools. There are beaches of both black (volcanic) and golden sands while orchids and untamed subtropical vegetation grow in the valleys. Guadeloupe is to the north and Martinique to the south.

LANGUAGE: The official language is English, but a Creole French, the national language, is spoken by most of the population. A dictionary of this language is in preparation. Cocoy, a variant of English, is spoken in the region of Marigot and Wesley.

RELIGION: Roman Catholic majority.

TIME: GMT - 4.

ELECTRICITY: 220/240 volts AC, 50Hz.

COMMUNICATIONS: Telephone: IDD available. Country code: 1 809. Outgoing international code: 1 for USA, Canada and *most* Caribbean islands; 011 for other countries. **Fax:** Services are available through the Cable & Wireless Company. Opening hours: 0700-2000 Monday to Saturday. **Telex:** Services are also available through Cable & Wireless; for opening hours see above. **Post:** There are no *Poste Restante* facilities. Post offices are open 0830-1300 and 1430-1700 Monday; 0830-1300 and 1430-1600 Tuesday to Friday. **Press:** Newspapers are in English. These include *The New Chronicle* (published every Friday), *The Tropical Star* (every Wednesday) and the *Official Gazette*.

BBC World Service and Voice of America frequencies: From time to time these change. See the section *How to Use this Book* for more information.

BBC:

| MHz | 17.84 | 15.22 | 9.915 | 5.975 |

Voice of America:

| MHz | 15.21 | 11.70 | 6.130 | 0.930 |

PASSPORT/VISA

Regulations and requirements may be subject to change at short notice, and you are advised to contact the appropriate diplomatic or consular authority before finalising travel arrangements. Details of these may be found at the head of this country's entry. Any numbers in the chart refer to the footnotes below.

	Passport Required?	Visa Required?	Return Ticket Required?
Full British	Yes	No	Yes
BVP	Not valid/2	-	-
Australian	Yes	No	Yes
Canadian	1	No	Yes
USA	1	No	Yes
Other EU (As of 31/12/94)	Yes	No	Yes
Japanese	Yes	No	Yes

PASSPORTS: [1] Valid passport required by all except nationals of Canada and the USA who must have suitable ID and return or onward tickets.

British Visitors Passport: [2] Not accepted. Although the immigration authorities in this country may in certain circumstances accept British Visitors Passports for persons arriving for holidays or unpaid business trips of up to 3 months, travellers are reminded that no formal agreement exists to this effect and the situation may, therefore, change at short notice. In addition, UK nationals using a BVP and returning to the UK from a country with which no such formal agreement exists may be subject to delays and interrogation by UK immigration.

VISAS: Not required for a stay of up to 21 days (*see note below). For an extension, visitors should apply to the Immigration Department at the Police Headquarters in Roseau, Dominica.

Application to: Dominica High Commission. For address, see top of entry.

Temporary residence: Those applying for temporary residence must obtain a work permit.

Note [*]: However, nationals of the former Communist bloc countries and nationals of African states outside the Commonwealth should enquire at the nearest Embassy or High Commission with regard to visa requirements.

MONEY

Currency: East Caribbean Dollar (EC$) = 100 cents. Notes are in denominations of EC$100, 20, 5 and 1. Coins are in denominations of 50, 25, 10, 5, 2 and 1 cents. US Dollars are also legal tender.

Credit cards: Visa and Access/Mastercard (limited) are accepted. Check with your credit card company for details of merchant acceptability and other services which may be available.

Travellers cheques: Accepted by most hotels.

Exchange rate indicators: The following figures are included as a guide to the movements of the EC Dollar against Sterling and the US Dollar:

Date:	Oct '92	Sep '93	Jan '94	Jan '95
£1.00=	4.27	4.13	3.99	4.22
$1.00=	*2.70	*2.71	*2.70	*2.70

Note [*]: The Eastern Caribbean Dollar is tied to the US Dollar.

Currency restrictions: Unlimited import of local and foreign currency, subject to declaration on arrival. Export of both is limited to the amount declared on import.

Banking hours: 0800-1500 Monday to Thursday; 0800-1700 Friday.

DUTY FREE

The following goods may be imported into Dominica without incurring customs duty:
200 cigarettes or 2 packets of tobacco or 24 cigars; 2 bottles of alcoholic beverage.

PUBLIC HOLIDAYS

Jan 2 '95 For New Year's Day. **Feb 27-28** Carnival. **Apr 14** Good Friday. **Apr 17** Easter Monday. **May 1** May Day. **Jun 5** Whit Monday. **Aug 7** August Monday. **Nov 3** National Day. **Nov 4** Community Service Day. **Dec 25** Christmas. **Dec 26** Boxing Day. **Jan 1 '96** New Year's Day. **Apr 5** Good Friday. **Apr 8** Easter Monday. **May 1** May Day. **May 23** Whit Monday.

HEALTH

Regulations and requirements may be subject to change at short notice, and you are advised to contact your doctor well in advance of your intended date of departure. Any numbers in the chart refer to the footnotes below.

	Special Precautions?	Certificate Required?
Yellow Fever	No	1
Cholera	No	No
Typhoid & Polio	2	-
Malaria	No	-
Food & Drink	3	-

[1]: A yellow fever vaccination certificate is required from travellers over one year of age coming from infected areas.

[2]: Polio immunisation is recommended; the risk of typhoid fever is uncertain, but vaccination is recommended.

[3]: Mains water is normally chlorinated, and whilst relatively safe may cause mild abdominal upsets. Bottled water is available and is advised for the first few weeks of the stay. Drinking water outside main cities and towns may be contaminated and sterilisation is advisable. Milk is pasteurised and dairy products are safe for consumption. Local meat, poultry, seafood, fruit and vegetables are generally considered safe to eat.

Health care: Health insurance is recommended.

TRAVEL - International

AIR: The main airline to serve Dominica is *LIAT (LI)*. Others include *Air Caraibes, Air Martinique* and *Air Guadeloupe.*

Approximate flight times: From Roseau to *London* via Antigua is approximately 10 hours (depending on length of stopover), to *Los Angeles* is 10 hours and to *New York* is 7 hours.

International airports (turbo-prop only): *Melville Hall (DOM)* is approximately 56km (35 miles) northeast of Roseau.
Canefield (DCF) is approximately 5km (3 miles) north of Roseau.

SEA: *Geest* and several other island-hopping freight lines stop in Dominica. Generally, passenger accommodation is comfortable but numbers are limited, so book well in advance. The *Caribbean Express*, a scheduled ferry service, offers boat connections on a 200-seat catamaran; connections can be made from Guadeloupe, Martinique and Les Saintes. Other cruise liners stop at Woodbridge Bay, 5km (3 miles) outside Roseau. A new cruise ship jetty has been developed and opened at Prince Rupert Bay, Portsmouth.

TRAVEL - Internal

ROAD: There are more than 700km (450 miles) of well-maintained roads on the island and there is little traffic outside Roseau. Traffic drives on the left. **Bus:** Service exists but is unpredictable. **Taxis** and **minibuses** are the most efficient means of road transport. **Car hire:** Available, but roads can be difficult. Jeep tours operated by local firms offer the best means of sightseeing; all vehicles chartered for this purpose must be hired for at least three hours. **Documentation:** International Driving Permit recommended. A valid foreign licence can be used to get a Temporary Visitor's Permit.

JOURNEY TIMES: The following chart gives approximate journey times (in hours and minutes) from Roseau to other places in Dominica.

	Road
Canefield Airport	0.15
Melville H. A'port	1.00
Portsmouth	0.50

ACCOMMODATION

HOTELS: The number of hotels has expanded in recent years; most of the hotels are small- to medium-sized, and well-equipped; the largest of them has 98 rooms. There are three hotels at the fringe of an area designated as a National Park. Information can be obtained from the Dominica Hotel Association, PO Box 384, Roseau. Tel: 448 6565. Fax: 448 0299. The Association also provides assistance in organising conferences and conventions in Dominica. **Grading:** Many of the hotels offer accommodation according to one of a number of 'Plans' widely used in the Caribbean; these include Modified American Plan (MAP) which consists of room, breakfast and dinner and European Plan (EP) which consists of room only.

APARTMENTS/COTTAGES: These offer self-catering, full service and maid service facilities and are scattered around the island.

GUEST-HOUSES: There is a variety of guest-houses and inns around the island which offer a comfortable and very friendly atmosphere. There is a 10% government tax and 10% service charge on rooms.

CAMPING/CARAVANNING: Not encouraged at the present time, though sites may be designated in future. Overnight safari tours are run by local operators.

RESORTS & EXCURSIONS

Roseau, on the southwest coast, is the main centre for visitors. From hotels around here it is possible to arrange jeep safari tours for seeing the hinterland of the country. Canoe trips up the rivers can also be arranged. The beaches are mainly of black volcanic sand, but there are a few white-sand beaches on the northeast of this island. Sports facilities include scuba diving, sailing and sport fishing.

Morne Trois Pitons National Park, covering 7000 hectares (17,000 acres) in the south-central part of Dominica, was established in July 1975. Places of interest in the park include the *Boiling Lake*, the second-largest in the world which was discovered in 1922, and the *Emerald Pool, Middleham Falls, Sari Sari Falls, Trafalgar Triple Waterfalls, Freshwater Lake, Boeri Lake* and the *Valley of Desolation*.

Cabrits Historical Park was designated a park in 1987. Attractions include the **Cabrits Peninsular** which contains the historical ruins of *Fort Shirley* and *Fort George*, 18th- and early 19th-century forts, and a museum at Fort Shirley. The usual touring spots in addition to the above include the **Carib Indian Territory**, the *Sulphur Springs*, the *Central Forest Reserve, Botanical Gardens, Titou Gorge, L'Escalier Tête Chien*, several areas of rainforest and a variety of fauna and flora.

SOCIAL PROFILE

FOOD & DRINK: In general it is wise to order the speciality of the house or of the day to ensure freshness. Island cooking includes Creole, Continental and American. Creole dishes include *tee-tee-ree* (tiny freshly spawned fish), *lambi* (conch), *agouti* (a rodent), *manicou*, pig and wild pigeon (smoked meats), and *crabbacks* (backs of red and black crabs stuffed with seasoned crab meat). *Bello Hot Pepper Sauce* is made locally and served everywhere with almost everything. Food prices on Dominica are usually reasonable. Restaurants close at about 2400 weekdays and are open later at weekends. Root vegetables, such as yams and turnips, are often referred to as 'provisions' on a menu. **Drink:** Island fruit juices are excellent as are rum punches, particularly Anchorage Hotel's coconut rum punch (made from fresh coconut milk, sugar, rum, bitters, vanilla and grenadine). *Sea moss* is a non-alcoholic beverage made from sea moss or seaweed, with a slightly minty taste. Spirits, local rum especially, are inexpensive. Wines (mainly French and Californian), are expensive. There is a wide choice of

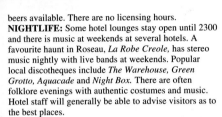

WORLD TRAVEL ATLAS

As well as a complete set of conventional plates, the World Travel Atlas contains a wealth of specialist maps and charts designed specifically for use by the travel trade and students of travel and tourism.

The only atlas of its kind, the World Travel Atlas has quickly established itself as an essential reference work for all those connected with the world of travel.

Caribbean Resorts ● World Cruise Routes ● Spanish Resorts ● World Climate ● World Natural and Cultural Heritage Maps ● World Health ● World Driving ● Italian Resorts ● International Tourism Statistics ● Main Airports of the World ● Greek Islands ● UK & Mediterranean clean beaches

COLUMBUS PRESS

Call Columbus Press for further details on (0171) 417 0700 or fax (0171) 417 0710.

---

beers available. There are no licensing hours.

NIGHTLIFE: Some hotel lounges stay open until 2300 and there is music at weekends at several hotels. A favourite haunt in Roseau, *La Robe Creole,* has stereo music nightly with live bands at weekends. Popular local discotheques include *The Warehouse, Green Grotto, Aquacade* and *Night Box.* There are often folklore evenings with authentic costumes and music. Hotel staff will generally be able to advise visitors as to the best places.

SHOPPING: There is no duty-free shopping, but there are some excellent buys to be found among native handicrafts including hats, bags and rugs made from vetiver grass joined with wild banana strands. The *Carib Reserve Crafts Centre* produces bags made from two layers of reeds that are buried in the ground to achieve a 3-colour effect and covered with a layer of broad banana-type leaf to make them waterproof. There are also two clothing companies and the denim jeans bought here are cheaper than on the other islands to which they are exported. **Shopping hours:** 0800-1300 and 1400-1600 Monday to Friday; 0800-1300 Saturday.

SPORTS: Scuba and **snorkelling** equipment may be hired through hotels and local tour operators. There are facilities for **parasailing, windsurfing** and **water-skiing** at many seaside hotels. Fifteen-minute parasailing flights are available for parties of four or more. Windsurf boards may be hired. Speedboats can be hired for water-skiing. **Motor boats** and **sailing boats** can be chartered at the Anchorage Hotel or through tour operators. **Angling** charters can be arranged for parties of fishermen through the Anchorage Hotel, which also operates a sports tour that includes **horseriding** on a mountain farm. There are a variety of other tours on offer for flora, fauna and **hiking** enthusiasts. Better hotels have swimming pools and of course the sea is warm and clear for **swimming. Tennis** and **squash** facilities are available at some hotels.

SPECIAL EVENTS: Jul 23-29 '95 *DOMFESTA* (the Dominican Festival of Arts, when everyone dresses in national costume). **Oct 22** Heritage Day. **Oct 23** Creole Day. **Nov 3** National Independence Day. **Nov 4** National Day of Community Service. **Feb '96** *Carnival* takes place just before Lent and is preceded by two weeks of celebrations, culminating in an explosion of parades, with the streets filled with costumed bands, dancing and music. Contact the Tourist Board for exact dates.

SOCIAL CONVENTIONS: Casual dress is normal, but swimwear and shorts are not worn on the streets in town. Evening clothes are informal but conservative. The Catholic Church is one of the most dominant social influences. **Photography:** Visitors should ask 'OK – Alright?' (the accepted opening gambit in a conversation) as a courteous gesture before taking photographs of local people. **Tipping:** A 10% service charge is added by most hotels and some restaurants. Other less touristic places do not add service to the bill and therefore tipping is discretionary; 10-15% of the bill is acceptable. Taxi rates are set by law and therefore taxi drivers do not expect tips.

BUSINESS PROFILE

ECONOMY: Roughly 60% of the island is under cultivation, with bananas, coconuts, citrus fruits and cocoa being the main produce. The Dominican economy has a little light industry, producing vegetable oil, canned juices, cigarettes and soap, but relies mainly on its agriculture. During the late 1980s, the dominant enterprises went into deficit which prompted urgent efforts to diversify the

island's economic base. Industrial development has been hampered, however, by the lack of an adequate infrastructure. Tourism, meanwhile, is not as developed in Dominica as elsewhere in the Caribbean, and Dominica was comparatively tardy in joining the Caribbean economic community CARICOM, largely due to fears about the consequences of opening its inefficient industry up to competition from the rest of the Community. Equipped with guarantees about their protection, however, Dominica finally joined. A series of grants and soft loans have been provided by the UK and the European Union to assist Dominica through this difficult stage in its development. The island's largest trading partners are the UK, the USA, Canada and Japan; Barbados and Guadeloupe are the largest within the Caribbean region.

BUSINESS: Government office hours: 0800-1300 and 1400-1700 Monday; 0800-1300 and 1400-1600 Tuesday to Friday.

COMMERCIAL INFORMATION: The following organisations can offer advice: Dominica Association of Industry and Commerce (DAIC), PO Box 85, 15 King George V Street, Roseau. Tel: 448 2874. Fax: 448 6868; *or* Dominica Export-Import Agency (Dexia), PO Box 173, Roseau. Tel: 448 2780. Fax: 448 6308. Telex: 8626.

CLIMATE

Hot, subtropical climate throughout the year. The main rainy season is between June and October, when it is hottest.

Required clothing: Lightweight cottons and linens. Waterproofing is advisable throughout most of the year.

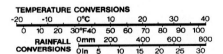

TEMPERATURE CONVERSIONS

-20	-10	0°C	10	20	30	40
0	10 20	30°F40	50 60 70	80 90	100	

RAINFALL CONVERSIONS

0mm	200	400	600	800
0in 5	10	15	20	25 30

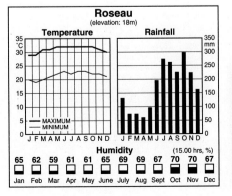

Roseau
(elevation: 18m)

Temperature — Rainfall

— MAXIMUM
— MINIMUM

J F M A M J J A S O N D   J F M A M J J A S O N D

Humidity (15.00 hrs, %)

Jan	Feb	Mar	Apr	May	June	July	Aug	Sept	Oct	Nov	Dec
65	62	59	61	61	65	69	69	67	70	70	67

□ *international airport*

100km
50mls

Atlantic Ocean

Caribbean Sea

S. AMERICA

DOMINICAN REPUBLIC

HAITI

Puerto Plata
Cabo Francés Viejo
● Santiago
Samaná Pen.
La Vega ● San Francisco de Macorís
San Juan ● Pico Duarte 3175m
Vaque del Norte
Vaque del Sur
SANTO DOMINGO
La Romana
Cabo Engaño
San Pedro de Macorís
● Barahona
L. de Enriquillo
◇ Cabo Beata

Caribbean Sea

DAB-M78

Location: Caribbean, island of Hispaniola, east of Cuba.

Secretaría de Estado de Turismo
Avenida Mexico esq., 30 de Marzo, Santo Domingo, DN, Dominican Republic
Tel: 689 3655. Fax: 682 3806. Telex: 3460303.

Dominican Tourism Promotion Council
Desiderio Arias 24, Bella Vista, Santo Domingo, Dominican Republic
Tel: 535 3276. Fax: 535 7767.
USA Mailing address: EPS No. A-355, PO Box 02-5256, Miami, FL 33102-5256

Honorary Consulate of the Dominican Republic
6 Queens Mansions, Brook Green, London W6 7EB
Tel: (0171) 602 1885. Opening hours: 1000-1300 Monday to Friday.
Tourist information is available on written request. Enclose a stamped, self-addressed envelope and £1 in cash or stamps.

British Consulate
Saint George School, Abraham Lincoln 552, Santo Domingo, DR, Dominican Republic
Tel: 540 3132. Fax: 562 5015.
Consulates in: Santo Domingo and Puerto Plata.

Embassy of the Dominican Republic
1715 22nd Street, NW, Washington, DC 20008
Tel: (202) 332 6280. Fax: (202) 265 8057.

Dominican Tourist Office Information Centre
11th Floor, 1 Times Square Plaza, 7th Avenue, 42nd Street, New York, NY 10036
Tel: (212) 575 4966. Fax: (212) 575 5448. Telex: 427051 (a/b DTIC UI).

Embassy of the United States of America
Unit 5500, Calle César Nicolás Pensón & Calle Leopoldo Navarro, Santo Domingo, DN, Dominican Republic
Tel: 541 2171 *or* 541 8100. Fax: 686 7437. Telex: 3460013.

General Consulate of the Dominican Republic
Suite 241, 1055 St Mathieu Central Tower, Montréal, Québec H3H 2S3
Tel: (514) 933 9008. Fax: (514) 933 2070.
Consulates in: Edmonton, St John, St John's and Vancouver.

Timatic

Health	
GALILEO/WORLDSPAN:	TI-DFT/SDQ/HE
SABRE:	TIDFT/SDQ/HE

Visa	
GALILEO/WORLDSPAN:	TI-DFT/SDQ/VI
SABRE:	TIDFT/SDQ/VI

For more information on Timatic codes refer to Contents.

Canadian Embassy
PO Box 2054, Máximo Gómez 30, Santo Domingo 1, Dominican Republic
Tel: 689 0002. Fax: 682 2691. Telex: 3460270.

AREA: 48,422 sq km (18,696 sq miles).
POPULATION: 7,749,717 (1994 estimate).
POPULATION DENSITY: 148.1 per sq km.
CAPITAL: Santo Domingo. **Population:** 2,609,005 (1994).
GEOGRAPHY: The Dominican Republic is in the Caribbean, sharing the island of Hispaniola with Haiti and constituting the eastern two-thirds of land. The landscape is forested and mountainous, with valleys, plains and plateaus. The soil is fertile with excellent beaches on the north, southeast and east coasts, rising up to the mountains.
LANGUAGE: Spanish is the official language. English is widely spoken.
RELIGION: Roman Catholic; small Protestant and Jewish minorities.
TIME: GMT - 4.
ELECTRICITY: 110 volts AC, 60Hz. American-style 2-pin plugs are in use.
COMMUNICATIONS: Telephone: Full IDD available. Country code: 1 809. Outgoing international code: 011. **Fax:** There are facilities at most locations. Most hotels offer this service. **Telex/telegram:** Telexes and telegrams may be sent from RCA Global Communications Inc., Santo Domingo, or from ITT-America Cables and Radio Inc., Santo Domingo. Large hotels have facilities. **Post:** Airmail takes about seven days to reach western Europe. It is advisable to post all mail at the Central Post Office in Santo Domingo to ensure rapid handling. **Press:** All daily papers are in Spanish. The English-language *Santo Domingo News* is published weekly on Wednesday and may be obtained in hotels. *Dominicana News*, a monthly Tourism Promotion Council publication, has the main Dominicana tourism industry items.
BBC World Service and Voice of America frequencies: From time to time these change. See the section *How to Use this Book* for more information.

BBC:

MHz	17.84	15.22	9.915	5.975
Voice of America:				
MHz	15.21	11.91	6.130	9.590

PASSPORT/VISA

Regulations and requirements may be subject to change at short notice, and you are advised to contact the appropriate diplomatic or consular authority before finalising travel arrangements. Details of these may be found at the head of this country's entry. Any numbers in the chart refer to the footnotes below.

	Passport Required?	Visa Required?	Return Ticket Required?
Full British	Yes	1	Yes
BVP	Not valid	-	-
Australian	Yes	4	Yes
Canadian	Yes	4	Yes
USA	Yes	4	Yes
Other EU (As of 31/12/94)	Yes	1/2	Yes
Japanese	Yes	3	Yes

PASSPORTS: Valid passport required by all. The passport has to remain valid for 6 months after departure.
British Visitors Passport: Not acceptable.
VISAS: Required by all except:
(a) **[1]** nationals of Denmark, Greece, Italy, Spain and the UK as tourists only for a maximum of 90 days;
(b) **[2]** nationals of Belgium, France and its overseas departments and territories, Germany, Ireland, Luxembourg, The Netherlands, Portugal and foreign nationals who are legal residents of Denmark, France, UK, Germany, Greece, Ireland, Italy, The Netherlands, Portugal and Spain in possession of a valid passport and a Tourist Card – cost £10 and valid for 60 days from date of entry;
(c) **[3]** nationals of Japan as tourists only for a maximum of 90 days;
(d) nationals of Argentina, Austria, Ecuador, Finland, Iceland, Israel, South Korea, Liechtenstein, Norway, Sweden and Uruguay as tourists only for a maximum of 90 days;
(e) **[4]** nationals of Australia, any legal resident of Canada and any legal resident of the USA (including Puerto Rico and the Virgin Islands) in possession of a valid passport and a Tourist Card – cost £10 and valid for 60 days from date of entry;
(f) nationals of Albania, Andorra, Antigua & Barbuda, Bahamas, Barbados, Brazil, Bulgaria, Costa Rica, Croatia, Czech Republic, Dominica, Hungary, Jamaica, Mexico, Monaco, Paraguay, Poland, Romania, St Lucia, St Vincent & the Grenadines, San Marino, Slovak Republic, Slovenia, Suriname, Switzerland, Trinidad & Tobago, Turks and Caicos Islands, any legal resident of Venezuela and Yugoslavia (Serbia and Montenegro) in possession of a valid passport and a Tourist Card – cost £10 and valid for 60 days from date of entry.
Note: Persons who were born in Cuba are not allowed to enter the Dominican Republic without a visa or a re-entry permit, even if holding a passport of another nationality but keeping their Cuban nationality. Contact the Embassy for further information. For addresses, see top of entry.
Types of visa: Tourist visa costs £12. There are also Business and Student visas. All visas have to be authorised by the authorities in the Dominican Republic and take anything up to 8 weeks to obtain unless requested by cable (the cost of which must be paid by the applicant).
Validity: Tourist visa is valid for 90 days and single-entry only. Business and Student visas are valid for up to a year.
Application to: Consulate (or Consular section of Embassy). For addresses, see top of entry.
Application requirements: (a) 5 application forms. (b) 5 passport-size photos. (c) Proof of sufficient funds to cover stay. (d) Postal applications should be accompanied by a stamped, self-addressed envelope.
Working days required: 6-8 weeks.
Temporary residence: Consult the Embassy to enquire about Residence visas.
Note: The month in the date of birth should be spelled out so as to avoid confusion when entered in the visa.

MONEY

Currency: Dominican Republic Peso (RD$) = 100 centavos. Notes are in denominations of RD$1000, 500, 100, 50, 20, 10, 5 and 1. Coins are in denominations of RD$1, 50, 25, 10, 5 and 1 centavos.
Currency exchange: The Peso is not available outside of the Dominican Republic. Currencies of the USA, Canada, France, Germany, Italy, Japan, Mexico, The Netherlands, Spain, Switzerland, UK and Venezuela may be converted into local currency. At departure all unspent local currency should be reconverted into US Dollars at any bank. All exchange must be done through official dealers such as banks and hotels approved by the Central Bank.
Credit cards: Access/Mastercard, American Express, Diners Club and Visa are accepted. Check with your credit card company for details of merchant acceptability and other services which may be available.
Travellers cheques are accepted by some banks.
Exchange rate indicators: The following figures are included as a guide to the movements of the Dominican Peso against Sterling and the US Dollar:

Date:	Oct '92	Sep '93	Jan '94	Jan '95
£1.00=	20.19	19.90	18.46	20.69
$1.00=	12.73	13.03	12.48	13.22

Currency restrictions: Import and export of local currency is prohibited. Free import of foreign currency allowed but subject to declaration; export is limited to the amount declared.
Banking hours: 0800-1600 Monday to Friday.

DUTY FREE

The following goods may be imported into the Dominican Republic without incurring customs duty:
200 cigarettes or tobacco products to the value of US$5; 1 bottle of alcohol (opened) to the value of US$5; a reasonable amount of perfume; gifts up to a value of US$100.
Prohibited items: Agricultural and horticultural products.

PUBLIC HOLIDAYS

Jan 1 '95 New Year's Day. **Jan 6** Epiphany. **Jan 21** Our Lady of Altagracia. **Jan 26** Duarte. **Feb 27** Independence Day. **Apr 14** Good Friday and Pan-American Day. **May 1** Labour Day. **Jul 16** Foundation of Sociedad la Trinitaria. **Aug 16** Restauration Day. **Sep 24** Our Lady of Mercedes. **Oct 12** Columbus Day. **Oct 24** United Nations Day. **Nov 1** All Saints' Day. **Dec 25** Christmas Day. **Jan 1 '96** New Year's Day. **Jan 6** Epiphany. **Jan 21** Our Lady of Altagracia. **Jan 26** Duarte. **Feb 27** Independence Day. **Apr 5** Good Friday. **Apr 14** Pan-American Day.

HEALTH

Regulations and requirements may be subject to change at short notice, and you are advised to contact your doctor well in advance of your intended date of departure. Any numbers in the chart refer to the footnotes below.

	Special Precautions?	Certificate Required?
Yellow Fever	No	No
Cholera	No	No
Typhoid & Polio	1	-
Malaria	2	-
Food & Drink	3	-

[1]: Polio is endemic. The risk of contracting typhoid is uncertain; vaccination is strongly advised.
[2]: Malaria risk, exclusively in the malignant *falciparum* form, exists throughout the year in Barahona Municipio and Cabral Municipio (Barahona Prov.), Dajabón Prov., Jimaní Municipio (Independencia Prov.), Pedernales Municipio (Pedernales Prov.), Comendador (Elias Piña Prov.) and Montecristi Prov.
[3]: All water should be regarded as being potentially contaminated and sterilisation should be considered essential. Water used for drinking, brushing teeth or making ice should have first been boiled or otherwise sterilised. Milk is pasteurised. Powdered or tinned milk is available. Only eat well-cooked meat and fish, preferably served hot. Pork, salad and mayonnaise may carry increased risk. Vegetables should be cooked and fruit peeled.
Rabies is present. For those at high risk, vaccination before arrival should be considered. If you are bitten abroad seek medical advice without delay. For more information consult the *Health* section at the back of the book.
Bilharzia (schistosomiasis) is present. Avoid swimming and paddling in fresh water.
Hepatitis A is present, precautions strongly advised.
Health care: Health insurance (to include emergency repatriation) is strongly recommended.

TRAVEL - International

AIR: The Dominican Republic's national airline is *Compañía Dominicana de Aviación C por A (DO).*
Approximate flight time: From London to Santo Domingo is 11 hours (including stopover).
International airports: *Santo Domingo (SDQ)* (Internacional de las Americas), 30km (18 miles) east of the city (travel time – 30 minutes). Taxi services are available to Santo Domingo. Airport facilities include outgoing duty-free shop with perfumes, designer fashions, cigarettes, cameras and spirits; post office; bank/bureau de change (24 hours); restaurants and bars (some are open 24 hours) and car hire *(Avis, National, Nelly, Hertz, Honda, Budget,* etc*).*
Puerto Plata International Airport (POP) (La Union). Airport facilities include outgoing duty-free shop with perfumes, spirits, cameras and cigarettes; banking and exchange facilities (0800-1730); restaurant (0800-1900); bar (0800-1900) and car hire *(Avis).*
Punta Cana International Airport is 10-30 minutes travel time from the Punta Cana and Bávaro resorts. Airport facilites include gift shops, duty-free shop and taxi.
Departure tax: US$10 on all international flights. Passengers in direct transit and children under two years of age are exempt. **Note:** When buying an international air ticket in the Dominican Republic a tax of at least RD$3139 (approx £160 on a one-way ticket) and at least RD$2671 (approx £135 on a return ticket) is levied on the carrier by the Government. This expense is passed on directly to the customer on the price of the ticket. If the ticket is bought outside the Dominican Republic there is no tax.
SEA: *Commodore Cruise Lines, Carnival Cruise Lines, Family Cruise Lines, Regent Holidays, Flagship Line, Norwegian American* and *Holland America* stop at the north coast. A cruise port was opened recently in Santo Domingo.

TRAVEL - Internal

AIR: There are some regular flights between Santo Domingo, Santiago, Samaná, Punta Cana and Puerto Plata by *Bávaro Sun Flight* or *Dorado Air.* Planes may also be chartered. For more information, contact the airlines directly.
ROAD: Traffic drives on the right. There is a reasonable network of roads, including the *Sanchez Highway* running westwards from Santo Domingo to Elias Pina on the Haitian frontier; the *Mella Highway* extending eastwards from Santo Domingo to Higuey in the southeast; and the *Duarte Highway* running north and west from Santo Domingo to Santiago and to Monte Cristi on the northwest coast. Not all roads in the Dominican Republic are all-weather and 4-wheel-drive vehicles are recommended for wet weather. Checkpoints near military installations are ubiquitous, though no serious difficulties have been reported (those near the Haitian border are most likely to be sensitive). **Bus:** Cheap and efficient air-conditioned bus and coach services run from the capital to other major towns. **Car hire:** There are several car hire companies in Santo Domingo (including *Hertz* and *Avis*). Minimum age for car hiring is 25. A national or international licence can be used, but are only valid for 90 days. Credit cards are recommended for car hire transactions. **Documentation:** Foreign driving licence accepted.
URBAN: Santo Domingo has flat-fare bus and minibus services, and an estimated 7000 shared taxis called *Carro de Conchos*. These operate a 24-hour service, stop on demand and charge higher fares. In old Santo Domingo the streets are narrow with blind corners so care should be taken, particularly as Dominican drivers have a tendency to use their horns rather than their brakes. Horse-drawn carriages are available for rent in most cities for tours around parks and plazas.
JOURNEY TIMES: The following chart gives approximate journey times (in hours and minutes) from Santo Domingo to other major cities and towns in the Dominican Republic.

	Air	Road
Santiago	0.30	2.00
Puerto Plata	0.45	3.15
Samanà	0.35	4.30
La Romana	0.25	1.45
Punta Cana	0.30	4.15
Barahona	-	4.00

ACCOMMODATION

HOTELS: There are many hotels in the Dominican Republic and extensive development is under way. The southeast coast is noted for its modern hotels and beautiful beaches. In the capital the choice runs from clean, neat and cheap to plush, with rates remaining the same all year because of steady business traffic. At resort hotels winter prices are higher and in summer prices drop by up to 10%. Hotels outside Santo Domingo and La Romana are considerably less expensive whatever the season. Service charge and a 13% government tax will be added to all bills. **Grading:** There is a 5-star grading system, but visitors should note that even the highest grade is somewhat lower in standard than is general in the Caribbean.
GUEST-HOUSES: Guest-houses are very economical, and best found after arrival in the country.
SELF-CATERING: Self-catering establishments are available in Puerto Plata at very reasonable rates.
CAMPING: There are no official sites, and camping is only possible in rural areas after obtaining permission from the landowner. National Parks are also available for camping with the permission of the National Parks Office.

RESORTS & EXCURSIONS

Santo Domingo: The colonial section has been carefully restored to retain its original charm, and is home to the first university, cathedral and hospital built in the New World. The modern city of Santo Domingo, by contrast, is a thriving port city, equipped with discotheques, gambling casinos, shops and the *Cultural Plaza* which houses the *Gallery of Modern Art* and the *National Theatre.* Just a few miles east of the city is a remarkable cave complex, *Los Tres Ojos de Agua (The Three Eyes of Water)*, so-called because it contains three turquoise lagoons on three different levels, each fed by an underground river and surrounded by countless stalactites, stalagmites and lush tropical vegetation.
One hour 45 minutes east of Santo Domingo is the city of **La Romana**, home to the understated elegance and graceful charm of the 7000-acre *Casa de Campo* resort, designed by Oscar de la Renta. Nestled within the resort is *Altos de Chavon,* a reconstructed 15th-century Mediterranean-style village for culture and art which is perched high on a cliff overlooking the tropical *Chavon River* and Caribbean Sea. To stage major events, Altos de Chavon hosts a 5000-seat Greek amphitheatre, built in the traditional design of Epidauros.
The Northern, or **Amber Coast**, is so named because some of the most beautiful amber in the world is mined here. The *Amber Museum* houses a good display of unusual amber pieces found in this area.
Puerto Plata (the Silver Port) has some of the finest beaches of the Caribbean Islands. The Atlantic coast of the country is renowned for its miles of unspoilt beaches that surround Puerto Plata, the most popular being **Sosúa**. Just two miles from the town is the *Playa Dorada* resort complex, within which is the *Jack Tar Village* resort. Just outside the Playa Dorada complex, in Puerto Plata, is the *Costambar Beach Resort,* with 5km (3 miles) of beach. *Mount Isabel de Torres* features a cable car which climbs over 760m (2500ft) above sea level. The breathtaking view of the Atlantic and the port of Puerto Plata is well worth the 7-minute climb up to the top of the mountain. 10 sq km (4 sq miles) of botanical gardens can be explored here. **Rio San Juan** is still a virgin land awaiting the adventurer to discover *Playa Grande* (with a few resorts under construction) and the beautiful *Playa Caletón* and the *Gri-Gri* lagoon.
The **Samaná Peninsula** is located on the northern portion of the island, approximately two hours from Puerto Plata's international airport. Samaná, with its transparent blue waters, miles of unspoilt beaches, and dozens of caves waiting to be explored, is a romantic paradise. Other resorts; *The Gran Bahia Beach Resort, Cayo Levantado* and *El Portillo Beach Club.*
San Cristobal, where the first constitution was signed on November 6, 1844, is probably the most visited city particularly by those wishing to get a closer look at the historical events linked to Trujillo's life, a dictator who governed the country with an iron fist from 1930-61. In the church and *Caves of Santa María* the patrons saint's day is celebrated with drums and dance rituals.
Azua De Compostela was founded in 1504 by Diego Velázquez, who later conquered and destroyed Cuba on three different occasions by fire. In particular, the ruins of the colonial city in *Pueblo Viejo* are well worth a visit.
The popular destination of **Barahona** is a humid land with beautiful beaches of white sand. Particularly *Cabritos Island*, a national park in the centre of *Lake Enriquillo*, is the greatest preserve of the wild American Crocodile, large populations of flamingoes and two species of iguana.
POPULAR ITINERARIES: 5-day: (a) Santo Domingo–Samaná–Rio San Juan–Sosúa–Puerto Plata–Santo Domingo. (b) Santo Domingo–San Cristobal–Azua–Barahona–Santo Domingo.

SOCIAL PROFILE

FOOD & DRINK: Native Dominican cooking combines Spanish influences with local produce. Beef is expensive (Dominicans raise fine cattle, but most is exported) and local favourites are pork and goat meat. There is plenty of fresh fish and seafood, island-grown tomatoes, lettuce, papaya, mangoes and passion fruit and all citrus fruits are delicious. Local dishes include *la bandera* (meaning 'the flag', comprising white rice, red beans, stewed meat, salad and fried green plaintain), *chicharrones* (crisp pork rind), *chicharrones de pollo* (small pieces of fried chicken), *casava* (fried yuca), *moro de habicuelas* (rice and beans), *sopa criolla dominicana* (native soup of meat and vegetables), *pastelon* (baked vegetable cake) and *sancocho* (stew with anything up to 18 ingredients). **Drink:** *Presidente* (Dominican beer) is very good, as are rum drinks such as the local *Brugal* or *Bermudez. Rum añejo* (old, dark rum) with ice makes a good after-dinner drink. Native coffee is excellent and very strong. Locally-produced beer and rums are cheaper than imported alcohol which tends to be expensive.
NIGHTLIFE: Choice varies from a Las Vegas-style review, discotheques and casinos to a quiet café by the sea in Santo Domingo. Hotels offer more traditional shows including folk music and dancing. Popular dances are the *merengue,* accompanied by a 3-man group called *perico ripiao,* and the *salsa*. The *Malécon*, along a seaside boulevard in Santo Domingo, is known as the world's longest discotheque. Concerts and other cultural events are often held at the *Casa de Francia* and *Plaza de la Cultura* in Santo Domingo, among others.
SHOPPING: Best buys are products made on the island including amber jewellery and decorative pieces which are a national speciality, some pieces encasing insects, leaves or dew drops within ancient petrified pine resin. Larimar or Dominican turquoise is another popular stone. Milky blue and polished pink pieces of conch shell are also made into jewellery. Rocking chairs, wood carvings, macramé, baskets, limestone carvings and tortoiseshell also make good buys. **Shopping hours:** 0830-1200 and 1400-1800 Monday to Saturday.
SPORT: Swimming: Although some shores are rough and rocky, magnificent stretches of beach can be found and many of the hotels have pools. **Scuba diving** and **snorkelling:** *Actividades Acuáticas SA* is one of the fully equipped companies in Santo Domingo and *Mundo Submarino,* where only experienced divers can arrange half-day and all-day trips. Snorkelling gear can be borrowed or rented from resort hotels. **Sailing:** Small sailing craft are available through hotels in Santo Domingo and most other resorts in the country. **Fishing:** Charter boats are available through hotels for offshore fishing for marlin, sailfish, dorado, benittos and other game fish. River fishing in flat-bottomed boats with guides can be hired at La Romana, Boca de Yuma and on the north coast. **Tennis:** There are many tennis courts and La Romana boasts a 10-court hillside village. **Golf:** There are championship golf courses at La Romana with other courses near Puerto Plata and the Santo Domingo

Country Club. **Horseriding:** Dominicans love horseriding and their country offers possibly the best riding in the Caribbean. Regular polo games are held at Sierra Prieta in Santo Domingo and at Casa de Campo near La Romana where guests can join in the twice-weekly competitions. **Baseball:** This is another Dominican passion. The professional winter season runs from October to January. Ask locals or look in the local paper for schedules and the nearest game.

SPECIAL EVENTS: The following is a selection of the major festivals and other special events celebrated annually in the Dominican Republic. For a complete list contact the Consulate or the Tourism Promotion Council in Santo Domingo.

Apr '95 *Dominican Gastronomic Festival,* Santo Domingo. **Jun** *Cabeza de Toro International* (fishing tournament), Higuey. **Jul** *Santo Domingo Merengue Festival.* **Oct** *Puerto Plata Merengue Festival.* **Dec** *Santo Domingo International Marathon.* **Feb '96** *Carnival,* Santo Domingo and other parts of the country.

In addition to the above, various saint's days are celebrated in different places throughout the year.

SOCIAL CONVENTIONS: The Dominican lifestyle is more American than Latin, with short siestas and without long, late lunches. The non-Latin ambience is indicated by the fact that, though the culture is rich in Roman Catholic and Spanish influences, 72-hour divorces may be obtained. Daytime dress is generally casual but beachwear and shorts are only acceptable in resorts and at pools. Evenings tend to be smarter with jackets (although not necessarily ties) recommended for men at better restaurants, hotels and for social functions. **Tipping:** Hotel and restaurant bills automatically include a 10% service charge but an additional tip may be given as an appreciation of good service. Taxi drivers on the fixed routes do not expect tips.

BUSINESS PROFILE

For many years sugar was Dominicana's main export item, along with coffee, tobacco and cocoa. However due to the last decade's world market decline in traditional agricultural crops, metals and ores, including ferro-nickel, gold and silver, have become the other main exports. Oil exploration concessions have been granted, but no deposits have been found to date. Coal deposits have been found but are yet to be exploited. Manufacturing industry is confined to building materials, consumer goods and light engineering. Tourism development which was initiated at the beginning of the 1980s is having a major impact on the Dominican economy today: 17% of the GNP and making up more than 50% of the total hard currency earnings of the country. Dominicana boasts over 25,000 hotel rooms, making it the largest room supply in the entire Caribbean. The USA buys most of Dominicana's sugar exports and provides about 30% of imports. Japan is another major source of imports. Trade with the EU is increasing after Dominicana joined the Lomé agreement in 1989.

BUSINESS: It is usual for business people to dress smartly and to deal formally with each other at first, although the general atmosphere is informal. Spanish is the main business language and a knowledge of it will be of assistance. Enquire at hotel for interpreter services. **Office hours:** 0830-1200 and 1400-1800 Monday to Friday. **Government office hours:** 0730-1430 Monday to Friday. **COMMERCIAL INFORMATION:** The following organisation can offer advice: Cámara de Comercio y Producción del Distrito Nacional, Apartado Postal 815, Arz. Nouel 206, Santo Domingo, DN. Tel: 682 7206. Fax: 685 2228. There are also official Chambers of Commerce in the larger towns.

CLIMATE

Hot with tropical temperatures all year. Rainy season is from June to October. Hurricanes may sometimes occur during this time.

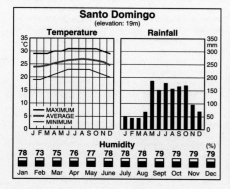

Santo Domingo (elevation: 19m)

Humidity (%)
78 73 75 76 77 78 78 78 78 79 79 79 79
Jan Feb Mar Apr May June July Aug Sept Oct Nov Dec

Location: South America.

Asociación Ecuatoriana de Agencias de Viajes y Turismo (ASECUT)
Casilla 1210, Edificio Banco del Pacifico, 5° Piso, Avenida Amazonas 720 y Veintimilla, Quito, Ecuador
Tel: (2) 503 669. Fax: (2) 285 872. Telex: 2749.
Corporación Ecuatoriana de Turismo
PO Box 2454, Reina Victoria 514 y Roca, Quito, Ecuador
Tel: (2) 527 002 *or* 523 044. Fax: (2) 568 198. Telex: 21158 (a/b DITUR-ED).
Embassy of the Republic of Ecuador
Flat 3B, 3 Hans Crescent, Knightsbridge, London SW1X 0LS
Tel: (0171) 584 1367. Fax: (0171) 823 9701. Opening hours: 0930-1300 Monday to Friday.
British Embassy
Casilla 314, Calle González Suárez 111, Quito, Ecuador
Tel: (2) 560 669 *or* 560 670/1 *or* 237 363 (Consular section). Fax: (2) 560 729 *or* 560 730. Telex: 2138 (a/b PRODQT ED).
Consulates in: Guayaquil, Cuenca and Galápagos.
Embassy of the Republic of Ecuador
2535 15th Street, NW, Washington, DC 20009
Tel: (202) 234 7200. Fax: (202) 667 3482.
Embassy of the United States of America
Avenida 12 Octubre y Patria, Quito, Ecuador
Tel: (2) 562 890 *or* 561 749. Fax: (2) 502 052.
Consulate in: Guayaquil.
Embassy of the Republic of Ecuador
Suite 1311, 50 O'Connor Street, Ottawa, Ontario K1N 6L2
Tel: (613) 563 8306. Fax: (613) 235 5776.
Consulates in: Montréal, Calgary, Toronto and Vancouver.
Consulate of Canada
Edificio Torres de la Merced, 21°, Oficina 6, General Cordova 800 y Victor Manuel Rendon, Guayaquil, Ecuador
Tel: (4) 566 747. Fax: (4) 314 562. Telex: 42513.

AREA: 272,045 sq km (104,506 sq miles).
POPULATION: 11,078,400 (1991).
POPULATION DENSITY: 40.7 per sq km (1991).

Timatic	Health
	GALILEO/WORLDSPAN: **TI-DFT/UIO/HE**
	SABRE: **TIDFT/UIO/HE**
	Visa
	GALILEO/WORLDSPAN: **TI-DFT/UIO/VI**
	SABRE: **TIDFT/UIO/VI**

For more information on Timatic codes refer to Contents.

CAPITAL: Quito. **Population:** 1,100,847.
GEOGRAPHY: Ecuador is bounded to the north by Colombia, to the east and south by Peru, and to the west by the Pacific Ocean. There are three distinct zones: the *Sierra* or uplands of the Andes, running from the Colombian border in the north to Peru in the south, of which there are two main ranges, the Eastern and Western Cordilleras (divided by a long valley); the *Costa,* a coastal plain between the Andes and the Pacific with plantations of bananas, cacao, coffee and sugar; and the *Oriente,* the upper Amazon basin to the east, consisting of tropical jungles threaded by rivers. The latter, although comprising 36% of Ecuador's land area, contains only 3% of the population. Colonisation is, however, increasing in the wake of the oil boom.
LANGUAGE: Spanish with Quechua or Indian dialects. Some English is spoken.
RELIGION: 90% are nominally Roman Catholic.
TIME: GMT - 5 (Galapagos Islands GMT - 6).
ELECTRICITY: 110 volts AC, 50Hz.
COMMUNICATIONS Telephone: IDD is available. Country code: 593. Outgoing international code: 00. Callers should note that even if the person called is not there a charge may still be made. **Telex/telegrams:** Main hotels in Guayaquil, Quito and Cuenca have telex booths. There is also a service at the offices of IETEL *(Instituto Ecuatoriano de Telecommunicaciones).* Telegrams may be sent from the chief telegraph office in main towns. There is a 24-hour service in Quito, and a service until 2000 at some hotels. **Post:** Airmail to western Europe and the USA takes up to a week, but incoming deliveries are less certain. **Press:** Dailies are in Spanish and include *El Comercio* and *Hoy,* published in Quito; and *El Telégrafo* and *El Universo,* published in Guayaquil.
BBC World Service and Voice of America frequencies: From time to time these change. See the section *How to Use this Book* for more information.

BBC:

MHz	17.84	15.22	9.915	9.590

Voice of America:

MHz	18.82	15.18	9.525	1.735

PASSPORT/VISA

Regulations and requirements may be subject to change at short notice, and you are advised to contact the appropriate diplomatic or consular authority before finalising travel arrangements. Details of these may be found at the head of this country's entry. Any numbers in the chart refer to the footnotes below.

	Passport Required?	Visa Required?	Return Ticket Required?
Full British	Yes	No	Yes
BVP	Not valid	-	-
Australian	Yes	No/2	Yes
Canadian	Yes	No/2	Yes
USA	Yes	No/2	Yes
Other EU (As of 31/12/94)	Yes	No/1/2	Yes
Japanese	Yes	No/2	Yes

PASSPORTS: Valid passport required by all except nationals of Colombia with an identity card.
Note: Passports must be carried at all times.
British Visitors Passport: Not acceptable.
VISAS: Required by:
(a) **[1]** nationals of France (nationals of all other EU countries do not need a visa for stays of up to 90 days);
(b) nationals of China, Cuba, North Korea, South Korea, Taiwan (China), Vietnam and Indian and Pakistani nationals of the Sikh religion;
(c) **[2]** all nationals wishing to remain in Ecuador for between 3 and 6 months for business reasons. The cost of the visa will be approximately US$50.
Types of visa: Tourist, Business, Transit or Student (it is illegal to study on a Tourist visa).
Application to: Consulate (or Consular section at Embassy). For addresses, see top of entry.
Application requirements: (a) 4 passport-size photos. (b) Valid passport. (c) US$50 for Student and Business visas. (d) Letter from universities sending and receiving student needed for Student visa. (e) Letter from company sending and receiving businessperson required for Business visa.
Working days required: Applications in person – 5.
Temporary residence: Persons wishing to stay longer than 6 months should apply to the Consulate for details of the procedures to be followed.

MONEY

Currency: Sucre (Su) = 100 centavos. Notes are in denominations of Su10,000, 5000, 1000, 500, 100, 50, 20, 10 and 5. Coins are in denominations of Su50, 20, 10, 5 and 1.
Currency exchange: It is strongly advised to take US

Dollar travellers cheques and currency, as these are the most easily negotiated in Ecuador (though some difficulty may be experienced outside of main towns). The rate of commission varies between 1% and 4%, so it is worth shopping around. *Rodrigo Paz* bureaux de change are recommended as being reliable.
Credit cards: Access/Mastercard, American Express, Visa and Diners Club are accepted. Check with your credit card company for details of merchant acceptability and other services which may be available. The American Express office in Avenida Amazonas, Quito is very helpful to foreign travellers.
Travellers cheques: US Dollar travellers cheques are easily changed into US Dollar banknotes at the *cambios*. US Dollar travellers cheques are generally more easily negotiable than Sterling. See also *Currency exchange* above.
Exchange rate indicators: The following figures are included as a guide to the movements of the Sucre against Sterling and the US Dollar (free market rates):

Date:	Oct '92	Sep '93	Jan '94	Jan '95
£1.00=	2977.17	2791.65	2812.20	3555.60
$1.00=	875.97	1828.19	1900.78	2272.67

Currency restrictions: There are no restrictions on the import and export of either local or foreign currency.
Banking hours: 0900-1330 Monday to Friday; some banks are also open 0900-1330 Saturday.

DUTY FREE

The following goods may be imported into Ecuador without incurring customs duty:
300 cigarettes or 50 cigars or 200g of tobacco; 1 litre of alcohol; a reasonable amount of perfume.
Note: Prior permission is required for the import of firearms, ammunition, narcotics, fresh or dry meat and meat products, plants and vegetables.

PUBLIC HOLIDAYS

Jan 1 '95 New Year's Day. **Jan 6** Epiphany. **Feb 27-28** Carnival. **Apr 13** Holy Thursday. **Apr 14** Good Friday. **Apr 15** Easter Saturday. **May 1** Labour Day. **May 24** Battle of Pichincha. **Jul 24** Birthday of Simón Bolívar. **Aug 10** Independence of Quito. **Oct 9** Independence of Guayaquil. **Oct 12** Discovery of America. **Nov 1** All Saints' Day. **Nov 2** All Souls' Day. **Nov 3** Independence of Cuenca. **Dec 6** Foundation of Quito. **Dec 25** Christmas Day. **Jan 1 '96** New Year's Day. **Jan 6** Epiphany. **Apr 4** Holy Thursday. **Apr 5** Good Friday. **Apr 6** Easter Saturday.
Note: Check with Tourist Board or Embassy for exact details.

HEALTH

Regulations and requirements may be subject to change at short notice, and you are advised to contact your doctor well in advance of your intended date of departure. Any numbers in the chart refer to the footnotes below.		
	Special Precautions?	**Certificate Required?**
Yellow Fever	Yes	1
Cholera	Yes	2
Typhoid & Polio	Yes	-
Malaria	3	-
Food & Drink	4	-

[1]: Vaccination certificate is required from all travellers over one year of age arriving from infected areas. Travellers arriving from non-endemic zones should note that vaccination is strongly recommended for travel outside the urban areas, even if an outbreak of the disease has not been reported and they would normally not require a vaccination certificate to enter the country.
[2]: Following WHO guidelines issued in 1973, a cholera vaccination certificate is no longer a condition of entry to Ecuador. However, cholera is a serious risk in this country and precautions are essential. Up-to-date advice should be sought before deciding whether these precautions should include vaccination as medical opion is divided over its effectiveness. See the *Health* section at the back of the book.
[3]: Malaria risk, predominantly in the benign *vivax* form, exists throughout the year below 1500m in the provinces of Esmeraldas, Guayas, Manabí, El Oro, Los Ríos, Morona Santiago, Napo, Pastaza, Sucumbíos, Zamora Chinchipe and Pichincha. Chloroquine-resistant *falciparum* has been reported.
[4]: All water should be regarded as being potentially contaminated. Water used for drinking, brushing teeth or making ice should have first been boiled or otherwise sterilised. Bottled water is available. Milk is unpasteurised and should be boiled. Powdered or tinned milk is available and is advised, but make sure that it is

reconstituted with pure water. Avoid dairy products which are likely to have been made from unboiled milk. Only eat well-cooked meat and fish, preferably served hot. Pork, salad and mayonnaise may carry increased risk. Vegetables should be cooked and fruit peeled.
Hepatitis is widespread and inoculation with gamma globulin is highly recommended.
Rabies is present. For those at high risk, vaccination before arrival should be considered. If you are bitten abroad seek medical advice without delay. For more information consult the *Health* section at the back of the book.
Health care: Medical facilities outside the major towns are extremely limited. Health insurance (to include emergency repatriation) is recommended.

TRAVEL - International

AIR: Ecuador's national airlines are *SAN (MM)* and *TAME (EQ)*.
Approximate flight times: From Quito to *London* is 17 hours, to *Los Angeles* is 9 hours and to *New York* is 9 hours 30 minutes.
International airports: *Quito (UIO)* (Mariscal Sucre) is 8km (5 miles) from the city. There is a bus to the city every 20 minutes from 0600-2300. Return is from Ave 10 de Agosto. Taxis are available.
Guayaquil (GYE) (Simón Bolívar) is 5km (3 miles) from the city. There are bus and taxi services into the city.
Departure tax: US$25 payable in US Dollars.
SEA: There are regular passenger/cargo services from Europe, including *Hamburg-South American, Royal Netherlands, Knutsen* and *Johnson Lines,* which take 20-22 days from Rotterdam and Le Havre. Others sail from Antwerp, Genoa and Liverpool, and the US West Coast (*Delta Line Cruises*). Guayaquil is the main port for both passengers and freight.
ROAD: The Pan-American Highway bisects the country from the Colombian border at Rumichaca south to Quito and on to Riobamba, Cuenca, Loja, and ending at Macará near the border with Peru. See also *Road* in the *Travel – Internal* section below. **Bus:** *TEPSA* buses connect with several countries.

TRAVEL - Internal

AIR: The national airlines *SAN-Saeta (MM)* and *TAME (EQ)* fly frequently between Guayaquil and Quito. A number of small airlines serve the coast and eastern part of the country. Flying is the usual mode of transport for intercity travel. Other airports include *Cuenca, Manta, Esmeraldas, Lago Agrio* and *Coca.*
Departure tax: 12% of the ticket price for domestic departures.
Galapagos Islands: There are daily flights at 1300 to the Galapagos Islands on national airlines from both Quito and Guayaquil; note that non-Ecuadoreans have to pay more for their tickets on this route (US$40 is charged for visiting any national park).
SEA/RIVER: Ecuador's rocky coastline makes coast-hopping an inefficient and perhaps dangerous means of transport for the visitor. Several navigable rivers flow westwards into the Amazon basin, but this region is often closed to visitors due to a territorial dispute with Peru. Dugout canoes, which carry up to about 25 people, are widely used as a means of transport in roadless areas, particularly in the Oriente jungles and in the northwest coastal regions. There are few passenger services between the mainland and the *Galapagos Islands*; once there, however, tourist boats, local mail steamers and hired yachts may be used to travel between islands.
RAIL: Children under three travel free. Children aged three to eleven pay half fare. The journey from Guayaquil to Quito offers spectacular views, as the train climbs to 3238m (10,623ft) in 80km (50 miles), reaching its highest point at Urbina (3609m/11,841ft). For railway engineering enthusiasts the construction will be of interest, travelling through the Alausí loop and the Devil's Nose double zigzag.
ROAD: Traffic drives on the right. An extensive network of roads spreads out from the main north–south axis of the Pan-American Highway. The Government and *PetroEcuador* are developing highways into the Oriente. In general, road improvements are being put into effect rapidly but, due to the effect of earthquakes and flooding (in the south) during the last ten years, conditions remain variable; potholes and cracks in the road are sometimes sizeable. The roads between Quito and Guayaquil and between Quito, Latacunga, Ambato and Riobamba are completely paved. A road connects Quito, Otavalo, Ibarra and Tulcan. Tulcan is the frontier with Colombia. **Bus:** *TEPSA* buses connect with several countries. Bus travel has improved greatly and is generally more convenient than in the other Andean countries, as distances are shorter and there are more paved roads. The bus service between Quito and Guayaquil and from Quito to the main cities of the highlands needs reservations.

Car hire: *Avis, Budget, National* and *Hertz* car rentals all operate in Ecuador. **Documentation:** International Driving Permit is required.
URBAN: Quito and Guayaquil have bus and minibus services operating at flat fares.
JOURNEY TIMES: The following chart gives approximate journey times from Quito (in hours and minutes) to other major cities/towns in Ecuador.

	Air	Road	Rail
Guayaquil	0.50	7.00	7.00
Cuenca	1.30	9.30	-
Ambato	-	2.30	-
Riobamba	-	3.30	3.00
Esmeraldas	1.00	7.00	-
Puerto Ayora	2.30	-	-

ACCOMMODATION

HOTELS: Hotel rooms should be booked at least a week in advance. Outside the main towns a more or less standard price is charged per person for one night in a *provision residencia*, or a hotel. There is, however, a minimum charge per person. A 10% service charge and 5% tax are added to upper- and middle-range hotel bills. Cheaper hotels usually charge 5% at the most. Hotel accommodation is very limited on the Galapagos Islands. Further information is available through the national hotel association, Asociación Hotelera del Ecuador, Avenida América 5378, Quito. Tel: (2) 453 942. **Grading:** Hotels in Ecuador have been graded into three main categories according to standard and price bracket. All categories provide at least basic facilities.
CAMPING/CARAVANNING: Camping facilities in Ecuador are run by American or European agencies, but these are very limited. There are two campsites on the Galapagos Islands.

RESORTS & EXCURSIONS

For the purposes of this section, the country has been divided up into six principal areas: **Quito, The Cities of the Andean Highlands, Guayaquil, The Littoral, The Oriente** and the **Galapagos Islands.**
Quito: The capital city has a setting of great natural beauty, overshadowed by the volcano *Pichinca* with its twin peaks of *Ruca* and *Guagua*. The city has preserved much of its Spanish colonial character, the cathedral in the *Plaza Independencia* and the many old churches and monasteries being among the most notable instances of this. Also in the Plaza is the *Municipal Palace*, the *Archbishop's Palace* and the *Government Palace*. Many of the city's famous churches and monasteries contain priceless examples of Spanish art and sculpture, particularly the convent of *San Francisco* and the Jesuit church of *La Compania*. Other places in Quito worth visiting include the *Alameda Park*, the *Astronomical Observatory*, the *School of Fine Arts* and the modern *Legislative Palace*. As the cultural and political capital, Quito has a number of museums of colonial and modern art.
The Cities of the Andean Highlands: The Pan-American Highway traverses the country from north to south, a spectacular route which passes through all the principal cities of the Andean Highlands. **Tulcan**, centre of a rich farming area, is the northernmost of these. Further south is **Chota,** still inhabited by the descendants of former slaves who retain some of their tribal customs. The peak of *Mount Imbabura* signals the approach to the valley of *Otavalo*, the town of the same name being famed for its craftwork and Indian market. Approaching **Quito**, one passes a granite monument which marks the Equator. South of Quito, the region of **Latacunga** and **Ambato** has much fine scenery, marked by an avenue of volcanos. The next city, **Cuenca,** was founded in 1577, and still contains many examples of Spanish colonial architecture. Contrasting with this, a vast cathedral has recently been built. Interesting provincial towns surrounding Cuenca include **Ingapirca**, an ancient Inca settlement. In the highlands of southern Ecuador, **Loja** is the last city of importance on the Pan-American Highway, being originally a trading station on the Spanish 'gold road'.
Guayaquil: Ecuador's biggest city, it is also the chief port and commercial centre. A good starting point for sightseeing is the *Rotonda*, the city's most historic landmark, which faces the beautiful garden promenade of *Paseo de las Colonias*. Across the *Malecon Boulevard* are the *Government Palace* and city hall, while at the northern end one can find the ancient fortress of *La Planchada*. Other places of interest include the *Church of Santo Domingo*, the old residential section of *Las Penas* and the *Municipal Museum*.
The Littoral: This is a narrow coastal belt, 560km (350 miles) in length. The chief ports provide visitors with some of the best resorts for deep-sea fishing on the west coast. Particularly attractive are the towns of **Playas**

Posoria and **Salinas,** while **Esmeraldas,** one of the country's most important ports, is also known for its beautiful beaches. The region of **Santo Domingo de los Colorados,** situated some 90km (55 miles) west of Quito, is the domain of the Colorados Indians who still practise many of their ancient customs.

The Oriente: The Oriente is a primeval world of virgin forests and exotic flora and fauna, still mainly inhabited by the Indians. The principal towns of the area are **El Puyo, Tena, Macas, Lago Agrio, Sucúa** and **Zamora.** Tourist excursions are available along the rivers, which provide the principal method of transport. **Baños** is worth visiting, taking its name from the numerous springs and pools of hot and cold mineral waters. It is also the gateway to the **Amazon region,** passing through the spectacular gorge of the *River Pastaza*. From Baños, one may climb up *Cotopaxi* which, at 5896m (19,344ft), is the highest active volcano in the world. Other volcanoes include *Chimborazo* and *Tungurahua*. All have refuges at the snow-line where intrepid walkers can make overnight stays.

Galapagos Islands: Situated about 800km (500 miles) west of the Ecuadorian mainland, the islands are bleak, barren and rocky. Made famous by Charles Darwin's scientific voyage in the 'Beagle' during the last century, the islands' unique wildlife – which includes giant tortoises, lizards and iguanas – remains the most interesting feature for the modern-day visitor. The islands have been turned into a national park in an attempt to preserve their natural state, and in 1978 UNESCO declared the Galapagos to be 'the universal natural heritage of humanity'. Accommodation and travel can generally be arranged either inclusively from the visitor's home country or through local tour operators once in Ecuador. (Shop around and take advice before booking; quality of service and reliability vary greatly.) Accommodation is extremely limited and food is not cheap. There are a few small restaurants. Boat trips around the islands can be arranged locally.

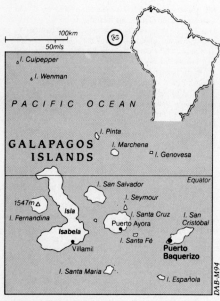

SOCIAL PROFILE

FOOD & DRINK: Avoid unpeeled fruits and raw vegetables. Best of the jungle fruits include *chirimoya,* with a delicious custard-like inside; *mamey,* which has a red, sweet, squash-like meat; and *pepinos,* a sweet white and purple striped cucumber-like fruit. Specialities include *llapingachos* (pancakes with mashed potato and cheese); shrimp or lobster *ceviche; locro* (stew of potatoes and cheese); *humitas* (flavoured sweetcorn tamale); and the national delicacy of baked guinea pig. Restaurants have waiter service and there are café-style bars. **Drink:** Ecuador has some of the best beer in South America. International drinks and whiskies are available but expensive. An Ecuadorian speciality is a unique fruit juice called *naranjilla* – a taste somewhere between citrus and peach. Good Chilean wine is available, but is expensive. The best local drink is *paico,* made from fresh lemon. There are no licensing hours.

NIGHTLIFE: There is little nightlife except in Quito and Guayaquil, where there are excellent restaurants and other attractions. In smaller towns, social life takes place in the home and in private clubs. The cinema is the most popular entertainment.

SHOPPING: Bargaining is acceptable in small shops and in markets, but prices are usually fixed in 'tourist stores'. A few stores around the major hotels have fixed prices. In the Province of Azuay, the cities of Cuenca and Gualaceo offer a wide variety of handicrafts at *ferias* or special market days. The top attractions are the ferias of Otavalo, Ambato, Latacunga, Saquisili and Riobamba, held once a week. They offer the visitor excellent bargains for Indian crafts and silver. Principal silver stores are in Quito. Special purchases include native woodcarvings, varnished and painted ornaments made of bread dough, Indian tiles, woollen and orlon rugs, blankets, baskets, leather goods, *shigras* (shoulder bags) and handloomed textiles, aboriginal art and native weapons. **Shopping hours:** 0900-1300 and 1500-1900 Monday to Friday. Some shops may also open Saturday and Sunday.

SPORT: Soccer: Football is one of the main national sports. *Pelota de Guante* (or *gloveball*) is played with a heavy ball and leather glove. **Golf and tennis:** Popular around Quito and on the coast. **Horseriding and hiking:** Especially recommended in the *Sierra* country. Jungle tours are offered. **Watersports: Swimming, fishing** (the game fishing off the west coast is particularly good), **sailing** and **diving** are all available.

SPECIAL EVENTS: The following is a selection of the major festivals and other special events celebrated annually in Ecuador:
Apr 5-8 '95 *Holy Week.* **May 24** *Battle of Pichincha.* **Jun** *Corpus Christi* (harvest festivals in mountain villages). **Jun 24** *Feast of John the Baptist,* especially in Otavalo. **Jul 24** *Simón Bolívar's Birthday.* **Aug 10** *Independence Day.* **Sep (first two weeks)** *Yamor's Festival* (native masks, costumes and dances), Otalavo. **Sep 20-26** *Bananas Fair,* Machala. **Sep** *Lakes Festival,* Ibarra. **Oct 9** *International Fair,* Guayaquil (celebration of town's independence). **Nov 2** *All Souls' Day* (visits to cemeteries). **Dec 24** *Christmas Eve* (costume pageants). **Dec 31** *New Year's Eve* (effigies of old year's events burnt in streets). **Feb '96** *Carnival* (3-day national celebration).

SOCIAL CONVENTIONS: Casual wear is widely acceptable, but business people are expected to dress smartly. Smart clothes are often required when visiting hotel dining rooms and better restaurants. Beachwear should only be worn on the beach and revealing clothes should not be worn in towns. Smoking is widely accepted. **Photography:** A tip may be requested if you wish to take someone's photograph. **Tipping:** 10% service charge is usually added to the bill in hotels and restaurants. Taxi drivers do not expect tips.

BUSINESS PROFILE

ECONOMY: Ecuador's economy rests on the twin pillars of oil and agriculture, both of which have undergone widely fluctuating fortunes in recent years. Ecuador is the world's largest exporter of bananas, and also grows coffee, cocoa, palm oil and sugar in significant quantities. Fishing is another important sector. Agricultural growth has been stunted by the continuing use of relatively primitive methods: industry has received the bulk of available investment capital in recent years. Crude oil production grew rapidly during the 1970s until, by the end of the decade, it was the largest single export earner and Ecuador had joined OPEC. It left the organisation in 1985 in an effort to boost exports still further because the Government felt that the allocated OPEC quota was too low. When the world oil price declined sharply shortly afterwards, Ecuador lost substantially. A major earthquake then disrupted production yet further. In the last three years, Ecuador has altered its previous, somewhat isolationist foreign and trade policy and now actively encourages foreign investment to broaden its industrial base, which is concentrated in light manufacturing and consumer products. Indeed, the Government threatened to leave the Andean Pact, the economic bloc comprising Bolivia, Colombia, Peru and Venezuela, unless it adopted a more liberal attitude to inward investment. Ecuador is also a member of ALADI (Asociacíon Latinoamericana de Integracion). The USA are the largest single trading partner, accounting for 50% of Ecuadorean exports and supplying around one-third of imports. Other significant importers are Japan, Germany, Brazil, the UK and Italy.

BUSINESS: Business is conducted in Spanish. Appointments should be made in advance and may be subject to last-minute changes, particularly in the case of ministers and government officials. Sales approaches should be low key. The best months are October to mid-December and mid-January to June. **Office hours:** 0900-1300 and 1500-1900 Monday to Friday; 0830-1230 Saturday.

COMMERCIAL INFORMATION: The following

organisation can offer advice: Federación Nacional de Cámaras de Comercio del Ecuador, Avenida Olmedo 414, Casila y Boyacá, Guayaquil. Tel: (4) 323 130. Fax: (4) 323 478. Telex: 3466.

CONFERENCES/CONVENTIONS: For more information, contact Centro de Exposiciones Quito, Avenidas Amazonas y Atahualpa, Quito. Tel: (2) 444 694. Fax: (2) 449 846.

CLIMATE

Warm and subtropical. Weather varies within the country due to the Andes mountain range and coastal changes. Andean regions are cooler and it is especially cold at nights in the mountains. Rainfall is high in coastal and jungle areas.

Required clothing: Lightweight cottons and linens, and rainwear in subtropical areas. Warmer clothes are needed in upland areas.

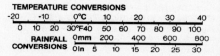

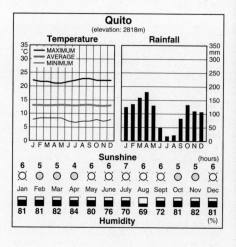

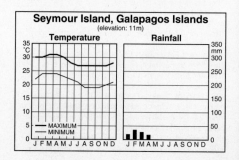

Egypt

□ international airport

Location: Middle East, north Africa.

Note: Egyptian extremist groups seeking to overthrow the Government have staged violent attacks against Egyptian police and security officials, Egyptian Christians, moderate muslim intellectuals and foreign tourists. The majority of these attacks have taken place in the southern provinces of Assiyut, Minya and Qena, which lie between Cairo and Luxor. All surface travel through these provinces is considered dangerous. For up-to-date information, contact the FCO Travel Advice Unit. Tel: (0171) 270 4129.
Sources: US State Department – October 7, 1994.

Egyptian General Authority for the Promotion of Tourism
Misr Travel Tower, Abasseia Square, Cairo, Egypt
Tel: (2) 823 570 *or* 282 8430. Telex: 20799.

Embassy of the Arab Republic of Egypt
26 South Street, London W1Y 8EL
Tel: (0171) 499 2401. Fax: (0171) 355 3568. Telex: 23650 (a/b BOSTAN G). Opening hours: 0930-1730 Monday to Friday.

Egyptian Consulate
2 Lowndes Street, London SW1X 9ET
Tel: (0171) 235 9719. Opening hours: 1000-1200 Monday to Friday for personal applications; afternoons only for the collection of visas.

Egyptian State Tourist Office
Egyptian House, 170 Piccadilly, London W1V 9DD
Tel: (0171) 493 5282. Fax: (0171) 408 0295. Opening hours: 0930-1630 Monday to Friday.

British Embassy
Sharia Ahmad Raghab, Garden City, Cairo, Egypt
Tel: (2) 354 0852/9. Fax: (2) 354 0859. Telex: 94188 (a/b UKEMB UN).
Consulates in: Alexandria, Suez, Port Said and Luxor (honorary).

Embassy of the Arab Republic of Egypt
3521 International Court, NW, Washington, DC 20008
Tel: (202) 895 5400. Fax: (202) 244 4319.

Egyptian Tourist Authority
630 Fifth Avenue, New York, NY 10111
Tel: (212) 332 2570. Fax: (212) 956 6439.

Embassy of the United States of America
North Gate 8, Kamal El-Din Salah Street, Cairo, Egypt
Tel: (2) 355 7371. Fax: (2) 357 3200. Telex: 93773.

Embassy of the Arab Republic of Egypt
454 Laurier Avenue East, Ottawa, Ontario K1N 6R3
Tel: (613) 234 4931. Fax: (613) 234 9347.
Consulate in: Montréal.

Egyptian Tourist Authority
1253 McGill College Avenue, Suite 250, Montreal, PQ H3B 2Y5

Tel: (514) 861 4420. Fax: (514) 861 8071.

Canadian Embassy
PO Box 2646, 6 Sharia Muhammad Fahmi el-Sayed Street, Garden City, Cairo, Egypt
Tel: (2) 354 3110. Fax: (2) 356 3548. Telex: 92677.

AREA: 997,739.5 sq km (385,229 sq miles).
POPULATION: 53,153,000 (1990 estimate).
POPULATION DENSITY: 53.3 per sq km.
CAPITAL: Cairo (El Qahira). **Population:** 6,052,836 (1986).
GEOGRAPHY: Egypt is bounded to the north by the Mediterranean, to the south by the Sudan, to the west by Libya, and to the east by the Red Sea and Israel. The River Nile divides the country unevenly in two, while the Suez Canal provides a third division with the Sinai Peninsula. Beyond the highly cultivated Nile Valley and Delta, a lush green tadpole of land that holds more than 90% of the population, the landscape is mainly flat desert, devoid of vegetation apart from the few oases that have persisted in the once fertile depressions of the Western Desert. Narrow strips are inhabited on the Mediterranean coast and on the African Red Sea coast, but coastal Sinai is as barren as its interior. The coast south of Suez has fine beaches and the coral reefs just offshore attract many divers. The High Dam at Aswan now controls the annual floods that once put much of the Nile Valley under water; it also provides electricity.
LANGUAGE: Arabic is the official language. English and French are widely spoken.
RELIGION: Islam is the predominant religion. All types of Christianity are also represented, especially the Coptic Christian Church.
TIME: GMT + 2 (GMT + 3 from May 1 to September 30).
ELECTRICITY: Most areas 220 volts AC, 50Hz. Certain rural parts still use 110-380 volts AC.
COMMUNICATIONS: Telephone: Full IDD is available. Country code: 20. Outgoing international code: 00. International telephone calls should be ordered in advance, as the service is subject to delays. **Fax:** Several of the major hotels in Cairo have introduced fax facilities; check with the hotel concerned before travelling. **Telex/telegram:** 24-hour telex facilities are available at 19 El Alfi Street, Cairo; 26 July Street, Zamalek; 85 Abdel Khalek Sarwat Street, Attaba; El Tayaran Street, Nasser City; and at major hotels. International telex and telegram services are available from the Central Post Offices in Cairo, Alexandria, Luxor and Aswan and main hotels. **Post:** The postal system is efficient for international mail. Airmail to Western Europe takes about five days. There are *Poste Restante* facilities at the Central Post Office; a small fee is charged when mail is collected. All post offices are open daily 0900-1400 except Friday, and the Central Post Office in Cairo is open 24 hours. **Press:** The most influential Egyptian daily is *Al-Ahram*, others include *Al-Akhbar* and several weekly and periodical publications. The English-language daily newspaper is the *Egyptian Gazette*, and *The Middle East Observer* is the main weekly English-language business paper.
BBC World Service and Voice of America frequencies: From time to time these change. See the section *How to Use this Book* for more information.
BBC:

| MHz | 17.64 | 15.07 | 12.09 | 1.323 |

A service is also available on 648kHz and 1323kHz.
Voice of America:

| MHz | 21.45 | 11.82 | 9.700 | 6.060 |

PASSPORT/VISA

Regulations and requirements may be subject to change at short notice, and you are advised to contact the appropriate diplomatic or consular authority before finalising travel arrangements. Details of these may be found at the head of this country's entry. Any numbers in the chart refer to the footnotes below.

	Passport Required?	Visa Required?	Return Ticket Required?
Full British	Yes	Yes	Yes
BVP	Not valid	-	-
Australian	Yes	Yes	Yes
Canadian	Yes	Yes	Yes
USA	Yes	Yes	Yes
Other EU (As of 31/12/94)	Yes	Yes	Yes
Japanese	Yes	Yes	Yes

Restricted entry and transit: The Government of the Arab Republic of Egypt may refuse admission and transit to nationals of Algeria, Morocco, Tunisia, Iran, Iraq, Lebanon and Palestinians. Some applications for visas by nationals of these countries may be accepted, but they will have to wait at least one month for the visa to be processed.

PASSPORTS: Valid passport required by all. Passports should be valid for at least 6 months beyond the period of intended stay in Egypt.
British Visitors Passport: Not accepted.
VISAS: Required by all except:
(a) nationals of Bahrain, Djibouti, Guinea, Libya, Mauritania, Oman, Qatar, Saudi Arabia, Sudan, United Arab Emirates and Yemen for a stay not exceeding 90 days;
(b) nationals of Jordan (if holding a passport valid for at least 5 years) for a stay not exceeding 30 days.
Note: Requirements for visas and other regulations are subject to change at short notice; check with the appropriate authority before travelling.
Types of visa: Tourist and Business (both have Single- and Multiple-entry types). Fees vary considerably according to nationality.
Cost: *Tourist* (UK nationals): Single-entry – £15; Multiple-entry – £18. *Business* (UK nationals): Single-entry – £53; Multiple-entry – £91, provided a business letter is forwarded. *Tourist* (Canadian nationals): Single-entry – £40; Multiple-entry – £70. *Business* (Canadian nationals): Single-entry – £70; Multiple-entry – £70. Payment of fees by cash or postal orders only. Cheques will not be accepted. US nationals pay a standard rate of £12 for visas of any type. Other nationals should check with the appropriate Consulate (or Consular section of Embassy) for costs of visas. Visa fees are per passport, not per person.
Validity: Varies, but visas are usually easy to renew within the country.
Application to: Consulate (or Consular section at Embassy). For addresses, see top of entry.
Application requirements: (a) 1 passport-size photograph. (b) Valid passport. (c) Application form. (d) Business letter for Business visa.
Working days required: Up to 1 month.
Note: All visitors must register with the police within a week of arrival in the country. This registration is generally done by the hotel.

MONEY

Currency: Egyptian Pound (£E) = 100 piastres. Notes are in denominations of £E100, 20, 10, 5 and 1, and 50, 25, 10 and 5 piastres. Coins are in denominations of 20, 10, 5, 2 and 1 piastres.
Currency exchange: There are five national banks and 78 branches of foreign banks.
Credit cards: Access/Mastercard, American Express, Diners Club and Visa are accepted. Check with your credit card company for details of merchant acceptability and other services which may be available.
Exchange rate indicators: The following figures are included as a guide to the movements of the Egyptian Pound against Sterling and the US Dollar:

Date	Oct '92	Sep '93	Jan '94	Jan '95
£1.00=	5.24	5.13	4.99	5.32
$1.00=	3.30	3.36	3.37	3.40

Currency restrictions: There are no restrictions on the import of foreign currency provided it is declared on an official customs form. The export of foreign currency is limited to the amount declared on arrival. The import and export of local currency is limited to £E100.
Banking hours: 0800-1400 Sunday to Thursday.

DUTY FREE

The following goods may be imported into Egypt without incurring customs duty:
200 cigarettes or 25 cigars or 200g of tobacco; 2 litres of alcoholic beverages; a reasonable amount of perfume or eau de cologne; gifts up to the value of £E500.
Note: All cash, travellers cheques, credit cards and gold over £E500 must be declared on arrival.
Prohibited items: Drugs, firearms and cotton; for a full list, contact the Egyptian State Tourist Office.

PUBLIC HOLIDAYS

Jan 1 '95 New Year's Day. **Mar 2-4** Bairam Feast. **Apr 25** Sham el-Nassim, Sinai Liberation Day. **May 1** Labour Day. **May 10-14** The Grand Feast. **Jun 1** Islamic New

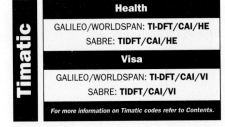

Year. **Jun 18** Liberation Day. **Jul 23** Revolution Day. **Aug 9** Prophet's Birthday. **Oct 6** Armed Forces Day. **Dec 23** Victory Day. **Jan 1 '96** New Year's Day. **Feb 21-23** Bairam Feast. **Apr 25** Sinai Liberation Day. **Apr 29-May 2** The Grand Feast.

Note: Muslim festivals are timed according to local sightings of various phases of the Moon and the dates given above are approximations. During the lunar month of Ramadan that precedes Eid al-Fitr, Muslims fast during the day and feast at night and normal business patterns may be interrupted. Many restaurants are closed during the day and there may be restrictions on smoking and drinking. Some disruption may continue into Eid al-Fitr itself. Eid al-Fitr and Eid al-Adha may last anything from two to ten days, depending on the region. For more information see the section *World of Islam* at the back of the book.

HEALTH

Regulations and requirements may be subject to change at short notice, and you are advised to contact your doctor well in advance of your intended date of departure. Any numbers in the chart refer to the footnotes below.

	Special Precautions?	Certificate Required?
Yellow Fever	No	1
Cholera	Yes	2
Typhoid & Polio	Yes	-
Malaria	3	-
Food & Drink	4	-

[1]: A yellow fever vaccination certificate is required from travellers over one year of age coming from infected areas (see below). Those arriving in transit from such areas without a certificate will be detained at the airport until their onward flight departs. The following countries and areas are regarded by the Egyptian health authorities as being wholly infected with yellow fever: all countries in mainland Africa south of the Sahara with the exception of Lesotho, Mozambique, Namibia, South Africa, Swaziland and Zimbabwe (and including Mali, Mauritania, Niger and Chad); Sudan south of 15°N (location certificate issued by a Sudanese official is required to be exempt from vaccination certificate); São Tomé e Principe; Belize, Bolivia, Brazil, Colombia, Costa Rica, Ecuador, French Guiana, Guatemala, Guyana, Honduras, Nicaragua, Panama, Peru, Suriname, Trinidad & Tobago and Venezuela.

[2]: Following WHO guidelines issued in 1973, a cholera vaccination certificate is no longer a condition of entry to Egypt. However, cholera is a risk in this country and precautions are advised. Up-to-date advice should be sought before deciding whether these precautions should include vaccination as medical opinion is divided over its effectiveness. See the *Health* section at the back of the book.

[3]: Malaria risk, almost exclusively in the benign *vivax* form, exists from June to October in rural areas of the Nile Delta, El Faiyoum area (malignant *falciparum* form), the oases and part of Upper Egypt. There is no risk in Cairo or Alexandria at any time.

[4]: Mains water is normally chlorinated, and whilst relatively safe may cause mild abdominal upsets. Bottled water is available and is advised for the first few weeks of the stay. Milk is unpasteurised and should be boiled. Powdered or tinned milk is available and is advised, but make sure that it is reconstituted with pure water. Avoid dairy products which are likely to have been made from unboiled milk. Only eat well-cooked meat and fish, preferably served hot. Pork, salad and mayonnaise may carry increased risk. Vegetables should be cooked and fruit peeled. Drinking water outside main cities and towns carries a greater risk and should always be sterilised.

Rabies is present. For those at high risk, vaccination before arrival should be considered. If you are bitten abroad seek medical advice without delay. For more information consult the *Health* section at the back of the book.

Bilharzia (schistosomiasis) is present. Avoid swimming and paddling in fresh water. Swimming pools which are well-chlorinated and maintained are safe.

Health care: Public hospitals and chemists are open to tourists. Health insurance is strongly advised.

TRAVEL - International

AIR: The national airline is *Egyptair (MS)*. Charter services fly direct from Gatwick to Egypt.

For free advice on air travel, call the Air Travel Advisory Bureau in the UK on (0171) 636 5000 (London) *or* (0161) 832 2000 (Manchester).

Approximate flight times: From *London* to Cairo is 4 hours 45 minutes and to Luxor is 5 hours 35 minutes. From *Los Angeles* to Cairo is 16 hours 40 minutes, from *New York* is 14 hours 35 minutes, from *Singapore* is 11 hours 45 minutes, and from *Sydney* is 21 hours 30 minutes.

International airports: *Cairo International (CAI)*, 22.5km (14 miles) northeast of the city at Heliopolis (minimum travel time – 30 minutes, much longer during the rush hour). There are coach services every 5-6 minutes, and taxis are available to the city centre and the main hotels. Special limousines are offered by local and international operators, also hotel cars. Airport facilities include an incoming and outgoing 24-hour duty-free shop selling a wide range of goods, several 24-hour car hire firms, post office, 24-hour bank/bureau de change, restaurants (0900-2100 in the departure lounge and 24 hours outside the airport), 24-hour bar, hotel reservation service, souvenir shops, bookshop and travel insurance services.

El Nouzha (ALY) is 7km (4 miles) southeast of Maydan al-Tahir (Alexandria). Regular bus services to downtown Alexandria and to Cairo. Special limousine and local taxis, plus hotel cars, are available. Airport facilities include a 24-hour incoming and outgoing duty-free shop, 24-hour car hire, 24-hour bank and exchange services, and a 24-hour bar and restaurant.

Luxor Airport (LXR) is 5.5km (3.5 miles) from Luxor. There is a regular bus service to the city centre. Special limousine and local taxi services are available. Airport facilities include car hire, bank and exchange services, and a bar and restaurant.

Departure tax: £E21.

SEA: The main coastal ports are Alexandria, Port Said and Suez. Ferries operated by *Adriatica (Sealink)* sail from Venice, Italy to Alexandria via Piraeus once a week June 21-September 27, and roughly once a week for the remainder of the year. *Stability Line* operates from Venice and Brindisi to Alexandria three times a week. A car ferry service goes from Genoa, Italy to Alexandria. The *Saudi Sea Transport Company* runs a regular car ferry service between Suez and Jeddah. A steamer service travels thrice-weekly up the Nile between Wadi Halfa (Sudan) and Aswan. The *Black Sea Shipping Company* sails from Odessa. Other main passenger lines are: *Grimaldi/Siosa, Rashid* and *Prudential;* and *Soviet Lines* (cruise ships).

RAIL: There are no international rail links to any of Egypt's northern neighbours. The railheads at Aswan and Wadi Halfa (Sudan) are connected by a ferry across Lake Nasser.

ROAD: The road border between Libya and Egypt has now been re-opened. There is a route to Cairo from Israel via El Arish and Port Said, Suez or Ismailia. Group taxis are available from the Israeli border. Also daily coaches leave early in the morning from Tel Aviv and Ashkelon in Israel via El Arish to Cairo and *vice versa*. Fares are US$25 one way and US$45 return.

TRAVEL - Internal

AIR: *Egypt Air* operates daily flights between Cairo, Alexandria, Luxor, Aswan, Abu Simbel, New Valley and Hurghada. For information on schedules, contact local offices. *Air Sinai* operates services on the following routes: Cairo to *Tel Aviv;* Cairo to *El Arish;* Cairo to *St Catherine* and *Eilat* (1 hour 15 minutes); and Cairo to *Ras El Nakab, Luxor* and *Sharm el-Sheikh.*

SEA/RIVER: There is a hydrofoil service linking Hurghada with Sharm el-Sheikh in Sinai. There are also two new ferries operating a daily ferry service (travel time – 5-6 hours). For more information, contact Red Sea Cruises Company in Hurghada, or the Egyptian Land Company in Cairo at Champolion Street. Tel: (2) 741 467 *or* 751 563. The traditional Nile sailing boats, *feluccas,* can be hired by the hour for relaxed sailing on the Nile. The Sudanese railway system operates a steamer service from Aswan to Wadi Halfa. Regular Nile cruises operate between Luxor and Aswan, and sometimes between Cairo and Aswan usually for the following periods: four nights, five days (standard tour); six nights, seven days (extended tour), and 14 nights, 15 days (full Nile cruise). There are over 160 individually-owned boats of all categories operating on the Nile.

RAIL: A comprehensive rail network offering a high standard of service is operated along an east–west axis from Sallom on the Libyan border to Alexandria and Cairo, and along the Nile to Luxor, Aswan and Abu Simbel. There are also links to Port Said and Suez. There are frequent trains from Cairo to Alexandria, and also several luxury air-conditioned day and night trains with sleeping and restaurant cars from Cairo to Luxor and Aswan for the Nile Valley tourist trade. Children under 4 years travel free. Children aged 4-9 years pay half fare. Holders of Youth Hostel cards can get reductions. Vouchers may be obtained on presentation of a membership card from the *Egyptian Youth Hostels Travel Bureau*, 7 Sharia Dr Abdel Hamid Saiid, Maarouf, Cairo. Tel: (2) 758 099. For details of other possible reductions, contact the Tourist Office.

ROAD: Traffic drives on the right. Besides the Nile Valley and Delta, which hold an extensive road network, there are paved roads along the Mediterranean and African Red Sea coasts. The road looping through the Western Desert oases from Asyut to Giza is now fully paved. The speed limit is usually 90kmph (56mph) on motorways and 100kmph (63mph) on the desert motorway from Cairo to Alexandria (there are substantial fines for speeding). Private motoring in the desert regions is not recommended without suitable vehicles and a guide. For more details, contact the *Egyptian Automobile Club* in Cairo. **Bus:** The national bus system serves the Nile Valley and the coastal road. Main routes are from Cairo to St Catherine, Sharm el-Sheikh, Dahab, Ras Sudr, El-Tour, Taba and Rafah; from Suez to El-Tour and Sharm el-Sheikh; and from Sharm el-Sheikh to Taba, Newiba, El-Tour, Dahab and St Catherine. **Taxi:** Taxis are available in all the larger cities and are metered (see also *Urban* below). Long-distance group taxis for all destinations are cheap. Fares should be agreed in advance. **Car hire:** Car hire is available through *Avis, Hertz, Budget* and local companies. **Documentation:** Visitor's own insurance and an International Driving Permit or national driving licence are required to drive any motor vehicle. *Carnet de Passage* or a suitable deposit is necessary for the temporary import of visitor's own vehicle. All vehicles (including motorcycles) are required by law to carry a fire extinguisher and a red hazard triangle.

URBAN: The government-owned *Cairo Transport Authority* runs buses and tram services in Cairo and also operates cross-Nile ferries. There is a central area flat fare. In addition, there are other buses and fixed-route shared taxi and minibus services run by private operators. Vehicles normally wait at city terminals to obtain a full load, but there are frequent departures. Fares are three to four times higher than on the buses. Cairo's suburban railways have been upgraded to provide a rapid transit network, including Africa's first underground railway. Alexandria also has buses and tramways, with first- and second-class accommodation and distance-regulated fares.

JOURNEY TIMES: The following chart gives approximate journey times (in hours and minutes) from Cairo to other major cities/towns in Egypt.

	Air	Road	Rail	River
Alexandria	0.30	3.00	2.30	-
Luxor	1.00	12.00	17.00	b
Aswan	2.00	16.00	19.00a	b
Port Said	0.45	3.00	3.00	-
St Catherine	0.30	4.00	-	-
Hurghada	1.00	8.00	-	-
Sharm el-Sh'k	1.30	7.00	-	-
Marsa Matr'h	1.30	5.00	9.00	-
Areish	1.00	5.00	9.00	-
Ismailia	-	2.00	2.30	-
Suez	-	4.00	4.00	-
New Valley	2.00	12.00	-	-

Note: [a] Overnight journey. **[b]** For further information, see *Sea/River* above.

ACCOMMODATION

Tourism is one of Egypt's main industries, and accommodation is available around all the major attractions and the larger cities. Egypt has all types of accommodation on offer, from deluxe hotels to youth hostels, at prices to suit all pockets.

HOTELS: The main cities have quality hotels moderately priced, which *must* be booked well in advance, especially during the winter months. Smaller hotels are very good value. In 1991 hotel capacity in Egypt had reached 413 hotels and 158 floating hotels with 46,620 rooms and 6504 cabins. Of these hotels over 300 belong to the Egyptian Hotel Association, 8 El Sad El Ali Street, Dokki, Cairo. Tel: (2) 712 134 *or* 348 8468. Fax: (2) 360 8956. Telex: 92355 (a/b ANIS UN).

Grading: The Egyptian Hotel Association grades member hotels on a scale from **5-** to **1-star.**

Note: Hotel bills are subject to a tax and service charge of 12%.

CAMPING/CARAVANNING: Travel through the desert wilderness is available through local tour operators. It should be borne in mind that desert travel is extremely hazardous without an experienced guide, ample supplies of water, and a vehicle in good mechanical condition. There are only a few official campsites in the country. Tourists are advised to contact the local Tourist Offices on arrival for further details. The tourist office in Cairo is at 5 Adly Street, Cairo. Tel: (2) 391 5590 *or* 391 8554 *or* 390 3613. There is also an office at Cairo International Airport.

RESORTS & EXCURSIONS

The major attractions in Egypt are Cairo, Alexandria and the northern coast, Nile cruises, Luxor, Abu Simbel, Aswan and the Pharaonic treasures, the Sinai peninsula, and the fabulous Red Sea coastline. Egypt's combination of beach resorts and ancient heritage make it one of the most exciting holiday centres within easy reach of Europe.

Cairo

The capital is a city of astonishing diversity and vitality, uniting elements of Africa, the Orient and Western Europe. Sprawling around the Nile and up towards the Delta, Cairo has a population of 14 million and needs several days to visit properly.

The *Egyptian Museum* contains the largest, and one of the most impressive, collections of Pharaonic and Byzantine art and sculpture from the surrounding area. The witty statues of Akhenaten alone justify a visit, and of course the museum houses the celebrated treasures of Tutankhamun, a minor Pharaoh who ruled for a few years a millenium before Christ. Nearby is *Tehrir (Revolution) Square*, the focal point of downtown Cairo. This area, characterised by tall French neo-classical city blocks, was built in the middle of the 19th century by Pasha Ismail, whose ambitious plans to modernise his country reduced it to a state of bankruptcy (which lasted until Nasser came to power in 1952). The *Cairo Tower*, near the Gezira Sports Club on an island in the Nile, affords a wonderful view of the city; it stands amidst the elegant town-houses of a wealthy neighbourhood that bears a striking resemblance to London's St John's Wood. By contrast there is the hustle and bustle of the *Khan-el-Khalili Bazaar*, where one can bargain for traditional leather work, brassware and excellent inexpensive tailor-made clothing. It is set in an area of narrow winding streets where the local inhabitants will always approach the traveller in the hope of doing a little business. A trip around Old Cairo is an enchanting return to a former age, and there are many fine examples of Islamic art and architecture. The *Citadel* and nearby *Al Rif'ai* and *Sultan Hassan* mosques should not be missed but numerous less well-known attractions may be found around almost every corner (Cairo has over 1000 mosques). There is also a *Coptic and Islamic Museum*. In Pharaonic times, the east bank of the Nile was for the living and the west for the dead. Today's west bank is the most modern part of the city – site of the university, the wealthy suburb of Zamalek and the apartment blocks of Dokki – but where the city stops, the Egypt of the *fellahin* (peasants) abruptly starts – date palms, canals, mud villages and lush green fields. To the south, the transition is even more startling. An area of casinos and luxury hotels suddenly gives way to rolling sand dunes and, towering above them, the magnificent pyramids of *Giza*. There are three, the largest being over 137m (450ft) high and containing some three million huge blocks of stone. One can explore deep inside the pyramids by means of labyrinthine tunnels and staircases. Adjacent is the massive *Sphinx*, much admired by Alexander, Caesar, Cleopatra and Napoleon. Camels and horses may be hired and there is a golf course nearby, the night skyline is illuminated by a light show (an unusual but effective way to see the pyramids and Sphinx). **Helwan**, a famous winter resort and health spa, is 30km (18 miles) from Cairo. At nearby **Sakkara**, the step pyramids of *Zoser* are even older than those at Giza and there are fine wall reliefs, particularly in the *Necropolis*. Donkey rides can be taken to Sakkara from Giza. 50km (30 miles) further south is **Al Faiyoum**, a salt-water lake visited by Herodotus in 450BC (malaria is a serious risk here).

Nile Cruises

A number of tour operators offer Nile cruises, the majority operate from **Luxor** to **Aswan** or vice versa. Some trips include an extension to **Abydos** and **Denderha**. The Luxor/Aswan cruise lasts four nights/five days; the cruise which includes Abydos and Denderha six nights/seven days; while one or two companies operate long tours on special departure dates only to **Minia** (a charming town with Roman, Greek and Pharaonic ruins) and/or through to **Cairo**.
There are numerous cruise steamers on the Nile, and the majority operate to a very high standard of service. According to the particular vessel used they carry from between 50 to 100 passengers, with the facilities varying according to size of the individual vessel. Contacting a specialist operator is recommended for choosing a Nile cruise. Normally visitors can only book the complete package through the tour operators. Traditional *felluccas* may also be chartered.

The Northern Coast

Alexandria is more modern than Cairo but is graced by numerous Hellenistic and Roman relics from the age when it was the cultural capital of Europe. It remains a popular holiday resort for Egyptians.
The northern beaches stretch from the Libyan border to the Nile Delta and along the north of **Sinai**. West of Alexandria, the coast road takes one to the **Mersa Matruh** resort, which has a very fine beach; from there it is possible to head inland to visit the **Siwa Oasis** (site of Amun's oracle, visited by Herodotus and Alexander the Great) on the Libyan border. There are other fine beaches at **El Alamein** (where World War II relics are on view), **Baltim, Gamasa, Sidi Kreir** and **Ras El Bar**, where the temperatures are warm enough for bathing until November.

Luxor

Luxor – Homer's 'Hundred-gated Thebes' – is about 500km (300 miles) south of Cairo and contains a vast conglomeration of ancient monuments: the *Temples of Amon* at **Karnak;** colossal statues, obelisks and halls (there is, as at Giza, a *son et lumière* show); the *Valley of the Queens* and the *Valley of the Kings*, where 64 of the Pharaohs are depicted in an enormous relief hewn from the rock. The other temples, tombs and monuments are equally awe-inspiring. Since 1988 visitors have had the opportunity to view these monuments from a hot-air balloon. Many specialist guidebooks are available; the Egyptian State Tourist Office will also be able to supply more detailed information.

Aswan

As well as being a beautiful winter resort with many hotels, Aswan has a huge array of temples, monasteries, the *Elephantine Island's* ancient *Nilometre*, and the *Aswan High Dam*, one of the three largest dams in the world. 2km (1.2 miles) south of Aswan is *Philae*, a classical temple considered to be sufficiently important to be saved from the flooding caused by the opening of the Dam. Further to the south is **Abu Simbel** – surviving largely thanks to a UNESCO-backed project in the 1960s – with the two magnificent temples of Rameses II. 120km (75 miles) north of Aswan is the temple of **Edfu**, one of the best preserved in Egypt. There are three weekly sailings from Aswan down the Nile into the Sudan.

Sinai & The Red Sea

Sinai's diving resorts include **Ras Mohammed, Sharm el-Sheikh, Dahah, Neweiba** and **Arish**, most with diving centres offering lessons at all levels. The views across the Gulf of Aqaba to the Saudi Mountains are breathtaking and temperatures are warm until very late in the year. Other watersports are on offer and the whole Sinai east coast has beach resorts with hotels and beach huts where the desert merges into beach fringed by palm trees. **Ras Mohammed,** the southernmost point of the peninsula, is the site of the world's most northerly mangrove forest. In the interior there are the rugged and scenic Sinai Mountains, amongst which is the **Mount Sinai** of the Bible. Nearby is the famous **St Catherine's Monastery.** This was first settled by hermits in the 4th century and attracted an increasing number of pilgrims, particularly after the construction of a sanctuary in 337. Almost every subsequent century saw additions to the architecture of the settlement, as well as intermittent periods of decline and abandonment. Many of the bequests made to the monastery over the years are also on display in the museum. Other attractions in Sinai include Saladin's massive **Qalaat al-Gundi** fortress, one of the region's many reminders of the Crusaders' presence in the Middle East during the 12th and 13th centuries; and **Al-Tur,** on the Red Sea, capital of South Sinai.
The newest tourist attraction in Egypt is perhaps the western coast of the Red Sea. **Hurghada**, some 400km (250 miles) south of Suez, is a well-equipped diving resort with marvellous coral reefs. There is a modern tourist village at **El Gufton** nearby.
POPULAR ITINERARIES: 5-day: Luxor–Aswan–Hurghada (Nile River cruise). **7 day:** Cairo–Abu Simbel–Aswan–Luxor–Sinai–Sharm el-Sheikh.

SOCIAL PROFILE

FOOD & DRINK: Egyptian cuisine is excellent, combining many of the best traditions of Middle Eastern cooking, and there are both large hotel restaurants and smaller specialist ones throughout the main towns. Some of the larger hotels in Cairo and its environs have excellent kitchens serving the best cosmopolitan dishes. In the centre of Cairo, American-style snack bars are also spreading. Local specialities include bean dishes (*foul*), kebabs and *humus* (chickpeas). Restaurants have waiter service, with table service for bars. **Drink:** Although Egypt is a Muslim country, alcohol is available in café-style bars and good restaurants.
NIGHTLIFE: Sophisticated nightclubs, discotheques, and good restaurants can be found in Cairo and Alexandria. There is nightlife in Luxor and Aswan, including barbecues along the Nile.
SHOPPING: The most interesting shopping area for tourists in Cairo is the old bazaar, *Khan-el Khalili*, specialising in reproductions of antiquities. Jewellery, spices, copper utensils and Coptic cloth are some of the special items. There are also modern shopping centres available, particularly near Tehrir Square. **Shopping hours:** *Winter:* 0900-2100 every day except Friday (Islamic Sabbath). During Ramadan, hours vary, with shops often closing on Sunday as well. *Summer:* 0900-1400 and 1700-2100 Saturday to Thursday.
SPORT: Tennis, golf, croquet and **horseriding** clubs are found in both Alexandria and Cairo. For details, ask at the hotel. There is a public golf club at the foot of the

DAB-M416

1000km
500mls

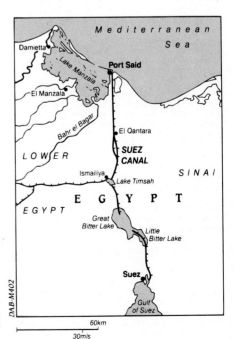

DAB-M402

60km
30mls

Giza pyramids. **Watersports:** There are very fine coral reefs in Egyptian waters and **diving** facilities are being expanded year by year. The longest established resorts are on the Gulf of Aqaba, Sharm el-Sheikh, Dahab and Neweiba, but specialist diving clubs have opened up on the Red Sea coast at Hurghada and Ras Mohammed. Equipment may be hired and training is available at all levels of ability. See also *Resorts & Excursions* above, or contact the Egyptian State Tourist Office (address above).
Note: The Red Sea coral reefs are all protected and persons removing 'souvenirs' will incur heavy fines.
SPECIAL EVENTS: The following is a selection of the major festivals and other special events celebrated in Egypt during 1995/96. For a complete list, contact the Egyptian State Tourist Office.
Jun '95 *International Wind Surfing Festival,* Hurgada/Red Sea. **Jul** *Sayed Noiser Weight Lifting Festival,* Cairo. **Aug** *Wafa El Nil.* **Sep** *International Cycling Race,* Cairo. **Oct 22** *Coronation of Ramases II.* **Oct** *International Yachting Festival,* Cairo; *Pharaoh Rally Festival,* National. **Nov** *Festival of Tut-Ankh-Amun.* **Nov** *Arab Horse Breeding Festival,* Zahra. **Nov** *International Fishing Competition,* Sharm el-Sheikh/South Sinai. **Dec** *International Rowing Race,* Luxor.
SOCIAL CONVENTIONS: Islam is the dominant influence and many traditional customs and beliefs are tied up with religion. The people are generally courteous and hospitable and expect similar respect from visitors. Handshaking will suffice as a greeting. Because Egypt is a Muslim country, dress should be conservative and women should not wear revealing clothes particularly when in religious buildings and in towns (although the Western style of dress is accepted in the modern nightclubs, restaurants, hotels and bars of Cairo, Alexandria and other tourist destinations). Official or social functions and smart restaurants usually require more formal wear. Smoking is very common. **Photography:** Tourists will have to pay a fee of £E25 per day to take photographs inside pyramids, tombs and museums. **Tipping:** 10-12% is added to hotel and restaurant bills but an extra tip of 5% is normal. Taxi drivers generally expect 10%.

BUSINESS PROFILE

ECONOMY: On taking power in the 1950s, Nasser quickly instituted a Soviet-style command economy which was closed to Western investment. After his death, his chosen model was gradually dismantled, particularly under Sadat, who followed a policy of *infitah* (openness) towards investment. The Egyptian economy underwent high growth during the 1970s with the rapid expansion of the oil industry, tourism and Suez canal use (with consequent increase in tariff revenues). Tourist revenues have recently slumped, however, in the wake of a terrorist campaign credited to militant Islamists. However, with the fall in the oil price, Egypt suffered a massive drop in revenues and a severe shortage of foreign currency. The unwieldy and inefficient public sector, which appears all but unreformable, soaks up much of this. Egypt's major industries are textiles, fertilisers, rubber products and cement. There is one major steelworks and several vehicle assembly plants. Agriculture, which generates around 20% of Gross National Product, is largely dependent on cotton, which puts considerable strain on the Nile waters in addition to that imposed by the rapidly growing population, over 90% of whom live within a few miles of the river. The country's major trading partners are the United States and the larger of the European Union economies (Germany, France, Italy and the UK). In 1987 Romania was the second largest export market. The Government is gradually attempting to cut subsidies on foodstuffs, electricity and oil, although many of the poorer Egyptians depend on these and previous attempts to reduce them have met with riots. The country is second only to Israel in the amount of aid it receives from the USA. Since the Gulf War, Egypt has benefited economically from its improved standing in the international community. Egypt's main economic challenge now is the ability of its trade sector to respond to changed conditions in the former Soviet Union and Eastern Europe, formerly its largest export market.
BUSINESS: Suits are expected for business persons and Muslim customs should be respected. English and French are widely spoken in business circles, but business cards in Arabic are appreciated. **Government office hours:** 0900-1400 Saturday to Thursday.
COMMERCIAL INFORMATION: The following organisations can offer advice: Egyptian-British Chamber of Commerce, PO Box 4EG, Kent House, Market Place, London W1A 4EG. Tel: (0171) 323 2856. Fax: (0171) 323 5739; *or*

Alexandria Chamber of Commerce, Sharia el-Ghorfa Altogariya, Alexandria. Tel: (3) 809 339. Telex: 4180; *or*
Cairo Chamber of Commerce, 4 Sharia Midan el-Falaki, Cairo. Tel: (2) 355 8261. Fax: (2) 356 3603. Telex: 927753.
CONFERENCES/CONVENTIONS: Cairo has many hotels and three large meeting halls (seating up to 2000 people) which are equipped for use as conference centres. The new Cairo International Conference Centre, 12km (7 miles) east of Cairo International Airport, has seating for 2500 people, with an exhibition hall, banquet hall and comprehensive facilities. There is also a new convention centre at Alexandria University, which has a main hall with seating for 2400. In 1992 the American Society of Travel Agents (ASTA) held its congress in Cairo. Over 8000 delegates attended. For more information on conference facilities in Egypt, contact the tourist office, or Cairo International Conference Centre, El-Nasr Road, Autostrade, Nasr City. Tel: (2) 263 4632 *or* 263 4645. Fax: (2) 263 4640. Telex: 20607; *or* Egyptian General Company for Tourism and Hotels, 4 Latin America Street, Cairo. Tel: (2) 302 6470. Telex: 92363.

CLIMATE

Hot, dry summers with mild, dry winters and cold nights. Rainfall is negligible except on the coast. In April the hot, dusty *Khamsin* wind blows from the Sahara.
Required clothing: Lightweight cottons and linens during summer with warmer clothes for winter and cooler evenings.

TEMPERATURE CONVERSIONS

-20	-10	0°C	10	20	30	40

0	10	20	30°F40	50	60	70	80	90	100
RAINFALL 0mm 200 400 600 800
CONVERSIONS 0in 5 10 15 20 25 30

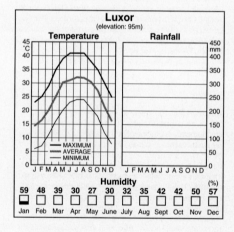

Luxor
(elevation: 95m)

Humidity (%)

59	48	39	30	27	30	32	35	42	42	50	57
Jan	Feb	Mar	Apr	May	June	July	Aug	Sept	Oct	Nov	Dec

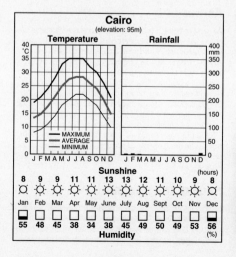

Cairo
(elevation: 95m)

Sunshine (hours)

8	9	9	11	11	13	13	12	11	10	9	8
Jan	Feb	Mar	Apr	May	June	July	Aug	Sept	Oct	Nov	Dec
55	48	45	38	34	38	45	49	50	49	53	56

Humidity (%)

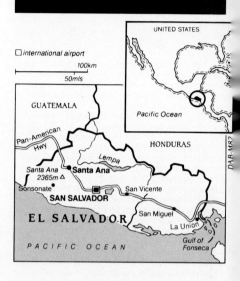

El Salvador

□ *international airport*
100km
50mls

Location: Central America.

Note: The Peace Accords signed in 1992 between the government of El Salvador and the FMLN have brought a halt to fighting in El Salvador. Areas formerly considered dangerous are now open for travel. In view of the country's recent history of extreme political unrest and instability, however, visitors are advised to drive with their doors locked and windows raised, and to avoid travel on unpaved roads at all times because of random banditry, carjackings, criminal assaults and lack of police and road service facilities. Most robberies and assaults, some resulting in fatalities, occur during the evening or early morning hours. Travellers with conspicuous amounts of luggage, top-of-the-line model cars and foreign licence plates are particularly vulnerable, even in the capital. Many Salvadorans are armed and gun battles are not infrequent. *Sources: US State Department – September 2, 1994.*

Instituto Salvadoreño de Turismo (ISTU)
Calle Rubén Dario 619, San Salvador, El Salvador
Tel: 222 8000. Fax: 222 1208. Telex: 20775.
Embassy of the Republic of El Salvador
5 Great James Street, London WC1N 3DA
Tel: (0171) 430 2141. Fax: (0171) 430 0484. Opening hours: 1000-1700 (general enquiries) and 1000-1400 (visa enquiries) Monday to Friday.
British Embassy
PO Box 1591, Paeso General Escalón 4828, San Salvador, El Salvador
Tel: 298 1763. Fax: 298 3328. Telex: 20033 (a/b PRODROME).
Consulate General and Embassy of the Republic of El Salvador
2308 California Street, NW, Washington, DC 20008
Tel: (202) 265 9671. Fax: (202) 328 0563
Embassy of the United States of America
Unit 3116, Final Blvd, Station Antiguo Cuscatlan, San Salvador, El Salvador
Tel: 278 4444. Fax: 278 6011. Telex: 20657.
Embassy of the Republic of El Salvador
209 Kent Street, Ottawa, Ontario K2P 1Z8
Tel: (613) 238 2939. Fax: (613) 238 6940.
Canadian Consulate
Apartado Postal 3078, 111 Avenida Las Palmas, Colonia San Benito, San Salvador, El Salvador
Tel: 224 1648. Fax: 279 0765.

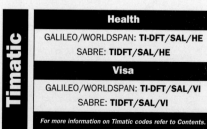

Timatic

Health	
GALILEO/WORLDSPAN: **TI-DFT/SAL/HE**	
SABRE: **TIDFT/SAL/HE**	
Visa	
GALILEO/WORLDSPAN: **TI-DFT/SAL/VI**	
SABRE: **TIDFT/SAL/VI**	

For more information on Timatic codes refer to Contents.

AREA: 21,041 sq km (8124 sq miles).
POPULATION: 5,251,678 (1990 estimate).
POPULATION DENSITY: 249.6 per sq km.
CAPITAL: San Salvador. **Population:** 494,089 (1989 estimate).
GEOGRAPHY: El Salvador is located in Central America and is bordered north and west by Guatemala, north and east by Honduras and south and west by the Pacific Ocean. Most of the country is volcanic uplands, along which run two almost parallel rows of volcanoes. The highest are Santa Ana at 2365m (7759ft), San Vicente at 2182m (7159ft) and San Salvador at 1943m (6375ft). Volcanic activity has resulted in a thick layer of ash and lava on the highlands, ideal for coffee planting. Lowlands lie to the north and south of the high backbone.
LANGUAGE: The official language is Spanish. English is widely spoken.
RELIGION: 99% Roman Catholic and some other Christian denominations.
TIME: GMT - 6.
ELECTRICITY: 110 volts AC, 60Hz.
COMMUNICATIONS: Telephone: IDD available. Country code: 503. IDD is available to Europe, the USA and certain international ports. **Telex:** May be sent from ANTEL. **Post:** Airmail to Europe takes up to seven days. Post office hours: 0900-1600 Monday to Friday. **Press:** Four daily newspapers are published in San Salvador, including *Diario de Hoy* and *La Prensa Gráfica.* There are several provincial papers. The *El Salvador News Gazette* is printed in English.
BBC World Service and Voice of America frequencies: From time to time these change. See the section *How to Use this Book* for more information.

BBC:				
MHz	**17.84**	**15.22**	**9.590**	**5.975**
Voice of America:				
MHz	**15.21**	**11.70**	**6.130**	**0.930**

PASSPORT/VISA

Regulations and requirements may be subject to change at short notice, and you are advised to contact the appropriate diplomatic or consular authority before finalising travel arrangements. Details of these may be found at the head of this country's entry. Any numbers in the chart refer to the footnotes below.

	Passport Required?	Visa Required?	Return Ticket Required?
Full British	Yes	No	No
BVP	Not valid	-	-
Australian	Yes	Yes	Yes
Canadian	Yes	Yes/2	Yes
USA	Yes	Yes/2	Yes
Other EU (As of 31/12/94)	Yes	1	Yes
Japanese	Yes	No	Yes

Restricted entry: Contact the El Salvador Embassy directly for the latest information on current restrictions.
PASSPORTS: Valid passport required by all.
British Visitors Passport: Not accepted.
VISAS: Required by all except:
(a) **[1]** nationals of Belgium, Denmark, Germany, Ireland, Italy, Luxembourg, The Netherlands, Spain and the UK (all other EU nationals *do* require a visa);
(b) **[2]** nationals of Canada and the USA require a Tourist Card allowing them stays not exceeding 90 days.
(c) nationals of Mexico require a Tourist Card allowing them stays not exceeding 90 days.
(d) nationals of Argentina, Austria, Chile, Colombia, Costa Rica, Finland, Guatemala, Honduras, Iceland, Liechtenstein, Monaco, Nicaragua, Norway, Panama, Sweden and Switzerland;
(e) nationals of Japan.
Types of visa: Tourist and Business. Cost: £20 each.
Validity: Business and Tourist: up to 90 days. Visas can be renewed at the Immigration Office in El Salvador.
Application to: Consulate (or Consular section at Embassy). For addresses, see top of entry.
Application requirements: (a) Application form. (b) Passport-size photo. (c) Valid passport.
Working days required: Business visas – 48 hours. Tourist visas – 10 working days.
Temporary residence: Apply to Ministry of Interior in San Salvador.

MONEY

Currency: Colón, ES¢ (colloquially 'Peso') = 100 centavos. Notes are in denominations of ES¢100, 50, 25, 10, 5, 2 and 1. Coins are in denominations of ES¢1, and 50, 25, 10, 5, 3, 2 and 1 centavos. Prices are sometimes shown in US Dollars.
Currency exchange: The legal rate of exchange is 8 Colónes to the US Dollar. Banks generally charge 1 Colón for changing money and cheques. A black market operates for US Dollars (cash only) at the borders and in the capital outside the new post offices, but this is strictly prohibited.
Credit cards: American Express, Visa and Access/ Mastercard are widely accepted, whilst Diners Club has more limited use. Check with your credit card company for details of merchant acceptability and other services which may be available.
Travellers cheques: These may be cashed at any bank or hotel on production of a passport.
Note: Visitors should reconvert all unspent Colónes before entering Guatemala or Honduras, as they are neither exchanged or accepted in these countries.
Exchange rate indicators: The following figures have been included as a guide to the movements of the Colón against Sterling and the US Dollar:

Date:	**Oct '92**	**Sep '93**	**Jan '94**	**Jan '95**
£1.00=	**13.83**	**13.29**	**12.84**	**13.71**
$1.00=	**8.71**	**8.70**	**8.68**	**8.76**

Currency restrictions: Import of foreign currency is free, subject to declaration. Export of foreign currency is limited to the amount declared on import. On leaving the country Salvadorean Colónes can be exchanged.
Banking hours: 0900-1300 and 1345-1600 Monday to Friday.
Note: All banks are closed for balancing on Jun 29-30 and Dec 30-31.

DUTY FREE

The following goods may be imported into El Salvador without incurring customs duty:
200 cigarettes or 50 cigars; 2 litres of alcoholic beverage; up to 6 units of perfume; gifts to the value of US$500.

PUBLIC HOLIDAYS

Jan 1 '95 New Year's Day. **Apr 14-17** Easter. **May 1** Labour Day. **Jun 15** Corpus Christi. **Aug 4-6** San Salvador Festival. **Sep 15** Independence Day. **Oct 12** Discovery of America. **Nov 2** All Souls' Day. **Nov 6** For First Call for Independence Day. **Dec 24-25** Christmas. **Jan 1 '96** New Year's Day. **Apr 5-8** Easter.

HEALTH

Regulations and requirements may be subject to change at short notice, and you are advised to contact your doctor well in advance of your intended date of departure. Any numbers in the chart refer to the footnotes below.

	Special Precautions?	Certificate Required?
Yellow Fever	No	1
Cholera	No	No
Typhoid & Polio	Yes	-
Malaria	2	-
Food & Drink	3	-

[1]: A yellow fever vaccination certificate is required from travellers over six months of age coming from infected areas.
[2]: Malaria risk, predominantly in the benign *vivax* form, exists all year throughout the country, but is greater below 600m in the rainy season (May to October).
[3]: All water should be regarded as being potentially contaminated. Water used for drinking, brushing teeth or making ice should have first been boiled or otherwise sterilised. Milk is unpasteurised and should be boiled. Powdered or tinned milk is available and is advised, but make sure that it is reconstituted with pure water. Avoid dairy products which are likely to have been made from unboiled milk. Only eat well-cooked meat and fish, preferably served hot. Pork, salad and mayonnaise may carry increased risk. Vegetables should be cooked and fruit peeled.
Rabies is a serious risk in El Salvador. It is primarily transmitted by dogs and bats, but persons bitten by any animal should seek medical attention promptly. For persons at high risk of exposure on a continuing basis, it may be advisable to have a course of rabies vaccine. Persons taking animals to El Salvador should be certain that the animals are immunised against rabies. See the *Health* section at the back of the book.
Health care: There about 50 state-run hospitals with a total of more than 7000 beds. Health insurance is strongly advised.

TRAVEL - International

AIR: El Salvador's national airline is *TACA International Airlines (TA).*
Approximate flight time: From London to El Salvador *excluding* stopover time in USA (usually overnight) is 10 hours 20 minutes.
International airport: *San Salvador (SAL)* (El Salvador International) is 44km (27 miles) from the city. Airport facilities include a restaurant, duty-free shops and car hire. Coach travel to the city is available 0600-1900. Taxis to the city are also available.
Departure tax: US$17 is payable when leaving the country via the airport at any time of day or night.
SEA: The principal ports are *La Union, La Libertad* and *Acajutla* on the Pacific coast.
RAIL: There are rail links to Guatemala. Contact the Embassy for passage details.
ROAD: There are frequent buses from San Salvador to Guatemala City. Scheduled services to Honduras have been suspended, but local buses travel as far as the border. If arriving at the border during off-duty hours (from 1200-1400 and 1800-0800, and from 1200 Saturday to 2000 Monday) a duty must be paid in exact cash notes.

TRAVEL - Internal

AIR: Services are available from San Salvador to San Miguel, La Unión and Usulután.
RAIL: There are over 600km (372 miles) of railways, linking San Salvador with Acajutla, Cutuco, San Jeronimo and Angiuatu.
ROAD: Traffic drives on the right. There are more than 12,000km (7440 miles) of roads around the country; a third of this network is either paved or improved to allow all-weather use. **Bus:** A good service exists between major towns. **Car hire:** Car rental is available from San Salvador. **Documentation:** A National or International Driving Permit is required. A vehicle may remain in the country for 30 days, and for a further 60 days on application to the Customs and Transport authorities.
URBAN: Bus: City buses offer a good service, but are often crowded. **Taxi:** Plentiful but not metered, so it is advisable to agree the fare beforehand. Large hotels have their own taxi services.
JOURNEY TIMES: The following chart gives approximate journey times (in hours and minutes) from San Salvador to other major cities/towns in El Salvador.

	Road
Costa del Sol	0.50
Santa Ana	1.15
San Miguel	3.00

ACCOMMODATION

HOTELS: The main hotels are in the capital, and accommodation should be booked in advance. The situation for foreign visitors remains unstable, and advice should be sought from the Embassy. Lake Coatepeque is a popular resort which has good hotels, restaurants and lodging houses. **Grading:** Hotels in El Salvador can be classified into three groups: deluxe, first-class and smaller hotels.

RESORTS & EXCURSIONS

San Salvador: Situated 680m (2240ft) above sea level, San Salvador, which is the second largest city in Central America, is the capital. It has an estimated population of over 800,000. Founded by the Spaniard Gonzalo De Alvarado in 1545, the city is a blend of modern buildings and colonial architecture, broad plazas and monuments, amusement parks and shopping centres. Downtown are the most important public buildings. Standing within a short distance of each other are the *Cathedral*, the *National Palace,* the *National Treasury* and the *National Theatre.* Among the churches to be seen are *St Ignatius Loyola,* once the *Shrine of the Virgin of Guadeloupe,* with its traditional Spanish colonial façade. The amusement park on San Jacinto Mountain can be reached by cable car and gives a panoramic view of the city. *Balboa Park* and the 1200m (3900ft) rock formation, the *Devil's Doorway,* also give a bird's-eye view.
Elsewhere: Excursions can be made by road to **Panchimalco**, around which live the Pancho Indians (pure-blooded descendants of the original Pipil tribes, who retain many of their old traditions and dress); to *Lake Ilopango*, worth a visit for its extraordinary scenery; and to the volcanoes of *San Salvador* and *Izalco* (1910m/6270ft).
The town of **Ilobasco** is renowned for its beauty and its craftwork. The *Tazumal Ruins,* situated in the city of **Chalchuapa,** 78km (46 miles) from San Salvador, are worth a visit, as are the *San Andres Ruins.*
El Salvador has a 320km (200-mile) Pacific Coast with resort hotels, unspoiled beaches, fishing villages and pine views. The best resorts tend to be found along the *Costa del Sol*, easily accessible via a modern highway.
For an inland resort, the region of *Lake Coatepeque* at the foot of the *Santa Ana Volcano* is recommended. It has good hotels, restaurants and lodging houses.

SOCIAL PROFILE

FOOD & DRINK: There are numerous Chinese, Mexican, Italian, French and local restaurants, plus several fast-food chains. The food market (one of the biggest and cleanest in Latin America) has many stalls selling cheap food.
NIGHTLIFE: San Salvador has a few nightclubs and cocktail lounges with dinner and dancing, some of which require membership. There are many cinemas, some showing English-language films with subtitles; there are also some 'juke box' dance-halls and theatres.
SHOPPING: Various goods can be bought at the *Mercado Cuartel* crafts market, including towels in Maya designs.
Shopping hours: 0900-1200 and 1400-1800 Monday to Friday; 0800-1200 Saturday.
SPORT: Visitors can watch or take part in **bowling, mini-golf, football** (played regularly at San Salvador's stadium), **horseracing** and **motor-racing**. Basketball, tennis, **swimming, fishing, target shooting, wrestling, boxing** and **sailing boat racing** are available in private clubs only.
SPECIAL EVENTS: For full details of special events and festivals in El Salvador, contact the National Tourism Institute or Embassy (for addresses, see top of entry).
SOCIAL CONVENTIONS: Conservative casual wear is acceptable. **Photography:** Sensitive (eg military) areas should not be photographed. **Tipping:** 10% in hotels and restaurants. 15% is appropriate for smaller bills. Taxi drivers do not expect tips, except when the taxi has been hired for the day.

BUSINESS PROFILE

ECONOMY: The civil war, together with drought and flooding, has caused economic decline in El Salvador's mainly agricultural economy. The principal commercial crop is coffee, which is the country's major export earner. Other important crops are cotton, sugar, maize, beans and rice. There is a sizeable manufacturing sector – the largest in Central America – which is engaged in producing footwear, textiles, leather goods and pharmaceuticals. El Salvador has a substantial foreign debt and relies heavily on United States aid and loans from the International Monetary Fund. El Salvador is a member of the Central American Common Market. The recent political settlement in El Salvador has been accompanied by the provision of a stand-by facility from the IMF to support an economic programme aimed at reducing inflation to single figures, strengthening the balance of payments and achieving 3-4% economic growth. The USA is the country's largest trading partner, followed by Guatemala, Germany and Japan.
BUSINESS: Business people are expected to wear suits. Although some local business people speak English, a good knowledge of Spanish is important. Visiting cards are essential. The best months for business visits are September to March, avoiding the Christmas period.
Office hours: 0800-1230 and 1430-1730 Monday to Friday.
COMMERCIAL INFORMATION: The following organisation can offer advice: Cámara de Comercio e Industria de El Salvador, Apartado 1640, 9a Avenida Norte y 5a Calle Poniente, San Salvador. Tel: 271 2055. Fax: 271 4461. Telex: 20753.

CLIMATE

Hot, subtropical climate affected by altitude. Coastal areas are particularly hot, with a rainy season between May and October. Upland areas have a cooler, temperate climate.
Required clothing: Lightweight cottons and rainwear during the wet season in coastal areas. Waterproof clothing is advisable all year round.

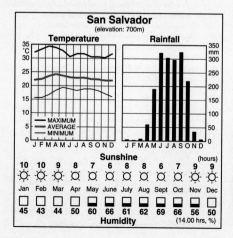

San Salvador
(elevation: 700m)

Equatorial Guinea

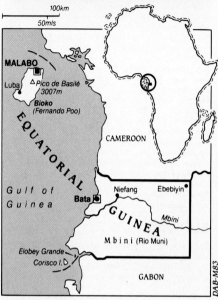

100km
50mls

MALABO
Luba △Pico de Basilé 3007m
Bioko (Fernando Poo)
CAMEROON
EQUATORIAL
Gulf of Guinea
Bata Niefang Ebebiyin
GUINEA
Mbini
M b i n i (Rio Muni)
Elobey Grande
Corisco I.
GABON

DAB-M83

□ *international airport*

Location: West Africa, Gulf of Guinea.

Embassy of the Republic of Equatorial Guinea
6 rue Alfred de Vigny, 75008 Paris, France
Tel: (1) 47 66 44 33 *or* 47 66 95 70. Fax: (1) 47 64 94 52.
British Consulate
Apartado 801, World Bank Compound, Malabo, Equatorial Guinea
Tel: 2400. Telex: 5403.
Embassy of the United States of America
Calle de los Ministros, PO Box 597, Malabo, Equatorial Guinea
Tel: 2406 *or* 2507 *or* 2185. Fax: 2164.
Embassy of Equatorial Guinea
57 Magnolia Avenue, Mount Vernon, NY 10553, USA
Tel: (914) 738 9584 *or* 667 6913. Fax: (914) 667 6838.
The Canadian Embassy in Libreville deals with enquiries relating to Equatorial Guinea (see *Gabon* later in this book).

AREA: 28,051 sq km (10,830 sq miles).
POPULATION: 348,000 (1990 estimate).
POPULATION DENSITY: 12.4 per sq km.
CAPITAL: Malabo. **Population:** 33,000 (1986).
GEOGRAPHY: Equatorial Guinea is bordered to the south and east by Gabon, to the north by Cameroon and to the west by the Gulf of Guinea. The country also comprises the island of Bioko, formerly Fernando Poo, 34km (21 miles) off the coast of Cameroon, and the small offshore islands of Corisco, Great Elobey, Small Elobey and Pagalu. The mainland province, Mbini, is mainly forest, with plantations on the coastal plain and some mountains. Bioko rises steeply to two main peaks in the north and south. The southern area is rugged and inaccessible. Cultivation and settlements exist on the other slopes; above the farming land, the forest is thick. The beaches around the islands are extremely beautiful.
LANGUAGE: Spanish is the official language. African dialects including Fang and Bubi are spoken.
RELIGION: No official religion, but the majority are mainly Roman Catholic, with an Animist minority.
TIME: GMT + 1.
ELECTRICITY: 220/240 volts AC.
COMMUNICATIONS: Telephone: IDD is available. Country code: 240. Operator assistance may be required when making international calls from the country. **Post:** Service to Western Europe takes up to two weeks. **Press:** Equatorial Guinea has two dailies, *Ebano* in Spanish and *Potopoto* in Fang.
BBC World Service and Voice of America frequencies: From time to time these change. See the section *How to Use this Book* for more information.
BBC:

| MHz | 17.79 | 15.40 | 15.07 | 9.410 |

Voice of America:

| MHz | 21.49 | 15.60 | 9.525 | 6.035 |

PASSPORT/VISA

Regulations and requirements may be subject to change at short notice, and you are advised to contact the appropriate diplomatic or consular authority before finalising travel arrangements. Details of these may be found at the head of this country's entry. Any numbers in the chart refer to the footnotes below.

	Passport Required?	Visa Required?	Return Ticket Required?
Full British	Yes	Yes	Yes
BVP	Not valid	-	-
Australian	Yes	Yes	Yes
Canadian	Yes	Yes	Yes
USA	Yes	Yes	Yes
Other EU (As of 31/12/94)	Yes	Yes	Yes
Japanese	Yes	Yes	Yes

PASSPORTS: Valid passport required by all.
British Visitors Passport: Not accepted.
VISAS: Required by all.
Types of visas: Business and Tourist. Cost: FFr350.
Validity: Enquire at Consulate or Embassy.
Application to: Consulate (or Consular section at Embassy). For address, see top of entry. Applications should be made well in advance (at least 2 months), unless application is made directly from Paris where it takes 2 days.
Exit permit: Necessary only if visa has run out. This can normally be arranged at the airport.

MONEY

Currency: CFA Franc (CFA Fr) = 100 centimes. Notes are in denominations of CFA Fr10,000, 5000, 1000, 500 and 100. Coins are in denominations of CFA Fr500, 100, 50, 25, 10, 5, 2 and 1. The country is part of the French Monetary Area and notes of the formerly used currency Ekuele (Ek) should not be accepted as they are worthless.
Note: At the beginning of 1994, the CFA Franc was devalued against the French Franc.
Credit cards: Diners Club is accepted on a limited basis. Check with your credit card company for details of merchant acceptability and other services which may be available.
Exchange rate indicators: The following figures are included as a guide to the movements of the CFA Franc against Sterling and the US Dollar:

Date:	Oct '92	Sep '93	Jan '94	Jan '95
£1.00=	413.75	433.87	436.79	834.94
$1.00=	260.71	284.14	295.22	533.67

Currency restrictions: The import of local currency is unrestricted. Export of local currency is limited to CFA Fr3000. It is worth remembering that CFA Franc notes cannot easily be exchanged outside the CFA Franc area. There are no restrictions on the import and export of foreign currency.
Banking hours: 0800-1200 Monday to Saturday.

DUTY FREE

The following goods may be imported into Equatorial Guinea without incurring customs duty:
200 cigarettes or 50 cigars or 250g of tobacco; 1 litre of wine; 1 litre of alcoholic beverage; a reasonable amount of perfume.
Prohibited items: Spanish newspapers.

PUBLIC HOLIDAYS

Jan 1 '95 New Year's Day. **Mar 5** Independence Day. **Apr 14** Good Friday. **Apr 17** Easter Monday. **May 1** Labour Day. **May 25** OAU Day. **Dec 10** Human Rights Day. **Dec 25** Christmas. **Jan 1** '96 New Year's Day. **Mar 5** Independence Day. **Apr 5** Good Friday. **Apr 8** Easter Monday.

Timatic

Health	
GALILEO/WORLDSPAN: **TI-DFT/SSG/HE**	
SABRE: **TIDFT/SSG/HE**	
Visa	
GALILEO/WORLDSPAN: **TI-DFT/SSG/VI**	
SABRE: **TIDFT/SSG/VI**	

For more information on Timatic codes refer to Contents.

HEALTH

	Special Precautions?	Certificate Required?
Yellow Fever	Yes	1
Cholera	Yes	2
Typhoid & Polio	Yes	-
Malaria	3	-
Food & Drink	4	-

Regulations and requirements may be subject to change at short notice, and you are advised to contact your doctor well in advance of your intended date of departure. Any numbers in the chart refer to the footnotes below.

[1]: A yellow fever vaccination certificate is required from all travellers coming from infected areas. Travellers arriving from non-endemic zones should note that vaccination is strongly recommended for travel outside the urban areas, even if an outbreak of the disease has not been reported and they would normally not require a vaccinaito certificate to enter the country.
[2]: Following WHO guidelines issued in 1973, a cholera vaccination certificate is no longer a condition of entry to Equatorial Guinea. However, cholera is a serious risk in this country and precautions are essential. Up-to-date advice should be sought before deciding whether these precautions should include vaccination as medical opinion is divided over its effectiveness. See the *Health* section at the back of the book.
[3]: Malaria risk, predominantly in the malignant *falciparum* form, exists all year throughout the country. Resistance to chloroquine has been reported.
[4]: All water should be regarded as being potentially contaminated. Water used for drinking, brushing teeth or making ice should have first been boiled or otherwise sterilised. Milk is unpasteurised and should be boiled. Powdered or tinned milk is available and is advised, but make sure that it is reconstituted with pure water. Avoid dairy products which are likely to have been made from unboiled milk. Only eat well-cooked meat and fish, preferably served hot. Pork, salad and mayonnaise may carry increased risk. Vegetables should be cooked and fruit peeled.
Bilharzia (schistosomiasis) is present. Avoid swimming and paddling in fresh water. Swimming pools which are well-chlorinated and maintained are safe.
Health care: Medical insurance including emergency repatriation is strongly advised.

TRAVEL - International

AIR: Equatorial Guinea's national airline is *Aerolíneas Guinea Ecuatorial*, which operates regular services to some neighbouring countries. *Iberia Airlines* of Spain run direct flights from Madrid to Malabo twice a week.
Approximate flight time: From Madrid to Malabo is 8 hours 40 minutes.
International airports: There are international airports at *Malabo (SSG)*, 7km (4 miles) from the city centre, and *Bata*, 6km (3.7 miles) from the city centre.
Departure tax: In general CFA Fr4000, but note that this will vary according to flight, route and class of travel.
SEA: The main ports are Malabo and Bata, with sailings to Spain and the Canary Islands.
ROAD: Roads link Equatorial Guinea with Cameroon and Gabon (bush taxis are available), although road surfaces are not always good. Most travellers enter from Douala in Cameroon.

TRAVEL - Internal

AIR: There are flights between Malabo and Bata every day except Sunday, and it is advisable to book in advance. Light aircraft can be chartered in Malabo with international pilot's qualifications.
Departure tax: CFA Fr1000.
SEA: There is a ferry between Malabo, Bata and Douala. The trip takes about 12 hours. There are four classes of fare.
ROAD: There are few tarred roads in the country. On Bioko, the north is generally better served with tarred roads. Bush taxis connect Malabo with Luba and Riaba and can be hired hourly or daily. There are no car rental facilities.

ACCOMMODATION

Only in Malabo and Bata are the hotels of an acceptable standard for the majority of European travellers. For more information, contact the Embassy in Paris.

RESORTS & EXCURSIONS

Equatorial Guinea is still recovering from the effects of the Macias Nguema dictatorship. The capital, **Malabo**, is a shabby but attractive town, with old Spanish colonial architecture. The *Spanish Cultural Centre* is worth a visit. *Mount Malabo* overlooks the city. **Luba** (an hour's drive from Malabo) has some lovely and deserted beaches.

SOCIAL PROFILE

FOOD & DRINK: There are very few restaurants in Equatorial Guinea and those that exist are mainly restricted to Malabo and Bata, and do not necessarily open every day.
SHOPPING: Shopping hours: 0800-1830 Monday to Friday; 0900-1400 Saturday.
SOCIAL CONVENTIONS: Foreign visitors (especially Europeans) are a comparative rarity in Equatorial Guinea and are liable to be met with much curiosity and, possibly, suspicion. Foreign cigarettes are appreciated as gifts. A knowledge of Spanish is useful. **Photography:** A permit is required. Care should be taken when choosing subjects. **Tipping:** Unless service charges are added to bills, 10-15%.

BUSINESS PROFILE

ECONOMY: Equatorial Guinea produces timber, coffee and bananas for export, and is just self-sufficient in other basic food products. Cocoa production is being re-established on Bioko Island after serious disruption which followed a long period of political instability. Industry is virtually non-existent. There are thought to be mineral deposits inland, including gold and uranium, but prospecting is hampered by the lack of transport systems in the country. Offshore drilling has located deposits of natural gas and preliminary surveys carried out with French and Spanish cooperation in 1984 suggest the presence of oil. Spain remains Equatorial Guinea's principal trading partner, followed by France, Germany and Italy. The country is a member of the Central African Customs and Economic Union, UDEAC, and the CFA Franc Zone. Equatorial Guinea receives large injections of foreign aid from a variety of bilateral and multilateral sources.
BUSINESS: Jackets and ties are only necessary for governmental business. The best time to visit is December to January. Since joining the CFA Franc Zone, external trade has increased. However, it is essential to speak some Spanish as there is no interpreter service and French and pidgin English are only occasionally used. Accommodation arrangements are best made through contacts in Equatorial Guinea.
Office hours: 0800-1700 Monday to Friday.
COMMERCIAL INFORMATION: The following organisation can offer advice: Cámara de Comercio, Agrícola y Forestal de Malabo, Apartado 51, Malabo. Tel: 151.

CLIMATE

Tropical climate all year round. Rainfall is heavy for most of the year, decreasing slightly in most areas between December and February.
Required clothing: Lightweight cottons and linens.

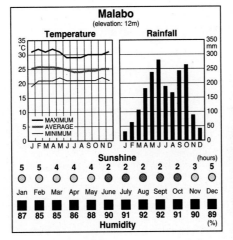

Malabo
(elevation: 12m)

Eritrea

Location: Northeast Africa, on the Red Sea coast.

Note: The northern Ethiopian province of Eritrea declared independence after a referendum in May 1993.

Eritrean Tour Service (ETS)
National Avenue 61, Asmara, Eritrea
Tel: (1) 119 999.
Department of Trade, Industry and Tourism
PO Box 1844, Asmara, Eritrea
Tel: (1) 127 806. Fax: (1) 110 586.
Eritrean Consulate in the UK
96 White Lion Street, London N1 9PF
Tel: (0171) 713 0096. Fax: (0171) 713 0161. Opening hours: 0930-1230 and 1400-1730 Monday to Friday.
Embassy of the United States of America
34 Zera Yacob Street, PO Box 211, Asmara, Eritrea
Tel: (1) 120 004. Fax: (1) 127 584.
Embassy of the State of Eritrea
Suite 400, 910 17th Street, NW, Washington, DC 20006
Tel: (202) 429 1991. Fax: (202) 429 9004.
Deals with enquiries from Canada.
The Canadian Embassy in Addis Ababa deals with enquiries relating to Eritrea (see *Ethiopia* later in this book).

AREA: 124,000 sq km (48,000 sq miles).
POPULATION: 3,500,000 (1992 estimate).
POPULATION DENSITY: 21 per sq km.
CAPITAL: Asmara. **Population:** 350,000 (1992).
GEOGRAPHY: Eritrea stretches along the Red Sea. To the south it borders Ethiopia, to the southeast Djibouti and to the east Sudan. The low-lying coastal area is very humid. The mountainous interior is largely cultivated.
LANGUAGE: Arabic and Tigrinya are the official languages. Various dialects such as Afar, Bilen, Kunama, Nara, Saho and Tigre are also spoken. English and Italian are the most commonly spoken foreign languages.
RELIGION: 50% Ethiopian Orthodox and 50% Muslim.
TIME: GMT + 3.
ELECTRICITY: 110 volts AC in Asmara; a different voltage exists outside the capital. There are occasional power surges.
COMMUNICATIONS: Telephone: IDD is available to Asmara, Massawa and Assab. Country code: 291. Operator assistance may be required when making international calls. All larger cities are connected via the internal system. **Telex/telegram:** International services are available in the telex office in Asmara. **Post:** International post services have not been resumed with all countries. Delays are likely. **Press:** The daily, *Hibret*, is published in Tigrinya. *Hadas Eritrea* is published twice-weekly in

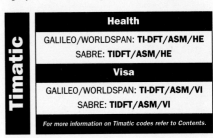

Timatic

Health		
GALILEO/WORLDSPAN: **TI-DFT/ASM/HE**		
SABRE: **TIDFT/ASM/HE**		

Visa		
GALILEO/WORLDSPAN: **TI-DFT/ASM/VI**		
SABRE: **TIDFT/ASM/VI**		

For more information on Timatic codes refer to Contents.

Arabic and Tigrinya. English-language newpapers and magazines are rare.
BBC World Service and Voice of America frequencies: From time to time these change. See the section *How to Use this Book* for more information.

BBC:

MHz	21.47	17.64	15.42	9.630

A service is also available on 1413kHz (0100-0500 GMT).

Voice of America:

MHz	21.49	15.60	9.525	6.035

PASSPORT/VISA

Regulations and requirements may be subject to change at short notice, and you are advised to contact the appropriate diplomatic or consular authority before finalising travel arrangements. Details of these may be found at the head of this country's entry. Any numbers in the chart refer to the footnotes below.

	Passport Required?	Visa Required?	Return Ticket Required?
Full British	Yes	Yes	Yes
BVP	Not valid	-	-
Australian	Yes	Yes	Yes
Canadian	Yes	Yes	Yes
USA	Yes	Yes	Yes
Other EU (As of 31/12/94)	Yes	Yes	Yes
Japanese	Yes	Yes	Yes

PASSPORTS: Valid passport required by all.
British Visitors Passport: Not accepted.
VISAS: Required by all except nationals of Eritrea with proof of national identity.
Types of visas: Business and Tourist (Single- or Multiple-entry) and Transit. Cost – *Single-entry*: £15, *Multiple-entry*: £25. Passengers who do not leave the airport do not need a Transit visa.
Validity: Single-entry visas are valid for 4 weeks from date of issue for stays of up to 4 weeks. Multiple-entry visas are valid for 6 months. Extensions are possible. Apply to the Foreign Ministry in Asmara.
Application to: Consulate (or Consular section at Embassy). For addresses, see top of entry.
Application requirements: (a) Application form. (b) Valid passport. (c) 1 passport-size photo. (d) For Business visa, a company letter stating reason for visit. (e) Fee. (f) Stamped, self-addressed envelope for postal applications.
Working days required: 1 day for applications in person.

MONEY

Currency: The Ethiopian Birr is used in Asmara, in the interior and on the southern coast. The Sudanese Dinar is in circulation in the northern and western parts of Eritrea. Ethiopian Birr (Br) = 100 cents. Notes are in denominations of Br100, 50, 10, 5 and 1. Coins are in denominations of 50, 25, 10, 5 and 1 cents. Sudanese Dinar (SDD) = 100 piastres. Notes are in denominations of Sud£100, 50, 20, 10, 5 and 1, and 50 and 25 piastres. Coins are in denominations of 50, 10, 5, 2 and 1 piastres.
Currency exchange: US Dollar bills are the most convenient form of exchange.
Credit cards: Mastercard and Diners Club are accepted on a limited basis. Check with your credit card company for details of merchant acceptability.
Exchange rate indicators: The following is included as a guide to the movements of the Birr against Sterling and the US Dollar:

Date:	Oct '92	Sep '93	Jan '94	Jan '95
£1.00=	7.82	7.57	7.28	8.47
$1.00=	4.93	4.96	4.92	5.42

The following is included as a guide to the movements of the Sudanese Dinar against Sterling and the US Dollar:

Date:	Jan '95
£1.00=	48.62
$1.00=	31.09

Currency restrictions: Import and export of local or foreign currency is unrestricted. Amounts should be declared.
Banking hours: 0800-1130 and 1300-1600 Monday to Friday; 0800-1200 Saturday.

DUTY FREE

The following goods may be imported into Eritrea without incurring customs duty:
A reasonable amount of items for personal use.

PUBLIC HOLIDAYS

Jan 1 '95 New Year's Day. **Jan 6** Epihany. **Mar 3** Eid al-Fitr (End of Ramadan). **May 10** Eid al-Adha (Feast of the Sacrifice). **May 24** Liberation Day. **Jun 20** Martyrs' Day. **Sep 1** Anniversary of the Start of the Armed Struggle. **Sep** Meskel. **Dec 25** Christmas. **Jan 1 '96** New Year's Day. **Jan 6** Epiphany. **Feb 22** Eid al-Fitr (End of Ramadan).

Note: Muslim festivals are timed according to local sightings of various phases of the Moon and the dates given above are approximations. During the lunar month of Ramadan that precedes Eid al-Fitr, Muslims fast during the day and feast at night and normal business patterns may be interrupted. Some disruption may continue into Eid al-Fitr itself. Eid al-Fitr and Eid al-Adha may last anything from two to ten days, depending on the region. For more information see the section *World of Islam* at the back of the book.

HEALTH

Regulations and requirements may be subject to change at short notice, and you are advised to contact your doctor well in advance of your intended date of departure. Any numbers in the chart refer to the footnotes below.

	Special Precautions?	Certificate Required?
Yellow Fever	Yes	1
Cholera	Yes	2
Typhoid & Polio	Yes	-
Malaria	3	-
Food & Drink	4	-

[1]: A yellow fever vaccination certificate is required from travellers over one year of age coming from infected areas. Travellers arriving from non-endemic zones should note that vaccination is strongly recommended for travel outside the urban areas, even if an outbreak of the disease has not been reported and they would normally not require a vaccination certificate to enter the country.
[2]: Following WHO guidelines issued in 1973, a cholera vaccination certificate is no longer a condition of entry to Eritrea. However, cholera is a serious risk in this country and precautions are essential. Up-to-date advice should be sought before deciding whether these precautions should include vaccination as medical opinion is divided over its effectiveness. See the *Health* section at the back of the book.
[3]: Malaria risk exists throughout the year in all areas below 2000m. Highly chloroquine-resistant *falciparum* has been reported.
[4]: All water should be regarded as being potentially contaminated. Water used for drinking, brushing teeth or making ice should have first been boiled or otherwise sterilised. Milk is unpasteurised and should be boiled. Powdered or tinned milk is available and is advised, but make sure that it is reconstituted with pure water. Avoid dairy products which are likely to have been made from unboiled milk. Only eat well-cooked meat and fish, preferably served hot. Pork, salad and mayonnaise may carry increased risk. Vegetables should be cooked and fruit peeled.
Rabies is present. For those at high risk, vaccination before arrival should be considered. If you are bitten abroad seek medical advice without delay. For more information, consult the *Health* section at the back of the book.
Bilharzia (schistosomiasis) is present. Avoid swimming and paddling in fresh water. Swimming pools which are well-chlorinated and maintained are safe. *Hepatitis* and *Tetanus* vaccinations are recommended. *Meningitis* is a risk, depending on the area visited and time of year.
Health care: Time is needed to acclimatise to the high altitude and low oxygen level. Those who suffer from heart ailments or high blood pressure should consult a doctor before travelling. Medical services are adequate throughout the country: however, modern facilities are not always available and supplies can be irregular. Visitors should bring a supply of any necessary drugs and prescriptions. Chemists can be found in larger towns. Solutions for contact lenses are not available. The country has an extensive network of health workers. Regional and district clinics and the central hospital in Asmara deal with emergencies. Health insurance is strongly advised.

TRAVEL - International

AIR: Eritrea has, as yet, no national airline. Asmara is the only international airport, with flights from Addis Ababa (daily), Frankfurt/M, Jeddah, Rome (twice-weekly), Riyadh and London with *Ethiopian Airlines (ET)*; from Frankfurt/M and Cairo with *Lufthansa;* and from Kassala and Khartoum with *Sudan Airways.*
Approximate flight time: From Addis Ababa to Asmara is 1 hour.
International airports: *Asmara* (Yohannes IV) is about 9km (6 miles) from the city. Buses go to the city centre. Taxis are also available.
Departure tax: Br50 for international departures, plus Br3 security charge.
SEA: Regular sailings between European ports and Massawa or Assab on regional shipping lines. Parts of the important port of Massawa were destroyed during the war for independence.

TRAVEL - Internal

AIR: Internal airports are Asmara, Massawa and Assab. There is no service between them at present.
RAIL: There are no railway tracks.
ROAD: The infrastructure suffered badly during the protacted fighting. Repairs and a modernisation programme are currently underway. Reasonable roads still connect all business centres and holiday resorts. Four-wheel-drive vehicles are recommended on all other roads and tracks. An extension of the existing road system is planned. Traffic drives on the right. **Bus:** Services connect all larger towns and cities. **Taxi:** These can be found in the capital and at the airport. Fares should be negotiated in advance. **Car hire:** Rental cars can be booked through the Eritrean Tour Service (ETS) (for address, see top of entry) or through Africa Garage, Ras Wolde Butul 29, Asmara. Tel: (1) 111 755.

ACCOMMODATION

The capital Asmara has five hotels which sometimes also offer seminar rooms and small exhibition spaces. Accommodation can also be found in Massawa (two hotels) and in Keren (one hotel). Meals are available in all hotels. There are also hotels in smaller towns; prices are, in general, slightly lower than those in the main centres. When making reservations, check for service charges and sales taxes. Hotel bills must be paid in hard currency.

RESORTS & EXCURSIONS

Eritrea's capital **Asmara** was only a small cluster of villages at the beginning of the 19th century. In 1897 the Italian colonial government moved the administration from Massara. Today, Italian architecture prevails in the city. The magnificent *Cathedral* (1922), built in the Lombardian style, is not far from a bustling market. Fruit and vegetables, bric-a-brac, spices, used furniture, ceramics, handicrafts and clothes are sold on the stalls. There are a number of churches and mosques which can be visited. Marble from the Carrara quarry was used to build the largest mosque, *Khalufa el Rashidin*. Gold and silver jewellery is on offer at the nearby market. Palms and colourful bougainvillea line the main avenues. The *National Avenue* is the major thoroughfare of the city; an ideal place to meet people and enjoy the numerous cafés and bars. The Avenue is also the address for the *Government Administrative Centre*, the *Asmara Theatre* (built 1918), the *Catholic Cathedral* and the *Town Hall.* The former residence of the colonial rulers, the *Ghibi* or palace, is used today as the *National Museum.* The *University* and the *Mai Jahjah Fountain* are also interesting.
The road from Asmara to Massawa, 105km (65 miles), is both spectacular and beautiful. It descends from 2438m (8000ft) to sea level, with hairpin bends on the escarpment, and magnificent views over the coastal desert strip. It passes the famous Orthodox *Monastery of Debre Bizen*. **Massawa** was an important centre in ancient times and remains, to this day, the largest natural deep-water port on the Red Sea. If Asmara is an 'Italian' city, Massawa is 'Turko-Egyptian', reflecting the periods of Ottoman and Egyptian rule from the 16th century to the late 1800s. Dams connect the islands of Batsa and Twalet with the main part of the city. The port and the old town of **Batsa** were damaged during the civil war but are still impressive. The *Iman Hanbeli Mosque* escaped damage. *Batsa island* is a good area for restaurants, cafés and bars; visitors can take a small boat to *Sheikh Said Island* (also known as Isola Verde), a favourite picnic spot. **Twalet** has fine examples of Italian architecture. Here, also, is a badly damaged *Ghibi* or palace. It was originally built in the 15th century, but has been much altered and restored since then. It was badly damaged in the recent war and is again in need of restoration. The *Port Club* has a restaurant, a museum, a small library and sporting facilities.
North of Massawa is the white sandy beach of *Gergussum.* It is a good place to sunbathe or swim. From here it is not far to **Emberemi**, famous for the mausoleums of Sheikh el Amin and Muhammad Ibn Ali. It is an important pilgrimage site. **Keren**, in the Province of Senhit, is like a miniature Asmara. The *Forto* was built during the Turkish period. Also of interest are the religious sites of the *Tomb of Said Abu Bakr el Mirgani* and the *Mariam de Arit. Debre Sina*, near Elabered on the Asmara–Keren road, is also a noteworthy monastery. The modern city of **Assab** in the southeasterly Province of Denkalia has lots of beaches. The Turkish and Egyptian colonial periods left numerous interesting buildings and sites in **Agordet** (Barka Province). Here is situated the tomb of Said Mustafa wad Hasan. *Qohaito, Matera* and *Rora Habab* are also important archaeological sites.
The *Dahlak Archipelago,* consisting of hundreds of islands in the Red Sea near Massawa, is protected as a Marine National Park, but is difficult to achieve access to at present.

SOCIAL PROFILE

FOOD & DRINK: Italian cuisine dominates in the restaurants of the larger cities. Massawa is renowed for its excellent seafood especially prawns and lobster. Local specialities are often very spicy. **Drink:** Tea and expresso are drunk black with a lot of sugar. In some regions coffee is served with ginger or black pepper and sugar. Fruit juices (banana, mango and papaya) are available.

SHOPPING: Good buys are gold and silver jewellery (sold by weight), woodcarvings, leather items, spears, drums, carpets and wicker goods. In market places a certain amount of bargaining is expected, but prices at shops in towns are usually fixed. **Shopping hours:** 0800-1300 and 1500-2000 Monday to Saturday (regional variations occur).

SPORT: Swimming: Good facilities on the coast with pleasant water temperatures. The 1000km (625 miles) of beaches are clean and uncrowded. **Diving** is excellent. **Trekking, mountain climbing** and **fishing** can be arranged.

SOCIAL CONVENTIONS: Casual wear is suitable for most places, but visitors should dress modestly. Private informal entertaining is very common. **Tipping:** Hotels and restaurants add a 10% service charge. Tipping is a fairly frequent custom, but amounts are small. Taxi drivers do not expect a tip.

BUSINESS PROFILE

ECONOMY: Years of civil war have left Eritrea, which was until 1991 the northernmost province of Ethiopia, with its economy in parlous condition. There is, moreover, little statistical information about its performance. Agriculture sustains the bulk of the population with indigenous grains, maize, wheat and sorghum as the main crops. Reconstruction of this sector has been hampered by the legacy of the war (damage to land, mines, lack of equipment) and poor rainfall, and the country thus relies on substantial international aid to ward off starvation. The small industrial economy has also suffered severely: the principal industries, which produce glass, cement, footwear and textiles, are operating well below capacity due to lack of machinery and/or the wherewithal to repair it. In the future, the Government is hoping to develop fishing and mineral industries – there are thought to be significant oil and gas deposits within Eritrea's territorial waters – as part of its reconstruction programme. All of this depends on aid and foreign investment, and the Government now avows free market policies in order to attract both. Doners and investors remain suspicious, however, of the former socialist rhetoric of the new governing party and have been somewhat slow to respond. The International Development Association and the Italian government have provided the most so far, while the Eritreans have been holding talks with a wide range of individual governments and multinational institutions.

BUSINESS: Local business people tend to speak English or Italian. A knowledge of French can also be useful. Business cards are not always exchanged. May-October is best for business visits. **Office hours:** 0800-1200 and 1400-1700 Monday to Friday; 0800-1400 Saturday (Asmara). In other towns hours may vary slightly.

CLIMATE

Central plateau: May has the highest temperatures with 30°C. Temperatures can fall as low as freezing between December and February. The short rainy season is March-April and the main one from the end of June to the beginning of September. *Coastal areas:* June-August sees the highest temperatures (25-40°C). Temperatures rarely fall below 18°C. The northern coast has a rainy season (December-February); rainfall is scarce in the southern coastal strip. *Western plateau:* Hottest season April-June with temperatures up to 40°C, December is the coldest month (around 12°C). There are dramatic temperature differences between day and night. Rainy seasons similar to the central plateau.

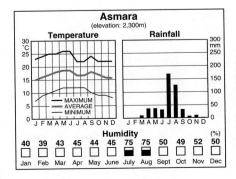

Asmara
(elevation: 2,300m)

Temperature / Rainfall / Humidity

	Jan	Feb	Mar	Apr	May	June	July	Aug	Sept	Oct	Nov	Dec
Humidity (%)	40	39	43	45	44	45	75	75	50	49	52	50

MAXIMUM / AVERAGE / MINIMUM

Estonia

□ *international airport*

Location: Northern Europe.

Estonian Tourist Board
Pikk Street 71, EE-0001 Tallinn, Estonia
Tel: (2) 601 700. Fax: (2) 452 883.
Embassy of the Republic of Estonia
16 Hyde Park Gate, London SW7 5DG
Tel: (0171) 589 3428. Fax: (0171) 589 3430. Opening hours: 0900-1230 and 1400-1600 Monday, Tuesday, Thursday and Friday. *Visa section:* Opening hours: 0930-1230.
British Embassy
Kentmanni 20, EE-0001 Tallinn, Estonia
Tel: (3726) 313 353 *or* 313 461/2. Fax: (3726) 313 354. Telex: 173974.
Embassy of the Republic of Estonia
Suite 1000, 1030 15th Street, NW, Washington, DC 20005
Tel: (202) 789 0320. Fax: (202) 789 0471.
Consulate of the Republic of Estonia
Suite 2415, 630 Fifth Avenue, New York, NY 10111
Tel: (212) 247 1450. Fax: (212) 262 0893.
Embassy of the United States of America
Kentmanni 20, EE-0001 Tallinn, Estonia
Tel: (2) 312 021-4. Fax: (2) 312 025.
Consulate General of the Republic of Estonia
Suite 202, 958 Broadview Avenue, Toronto, Ontario M4K 2R6
Tel: (416) 461 0764. Fax: (416) 461 0448.
Orav Travel
5650 Yonge Street, North York, Ontario M2M 4G3
Tel: (416) 221 4164. Fax: (416) 221 4885.
The Canadian Embassy in Riga deals with enquiries relating to Estonia (see *Latvia* later in this book).

AREA: 45,226 sq km (17,462 sq miles).
POPULATION: 1,565,662 (1989).
POPULATION DENSITY: 34.5 per sq km.

Timatic

Health
GALILEO/WORLDSPAN: **TI-DFT/TAY/HE**
SABRE: **TIDFT/TAY/HE**

Visa
GALILEO/WORLDSPAN: **TI-DFT/TAY/VI**
SABRE: **TIDFT/TAY/VI**

For more information on Timatic codes refer to Contents.

CAPITAL: Tallinn. **Population:** 497,766.
GEOGRAPHY: Estonia is the most northerly of the three Baltic Republics and is bordered to the north and west by the Baltic Sea, to the East by the Russian Federation and to the south by Latvia. The country is one of great scenic beauty with many forests, more than 1400 lakes and 1500 islands. Smaller than Lithuania and Latvia, it has nevertheless the longest coastline of all the Baltic States.
LANGUAGE: Estonian is the official language. A large minority speak Russian. The Government has pledged to provide all non-ethnic Estonians with one year's free tuition in the Estonian language. Since independence the indiscriminate use of Russian could on occasion cause offence. English should be used if unsure.
RELIGION: Predominantly Protestant (Lutheran).
TIME: GMT + 2 (GMT + 3 from last Sunday in March to Saturday before last Sunday in September).
ELECTRICITY: 220 volts AC, 50Hz. European-style 2-pin plugs are in use.
COMMUNICATIONS: Telephone: IDD service is available. Country code: 372. Outgoing international code: 810. **Post:** Post to Western Europe takes up to six days. **Press:** Newspapers are published in Estonian. The English-language newspaper *The Baltic Independent* is published weekly.
BBC World Service and Voice of America frequencies: From time to time these change. See the section *How to Use this Book* for more information.

BBC:

MHz	15.07	12.09	9.410	6.195

Voice of America:

MHz	11.97	9.670	6.040	5.995

PASSPORT/VISA

Regulations and requirements may be subject to change at short notice, and you are advised to contact the appropriate diplomatic or consular authority before finalising travel arrangements. Details of these may be found at the head of this country's entry. Any numbers in the chart refer to the footnotes below.

	Passport Required?	Visa Required?	Return Ticket Required?
Full British	Yes	No	No
BVP	Valid	No	No
Australian	Yes	No	No
Canadian	Yes	No	No
USA	Yes	No	No
Other EU (As of 31/12/94)	Yes	1	No
Japanese	Yes	No	No

PASSPORT: Required by all.
British Visitors Passport: Accepted.
VISA: Required by all except:
(a) nationals of countries referred to in the chart above;
(b) **[1]** nationals of Denmark (all other EU nationals, other than the UK, *do* require a visa);
(c) nationals of Andorra, Bulgaria, Czech Republic, Hungary, Latvia, Liechtenstein, Lithuania, Monaco, New Zealand, Poland, San Marino, Slovak Republic and Vatican City. For the latest information, contact the relevant authorities at least 3 weeks before travelling.
Types of visa: Tourist and Transit. Cost: *Transit* – £5, *Single-entry* – £10, *Multiple-entry* – £30.
Validity: *Transit* – 3 days, *Single-entry* – 1 month and *Multiple-entry* – 12 months. In some cases visas for Estonia are also valid for Latvia and Lithuania.
Applications to: Consulate (or Consular section of Embassy). For addresses, see top of entry.
Application requirements: (a) Completed application form. (b) Valid passport. (c) 1 passport-size photo. (d) Company letter for business travellers.
Working days required: 1 day for applications in person; postal applications take 2 days.

MONEY

Currency: 1 Kroon = 100 sents. Roubles and kopeks are no longer accepted. Notes are in denominations of 500, 100, 50, 25 *or* 20, 2 and 1 kroon. Coins are in denominations of 1 kroon, and 20, 5, 2 and 1 sents. US Dollars and Deutschmarks are widely accepted, especially in major hotels and by car rental firms.
Currency exchange: The value of the kroon has been pegged to the Deutschmark at a rate of 8 kroons = DM1 with a 3% band allowed for fluctuation.
Credit cards: Credit cards are accepted on a very limited basis. Check with your credit card company for details of merchant acceptability and other services which may be available.
Exchange rate indicators: The following figures are

included as a guide to the movements of the Estonian Kroon against Sterling and the US Dollar:

Date:	Oct '92	Sep '93	Jan '94	Jan '95
£1.00=	19.54	20.05	20.50	19.36
$1.00=	12.31	13.13	13.86	12.37

Currency restrictions: The import and export of local and foreign currency is unrestricted. Amounts over DM1000 must be declared on arrival.
Banking hours: 0930-1730 Monday to Friday.

DUTY FREE

The following goods may be imported into Estonia without incurring customs duty:
200 cigarettes or 20 cigars or 250g tobacco; 1 litre of spirits and 1 litre of wine; 10 litres of beer.

PUBLIC HOLIDAYS

Jan 1 '95 New Year's Day. **Feb 24** Independence Day. **Apr 14** Good Friday. **May 1** Labour Day. **Jun 23** Victory Day (Anniversary of the Battle of Võnnu). **Jun 24** Midsummer Day. **Dec 25-26** Christmas. **Jan 1 '96** New Year's Day. **Apr 5** Good Friday.

HEALTH

Regulations and requirements may be subject to change at short notice, and you are advised to contact your doctor well in advance of your intended date of departure. Any numbers in the chart refer to the footnotes below.		
	Special Precautions?	Certificate Required?
Yellow Fever	No	No
Cholera	No	No
Typhoid & Polio	No	-
Malaria	No	-
Food & Drink	No	-

Rabies is present. For those at high risk, vaccination before arrival should be considered. If you are bitten abroad, seek medical advice without delay. For more information, consult the *Health* section at the back of the book.
Health care: Medical insurance is recommended.

TRAVEL - International

AIR: Estonia's national airline is *Estonian Airlines*. There are direct weekly flights on Saturday from Frankfurt/M in Germany to Tallinn and indirect flights to Tallinn via Moscow, Helsinki or Stockholm from all major European cities. Connections to the USA are via Helsinki and New York or Los Angeles.
International flight times: From *London* to Tallinn takes approximately 5 hours (via Helsinki). From *Frankfurt/M* to Tallinn takes about 2 hours 30 minutes. From *Los Angeles* to Tallinn takes approximately 22 hours (via Helsinki). From *New York* to Tallinn takes approximately 13 hours 30 minutes (via Helsinki).
International airport: *Tallinn* (TLL) is located 4km (2.5 miles) southeast of the city. Flight information is in operation 24 hours (tel: (2) 211 092). Bus no. 22 runs between the city and the airport (travel time – 20 mins.); taxis are also available. The airport facilities include bank (0900-1700), duty-free shops (0900-1800), shops (0900-1800) and car rental (*Avis*, tel: (2) 215 602 or 212 735; *Europcar*, tel: (2) 219 031 or 441 637).
SEA: The *Finnjet* runs daily from Travemünde in Germany to Helsinki, where it connects with the *Tallink* to Tallinn (travel time from Helsinki – 4 hours). The *Nord Estonia* runs from Stockholm in Sweden to Tallinn three to four times a week. The crossing takes 14 hours.
RAIL: Estonia has an underdeveloped rail system although there are links to Riga (Latvia), Vilnius (Lithuania) and the Russian Federation. There are daily trains from Berlin (Germany) to Riga with connections to Tallinn. The *Eurotrain Explorer Pass* for the Baltic States is an attractive option for young people offering free travel on the networks of all three Baltic states. It is available for 7 (£13), 14 (£18) or 21 days (£25); eligible for students with relevant identification, those under 26, as well as teachers and academics and their accompanying spouses.
ROAD: There are direct routes along the Baltic coast into Latvia and Lithuania and also east into the Russian Federation. Routes are via Poland and Belarus or Poland and Lithuania; border points: Terespol (Poland)–Brest (Belarus) and Ogrodniki (Poland)–Lazdijai (Lithuania).

TRAVEL - Internal

AIR: There are domestic flights from Tallinn to the islands of Saaremaa, Hiiumaa and also to the southern town of Tartu.
RAIL: The rail system is underdeveloped but most major cities are connected to the network. Rail services to Tartu take about 3 hours 30 minutes from Tallinn.
SEA/RIVER: Ferries connect the mainland with the larger islands and boats operate on Lake Peipus and the Emajõgi River.
ROAD: Estonia has a high density of roads although there are few major highways. Cautious driving is generally recommended since even on motorways encounters with cyclists and horse-drawn carts are not infrequent. Signs are not illuminated and fairly small, so driving at night is best avoided. Lead-free and 4-star petrol are as yet only available in Narva, Pärnu and Tallinn, but the network of modern Western-style petrol stations is steadily being expanded. Payment is in local currency only, although credit cards may be accepted on occasion. The Finnish-owned *Yellow Angels* offer breakdown services on the Via Baltica that connects Tallinn, Riga and Vilnius. It is best to remember that spare parts are not always readily available. Traffic drives on the right. **Bus:** There is a wide network covering most of the country including express services. Prices are very low and buses are still the most important means of transport. **Taxi:** State taxis, usually light green or light yellow *Volgas*, have fixed prices. Private taxis must display the name of the company and their number on the roof. Fares should be agreed upon beforehand, payment is often made in Dollars or Deutschmarks. *Marshrut-taxis* are minibuses which operate on fixed routes stopping on request. They can take up to 10 people. **Car hire:** Can be arranged through *Hertz* at Tartu mnt. 13, Tallinn. Tel: (2) 421 003 *or* 424 254. **Regulations:** Speed limits are 100kmph (63mph) on motorways, 90kmph (56mph) on other roads and 60kmph (37mph) in built-up areas. The consumption of alcohol while driving is strictly forbidden. **Documentation:** European nationals should be in possession of the new European driving licence.
URBAN: Taxis in Tallinn are inexpensive. All parts of the city can also be reached by bus and tram.

ACCOMMODATION

HOTELS: Since independence there has been a scramble from Western firms to turn the old state-run hotels into modern Western-standard enterprises. There have already been successful Estonian/Finnish joint ventures such as the Palace Hotel in Tallinn, which offers every comfort to be expected from a modern Western hotel catering to both tourists and business travellers, such as satellite television, cocktail lounge and conference facilities. Tallinn currently has two 4- and two 3-star hotels. Many more such joint ventures with firms from all over Western Europe and the United States will ensure that the standard of accommodation in Estonia rapidly reaches Western European levels. Outside Tallinn, which for the time being is the main location of the current expansion, Estonia enjoys an adequate range of acceptable accommodation, left over from the pre-independence days, including large hotels and smaller pension-type establishments. For more details, contact the Embassy (address at beginning of entry).
YOUTH HOSTELS: The majority of youth hostels have saunas and seminar facilities. For further information, contact Estonian Youth Hostels, Kentmanni 20, EE-0001 Tallinn. Tel: (2) 442 898 *or* 441 096. Fax: (2) 446 971.
CAMPING: There are four campsites in Estonia. These are as follows: Camping & Motel Peoleo, 12km (7.5 miles) south of Tallinn; Camping Kernu, 40km (25 miles) south of Tallinn; Motel Valgerrand in Pärnu; and Camping Malvaste on the island of Malvaste.

RESORTS & EXCURSIONS

Tallinn, an ancient Hanseatic city and the capital of Estonia, has a wealth of historical and architectural monuments, particularly in the old town centre which is dominated by the soaring steeple of the medieval *Town Hall* (14th-15th centuries), the oldest in northern Europe. At least two-thirds of the original *City Wall* still stands and a superb view of the narrow streets, the gabled roofs and the towers and spires of old Tallinn is afforded from *Toompea Castle*, situated on a cliff-top. A favourite recreation spot is *Kadriorg Park*, which contains the palace built for Peter the Great.
About two hours drive from Tallinn is **Pärnu**, a small town situated on the banks of the Pärnu River where it

emerges into the Riga Bay. Established in the 13th century, the town is known as a seaport and a health resort. Among its attractions are its theatre and its 3km-long (2-mile) sandy beach which is very popular with Estonians.
Tartu is Estonia's second largest city and lies about 176km (110 miles) from Tallinn on the *Emajõgi River*. The city has a very old university and other sights include the *Vyshgorod Cathedral* (13th-15th centuries), the *Town Hall* (18th century) and the university's *Botanical Garden*.
Narva is one of the oldest towns in Estonia. Situated on the western banks of the Narva River, it was first mentioned in the chronicle of Novorod. The *Herman Castle* is the oldest architectural monument and the city museum which is situated in the castle are well worth seeing.
Haapsalu is a small town of the western coast and has been a well-known resort since the 19th century. It is the ideal place to get away from it all with its romantic wooden houses and tree-lined avenues.
Saaremaa is the largest island in Estonia. One can see old windmills, stone churches, fishing villages and a restored Episcopal castle dating back to the 13th century.
Mustvee, situated on the shores of the beautiful and vast *Lake Peipsi,* and **Kuremäe,** the site of the only functioning convent in Estonia, are also well worth a visit.

SOCIAL PROFILE

FOOD & DRINK: Hors d'oeuvres are very good and often the best part of the meal. Local specialities include *sult* (jellied veal), *taidetud basikarind* (roast stuffed shoulder of veal) and *rossolye* (vinaigrette with herring and beets). Braised goose stuffed with apples and plums is also a Baltic speciality.
NIGHTLIFE: Tallinn is used to entertaining day-trippers from over the water in Finland and has a wide range of restaurants, cafés and bars. There is also an opera and ballet theatre.
SHOPPING: Amber and local folk-art are good buys.
SPORT: Basketball is very popular, as is **cross-country skiing** and **football**.
SPECIAL EVENTS: The following is a selection of major events and festivals. For further information contact the Estonian Embassy or the tourist office.
May '95 *Cultural Days '95,* Tartu. **Jun** *Pärnu Music Festival.* **Jun-Jul** *Music Week,* Tallinn. **Jul** *Rock Summer,* Tallinn. **Jul-Aug** *International Organ Festival,* Tallinn. **Sep** *International Festival of Flowers,* Tallinn. **Oct** *Jazz Festival,* Tallinn. **Nov** *International Festival of New Music, NYYD '95,* Tallinn. **Dec** *Christmas Fair* in the Old Centre of Tallinn.
The weekly publication *Tallinn this Week* also lists events.
SOCIAL CONVENTIONS: Handshaking is customary. Normal courtesies should be observed. The Estonians are proud of their culture and their national heritage and visitors should take care to respect this sense of national identity. **Tipping:** Taxi fares and restaurant bills include a tip.

BUSINESS PROFILE

ECONOMY: Economic autonomy was a key demand from Estonia during the negotiations which led to its independence. The establishment of an Estonian currency, the kroon, and the introduction of export quotas on wood, leather and fur, three of the republic's major products, were important moves en route to full sovereignty. The Baltic States are generally more prosperous than the CIS, benefiting from a tradition of trading activity in the Baltic and serving as a transit point for goods flowing to and from the CIS. In the short term, the Baltic States are looking to improve their economic links with Scandinavia and the EU. Other than oil-shale, which is present in significant quantities and provides the basis of the country's power generation, Estonia has few raw materials of its own and relies mostly on imported commodities to produce finished goods. Light machinery, electrical and electronic equipment and consumer goods are the main products. Fishing, forestry and dairy farming dominate the agricultural sector. Estonia's infrastructure, particularly the road network, is well-developed by regional standards. In June 1992, Estonia became the first former Soviet republic to introduce its own currency, the kroon, which is now the only legal tender and is fixed in value to the Deutschmark. The Estonian move was watched with great interest by other republics, many of whom later introduced their own currencies. The Government's economic policies are now beginning to bear fruit after several years of sharp decline in economic performance. Inflation has dropped to single figures. Privatisation continues apace with 80% of companies having been transferred to the private sector by 1994. Like its Baltic neighbours, Estonia aspires to eventually join the European Union. Economic contacts with the EU and EFTA have already been established, and Estonia has joined the IMF, World Bank and the European Bank for Reconstruction and Development.

BUSINESS: Prior appointments are necessary. Business is conducted formally. Business cards are exchanged after introduction. **Office hours:** 0830-1830 Monday to Friday.

COMMERCIAL INFORMATION: The following organisation can offer advice: Chamber of Commerce and Industry of the Republic of Estonia, Toomkooli Street 17, EE-0106 Tallinn. Tel: (2) 444 929. Fax: (2) 443 656. Telex: 173254.

CLIMATE

Temperate climate, but with considerable temperature variations. Summer is warm with relatively mild weather in spring and autumn. Winter, which lasts from November to mid-March, can be very cold. Rainfall is distributed throughout the year with the heaviest rainfall in August. Heavy snowfalls are common in the winter months.

TEMPERATURE CONVERSIONS

-20	-10	0°C	10	20	30	40

0	10	20	30°F	40	50	60	70	80	90	100

RAINFALL CONVERSIONS

0mm	200		400		600		800
0In	5	10	15	20	25	30	

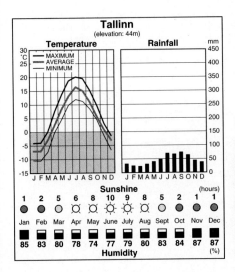

Tallinn
(elevation: 44m)

Ethiopia

☐ international airport

500km
300mls

Location: Northeast Africa.

Note: The transitional government which came to power in September 1991, following two decades of civil war, has achieved a measure of success in managing regional conflicts and consolidating central authority. However, some outlying areas of the country continue to experience lawlessness and there are scattered reports of low-level civil strife, which increase in major population centres during the period leading up to the Constituent Assembly elections. There have also been increased reports of armed clashes between various opposition elements and government forces in outlying areas of Jijiga, the western area of Nekemte and in the east around Harar. However, these reports are unconfirmed. Many people have been injured in land-mines and other anti-personnel devices which litter the countryside, particularly in areas east and south of Harar. Travel on paved roads is generally safer and areas off the pavement around bridges or water crossings can also be hazardous. Pickpocketing is rampant and incidents of banditry are not uncommon in the southernmost areas, along the Kenyan border and as far north as Woleyita, particularly on roads outside major towns or cities. Attacks may be violent and some people have been killed.
Source: US State Department — May 9, 1994.

Ethiopian Commission for Hotels and Tourism
PO Box 2183, Addis Ababa, Ethiopia
Tel: (1) 517 470. Fax: 513 899. Telex: 21067.

Embassy of Ethiopia
17 Princes Gate, London SW7 1PZ
Tel: (0171) 589 7212. Opening hours: 0900-1300 (visa applications) and 1500-1700 (visa collections) Monday to Friday.

British Embassy
PO Box 858, Fikre Mariam Abatechan Street, Addis Ababa, Ethiopia

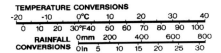

Timatic

Health
GALILEO/WORLDSPAN: **TI-DFT/ADD/HE**
SABRE: **TIDFT/ADD/HE**
Visa
GALILEO/WORLDSPAN: **TI-DFT/ADD/VI**
SABRE: **TIDFT/ADD/VI**

For more information on Timatic codes refer to Contents.

Tel: (1) 612 354. Fax: (1) 610 588. Telex: 21299 (a/b PROAD ET).
Embassy of the Ethiopian Transitional Government
2134 Kalorama Road, NW, Washington, DC 20008
Tel: (202) 234 2281/2. Fax: (202) 328 7950.
Embassy of the United States of America
PO Box 1014, Entoto Street, Addis Ababa, Ethiopia
Tel: (1) 550 666. Fax: (1) 552 191. Telex: 21282.
Embassy of Ethiopia
Suite 210, 151 Slater Street, Ottawa, Ontario K1P 5H3
Tel: (613) 235 6637 *or* 235 6790. Fax: (613) 235 4638.
Canadian Embassy
PO Box 1130, Old Airport Area, Higher 23, Kebele 12, House number 122, Addis Ababa, Ethiopia
Tel: (1) 713 022. Fax: (1) 713 033. Telex: 21053 (a/b DOMCAN ET).

AREA: 1,235,000 sq km (435,000 sq miles).
POPULATION: 50,000,000 (1993 estimate).
POPULATION DENSITY: 40.5 per sq km.
CAPITAL: Addis Ababa. **Population:** 1,412,577 (1984).
GEOGRAPHY: Ethiopia is situated in northeast Africa, bordered by Eritrea, Sudan, Kenya, Somalia and Djibouti. It is the tenth-largest country in Africa and about twice the size of France. The central area is a vast highland region of volcanic rock forming a watered, temperate zone surrounded by hot, arid, inhospitable desert. The Great Rift Valley, which starts in Palestine, runs down the Red Sea and diagonally southwest through Ethiopia, Kenya and Malawi. The escarpments on either side of the country are steepest in the north where the terrain is very rugged. To the south, the landscape is generally flatter and more suited to agriculture.
LANGUAGE: Amharic is the official language, although about 80 other native tongues are spoken, including Galla in the south. English is the second official language. Italian and French are still widely spoken.
RELIGION: Christianity (Ethiopian Orthodox Church and the Coptic Church), mainly in the north; Islam, mainly in the east and south.
TIME: GMT + 3.
ELECTRICITY: 220 volts AC, 50Hz.
COMMUNICATIONS: Telephone: IDD is available. Country code: 251. Calls out of Ethiopia must be made through the international operator. **Fax:** Facilities are available in major hotels. **Telex/telegram:** International services from local offices and hotels in Addis Ababa and telex offices in Asmara. Telexes may also be sent from the Head Office of the Addis Ababa region of the Telecommunications Services at Churchill Road, opposite Ras Hotel. **Post:** Service to and from Europe takes up to two weeks. **Press:** Newspapers published in the capital include *Addis Zemen.* The English-language daily in Ethiopia is *The Ethiopian Herald.* Other periodicals are also available.
BBC World Service and Voice of America frequencies: From time to time these change. See the section *How to Use this Book* for more information.
BBC:

MHz	21.47	17.64	15.42	9.630

A service is also available on 1413kHz (0100-0500 GMT).
Voice of America:

MHz	21.49	15.60	9.525	6.035

PASSPORT/VISA

Regulations and requirements may be subject to change at short notice, and you are advised to contact the appropriate diplomatic or consular authority before finalising travel arrangements. Details of these may be found at the head of this country's entry. Any numbers in the chart refer to the footnotes below.

	Passport Required?	Visa Required?	Return Ticket Required?
Full British	Yes	Yes	Yes
BVP	Not valid	-	-
Australian	Yes	Yes	Yes
Canadian	Yes	Yes	Yes
USA	Yes	Yes	Yes
Other EU (As of 31/12/94)	Yes	Yes	Yes
Japanese	Yes	Yes	Yes

Prohibited entry and transit: Entry into Ethiopia can normally only be made by air transport via Addis Ababa international airport and special permission is necessary for any other entry.
PASSPORTS: Required by all.
British Visitors Passport: Not accepted.
VISAS: Required by all except nationals of Kenya, Djibouti, Eritrea and Sudan for a period of up to 3 months.
Types of visa: *Business:* Cost – £40; *Transit:* Cost – £39;

Tourist: Cost – £39. Transit visas are not required by those continuing their journey to a third country and not leaving the airport.
Validity: 2 months.
Application to: Consulate (or Consular section at Embassy). For addresses, see top of entry.
Application requirements: (a) Completed application form. (b) Valid passport. (c) 2 passport-size photos. (d) Covering letter if purpose of visit is business. (e) Fee.
Working days required: Immediate (in person); 2 days (postal).
Exit permit: Required by all nationals of Ethiopia and visitors staying more than 15 days in the country.

MONEY

Currency: Ethiopian Birr (Br) = 100 cents. Notes are in denominations of Br100, 50, 10, 5 and 1. Coins are in denominations of 50, 25, 10, 5 and 1 cents.
Currency exchange: US Dollar bills are the most convenient currency to exchange.
Credit cards: Access/Mastercard and Diners Club are accepted on a very limited basis (only the Hilton Hotel is certain to accept them). Check with your credit card company for details of merchant acceptability and other services which may be available.
Exchange rate indicators: The following figures have been included as a guide to the movements of the Birr against Sterling and the US Dollar:

Date:	Oct '92	Sep '93	Jan '94	Jan '95
£1.00=	7.82	7.57	7.28	8.47
$1.00=	4.93	4.96	4.92	5.42

Currency restrictions: The import and export of local currency is limited to Br100. Foreign currency is unlimited but must be declared on arrival.
Banking hours: 0800-1130 and 1300-1600 Monday to Friday; 0800-1200 Saturday. Cash must be withdrawn before 1100 in the morning, and before 1500 in the afternoon.

DUTY FREE

The following goods may be imported into Ethiopia without incurring customs duty:
100 cigarettes or 50 cigars or 225g of tobacco; 1 litre of spirits; 2 bottles or half a litre of perfume; gifts up to the value of Br10.

PUBLIC HOLIDAYS

Jan 7 '95* Christmas. **Jan 19*** Epiphany. **Mar 2** Battle of Adowa. **Mar 3** Eid al-Fitr (End of Ramadan). **Apr 6** Victory Day. **Apr 17*** Palm Monday. **Apr 21*** Good Friday. **April 24*** Easter Monday. **May 1** May Day. **May 10** Eid al-Adha/Arafat (Feast of the Sacrifice). **Aug 9** Mouloud (Prophet's Birthday). **Sep 11** New Year's Day. **Sep 27*** Feast of the True Cross. **Jan 7 '96*** Christmas. **Jan 19*** Epiphany. **Feb 22** Eid al-Fitr (End of Ramadan). **Apr 6** Victory Day. **Apr*** Palm Sunday. **Apr*** Good Friday. **Apr*** Easter Monday.
Note [*]: Indicates Coptic holidays. (a) Ethiopia still uses the Julian calendar, which is divided into 12 months of 30 days each, and a 13th month of five or six days at the end of the year; hence the date for Christmas. The Ethiopian calendar is seven years and eight months behind our own. (b) Muslim festivals are timed according to local sightings of various phases of the Moon and the dates given above are approximations. During the lunar month of Ramadan that precedes Eid al-Fitr, Muslims fast during the day and feast at night and normal business patterns may be interrupted. Some disruption may continue into Eid al-Fitr itself. Eid al-Fitr and Eid al-Adha may last anything from two to ten days, depending on the region. For more information see the section *World of Islam* at the back of the book.

HEALTH

Regulations and requirements may be subject to change at short notice, and you are advised to contact your doctor well in advance of your intended date of departure. Any numbers in the chart refer to the footnotes below.		
	Special Precautions?	**Certificate Required?**
Yellow Fever	Yes	1
Cholera	Yes	2
Typhoid & Polio	Yes	-
Malaria	3	-
Food & Drink	4	-

[1]: A yellow fever vaccination certificate is required from travellers over one year of age coming from infected areas. Travellers arriving from non-endemic zones should note that vaccination is strongly recommended for travel outside the urban areas, even if an outbreak of the disease has not been reported and they would normally not require a vaccination certificate to enter the country.
[2]: Following WHO guidelines issued in 1973, a cholera vaccination certificate is no longer a condition of entry to Ethiopia. However, cholera is a serious risk in this country and precautions are essential. Up-to-date advice should be sought before deciding whether these precautions should include vaccination as medical opinion is divided over its effectiveness. See the *Health* section at the back of the book.
[3]: Malaria risk exists throughout the year in all areas below 2000m. Highly chloroquine-resistant *falciparum* is reported.
[4]: All water should be regarded as being potentially contaminated. Water used for drinking, brushing teeth or making ice should have first been boiled or otherwise sterilised. Milk is unpasteurised and should be boiled. Powdered or tinned milk is available and is advised, but make sure that it is reconstituted with pure water. Avoid dairy products which are likely to have been made from unboiled milk. Only eat well-cooked meat and fish, preferably served hot. Pork, salad and mayonnaise may carry increased risk. Vegetables should be cooked and fruit peeled.
Rabies is present. For those at high risk, vaccination before arrival should be considered. If you are bitten abroad, seek medical advice without delay. For more information, consult the *Health* section at the back of the book.
Bilharzia (schistosomiasis) is present. Avoid swimming and paddling in fresh water. Swimming pools which are well-chlorinated and maintained are safe.
Meningitis risk is present, depending on area visited and time of year.
Health care: The high altitude and low oxygen level of much of Ethiopia needs time to be acclimatised to. Those who suffer from heart ailments or high blood pressure should consult a doctor before travelling. See also the section on *Health* at the back of this book. Health insurance is strongly advised.

TRAVEL - International

AIR: Ethiopia's national airline is *Ethiopian Airlines (ET)*.
Approximate flight time: From London to Addis Ababa is 10 hours 35 minutes.
International airports: *Addis Ababa (ADD)* (Bole International) is 8km (5 miles) southeast of the city (travel time – 20 minutes). Coach service departs every 15 minutes to the city. There are full duty-free facilities at the airport and also car rental, banks and bureaux de change, post office, hotel reservation points and a restaurant and bar.
Departure tax: US$10, payable in US Dollars only.
SEA: There are regular sailings between European ports and Massawa or Assab in Eritrea.
RAIL: A 784km (487-mile) rail service between Djibouti and Addis Ababa is run jointly by the two governments; the service is currently closed to visitors.
ROAD: The main route is via Kenya. There is an all-weather road from Moyale on the border via Yabelo, Dila and Yirga to Addis Ababa.

TRAVEL - Internal

Note: *Travel passes* are required for those wishing to travel outside of Addis Ababa. Only guided tourism is permitted; travelling alone is discouraged. In the smaller towns the locals may may expect a small payment in return for being photographed.
AIR: *Ethiopian Airlines* runs internal flights to over 40 towns, although services may be erratic.
Departure tax: Br5.
RAIL: The only operative line runs between Addis Ababa and Djibouti, via Dire Dawa.
ROAD: A good network of all-weather roads exists to most business and tourist centres. Otherwise, 4-wheel-drive vehicles are recommended. Frequent fuel shortages can make travel outside Addis Ababa very difficult. Vehicle travel after dark outside Addis Ababa is risky. Traffic drives on the right. **Bus:** Services are run by the Government and private companies and they operate throughout the country. The bus terminus can provide schedules and tickets, although it is unusual for tourists to attempt to use this service. **Taxi:** Available in Addis Ababa. Painted blue and white, they offer service on a shared basis. Fares should be negotiated

before travelling. **Car hire:** Available in Addis Ababa from *National Tour Operations*. Tel: (1) 444 838. Telex: 21370. **Documentation:** A British driving licence is valid for up to one month, otherwise the visitor needs to obtain a temporary Ethiopian driving licence on arrival.

ACCOMMODATION

Good hotels can be found in Addis Ababa and other main centres and some offer facilities for small exhibitions and conferences. There are hotels in the other larger towns; prices are, in general, slightly lower than those in the main centres. There is a 10% service charge and a 2% government tax on all accommodation. For more information, contact the Ethiopian Commission for Hotels and Tourism (address at top of entry).

RESORTS & EXCURSIONS

Addis Ababa is at an altitude of 2440m (8000ft) in the central highlands. Places of interest include the university, *St George's Cathedral*, the *Ethnology Museum*, the *Menelik Mausoleum*, the *Trinity Church*, the *Old Ghibbi Palace* and the market, one of the largest in Africa.
Aksum lies in the north and was the ancient royal capital of the earliest Ethiopian kingdom. It is renowned for multi-storeyed ancient carved granite obelisks, for important archaeological remains and for the church, which claims to house the Lost Ark of the Covenant.
Gondar was the capital of Ethiopia from 1732 to 1855 and is the site of many ruined castles.
Lalibela is famous for its 12th-century, rock-hewn churches.
Harar is a famous Moslem walled city and the centre for the coffee trade. **Dire Dawa**, near Harar, is an important trading centre on the Addis Ababa–Djibouti railway line.
National Parks: There are seven national parks in Ethiopia: the *Simien National Park* (in the northern mountain massif); the *Awash National Park* (east of the capital); the *Omo and Mago National Parks* (southwest of the capital); the *Langeno and Shala-Abijata Lakes National Parks* (south of the capital); and the *Bale Mountains National Park,* on high southern moorland country, which has its own unique flora and fauna.

SOCIAL PROFILE

FOOD & DRINK: Menus in the best hotels offer international food and Addis Ababa also has a number of good Chinese, Italian and Indian restaurants. Ethiopian food is based on dishes called *we't* (meat, chicken or vegetables, cooked in a hot pepper sauce) served with or on *injera* (a flat spongy bread). Dishes include *shivro* and *misir* (chick peas and lentils, Ethiopian style) and *tibs* (crispy fried steak). There is a wide choice of fish including sole, Red Sea snapper, lake fish, trout and prawn. Traditional restaurants in larger cities serve food in a grand manner around a brightly coloured basket-weave table called a *masob*. Before beginning the meal guests will be given soap, water and a clean towel, as the right hand is used to break off pieces of *injera* with which the *we't* is gathered up. Cutlery is not used. **Drink:** Ethiopian coffee from the province of Kaffa, with a little rye added for extra aroma, is called 'health of Adam'. Local red and dry white wines are worth trying. *Talla* (Ethiopian beer) has a unique taste and European-style lager is widely available. *Kaitaka* (a pure grain alcohol), cognac (a local brandy) and *tej* (an alcoholic drink based on fermented honey) are unique.
SHOPPING: Special purchases include local jewellery (sold by the actual weight of gold or silver), woodcarvings, illuminated manuscripts and prayer scrolls, wood and metal crosses, leather shields, spears, drums and carpets. In market places a certain amount of bargaining is expected, but prices at shops in towns are fixed. **Shopping hours:** 0800-1230 and 1530-1930 Monday to Friday (with local variations).
SPORTS: Wildlife **safaris** to the national parks are organised by a number of tour operators. For details, contact the Embassy or Tourism Commission. There is excellent **swimming** in the lakes of the Rift Valley, especially Lake Langano (but beware of bilharzia – enquire locally).
SOCIAL CONVENTIONS: Casual wear is suitable for most places, but Ethiopians tend to be fairly formal and conservative in their dress. Private informal entertaining is very common. **Tipping:** In most hotels and restaurants a 10% service charge is added to the bill. Tipping is a fairly frequent custom, but amounts are small.

BUSINESS PROFILE

ECONOMY: The economy is largely dependent on subsistence agriculture. Coffee is the largest single export earner, the bulk of which is bought by the USA, and Ethiopia also produces some oil derivatives for overseas sale. Germany is Ethiopia's other main export market. Ethiopia is one of the world's least developed countries, with a hostile climate, poor infrastructure and a dearth of skilled labour. With the civil war over, Ethiopia faces a vast reconstruction task under unusually difficult conditions and is further hampered by extensive war damage and huge debts. The Mengistu regime took large parts of the economy into state ownership, a process which the new government of Meles Zenawi has committed itself to reversing.
BUSINESS: Business persons should wear suits and ties for business visits. English is widely used for trade purposes but Italian and French are also useful. Nonetheless, knowledge of a few words of Amharic will be appreciated. Some of the more useful are *Tena Yistillign* – 'Hello'; *Ishi* – 'Yes'; *Yellem* – 'No'; and *Sint new* – 'How much is this?' Normal courtesies should be observed and business cards can be used. Best months for business visits are October to May.
Office hours: 0800-1200 and 1300-1600 Monday to Friday, 0800-1200 Saturday.
COMMERCIAL INFORMATION: The following organisations can offer advice: Ministry of External Economic Cooperation, PO Box 2559, Addis Ababa. Tel: (1) 151 066. Telex: 21320; *or* Commercial Bank of Ethiopia, PO Box 255, Unity Square Road, Addis Ababa. Tel: (1) 515 000. Telex: 21037; *or* Ethiopian Chamber of Commerce, PO Box 517, Mexico Square, Addis Ababa. Tel: (1) 518 240. Telex: 21213; *or* Ethiopian Trade Promotions Section, 17 Princes Gate, London SW7 1PZ. Tel: (0171) 589 3069.

CLIMATE

Hot and humid in the lowlands, warm in the hill country and cool in the uplands. Most rainfall is from June to September.
Required clothing: The lightest possible clothing in lowland areas; medium- or light-weight in the hill country. Warm clothing may be needed at night to cope with the dramatic temperature change.

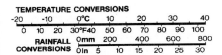

TEMPERATURE CONVERSIONS

-20	-10	0°C	10	20	30	40

0	10	20	30°F40	50	60	70	80	90	100

RAINFALL CONVERSIONS

0mm	200	400	600	800
0in	5	10	15	20	25	30

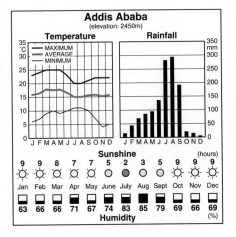

Addis Ababa
(elevation: 2450m)

Temperature / Rainfall

Sunshine (hours)

| 9 | 9 | 8 | 7 | 7 | 5 | 2 | 3 | 5 | 9 | 9 | 9 |
Jan Feb Mar Apr May June July Aug Sept Oct Nov Dec

| 63 | 66 | 66 | 71 | 74 | 83 | 85 | 79 | 69 | 66 | 69 |
Humidity (%)

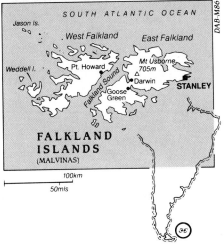

Falkland Islands

SOUTH ATLANTIC OCEAN
Jason Is.
West Falkland   East Falkland
Pt. Howard   Mt Usborne 705m
Weddell I.   Darwin   STANLEY
Goose Green
FALKLAND ISLANDS (MALVINAS)
100km
50mls
DAB·M86

Location: South Atlantic.

Falkland Islands Tourist Board
56 John Street, Stanley, East Falkland
Tel: 22215. Fax: 22619. Telex: 2433.
Falkland Islands Government Office *and* **Tourist Board**
Falkland House, 14 Broadway, London SW1H 0BH
Tel: (0171) 222 2542 *or* 377 0566. Fax: (0171) 222 2375.
This is not a Diplomatic Mission, as the Falkland Islands are a Crown Colony. The office helps to promote trade and investment in the Islands; in dissemination of information to the media and general public on Falkland matters and policy; in processing and assistance of immigrants; and in promoting the Falklands' interest in all respects.

AREA: 12,173 sq km (4700 sq miles).
POPULATION: 2121 (1991).
POPULATION DENSITY: 0.2 per sq km.
CAPITAL: Stanley. **Population:** 1643 (1990).
GEOGRAPHY: The Falkland Islands are located 560km (350 miles) off the east coast of South America and consist of two main islands and hundreds of small outlying islands, amounting to about two and a half million acres. Generally the main islands are mountainous in the northern areas and low lying and undulating in the south. The highest mountain is Mount Usborne at 705m (2313ft).
LANGUAGE: English.
RELIGION: Christian.
TIME: GMT - 4 (GMT - 3 from second Sunday in September to third Saturday in April).
ELECTRICITY: 240 volts AC, 50Hz.
COMMUNICATIONS: Telephone/telex: IDD available. Country code: 500. Outgoing international code: 0. External communication links are provided by Cable and Wireless plc. Telephone and telex links to the Islands, which are by satellite, provide clear and rapid links to the outside world. The Cable and Wireless office is open daily 0800-2000 for acceptance of traffic and sale of phone cards for use in the international telephone service booths situated in the office. **Fax:** A newly installed system spanning the Islands provides international direct-dialling facilities, together with telex, facsimile and high-speed data services. **Radio:** Remote areas keep in contact by radio. **Post:** Airmail to Europe takes four to seven days to arrive. **Press:** There are no daily papers on the Falkland Islands, but *Penguin News* (fortnightly) is published in Stanley and all British national newspapers are also available. *The Falkland*

Health

Timatic

GALILEO/WORLDSPAN: **TI-DFT/MPN/HE**
SABRE: **TIDFT/MPN/HE**

Visa

GALILEO/WORLDSPAN: **TI-DFT/MPN/VI**
SABRE: **TIDFT/MPN/VI**

For more information on Timatic codes refer to Contents.

Islands Gazette is a government publication.
BBC World Service and Voice of America frequencies: From time to time these change. See the section *How to Use this Book* for more information.

BBC:				
MHz	15.26	15.19	11.75	9.915
Voice of America:				
MHz	15.21	11.58	9.775	5.995

PASSPORT/VISA

Regulations and requirements may be subject to change at short notice, and you are advised to contact the appropriate diplomatic or consular authority before finalising travel arrangements. Details of these may be found at the head of this country's entry. Any numbers in the chart refer to the footnotes below.

	Passport Required?	Visa Required?	Return Ticket Required?
Full British	Yes	No	Yes
BVP	Not valid	-	-
Australian	Yes	No	Yes
Canadian	Yes	No	Yes
USA	Yes	No	Yes
Other EU (As of 31/12/94)	Yes	No	Yes
Japanese	Yes	Yes	Yes

PASSPORTS: Valid passports required by all.
British Visitors Passport: Not accepted.
VISAS: Required by all except nationals of EU and Commonwealth countries, Chile, Finland, Iceland, Liechtenstein, Norway, San Marino, Sweden, Switzerland and Uruguay.
Note: All nationals are required to complete visitor forms.
Application to: Falkland Islands Government Office. For address, see top of entry.

MONEY

Currency: Falkland Islands Pound (FI£) = 100 pence. Notes are in denominations of FI£50, 20, 10 and 5. Coins are in denominations of FI£1, and 50, 10, 5, 2 and 1 pence. This currency is equivalent to Sterling and Sterling notes and coins are also in use on the Islands.
Currency exchange: Exchange facilities are available in Stanley and the Standard Chartered Bank. British Pound Sterling cheques up to £50 from Barclays, Lloyds, Midland and National Westminster banks can be cashed on production of a valid cheque card. Falklands currency cannot be exchanged anywhere outside the Islands.
Credit cards: Not widely accepted.
Travellers cheques: May be changed at the Standard Chartered Bank and at some commercial outlets.
Exchange rates: For a guide to the movement of the US Dollar against the Falkland Islands Pound, see the *United Kingdom* section later in the book (FI£1 = UK£1).
Currency restrictions: As for the United Kingdom.
Banking hours: 0830-1200 and 1330-1500 Monday to Friday.

DUTY FREE

Allowances are as for the United Kingdom.
Prohibited items: Uncooked meat, unboned cured meat and plants can only be imported under licence. It is forbidden to carry livestock at any time on incoming aircraft. There are no restrictions on fruit and vegetables from the United Kingdom for human consumption, or on any dairy produce and dried and tinned vegetables for human consumption.

PUBLIC HOLIDAYS

Jan 1 '95 New Year's Day. **Apr 14** Good Friday. **Apr 21** Queen's Birthday. **Jun 14** Liberation Day. **Aug 14** Falkland Day. **Oct 5** Bank Holiday. **Dec 8** Anniversary of the Battle of the Falkland Islands. **Dec 25-29** Christmas. **Jan 1 '96** New Year's Day. **Apr 5** Good Friday. **Apr 21** Queen's Birthday.

HEALTH

Regulations and requirements may be subject to change at short notice, and you are advised to contact your doctor well in advance of your intended date of departure. Any numbers in the chart refer to the footnotes below.

	Special Precautions?	Certificate Required?
Yellow Fever	No	No
Cholera	No	No
Typhoid & Polio	No	-
Malaria	No	-
Food & Drink	No	-

WORLD TRAVEL ATLAS

As well as a complete set of conventional plates, the World Travel Atlas contains a wealth of specialist maps and charts designed specifically for use by the travel trade and students of travel and tourism.
The only atlas of its kind, the World Travel Atlas has quickly established itself as an essential reference work for all those connected with the world of travel.

Caribbean Resorts ● World Cruise Routes ● Spanish Resorts ● World Climate ● World Natural and Cultural Heritage Maps ● World Health ● World Driving ● Italian Resorts ● International Tourism Statistics ● Main Airports of the World ● Greek Islands ● UK & Mediterranean clean beaches

COLUMBUS PRESS

Call Columbus Press for further details on (0171) 417 0700 or fax (0171) 417 0710.

Health care: Hospital, dental and other medical treatments are usually free, as are prescribed medicines and ambulance travel.

TRAVEL - International

AIR: Travel to and from the Islands is by courtesy of the UK Ministry of Defence. Departures are by Tristar from *Brize Norton*, Oxfordshire, in the UK, with civilian bookings made through the Falkland Islands Government Office. Flights from the UK are via Ascension Island. Return to the UK is arranged through Falkland Island Co. in Stanley. *Aerovías DAP* fly weekly from Punta Arenas in southern Chile to Stanley.
Approximate flight time: From *Brize Norton* to Mount Pleasant is 18 hours, from *Punta Arenas* is 4 hours 30 minutes.
International airport: *Mount Pleasant Airport (MPN)* is about 56km (35 miles) from Stanley. There are duty-free facilities at the airport. Regular buses from the airport go to the capital.

TRAVEL - Internal

AIR: Most of the settlements and offshore islands in the Falklands can be reached by light aircraft. This service is run by the *Falkland Islands Government Air Service (FIGAS)* (tel: 27219; fax: 27309) which operates five Islander aircraft from the airport. There are no fixed schedules but daily flights operate to all parts of the Islands, subject to demand.
SEA: Boats may be chartered for day trips from Stanley and elsewhere in the Islands. Some settlements may be able to offer the use of landing vessels or other crafts to reach the outlying Islands.
ROAD: Outside the capital, overland travel is very difficult as the roads are bad and vehicles frequently get bogged down. There is one road linking Stanley and the Mount Pleasant airport complex. Land-Rovers are the best form of transport in this terrain. **Bus:** There are routes to and from the airport, also in and around Stanley. **Taxi:** A taxi service is available. **Car hire:** Land-Rovers and other vehicles can be rented.
JOURNEY TIMES: The following chart gives approximate journey times from Stanley to other islands in the surrounding area.

	Air	Road
Mount Pleasant	0.15	0.50
Pebble Island	0.40	-
Port Howard	0.40	-
Sea Lion Island	0.30	-

ACCOMMODATION

Accommodation is limited and must be booked in advance. There are hotels, lodges and boarding houses in the Falkland Islands. There are two hotels in Stanley, and lodges at Darwin, Pebble Island, Port Howard, San Carlos and Sea Lion Island. Self-catering accommodation is also available throughout the Islands. All ground arrangements can be made through Stanley Services Limited, Stanley. Tel: 22624. Fax: 22623. Telex: 2438.
Grading: Although there is no formal grading system, the hotels and lodges fall roughly within the British 2- to 3-crown categories, as used by the English Tourist Board. Contact the Tourist Board for full details.

RESORTS & EXCURSIONS

For the purpose of this guide the Falkland Islands and the surrounding islands have been divided into four sections: Stanley, coastal areas, inland areas and

British battle sites.
Stanley has pubs, snack bars and restaurants, and there is a golf and race course. The houses on the seafront overlook Stanley Harbour where many different sea birds can be seen. The *Government House*, *Stanley Museum* and the *Cathedral* are also worth visiting.
Coastal areas: These offer a chance (in good weather) to explore ships and wrecks abandoned over the years in the often fierce weather conditions that characterises the local waters. 19th-century sailing ships and iron vessels (some of which remain in use for storage) can be seen at Stanley and Darwin; Stanley used to be a safe anchorage for whalers and merchant vessels travelling around the Horn, though not all of them made it – if conditions are good it may be possible to arrange a dive to see the underwater wrecks. The marine birdlife is varied, including the famous penguins; the views in winter are made more spectacular by the winter waves, 'grey beards', that can reach a height of 4.5m (15ft).
Inland areas: Here there is a chance to view the varied wildlife, and activities such as fishing, horseriding and walking can be enjoyed often in complete solitude. The Falklands are developing as a tourist area, giving people the opportunity to experience the natural beauty of the Islands.
British battle sites: Many visitors come to the Islands to see places made known by the events of the Falkland Islands conflict. As well as the battlefields at Goose Green, San Carlos, Fitzroy, Pebble Island, Mount Tumbledown and Stanley itself, there are also military cemeteries, memorials and museums.

SOCIAL PROFILE

FOOD & DRINK: Almost everything is home cooked and many traditional recipes have been handed down through several generations. Food, generally British in character, includes large 'camp breakfasts' and *smoko* (tea and coffee with homemade cakes) with lunch and dinner.
NIGHTLIFE: There is a variety of clubs and societies which welcome visitors. There are several pubs in Stanley, as well as restaurants and cafés.
SHOPPING: Costs tend to be high as so much has to be imported, though smaller luxury goods may be cheaper. There is a good range of shops in Stanley selling the same type of goods found in a small town in Britain and a variety of souvenirs. Fresh vegetables are available all year round but many Islanders are virtually self-sufficient. Photographers should purchase their film before arrival on the island. **Shopping hours:** 0800-1700 Monday to Friday.
SOCIAL CONVENTIONS: The lifestyle in the Falkland Islands resembles that of a small English or Scottish village/town and communities on the Falkland Islands are highly self-contained. The influx of the British Forces has obviously had an effect on the Islands. More people now visit the Islands (for a variety of reasons – see *Resorts & Excursions*) and the islanders themselves have benefited from the additional amenities offered by the forces. The Government runs a radio station for the islanders (FIBS), in conjunction with the British Forces Broadcasting Service; this broadcasts all day on FM and medium wave. The forces also run a limited closed-circuit television network in Stanley, another example of the close links that have built up between the Islands and the British Forces/government. The population is very keen to remain under British sovereignty. **Tipping:** If no service charge has been added to the bill, 10% is appropriate. Taxi drivers expect a tip.

BUSINESS PROFILE

ECONOMY: The economy is dominated by fishing and sheep-farming, which is the major employer; wool is the principal export earner, and most of it is sold in Britain. The poor quality of the land precludes crop-growing on any scale larger than allotment. Productivity in sheep-farming has improved sharply since the mid-1980s with the division of the land into smaller working units, coupled with incentives for new farmers to work them. There have been several investigations into the possibilities of broadening the base of the economy. Fishing seems to be the most promising sector, and the British government has expanded the exclusion zone around the Islands, partly with this in mind. The Islands also seem destined to become an important staging post en route to Antarctica, as and when full-scale development begins there in earnest. Trade is almost entirely with the United Kingdom. Commercial links with Argentina were severed after the South Atlantic War in 1982. Since their resumption, trade with Argentina has surpassed previous levels and continues to grow, albeit slowly. The pace has quickened during the last few years and, despite the adamant British refusal to discuss sovereignty, Anglo-Argentinian relations have improved appreciably and especially at the economic and trade level. Fisheries control and aircraft landing rights have already been agreed, but there is concern on the Islands about Argentina's sale of regional fishing licenses, starting in 1993, which both breaks the Islands' prior monopoly and threatens further depletion of the already dwindling stocks.
BUSINESS: The Falkland Islands Development Corporation (FIDC), Stanley, can supply information on business opportunities. Punctuality for meetings is expected.
COMMERCIAL INFORMATION: The following organisation can offer advice: Falkland Islands Development Corporation (FIDC), Stanley. Tel: 27211. Fax: 27210. Telex: 2433.

CLIMATE

The climate is temperate and largely conditioned by the surrounding sea being cooled by the Antarctic Current.
Required clothing: Much as for the UK; woollens and warm clothing should always be on hand.

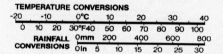

TEMPERATURE CONVERSIONS

-20	-10	0°C	10	20	30	40

0	10	20	30°F40	50	60	70	80	90	100

RAINFALL CONVERSIONS

0mm	200	400	600	800

0in	5	10	15	20	25	30

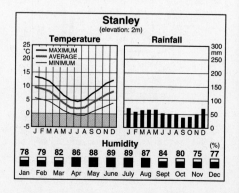

Stanley (elevation: 2m)

Temperature / Rainfall / Humidity

□ international airport

Location: South Pacific; Melanesia.

Ministry of Tourism
GPO Box 1260, Suva, Fiji
Tel: 312 788. Fax: 302 060.
Fiji Visitors Bureau
PO Box 92, Suva, Fiji
Tel: 302 433. Fax: 300 970. Telex: 2180.
Embassy of the Republic of Fiji
34 Hyde Park Gate, London SW7 5DN
Tel: (0171) 584 3661. Fax: (0171) 584 2838. Opening
hours: 0930-1730 Monday to Thursday; 0930-1600
Friday.
British Embassy
PO Box 1355, Victoria House, 47 Gladstone Road, Suva,
Fiji
Tel: 311 033. Fax: 301 406. Telex: 2129 (a/b
PRODROME FJ).
Fiji Embassy
Suite 240, 2233 Wisconsin Avenue, NW, Washington,
DC 20007
Tel: (202) 337 8320. Fax: (202) 337 1996.
Fiji Visitors Bureau
577 West Century Boulevard, Los Angeles, CA 90045
Tel: (310) 568 1616. Telex: 759972.
Embassy of the United States of America
PO Box 218, 31 Loftus Street, Suva, Fiji
Tel: 314 466. Fax: 300 081. Telex: 2255.
Fiji Consulate
1840 Clark Drive, Vancouver, British Columbia V5N
3G4
Tel: (604) 254 5544.
Canadian Consulate
PO Box 2193, 7th Floor, LICI Building, Butt Street,
Suva, Fiji
Tel: 300 589. Fax: 300 296.

AREA: 18,333 sq km (7078 sq miles).
POPULATION: 746,326 (1991 estimate).
POPULATION DENSITY: 40.6 per sq km.
CAPITAL: Suva. **Population:** 69,665 (1986).
GEOGRAPHY: Fiji is located in the South Pacific,
3000km (1875 miles) east of Australia and about 1930km
(1200 miles) south of the Equator. It comprises 322

Timatic	
Health	
GALILEO/WORLDSPAN: **TI-DFT/NAN/HE**	
SABRE: **TIDFT/NAN/HE**	
Visa	
GALILEO/WORLDSPAN: **TI-DFT/NAN/VI**	
SABRE: **TIDFT/NAN/VI**	
For more information on Timatic codes refer to Contents.	

islands, 105 of which are uninhabited (some are little
more than rugged limestone islets or tiny coral atolls).
The two largest are Viti Levu and Vanua Levi, extinct
volcanoes rising abruptly from the sea. There are
thousands of streams and small rivers in Fiji, the largest
being the Kioa River on Viti Levu, which is navigable
for 128km (80 miles). Mount Victoria, also on Viti Levu,
is the country's highest peak, at 1322m (4430ft).
LANGUAGE: The main languages are Fijian and Hindi.
English is widely spoken.
RELIGION: Methodist and Hindu with Roman Catholic
and Muslim minorities. A strictly fundamentalist
Methodist version of Christianity is enshrined in and
informs the Fijian Constitution.
TIME: GMT + 12.
ELECTRICITY: 240 volts AC, 50Hz. Larger hotels
also have 110-volt razor sockets.
COMMUNICATIONS: Telephone: IDD is available.
Country code: 679. International calls can be made from
hotels via an operator, or from the Fiji International
Telecommunications (*FINTEL*) office in Victoria Parade
in Suva. **Fax:** The *FINTEL* office in Victoria also offers
fax services. Major hotels have facilities.
Telex/telegram: Facilities are available at major hotels
in Suva and at the Fiji International Telecommunication
Ltd office on Victoria Parade. **Post:** Airmail to Europe
takes up to ten days. Post office hours: 0800-1630
Monday to Friday; 0800-1300 Saturday. **Press:** A
number of newspapers are published in Fijian and Hindi
including the *Fiji Post* and the *Island Business*. The main
English-language daily is the *Fiji Times*, which claims to
be 'the first newspaper published in the world today' – a
reference to Suva's position just to the west of the
International Date Line. *Fiji Magic* is the tourist
newspaper, which may be of interest to visitors.
**BBC World Service and Voice of America
frequencies:** From time to time these change. See the
section *How to Use this Book* for more information.

BBC:				
MHz	17.83	15.34	11.95	9.740
Voice of America:				
MHz	18.82	15.18	9.525	1.735

PASSPORT/VISA

Regulations and requirements may be subject to change at short notice, and you are advised to contact the appropriate diplomatic or consular authority before finalising travel arrangements. Details of these may be found at the head of this country's entry. Any numbers in the chart refer to the footnotes below.

	Passport Required?	Visa Required?	Return Ticket Required?
Full British	Yes	No	Yes
BVP	Not valid	-	-
Australian	Yes	No	Yes
Canadian	Yes	No	Yes
USA	Yes	No	Yes
Other EU (As of 31/12/94)	Yes	1	Yes
Japanese	Yes	No	Yes

PASSPORTS: Valid passport required by all. All
passports must be valid for at least 4 months from the
date of entry.
British Visitors Passport: Not accepted.
VISAS: Required by all except:
(a) nationals of countries shown in the chart above;
(b) nationals of Commonwealth countries;
(c) **[1]** nationals of EU countries (except nationals of
Portugal who *do* need visas);
(d) nationals of Argentina, Austria, Brazil, Chile,
Columbia, Finland, Iceland, Indonesia, Israel, South
Korea, Liechtenstein, Mexico, Norway, Paraguay,
Peru, Philippines, Sweden, Switzerland, Taiwan,
Thailand, Tunisia, Turkey, Uruguay, Venezuela and
Western Samoa.
Types of visa: Single- or Multiple-entry. Cost depends
on rate of exchange (currently £25 for Single-entry and
£49 for Multiple-entry). Transit visas are not required
if stay in Fiji does not exceed 3 hours, the visitor does
not leave the airport and has confirmed onward tickets.
Validity: 30 days, but can be extended for an
additional 6 months on application to Immigration
Dept, Fiji.
Application to: Consulate (or Consular section at
Embassy). For addresses, see top of entry.
Application requirements: (a) Valid passport. (b)
Application form(s). (c) 2 passport-size photos. (d)
Sufficient funds to cover duration of stay. (e)
Onward/return air ticket. (f) Fee.
Working days required: In person – 3 days; by post –
2 weeks.
Temporary residence: Enquiries should be directed to
the Embassy of Fiji or the Ministry of Home Affairs,
Government Building, Suva.

MONEY

Currency: Fijian Dollar (F$) = 100 cents. Notes are in
denominations of F$20, 10, 5, 2 and 1. Coins are in
denominations of 50, 20, 10, 5, 2 and 1 cents.
Currency exchange: Exchange facilities are available at
the airport and at trading banks.
Credit cards: Access/Mastercard, American Express,
Diners Club and Visa are accepted at a small number of
establishments. Check with your credit card company for
details of merchant acceptability and other services
which may be available.
Exchange rate indicators: The following figures are
included as a guide to the movements of the Fijian Dollar
against Sterling and the US Dollar:

Date:	Oct '92	Sep '93	Jan '94	Jan '95
£1.00=	2.40	2.36	2.28	2.20
$1.00=	1.51	1.55	1.54	1.40

Currency restrictions: There are no restrictions on the
import of foreign or local currency. Unspent local
currency can be re-exchanged on departure up to the
amount of foreign currency imported. The export of local
currency is limited to F$100. The export of foreign
currency as cash is limited to the equivalent of F$500.
Banking hours: 0930-1500 Monday to Thursday; 0930-
1600 Friday.

DUTY FREE

The following items may be imported by people over 17
years of age into Fiji without incurring customs duty:
*500 cigarettes or 500g of tobacco goods; 2 litres of
spirits or 4 litres of wine or 4 litres of beer; goods to the
value of F$400.*
Prohibited items: All categories of firearms,
ammunition and all narcotics. Fruit or plants may be
confiscated on entry.

PUBLIC HOLIDAYS

Jan 1 '95 New Year's Day. **Apr 14-17** Easter. **May 30**
Ratu Sir Lala Sukuna Day. **Jun 13** Queen's Official
Birthday. **Jul 24** Constitution Day. **Aug 9** Prophet's
Birthday. **Oct 9** For Independence Day. **Nov 3** Diwali.
Dec 25-26 Christmas Holiday. **Jan 1 '96** New Year's
Day. **Apr 5-8** Easter.
Note: Muslim festivals are timed according to local
sightings of various phases of the moon and therefore
dates can only be approximations.

HEALTH

Regulations and requirements may be subject to change at short notice, and you are advised to contact your doctor well in advance of your intended date of departure. Any numbers in the chart refer to the footnotes below.

	Special Precautions?	Certificate Required?
Yellow Fever	No	1
Cholera	No	-
Typhoid & Polio	Yes	-
Malaria	No	-
Food & Drink	2	-

[1]: A yellow fever vaccination certificate is required
from travellers over one year of age arriving from
infected areas.
[2]: Mains water is normally heavily chlorinated, and
whilst relatively safe may cause mild abdominal upsets.
Bottled water is available and is advised for the first few
weeks of the stay. Milk is pasteurised and dairy products
are safe for consumption. Local meat, poultry, seafood,
fruit and vegetables are generally considered safe to eat.
Health care: The main hospitals are located in Suva,
Sigatoka, Lautoka, Ba, Savusavu, Taveuni, Labasa and
Levuka, with clinics and medical representations
elsewhere throughout the islands. Medical insurance is
recommended.

TRAVEL - International

AIR: *Air Pacific (FJ)* and *Polynesian Airways (PH)* are
the main international airlines which serve Fiji.
Polynesian Airways offer a 'Polypass' which allows the
holder to fly anywhere on the airline's network: Sydney
(Australia), Auckland (New Zealand), American Samoa,
Cook Islands, Vanuatu, Western Samoa, New Caledonia,
Fiji and, on pay-ment of a supplement, Tahiti. The pass is
valid for 30 days.
Approximate flight times: From *London* to Nadi is 27
hours 45 minutes (plus connection/stopover time), from
Los Angeles 11 hours and from *Sydney* is 3 hours 45
minutes.
International airports: *Nadi (NAN)* is 5km (3 miles)
from the town of the same name. Airport facilities

include a 24-hour, 7-day bank (BNZ); an outgoing duty-free shop; bar; restaurant; left luggage office; post office and car hire.
Suva (SUV) is actually at Nausori, 21km (13 miles) from Suva.
Nadi is where most international flights arrive, while Suva is the hub of the internal flight network. Buses and taxis are available at both airports.
Departure tax: F$10. Children under 12 years of age are exempt.
SEA: The international ports are Suva and Lautoka (Viti Levu). Passenger lines serving Fiji are *Polish Ocean, CTC, Cunard, Norwegian America, P&O, Princess Cruises, Royal Viking Line* and *Sitmar. Royal Interocean* is a cargo line which also carries passengers. There are regular sailings to Tuvalu, Kiribati, Western Samoa and Nauru.

TRAVEL - Internal

AIR: *Air Pacific (FJ)* operates shuttle services between Nadi and Suva (Nausori) and regular flights to Vanua Levi, Labasa and Taveuni. The flight time from Nadi to Suva is approximately 30 minutes. Tel: 386 444 (Suva) or 72422 (Nadi).
Fiji Air operates from Suva to Coral Coast resorts, Ovalau, Vatakoula, Bafour, Lakeba in the Lau group, Gau Island and Ba. A 'Discover Fiji' ticket is available which gives virtually unlimited flights (Rotuma and Funafuti in Tuvalu not included) for ten days. Tel: 301 524 (Suva) or 72521 (Nadi). *Sunflower Air* operates four flights daily to Malololaitai (for Musket Cove and Plantation Village), and three daily to Pacific Harbour Resort. There are less frequent departures to Kadavu, Labasa, Taveuni and Savusavu. Tel: 73408 (Nadi). *Pacific Crown Aviation* operates a helicopter out of Suva which is available for charter.
SEA: Government and local shipping companies operate freight and passenger services linking the outer islands. Cruises to offshore islands leave Nadi/Lautoka and Suva. A ferry goes back and forth regularly from Suva to Labasa, and to Ovalau and Koro Island. Yachts and cabin cruisers are available for charter. Inter-island trips can take anything from a few hours to a few weeks, and are generally very inexpensive. In general, timetables are not posted. Persons wishing to travel about the islands in this way should enquire at the offices of one of the local shipping agents, being sure to confirm all arrangements with the captain once the vessel is in port. A number of roll-on/roll-off ferries now operate between the major islands, greatly reducing journey times. These boats can take between 300 and 500 passengers and have a full range of facilities, including bar, TV lounge and snack bar.
ROAD: Traffic drives on the left. There are about 3100km (1950 miles) of roads, 1100km (700 miles) of which are usable all year round. Traffic drives on the left. The approximate driving time from Nadi to Suva is three hours (on a tar-sealed road). The main roads on Viti Levu follow the coast, linking the main centres. **Bus:** Services operate across Viti Levu and the other main islands between all towns and on suburban routes. Express air-conditioned buses operate between Suva and Nadi and between Suva and Lautoka. **Taxi:** These are metered in towns. A fare table for long distances is required. **Car hire:** Car rental is available. **Documentation:** Foreign driving licence accepted.

ACCOMMODATION

HOTELS: There are a good number of luxury hotels, the majority of which are located in Nadi, Sigatoka, Douba, Suva, Raki Raki, Tavua and Lautoka and off Viti Levu at Savusavu and Ovalau. There are also many small, inexpensive hotels throughout the islands. Increasing numbers of establishments are offering dormitory accommodation at cheap rates. Small resort islands include Beachcomber, Treasure, Castaway, Mana and Plantation Islands. A 5% hotel tax is levied on all hotel services charged to guests' accounts, including meals in hotel restaurants. For information, contact the Fiji Visitors Bureau at the address above (listings of hotels, their cost and facilities can be supplied); or the Fiji Hotel Association, PO Box 13560, 42 Gornie Street, Suva. Tel: 302 975 or 302 980. Fax: 300 331. **Grading:** A star system is used to indicate the price range, as follows: **3-star** (deluxe price range), **2-star** (medium price range) and **1-star** (budget price range).
GUEST-HOUSES: These are known locally as *Budgetels* and are clean, comfortable and most have a licensed bar, pool and restaurant; some are air-conditioned with kitchenettes. There is a youth hostel in Suva.

RESORTS & EXCURSIONS

There are many scenic and historic attractions in Fiji, including trips to copra, ginger, sugar cane and cocoa plantations. The capital, **Suva**, has many old shops and markets with various foods, artefacts, handicrafts and especially seafood. Places of historic interest include the *National Museum,* situated in the lush surrounds of *Thurston Gardens* next to *Government House* and the old *Parliament Buildings*. Other sites of interest on Fiji include the *Cultural Centre* at **Orchid Island,** just outside of Suva, the mysterious earthworks at **Taveuni** and the old colonial houses (situated around Fiji). The ethnic variety of Fiji society can be seen mainly in the towns. There are powerfully built Fijians dressed in wrap-around *sulus,* numerous Indians, men in Western clothes, women wearing colourful *saris* and a scattering of European, Chinese and other Pacific Islanders. One tradition of both the Indians and Fijians is the practice of fire-walking. Fijian fire-walking has its origin in legend, while Indian fire-walking is done for religious reasons; although tourists can pay to see these ceremonies, the ritual remains a religious penance and not merely a tourist attraction. Cruises on large schooners or yachts to the different islands can be arranged, and tours around the main islands in comfortable coaches are also available. For the hardier, hiking in the mountains with dramatic views of the islands is another option.

SOCIAL PROFILE

FOOD & DRINK: International cuisine is available, but the local cooking is Fijian and Indian. Local dishes include *kakoda* (a marinated local fish steamed in coconut cream and lime), *raurau* (a taro leaf dish), *kassaua* (tapioca, often boiled, baked or grated and cooked in coconut cream with sugar and mashed bananas), and *duruka* (an unusual asparagus-like vegetable in season during April and May). Breadfruit is also common. Indian curries are served in all major hotels. A number of hotels and restaurants also serve the Fijian *lovo* feast of meats, fish, vegetables and fruit cooked in covered pits. Table service is normal, although some establishments offer buffet-style food at lunchtime. Hotels often serve meals to non-residents.
Drink: A wide range of drinks are available. Local beers are *Carlton,* brewed in Suva, and *Fiji Bitter,* brewed in Lautoka. Local wines include *Meridan Moselle* and *Suvanna Moselle.* South Pacific Distilleries produce *Bounty Fiji Golden Rum, Old Club Whisky, Booth's Gin* and *Cossack Vodka.* Throughout Fiji the drinking of *yaqona* (pronounced yanggona) or *kava* is common. In the past the drink was prepared by virgins, who chewed the root into a soft pulpy mass before adding water. It is made from the root of the pepper plant and the *yaqona* drinking ceremony is still important in the Fijian tradition, although it has also become a social drink. Bars and cocktail lounges have table and/or counter service. Only licensed restaurants, clubs and hotel bars can serve alcohol.
NIGHTLIFE: Major hotels and resorts have live bands and dancing during the evening. There are also a number of nightclubs with entertainment, especially in Suva. Cinemas show English-language and Indian films with programmes listed in the local newspapers. Most of Fiji's social life, however, is in private clubs and visitors can obtain temporary membership through hotels. Hotels offer Fijian entertainment (*mokeo*) on a rotation basis and details can be obtained from most hotel receptions.
SHOPPING: Favourite buys are filigree jewellery, woodcarvings (such as *kava* bowls) and polished coconut shells, sea shells, woven work (such as mats, coasters, hats, fans and trays), tapa cloth and pearls. Most items are reasonably priced and bargaining is not a rule in shops. Some shopkeepers will give a discount with large purchases. Duty-free items are available and include cameras, televisions, watches, binoculars, clocks, lighters, hi-fi equipment, pewter, crystal and porcelain. **Shopping hours:** 0800-1700 Monday to Friday, some shops have half-day closing on Wednesday and are open later Friday; 0800-1300 Saturday.
SPORT: Fishing: Fully equipped launches operate from the Beachcomber Travelodge, Fijian, Korolevu Beach and Regent of Fiji hotels. **Water-skiing** is also available. **Golf:** There are 18-hole courses in Suva and at Pacific Harbour. Nadi, Lautoka, Ba, Vatukaula, Nausori and Labasa have 9-hole courses. Private clubs welcome visitors if arrangements are made with the club secretary first. **Scuba diving & snorkelling:** The most popular diving area is Astrolabe Lagoon near Kadavu Island. Equipment can be hired at Tradewinds Marina, Suva, and at the Regent of Fiji Hotel and Mana Island Resort. **Surfing:** Dangerous reef waves prevent

surfing in Fiji. **Horseriding:** Horses and equipment are available at several resorts. **Spectator sports:** From May to October **rugby, football, hockey** and **netball** are the main sports. The **cricket** and **tennis** seasons begin after October.
SPECIAL EVENTS: The following is a selection of the major festivals and other special events celebrated annually in Fiji. For a complete list, contact the Fiji Visitors Bureau.
Jul *Bula Festival*, Nadi. **Aug** *Hibiscus Festival,* Suva. **Sep** *Sugar Festival,* Lautoka. **Oct/Nov** *Diwali* (Festival of Lights).
SOCIAL CONVENTIONS: Fijians are a very welcoming, hospitable people and visitors should not be afraid to accept hospitality. Normal courtesies should be observed when visiting someone's home. Informal casual wear is widely acceptable. Swimsuits are acceptable on the beach and around swimming pools, but should not be worn in towns. Smoking is only restricted where specified. **Tipping:** Only necessary for very special services and then only a small tip is required.

BUSINESS PROFILE

ECONOMY: The economy is largely agricultural, with sugar as the main product, although tourism is rapidly increasing in importance. Together, these make up about 90% of Fiji's foreign export earnings, although tourism has been damaged somewhat by the political upheaval since 1987. Copra, once the second most important product, has been overtaken by gold, fish and timber. Low-grade copper deposits have been discovered, though it is not clear whether or not these will be exploited. There are a number of light industrial enterprises producing goods such as cement, paint, cigarettes, biscuits, flour, nails, barbed wire, furniture, matches and footwear mainly for domestic consumption. The Government is also looking to attract manufacturers for export by offering tax incentives: textiles have started to develop under this regime and it is hoped that shipping services (repair yards, boatbuilding) as well as the timber industry will develop along the same lines. Trade and commerce in Fiji have traditionally been dominated by the Indian population; this is likely to persist despite the anti-Indian military coup of 1987. Fiji's largest trading partners are Australia, New Zealand, Japan, the USA and the UK.
BUSINESS: Lightweight or tropical suits are acceptable.
Office hours: 0800-1630 Monday to Friday (some businesses close half an hour earlier Friday).
COMMERCIAL INFORMATION: The following organisation can offer advice: Suva Chamber of Commerce, PO Box 337, 2nd Floor, G B Hari Building, 12 Pier Street, Suva. Tel: 313 122. Fax: 300 953.

CLIMATE

Tropical. Southeast trade winds from May to October bring dry weather. The rainy season is from December to April.
Required clothing: Lightweight for summer, rainwear for the wet season.

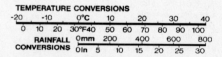

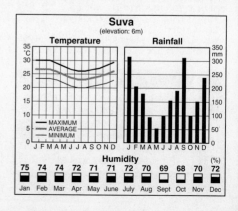

Finland

Location: Scandinavia, Europe.

Matkailun edistämiskeskus (Tourist Board)
PO Box 625, Töölönkatu 11, 00101 Helsinki, Finland
Tel: (0) 403 011. Fax: (0) 40 30 13 33. Telex: 122690.

Embassy of the Republic of Finland
38 Chesham Place, London SW1X 8HW
Tel: (0171) 235 9531. Fax: (0171) 235 3680. Telex:
24786 (a/b FINAMB G). Opening hours: 0830-1630
Monday to Friday (0900-1200 for visa applications).

Finnish Tourist Board
30-35 Pall Mall, London SW1Y 5LP
Tel: (0171) 839 4048 *or* 930 5871 (trade only). Fax:
(0171) 321 0696. Opening hours: 0900-1700 Monday to
Friday.

British Embassy
Ita inen Puistotie 17, 00140 Helsinki, Finland
Tel: (0) 661 293. Fax: (0) 661 342 *or* 661 943.
Consulates in: Jyväskylä, Kotka, Kuopio, Mariehamn,
Oulu (Uleåborg), Pori (Bjorneborg), Tampere
(Tammerfors), Turku and Vaasa (Vasa).

Embassy of the Republic of Finland
3301 Massachusetts Avenue, NW, Washington, DC 20008
Tel: (202) 298 5800. Fax: (202) 298 6030.

Finnish Tourist Board
655 Third Avenue, New York, NY 10017
Tel: (212) 949 2333. Fax: (212) 983 5260. Telex: 620681
(a/b SCANDIA).

Embassy of the United States of America
Itäinen Puistotie 14A, 00140 Helsinki, Finland
Tel: (0) 171 931. Fax: (0) 174 681. Telex: 121644 (a/b
USEMB SF).

Embassy of the Republic of Finland
Suite 850, 55 Metcalfe Street, Ottawa, Ontario K1P 6L5
Tel: (613) 236 2389. Fax: (613) 238 1474.
Consulates in: Calgary, Edmonton, Halifax, Montréal,
Québec, Regina, St John, Sault Ste Marie, Sudbury,
Thunder Bay, Timmins, Toronto, Vancouver and
Winnipeg.

Finnish Tourist Board
PO Box 246, Station Q, Suite 604, 1200 Bay Street,
Toronto, Ontario M4T 2M1
Tel: (416) 964 9159. Fax: (416) 964 1524.

Canadian Embassy
PO Box 779, P. Esplanadi 25B, 00100 Helsinki, Finland
Tel: (0) 171 141. Fax: (0) 601 060.

AREA: 338,145 sq km (130,559 sq miles).
POPULATION: 5,029,002 (1991 estimate).
POPULATION DENSITY: 14.9 per sq km.
CAPITAL: Helsinki. **Population:** 502,000 (1993
estimate).
GEOGRAPHY: Finland is situated in Scandinavia in
the far north of Europe. Bounded to the west by
Sweden and the Gulf of Bothnia, to the north by
Norway, to the east by the Russian Federation and to
the south by the Gulf of Finland, it is the fifth largest
country in Europe. There are about 30,000 islands off
the Finnish coast, mainly in the south and southwest,
and inland lakes containing a further 98,000 islands.
The Saimaa lake area is the largest inland water system
in Europe. 10% of the total land area is water, and 65%
forest, the country being situated almost entirely in the
northern zone of a coniferous forest. In the south and
southwest the forest is mainly pine, fir and birch. In
Lappland, in the far north, trees become more sparse
and are mainly dwarf birch. 8% of the land is
cultivated.
LANGUAGE: The official language is Finnish, which
is spoken by 93.6% of the population. Swedish is
spoken by 6% of the population. About 1700 people
speak Same (Lapp language). English is taught as the
first foreign language from the age of eight.
RELIGION: 90% Lutheran, 10% others including
Finnish Orthodox, Baptists, Methodists, Free Church,
Roman Catholic, Jews and Muslims.
TIME: GMT + 2 (GMT + 3 from last Saturday in
March to Saturday before last Sunday in September).
ELECTRICITY: 220 volts AC, 50Hz. Continental 2-
pin plugs are standard.
COMMUNICATIONS: **Telephone:** Full IDD is
available. Country code: 358. Outgoing international
code: 990. For international enquiries made from
within Finland, callers should dial 92020; tariff
information is available on 92023. Local calls made in
telephone boxes require F Mk1 or F Mk5 coins. **Fax:**
Many hotels and businesses have fax facilities. Also
available in larger post offices in Helsinki.
Telex/telegram: There are telex services at the Central
Post Office (see below for address). Telegrams can be
left with the nearest post office or hotel desk. **Post:**
Letters and postcards sent by airmail usually take about
three days to reach destinations within Europe. Stamps
are available from post offices, book and paper shops,
stations and hotels. Visitors can have mail sent to them
Poste Restante, Central Post Office, Mannerheimintie
11, Helsinki, which is open 0800-2200 Monday to
Saturday; 1100-2200 Sunday. Generally, post offices
are open 0900-1700 Monday to Friday, closed
Saturday. During winter many town offices are open
0900-1800. **Press:** There are over 90 daily newspapers
including: *Uusi Suomi, Helsingin Sanomat, Ilta-
Sanomat* and *Iltalehti. Seura* is a monthly illustrated
news magazine and is one of several periodicals.
Kauppalehti is one of the leading business newspapers.
There are no English-language newspapers published
in Finland, but most UK and American daily
newspapers are available.
**BBC World Service and Voice of America
frequencies:** From time to time these change. See the
section *How to Use this Book* for more information.

BBC:

MHz	15.07	12.09	9.410	6.195

Voice of America:

MHz	11.97	9.670	6.040	5.995

PASSPORT/VISA

Regulations and requirements may be subject to change at short notice, and you are advised to contact the appropriate diplomatic or consular authority before finalising travel arrangements. Details of these may be found at the head of this country's entry. Any numbers in the chart refer to the footnotes below.

	Passport Required?	Visa Required?	Return Ticket Required?
Full British	1	2	No
BVP	Valid	No	No
Australian	Yes	No	No
Canadian	Yes	No	No
USA	Yes	No	No
Other EU (As of 31/12/94)	1	No	No
Japanese	Yes	No	No

PASSPORTS: Valid passport required by all except the
following nationals provided they hold a valid national
ID card:
(a) Iceland, Norway and Sweden;
(b) [1] Belgium, Denmark, France (and overseas
territories), Germany, Italy, Luxembourg, The
Netherlands, and the UK with a BVP;
(c) Austria, Liechtenstein and Switzerland.
British Visitors Passport: Acceptable. The sum
duration of trips to Finland, Norway, Denmark, Sweden
and Iceland using a BVP must not exceed 3 months in
any 6-month period.
VISAS: Required by all except:
(a) nationals shown on the chart above, but [2] holders of
British Hong Kong passports *do* require a visa;
(b) nationals of Andorra, Argentina, Austria, Bahamas,
Barbados, Belize, Bermuda, Bolivia, Botswana, Brazil,
Chile, Colombia, Costa Rica, Côte d'Ivoire, Croatia,
Cuba, Cyprus, Czech Republic, Dominica, Dominican
Republic, Ecuador, El Salvador, Fiji, Grenada,
Guatemala, Honduras, Hungary, Iceland, Israel, Jamaica,
Kenya, South Korea, Lesotho, Liechtenstein, Malawi,
Malaysia, Malta, Mauritius, Mexico, Monaco, Namibia,
New Zealand, Nicaragua, Niger, Norway, Panama,
Paraguay, Peru, Poland, San Marino, Seychelles, St
Vincent & the Grenadines, Singapore, Slovak Republic,
Slovenia, Suriname, Swaziland, Sweden, Switzerland,
Tanzania, Thailand, Trinidad & Tobago, Uganda,
Uruguay, Vatican City and Zambia.
Visas are required for stays exceeding 3 months and for
all who wish to work during their stay except nationals of
Denmark, Iceland, Norway and Sweden.
Types of visa: Tourist, Transit and Business – cost: £12.
Validity: 3 months for Tourist visa; up to 5 days for
Transit visa. Applications for renewal or extension
should be made to the Embassy or Authorities in Finland.
Application to: Consulate (or Consular section at
Embassy). For addresses, see top of entry.
Application requirements: (a) Application form. (b) 2
passport-size photos. (c) Valid passport. (d) Possible
invitation from either a family or business company.
Working days required: 2-3 days. Some applications
might be referred to the Finnish Ministry of the Interior.
Allow 2-3 weeks.
Temporary residence: Apply to Finnish Embassy.
Work permits and Residence permits should be arranged
well in advance.
Note: Those wishing to visit the CIS from Finland are
advised to obtain their visa in their country of origin;
applications made in Helsinki take at least 8 weeks.

MONEY

Currency: Markka (F Mk) = 100 penniä. Notes are in
denominations of F Mk1000, 500, 100, 50 and 10.
Coins are in denominations of F Mk10, 5 and 1, and 50,

20 and 10 penniä.

Currency exchange: Foreign currency and travellers cheques can be exchanged in banks and currency exchange offices at ports, stations and airports.

Credit cards: Access/Mastercard, American Express, Diners Club and Visa enjoy wide acceptance. Check with your credit card company for details of merchant acceptability and other services which may be available. Up-to-date information is available in Helsinki on tel: (0) 12511 *(American Express)*, (0) 693 991 *(Diners Club)* or (0) 692 2439 *(other cards)*.

Travellers cheques: American Express travellers cheques are accepted throughout the country.

Exchange rate indicators: The following figures are included as a guide to the movements of the Markka against Sterling and the US Dollar:

Date:	Oct '92	Sep '93	Jan '94	Jan '95
£1.00=	7.71	8.80	8.57	7.41
$1.00=	4.86	5.76	5.79	4.41

Currency restrictions: Unrestricted import and export of both local and foreign currency.

Banking hours: 0915-1615 Monday to Friday.

DUTY FREE

The following items may be imported into Finland by:
(a) Passengers aged 16 and over without incurring customs duty: *200 cigarettes or 250g of other tobacco products* **[1]**; *manufactured tobacco and cigarette rolling papers for making up to 200 cigarettes; non-commercial goods to a value of F Mk1500* **[2]**.
(b) Passengers aged 18 and over without incurring customs duty: *cigarettes, tobacco products, cigarette rolling papers, etc – as above; non-commercial goods – as above; 2 litres of beer and 2 litres of other mild alcoholic drinks (less than 21% by volume).*
(c) Passengers aged 20 and over without incurring customs duty: *cigarettes, tobacco products, cigarette rolling papers, etc – as above; non-commercial goods – as above; 2 litres of beer and 2 litres of other mild alcoholic drinks (less than 21% by volume)* or *2 litres of beer and 1 litre of strong alcoholic drinks.*

Note: [1] 400 cigarettes or 500g of other tobacco products if arriving from outside Europe. **[2]** Goods may include foodstuffs up to a weight of 15kg, of which no more than 5kg should be edible fats (of which no more than 2.5kg should be butter).

Controlled items: The import and export of food, plants, medicines, firearms and works of art are subject to certain restrictions and formalities. In general, dogs and cats may be imported, provided they are accompanied by a certificate issued by a competent veterinary surgeon to the effect that 30 days prior to entry, and within the previous year, they have been vaccinated against rabies. The certificate must be in Finnish, Swedish, English or German. Dogs and cats from rabies-free countries (Sweden, Norway, Iceland, UK, Ireland, Australia and New Zealand) do not require a certificate if imported direct. The importation of drinks containing more than 60% alcohol by volume is prohibited. Contact the Finnish Tourist Board for further details (for address, see top of entry).

PUBLIC HOLIDAYS

Jan 1 '95 New Year's Day. **Jan 6** Epiphany. **Apr 14** Good Friday. **Apr 17** Easter Monday. **May 1** Labour Day. **May 25** Ascension Day. **Jun 5** Whitsun. **Jun 23-24** Midsummer's Day. **Nov 4** All Saints' Day. **Dec 6** Independence Day. **Dec 24-26** Christmas. **Jan 1 '96** New Year's Day. **Jan 6** Epiphany. **Apr 5** Good Friday. **Apr 8** Easter Monday.

Note: Shops and offices usually close earlier on the eve of a public holiday.

HEALTH

Regulations and requirements may be subject to change at short notice, and you are advised to contact your doctor well in advance of your intended date of departure. Any numbers in the chart refer to the footnotes below.

	Special Precautions?	Certificate Required?
Yellow Fever	No	No
Cholera	No	No
Typhoid & Polio	No	-
Malaria	No	-
Food & Drink	No	-

Health care: There are no vaccination requirements for any international traveller. There is a Reciprocal Health Agreement with the UK but, although consultation at a health centre is usually free, charges will be made for hospital and dental treatment, and prescribed medicines. Some of these charges may, however, be partially refunded by the Finnish Sickness Insurance Institute – enquire at a local office before leaving. For emergencies in Helsinki, dial 000; for other regions, enquire at hotels.

TRAVEL - International

AIR: The national airline of Finland is *Finnair (AY)*. For free advice on air travel, call the Air Travel Advisory Bureau in the UK on (0171) 636 5000 (London) *or* (0161) 832 2000 (Manchester).

Approximate flight times: From *London* to Helsinki is 2 hours 55 minutes, from *New York* is 8 hours, from *San Francisco* is 10 hours 10 minutes, from *Singapore* is 14 hours, from *Toronto* is 8 hours 45 minutes and from *Zurich* is 2 hours 55 minutes.

International airports: *Helsinki (HEL)* (Helsinki-Vantaa) is Finland's principal international airport, 20km (12 miles) north of the city (travel time – 25 minutes). Facilities include bank (0700-2300), duty-free shop, car rental, hotel, VIP lounge, a 24-hour electronic information system with four channels, conference rooms, restaurants, cafés and cafeteria bars. There are various charges for short- and long-term car parking. There is a coach service to the city every 15 minutes. A bus service runs two to four times an hour up until 2300. Taxi services are available. Some Helsinki hotels run courtesy coaches. The other international airports are *Jyväskylä (JYV)*, 21km (13 miles) from the city; *Kemi (KEM)*, 6km (4 miles) from the city; *Kokkola (KOK)*, 22km (14 miles) from the city; *Oulu (OUL)*, 15km (9 miles) from the city; *Rovaniemi (RVN)*, 10km (6 miles) from the city; *Tampere (TMP)*, 15km (9 miles) from the city; *Turku (TKU)*, 7km (4 miles) from the city; and *Vaasa (VAA)*, 12km (7 miles) from the city.

SEA: *Finnjet-Silja Line* car ferry *GTS Finnjet* sails from Travemünde on the Baltic coast of Germany to Helsinki with further connections from Lübeck. Car ferries sail daily from Stockholm and other Swedish ports on the *Silja, Vaasalaivat-Vaasaferries* and *Viking* Lines. Other major ports are Turku, Naantali and Vaasa. Cruise lines with ships putting in to Finnish ports are *Royal Viking, Sally Line, Kristina Cruises, Eckerö Line, Birka Line, Jakob Line, KG Line, M/S Konstantin Simonov Cruises, Polferries, Saimaa Lines, Anedin Line, TUI Viking, CTC, Norwegian American* and *Lauro*.

RAIL: Rail-sea links exist from Hamburg, Copenhagen and Stockholm to Helsinki or Turku. There is a rail connection between Haparanda/Tornio in the north from Sweden, and daily trains to Moscow and St Petersburg.

ROAD: Most direct road routes include sea ferry links from Sweden or Germany, though there is a northern land link via northern Norway or Sweden to Finnish Lappland, which involves travel within the Arctic Circle. **Coaches:** There are coach services from many European cities, including direct services from London to Helsinki or Turku and Gothenburg with a sea link from Sweden.

TRAVEL - Internal

AIR: There are 20 domestic airports in Finland. *Finnair* runs an excellent network of domestic services.

Cheap tickets: There are a variety of money-saving offers available. These include: *Finnair Holiday Ticket*, giving unlimited travel for 15 days (available to non-residents of Finland), which is available before departure to those who have a ticket for Finland; *Family discount* (one full fare plus 25-75% discounts for other members); *Group discounts* which vary between 15% and 35%, depending on the size of the group; *Senior Citizen's discounts* giving 50% discount (with some restrictions) for persons over 65; *Youth reduction* giving 50% discount (with some restrictions) for persons aged 12-23. There are special 'Midnight Sun' return flights to Rovaniemi between June 15 and July 15. Contact Finlandia Travel Agency (3rd Floor, 227 Regent Street, London W1R 7DB; tel: (0171) 409 7334; fax: (0171) 409 7733) or the Finnish Tourist Board for further information.

RIVER/LAKE: Traffic on the inland waterways is serviced by lake steamers and motor vessels. There is a wide choice of routes and distances. Popular routes are the 'Silver Line' between Hämeenlinna and Tampere; the 'Poet's Way' between Tampere and Virrat, and the Saimaa Lake routes. There are regular services also on Lake Päijänne and Lake Inari. On Lake Pielinen there are regular services, also by car ferry. Overnight accommodation in small cabins and meals and refreshments are available on lake steamers.

RAIL: There is 6000km (3700 miles) of rail network with modern rolling stock. Rail travel is cheap and efficient. In 1990 a fast train with a maximum speed of 140kmph (90mph) was introduced. Seat reservations are required for 'EP' express trains. Main rail connections run car-sleeper trains. Seats can be booked for a small extra charge. Tickets are valid for one month. Return fares are exactly double the price of a single fare. Children under 6 years of age travel free of charge, children 6-16 pay half price.

Cheap fares: Special tickets offering discounts are available including: *Group tickets* (minimum of three people), giving 20% discount, valid for one month; *Finnrail pass*, giving unlimited travel for 3, 5 or 10 days, first- or second-class; *Finnish Senior Citizen's Rail Card* for persons over 65 years of age can be bought at any Finnish rail station, entitling the holder to a 50% discount (passport has to be shown); *Scanrail Card*, valid for 21 days for travel in the Scandanavian countries with reductions of 25-50% for young people according to age; *Interrail Ticket*, valid in Finland as well as the rest of Europe; *Eurail Passes* are also accepted.
For further details and reservations, contact the Finnish Tourist Board (for address, see top of entry).

ROAD: There are 75,000km (46,000 miles) of road. The main roads are passable at all times and are surfaced with asphalt or oil and sand. There are weight restrictions on traffic from April to May in southern Finland, and from May to early June in northern Finland. Traffic drives on the right. Horn-blowing is frowned upon. In some areas warnings of elk, deer and reindeer crossing will be posted. Drivers involved in an elk or reindeer collision should report the event to the Police immediately. Better still, they should take care to avoid collisions as there is not much difference between the consequences of a car/elk (etc) collision and a car/car collision. **Bus:** This is an excellent means of transport. There are more than 300 express services daily from Helsinki and connections can be made to the most remote and isolated parts of the country. In Lappland, buses are the major means of surface travel. Bus stations have restaurants and shops. Baggage left at one station is dispatched to its destination, even when bus transfers and different bus companies are involved. One child under four is carried free (children 4-11 years pay half fare). Seats for coaches can be reserved in advance by paying the full fare and reservation fee. Timetables are widely available. **Cheap fares:** Group tickets are sold for groups travelling at least 75km (46 miles) and including at least four persons. Group discount is 20% for groups of five to nine people and 30% for larger groups. A family reduction is given with at least three paying members travelling together. The state post office also runs a bus service with routes that serve the rural areas. **Taxi:** Available in every city and from airports or major hotels. Taxi drivers are not tipped. **Car hire:** Cars can be rented in Helsinki and other places. Normally, the hiring party should be at least 19-25 years of age and have at least one year's driving experience. The rates usually include oil, maintenance, liability and insurance, but no petrol. A few caravans are for hire. **Regulations:** Seat belts must be worn by the driver and all front-seat passengers over 15. Children under 15 years of age must travel in the back. Outside of towns, car headlights must be kept on at all times. In towns they must be used in dim, dark or rainy conditions. Cars towing caravans may not exceed 80kmph (50mph). Cars and caravans must have the same tyres. Studded tyres are allowed from October 1 to April 30 or when weather conditions are appropriate. During December to January snow tyres are recommended for vehicles under 3.5 tonnes. It is possible to hire tyres. Further information can be obtained from *Autoliitto* (Automobile and Touring Club of Finland), Hämeentie 105A, 00101 Helsinki. Tel: (0) 774 761. Fax: (0) 77 47 64 44. If involved in an accident, immediately contact the Finnish Motor Insurer's Bureau *(Liikennevakuutusyhdistys)*, Bulevardi 28, 00120 Helsinki. Tel: (0) 19251. **Documentation:** National driving licence or International Driving Permit and insurance required.

URBAN: Efficient and integrated bus, metro and tramway services, suburban rail lines and ferry services to Suomenlinna Islands are operated in Helsinki. A common fares system applies to all the modes (including the ferries) with a zonal flat fare and free transfer between services. Multi-trip tickets are sold in advance, as are various passes. The peninsular location of the city has led to an emphasis on public transport. Tram no. 3 passes most of the main tourist attractions – a free brochure in English is available for those who wish to take the trip. **Helsinki Card:** This is available for one, two or three days. Once purchased, it gives free travel on public transport and free entry to about 50 museums and other sights in the city. Enquire at the Tourist Board for prices and further details.

JOURNEY TIMES: The following chart gives approximate journey times (in hours and minutes) from Helsinki to other major cities/towns in Finland.

	Air	Road	Rail
Tampere	0.35	2.50	2.15
Turku	0.30	2.40	2.16
Rovaniemi	1.15	-	12.00

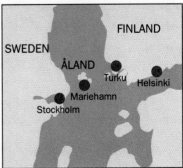

ACCOMMODATION

HOTELS: Most Finnish hotels and motels all have modern conveniences. They are quite new and invariably have saunas and many have swimming pools. The price level varies from district to district, being higher in Helsinki and some areas of Lappland.
Many hotels and motels usually include breakfast in their rates. The service fee is usually included in the bill and is 15% of the room rate, for meals and drinks it is 14% on weekdays and 15% on Friday evenings, Saturdays, Sundays, holidays and the eve of holidays.
Advance reservations are advisable in the summer months (users of the Finncheque system should see below). Details of hotels are listed in the brochure *Hotels, Motels and Hostels in Finland*, available from Finnish Tourist Board offices. See also their publication *Finland Handbook* which gives, among other invaluable information, full details of accommodation in Finland and addresses of booking agencies.
A hotel cheque system called Finncheque offers the opportunity to travel from hotel to hotel in summer. There are 160 hotels in 80 locations to choose from. Only the first night can be reserved in advance. Reservations to the next hotel are free of charge. Finncheques are personal and are available from accredited agents abroad, and in the UK from the Finlandia Travel Agency, 3rd Floor, 227 Regent Street, London W1R 7DB. Tel: (0171) 409 7334. Fax: (0171) 409 7733. Accommodation at reduced rates is often possible at weekends, especially for groups and during weekends. Reductions are also possible for guests participating in special schemes run by hotel chains throughout Scandinavia. The *Finland Handbook* gives details. The Finnish Hotel, Restaurant and Cafeteria Association (tel: (0) 176 455; fax: (0) 171 430) and the Hotel and Restaurant Council (tel: (0) 632 488; fax: (0) 632 813) are at Merimiehenkatu 29, 00150 Helsinki. **Children:** If an extra bed is required for a child there is a supplementary charge. No charge is made for children under 15 if an extra bed is not required.
Summer hotels: During summer (June 1 to August 31), when the universities are closed, the living quarters of the students become available to tourists. These are modern and clean and become the 'summer hotels' of Finland. They are located around the country in major cities. The price level of summer hotels is less than that of regular hotels. **Grading:** There is a hotel grading scheme linked to the Finncheque system. For *Category I* and *II* hotels (the former being the more expensive) the price includes accommodation in a double room, breakfast and service. For *Category III* hotels the price includes a self-service or packed lunch.
GUEST-HOUSES: A *gasthaus* in Finland is usually a privately-run family business. It is generally a small hotel with dining facilities for 20-50 people. In country areas the term may describe a restaurant with some accommodation available. For information, contact Finlandia Hotels, Merimiehenkatu 29, 00150 Helsinki. Tel: (0) 148 8987. Fax: (0) 148 8987. Bed & breakfast accommodation ranges from rooms in main buildings to cottages and outbuildings. There is no charge for children under four, and there are discounts of 50% for children aged 4-12 years. For further information, contact Lomarengas ry, Malminkaari 23, 00700 Helsinki. Tel: (0) 35 16 13 21. Fax: (0) 35 16 13 70.
FARMHOUSE HOLIDAYS: More than 150 farmhouses take guests on a bed & breakfast and full- or half-board basis. They are in rural settings and almost always close to water. The guest rooms may be without modern conveniences, but are clean and there is usually a bathroom in the house. Some farms also have individual cottages for full-board guests, or apartments with kitchen, fridge and electric stove for those wishing to cater for themselves. The guests can join the farm family for meals, take a sauna twice a week, row, fish, walk in the forests or join in the work of the farm. Full-board rates include two hotel meals, coffee twice a day and a sauna twice a week, children 50-75% reduction. The majority of farms are in central and eastern Finland, some on the coast and in the Åland Islands.
Grading: Farmhouses are graded on a scale from 1 to 5 stars.
5-star: These are similar to 4-star, but separate facilities are available to each family.
4-star: These are farms where guest facilities are well furnished. Buildings and surroundings have been designed with the guest in mind and recreational opportunities are provided. WCs and showers are provided with a maximum of eight users per unit.
3-star: These are working farms with dedicated facilities for vacationing guests. Furnishings and decor are good. WCs and showers are in the same building with a maximum of ten users per unit.
2-star: These are primarily working farms. However, attention has been given to the comfort of guest facilities. WCs and showers are in the same building or in a separate service building.
1-star: These are very basic. There is usually electricity and heating. There will be either an outhouse or a WC and shower in a separate building.
SELF-CATERING: There are over 200 Holiday Villages in Finland, many in the luxury class with all modern conveniences. These villages consist of self-contained first-class bungalows by a lake and offer varied leisure activities, such as fishing, rowing, hiking and swimming. The best villages are open all the year round and can be used as a base for winter holidays and skiing. Some of the villages also have hotels and restaurants. Those in the top-price bracket have several rooms, TV and all modern conveniences.
There are also about 5000 individually-owned holiday cottages for hire, ranging from the humblest fishing hut on the coast or in the archipelago to the luxury villas of the inland lakes. They are all furnished and have cooking utensils, crockery and bed-linen as well as fuel for heating, cooking and lighting and in many cases a sauna and a boat. Most cottages inland are near a farm where the tourist can buy food. Reductions are available out of season. Enquire at tourist offices for details.
Grading: Only some of the holiday organisations have classifications. Where they exist they are as follows:
5-star: Cottage with at least two bedrooms, sitting room, kitchen, sauna (with dressing room), shower and toilet. Electricity and every modern convenience. Living space is at least 24 sq metres. Private rowing boat.
4-star: Cottage with at least two bedrooms, sitting room, kitchen, sauna, shower and toilet. Electricity. Living space is at least 24 sq metres. Private rowing boat.
3-star: Cottage with at least a bedroom, sitting room/kitchen or kitchenette, sauna, shower and toilet/privy. Electricity. Living space is at least 24 sq metres. Private rowing boat.
2-star: Cottage with at least sitting room, bed alcove, cooking facilities, well, sauna (own or shared) and privy. Living space is at least 12 sq metres. One rowing boat for two cottages at most.
1-star: Cottage with sitting room, cooking facilities, well, sauna (own or shared), shower and private section in jointly-used privy. Living space is at least 12 sq metres. Rowing boat available.
YOUTH HOSTELS: There are about 160 youth hostels in Finland. Many of them are only open in the summer from June 10 to August 15, and about 50 of them are also open in winter. Some of the hostels are in empty educational establishments, with accommodation and fairly large rooms, but a lot of them also offer 'family rooms'. The hostels do not in general provide food, but coffee and refreshments are available at most and some have self-service kitchens. There are no age restrictions and motorists may use the hostels. Sheets can be hired. All youth hostels accept Finncheques. For more information, contact The Finnish Youth Hostel Association, Yrjönkatu 38B, 00100 Helsinki. Tel: (0) 694 0377. Fax: (0) 693 1349. Telex: 122192 (a/b SUMHO SF).
Grading: Youth hostels are classified into three categories according to their facilities. The **3-star** category 'Finnhostels' provide facilities for courses and conferences. **2-** and **1-star** hostels meet basic international requirements.
CAMPING/CARAVANNING: There are about 350 campsites in Finland. The majority have cooking facilities, kiosks and canteens where food, cigarettes and sweets can be bought. Campsites are generally along waterways, within easy reach of the main roads and towns. Camping anywhere other than in official campsites is forbidden without special permission from the landowner. The camping season starts in late May or early June and ends in late August or early September. In southern Finland it is possible to sleep under canvas for about three months and in the north for about two months. Most campsites have indoor accommodation, camping cottages, and holiday cottages suitable for family accommodation. Prices depend on the classification of the campsite and are charged for a family, ie children, two adults, car, tent and trailer. The charge includes the basic facilities such as cooking, washing, etc. If a camper has an international camping card (FICC) he does not require a national camping card. Further details are given in the booklet *Finland, Camping and Youth Hostels* available at the Finnish Tourist Board Offices or Information, Camping Department, PO Box 776, Mikonkatu 25, 00101 Helsinki. Tel: (0) 170 868. Fax: (0) 654 358. Telex: 122619 (a/b FTATA SF).
Grading: The standard of sites varies and they are classified into the following three grades:
3-star: Covered cooking area, fire-lighting area, main drainage, toilets, washroom with hot water, washing and ironing facilities, play and ball areas, site guarded on a 24-hour basis.
2-star: Covered cooking area, fire-lighting area, main drainage, toilets, washing and washing-up facilities, showers, play area, site guarded at night.
1-star: Covered cooking area, fire-lighting area, main drainage, toilets, washing-up facilities.

RESORTS & EXCURSIONS

Over the country as a whole there are marked differences in climate and landscape, with corresponding regional variations in traditions, culture and food. Seasonal variations are particularly marked in the north; in Lappland, for instance, the winter sports season lasts until May, and the midnight sun shines night and day for the whole of June and part of July. Autumn is also worth seeing, for in September the first frosts produce the vivid colours of 'Ruska'. In south Finland spring comes earlier and summer is longer. At Midsummer daylight lasts for 19 hours and in summer there are generally many hours of warm sun.

Helsinki Metropolitan Area

There are about 770,000 inhabitants in the Helsinki Metropolitan Area, making it the most densely populated region in Finland. The area comprises four towns, **Helsinki** (the capital), **Espoo**, **Vantaa** and **Kauniainen**. However, only half of the 800 sq km (300 sq miles) that it occupies is actually developed. The rest consists of parks, forests, shoreline, and lakes with almost a feeling of the countryside. In many places there are historical sights – old manors and churches – as well as buildings by the best-known of Finnish architects including *Dipoli Hall* at the *Helsinki University of Technology* in **Otaniemi**, an internationally acknowledged 20th-century masterpiece.

Finnish Archipelago and Åland Islands

Finland is surrounded in the south, southwest and west by the *Baltic*, the *Gulf of Finland* and the *Gulf of Bothnia*. The coastline is extremely indented and its total length is 4600km (2760 miles). Around the coast is a vast archipelago of thousands of islands of varying sizes.
The coast and archipelago are largely composed of granite rocks, either grey or red, but nowhere do they rise very high. In many places there are long unspoiled sandy beaches. There are no tides to speak of, so the appearance of the seashore does not differ much from the lakeshores. In addition the seawater is not very salty as very little water of high salt content passes through the Danish straits, and the many rivers as well as the rainfall contribute more water to the Baltic than is lost by evaporation. A special feature of the Baltic is that the land is constantly rising from the sea, as much as 9mm a year in the narrow part of the Gulf of Bothnia, a long-term result of the end of the Ice Age. The archipelago can be explored by local cruises from many coastal towns. Southwest Finland and the Åland Islands are the warmest part of the country and more deciduous trees grow here. Fruit and vegetables are extensively cultivated and 20% of the country's fields are here.
For historical reasons a large proportion of the Swedish-speaking population of Finland lives in this region and is concentrated in the Åland Islands, the **Turku archipelago** and on the south coast. The region is often spoken of as the cradle of Finnish civilisation and the area has a larger concentration of granite churches and manors than elsewhere.
Resorts: Ekenäs, Hamina, Hanko, Hyvinkää, Hämeenlinna, Kotka, Kouvola, Kuusankoski, Lohja, Mariehamn and Åland Islands, Naantali, Pargas, Pori, Porvoo, Rauma, Riihimäki, Turku, Uusikaupunki.

Finnish Lakeland

The majority of Finland's 180,000 lakes are situated between the coastal area of about 100km (60 miles) in width and the eastern frontier. The lakes are a veritable maze with their profusion of bays, headlands and islands. Sometimes they open out into broader waters. They are linked to each other by rivers, straits and canals forming waterways which in former times were a principal means of communication. Nowadays they are attractive routes for the tourist. As the lakes are usually shallow and the surrounding land is not high the water soon becomes warm in summer. A very large number of summer festivals of all kinds take place in the lakeland area, often in beautiful country settings.

Western Lakeland

Jyväskylä, Tampere, Lahti, Hämeenlinna region. This area comprises two major waterways, the oldest of which, the Finnish *Silverline,* runs between Hämeenlinna, birthplace of Sibelius, and Tampere, through fertile agricultural lands with a fairly dense population. Lahti, a winter sports centre, lies at one end of *Lake Päijänne* where the land is higher and steep rocky cliffs rise to as much as 200m (650ft). At the other end is Jyväskylä, famous for its modern architecture.

Eastern Lakeland

The eastern region is dominated by *Lake Saimaa,* a vast area of water with a profusion of interconnected lakes. Dotted over their surface are no less than 33,000 islands and the shoreline is 50,000km (80,000 miles) long. A network of waterways leads from one to the other of the lively Savo towns such as **Savonlinna** with its medieval *Olavinlinna Castle*, the best preserved in Scandinavia. At Olavinlinna Castle, the Savonlinna Opera Festival is held annually in July. In addition to operas performed to international standards, there are a number of musical concerts. **Kuopio** is known for its food speciality 'kalakukko'.

Forest Finland

The remoteness of Forest Finland has meant that the beauty of the wild, vast forests, rivers and lakes has remained unspoiled. It is a popular area for canoe and hiking trips, and rapid-shooting.

Northern Karelia, the southernmost part of Forest Finland, lies in the 'bulge' to the east of *Lake Pielinen*. The *Koli Heights* (347m/1138ft), the highest point in Northern Karelia, overlook the lake. A large percentage of the Finnish Orthodox population lives in Karelia, and the region has preserved its own special character, customs and food. One speciality is known far beyond the region, the 'Karjalan piirakka', Karelian pasty.

Kainuu, the district round *Lake Oulujärvi*, is wild and beautiful with vast forests, marshes, deep lakes and rapids. **Vuokatti**, near Sotkamo village, specialises in cross-country skiing.

Resorts: Iisalmi, Imatra, Joensuu, Jyväskylä, Kajaani, Kuopio, Lahti, Lappeenranta, Lieksa, Mikkeli, Nurmes, Outokumpu, Savonlinna, Tampere, Valkeakoski, Varkaus.

Ostrobothnia

The west coast area of Ostrobothnia with its long sandy beaches (of which the dunes of *Kalajoki* are the best known), is an agricultural region with a sunny climate and less rain than elsewhere. There are islands between **Vaasa** and **Kokkola** with old fishermen's villages.

Hailuoto Island, with its interesting fauna, can be reached by ferry from **Oulu**, the area's chief commercial and university centre.

Picturesque old wooden houses are still a living part of the coastal towns. Traditions are maintained in many local festivals where 'Pelimannit' play music handed down from father to son. A number of Swedish-speaking Finns live on the coast. **Seinäjoki** has administrative buildings designed by Alvar Aalto. 80km (130 miles) southeast of Seinäjoki is **Ähtäri Wildlife Park**.

The region just south of the Arctic Circle along the eastern frontier is centred round **Kuusamo**. In **Oulanka National Park rivers** with rapids run through gorge-like valleys. Seine fishing (using vertical nets) takes place on *Lake Kitkajärvi*. In summer there are numerous hiking routes. *Ruka Fell* is a popular winter sports centre.

Resorts: Jakobstad, Kokkola, Oulu, Raahe, Seinäjoki, Vaasa.

Lappland

Finnish Lappland is a place for those who wish to enjoy the peace and quiet of a remote area either in the comfort of first-class accommodation out in the wilds or in more primitive conditions. Lappland can offer gastronomic delights such as salmon and reindeer prepared in many ways, and the rare golden cloudberry. It is a very large area of 100,000 sq km (38,000 sq miles). Between the many rivers are vast uninhabited areas and swamps. In the valleys pine and spruce grow, but the most northerly regions are treeless tundra or low fell birch scrub. Many fells have gently rounded treeless tops.

There are only four towns in the province: **Rovaniemi** (the provincial capital), **Kemijärvi**, **Tornio** and **Kemi**. The whole of the rest of Lappland is a very sparsely populated area with a density of only slightly over two persons per sq km. Of the 200,000 inhabitants, about 3900 are Lapps and 600 Skolt Lapps, the latter belonging to the Orthodox church. About 200,000 reindeer roam freely on the fells. They are the property of 5800 different owners. There are reindeer round-ups from September to January. Special reindeer-driving competitions take place in March with participants from all over Lappland.

As regards scenery and communications, Lappland can be roughly divided into two areas: Eastern and Western Lappland.

Eastern Lappland

Suomutunturi, on the Arctic Circle, is a well-known winter sports centre, as are also **Pyhätunturi, Luostotunturi** and **Saariselkä Fells**. At **Porttikoski** and **Simo** there are traditional lumberjack competitions in summer. Further north **Tankavaara** is a gold-panning centre. **Inari** village lies on the third-largest lake in Finland, *Lake Inari* with 3000 islands, on one of which there is an old Lapp sacrificial palace. The *Sami Museum* is devoted to the history of the Lapps. In the wilds lies *Pielpajärvi Church*. The *River Lemmenjoki* flows into Lake Inari and is another well-known gold-panning region. The **Lemmenjoki National Park** has marked routes for hikers.

Western Lappland

The scenery differs from Eastern Lappland and the ground is higher. The fells rise in bare and impressive ranges. Among the best known are *Yllästunturi, Olostunturi* and *Pallastunturi.* All of them are winter sports centres but are attractive also at other seasons, especially for hiking. *Haltia Fell*, the highest in Finland, at 1300m (4265ft) and *Saana Fell*, 1029m (3376ft), lie on the border between Finland, Norway and Sweden. In the north is the Lapp village of **Hetta**, scene of colourful festivities on Lady Day in March.

Resorts: Kemi, Kemijärvi, Rovaniemi, Tornio.

Winter Sports

Skiing is the main activity in the Finnish winter. All over the country there are marked and often illuminated ski tracks of varying length and difficulty setting out from near the centre of towns. The tracks lead through the forest and over snow to covered frozen lakes and the sea. **Cross-country skiing** can be enjoyed in south and central Finland up to the end of March. In Lappland the season lasts to the end of May and then there are 14-16 hours of sunshine. Winter begins in earnest when the snow comes to stay, that is, in Lappland at the end of October and elsewhere in November and December. By the end of winter in the north and northeast the snow is about 70cm (2ft) deep. Avalanches are rare even in the fells. The lakes and ground freeze in Lappland in October and elsewhere in November or December. The coastal waters freeze in December. The temperature eventually falls well below zero but it does not feel unbearably cold because the air is dry. Finnish buildings are constructed to keep in the warmth with insulated walls, double windows and efficient central heating. Winter weather seldom affects transport, either by land or in the air, so services run according to timetables. Sea connections are easily maintained by the use of powerful ice-breakers. By January the days are getting longer and the pace increases so that by April there are well over 12 hours of daylight even in Helsinki, and the sun is warm. The snow starts to melt at the beginning of March and in Lappland at the beginning of April. In south Finland the ground is clear of snow by April and in north Finland by May. The ice disappears in south Finland by the beginning of May and in north Finland by the end of May.

Skiing centres: *The North* – Pallastunturi, Saariselkä, Olostunturi, Yllästunturi, Rovaniemi; *The Centre* – Suommu, Ruka, Isosyöte, Vuokatti, Ruuponsaari, Koli, Summassaari, Ahtäri, Jyväskylä, Joutsa; *The South* – Ellivuori, Messilä, Hyvinkää, Lahti.

POPULAR ITINERARIES: 5-day: Helsinki–Turku–Tampere–Kuopio–Helsinki. **7-day:** Helsinki–Rovaniemi–North Cape.

SOCIAL PROFILE

FOOD & DRINK: Potatoes, meat, fish, milk, butter and rye bread are the traditional mainstays of the Finnish diet, but food in Finland has been greatly influenced both by Western (French and Swedish) and Eastern (Russian) cooking. Tourists can rely on excellent fresh fish dishes on menus. Examples are pike, trout, perch, whitefish, salmon and Baltic herring. All are in abundance most of the year. Crayfish (a Finnish speciality) is available from July to August. One should also try reindeer meat, smoked or in other forms. Regional dishes include also *kalakukko,* a kind of fish and pork pie, baked in a rye flour crust, and *karjalan piirakka,* a pasty of rye flour stuffed with rice pudding or potato and eaten with egg butter. Various kinds of thick soups are also popular.

In restaurants *(ravintola)* the menu is Continental with several Finnish specialities. Restaurant prices are moderate if the set menu is chosen. Most restaurants have a special menu for children, or other half-price meals. Inexpensive lunches are served at places called *kahvila* and *baari* (the latter is not necessarily a licensed bar). Information about **gourmet trails** may be obtained from Finnish Tourist Board offices; two are planned – for east and west Finland. The trails have been designed so that both can be covered in two to four days. Visitors on the trails will visit a variety of eating places from large chain hotels to inns and farmhouses, with the emphasis on the smaller, more personal places. Additionally in Lappland *Lappi à la carte* consists of three gourmet routes. An English route map with details is available from the Tourist Board. **Drink:** Restaurants are divided into two classes: those serving all kinds of alcohol and those serving only beers and wines. Waiter service is common although there are many self-service snack bars. Bars and cafés may have table and/or counter service and all internationally known beverages are available. The Finnish berry liqueurs, *mesimarja* (arctic bramble), *lakka* (cloudberry), and *polar* (cranberry), as well as the Finnish vodka (usually served ice cold with meals), are well worth trying. Finnish beer (grades III and IV A), is of a high quality and mild beers are served in most coffee bars. There are strict laws against drinking and driving. In restaurants beer is served from 0900 and other liquor from 1100. All alcohol is served until half an hour before the restaurant closes. Nightclubs are open to serve drinks until 0200 or 0300. Service begins at 1100 and continues until the restaurant closes. The age limit for drinking is 18 years, but consumers must be 20 before they can buy the stronger alcoholic beverages.

Restaurant classification: Prices for alcohol vary according to the restaurants classification.

E: Elite price category.

G: General price category.

S: Self-service price category.

A: Fully licensed.

B: Licensed for beer and wine.

SHOPPING: Finnish handicrafts, jewellery, handwoven *ryijy* rugs, furniture, glassware, porcelain, ceramics, furs and textiles are amongst the many Finnish specialities. Excellent supermarkets and self-service shops can be found all over the country. Helsinki railway station has the first underground shopping centre in the country, where the shops are open 0800-2200 (1200-2200 Sunday and holidays). At the Katajanokka boat harbour there is a shop selling glass, china, wooden articles and textiles. **Duty free:** Anyone permanently resident outside Scandinavia can claim back purchase tax at the time of departure. Repayment can be made (on presentation of a special cheque provided by the retailer) at the following gateways: Helsinki, Turku, Tampere, Mariehamn, Vaasa and Rovaniemi airports; on board ferries and ships operated by *Silja Line, Viking Line, Vaasaferries* and *Polferries*; and at the main checkpoints on the land borders with Sweden, Norway and the Russian Federation. For further information on tax-free shopping, contact European Tax Free Shop of Finland, Yrjönkatu 29D, 00100 Helsinki. Tel: (0) 693 2433. **Shopping hours:** 0900-2000 Monday to Friday; 0900-1600 Saturday and 1000-1600 most Sundays.

SPORT: Riding, **hiking**, **golf**, **tennis**, **squash**, **archery** and **gold-panning** are all available. **Tennis:** It is estimated that one person in 20 in Finland plays tennis. There are over 1300 (mostly clay) outdoor courts and 350 indoor courts in the country. Many tourist centres have a court of their own. It can be difficult to hire equipment, so visitors are advised to bring their own. Many centres offer tennis courses lasting from three to seven days. Packages include accommodation and insurance. **Golf:** The main golf season runs from May to October, although in Rovaniemi (and perhaps in other areas) the visitor is invited to play snow golf in winter. There are both 9- and 18-hole golf courses with the best being in the region of Helsinki. **Skiing:** The peak season in south and central Finland is from January to March. Ski centres in this region include Ellivuori in Vammala, Lahti, Joutsa, Kuopio, Lieksa and Saarijärvi. These centres offer *après-ski* entertainment as well. In Lappland the ski season lasts from late autumn to April, the most popular time being March and April (see *Winter Sports* section in *Resorts & Excursions*). **Cycling** is very good and bicycle races are popular. Ready-planned cycle routes are available, some of which follow old country roads whilst others follow the special cycle lanes in various cities. Along planned routes campsites, hostels and other forms of accommodation are available. Cycles can be hired from a variety of outlets including campsites, hotels, holiday villages, hotels, hostels and tourist information offices. Local tourist offices can provide details. **Fishing** takes place both in the sea and in the many inland lakes and waterways. The sea round Finland has a low salt content with the result that those fishing in the coastal region can catch both sea and freshwater fish in the same area. Foreign visitors over 18 years are required to purchase a general fishing licence (valid for one year) for all areas of Finland apart from the Åland Islands. This is obtainable from postal bank offices and from post offices. In addition, permission from owners of fishing waters must be obtained. Some northern municipalities have their own fishing licences.

Watersports: There are plenty of opportunities for **swimming**, **boating**, **canoeing**, **water-skiing** and **windsurfing**. There are about 26 water-skiing clubs in the Finnish Water-ski Association, about 30 windsurfing clubs, and boats may be hired at campsites, holiday villages and hotels. **Diving:** There are no commercial dive centres in Finland, but, in spite of the relatively low temperatures, the clear waters and absence of dangerous currents and poisonous fauna and flora along the south and southwest coast of Finland make the area ideal for the prepared diver; those who are interested should contact the Finnish Sport Divers' Association, Radiokatu 20, 00240 Helsinki. Tel: (0) 158 2258. Fax: (0) 158 2516. Telex: 121797 (a/b SVUL SF). **Boating:** Only experienced sailors with up-to-date charts (which are readily available) should navigate the Finnish archipelago in which there are many hidden rocks. A number of sailing courses are run by sailing schools approved by the Finnish Yachting Association. Instruction is given in Finnish but many instructors speak English, German or Swedish. Further information can be obtained from the Finnish Yachting Association, Radiokatu 20, 00240 Helsinki. Tel: (0) 1581. Fax: (0) 158 2369. Telex: 121797 (a/b SVUL SF). Lake cruises from a few hours to a couple of days can be taken from June to August using vessels ranging from romantic steamers to modern hydrofoils. **Canoeing:** The best canoeing waters are among the Finnish lakes which are linked in long chains by short channels with strong currents. In remote areas it is advisable to take a guide. Coastal canoeing is generally safe, but only the most experienced canoeists should attempt a sea-going trip. City tourist offices can supply ready-planned canoeing routes. All canoeists should use charts of the coastal regions and inland waterways. Further information can be obtained from the Finnish Canoe Association, Radiokatu 20, 00240 Helsinki. Tel: (0) 158 2363. Fax: (0) 145 237. Telex: 121797 (a/b SVUL SF).

Survival courses: These are available in Kotka in February and March (where there are three tours each for a maximum of 15 people) and in Sotkamo from mid-August to the end of October (4-day survival courses for 4-12 people). The Kotka course, taking place in mid-winter, is the tougher and, although insurance is included in the price, participants are recommended to take out additional insurance.

SPECIAL EVENTS: The following is a selection of the major festivals and special events celebrated in Finland during 1995/96. For a complete list, contact the Finnish Tourist Board.
Mar 8-12 '95 *International Short Film Festival*, Tampere. **Apr 20-23** *Jazz Espoo Festival*, Espoo. **May 14-19** *International Sibelius Conductors' Competition*, Helsinki. **Jun** *Jyväskylä Arts Festival; Karelian Hunting Fair*, Lieksa. **Jun-Jul** *Korsholm Music Festival*, Mustasaari. **Jul-Aug** *Häme Castle Children's Festival*, Hämeenlinna. **Jul 7-9** *Härmä Mischief*, Alahärmä. **Aug 6** *World Speedway Championships*, Tampere. **Aug 18-26** *World Rowing Championships*, Tampere. **Mar 10 '96** *Tar Skiing Race*, Oulu.
SOCIAL CONVENTIONS: Handshaking is customary. Normal courtesies should be observed. It is customary for the guest to refrain from drinking until the host or hostess toasts their health with a 'skol'. Casual dress is acceptable. Black tie will usually be specified when required. Finns appear sometimes to be rather reserved and visitors should not feel alarmed if there is a lack of small talk during the first half hour or so. **Tipping:** 15% service charge included in the bill in hotels. Restaurants and bars have 14% service charge on weekdays and 15% on weekends and holidays. The obligatory cloakroom or doorman fee is usually clearly indicated. Taxi drivers, washroom attendants and hairdressers are not tipped.

BUSINESS PROFILE

ECONOMY: Finland is a highly industrialised country, producing a wide range of industrial and consumer goods. Timber and related industries form the backbone of the economy, accounting for 40% of all Finnish exports, but the country is consequently vulnerable to fluctuations in the world market prices and demand levels for timber, paper, and finished products such as furniture. Agriculture is relatively important by the standards of most European industrialised economies, despite the country's climatic and geographical conditions which allow a very short growing season, giving Finland virtual self-sufficiency in basic foodstuffs such as grains, dairy products and root crops. The largest industrial sector is engineering, and although traditional 'metal bashing' industries have been in a strong position by world standards, there has nonetheless been a decline which threw Finland into an unprecedented recession at the turn of the 1990s. Industry is heavily dependent on imported components, which should merit increased attention from British firms. Paper, chemicals,

woodworking, metal ores and textiles are Finland's other major export industries. Apart from engineering products, consumer goods are the country's main imported products. Through its geographical position and political neutrality, Finland has enjoyed the benefits of trade with both East and West, and is well placed to take up new opportunities in Eastern Europe and the CIS. Finland is a long-standing member of the European Free Trade Association (EFTA) which started life as a rival trading bloc to the EEC and, since 1992, has a trade agreement with it under the auspices of the European Economic Area. Nonetheless, full membership of the EU remained a key aspiration of the Finns and, as in 1992, a formal application was lodged with Brussels. This was accepted, and along with Sweden and Austria, Finland joined the EU in the latest tranche of entries on January 1, 1995.
BUSINESS: Businessmen are expected to dress smartly. Most Finnish business people speak English and/or German. Finnish is a complex language related to Hungarian and Estonian; details of available courses may be obtained from the Council for the Instruction of Finnish for Foreigners, Pohjoisranta 4 A 4, 00170 Helsinki. Local tourist boards and travel agents will be able to assist in finding translation services. Punctuality is essential for business and social occasions. Calling cards are common. Best months for business visits are February to May and October to December. **Office hours:** 0800-1615 Monday to Friday.
COMMERCIAL INFORMATION: The following organisation can offer advice: Finland Trade Centre, 30-35 Pall Mall, London SW1Y 5LP. Tel: (0171) 747 3000. Fax: (0171) 747 3007; *or* Keskuskauppakamari (Central Chamber of Commerce of Finland), PO Box 1000, Fabianinkatu 14, 00101 Helsinki. Tel: (0) 650 133. Fax: (0) 650 303. Telex: 123814.
CONFERENCES/CONVENTIONS: Finland is among the world's top 20 conference destinations. In addition to conference centres and hotels there are cruise ships offering conference facilities. Information may be obtained from Helsinki Congress Marketing, Fabianinkatu 4 B 11, 00130 Helsinki. Tel: (0) 6511 500. Fax: (0) 654 705. In addition there are several Finnish congress organisers and travel agencies with congress departments. The Finnish Tourist Board can supply details.

CLIMATE

Temperate climate, but with considerable temperature variations (see below). Summer is warm with relatively mild weather in spring and autumn. Winter, which lasts from November to mid-March, is very cold. In the north (see the chart for Sodankyla), the snow cover lasts from mid-October until mid May, but in the brief Arctic summer there may be up to 16 hours of sunshine a day. Rainfall is distributed throughout the year with snow in winter, but the low humidity often has the effect of making it seem warmer than the temperature would indicate (even in Lappland the temperature can rise to over 30°C). During warm weather, gnats and mosquitos can be a hazard, particularly in the north of the country. Bring a good supply of insect repellant. The *Midnight Twilight* season lasts for two months in the north during winter.

Required clothing: Light- to medium-weights in warmer months. Medium- to heavy-weights in winter, with particularly warm clothing needed for the Arctic north. Waterproofing is essential throughout the year.

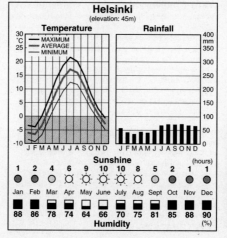

France

□ *international airport*

Location: Western Europe.

Note: For information on Overseas Departments, Overseas Territories and Overseas Collectivités Territoriales, consult the section on *French Overseas Possessions* below (after the entry for French Guiana).

Maison de la France (Tourist Information Agency)
8 avenue de l'Opéra, 75001 Paris, France
Tel: (1) 42 96 10 23. Fax: (1) 42 86 08 94. Telex: 214260.
Direction des Industries Touristiques
2 rue Linois, 75740 Paris, Cedex 15, France
Tel: (1) 44 37 36 00. Fax: (1) 44 37 36 36. Telex: 870974.
Embassy of the French Republic
58 Knightsbridge, London SW1X 7JT
Tel: (0171) 201 1000. Fax: (0171) 259 6498. Telex: 261905 (a/b FRALON).
French Consulate General (Visa Section)
PO Box 57, 6A Cromwell Place, London SW7 2EW
Tel: (0171) 838 2050. Information Service: (0898) 200 289 (calls are charged at the higher rate of 39p/49p per minute). Fax: (0171) 838 2046. Telex: 924153. Opening hours: 0900-1130 (and 1600-1630 for visa collection only) Monday to Friday (except French and British national holidays).
Consulate in: Scotland (tel: (0131) 225 7954)
French Embassy (Cultural Section)
23 Cromwell Road, London SW7 2DQ
Tel: (0171) 838 2055. Fax: (0171) 838 2088. Opening hours: 0930-1300 and 1430-1700 Monday to Friday.
French Government Tourist Office
178 Piccadilly, London W1V 0AL
Tel: (0891) 244 123 (France Information Line; calls are charged at the higher rate of 39/49p per minute). Fax: (0171) 493 6594. Telex: 21902. Opening hours: 0900-1700 Monday to Friday.
British Embassy
35 rue du Faubourg St Honoré, 75383 Paris, Cedex 08, France
Tel: (1) 42 66 91 42. Fax: (1) 42 66 95 90. Telex: 650264 (a/b INFORM).

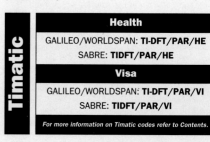

Health	
GALILEO/WORLDSPAN: **TI-DFT/PAR/HE**	
SABRE: **TIDFT/PAR/HE**	
Visa	
GALILEO/WORLDSPAN: **TI-DFT/PAR/VI**	
SABRE: **TIDFT/PAR/VI**	

For more information on Timatic codes refer to Contents.

Timatic

British Consulate General
9 avenue Hoche, 75008 Paris, France
Tel: (1) 42 66 38 10. Fax: (1) 40 76 02 87. Telex: 651018 (a/b CONSUL).
(All post should be addressed to the British Embassy.)
Consulates in: Biarritz, Bordeaux, Lille, Calais, Boulogne-sur-Mer, Cherbourg, Dunkirk, Lyon, Marseille, Le Havre, Nantes, Nice, St Malo-Dinard, Toulouse, Cayenne (French Guiana), Fort de France (Martinique), Papeete (Tahiti), Pointe-à-Pitre (Guadeloupe) and Réunion.
Embassy of the French Republic
4101 Reservoir Road, NW, Washington, DC 20007
Tel: (202) 944 6000 *or* 944 6200 (Consular section). Fax: (202) 944 6072.
Consulates in: Atlanta, Boston, Chicago, Detroit, Houston, Los Angeles, Miami, New Orleans, New York, San Francisco and Washington.
French Government Tourist Office
444 Madison Avenue, New York, NY 10020-2451.
Tel: (212) 838 7800. Information Line: (1 900) 990 0040 (calls are charged at 50¢ per minute). Fax: (212) 838 7855.
Embassy of the United States of America
2 avenue Gabriel, 75382 Paris, Cedex 08, France
Tel: (1) 42 61 80 75 *or* 42 96 12 02. Fax: (1) 42 66 97 83. Telex: 285221 (a/b AMEMB).
Consulates in: Bordeaux, Lyon, Marseille, Martinique and Strasbourg.
Embassy of the French Republic
42 Sussex Drive, Ottawa, Ontario K1M 2C9
Tel: (613) 789 1795. Fax: (613) 789 3484.
Consulates in: Calgary, Chicoutimi, Edmonton, Halifax, Moncton, Montréal, North Sydney, Québec, Regina, Rouyn-Noranda, St John's, Saskatoon, Sudbury, Toronto, Vancouver, Victoria, Whitehorse and Winnipeg.
French Government Tourist Office
Suite 490, 1981 McGill College, Montréal, Québec H3A 2W9
Tel: (514) 288 4264. Fax: (514) 845 4868.
Canadian Embassy
35 avenue Montaigne, 75008 Paris, France
Tel: (1) 44 43 29 00. Fax: (1) 44 43 29 99. Telex: 651806.
Consulates in: Lyon, St Pierre (St Pierre et Miquelon), Strasbourg and Toulouse.

AREA: 543,965 sq km (210,026 sq miles).
POPULATION: 57,049,000 (1991).
POPULATION DENSITY: 104.1 per sq km.
CAPITAL: Paris. **Population:** 2,152,423 (1990).
GEOGRAPHY: France, the largest country in Europe, is bounded to the north by the English Channel *(La Manche),* the northeast by Belgium and Luxembourg, the east by Germany, Switzerland and Italy, the south by the Mediterranean (with Monaco as a coastal enclave between Nice and the Italian frontier), the southwest by Spain and Andorra, and the west by the Atlantic Ocean. The island of Corsica, southeast of Nice, is made up of two *Départements.* The country offers a spectacular variety of scenery, from the mountain ranges of the Alps and Pyrénées to the attractive river valleys of the Loire, Rhône and Dordogne and the flatter countryside in Normandy and on the Atlantic coast. The country has some 2900km (1800 miles) of coastline.
LANGUAGE: French is the official language, but there are many regional dialects. Basque is spoken as a first language by some people in the southwest, and Breton by some in Brittany. Many people, particularly those connected with tourism in the major areas, will speak at least some English.
RELIGION: Approximately 90% Roman Catholic with a Protestant minority. Almost every religion has at least some adherents.
TIME: GMT + 1 (GMT + 2 from last Sunday in March to Saturday before last Sunday in September).
ELECTRICITY: 220 volts AC, 50Hz. 2-pin plugs are widely used; adaptors recommended. Old hotels may still use 110 volts.
COMMUNICATIONS: Telephone: Full IDD is available. Country code: 33. Outgoing international code: 19. Card-only telephones are now common, the pre-paid cards being purchased from post offices or *Tabacs.* International calls are cheaper between 2230-0800 Monday to Friday, and from 1400 Saturday to 0800 Monday. Calls can be received from all phone boxes showing the sign of a blue bell. **Fax:** Services are widely available; many hotels have facilities. **Telex:** There are public telex offices at 7 place de la Bourse and 7 rue Feydeau, 75002 Paris, which are open 24 hours a day, and telex facilities in the central post offices of most major towns, or in the offices of private companies, who will require an international telex credit card to charge the cost. The country code for telex is 42F. **Post:** Stamps can be purchased at post offices and *Tabacs.* Post normally takes a couple of days to reach its destination within Europe. Post office opening hours: 0800-1900 Monday to Friday; 0800-1200 Saturday. **Press:** There are many daily newspapers, the most prominent being *Le Monde, Libération, France-Soir* and *Le Figaro.* Outside the Ile-de-France, however, these newspapers are not nearly as popular as the provincial press.
BBC World Service and Voice of America frequencies: From time to time these change. See the section *How to Use this Book* for more information.

BBC:				
MHz	**17.64**	**12.09**	**9.760**	**0.648**
Voice of America:				
MHz	**15.20**	**9.670**	**6.040**	**5.995**

PASSPORT/VISA

Regulations and requirements may be subject to change at short notice, and you are advised to contact the appropriate diplomatic or consular authority before finalising travel arrangements. Details of these may be found at the head of this country's entry. Any numbers in the chart refer to the footnotes below.

	Passport Required?	Visa Required?	Return Ticket Required?
Full British	1	No	*
BVP	Valid	-	*
Australian	Yes	Yes	*
Canadian	Yes	No	*
USA	Yes	No	*
Other EU (As of 31/12/94)	2	No	*
Japanese	Yes	No	*

Note: The French Consulate General is currently working on new visa regulations. It will therefore be necessary to check with the Consulate (or Consular section of Embassy) before departure.
PASSPORTS: Valid passport required by all except:
(a) **[1]** nationals of the UK provided they are in possession of a British Visitors Passport or a 60-hour British Excursion Document;
(b) **[2]** nationals of Belgium, Germany, Italy, Luxembourg, The Netherlands and Spain provided they are in possession of a passport expired for a maximum of 5 years or a valid national ID card;
(c) nationals of Andorra, Liechtenstein, Monaco and Switzerland, provided they are in possession of a passport expired for a maximum of 5 years or a valid national ID card.
Note [*]: It is advised that passengers hold return or onward tickets although this is not an absolute requirement.
British Visitors Passport: A British Visitors Passport can be used for holidays or unpaid business trips to France (including Corsica). For further information, see the *Passport/Visa* section of the introduction at the beginning of the book.
VISAS: Required by all except:
(a) nationals of countries shown in the chart above;
(b) nationals of Andorra, Argentina, Austria, Brunei, Chile, Cyprus, Czech Republic, Finland, Hungary, Iceland, †Israel, South Korea, Liechtenstein, Malta, Monaco, New Zealand, Norway, Poland, San Marino, Singapore, Slovak Republic, Slovenia, Sweden, Switzerland and Vatican City provided the stay does not exceed 3 months in metropolitan France or 30 days in French overseas territories.
Notes: British citizens who have retained their Commonwealth passports may require a visa. Check with the visa section of the Consulate for details.
[†] Israeli nationals *do* require a visa to visit French overseas territories.
Types of visa: Transit (cost £7-8); Short-stay single or Multiple-entry (cost £23-28); stays for over 90 days (cost £75-80). Prices alter with the fluctuation of the exchange rate, so check for the exact price before travelling.
Note: Payment for visas may only be made using cash.
Validity: Transit visas are valid for 1-5 days, excluding day of arrival; Short-stay visas are valid for up to 3 months. For procedure regarding renewal, apply to French Consulate.
Application to: Consulate (or Consular section at Embassy). For addresses, see top of entry.
Application requirements: (a) Valid passport. (b) Up to 3 application forms. (c) Up to 3 passport-size photos. (d) Return ticket to country of residence. (e) In certain cases travellers may require evidence of hotel reservations, business appointments, invitation from relatives, and means of support.
Note: Postal applications are *not* acceptable.
Working days required: For most nationals, 24 hours. However, nationals of Eastern European countries must allow 28 days, and nationals of Middle Eastern countries, or those with refugee travel documents, should allow 2 months.
Temporary residence: A Work Permit may often have to be obtained in France. For full details, enquire at the French Consulate.

MONEY

Currency: French Franc (FFr) = 100 centimes. Notes are in denominations of FFr500, 200, 100, 50, 20 and 10. Coins are in denominations of FFr20, 10, 5, 2 and 1, and 50, 20, 10 and 5 centimes.
Currency exchange: Some first-class hotels are authorised to exchange foreign currency. Also look for the French equivalent of the Trustee Savings Bank, 'Crédit Mutuel' or 'Crédit Agricole', which have longer opening hours. Shops and hotels are prohibited from accepting foreign currency by law. Many UK banks offer differing exchange rates depending on the denominations of French currency being bought or sold. Travellers should check with their banks for details and current rates.
Credit cards: American Express, Diners Club and Visa are widely accepted. Check with your credit card company for details of merchant acceptability and other services which may be available.
Travellers cheques: Accepted almost everywhere.
Exchange rate indicators: The following figures are included as a guide to the movements of the French Franc against Sterling and the US Dollar:

Date:	**Oct '92**	**Sep '93**	**Jan '94**	**Jan '95**
£1.00=	**8.28**	**8.68**	**8.74**	**8.35**
$1.00=	**5.21**	**5.68**	**5.90**	**5.34**

Currency restrictions: The import and export of of local and foreign currency is unrestricted. Amounts over FFr50,000 have to be declared.
Banking hours: 0900-1200 and 1400-1600 Monday to Friday. Some banks close on Monday. Banks close early (1200) on the day before a bank holiday; in rare cases, they may also close for all or part of the day after.

DUTY FREE

The following goods may be imported into France without incurring customs duty by:
(a) Passengers over 17 years of age entering from countries outside the EU:
200 cigarettes or 50 cigars or 100 cigarillos or 250g of tobacco; 1 litre of spirits of more than 22% or 2 litres of alcoholic beverage up to 22%; 2 litres of wine; 50g of perfume and 250ml of eau de toilette; other goods to the value of FFr300 (FFr150 per person under 15 years of age).
(b) Passengers over 17 years of age entering from an EU country:
300 cigarettes or 75 cigars or 150 cigarillos or 400g of tobacco; 1.5 litres of spirits of more than 22% or 3 litres of spirits or sparkling wine up to 22%; 5 litres of wine; 75g of perfume and 375ml of eau de toilette; other goods to the value of FFr4200 (FFr1100 per person under 15 years of age).
(c) Passengers over 17 years of age entering from an EU country with duty-paid goods:
800 cigarettes or 400 cigarillos or 200 cigars or 1kg of tobacco; 90 litres of wine (including up to 60 litres of sparkling wine); 10 litres of spirits; 20 litres of intermediate products (such as fortified wine); 110 litres of beer.
Prohibited items: Gold objects, other than personal jewellery below 500g in weight.

PUBLIC HOLIDAYS

Jan 2 '95 For New Year's Day. **Apr 17** Easter Monday. **May 1** Labour Day. **May 8** Liberation Day. **May 25** Ascension Day. **Jun 5** Whit Monday. **Jul 14** National Day, Fall of the Bastille. **Aug 15** Assumption. **Nov 1** All Saints' Day. **Nov 11** Remembrance Day. **Dec 25** Christmas Day. **Jan 1 '96** New Year's Day. **Apr 8** Easter Monday.
Note: In France the months of July and August are traditionally when the French take their holidays. For this reason the less touristic parts of France are quiet during these months, while coastal resorts are very crowded.

HEALTH

Regulations and requirements may be subject to change at short notice, and you are advised to contact your doctor well in advance of your intended date of departure. Any numbers in the chart refer to the footnotes below.

	Special Precautions?	Certificate Required?
Yellow Fever	No	No
Cholera	No	No
Typhoid & Polio	No	-
Malaria	No	-
Food & Drink	No	-

Rabies is present. For those at high risk, vaccination before arrival should be considered. If you are bitten abroad seek medical advice without delay. For more information, consult the *Health* section at the back of the book.

Health care: There is a Reciprocal Health Agreement with the UK. On presentation of Form E111 at an office of the *Caisse Primaires d'Assurance Maladie* (Sickness Insurance Office), UK citizens are entitled to a refund of 70-80% of charges incurred for dental and medical (including hospital) treatments and prescribed medicines. The standard of medical facilities and practitioners in France is very high but so are the fees, and health insurance is recommended – even for UK citizens: a lot of paperwork is involved in obtaining refunds.

TRAVEL - International

AIR: The national airlines are *Air France (AF)* and *Air Inter (IT)*.

For free advice on air travel, call the Air Travel Advisory Bureau in the UK on (0171) 636 5000 (London) *or* (0161) 832 2000 (Manchester).

Approximate flight times: From London to *Paris* is 1 hour 5 minutes; to *Nice* and *Marseille* is 2 hours.
From *Los Angeles* to Paris is 15 hours 5 minutes.
From *New York* to Paris is 8 hours (3 hours 45 minutes by Concorde).
From *Singapore* to Paris is 15 hours 5 minutes.
From *Sydney* to Paris is 25 hours 5 minutes.
International airports: *Paris-Charles de Gaulle (PAR/CDG)* is 23km (14.5 miles) northeast of the city. It is also known as *Roissy-Charles de Gaulle*. There is a coach to the city every 15 minutes up to 2300. Buses and trains run to Paris Gare du Nord or Châtelet every 15-20 minutes up to 2350. There are taxis to the city. Duty-free facilities are available.
Paris-Orly (PAR/ORY) is 15km (9 miles) south of the city. Coaches run to the city every 20 minutes, buses every 15 minutes to place Denfert Rochereau (travel time – 25 minutes) from outside Orly Ouest. Taxis are available. Hotel courtesy coaches run to Hilton Orly and PLM Orly. *RER/SNCF Orly-Rail* trains run every 15 minutes from 0530-2330 (travel time – 40 minutes).
Bordeaux (Merignac) *(BOD)* is 12km (7.3 miles) west of the city. There are coaches, buses and taxis to the city. Duty-free facilities are available.
Lille (Lesquin) *(LIL)* is 15km (9 miles) southeast of the city. Coaches are available to the city, as well as taxis. Duty-free facilities are also available.
Lyon (Lyon/Satolas) *(LYS)* is 30km (19 miles) east of the city. Coaches or taxis are available to the city. Duty-free facilities are also available.
Marseille (Marseille-Marignane) *(MRS)* is 25km (15.5 miles) northwest of the city. Coach service only departs to the city. Duty-free facilities are available.
Nice (Nice-Côte d'Azur) *(NCE)* is 7km (4 miles) west of the city. Coach to the city departs every 15-30 minutes until 2315. Bus no. 9/10 departs every 20 minutes until 2000. Taxis to the city are available, as are duty-free facilities.
Toulouse (Blagnac) *(TLS)* is 7km (4 miles) northwest of the city. Coaches to the city depart every 45 minutes (24-hour service). Taxis are available to the city.
There are also small airports with some international flights at Biarritz, Caen, Deauville (St Gatien), Le Havre, Montpellier, Morlaix, Nantes, Rennes and Quimper.
THE CHANNEL TUNNEL
Road vehicles: All road vehicles are carried through the tunnel in *Le Shuttle* running between the two terminals, one near Folkestone in Kent, with direct access from the M20, and one just outside Calais with links to the A16/A26 motorway (Exit 13). Each shuttle is made up of 12 single- and 12 double-deck carriages, and vehicles are directed to single-deck or double-deck shuttles depending on their height. The first phase of commercial operation of the tourist Shuttle is for cars and motorcycles. Facilities for coaches, minibuses, caravans, campervans and other vehicles over 1.85m (6.07ft) as well as bicycles were due to become operational in spring 1995. Passengers generally travel with their vehicles. Heavy goods vehicles are carried on special shuttles with a separate passenger coach for their drivers. Terminals and shuttles are well-equipped for disabled passengers and Passenger Terminal buildings contain duty-free shops,

restaurants, bureaux de change and other amenities. The journey takes about 35 minutes from platform to platform and about one hour from motorway to motorway. In January 1995, shuttles ran hourly 24 hours per day with a projected increase to twice hourly in March and four times (in peak hours) by summer 1995. Services run every day of the year. The reservation system was due to be replaced by a turn-up-and-go service in April 1995. By contacting Eurotunnel Customer Services in Coquelle (tel: 21 00 61 00; fax: 21 00 60 92) as they approach the French terminal, motorists can find out when the next shuttle leaves and how busy the service is. Motorists pass through customs and immigration before they board the shuttle without further checks on arrival. Fares are charged according to length of stay and time of year. The price remains constant throughout the day and applies to the car, regardless of the number of passengers or size of the car. Introductory fares valid until March 30, 1995 were: Day Return: £49 (FFr390); 5-Day Return: £75 (FFr620); Standard Return: £136 (FFr1140). Lower rates apply to motorcycles. Tickets may be purchased in advance from travel agents, or from Eurotunnel Customer Services in France or the UK with a credit card. For further information, contact Eurotunnel Customer Services in the UK on (01303) 271 100.

Direct Rail links: The direct Eurostar train link through the Channel Tunnel between London and Lille, Brussels or Paris started operating on November 14, 1994. *Eurostar* is a service provided by the railways of Belgium, the United Kingdom and France, operating direct high-speed trains from Paris *(Gare du Nord)* to London *(Waterloo International)* and to Brussels *(Midi)*. It takes 3 hours from Paris to London. When the high-speed rail link from London through Kent to the tunnel is operational (expected to be in the year 2002), the travel time between the two capitals will be reduced to two and a half hours. It takes 3 hours 15 minutes from London to Brussels (2 hours 40 minutes with the completion of the high-speed Belgian link in 1997/98). A direct service to Lille (travel time – 2 hours 10 minutes) runs once daily from Waterloo. Services, including overnight sleeper trains, will also run from major regional centres. Access to the entire British railway network will be provided, bringing many British business centres within a comfortable day's journey. Plans also envisage the use of London's St Pancras station by Eurostars travelling north of London, and also as a second London terminus. The Eurostar trains are equipped with standard-class and first-class seating, buffet, bar and telephones, and will be staffed by multi-lingual, highly trained personnel. Pricing is competitive with the airlines, and range from *Discovery Gold* (first class) to *Discovery Special* (standard class). Whilst the latter offer the best value, tickets must be booked at least 14 days before travel, cannot be exchanged or refunded and are subject to availability. *Discovery* tickets, also standard class, can be exchanged or refunded, but prices are higher. Children aged between 4-11 years benefit from a special fare in first class as well as in standard class. Children under 4 years old travel free but cannot be guaranteed a seat.

Wheelchair users and blind passengers together with one companion get a special fare. For more information, contact Eurostar Enquiries, EPS House, Waterloo Station, London SE1 8SE (tel: (0181) 784 1333). Telephone reservations may be made by travel agents on (01233) 617 599 and by members of the public on (01233) 617 575. For information on special fares for groups of at least ten people, telephone (0171) 922 6049. All enquiries in France should be made to SNCF in Paris. Tel: (1) 45 82 50 50.
SEA: The following companies run regular cross-channel ferries: *Brittany Ferries* from Plymouth to Roscoff and from Portsmouth to St Malo; *Commodore Shipping Services* from Jersey to St Malo; *Condor Hydrofoil* from Jersey, Guernsey, Sark and Alderney to St Malo; *Emeraude Ferries* from Jersey to St Malo; *Hoverspeed* from Dover to Boulogne and Calais, with train and coach to Paris; *Sally Line* from Ramsgate to Dunkirk; *Sealink* from Dover and Folkestone to Calais, Dover to Dunkirk, Folkestone to Boulogne and Newhaven to Dieppe; and *P&O* from Dover to Boulogne and Calais, and Portsmouth and Southampton to Calais, Cherbourg and Le Havre. These companies offer a variety of promotional fares and inclusive holidays for short breaks and shopping trips.
Passenger and roll-on/roll-off ferry links to and from North Africa and Sardinia are provided by the *Société Nationale Maritime Corse-Mediterranée (SNCM)* (see below in *Travel – Internal*).
RAIL: For cross-channel services, see *Direct Rail links* above. International trains and through coaches run from the channel ports and Paris to destinations throughout Europe. For up-to-date routes and timetables, contact *French Railways (SNCF)* or (in the UK) *British Rail International*. There is also a special bargain-price ticket combining air and rail travel. Flights depart from one of 16 airports in the UK and Ireland to Paris, and then on to a choice of 3000 destinations in France by train. Further information on these tickets can be obtained through *Air France* or *French Railways*.
ROAD: There are numerous and excellent road links with all neighbouring countries. See above for **car ferry** information. See below for information concerning **documentation** and **traffic regulations**.
The following companies run regular **coach** services to France from the UK: *Eurolines* and *National Express/Riviera Express*.

TRAVEL - Internal

AIR: *Air Inter* is the national domestic airline flying between Paris (from both Orly and Charles de Gaulle airports) and 45 cities and towns. It also connects regional airports including those in Corsica with those on the mainland. Details of all internal flights are available from *Air France*.
Note: *Air Inter's* 'Horaires et Tarifs' gives all flight information, as well as travel arrangements to and from all airports. Details of independent airlines may be obtained from the French Government Tourist Office.
SEA/RIVER: There are almost 9000km (5600 miles) of navigable waterways in metropolitan France, and all of these present excellent opportunities for holidays. Cruising boats may be chartered with or without crews, ranging in size from the smallest cabin cruiser up to converted commercial barges *(péniches)*, which can accommodate up to 24 people and require a crew of eight. Hotel boats, large converted barges with accommodation and restaurant, are also available in some areas, with a wide choice of price and comfort. For further information, contact the national or regional tourist board.
The main canal areas are the north (north and northeast of Paris) where most of the navigable rivers are connected with canals; the Seine (from Auxerre to Le Havre, but sharing space with commercial traffic); the east, where the Rhine and Moselle and their tributaries are connected by canals; in Burgundy, where the Saône and many old and picturesque canals crisscross the region; the Rhône (a pilot is recommended below Avignon); the Midi (including the Canal du Midi, connecting the Atlantic with the Mediterranean); and Brittany and the Loire on the rivers Vilaine, Loire, Mayenne and Sarthe and the connecting canals. Each of these waterways offer a magnificent variety of scenery, a

means of visiting many historic towns, villages and sites and, because of the slow pace (8kmph/5mph), an opportunity to learn much about rural France.
State-run car ferries known as *'BACs'* connect the larger islands on the Atlantic coast with the mainland; they also sail regularly across the mouth of the Gironde. The island of Corsica is served by passenger and roll-on/roll-off ferries operated by the *Société Nationale Maritime Corse-Mediterranée (SNCM)*, 61 boulevard des Dames, 13002 Marseille. Tel: 91 56 32 00. Telex: 440068. Services run from Marseille and Nice to Ajaccio, Propriano and Bastia on the island.

RAIL: *French Railways (SNCF)* operate a nationwide network with 34,600km (21,500 miles) of line, over 12,000km (7500 miles) of which has been electrified. *TGV (Train à Grande Vitesse)* is the fastest train in the world, running on new high-speed lines from Paris to Brittany and southwest France at 300kmph (186mph) and to Lyon and the southeast at 270kmph (168mph).
The *SNCF* is divided into five systems (East, North, West, Southeast and Southwest). The transport in and around Paris is the responsibility of a separate body, the *RATP* at 53 ter quai des Grands-Augustins, 75006 Paris. Tel: (1) 43 46 14 14 (general information). This provides a fully integrated bus, rail and métro network for the capital.

Tickets bought abroad: There is a range of special tickets on offer to foreign visitors, which usually have to be bought before entering France; some, such as the *France Rail'n'Drive Pass,* are only available in North America; others are unique to Australia and New Zealand. There are also special European *Rail and Drive* packages. The *France Railpass* gives the holder free travel on any four days within a period of 15 days, or nine days within any one month; it is only sold outside France. Contact *SNCF* for details. Holders of the ticket are also entitled to reduced car hire rates at over 200 railway stations, a reduced entrance fee to a large number of historic buildings, a free return ticket from the Paris airports to the city centre, travel concessions on the Paris métro and buses, and reduced prices for many other services and facilities. In addition, holders of this ticket do not need to pay supplements applied to Trans Europe-Expresses (TEEs) and some TGVs. It does not, however, include seat reservation charges (compulsory on TEE and TGV trains) and supplements for sleeping accommodation.

Tickets bought in France: It is important to validate *(composter)* tickets bought in France by using the orange automatic date-stamping machine at the platform entrance.
Note: There are various different kinds of tickets (including Family and Young Person's Tickets) offering reductions which can usually be bought in France. In general, the fares charged will depend on what day of the week and what time of the day one is travelling; timetables giving further details are available from *SNCF* offices.
The Blue, White and Red Tariff Calendar: The *French Railways'* tariff calendar is colour-coded; the colour of a particular period can affect the price of the ticket. The system of special fares, reductions, restrictions and so on is complex, as one would expect from such a highly sophisticated railway network. Enquire at *SNCF* offices for more details. The following breakdown of the tariff is included as a guide:
Blue (Off-peak): Normally 1200 Monday to 1200 Friday; 1200 Saturday to 1500 Sunday.
White (Standard): Normally 1200 Friday to 1200 Saturday; 1500 Sunday to 1200 Monday, plus some public holidays.
Red (Peak): About 20 days in the year when no reduction is available. Apply to *French Railways* in London or any *SNCF* station for details.
Motorail (car sleeper) services are operated from Boulogne, Calais, Dieppe and Paris to all main holiday areas in both summer and winter. Motorail information and booking from *French Railways* (address above).
Ancillary services include coach tours and excursions throughout France, self-drive car hire and bicycle hire.
Skiing holidays: *SNCF*, in association with the French Association of Resorts Sports Goods Retailers (AFMASS), organise skiing holidays. Packages are marketed only in France, contact *SNCF* on arrival.
For all services: Full information is available from *French Railways (SNCF)*. In the UK, timetables, fares, information and bookings can also be obtained through principal British Rail Travel Centres.
ROAD: France has over 6000km (3728 miles) of motorways *(autoroutes),* some of which are free whilst others are toll roads *(autoroutes à péage).* Prices vary depending on the route, and caravans are extra. There are more than 28,000km (17,500 miles) of national roads *(routes nationales).* Motorways bear the prefix 'A' and

national roads 'N'. Minor roads (marked in yellow on the Michelin roadmaps) are maintained by the *Départements* rather than by the Government and are classed as 'D' roads. It is a good idea to avoid travelling any distance by road on the last few days of July/first few days of August and the last few days of August/first few days of September, as during this time the bulk of the holiday travel takes place, and the roads can be jammed for miles. A sign bearing the words *Sans Plomb* at a petrol service station indicates that it sells unleaded petrol. The *Bison Futé* map provides practical information and is available from the French Government Tourist Office.
Bus: There are very few long-distance bus services in France apart from *Europabus,* about which information may be obtained from national British Rail Travel Centres. Local services outside the towns and cities are generally adequate. Information and timetables are only available locally.
Car hire: A list of agencies can be obtained at local tourist offices (Syndicats d'Initiative or Offices de Tourisme). Fly-drive arrangements are available through all major airlines. *French Railways* also offer reduced train/car-hire rates. Their 'France Vacances' pass offers free car hire to first-class passengers.
Caravans: These may be imported for stays of up to six months. There are special requirements for cars towing caravans which must be observed. Contact the French Government Tourist Office for details.
Regulations: Traffic drives on the right. The minimum age for driving is 18. Speed limits are 60kmph (37mph) in built-up areas, 90kmph (56mph) outside built-up areas, 110kmph (68mph) on dual carriageways separated by a central reservation, and 130kmph (81mph) on motorways. Visitors who have held a driving licence for under one year may *not* travel faster than 90kmph (56mph) or any lower speed limit. Seat belts must be worn by all front-seat passengers. Under-tens may not travel in the front seat. A red warning triangle must be carried for use in the event of a breakdown. All headlamp beams must be adjusted for righthand drive and UK drivers are advised to apply a yellow covering to their headlamps (available from any AA or motoring shop). Snowchains are widely available, for hire or to buy. The police in France can and do fine motorists on the spot for driving offences such as speeding. Random breath tests for drinking and driving are used. *Priorité à droite:* Particularly in built-up areas, the driver *must* give way to

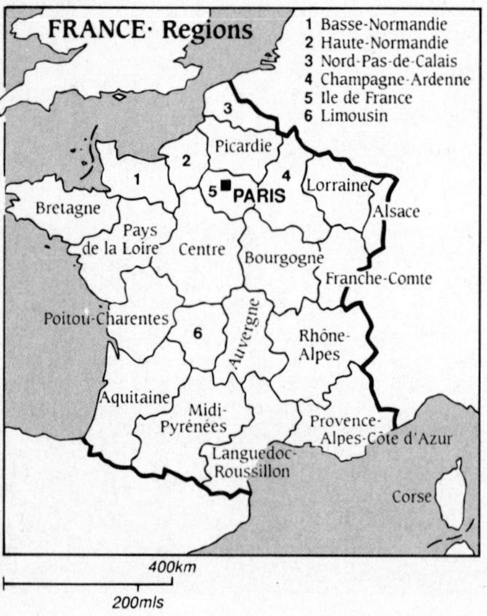
FRANCE· Regions
1 Basse-Normandie
2 Haute-Normandie
3 Nord-Pas-de-Calais
4 Champagne-Ardenne
5 Ile de France
6 Limousin
Picardie
PARIS
Lorraine
Alsace
Bretagne
Pays de la Loire
Centre
Bourgogne
Franche-Comte
Poitou-Charentes
Auvergne
Rhône-Alpes
Aquitaine
Midi-Pyrénées
Provence-Alpes-Côte d'Azur
Languedoc-Roussillon
Corse
DAB-M277
400km
200mls

anyone coming out of a side-turning on the right. The *priorité* rule no longer applies at many roundabouts – the driver should now give way to cars which are already on the roundabout with the sign *vous n'avez pas la priorité*. Watch for signs and exercise great caution. All roads of any significance outside built-up areas have right of way, known as *Passage Protégé*, and will normally be marked by signs consisting either of an 'X' on a triangular background with the words 'Passage Protégé' underneath, or a broad arrow, or a yellow diamond. For further details on driving in France, a booklet called *Welcome on the French Motorways* is available free from French Government Tourist Offices.

Documentation: A national driving licence is acceptable. EU nationals taking their own cars to France are *strongly advised* to obtain a Green Card. Without it, insurance cover is limited to the minimum legal cover in France; the Green Card tops this up to the level of cover provided by the car owner's domestic policy. The car's registration documents must also be carried.

URBAN: Urban public transport is excellent. There are comprehensive bus systems in all the larger towns. There are also tramways, trolleybuses and a métro in Marseille; trolleybuses, a métro and a funicular in Lyon; and the world's first automated driverless train in Lille (where there is also a tramway). There are tramway services in St Etienne and Nantes and trolleybuses in Grenoble, Limoges and Nancy. The systems are easy to use, with pre-purchase tickets and passes. Good publicity material and maps are usually available.

Paris has the best urban transport network in the world. *Métro:* The dense network in the central area makes the métro the ideal way to get about in Paris. When changing trains, look for the *Correspondances* sign on the platform. As each line is identified by the names of its termini, one should know the final destination of the train one wishes to catch and then follow the appropriate signs: *Direction – Créteil*, for example, would be the sign to follow for stations between *Balard* and *Créteil* when travelling from west to east. Each line also has a number, which is seldom used to identify it. There are maps on station platforms, and inside the trains. Buy a *carnet* of ten tickets rather than buying each singly. However long the journey and however many changes, one flat-fare ticket will suffice each time, except on the suburban portion of certain lines. First trains leave at about 0500, last trains at about 0030. A *Paris Visite* allows unlimited travel on most forms of public transport in Paris for a period of three to five consecutive days.

Rail: *RER* (fast suburban services). *Line A:* St Germain-en-Laye to Boissy-St Leger or Marne-la-Vallée; *Line B:* Remy-les-Chevreuses to Roissy via Châtelet-les-Halles and the Gare du Nord; *Line C:* Gare d'Orleans-Austerlitz to Versailles. These lines are divided into fare stages and these vary according to distance, except within the metropolitan area where the same system applies as on the métro. There is also an extensive network of conventional suburban services run by the state *SNCF* rail system, with fare structure and ticketing integrated with the other modes of public transport.

Bus: The same tickets are used as on the métro, but bus routes are divided into fare stages *(sections)*. Inside Paris, one ticket covers up to two fare stages and two cover two or three stages or more. The first bus leaves at 0600 and the last bus at 2100, except on certain lines which run until 0030. Timetables are posted up at bus stops and in bus shelters. Fares and tickets have been standardised with those of private operators in the suburban areas. 2- to 4- or 7-day passes *(Billets de Tourisme)* entitle travellers to any number of journeys for the corresponding number of days on all Paris bus and métro lines (first-class on métro and *RER/RATP*), with the exception of minibuses, special bus services, and *RER/SNCF* lines. These are available in Paris from RATP Tourist Offices at 53 ter quai des Grands-Augustins (tel: (1) 40 46 41 41) and place de la Madeleine (VIA International, tel: (1) 42 05 12 10) or from 50 of the métro stations, all seven main-line railway stations and certain banks. *Carte Orange* monthly passes (for which a passport-size photograph is required) are valid for any number of journeys for a calendar month within a given radius on Paris buses, métro and *RER*, suburban (*SNCF*) railways and some suburban buses *(RATP)*. These are available at any Paris or suburban railway or métro station, Paris bus stations and certain specially licensed shops. Children under four years of age travel free on buses and underground, while children between 4-12 years travel half-price.

Taxi: Day and night rates are shown inside each cab. There are extra charges on journeys to and from racecourses, stations and airports and for luggage.

Private car: In the centre of Paris there are parking meters; otherwise parking time is restricted *(zone bleue)*. Car parks charging a fee are plentiful all over Paris and on the outskirts.

ACCOMMODATION

HOTELS: Room and all meals, ie full-board or 'pension' terms, are usually offered for a stay of three days or longer. Half-board or 'demi-pension' (room, breakfast and one meal) terms are usually available outside the peak holiday period. They are not expensive but adhere to strict standards of comfort. Hotels charge around 30% extra for a third bed in a double room. For children under 12, many chains will provide another bed in the room of the parents free. *Logis de France* are small- or medium-sized, inexpensive and often family-run hotels which provide good, clean, basic and comfortable accommodation with a restaurant attached. They publish a guide listing all the hotels and the amenities offered. *Relais-Châteaux* are châteaux hotels. Further information can be obtained from the Fédération Nationale de l'Industrie Hôtelière, 22 rue d'Anjou, 75008 Paris. Tel: (1) 44 95 86 00. Fax: (1) 47 42 15 20.

Paris: Hotel bookings can be made in person through tourist offices at stations or at the Paris Tourist Office, 127 avenue des Champs-Elysées, 75008 Paris. Tel: (1) 49 52 53 54. Fax: (1) 49 52 53 00. Further information on hotels and other accommodation in France is available through the Fédération Nationale des Logis de France, 83 avenue d'Italie, 75013 Paris. Tel: (1) 45 84 83 84. Fax: (1) 44 24 08 74. Telex: 202030.

Guides: The *Michelin Guides* to France are extremely useful, with up-to-date prices, opening dates and town plans. *Hotels de Tourisme* publish an annual directory of its members available from the French Government Tourist Office. An official guide to all French graded hotels is available, as well as regional lists, the *Logis de France* guide and various chain/association guides from the French Government Tourist Office and bookshops. The Tourist Office publishes guides to hotels in Paris and the Ile-de-France, available free of charge.

Grading: *Hôtels de Tourisme* are officially graded into five categories according to the quality of the accommodation, as are also the *Motels de Tourisme*. Gradings, which are fixed by government regulation and checked by the *Préfecture* of the *Départements*, are as follows:

4-star L: Luxury. **4-star:** Deluxe. **3-star:** First class. **2-star:** Standard. **1-star:** Budget.

Logis de France are subject to a specific code usually above basic requirements for their grade and are inspected regularly to ensure that they conform to the standards laid down.

SELF-CATERING: *Gîtes de France* are holiday homes (often old farmhouses) in the country, all of which conform to standards regulated by the non-profitmaking National Federation. Over 1500 *gîtes* have been reserved for the British section of the *Gîtes de France*. Annual membership gives access to full booking service including ferry crossings at reduced rates, overnight hotel bookings and fully illustrated handbook. The London booking service will confirm any booking within two weeks. Full information in the UK is available from *Gîtes de France* (Farm Holidays in France Ltd), 178 Piccadilly, London W1V 9BD. Tel: (0171) 493 3480. Fax: (0171) 495 6417.

Villas, Houses and Apartments Rental: Villas and houses can be rented on the spot. Local *Syndicats d'Initiative* can supply a complete list of addresses of local rental agencies. Tourists staying in France for over a month may prefer to live in an apartment, rather than in a hotel. For information about apartments to rent, apply to: Fédération Nationale des Agents Commerciaux et Mandataires (FNAICM) in Paris. Tel: (1) 42 93 61 24.

CHATEAUX HOLIDAYS: An association, *Château-Accueil*, publishes a list of châteaux offering accommodation suitable for families. Contact the Tourist Office for further information.

CAMPING/CARAVANNING: There are 7000 campsites throughout France. A few have tents and caravans for hire. Prices vary according to location, season and facilities. All graded campsites will provide water, toilet and washing facilities. Touring caravans may be imported for stays of up to six consecutive months. There are 100 British companies offering camping holidays in France. The French Government Tourist Office has a full list of tour operators who run all types of tours, including camping and special interest holidays. The following camping and caravan site is open throughout the year: Paris-Ouest Bois de Boulogne, route du Bord de l'Eau, 75016 Paris.

Note: Cars towing caravans are not allowed to drive within the boundaries of the *périphérique* (the Paris ring road).

YOUTH HOSTELS: There are hundreds of these in France, offering young people very simple accommodation at very low prices. There are hostels in all major towns. Stays are usually limited to three or four nights or a week in Paris. Hostels are open to all members of the National Youth Hostel Association upon presentation of a membership card. Lists are available from national youth hostel organisations.

RESORTS & EXCURSIONS

Tourism is an industry of considerable importance in France and anything more than the briefest sketch of her many attractions is beyond the scope of this book. This section has been divided into a number of sub-sections by region, each containing basic descriptions of regional cuisine, culture, history and scenery: Paris & Ile-de-France; Brittany; Normandy; Nord, Pas de Calais & Picardy; Champagne & Ardennes; Lorraine, Vosges & Alsace; Burgundy & Franche-Comté; Auvergne & Limousin; Val de Loire; Western Loire; Aquitaine & Poitou-Charentes; Languedoc-Roussillon; Rhône/Savoie & Dauphiny; Midi-Pyrénées; Côte d'Azur & Provence; Corsica. Because of historical circumstances interesting places to visit are often situated along the courses of rivers; for instance the Loire, the Rhône, the Seine or the Dordogne. This, effectively, often provides ready-made itineraries for the visitor.

Note: The enclave of Monaco has its own entry in the *World Travel Guide*, as do the French Overseas Departments and many of the other French overseas possessions; see the *Contents* pages for details.

Paris & Ile-de-France

Paris is one of the world's great cities and is easy to negotiate even on the first visit. The *périphérique* and *boulevard circulaire* ring roads enclose a core of 105 sq km (40 sq miles) which is small enough to walk across in an afternoon. There is an extensive (and cheap) métro network, now augmented by an efficient rapid transit system (the *RER*). The ring roads roughly follow the line

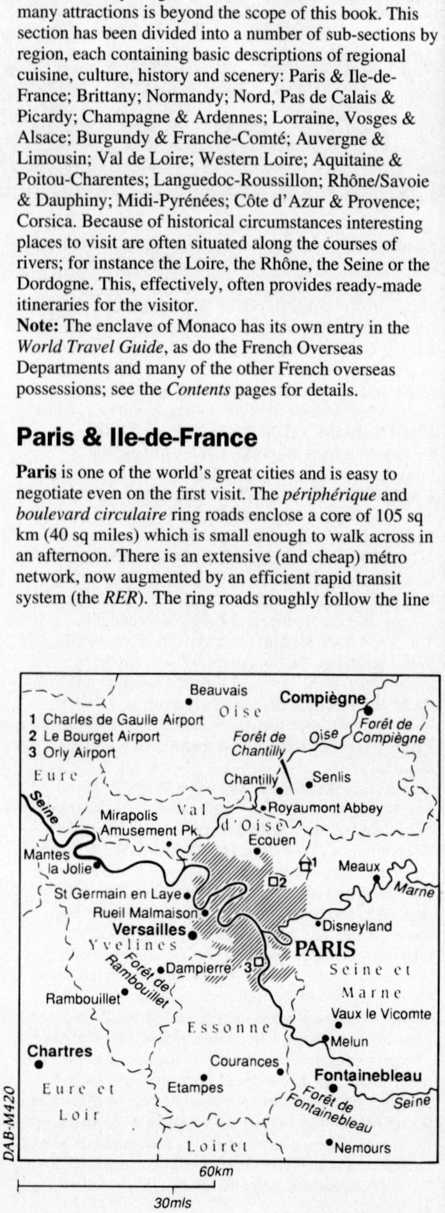
1 Charles de Gaulle Airport
2 Le Bourget Airport
3 Orly Airport
Beauvais
Oise
Compiègne
Forêt de Chantilly
Forêt de Compiègne
Eure
Chantilly
Senlis
Seine
Mirapolis Amusement Pk
Val d'Oise
Royaumont Abbey
Ecouen
Mantes la Jolie
Meaux
Marne
St Germain en Laye
Rueil Malmaison
Versailles
Disneyland
Yvelines
PARIS
Forêt de Rambouillet
Dampierre
Seine et Marne
Rambouillet
Vaux le Vicomte
Essonne
Melun
Chartres
Courances
Fontainebleau
Eure et Loir
Etampes
Forêt de Fontainebleau
Seine
Loiret
Nemours
DAB-M420
60km
30mls

PARIS VISITE

THE PASS THAT MAKES PARIS YOUR CUSTOMERS PLAYGROUND

PARIS VISITE IS an all in travel pass – valid for 2, 3 or 5 days – giving you free access to every part of the city and its surrounding areas, up to Euro Disney ® Resort, Roissy-Charles-de-Gaulle and Orly airports, Versailles...

PARIS VISITE offers unlimited travel on Metro, buses, RER, Ile de France trains, funiculaire de Montmartre, Orlybus, Roissybus.... and extra privileges as first class travel on the RER and SNCF systems throughout the Paris area and reductions at some of the capital's major tourist sites.

For more information and tickets purchasing, contact:
RATP
Unité Vente – Département Commercial
124, rue du Mont Cenis
F 75889 PARIS Cedex 18
Tel: 33 1 49 25 61 92
Fax: 33 1 49 25 63 44

of the 19th-century city walls and within them are most of the well-known sights, shops and entertainments. Beyond the ring roads is an industrial and commercial belt, then a broad ring of suburbs, mostly of recent construction.

There are more than 80 museums and perhaps 200 art galleries in Paris. *La Carte* is a pass providing free admission to about 60 national and municipal museums in the Paris area. Visitors should note that most museums are closed for public holidays and for one day in the working week, usually Monday or Tuesday. Admission is half price on Sunday; concessions are available for those under 25 and persons over 65 years. The tourist office can supply details.

Central Paris contains fine architecture from every episode in a long and rich history (including the present) together with every amenity known to science and every entertainment yet devised. The oldest neighbourhood is the **Ile-de-la-Cité**, an island on a bend in the Seine where the *Parisii*, a Celtic tribe, settled in about the 3rd century BC. The river was an effective defensive moat and the *Parisii* dominated the area for several centuries before being displaced by the Romans in about 52BC. The island is today dominated by the magnificent cathedral of *Notre-Dame*. Beneath it is the *Crypte Archéologique*, housing well-mounted displays of Paris' early history. Having sacked the Celtic city, the Gallo-Romans abandoned the island and settled on the heights along the **Rive Gauche** (Left Bank), in the area now known as the *Latin Quarter* (Boulevards St Michel and St Germain). The naming of this district owes nothing to the Roman city: when the university was moved from the *Cité* to the left bank in the 13th century, Latin was the common language among the 10,000 students who gathered there from all over the known world. The *Latin Quarter* remains the focus of most student activity (the *Sorbonne* is here) and there are many fine bookshops and commercial art galleries. The *Cluny Museum* houses some of the finest medieval European tapestries to be found anywhere, including 'The Field of the Cloth of Gold'. At the western end of the Boulevard St Germain is the *Orsay Museum*, a superb collection of 19th- and early 20th-century art located in a beautifully reconstructed railroad station.

Other Left Bank attractions include the *Panthéon*, the basilica of *St Séverin*, the *Palais* and *Jardin de Luxembourg*, the *Hôtel des Invalides* (containing

Napoleon's tomb), the *Musée Rodin* and *St Germain-des-Prés*. Continuing westwards from the Quai d'Orsay past the *Eiffel Tower* and across the Seine onto the Right Bank, the visitor encounters a collection of museums and galleries known as the *Trocadero*, a popular meeting place for young Parisians. A short walk to the north is the *Place Charles de Gaulle*, known to Parisians as the *Etoile* and to tourists as the site of the *Arc de Triomphe*. It is also at the western end of that most elegant of avenues, the **Champs-Elysées** (Elysian Fields), justly famous for its cafés, commercial art galleries and sumptuous shops. At the other end of the avenue, the powerful axis is continued by the *Place de la Concorde*, the *Jardin des Tuileries* (where model sailing boats may be rented by the hour) and finally the Louvre.

The *Palais du Louvre* is in the process of reconstruction and reorganisation. The most controversial addition to the old palace, a pyramid with 666 panes of glass, juxtaposes the ultra-modern with the classical façade of the palace. The best time to see the pyramid is after dark, when it is illuminated. The Richelieu Wing of the palace was inaugurated by President Mitterrand in November 1993, marking the completion of the second stage of the redevelopment programme. By 1996, a labyrinth of subterranean galleries will be fully functioning, providing display areas, a conference and exhibition centre, design shops and restaurants. The Carrousel and Tuileries Gardens will also be re-landscaped in the final stage of the redevelopment programme.

North of the Louvre are the *Palais Royal*, the *Madeleine* and *l'Opéra*. To the east is *Les Halles*, a shopping and commercial complex built on the site of the old food market. It is at the intersection of several métro lines and is a good starting point for a tour of the city. There are scores of restaurants in the maze of small streets around Les Halles; every culinary style is practised at prices to suit every pocket. Further east, beyond the Boulevard Sebastopol, is another controversial newcomer, the post-modern *Georges Pompidou Centre of Modern Art* (also known as the *Beaubourg*). It provides a steady stream of surprises in its temporary exhibition spaces (which, informally, include the pavement outside, where lively and often bizarre street-performers gather) and houses a permanent collection of 20th-century art. The *Centre Pompidou* is Paris' premier tourist attraction, having surpassed the Eiffel Tower in popularity in its first year. East again, in the Marais district, are the *Carnavalet* and

Picasso Museums, housed in magnificent town houses dating from the 16th and 18th centuries respectively. One of the best-known districts in Paris is **Montmartre**, which stands on a hill overlooking the Right Bank. A funicular railway operates on the steepest part of the hill, below *Sacré-Coeur*. Local entrepreneurs have long capitalised on Montmartre's romantic reputation as an artist's colony and if visitors today are disappointed to find it a well-run tourist attraction, they should bear in mind that it has been exactly that since it first climbed out of poverty in the 1890s. The legend of Montmartre as a dissolute cradle of talent was carefully stage-managed by Toulouse-Lautrec and others to fill their pockets and it rapidly transformed a notorious slum into an equally notorious circus. An earlier Montmartre legend concerns St Denis. After his martyrdom, he is said to have walked headless down the hill. The world's first Gothic cathedral, *St Denis*, was constructed on the spot where he collapsed. Just north of **Belleville** (a working class district that produced Edith Piaf and Maurice Chevalier) at *La Villete*, is one of Paris' newer attractions, the *City of Science and Technology*. The most modern presentation techniques are used to illustrate both the history and the possible future of man's inventiveness; season tickets are available. One of the great pleasures of Paris is the great number of sidewalk cafés, now glass-enclosed in wintertime, which extends people-watching to a year-round sport in any part of the town. There are as many Vietnamese and Chinese restaurants as there are French cafés. North African eating places also abound, and dozens of American Tex-Mex eateries are scattered throughout the city. Bric-a-brac or *brocante* is found in a

PARIS

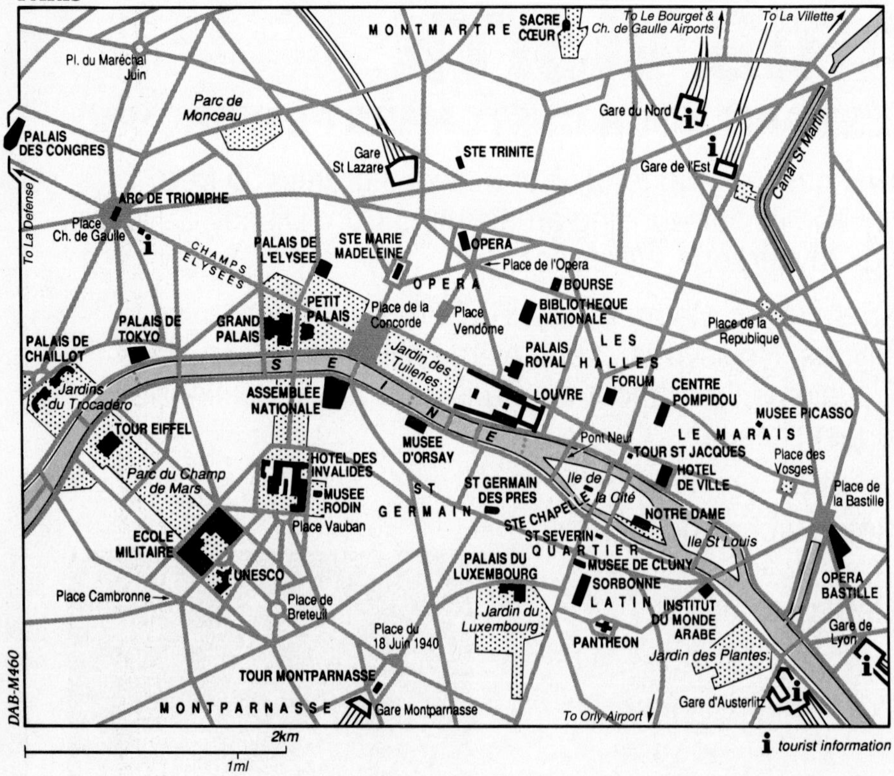
MONTMARTRE
SACRE CŒUR
To Le Bourget & Ch. de Gaulle Airports
To La Villette
Pl. du Maréchal Juin
Parc de Monceau
PALAIS DES CONGRES
Gare St Lazare
STE TRINITE
Gare du Nord
Gare de l'Est
Canal St Martin
To La Defense
ARC DE TRIOMPHE
Place Ch. de Gaulle
CHAMPS ELYSEES
PALAIS DE L'ELYSEE
STE MARIE MADELEINE
OPERA
Place de l'Opera
BOURSE
BIBLIOTHEQUE NATIONALE
PETIT PALAIS
Place de la Concorde
Place Vendôme
Place de la Republique
PALAIS DE TOKYO
GRAND PALAIS
PALAIS DE CHAILLOT
Jardin des Tuileries
PALAIS ROYAL
LES HALLES
FORUM
CENTRE POMPIDOU
SEINE
Jardins du Trocadéro
ASSEMBLEE NATIONALE
LOUVRE
MUSEE PICASSO
TOUR EIFFEL
MUSEE D'ORSAY
Pont Neuf
LE MARAIS
TOUR ST JACQUES
Place des Vosges
Parc du Champ de Mars
HOTEL DES INVALIDES
MUSEE RODIN
ST GERMAIN DES PRES
Ile de la Cité
HOTEL DE VILLE
Place de la Bastille
Place Vauban
ST GERMAIN
STE CHAPELLE
NOTRE DAME
ECOLE MILITAIRE
ST SEVERIN
Ile St Louis
PALAIS DU LUXEMBOURG
QUARTIER LATIN
MUSEE DE CLUNY
UNESCO
SORBONNE
OPERA BASTILLE
Place Cambronne
Place de Breteuil
Jardin du Luxembourg
INSTITUT DU MONDE ARABE
Gare de Lyon
Place du 18 Juin 1940
PANTHEON
Jardin des Plantes
TOUR MONTPARNASSE
MONTPARNASSE
Gare Montparnasse
To Orly Airport
Gare d'Austerlitz
DAB-M460
2km
1ml
i tourist information

number of flea markets (*marché aux puces*) on the outskirts of town, notably at the Porte de Clignancourt. There are several antique centres (*Louvre des Antiquaires*, *Village Suisse,* etc) where genuine antique furniture and other objects are on sale. Amongst the larger department stores are the *Printemps* and the *Galeries Lafayette* near the Opéra, the *Bazaar Hôtel de Ville (BHV)* and the *Samaritaine* on the Right Bank and the *Bon Marché* on the Left Bank. The remains of the great forests of the **Ile-de-France** (the area surrounding Paris) can still be seen at the magnificent châteaux of *Versailles*, *Rambouillet* and *Fontainebleau* on the outskirts of Paris.

The **Euro Disney Resort** lies to the east of the capital, a complete vacation destination located at Marne-la-Vallée, 32km (20 miles) from Paris. The site has an area of 1943 hectares (5000 acres), one-fifth of the size of Paris, and includes hotels, restaurants, a campsite, shops, a golf course and has as its star attraction the *Euro Disneyland Theme Park.* Inspired by previous theme parks, Euro Disneyland features all the famous Disney characters plus some new attractions especially produced to blend with its European home. The site is easily accessible by motorway, regional and high-speed rail services, and by air. Euro Disney lies between two major international airports: *Roissy-Charles de Gaulle* and *Orly.*

Brittany

Brittany comprises the *Départements* of Côtes-du-Nord, Finistère, Ille-et-Villaine and Morbihan. Fishing has long been the most important industry and the rocky Atlantic coastline, high tides and strong, treacherous currents demand high standards of seamanship. At Finistère (*finis terrea* or Land's End) the Atlantic swell can drive spouts of water up to 30m (100ft) into the air. The coastal scenery is particularly spectacular at *Pointe du Raz* and *Perros-Guirec*. The Gauls arrived on the peninsular in about 600BC. Little is known about their way of life or why they constructed the countless stone monuments to be found throughout Brittany – cromlechs, altars, menhirs and dolmans (**Carnac** is the supreme example of this). They were displaced by the Romans during the reign of Julius Caesar, who, in turn, were displaced by Celts arriving from Britain in AD460. The Celts named their new land Brittanica Minor and divided it into the coastal area, *l'Ar Mor* (the country of the sea), and the inland highlands, *l'Ar Coat* (the country of the woods). The two areas in Brittany are still referred to as **l'Amor** and **l'Argoat.** The Celts were master stonemasons, as may be seen by the many surviving *calvaires*, elaborately carved stone crosses. Brittany emerged from the Dark Ages as an independent duchy. A series of royal marriages eventually brought Brittany into France and by 1532 the perpetual union of the Duchy of Brittany with France was proclaimed. Despite its rugged coastline, it is possible to enjoy a conventional beach holiday in Brittany. The *Emerald Coast*, a region of northern Brittany centred on **Dinard**, has many fine bathing beaches. The beach resorts are often named after little-known saints: *St Enogat, St Laumore, St Brill, St Jacut, St Cast,* etc. There are also bathing beaches in the bay of St Brieuc, including **Val André, Etables** and **St Quay**. Brittany's main attractions are her wild beauty and the unique Breton culture. In general, coastal areas have retained a more characteristically Breton way of life than the hills inland. Elaborate Breton head-dresses are still worn in some parts, the style varying slightly from village to village. Breton religious processions and the ceremonies of the *pardons* that take place in a number of communities at various times of the year may have changed little since Celtic times. In the region around **Plouha** many of the inhabitants still speak Breton, a language evolved from Celtic dialects. The coast from **Paimpol** consists of colossal chunks of rock, perilous to shipping, as the many lighthouses suggest. The very pleasant villages and beaches of **Perros-Guirec**, **Trégastel** or **Trébeurden** contrast with the wild and rocky shoreline.

Near the base of the peninsula, at **Aber Vrac'h** and **Aber Benoit**, the ocean is caught and churned up in deep, winding chasms penetrating far inland. Further along the coast is the huge and sprawling port of **Brest**, possessing one of Europe's finest natural harbours which has a 13th-century castle. The canal running from Brest to **Nantes** makes a very pleasant journey either by hired boat or walking or on horseback, although not all of the route is navigable by water. The interior consists of wooded hills and farms, *buttes* (knolls) with fine views, short rivers and narrow valleys. Many of the so-called mountains are merely undulating verdant dunes, barely 300m (1000ft) high. They are, nonetheless, remnants of the oldest mountain chain on the planet. Breton architecture is perhaps more humble than in other parts of France, being more akin to that of a village in England or Wales. Inland, there are several impressive castles and many walled towns and villages. The churches are small and simple. For the most part, Brittany benefits from the warmth of the Gulf Stream all year round, but the tourist season runs from June to September. The countryside blazes with flowers in the spring, attracting many varieties of birdlife. The city of **Rennes**, the ancient capital of Brittany, is a good base from which to explore the highlands; sights include the *Palais de Justice,* the castle, the *Musée des Beaux-Arts* and the *Musée de Bretagne,* which seeks to preserve and foster all things Breton. Some of Brittany's most productive farms are close to the northern shore. Fertilized with seaweed, they produce fine potatoes, cabbage, cauliflower, artichokes, peas, string beans and strawberries. The quality of locally produced ingredients lends itself to the simple Breton cuisine, which brings out natural flavours rather than concealing them with elaborate sauces. Raw shellfish (including oysters), lobster, lamb and partridge are particularly good. The salt meadows of lower Brittany add a distinctive flavour to Breton livestock and game. *Crêpes* (pancakes) are a regional speciality and there are two distinct varieties: a sweet dessert *crêpe* served with sugar, honey, jam, jelly or a combination (eg *suzette*); and the savoury *sarrasin* variety, made from buckwheat flour and served with eggs, cheese, bacon or a combination of several of these (the *crêpe* is folded over the ingredients and reheated). They can be bought ready-made in the local shops. Little or no cheese is produced in Brittany, but some of the finest butter in the world comes from here – it is slightly salted, unlike the butter from the other regions of France. Cider is frequently drunk with food, as well as wine. The popular wine, *Muscadet,* comes from the extreme southern point of Brittany, at the head of the Loire Estuary, near Nantes. It is a dry, fruity white wine that goes very well with shellfish, especially oysters.

Normandy

Normandy contains five *Départements*: Seine Maritime, Calvados, Manche, Eure and Orne, all but the last two touching on the sea. Its southern border is the *River Couesnon* which has, over the years, shifted its course as it flows over almost flat country, gradually moving south of **Mont-Saint-Michel,** one of Europe's best-known architectural curiosities. Mont-Saint-Michel and its bay are on the Natural and Cultural World Heritage List drawn up by UNESCO. The tides are phenomenal. At their peak, there is a difference of about 15m (50ft) between the ebb and the flow, the height of a 5-storey building. The sands in the bay are flat and, when the tides are at their highest, the sea runs in over a distance of some 24km (15 miles) forming a wave about 70cm (2ft) deep. The sandbank changes from tide to tide and if the legend of the sea entering the bay at the speed of a galloping horse is perhaps a slight exaggeration, the danger of quicksand is real enough. The present *Abbey of Saint-Michel* was built in the 8th century by Bishop Aubert; his skull bears the mark of the finger of Saint Michel, the archangel Michael. **Cabourg** is the Balbec in Proust's novels. De Maupassant and Flaubert included Norman scenes in their novels and Monet, Sisley and Pissaro painted scenes of the coast and the countryside. **Deauville** – with its beach, casino, golf course and race track – is the social capital of the area. **Bayeux** is worth a visit for the fantastic tapestry – there is nothing like it in the world. The landing beaches and Second World War battlefields are remembered by excellent small museums in **Arromanches** (the landings), and Bayeux (battle of Normandy). There is also a 'peace museum' in **Caen**, with its beautiful Romanesque church and ruins of an enormous castle, founded by William the Conqueror. Other monuments worth visiting include the 14th-century *Church of St Etienne,* the *Church of St Pierre* (Renaissance) and the *Abbaye aux Dames*. There is also a museum of local crafts from the Gallo-Roman period to the present.

The cross-Channel terminus and port of **Dieppe** has attractive winding streets and a 15th-century castle, housing the *Musée de Dieppe.* There are some beautiful châteaux in Normandy, particularly along the route between Paris and Rouen. They include the *Boury-en-Vexin, Bizy at Vernon, Gaillon, Gaillard-les-Andelys, Vascoeuil* and *Martinville*. Along the same route are found a number of other sites classed *monument historique*; the *Claude Monet House* and garden in **Giverny**, the *Abbey de Martemer* (Lisors) and the village of **Lyon-la-Fôret**. All of these merit a detour. The ancient capital of **Rouen** has restored ancient streets and houses, including the *Vieille Maison* of 1466 and the *place du Vieux-Marché,* where Jeanne d'Arc was burnt in 1432. There is a magnificent 13th-century cathedral (the subject of a series of paintings by Monet), as well as many fine museums and churches, including *St Ouen* and *St Maclou*. The cloister of St Maclou was a cemetery for victims of the Great Plague. The old port of **Honfleur,** with its well-preserved 18th-century waterfront houses, is also well worth a visit.

Normandy is a land of farmers and fishermen and is one of the finest gastronomic regions of France. Here is produced the finest butter in the world, a thick fresh cream and excellent cheeses, including the world-famous *Camembert*, *Pont l'Evêque* and *Liverot*. Both crustaceans and saltwater fish abound; *sole Normande* is one of the great dishes known to the gastronomic world. There is also lobster from Barfleur, shrimp from Cherbourg and oysters from Dive-sur-Mur. Inland one finds ducks from Rouen and Nantes, lamb from the salt meadows near Mont-Saint-Michel, cream from Isigny, chicken and veal from the Cotentin, and cider and calvados (applejack) from the Pays d'Auge.

Hôtels Berlioz Bastille

More than
20 NEW OR RENOVATED HOTELS IN THE HEART OF PARIS

★★ *and* ★★★ *high standards of accomodation.*

We are your PRIVILEGED PARISIAN INCOMING AGENTS and provide
additionnal services: transfers, meals, tours...

Be sure to receive the BEST RATES FOR YOUR STAY.

WE AWAIT YOUR REQUESTS!

phone: 33 (1) 44 64 78 78
fax: 33 (1) 44 64 76 88

4, rue Claude Tillier - 75012 Paris - France

Nord, Pas de Calais & Picardy

Northern France is made up of the *Départements* of Nord/Pas de Calais (French Flanders) and Somme-Oise Aisne (Picardy).

Amiens, the principal town of Picardy, has a beautiful 13th-century cathedral, which is one of the largest in France. The choirstalls are unique. The nearby *Quartier Saint Leu* is an ancient canal-side neighbourhood.

Beauvais is famous for its Gothic *Cathedral of St Pierre* (incorporating a 9th-century Carolingian church) which would have been the biggest Gothic church in the world, if it had been completed. Its 13th-century stained glass windows are particularly impressive. There is also a fine musuem of tapestry.

Compiègne is famous for its *Royal Palace,* which has been a retreat for the French aristrocracy from the 14th century onwards and where Napoleon himself lived with his second wife, Marie-Louise. There are over a thousand rooms within the palace and the bedrooms of Napoleon and his wife, preserved with their original decorations, are well worth viewing for their ostentatiously lavish style. Surrounding the town and palace is the *Forest of Compiègne,* where the 1918 Armistice was signed, and which has been a hunting ground for the aristocracy for hundreds of years – a wander through its dark and tranquil interior is an exceptionally pleasant experience. The town also has a fine *Hôtel de Ville* and a *Carriage Museum* is attached to the Palace.

The château of **Chantilly** now houses the *Musée Condé* and there are impressive Baroque gardens to walk around, as well as a 17th-century stable with a 'live' *Horse Museum.* The town of **Arras**, on the *River Scarpe*, has beautiful 13th- and 14th-century houses and the lovely *Abbey of Saint Waast.* There are pretty old towns at **Hesdin** and **Montreuil** (with its ramparts and citadel).

Boulogne is best entered by way of the lower town with the 13th-century ramparts of the upper town in the background; the castle next to the basilica of *Notre Dame* is impressive.

Le Touquet is a pleasant all-year-round coastal resort town with 10km (6 miles) of sandy beaches. The port of **Calais**, of great strategic importance in the Middle Ages, is today noted for the manufacture of tulle and lace, as well as being a cross-Channel ferry terminus. Nearby, the village of **Sangatte** has become a significant site, being the channel tunnel entrance on the French mainland.

The further north one goes, the more beer is drunk and used in the kitchen, especially in soup and *ragoûts.* Wild rabbit is cooked with prunes or grapes. There is also a thick Flemish soup called *hochepot* which, literally, has everything in it but the kitchen sink. The cuisine is often, not surprisingly, sea-based – *matelotes* of conger eel and *caudière* (fish soup). Shellfish known as *coques*, 'the poor man's oyster', are popular too. The *marolles* cheese from Picardy is made from whole milk, salted and washed down with beer. Flanders, although it has a very short coastline, has many herring dishes, *croquelots* or *bouffis,* which are lightly salted and smoked. *Harengs salés* and *harengs fumés* are famous and known locally as *gendarmes* ('policemen').

Champagne & Ardennes

The chalky and rolling fields of Champagne might have remained unsung and unvisited, had it not been for an accident of history. Towards the end of the 17th century a blind monk, tending the bottles of mediocre wine in the cellars of his abbey at Hautviliers, discovered that cork made a fine stopper for aging his wine. After the first fermentation, cork kept air, the enemy of aging wine, from his brew. But it also trapped the carbon dioxide in the bottle and when he pulled the cork it 'popped'. At that moment, some say, the world changed for the better. 'I am drinking the stars,' he is said to have murmured as he took the first sip of champagne the world had ever known. This northeastern slice of France is composed of the *Départements* of Ardennes, Marne, Aube and Haute Marne. On these rolling plains many of the great battles of European history have been fought, including many in the First and Second World Wars. The Ardennes was once known as the 'woody country' where Charlemagne hunted deer, wild boar, small birds and game in the now vanished forests. The area has three main waterways: the *Seine,* the *Aube* and the *Marne.* The **Marne Valley** between Ferté-sous-Jouarre and Epernay is one of the prettiest in France. Forests of beech, birch, oak and elm cover the high ground, vines and fruit trees sprawl across the slopes and corn and sunflowers wave in the little protected valleys. The valleys form a long fresh and green oasis, dotted with red-roofed villages. In 496 Clovis, the first king of France, was baptised in the cathedral in **Rheims**. From Louis VII to Charles X, the kings of France made it a point of honour to be crowned in the city where the history of the country really began. Rheims and its cathedral have been destroyed, razed, and

rebuilt many times over the centuries. The *Church of St Rémi,* even older than the cathedral, is half Romanesque, half Gothic in style. The most remarkable feature is its great size, comparable to that of Notre Dame de Paris. Beneath the town and its suburbs there are endless caves for champagne. **Epernay** is the real capital of champagne, the drink. Here, 115km (72 miles) of underground galleries in the chalk beneath the city store the wine for the delicate operations required to make champagne. These include the blending of vintages, one of the most important tasks in the creation of champagne. It is left to age for at least three years. Aside from champagne as the world knows it, there is an excellent *blanc de blanc champagne nature*, an unbubbly white wine with a slight bite and many of the characteristics of champagne. The perfect Gothic style of the cathedral of *St Etienne* in **Châlons-sur-Marne** has preserved the pure lines of its 12th-century tower. Nearby, the little town of **St Ménéhould**, almost destroyed in 1940, has contributed to the gastronomic world recipes for pigs' feet and carp, but historically it is known for the fact that the postmaster, in 1791, recognised Louis XVI fleeing from Paris with his family and reported him.

Before the annexation of Franche-Comté and Lorraine, **Langres** was a fortified town. Its Gallo-Roman monuments, its 15th- and 17th-century mansions and its religious architecture make it well worth a visit. **Troyes**, ancient capital of the Champagne area, has a beautifully preserved city centre with a Gothic cathedral, dozens of churches and 15th-century houses and a system of boulevards shaped like a champagne cork. The city also boasts the *Musée d'Art Moderne* in the old Bishops' Palace – a private collection of modern art, including works by Bonnard, Degas and Gauguin.

There are beautiful lakes in the Champagne-Ardenne region, the largest being *Lac du Der-Chantecoq.* The *Fôret d'Orient* has a famous bird sanctuary. There is no school of cooking founded on the use of champagne, but locally there are a few interesting dishes that include the wine. Châlons-sur-Marne has a dish that involves cooking chicken in champagne. It goes well in a sauce for the local trout; kidneys and pike have also been fried in champagne.

Lorraine, Vosges & Alsace

This part of France is made up of two historic territories, *Alsace* and *Lorraine,* in which there are six *Départements*: Vosges, Meurthe-et-Moselle, Meuse, Moselle, Bas-Rhin, Haut-Rhin and the territory of Belfort. These territories have see-sawed from French to German control during conflicts between the two countries for centuries. The major cities of the area are

Strasbourg, Metz, Nancy and Colmar. **Strasbourg,** by far the largest and most important, has been for centuries what its name suggests: a city on a highway – the highway being the east–west trade (and invasion) route and the north–south river commerce. Today it is the headquarters of the Council of Europe, but it is rich in historic monuments and architecture and possesses a magnificent cathedral.

Metz, a Gallo-Romaine city, is situated in a strategic position as a defence point and is also a crossroads of trade routes. It contains some elegant medieval walls, arches and public buildings, but its pride is the *Cathedral of St Etienne.* **Nancy** is best known for its perfectly proportioned *Place Stanislas*, gracefully surrounded with elegant wrought-iron gates. The history of Lorraine is excellently documented in the town's museum. A visit to **Colmar** can be a pleasant glimpse into the Middle Ages, and it is one of the most agreeable cities in Alsace, as well as being capital of the Alsatian wine country. The narrow, winding, cobbled streets are flanked by half-timbered houses, painstakingly restored by the burghers of the city. The 13th-century *Dominican Convent of Unterlinden,* now a museum, contains some important works from the 15th and 16th centuries, including the exquisite *Grünewald triptych.*

Colmar is a perfect place from which to set out along the *Wine Route,* stopping at many of the appealing towns along the way to taste the local wine. **Turckheim**, just outside Colmar, has some of the best-preserved array of 15th- and 16th-century houses in the district and a town crier takes visitors through the streets at night to recall the atmosphere of old. The town of **Eguisheim,** with its Renaissance fountain and monument in the village square, is also a charming Alsatian town with many historic houses and wine cellars open to the public for wine-tasting. **Kayersberg** (the birthplace of Dr Albert Schweitzer, whose house has been turned into a museum with momentoes of his work and life) also has some castle ruins on a hill overlooking the town and a picturesque stream that meanders through the town. A particularly popular town with tourists is **Riquewihr**, with its 13th- and 14th-century fortifications and belfry tower and its many medieval houses and courtyards. **St Hippolyte** is another picturesque wine-tasting town at the foot of the *Haut-Koenigsbourg Castle,* a sprawling and impressive medieval castle where Jean Renoir filmed *La Grande Illusion.*

Steer-yourself boats are readily available for canal cruising in a number of locations. There are also regularly scheduled *Rhine* river and canal tours daily all summer; several hotel boats ply these waterways as well. Sightseeing helicopters and balloons make regular flights, weather permitting. Several sentimentally ancient steam trains make regular circuits including **Rosheim/Ottrat** (on the wine trail); at **Andolsheim** a steam train runs along the *Canal d'Alsace* between Cernay and Soultz.

Throughout Alsace there are artisans' workshops, including glass and wood painting at **Wimmenau** and pottery in **Betschdorf** where studios and shops are open to the public. Organised walking tours that include overnight stops and meals *en route* are arranged from Colmar and **Mulhouse.** Bicycle trails are marked along the Rhine where bicycles are readily available for hire. **Belfort**, a major fortress town since the 17th century, commands the *Belfort gap,* or *Burgundy gate,* between the *Vosges* and the *Jura* mountains. Dominating the routes from Germany and Switzerland, it became famous during the Franco-Prussian war of 1870-71 when it withstood a 108-day siege. This is commemorated by a huge stone statue, the *Lion of Belfort,* by Bartholdi, the creator of the Statue of Liberty. The *route de vin* lies between the Rhine and a low range of pine-covered mountains called the **Vosges.** The flat, peaceful plain is covered with orchards and vineyards. Lovely, rural villages dot the landscape, their church spires piercing the horizon. The wines of Alsace have a long history, the Alsatian grapes being planted before the arrival of the Romans. It has never been clearly understood where they originated; unlike other French wines, these depend more on grape type than soil or processing. Almost exclusively white with a fruity and dry flavour, they make an excellent accompaniment to the local food. Beer also goes well with Alsatian food, and as might be expected, good beer is brewed in both the Alsace and the Lorraine areas. There are famous and popular mineral water sources in **Contrexéville** and **Vittel** (also a spa town). They were well known and appreciated by the Romans and today are the most popular in France. One of the food specialities of Alsace is *truite bleue,* blue trout, which is simply boiled so fresh as to be almost alive when tossed into the water. The swift rivers provide gamey trout and they can be fished by visitors if permits are obtained (at any city hall). The cooking is peppery and hearty and quite unlike that of any other French region. *Munster,* a strong winter cheese, is usually served

STRASBOURG

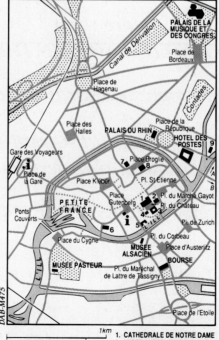

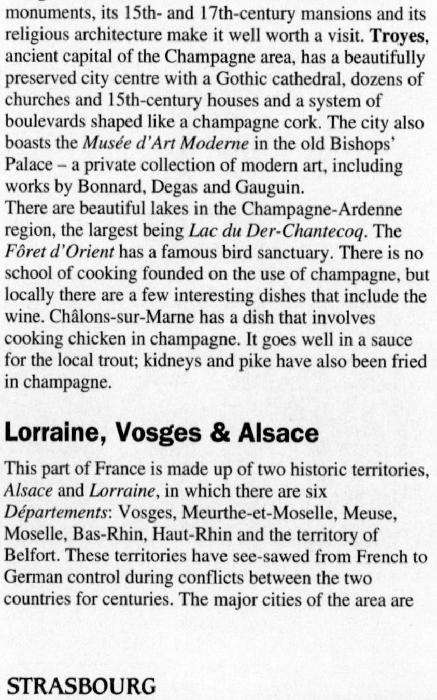

```
         1km
    ──────────────
      ½ ml
```

i *tourist information*

A. To European Parliament,
   Council of Europe &
   Commission on Human Rights
B. To Zoological Museum &
   Botanic Gardens

1. CATHEDRALE DE NOTRE DAME
2. LYCEE FUSTEL DE COULANGES
3. CHATEAU DES ROHAN
4. MUSEE DE L'ŒUVRE N. DAME
5. MUSEE HISTORIQUE
6. ST THOMAS
7. BANQUE DE FRANCE
8. HOTEL DE VILLE
9. ST PAUL

with caraway seeds. Lorraine and Alsatian tarts are made with the excellent local fruits: *mirabelles* (small, yellow plums), cherries, pears, etc. Each of these fruits also makes a world-renowned *eau-de-vie*, a strong white alcohol liqueur which is drunk as a digestive after a heavy meal. Lorraine is famous for *quiche lorraine* made only in the classical manner: with cream, eggs and bacon. Nancy has a *boudin* (blood sausage), although this is found in all parts of France.

Burgundy & Franche-Comté

Burgundy begins near **Auxerre,** a small medieval town with a beautiful Gothic cathedral, and extends southward to the hills of Beaujolais just north of Lyon. The *Départements* are the Yonne, Côte d'Or, Nièvre and the Saône-et-Loire. Driving through this region, one seems to be traversing a huge *carte des vins*: Mersault, Volnay, Beaune, Aloxe Corton, Nuits-Saint-Georges, Vosne-Romanée and Gevrey-Chambertin. This vast domain of great wines was for 600 years an independent kingdom, at times as strong as France itself, enjoying its heydey in the 15th century. Throughout a stormy history, however, Burgundy's vineyards survived thanks in large part to the knowledge, diligence and good taste of its monks. Several of the orders owned extensive vineyards throughout the region, among them the Knights of Malta, Carthusians, Carmelites and, most importantly, the Benedictines and Cistercians. As a result the 210km (130-mile) length of Burgundy is peppered with abbeys, monasteries and a score of fine Romanesque churches, notably in *Fontenay, Vézelay, Tournus* and *Cluny*. There are also many fortified châteaux. **Dijon**, an important political and religous centre during the 15th century, has several fine museums and art galleries, as well as the *Palais des Ducs*, once the home of the Dukes of Burgundy. There are also elegant restored town houses to be visited, dating from the 15th to the 18th century, and a 13th-century cathedral. The towns of **Sens** and **Macon** both possess fine churches dating from the 12th century. The region of Franche-Comté is shaped like a fat boomerang and is made up of the *Départements* of Doubs, Jura and Haute Saône. The high French Jura Mountains, rising in steps from 245-11,785m (800-5850ft), run north to south along the French-Swiss border. To the west is the forested Jura plateau, the vine-clad hills and eventually the fertile plain of northern Bresse, called the *Finage.* The heights and valleys of the Jura are readily accessible and, in the summertime, beautifully green, providing pasture land for the many milk cows used in the production of one of the great mountain cheeses: *Comté*. There are many lovely (and romantically named) rivers in this region – Semouse, Allance, Gugeotte, Lanterne, Barquotte, Durgeon, Colombine, Dougeonne, Rigotte and Romaine (named by Julius Caesar). They weave and twist, now and then disappearing underground to reappear again some miles away. All these physical characteristics combine to make Franche-Comté an excellent region for summer vacations and winter sports.

Val de Loire

The 'centre' of France from Chartres to Châteauroux and from Tours to Bourges includes the *Départements* of Eure-et-Loir, Loiret, Loir-et-Cher, Indre, Indre-et-Loire and Cher. The Central Loire includes the famous *Châteaux* country, perhaps the region most visited by foreign tourists to France. Through it flows a part of the *Loire River*, the longest river in France, and considered to be its most capricious, often reducing to a mere trickle of water in a bed of sand. It has been called a 'useless' great river, because it drives no turbines or mill wheels and offers few navigable waterways. It could be said that the Loire serves only beauty and each of its tributaries has its own character. The *Cher* is a quiet, slow-moving river, flowing calmly through grassy meadows and mature forests. The château of **Chenonceaux** stands quite literally *on* the river; a working mill in the early medieval period when the Cher flowed more vigorously, it was transformed into perhaps the most graceful of all French châteaux, its court rooms running clear from one bank to the other on a row of delicate arches. Chenonceaux's development owed much to a succession of beautiful and powerful noblewomen, and its charm is of an undeniably feminine nature. The *Indre* is a river of calm reflections. Lilies abound and weeping willows sway on its banks. The château at **Azay-le-Rideau** was designed to make full use of these qualities and stands beside several small man-made lakes, each reflecting a different aspect of the building. Water is moved to and from the river and between the lakes through a series of gurgling channels. The water gardens and its reflections of the intricately carved exterior more than compensate for the rather dull interior. The *Vienne* is essentially a broad stream. It glides gracefully beneath the weathered walls of old **Chinon**, where several important chapters in French history were acted out. The château of **Blois**, which is one of the finest architecturally speaking, is certainly the most interesting in terms of history. It stands in the centre of the ancient town of the same name, towering over the battered stone houses clustered beneath its walls. **Chambord**, several miles south of the Loire, is the most substantial of the great châteaux. Standing in a moat in the centre of a vast lawn bordered by forests, the body of the building possesses a majestic symmetry. In contrast, the roofscape is a mad jumble of eccentric chimneys and apartments. Some have attributed the bizarre double-helix staircase to Leonardo da Vinci. The five châteaux described in outline above are generally ranked highest amongst the Loire châteaux and form the core of most organised tours. There are, of course, dozens more that can be visited and it is even possible to stay overnight in several. Contact the Tourist Office for more information. The Loire Valley is very warm and crowded with tourists in summer.

Besides châteaux, there is much else of interest in the Val de Loire and surrounding districts. There are magnificent 13th-century cathedrals in **Chartres** and **Tours**, as well as abbeys and mansions and charming riverside towns and villages.

Other places of outstanding interest include **Orléans**, famous for its associations with Jeanne d'Arc, with a beautiful cathedral, the *Musée des Beaux Arts* and 16th-century *Hôtel de Ville;* and **Bourges**, a 15th-century town, complete with maisons and museums and the *Cathedral of St Etienne.* The charming little town of **Loches**, southeast of Tours, has a fine château and an interesting walled medieval quarter. It was in the heartland of the **Touraine** where the true cuisine of France developed (Touraine was given the name 'the garden of France').

Western Loire

The region of the Western Loire comprises the *départements* of Loire-Atlantique, the Vendée, Maine et Loire, Sarthe and Mayenne. The Vendée and the Loire-Atlantique share a beautiful and wild coastline with Brittany. There are 305km (190 miles) of sandy beaches. Inland, the mild climate makes for beautiful mature pastures, often made more attractive by clumps of wild camelias and roses.

In the Western Loire, **La Baule**, a summer resort with a fine, seemingly endless beach, is a pleasant town with winding streets and giant pines, excellent hotels, restaurants and a casino. It has an unusually mild microclimate and is exceptionally warm for the region. **Le Mans**, famous for its racetrack, is an historic old town built on a hill overlooking the west bank of the *Sarthe.* The 12th-century choir in the *Cathedral of Saint-Julian* is one of the most remarkable in France. The magnificent 13th- and 14th-century stained glass is also impressive. Most of the Sarthe Valley consists of beautifully wooded hills, divided by the thick hedges that are seasonally draped with wild roses, honeysuckle, or large juicy blackberries. In May or early June the apple and pear blossoms blend with the hawthorn; the orchards are in bloom and the fields and forests are rich and green. These two months are most attractive and the weather at that time is usually favourable; the autumn is less dry but as a rule usually remains pleasant through October.

Nantes, on the coast of the Loire-Atlantique, is a thriving commercial and industrial centre. There is a medieval castle, which also houses the *Musée d'Art Populaire,* a display of Breton costumes; a 15th-century cathedral; and a naval museum. Upstream from Nantes, the town of **Angers** contains some spectacular tapestries. In the castle can be seen 'St John's Vision of the Apocalypse' (14th century) and in the *Hôpital St Jean*, Jean Lurcat's 'Chant du Monde' (20th century). The Hôpital itself is very beautiful and there are several museums and art galleries in the town worth a visit, as well as the magnificent castle/fortress and the cathedral.

The regional cuisine has the advantages of excellent vineyards, an abundance and variety of fish from the Loire and its tributaries, plentiful butter and cheese, fruits and vegetables and easily available game from the forests. In general, the wines of the Loire all have a clean refreshing taste that makes them ideal for light lunches or as an *apéritif.*

Aquitaine & Poitou-Charentes

This area of sunshine and Atlantic air in the southwest of France includes the *Départements* of Deux Sèvres, Vienne, Charente-Maritime, Charente, Gironde, Dordogne, Lot-et-Garonne, Landes and Pyrénées Atlantiques, the latter on the Spanish border. The coastline has 270km (170 miles) of beaches and the 30km (20 miles) or so from **Hossegor** to **Hendaye** fall within the Basque area and offer some of the best surfing in Europe. North of Bordeaux the region of Guyenne is sometimes referred to as 'west-centre' as if it were a clearly defined part of France, yet a diversity of landscapes and an extraordinary mixing and mingling of races exists here – Celts, Iberians, Dutch and Anglo Saxons, to name a few. The linguistic frontier between the *langue d'oie* and *langue d'oc* runs between **Poitiers** (former capital of the Duchy of Aquitaine) and **Limoges**, creating a dialect which developed from both. These people have in common the great north–south highway, the important line of communication between the Parisian basin and the Aquitaine basin. Throughout the centuries it was the route of many invaders: Romans, Visigoths, Alemanni, Huns, Arabs, Normans, English, Huguenots and Catholics all moved along it. **Biarritz** and **Bayonne** are both resorts on the Aquitaine/Basque coast, close to the Spanish border. Biarritz has been famous as a cosmopolitan spa-town since the 19th century, when it was popular with European aristocracy. There are several sheltered beaches, as well as a casino. Bayonne, a few kilometres up the coast but slightly inland, is a typical Basque town which is worth a visit. There is a 13th-century cathedral and two museums (one of them devoted to Basque culture). **Bordeaux** is on the *Garonne River* just above where it joins the Dordogne, the two streams forming an estuary called the *Gironde* which forms a natural sheltered inland harbour. It is flanked on both sides by vineyards as far as the eye can see. The combination of great wines and great wealth made Bordeaux one of the gastronomic cities of France and the city offers an impressive sight from the stone bridge with 17 arches that crowns the enormous golden horn which

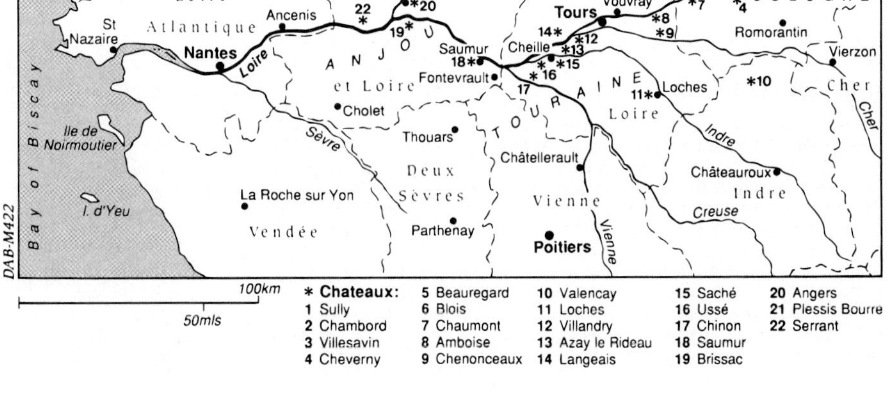

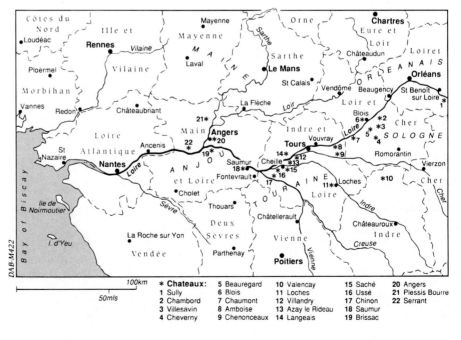

Côtes du Nord
Loudéac
Ille et Vilaine
Rennes
Vilaine
Mayenne
Laval
Orne
Sarthe
Le Mans
Chartres
Eure et Loir
Châteaudun
Loiret
Orléans
St Benoît sur Loire
Ploërmel
Morbihan
Vannes
Redon
Châteaubriant
St Calais
Vendôme
Beaugency
La Flèche
Loir et Cher
Blois
Sologne
Cher
Loire Atlantique
Ancenis
Maine et Loire
Angers
St Nazaire
Nantes
Loire
Anjou
Saumur
Cheille
Fontevrault
Indre et Loire
Tours
Vouvray
Romorantin
Vierzon
Touraine
Loches
Cholet
Sèvre
Thouars
Châtellerault
Châteauroux
Indre
Creuse
Ile de Noirmoutier
I. d'Yeu
Bay of Biscay
La Roche sur Yon
Vendée
Deux Sèvres
Parthenay
Vienne
Poitiers
DAB-M422
100km
50mls
* Chateaux:
1 Sully
2 Chambord
3 Villesavin
4 Cheverny
5 Beauregard
6 Blois
7 Chaumont
8 Amboise
9 Chenonceaux
10 Valencay
11 Loches
12 Villandry
13 Azay le Rideau
14 Langeais
15 Saché
16 Ussé
17 Chinon
18 Saumur
19 Brissac
20 Angers
21 Plessis Bourre
22 Serrant

forms the harbour. The second largest city of France in area, the fourth in population, the fifth port, it was described by Victor Hugo with the words: 'Take Versailles, add Antwerp to it, and you have Bordeaux'. Its magnificent geographical position and unsurpassed vineyards belie Hugo's simplification. The city is the commercial and cultural centre for all of the southwest. South of Bordeaux along the coast is a strip of long sandy beaches backed by lagoons, some communicating with the sea, some shut off from it. Just at the back of this is the **Landes**, covered with growths of scrubby pine. Here in the marshes the shepherds walk on stilts. The hilly region between the *Adour* and Garonne rivers comprises the inland part of Gascony, first known as *Aquitania Propria* and later as *Novem Populena*. It was inhabited by Vascones, or Basques who, since prehistoric times, had lived in this area and south of the Pyrénées. In the south the Basque language has survived to this day, but the northern part of the area became known as Vasconia and then **Gascony**, a name made famous by the swashbuckling Gascons of literature; Cyrano de Bergerac, d'Artagnan of 'The Three Musketeers' and *le vert gallant* – Henri IV. In the centre of Gascony is the old countship of **Armagnac** which, like Cognac, provides the world with a magnificent brandy that bears the name of the region. The difference between the two stems from several factors: the type of grape used, the soil, the climate, the method of distilling the wine and the variety of wood used in the maturing casks. Armagnac is still made by local artisans and small farmers. The quality and taste varies much more than Cognac, but it inevitably retains its fine flavour.

The **Dordogne** (and neighbouring Lot) is the area where traces of prehistoric (Cro-Magnon) man abound. The *Dordogne River* itself, one of the most beautiful of all French rivers, flows swiftly through the region, its banks crowded with old castles and walled towns. In **Montignac** the fabulous painted caves of *Lascaux* are reproduced in the exact proportions and colours of the original, a few miles away. The reproduction was necessary as the original deteriorated rapidly when exposed to the heat and humidity of visitors. A highly interesting and informative museum and zoo of prehistoric artefacts and animals has been created in *le Thot* a few miles from Agen. The area around **Perigueux** is a country of rivers and castles – very different from those on the Loire as these are older and, for the most part, fortified defence points against medieval invaders. There are facilities for renting horse and gypsy wagons (*roulotte à chevaux*) for slow-moving tours of the region. Along with hiking treks, river boating and bicycling tours, it offers a relaxed way to explore this beautiful land.

It is possible in Aquitaine and Poitou-Charentes to find pleasant hotels and *auberges* for an overnight or few days' stay. They range from *gîtes* and *chambre d'hôtes* – a farm bed & breakfast programme – to châteaux hôtels with elegant restaurants. There are no less than 150 *chambres d'hôtes* stopovers in the Poitou-Charentes region alone, including many on the coast, near beaches and pleasure ports. The area of Poitou-Charentes has lovely mature woodland and an attractive coast where oysters are cultivated. The *Charente-Maritime* is known as 'the Jade Coast', with **Royan** to the south (a fine modern resort with 13km/8 miles of fine sand beaches) and **La Rochelle** to the north. The rivers of the region offer quiet scenic walks or boating trips. The centre of the *Département* of Charente, amid low, rolling hills covered with copses of trees and vineyards, is a little town of only 22,000 inhabitants whose name is known all over the world. Here, in an area of some 150,000 acres, the only brandy that can be called *Cognac* is produced. Use of the name is forbidden for brandy which is made elsewhere or from other than one of the seven officially accepted varieties of grape. The *Valois Château*, located here, was the birthplace of Francis I. The ancient port of **La Rochelle**, from which many pioneers left to explore the new world, is today a popular vacation and sailing port.

Close by, the offshore islands of **Oléron** and **Ré** are both connected to the mainland by bridges.

Auvergne & Limousin

West of the Rhône are the volcanic highlands of the **Massif Central**, historically known as Auvergne and consisting today of the *Départements* of Haute-Loire, Cantal, Pay-de-Dôme and Allier. The Limousin region to the west comprises Haute-Vienne, Creuse and Corrèze. Architecturally, Auvergne is rich in châteaux and churches (especially in the Allier and Loire gorges) and is noted for its colourful, rich and mysterious nature. The *National Park* here offers magnificent walking country – a land of water, mountains, plains and extinct volcanoes (the Cantal crater may once have been 30km/20 miles wide). There are ten spa resorts within its boundaries, as well as many lakes, rivers and forests. The high plateaus of *Combrailles, Forez* and *Bourbonnais* are very beautiful.

Clermont-Ferrand, which is the political and economic nucleus for the whole of the Massif Central, is a lively and sprawling town and the birthplace of the Michelin tyre empire. Much of the town's architecture (especially in the older parts of the Clermont area) is black, because of the local black volcanic rock. There is a 13th-century Gothic cathedral and a 14th-century Romanesque basilica, as well as several museums. The town makes a very good base for exploring the beautiful areas around it.

There are plenty of good hôtels, *gîtes d'hôtes*, and *gîtes de France* throughout the region. The cuisine is splendid, including *cornet de Murat* (pastries), *pounti, truffades* and the St Nectaire cheeses.

The 2000-year-old regional capital of Limousin, **Limoges**, is an important rail and route crossroad, famous for the production of an extremely fine porcelain. The nearby city of **Aubusson** is noted for its tapestries (a local tradition dating back to the 8th century). Both cities are also famous for their enamel.

Languedoc-Roussillon

The combined territories of Languedoc and Roussillon include five *Départements*: Aude, Gard, Hérault, Lozère and Pyrénées-Oriental. The area has been French since the 13th century and the name *languedoc* comes from *lang d'oc* or language in which 'yes' is *oc* (as opposed to *langue d'oie* the language in which 'yes' is *oui)*. This ancient language is still heard throughout the south of France, on both sides of the Rhône. The Mediterranean coast between **Perpignan** (the ancient capital of the Kings of Mallorca) and **Montpellier** now has one of the most modern holiday complexes in Europe, including the resorts of **La Grande Motte, Port Leucate** and **Port Bacarès**. More wine is produced in Languedoc-Roussillon than any other place in the world. The vineyards, started in the Roman era and producing red, white and rosé wine, begin in the **Narbonne** area, run past **Béziers** (the wine marketing centre for the region) and on to **Montpellier**. Once an important seaport which imported spices (its name derives from 'the Mount of Spice Merchants'), the city is an important intellectual and university centre with five fine museums, impressive 17th- and 18th-century architecture and a superb summer music festival. There are a great variety of other attractions in this warm southland. The Roman (and some Gallic) ruins are often magnificent; the *Maison Carré, Diana's Temple* and the *Roman Arena* in **Nîmes**, the Rome of the Gauls, are among the finest examples of Greco-Roman architecture to be found today. The 2000-year-old *Pont de Gard* is one of man's greatest architectural accomplishments and certainly merits a special trip. There is the medieval city of **Aigues-Mortes** which would still be recognizable to St Louis and his crusaders, for it was from here they embarked for the east; and the crenelated walled city of **Carcassonne** and towers of **Uzès** are unmissable.

The *Canal du Midi*, ideal for steer-yourself canalling, is a tranquil waterway, largely abandoned by commerce, that connects the Atlantic with the Mediterranean. It runs through the sleepy village of **Castelnaudary**, famous for its *cassoulet*, past the citadel of Carcassonne and on through Montpellier.

Rhône, Savoie & Dauphiny

This region includes the French Alps and their foothills, and the vast long valleys of the Rhône and Saône rivers. The *Départements* are Loire, Rhône, Ain, Ardèche, Drôme, Isère, Savoie and Haute-Savoie.

Lyon, in the deepest part of the Rhône valley, has a proud gastronomic tradition. As France's second city, Lyon is a major cultural, artistic, financial and industrial centre, with international festivals and trade fairs. The *Cathedral of St Jean* is well worth a visit, as are the Roman remains of the city, and the *Musée de la Civilisation Gallo-Romaine*. The French Alps stretch across Savoie and Dauphiny on the border with Italy. Napoleon came this way after escaping from Elba in 1815. Landing with 100 men near Cannes, he intended to march along the coast to Marseille and up the Rhône Valley to Lyon and Paris, but he received reports that the population on that route was hostile and was forced instead to head inland through the mountains. They reached **Gap** (150km/93 miles from the coast) in four days, **Grenoble** a few days after and arrived in Paris (1152km/715 miles from Cannes) in 20 days with a large and loyal army in tow. It is possible to retrace his route, which passes through much beautiful scenery; each stopping place is clearly marked. The Alps have demanded much of France's engineers and some of the roads and railways are themselves tourist attractions. Notable examples include the 9km (6-mile) steam locomotive run from *La Rochette* to *Poncharra* (about 40km/24 miles from Grenoble); and the 32km (19-mile) track (electrified in 1903) from *Saint-Georges-de-Commiers* to *la Mira* (near Grenoble), with 133 curves, 18 tunnels and 12 viaducts. As in most mountainous regions of the world, white-water boating *(randonnées nautiques)* can be enjoyed on many of the Alpine rivers. Hiking is popular and well organised, utilising the GR *(grandes randonnées* or main trails) maps that show where the official marked trails pass. The rivers racing from the Alpine heights into the Rhône provide a great deal of electrical power and good opportunities for trout fishing. The *Fédération des associations agréées de Pêche et de Pisciculture de la Drôme* in Valence can lead a fisherman to the right spot (HQ in Valence, but branches in 36 cities). Skiing, however, is the principle sport in the French Alps. The best skiing is found, for the most part, west of Grenoble and south of Lake Geneva. All the resorts are well-equipped, provide warm, comfortable lodgings and good food. Some specialise in skiing the year round, but almost all have summer seasons with facilities such as golf courses, tennis courts, swimming pools and natural lakes. At the lake resort of **Annecy**, there is an unusual *Bell Museum* with a very fine restaurant attached; international festivals of gastronomy are held throughout the year.

Midi-Pyrénées

The Midi-Pyrénées area, with its magnificent mountain scenery, lies between Aquitaine to the west and Languedoc-Roussillon to the east. It encompasses part of the Causses, the high plateau country and most of Gascony. Included in it are the *Départements* of Lot, Aveyron, Tarn-et-Garonne, Tarn, Gers, Haut-Garonne, Ariège and Haute Pyrénées. This is a land of plains dotted with hillocks, sandy stretches, moors and pine woods, desolate plateaux cleft by magical grottoes, and little valleys covered with impenetrable forests. The northeastern section is a rough, mountainous land, known as the *Rouergue*. It is situated on the frontier of Aquitaine, formed by the plateau of the *Causse,* where game and wild birds feed on the thyme and juniper growing wild in the chalky soil. As a result, these little animals and birds develop a delicious and individual flavour. The principal town, **Rodez**, is severe and beautiful. The crenelated summit of its red tower, one of the marvels of French Gothic architecture, rises above a confusion of narrow streets and small squares. From here there are views of the high plateaux beyond the Aveyron, a majestically stark landscape of granite outcrops and steep ravines. The villages and farmhouses, built of local rock, often mimic the rock formations to the extent that they are all but invisible to outsiders.

To the southeast is **Millau**, gateway to the Tarn gorges, and to the south lies **Roquefort** with its windy caves that store the famous ewe's-milk cheese. These damp cold winds are the secret that has created the 'cheese of kings and the king of cheeses'. **Auch** was the ancient metropole of the Roman *Novem Populena*, one of the most important towns in Gaul, long rivalling *Burdigala* (Bordeaux) in importance. The cathedral has two Jesuit towers, choirstalls carved in solid oak and a 16th-century stained glass window. The people of Auch have erected a statue to *le vrai d'Artagnan* ('the real d'Artagnan'), the famous Gascon musketeer immortalised by Dumas. **Cahor**, situated on a peninsula formed by the *River Lot*, has a famous bridge, *Pont Valentré,* with its six pointed arches and three defensive towers rising 40m (130ft) above the river. It is the most magnificent fortified river span that has survived in Europe and was begun in 1308. Legend has it that the construction work was plagued with problems and the bridge still remained unfinished after 50 years. Then one of the architects made a pact with the devil and the bridge was finished without another hitch. A small figure of the devil is still visible on the central tower. A fine, very dark red wine bears the name *Cahors*. It is made from grapes of the Amina variety brought in from Italy in Roman times. **Toulouse**, one of the most interesting cities of France, is an agricultural market centre, an important university town, an aero-research centre and one of the great cities of French art (it has seven fine museums). After the Middle Ages the stone quarries in the region were exhausted so the city was built with a soft red brick which seems to absorb the light. As a result it is called the *Ville Rose* and is described as 'pink in the light of dawn, red in broad daylight and mauve by twilight'. There are many beautiful public buildings and private dwellings, like the 16th-century Renaissance *Hôtel d'Assezat* and one known as the *Capitole*, now used as a city hall. The finest Romanesque church in southern France is here. The first Gothic church west of the Rhône was built in Toulouse, the *Church of the Jacobins*; and the first Dominican monastery was founded in Toulouse by Saint Dominic

Mieux dans sa tête
Mieux dans son corps

Stress, insomnia and nervous tension can be a part of everyone's daily life. The spa of Néris-les-Bains can help you regain a sense of calm, balance and joie de vivre. In the welcoming and peaceful surroundings of the Auvergne in central France, Néris enjoys all the natural resources necessary to put you back on your feet.

A visit to the spa at Néris-les-Bains is particularly recommended for those suffering from psychosomatic and neurological conditions as well as rheumatism and those needing occupational therapy. The mineral water of Néris is very rich in oligo-elements and has proven sedative properties, promoting a sense of equilibrium and calm, as well as significant healing and purifying effects. Used in external hydrotherapy, it provides the major therapeutic benefit of the cure.

Over the past decade the spa has been renovated and modernised:

• Priority has been given to hygiene: cubicles are disinfected after each use by means of an anti-microbe network and all the floors are cleaned mechanically.

• The springs are equipped with the latest balneotherapy technology combining comfort and effectiveness: underwater physiotherapy and massage, jet baths and showers, steam rooms, arm and foot baths and seaweed treatment.

• A team of professional attendants will take care that nothing mars your visit.

• All treatments are tailored to your individual requirements and expectations to ensure a profound sense of relaxation and well-being.

More and more people are discovering Néris, the No One spa in France for the treatment of psycho-somatic and neurological conditions. We are therefore expending a lot of energy to ensure that you enjoy exceptional therapeutic comfort, rigorous standards of hygiene and personalised care in a warm and welcoming atmosphere. Néris-les-Bains offers a wide range of accommodation with hotels of all classes, camp sites and family gîtes at your disposal. There is a variety of entertainments including a casino, open-air festivals and balls, theatre, golf, tennis, horse riding, fishing and walks in the 15 hectares of parks as well as specially conceived historic walks around the town. In this way the total environment of the town will contribute effectively to your recuperation.

Néris-les-Bains

For more information phone +33 70 03 10 39 (spa) or +33 70 03 11 03 (tourist office)

himself. Toulouse is a vibrant city with much activity, with its long rue Alsace-Lorraine being its axis. It is here in the early evenings that Toulousians and visitors alike sit for an apéritif at one of the large sidewalk cafés. The region was an important part of the Roman Empire, subjected for 800 years to Arabic influence (the Moors holding substantial parts of Spain just across the Pyrénées) and the cuisine has therefore developed from both Roman and Arabic. Toulouse sausage, a long fat soft sausage whose filling must be chopped by hand, is one of the ingredients of the local *cassoulet* as well as a very popular dish in its own right. **Albi** is another red-brick city, smaller but no less interesting than Toulouse, located on the *River Tarn.* The first extraordinary thing about Albi is its brick church. Albi was the centre of violent religious wars (the Albigenaise Heretics resisted the Catholic crusaders for decades). The mammoth red-brick *Cathedral of Sainte Cécile*, towering above all the other buildings of the town, was built as a fortress to protect the cruel bishop who imposed the church on the populace. Inside is a vast hall, subdivided by exquisite stonework embellished with statues. The nearby 13th-century *Palace of the Archbishop* (also fortified) is now a museum containing the largest single collection of the works of Toulouse-Lautrec. The town of **Lourdes** has acted as a magnet for the sick in need of miracle cures, ever since the visions of Bernadette Soubirous in the mid-19th century. Apart from the famous grotto, there is a castle and a museum.

Côte d'Azur & Provence

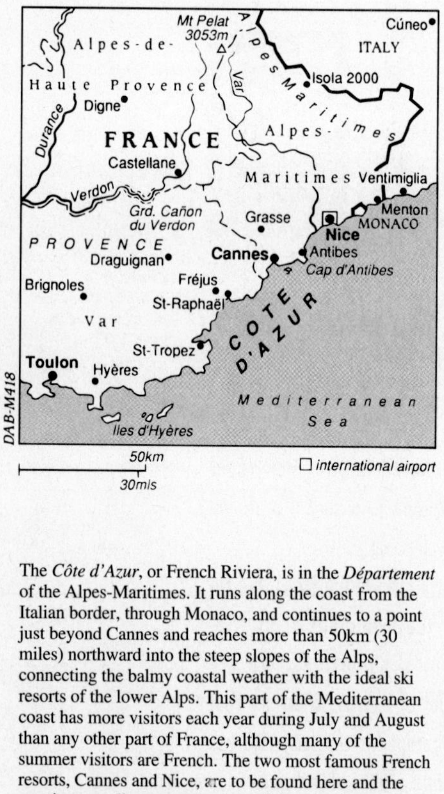

The *Côte d'Azur*, or French Riviera, is in the *Département* of the Alpes-Maritimes. It runs along the coast from the Italian border, through Monaco, and continues to a point just beyond Cannes and reaches more than 50km (30 miles) northward into the steep slopes of the Alps, connecting the balmy coastal weather with the ideal ski resorts of the lower Alps. This part of the Mediterranean coast has more visitors each year during July and August than any other part of France, although many of the summer visitors are French. The two most famous French resorts, Cannes and Nice, are to be found here and the area is generally accepted as one of the most beautiful resort spots in the world. It well deserves its immense popularity – with artists (Matisse, Picasso, Chagall and Dufy) as well as tourists. The palm trees, blue sea, beautiful beaches, sparkling cities and villages with their splendid residences against the backdrop of the high green mountains have impressed visitors since the 18th century when the crochety doctor-cum-novelist, Tobias Smollet, paid a visit and described it in his *Travels in France and Italy.* The weather is wonderful with long, hot and sunny summers. There is plenty of diversion here, especially in the spring, summer and early autumn months. The coastal resort towns include **Cannes**, made popular as a resort by Lord Brougham in the 19th century when, because of a plague in Nice, he was forced to stop here; **Nice**, itself, the largest metropolis on the coast, a thriving commercial city as well as a year-round resort (the annual carnival and battle of roses perhaps date back to 350BC); **Napoule Plage**, a small and exclusive resort with several sandy beaches, a marina and a splendid view of the rolling green *Maure Mountains*; **Golfe-Juan**, now a popular resort town with many expensive mansions and hotels; **Juan-les-Pins**, with a neat harbour, beaches and pine forests in the hills which protect the village from the winds in both summer and winter; **Antibes** and **Cap d'Antibes**, very popular but expensive resorts; **Villefranche-sur-Mer**, a deep-water port which has been used by pleasure yachts and navies for centuries; **St-Jean-Cap-Ferrat**, an exclusive and expensive resort consisting of great private mansions and seaside estates; **Beaulieu**, much less exclusive, yet a fine resort town; **Menton** (near the Principality of Monaco), once a fishing village and citrus-fruit-producing area, now a pleasant vacation resort. The Côte d'Azur is an extraordinary playground with every kind of amusement. There are excellent museums, historic places dating from the pre-Christian era to the present day, hills, mountains, lakes and rivers, gorges and alpine skiing trails. The entire area has a generous supply of good, comfortable hotels as well as luxury châteaux, restaurants with every sort of food, and good drinking bars everywhere. One of the greatest museums in the world, the *Maeght Foundation*, is located in **St-Paul-de-Vence**. Picasso, Braque, Matisse and Léger museums also exist and there is plenty of beautiful foothill countryside to explore. Resorts further along the coast from Cannes include **St Tropez**, a terribly crowded, hard to reach yet fashionable village; **Port Grimaud**, the first of the custom-built 'fishing village' resorts (and now old enough to look almost like the real thing); **Ste Maxime**, a fashionable but crowded resort with fine beaches and harbour; **Fréjus**, which was a port when the Greeks were settling in the Mediterran-ean basin 'like frogs around a pond' and which is less fashionable than most of its neighbours; and **St Raphael**, at one time a Roman resort, and now a comfortable middle-class vacation town. **Grass,** just north of Cannes, is a charming hilltop town famed for its perfume.

Spectacular weather is one of the major attractions of *Provence*, whose *Départements* comprise Hautes Alpes, Alpes de Hautes Provence, Var, Vaucluse and Bouches du Rhône. The deep blue skies of summer are seldom clouded, although there is some rain in spring and autumn. The only inhospitable element is the *Mistral*, a wind that sometimes roars down the Rhône Valley, often unrelenting for three or four days. When the Romans arrived in Gaul, they were so delighted with the climate of the Bouches du Rhône that they made it a province rather than a colony, which was more usual.

The varied flora that have taken root in this land have given it the hues of pewter, bronze, dark green and vibrant green. The sun has baked the dwellings to shades of ochre and rose while the deep red soil has provided tiles that remain red, defying the searing rays of the Midi sunshine. The towns, their architecture, stones and tiles all blend subtly throughout Provence with the majestic plane trees in the streets and squares. Their long heavy trunks of mottled greys and the graceful vaulting of the heavily leafed branches create a peculiar atmosphere not found anywhere else. These are the principal adornment of most of the cities, market towns and villages, casting a deep blue shade on the inhabitants, the mossy fountains, café terraces, and games of *pétanque*. The eras of Greek and Roman domination of Provence have left monuments scattered across the countryside. They include walled hill towns, triumphal arches, theatres, colosseums, arenas, bridges and aquaducts. Christianity brought the *Palace of the Popes* in **Avignon**, many churches and hundreds of roadside shrines or 'oratories' which have given the name *oradour* to many communities along the Rhône. Christian art of the highest quality is scattered throughout the area from *Notre-Dame-des-Doms* in Avignon to *Notre-Dame-du-Bourg* in **Digne** in the centre of the lower alps. The pilgrims throughout the territory built wonderful churches typified by graceful semi-circular arches, round rose windows, statues of Christ surrounded by evangelists, saints, the damned in chains, and processions of the faithful. These are carved in stone so worn by the sun and wind they almost have the quality of flesh.

Many of the towns and villages are marked by a fortified castle and watchtower to guard against the coming of the Saracens, the Corsairs of the Rhône and marauding bands. For this was the invasion route, by land from the north and by sea from the south. *Tarascon, Beauclair, Villeneuve, Gourdon, Entrevaux, Sisteron* and many others had their 'close' and tower situated high above the river or overlooking the sea. **Marseille** was founded by the Greeks (they called it Massalia) and used as a base for their colonisation of the Rhône Valley. Today, it is France's most important commercial port on the Mediterranean and consequently is of a primarily industrial nature. Nonetheless, there are sites of interest to the conventionally minded tourist – the old port, the hilltop church of *Notre-Dame-de-la-Garde*, many fine restaurants (especially for seafood), several museums, Le Corbusier's *Unité d'Habitation*, the *Hospice de la Vieille Charité* and, of course, the *Château d'If*, one of the most notorious of France's historic island fortresses.

Vast oil refineries and depots dominate the sparsely populated salt flats and marshes to the north and west of the city, but the land is not yet dead. It is the perfect habitat for several species of birds found in only a few other places in Eastern Europe, including bustards and nightjars. On the far side of the Rhône is the marshy area known as the **Camargue**, long used for the breeding of beef cattle and horses, for the evaporation of sea water to make salt, and more recently for growing rice. The cattle breeders, or cowboys, are armed with lances instead of lassos. Vast flocks of waterbirds nest here in a national bird reserve, among them pink flamingos and snow-white egrets. When, in 123BC, Consul Sextias Calvinus established a camp beside some warm springs in the broad lower Rhône Valley, it was named Aquae Sextiae – today known as **Aix-en-Provence.** Other interesting ancient sites are the ruined Roman aqueduct at **Pont du Gard** and the amphitheatre in **Arles**. This whole region is also fascinating since it was frequently painted by the great Post-Impressionist painters Cézanne and Van Gogh. The combination of gentle light and breathtaking scenery finds echoes throughout the art galleries of the world. Near Arles is **Les Baux**, a haunting and mysterious deserted, medieval hilltop village. The many olive trees found throughout Provence provide a popular fruit and one of the important staples of the local cuisine, a fine olive oil used extensively in the cooking of local food. Garlic, though not exclusively associated with Provence, is used more here than in any other part of France. It is sometimes called 'the truffle of Provence'. A third element, tomato, seems to get into most of the delicious Provençal concoctions as well. The cooking here varies from region to region. In the Camargue a characteristic dish is *estouffade de boeuf.* Marseille is noted for a dish called *pieds et paquets* ('feet and packages') which consists of sheeps' tripe stuffed with salt pork and cooked overnight in white wine with onions, garlic and parsley. *Tripe á la Niçoise* is similar, but nonetheless individual. Perhaps the most typical dish and one found in most parts of Provence is *tomates provençales*, a heavenly concoction with all the Provençal specialities: olive oil, garlic and parsley baked in and on a tomato. This combination can also be applied to courgettes (zucchini) and aubergines (egg plant). All of these vegetables, along with sweet peppers, are found in the most famous Provençal vegetable *ragoût* known, for some long lost reason, as *ratatouille*, this too being well laced with garlic and of course cooked in olive oil. Mayonnaise, also, well mixed with Provençal garlic, becomes *aioli,* which is served with boiled vegetables and/or fish. Quail, thrush, trout and crayfish were, not so long ago, the mainstays of the Provençal table, but stocks have declined and these dishes are now rarely served. *Gigot* (leg of lamb) is a more common local speciality. Surviving into the era of *nouvelle cuisine* and still the pride of the Provençal coast is the famous fish stew called *bouillabaisse*. Like *cassoulet* in Languedoc there are several versions, each claiming to be the 'authentic' one. The ingredients are not vastly different – having to do with the amount of saffron or the inclusion or exclusion of certain fish.

Few wines are grown in Provence, although some are quite good, especially those originating in the Lubéron. The four districts that have been granted recognition are best known for their rosé wines: *Cassis, Bandol, Bellet* and *la Palette.* They are all on the coast, except la Palette which is near Aix.

Corsica

The island of Corsica is made up of two French *Départements*: Haute Corse (upper Corsica) and Corse du Sud (south Corsica). The 8720 sq km (3367 sq miles) are inhabited by not many more than 250,000 people. It is one of the very few places left in Europe that is not invaded by campers and trailers during the vacation season and its charm lies in this unspoiled and rugged atmosphere. The name Corsica, or *Corse*, is a modernisation of *Korsai*, believed to be a Phoenician word meaning 'covered with forests'. The Phoenician Greeks landed here 560 years before the Christian era to disturb inhabitants who had probably originated in Liguria. From that time on, Corsica has been fought for, or over, creating a bloody history probably unparalleled for such a small area. The Greeks were followed by the Romans, then the Vandals, Byzantines, Moors and Lombards. In 1768 Genoa sold Corsica to France and its 2500 years of disputed ownership ended. In spite of its extensive and colourful history it is of course best known as the birthplace of Napoléon Bonaparte. The island has been described as 'a mountain in the sea', for when approached by sea that is exactly what it looks like. A strange land, the mountains rise abruptly from the western shore where the coast is indescribably beautiful with a series of capes and isolated beachless bays; along its entire length rock and water meet with savage impact. The coastline, unfolded, is about 992km (620 miles) long. Corsica consists of heaths, forests, granite, snow, sand beaches and orange trees. This combination has

produced a strange, fiery, lucidly intellectual and music-loving race of people, both superstitious and pious at the same time. The interior is quite undeveloped, with mountains, and dry scrubby land overgrown with brush called *maquis* (from the local *maccia* which means 'brush'). It is a dry wilderness of hardy shrubs – arbutus, mastic, thorn, myrtle, juniper, rosemary, rock rose, agave, pistachio, fennel, heather, wild mint and ashphodel, 'the flower of hell'. During the German occupation of France (1940-44) resistance fighters were given the name *maquis* from the association of the wild country in which they hid, much as the savage backlands of Corsica provided at one time comparatively safe shelter for the island bandits. There is a desolate grandeur about the *maquis*, while on the other hand the rugged beauty of Corsica's magnificent mountain scenery is anything but desolate.
A considerable amount of forested area remains, although since discovered by the Greeks it has been frequently raided for its fine, straight and tall *laricio* pine that seems to thrive only here. They have been known to grow as high as 60m (200ft), perfect for use as masts and are still used as such. Corsica is also rich in cork oaks, chestnuts and olives. There is a *Regional Nature Conservation Park* on the island. North of the eastern plain are the lowlands, principally olive groves, known as *La Balagne*, the hinterland of Calvi and l'Ile Rousse. To the south is the dazzling white city of **Ajaccio**, full of Napoleonic memorabilia. The town runs in a semicircle on the calm bay, set against a backdrop of wooded hills. At the foot of the cape at the northern end of the island is the commercial, but none the less picturesque, town of **Bastia**, with its historic citadel towering over the headland. The old town has preserved its streets in the form of steps connected by vaulted passages, converging on the *Vieux port*. The port itself, with a polyglot population, is busy all year round. A little further north, the terraced *St Nicholas Beach,* shaded by palm trees and covered with parasols and café tables, separates the old port from the new. The new port, just beyond, is the real commercial port of the island. Corsican cuisine is essentially simple, with the sea providing the most dependable source of food, including its famous lobster. Freshwater fish abound in the interior and, as is to be expected, the *maquis* is game country. The aromatic herbs and berries add a particularly piquant flavour to the meat. Among the game available, *sanglier* and *marcassin* – young and older wild boar – turn up in season either roasted, stewed in a *daube* of red wine, or with a highly spiced local sauce *pibronata.* Sheep and goats are plentiful. Pigs, fed on chestnuts, are common at the Corsican table and they make an unusually flavoured ham. The extremes of the Corsican climate limit the variety of vegetables available. The Corsicans like hot and strong flavours that use even more herbs than are used in Provence. They like to shock with hot peppers and strong spices. A fish soup called *dziminu*, much like *bouillabaise* but much hotter, is made with peppers and pimentos. Inland freshwater fish is usually grilled and the local eels, called *capone*, are cut up and grilled on a spit over a charcoal fire. A peppered and smoked ham, called *prizzutu*, resembles the Italian *prosciutto*, but with chestnut flavour added. A favourite between-meal snack is *figatelli*, a sausage made of dried and spiced pork with liver. Placed between slices of a special bread, these are grilled over a wood fire. Red wine is available in abundance, but white and rosé are also produced on the island.
POPULAR ITINERARIES: 5-day: (a) Paris–Chartres–Blois–Chambord–Amboise–Chenonceaux–Azay-le-Rideau–Chinon–Tours–Paris. (b) Avignon–Pont du Gard–Arles–Les Baux–Aix-en-Provence–Avignon. (c) Paris–Giverny–Rouen–Honfleur–Bayeux–Mont-Saint-Michel–Paris. **7-day:** (a) Dieppe–Rouen–Chartres–Orléans–Tours–Saumur–Angers–Le Mans–Honfleur–Dieppe. (b) Nice–Antibes–Cannes–Grasse–Digne–Avignon–Les Baux–Arles–Aix-en-Provence–St Tropez–St Raphael–Nice.

SOCIAL PROFILE

FOOD & DRINK: With the exception of China, France has a more varied and developed cuisine than any other country. There is almost complete unanimity of opinion that French food is the best in the Western world. The vegetables, cheese, butter and fruit eaten in a French restaurant are usually fresh, although with the mushrooming of cafeterias and fast-food establishments, quality is no longer always reliable. The simple, delicious cooking for which France is famous is found in the old-fashioned bistro and restaurant. There are two distinct styles of eating in France. One is of course 'gastronomy' *(haute cuisine),* widely known and honoured as a cult with rituals, rules and taboos. It is rarely practised in daily life, partly because of the cost and the time which must be devoted to it. The other is family-style cooking, often just as delicious as its celebrated counterpart. It is the style of cooking experienced daily by the majority of French people and is the result of a carefully maintained family tradition. Almost all restaurants offer two types of meal: *à la carte* (extensive choice for each course and more expensive) and *le menu* (a set meal at a fixed price with dishes selected from the full *à la carte* menu). At simple restaurants the same cutlery will be used for all courses. The tourist office publishes a guide to restaurants in Paris and the Ile-de-France. Many restaurants close for a month during the summer, and one day a week. It is always wise to check that a restaurant is open, particularly on a Sunday. Costs are not necessarily high. Generally speaking, mealtimes in France are strictly observed. Lunch is as a rule served from noon to 1330, dinner usually from 2000-2130, but the larger the city, the later the dining hour.
Dishes include *tournedos* (small steaks ringed with bacon), *châteaubriand, entrecôte* (rib steak) served with *béarnaise* (delicate sauce with egg base), *gigot de pre-salé* (leg of lamb roasted or broiled) served with *flageolets* (light green beans) or *pommes dauphines* (deep-fried mashed potato puffs). Other dishes include *brochettes* (combinations of cubed meat or seafood on skewers, alternating with mushrooms, onions or tomatoes) or *ratatouille niçoise* (stew of courgettes, tomatoes and aubergines braised with garlic in olive oil); *pot-au-feu* (beef boiled with vegetables and served with coarse salt) and *blanquette de veau* (veal stew with mushrooms in a white wine/cream sauce). In the north of France (Nord/Pas de Calais and Picardy) fish and shellfish are the star features in menus – oysters, *moules* (mussels), *coques* (cockles) and *crevettes* (shrimps) are extremely popular. In Picardy duck pâtés and *Ficelle picarde* (ham and mushroom pancake) are popular. In the Champagne-Ardenne region there are the hams of Rheims and de Sanglier (wild boar). Among the fish specialities in this area are *écrevisses* (crayfish) and *brochets* (pike). Alsace and Lorraine are the lands of *choucroute* and *kugelhof* (oven-baked buns), *quiche lorraine* and *tarte flambée* (onion tart). Spicy and distinctive sauces are the hallmark of Breton food, and shellfish is a speciality of the region, particularly *homard à l'amoricaine* (lobster with cream sauce). Lyon, the main city of the Rhône Valley, is the heartland of French cuisine, though the food is often more rich than elaborate. A speciality of this area is *quenelles de brochet* (pounded pike formed into sausage shapes and usually served with a rich crayfish sauce). Bordeaux rivals Lyon as gastronomic capital of France. Aquitaine cuisine is based on goosefat. A reference to 'Perigord' will indicate a dish containing truffles. Basque chickens are specially reared. In the Pyrénées, especially around Toulouse, visitors will find salmon and *cassoulet,* a hearty dish with beans and preserved meat. General de Gaulle once asked, with a certain amount of pride, how it was possible to rule a country which produced 365 different kinds of cheese; some of the better known are Camembert, Brie, Roquefort, Reblochon and blue cheeses from Auvergne and Bresse. Desserts include: *soufflé grand-marnier, oeufs à la neige* (meringues floating on custard), *mille feuilles* (layers of flaky pastry and custard cream), *Paris-Brest* (a large puff-pastry with hazelnut cream), *ganache* (chocolate cream biscuit) and fruit tarts and flans.
For more information on the specialities from the various regions of France, consult the regional entries above.
Drink: Countless books have been written on the subject of French wine, and space here does not permit any major addition to the vast corpus of literature, which ranges from the scientific and learned to the emotional and anecdotal. Wine is by far the most popular alcoholic drink in France, and the choice will vary according to region. Cheap wine *(vin ordinaire)*, worth a try at FFr4 upwards, can be either very palatable or undrinkable, but there is no certain way of establishing which this is likely to be before drinking. Wines are classified into AC *(Appellation Controllée),* VDQS *(Vin delimité de qualité superieure), Vin de Pays* and *Vin de Table*. There are several wine-producing regions in the country; some of the more notable are Bordeaux, Burgundy, Loire, Rhône and Champagne. In elegant restaurants the wine list will be separate from the main menu, but in less opulent establishments will be printed on the back or along the side of the *carte*. The waiter will usually be glad to advise an appropriate choice. In expensive restaurants this will be handled by a *sommelier* or wine steward. If in doubt, try the house wine; this will usually be less expensive and will always be the owner's pride. Coffee is always served after the meal (not with the desert), and will always be black, in small cups, unless a *café au lait* (or *à crème)* is requested. The bill *(l'addition)* will not be presented until it is asked for, even if clients sit and talk for half an hour after they have finished eating. Liqueurs such as Chartreuse, Framboise and Genepi (an unusual liqueur made from a local aromatic plant) are available. Many of these liqueurs, such as *eau de vie* and *calvados* (applejack) are very strong and should be treated with respect, particularly after a few glasses of wine. A good rule of thumb is to look around and see what the locals are drinking. Spirit measures are usually doubles unless a *baby* is specifically asked for. There is also a huge variety of aperitifs available. A typically French drink is *pastis,* such as Ricard and Pernod. The region of Nord/Pas de Calais and Picardy does not produce wine, but brews beer and cider. Alsace is said to brew the best beer in France but fruity white wines, such as Riesling, Traminer and Sylvaner, and fine fruit liqueurs, such as Kirsch and Framboise, are produced in this area. The wines from the Champagne region of the Montagne de Reims district are firm and delicate (Vevenay Verzy), or full bodied and fully flavoured (Bouzy and Ambonnay). The legal age for drinking alcohol in a bar/café is 18. Minors are allowed to go into bars if accompanied by an adult but they will not be served alcohol. Hours of opening depend on the proprietor but generally bars in minor towns and resorts are open throughout the day; some may still be open at 0200. Smaller towns tend to shut earlier. There are also all-night bars and cafés.
NIGHTLIFE: In Paris nightclubs and discos there is sometimes no entry fee although drinks are more expensive. Alternatively, the entrance price sometimes includes a *consommation* of one drink. As an alternative to a nightclub, there are many late-night bars. Tourist offices publish an annual and monthly diary of events available free of charge. Several guides are also available which give information about entertainments and sightseeing in the capital. Some of the best are *Pariscope, 7 à Paris, Officiel des Spectacles* and the English-language *Passion.* In the provinces the French generally spend the night eating and drinking, although in the more popular tourist areas there will be discos and dances. All weekend festivals in summer in the rural areas are a good form of evening entertainment. There are over 130 public casinos in the country.
SHOPPING: Special purchases include laces, crystal glass, cheeses, coffee and, of course, wines, spirits and liqueurs. Arques, the home of Crystal D'Arques, is situated between St Omer and Calais, en route to most southern destinations. Lille, the main town of French Flanders, is known for its textiles, particularly fine lace. Most towns have fruit and vegetable markets on Saturday. Hypermarkets, enormous supermarkets which sell everything from foodstuffs and clothes to hi-fi equipment and furniture, are widespread in France. They tend to be situated just outside a town and all have parking facilities. **Shopping hours**: Department stores are open 0900-1830/1930 Monday to Saturday. Food shops are open 0700-1830/1930. Some food shops (particularly bakers) are open Sunday mornings, in which case they will probably close on Monday. Many shops close all day or half-day Monday. Hypermarkets are normally open until 2100 or 2200.
SPORT: Almost every kind of sport, for spectators and participants, is available in the country, ranging from the thrills and passion of an international **rugby** match to a

quiet game of **boules** in a sleepy village square. **Tennis** facilities are widespread, although they may be reasonably expensive. **Horseriding** is very popular. **Golf** courses are becoming common, particularly in the south. Game **shooting** permits are required from local *gendarmerie*. **Horseracing** is a popular spectator sport, as are rugby and **football**. **Sailing** and **boating** is available in the English Channel, Bay of Biscay, Riviera and major rivers (Loire, Rhône, Saône). Cruising boats may be rented on the Rhône, Canal du Midi and Burgundy Canal. Yachts proliferate, especially in the south. There are thousands of miles of carefully marked **hiking** trails in France. They are known as *Sentiers de Grande Randonnée*, and are generally marked on maps. **Winter sports:** The French and Swiss Alps contain some of the best **ski resorts** in the world. There are over 480km (300 miles) of ski *piste*, over 150 ski lifts, innumerable ski schools and quality resort facilities. All the major resorts offer skiing package holidays. The season runs from early December to the end of April. The height of the season is during February and March, as is reflected in the higher prices. (See *Resorts & Excursions* for further details.) The French Government Tourist Office will also be able to supply a wide range of literature on this subject.

SPECIAL EVENTS: The following is a selection of the major festivals and other special events celebrated during 1995 in France. For a complete list, contact the French Government Tourist Office which publishes a handbook giving full details of the wide range of festivals and special events in France during 1995/96; free copies are available on request.

Apr 22-23 '95 **Le Mans* (24-hour motor race). **Apr 27-May 8** *Foire de Paris*. **May 17-28** *Cannes Film Festival*. **May 29-Jun 11** *Rolland Garros International Tennis Tournament*, Paris. **Jun 2-Jul 1** *Music Festival*, Strasbourg. **Jun 11-18** *Paris Air Show*. **Jul 1-15** *"Halle That Jazz" Festival*, La Villette, Paris. **Jul 1-23** *Tour de France*. **Jul 2** *French Grand Prix (Formula 1)*, Magny-Cours Circuit, Nevers. **Jul 7-31** *Avignon Festival*. **Jul 11-24** *Aix-en-Provence Festival*. **Jul 14** *Bastille Day*. **Jul 15-Aug 19** *Music Festival*, Vézère (Château du Saillant). **Jul 17-23** *Fêtes de Cornouailles*, Quimper. **Jul (2nd fortnight)** *Jazz Festival*, Antibes. **Aug 5-13** *Celtic Festival*, Lorient. **Sep 9** *Médoc Marathon*. **Sep 16-17** *"Bol d'Or" Motorcycle Endurance Race*, Le Castellet. **Oct 1** *Grand Prix de l'Arc de Triomphe* (horseraces), Paris. **Oct 7-15** *Fair of Contemporary Art*, Espace Tour Eiffel, Paris. **Oct 28-29** *Gastronomic Fair*, Romorantin. **Nov** *Gastronomic Fair*, Dijon. **Nov 15** *Release of Beaujolais Nouveau*. **Dec 1-11** *International Boat Show*, Paris.

Note [*]: Throughout the year there are several motor racing events in Le Mans, as well as trade fairs in various parts of the country; there are also many local festivals and fairs (which usually preserve their original agricultural purpose).

SOCIAL CONVENTIONS: Handshaking and, more familiarly, kissing both cheeks, are the usual form of greeting. The form of personal address is simply *Monsieur* or *Madame* without a surname and it may take time to get to first-name terms. At more formal dinners it is the most important guest or host who gives the signal to start eating. Meal times are often a long, leisurely experience. Casual wear is common but the French are renowned for their stylish sportswear and dress sense. Social functions, some clubs, casinos and exclusive restaurants warrant more formal attire. Evening wear is normally specified where required. Topless sunbathing is tolerated on most beaches but naturism is restricted to certain beaches – local tourist offices will advise where these are. Smoking is prohibited on public transport and in cinemas and theatres. Tobacconists display a red sign in the form of a double cone, usually located in cafés. A limited choice of brands can be found in restaurants and bars. **Tipping:** 12-15% service charge is normally added to the bill in hotels, restaurants and bars, but it is customary to leave small change with the payment; more if the service has been exceptional. Other services such as washroom attendants, beauticians, hairdressers and cinema ushers expect tips. Taxi drivers expect 10-15% of the meter fare.

BUSINESS PROFILE

ECONOMY: France has the fourth strongest capitalist economy in the world, after the USA, Japan and Germany. It has a wide industrial and commercial base, covering everything from agriculture to light and heavy industrial concerns, the most advanced technology and a burgeoning service sector. France is Western Europe's leading agricultural nation with over half of the country's land area devoted to farming. Wheat is the most important crop; maize, sugar beet and barley are also produced in large quantities. The country is

self-sufficient in these (which are produced in sufficient surplus for major exports) and the majority of other common crops. The livestock industry is also expanding rapidly. As is well known, France is one of the world's leading wine producers. Despite criticism from some quarters (not least Britain) that French agriculture is inefficient, the sector has regularly turned in good profit margins and a sound export performance. With the emergence of newly industrialised countries, especially the 'Tiger economies' of the Pacific basin, France's share of the world market for industrial products has declined in recent years. Nonetheless, French companies retain a strong presence in many industries, particularly steel, motor vehicles, aircraft, mechanical and electrical engineering, textiles, chemicals and food-processing. In advanced industrial sectors, France has a nuclear power industry sufficiently large to meet over half of the country's energy requirements (coal mining, once important, is in terminal decline), and is a world leader in computing and telecommunications. Service industries have not developed as far as in Britain with the exception of tourism, which has long been a major foreign currency earner, although the financial services industry has undergone rapid growth in the last few years. The Government has initiated a programme of privatisation to slim down the country's large industrial public sector. Oil and finance companies (including some of the banks nationalised in the 1980s) have been sold off, although the programme as a whole is not as aggressive or widespread as in Britain. France was a founder member of the European Community and has benefited greatly from its participation.

BUSINESS: Business people should wear conservative clothes. Prior appointments are expected and the use of calling cards usual. While a knowledge of French is a distinct advantage in business dealings, it is considered impolite to start a conversation in French and then have to revert to English. Business meetings tend to be formal and business decisions are only taken after lengthy discussion with many facts and figures to back up sales presentation. Business entertaining is usually in restaurants. Avoid mid-July to mid-September for business visits. **Office hours:** Generally 0900-1200 and 1400-1800 Monday to Friday.

COMMERCIAL INFORMATION: The following organisations can offer advice: Chambre de Commerce et d'Industrie de Paris, 27 avenue de Friedland, 75382 Paris, Cedex 08. Tel: (1) 42 89 70 00. Fax: (1) 42 89 78 68. Telex: 650100l; *or*
Franco-British Chamber of Commerce, 110 rue de Longchamps, 75016 Paris. Tel: (1) 44 05 32 88. Fax: (1) 44 05 32 99; *or*
Direction Générale des Douanes et Droits Indirects, Division des Autorisations Commerciales (Importations), 8 rue de la Tour des Dames, 75009 Paris. Tel: (1) 44 63 25 25. Fax: (1) 44 63 27 60.

CONFERENCES/CONVENTIONS: Paris is the world's leading conference city (in 1986 it hosted 358 conventions), with the total amount of seating available (over 100,000 seats) exceeding that of any rival city. Also in demand are the Riviera towns of Nice and Cannes (the Acropolis Centre in Nice being the largest single venue in Europe); other centres are Lyon, Strasbourg and Marseille. The Business Travel Club (CFTAR) is a government-sponsored association of cities, departments, hotels, convention centres and other organisations interested in providing meeting facilities and incentives; it has over 80 members. Enquiries should be made through the French Government Tourist Office, which in several cities has a special department for business travel; these include London, Frankfurt/M, Düsseldorf, Milan, Madrid and Chicago. The following organisations can offer advice: Maison de la France, Conference and Incentive Department, 178 Piccadilly, London W1V 0AL. Tel: (0171) 629 1272. Fax: (0171) 493 6594; *or* Representation Plus, 375 Upper Richmond Road West, London SW14 7NX. Tel: (0181) 392 1580. Fax: (0181) 392 1318.

CLIMATE

A temperate climate in the north; northeastern areas have a more continental climate with warm summers and colder winters. Rainfall is distributed throughout the year with some snow likely in winter. The Jura Mountains have an alpine climate. Lorraine, sheltered by bordering hills, has a relatively mild climate.
Mediterranean climate in the south; mountains are cooler with some snow in winter.
The Atlantic influences the climate of the western coastal areas from the Loire to the Basque region; the weather is temperate and relatively mild with rainfall distributed throughout the year. Summers can be very hot and sunny. Inland areas are also mild and the French slopes of the

Pyrénées are reputed for their sunshine record. Mediterranean climate exists on the Riviera, Provence and Roussillon. Weather in the French Alps is variable. Continental weather is present in Auvergne, Burgundy and Rhône Valley. Very strong winds (such as the *Mistral*) can occur throughout the entire region.
Required clothing: European, according to season.

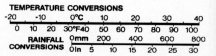

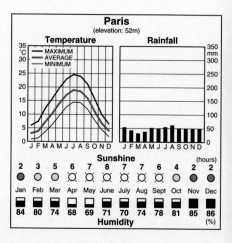

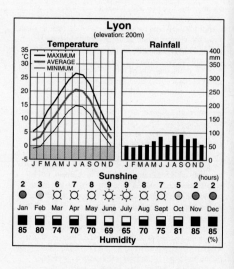

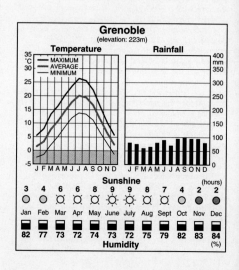

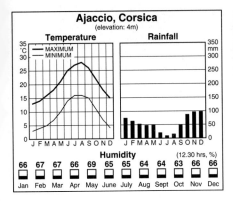

Ajaccio, Corsica
(elevation: 4m)

Temperature | **Rainfall**

MAXIMUM / MINIMUM

Humidity (12.30 hrs, %)

	Jan	Feb	Mar	Apr	May	June	July	Aug	Sept	Oct	Nov	Dec
	66	67	67	66	69	65	65	64	64	63	66	66

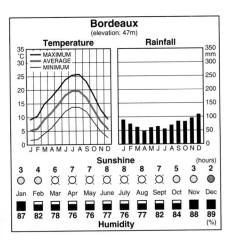

Bordeaux
(elevation: 47m)

Temperature | **Rainfall**

MAXIMUM / AVERAGE / MINIMUM

Sunshine (hours)

	Jan	Feb	Mar	Apr	May	June	July	Aug	Sept	Oct	Nov	Dec
Sunshine	3	4	6	7	8	8	8	8	7	5	3	2
Humidity	87	82	78	76	76	77	76	77	82	84	88	89

Humidity (%)

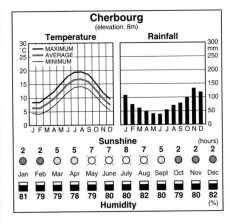

Cherbourg
(elevation: 8m)

Temperature | **Rainfall**

MAXIMUM / AVERAGE / MINIMUM

Sunshine (hours)

	Jan	Feb	Mar	Apr	May	June	July	Aug	Sept	Oct	Nov	Dec
Sunshine	2	2	5	5	7	7	7	8	7	5	2	2
Humidity	81	79	79	78	79	80	80	82	80	79	80	82

Humidity (%)

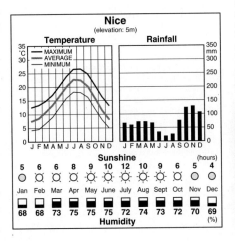

Nice
(elevation: 5m)

Temperature | **Rainfall**

MAXIMUM / AVERAGE / MINIMUM

Sunshine (hours)

	Jan	Feb	Mar	Apr	May	June	July	Aug	Sept	Oct	Nov	Dec
Sunshine	5	6	6	8	9	10	12	10	9	6	5	4
Humidity	68	68	73	75	75	75	72	74	73	72	70	69

Humidity (%)

French Guiana

200km
100mls

ATLANTIC OCEAN

SURINAME

FRENCH GUIANA

BRAZIL

St Laurent · Sinnamary · Iles du Salut : Devil's I. · **Kourou** · Délices · **CAYENNE** · Kaw · Régina · Ouaqui · Bienvenue · Maroni · Itani · Mana · Oyapock

Mitaraca 690m · Serra Tumucumaque

DAB-M90

☐ *international airport*

Location: South America, northeast coast.

Agence Régionale du Tourisme de la Guyane
BP 801, 12 rue de Lalouette, 97338 Cayenne, French Guiana
Tel: 300 900. Fax: 309 315. Telex: 910356.
French Consulate General (Visa Section)
PO Box 57, 6A Cromwell Place, London SW7 2EW
Tel: (0171) 838 2050. Information Service: (0898) 200 289 (calls are charged at the higher rate of 39p/49p per minute). Fax: (0171) 838 2046. Telex: 924153. Opening hours: 0900-1130 (and 1600-1630 for visa collection only) Monday to Friday (except French and British national holidays).
The French Embassies in Washington, DC and Ottawa deal with enquiries relating to French Guiana (see the entry on *France* earlier in the book).
British Honorary Consulate
16 avenue Président Monnerville, Cayenne, French Guiana
Tel: 311 034 *or* 304 242. Fax: 304 094. Telex: NCH 910365 FG.

AREA: 91,000 sq km (35,135 sq miles).
POPULATION: 114,808 (1990).
POPULATION DENSITY: 0.8 per sq km.
CAPITAL: Cayenne. **Population:** 41,667 (1990).
GEOGRAPHY: French Guiana is situated on the northeast coast of South America and is bordered by Brazil to the south and the east and by Suriname to the west. The southern Serra Tumucumaque Mountains are part of the eastern frontier, whilst the rest is formed by the River Oyapock. Suriname is to the west along the rivers Maroni-Itani and to the north is the Atlantic coastline. Along the coast runs a belt of flat marshy land behind which the land rises to higher slopes and plains or savannah. The interior is comprised of equatorial jungle. Off the rugged coast lie the Iles du Salut and Devil's Island. Cayenne, the capital and chief port, is on the island of the same name at the mouth of the Cayenne River.

Timatic

Health
GALILEO/WORLDSPAN: **TI-DFT/CAY/HE**
SABRE: **TIDFT/CAY/HE**

Visa
GALILEO/WORLDSPAN: **TI-DFT/CAY/VI**
SABRE: **TIDFT/CAY/VI**

For more information on Timatic codes refer to Contents.

LANGUAGE: The official language is French, though most of the population speak a Creole *patois*. English is widely spoken.
RELIGION: Roman Catholic.
TIME: GMT - 3.
ELECTRICITY: 220/127 volts AC, 50Hz.
COMMUNICATIONS: Telephone: IDD available. Country code: 594. Outgoing international code: 19 (16 for France). **Fax:** Facilities are widely available. **Telex:** There are facilities in Cayenne. **Press:** The daily newspapers include *France Guyane* and *La Presse de Guyane*. There are no English-language newspapers.
BBC World Service and Voice of America frequencies: From time to time these change. See the section *How to Use this Book* for more information.
BBC:

MHz	17.84	9.915	7.325	5.975

Voice of America:

MHz	15.21	11.74	9.815	6.030

PASSPORT/VISA

The regulations for tourist and Business visas are the same as for France (see the *Passport/Visa* section for France above). Visitors should specify that they wish to visit French Guiana when they make their application.

MONEY

Currency: French Franc (FFr) = 100 centimes. Banknotes are in denominations of FFr500, 200, 100, 50 and 20. Coins are in denominations of FFr10, 5, 2 and 1, and 50, 20, 10 and 5 centimes.
Currency exchange: The *Banque de la Guyane* will exchange money (not Saturday). There are no exchange facilities at the airport. There are two currency exchange offices in Cayenne (*Guyane Changes* and *Change Caraïbes*).
Credit cards: Visa, Eurocard, Mastercard and *Carte Bleue* are accepted. At present, American Express is not. Check with your credit card company for details of merchant acceptability and other services which may be available.
Travellers cheques: These are only accepted in a few places in Cayenne and Kourou.
Currency exchange rates: As for France.
Currency restrictions: As for France.
Banking hours: 0745-1130 and 1500-1700 Monday to Friday.

DUTY FREE

As for France.

PUBLIC HOLIDAYS

Jan 1 '95 New Year's Day. **Feb 22-28** Lenten Carnival. **Apr 14-17** Easter. **May 1** Labour Day. **May 25** Ascension Day. **Jun 5** Whit Monday. **Jul 14** National Day. **Nov 11** Armistice Day. **Dec 25** Christmas Day. **Jan 1 '96** New Year's Day. **Feb/Mar** Lenten Carnival. **Apr 5-8** Easter.

HEALTH

Regulations and requirements may be subject to change at short notice, and you are advised to contact your doctor well in advance of your intended date of departure. Any numbers in the chart refer to the footnotes below.

	Special Precautions?	Certificate Required?
Yellow Fever	Yes	1
Cholera	No	No
Typhoid & Polio	Yes	-
Malaria	2	-
Food & Drink	3	-

[1]: A yellow fever vaccination certificate is required from travellers over one year of age coming from all countries.
[2]: Malaria risk, predominantly in the malignant *falciparum* form, exists all year throughout French Guiana. Resistance to chloroquine has been reported.
[3]: Mains water is normally heavily chlorinated, and whilst relatively safe, may cause mild abdominal upsets. Bottled water is available and is advised for the first few weeks of the stay. Drinking water outside main cities and towns is likely to be contaminated and sterilisation is considered essential. Milk is unpasteurised and should be boiled. Powdered or tinned milk is available and is

advised, but make sure that it is reconstituted with pure water. Avoid dairy products which are likely to have been made from unboiled milk. Local meat, poultry, seafood, fruit and vegetables are generally considered safe to eat.

Rabies is present. For those at high risk, vaccination before arrival should be considered. If you are bitten abroad, seek medical advice without delay. For more information, consult the *Health* section at the back of the book.

Health care: There are medical facilities in Cayenne but very little elsewhere. Full health insurance is essential.

TRAVEL - International

AIR: French Guiana's national airline is *Air Guyane*, though it does only offer internal services.
Approximate flight time: From London to Cayenne is 11 hours 30 minutes.
International airport: *Cayenne (CAY)* (Rochambeau), 17km (11 miles) southwest of the city. Taxis are available to the city, or hotel. Limited facilities at the airport include currency exchange and car rental.
SEA: Cayenne is a regular port of call for ships of *Compagnie Générale Maritime* (France).
ROAD: A road runs along the coast from Guyana through Suriname to French Guiana, but it is impassable during the rainy season. There is an all-weather road connecting Cayenne with St Laurent. It is possible to drive from Cayenne to Paramaibo, but given the risk of theft, it is safer to leave one's car at St Laurent and take public transport (minibus) to Paramaibo. The Cayenne district is served by a good road system.

TRAVEL - Internal

AIR: *Air Guyane* serves the interior of the country from Cayenne. Bookings may only be made at the *Air Guyane Voyages* agency.
SEA/RIVER: There are numerous coastal and river transport services. Contact local authorities for information.
ROAD: There is a road along the coast from Cayenne to Kourou and beyond. Traffic drives on the right. **Bus:** Services operate along the coast. **Taxi:** Available in Cayenne. **Car hire:** Available at the airport or Cayenne.
Documentation: An International Driving Permit is recommended, although it is not legally required.

ACCOMMODATION

HOTELS: Since French Guiana was chosen as a site for European space development, a number of well-appointed air-conditioned hotels have been built. Cayenne, Kourou and St Laurent du Maroni all offer adequate, comfortable accommodation, but prices are higher than in Guyana or Suriname. Guest-houses and *gîtes* (cottages) are cheaper alternatives.
CAMPING/CARAVANNING: Only inland camping is available, sleeping on hammocks strung from the walls of a *carbet* (a jungle version of a shack).

RESORTS & EXCURSIONS

Cayenne: The capital and chief port. Points of interest include the Jesuit-built residence of the Prefect in the *Place de Grenoble,* the *Canal Laussat* (built in 1777), and the *Botanical Gardens.* There are also bathing beaches, the best of which is *Montjoly.*
Kourou: The main *French Space Centre* was built here which makes Kourou something of a European enclave. There are several restaurants and two good hotels. Tourist attractions include bathing, fishing and the *Sporting and Aero Club.*
Iles du Salut: These islands include the notorious *Devil's Island* where political prisoners were held. There is a hotel (an ex-mess hall for the prison warders) on **Ile Royale.**
Haut-Maroni and Haut-Oyapoc: Visits to Amerindian villages in these areas are restricted; permission must be obtained from the Préfecture in **Cayenne** before arrival in the country.

SOCIAL PROFILE

FOOD & DRINK: There is a fairly good selection of restaurants and hotel dining rooms offering a number of different cuisines. The majority of them are in Cayenne although French and Continental, Vietnamese, Chinese, Creole and Indonesian restaurants can be found elsewhere.

NIGHTLIFE: There are nightclubs in Cayenne, Kourou and St Laurent du Maroni. Cayenne also has three cinemas featuring French-language films. A cinema can also be found in Kourou.
SHOPPING: Within the past few years a great many new boutiques have opened offering a wide range of merchandise. Good buys are basketry, hammocks, pottery, wood sculpture and gold jewellery.
SPORT: Fishing: Sea-fishing is good from rocks; canoes are also available. **Swimming:** Safe around Ile de Cayenne and some hotels have pools. **Water-skiing:** Facilities are available in Kourou. **Tennis:** There are courts in Cayenne and some hotels have courts.
Pioneering/hiking: There are river trips and treks into the interior and jungle shelters are available for overnight stops. A special permit is necessary from the Préfecture in Cayenne.
SOCIAL CONVENTIONS: Conservative casual wear is suitable almost everywhere. On beaches, modest beachwear is preferred. Normal social courtesies should be adhered to. **Tipping:** In hotels and restaurants a 10% tip is usual. Taxi drivers are not tipped.

BUSINESS PROFILE

ECONOMY: French Guiana's economy is heavily dependent on that of France itself, especially for imports of food and manufactured goods. It also receives large injections of development aid. Most of the workforce is engaged in the agricultural sector, principally forestry and fisheries. The country has valuable reserves of timber, but these have yet to be exploited fully because of lack of investment and poor infrastructure, especially roads. The development of mineral resources, which are thought to be present in commercially significant quantities, suffers from the same considerations. Tourism is similarly affected but has shown steady growth. One notable asset, acquired by virtue of French Guiana's geographical position near the Equator, is the European Space Agency satellite launch facility at Kourou which has brought some economic benefits to the country. French Guiana has a vast trade imbalance, with imports exceeding exports by a factor of 12. Other than France (which controls 60% of the export business to French Guiana), Trinidad & Tobago, the USA, Germany and Japan are the country's major trading partners. Trade with the UK is insignificant.
BUSINESS: Lightweight suits are required. English will be understood by practically everyone, although a working knowledge of French may be of assistance. The best time to visit is August to November. **Office hours:** 0800-1300 and 1500-1800 Monday to Friday.
COMMERCIAL INFORMATION: The following organisation can offer advice: Chambre de Commerce de la Guyane, BP 49, 97321 Cayenne. Tel: 303 000. Fax: 310 211. Telex: 910537.

CLIMATE

Tropical. Dry season is August to December; rainy season is January to June. May and June are marked by particularly heavy rainfall. Hot all year round, with cooler nights.
Required clothing: Tropical lightweights and rainwear.

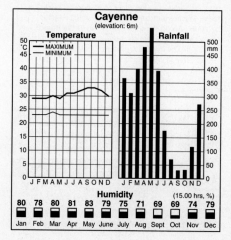

Cayenne
(elevation: 6m)

	Temperature		Rainfall	
	MAXIMUM			
	MINIMUM			

Humidity (15.00 hrs, %)

Jan	Feb	Mar	Apr	May	June	July	Aug	Sept	Oct	Nov	Dec
80	78	80	81	83	79	75	71	69	69	74	79

Note: Scattered throughout the world are several French *Départements, territoires d'outre-mer* and *Collectivités Territoriales.* Most of these have their own sections in the *World Travel Guide,* but basic information is given for the others. Further information on all of the Possessions can be obtained from the French embassies listed at the top of the *France* entry earlier in this book, and from:
Maison de la France (Tourist Information Agency)
8 avenue de l'Opéra, 75001 Paris, France
Tel: (1) 42 96 10 23. Fax: (1) 42 86 08 94. Telex: 214260.
French Government Tourist Office
178 Piccadilly, London W1V 0AL
Tel: (0891) 244 123 (France Information Line; calls are charged at the higher rate of 39/49p per minute). Fax: (0171) 493 6594. Telex: 21902. Opening hours 0930-1300 and 1430-1700 Monday to Friday.
French Government Tourist Office
444 Madison Avenue, New York, NY 10020-2451
Tel: (212) 838 7800. Information Line: (1 900) 990 0040 (calls are charged at 50¢ per minute). Fax: (212) 838 7855.
French Government Tourist Office
Suite 490, 1981 McGill College, Montréal, Québec H3A 2W9
Tel: (514) 288 4264. Fax: (514) 845 4868.
Ministry of Overseas Departments and Territories
27 rue Oudinot, 75358 Paris 08 SP, France
Tel: (1) 47 83 01 23. Fax: (1) 47 06 19 27.

French Overseas Deparments

There are four *départements d'outre-mer,* each one an integral part of the French Republic. Despite the greater autonomy achieved with the formation of their own individual Regional Councils in 1974, each French Overseas Department still returns elected representatives to the Senate and National Assembly in Paris, as well as to the European Parliament in Strasbourg.

GUADELOUPE and **MARTINIQUE** are in the Caribbean (also including the islands of St Martin and St Barthélemy); see the separately listed entries for these further on in this book.

FRENCH GUIANA is on the northwest coast of South America; see the separately listed entry above.

REUNION is in the Indian Ocean; see the separately listed entry further on in this book.

French Overseas Territories

Like the French Overseas Departments above, the four *territoires d'outre-mer* are integral parts of the French Republic. However, each one is administered by an appointed representative of the French government, and the level of autonomy is restricted.

TAHITI is in the central South Pacific; see the separately listed entry below.

FRENCH SOUTHERN & ANTARCTIC TERRITORIES consist of a thin slice of the Antarctic mainland and a few small islands. The total area is 439,797 sq km (169,805 sq miles). The territory is used mainly for scientific purposes, although fishing in the area is important.

NEW CALEDONIA is in the South Pacific, east of Australia; see the separately listed entry further on in this book.

WALLIS AND FUTUNA ISLANDS
Location: Southwest Pacific between Fiji, Tuvalu and Western Samoa. **Area:** 274 sq km (106 sq miles). **Population:** 13,705 (1990). **Population Density:** 50 per sq km. **Capital:** Mata-Utu (Wallis Island). **Population:**

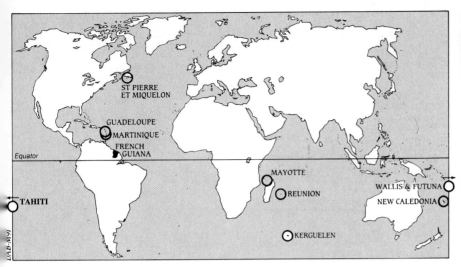

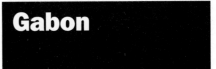

Gabon

☐ *international airport*

815 (1983). **Religion:** Roman Catholic. **Time:** GMT +
12. **Health:** Vaccinations against typhoid, tetanus and
paratyphoid are advised. There is a hospital in the capital.
Travel: The main airport (Hihifo) is on Wallis Island,
5km (3 miles) from Mata-Utu. Approximate flight time
from London is 29 hours. There is also an airport in
Futuna in Alo in the southeastern part of the island. *Air
Calédonie (New Caledonia)* is the main airline serving
the Islands. There is a weekly flight from Wallis Island to
Nouméa (New Caledonia), and a thrice-weekly service
from Wallis to Futuna. Boat services operate from New
Caledonia and between the islands. Minibus services
operate on Futuna and car hire is available. However, the
only surfaced roads are in Mata-Utu. **Accommodation:**
There are a small number of hotels on the islands; contact
the **French Government Tourist Office** (for address,
see top of entry) for details of booking accommodation
and other information.

Overseas Collectivités Territoriales

The administration of the two *collectivités territoriales*
shares aspects of both the above categories: an integral
part of the French Republic, they are administered by an
appointed representative of the French government, and
yet at the same time they return elected representatives to
the Senate and National Assembly in Paris, as well as to
the European Parliament in Strasbourg.

MAYOTTE is part of the Comoros archipelago off the
northwest corner of Madagascar. The island is claimed by
the Federal Republic of the Comoros (which unilaterally
declared independence from France in 1975), although
residents have maintained that they wish to retain their
close links with France. Various attempts have been made
by international organisations, including the United
Nations, to resolve the situation, although both the
islanders and the French government are in favour of
maintaining Mayotte's special status. An airport and a
deep-water port are being built, aided by French funding,
with the intention of developing a tourist industry.
Area: 374 sq km (144 sq miles). **Population:** 94,410
(1991). **Capital:** Dzaoudzi. **Population:** 5865 (1985).
Health: There are no vaccination requirements for any
international traveller, although precautions against
malaria are advised. Only bottled water should be drunk.
Travel: The main airport is *Pamandzi* on the island of the
same name; services are available from Paris, the Comoros
Islands and Réunion. There is a regular boat service to
Mayotte, and there are approximately 110km (70 miles) of
tarred roads on the island. **Accommodation:** There are a
small number of hotels on the islands; contact the **French
Government Tourist Office** for details of booking
accommodation, and for other information contact the
Comité Territorial du Tourisme de Mayotte, BP 169,
Mamoudzou, 97600 Mayotte. Tel: 610 909. Fax: 610 346.

ST PIERRE ET MIQUELON comprise a group of small
islands which lie off the southern coast of Newfoundland.
Previously enjoying Departmental status, the islands have
since 1955 been a part of the *collectivités territoriales*,
partly as a result of a dispute with Canada over fishing and
mineral rights in the area.
Area: 242 sq km (93 sq miles). **Population:** 6392 (1990).
Capital: St Pierre. **Population:** 5683 (1990); almost all of
the population live in the capital or elsewhere on the small

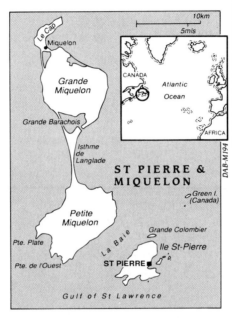

island of the same name. **Time:** GMT -3 (GMT -2 from
first Sunday in April to Saturday before last Sunday in
October). **Country code:** 508. **Outgoing international
code:** 19. **Health:** No special precautions are required.
Travel: The islands' airport is *St Pierre* which has
international flights from Paris via Montréal or Halifax
(stopovers are generally not permitted). The main airlines
serving St Pierre are *Air Saint Pierre* and *Atlantic Airways*.
Boat services operate between the islands and to Canada.
Buses, taxis and hired cars are available.
Accommodation: Hotels and guest-houses are available
on the island; for details of booking accommodation and
other information, contact the **Agence Régionale du
Tourisme**, BP 4274, rue du 11 Novembre, 97500 St
Pierre. Tel: 412 222. Fax: 413 355. Telex: 914437.
Information can also be obtained from the **French
Government Tourist Office**; for address, see top of entry.

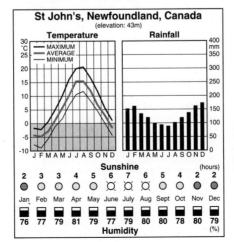

Location: West Coast of Central Africa.

Office National Gabonais du Tourisme
PO Box 161, Libreville, Gabon
Tel: 722 182.
Embassy of the Gabonese Republic
27 Elvaston Place, London SW7 5NL
Tel: (0171) 823 9986. Fax: (0171) 584 0047. Telex:
919418. Opening hours: 0900-1500 Monday to Friday.
British diplomatic and commercial representation:
The British Embassy in Gabon closed in July 1991.
*The West African Department of the Foreign &
Commonwealth Office is currently handling consular and
commercial enquiries for Gabon.*
Tel: (0171) 270 2516. Fax: (0171) 270 2946.
Embassy of the Gabonese Republic
2034, 20th Street, NW, Washington, DC 20009
Tel: (202) 797 1000. Fax: (202) 332 0668.
Embassy of the United States of America
BP 4000, boulevard de la Mer, Libreville, Gabon
Tel: 762 003/4 *or* 743 492. Fax: 745 507. Telex: 5250.
Embassy of the Gabonese Republic
BP 368, 4 Range Road, Ottawa, Ontario K1N 8J5
Tel: (613) 232 5301 *or* 232 5302. Fax: (613) 232 6916.
Telex: 053-4295.
Canadian Embassy
PO Box 4037, Libreville, Gabon
Tel: 743 464 *or* 743 465. Fax: 743 466. Telex: 5527 (a/b
DOMCAN GO) .

AREA: 267,667 sq km (103,347 sq miles).
POPULATION: 1,206,000 (1985 estimate).
POPULATION DENSITY: 4.5 per sq km.
CAPITAL: Libreville. **Population:** 352,000 (1988).

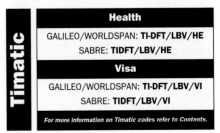

Health	
GALILEO/WORLDSPAN: **TI-DFT**/LBV/HE	
SABRE: **TIDFT**/LBV/HE	
Visa	
GALILEO/WORLDSPAN: **TI-DFT**/LBV/VI	
SABRE: **TIDFT**/LBV/VI	

For more information on Timatic codes refer to Contents.

St John's, Newfoundland, Canada
(elevation: 43m)

Temperature — MAXIMUM, AVERAGE, MINIMUM
Rainfall

Sunshine (hours): 2 3 3 4 5 6 7 6 5 4 2 2
Jan Feb Mar Apr May June July Aug Sept Oct Nov Dec

Humidity (%): 76 77 79 81 79 77 79 80 80 78 80 79

GEOGRAPHY: Gabon is bordered to the west by the Atlantic Ocean, to the north by Equatorial Guinea and Cameroon, and to the east and south by the Congo Republic. The 800km-long (500-mile) sandy coastal strip is a series of palm-fringed bays, lagoons and estuaries. The lush tropical vegetation (which covers about 82% of the interior) gives way in parts to the savannah. There are many rivers and they remain the main communication routes along which settlements have grown. Of the 40 or so Bantu tribes, the largest are the Fang, Eshira, Mbele and Okande. Only a small percentage of native Gabonese live in the towns, as the population is concentrated in the coastal areas and the villages along the banks of the many rivers, following a more traditional rural style of life.

LANGUAGE: The official language is French. The principle African language is Fang. Eshira is spoken by a tenth of the population. Bantu dialects spoken include Bapounou and Miene.

RELIGION: About 75% Christian, the remainder are Muslim and animist religions.

TIME: GMT + 1.

ELECTRICITY: 220 volts AC, 50Hz.

COMMUNICATIONS: Telephone: IDD is available. Country code: 241. No area codes required. Outgoing international code: 00. **Telex:** Facilities are available at the main post office in Libreville and major hotels. **Post:** Airmail from Gabon takes at least a week to Western Europe. Urgent letters should be sent by special delivery to ensure their safe arrival. Post office opening hours are 0800-1200 and 1430-1800 Monday to Friday. **Press:** There are two dailies, the *Gabon-Matin* and *L'Union*. There are several periodicals, published mainly on the topics of the Government and the economy. Official bulletins are published in French, and have limited circulations.

BBC World Service and Voice of America frequencies: From time to time these change. See the section *How to Use this Book* for more information.

BBC				
MHz	21.66	17.88	15.40	9.600
Voice of America:				
MHz	21.49	15.60	9.525	6.035

PASSPORT/VISA

Regulations and requirements may be subject to change at short notice, and you are advised to contact the appropriate diplomatic or consular authority before finalising travel arrangements. Details of these may be found at the head of this country's entry. Any numbers in the chart refer to the footnotes below.

	Passport Required?	Visa Required?	Return Ticket Required?
Full British	Yes	Yes	Yes
BVP	Not valid	-	-
Australian	Yes	Yes	Yes
Canadian	Yes	Yes	Yes
USA	Yes	Yes	Yes
Other EU (As of 31/12/94)	Yes	Yes	Yes
Japanese	Yes	Yes	Yes

Restricted entry: Nationals of Angola, Cape Verde, Cuba, Ghana, Guinea-Bissau, Haiti and Israel will be refused admission unless transiting by the same aircraft.

PASSPORTS: Valid passport required by all except nationals of Cameroon, Central African Republic, Chad, Congo and Equatorial Guinea, who must have a return ticket and national ID card or passport expired for less than 5 years.

British Visitors Passport: Not accepted.

VISAS: Required by all except nationals of Cameroon, Central African Republic, Chad, Congo, Côte d'Ivoire, Senegal and Togo.

Types of visa: Visitors and Transit. Cost: £20.

Validity: *Visitors:* 3 months. *Transit:* Not required by those who continue their journey to a third country by the same or connecting aircraft within 24 hours. Tickets must be held with reserved seats and other documents for their onward journey.

Application to: Consulate (or Consular section at Embassy). For addresses, see top of entry.

Application requirements: *Business visa:* Letter from company. *Tourist visa:* (a) 3 passport-size photographs. (b) 3 forms. (c) Fee.

Working days required: 2-4 weeks. Postal applications must include a registered stamped, self-addressed envelope.

MONEY

Currency: CFA Franc (CFA Fr) = 100 centimes. Notes occur in denominations of CFA Fr10,000, 5000, 1000 and 500 (the smallest of these is not negotiable in the UK). Coins are in denominations of CFA Fr500, 100, 50, 25, 10, 5, 2 and 1.

Note: At the beginning of 1994, the CFA Franc was devalued against the French Franc.

Currency exchange: Gabon is part of the French Monetary Area and the CFA Franc is legal tender in all other former French Equatorial African countries (Chad, Congo, Central African Republic, Cameroon and Equatorial Guinea).

Credit cards: Limited use of Visa, American Express and Access/Mastercard. Diners Club is more widely accepted; however, in general, the use of credit cards in Gabon remains relatively limited. Check with your credit card company for merchant acceptability and other facilities which may be available.

Travellers cheques: French Franc cheques are more readily converted than those in Sterling.

Exchange rate indicators: The following figures are included as a guide to the movements of the CFA Franc against Sterling and the US Dollar:

Date:	Oct '92	Sep '93	Jan '94	Jan '95
£1.00=	413.75	433.87	436.78	834.94
$1.00=	260.71	284.14	295.22	533.67

Currency restrictions: Import of foreign and local currency is unlimited, subject to declaration. Export of local currency is limited to CFA Fr200,000. Export of foreign currency is limited to the amount declared on arrival.

Banking hours: 0730-1130 and 1430-1630 Monday to Friday.

DUTY FREE

The following goods may be imported into Gabon by persons of 17 and over without incurring customs duty: *200 cigarettes or 50 cigars or 250g of tobacco (females – cigarettes only); 2 litres of alcoholic beverage; 50g of perfume; gifts up to CFA Fr5000.*

Controlled items: Guns and ammunition require a police permit.

PUBLIC HOLIDAYS

Jan 1 '95 New Year's Day. **Mar 3** Eid al-Fitr (End of Ramadan). **Mar 12** Renovation Day. **Apr 17** Easter Monday. **May 1** Labour Day. **May 10** Eid Al-Adha (Feast of the Sacrifice). **Jun 5** Whit Monday. **Aug 9** Mouloud (Prophet's Birthday). **Aug 17** Anniversary of Independence. **Nov 1** All Saints' Day. **Dec 25** Christmas Day. **Jan 1 '96** New Year's Day. **Feb 22** Eid al-Fitr (End of Ramadan). **Mar 12** Renovation Day. **Apr 8** Easter Monday. **Apr 29** Eid al-Adha (Feast of the Sacrifice).

Note: Muslim festivals are timed according to local sightings of various phases of the Moon and the dates given above are approximations. During the lunar month of Ramadan that precedes Eid al-Fitr, Muslims fast during the day and feast at night and normal business patterns may be interrupted. Some disruption may continue into Eid al-Fitr itself. Eid al-Fitr and Eid al-Adha may last anything from two to ten days, depending on the region. For more information see the section *World of Islam* at the back of the book.

HEALTH

Regulations and requirements may be subject to change at short notice, and you are advised to contact your doctor well in advance of your intended date of departure. Any numbers in the chart refer to the footnotes below.

	Special Precautions?	Certificate Required?
Yellow Fever	Yes	1
Cholera	Yes	2
Typhoid & Polio	Yes	-
Malaria	3	-
Food & Drink	4	-

[1]: A yellow fever vaccination certificate is required from all travellers over one year of age.

[2]: Following WHO guidelines issued in 1973, a cholera vaccination certificate is not a condition of entry to Gabon. However, cholera is a serious risk in this country and precautions are essential. Up-to-date advice should be sought before deciding whether these precautions should include vaccination as medical opinion is divided over its effectiveness. See the *Health* section at the back of the book.

[3]: Malaria risk, predominantly in the malignant *falciparum* form, exists all year throughout the country. Resistance to chloroquine has been reported.

[4]: All water should be regarded as potentially contaminated. Water used for drinking, brushing teeth or making ice should have first been boiled or otherwise sterilised. Milk is unpasteurised and should be boiled. Powdered or tinned milk is available and is advised, but make sure that it is reconstituted with pure water. Avoid dairy products which are likely to have been made from unboiled milk. Only eat well-cooked meat and fish, preferably served hot. Pork, salad and mayonnaise may carry increased risk. Vegetables should be cooked and fruit peeled.

Bilharzia (schistosomiasis) is present. Avoid swimming and paddling in fresh water. Swimming pools which are well-chlorinated and maintained are safe.

Rabies is present. For those at high risk, vaccination before arrival should be considered. If you are bitten abroad seek medical advice without delay. For more information consult the *Health* section at the back of the book.

Health care: Travellers in rural areas should take a first-aid kit with anti-tetanus and anti-venom serums. Medical facilities are limited. Full health insurance is essential.

TRAVEL - International

AIR: Gabon's national airline is *Air Gabon (GN)*.

Approximate flight time: From London to Libreville is 10 hours 30 minutes.

International airport: Libreville (LBV) is 12km (7 miles) north of the city (travel time – 10 minutes). Airport facilities include bureaux de change (0830-1130; 1430-1730), shops (0800-2400), tourist information (open during operational hours), car rental (*Avis, Europcar, Hertz* and *Eurafrique*), hotel reservation desk and duty-free shops. Taxis are available. There are also local airports at *Franceville* and *Port Gentil (POG)*.

TRAVEL - Internal

AIR: There are nearly 200 airstrips. *Air Gabon* is the domestic airline and operates regular flights from Libreville, Oyem, Mitzic and other cities.

SEA: There are ferries and river barges running for example from Lambaréné to Port Gentil and Libreville to Port Gentil.

RAIL: The *Trans-Gabon Railway* connects Libreville with Ndjole, Booué and Masuku (Franceville), with extensions under construction to Belinga in the north. Children under 4 years travel for free. Children aged fom 4 to 11 years pay half fare.

ROAD: Traffic drives on the right. There are nearly 5000km (3100 miles) of road, but only 500km (310 miles) are tarred. Most of the country consists of impenetrable rainforest and the roads are generally of a poor standard. Road travelling in the rainy season is inadvisable. There is no road connection between the second largest city of Port Gentil and Libreville, or any other part of the country. **Bus:** Inter-urban travel is mainly by minibus or pick-up truck. Daily minibus services run from Libreville to Lambaréné, Mouila, Oyem and Bitam (the last two usually involving night stops). Seats for these and other less frequent routes can be obtained from a broker, *Gabon Cars*, in Libreville. This is not, however, normally necessary for the main routes as seats will be readily available in the 'bus station' near the central market 0600-0800. There are also conventional buses on the Mouila route and other services out of Mouila. **Car hire:** Cars may be hired from main hotels and airports. **Documentation:** International Driving Permit is advised and international insurance is required.

URBAN: There are extensive shared taxis. There are bus services in Port Gentil and Masuku (Franceville), and shared taxis in other centres. Taxi rates vary.

ACCOMMODATION

HOTELS: There are five high-class hotels in Libreville and also first-class hotels in Port Gentil, Masuku (Franceville), Mouila, Lambaréné, Oyem, Koulamoutou, Makokou and Tchibanga but, like most of the accommodation in Gabon, they are expensive. Tourist facilities, including comfortable accommodation, are being expanded throughout the country, especially along the coast and in towns close to the National Parks. There are hotels in other major cities and towns. These hotels will accept most major credit cards. For further information, contact Direction Generale de l'Hôtellerie et du Contrôle des Hotels, PO Box 403, Libreville. Tel: 738 380.

CAMPING: Free but limited. Use with caution.

RESORTS & EXCURSIONS

The main cities in Gabon are **Libreville, Port Gentil, Lambaréné, Moanda, Oyem, Mouila** and **Franceville. Libreville** is a lively and charming capital, beside the ocean. Its white buildings contrast with the green of the nearby equatorial forest. Sights include the artcraft village and the *National Museum,* which contains some of the most beautiful woodcarvings in Africa, especially the indigenous Fang style of carving which influenced Picasso's figures and busts. You can also see the delightful *Peyrie Gardens,* in the heart of the city; the popular quarters of *Akebe* and *Nombakele,* the harbour, the *Cathedral of St Michel* and the *Mount Bouet Market.* There are city tours conducted in French.
Elsewhere: A route winds through a forest of giant trees from Libreville to **Cape Esterias,** where the rocks abound with sea urchins, oysters and lobsters. It is a good place to swim. It is possible to go to the *Kinguele Falls* on *M'Bei River* or to **Lambaréné,** the town made famous by Doctor Schweitzer. His hospital is open to visitors and a tour on *Evaro Lake* can be organised. Trips are available down the rapids of the **Okanda** region. Further south, the villages of **M'Bigou** and **Eteke** are famous for their local crafts and gold mines and, to the west, the enchanting **Mayumba** set between sea and lake. Eastwards, the region of **Bateke Plateau** comprises savannah and forest galleries, and tumultuous rivers spanned by liana bridges, such as the one at **Poubara.** Game and wildlife include forest elephants, buffaloes, sitatunga, river hogs, gorillas, panthers, crocodiles, monkeys and parrots. For the deep-sea fishermen, shark, barracuda, tarpon, scad, tuna and ray can all be caught. In the **Sette-Cama, Iguela** and **N'Dende** zones, hunters going on safari can hire guides experienced in tracking and approaching the game. For those armed only with camera and video-camera, there is the *Lope* reserve and two national parks, *Wonga-Wongue* and *Moukalaba.*

SOCIAL PROFILE

FOOD & DRINK: Most hotels and restaurants serve French and continental-style food and are expensive. Gabonese food is distinctive and delicious, but not always readily available, as many restaurants are Senegalese, Cameroonian and Congolese. **Drink:** Licensing hours are similar to those in France.
NIGHTLIFE: There are nightclubs in Libreville with music and bars. Food is often served, although this can be expensive. There are also casinos in the *Inter-Continental Hotel* and the *Meridien Rendama Hotel.*
SHOPPING: In Libreville there are two bustling markets at Akebe-Plaine, Nkembo and Mon-Bouet. Stone carvings can be bought on the outskirts of both, fashioned by a group of carvers who have adapted traditional skills for the tourist market. Crafts from local villages can also be bought from stalls in the streets or from the villagers themselves. African (Fang) mask carvings, figurines, clay pots and traditional musical instruments can also be bought. **Shopping hours:** 0800-1200 and 1500-1900 Monday to Saturday. Some shops close on Monday.
SPORT: Swimming: Although a few hotels have pools, the beaches on the Atlantic coast offer ideal bathing conditions. **Water-skiing:** Port Gentil at the mouth of the River Ogooue and Libreville have beaches with facilities for water-skiing and other **watersports.** Mayumba in the south and Cap Esterias, 35km (22 miles) from Libreville are popular watersports centres at weekends. **Skindiving:** Perroquet and Pointe Denis both offer good skindiving. **Tennis:** Courts available in Libreville and Port Gentil. **Safaris:** Trips can be made to the Okanda National Park and other parks in the savannah region, all of which are rich in wildlife. Details can be obtained from the Tourist Office in Gabon. **Fishing:** Many of the rivers offer excellent fishing; equipment can be hired at Port Gentil. Fish abound in Gabonese rivers and lakes, but the fishermen can find the largest variety along the coast and in the numerous lagoons located at the mouth of Ogooue.
SOCIAL CONVENTIONS: Dance, song, poetry and myths remain an important part of traditional Gabonese life. **Photography:** It is absolutely forbidden to photograph military installations. In general, permission to photograph anything should be requested first, to prevent misunderstandings. **Tipping:** Should be 10%-15% unless service is included in the bill.

BUSINESS PROFILE

ECONOMY: Oil reserves and mineral deposits have allowed Gabon to develop into one of Africa's most

successful economies. There is a small manufacturing base engaged in oil refining and the production of plywood, paints, varnishes and detergents, dry batteries, cement, cigarettes and textiles. Future growth in this sector is likely to be limited by a shortage of skilled labour, high costs and inadequate infrastructure. The main economic priority at present is agriculture; Gabon produces coffee, sugar cane, rubber and some crops. Efforts are under way to stimulate growth in these and other industries, notably fishing which is much under-exploited. The other sector with potential is the timber industry, since Gabon has considerable afforested areas. Gabon is a member of the Central African economic and customs union, UDEAC, and of the CFA Franc Zone. The country has a large balance of payments surplus, and oil contributes 80% of export earnings. The potential for future growth is considerable, although recent setbacks, principally falling raw material prices, have forced the Government to accept an IMF-financed Structural Adjustment Programme. A joint debt-relief programme has been arranged with neighbouring Cameroon and Congo. Manufactured goods, transport equipment and foodstuffs are the main imports. The country's main trading partners are in the industrialised West, with France the largest followed by the USA, Japan and Germany.
BUSINESS: Tropical suits are required. French is the principal language used in business circles. Translators and interpreters are available through the Embassy. Strong business ties remain with France despite competition from the USA and Japan. **Office hours:** 0730-1200 and 1430-1800 Monday to Friday.
COMMERCIAL INFORMATION: The following organisations can offer advice: Chambre de Commerce, d'Agriculture, d'Industrie et des Mines du Gabon, BP 2234, Libreville. Tel: 722 064. Fax: 746 477. Telex: 5554; *or*
Ministry of Commerce, Industry and Scientific Research, BP 3906, Libreville. Tel: 763 055. Telex: 5347.
CONFERENCES/CONVENTIONS: Further information can be obtained from the Comité National des Fêtes et Conferences (COMINAFC), PO Box 882, Libreville. Tel: 761 766.

CLIMATE

Equatorial with high humidity. The dry season is from mid-May to mid-September, and the main rainy season is from February to April/May.
Required clothing: Lightweight tropical, with raincoats advised during the rainy season.

TEMPERATURE CONVERSIONS

-20	-10	0°C	10	20	30	40

0	10	20	30°F40	50	60	70	80	90	100

RAINFALL CONVERSIONS

0mm	200		400		600		800

0In	5	10	15	20	25	30

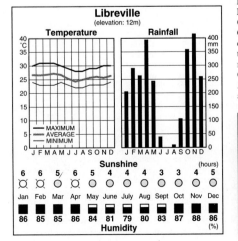
Libreville
(elevation: 12m)

The Gambia

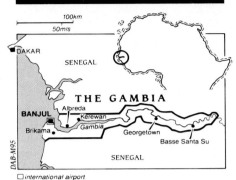

□ *international airport*

Location: West Africa.
Note: in July 1994, the democratic government of the Gambia was overthrown in a military coup. A counter-coup was attempted in November 1994 that resulted in significant loss of life among military personnel. The situation remains unsettled, particularly in Banjul, the capital, and Kombo Saint Mary Division, including Bakau, Fajara, Serrekunda, Yundum and areas near the airport. Army positions are best approached with caution, especially roadblocks and road checkpoints; uniformed soldiers and police officers expect their instructions to be heeded. It is advisable to avoid the traffic control point on Atlantic Raod, near Fajara barracks, Balau. In the event of civil disturbances of fighting among security forces, visitors may wish to seek shelter and remain indoors.
Source: US State Department – November 25, 1994.

Ministry of Information and Tourism
New Admin. Building, Banjul, The Gambia
Tel: 227 881/2. Telex: 2204.
High Commission of the Republic of The Gambia
57 Kensington Court, London W8 5DG
Tel: (0171) 937 6316/7/8. Fax: (0171) 937 9095. Telex: 911857. Opening hours: 0930-1700 Monday to Thursday; 0900-1300 Friday.
Gambia National Tourist Office
Address and fax as for High Commission.
Tel: (0171) 376 0093. Opening hours: 0930-1700 Monday to Thursday; 0900-1300 Friday.
British High Commission
PO Box 507, 48 Atlantic Road, Fajara, Banjul, The Gambia
Tel: 495 133/4 *or* 495 578. Fax: 496 134. Telex: 2211 (a/b UK REP GV).
Embassy of the Republic of The Gambia
Suite 1000, 1155 15th Street, NW, Washington, DC 20005
Tel: (202) 785 1399 *or* 785 1379 *or* 785 1425. Fax: (202) 785 1430.
Also deals with enquiries from Canada.
Embassy of the United States of America
PO Box 19, Kairaba Avenue, Fajara, Banjul, The Gambia
Tel: 392 856 *or* 392 858. Fax: 392 475.
The Canadian High Commission in Dakar deals with enquiries relating to The Gambia (see *Senegal* later in this book).

AREA: 11,295 sq km (4361 sq miles).
POPULATION: 800,000 (1988 estimate).
POPULATION DENSITY: 70.8 per sq km.
CAPITAL: Banjul. **Population:** 47,000 (1986).
GEOGRAPHY: The Gambia is situated on the Atlantic coast at the bulge of Africa. The country consists of a thin ribbon of land, at no point wider than 50km (30 miles), running east–west on both banks of the River Gambia. The Gambia is bounded to the west by the Atlantic Ocean and on all other sides by Senegal. It is also the smallest and westernmost African nation. The

Health	
GALILEO/WORLDSPAN: **TI-DFT/BJL/HE**	
SABRE: **TIDFT/BJL/HE**	

Visa	
GALILEO/WORLDSPAN: **TI-DFT/BJL/VI**	
SABRE: **TIDFT/BJL/VI**	

For more information on Timatic codes refer to Contents.

Timatic

country mainly consists of a low plateau which decreases in height as it nears the Atlantic coast. The plain is broken in a few places by low flat-topped hills and by the river and its tributaries. The area extending from MacCarthy Island, where Georgetown is located, to the eastern end of the country is enclosed by low rocky hills. The coast and river banks are backed mainly by mangrove swamps, while the lower part of the river has steep red ironstone banks which are covered with tropical forest and bamboo. Away from the river the landscape consists of wooded, park-like savannah, with large areas covered by a variety of trees such as mahogany, rosewood, oil palm and rubber. On the coast the river meets the Atlantic with impressive sand cliffs and 50km (30 miles) of broad, unspoiled beaches, palm-fringed and strewn with shells. These silver sand beaches are one of The Gambia's main attractions for visitors seeking an escape from the European winter.

LANGUAGE: The official language is English. Local languages are Mandinka, Fula, Wollof, Jola and Serahule.

RELIGION: Over 80% Muslim, with the remainder holding either Christian or Animist beliefs.

TIME: GMT.

ELECTRICITY: 220 volts AC, 50Hz. Plugs are either round 3-pin or square 3-pin (15 or 13 amps).

COMMUNICATIONS: Telephone: IDD is available. Country code: 220. Outgoing international code: 00. The country has an automatic telephone-system. **Fax:** There are nine GAMTEL offices in Banjul offering this service, some on a 24-hour basis. **Telex/telegram:** Services are run by GAMTEL, Cameron Street, Banjul. There are several GAMTEL branches in Banjul with telex stations. **Post:** Post office hours: 0800-1300 Monday to Friday; 0800-1100 Saturday. **Press:** Newspapers are English-language and include *The Gambia Weekly* (which appears every Friday), *The Nation, The Gambia Times* and *Gambia Onwards.*

BBC World Service and Voice of America frequencies: From time to time these change. See the section *How to Use this Book* for more information.

BBC:

| MHz | 17.79 | 15.40 | 15.07 | 9.410 |

Voice of America:

| MHz | 21.49 | 15.60 | 9.525 | 6.035 |

PASSPORT/VISA

Regulations and requirements may be subject to change at short notice, and you are advised to contact the appropriate diplomatic or consular authority before finalising travel arrangements. Details of these may be found at the head of this country's entry. Any numbers in the chart refer to the footnotes below.

	Passport Required?	Visa Required?	Return Ticket Required?
Full British	Yes	1	Yes
BVP	Not valid	-	-
Australian	Yes	No	Yes
Canadian	Yes	No	Yes
USA	Yes	Yes	Yes
Other EU (As of 31/12/94)	Yes	1	Yes
Japanese	Yes	Yes	Yes

PASSPORTS: Valid passport required by all.
British Visitors Passport: Not acceptable.
VISAS: Required by all except:
(a) those referred to in the chart above;
(b) nationals of Commonwealth countries;
(c) nationals of Benin, Burkina Faso, Cape Verde, Côte d'Ivoire, Guinea Republic, Guinea-Bissau, Mali, Mauritania, Niger, Senegal and Togo;
(d) **[1]** nationals of Belgium, Denmark, Germany, Greece, Italy, Ireland, Luxembourg, The Netherlands, Spain and the UK (for the purposes of tourism only) for visits of up to 3 months;
(e) nationals of Finland, Iceland, Norway, San Marino, Sweden, Tunisia and Turkey for visits of up to 3 months.
Types of visa: Tourist and Business visas are £20. Collective visas are obtainable for organised groups.
Validity: Normally 90 days.
Application to: Consulate (or Consular section at Embassy or High Commission). For addresses, see top of entry.
Application requirements: (a) Valid passport. (b) 2 application forms. (c) 2 passport-size photos. (d) Yellow fever vaccination certificate for all those nationals arriving from endemic or infected areas.
Working days required: Often within 48 hours. Postal applications need recorded, stamped, self-addressed envelope.
Temporary residence: Refer enquiries to the Gambian Embassy or High Commission.

MONEY

Currency: Gambian Dalasi (Di) = 100 bututs. Notes are in denominations of Di50, 25, 10, 5 and 1. Coins are in denominations of Di1 and 50, 25, 10, 5 and 1 bututs.
Credit cards: Access and Visa both have limited acceptance. Check with your credit card company for details of merchant acceptability and other services which may be available.
Travellers cheques: US Dollar and Sterling travellers cheques are equally acceptable.
Exchange rate indicators: The following figures are included as a guide to the movements of the Dalasi against Sterling and the US Dollar:

Date:	Oct '92	Sep '93	Jan '94	Jan '95
£1.00=	13.13	14.23	12.40	15.12
$1.00=	8.27	9.32	8.38	9.66

Currency restrictions: The thriving black market for hard currency is officially discouraged, and visitors must complete a currency declaration form on arrival. Currency from Algeria, Ghana, Guinea, Mali, Morocco, Nigeria, Sierra Leone and Tunisia is neither accepted nor exchanged. There are no restrictions on the import of other foreign currencies; export is limited to the amount imported. CFA Francs are accepted. Local currency may be difficult to exchange outside the country.
Banking hours: 0800-1330 Monday to Thursday; 0800-1200 Friday.

DUTY FREE

The following goods may be imported into The Gambia without incurring customs duty:
200 cigarettes or 50 cigars or 250g of tobacco (or mixed to the same total quantity); 1 litre of spirits; 1 litre of beer or wine; goods up to a value of Di1000.

PUBLIC HOLIDAYS

Jan 3 '95 For New Year's Day. **Feb 18** Independence Day. **Mar 3** Eid al-Fitr (End of Ramadan). **Apr 14-17** Easter. **May 1** Labour Day. **May 10** Eid al-Adha (Feast of the Sacrifice). **Aug 9** Mouloud (Prophet's Birthday). **Aug 15** Assumption. **Dec 25** Christmas Day. **Jan 1 '96** New Year's Day. **Feb 18** Independence Day. **Feb 22** Eid al-Fitr (End of Ramadan). **Apr 5-8** Easter. **Apr 29** Eid al-Adha (Feast of the Sacrifice).
Note: Muslim festivals are timed according to local sightings of various phases of the Moon and the dates given above are approximations. During the lunar month of Ramadan that precedes Eid al-Fitr, Muslims fast during the day and feast at night and normal business patterns may be interrupted. Many restaurants are closed during the day and there are restrictions on smoking and drinking. Some disruption may continue into Eid al-Fitr itself. Eid al-Fitr and Eid al-Adha may last anything from two to ten days, depending on the region. For more information see the section *World of Islam* at the back of the book.

HEALTH

Regulations and requirements may be subject to change at short notice, and you are advised to contact your doctor well in advance of your intended date of departure. Any numbers in the chart refer to the footnotes below.

	Special Precautions?	Certificate Required?
Yellow Fever	Yes	1
Cholera	Yes	2
Typhoid & Polio	Yes	-
Malaria	3/Yes	-
Food & Drink	4/Yes	-

[1]: A yellow fever vaccination certificate is required from all travellers over one year of age arriving from endemic or infected areas. Travellers arriving from non-endemic zones should note that vaccination is strongly recommended for travel outside the urban areas, even if an outbreak of the disease has not been reported and they would normally not require a vaccination certificate to enter the country.
[2]: Following WHO guidelines issued in 1973, a cholera vaccination certificate is no longer a condition of entry to The Gambia. However, cholera is a serious risk in this country and precautions are essential. Up-to-date advice should be sought before deciding whether these precautions should include vaccination as medical opinion is divided over its effectiveness. See the *Health* section at the back of the book.
[3]: Malaria risk, predominantly in the malignant *falciparum* form, exists all year throughout the country. Chloroquine resistance has been reported. Travellers should consult their doctors for medical advice.
[4]: All water should be regarded as being potentially

contaminated. Water used for drinking, brushing teeth or making ice should have first been boiled or otherwise sterilised. Milk is unpasteurised and should be boiled. Powdered or tinned milk is available and is advised, but make sure that it is reconstituted with pure water. Avoid dairy products which are likely to have been made from unboiled milk. Only eat well-cooked meat and fish, preferably served hot. Pork, salad and mayonnaise may carry increased risk. Vegetables should be cooked and fruit peeled.
Bilharzia (schistosomiasis) is present. Avoid swimming and paddling in fresh water. Swimming pools which are well-chlorinated and maintained are safe.
Rabies is present. For those at high risk, vaccination before arrival should be considered. If you are bitten abroad, seek medical advice without delay. For more information, consult the *Health* section at the back of the book.
Health care: Visitors are advised to bring good supplies of sun-screen lotion, insect repellent and anti-stomach upset medicines; all of these may be needed and they can prove expensive or, in some cases, impossible to buy in The Gambia. The Government provides both therapeutic and preventative medical and health services, and plays a dominant role in health services. There are two government-run hospitals: one in Banjul, the Royal Victoria Hospital, with children's and maternity wards; and the other at Bansang (Bansang Hospital), which is located about 320km (200 miles) upriver. Other medical facilities run by the Government include Alatentu (a leprosy hospital), an infirmary, a mental hospital and a tuberculosis sanatorium. The Medical Research Centre at Fajara (opposite the British High Commission) provides good facilities as well. Maternal and child-welfare services have been extended to most parts of the country. Health insurance is advised.

TRAVEL - International

AIR: The main airlines to serve The Gambia are *British Airways (BA)* and *Sabena (SN)*. The Gambia's national airline is *Gambian Airways (GM)*, head office in Banjul.
Approximate flight time: From London to Banjul is approximately 5 hours 30 minutes (direct).
International airport: *Banjul (BJL)* (Yundum International) is 29km (18 miles) southwest of the city. Taxis are available to the city. During 1989, NASA upgraded airport facilities and it is now an emergency space-shuttle landing site.
Departure tax: Gambian passport holders – Di50. Other passengers including non-Gambian residents – Di15.

TRAVEL - Internal

RIVER: The River Gambia provides excellent connections to all parts of the country. The ferry from Barra Point to Banjul runs every two hours in either direction and takes about 30 minutes. There is also a weekly ferry from Banjul to Basse, 390km (240 miles) away; the journey takes about a day and the length of stay at intermediate stops varies.
ROAD: Traffic drives on the right. There are slightly over 3000km (2000 miles) of roads in the country, about 450km (280 miles) of which are paved. Roads in and around Banjul are mostly bituminised, but unsealed roads often become impassable in the rainy season. Road construction programmes include the new link from Banjul to Serrekunda and the proposed link from Lamin Koto to Passimas. **Collective taxis:** These can be hired from Barra to Dakar. It is advisable to settle taxi fares in advance. **Car hire:** This is possible, check with company for details before travelling. **Documentation:** An International Driving Permit will be accepted for a period of three months. A valid UK licence can be used for a short visit.

ACCOMMODATION

Several Gambian hotels are geared primarily to package tours. Accommodation is often booked up in the tourist season (November to May), and confirmation of advance booking should be sought. Most of the hotels are self-contained complexes set in spacious gardens and will generally cater for most tourist needs. Bedrooms will not always be air-conditioned. For further information, contact the Gambian National Tourist Office (address at top of entry).
The number of hotels has increased greatly in recent years and is expected to continue; in 1967 there were only two hotels with a total of 52 beds, whereas now there are over 20 with 4500 beds, both in Banjul and along the coast. 75% of establishments belong to the Gambia Hotel Association which can be contacted c/o The Atlantic Hotel, PO Box 296, Marina Parade, Banjul. Tel: 228 601/6. Fax: 227 861. Telex: 2250 (a/bGV).

RESORTS & EXCURSIONS

The Gambia is Africa's smallest nation, but nonetheless offers landscapes and attractions of great diversity – broad, sandy beaches on the Atlantic, lush tropical forests, swamps and marshes and large areas of wooded savannah.

Banjul & The Coast

The *River Gambia* is several miles wide at its mouth near **Cape St Mary**. It narrows to 5km (3 miles) at Banjul (known as Bathurst in pre-independence days), which is situated on **St Mary's Island** and has a deep sheltered harbour. **Banjul** is the only sizeable town in the country and is the seat of government. There is an interesting *National Museum*. The area around *MacCarthy Square* has a colonial atmosphere, with pleasant 19th-century architecture. Nearby is the craft market. Souvenirs can also be bought at *bengdulalu* (singular: *bengdula*) near the Wadner Beach, Sunwing and Fajara hotels, at the Senegambia Hotel and at Kotu beach. *Bengdula* in the Mandinka language means a 'meeting place' and is a shopping area consisting of African-style stalls, usually built near hotels. Local handicrafts of a large variety can be bought at *bengdulalu*. The Atlantic coast to the south of Banjul boasts some of the finest beaches in all Africa with no less than 15 hotels in the **Banjul**, **Kombo** and **St Mary** area. They are served by the international airport at **Yundum**, a few miles from the capital.

The River Gambia

This is the dominant feature of the country and is the major method of transportation and irrigation as well as providing opportunities for fishing, boating and sailing. It is possible to take boat trips up the river. Most remarkable is the abundance and variety of birdlife along the shores. Particularly well worth visiting is the *Abuko Nature Reserve*, which has crocodiles, monkeys, birds and antelope. Details of cruises can be found on hotel noticeboards. Banjul is the starting point for coach and river trips to all parts of the country and coastline. The whole river and the numerous creeks (known locally as *bolongs*) which join it, are fascinating to the bird lover and the student of nature.
THE RIVER MOUTH: *Fort Bullen* at **Barra Point** was built by the British 200 years ago to cover the approaches to Banjul and the river, succeeding *James Island Fortress* (destroyed by the French) as the main point of defence in the colony. It can be reached by direct ferry from the capital. **Oyster Creek** is the centre of an area of creeks and waterways which can be visited from Banjul.
UP-RIVER FROM BANJUL: Albreda was the main French trading post before they withdrew from The Gambia. Nearby is the village of **Juffure**, home of the ancestors of black American writer Alex Haley, author of 'Roots'. Visitors who want to see more of the countryside may cross by ferry from Banjul to Barra and travel by road to Juffure and Albreda (the journey lasts about 50 minutes), and then by canoe to **James Island** in the calm waters of the River Gambia. **Tendaba** is a new holiday centre, 160km (100 miles) from Banjul by river or road. Further upriver, the fascinating circles of standing stones around **Wassau** have now been identified as burial grounds more than 1200 years old. **Georgetown** was the 'second city' of colonial days, and is still the administrative and trading centre of the region. **Basse Santa Su** is the major trading centre for the upper reaches of the Gambia River. Handsome trading houses built at the turn of the century can be seen there. By the riverside at **Perai Tenda** can be found a multitude of abandoned shops formerly operated by European, Gambian and Lebanese merchants in the days when up-river commerce offered substantial profits for private traders.

SOCIAL PROFILE

FOOD & DRINK: Western food is available at most tourist hotels and restaurants, and some also serve Gambian food. Recommended dishes include *benachin* (also called 'Jollof Rice', a mixture of spiced meat and rice with tomato puree and vegetables), *base nyebe* (rich stew of chicken or beef with green beans and other vegetables), *chere* (steamed millet flour balls), *domodah* (meat stewed in groundnut puree and served with rice), *plasas* (meat and smoked fish cooked in palm oil with green vegetables) served with *fu-fu* or mashed *cassava churq-gerteh* (a sweet porridge consisting of pounded groundnuts, rice and milk). Local fruits like mangoes, bananas, grapefruit, papayas and oranges are delicious and are available in the markets. **Drink:** A good selection of spirits, beers and wines is available. Local fresh fruit juice is delicious.
NIGHTLIFE: In general the nightlife is subdued,

although there are nightclubs in Banjul, Farjara, Bakau and Serrekunda. Gambian ballet, drumming, dancing and fire-eating displays are organised at a hotel every week.
SHOPPING: Souvenirs can be bought in Banjul at the craft market across from MacCarthy Square and at *bengdulalu* (see *Resorts & Excursions* above). One of the most popular purchases is the *Gambishirt*, made of printed and embroidered cotton cloth, mostly in bright colours. Some of the souvenirs are gaudy, others exceedingly attractive. Woodcarvings, beaded belts, silver and gold jewellery, and ladies handbags are also popular items. Other West African handicrafts made of straw, beads, leather, cloth or metal can be purchased here. **Shopping hours:** 0900-1200 and 1400-1700 Monday to Thursday; 0900-1300 Friday and Saturday.
SPORT: Swimming: The estuary of the River Gambia on the Atlantic coast provides miles of magnificent beaches with warm seas throughout the year. Caution is necessary due to strong currents, but the beach at Cape St Mary is safe for both children and adults. **Water-sports:** Atlantic resorts cater for **windsurfing** and **surfing**.
Fishing: Both sea and river fishing is good all year, particularly line-fishing from the beaches. Several sport-fishing boats are available for sea-angling trips. **Sailing:** The Gambia Sailing Club at Banjul welcomes visitors. A notable event is the race to Dog Island; in addition, regattas are organised on special occasions. **Golf:** The Banjul Golf Club has an 18-hole golf course at Fajara near the Atlantic coast. International meetings are organised every year. **Wrestling:** The traditional national sport; contests can be watched in most towns and villages. **Birdwatching:** Very popular in The Gambia; the country has one of the largest number of bird species per square mile in the world. **Tennis** courts are available at some hotels, while details of the location of other courts are available from the Tourist Information Office or most hotel receptions. Tennis clubs include The Cedar Club near Serekunda and the Reform Club in Banjul. *Bouts* (a traditional sport) can be seen on most weekends in Banjul and its suburbs, Serekunda and Bakau. Inter-club **cricket** is played in league matches organised by the Gambia Cricket Association which also organises international matches. A league **football** championship is organised by the Gambia Football Association.
SPECIAL EVENTS: There are big celebrations at Christmas, and also during the Muslim festivals of *Tabaski* and *Koriteh*, but dance or acrobatic street shows can be seen at any time of the year.
SOCIAL CONVENTIONS: Handshaking is a common form of greeting; 'Nanga def' ('How are you?') is the traditional greeting. Gambians are extremely friendly and welcoming and visitors should not be afraid to accept their hospitality. Many Gambians are Muslim and their religious customs and beliefs should be respected by guests; however most understand the English customs and language. Visitors should remember that the right hand only should be used for the giving or receiving of food or objects. Casual wear is suitable although beachwear should only be worn on the beach or at the poolside. Only the very top-class dining rooms encourage guests to dress for dinner. Despite the effects of tourism, traditional culture in music, dancing and craftsmanship still flourishes in the many villages on both banks of the River Gambia. **Tipping:** 10% service charge is sometimes included in hotel and restaurant bills.

BUSINESS PROFILE

ECONOMY: The economy of The Gambia is historically agricultural, with groundnuts (in the form of nuts, oil and cattle cake) accounting for well over 90% of total exports. Agriculture, forestry and fishing provide a

living for 85% of the people and contribute about 59% of the Gross Domestic Product, whereas the industrial sector contributes less than 3%. In the past few years the tourist industry has grown rapidly, and is the most dynamic sector of the economy; the number of tourists has grown from 660 in 1965 to over 25,000 in 1975 and to nearly 112,986 in 1988/9, contributing 10% of the GDP. Another big cash earner is The Gambia Port Authority. There is great potential in the fisheries sector, and the Government, with United Nations Development Programme (UNDP) assistance, is encouraging improved methods and the modernisation of boats. General policy is concerned with trying to broaden the economic base, and there is much excitement about the results of recent seismic surveys which indicate the presence of oil and gas deposits. Gambian economic development has been jeopardised, however, following the military coup in the summer of 1994 which overthrew the long-standing government of Dawda Jawara. Advice by West European governments to their own citizens to avoid the Gambia for the forseeable future has devastated the tourist industry. Bilateral and multilateral aid subventions have also been halted with the object of putting pressure on the military government to effect a speedy return to civilian government. The Gambia is a member of the Economic Community of West African States (ECOWAS).
BUSINESS: Businessmen wear jackets and ties for business meetings. A personal approach is important in Gambian business circles. Punctuality is appreciated and it is advisable to take calling cards, although their use is not widespread. **Office hours:** 0900-1600 Monday to Thursday; 0900-1200 Friday and Saturday.
COMMERCIAL INFORMATION: The following organisation can offer advice: Gambia Chamber of Commerce and Industry, PO Box 33, 78 Wellington Street, Banjul. Tel: 227 765

CLIMATE

The Gambia is generally recognised to have the most agreeable climate in West Africa. The weather is subtropical with distinct dry and rainy seasons. From mid-November to mid-May coastal areas are dry, while the rainy season lasts from June to October. Inland the cool season is shorter and daytime temperatures are very high between March and June. Sunny periods occur on most days even in the rains.

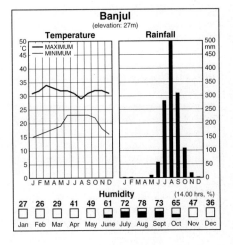

Banjul
(elevation: 27m)

Humidity											(14.00 hrs, %)
27	26	29	41	49	61	72	78	73	65	47	36
Jan	Feb	Mar	Apr	May	June	July	Aug	Sept	Oct	Nov	Dec

☐ *international airport*

Location: Caucasus, north of Turkey.

Note: Georgia became a member of the CIS in October 1993. Increased political stability and a recent crackdown on crime mean that visits to most parts of Georgia can now be made in relative safety, although travel at night outside the capital Tbilisi should still be avoided if possible. Travel to the regions of Abkhazia and South Ossetia should be strictly avoided, as the security situation is unpredictable. Uncontrolled possession of firearms is still widespread throughout Georgia. Heating, lighting and basic foodstuffs are frequently unavailable due to acute energy shortages.
Source: Foreign Office Travel Advice Unit – December 5, 1994.

Ministry of Foreign Affairs
Chitadze Street 4, 380008 Tbilisi, Georgia
Tel: (8832) 997 249.
Intourist
219 Marsh Wall, Isle of Dogs, London E14 9PD
Tel: (0171) 538 8600. Fax: (0171) 538 5967.
Georgian Embassy
Am Kurpark 6, 53177 Bonn, Federal Republic of Germany
Tel: (288) 957 510. Fax: (288) 99 57 51 20.
Georgian Embassy
Suite 424, 1511 K Street, NW, Washington, DC 20005
Tel: (202) 393 6060 *or* 393 5959.
Intourist USA Inc
Suite 603, 610 Fifth Avenue, New York, NY 10020
Tel: (212) 757 3884/5. Fax: (212) 459 0031.
Embassy of the United States of America
25 Ulitsa Atoneli, 380026 Tbilisi, Georgia
Tel: (8832) 989 968. Fax: (8832) 933 759. Telex: 210212.
France, Germany, Israel and Turkey also have embassies in Tbilisi, all temporarily housed in the Metekhi Palace Hotel (tel: 744 623).
Intourist
Suite 630, 1801 McGill College Avenue, Montréal, Québec H3A 2N4
Tel: (514) 849 6394. Fax: (514) 849 6743.
The Canadian Embassy in Ankara deals with all enquiries relating to Georgia (see *Turkey* later on in the book).

AREA: 70,000 sq km (27,000 sq miles).
POPULATION: 5,471,000 (1991).
POPULATION DENSITY: 78.2 per sq km.

Timatic	Health	
	GALILEO/WORLDSPAN: **TI-DFT/TBS/HE**	
	SABRE: **TIDFT/TBS/HE**	
	Visa	
	GALILEO/WORLDSPAN: **TI-DFT/TBS/VI**	
	SABRE: **TIDFT/TBS/VI**	
	For more information on Timatic codes refer to Contents.	

CAPITAL: Tbilisi. **Population:** 1,268,000 (1990).
GEOGRAPHY: Georgia is bordered by the Russian Federation, Turkey, Armenia, Azerbaijan and the Black Sea. The state is crossed by the ranges of the Greater Caucasus (highest peak: Mt Shkhara, 5068m/16,627ft). Enclosed high valleys, wide basins, health spas with famous mineral waters, caves and waterfalls combine in this land of varied landscapes and striking beauty.
LANGUAGE: Predominantly Georgian. Russian, Ossetian and Abkhazian are also spoken.
RELIGION: Christian majority, mainly Georgian Orthodox church. Also Eastern Orthodox, Muslim, Jewish and other Christian denomination minorities.
TIME: GMT + 3 (GMT + 4 from last Sunday in March to the Saturday before last Sunday in September).
COMMUNICATIONS: Telephone: IDD is in theory available to Tbilisi (although in practice it is almost impossible to get through, and lines are of very poor quality). Country code: 7. However, the country code is due to change to 955 in 1995. All outgoing calls from Georgia, except to other parts of the CIS, must be made through the operator and long waits are inevitable. It is often possible to secure better service by mentioning that one is a foreigner and offering to pay a special premium rate. Many businessmen and journalists now use satellite links to overcome the considerable problems of ordinary telephone communication. The Metekhi Palace Hotel is equipped with its own satellite phones. **Post:** International postal services are severely disrupted. Long delays are inevitable and parcels containing anything of value are unlikely to arrive intact. Registering post may increase its chances of reaching its destination, but not necessarily the speed of delivery. **Media:** The *Georgian News Agency* is located at Pr. Rustaveli 42, 380008 Tbilisi. **Radio/TV:** The *Department of Television and Radio Broadcasting* is at Kostava 68, 380071, Tbilisi. Tel: (8832) 362 460. *Radio Tbilisi* broadcasts in Georgian, Russian, Azerbaijani, Armenian and English, while Tbilisi television only has programmes in Georgian and Russian. **Press:** The principal dailies are *Droni, Sakartvelos Respublika* and *Novaya Gazeta. Georgian Times* is a recently launched English-language weekly. Foreign newspapers are available from some hotels. During the period of Gamsakhurdia's presidency, the Government retained a firm control of the media, allowing very little material which dissented from official government policy to appear. Since the demise of Gamsakhurdia the press has enjoyed greater freedom, but television and radio still operate primarily as organs of government propaganda.
BBC World Service frequencies: From time to time these change. See the section *How to Use this Book* for more information.
BBC:

MHz	17.64	12.09	9.410	6.195

PASSPORT/VISA

Regulations and requirements may be subject to change at short notice, and you are advised to contact the appropriate diplomatic or consular authority before finalising travel arrangements. Details of these may be found at the head of this country's entry. Any numbers in the chart refer to the footnotes below.

	Passport Required?	Visa Required?	Return Ticket Required?
Full British	Yes	Yes	Yes
BVP	Not valid	-	-
Australian	Yes	Yes	Yes
Canadian	Yes	Yes	Yes
USA	Yes	Yes	Yes
Other EU (As of 31/12/94)	Yes	Yes	Yes
Japanese	Yes	Yes	Yes

Note: The Consulate/Embassies of the Russian Federation no longer issue tourist visas valid for Georgia.
PASSPORTS: Valid passport required by all. British passports must be valid for 10 years and for at least 6 months after returning from Georgia.
British Visitors Passport: Not accepted.
VISAS: Required by all except resident nationals of Bulgaria and Hungary.
Types of visa: Entry/exit Tourist; Business (for business or educational visits, trade fairs and exhibitions); and Transit (see below). Cost: US$30 at Georgian Embassies. Presently, nationals of countries where there is no Georgian diplomatic representation may obtain visas for US$30 at the airport, however it is not known how long this service will be available and travellers are advised to check with a Georgian Embassy or Consulate before travelling. Tour operators charge £10 plus VAT for obtaining visas for their clients. Generally, all visa types need proof of accommodation. Travellers with Transit visas are allowed a maximum of 48 hours to transit,

provided they are in possession of confirmed onward travel documentation and valid entry requirement for the onward destination. Passengers may leave the airport under certain conditions on a Transit visa, but anyone intending independent excursions must obtain a full visa.
Application to: Consulate (or Consular section at Embassy). For addresses, see top of entry.
Application requirements: *Tourist visa:* (a) Completed application form. (b) 3 recent identical passport photos. (c) Photocopy of the first 5 pages of a valid passport, trimmed to actual size (if British visitors hold a EU-format passport, pages 32 and 33 must also be photocopied). (d) A copy of a voucher (exchange order) issued by an authorised travel company with indication of reference number, names, dates of entry and exit, itinerary, means of transportation, class of services and amount of money paid by the client. (e) Fee.
Business visa: (a) Completed application form. (b) 3 recent identical passport photos. (c) Photocopy of first 5 pages (plus 32 and 33 if EU-format) of a valid passport. (d) An introductory letter from company or firm indicating the purpose, itinerary, organisation to be visited, period of stay and exact departure dates of flights. (e) An invitation from the organisation, department or institution to be visited in Georgia. (f) Fee. All postal applications must be accompanied by a large stamped, self-addressed envelope.
Those who are travelling in groups (standard Intourist tours, coach tours, international competitions, package tours, cruises) should submit all documentation to the tour operator making the travel arrangements. Applications should be made directly to the nearest Intourist office.
For visits to relatives/friends in Georgia, enquire at the Consulate for details of application procedures.
Working days required: Applications for visas may not be made earlier than 3 months before departure whether by post or personal visit. Visas at the Georgian Embassy take 1 week to process and cost US$30 (same-day visas can be arranged for US$100 and visas which take 3-4 days can be arranged for US$50).

MONEY

Currency: At present Georgia remains in the Rouble Zone but a national currency, the 'Lary' is to be introduced in 1995. In April 1993 a cash crisis in the republic forced the Government to introduce Georgian coupons, printed in denominations of 5, 10, 50, 100, 1000, 5000 and 10,000, originally valued on a par, and to circulate in parallel with the Rouble. Georgia has almost no gold or hard currency reserves, and as a result the coupon has failed to hold its value against the Rouble.
Credit cards: Credit cards are acceptable in certain hotels.
Currency exchange: US Dollars or Deutschmarks are widely welcomed. Sterling is less readily recognised (there is a tendency to assume that the Pound Sterling is equivalent to the US Dollar). Visitors are advised to carry notes in small denominations, as the chance of being offered change is remote. All bills are settled in cash; cheques are never used. Money changed officially may in theory be reconverted on leaving the country, but only on payment of a substantial commission and on production of proof of the original exchange transaction. In view of this and the constant fluctuations in the exchange rate, visitors are advised to change relatively small amounts of money as it is required. There is unlikely to be any substantial difference between rates offered by banks, bureaux de change or illegal street traders.
Currency restrictions: The import and export of local currency is prohibited. Foreign currency must be declared on arrival. The export of foreign currency is limited to the amount declared.
Banking hours: In theory, banks open 1000-1700 Monday to Friday, closing for an hour at some time in the middle of the day. In practice, given the almost total breakdown of civil society in the republic, opening hours are unpredictable.

DUTY FREE

The following goods may be imported into the Commonwealth of Independent States without incurring customs duty:
250 cigarettes or 250g of tobacco products; 1 litre of spirits; 2 litres of wine; a reasonable quantity of perfume for personal use; gifts up to a value of Rub1000.
Note: On entering the country, tourists must complete a customs declaration form which must be retained until departure. This allows for the import of articles intended for personal use, including currency and valuables (such as jewellery, cameras, computers, etc) which must be registered on the declaration form. Customs inspections can be long and detailed.

Prohibited imports: Military weapons and ammunition, narcotics and drug paraphernalia, pornography, loose pearls and anything owned by a third party that is to be carried in for that third party. If you have any query regarding items that may be imported, an information sheet is available on request from Intourist.
Prohibited exports: As prohibited imports, as well as annulled securities, state loan certificates, lottery tickets, works of art and antiques (unless permission has been granted by the Ministry of Culture), saiga horns, Siberian stag, punctuate and red deer antlers (unless on organised hunting trip), and punctuate deer skins.

PUBLIC HOLIDAYS

Jan 1 '95 New Year's Day. **Jan 7** Orthodox Christmas. **Apr 21-24** Orthodox Easter. **May 26** Independence Day. **Aug 28** St Marian's Day. **Oct 14** Khetkhob (Ancient Capital of Georgia Day). **Nov 23** St George's Day. **Jan 1 '96** New Year's Day. **Jan 7** Orthodox Christmas. **Apr 12-15** Orthodox Easter.

HEALTH

Regulations and requirements may be subject to change at short notice, and you are advised to contact your doctor well in advance of your intended date of departure. Any numbers in the chart refer to the footnotes below.

	Special Precautions?	Certificate Required?
Yellow Fever	No	No
Cholera	No	No
Typhoid & Polio	Yes	-
Malaria	No	-
Food & Drink	1	-

[1]: All water should be regarded as being a potential health risk. Water used for drinking, brushing teeth or making ice should have first been boiled or otherwise sterilised. Milk is pasteurised and dairy products are safe for consumption. Only eat well-cooked meat and fish, preferably served hot. Pork, salad and mayonnaise may carry increased risk. Vegetables should be cooked and fruit peeled.
Rabies is present. For those at high risk, vaccination before arrival should be considered. If you are bitten abroad, seek medical advice without delay. For more information consult the *Health* section at the back of the book.
Health care: The health service, now in a state of collapse, does provide free medical treatment for all citizens in principal. If a traveller becomes ill during a booked tour in the CIS, emergency treatment is free, with small sums to be paid for medicines and hospital treatment. If a longer stay than originally planned becomes necessary because of the illness, the visitor has to pay for all further treatment. Due to the present state of medical services, emergency evacuation travel insurance is recommended for all travellers. It is also advisable to take a supply of those medicines that are likely to be required (but check first that they may be legally imported) as medicines can prove very difficult to get hold of.

TRAVEL - International

AIR: Regular flights are available from Vienna, Frankfurt/M, Cologne, Paris, Tel Aviv, Ankara and Thessaloniki. It is also possible to fly via Moscow. Transfer from Moscow's Sheremetevo International Airport to Vnukovo Airport may entail a stopover in Moscow. Flights to Georgia can be subject to long delays and cancellations.
International airport: The airport is 18km (11 miles) east of Tbilisi city centre. Taxis and buses run into town. The airport itself has very few facilities.
SEA: The main ferry ports are Batumi and Sukhumi. Fighting in Abkhazia has put Sukhumi out of action indefinitely. Batumi continues to provide international connections with the Black Sea and Mediterranean ports.
RAIL: Tbilisi has railway connections with Azerbaijan, Armenia (with the line continuing into eastern Turkey), Moscow in the Russian Federation (with the main tracks running along the Black Sea coast), Iran and Turkey (see *Rail – Internal* for further information).

TRAVEL - Internal

RAIL: In total, Georgia has almost 1500km (932 miles) of railway. However, lines are currently single-track and slow, and rolling stock is antiquated. The Government has now restored order on the railway, which had suffered from fuel shortages, armed attacks on trains, sabotage of track and bridges and the fighting in Abkhazia, and there is now a fundamentally sound infrastructure. However, rail passengers are advised to store their valuables in the compartment under the seat/bed and to not leave the compartment unattended. It is also a good idea to ensure the compartment door is secure from the inside by tying it closed with wire or strong cord. Reservations are required for all trains. There are two classes of trains, primarily distinguished by the comfort of the seats. Children under five years of age travel free and children from five to nine years of age pay half fare.
ROAD: Georgia has approximately 20,000km (12,428 miles) of asphalted roads, and there is an ambitious project to construct a motorway connecting the Black Sea ports to the border with Azerbaijan, passing through Tbilisi. Travellers attempting to drive around Georgia independently should be aware that it is difficult to buy fuel without highly specialised local knowledge and that an adequate supply of fuel should be obtained in Tbilisi beforehand. Also, reliable road maps or signposts do not exist. **Buses** provide a reliable if uncomfortable service between towns within the republic.
URBAN: Tbilisi is served by buses, trolleybuses and a small underground system. It is common practice to flag down private cars as well as official taxis, but fares should always be negotiated in advance, bearing in mind the likelihood that rates set for foreigners will be unreasonably high. In view of the rising crime rate, foreigners should take precautions before getting into a car and it is generally safer to use officially marked taxis which should not be shared with strangers. It is inadvisable to take a ride if there is already more than one person in the car.

ACCOMMODATION

Hotels formerly run by Intourist are mostly very run down, with poor security and low standards of hygiene and comfort. The Hotel Tbilisi, built in 1914 and until recently retaining an atmosphere of faded grandeur, with dusty potted palms and an extravagantly carved foyer, was unfortunately gutted by fire in 1992, and has yet to be renovated. The Austrian-run Metekhi Palace is the only hotel which can lay claim to international standards. Accommodation is luxurious, with an indoor swimming pool, satellite phones, business centre, health club and numerous bars and restaurants. Prices are correspondingly high.

RESORTS & EXCURSIONS

Tbilisi: The capital of Georgia stands on the banks of the River Mtkvari, in a valley surrounded by hills. It is best seen from the top of *Mount Mtatsminda.* With its warm climate, stone houses built around vine-draped courtyards, and winding streets, the city had a lively, Mediterranean atmosphere even during the Soviet period. The old city, spreading out from the south bank of the river, has numerous frescoed churches (the most noteworthy being the 6th-century *Sioni Cathedral),* 19th-century houses with arcaded open galleries on the upper floors, a castle and a surprising number of cafés and enticing tourist shops selling locally produced arts and crafts. *Prospekt Rustaveli,* Tbilisi's main thoroughfare, features an assortment of stylish public buildings testifying to the city's prosperity at the turn of the century. The *Georgian State Museum* on Prospekt Rustaveli houses a collection of icons, frescoes and porcelain, as well as an outstanding display of jewellery discovered in pre-Christian Georgian tombs. The *Georgian State Art Museum,* in the centre of town, includes many works by the much-loved 19th-century 'primitive' artist, Niko Pirosmani. The *Narikala Fort,* first established by the Persians in the 4th century AD and most recently rebuilt in the 17th century, is a good vantage point for views over the old city. Visitors can still experiment with health-giving sulphur baths in a domed, oriental-style 19th-century bath house just north of the Metekhi Bridge. The open-air *Museum of Popular Life and Architecture,* located in a western suburb, has interesting examples of rural buildings and artefacts. Davit Aghmashenebeli Prospekt is the base for the *Georgian State Philharmonic Orchestra* and the internationally known *Georgian National Dance Troupe.*
Mtskheta, 20km (12 miles) to the northwest, predated Tbilisi as the capital of Iveria, until the 5th century AD, and remained the centre of Georgian Christianity until the 12th century. The 15th-century *Sveti Tskhoveli* (Pillar of Life) *Cathedral,* standing at the confluence of the Mtkvari and Aragvi rivers, was the holiest place in old Georgia. According to legend, the church is built on the spot where Christ's crucifixion robe was dropped to the ground in 328AD, having been brought from Jerusalem by a local Jew. The existing church has some impressive royal tombs, a fine icon stand and distinctive carved decoration, including bulls' heads and semi-pagan fertility symbols. Also of interest are the *Samtavro Convent* (founded in the 11th century and still functioning) and the *Dzhvari Cathedral,* the design of which became a prototype for Georgian ecclesiastical architecture.
Sukhumi, the capital of Abkhazia in the far northwest of Georgia, was until recently a relaxed, sunny port/resort, renowned for its beaches fringed with palms and eucalyptus trees, lively open-air cafés and cosmopolitan population. The ruined 11th-century *Castle of the Georgian Bagratid King,* the *Botanical Gardens, Shroma Cave* with its amazing stalactites and stalagmites and the monkey-breeding farm were particular favourites among visitors.
Abkhaz, Georgians, Greeks, Russians, Turks and others lived here in apparent harmony until recent years when the city was overtaken by civil war and thousands of refugees fled. Now tourists are advised not to venture here.
Gagra and **Pitsunda,** which used to be Abkhazia's most thriving holiday resorts, are also out of bounds as tourist destinations.
The **Georgian Military Highway,** leading 220km (137 miles) from Tbilisi to **Vladikavkaz** (formerly Ordzhonikidze) in North Ossetia (now part of the Russian Federation) was built by the Russians in the 19th century to help them control their recently conquered Georgian territories. The road winds through the dramatic mountain scenery of the high Caucasus, apparently little changed since the 19th-century novelist Lermontov described the route in *Hero of our Time.* Sites of interest along the road include the 14th-century *Tsminda Sameba* (Holy Trinity) *Church,* overlooking the mountain town of **Kazbegi,** and the city of Mtskheta (see above).
Gori, 95km (59 miles) west of Tbilisi, was the birthplace of Iosif Dzhugashvili, better known to the world as Stalin. The town has the last surving public statue of Stalin in the former USSR, as well as a park and a museum devoted to Stalinist hagiography. The latter has been 'temporarily' closed for several years, ostensibly for renovation, but more probably to give the curators pause to decide how to display their exhibition in view of prevailing attitudes to the local hero. It also contains the ruins of a 12th-century fortress and a 16th-century church dedicated to St George. 10km (6 miles) east of Gori is **Uplistsikhe,** a large complex of natural caves. Inhabited from the 6th century BC to the 14th century AD, the caves were gradually transformed into increasingly sophisticated dwellings, shops and public buildings, including a theatre, dungeons and enormous wine cellars. The *Atenis Sioni Church,* 10km (6 miles) south of Gori, stands in a beautiful setting and is highly prized for its 11th-century stonecarvings and frescoes. **Bordzhomi,** 150km (93 miles) west of Tbilisi, is a spa town producing much acclaimed mineral water. It is possible to hike in the hills surrounding Bordzhomi. **Bakuriani** is located 29km (18 miles) southeast of Bordzhomi at an altitude of 1700m (5580ft). Before the current breakdown of order, Georgian tourist authorities were working to promote the *studarui* on the Georgian Military Highway as an international ski resort, proclaiming its clean air, uncrowded slopes and marvellous setting. There is a luxury hotel complex run by the same company that owns the Metekhi Palace in Tbilisi. 10km (6 miles) from Bakuriani, heading towards Bordzhomi, is the 12th-century *Daba Monastery,* and nearby a 60m (197ft) waterfall. During the summer it is also possible to visit *Lake Tabatskuri,* sunk into a hollow high in the mountains.
Batumi, a seaside resort and port in the southwest of the republic, is the capital of the Adzharian Autonomous Republic. Close to the Turkish border, the town has a decidedly Turkish character, with a mosque and 19th-century bath house. However its charm lies less in any particular sights than in its lush, subtropical setting, among citrus groves and tea plantations, with mountains rising up from the edge of the sea. The museum (with its superb national costume collection), the circus, the park and the theatre are also well worth visiting.

SOCIAL PROFILE

FOOD & DRINK: According to Georgian legend, when God was distributing land among the peoples of the world the Georgians were so busy eating and drinking, they lost their place in the queue and there was no land left for them. But then they invited God to join the party, and he enjoyed himself so immensely he gave them all the choicest bits of land he had been saving for himself. Georgians pride themselves, with some justification, as the *bons viveurs* of the former Soviet Union, and their culinary tradition has survived better than most the dead hand of Soviet mass-catering. The cuisine makes extensive use of walnuts, which are used to thicken soups and sauces (anything including the word *satsivi* will be

UK STD CODES

As of 16 April 1995, the UK STD codes will change. Insert a 1 after the first zero in the old STD code, eg. 071 becomes 0171.

There are five exceptions:

CITY	NEW CODE	+ PREFIX
Bristol	0117	9
Leicester	0116	2
Leeds	0113	2
Nottingham	0115	9
Sheffield	0114	2

served in a rich sauce flavoured with herbs, garlic, walnuts and egg). Walnuts also feature as desserts, coated in caramelised sugar *(gozinaki),* or in *churchkhela,* when they are threaded on string then dipped in thickened, sweetened grape juice which is subsequently dried into chewy, flavoursome 'candles'. There is less emphasis on lamb to the exclusion of other kinds of meat than in other parts of the Caucasus. Roast suckling pig is often served, and beef and chicken are grilled or casseroled in various sauces, one of the commonest forms being *chakhokhbili,* a stew involving herbs, tomatoes and paprika. Meals usually start with an array of hot and cold dishes which may include spicy grilled liver and other offal, *lobio* (a bean and walnut salad), marinated aubergines, *pkhali* (made from young spinach leaves pounded together with spices), *khachapuri* (consisting of layers of flat bread alternated with melting cheese), not to mention assorted fresh and pickled vegetables and cured meat *(basturma).* Cafés, restaurants and street food traditions are all better established in Georgia than in many of the other former Soviet republics, and the markets are full of locally grown fruit and vegetables. Privately-run restaurants, cafés and bars, which began to thrive during the Gorbachev period, have all been badly hit by the post-independence breakdown in civil order. **Drink:** Both red and white wine is produced in Georgia. *Kindzmareuli,* a fruity, red wine, is reputed to have been Stalin's favourite tipple. *Tsinandali* is a dry white wine, as is *Gurdzhaani. Akhasheni* and *Teliani* are two of the commoner red wines, fruity and dry respectively.

NIGHTLIFE: Any semblance of nightlife in the republic now survives primarily in international hotels. The Georgian State Dancers are highly praised but only occasionally to be glimpsed in Tbilisi, being almost constantly on tour earning foreign currency for the Government. The Rustaveli Georgian Drama theatre also has a good reputation and is particularly renowned for its Shakespeare productions. There is a casino in the Iveria hotel.

SHOPPING: Georgian ceramics, embroidery and jewellery are all distinctive, and may be bought in art salons or special tourist shops. Visitors may also develop a liking for locally produced wines and brandies. Antiques such as rugs and icons attract a heavy export duty and must be licenced for export by the Ministry of Culture. Goods acquired in markets or from private individuals will not come with an export licence, whereas official tourist shops usually take responsibility for certification.

SPORT: Sport, in particular **football,** was an important focus of national pride during the Soviet period. Since independence, however, Georgia has withdrawn from leagues within the CIS but now participates in international sports events. Social and political chaos has put a stop to the majority of sporting activity in the republic.

SOCIAL CONVENTIONS: Georgians pride themselves on their reputation for gregariousness and hospitality. Foreigners sitting in restaurants are likely to have unsolicited bottles of brandy or wine bestowed on them by complete strangers. They will then be expected to raise (and empty) their glasses in response to an endless string of elaborate toasts, preferably interpolating a few suitably enthusiastic toasts of their own into the sequence. Visitors may also be entertained in private homes. On such occasions gifts such as chocolate, flowers or alcohol are well received. On social occasions foreign women will find themselves the object of immense flattery. Those finding such attentions oppressive should avoid giving any hint of

encouragement. A tradition of violent crimes of honour and blood feuds has survived in Georgian society, and may to some degree be seen as influential in the inter-ethnic bloodlettings seen in the republic in recent years. On a more practical level, visitors should be aware that it has become the norm for most men in Georgia to carry firearms, and banditry and street crime have increased. Anyone travelling in the republic should be cautious when venturing out after dark, carry as few valuables as possible, and accept the risk of being robbed and possibly attacked.

BUSINESS PROFILE

ECONOMY: Like all the former Soviet republics, Georgia has suffered profound economic setbacks during the years following the collapse of the USSR. Disruption of the centrally organised Soviet trade and supply networks, political instability and the ruinously expensive civil wars in Abkhazia and South Ossetia have led to hyperinflation, now over 50% per month and rising, and a slump in production. The war in Abkhazia added to Georgia's woes by closing off road and rail routes, vital to Georgia for supplies of fuel, raw materials and food from Russia. In view of Georgia's lack of any substantial hard currency or gold reserves, the introduction of a new national currency, the Lary, proposed for early 1995, is unlikely to go far towards slowing down inflation. In the long term Georgia may have genuine economic potential as a tourist destination, boasting an attractive, relatively unspoilt coastline, a large number of spas and resorts, wonderful mountain scenery, a pleasant climate and good food and drink. There are plans to reduce Georgia's dependence on energy imports by exploiting domestic reserves of coal, oil and peat. The republic's industrial sector is dominated by shipbuilding, food-processing and fertiliser production. Within the Soviet Union, Georgia survived primarily as an exporter of agricultural commodities such as tea, fruit (citrus fruit in particular), wine, tobacco and vegetables. As a signatory of the treaty on regional cooperation signed at the Black Sea conference in 1992, Georgia hopes eventually to establish trade links with neighbouring states, in particular Turkey, outside the CIS.

COMMERCIAL INFORMATION: The following organisation can offer advice: Chamber of Commerce and Industry of Georgia, Prospekt I, Chavchavadze 11, 380079 Tbilisi. Tel: (8832) 230 045 *or* 220 709. Fax: (8832) 235 760. Telex: 212183.

CLIMATE

Hot summers with mild winters, particularly in the soutwest. Low temperatures are common in alpine areas. Heaviest rainfall exists in the subtropical southwest.

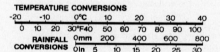

TEMPERATURE CONVERSIONS

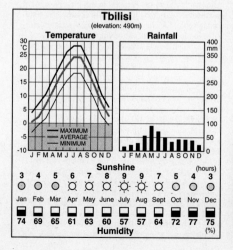

Tbilisi
(elevation: 490m)

Germany
(Federal Republic of)

☐ international airport

Location: Western/Central Europe.

Deutsche Zentrale für Tourismus e.V. (DZT)
Beethovenstrasse 69, 60325 Frankfurt/M, Federal Republic of Germany
Tel: (69) 75720. Fax: (69) 751 903.
Embassy of the Federal Republic of Germany
23 Belgrave Square, 1 Chesham Place, London SW1X 8PZ
Tel: (0171) 824 1300. Fax: (0171) 235 0609. Telex: 21560 (a/b AALDNE G).
Consulate: Tel: (0891) 331 166 (recorded visa information; calls are charged at the higher rate of 39p/49p per minute) *or* (0171) 824 1465/6. Fax: (0171) 824 1449. Opening hours: 1400-1700 Monday to Thursday; 1400-1530 Friday.
General Consulates in: Manchester (tel: (0161) 237 5255; fax: (0161) 237 5244) *and* Edinburgh (tel: (0131) 337 2323; fax: (0131) 346 1578).
German National Tourist Office
Nightingale House, 65 Curzon Street, London W1Y 8NE
Tel: (0891) 600 100 (recorded information; calls are charged at the higher rate of 39p/49p per minute) *or* (0171) 493 0080 (general enquiries) *or* 495 0081 (trade only). Fax: (0171) 495 6129. Opening hours: 1000-1700 Monday to Friday; 1000-1200 and 1500-1600 Monday to Friday for telephone enquiries.
British Embassy
Friedrich-Ebert-Allee 77, 53113 Bonn, Federal Republic of Germany
Tel: (228) 234 061. Fax: (228) 234 070 *or* 237 058. Telex: 886887 (a/b BRINF D).
Consulates in: Düsseldorf, Frankfurt/M, Hamburg, Bremen, Nuremberg, Hannover, Munich, Stuttgart, Kiel and Berlin.

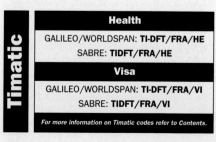

Timatic

Health		
GALILEO/WORLDSPAN: TI-DFT/FRA/HE		
SABRE: TIDFT/FRA/HE		

Visa		
GALILEO/WORLDSPAN: TI-DFT/FRA/VI		
SABRE: TIDFT/FRA/VI		

For more information on Timatic codes refer to Contents.

Embassy of the Federal Republic of Germany
4645 Reservoir Road, NW, Washington, DC 20007-1998
Tel: (202) 298 4000 (automatic information system) *or* 298 8140 (switchboard). Fax: (202) 298 4249 *or* 333 8506. Telex: 64418 (a/b AAWN UW) *or* 197685 (a/b AAWN UT).
General Consulates in: Atlanta, Boston, Chicago, Detroit, Houston, Los Angeles, Miami, New York (tel: (212) 308 8700), San Francisco and Seattle.

German National Tourist Office
52nd Floor, 122 East 42nd Street, New York, NY 10168
Tel: (212) 661 7200. Fax: (212) 661 7174.

Embassy of the United States of America
Deichmanns Aue 29, 53179 Bonn, Federal Republic of Germany
Tel: (228) 339-1. Fax: (228) 339-2663.
Consulates in: Berlin, Frankfurt/M, Hamburg, Munich, Stuttgart and Leipzig.

Embassy of the Federal Republic of Germany
PO Box 379, Postal Station 'A', 14th Floor, 275 Slater Street, Ottawa, Ontario K1N 8V4
Tel: (613) 232 1101/2/3/4/5. Fax: (613) 594 9330. Telex: 534226 (a/b AA OTT CA) *or* 533122 (a/b GERMANEMB OTT).
Consulates in: Calgary, Fort St John, Halifax, Kitchener, London, Montréal, Regina, St John's, Toronto, Vancouver and Winnipeg.

German National Tourist Office
Suite 604, North Tower, 175 Bloor Street East, Toronto, Ontario M4W 3R8
Tel: (416) 968 1570. Fax: (416) 968 1986.

Canadian Embassy
Friedrich-Wilhelm-Strasse 18, 53113 Bonn, Federal Republic of Germany
Tel: (228) 968-0. Fax: (228) 968-3904. Telex: 886421 (a/b DOMCA D).
Consulates in: Berlin, Düsseldorf and Munich.

AREA: 356,854 sq km (137,817 sq miles).
POPULATION: 80,980,343 (1992).
POPULATION DENSITY: 227 per sq km.
CAPITAL: Berlin. **Population:** 3,446,031 (1992).
Administrative Capital: Bonn. **Population:** 296,244 (1992). The move of the administration to Berlin should be completed by the end of 2002. However, eight ministries are to remain in Bonn, therefore creating two administrative capitals. The *Bundesrat* (upper house) will remain in Bonn.
GEOGRAPHY: The Federal Republic of Germany shares frontiers with Austria, Belgium, the Czech Republic, Denmark, France, Luxembourg, The Netherlands, Poland and Switzerland. The northwest of the country has a coastline on the North Sea with islands known for their health resorts, while the Baltic coastline in the northeast stretches from the Danish to the Polish border. The country is divided into 16 states *(Bundesländer)* including the formerly divided city of Berlin. The landscape is exceedingly varied, with the Rhine, Bavaria and the Black Forest being probably the three most famous features of western Germany. In eastern Germany the country is lake-studded with undulating lowlands which give way to the hills and mountains of the Lausitzer Bergland, the Saxon Hills in the Elbe Valley and the Erzgebirge, whilst the once divided areas of the Thuringian and Harz ranges in the central part of the country are now whole regions again. River basins extend over a large percentage of the eastern part of Germany, the most important being the Elbe, Saale, Havel, Spree and Oder. Northern Germany includes the states of Lower Saxony (Niedersachsen), Schleswig-Holstein, Mecklenburg-West Pomerania and the city states of Bremen and Hamburg. The western area of the country consists of the Rhineland, the industrial sprawl of the Ruhr, Westphalia (Westfalen), Hesse (Hessen), the Rhineland-Palatinate (Rheinland-Pfalz) and the Saarland. In the southern area of the country are the two largest states, Baden-Württemberg and Bavaria (Bayern), which contain the Black Forest (Schwarzwald), Lake Constance (Bodensee) and the Bavarian Alps. Munich (München), Stuttgart and Nuremberg (Nürnberg) are the major cities. The eastern part of the country is made up of the states of Thuringia, Saxony, Brandenburg, Saxony-Anhalt and Berlin. The major cities in eastern Germany are Dresden, Leipzig, Erfurt, Halle, Potsdam, Schwerin and Rostock. Apart from Leipzig and Rostock these are also all recently reconstituted state-capitals.
LANGUAGE: German. English is widely spoken and French is also spoken, particularly in the Saarland. In the north of Schleswig-Holstein, Danish is spoken by the Danish minority and taught in schools. Regional dialects often differ markedly from standard German.
RELIGION: Approximately 51% Protestant, 36% Roman Catholic and other non-Christian denominations.
TIME: GMT + 1 (GMT + 2 from last Sunday in March to Saturday before last Sunday in September).
ELECTRICITY: 220 volts AC, 50Hz. European-style round 2-pin plugs are in use. Lamp fittings are screw type.
COMMUNICATIONS: Telephone: Full IDD is available. Country code: 49. Outgoing international code: 00. National and international calls can be made from coin- or card-operated telephone booths. There are already 2200 card-operated public telephones in the new eastern states. Calls can be made from post offices. Cheap rate applies between 1800-0800 Monday to Friday and all day Saturday and Sunday. **Fax:** Facilities are increasingly available in east Germany. **Telex/telegram:** Fully automatic telex and telecommunications services are available throughout the country. Telegrams can be sent during opening hours from all post offices. Public telex facilities are available at Fernmeldeamt 1, Winterfeldstrasse 21, 10781 Berlin; and Pressehaus 1, Heussallee 2-10, 53113 Bonn. **Post:** Stamps are available from hotels, slot machines and post offices. A 5-figure postal code is used on all internal addresses. *Poste Restante* mail should be addressed as follows: recipient's name, Postlagernd, Hauptpostamt, post code, name of town. Post office hours: 0900-1800 Monday to Friday and 0900-1200 Saturday. Smaller branches may close for lunch. **Press:** Newspapers are free of government control. The most influential dailies include the *Süddeutsche Zeitung, Die Welt* and the *Frankfurter Allgemeine Zeitung.* The most widely read of the weekly publication are *Der Spiegel* and *Die Zeit.* Some new or revamped newspapers, such as *Super* and *Berliner Kurier*, have emerged out of eastern Germany and are competing well with western German papers. Most major English newspapers and international magazines are also available in Germany.
BBC World Service and Voice of America frequencies: From time to time these change. See the section *How to Use this Book* for more information.

BBC:

MHz	**15.07**	**12.09**	**9.750**	**6.180**

A service is also available on 648kHz. A service for Greater Berlin is available on 90.2FM.

Voice of America:

MHz	**15.20**	**9.760**	**6.040**	**5.995**

PASSPORT/VISA

Regulations and requirements may be subject to change at short notice, and you are advised to contact the appropriate diplomatic or consular authority before finalising travel arrangements. Details of these may be found at the head of this country's entry. Any numbers in the chart refer to the footnotes below.

	Passport Required?	Visa Required?	Return Ticket Required?
Full British	1	No	No
BVP	Valid	No	No
Australian	Yes	No	Yes
Canadian	Yes	No	Yes
USA	Yes	No	Yes
Other EU (As of 31/12/94)	2	No	No
Japanese	Yes	No	Yes

PASSPORTS: Valid passport required by all except:
(a) **[1]** nationals of the UK holding a BVP;
(b) **[2]** holders of national ID cards issued to nationals of Belgium, Denmark, France, Germany, Greece, Ireland, Italy, Luxembourg, The Netherlands, Portugal and Spain;
(c) holders of national ID cards issued to nationals of Austria, Finland, Iceland, Liechtenstein, Malta, Monaco, Norway, San Marino, Sweden and Switzerland.
Note: (a) Nationals of *all* countries arriving in the Federal Republic of Germany wishing to take up employment must be in possession of a full passport. (b) Holders of British passports with the endorsement *British Citizen*, and holders of British passports issued before January 1, 1983, with the endorsement *'Holder has the right of abode in the United Kingdom'* may enter without a visa. Holders of other British passports may require a visa and should consult the Embassy before making any definite travel arrangements.
British Visitors Passport: Valid. A BVP can be used for holidays or unpaid business trips of up to 3 months.
VISAS: Required by all except:
(a) nationals of countries referred to in the chart above;
(b) nationals of countries also referred to above under passport exemptions;
(c) nationals of Andorra, Argentina, Bolivia, Brazil, Brunei, Chile, Colombia, Cook Islands, Costa Rica, Croatia, Cyprus, Czech Republic, Ecuador, El Salvador, French Guiana, Guadeloupe, Guam, Guatemala, Honduras, Hungary, Israel, Jamaica, Kenya, South Korea, Macau, Malawi, Malaysia, Martinique, Mexico, New Caledonia, New Zealand, Niue, Panama, Paraguay, Peru, Poland, Puerto Rico, Réunion, St Pierre & Miquelon, Singapore, Slovak Republic, Slovenia, Tahiti, Uruguay, Vatican City and Venezuela.
Nationals of other countries, including children under 16 years of age, require a visa.
Types of visa: Entry: £8.10. Transit: £2.20. Residence: enquire at Embassy for details.
Validity: *Entry:* normally up to 3 months (see also *Working days required* below). *Transit:* 12 hours.
Application to: Consulate (or Consular section at Embassy). For addresses, see top of entry.
Application requirements: (a) Application form(s) (number dependent on nationality of applicant). (b) Photo(s) (number dependent on nationality of applicant). (c) Proof of adequate means of support during stay. (d) Proof of medical insurance.
Working days required: For UK residents applying in the UK, visas will normally be issued within 24 hours. If the stay is likely to be for more than 3 months, applications should be made at least 6 weeks in advance of the intended date of departure. Visa applications by non-residents have to be referred to the German Embassy in the applicant's home country, and may take up to 8 weeks to be issued.
Temporary residence: Residence permits may be obtained from the Aliens Office of the local council in Germany, no later than 3 months after entry. Nationals of EU and EFTA countries and the USA may apply for a residence permit after entry.
Work permits: British citizens have the right to look for work or to take up a job previously obtained in the Federal Republic of Germany without a work permit. A residence permit must, however, be obtained for stays of over 3 months (see above). There are special regulations for nationals of EU countries, Iceland, Liechtenstein, Norway, Switzerland and the USA. A booklet, *Residence and Work in Germany,* is obtainable from the Embassy.

MONEY

Currency: Deutsche Mark (DM) = 100 pfennigs. Notes are in denominations of DM1000, 500, 200, 100, 50, 20, 10 and 5. Coins are in denominations of DM5, 2 and 1, and 50, 10, 5, 2 and 1 pfennigs.
Credit cards: Credit cards are accepted in 60% of all shops, petrol stations, restaurants and hotels. Nationals of other Western European countries, Canada and the USA and will find less credit card availability than they are used to in their own countries and it is advisable to carry cash or Eurocheques as well. All major credit cards are accepted. Check with your credit card company for details of merchant acceptability and other services which may be available.
Eurocheques are accepted up to a value of DM400. They can be exchanged in building societies, banks and post offices.
Travellers cheques: These can be changed at banks, post offices, railway stations, travel bureaux and hotels. Generally they provide the best rate of exchange.
Exchange rate indicators: The following figures are included as a guide to the movements of the Deutsche Mark against Sterling and the US Dollar:

Date:	**Oct '92**	**Sep '93**	**Jan '94**	**Jan '95**
£1.00=	**2.44**	**2.46**	**2.57**	**2.44**
$1.00=	**1.54**	**1.61**	**1.74**	**1.58**

Currency restrictions: There are no restrictions on the import or export of either local or foreign currency.
Banking hours: Generally 0830-1300 and 1400/1430-1600 Monday to Friday; Thursday until 1730 in main cities. Main branches do not close for lunch.

DUTY FREE

The following goods may be imported into the Federal Republic of Germany without incurring customs duty by:
(a) Visitors residing in an EU country:
300 cigarettes or 150 cigarillos or 75 cigars or 400g of tobacco; 1.5 litres of spirits with an alcohol content exceeding 22% by volume or 3 litres of spirits or liqueurs with an alcohol content not exceeding 22% by volume or 3 litres of sparkling wine or liqueur wine; 5 litres of any other wine; 1kg of coffee or 400g of coffee extract or essence; 200g of tea or 80g of tea extract or essence; 75g

LUDWIG-MAXIMILIANS-UNIVERSITY MUNICH

Faculty of Medicine, Dean: Prof. Dr. Dr. h. c. Klaus Peter

KLINIKUM   GROSSHADERN

Marchioninistr. 15
D-81377 München 70
Tel. 0 89 / 70 95 - 1
Fax 0 89 / 700 44 18

Anesthesiology	Prof. Dr. Dr. h. c. Klaus Peter
Cardiosurgery	Prof. Dr. Bruno Reichart
Gynecology and Obstetrics	Prof. Dr. Hermann Hepp
Internal Medicine	
Clinic I	Prof. Dr Gerhard Steinbeck
Clinic II	Prof. Dr. Gustav Paumgartner
Clinic III	Prof. Dr. Wolfgang Wilmanns
Neurology	Prof. Dr. Thomas Brandt
Neurosurgery	Prof. Dr. Hans-Jürgen Reulen

Nuclear Medicine	Prof. Dr. Klaus Hahn
Orthopaedic Surgery	Prof. Dr. H. J. Refior
Otorhinolaryngology	Prof. Dr. Ernst Kastenbauer
Physical Medicine and Rehabilitation	Prof. Dr. Edward Senn
Surgery	Prof. Dr. F. W. Schildberg
Urology	Prof. Dr. Alfons Hofstetter
Radiology	Prof. Dr. Maximilian Reiser
Radiotherapy	Prof. Dr. Eckhart Dühmke
Clinical Chemistry	Prof. Dr. Dietrich Seidel

KLINIKUM   INNENSTADT

Ziemssenstr. 1
D-80336 München 2
Tel. 0 89 / 51 60 - 1
Fax 0 89 / 51 60 - 51 99

Children's Hospital	Prof. Dr. H. B. Hadorn, Prof. Dr. Dietrich Reinhardt
Pediatric Surgery	Prof. Dr. Ingolf Joppich
Dentistry/Oral Surgery	Prof. Dr. Dr. D. Schlegel, Prof. Dr. Reinhard Hickel
	Prof. Dr. W. Gernet, Prof. Dr. Ingrid Rudzki-Janson
Dermatology	Prof. Dr. Gerd Plewig
Gynecology and Obstetrics	Prof. Dr. Günther Kindermann
Internal Medicine	Prof. Dr. Peter C. Scriba, Prof. Dr. Detlef Schlöndorff
Infection & Tropical Disease	Prof. Dr. Thomas Löscher

Occupational Medicine	Prof. Dr. Günter Fruhmann
Ophthalmology	Prof. Dr. Anselm Kampik
Psychiatry	Prof. Dr. Hanns Hippius
	Prof. Dr. Hans-Jürgen Möller
Surgery	Prof. Dr. Leonhard Schweiberer
Forensic Medicine	Prof. Dr. Wolfgang Eisenmenger
Immunology	Prof. Dr. Gert Riethmüller
Microbiology	Prof. Dr. G. Ruckdeschel (komm.)

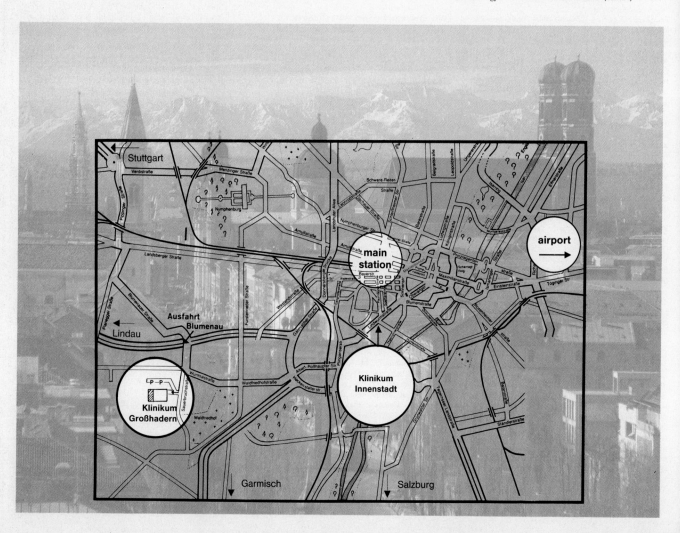

The Katharinen Hospital

The Katharinen Hospital is the Largest hospital in the Stuttgart area, the central (main) hospital.
Teaching Hospital of Tübingen University with 954 beds, 21 departments and institutes in a central location, focal point of in- and out-patient treatment of the population in and around Stuttgart.

Katharinen Hospital, Kriegsbergstrasse, 70147 Stuttgart, Abteilung 1
Tel: 49 711 278 2001, Fax: 49 711 278 2009

---

of perfume and 375ml of eau de toilette; personal goods (including foodstuffs) to the value of DM1235, of which no more than DM115 worth may originate from non-EU states.
(b) Visitors residing in a European non-EU country:
200 cigarettes or 100 cigarillos or 50 cigars or 250g of tobacco; 1 litre of spirits with an alcohol content exceeding 22% by volume or 2 litres of spirits or liqueurs with an alcohol content not exceeding 22% by volume or 2 litres of sparkling or liqueur wine; 2 litres of any other wine; 500g of coffee or 200g of coffee extract or essence; 100g of tea or 40g of tea extract or essence; 50g of perfume and 250ml of eau de toilette; personal goods to the value of DM115.
(c) Visitors entering from an EU country with duty-paid goods:
800 cigarettes and 400 cigarillos and 200 cigars and 1kg of tobacco; 90 litres of wine (including up to 60 litres of sparkling wine); 10 litres of spirits or liqueur with an alcohol content exceeding 22% by volume; 20 litres of intermediate products (such as fortified wine); 110 litres of beer.
(d) Visitors entering from a non-European country:
400 cigarettes or 100 cigars or 500g of tobacco; wines, spirits and perfume as for European non-EU countries.
Note: (a) The tobacco and alcohol allowances are granted only to those over 17 years of age, and the coffee allowances only to those over 15. (b) Wine in excess of the above allowances imported for personal consumption and valued at less than DM250 will be taxed at an overall rate of 15%; this includes 14% import turnover tax.

PUBLIC HOLIDAYS

Jan 1 '95 New Year's Day. **Jan 6** Epiphany [1]. **Apr 14-17** Easter. **May 1** Labour Day. **May 25** Ascension Day. **Jun 5** Whit Monday. **Jun 15** Corpus Christi [2]. **Aug 15** Ascension of the Virgin Mary [3]. **Oct 3** Day of Unity. **Oct 31** Reformation Day [4]. **Nov 1** All Saints' Day [5]. **Nov 22** Day of Prayer and Repentance. **Dec 25-26** Christmas. **Jan 1 '96** New Year's Day. **Jan 6** Epiphany [1]. **Apr 5-8** Easter.
Note: (a) In addition, Carnival (Rose) Monday, which is not an official public holiday, is celebrated on **Feb 27 '95** and **Feb 20 '96**. (b) The holidays indicated with footnotes are Roman Catholic feast days and are celebrated only in the areas indicated: [1] Baden-

Württemberg, Saxony-Anhalt and Bavaria only; [2] Baden-Württemberg, Saarland, North Rhine-Westphalia, Rhineland-Palatinate, Hesse, Bavaria and Catholic areas of Thuringia only; [3] Saarland and Catholic areas of Bavaria only; [4] Brandenburg, Mecklenburg-West Pomerania, Saxony-Anhalt and evangelical areas of Thuringia only; [5] Baden-Württemberg, North Rhine-Westphalia, Saarland, Rhineland-Palatinate, Bavaria and Catholic areas of Thuringia only.

HEALTH

Regulations and requirements may be subject to change at short notice, and you are advised to contact your doctor well in advance of your intended date of departure. Any numbers in the chart refer to the footnotes below.

	Special Precautions?	Certificate Required?
Yellow Fever	No	No
Cholera	No	No
Typhoid & Polio	No	-
Malaria	No	-
Food & Drink	1	-

[1]: Tap water is considered safe to drink. Milk is pasteurised and dairy products are safe for consumption. Local meat, poultry, seafood, fruit and vegetables are generally considered safe to eat.
Rabies is present; look out for 'Tollwut' signs. For those at high risk, vaccination before arrival should be considered. If you are bitten abroad, seek medical advice without delay. For more information consult the *Health* section at the back of the book.
Health care: There is a Reciprocal Health Agreement with the UK. On presentation of the form E111 (see the *Health* section at the back of the book), UK citizens are entitled to free medical and dental treatment. Prescribed medicines and hospital treatment must be paid for. Private insurance is recommended for specialist medical treatment outside the German National Health Service, which can be very expensive.
Surgery hours are generally 1000-1200 and 1600-1800 (not Wednesday afternoon, Saturday or Sunday). The emergency telephone number is 112; additionally, there is an emergency call-out service out of surgery hours (1800-0700). Chemists are open 0900-1800 Monday to

Friday and 0900-1200 Saturday. All chemists give alternative addresses of services available outside the normal opening hours.
There are 350 officially recognised medical spas and watering places with modern equipment providing therapeutic treatment and recreational facilities for visitors seeking rest and relaxation. A list of the spas and health resorts and various treatments can be ordered from the German National Tourist Office, or directly from Deutschen Bäderverband e.V. (German Spas Association), Schumannstrasse 111, 53113 Bonn. Tel: (228) 262 010. Fax: (228) 215 524.

TRAVEL - International

AIR: The national airline is *Lufthansa (LH)*.
For free advice on air travel, call the Air Travel Advisory Bureau in the UK on (0171) 636 5000 (London) *or* (0161) 832 2000 (Manchester).
Approximate flight times: From *London* to Hamburg, Bremen or Hannover is 1 hour 20 minutes; to Cologne/Bonn is 1 hour 10 minutes; to Frankfurt/M is 1 hour 25 minutes; to Nuremberg is 2 hours 30 minutes (with one stop); and to Munich is 1 hour 40 minutes. From *Los Angeles* to Frankfurt/M is 14 hours 50 minutes, from *New York* is 8 hours 20 minutes, from *Singapore* is 14 hours 5 minutes and from *Sydney* is 24 hours 55 minutes.
International airports: Note: The Stuttgart airport will be partly closed from Jul 31-Oct 4 '95. This will affect some charter flight connections as well as landing/starting facilities for large aircraft.
Berlin-Tegel (BER) (Otto Lilienthal) is 8km (5 miles) northwest of the city (travel time – 20 minutes). Airport facilities include duty-free shop, bank/bureau de change, left luggage (0530-2200), 24-hour medical facilities, post office (0630-2100), restaurant (0600-2200), bars (0600-2200), snack bar (0515-2300), shops, tourist information, conference rooms, hotel reservation and car hire. Bus no. 109 goes to the city every 5-10 minutes from 0500-2400; return is from Bahnhof Zoo or Budapester Strasse. There is a 24-hour taxi service and a bus service every 30 minutes from *Berlin Tegel* airport to east Berlin *Schönefeld* airport.
Berlin-Schönefeld (SXF) is 20km (12 miles) southeast of the city (travel time – 1 hour). Airport facilities include duty-free shop, bank/bureau de change (0800-2200), post

office (0800-1800), restaurant (0600-2200), 24-hour left luggage, 24-hour medical facilities, 24-hour nursery, 24-hour snack bar, 24-hour hotel reservation, 24-hour tourist information and car hire. S-Bahn no. S9 departs to the city (to *Westkreuz*) via Alexanderplatz and Bahnhof Zoo; also S10 (via *Ostkreuz*) runs via Oranienburg and S45 (every 20 minutes, to Westend). Further connections with the regional train services R1, R2 and R12 are available at the same tariff as the S-Bahn. Bus no. 171 runs between U-Bahn Station Rudow (Line 7) and the airport. 24-hour taxi service is available to the city. A main line railway station is a 5-minute walk from the airport; from here connections to major German cities and to Basel, Budapest, Prague and Vienna are possible.
Berlin-Tempelhof is 6km (4 miles) southeast of the city centre (travel time – 20 minutes). Airport facilities include duty-free shop, left luggage (0600-2200), 24-hour medical facilities, bank/bureau de change, snack bar (0600-2130), other shops and car hire. Bus no. 119 departs every 10 minutes to the city. The underground lines 6 and 7 run every 2-10 minutes (travel time – 15 minutes). Taxis are available.
Leipzig/Halle (LEJ) is 20km (12 miles) northwest of the city (travel time – 30 minutes). Coach departs to the city. Return is from the main railway station and major hotels. 24-hour taxi services are available to the city. Airport facilities include duty-free shop (0800-1800), conference centre, bank (0900-2100), post office (0800-1700), snack bar (0800-2100), medical facilities (0600-1800), tourist information and restaurant (0800-2100).
Dresden (DRS) (Klotsche) is 10km (6 miles) from Dresden (travel time – 25 minutes). Daily bus services are available to the city.
Bremen (BRE) (Neuenland) is 3km (2 miles) from the city (travel time – 10 minutes). There is a duty-free shop, bank (0900-1630), bureau de change (0630-1930), conference centre, car hire and hotel reservation. Tram no. 5 takes approximately 12 minutes to the city centre (main railway station). Services run every 5-15 minutes Monday to Saturday, and every 15-30 minutes Sunday. There is a 24-hour taxi service.
Cologne (Köln/Bonn) (CGN) (Wahn) is 14km (9 miles) southeast of Cologne, and 21km (13 miles) northeast of Bonn (travel time – 25 and 35 minutes respectively). There is a duty-free shop, tourist information, conference centre, car hire, restaurant (1100-2000), bar (0600-2300), bank/building society and shops. Express bus no. 170 goes to Cologne every 15-30 minutes. Express bus no. 670 goes to Bonn every 20 minutes from 0605-1945, every 30 minutes until 2345. Return is from Stadthaltestelle am Hauptbahnhof (bus station near the main railway station) from 0524-2255. There is a 24-hour taxi service at the airport.
Düsseldorf (DUS) (Lohausen) is 13km (8.5 miles) north of the city. Airport facilities include a duty-free shop (0420-2130), bank (0630-2130), 24-hour medical facilities, post office, restaurant (0600-2359), bars (0430-2130), snack bar (0430-2130), tourist information, car hire and conference rooms. A train goes to the city every 20 minutes (the airport station is under the arrival hall). Return is from Hauptbahnhof (main railway station) every 30 minutes from 0500-2309. An S-Bahn connection (S7) every 20-30 minutes and bus no. 727 are available as well. Taxis run a 24-hour service to Düsseldorf.
Frankfurt/M (FRA) (Rhein/Main) is 12km (7 miles) southwest of the city. Facilities include left luggage (0630-2200), 24-hour medical facilities, duty-free shops, banks (0700-2130), restaurants, bars, snack bars, shops, tourist information, Airport Conference Centre (23 conference rooms), post office (0600-2200), tourist information (0800-2100) and car hire. Travel to and from the city is by buses no. 61 and 62 every 20 minutes, returning from Hauptbahnhof. Lines S14 (every 20 minutes) and S15 (every 10 minutes) go to the city from 0415-0044 (the station is underneath the arrival hall). S-Bahn S14 also goes directly to Mainz and Wiesbaden (travel time – 40 minutes). The airport has its own InterCity train station which also offers international services (Switzerland, Austria and Hungary). The *Lufthansa Courtesy Airport Bus* connects with Mannheim (travel time – 1 hour) and Heidelberg (travel time – 1 hour). There is a 24-hour taxi service to Frankfurt. The *Lufthansa Airport Express* runs four times a day to Düsseldorf Airport (travel time – 2 hours 45 minutes) and to Stuttgart (travel time – 1 hour 25 minutes). This service is only available to passengers who present a confirmed airline ticket.
Hamburg (HAM) (Hamburg-Fuhlsbüttel) is 12km (7.5 miles) north of the city centre (travel time – 25 minutes). Airport facilities include duty-free shop, bank (0600-2230), shops, restaurants (0530-2200), snack bar, post office (0700-2000) and tourist information. Coaches go to the city every 20 minutes from 0600-2300, returning from Zentral Omnibus Bahnhof Kirchenallee. Buses no. 109, 31 (express) and 606 (nightbus) go to the city every 20 minutes (hourly throughout the night) from 0500-2400, returning from Hauptbahnhof and Stephansplatz. Express bus no. 110 runs every 10 minutes to Ohlsdorf station (travel time – 9 minutes). A 24-hour taxi service is available.
Hannover (HAJ) (Langenhagen) is 11km (7 miles) north of the city (travel time – 30 minutes). There is a duty-free shop, 24-hour lockers, 24-hour medical facilities, banks/bureau de change (0630-2100 Mon-Fri, 0900-1730 Sat-Sun), bars (0600-1900), snack bar, post office, restaurants and car hire. Express bus no. 60 goes to the city every 20-30 minutes from 0520-2300, returning from the city air terminal at the main railway station (Ernst-August-Platz). A 24-hour taxi service runs to Hannover.
Munich (MUC) (Franz Joseph Strauss) is 28.5km (18 miles) northeast of the city (travel time – 38 minutes). Facilities include duty-free shop, 24-hour left luggage, 24-hour medical facilities, snack bar (0400-2200), restaurants, post office, banks, conference centre, car hire and bars. Direct link with the S-Bahn S8 runs every 20 minutes from Hauptbahnhof (0313-0033; return 0355-0115). The Airport City Bus runs every 20 minutes from 0625-2325 to the Hauptbahnhof and every 30 minutes from 0515-2330; further bus services are available. The lines S1 and S6 running to the city offer interchange with underground, bus and tram services. Coach Oberbayern runs every 10 minutes to the city centre.
Münster-Osnabrück (MSR) is 25km (16 miles) from the city. There is a duty-free shop. Buses go to Münster (travel time – 30 minutes) and Osnabrück (travel time – 35 minutes). Taxis take 40 minutes.
Nuremberg (NUE) is 7km (4.5 miles) north of the city centre. There is a duty-free shop, 24-hour lockers, business centre, 24-hour medical facilities, bars (0500-2000), snack bar (0430-2000), post office (0630-1750 Mon-Fri, 0630-1200 Sat), restaurants (1100-2300) and car hire. The Airport Express runs every 30 minutes to the Hauptbahnhof 0500-2330. There is a 24-hour taxi service. Bus no. 32 goes to Thon with interchanging bus no. 30 to Erlangen (travel time – 20 minutes) as well as trams no. 4 and 9. Taxis are available.
Saarbrücken (SCN) (Ensheim) is 16km (10 miles) from the city centre. There is an hourly bus service to the city and taxis are also available.
Stuttgart (STR) (Echterdingen) is 14km (9 miles) south of the city (travel time – 35 minutes). There are duty-free shops (0430-2359), 24-hour lockers, conference centre, 24-hour medical facilities, bank/bureau de change (0730-2100), bars (0530-2359), post office (0700-2000 Mon-Sat, 1000-1300 Sun), restaurant (0530-2300) and car hire. Express bus connection (Line A) goes direct to the main station every 20 minutes from 0625-2325. Return is from the city Air Terminal from 0525-2255. An S-Bahn link (lines S2 and S3) is available with trains running at 10-minute intervals. Bus nos. 33, 7600 and 7556 also connect with the city. There is a 24-hour taxi service to Stuttgart.
SEA: The following shipping lines serve routes to Germany from the UK:
Scandinavian Seaways: Harwich–Hamburg.
Sealink: Harwich–Hook of Holland, Dover–Calais, Folkestone–Boulogne, Newhaven–Dieppe.
P&O European Ferries: Felixstowe–Zeebrugge, Dover–Calais, Portsmouth–Le Havre, Portsmouth–Cherbourg, Dover–Boulogne, Dover–Ostend.
Olau Line: Sheerness–Flushing (Holland).
North Sea Ferries: Hull–Rotterdam, Hull–Zeebrugge.
Sally Line: Ramsgate–Dunkirk.
Hovercraft: Dover–Boulogne/Calais.
Ferry connections also exist from Germany to The Netherlands, Norway, Denmark, Sweden, Finland, the Russian Federation, Latvia and Lithuania.
RAIL: Routes from London are from London Victoria via Dover and Ostend, or London Liverpool Street to Hook of Holland via Harwich. Travel time to Cologne/Bonn is around 10 hours.
There are excellent connections between the Federal Republic of Germany and other main European cities. A number of scenic rail journeys begin in Germany and go to Austria or Switzerland, such as the routes through the Black Forest: Frankfurt–Offenburg–Singen–Schaffhausen and Würzburg–Zürich. For more information, contact German Rail in London at Suite 4, 23 Oakhill Grove, Surbiton, Surrey KT6 6DU. Tel: (0181) 390 8833 (general enquiries) *or* 399 1097 (freight only) *or* (0891) 887 755 (recorded information; calls are charged at the higher rate of 39p/49p per minute). Fax: (0181) 399 4700.
ROAD: Germany is connected to all surrounding countries by a first-class network of motorways and trunk roads. Regular coach services to the Federal Republic of Germany from the UK are operated at present by *Eurolines* (tel: (0171) 730 0202 *or* 730 8235) to Berlin, Cologne, Frankfurt/M, Dortmund, Hannover and Munich; and by *Transline* (tel: (01708) 864 911; fax: (01708) 865 715) every Thursday and Sunday. In every major city there are *Mitfahrerzentralen* (car sharing

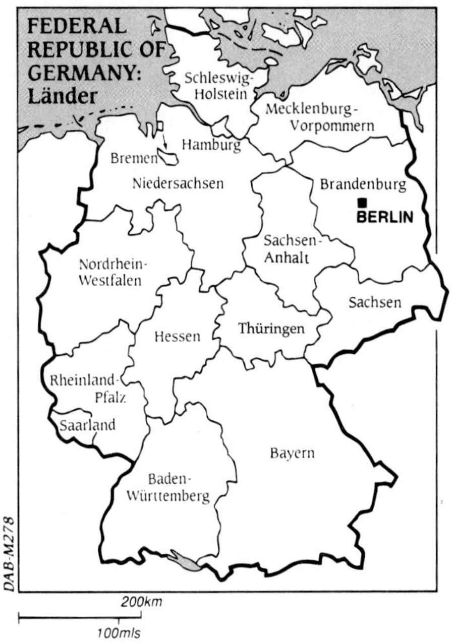
FEDERAL REPUBLIC OF GERMANY: Länder
Schleswig-Holstein
Mecklenburg-Vorpommern
Hamburg
Bremen
Niedersachsen
Brandenburg
BERLIN
Sachsen-Anhalt
Nordrhein-Westfalen
Sachsen
Hessen
Thüringen
Rheinland-Pfalz
Saarland
Bayern
Baden-Württemberg
DAB-M278
200km
100mls

agencies, see Yellow Pages) which offer shared car travelling to all European cities on the basis of shared costs; an agency fee is charged.
See below for information on **documentation** and **traffic regulations.**

TRAVEL - Internal

AIR: Internal services are operated by *Lufthansa* and several regional airlines. Frankfurt/M is the focal point of internal air services and all airports in the Federal Republic of Germany can be reached in an average of 50 minutes flying time. There are several airports in the country apart from those listed above which offer internal air services. Helgoland, Sylt and some other Friesian Islands are served by seasonal services operated by regional airlines or air taxi services. Connections by air are run daily from Berlin, Bremen, Cologne/Bonn, Düsseldorf, Frankfurt/M, Hamburg, Hannover, Munich, Nuremberg, Stuttgart and Westerland/Sylt (summer only). The majority of western airports offer daily flights to Leipzig and several flights a week to Dresden.
SEA/RIVER: Regular scheduled boat services operate on most rivers, lakes and coastal waters, including the Danube, Main, Moselle, Rhine, Neckar and the Weser, and also on Ammer See, Chiemsee, Königssee and Lake Constance. Ferry services are operated on Kiel Fjord and from Cuxhaven to Helgoland and to the East and North Friesian Islands as well as to Scandinavian destinations. Besides these scheduled services, special excursions are available on all navigable waters. The *KD German Rhine Line* covers the Rhine, Main and Moselle rivers, and has 19 comfortable ships which operate daily from April to late October. Tours with entertainment on board and excursions are arranged as well as cruises between The Netherlands and Switzerland and on the Moselle. In conjunction with the *'White Fleet' Dresden*, the KD also organises cabin cruises on the Elbe between Dresden and Hamburg. The *'White Fleet'* offers 30 scheduled services and short trips around Berlin. Further routes include the rivers Saale and Elbe, several lakes and the Mecklenburger Lake District. *Hapag-Lloyd* operates cruises of 7-21 days from Bremerhaven, Hamburg and Kiel in summer. Lake Constance (Europe's third-largest inland lake) is served by regular steamers, pleasure boats and car ferries between the German, Swiss and Austrian shores. The *Bodensee Pass* gives 50% reductions to visitors throughout the Lake Constance area. This includes scheduled ferry services offered by the German, Swiss and Austrian railways as well as some bus, local train and mountain railway routes. The pass is valid for either 15 days or one year. Children up to 6 years of age travel free. In addition to the pass, there is a Family Ticket which is available free of charge and allows children between 6-16 years of age free travel; unmarried young persons between 16-26 years of age pay half. In both cases they have to be accompanied by a parent. The Family Ticket is only valid on boats and together with the *Bodensee Pass.*
RAIL: It will take some time before the rail network in eastern Germany is brought up to western standards, though modernisation programmes are underway. Connecting the east and west German systems will

Gaming as we prefer it
in Germany

near-by to Düsseldorf (distance 60–70 km)
open from 3.00 p.m. to 2.00 a.m.

Spielbank Hohensyburg ♜
DORTMUND

Hohensyburgstrasse 200 · 4600 Dortmund 30 · Tel. 02 31/77 40-0
The new dimension of gaming in Germany, placed in a traditional park landscape
neighbouring the famous industrial region "Ruhrgebiet".
Outstanding offers by excellent gastronomy, congress and convention facilities.
Gaming offer: 18 French Roulette / 1 American Roulette / 2 Baccara / 5 Black Jack / 160 Slots

Internationales Spielcasino Aachen ♣

Monheimsallee 44 · 5100 Aachen · Tel. 02 41/18 08-0
Classical Casino in a historical building with modern elegance and atmosphere of excellent life-style.
In the neighbourhood of a congress center and a first class hotel.
Outstanding gastronomy and convention facilities.
Gaming offer: 12 French Roulette / 1 American Roulette / 5 Black Jack / 2 Baccara / 60 Slots

You are also cordially welcome to our casinos:

Spielcasino Bad Oeynhausen · Bremer Spielbank · Spielbank Kassel
Casino Berlin · Casino Dresden · Casino Leipzig · Casino Rostock

Westdeutsche Casino Group

require large investments. Berlin's inclusion in the IC/EC/ICE network which at present runs on eight axes is becoming more intensive. Several InterCity and one ICE connections are on offer running every 1-2 hours on the following routes: Berlin–Frankfurt/M–Karlsruhe, Berlin–Cologne–Basel, Munich–Frankfurt/M–Berlin (ICE) and Hamburg–Berlin–Dresden with direct links to Prague. The *ICE-Business-Sprinter* runs non-stop on the following routes: Frankfurt/M–Hannover, Wiesbaden–Hannover, Frankfurt/M–Hamburg, Wiesbaden–Hamburg, Mannheim–Hamburg, Karlsruhe–Hamburg and Frankfurt/M–Munich. Seats on these services have to be booked in advance; yearly ticket holders can use the Sprinters without surcharge. Generally, reservations are advised on all services. Children under 4 years of age travel free of charge; those aged 4-11 pay half fare. For latest information leaflets, contact German Rail or the German National Tourist Office.

The *Deutsche Bahn AG* (DB) operates some 32,684 passenger trains each day over a 40,800km (25,500-mile) network and many international through services. Work on the 3200km (2000-mile) fast-train network has already started and should be completed by 2010. The network does not radiate around the capital as the federal structure provides an integrated system to serve the many regional centres. *InterCity Express, InterCity, EuroCity* and *InterRegio* departure and arrival times are coordinated with each other. More than 50 cities, including Berlin, Leipzig, Erfurt and Dresden, are served hourly by *InterCity* trains; regional centres are connected every two hours (west Germany) or every 2-4 hours in the new federal states through the *InterRegio* system. Details of up-to-date prices, and where tickets can be bought, are available from German Rail or the Tourist Office.

With a railway network as complex, modern and sophisticated as that in the western part of the Federal Republic of Germany, it is obviously impossible to give all the details of the main routes, facilities, timetables, fares and reductions which are available. The following section gives brief descriptions of the major special fares and tickets which are currently on offer. Some of these can only be obtained in Germany. Other new schemes, or modifications to existing ones, may be introduced in the future.

The introduction of the new high-speed *InterCity Express*, travelling at 280kmph (175mph), reduced travel times between the major centres immensely. The service is operating hourly only on some connections at the moment; a supplement is payable. The extensive InterCity network (300 trains per day) connects the major centres at hourly intervals, and ensures swift interchange between trains. A supplement of £5 (DM12) is also charged for first- or second-class on *InterCity* and *EuroCity* trains. Smaller towns are linked by the 26 *InterRegio* lines at 2-hour intervals. Supplementing the system of these longer-distance trains are several commuter networks in larger cities.

Facilities and services: Buffet cars with some seating for light refreshments and drinks are provided on *InterRegio (IR)* trains. Most *InterCity* and *EuroCity* trains carry a 48-seat restaurant, offering a menu and drinks throughout the journey. The newer generation *InterCity Express* trains combine both of the above-mentioned facilities, offering a selection of snacks and menu in their restaurant cars. First-class passengers are provided with 'at-your-seat' service. The *InterCity Express* also provides a service car with conference compartment, card telephones and fully equipped office (photocopier, fax, etc). **Sleeping cars:** Many have showers, and air-conditioning is provided on most long-distance overnight trains. Beds are bookable in advance. Some trains provide couchettes instead. Sleeping-car attendants serve refreshments. Seat reservations should be made for all long-distance trains well in advance. When reserving a seat on *InterCity, EuroCity* and *InterCity Express* trains specify *Grossraumwagen*, which is a carriage with adjustable seats and without compartments, or *Abteilwagen,* which is made up of compartments. **Bicycle hire:** At approximately 260 stations in areas suited for cycle tours, the *DB* operates a bike hire service (ticket holders have special reduced rates). **Mountain railways:**

Travel to Germany's oldest sights with its most comfortable train.

Unternehmen Zukunft
Deutsche Bahn

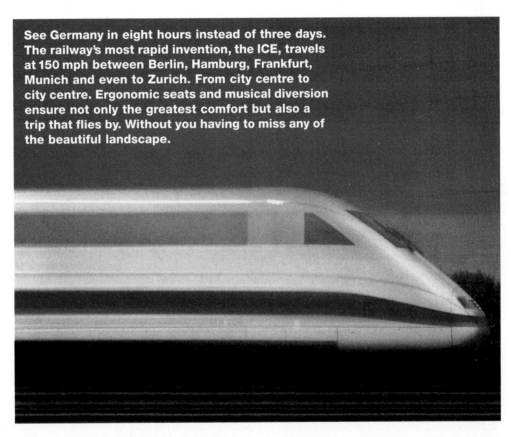

See Germany in eight hours instead of three days. The railway's most rapid invention, the ICE, travels at 150 mph between Berlin, Hamburg, Frankfurt, Munich and even to Zurich. From city centre to city centre. Ergonomic seats and musical diversion ensure not only the greatest comfort but also a trip that flies by. Without you having to miss any of the beautiful landscape.

Cable cars, chairlifts or cogwheel railways serve all popular mountain sites.
Saverticket: Available for a return journey on one weekend or within one month.
Supersaverticket: Available for a return journey on a Saturday or within one month (not valid Friday, Sunday and during peak days).
EURO DOMINO: *EURO DOMINO* tickets, which enable holders to make flexible travel arrangements, are valid in 26 European countries including the ferry service from Brindisi (Italy) to Igoumenitsa (Greece). They have to be bought in the country of residence for which a valid passport or other form of ID has to be shown. First- and second-class tickets are available for travellers over 26 years of age; for passengers under 26, only second-class is available (at £98 for 3 days, £107 for 5 days and £148 for 10 days). The tickets for travellers over 26 years of age are also valid for 3 (at £196 first-class, £131 second-class), 5 (at £216 first-class, £144 second-class) or 10 days (at £295 first-class, £198 second-class) within a month. Discounted holders get a discount of 25% on rail travel in the country of origin or in all countries which comply with the system. Discounted *EURO DOMINO* tickets are on offer for persons under 26 years of age. Children between 4-12 days pay half and get a 50% discount, children under four travel free. The German variety of the ED-ticket is valid on the complete network of the *DB*; all *InterCity* trains, including the *InterCity Express,* can be used without paying a

supplement. Motorail is exempt. Where seat reservation is required, a reduced fee is charged; the usual rates apply for couchette and sleeping-cars.
Inter-Rail: Available to those under 26. Four different tickets are available. Europe is split into seven zones (A-G) and the pass is valid for an unlimited number of train journeys in the zones chosen. The *Global Pass* is valid for one month in all seven zones (28 countries, including Morocco, Turkey and the ferry connection Brindisi–Patras). Other tickets cover just one zone (2-7 countries, 15 days validity), two zones (6-10 countries, one month validity) and three zones (9-15 countries, one month validity). Reductions of 50% are offered in the country of residence for travel to the border and back as well as transit journeys. The Inter-Rail ticket is only available for second-class travel and does not include the use of certain services such as the *X2000* in Sweden, the *Pendolino* in Italy or the *AVE* in Spain.
Tramper Monthly Ticket: Available to all persons under 23 and to all students under 27. It is valid for a month, and gives unlimited free use of all rail services in the Federal Republic of Germany. A passport and a loose passport-size photo are needed when purchasing one. These tickets are available in Germany only. Bicycles are transported free of charge.
BahnCard: The BahnCard ticket offers half-price rail travel with a choice of first- or second-class and is valid for one year. It costs DM440 (approximately £170) for first class or DM220 (approximately £85) for second

class. In addition, there are reduced versions for married couples, families, senior citizens, young people and children.

Rail Europe Senior (RES) Card: This offers considerable savings (up to 30%) on rail travel for senior citizens over 60 on international (cross border) journeys. The card is available from British Rail travel centres and major railway stations. In Germany it is only valid in conjunction with the *BahnCard* (see above). It is valid for one year or the remaining validity of the BahnCard. This card is superseding the old Senior Citizen's Railcard.

EURO-MINI-GROUP: A return ticket for groups of 2-5 people with at least one person under 16 years of age and one adult among them. This ticket is valid for two months and gives a 25% reduction for adults and 50% for children.

Good Evening Ticket: This ticket is available only in Germany. It offers travel on nearly all routes within Germany for a flat fare between 1900-0200 daily except Christmas, Easter and other major travelling dates. The ticket has to be bought at the station of departure.

Motorail: The German Railway has a fully integrated motorail network, connecting with the rest of the European motorail network. Trains run mostly during the summer and at other holiday periods; most have sleeper, couchette and restaurant/buffet cars.

German Rail Passes available outside Germany: There are certain discount rail passes that can only be purchased outside Germany. The *Wunder Flexipass,* available through worldwide travel agencies and Rail Europe, entitles travellers to four days of unlimited first-class travel plus one day's car rental within a 21-day period. The following rail passes can only be purchased through German Rail offices and travel agencies outside Europe: *German Railpass* (valid for 5, 10 or 15 days for either first- or second-class travel), *German Rail Youthpass* (second-class travel for travellers under 26 years of age), *German Rail Twinpass* (for two persons travelling together, first- or second-class, for 5, 10 or 15 days), German Rail Regional Pass (valid in your choice of one of Germany's 15 regions for unlimited travel for 5 days (£85 first-class or £54 second-class) or 10 days (£128 first-class and £85 second-class) within a 21-day period) and the *German Rail and Car Pass* (offering five days of unlimited rail travel within Germany plus three days of car hire with unlimited mileage; prices vary according to whether the pass covers one or two people, the class of rail travel and the category of car).

ROAD: Traffic drives on the right. The western part of the Federal Republic of Germany is covered by a modern network of motorways *(Autobahnen)* extending over 10,500km (6563 miles). There are over 487,000km (303,000 miles) of roads in all, and every part of the country can be reached by motorists. Use of the network is free at present, but the introduction of a road toll is being discussed. A final decision is to be made during 1995. Lead-free petrol is obtainable everywhere. The breakdown service of the ADAC is available throughout the country, though in the new states the *Auto Club Europa (ACE)* and the *Allgemeine Deutsche Motorsportverband (ADMV)* also provide a service. Help is given free of charge to members of affiliated motoring organisations, such as the AA, and only parts have to be paid for. Breakdown services, including a helicopter rescue service, are operated by the *ADAC* (German automobile association). In the event of a breakdown, use emergency telephones located along the motorway. When using these telephones ask expressly for road service assistance ('Strassenwachthilfe'). In almost all cases, the number to dial for emergency services is 110 (in some of the eastern states it is still 155; if in doubt dial the fire brigade, 112). The tourist office publishes the booklet *Autobahn-Service* giving information on all the facilities and services available on the motorways throughout the country.

Note: Although motorways in eastern Germany are of a reasonable standard, many secondary roads are still poorly surfaced and in a state of disrepair. It will take time before they are brought up to Western standards.

Bus: Buses serve villages and small towns, especially those without railway stations. Operated by the Post, German Railways or private firms, they only tend to run between or to small places and there are few long-distance services. *Europabus/Deutsche Touring* runs services on special scenic routes such as the *Romantic Road* (Wiesbaden/Frankfurt to Munich/Füssen) and the *Castle Road* between Mannheim/Heidelberg to Rothenburg and Nuremberg.

Taxi: These are available everywhere. Watch out for waiting-period charges and surcharges. All taxis are metered.

Car hire: Self-drive cars are available at most towns and at over 40 railway stations. Chauffeur-driven cars are available in all large towns. Rates depend on the type of car. Some firms offer weekly rates including unlimited mileage. VAT at 15% is payable on all rental charges. On request, cars will be supplied at airports, stations and hotels. It may be difficult to use credit cards at petrol stations.

Several airlines, including *Lufthansa*, offer 'Fly-drive'. Contact the National Tourist Office for details.

Motoring organisations: The *Allgemeiner Deutscher Automobil Club* (ADAC) based in Munich and the *Automobilclub von Deutschland* (AvD) based in Frankfurt/M have offices at all major frontier crossings and in the larger towns. They will be able to assist foreign motorists, particularly those belonging to affiliated motoring organisations. They also publish maps and guidebooks which are available at their offices. ADAC operates an emergency service to relay radio messages to motorists. In both winter and summer there are constant radio reports on road conditions and traffic. They will also rent snow chains.

Regulations: Traffic signs are international. Speed limits in western Germany are 50kmph (31mph) in built-up areas and 100kmph (62mph) on all roads outside built-up areas. Motorways *(Autobahnen)* and dual carriageways have a recommended speed limit of 130kmph (81mph). Speed limits in eastern Germany vary according to the condition of the road. Although officially the same as in western Germany since January 1993, some motorways and dual carriageways still carry a 100kmph (62mph) speed limit. Children under 12 must travel in a special child seat in the back. Seat belts must be worn in the front and back. All visitors' cars must display vehicle nationality plates. Fines can be imposed for running out of petrol on a motorway. The warning triangle and a first-aid box are compulsory. The nationwide alcohol limit is 0.8‰. Disabled drivers should be warned that, although Germany is well-organised for the disabled traveller, a disabled badge or car sticker as used in the UK will not entitle the disabled motorist to park freely in Germany.

Documentation: Foreign travellers may drive their cars for up to one year if in possession of a national licence or International Driving Permit and car registration papers. Insurance is legally required. EU nationals taking their own cars are strongly advised to obtain a Green Card. Without it, insurance cover is limited to the minimum legal cover; the Green Card tops this up to the level of cover provided by the car owner's domestic policy.

URBAN: Good public transport services exist in all towns. All urban areas have bus services, and these are supplemented in a number of larger cities by underground and suburban railway trains. In many towns, block tickets for several journeys can be purchased at reduced rates and unlimited daily travel tickets are available. In many larger cities tickets for a local transport journey have to be purchased from ticket machines before you board the suburban train *(S-Bahn)*, underground *(U-Bahn)*, bus or tram. There are numerous sophisticated vending machines which service all the main boarding points and a wide range of relevant maps and leaflets are available to travellers. Although there is often no conductor on trams and underground trains, inspections are frequent and passengers without valid tickets will be fined on the spot. Timetables and brochures are available at stations.

Berlin: The city's excellent public transport includes an extensive network of buses, underground and S-Bahn which is supplemented by the regional services of the Deutsche Reichsbahn (lines R1-14). In the eastern part of the city, tram services and the ferries of the Berliner Verkehrs-Betriebe, BVG (Berlin Public Transport), in conjunction with east Berlin's 'White Fleet', provide further services. The underground lines 1 and 9 run a 24-hour service Friday night to Saturday and Saturday night to Sunday. The Berlin-Ticket is valid for 24 hours for unlimited travel on bus, underground, S-Bahn and the BVG ferries. The special BVG-excursion coaches are exempt. Holders of the Combined Day-Ticket enjoy unlimited travel with bus, underground and S-Bahn as well as on the complete ferry network of either organisation. A special Weekly Ticket with a validity of 7 days can only be obtained at Bahnhof Zoo. Further details are available from the information desks of the BVG.

Note: Pedestrians should be aware that it is an offence to cross a road when the pedestrian crossing lights are red, even if there is no traffic on the road. On-the-spot fines for offenders are common.

JOURNEY TIMES:

(1) The following chart gives approximate journey times (in hours and minutes) from **Berlin** to other major cities and towns in the Federal Republic of Germany.

	Air	Road	Rail
Hamburg	0.45	4.00	4.45
Cologne	1.05	7.00	7.10
Frankfurt/M	1.10	6.30	8.00
Munich	1.20	7.00	10.10
Dresden	-	2.30	3.00
Leipzig	-	2.00	2.30
Erfurt	-	4.30	5.00
Rostock	-	2.30	3.00

(2) The following chart gives approximate journey times (in hours and minutes) from **Bonn** to other major cities and towns in the Federal Republic of Germany.

	Air	Road	Rail	River
Hamburg	0.55	4.00	4.30	-
Hannover	-	3.00	3.15	-
Frankfurt/M	0.40	2.20	2.00	a
Düsseldorf	-	1.00	0.45	-
Cologne	b	0.20	0.15	0.40
Stuttgart	0.50	4.00	3.30	-
Munich	1.00	7.00	6.00	-
Berlin	1.05	8.00	8.00	-
Leipzig	-	7.00	9.00	-
Dresden	1.45	8.00	13.00	-

[a]: There is a hydrofoil service (not daily) between Cologne and Mainz via Koblenz and Bonn which takes about 3 hours 30 minutes.

[b]: Cologne and Bonn share the same airport; see the *Air* section in *Travel – International* above for details.

Note: All the above times are average times by the fastest and most direct route, by motorways in the case of road journeys, and by the quickest hydrofoil service for the time by river. The slow boat from Bonn to Cologne, for instance, takes three hours.

ACCOMMODATION

HOTELS: There is a good selection of hotels in the Federal Republic of Germany and comprehensive guides can be found at the German National Tourist Office. They can also provide the German Hotel Association Guide, published by the Deutscher Hotel- und Gaststättenverband (DEHOGA), Kronprinzenstrasse 46, 53173 Bonn. Tel: (228) 82008-0. Fax: (228) 82008-46. Telex: 885489. This association counts some 50% of establishments offering accommodation in Germany among its membership and can supply further information on accommodation in Germany. A special accommodation guide for the disabled is available through BAG 'Hilfe für Behinderte', Kirchfeldstrasse 149, 40215 Düsseldorf; or BVB, Alt Krautheimerstrasse 17, 74238 Krautheim/Jagst. Some hotels are situated in old castles, palaces and monasteries. Alongside these are modern, comfortable hotels and well-planned and purpose-built premises. Examples of accommodation for a family on holiday is a country inn offering bed, breakfast and meal. More demanding visitors are also well catered for with medium to luxury hotels. The German hotel trade is extremely well-equipped with facilities from swimming pools and saunas to exercise gyms. When touring the country with no fixed itinerary, it is obviously often difficult to make reservations in advance. Watch out for *Zimmer Frei* (Vacancies) notices by the roadside, or go to the local Tourist Office (usually called *Verkehrsamt*). Visitors should try to get to the town where they want to stay the night by 1600, particularly in summer. **Grading:** Hotels are not graded as such, but every establishment offering accommodation falls into a particular category which stipulates rigid criteria regarding facilities offered. The categories are as follows:

Hotel: Must be accessible to all persons; must provide accommodation and at least one restaurant for guests and non-guests. It must also have a number of rooms for common use by all residents such as a lounge etc. 27% of establishments fall into this category.

Gasthof: A 'Gasthof' (inn) must provide the same facilities as a hotel except for the common rooms such as a lounge etc. 30% of establishments fall into this category.

Pension: A 'Pension' must provide accommodation and food only for guests. It does not have to provide a restaurant for non-residents nor does it have to provide any common rooms. 16% of establishments fall into this category.

Hotel garni: Provides accommodation and breakfast only for guests. 27% of establishments fall into this category.

HISTORIC HOLIDAYS: Information about holidays in castles, stately mansions and historic hostelries may be obtained by contacting the National Tourist Office or by writing to Gast im Schloss e.V., Geschäftsstelle D4, 9-10, Postfach 120620, 68057 Mannheim. Tel: (621) 12662-0. Fax: (621) 12662-12.

SELF-CATERING: All-in self-catering deals are available that include sea travel to a German or other Channel port, and accommodation at the resort. The latter might be in anything from a farmhouse to a castle. Details are available from the German National Tourist Office.

FARMHOUSES: The booklet *Urlaub auf dem Bauernhof* (*Holidays at the Farm*) is published in conjunction with the German Agricultural Society and can be obtained from *DLG-Verlag*, Eschborner

Landstrasse 122, 60489 Frankfurt/M. Tel: (69) 24788-455. Fax: (69) 24788-480. *Agrartour GmbH* offers agricultural studies. For more information, contact Agrartour GmbH, Eschborner Landstrasse 122, 60489 Frankfurt/M. Tel: (69) 24788-491. Fax: (69) 24788-495. Regional guides on most tourist regions can also be obtained from the Tourist Office. All aforementioned booklets are published in German only. A basic knowledge of German will be required for such a holiday. Information and catalogues can also be obtained from *Arbeitsgemeinschaft Urlaub auf dem Bauernhof*, Godesberger Allee 142-148, 53175 Bonn. Tel: (228) 8198-0. Fax: (228) 8198-231. A catalogue with addresses in the whole of the country, including 2000 addresses in the eastern part, can be ordered from Landschriftenverlag GmbH Bonn, Zentrale für den Landurlaub, Heerstrasse 73, 53111 Bonn. Tel: (228) 631 284/5. Fax: (228) 631 286. It costs DM17.50 and is published annually in December.

YOUTH HOSTELS: There are 640 youth hostels throughout both eastern and western Germany. They are open to members of any Youth Hostel Association affiliated to the International Youth Hostel Association. Membership can be obtained from the YHA or *Deutsches Jugendherbergswerk* (German Youth Hostel Organisation), Bismarckstrasse 8, 32756 Detmold (postal address: Postfach 1455, 32704 Detmold). Tel: (5231) 7401-0. Fax: (5231) 7401-49. Reservation is advised during the high season (and throughout the year in major cities).

CAMPING/CARAVANNING: There are well over 2500 campsites in the Federal Republic of Germany. They are generally open from April to October, but 400 sites, mostly in winter sports areas, stay open in the winter and have all necessary facilities. (Campsites in the eastern part of the country are of a very basic standard.) The permission of the proprietor and/or the local police must always be sought before camp is pitched anywhere other than a recognised campsite. It is not normally possible to make advance reservations on campsites. A free map/folder giving details of several hundred selected campsites throughout the country is available from the German National Tourist Board. The German Camping Club publishes a camping guide of the best sites in Germany; contact *Deutscher Camping-Club (DCC)*, Mandlstrasse 28, 80802 München. Tel: (89) 380142-0. Fax: (89) 334 737. The *AA Guide to Camping and Caravanning on the Continent* lists nearly 2000 European campsites, including a large section on Germany.

RESORTS & EXCURSIONS

Situated at the crossroads of Europe, the scenery of the Federal Republic of Germany is enormously varied and includes sandy beaches, towering mountains, forests, lakes and settlements ranging from medieval villages to some of Europe's greatest cities. Every region offers different foods and a wide range of wines and local beers. The country is divided into 16 states (*Bundesländer*). The north includes the North Sea coast and the East Friesian Islands, Schleswig-Holstein, the city-states of Hamburg and Bremen, as well as the Weser Valley, Lüneburg Heath and the Harz Mountains. The central western area of the country consists of the Rhineland region, the industrial sprawl of the Ruhr, the varied landscapes of Westphalia, the wine region Rhineland-Palatinate, the Saarland and the state of Hesse with its German fairytale road. The Black Forest can be found in the south and is part of the state of Baden-Württemberg. Areas of touristic interest in this state include the Neckar Valley, Swabia and Lake Constance. Munich (München) is the capital of Bavaria. The main tourist regions are the Bavarian Forest to the east with the first German national park near the border with the Czech Republic, Franconia to the north, Upper Bavaria and the Alps to the south and the Allgäu region. Bavaria is the most popular tourist destination for nationals and visitors. The Baltic coast with its resorts is the most popular holiday region in the east, followed by the Thuringian Forest, the northern lake district, Saxon Hills, the Harz Mountains and the Zittauer Gebirge. More detailed information on the various regions and cities in the Federal Republic of Germany follows.

The Rhineland

The Rhineland is Germany's oldest cultural centre. Names such as Cologne, Aachen and Mainz are synonymous with soaring Gothic architecture and with the history and lives of many of the great names of Western Europe. However, the area consists of more than a mere series of riverside towns. Here too are the vast plains of the Lower Rhine farmlands, the crater lakes of the **Eifel Hills,** the **Bergische Land** with its lakes and *Altenberg Cathedral* and the **Siebengebirge.** Visitors are attracted to the Rhineland and the **Moselle Valley** not

only for their beauty and romanticism, but also for the convivial atmosphere engendered by wine and song, after all 'Rhineland is Wineland'. Like most of its tributaries, the Rhine is lined with vineyards wherever the slopes face the sun. Alternating with the vineyards are extensive orchards which, in spring, are heavy with blossom. The **Ahr Valley** in the Eifel region is particularly famous for its lush scenery and its red wine; nearby is the famous **Nürburgring** racing circuit. **Trier,** the oldest German town close to the Luxembourg border, is situated on the River Moselle. The city houses the most important Roman ruins north of the Alps. Following the River Moselle eastwards towards Koblenz are several towns well-known among wine connoisseurs – **Bernkastel-Kues, Kröv, Beilstein** and **Cochem.** The Rhine Valley between Cologne and Mainz is world famous for its wines and wine festivals during the autumn. *Eltz Castle,* located deep in the woods near the Elzbach River, can be reached after a 40-minute walk and has one of the best-preserved and impressive Middle Age castle interiors in Germany. The Rhine Gorge's numerous castles include *Stolzenfels, Marksburg Castle, Rheinfels* at **St Goar** and the *Schönburg Castle* at **Oberwesel.** Along the Cologne–Mainz route the *KD German Rhine Line* operates boats between Good Friday and the end of October enabling the passenger to enjoy the view of both sides of the river with vineyards and picturesque villages lining the banks.

The main cities on the Rhine, from north to south, are as follows:

Düsseldorf is one of the great cities of the German industrialised north, an important commercial and cultural centre and the capital of the state of North Rhine-Westphalia (Nordrhein-Westfalen); the city in fact developed over 700 years from a small fishing village at the mouth of the Düssel River to become the country's leading foreign trade centre. The city is extremely prosperous with a fine opera house as well as many concert halls, galleries and art exhibitions. There are over 20 theatres and 17 museums, including the *State Art Gallery of North Rhine-Westphalia,* the *Kunsthalle* (City Exhibition Hall) and the late Baroque *Benrath Palace.* The major exhibition centre is to the north of Hofgarten, which has been staging trade fairs since the time of Napoleon. The heart of the city is the *Königsallee* or 'Kö', a wide boulevard bisected by a waterway and lined with trees, cafés, fashionable shops and modern shopping arcades. Nearby are the botanical gardens, the *Hofgarten,* the Baroque *Jägerhof Castle* and the state legislature. Other attractions include the remains of the 13th-century castle, *St Lambertus Church,* the rebuilt 16th-century *Town Hall, Benrath Palace* in southern Düsseldorf and the many gardens and lakes both in the city and in the suburbs.

Cologne (Köln) is an old Roman city and an important cultural and commercial centre holding many trade fairs each year. Attractions include the *Cathedral of St Peter and St Mary* (13th-19th century); the golden reliquary of the Three Magi; the Romanesque churches of *St Pantaleon, St George, St Apostein, St Gereon* and *St Kunibert;* the Gothic churches of *St Andreas* and the *Minoritenkirche* and *Antoniterkirche;* the medieval city wall and the *Roman-Germanic Museum.* Several

examples of Roman art have been preserved, among them the Dionysus mosaic, the *Praetorium,* the sewage system and the catacombs. The *Wallraf-Richartz Museum* (paintings) is located in a controversial modern building next to the main railway station and the river. Worth a visit is the *Schnütgen Museum* (medieval ecclesiastical art); the zoo; and the *Rhine Park* with 'dancing fountains'. The city is a major starting point for boat trips on the Rhine. It also has a famous carnival. The *Altstadt* (old town) has been lovingly reconstructed and can be enjoyed on foot as can the extensive pedestrian shopping zone.

Aachen (Aix-La-Chapelle), a beautiful spa town and the old capital city of the empire of Charlemagne, is not actually on the Rhine, being situated about 50km (30 miles) west of Cologne. It is actually located at the border of three countries – the Federal Republic of Germany, Belgium and The Netherlands – and a short distance from the city is a point where a person can stand in all three countries at once. Attractions in Aachen include the Cathedral *(Kaiserdom);* Charlemagne's marble throne; the *Octagonal Chapel;* the *Town Hall* built between 1333 and 1370 on the ruins of the imperial palace, with Coronation Hall and Charlemagne frescoes; *Suermond Museum* (paintings, sculptures); and the elegant fountains of sulphurous water, bearing witness to the spa status of the city. In July, an international riding, jumping and driving tournament occurs.

The over 2000-year-old university town and longstanding federal capital **Bonn** will become the second capital of the country, even when the move of 10 ministries to Berlin is complete, as the *Bundesrat* (upper house) and some administration is to remain. South of the actual city is the former spa of *Bad Godesberg,* which is now part of Bonn. It is also the embassy district and offers a good selection of international restaurants and shops. Attractions include the *Cathedral* (11th-13th centuries) and cloisters; *Kreuzberg Chapel,* approached by a flight of 'holy steps'; *Schwarzrheindorf Church* (two storied: 1151); *Town Hall* (1737) and market square; art collections in the *Godesburg* (1210); *Redoute* (1792); *Poppelsdorf Palace* (1715-40) and botanical garden; the *Beethoven Museum* in the house where he was born, and much general theatrical and musical activity associated with the life and work of the great composer; *Pützchens Market* (September); the *University* (1725) and *Hofgarten.* Excursions can be made from Bonn to the *Siebengebirge,* the *Ahr Valley, Brühl Castle* and the *Nürburgring.* The city also has many parkland areas, such as the *Kottenforst, Venusberg* and *Rhine Promenade.* In keeping with old tradition, the beginning of May sees the festival of *The Rhine in Flames.*

DÜSSELDORF

A. ST ANDREAS
B. KUNSTSAMMLUNG NORDRHEIN-WESTFALEN
C. KUNSTHALLE
D. OPER
E. THYSSEN-HAUS
F. MANNESMAN-HAUS

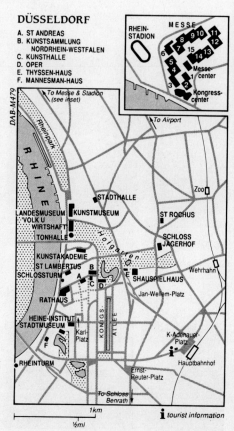

ℹ *tourist information*

Phantasialand

Brühl near Cologne

Brühl · Berggeiststr. 31- 41 · 50321 Brühl · Germany
Info-Tel.: 0 10 49 - 22 32 - 3 61 04
Fax: 0 10 49 - 22 32 - 3 62 36

As from 1st April to 31st October PHANTASIALAND
is opened daily from 9.00 a.m. to 6.00 p.m.
Ticket offices close at 4.00 p.m.

PHANTASIALAND is easily accessible via the motorway
BAB 553 (motorway exit Brühl-Süd),
and is directly off the trunk road B 51, situated right
between Cologne and Bonn.

**Take a break from everyday life and
immerse yourself in the world of fantasy.**

PHANTASIALAND is situated right in the
heart of North Rhine-Westphalia, in Brühl
near Cologne on the A 553, in the direction
of Euskirchen. Lots of fun for young and old
awaits the visitor; boredom has absolutely
no chance here. Treat yourself to a whole
day of absolute pleasure, from 1 April to 31
October, daily from 9-18 h, in the land of
boundless possibilities.

NEW Set off on an unbelievable trip
through space.

GALAXY, one of the most modern and
lavish attractions, is unique in Europe.
Experience the sensational combination of
lightning flight simulation and special
IMAX®-HD-film effects.

Sixteen shuttles await all young and old
hobby astronauts. Due to territorial protection all over Europe GALAXY is an exclusive
thrill for the next few years, just for visitors
to PHANTASIALAND.

Apart from GALAXY there is, of course,
much more to see and do. A mixture of
tranquillity, hilarity and exhilaration. The
varied range of shows alone, especially
Europe's most successful super-magic-
show, PHANTASIALAND Jubilee, will not
fail to fascinate you.

Koblenz is situated at the confluence of the Rhine and the Moselle. From the *Ehrenbreitstein Fortress* (1816-32) visitors have a spectacular view over the *Deutsches Eck Monument* to German unity and the Rhine and Moselle rivers. Other attractions include *Monastery Church* (12th-13th centuries); former *Electors' Palace; Collegiate Church of St Florin* (12th century with a 14th-century chancel); and *Church of Our Lady* (12th century with a 15th-century chancel). Ehrenbreitstein also houses a *Beethoven Museum.*
Rüdesheim, on the Rhine south of Koblenz, is famous for its *Drosselgasse,* a famous narrow lane with many little wine bars and pubs, some serving the delicious Rüdesheimer Kaffee (brandy coffee). A cable car from Rüdesheim takes visitors up to the beautiful *Niederwald Castle,* a starting point for walks in the Taunus range. It is also a popular starting point for many of the Rhine cruises. Almost midway between Rüdesheim and Koblenz is the Rhine's symbol, *Lorelei Rock,* which has evoked many songs and legends about it.
Trier on the Moselle is, as its name indicates, not on the Rhine but on its tributary, the Moselle. It is situated on the Luxembourg frontier about 100km (60 miles) southwest of Koblenz. It is the oldest city in Germany, a Roman imperial capital in the 3rd and 4th centuries AD, and has been declared a UNESCO World Heritage site. Attractions include *The Porta Nigra* (city gate, 2nd century); *Roman Imperial Baths; Basilica; Amphitheatre; Cathedral* (4th century); Gothic *Church of Our Lady; Simeonstift* with 11th-century cloisters; *Church of St Matthew* (Apostle's grave); *Church of St Paulinus* (designed by Balthasar Neumann); *Regional Museum; Episcopal Museum; Municipal Museum; Municipal Library* (with notable manuscripts); and the house where Karl Marx was born.
Mainz is the capital of the Rhineland-Palatinate, a university town and episcopal see dating back 2000 years, situated on the rivers Rhine and Main. Attractions include the international museum of printing *(Gutenberg Museum);* the 1000-year-old *Cathedral; Electors' Palace; Roman Jupiter Column* (AD67); *'Sparkling Hock' Museum; Citadel* with monument to the General Nero Claudius Drusus; old half-timbered houses; *Mainzer Fassenacht* (carnival); and the *Wine Market* (late August and early September). The sunny slopes of the Rhinegau Hills are the centre of one of the world's most famous wine-producing regions.

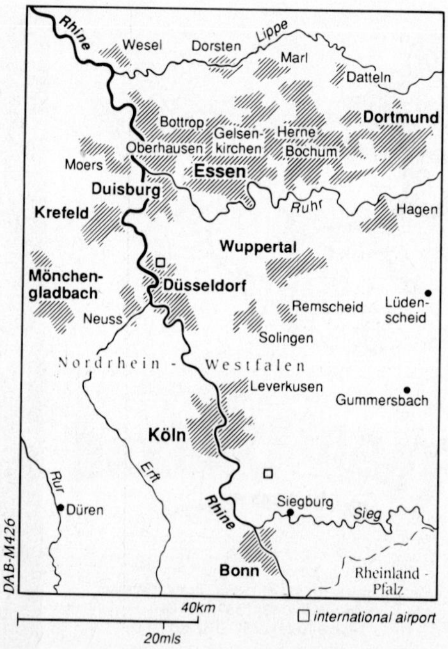

North Germany

Undiscovered by many holidaymakers, the northern region, although relatively flat, offers pleasant scenery with gently rolling hills, lake country and fine sandy beaches and dunes in the state of Schleswig-Holstein.
Hamburg is the second-largest city in the Federal Republic of Germany with a population of 1.6 million people. It is a city-state, forming with Lübeck, Bremen and Rostock the ancient *Hanseatic League* of ports, and Hamburgers have always been proud of their independence. An overall impression can be gained on a sightseeing tour, starting at the Hauptbahnhof. The Baroque *Church of St Michaelis* (der Michel), the *Town Hall* with its distinctive green roof, the elegant *Hanseviertel,* the *Alster Arcades* and the *Alster Lake,* the biggest lake inside a city in Europe, are the city's principal sights. Museums of interest include the domed Hamburg Art Gallery *(Kunsthalle),* the *Historical Museum,* the *Decorative Arts and Crafts Museum* and the *Altonaer Museum.* Hamburg is equally well-endowed with theatres including the Hamburg State Opera *(Hamburgische Staatsoper),* the German Theatre *(Deutsches Schauspielhaus)* and the North German dialect *(Plattdeutsch)* theatre, the *Ohnsorgtheater.* In the heart of the city is the *Planten un Blomen* park near the Congress Centrum Hamburg, which is renowned for its fountain displays during the summer; in the evenings at 2200 the display is accompanied by a sound and light show. During a daytime visit to the park, the *Television Tower* should not be missed. For a small charge, visitors can take the lift to the top platform and enjoy a view of the city, the harbour, the northern districts and the surrounding countryside. Just below is a restaurant which turns full circle in an hour enabling every vantage point to be enjoyed at the diners' leisure. Not far from the Television Tower, next to the Feldstrasse underground station, the large *Dom* funfair takes place several times a year. From Feldstrasse it is not far to the famous St Pauli district which includes the notorious *Reeperbahn.* After dark this area comes alive – though it might be different if the FC St Pauli football team is playing at home – with neon lights, music, crowds, theatres (it is here that the German production of *Cats* was staged) and doormen trying to attract people into their establishments. After a long night out, revellers congregate at the *Fischmarkt,* which opens at 6.30am, where freshly-caught fish, fruit, vegetables and plants are on sale. A trip through the Harbour is recommended and a wide range of tours is available. Hamburg enjoys unrivalled shopping facilities with pedestrian shopping streets, elegant arcades, fine department stores and street cafés concentrated in the area between the main railway station and the *Gänsemarkt.* Refuge from a hectic day's shopping can be sought by hiring a rowing boat or a paddle boat (a deposit has to be left) and exploring the Alster and the intricate network of canals (Hamburg has more bridges than Venice) which extend throughout the city. On Sundays a stroll on the banks of the River Elbe is a favourite pastime or a visit to the Museum Harbour at *Övelgönne.* The numerous cafés and restaurants make sure that nobody overdoes the walking.
Bremen, also a city-state with over half a million inhabitants, is the oldest German maritime city, having been a market town since AD965. The oldest buildings are clustered around the market like the Gothic *Rathaus* (1405-1410). In front of it stands the *Roland,* the statue of a medieval knight and symbol of the city. The extensive pedestrian zone includes a sculpture of the *Bremer Stadtmusikanten,* made famous in the fairytale by Grimm. Also part of this is the *Schnoorviertel,* a district which has retained its medieval charm with narrow cobbled streets, now housing art galleries and exclusive shops. In **Schleswig-Holstein** is Germany's 'Little Switzerland' and the dukedom of Lauenburg, an area of quiet meadows and wooded hills. Glistening among them are the blue waters of innumerable lakes and fjords reaching deep into the interior of this state. A trip could also include visits to tiny undiscovered towns such as **Ratzeburg** and **Mölln** or to one of a string of Baltic resorts such as **Timmendorfer Strand, Grömitz, Damp 2000** and **Schönhagen,** whose golden, sandy beaches attract crowds of visitors every summer. **Lübeck,** whose picturesque oval-shaped old town, ringed by water, still has many reminders of the city's political and commercial golden age in the Middle Ages, claims the title of the most beautiful town of northern Germany. The historic town centre is to become completely pedestrianised. The *Holsten Gate,* the *Rathaus* and the many examples of northern red-brick town houses are part of the historic heritage. The famous novel 'The Buddenbrooks' by Thomas Mann was set here. The *Buddenbrook House* contains the Heinrich and Thomas Mann Centre giving information on the life and works of both. **Flensburg,** the most northerly town in the Federal Republic of Germany, has architecture dating back to the 16th century and for many years of its history was part of Denmark. Just south of Flensburg is **Kappeln an der Schlei,** a picturesque small town between the Fjord and the Baltic. Every hour during the summer the traffic comes to a halt when the rotating bridge allows sail and fishing boats to pass. At the beginning of the season in May the *Heringstage* lure visitors to taste the town's speciality: herring. Along the Schlei lies the old Viking town of *Haithabu* – the interesting museum is well worth a visit. Further south, still on Schleswig-Holstein's east coast, is the state's capital **Kiel.** It is a modern city with a large university, and is located on the Nord-Ostsee (Kiel) Canal which connects the North Sea with the Baltic. Annually in June yachting and sailing enthusiasts flock to the *Kieler Woche.* Currently the main yachting centre of the Federal Republic of Germany, it offers excellent facilities. The western coast of Schleswig-Holstein is constantly pounded by waves and large systems of dykes protect the country from the worst. Sea breezes, a wealth of bird species and nature reserves make the **North Friesian Islands** of *Sylt, Föhr* and *Amrum* a favourite for nature holidays. Ferries connect with the numerous *Halligen,* small flat islets off the coast.
East Friesland consists of a wide plain interspersed by ranges of tree-covered hills known for their health resorts and modern spa facilities, as well as their fine sandy beaches. The car-free East Friesian Islands also offer relaxed health holidays. Sea air and scenery along the coast guarantee a happy and restful holiday atmosphere. In contrast is **Lower Saxony** with its large nature reserve between the rivers Elbe and Aller. The countryside comprises moorlands with wide expanses of heather, grazing sheep, clumps of green birch trees and junipers. Of interest in this area are the half-timbered houses of **Celle** and **Lüneburg**. Further west is the town of **Oldenburg**, the economic and cultural centre of the region between the Ems and the Weser; to the north is the spa town of **Wilhelmshaven**, which has as its speciality relaxing and therapeutic mud baths. It is also the starting point for many tours along the East Friesland coast and the off-lying islands.
Westphalia extends from the Rhine to the Weser Valley. For many, Westphalia conjures up images of the industrial Ruhr Valley, but the region is also one of outstanding natural beauty, historical interest and moated castles. Areas of particular interest include the **Teutoburger Forest** with its nature reserves; **Münsterland**, with the ancient episcopal *See of Münster* (whose attractions include the Gothic *Town Hall* where the Peace of Westphalia, which brought to an end the horrors of the Thirty Years' War, was signed in 1648); and the **Sauerland Region**, a peaceful area of lakes, forests and hills, providing good skiing in the winter and beautiful walking country at any time of the year.
South of Münster is the industrial area of the **Ruhr**. Made up of several large cities all merging into each other to form one enormous conurbation, the *Ruhrgebiet* is, despite its heavily industrial character, a vibrant centre of culture with many museums, theatres, art galleries and opera houses and the area also has a large number of parks providing refuge from the industrial landscape. The older buildings, surviving or restored, as well as other occasional examples are reminders of the days when the cities were only small towns, separated by fields and open rolling countryside. The main cities of the Ruhr are (going west to east): **Krefeld**; **Duisburg**, Germany's largest internal port; **Mühlheim**; **Essen**, in the heart of the region; **Bochum**; and **Dortmund**, centre of Germany's brewing industry. South of the Ruhr and bordering the beautiful Siegerland and Sauerland regions is **Wuppertal,** which, stretched out along its own valley, is home to a unique suspension railway urban transit system, the *Schwebebahn.*
The state capital of Lower Saxony, **Hannover,** hosts the renowned Hannover Trade Fair. The 'Big City in the Park' is also an important internal crossroads with interesting sights. Attractions include the *Herrenhausen Castle* and the Baroque *Royal Gardens of the Duke Georg von Calenberg.* The annual music and theatre festival, which is performed on open-air stages within the garden, attracts many visitors each summer. The city also has a 14th-century market church, the *Marienkirche* (14th century), several museums and a 15th-century town hall with the famous gable. There are also numerous museums, espcially the *Sprengel Museum* near the Masch Lake is becoming an important centre for modern art.
Romantic Germany can be found in the **Weser Valley**, where there are fairytale towns such as **Hameln** (Hamlyn), famed for the tale of the Pied Piper. A play about the infamous piper is re-enacted during the summer months every Sunday at noon. The town has several buildings in Weser Renaissance style. Here is also the romantic area of the **Weserbergland** with numerous hill ranges and deep forests.

Central Germany

East of the Rhineland-Palatinate lies the state of **Hesse**, the capital city of which is Wiesbaden. The northern part of Hesse – *Kurhesse-Waldeck* – boasts lakes, forests and state-recognised health resorts. Hesse is also known for its many rural villages with half-timbered houses and their old customs are observed to this day. The *German Fairy Tale Road* leads through some of these towns.
Schwalmstadt, the home of 'Little Red Riding Hood', is a town where people still wear traditional costumes to church on Sunday and at folk festivals. In the Reinhardswald, *Sababurg* – now a castle-hotel – inspired the Brothers Grimm to write the 'Sleeping Beauty' story. The **Lahn**, a tributary of the Rhine, is much visited for

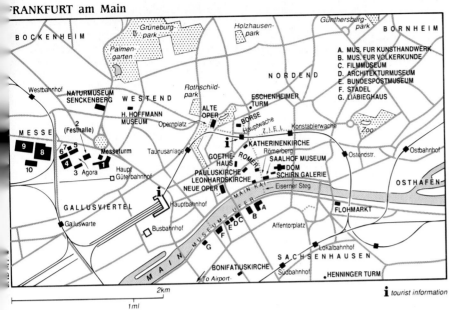

FRANKFURT am Main

2km
1ml

A. MUS. FUR KUNSTHANDWERK
B. MUS. FUR VÖLKERKUNDE
C. FILMMUSEUM
D. ARCHITEKTURMUSEUM
E. BUNDESPOSTMUSEUM
F. STÄDEL
G. LIABIEGHAUS

i tourist information

romantic scenery in *Nassau, Wetzlar, Limburg* and at the *Schaumburg Castle.* Also on this river is the old university town of **Marburg** which attracts visitors from all over the world.

Wiesbaden is the capital of the state of Hesse. It is an international spa and congress centre in the Taunus and on the Rhine; the spas specialise in the treatment of rheumatism. Attractions include the *Kurhaus* and casino; the *Wilhelmstrasse,* with elegant shops and cafés; *Hesse State Theatre;* the *Neroberg* (245m/804ft, with high-rack railway); the *Greek Chapel;* international riding and jumping championships in the grounds of *Biebrich Palace* at Whitsun; boat trips on the Rhine; and woodland walks.

Darmstadt is situated a few miles to the east of the Rhine. Attractions include the *Palace* (16th and 17th centuries); *Prince George Palace* (18th century) with porcelain collection; *Regional Museum; Luisenplatz* with *Ludwigsäule;* artists' colony on *Mathildenhöhe;* *'Wedding Tower'* and *Russian Chapel; National Theatre* on the Marienplatz; and *Kranichstein Hunting Lodge* with hunting museum and hotel.

The city of **Frankfurt am Main** is a major financial, commercial and industrial centre situated at the crossroads of Germany. Its soaring skyline has led to the nickname of 'Mainhattan'. Although almost all of the city was destroyed in 1944, many of the buildings in the Old Town have been carefully restored. The *Römer,* the town hall and crowning place of the German emperors since 1562, has been rebuilt from scratch. Some ancient buildings survived the war, including part of the cathedral and the 13th-century chapel that once adjoined *Frederick Barbarossa's Palace.* In the *City Museum* there is a perfect scale model of the old town and also the astonishing city silver. The stark *Paulus Church* was home to the first German parliament in 1848. Other attractions elsewhere in the city include the zoo, the birthplace of Goethe, the *Opera House,* the suburbs of *Sachsenhausen* and *Hoechst,* both formerly towns in their own right, and the *Messe,* the exhibition halls complex. Art enthusiasts should pay a visit to the *Natural History Museum* with its extensive *Städel* paintings.

Further south is the rolling hill country of the **Odenwald,** a region rich in legend and folklore and renowned for its hiking facilities. The western slopes are traversed by the *Bergstrasse.* The region is noted for its particularly mild climate which permits the cultivation of a wide range of flowers and fruit. The Odenwald can be explored by way of two routes; the *Nibelungenstrasse* and the *Siegfriedstrasse.* Places worth visiting include **Erbach,** which has a Baroque palace and a medieval watchtower; **Michelstadt** with its half-timbered *Town Hall* and basilica; the resort of **Lindenfels;** and the spa town of **Bad König.** Northwest of Frankfurt and north of Wiesbaden is the wooded hill country of the **Taunus,** a ski centre during the winter. Resorts here include the old town of **Oberursel,** the spa town of **Bad Homburg** and, nearby, the preserved Roman fort of **Saalburg,** situated on the line which marked the old frontier of the Roman Empire.

Northeast of Frankfurt is the Baroque town of **Fulda,** gateway to the Rhön region. Some of the buildings here date back to the 9th century. Further north is **Kassel,** home of the *Grimm Brothers Museum,* and the *Wilhelmshöhe Palace* with its magnificent grounds.

The Southwest

The two southern states of the Federal Republic of Germany are also the largest; **Bavaria** and **Baden-Württemberg.**
In the north of **Baden-Württemberg** is the *Neckar Valley.* The most famous place on the river is Germany's oldest university town, **Heidelberg,** which is dominated by the ruins of its famous 14th-century castle. For many the city personifies the era of Romanticism. Other attractions include the 'Giant Cask' in the cellar holding 220,000 litres (48,422 gallons); *Apothecaries' Museum; Church of the Holy Ghost; St Peter's Church; Karlstor Gate;* and wine taverns. The castle there remains partly Renaissance, partly Gothic and Baroque in style; serenade concerts are played during the summer in the courtyard. Vineyards are located along the Neckar Valley, around castles such as *Gutenberg, Hornberg* and *Hirschhorn,* which offer splendid views across the landscape. To the east of Heidelberg, another scenic route begins, the 280km-long (175-mile) *Castle Road* going to Nuremberg in Bavaria. This route follows the river, branching off at **Heilbronn** and continuing east to medieval places such as **Rothenburg** and **Ansbach** in Bavaria. Further to the south is the *Swabian Jura,* the limestone plateau between the Black Forest and Europe's longest river, the Danube. Places to visit include the *Hohenzollern Castle* near **Hechingen, Beuren Abbey** and the *Bären Caves.* Picturesque towns are **Urach** and **Kirchheim unter Teck.** Albert Einstein's birthplace, **Ulm,** houses the world's tallest cathedral spire (161m/528ft). Following the road from Ulm one reaches **Reutlingen** and **Blaubeuren** with a fine abbey which is well worth a visit. Another remarkable Baroque church can be found at **Zwiefalten.** In the southwestern corner of the state, the Rhine acts as a natural border between France and Germany and there lies the **Black Forest.** Walking enthusiasts will enjoy the air filtered by the large pine tree forests, the mountainous scenery and the beautifully situated lakes in the south such as *Titisee* and *Schluchsee.* The Black Forest is well known for its mineral springs whose healing powers were first recognised by the Romans. Its chief spa, **Baden-Baden,** was the summer capital of Europe during the last century. Travellers still flock to this delightful town to 'take the waters', which may be inhaled as a vapour, bathed in or simply drunk. Fortified by the water's therapeutic powers, one can take advantage of the town's many sporting facilities. For the less energetic, the evening could be spent playing roulette or baccarat in a casino which Marlene Dietrich herself regarded as the most elegant in the world. Other attractions include the Baroque *Kleine Theater, National Art Gallery,* ruins of the *Roman Baths,* the *Margravial Palace* (museum), 15th-century *Collegiate Church, Russian Church, Romanesque Chapel,* parks and gardens, *Lichtentaler Allee,* tennis, riding, 18-hole golf course, winter sports, international horseracing weeks at Iffezheim and a modern congress hall. There are also many charming villages and resorts in the surrounding area that are well worth visiting, principally **Freudenstadt,** which claims to have more hours of sunshine than any other German town, and the climatic spa of **Triberg,** with its 162m-high (531ft) waterfalls and swimming pool surrounded

by evergreens.
The other main towns and cities in the region not mentioned above are as follows:
Mannheim is a commercial, industrial and cultural centre on the confluence of the rivers Rhine and Neckar. Attractions include the former *Electors' Palace,* now the university; *Municipal Art Gallery; Reiss Museum* in the old arsenal; the old *Town Hall* and *Market Square;* and the *National (Schiller) Theatre.*
Saarbrücken is mainly a modern industrial city, the capital of the Saarland, situated about 140km (90 miles) west of Mannheim on the French frontier. Attractions include the *Church of St Ludwig and Ludwigsplatz* (1762-75); the *Collegiate Church of St Arnual* (13th and 14th centuries); a palace with grounds and a Gothic church; and a Franco-German garden with a miniature town *(Gulliver's Miniature World).*
Stuttgart is the capital of Baden-Württemberg. Often referred to as 'the largest village in Europe', Stuttgart is a green and open city surrounded by trees and vineyards with only a quarter of its area built on. Two of its major industries are the manufacture of Mercedes cars and the publishing industry. Attractions include the modern *Staatsgalerie;* the *Prinzenbau* and *Alte Kanzlei* on the *Schillerplatz;* the *Neues Schloss,* a vast palace which served as the residence for the kings of Württemberg and has been painstakingly restored after 1945; *Württemberg Regional Museum; Daimler-Benz Automobile Museum;* 15th-century *Collegiate Church; TV Tower* (193m/633ft high); *Killesberg Park; Ludwigsburg Palace; Wilhelma Zoo;* botanical gardens; theatre (ballet); and mineral-water swimming pools. The Stuttgart Ballet and the Stuttgart Chamber Orchestra are renowned the world over.
Freiburg is the gateway to the Black Forest, an archepiscopal see and an old university town. The Gothic *Cathedral* (12th-15th centuries) has a magnificent tower (116m/380ft) and is accepted as an architectural masterpiece. Other attractions include the historic red 'Kaufhaus' on the Cathedral Square (1550); *Augustinian Museum;* Germany's oldest inn, the *Roten Bären;* and many excellent wine taverns. The city is noted for its trout and game dishes and because of several ecological experiments it was named the Green Capital of Germany. The nearby *Schauinsland Mountain* (1284m/4213ft) can be reached by cable-car. Nearby **Todtnauberg** in the Upper Black Forest is the highest situated resort in the Black Forest (1006m/3300ft) and a perfect observation point is the *Belchen* summit nearby. The highest mountain is the *Feldberg* whose slopes are frequented during the winter season by skiers and other winter sports enthusiasts.
Konstanz is a German university and cathedral town on the *Bodensee* (Lake Constance) which marks the border between Austria, Switzerland and the Federal Republic of Germany. Konstanz is a frontier anomaly, a German town on the Swiss side of the lake, completely surrounded by Swiss territory except for a strip on the waterfront. Attractions include the *Konzilsgebäude* (14th century); Renaissance *Town Hall* (16th century); historic old *Insel Hotel* (14th century); *Barbarossa-Haus* (12th century); *Hus-Haus* (15th century); and the old town fortifications *Rheintorturm, Pulverturm* and *Schnetztor.* The town has theatres, concert halls, a casino, and hosts an international music festival as well as the *Seenachtsfest,* a lake festival. *Reichenau,* an island with a famous monastery, and the island of *Mainau,* with stilted buildings, make an interesting day trip.
The Bavarian town of **Lindau** is a former free imperial city on an island in Lake Constance. It has a medieval town centre and an old *Town Hall* (1422-35). Other attractions include *Brigand's Tower, Mang Tower* (old lighthouse), *Cavazzen House* (art collection), *Heidenmauer Wall, St Peter's* with Holbein frescoes; harbour entry (new lighthouse); international casino; and boat trips. Opposite the town of Konstanz is **Meersburg,** an old town with two castles. Here is also the *German Newspaper Museum* which covers the history of the German-language press on its three floors. The museum is only open during the summer. As an area Lake Constance is the focal point of a delightful holiday district, rich in art treasures and facilities for outdoor activities.
Ulm is famous above all for its soaring Gothic *Cathedral* (768 steps in the 161m/528ft tower; choir stalls by J. Syrlin). Other attractions include the beautiful *Town Hall* with famous ornamental clock; *Corn Exchange* (1594); *Schuhaus* (1536); *Schwörhaus* (1613); old fishermen's quarter with city wall and *Metzgerturm* (butchers tower); *Wiblingen Monastery,* Baroque library; *Museum of Bread;* and the *Municipal Museum* with local works of art.
Heilbronn is a former imperial city, surrounded by vineyards and situated on the *Castle Road.* The Renaissance *Town Hall* has an outside staircase, clock, gable and artistic clock. Other attractions include the

16th-century *Käthchen House* and the Gothic *Kilian Church* with the 62m-high (203ft) tower (1513-29). The town is also a good base for excursions into the *Neckar Valley.*

Tübingen, south of Stuttgart, is a world-famous romantic university town on the River Neckar. The old town centre is undamaged. Attractions include the *Castle of the Count Palatine* (1078); late Gothic *Collegiate Church* (1470) with royal burial place; *Market Square* with *Town Hall* (1453); picturesque Neckar front; *Hölderlin Tower;* site of former student lock-up (1514); old and new lecture theatres *(Aula)* of the university; and memorials to Johannes Kepler, Hegel, Schelling, Hölderlin, Mörike, Hauff and Uhland who studied at the theological seminar of the university.

Bavaria

Bavaria consists of four main tourist areas: the *Bavarian Forest* and *East Bavaria; Swabia* and the *Allgäu* in the southwest; *Upper Bavaria* with the German part of the Alps in the south; and *Franconia,* the northern region of Bavaria. The various landscapes feature towering mountains, lakes, forests and many resorts.

In the **Upper Bavaria** region the best-known places include **Garmisch-Partenkirchen, Berchtesgaden, Mittenwald** and **Oberammergau,** home of the Passion Play. One of the most spectacular feasts of architecture that epitomises the fairytale landscape of Bavaria is *Neuschwanstein Castle,* built by Ludwig II of Bavaria. Constructed on the ridge of a mountain valley surrounded by snowcapped peaks, it is a vision from fairyland while at night it changes into the perfect home for Count Dracula.

The vast **Bavarian Forest** can be found in the eastern part of Bavaria bordering the Czech Republic, and site of the first national park. This still unspoiled and peaceful region offers much for those who enjoy outdoor activities and especially walking. Old historic towns such as the three river town of **Passau** and the 2000-year-old **Regensburg** provide interesting contrasts to the nature reserves and the **German National Park.** Numerous art treasures can be found in the northern part of Bavaria – the **Franconia** region. Its main attractions include medieval and historic old towns such as **Coburg,** home of Prince Albert; the cathedral town of **Bamberg; Bayreuth,** which stages an annual *Wagner Opera Festival;* and **Würzburg,** with its world-famous Baroque palace, set on the River Main amongst the Franconian vineyards. **Nuremberg** (Nürnberg), the main city in this region, is a modern metropolis and yet the centre of the town has retained its traditional style. The many valleys, forests, lakes and castles of the Swiss Franconian area and the *Fichtel Mountains,* combined with the nature reserves in the *Altmühl Valley,* make Franconia an ideal holiday centre.

Connecting the northern area of Bavaria with the south is the most famous of all the German scenic roads – the *Romantic Road.* The towns along the way give visitors an excellent insight into the region's history, art and culture. Places of particular interest are the aforementioned Würzburg; medieval **Rothenburg, Dinkelsbühl** and **Nördlingen; Augsburg,** founded in 15BC by the Romans; the pilgrimage church *Wieskirche* in the meadows; *Steingaden Abbey;* and the most popular site of *Neuschwanstein Castle* near the village of **Schwangau.**

The main towns and cities in Bavaria are as follows: The Bavarian capital **Munich** (München) is the third-largest German city with 1.2 million inhabitants and a major international artistic and business centre. The 800-year-old city is renowned for its numerous interesting museums and several fine Baroque and Renaissance churches. The *Alte Pinakothek* is home to the largest collection of Rubens paintings in the world; directly opposite is the *Neue Pinakothek* with a collection of modern paintings. The *German Museum* (natural science and technology) with planetarium and a life-size coal mine is also interesting for children. Worth a visit is the *Lenbach Gallery* in the impressive villa of the Munich 'Painter Viscount'. Only a short walk away is the *Glyptothek* on the Königsplatz, housing Greek and Roman sculptures. Other attractions include the *Royal Palace* and *Royal Treasury; Bavarian National Museum* and others; the *Church of Our Lady; the Theatinerkirche* and *Asamkirche;* and the *Church of St Michael.* The *Marienplatz* is surrounded by the New and Old Town Hall and the restored *Mariensäule.* Every day at 1100 a large group watches the carillion depicting the Schäfflertanz. The site of the 1972 Olympic Games, the facilities are now used by the residents of the city. The *Olympia Park* with its stadium and the 300m (1000ft) tower are now used as a recreational area. Munich is also the setting for the most famous of all German events, the *Oktoberfest* beer festival. This has its origins in 1810 when Crown Prince Ludwig of Bavaria married Princess

Therese von Sachsen-Hildburghausen. The people liked the festival so much that it became a regular feature and now takes place annually for two weeks – the first Sunday in October is always the last day of the festival. The nine Munich breweries all have their own beer tents, serving their beer exclusively. The city has many famous beer cellars, including the *Hofbräuhaus* and the *Mathäser Bierstadt,* the largest in the world. The district of *Schwabing* has been the city's artists' colony since the 1920s and is still recommended for its good shopping, cafés, small theatres and stalls along the Leopoldstrasse. An escape from the city is offered by the *Englischer Garten,* one of the largest parks in Europe. Right in the middle stands the Chinese Tower surrounded by traditional beer gardens. The many theatres include the *National Theatre* (opera house), the Rococo theatre built by Cuvilliés and the *Schauspielhaus* (playhouse). The *Nymphenburg Palace* is home to a portait gallery and a famous collection of china. The *Fasching* (carnival) season reaches its peak during February with several balls and other festivities; but the *Auer Dult,* a funfair and flea market, takes place three times a year.

Augsburg, founded in AD15 by the Romans, lies northwest of Munich and was once the financial centre of Europe. It is also the city where the Fuggers, a famous medieval aristocratic family and great patrons of the arts, resided. Here, in 1555, the Peace Treaty was signed which halted the German religious conflicts during the Reformation. It also boasts the oldest council housing in the world, dating back to 1519. Other attractions include the *Cathedral* (807 Romanesque/1320 Gothic) with 12th-century stained-glass windows and 11th-century bronze door; *St Anna's Church* (16th-century Luther memorial); *Town Hall* (1615); *Perlach Tower;* Baroque fountains (16/17th centuries); *Arsenal; City Gates* (14-16th centuries); *Schaezler Palace* and Rococo banquet hall (18th century) with German Baroque gallery and an Old German gallery with paintings by Holbein and Dürer; *Maximilian Museum; Roman Museum;* and *Mozart House.*

Bamberg is an old imperial town and bishopric, built on seven hills, with many medieval and Baroque buildings. Attractions include the *Imperial Cathedral* (13th century) with famous 'Bamberger Reiter' sculpture, reliefs, royal tombs and Veit Stoss altar; the old *Town Hall;* picturesque fishermen's dwellings (*'Little Venice'); Old Royal Palace, New Palace* (picture gallery) and rose garden; and *Michaelsberg Monastery.*

Bayreuth is mainly famous for its *Wagner Opera Festival* which takes place every year from late July to August. Other attractions, many of which are connected with the life and works of the composer, include the *Festival Theatre* (1872-1876), *Villa Wahnfried* (Wagner's home, now a museum), *Wagner Memorial* ('Chiming Museum'), *Freemasons' Museum,* Wagner's grave in the Court Gardens; the *Old* and the *New Palace,* the former residence of the Margraves; *Opera House* (largest European Baroque stage); *Eremitage* (park); and the parish church. The city is also a convenient base for excursions into the *Fichtel Mountains, Oberpfälzer Woods* and the 'Franconian Switzerland'.

Nuremberg (Nürnberg) is a mainly modern city which has, nevertheless, managed to retain much of its medieval centre. The *Church of St Lawrence* and the *Church of St Sebald* are built in the typical red sandstone of the region. Attractions include the *Imperial Castle* with the old stables today used as a Youth Hostel; the *City Wall* (over 5km/3 miles long) with 46 watchtowers; *Dürer's house; Museum of Toys; Fembohaus* (municipal museum); *Germanic National Museum; Museum of Transport;* 'Old Nürnberg', a guild hall; *Town Hall;* the *'Schöne Brunnen'* fountain with mechanical clock; *Church of Our Lady* and the zoo (dolphin pool). The international toy fair and the famous Christmas Fair, *Christkindlmarkt,* also attract many visitors.

Passau is situated at the confluence of the Danube, Inn and Ilz rivers. Attractions include the Baroque *Cathedral* with the world's largest church organ; *Bishop's Palace* with Rococo staircase; *Oberhaus* and *Niederhaus* fortresses (13th-14th centuries); and Inn quay with Italian architecture.

Regensburg is about 80km (50 miles) northeast of Munich, a city which can trace its roots back to the 1st century AD. Attractions of the old episcopal city include the *Cathedral* (with its famous 'Regensburger Domspatzen' choir); *St Emmeram's Church* (with many crypts and tombs); the *'Scottish Church'* (with its Romanesque portal); *Old Chapel; Palace Niedermünster* (excavations); *Porta Praetoria* (North Gate); 12th-century stone bridge; *Old Town Hall* with the Imperial Chamber; fine patrician residences; *Palace of the Princes of Thurn and Taxis;* and museums.

The old Franconian imperial town **Rothenburg o.d.T.** is famous for its well-preserved medieval atmosphere. It is possible to walk along its two miles of encircling walls with over 30 gates and towers, overlooking the

magnificent patrician houses. Other attractions include the *Town Hall* (16th-17th centuries); *Church of St Jacob* with altar by Riemenschneider (circa 1500); the *Plönlein;* 'Meistertrunk' clock; extensive network of footpaths; and traditional medieval inns.

The northern Bavarian town **Würzburg,** about halfway between Frankfurt/M and Nuremberg, nestles between vineyards famous for their *Bocksbeutel* (specially formed bottle). The *Festung Marienberg* (fortress) offers a spectacular view over the city and its numerous spires. Walking across the 15th-century *Old Main Bridge,* with statues of the Franconian apostles of Lilian, Totnan and Kolonat, the view is dominated by the imposing Romanesque *Cathedral.* Attractions include the *Mainfränkisches Museum,* housed in the former arsenal with examples of the work of Riemenschneider (1460-1531), and the *Marienkirche,* built in AD706 and one of the oldest churches in the country. The Baroque Castle-Palace *(Residenz),* designed by Balthasar Neumann taking Versailles as a model, is supposedly one of the most elaborate buildings in the country. Candlelit Mozart concerts take place during the summer months in the *Emperor's Hall* and the *Hofgarten.* The grand staircase with the painting by Tiepolo here is regarded as one of the finest examples of the Baroque style in Europe. The *Käppele,* another Baroque building, was also designed by Balthasar Neumann. The town library and tourist information found a home in the *Haus zum Falken* (Falcon House), which has an impressive Rococo façade. Relaxation and diversion from sightseeing are provided by the numerous wine bars – the *Stachel* (thorn) was built in 1413 – cafés and restaurants. Nearly the whole of the city centre is a pedestrian zone, only disturbed by the passage of trams.

Berlin

Berlin is the largest city in Germany. It is also the country's capital and the future seat of Government. The move of several ministries is to be completed by 2002. Its location at the heart of Central Europe and the disappearance of the Iron Curtain are sure to mean that its importance in Europe can only increase, while its location within Germany is liable to shift the country's centre of gravity eastwards. Since November 1989 when the Wall came down, nearly 100 streets have been reconnected, disused 'ghost' stations on the underground and overground suburban railways have sprung back to life and the watchtowers, dogs and barbed wire that divided the city, the country and indeed the continent for 28 years have virtually disappeared; nevertheless the two parts of the city remain very different places. Although this is largely due to the economic contrast between West and East, the two halves of the city have never been of a uniform character. The east contains the densely populated, urban proletarian quarters of **Mitte, Pankow, Prenzlauer Berg** and **Friedrichshain** which inspired the theatre of Erwin Piscator and Bertold Brecht, although west Berlin also had its working-class quarters like the **Wedding, Neukölln** and **Kreuzberg** (the latter is known for its pubs and the high proportion of Turkish nationals whose shops dominate the streets). In comparison, the green and leafy areas of **Charlottenburg** and **Zehlendorf** exude a more bourgeois atmosphere. After the city was occupied by the four post-war victorious powers, the two halves diverged even more as West Berliners broke away from their past and embraced the idea of a new, intensely Western, Americanised city. At the same time their fellow citizens in the east chose instead to retain what remained of the old Berlin. It is for this reason that the eastern half of the city arguably gives a more accurate image of what Berlin was like in the 1920s and 30s, although visitors have to move slightly away from the city centre with its awkward juxtaposition of ponderous Prussian monuments and monolithic post-war social-realist architecture, in order to find the quarters that, despite wartime destruction followed by decades of decay, nevertheless retain a vestige of the atmosphere of the pre-war capital. **Alexanderplatz,** immortalised in Alfred Döblin's 1929 novel *Berlin Alexanderplatz,* was one of the main centres of the old 1920s Berlin as well as of post-war East Berlin. It is likely with time to re-emerge as an important focal point in the newly united city, although through relentless modernisation it has changed character completely and is now a bustling if faceless area of cafés, hotels and the 365m-high (1190ft) Television Tower *(Fernsehturm)* which dominates the skyline of the city. The oldest church in Berlin, the *Nikolai Church* (13th century), lent its name to the surrounding district, the **Nikolaiviertel.** This part of the city is an example for well-planned city restoration; it suffered tremendously during the war and was rebuilt partly with historic details, partly with modern façades, on the occasion of the 750th Anniversary of Berlin. Sweeping westwards away from Alexanderplatz is **Unter den Linden,** which Frederick

BERLIN

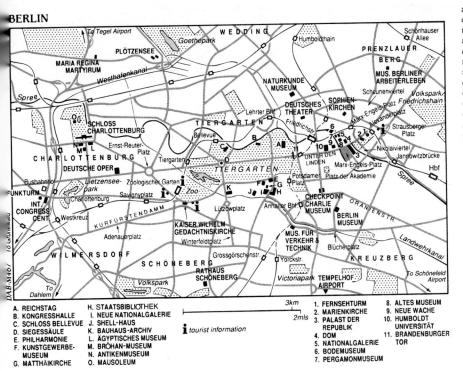

A. REICHSTAG	H. STAATSBIBLIOTHEK
B. KONGRESSHALLE	I. NEUE NATIONALGALERIE
C. SCHLOSS BELLEVUE	J. SHELL-HAUS
D. SIEGESSÄULE	K. BAUHAUS-ARCHIV
E. PHILHARMONIE	L. ÄGYPTISCHES MUSEUM
F. KUNSTGEWERBE-MUSEUM	M. BRÖHAN-MUSEUM
G. MATTHÄIKIRCHE	N. ANTIKENMUSEUM
	O. MAUSOLEUM

1. FERNSEHTURM
2. MARIENKIRCHE
3. PALAST DER REPUBLIK
4. DOM
5. NATIONALGALERIE
6. BODEMUSEUM
7. PERGAMONMUSEUM
8. ALTES MUSEUM
9. NEUE WACHE
10. HUMBOLDT UNIVERSITÄT
11. BRANDENBURGER TOR

i tourist information

3km
2mls

the Great saw as the centrepiece of his royal capital and which changed from one of the premier thoroughfares of the old unified city to the showpiece of the German Democratic Republic, lined with restored monumental buildings and diplomatic delegations to the former capital of the GDR. However, for nearly 30 years it was in fact a dead-end, a monumental avenue cut off by the Wall. At its western end, the *Brandenburger Gate* (*Brandenburger Tor*) has been the supreme symbol of the city of Berlin (and even of elusive German nationhood) since its completion in 1791. Situated just within the old boundaries of East Berlin the view of the Brandenburg Gate from the West was for nearly 30 years obscured by the Wall which ran directly in front of it and as such it became an eloquent symbol of post-war European division. Now, for the first time since 1961, it is accessible from both East and West and is perhaps the most potent evocation of the peaceful revolution of 1989. The deceptively benign-looking *Berlin Wall* has all but gone and walkers and cyclists now roam along what was so recently known as the *Todesstreifen* or *Death Strip*. Quite a few tourists were able to buy 'their own' piece of the Wall, other parts can now be seen in several museums.

Berlin is not just an industrial city but also a cultural and scientific capital with several universities. It houses three opera houses, 53 theatres and more than 100 cinemas. East Berlin has a rich array of museums, most of which can be found on *Museumsinsel* (Museum Island) in a fork of the *River Spree*. The most famous is the *Pergamon Museum* which houses works of classical antiquity such as the *Pergamon Altar*, and art of the Near East, Islam and the Orient. Among the many museums in the west are the *Ägyptisches Museum* (Egyptian Museum) at Charlottenburg, which contains the world-famous bust of Queen Nefertiti; the museums at Dahlem housing the major part of the Prussian State art collections; and the *Berlin Museum* in the old Supreme Court Building in Kreuzberg. The restored *Martin-Gropius-Bau* houses changing art exhibitions and the Berlin Gallery, with exhibits of the Jewish collection of the Berlin Museum and 20th-century paintings. Nearby is the **Prinz Albrecht Area** which is to become an international monument and memorial, as the building of the Gestapo, later the *Reichssicherheitshauptamt*, stood here. The exhibition entitled *Topography of Terror* documents this part of the history. The planned *Kulturforum* is to be constructed next to the *National Gallery* (designed by Mies van der Rohe), the Philharmonic, the Chamber Music Hall and other museums, and will be developed as a cultural centre for the city.

One of the major cultural attractions of the eastern part of Berlin is the *Deutsche Staatsoper* staging highly impressive performances in a superbly refurbished classical setting. However, with the demise of the German Democratic Republic, subsidies are no longer guaranteed and the Opera's future is uncertain as ticket prices are forced to conform to market rates.

Nevertheless, Berlin's cultural scene will no doubt continue to draw visitors from all over the world. The arguably finest concert hall is part of the *Schauspielhaus Berlin*, designed by the famous architect Karl Friedrich Schinkel. At 1200, 1500 and 1900, visitors can enjoy the carillon of the tower of the *French Cathedral*. Other attractions are as diverse as the *Berlin Festival* in September, the *Jazz Festival* in the autumn, the *Berlinale* in February, the Philharmonic Concerts and the thriving 'alternative' theatre.

Venturing west from the Opera along Unter den Linden and through the *Tiergarten* the visitor will eventually arrive at the heart of West Berlin, the *Kurfürstendamm*, popularly referred to as the 'Ku'damm'. As with so many features of this once divided city it is all too easy to attribute symbolic significance to the 'Ku'damm', for in a sense it is the embodiment of the glitzy materialistic West and of the differences created by the two systems which co-existed in Berlin for 40 years. Pulsating with traffic and people 24 hours a day and lined with cafés and shops, despite unification it still seems a thousand miles away from the bleak Alexanderplatz in the other half of the city. After taking time to sit in a café for a while and watch the crowds go by, strolling eastwards along the Ku'damm one will come to the *Kaiser-Wilhelm-Gedächtniskirche*. Preserved as a ruin after the destruction of the Second World War it is a stark reminder of the city's suffering from bombardment and its post-war rebirth. Not far from here also are the *Europa Center*, containing shops, nightlife and a rooftop café with a splendid view of the whole city, and the world-renowned department store, the *KaDeWe* (short for *Kaufhaus des Westens*). Other attractions of the western half of the city include: the *Siegesäule* (Victory Column), built at the order of Kaiser Wilhelm I two years after victory in the Franco-Prussian War of 1871; and the *Tiergarten*, an English-style park in the heart of the city. The *Reichstag*, reconstructed after 1945 and containing a fascinating exhibition, *Fragen an die Deutsche Geschichte* (Questioning German History), is to undergo another round of modernisation before the ministries can move in. *Schloss Charlottenburg*, the splendid Baroque and Rococo summer home of Frederick, was the former summer home of the king outside Berlin. The Palace Park is ideal for long walks. The *Gedenkstätte Plötzensee* is a memorial to more than 2500 members of the resistance who were executed next to the *National Gallery* and generally to the German resistance during the Nazi regime.

Since the 1920s, when the city immortalised by Christopher Isherwood in *Goodbye to Berlin* enjoyed a reputation for decadence and radicalism which attracted people from all over Europe, Berlin has been known for its vibrant, flamboyant nightlife. This was fostered after the forming of the Federal Republic as, cut off from the rest of the country, West Berlin strived to attract and nurture an alternative culture, a radical political awareness and an adventurous creativity. Several alternative projects have gained increasing attention,

among them the old *UFA-Factory* with cinema, circus, café, bakers and more, and the *Ökodorf e.V.* (centre and meeting place for people involved in ecological activities). Another of those is the first women-only hotel *artemisia* in Europe. Although Sally Bowles and her like may no longer be found revelling through the night in a smoke-filled cabaret on the Tauentzien, Berlin is still a city that is open 24 hours a day with an unrivalled range of nightclubs, bars, restaurants, cabarets and *Kneipen* (pubs), catering for every taste and budget. There are excellent twice-monthly listings guides, *Prinz*, *Tip* and *Zitty*, as well as *Oxmox* (monthly), giving details of everything going on in the city, including east Berlin. Published on alternate weeks, they are available from any news kiosk. Diversion from the city life can be easily found as the city boundaries include numerous recreational areas, such as the *Pfaueninsel* (peacock island), now a nature reserve; the *Spandauer* and *Tegler Forests* and the *Grunewald*. The People's Park *Friederichshain* in the eastern part of the city is simultaneously the largest and oldest park in east Berlin.

Mecklenburg-West Pomerania

The state of **Mecklenburg-West Pomerania** contains the longest stretch of the Baltic coast in Germany. The northeast city of **Neubrandenburg** on Lake Tollense is an example of a well-preserved medieval city with a city wall, moat and towers. The city centre is surrounded by a circular city wall with four city gates, three moats and several *Wiekhäuser* (fortifications). The university and old *Hanseatic* town of **Rostock** lies on the Baltic coast. The university was founded in 1419 and was the first university in Northern Europe. Attractions in the city include the elegant burghers' houses in *Thälmann Square*, the 15th-century *Town Hall*, the late Gothic *Marien Church* with its 15th-century astronomical clock and Baroque organ and the district of *Warnemünde* with its fishing harbour. The city was somewhat of a showpiece for the regime of the former GDR and has monumental housing complexes which are now the source of many of the city's problems. **Greifswald**, a small university town east of Rostock, has original 15th-century burghers' houses and part of a medieval fishing village. Birthplace of the famous German painter Caspar David Friedrich, the city's appearance was radically altered in the post-war period through the construction of new residential areas and industrial zones. The 'White Fleet' of passenger boats serves all the coastal ports, and calls at **Hiddensee Island**, an island with no cars and a large protected bird colony. The island of **Rügen**, with its nature reserve and famous chalk cliffs, is the largest island in Germany and is a popular holiday destination. From here there are connecting ferries to the Republic of Lithuania in the eastern Baltic region.

Schwerin was founded in 1160 and is still a charming town today. *Schwerin Castle*, on the lake of the same name and surrounded by a terraced garden crossed by a canal, was for many decades the residence of the Dukes of Mecklenburg and is one of the finest examples of German Gothic architecture. In the historic old quarter of the city is the well-preserved Gothic *Cathedral*, the *Town Hall* and an interesting museum with collections of French, German and Dutch paintings from the 17th, 18th and 19th centuries.

March of Brandenburg

Graphically described by the 19th-century German writer Theodor Fontane, the area of the **March of Brandenburg** that surrounds Berlin is a region of birch and pine forests and open horizons. The picturesque **Spreewald** lies south of Berlin and offers numerous waterways to be explored by boat and tranquil hamlets such as **Bückchen** to be discovered. Flat-bottomed barge is still the main means of transport in this region, as it has been for centuries. At **Lehde** there is a museum of original houses and farm buildings, complete with interiors. There are also several examples of the culture of the *Sorben*, a resident Slavic minority. **Potsdam**, although lacking many of its former attractions, has preserved several 18th-century buildings. The city also boasts three extensive parks, the *Neuen Garten* with the marble palace (closed for modernisation) and *Schloss Cecilienhof* (the Potsdam Conference took place here), the *Babelsberg* (park designed by the Prince of Pückler-Muskau) and naturally *Sanssouci* containing a gilded tea-house, and *Sanssouci Palace*, built on the instructions of Frederick the Great by Knobelsdorff. This, the favourite palace of Frederick the Great, is definitely a must for every visitor. The picture gallery next door to the palace contains many old masters. The *Dutch Quarter* of the city should also not be missed. Traces of Frederick the Great are also to be found at **Rheinsberg**, which was immortalised by Kurt Tucholsky's tale of the same name. The interior of the

The

DRESDEN PHILHARMONIC

Music Director: Michel Plasson
Principal Guest Conductor: Juri Temirkanov

Representatives of Saxonian orchestral culture, a proud tradition of 450 years of music making

The Orchestra's hallmarks are performances of interesting new pieces and the revival of important neglected works. Its traditional concerts with great choral symphony and opera concertante enjoy great popularity. The sheer virtuosity and musicality, subtle expressiveness, wide ranging dynamics and a vivid sound make every concert with the Dresden Philharmonic a memorable occasion.

Dresden Philharmonic
im Kulturpalast am Altmarkt
Postfach 120 368, 01005 Dresden, Germany.
Telephone 0351/4866 306 (24 hours),
0351/4866 286.

beautifully situated castle is still undergoing restoration, but visits are possible. One of the towers houses a Tucholsky Memorial. The *Cavalier House* has been home to a music academy since 1991 which concentrates on period music and the music played at the court of Crown Prince Frederick. The **Schorfheide** is an area of forest north of Berlin. Beavers, otters and eagles have claimed this picturesque area as their own. In the centre of this landscape of birches and pines lies the *Werbellin Lake*. Any visit to the region should also include a visit to the former Cistercian *Monastery of Chorin*, where in the summer concerts are staged.

Saxony, Saxony-Anhalt and Thuringia

Magdeburg, an industrial town to the southwest of Berlin, contains the *Statue of the Magdeburg Knight*, a *Cathedral* dating from AD955 and the *Monastery of Our Lady*. The attractive town of **Quedlinburg**, 55km (34 miles) southwest of Magdeburg, has many 16th-century half-timbered houses such as the *Finkenherd* and a Renaissance *Town Hall* that have been restored to their original condition. Among the towering scenery of the **Harz Mountains**, a region ideal for walking and winter sports holidays and dotted with villages noted for their attractive carved timber-fronted houses, lies the town of **Wernigerode** whose castle and 16th-century *Town Hall* endow it with a fairytale air. There is a museum of church relics here. On a walk the visitor can see half-timbered houses of six centuries, among them the *Crooked House*. The Harz is also one of the most beautiful hiking areas in Germany; since December 1989, hikers can enjoy the *Brocken* (highest point of the Harz) again. **Stolberg** is often described as the 'Pearl of the South Harz region' and contains characteristic half-timbered houses and a *Town Hall* dating back to 1492 which contains no inner staircase. Just to the south lies the city of **Halle**, where Martin Luther often preached in the *Marienkirche* in the *Market Square*. Handel was born here in 1685, and is commemorated by an annual festival. One of the most famous Reformation towns is nearby **Wittenberg**, where Martin Luther nailed his '95 Theses Against Indulgences' to the door of the castle church in 1517. Numerous magnificent buildings from the 16th-century, *Luther's House*, the *Melanchton House*, the *Castle Church* and the buildings of the former *University*

bear witness to the town's historical significance. South of Halle lies the historic town of **Naumburg** with its beautiful late Romanesque/early Gothic *Cathedral of St Peter and St Paul*. A trip from here into the old Hanseatic towns of **Salzwedel**, **Stendal** and **Tangermünde** to see the medieval fortifications is especially recommended.

Thuringia lies between Saxony and Hesse. The wooded heights and slate mountains of the *Thuringian Forest* make this region an ideal area for walking. The most famous route for hiking is the *Rennsteig* which stretches for over 168km (105 miles). The entire region of the Rennsteig is a protected zone and is therefore immune to any industrial or urban development. The walker will come across many rare plants and birds such as the capercaillie and the black grouse. A flourishing craft industry and winter sports facilities centred in **Suhl** are further attractions which draw visitors to the region. **Eisenach**, the birthplace of Johann Sebastian Bach, contains the oldest *Town Gate* in Thuringia and the Romanesque *Nikolai Church*. The town is dominated by the *Wartburg Castle* where Martin Luther sought refuge and translated the New Testament into German. The small town of **Rudolstadt** was known for its cultural life during the Renaissance, hosting plays of the Weimar Court Theatre, directed by Goethe, and founding a renowned court orchestra in 1635 which attracted many of the best classical musicians. It is now a popular stop along *Thuringia's Classic Road*. **Arnstadt**, where the young Johann Sebastian Bach was an organist in Arnstadt church, is often described as the gateway to the Thuringia Forest, with its lush hiking trails and magnificent views.

The southern 1000-year-old town of **Weimar** was home of many great men, including Luther, Bach, Liszt, Wagner and Schiller. A great cultural centre of the past, the city experienced its golden age in the 18th and 19th century. Goethe lived here for 50 years and was a major influence as a civil servant, theatre director and poet. Goethe's house is now the *National Museum*. Literature enthusiasts should not miss the *Goethe and Schiller Archive*. Bach was Court Organist and Court Concertmaster, Liszt and Richard Strauss were each director of music. There is documentation of their private and public lives kept in hotels and museums in the town. A gruesome museum commemorates the nearby site of **Buchenwald** concentration camp. Other noteworthy sites

in the region are **Gera** with its Renaissance *Town Hall* and fine *Burghers' Houses*, the old university town of **Jena**, the castle ruins at **Friedrichsroda**, the imperial city **Nordhausen** with its late Gothic *Cathedral* and Renaissance *Town Hall*, the picturesque town of **Mühlhausen**, and **Erfurt** with its well-preserved town centre which is on the UNESCO list of monuments. Saxony, too, has much to offer the visitor. To the southeast of Halle lies **Leipzig**, a city with a fascinating history. Lenin printed the first issues of his Marxist newspaper here. Lessing, Jean-Paul Sartre and Goethe all studied at the university. Leipzig is a town of music and books; 38 publishers have their houses here. It is the birthplace of Wagner, Mendelssohn was director of music and Bach was choirmaster at *St Thomas' Church* between 1723 and 1750 (St Thomas' Church has been completely restored, as has the 16th-century *Town Hall*). Johann Sebastian Bach's church choir still exists, and is of an excellent standard, as is the city's *Gewandhaus* Orchestra. The old *University* (1407), the famous *Auerbachs Cellar* and the *Kaffeebaum*, the most famous of the city's cafés, are further attractions in the city. Today Leipzig is known throughout the world for its international trade fairs.

To the southeast of Leipzig, in Southern Saxony, are Meissen and Dresden. **Meissen** is the oldest china manufacturing town in Europe, famous for its fine Meissen china. Visitors may tour the factory. When wandering through the narrow streets and alleyways of the city the visitor will feel transported back to a former age. The *Albrechtsburg Cathedral* (1485) and the *Bishop's Castle* tower above the city. Meissen is also the centre of a wine-growing region.

With over half a million inhabitants **Dresden** is one of the largest towns in southeast Germany. Its heyday was in the 17th and 18th centuries when August the Strong and subsequently his son August III ruled Saxony. The most famous building in the city is the restored *Zwinger Palace*, which contains many old masters in its picture gallery, among them the *Sistine Madonna* by Raphael. Dresden was often referred to as 'Florence on the Elbe' until allied bombings destroyed so much of the Baroque magnificence of the city in the Second World War. However, some of the finest buildings, such as the Catholic *Hofkirche*, the *Palace Church*, the *Semper Opera* and the *Green Vault* treasure chamber of the Saxon Princes, either survived the bombings or have

been restored in the intervening period, while the ruins of the *Frauenkirche* are a constant reminder of the horror unleashed on the city in 1944. Other attractions include the *Arsenal,* which has a vast collection of armour and weapons from the Middle Ages to the present day, the fountains in the *Pragerstrasse,* the old market, the Philharmonic Orchestra and the *Kreuz* Choir.
The **Erzgebirge** region near Dresden forms the border with the Czech Republic. Its mountainous wooded landscape makes it ideal for walkers in the summer and skiers in the winter. **Sächsische Schweiz** *(Saxon Switzerland),* the sandstone mountain range with its unique cliff formations, is visited every year by tourists from all over Germany and is to become a national park. **Chemnitz** (formerly Karl-Marx-Stadt) is the main town in the region. It was heavily destroyed during the war and only a few of the historic buildings remain. These are the *Old Town Hall* (16th century) and the 800-year-old *Red Tower*; others are **Freiberg**, **Kuchwald**, with its open-air theatre, and **Seiten** with its toy museum. **Zwickau** is the birthplace of Robert Schumann and is home to a late Gothic *Cathedral,* a *Town Hall* dating back to 1403 and numerous old burghers' houses.
The Dresden and Cottbus districts contain the minority **Sorbs**, descendants of a 6th-century slavic people. Sorb-language newpapers and broadcasts combine with teaching in local schools to retain the Sorb culture.
POPULAR ITINERARIES: 5-day: Rüdesheim–Lorelei Rock–St Goar–Koblenz–Bonn–Cologne (Rhine Cruise). **7-day:** (a) Heidelberg–Würzburg–Nuremberg–Regensburg–Neuschwanstein Castle (The Romantic Road). (b) Heidelberg–Heilbronn–Nuremberg (The Castle Road). (c) Erfurt–Weimar–Jena–Eisenach–Rudolstadt–Arnstadt (Thuringia's Classic Road).

SOCIAL PROFILE

FOOD & DRINK: The main meal of the day in Germany tends to be lunch with a light snack eaten at about seven in the evening. Breakfast served in homes and hotels usually consists of a boiled egg, bread rolls with jam, honey, cold cuts and cheese slices. Available from snack bars, butcher shops, bakers and cafés are grilled, fried or boiled sausages *(Bratwurst)* with a crusty bread roll or potato salad (costing approximately DM6, depending on facilities). There are also bread rolls filled with all kinds of sausage slices, hot meat filling (such as *Leberkäse*), pickled herring, gherkins and onion rings or cheese. In bakeries, *Strudel* with the traditional apple filling, a variety of fruits and *fromage frais,* is available. There is also an astonishingly wide variety of breads. A set menu meal (available from DM20) in a simple *Gasthof* or café usually includes three courses: a soup is the most popular starter. The main meal consists of vegetables or a salad, potatoes, meat and gravy. For puddings there is often a sweet such as a *blancmange,* fruit or ice cream. Restaurants often serve either beer or wine. Cakes and pastries are normally reserved for the afternoon with *Kaffee und Kuchen* ('coffee and cakes') taken at home or in a café. Cafés serving *Kaffee und Kuchen* are not only to be found in cities, towns and villages but also at or near popular excursion and tourist spots. International speciality restaurants such as Chinese, Greek, Turkish and others can be found everywhere in the western part of the country. Waiter or waitress service is normal although self-service restaurants are available. Bakeries and dairy shops specialise in lighter meals if preferred. *Local regional specialities* cover an enormous range:
Frankfurt and Hesse: *Rippchen mit Sauerkraut* (spare ribs) and of course *Frankfurter* sausages and *Ochsenbrust* with green sauce, *Zwiebelkuchen* (onion flan) and *Frankfurter Kranz* cream cake.
Westphalia and Northern Rhineland: *Rheinischer Sauerbraten* (beef marinaded in onions, sultanas, pimento, etc), *Reibekuchen* (potato fritters), *Pfeffer-Potthast* (spiced beef with bay leaves) and *Moselhecht* (Moselle pike with creamy cheese sauce). Westphalia is also famous for its smoked ham, sausages and bread such as *Pumpernickel.*
Stuttgart and Baden: *Schlachtplatte* (sauerkraut, liver sausage and boiled pork). A variety of pastas are served such as *Maultaschen* (a type of ravioli) and *Spätzle* (noodles), as well as *Eingemachtes Kalbfleisch* (veal stew with white sauce and capers) and *Schwarzwälder Kirschtorte* (Black Forest gateau).
Munich and Bavaria: *Leberkäs* (pork and beef loaf), as well as a variety of dumplings, *Spanferkel* (suckling pig), the famous *Weisswurst* (white sausages), *Strudel, Leberknödelsuppe* (liver dumplings soup), *Nürnberger Lebkuchen* (gingerbread) and from the same town grilled *Rostbratwurst* sausages.
Hamburg and Northern Germany: *Hamburger Aalsuppe* (eel/lobster/crayfish soup), *Labskaus* (hotpot with fried eggs), *Rote Grütze mit Sahne oder Vanillesosse* (fruit compote served with cream or custard), smoked eel, *Rumtopf* (fruit marinaded in rum), Lübecker marzipan, *Heidschnuckenbraten* (Lüneburg Heath mutton), fish with green sauce, *Bauernfrühstück* (omelette with fried potatoes, tomatoes and onions) and bread rolls filled with fish or prawns as a snack.
Bremen: *Kohl und Pinkel* (kale and sausages), *Matjes Hering* (white herring), eel soup and *Hannoversches Blindhuhn* (hotpot with bacon, potatoes, vegetables and fruit).
Berlin: *Eisbein mit Sauerkraut* (leg of pork) and mashed potatoes, *Bouletten* (hamburgers), *Kartoffelpuffer* (potato fritters), *Eierpfannkuchen* (pancakes), *Berliner Pfannkuchen* (doughnut), and *Berliner Weisse mit Schuss* (beer with a dash of something – usually raspberry syrup).
March of Brandenburg: *Teltower Rübchen* (swedes), *Mohnprielen* and *Mohnstriezel* (pastries with poppy seeds), *Morchelgerichte* (mushroom dishes), Oder crabs, *Eberswalder Spritzkuchen* (doughnuts), *Schwarzsauer mit Backpflaumen und Klößen* (black pudding with prunes and dumplings).
Saxony: *Leipziger Allerlei* (vegetables in white sauce), *Dresdner Stollen* (German christmas cake) and *Speckkuchen* (bacon flan).
Saxony-Anhalt: *Lehm und Stroh* (sauerkraut with mushy peas), *Köhlersuppe* (croutons, suet, onions and mushrooms), *Speckkuchen mit Eiern und Kümmel* (bacon flan with eggs and caraway seeds). *Zerbster Brägenwurst* (sausage) with Bitterbier. *Baumkuchen* (literally tree cake, the thin layers of pastry are like the rings of trees).
Thuringia: *Thüringer Rostbratwürste* (grilled sausages), *Hefeplinsen* (pancakes with raisins) with sugar or jam. Apple, plum, poppy seed, *fromage frais* or onion crumbles. There are numerous mushroom dishes, which are called *Schwämm.*
Mecklenburg-West Pomerania: *Plum'n un Klüt* (plums and dumplings), *Spickbost* (smoked goose breast).
Drink: Bars can either have table service and/or counter service, although customers will often find that the drinks bought are simply marked down on a beer mat to be paid for on leaving. The legal age for drinking alcohol in a bar or café is 18. Minors are allowed to go into a bar if accompanied by an adult but they will not be served alcohol. Opening hours depend on the proprietor but generally bars in major towns and resorts are open all day and close around midnight or later. Exceptions are Berlin and Hamburg where every pub can open for 24 hours. The national drink is **beer** in its many forms. Regional flavours vary from light *pilsner*-type lagers to heavy stouts. Two of particular note are *Bayrisches G'frornes* (frozen beer) and *Weizenbier* from Bavaria and *Mumme* (bittersweet beer without hops) to be found in Hannover.
German **wines** are among the finest in the world. Some of the most famous are grown in the Rhine and the Moselle Valley but also in the Ahr region, Nahe, Franconia and Baden area. Try *Äppelwoi* (cider) in Frankfurt/M, *Cannstatter* (white wine) in Stuttgart, *Kirschwasser* (cherry schnapps) in Baden, and *Würzburger* (dry white wine) in Würzburg.
NIGHTLIFE: In all larger towns and cities in western Germany and also in the major eastern cities visitors will have the choice between theatre, opera (Hamburgische Staatsoper, Deutsche Oper Berlin and the National Theatre in Munich are some of the most famous names), nightclubs, bars with live music and discos catering for every taste. Berlin, in particular, is famous for its large selection of after-hours venues. Traditional folk music is found mostly in rural areas. There are *Bierkellers* in the south and wine is drunk in small wine cellars in the Rhineland Palatinate, Franconia and Baden region.
SHOPPING: Special purchases include precision optical equipment such as binoculars and cameras, porcelain, handmade crystal, silver, steelware, Solingen knives, leatherwear, sports equipment, toys from Nuremberg and Bavarian *Loden* cloth. Special purchases in eastern Germany include musical instruments, wooden carved toys from the Erzgebirge Mountains, and Meissen china (the workshops in Meissen are open to the public).
Shopping hours: 0800/0900-1800/1830 Monday to Wednesday and Friday; 0900-2030 Thursday and 0900-1330/1400 Saturday. Smaller shops may close 1300-1500 for lunch. On the first Saturday of each month shops are open until 1600.
SPORT: The Federal Republic of Germany has extensive sports facilities with a sports field or stadium in all larger towns. League **football** matches take place on Saturday afternoons. International matches also take place from time to time: the national team were world champions in 1990, a title they previously won in 1954 and 1974, as well as having been runners-up in 1966, 1982 and 1986. **Racecourses** can be found at Baden-Baden, Hamburg, Munich and Frankfurt/M. **Horseriding** is very popular and hotels with riding facilities are located in all tourist regions. National centres are Verden and Warendorf (National Stud). There are over 200 major **golf** courses. The northern coastline and the extensive rivers and lakes provide **sailing, swimming** and both sea and river **fishing**. A fishing permit is needed (costing approximately DM15 a day). Fishing is particularly good on inland waterways; fishing and sailing are also popular at the Bay of Lietzow on the Baltic coast. The Baltic coast has many beaches. All resorts and larger towns in the Federal Republic of Germany have swimming pools. **Winter sport** resorts are mainly in the Suhl area in the south of the country. The main resort is Oberhof, which offers excellent **ski-jumping** and **tobogganing**. **Ice hockey** and **skating** are both popular. **Skiing:** In Bavaria, skiing is available at resorts such as *Garmisch-Partenkirchen, Berchtesgaden, Oberstdorf, Inzell, Reit im Winkl,* as well as in the southern mountains. Other areas are the Harz Mountains, the Black Forest and the Bavarian Forest. The season runs from November to April. **Curling** is especially popular in Upper Bavaria. Other popular sports include **tennis, squash** and **windsurfing**. **Cycling** is increasingly popular and cycling paths ensure that even in cities cycling is a safe form of transport. Push-bikes are available from certain railway stations for hire and a list of these railway stations is available through DB or GNTO. Organised holidays can be booked through: *Rotalis Reisen per Rad,* PO Box 100244, 80593 Baldham near Munich (tel: (8106) 7175) and other organisations. Further information is available from the Allgemeiner Deutscher Fahrrad-Club e.V. (German Cycling Club) (ADFC), Hollerallee 23, 28209 Bremen. Tel: (421) 346 290. **Walking areas:** The Harz Mountains, Black Forest and the Bavarian Forest are some of the best. The network of marked trails amounts to 132,000km (82,500 miles) and also in the eastern states enthusiasts can find new trails. The District of Templin in the March of Brandenburg provides 480km (300 miles) of paths. The Deutsche Alpenverein (German Alps Club) maintains several huts in the Alps and the other ranges. It also organises tours and courses in **rock climbing**. The Saxon Hills between Dresden and Bad Schandau, with more than 1000 prepared routes, provide good training for aspiring climbers. Excellent facilities can also be found in Oberhof.
SPECIAL EVENTS: Hundreds of annual festivals are celebrated throughout the country and full details can be obtained from the Tourist Board. The following list is a selection of those events celebrated in 1995/96:
Mar 17-Apr 17 '95 *Frühlingsdom* (folk festival and funfare), Hamburg. **Apr 8-May 1** *Frühjahrs-Dippemess* (folk festival), Frankfurt/M. **Apr 15-May 1** *Spring Fair,* Aachen. **Apr 16-17** *Easter Festival,* Potsdam. **Apr 20-23** *Shakespeare Festival,* Weimar. **Apr 22-May 14** *Spring Market,* Leipzig. **May 1-31** *International May Music Festival,* Wiesbaden. **May 5-7** *Harbour Anniversary,* Hamburg. **May 6** *The Rhine in Flames,* Bonn to Linz/Rhine. **May 6-Jun 4** *Lake Constance Festival,* Konstanz. **May 12-21** *International Festival of Old Music,* Stuttgart. **May 19-21** *City Festival,* Münster. **May 20-Jun 5** *Music Festival,* Dresden. **May 26-27** *City Festival,* Bremen. **May 27-28** *International Rum Regatta,* Flensburg. **May 31-Jun 13** *Gewandhaus Festival and 'Allerleipzing' Cultural Festival,* Leipzig. **Jun 2-5** *International Jazz Festival,* Moers. **Jun 2-6** *75th Handel Festival,* Göttingen. **Jun 3-24** *Mozart Festival,* Würzburg. **Jun 5-20** *Film Festival,* Potsdam. **Jun 9-11** *City Festival,* Leipzig. **Jun 9-12** *Wine Festival,* Freiburg. **Jun 16-25** *Marksmen's Fair,* Hildesheim, near Hannover. **Jun 17-18** *Celebration of the 837th Anniversary of the City's Foundation,* Munich. **Jun 17-25** *Kiel Week* (world's largest sailing event), Kiel. **Jun 20-25** *Richard Strauss Festival,* Garmisch-Partenkirchen. **Jun 23-Jul 2** *Festival Week Marking the 777th Anniversary of the Town Charter,* Rostock. **Jun 24-Jul 1** *Munich Film Festival.* **Jun 30-Jul 9** *875th Anniversary celebrations,* Freiburg. **Jul 1** *The Rhine in Flames,* Rüdesheim. **Jul 1-9** *Bach Festival,* Berlin. **Jul 20-24** *1200th Anniversary of Town's Foundation,* Waibstadt. **End of Jul-End of Aug** *Wagner Festival,* Bayreuth. **Aug 11-20** *International Summer Festival,* Bremen. **Aug 18-21** *Wine Festival,* Rüdesheim. **Aug 25-Sep 3** *1000th Anniversary celebrations,* Ilsenberg. **Sep 16-Oct 1** *Oktoberfest Beer Festival,* Munich. **Sep 28-Oct 8** *Cannstatt Folk Festival,* Stuttgart. **Oct 2-22** *Holsten Cup Tennis,* Berlin. **Oct 12-22** *European Humour and Satire Festival (Laughter Fair),* Leipzig. **Oct 14-29** *Freimarkt* (folk festival), Bremen. **Nov 3-Dec 3** *Winterdom* (folk festival and funfair), Hamburg. **Nov 11** *750th Anniversary as a Free Imperial Town,* Regensburg. **Late Nov-late Dec** *Christmas markets,* various towns. **Feb 20 '96** *Carnival Processions,* Mainz, Cologne, Düsseldorf.
SOCIAL CONVENTIONS: Handshaking is customary. Normal courtesies should be observed and it is common to be offered food and refreshments when visiting someone's home. When eating a meal it is considered impolite to leave the left hand on your lap when using the

right hand for soup etc. The left hand should rest lightly on the table. Before eating it is normal to say *Guten Appetit* to the other people at the table to which the correct reply is *Ebenfalls*. It is customary to present the hostess with unwrapped flowers (according to tradition, one should always give an uneven number and it is worth noting that red roses are exclusively a lover's gift). Courtesy dictates that when entering a shop, restaurant or similar venue, visitors should utter a greeting such as *Guten Tag* (or *Grüss Gott* in Bavaria) before saying what it is that they want; to leave without saying *Auf Wiedersehen* can also cause offence. Similarly, when making a telephone call, asking for the person you want to speak to without stating first who you are is considered rude. Casual wear is widely acceptable, but more formal dress is required for some restaurants, the opera, theatre, casinos and important social functions. Evening wear is worn when requested. Smoking is prohibited where notified and on public transport and in some public buildings. Visitors should be prepared for an early start to the day with shops, businesses, schools, etc opening at 0800 or earlier. It is very common practice to take a mid-afternoon stroll on Sunday, so that town and city centres at this time are often very animated places, in stark comparison with Saturday afternoons when, due to early closing of the shops, town centres can seem almost deserted. **Tipping:** Service charge on hotel bills. Restaurant bills in the west include 10% service charge, it is customary to round up to the nearest figure. It is also customary to tip taxi drivers, hairdressers and cloak-room attendants.

BUSINESS PROFILE

ECONOMY: From the ruins of the Third Reich, both parts of divided post-war Germany emerged over the next two decades as the economic powerhouses of their respective European blocs. The unified German economy is now the third most productive in the world with a GDP of US$1.6 trillion (£850 billion). The bulk of this achievement was in the West (the pre-unification Federal Republic), where it is still referred to as the 'Wirtschaftswunder' (economic miracle). The Western economy is essentially industrial, with large chemical and car manufacturing plants, mechanical, electrical and electronic engineering, and rapidly growing advanced technology and service sectors in computing, biotechnology, information processing and media. The East's (former Democratic Republic's) economy never dominated COMECON – the Soviet bloc Council for Mutual Economic Assistance – in the way that the West did the EC: the former USSR economy overshadowed all of its East European neighbours. However, the East did achieve the highest growth and per capita income within the bloc, and developed major trading links both within and outside COMECON. Lacking raw materials, the core of its trade exchanged manufactured goods for Polish coal and Soviet oil and gas but, by the time of reunification, 30% of East German trade was conducted outside the bloc. Its geographical position and special relationship with West Germany, coupled with a strong industrial base, motivated this process. Although the East was undoubtedly economically successful by Eastern European standards, reunification illustrated starkly, almost brutally, how far Eastern Europe had fallen behind the West. Optimists, particularly among the old FRG's political leadership, declared brightly that West German industry would smoothly sweep up the more efficient and modern industries in the East while a large injection of corporate investment from the same quarter would account for any excess or redundant capacity in the GDR economy. Western business executives were far more sceptical. While they appreciated the new market opportunities, they concluded that demand in the East could be met by increasing their existing production levels and shipping the goods eastwards rather than 'greenfield' investment or purchasing ailing, incompatible and costly GDR industries. There have been some notable exceptions to this trend: Volkswagen took under their wing the manufacturers of the legendary Trabant motor car, but most of the inward investment has been in relatively underdeveloped service industries such as media, advertising and management services. Though welcome, this is inadequate. Eastern economic development cannot be based on services alone; some industrial base is necessary. The Bonn government also hoped that the instant conversion of the GDR's Ostmark into Deutschmarks at the artificial rate of one-to-one (as against a true market rate of between 5 and 10 Ostmarks to DM1) would stimulate the eastern economy by putting more money into Eastern pockets. Unfortunately, the newly affluent Eastern consumers showed more interest in buying imported goods than home-grown ones. Most economic analysts believe that the currency conversion and other decisions were serious misjudgements conceived during the heady rush towards unification. By

1991, it was clear that the Eastern economy, were it standing alone, would collapse. Output had fallen to 35% of pre-unification levels and unemployment, and workers on 'zero short-time working' (effectively redundancy on full pay) accounted for half the workforce. The economy as a whole has weathered the global recession of the early 1990s fairly well. Growth has slowed but is still occurring. There is confidence that the underlying strength of the economy is such that the East will eventually be pulled up to approximate economic parity with the West, perhaps over the space of a decade. However, many policy planners are becoming seriously worried about the cost of this mammoth enterprise. Many billions of Deutschmarks have been pumped into the development of the former East since reunification in 1989, causing a huge drain on German resources. More recently, severe spending cuts have been introduced and the *Bundesregierung* (federal government) has managed to resist pressure from other European governments to cut interest rates. German trade with Eastern Europe has grown relatively quickly compared to other routes; otherwise no change in German trade patterns should be expected. The main UK exports are office and data-processing equipment, electrical goods and machinery and oil; vehicles and various types of machinery comprise the bulk of UK imports.

BUSINESS: Business people are expected to dress smartly. English is spoken by many local business people, but it is an advantage to have a working knowledge of German, or an interpreter. Appointments should be made well in advance, particularly in the summer. Appointments may be suggested slightly earlier in the day than is often the custom in the UK. Once made, appointment times should be strictly adhered to. Some firms may close early Friday afternoon. Always use titles such as *Herr Doktor*, or *Frau Doktor* when addressing business contacts. Punctuality is essential for business visits. **Office hours:** 0800-1600 Monday to Friday.

BUSINESS IN THE NEW STATES: 45 years of central planning have left the economy of what is now the eastern half of the Federal Republic of Germany in a weak state with numerous uneconomic companies, a lack of essential investment in up-to-date technology and distorted markets (see *Economy* section above). However, together with the EU Commission, the German government is attempting to encourage investment in the eastern half of the country in order to expedite the reconstruction (*Wiederaufbau*) of the economy there and to raise material conditions to the same high standards of western Germany. To this end the Government has set up investment incentives which, they stress, are available on equal terms to both German and foreign investors alike and the European Recovery Programme Fund (formerly the Marshall Fund) has been extended to cover what was previously the German Democratic Republic. Information about the various schemes is available from the Department of Trade and Industry in London *or* from the various banks administering the incentive programmes for the Federal Government. They are as follows:

European Recovery Programme (Berliner Industrie Bank), Landecker Strasse 2, 14199 Berlin. Tel: (30) 820 030. Fax: (30) 824 3003.
Bank for Reconstruction (Kreditanstalt für Wiederaufbau), Palmengartenstrasse 5-9, 60325 Frankfurt/M. Tel: (69) 7431-0. Fax: (69) 7431-2944. European Recovery Programme credits for modernisation, effluent treatment and clean-air programmes plus its own investment credit scheme.
German Equalisation Bank (Deutsche Ausgleichsbank), Wielandstrasse 4, 53173 Bonn. Tel: (228) 831-0. Fax: (228) 831-255. European Recovery Programme credits for start-ups, waste management and energy-saving programmes plus its own investment credit scheme.
Consulates in the Federal Republic of Germany can also advise potential investors (see beginning of the entry).
COMMERCIAL INFORMATION: The following organisations can offer advice: German-British Chamber of Industry and Commerce, Mecklenburg House, 16 Buckingham Gate, London SW1E 6LB. Tel: (0171) 233 5656. Fax: (0171) 233 7835. *(This organisation also has branch offices in most major Western European capitals); or*
Deutscher Industrie- und Handelstag (Association of German Chambers of Industry and Commerce), Adenauerallee 148, 53113 Bonn. Tel: (228) 104-0. Fax: (228) 104-158.
The organisation affiliates 69 Chambers of Industry and Commerce. There are also Chambers of Industry and Commerce in all major German towns and a regional Chamber of Commerce for each of the states.
CONFERENCES/CONVENTIONS: The western part of Germany can offer a highly developed and well-equipped network of conference destinations. For

information, contact the German Convention Bureau, Gebäude 303, Lufthansa-Basis, 60528 Frankfurt/M. Tel: (69) 951 092. Fax: (69) 951 192.
Founded in 1973 the Bureau is a non-profitmaking organisation sponsored by Germany's major convention cities, hotels, travel agents and carriers, as well as the country's leading travel and tourist associations, including the German National Tourist Board, Lufthansa and the German Railways.

CLIMATE

Temperate throughout the country with warm summers and cold winters, but prolonged periods of frost or snow are rare. Rain falls throughout the year.
Required clothing: European clothes with light- to medium-weights in summer, medium- to heavy-weights in winter. Waterproofing is needed throughout the year.

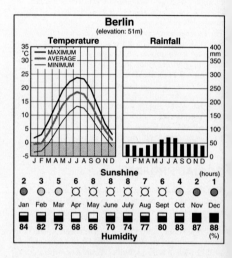

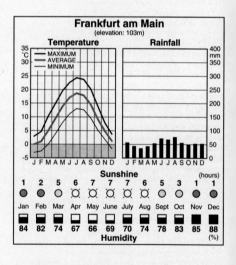

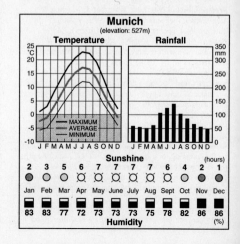

Ghana

Location: West Africa.

Ghana Tourist Board
PO Box 3106, Tesano, Nsawam Road, Accra, Ghana
Tel/Fax: (21) 231 779. Telex: (94) 2143 TOURISM.

Ghana Tourist Development Company
PO Box 8710, Accra, Ghana
Tel: (21) 772 084. Fax: (21) 772 093.

Ghana High Commission (Education and Visas)
104 Highgate Hill, London N6 5HE
Tel: (0181) 342 8686. Fax: (0181) 342 8566/70. Telex: 21370. Opening hours: 0930-1300 Monday to Friday (Visa section).

Ghana High Commission (Tourist Information)
102 Park Street, London W1Y 3RJ
Tel: (0171) 493 4901. Fax: (0171) 629 1730. Opening hours: 0930-1300 and 1400-1730 Monday to Friday.

British High Commission
PO Box 296, Osu Link, off Gamel Abdul Nasser Avenue, Accra, Ghana
Tel: (21) 221 665 *or* 669 585. Fax: (21) 664 652. Telex: 2323 (a/b UKREP GH).

Embassy of the Republic of Ghana
3512 International Drive, NW, Washington, DC 20008
Tel: (202) 686 4520. Fax: (202) 686 4527.

Ghana Permanent Mission to the United Nations (Visas and Tourist Information)
19 East 47th Street, New York, NY 10017
Tel: (212) 832 1300.

Embassy of the United States of America
PO Box 194, Ring Road East, Accra, Ghana
Tel: (21) 775 348/9 *or* 775 297/8. Fax: (21) 776 008.
Telex: 2579 (a/b EMBUSA GH).

Embassy of the Republic of Ghana
1 Clemow Avenue, Ottawa, Ontario K1S 2A9
Tel: (613) 236 0871/3. Fax: (613) 236 0874.

Canadian Embassy
PO Box 1639, 42 Independence Avenue, Accra, Ghana
Tel: (21) 773 791 *or* 228 555/6. Fax: (21) 773 792.
Telex: 2024.

AREA: 238,537 sq km (92,100 sq miles).
POPULATION: 15,400,000 (1991 estimate).
POPULATION DENSITY: 64.6 per sq km.
CAPITAL: Accra. **Population:** 867,459 (1984).
GEOGRAPHY: Ghana is situated in West Africa and is a rectangular-shaped country bounded to the north by Burkina Faso, the east by Togo, the south by the Atlantic Ocean and the west by the Côte d'Ivoire. A narrow grassy plain stretches inland from the coast, widening in the east, while the south and west are covered by dense rainforest. To the north are forested hills beyond which is dry savannah and open woodland. In the far north is a plateau averaging 500m (1600ft) in height. In the east the Akuapim Togo hills run inland from the coast along the Togo border. The Black and White Volta rivers enter Ghana from Burkina Faso merging into the largest man-made lake in the world, Lake Volta. Ghana's coastline is dotted with sandy palm-fringed beaches and lagoons.
LANGUAGE: The official language is English. Local African languages are widely spoken, including Twi, Fante, Ga and Ewe.
RELIGION: Christian, Muslim and traditional beliefs. All forms of religion have a strong influence on Ghanaian life.
TIME: GMT.
ELECTRICITY: 220 volts AC, 50Hz; usually 3-pin plugs. Single phase, 3-pin plugs are used in larger buildings. Older buildings have 2-pin plugs. Light bulbs are of the bayonet type.
COMMUNICATIONS: Telephone: IDD service has recently become available to major cities. Country code: 233. Outgoing international code: 00. Rehabilitation and modernisation are still in progress. **Fax:** There is a 24-hour fax service in Accra. **Telex/telegram:** Services are available from Post & Telecommunications Corporation, High Street, Accra and Stewart Avenue, Kumasi. There are three charge rates. **Post:** Airmail letters to Europe may take two weeks or more to arrive. **Press:** Daily newspapers are in English and include *The Ghanaian Times*, *The People's Daily Graphic* and *The Pioneer*.
BBC World Service and Voice of America frequencies: From time to time these change. See the section *How to Use this Book* for more information.

BBC:

MHz	17.79	15.40	12.09	9.600

Voice of America:

MHz	21.48	15.58	9.575	6.035

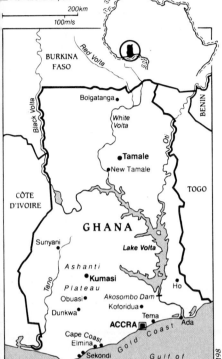

Palms and sand beaches near Cape Coast, Gulf of Guinea

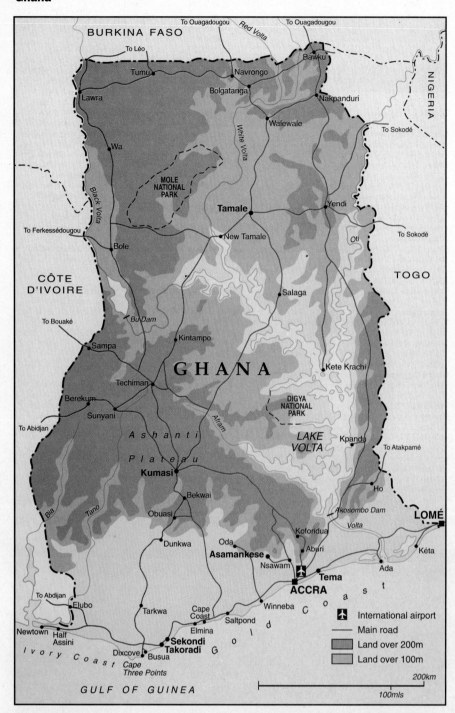

business the applicant will be conducting in Ghana). (d) 4 passport-size photos.
Non-Commonwealth nationals: (a) Valid passport. (b) Application form. (c) 4 passport-size photos.
Working days required: 2.
Note: Business travellers involved in diamond or scrap-metal industries must have their applications referred to Accra and should allow a month for processing.
Temporary residence: Application with sufficient notice to be made to High Commission or Embassy.

MONEY

Currency: Cedi (¢) = 100 pesewas. Notes are in denominations of ¢1,000, ¢500, ¢200, ¢100, ¢50. Coins are in denominations of ¢100, ¢50, ¢20, ¢10 and ¢5.
Currency exchange: The Ghanaian Cedi is pegged to the US Dollar but, as indicated in the exchange rate indicators below, it has been subject to frequent devaluations. Foreign currency must be exchanged with authorised dealers only (eg banks and Forex Bureaux).
Credit cards: Limited use of Diners Club, Visa and Access/Mastercard. Check with your credit card company for details of merchant acceptability and other services which may be available.
Exchange rate indicators: The following figures are included as a guide to the movements of the Cedi against Sterling and the US Dollar:

Date:	Oct '92	Sep '93	Jan '94	Jan '95
£1.00=	773.08	1005.00	1400.00	1800.00
$1.00=	487.14	658.15	905.00	1000.00

Currency restrictions: Free import of foreign currency, subject to declaration (on exchange control form T5 which must be retained to record transactions). Export of foreign currency is limited to the amount declared on import. The import and export of local currency is limited to ¢3000 and should be recorded in passport. Unused local currency can be re-exchanged on proof of authorised exchange, and visitors are advised to retain all currency exchange receipts.
Banking hours: 0830-1400 Monday to Thursday and 0830-1500 Friday. A few city branches are open from 0830-1200 Saturday.

DUTY FREE

The following goods may be imported into Ghana by persons aged 16 and over without incurring customs duty:
400 cigarettes or 100 cigars or 1lb of tobacco; 1 litre of spirits and 1 litre of wine; 200g of perfume; toiletries and small food items.
Prohibited items: Animals; firearms; ammunition; explosives; milk with a high fat content and mercury.

PUBLIC HOLIDAYS

Jan 1 '95 New Year's Day. **Jan 7** Fourth Republic Anniversary. **Mar 6** Independence Day. **Apr 14-17** Easter. **May 1** Labour Day. **Jul 1** Republic Day. **Dec 25-26** Christmas. **Dec 29** Bank Holiday. **Jan 1 '96** New Year's Day. **Jan 7** Fourth Republic Anniversary. **Mar 6** Independence Day. **Apr 5-8** Easter.

HEALTH

Regulations and requirements may be subject to change at short notice, and you are advised to contact your doctor well in advance of your intended date of departure. Any numbers in the chart refer to the footnotes below.

	Special Precautions?	Certificate Required?
Yellow Fever	Yes	1
Cholera	Yes	2
Typhoid & Polio	Yes	-
Malaria	3	-
Food & Drink	4	-

[1]: A yellow fever vaccination certificate is required by all.
[2]: A cholera vaccination certificate is recommended if coming from an infected or endemic area, and

PASSPORT/VISA

Regulations and requirements may be subject to change at short notice, and you are advised to contact the appropriate diplomatic or consular authority before finalising travel arrangements. Details of these may be found at the head of this country's entry. Any numbers in the chart refer to the footnotes below.

	Passport Required?	Visa Required?	Return Ticket Required?
Full British	Yes	Yes	Yes
BVP	Not valid	-	-
Australian	Yes	Yes	Yes
Canadian	Yes	Yes	Yes
USA	Yes	Yes	Yes
Other EU (As of 31/12/94)	Yes	Yes	Yes
Japanese	Yes	Yes	Yes

PASSPORTS: Valid passport required by all except nationals of Benin, Burkina Faso, Cape Verde, Côte d'Ivoire, Gambia, Guinea Republic, Guinea-Bissau, Mali, Mauritania, Niger, Nigeria, Senegal, Sierra Leone, Togo and Zimbabwe holding some proof of national identity.
British Visitors Passport: Not acceptable.
VISAS: Required by all except nationals of Benin,

Burkina Faso, Cape Verde, Côte d'Ivoire, Gambia, Guinea Republic, Guinea-Bissau, Mali, Mauritania, Niger, Nigeria, Senegal, Sierra Leone, Togo and Zimbabwe.
Note: Visas can also be issued on arrival at the Kotoka International Airport, Accra, provided the applicant gives a 2-week prior written notification to either the Director, Ghana Immigration Service, Accra, or The Executive Director, Ghana Tourist Board, Box 3106, Accra.
Types of visa: Single-entry, Multiple-entry and Transit. An Entry visa is required for all non-Commonwealth nationals not mentioned above. An Entry Permit is required for all Commonwealth nationals.
Cost: All visas (including Transit visas) and permits cost £15.00; Multiple-entry visas cost £35.00.
Validity: Valid for 3 months from the date of issue. However, length of stay is at the discretion of airport officials and only one month is guaranteed. Visas may be extended when in Ghana.
Application to: Consulate (or Consular section at Embassy or High Commission). For addresses, see top of entry.
Application requirements: *British and Commonwealth nationals:* (a) Valid passport. (b) Completed entry permit application form. (c) Evidence of return ticket and/or a letter of guarantee from a company in support of the application (the letter should explain the nature of

vaccination is strongly recommended. Cholera is a serious risk in this country and precautions are essential. See the *Health* section at the back of the book.

[3]: Malaria risk, predominantly in the malignant *falciparum* form, exists all year throughout the country. Malaria precaution is advised.

[4]: All water should be regarded as being potentially contaminated. Water used for drinking, brushing teeth or making ice should have first been boiled or otherwise sterilised. Milk is unpasteurised and should be boiled. Powdered or tinned milk is available and is advised, but make sure that it is reconstituted with pure water. Avoid dairy products which are likely to have been made from unboiled milk. Only eat well-cooked meat and fish, preferably served hot. Pork, salad and mayonnaise may carry increased risk. Vegetables should be cooked and fruit peeled.

Bilharzia (schistosomiasis) is present. Avoid swimming and paddling in fresh water. Swimming pools which are well-chlorinated and maintained are safe.

Rabies is present. For those at high risk, vaccination before arrival should be considered. If you are bitten abroad, seek medical advice without delay. For more information consult the *Health* section at the back of the book.

Health care: Health insurance is advised. Medical facilities exist in all the regional capitals as well as in most towns and villages.

TRAVEL - International

AIR: Ghana's national airline is *Ghana Airways (GH)*. It provides flights from Accra to London three times a week. Other airlines flying to Accra include *Aeroflot, Air Afrique, Balkan, British Airways, Egypt Air, Ethiopian Airlines, KLM, Nigeria* and *Swissair*.

Approximate flight time: From London to Accra is 6 hours 30 minutes (direct) *or* 8 hours 25 minutes (with stopover in Kano).

International airport: *Accra 'Kotoka' (ACC)*, 10km (6 miles) north of Accra (travel time – 20 minutes). Taxis to the city are available. Work has started on upgrading the airport.

Departure tax: US$10.

SEA: Ghana has two deep-water ports, one at Takoradi, the other at Tema.

ROAD: A coast road links Lagos, Cotonou and Lomé to Accra. The best internal road from Abidjan (Côte d'Ivoire) runs inland through Kumasi. The road from Burkina Faso crosses the border at Navrongo. Long-distance taxis operate between Ghana and neighbouring countries. See below for information on **documentation.**

TRAVEL - Internal

AIR: There are domestic airports in Kumasi, Tamale and Sunyani.

RAIL: The rail network is limited to a 1000km (600-mile) loop by the coast connecting the cities Accra, Takoradi and Kumasi and several intervening towns. Trains run at least twice a day on all three legs of this triangle. There are two classes of ticket. Passenger cars are not air-conditioned. Children under three years of age travel free. Half-fare is charged for children aged 3-11.

ROAD: There are almost 32,000km (21,000 miles) of roads in Ghana of which 6000km (3700 miles) are paved. Traffic drives on the right. **Car hire:** Available from *Hertz/Avis* and local agencies but extremely expensive, whether with or without driver. **Coach:** State-run coach services connect all major towns. **Documentation:** An International Driving Permit is recommended, although it is not legally required. A British driving licence is valid for 90 days.

URBAN: Two major road improvement projects are underway in Accra and Kumasi as an attempt to improve traffic flow in these cities. Accra has extensive bus services operated by the City Transport Authority, although more than half of the journeys are operated by private services which run small buses *(Moto-way)*, minibuses *(Tro-Tro)* – of which there are 120,000 – and wooden-body trucks *(Mammy Wagons)*. There are over 300,000 conventional taxis. Drivers do not generally expect tips.

ACCOMMODATION

HOTELS: There are three international chain hotels in Ghana, all located in the capital; The Labadi Beach Hotel managed by the Metropole of UK; Golden Tulip, managed by Golden Tulip, the Netherlands and The Novotel managed by Accra/Novotel, France. In addition to these there are international-standard hotels, hostels and guest-houses throughout the country and mainly concentrated in the urban centes. **Grading:** Hotels, hostels and guest-houses are star-graded and licensed by the Ghana Tourist Board.

Top picture: Kwame Nkrumah Memorial, Accra. Above: Elmina Fort & Castle, Central Ghana

HOST-BASED VISITS: In the past it has been possible to obtain accommodation in outlying villages by negotiating with the Headman. A new venture, *Insight Travel*, offers visitors the opportunity of staying with Ghanaians and sharing village activities such as working on the family farm, learning local music or dance, and participating in community events. Excursions can also be arranged. All hosts (who come from a variety of backgrounds including business, teaching and government service) have homes in or around Kumasi in the Ashanti region of Ghana. Holidays are organised in conjunction with *Adehye Tours* in Ghana. In the UK, contact the Africa Travel Shop, 4 Medway Court, Leigh Street, London WC1H 9QX. Tel: (0171) 387 1211; *or* Insight Travel, 6 Norton Road, Garstang, Preston, Lancashire PR3 1JY. Tel: (01995) 606 095. Costs of holidays are usually around £500 per person, plus flight.
CAMPING: Camping in national parks is encouraged, but only for the very adventurous, as it can be dangerous. In game reserves visitors must be accompanied by an armed guide.

RESORTS & EXCURSIONS

For the purposes of this guide, the country has been divided into three regions: Greater Accra, Kumasi Ashanti and the West Coast. This does not necessarily reflect administrative or tribal boundaries.

Greater Accra Region

Accra: The *National Museum* has a large collection of Ghanaian art. The *Makola Market*, a large and busy open-air market, is located on Kojo Thompson Road. Traders from surrounding villages bring their wares every day. The *Centre for National Culture* is an arts centre and crafts market, where crafts, *kente* and other traditional cloths can be purchased. The *Kwame Nkrumah Mausoleum*, on the High Street, is a magnificent monument to the first President of Ghana. The *National Theatre* is a Chinese showpiece and the venue for musical shows, plays, dances and conferences.
Aburi: 38km (24 miles) to the north of Accra in the *Akwapim Hills*, *The Sanatorium* (now a rest house), built there in the 19th century, is indicative of the refreshing climate. The *Botanical Gardens,* planted by British naturalists in colonial days, has a comprehensive array of subtropical plants and trees. **Ada** is a popular resort at the mouth of the Volta, where Ghanaians and tourists go for watersports. A luxury hotel has recently been built here. Swimming is safe in the river mouth. Anglers have the opportunity to catch barracuda and Nile perch. Nearby are the salt marshes of the *Songow Lagoon,* famous for their birdlife.
Shai Hills Game Reserve: A comparatively small reserve some 50km (30 miles) by road from Accra. Horses may be hired here to explore the park.

Kumasi Ashanti Region

Kumasi is the historic capital of the Ashanti civilisation, where ruins of the *Maryha Palace* and the *Royal Mausoleum* burnt down by Lord Baden-Powell may be examined. The *Cultural Centre* is a complex comprising a museum, library and outdoor auditorium largely devoted to the Ashanti. There is also a *'Living Museum'*, a farm and reconstituted village, where craftsmen such as potters, goldsmiths and sculptors can be seen at work using traditional methods. Of particular interest are weavers making the vividly coloured kente cloth, the ceremonial dress of the region.
Owabi Wildlife Sanctuary: Located to the west, close to Kumasi. Further to the northeast is the *Boufom Wildlife Sanctuary* containing the spectacular *Banfabiri Falls*. To the south is the pleasant gold-mining city of **Obuasi**.
Akosombo: Originally built to house construction workers when the Volta River was dammed to form the largest man-made sheet of water on earth, Akosombo is now developing as a holiday centre, particularly for watersports. The waterway stretches for two-thirds of the length of the country. A round trip on the car ferry to **Kete-Kachi** takes a day; alternatively one can take the 3-day trip to the northern capital of **New Tamale** at the head of the lake. There are facilities for sailing, water-skiing and other watersports.
Mole National Park: The best equipped of the reservations in Ghana. The visitor can go either on foot or hire a Land-Rover, but must always be accompanied by a guide. Routes are planned to take in species of antelope, monkeys, buffalo, warthog and, more rarely, lions and elephants, which have been introduced into the region. Unlike many African game reserves the visitor is allowed to camp and explore the area at will, rather than being confined to a car on a set route. Tourist facilities exist at the entrance to the park; these include a motel with restaurant.

Top picture: Warrior Statue, Ashanti region. Above: Woodcarving village, Ashanti region.

PHOTO CREDIT: BOB BURCH

Cocoa trees on plantation, TAFO Cocoa Research Institute, Eastern Ghana

West Coast

At **Dixcove** there is a fish market and a 17th-century British fort. Nearby **Busua** is a tropical beach with palms and with spectacular Atlantic breakers; however, as with much of the Ghanaian coast, swimming is unsafe due to the treacherous undertow of the waves. In this area there are to be found small rocky inlets which are safe for swimming. **Elmina** ('the mine'), the first Portuguese settlement in Ghana, has an intact 15th-century fort. This resort is popular with Ghanaians.
Fort St Jago, on a hill overlooking the castle, and **Cape Coast Castle** (which served as the seat of the British administration in the then Gold Coast until the administration was moved to the *Osu Castle* in Accra) have been declared World Heritage Monuments by the World Heritage Foundation under UNESCO.

SOCIAL PROFILE

FOOD & DRINK: International food is available in most large hotels and many restaurants serve a range of local traditional foods. On the coast, prawns and other seafood are popular. Dishes include traditional soups (palmnut, groundnut), *Kontomere* and *Okro* (stews) accompanied by *fufu* (pounded cassava), *kenkey* or *gari*.

In Accra there are also restaurants serving Middle Eastern, Chinese, French and other European cuisine.
Drink: Local beer (which is similar to lager) and spirits are readily available.
NIGHTLIFE: In Accra and other major centres there are nightclubs with Western popular music and Afro beat.
SHOPPING: Almost all commodities, including luxury items, can be found in the shops and markets. Artefacts from the Ashanti region and northern Ghana can be bought along with attractive handmade gold and silver jewellery. Modern and old African art are also available (although prices are expensive), in particular Ashanti stools and brass weights formerly used to measure gold. In all the northern markets, earthenware pots, leatherwork, locally woven shirts and *Bolgatanga* baskets woven from multi-coloured raffia are sold. **Shopping hours:** 0800-1200 and 1400-1730 Monday, Tuesday, Wednesday, Thursday and Friday; 0800-1300 Saturday.
SPORT: Golf: There are courses at Achimota, Accra and Kumasi. **Watersports:** For those in search of **sailing** or **water-skiing** there are a number of centres with good facilities, particularly on Lake Volta where there is a yacht club at Akosombo, and at Ada on the mouth of the Volta. Another exhilarating experience is to be taken out over the surf in a local fishing boat. Although Ghana's coast offers miles of sandy beaches, bathing can be

dangerous. Near Accra there are three **swimming** pools within yards of the surf. Ada, at the mouth of the Volta, also offers safe swimming with less risk of bilharzia, but it is not advised to swim upstream. **Spectator sports:** Ghanaians are keen **footballers, tennis players** and **boxers.** Another popular sport is **horseracing** at the Accra racecourse every Saturday.
SPECIAL EVENTS: Ghanaian festivals are well worth seeing with drumming, dancing and feasting. Every part of the country has its own annual festivals for the affirmation of tribal values, the remembrance of ancestors and past leaders, and the purification of the state in preparation for another year. The most impressive national celebrations are on the following days:
Mar 6 '95 *Independence Day*, Accra. **Jan 7 '96** *Fourth Republic Anniversary.* **Mar 6** *Independence Day,* Accra.
SOCIAL CONVENTIONS: Ghanaians should always be addressed by their formal titles unless they specifically request otherwise. Handshaking is the usual form of greeting. **Tipping:** When a service charge is not included, a 10% tip is usual.

BUSINESS PROFILE

ECONOMY: Agriculture occupies most of the working population, while mining for diamonds and other minerals is a major employer and an important foreign currency earner. The fishing industry developed significantly during the 1980s, with a relatively modern fleet operating alongside traditional canoe fishing. However, the economy has suffered throughout the last decade from the low world price for cocoa, the principal cash crop. Ghana is a member of the Economic Community of West African States. During the last few years it has also been a test bed for a new kind of economic development programme arranged and supervised by the International Monetary Fund (IMF) and the World Bank. Termed the Structural Adjustment Programme, it involves measures to liberalise the economy, remove trade barriers and state intervention in industry and maintain firm budgetary control. Although similar to previous IMF/World Bank packages in content, it has the benefit for developing countries of being stretched over a longer period and is thus less drastic in its impact. It is generally considered to have been a success in Ghana and has since been applied elsewhere. The rural economy has especially benefited: this has contributed to Ghana's present self-sufficiency in food. The UK is the largest trading partner, accounting for 20% of Ghana's exports and nearly 30% of imports. Ghana received US$600m in multi- and bi-lateral aid in 1989 of which the UK contributed £30m directly. Nigeria, the USA, Germany, Japan and The Netherlands are other important trading partners.
BUSINESS: Appointments are customary and visitors should always be punctual for meetings. Best time for business visits is from September to April. **Office hours:** 0800-1200 and 1400-1700 Monday to Friday.
COMMERCIAL INFORMATION: The following organisation can offer advice: Ghana National Chamber of Commerce, PO Box 2325, Accra. Tel: (21) 662 427. Fax: (21) 662 210. Telex: 2687.

CLIMATE

A tropical climate, hot and humid in the north and in the forest land of Ashanti and southwest plains. The rainy season is April to July. On the coast there is no real seasonal change.
Required clothing: Tropical lightweight clothing. Sunglasses are essential.

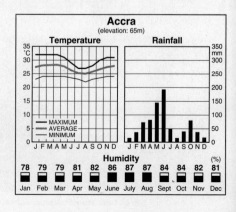

Accra
(elevation: 65m)

	Humidity										(%)
78	79	79	81	82	86	87	87	84	84	82	81
Jan	Feb	Mar	Apr	May	June	July	Aug	Sept	Oct	Nov	Dec

Gibraltar

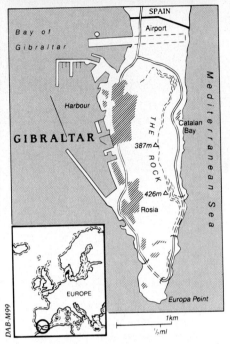

Bay of Gibraltar

Harbour

GIBRALTAR

THE ROCK

387m

426m

Rosia

SPAIN

Airport

Catalan Bay

Mediterranean Sea

Europa Point

EUROPE

1km

½ml

DAB-M99

Location: Western entrance to the Mediterranean, southern tip of Europe.

Gibraltar Information Bureau
Duke of Kent House, Cathedral Square, Gibraltar
Tel: 74950. Fax: 74943.
Diplomatic representation: Gibraltar's foreign affairs are handled by the UK Foreign and Commonwealth Office, King Charles Street, London SW1A 2AH. Tel: (0171) 270 2862. All other enquiries should be made to the Gibraltar Information Bureau.
UK Passport Office
Clive House, 70-78 Petty France, London SW1 9HD
Tel: (0171) 271 8552/8.
Gibraltar Information Bureau
Arundel Great Court, 179 The Strand, London WC2R 1EH
Tel: (0171) 836 0777. Fax: (0171) 240 6612. Opening hours: 0900-1730 Monday to Friday.
Gibraltar Information Bureau
Suite 710, 1155 15th Street, NW, Washington, DC 20005
Tel: (202) 452 1108. Fax: (202) 872 8543.

AREA: 6.5 sq km (2.5 sq miles).
POPULATION: 28,074 (1991 estimate).
POPULATION DENSITY: 4319.2 per sq km.
CAPITAL: Gibraltar.
GEOGRAPHY: Gibraltar is a large promontory of jurassic limestone, situated in the western entrance to the Mediterranean. The 5km-long (3 mile) rock contains 143 caves, over 48km (30 miles) of road and as many miles of tunnels. The highest point of the Rock is 425m (1400ft) above sea level. An internal self-governing British Crown Colony, Gibraltar has given its name to the Bay and the Straits which it overlooks. Spain is to the north and west and Morocco is 26km (16 miles) to the south.
LANGUAGE: English and Spanish are the official

languages.
RELIGION: 77% Roman Catholic, with Church of England, Church of Scotland, Jewish, Hindu and other minorities.
TIME: GMT + 1 (GMT + 2 from last Sunday in March to Saturday before last Sunday in September).
ELECTRICITY: 220/240 volts AC, 50Hz.
COMMUNICATIONS: Telephone: IDD is available. Country code: 350. Outgoing international code: 00.
Fax: Facilities are available in some hotels.
Telex/telegram: Enquire for both at Gibtel, 60 Main Street, or after office hours at Mount Pleasant, 25 South Barracks Road. There are two telex offices. **Post:** Airmail within Europe takes between one and five days. Airmail flights are usually daily. There is a *Poste Restante* facility at the main post office in Main Street. Post office hours: 0900-1515 Monday to Friday (0900-1700), and 1000-1300 Saturday. **Press:** Newspapers are in English; most are published weekly. *The Gibraltar Chronicle* (est. 1801) is the only daily.
BBC World Service and Voice of America frequencies: From time to time these change. See the section *How to Use this Book* for more information.
BBC:

MHz	17.70	15.07	12.09	6.195

Voice of America:

MHz	15.20	9.760	6.040	5.995

PASSPORT/VISA

Regulations and requirements may be subject to change at short notice, and you are advised to contact the appropriate diplomatic or consular authority before finalising travel arrangements. Details of these may be found at the head of this country's entry. Any numbers in the chart refer to the footnotes below.

	Passport Required?	Visa Required?	Return Ticket Required?
Full British	1	No	No
BVP	Valid	-	-
Australian	Yes	No	No
Canadian	Yes	No	No
USA	Yes	No	No
Other EU (As of 31/12/94)	2	No	No
Japanese	Yes	No	No

PASSPORTS: Required by all except:
(a) **[1]** British nationals, provided they are in possession of a BVP;
(b) **[2]** EU nationals in possession of a national identity card (with the exception of nationals of Spain and Portugal who *do* require a passport).
British Visitors Passport: Acceptable, but visitors cannot take excursions into Morocco unless in possession of a full passport.
VISAS: Required by nationals of Afghanistan, Albania, Algeria, Angola, Bangladesh, Benin, Bhutan, Bosnia-Herzegovina, Bulgaria, Burkina Faso, Cambodia, Cameroon, Cape Verde, Central African Republic, CIS, Comoro Islands, Chad, China, Congo, Cuba, Djibouti, Egypt, Equatorial Guinea, Ethiopia, Gabon, Guinea Republic, Guinea-Bissau, Haiti, India, Indonesia, Iran, Iraq, Jordan, Laos, Lebanon, Liberia, Libya, Former Yugoslav Republic of Macedonia, Madagascar, Mali, Mauritania, Mongolia, Morocco, Mozambique, Myanmar, Nepal, Nigeria, Oman, North Korea, Pakistan, Philippines, Romania, Rwanda, Sao Tomé e Príncipe, Saudi Arabia, Senegal, Somalia, Sudan, Syria, Taiwan, Togo, Tunisia, Turkey, Uganda, Vietnam, Yemen, Yugoslavia (Serbia and Montenegro) and Zaïre. Contact the Foreign and Commonwealth Office for latest information.
Applications to: Any British visa-issuing post abroad or in the UK, or the Visa section of the UK Passport Office in London (address above).
Note: (a) All nationals who require a visa to enter the UK need a separate visa to enter Gibraltar. (b) Visa requirements for other nationals wishing to visit Gibraltar are subject to frequent change at short notice and travellers should contact the UK Passport Office (address above) for up-to-date information.
Temporary residence: Persons must obtain prior permission from the Government of Gibraltar if wishing to work (nationals of EU countries are exempt).

MONEY

Currency: Gibraltar uses the pound Sterling. Gib£1 = 100 new pence. The Gibraltar government issues banknotes of Gib£50, 20, 10, 5 and 1 for local use only. Coinage is the UK coinage with a different reverse design. The Gibraltar government also issues their own coins. All UK notes are accepted.
Currency exchange: All international travellers cheques and credit cards are accepted. UK Postcheques are

accepted in post offices, but not Girobank cheques. Tourists from the UK are strongly advised to change their unspent Gibraltar pounds into UK pound notes at parity in Gibraltar before departure; UK banks charge for exchanging the Gibraltar Pound.
Banking hours: 0900-1530 Monday to Thursday, 0900-1530 and 1630-1800 Friday.

DUTY FREE

The following goods may be taken into Gibraltar without incurring Customs duty:
200 cigarettes or 100 cigarillos or 50 cigars or 250g of tobacco; 2 litres of fortified or sparkling wine or 1 litre of spirits, liqueurs and cordials or 2 litres of still wine; 50g of perfume and 250ml of eau de toilette; goods to a total value of £32.

PUBLIC HOLIDAYS

Jan 2 '95 For New Year's Day. **Mar 14** Commonwealth Day. **Apr 14** Good Friday. **Apr 17** Easter Monday. **May 1** May Day. **May 29** Spring Bank Holiday. **Jun 14** Queen's Official Birthday. **Aug 28** Late Summer Bank Holiday. **Dec 26-27** Christmas. **Jan 1 '96** New Year's Day. **Mar 14** Commonwealth Day. **Apr 5** Good Friday. **Apr 8** Easter Monday.

HEALTH

Regulations and requirements may be subject to change at short notice, and you are advised to contact your doctor well in advance of your intended date of departure. Any numbers in the chart refer to the footnotes below.

	Special Precautions?	Certificate Required?
Yellow Fever	No	No
Cholera	No	No
Typhoid & Polio	No	-
Malaria	No	-
Food & Drink	1	-

[1]: Mains water is normally chlorinated, and whilst relatively safe may cause mild abdominal upsets. Bottled water is available and is advised for the first few weeks of the stay. Milk is pasteurised and dairy products are safe for consumption. Local meat, poultry, seafood, fruit and vegetables are generally considered safe to eat.
Health care: Gibraltar is a British Crown Colony and UK citizens are entitled to free treatment in public wards at St Bernard's Hospital and at Casemates Health Centre on presentation of a UK passport during stays of up to 30 days in the colony. Other EU nationals are similarly entitled on presentation of form E111. Medical treatment elsewhere and prescribed medicines must be paid for. Dental treatment must also be paid for but extractions are undertaken for only a nominal charge at St Bernard's Hospital during normal weekday working hours.
Note: Passengers travelling from Gibraltar to Spain or Morocco are advised to refer to the *Health* entry for those countries.

TRAVEL - International

AIR: *GB Airways (GT)* operates direct services to Gibraltar from Europe and Africa.
Approximate flight time: From London to Gibraltar is 2 hours 45 minutes.
International airport: *Gibraltar (GIB)* (North Front) is 2km (1.6 miles) north of the town centre. A bus to the centre departs every 15 minutes from 0900-2130. Return is from the Market Place bus stop. Taxis and courtesy coaches are available. There are duty-free facilities.
SEA: International cruises are run by *CTC, P&O, BI, Polish Ocean, Costa, Norwegian American, Norwegian Cruises/Union Lloyd* and *TVI Cruises*. There is a regular ferry service to Tangier, Morocco.
ROAD: The only international land access is the frontier with Spain at La Linea. There are no caravanning or camping facilities, and sleeping in vehicles is not permitted.

TRAVEL - Internal

ROAD: Traffic drives on the right. **Bus:** There are good local bus services operating at frequent intervals. **Taxi:** There are plenty of taxis and the driver is required by law to carry and produce on demand a copy of the taxi fares. **Car hire:** Both self-drive and chauffeur-driven cars are available. Touring outside Gibraltar can also be arranged. **Documentation:** Third Party insurance is compulsory. A UK driving licence is accepted.
JOURNEY TIMES: The following chart gives approximate journey times (in hours and minutes) from

Gibraltar to major foreign cities.

	Air	Road	Rail	Sea
London	2.45	-	-	-
Tangier	0.20	-	-	2.00
Malaga	-	2.00	-	-
Madrid	-	12.00	10.00	-

ACCOMMODATION

HOTELS: Hotels range from luxury establishments with lounges, terrace shops, bars and swimming pools, to more modest hotels. Summer rates are in force from April 1 to October 31. More information may be obtained from the Gibraltar Information Bureau on request.
CAMPING: Camping is not permitted; however, beach tents or beach umbrellas may be rented from villagers at Catalan Bay. These will include two deck chairs. Tent supplies and space for pitching on, however, is limited and it is advisable to book well in advance. Tents can only be used during the day.

RESORTS & EXCURSIONS

The town of Gibraltar is an 18th-century British Regency town built on a 15th-century Spanish town which was, in turn, built on a 12th-century Moorish town. The principal tourist sites and places of interest are:
St Michael's Cave, situated 300m (1000ft) above sea level, was known to the Romans for its spectacular stalactites and stalagmites. It is part of a complex series of interlinked caves including *Leonora's Cave* and *Lower St Michael's Cave.* Today it is used for concerts and ballet.
The *Upper Galleries,* hewn by hand from the Rock in 1782, house old cannon and tableaux evoking the Great Siege (1779-1783).
The *Apes' Den* is the home of the famous Barbary Apes, which are in fact not apes but tailless macaque monkeys. The *Gibraltar Museum* contains caveman tools and ornaments excavated from the Rock's caves, including a replica of the Gibraltar Skull, the first Neanderthal skull found in Europe (1848). There are also exhibits from the Phoenician, Greek, Roman, Moorish, Spanish, and British periods of the Rock's history; a comprehensive collection of prints and lithographs; a collection of weapons, 1727-1800; a large-scale model of the Rock made in 1865; and displays of fauna and flora. The museum itself was built above a fine, complete 14th-century *Moorish Bath House.*
Other sites of interest are: the 14th-century keep of the much-rebuilt *Moorish Castle;* the *Shrine of Our Lady of Europe,* a mosque before conversion to a Christian chapel in 1462, housing the 15th-century image of the Patroness of Gibraltar; the ancient *Nun's Well,* a Moorish cistern; *Parson's Lodge Battery* (1865), above Rosia Bay; *The Rock Buster,* an 100-ton gun; the 18th-century *Garrison Library; Trafalgar Cemetery; Alameda Gardens; Europa Point,* just 26km (16 miles) from Africa; the almost complete *city walls,* dating in part from the Moorish occupation.
Some popular tourist activities in Gibraltar are: the cable-car trip to the top of the Rock, stopping at the Apes' Den on the way up; the *Convent,* residence of the Governor, and formerly a 16th-century Franciscan Monastic house;

the *Guided Walking Tour of Places of Worship,* Wednesdays at 1000, including visits to Gibraltar's two cathedrals, a synagogue, the Garrison chapel, the Presbyterian church and the Methodist chapel – all buildings of historical interest; the guided walking tour around the city walls, every Friday at 1030; and the *Mediterranean Steps Walk* which starts at *O'Hara's Battery* (the highest point in Gibraltar), snakes down the eastern cliff and around the southern slopes to the western side of the Rock.
Gibraltar has five beaches. On the east side are *Eastern Beach, Catalan Bay* and, towards the south, *Sandy Bay,* where the Rock is very sheer and parking difficult. *Little Bay,* a pebble beach, and *Camp Bay/Keys Promenade* are on the western coast.
Day trips to Ronda, Malaga and Jerez in Andalucia, Spain can be arranged from Gibraltar, as can day trips by air to Tangier and other Moroccan cities (see the entry for *Spain* below for further information on Andalucia). The Gibraltar Information Bureau is in Cathedral Square. The staff will advise on tours and excursions and where to buy tickets.

SOCIAL PROFILE

FOOD & DRINK: There are bars and bistros throughout the town and at the Marina, operating under Mediterranean licensing hours and selling British beer. Restaurants cover the whole price range. Gibraltar's geographical location and its history as a British colony means that it can offer a large selection of British dishes as well as French, Spanish, American, Moroccan, Italian, Chinese and Indian cuisine. **Drink:** Spirits and tobacco are substantially cheaper than in the UK for identical brands. All types of alcoholic drinks are served, including draught beer (served at the *Gibraltar Arms*).
NIGHTLIFE: Gibraltar has a number of discos and nightspots open until the early hours of the morning. The casino complex includes a restaurant, nightclub, roof restaurant (summer) and gaming rooms, and is open from 0900 to the early hours.
SHOPPING: All goods are sold in Gibraltar at reduced-tax prices, and free of VAT. The majority of shops are in or near Main Street. Silk, linen, jewellery, perfumes, carvings, radios, leatherwork, electronic and photographic equipment, cashmere and watches can be bought. **Shopping hours:** 1000-1900 Monday to Friday and 1000-1300 Saturday.
SPORT: Many forms of **watersports** are available in Gibraltar. Pier **fishing** facilities are available and there are charter boats for hire, although deep-sea fishing (for blue shark and swordfish) is not always available at short notice. For a more leisurely sport, go on a boat trip to see and photograph the dolphins in the Bay. **Scuba diving** is a growing sport. There is also **parasailing** and **water-skiing.**
SPECIAL EVENTS: The following is a selection of major festivals and other special events celebrated in Gibraltar during 1995. For a complete list with exact dates, contact the Gibraltar Information Bureau.
May '95 *Annual Flower Show.* **Jun** *International Festival of Music and Performing Arts.* **Sep** *Battle of Britain Ceremony.* **Oct** *Trafalgar Day Ceremony.* **Nov-Dec** *Gibraltar Annual Drama Festival.*
SOCIAL CONVENTIONS: Gibraltar is a strongly traditional society with an attractive blend of British and Mediterranean customs. **Tipping:** Normally a 10-15% tip is given.

BUSINESS PROFILE

ECONOMY: The main sources of income are tourism and offshore financial services. The British armed forces, who have bases and ship repair and docking facilities on the Rock, are the other principal earners. The construction industry is also important. The economy is affected to a large extent by the state of relations with Spain and, in particular, the level of border crossings. At present, these are almost wholly unrestricted with the result that many native Gibraltarians work in Spain and a significant number of Spaniards have jobs on the Rock. The UK is naturally the largest source of imports. Gibraltar is not an exporter as such but earns foreign exchange through re-export, mainly into Spain. The island is also endeavouring to develop an 'offshore' financial services industry but apparently fears obstruction by Spain.
BUSINESS: English is normally used for business, but Spanish may be used for business connected with Spain.
Office hours: 0900-1300 and 1500-1800 Monday to Friday. **Government office hours:** Generally 0845-1315 and 1415-1730 Monday to Thursday, and 0845-1315 and 1415-1715 Friday; but hours vary according to department and season.
COMMERCIAL INFORMATION: The following organisation can offer advice: Gibraltar Chamber of Commerce, PO Box 29, Suite 11, Don House, 30-38 Main Street. Tel: 78376. Fax: 78403. Telex: 2151. Information is also available from the Gibraltar Information Bureau.
CONFERENCES/CONVENTIONS: Facilities at hotels for conferences and conventions continue to be developed. Europort Gibraltar, an 82,000 sq m (212,000 sq ft) financial complex, offers extensive office and conference facilities. St Michael's Cave (see *Resorts & Excursions* above) offers an absolutely unique and scenic location for meetings. Contact the Gibraltar Information Bureau for further information.

CLIMATE

Warm throughout the year, with hot summers and mild winters with no snow. Summer (May to September) can be very hot and humid.
Required clothing: Lightweights for summer and mediumweights for winter months.

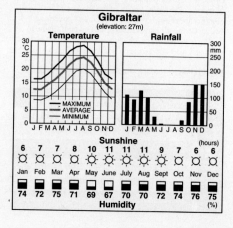

Greece

□ *international airport*

Location: Southeast Europe.

Ellinikos Organismos Tourismou (EOT) (National Tourist Organisation of Greece)
PO Box 1017, Odos Amerikis 2, 105 64 Athens, Greece
Tel: (1) 322 3111/19. Fax: (1) 322 2841. Telex: 215832.
Hellenic Association of Travel and Tourism Agents (HATTA)
11 Iossif Rogon Street, 117 43 Athens, Greece
Tel: (1) 923 4143 *or* 923 1198. Fax: (1) 923 3307.

Embassy of the Hellenic Republic
1A Holland Park, London W11 3TP
Tel: (0171) 221 6467. Fax: (0171) 243 3202. Opening hours: 1000-1400 Monday to Friday.
National Tourist Organisation of Greece (GNTO)
4 Conduit Street, London W1R 0DJ
Tel: (0171) 734 5997. Fax: (0171) 287 1369. Telex: 21122 (a/b GR TOUR G). Opening hours: 0930-1700 Monday to Thursday, 0930-1630 Friday.
Also deals with enquiries regarding conferences and conventions.
British Embassy
Odos Ploutarchou 1, 106 75 Athens, Greece
Tel: (1) 723 6211/9. Fax: (1) 724 1872. Telex: 216440 (a/b LION GR).
Consulates in: Crete, Corfu, Patras, Rhodes, Salonika, Samos, Syros and Volos.
Embassy of the Hellenic Republic
2221 Massachusetts Avenue, NW, Washington, DC 20008
Tel: (202) 939 5800. Fax: (202) 939 5824.
Consulates in: Atlanta, Boston, Chicago, Houston, Los Angeles (tel: (213) 385 1447), New Orleans, New York (tel: (212) 988 5500) and San Francisco.
National Tourist Organisation of Greece
Olympic Tower, 645 Fifth Avenue, New York, NY 10022
Tel: (212) 421 5777. Fax: (212) 826 6940. Telex: 2366489 (a/b NATOUR).
Embassy of the United States of America
Leoforos Vasilissis Sophias 91, 101 60 Athens, Greece
Tel: (1) 721 2951 *or* 721 8401. Fax: (1) 645 6282. Telex: 215548.
Consulate in: Thessaloniki.
Embassy of the Hellenic Republic
76-80 MacLaren Street, Ottawa, Ontario K2P 0K6
Tel: (613) 238 6271. Fax: (613) 238 5676.
Consulates in: Montréal, Toronto and Vancouver.
Greek National Tourist Organisation
Main Level, 1300 Bay Street, Toronto, Ontario M5R 3K8
Tel: (416) 968 2220. Fax: (416) 968 6533. Telex: 06218604.

Office National du Tourisme Grec
1233 de la Montagne, Montréal, Québec H3G 1Z2
Tel: (514) 871 1535. Fax: (514) 871 1498.
Canadian Embassy
Odos Ioannou Gennadiou 4, 115 21 Athens, Greece
Tel: (1) 725 4011. Fax: (1) 725 3994. Telex: 215584 (a/b DOM GR).

AREA: 131,944 sq km (50,944 sq miles).
POPULATION: 10,300,000 (1992 estimate).
POPULATION DENSITY: 77.1 per sq km.
CAPITAL: Athens. **Population:** 4,000,000 (1993).
GEOGRAPHY: Greece is situated in southeast Europe on the Mediterranean. The mainland consists of the following regions: Central Greece, Peloponnese, Thessaly (east/central), Epirus (west), Macedonia (north/northwest) and Thrace (northwest). Euboea, the second largest of the Greek islands, lying to the northeast of the central region, is also considered to be part of the mainland region. The Peloponnese peninsula is separated from the northern mainland by the isthmus of Corinth. The northern mainland is dissected by high mountains (such as the Pindus) that extend southwards towards a landscape of fertile plains, pine-forested uplands and craggy, scrub-covered foothills. The islands account for one-fifth of the land area of the country. The majority are thickly clustered in the Aegean between the Greek and Turkish coasts. The Ionian Islands are the exception; they are scattered along the west coast in the Ionian Sea. The Aegean archipelago includes the Dodecanese, lying off the Turkish coast, of which Rhodes is the best known; the Northeast Aegean group, including Lemnos, Lesbos, Chios, Samos and Ikaria; the Sporades, off the central mainland; and the Cyclades, 39 islands of which only 24 are inhabited. Crete, the largest island, is not included in any formal grouping.
For fuller descriptions of these regions and islands, see below under *Resorts & Excursions*.
LANGUAGE: Greek. Most people connected with tourism will speak at least some English, German, Italian or French.
RELIGION: 97% Greek Orthodox, with Muslim, Roman Catholic and Jewish minorites.
TIME: GMT + 2 (GMT + 3 from last Sunday in March to Saturday before last Sunday in September).
ELECTRICITY: 220 volts AC, 50Hz. Round 2-pin plugs are used.
COMMUNICATIONS: Telephone: IDD is available throughout the mainland and islands. Country code: 30, followed by (1) for Athens, (31) for Thessaloniki, (81)

Olympia

for Heraklion and (661) for Corfu. Outgoing international code: 00. **Fax:** Main post offices and large hotels have facilities. **Telex/telegram:** There are telex/telegram facilities in main post offices and large hotels in all Greek cities and the major islands. **Post:** All letters, postcards, newspapers and periodicals will automatically be sent by airmail. There are *Poste Restante* facilities at most post offices throughout the country. Advance notice is required at all Athens branches except for the central office at 180 Eolou Street. A passport must be shown on collection. Post office hours: 0800-1400 Monday to Friday and 0800-1330 Saturday. **Press:** There are 18 daily newspapers in Athens including *Eleftheros Typos*, *Ta Nea* and *Eleftherotyia*. *Athens News* and *Greece Today* are both published daily in English.

BBC World Service and Voice of America frequencies: From time to time these change. See the section *How to Use this Book* for more information.
BBC:

| MHz | 17.64 | 15.07 | 9.410 | 6.18 |

A service for the Greek islands is available on 1323kHz/226.7m.
Voice of America:

| MHz | 15.205 | 9.760 | 6.040 | 5.995 |

A service is also available on 792kHz/379m.

PASSPORT/VISA

Regulations and requirements may be subject to change at short notice, and you are advised to contact the appropriate diplomatic or consular authority before finalising travel arrangements. Details of these may be found at the head of this country's entry. Any numbers in the chart refer to the footnotes below.

	Passport Required?	Visa Required?	Return Ticket Required?
Full British	Yes/1	No/2	No
BVP	Valid	No	No
Australian	Yes	No	No
Canadian	Yes	No	No
USA	Yes	No	No
Other EU (As of 31/12/94)	1	No	No
Japanese	Yes	No	No

PASSPORTS: Passport valid for 6 months required by all except **[1]** EU nationals with a valid national ID card, and UK nationals provided they hold a BVP, for a stay of up to 3 months (Portuguese nationals for a stay of up to 2 months) who have sufficient funds for their length of stay.
British Visitors Passport: Valid.
VISAS: Required by all except:
(a) nationals of the countries referred to in the chart above for a period of up to 3 months (**[2]** including holders of British passports, but with the exception of citizens of British Dependent Territories, and citizens of Hong Kong, who should see (d) below);
(b) nationals of Andorra, Antigua & Barbuda, Argentina, Austria, Cyprus, Czech Republic, Ecuador, Finland, Hungary, Iceland, Israel, Liechtenstein, Malta, Mexico, Monaco, New Zealand, Nicaragua, Norway, San Marino, St Kitts & Nevis, Slovak Republic, South Korea, Sweden, Switzerland, Taiwan (China) and Zimbabwe for a period of up to 3 months;
(c) nationals of Brazil, Chile and Uruguay for a period of up to 2 months;
(d) nationals of Hong Kong and Peru for a period of up to 1 month;
(e) nationals of Singapore for a period of up to 2 weeks.
Types of visa: Tourist and Transit. Cost varies according to nationality, and can be anything from £14-£45.
Validity: Up to 3 months, depending on nationality. Transit visas are valid for up to 4 days.

Timatic

Health	
GALILEO/WORLDSPAN:	TI-DFT/ATH/HE
SABRE:	TIDFT/ATH/HE

Visa	
GALILEO/WORLDSPAN:	TI-DFT/ATH/VI
SABRE:	TIDFT/ATH/VI

For more information on Timatic codes refer to Contents.

GREECE

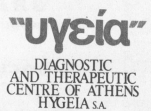

Application to: Visa or Consular section at Embassy. For addresses, see top of entry.
Application requirements: Applications in person only: (a) Completed application form with stamped, self-addressed envelope. (b) Sufficient funds to cover stay. (c) Fee. (d) Valid passport. (e) Passport-size photo. (f) Return or onward ticket.
Working days required: 1-2 days.
Temporary residence: Apply to the Aliens Department in Athens, 173 Alexandras Avenue, 155 22 Athens. Tel: (1) 646 8103, ext. 379.
Important note: Persons arriving in and departing from Greece on a charter flight risk having the return portion of their ticket invalidated by the authorities if, at any time during their stay, they leave Greece and remain overnight or longer in another country.

MONEY

Currency: Drachma (Dr). Notes are in denominations of Dr5000, 1000, 500, 100 and 50. Coins are in denominations of Dr100, 50, 20, 10, 5, 2 and 1.
Currency exchange: Foreign currencies and travellers cheques can be exchanged at all banks, savings banks and bureaux de change. Exchange rates can fluctuate from one bank to another. Many UK banks offer differing exchange rates depending on the denominations of Greek currency being bought or sold. Check with banks for details and current rates. Generally banks in Greece charge a commission of 2% with a minimum of Dr50 and a maximum of Dr4500 on the encashment of travellers cheques.
Credit cards: Diners Club, Visa, American Express, Access/Mastercard and other major credit cards are widely accepted (although less so in petrol stations). Check with your credit card company for details of merchant acceptability and other services which may be available.
Travellers cheques: All major currencies are widely accepted and can be exchanged easily at banks.
Exchange rate indicators: The following figures are included as a guide to the movements of the Drachma against Sterling and the US Dollar:

Date:	Oct '92	Sep '93	Jan '94	Jan '95
£1.00=	315.52	350.82	368.91	376.42
$1.00=	98.82	229.75	249.35	240.60

Currency restrictions: Import of foreign currency is free, subject to declaration of amounts greater than US$1000 (non-appliance will result in fines, confiscation and confinement). Export of foreign currency is limited to the amount declared on import. The import of local currency is limited to Dr100,000 for foreign nationals and DR40,000 for Greek nationals and the export to Dr20,000.
Banking hours: 0800-1400 Monday to Friday. Many banks on larger islands stay open in the afternoon and some during the evening to offer currency exchange facilities during the tourist season. The GNTO bureau in Athens can give full details.

DUTY FREE

The following goods may be imported into Greece by visitors without incurring customs duty by:
(a) Passengers from EU countries:
*300 cigarettes or 75 cigars or 150 cigarillos or 400g of tobacco; *1.5 litres of alcoholic beverages or 5 litres of liqueurs, still and sparkling wines; 75g of perfume and 375ml of eau de cologne; 1kg of coffee or 400g of coffee extract; 200g of tea or 80g of tea extract; gifts up to a total value of Dr137,000 provided no single item has a value of over Dr77,500 (children under 15 are allowed up to Dr34,000).
(b) Passengers from other countries:
*200 cigarettes or 50 cigars or 100 cigarillos or 250g of tobacco; *1 litre of alcoholic beverage or 2 litres of wine; 50g of perfume and 250ml of eau de cologne; 500g of coffee or 200g of coffee extract; 100g of tea or 40g of tea extract; gifts up to a total value of Dr10,500 (children under 15 are allowed up to Dr5500).
(c) Passengers entering from an EU country with duty-paid goods:
*800 cigarettes and 400 cigarillos and 200 cigars and 1kg of tobacco; *90 litres of wine (including up to 60 litres of sparkling wine); 10 litres of spirits; 20 litres of intermediate products (such as fortified wine); 110 litres of beer.
Note: Although there are now no legal limits imposed on importing duty-paid tobacco and alcoholic products from one EU country to another, travellers may be questioned at customs if they exceed the above amounts and may be asked to prove that the goods are for personal use only.
[*] The tobacco and alcoholic allowances listed above are not available to passengers under the age of 18.
Restricted items: It is forbidden to bring in plants with soil, and windsurfboards (unless a Greek national

residing in Greece guarantees it will be re-exported).
Note: The export of antiquities is prohibited without the express permission of the Archaeological Service in Athens. Those who ignore this will be prosecuted.

PUBLIC HOLIDAYS

Jan 1 '95 New Year's Day. **Jan 6** Epiphany. **Mar 6** Shrove Monday. **Mar 25** Independence Day. **Apr 21** Good Friday. **Apr 23** Easter Sunday. **Apr 24** Easter Monday. **May 1** Labour Day. **Jun 12** Holy Spirit Day. **Aug 15** Assumption. **Oct 28** Ohi Day. **Dec 25-26** Christmas. **Jan 1 '96** New Year's Day. **Jan 6** Epiphany. **Feb 26** Shrove Monday. **Mar 25** Independence Day. **Apr 12** Good Friday. **Apr 14** Easter Sunday. **Apr 15** Easter Monday.

HEALTH

Regulations and requirements may be subject to change at short notice, and you are advised to contact your doctor well in advance of your intended date of departure. Any numbers in the chart refer to the footnotes below.

	Special Precautions?	Certificate Required?
Yellow Fever	No	1
Cholera	No	No
Typhoid & Polio	No	-
Malaria	No	-
Food & Drink	2	-

[1]: A yellow fever vaccination certificate is required from travellers over six months of age coming from infected areas.
[2]: Mains water is normally chlorinated, and whilst relatively safe may cause mild abdominal upsets. Bottled water is available and is advised for the first few weeks of the stay. Milk is pasteurised and dairy products are safe for consumption. Local meat, poultry, seafood, fruit and vegetables are generally considered safe to eat. *Rabies* is present. For those at high risk, vaccination before arrival should be considered. If you are bitten abroad seek medical advice without delay. For more information consult the *Health* section at the back of the book.
Health care: There is a Reciprocal Health Agreement with the UK, but it is poorly implemented and it is essential to take out holiday insurance. Refunds for medical treatment are theoretically available from the Greek Social Insurance Foundation on presentation of form E111 (see the *Health* section at the back of the book).
Chemists can diagnose and supply drugs. There are often long waits for treatment at public hospitals. Hospital facilities on outlying islands are sometimes sparse, although many ambulances without adequate facilities have air ambulance backup.

TRAVEL - International

AIR: Greece's national airline is *Olympic Airways (OA)*. For free advice on air travel, call the Air Travel Advisory Bureau in the UK on (0171) 636 5000 (London) or (0161) 832 2000 (Manchester).
Approximate flight times: From *London* to Athens is 3 hours 15 minutes; to Rhodes is 3 hours 45 minutes; to Corfu is 3 hours 5 minutes; to Heraklion is 3 hours 45 minutes; and to Skiathos is 3 hours 20 minutes.
From *Los Angeles* to Athens is 18 hours 35 minutes.
From *New York* to Athens is 10 hours 10 minutes.
From *Singapore* to Athens is 11 hours 25 minutes.
From *Sydney* to Athens is 22 hours 5 minutes.
International airports: *Athens (ATH)* (Hellinikon) is 14km (9 miles) from the city. There are two air terminals: The East, which is for international and charter flights by international airlines; and the West, which is only for *Olympic Airways* flights. Express Bus no. 91 runs to the East and West terminals from Sintagma Square or Stadiou Street in Athens every 30-40 minutes from 0600-0020 and every hour from 0130-0530. Taxi services are available to the city centre; meters start at Dr200 and there is a surcharge of approximately Dr260 for taxis from the airport and Dr50 for each piece of luggage over 10kg. Airport facilities include a duty-free shop, car hire *(Avis, Budget, Hertz, InterRent)*, 24-hour bank and bureau de change, bar and restaurant facilities. *Heraklion (HER)* (Crete) is 5km (3 miles) from the city. Bus and taxi services are available. Airport facilities include a cafeteria and a duty-free shop.
Thessaloniki (SKG) (Micra) is 16km (10 miles) from the city. Regular coach and taxi services are available. There is a duty-free shop, cafeteria and bar.
Corfu (CFU) (Kerkira) is 3km (2 miles) from the city. Regular coach and taxi services are available. There is a duty-free shop, cafeteria and bar.

Rhodes (RHO) (Paradisi) is 16km (10 miles) from the city. Coach and taxi services are available. Airport facilities include a duty-free shop, car hire *(Avis, Rent-a-car)*, bank and bureau de change, café and a 24-hour bar. There are also international airports at *Chania (CHQ)*, *Kalamata (KLX)*, *Karpathos (AOK)*, *Kavala (KVA)*, *Kefalonia (EFL)*, *Kos (KGS)*, *Lesbos (Mytilini) (MJT)*, *Mykonos (JMK)*, *Preveza (Aktion) (PVK)*, *Salonika (SKG)*, *Samos (SMI)*, *Skiathos (JSI)*, *Thira (Santorini) (JTR)* and *Zakynthos (ZTH)*, most of which predominately serve summer traffic.
SEA: The major Greek ports are Piraeus, Thessaloniki and Volos, Igoumenitsa, Heraklion, Corfu, Patras and Rhodes. Shipping and ferryboat lines link these ports with Egypt, Italy, Cyprus, Syria, Israel, Turkey and Russia. Greek ports are used by a number of cruise lines including *Epirotiki, K Lines, Carpas Cruises, Costa, Chandris, Mediterranean Passenger Services, Med Sun Lines, Royal Cruise Line, Sun Line* and *Swan Hellenic.* The GNTO can give full details.
A car ferry links the Italian ports of Brindisi and Ancona with Patras and Piraeus. There are services from Igoumenitsa to Bari, Brindisi and Trieste; Heraklion to Ancona and Brindisi; Corfu to Bari, Brindisi and Trieste; Rhodes to Ancona. Ferries also run from Piraeus to Alexandria in Egypt, to Haifa in Israel and to Istanbul in Turkey. During the summer months there are also services between Ithaca to Brindisi and Cephalonia to Brindisi. A subsidiary of *DFDS* operates a scheduled car-ferry service from Alexandria (Egypt) via Heraklion to Patras and on to Ancona.
RAIL: The national railway company is *Hellenic State Railways (OSE)*. The following continental rail services run from London to Athens:
Acropolis Express: London–Paris–Milan–Trieste–Belgrade*–Athens.
Hellas Express: London–Amsterdam–Cologne–Bonn–Stuttgart–Munich–Salzburg–Zagreb*–Belgrade*–Nis*–Athens.
Interail tickets, for those aged 26 and under, include rail travel within Greece, but a supplement will be added for couchettes; the ticket does not include the cost of ferries between other countries or islands, but certain shipping lines offer a discount to ticket holders. The **Eurailpass** (for first-class travel) and the **Eurailpass Youthpass** (for persons aged 26 and under) also cover rail travel in Greece. The **Saver Ticket** is available for groups of 3-5 persons, which is valid for 15 days, 21 days or 1 month. Check with the companies concerned for details.
ROAD: It is possible to ferry cars across to one of the major ports of entry or to enter overland. Points of overland entry are Evzoni, 550km (342 miles) from Athens, and Niki, 632km (393 miles) from Athens, in The Former Yugoslav Republic of Macedonia*; Promahonas in Bulgaria, 736km (457 miles) from Athens; Kastanies, 999km (621 miles) from Athens; and Kipi, 892km (554 miles) from Athens. From Yugoslavia* the route is via Italy (Trieste), Austria (Graz) and Belgrade. The journey from northern France to Athens is over 3200km (2000 miles). For car-ferry information, see entry on *Sea* above.
Bus: There are routes from Athens via Thessaloniki to Sofia, Paris, Dortmund and Istanbul. Information and bookings are available from terminals in Athens at 6 Sina Street; 1 Karolou Street and 17 Filellinon Street; also at Thessaloniki rail station. See below under *Travel – Internal* for information on **documentation** and **traffic regulations.**
Note [*]: At the time of writing, due to the present situation of war in the former Yugoslavia, it is extremely unwise and dangerous to take any route through what was Yugoslavia. Consult the GNTO for advice on alternative routes.

TRAVEL - Internal

AIR: The national airline, *Olympic Airways (OA)*, has its own terminal (Athens West) and flies from *Athens* to Alexandroupolis, Chania (Crete), Chios, Heraklion, Ioannina, Kalamata, Kassos, Kastelorica, Kastoria, Kavala, Kefaloniá, Kerkira (Corfu), Kos, Kozani, Kithira, Larissa, Leros, Memnos, Mytilini, Milos, Mykonos, Paros, Preveza Aktion, Pyrgos, Rhodes, Samos, Santorini (Thira), Skiathos, Sitia, Skiros, Siros, Thessaloniki, Volos and Zakinthos; from *Rhodes* to Heraklion, Karpathos, Kassos, Kastelorico, Kos, Leros, Mykonos, Paros, Sitia and Santorini (Thira); from *Chios* to Mykonos, Samos and Thessaloniki; from *Heraklion* to Santorini (Thira), Mykonos and Paros; from *Karpathos* to Kassos and Sitia; from *Kefaloniá* to Zakinthos; from *Kerkira* to Kefaloniá, Preveza and Zakinthos; from *Kos* to Leros and Samos; from *Mykonos* to Mytilini; and from *Thessaloniki* to Chania, Heraklion, Ioannina, Kos, Larissa, Lemnos, Mytilini, Rhodes, Samos and Skiathos.
SEA: It is both cheap and easy to travel around the islands. There are ferry services on many routes, with sailings most frequent during the summer. Tickets can be

bought from the shipping lines' offices located around the quaysides. In major ports the larger lines have offices in the city centre. There are three classes of ticket (First class, Second class and Tourist Class) which offer varying degrees of comfort; couchette cabins can be booked for the longer voyages or those wishing to avoid the sun. Most ships have restaurant facilities. During high season it is wise to buy tickets well in advance, as inter-island travel is very popular.

Ferry routes: From **Piraeus** there are regular sailings to the following (figures in brackets are approximate journey times in hours and minutes, although journey lengths vary according to whether the ferry reaches its destination using a direct route or stops at islands in between Piraeus and its final port of call):

Agios Kirikos (Ikaria) (8 hrs); Agios Nikolaos (Crete) (13 hrs 30 mins); Amorgos (Cyclades); Anafi (Cyclades) (18 hrs 40 mins); Astipalaia (Dodecanese) (13 hrs); Chalki (Halki) (Dodecanese) (30 hrs 30 mins); Chania (Crete) (12 hrs); Chios (11 hrs); Donoussa (Cyclades) (from 10 hrs 30 mins to 26 hrs 15 mins); Elafonissos (10 hrs); Folegandros (Cyclades) (12 hrs); Geraka (Peloponnese); Gytheion (Peloponnese) (17 hrs); Heraklia (Iraklia) (Cyclades) (from 15 hrs 40 mins to 21 hrs); Heraklion (Crete) (12 hrs); Santorini (Cyclades) (11 hrs 30 mins); Ios (Cyclades) (11 hrs); Kalimnos (Dodecanese) (12 hrs); Karlovassi (Samos) (10 hrs); Karpathos (Dodecanese) (26 hrs); Kassos (Dodecanese) (23 hrs 30 mins); Kimolos (Cyclades) (8 hrs); Kythira (Peleponnese) (9 hrs 45 mins); Kythnos (Cyclades) (4 hrs); Kos (Dodecanese) (14 hrs); Koufonissia (Cyclades) (from 14 hrs 30 mins to 23 hrs); Leros (Dodecanese) (10 hrs); Milos (Cyclades) (8 hrs); Monemvassia (Peloponnese) (6 hrs); Mykonos (Cyclades) (5 hrs 50 mins); Mytilini (14 hrs); Naxos (Cyclades) (8 hrs); Neapolis (Peloponnese) (8 hrs 25 mins); Nissiros (Dodecanese) (22 hrs 30 mins); Paros (Cyclades) (7 hrs); Patmos (Dodecanese) (8 hrs); Portokagio (Peloponnese) (6 hrs 30 mins); Rhodes (14 hrs); Samos (Vathi) (12 hrs); Santorini (Thira) (Cyclades) (12 hrs); Schinoussa (Cyclades) (from 15 hrs 20 mins to 23 hrs); Serifos (Cyclades) (5 hrs); Sifnos (Cyclades) (5 hrs 30 mins); Sikinos (Cyclades) (10 hrs 30 mins); Sitia (Crete) (14 hrs); Symi (Dodecanese) (26 hrs 30 mins); Syros (Cyclades) (4 hrs 30 mins); Thessaloniki (14 hrs); Tilos (Dodecanese) (29 hrs); Tinos (Cyclades) (4 hrs 45 mins); and Vathi (Samos) (12 hrs). Check sailing times either with individual lines, the National Tourist Organisation of Greece, or in Piraeus upon arrival in Greece.

There are also services from **Piraeus** or **Zea** to the Saronic Gulf: Aegina, Methana, Poros, Hydra (Idra), Ermioni, Porto-Heli and Spetses; and also to Leonidio, Monemvassia, Nauplia, Neapolis-Kithira, Tolo and Tiros.

Local services from **Rafina** (near Athens) to Gavrion (Andros), Karistos (Euboea), Marmari (Euboea), Mesta (Chios), Mykonos, Naxos, Paros, Syros and Tinos.

Other routes include Agia Marina–Nea Styra; Perama–Salamis; Rio–Antirio; Aedipsos–Arkitsa; Eretria–Oropos; Glifa–Agiokambos; Patras–Ithaca; Patras–Sami; Patras–Corfu; Patras–Paxi; Preveza–Aktion; Igoumenitsa–Corfu; Corfu–Paxi; Kyllini–Zante; Kyllini–Cephalonia (Poros); Kavala–Thassos (Limenas); Kavala–Thassos (Prinos); Keramoti–Thassos; and Alexandroupolis–Samothrace.

A **hydrofoil** service (the 'Flying Dolphins') offers a fast and efficient service from Piraeus, travelling throughout the islands. Although this is slightly more expensive than travelling by ferry, journey times are cut drastically. There are also fast hydrofoil services from Zea Marina, Lavrio, Agios Konstandinos, Volos, Kimi (Euboea), Thessaloniki and Gytheion. For further information, contact the Flying Dolphins, 69 Akti-Miaouli, Athens. Tel: (1) 453 6107/4 *or* 453 7107/61. Fax: (1) 453 5403.

Numerous types of yachts and sailing vessels can be chartered or hired with or without crews. 'Flotilla holidays' are popular, and the GNTO has a full list of companies running this type of holiday.

RAIL: There are two main railway stations in Athens: *Larissa* (with trains to Northern Greece, Evia and Europe) and *Peloponnissos* (with trains to the Peloponnese). **North:** Regular daily trains from Athens to Thessaloniki, Thebes, Livadia, Paleofarsala, Larissa, Plati, Edessa, Florina, Seres, Drama, Komotini, Halkida and Alexandroupolis (connections from Thessaloniki and Larissa). **South:** Athens to Corinth, Xylokastra, Patras, Mycenae, Olympia, Argos, Tripoli, Megalopolis and Kalamata. Train information and tickets are available from 1 Karolou Street, 10437 Athens (tel: (1) 522 2491) or from 6 Sina Street (tel: (1) 362 4402).

Cheap fares: 20% rebate on return fares. Touring cards lasting 10, 20 and 30 days entitle the holder to unlimited travel on trains (second class) and on *CH* buses for a reduced cost (further reductions for groups). Prices depend on the number of passengers and duration of validity. Other reductions available include *Senior Passes* (for national transport: see below), *Interail Senior* and *Junior Cards*, and, for passengers residing outside Europe, *Eurailpass* and *Eurail Youthpass* cards.

Vergina Flexi-Pass: Entitles the holder to unlimited first-class rail travel in Greece for a period of 3-5 days (valid for one month) or 10 days (valid for two months). The pass also includes entitlement to a one-day cruise, an archaeological tour in Athens, one night's accommodation in Athens, a meal on an intercity train, a sleeping berth and breakfast on the overnight train from Athens to Thessaloniki (or vice versa) and other benefits. Discounts are offered to holders under 26. For further information, telephone or fax (1) 524 0996.

Senior Cards: Entitle passengers to: (a) 50% reduction on rail travel and *CH* buses. (b) Five single journeys free of charge, provided dates do not coincide with *either* the ten days before and after Easter *or* the ten days before and after Christmas. The cards are valid for one year.

Group Tickets: Entitle passengers to a 30% reduction for groups of at least 10 persons.

For further information on the above schemes, contact the GNTO.

ROAD: Greece has a good road network on the whole, totalling approximately 50,000km (31,069 miles), mostly paved. Traffic drives on the right. Examples of some distances from Athens: to Thessaloniki, 511km (318 miles); to Corinth, 85km (53 miles); to Igoumenitsa, 587km (365 miles); and to Delphi, 165km (103 miles).

Bus: Buses link Athens and all main towns in Attica, northern Greece and the Peloponnese. Service on the islands depends on demand, and timetables should be checked carefully. Some islands do not allow any kind of motorised transport, in which case islanders use boats, or donkeys and carts to travel around; these are also worth finding out about. Fares are cheap. *Hellenic State Railways (OSE)* run bus services to northern Greece from the Karolou Street terminus and to the Peloponnese from the Sina Street station.

Bus information: There are two terminals in Athens: Terminal A and Terminal B. For information on buses from Athens to the provinces, enquire at Terminal A, 100 Kifissou Street, Athens *or* Terminal B, 260 Liossion Street, Athens.

Taxi: Rates are per km and are very reasonable, with extra charge for fares to/from stations, ports and airports. Taxis run on a share basis, so do not be surprised if the taxi picks up other passengers for the journey. There is an additional charge from 0100-0600, with double fare from 0200-0400.

Car hire: Most car hire firms operate throughout Greece. For details, contact the GNTO. Reservations can be made by writing or telephoning the car hire agency direct, or through the Association of Car Rental Enterprises, 314 Syngou Avenue, Athens. Tel: (1) 951 0921.

Regulations: The minimum age for driving is 17. Children under 10 must sit in the back seat. Seat belts must be worn. There are fines for breaking traffic regulations. The maximum speed limit is 100kmph (60mph) on motorways, 80kmph (49mph) outside built-up areas and 50kmph (31mph) in built-up areas. There are slightly different speed limits for motorbikes. It is illegal to carry spare petrol in the vehicle. EU nationals may import a foreign-registered car, caravan, motorcycle, boat or trailer for a maximum of six months.

Documentation: A national driving licence is acceptable for EU nationals. EU nationals taking their own cars to Greece *must* obtain a Green Card, to top up the insurance cover to that provided by the car owner's domestic policy. It is no longer a legal requirement for visits of less than three months, but without it, insurance cover is limited to the minimum legal cover in Greece. The car registration documents have to be carried at all times. Nationals of non-EU countries may need an International Driving Licence and should contact *ELPA*. *ELPA* (Grecian Automobile Touring Club) has organised a **road assistance** service on main roads, conditions of which have vastly improved. Contact *ELPA*, 2-4 Messogion Avenue, 115 27 Athens. Tel: (1) 779 1615, or in an emergency, dial 104 *or* 174. There are good repair shops in big towns and petrol is easily obtainable.

JOURNEY TIMES: The following chart gives approximate journey times (in hours and minutes) from Athens to other major cities/islands in Greece.

	Air	Road	Sea
Corfu	0.50	*11.00	-
Crete	0.50	-	12.00
Mykonos	0.45	-	5.50
Rhodes	0.55	-	14.00
Thessaloniki	0.50	8.00	14.00
Thira	0.40	-	12.00

Note [*]: The journey time by road to Corfu includes a sea crossing from Patras.

ACCOMMODATION

HOTELS: The range of hotels can vary greatly both among the islands and on the mainland, from high class on larger islands and mainland to small seasonal chalets. Booking for the high season is essential. *Xenia* hotels are owned and often run by the GNTO. Small family hotels are a friendly alternative to the hotel chains. The Panhellenic Hotel Hoteliers Association has branches in Athens, Heraklion, Rhodes Town, Corfu Town and Thessaloniki. Hotel reservations can be made by writing directly to the hotels, through a travel agent, or through writing, faxing or phoning the Hellenic Chamber of Hotels, 24 Stadiou Street, 105 64 Athens. Tel: (1) 331 0022/6. Fax: (1) 322 5449. Reservations can also be made in person at the Hellenic Chamber of Hotels inside the National Bank of Greece on 2 Karageorgi Street. Tel: (1) 323 7193. Opening hours: 0830-1400 Monday to Thursday, 0830-1330 Friday and 0900-1230 Saturday.

Grading: Hotels are all officially classified as **Luxury** or rated on a scale from **A** to **E**. The category denotes what facilities must be offered and the price range that the hotelier is allowed to charge.

SELF-CATERING: Furnished rooms in private houses, service flats, apartments and villas are available. On most of the Greek islands, rooms in private homes are an extremely popular form of accommodation and can usually be arranged on the spot. All types of accommodation can be arranged through tour operators in this country. The GNTO can provide a full and up-to-date list on request. **Grading:** As for hotels.

TRADITIONAL SETTLEMENTS: There are traditional settlements and hostels on Makrinitsa (Pilion), Vizitsa (Pilion), Milies (Pilion), Ia (Santorini), Mesta (chios), Psara Island, Areopolis (Mani), Vathia (Mani), Papingo (Epirus), Koriskades (Central Greece), Monemvasia (Peloponnese) and Gythion (Peloponnese) which offer single, double or triple bedrooms with shower, or a 4-bed house. **Grading:** As for hotels.

CAMPING/CARAVANNING: There is a wide network of official campsites. For details contact the GNTO. It is not permitted to camp anywhere except registered sites.

YOUTH HOSTELS: These can be found in Athens at 57 Kypselis Street, tel: (1) 822 5860; and at 52 Peoniou Street (tel: (1) 522 2530). There are 25 others throughout the country. An International Youth Hostel Membership Card can be obtained for approximately Dr1300 from the Greek Youth Hostels Association, 4 Dragatsaniou Street, 105 59 Athens. Tel: (1) 323 4107 *or* 323 7590.

Note: Tourist police in the main tourist destinations of Greece are specially trained to assist visitors with accommodation, maps, timetables, details of places to visit or special events. All wear flag badges denoting which language(s) they are able to speak; do not hesitate to ask for help.

RESORTS & EXCURSIONS

For the purposes of clarity, information on *Resorts & Excursions* within Greece has been divided into 13 regional sections. These do not necessarily reflect administrative boundaries.

Note: Some of the beaches and seas of Greece are host to the threatened Loggerhead Turtle and the Monk Seal; visitors who find themselves in areas where they breed should keep their distance, behave quietly (this includes car noise), avoid leaving rubbish which may be dangerous (for example turtles may die after eating plastic bags which they mistake for jellyfish) and at night avoid showing lights.

Attica

Athens is in the region of Attica, which is characterised by calm beaches, and the pinewoods and thyme-covered slopes of Mount *Parnes, Hymettus* and *Pentelico*. The city of Athens is dominated by the flat-topped hill of the **Acropolis,** site of the 2400-year-old *Parthenon,* one of the most famous classical monuments in the world (which is beautifully lit at night by a mass of coloured lights), the *Theatre of Dionysius,* the *Doric Temple of Heiphaistos*, the *Roman Forum*, *Hadrian's Arch*, and the waterclock of Andronikos Kyrrhestes, commonly known as the *Tower of the Winds*. On the far side of the Acropolis is the restored *Odeon of Herod Atticus*, a superb theatre in which the open-air plays of the International Athens Festival are held from June to September. In the centre of Athens there are modern shops, restaurants, international-class hotels and nightclubs. The old quarter of the town, **Plaka**, which spreads around the Acropolis, provides a picturesque contrast with its famed flea market, small tavernas, craft shops and narrow winding alleys. **Piraeus**, lying at the innermost point of the *Saronic Gulf* just outside Athens, is the main port of the town. From here ferries leave regularly for the islands and other points along the coast. An electric train service connects Athens and Piraeus.

SOUTHWARDS ALONG THE WEST COASTLINE: The **Apollo Beach** is one of the best developed tourist areas, stretching from Piraeus as far as Cape Sounio at the southern tip of the promontory. Marinas, well-appointed swimming beaches, small bays, modern hotel complexes, rented flats, numerous tavernas which specialise in seafood, luxury-class restaurants and nightclubs are all attractions of the area.

Cape Sounio, 69km (43 miles) from Athens, is a towering promontory which dominates the landscape for miles around. Here the superb ruins of the *Temple of Poseidon,* surrounded by steep access paths, crown the cape. Other resorts (and their distance from Athens) include: **Paelo Faliro** (8km/5 miles), **Alimos** (11km/7 miles), **Glifada** (17km/11 miles), **Voula** (18.5km/11.5 miles), **Kavouri** (23km/14 miles), **Vouliagmeni** (24km/15 miles), *Vouliagmeni Lake* (a natural lake with medicinal waters, set in beautiful surroundings) (26km/16 miles), **Varkiza** (28km/17 miles), **Lagonissi** (40km/25 miles) and **Anavissos** (51km/32 miles).

NORTHWARDS AROUND THE GULF OF CORINTH: Kineta (55km/34 miles from Athens), a coastal resort with an extensive beach, lies on the *Saronic Gulf* and can be reached on the Old Corinth road. **Porto Germeno** (73km/45 miles from Athens), **Psatha** (67km/42 miles) and **Alepohori** (61km/38 miles) are typical Attic villages, set in thick pinewoods, bordering on the *Gulf of Corinth.* Sheltered bays provide excellent swimming. Accommodation is available and there are numerous restaurants specialising in fish dishes.

THE EAST COAST OF ATTICA: Stretching from Cape Sounio to **Skala Oropou,** there are a succession of resorts, set amid pinewoods. These include (all distances are from Athens) **Lavrio** (52km/32 miles), **Porto Rafti** (38km/24 miles), **Loutsa** (30km/19 miles), **Rafina** (28km/17 miles), **Mati** (29km/18 miles), **Agios Andreas** (31km/19 miles), **Nea Makri** (33km/21 miles), **Schinias** (44km/27 miles), **Agia Marina** (47km/29 miles) and **Agii Apostoli** (44km/27 miles). In general, there is a wide choice of hotels, rooms to rent, restaurants and tavernas.

THE SARONIC GULF AND ISLANDS: The Saronic Gulf stretches from the Attica coastline to the Peloponnese shores. The best known islands here are **Aegina, Salamis, Poros, Hydra, Spetses, Dokos, Spetsopoula** and the islets of **Angistri** and **Moni.** The Gulf is served by passenger ships, car ferries and fast-sailing hydrofoils. Passenger ships sail from the central harbour at **Piraeus** for Aegina, Methana, Poros, Hermione (Eermioni), Hydra and Spetses, while car ferries sail to Aegina, Methana and Poros. Special timetables cover small motorship sailings to **Agia Marina** and **Souvala** on the island of Aegina. Further information can be obtained from Piraeus Central Port

Authority. Tel: (1) 452 0910. Fast hydrofoil services supplement steamer services. For Aegina, sailings are from the central harbour at Piraeus. For Methana, Poros, Hydra, Hermione, Porto-Heli, Spetses, Leonidio, Nauplia, Kythera, Neapolis and Monemvassia, sailings are from the Zea Marina, close to Piraeus. A local Piraeus bus connects the terminus with Zea Marina. One-day cruises to the islands of Aegina, Poros and Hydra leave daily throughout the year from Flisvos Marina at Paleo Faliro.

Salamis, close to Piraeus, enjoys a frequent shuttle service by motor-sailing vessels, *caiques,* from nearby Piraeus and from **Perama** across the Straits. The island has good roads and a network of bus and taxi services. At **Eandio** there are the remains of ancient *Telamon.* Sandy beaches are at **Kaki Vigla, Moulki, Kanakia** and **Peristeria.** There are no large hotels.

Aegina (Egina) is a favourite among holidaymakers for its excellent beaches, clear seas and fine climate. The terrain is flat and cycling is popular. Other means of transport are buses, taxis and horsedrawn carriages. There are beauty spots and beaches at **Plakakia, Agia Marina, Faros** and **Marathonas. Angistri** and **Moni** are two small wooded islands which offer opportunities for excursions.

Methana, jutting out from the Peloponnese peninsula, is renowned for its medieval springs at Methana town and modernised hydrotherapy installations run by the National Tourist Organisation. Methana attracts a large number of visitors every year.

Poros is a thickly wooded island lying just off the Peloponnesian mainland township of **Galatas.** It is made up of two islands, linked by a narrow neck of land: **Calavria** and **Sphaeria** on which the town of Poros is built. Ferries leave for the mainland where there is a famous lemon grove and the remains of ancient Trizina, the legendary birthplace of Theseus. Sandy beaches, at **Askeli** and **Neorio,** are also accessible by ferry.

Hydra is a cosmopolitan island offering an active nightlife. Beaches are at **Kamina, Molos, Palamida, Bisti** and **Mandraki** and the sea cave of *Bariami* has been converted into a swimming pool; many beaches are more easily reached by boat. The island does not allow any motorised transport. There is only a small number of hotel rooms and most visitors hire or own their accommodation. A large (closed) monastery is centred at the highest point of the island.

Spetses lies at the southern extremity of the Saronic Gulf. It has long been a holiday resort and has good hotels and entertainment facilities. Seaside resorts include *Zogeria, Agia Marina, Agia Anangiri* and *Agia Pasaskevi.*

Central Greece

North of Attica is the region of Central Greece, mountainous and dry in the interior, yet temperate along the coast. Near the main road from Athens to Delphi lie the southern slopes of **Mount Parnassus,** which towers 2457m (8061ft) over the Gulf of Corinth. Here the land forms a natural stone amphitheatre which houses the *Sanctuary of Apollo,* one of the most famous archaeological sites in Greece. There is also a newly developed ski centre, *Parnassus Ski Centre,* accessible from **Arahova, Amfiklia** and **Eftalofos,** which has modern ski facilities, restaurants, a first-aid centre and a ski school. **Livadia,** built into the foothills of Mount Helikon, was famous in ancient times for the *Oracle of Trophonios Zeus* and the two *Springs of Forgetfulness (Lethe)* and *Memory (Mnemonyne)* to the north of the town. **Delphi** (176km/109 miles from Athens) can be reached by road through Boeotia via Livadia and Arahova. This is the site of the famous Oracle, where rulers of Greece came for many centuries for political and moral guidance. The centre of the complex of temples is the *Doric Temple of Apollo* dating from the 4th century BC. *The Delphi Museum* contains the superb statue of the Charioteer, circa 475BC. **Itea,** ancient Chalkion, lies on the northern coast of the Gulf of Corinthia. There is an excellent beach that skirts the olive trees and a good road leads to **Kira** where the remains of the ancient pier can still be seen at the bottom of the sea. Good bathing spots in **Phokida** include *Itea, Kira, Galaxidi, Eratini,* and the small islands of **Trizonia** and **Ai-Gianis.** There are a number of spa towns in Central Greece, such as **Thermopiles, Kamena Vourla, Plastistomo** and **Loutra Ipatis.** West of **Karpenissi** (built on the foothills of Mount Timfristos at an altitude of 960m/2438ft) can be found the picturesque mountain villages of **Fragista, Granitsa** and **Agrafa,** which are covered in snow during the winter.

The Peloponnese

Corinth is the most convenient starting point for a tour of the seven provinces of the **Peloponnese,** separated from central Greece by the *Canal of Corinth.*

Corinth was once a city state rival of Athens and a powerful maritime state. The old town of Corinth, destroyed by earthquake in 1858, was built up only to be destroyed again in 1928. The modern city, despite its beautiful location, is unremarkable. 8km (5 miles) away, on the northern slopes of *Akorinthos Mountain,* are the ruins of ancient Corinth, the capital of Roman Greece, where well-preserved Roman remains and the columns of the temple of Apollo are still to be seen. South of Corinth lies the impressive open-air theatre of Epidaurus, which offers performances at weekends during the Epidaurus Festival from July to August. Other archaeological sites in the area include the famous *Lion Gate* at **Mycenae,** where it is possible to stay overnight in the pavilion; the ancient temple, theatre and sanctuary at **Argos;** and the *Heraion* near the village of **Perahora.** There are museums at Corinth, **Nauplia** and **Epidaurus.**

WEST AND SOUTHWEST FROM CORINTH: From Corinth the coast road passes the villages of **Vrahati, Kokkoni** and **Kiato** before it reaches the popular coastal resort of **Xylokastra,** where there is a magnificent view of the *Parnassus* and *Elikon* mountains. After the *Kiato Bridge,* a road leads high into the mountains and the extensive fir forests round **Goura.** Another mountain road leads inland from Xylokastra to the cool alpine climate of **Trikala** at *Mount Zira,* the main ski centre of the south.

WESTERN PELOPONNESE: Scores of bays and sandy beaches deck the coastline. Several beaches, including *Katakolo* and *Agios Andreas* (to the west of Pirgos) and *Kourouta* and *Kyllini* (to the north), offer modern amenities. **Patras** is a thriving commercial and industrial centre, the third most important town in Greece and its main western port. Distinctive for its arcaded streets, Patras is also a pleasant seaside resort with some good hotels. It is an ideal base for visitors to the region. West of Patras is *Lapas* and, further south, are *Kourouta* and *Palouki* beaches, connected by a daily bus to **Amaliada.**

At **Kyllini** there are mineral springs, hydropathic installations and a number of new hotels. With a public beach, it is a lively resort as well as a spa. East of Patras there are beaches at **Psathopirgos, Lambiri, Longos, Selianitika, Kounoupeli** and **Kalogria.** A tiny train climbs up the *Vouraikos Gorge* from **Diakofto** to **Kalavanta.** Other resorts include **Vartholomio, Niko Leika** (Egio), **Lakopetra** and **Metoni.** A road runs 77km (48 miles) southeast of Patras through superb mountain scenery to **Kalavrita. Olympia,** the original site of the games where the flame is still lit, can be reached by the mountain road from Kalavrita. At Olympia, there are the

ATHENS

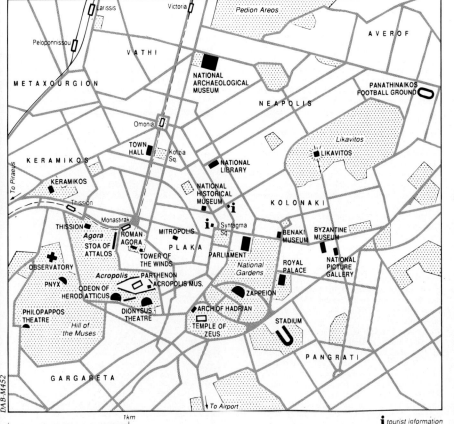

1 *tourist information*

1km

½ml

DAB-M452

ruins of Atlas, a museum of the *Olympic Games* and two archaeological museums. Olympia can be reached (a) by car along the coast of **Ahaia** or from **Tripoli** in the central Peloponnese – both of the drives are very interesting, so it would be worth trying the 334km (208-mile) coastal route via Patras and Pirgos one way, returning via Tripoli; (b) by train (Athens–Patras–Pirgos–Olympia).

From Olympia the road turns east and follows the Alfios River through the wild Arcadian Mountains. There is a spa at **Loutra**. The road becomes hair-raising with a sheer drop of 300m (1000ft) after **Isounda**, and should only be attempted by the adventurous. The main road from Olympia to Tripoli is less treacherous, going down from the mountains to the plain of Tripoli.

At **Bassae** is the well-preserved temple of the Epicurian Apollo. At **Kaifa** there is a hot-spring resort built on an island in the middle of the lake. The picturesque coast of the western Peloponnese offers plenty of opportunities for swimming. Between Kyllini and Kiparissia, the beaches at **Kastro, Loutra Kyllinis, Kourouta, Skafidia, Katakolo, Kaifa** and **Kiparissia** are popular.

SOUTHEAST OF CORINTH: There are beaches at **Loutraki**, a well-known resort with restaurants, modern shops, hotels and cinemas; **Nea Kios** near Argos; **Assini Kosta** in the south and **Tolo.** On the southern tip of the promontory, southeast of Corinth, is the resort of **Porto-Heli**, which has attractive beaches, some quite unspoilt, and good swimming. With a good road network – making trips to interesting places such as **Nauplia** and **Epidaurus** convenient – ample hotel accommodation, and many opportunities for watersports, Porto-Heli is a popular summer resort. There is a sea connection between Porto-Heli and the Saronic Gulf Islands and a ferry from the island of Spetses. On the east coast **Nafplio** is a well-preserved Venetian town which overlooks a lovely bay.

SOUTHERN PELOPONNESE: The once powerful city state of **Sparta** is notorious in ancient history for the austerity of its regime, but it is now a provincial town with parks, broad avenues and a pleasant atmosphere. At **Mystra**, 4km (2.5 miles) away, lie the ruins of a Byzantine city and, to the north, are the *Taigetos* and *Parnon* mountains. South of Sparta, the port of **Githio** is a good starting point for exploring the Mani area. There are caves with underground lakes and rivers at **Glifada** and **Alepotripa** in the Diros region. The island of **Kythera** (Kithira) lies 14 nautical miles off **Kavo Maleas** on the southernmost tip of the Peloponnese. Ships dock at **Agia Pelagia** near a beautiful stretch of coastline and bathing beach. The capital, Kythera, 30km (19 miles) south, is easily reached on the main roadway which crosses the island. It is a neat hamlet, built on a hillside overlooking the sea, which is crowned by a Venetian castle. **Kapsali** is the main harbour. Other resorts include **Anarnti, Areopolis, Gytheion** and **Monemvassia.**

Euboea

The island of **Euboea** (or **Evia**) is the second largest in Greece after Crete. A main highway and ferryboats from several terminals connect this island, of great natural beauty and scenic variety, to the mainland. Euboea is brisk with tourist traffic, but there are still many peaceful and unspoilt villages. There are large fertile valleys, sandy beaches, organised bathing facilities, secluded coves and wooded mountainsides, ideal for climbing. Resorts include **Halkida, Malakonta, Lefkanti, Kambos, Amarinthos, Almiropotamos, Marmari, Honeftiko, Limni, Agiokambos, Edipsos, Agios Georgios, Nea Stira, Karistos, Kimi** and **Rovies.**

On the other side of the Northern Euboean Gulf is the prefecture of **Fthiotida** with mountains, valleys, rivers, numerous medicinal springs, woodland, and sandy beaches. There are some excellent beaches at **Kamena Vourla,** one of the best-known and most frequented spas. **Skala** also has fine bathing beaches and, west of **Lamia**, the capital of the region, is the *Ipati Spa* with modern hydrotherapy facilities.

Winter sports enthusiasts should visit the *Mount Parnassus Winter Sports Resort*, 27km (17 miles) from **Arachova** and 17km (11 miles) from **Amfiklia**. The GNTO installations are located at **Fterolaka** and at **Kelaria**, at an altitude of 1600-2250m (5250-7380ft). The centre is open daily from December to April between 0900-1600. In **Gerondovrahos,** at an altitude of 1800m (5910ft) on *Mount Parnassus,* there is a ski centre run by the Athenian Ski Club.

Other resorts include **Agios Konstandinos, Arkitsa** and **Livanates.**

Thessaly

The fertile plain of **Thessaly** in Central Greece is surrounded by *Mount Pindus, Olympus, Pelion, Orthrys, Ossa* and *Agrapha.* The *River Pinios*, flowing down from the western slopes of the Pindus, cuts Thessaly in two and, passing through the valley of **Tempi**, meets the sea. **Olympus**, home of the immortal gods and land of the Centaurs, is only one of the many places in Thessaly where relics of ancient Greece can be seen and, on the western edge of the plain of Thessaly, just as the Pindus range begins to form, there are 24 perpendicular rocks on which Byzantine monks built their monastic community, the *Meteora*, about 600 years ago.

Nearby resorts include **Agiokambos, Elati, Kalambaka, Kardista, Larissa, Neraida, Smokovo** and **Trikala.**

At the northernmost point of *Pagassitikos Bay* is the port of **Volos**, traditionally the launching place of Jason and the Argonauts in their search for the Golden Fleece. There are several seaside villages along the *Pagasitic Gulf*, including **Agria**, 7km (4 miles) southeast of Volos. Northeast of Volos, there are hill villages and seaside towns on the Aegean; notably **Portaria, Makrinitsa, Hania, Zagora, Horefto, Ai-Gianis** and **Tsangarada.** Other coastal resorts include **Afissos, Agios Loanis, Agios Lavrendis, Alikes, Kala Nera, Milies, Vizitsa** (where there are traditional mansions, some of which are being renovated by the GNTO as guest-houses), **Tri Keri, Nea Anhialos, Platania** and **Milopotapos.**

There are winter sports centres on *Mount Pelion.*

Epirus

Epirus, the northwest corner of the Greek peninsula, is the most mountainous region in Greece. **Parga** lies 77km (48 miles) from **Preveza** and 90km (56 miles) from Arta. It is a small, picturesque town built in a semi-circle round the bay. Flanked by small inlets, coves, sandy beaches and islets, Parga is surrounded by wooded hills. Going north out of **Janene,** the road leads through the **Vikos Gorge**, the canyon formed by the *River Aoos*, which houses 46 pretty villages, known as the **Zagorokozia.** The Gorge is set in the *Vikos-Aoos National Park,* where the small villages of **Micro** and **Mega Papingo** are also located.

There are resorts at **Arta, Dodoni, Igoumenitsa, Janene, Katrossikia, Metsovo, Plataria, Preveza** and **Skamneli.** Roman ruins can be seen at **Nikopolis, Kassopi, Messopotamos** and **Dodoni.**

Macedonia

Macedonia stands slightly apart from the rest of the country. Part of Greece for little more than two generations, its scenery and climate have more in common with the adjoining Balkans. Though bitterly cold in winter, this is still a particularly beautiful part of Greece, rich in historical monuments and archaeological sites. In the area around **Florina**, are the lakes including the dramatic *Prespa* basin. **Grevena**, in the southern part of Macedonia, is mountainous, with the **Pindus** range rising to the west and the **Hassia** range to the north. The unspoilt villages in the area are ideal for those in search of peace and quiet.

Platamonas, on the west coast, is a popular summer resort, with camping grounds and supervised swimming beaches.

Other northern resorts include **Aridea, Gianitsa, Edessa, Skidra, Drossopigi, Nermfeon** and **Kastoria.** In the south, there are more resorts at **Perivoli, Kozani, Neapolis Petrana, Ptolemaida, Siatista, Naoussa** and **Veria.** Coastal resorts include **Katerini, Korinos, Lertokana, Litokoro, Makrigialos, Methoni, Paralia** and **Plaka.** One of Greece's largest sports centres is at **Kato Vermio** (Seli), near Naoussa.

Thessaloniki is the second-largest city in Greece. A modern coastal town, it contains much Byzantine art as well as churches and museums including the superb *Archaeological Museum.* The neighbouring villages and suburbs offer good walks and cafés, but beaches are often unclean. There are many historical sites in Thessaloniki, including the *Arch of Galerius* built in AD297; ruins of the *Roman agora* (which are still being excavated), Roman market, theatre and Roman baths; **Exedra** close to the *Egnatian Way;* **Nymphaion,** the circular building whose cisterns now serve as the chapel of *Agios Ioannis Prodromis*; the *Rotunda* and the fine churches including the 8th-century *Ayia Sofia*. The newly-restored and striking *White Tower* affords an excellent view.

Northeast of Thessaloniki is the mountainous and wooded peninsula of **Halkidiki** (Chalcidice), the highlight of eastern Macedonia. There are numerous archaeological sites, including the *Temple of Zeus Ammon* on the shore at **Kalithea** and the ruins of ancient *Olynthos* on **Kassandra**. The countryside, with pinewoods and olive groves, is ideal for peaceful walks. Kassandra and **Sithonia** shelter the north's best beaches and are both fast-growing holiday destinations. Here also is the religious community of *Mount Athos,* which can only be visited by men with a special permit. No women are allowed in. This is issued by the Ministry of Foreign Affairs (tel: (1) 361 0581) or by the Ministry of Northern Greece, Directorate of Civil Affairs at Odos El Venizelou 48, Thessaloniki. Tel: (31) 264 321. Overnight stays are forbidden for those without proven religious or scientific interests in the area.

In east Macedonia, on the road from **Drama** to Kavala, lies **Philippi**. Named after the father of Alexander the Great, it is known to be the site of the defeat of Caesar's murderers, Brutus and Cassius, by Octavius in 42BC, and of the first recorded preaching of St Paul in Greece. Today it is one of Macedonia's most extensive archaeological sites.

Thassos lies off the coast of eastern Macedonia. It is thickly wooded with plane, oak, cedar and olive groves. Thassos has good beaches for swimming and fishing at **Makriamos, Arhangelos, Agios Ioannis, Limenas, Potos** and **Pefkari.** The islet of **Thassopoula** just offshore can be reached by caique. On the north shore is the capital, **Limenas**, which has a museum. There are archaeological sites nearby including the *Temple of Pythian Apollo*, the agora, the theatres and the *Choregic Monument* set inside the sanctuary of Dionysus. **Thassos** can be reached by ferry from Keramoti or Kavala on the mainland.

Kavala is a modern, commercial seaside port which still retains many traditional features, particularly in the town centre. There are hotels, beaches, museums, restaurants and tavernas as well as an aqueduct and Byzantine citadel. Boats can be hired for fishing, water-skiing and sailing. Popular sandy beaches are at **Kalamitsa, Batis** and **Toska,** and secluded ones at **Iraklitsa** and **Peramos.** There are also some little-known stalactite and stalagmite caves and many archaeological sites nearby. **Mount Pangaion** is a good area for hunting and climbing.

Thrace

Going east from Macedonia the villages become more oriental in style. **Xanthi** is an attractive small town clinging to the hilly sides of the *Eskeje Remma Valley.* Southwest of Xanthi is **Avdira**. Nearby **Lagos**, built on the narrow strip of land in the lagoon, is rich in wildfowl. One of the best northern beaches is 8km (5 miles) east of **Fanari.** The main road dips down to the coast before going inland again to **Komotini**, further east, then follows the coast via **Nia Hili** to **Alexandroupolis**, which has an archaeological museum of local finds. North from here is **Soufli**, famous for its silks.

The Ionian Islands

The Ionian Islands lie off the west coast of mainland Greece. Comparatively isolated from each other in the past, each of the six islands has developed differently. **Corfu (Kerkira)** is the northernmost island of western Greece. Its natural beauty has led to a degree of commercialisation. The capital, also called Corfu, has two small harbours with large Venetian fortresses. With Italian, French and English influences evident in its architecture, Corfu is a typical Ionian island town. It is made up of wide avenues and large squares, among them the graceful *Spianada* or esplanade, cobbled alleyways, arches and colonnades. Recommended sights are the *Archaeological Museum*, which houses

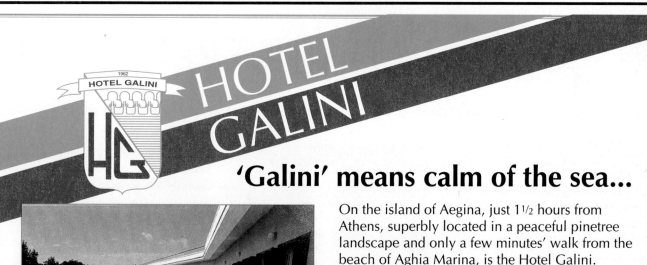

finds from local archaeological excavations; the *Museum of Asiatic Art*; the *Town Hall*, a splendid example of Venetian architecture (built in 1663); the 12th-century Byzantine *Church of St Jason and Sosipater* and the *Church of St Spyridon*. Good roads lead out of Corfu town to excellent harbours suitable for swimming and fishing, such as **Roda**, **Kassiopi** and **Douloura**, and to traditional inland villages such as **Ano Korakiana, Ano Garouna, Doukades, Agii Douli** and **Pelekas** where, from the top of its rocky hill, the sunset can be superb. In the region of Pelekas lies *Ropa's Meadow* (Livaditou Ropa), Corfu's excellent golf course. On the western side of the island the roads thread their way through olive and orange groves, pine trees and cypresses. Resorts on Corfu include **Kanoni**, where a narrow causeway leads to the *Monastery of Vlaherni;* **Perama; Benitses; Moraitika; Messongi; Dassia; Gouvia; Gastouri** and the museum palace *The Achilleion*, partly converted into a casino; **Ipsos** and **Paleokastritsa.**

Paxi, as yet undeveloped, is the smallest of the Ionians and has quiet sandy beaches, bays, rocky promontories and caves. Dense grapevines and olive groves cover the island. The main resort is *Giaios* (or Paxi), on the east coast. Excursions can be made to **Andipaxi**, a tiny island 5km (3 miles) to the south of Paxi.

Levkas (Lefkada), joined by a narrow strip of land to the Greek mainland, is a green and fertile island which is surrounded by many islets. Excursions, involving some mountain climbing, can be made in the centre of Levkas, near the *Stavrota Mountain*. There is good swimming and fishing in the villages of **Agios Nikitas** on the northwestern coast, **Ligia** on the southeastern coast or **Vassiliki** (which is also popular with windsurfers) on the southwestern coast.

Cephalonia (Kefalonia) has beaches at **Makri** and **Plati, Yialos, Skala, Fiskardo** and in the Palli district close to the *Monastery of Kepourio*. The mountainous scenery (including the 1600m/5250ft *Mount Enos*) is dramatic and the island has a good network of roads. At **Assos** there is a castle and in the capital, **Argostoli**, an *Archaeological Museum* and *Folk Art Museum*.

Ithaca (Ithaki) is close to Cephalonia, and is well known for being the island home of the great Odysseus, hero of the Trojan war. The small and mountainous island is renowned for its coves. **Vathi**, the capital, is small, and its white houses fan out in a mounting semi-circle at one end of the bay. There are beaches at **Kuoni**, south of *Frikies*, and from here there is a road going to *Loizos' cave*, where traces of the worship of Artemis, Hera and Athena have been found.

Zante (Zakinthos) is the southernmost island in the Ionian group. Zante is also the name of the capital, where in the town museum there are Ionian historic treasures. In the southeast is the huge bay of *Laganas*, where there are numerous hotels and restaurants and lively nightlife. There are more sandy beaches at **Argassi, Alikes** and **Tsilivi**, 3km (2 miles) from the town of Zante.

Crete

The largest and most southerly Greek island, Crete is rich in historical remains and scenic variety. Along the northern shores there are modern resorts. Alongside lie the scattered remains of older civilizations – Minoan palaces, Byzantine churches, Venetian castles and sites of more recent struggles. Crete is divided into four prefectures – **Chanea** (Hania), **Rethymnon** (Rethimno), **Heraklion** (Iraklio) and **Agios Nikolaos** – and has a good road network and regular communications.

Heraklion, the largest and busiest town on the island, has a variety of nightlife and sightseeing to offer. In the prefecture of Heraklion are three of the most important Minoan centres – *Knossos, Phaestos* and *Malia*. Crete is well known as the setting for the battle between Theseus and the Minotaur, and the ruins of Knossos are popularly held to be the site of the labyrinth.

East of Heraklion is **Agios Nikolaos**, one of the best-known holiday resorts on the island. As a result it is very crowded in the high season. Much of the east coast of Crete has been developed specifically as a tourist area and is a popular target for package tours. The prefecture of Rethymnon combines the gentle scenery of the northern and southern coastlines with the precipitous gorges of the *Idi* and *White Mountains*. The main town, **Rethymnon**, on the northern coast, is an hour and a half's bus ride west from the airport. There is a well-preserved Venetian fort behind the harbour and, like the other large towns on the north coast, Venetian influence is apparent in the architecture.

In the Lasithi region, **Elounda** and **Ierapetra** are the most developed resorts and, at the western end of the island, is the fertile region of Chanea (Xania). **Chanea**, the main town, has a mixture of modern, neo-classical and Venetian architecture. Places to visit are the popular

seaside resorts of **Plátanos, Máleme** and **Kolimbari;** the freshwater springs at **Falarsana;** and the *Samaria Gorge*, the longest in Europe.

Other resorts include **Agia Galini, Agia Mannia, Agia Plagia, Amnissos, Amoudara, Gouves, Kokini Hani, Limenas Hersonissou, Malia, Seteia** and **Stalida.**

The Dodecanese

This cluster of 12 islands lies to the southeast of the Greek mainland. Distances between the islands are fairly small, so visitors can easily hop from one to another, swapping, say, the relative sophistication of Rhodes and Kos for the calmer and simpler life on **Tilos** or **Astipalaia.**

Rhodes is one of the most popular and best-developed islands in the Mediterranean. It offers international-class hotels, varied nightlife, sports facilities and duty-free shopping. It has 370km (230 miles) of coastline and a good, well-surfaced road network. Bus services bring most of the towns and villages within easy reach of the capital. Travel agents organise daily sightseeing trips to the archaeological sites and beauty spots. Rhodes is 267 nautical miles from Piraeus and is connected by boat services. Rhodes airport is international and there are daily direct flights from Athens. The main town, also called Rhodes, lies on the very northern tip of the island. It is made up of two distinct parts, the new town and the old town which stands within the walls of the medieval fortress. The 15th-century *Knight's Hospital* is now an archaeological museum which houses the celebrated *Aphrodite of Rhodes*. The *Palace of the Grand Masters* also has a splendid collection. 2km (1.2 miles) to the west of Rhodes town lies the *Acropolis* of ancient Rhodes. Many impressive ruins can still be seen, including the *Temple of Apollo* and a theatre and stadium, which date back to the 2nd century BC.

At **Filerimos**, 15km (9 miles) from Rhodes, lie the ruins of ancient *Ialisos*. The view from the *Acropolis* is spectacular. Ancient **Kameiros**, 25km (16 miles) southwest of Ialisos, is one of the few archaeological sites in Greece where many buildings and monuments

from the Hellenistic period can still be seen. 56km (35 miles) to the southeast of Rhodes is *Lindos*, with its well-preserved remains scattered on the ancient Acropolis.

Rhodes is a favourite for sports enthusiasts: there is good fishing at the resorts of **Lindos, Kameiros** and **Genadi** and there are facilities for water-skiing, sailing, tennis, basketball and golf at sports grounds and clubs all over the island.

There are other resorts at **Faliraki, Ixia, Kalithea, Kremasti, Afandou Golf, Ialisos, Kritinia** and **Profitis Elias.**

Conducted tours: By coach – half-day: daily tour of the town, excursions to Lindos, Kamiros, Ialisos, **Butterfly Valley** and 'Rhodes By Night' which includes an evening meal and folk dances. There is also a whole-day tour of Byzantine antiquities.

Cruises: A whole-day cruise along the east coast of Rhodes to Simi and **Panormitis** and conducted tours to Kos, Halki, Tilos, Nissiros and Patmos.

Excursions by air: To Athens, Nauplia, Epidaurus, Corinth (two days), Heraklion (museum), Knossos, Phaestos, Gortys and Agia Triada (three days).

Inter-island connections by air: Flights are available between Rhodes and Kos, Karpathos, Heraklion (Crete), Mykonos, Thira (Santorini) and Kassos.

Cos (Kos) is a fertile island with a mild climate, sandy beaches (some of which have black volcanic sand) and ample hotel accommodation. Most places of historical and sightseeing interest lie within the pretty main town of the same name, and its immediate surroundings, and can be visited easily on foot or by hiring a bicycle. The *Plane Tree of Hippocrates*, a massive tree with a trunk 12m (39ft) in circumference, is near here, as is the castle of the *Knights of St John*, an impressive example of medieval defensive architecture with its double wall and moat; an ancient agora with remains of Greek buildings of the 4th to 2nd centuries BC; the *Temple of Dionysus*; the *Odeon;* a restored Roman villa with mosaic decorations; some Roman baths; and a *Gymnasium* of the Hellenistic period (2nd century BC) with a restored colonnade of Xytos. The beaches towards **Lambi**, to the north of Kos, and towards **Agios Fokas**, to the south, are being developed. Places to visit include **Asfendiou, Kardamena, Pili,** the old fortress at **Palio Pili,** the fishing villages of **Marmari** and **Mastihari, Kefalos** with its pleasant beach and **Palatia** where ruins of *Astipalaia,* the ancient capital of Kos, survive.

Other resorts include **Antimahia, Lambi Milos Lappa** and **Psalidi.**

There are frequent daily flights to the mainland, and frequent connections by ship to Piraeus. Local steamship lines link Kos with Rhodes and Kalimnos and with Nissiros.

Conducted Tours: There is a daily coach tour of the island.

Cruises: There are day cruises to **Kalimnos,** Nissiros (with a visit to its volcano), **Patmos** (with a visit to the monastery and *Grotto of St John the Baptist*) and to **Pserimos** and its splendid swimming beach.

Patmos lies 140 nautical miles from Piraeus, with which it is connected by steamship services. It is also linked with the Dodecanese group of islands by an inter-island boat service. The nearby isles of **Fourni, Lipsi** and **Leros** are easily accessible from Patmos. The island, a place of pilgrimage, is dominated by the massive and formidable *Monastery of St John the Divine* in **Hora.** The 'sacred grotto', where St John received and dictated 'Revelations', is enshrined in the *Church of the Apocalypse,* just below the Monastery. Hora, the island capital, lies 2km (1.2 miles) away from the port of **Skala** and can be reached by bus or taxi. It is an extraordinary sight: whitewashed houses arranged along maze-like alleys too narrow for cars, clustered around the base of the monastery. Patmos has fine beaches at Grikos, Meloi, Netia, Diakofit and around *Kambos Bay,* which can be reached by motor launch or by car from Skala. Excursions to the monasteries of *Panagia Apolou* and *Panagia Geranou* are particularly pleasant.

Kalimnos lies 180 nautical miles from Piraeus, with which it is connected by regular steamship services. An inter-island boat service also links Kalymnos with other islands of the Dodecanese. Rocky and barren on the whole, Kalymnos is famous for its sponge fishing – a tradition which is expressed in many folk songs and local dances. Along the west coast of the island there are several resorts, including **Linaria, Mirties** and **Massouri.** Excursions can be made to the stalagmite and stalactite *Grotto of Spilia Kefalas* (35 minutes by motor launch); to the health springs at **Therma** (1km/0.6 miles to the south of the Kalymnos town); and to **Horio,** the old capital which stands below the medieval castle. Near Horio are the remains of the Franco-Byzantine fortress, *Pera-Kastro,* and the traces of the *Church of Christ of Jerusalem,* built towards the end of the 4th century AD. To the southwest lie the monasteries of *Evangelistria* and *Agia Ekaterini,* both of which have guest-houses. There are boat trips to the nearby isles of **Telendos** and **Pserimos,** ideal for swimming and fishing.

Simi, a predominantly rocky island, lies 235 nautical miles from Piraeus and 25 nautical miles from Rhodes. The steamship line that serves the rest of the Dodecanese calls at Simi. The beach at **Pedi** is good for swimming and the bays of *Nanou, Marathoundas* and *Niborio* can be reached by motor launch. Nearby are the deserted islands of **Seskli** and **Nemo,** ideal for fishing.

Karpathos is a mountainous island with fertile valleys and plains. Piraeus lies 227 nautical miles away while Rhodes, with which it is connected by steamship and summer flights, is only 89 nautical miles away. The island capital, **Pigadia,** lies in a wide, curving bay on the east coast. Its small port of **Possi** is a natural harbour and there are good beaches nearby. Transport is provided by buses and taxis while motor launches serve the coastal areas. Attractive spots are **Aperi, Volada, Mirtonas, Othos, Messohori** and its beautiful bathing beach, *Agia Marina,* the fishing port **Finiki,** and **Arkassa.** The northern part of Karpathos is dominated by the densely forested mountain of *Profitis Ilias* (1140m/3740ft). From the small harbour of **Diafani,** on the northern coast, a road will take you to **Olimbos,** a charming village where ancient traditions and customs are very much alive. Excursions can be made to the northern headland of Karpathos and the tiny isle of **Saria,** where the remains of the ancient city of **Nissiros** can be seen (access is by motor launch from Diafani), and to **Kira-Panagia,** a picturesque bay with a fine beach and monastery.

Leros, a mountainous but extensively cultivated island, lies 169 nautical miles from Piraeus. Excursions can be made to the coastal villages of **Agia Marina, Koukouli, Kithoni, Panagies, Blefouti, Gourna, Lepida** and **Temenia.** Traces of the island's past glory include the Franco-Byzantine fort overlooking the capital town, **Platanos,** and the ruins of the Byzantine castle on *Mount Kasteli,* to the northwest. **Leros** is ideal for fishing and small craft can be hired. Laki, one of the largest natural harbours in the Mediterranean, lies 3km (2 miles) from Platanos. The villages of Leros can be reached by taxi along well-paved roads. Old customs and traditions also survive on Leros: the celebrations at Carnival time are reminiscent of the ancient Dionysian festivities.

Tilos, lying 290 nautical miles from Piraeus and only 49 nautical miles northwest of Rhodes, is an island neglected by tourists. It is a hilly island with many isolated and unspoilt beaches. Its few inhabitants live at **Livadia,** a natural port, and at **Megalo Horio** which is crowned by a medieval castle. There are good bathing beaches at Livadia, *Agios Antonios* and *Plaka.* Mules and donkeys are the major forms of transport. Almost all coastal regions offer splendid fishing and boats are available for hire.

Nissiros is connected with Piraeus (200 nautical miles) and Rhodes (60 nautical miles) by regular steamship service. Only 42 sq km (16 sq miles) in area, Nissiros seems larger, due to the massive bulk of its inactive volcano which towers over the island. The capital, **Mandraki,** is built below the medieval castle and *Monastery of Panagia Spiliani.* 8km (5 miles) southwest of Mandraki lie the remains of the ancient Acropolis with its Pelasgian walls, still well preserved in many places. The fishing village of **Pali** has a good beach where there is excellent swimming.

Halki, a small hilly island with many unspoilt beaches, lies 302 nautical miles from Piraeus and 35 nautical miles from Rhodes. The steamship line, which serves all the small islands of the Dodecanese, calls at Halki. There are no cars or buses on this peaceful island but horses and small motorboats can be hired. The small population of Halki busies itself with fishing and sponge diving. The

Masked dancing

capital, **Niborio,** is built in tiers, and from the midst of its squat white houses rises the tall bell-tower of **Agios Nikolaos.** Nissiros's best bathing beach is nearby.

Kastelorizo (Megisti), the easternmost of the islands in the Aegean Sea, is a mere 9 sq km (6 sq miles) in area. It is connected to nearby Rhodes by a twice-weekly boat. Above the houses, on a high rock, rises an old castle which the Knights of St John reconstructed in the 14th century. The fascinating *Grotto of Parasta,* which can be reached by boat, is to the southeast of the island. There are beaches next to the harbour at **Agios Stefanos** and on the uninhabited isle of **Agios Georgios** (10 minutes by motorboat).

Astipalaia, mountainous but fertile, has a coastline 110km (68 miles) long, indented with beautiful bays. It can be reached from Piraeus, 165 nautical miles away, by the steamship line which links the Dodecanese. Astipalaia offers peace and quiet. The capital, also called Astipalaia, is dominated by its Franco-Byzantine castle. The most beautiful parts of the island are **Livadi** and **Maltezana** where there are fine sandy beaches.

Kassos lies between Crete and Karpathos from which it is separated by only 3 nautical miles. Piraeus is 215 nautical miles away and Rhodes 94 nautical miles. Like all the small islands in the Dodecanese group it is served by an inter-island steamship line. **Emborios,** the port, and **Fri,** the principal town, are picturesque. **Selai,** a cave

to the west of the village of **Agia Marina,** is filled with stalactites of various formations. Nearby there are remains of an ancient wall. Non-asphalt roads and country paths lead to pretty villages such as **Panagia, Arvanitohori** and **Poli.** The isle of **Armathia** can be reached by boat.

Climate: In the summer months (June to September) the temperature averages between 25°-31°C. In the winter (October to May) the temperature normally averages between 12°-17°C.

Northeast Aegean Islands

This group of islands, fairly widely scattered in the waters of the northeast Aegean, includes **Chios** (Hios), **Samos, Lesbos** (Lesvos), **Lemnos** (Limnos), **Ikaria** and the smaller islets around them.

Lemnos, 188 nautical miles from Piraeus, is still relatively unknown to the main tourist stream. **Mirina,** its capital, is built over the ancient city of the same name and has a museum housing exhibits from the island's history. There is a swimming beach nearby. At **Nea Koutali,** pinewoods reach down to the sea. Exactly opposite Nea Koutali, on the eastern shore of the large bay, is **Moudros,** a charming town with attractive houses, a stately church and good beaches. Shellfish and strong local wine are specialities. Lemnos is linked to

Athens and Thessaloniki by air, and to Kimi, Agios Efstratios, Kavala, Samonthraki, Alexandroupolis, Mytilini, Thessaloniki, Agios Konstantinos and the islands of the Sporades and the Dodecanese by steamer service.

Lesbos is 118 nautical miles from Piraeus and is the largest island in this group, with vast olive groves, shady pinewoods, good beaches and picturesque monasteries. The capital, **Mytilini**, has a bathing beach with good facilities at *Tzamakia*. There are other beaches at **Vateron, Petra, Skala Eftalou, Agios Issidoros** (pebble beach) and along the *Gulf of Kaloni* on the east coast of the island. At **Loutra Thermis** there are therapeutic springs which have been known since antiquity. **Mithimna**, or Molivos, in the north of the island, is a meeting place for artists from all over the world. Lesbos is linked to Athens by air and to Piraeus, Thessaloniki, Moudania, Leros, Kos, Kalimnos, Patmos, Rhodes, Skiathos, Samos, Chios, Lemnos, Agios Efstratios and Agios Konstantinos by steamer service.

Chios (Hios), 153 nautical miles from Piraeus, is dominated by two mountains, the *Profitis Elias* and *Oros*. The capital town Chios lies on the eastern shore, very close to the coastline of Turkish Ionia. The port has a dual character – the old waterfront with its small, distempered houses and numerous fishing smacks, and the new quays behind which stand modern buildings and

busy patisseries. The archaeological museum, located behind the quay warehouses, contains interesting exhibits. There is also a museum of modern Greek sculpture and the fine churches of *Agios Issidoros* and *Agios Andreas*. There are good beaches at **Karfa, Marmaro, Nago, Pandorikias, Langada** and **Emborios** (black pebbles) and near the *Monastery of Agia Markella*. Villages in the south of the island still have a medieval appearance. The village of **Mesta** is one of the traditional settlements which the National Tourist Organisation has turned into small guest-houses. A medieval settlement, it has suffered little damage and change in the course of centuries. The port serving Mesta is **Passalimani**, a small fishing village, where there are rooms to let. Small vessels from Chios sail to the historic island of **Psara** with its unfrequented beaches, rich fishing grounds and the *Kimissis Theotokou Monastery*. The one port and village on the island has a guest-house. Small vessels also sail to the **Inoussai Islands**, another secluded refuge with sandy beaches and small tavernas. Chios is linked to Athens by air and to Piraeus by ferryboat. Steamer services also operate from Thessaloniki, the Dodecanese and Sporades, but on a less frequent schedule. There are also connections with Lemnos, Ikaria, Samos, Kavala and Crete. Mesta is linked with Rafina.

Samos, 174 nautical miles from Piraeus, is a land of

forested hills, olive groves, vineyards and meadows. Samos, the island's capital, has undergone extensive development but has retained many elegant buildings and museums. A short road links the port area with **Vathi**, the old quarter built on the slopes of the red clay hills behind the port. From Samos town a good asphalt road runs the length of the island's coast to **Karlovassi**, passing the beaches at **Kokan, Tsarmadou, Aviakia, Darlovossi** (pebble) and **Potami**, 2km (1 mile) beyond. To the west are the beaches at **Votsalakia** and **Hrissi Amnos**, probably the best on the island. There are well-appointed beaches at **Psili Ammos** and **Possidonion**, on the south-east coast, at **Gangos** and along the *Cape of Kotsika*. Close to the eastern shore lie the islets of **Agios Nikolaos, Prassonissi** and **Vareloudi**, excellent for snorkel fishing.

There are flights to Samos from Athens and a regular steamer service from Piraeus. Steamer services also operate from Thessaloniki, Kavala, Agios Efstratios, Chios, Kalimnos, Kos, Lemnos, Leros, Mudania, Mytilini, Patmos, Rhodes, Chalki, Karpathos, Kassos, Anafi, Santorini, Milos and Folegandros, but on a less frequent schedule. There are also sailings twice or three times a week for the islet of Fourni.

Ikaria is 143 nautical miles from Piraeus and lies between Samos and Andros. The southern side of the island is steep and rocky but the northern shore is lined

Thassos

with good bathing beaches. The main port and capital is
Agios Kirikos. There are thick pinewoods, streams and a
sandy beach at **Armenistis** and a spa at **Therma**. At
Therma Lefkadas there are hot medicinal springs.
Motorboats can be chartered to **Fanari**, on the
northeastern corner of the island, and to the small island
of **Fourni**, famous for its lobsters, *raki*, honey and an
exceptional sandy beach. There is a Piraeus–Ikaria
steamer service but, as an alternative, fly to Samos and
from there pick up the steamer service to Ikaria.

The Sporades

Across the waters from the eastern coast of mainland
Greece are the four islands of the Sporades – **Skiathos**,
Skopelos, **Alonissos** and **Skiros**. The islands are
becoming very popular and it is advisable to book early,
especially in the high season. In addition to hotels, there
are villas and rooms to rent from individual families. A
list of private lodgings can be obtained from the local
tourist police.
Skiathos is 41 nautical miles from the town of **Volos.**
The island is green and idyllic, with 70 sandy inlets,
several bays and three harbours. Its highest wooded
summit rises to 438m (1437ft). Nine smaller islands
surround Skiathos. Two of these, the **Tsougries**, lie
across the main harbour, offering safe anchorage to boats
and a small marina for yachts. The main town, also called
Skiathos, was built in 1830 on two low hills. It is the hub
of the tourist summer season, with several hotels, villas
and rooms to let. There is a good road which hugs the
southern coast with its many bays, linking the town with
Koukounaries, the famous pine grove. Another way to
get around Skiathos is by motor launch. They run at
regular intervals to the more popular beaches for a
moderate fare. There are also motorboats for hire. The

nights in Skiathos are especially lively, with tavernas,
bars and discotheques. There are beaches at
Koukounaries, Mandraki, Lalaria (pebble beach) and
Agia Eleni. Worth visiting is the ancient walled town of
Kastro, northeast of Skiathos town. Skiathos has many
facilities for tourists including a marina with a supply
station, a medical centre, tourist police and a garage for
light car repairs.
Skopelos is 58 nautical miles from Volos. The island has
small bays, golden sands and slopes covered with olive
trees, churches and monasteries. The main town of
Skopelo, a seaport with narrow cobbled streets and a
sandy beach, is quieter than Skiathos. There are beaches
which have shallow and safe waters for children at
Stafylos Cove; at **Limnonari** – to which one crosses by
boat from **Agnondas**; at **Panormos**, a wind-protected
bay; at **Milia** and **Elios;** and at **Loutraki,** the *Glossa
port.* For those who prefer shingle beaches, there is *Agios
Konstandinos.* The *Tripiti Grotto* is also worth visiting.
Alonissos is 62 nautical miles from Volos. The centre of
the island has been submerged, leaving two small islets
and several smaller ones still. A rock mass called
Psathoura, where there are several grottos with
stalactites, is all that remains of ancienti Alonissos. With
only 10km (6 miles) of roads on Alonissos, the best way
of getting about is by motorboat, sharing the fare. These
ply between the islands and beaches and excursion sites.
The beaches at **Kokkinokastro,** *Palavodimos, Steni
Vala, Ai-Nikolas* and *Kalamakia*, are 30 minutes by
caique from the small port of **Patitri** and offer excellent
bathing. On some of the surrounding, virtually
uninhabited isles there are isolated, good beaches but no
amenities. There are guest-houses and rooms to rent as
well as bungalows and small hotels. Other services
include a medical centre, port authority, customs, police
and motorboat rentals for fishing trips and excursions.

Cyclop's Cave, decorated with stalactites and
stalagmites, is to be found on the island of **Gioura**.
Psathoura has remains of an ancient city, most of which
are submerged. Divers will see traces of streets, houses
and windows in shallow waters. When the sea is calm
they can be seen from the surface.
Skiros (Skyros) is 25 nautical miles from Kimi, in
Euboea, and 118 nautical miles from Piraeus. The
island's main port is **Linaria** and there are beaches
nearby at **Magazia, Molos** and **Girismati.** The more
distant beaches of *Ahili, Aspi, Kalamitsa, Pefkos, Atsitsa,
Tris Boukes* and *Aherounes* also offer good bathing and
can be reached by car. However, only the road to Ahili,
Aspi and Aherounes is asphalt. *Atsitsa* and *Pefkos* are
more islolated beaches. In most places there are small
tavernas by the sea and, in summer, cruises round the
island with small boats are organised.
Climate: In the summer months (June to September) the
temperature averages between 23°-27°C. In the winter
(October to May) the temperature averages between 10°-
20°C.

The Cyclades

Kea (Tzia), 42 nautical miles from Piraeus, is dotted
with small, cultivated valleys, sandy beaches, fruit
orchards, clusters of whitewashed houses, quaint villages
and a large number of churches. A short distance inland
from the port of **Korissia** lies **Hora,** with its 15 churches
and elegant archways. Several windmills, chapels and
notable monasteries are scattered around the island's
countryside. One is the famous *Convent of Panagia
Kastriani*, overlooking *Otzia Bay.* Archaeological sites
include one close to the *Vourkari* fishing hamlet. At
Koundouro and **Pisses** there are good swimming
beaches.
Kithnos (Kythnos) is 54 nautical miles from Piraeus. A
small island, its harsh landscape is softened by the dashes
of green provided by vineyards and fig trees. It has two
harbours, **Loutra** and **Merihas**, both sheltered
anchorages. Clinging to the barren hillside is **Hora** (this
is the name usually given to the main township or head
village) also known as **Messaria.** White Cycladic
cottages, churches with frescoes and icons and the
spontaneous hospitality of the islanders combine to make
Kithnos increasingly popular with visitors in search of
beauty and quiet. Loutra gets its name from the well-
known warm medicinal springs in the area. Sites worth
visiting include the monasteries of *Panagia tou Nikou*
and *Panagia tis Kanalas.*
Serifos is 70 nautical miles from Piraeus. Ships calling at
the island anchor at **Livadi** which is surrounded by
gardens and orchards. From here the road climbs up to
Hora where flagstones pave the narrow alleys, lined by
typically Cycladic houses and churches. Higher still
stands the old Venetian fortress. Attractive beaches are to
be found at **Mega Livadi** and **Koutalas.**
Sifnos is 82 sq km (52 sq miles) in area. An attractive
drive inland from the port of **Kamares** leads to the
capital **Apollonia,** which echoes back to the time the god
Apollo was worshipped there. In the modern town, many
houses retain their distinctive Cycladic character. There
are a number of notable churches and a folkloric
museum. The medieval atmosphere in the old capital,
Kastro, is striking. There is an archaeological collection
in the *Roman Catholic Cathedral.* The villages of
Artemonas and **Exambela** are built on gently undulating
hills amid picturesque windmills. It is estimated that
there are 365 churches and chapels on Sifnos.
Monasteries such as those of *Ai Yanni tou Moungou,
Agios Symeon, Ai Lia* and *Panagia Hrissopigi* are of
interest.
Kimolos, 88 nautical miles from Piraeus, is an island of
white chalk cliffs. Ships call at the harbour of **Pstahi.** In
the capital, **Kimolos,** houses are smothered with flowers
and the streets are laid with decorated flagstones. The
indented coastline is lined with fine, sandy beaches.
There are hot natural springs at **Prassa**, and a submerged
city off the coast at **Koftou** is of archaeological interest.
Milos is 82 nautical miles from Piraeus. This beautiful
island is inseparably associated with Venus, the goddess
of love. **Adamas,** on the eastern shore, is the island's
port. The icons of the *Church of Agia Trias* are
noteworthy. **Plaka,** the island's typically Cycladic
capital, is overlooked by the remains of a Frankish castle
and the 13th-century Byzantine *Church of Thalassistra.*
The *Archaeological Museum* houses ceramics from the
island dating back to the 6th millenium BC, and the
Folkloric Museum contains examples of popular art.
There are extensive early Christian catacombs near the
small village of **Tripiti.** Attractive swimming beaches
include those at **Chivadolimni, Pollonia** and **Adamas**
and excursions can be made in small craft to the
Glaronissia; to volcanic islets with remarkable caves and
crystalline rocks; to the *Sykia Sea Cave* with its gaily
coloured sea bed; and to the islet of **Andimilos.**

Andros is 85 nautical miles from Piraeus. The island is green with pine-clad hills, olive groves and vineyards. Its port is **Gavrion** and its capital Andros, an attractive town with numerous mansions in the neo-classical style, hotels, clubs, the noteworthy *Maritime Museum*, as well as an *Archaeological Museum* with ceramics from ancient Agora and a rich collection of finds from the excavations on the island, dating back to the Geometric, Classical and Hellenistic Periods. There are fine swimming beaches all over the island, including *Gavrion, Batsi, Nimborio* and *Korthion.* At **Paleopolis** there are remains of ancient walls, a theatre and stadium. The *Panachrantou Monastery* at **Falika** and the Byzantine *Church of Taxiarchon* in **Messaria** are worth a visit. **Apikia** is well-known for its mineral springs.

Tinos, 86 nautical miles from Piraeus, is a focus of pilgrimages celebrating the Annunciation (March 25) and the Dormition (August 15) when thousands of pilgrims flock to this sacred island to attend celebrations in honour of the Virgin Mary at the marble *Church of the Evangelistria.* There is also a *Byzantine Museum,* and the *Archaeological Museum,* exhibiting finds from the ancient temples of Poseidon and Amphitrite. Buses connect the villages with the town of **Tinos.** The island's fine beaches include *Agios Fokas* and *Kionia,* very close to the town, and **Kolibithra,** on the northern coast. At **Kionia** there are also traces of ancient settlements.

Siros (Syros) is 80 nautical miles from Piraeus, lying at the heart of the Cycladic complex. Its capital and main port **Ermoupolis** is also the capital of the Cyclades. It has many notable buildings in the neo-classical style, such as the town hall and the customs house, as well as a fine theatre, spacious public squares and impressive churches. Upper Syros retains a strong medieval flavour with city walls, narrow cobbled streets and arcades.

Mykonos (Mikonos) is 95 nautical miles from Piraeus. Renowned for its many windmills, catching the brisk 'meltemi' breezes, this barren island is a very popular holiday resort. Mykonos town comprises a modern harbour, whitewashed alleys, churches in the distinctive local style, shops selling local arts and crafts, small tavernas, cafés and discotheques. The *Paraportiani Church* near the quay is considered to be an architectural masterpiece. The *Archaeological Museum* exhibits finds excavated from the necropolis on the nearby islet of **Rineia.** There is also a *Museum of Popular Art.* Interesting excursions can be made to the monasteries of *Agios Panteleimon,* close to **Hora,** and the *Tourliani Monastery* at **Ano Mera.** Beaches range from cosmopolitan to secluded, and include *Agios Stefanos, Kalafatis, Platis Yialos* and *Ornos.* The best beaches, however, are on the south side of the island and can be reached by caique from Plati Yialos. They are *Paradise, Super Paradise, Agrari* and *Elia.* From Mykonos, there is a boat service to the island of **Delos.**

Delos (Dilos) was a sacred island in ancient times, and is said to have been the birthplace of Apollo and Artemis. The island has many archaeological sites, such as the *Lions Way* and the three temples of Apollo. A museum exhibits archaic, Classical, Hellenistic and Roman sculptures, including the *Archaic Sphinx of the Naxians* and *Acroteria* (Victories) from the *Temple of the Athenians.*

Paros is 90 nautical miles from Piraeus. The island's hinterland has undulating hills that contain the famous Parian marble. **Parikia**, the island's capital and main port, is built on the site of the ancient city. It is the custom on the island to have doors and windows open in the houses as a sign of welcome to strangers visiting the island. A narrow, stone-paved alley leads to one of the most impressive shrines in Christendom, the *Ekatondapiliani* or *Katapoliani* church. At **Kolimbithres** the rugged coast forms inlets with golden sands. There are attractive swimming beaches at **Drios, Alikes** and **Piso Livadi.** Of the island's monasteries, *Zoodohos Pigi Longovarda* and *Christou Tou Dassous* are the most significant.

Antiparos is separated from Paros by a narrow channel. The main attraction on this small island is its famous cave with stalactites; this can be reached by pack animals which carry visitors from the beach. There are many deserted beaches.

Thira (Santorini) is 127 nautical miles from Piraeus. Vast geological upheavals gave this Cycladic island its unique form – a steep plateau with sheer cliffs which rises from the sea. Because of its height and shape, there is often a warm, romantic wind that blows through the island. A funicular railway, pack mules or donkeys carry visitors up from the harbour of **Skala** to the island's capital Thira, a picturesque town with twisting alleys, arcades, a museum and an old Frankish quarter. It is also a good vantage point from which to view the **Kamenes,** two jet black volcanic islets in the bay that can be visited by light craft, as can **Therasia** (Thirassia), the second largest island of the Santorini group. There are some interesting archaeological remains in Ancient Thira

Mani

which has witnessed the passage of Phoenicians, Dorians, Romans and Byzantines. There are remains of a cluster of houses, a market place, baths, theatres, temples, tombs and early Christian relics. **Akrotiri** is also of great interest for the relics of the Minoan civilisation which have been excavated there. The *Monastery of Profitas Ilias* on the island's summit and the swimming beaches of *Perissa* and *Kamazi* are other attractions.

Naxos, 106 nautical miles from Piraeus, is the largest and most fertile island in the Cyclades group. Everywhere lies evidence of the island's long history: the *Temple of Apollo;* the immense gateway on the tiny islet of **Palatia,** linked to the main island by a causeway; Mycenaean tombs; a museum; remains of a Mycenaean settlement at **Grotta** (Cave); a castle; and historical churches. The village of **Halki** has a medieval fortress and several Byzantine churches. From **Naxos Town** the road leads inland to the village of **Sangri** from where one can visit the famous *Himaros Tower,* one of the best-preserved monuments of the Hellenistic period. There are many sandy beaches, such as at **Apollonas, Kastraki, Vigla** and **Agios Georgios.**

Ios, 114 nautical miles from Piraeus, is an extremely popular and busy island. Close to the small harbour of **Ormos,** where fishing smacks and yachts anchor, lies the attractive swimming beach of *Yalos;* other pleasant beaches are at **Koumbaras, Manganavi** and **Psathi.**

Amorgos, where the cities of Minoa, Arkesini and Aegiali once flourished, has several ruins of archaeological interest. There is a harbour in **Katapola** and, in **Hora,** whitewashed houses are built up a rocky slope. In the same area lies **Panagia Exohoriani** where a fiesta is held on August 15 every year. At **Plakoto** there are remains of an ancient tower and of a temple. There are good beaches at **Agios Panteleimon, Kato Akrotiri,**

Agia Anna and **Agia Paraskevi.**

Sikinos-Folegandros: These islands lie close to Ios and are attractive for their genuine island life and solitude. **Hora** is the only sizeable village on Sikinos. Its cottages are built in the distinctive island style along narrow alleys and there is a fine cathedral church. Attractions include the castle and *Hrissopigi Monastery,* built like a fortress. There is a good swimming beach at **Spillia. Folegandros** is an island of wild beauty, rugged and barren. There are some sandy beaches tucked away among the rocks, such as at **Karavostassi** on the southeastern coast of the island. **Panagia** has an interesting church and at **Hrissospilia** there is a cave with stalactites, stalagmites and ancient ruins.

Anafi, the most southerly of the Cycladic group of islands, has a rocky shoreline with many creeks. There are several smaller, attractive islands which people in search of the 'genuine article' are gradually discovering. **Schinoussa** with its extremely picturesque, tiny harbour; **Mersinia** or **Donoussa** with its superb sandy beaches; and the Koufonissia group of **Keros** and **Heraklia** – all of them are very modest in size and provide peaceful anchorages.

POPULAR ITINERARIES: 7-day: (a) Athens–Corinth–Mycenae–Nafplion–Epidaurus–Olympia–Delphi. (b) Athens–Delphi–Meteora–Thessaloniki–Phillipi–Kavala–Vergina. (c) Piraeus–Mykonos–Santorini–Crete–Rhodes–Patmos.

SOCIAL PROFILE

FOOD & DRINK: Restaurant and taverna food tends to be very simple, rarely involving sauces but with full use of local olive oil and charcoal grills. Dishes like *Dolmades* (stuffed vine leaves), *Moussaka, Kebabs* and *Avgolemono* (soup) can be found everywhere.

Taramosalata and a variety of seafood dishes, especially squid *(Kalamari)* or octopus, are excellent. Salads are made with the local cheese *(Fetta)* and fresh olive oil. Olives are cheap and plentiful. All restaurants have a standard menu which includes the availability and price of each dish. A good proportion of the restaurants will serve international dishes. Hours are normally 1200-1500 for lunch and 2100-2400 for dinner. Waiter service is usual. **Drink:** One of the best-known Greek drinks is *Retsina* wine, made with pine-needle resin. Local spirits include *Ouzo*, an aniseed-based clear spirit to which water is added. Local brandy is sharp and fiery. Greek coffee is served thick and strong, and sugared according to taste. Greek beer is a light *Pilsner* type. Visitors may be required to pay for each drink if seated some way from the bar. **Opening hours** vary according to the region and local laws.

NIGHTLIFE: This is centred in main towns and resorts with concerts and discotheques. Nightclubs featuring Greek Bouzouki music are extremely popular. There are some casinos in Greece, such as the Mont Parnes Casino in Athens, the Corfu Casino in Corfu and the Casino at the Grand Hotel Astir in Rhodes.

SHOPPING: Special purchases include lace, jewellery, metalwork, pottery, garments and knitwear, furs, rugs, leather goods, local wines and spirits. Athens is the centre for luxury goods and local handicrafts. The flea markets in Monastiraki and Plaka, below the Acropolis, are all crowded in high season. Regional specialities include silver from Ioannina, ceramics from Sifnos and Skopelos, embroidery from Skiros, Crete, Rhodes and the Ionian Islands, fur from Kastoria, alabaster from Crete and *flokati* rugs from the Epirus region. **Note:** There is a temptation to buy fake antiques, especially archaeological items. It is in fact illegal to export any item of real antiquity.

Shopping hours: These vary according to the season and location, but a rough guide follows: 0900-1700 Monday and Wednesday; 0830-1530 Saturday; and 0900-1400 and 1730-1900 Tuesday, Thursday and Friday.

Note: Most holiday resort shops stay open late in the evening.

SPORT: Athens has one **golf** club, the Glifada Golfcourse & Club. There are also clubs on Rhodes, Corfu and Halkidiki. There are many **tennis** clubs throughout Greece, including Thessaloniki, Halkidiki, Patras, Crete, Rhodes, Larissa and 15 in the Athens metropolitan area. For further information on tennis courts in Greece, contact the EFOA Association, 8 Omirou Street, Athens. Tel: (1) 323 0412. There are some **horseriding** clubs in Greece (five in Attica, two in Thessaloniki and one in Corfu). **Hunting:** Those who wish to shoot in Greece must have a special licence. **Mountaineering** is becoming increasingly popular and there is scope for **hill walking** and **climbing**. Further information is available from the Hellenic Alpine Club, 7 Karageorgr Servias Street, Athens. Tel: (1) 323 4555. There are over 7000 karstic cave formations in the country, the majority in Crete. Further information on these caves is available from the Hellenic Speleogical Society, 8 Mantearou Street, 10672 Athens. Tel: (1) 361 7824. **Skiing** centres are open December to March in a number of areas. Contact the GNTO for details.

Watersports: There are excellent facilities along all coastlines of the mainland and particularly in the islands. Most major hotels can help with arrangements. Water-skiing is especially popular and there are 30 water-ski schools in Greece with restaurants and child-care facilities. Speed boats are also available for hire. For further information, contact the Water-Skiing Association, 32 Stournara Street, Athens. Tel: (1) 523 1875. **Scuba diving:** The use of breathing apparatus is prohibited in many areas: check with port authorities. For a full list of areas where scuba diving is permitted, contact the GNTO or the Hellenic Federation of Underwater Activities, Post Office of West Airport, 16604 Helleniko, Athens. Tel: (1) 981 9961. **Fishing:** Greek waters offer good fishing, particularly during the summer and autumn. Boats and equipment can be found in most villages. For further information, contact Amateur Anglers and Maritime Sports Club, Akti

Moutopoulou, Piraeus. Tel: (1) 451 5731.

SPECIAL EVENTS: The following is a selection of the major annual festivals and special events celebrated in Greece during 1995/96. For a complete list, contact the GNTO.

Mar '95 *Carnival* (marks the beginning of Lent with celebrations throughout the country), particularly in Naoussa, Veria, Kozani, Skiros, Chios, Galaxidi and Thebes. **Apr** *Holy Week* (religious processions and ceremonies throughout the country). **May** *Folklorist Festival,* Eleusis. **May 21-23** *Anastenaria* (fire-walking ritual), Serres and Thessaloniki. **Jun** *Lassithi* (village folkore festival), Crete; *Rally Acropolis,* Athens; *Eleftheria Festival,* Kavala. **Late Jun-beginning of Jul** *Navy Week,* throughout Greece. **Late Jun-Sep** *Athens Festival* (opera, ballet, classical and contemporary music at the Herod Atticus Odeon); *Patras Festival* (ancient and modern drama, ballet, and concerts). **Late Jun-Aug** *Epidaurus Festival* (classical drama at the Epidaurus Ancient Theatre). **Jul** *International Sailing Regatta; Aegean Sailing Week,* Athens; *Cultural Festival,* Preveza. **Mid-Jul** *Wine Festival,* Rethymnon (Crete). **End Jul** *Music Festival,* Ithaka. **Jul-Aug** *Philippi and Thassos Festival* (ancient drama, ballet and concerts); *Sun and Stone Festival* (Greek folk dancing), Nea Karvali. **Jul-Sep** *Epirotika Festival* (drama, music and paintings), Ioannina. **Aug** *Epirotika Festival,* Janene; *Hippokraetia Festival,* Kos; *Olympus Festival,* Litohoro. **Late Aug-mid Sep** *Wine Festival,* Patras. **Sep** *Thessaloniki International Trade Fair.* **Oct** *Demetria Festival* (theatre, music, opera and ballet), Thessaloniki; *International Days of Music; Greek Film Festival,* Macedonia; *International Open Marathon,* Athens. **Nov** *Philoxenia* (tourism trade show), Thessaloniki; *Tsikoudia Festival* (Greek liqueur-tasting), Crete.

SOCIAL CONVENTIONS: Visitors to Greece will find the Greeks to be well aware of a strong historical and cultural heritage. Traditions and customs differ throughout Greece, but overall a strong sense of unity prevails. The Greek Orthodox Church has a strong traditional influence on the Greek way of life, especially

in more rural areas. The throwing back of the head is a negative gesture. Dress is generally casual. Smoking is prohibited on public transport and in public buildings.
Tipping: 12-15% is usual.

BUSINESS PROFILE

ECONOMY: Traditionally agricultural, accession to the European Union gave a new impetus to the Greek economy, particularly the industrial sectors of textiles, clothing and shoes, cement, mining and metals, chemicals, steel and processed agricultural products. Tourism, the most important service industry, boomed during the 1980s and is expected to continue growing during the 1990s, with over ten million tourists visiting the country in 1994. Shipping is also an important source of income, with Greece having one of the largest merchant fleets in the world. Greek enterprises have consistently found difficulty penetrating European markets, however, because of the comparatively small scale of the majority of businesses. The country produces large quantities of wheat, barley, maize, tobacco and fruit for export. Compared to the rest of Western Europe, Greece is both poor and underdeveloped (20% of the working population work the land – a very high proportion by EU standards) but it experienced rapid growth during the 1970s which continued, albeit at a slower rate, through the 1980s. The EU takes about 65% of Greek trade. Outside the European Union, Saudi Arabia (oil), Japan and the USA are the country's major trading partners. Large EU loans have been provided in the last couple of years to keep the economy solvent. Public deficits and a high national debt are the economic challenges facing successive Greek governments.
BUSINESS: Formal suits are expected. French, German and English are often spoken as well as Greek.
COMMERCIAL INFORMATION: The following organisation can offer advice: Athens Chamber of Commerce, Odos Akademias 7, 106 71 Athens. Tel: (1) 360 2411. Fax: (1) 360 7897 or 361 6464. Telex:

215707.
CONFERENCES/CONVENTIONS: Enquiries can be made to the GNTO.

CLIMATE

Greece has a warm Mediterranean climate. In summer, dry hot days are often relieved by stiff breezes, especially in the north and coastal areas. Athens can be stiflingly hot, so visitors should allow time to acclimatise. The evenings are cool. Winters are mild in the south but much colder in the north. November to March is the rainy season.
Required clothing: Lightweight clothes during summer months, including protection from the midday sun. Light sweaters are needed for evenings. Rainproofs are advised for autumn. Winter months can be quite cold, especially in the northern mainland, so normal winter wear will be required.

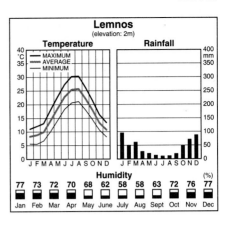

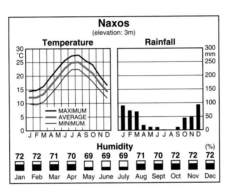

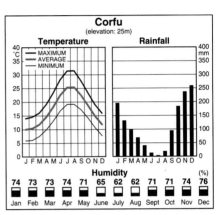

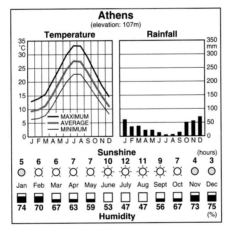

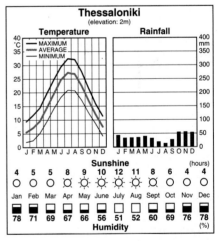

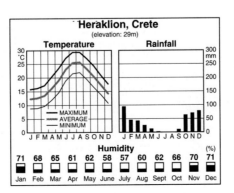

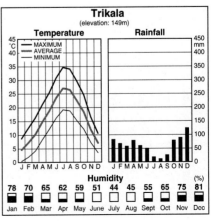

Greenland

Location: South Arctic/North Atlantic.

Important note: The arctic weather conditions in Greenland may cause delays and interruptions in transport services or changes to planned itineraries. In some cases, this may result in additional hotel accommodation or helicopter/ship transportation costs. Such expenses *must* be paid by the traveller at the time. Tour operators and airlines are unable to accept responsibility for expenses resulting in any such delays, but tour companies will normally be able to give refunds for services, transport, accommodation, etc which were paid for in advance, but which they were not able to provide. These refunds, where applicable, will only be made after the end of the trip. It is, therefore, very important to retain all unused vouchers or tickets. *It is strongly recommended that travellers take as much money as possible with them in order to cover expenses which may arise as a result of unforeseen delays.*

Greenland Tourism A/S
PO Box 1552, DK-3900 Nuuk, Greenland
Tel: 22888. Fax: 22877.
Greenland Tourism A/S
Box 2151, 52 Pilestræde, DK-1016 Copenhagen K, Denmark
Tel: 33 13 69 75.
For Diplomatic Representation, see Royal Danish Embassies in the entry for *Denmark* earlier in the book.
Danish Tourist Board
55 Sloane Street, London SW1X 9SY
Tel: (0171) 259 5958/9. Opening hours: 1100-1600 Monday to Friday.

Timatic	Health
	GALILEO/WORLDSPAN: **TI-DFT/SFJ/HE**
	SABRE: **TIDFT/SFJ/HE**
	Visa
	GALILEO/WORLDSPAN: **TI-DFT/SFJ/VI**
	SABRE: **TIDFT/SFJ/VI**
	For more information on Timatic codes refer to Contents.

British Honorary Consulate
PO Box 1073, Royal Greenland, Vestervig 45, DK-3900 Nuuk, Greenland
Tel: 24422. Fax: 22409. Telex: 90437 (a/b PROGHB GD).
Grønlands Hjemmestyre
(Greenland Home Rule Government)
PO Box 1015, DK-3900 Nuuk, Greenland
Tel: 23000. Fax: 25002. Telex: 90613.
Canadian Consulate
PO Box 1012, DK-3900 Nuuk, Greenland
Tel: 28888. Fax: 27288. Telex: 90602.

AREA: 2,175,600 sq km (840,000 sq miles).
POPULATION: 55,385 (1992).
POPULATION DENSITY: 0.03 per sq km.
CAPITAL: Nuuk (formerly Godthåb). **Population:** 12,233 (1991).
GEOGRAPHY: Greenland is the world's biggest island (if Australia is counted as a continent). The surrounding seas are either permanently frozen or chilled by the mainly cold currents caused by the meeting of the Arctic and the North Atlantic Oceans. The inland area is covered with ice, stretching 2500km (1500 miles) north–south and 1000km (600 miles) east–west. In the centre, the ice can be up to 3km (2 miles) thick. The ice-free coastal region, which is sometimes as wide as 200km (120 miles), covers a total of 341,700 sq km (131,900 sq miles), and is where all of the population is to be found. This region is intersected by deep fjords which connect the inland ice area with the sea. The Midnight Sun can be seen north of the Arctic Circle; the further north one is, the more the Midnight Sun will be in evidence. The arctic night in the winter results in a continuous twilight and, in the far north of the country, complete darkness. The Northern Lights can be seen during the autumn and winter months.
LANGUAGE: The official languages are Greenlandic, an Inuit (Eskimo) language, and Danish. Greenlanders connected with tourism will normally speak at least some English.
RELIGION: Church of Greenland (part of the Protestant Church of Denmark) and Danish. There is a Roman Catholic church in Nuuk.
TIME: East Greenland/Mesters Vig: GMT (summer and winter).
Scoresby Sound: GMT - 1 (GMT from last Sunday in March to Saturday before last Sunday in September).
Ammassalik and west coast: GMT - 3 (GMT - 2 from last Sunday in March to Saturday before last Sunday in September).
Thule area: GMT - 4 (GMT - 3 from April to October).
ELECTRICITY: 220 volts AC, 50Hz.
COMMUNICATIONS: Telephone: IDD is available. Country code: 299. There are no area codes. Outgoing international code: 009. There are no telephone boxes in Greenland, but calls can be made from hotels. **Telegram:** All towns have a telegraph station. **Post:** Greenland produces its own stamps which are popular among collectors. Post from Greenland takes about four to five days to reach Europe. Post office hours: 0900-1500 Monday to Friday. **Press:** There are no daily newspapers in Greenland, but there are two weekly publications and one monthly.
BBC World Service and Voice of America frequencies: From time to time these change. See the section *How to Use this Book* for more information.
BBC:

MHz	12.10	9.410	6.195	3.955

Voice of America:

MHz	11.97	9.670	6.040	5.995

PASSPORT/VISA

The regulations for tourist and Business visas are the same as for Denmark (see the *Passport/Visa* section for Denmark above). Visitors should specify that they wish to visit Greenland when they make their application. Special permits are necessary for persons wishing to visit Kranak, the military zone around Thule. Applications should be made to The Greenland Home Rule Government – Denmark Bureau, PO Box 2151, 52 Pilestræde, DK-1016 Copenhagen. Tel: 33 13 42 24.

MONEY

Currency: Danish Krone (DKr) = 100 øre. Notes are in denominations of DKr1000, 500, 100 and 50. Coins are in denominations of DKr20, 10, 5, 2 and 1, and 50 and 25 øre.
Currency exchange: Cheques drawn on Danish banks or on Eurocheque cards can be cashed at banks. Travellers

cheques and cash can also be exchanged. There are two Greenland banks, *Nuna Bank* (PO Box 1031, Skibshavns-vej 33, DK-3900 Nuuk) and *Grønlandsbanken* (PO Box 1033, DK-3900 Nuuk). *KNI* represents the banks in other towns and villages.
Note: There is no banking service in Søndre Strømfjord at present.
Credit cards: Limited use of American Express and Diners Club. Credit cards are not widely accepted; check with your credit card company for merchant acceptability and other facilities which may be available.
Travellers cheques: Cheques in major currencies may be exchanged as indicated above.
Exchange rate indicators: The following figures are included as a guide to the movements of the Danish Krone against Sterling and the US Dollar:

Date:	Oct '92	Sep '93	Jan '94	Jan '95
£1.00=	9.36	10.14	10.05	9.52
$1.00=	5.89	6.64	6.90	6.09

Currency restrictions: None.
Banking hours: 0930-1600 Monday to Wednesday and Friday, 0930-1800 Thursday.

DUTY FREE

The following goods may be imported into Greenland without incurring customs duty:
200 cigarettes or 250g of tobacco and 200 cigarette papers (travellers must be over 15); 1 litre of spirits or 2 litres of fortified wine and 2 litres of ordinary wine (travellers must be over 18).
These goods must be carried by the traveller personally.
Prohibited items: Pistols, fully- or semi-automatic weapons, narcotics and live animals. Hunting rifles require a licence; apply to the carrying airline.

PUBLIC HOLIDAYS

Jan 1 '95 New Year. **Apr 13** Maundy Thursday. **Apr 14** Good Friday. **Apr 17** Easter Monday. **May 12** Common Prayer's Day. **May 25** Ascension Day. **Jun 5** Whit Monday *and* Constitution Day. **Jun 21** National Day. **Dec 24-26** Christmas. **Dec 31-Jan 1 '96** New Year. **Apr 4** Maundy Thursday. **Apr 5** Good Friday. **Apr 8** Easter Monday.

HEALTH

Regulations and requirements may be subject to change at short notice, and you are advised to contact your doctor well in advance of your intended date of departure. Any numbers in the chart refer to the footnotes below.

	Special Precautions?	Certificate Required?
Yellow Fever	No	No
Cholera	No	No
Typhoid & Polio	No	-
Malaria	No	-
Food & Drink	No	-

Rabies is present. For those at high risk, vaccination before arrival should be considered. If you are bitten abroad seek medical advice without delay. For more information, consult the *Health* section at the back of the book.
Health care: No vaccinations or certificates are required for entry into Greenland. There are hospitals and dentists in all towns. Although medical services are generally free, medical insurance is advisable, particularly as charges are made for dental treatment. Travellers are also advised to bring their own medicines and prescribed drugs, as these can often be difficult to obtain in Greenland.

TRAVEL - International

AIR: Flying to Greenland by scheduled services will usually involve a stopover in Iceland or Denmark; contact *Scandinavian Airlines System (SAS)* or *Greenlandair (GL)*.
Approximate flight time: From London to Greenland is 5 hours 30 minutes (including stopover in Copenhagen).
International airports: There are international airports at: *Søndre Strømfjord (SFJ)*, served from Copenhagen by *SAS*;
Narsarsuaq (UAK), served from Copenhagen by *Greenlandair* and from Iceland by *Icelandair*;
Kulusuk, served from Iceland by *Icelandair*;
Ilulissat, served from Iceland by *Icelandair* and *Greenlandair*;
Nuuk, served from Iceland by *Greenlandair* and from

Canada/Frobisher Bay by *First Air*.
Services are generally more frequent during the summer months. Connections can then be made to other parts of the country.
Note: By far the most common, and recommended, method of visiting Greenland is with a tour operator. Stories of people travelling independently and subsequently finding themselves in trouble are not uncommon. Only travellers already familiar with the country are advised to make the journey by themselves.

TRAVEL - Internal

AIR: Local services are operated by *Grønlandsfly (GL)* using both planes and helicopters. For further information, contact PO Box 1012, DK-3900 Nuuk. Tel: 28888. Fax: 27288. Telex: 90602. The frequency of departure on all routes is variable, and it is advisable to make reservations well in advance. Reservations made outside Greenland will take some time to confirm.
SEA: Between May and January, *KNI* boats operate services along the west coast. In addition, all villages are served by local boats connecting them with the nearest town, but space may be limited. Boats in some towns may be available for hire, with a skipper.
RAIL/ROAD: There are no railways in Greenland and no roads suitable for travelling from town to town. Air and seacraft are the most practical means of travel for the inexperienced visitor.
DOG SLEDGES: In Sisimiut, Aasiaat, Ilulissat and Ammassalik, dog sledges can be hired by the day, or for longer periods. **Note:** It is important to remember that sledge dogs are usually only semi-tame. This is just one reason why dog sledges should be given right of way at all times. Take particular care, as they are almost totally silent.
JOURNEY TIMES: The following chart gives approximate journey times (in hours and minutes) from Nuuk to other major cities/towns in Greenland.

	Air	Sea
Disko Bay	2.50	48.00
South Greenland	1.50	48.00
East Greenland	3.00	-

ACCOMMODATION

HOTELS: There are hotels in the major towns, but only those in Ammassalik, Ilulissat, Maniitsoq, Narsarsuaq, Narsaq, Nuuk, Qasigiannguit, Qaqortoq, Sisimiut, Søndre Strømfjord and Ummannaq approach European standards. There is no public accommodation in Upernavik, Thule or Scoresbysund. All reservations should be made in advance; contact Greenland Tourism or the Danish Tourist Board for telephone and telex numbers. For further information on accommodation, contact the CHR (Association of Hotels and Restaurants in Greenland), PO Box 73, DK-3900 Nuuk. Tel: 21500. Fax: 24340.
CAMPING: There are no official campsites, but most places have specific areas for tent-pitching. Camping is permitted everywhere except on ruins and on cultivated land in south Greenland.
YOUTH HOSTELS: Youth hostel accommodation is available in Narsarsuaq, Narsaq, Julianehåb, Nuuk and Jakobshavn. Elsewhere in south Greenland it is possible to stay overnight in mountain huts – contact the local tourist office.

RESORTS & EXCURSIONS

Organised excursions can be arranged from every town in Greenland, and especially **Nuuk, Narsaq, Ilulissat, Sisimiut** and **Narsarsuaq**. For information on all-inclusive tours/package tours, hiking and hotels, contact Greenland Tourism or the Danish Tourist Board for a list of tour operators.
Greenland is not a country for those seeking an ordinary holiday. It is a place of wild and rugged scenery and clear clean air. The region may be seen on foot, by boat, by plane, by helicopter or by dog sledge according to the season and the terrain.
Mountain walking: It is advisable to have a guide for mountain walking. Mountain huts are often available, particularly in the region of the *Narsaq* and *Qaqortoq* peninsulas and *Vatnahverfi*. Walking tours in the central western coastal area can be organised by contacting Greenland Travel, PO Box 130, DK-1004 Copenhagen K. Group tours, usually with a guide, are operated by a number of tour-operators. Enquire with Greenland Tourism (see top of entry for addresses).
Main tourist centres: Nuuk, the capital, has a population of 12,233, and is overlooked by *Sermitsiaq Mountain*. One of the major attractions is the

Greenland National Museum. It is situated near the entrance to a large fjord complex with steep mountains, lush valleys and a few small villages.
Narsarsuaq and **Qagsiarsuk** in southern Greenland was the area first settled by the Viking Eric the Red 1000 years ago. Many ruins from this epoch of Greenland's history still survive.
Ilulissat (Jakobshavn) in west Greenland (Disko Bay) has many modern as well as traditional buildings, and is surrounded by spectacular scenery. Knud Rasmussen's house is worth a visit. Motor-trips to nearby trading stations can sometimes be arranged.
Julianehåb is the largest town in south Greenland and the area's administrative centre. The town has several houses of historical interest and a museum. Excursions can be arranged by the local tourist office.
Narsaq tourist office also arranges regular excursions. The area between **Søndre Strømfjord** and **Sisimiut** is good for walking in summer and for dog-sledge expeditions in winter. Cross-country skiing can also be arranged.
There is a small *Inuit* (Eskimo) museum at **Qaqortoq**, which includes an exact copy of a turf-built house. There are minor local museums in most towns. The country also has many ruins of old Norse settlements and Eskimo houses. For further details, contact tour operators, the Danish Tourist Board or local tourist offices in Greenland.
Note: No finds may be removed from ancient monuments, which are all protected areas.

SOCIAL PROFILE

FOOD & DRINK: Most hotels have restaurants of a good standard, where Danish food and Greenland specialities are served. Reindeer meat (caribou), musk ox, fowl, shrimps and fish are the most popular local food. Prices are similar to Denmark.
SHOPPING: The range of goods available is similar to that in an ordinary Danish provincial town, but prices are in general slightly higher. Special purchases include bone and soapstone carvings, skin products and beadwork. The Greenland Home Rule Administration can provide information on claiming tax back on items purchased in Greenland. **Shopping hours:** 0900-1730 Monday to Friday, 0830-1300 Saturday. These will vary from region to region.
SPORT: During the summer period anglers come to Greenland for the superb Arctic **fishing** in the rivers and fjords. Fishing permits can be obtained from the local tourist offices. Persons fishing without a licence are liable to a fine and confiscation of equipment. Interested persons should contact the local tourist offices for detailed information. **Mountaineering** or **glacier scaling** can be performed by experienced mountaineers and skiers, while actual expeditions need a permit from the Danish Polar Centre, Hausergade 3, DK-1128 Copenhagen K. The country also offers excellent opportunities for those interested in activities such as **geology, botany** and **ornithology**. Maps of the coastal area (scale 1:250,000) can be purchased from the Kort og Matrikelstyrelsen, Proviantgaarden, Rigsdagsgaarden 7, DK-1218 Copenhagen K. **Photography:** A UV or skylight filter and a lens shade should always be used. In winter, the camera must be polar-oiled. It is advisable to bring your own films. Film cannot be developed in Greenland.
SPECIAL EVENTS: The return of the sun after the arctic night is celebrated in north Greenland. In Ilulissat, this takes place around January 13. At Easter time dog-sledge races take place in several north Greenland towns. Every summer there is a sheepfarmers' show in the south.
SOCIAL CONVENTIONS: Life is generally conducted at a more relaxed pace than is usual in northern Europe, as exemplified by the frequent use of the word *imaqa* – 'maybe'. Until recently, foreign visitors were very rare. The name of the country in Greenlandic is *Kalaallit Nunaat*, meaning 'Land of the People'. **Photography:** Throughout the country there is a ban on taking photographs inside churches or church halls during services. **Tipping:** Service charge is usually added to the bill. Tips are not expected.

BUSINESS PROFILE

ECONOMY: Fish and fish products, especially shrimps, are the territory's most valuable exports. Greenland withdrew from the then European Community in February 1985 over the issue of the fisheries policy. EU member states retain the right to fish within the declared exclusion zone in exchange for a cash payment of around US$25 million per annum; this compensates, in part, for the loss of development aid and

Greenland retains preferential access to EU markets. Although there are plans to develop the island's mineral deposits of iron ore, uranium, zinc, lead and coal, the economy ultimately depends on large subsidies from the Danish central government. Denmark retained a monopoly on trade with Greenland until 1950 and continues to dominate its trading patterns. The KNI – the Royal Greenland Trade Department – organises transport, supplies and production in the country. Germany, Norway, the USA and France are the other significant trading partners.
BUSINESS: Suits should be worn. A knowledge of Danish is extremely useful. **Office hours:** 0900-1500 Monday to Friday.
COMMERCIAL INFORMATION: The following organisation can offer advice: Kalaallit Niuerfiat (KNI) – Greenland Trade, PO Box 1008, DK-3900 Nuuk. Tel: 25211. Fax: 24431.
CONFERENCES/CONVENTIONS: For information on conferences and conventions, contact Greenland Travel, PO Box 130, DK-1004 Copenhagen K. Tel: 33 13 10 11. Fax: 33 13 85 92.

CLIMATE

Greenland has an Arctic climate, but owing to the size of the country there are great variations in the weather. As the climate graph below shows, winters can be severe and the summers comparatively mild, particularly in areas which are sheltered from the prevailing winds. Precipitation, mostly snow, is moderately heavy around the coast. The north of the country, and much of the interior, enjoys true Arctic weather, with the temperature only rising above freezing for brief periods in the summer.
Note: Conditions in all parts of the country can become hazardous when there is a combination of a low temperature and a strong wind. Local advice concerning weather conditions should be followed very carefully. Nevertheless, the summer months are suitable for a wide range of outdoor activities.
Required clothing: Good quality windproof and waterproof clothes, warm jerseys and moulded sole shoes at all times of the year; also some slightly thinner clothes – it is important to be able to change clothing during a day's climbing as temperatures can vary greatly during one day. Sunglasses and protective sun lotion are strongly advised. Extra warm clothes are necessary for those contemplating dog-sledge expeditions. Extra clothes are not always available for hire in Greenland.

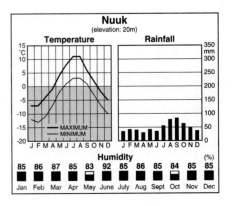

Grenada

Location: Caribbean, Windward Islands.

Grenada Board of Tourism
PO Box 293, The Carenage, St George's, Grenada
Tel: 440 2001. Fax: 440 6637.
Grenada High Commission
1 Collingham Gardens, London SW5 0HW
Tel: (0171) 373 7809. Fax: (0171) 370 7040. Opening
hours: 0930-1330 and 1430-1730 Monday to Friday.
Grenada Board of Tourism
Address as above
Tel: (0171) 370 5164/5. Fax: (0171) 244 0177. Opening
hours: 0930-1730 Monday to Friday.
British High Commission
14 Church Street, St George's, Grenada
Tel: 440 3222 *or* 440 3536. Fax: 440 4939. Telex: 3419
(a/b UKREP GA).
Embassy of Grenada
1701 New Hampshire Avenue, NW, Washington, DC
20009
Tel: (202) 265 2561. Fax: (202) 265 2468.
Grenada Board of Tourism
Suite 900D, 820 2nd Avenue, New York, NY 10017
Tel: (212) 687 9554. Fax: (212) 573 9731.
Embassy of the United States of America
PO Box 54, Point Salines, St George's, Grenada
Tel: 444 1173-8. Fax: 444 4820.
Consulate General of Grenada
Suite 830, 439 University Avenue, Toronto, Ontario
M5G 1Y8
Tel: (416) 595 1343. Fax: (416) 565 8278.
Grenada Board of Tourism
Address as above
Tel: (416) 595 1339. Fax: (416) 565 8278.
**The Canadian High Commission in Bridgetown deals
with enquiries relating to Grenada (see *Barbados*
earlier in the book).**

AREA: 344.5 sq km (133 sq miles).
POPULATION: 95, 343 (1993 estimate).

POPULATION DENSITY: 276.7 per sq km.
CAPITAL: St George's. **Population:** 4788 (1981
estimate).
GEOGRAPHY: Grenada is located in the Caribbean.
The island is of volcanic origin and is divided by a
central mountain range. It is the most southerly of the
Windward Islands. Agriculture is based on nutmeg,
cocoa, sugar cane and bananas. Tropical rainforests,
gorges and the stunning beauty of dormant volcanoes
make this a fascinating and diverse landscape with some
of the finest beaches in the world. Carriacou and some of
the other small islands of the Grenadines are also part of
Grenada.
LANGUAGE: English.
RELIGION: Christian: Roman Catholic 64%, Anglican
22%, Methodist 3%, Seventh Day Adventists 3%.
TIME: GMT - 4.
ELECTRICITY: 220/240 volts AC, 50Hz.
COMMUNICATIONS: Telephone: Full IDD service.
Country code: 1 809. No area codes are in use. **Fax:**
Cable and Wireless provide a service in St George's.
Telex/telegram: International Cable & Wireless (West
Indies) Limited offer telegraphic and telex services 0700-
1900 Monday to Friday, and 0700-1000 and 1600-1800
public holidays and Sunday. **Post:** The post office in St
George's is open 0800-1600 Monday to Friday and 0800-
1200 Saturday. **Press:** All newspapers are printed weekly
in English. They include *The Grenada Voice*, *Grenada
Today* and *The Informer*.
**BBC World Service and Voice of America
frequencies:** From time to time these change. See the
section *How to Use this Book* for more information.
BBC:

MHz	17.84	15.22	9.915	6.195
Voice of America:				
MHz	15.21	11.70	9.590	5.995

PASSPORT/VISA

*Regulations and requirements may be subject to change at short notice, and you
are advised to contact the appropriate diplomatic or consular authority before
finalising travel arrangements. Details of these may be found at the head of this
country's entry. Any numbers in the chart refer to the footnotes below.*

	Passport Required?	Visa Required?	Return Ticket Required?
Full British	No	No	Yes
BVP	Not valid/1	-	-
Australian	Yes	No	Yes
Canadian	No	No	Yes
USA	No	No	Yes
Other EU (As of 31/12/94)	Yes	No	Yes
Japanese	Yes	No	Yes

PASSPORTS: Valid passport required by all except:
(a) nationals of Canada, the UK and the USA in
possession of two forms of valid ID (eg driving
licence, birth certificate or electoral registration, one of
which must have a photo) for stays of up to 3 months;
(b) nationals of Dominica, St Vincent & the
Grenadines and St Lucia, with acceptable
identification.
British Visitors Passport: [1] Not officially accepted.
Although the immigration authorities of this country
may in certain circumstances accept British Visitors
Passports for persons arriving for holidays or unpaid
business trips of up to three months, travellers are
reminded that no formal agreement exists to this effect
and the situation may, therefore, change at short notice.
In addition, UK nationals using a BVP and returning to
the UK from a country with which no such formal
agreement exists may be subject to delays and
interrogation by UK immigration.
VISAS: Required by all except:
(a) nationals of countries shown in the chart above;
(b) those who continue their journey to a third
destination within 14 days, providing they hold an
onward ticket;
(c) nationals of Commonwealth countries (except
nationals of Cyprus and Pakistan who *do* need visas);
(d) nationals of Austria, Bulgaria, Chile, Czech
Republic, Finland, Iceland, Israel, South Korea,
Liechtenstein, Norway, Poland, Slovak Republic,
Sweden, Switzerland, Taiwan (China) and Venezuela;
(e) visitors holding a re-entry permit.
Types of visa: Tourist and Business. Cost: £10.
Validity: Up to 3 months.
Application to: Consulate (or Consular section at
Embassy or High Commission) well in advance of
intended day of departure. For addresses, see top of
entry.
Application requirements: (a) Valid passport. (b)
Completed application forms. (c) 2 passport-size

photographs. (d) Fee payable by cash or postal order.
(e) Stamped-self-addressed envelope. (f) For Business
visas, letter from contact in Grenada.

MONEY

Currency: Eastern Caribbean Dollar (EC$) = 100 cents.
Notes are in denominations of EC$100, 20, 5 and 1.
Coins are in denominations of EC$1, and 50, 25, 10, 5, 2
and 1 cents.
Currency exchange: The Grenada National Bank, the
Grenada Co-operative Bank, Barclays Bank
International, the Royal Bank of Canada, Grenada Bank
of Commerce and the Bank of Nova Scotia are all found
on the island.
Credit cards: American Express and Visa are widely
accepted, whereas Access/Mastercard and Diners Club
acceptance is less common. Some shops and car hire
companies may not accept credit cards. Check with your
credit card company for details of merchant acceptability
and other services which may be available.
Travellers cheques: Widely accepted.
Exchange rate indicators: The following figures are
included as a guide to the movements of the Eastern
Caribbean Dollar against Sterling and the US Dollar:

Date:	Oct '92	Sep '93	Jan '94	Jan '95
£1.00=	4.27	4.13	3.99	4.22
$1.00=	*2.70	*2.70	*2.70	*2.70

Note [*]: The Eastern Caribbean Dollar is tied to the US
Dollar.
Currency restrictions: Free import of local currency is
subject to declaration. Export limited to amount declared
on import. No restrictions on import or export of foreign
currency.
Banking hours: 0800-1400 Monday to Thursday, 0800-
1300 and 1430-1700 Friday.

DUTY FREE

The following goods may be imported into Grenada
without incurring customs duty:
*200 cigarettes or 50 cigars or 250g of tobacco; 1 quart
wine or spirits; a reasonable amount of perfume.*

PUBLIC HOLIDAYS

Jan 1 '95 New Year's Day. **Feb 7** Independence Day.
Apr 14 Good Friday. **Apr 17** Easter Monday. **May 1**
Labour Day. **Jun 5** Whit Monday. **Jun 13** Corpus
Christi. **Aug 2-3** Emancipation Day. **Oct 25**
Thanksgiving Day. **Dec 25-26** Christmas. **Jan 1 '96** New
Year's Day. **Feb 7** Independence Day. **Apr 5** Good
Friday. **Apr 8** Easter Monday.

HEALTH

*Regulations and requirements may be subject to change at short notice, and
you are advised to contact your doctor well in advance of your intended date of
departure. Any numbers in the chart refer to the footnotes below.*

	Special Precautions?	Certificate Required?
Yellow Fever	No	1
Cholera	No	No
Typhoid & Polio	Yes	-
Malaria	No	-
Food & Drink	2	-

[1]: A yellow fever vaccination certificate is required
from all travellers over one year of age coming from
infected areas.
[2]: Mains water is normally chlorinated and relatively
safe. Bottled water is available. Milk is pasteurised and
dairy products are safe for consumption. Local meat,
poultry, seafood, fruit and vegetables are generally
considered safe to eat.
Health care: Medical facilities are adequate. Health
insurance is advised.

TRAVEL - International

AIR: The main airlines to serve Grenada are *American
Airlines Caledonian Airways (AA), LIAT (LI), British
Airways (BA)* and *BWIA International (BW)* which offer
connections with Grenada from other Caribbean islands.
Approximate flight times: From Grenada to *London*
(via Barbados) is 9 hours, to *Los Angeles* is 9 hours and
to *New York* is 5 hours.
International airport: *Point Salines (GRN)* airport is
close to St George's, and there are taxis operating

between the airport and the capital. Facilities include duty-free and handicraft shops, snack bars and boutiques. **Departure tax:** EC$35 per adult, payable in cash on departure for all international flights. EC$17.50 is charged for children 5-10 years of age.
SEA: St George's, considered the most picturesque port in the Caribbean, is port of call for many cruise lines, including *Cunard, Costa, TUI Cruises, Royal Viking* and *CTC. Geest Lines* sail from the UK via Barbados, stopping at St Vincent and St Lucia or Dominica on the return trip. 70% (197,775) of tourist arrivals are cruise-ship passengers. Inter-island schooners sail to Carriacou, Petit Martinique and Isle de Ronde up to four times weekly. Check at a local tourist office for times and fares.

TRAVEL - Internal

SEA: Grenada has a very large fleet of charter yachts, from large professional vessels to smaller bare-boat charters. Round-island trips are very popular. Arrangements can be made via the Tourist Board in Grenada.
ROAD: Roads are narrow and winding. Traffic drives on the left. **Bus:** These are cheap but slow. **Taxi:** Taxis are the most efficient means of transport. **Car hire:** A large range of vehicles is available in St George's or St Andrew's. Credit cards are not always accepted by car hire companies. **Documentation:** A temporary licence to drive (costing approximately EC$60) is available from local authorities on presentation of a valid British or Northern Ireland driving licence. An International Driving Permit is recommended, although it is not legally required.
JOURNEY TIMES: The following chart gives approximate journey times (in hours and minutes) from St George's to other major cities/islands in Grenada.

	Air	Road	Sea
Grenville	-	0.35	-
Carriacou	0.20	-	3.30

ACCOMMODATION

HOTELS: Grenada offers a variety of modern, luxurious hotels. Pre-booking is essential. A 10% service charge and 8% government tax is added to all hotel bills. Contact the National Tourist Office for details and exact price listings. Further information is available from the Grenada Hotel Association, PO Box 440, St George's. Tel: 444 1353. Fax: 444 4847.
GUEST-HOUSES: There are a few guest-houses, some of which offer self-catering facilities.
SELF-CATERING: There is a growing number of apartments and villas available for rent. Contact the Grenada Board of Tourism for details.

RESORTS & EXCURSIONS

St George's: *The Carenage,* a picturesque inner harbour with 18th-century warehouses and restaurants, the botanical gardens, the zoo and *Fort George* (built by the French in 1705) are all worth a visit. See also the outer harbour, *St Andrew's Presbyterian Church* and *Fort Frederick.*
Spice Country: On the way here, north from the capital, visitors pass through some of the prettiest fishing villages on the island. Hidden among the red roofs of **Gouyave** is

the factory where spices are sorted, dried and milled. The *Dougaldston Estate* is a traditional plantation in the centre of the nutmeg- and cocoa-growing region.
Sauteurs/Morne des Sauteurs: From these rocks the last of the island's Carib Indians plummeted to their deaths in 1650.
Levera Bay & Grande Anse: Two of the island's best beaches.
Grand Etang: Extinct volcano cradling a beautiful 30-acre blue lake.
Annandale Falls: A 15m (50ft) cascade that flows into a mountain stream.
Carriacou: In 'the Grenadines of Grenada', this is a yachtsman's paradise.

SOCIAL PROFILE

FOOD & DRINK: Local specialities include seafood and vegetables, *calaloo soup,* crabs, conches *(lambi)* and avocado ice-cream. Most hotels and restaurants offer international cuisine, serving a large variety of tropical fish and English, Continental, American and exotic West Indian food. **Drink:** A local company supplies a wide variety of local fruit juices and nectars. The local rum and beer, *Carib,* is excellent. Bars are stocked with most popular wines and spirits, including various brands of whisky, rum and brandy. In past times, casks containing Grenadian rum were stamped with the words 'Georgius Rex Old Grenada', the acronym GROG formed from these words is said to be the origin of the navy word 'grog'.
NIGHTLIFE: Based in hotels, with discos, organised shows and cabarets.
SHOPPING: Special purchases include spices, straw goods, printed cottons and other fabrics. There are a number of duty-free shops selling quality goods from all over the world. **Shopping hours:** 0800-1600 Monday to Friday, 0800-1200 Saturday.
SPORT: Golf and **tennis:** Both available either independently or through hotels. **Watersports:** Equipment for all watersports is available. **Yachting:** This is extremely popular. A number of major yacht races and regattas are held throughout the year. A variety of small and large craft may be rented. Contact the Grenada Board of Tourism for details. **Fishing:** A major fishing tournament is held in January.
SPECIAL EVENTS: There are several yachting and fishing events throughout the year; in addition, public holidays are usually accompanied by some form of special event or celebration. The following is a selection of the major festivals and special events celebrated in Grenada during 1995. For full details of events, contact the Grenada Board of Tourism.
Mar 6-7 '95 *Carriacou Carnival.* **Mar 12-18** *St Patrick's Day Fiesta Celebrations.* **Apr 14-17** *Easter Dinghy Races and Kare Fishing Competition.* **Apr 23-30** *St Mark's Day Fiesta.* **Jul 16-22** *Grenada Celebrates The Family Week.* **Aug 5-8** *Carriacou Regatta.* **Aug 6-8** *Rainbow City Festival.* **Aug 11-15** *Grenada Carnival.* **Oct 21-22** *Carib Beer Yacht Regatta.*
SOCIAL CONVENTIONS: Local culture reflects the island's history of British and French colonial rule and, of course, the African cultures imported with the slaves – African influence is especially noticeable on the island of Carriacou in the Big Drum and in Grenada with the Shango dance. The Roman Catholic Church also exerts a strong influence on the way of life. Local people are generally friendly and courteous. Dress is casual and informal but beachwear is not welcome in town.

BUSINESS PROFILE

ECONOMY: The Grenadian economy is predominantly agricultural and centred on the production of spices. The principal exports are nutmeg, cocoa, bananas and sugar cane. Earnings from all these products have varied substantially according to fluctuations in the world market. Repeated attempts to broaden the base of the economy (such as developing the fishing industry) have failed to yield dividends. Local industry is minimal and has scarcely expanded at all since the mid-1980s. The most important single economic activity is tourism. Grenada relies on extensive foreign aid from the USA, the UK, Canada and the European Union. The UK and the USA are the island's main trading partners.
BUSINESS: All correspondence and trade literature is in English. **Office hours:** 0800-1200 and 1300-1600 Monday to Friday.
COMMERCIAL INFORMATION: The following organisation can offer advice: Grenada Chamber of Industry and Commerce, PO Box 129, Decaul Building, Mount Gay, St George's. Tel: 440 2937. Fax: 440 6627.
CONFERENCES/CONVENTIONS: Eight hotels offer facilities, seating from 25-300 persons. For details contact the Ministry of Tade, Lagoon Road, St George's. Tel: 440 2101. Fax: 440 4115.

CLIMATE

Tropical. The dry season runs from January to May. The rainy season runs from June to December.
Required clothing: Tropical lightweights and cool summer clothing.

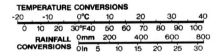

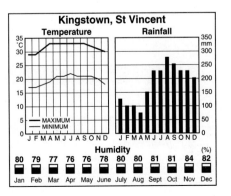

Guadeloupe

Location: Caribbean, at the arc of the Leeward group of islands of the Lesser Antilles.

Office du Tourisme
BP 1099, 5 square de la Banque, 97181 Pointe-à-Pitre, Guadeloupe
Tel: 820 930. Fax: 838 922. Telex: 919715.
Embassy of the French Republic
58 Knightsbridge, London SW1X 7JT
Tel: (0171) 201 1000. Fax: (0171) 259 6498. Telex: 261905 (a/b FRALON).
French Consulate General (*Visa Section*)
PO Box 57, 6A Cromwell Place, London SW7 2EW
Tel: (0171) 838 2050. Information Service: (0898) 200 289 (calls are charged at the higher rate of 39/49p per minute). Fax: (0171) 838 2046. Telex: 924153. Opening hours: 0900-1130 (and 1600-1630 for visa collection only) Monday to Friday (except French and British national holidays).
Consulate in: Scotland (tel: (0131) 225 7954).
French Embassy (*Cultural Section*)
23 Cromwell Road, London SW7 2DQ
Tel: (0171) 838 2055. Fax: (0171) P838 2088. Opening hours: 0930-1300 and 1430-1700 Monday to Friday.
French Government Tourist Office
178 Piccadilly, London W1V 0AL
Tel: (0891) 244 123 (France Information Line; calls are charged at the higher rate of 39/49p per minute). Fax: (0171) 493 6594. Telex: 21902. Opening hours: 0900-1700 Monday to Friday.
Caribbean Tourism
Vigilant House, 120 Wilton Road, London SW1V 1JZ
Tel: (0171) 233 8382. Fax: (0171) 873 8551. Opening hours: 0930-1730 Monday to Friday.

British Consulate
BP 2041, Zone Industrielle de Jarry, 97192 Pointe-à-Pitre Cedex, Guadeloupe
Tel: 266 429. Telex: 019779 (a/b OUVRE GL).
Embassy of the French Republic
4101 Reservoir Road, NW, Washington, DC 20007
Tel: (202) 944 6000 *or* 944 6200 (Consular section). Fax: (202) 944 6072.
Consulates in: Atlanta, Boston, Chicago, Detroit, Houston, Los Angeles, Miami, New Orleans, New York, San Francisco and Washington.
Embassy of the French Republic
42 Sussex Drive, Ottawa, Ontario K1M 2C9
Tel: (613) 789 1795. Fax: (613) 789 3484.
Consulates in: Calgary, Chicoutimi, Edmonton, Halifax, Moncton, Montréal, North Sydney, Québec, Regina, Rouyn-Noranda, St John's, Saskatoon, Sudbury, Toronto, Vancouver, Victoria, Whitehorse and Winnipeg.
French Government Tourist Office
Suite 700, 30 St Patrick Street, Toronto, Ontario M5T 3A3
Tel: (416) 593 4723. Fax: (416) 979 7587.
French Government Tourist Office
Suite 490, 1981 McGill College, Montréal, Québec H3A 2W9
Tel: (514) 288 4264. Fax: (514) 845 4868.

AREA: Total: 1780 sq km (687 sq miles). **Basse-Terre:** 839 sq km (324 sq miles). **Grand-Terre:** 564 sq km (218 sq miles). **Marie-Galante:** 150 sq km (58 sq miles). **La Désirade:** 29.7 sq km (11.5 sq miles). **Les Saintes:** 13.9 sq km (5.4 sq miles). **St Barthélemy:** 95 sq km (37 sq miles). **St Martin** (which shares the island with St Maarten, part of the Netherlands Antilles): 88 sq km (34 sq miles).
POPULATION: 387,034 (1990).
POPULATION DENSITY: 217.4 per sq km.
CAPITAL: Basse-Terre (administrative). **Population:** 14,107 (1990). Pointe-à-Pitre, on Grande Terre (commercial centre). **Population:** 26,083 (1990).
GEOGRAPHY: Guadeloupe comprises Guadeloupe proper (Basse-Terre), Grande-Terre (separated from Basse-Terre by a narrow sea channel) and five smaller islands. Basse-Terre has a rough volcanic relief whilst Grande Terre is flat and chalky. All the islands have beautiful white- or black-sand palm-fringed beaches. There are also many lush mountainous areas with stunning and unspoiled tropical scenery.
LANGUAGE: The official language is French. The *lingua franca* is Creole. *Patois* and English are also widely spoken.
TIME: GMT - 4.
RELIGION: The majority are Roman Catholic, with a minority of predominantly Evangelical protestant groups.
ELECTRICITY: 110 or 220 volts AC, 50Hz.
COMMUNICATIONS: Telephone: IDD is available. Country code: 590. Outgoing international code: 19. Good internal network. There are no area codes. **Telex:** Facilities available in the capital. **Post:** Airmail takes about a week to reach Europe. **Press:** Newspapers are all in French. The main daily is *France-Antilles*.
BBC World Service and Voice of America frequencies: From time to time these change. See the section *How to Use this Book* for more information.
BBC:

MHz	17.84	15.22	9.915	6.195
Voice of America:				
MHz	15.21	11.70	6.130	0.930

PASSPORT/VISA

The regulations for tourist and Business visas are the same as for France (see the *Passport/Visa* section for France above). Visitors should specify that they wish to visit Guadeloupe when they make their application.

MONEY

Currency: French Franc (FFr) = 100 centimes. Notes are in denominations of FFr500, 200, 100, 50 and 20. Coins are in denominations of FFr20, 10, 5, 2 and 1, and 50, 20, 10 and 5 centimes.
Credit cards: Access/Mastercard (limited), Diners Club, American Express and Visa are accepted. Check with your credit card company for details of merchant acceptability and other services which may be available.
Travellers cheques are accepted in most places, and may qualify for discount on luxury items. US and Canadian dollars are also accepted in some places.
Exchange rate indicators: The following figures are included as a guide to the movements of the French Franc against Sterling and the US Dollar:

Date:	Oct '92	Sep '93	Jan '94	Jan '95
£1.00=	8.28	8.68	8.74	8.35
$1.00=	5.21	5.68	5.90	5.34

Currency restrictions: As for France.

DUTY FREE

Guadeloupe is an Overseas Department of France, and the duty-free allowances are therefore the same as for France.

PUBLIC HOLIDAYS

Jan 2 '95 For New Year's Day. **Feb** Lenten Carnival. **Apr 17** Easter Monday. **May 1** Labour Day. **May 8** Liberation Day. **May 25** Ascension Day. **Jun 5** Whit Monday. **Jul 14** National Day, Fall of the Bastille. **Jul 21** Victor Schoëlcher Day. **Aug 15** Assumption. **Nov 1** All Saints' Day. **Nov 11** Remembrance Day. **Dec 25** Christmas Day. **Jan 1 '96** New Year's Day. **Feb/Mar** Lenten Carnival.

HEALTH

Regulations and requirements may be subject to change at short notice, and you are advised to contact your doctor well in advance of your intended date of departure. Any numbers in the chart refer to the footnotes below.

	Special Precautions?	Certificate Required?
Yellow Fever	No	1
Cholera	No	No
Typhoid & Polio	Yes	-
Malaria	No	-
Food & Drink	2	-

[1]: A yellow fever vaccination certificate is required by travellers over one year of age arriving from an infected or endemic zone.
[2]: Mains water is chlorinated and whilst relatively safe, may cause mild abdominal upsets. Bottled water is available and is advised for the first few weeks of stay. Drinking water outside main cities and towns may be contaminated and sterilisation is advised. Milk is pasteurised and dairy products are safe for consumption. Local meat, poultry, seafoods and fruit are generally considered safe to eat.
Bilharzia (schistosomiasis) is present. Avoid swimming and paddling in fresh water. Swimming pools, which are well maintained and chlorinated, are safe.
Health care: A Reciprocal Health Agreement exists between France and the UK. However, the benefits which go with this agreement may not be fully available in Guadeloupe. Check with your doctor before departure.

TRAVEL - International

AIR: Guadeloupe's national airline is *Air Guadeloupe*.
Approximate flight times: From Guadeloupe to *London* is 12 hours 40 minutes (including a stopover time of one hour in Paris), to *Los Angeles* is 9 hours and to *New York* is 6 hours.
International airport: Pointe-à-Pitre (PTP) (Raizet), 3km (2 miles) from Pointe-à-Pitre.
SEA: Guadeloupe is a point of call for the following international cruise operators: *Chandris, Holland America, Royal Caribbean, Cunard, Sun Line, Sitmar, TUI Cruises* and *Princess Cruises*. Many ships ply between Guadeloupe and Martinique, and also connect with Miami and San Juan.

TRAVEL - Internal

AIR: *LIAT, Air Antilles, Air Guadeloupe, Windward Island Airlines* and *BWIA* connect Guadeloupe with the smaller islands in the group. *Air France* also offers a limited inter-island service. There are domestic airports on the islands of Marie-Galante, La Désirade and St Barthélemy.
SEA: Regular ferry services ply around the islands.
ROAD: There is a good public **bus** service, **taxi** services and many **car and van rental** companies.
Documentation: National driving licence is sufficient, but at least one year's driving experience is required. An International Driving Licence is advised.

ACCOMMODATION

HOTELS: There is a good selection of hotels on Guadeloupe, ranging from first-class beach resorts to country inns. The accommodation on the outlying islands can be interesting, but may be very basic. At present there are over 3000 rooms throughout the group. The tax on hotel rates is 5-7%, rising to 20-30% in the high season (mid-December to mid-April). The Relais de la Guadeloupe provides a central booking service.
Grading: 3- and 4-star hotels offer sporting and cultural

activities in addition to board and lodging. There are also two particular categories of hotel: Hibiscus (H) and Alamandas (A). Hibiscus hotels are 2- or 3-star establishments usually run as a family affair. Alamandas hotels are sophisticated 1- or 2-star establishments. Many hotels in the Caribbean offer accommodation according to one of a number of plans: **FAP** is Full American Plan; room with all meals (including afternoon tea, supper, etc). **AP** is American Plan; room with three meals. **MAP** is Modified American Plan; breakfast and dinner included with the price of the room, plus in some places British-style afternoon tea. **CP** is Continental Plan; room and breakfast only. **EP** is European Plan; room only.
SELF-CATERING: Villas and cottages may be rented. Obtain further information from the tourist office.

RESORTS & EXCURSIONS

Pointe-à-Pitre, the commercial capital of Guadeloupe, is a gracious town with a pleasant square at its core, the *Place de la Victoire*, which is surrounded by a busy market and, further out, the docks. It is an active, lively port with many narrow streets to explore. The *Pavillion d'Exposition de Bergevin* and the *Centre Cultural Remy Nainsouta* are two interesting museums in the town. On **Basse-Terre**, *Saint Marie de Capesterre* where Columbus landed should be visited, as should the Hindu temple to its south, where it may be possible to see religious ceremonies taking place. The small town of **Trois Rivières** has a collection of interesting Indian relics which could easily be visited on the way to the **National Park** near **St Claude**. This 74,000-acre park, of great natural beauty, is situated at the base of *La Soufrière*, an inactive volcano. In the rainforests there are some good walking and picnic areas which make a pleasant alternative to lying on the islands' fine beaches. The town of **Basse-Terre** itself is a beautiful old French colonial town, situated at the foot of La Soufrière. The *St Charles Fort* is of French military architecture, built in 1605 and now restored into a museum. The cathedral and market place are also worth seeing. At *Fort Fleur de L'Epée* on **Grande-Terre** there are some fascinating underground caves and to the north of these is the old sugar town of **Sainte Anne**. The other islands of **Marie-Galante, La Désirade** and **Les Saintes** are visited less frequently and are best suited to the resourceful traveller. La Désirade, quiet and undeveloped, is known for its seafood. Les Saintes are a string of tiny islands, only two of which are inhabited, **Terre-de-Haut** and **Terre-de-Bas.** These are both very attractive and have a selection of modestly priced hotels. Marie-Galante has a number of good hotels and beaches. Its old and crumbling mills are reminders of its history as a major sugar plantation.

SOCIAL PROFILE

FOOD & DRINK: Predominantly seafood, cooked in French, Creole, African, Hindu or South-East Asian styles. Dishes include lobster, turtle, red snapper, conch and sea urchin. Island specialities include stuffed crab, stewed conch, roast wild goat, jugged rabbit and broiled dove. The spicy flavour of Creole cuisine is unique. The more formal restaurants will require appropriate dress. **Drinks** include a great supply of French wines, Champagnes, liqueurs and local rum. A local speciality, *Rum Punch* (a brew of rum, lime, bitter and syrup), is a must. There are no licensing restrictions.
NIGHTLIFE: There are plenty of restaurants, bars and discotheques, with displays of local dancing and music. The famous dance of the island is called the *Biguine,*

where colourful and ornate Creole costumes are still worn.
SHOPPING: Worthwhile purchases are French imports, including perfume, wine, liqueurs and Lalique crystal. Local items include fine-flavoured rum, straw goods, bamboo hats, voodoo dolls, and objects of aromatic Vetevier root. Travellers cheques give a 20% discount in some shops. **Shopping hours:** 0830-1300 and 1500-1800 Monday to Friday, 0830-1300 Saturday.
SPORT: All **watersports** are available somewhere on Guadeloupe, but they may be less well developed than on some of the other Caribbean islands. The **swimming** and **snorkelling** are excellent, as is the **fishing** (including deep-sea, harpoon fishing). Some of the beaches are for nude and topless sunbathing. **Small-boat sailing** is popular as well as **water-skiing. Tennis, golf** (at the famous 18-hole course of Saint-Françoise, at Le Méridien hotel, designed by R. Trent Jones), **horseriding, hiking** and **mountain climbing** are all possibilities in Guadeloupe.
SPECIAL EVENTS: There are many local festivals and special events, both Roman Catholic and Creole. For details, contact the French Government Tourist Board.
SOCIAL CONVENTIONS: The atmosphere is relaxed and informal. Casual dress is accepted everywhere, but formal dress is needed for dining out and in nightclubs. **Tipping:** 10% is normal.

BUSINESS PROFILE

ECONOMY: Guadeloupe's economy is relatively diverse by regional standards – with agriculture, light industry and tourism – but remains heavily dependent on French aid. Sugar has been the principal export earner, but both production and revenues have declined during the 1980s. Bananas have now replaced sugar as the main export product. Coffee, cocoa and vanilla are the other important cash crops. Tourism is a key and fast-growing sector, although it has suffered from a general downturn in the Caribbean and from the effects of hurricanes. France supplies most of the island's imports and takes three-quarters of its exports.
BUSINESS: Lightweight suits, safari suits, and shirt and tie are recommended for business meetings. Best times to visit are January to March and June to September. Much of the island's business is connected to France. **Office hours:** 0800-1700 Monday to Friday, 0800-1200 Saturday.
COMMERCIAL INFORMATION: The following organisation can offer advice: Chambre de Commerce et d'Industrie de Pointe-à-Pitre, BP 64, rue F Eboué, 97152 Pointe-à-Pitre. Tel: 900 808. Fax: 902 187. Telex: 919780.

CLIMATE

Warm weather throughout the year with the main rainy season occurring from June to October. Showers can, however, occur at any time although they are usually brief. The humidity can be exceedingly high at times.
Required clothing: Lightweights with warmer top layers for the evenings; showerproofs are advisable.

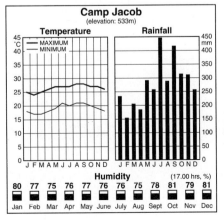

TEMPERATURE CONVERSIONS

-20	-10	0°C	10	20	30	40

0	10	20	30°F 40	50	60	70	80	90	100

RAINFALL CONVERSIONS

0mm	200		400		600		800

0in	5	10	15	20	25	30

Camp Jacob
(elevation: 533m)
Temperature / Rainfall

Humidity (17.00 hrs, %)

80	77	75	76	77	76	76	75	78	81	79	81
Jan	Feb	Mar	Apr	May	June	July	Aug	Sept	Oct	Nov	Dec

Guam

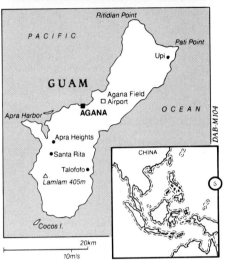

Location: Western Pacific, Micronesia.

Guam Visitors Bureau
PO Box 3520, Suite 201-205, Boon's Building, 1270 North Marine Drive, Upper Tumon, Agaña, Guam 96911
Tel: 646 5278/9. Fax: 646 8861. Telex: 6432.
The Embassy of the United States of America in London deals with enquiries relating to Guam (see *United Kingdom* **later in the book).**
The Embassy of the United States of America in Ottawa deals with enquiries relating to Guam (see *Canada* **earlier in the book).**
AREA: 549 sq km (212 sq miles).
POPULATION: 133,152 (1990 estimate).
POPULATION DENSITY: 242.5 per sq km.
CAPITAL: Agaña. **Population:** 5000 (1983). Tamuning is the commercial centre.
GEOGRAPHY: Guam is the largest and most southerly island of the Marianas archipelago. It is a predominantly hilly island and its northern end is a plateau of rolling hills and cliffs rising 152m (500ft) above sea level. The cliffs are tunnelled with caves. The island narrows in the middle, with the southern half widening into a land of mountains and valleys cut by streams and waterfalls. The most sheltered beaches are on the western coast.
LANGUAGE: English and Chamorro. Japanese and Tagalog are also widely spoken.
RELIGION: Christian; 90% Roman Catholic.
TIME: GMT + 10.
ELECTRICITY: 120 volts AC, 60Hz.
COMMUNICATIONS: Telephone: Overseas telecommunications facilities are available in Agaña. Country code: 671. Outgoing international calls must go through the operator. **Fax:** Many hotels have facilities. **Post:** Post offices are open 0830-1700 Monday to Friday, 0900-1200 Saturday. **Press:** The English-language daily newspaper is *The Pacific Daily News.*
BBC World Service and Voice of America frequencies: From time to time these change. See the section *How to Use this Book* for more information.

BBC:				
MHz	17.83	15.36	11.95	9.740
Voice of America:				
MHz	18.82	15.18	9.525	1.735

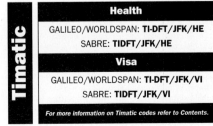

PASSPORT/VISA

Passports are required by all except those entering directly from the USA. Those arriving from any other country must comply with the passport and visa requirements for the USA (see *USA* later in this book). All enquiries should be addressed to the relevant US Embassy.

MONEY

Currency: US Dollar (US$) = 100 cents. See the *USA* section below for information on currency exchange, exchange rates, etc.
Credit cards: Most major credit and charge cards are widely accepted on Guam.
Banking hours: 1000-1500 Monday to Thursday, 1000-1800 Friday.

DUTY FREE

The list of goods exempted from payment of customs duty is the same as for the USA, as is the list of prohibited and restricted goods. See the *Duty Free* section in the general *USA* entry later in the book.

PUBLIC HOLIDAYS

Jan 1 '95 New Year's Day. **Feb 13** For George Washington's Birthday. **Mar 6** Guam Discovery Day. **May 22** Memorial Day. **Jul 4** Independence Day. **Sep 4** Labor Day. **Nov 23** Thanksgiving Day. **Dec 25** Christmas Day. **Jan 1 '96** New Year's Day. **Feb 12** For George Washington's Birthday. **Mar 6** Guam Discovery Day.

HEALTH

Regulations and requirements may be subject to change at short notice, and you are advised to contact your doctor well in advance of your intended date of departure. Any numbers in the chart refer to the footnotes below.

	Special Precautions?	Certificate Required?
Yellow Fever	No	No
Cholera	No	No
Typhoid & Polio	Yes	-
Malaria	No	-
Food & Drink	1	-

[1]: Mains water is normally chlorinated, and whilst relatively safe may cause mild abdominal upsets. Bottled water is available and is advised for the first few weeks of the stay. Milk is pasteurised and dairy products are safe for consumption. Local meat, poultry, seafood, fruit and vegetables are generally considered safe to eat.
Health care: Health insurance is strongly advised. There are four hospitals.

TRAVEL

AIR: Several air taxi companies operate scheduled air commuter services daily between Saipan, Rota and Guam.
Approximate flight time: From Guam to London is 14 hours 30 minutes.
International airport: *Agaña Field Naval Station* is 5km (3 miles) from the city. Taxis are available.
Departure tax: US$5.
SEA: Guam is a port of call for the following shipping lines: *Dominion Far East, Flagship Cruises, Kyowa, Daiwa, Micronesia Transport, American President, Sea-Land Services, Austfreight* and *Sitmar*.
ROAD: Bus: A reasonable service is available on a limited number of routes. **Taxi:** Fares are metered. **Car hire:** Available through most major companies. Charges are based on time and mileage plus insurance.
Documentation: An International Driving Permit is required.

ACCOMMODATION

HOTELS: Over the past decade tourism has been growing rapidly and, to cater for this, numerous hotels have been built offering a good range of facilities to suit most tastes and pockets. Many hotels cater almost exclusively for Japanese tourists. For more details, contact the US Embassy.
CAMPING: Camping is permitted on beaches and in some parks; some places are better avoided and the camper is advised to take advice. Information can be obtained from the US Embassy.

RESORTS & EXCURSIONS

Guam is the largest island in Micronesia and, due to the large US Naval presence, the most cosmopolitan and energetic. Spain ruled the islands for nearly 250 years and **Agaña**, the capital, has many historic buildings dating from this era. Also of interest are buildings from the Spanish colonial period and the relics of the Chamorro period (a culture which remains alive today, albeit much modified, in about 55,000 persons). Many attractions are geared towards American GIs at the local US military base.
Tumon Bay, just up the coast from Agaña, is the main tourist centre. There are fine coral reefs around the coast. The interior is mountainous, particularly in the south. There are several spectacular cliffs on the north coast. There are three botanical gardens in Guam: the *Inarajan Shore Botanical Garden* by the sea in the southern part of the island; the *Nano Fall Botanical Gardens* in **Agat**, where swimming can be enjoyed in the Nano River under rushing cascades; and the *Pineapple Plantation* in **Yigo**. There are also many parks in Guam, some dedicated to the war years, such as the *South Pacific Memorial Park* in Yigo, commemorating those killed in the Second World War, and the *War in the Pacific National Historical Park*, the location of five World War II battle sites with a museum of war photos and relics. Guam has another small museum with sections dedicated to Chamorro culture, natural history and the Japanese soldier who hid in the interior until 1972, unaware that World War II was over. As most tourists to Guam are Japanese, many sites commemorate the war years. Other parks include *Latte Park*, located at the bottom of Kasamata Hill; and *Merico Pier Park*, with recreational facilities for watersports and the location of the *Merico Water Festival* held every August. It is also the gateway to **Cocos Island**, a beautiful 100-acre resort surrounded by a clear lagoon and accessible by speedboat or glass-bottomed boat. Beach parks include *Talofofo Bay Beach Park*, located at the mouth of the Talofofo River and a surfers' paradise; and *Ipao Beach Park*, once the location of an ancient Chamorro settlement, later a penal and leper colony, and now one of Guam's most popular recreational areas.

SOCIAL PROFILE

FOOD & DRINK: Guamanian cooking is very similar to Spanish cuisine. The wide selection of restaurants feature American, European, Chinese, Filipino, Indonesian, Japanese, Korean and Mexican food.
NIGHTLIFE: A choice of nightclubs feature music and dancing. Major hotels frequently stage shows with singers and musicians from the US mainland and, during the autumn, winter and spring, the *Guam Symphony & Choral Society* performs monthly. There are a number of cinemas in Agaña, most showing recent US films. Dance shows and dinner cruises are also available.
SHOPPING: The Agaña Shopping Center sells local goods but Mark's Shopping Center on the west side of Agaña and Gibson's Shopping Center at Tamuning have a wider selection of merchandise. Good buys in Guam include watches, perfume, jewellery, liquor, china, stereo equipment and cameras (Kimura Camera in the ITC Building in Agaña is excellent for both new cameras and repairs to old ones). **Shopping hours:** 1000-2100 Monday to Saturday, 1200-1800 Sunday.
SPORT: Fishing: Reef fishing with net and rod is popular, as is spearfishing for groupers and skipjacks and deep-sea fishing for marlin, tuna, wahoo, barracuda, bonito and sailfish. **Surfing:** Facilities are available at coastal resorts. **Golf:** There are several 18-hole courses. The Windward Hills Course has a clubhouse and pool, as does the Country Club of the Pacific. Visitors are welcome at both. **Skindiving/snorkelling:** Fully-equipped boats may be chartered. **Swimming:** Many hotels have swimming pools; the west coast offers safe bathing. **Spectator sports:** Greyhound races are held three times a week. Cockfights are staged (legally) every weekend and on public holidays at the *Sport-O-Dome* in Tamuning, 1000-2400 (betting allowed).
SPECIAL EVENTS: Each village has its own fiesta to celebrate its patron saint. They are celebrated on the weekend closest to the *Saint's Day* and show the strong Spanish influence on local culture. *Liberation Day* (July 21) is celebrated with fireworks, feasts and one of the year's most impressive parades (the other is on December 8 in honour of the Immaculate Conception). The *Merico Water Festival* is held every August with various watersports events.
SOCIAL CONVENTIONS: Western customs are well understood – for the visiting Westerner it is quite likely that it will not be the customs of the locals that have to be observed, but those of the visiting Japanese who make up 80% of the island's tourists. The most evident Chamorro

legacy is the Chamorro language and a range of facial expressions, called 'Eyebrow', which virtually constitutes a language of its own.

BUSINESS PROFILE

ECONOMY: Guam exports copra, fish and handmade goods. A petroleum refinery and a handful of light industries have been in operation since the early 1970s. The island is also an important re-export centre for distribution of goods throughout the Pacific, particularly to Micronesia. Tourism, mostly from Japan, is expanding rapidly. Government policy presently concentrates on attracting foreign investment, especially from Asian manufacturers, in order to develop an industrial base for the economy. The viability of Guam as an offshore financial centre is currently under investigation.
COMMERCIAL INFORMATION: The following organisation can offer advice: Guam Chamber of Commerce, PO Box 283, 102 Ada Plaza Center, Agaña, GU 96910. Tel: 472 6311. Fax: 472 6202.

CLIMATE

Tropical, with dry and rainy seasons. The hottest months precede the rainy season, which is July to November.
Required clothing: Casual lightweight clothing, with waterproof wear needed for the rainy season.

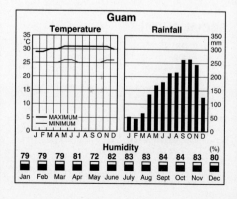

Guam — Temperature / Rainfall

	Jan	Feb	Mar	Apr	May	June	July	Aug	Sept	Oct	Nov	Dec
Humidity (%)	79	79	79	81	72	82	83	83	84	84	83	80

Guatemala

331

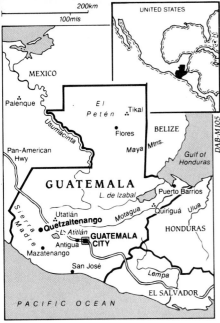

☐ *international airport*

Location: Central America.

Note: Although negotiations are continuing between the government of Guatemala and guerrilla leaders to end a 33-year armed conflict, there are still occasional encounters between Guatemalan army and guerrilla forces in the departments of El Quiche, Northern Alta Verapaz, Huehuetenango, San Marcos, Peten, Escuintla, Suchitepequez, Santa Rosa and Sacatepequez. There are occasional guerrilla roadblocks on the roads between Guatemala City and the border of El Salvador, as well as along the Pacific coast. However, visitors to major tourist destinations rarely come into contact with guerrilla or military forces.
Source: US State Department – September 30, 1994.

Guatemala Tourist Commission
7 Avenida 1-17, Centro Cívico, Zona 4, Guatemala City, Guatemala
Tel: (2) 311 333. Fax: (2) 318 893. Telex: 5532 (a/b INGUAT GU).

Embassy of the Republic of Guatemala
13 Fawcett Street, London SW10 9HN
Tel: (0171) 351 3042. Fax: (0171) 376 5708. Opening hours: 1000-1400 Monday to Friday.

British Embassy
7th Floor, Edificio Centro Financerio, Tower Two, 7a Avenida 5-10, Zona 4, Guatemala City, Guatemala
Tel: (2) 321 601/2/4. Fax: (2) 341 904. Telex: 5686 (a/b BRITON GU).

Embassy of the Republic of Guatemala
2220 R Street, NW, Washington, DC 20008
Tel: (202) 745 4952/3/4. Fax: (202) 745 1908.

Embassy of the United States of America
Avenida La Reforma 7-01, Zona 10, Guatemala City, Guatemala
Tel: (2) 311 541/55. Fax: (2) 318 885.

Embassy of the Republic of Guatemala
Suite 1010, 130 Albert Street, Ottawa, Ontario, K1P 5G4
Tel: (613) 233 7188 (Consular section). Fax: (613) 233 0135.

Timatic

Health
GALILEO/WORLDSPAN: **TI-DFT/GUA/HE**
SABRE: **TIDFT/GUA/HE**

Visa
GALILEO/WORLDSPAN: **TI-DFT/GUA/VI**
SABRE: **TIDFT/GUA/VI**

For more information on Timatic codes refer to Contents.

Guatemala Tourist Commission (INGUAT)
SACA Information Centre, 72 McGill Street, Toronto, Ontario M5B 1H2
Tel: (416) 348 8597. Fax: (416) 348 8597.

Canadian Embassy
PO Box 400, 10 Avenida 21-25, Zona 14, Guatemala City, Guatemala
Tel: (2) 336 102. Fax: (2) 336 148. Telex: 5206 (a/b CANADA GU).

AREA: 108,429 sq km (42,042 sq miles).
POPULATION: 9,453,953 (1991 estimate).
POPULATION DENSITY: 86.8 per sq km.
CAPITAL: Guatemala City. **Population:** 1,095,677 (1991 estimate).
GEOGRAPHY: Guatemala is located in Central America and shares borders with Mexico, Belize, Honduras and El Salvador. The landscape is predominantly mountainous and heavily forested. A string of volcanoes rises above the southern highlands along the Pacific, three of which are still active. Within this volcanic area are basins of varying sizes which hold the majority of the country's population. The region is drained by rivers flowing into both the Pacific and the Caribbean. One basin west of the capital has no river outlet and thus has formed Lake Atitlán, which is ringed by volcanoes. To the northwest, bordering on Belize and Mexico, lies the low undulating tableland of El Petén, 36,300 sq km (14,000 sq miles) of almost inaccessible wilderness covered with dense hardwood forest. This area covers approximately one-third of the national territory, yet contains only 40,000 people.
LANGUAGE: The official language is Spanish. English is widely spoken in Guatemala City. Over 20 indigenous languages are also spoken.
RELIGION: Mostly Roman Catholic and about 25% Protestant.
TIME: GMT - 6.
ELECTRICITY: 110 volts AC, 60Hz. There are some regional variations.
COMMUNICATIONS: Telephone: IDD is available. Country code: 502. Outgoing international code: 00. Telephone calls to Europe are slightly cheaper between 1900 and 0700. **Fax:** Some hotels have facilities.
Telex/telegram: Telex facilities are available in Guatemala City; local telegrams can be sent from the central post office. Urgent telegrams are charged at double the ordinary rate. **Post:** Airmail to Europe takes 6-12 days. **Press:** All newspapers are in Spanish. Publications include *El Gráfico, Prensa Libra* and *La Hora*.
BBC World Service and Voice of America frequencies: From time to time these change. See the section *How to Use this Book* for more information.
BBC:

| MHz | 17.84 | 15.22 | 7.325 | 5.975 |
Voice of America:
| MHz | 15.21 | 11.58 | 9.775 | 5.995 |

PASSPORT/VISA

Regulations and requirements may be subject to change at short notice, and you are advised to contact the appropriate diplomatic or consular authority before finalising travel arrangements. Details of these may be found at the head of this country's entry. Any numbers in the chart refer to the footnotes below.

	Passport Required?	Visa Required?	Return Ticket Required?
Full British	Yes	No	Yes
BVP	Not valid	-	-
Australian	Yes	Yes	Yes
Canadian	Yes	Yes/2	Yes
USA	Yes	Yes/2	Yes
Other EU (As of 31/12/94)	Yes	1	Yes
Japanese	Yes	No	Yes

Restricted entry: Nationals from the following countries require special authorisation from the Department of Immigration in Guatemala prior to applying for a visa: Afghanistan, Albania, Angola, Algeria, Bahrain, Bangladesh, Benin, Bhutan, Bolivia, Bosnia-Hercegovina, Botswana, Brunei, Bulgaria, Cambodia, Central African Republic, China, CIS, Congo, Croatia, Cuba, Czech Republic, Djibouti, Dominican Republic, Equatorial Guinea, Estonia, Ethiopia, Guyana, Haiti, Hong Kong, Hungary, India, Indonesia, Iran, Iraq, Jordan, Kenya, North Korea, Kuwait, Laos, Latvia, Lebanon, Liberia, Libya, Lithuania, Former Yugoslav Republic of Macedonia, Malawi, Malaysia, Maldives, Mali, Mauritania, Mongolia, Mozambique, Myanmar, Namibia, Nepal, Oman, Pakistan, Peru, Philippines, Poland, Qatar, Romania, Rwanda, Saudi Arabia, Singapore, Slovak Republic, Slovenia, Syria, Somalia, Sudan, Suriname, Sri Lanka, Tanzania, Thailand, Tunisia, Turkey, Uganda, Vietnam, Yugoslavia (Serbia

and Montenegro), Yemen, Zaïre, Zambia and Zimbabwe. Details of passport, profession, purpose of visit, family or business contact in Guatemala, return ticket and evidence of means of support are all required. Enquire at Consulate (or Consular section at Embassy) for further details, as the specified nationalities may be subject to change at short notice. Authorisation will take 3-4 weeks.
PASSPORTS: Required by all.
British Visitors Passport: Not accepted.
VISAS: Required by all except:
(a) **[1]** nationals of EU countries (except Greece, Ireland and Portugal who *do* need visas) for a stay of one month with a possible extension to three months;
(b) nationals of Andorra, Argentina, Austria, Belize, Costa Rica, Ecuador, El Salvador, Finland, Honduras, Israel, Japan, Liechtenstein, Monaco, Nicaragua, Norway, San Marino, Sweden, Switzerland, Uruguay and Vatican City for stays of one month with possible extension to three months.
Note [2]: Nationals of Canada, Mexico and the USA entering Guatemala *by air* do not need a visa. They will be issued with a Tourist Card at Guatemala airport.
Types of visa: Visitors (tourist) and Business. Both are valid for 30 days from date of entry, but must be used within 30 days of issue. Cost: £7.
Application to: Guatemalan Consulate (or Consular section at Embassy). For addresses, see top of entry.
Application requirements: *For Tourist visa:* (a) 1 application form. (b) 1 passport-size photo. (c) Valid passport. *For Business visa:* (a) 2 application forms. (b) 2 passport-size photos. (c) Letter from applicant's company in duplicate. (d) Valid passport.
Note: Passengers from Guinea and Nigeria should present a valid certificate of vaccination against yellow fever or they will be subject to five days of quarantine on arrival.
Working days required: 1.

MONEY

Currency: Quetzal (Q) = 100 centavos. Notes are in denominations of Q100, 50, 20, 10, 5 and 1, and 50 centavos. Coins are in denominations of 25, 10, 5 and 1 centavos.
Currency exchange: From November 1989 the exchange rate ceased to be fixed. It may be difficult to negotiate notes which are torn.
Credit cards: Visa and American Express are accepted, whilst Diners Club and Access/Mastercard have a more limited acceptance. Check with your credit card company for details of merchant acceptability and other services which may be available.
Travellers cheques: Accepted by most banks and most good hotels, although the visitor may experience the occasional problem. Travellers cheques in US Dollars are recommended.
Exchange rate indicators: The following figures are included as a guide to the movements of the Quetzal against Sterling and the US Dollar (official rates):

Date:	Oct '92	Sep '93	Jan '94	Jan '95
£1.00=	8.33	8.91	8.57	8.77
$1.00=	5.25	5.84	5.79	5.60

Currency exchange: There are no restrictions on the import or export of either local or foreign currency.
Banking hours: 0900-1500 Monday to Friday.

DUTY FREE

The following goods may be imported by persons over 18 years of age into Guatemala without incurring customs duty:
80 cigarettes or 3.5 oz of tobacco; 1.5 litres (2 bottles) of alcohol (opened); 2 bottles of perfume (opened).

PUBLIC HOLIDAYS

Jan 1 '95 New Year's Day. **Apr 14-17** Easter. **Jun 30** Anniversary of the Revolution. **Sep 15** Independence Day. **Oct 20** Revolution Day. **Nov 1** All Saints' Day. **Dec 24** Christmas Eve. **Dec 25** Christmas Day. **Dec 31** New Year's Eve. **Jan 1 '96** New Year's Day. **Apr 5-8** Easter.

HEALTH

Regulations and requirements may be subject to change at short notice, and you are advised to contact your doctor well in advance of your intended date of departure. Any numbers in the chart refer to the footnotes below.

	Special Precautions?	Certificate Required?
Yellow Fever	No	1
Cholera	No	No
Typhoid & Polio	Yes	-
Malaria	2	-
Food & Drink	3	-

[1]: A yellow fever vaccination certificate is required from travellers over one year of age coming from countries with infected areas.
[2]: Malaria risk exists throughout the year below 1500m in the *departamentos* of: Alta Verapaz, Baja Verapaz, Chimaltenango, El Petén, El Quiché, Huehuetenango, Izabal, San Marcos, Santa Rosa and Sololá.
[3]: All water should be regarded as being potentially contaminated. Water used for drinking, brushing teeth or making ice should have first been boiled or otherwise sterilised. Milk is unpasteurised and should be boiled. Powdered or tinned milk is available and is advised, but make sure that it is reconstituted with pure water. Avoid dairy products which are likely to have been made from unboiled milk. Only eat well-cooked meat and fish, preferably served hot. Pork, salad and mayonnaise may carry increased risk. Vegetables should be cooked and fruit peeled.
Rabies is present. For those at high risk, vaccination before arrival should be considered. If you are bitten abroad, seek medical advice without delay. For more information consult the *Health* section at the back of the book.
Altitude sickness may be experienced in higher places, and exertion should be avoided.
Hepatitis inoculation is highly recommended.
Health care: There are good medical facilities in Guatemala City, but insurance is strongly advised.

TRAVEL - International

AIR: Guatemala's national airline is *Aviateca (GU)*.
Approximate flight times: From Guatemala to *London* is 8 hours (plus stopover time in Miami or Madrid), to *Los Angeles* is 6 hours and to *New York* is 7 hours.
International airport: *Guatemala City (GUA)* (La Aurora), 7km (4 miles) south of the city. Airport facilities include car hire, vaccination centre, duty-free shop, bar, buffet, restaurant, bank, tourist information, telephones and bureaux de change. A bus to the city runs every 30 minutes. Taxi services to Guatemala City are available.
Departure tax: Q50 is levied on all international flights.
SEA: There are several international passenger services from North America, the Far East and Europe to Santo Tomás in Mexico. Cargo services run to the Pacific ports of San José and Champerico. There are also seven direct lines linking Guatemala with the Far East.
RAIL: There is a daily rail link between the Pacific and Caribbean coasts from Guatemala City to Puerto Barrios, and a daily link via Mazatenango from Guatemala City to Mexico (although an overnight stay is necessary at the border). No meals are served on these trains.
ROAD: The Inter-American Highway runs through Guatemala from Mexico in the north and El Salvador in the south. **Bus:** There are bus services from Mexico and El Salvador, Nicaragua, Costa Rica and Panama. The route south is liable to disruption due to the political situation in this part of Central America. Border crossings can be subject to considerable delays. The buses used by some companies are comfortable and air-conditioned, but it is vital to book as far in advance as possible *for every stage of the journey.*

TRAVEL - Internal

AIR: Air transport is by far the most efficient means of internal travel since there are over 380 airstrips. *Aviateca (GU)*, *Aeroquetzal* and *Aerovias* run daily flights from Guatemala City to Petén. Private charter flights are available.
ROAD: Traffic drives on the right. There is an extensive road network but less than a third of the roads are all-weather. Many of the roads are made from volcanic ash, and therefore very muddy during the rains. There are, however, about 13,000km (8000 miles) of first- and second-class roads in the country with paved highways from Guatemala City to the principal towns in the interior and to both the Atlantic and Pacific ports. **Bus:** The network of regular bus services between major towns is cheap but crowded. **Taxi:** Flat rate for short or long runs within the city although prices tend to be expensive. Cars can also be hired by the hour. Vehicles must be summoned by phone as they do not cruise for hire. There are ranks at the main international hotels. Tipping is discretionary (5-10%). **Car hire:** *Hertz* (tel: (2) 311 711), *Avis* (tel: (2) 310 017), *Europcar International* (tel: (2) 318 365) and local firms exist in Guatemala City. Rates are low, but insurance is extra. It is also possible to hire motorcycles.
Documentation: A local licence will be issued on production of visitor's own national driving licence.
URBAN: Guatemala City and major towns have limited, but cheap and regular, bus services.

ACCOMMODATION

HOTELS: There are many hotels in Guatemala City to suit every pocket and taste. Antigua (the capital until largely destroyed by earthquakes in 1773, a fate which also befell the present capital in 1976) also has a good choice of hotels. Puerto Barrios, Chichicastenango, Quetzaltenango, Panajachel (near Lake Atitlán) and Coban also have a reasonable selection of hotels, although elsewhere accommodation is more limited. Throughout the country standards are inconsistent. Most hotels charge a 17% room tax. Registered hotels are required to display room rates; the Tourist Office in Guatemala City will deal with complaints. **Tipping:** 10-15% is normal in hotels where service has not been included.
PENSIONS/GUEST-HOUSES: Most large towns have guest-houses and boarding houses offering inexpensive accommodation.
CAMPING: There are campsites throughout the country although facilities are basic. A popular excursion is to stay overnight on camping grounds on the still-active Pacaya volcano to see the glow of the ashes and lava from the volcano's eruptions. Around Lake Atitlán camping is permitted only in designated areas.

RESORTS & EXCURSIONS

Guatemala City and its environs: The city lies at the edge of a plateau cut by deep ravines. The old quarter with its low colonial houses is situated in the northern part of the city. A Plaza called *Parque Central* lies at its heart and is bordered by the *National Palace*, the *Cathedral*, the *National Library* and an arcade of shops. In the south of the city, close to the airport and the national racecourse, is *Parque La Aurora*, which contains the zoo, the *Archaeological Museum* and the *Handicrafts Museum*. Churches to visit include the cathedral, *Cerro de Carmen, La Merced, Santo Domingo, Santuario Expiatorio, Las Capuchinas, Santa Rosa* and *Capilla de Yurrita*.
Outside Guatemala City is **Antigua**, a beautifully situated town which was, before its destruction in an earthquake, considered to be the most splendid in Central America. Monuments that survived include the *Plaza de Armas*, the *Cathedral*, the *University of San Carlos* and the *San Francisco Church*.
Three nearby volcanoes, *Volcán de Agua, Volcán de Acatenango* and *Volcán de Fuego*, all offer incomparable views of the city and surrounding countryside.
On the route to Guatemala City: Quiriguá is remarkable for its memorials of the ancient Mayan Empire while **Zacapa**, **Chiquimula** and **Esquipular** have some of the finest colonial churches in the Americas.
Caribbean coast: The port of **Puerto Barrios** has the nearby beach of *Escobar* to recommend it. Inland from here is *Lake Izabal* which has the Spanish fort of *San Felipe* and is a reserve for some of the earth's rarest mammals.
San José: The country's second largest port where fishing and swimming are available. An interesting journey can be taken through the *Chiquimula Canal* by launch from the old Spanish port of *Iztapa*, which is now a bathing resort.
Lake Atitlán: One of the most beautiful lakes in the world, surrounded by purple highlands and olive-green mountains and with over a dozen villages on its shores. Visitors can stay at or near **Panajachel**. Water-skiing, swimming and boating are all available.
Western Guatemala: Totonicapán is a thriving industrial town whose local pottery is for sale throughout the country. Its market is considered to be one of the cheapest in Guatemala. **Momostenango** is the centre for blanket weaving.
Quetzaltenango: The most important city in western Guatemala, set amongst a group of high mountains and volcanoes. It is a modern city, but it also has narrow colonial streets, broad avenues, fine public buildings and a magnificent plaza.
Flores: Lies in the heart of the Petén forests, built on an island in the middle of the beautiful *Lake Petén*.
Itza: *Tikal*, the great Mayan ruins of vast temples and public buildings. At least two days are needed to see them all.
Sayaxche: A good centre for visiting the Petén, whether the interest is in wildlife or Mayan ruins. The best of the latter are *Seibal, Itzan, Dos Pilas, Yaxha* and *Uaxactun*.

SOCIAL PROFILE

FOOD & DRINK: There is a variety of restaurants and cafés serving a wide selection of cooking styles including American, Argentine, Chinese, German, Italian, Mexican and Spanish. Fast-food chains also have outlets here and there are many continental-style cafés. The visitor should note that food varies in price rather than quality.
NIGHTLIFE: In Guatemala City in particular there are nightclubs and discotheques with modern music and dance. Guatemala is the home of *marimba* music which can be heard at several venues. In the cities the *marimba* is a huge elaborate xylophone with large drum sticks played by four to nine players. In rural areas the sounding boxes are made of different shaped gourds *(marimbas de tecomates)*. There are also theatres and numerous plays in English and other cultural performances. Films with English and Spanish subtitles are often shown in major towns.
SHOPPING: Special purchases include textiles, handicrafts, jewellery, jade carvings, leather goods, ceramics and basketry. Markets are best for local products and bargaining is necessary. Coban is the cheapest place to buy silverware. **Shopping hours:** 0930-1730 Monday to Saturday.
SPORT: Swimming: North of the capital is the Parque Minerva where there are two swimming pools. There are pools at Ciudad Olímpica, and *Baños del Sur* has large hot baths in Guatemala City and some hotels. **Bowling:** 10-pin bowling and billiards can be played at Bolerama 0-61, Zona 4 in the city. **Basketball/baseball:** Courts at the Parque Minerva. **Golf:** There is an 18-hole golf course at the Guatemala Country Club, 8km (5 miles) from the city. **Tennis** can be played at the Guatemala Lawn Tennis Club and the Mayan Club.
SOCIAL CONVENTIONS: Guatemala is the most populated of the Central American republics and is the only one which is predominantly Indian, although the Spanish have had a strong influence on the way of life. Full names should be used when addressing acquaintances, particularly in business. Dress is conservative and casual wear is suitable except in the smartest dining rooms and clubs. **Tipping:** 10-15% is normal in restaurants where service has not been included.

BUSINESS PROFILE

ECONOMY: Coffee is the leading export in this largely agricultural economy, accounting for about one-third of foreign earnings. Other major crops are sugar cane, bananas, cardamom and cotton. Guatemala boasts the largest manufacturing sector in Central America, producing processed foods, textiles, paper, pharmaceuticals and rubber goods. Oil deposits, first discovered in the mid-1970s, are being exploited by American concerns but the country remains a marginal producer and continues to rely heavily on imported oil. Poor weather and the civil war have disrupted economic development during the last two decades, although Guatemala has received solid support from the United States and international institutions such as the Inter-American Development Bank and the IMF. The USA are substantially Guatemala's largest trading partner, followed by El Salvador, Honduras, Mexico and some EU countries, notably Germany and Italy.
BUSINESS: Guatemalan businessmen tend to be rather formal and conservative. Normal courtesies should be observed and appointments should be made. Punctuality is appreciated and calling cards can be useful. **Office hours:** 0800-1800 Monday to Friday, 0800-1200 Saturday.
COMMERCIAL INFORMATION: The following organisation can offer advice: Cámara de Comercio de Guatemala (Chamber of Commerce), 10a Calle 3-80, Zona 1, Guatemala City. Tel: (2) 82681. Fax: (2) 514 197. Telex: 5478.

CLIMATE

Guatemala's climate varies according to altitude. The coastal regions and the northeast are hot throughout the year, while the highlands have a much more temperate climate. The rainy season is from June to October, and the rest of the year is quite dry. Temperatures fall sharply at night.
Required clothing: Lightweight tropicals. Jacket or light woollens for night.

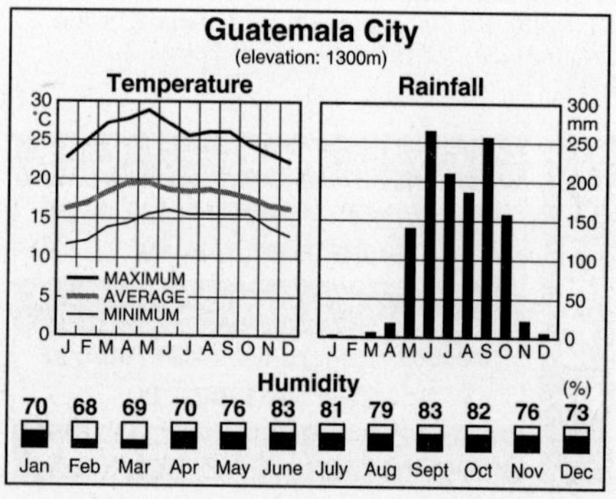
Guatemala City
(elevation: 1300m)
Temperature
Rainfall
°C
mm
MAXIMUM
AVERAGE
MINIMUM
J F M A M J J A S O N D
J F M A M J J A S O N D
Humidity
(%)
70 68 69 70 76 83 81 79 83 82 76 73
Jan Feb Mar Apr May June July Aug Sept Oct Nov Dec

Guernsey

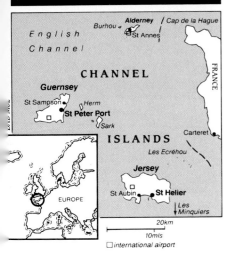

☐ *international airport*

Location: English Channel, off the northern coast of France.

Guernsey Tourist Office
PO Box 23, White Rock, St Peter Port, Guernsey, Channel Islands GY1 3AN
Tel: 726 611 (administration) *or* 723 552 (information). Fax: 721 246 *or* 714 951. Telex: 4191612.

AREA: 65 sq km (25 sq miles).
POPULATION: 58,000.
POPULATION DENSITY: 892.3 per sq km.
CAPITAL: St Peter Port.
GEOGRAPHY: Guernsey is situated in the Gulf of St Malo, 50km (30 miles) from the coast of France and 130km (80 miles) from the south coast of England. The cliffs on the south coast rise to 80m (270ft), from which the land slopes away gradually to the north. Guernsey is an ideal centre for excursions to the other Channel Islands and France.
LANGUAGE: English is the official language. Norman *patois* is spoken in some parishes.
RELIGION: Church of England, Baptist, Congregational and Methodist.
TIME: GMT (GMT + 1 from March to October).
ELECTRICITY: 240 volts AC, 50Hz.
COMMUNICATIONS: Telephone: To telephone Guernsey from the UK the STD code is 01481; calls from overseas must be made using the UK country code: 44. Outgoing international code: 00. **Post:** Only Guernsey stamps will be accepted on outgoing mail. The main post office is at Smith Street, St Peter Port. Post boxes are painted blue. **Press:** The local newspapers are *The Guernsey Evening Press* (daily except Sunday) and *The Weekender*. English, French, German, Dutch and Italian newspapers are also available at newsagents.

PASSPORT/VISA

Passport and Visa requirements are the same as those for the rest of the UK. See the *United Kingdom* section later in this book.

MONEY

Currency: Pound Sterling (£) = 100 pence. Notes are in denominations of £50, 20, 10, 5 and 1. Coins are in denominations of £1, and 50, 20, 10, 5, 2 and 1 pence. All UK notes and coins are legal tender, and circulate with the Channel Islands issue.
Note: Channel Islands notes and coins are not accepted in

the UK, although they can be reconverted at parity in UK banks.
Currency exchange: Foreign currencies can be exchanged at bureaux de change, in banks and at many hotels.
Credit cards: Access/Mastercard, American Express, Diners Club and Visa are all widely accepted. Check with your credit card company for details of merchant acceptability and other services which may be available.
Travellers cheques: These are widely accepted.
Exchange rates: The following is included as a guide to the movement of Sterling against the US Dollar:

Date:	Oct '92	Sep '93	Jan '94	Jan '95
$1.00=	0.63	0.65	0.68	0.64

Banking hours: 0930-1530 Monday to Friday. Some banks are open later on weekdays and on Saturday morning.

DUTY FREE

The Channel Islands are largely a duty-free zone. The following goods may be exported from Guernsey without incurring customs duty in the UK:
200 cigarettes or 50 cigars or 250g of tobacco; 1 litre of alcoholic beverages if over 22% proof or 2 litres of sparkling or fortified wines; 2 litres of still table wine; 600ml of perfume and 250ml of eau de toilette; other goods to a value of £136.
Note: (a) [*] No limit for goods brought in from an EU country. (b) There is a total ban on the importation of animals other than from the UK or other Channel Islands.

PUBLIC HOLIDAYS

Jan 1 '95 New Year's Day. **Apr 14** Good Friday. **Apr 17** Easter Monday. **May 8** For May Day. **May 9** Liberation Day (commemorating the arrival of the British Forces to the Island at the end of the Second World War). **May 29** Spring Bank Holiday. **Aug 7** Summer Bank Holiday. **Aug 28** Late Summer Bank Holiday. **Dec 25** Christmas Day. **Dec 26** Boxing Day. **Jan 1 '96** New Year's Day. **Apr 5** Good Friday. **Apr 8** Easter Monday.

HEALTH

Regulations and requirements may be subject to change at short notice, and you are advised to contact your doctor well in advance of your intended date of departure. Any numbers in the chart refer to the footnotes below.

	Special Precautions?	Certificate Required?
Yellow Fever	No	No
Cholera	No	No
Typhoid & Polio	No	-
Malaria	No	-
Food & Drink	No	-

Health care: Guernsey has a large hospital (Princess Elizabeth Hospital) and many medical and dental practices. There is a Reciprocal Health Agreement with the UK (Guernsey is a Crown Dependency and not strictly part of the UK). On presentation of proof of residence in the UK (driving licence, NHS card, etc), UK citizens are entitled to free hospital and other medical treatment, free emergency dental treatment and free travel by ambulance; most prescribed medicines must be paid for. Medical insurance is recommended.

TRAVEL - International

AIR: Approximate flight time: From London to Guernsey is 45 minutes. Guernsey can be reached all year round from various locations on mainland Britain, Dinard and Cherbourg, and during the summer from Amsterdam, Dortmund, Düsseldorf, Frankfurt/M, Hamburg, Paderborn/Lippstadt, Paris, Stuttgart and Zurich.
International airport: *Guernsey (GCI)*, 5km (3 miles) from St Peter Port (travel time – 20 minutes). Bus and taxi services are available to the town.
SEA: *British Channel Island Ferries* have been acquired by *Condor* and all services form Poole (Dorset) have now ceased. They now only operate ferry services out of Weymouth. *Condor Hydrofoil* operates seasonal services from Weymouth and St Malo. Services from France include *Channiland,* operating from Cherbourg, and *Emeraude Lines* operating from St Malo, Portbail, Carteret, St Quay Portrieux and Granville. Day excursions are available daily to Herm and Sark by boat. Inter-island services are also available from *Aurigny Air Services* and *Condor Hydrofoil.*

TRAVEL - Internal

ROAD: Bus: A comprehensive bus service serves all parts of the island. A variety of island tours are also

available during the summer. **Car hire:** There are many car hire companies available on Guernsey, with rates that compare favourably with the UK. There is an unlimited mileage allowance. Coach hire for large parties is also available. **Bicycle hire:** Available from various firms for daily or weekly hire. **Regulations:** Driving is on the left. Maximum speed limit is 35mph (56kmph). Parking is free, although time limits are imposed. If these are exceeded, a fine of £10 is charged. **Documentation:** A full national driving licence is required.
JOURNEY TIMES: The following chart gives approximate journey times (in hours and minutes) from St Peter Port to the neighbouring Channel Islands.

	Air	Sea
Alderney	0.15	-
Herm Island	-	0.20
Jersey	0.15	1.00
Sark Island	-	0.40

ACCOMMODATION

A full colour brochure of all accommodation is available from the Guernsey Tourist Office (address at top of entry). The Guernsey government has a scheme for the compulsory inspection and grading of hotels to ensure standards of accommodation are maintained and improved.
HOTELS: A large selection of well-maintained hotels, offering facilities for the single or group visitor, is available. Over 94% of the rooms have ensuite facilities. All have at least a washbasin and hot and cold running water in all rooms. Advance booking is advisable during the summer period. For the brochure mentioned above, contact the Guernsey Tourist Office or the Guernsey Hotel and Tourism Association (GHATA), c/o Guernsey Chamber of Commerce, States Arcade, Market Street, St Peter Port. Tel: 713 583. Fax: 710 755.
Grading: All hotels are graded, being given a number of Crowns (with 5 Crowns given as the highest grade) according to the facilities offered. Some registered hotels have either not been awarded any Crowns or are awaiting their assessment.
5 Crowns: All bedrooms contain a fixed bath and WC en suite; most offer central heating, indoor or outdoor swimming pool, baby listening service, special diets, special rates and are open throughout the year.
4 Crowns: All bedrooms contain a fixed bath and shower and WC en suite; many offer central heating, indoor or outdoor swimming pool, baby listening service, special diets, special rates and are open throughout the year.
3 Crowns: 75% of rooms must contain a fixed bath or shower and WC en suite; several offer all or some of the following: central heating, indoor or outdoor swimming pool, baby listening service, special diets, special rates and are open throughout the year.
2 Crowns: 50% of rooms must contain a fixed bath or shower and WC en suite; several offer all or some of the following: central heating, indoor or outdoor swimming pool, baby listening service, special diets, special rates and are open throughout the year.
1 Crown: 25% of rooms must contain a fixed bath or shower and WC en suite; some may offer the following: central heating, indoor or outdoor swimming pool, baby listening service, special diets, special rates and are open throughout the year.
For further information, contact the Guernsey Hotel and Tourism Association.
GUEST-HOUSES: These are normally family-run establishments, providing a good standard of accommodation in a homely atmosphere. This can be based on full-board, half-board or bed & breakfast, according to the visitor's requirements. A number of these have residential liquor licences. **Grading:** All are graded A-D, with A offering the best service.
SELF-CATERING: Units are graded A-C according to size, number of persons accommodated, standards and amenities offered.
CAMPING: There are four official campsites at various locations around the island. Full details are available from the Tourist Office. Visitors are not permitted to bring caravans into Guernsey.

RESORTS & EXCURSIONS

St Peter Port is an attractive harbour town with narrow streets leading uphill from the sea. It has all the character of a traditional fishing village, complete with boats bobbing about in the harbour. The town church has a 12th-century chancel, a 15th-century south chapel and the interior dates back to 1886. Just above the *French Halles* are the *Guille-Alles Library*. The *Island Museum* at **Candie** won 'Museum of the Year' award in 1979 (open 1030-1730 daily).
Nearby *Castle Cornet* overlooks the harbour. Built during the reign of King Stephen, it has been the scene of many historic battles and bears the military stamp of

ST PETER PORT

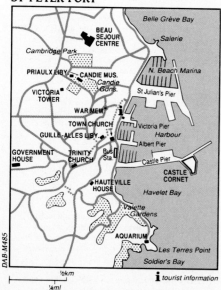

i tourist information

many eras, from Norman times through to the German occupation during the Second World War. The castle also contains the *Royal Guernsey Militia Museum,* a *Maritime Museum* and attractive gardens (open 1030-1730 daily, April to October).
Hauteville House, on the south side of St Peter Port at the top of the hill, was the home of French writer Victor Hugo from 1855-1870. The French coast can be seen from the window of his study, and it was here that he wrote *The Toilers of the Sea.* Hugo's statue stands in *Candie Gardens,* which is also the location of the oak he planted, now a symbol of European unity. The miniature botanical gardens also contain subtropical plants, trees and shrubs, all grown in the open.
The *Dolmens* (tombs of prehistoric tribes) are also worth seeing, with examples scattered around the island. Among the more notable are *Déhus Dolmen,* near the yacht marina in the **Vale,** *La Varde Dolmen* at the Pembroke end of **L'Ancresse Common,** *Le Creux Faies* at **L'Erée,** and *La Catioroc,* on a mound overlooking **Perelle Bay** (said to be a former meeting place for Guernsey witches).
Among the castles are *Ivy Castle* near **Le Bouet,** a Norman stronghold built before the Norman Conquest of England, and *Vale Castle* at **St Sampson,** whose origins are lost in time, where a Russian garrison was stationed circa 1805. There are fortifications at *Fort Pezerie, Fort Grey, Fort Saumerez* and *Fort George.* Martello Towers are to be found scattered around the island.
Few of the fortifications made by the Nazis remain, most of these being on the cliffs. The underground hospital at **St Andrews** is the largest German structure in the Channel Islands, and this is now a tourist attraction. The *Occupation Museum* at the **Forest** contains many relics and a glimpse into life during the German occupation. The cliffs around the island make a pleasant walk, and lead to many bays, most of which are suitable for bathing and accessible from the cliffs. Inland one finds many pleasant walks. The *Water Lanes* leading to the shore are also worth seeing, particularly at **Moulin Huet** and **Petit Bôt.** The *Chapel* at **Les Vauxbelets** is the smallest church in the world, with space for a priest and a congregation of two.

SOCIAL PROFILE

FOOD & DRINK: Guernsey is famous for its food and the island has a wide variety of restaurants ranging from traditional French and English cuisine to Italian, Indian and Chinese. The local speciality is shellfish, with freshly caught lobsters, crabs and scallops forming the basis of many dishes. Table service is normal in restaurants, with counter service in bars. There are two self-service restaurants in St Peter Port. **Drink:** A wide variety of alcoholic beverages is available and spirits, beers and wines are relatively cheap compared to the mainland. Eating out is also excellent value for money as there is no VAT. Bars may open between 1030 and 2345 daily except Sunday.
NIGHTLIFE: Discotheques are located in various parts of the island, whilst live music and cabarets are organised by some hotels during the summer season. The Beau Sejour Leisure Centre at St Peter Port contains a cinema, theatre, bars and café.
SHOPPING: There is no VAT but a Guernsey Bailiwick tax is imposed on certain goods such as spirits, wines,

beers and tobacco. Prices of luxury goods are relatively cheaper than in the UK, although the overall cost of foodstuffs is higher. Special purchases include Guernsey's local pottery and crafts. **Shopping hours:** 0900-1730 Monday to Saturday. Early closing is on Thursday, although most shops will stay open. Some shops open in the evening during summer months.
SPORT: The Beau Sejour Leisure Centre caters for a wide variety of sports, including **tennis, squash, swimming, badminton, bowls,** five-a-side **football, roller skating, keep-fit** classes and **snooker.** Windsurfing boards are available for hire from Cobo and L'Ancresse bays. The Island has an 18-hole **golf** course; **horseriding, go-karting, sailing, flying** and **fishing** (including wreck fishing) are also available.
SPECIAL EVENTS: Below are a selection of special events in Guernsey. For full details of special events and festivals celebrated during 1995/96, contact the Guernsey Tourist Office.
Apr 25-27 '95 *Salon Culinaire.* **May 4-11** *Rolls Royce Enthusiasts Club Rally.* **May 8** *Liberation Historic Transport Show.* **May 9** *Liberation Day.* **May 29** *La Chevauchée.* **Jun 25-Jul 1** *Guernsey Square Dance Festival.* **Jul 5** *Viaer Marchi.* **Jul 14** *Round Table Harbour Carnival.* **Jul 22-30** *St Peter Port Town Carnival.* **Jul 31-Aug 6** *Guernsey International Folk Festival.* **Aug 5** *Rocquaine Regatta.* **Aug 9-10** *South Show.* **Aug 16-17** *West Show.* **Aug 25-26** *North Show.* **Sep 9** *Kite Fly '95.* **Sep 11-17** *Battle of Britain Week.* **Sep 23-Oct 21** *Guernsey Festival.* **Oct 15-21** *Chess Festival.*
SOCIAL CONVENTIONS: Handshaking is the customary form of greeting and normal social courtesies should be observed when visiting someone's home. It is not usual to start eating until everyone is served. If invited to someone's home, a small present such as flowers or chocolates is appreciated. Casual wear is acceptable in most places. Smoking is not allowed on buses. **Tipping:** 10-12% is normal, except where a service charge is included.

BUSINESS PROFILE

ECONOMY: Finance, tourism and agriculture are the main contributors to Guernsey's buoyant economy. The island has gradually been developed as an offshore financial centre: several London merchant banks are now incorporated here to take advantage of tight disclosure laws and low taxes. Flowers and tomatoes are the main exports and are internationally renowned.
BUSINESS: Business people are generally expected to dress smartly, with a suit and tie for men. Appointments should be made and calling cards are customary. Business is conducted in English. **Office hours:** 0900-1700 Monday to Friday.
COMMERCIAL INFORMATION: The following organisation can offer advice: Guernsey Chamber of Commerce, States Arcade, Market Square, St Peter Port GY1 1HD. Tel: 727 483. Fax: 710 755.
CONFERENCES/CONVENTIONS: Approximately 100 conferences are held in Guernsey each year, with the total number of delegates being between 10,000 and 12,000 per annum; the maximum recommended conference size is 750. Organisers can obtain advice from the Conference Manager at the Guernsey Tourist Office (see address at beginning of entry).

CLIMATE

The most popular holiday season is from Easter to October, with temperatures averaging 20-21°C. These months give an average of 200 and 260 hours of sunshine. Rainfall is mainly during the cooler months. The sea is 17°C on average during the summer.
Required clothing: Normal beach and holiday wear for summer, with some warmer clothing as there are often sea breezes. Warm winter wear and rainwear are advised.

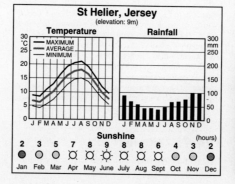

St Helier, Jersey
(elevation: 9m)

Guinea Republic

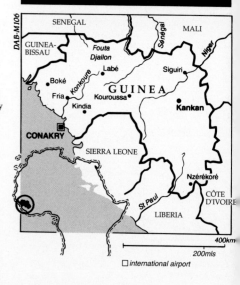

□ *international airport*

Location: West Africa.

Secrétariat d'Etat au Tourisme et à l'Hôtellerie
BP 1304, square des Martyrs, Conakry, Guinea
Tel: 442 606.
Embassy of the Republic of Guinea
51 rue de la Faisanderie, 75016 Paris, France
Tel: (1) 47 04 81 48 *or* 45 53 85 45. Fax: (1) 47 04 57 65.
Telex: 648497.
British Consulate
BP 834, Conakry, Guinea
Tel: 461 734 *or* 465 361 *or* 443 442. Fax: 444 215.
Telex: 22294.
Embassy of the Republic of Guinea
2112 Leroy Place, NW, Washington, DC 20008
Tel: (202) 483 9420. Fax: (202) 483 8688.
Embassy of the United States of America
BP 603, 2nd Boulevard and 9th Avenue, Conakry, Guinea
Tel: 411 520/1/3. Fax: 411 522.
Embassy of the Republic of Guinea
483 Wilbrod Street, Ottawa, Ontario K1N 6N1
Tel: (613) 789 8444. Fax: (613) 789 7560.
Canadian Embassy
PO Box 99, Conakry, Guinea
Tel: 412 395. Fax: 414 236. Telex: 2170.

AREA: 245,857 sq km (94,926 sq miles).
POPULATION: 5,718,000 (1990).
POPULATION DENSITY: 20.6 per sq km.
CAPITAL: Conakry. Population: 800,000 (1986 estimate).
GEOGRAPHY: The Republic of Guinea is located in West Africa and bounded to the northwest by Guinea-Bissau, the north by Senegal and Mali, the east by Côte d'Ivoire, the south by Liberia and the southwest by Sierra Leone. Guinea's many rivers supply water to much of West Africa. The River Niger flows north from the southern highlands into Mali before turning south again through Niger and Nigeria. The coastal plain is made up of mangrove swamps, while inland are the Fouta Djaleon hills which form several distinct ranges and plateaux over the whole of western Guinea. In the northeast, savannah plains of the Sahel region stretch into Mali. To the south are mountains known as the Guinea Highlands.
LANGUAGE: French is the official language. Susu, Malinké and Fula are local languages.
RELIGION: Muslim, Animist and Christian. The

Timatic

Health	
GALILEO/WORLDSPAN:	**TI-DFT/CKY/HE**
SABRE:	**TIDFT/CKY/HE**

Visa	
GALILEO/WORLDSPAN:	**TI-DFT/CKY/VI**
SABRE:	**TIDFT/CKY/VI**

For more information on Timatic codes refer to Contents.

majority (approx 75%) of the population are Muslim.
TIME: GMT.
ELECTRICITY: 220 volts, 50Hz.
COMMUNICATIONS: Telephone: IDD service is available. Country code: 224. The communication is relatively poor and outgoing international calls must be made through the operator. Limited telephone and fax lines are usually available 1800-0600. **Telex:** There are facilities at the Hotel de l'Indépéndence and Grand Hotel de l'Unité. **Post:** There are numerous post offices in the capital. **Press:** The weekly newspaper is *Horoya*. Two official publications, *Journal Official de Guinée* and *Le Travailleur de Guinée,* are published in French.
BBC World Service and Voice of America frequencies: From time to time these change. See the section *How to Use this Book* for more information.

BBC:				
MHz	**17.79**	**15.40**	**15.07**	**9.600**
Voice of America:				
MHz	**21.49**	**15.60**	**9.525**	**6.035**

PASSPORT/VISA

Regulations and requirements may be subject to change at short notice, and you are advised to contact the appropriate diplomatic or consular authority before finalising travel arrangements. Details of these may be found at the head of this country's entry. Any numbers in the chart refer to the footnotes below.

	Passport Required?	Visa Required?	Return Ticket Required?
Full British	Yes	Yes	Yes
BVP	Not valid	-	-
Australian	Yes	Yes	Yes
Canadian	Yes	Yes	Yes
USA	Yes	Yes	Yes
Other EU (As of 31/12/94)	Yes	Yes	Yes
Japanese	Yes	Yes	Yes

Restricted entry: Journalists may visit the Republic of Guinea by government invitation only.
PASSPORTS: Valid passport required by all.
British Visitors Passport: Not accepted.
VISAS: Required by all except nationals of Algeria, Benin, Burkina Faso, Cape Verde, Côte d'Ivoire, Cuba, Egypt, Gambia, Ghana, Guinea-Bissau, Liberia, Mali, Mauritania, Morocco, Niger, Nigeria, Romania, Senegal, Sierra Leone, Tanzania, Togo and Tunisia.
Types of visa: Tourist, Business and Transit. Transit visas are not required by those continuing their journey by the same aircraft and not leaving the airport.
Application to: Embassy (or Consular section at Embassy). For addresses, see top of entry.
Application requirements: (a) 2 application forms. (b) 2 passport-size photographs. (c) Passport with a remaining validity of 6 months after intended length of stay.
Working days required: 5 weeks.

MONEY

Currency: Guinea Franc (FG) = 100 centimes. Notes are in denominations of FG5000, 1000, 500, 100, 50 and 25.
Currency exchange: Hotels will accept some foreign currencies in payment. Inter-bank fund transfers are frequently difficult, if not impossible, to accomplish.
Credit cards: Limited use of Access/Mastercard. Check with your credit card company for details of merchant acceptability and other services which may be available.
Exchange rate indicators: The following figures are included as a guide to the movements of the Guinea Franc against Sterling and the US Dollar:

Date:	**Oct '92**	**Sep '93**	**Jan '94**	**Jan '95**
£1.00=	**1284.64**	**1243.20**	**1199.75**	**1566.80**
$1.00=	***809.48**	**814.15**	**810.92**	**1001.47**

Note [*]: The rate given is the public transaction rate.
Currency restrictions: Import or export of local currency is prohibited. Import of foreign currency is unlimited but must be declared on arrival; export is limited to the amount declared on arrival.
Banking hours: 0830-1230 and 1430-1630 Monday to Friday.

DUTY FREE

The following goods may be imported into Guinea without incurring customs duty:
1000 cigarettes or 250 cigars or 1kg of tobacco; 1 bottle of alcohol (opened); a reasonable amount of perfume.

PUBLIC HOLIDAYS

Jan 1 '95 New Year's Day. **Mar 2** Eid al-Fitr (End of Ramadan). **Apr 17** Easter Monday. **May 1** Labour Day. **Aug 9** Mouloud (Prophet's Birthday). **Aug 27** Anniversary of Women's Revolt. **Sep 28** Referendum Day. **Oct 2** Republic Day. **Nov 1** All Saints' Day. **Nov 22** Day of 1970 Invasion. **Dec 25** Christmas Day. **Jan 1 '96** New Year's Day. **Feb 22** Eid al-Fitr (End of Ramadan). **Apr 8** Easter Monday.
Note: Muslim festivals are timed according to local sightings of various phases of the Moon and the dates given above are approximations. During the lunar month of Ramadan that precedes Eid al-Fitr, Muslims fast during the day and feast at night and normal business patterns may be interrupted. Many restaurants are closed during the day and there may be restrictions on smoking and drinking. Some disruption may continue into Eid al-Fitr itself. Eid al-Fitr may last anything from two to ten days, depending on the region. For more information see the section *World of Islam* at the back of the book.

HEALTH

Regulations and requirements may be subject to change at short notice, and you are advised to contact your doctor well in advance of your intended date of departure. Any numbers in the chart refer to the footnotes below.

	Special Precautions?	Certificate Required?
Yellow Fever	Yes	1
Cholera	Yes	2
Typhoid & Polio	Yes	-
Malaria	Yes/3	-
Food & Drink	4	-

[1]: A yellow fever vaccination certificate is required from travellers over one year of age coming from infected areas. Travellers arriving from non-endemic zones should note that vaccination is strongly recommended for travel outside the urban areas, even if an outbreak of the disease has not been reported and they would normally not require a vaccination certificate to enter the country.
[2]: Following WHO guidelines issued in 1973, a cholera vaccination certificate is no longer a condition of entry to Guinea. However, cholera is a serious risk in this country and precautions are essential. Up-to-date advice should be sought before deciding whether these precautions should include vaccination as medical opinion is divided over its effectiveness. See the *Health* section at the back of the book.
[3]: A malaria risk, predominantly in the malignant *falciparum* form, exists all year throughout the country. Resistance to chloroquine has been reported.
[4]: All water should be regarded as being potentially contaminated. Water used for drinking, brushing teeth or making ice should have first been boiled or otherwise sterilised. Only eat well-cooked meat and fish, preferably served hot. Pork, salad and mayonnaise may carry increased risk. Vegetables should be cooked and fruit peeled.
Rabies is present. For those at high risk, vaccination before arrival should be considered. If you are bitten abroad, seek medical advice without delay. For more information, consult the *Health* section at the back of the book.
Bilharzia (schistosomiasis) is present. Avoid swimming and paddling in fresh water. Swimming pools which are well-chlorinated and maintained are safe.
Meningitis, hepatitis, filariasis and *onchocerciasis* (river blindness) can occur.
Health care: Health insurance is essential. There are rudimentary medical, dental and optical facilities in Conakry. Doctors and hospitals expect immediate cash payment for health services.

TRAVEL - International

AIR: Guinea's national airline is *Air Guinée (GI)*. There are regular air connections with Guinea-Bissau, Nigeria, Congo, Ghana, Morocco, Gambia, France and Belgium.
Approximate flight time: From London to Conakry is 9 hours (including stopover time in Paris or Brussels of up to 3 hours).
International airport: *Conakry (CKY)*, 13km (8 miles) southwest of the city. Taxis are available to the city.
Departure tax: FG9000 (approx. US$10).
Note: Foreigners at Conakry Airport are particular targets for pickpockets and persons posing as officials who will offer assistance and then make off with bags, purses and wallets. Being met at the airport by travel agents, business contacts, family members or friends avoids this possibility.
SEA: The principal shipping lines calling at Conakry are *Lloyd Triestino, DSS Line (UK)* and *Polish Ocean Lines.*
ROAD: Roads link Freetown (Sierra Leone) with Conakry and with Ganta on the Liberian border; and Bamako (Mali) with Siguiri and Kankan. Roads from Liberia and Mali can be difficult. Buses operate from Tambacomda (Senegal) and Bamako (Mali). See also *Travel – Internal* below.

TRAVEL - Internal

AIR: *Air Guinée* operates internal services to some of the main towns, such as Conakry, Labé, Kankan, Boké, Kissidougou, Macenta, Nzérékoré and Siguiri.
Departure tax: FG4800 for all domestic flights.
RAIL: A twice-weekly passenger service connects Conakry, Kindia and Kankan. There are also five trains a week between Port Kamsar and Sangaredi. There is a limited buffet service. Discounts for children and international rail connections do not exist. In general, rail travel is not recommended.
ROAD: Roads are in poor condition and little used, and the minor roads are overgrown with bush. However, improvements are currently under way. Travel by road is often impossible in the rainy season (May-Oct). The roads between Conakry (via Kindia) and Kissidougou and from Boké to Kamsar are both paved, as is the road to Freetown. **Taxi:** These are available, although fares should be negotiated in advance. **Documentation:** International Driving Permit required.
URBAN: Buses and taxis operate cheaply within Conakry. It is not necessary to tip taxi drivers.

ACCOMMODATION

HOTELS: In Conakry there are a few highly priced hotels of an adequate standard. Kankan also has a few hotels. Accommodation should be booked well in advance with written confirmation.
REST HOUSES: These are available in most of the major towns; enquire locally.
CAMPING: Not allowed in Guinea.

RESORTS & EXCURSIONS

In 1958, when it declared independence from France, Guinea became an isolated and secretive country. However, after the death of the dictator Sekou Touré in 1984, Guinea began, slowly, to allow tourists through its once stubbornly closed doors. Yet it is still one of the least visited countries in Africa and it can be difficult, despite declarations to the contrary, to acquire visas. Guinea's main attraction to tourists is its relatively undisturbed countryside. Its landscape varies from mountains to plains and from savannahs to forests, and the three great rivers of West Africa – the Gambia, the Senegal and the Niger – all originate here. The **Fouta Djallon** highlands are well known for their picturesque hills, offering superb views, and the rolling valleys and waterfalls, which are all presided over by the mostly Muslim population of Fula herders and farmers. In the eastern region of Guinea lie many historical towns with echoes and remnants of medieval empires. In the south is the **Guinée Forestière,** a highland area of rainforest and old pre-Islamic tribes.
The capital, **Conakry,** is located on the island of Tumbo and is connected to the Kaloum Peninsula by a 300m-long (984ft) pier. The city is well laid-out, its alleys shaded by mangrove and coconut palm trees. The *Cathedral,* built in the 1930s and located in the town centre, is well worth viewing. There is also a *National Museum.* The *Kakimbon Caves* in the village of **Ratoma,** now a suburb of Conakry, are the source of many interesting legends and are bestowed with great religious significance by the local Baga people. The **Iles de Los,** off the Kaloum Peninsula, are well recommended as a tourist destination and are easily accessible from Conakry. About 150km (93 miles) outside Conakry is the picturesque *Le Voile de la Marée,* nestled at the bottom of a 70m-high (230ft) rock from which the River Sabende plunges, amidst lush vegetation, into a deep pond. In **Pita,** located between Dalaba and Labé, the *Kinkon Falls* can be found which produce 150m (492ft) of cascading water.
There are no national parks in Guinea, but wildlife can best be seen in the northeast savannahs between the Tinkisso River and the Mali border, in the foothills of the Fouta Djaleon and in the southeast.

SOCIAL PROFILE

FOOD & DRINK: Restaurants, except in the capital where Western-style food is available, generally serve local dishes including *jollof rice,* stuffed chicken with groundnuts, and fish dishes. These are usually served with rice and may be spicy. Staples are cassava, yams and maize. Guineans are fond of very hot maize soup, served from calabashes. **Drink:** Main hotels, mostly in the capital, have reasonable restaurants where a wide variety of alcoholic beverages are served, including good West African brands of beer. This is also available in local bars.
NIGHTLIFE: Although there are theatres, nightclubs and cinemas, Guineans prefer to make their own entertainment. In the streets people can often be seen

gathered together to dance, sing and play traditional musical instruments or home-made guitars. Conakry is a dynamic centre for music and the singing of the Kindia people is renowned.

SHOPPING: Although department stores in the major cities are poorly stocked, local markets sell a unique display of goods. Special purchases include brightly coloured, distinctive Guinean clothes, woodcarvings, leather rugs in bold black-and-white designs, skins, locally produced records, calabashes and jewellery.
Shopping hours: 0900-1800 Monday to Saturday.
SPORT: In Landreah is the 28 September Stadium where a number of sporting events are held. **Football** is the most popular sport and the national team is more than competent. **Swimming:** There are one or two beaches on the Iles de Los (which lie just off the coast near Conakry), but currents can be strong and swimmers are advised to exercise care and follow local advice.
SOCIAL CONVENTIONS: Although Muslim customs are less strict than in the Arab world, beliefs and traditions should be respected by tourists. Casual dress is acceptable. Street crime is relatively common.
Photography: A permit (applied for in advance) has to be obtained from the Ministère de l'Intérieur et de la Securité. **Tipping:** A 5% service charge will usually be included in the bill.

BUSINESS PROFILE

ECONOMY: Most of the population is engaged in subsistence agriculture. Until 1984 the economy functioned under centralised state control. The regime which took over has endeavoured to decentralise economic control and production which, apart from agriculture, is concentrated in mining. Guinea has substantial reserves of bauxite – which accounts for over 90% of export earnings – and diamonds which suffered from low world demand during the late 1970s and early 1980s, but the sector has now recovered. The country's natural resources have helped to secure extensive foreign aid to bolster the economy: this previously derived from the former Soviet Union but now comes largely from Western donors. Guinea has also benefited from growing regional cooperation: Cameroon, for example, processes much of the bauxite ore to produce aluminium. Guinea is a member of both the Mano River Union (with Liberia and Sierra Leone) and of the Gambia River Development Organisation (with Gambia and Senegal). France (Guinea's major importer) and the USA are the destinations for 20% of the country's exports.
BUSINESS: Appointments should be made in advance. Tropical-weight suits and ties are worn by some business visitors, but these are not essential. A knowledge of French is advisable. **Office hours:** 0800-1630 Monday to Thursday, 0800-1300 Friday.
COMMERCIAL INFORMATION: The following organisation can offer advice: Chambre de Commerce, d'Industrie et d'Agriculture de Guinée, BP 545, Conakry. Tel: 444 495. Telex: 609.

CLIMATE

The climate is tropical and humid with a wet and a dry season. Wet season lasts from May to October; dry season lasts from November to April.
Required clothing: Tropical or washable cottons throughout the year. A light raincoat or umbrella is needed during the rainy season.

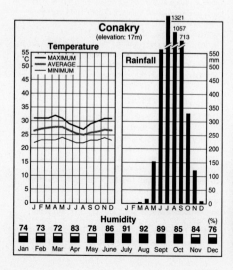

Conakry
(elevation: 17m)
Temperature
Rainfall

Humidity

□ international airport

Location: West Africa.

Centro de Informação e Turismo
CP 294, Bissau, Guinea-Bissau.
Consulate General of the Republic of Guinea-Bissau
8 Palace Gate, London W8 4RP
Tel: (0171) 589 5253. Fax: (0171) 589 9590. Opening hours: 1000-1300 Monday to Friday.
Embassy of the Republic of Guinea-Bissau
Avenue Franklin Roosevelt 70, 1050 Brussels, Belgium
Tel: (2) 647 0890. Fax: (2) 640 4312. Telex: 64731.
British Consulate
Mavegro International, CP 100, Bissau, Guinea-Bissau
Tel: 211 529. Telex: 259 (a/b MAVEGRO BI).
Embassy of the Republic of Guinea-Bissau
Mezzanine Suite, 918 16th Street, NW, Washington, DC 20006
Tel: (202) 872 4222. Fax: (202) 872 4226.
Embassy of the United States of America
Bairro de Penha, CP297, Codex 1067, Bissau, Guinea-Bissau
Tel: 252 273/4/5/6. Fax: 252 282.
The Canadian Embassy in Dakar deals with enquiries relating to Guinea-Bissau (see *Senegal* later in the book).

AREA: 36,125 sq km (13,948 sq miles).
POPULATION: 943,000 (1989 estimate).
POPULATION DENSITY: 26.1 per sq km.
CAPITAL: Bissau. **Population:** 109,214 (1979).
GEOGRAPHY: Guinea-Bissau (formerly Portuguese Guinea) is located in West Africa, and is bounded to the north by Senegal and to the south by the Republic of Guinea. It encompasses the adjacent Bijagós Islands and the island of Bolama. The country rises from a coastal plain broken up by numerous inlets through a transitional plateau to mountains on the border with Guinea. Thick forest and mangrove swamp cover the area nearest the Atlantic Ocean. Savannah covers the inland areas.
LANGUAGE: Official language is Portuguese. The majority of the population speak Guinean Creole. Balante and Fulani languages are also spoken.
RELIGION: 30% Muslim, 66% Animist and 4% Christian.
TIME: GMT.
ELECTRICITY: Limited electricity supply on 220 volts AC, 50Hz.
COMMUNICATIONS: Telephone: IDD is available.

Timatic

Health	
GALILEO/WORLDSPAN: **TI-DFT/BXO/HE**	
SABRE: **TIDFT/BXO/HE**	

Visa	
GALILEO/WORLDSPAN: **TI-DFT/BXO/VI**	
SABRE: **TIDFT/BXO/VI**	

For more information on Timatic codes refer to Contents.

Country code: 245. Outgoing international calls must go through the operator. It is difficult to find public telephones or to receive international calls. Telephone services are also expensive. **Telex:** Facilities are available at the main post office in Bissau. International telex code: BI. **Press:** There are no English-language papers. *Nô Pintcha* and *Voz da Guiné* are published daily.
BBC World Service and Voice of America frequencies: From time to time these change. See the section *How to Use this Book* for more information.
BBC:

MHz	17.79	15.40	15.07	9.410

Voice of America:

MHz	21.49	15.60	9.525	6.035

PASSPORT/VISA

Regulations and requirements may be subject to change at short notice, and you are advised to contact the appropriate diplomatic or consular authority before finalising travel arrangements. Details of these may be found at the head of this country's entry. Any numbers in the chart refer to the footnotes below.

	Passport Required?	Visa Required?	Return Ticket Required?
Full British	Yes	Yes	Yes
BVP	Not valid	-	-
Australian	Yes	Yes	Yes
Canadian	Yes	Yes	Yes
USA	Yes	Yes	Yes
Other EU (As of 31/12/94)	Yes	Yes	Yes
Japanese	Yes	Yes	Yes

PASSPORTS: Valid passport required by all.
British Visitors Passport: Not accepted.
VISAS: Required by all except nationals of Benin, Burkina Faso, Cape Verde, Côte d'Ivoire, Cuba, Gambia, Ghana, Guinea, Liberia, Mali, Mauritania, Niger, Nigeria, Senegal, Sierra Leone and Togo.
Visas can be extended in Bissau Central Police Station. Contact Embassy for details.
Application to: Consulate (or Consular section at Embassy). For addresses, see top of entry.
Application requirements: (a) 2 completed application forms. (b) 2 passport-size photos. (c) Passport.
Working days required: Applications should be made 1 day in advance; same day if applying in the UK.

MONEY

Currency: Guinea-Bissau Peso (GBP) = 100 centavos. Notes are in denominations of GBP5000, 1000, 500, 100 and 50. Coins are in denominations of GBP20, 5, 2.5 and 1, and 50 centavos.
Currency exchange: US currency in small denominations is the most useful for exchange into Guinea-Bissau Pesos. Inter-bank fund transfers are frequently difficult and time-consuming to accomplish.
Credit cards: Limited use of Access in the capital, but check with your credit card company for details of merchant acceptability and other services which may be available.
Travellers cheques: These are rarely accepted. They can sometimes be cashed at banks. There is a fixed rate of commission on all transactions.
Exchange rate indicators: The following figures are included as a guide to the movements of the Guinea-Bissau Peso against Sterling and the US Dollar:

Date:	Oct '92	Sep '93	Jan '94	Jan '95
£1.00=	7907.50	7652.50	7385.00	21215.1
$1.00=	4982.67	011.46	4991.55	13560.3

Currency restrictions: Import and export of local currency is prohibited. There are no restrictions on the import of foreign currency, export is limited to the amount declared on arrival.
Banking hours: 0730-1000 Monday to Friday.

DUTY FREE

The following goods can be imported into Guinea-Bissau without incurring customs duty:
2.5 litres of alcoholic beverages (non-Muslims only); a reasonable quantity of tobacco products and perfume in opened bottles.
Restricted items: Alcohol.

PUBLIC HOLIDAYS

Jan 1 '95 New Year's Day. **Jan 20** Death of Amílcar Cabral. **Mar 2** Korité (End of Ramadan). **May 1** Labour Day. **May 10** Tabaski (Feast of the Sacrifice). **Aug 3** Anniversary of the Killing of Pidjiguiti. **Sep 24** National

Day. **Nov 14** Anniversary of the Movement of Readjustment. **Dec 25** Christmas. **Jan 1 '96** New Year's Day. **Jan 20** Death of Amílcar Cabral. **Feb 22** Korité (End of Ramadan). **Apr 29** Tabaski (Feast of the Sacrifice). **Note:** Muslim festivals are timed according to local sightings of various phases of the Moon and the dates given above are approximations. During the lunar month of Ramadan that precedes Korité, Muslims fast during the day and feast at night and normal business patterns may be interrupted. Many restaurants are closed during the day and there may be restrictions on smoking and drinking. Some disruption may continue into Korité itself. Korité and Tabaski may last anything from two to ten days, depending on the region. For more information see the section *World of Islam* at the back of the book.

HEALTH

Regulations and requirements may be subject to change at short notice, and you are advised to contact your doctor well in advance of your intended date of departure. Any numbers in the chart refer to the footnotes below.

	Special Precautions?	Certificate Required?
Yellow Fever	Yes	1
Cholera	Yes	2
Typhoid & Polio	Yes	-
Malaria	3	-
Food & Drink	4	-

[1]: A yellow fever vaccination certificate is required from travellers over one year of age coming from infected areas and from the following countries: all mainland African countries lying wholly or in part between 20°N and 20°S (except Sudan, Cameroon, Malawi, Namibia, Botswana and Zimbabwe); and – in Latin America – Bolivia, Brazil, Colombia, Ecuador, French Guiana, Guyana, Panama, Peru, Suriname and Venezuela. Travellers arriving from non-endemic zones should note that a vaccination is strongly recommended for travel outside the urban areas, even if an outbreak of the disease has not been reported and they would normally not require a vaccination certificate to enter the country.
[2]: Following WHO guidelines issued in 1973, a cholera vaccination certificate is no longer a condition of entry to Guinea-Bissau. However, cholera is a serious risk in this country and precautions are essential. Up-to-date advice should be sought before deciding whether these precautions should include vaccination as medical opinion is divided over its effectiveness. See the *Health* section at the back of the book.
[3]: Malaria risk, predominantly in the malignant *falciparum* form, exists all year throughout the country. Resistance to chloroquine has been reported.
[4]: All water should be regarded as being potentially contaminated. Water used for drinking, brushing teeth or making ice should have first been boiled or otherwise sterilised. Only eat well-cooked meat and fish, preferably served hot. Pork, salad and mayonnaise may carry increased risk. Vegetables should be cooked and fruit peeled.
Rabies is present. For those at high risk, vaccination before arrival should be considered. If you are bitten abroad seek medical advice without delay. For more information consult the *Health* section at the back of the book.
Bilharzia (schistosomiasis) is present. Avoid swimming and paddling in fresh water. Swimming pools which are well-chlorinated and maintained are safe.
Meningitis, hepatitis, filariasis and *onchocerciasis* (river

blindness) can occur.
Health care: Health insurance is essential. Medical facilities in Guinea-Bissau are extremely limited and medicines are often unavailable. Doctors and hospitals often expect immediate cash payment for health services.

TRAVEL - International

AIR: Guinea-Bissau's national airline is *Transportes Aéreos da Guiné Bissau*. Other airlines that fly direct to Bissau include *TAP Air Portugal (TP)*, *Europe Aero Service (EAS)* and *Aeroflot (SU)*.
Approximate flight time: From *London* to Bissau is 10 hours 20 minutes (including stopover of 1 hour 30 minutes, often in Lisbon). There are daily flights from *Lisbon* to Bissau.
International airport: *Bissau (BXO)* (Bissalanca), 11km (7 miles) from the city (travel time – 30 minutes). Taxi service is available to the city.
SEA/RIVER: Ferries running between coastal and inland ports form an important part of the transport system, especially as roads are often impassable (see *Sea/River* in *Travel – Internal* below). The main port is Bissau. This and four inland ports are currently being expanded and upgraded. A new commercial river port is planned at N'Pungda.
ROAD: Travellers should check that overland entry is allowed before embarking (the usual route of entry is by plane from Conakry in the Guinea Republic); entry from Senegal is not recommended. New roads are planned to link Guinea-Bissau with several neighbouring states.

TRAVEL - Internal

AIR: There are 60 small airfields. The national airline provides internal flights, including the outlying islands.
SEA/RIVER: Most towns are accessible by ship. Riverboats can reach almost all areas; there are ferries from Bissau to Bolama (often irregular due to tides) and Bissau to Bafatá, calling at smaller towns en route. Coast-hopping ferries go from the north coast to Bissau.
ROAD: There are more than 3000km (1850 miles) of roads, one-fifth tarred and a similar proportion improved for all-weather use. Improvements are planned. There are local and long-distance **taxis** and **buses** (the latter offer limited services). **Documentation:** An International Driving Permit is recommended, although it is not legally required. A temporary driving licence is available from local authorities on presentation of a valid British driving licence.

ACCOMMODATION

HOTELS: Several new hotels include the 4-star Sheraton in north Bissau with 175 rooms and the 24 Septembre Hotel. There is also a brand new leisure hotel on the island of Maio that can be reached by ferry from Bissau, and another hotel is being built in the north on the beach of Varella. Guinea-Bissau also offers some small, inexpensive hotels. Accommodation should be booked in advance. Tariffs are liable to change at any time, therefore confirmation of booking is essential.
CAMPING: There are no designated campsites and camping is not recommended.

RESORTS & EXCURSIONS

Until recently, Guinea-Bissau was well off the tourist route, but efforts have been made to encourage visitors to this beautiful country.
The capital, **Bissau**, is a small and pleasant town of about 50,000 people. The *Museum of African Artefacts* is

fantastic.
Bolama, the original capital of Guinea-Bissau, is now a rather attractive ruin, and the island is worth seeing, with good beaches. **Bubaque** is another island of interest. All the coastal islands are unspoiled.

SOCIAL PROFILE

FOOD & DRINK: Guinea-Bissau's few small hotels offer cheap excellent food including *jollof rice*, chicken and fish dishes. Staples are cassava, yams and maize.
SHOPPING: Locally made artefacts and carvings can be found in the markets. There are also some modern shops in Bissau. **Shopping hours:** 0730-1200 and 1600-1900 Monday to Friday.
SPORT: Swimming: Seas are warm and offer good bathing and swimming. However, bathers should not venture out of their depth in some parts as currents can be strong. **Fishing:** Some of the rivers and the sea offer excellent fishing, although facilities have not been developed.
SOCIAL CONVENTIONS: Casual wear is widely accepted. Social customs should be respected, particularly in Muslim areas. Petty thievery and pickpocketing are increasingly common, particularly at the airport, in markets and at public gatherings.
Photography: Visitors should request permission from security personnel before photographing military or police installations. **Tipping:** 10% is an acceptable amount, although not encouraged.

BUSINESS PROFILE

ECONOMY: Rice is the staple food in this poor, largely subsistence economy. The main cash crops are groundnuts, cashews and palm kernels. Timber is the only significant industry. Cotton production is being developed with EU assistance; a sugar complex is planned and the fishing industry has been earmarked for major expansion. The possible exploitation of oil and bauxite deposits is being considered. In the short term, it seems little can be done to lighten the country's massive foreign debt. Guinea-Bissau will continue to rely on large quantities of foreign aid, of which it is among the highest per capita recipients in the world. France, Portugal, Italy and Thailand are Guinea-Bissau's largest trading partners. An attempt is now being made to revitalise the economy through the financing of infrastructure programmes.
BUSINESS: Businessmen wear safari suits (bush jackets without a tie). A knowledge of Portuguese is useful as only a few executives speak English. Visits during Ramadan should be avoided.
COMMERCIAL INFORMATION: For further information contact: Associação Comercial e Industrial e Agricola da Guiné-Bissau, Bissau.

CLIMATE

The climate is tropical, with a wet season from May to November. The dry season is from December to April, with hot winds from the interior. Humidity is high from July to September. Temperatures vary with altitude and distance from the coast.
Required clothing: Tropical lightweight cotton clothes and raincoat for the rainy season.

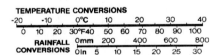

TEMPERATURE CONVERSIONS

-20	-10	0°C	10	20	30	40
0	10	20	30°F 40	50 60	70 80 90	100

RAINFALL 0mm 200 400 600 800
CONVERSIONS 0In 5 10 15 20 25 30

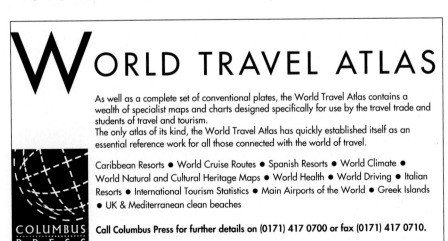
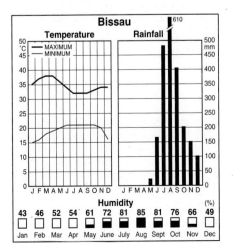

☐ *international airport*

Location: South America, northeast coast.

Tourism Association of Guyana
Hotel Tower, 74-75 Main Street, Georgetown, Guyana
Tel: (2) 72011/5. Fax: (2) 65691 *or* 56021.
Guyana Overland Tours
PO Box 10173, 48 Prince's and Russell Streets,
Charlestown, Georgetown, Guyana
Tel: (2) 69876.
High Commission for the Co-operative Republic of Guyana
3 Palace Court, Bayswater Road, London W2 4LP
Tel: (0171) 229 7684/8. Fax: (0171) 727 9809. Opening
hours: 0930-1730 Monday to Friday (except national and
UK holidays); 0930-1430 Monday to Friday (visas).
Caribbean Tourism
Vigilant House, 120 Wilton Road, London SW1V 1JZ
Tel: (0171) 233 8382. Fax: (0171) 873 8551. Opening
hours: 0930-1730 Monday to Friday.
British High Commisson
PO Box 10849, 44 Main Street, Georgetown, Guyana
Tel: (2) 65881/2/3/4. Fax: (2) 53555. Telex: 2221 (a/b
UKREP GY).
Embassy of the Co-operative Republic of Guyana
2490 Tracy Place, NW, Washington, DC 20008
Tel: (202) 265 6900/01. Telex: 64170.
Consulate General of the Co-operative Republic of Guyana
3rd Floor, 866 UN Plaza, New York, NY 10017
Tel: (212) 527 3215.
Embassy of the United States of America
PO Box 10507, 99-100 Young and Duke Streets,
Kingston, Georgetown, Guyana
Tel: (2) 54900 *or* 57963 (24-hour). Fax: (2) 58497.
Telex: 2213 (a/b AMEMSY GY).
High Commission for the Co-operative Republic of Guyana
Suite 309, Burnside Building, 151 Slater Street, Ottawa,
Ontario K1P 5H3
Tel: (613) 235 7249/7240. Fax: (613) 235 1447.
Consulate in: Toronto.
Canadian High Commission
PO Box 10880, High and Young Streets, Georgetown,
Guyana

	Health	
	GALILEO/WORLDSPAN: **TI-DFT/GEO/HE**	
	SABRE: **TIDFT/GEO/HE**	
	Visa	
	GALILEO/WORLDSPAN: **TI-DFT/GEO/VI**	
	SABRE: **TIDFT/GEO/VI**	

For more information on Timatic codes refer to Contents.

Timatic

Tel: (2) 72081/5 *or* 58337. Fax: (2) 58380. Telex: 2215
(a/b DOMCAN GY).

AREA: 214,969 sq km (83,000 sq miles).
POPULATION: 739,553 (1991 estimate).
POPULATION DENSITY: 3.4 per sq km.
CAPITAL: Georgetown. **Population:** 72,049 (1976).
GEOGRAPHY: Guyana lies in the northeast of South
America, bordered by Venezuela to the west, Suriname
to the southeast and Brazil to the south. It is bordered by
the Atlantic Ocean to the north and east. The word
'Guiana' (the original spelling) means 'land of many
waters' and the name was well chosen, for there are over
1600km (965 miles) of navigable rivers in the country.
The interior is either high savannah uplands (such as
those along the Venezuelan border, called the *Rupununi,*
and the *Kanaku Mountains* in the far southwest), or thick,
hilly jungle and forest, which occupy over 85% of the
country's area. The narrow coastal belt contains the vast
majority of the population, and produces the major cash
crop, sugar, and the major subsistence crop, rice. One of
the most spectacular sights to be seen in the interior is the
towering Kaieteur Falls along the Potaro River, five
times the height of Niagara. The country has 322km (206
miles) of coastline. Nearly 25% of the population lives in
or near Georgetown.
LANGUAGE: English is the official language but Hindi,
Urdu and Amerindian are also spoken.
RELIGION: 50% Christian, 35% Hindu, less than 10%
Muslim.
TIME: GMT - 4.
ELECTRICITY: 110 volts AC, 60Hz.
COMMUNICATIONS: Telephone: IDD is available to
main towns and cities. Country code: 592. Outgoing
international code: 001. **Fax:** Facilities are available at
the Guyana Telephone and Telegraph Company, the
Bank of Guyana Building in Georgetown and some
hotels. **Telex/telegram:** Available at the Guyana
Telephone and Telegraph Company and Bank of Guyana
Building. Certain hotels also have facilities. **Press:** The
daily state-owned newspaper is *The Guyana Chronicle.*
There is also *The Mirror* as well as the independent
Stabroek News, published every day except Monday.
**BBC World Service and Voice of America
frequencies:** From time to time these change. See the
section *How to Use this Book* for more information.
BBC:

MHz	17.84	15.22	7.325	5.975

Voice of America:

MHz	15.21	11.58	9.775	5.995

PASSPORT/VISA

Regulations and requirements may be subject to change at short notice, and you are advised to contact the appropriate diplomatic or consular authority before finalising travel arrangements. Details of these may be found at the head of this country's entry. Any numbers in the chart refer to the footnotes below.

	Passport Required?	Visa Required?	Return Ticket Required?
Full British	Yes	No	Yes
BVP	Not valid	-	-
Australian	Yes	No	Yes
Canadian	Yes	No	Yes
USA	Yes	No	Yes
Other EU (As of 31/12/94)	Yes	No	Yes
Japanese	Yes	No	Yes

PASSPORTS: Valid passport required by all.
British Visitors Passport: Not acceptable.
VISAS: Required by all except:
(a) nationals in the chart above for stays of up to 30 days;
(b) persons of Guyanese birth with foreign passports
provided their passports clearly indicate place of birth or
they have other satisfactory documentary evidence;
(c) nationals of the CARICOM countries, ie Antigua &
Barbuda, Bahamas, Barbados, Belize, Dominica,
Grenada, Jamaica, Montserrat, St Kitts & Nevis, St
Lucia, St Vincent & the Grenadines, Suriname and
Trinidad & Tobago, provided they hold onward or return
tickets and sufficient funds for duration of stay;
(d) nationals of Finland, North Korea, South Korea, New
Zealand, Norway and Sweden.
Types of visa: Single-entry, Multiple-entry; Transit.
Entry fees vary according to nationality of applicant,
since they are charged on a reciprocal basis.
Validity: Visas are valid for 3 months from date of issue.
Length of stay and extension is at the discretion of the
Immigration Office.
Application to: Consulate (or Consular section at
Embassy or High Commission). For addresses, see top of
entry.
Application requirements: (a) Application form. (b) 2
passport-size photos. (c) Evidence of sufficient funds to

cover length of stay. (d) Passport, valid for at least 6
months prior to travel. (e) Business letter or letter of
invitation.
Working days required: Applicants should contact
Embassy or High Commission at least 1 week in advance
of travel to Guyana, although it may only take 2 days to
process.
Temporary residence: Permission must be obtained
from Minister of Home Affairs, Guyana.

MONEY

Currency: Guyana Dollar (Guy$) = 100 cents. Notes are
in denominations of Guy$500, 100, 20, 10, 5 and 1.
Coins are in denominations of 50, 25, 10, 5 and 1 cents.
Due to the rate of inflation most transactions involve
notes only.
Currency exchange: Banks offer exchange facilities.
Bureaux de change offer free conversion of currencies.
Credit cards: American Express, Visa, Access/Master-
card and Diners Club enjoy limited acceptance (eg at the
Forte Crest and Tower hotels and some stores). Check
with your credit card company for details of merchant
acceptability and other services which may be available.
Travellers cheques: The exchanging of these can lead to
great complications, and for this reason they are not
recommended for those who may wish to change money
in a hurry.
Exchange rate indicators: The following figures are
included as a guide to the movements of the Guyana
Dollar against Sterling and the US Dollar:

Date:	Oct '92	Sep '93	Jan '94	Jan '95
£1.00=	198.46	192.85	186.10	222.02
$1.00=	125.06	126.29	125.79	141.91

Currency restrictions: The import or export of foreign
currency over the equivalent of US$10,000 must be
declared. The Guyana Dollar is not negotiable abroad.
Banking hours: 0800-1200 Monday to Thursday, 0800-
1200 and 1530-1700 Friday.

DUTY FREE

The following goods can be imported (by persons over 16
years of age) into Guyana without incurring customs duty:
*200 cigarettes or 50 cigars or 225g tobacco; spirits not
exceeding 570ml; wine not exceeding 570ml; a
reasonable amount of perfume.*

PUBLIC HOLIDAYS

Jan 1 '95 New Year's Day. **Feb 23** Mashramani
(Republic Day). **Mar 3** Eid al-Fitr (End of Ramadan).
Apr 14 Good Friday. **Apr 17** Easter Monday. **May 1**
Labour Day. **May 5** Indian Heritage Day. **May 10** Eid al-
Adha (Feast of the Sacrifice). **Jun 26** Caribbean Day.
Aug 7 Freedom Day. **Aug 9** Yum an-Nabi (Prophet's
Birthday). **Oct/Nov** Deepavali. **Dec 25-26** Christmas.
Jan 1 '96 New Year's Day. **Feb 22** Eid al-Fitr (End of
Ramadan). **Feb 23** Mashramani (Republic Day). **Apr 5**
Good Friday. **Apr 8** Easter Monday.
Note: (a) Muslim festivals are timed according to local
sightings of various phases of the Moon and the dates
given above are approximations. During the lunar month
of Ramadan that precedes Eid al-Fitr, Muslims fast
during the day and feast at night and normal business
patterns may be interrupted. Many restaurants are closed
during the day and there may be restrictions on smoking
and drinking. Some disruption may continue into Eid al-
Fitr itself. Eid al-Fitr and Eid al-Adha may last anything
from two to ten days, depending on the region. For more
information see the section *World of Islam* at the back of
the book. (b) Hindu festivals are declared according to
local astronomical observations and it is only possible to
forecast the month of their occurrence.

HEALTH

Regulations and requirements may be subject to change at short notice, and you are advised to contact your doctor well in advance of your intended date of departure. Any numbers in the chart refer to the footnotes below.

	Special Precautions?	Certificate Required?
Yellow Fever	Yes	1
Cholera	No	-
Typhoid & Polio	Yes	-
Malaria	2	-
Food & Drink	3	-

[1]: A yellow fever vaccination certificate is required
from travellers coming from infected areas and from the
following countries: Angola, Belize, Benin, Bolivia,
Brazil, Burkina Faso, Burundi, Cameroon, Central
African Republic, Chad, Colombia, Congo, Costa Rica,
Côte d'Ivoire, Ecuador, French Guiana, Gabon, Gambia,

Ghana, Guatemala, Guinea, Guinea-Bissau, Honduras, Kenya, Liberia, Mali, Nicaragua, Niger, Nigeria, Panama, Peru, Rwanda, São Tomé e Príncipe, Senegal, Sierra Leone, Somalia, Suriname, Togo, Uganda, Venezuela, Tanzania and Zaïre. Travellers arriving from non-endemic zones hould note that vaccination is strongly recommended for travel outside the urban areas, even if an outbreak of the disease has not been reported and they would normally not require a vaccination certificate to enter the country.

[2]: Malaria risk exists throughout the year in the northwest region and areas along the Pomeroon River. Chloroquine-resistant *falciparum* is reported. **Note:** Sleeping under a mosquito net is recommended, especially in Georgetown, as are insect repellants.

[3]: Mains water is normally chlorinated in main cities, and whilst relatively safe may cause mild abdominal upsets. Bottled water is available and is advised for the first few weeks of the stay. Milk is unpasteurised and should be boiled. Powdered or tinned milk is available and is advised, but make sure that it is reconstituted with pure water. Avoid dairy products which are likely to have been made from unboiled milk. Local meat, poultry, seafood, fruit and vegetables are generally considered safe to eat.

Health care: Health insurance is recommended. Hospital treatment in Georgetown is free, but doctors will charge for an appointment. Medical care and prescription drugs are limited and sanitary conditions are poor in many medical facilities. Travellers are advised to bring prescription medicines sufficient for their length of stay.

TRAVEL - International

AIR: Guyana's national airline is *Guyana Airways Corporation* (GY).

Approximate flight time: From London to Guyana is 10 hours (via Antigua or Port of Spain – no direct flights).

International airport: *Georgetown (GEO)* (Timehri) is 28km (17 miles) from the city (travel time – 35 minutes). Coach to the city is available. An irregular and crowded bus service to the city is also available. Taxis meet every plane. There are duty-free facilities at Georgetown Airport but the opening hours are erratic. The bank is open 0800-1400.

Departure tax: Guy$1500 is levied on all international departures; transit passengers and children under seven years of age are exempt.

SEA: The *Royal Netherlands Line* and the *Europe West Indies Line* sail every two weeks from Europe and New York or New Orleans. Numerous schooners sail between Guyana and the Caribbean islands, but schedules are erratic. For details contact local ports. Up to 12 passengers are carried by cargo vessels run by the *Royal Netherlands Steamship Company* which ply from London, Southampton and Liverpool to Georgetown. Following recent improvements in relations with Suriname, a ferry service across the Berbice River now links the two countries.

RAIL: There are no passenger rail services.

ROAD: International road links are currently limited to a short stretch across the Brazilian border as far as Lethem. The only reliable link from there to Georgetown is by air. There are plans to extend the road from Linden as far as the Brazilian border and to establish a car ferry service across the Courantyne River to Suriname. It is uncertain if there is a reliable route to Venezuela.

See below for information on **documentation**.

TRAVEL - Internal

AIR: The only reliable means of travelling into the interior is by air. *Guyana Airways Corporation* operates scheduled services between Georgetown and other main centres. Flights to the Kaieteur Falls are run once a week by *Guyana Airways Corporation*, but there can be problems securing a reservation, and the schedule leaves little time for sightseeing. Group charters are the most practical arrangement. The charter of Bretton Norman Islander airplanes is available from *Guyana Aviation Group*, Georgetown Airport. *Guyana Overland Tours* run a 6-day trip on the first Tuesday of every month for groups of ten or more, but require at least one month's notice.

SEA/RIVER: Guyana has 1000km (600 miles) of navigable inland waterways, the most notable being the Mazaruni, Essequibo, Potaro, Demerara and Berbice rivers. Government steamers communicate with the interior up the Essequibo and Berbice rivers, but services can be irregular due to flooding. The Government also runs a coast-hopping service from Georgetown to several northern ports. Smaller craft operate where there is sufficient demand throughout the country.

RAIL: Mining concerns operate railways, but there are no scheduled passenger services.

ROAD: Traffic drives on the left. All-weather roads are concentrated in the eastern coastal strip, although there is now a road inland as far as Linden and there are plans to extend it as far as the Brazilian border. The coastal road linking Georgetown, Rossignol, New Amsterdam and Crabwood Creek (Courantyne) is fairly good, but generally road conditions are poor. Because of Guyana's many rivers, most journeys of more than a few miles outside the capital will involve ferries and the attendant delays. **Bus:** Georgetown's Stabroek market is the terminus for buses operated by the *Guyana Transport Company*. These are regular but generally crowded. Areas served: Linden, Timehri (international airport) and Patentia (all hourly), Rossignol (11 a day) and Parika (15 a day). Services from Vreed en Hoop to Parika operate in conjunction with the passenger-ferry service across the Demerara to Georgetown; services from New Amsterdam to Crabwood Creek operate in conjunction with ferries across the Berbice River. Rival 'tapir' minibuses also operate on some of the routes. There are a number of up-country bus links, some run by the mining companies. Bush buses to Isano, Mahdia and Tumatumari are run weekly by the *Transport and Harbours Department,* connecting with the steamer at Bartica. **Taxi:** It is advisable to travel by taxi at night. Vehicles are plentiful. There is a standard fare for intercity travel; night fares are extra. For longer trips, fares should be agreed before departure. A 10% tip is usual in taxis. **Car hire:** Limited availability from local firms in Georgetown.

Documentation: Foreign licence or International Driving Permit is accepted.

Note: There are often serious petrol shortages in Guyana, which can make travelling long distances by car hazardous.

ACCOMMODATION

HOTELS: There are some good hotels in Georgetown, of which the Forte Crest Hotel conforms to international standards. Others of a reasonable standard include the Tower Hotel, the Park Hotel and the Woodbine Hotel. There are no high-season charges. Nature lovers can stay in cabins at the interior resorts and camps. As power cuts are common, it is advisable to take a torch.

GUEST-HOUSES: Ranch, by invitation only.

CAMPING/CARAVANNING: There are no camping facilities.

RESORTS & EXCURSIONS

Georgetown: The 19th-century wooden houses supported on stilts and charming green boulevards laid out along the lines of the old Dutch canals give the capital a unique character. Some of the more impressive wooden buildings dating from the colonial past include the city hall, *St George's Cathedral*, the *Law Courts* and the *State House*. The *Botanical Gardens,* which cover 120 acres, have a fine collection of palms, orchids and lotus lilies; nearby is the new *Cultural Centre* which contains what is probably the best theatre in the Caribbean. Also worth visiting is the *Natural History Museum*, which contains an up-to-date display of all aspects of Guyanese life and culture and the *Walter Roth Anthropological Museum*.

Bartica: At the junction of the Essequibo and Mazaruni rivers is the 'take-off' town for the gold and diamond fields, *Kaieteur Falls* and the rest of the interior. A visit to the Kaieteur Falls in the **Kaieteur National Park** is particularly recommended; situated on the Potaro River, it ranks with Niagara, Victoria and Iquazú in majesty and beauty.

SOCIAL PROFILE

FOOD & DRINK: The food in hotels and restaurants reflects the range of influences on Guyanese society. From India came curries, especially mutton, prawn or chicken, and Africa contributed dishes such as *foo-foo* (plantains made into cakes) and *metemgee* (edows, yams, cassava and plantains cooked in coconut milk and grated white of coconut). Portuguese garlic pork and Amerindian pepperpot are specialities. On the menus of most restaurants one may find chicken, pork and steak and, most of the time, shrimp. The best Chinese food in the country can be found in Georgetown. **Drink:** It is best to drink bottled water in Guyana. Local rum, known as Demerara rum, is well worth trying, while the local beer is *Banks*.

NIGHTLIFE: There are numerous nightclubs and bars in Georgetown.

SHOPPING: Stabroek Market in Georgetown has local straw hats, baskets, clay goblets and jewellery. Other shops sell Amerindian bows and arrows, hammocks, pottery and salad bowls. Government-run shops sell magnificent jewellery, utilising local gold, silver, precious and semi-precious stones. Prices are very low for the quality of goods. **Shopping hours:** 0800-1130 and 1300-1600 Monday to Friday; 0800-1130 Saturday.

Note: It is absolutely essential to ensure that receipts and correct documentation are retained, otherwise visitors may experience difficulty when clearing customs.

SPORT: Cricket and **hockey** are both popular, and the Bourda is one of the most attractive cricket grounds in the area. **Shooting:** Night hunting from boats is often a feature of coastal river fishing, and small local deer and capybara are often encountered. Licence for use of firearms and ammunition must be requested one month before arrival. **Riding:** Horses are available at Manari Ranch in the Rupununi Savannahs. **Fishing:** The rivers and the interior abound in game fish, the best known of which is the man-eating piranha (called locally *perai).* The most sought after by the sportsman is the *lucanni,* a fish similar to the large-mouth bass. Most of the interior rivers are difficult for the more casual visitor to get to, but those who book in advance can reach them by air. Some of the coastal rivers within reach of Georgetown are also good for fishing, although it is wise to stay overnight in the fishing grounds, as the best are 4-5 hours' drive from the city. Fishing licences are required.

SPECIAL EVENTS: Annual carnival celebrations coincide with Mashramani (Republic Day) in February.

SOCIAL CONVENTIONS: In Georgetown it is wise to exercise care when travelling after dark and to avoid obtrusive displays of wealth. Most crimes against people and property occur in the major business and shopping districts of Georgetown, in and around the two major indoor/outdoor markets of Stabroek and Bourda, and in the vicinity of the two major hotels most frequented by tourists and other foreigners (the Tower and Forte Crest). Hospitality is important to the Guyanese and it is quite common for the visitor to be invited to their homes. Informal wear is widely acceptable, but men should avoid wearing shorts. **Tipping:** 10% at hotels and restaurants.

BUSINESS PROFILE

ECONOMY: Apart from agriculture – which allows Guyana self-sufficiency in sugar, rice, vegetables, fruit, meat and poultry – bauxite mining is the main economic activity in Guyana. Bauxite, sugar cane and rice are Guyana's largest exports. Gold and diamonds are the other important mining industries. Forests cover 80% of the land area, but timber has yet to assume any great economic importance. The economy has recovered from near-total collapse in 1982 with the benefit of large amounts of foreign aid under bilateral arrangements and from multinational sources including the International Monetary Fund. The UK, the USA, Canada and Germany are Guyana's main export markets. Guyana's US$220-million annual import bill is shared between the USA (30%), the UK (13%), Japan (4.5%), Trinidad & Tobago, Indonesia and others. Guyana is a founder member of CARICOM, the Caribbean economic union.

BUSINESS: Appointments should be made and punctuality is appreciated. Calling cards are useful. The pace of business and general attitudes are very Caribbean-orientated. It is, however, wise to bear in mind that the country is very much part of South America, the ties with the Caribbean being more a hangover from British colonial days than a reflection of Guyanese popular consciousness. **Office hours:** 0800-1200 and 1300-1630 Monday to Friday.

COMMERCIAL INFORMATION: The following organisations can offer advice: Guyana Manufacturer's Association, 62 Main Street, Cummingsburg, Georgetown. Tel: (2) 74295. Fax: (2) 70670; *or*

Georgetown Chamber of Commerce and Industry, PO Box 10110, 156 Waterloo Street, Cummingsburg, Georgetown. Tel: (2) 63519; *or*

Ministry of Trade, Tourism and Industry, Urquhart Street, Georgetown. Tel: (2) 62505. Telex: 2288.

CLIMATE

Guyana's climate is warm and tropical throughout the year. The rainfall is generally high for most of the year, as is the humidity. November to January and April to July are the rainy seasons, while in coastal areas the climate is tempered by sea breezes.

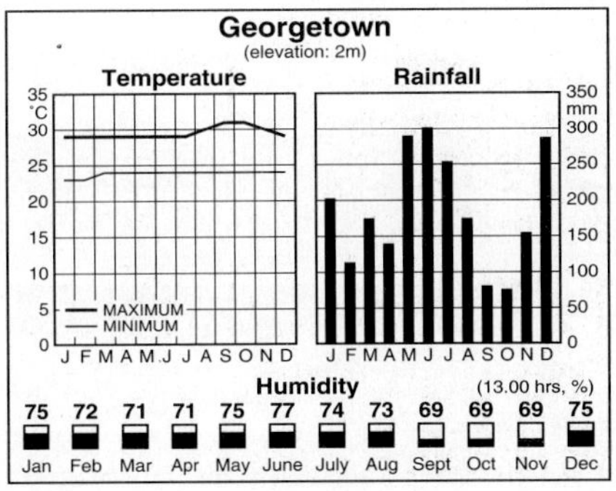
Georgetown
(elevation: 2m)
Temperature
Rainfall
35 °C 30 25 20 15 10 5 0
350 mm 300 250 200 150 100 50 0
MAXIMUM
MINIMUM
J F M A M J J A S O N D
J F M A M J J A S O N D
Humidity
(13.00 hrs, %)
75 72 71 71 75 77 74 73 69 69 69 75
Jan Feb Mar Apr May June July Aug Sept Oct Nov Dec

□ *international airport*

Location: Caribbean; island of Hispaniola.

Note: Some commercial airlines have resumed services to Haiti. Foreigners in Haiti are at risk from criminal attacks, particularly in urban areas, owing to their relative affluence. There are continued shortages of electrical power and fuel. Those who intend to visit should contact their consular representatives in Port-au-Prince for advice.
Source: FCO Travel Advice Unit – October 20, 1994.

Office National du Tourisme d'Haiti
avenue Marie-Jeanne, Port-au-Prince, Haiti
Tel: 221 729. Telex: 0206.
Embassy of the Republic of Haiti
BP 25, 160A avenue Louise, B-1050 Brussels, Belgium
Tel: (2) 649 7381. Fax: (2) 640 6080.
Caribbean Tourism
Vigilant House, 120 Wilton Road, London SW1V 1JZ
Tel: (0171) 233 8382. Fax: (0171) 873 8551. Opening hours: 0900-1730 Monday to Friday.
British Consulate
PO Box 1302, Hotel Montana, Port-au-Prince, Haiti
Tel: 73969. Fax: 74048. Telex: 2030259.
Embassy of the Republic of Haiti
2311 Massachusetts Avenue, NW, Washington, DC 20008
Tel: (202) 332 4090/1/2. Fax: (202) 745 7215. Telex: 440202.
Consulate General of Haiti
60 East 42nd Street, New York, NY 10017
Tel: (212) 697 9767.
Embassy of the United States of America
BP 1761, boulevard Harry Truman, Port-au-Prince, Haiti
Tel: 220 200. Fax: 231 641.
Embassy of the Republic of Haiti
Suite 212, Place de Ville, Tower B, 112 Kent Street, Ottawa, Ontario K1P 5P2
Tel: (613) 238 1628/9. Fax: (613) 238 2986.

Canadian Embassy
BP 826, Edifice Banque Nova Scotia, route de Delmas, Port-au-Prince, Haiti
Tel: 232 358. Fax: 238 720. Telex: 20069.

AREA: 27,750 sq km (10,714 sq miles).
POPULATION: 6,625,000 (1991 estimate).
POPULATION DENSITY: 238.7 per sq km.
CAPITAL: Port-au-Prince. **Population:** 738,342 (1984).
GEOGRAPHY: Haiti is situated in the Caribbean and comprises the forested mountainous western end of the island of Hispaniola, which it shares with the Dominican Republic. Its area includes the Ile de la Gonâve, in the Gulf of the same name; among other islands is La Tortue off the north peninsula. Haiti's coastline is dotted with magnificent beaches, between which stretches lush subtropical vegetation, even covering the slopes which lead down to the shore. Port-au-Prince is a magnificent natural harbour at the end of a deep horseshoe bay.
LANGUAGE: The official languages are French and Creole. English is widely spoken in tourist areas.
RELIGION: Roman Catholic with Protestant minorities. Voodooism (an African religion) is still found in Haiti, despite the largely Christian population. Considered by some to be 'black magic', voodooism is a folk religion, manifested by a series of complex ritual drawings, songs and dances.
TIME: GMT - 5 (GMT - 4 from first Sunday in April to Saturday before last Sunday in October).
ELECTRICITY: 110 volts AC, 60Hz.
COMMUNICATIONS: Telephone: IDD available. Country code: 509. There are no area codes. Outgoing international code: 00. The internal service is reasonable. **Telex:** International telex facilities are available at main hotels and at offices of TELECO. **Post:** Airmail to Europe takes up to a week. The main post office in Port-au-Prince, Cité de l'Exposition, is in place d'Italie. Post office hours: 0800-2000 Monday to Friday and 0830-1200 Saturday. Letters posted after 0900 will not be despatched until the following working day. **Press:** The three main dailies are *Le Matin*, *Le Nouvelliste* and *Panorama*.
BBC World Service and Voice of America frequencies: From time to time these change. See the section *How to Use this Book* for more information.
BBC:

| MHz | 17.84 | 15.22 | 9.915 | 7.325 |

Voice of America:

| MHz | 21.49 | 15.60 | 9.525 | 6.035 |

PASSPORT/VISA

Regulations and requirements may be subject to change at short notice, and you are advised to contact the appropriate diplomatic or consular authority before finalising travel arrangements. Details of these may be found at the head of this country's entry. Any numbers in the chart refer to the footnotes below.

	Passport Required?	Visa Required?	Return Ticket Required?
Full British	Yes	2	Yes
BVP	Not valid	-	-
Australian	Yes	Yes	Yes
Canadian	No/1	No	Yes
USA	No/1	No	Yes
Other EU (As of 31/12/94)	Yes	Yes	Yes
Japanese	Yes	Yes	Yes

PASSPORTS: [1] Valid passport required by all except nationals of Canada and the USA over 18 years of age holding proof of citizenship (birth certificate etc) and another official document with photograph and proof of nationality for a stay of up to 30 days. However, due to recent political developments between the USA and Haiti, the US Embassy is advising *all* nationals to be in possession of a passport on entering Haiti.
British Visitors Passport: Not accepted.
VISAS: Required by all except:
(a) [2] nationals of the UK holding passports that indicate right of abode in the UK (ie holders of British Commonwealth passports *may* require visas);
(b) nationals of Argentina, Austria, Israel, Liechtenstein, Monaco, Norway, South Korea, Sweden and Switzerland for a stay not exceeding 90 days;
(c) nationals of USA and Canada for a stay of up to 90 days;
(d) travellers in transit who do not leave the airport.
Types of visa: Tourist, Business and Transit.
Cost: BFr800.
Validity: 3 months. For a stay of 90 days, return or onward tickets are needed.
Application to: Consulate (or Consular section at Embassy). For addresses, see top of entry.
Application requirements: (a) 2 photos. (b) Valid passport. (c) Fee. (d) Letter of confirmation from

company for Business visa.
Temporary residence: Contact Embassy of the Republic of Haiti.
Note: A Government *Head Tax* of US$25 is levied on all non-residents who are leaving Haiti after a stay of more than 72 hours.

MONEY

Currency: Gourde (Gde) = 100 centimes. Notes are in denominations of Gde500, 250, 100, 50, 10, 5, 2 and 1. Coins are in denominations of 50, 20, 10 and 5 centimes. US currency also circulates (the Gourde is tied to the US Dollar).
Currency exchange: US Dollars are accepted and exchanged everywhere. Other foreign currencies are accepted for exchange only by some banks.
Credit cards: American Express is widely accepted; Diners Club has more limited use. Check with your credit card company for details of merchant acceptability and other services which may be available.
Travellers cheques: Accepted by most major shops and banks.
Exchange rate indicators: The following figures are included as a guide to the movements of the Gourde against Sterling and the US Dollar:

Date:	Oct '92	Sep '93	Jan '94	Jan '95
£1.00=	6.64	18.37	17.72	29.85
$1.00=	0.48	12.03	11.98	19.08

Currency restrictions: There are no restrictions on the import and export of foreign or local currency.
Banking hours: 0900-1300 Monday to Friday.

DUTY FREE

The following goods can be imported into Haiti without incurring customs duty:
200 cigarettes or 50 cigars or 250g of tobacco; 1 litre of spirits; small quantity of perfume or eau de toilette for personal use.
Note: In addition, Haitian nationals and foreign residents may bring in, for their personal use, new goods with a total value not exceeding US$200.
Prohibited goods: Coffee, matches, methylated spirits, pork, all meat products from Brazil and the Dominican Republic, drugs and firearms (except sporting rifles with prior permission).

PUBLIC HOLIDAYS

Jan 1 '95 Independence Day. **Jan 2** Heroes of Independence Day. **Feb 27** Shrove Monday. **Feb 28** Shrove Tuesday. **Apr 14** Good Friday; Pan-American Day/Bastilla's Day. **May 1** Labour Day. **May 18** Flag Day. **May 22** National Sovereignty. **Aug 15** Assumption. **Oct 24** United Nations Day. **Nov 2** All Souls' Day (half-day). **Nov 18** Army Day. **Dec 5** Discovery Day. **Dec 25** Christmas Day. **Jan 1 '96** New Year's Day. **Jan 2** Heroes of Independence Day. **Feb 20** Shrove Tuesday. **Apr 5** Good Friday. **Apr 14** Pan-American Day/Bastilla's Day.

HEALTH

Regulations and requirements may be subject to change at short notice, and you are advised to contact your doctor well in advance of your intended date of departure. Any numbers in the chart refer to the footnotes below.

	Special Precautions?	Certificate Required?
Yellow Fever	No	1
Cholera	No	No
Typhoid & Polio	Yes	-
Malaria	2	-
Food & Drink	3	-

[1]: A yellow fever vaccination certificate is required from travellers coming from infected areas.
[2]: Malaria risk, in the malignant *falciparum* form, exists throughout the year below 300m in suburban and rural areas. Malaria prophylaxis is highly recommended.
[3]: All water should be regarded as being potentially contaminated. Water used for drinking, brushing teeth or making ice should have first been boiled or otherwise sterilised. Milk is unpasteurised and should be boiled. Powdered or tinned milk is available and is advised, but make sure that it is reconstituted with pure water. Avoid dairy products which are likely to have been made from unboiled milk. Only eat well-cooked meat and fish, preferably served hot. Pork, salad and mayonnaise may carry increased risk. Vegetables should be cooked and

fruit peeled.
Rabies is present. For those at high risk, vaccination before arrival should be considered. If you are bitten abroad, seek medical advice without delay. For more information, consult the *Health* section at the back of the book.
Health care: Health insurance providing cover for repatriation in the event of serious illness is strongly recommended. Medical facilities are fairly good. The local herb tea is said to be good for stomach upsets.

TRAVEL - International

AIR: There are good connections with the USA, the West Indies and France.
Approximate flight times: From Port-au-Prince to *London* is 8 hours, to *Los Angeles* is 9 hours, to *New York* is 5 hours and to *Singapore* is 33 hours (with good connections).
International airport: *Port-au-Prince (PAP)* (Mais Gaté) is 13km (8 miles) east of the city (travel time – 25 minutes). There is a snack bar, duty-free shop, bank, bar and car hire facilities. Taxis are available to the city.
Departure tax: US$25; transit passengers and children under two years of age are exempt.
SEA: Cap-Haïtien and Port-au-Prince are both ports of call for a number of cruise lines: *Norwegian American, Royal Caribbean, Commodore Cruise/Cosmos* and *Holland America.*

TRAVEL - Internal

AIR: There are scheduled routes between Port-au-Prince and Cap-Haïtien; and Port-au-Prince and Santo Domingo. Reservations should be double checked as delays and cancellations are common. Planes may be chartered.
SEA: Sailing trips can be arranged from Port-au-Prince to beaches around the island, including glass-bottomed boat trips over Sand Cay Reef.
RAIL: There is no rail system.
ROAD: During the 1980s all-weather roads were constructed from Port-au-Prince to Cap-Haïtien and Jacmel. **Bus:** Services depart from Port-au-Prince to Cap-Haïtien, Jacmel, Jérémie, Hinche, Les Cayes and Port-de-Paix on an unscheduled basis. **Taxi:** Station-wagons *(camionettes)* run between Port-au-Prince and Pétionville, as well as some other towns. Tipping is unnecessary. **Car hire:** Available independently in Port-au-Prince and Pétionville, or through hotels and the airport. Petrol can be very scarce outside Port-au-Prince. All hired cars' registration numbers begin with 'L'. **Documentation:** Some foreign driving licences are acceptable for up to three months, after which a local permit is necessary. However, most will need an International Driving Permit.
URBAN: Bus: *Tap-taps,* which run within Port-au-Prince with a standard rate for any journey, are colourful but crowded. **Taxi:** Unmetered, with fixed route prices, otherwise fares agreed in advance. Taxi licence plates begin with the letter 'P'. Shared taxis *(publiques)* are the cheapest form of taxi service in the towns. Drivers can be hired for tours by the hour or the day with price negotiated.

ACCOMMODATION

Accommodation is limited in Haiti. Existing facilities include modest small inns, guest-houses and palatial-style hotels. The majority of accommodation is in Port-au-Prince and Pétionville, while the beach hotels are north of the capital on the road to St Marc or west towards Petit-Gonâve. Accommodation is also to be found in Cap-Haïtien, Jacmel, the Gonâve Bay area, Les Cayes and the Petit-Gonâve beach area. Swimming pools and air-conditioning are essential in central hotels where the heat can become severe. All resorts offer substantial reductions between April 16 and December 15. A 10% service charge and 5% room tax will be added to all hotel bills. For more information contact the Association Hôtelière et Touristique d'Haiti, c/o Hotel Montana, BP 2562, rue F Cardozo, route de Pétionville, Port-au-Prince. Tel: 571 920. Telex: 20493.
Note: It is vital to make reservations well in advance for the Carnival period (see *Special Events* in the *Social Profile* section below).

RESORTS & EXCURSIONS

The capital, **Port-au-Prince,** is a bustling city with a population of over half a million. Places to visit include the busy *Iron Market,* the two cathedrals, the *Museum of Haitian Art,* the *Statue of the Unknown Slave,* the *Gingerbread Houses* and the *Defly Mansion.* The hillside suburb of *Pétionville* offers a calmer respite and some of the city's best dining, gallery-hopping and nightlife.
Cap-Haïtien and the North Coast: On Christmas Eve 1492, Columbus ran aground on the north coast of Hispaniola near the present-day site of *Cap-Haïtien.* The wreck of the Santa Maria lies nearby. Today, communications in the region are more convenient, and Cap-Haïtien is only 40 minutes by plane from the capital. The town nestles at the foot of lush green mountains and is surrounded by several fine beaches. The *Citadelle* is not to be missed – a remarkable fortress in the mountains, 40km (25 miles) south of Cap-Haïtien, and the nearby ruins of *Sans Souci Palace.* A half-hour drive leads to the village of **Milot,** gateway to the Citadelle and site of the palace ruins. Versailles was the model for *Sans Souci,* and the ruins still suggest a link.
Jacmel and the South Coast: With the completion of a well-marked road over the mountains several years ago, the drive to Jacmel is now a pleasant two hours or less through breathtaking scenery. There are several beaches in this region. High in the mountains, south of the capital, is the town of **Kenscoff,** much favoured by Haitians as a summer resort.

SOCIAL PROFILE

FOOD & DRINK: The French cuisine is good and the Creole specialities combine French, tropical and African influences. Dishes include Guinea hen with sour orange sauce, *tassot de dinde* (dried turkey), *grillot* (fried island pork), *diri et djondjon* (rice and black mushrooms), *riz et pois* (rice and peas), *langouste flambé* (local lobster), *ti malice* (sauce of onions and herbs), *piment oiseau* (hot sauce) and *grillot et banane pese* (pork chops and island bananas). Sweets include sweet potato pudding, mango pie, fresh coconut ice cream, cashew nuts and island fruits. **Drink:** French wine is available in the better restaurants. The island drink is rum and the best is probably 'Barbancourt', made by a branch of Haiti's oldest family of rum and brandy distillers.
NIGHTLIFE: There is plenty of choice ranging from casinos to African drum music and modern Western music and dance. There is something happening in at least one major hotel every evening with the main attraction being folkloric groups and voodoo performances. On Saturday nights *bamboche,* a peasant-style dance, can be seen in one of the open-air dance halls. Hotels can give further up-to-date information on local nightlife.
SHOPPING: Bargaining at the Iron Market is recommended where good and bad quality local items can be bought, including carvings, printed fabrics, leatherwork, paintings (particularly in the naïf style, for which Haiti is famous), straw hats, seed necklaces and jewellery, cigars and foodstuffs. Port-au-Prince has a good selection of shops and boutiques selling a wide range of local and imported items. Bargaining is an accepted practice. **Shopping hours:** 0800-1200 and 1300-1600 Monday to Friday, 0800-1200 Saturday.
SPORT: Watersports: Kyona and Ibo beaches (Ibo is on Cacique Isle) are best for **swimming, snorkelling, spearfishing, sailing, boomba racing** in native dugout canoes and **water-skiing. Fishing:** La Gonâve is a popular location for fishermen. **Hunting:** Best season is from October to April, especially for duck shooting, when there are 63 varieties gathered on Haiti's lakes and *étangs* (ponds). Permission to bring firearms into Haiti is necessary and can be obtained from the Chief of Army, Grand Quartier General, Port-au-Prince. **Golf:** There is a 9-hole course at the Pétionville Club. **Tennis:** Courts can be found at Pétionville Club, El Rancho, Ibo Beach, Ibo Lake, Kaloa Beach, Royal Haitian hotels, Habitation Le Clerc and at the Club Med in Montraus. **Spectator sports: Football** is the favourite national sport, followed by **basketball. Cockfighting** can be seen every Saturday and Sunday in the circular Gaguere. There are also many informal cockfights throughout the island.
SPECIAL EVENTS: The principal annual festivals are the *Carnival,* held throughout Haiti three days before Ash Wednesday; the *Ra Ra,* held in Leogane from Ash Wednesday to Easter; and the *Pan-American Discovery Day* celebrations held on December 5 to celebrate Columbus' landfall on the north coast. For a complete list of carnivals and festivals held during 1995/96, contact the Office National du Tourisme d'Haiti.
SOCIAL CONVENTIONS: Informal wear is acceptable, although scanty beachwear should be confined to the beach or poolside. Only the most elegant dining-rooms encourage guests to dress for dinner. **Tipping:** 10% service charge is added to hotel and restaurant bills. Taxi drivers do not expect tips.

BUSINESS PROFILE

ECONOMY: Haiti's average income is the lowest in the Western hemisphere by a considerable margin (US$360 per annum, 1987 figures) and exacerbated by vast disparities between the incomes of rich and poor. The World Bank estimates that 85% of the people live below the absolute poverty line. Two-thirds of the employed population work in agriculture, mainly in the coffee plantations which generate 25% of Haiti's export earnings. Sugar cane, sweet potatoes, cocoa and sisal are also grown for export. Coffee earnings suffered from droughts during the 1980s and the collapse in the world price. Market factors also affected receipts from bauxite mining, another key economic sector which at one stage ground to a complete halt. Tourism, once promising, has all but vanished. Haiti relies for most of its finance on overseas aid, particularly from the USA, although the Americans have occasionally proved reluctant to give money which simply disappears with monotonous regularity: the fall of the sickeningly corrupt Duvalier Dynasty improved the situation somewhat. This trend was interrupted with the ousting of President Aristide and the imposition of a trade embargo on the military dictatorship of General Cedras. It is hoped that with the re-instatement of Aristide after the 1994 intervention of the American military and the subsequent lifting of the trade embargo, there will be an increase in economic growth. Industry cannot develop to any great extent until some semblance of an infrastructure has been built. The bulk of Haiti's trade takes place with the USA.
BUSINESS: It is usual to wear a suit for initial or formal calls. The British Trade Correspondent can put visitors in touch with a reliable English-French translator if required. Business visitors are generally entertained to lunch or dinner by their agents or important customers and should return invitations either at their hotel or a restaurant. Best time to visit is November to March. **Office hours:** 0700-1600 Monday to Friday.
COMMERCIAL INFORMATION: The following organisation can offer advice: Chambre de Commerce et d'Industrie de Haiti, Boîte Postale 982, Port-au-Prince. Tel: 222 475. Fax: 220 281.

CLIMATE

Tropical, with intermittent rain throughout the year. Much cooler temperatures exist in hill resorts and there is a high coastal humidity.
Required clothing: Tropical lightweights with rainwear and warm clothing for hill regions.

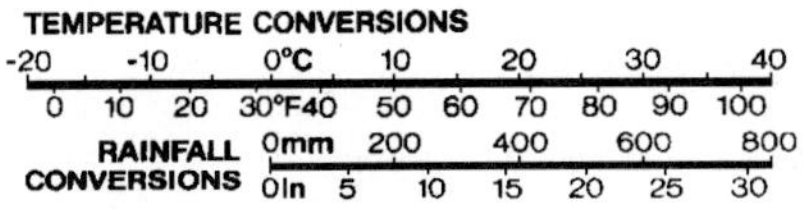
TEMPERATURE CONVERSIONS
-20 -10 0°C 10 20 30 40
0 10 20 30°F40 50 60 70 80 90 100
RAINFALL 0mm 200 400 600 800
CONVERSIONS 0In 5 10 15 20 25 30

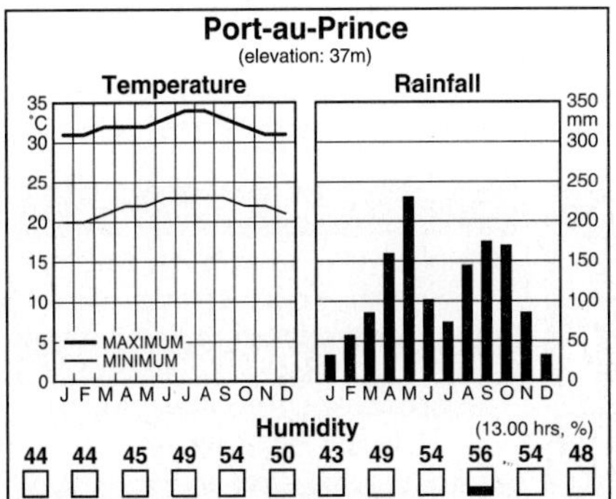
Port-au-Prince
(elevation: 37m)
Temperature
Rainfall
MAXIMUM
MINIMUM
Humidity
(13.00 hrs, %)
44 44 45 49 54 50 43 49 54 56 54 48
Jan Feb Mar Apr May June July Aug Sept Oct Nov Dec

Honduras

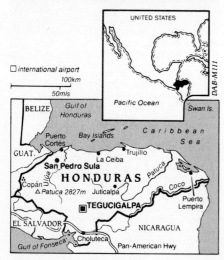

□ *international airport*
100km
50mls

UNITED STATES

Pacific Ocean

BELIZE
Gulf of Honduras
Swan Is.
GUAT.
Puerto Cortés
Bay Islands
Caribbean Sea
La Ceiba
Trujillo
San Pedro Sula
Copán
HONDURAS
Patuca
△ Patuca 2827m
Juticalpa
Coco
Puerto Lempira
TEGUCIGALPA
EL SALVADOR
NICARAGUA
Choluteca
Gulf of Fonseca
Pan-American Hwy

Location: Central America.

Instituto Hondureño De Turismo
Apartado Postal 3261, Centro Guanacaste, Barrio
Guanacaste, Tegucigalpa, Honduras, Ca
Tel: 383 975. Fax: 382 102.
Embassy of The Republic of Honduras *and* **Consulate
General**
115 Gloucester Place, London W1H 3PJ
Tel: (0171) 486 4880. Fax: (0171) 486 4880 (outside
office hours). Opening hours: 1000-1600 Monday to
Friday.
British Embassy
Apartado Postal 290, Edificio Palmira, 3° Piso, Colonia
Palmira, Tegucigalpa, Honduras, Ca
Tel: 325 429 *or* 320 612 *or* 320 618. Fax: 325 480.
British Consulate
Apartado Postal 298, Terminales de Puerto Cortés, San
Pedro Sula, Honduras, Ca
Tel: 542 600. Telex: 5513.
Embassy of The Republic of Honduras
3007 Tilden Street, NW, Washington, DC 20008
Tel: (202) 966 7702 *or* 966 2604 *or* 966 5008 *or* 966
4596. Fax: (202) 966 9751.
Embassy of The United States of America
Avenido La Paz, Postal 3453, Tegucigalpa, Honduras, Ca
Tel: 369 320 Fax: 385 114.
Embassy of The Republic of Honduras
Suite 300-A, 151 Slater Street, Ottawa, Ontario K1P 5H3
Tel: (613) 233 8900. Fax: (613) 232 0193.
Consulates in: Montréal, Québec, Toronto and
Vancouver.
Canadian Consulate
Apartado Postal 3552, Edificio Comercial Los Castonos,
60 Piso, Boulevard Morazan, Tegucigalpa, Honduras, Ca
Tel: 314 545 *or* 314 551. Fax: 315 793. Telex: 1683 (A/B
DOMCAN HO).

AREA: 111,888 sq km (43,277 sq miles).
POPULATION: 4,915,900 (1991 estimate).
POPULATION DENSITY: 43.9 per sq km.
CAPITAL: Tegucigalpa, DC. **Population:** 670,100
(1991 estimate).
GEOGRAPHY: Honduras shares borders in the
southeast with Nicaragua, in the west with Guatemala,
and in the southwest with El Salvador. To the north lies

the Caribbean and to the south the Pacific Ocean. The
interior of the country comprises a central mountain
system running from east to west, cut by rivers flowing
into both the Caribbean and Pacific. The lowlands in the
south form a plain along the Pacific coast. The Gulf of
Fonseca in the southwest contains many islands which
have volcanic peaks. The large fertile valleys of the
northern Caribbean lowlands are cultivated with banana
plantations. However, large areas of land in Honduras are
unsuitable for cultivation, and communications tend to be
difficult. The majority of the population lives in the
western half of the country, while the second largest
concentration of people is in the Cortés area which
extends northwards from Lake Yojoa towards the
Caribbean.
LANGUAGE: Official language is Spanish. English is
widely spoken by the West Indian settlers in the north
and on the Bay Islands off the Caribbean coast.
RELIGION: Roman Catholic majority; Evangelist and
Mormon.
TIME: GMT - 6.
ELECTRICITY: 110/220 volts AC, 60Hz.
COMMUNICATIONS: Telephone: Services between
Honduras and Western Europe are available. IDD is
available. Country code: 504. Outgoing international
code: 00. **Fax:** Empresa Hondureña de
Telecomunicaciones (*HONDUTEL*) offer a service.
Telex/telegram: Ordinary and letter telegrams
(minimum 22 words) may be sent. A telex service is
operated by *HONDUTEL* and the Tropical Radio
Company. **Post:** Airmail to Western Europe takes
between four and seven days. Post office hours: 0800-
1200 and 1400-1800 Monday to Saturday. **Press:** Daily
newspapers are in Spanish, and include *El Heraldo, La
Prensa, La Tribuna* and *El Tiempo*. The weekly
Honduras This Week is published in English.
**BBC World Service and Voice of America
frequencies:** From time to time these change. See the
section *How to Use this Book* for more information.
BBC:

MHz	17.84	15.22	9.590	5.975

Voice of America:

MHz	15.21	11.74	9.815	6.030

PASSPORT/VISA

*Regulations and requirements may be subject to change at short notice, and you
are advised to contact the appropriate diplomatic or consular authority before
finalising travel arrangements. Details of these may be found at the head of this
country's entry. Any numbers in the chart refer to the footnotes below.*

	Passport Required?	Visa Required?	Return Ticket Required?
Full British	Yes	No/1	Yes
BVP	Not valid	-	-
Australian	Yes	No/1	Yes
Canadian	Yes	No/1	Yes
USA	Yes	No/1	Yes
Other EU (As of 31/12/94)	Yes	No/1	Yes
Japanese	Yes	No/1	Yes

PASSPORTS: Valid passport required by all.
British Visitors Passport: Not accepted.
VISAS: Required by all except:
(a) nationals referred to in the chart above;
(b) nationals of Argentina, Austria, Chile, Curaçao, Costa
Rica, El Salvador, Finland, Guatemala, Iceland,
Liechtenstein, Malta, Monaco, New Zealand, Norway,
Panama, San Marino, Sweden, Switzerland, Uruguay and
Vatican City;
(c) those in transit continuing their journey within 48
hours.
Note [1]: If travelling on official government business, a
courtesy visa must be held which is supplied by the
Consular section of the Embassy free of charge.
Types of visa: Business and Tourist visas; cost – £10.
Validity: Up to 1 month.
Application to: Consulate (or Consular section at
Embassy). For addresses, see top of entry.
Application requirements: (a) Valid passport. (b) 1
passport-size photo. (c) Completed application form. (d)
Business letters where applicable.
Exit permit: Required by all visitors staying longer than
90 days.

MONEY

Currency: Lempira (L) = 100 centavos. Notes are in
denominations of L100, 50, 20, 10, 5, 2 and 1. Coins are
in denominations of 50, 20, 10, 5, 2 and 1 centavos. A
real is one-eighth of a Lempira, and is used colloquially,
though there is no such coin.

Currency exchange: Sterling cannot normally be
exchanged, even in banks; visitors should therefore take
US Dollar travellers cheques.
Credit cards: Access/Mastercard, American Express,
Diners Club and Visa are accepted. Check with your
credit card company for details of merchant acceptability
and other services which may be available.
Travellers cheques: Normally accepted by Banco De
Ahorro Hondureño. All other banks will only cash
travellers cheques which are accredited to them (but not
for US currency).
Exchange rate indicators: The following figures are
included as a guide to the movements of the Lempira
against Sterling and the US Dollar:

Date:	Oct '92	Sep '93	Jan '94	Jan '95
£1.00=	9.36	10.67	10.86	14.56
$1.00=	5.89	6.98	7.36	9.30

Note: The exchange rate, which was pegged to the US
Dollar, has been allowed to float since 1990.
Currency restrictions: No restrictions on import, but
US Dollars must be declared. No restrictions on export of
foreign currency except US Dollars up to the amount
declared.
Banking hours: 0900-1500 Monday to Friday.

DUTY FREE

The following goods may be imported into Honduras
without incurring customs duty:
*200 cigarettes or 100 cigars or 1lb of tobacco; 2 bottles
of alcoholic beverage; a reasonable amount of perfume
for personal use; gifts up to a total value of US$50.*

PUBLIC HOLIDAYS

Jan 1 '95 New Year's Day. **Apr 13** Maundy Thursday.
Apr 14 Good Friday; Pan-American Day. **May 1** Labour
Day. **Sep 15** Independence Day. **Oct 3** Birth of General
Morazán. **Oct 12** Discovery of America Day. **Oct 21**
Armed Forces Day. **Dec 25** Christmas Day. **Dec 31** New
Year's Eve. **Jan 1 '96** New Year's Day. **Apr 4** Maundy
Thursday. **Apr 5** Good Friday. **Apr 14** Pan-American Day.

HEALTH

*Regulations and requirements may be subject to change at short notice, and
you are advised to contact your doctor well in advance of your intended date of
departure. Any numbers in the chart refer to the footnotes below.*

	Special Precautions?	Certificate Required?
Yellow Fever	Yes	1
Cholera	Yes	-
Typhoid & Polio	Yes	-
Malaria	2	-
Food & Drink	3	

[1]: A yellow fever vaccination certificate is required
from all travellers arriving from infected areas.
[2]: Malaria risk, in the benign *vivax* form, exists
throughout the year in Departments of Atlántida,
Choluteca, Colón, Cortés, Gracias a Dios, Olancho, Islas
de la Bahía, Valle and Yoro; especially in rural areas.
[3]: All water should be regarded as being potentially
contaminated. Water used for drinking, brushing teeth or
making ice should first be boiled or otherwise sterilised.
Milk is unpasteurised in rural areas and should be boiled.
Powdered or tinned milk is available and is advised, but
make sure that it is reconstituted with pure water. Avoid
dairy products which are likely to have been made from
unboiled milk. Only eat well-cooked meat and fish,
preferably served hot. Pork, salad and mayonnaise may
carry increased risk. Vegetables should be cooked and
fruit peeled.
Rabies is present. For those at high risk, vaccination
before arrival should be considered. If you are bitten
abroad, seek medical advice without delay. For more
information, consult the *Health* section at the back of the
book.
Health care: Health insurance is recommended. There
are hospitals in Tegucigalpa and all the large towns.
Mosquito nets are recommended for coastal areas.

TRAVEL - International

AIR: The national airline of Honduras is *SAHSA*
(*Servicios Aéreos de Honduras*). A sales tax of 10% is
payable on international bookings for tickets issued in
Honduras.
Approximate flight times: From *London* to Honduras is
12 hours 30 minutes. (There are no direct flights from

London; connections are generally via Miami or Houston.)
From *New York* to Honduras is 8 hours.
International airport: *Tegucigalpa (TGU)* (Toncontin), 7km (4 miles) southeast of the city. Airport facilities include bar, restaurant, duty-free shop, bank, post office, vaccination centre and car hire.
There are also local airports at *San Pedro Sula (SAP)* (Dr Ramón Villeda Morales), *Islas de la Bahía (ROA)*, at *La Ceiba (LCE)* (Goloson) and at *Roatan, Islas de la Bahia (ROA)* (Dr Juan Manuel Galvez).
Departure tax: L95, or its equivalent in US Dollars, is levied on all passengers over 12 years.
SEA: The principal ports on the Atlantic and Caribbean coastline are Puerto Cortés, Tela, La Ceiba and Trujillo. The principal ports on the Pacific coastline are Amapala and El Henecan. Sailings to Puerto Cortés from Europe are frequent. Ships operated by *Harrison Line, Carol Line, Cie Generale Transatlantique, Hapag-Lloyd, The Royal Netherlands Steamship Company* and vessels owned or chartered by the *United Fruit Company* and *Standard Fruit Company* sometimes have limited passenger accommodation.
RAIL: There are no rail services between Honduras and neighbouring countries.
ROAD: Road routes run from El Salvador and Nicaragua via the Pan-American Highway, and from Guatemala on the Western Highway. Visas must be obtained before the journey is undertaken. Border crossings can be fraught with delay. **Bus:** The *Ticabus* company runs international services to all Central American capitals, but these comfortable coaches are often booked days in advance.

TRAVEL - Internal

AIR: Local airlines (*SAHSA, Aéreoservicios* and *Islena Airline*) operate daily services which link Tegucigalpa and other principal towns. *Islena Airline* runs services to Utila, the cheapest Bay Island (off the Caribbean coast). Apart from Tegucigalpa, the main airports are *Dr Ramón Villeda Morales Airport,* 17km (11 miles) from the centre of San Pedro Sula, and the airport at La Ceiba. Over 30 smaller airfields handle light aircraft and commercial aviation. There is a hospitals and airport tax of 2.5% on domestic journeys for tickets issued in Honduras.

SEA: Ferries operate between ports on the Atlantic, Pacific and Caribbean coastlines. For details contact local port authorities. There are sailings from La Ceiba and Puerto Cortés to the Bay Islands several times a week. Arrangements must be made with local boat owners.
RAIL: There are only three railways, confined to the northern coastal region and mainly used for transport between banana plantations.
ROAD: There is a total of 11,790km (7369 miles) of roads of which 8364km (5228 miles) are all-weather, and 2383km (1489 miles) are paved. However, internal air transport is much more convenient for business visitors. An all-weather road exists from Tegucigalpa to San Pedro Sula, Puerto Cortés, La Ceiba and towns along the Caribbean coast, as well as to the towns around the Gulf of Fonseca in the south. **Bus:** Local lines run regular services to most large towns, but the services are well used and booking in advance is essential. On the whole the services are very cheap. **Taxi:** Not metered, and run on a flat rate within cities. For other journeys, fares should be agreed before commencing journey. **Car hire:** Self-drive cars are available at the airport.
Documentation: Both international or foreign driving licences are accepted.
JOURNEY TIMES: The following chart gives approximate journey times (in hours and minutes) from Tegucigalpa to other major cities/towns in Honduras.

	Air	Road
Comayagua	-	1.00
Siguatepeque	-	2.30
San Pedro S.	0.25	3.30
Choluteca	-	2.30
La Ceiba	0.35	5.00
Bay Islands	0.40	*7.00
Sta Rosa de Copán	6.00	-
Puerto Cortés	-	4.00

Note [*]: Includes sea crossing of 2 hours.

ACCOMMODATION

HOTELS: Reasonable hotels are available in both Tegucigalpa and San Pedro Sula (where the rates are lower, but standards equivalent to those in the capital are maintained). Elsewhere both rates and standards of comfort are somewhat lower. The Instituto Hondureño de Turismo (address at beginning of entry) can supply lists of hotels with accommodation details. For further

information, contact the Honduran Hotel Association, Edificio Midence Soto, 12, Piso No 1214, Tegucigalpa. Tel: 370 982. **Grading:** Hotels are split into three categories (upper, middle and lower) according to standard.

RESORTS & EXCURSIONS

Tegucigalpa, the capital, was originally founded as a mining camp in 1524. Unlike so many of Central America's cities, Tegucigalpa has never been subjected to the disasters of earthquake or fire and so retains many traditional features. Visitors to the capital should plan to visit the city's impressive parks, particularly *Concordia* where models of Copan's Mayan architecture are displayed, and the *United Nations Park* for a spectacular view of the city. Also recommended is a visit to neighbouring **Comayagua,** former capital of Honduras and now a colonial masterpiece of cobbled streets, tiny plazas and whitewashed homes.
The Caribbean Coast: Two coastal towns are important to tourists and commercial visitors: La Ceiba and Trujillo. **La Ceiba,** which lies at the foot of the towering 1500m (5000ft) **Pico Bonito,** still a major banana port, now looks to tourism as a future major industry. There are good hotels and beaches, and a new international airport, one of the city's major assets.
Trujillo was once a thriving port and the old capital of colonial Honduras. Trujillo today offers many old Spanish buildings, a fascinating pirate history and superb tropical beaches. New resorts and subdivisions are now opening in the Trujillo area.
Bay Islands: 50km (30 miles) off the Caribbean coast of Honduras lies the exotic archipelago of the Bay Islands. Consisting of three major islands (Roatan, Guanaja and Utila) and several smaller islands, the Bay Islands have a history that spans the ancient Mayan civilisation, early Spanish exploration, colonial buccaneers and the British Empire. **Roatan** and **Guanaja** are hilly, tropical islands, protected by a great coral reef which provides fine skindiving. **Utila** offers wide expanses of sandy beach and is ringed by tiny cays surrounded by palm trees.
San Pedro Sula is a fast-growing banana, sugar manufacturing and distribution centre for the entire north coast, Today San Pedro Sula boasts a new airport, first-class hotels and several excellent restaurants.

WORLD TRAVEL ATLAS

As well as a complete set of conventional plates, the World Travel Atlas contains a wealth of specialist maps and charts designed specifically for use by the travel trade and students of travel and tourism.
The only atlas of its kind, the World Travel Atlas has quickly established itself as an essential reference work for all those connected with the world of travel.

Caribbean Resorts ● World Cruise Routes ● Spanish Resorts ● World Climate ● World Natural and Cultural Heritage Maps ● World Driving ● Italian Resorts ● International Tourism Statistics ● Main Airports of the World ● Greek Islands ● UK & Mediterranean clean beaches

COLUMBUS PRESS

Call Columbus Press for further details on (0171) 417 0700 or fax (0171) 417 0710.

The ancient city of **Copán** is 171km (106 miles) from San Pedro Sula. The *Copán Ruins Archaeological Park* in western Honduras is the best remaining testament to the culture of the Mayan Indians. Among the best of the ruins are the magnificent *Acropolis* composed of courts and temples, the *Great Plaza*, a huge amphitheatre, and the *Court of the Hieroglyphic Stairway*. Near the *Great Acropolis* recent archaeological work has brought to light invaluable excavations.

SOCIAL PROFILE

FOOD & DRINK: There is a wide variety of restaurants and bars in Tegucigalpa and the main cities. Typical dishes include *curiles* (seafood), *tortillas, frijoles, enchiladas, tamales, de elote* (corn tamales), *nacatamales, tapado, yuca con chicharron* and *mondongo.* Typical tropical fruits include mangoes, papayas, pineapples, avocados and bananas.
NIGHTLIFE: There are cinemas and some discotheques in the main cities.
SHOPPING: Local craftsmanship is excellent and inexpensive. Typical items include woodcarvings, cigars, leather goods, straw hats and bags, seed necklaces and baskets. **Shopping hours:** 0830-1130 and 1330-1730 Monday to Saturday.
SPORT: Fishing: There is good fishing on both coasts and Lake Yojoa offers some of the best bass fishing in the world. **Scuba/snorkelling:** Excellent diving in the clear waters of the Bay Islands, teeming with coral and tropical fish. Some hotels include rental of equipment in price. **Golf:** An increasingly popular sport, with courses available in most major populated areas. **Swimming:** Safe swimming can be done on both seaboards where beautiful sandy beaches are found. **Spectator sports: Football** is the most popular national sport followed closely by **baseball.** Others include **basketball, boxing** and **bowling.**
SPECIAL EVENTS: The following special events are celebrated in Honduras during 1995/96. For further information, contact the Embassy.
Mar/Apr '95 *Holy Week.* **Apr** *Pine Festival.* **May (3rd Saturday)** *Great National Carnival.* **Jun 29** *St Peter.* **Aug (last Saturday)** *Carnival of Maize.* **Dec 8** *Our Lady of Conception.* **Dec 12** *Our Lady of Guadaloupe.* **Jan 15 '96** *Our Lord of Esquipulas.* **Feb 3** *Our Lady of Suyapa.* **Feb (3rd Saturday)** *National Coffee Festival.*
SOCIAL CONVENTIONS: There are strong Spanish influences, but the majority of the population are mestizo, mainly leading an agricultural way of life with a low standard of living. Many rural communities can still be found living a relatively unchanged, traditional lifestyle. Normal social courtesies should be observed. It is customary for a guest at dinner or someone's home to send flowers to the hostess, either before or afterwards. Conservative casual wear is widely acceptable with dress tending to be less conservative in coastal areas. Beachwear and shorts should not be worn away from the beach or poolside. Men are required to wear dinner jackets for formal social occasions. Hotels, restaurants and shops include a 7% sales tax on all purchases.
Tipping: Service is included in most restaurant bills. In hotels, cafeterias and restaurants 10-15% of the bill is customary where service is not included. Porters and cab drivers should be tipped when helping with the luggage (L0.50 to L1).

BUSINESS PROFILE

ECONOMY: Honduras relies on agriculture and timber. The main agricultural products are bananas, beans,

coffee, cotton, maize, rice, sorghum and sugar; there is some dairy and beef farming. Apart from wood and wood products, light industries produce a variety of consumer goods. Both sectors have experienced difficulties during the 1980s, with export earnings especially badly hit by low world prices and slack demand within the Central American Common Market of which Honduras is a member. The economy is propped up to a large degree by various forms of US-sponsored aid – both direct and multilateral (through the IMF, Inter-American Development Bank and others) – as the country became increasingly militarised under US prompting. Mining of zinc, lead, copper, gold and silver are growing, but as yet contribute only a small proportion of gross domestic product. The USA is responsible for slightly over half of all Honduran trade.
BUSINESS: It is customary to address a professional person by his or her title, particularly on first meeting or during early acquaintance. Business people are generally expected to dress smartly and some dining rooms require men to wear a jacket. There are very few local interpreter or translation services available. Though many businessmen throughout the country also speak English, correspondence should be in Spanish. **Office hours:** 0800-1200 and 1400-1700 Monday to Friday, 0800-1100 Saturday.
COMMERCIAL INFORMATION: The following organisations can offer advice: Federación de Cámaras de Comercio e Industrias de Honduras (FEDECAMARA), Apartado Postal 3393, Edificio Castañito 2° Nivel, 6a Avenida, Colonia Los Castaños, Tegucigalpa. Tel: 321 870. Fax: 326 083; *or* Cámara de Comercio e Industrias de Tegucigalpa, Frente Edificio Hondutel, Colonia Miraflores, Tegucigalpa. Tel: 328 210 *or* 328 110 *or* 312 740. Fax: 312 049.

CLIMATE

The climate is tropical, with cooler, more temperate weather in the mountains. The north coast is very hot with rain throughout the year, and though the offshore breezes temper the climate, the sun is very strong. The dry season is from November to April and the wet season runs from May to October. Humidity figures are not available.
Required clothing: Lightweight cottons and linens; warmer clothes are recommended between November and February and in the mountains. Waterproofs are needed for the wet season.

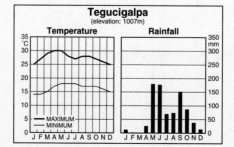

Tegucigalpa
(elevation: 1007m)
Temperature   Rainfall
MAXIMUM
MINIMUM

Hong Kong

□ *international airport*
20km
10mls
CHINA

Location: Far East.

Hong Kong Tourist Association
Head Office, 35th Floor, Jardine House, 1 Connaught Place, Hong Kong
Tel: 801 7111 *or* 801 7177. Fax: 810 4877.
Hong Kong Government Office
6 Grafton Street, London W1X 3LB
Tel: (0171) 499 9821. Fax: (0171) 495 5033 *or* 493 1964. Opening hours: 0930-1300 and 1400-1730 Monday to Friday.
Hong Kong Tourist Association
125 Pall Mall, London SW1Y 5EA
Tel: (0171) 930 4775. Fax: (0171) 930 4777. Opening hours: 0930-1730 Monday to Friday.
UK Passport Office
Clive House, 70-78 Petty France, London SW1
Tel: (0171) 279 3434.
British Trade Commission
9th Floor, Bank of America Tower, 12 Harcourt Road, Hong Kong
Tel: 523 0176. Fax: 845 2870. Telex: 73031 (a/b UK TRADE).
Hong Kong Tourist Association
5th Floor, 590 Fifth Avenue, New York, NY 10036-4706
Tel: (212) 869 5008/9.
General Consulate of the United States of America
26 Garden Road, Hong Kong
Tel: 523 9011. Fax: 845 1598. Telex: 63141 (a/b USDOC HX).
Hong Kong Tourist Association
Suite 909, 347 Bay Street, Toronto, Ontario M5H 2R7
Tel: (416) 366 2389. Fax: (416) 366 1098.
Office of the Commission for Canada
GPO Box 11142, 11-14th Floors, One Exchange Square, 8 Connaught Place, Hong Kong
Tel: 810 4321 *or* 810 0880. Fax: 810 6736. Telex: 73391 (a/b DOMCA HX).

AREA: 1076 sq km (415 sq miles).
POPULATION: 5,757,900 (1992 estimate).
POPULATION DENSITY: 5385 per sq km.
GEOGRAPHY: Hong Kong is located in the Far East, just south of the tropic of Cancer. Hong Kong Island is 32km (20 miles) east of the mouth of Pearl River and 135km (84 miles) southeast of Canton. It is separated from the mainland by a good natural harbour. Hong Kong Island was ceded to Britain by the Treaty of Nanking (1842); and the Kowloon Peninsula (south of Boundary Street and Stonecutters Island) by the Convention of Peking (1860). The area of Boundary Street to Shenzhen River and 235 islands, now known as the New Territories, were leased to Britain in 1898 for a period of 99 years. The New Territories (plus 235 islands) comprise 891 sq km (380 sq miles). Shortage of land suitable for development has led to reclamation from the sea, principally from the seafronts of Hong Kong Island and Kowloon.
LANGUAGE: Chinese is the official language with

Cantonese most widely spoken. English is spoken by many, particularly in business circles. English-speaking policemen have a red flash on their shoulder lapels.
RELIGION: Buddhist, Confucian, Taoist, with Christian and Muslim minorities, but there are also places of worship for most other religious groups.
TIME: GMT + 8.
ELECTRICITY: 200 volts AC, 50Hz.
COMMUNICATIONS: Telecommunications services are as sophisticated and varied as one might expect in an advanced Western-style economy (including radio-paging and viewdata). **Telephone:** Directory enquiries services are computerised. For directory enquiries, dial 10181 (English) or 1083 (Chinese). Full IDD is available. Country code: 852. Outgoing international code: 001. Local public telephone calls cost HK$1. **Fax:** Hong Kong Telecommunications Ltd and the post office provide services. Bureaufax and international services are also available. **Telex/telegram:** Public telex facilities are available on Hong Kong Island at the Hong Kong Telecommunications office, New Mercury House, 22 Fenwick Street, Wan Chai, and Hermes House, Middle Road, Kowloon and at larger hotels. **Post:** Regular postal services are available. Airmail to Europe takes three to five days. *Poste Restante* facilities are available. Post office hours: 0800-1800 Monday to Friday, 0800-1400 Saturday. **Press:** English-language dailies include *Asian Wall Street Journal, Hong Kong Standard, International Herald Tribune* and *South China Morning Post.*
BBC World Service and Voice of America frequencies: From time to time these change. See the section *How to Use this Book* for more information.

BBC:				
MHz	**6.750**			
Voice of America:				
MHz	**15.43**	**11.72**	**5.985**	**1.143**

PASSPORT/VISA

Regulations and requirements may be subject to change at short notice, and you are advised to contact the appropriate diplomatic or consular authority before finalising travel arrangements. Details of these may be found at the head of this country's entry. Any numbers in the chart refer to the footnotes below.

	Passport Required?	Visa Required?	Return Ticket Required?
Full British	Yes	No/1	Yes
BVP	Not valid	-	-
Australian	Yes	No/2	Yes
Canadian	Yes	No/2	Yes
USA	Yes	No/3	Yes
Other EU (As of 31/12/94)	Yes	No/3/4	Yes
Japanese	Yes	No/3	Yes

PASSPORTS: Valid passport required by all. Passports must be valid for at least 6 months after the period of intended visit.
British Visitors Passport: Not acceptable.
Note: Since October 1980, all visitors must carry some form of official identification *at all times*. For UK visitors this should be a valid passport. The police make random checks and those without identification are liable to face prosecution.
VISAS: Required by all except:
(a) **[1]** British passport holders for visits not exceeding 12 months;
(b) **[2]** nationals of Australia, Canada and other Commonwealth countries for visits not exceeding 3 months (*except* nationals of Bangladesh and Pakistan who need visas for visits exceeding 1 month);
(c) **[3]** nationals of Germany, Greece, Japan and USA, for visits not exceeding 1 month;
(d) **[4]** nationals of Belgium, Denmark, France, Ireland, Italy, Luxembourg, The Netherlands, Portugal and Spain for visits not exceeding 3 months;
(e) nationals of Andorra, Austria, Brazil, Chile, Colombia, Ecuador, Israel, Liechtenstein, Monaco, Norway, San Marino, Sweden, Switzerland and Turkey for visits not exceeding 3 months;
(f) nationals of Argentina, Bolivia, Costa Rica (except holders of a provisional passport who *do* require a visa), Dominican Republic, El Salvador, Finland, Guatemala, Honduras, Iceland, Mexico, Morocco, Nepal, Nicaragua, Panama, Paraguay, Peru, South Africa, Tunisia, Uruguay and Venezuela for visits not exceeding 1 month;
(g) nationals of Algeria, Angola, Bahrain, Benin, Bhutan, Bosnia-Hercegovina, Burkina Faso, Burundi, Cameroon, Cape Verde, Central African Republic, Chad, Comoros, Congo, Côte d'Ivoire, Croatia, Djibouti, Egypt, Equatorial Guinea, Estonia, Ethiopia, Former Yugoslav Republic of Macedonia, Federated States of Micronesia, Gabon, Guinea Republic, Guinea-Bissau, Haiti, Indonesia, Jordan, South Korea, Kuwait, Latvia, Liberia, Lithuania, Madagascar, Mali, Marshall Islands, Mauritania, Mozambique, Namibia, Niger, Oman, Philippines, Poland, Qatar, Rwanda, São Tomé e Príncipe, Saudi Arabia, Senegal, Sierra Leone, Slovenia, Suriname, Thailand, Togo, United Arab Emirates, US Trust Territory of Pacific Islands (holders of US Trust Territory passports only), Vatican City, Yemen and Zaïre for visits not exceeding 14 days.
Note: Nationals of countries which formerly comprised Eastern Europe, and Afghanistan, Cambodia, China, CIS, Cuba, Djibouti, Iran, Iraq, North Korea, Laos, Lebanon, Libya, Mongolia, Myanmar (Burma), Namibia, Somalia, Sudan, Syria, Taiwan (China) and Vietnam, require visas. For clarification or further information, consult the Hong Kong Immigration Department (address below under *Commercial Information*) or their booklet *Do you need a Visa for Hong Kong?* (also available from the Hong Kong Government Office in London). For address, see top of entry.
Application to: British Consulate (or Consular section at British Embassy or High Commission) or, if applying in the UK, the UK Passport Office.

MONEY

Currency: Hong Kong Dollar (HK$) = 100 cents. Notes are in denominations of HK$1000, 500, 100, 50 and 20. Coins are in denominations of HK$5, 2 and 1, and 50, 20 and 10 cents.
Currency exchange: Foreign currency can be changed in banks, hotels, bureaux de change and shops.
Credit cards: Access/Mastercard, American Express, Diners Club and Visa are widely accepted. Check with your credit card company for details of merchant acceptability and other services which may be available.
Travellers cheques: Accepted almost everywhere.
Exchange rate indicators: The following figures are included as a guide to the movements of the Hong Kong Dollar against Sterling and the US Dollar:

Date:	**Oct '92**	**Sep '93**	**Jan '94**	**Jan '95**
£1.00=	**2.26**	**11.86**	**11.43**	**12.10**
$1.00=	**7.73**	**7.77**	**7.72**	**7.74**

Currency restrictions: There are no restrictions.
Banking hours: 0900-1630 Monday to Friday, 0900-1330 Saturday.

DUTY FREE

The following goods may be imported into Hong Kong without incurring customs duty:
200 cigarettes or 50 cigars or 250g of tobacco; 1 litre bottle of wine or spirits; 60ml perfume.
Note: (a) If arriving from Macau, duty-free imports for Macau residents are limited to half the above cigarette, cigar and tobacco allowance. (b) Aircraft crew and passengers in direct transit via Hong Kong are limited to 20 cigarettes *or* 57g of pipe tobacco. (c) The import of animals is strictly controlled. (d) Firearms must be declared upon entry and handed into custody until departure. (e) Non-prescribed drugs may not be brought in without a doctor's certificate of use.

PUBLIC HOLIDAYS

Jan 1 '95 First weekday in January. **Jan 31-Feb 2** Lunar New Year. **Apr 5** Ching Ming Festival. **Apr 14-17** Easter. **Jun 2** Tuen Ng (Dragon Boat Festival). **Jun 17-19** Queen's Official Birthday. **Aug 26** Last August Saturday. **Aug 28** Liberation Day. **Sep 9** Mid-Autumn Festival. **Nov 1** Chung Yeung Festival. **Dec 25-26** Christmas. **Jan 1 '96** New Year's Day. **Feb 19-21** Lunar New Year. **Apr 5** Ching Ming Festival. **Apr 5-8** Easter.
Note: Some of the above dates are provisional only. Travellers should confirm them closer to the time of visit.

HEALTH

Regulations and requirements may be subject to change at short notice, and you are advised to contact your doctor well in advance of your intended date of departure. Any numbers in the chart refer to the footnotes below.

	Special Precautions?	Certificate Required?
Yellow Fever	No	No
Cholera	No	No
Typhoid & Polio	Yes	-
Malaria	1	-
Food & Drink	2	-

[1]: There may be an occasional risk of malaria in rural areas.
[2]: All water direct from government mains in Hong Kong exceeds the United Nations World Health Organisation standards and is fit for drinking. However, all hotels also provide bottled water in guest rooms. Milk is pasteurised and dairy products are safe for consumption. Local meat, poultry, seafood, fruit and vegetables are generally considered safe to eat.
Health care: There is a Reciprocal Health Agreement with the UK, but it is of a limited nature. On presentation of a valid passport *and* an NHS card, free emergency treatment is available at certain hospitals and clinics. Small charges are made for all other services and treatment. All visitors are advised to take out private health insurance. Hotels have a list of government-accredited doctors. First-class Western medicine is practised. Excellent dental care is available.

TRAVEL - International

AIR: The main airline to serve Hong Kong is *Cathay Pacific (CX).*
For free advice on air travel call the Air Travel Advisory Bureau in the UK on (0171) 636 5000 (London) *or* (0161) 832 2000 (Manchester).
Approximate flight times: From Hong Kong to *London* is 13 hours 35 minutes, to *Los Angeles* is 16 hours 25 minutes, from *New York* is 18 hours 45 minutes, to *Singapore* is 3 hours 30 minutes and to *Sydney* is 7 hours 40 minutes.
International airport: *Hong Kong International* (HKG) (Kai Tak) is 7.5km (4.5 miles) from central Hong Kong. Airport facilities include an outgoing duty-free shop, a wide range of car hire companies, banks, and 24-hour bars and restaurants. All the above are open 0600-2400. Airbus A1 (circular route) runs to Kowloon (travel time – 20 minutes); Airbus A2 runs to central Hong Kong every 15 minutes; Airbus A3 (circular route) runs to Causeway Bay (travel time – 30 minutes); taxis are plentiful.
Departure tax: Adults pay HK$50; children under 12 are exempt.
SEA: Lines serving the port of Hong Kong are as follows: *Norwegian America, Royal Viking, CTC, Sitmar* and *Lindblad Travel.* Hovercrafts link Hong Kong with China; there are also a number of ships sailing to major Chinese ports, although these are less frequent. Enquire locally for details.
Travel to Macau: *Journey times:* by jetfoil – 55 minutes; by hydrofoil – 75 minutes. See also the section on *Macau* below.
RAIL: The *Kowloon–Canton Railway (KCR)* operates a service jointly with *Chinese Railways* from Kowloon to Canton (Guanzhou), four times a day. There are also services from Hong Kong to Foshan and Changping. Restaurant cars are only available if travelling first class. Local KCR trains run regularly (every 3-20 minutes) to Lo Wu, the last stop before the Chinese border. It is possible to then cross the border to Shenzhen, the first city in China over the border. To go as far as Lo Wu, it is necessary to hold a visa for China, otherwise it is only possible to get to Sheung Shui. Children under 3 travel free. Children aged 3-9 pay half fare.

TRAVEL - Internal

SEA: Cross-harbour passenger services (shortest route 7-10 minutes) are operated by *Star Ferries* (sailing every 5 minutes) from 0630-2330. There are frequent passenger and vehicle services on other cross-harbour routes. *Wallah wallahs* (small motorboats) provide 24-hour service. The outlying islands are served daily by ferries and hydrofoils. However, the opening of the Cross Harbour Tunnel means that *wallah wallahs* are decreasing in popularity.
Tours of the harbour and to Aberdeen and Yaumatei typhoon shelters are available by *Watertours* junks, and visits to outlying islands are possible by public ferry.
RAIL/METRO: *Mass Transit Railway (MTR)* has four lines and provides a cross-harbour link. It is more expensive than the ferry, but quicker, particularly for those travelling further into Kowloon than Tsimshatsui. An MTR Tourist Ticket is available, valid for HK$25 worth of travel. For visitors staying for a week or more it is worth getting a HK$70 or HK$120 ticket, which will provide travel up to that value. They are more convenient than buying a ticket for each journey travelled, and also work out slightly cheaper. The only other railway line in the colony is the Kowloon–Canton Railway (KCR)

Timatic

Health
GALILEO/WORLDSPAN: **TI-DFT/HKG/HE**
SABRE: **TIDFT/HKG/HE**
Visa
GALILEO/WORLDSPAN: **TI-DFT/HKG/VI**
SABRE: **TIDFT/HKG/VI**

For more information on Timatic codes refer to Contents.

which has 13 stations within Hong Kong. Trains run between 0552-0012.
ROAD: Traffic drives on the left. **Bus:** Routes run throughout the territory, with cross-harbour routes via the tunnel. These, however, are often very crowded. Air-conditioned coaches operate along certain Hong Kong and Kowloon routes. Maxicabs, however, operate on fixed routes without fixed stops. **Minibus:** These can pick up passengers and stop on request except at regular bus stops and other restricted areas. **Trams:** Only available on Hong Kong Island. *Peak Tram* on the Island is a cable tramway to the upper terminus on Victoria Peak, 400m (1300ft) high. **Taxi:** Plentiful in Hong Kong and Kowloon. There is an extra charge (HK$20) for the Cross Harbour Tunnel. Red taxis serve Hong Kong Island and Kowloon, green ones the New Territories, and blue ones Lantau Island. Many drivers speak a little English, but it is wise to get your destination written in Chinese characters. **Rickshaws:** Gradually disappearing and are now purely a tourist attraction. It is advisable to agree the fare in advance. **Car hire:** A wide selection of self-drive and chauffeur-driven cars are available, although car hire is not that popular in Hong Kong.
Documentation: An International Driving Permit is recommended, although it is not legally required. A valid national licence is accepted for up to 12 months. Minimum age is 18 years. Third Party insurance is compulsory.
JOURNEY TIMES: The following chart gives approximate journey times (in hours and minutes) from the Hong Kong Island terminals to main tourist districts and outlying islands.

	Road	**Metro**	**Sea**
Kai Tak	0.35	-	-
Kowloon	0.20	0.04	0.10
Causeway Bay	0.10	-	-
Lantau Is.	-	-	1.00
Aberdeen	0.20	-	-
Cheung Chau	-	-	1.00

ACCOMMODATION

HOTELS: There is an excellent selection of hotels, but due to intensifying interest on the part of visitors wanting to see the colony before it reverts to Chinese control (June 1997), hotels are becoming increasingly booked up. Advance booking is strongly advised, especially in the peak periods March to April and October to November. Since 1988 there have been 19 hotels and 9000 new rooms opened and by 1995 there will be an estimated 35,494 rooms. Consequently the high occupancy rates and premium prices should be a thing of the past. Guest-house accommodation is also available. 10% service charge and 5% government tax are added to the bill. Many hotels are members of the Hong Kong Tourist Association (address at top of entry). 75 hotels belong to the Hong Kong Hotels Association, 508-511 Silvercord Tower II, 30 Canton Road, Kowloon. Tel: 375 3838. Fax: 375 7676. **Grading:** Though there is no grading structure as such, hotel members of the HKTA fall into one of four categories: **High Tariff A Hotels** (17 members); **High Tariff B Hotels** (28 members); **Medium Tariff Hotels** (27 members); **Hostels/Guest-houses** (10 members).
SELF-CATERING: Resort houses on the outlying islands can be hired.
CAMPING/CARAVANNING: Permitted in the countryside, though permission is required within the Country Park protection area.
YOUTH HOSTELS: There are four main YMCA/YWCAs in Hong Kong. The YMCA in Kowloon is at 41 Salisbury Road, Tsimshatsui, Kowloon. Tel: 369 2211. For details contact the tourist office. There are numerous youth hostels in Hong Kong, all of which are outside the city. Contact Hong Kong Youth Hostels Association Ltd, Room 225-226, Block 19, Shek Kip Mei Estate, Sham Shuipo, Kowloon. Tel: 788 1638.

RESORTS & EXCURSIONS

Hong Kong is a major tourist destination as well as being one of the world's major business centres. This tax-free, bustling port and commercial centre has many luxury hotels and lesser hostelries which are used as bases to explore Hong Kong, the New Territories and the many small islands. Transportation is modern and well organised and most tours and sightseeing trips are completed in time for the tourist to be back in Hong Kong the same day. A tour of the New Territories takes about six hours, one of Hong Kong Island about four. Other popular excursions include sport and recreation tours and night tours, such as a dinner cruise and a tram tour with cocktails served. Contact the Tourist Association in London, or in Hong Kong (for addresses and phone numbers, see top of entry) for further details.

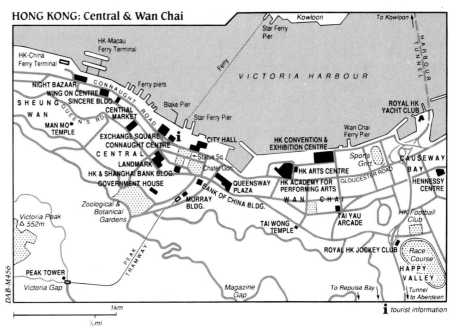

HONG KONG: Central & Wan Chai

tourist information

Places worth visiting include: *Sung Dynasty Village* – a recreation of a 1000-year-old Chinese village; *Tsimshatsui* – shops, restaurants and a space museum in a vast complex; nightly planetarium 'sky shows'; the harbour and its magnificent skyline (tours of the harbour can be made by junk); *The Peak* – take a tram to the 'top' of Hong Kong Island for exceptional views and the Chinese Peak Tower Village at its upper terminus with restaurant and coffee shop; the night markets; *Ocean Park,* with performing dolphins and killer whales; the floating restaurants; *Repulse Bay,* with the *Tin Hau Temple* overlooking the beach; *Stanley Market;* the New Territories countryside; tranquil rural beauty near the Chinese border; the Chinese markets; *Miu Fat Monastery, Ching Chung Koon* and many other splendid Chinese temples; the fishing villages; *Sea Ranch* – a luxury resort and country club with beaches on **Lantau Island** and the splendid *Po Lin Monastery,* also on Lantau Island. Many of the islands have delightful beaches to escape the hubbub of the city – *Lantau, Lamma* and *Cheung Chau* are just three of these. *Special Interest Tours:* A wide variety of these are available, and the Hong Kong Tourist Association provides a booklet giving details.

SOCIAL PROFILE

FOOD & DRINK: Hong Kong is one of the great centres for international cooking. Apart from Chinese food, which is superb, there are also many Indian, Vietnamese, Filipino, Singapore/Malaysian and Thai restaurants. It is the home of authentic Chinese food from all the regions of China, which may be sampled on a sampan in Causeway Bay, on a floating restaurant at Aberdeen, in a Kowloon restaurant, in a street market or at a deluxe hotel. Hotels serve European and Chinese food but there are also restaurants serving every type of local cuisine.
Chinese regional variations on food include Cantonese, Northern (Peking), Chiu Chow (Swatow), Shanghai, Sichuan and Hakka. Cantonese is based on parboiling, steaming and quick stir-frying to retain natural juices and flavours. The food is not salty or greasy and seafoods are prepared especially well, usually served with steamed rice. Specialities include *Dim Sum* (savoury snacks, usually steamed and served in bamboo baskets on trolleys). These include *Cha siu bao* (barbecue pork bun), *Har gau* (steamed shrimp dumplings) and *Shiu mai* (steamed and minced pork with shrimp). The emphasis in Northern food is on bread and noodles, deep-frying and spicy sauces. Specialities include *Peking duck* and hotpot dishes. Shanghainese food is diced or shredded, stewed in soya or fried in sesame oil with pots of peppers and garlic. *Chiu Chow* is served with rich sauces and Hakka food is generally simple in style with baked chicken in salt among the best dishes. Sichuan food is hot and spicy with plenty of chillies. A speciality is barbecued meat.
Drink: The Chinese do not usually order a drink before dinner. Popular Chinese wines and spirits are *Zhian Jing* (a rice wine served hot like *Sake), Liang hua pei* (potent plum brandy), *Kaolian* (a whisky) and *Mao toi.* Popular beers are the locally brewed *San Miguel* and *Tsingtao* (from China) with imported beverages widely available.

NIGHTLIFE: There are many nightclubs, discotheques, hostess clubs, theatres and cinemas. Cultural concerts, plays and exhibitions can be seen at Hong Kong's City Hall which also has a dining room, ballroom and cocktail lounge. The Hong Kong Cultural Centre, including a 2100-seat Concert Hall, 1750-seat Grand Theatre, a studio theatre with 300-500 seats and restaurants, bars and other facilities, has become the major venue for cultural concerts, plays and operas. Hong Kong Art Centre in Wan Chai supplements the City Hall's entertainment with culture in the form of Chinese opera, puppet shows, recitals and concerts. American, European, Chinese and Japanese films with subtitles are shown at a number of good air-conditioned cinemas. Two daily papers, the *Hong Kong Standard* and the *South China Morning Post,* contain details of entertainment. An unusual event to watch is night horse-racing held Wednesday nights from September to May. For further details, contact the Hong Kong Tourist Association.
SHOPPING: Whether one is shopping in modern air-conditioned arcades or more traditional street markets, the range of goods available in Hong Kong is vast. Many famous-name shops have opened in Hong Kong, bringing the latest styles in great variety. Places that display the HKTA sign (Hong Kong Tourist Association) are the best guarantee of satisfaction. Bargaining is practised in the smaller shops and side stalls only. There are excellent markets in Stanley on Hong Kong Island, which is in a beautiful setting in a small village on the coast, and in Temple Street, Kowloon, which is a night market.

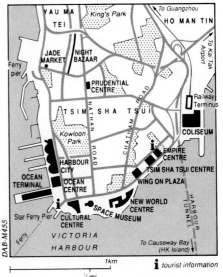

HONG KONG: Kowloon

tourist information

Tailoring is first class. Except for a few items such as liquor and perfume, Hong Kong is a duty-free port.
Shopping hours: Hong Kong Island (Central & Western): 1000-1800 (1000-2000 along Queen's Road). Hong Kong Island (Causeway Bay & Wan Chai): 1000-2130. Kowloon (Tsimshatsui & Yan Ma Tei): 1000-1930. Kowloon (Mongkok): 1000-2100. Many shops are open Sunday.
SPORT: Spectator sports are **soccer, rugby** and **cricket**. Jogging facilities are provided by some hotels. The Clinic at Adventis Hospital holds jogging sessions every Sunday. There are also good facilities for **squash, golf, tennis, hiking, riding, bowling** and **ice skating**, as well as health-centre facilities available. There are over 30 highly-acclaimed beaches throughout the territory. Excellent **skindiving, water-skiing** and **sailing** are available. **Horserace** meetings, at which vast sums of money change hands, are held from September to May Saturday or Sunday afternoon and Wednesday evening. The two main **racecourses** are at Happy Valley (Hong Kong Island) and Shatin (New Territories). For details, contact the Royal Hong Kong Jockey Club. There are also many massage parlours, although these vary in respectability.
SPECIAL EVENTS: The following is a selection of the major festivals and special events celebrated in Hong Kong during 1995. For a complete list, with exact dates, contact the Tourist Association.
Mar 1-5 '95 *Hong Kong Arts Festival.* **Mar 2** *Birthday of To Tei Kung.* **Mar 19** *Birthday of Koon Yam.* **Mar 25-26** *Cathay Pacific/Hong Kong Bank Invitation Seven-A-Side Rugby Tournament.* **Apr 2** *Birthday of Pak Tai.* **Apr 5** *Ching Ming Festival.* **Apr 15** *San Fernando Race* (sailing). **Apr 22** *Birthday of Tin Hau.* **Apr** *19th Hong Kong International Film Festival.* **May 7** *Birthday of Lord Buddha; Birthday of Tam Kung.* **May 20-21** *Spring Regatta.* **Jun 2** *Tuen Ng (Dragon Boat) Festival.* **Jun 10** *Birthday Kwan Tai.* **Jun 10-11** *Hong Kong Dragon Boat Festival International Races.* **Jul** *International Arts Carnival.* **Sep 9** *Mid-Autumn Festival.* **Oct** *Cathay Pacific/Wharf Holdings International Cricket Sixes.* **Nov 1** *Chang Yeung Festival.*
Note: A festival in Hong Kong is a major event on a scale hardly understood in the West. During Chinese New Year festivities, there is total disruption of everyday life.
SOCIAL CONVENTIONS: Handshaking is the common form of greeting. In Hong Kong the family name comes first, so Wong Man Ying would be addressed as Mr Wong. Most entertaining takes place in restaurants rather than in private homes. Usually informal and normal courtesies should be observed when visiting someone's home. During a meal a toast is often drunk saying *Yum Sing* at each course. There may be up to 12 courses served in a meal, and although it is not considered an insult to eat sparingly, a good appetite is always appreciated and it is considered cordial to taste every dish. It is customary to invite the host to a return dinner. Informal wear is acceptable. Some restaurants and social functions often warrant formal attire. Smoking is widely acceptable and only prohibited where specified.
Tipping: Most hotels and restaurants add 10% service charge and an additional 5% gratuity is also expected. Small tips are expected by taxi-drivers, doormen and washroom attendants.

BUSINESS PROFILE

ECONOMY: Under the terms of the Sino-British agreement, Hong Kong's existing economic system will be preserved for at least 50 years. Hong Kong has the archetypal 'Tiger economy', the appellation now afforded to the fast-growing economies of the Pacific Basin. Its mainstays are light manufacturing industry, financial services and shipping, the latter assisted by Hong Kong's fine natural port. The manufacturing sector has thriving textile and consumer electronics industries, employing almost half the workforce and producing three-quarters of Hong Kong's export income. The colony is also the world's leading producer of children's toys. The economy suffered some loss of business confidence in the wake of the 1984 Sino-British agreement and as a result of subsequent bilateral developments and, events inside China (such as the Tian-an-Men Square shootings) in 1989. The growth rate, which averaged 8% in the 1980s, slipped to between 2-3% at the beginning of the 1990s, with inflation reaching double figures, but the economy remains vibrant and has received a substantial boost from the recently constructed airport construction project. Hong Kong is the world's 11th largest trading economy and its major trading partner is China, followed by Japan, Taiwan, the UK and the USA. Declining trade with the USA in recent years has been offset by growth in European markets, especially Germany. The best guarantor of Hong Kong's economic future is the continuing prosperity of the

Special Economic Zones in southern China which are Hong Kong's immediate neighbours. Provided the status of these Zones is maintained, Hong Kong will be more or less merged into them: as one Hong Kong businessman put it, 'the border will effectively move north' to the northern boundaries of the Special Economic Zones. Much will depend on the successful completion of major and much-needed infrastructure projects. As well as the Chek Lap Lok airport, tenders have been sought for a new £1-billion container port at Kwai Chung, which Hong Kong will need in order to maintain its dominant role as a transport hub for Chinese trade (Hong Kong currently handles about 60% of China's export traffic). While there remain widespread worries about Hong Kong's political future, the territory's business community is well aware that the evidence from the rest of the region, and indeed from Hong Kong's own recent experience, is that democracy is not a necessary precursor for economic success.
BUSINESS: Business people are generally expected to dress smartly. Local business people are usually extremely hospitable. Appointments should be made in advance and punctuality is appreciated. Business cards are widely used with a Chinese translation on the reverse. Most top hotels provide business centres for visiting business people, with typing, duplication, translation and other services. **Office hours:** 0900-1300 and 1400-1700 Monday to Friday, 0900-1230 Saturday. Some Chinese offices open earlier than 0930 and close later than 1700.
COMMERCIAL INFORMATION: The following organisations can offer advice: Immigration Department of the Hong Kong Government, 7 Gloucester Road. Tel: 523 0176; *or*
Hong Kong General Chamber of Commerce, PO Box 852, 22nd Floor, United Centre, 95 Queensway. Tel: 529 9229. Fax: 527 9843. Telex: 83535.
CONFERENCES/CONVENTIONS: The Hong Kong Convention and Incentive Travel Bureau is a division of the Hong Kong Tourist Association (for addresses, see top of entry) which specialises in promoting Hong Kong as a leading venue with a special East/West position; it publishes lavish and detailed brochures showcasing the region for conference and incentive planners, together with a glossy catalogue of promotional material and a directory of associations and societies in Hong Kong. There were 245 association conferences, 57 exhibitions, 315 corporate meetings and 517 incentive group meetings in 1991, mostly with participants from the Pacific Basin (including the USA); Europe, the UK and Germany also figured significantly. There are venues with seating for up to 12,500 persons. For further information, contact the Hong Kong Tourist Association.

CLIMATE

Hong Kong experiences four distinct seasons, with the climate influenced in winter by the north-northeast monsoon and in summer by the south-southwest monsoon. Summers are very hot, with the rainy season running from June to August. Spring and autumn are warm with occasional rain and cooler evenings. Winter can be cold, but most days are mild. There is a risk of typhoons from July to September.
Required clothing: Lightweight cottons and linens are worn during the warmer months, with warmer clothes for spring and autumn evenings. It should be noted that even during the hottest weather, a jacket or pullover will be required for the sometimes fierce air-conditioning indoors. Warm mediumweights are best during winter. Waterproofing is advisable during summer rains.

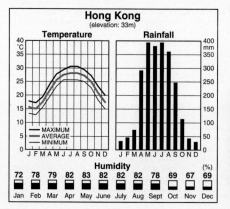

Hong Kong
(elevation: 33m)

	Temperature	Rainfall	

MAXIMUM
AVERAGE
MINIMUM

Humidity

72	78	79	82	83	82	82	82	78	69	67	69	(%)
Jan	Feb	Mar	Apr	May	June	July	Aug	Sept	Oct	Nov	Dec	

Hungary

Location: Central Europe.

Országos Idegenforgalmi Hivatal (OIH) (Hungarian Tourist Board)
Vigadó u. 6, 1051 Budapest, Hungary
Tel: (1) 118 0750. Fax: (1) 118 5241. Telex: 225182.
Embassy of the Hungarian Republic
35 Eaton Place, London SW1X 8BY
Tel: (0171) 235 4048 *or* 235 7191. Fax: (0171) 823 1348.
Opening hours: 0900-1700 Monday to Thursday, 0830-1600 Friday. *Consulate:* Tel: (0171) 235 2664. Opening hours: 1000-1230 Monday to Friday.
Hungaria (Hungarian Tourist Board representatives)
PO Box 4336, London SW18 4XE
Tel: (0181) 871 4009 (administration) *or* (0891) 171 200 (24 hours – calls are charged at the higher rate of 39/49p a minute). Fax: (0181) 871 4009 *or* (0891) 669 970 (24 hours – calls are charged at the higher rate of 39/49p a minute).
British Embassy
Harmincad Ucta 6, Budapest V, Hungary
Tel: (1) 266 2888 *or* 266 2046. Fax: (1) 266 0907. Telex: 224527 (a/b BRIT H).
Embassy of the Hungarian Republic
3910 Shoemaker Street, NW, Washington, DC 20008
Tel: (202) 362 6730. Fax: (202) 966 8135.
IBUSZ (Hungarian Tourist Board representatives)
Suite 1120, 250 West 57th Street, New York, NY 10107
Tel: (212) 586 5230. Fax: (212) 581 7925.
Embassy of the United States of America
Unit 1320, V. Szabadság tér 12, 1054 Budapest, Hungary
Tel: (1) 112 6450. Fax: (1) 132 8934. Telex: 224222.
Embassy of the Hungarian Republic
7 Delaware Avenue, Ottawa, Ontario K2P 0Z2
Tel: (613) 232 1711 *or* 232 1549 *or* 232 3209 (Consular section). Fax: (613) 232 5620.
Consulates in: Montréal, Toronto, Vancouver and Calgary.
Canadian Embassy
Budakeszi ut. 32, 1121 Budapest, Hungary
Tel: (1) 176 7312 *or* 176 7512 *or* 176 7711/2. Fax: (1) 176 7689. Telex: 224588.

AREA: 93,030 sq km (35,919 sq miles).
POPULATION: 10,337,000 (1992 estimate).
POPULATION DENSITY: 111.1 per sq km.
CAPITAL: Budapest. **Population:** 1,992,343 (1992).
GEOGRAPHY: Hungary is situated in Central Europe, sharing borders to the north with the Slovak Republic, to

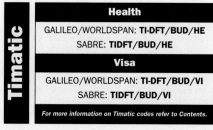

Health	
GALILEO/WORLDSPAN:	**TI-DFT/BUD/HE**
SABRE:	**TIDFT/BUD/HE**

Visa	
GALILEO/WORLDSPAN:	**TI-DFT/BUD/VI**
SABRE:	**TIDFT/BUD/VI**

For more information on Timatic codes refer to Contents.

HUNGUEST

HUNGARIAN HOLIDAY PLANNING AND
PROPERTY MANAGEMENT CO. LTD.

HUNGUEST
Co. Ltd.

Our company is the largest hotel-chain in Hungary. It owns more than 260 hotels with rich experience in the field of cater–ing. Our hotels are located in the most beautiful and most popular holiday resorts in Hungary, thus the guests visiting there can spend their time of rests in various way. A part of our hotels operates as health hotels, where medical and health services are also available. Our company limited by shares sells sleeping places through "HUNGUEST TRAVEL" Travel Agency.

NEMZETI ÜDÜLÉSI ÉS UTAZÁSI IRODA

Addresses and phone numbers of our Budapest Sales Offices:
H-1068 Budapest, Dózsa György út 84/b.   Phone: /00 36 1/ 122-8893;   /00 36 1/ 142-8307
H-1063 Budapest, Bajcsy-Zsilinszky ut 55.   Phone: /00 36 1/ 131-4343

Spend some agreeable weeks in Budapest and at Lake Balaton

Spend some agreeable weeks in Budapest and at Lake Balaton in the comfortable and well-furnished Radio Inn hotels of the Department of Organised Holidays of the Hungarian Radio.

Radio Inn Budapest is situated in the heart of the city, in a diplomatic quarter full of trees and parks. Our guests can enjoy the comfort of a single room or two-roomed apartments with kitchen, bathroom, telephone and a colour television with satellite programmes. They can have a rest in the spacious garden and the inner court of the hotel. For groups, breakfast and cold buffet

dinner can be ordered at the dining hall. **Radio Inn Siófok** is situated just on the shore of Lake Balaton, in the middle of a wonderful park. There are double rooms with two extra beds, bathroom, colour television with satellite and video programmes, telephone and mini-bar. In the restaurant, breakfast, partial or full board is available. Children's playground and sports facilities, including a tennis court, complete the guests' leisure time. Upon request, both hotels can offer various programmes: sightseeing, excursions to the Hungarian 'Puszta' plain, folklore programmes etc.

Both provide an atmosphere of intimacy and agreeable surroundings far from crowded cities, and at low prices.

Radio Inn Budapest
Benczur utca 19.
H – 1800 Budapest
Tel: (36-1) 3220 237
Fax: (36-1) 1228 284

Radio Inn Siófok
Beszédes József sétány 77.
H – 8600 Siófok
Tel: (36-84) 311634
Fax: (36-84) 313832

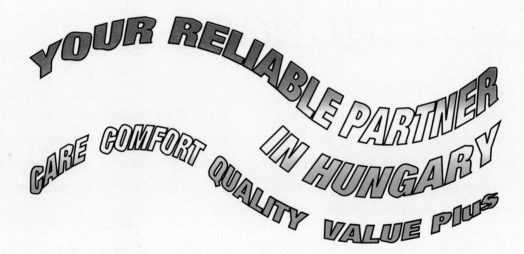

the northeast with Ukraine, to the east with Romania, to the south with Croatia and Yugoslavia and to the west with Austria and Slovenia. There are several ranges of hills, chiefly in the north and west. The Great Plain *(Nagyalföld)* stretches east from the Danube to the foothills of the Carpathian Mountains in the CIS, to the mountains of Transylvania in Romania, and south to the Fruska Gora range in Croatia. Lake Balaton is the largest unbroken stretch of inland water in Central Europe.
LANGUAGE: Hungarian (Magyar) is the official language. German is widely spoken. Some English and French is spoken, mainly in western Hungary.
RELIGION: 65% Roman Catholic, 20% Protestant. Eastern Orthodox and Jewish minorities. There is no official national religion.
TIME: GMT + 1 (GMT + 2 from last Sunday in March to Saturday before last Sunday in September).
ELECTRICITY: 220 volts AC, 50Hz.
COMMUNICATIONS: Telephone: IDD available. Country code: 36. Outgoing international code: 00. Local public telephones are operated by a Ft5 coin. Red phones are for international calls. **Telex:** Facilities available from major hotels and the main post office in Budapest, Petőfi Sándor Utca (0700-2100). **Post:** Airmail takes three days to one week to reach other European destinations. In addition to the main post office, the offices at West and East railway stations in Budapest are open 24 hours a day. Stamps are available from tobacconists as well as post offices. Post office hours: 0800-1800 Monday to Friday, 0800-1400 Saturday.
Press: In 1988 censorship laws were relaxed and since 1989 private ownership of publications has been permitted. National dailies include *Népszabadság, Magyar Hirlap* and *Népszava.* English-language newspapers include the *Daily News, Budapest Week, Budapest Sun, Budapest Business Journal* and *New Hungarian Quarterly.*
BBC World Service and Voice of America frequencies: From time to time these change. See the section *How to Use this Book* for more information.

BBC:				
MHz	**15.07**	**12.09**	**9.410**	**6.180**
Voice of America:				
MHz	**9.670**	**6.040**	**5.995**	**1.197**

PASSPORT/VISA

Regulations and requirements may be subject to change at short notice, and you are advised to contact the appropriate diplomatic or consular authority before finalising travel arrangements. Details of these may be found at the head of this country's entry. Any numbers in the chart refer to the footnotes below.

	Passport Required?	Visa Required?	Return Ticket Required?
Full British	Yes	No	No
BVP	Not valid	-	-
Australian	Yes	Yes	No
Canadian	Yes	No	No
USA	Yes	No	No
Other EU (As of 31/12/94)	Yes	No/1	No
Japanese	Yes	Yes	No

PASSPORTS: Valid passport required by all. All passports must be valid for at least 6 months.
British Visitors Passport: Not accepted.
VISAS: Required by all except:
(a) nationals of the countries referred to in the chart above for a stay of up to 90 days, and nationals of the UK who may stay for up to 6 months ([**1**] except nationals of Spain who *do* need a visa);
(b) nationals of Argentina, Austria, Bulgaria, Chile, Costa Rica, Ecuador, Finland, Iceland, Israel, South Korea, Liechtenstein, Monaco, Norway, Poland, Seychelles, South Africa, Sweden, Switzerland and Uruguay for a stay of up to 90 days;
(c) nationals of the CIS (with the exception of citizens of Uzbekistan who *do* need a visa), Croatia, Cuba, Cyprus, Czech Republic, Malaysia, Malta, Nicaragua, Romania, San Marino, Slovak Republic, Slovenia and Yugoslavia (Serbia and Montenegro) for a stay of up to 30 days;
(d) nationals of Singapore for a stay of up to 14 days.
Types of visa: Single-entry Tourist, Transit or Business (£12 plus pre-paid registered envelope); Double-transit or Double-entry visa (£24); Multiple-entry visa (£40).
Note: Visa fees must be paid in cash or by postal order; cheques are unacceptable. Visas are free for nationals of China, India, Iran and Sri Lanka (but the telex fee of £16 must still be paid).
Validity: *Entry visa* (Tourist and Business) – valid for 30-day stay within 6 months of the date of issue. *Transit visa* – valid for 48-hour stay within 6 months from date of issue. *Multiple-entry visa* – valid for multiple entries into Hungary within 6 months from the date of issue.
Application to: Consulate (or Consular section at Embassy). For addresses, see top of entry. Visas are not issued at road border points or at Budapest Airport.
Application requirements: (a) 3 recent, identical passport-size photos. (b) Valid passport. (c) Completed visa application form. (d) Fee. (e) Written invitation from Hungary if Business visa (endorsed by the Hungarian police). (f) Return ticket (whether for air or rail). (g) £14 per passport for postal applications. (h) Stamped self-addressed, registered or recorded envelope for postal applications. (i) Bank statement proving adequate financial situation. (j) Confirmation of hotel/youth hostel/camping/motel reservation in Hungary or letter of invitation from friends or relatives living in Hungary. (k) telex fee of £16 for visa application to be sent to Hungary for approval.
Working days required: A visa may be obtained 48 hours after approval in Hungary, which takes approximately 2-3 weeks. Nationals of Australia, Hong Kong, Japan, New Zealand, Taiwan (China) and some South and Central American countries may receive their visas in a short procedure or even on the same day. Nationals eligible for short procedure may even ask for an immediate visa which may be issued in one hour for an extra fee of £5.
Note: Within 48 hours of arrival visitors who will be staying for more than 30 days must register with the police (the hotel will handle this); if staying in a private residence with friends there is no requirement to register.

MONEY

Currency: Forint (Ft) = 100 fillér. Notes are in denominations of Ft5000, 1000, 500, 100, 50 and 20. Coins are in denominations of Ft20, 10, 5, 2 and 1, and 50, 20 and 10 fillér. A large number of commemorative coins in circulation are legal tender.
Currency exchange: Currency can be exchanged at hotels, banks, airports, railway stations, travel agencies and some restaurants. Retain all exchange receipts, as it is illegal to change money on the black market.
Credit cards: Access/Mastercard, American Express, Diners Club and Visa are accepted. Check with your credit card company for details of merchant acceptability and other services which may be available.
Travellers cheques: Widely accepted in stores and banks.
Exchange rate indicators: The following figures are included as a guide to the movements of the Forint against Sterling and the US Dollar:

Date:	**Oct '92**	**Sep '93**	**Jan '94**	**Jan'95**
£1.00=	**125.90**	**143.80**	**149.06**	**177.02**
$1.00=	**79.33**	**94.17**	**100.75**	**113.15**

Currency restrictions: Import of local currency is limited to Ft500; up to Ft1000 may be exported *(check with Embassy or local banks before departure).* Unlimited import of foreign currency, provided the amount is declared. Export of foreign currency is limited to the amount declared on import. There is no compulsory money exchange. Hungarian currency can be exchanged for up to 50% of the officially exchanged sum (but not more than US$100) at any authorised office or branch of the National Savings Bank.
Banking hours: 0900-1400 Monday to Friday, 0900-1200 Saturday.

DUTY FREE

The following may be imported into Hungary by persons over 16 years of age without incurring customs duty: *250 cigarettes or 50 cigars or 250g of tobacco; 1 litre of alcoholic beverage and 2 litres of wine; 250g of perfume; gifts to the value of Ft8000.*

PUBLIC HOLIDAYS

Jan 1 '95 New Year's Day. **Mar 15** Anniversary of 1848 uprising against Austrian rule. **Apr 17** Easter Monday. **May 1** Labour Day. **Jun 5** Whit Monday. **Aug 20** Constitution Day. **Oct 23** Day of Proclamation of the Republic. **Dec 25-26** Christmas. **Jan 1 '96** New Year's Day. **Mar 15** Anniversary of 1848 uprising against Austrian rule. **Apr 8** Easter Monday.

HEALTH

Regulations and requirements may be subject to change at short notice, and you are advised to contact your doctor well in advance of your intended date of departure. Any numbers in the chart refer to the footnotes below.

	Special Precautions?	Certificate Required?
Yellow Fever	No	No
Cholera	No	No
Typhoid & Polio	No	-
Malaria	No	-
Food & Drink	1	-

[**1**]: Mains water is normally chlorinated, and whilst relatively safe may cause mild abdominal upsets. Bottled water is available and is advised for the first few weeks of the stay. Milk is pasteurised and dairy products are safe for consumption. Local meat, poultry, seafood, fruit and vegetables are generally considered safe to eat.
Rabies is present. For those at high risk, vaccination before arrival should be considered. If you are bitten abroad seek medical advice without delay. For more information, consult the *Health* section at the back of the book.
Health care: There is a Reciprocal Health Agreement with the UK. On presentation of a UK passport, treatment is free at hospitals, 'poly-clinics' and doctor's surgeries. For emergencies, call 04. Charges will be made for dental and ophthalmic treatment and for prescribed medicines. For an emergency dental service, call 330 189. Chemists are open in the capital from 0800-1000. There are chemists with a 24-hour emergency service open in every district.

TRAVEL - International

AIR: The national airline is *Malév (MA)*, operating flights to 37 cities.
For free advice on air travel, call the Air Travel Advisory Bureau in the UK on (0171) 636 5000 (London) *or* (0161) 832 2000 (Manchester).
Approximate flight time: From Budapest to London is 2 hours 40 minutes.
International airport: *Budapest Ferihegy (BUD)*, 16km (10 miles) from the city (travel time – 30 minutes). There are now two terminals, one of which is used exclusively by *Malév, Air France* and *Lufthansa.* Facilities include a duty-free shop, florist, newsagent, restaurant and bar, bureaux de change, banks, tourist information centre, gift shop and post office (November-March: 0800-1600; April-October: 0800-1930). Regular coach and bus services are available to the city, costing approx. Ft200 for the centrum bus and approx. Ft400-500 for the airport minibus. Taxis are available at all times. The major car hire companies are represented.
RIVER: From April 4 to October 1 there is a daily hydrofoil service run by *MAHART* between Vienna and Budapest (except Sunday). The journey costs approx. US$75 and takes six hours. Reservations must be made at least 21 days in advance to avoid a US$20 surcharge. 20kg of luggage may be carried free of charge.
Passengers arriving by boat are advised to reserve a taxi through the shipping line, as none are readily available on the dock.
RAIL: Links with the rest of Europe are good and there are three international trains daily to Budapest. Inter-Rail, Eurotrain and RES concessions are valid on the Hungarian State Railways *(MAV).* Between Dresden and Budapest there is a car transport system. The *Orient Express* offers a good route from Paris overnight via Stuttgart, Munich and Vienna, reaching Budapest at 2030. There are first- and second-class day carriages from Paris through to Budapest and also first- and second-class sleeping cars on four days a week with a dining car from Stuttgart. Other international routes include Budapest–Belgrade, Budapest–Moscow, Budapest–Prague and Budapest–Venice–Rome.
The *Wiener Waltzer* from Basel travels via Zurich, Salzburg and Vienna to Budapest, arriving at 1430. First- and second-class day carriages run from Basel through to Budapest and both sleeping cars and couchettes (the latter second-class only) as far as Vienna. There is a minibar service in Switzerland and Austria, and a dining car in Hungary.
The most convenient route from London is via Dover/Ostend joining *Ostend/Vienna Express* with sleeping cars and couchettes to Vienna.
Luggage allowances: 35kg for adults, 15kg for children.
Note: Travellers leaving Hungary by train must pay their fare in convertible currency. Most generally recognised international concessionary tickets are accepted in Hungary; contact *MAV* for details. Seat reservations are strongly advised for all services.
ROAD: Route via The Netherlands, Belgium and Austria and from Vienna via the E5 Transcontinental Highway which passes near Bratislava (Slovak Republic). Bus connections are available from most major European cities.

TRAVEL - Internal

AIR: Internal air services are operated by *Danube Air* which flies from *Budaors Airport*, 16km (10 miles) from the centre of Budapest. 6-, 8-, 10- and 14-seater turbo-prop and jet aircraft are used and the service connects the capital with about 12 towns and cities throughout Hungary.

RIVER/LAKE: There are regular services on the Danube and Lake Balaton from spring to late autumn. *MAHART* and the *Budapest Travel Company (BKV)* also operate ferries in the city centre, the Roman Embankment (*Római Part*) and at some crossing points.
Ferry services on the Danube, suitable for cars and buses, operate hourly between Esztergom and Párkány (Sturovo) throughout the year (except for when the river is frozen) 0800-1800 daily.
On Lake Balaton, a ferry operates during the summer at 40-minute intervals daily between Tihanyrév and Szántódrév 0620-2400; at other times of the year the service runs 0630-1930.
RAIL: Services are operated by *MAV*. Tel: (1) 122 2660 *or* 141 3023. All main cities are linked by efficient services but facilities are often inadequate. Supplements are payable on express trains. Reservations for express trains are recommended, particularly in summer. Tickets can be bought 60 days in advance on domestic railway lines, as can seat reservations. The most popular tourist rail routes are Budapest–Kecskemet–Szeged–Budapest and Budapest–Siofok–Lake Balaton.
Cheap fares: Concessions are available for groups (minimum of six persons), those under the age of 26 and for pensioners (women of 55 years of age or over and men of 60 years or over). Children aged 4-12 pay half fare. Children under 4 travel free. Balaton and Tourist Season Tickets (7-10 days) are also available. Contact *MAV* for details. The *Hungarian Flexipass*, sold by travel agents worldwide and by Rail Europe, offers unlimited first-class train travel for 5 days in a 15-day period or for 10 days in a 30-day period.
ROAD: Traffic drives on the right. There are eight arterial roads in the country: all but the M8 start from central Budapest. No tolls are charged. From Budapest the two main highways are the M1 from Györ to Vienna and the M7 along Lake Balaton. The M3 connects Budapest with eastern Hungary. Generally the road system is good. **Bus:** Budapest is linked with major provincial towns. Tickets are available from *Volán* long-distance bus terminal, Budapest, and at *IBUSZ* and *Volán* offices throughout the country. A bus season ticket is also available. **Car hire:** Available at *Ferihegy Airport* or at *IBUSZ, Volán, Express* and Budapest tourist offices as well as at major hotels. **Regulations:** Speed limits are 60kmph (37mph) in built-up areas, 80kmph (50mph) on main roads, 100kmph (62mph) on highways and

120kmph (75mph) on motorways. Seat belts are compulsory. Petrol stations are infrequent and there are no special tourist petrol coupons. There is a total alcohol ban when driving; severe fines are imposed for infringements. It is obligatory to keep headlights dipped at all times when on the open road. **Breakdowns:** The Hungarian Automobile Club (24-hour emergency helpline tel: (1) 115 1220) operates a breakdown service on main roads at weekends and a 24-hour service on motorways. **Documentation:** International Driving Permit and Green Card insurance necessary.
URBAN: There is good public transport in all the main towns. Budapest has bus, trolleybus, tramway, suburban railway (*HEV*), a 3-line metro and boat services. The metro has ticket barriers at all stations. The bus-trolleybus-tramway system has pre-purchase flat fares with ticket puncher on board. Day passes are available for all the transport modes in the city. Trams and buses generally run from about 0430-2300. Some night services also operate. The metro runs from 0430-2310 and stations can be identified by a large 'M'. There is also a cogwheel railway (Városmajor–Széchenyi Hill), a *Pioneers' Railway* (Hüvösvölgy–Széchenyi Hill), a chairlift and a funicular. There are tramways in some of the other towns, or else good bus services. Day passes are available in Budapest.
JOURNEY TIMES: The following chart gives approximate journey times (in hours and minutes) from Budapest to other major cities/towns in Hungary.

	Road	Rail
Sopron	3.30	3.25
Miskolc	3.00	2.20
Pécs	3.00	3.00
Szeged	2.00	2.20
Szentendre	0.30	0.40
Lake Balaton	2.00	2.15

ACCOMMODATION

HOTELS: In all classes of hotel, visitors from the West can expect to be made very welcome and service will usually be friendly and smooth. In addition to hotels, there are Tourist Hostels, which provide simple accommodation usually in rooms with four or more beds. For information contact: Hungarian Hotel Association – Secretariat, H-1123 Budapest, Jagello-u 1/3, Novotel

Convention Centre. Tel: (1) 166 9462. Fax: (1) 122 3854.
Grading: Hungarian hotels are classified by use of a star rating system. **5-** and **4-star** hotels are luxury class and are generally extremely comfortable. **3-star** hotels are comfortable but less luxurious and offer good value for money. **2-** and **1-star** hotels are generally adequate and clean.
GUEST-HOUSES: Available almost everywhere. Paying-guest accommodation is an inexpensive and excellent way of getting to know the people. Renting often includes bathroom but not breakfast. Such accommodation can be booked through tourist offices once in Hungary. Applications should be made well in advance.
SELF-CATERING: Bungalows with two rooms, fully equipped, can be rented at a large number of resorts. Full details and rates can be obtained from tourist offices in Hungary or abroad.
CAMPING/CARAVANNING: Camping is forbidden except in the specially designated areas. Booking is through Hungaro Well, Mogyoródi ut 21, H-1146 Budapest, tel/fax: (1) 140 2064, or through travel agencies. Most of the sites cater only for campers bringing in their own equipment. Caravans are permitted in all sites that have power points; a parking charge is made. Young people between 6-16 pay half price and there is no charge for children under the age of six.
Grading: There are four categories of site, designated **I, II, III** and **IV**, according to the amenities provided, and most are open from May to September.
YOUTH HOSTELS: There are ten in Budapest and 14 in other towns. Hostels are open all day and beds cost around US$6. For further information, contact Express Youth and Student Travel Bureau, V Szabadság tér 16, Budapest 1395. Tel: (1) 131 7777.

RESORTS & EXCURSIONS

The country has, for convenience, been divided into five regions.

Budapest & the Danube

The capital city of **Budapest,** situated on one of the most beautiful areas of the Danube, is made up of two parts – *Buda* and *Pest*. The former is the older, more graceful

part, with cobbled streets and medieval buildings; the latter is the commercial centre. The capital is a lively city which has long been a haven for writers, artists and musicians. In the *Buda* section can be found *Gellert Hill* which gives a wonderful view of the city, river and mountains; on the hill is the *'Citadella'*, a stone fort. *The Royal Palace,* bombed during the Second World War and now reconstructed, houses the *National Gallery* with collections of fine Gothic sculpture and modern Hungarian art (including many paintings by Mihaly Munkácsy), and the *Historical Museum of Budapest,* containing archaeological remains of the old city, and furnishings, glass and ceramics from the 15th century. Also in the Buda region is the *Fisherman's Bastion* – so called because it was the duty of the fishermen of the city to protect the northern side of the Royal Palace during the Middle Ages – and *Matthias Church* with its multicoloured tiled roof.

On the *Pest* side are the *Parliament;* the *Hungarian National Museum,* containing remarkable treasures including the oldest skull yet found in Europe and Liszt's gold baton; the *Belvárosi Templom,* Hungary's oldest church, dating back to the 12th century; the *Museum of Fine Arts* housing European paintings; the *Ethnographic Museum;* and *Margaret Island,* connected to both Buda and Pest by a bridge. The whole island is a park with a sports stadium, swimming pool, spas, a rose garden and fountains. Budapest has about 100 hot springs; one is in the city zoo, much to the delight of the local hippo population who breed there very successfully.

Upstream from Budapest is **Szentendre,** an old Serbian market town where the Hungarian painter Károly Ferenczy did most of his work; there is a museum named after him containing historical, archaeological and ethnographic collections as well as paintings. The *Serbian Museum for Ecclesiastical History* contains many fine examples of ecclesiastical art from the 14th to the 18th centuries. There are many good exhibitions in the city, particularly of the ceramics of Margit Kovács.

Visegrád, a few miles further upriver, was once a royal stronghold, but is now a tourist resort. The 15th-century summer palace has been excavated and restored. The *King Matthias Museum* housed in a Baroque mansion displays many archaeological discoveries.

Esztergom was originally a Roman outpost; it later became the residence of Magyar kings in the 12th and 13th centuries. The *Cathedral,* the *Museum of the Stronghold of Esztergom* and the *Christian Museum of Esztergom,* containing some of Hungary's finest art collections, are worth visiting.

Lake Balaton & the West

The lake is a popular holiday region, not least because of its sandy beaches and shallow waters, with an average depth of only 3.5m (11ft). The surrounding countryside consists mainly of fertile plains dotted with old villages. Further west, towards the Austrian border, the terrain becomes more hilly and forested.

Székesfehérvár, between the lake and Budapest, has a 17th-century *Town Hall* in the Baroque style, as well as the *Zichy Palace* and the *Garden of Ruins* – an open-air museum.

Siófok, on the south shore of the lake, has some of the sandiest beaches and best facilities for tourists.

Keszthely is a pleasant old town containing the *Georgikon,* founded in the 18th century, the first agricultural college in Europe; the *Helikon Library*; and the *Balaton Museum.*

Balatonfüred is a well-known health resort with 11 medicinal springs.

Veszprém, 10km (6 miles) north of *Lake Balaton,* built on five hills, is a pretty town with cobbled streets. It is the home of the *Var Museum,* an *Episcopal Palace* and the 15th-century *Gizella Chapel.*

Further west, the main towns are **Szombathely** (which claims to be the oldest town in Hungary) and **Zalaegerszeg.** Szombathely has superb examples of Romanesque stonework.

Sopron, close to the Austrian frontier, is built on its old Roman foundations, and reminders of the region's history are still very much in evidence. Among the sights here are the *Fire Tower,* the *Liszt Museum* and the ancient quarry at **Fertörákos.**

Nearby is the spa town of **Balf** and the Baroque castle of *Fertöd,* recently restored to its original condition.

Two other towns worth visiting in this region are the walled town of **Köszeg,** and the riverside town of **Györ,** on the main Budapest–Vienna highway. About 18km (11 miles) southeast of Györ is the ancient hilltop monastery of *Pannonhalma,* with a library containing over a quarter of a million books.

The Great Plain Area

This region covers more than half the country, and contains thousands of acres of vineyards, orchards and farmland.

Kecskemét, 85km (53 miles) southeast of the capital, is the home town of the composer Zoltán Kodály. Although an industrial town in many respects, it still has some fine examples of peasant architecture, and of crafts in the *Naive Artists and Katona Jozsef Museum.* There is an artists' colony, and it is also a centre for folk music. Outside the town is the *Kiskunság National Park* with the *Shepherd Museum* showing how animals and people lived in earlier times.

Szeged is the economic and cultural centre of this region. It is famed for its Festival of Opera, Drama and Ballet held in July and August. Here, too, is Hungary's finest Greek Orthodox (Serbian) church.

Baja is a small, picturesque town on the banks of both the Danube and Sugovica rivers. It has many small islands, some old churches and an artists' colony.

Southern Hungary

Pécs, the main town of this region, contains much architecture dating back to the Middle Ages. The area was also colonised by the Romans, and there are many archaeological sites and museums containing relics from this period; in addition, the Turkish conquest of Hungary during the 16th century has left Pécs, like so many other Hungarian cities, with many glorious examples of Ottoman architecture. Principal amongst these is the *Mosque of Pasha Hassan Yakovali.*

Mohács, on the Danube, was the site of the battle in 1526 at which the Turks gained control of Hungary. The battlefield has now been turned into a memorial park.

Kalocsa is a town of museums where many aspects of Hungarian folklore are preserved. South of Kalocsa is the *Forest of Gemenc,* a government-protected nature reserve and the home of many varieties of plant and animal life.

The Northern Highlands

Miskolc, Hungary's second biggest city, is situated near the Slovak border. Primarily industrial, the city has nevertheless several points of interest, including medieval architecture and the warren of man-made caves

in the *Avas Hills* near the city centre. Nearby are the beautiful *Bükk Mountains.*
Eger, one of the country's oldest cities, has nearly 200 historical monuments, including the *Minaret.*
Due east of Miskolc is **Tokaj,** the centre of the most famous wine-producing region of the country. Halfway between Tokaj and the Slovak border is the spectacular castle of *Sárospatak,* one of Hungary's greatest historical monuments.
POPULAR ITINERARIES: 5-day: (a) Szentendre–Visegrád–Esztergom–Györ–Sopron. (b) Eger–Miskolc–Tokaj. **7-day:** (a) Székesfehérvár–Veszprém–Balatonfüred–Zalaegerszeg–Keszthely–Siofok (Lake Balaton). (b) Kecskemét–Szeged–Baja–Mohács–Pécs (Great Plain and the South).

SOCIAL PROFILE

FOOD & DRINK: There is a good range of restaurants. Table service is common, although there are many inexpensive self-service restaurants. A typical menu offers two or three courses at inexpensive rates. Fine dairy and pastry shops *(cukrászda)* offer light meals. Specialities include *halászlé* (fish soups) with pasta and Goulash *gulyás* soup. Western goulash is called *pörkölt* or *tokány.* Stuffed vegetables, sweet cakes, *gundel palacsinta* (pancake) and pastries are also popular.
Drink: *Eszpresszó* coffee bars and *Drink* bars offer refreshments. *Gerbeaud's* is probably Budapest's most famous coffee-house. *Tokaji* (strong dessert wine) or Bull's Blood (strong red wine) are recommended. *Pálinka* or *barack* (apricot brandy) is a typical liqueur. Imported beers and soft drinks are also available. There are no licensing hours, but the legal age for drinking in a bar is 18 years. Minors are allowed to go into bars but will not be served alcohol.
NIGHTLIFE: Budapest has many nightclubs, bars and discos. There is a casino in the Budapest Hilton, and one on the river in front of the Forum. Cinemas in major towns show many English films. During summer months the popular Lake Balaton resort has a lively nightlife. Western Hungary in particular has a lot of very good wine cellars. Visitors would do well to search out traditional folk music and dancing, as the gypsy music which is so common in bars is not considered the 'true' folk tradition of the country. The magnificent Budapest Opera House stages regular performances, and seats are (by Western standards) exceedingly cheap.
SHOPPING: Special purchases include embroideries, Herend and Zsolnay porcelain, and national dolls.
Shopping hours: 1000-1800 Monday to Friday, 1000-1300 Saturday. Food shops are open from 0700-1900 Monday to Friday, 0700-1400 Saturday.
SPORT: Details of **hunting** seasons and licences are available from, MAVAD Rt., Uri u. 39, H-1014 Budapest. Tel: (1) 201 6445. Fax: (1) 201 6371. Holidays for **horseriding** enthusiasts, including cross-country tours and a stay on a stud farm, are available from IBUSZ Hobby and Horseriding Dept, Ferenciek tere 10, H-1364 Budapest. Tel: (1) 118 2967. Fax: (1) 118 2916. **Sailing** and **rowing** are available on Lake Balaton and the Danube (details available from IBUSZ). **Skiing** is popular in the Buda Hills, near Budapest, centred on Szabadsághegy. **Ice skating** is another popular winter sport.
SPECIAL EVENTS: The following is a selection of some of the major festivals and special events celebrated annually in Hungary.
Mar 10-Apr 2 '95 *Budapest Spring Festival.* **May 7-31** *Balaton Festival,* Lake Balaton. **Jun 25** *International Dixieland Festival,* Miskolc-Diósgyör. **Jul 8-9** *Palace Festival,* Visegrád. **Jul-Aug** *Budapest Open-Air Theatre; Szeged Open-Air Theatre; Szentendre Summer Festival.* **Aug 5-6** *Eszerházi Celebration,* Fertöd. **Aug 10-19** *BudaFest,* Budapest. **Aug 20** *Craft Festival,* Budapest; *International Flower Carnival,* Debrecen; *Bridge Fair,* Hortobágy. **Sep 8-10** *Lipizzan Equestrian Festival,* Szilásvárad. **Sep 13-17** *International Wine Festival,* Budapest. **Dec 31** *New Year's Eve in the Opera,* Budapest.
There are also International Trade Fairs in May and September. The many music and folklore festivals normally take place from July to August.
SOCIAL CONVENTIONS: Most Hungarians enjoy modern music and dance, although older people still preserve their old traditions and culture, particularly in small villages. Handshaking is customary. Both Christian name and surname should be used. Normal courtesies should be observed. At a meal, toasts are usually made and should be returned. A useful word is *egészségünkre* (pronounced Ay-gash-ay-gun-gre), meaning 'your health'. Very few people speak English outside hotels and big restaurants and consequently they are unable to help visitors much. A knowledge of German is very useful. Gifts are acceptable for hosts as a token of thanks, particularly when invited for a meal. Casual wear is acceptable in most places, with the exception of

expensive restaurants and bars. Formal attire should be worn for important social functions, but it is not common practice to specify dress on invitations. Smoking is prohibited on public transport in towns and public buildings. Travellers may smoke on long-distance trains.
Photography: Military installations should not be photographed; other restrictions will be signposted.
Tipping: Not obligatory, although 10-15% is normal for most services.

BUSINESS PROFILE

ECONOMY: Before the political upheaval in Central and Eastern Europe during 1989, Hungary had gone furthest of all the socialist bloc countries in decentralising and deregulating the economy. Although this brought considerable dividends in the form of constant economic growth and ready availability of foodstuffs and consumer goods, it allowed the Government to build up a large overseas debt and stimulated unprecedented price inflation. Hungary is poor in natural resources other than bauxite, natural gas and some oil. For this reason, it relies especially heavily on foreign trade which, according to Government information, accounts for half of gross national product – an extraordinarily high proportion. Hungary has a fairly well-developed industrial economy concentrated in chemicals, plastics, pharmaceuticals, fertilisers, computers and telecommunications, mining, construction and aluminium (from the bauxite deposits). The country has also traditionally been an exporter of agricultural produce, particularly fruit and vegetables, maize and wheat, sugar beet, potatoes and livestock. The Government has earmarked this sector for attention in future economic development, with one eye on the future membership of the European Union. Hungary has eschewed the 'big bang' road to capitalism and opted for a more gradual transition to a market economy. Price controls have largely been removed and a programme of privatisation is under way, starting with the retail and property sectors. As a result of the development of the market economy and the measures aimed at liberalisation and deregulation, the number of business organisations with legal entities rose from 29,470 in 1990 to 85,638 by the end of 1993. The private commercial sector and capital markets are developing steadily. According to government figures, by mid-1994 the share of the private sector in GDP reached 50%. Foreign investment has picked up largely as a result of the liberalisation of trade through agreements with the EU, EFTA and CEFTA (Poland, Czech Republic and Slovak Republic) and the number of Hungarian companies with foreign participation (joint ventures) grew to over 21,000 by mid-1994.
BUSINESS: Business people are expected to dress smartly. Local business people are generally friendly and hospitable and it is usual for visitors to be invited to lunch or dinner in a restaurant. Business cards are widely distributed and visitors are well advised to have a supply available in Hungarian. Best months for business visits are September to May. Appointments should always be made. Interpreter and translation services may be booked through IBUS. **Office hours:** 0830-1700 Monday to Friday.
COMMERCIAL INFORMATION: The following organisation can offer advice: Magyar Gazdasági Kamara (Hungarian Chamber of Commerce), PO Box 106, H-1389 Budapest. Tel: (1) 153 3333. Fax: (1) 153 1285.
CONFERENCES/CONVENTIONS: The following organisation can offer advice: Hungarian Convention Bureau, Kelskeméti u. 14, H-1053 Budapest. Tel: (1) 138 4351. Fax: (1) 117 5057.

CLIMATE

There are four seasons, with a very warm summer from June to August. Spring and autumn are mild, while winters are very cold. Rainfall is distributed throughout the year with snowfalls in winter.

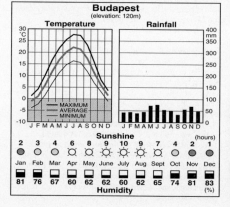

Budapest
(elevation: 120m)

	Temperature		Rainfall	
	MAXIMUM	AVERAGE	MINIMUM	
Sunshine				(hours)
Jan	2	Feb 3	Mar 4	Apr 6	May 8	June 9	July 10	Aug 9	Sept 7	Oct 4	Nov 2	Dec 1
Humidity	81	76	67	60	62	62	60	65	74	81	83	(%)

Iceland

Location: North Atlantic, close to Arctic Circle.

Iceland Tourist Board
Laekjargata 3, 101 Reykjavík, Iceland
Tel: (1) 27488. Fax: (1) 624 749. Telex: 3169.
Embassy of the Republic of Iceland
1 Eaton Terrace, London SW1W 8EY
Tel: (0171) 730 5131/2. Fax: (0171) 730 1683. Telex: 918226 (a/b ICEMBY G). Opening hours: 0900-1600 Monday to Friday.
Iceland Tourist Bureau/Icelandair
172 Tottenham Court Road, London W1P 9LG
Tel: (0171) 388 5346 *or* 388 7550 (tourist information) *or* 388 5599 (Icelandair reservations). Fax: (0171) 387 5711. Telex: 23689. Opening hours: 0900-1700 Monday to Friday.
British Embassy
PO Box 460, Laufásvegur 49, 121 Reykjavík, Iceland
Tel: (1) 15883/4. Fax: (1) 27940. Telex: 2037 (a/b UKREYK IS).
British Vice-Consulate
Glerargata 26, Akureyri, Iceland
Tel: (6) 21165.
Embassy of the Republic of Iceland
2022 Connecticut Avenue, NW, Washington, DC 20008
Tel: (202) 265 6653/4/5. Fax: (202) 265 6656.
Consulates in: Atlanta, Bayamon (Puerto Rico), Boston, Chicago, Dallas, Detroit, Harrisburg, Houston, Dallas, Los Angeles, Miami, Minneapolis, New York (tel: (212) 686 4100), Portland, San Francisco, Seattle and Tallahassee.
Iceland Tourist Board
655 Third Avenue, New York, NY 10017
Tel: (212) 949 2333. Fax: (212) 983 5260.
Embassy of the United States of America
PO Box 40, Laufásvegur 21, 101 Reykjavík, Iceland
Tel: (1) 629 100. Fax: (1) 629 139.
Consulate General of the Republic of Iceland
Suite 300, 246 Queen Street, Ottawa, Ontario K1P 5E4
Tel: (613) 238 7412. Fax: (613) 238 1799.
Consulates in: Calgary, Edmonton, Halifax, Montréal, Regina, St John's, Toronto, Vancouver and Winnipeg.
Consulate General of Canada
PO Box 8094, Suöurlandsbraut 10, 108 Reykjavík, Iceland
Tel: (1) 680 820. Fax: 680 899. Telex: 94014879.

Health	
GALILEO/WORLDSPAN:	**TI-DFT/REK/HE**
SABRE:	**TIDFT/REK/HE**
Visa	
GALILEO/WORLDSPAN:	**TI-DFT/REK/VI**
SABRE:	**TIDFT/REK/VI**

For more information on Timatic codes refer to Contents.

Timatic

AREA: 103,000 sq km (39,769 sq miles).
POPULATION: 262,193 (1992 estimate).
POPULATION DENSITY: 2.5 per sq km.
CAPITAL: Reykjavík. **Population:** 100,850 (1992 estimate).
GEOGRAPHY: Iceland is a large island in the 'North Atlantic close to the Arctic Circle and includes islands to the north and south. The landscape is wild, rugged and colourful, with black lava, red sulphur, hot blue geysers, grey and white rivers with waterfalls and green valleys. Iceland's coastline is richly indented with bays and fjords, and its varied and dramatically rugged land has a total surface area of slightly under 104,000 sq km (40,000 sq miles). The whole of the central highland plateau of the island is a beautiful but barren and uninhabitable moonscape; so much so that the first American astronauts were sent there for pre-mission training. Five-sixths of the area of Iceland are uninhabited, the population being concentrated on the coast, in the valleys and in the plains of the southwest and southeast of the country. More than half the population live in or around Reykjavík, the capital. Iceland is one of the most active volcanic countries in the world. Hekla, in the south of Iceland, is the most famous and magnificent volcano of them all. It has erupted no fewer than 16 times since Iceland was settled, and throughout the Middle Ages was considered by European clergymen as one of the gateways to Hell itself. Another volcano, Snæfellsnes, fired Jules Verne's imagination to use its crater as the point of entry for his epic tale *Journey to the Centre of the Earth.* Iceland's highest and most extensive glacier is Vatnajökull at 8500 sq km (3300 sq miles), the largest in Europe.
LANGUAGE: The official language is Icelandic. English (which is taught in schools) and Danish are widely spoken.
RELIGION: Lutheran, with a Catholic minority.
TIME: GMT.
ELECTRICITY: 220 volts AC, 50Hz. Plug fittings are normally 2-pin with round section pins 4mm in diameter with centres 2cm apart. Lamp fittings are screw-type. Almost all the power is generated by thermal hydro-electric stations.
COMMUNICATIONS: Telephone: Full IDD service is available. Country code: 354. Outgoing international code: 90. **Fax:** Public facilities are available at the main telephone headquarters in Austurvoll Square and in most

hotels and offices. **Telex/telegram:** Telexes can be sent from post offices as well as from some major hotels and the telecommunications centre in Austurvoll Square (open daily). There is a 24-hour telegram service from the Telegraph Office in Reykjavík. **Post:** There is an efficient airmail service to Europe. Post offices are open 0830-1630 Monday to Friday. The post office at Austurstræti is open June-September additionally 1000-1400 Saturday. **Press:** The most popular newspapers are *Morgunbladid, DV* and *Tíminn.* There are no English-language dailies printed in Iceland, but an English-language magazine, *News from Iceland,* is available.
BBC World Service and Voice of America frequencies: From time to time these change. See the section *How to Use this Book* for more information.
BBC:

MHz	15.07	12.09	9.410	6.180

Voice of America:

MHz	11.97	9.670	6.040	5.990

PASSPORT/VISA

Regulations and requirements may be subject to change at short notice, and you are advised to contact the appropriate diplomatic or consular authority before finalising travel arrangements. Details of these may be found at the head of this country's entry. Any numbers in the chart refer to the footnotes below.

	Passport Required?	Visa Required?	Return Ticket Required?
Full British	1	No	Yes
BVP	Valid	No	Yes
Australian	Yes	No	Yes
Canadian	Yes	No	Yes
USA	Yes	No	Yes
Other EU (As of 31/12/94)	1	No	Yes
Japanese	Yes	No	Yes

PASSPORTS: Valid passport required by all except:
(a) [1] nationals of Belgium, Denmark, France, Germany, Italy, Luxembourg and The Netherlands holding a national ID card or, in the case of nationals of the UK, a valid BVP;
(b) nationals of Finland, Iceland, Norway and Sweden travelling between those countries;
(c) nationals of Austria, Liechtenstein and Switzerland

travelling as tourists and holding a valid national ID card.
British Visitors Passport: Acceptable. A BVP is valid for holidays or unpaid business trips to Iceland for a period not exceeding 3 months. Trips to Iceland, Denmark, Norway, Sweden or Finland must add up to less than 3 months in any 9-month period.
VISAS: Required by all except:
(a) nationals of countries referred to on the chart above;
(b) nationals of Scandinavian countries;
(c) nationals of Anguilla, Antigua & Barbuda, Austria, Bahamas, Barbados, Bermuda, Botswana, Brazil, Brunei, Cayman Islands, Chile, Cyprus, Czech Republic, Dominica, Falkland Islands, Fiji, Gambia, Gibraltar, Grenada, Guyana, Hong Kong, Hungary, Israel, Jamaica, Kiribati, South Korea, Lesotho, Liechtenstein, Malawi, Malaysia, Malta, Mauritius, Mexico, Monaco, Montserrat, New Zealand, Poland, St Helena, St Kitts & Nevis, St Lucia, St Vincent & the Grenadines, San Marino, Seychelles, Singapore, Slovak Republic, Slovenia, Solomon Islands, Swaziland, Switzerland, Tanzania, Trinidad & Tobago, Turks & Caicos Islands, Tuvalu, Uruguay, Vanuatu, Vatican City and Virgin Islands for a stay of up to 3 months.
Types of visa: *Entry* (cost £10).
Validity: Up to 3 months. For extensions apply to nearest police authority in Iceland.
Application to: Consulate (or Consular section at Embassy). For addresses, see top of entry.

Application requirements: (a) Completed visa application form. (b) 2 passport-size photos. (c) Valid passport. (d) Return or onward ticket to a country to which the applicant has a legal right of entry. (e) For postal applications, a stamped-self-addressed envelope.
Working days required: Minimum 5 days by post or personal visit.
Temporary residence: Enquire at Icelandic Embassy.

MONEY

Currency: Iceland Krona (IKr) = 100 aurar. Notes are in denominations of IKr5000, 1000, 500 and 100. Coins are in denominations of IKr50, 10, 5 and 1, and 50 and 10 aurar.
Credit cards: Visa, Access/Mastercard, Diners Club and American Express are widely accepted. Check with your credit card company for details of merchant acceptability and other services which may be available.
Travellers cheques: Widely used.
Exchange rate indicators: The following figures are included as a guide to the movements of the Krona against Sterling and the US Dollar:

Date:	Oct '92	Sep '93	Jan '94	Jan '95
£1.00=	91.45	106.21	107.15	107.27
$1.00=	57.63	69.55	72.42	68.57

Currency restrictions: There is no limit to the import of foreign and local currency. The export of local currency is limited to IKr17,000. The export of foreign currency is limited to the amount imported.
Banking hours: 0915-1600 Monday to Friday.

DUTY FREE

The following goods may be imported into Iceland by passengers of 16 years of age and over (tobacco products) or 20 years of age and over (alcoholic beverages) without incurring customs duty:
200 cigarettes or 250g of tobacco products; 1 litre of spirits and 1 litre of wine (under 21% proof) or 1 litre of spirits and 6 litres of beer (8 litres of Icelandic beer).
Note: All fishing equipment must be disinfected and a veterinary certificate obtained within seven days of arrival.
Prohibited items: Drugs, firearms and uncooked meats.

PUBLIC HOLIDAYS

Jan 1 '95 New Year's Day. **Apr 13** Maundy Thursday. **Apr 14** Good Friday. **Apr 17** Easter Monday. **May 25** Ascension Day. **Jun 5** Whit Monday. **Jun 19** For National Day. **Aug 7** Bank Holiday. **Dec 24-26** Christmas. **Dec 31** New Year's Eve. **Jan 1 '96** New Year's Day. **Apr 4** Maundy Thursday. **Apr 5** Good Friday. **Apr 8** Easter Monday.

HEALTH

Regulations and requirements may be subject to change at short notice, and you are advised to contact your doctor well in advance of your intended date of departure. Any numbers in the chart refer to the footnotes below.

	Special Precautions?	Certificate Required?
Yellow Fever	No	No
Cholera	No	No
Typhoid & Polio	No	-
Malaria	No	-
Food & Drink	No	-

Health care: All hospitals have excellent standards of medical service. There is a Reciprocal Health Agreement with the UK. On presentation of a UK passport or NHS card, all in-patient treatment at hospitals and emergency dental treatment for children aged 6-15 is free. Other medical and dental treatment, prescribed medicines and travel by ambulance must be paid for.

TRAVEL - International

AIR: The national airline is *Icelandair (FI)*.
Approximate flight times: From Iceland to *London* is 2 hours 50 minutes and to *Glasgow* is 2 hours 10 minutes.
International airport: *Keflavik (REK)*, 45km (28 miles) southwest of Reykjavík (travel time – 45 minutes). Airport facilities include bus services, departing after the arrival of each flight; taxi services; a duty-free shop selling a wide range of goods, including Icelandic handmade items such as sweaters; banking and exchange facilities, open on arrival of all scheduled services; restaurants and bars open 0700-2300 and car hire (*Icelandair*) offices. For further details on car hire, see the *Road* section below. There are international flights from major European and North American destinations, although some of these operate only seasonally. Flights are operated to the Faroe Islands and Greenland during the summer months. For further details, contact *Icelandair* (for address, see top of entry).
SEA: Weekly direct services run between Reykjavík and Immingham (Humberside). Although designed for cargo, the ships have six cabins with bathroom. The voyage takes approximately three days. Full details are available from *Regent Holidays* (tel: (01983) 864 212 *or* 864 225).

TRAVEL - Internal

AIR: *Icelandair (FI)* runs domestic services throughout the island to ten major destinations which link with regional carriers in the west, north and east of the country. There are 12 local airports. *Icelandair* also offers a variety of special air packages for the internal traveller. These include *Air Rover, Air/Bus Rover* and *Fly As You Please.* For further details, contact the local office.
SEA: Ferry services serve all coastal ports in summer, although weather curtails timetables in winter. There is a regular passenger-/car-ferry service between Reykjavík and Akranes.
RAIL: There is no railway system in Iceland.
ROAD: Roads serve all settlements. The 12,000km (7500 miles) of roads are mostly gravel rather than tarred. Traffic drives on the right. **Bus:** Services are efficient and cheap, connecting all parts of the island during the summer. In winter, buses operate to a limited number of destinations. Holiday tickets *(Omnibus Passport)* and *Air/Bus Rovers* are valid for unlimited travel by scheduled bus services; also *Full-Circle Passports* are available, valid for circular trips around Iceland (without any time limit). **Taxi:** Available from all hotels and airports. **Car hire:** Car rental services are available from Reykjavík, Akureyri and many other towns. **Note:** Drivers who are used to reliable, well-surfaced roads and regular road markings should think twice before hiring self-drive cars in Iceland, particularly if they are going to be driving away from the main centres. **Documentation:** Drivers must be over 20 years of age. An International Driving Permit is recommended, although it is not legally required. A temporary licence to drive is available from local authorities on presentation of a valid British or Northern Ireland driving licence.
JOURNEY TIMES: The following chart gives approximate journey times (in hours and minutes) from Reykjavík to other major cities/towns in Iceland.

	Air	Road	Sea
Isafjordur	0.50	10.00	-
Saudakrokur	0.45	4.30	-
Akureyri	0.55	6.00	-
Husavik	1.00	7.00	-
Höfn	0.65	9.30	-
Vestmanna Is.	0.30	*1.00	6.00
Egilsstadir	0.70	14.00	-

Note [*]: To Thorlakshofn, then sea crossing.

ACCOMMODATION

HOTELS: These are not classified but most have rooms with private bathroom or shower, telephone, radio and TV on request. The more expensive ones also have hairdressers, shops and beauty parlours. Hotel or hostel accommodation is available in most areas. For further information, contact the Icelandic Hotel and Restaurant Association, Hafnarstraeti 20, 101 Reykjavík. Tel: (1) 27410. Fax: (1) 27478.
PENSIONS & GUEST-HOUSES: These are available in the larger towns. Rooms are also available in private houses with breakfast included in the cost.
FARMHOUSE HOLIDAYS: Fairly widely available; contact the Iceland Tourist Bureau for details. Full board (three meals daily) is included. Reductions are available for children.
CAMPING/CARAVANNING: The inhospitable interior and unpredictable weather do not lend themselves to favourable camping conditions. The best method is to exploit the interior using the coastal ports as a base rather than camping outside the towns.
The best-equipped camping grounds are to be found in Reykjavík, Husafell, Isafjordur, Varmahlid, Akureyri, Myvatn, Eglisstadir, Laugarvatn, Thingvellire, Jokulsargljufur and Skaftafell. In some places camping is restricted to certain specially marked areas, while elsewhere camping is generally free. Campers, however, must request permission from the local farmer to camp on any fenced and/or cultivated land.
YOUTH HOSTELS: Youth hostels are open in Reykjavík, Leirubakki, Fljotsdalur, Vestmannaeyjar, Reynisbrekka, Höfn in Hornafjordur, Stafafell, Berunes, Seydisfjordur, Husey, Akureyri, Blonduos, Isafjordur and Breidavik. Many country hostels provide overnight accommodation for travellers bringing their own sleeping bags or bedrolls for a fee. In uninhabited areas there are a number of huts, owned by the touring club of Iceland, where travellers can stay overnight. They must observe regulations posted in the huts and bring their own sleeping bags and food. Groups travelling with the club always have priority over others. For more information, contact the Icelandic Youth Hostel Association, Sundlaugaveg 34, 105 Reykjavík. Tel: (1) 38110.

RESORTS & EXCURSIONS

Only the coastal regions of Iceland are inhabited. Probably the best way to enjoy the tourist attractions is to take one of the coach tours which are arranged all over the island and use the coastal towns as a base. The main fjord areas are in the far northwest and southeast while along the southern coastline are sandy beaches, farmlands, waterfalls and glaciers. The central region consists of spectacular highland plateaux, volcanoes, glaciers and mountains. Waterfalls abound in Iceland and, with the many glacial streams and rivers in the country, are among the largest in Europe. *Gullfoss* – the 'Golden Waterfall' – near **Geysir**, is always a favourite visit for tourists.
Reykjavík and the South: Reykjavík is the world's most northerly capital (although Nuuk in Greenland runs a close second). It is set on a broad bay, surrounded by mountains, and is in an area of geothermal hot springs providing it with a natural central heating system and pollution-free environment. It is a busy city of around 100,000 inhabitants and has a combination of old-fashioned wooden architecture and very modern buildings. There are nightclubs, art galleries and museums. Flights can be booked to visit the **Vestmanna Islands** off the south coast, and **Heimay**, where a recent volcanic eruption partially destroyed the town. Also there are trips to the hot springs and geysers of the area. *Reykjavík Excursions* operate daily excursions from the capital throughout the southwest part of Iceland as well as city sightseeing tours and special itineraries.
The Western Fjords: There are coach trips from Reykjavík to visit the small fishing villages and towns along the fjords in the northwest: **Kroksfardarnes, Holmavik, Korksfjaroarnes, Orlygshofn** and **Isafjordur.** The road climbs over mountain passes between each new fjord, stopping at Iceland's only whaling station, the *Museum of Farm Implements and Fishing Equipment* between Orlygshofn and Isafjordur and the *Dynjandi Waterfall.* Accommodation on these trips is in community centres and schools for those with sleeping bags. For further information, contact Isafjordur Tourist Office. Tel: (4) 3457.
The Central Highlands: A number of Icelandic tour companies operate 'safaris' in specially constructed overland buses into the mountainous interior. These are camping tours, and tents are provided. Sleeping bags can be bought or rented. Also recommended are warm clothing, hiking shoes, rubber boots and swimsuits for bathing in the warm pools. The tours go through lava beds, sandy deserts and rivers, passing glacial lakes with floating icebergs, glaciers, vast icefields, mountain ranges, crevasses and extinct volcanoes, and the *Skaftafell National Park.*
Akureyri and the North: Akureyri is the country's second most important town and is the commercial centre of a mainly agricultural region. There are museums of folklore and natural history in the town itself and coach tours to visit *Lake Myvatn*, an important bird sanctuary with many rare species, surrounded by lava formations, volcanoes and craters. *Nordair* offers a midnight sun trip flight to **Grimsey**, an offshore island which is within the Arctic Circle. Other places within easy reach of Akureyri include **Dimmuborgir,** the *Dettifoss* and *Godafoss* waterfalls and the *Myvatn* district, where there are hot pools for bathing. The temperature of some of these pools has risen recently making them uncomfortable for bathing, but others are still usable.
Höfn and the Southeast: This is an area of increasing tourist development. From Höfn, a fishing village on the southeast coast, sightseeing trips leave for *Jokullon,* a river lake at the mouth of the largest glacier in Europe, *Vatnajökull.* A journey over the glacier in a heated snowmobile is possible. Höfn also has horseriding facilities.

SOCIAL PROFILE

FOOD & DRINK: Icelandic food in general is based on fish and lamb, as well as owing much to Scandinavian and European influences. The salmon of Iceland is a great delicacy, served in many forms, one of the most popular being *graflax*, a form of marination. Fishing is Iceland's most important export, accounting for some 80% of the country's gross national product. There is also a heavy emphasis on vegetables grown in greenhouses heated by the natural steam from geysers. Specialities include *hangikjot* (smoked lamb), *hardfiskur* (dried fish), *skyr* (curds) and Icelandic *sild* (herring and salmon). There have been some welcome additions to the selection of eating places in Reykjavík and there is now a small but attractive choice of restaurants to cater for all pockets with new tourist menus. **Drink:** Bars have table and/or counter service, and will serve coffee as well as alcohol. In coffee shops you pay for the first cup; you help yourself to subsequent cups. There is a wide selection of European spirits and wines. *Brennivin* (a potent variation of aquavit made from potatoes) is a local drink.

NIGHTLIFE: Nightclubs and cinemas exist in major centres. Leading theatres are the National Theatre and the Reykjavík Idno Theatre, closed in summer, but during the tourist season there is an attractive light entertainment show in English called 'Light Nights' with traditional Icelandic stories and folk songs. The Iceland Symphony Orchestra gives concerts every two weeks at the University Theatre during the season September to June.

SHOPPING: Fluffy, earth-coloured *Lopi* wool blankets and coats, jackets, hats and handknits are synonymous with Iceland. Several local potters handthrow earthenware containers in natural colours. Crushed lava is a common addition to highly glazed ceramic pieces which are popular as souvenirs. The duty-free shop at Keflavik Airport sells all of these products, as does the Iceland Tourist Bureau souvenir shop in Reyjkavík.
Shopping hours: 0900-1800 Monday to Friday, 0900-1300/1600 Saturday.

SPORT: Ornithology: Lake Myvatn in northern Iceland is apparently the most fertile spot on the globe at that latitude and is a favourite breeding ground for many species of birdlife, particularly waterfowl. **Fishing:** The salmon fishing in Iceland is widely regarded as being among the best in world. Trout and charr may also be caught. There are many opportunities for **walking holidays** and **natural history tours;** enquire at the Tourist Bureau. **Pony trekking** holidays rely on the services of the sure-footed Icelandic horse, a descendant of the original Viking horse brought over from Norway over 1100 years ago. **Swimming** is very popular in Iceland – surprisingly mostly outdoors – since there are many natural and man-made pools, heated by geothermal springs, a natural phenomenon common in Iceland. In fact the word 'geyser' was derived from the Icelandic word *Geysir,* which is the name of Iceland's famous spouting hot spring in the southwest of the country. The main spectator sports are **soccer, handball, basketball** and **field athletics**.

SPECIAL EVENTS: The following is a selection of the major festivals and special events celebrated in Iceland during 1995/96. For a complete list, contact the Iceland Tourist Bureau.
Apr 18-19 '95 Handball: *Iceland v. Portugal,* Reykjavík. **Apr 20** *First Day of Summer Celebrations,* throughout country. **End Apr** *Donald Duck Ski Tournament for children,* Hlióarfjall and Reykjavík. **May 7-21** *World Championship Handball,* Reykjavík, Hafnarfjorour, Kópavogur, Akureyri. **Jun** *Reykjavík Games.* **Jun 11** *Seafarers' Day,* Reykjavík and all fishing ports. **Jun 17** *Independence Day Celebrations,* throughout country. **Jun 23-25** *Arctic Open Midsummer Night Golf Tournament,* Akureyri. **Jun 24-Aug 30** *Light Nights* (theatre and audio-visual presentation based on Icelandic folklore, performed in English with summaries in other languages), Reykjavík. **Jun-Aug** *Exhibition of works belonging to the National Gallery of Iceland,* Reykjavík; *Arbœr Folk Museum* (open air display), Reykjavík. **Jul** *Akureyri Guitar Festival.* **Jul-Aug** *Skálholt Church Music Festival.* **Aug** *Icelandic Cup Annual Athletic Games,* Reykjavík. **Aug 4-7** *Westman Islands Festival; Siglufjörour Herring Festival.* **Aug 20** *Reykjavík Marathon.* **Sep 16-Oct 1** *Nordic Tapestry Exhibition,* Reykjavík.
SOCIAL CONVENTIONS: Visitors will find Iceland is a classless society with a strong literary tradition. Handshaking is the normal form of greeting. An Icelander is called by his first name because his surname is made up of his father's Christian name plus 'son' or 'daughter' (eg John, the son of Magnus, would be called John Magnusson, while John's sister, Mary, would be known as Mary Magnusdóttir). People are addressed as *Fru* (Mrs) and *Herra* (Mr). Visitors will often be invited to homes especially if on business and normal courtesies should be observed. Icelanders pay careful attention to their appearance and, as for most Western countries, casual wear is widely acceptable although unsuitable for smart and social functions. **Tipping:** Service charges are included in most bills and extra tips are not expected.

BUSINESS PROFILE

ECONOMY: Iceland is short of indigenous raw materials and thus relies heavily on foreign trade to keep its relatively successful economy ticking over. Exports of goods and services account for over one-third of the gross national product. The largest proportion of these derive from fisheries and related products such as fishmeal and oil. The economy is thus particularly

susceptible to fluctuating world prices in this commodity and maintains a broad fisheries exclusion zone (320km/200 miles) to protect its earnings. Other sources of revenue come from sale of minerals such as aluminium, ferro-silicon, cement and nitrates used in fertilisers. Light industry is developing steadily and producing knitwear, blankets, textiles and paint. The major problem in the economy of recent years has been the fall-out from the wholesale liberalisation of trade with the European Union and the European Free Trade Association, the grouping of non-EU European countries of which Iceland is a member, which left some local companies unable to compete in some products such as furniture and household goods. The former EC and EFTA agreed the creation of a free-trade zone, the European Economic Area, in October 1991. Iceland's principal import suppliers are, in order of importance, Germany, Denmark, Norway and the UK. The UK, the USA and Germany are the country's main export markets.
BUSINESS: Business people are expected to dress smartly. Local business people are conservative but very friendly and most speak English. Previous appointments are not generally necessary, but visits between May and September should be planned in advance as many local business people travel abroad at this time. The telephone directory is listed by Christian name. **Office hours:** 0900-1700 Monday to Friday. Most offices are closed Saturday. Some firms close down completely for an annual 3-week holiday; this is usually in July.
COMMERCIAL INFORMATION: The following organisation can offer advice: Verzlunarrád Islands (Chamber of Commerce), Hús verslunarinnar (House of Commerce), 103 Reykjavík. Tel: (1) 676 666. Fax: (1) 686 564. Telex: 2316.
CONFERENCES/CONVENTIONS: There are several large hotels in Reykjavík equipped for conferences and business meetings, while smaller conferences may be held at venues outside the capital. For further information, contact the Iceland Convention and Incentive Bureau, PO Box 1700, Posthusstraeti 9, 121 Reykjavík (tel: (1) 626 070; fax: (1) 626 073); *or* the Iceland Tourist Board (for address, see top of entry).

CLIMATE

Iceland's climate is tempered by the Gulf Stream. Summers are mild and winters rather cold. The colourful *Aurora Borealis* (Northern Lights) appear from the end of August. From the end of May to the

beginning of August, there are nearly 24 hours of perpetual daylight in Reykjavík, while in the northern part of the country the sun barely sets at all. Winds can be strong and gusty at times and there is the occasional dust storm in the interior. Snow is not as common as the name of the country would seem to suggest, and in any case does not lie for long in Reykjavík; it is only in north Iceland that skiing conditions are reasonably certain. However, the weather is very changeable at all times of the year, and in Reykjavík there may be rain, sunshine, drizzle and snow in the same day. The air is clean and pollution-free, with no smog at all times of the year.
Required clothing: Lightweights in warmer months, with extra woollens for walking and the cooler evenings. Medium- to heavy-weights are advised in winter. Waterproofing is recommended throughout the year.

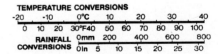

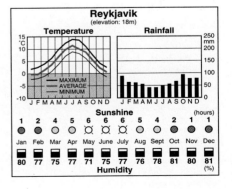

Location: Indian sub-continent.

Note: At the time of writing the Foreign Office advises against travel to the Kashmir Valley due to civil unrest.

Department of Tourism of the Government of India Ministry of Tourism
Transport Bhavan, Parliament Street, New Delhi 110 001, India
Tel: (11) 371 414. Fax: (11) 371 0518. Telex: 3166527.
India Tourism Development Corporation Ltd
SCOPE Complex, 6th Floor, Core VIII, 7 Lodi Road, New Delhi 110 003, India
Tel: (11) 436 0303. Fax: (11) 436 0233. Telex: 3174040.
Office of the High Commissioner for India
India House, Aldwych, London WC2B 4NA
Tel: (0171) 836 8484. Fax: (0171) 836 4331. Telex: 263581.
Visas: tel: (0171) 836 0990 *or* (0891) 880 800 *or* (0891) 444 544 (recorded information – calls are charged at the higher rate of 39/49p per minute). Opening hours: 0930-1300 and 1400-1700 Monday to Friday (0930-1300 for visa application and 1630-1730 for collection).
Government of India Tourist Office
7 Cork Street, London W1X 2LN
Tel: (0171) 437 3677 *or* (0181) 812 0929 (brochure request line). Fax: (0171) 494 1048. Opening hours: 0930-1300 and 1400-1800 Monday to Friday.

British High Commission
Chanakyapuri, New Delhi 211 100, India
Tel: (11) 601 371. Fax: (11) 609 940. Telex: 3165125 (a/b BHC IN).
Deputy High Commissions in: Bombay, Calcutta and Madras.
Embassy of India
2107 Massachusetts Avenue, NW, Washington, DC 20008
Tel: (202) 939 7000. Fax: (202) 939 7027.
Government of India Tourist Office
Suite 15, 30 Rockefeller Plaza, North Mezzanine, New York, NY 10112
Tel: (212) 586 4901/2/3. Fax: (212) 582 3274.
Embassy of the United States of America
Shanti Path, Chanakyapuri, New Delhi 110 021, India
Tel: (11) 600 651. Fax: (11) 687 2028 *or* 687 2391. Telex: 3182065 (a/b USEM IN).
Consulates in: Bombay, Calcutta and Madras.
High Commission for India
10 Springfield Road, Ottawa, Ontario K1M 1C9
Tel: (613) 744 3751/2/3. Fax: (613) 744 0913. Telex: 0534172.
Consulates in: Toronto and Vancouver.
India Government Tourist Office
Suite 1003, 60 Bloor Street West, Toronto, Ontario M4W 3B8
Tel: (416) 962 3787/8. Fax: (416) 962 6279.
Canadian High Commission
PO Box 5207, 7/8 Shantipath, Chanakyapuri, New Delhi 110 021, India
Tel: (11) 687 6500. Fax: (11) 687 6579. Telex: 03172363 (a/b DMCN IN).
Consulate in: Bombay.

AREA: 3,287,262 sq km (1,269,218 sq miles).
POPULATION: 846,302,688 (1991).
POPULATION DENSITY: 257.4 per sq km.
CAPITAL: New Delhi. **Population:** 7,206,704 (1991).
GEOGRAPHY: India shares borders to the northwest with Pakistan, to the north with China, Nepal and Bhutan, and to the east with Bangladesh and Myanmar. To the west lies the Arabian Sea, to the east the Bay of Bengal and to the south the Indian Ocean. Sri Lanka lies off the southeast coast, and the Maldives off the southwest coast. The far northeastern states and territories are all but separated from the rest of India by Bangladesh as it extends northwards from the Bay of Bengal towards Bhutan. The Himalayan mountain range to the north and the Indus River (west) and Ganga River (east) form a physical barrier between India and the rest of Asia. The country can be divided into five regions: Western, Central, Northern (including Kashmir and Rajasthan), Eastern and Southern.
LANGUAGE: The universal national language is English. The States are free to decide their own regional languages for internal administration and education. There are 14 official languages in India. About 50% of the population are Hindi speakers. The Muslim population largely speak Urdu. Other northern regional languages widely used are Punjabi, Bengali, Gujerati and Oriya. In the south, Tamil and Telegu are widely used, although other regional languages are Marathi, Kannada and Malayalam.
RELIGION: 83.5% Hindu, 10.7% Muslim, 1.8% Sikh, 2.6% Christian, 0.7% Buddhist, 0.7% others.
TIME: GMT + 5.30.
ELECTRICITY: Usually 220 volts AC, 50Hz. Some areas have a DC supply. Plugs used are of the round 2- and 3-pin type.
COMMUNICATIONS: Telephone: IDD service is widely available all over India. Otherwise calls must be placed through the international operator. Country code: 91. Outgoing international code: 00. **Fax:** Facilities are available in most 5-star hotels and some offices of the Overseas Communication Service in large cities. **Telex/telegram:** International 24-hour service from large hotels and telegraphic offices in major cities. **Post:** Airmail service to Western Europe takes up to a week. Stamps are often sold at hotels. **Press:** There are numerous local dailies published in several languages. Many newspapers are in English, the most important include *The Times of India*, *Indian Express*, *Hindu*, *The Hindustan Times*, *The Economic Times* and *The Statesman*.
BBC World Service and Voice of America frequencies: From time to time these change. See the section *How to Use this Book* for more information.
BBC:

MHz	17.79	15.31	11.75	9.740

A service is also available on 1413kHz.
Voice of America:

MHz	21.55	15.42	9.760	6.070

PHOTO CREDIT: DANIEL WHITE

Saddhu, Varanasi

DAB-M115

1000km
500mls

☐ *international airport*

FOR SUN WORSHIPPERS OF ALL AGES

Throughout the centuries India's beaches have attracted generations of sun worshippers. At Konark in Orissa for example, devotees of Surya the sun god erected a stupendous temple in the form of a massive twelve-wheeled chariot drawn by seven horses.

Further south, at Mahabalipuram, the renowned eighth century shore temple was dedicated to Vishnu, the Supreme Being, originally a manifestation of solar energy.

In the late twentieth century new kinds of temples have been built along India's shores, dedicated to the needs of the sybarite. Some, like those at Goa, Kovalam in Kerala or Fisherman's Cove near Mahabalipuram, are splendid beach resorts offering first class accommodation and facilities. Others, such as the beach pavilions on the treasured islands of the Lakshadweep, are closer to nature but no less comfortable.

There are hundreds and hundreds of kilometres of beaches - you'll worship in India. Phone us on 081-812 0929 for our free colour brochure or see your travel agent for details.

INDIAhhh

ONLY 9 HOURS AWAY

PASSPORT/VISA

Regulations and requirements may be subject to change at short notice, and you are advised to contact the appropriate diplomatic or consular authority before finalising travel arrangements. Details of these may be found at the head of this country's entry. Any numbers in the chart refer to the footnotes below.

	Passport Required?	Visa Required?	Return Ticket Required?
Full British	Yes	Yes	No
BVP	Not valid	-	-
Australian	Yes	Yes	No
Canadian	Yes	Yes	No
USA	Yes	Yes	No
Other EU (As of 31/12/94)	Yes	Yes	No
Japanese	Yes	Yes	No

PASSPORTS: Valid passport required by all.
British Visitors Passport: Not accepted.
VISAS: Required by all except nationals of Bhutan and Nepal, who may enter for up to 3 months providing the visit is not for business.
Types of visa: Tourist, Business and Transit. Prices vary according to length and purpose of stay (travellers should consult the High Commission or Embassy for details). With the exception of nationals of Afghanistan, China, Iran and South Africa, Transit visas are not required for passengers whose tickets show they intend to continue their journey from the airport, providing they do not leave the airport, and providing they continue their journey within 72 hours (24 hours if travelling via Bombay). Nationals of Pakistan must travel via Amritsar, Delhi or Bombay airports, continuing their journey the same day, and they are not allowed to leave the airport. Nationals of Bangladesh may require a visa if they have to leave the airport for a connecting flight. Restricted Area Permits are needed to visit some areas (see *Restricted and protected areas* below).
Validity: *Tourist* – 3 months (cost £13); *Tourist* – up to six months (cost £26); *Business* – up to one year (cost £32). The 3-month Tourist visa has to be used within three months from the date of issue.
Application to: Consulate (or Consular section at High Commission or Embassy). For addresses, see top of entry.
Application requirements: (a) Sufficient funds to cover duration of stay. (b) Business visa applicants should present letter from company. (c) Valid passport. (d) 3 passport-size photos.
Note: Postal applications should enclose payment in postal orders only.
Working days required: Personal visits – 2 days; by post – 3-4 weeks.
Temporary residence: Prior permission should be sought before entry into India.
Restricted and protected areas: Certain parts of the country have been designated protected or restricted areas that require special permits and in some cases prior government authorisation which is easily obtained. Intent to visit a specific restricted region should be indicated when applying for a visa and a permit will be granted to visit that region only. *Passengers are advised to check with the Government of India Tourist Office (GITO) for up-to-date information before departure.*
The following regions in the specified states (in brackets) can be visited with a special permit:
Itanagar, Ziro, Along, Pasighat, Miao and Namdapha (all in Arunachal Pradesh); Kaziranga National Park, Manas Bird Sanctuary, Guwahati City and Kamakhya Temple, Sibsagar and Jatinga Bird Sanctuary (all in Assam); Loktak Lake, Imphal, Moirang, INA Memorial, Keibul Deer Sanctuary and Waithe Lake (all in Manipur); Shillong, Barapani, Cherapunji, Mawsyram, Jakeran, Ranikor, Thadlaskein, Nartiang, Tura and Siju (all in Meghalaya); Vairangate, Thingdawl and Aizawl (all in Mizoram); Gangtok, Rumtek, Phodang, Pemayangtse and Zongri/West Sikkim (all in Sikkim); Pooh–Khab–Sumdho–Dhankar–Tabo–Gompa–Kaza route, Morang–Dabling route, Kaza–Kibber–Prangla Pass–Baralacha–Keylong–Manall route (all in Himachal Pradesh); Dharma Ghati, Joling Kong area, Sobla, Dharchula, Chaudas, Nanda Devi Sanctuary, Niti Ghati and Kalindi Khal/Chamoli and Uttar Kashi districts, and areas around Milam Glacier (all in Uttar Pradesh); Municipal area, Port Blair, Havelock Island, Long, Neil Island, Mayabunder, Diglipur, Rangat, Jolly Buoy, South Cinque, Red Skin, Mount Harriet and Madhuban (all in Andaman & Nicobar Islands); and Bangaram (Lakshadweep).

MONEY

Currency: Rupee (RS) = 100 paise. Notes are in denominations of RS500, 100, 50, 20, 10, 5, 2 and 1. Coins are in denominations of RS2 and 1, and 50, 25, 20, 10 and 5 paise.
Currency exchange: Currency can only be changed at banks or authorised money changers.
Credit cards: Access/Mastercard, American Express, Diners Club and Visa are accepted. Check with your credit card company for details of merchant acceptability and other services which may be available.
Travellers cheques: These are widely accepted and may be changed at banks.
Exchange rate indicators: The following figures are included as a guide to the movements of the Rupee against Sterling and the US Dollar:

Date:	Oct '92	Sep '93	Jan '94	Jan '95
£1.00=	45.00	48.00	46.41	49.08
$1.00=	28.36	31.44	31.37	31.37

Currency restrictions: Import and export of local currency is prohibited, except for Rupee travellers cheques. Foreign currency may be exported up to the amount imported and declared. All foreign currency must be declared on arrival if value is over US$10,000, and when exchanged the currency declaration form should be endorsed, or a certificate issued. The form and certificates must be produced on departure to enable reconversion into foreign currency. Changing money with unauthorised money changers is not, therefore, advisable.
Banking hours: 1000-1400 Monday to Friday; 1000-1200 Saturday.

DUTY FREE

The following goods may be imported into India by passengers over 17 years of age without incurring customs duty:
200 cigarettes or 50 cigars or 250g of tobacco; 1 litre of alcoholic beverage; 250ml of eau de toilette; goods for personal use or gifts to a value of RS600 (foreign passport holders) or RS2600 (Indian passport holders).
Prohibited items: Narcotics, plants, gold and silver bullion and coins not in current use are prohibited.

PUBLIC HOLIDAYS

Jan 26 '95 Republic Day. **Mar 3** Eid al-Fitr (End of Ramadan). **Apr 13** Mahavir Jayanti. **Apr 14** Good Friday. **May 11** Idu'l Zuha/Bakrid (Feast of the Sacrifice). **May 14** Buddha Purnima. **Aug 10** Milad-un-Nabi (Id-e-Milad). **Aug 15** Independence Day. **Oct 2** Mahatma Gandhi's Birthday. **Oct 3** Vijaya Dasami; Dussera; Ramlila. **Oct 23** Deepavali (Diwali). **Nov 7** Guru Nanak's Birthday. **Dec 25** Christmas Day. **Jan 26 '96** Republic Day. **Feb 22** Eid al-Fitr (End of Ramadan). **Mar/Apr** Mahavir Jayanti. **Apr 5** Good Friday. **Apr 29** Idu'l Zuha/Bakrid (Feast of the Sacrifice).
Notes: (a) Public holidays in India tend to be observed on a strictly regional basis. Only the secular holidays of Republic Day, Independence Day and Mahatma Gandhi's Birthday are universally observed. All others are dependent on region and religion, although on major religious festival days government offices will be closed nationwide. In addition, there are numerous festivals and fairs which are also observed in some States as holidays, the dates of which change from year to year. For more details, contact the Government of India Tourist Office. See also under the heading *Special Events* in the *Social Profile* section. (b) Muslim festivals are timed according to local sightings of various phases of the Moon and the dates given above are approximations. During the lunar month of Ramadan that precedes Eid al-Fitr, Muslims fast during the day and feast at night and normal business patterns may be interrupted. Many restaurants are closed during the day and there may be restrictions on smoking and drinking. For more information see the section *World of Islam* at the back of the book.

HEALTH

Regulations and requirements may be subject to change at short notice, and you are advised to contact your doctor well in advance of your intended date of departure. Any numbers in the chart refer to the footnotes below.

	Special Precautions?	Certificate Required?
Yellow Fever	Yes	1
Cholera	Yes	2
Typhoid & Polio	Yes	-
Malaria	3	-
Food & Drink	4	-

[1]: Any person (including infants over six months old) arriving by air or sea without a yellow fever certificate is detained in isolation for a period of up to 6 days if arriving within 6 days of departure from or transit through an infected area (30 days if travelling by ship). When a case of yellow fever is reported from any country, that country is regarded by the Government of India as being infected and is added to the list below. The following countries are regarded as being infected: Angola, Benin, Bolivia, Brazil, Burkina Faso, Burundi, Cameroon, Central African Republic, Chad, Colombia, Congo, Côte d'Ivoire, Ecuador, Equatorial Guinea, Ethiopia, French Guiana, Gabon, Gambia, Ghana, Guinea, Guinea-Bissau, Guyana, Kenya, Liberia, Mali, Niger, Nigeria, Panama, Peru, Rwanda, São Tomé e Príncipe, Senegal, Sierra Leone, Somalia, Sudan, Suriname, Tanzania, Togo, Trinidad & Tobago, Uganda, Venezuela, Zaïre and Zambia.
[2]: Travellers proceeding to countries that impose restrictions for arrivals from India or from an infected area in India on account of cholera are required to possess a certificate. An inoculation against cholera is recommended. See the *Health* section at the back of the book.
[3]: Malaria risk exists, mainly in the benign *vivax* form, throughout the year in the whole country excluding parts of the states of Himachal Pradesh, Jammu and Kashmir, and Sikkim. High resistance to chloroquine is reported in the malignant *falciparum* form.
[4]: All water should be regarded as being potentially contaminated. Water used for drinking, brushing teeth or making ice should have first been boiled or otherwise sterilised. Milk is unpasteurised and should be boiled. Powdered or tinned milk is available and is advised, but make sure that it is reconstituted with pure water. Avoid dairy products which are likely to have been made from unboiled milk. Only eat well-cooked meat and fish, preferably served hot. Pork, salad and mayonnaise may carry increased risk. Vegetables should be cooked and fruit peeled.
At the end of September 1994, there were outbreaks of the *bubonic plague* in the town of Surat. Visitors are advised to check with their national health authority prior to travel. For further information, consult the *Health* section at the back of the book.
Meningitis is present in some areas at certain times of the year. Vaccination is advisable.
Rabies is present. For those at high risk, vaccination before arrival should be considered. If you are bitten abroad, seek medical advice without delay. For more information, consult the *Health* section at the back of the book.
Health care: It is advisable to bring specific medicines from the UK. There are state-operated facilities in all towns and cities and private consultants and specialists in urban areas. In Sikkim, there are four district hospitals at Singtam, Gyalshing, Namchi and Mangan and one central hospital at Gangtok supplemented by small dispensaries and centres.
On leaving India: Visitors leaving for countries which impose health restrictions on arrivals from India are required to be in possession of a valid certificate of inoculation and vaccination. There is no health check-up of passengers leaving by air or sea.

TRAVEL - International

AIR: India's national airline is *Air India (AI).*
For free advice on air travel, call the Air Travel Advisory Bureau in the UK on (0171) 636 5000 (London) *or* (0161) 832 2000 (Manchester).
Approximate flight times: From *London* to Delhi is 9 hours, to Calcutta is 12 hours, to Madras is 12 hours 30 minutes and to Bombay is 9 hours.
From *Los Angeles* to Delhi is 25 hours 30 minutes.
From *New York* to Delhi is 18 hours.
From *Singapore* to Delhi is 5 hours.
From *Sydney* to Delhi is 10 hours.
International airports: *Bombay (BOM)* is 29km (18 miles) north of the city (travel time – 40 minutes). There is a coach to the *Air India* office and major hotels. Taxi services go to the city. Taxi fares should have fixed rates from the airport to the city. Public transport is also available in the form of the *EATS* bus service and local buses. Other facilities include a retiring room for passengers in transit and a child-care lounge.
Calcutta (CCU) is 13km (11 miles) northeast of the city (travel time – 60 minutes). There is a 24-hour coach

Timatic

Health
GALILEO/WORLDSPAN: **TI-DFT/DEL/HE**
SABRE: **TIDFT/DEL/HE**

Visa
GALILEO/WORLDSPAN: **TI-DFT/DEL/VI**
SABRE: **TIDFT/DEL/VI**

For more information on Timatic codes refer to Contents.

service to *Indian Airlines* city office and major hotels. A bus goes every 10 minutes 0530-2200. Taxi services go to the city. There is a 24-hour post office, bars, duty-free shops and restaurants available.
Delhi (DEL) (Indira Gandhi International) is 16km (10 miles) from the city (travel time – 45 minutes). There are coach, bus and taxi services to the city. There are 24-hour duty-free shops and restaurants.
Madras (MAA) is 18km (14 miles) southwest of the city (travel time – 40 minutes). A coach meets all flight arrivals 0900-2300. There is a train every 20-30 minutes from 0500-2300. Bus no. 18A runs every 25 minutes from 0500-2200. Taxi services go to the city.
Airport facilities: All the above airports have money exchange facilities, tourist information offices and hotel reservation services.
Note: *Ahmedabad Airport* is being upgraded as an international airport.
Departure tax: RS300 in *Bombay, Delhi* and *Madras.*
SEA: The main passenger ports are Bombay, Calcutta, Cochin, Madras, Calicut, Panaji (Goa) and Rameswaram (the main departure point for the sea crossing to Sri Lanka; passenger services are presently suspended due to the political situation in Sri Lanka).
Indian ports are also served by several international shipping companies and several cruise lines. There are, however, no regular passenger liners operating to South-East Asia.
RAIL: Note: This section gives details of the major overland routes to neighbouring countries (where frontiers are open); in most cases these will involve road as well as rail travel. Details should be checked with the GITO as they may be subject to change.
Connections to Pakistan are currently only possible between Amritsar and Lahore (New Delhi–Amritsar–Lahore–Hyderabad–Karachi).
The most practical and popular route to Nepal is by train to Raxaul (Bihar) and then by bus to Kathmandu or by train to Gorakphur (or by bus if coming from Varanasi) and then by bus to Kathmandu crossing the border at Sunauli; also, by train to Nautanwa (UP) and then by bus to Kathmandu/Pokhara, or Bhairawa to Lumbibi for Pokhara. It is also possible to make the crossing from Darjeeling by bus to Kathmandu across the southern lowlands.
The best way of reaching Bhutan is by train to Siliguri, then bus to Phuntsholing. There is also an airlink from Calcutta to Paro by *Druk Air.*
To Bangladesh, the best route is Calcutta to Bangaon (West Bengal) by train, rickshaw across the border to Benapol, with connections via Khulna or Jessore to Dhaka. Another route is from Darjeeling via Siliguri, then train or bus from Jalpaiguri to Haldibari.
Travel to Sri Lanka is possible on the following link: Madras–Rameswaram–Talaimannar–Colombo Fort. This includes a ferry crossing from Rameswaram.
Currently no land frontiers are open between India and Myanmar or the People's Republic of China.
ROAD: Of late, the overland route from Europe to India has become very popular, but travellers should have accurate information about border crossings, visa requirements and political situations en route. Several 'adventure holiday' companies arrange overland tours and buses to India. For information on overland routes to neighbouring countries, consult the *Rail* section above.

TRAVEL - Internal

AIR: The domestic airline is *Indian Airlines.* The network connects over 70 cities. *Indian Airlines* also operate regular flights to the neighbouring countries of Pakistan, Nepal, Bangladesh, Sri Lanka, Afghanistan, the Maldives, Singapore and Thailand.
Special fares: There are various special *Indian Airlines* fares available to foreign nationals and Indian nationals residing abroad. All are available throughout the year, and may be purchased either abroad or in India, where payment is made in a foreign convertible currency (such as US Dollars or Sterling). With the exception of the Youth Fare India (see below), discounts of 90% are available for children under two years, and of 50% for children aged 2-12. Full details of all the special fares are contained in the *See India Travel Schemes* brochure, available from the GITO. A summary of each is given below.
Discover India costs US$400 and is valid for 21 days from first flight, offering unlimited economy-class travel on all domestic *Indian Airlines* services. No stop may be visited more than once, except for transfer.
Youth Fare India is valid for 120 days, offering a 25% discount on the normal US Dollar fare. It is available to those aged 12-30 at the commencement of travel for journeys on economy/executive class of domestic air services and Indo-Nepal services.
South India Excursion is valid for 21 days from the first flight on *Indian Airlines,* offering economy-class (up to 30% off the normal US Dollar fare) travel between any or all of the south India stations of Madras, Trichi, Madurai, Trivandrum, Cochin, Coimbatore and Bangalore. For individual passengers, this fare must be combined with fares from the Maldives or Sri Lanka to India via Madras, Tiruchirapalli or Trivandrum.
India Wonderfares (North, South, East and West) cost US$200 and are valid for seven days, offering economy-class travel between main centres in India. No town may be visited more than once, except for transfer.
SEA/RIVER: There are ferries from Calcutta and Madras to Port Blair in the Andaman Islands, and from Cochin and Calicut to the Lakshadweep Islands. Services are often seasonal, and are generally suspended during the monsoon. One particularly attractive boat journey is the 'backwaters' excursion in the vicinity of Cochin in Kerala. Several local tours are available.
RAIL: The Indian internal railway system is the largest in Asia and the second-largest in the world. There are 60,900km (37,850 miles) of track, over 7000 stations and over 11,000 locomotives, including 5000 steam engines. Rail travel is relatively inexpensive. Express services link all the main cities and local services link most other parts of the country. Buses connect with trains to serve parts of the country not on the rail network. Children 5-11 years of age pay half price, children under five travel free.
There are five classes of travel: first-class air-conditioned, second-class air-conditioned, air-conditioned chair car, first-class and second-class. Major trains carry restaurant cars. Important routes run as follows: Bombay–Ahmadabad (five a day), Bombay–Allahabad (five a day), Bombay–Bangalore–Mysore (two a day), Bombay–Calcutta (three a day), Bombay–Madras (three a day), Bombay–New Delhi (four a day), Bombay–Patna (five a day), Bombay–Pune (five a day); Calcutta–Allahabad (three a day), Calcutta–New Jalpaiguri–Darjeeling (Toy Train, one a day), Calcutta–Madras (three a day), Calcutta–New Delhi (three a day); Delhi–Agra (Taj Express, five a day), Delhi–Ahmadabad (four a day), Delhi–Allahabad (five a day), Delhi–Jaipur (five a day), Delhi–Madras (three a day); Madras–Ernakulam–Cochin (one a day).
Special fares: There is a special **Indrail Pass** consisting of a single non-transferable, non-refundable ticket which enables a visitor to travel on any train without restriction within the period of validity. It is sold only to foreign nationals and Indians residing abroad holding a valid passport, and replaces all other concessional tickets. Payment is accepted only in foreign currency (US Dollars or Sterling). Children between 5-12 years of age are entitled to a **Child Indrail Pass,** and pay roughly half the normal fare. Children under five years of age travel free. The normal free *baggage allowances* are 70kg air-conditioned class, 50kg first-class/AC Chair Car and 35kg second-class. **Child Indrail Pass** holders are entitled to half the above allowances. Holders of an **Indrail Pass** are exempted from all reservation fees, sleeping car charges, express train meal charges and other costs. *Validity:* A ticket can be used within one year of its issue. Validity period is from the date of commencement of the first journey up to midnight of the date on which validity expires. The ticket must be used within one year of its issue. *Advance reservation* is essential, particularly on overnight journeys, arranged through travel agents. Reservations are on a first-come-first-served basis. For individuals or small groups a 2/3-month notice should suffice; during summer months a longer period is desirable to ensure reservations for the entire itinerary. Reservations can be made up to 360 days in advance. **Indrail** passes can be reserved in the UK from *SD Enterprises.* Tel: (0181) 903 3411.
Palace on Wheels: Expensively decorated Edwardian-style luxury steam train. Each coach consists of saloon, four sleeping compartments with upper and lower berth, bathroom, shower, toilet and small kitchen. Room service is available. There is a dining car, a bar, an observation car and a fully-equipped first-aid centre. Tariff includes cost of travel; full catering; elephant, camel and boat rides; conducted sightseeing tours; and entrance fees.
Itinerary:
Delhi–Jaipur–Udaipur–Jaisalmer–Jodhpur–Bikaner–Delhi.
Bookings: Several tour operators/travel agents organise escorted tour facilities which includes the *Palace on Wheels.*
Interesting is also a journey on the 'Toy Train', a narrow-gauge rail line completed in 1881. Covering the route Calcutta–New Jalpaiguri–Darjeeling in 8 hours, it crosses over 500 bridges and offers ample opportunity for photos as the pace is quite leisurely. There is one daily train in either direction.
ROAD: Traffic drives on the left. An extensive network of **bus** services connects all parts of the country, and is particularly useful for the mountainous regions where there are no rail services. Details of routes may be obtained from the local tourist office. **Tourist cars:** There are a large number of chauffeur-driven tourist cars (some air-conditioned) available in important tourist centres of India. These unmetered tourist cars run at a slightly higher rate than the ordinary taxis, and are approved by the GITO. Self-drive cars are not generally available. **Documentation:** A 'Carnet de Passage' with full insurance and Green Card are required. An International Driving Permit is recommended. A temporary licence to drive is available from local authorities on presentation of a valid national driving licence.
URBAN: Taxis and **auto rickshaws** are available in large cities and fares should be charged by the kilometre. They do not always have meters but, where they do, visitors should insist on the meter being flagged in their presence. Fares change from time to time and therefore do not always conform to the reading on the meter, but drivers should always have a copy of the latest fare chart available for inspection. Public transport is often crowded and can be uncomfortable. For those interested, *Bombay Electric Supply & Transport (BEST)* is one of the best public transport operators in India.
JOURNEY TIMES: The following chart gives approximate journey times (in hours and minutes) from Delhi to other major cities/towns in India.

	Air	Road	Rail	Sea
Bombay	1.50	28.00	17.30a	-
Calcutta	2.00	30.00	18.00b	-
Madras	3.00	45.00	32.00	-
Hyd'bad	1.55	40.00	24.00	-
Agra	0.40	4.30	3.15	-
Jaipur	0.40	6.00	5.15	-
Jammu	1.50	14.45	16.00	-
Triv'rum	5.00c	62.00	60.00	-
Patna	1.30	22.00	16.00	-
Port Blair	5.05c	-	-	d

[a] Time by express (not daily); normal train takes 23 hours. **[b]** Time by express (not daily); normal train takes 25 hours. **[c]** Does not include stopover in Madras. **[d]** Boat journey from Madras takes 3-4 days.
Note: Further information (including route maps, times of express trains and more detailed journey-time charts) may be found in the official *India* brochure, available free from the Government of India Tourist Office.

ACCOMMODATION

For all sections, contact the GITO for detailed information.
HOTELS: Modern Western-style hotels are available in all large cities and at popular tourist centres. Usually they offer a choice of first-class Western and Indian cuisine. Hotel charges in India are moderate compared to those in many other countries. A 10% service charge and a 7-20% 'luxury tax' is normally added to bills.
A full list of Government Approved Hotels, Palace Hotels and ITDC (Ashok) Travellers' Lodges is available from the Government of India Tourist Office or contact the Federation of Hotel and Restaurant Associations of India, M-75 (Market), Greater Kailash II, New Delhi 110048. Tel: (11) 641 1779 *or* 646 4194. Fax: (11) 646 194. **Grading:** Hotels range from **5-star deluxe, 5-** and **4-star** hotels, which are fully air-conditioned with all luxury features, **3-star** hotels, which are functional and have air-conditioned rooms, to **2-** and **1-star** hotels, which offer basic amenities.
TOURIST BUNGALOWS: There are tourist bungalows (known as holiday homes in Maharashtra and Gujarat, and tourist lodges in West Bengal) at almost every tourist centre in the country, under the control of the respective State Government Tourist Development Corporation, except in the metropolitan cities of Delhi, Calcutta, Madras, Bombay and Bangalore. These include a clean single, double and family room, most with a bath and general canteen. At holiday homes and certain tourist cottages there are kitchen facilities. Bookings should be made (a deposit will be required) with the managing director of the respective corporation, or with the manager of the bungalow.
HOUSEBOATS: These are peculiar to Srinagar. Moored on the banks of the river Jhelum and the Dal and Nagin lakes, they range from 24-38m (79-125ft) in length and 3-6m (10-20ft) in width. There are two living rooms, two or three bedrooms, bathrooms, and hot and cold running water. The boats have every comfort and are sumptuously furnished with all modern amenities: electricity, crockery, cutlery, radios and decks for bathing. Smaller boats can be punted about and moored at different places. Each houseboat has a paddle boat for crossings and an attached kitchen-boat which also serves as quarters for the staff. Reductions are available for children and, in the lower two categories, for lodging only. **Grading:** There are four categories: **deluxe, A, B** and **C.**

CAMPSITES: These are to be found throughout India. Full addresses may be obtained from the GITO or the YMCA Tourist Association, Cum Programme Centre, Jai Singh Road, New Delhi 110 001. Tel: (11) 311 915. Telex: 62547.

YOUTH HOSTELS: These provide a convenient and cheap base for organised tours, trekking, hiking or mountaineering. The Department of Tourism has set up 16 hostels, spread throughout every region, ideally placed for exploring both the plains and the hill stations. Each has a capacity for about 40 beds or more, segregated roughly half and half into male and female dormitories. Beds with mattresses, bedsheets, blankets, wardrobe with locks, electric light points, member kitchen utensils and parking areas are available at each hostel.

RESORTS & EXCURSIONS

India has a rich history and the palaces, temples and great cities of its ancient cultures cannot fail to grip the imagination. In the spring particularly, the big cities come alive with concerts, plays, parties and exhibitions. Among the most spectacular hill stations (mountain resorts which make ideal destinations in summer) are **Simla** (once the Imperial summer capital), **Mussoorie, Ranikhet** and **Nainital** (within reach of Delhi), and West Bengal's magnificent resort, **Darjeeling** – which offers a breathtaking view of the whole *Kanchenjunga* range. Along the fabled coasts of **Malabar** and **Coromandel**, unspoiled sandy beaches stretch for miles. Skiing is possible in the silent snowbound heights of *Gulmarg* and *Kufri* in the Himalayas.

The North

Delhi has two parts: **New Delhi**, India's capital and the seat of government, is a 20th-century city, offering wide tree-lined boulevards, spacious parks and the distinctive style of Lutyen's architectural design; 'Old' **Delhi**, on the other hand, is a city several centuries old, teeming with narrow winding streets, temples, mosques and bazaars. Notable sites are the *Red Fort* and the nearby *Jama Masjid* (India's largest mosque) and the *Qutab Minar's* soaring tower. Delhi attracts the finest musicians and dancers offering an ideal opportunity to hear the *sitar, sarod* and the subtle rhythm of the *tabla,* and to see an enthralling variety of dance forms, each with its own costumes and elaborate language of gestures. Theatres and cinemas show films from all over India, and the city has some of the country's finest restaurants offering many styles of regional cuisine.

Delhi lies at the apex of the *'Golden Triangle'* – an area filled with ancient sites and monuments. In the southwest lies **Agra**, city of the fabled *Taj Mahal.* This magnificent mausoleum was built by Shah Jahan as a monument to his love for his wife, Mumtaz, who died in childbirth. Shah Jehan was later imprisoned by his own son in the nearby *Red Fort.* Other important landmarks are *Akbar's Palace,* the *Jahangir Mahal,* the octagonal tower *Mussumman Burj* and the *Pearl Mosque.* Nearby is **Fatehpur Sikri,** the town Akabar built as his new capital but abandoned after only a few years. This town is now no more than a ghost town.

The southwestern pivot of the triangle is **Jaipur**, gateway to the desert state of Rajasthan. Known as the 'Pink City' because of the distinctive colour of its buildings, Jaipur is a town of broad, open avenues and many palaces. The *Amber Palace,* just outside the city is particularly beautiful as is the façade of the *Palace of the Winds* within the city walls. To the southwest is **Udaipur**, famed for its *Lake Palace Hotel,* built on an island in the lake, while to the north, in the centre of the Rajasthan desert, is **Jodhpur**, with its colourful, winding lanes and towering fortress. Near **Ajmer** is the small lakeside town of **Pushkar**. It is a site of religious importance for Hindus and it is here that every November the fascinating *Camel Fair* is held. **Jaisalmer** is a charming oasis town, once a resting place on the old caravan route to Persia. Among its attractions are the camel treks out into the surrounding desert.

To the south of the 'Golden Triangle' is the huge state of **Madhya Pradesh**. Its greatest attractions lie close to the northern frontier. Less than 160km (100 miles) from Agra is the great ruined fortress at **Gwalior.** To the east lies **Khajuraho** with its famous temples and friezes of sensuously depicted figures – a must for any visitor.

To the east of Delhi is the state of **Uttar Pradesh**, through which flows the sacred *River Ganga.* Built along its bank is the wondrous city of **Varanasi**, India's holiest Hindu location. The town itself is a maze of winding streets, dotted with temples and shrines. Lining the river are a series of ghats which, at dawn, are thronged with pilgrims and holy men performing ritual ablutions and prayers.

Less than 320km (200 miles) to the north of Delhi is **Simla**, the greatest of all hill stations, surrounded by finely scented pine forests and the rich beauty of the *Kulu Valley.*

In the far north, reaching into Central Asia, is the extensive mountain region of **Kashmir**, an area long established as a popular summer resort, and the valley of the *River Jhelum.* The gateway to the region is **Jammu**, a town surrounded by lakes and hills. The temples of *Rambireshwar* and *Raghunath* number among its most impressive sights. Jammu is the railhead for **Srinagar**, the ancient capital of Kashmir, and favourite resort of the Mughal emperors. It was they who built the many waterways and gardens around *Lake Dal,* complementing the natural beauty of the area. Among the attractions are the houseboats where visitors can live on the lakes surrounded by scenery so beautiful it is known as 'paradise on earth'.

Srinagar is also a convenient base for trips to **Gulmarg** and **Pahalgam.** Gulmarg offers fine trout fishing, and enjoys the distinction of having the highest golf course in the world. From here there are good views of *Nanga Parbat,* one of the highest mountains in the world. It is well placed as a starting point for treks into the hills and mountains. *Pahalgam* is another popular hill resort and base for pilgrimages to the sacred cave of *Amar Nath.*

More exotic, though less accessible, is the region of Ladakh, beyond the Kashmir Valley. It is a mountainous land on the edge of the Tibetan Plateau which is still largely Tibetan in character. The capital, **Leh**, is situated high in the Karakouram mountain range, through which passed the old *Silk Road* from China to India and Europe.

INDIA: States
A Arunachal Pradesh
H Haryana
Ma Manipur
Me Meghalaya
Mi Mizoram
N Nagaland
T Tripura
Jammu & Kashmir
Himachal Pradesh
Punjab
NEW DELHI
Sikkim
Rajasthan
Uttar Pradesh
Assam
Bihar
Gujarat
Madhya Pradesh
Tropic of Cancer
Maharashtra
Orissa
West Bengal
Andhra Pradesh
Karnataka
Tamil Nadu
Kerala
Union Territories:
1 Chandigarh
2 Delhi
3 Goa, Daman & Diu
4 Dadra & Nagar Haveli
5 Pondicherry
6 Lakshadweep
7 Andaman & Nicobar Is.
DAB-M279
1000km
500mls

The West

The principal metropolis of Western India is **Bombay**, the capital of the state of **Maharashtra,** a bustling port and commercial centre, with plate-glass skyscrapers and modern industry jostling alongside bazaars and the hectic streetlife. Many of the country's films are made in the famous Bombay studios. The city also boasts one of the finest race tracks in India, the Mahalaxmi course. There is a pleasant seafront with a palm-lined promenade and attractive beaches such as *Juhu, Versova, Marve, Madh* and *Manori.* On the waterfront is Bombay's best-known landmark, the *Gateway to India,* whence boats leave on the 10km (6-mile) journey across the busy harbour to the **Elephanta Island**. The island is famous for the 8th-century cave temples, on whose walls are large rock carvings, the finest of which is the 3-faced *Maheshmurti,* the great Lord.

To the north lies the state of **Gujarat,** renowned for its silks, as the birthplace of Mahatma Gandhi, and as the last refuge of the Asian lion, found deep in the *Gir Forest.* **Ahmadabad**, in the east of the state, is the principal textile city of India, producing silks which are famous throughout the world. Ahmadabad is also the site of *Sabarmati Ashram,* founded by Mahatma Gandhi, from where his ideology of non-violence is still promoted. Gandhi's birthplace is some 320km (200 miles) to the west, in the fishing village of **Porbandar**.

To the east of Bombay is **Aurangabad**, the starting point for visits to two of the world's most outstanding rock-cut temples. The Buddhist cave temples at **Ajanta** date back at least 2000 years. Cut into the steep face of a deep rock gorge, the 30 caves contain exquisite paintings depicting daily life at that time.

The caves at **Ellora** depict religious stories and are Hindu, Buddhist and Jain in origin. The *Temple of Kailasa* is the biggest hewn monolith temple in the world. Southeast of Bombay are several fine hill stations, notably **Matheran** with its narrow gauge trains, **Mahabaleshwar** and **Pune** with its peaceful *Bund Gardens.*

Further to the south lies **Goa.** The 100km-long (60-mile) coastline offers some of the finest beaches in the subcontinent. Goa was Portuguese until 1961, and there is also a charming blend of Latin and Indian cultures. **Panaji**, the state capital, is one of the most relaxed and elegant of India's cities. The town is dominated by the huge *Cathedral of the Immaculate Conception,* but the shops, bars and pleasant streets are its main attraction. 'Old Goa', only a bus ride away from Panaji, displays a bewildering variety of architectural styles. Buildings of note include the *Basilica* and the *Convent and Church of St Francis of Assisi.* In nearby **Ponda** is the 400-year-old *Temple of Shri Mangesh,* which is said to be the oldest Hindu shrine.

Accommodation in the region includes the luxury resort of **Aguada**, the Taj holiday village and the Aguada hermitage. There are also good, simple hotels and cottages for rent in villages along the coastline, notably **Calangute, Baya** and **Colva.**

Goa also has several wildlife sanctuaries, including *Bondla* in the hills of western *Ghats,* where wild boar and sambar can be seen in their natural habitat. The region is famous for its food – an array of dishes, both Indian and Portuguese – as well as for its colourful festivals, including the spectacular Carnival held on the three days leading up to Ash Wednesday.

The South

The south is the part of India least affected by incursions of foreign cultures through the centuries. It is here that Indian heritage has survived in its purest form.

The regional capital is **Madras**, India's fourth-largest city. Madras is the cradle of the ancient Dravidian civilisation, one of the oldest articulate cultures in the world. It is also home of the classical style of Indian dancing and a notable centre of temple sculpture art. Sprawling over 130 sq km (50 sq miles), the metropolis has few tall buildings and enjoys the relaxed ambience of a market town rather than the bustle of a huge city. From *Madras Lighthouse* there is a fine view of the city that includes many churches which tell of the city's strong Christian influence, first introduced in AD78 when the apostle St Thomas was martyred here.

Madras, however, is largely a commercial city and the centre of the area's rail, air and road networks, and serves as a good starting point from which to explore the south. Within the region are several important religious centres, notably **Kanchipuram**, which has an abundance of temples, and whose striking *gopurams,* or gateways, are decorated with sculptures of gods and goddesses. Inland is **Madurai**, with a large and bustling temple, and **Thanjavur**. Also worth visiting is **Tiruchirapalli**, which has a fortress built atop a strange boulder-shaped hill that dominates the town.

Further south, along the coast, is **Pondicherry**, an attractive town with a distinctive French style, and beyond, **Rameswarum**, once the ferry link to Sri Lanka.

To the west lies the state of **Kerala,** where many of India's major coastal resorts are to be found. Among the finest is **Kovalam**, offering unspoilt beaches and a new complex of modern amenities, including luxury bungalows and a 5-storey hotel with swimming pool. Only a few miles away is **Trivandrum**, the state capital with its famous *Padmanabhaswamy Temple.* Further inland is the *Periyar Game Sanctuary* which has a rich and varied wildlife. Other resorts include *Cranganorre, Alleppey* and *Cochin.*

Further to the north is the state of **Karnataka**, which has fine, unexplored beaches at **Karwar**, **Mahe** and **Udipi**. The state's capital is **Bangalore**, an affluent city which is the centre of electronics and engineering industries, but has many charming parks and gardens. To the southwest lies **Mysore**, where incense is manufactured, and where you can stay in the *Lalitha Mahal Hotel,* previously the home of a Maharaja.

Karnataka has a number of important religious and historical sites, including the ruins at **Hampi** to the north of Bangalore, and the vast statue of Lord Bahubali at *Sravanabelagola,* north of Mysore.

To the east of Karnataka is the state of **Andhra Pradesh**, with its capital at **Hyderabad**, offering a well-stocked one-man museum. 220km (350 miles) to the east is **Visakhapatnam**, the fourth-largest port. Far away to the east across the Bay of Bengal are the **Andaman Islands**, a lushly forested archipelago which has exotic plant life and a wide variety of corals and tropical fish, making it a major attraction for snorkelling enthusiasts. The islands' capital, **Port Blair**, can be reached from Madras and Calcutta by boat or air.

The East

The largest city in India and hub of the east is **Calcutta**. Established as a British trading post in the 17th century, it grew rapidly into a vibrant centre. Its colonial heritage is reflected in the buildings of Chowringhee Street and Clive Street, now Jawaharlal Nehru Road and Netaji Subhash Road. The city is filled with life and energy. It is a major business centre and offers fine markets and bazaars. It is also the centre of much of the country's creative and intellectual activity, including the sub-continent's finest film-makers. Central Calcutta is best viewed from the *Maidan,* the central area of parkland where early morning *yoga* sessions take place. The city's *Indian Museum* is one of the finest in Asia. Other attractions include the white marble *Victoria Memorial,* the *Octherlony Institute* and the headquarters of the Rama Krishna movement. Across the river are the *Kali Temple of Dakshineshwasar* and the *Botanical Gardens.* To the west is the state of Bihar, with the religious centre of **Bodhgaya,** a sacred place for both Hindus and Buddhists. To the south, in the state of Orissa, are three temple cities. Foremost is **Bhubaneswar**, a town in which there once stood no less than 7000 temples, 500 of which have survived. Largest of these is the great *Lingaraja Temple,* dedicated to Lord Shiva. A short journey away to the south of Bhubaneswar lies **Puri**, one of the four holiest cities in India, now being developed as a beach resort. In June and July Puri stages one of India's most spectacular festivals, the *Rath Yatra* or 'Car Festival', at which pilgrims pay homage to images of gods drawn on massive wooden chariots. A short distance along the coast to the north is **Konarak**, known for its 'Black Pagoda' – a huge solitary temple to the sun god in the form of a chariot drawn by horses. The sculpture has a sensuous nature similar to that of Khajuraho, and is counted amongst the finest in India.

To the north of Calcutta is one of the great railway journeys of the world, the 'Toy Train' to **Darjeeling**. The last part of the line runs through jungle, tea gardens and pine forests. Darjeeling straddles a mountain slope which drops steeply to the valley below, and commands fine views of *Kanchenjunga* (8586m/28,169ft), the third-highest mountain in the world. It is the headquarters of the Indian Mountaineering Institute, as well as the birthplace of Sherpa Tenzing. It is also a world-renowned tea-growing centre.

A bus journey of two and a half hours takes one to **Kalimpong**, a bazaar town at the foot of the Himalayas. From here a number of treks can be made to places offering fine panoramas of the mountains. Further north is the mountain state of **Sikkim**. The capital, **Gangtok**, lies in the southwest. The main activity for visitors is trekking, although it is still in its infancy and facilities are minimal. At the moment travel for non-Indian residents is limited. Trekking is allowed only to groups, while individuals may only visit Gangtok, **Rumtek** and **Phodom**. The nearest railheads are Darjeeling and Siliguri, on the slow but spectacular line of India's northeast frontier railway.

Even further to the east are the states of **Assam** and **Meghalaya**. Assam is famous for tea and wildlife reserves, and can be reached from the state capital of **Gauhati**. The tiger reserve of *Manas* is also rich in other varieties of wildlife, while in **Kaziranga** it is possible to see the one-horned rhinoceros of India.

Shillong, the capital of Meghalaya, is the home of the Khasi people. The region is filled with pine groves, waterfalls and brooks and is described as the 'Scotland of the East'.

Beach Resorts

India's coast has some of the most beautiful beaches in the world. Below are listed both well-known resorts, such

Treasures of Goa

Swaying palms, miles of golden sand, lush greenery, an incredible cultural heritage, magnificent churches, temples and monuments; a unique cultural synthesis of east and west, a rare blend of yesterday and tomorrow. Such are the treasures of Goa. Come and discover them yourself.

Church (16th Century)

Temple (13th Century)

Issued by:
DIRECTORATE OF TOURISM
Government of Goa
Panaji, 403 001 GOA, India.
Tel: +91 832 - 225583 / 224757

GOA TOURISM DEV. CORPN. LTD.
Trionora Apartments, Panaji 403 001 GOA, India.
Tel: +91 832 226728 / 226515 / 224132
Fax: +91 832 223926

as Goa, and several intriguing lesser-known beaches. Hotel facilities and accommodation are also indicated. Further information may be obtained by consulting other sections in *Resorts & Excursions* above.
Major beaches include:
Goa: Calangute, Baga Beach and Colva Beach. *5-star hotels with private beaches:* Fort Aguada Beach Resort, Oberoi Bogmalo Beach and Cidade de Goa. It has reasonably priced hotels, tourist cottages, a tourist resort and youth hostels.
Bombay: Juhu Beach. 5-star hotel complex. Crowded.
Kovalam: Ashok Beach resort. 5-star hotel complex, including beach cottages, Halcyon Castle and Kovalam Palace Hotel. Hotel Samudra, Kerala Tourism Development Corporation, is reasonably priced.
Madras Region: Fisherman's Cove at Covelong beach resort; shore cottages by the shore temples at **Mamallapuram**. Mamallapuram beach resort.
Puri: 3- and 4-star hotels, tourist bungalows, youth hostels. Major Hindu pilgrim centre.
Lesser-known beaches include:
Gujarat: Tithal, Ubhrat, Hajira, Diu (UT), Daman (UT), Chorwad, Dahanu and Dwarka. Cheap hotels, holiday homes. **Maharashtra:** Off Bombay – Madh, Marve and Manori. Cheap hotels – Murud Janjira. Holiday homes – Erangal. **Goa:** Karwar, Ankola, Gokarna, Honnavar and Bhatkal. **Karnataka:** Ullal (smaller beach resort, Summer Sands, cottages), Udupi (Hindu pilgrim centre), Mahe (UT) and Mangalore.

Kerala: Cannanore, Quilon, Varkala. **Tamil Nadu:** Kanya Kumari, Tiruchendur, Rameswaram, Karikal (UT) and Pondicherry (UT). **Andhra Pradesh:** Maipadu, Machilipatnam, Mangiripundi and Bheemunipatnam. **Orissa:** Golpalpur on Sea, Oberoi Hotel, tourist bungalows. **West Bengal:** Digha – reasonably priced hotels, tourist bungalows.
Note: UT = Union Territory.

Hill Stations

Hill stations have long been popular among Indians and foreign visitors alike for providing a relaxing and salubrious retreat from the heat of the plains. Further information on some of the places mentioned here may be found by consulting other sections in *Resorts & Excursions* above.
The most popular hill stations include:
Kashmir: Leh in Ladakh, Srinagar, Pahalgam, Gulmarg for lakes, houseboats, good hotels, tourist reception centres. **Himachal Pradesh:** Simla (various types of hotels, tourist bungalows), nearby Kufri (winter sports centre, skating rink, skiing facilities), Kulu, Manali (reasonably priced hotels, log huts, travellers lodges and tourist bungalows). **Uttar Pradesh:** Nainital boasts a lake boat club, Almora, Ranikhet (reasonably priced hotels, tourist bungalows, clubs, youth hostels), Mussoorie, Ropeway (hotels and tourist bungalows). **West Bengal:** Darjeeling, RA, Kalimpong for

Victoria Memorial, Calcutta

mountaineering. **Meghalaya:** Shillong. **Sikkim:** Gangkok (RA, hotels). **Tamil Nadu:** Ootacamund, Udagamandalam, Kodaikanal, Silvery Lake – hotels, tourist bungalows.
Lesser-known hill stations include:
Himachal Pradesh: Dalhousie, Dharamsala, Nahan, Paonta Saheb, Keylong, Chamba and Kangra. **Kashmir:** Sonamarg, Batote. **Uttar Pradesh:** Dehra Dun, Lansdown. **West Bengal:** Mirik. **Madhya Pradesh:** Pachmarhi. **Maharashtra:** Mahabaleshwar, Panchgani, Panhala, Matheran, Lonavla and Khandala. **Gujarat:** Saputara. **Rajasthan:** Mount Abu. **Tamil Nadu:** Yercaud, Coonoor, Kotagiri. **Kerala:** Ponmundi, Munnar. **Karnataka:** Mercara. **Andhra Pradesh:** Horseley Hills. **Meghalaya:** Shillong. **Bihar:** Netarhat.

Trekking

Trekking conjures up visions of the spectacular northern and eastern Himalayas, the mist-strewn Western Ghats or the blue tranquillity of the Nilgiri Hills. India is the ideal destination for a trekking holiday, offering everything from short and easy excursions to the long challenges of the snowy peaks. Trekking requires the stamina to walk long hours and the mental agility to adapt to a spectacular and ever-changing landscape.
The highest mountain range on earth – the Himalayas – form 3500km (2200 miles) of India's northern and eastern frontiers. The spectacle of the snow-capped peaks, glaciers, pine-forested slopes, rivers and lush meadows of wild flowers cannot be equalled. Peninsular India offers natural beauty of another kind, clothed in

green woodland and fragrant orchards.
Below is a description of the most important trekking areas in India, and also a section devoted to general trekking information and sources of further information.
JAMMU & KASHMIR: Jammu & Kashmir is India's northernmost state, and the one which is best-known for trekking. It is an extravagantly beautiful land of flower-spangled meadows, wild orchards, spectacular coniferous forests, icy mountain peaks and clear streams and rivers. The capital, **Srinagar,** is the base for many treks, notably to the blue Zabarwan Hills and Shankaracharya Hill. The three other main bases in Jammu & Kashmir are **Pahlagam** (100km/62 miles from Srinagar) in the *Lidder Valley,* the base for treks to sacred *Amarnath, Aru, Lidderwat* and the glacial lakes of *Tarsar* and *Tulian;* **Gulmarg** (51km/32 miles from Srinagar), from where treks can be made to the crystal tarns of *Apharwat* and *Alpather,* the upland lakes of *Vishansar* and *Gangabal* and the *Thajiwas Glacier;* and **Sonamarg,** in the *Sindh Valley,* the base for treks into the surrounding mountains. Srinagar is also the roadhead for trips into the arid plateau of *Ladakh,* a country of perpetual drought, the home of wild asses and yaks and with high ranges that have some of the largest glaciers in the world outside the polar regions. **Leh,** the divisional capital, lies on an ancient *Silk Road* and is the base for spectacular treks across this remarkable landscape.
Further south, excellent trekking may be had in the vicinity of Jammu, the railhead to the *Kashmir Valley.* The three main centres are **Kishtwar, Doda** and **Poonch.**
HIMACHAL PRADESH: The landscape of this province ranges from the barren rocks and raging torrents

of the valleys of *Spiti* and *Lahaul* in the north to the southern orchard country of *Kangra* and *Chamba.* Treks from **Manali** include the *Bhaga River* to **Keylong,** and then on to the *Bara Shigri* glacier or over the *Baralacha Pass* to Leh (see above). **Kullu,** in the centre of the province, is set in a narrow valley between the towering Himalayas and the *River Beas,* and is famous for its temples and religious festivals. Treks from here traverse terraced paddy fields and on to remoter regions of snow and ice. The view from the *Rohtang Pass* is particularly spectacular. The town of **Dharamsala,** in the *Kangra Valley* area, is the base for treks into the *Bharmaur Valley* over the *Indrahar Pass,* and on to other still higher passes beyond. **Chamba,** situated on a mountain above the *Ravi River,* is named after the fragrant trees which flourish around its richly carved temples. Treks from the nearby town of **Dalhousie** lead to the glacial lake of *Khajjiar* and to the passes of *Sach* and *Chini.* **Shimla,** once the summer capital of the British, is a high hill station and the base for treks into *Kullu Valley* via the *Jalori Pass* and on to the Kalpur and Kinnaur valleys.
GARHWAL: Set high in the *Garhwal Himalayas,* this region (which is sometimes referred to as the Uttarakhand) abounds in myths and legends of the Indian gods. It is also where the source of the life-giving 'Ganga' is to be found; indeed, many of the great rivers of northern India have their headwaters in this land of lush valleys and towering snow-ridged peaks.
Mussoorie, a hill station much used by the British to escape the searing heat of the plains, is an excellent base for treks into the *Gangotri* and *Yamounotri* valleys. The source of the Ganga at *Gaumukh* can also be reached from here. Another hill station, **Rishikesh,** is situated just north of the sacred city of **Hardwar,** and is the base for treks to another holy shrine, *Badrinath.* A particularly rewarding stop en route to Badrinath is the breathtaking *Valley of Flowers,* which is in full bloom in August. Other destinations include *Hemkund Lake, Mandakini Valley* and *Kedarnath,* one of the 12 Jyotirlings of Lord Shiva with a beautiful temple.
KUMAON: This region, which stretches from the Himalayas in the north to the green foothills of Terai and Bhabar in the south, consists of the three northeastern Himalayan districts of Uttar Pradesh, all of which are particularly rich in wildlife. One of the major trekking centres is **Almora,** an ideal base for treks into pine and rhododendron forests with dramatic views of stark, snow-capped mountains. The *Pindiri Glacier* and the valley of *Someshwar* can be reached from here. Another base is **Nanital,** a charming, orchard-rich hill station. It is the base for short treks to **Bhimtal, Khurpatal** and *Binayak Forest.* **Ranikhet,** with a magnificent view of the central Himalayas, is the base for treks to **Kausani.** The view from here is one of the most spectacular in India, and inspired Mahatma Gandhi to pen his commentary on the Gita-Anashakti Yoga.
DARJEELING AND SIKKIM: Dominated by the five summits of mighty *Kanchenjunga,* the Darjeeling and Sikkim area of the Eastern Himalayas is also a region of gentle hills and dales, pine forests, turquoise lakes and babbling streams. One of the best ways of arriving in the area is by the 'Toy Train' from New Jalpaiguri. The town of **Darjeeling** is the home of the Everest-climber Tenzing Norgay and also of the Himalayan Mountaineering Institute, and is the base for both low- and high-level treks. Destinations include *Tiger Hill* (offering a breathtaking view of the Himalayas), and the peaks of *Phalut, Sandakphu, Singalila* and *Tanglu.* To the north, Sikkim is a wonderland of ferns and flowers, birds and butterflies, orchids and bamboos, forests of cherry, oak and pine, all set among slowly flowing rivers, terraced paddy fields and blazing rhododendrons. Deep in the interior are Sikkim's famous monasteries, their white prayer flags fluttering against a deep blue sky. The capital is **Gantok,** a convenient base for treks into the mysterious north and east of the region, to sacred *Yaksum, Pemayangtse* and the mountains near **Bakkhim** and **Dzongri.**
ARAVALLI HILLS: The Aravallis, remnants of the oldest mountain range in the sub-continent, resemble outcroppings of rocks rather than mountains and are virtually barren except for thorny acacias and date palm groves found near the oases. The main resort in the region, *Mount Abu,* stands on an isolated plateau surrounded by rich green forest. A variety of one-day treks are available from here, all of which afford the opportunity to visit some of the remarkable temples in the region, notably *Arbuda Devi Temple,* carved out of the rock face and offering spectacular views across the hills. **Guru Shikhar, Gaumukh** and *Achalgarh Fort* can all be reached during one-day treks from Mount Abu.
SATPURA RANGE: This range straddles central India and forms the northern border of the *Deccan.* The main hill station is **Pachmarhi,** a beautiful resort of green forest glades and deep ravines overlooking red sandstone hills. Short treks can be had from here to the *Mahadeo*

and *Dhupgarh* peaks.

WESTERN GHATS: The Western Ghats run parallel to the west coast of India from the River Tapti to the southernmost tip of the sub-continent. The mountains are lush and thickly forested and although they cannot claim to have the awesome majesty of the great Himalayas, the region has many features of great natural beauty. The hill station of **Mahabaleshwar**, in the north of the range, is the highest in the area and is considered an ideal base for trekkers. Other popular bases and trekking destinations include **Lonavala**, **Khandala**, **Matheran** and **Bhor Ghat**, a picturesque region of waterfalls, lakes and woods. Further south in Karnataka is **Coorg**, perched on a green hilltop and surrounded by mountainous countryside. **Madikeri** is a take-off point for treks in this region. The *Upper Palani* hills in Tamil Nadu are an offshoot of the Ghats, covered in rolling downs and coarse grass. **Kodaikanal** is the attractive base for two short treks to *Pilar Rock* and *Green Valley View*. **Courtallam**, also in Tamil Nadu, is surrounded by dense vegetation and coffee and spice plantations; rich in wildlife, it is also one of the most beautiful areas of the Western Ghats.

NILGIRIS: The gentle heights of southern India, a world away from the daunting Himalayas, are friendly and approachable with treks made simple by moderate altitudes and a pleasant climate. Sometimes known as the *Blue Mountains* because of their lilac hue, they are noted for their orange orchards, tea gardens, wooded slopes and tranquil lakes. There are three major trekking centres here: **Ootacamund** (popularly known as Ooty) is the base for walks to the *Wenlock Downs*, the *Kalahatti Falls* and *Mudumali Game Sanctuary;* **Coonor**, conveniently situated for *Drogg's Peak* and *Lamb's Rock;* and **Kotagiri**, the oldest of the three, whose sheltered position enables it to offer many shaded treks to explore the tranquillity of the Nilgiris.

GENERAL TREKKING INFORMATION: Essential equipment: Tent, sleeping bag, foam/inflatable mattress, rucksack, umbrella (doubles as a walking stick), sun-hat, dark glasses, toilet requirements. **Clothing:** Wind-proof jacket, down jacket, trousers, shirts, woollen pullover, woollen underwear (for high altitudes), and gloves. **Footwear:** Be sure to take a light, flexible and comfortable pair of trekking boots (two pairs should be taken for longer treks) and at least three pairs of woollen socks. Use talc to keep feet dry. **First-aid kit:** Sterilised cotton wool, bandages, antiseptic ointment, water purification tablets, pills, etc for common ailments (such as cough, cold, headache, stomach ache, etc), eye lotion, anti-sunburn cream, a hot stimulant for emergencies, and morphia salt tablets to avoid cramps. **Miscellaneous:** Torch, thermos/water bottle, insect repellant, mirror, cold cream, lip-salve, walking stick, spare boot laces, sewing kit, tinned and dehydrated food. **Food & accommodation:** Board and lodging accommodation is available on all trekking routes. **Permits:** No system of issuing Trekking Permits exists in India. Trekkers are, however, reminded that it is forbidden to enter Restricted and Protected Areas without the correct documentation. Consult the GITO before departure or local tourist offices on arrival in India to ascertain what restrictions may apply and what documentation may be required. **Season:** This varies from region to region; check with the GITO for further information. In general, the season runs from April to June and September to November. It is possible to undertake treks in the valleys of Lahaul, Pangi and Zanskar and in Ladakh during the rainy season (June to August), as these areas receive minimal precipitation. **Mountaineering:** Permission for mountaineering *must* be obtained from the Indian Mountaineering Foundation, Anand Niketan, Beneto Juarez Road, New Delhi 110 021.

Wildlife

The Indian peninsula is a continent in itself, the geographical diversity of which has resulted in a vast range of wildlife, with over 350 species of mammals and 1200 species of birds in the country. Each region has something special to offer: the **hangul** is restricted to the valley of Kashmir in northern India, the **rhino** is found in isolated pockets along the Brahmaputra River in the east, the **black langur** in the Western Ghats, and Western India is the home of the last remaining **Asiatic lions**. Two of India's most impressive animals, the **Bengal** (or Indian) **tiger** and the **Asiatic elephant** are still found in most regions, though their population has shrunk drastically.

Most of India's wildlife finds refuge in over 200 sanctuaries and parks around the country. The following list refers to some of the more important of these. Accommodation often needs to be booked in advance, either by direct application or through the local State TDC or the controlling authority of the respective park.

Tibetan monk, Darjeeling

The GITO produces a map *(Wildlife – India)* which contains fuller details on these points.

NORTHERN INDIA

Dachigam Wildlife Sanctuary (Kashmir): Broad valley; mountain slopes; rare hangul deer, black and brown bear, leopard; heronry.

Govind Sagar Bird Sanctuary (Himachal Pradesh): Bird sanctuary with crane, duck, goose and teal.

Corbett National Park (Uttar Pradesh): Himalayan foothills near Dhikala; Sal forest and plains; tiger, elephant, leopard and rich birdlife. Excellent fishing in Ramganga River.

Dudhwa National Park (Uttar Pradesh): Nepal border; tiger, sloth bear and panther.

Flower Valley National Park (Uttar Pradesh): When in bloom this 'roof garden' at 3500m (11,500ft) is a glorious blaze of colour. Permits are required to enter.

Sariska National Park (Rajasthan): About 200km (125 miles) from Delhi. Forest and open plains; sambar (largest Indian deer), cheetal (spotted deer), nilgai (Indian antelope), black buck, leopard and tiger; good night-viewing.

Ranthambhor (Sawai Madhopur – Rajasthan): Hill forest, plains and lakes; sambar, chinkara (Indian gazelle), tiger, sloth bear, crocodiles and migratory water-birds.

Bharatpur National Park (Keoloadeo Ghana Bird Sanctuary) (Rajasthan): India's most outstanding bird sanctuary; many indigenous water-birds; huge migration from Siberia and China; crane, goose, stork, heron, snakes, birds, etc.

Bandhavgarh National Park (Madhya Pradesh):

Situated in the Vindhyan Mountains, this park has a wide variety of wildlife including panther, sambar and gaur.

Kanha National Park (Madhya Pradesh): Sal forest and grassland; only home of barasingha (swamp deer), tiger, cheetal and gaur.

Shivpuri National Park (Madhya Pradesh): Open forest and lake; chinkara, chowsingha (4-horned antelope), nilgai, tiger, leopard and water-birds.

EASTERN INDIA

Kaziranga National Park (Assam): Elephant grass and swamps; one-horned Indian rhinoceros, water buffalo, tiger, leopard, elephant, deer and rich birdlife. Elephant transport is available within the park.

Manas Wildlife Sanctuary (Assam): On the Bhutan border, rainforest, grassland and river banks; rhino, water buffalo, tiger, elephant, golden langur and water-birds; fishing permitted.

Palamau Tiger Reserve (Bihar): Rolling, forested hills; tiger, leopard, elephant, sambar, jungle cat, rhesus macaque (monkey) and occasionally wolf.

Hazaribagh National Park (Bihar): Sal forested hills; sambar, nilgai, cheetal, tiger, leopard and occasionally muntjac (larger barking deer).

Sundarbans Tiger Reserve (West Bengal): Mangrove forests; tiger, fishing cat, deer, crocodile, dolphin and rich birdlife. Transport: access and travel by chartered boat.

Jaldapara Wildlife Sanctuary (West Bengal): Tropical forest and grassland; rhino, elephant and rich birdlife.

Similipal Tiger Reserve (Orissa): Immense Sal forest; tiger, elephant, leopard, sambar, cheetal, muntjac and chevrotain.

SOUTHERN INDIA

Periyar Wildlife Sanctuary (Kerala): Large artificial lake; elephant, gaur, wild dog, black langur, otters, tortoises and rich birdlife including hornbill and fishing owl. Viewing by boat.

Vedanthangal Water Birds Sanctuary (Tamil Nadu): One of the most spectacular breeding grounds in India. Cormorant, heron, stork, pelican, grebe and many others.

Point Calimere Bird Sanctuary (Tamil Nadu): Particularly noted for its flamingo, also for heron, teal, curlew and plover, black buck and wild pig.

Pulicat Bird Sanctuary (Andhra Pradesh): Flamingo, grey pelican, heron and tern.

Dandeli National Park (Karnataka): Park with bison, panther, tiger and sambar. Easily accessible from Goa.

Jawahar National Park (includes **Bandipur** and **Nagarhole National Parks** (Karnataka), and the Wildlife Sanctuaries of **Mudumalai** (Tamil Nadu) and **Wayanad**, Kerala): Extensive mixed forest; largest elephant population in India, leopard, gaur, sambar, muntjac and giant squirrel. Birds include racquet-tailed drongo, trogon and barbet.

WESTERN INDIA

Krishnagiri Upavan National Park (Maharashtra): Formerly known as Borivli, this park protects an important scenic area close to Bombay. Kanheri Caves and Vihar, Tulsi and Powai lakes; water-birds and smaller types of wildlife. Lion Safari Park nearby.

Tadoba National Park (Maharashtra): Teak forests and lake; tiger, leopard, nilgai and gaur. Night-viewing.

Sasan Gir National Park (Gujarat): Forested plains and lake; only home of Asiatic lion, sambar, chowsingha, nilgai, leopard, chinkara and wild boar.

Nal Sarovar Bird Sanctuary (Gujarat): Lake; migratory water-birds; indigenous birds include flamingo.

Little Rann of Kutch Wildlife Sanctuary (Gujarat): Desert; herds of khur (Indian wild ass), wolf and caracal.

Velavadar National Park (Gujarat): New Delta grasslands; large concentration of black buck.

POPULAR ITINERARIES: 5-day: (a) Delhi–Agra–Jaipur. (b) Calcutta–Darjeeling–Sikkim. **7-day:** (a) Delhi–Agra–Khajuraho–Varanasi–Delhi. (b) Bombay–Aurangabad–Jaipur–Delhi. (c) Bombay–Bangalore–Goa. (d) Madras–Bangalore–Trivandrum–Bombay.

SOCIAL PROFILE

FOOD & DRINK: The unforgettable aroma of India is not just the heavy scent of jasmine and roses on the warm air. It is also the fragrance of spices so important to Indian cooking – especially to preparing curry. The word 'curry' is an English derivative of *kari,* meaning spice sauce, but curry does not, in India, come as a powder. It is the subtle and delicate blending of spices such as turmeric, cardamom, ginger, coriander, nutmeg and poppy seed. Like an artist's palette of oil paints, the Indian cook has some 25 spices (freshly ground as required) with which to mix the recognised combinations or *masalas.* Many of these spices are also noted for their medicinal properties. They, like the basic ingredient, vary from region to region. Although not all Hindus are vegetarians, vegetable dishes are more common than in Europe, particularly in southern India. Broadly speaking, meat dishes are more common in the north, notably, *Rogan Josh* (curried lamb), *Gushtaba* (spicy meat balls in yoghurt) and the delicious *Biryani* (chicken or lamb in orange-flavoured rice, sprinkled with sugar and rose water). Mughlai cuisine is rich, creamy, deliciously spiced and liberally sprinkled with nuts and saffron. The ever-popular *Tandoori* cooking (chicken, meat or fish marinated in herbs and baked in a clay oven) and kebabs are also northern cuisine. In the south, curries are mainly vegetable and inclined to be hotter. Specialities to look out for are *Bhujia* (vegetable curry), *Dosa, Idli* and *Samba* (rice pancakes, dumplings with pickles, and vegetable and lentil curry), and *Raitas* (yoghurt with grated cucumber and mint). Coconut is a major ingredient of southern Indian cooking. On the west coast there is a wide choice of fish and shellfish: *Bombay duck* (curried or fried bomble fish) and *Pomfret* (Indian salmon) are just two. Another speciality is the Parsi *Dhan Sak* (lamb or chicken cooked with curried lentils) and *Vindaloo* (vinegar marinade). Fish is also a feature of Bengali cooking as in *Dahi Maach* (curried fish in yoghurt flavoured with turmeric and ginger) and *Malai* (curried prawn with coconut). One regional distinction is that, whereas in the south rice is the staple food, in the north this is supplemented and sometimes substituted by a wide range of flat breads, such as *Pooris, Chapatis* and *Nan.* Common throughout India is *Dhal* (crushed lentil soup with various additional vegetables), and *Dhai,* the curd or yoghurt which accompanies the curry. Besides being tasty, it is a good 'cooler'; more effective than liquids when things get too hot.

Sweets are principally milk-based puddings, pastries and

Tea pickers, Darjeeling

pancakes. Available throughout India is *Kulfi,* the Indian ice cream, *Rasgullas* (cream cheese balls flavoured with rose water), *Gulab Jamuns* (flour, yoghurt and ground almonds), and *Jalebi* (pancakes in syrup). Besides a splendid choice of sweets and sweetmeats, there is an abundance of fruit, both tropical – mangoes, pomegranates and melons – and temperate – apricots, apples and strawberries. Western confectionery is available in major centres. It is common to finish the meal by chewing *Pan* as a digestive. Pan is a betel leaf in which are wrapped spices such as aniseed and cardamom. Besides the main dishes, there are also countless irresistible snacks available on every street corner, such as *Samosa, Fritters, Dosa* and *Vada.* For the more conservative visitor, Western cooking can always be found. Indeed, the best styles of cooking from throughout the world can be experienced in the major centres in India.

Drink: Tea is India's favourite drink and many of the varieties are enjoyed throughout the world. It will often come ready-brewed with milk and sugar unless 'tray tea' is specified. Coffee is increasingly popular. *Nimbu Pani* (lemon drink), *Lassi* (iced buttermilk) and coconut milk

straight from the nut are cool and refreshing. Soft drinks (usually sweet) and bottled water are widely available, as are Western alcoholic drinks. There is a huge variety of excellent Indian beer. There is also good Indian made gin, rum and brandy.

Restaurants have table service and, depending on area and establishment, will serve alcohol with meals. Most Western-style hotels have licensed bars. Visitors will be issued All India Liquor Permits on request by Indian Embassies, Missions or Tourist Offices or from the Tourist Office in London. Currently, only Gujarat imposes prohibition, but this may change; check with the Tourist Office for up-to-date information. In almost all big cities in India certain days in the week are observed as dry days when the sale of liquor is not permitted. Tourists may check with the nearest local tourist office for the prohibition laws/rules prevailing in any given state where they happen to be travelling or intend to travel.

NIGHTLIFE: India has generally little nightlife as the term is understood in the West, although in major cities a few Western-style shows, clubs and discos are being developed. In most places the main attraction will be

quickly. Cloths include silks, cottons, *himroos,* brocades, chiffons and *chingnons.* **Jewellery:** This is traditionally heavy (particularly *kundan* from Rajasthan) and stunningly elaborate. Indian silverwork is world-famous. Gems can be bought and mounted. Apart from diamonds, other stones include lapis lazuli, Indian star rubies, star sapphires, moonstones and aquamarines. Hyderabad is one of the world's leading centres for pearls.

Handicrafts and leatherwork: Once again, each area will have its own speciality; the range includes fine bronzes, brasswork (often inlaid with silver), canework and pottery. Papier mâché is a characteristic Kashmir product, some decorated with gold leaf. Marble and alabaster inlay work, such as chess sets and ornamental plates, are a speciality of Agra. Good leatherwork buys include open Indian sandals and slippers. **Woodwork:** Sandalwood carvings from Karnataka, rosewood from Kerala and Madras, Indian walnut from Kashmir. **Other buys:** Foods such as pickles, spices and Indian tea, and perfumes, soap, handmade paper, Orissan playing cards and musical instruments.

Shopping hours: 0930-1800 Monday to Saturday in most large stores.

Note: It is forbidden to export antiques and art objects over 100 years old, animal skins or objects made from skins.

SPORTS: A wide range of activities is available in India, ranging from **horseracing** at Calcutta to **fishing** in Kashmir, and from **golf** to **polo.** The great Indian sport, though, is **cricket.** Interest in the game reaches almost fever pitch, particularly during the winter test season when the country's national team is in action in all the major cities. Club matches can also be seen in almost every town. **Skiing** is fast becoming a popular sport, and facilities are offered by some resorts in the north of the country (including Gulmarg and Kufri), set in some of the most beautiful mountain landscape in the world. **River running** is another young sport in India; the snow-fed mountain rivers of the northern Himalayas place them among the best regions in the world for this sport. **Camel safaris** can be taken in the Thar desert and range from 1-15 days' duration; an ideal way to visit this fascinating region. Delhi is the country's centre for **rock climbing,** also available in the Aravalli Hills and the Western Ghats. **Hang gliding, ballooning** and **gliding** are also becoming more widely available for those who wish to obtain a bird's-eye view of some of the landscape. **Motor rallying** is an excellent sport for participants and spectators alike. The most notable, and demanding, event is the *Himalayan Car Rally.* Most large hotels have swimming pools, and there are facilities for a wide range of **watersports** including **sailing, rowing** and **water-skiing** at seaside resorts. The Andaman Islands in particular are noted for their **scuba diving. Fishing** is also available, particularly in the Kangra Valley and Simla, in Darjeeling and Orissa and throughout the Himalayas. Tackle can often be hired from local fishing authorities. Check with the local tourist office for details of seasons and licences. **Golf** enthusiasts will find many courses open to visitors throughout India; enquire at major hotels for details of temporary membership. *Calcutta Amateur Golf Championships* attract large numbers of serious golfers in the east; the standards are high, and for those interested, temporary membership is available from the Royal Calcutta Golf Club. Srinagar and Gulmarg have good courses and hold tournaments in the spring and autumn. The course at Shillong is widely regarded as being one of the most beautiful in the world. Other participating sports include **horseriding** in hill stations and **tennis** and **squash,** available in hotels and private clubs. Spectator sports include **football,** interest in which is increasing, while **polo** and **hockey** are sports at which the Indians have long excelled, winning many Olympic gold medals in the latter. For information on **trekking,** see the section above.

SPECIAL EVENTS: Below is a selection from the hundreds of Indian festivals celebrated throughout 1995/6. Public holidays are indicated PH. All the festivals are nationwide unless otherwise stated.
Mar 17 '95 *Holi,* mainly in the northern part of India.
Jun 9 *Muharram,* particularly Lucknow. **Jun 30** *Rath Yatra* (temple festival in honour of Lord Jagannah (Lord of the Universe) with three colossal chariots drawn from Puri temple by thousands of pilgrims), mainly Orissa.
Aug 15 *Independence Day* (PH). **Sep 6** *Onam* (harvest festival; spectacular snake boat races in many parts of Kerala), Kerala. **Oct 1-2** *Durgapuja.* **Oct 3** *Dussehra* (also known as Ram Lila/Delhi, Durga Puja/Bengal or Navaratri/southern India). **Oct 23** *Diwali* (magnificent illuminations and fireworks). **Nov 7** *Pushkar Fair.* **Dec 25** *Christmas Day* (PH, mostly in Goa, Bombay and Tamil Nadu). **Jan '96** *Pongal* (harvest festival), mainly Tamil Nadu, Andhra Pradesh and Karnataka. **Jan 26** *Republic Day* (PH, grand military parade and procession of dancers especially in Delhi).

cultural shows featuring performances of Indian dance and music. The Indian film industry is the largest in the world, now producing three times as many full-length feature films as the USA. Bombay and Calcutta are the country's two 'Hollywoods'. Almost every large town will have a cinema, some of which will show films in English. Music and dancing are an important part of Indian cinema, combining with many other influences to produce a rich variety of film art. Larger cities may have theatres staging productions of English-language plays.

SHOPPING: Indian crafts have been perfected over the centuries, from traditions and techniques passed on from generation to generation. Each region has its own specialities, each town its own local craftspeople and its own particular skills. Silks, spices, jewellery and many other Indian products have long been acclaimed and widely sought; merchants would travel thousands of miles, enduring the hardships and privations of the long journey, in order to make their purchases. Nowadays, the marketplaces of the sub-continent are only eight hours away, and for fabrics, silverware, carpets, leatherwork and antiques, India is a shopper's paradise. Bargaining is expected, and the visitor can check for reasonable prices at state-run emporiums. **Fabrics:** One of India's main industries, its silks, cottons, and wools rank amongst the best in the world. Of the *silks,* the brocades from Varanasi are among the most famous; other major centres include Patna, Murshidabad, Kanchipuram and Surat. Rajasthan *cotton* with its distinctive 'tie and dye' design is usually brilliantly colourful, while Madras cotton is known for its attractive 'bleeding' effect after a few washes. Throughout the country may be found the *himroo* cloth, a mixture of silk and cotton, often decorated with patterns. Kashmir sells beautiful *woollens,* particularly shawls. **Carpets:** India has one of the world's largest carpet industries, and many examples of this ancient and beautiful craft can be seen in museums throughout the world. Kashmir has a long history of carpet-making, influenced by the Persians. Pure wool and woven wool and silk carpets are exquisitely made, and though fairly expensive, they are marked up sharply by the time they reach the west. Each region will have its own speciality; one such are the distinctive, brightly coloured Tibetan rugs, available mainly in Darjeeling. **Clothes:** Clothes are cheap to buy, and can be tailor-made in some shops, usually very

Note: Besides the above festivals there are hundreds of festivals and fairs which are of regional significance, celebrated with equal pomp and colour. The most authentic of these are the following: The Temple Festivals in southern India, a list of which is often available at GITOs. Festivals at Ladakh in Kashmir. Festivals in Rajasthan; a visitor will be unlucky to visit Rajasthan at a time when a festival of some kind is not either in progress or about to take place. The visitor may also be lucky enough to witness dancing at a village festival or a private wedding.

SOCIAL CONVENTIONS: The Indian Hindu greeting is to fold the hands and tilt the head forward to *namaste*. Indian women prefer not to shake hands. All visitors are asked to remove footwear when entering places of religious worship. The majority of Indians remove their footwear when entering their houses, and the visitor should follow suit accordingly. Because of strict religious and social customs, visitors must show particular respect for traditions when visiting someone's home. Many Hindus are vegetarian and many, especially women, do not drink alcohol. Sikhs and Parsees do not smoke and it is important for guests to follow all local customs. Small gifts are acceptable as tokens of gratitude for hospitality. Women are expected to dress with sobriety. Short skirts and tight or revealing clothing should not be worn, since this will generally only attract unwelcome attention. Business people are not expected to dress formally except for meetings and social functions. Trained English-speaking guides are available at fixed charges at all important tourist centres. Guides speaking French, Italian, Spanish, German, Russian or Japanese are available in some cities. Consult the nearest GITO. Unapproved guides are not permitted to enter protected monuments, and tourists are therefore advised to ask for the services of guides who carry a certificate issued by the Department of Tourism. **Photography:** Formalities are mainly in regard to protected monuments and the wildlife sanctuaries. Special permission of the Archaeological Survey of India, New Delhi, must be sought for use of tripod and artificial light to photograph archaeological monuments, and photographs of the wildlife sanctuaries are allowed on payment of a prescribed fee which varies from one sanctuary to another. Contact the nearest GITO. **Tipping:** It is usual to tip porters 20-25 paise per bag and waiters, guides and drivers 10% where service is not included.

BUSINESS PROFILE

ECONOMY: India is a country of astonishing poverty coupled with a comparatively well-developed industrial economy which has invested much in advanced technology initiatives such as digital communications and space research. The country rates in the top dozen in the world by gross national product and is one of the highest in terms of investing national wealth in industrial projects. Roughly two-thirds of the population are involved in agriculture, both subsistence – mainly cereals – and cash crops, including tea, rubber, coffee, cotton, jute, sugar, oilseeds and tobacco. The agricultural sector has been severely affected, however, by frequent droughts during the 1980s and early 1990s, particularly as harvests depend almost entirely on the annual monsoon. India has some oil deposits which are now playing a growing role in the economy as well as assisting the balance of payments deficit, which constantly hampers the country's economic development. India's industrial base has expanded greatly in the last two decades with major developments in heavy engineering – especially transport equipment, a major export earner – iron and steel, chemicals and electronics. The 1990 Gulf crisis caused significant damage to the Indian economy through the loss of two of its most important trading partners, the increase in the price of imported oil, the loss of remittances from Indian workers in both Iraq and Kuwait and their return home, which put a sudden strain on the labour market. In 1992 and 1993, a series of natural disasters proved to be major obstacles to economic growth while political difficulties have prevented the Rao government from tackling the public sector. Japan and the CIS are India's major trading partners among a wide range of extensive bilateral economic relations stretching from Australia and the Pacific Basin through Western Europe to the USA, Canada and Brazil.

BUSINESS: English is widely used in commercial circles, so there is little need for interpreter and translation services. Business cards are usually exchanged. All weights and measures should be expressed in metric terms. Indian businessmen welcome visitors and are very hospitable. Entertaining usually takes place in private clubs. The best months for business visits are October to March, and accommodation should be booked in advance. **Office hours:** 0930-1730 Monday to Friday; 0930-1300 Saturday.

Sikkim

COMMERCIAL INFORMATION: The following organisations can offer advice: Ministry of Commerce, Udyog Bhavan, New Delhi 110 011. Tel: (11) 301 6664. Fax: (11) 301 3583. Telex: 3163233; *or*
Ministry of External Affairs, South Block, New Delhi 110 011. Tel: (11) 301 2318. Telex: 3161880; *or*
Associated Chambers of Commerce and Industry of India (ASSOCHAM), 2nd Floor, Allahabad Bank Building, 17 Parliament Street, New Delhi 110 001. Tel: (11) 310 704. Fax: (11) 312 193. Telex: 3161754; *or*
Federation of Indian Chambers of Commerce and Industry, Federation House, Tansen Marg, New Delhi 110 001. Tel: (11) 331 9251. Fax: (11) 332 0714. Telex: 3162521; *or*
Indian Chamber of Commerce, India Exchange, 4 India Exchange Place, Calcutta 700 001. Tel: (33) 203 243. Fax: (33) 204 495. Telex: 217432.

CONFERENCES/CONVENTIONS: The main congress and exhibition centres in the country are Delhi, Bombay, Calcutta, Madras, Agra, Jaipur, Udaipur, Varanasi, Bhubeneswar, Hyderabad, Bangalore and Panaji. In addition, top-class hotels and auditoria with convention and conference facilities are found throughout the country. *Air India, Indian Airlines* and leading hoteliers and travel agents are members of the International Congress and Conference Association

(ICCA) and together they provide all the services required for an international event, including the organising of pre- and post-conference tours. There are two particularly useful booklets which give information on India in general, and in particular on conference facilities, called *Conventionally Yours* and *India: an Unusual Environment for Meetings,* available from the GITO. For further information, contact the India Convention Promotion Bureau (ICPB), Room 233, Ashok Hotel, Chanakyapuri, New Delhi 110021. Tel: (11) 687 3612. Fax: (11) 687 3216.

CLIMATE

Hot tropical weather with variations from region to region. Coolest weather lasts from November to mid-March, with cool, fresh mornings and evenings and dry, sunny days. Really hot weather, when it is dry, dusty and unpleasant, is between April and June. Monsoon rains occur in most regions in summer between June and September.

Western Himalayas: Srinagar is best from March to October; July to August can be unpleasant; cold and damp in winter. Simla is higher and therefore colder in winter and places like Pahalgam, Gulmarg and Manali

recommended that the area is avoided.
Required clothing: Lightweight cottons and linens. Waterproofing is advisable throughout the year and essential in monsoons, usually from mid-June to mid-October. Warmer clothes are useful for cooler evenings.

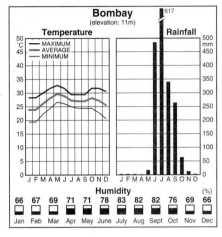

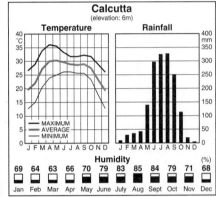

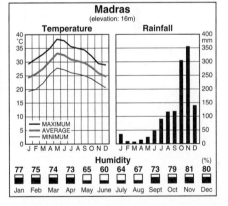

are usually under several feet of snow (December to March) and temperatures in Ladakh can be extremely cold. The road to Leh is open from June to October.
Required clothing: Light- to medium-weights are advised from March to October, with warmer wear for winter. Weather can change rapidly in the mountains, therefore it is important to be suitably equipped. Waterproofing is advisable.
Northern Plains: Extreme climate, warm inland from April to mid-June falling to almost freezing at night in winter, between November and February. Summers are hot with monsoons between June and September.
Required clothing: Lightweight cottons and linens in summer with warmer clothes in winter and on cooler evenings. Waterproofing is essential during monsoons.
Central India: Madhya Pradesh State escapes the very worst of the hot season, but monsoons are heavy between July and September. Temperatures fall at night in winter.
Required clothing: Lightweights are worn most of the year with warmer clothes during evenings, particularly in winter. Waterproofed clothing is advised during monsoon rains.
Western India: November to February is most comfortable, although evenings can be fairly cold. Summers can be extremely hot with monsoon rainfall

between mid-June and mid-September.
Required clothing: Lightweight cottons and linens are worn most of the year with warmer clothes for cooler winters, and waterproofing is essential during the monsoon.
Southwest: The most pleasant weather is from November to March. Monsoon rains fall between late April and July. Summer temperatures are not as high as Northern India, although humidity is extreme. There are cooling breezes on the coast. Inland, Mysore and Bijapur have pleasant climates with relatively low rainfall.
Required clothing: Lightweights are worn all year with warmer clothes for cooler evenings, particularly in winter. Waterproofing is advised during the monsoon.
Southeast: Tamil Nadu experiences a northeast monsoon between October and December and temperatures and humidity are high all year. Hills can be cold in winter. Hyderabad is hot, but less humid in summer and much cooler in winter.
Required clothing: Lightweight cottons and linens. Waterproofing is necessary during the monsoon. Warmer clothes are worn in the winter, particularly in the hills.
Northeast: March to June and September to November are the driest and most pleasant periods. The rest of the year has extremely heavy monsoon rainfall and it is

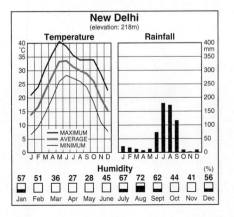

Indonesia

East Timor incorporated into Indonesia July 1976

☐ *international airport*

Location: South-East Asia.

Note: Periodically, limited civil unrest resulting in violence has occurred in the province of Aceh, located in the far northern tip of Sumatra, and in the occupied Province of East Timor, located 480km (300 miles) north of Australia. In the Province of Irian Jaya, certain regions require special permits to visit. Permits can be obtained from police authorities in Indonesia.
Source: US State Department – November 25, 1994.

**Direktorat Jenderal Pariwisata Indonesia
(Directorate-General of Tourism)**
81 Jalan Kramat Raya, Jakarta 10450, Indonesia
Tel: (21) 310 3117. Fax: (21) 310 1146. Telex: 61525.
Embassy of the Republic of Indonesia
38 Grosvenor Square, London W1X 9AD
Tel: (0171) 499 7661. Fax: (0171) 491 4993. Telex: 28284 (a/b INDONEG). Opening hours: 1000-1300 and 1430-1600 Monday to Friday.
Indonesia Tourist Board
3-4 Hanover Street, London W1R 9HH
Tel: (0171) 493 0030. Fax: (0171) 493 1747. Opening hours: 0900-1700 Monday to Friday.
British Embassy
Jalan M H Thamrin 75, Jakarta 10310, Indonesia
Tel: (21) 330 904. Fax: (21) 314 1824 *or* 390 2726.
Consulates in: Medan and Surabaya.
Embassy of the Republic of Indonesia
2020 Massachusetts Avenue, NW, Washington, DC 20036
Tel: (202) 775 5200. Fax: (202) 775 5365.
Consulate General of Indonesia
5 East 68th Street, New York, NY 10021
Tel: (212) 879 0600. Fax: (212) 570 6206 (visas and tourist information).
Indonesian Tourist Promotion Office
3457 Wilshire Boulevard, Los Angeles, CA 90010
Tel: (213) 387 2078. Fax: (213) 380 4876.
Also deals with enquiries from Canada.
Embassy of the United States of America
PO Box 1, Medan Merdeka Selatan 5, Jakarta, Indonesia
Tel: (21) 360 360. Fax: (21) 386 2259. Telex: 44218.
Consulates in: Medan and Surabaya.
Embassy of the Republic of Indonesia
287 MacLaren Street, Ottawa, Ontario K2P 0L9
Tel: (613) 236 7403. Fax: (613) 563 2858.
Consulates in: Toronto, Vancouver and Edmonton.
Canadian Embassy
PO Box 1052, 5th Floor, WISMA Metropolitan, Jalan Jendral Sudirman, Jakarta 10010, Indonesia
Tel: (21) 525 0709. Fax: (21) 571 2251. Telex: 65131 (a/b DMCAN IA).

AREA: 1,904,569 sq km (735,358 sq miles).
POPULATION: 182,000,000 (1991 estimate, including East Timor).
POPULATION DENSITY: 93.7 per sq km.
CAPITAL: Jakarta (Java). **Population:** 7,347,800 (1990 estimate).
GEOGRAPHY: Indonesia is made up of six main islands, Sumatra, Java, Sulawesi, Bali, Kalimantan (part of the island of Borneo) and Irian Jaya (the western half of New Guinea), and 30 smaller archipelagos, in total 13,677 islands. 3000 of these islands are inhabited and stretch over 4828km (3000 miles), most lying in a volcanic belt with more than 300 volcanoes, the great majority of which are extinct. The landscape varies from island to island, ranging from high mountains and plateaux to coastal lowlands and alluvial belts.
LANGUAGE: Bahasa Indonesian (a variant of Malay) is the national language, but each ethnic group has its own language, and altogether more than 250 dialects are spoken. The older generation still speak Dutch as a

second language, but a large number of younger people now speak some English.
RELIGION: There is a Muslim majority of about 87%, with Christian, Hindu (mainly in Bali) and Buddhist minorities. Animist beliefs are held in remote areas.
TIME: Indonesia spans three time zones:
Bangka, Billiton, Java, West and Central Kalimantan, Madura and Sumatra: GMT + 7.
Bali, Flores, South and East Kalimantan, Lombok, Sulawesi, Sumba, Sumbawa and Timor: GMT + 8.
Aru, Irian Jaya, Kai, Moluccas and Tanimbar: GMT + 9.
ELECTRICITY: Generally 110 volts AC, 50Hz, but 220 volts AC, 50Hz, in some areas, including Jakarta. 220-volt supplies are gradually superseding 110-volt supplies.
COMMUNICATIONS: Telephone: IDD is available to main cities. Country code: 62 (followed by 22 for Bandung, 21 for Jakarta, 61 for Medan, and 31 for Surabaya). Outgoing international code: 00.
Telex/telegram: Public telex facilities are operated from the Directorate General for Post and Communications in Jakarta (24 hours), and also from some major hotels and at the chief telegraphic offices in Semarang, Yogjakarta, Surabaya and Denpasar. Telegrams can be sent from any telegraphic office; in Jakarta facilities are available 24 hours a day, but services outside Jakarta are less efficient.
Post: Airmail to Western Europe takes up to ten days. Internal mail is fast and generally reliable by the express service (*Pos KILAT*), but mail to the outer islands can be subject to considerable delays. **Press:** There are several English-language newspapers in Jakarta and on the other islands, notably *The Indonesian Times, Indonesian Observer* and *The Jakarta Post.*
BBC World Service and Voice of America frequencies: From time to time these change. See the section *How to Use this Book* for more information.
BBC:

MHz	17.83	11.95	9.740	6.195

Voice of America

MHz	18.82	15.18	9.525	1.735

PASSPORT/VISA

Regulations and requirements may be subject to change at short notice, and you are advised to contact the appropriate diplomatic or consular authority before finalising travel arrangements. Details of these may be found at the head of this country's entry. Any numbers in the chart refer to the footnotes below.

	Passport Required?	Visa Required?	Return Ticket Required?
Full British	Yes	No/3	Yes
BVP	Not valid	-	-
Australian	Yes	1/3	Yes
Canadian	Yes	No/3	Yes
USA	Yes	No/3	Yes
Other EU (As of 31/12/94)	Yes	2/3	Yes
Japanese	Yes	No/3	Yes

Restricted entry: Portuguese nationals will be refused entry under all circumstances; nationals of Israel require special permission.
PASSPORTS: Valid passport required by all; expiry date must be at least 6 months after date of entry.
British Visitors Passport: Not acceptable.
VISAS: Tourist visas are required by all except the following, providing stay does not exceed 60 days:
(a) nationals of countries referred to in the chart above;
(b) **[1]** Australian nationals (other than journalists who *do* require visas);

(c) **[2]** nationals of EU countries, with the exception of Portugal (see *Restricted entry* above);
(d) nationals of Argentina, Austria, Brazil, Brunei, Chile, Egypt, Finland, Hungary, Iceland, South Korea, Kuwait, Liechtenstein, Malaysia, Malta, Mexico, Monaco, Morocco, New Zealand, Norway, Philippines, Saudi Arabia, Singapore, Sweden, Switzerland, Taiwan (China), Thailand, Turkey, United Arab Emirates, Venezuela and Yugoslavia (Serbia and Montenegro);
(e) nationals of any country (except South Africa) travelling to Indonesia for conference purposes who have documentary proof of approval from the Indonesian government (also valid for tourist purposes).
Note: [3] (a) All business visitors and all those visiting relatives or friends (ie not staying in a hotel) require a Business or Social visa, whatever their nationality. (b) All tourists wishing to stay longer than 30 days must obtain visas in advance of visit. (c) All children travelling with parents who require visas must also have visas, even if travelling on their parents' passports. (d) Travellers in transit may remain in the airport for up to 8 hours without a Transit visa.
Types of visa: Tourist (£10), Business (£15 for 4 weeks, £30 for 5 weeks), Social (cost as for Business) and Transit (£10). Business and Social visas are free to those not needing Tourist visas (as listed above). Re-entry permit visas cost £25.
Validity: *Tourist* – 2 months; *Business* and *Social* – 3 months.
Application to: Consulate (or Consular section at Embassy). For addresses, see top of entry. Visas will not be issued on arrival.
Application requirements: (a) Passport valid for at least 6 months after entry date. (b) Application form. (c) 3 passport-size photos. (d) Sufficient funds to cover duration of stay. (e) Onward or return tickets, which may be purchased at point of entry.
Working days required: Minimum 3, for applications made by post or in person.
Temporary residence: Application to be made to the Consular department at the Indonesian Embassy.
Note: People wishing to travel to Irian Jaya must obtain a special permit from the State Police Headquarters in Jakarta or regional police headquarters. Issue of the permit may take two days.
Gateways: Entry and exit must be made from one of the following ports: *Air:* Polonia (Medan), Batubesar (Batam), Simpang Tiga (Pekanbaru), Soekarno Hatta International (Jakarta), Ngurah Rai (Bali), Sam Ratulangie (Manado), Pattimura (Ambon), Frans Kaisiepo (Blak), El Tan (Kupang), Supadio (Pontianak), Sepinggan (Balikpapan) and Juanda (Surabaya). *Sea:* Belawan (Medan), Batu Ampar (Batam), Tanjung Emas (Semarang), Tanjung Priok (Jakarta), Tanjung Perak (Surabaya), Benoa and Padang Bai (Bali), Yos Sudarso (Ambon), Bitung (Manado), Sekupang (Batam) and Tangjung Pinang (Riau).

MONEY

Currency: Rupiah (Rp) = 100 sen. Notes are in denominations of Rp50,000, 10,000, 5000, 1000, 500 and 100. Coins are in denominations of Rp100, 50, 25, 10 and 5.
Currency exchange: Though in the main centres for tourism there should be no difficulty exchanging major currencies, problems may occur elsewhere. The best currency for exchange purposes is the US Dollar.
Credit cards: Access/Mastercard, American Express and Visa are accepted. Check with your credit card company for details of merchant acceptability and other services which may be available.

Timatic

Health	
GALILEO/WORLDSPAN:	**TI-DFT/CGK/HE**
SABRE:	**TIDFT/CGK/HE**
Visa	
GALILEO/WORLDSPAN:	**TI-DFT/CGK/VI**
SABRE:	**TIDFT/CGK/VI**

For more information on Timatic codes refer to Contents.

Travellers cheques: Limited merchant acceptance but can be easily exchanged at banks and larger hotels.
Exchange rate indicators: The following figures are included as a guide to the movements of the Rupiah against Sterling and the US Dollar:

Date:	**Oct '92**	**Sep '93**	**Jan '94**	**Jan '95**
£1.00=	**3318**	**3221**	**3123**	**3439**
$1.00=	**2091**	**2109**	**2111**	**2199**

Currency restrictions: There are no restrictions on the import or export of foreign currency. The import and export of local currency is limited to Rp50,000, which must be declared. Local currency may be exchanged on departure.
Banking hours: 0800/0830-1200/1400 Monday to Saturday.

DUTY FREE

The following goods may be imported into Indonesia by travellers over 18 years of age without incurring customs duty:
(a) For a one-week stay:
200 cigarettes or 50 cigars or 100g of tobacco; less than 2 litres of alcohol (opened); a reasonable amount of perfume; gifts up to the value of US$100.
(b) For a 2-week stay:
400 cigarettes or 100 cigars or 200g of tobacco; alcohol, perfume and gifts as above.
(c) For a stay of more than two weeks:
600 cigarettes or 150 cigars or 300g of tobacco; alcohol, perfume and gifts as above.
Note: Cameras and jewellery must be declared on arrival. It is prohibited to import weapons, ammunition, non-prescribed drugs, television sets, Chinese publications and medicines, and pornography.

PUBLIC HOLIDAYS

Jan 1 '95 New Year's Day. **Mar 3** Eid al-Fitr (End of Ramadan). **Apr 14** Good Friday. **May 10** Eid al-Adha (Feast of the Sacrifice). **May 25** Ascension Day. **May 31** Muharram (Islamic New Year). **Aug 9** Mouloud (Prophet's Birthday). **Aug 17** Indonesian National Day. **Dec 20** Ascension of the Prophet. **Dec 25** Christmas Day. **Jan 1 '96** New Year's Day. **Feb 22** Eid al-Fitr (End of Ramadan). **Apr 5** Good Friday.
Note: (a) Muslim festivals are timed according to local sightings of various phases of the Moon and the dates given above are approximations. During the lunar month of Ramadan that precedes Eid al-Fitr, Muslims fast during the day and feast at night and normal business patterns may be interrupted. Many restaurants are closed during the day and there may be restrictions on smoking and drinking. Some disruption may continue into Eid al-Fitr itself. Eid al-Fitr and Eid al-Adha may last anything from two to ten days, depending on the region. For more information see the section *World of Islam* at the back of the book. (b) There are also Buddhist festivals timed according to phases of the moon.

HEALTH

Regulations and requirements may be subject to change at short notice, and you are advised to contact your doctor well in advance of your intended date of departure. Any numbers in the chart refer to the footnotes below.

	Special Precautions?	Certificate Required?
Yellow Fever	No	1
Cholera	Yes	2
Typhoid & Polio	Yes	-
Malaria	3	-
Food & Drink	4	-

[1]: A yellow fever vaccination certificate is required from travellers coming from infected areas and from those countries that have in the past been classified as endemic or infected areas.
[2]: Following WHO guidelines issued in 1973, a cholera vaccination certificate is no longer a condition of entry to Indonesia. However, cholera is a serious risk in this country and precautions are essential. Up-to-date advice should be sought before deciding whether these precautions should include vaccination as medical opinion is divided over its effectiveness. See the *Health* section at the back of the book.
[3]: Malaria risk exists in the malignant *falciparum* form throughout the year everywhere except parts of Java-Bali, Jakarta municipality and other big cities. The existing form is reported to be 'highly resistant' to chloroquine and 'resistant' to sulfadoxine/pyrimethane.
[4]: All water should be regarded as being a potential health risk. Water used for drinking, brushing teeth or making ice should have first been boiled or otherwise sterilised. Milk is unpasteurised and should be boiled. Powdered or tinned milk is available and is advised, but make sure that it is reconstituted with pure water. Avoid dairy products which are likely to have been made from unboiled milk. Only eat well-cooked meat and fish, preferably served hot. Salad and mayonnaise may carry increased risk. Vegetables should be cooked and fruit peeled.
Rabies is present. For those at high risk, vaccination before arrival should be considered. If you are bitten abroad, seek medical advice without delay. For more information, consult the *Health* section at the back of the book.
Bilharzia (schistosomiasis) is present in central Sulawesi. Avoid swimming and paddling in fresh water. Swimming pools which are well-chlorinated and maintained are safe.
Health care: Health insurance, to include emergency repatriation cover, is advised. Adequate routine medical care is available in all major cities, but emergency services are generally inadequate outside major cities.

TRAVEL - International

Note: For a list of the air and sea ports which may be used to enter and exit Indonesia, see the end of the *Passport/Visa* section above.
AIR: Indonesia's national airline is *Garuda Indonesia (GA).*
For free advice on air travel, call the Air Travel Advisory Bureau in the UK on (0171) 636 5000 (London) *or* (0161) 832 2000 (Manchester).
Approximate flight times: From *London* to Jakarta is 20 hours 20 minutes and to Bali is 22 hours 15 minutes (with a good connection in Jakarta). From *Los Angeles* to Jakarta is 24 hours 20 minutes. From *New York* to Jakarta is 30 hours via Europe or 31 hours via Los Angeles. From *Singapore* to Jakarta is 1 hour 35 minutes. From *Sydney* to Jakarta is 7 hours 55 minutes.
International airports: *Jakarta (CGK)* (Soekarno Hatta) is 20km (12 miles) northwest of the city (travel time – 45 minutes). Airport facilities include banks/bureaux de change, a post office, duty-free shops, gift shops, restaurants, snack bars (all open 1 hour before and after flights), car rental *(Hertz)* and 24-hour medical/vaccination facilities. A bus goes to the city every 30 minutes 0630-2100. Buses leave Jakarta from Gambir railway station and from Rawamangun and Blok M bus stations. Taxis are also available to the city centre at a cost of approximately Rp12,000. A regular bus shuttle goes to Jakarta's second airport, *Halim Perdana Kusuma (HLP)*, 13km (8 miles) southeast of the city (travel time – 45 minutes).
Denpasar (DPS) (Ngurah Rai), 13km (8 miles) south of the city, is the main airport on Bali (travel time to city – 15 minutes). There are duty-free facilities at the airport. A bus goes to the city every 5 minutes 0400-2000. Return is from Jegal bus station, Imam Bonjal Street. Taxis are available to the city and to Kuta, Logian, Sanur and Nusadua.
Departure tax: Varies according to departure point. It is Rp21,000 from Jakarta for international flights and Rp20,000 from Denpasar.
SEA: International ports are Belawan (Sumatra), Denpasar (Bali), Tanjung Priok (Java), Padang Bay (Bali), Surabaya (Java) and Tandjung Pinang.
Passenger lines: *CTC, Cunard, Dominion Far East, Lindblad, Norwegian American, Pacific International, P&O, Royal Viking, Sitmar* and *Windjammer Cruises.*
Cargo/passenger lines: *American President Lines, Austasia, Ben Shipping, Golden Line, Lykes, Polish Ocean* and *Royal Interocean.*
RAIL: There is a daily sea and rail service between Belawan and Penang (West Malaysia) operated by *National Railroad of Indonesia.*
ROAD: Indonesia's international land borders are between Kalimantan and the Malaysian states of Sarawak and Saba on the island of Borneo, and Irian Jaya and Papua New Guinea. There are no road links with Saba and the few (poorly maintained) roads to Sarawak are not recognised as gateways to Indonesia. Access through the forests of Papua New Guinea is virtually impossible (assuming it was allowed).

TRAVEL - Internal

AIR: Indonesia has a good internal air system linking most of the larger towns to Jakarta. *Kemayoran*, Jakarta's domestic airport, is 3km (2 miles) from the city. Domestic operators include: *Bouraq Indonesia Airlines, Garuda Indonesia, Merpati Nusantara Airlines* and *Sempati.*
Visit Indonesia Air Pass: This gives access to varying numbers of cities depending on the ticket bought. Contact *Garuda Indonesia* for prices and further information.
Departure tax: Varies according to point of departure. It is Rp8000 from Jakarta and Rp7000 from Denpasar.
SEA: Sailings are available to Sumatra, Sulawesi and Kalimantan. Ferries between Ketapangan, Java, Gilimanuta and Bali depart regularly.
RAIL: Children under 3 travel free. Children between the ages of 3 and 7 pay half fare. There is a total of nearly 7000km (4350 miles) of track on Sumatra, Madura and Java. In Sumatra trains connect Belawan, Medan and Tanjong Balai/Rantu Prapet (two or three trains daily) in the north, and Palembang and Panjang (three trains daily) in the south. An extensive rail network runs throughout Java. The *Bima Express*, which has sleeping and restaurant cars, links Jakarta and Surabaya; there are also other express services. There are three classes of travel, but first-class exists only on principal expresses. There is some air-conditioned accommodation.
ROAD: Traffic drives on the left. There are over 219,000km (136,875 miles) of roads in the country, of which about 13,000km (8125 miles) are main or national roads and 200km (125 miles) are motorway. There are good road communications within Java and to a lesser extent on Bali and Sumatra. The other islands have a poor road system, although conditions are improving with tourism becoming more important. **Bus:** There are regular services between most towns. Bus trips can be made from Jakarta to Bali (two days). Indonesia is the land of *jam karet* (literally 'rubber time') and complicated journeys involving more than a single change should not be attempted in a day. Bus fares are about the same as third-class rail. Vehicles can be extremely crowded. The crew includes three conductors who also act as touts. There are 'Bis Malam' night-buses on a number of routes, running in competition with the railways. Pre-booking is essential. **Taxi:** Available in all cities. All taxis are metered. Outside Jakarta, the *bajaj,* a bicycle rickshaw, can be hired by the journey or by the hour. **Car hire:** Available with local agents.
Documentation: An International Driving Permit is required.
URBAN: Jakarta is the only city with an established conventional bus service of any size. Double-deckers are operated. In Jakarta and other major towns the *helecak,* a motorised rickshaw, offers cheaper transport than taxis. Fares should be bargained for. As well as taxis, there are also *bajajs,* pedicabs and other minibus-type services.

ACCOMMODATION

International hotels are found only in major towns and tourist areas. Several of these have business centres with a variety of services. High hotel taxes are charged (10% service, plus 10% government tax). Resort hotels on Bali vary from international class, luxury hotels to beach cottages along the shore. Most hotels have pools and can supply most leisure equipment. **Grading:** All hotels are graded according to facilities.

RESORTS & EXCURSIONS

For the purposes of this section the country has been divided into the main tourist areas, these being: Java, Sulawesi, Sumatra, Eastern Indonesia, Bali and Lombok.

Java

The capital city of **Jakarta** retains much from the colonial Dutch and British periods, with many fine colonial-style buildings and the recently restored 'old quarter'. The *National Monument* towers 140m (450ft) above the Merdeka Square and is crowned with a 'flame' plated in pure gold. The *Central Museum* has a fine ethnological collection including statues dating from the pre-Hindu era. Worth visiting is the *Portuguese Church,* completed by the Dutch in 1695, which houses a magnificent and immense Dutch pump organ. The modern *Istiqlal Mosque* in the city centre is one of the largest in the world. There is an antiques market on Jalan Surabaya and batik factories in the Karet.
Throughout the island, puppet shows are staged in which traditional *wayang gotek* and *wayang Kulit* marionettes act out stories based on well-known legends; performances can sometimes last all night. 13km (8 miles) from Yogyakarta is the **Prambana** temple complex, built in honour of the Hindu gods Shiva, Brahma and Vishnu, which includes the 10th-century *Temple of Loro Jonggrang* and said to be the most perfectly proportioned Hindu temple in Indonesia. At the temple there are also open-air performances of Ramayana ballet which involve hundreds of dancers, singers and *gamelan* musicians. Perched on a hill to the west of Yogyakarta is **Borobudur**, probably the largest Buddhist sanctuary in the world, which contains more than 5km (3 miles) of relief carvings. The *Royal Mangkunegaran Palace* in Surakarta is now used as a museum and has displays of dance ornaments, jewellery and 19th-century carriages used for royal occasions.

Mount Bromo in the east of Java is still very active and horseback treks to the crater's edge can be made from nearby Surabaya. During August and September **Madura** is a venue for a series of bullock races which culminate in a 48-hour non-stop carnival celebration in the town of **Pamekasan.**

Sulawesi

Unofficially known as 'Orchid Island', Sulawesi is a land of high mountains, misty valleys and lakes. In the south is *Bantimurung Nature Reserve* which has thousands of exotic butterflies. The island has geysers and hot springs, the most celebrated of which are at Makule, Karumengan, Lahendong, Kinilow and Leilem. **Torajaland** is known as the 'Land of the Heavenly Kings' and its people are noted for their richly-ornamented houses and custom of burying the dead in vertical cliffside tombs. **Ujung Pandang**, formerly Makassar, is celebrated for the *Pinsa Harbour* where wooden schooners of the famous Buganese seafarers are moored. **Fort Rotterdam**, built by Sultan Ala in 1660 to protect the town from pirates, is now being restored. Racing is a popular island activity; there is horseracing and bullock-racing and at *Ranomuut* there are races with traditional horse-drawn carts *(bendi).*

Sumatra

Sumatra is the second-largest island in Indonesia, straddling the Equator, with a volcanic mountain range, hot springs, unexplored jungle and vast plantations. There are many reserves established to protect the indigenous wildlife from extinction. *Mount Loeser Reserve, Bengkulu* and *Gedung Wani* organise supervised safaris enabling visitors to see at close hand tigers, elephants, tapirs and rhinos. *Lake Toba*, once a volcanic crater, is 900m (3000ft) above sea level and has an inhabited island in the middle. *Lingga* village near **Medan** is a traditional Karonese settlement with stilted wooden houses which have changed little through the centuries. At **Bukkitinggi** is the old fortress of *Fort de Kock* and nearby a zoo, market, a renovated rice barn and the *Bundo Kandung Museum.* The best beaches are on the east coast.

Eastern Indonesia

Indonesia is made up of almost 14,000 islands. The wildest and least visited of these are in the east, gathered in two great archipelagos north and south of the treacherous Banda Sea.
MOLUCCAN ARCHIPELAGO: Also known as the Maluku Archipelago, it is made up of 1000 islands, many uninhabited and the rest so isolated from each other and (since the decline of the spice trade) from the outside world that each has its own culture and very often its own language.
Halmahera is the largest island in the Moluccan group and one of the most diverse. On the coast are relic populations of all the great powers who competed for domination of the Spice Trade – Arabs, Gujuratis, Malays, Portuguese and Dutch – whilst inland the people speak a unique language that has little or nothing in common even with other unique, but related, languages on the more remote islands. **Morotai**, to the north, was the site of a Japanese air base during the Second World War, but is now engaged in the production of copra and cocoa products. **Ternate** and **Tidore**, tiny volcanic islands off the west coast of Halmahera, were once the world's most important source of cloves and consequently amassed far more wealth and power than their size would seem to merit. The Sultanate of Ternate was an independent military power of considerable muscle before the arrival of the Portuguese, exerting influence over much of South-East Asia. Both islands are littered with the remains of this and the equally strident colonial era and draw more tourists than their larger neighbour. Further south, **Ambon** was another important centre of the clove trade and has over 40 old Dutch fortresses dating from the early 17th century. **Banda**, in the middle of the Banda Sea, is often referred to as the original 'Spice Island' and is famous as a nutmeg-growing centre.
NUSA TENGARRA ARCHIPELAGO: Nusa Penida was at one time a penal colony but now attracts visitors to its dramatic seascapes and beaches. **Komodo** is home of the world's largest and rarest species of monitor lizard, while **Sumba** is noted for its beautiful *Ikat* cloth. The islands north of **Timor** – including Solor, Lembata, Adonara, Alor, Wetar and Pantar – are rarely visited by tourists: there are many old fortresses on the islands and from here seafarers used to set sail on whale hunts. Timor itself is out of bounds to tourists because of the bloody and protracted war with separatists in the east of the island. The cultures on **Roti, Ndau** and **Sawu** have

apparently changed little since the Bronze Age, yet the islands' inhabitants are renowned as musicians and palm weavers. The **Terawangan Islands** are a small group with beautiful beaches and coral gardens. **Lucipara** has excellent waters for snorkelling. **Kangean, Tenggaya, Bone Rate** and **Tukang Besi** are a group of isolated atolls in the Flores and Banda seas epitomising everyone's idea of a tropical paradise.
IRIAN JAYA: The western part of the island of New Guinea, this is one of the last great unexplored areas of the world. Even today, visiting ships are often greeted by flotillas of warriors in war canoes. All those intending to visit Irian Jaya must obtain special permits from State Police Headquarters in Jakarta.

Bali

The landscape of Bali, 'Island of the Gods', is made up of volcanic mountains, lakes and rivers, terraced ricefields, giant banyans and palm groves and, on the coast, bays ringed with white sandy beaches. The island lies a short distance from the eastern coast of Java, across the Strait of Bali. Although its total area is only 2095 sq km (1309 sq miles) the island supports a population of approximately two and a half million. Unlike the rest of Indonesia, the predominant religious faith is Hinduism, though in a special form known as 'Agama-Hindu'. Stretching east to west across the island is a volcanic chain of mountains, dominated by the mighty *Gunung Agung* (Holy Mountain) whose conical peak soars more than 3170m (10,400ft) into the sky. North of the mountains, where the fertility of the terrain permits, is an area devoted to the production of vegetables and copra. The fertile rice-growing region lies on the central plains. The tourist areas are in the south, around **Sanur Beach** and at **Kuta**, which lies on the other side of a narrow isthmus.
The island has thousands of temples – the exact number has never been counted – ranging from the great 'Holy Temple' at **Besakih** to small village places of worship. Of the many festivals, most are held twice a year and involve splendid processions, dances and daily offerings of food and flowers made to the gods. Cremations are also held in great style, though their cost is often almost prohibitive for the average Balinese family.
Denpasar is the island's capital. Sights include the *Museum*, a new art centre and the internationally recognised *Konservatori Kerawitan*, one of the major centres of Balinese dancing. The *Sea Temple of Tanah Lot* on the west coast (a short drive from Kediri) is one of the most breathtaking sights of Bali. *Goa Gajah* (Elephant Cave) near Bedulu is a huge cavern with an entrance carved in a fantastic design of demonical shapes, animals and plants, crowned by a monstrous gargoyle-like head. The *Holy Springs of Tampaksiring* are believed to possess curative properties and attract thousands of visitors each year.
Serangan Island is also known as Turtle Island because of the turtles kept there in special pens. The island lies south of Sanur and can be reached by sail boat or, at low tide, on foot. Every six months the island becomes the scene of a great thanksgiving ceremony in which tens of thousands take part.
The sacred monkey forest at **Sangeh** is a forest reserve which, as well as being the home of a variety of exotic apes, also has a temple. **Penelokan** is a splendid vantage point for views of the black lava streams from *Mount Batur*. It is also possible to sail across the nearby *Lake Batur* to Trunyan for a closer look at the crater. North of Kintamani, at an altitude of 1745m (5725ft), lies the highest temple on the island, *Penulisan. Pura Besakih*, a temple which dates back originally to the 10th century, stands high on the volcanic slopes of Gunung Agung. Nowadays, it is a massive complex of more than 30 temples, and the setting for great ceremonial splendour on festival days. **Padangbai** is a beautiful tropical coastal village, where lush vegetation backs a curving stretch of white, sandy beach. It is also the island's port of call for giant cruise liners. *Goa Lawah* lives up to its name ('bat cave' in the local tongue), a safe and holy haven for thousands of bats which line every inch of space on its walls and roof. Non bat-lovers should avoid moonlight strolls in the area, as the animals leave for food sorties at night. *Kusambe* is a fishing village with a black sand beach. *Lake Bratan* is reached via a winding road from Budugul. The shimmering cool beauty of the lake and its pine-forested hillsides is an unusual sight in a tropical landscape.

Lombok

Fifteen minutes flight (or a ferry trip) away is Lombok, an unspoilt island whose name means 'chilli pepper'. Its area is 1285 sq km (803 sq miles). The island possesses one of the highest volcanic mountains in the Indonesian archipelago, *Mount Rindjani*, whose cloud-piercing peak

soars to 3745m (12,290ft). The population of about 750,000 is a mixture of Islamic Sasaks, Hindu Balinese and others of Malay origin. The two main towns are **Mataram**, the capital, and the busy port of **Ampenan**; both are interesting to explore. The south coast is rocky. The west, with shimmering rice terraces, banana and coconut groves and fertile plains, looks like an extension of Bali. The east is dry, barren and desert-like in appearance. The north, the region dominated by Mount Rindjani, offers thick forests and dramatic vistas. There are also some glorious beaches, some of white sand, others, such as those near Ampenan, of black sand. At **Narmada**, reached by an excellent east–west highway, is a huge complex of palace dwellings, complete with a well containing 'rejuvenating waters', built for a former Balinese king. At **Pamenang** visitors can hire a boat and go skindiving, entering a clear-water world of brilliantly coloured coral and inquisitive tropical fish.

Indonesian Culture

Dancing is considered an art, encouraged and practised from very early childhood. The extensive repertoire is based on ancient legends and stories from religious epics. Performances are given in village halls and squares, and also in many of the leading hotels by professional touring groups. The dances vary enormously, both in style and number of performers. Some of the more notable are the *Legong*, a slow, graceful dance of divine nymphs; the *Baris*, a fast moving, noisy demonstration of male, warlike behaviour; and the *Jauk*, a riveting solo offering by a masked and richly costumed demon. Many consider the most dramatic of all to be the famous *Cecak* (Monkey Dance) which calls for 100 or more very agile participants.
Art centres: The village of *Ubud* is the centre of Bali's considerable art colony and contains the galleries of the most successful painters, including those of artists of foreign extraction who have settled on the island. Set in a hilltop garden is the *Museam Puri Lukistan* (Palace of Fine Arts) with its fine display of sculpture and paintings in both old and contemporary styles. *Kamasan*, near Klungkung, is another centre, but the painting style of the artists is predominantly *wayang* (highly stylised). Other artistic centres include *Celuk* (gold and silver working), *Denpasar* (woodworking and painting) and *Batubulan* (stone carving).

SOCIAL PROFILE

FOOD & DRINK: Almost every type of international cuisine is available in Jakarta, the most popular being Chinese, French, Italian, Japanese and Korean. Indonesia's spices make its local cuisine unique. Specialities include: *rijstafel* (an Indonesian-Dutch concoction consisting of a variety of meats, fish, vegetables and curries), *sate* (chunks of beef, fish, pork, chicken or lamb cooked on hot coals and dipped in peanut sauce), *sate ajam* (broiled, skewered marinated chicken), *ajam ungkap* (Central Java; deep-fried, marinated chicken), *sate lileh* (Bali; broiled, skewered fish sticks), *ikan acar kuning* (Jakarta; lightly marinated fried fish served in a sauce of pickled spices and palm sugar), *soto* (a soup dish with dumpling, chicken and vegetables), *gado-gado* (Java; a salad of raw and cooked vegetables with peanut and coconut milk sauce), *babi guling* (Bali; roast suckling pig) and *opor ajam* (boiled chicken in coconut milk and light spices). Indonesians like their food highly spiced and the visitor should always bear this in mind. In particular look out for the tiny, fiery hot, red and green peppers often included in salads and vegetable dishes. A feature of Jakarta are the many *warungs* (street stalls). Each specialises in its own dish or drink, but the traveller is probably best advised not to try them without the advice of an Indonesian resident. There are restaurants in the hotels which, along with many others, serve European, Chinese and Indian food.
NIGHTLIFE: Jakarta nightclubs feature international singers and bands and are open until 0400 during weekends. Jakarta has over 40 cinemas and some English-language and subtitled films are shown. There are also casinos, and theatres providing cultural performances. Many of the larger hotels, particularly in Bali, put on dance shows accompanied by the uniquely Indonesian Gamelan Orchestras. Throughout the year many local moonlight festivals occur; tourists should check locally. Indonesian puppets are world famous and shows for visitors are staged in various locations.
SHOPPING: Favourite buys are batik cloth, woodcarvings and sculpture, silverwork, woven baskets and hats, bamboo articles, krises (small daggers), paintings and woven cloth. At small shops bartering might be necessary. **Shopping hours:** 0830-2000 Monday to Saturday. Some shops open Sunday.

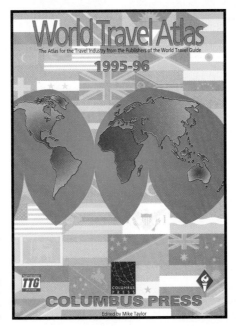
SPORT: Golf: There are courses at the major tourist destinations. **Skating:** There is an ice-skating rink at Jalan Pintu Gelora VII, Senayan. **Watersports:** The Putri Skindiving Centre, Tanjung Priok, can organise trips and rents out equipment. Swimming is safe at the beaches and many hotels have pools. **Horseriding:** The Jakarta International Saddle Club maintains a complex of sports facilities where riding lessons are available. **Spectator sports:** Horseraces are held every Sunday afternoon at Pulo Mas, JLJ Ahmed Yani. Jai Alai (a form of Basque pelota) is played daily at Hailai Jaya Ancol, Bina Ria, Tanjung Priok. Chinese shadow-boxing competitions can be watched at Loka Sari and JL Mangga Besar. There are fully-equipped watersports centres on Java, one at '1000 Islands' north of Jakarta, another at Surabaya.
SPECIAL EVENTS: There are a number of festivals which take place during the year, the dates of which often vary according to the Hindu or Buddhist calendars. Bali stages some magnificent festivals all year round. Festival calendars can be obtained on arrival. The Sultan's birthday in mid-December is celebrated by a fair and festival in Yogyakarta, Java. Some of the more important events throughout the year are listed below (for exact dates contact the tourist office):
Feb *Pasola Jousting Tournament*, Sumba Island; *Nyale Festival*, South Lombok. **Mar-Apr** *Maleman Sriwedari*, a month-long traditional night fair, Central Java. **Apr** *Mappanre Tasi Ceremony*, South Kalimantan. **May** *Jakarta Festival*. **Jun** *Paper Kite Festival*, Pangandaran Beach. **Jun-Jul** *Bali Arts Festival*; *Lake Toba Festival*, North Sumatra. **Jul** *Bunaken Festival*, North Sulawesi; *Tabuik*, West Sumatra; *Art Festival*, Banda Aceh; *Art Festival*, South Sulawesi; *Tabot*, Bengkulu. **Jul-Aug** *Darwin, Australia to Ambon Yacht Competition*, Ambon. **Aug** *Bidar Canoe Race*, South Sumatra; *Pacu Jalur*, Riau; *The Lake of Poso Festival*, Central Sulawesi. **Sep** *Grebeg Maulid*, Yogyakarta; *Erau Festival*, East Kalimantan. **Nov** *Kesodo Ritual Ceremony*, East Java.
SOCIAL CONVENTIONS: Indonesia encompasses no fewer than 250 separate languages and dialects, many of them as different from each other as Welsh is from English. Since independence many have developed a strong sense of national pride, and maintain traditions of dance, painting, woodcarving and stonecarving. Social courtesies are often fairly formal. In particular, when drink or food is served, it should not be touched until the

host invites the guest to do so. Never pass or accept anything with the left hand. Indonesians are polite and will extend endless courtesies to foreigners whom they trust and like. When invited home, a gift is appreciated (as long as it is given with the right hand). Informality is normal, but a few smart establishments encourage guests to dress for dinner. Safari suits are acceptable on formal occasions and for business wear. Muslim customs, especially those concerning female clothes, should be observed. **Tipping:** Not compulsory. 10% is customary except where a service charge is included in the bill. Porters expect Rp500 per bag.

BUSINESS PROFILE

ECONOMY: Oil and gas are the backbone of the Indonesian economy, providing half of both domestic product and export earnings. Revenues are now set to decline steadily and the Government is seeking to broaden the country's economic base. The country has immense potential with reserves of tin, bauxite, nickel, copper and gold; it is also one of the world's leading producers of rubber and a major source of tea and coffee. Two-thirds of the land is covered by forest but the Government has banned further commercial logging operations. In the last two decades, the Government has concentrated on building up a manufacturing sector, which it has done with notable success. Manufactured exports have now reached US$5 billion in value annually - on a par with oil and gas earnings. Further economic growth, in manufacturing particularly, may be stalled, however, by a recent fall in inward investment: this is the result of growing competition for foreign capital from elsewhere in the region and unusually high hidden business costs. Japan is the country's major trading partner, supplying manufactured goods in exchange for raw materials. The pattern of trade with the USA, Singapore and Germany is similar.
BUSINESS: Business dealings should be conducted through an agent and tend to be slow. Visiting cards are widely used. Literature should be in English, but prices should be quoted in US Dollars as well as Sterling. **Office hours:** 0700/0900-1500/1700 Monday to Friday. Some offices are open Saturday mornings. **Government office hours:** 0800-1500 Monday to Thursday, 0800-

1130 Friday and 0800-1200 Saturday.
COMMERCIAL INFORMATION: The following organisation can offer advice: Kamar Dagang dan Industri Indonesia (KADIN) (Indonesian Chamber of Commerce and Industry), 3rd-5th Floors, Chandra Building, Jalan M H Thamrin 20, Jakarta 10350. Tel: (21) 324 000. Fax: (21) 310 6098. Telex: 61262.
CONFERENCES/CONVENTIONS: For information or assistance in organising a conference or convention in Indonesia, contact the Directorate of International Relations & Conventions, 81 Jalan Kramat Raya, Jakarta. Tel: (21) 310 3117 ext. 126/186. Fax: (21) 310 1146.

CLIMATE

Tropical climate varying from area to area. The eastern monsoon brings the driest weather (June to September), while the western monsoon brings the main rains (December to March). Rainstorms occur all year. Higher regions are cooler.
Required clothing: Lightweights with rainwear. Warmer clothes are needed for cool evenings and upland areas.

Iran

800km
400mls
□ international airport

Location: Middle East.

Ministry of Culture and Islamic Guidance:
Iran Touring and Tourism Organisation
864 Walle-Ahd Street, Walle-Ahd Square, Tehran
Tel: 620 160 *or* 303 582. Fax: 656 800.

Iran National Tourist Organisation (INTO)
191 Motahari Avenue, Doctor Mofatteh Crossroads,
Tehran 15879
Tel: (21) 896 062 *or* 893 4444 *or* 892 212. Fax: (21) 895 884.

Embassy of the Islamic Republic of Iran
16 Prince's Gate, London SW7 1PT
Tel: (0171) 584 8101. Fax: (0171) 589 4440.

Iranian Consulate
50 Kensington Court, Kensington High Street, London W8 5DB
Tel: (0171) 937 5225 *or* 795 4949 (for visa enquiries).
Fax: (0171) 938 1615. Opening hours: 0900-1330 Monday to Thursday; 0900-1230 Friday.

Iran Travel and Consular Services (ITCS)
37A Kensington High Street, London W8 5ED
Tel: (0171) 937 2288. Fax: (0171) 937 6868.
(Provides vias, ticketing, hotel booking and travel insurance service).

British Embassy
PO Box 11365-4474, 143 Ferdowsi Avenue, Tehran 11344, Iran
Tel: (21) 675 011 (8 lines). Fax: (21) 678 021. Telex: 212493 (a/b PROD IR).

Embassy of the Islamic Republic of Iran
245 Metcalfe Street, Ottawa, Ontario K2P 2K2

Tel: (613) 235 4726 *or* 233 4726 (Consular section). Fax: (613) 232 5712.
Canadian Embassy
PO Box 11365-4647, 57 Shahid Javad-e-Sarfaraz (Daryaye-Noor), Ostad-Motahari Avenue, Tehran, Iran
Tel: (21) 622 623-6. Fax: (21) 623 202. Telex: 212337 (a/b MCAN IR).

AREA: 1,648,000 sq km (636,296 sq miles).
POPULATION: 55,840,000 (1991).
POPULATION DENSITY: 33.9 per sq km.
CAPITAL: Tehran. **Population:** 6,042,584 (1986).
GEOGRAPHY: Iran is located in the Middle East, bounded to the north by the CIS and the Caspian Sea, the east by Afghanistan and Pakistan, the south by the Persian Gulf and the Gulf of Oman, and the west by Iraq and Turkey. The centre and east of the country is largely barren undulating desert, punctured by *qanats* (irrigation canals) and green oases, but there are mountainous regions in the west along the Turkish and Iraqi borders and in the north where the Elburz Mountains rise steeply from a fertile belt around the Caspian Sea.
LANGUAGE: Persian *(Farsi)* is the most widely spoken language. Arabic is spoken in Khuzestan in the southwest, and Turkish in the northwest around Tabriz. English, French and (to a lesser extent) German are spoken by many businessmen and officials.
RELIGION: Predominantly Islamic; mostly Shi'ite, with a minority of Sunnis. The 1976 census recorded 300,000 Christians, 80,000 Jews and 30,000 Zoroastrians.
TIME: GMT + 3.5 (GMT + 4.5 from March to September).
ELECTRICITY: 220 volts AC, 50Hz. Plugs have two round pins.
COMMUNICATIONS: Telephone: IDD service available. Country code: 98. Outgoing international code: 00. Telephone booths are yellow. **Telex/telegram:** Facilities are available at the Central Telegraph Office, Meydan Sepah, Tehran. There are three charge bands. There are also telex facilities at the major hotels. **Post:**

Airmail to Western Europe can take at least two weeks. The Central Post Office in Tehran is on Sepah Avenue. Post boxes are yellow. Stamps can be bought at some cigarette kiosks. Post office hours: Generally 0730-1400 Saturday to Thursday, but some main post offices stay open until 1900. **Press:** Officially the press is free, but in practice it is highly censored. The main English-language daily is the *Tehran Times*.
BBC World Service and Voice of America frequencies: From time to time these change. See the section *How to Use this Book* for more information.
BBC:

MHz	15.57	11.76	9.740	1.413
Voice of America:				
MHz	15.44	11.90	9.700	9.530

PASSPORT/VISA

Regulations and requirements may be subject to change at short notice, and you are advised to contact the appropriate diplomatic or consular authority before finalising travel arrangements. Details of these may be found at the head of this country's entry. Any numbers in the chart refer to the footnotes below.

	Passport Required?	Visa Required?	Return Ticket Required?
Full British	Yes	Yes	Yes
BVP	Not valid	-	-
Australian	Yes	Yes	Yes
Canadian	Yes	Yes	Yes
USA	Yes	Yes	Yes
Other EU (As of 31/12/94)	Yes	Yes	Yes
Japanese	Yes	Yes	Yes

Entry restrictions: Nationals of Israel will be refused entry under all circumstances. Women judged to be dressed immodestly will be refused entry.

PASSPORTS: Valid passport required by all.
British Visitors Passport: Not acceptable.
VISAS: Required by all except nationals of the Former Yugoslav Republic of Macedonia and Turkey (for a stay not exceeding 3 months).
Types of visa: Entry, Transit, Multiple, Pilgrimage and Business. Fee varies according to nationality of applicant and type of visa.
Note: (a) A visa cannot be issued for passports which have a validity of less than 6 months. (b) All foreigners must register with the police within 48 hours of arrival. (c) Exit permits required by all (often included with visa).
Validity: *Entry visa:* up to 3 months from date of authorisation. *Transit visa:* maximum of 7 days. Applications for renewal or extension should be made to the Iranian Embassy.
Application to: Consulate (or Consular section at Embassy). For addresses, see top of entry.
Application requirements: (a) 2 completed application forms. (b) 3 passort-size photos. (c) Stamped, self-addressed envelope, if passport sent by post. (d) Fee. (e) Holders of British passports applying for a Transit visa must provide a letter of recommendation from the British Foreign and Commonwealth Office in London. All other nationals must provide a similar letter from the appropriate Embassy. (f) Applicants for a Business visa must have the authorisation of the Iranian Ministry of Foreign Affairs (to be obtained via business associates in Iran).
Note: A return ticket must be purchased before travelling to Iran. Those buying their outward ticket from Iran should provide a letter from an Iranian bank indicating that the equivalent in currency of the cost of the ticket has been exchanged. **Working days required:** Business visa – 1 week. Others – 4 weeks.
Temporary residence: All foreigners wishing to stay for more than 3 months must obtain a residence permit. Application must be made within 8 days of arrival to Police Headquarters or the Ministry of Foreign Affairs in Tehran.

MONEY

Currency: Iranian Rial (RL) = 100 dinars. Notes are in denominations of RL10,000, 5000, 2000, 1000, 500, 200 and 100. Coins are in denominations of RL50, 20, 10, 5, 2 and 1.
Exchange rate indicators: The following figures are included as a guide to the movements of the Iranian Rial against Sterling and the US Dollar:

Date:	Oct '92	Sep '93	Jan '94	Jan '95
£1.00=	104.15	231.00	2623.0	2705.5
$1.00=	65.63	151.28	1772.9	1729.3

Currency restrictions: There are no restrictions on the import of foreign currency if declared on arrival (there is a special form). Export of foreign currency is permitted up to the limit imported and declared. Import of local currency is allowed up to RL20,000; export of local currency up to RL5000. Any amount larger than this requires authorisation from the Central Bank. With one exception, all the Iranian banks were nationalised in June 1979. The number of foreign banks has fallen dramatically since the Revolution, but there are still around 30 in operation. Foreign visitors must convert the equivalent of US$300 into Iranian Rials.
Banking hours: 0730-1330 Saturday to Wednesday; 0800-1230 Thursday. Closed Friday.

DUTY FREE

The following goods may be imported into Iran without incurring customs duty:
200 cigarettes or equivalent in tobacco products; a reasonable quantity of perfume for personal use; gifts on which the import duty/tax does not exceed RL11,150.
Prohibited items: Alcohol, narcotics, guns and ammunition, aerial photo cameras, radio apparatus, fashion magazines and filmed, recorded or printed material carrying views contrary to those held by the Islamic Law.

TOURISM & PILGRIMAGE SECRETARIAT OF THE MINISTRY OF CULTURE & ISLAMIC GUIDANCE

		Telephone	Telefax
1	Headquarters	893002-5	8893710
2	Tourist Services Office	91072374	6432088
3	Planning & Technical Office	6432093	6432093
4	Research Centre for National & International Tourism	891297	891299
5	Cultural Centre for Iranian Expatriates	8893701-7	893009
6	Exhibitions and Propaganda Management	6468184	6468184

SELECTED TRAVEL AGENTS

	NAME	TELEPHONE	TELEFAX	ADDRESS
1	Organisation for National and International Tourism	651986 656715 657065	656800	Keshavarz Blvd, Opposite Pars Hospital, No. 154
2	Apadana	7506203 7504830 765745 765715 7502949	7506483 224567	Tehran – Dr. Sahriati Ave, Hogough Junction, Someyeh, No. 4
3	Armitza	846737 851670 851963	8709646	Tehran – Dr. Beheshti Ave., Mithra Street, Nos. 57/59
4	Dor-e- Donia	8825026 8820110	836395	Tehran – Ostad Nejat Elahi, Someyeh Junction, No. 94
5	Esteghlal	834871 8829934 8828871	8828985	Tehran – Someyeh Ave., No. 205
6	Galli Tour	650260 659116 655996	222765	Tehran – Keshavarz Blvd., Felestin North, No. 12
7	Ghoghnoos	830111 8827973 8829939		Tehran – Iranshahr North Ave., No. 146
8	Iran Tour	846737 851670 851963	836991 215052	Tehran – Mirza Shirazi Ave., No. 81
9	Jahan Seyr	3112872 6414622-3 6407457	6465472	Tehran – Vessal Shirazi, No. 103
10	Keyhan Safar	652345 8863722 655926 654860	88637230 224696	Tehran – Dr. Fatemi Ave., No. 117
11	Kiyan	825679 820563 824788 8806527	222893 836814	Tehran – Gha'em Magham Farahani, No. 89
12	Persepolis	820584 831011-3 828603		Tehran – Nejat Elahi Str., No. 100
13	Seyr-o-Safar	656113 654054 567402	8855280	Tehran – Vessal Shirazi, No. 235
14	Simorgh Iran	821555 833573 4407395		Tehran – Ferdowsi Square, Forsat Ave., Corner of Mehrzad, No. 98
15	Tehran Pope	8008634-5 8008645-6 628734 629403	627489	Tehran – Yousef Abad, Corner of 37th Ave.
16	Tehran Safar	937071 937325 938062 930402	930594 214503	Tehran – Sattar Khan, Opposite Namazi Sevon, No. 141

FIVE STAR-HOTELS IN TEHRAN & PROVINCES

	HOTEL	TELEPHONE	TELEFAX	TELEX	ADDRESS
1	Bozorg Azadi	8083021-9	8083039	214302, 212845	Tehran, Chamran Highway, Evin Intersection
2	Esteghlal	290011-5	292760	212510	Tehran – Vali Asr, Chamran Highway
3	Homa	683021-9	8017179	212798	Tehran – Vali Asr Ave., Vanak Square, Shahid Khodai'i Str.
4	Laleh	655021-9, 656021-9	655594	212300	Tehran – Dr. Fatemi Str., Adjacent to Water Company
5	Bozorg Enghelab Khazar – Mazandaran	(0291) 22001-11	(0291) 22012		Chaloos – Tonkabon, Namak Abroud
6	Abbasi Guest House – Esfahan	(031) 226011-9	(031) 226008	312431	Esfahan – Shahid Ayat ollah Madani Ave.
7	Homa – Khorassan	(051) 832001-9	(051) 838024	512010	Mashad – Ahmad Abad Ave.
8	Homa – Fars	(071) 28000-14	(071) 47123	332231	Shiraz – Meshgin Fam Ave.

Islamic Republic Of
IRAN

Islamic Republic Of
IRAN

الجمهورية الاسلامية في ايران

PUBLIC HOLIDAYS

Feb 11 '95 National Day–Fall of the Shah. **Mar 3** Eid al-Fitr (End of Ramadan). **Mar 20** Oil Nationalisation Day. **Mar 21-24** Now Ruz (Iranian New Year). **Apr 1** Islamic Republic Day. **Apr 2** Revolution Day. **May 10** Eid al-Adha (Feast of the Sacrifice). **Jun 4** Anniversary of Death of Imam Khomeini. **Jun 5** Anniversary of Iranian Popular Uprising. **Jun 9** Ashoura. **Jul 14** Martyrdom of Imam Ali. **Aug 9** Mouloud (Prophet's Birthday). **Dec 20** Leilat al-Meiraj (Ascension of the Prophet). **Feb 11 '96** National Day – Fall of the Shah. **Feb 22** Eid al-Fitr (End of Ramadan). **Mar** Now Ruz (Iranian New Year). **Mar 20** Oil Nationalisation Day. **Apr 1** Islamic Republic Day. **Apr 2** Revolution Day.
Note: Muslim festivals are timed according to local sightings of various phases of the Moon and the dates given above are approximations. During the lunar month of Ramadan that precedes Eid al-Fitr, Muslims fast during the day and feast at night and normal business patterns may be interrupted. Many restaurants are closed during the day and there may be restrictions on smoking and drinking. Some disruption may continue into Eid al-Fitr itself. Eid al-Fitr and Eid al-Adha may last anything from two to ten days, depending on the region. For more information see the section *World of Islam* at the back of the book.

HEALTH

Regulations and requirements may be subject to change at short notice, and you are advised to contact your doctor well in advance of your intended date of departure. Any numbers in the chart refer to the footnotes below.

	Special Precautions?	Certificate Required?
Yellow Fever	No	1
Cholera	No	No
Typhoid & Polio	Yes	-
Malaria	2	-
Food & Drink	3	-

[1]: A yellow fever vaccination certificate is required from travellers over one year of age coming from infected areas. Former endemic zones are considered to be infected.
[2]: Malaria risk, mainly in the benign *vivax* form, exists from March to November in Sistan-Baluchestan and Hormozgan provinces, the southern parts of Bakhtaran, Bushehr, Fars, Ilaru, Kohgiluyeh-Boyar, Lorestan, and Chahar Mahal-Bakhtiari governates, and the north of Khuzestan. Resistance to chloroquine has been reported in the malignant *falciparum* strain.
[3]: Mains water is normally chlorinated, and whilst relatively safe may cause mild abdominal upsets. Bottled water is available and is advised for the first few weeks of the stay. Pasteurised milk is available; unpasteurised milk should be boiled. Powdered or tinned milk is available and is advised, but make sure that it is reconstituted with pure water. Avoid dairy products which are likely to have been made from unboiled milk. Only eat well-cooked meat and fish, preferably served hot. Salad and mayonnaise may carry increased risk. Vegetables should be cooked and fruit peeled.
Rabies is present. For those at high risk, vaccination before arrival should be considered. If you are bitten abroad, seek medical advice without delay. For more information, consult the *Health* section at the back of the book.
Bilharzia (schistosomiasis) is present in southwestern Iran. Avoid swimming and paddling in stagnant water. Swimming pools which are well-chlorinated and maintained are safe.
Health care: Health facilities are limited outside Tehran. Medical insurance is essential.

TRAVEL - International

AIR: Iran's national airline is *Iran Air (IR)*.
Approximate flight time: From London to Tehran is 8 hours 5 minutes.
International airport: *Tehran (THR)* (Mehrabad) is

11km (7 miles) west of the city. Airport facilities include a 24-hour bank, 24-hour post office, 24-hour restaurant, snack bar, 24-hour duty-free shop, gift shops, 24-hour tourist information and first aid/vaccination facilities. Airline buses are available to the city for a fare of RL50 (travel time – 30 minutes). Taxis are also available to the city centre for approximately RL2500 (travel time – 30-45 minutes).
Departure tax: RL1500. Transit passengers remaining in the airport and children under seven years of age are exempt.
SEA: The main port was Khorramshahr, but this is now totally destroyed from the war with Iraq. Bandar Abbas and Bandar Anzelli are still in use as ports. *P&O* connects Iranian ports with Persian Gulf States and Karachi.
RAIL: Sleeping cars run once a week from Moscow and Ankara (Turkey) through to Tehran. The *Qom-Zahedan Line,* when completed, will link Europe with India. Several other lines connect from remote provinces. Frontier stations are Razi (for Turkey), Djolfa (for the CIS) and Kerman (for bus link with Pakistan). Contact the Embassy or *Iranian State Railways* (see below) for details.
ROAD: No reliable international through road links. There are various routes possible from Turkey and Pakistan, but these are not recommended. Cars can also be put on boats at Venice or Brindisi and picked up at Ezmir. For details of political conditions governing access, contact the Embassy.

TRAVEL - Internal

AIR: *Iran Air* runs services to Tehran, Tabriz, Esfahan, Shiraz, Mashhad, Khorramshahr, Zahedan and other major cities. *Aseman Air* also runs services to the major cities. The vast size of Iran makes internal flights the most practical method of transport.
Departure tax: RL1500 on all departures.
RAIL: The Trans-Iranian Railway is of relatively recent construction, being started in 1938. The main line links Bandar-e Khomaini at the bottom of the Persian Gulf to Bandar-e Torkman at the southeast of the Caspian Sea through Ahvaz, Dorud, Arak, Qom, Tehran and Sari. There are many areas in the mountains and the desert which can only be reached by rail. However, rail links are at present uncertain.
Rail services are operated by *Iranian State Railways,* Tehran. Tel: (21) 555 120 *or* 556 114. Telex: 213103. There are some air-conditioned trains, also sleeping and dining cars on many trains. Daily services run on all routes. There are slightly over 4560km (2830 miles) of rail track in the country; several new lines are under construction and others are being extended.
ROAD: The road network is extensive, with more than 33,000km (20,500 miles) of paved roads and 456km (283 miles) of motorways, but the quality is unreliable. The two main roads, the A1 and A2 (not wholly completed as yet), link the Iraqi and Pakistani borders and the Afghan and Turkish borders. Traffic drives on the right. **Bus:** Widespread, cheap and comfortable, although services tend to be erratic.
Taxi: Available in all cities. The urban taxis (orange or blue) will carry several passengers at a time and are much cheaper than the private taxis which only carry one person. Group taxis for up to ten people are available for intercity travel. Prices are negotiated beforehand and tipping is not necessary. **Car hire:** Available in most cities and from airports.

Documentation: An International Driving Licence is required. Personal insurance is also required. All motorists entering Iran must possess a *Carnet de Passage en Douane* or pay a large deposit.
URBAN: Tehran has an extensive bus system, including double-deckers. Tickets are bought in advance at kiosks. Plans for a 4-line metro were suspended after the 1979 revolution, and construction did not recommence until 1986.
JOURNEY TIMES: The following chart gives approximate journey times (in hours and minutes) from Tehran to other major cities/towns in Iran.

	Air	Road	Rail
Ahvaz	1.30	17.00	19.00
B. Abbas	1.55	28.00	-
Esfahan	1.00	8.00	9.00
Kerman	1.30	20.00	18.00
Mashhad	1.30	14.00	15.00
Shiraz	1.30	15.00	-
Tabriz	1.20	12.00	11.00

ACCOMMODATION

HOTELS: A number of hotels are available and there is a fair range of accommodation. The fact that a hotel bears the name of an internationally known chain does not necessarily imply any current management connection. Student accommodation is available in small hotels. Schools and private houses also offer accommodation.
CAMPING/CARAVANNING: There are limited camping facilities and off-site camping is discouraged. Registration with the police is required if camping.

RESORTS & EXCURSIONS

Tehran, the capital, is essentially a modern city, but the best of the old has been preserved. The *Sepahsalar Mosque* has eight minarets, from which the city can be viewed. The *Bazaar* (open every day except Friday and religious holidays) is one of the world's largest. An endless maze of vaulted alleys, everything from fine carpets to silver and copper ware to exotic aromatic spices can be found here. There is a separate section for each trade practised and craftsmen can be seen at their work.
Museums include the *Archaeological* (open 0900-1200 and 1300-1600 daily, 0800-1100 Friday; closed Tuesday), *Ethnological* (open 0800-1500 daily; closed Thursday and Friday), *Contemporary Art* (open 0900-1200 and 1300-1600 daily; closed Monday), *Glass and Ceramics* (open 0900-1200 and 1300-1600 daily; closed Monday), *Decorative Art* (open 0900-1200 and 1300-1600 daily; closed Monday) and *National Art* (open 0800-1600 daily; closed Thursday and Friday). More traditional towns, such as **Rey, Varamin, Qazvin** and **Shemshak**, are within easy reach of Tehran.
The town of **Tabriz** is the country's second-largest city, with a ruined but restored fine blue mosque built in 1465. The covered *Qaisariyeh Bazaar* dates back to the 15th century. About 22km (14 miles) from the salt lake is the town of **Rezaiyeh**, which claims to be the birthplace of Zoroaster. Other towns worth visiting include **Ardebil, Astara, Bandar, Enzeki** and **Rasht**.
The Golden Triangle is the name popularly given to the region enclosed by the ancient cities of Hamadan, Kermanshahan and Khorrambadad. This is a part of Iran which is particularly rich in historical associations; for many centuries the Silk Road passed through the pleasant

rolling countryside of the region, and there are several indications of settlements dating back over 6000 years. **Hamadan** was the summer capital of the Persian Emperors, although one of the few easily visible signs of the city's antiquity is the *Stone Lion,* dating back to the time of Alexander. **Kermanshahan** is a good base for visiting the *Taghe Bostan Grottoes,* which have several excellent bas-relief carvings. The site of the *Seleucid Temple of Artemis* is in **Kangavar;** it consists of massive fallen columns and is now being reconstructed.
Esfahan is the former capital of Persia. The city's most remarkable feature is its magnificent central square which is roughly seven times larger than San Marco in Venice. The mosques, palaces, bridges and gardens also deserve a visit. The *Friday Mosque* (Masjid-e Jomeh) is one of Iran's finest buildings. The *Shaikh Lotfullah Mosque* is famous for the stalactite effect of its northern entrance. There are also several good bazaars.
Shiraz is the capital of the Fars Province, and another of the country's ancient cities. Several of the buildings date back to the 9th century, and there are several excellent parks and gardens. 50km (30 miles) away is **Persepolis,** famous for the *Ceremonial Seat of Darius,* built on an enormous platform carved out of the Kuhe Rahmat.
Khorasan is a large province in the east where a great revival of learning occurred in the early Middle Ages. **Mashhad,** a former trading post on the *Silk Road*, is the capital of the region.
The city of **Kerman** in the southern desert region has several stunning mosques and a ruined citadel.

SOCIAL PROFILE

FOOD & DRINK: Rice is the staple food and the Iranians cook it superbly. Dishes include *chelo khoresh* (rice topped with vegetables and meat in a nut sauce), *polo chele* (pilau rice), *polo sabzi* (pilau rice cooked with fresh herbs), *polo chirin* (sweet-sour saffron-coloured rice with raisins, almonds and orange), *adas polo* (rice, lentils and meat), *morgh polo* (chicken and pilau rice), *chelo kababs* (rice with skewered meats cooked over charcoal), *kofte* (minced meat formed into meatballs), *kofte gusht* (meatloaf), *abgusht* (thick stew), *khoreshe badinjan* (mutton and aubergine stew), *mast-o-khier* (cold yoghurt-based soup flavoured with mint, chopped cucumber and raisins) and *dolmeh* (stuffed aubergine, courgettes or peppers). Most Iranian meals are eaten with a spoon and fork, but visitors may choose a Western dish and eat with a knife and fork. **Drink:** Fruit and vegetable juices are popular, as are sparkling mineral waters. Tea is also popular and drunk in the many tea-houses *(ghahve khane)*. The consumption of alcohol is strictly forbidden.
SHOPPING: While the shops offer a wide selection of quality goods, local items can be bought in the many bazaars. Purchases include hand-carved, inlaid woodwork, carpets, rugs, silks, leather goods, mats, tablecloths, gold, silver, glass and ceramics. Bargaining is customary.
SPORT: Water-skiing facilities are available at the Karadj Dam near Tehran. Hotel **swimming** pools are open to non-residents and an entrance fee is charged. Some hotels have **tennis** courts and instruction is available at the Amjadieh Sports Centre in Tehran. There are several **horseriding** clubs, particularly in Tehran. There is an 18-hole **golf** course in Tehran affiliated to the Hilton Hotel on Valiye Asr Avenue. **Skiing:** The skiing season is from January to March in the Elburz Mountains. Resorts include Abe Ali, 62km (38 miles) east of Tehran; the Noor Slope, 71km (44 miles) from the capital; Shemshak, 59km (37 miles) from Tehran, and Dizine near the town of Gatchsar. Equipment for hire and all the usual winter sports facilities are available.
Hunting licences are needed and safaris can often be organised through the hotel and the Tehran-based safari company. **Fishing:** Many streams are well stocked with trout including the Djaje-Rud, the Karadje and the Lar. The dammed lakes of the Karadje River and the Sefid Rud are also filled with fish. **Horseracing** meetings are held at the Park-e-Mellat, Tehran. **Polo** matches are played at the polo grounds on the Karadj road out of Tehran.
SOCIAL CONVENTIONS: Feelings about certain countries (such as the USA and the UK) run high, so the visitor should avoid contentious subjects. The Western-isation of the Iranian way of life has been arrested since the fall of the Shah, and Koranic law exercises a much more traditional influence over much of the populace. In general, Western influences are now discouraged. Handshaking is customary, but not with members of the opposite sex. Visitors should address hosts by their surname or title. Iranians are very hospitable and like to entertain. It is also customary to be offered tea, and guests are expected to accept such offers of hospitality. Because of Islamic customs, dress should be conservative and discreet, especially women's. Businessmen are expected to wear a suit and more formal attire is also

needed in smart dining rooms and for important social functions. During Ramadan, smoking, eating and drinking in public is prohibited between sunrise and sunset; however, facilities are always available in major hotels. **Tipping:** In large hotels, a 10-15% service charge is added to the bill. In restaurants *(chelokababis)* it is usual to leave some small change. Tipping is not expected in tea-houses or small hotels.

BUSINESS PROFILE

ECONOMY: The economy is undergoing major reconstruction after the phenomenal damage resulting from the war with Iraq. With the ruinous drain on resources – both financial and human – at an end, the country can now concentrate on rebuilding what was one of the region's most prosperous economies. Iran's wealth comes from oil, and has thus been affected by the low world price throughout the latter part of the 1980s as well as the heavy demand from the military, exacerbated by an international arms embargo which forced Iran's weapons buyers into black market deals at grossly inflated prices. The agricultural sector is important for the numbers of people that it employs, but it has performed poorly in recent years and Iran has to import large quantities of foodstuffs. This has contributed to the present high level of inflation, unofficially estimated at around 100%. The Rial has also declined sharply in value in the last ten years, further increasing the cost of imported goods. One of the most urgent problems facing the regime is how to arrest the steady decline in living standards that the country has experienced since the revolution. Difficult relations with the West have led the Iranian government to try to diversify its trading links: one beneficiary of this was the CIS, which signed a series of major deals with Iranian corporations. The Government's long-term plans call for a diversification of the economy, reducing the dependence on oil – 20% of which is sold to Japan – in favour of agriculture and light industry. Iran now faces its most severe economic test for many years: the future stability of the country may depend on its performance.
BUSINESS: Most Iranian businessmen speak English and are polite and conservative in manner and expect an appropriate response from visitors. Exchanging calling cards is normally restricted to senior people. Appointments should be made and punctuality is expected for business meetings. Business gifts are quite acceptable. **Office hours:** 0800-1400 Saturday to Wednesday; 0800-1200 Thursday.
COMMERCIAL INFORMATION: The following organisation can offer advice: Iran Chamber of Commerce, Industries and Mines, 254 Taleghani Avenue, Tehran. Tel: (21) 836 0319. Fax: (21) 882 5111. Telex: 213382.

CLIMATE

Dry and hot in summer, harsh in winter. Low annual rainfall.
Required clothing: Tropical attire is worn from April to October. Mediumweight clothing is advised from November to March.

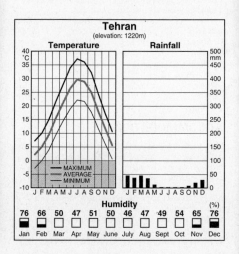

Tehran
(elevation: 1220m)

Temperature	Rainfall

MAXIMUM
AVERAGE
MINIMUM

J F M A M J J A S O N D   J F M A M J J A S O N D

Humidity (%)

76	66	50	47	51	50	46	47	49	54	65	76
Jan	Feb	Mar	Apr	May	June	July	Aug	Sept	Oct	Nov	Dec

Iraq

□ *international airport*

Location: Middle East.

Note: Some of the following information reflects the situation as it was before the Gulf War in the hope that if current issues were to be resolved, it would again prove to be useful. Conditions within the country remain unsettled and dangerous and travel to Iraq is discouraged by virtually all governments. Sanctions are still being applied by UN members, which severely restricts financial and economic activities within Iraq, including travel-related transactions. Regional conflicts continue in northern Iraq between Kurdish ethnic groups and Iraqi security forces. In southern Iraq, governmental repression of the Shia communities is severe.
Source: US State Department – September 15, 1994.

Iraqi Interests Section
21 Queen's Gate, London SW7 5JG
Tel: (0171) 584 7141/6. Fax: (0171) 584 7716. Opening hours: 0900-1530 Monday to Friday.
The Embassy of the Hashemite Kingdom of Jordan deals with enquiries relating to Iraq.
British Embassy
Zukak 12, Mahala 218, Hai al-Khelood, Baghdad, Iraq
Tel: (1) 537 2121-5. Telex: 213414 (a/b PRODRM K).
Presently closed due to the political situation.
Republic of Iraq Interests Section
c/o Embassy of Algeria, 1801 P Street, NW, Washington, DC 20036
Tel: (202) 483 7500. Fax: (202) 462 5066.
US Interests Section
c/o Embassy of Poland, PO Box 2447, Alwiyah, Baghdad, Iraq
Tel: (1) 719 6138/9 *or* 719 3791 *or* 718 1840.
Embassy of the Republic of Iraq
215 McLeod Street, Ottawa, Ontario K2P 0Z8
Tel: (613) 236 9177/8. Fax: (613) 567 1101.
Canadian Embassy
PO Box 323, Hay Al-Mansour, Mahalla 609, Street 1, House 33, Baghdad, Iraq
Tel: (1) 542 1459 *or* 542 1932/3. Telex: 212486 (a/b DMCAN IK).
Presently closed due to the political situation.

AREA: 438,317 sq km (169,235 sq miles).
POPULATION: 17,250,000 (1988).
POPULATION DENSITY: 39.4 per sq km.
CAPITAL: Baghdad. **Population:** 3,844,608 (1987).
GEOGRAPHY: Iraq shares borders with Turkey, Iran, the Gulf of Oman, Kuwait, Saudi Arabia, Jordan and Syria. There is also a neutral zone between Iraq and Saudi Arabia administered jointly by the two countries. Iraq's portion covers 3522 sq km (1360 sq miles). The country's main topographical features are the two rivers, the Tigris and the Euphrates, which flow from the Turkish and Syrian borders in the north to the Gulf in the

south. The northeast is mountainous, while in the west the country is arid desert. The land surrounding the two rivers is fertile plain, but the lack of effective irrigation has resulted in flooding and areas of marshland.
LANGUAGE: 80% Arabic, 15% Kurdish.
RELIGION: 45% Sunni Muslim, 50% Shia Muslim, with Druze and Christian minorities.
TIME: GMT + 3 (GMT + 4 from May 1 to September 30).
ELECTRICITY: 220 volts AC, 50Hz. Various 2- and 3-pin plugs are in use.
COMMUNICATIONS: Telephone: IDD service is available. Country code: 964. Outgoing international code: 00. **Telex/telegram:** There are facilities in Baghdad. Telegrams and telex messages can be sent from the telegraph office next to the post office in Rashid Street. Services are also available at major hotels. There is a 20% surcharge on telex tariffs. **Post:** Airmail between Western Europe and Iraq usually takes five to ten days, but can take longer. Avoid using surface mail. **Press:** Newspapers published in Arabic include *Ath-Thawra*, *Al-Iraq* and *Riyadhi*. Periodicals are also published. The main English-language daily is the *Baghdad Observer*.
BBC World Service and Voice of America frequencies: From time to time these change. See the section *How to Use this Book* for more information.
BBC:

| MHz | 21.47 | 15.07 | 11.76 | 9.410 |

A service is also available on 1413kHz and 702kHz (0100-0500 GMT).
Voice of America:

| MHz | 9.670 | 6.040 | 5.995 | 1.260 |

PASSPORT/VISA

Regulations and requirements may be subject to change at short notice, and you are advised to contact the appropriate diplomatic or consular authority before finalising travel arrangements. Details of these may be found at the head of this country's entry. Any numbers in the chart refer to the footnotes below.

	Passport Required?	Visa Required?	Return Ticket Required?
Full British	Yes	Yes	Yes
BVP	Not valid	-	-
Australian	Yes	Yes	Yes
Canadian	Yes	Yes	Yes
USA	Yes*	Yes	Yes
Other EU (As of 31/12/94)	Yes	Yes	Yes
Japanese	Yes	Yes	Yes

Note: The Embassy is currently issuing *Business visas* only and it is therefore not an option for tourists to travel to Iraq at the present time, due to the present trade embargo. The following information is given with regard to conditions before the Gulf War with the intention that it may prove useful in the event of diplomatic relations being resumed.
Entry restrictions: Holders of Israeli passports or other passports containing Israeli visas will be refused entry.
PASSPORTS: Required by all; must be valid for at least 3 months from date of issue of visa.
British Visitors Passport: Not acceptable
Note [*]: US passports are not currently valid for travel to, in or through Iraq and may not be used for that purpose unless a special validation has been obtained. Use of a US passport for such purposes without the requisite validation may be in violation of US law and may be punishable by a fine and/or imprisonment. For further information, contact the Office of Passport Policy and Advisory Services. Tel: (202) 955 0231/2.
VISAS: Required by all except nationals of Jordan (including Palestinians with Jordanian passports).
Types of visa and validity: *Business* (visits by invitation only): 3 months duration. *Transit:* required only if intending to leave the airport or if the stay in the airport will exceed 6 hours. *Tourist* visas are extremely difficult to acquire at the present time. Prices are available on application (£45 for visa). Visas should be applied for before entry into Iraq.
Application to: Consulate (or Consular section at Embassy). For addresses, see top of entry.
Application requirements: (a) Valid passport. (b) 2 passport-size photos. (c) 2 application forms. (d) Fee.
Working days required: 1 week from receipt of approval from Baghdad (which may take one month or more).
Exit permits: (a) Nationals of countries not belonging to the Arab League who wish to stay longer than 14 days or beyond the validity of their visa must obtain an *Arrival Notice* from the Directorate of Residents in Sa'adoun Street, Baghdad, within 14 days of arrival. Applicants must present a letter of support from their sponsors (usually a government office) and 2 photographs. The

Arrival Notice obviates the need for an *Exit Permit* unless the visit will exceed 30 days, in which case the applicant must obtain a further letter of support and possibly a *Residence Permit* (which itself will only be issued on presentation of a *Work Permit*). Heavy fines are imposed on those not adhering to these requirements and offenders may encounter great difficulty in leaving Iraq. (b) Nationals of Arab League countries must obtain an *Arab Affairs Card* from an Arab Affairs Office within 14 days of arrival. This also obviates the need for an *Exit Permit*.

MONEY

Currency: Iraqi Dinar (ID) = 20 dirhams = 1000 fils. Notes are in denominations of ID100, 50, 25, 10, 5 and 1, and 500 and 250 fils. Coins are in denominations of ID1, and 100, 50, 25, 10, 5 and 1 fils. A large number of commemorative coins has also been minted, some for everyday circulation, others for collectors. The Iraqi Dinar is pegged to the US Dollar.
Credit cards: These are not generally accepted.
Travellers cheques: These are not generally accepted.
Note: Foreign currency can be used at special duty-free shops in Baghdad up to a value of US$200. To obtain this concession, goods must be purchased within 20 days of arrival and passports must be produced.
Exchange rate indicators: The following figures are included as a guide to the movements of the Iraqi Dinar against Sterling and the US Dollar:

Date:	Oct '92	Sep '93	Jan '94	Jan '95
£1.00=	0.59	0.48	0.46	0.87
$1.00=	0.37	0.31	0.31	0.56

Currency restrictions: Import of local currency is allowed up to ID500. Import of foreign currency is unlimited, providing a declaration is made on arrival. However, Israeli currency is prohibited. Export of local currency is limited to ID25. Foreign currency export is restricted to the amount imported and declared.
Banking hours: 0800-1200 Saturday to Wednesday; 0800-1100 Thursday. Banks close at 1000 during Ramadan.

DUTY FREE

The following goods may be imported into Iraq without incurring customs duty:
200 cigarettes or 50 cigars or 250g tobacco; 1 litre of wine or spirits; 500ml of perfume (2 small opened bottles); other goods to the value of ID100, less the value of the above items.
Note: The import of typewriters as personal baggage is prohibited.

PUBLIC HOLIDAYS

Jan 1 '95 New Year's Day. **Jan 6** Army Day. **Feb 8** 14 Ramadan Revolution (Anniversary of the 1963 coup). **Mar 3** Eid al-Fitr (End of Ramadan). **May 10** Eid al-Adha (Feast of the Sacrifice). **May 31** Islamic New Year. **Jun 9** Ashoura. **Jul 14** Republic Day (Anniversary of the 1968 coup). **Aug 9** Mouloud (Prophet's Birthday). **Dec 20** Leilat al-Meiraj (Ascension of the Prophet). **Jan 1 '95** New Year's Day. **Jan 6** Army Day. **Feb 22** Eid al-Fitr (End of Ramadan).
Note: Muslim festivals are timed according to local sightings of various phases of the Moon and the dates given above are approximations. During the lunar month of Ramadan that precedes Eid al-Fitr, Muslims fast during the day and feast at night and normal business patterns may be interrupted. Many restaurants are closed during the day and there may be restrictions on smoking and drinking. Some disruption may continue into Eid al-Fitr itself. Eid al-Fitr and Eid al-Adha may last anything from two to ten days, depending on the region. For more information see the section *World of Islam* at the back of the book.

HEALTH

Regulations and requirements may be subject to change at short notice, and you are advised to contact your doctor well in advance of your intended date of departure. Any numbers in the chart refer to the footnotes below.

	Special Precautions?	Certificate Required?
Yellow Fever	No	1
Cholera	Yes	2
Typhoid & Polio	Yes	-
Malaria	3	-
Food & Drink	4	-

[1]: A yellow fever vaccination certificate is required from travellers coming from infected areas.
[2]: Following WHO guidelines issued in 1973, a cholera

vaccination certificate is not a condition of entry to Iraq. However, cholera is a serious risk in this country and precautions are essential. Up-to-date advice should be sought before deciding whether these precautions should include vaccination as medical opinion is divided over its effectiveness. See the *Health* section at the back of the book.
[3]: Malaria risk is almost entirely in the benign *vivax* form and exists from May to November below 1500m (4920ft) in some areas in the north (Arbil and Nineveh provinces).
[4]: All water should be regarded as being potentially contaminated. Water used for drinking, brushing teeth or making ice should have first been boiled or otherwise sterilised. Milk is unpasteurised and should be boiled. Powdered or tinned milk is available and is advised, but make sure that it is reconstituted with pure water. Avoid dairy products which are likely to have been made from unboiled milk. Only eat well-cooked meat and fish, preferably served hot. Pork, salad and mayonnaise may carry increased risk. Vegetables should be cooked and fruit peeled.
Note: All nationals entering Iraq for a period of five days or more are required to take an HIV blood test within the initial five days of entering the country. The hospitals in Baghdad designated to carry out the test and issue the certificate are Al Kindi, Al Kerama and Al Kadhimiya. Outside Baghdad, centres for preventative medicine in the governates should be approached. A medical certificate issued by Health Authorities outside Iraq is not valid and a fine of £500 will be incurred if this rule is not adhered to. People are advised to take their own syringes. Tour groups are able to show HIV test certificates issued in their own country.
Bilharzia (schistosomiasis) is present. Avoid swimming and paddling in fresh water. Swimming pools which are well-chlorinated and maintained are safe.
Rabies is present. For those at high risk, vaccination before arrival should be considered. If you are bitten abroad, seek medical advice without delay. For more information, consult the *Health* section at the back of the book.
Health care: Health insurance including emergency repatriation cover is essential. Basic modern medical care and medicines may not be available. Doctors and hospitals often expect immediate cash payment for services.

TRAVEL - International

Note: At present, all air travel into Iraq is prohibited due to UN sanctions held against Iraq. The following information is given with regard to conditions before the Gulf War with the intention that it may prove useful should sanctions be lifted and flights to Iraq resumed. The closest airport is Amman Airport in Jordan, from which there is a 15-hour air-conditioned coach ride into Baghdad. However, this journey is best made during the day and in a convoy, as the route passes through some reportedly dangerous territories within Iraq.
AIR: Iraq's national airline is *Iraqi Airways (IA).*
Approximate flight time: From London to Baghdad is 6 hours.
International airport: *Baghdad (BGW)* (Saddam International) is 18km (11 miles) south of the city (travel time – 20 minutes). Airport facilities include 24-hour banks, bureaux de change, post office, duty-free shops, bars, restaurants, snack bar, shops and first aid. Car rental is also available at the airport. Coach service is available to the city and returns from Damascus Street (100 minutes before flight departure). Taxi services go to the city with rates negotiable for shared taxis. There is a surcharge after 2200.
Departure tax: ID10; children under 12 years are exempt.
SEA: At present, all ports in Iraq are closed. Before the Gulf War, *Polish Ocean Lines* operated two routes: Amsterdam–Hamburg–Gdynia–Dubai; and Kuwait–Al Basrah.
RAIL: No services are running at present on the route into Iraq from Turkey and Syria.
ROAD: At present, only the borders from Turkey and Jordan are open to road travel. Before the Gulf War, principal international routes ran through Turkey, Syria and Jordan. Work on the Express Highway, an attempt to link Iraq with Kuwait, Syria and Jordan, has been suspended for the time being. For further information, contact the Embassy for up-to-date political conditions and border details.

TRAVEL - Internal

AIR: At the present time, there are no aircraft whatsoever allowed into Baghdad. However, before sanctions there were regular flights between Baghdad, Al Basrah and Mosul.
RAIL: Rail services are operated by the *State Enterprise for Iraqi Railways.* Tel: (1) 53 73 00 11. Telex: 212272. The country has over 2400km (1500 miles) of track, most of which is standard gauge. A further 300km (200 miles) or so is under construction. The principal route is from the Syrian border at Tel-Kotchek to Mosul, Baghdad and Al Basrah. Trains also run from Baghdad to Kirkuk and Arbil. A service operates three times daily between Baghdad and Al Basrah. Some sleeping cars, restaurants and air-conditioned accommodation are available.
Note: Many tracks were destroyed during the fighting and it is uncertain if any passenger services are running at all. Contact the *State Enterprise for Iraqi Railways* for up-to-date information.
ROAD: Traffic drives on the right. There are 25,000km (15,500 miles) of road. Principal routes are from Baghdad to Kirkuk, Arbil, Nineveh and Zakho; Baghdad to the Jordanian frontier; Baghdad to Kanaquin (Iranian border); Baghdad to Hilla and Kerbela; and Baghdad to Al Basrah and Safwan (Kuwait border). **Bus:** Services run from Baghdad and other main cities. **Taxi:** Services are available both in cities and for transit. Fares should be negotiated in advance. Metered taxis charge twice the amount shown on the meter. Tipping is not necessary.
Car hire: Available at the airport and in Baghdad.
Documentation: International Driving Permit required. Third Party insurance is necessary.
URBAN: Baghdad has an extensive bus system with double-deckers, and also private minibuses and shared taxis. Bus tickets should be pre-purchased at kiosks. A metro is under construction.

ACCOMMODATION

Mainly for business travellers. Modern hotel accommodation is limited and bookings should be made in advance. All prices are set by the Government for high-class hotels. Small hotels are also available for low budgets, but with a lower standard of facilities. Hotel bills are payable in foreign currency. A 10% service charge is usually added to the bill.

RESORTS & EXCURSIONS

Note: Many areas have suffered serious damage from the Gulf War and infrastructures once intact may be found to be severely damaged or non-existent.
BAGHDAD & ENVIRONS: In the capital, there is a striking contrast between the new buildings and the shabbier back streets. The Government aims to preserve the city's Islamic character by protecting the ruins of historic buildings such as the *Ike Abbasid Palace.* Long-established markets still trade. The museums of *Iraqi Folklore* and *Modern Art* are well worth visiting. The *River Tigris* is a central feature of the city.
Towns and excursions: South of the capital is **Babylon,** the great city once ruled by the Semitic King Hammirabi. The city, and particularly the famous *Hanging Gardens,* are now being restored.
NORTHERN/KURDISH REGION: Mountainous and forested area. **Note:** The enormous friction between the Government and the Kurds, who have established a *de facto* autonomous state in Iraqi Kurdistan, makes travel in this region inadvisable at present. Check with the British FCO Travel Advisory Service (tel: (0171) 270 4129) the current situation for up-to-date advice.
Towns and excursions: Kirkuk has assumed importance since the discovery of oil. It is famous for 'Eternal Fires', the endless burning of gas seepage. **Mosul** is the main northern town with the 13th-century *Palace of Qara Sariai* and the old *Mosque of Nabi Jirjis.* **Nineveh** is an ancient and rich archaeological site near Mosul. **Arbil** is probably the oldest continuously inhabited city in the world.

SOCIAL PROFILE

FOOD & DRINK: Restaurants serve both Middle Eastern and European dishes. Popular Iraqi dishes are *kubba, dolma* (vine leaves, cabbage, lettuce, onions, aubergine, marrow or cucumbers stuffed with rice, meat and spices), *tikka* (small chunks of mutton on skewers grilled on a charcoal fire), *quozi* (small lamb boiled whole and grilled, stuffed with rice, minced meat and spices and served on rice) and *masgouf* (fish from the Tigris, cooked on the river bank). Waiter service is usual. **Drink:** There is strict adherence to Islamic laws on the consumption of alcohol, which is available within the limits of religious laws. However, a permit for alcohol may be necessary. Effectively this means at international hotels only. Certain hotels prohibit the consumption of alcohol by visitors. During the lunar month of Ramadan smoking and drinking in public is not permitted.
NIGHTLIFE: Baghdad has nightclubs with cabaret, music and dancing, as do other main towns. There are also cinemas, theatres and bars.
SHOPPING: The long-established town markets sell copperware, silver, spices, carpets and brightly coloured rugs. In Baghdad the copper market is a centre of noisy activity with coppersmiths beating their pots into shape. **Shopping hours:** 0830-1300 and 1700-1900 Saturday to Thursday.
SOCIAL CONVENTIONS: Due to a long and varied history, Iraq is a culturally rich country. Today traditional Islamic culture predominates, with Koranic law playing an active role in the day-to-day life of the country, and visitors should be careful to respect this and act accordingly. Visitors should always address their hosts by full name and title. Traditional Arab hospitality is followed as a rule, in accordance with religious law. Conservative and discreet dress should be worn in observance of local Islamic laws. **Photography:** The summary execution of journalist Farzad Bazoft exemplifies the need for extreme caution when photographing anything of a sensitive nature. This includes photographs of local people (the Muslim religion does not allow the representation of human or animal images in any form); and, most importantly, any government installations, buildings or indeed anything else that may be considered off-limits to visitors. If in any doubt, do not take a photo. **Tipping:** Normal limit is 10-15%. Taxi drivers need not be tipped since the fare is agreed before the journey.

BUSINESS PROFILE

ECONOMY: The Iran-Iraq War brought a halt to many years of steady development of the economy fuelled by oil revenues from Iraq's major export commodity. Agriculture continues to employ most of the population, however, which has shown gradual improvement as government finance has assisted modernisation of farming with large irrigation schemes and mechanisation. The Government also used oil revenues to develop light industry on an import substitution principle, concentrating in recent years on textiles, chemicals and foodstuffs. Before the Gulf War, oil accounted for over 95% of export earnings, which came chiefly from Brazil, Japan, Spain, Turkey, the former Yugoslavia and Italy. Under the terms of the UN embargo imposed in the autumn of 1990, no trade whatsoever is permitted between Iraq and UN member states. Iraq now faces a poor economic situation with much of its oil industry and infrastructure destroyed by coalition bombing prior to the counter-invasion of Kuwait and later in January 1993 in response to non-compliance with the UN. Although reconstruction has proceeded at a surprisingly rapid pace, the normal economy is in turmoil and operating far below its pre-war levels. It has an enormous overseas debt which it has little chance of ever meeting, although this is proving to be a valuable negotiating card with key creditors like France and Russia who want repayment. In truth, it will be many years before Iraq will be able to reach the state of development which it had achieved by the mid-1980s. At present, the UN embargo is still in force and the principal UN Security Council members show little sign of allowing any relaxation. As long as the embargo remains, Iraq's economic prospects are very bleak.
BUSINESS: Formal courtesies are common and expected. Visiting cards are regularly exchanged and these are often printed in Arabic and English. Meetings may not always be on a person-to-person basis and it is often difficult to confine items to the business in progress as many topics may be discussed in order to assess the character of colleagues or traders. **Office hours:** 0800-1400 Saturday to Wednesday; 0800-1300 Thursday. Friday is the weekly day of rest when offices tend to be closed.
COMMERCIAL INFORMATION: Under normal circumstances the following organisation can offer advice: Federation of Iraqi Chambers of Commerce, Mustansir Street, Baghdad. Tel: (1) 888 6111.

CLIMATE

Summers are very hot and dry. Winters are warm with some rain.

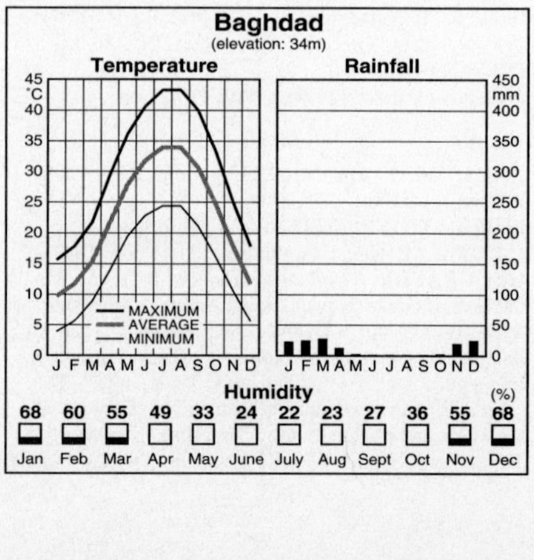
Baghdad
(elevation: 34m)
Temperature
Rainfall
°C
mm
MAXIMUM
AVERAGE
MINIMUM
J F M A M J J A S O N D
Humidity
(%)
68 60 55 49 33 24 22 23 27 36 55 68
Jan Feb Mar Apr May June July Aug Sept Oct Nov Dec

Ireland, Republic of

100km
50mls

□ *international airport*

Location: Europe, off the west coast of Britain.

Bord Fáilte Eireann
Baggot Street Bridge, Dublin 2, Ireland
Tel: (1) 676 5871. Fax: (1) 602 4100.
Embassy of the Republic of Ireland
17 Grosvenor Place, London SW1X 7HR
Tel: (0171) 235 2171. Fax: (0171) 245 6961. Telex: 916104.
Passport section: Tel: (0171) 245 9033. Fax: (0171) 493 9065.
Irish Tourist Board/Bord Fáilte
150-151 New Bond Street, London W1Y 0AQ
Tel: (0171) 493 3201. Fax: (0171) 493 9065. Opening hours: 0915-1715 Monday to Thursday and 0915-1700 Friday.
British Embassy
31-33 Merrion Road, Dublin 4, Ireland
Tel: (1) 269 5211. Fax: (1) 283 8423. Telex: 93717 (a/b UKDB EI).
Embassy of the Republic of Ireland
2234 Massachusetts Avenue, NW, Washington, DC 20008
Tel: (202) 462 3939. Fax: (202) 232 5993. Telex: 64160.
Consulates in: Boston, Chicago, New York (tel: (212) 319 2555) and San Francisco.
Irish Tourist Board
345 Park Avenue, New York, NY 10154
Tel: (212) 418 0800 (general enquiries) or (800) 223 6470.
Embassy of the United States of America
42 Elgin Road, Ballsbridge, Dublin 4, Ireland
Tel: (1) 668 7122. Fax: (1) 668 9946.
Embassy of the Republic of Ireland
170 Metcalfe Street, Ottawa, Ontario K2P 1P3
Tel: (613) 233 6281. Fax: (613) 233 5835.
Irish Tourist Board
Suite 1150, 160 Bloor Street East, Toronto, Ontario

M4W 1B9
Tel: (416) 929 2777. Fax: (416) 929 6783.
Canadian Embassy
65 St Stephen's Green, Dublin 2, Ireland
Tel: (1) 478 1988. Fax: (1) 478 1285. Telex: 93803.

AREA: 70,283 sq km (27,136 sq miles).
POPULATION: 3,547,000 (1991).
POPULATION DENSITY: 50.5 per sq km.
CAPITAL: Dublin. **Population:** 920,956 (1986).
GEOGRAPHY: The Republic of Ireland lies on the north Atlantic Ocean to the west and is separated from Britain by the Irish Sea to the east. The northeastern part of the island (Northern Ireland) is part of the United Kingdom. The country has a central plain surrounded by a rim of mountains and hills offering some of the most varied and unspoilt scenery in Europe – quiet sandy beaches, semi-tropical bays warmed by the Gulf Stream, and rugged cliffs make up the 5600km (3500 miles) of coastline.
LANGUAGE: Irish (Gaelic) is the official language, spoken by about 55,000 people (mostly in the west). The majority speak English.
RELIGION: Roman Catholic 95%, Protestant 5%.
TIME: GMT (GMT + 1 from last Sunday in March to 4th Saturday in October).
ELECTRICITY: 220 volts AC, 50Hz.
COMMUNICATIONS: Telephone: IDD is available. Country code: 353 followed by the area code, omitting the initial zero. Outgoing international code: 00. **Fax:** Many hotels have facilities. **Telex:** Telex services are fully automatic to the UK and the rest of Europe and are available from main post offices and hotels. **Post:** Irish postage stamps must be used on letters posted in the Republic. Post offices are open 0900-1730/1800 Monday to Friday; 0900-1300 Saturday. Sub-post offices close at 1300 one day of the week. The Central Post Office is in O'Connell Street, Dublin, and open 0800-2000 Monday to Friday for all business (1900 for parcels); 0800-2300 for sale of postage stamps, acceptance of telegrams, registered letters and express letters; 0900-1100 Sunday and public holidays for sale of stamps, acceptance of telegrams, registered letters and express letters; 0900-2000 for *Poste Restante* correspondence. **Press:** There are six daily newspapers published in Dublin including *The Irish Times,* the *Evening Press, Evening Herald* and the *Irish Independent;* and two in Cork. British dailies and Sunday papers are available.
BBC World Service and Voice of America frequencies: From time to time these change. See the section *How to Use this Book* for more information.
BBC:

MHz	17.64	12.09	9.750	6.195

Voice of America:

MHz	15.20	9.760	6.040	5.995

PASSPORT/VISA

Regulations and requirements may be subject to change at short notice, and you are advised to contact the appropriate diplomatic or consular authority before finalising travel arrangements. Details of these may be found at the head of this country's entry. Any numbers in the chart refer to the footnotes below.

	Passport Required?	Visa Required?	Return Ticket Required?
Full British	No/1	No	No
BVP	2	-	-
Australian	Yes	No	Yes
Canadian	Yes	No	Yes
USA	Yes	No	Yes
Other EU (As of 31/12/94)	1	No	No
Japanese	Yes	No	Yes

PASSPORTS: Valid passport required by all except:
(a) **[1]** nationals of EU countries provided they carry a national ID card or, for UK citizens, a BVP;
(b) nationals of Liechtenstein, Monaco and Switzerland, provided they hold a valid national ID card.
British Visitors Passport: [2] Accepted, although there is in fact no passport control between the UK and Northern Ireland and the Irish Republic. Passengers in transit through the UK are advised to hold onward or return tickets beyond Ireland to destinations outside the UK.
VISAS: Required by all except:
(a) nationals of countries referred to in the chart above;
(b) nationals of Andorra, Argentina, Austria, Bahamas, Barbados, Botswana, Brazil, Chile, Costa Rica, Cyprus, Czech Republic, Ecuador, El Salvador, Fiji, Finland, Gambia, Grenada, Guatemala, Guyana, Honduras, Hungary, Iceland, Israel, Jamaica, Kenya, South Korea, Lesotho, Malawi, Malaysia, Malta, Mauritius, Mexico,

Monaco, Nauru, New Zealand, Nicaragua, Norway, Panama, Paraguay, San Marino, Sierra Leone, Singapore, South Africa, Slovak Republic, Slovenia, Swaziland, Switzerland, Sweden, Tanzania, Tonga, Trinidad & Tobago, Uruguay, Vatican City, Venezuela, Western Samoa, Zambia and Zimbabwe.
Types of visa: Various categories, enquire at Embassy. Fee varies according to nationality and purpose of travel.
Application to: Consulate (or Consular section at Embassy). For addresses, see top of entry.
Application requirements: (a) 1 completed application form. (b) Fee. (c) Letters to substantiate purpose of visit. (d) Return ticket (advisable but not essential).

MONEY

Currency: Irish Punt (IR£) = 100 pence. Notes are in denominations of IR£100, 50, 20, 10 and 5. Coins are in denominations of IR£1, and 50, 20, 10, 5, 2 and 1 pence.
Credit cards: Access/Mastercard, American Express, Diners Club and Visa are all widely accepted. Check with your credit card company for details of merchant acceptability and other services which may be available.
Travellers cheques: Accepted throughout Ireland.
Exchange rate indicators: The following figures are included as a guide to the movements of the Irish Punt against Sterling and the US Dollar:

Date:	Oct '92	Sep '93	Jan '94	Jan '95
£1.00=	0.93	1.07	1.05	1.01
$1.00=	0.59	0.70	0.71	0.65

Currency restrictions: There are no restrictions on the import and export of local and foreign currencies.
Banking hours: 1000-1230 and 1330-1500 Monday to Friday. In Dublin, banks stay open until 1700 Thursday; there will also be one late opening night in other parts of the country, but the day will vary.

DUTY FREE

The following goods may be imported without incurring customs duty, as long as the items have *not* been bought in duty-free shops, thus avoiding tax:
(a) Goods obtained duty- and tax-paid in the EU:
*800 cigarettes or 400 cigarillos or 200 cigars or 1kg of tobacco; *10 litres of spirits (more than 22% proof), plus 20 litres of alcoholic drinks under 22% proof (eg fortified wine); *not more than 45 litres of wine (the amount of sparkling wine within this quantity must not exceed 30 litres); *not more than 55 litres of beer.*
Note: Although there are now no legal limits imposed on importing duty-paid tobacco and alcoholic products from one EU country to another, travellers may be questioned at customs if they exceed the above amounts and may be asked to prove that the goods are for personal use only.
(b) Goods obtained duty- and/or tax-free in the EU, or duty- and tax-free on a ship or aircraft, or goods obtained outside the EU:
*200 cigarettes or 100 cigarillos or 50 cigars or 250g of smoking tobacco; *1 litre of spirits (more than 22% proof) or 2 litres of other alcoholic beverages, including sparkling or fortified wine, plus 2 litres of table wine;* 50g of perfume and 250ml of eau de toilette; goods to the value of IR£34 (IR£17 for passengers under 15 years old).*
Note [*]: Tobacco and alcoholic beverages are only available to passengers over 17 years of age.

PUBLIC HOLIDAYS

Jan 2 '95 For New Year's Day. **Mar 17** St Patrick's Day. **Apr 14** Good Friday. **Apr 17** Easter Monday. **May 1** May Day. **Jun 5** Bank Holiday. **Aug 7** Bank Holiday. **Oct 30** Bank Holiday. **Dec 25** Christmas Day. **Dec 26** Boxing Day. **Jan 1 '96** New Year's Day. **Mar 17** St Patrick's Day. **Apr 5** Good Friday. **Apr 8** Easter Monday.

HEALTH

Regulations and requirements may be subject to change at short notice, and you are advised to contact your doctor well in advance of your intended date of departure. Any numbers in the chart refer to the footnotes below.

	Special Precautions?	Certificate Required?
Yellow Fever	No	No
Cholera	No	No
Typhoid & Polio	No	-
Malaria	No	-
Food & Drink	No	-

Health care: There is a Reciprocal Health Agreement with the UK. All prescribed medicines, and dental and medical treatment, are normally free (hospital treatment in public wards of health service hospitals is free if

arranged through a doctor). Local Health Boards arrange consultations with doctors and dentists. Evidence of residency in the UK is required, for example an NHS medical card or a driving licence, to take advantage of the agreement. Visitors should make it clear before treatment that they wish to be treated under the EU's social security regulations; it may be necessary to complete a simple statement to this effect.

TRAVEL - International

AIR: The Republic of Ireland's national airline is *Aer Lingus (EI)*.
For free advice on air travel, call the Air Travel Advisory Bureau in the UK on (0171) 636 5000 *(London) or* (0161) 832 2000 (Manchester).
Approximate flight time: From Dublin to London is 50 minutes. There are a wide range of promotional air fares to Ireland from main cities in Britain. An ever increasing number of airlines connect regional UK airports with Ireland.
International airports: *Dublin Airport* (DUB), 11km (7 miles) north of the city. The 41A city bus leaves Abbey Street every ten minutes (travel time – 25 minutes). Airport facilities include airside duty-free shop, car hire, bank, bureau de change, bar, restaurant, tourist information centre and chemist. Opening hours vary throughout the year with the majority of facilities open until 2100. Airport express coach departs to the city bus station every 20 minutes. Taxis are available to the city centre.
Shannon Airport (SNN), 26km (16 miles) west of Limerick (travel time – 25 minutes). Airport facilities include outgoing duty-free shop, bank, bureau de change, bar, restaurant and tourist information centre.
Cork Airport (ORK), 8km (5 miles) southwest of the city (travel time – 25 minutes). Bus services are available to and from both Limerick and Clare, approximately every hour. A daily express coach travels between Limerick and Shannon and between Galway and Shannon. Taxi service is available to Limerick. Airport facilities include outgoing duty-free shop, car hire, bar and restaurant. Facilities are open during operational hours. Buses travel between the city centre and airport. Taxis are available to the city centre.
Knock/Connaught Airport (NOC) (Horan International), 11km (7 miles) north of Claremorris (Co Mayo) receives international flights from the UK only. Airport facilities include duty-free shop, bar, restaurant and car hire (pre-booking advised). Bus and taxi services are available to Claremorris, from where onward rail and bus connections are available to the rest of the country.
Galway/Corrib Airport, 6.5km (4 miles) northeast of Galway City. Airport facilities include hotel and guest-house accommodation, bar, duty-free shop, exchange bureau and café. Taxi rank and car hire are available at scheduled flight times only.
SEA: Ferry routes from the UK are: Cairnryan and Stranraer to Larne (Northern Ireland) (2 hours 20 minutes); Douglas (Isle of Man) to Dublin (4 hours); Holyhead (Isle of Anglesey) to Dublin (3 hours 50 minutes) and Dun Laoghaire (3 hours 30 minutes); Fishguard to Rosslare (3 hours 30 minutes); Swansea to Cork (10 hours, May to September only); Pembroke to Rosslare (4 hours 15 minutes). There are also ferries from Le Havre and Cherbourg in France to Rosslare and from Le Havre to Cork.
B&I Line, Sealink Stena Line, Swansea-Cork Ferries and *P&O Ferries* all operate regular car ferry sailings to Ireland.
RAIL: Rail links serve Ireland from all the above ferry ports, as well as from Northern Ireland.

TRAVEL - Internal

AIR: *Aer Lingus* (as well as several other carriers) operate services throughout the country. Charter flights are also available. The Aran Islands are served by *Aer Aran* (from Galway).
Domestic airports: *Waterford* (WAT), 9km (6 miles) from the city centre. Bus and taxi services are available into Waterford. Car hire is also available (pre-booking advised).
Galway (GWY), approximately 8km (5 miles) from the city centre. Bus and taxi services available into Galway centre.
Sligo (SXL), 8km (5 miles) from Sligo. Essential facilities only. Taxis need prior booking. Bus and taxi services are available into Sligo. Essential facilities only.
Carrickfinn (CFN) in Co Donegal.
Kerry (Farranfore) (KIR) in Co Kerry, 19km (12 miles) from both Killarney and Tralee. Taxi services available to both these towns and to the nearby railway station. Car hire is also available.
As well as the airports listed above (and in *Travel –*

International), there are also various small licensed airstrips which receive passenger services; enquire at the Irish Tourist Board for details of operators and routes.
SEA: Ferry services run to the various west coast islands. Enquiries should be made locally.
RAIL: Rail services in the Republic are owned by *Iarnród Eireann (Irish Rail)*, and express trains run between the main cities. There are two classes of accommodation, with restaurant and buffet cars on some trains. Children under 5 travel free. Children aged 5-15 pay half fare. A range of rail-only and combined rail and bus *Explorer* tickets is available for unlimited travel within the Republic of Ireland or all Ireland. The *Eurorail* card system is valid in Ireland.
ROAD: The network links all parts of Ireland; road signs are international. Traffic drives on the left. **Bus:** Internal bus services are run by *Bus Eireann* (Irish Bus) which has a nationwide network of buses serving all the major cities and most towns and villages outside the Dublin area. Bus services in remote areas are infrequent. An 'Expressway' coach network complements rail services. The central bus station is in Store Street, Dublin. Unlimited travel *CIE* tickets can also cover bus routes.
Coach tours: Many companies offer completely escorted coach tours, varying in length and itinerary. Full-day and half-day guided tours are organised from the larger towns and cities. These run from May to October. Full details are available from *CIE* Tours International office. **Taxi:** Service is available in major cities. Cruising taxis are infrequent. Places to get taxis are at hotels, rail and bus stations or taxi stands. **Car hire:** Available from all air and sea ports as well as major hotels. All international hire companies are represented in Ireland, as well as local operators. Age requirements vary from a minimum of 21 to a maximum of 75 years. A full licence from the driver's home country is required, and the driver will normally be required to have had at least two years' experience. **Bicycle hire:** Ask for a Tourist Board leaflet.
Documentation: EU nationals taking cars into the Republic require: motor registration book (or owner's authority in writing); full EU driving licence or International Driving Permit; nationality coding stickers; and insurance cover valid for the Republic. *A Green Card is strongly recommended, as without it, insurance cover is limited to the minimum legal requirement in Ireland* – the Green Card tops this up to the cover provided by the visitor's domestic policy.
URBAN: Extensive bus services operate in Dublin. There is a new, fast suburban rail service (DART), connecting Howth and Bray, including a link to Dun Laoghaire (the ferry port). The *Dublin Explorer* ticket is valid for four days on all Dublin buses and DART suburban trains. This ticket may not be used before 0945, but there are no evening restrictions.
JOURNEY TIMES: The following chart gives approximate journey times (in hours and minutes) from Dublin to other major cities/towns in Ireland.

	Air	Road	Rail
Cork	0.40	4.30	3.15
Galway	0.35	4.00	3.00
Limerick	-	3.30	3.00
Shannon Airport	0.35	-	-
Waterford	0.30	3.00	2.40
Kilkenny	-	2.00	1.45
Killarney	-	5.30	3.30

ACCOMMODATION

There are many forms of accommodation in Ireland, ranging from hotels and guest-houses to farmhouses, town and country homes, holiday hostels, youth hostels, holiday centres and self-catering. Prices vary according to location, type of accommodation, facilities and season. The official Tourist Board guide to accommodation in hotels, guest-houses, town and country homes and farmhouses is available (price – £4). For details, apply to Bord Fáilte (Irish Tourist Board), addresses at top of entry.
HOTELS: There are 668 hotels inspected, approved and graded by Bord Fáilte and prices are fixed by the Tourist Board. Most hotels belong to the Irish Hotels Federation, 13 Northbrook Road, Dublin 6. Tel: (1) 497 6459. Fax: (1) 497 4613.
Grading: The Irish Tourist Board register and grade hotels as follows:
5* – Top grade of hotel. All rooms have private bathroom, many have suites. Dining facilities include top-class à la carte.
4* – All provide a high standard of comfort and service. All have private bathrooms.
3* – Medium-priced. Comfortable accommodation and good service. All have private bathrooms.
2* – Likely to be family operated with a limited but satisfactory standard of food and comfort. Most rooms will have a private bathroom.

1* – Hotels that are clean and comfortable with satisfactory accommodation and service.
GUEST-HOUSES: Guest-houses are smaller, more intimate establishments often under family management. There are over 209 guest-houses registered and inspected by the Irish Tourist Board. These range from converted country houses to purpose-built accommodation. Meals range from bed & breakfast to full board. The minimum number of bedrooms is five and the availability of meals is not a requirement.
Grading: The Irish Tourist Board registers and grades guest-houses as follows:
4* – Guest-houses which provide a very high standard of comfort and personal service. In most cases 4* guest-houses provide a good quality evening meal, hot and cold running water in all bedrooms. All premises have rooms with private baths.
3* – Guest-houses which provide a high standard of comfort and personal service. Hot and cold running water in all bedrooms. All premises have rooms with private baths.
2* – Guest-houses that are well furnished, offering very comfortable accommodation with limited, but good standard of food and service. Hot and cold running water in all bedrooms.
1* – Guest-houses that are clean and comfortable. Hot and cold running water in all bedrooms. Adequate bathroom and toilet facilities.
Ungraded premises: Hotels and guest-houses not sufficiently long in operation are left ungraded.
FARMHOUSES/TOWN & COUNTRY HOMES: There are 2853 town or country homes and 517 farmhouses offering bed & breakfast on a daily or weekly basis with other meals often provided.
Irish Homes: This informal type of accommodation gives visitors the opportunity to share in the life of an Irish family in an urban or country setting. They may live in a Georgian residence, a modern bungalow or a traditional cottage. A farmhouse holiday again gives scope for meeting the people and is especially suitable for children. Visitors can forget about city life and enjoy the everyday life of the farm. Either way it will be a relaxing and friendly holiday.
All homes and farmhouses that have been inspected and approved by the Irish Tourist Board are listed in the official guide, available from the Tourist Board. In addition to this, the Town and Country Homes Association and *Fáilte Tuaithe* (pronounced Foil-tya Too-ha), the Irish Farmhouse Association, produce their own annual guides to their members' houses. These are also available from the Irish Tourist Board in Britain and from tourist information offices throughout Ireland. For more information, contact: Fáilte Tuaithe (Irish Farm Holidays), 2 Michael Street, Limerick. Tel: (61) 400 700. Fax: (61) 400 717; *or* the Town and Country Homes Association, Donegal Road, Ballyshannon, Co Donegal. Tel: (72) 51377. Fax: (72) 51207. Telex: 40060.
SELF-CATERING: There are over 2507 self-catering establishments scattered throughout Ireland, listed by the Irish Tourist Board. Self-catering holidays are available for those who like to come and go as they please without any restrictions. There is self-catering accommodation to suit all tastes, including houses, self-contained apartments, cottages and caravans. There are even traditional-style thatched cottages which are fully equipped and located in carefully selected beauty spots.
CAMPING/CARAVANNING: Ireland's caravan and camping parks are inspected by the Irish Tourist Board. Those that meet minimum requirements are identified by a special sign and listed in an official guide which shows the facilities at each park. Firms offering touring caravans, tents and camping equipment for hire are included in the listing. There are 125 caravan-and camp-sites. The majority are open from May to September.
YOUTH HOSTELS: 48 youth hostels are operated by *An Oige* (Irish Youth Hostel Association), 61 Mountjoy Street, Dublin 7. Tel: (1) 830 4555. Fax: (1) 830 5808. Telex: 32988. They provide simple dormitory accommodation with comfortable beds and facilities for cooking one's own meals. Usage is confined to members of *An Oige* or other youth organisations affiliated to the International Youth Hostel Federation. Non-members can buy stamps at hostels entitling them to further hostel use.
HOLIDAY HOSTELS: 112 registered holiday hostels offer privately owned accommodation at reasonable prices. Dormitory-style sleeping accommodation and/or private bedrooms are available. Some provide meals, others breakfast only. For further information, contact the Irish Tourist Board.
HOLIDAY CENTRES: These centres offer a comprehensive holiday with a wide variety of amenities and facilities including self-catering units, indoor heated swimming pool and restaurant facilities. The centres are registered with the Irish Tourist Board.

RESORTS & EXCURSIONS

Ireland's coastline is 2200km (3500 miles) long, offering an astonishing variety of scenery and conditions, from the long, gently sloping strands of the east coast to the wild rocky headlands of the west. There are a number of well-equipped, popular resorts, but Ireland is still unspoilt by over-commercialisation. The majority of resorts – including some of the loveliest – are peaceful, unpretentious places ideal for family holidays. Some of the most spectacular beaches are uncrowded, even at the height of summer. Indeed, the whole country is noted for its relaxed pace of life. Amongst the many attractions are the many pre-Christian sites dotted all over the country.
There are over 50 Tourist Information Offices throughout the country who will be able to offer help, advice and suggestions regarding all aspects of holidays and travel in their regions. Offices are normally open 0900-1800 Monday to Friday and 0900-1300 Saturday, but these may vary according to local custom and circumstance. Offices at seaports and airports will generally keep extended hours during the summer months.
REGIONS: For the purpose of this survey the country has been divided into the following four regions:
The East Coast: Counties Dublin, Louth, Meath, Kildare, Wicklow, Wexford, Carlow, Waterford and Kilkenny.
The Southwest: Counties Cork, Kerry, Clare, Limerick and Tipperary.
The West: Counties Galway, Mayo, Sligo, Leitrim and Donegal.
The Lakelands: Counties Monaghan, Cavan, Longford, Westmeath, Roscommon, Offaly and Laois.

The East Coast (including Dublin)

This coast was, owing to its geographical situation, the region which felt most strongly the effects of colonisation, both by the Vikings from the 9th century onwards and by the English after the Anglo-Norman invasion of 1170. It is a rich and varied area with woods, beaches, cliffs, stately homes and ruined castles.
Dublin, the capital city of Ireland, is spread over the broad valley of the *River Liffey* around Dublin Bay in a great sweep of coast from the rocky brow of **Howth** in the north to the headland of **Dalkey** in the south, and sheltered by the *Wicklow Hills*. In addition to its imposing public buildings, Dublin is particularly rich in architecture of the 18th century with fine Georgian mansions, wide streets and spacious squares. There are fashionable shopping centres and a range of cultural and sporting entertainments. From the city it is just a short journey to the *Dublin Mountains* or to one of the beaches.
There are many public parks in Dublin, the most famous of which is *Phoenix Park* at the western edge of the city. Originally priory land, it became a royal deer park in the 17th century. It is home to the Irish President and the US ambassador to Ireland. The park is noted for the *Viceroy Lodge* and a 61m (200ft) obelisk erected in tribute to the Duke of Wellington in 1817. The park, with a

DUBLIN

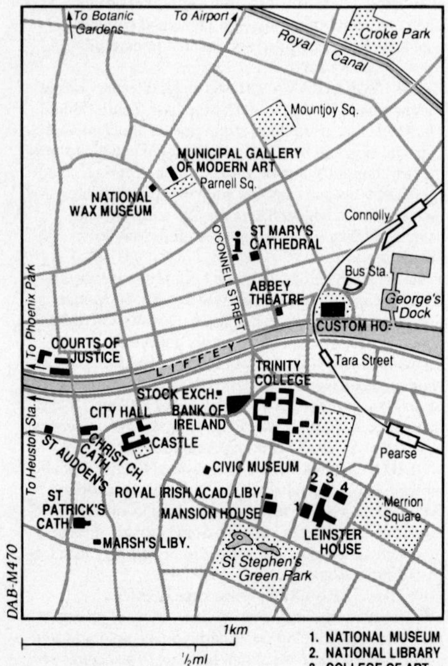
To Botanic Gardens
To Airport
Royal Canal
Croke Park
Mountjoy Sq.
MUNICIPAL GALLERY OF MODERN ART
Parnell Sq.
NATIONAL WAX MUSEUM
Connolly
O'CONNELL STREET
ST MARY'S CATHEDRAL
Bus Sta.
ABBEY THEATRE
George's Dock
CUSTOM HO.
To Phoenix Park
COURTS OF JUSTICE
LIFFEY
Tara Street
TRINITY COLLEGE
STOCK EXCH.
To Heuston Sta.
CITY HALL
BANK OF IRELAND
CHRIST CH. CATH.
ST AUDOEN'S
CASTLE
Pearse
CIVIC MUSEUM
ST PATRICK'S CATH.
ROYAL IRISH ACAD. LIBY.
MANSION HOUSE
Merrion Square
MARSH'S LIBY.
LEINSTER HOUSE
St Stephen's Green Park
DAB-M470
1km
½ml
i tourist information
1. NATIONAL MUSEUM
2. NATIONAL LIBRARY
3. COLLEGE OF ART
4. NATIONAL GALLERY

circumference of 11km (7 miles), has a network of roads and many quiet walks running through it. There is a zoo near the main entrance and an area known as *The Fifteen Acres* (but actually covering about 200), once the old duelling grounds, but now used as playing fields.
A full programme of sightseeing tours of Dublin (all year) and surrounding areas (in summer) is operated by *Bus Eireann*. Walking tours or 'Tourist Trails' are signposted in the city centre. These tours are contained in a special booklet giving maps and background information on points of interest along the routes and details of approved Dublin and national guides; for details of these and the many evening entertainments, see the daily newspapers or enquire at the Tourist Information Office.
Housed in the west wing of Leinster House, *The National Gallery* has over 2000 paintings. The National Museum has a collection of Irish antiquities from the Stone Age to medieval times. The most famous exhibits include the 8th-century Ardagh Chalice and Tara Brooch and the 12th-century Cross of Cong. There is also a room devoted to the Easter Rising and War of Independence. Other museums worth visiting include the *Dublin Civic Museum*; the *Municipal Gallery of Modern Art;* the *National Library of Ireland* and the *Royal Irish Academy Library. Trinity College Library* houses the 8th-century Book of Kells and the finest collection of early illuminated manuscripts in Ireland.
Trinity College is the city's most famous landmark. Founded by Elizabeth I in 1591, it is noted for its cobbled stone quadrangles and imposing grey college buildings. *Dublin Castle*, the seat of British administration from the 12th century to the 1920s, can be found on high ground west of Dame Street and *Christ Church Cathedral,* one of the city's finest historical buildings, located at the end of Lord Edward Street.
Dublin has facilities for most major sports. The national hurling and Gaelic football finals (September) and the Dublin Horse Show (August) are outstanding among the city's sporting events. There is horseracing at two suburban courses and at other venues within easy reach, rugby at Landsdowne Road and greyhound racing for most of the year on six evenings a week at one of the two Dublin tracks. The golfer has about 30 excellent courses to choose from. Sea bathing is available at nearby resorts, and there are municipal indoor heated swimming pools in the city and suburbs.
Theatre is always available in Dublin. The principal theatres are the *Abbey, Peacock, Gate, Gaiety, Olympia* and *New Eblana.* During the summer the Gaiety and the Olympia provide a season of variety and revue with well-known Irish and visiting artists, and occasional weeks of light opera and drama presented by first-class managements. The Gate is concerned mainly with producing the internationally recognised classics, and has a special feeling for the work of Irish writers of sophisticated comedy – such as Goldsmith, Sheridan, Wilde and Shaw. The New Eblana is a small theatre which has been acclaimed for its productions of modern plays.
The National Theatre of Ireland is the Abbey, where the programme consists almost entirely of new plays by Irish authors interspersed with revivals from the repertoire, which includes Yeats, Synge, O'Casey, Boucciault, Behan and Beckett. In the same building, the smaller *Peacock Theatre* provides the Abbey Players with an opportunity for experimental work.
The shows of *Lambert Mews Theatre* are directed and produced by the famous Lambert puppeteers. The theatre seats 100 people and is 10km (6 miles) from the city centre. Performances are nightly with two matinées weekly for children.
All these theatres perform Monday to Saturday; bookings should be made in advance.
The *Projects Arts Centre* presents drama, poetry readings and recitals at lunchtime and in the evening. These are very popular with student visitors (also open Sunday).
The *National Concert Hall*, Earlsport Terrace, provides high-quality concerts throughout the year.
Meath and **Louth** (the smallest of the 32 counties), between Dublin and the border, are lush and wooded counties with many fine beaches and, particularly in Louth, rugged cliffs rising out of the sea. The *Cooley Peninsula* in Louth has a beautiful coastline and is the setting of one of the oldest legends of Irish literature, the Táin Bó Cuailnge (the Cattle Raid of Cooley). Meath contains the greatest wealth of historical remains in the country including *Tara*, the seat of Celtic Ireland, 10th-century high crosses, and the largest Norman fortress in Ireland at *Trim.* **Wicklow,** south of the capital, is known as 'the Garden of Ireland'. It is also rich in stately homes and in reminders of Ireland's early medieval Christian heritage. In the hinterland of County Wicklow and County Dublin are the *Wicklow Mountains.* Further south from Wicklow is **Wexford,** also a fertile farming region, surrounded by hills and rivers and is famous for its Opera Festival.

EXCURSIONS: Newgrange, Dowth, Knowth and **Meath** are the most important of the group of around 40 Stone Age monuments known as the *Brú Na Bóinne.* These burial chambers, known as passage graves, predate the pyramids. The *Cooley Peninsula* (Louth) is good for hill walks. In the Dublin environs *Howth Castle* and *Malahide Castle,* **Dun Laoghaire** (pronounced 'Dun Leary'), **Russborough** and *Castletown House* and the Archbishop's ruined castle at **Swords** are all worth seeing. **Waterford** is a city with two cathedrals, exhibitions in the city hall and some interesting glassworks. The burial place of Richard Strongbow and his Irish wife Eva can be found here. A short distance from the city is the village of **Passage East,** where Richard landed in 1170, an event which was to bind together the fortunes of England and Ireland.
RESORTS: The eastern seaboard has some 400km (250 miles) of fine, silvery sand beaches running from the Mountains of Mourne to the port of Waterford.
Duncannon is a pleasant holiday town with a good beach and a rocky coast to the south. There is good walking and little traffic to the end of the peninsula. The area is ideal for those looking for isolated spots. The two finest sandy beaches are *Booley Strand* and *Dollar Bay*. **Fethard-on-Sea** is a quiet village on Hook Peninsula with a good beach. **Rosslare** is best known for its 10km (6-mile) beach backed by dunes and pleasant countryside.
Curracloe has a very long beach backed by interesting countryside. **Kilmuckridge** is known for its excellent beach with fine sand backed by *Old World Village.*
Blackwater is a picturesque village with a sandy beach.
Ballymoney is situated 5km (3 miles) north of Courtown. There is a good beach backed by dunes here. **Arklow,** a seaport town, has safe bathing from fine sandy beaches at *North and South Strands. Johnstown Strand* and *Ennereilly Strand* are also good bathing places. It has an amusement centre with swimming pool. **Brittas Bay** has an excellent beach of fine sand. **Dun Laoghaire** is a large, residential town with bathing, yachting, etc. There is a beach at *Seapoint* and outdoor pool open from May-August. The famous 'Forty-Foot' swimming place is at **Sandycove.** The beach at *Sandycove Harbour* is also popular. **Howth** is a fishing village. There is good bathing from *Balscadden Beach* (shingle) and *Claremont Strand* (sand). **Ireland's Eye,** a little island 2km (1 mile) offshore, has some delightful bathing coves. There is also an old stone church here on the site of a 6th-century monastery and an 18th-century Martello tower.
Portmarnock: Popular seaside resort with an excellent beach. **Malahide:** Popular seaside area with a good sandy beach. **Skerries** is a well-known north Dublin bathing place with a good beach and island rocks of that name.
Balbriggan is a coastal town with a good beach.
Blackrock in County Louth has a wide shallow beach and no cliffs. **Carlingford** has a small shingle and sand beach on *Carlingford Lough.* Nearby is the scenic village of **Omeath** with a shingle beach. **Donabate** has a ruined castle and safe sandy beaches and leads to **Lambay Island,** the scene of the first Viking raid in 795. **Rush:** Seaside resort with safe sandy beaches. **Clogher Head** has outstanding views of the Mountains of Mourne and Skerries. There is also a wide sandy beach safe for bathing. **Ardmore** is a charming resort with an extensive sandy beach. There is a medieval cathedral and round tower with spectacular views over Ardmore Bay.
Tramore, a busy seaside resort, has a 5km (3-mile) beach and excellent entertainment facilities. **Dunmore East** has an attractive harbour, headlands, cliffs and coves.

The Southwest

The counties of the southwest (Clare, Cork, Kerry, Limerick and Tipperary) comprise all of the ancient Kingdom of Munster and part of Connaught. This region includes the *River Shannon*, an area of great natural beauty and excellent fishing, countless lakes (including Lough Derg), ranges of rugged mountains such as the *Knockmealdowns,* the *Galtees* and rich fertile plains, as well as a staggering variety of historical and prehistoric remains.
EXCURSIONS: The Burren, a vast limestone plain, of great interest to botanists and archaeologists; hundreds of castles, ranging from the immaculate to the dilapidated; **Limerick**, Ireland's fourth-largest city, with Georgian buildings; the 13th-century *King John's Castle* and the 12th-century *St Mary's Cathedral; Bunratty Castle,* a few miles from Limerick, with its famous folk museum and medieval-style banquets; **Cashel**, one of the most important historical sites in the country; the beautiful countryside of the **Dingle Peninsula**, the westernmost point of Europe; the 'Ring of Kerry' road, taking in such places as **Killorglin** (with the Puck Fair in August), **Killarney, Valentia,** *Lough Currane,* the *Staigue Fort* and the *Standing Stones* at the *Shrubberies* near **Kenmare;** *Blarney Castle* and the *Blarney Stone,* near Cork; the city of **Cork** with *St Finbarr's Cathedral,* **Fota**

Island on the edge of the city, the old town, many churches, museums and art galleries; many quiet towns ringed with hills, such as **Bandon** and **Macroom; Tralee,** an attractive town with a good shopping centre and annual international 'Rose of Tralee' festival, and a good base for excursions to the west coast.
RESORTS: Beal: Long sandy beach on the Shannon estuary near **Ballybunion,** a leading holiday resort. A fine stretch of sand fronts the town, affording good and safe bathing. Good sporting and recreational facilities.
Ballyheigue: Quiet village, miles of sandy beach on a low lying peninsula. **Cloghane:** Fine beach situated beneath the eastern slopes of *Brandon Mountain.*
Ballyferriter/Dunquin: Magnificent scenery of sandy coves among rocky cliffs overlooking the **Blasket Islands. Ventry:** Long, safe sandy, beach 8km (5 miles) from Dingle. **Inch:** 6.5km (4-mile) strand on *Dingle Peninsula.* **Ballymona:** Sandy beach 5km (3 miles) from **Ballycotton. Glenbeigh:** 3km (2 miles) from Glenbeigh is *Rossdbeigh Strand.* Extensive sandy beach. Good bathing. **Valentia Island:** Situated less than a quarter of a mile offshore. Striking cliff scenery. Bathing and good sea fishing. Bridge from **Portmagee. Beginish Island:** In *Valentia Harbour;* has a fine strand. **Ballinskelligs:** Fine strand just outside the village. Attractions include boating, bathing, fishing and striking coastal scenery. **Waterville:** Good sandy beaches near the village. **Reenore:** Sandy beach within a few miles of Waterville. **Kells:** Pleasant sandy cove within easy reach of Waterville. **Castlecove:** Sandy beach situated amid rugged romantic scenery. **Sneem:** 15-minute drive to safe sandy beaches.
Parknasilla: Good bathing in nearby coves. Boating facilities. **Tahilla:** Secluded village in *Coongar Harbour.* **Kenmare:** Beautifully situated. Good bathing.
Ballydonegan: Fine beach with good bathing.
Castletownbere: Sheltered harbour. Small shingle beach nearby. **Glengariff:** Pleasant coastal resort. **Ballylickey:** Secluded sea inlet; fine scenery. **Bantry:** Well situated, sheltered by a background of hills. **Kilcrohane:** Secluded spot on *Dunmanus Bay.* **Ahakista:** Good bathing at coves and little strands nearby. **Barleycove:** Fine sandy beach.
Crookhaven: Charming harbour. **Goleen:** Secluded sandy beach. **Schull:** Sea and mountain scenery. Excellent for bathing, boating and rambling. **Ballydehob:** Small village with a quaint harbour. **Baltimore:** Shingle beach. Sailing and boat trips. **Castletownshend:** Pretty village in a secluded haven. **Union Hall:** Quaint fishing village. Shingle beach. **Glandore:** Attractive little resort popular for bathing. **Rosscarbery:** Quiet spot for a holiday. Good bathing. **Owenahincha Strand:** A favoured bathing place near Rosscarbery. **Castlefreke:** Safe sandy beaches in the area of Castlefreke.
Inchadoney: Situated 5km (3 miles) from Clonakilty. Offers good bathing from a sandy beach. **Clonakilty:** Many good places for swimming within easy reach of here, such as *Harbour View, Broad Strand, Inchadoney, Dooneen, Long Strand, Dunworley* and *Dunneycove.*
Courtmacsherry: A favourite seaside resort. Attractions include bathing, boating and tennis. **Garrettstown Strand:** Sandy beach. **Kinsale:** Good bathing nearby at *Summer Cove.* **Oysterhaven:** Small pebble beach. **Inch:** Fine sheltered sandy beach. **Ballycotton:** Fishing harbour. **Garryvoe:** Quiet spot with a fine stretch of sand.
Youghal: Popular resort. 8km (5 miles) of sandy beach. **Crosshaven:** Popular seaside resort.

The West Coast

The western and northwestern counties (Galway, Mayo, Sligo, Leitrim and Donegal) are the least anglicised part of the country, a land of thatched cottages and peat fires,

limestone plains and steep craggy cliffs, and of **Connemara,** a region of stark beauty which has long fired the imaginations of writers, poets and painters. The area is dominated by two spectacular mountain ranges, the *Twelve Bens* and *Maam Turks.* The northwest in particular consists of a rugged landscape of steep cliffs, often overlooking lonely islands, interspersed with sandy beaches. Inland the scenery is varied, ranging from the bleak mountains of **Donegal** to the lakes of **Leitrim.** The landscape is broken up by fertile valleys and dotted with ancient churches, prehistoric tombs and crumbling ruins. In County **Mayo,** the upland stretches from Lough Corrib and Killary Harbour in the south to the Mullet Peninsula in Killala Bay in the north. Traditional Ireland is very much in evidence here and the scenery is spectacular. The *Holy Mountain of Croagh Patrick* forms a mysterious conical shape and dominates the surrounding countryside for miles. The mountain is the place where St Patrick reputedly threw the reptiles out of Ireland and is now a place of pilgrimage; many thousands of people climb the mountain every year.
There are spectacular views from the mountain and on a good day the Twelve Bens mountain range and *Achill Island* can be seen. **Achill** is the largest off the Irish coast and has a beautiful 2km (1-mile) beach with fantastic rock formations at one end. The poet W B Yeats was a native of County **Sligo,** and his writings – which are commemorated annually in Sligo – provide the most eloquent and lyrical descriptions of this part of the country, with its mountains, lakes and golden coastal scenery. Yeats is buried in Drumcliff churchyard. Sligo is also, however, an area of outstanding archaeological interest. In the *Bricklieve Mountains* (at **Carrowkeel,** northwest of Ballinafad) is a Stone Age passage-grave cemetery. The *Stone of Cu* is a vast megalithic tomb to be found north of *Lough Gill* near **Fermoyle.** Cormac MacAirt, famous King of Ireland, was reputedly born and raised by a she-wolf in the *Caves of Kesh* in Keshcorran Hill.
The city of **Galway,** itself containing many examples of English, Spanish and French-influenced architecture, makes a convenient starting point for explorations in the west.
EXCURSIONS: The **Aran Islands** – Inishmore, Inishmaan and Inisheer – are accessible by air or boat from Galway, or short boat crossing from *Rossaveal.* They are Gaelic speaking and distinctive for the limestone rock similar to that found on the The Burren. Some of the earliest surviving examples of prehistoric fortifications are to be found here, together with many early Christian monastic settlements and a *Folk Museum.* The west coast is a particularly beautiful area of the country. **Westport,** one of the most attractive towns in the area, is unusual in that it was planned by the architect James Wyatt in the late 18th-century, and its most famous attraction is *Westport House,* a superb stately home situated by a lake. 4000 acres of Connemara have been designated as a national park. The principal attractions in this area include the *Maam Turk Mountains; Kylemore Abbey* and *Lough Mask Abbey. Lough Mask House* was notorious as the former home of one Captain Boycott, a man so unpopular with his tenants that nobody could work with him – hence the word 'boycott'.
Between Lough Corrib and Lough Mask is **Cong,** where the film 'The Quiet Man' was filmed. It is also the site of *The Cross of Cong,* a 12th-century Celtic cross made for Cong Abbey, a ruined Augustian Abbey also dating back to the 12th century. **Inishmurray Island,** 6.5km (4 miles) offshore has a 6th-century monastery and some well-preserved early Christian gravestones. W B Yeats was buried in the grounds of the 19th-century church at **Drumcliff,** once a monastic settlement founded by St

Colomba, a stone's throw from *Benbulben,* one of the most spectacular mountains in the country. Standing at 527m (1730ft), the mountain changes its face as you walk around it. *Lissadell House,* a typical aristocratic country home of the last century, is famous for its associations with Yeats.
RESORTS: The **Aran Islands:** Long sandy beaches at **Kilmurvey, Killeaney** and **Kilronan. Inisheer:** Fine sandy beaches. **Spiddal:** Four safe sandy beaches near Spiddal. **Inverin:** Seven sandy beaches within 5km (3 miles). **Carraroe:** Four sandy beaches nearby.
Lettermore: *Lettercallow Beach* and other small sandy beaches within driving distance. **Lettermullen:** Coral beach, 3km (2 miles) from Lettermullen and a 2km-long (1-mile) sandy beach at **Dynish** (5km/3 miles). **Carna:** Long sandy beaches at **Callowfeanish, Mweenish** and **Moyrus.** Short sandy beach at **Ardmore. Roundstone:** Fine strands at **Gurteen,** *Dog's Bay, Murvey Beach, Dolin Beach, Bunowen Beach, Aillebrack Beach, Dunloughan Beach, Mannin Beach* and *Coral Beach* composed of fragments of coraline with smooth rocks. **Cleggan:** Six safe sandy beaches close by, two within walking distance. **Clifden:** Holiday resort, excellent beaches close to town and at **Leagaun** (11km/7 miles). **Letterfrack:** Safe bathing at **Renvyle, Tullybeg** and **Lettergesh. Salthill:** Popular resort with many holiday amenities and good strands within 3km (2 miles).
Kinvara: 6km-long (3.5-mile) sandy beach *Traught Strand.* **Achill Island:** Safe sandy beaches at **Keel, Dooagh, Keem** and **Dugort. Ballina:** Long sandy beaches at **Bertragh, Carrowmore-Lackan, Ross Strand** and **Bunatrahir Strand. Belmullet:** Nine safe sandy beaches within easy driving distance. **Mulrany:** Good bathing strand. **Louisburgh:** 3km (2-mile) beach at *Old Head* and five more sandy beaches within driving distance. **Westport:** Bathing at **Bertra, Lecanvey** and **Kilsallagh. Lahinch:** Popular resort for bathing. Entertainment centre. Good recreational facilities. **Spanish Point:** A good sandy beach situated 3km (2 miles) west of **Milltown Malbay.** Recreational facilities. **Doolin:** Small village with thriving folk music events and a small sandy beach. **Silver Strand:** At **Freagh,** 3km (2 miles) north of Milltown Malbay, is a good, safe bathing place. **Kilkee:** Lovely resort built around a semi-circular bay; excellent bathing facilities; recreational facilities include golf, skindiving and sea fishing. **Moville:** Family resort by the shores of *Lough Foyle* on the *Inishowen Peninsula.* Fine coastal scenery. **Greencastle:** On Lough Foyle, 5km (3 miles) from Moville; good bathing beach. **Culdaff:** Secluded resort with a fine beach. Many beaches and cliffs along the coast. **Malin/Malin Head:** 6.5km (4 miles) north of **Cardonagh,** Malin Head is 14km (9 miles) further on. Malin Head is the most northerly point of Ireland affording superb coastal views. **Ballyliffen:** Secluded resort in beautiful surroundings. Bathing on the *Pollan Strand.* **Clonmany:** Village between hills and the sea. Fine coastal scenery. **Buncrana:** Well-developed holiday resort; fine scenery and recreational facilities. **Rathmullan:** Good bathing beach on the shore of *Lough Swilly.* **Portsalon:** On western shore of Lough Swilly near *Fanad Head.* Bathing, and fine cliff scenery. **Rosapenna:** Between Carrigart and Downings on *Rosguill Peninsula.* Ideal centre from which to tour. **Downings:** Quiet little resort with superb beaches and coastal scenery. **Carrigart:** On *Mulroy Bay* at foot of Rosguill Peninsula; beach surrounded by sandhills. **Dunfanaghy:** Well-equipped resort at *Sheephaven Bay;* splendid cliff scenery at *Horn Head.* **Portnablagh:** 2.5km (1.5 miles) from Dunfanaghy; excellent beach and bathing facilities; also beach at Marble Hill. **Gortahork:** Irish-speaking village under

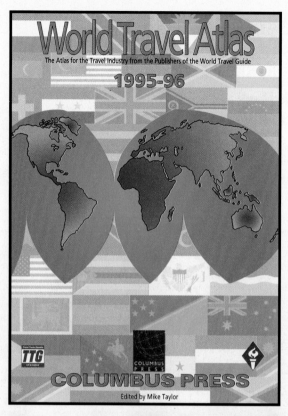

At Last – a Travel Atlas for the Travel Trade!

Have you ever picked up your atlas to discover that important resort you are looking for is not on the map? This is a common problem in the travel industry, as non-specialist atlases often do not recognise the particular needs of the busy travel agent. All too often they fail to show important travel resorts or destinations and are very poor on back-up tourist information. Such atlases are an embarrassment to our industry! But you don't have to put up with this any longer ...

At last – a travel atlas for the travel trade. We've taken a conventional atlas, then augmented it with over 100 plates – featuring over 6,000 resorts and attractions – all designed specifically for the travel industry. From cruises to climate, flight times to French resorts, cultural wonders to national parks, this is a publication that truly covers the world of travel. Armed with this easy-to-use atlas you will be able to give your clients the kind of advice they will return for, time after time!

New country frontiers. The world has changed much in recent years: is *your* atlas up to date? Eastern Europe, the CIS, South Africa – for your clients' business or leisure requirements, for staff training or general reference, this now the only atlas you'll need.

An atlas which has got its priorities right. Accuracy, relevance and ease of use make this a publication that will save you time and earn you money. Exhaustively indexed, meticulously researched and fully up to date, this is *the* atlas the travel industry has been waiting for. 'Excellent,' says one user, 'brilliant,' says another. What more can we say? Don't delay, order yours today!

Price: **£19.50.** (Bulk discounts available.)

For further information including details of hardback copies embossed with your company logo please contact Stephen Collins at the address above.

Columbus Press Limited
Columbus House, 28 Charles Square London N1 6HT, United Kingdom
Tel: +44 (0)171 417 0700. Fax: +44 (0)171 417 0710.

Muckish Mountain; departure point for *Tory Island.* **Derrybeg:** Secluded little resort with fine coastal scenery. **Bunbeg:** Peaceful resort sheltered by cliffs, within easy reach of many beauty spots; excellent sea bathing. **Burtonport:** Sheltered harbour; ideal for boating trips to nearby islands; rugged, rocky scenery. Strand at **Keadue** (5km/3 miles). **Aranmore Island:** 5km (3 miles) from mainland on rugged and complex coastline; cliff scenery, sea caves, bathing; may be reached by boat from **Burtonport. Dungloe:** Interesting geological curiosities; bathing in *Mahory Bay.* **Maas:** Conveniently situated between **Narin** and **Glenties;** ideal centre from which to tour the 'Highlands of Donegal'. **Narin** and **Portnoo:** Overlooking panoramic *Gweebarra Bay;* magnificent strand at Narin. **Rosbeg:** On the rugged shore of *Dawros Bay;* excellent beach and pleasant scenery. **Ardara:** Charming resort situated in a deep valley on *Loughros Mor Bay*; good touring centre. **Malinmore:** Pretty holiday resort with strand, 11km (7 miles) west of Carrick; impressive cliff scenery. **Carrick:** Ideal centre for boating and climbing; startling panoramic views from *Slieve League* seacliff (602m/1973ft). **Killybegs:** Fine natural harbour; fish-curing centre. **Inver:** On mouth of *Eany River* (Mountcharles – 6.5km/4 miles); good beach and bathing. **Mountcharles:** Overlooking *Donegal Bay* with charming scenery; sandy beach nearby. **Rossnowlagh:** Situated on Donegal Bay with excellent strand backed by gentle hills. **Bundoran:** One of Ireland's chief seaside resorts; on southern shore of Donegal Bay; lovely strand and all holiday amenities. **Mullaghmore:** Sheltered little resorts with superb bathing beach; sandhills. **Rosses Point:** Mainly noted for its championship golf course; fine strand. **Strandhill:** Popular resort at the foot of *Knocknarea Mountain.* **Enniscrone:** Popular family resort; excellent beach, surf bathing, salt-water baths.

The Lakelands

The Lakelands (Monaghan, Cavan, Longford, Westmeath, Roscommon, Offaly and Laois) are to be found in central Ireland, and the landscape ranges from fertile limestone plains and brown peat bogs to gently rolling hills and towering mountains which slope down to winding wooded valleys, moorlands and glens. Many of the counties can point to a turbulent past, owing to their geographical situation on the frontiers of the *Pale* (the area around Dublin) which made them a battleground for the recurring conflicts between the Irish clans and their English rulers. Nowadays, this mainly agricultural part of the country is considerably more peaceful, although Ireland's colourful, tempestuous and often tragic past is recalled here as elsewhere in the country in song, poetry, myths, legends and history. There are also several more concrete reminders, in the buildings and ruins which are dotted across the landscape, ranging from prehistoric burial mounds to 19th-century manor houses.

EXCURSIONS: *Dun a Ri Forest Park,* **Kingscourt;** *Killykeen Forest Park* and *Cuilcagh Mountain* (Cavan), source of the Shannon; *The Rock of Dunamase* and *Emo Court Gardens* near **Portlaoise;** old monastic settlement at **Fore,** and *Athlone Castle,* Co Westmeath; Goldsmith Country, Co Longford; Patrick Kavanagh Country, Co Monaghan; *Birr Castle* and old monastery at **Clonmacnois,** Co Offaly; *Lough Key Forest Park* and *Boyle Abbey* (both near Boyle), and *Roscommon Castle,* Co Roscommon; the 19th-century Cathedral at Longford; the city of **Kilkenny,** with its castle, museums, cathedral, a perfect Tudor merchant's house, and many other survivals from the city's influential past; the ruins of *Jerpoint Abbey* near **Thomastown**; *Dunmore Cave; Carton House* at **Maynooth** (Kildare), and the obelisk *Connolly's Folly* nearby; *White's Castle* at **Athy,** overlooking the *River Barrow;* the many lakes and rivers, offering possibilities for boating, fishing or merely a beautiful setting for a relaxing holiday.

POPULAR ITINERARIES: 5-day: (a) Dublin–Ardmore–Youghal–Cork–Killarney–Tralee–Dublin. (b) Dublin–Longford–Westport–Donegal–Carrick Derg–Dublin. **7-day:** (a) Dublin–Arklow–Wexford–Waterford–Cork–Limerick–Dublin. (b) Dublin–Mullingar–Athlone–Kilkee–Ennis–Limerick–Tipperary–Cork–Kinsale–Clonakikilty–Glengariff–Waterville–Killarney–Tralee.

SOCIAL PROFILE

FOOD & DRINK: Ireland is a farming country noted for its meat, bacon, poultry and dairy produce. The surrounding sea, inland lakes and rivers offer fresh fish including salmon, trout, lobster, Dublin Bay prawns, oysters (served with Guinness and wholemeal bread), mussels and periwinkles. Dublin has a wide selection of restaurants and eating places to suit every pocket, as do the other major towns. Table and self service are both common. The most typical Irish dishes will usually be found in a country restaurant, and include corned beef and carrots, boiled bacon and cabbage and Irish stew. Other local delicacies are *crubeens* (pigs trotters), *colcannon* (a mixture of potatoes and cabbage cooked together) and soda bread and soufflé made with *carrageen* (a variety of seaweed). Visitors should note that 'tea' is often almost a full meal with sandwiches and cakes.

DRINK: Pubs are sometimes called 'lounges' or 'bars' and there is often a worded sign outside the premises rather than the traditional painted boards found in Britain. Pubs and bars have counter service. The measure used in Ireland for spirits is larger than that used in Britain – an Irish double is equal to a triple in Britain.

Irish coffee is popular (glass of strong black coffee, brown sugar and whiskey with cream). Almost any drink is imported but the two most internationally distinctive products are *whiskey* (spelt with an 'e') and *stout.* Irish whiskey has a uniquely characteristic flavour and is matured in a wooden barrel for a minimum of seven years. Amongst the most popular brands are *Jamesons* and *John Powers Gold Label,* but others include *Paddy, Tullamore Dew, Old Bushmills, Middleton, Reserve* and *Hewitts.* Certainly as popular as whiskey is *stout* which is bottled or served from the tap. *Guinness,* one of the most famous, popular and distinctive drinks in the world, is found everywhere and *Murphy's* is almost as widely available. One of the most popular of lighter ales is *Smithwick's* or *Harp Lager,* also available everywhere. Liqueurs such as *Irish Mist* and *Bailey's* are both made from a base of Irish whiskey.

Licensing hours are 1030-2300 (2330 in summer) and until 2300 Sunday all year round. All bars close 1430-1630 Sunday.

NIGHTLIFE: Most towns have discos or dancehalls and many bars and pubs have live music and folk-singing, with professional ballad singers and groups who are often highly accomplished. Medieval castle banquets (such as those at Bunratty Castle) are very popular with visitors and there is a good choice of theatres and cinemas.

SHOPPING: Special purchases include hand-woven tweed, hand-crocheted woollens and cottons, sheepskin goods, gold and silver jewellery, Aran knitwear, linen, pottery, Irish crystal and basketry. **Shopping hours:** 0900-1730/1800 Monday to Saturday. Many towns have late night opening until 2000/2100 Thursday or Friday and smaller towns may have one early closing day a week. **Note:** It is possible to claim 'cashback' on goods bought in Ireland on leaving the country. For further information, contact the Revenue Commissioners (VAT Section), Castle House, South Great Georges Street, Dublin 2. Tel: (1) 872 9777, ext. 2440-3.

SPORT: The national sports are **Gaelic football** and **hurling**. There are 200 **golf** courses run by the Golfing Union of Ireland, and many people come to Ireland specifically for a golfing holiday, where the course rates are relatively cheap compared with the UK. The courses are set both by the sea and inland – two-thirds are 18-hole. Ample hotel and guest-house accommodation is available adjacent to most courses. Many of the larger hotels have **tennis** courts. **Equestrianism** is one of the principal tourist attractions of Ireland and facilities for **horseriding** are found all over the country. A full list of stables and riding holidays is available from the Irish Tourist Board. **Racecourses:** The principal racecourses are at Leopardstown, Fairyhouse (Irish Grand National every year), The Curragh (Irish Sweeps Derby) and Punchestown (also an international cross-country and 3-day-event riding course). **Football:** Although club football in Ireland is not of the highest standard, the national team has prospered considerably in recent years, reaching the quarter-finals of the 1990 World Cup and the second round in 1994. **Fishing:** Ireland has some of the best fishing of any country in the world, being blessed with uncounted miles of rivers and streams and over 5500km (3500 miles) of coastline. **Freshwater angling:** There is no closed season but March to October are the most suitable months for bream, rudd, roach, dace and perch. **Coarse angling:** There are new regulations regarding share certificates for coarse angling – consult the Irish Tourist Board for information. **Game fishing:** Generally the brown trout season is from mid-February or March until September 30. A licence is required for game fishing. Open salmon season is January 1 to September 7, according to district. A licence is essential, and generally a permit is also required. The best sea trout period is from June to September 30–October 12 in some areas. Salmon licences/permits also cover sea trout. **Sea angling:** There are new regulations regarding share certificates for coarse angling – check with the Irish Tourist Board. A day's boat fishing excursion can be organised. A wide range of fishing exists, from piers, rocks, in the surf or from boats. The Atlantic is particularly challenging, offering its own rewards for the angler who wishes to explore.

SPECIAL EVENTS: The following are some of the main festivals in Ireland during 1995. For full details, contact the Irish Tourist Board:

Apr 18-23 '95 *Pan Celtic Festival,* Tralee. **May 19-Jun 25** *County Wicklow Gardens Festival.* **Jul 2** *Budweiser Irish Derby Festival.* **Jul 19-30** *Galway Arts Festival.* **Aug** *August Puck Fair,* Killorglin. **Aug 8-12** *Kerrygold Dublin Horse Show.* **Aug 25-31** *Rose of Tralee International Festival.* **Sep 3** *All Ireland Hurling Final.* **Sep 8-10** *Clarenbridge Oyster Festival,* Clarenbridge, Co Galway. **Sep 17** *All Ireland Football Final.* **Oct 2-14** *Irish Life Dublin Theatre Festival.* **Oct 19-Nov 5** *Wexford Opera Festival.*

SOCIAL CONVENTIONS: The Irish are gregarious people, and everywhere animated *craic* (talk) can be heard. Oscar Fingal O'Flahertie Wills (better known as Oscar Wilde) once claimed: 'We are the greatest talkers since the Greeks'. Close community contact is very much part of the Irish way of life and almost everywhere there is an intimate small-town atmosphere. Visitors will find the people very friendly and welcoming no matter where one finds oneself in the country. A meal in an Irish home is usually a substantial affair and guests will eat well. Dinner is at midday and the evening meal is known as tea. Even in cities there is less formal wear than in most European countries and casual dress is widely acceptable as in keeping with a largely agricultural community. Women, however, often dress up for smart restaurants and social functions. Handshaking is usual, and modes of address will often be informal. Smoking is acceptable unless otherwise stated. **Tipping:** The customary tip in Ireland is 10-12%. Many hotels and restaurants add this in the form of a service charge indicated on the menu or bill. It is not customary to tip in bars unless you have table service when a small tip is advised. Tipping porters, taxi drivers, hairdressers, etc is customary but not obligatory.

BUSINESS PROFILE

ECONOMY: Ireland was not industrialised to the same degree as the rest of Europe, and only in the last few years has agriculture been overtaken as the largest single contributor to national product. Agriculture remains a key sector, however, and the Government is seeking to consolidate its role within the economy by modernisation and expansion of food-processing industries. Ireland's recent industrial development has been achieved by a deliberate policy of promoting export-led and advanced technology businesses, partly by offering attractive packages for foreign investors. Textiles, chemicals and electronics have performed particularly strongly. Promising oil and gas deposits have been located off the southern coast. Trade is dominated by the UK, which provides half of total imports and takes 40% of Ireland's exports. One major benefit of EU membership for Ireland, however, is that it has proved able to diversify its trade patterns.

BUSINESS: Business people should wear formal clothes for meetings. Local business people are very friendly and an informal business approach is most successful. However, it is advisable to make prior appointments and to allow enough time to complete business matters. Avoid business visits in the first week of May, during July, August and at Christmas or New Year.

COMMERCIAL INFORMATION: The following organisation can offer advice: Chambers of Commerce of Ireland, 22 Merrion Square, Dublin 2. Tel: (1) 661 2888. Fax: (1) 676 6043.

CONFERENCES/CONVENTIONS: For more information, contact the Irish Tourist Board or the Convention Bureau of Ireland, Bord Fáilte, Baggot Street Bridge, Dublin 2. Tel: (1) 676 5871. Fax: (1) 676 4760.

CLIMATE

The temperate climate is due to mild southwesterly winds and the Gulf Stream. Summers are warm, while temperatures during winter are much cooler. Spring and autumn are very mild. Rain falls all year.

Required clothing: Lightweights during summer with warmer mediumweights for the winter. Rainwear is advisable throughout the year.

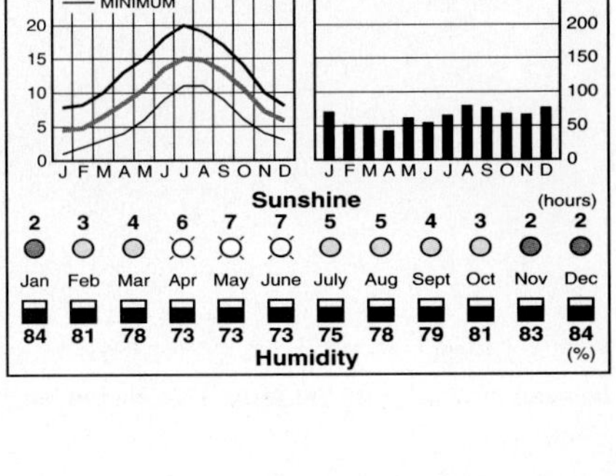

☐ international airport

Location: Eastern Mediterranean.

Ministry of Tourism
PO Box 1018, 24 King George Street, Jerusalem 91000, Israel
Tel: (2) 754 811. Fax: (2) 253 407 *or* 250 890. Telex: 26115.

Embassy of Israel
2 Palace Green, London W8 4QB
Tel: (0171) 957 9500. Fax: (0171) 957 9555. Opening hours: 1000-1300 Monday to Thursday; 1000-1200 Friday and Saturday.
Prior appointment necessary for personal visits.

Israel Government Tourist Office
18 Great Marlborough Street, London W1V 1AF
Tel: (0171) 434 3651. Fax: (0171) 437 0527. Opening hours: 1100-1400 Monday to Thursday (0900-1700 for telephone enquiries); 0900-1500 Friday (for telephone enquiries only).

British Embassy
192 Rehov Hayarkon, Tel Aviv 63405, Israel
Tel: (3) 524 9171/8. Fax: (3) 524 3313.

British Consulate General
6th Floor, Migdalor Building, 1 Ben Yehuda Street, Tel Aviv 63801, Israel
Tel: (3) 510 0166 *or* 510 0497 *or* 524 9171/2. Fax: (3) 510 1167. Telex: 371411 (a/b BRITA IL).
Consulate also in: Eilat.

Embassy of Israel
3514 International Drive, NW, Washington, DC 20008
Tel: (202) 364 5500. Fax: (202) 364 5610.
Consulates in: Atlanta, Boston, Chicago, Houston, Los Angeles, Miami, New York (tel: (212) 351 5200), Philadelphia and San Francisco.

Israel Government Tourist Office
19th Floor, 350 Fifth Avenue, New York, NY 10118
Tel: (212) 560 0600. Fax: (212) 629 4368. Telex: 23423021.
Israel Government Tourist Offices also in: Atlanta, Chicago, Dallas and Los Angeles.

Embassy of the United States of America
PO Box 100, 71 Rehov Hayarkon, Tel Aviv 09830, Israel
Tel: (3) 517 4338 *or* 517 4347 (after hours). Fax: (3) 663 449.

Embassy of Israel
Suite 1005, 50 O'Connor Street, Ottawa, Ontario K1P 6L2
Tel: (613) 567 6450. Fax: (613) 237 8865.
Consulates in: Montréal and Toronto.

Israel Government Tourist Office
Suite 700, 180 Bloor Street West, Toronto, Ontario M5S 2V6
Tel: (416) 964 3784. Fax: (416) 964 2420. Telex: 216217520.

Canadian Embassy
PO Box 6410, 220 Rehov Hayarkon, Tel Aviv 61063, Israel
Tel: (3) 527 2929. Fax: (3) 527 2333. Telex: 341293 (a/b CANAD IL).

Canadian Consulate
7 Rehov Havakuk, Tel Aviv 63505, Israel
Tel: (3) 544 2878/79/80 *or* 546 5810 *or* 546 5811.

AREA: 21,946 sq km (8473 sq miles).
POPULATION: 5,168,200 (1992 estimate).
POPULATION DENSITY: 230.9 per sq km.
CAPITAL: Jerusalem. **Population:** 544,200 (1991, including East Jerusalem).
GEOGRAPHY: Israel is on the eastern Mediterranean, bordered by Lebanon and Syria to the north, Jordan to the east, and Egypt to the south. The country stretches southwards through the Negev Desert to Eilat, a resort town on the Red Sea. The fertile Plain of Sharon runs along the coast, while inland, parallel to the coast, is a range of hills and uplands with fertile valleys to the west and arid desert to the east. The Great Rift Valley begins beyond the sources of the River Jordan and extends south through the Dead Sea (the lowest point in the world), and south again into the Red Sea, continuing on into Eastern Africa.
LANGUAGE: Hebrew and Arabic are the official languages. English is spoken in most places and French, Spanish, German, Yiddish, Russian, Polish and Hungarian are widely used.
RELIGION: Jewish (82%), Muslim (14%), with Christian (2.7%), Druze and other minorities (1.7%).
TIME: GMT + 2 (GMT + 3 from April to August).
ELECTRICITY: 220 volts AC, 50Hz. 3-pin plugs are standard; if needed, adaptors can be purchased in Israel.
COMMUNICATIONS: Telephone: Full IDD service. Country code: 972. Outgoing international code: 00. Local telephone directories are in Hebrew, but there is a special English-language version for tourists. **Fax:** This service is available at most 4- and 5-star hotels. Fax is increasingly used by Israeli business people.
Telex/telegram: Ordinary telex facilities are available to guests in most deluxe hotels in Jerusalem and Tel Aviv, and in main post offices. **Post:** Airmail to Europe takes up to a week. There are *Poste Restante* facilities in Jerusalem and Tel Aviv. Post office hours may vary but are generally: 0830-1230 and 1530-1830 Sunday to Thursday, 0800-1330 Wednesday and 0800-1200 Friday. All post offices are closed on Shabbat (Saturday) and holy days, although central telegraph offices are open throughout the year. **Press:** The main dailies are *Davar, Ha'aretz, Yediot Aharonoth* and *Ma'ariv*. Newspapers are printed in a variety of languages, including English. Political and religious affiliations are common. The English-language daily is the *Jerusalem Post* and the *Jerusalem Report* is published weekly.
BBC World Service and Voice of America frequencies: From time to time these change. See the section *How to Use this Book* for more information.

BBC:

MHz	21.47	15.57	1.323	0.639
Voice of America:				
MHz	9.700	9.530	7.205	6.060

Dome of the Rock with the Wailing Wall in the foreground, Jerusalem

Health
GALILEO/WORLDSPAN: **TI-DFT/TLV/HE**
SABRE: **TIDFT/TLV/HE**
Visa
GALILEO/WORLDSPAN: **TI-DFT/TLV/VI**
SABRE: **TIDFT/TLV/VI**
For more information on Timatic codes refer to Contents.

Timatic

HAV'A

HOLIDAY BROADENING YOUR HORIZONS.

THERE ARE PLENTY TO CHOOSE FROM.

Israel is a land of contrasts. One day you're relaxing on the golden, sandy beaches of the Mediterranean coast, the next you're riding in a jeep through the red, rocky craters and pillars of the Negev Desert.

If you choose to hike, you'll be following in the footsteps of nomadic tribes who've roamed the country for thousands of years. To really heighten the experience, have a ride on a camel, the ship of the desert.

Just a short journey away is the Dead Sea, where you can float 400 metres below sea level, the lowest point on the globe.

You don't have to travel far to see the different landscapes of Israel. It's only five hours away. If you would like further information call us free on 071-434 3651.

ISRAEL
HAV'A GREAT HOLIDAY

PASSPORT/VISA

Regulations and requirements may be subject to change at short notice, and you are advised to contact the appropriate diplomatic or consular authority before finalising travel arrangements. Details of these may be found at the head of this country's entry. Any numbers in the chart refer to the footnotes below.

	Passport Required?	Visa Required?	Return Ticket Required?
Full British	Yes	No/3	Yes
BVP	Not valid	-	-
Australian	Yes	No/2	Yes
Canadian	Yes	No/2	Yes
USA	Yes	No/2	Yes
Other EU (As of 31/12/94)	Yes	1	Yes
Japanese	Yes	No/2	Yes

PASSPORTS: Valid passport required by all. They must be valid for a minimum of 6 months after the intended date of arrival.

British Visitors Passport: Not accepted.

VISAS: All nationals require a stamp on arrival. Visas are required by all except:

(a) **[1]** nationals of *EU countries (*except* nationals of Germany if born before January 1, 1928 and nationals of Spain who have to pay a stamp fee);

(b) **[2]** nationals of Australia, Canada, Japan and USA;

(c) nationals of *Argentina, Austria, *Bahamas, Barbados, Bolivia, Brazil, Central African Republic, *Chile, *Colombia, *Costa Rica, *Cyprus, *Dominican Republic, *Ecuador, *El Salvador, Fiji, *Finland, Gibraltar, *Guatemala, *Haiti, Hong Kong, Hungary, *Iceland, Jamaica, South Korea, Lesotho, *Liechtenstein, Malawi, Malta, Mauritius, Mexico, *Monaco, Netherlands Antilles, *New Zealand, *Norway, Paraguay, Philippines, San Marino, Slovenia, South Africa, St Kitts & Nevis, Suriname, Swaziland, *Sweden, Switzerland, *Trinidad & Tobago and *Uruguay.

All other nationals must obtain visas prior to arrival, which *will* normally be entered in the passport, and must pay the standard fee.

Note: (a) All nationals listed above who do not require visas to enter Israel can obtain their stamps free of charge *if arriving by air at an international airport.* (b) **[*]** These nationals can obtain their stamp free of charge on arrival regardless of whether they enter by air or any other means of transport and at any port of entry. (c) **[3]** Nationals of British Dependent Territories *do* require a pre-arranged visa.

Types of visa: *Tourist/Entry:* £9, including postage. Visitors interested in stopping in Israel en route to other destinations may request 5-day *Transit visas*, which may be extended for a further ten days upon arrival in Israel. Transit visas are not required by those who continue their journey within 24 hours by the same or connecting flights. Passengers are allowed to leave the airport. Cruise ship passengers visiting Israel will be issued *Landing Cards,* allowing them to remain in the country for as long as the ship is in port. No visa applications are required. *Collective visas* are issued by Israeli diplomatic or consular missions for groups of no fewer than five and no more than 50.

Validity: Maximum is normally 3 months. Transit visas are for 5 days, which may be extended for another ten days on arrival in Israel. Visas may be extended (for a nominal fee) at offices of the Ministry of the Interior in the following locations: Afula, Akko (Acre), Ashqelon, Beersheba, Eilat, Hadera, Haifa, Herzliyya, Holon, Jerusalem, Nazareth, Netanya, Petah Tiqva, Ramat Gan, Ramla, Rehovot, Safed, Tel Aviv and Tiberias.

Application to: Consulate (or Consular section at Embassy). For addresses, see top of entry.

Application requirements: (a) Application form. (b) Passport-size photo. (c) Return ticket. (d) Foreign nationals in the UK must submit their residence and/or work permit along with a letter of reference.

Working days required: Depends on nationality.

Temporary residence: Apply to the Ministry of the Interior in Israel.

Note: As a concession to travellers intending to travel at a later date to countries inimical to Israel, entry stamps will, on request, be entered only on the entry form AL-17 and not on the passport. This facility is not available to those required to obtain their Israeli visas in advance.

MONEY

Currency: New Israel Shekel (NIS) = 100 new agorot (singular, agora). Notes are in denominations of NIS200, 100, 50, 20 and 10. Coins are in denominations of NIS5 and 1, and 50, 10 and 5 agorot.

Currency exchange: Foreign currency can only be exchanged at authorised banks and hotels. It is advisable to leave Israel with the minimum of Israeli currency. US Dollars, Sterling and Irish Punts are widely accepted. Payment in foreign currency exempts tourists from VAT on certain purchases and services.

Credit cards: All major credit cards are accepted.

Travellers cheques: These are widely accepted.

Exchange rate indicators: The following figures are included as a guide to the movements of the New Israel Shekel against Sterling and the US Dollar:

Date:	Oct '92	Sep '93	Jan '94	Jan '95
£1.00=	3.97	4.25	4.41	4.72
$1.00=	2.50	2.80	2.98	3.01

Currency restrictions: Visitors may import unlimited amounts of local and foreign currency. Foreign currency exchanged on arrival may be re-converted up to a maximum value of US$5000 or equivalent on the presentation of exchange receipts (at airport banks this is limited to US$500). These regulations are for non-residents only; residents should enquire at an Israel Government Tourist Office. Certain foreign currency regulations apply to travellers intending to enter Israel by land; they should seek advice before embarking.

Banking hours: 0830-1230 and 1600-1800 Sunday, Tuesday and Thursday; 0830-1200 Friday; 0830-1230 Wednesday and Monday.

DUTY FREE

The following goods may be imported into Israel by persons aged 17 years and over without incurring customs duty:

250 cigarettes or 250g of tobacco products; 1 litre of spirits; 2 litres of wine; 250ml of eau de cologne or perfume; gifts up to the value of US$150.

Note: Flowers, plants and seeds may not be imported without prior permission. Fresh meat may not be imported.

PUBLIC HOLIDAYS

Jan 16 '95 Tu B'Shevat (Arbor Day). **Mar 16** Purim (Feast of Lots). **Apr 15-21** Pesah (Passover). **May 4** Yom Ha'Atzmaut (Israel Independence Day). **May 28** Jerusalem Liberation Day. **Jun 4** Shavu'ot (Pentecost). **Aug 6** Tisha B'Av (Ninth of Av Fast). **Sep 25-26** Rosh Hashana. **Oct 4** Yom Kippur (Day of Atonement). **Oct 9**

ISRAEL GOVERNMENT TOURIST OFFICES OVERSEAS

AUSTRIA
Offizielles Israelisches
Verkehrsbüro,
Rossauer Lande 41/12
A-1090 Wien
Tel: +43-1-310-8174
Fax: +43-1-310-3917
Tlx: 47-115934

DENMARK
Den Israelske Stats Turistbureau
Vesterbrogade 6c
1520 København V
Tel: +45-33 11 97 11/11 96 79
Fax: +45-33 91 48 01

CANADA
180 Bloor St., West
Toronto, Ontario M5S 2V6
Tel: 416 964-3784
Fax: 416 961-3962

FEDERAL REPUBLIC OF GERMANY
Staatliches Israelisches
Verkehrsbüro
Bettinastr. 62, 7th Floor
60325 Frankfurt/Main
Tel: +49-69-752084
Fax: +49-69-746249

Staatliches Israelisches
Verkehrsbüro
Stollbergstr. 6
München 80539
Tel: +49-89-228-9568
Fax: +49-89-228-9569

Staatliches Israelisches
Verkehrsbüro
Kurfürstendamm 202
1000 Berlin AS
Tel: +49-30-883-6759/881-9685
Fax: +49-30-882-4093

FRANCE
Office National Israélien de Tourisme
14 rue de la Paix
Paris 75002
Tel: +33-1-42 61 01 97/42 61 03 67
Fax: +33-1-49 27 09 46
Tlx: 42-680940

HUNGARY
Izraeli Nagykovetsege
1026 Budapest 11,
Fullank U. 8
Tel: +36-1-176 7896/897
Fax: +36-1-176 0534

ITALY
Uffizio Nazionale Israeliano del
Turismo
Via Podgora 12/b
20122 Milano
Tel: +39-2-55187152
Fax: +39-2-55187062
Tlx: 43-324277

JAPAN
Israel Government Tourist Office
Kojimanchi Sannabcho Mansion 406
9-1, Sanbancho, Chiyoda-Ku,
Tokyo 102
Tel: +81-33-238-9081
Fax: +81-33-238-9077
Tlx: 2323359 IGTO TK J

NETHERLANDS
Israelisch Nationaal Verkehrsbureau
Wijde Kapelsteeg 2 (Hoek Rokin)
1012 NS Amsterdam
Tel: +31-20-624-9642/624-9325
Fax: +31-20-624-2651
Tlx: 44-14372

SOUTH AFRICA
Israel Government Tourist Office
5th Floor, Nedbank Gardens
33 Bath Avenue, Rosebank
PO Box 52560, Saxonwold 2132
Johannesburg
Tel: +27-11-788-1700
Fax: +27-11-447-3104

SPAIN
Oficina Nacional Israeli de Turismo
Gran Via 69 - Ofic 801
28013 Madrid
Tel: +34-1-559-7903, 559-4055
Fax: +34-1-542-6511

SWEDEN
Israeliska Statens Turistbyra
Sveavagen 28-30, 4 Tr.
Box 7554
10393 Stockholm 7
Tel: +46-8-213386/7
Fax: +46-8-217814
Tlx: 54-12742

SWITZERLAND
Offizielles Israelisches
Verkehrsbüro
Lintheschergasse 12
CH-8021 Zürich
Tel: +41-1-211-2344/5
Fax: +41-1-212-2036
Tlx: 45-813170

UNITED KINGDOM
Israel Government Tourist Office
18 Great Marlborough Street
London W1V 1AF
Tel: +44-171-434-3651
Fax: +44-171-437-0527

COMMISSIONER FOR NORTH AMERICA
Head Office & Northeast Region
350 Fifth Avenue
New York, NY 10118
Tel: 212 560-0600 (Head Office);
212 560-0639 (Northeast region)
Fax: 212 629-4368
Tlx: 23-423021

Midwest Region
5 South Wabash Avenue
Chicago, IL 60603
Tel: 312 782-4306
Fax: 312 782-1243
Tlx: 230-724389

Western Region
6380 Wilshire Blvd. Suite 1700
Los Angeles, CA 90048
Tel: 213 658-7462/3, 658-7240
Fax: 213 658-6543
Tlx: 23-6831135

South-Central Region
12700 Park Central Drive
Dallas, TX 75251
Tel: 214 991-9097/8
Fax: 214 392-3521

Southeast Region
1100 Spring St., N.W., Suite 440
Atlanta, GA 30309
Tel: 404 875-9924
Fax: 404 875-9926
Tlx: 230-542515

First Day of Sukkot (Tabernacles). **Oct 16** Simhat Torah (Rejoicing of the Law). **Dec 18** First Day of Hanukkah (Feast of Lights). **Feb 5 '96** Tu B'Shevat (Arbor Day). **Mar 5** Purim (Feast of Lots). **Apr 4-10** Pesah (Passover). **Apr 24** Yom Ha'Atzmaut (Israel Independence Day). **Note:** Jewish festivals commence on the evenings before the dates given above. Only the first and last days of Passover and Sukkot are officially recognised as national holidays, but there may be some disruption on intermediate dates; many shops and businesses will open, but close early. The Jewish religious day is Saturday – *Shabbat* – and begins at nightfall on Friday until nightfall on Saturday. Most public services and shops close early on Friday as a result. Muslim and Christian holidays are also observed by the respective populations. Thus, depending on the district, the day of rest falls on Friday, Saturday or Sunday.

HEALTH

Regulations and requirements may be subject to change at short notice, and you are advised to contact your doctor well in advance of your intended date of departure. Any numbers in the chart refer to the footnotes below.

	Special Precautions?	Certificate Required?
Yellow Fever	No	No
Cholera	No	No
Typhoid & Polio	Yes	-
Malaria	No	-
Food & Drink	1	-

[1]: Mains water is normally chlorinated, and whilst relatively safe, may cause mild abdominal upsets. Bottled water is available and is advised for the first few weeks of the stay. Drinking water outside main cities and towns may be contaminated and sterilisation is advisable. Milk is pasteurised and dairy products are safe for consumption. Local meat, poultry, seafood, fruit and vegetables are generally considered safe to eat. *Rabies* is present. For those at high risk, vaccination before arrival should be considered. If you are bitten abroad, seek medical advice without delay. For more information, consult the *Health* section at the back of the book.
Health care: Israel has excellent medical facilities and tourists may go to all emergency departments and first-aid centres. Health centres are marked by the red Star of David on a white background. Medical insurance is recommended.

TRAVEL - International

Note: Entry stamps will, on request, be entered only on the entry form AL-17 and not on the passport. This facility is not available to those required to obtain visas in advance (see *Passport/Visa* section above for details).
AIR: Israel's national airline is *El Al Israel Airlines (LY)*. For free advice on air travel, call the Air Travel Advisory Bureau in the UK on (0171) 636 5000 (London) *or* (0161) 832 2000 (Manchester).
Approximate flight times: From *London* to Tel Aviv is 4 hours 30 minutes and to Eilat is 5 hours. From *Los Angeles* to Tel Aviv is 17 hours 35 minutes, from *New York* is 11 hours 55 minutes, from *Singapore* is 10 hours 55 minutes and from *Sydney* is 14 hours 35 minutes.
International airport: *Tel Aviv (TLV)* (Ben Gurion International) is 14km (9 miles) from the city. An *Egged* Bus no. 475 runs every 15 minutes between 0500-2200, and *United Tours* shuttle bus no. 222 runs hourly 0400-2400 to Tel Aviv. There is also a taxi service. The *El Al* airline bus goes to the airport terminal in Tel Aviv. Departure depends on *El Al* arrivals. Duty-free facilities are available.
Departure tax: From Ben Gurion (except to Egypt) US$15, to Egypt US$11; from Eilat and Jerusalem US$7; from Rafiah NIS60.50; from Nitzana NIS15.10; from Taba NIS34.40. Children under two years of age are exempt.
SEA: Principal international passenger ports are Haifa and Ashdod. There are regular sailings of car/passenger ferries from Greece and Cyprus and cargo/passenger services from the USA (New York, Galveston) run by *Prudential Lines* and *Lykes Lines* to Haifa and Ashdod. Cruise lines run to Haifa from Venice and other Mediterranean ports. The *Grimaldi/Siosa Lines* run a service from Alexandria to Ashdod.
ROAD: On the whole, road access to Israel is somewhat limited. There are two crossing points from Egypt into Israel. Rafiah (Rafah), the main point of entry, is located some 50km (30 miles) southwest of Ashqelon. Four bus companies maintain services between Cairo and Tel Aviv and Jerusalem via Rafiah. *Egged* Bus no. 362 leaves Tel Aviv for the Rafiah terminal daily at 0850 and Rafiah for Tel Aviv at 1500. *Egged* Bus no. 100 leaves Tel Aviv for

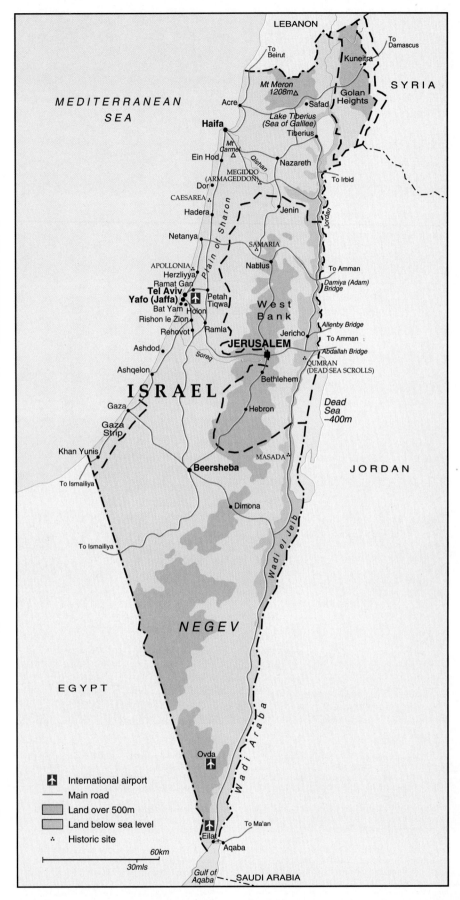

Cairo and Cairo for Tel Aviv daily at 0800. Taba, just south of Eilat, is open 24 hours a day and visitors may enter Israel on foot, by private car or in organised tour buses. Regular bus service is available between Taba, Santa Katerina (Sinai) and Cairo.
It is possible to travel from Jordan to the West Bank via the Allenby Bridge near Jericho, about 40km (25 miles) from Jerusalem, although travellers may be required to stop and be checked at any point. The Allenby Bridge

border opening hours are 0800-1600 Sunday to Thursday and 0800-1300 Friday. *Egged* buses and taxi service are also available to the bridge. At present, every tourist passing through here must obtain an entry visa to and an exit visa from Jordan. Exit fees are only payable on leaving for Jordan and are approximately US$26 (NIS78) per person (children up to the age of two years are exempt). Nationals of countries who are required to obtain an Israeli visa in advance should do so before

The Dead Sea

the border. Entry visas for Jordan or Israel will be provided on arrival at the respective border crossing point for all those who have organised pre-arranged visas. At present visas can only be organised through travel agents who will make the necessary arrangements through the travel agents representing them in the country issuing the visa. Lists of the visas issued will be passed to each crossing point every day. Travel agents are requested to coordinate the arrival time of buses with the management of the crossing point. Transfer of passengers between the Israeli and Jordanian checkpoints will be carried out by shuttle service (NIS2.5 per person). Transfers on foot will not be permitted. Border crossing hours are 0800-1830 Sunday to Thursday (closed Fridays and Saturdays and on Yom Kippur and the Jordanian festival on the first day of the Hijirah Calendar). Access is not allowed to Syria and Lebanon.
Note: Due to the peace process, border regulations are presently relaxing, but regulations are subject to changes in accordance with the changes made in the Peace Treaty with Jordan and changes are more than likely. Visitors are strongly advised to seek the most up-to-date advice on border crossings before travelling. For the latest information, contact the Israeli Tourist Office.

TRAVEL - Internal

AIR: A comprehensive service linking Tel Aviv with Eilat and all major cities is run by *Arkia/Israel Inland Airways (IZ)*.
SEA/LAKE: Ferries run across the Sea of Galilee (Lake Kinneret) from Tiberias on the west side to Ein Gev kibbutz on the eastern shore. Coastal ferries supply all ports. For details contact local port authorities.
RAIL: *Israel Railways* provides regular services between Tel Aviv and Herzliyya, Netanya, Hadera, Haifa, Akko (Acre) and Nahariyya, as well as a daily train between Tel Aviv and Jerusalem, which follows a particularly beautiful scenic route. Reserved seats may be ordered in advance. All passenger trains include a buffet car. There is no railway service on Shabbat (Saturday) and major holidays. For the latest schedule and fares, call (3) 542 1515 in Tel Aviv or (4) 564 564 in Haifa.
ROAD: Traffic drives on the right. An excellent system of roads connects all towns. Distances by road from Jerusalem to other cities are as follows: Tel Aviv 62km (39 miles), Tiberias 157km (97 miles), Eilat 312km (194 miles), Netanya 93km (58 miles), Dead Sea 104km (65 miles), Zefat 192km (120 miles) and Haifa 159km (99 miles). **Bus:** Two national bus systems, run by the *Egged* and *DAN* cooperatives, provide extensive services. The service is fast and efficient as well as cheap. With a few exceptions, services are suspended on religious holidays, and between sunset on Friday and sunset on Saturday (Shabbat). **Taxi:** Services are either run by companies or by individuals. There are both shared taxis (*sheruts*) and ordinary taxis. Taxi drivers are required by law to operate the meter. **Car hire:** Available in major cities. Hire fees are not cheap, and taxis are recommended for short journeys only. **Documentation:** Full driving licence and insurance are required. An International Driving Permit is recommended, although it is not legally required.
URBAN: *DAN* and *Egged* provide good local bus services in the main towns. Taxis are available.

ACCOMMODATION

From small, simple guest-houses to deluxe hotels, Israel offers a wide choice and high standards of accommodation. For a holiday with a difference, unique to Israel, there are *kibbutz country inns* in all parts of the country where one can find relaxed informality in delightful rural surroundings. Kibbutz Fly-Drive holidays are very popular and so are discovery tours by air-conditioned coach, staying at different hotels and kibbutzim to see the whole country.
HOTELS: There are approximately 300 hotels listed for visitors by the Ministry of Tourism. Prices vary according to season. It is best to book months in advance for Israel's high season (April to October) and for religious holiday seasons. 258 hotels are members of the Israel Hotel Association, PO Box 50066, 29 Ha'mered Street, Tel Aviv. Tel: (3) 517 0131. Fax: (3) 510 0197.
HOLIDAY/RECREATION VILLAGES: Located on the Mediterranean or the Red Sea Gulf, these villages provide accommodation usually in the form of small 2-bed cabins and bungalows. The standard fittings often include full air-conditioning and facilities. Most are only open between April and October and the emphasis is on casual living.
SELF-CATERING: Apartments and individual rooms are available on a rental basis throughout the country.
KIBBUTZ GUEST-HOUSES: All are clean and comfortable with modern dining rooms. Most have

visiting Jordan, as such visas cannot be obtained at the Allenby Bridge or in any Arab country.
The Arava Checkpoint crossing, 4km (3 miles) north of Eilat, is designated only as a temporary location for the passage of tourists who are not nationals of either Israel or Jordan. They are permitted to cross the border in both directions, that is from Israel to Jordan and return, and vice versa. *Egged* Bus no. 16 leaves every hour from the Central Bus Station in Eilat to the Arava checkpoint and returns. All nationals must have passports valid for at least six months from the date of crossing and a visa as required by each country. Visas to Jordan are issued at the Jordanian checkpoint and payment must be made in Jordanian Dinars. Individual tourists pay for a visa for a period of two weeks. Groups of 5-15 are exempt from payment, but still need a visa and must stay at least four nights in Jordan (if they stay less than five nights, they must pay a 4-dinar visa fee per person). A branch of the International Bank operates at the checkpoint during opening hours. Groups of 15 people are exempt from payment, but still need a visa and are not limited to any specific number of days or nights, provided that a Jordanian travel agent is waiting for them on the Jordanian side of the crossing point. Israel recognises Jordanian stamps in passports and visas and vice versa.

Tourists who wish to proceed to other Arab countries in addition to Jordan and Egypt should ask for the Israeli stamp on a separate paper or they will be refused entry. No Israeli or Jordanian registered vehicles will be permitted to cross the border. However, tourists' privately owned vehicles, registered in third countries, will be permitted to cross the border in accordance with existing regulations on each side concerning the type of vehicle permitted on each country's roads. The opening hours for the Arava border checkpoint are 0700-1400 Monday to Friday (closed Fridays and Saturdays and on Yom Kippur) and are likely to change.
The newly opened Jordan River Crossing can be crossed by holders of foreign passports valid for at least six months from the date of entry and persons with dual nationality as individuals or in groups; Israeli passport holders are permitted to visit Jordan in groups through travel agents only, who will make the necessary visa arrangements. A total of 300 Israelis per day are allowed to cross into Jordan at this point. All Israeli passport holders must obtain an exit permit from the Defence Forces. All UN cars (on official business or not) and vehicles with foreign registration will be permitted to cross freely without paying any fees; however, Israeli cars with diplomatic plates will not be permitted to cross

swimming pools (though it is wise to check that this is open to visitors) and provide a valuable insight into the style and aims of kibbutz life. Approximately 26 out of the 265 kibbutzim have guest-houses and each is located in a rural or scenic part of the country which is usually open all year. Further information is available from the Tourist Office.

CHRISTIAN HOSPICES: Throughout the country some 30 Christian hospices (operated by a variety of denominations) provide rooms and board at low rates. Although preference is given to pilgrimage groups, most will accommodate general tourists. They vary greatly in size and standards but all offer tourists basic accommodation in situations where hotels are full. Details are available from the Tourist Office.

CAMPING/CARAVANNING: The fine climate means Israel is a good country for camping, with campsites providing a touring base for each region. They offer full sanitary facilities, electric current, a restaurant and/or store, telephone, postal services, first-aid facilities, shaded picnic and camp-fire areas and day and night watchmen. They can be reached by bus, but all are open to cars and caravans. Most have tents and cabins, as well as a wide range of equipment for hire. All sites have swimming facilities either on-site or within easy reach. Hitch-hiking for campers is easy and popular, but one must compete for places with army personnel, who have priority over citizens. For further information, contact the Tourist Office.

YOUTH HOSTELS: Hostels in Israel can be dormitory, family bungalows, huts or modern cubicles and they are scattered all over the country in both urban and rural areas. For further details, write to the YHA, 2 Agron Street, Jerusalem (tel: (2) 245 875) or the IYHA, PO Box 1075, 3 Dorot Rishonim Street, Jerusalem 91009. Tel: (2) 252 706. Fax: (2) 235 220. Telex: 26580. Information is also available from the Tourist Office.

RESORTS & EXCURSIONS

Israel is a remarkable, fascinating and controversial country. For many it is, above all, the Holy Land. Religious attractions include the walk along the Via Dolorosa to the *Church of the Holy Sepulchre* in **Jerusalem** (the Holy City and cradle of Judaism, Christianity and Islam); the *Church of the Nativity* in **Bethlehem** and the *Church of the Annunciation* in **Nazareth**; the serenity of **Galilee** and the ride across the *River Jordan*, the river in which Jesus was baptised.
Tel Aviv: An exciting city offering commerce, culture and sandy beaches. The biggest attraction is the *Israeli Philharmonic Orchestra*. There are also several museums and the bustling *Carmel Market*. In 1950, **Jaffa** was united with Tel Aviv; situated a mile from the city, this is one of the oldest ports in the world. It has archaeological finds reaching back to the 3rd century BC, a beach, a lively nightlife in *Old Jaffa* and a flea market.
Jerusalem: For Jews, Christians and Muslims, this is one of the the most revered cities on earth. Attractions also exist for the more secular: everything from religious emblems and relics of antiquity to modern items of interest. Religious tours are available from West Jerusalem which include *Mount Zion* and the *Tomb of David*. Other sites are the *Tomb of Judges*, the memorial to the six million Jews who died in the Holocaust, and *Mea Shearim* ('the hundred gates'). In East Jerusalem visitors may follow the *Way of the Cross*, enter the *Church of the Holy Sepulchre*, and see the *Wailing Wall*, the *Dome of the Rock* and the Jaffa and Damascus gates.
Excursions: Three important excursions are to the *Hill of Rachel, En Karem* and *Abu Ghaush*.
The Negev: This area, once largely desert, is now being irrigated and farmed in a settlement movement started by, amongst others, David Ben Gurion. **Beersheba** and **Dimona** are both of interest, but **Eilat**, in particular, is the place for visitors. Eilat is the best-equipped seaside resort in the Middle East, and a paradise for underwater enthusiasts.
There are several attractive places in the coastal region; these include **Ashqelon** with the **Timna Valley National Park**, the *Sharon Valley* with its orange groves, historic **Caesarea**, and **En Hod**, the artists' village.
Haifa: Israel's leading seaport is both an industrial town and an ancient fortress. It is lively and interesting and provides a good starting point for visits to Galilee.
Galilee: Places of interest are the *Sea of Galilee* itself, **Nazareth**, the *Bet She'arim Catacombs*, **Megiddo**, **Tiberias** and the *Mount of Beatitudes*. The Tourist Office, together with a consortium of interested parties, is actively promoting Galilee as a tourist destination. Emphasis is being placed on the environment, sports, culture, history and health, with spa resorts (which have been used since Roman times) especially featured. The *Museum of Mediterranean Archaeology* celebrates many finds in the region.

The Negev Desert

The Dead Sea: 60km (41 miles) long and 17km (11 miles) wide, the Dead Sea is an inland lake lying 400m (1320ft) below sea level in the lower part of the Jordan Valley, flanked by the *Judean Mountains* to the west and the *Moab Mountains* to the east. It has more minerals and salt than any other body of water in the world and is renowned for its rejuvenating and health-giving properties. There are a number of health spas and resorts in the area. **Masada (Mezada),** on the left bank of the Dead Sea, is where the once luxurious palace of King Herod still stands, perched on a clifftop. It can be reached by cable car or a winding footpath and there is a breathtaking view of the Dead Sea and the pink mountains of Moab from here. Other interesting sights around the Dead Sea include **Mount Sodom,** a 13km-long (8-mile) mountain range made up of pure salt which has many caves with extraordinary hanging salt formations, and **Qumran,** where the famous Dead Sea Scrolls, written by Essene scribes, were discovered in ancient pottery jars.
The West Bank: In this troubled area are to be found **Hebron, Nablus** and **Samaria.** Consult with the Embassy or the Tourist Office before making any definite plans for visiting this area.
POPULAR ITINERARIES: 5-day: Tel Aviv–Jaffa–

Caesarea–Sharon Valley–Jerusalem–Masada–Nazareth–Tiberias–Sea of Galilee. **7-day:** Jerusalem–Bethlehem–Masada–Dead Sea–Eilat–Timna Valley National Park–Negev Desert.

SOCIAL PROFILE

FOOD & DRINK: Restaurants in Israel offer a combination of Oriental and Western cuisine, in addition to the local dishes. Some restaurants are expensive, though a high price does not necessarily mean a high standard. Table service is usual. There are many snack bars. Restaurants, bars and cafés catering to tourists must have menus in two languages (Hebrew plus French or English). Israeli cuisine is essentially a combination of Oriental and Western cuisine, plus an additional distinct flavour brought by the many and varied nationalities which make up the Israelis. Dishes such as Hungarian *goulash,* Russian *bortsch,* Viennese *schnitzel* or German *braten* are found next to Oriental items such as *falafel, humus, tahini, shashlik, kebabs* and Turkish coffee, as well as traditional Jewish dishes such as *gefilte* fish, chopped liver and chicken soup.
Kosher food: The Hebrew word *kosher* means food conforming to Jewish religious dietary laws. Milk,

cream or cheese may not be served together with meat in the same meal. Pork and shellfish are officially prohibited, but it is possible to find them on many menus.
Drink: The wines of Israel range from light white to dry red and sweet rosé. There is also a good choice of local brandies and liqueurs. Liqueurs include *Hard Nut* (a walnut concoction of Eliaz winery), *Sabra* (chocolate and orange) and *Arak* (an anise drink). Israeli beers are *Maccabee, OK* and *Gold Star.* A centre for liqueurs is the monastery at Latrun on the road between Jerusalem and Tel Aviv.
NIGHTLIFE: There are nightclubs and discotheques in most cities. Tel Aviv has a wealth of entertainment to divert the visitor and there are rock, jazz, folk and pop music clubs in all the main cities and resorts. Israeli folklore and dance shows can be seen everywhere, especially in the kibbutzim. The Israeli Philharmonic Orchestra can be heard at the ICC Binaynei Ha'ooma Hall in Jerusalem during the winter. A summer attraction is the *Israel Festival of International Music* and arts events. Cinema is popular in Israel and many cinemas screen three daily shows of international and local films (all Hebrew films are subtitled in English and French). Tickets for all events and even films can be bought in advance from ticket agencies and sometimes from hotels and tourist offices.
ARTS & CULTURE: There are art galleries all over Israel, with colonies of artists in the village of En Hod on Mount Carmel near Haifa, at Zefat and in Jaffa. Every large town has its museum; the *Israel Museum* in Jerusalem housing the Dead Sea Scrolls and the *Museum of the Diaspora* at Tel Aviv are internationally famous.
SHOPPING: There is a wide choice for shoppers in Israel; and in certain shops, especially in Arab markets, visitors can, and should, bargain. Tourists who buy leather goods at shops listed by the Ministry of Tourism and pay for them in foreign currency are exempt from VAT and receive a 25% discount on leather goods if these are delivered to them at the port of departure. Special purchases include jewellery, diamonds and other precious stones, ceramics, embroidery, glassware, wines, religious articles and holy books. 'Cashback' on purchased items can be claimed from the Department of Customs, 32 Agron Street, Jerusalem 944190.
Shopping hours: 0900-1900 Sunday to Thursday, some shops close 1300-1600; 0900-1300 Friday. Remember that the shopping facilities are both Israeli and Arabic, and are therefore governed by two different sets of opening hours and methods of business. Jewish stores observe closing time near sunset Friday evenings before *Shabbat* (Saturday) and Arabic stores close Friday. It takes a while to realise that Sunday is a normal working day unlike in Western countries. For shoppers, the Jewish stores are therefore open Friday, Arab markets Saturday and both are open Sunday when Christian stores close. Shops in the hotels are often open until midnight.
SPORT: Among annual sports events are the *Tel Aviv Marathon* and the *Kinereth Swimming Gala.* **Football, basketball** and **tennis** are popular. Many hotels have **tennis** courts, and there is a fine 18-hole **golf** course at Caesarea. **Horseriding** is available throughout the country. **Bicycling** and **skiing** are popular too. There are excellent facilities at kibbutz sportsgrounds and in cities. **Winter sports:** To many people's surprise there is a full skiing season at Mount Hermon, on the northern border. **Water sports: Swimming, surfing, sailing, water-skiing, yachting** and **fishing** are all available. All the large hotels have swimming pools. **Skindiving** and **aqualung diving** are especially popular in Eilat on the Red Sea coast with an excellent underwater observatory descending to the floor of the coral reef near the town. Eilat is a particularly good destination for winter sun for visitors from Western Europe.
Note: The Red Sea coastline has been designated a preservation area and any tourists found with 'souvenirs' such as coral will suffer severe fines from both the Israeli and Egyptian authorities.
SPECIAL EVENTS: In Bethlehem each Christmas there are Catholic, Protestant and Orthodox church services from December 24 to January 6. In Jerusalem, the Crucifixion and Resurrection of Christ are celebrated each Easter. The following is a selection of some of the other major festivals and special events celebrated during 1995/96 in Israel. For a complete list, contact the Israeli Government Tourist Office.
Mar 19-25 '95 *Spring Migration Birdwatcher's Festival,* Eilat. **Mar 26-Apr 4** *8th Arthur Rubenstein International Piano Master Competition,* Tel Aviv. **Apr 15-21** *Ein Gev Classical Festival,* Ein Gev; *Folk Music and Instrumental Festival,* Mevaseret and Zion. **Apr 23** *Mimouna.* **Apr 26-27** *Memorial Day for Martyrs and Heroes of the Holocaust,* Jerusalem. **May 3** *Official Ceremony Marking the Closing of Memorial Day and the Opening of Israel's 47th Independence Day Celebrations,* Jerusalem. **May 18** *Lag Ba'Omer* (picnics and sports activities). **May 18-Jun 10** *Israel Festival,* Jerusalem. **May 28** *Jerusalem Day celebrations.* **Jun 3-4** *Music Festival,* Abu Gosh. **Jun 19-22** *International Fair,* Tel Aviv. **Jun 20-Jul 7** *Mediterranean Festival,* Tel Aviv. **Jul 1-9** *International Folklore Festival.* **Jul 4-7** *Hot Air Balloon Festival,* Ayalon Valley. **Aug 7-17** *17th Zimriya World Assembly of Choirs,* Jerusalem. **Aug 11** *Tu Be'av Festivities.* **Oct 8-16** *Christian Celebration During the Feast of Tabernacles,* Jerusalem. **Oct 9-16** *Wine Festival,* Zichron Ya'akov and Rishon LeZion; *Jewish Folklore Festival and Chamber Music Festival,* Tel Aviv; *13th Workshop for Early Music Concerts,* Jerusalem and Tel Aviv; *11th International Film Festival,* Haifa; *Music Festival in the 'Land of 1000 Caves',* Beit Guvrin; *Israel Alternative Theatre Festival,* Acre; *Bedouin Festival,* Negev; *Music Festival,* Abu Gosh. **Oct 20-22** *Jewish Music Festival,* Merom Hagalil. **Nov 20-Dec 5** *International Guitar Festival.* **Dec 24-25** *International Christmas Choir Assembly,* Jerusalem, Nazareth and Bethlehem. **Mar 18 '96** *The King David Feast,* Jerusalem.
SOCIAL CONVENTIONS: Usually very informal, but in keeping with European style of hospitality. Visitors should observe normal courtesies when visiting someone's home and should not be afraid to ask questions about the country as most Israelis are happy to talk about their homeland, religion and politics. Often the expression *shalom* is used, which means 'peace' and is used instead of hello and goodbye. Dress is casual, but in Christian, Muslim and Jewish holy places modest attire is worn. For places such as the Western Wall visitors are given a cardboard hat to respect the religious importance of the site. Business people are expected to dress smartly, while plush restaurants, nightclubs and hotel dining rooms may require guests to dress for dinner. Formal evening wear is usually specified on invitations. It is considered a violation of the *Shabbat* (Saturday) to smoke in certain restaurants and many hotels. There is usually a sign to remind the visitor, and to disregard this warning would be regarded as discourteous to Orthodox Jews. **Tipping:** Less evident than in many other countries. A 10% service charge is added to restaurant, café and hotel bills by law.

BUSINESS PROFILE

ECONOMY: Israel has a diverse and sophisticated manufacturing economy which in many respects rivals that of Western Europe. Agriculture is relatively small – about 2.4% of gross domestic product – with citrus fruit as the main commodity and export earner. The industrial sector is concentrated in engineering, aircraft, electronics, chemicals, construction materials, textiles and food-processing. Mining is also small but is set to expand, with production of potash and bromine. There is a small indigenous oil industry. The infrastructure is well-developed and tourism, in which there has been considerable investment, is growing slowly but steadily. However, Israel suffers from a lack of natural resources, resulting in a large import bill, and very heavy defence expenditure. Offsetting that is a vast aid package from the USA, probably worth around US$5 billion per annum. The Labour government elected in 1992 will also benefit from a US$10-billion loan provision to finance housing resettlement. The economy has recovered from its major difficulties during the 1980s, which culminated in 1000% inflation and the almost total collapse of the Shekel, but growth is sluggish and any improvement in economic performance has been hampered by an inefficient state sector. The new Labour government seems less inclined than its predecessor to make extensive economic reforms. The USA is Israel's largest export market, followed by the UK. At present, trade restrictions due to the closure of the border between Israel and the West Bank and Gaza on October 19, 1994, are gradually being eased and may re-open fully within the near future. The success of the Israeli-Palestinian deal relies to a large extent on the economic viability of the two enclaves. This in turn will depend upon the fulfilment of promises of aid and economic support from the international community. The complexities of the situation have meant that the process has so far proved to be a slow and fraught one.
BUSINESS: Business can be frustrating, as in many instances it is difficult to get a positive reply to a straight question. However, perseverance will pay off. Appointments are usual, as is the use of business cards. Israelis tend not to be punctual and it is not uncommon to be kept waiting for as long as half an hour. Normal courtesies should be observed, although business meetings tend to be less formal than in Britain. **Office hours:** 0800-1300 and 1500-1800 Sunday to Thursday (November-May) and 0730-1430 Sunday to Thursday (June-October). Some offices are open half-day Friday.
COMMERCIAL INFORMATION: The following organisation can offer advice: Federation of Israeli Chambers of Commerce, PO Box 20027, 84 Hahashmonaim Street, Tel Aviv 67011. Tel: (3) 561 2444. Fax: (3) 561 2614. Telex: 33484 (a/b CHCOM IL).
CONFERENCES/CONVENTIONS: The Ministry of Tourism brochure *Picture a Perfect Convention* states that 'about two thousand years ago, some of the greatest conventions were held near Tiberias where it was recorded that five thousand were amply catered for'. Israel's record as a contemporary international conference centre began in 1963, and the country now attracts about 150 international meetings a year with 50,000 delegates; scientific and academic meetings account for about half the meetings, though religious and sporting events are on the increase. In 1992, 55% of meetings were held in Jerusalem. Apart from hotels and the convention centres in Jerusalem and Tel Aviv, opportunities exist to hold meetings in kibbutzim. For further information, contact the International Conventions Department, Ministry of Tourism, 24 King George Street, Jerusalem 91009. Tel: (2) 754 811. Fax: (2) 254 226.

CLIMATE

Mediterranean, with a pleasant spring and autumn. Winters in the north can be cool. Rain in winter is widespread, particularly in Jerusalem. Snow is rare. Summers can be very hot, especially in the south. The Red Sea resort of Eilat has a good climate for beach holidays all the year round.
Required clothing: Lightweight cottons and linens for warmer months are required. Mediumweights are recommended for winters, although on the Red Sea coast they are unlikely to be necessary during the day.

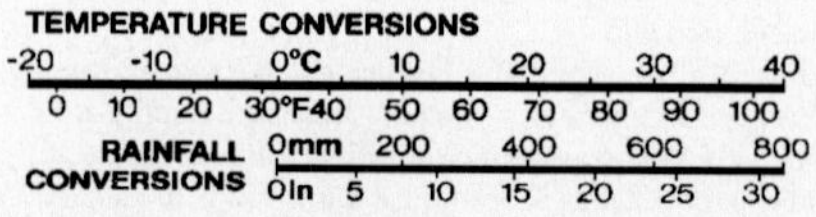

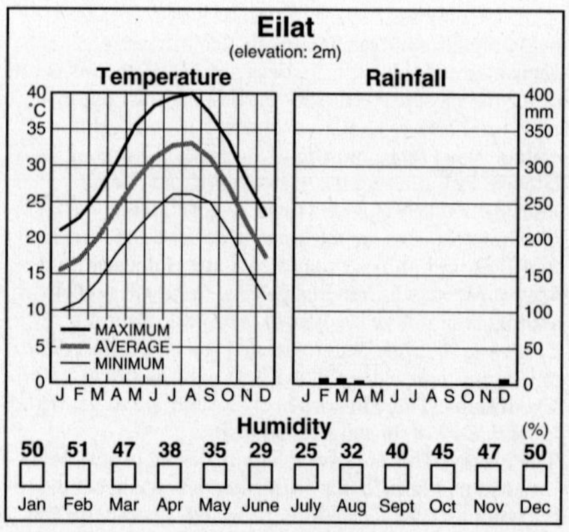

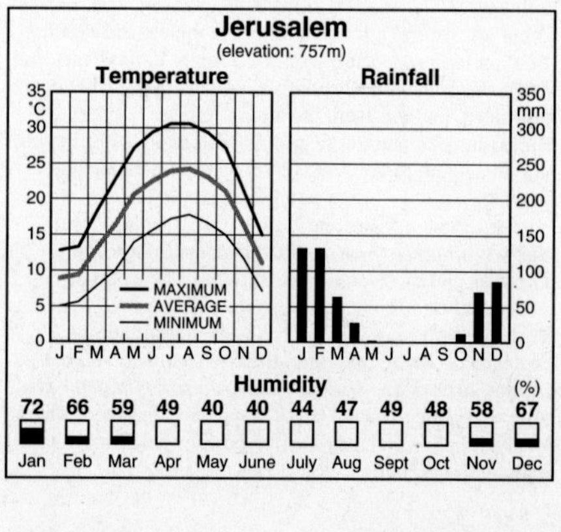

Top picture: Church on the Sea of Galilee. Above left: The Harbour, Jaffa, Tel Aviv. Above right: Traditional Bedouin in the Negev Desert.

Italy

400km
200mls

SWITZ.   AUS.
A L P S
Mt Blanc Milan
4807m   Trieste
Turin   Venice
Genoa   Bologna
MONACO Pisa Florence SAN MARINO
                        CROATIA
FRANCE Elba   Appennines Adriatic Sea
Corsica   Pescara
        ROME ■ ITALY
                Naples Bari
Sardinia   Vesuvius 1277m Pompei Brindisi
                        Taranto
        Tyrrhenian
            Sea
                    Reggio
                    di Calabria
        Palermo   Etna 3323m
        Sicily   Catania
Mediterranean Sea
ALG.   Pantelleria
TUNISIA   Linosa MALTA
                Lampedusa

EUROPE

DAB-M121

□ international airport

Location: Western Europe.

Ente Nazionale Italiano per il Turismo (ENIT)
Via Marghera 2, 00185 Rome, Italy
Tel: (6) 49711. Fax: (6) 496 3379. Telex: 680123.
Embassy of the Italian Republic
14 Three Kings Yard, Davies Street, London W1Y 2EH
Tel: (0171) 312 2200. Fax: (0171) 312 2230. Telex:
23520 (a/b ITADIPG).
Italian Consulate General
38 Eaton Place, London SW1 8AN
Tel: (0171) 235 9371 or 259 6322 (for recorded visa
information). Fax: (0171) 823 1609. Telex: 8950932.
Opening hours: 0900-1200 Monday to Friday.
Italian State Tourist Office (ENIT)
1 Princes Street, London W1R 8AY
Tel: (0171) 408 1254. Fax: (0171) 493 6695. Telex:
22402 (a/b ENIT GBG). Opening hours: 0900-1700
Monday to Friday.
British Embassy
Via XX Settembre 80A, 00187 Rome, Italy
Tel: (6) 482 5551 or 482 5441. Fax: (6) 487 3324. Telex:
626119 (a/b BREMB I).
Consulates in: Florence, Milan, Messina, Palermo, Turin,
Trieste, Genoa, Venice, Naples, Brindisi and Bari.
Embassy of the Italian Republic
1601 Fuller Street, NW, Washington, DC 20009
Tel: (202) 328 5500. Fax: (202) 462 3605. Telex: 64122.
Consulates in: Boston, Chicago, Detroit, Houston, Los
Angeles, Newark, New Orleans, New York (tel: (212)
737 9100), Miami, Philadelphia and San Francisco.
Italian State Tourist Office (ENIT)
Suite 1565, 630 Fifth Avenue, New York, NY 10111
Tel: (212) 245 4822. Fax: (212) 586 9249. Telex:
236024.
Embassy of the United States of America
Via Vittorio Veneto 119A, 00187 Rome, Italy
Tel: (6) 46741. Fax: (6) 488 2672. Telex: 622322 (a/b
AMBRMA).
Embassy of the Italian Republic
21st Floor, 275 Slater Street, Ottawa, Ontario K1P 5H9
Tel: (613) 232 2401/2/3. Fax: (613) 233 1484.

Consulates in: Calgary, Edmonton, Hamilton, Montréal,
Québec, Toronto, Winnipeg and Vancouver.
Italian State Tourist Office (ENIT)
Suite 1914, 1 place de Ville Marie, Montréal, Québec
H3B 2C3
Tel: (514) 866 7667. Fax: (514) 392 1429.
Canadian Embassy
Via G.B de Rossi 27, 00161 Rome, Italy
Tel: (6) 445 9811. Fax: (6) 4459 8750.

AREA: 301,277 sq km (116,324 sq miles).
POPULATION: 57,746,163 (1990 estimate).
POPULATION DENSITY: 191.7 per sq km.
CAPITAL: Rome. **Population:** 2,791,354 (1990).
GEOGRAPHY: Italy is situated in Europe and attached
in the north to the European mainland. To the north the
Alps separate Italy from France, Switzerland, Austria and
Slovenia.
Northern Italy: The Alpine regions, the Po Plain and the
Ligurian-Etruscan Appennines. Piemonte and Val
d'Aosta contain some of the highest mountains in Europe
and are good areas for winter sports. Many rivers flow
down from the mountains towards the Po Basin, passing
through the beautiful Italian Lake District (Maggiore,
Como, Garda). The Po Basin, which extends as far south
as the bare slopes of the Appennines, is covered with
gravel terraces and rich alluvial soil and has long been
one of Italy's most prosperous regions. To the east,
where the River Po flows into the Adriatic Sea, the plains
are little higher than the river itself; artificial (and
occasionally natural) embankments prevent flooding.
Central Italy: The northern part of the Italian peninsula.
Tuscany (Toscana) has a diverse landscape with snow-
capped mountains (the Tuscan Appennines), lush
countryside, hills and a long sandy coastline with
offshore islands. Le Marche, lying between the
Appennines and the Adriatic coast, is a region of
mountains, rivers and small fertile plains. The even more
mountainous *regioni* (administrative districts) of Abruzzo
and Molise are bordered by Marche to the north and
Puglia to the south, and are separated from the
Tyrrhenian Sea and to the west by Lazio and Campania.
Umbria is known as the 'green heart of Italy', hilly with
broad plains, olive groves and pines. Further south lies
Rome, Italy's capital and largest city. Within its precincts
is the Vatican City (see separate entry on *Vatican City*).
Southern Italy: Campania consists of flat coastal plains
and low mountains, stretching from Baia Domizia to the
Bay of Naples and along a rocky coast to the Calabria
border. Inland, the Appennines are lower, mellowing into
the rolling countryside around Sorrento. The islands of
Capri, Ischia and Procida in the Tyrrhenian Sea are also
part of Campania. The south is wilder than the north,
with mile upon mile of olive trees, cool forests and
rolling hills. Puglia, the 'heel of the boot', is a landscape
of volcanic hills and isolated marshes. Calabria, the 'toe',
is heavily forested and thinly populated. The Calabrian
hills are home to bears and wolves.
The Islands: Sicily (Sicilia), visible across a 3km (2-
mile) strait from mainland Italy, is fertile but
mountainous with volcanoes (including the famous
landmark of Mount Etna) and lava fields, and several
offshore islands. Sardinia (Sardegna) has a mountainous
landscape, fine sandy beaches and rocky offshore islands.
For more information on each region, see the *Resorts &
Excursions* section below.
LANGUAGE: Italian is the official language. Dialects
are spoken in different regions. German and Ladin are
spoken in the South Tyrol region (bordering Austria).
French is spoken in all the border areas from the Riviera
to the area north of Milan (border with France and
Switzerland). Slovenian is spoken in the provinces
bordering Slovenia. English, German and French are also
spoken in the biggest cities and resorts by people
connected with tourism.
RELIGION: Roman Catholic with Protestant minorities.
TIME: GMT + 1 (GMT + 2 from last Sunday in March
to Saturday before last Sunday in September).
ELECTRICITY: 220 volts AC, 50Hz.
COMMUNICATIONS: Telephone: Full IDD service
available. Country code: 39 (followed by 6 for Rome, 2
for Milan, 11 for Turin, 81 for Naples, 41 for Venice and
55 for Florence). Outgoing international code: 00.
Telephone kiosks accept Lit100 and Lit200 coins, as well
as *gettoni*, tokens which are available at tobacconists and
bars. There are some card phones, and phonecards can be
purchased at post offices, tobacconists and certain
newsagents. **Fax:** Some hotels have facilities.
Telex/telegram: Telex facilities are available at the main
post offices. Telex code: 43. Italcable operates services
abroad, transmitting messages by cable or radio. Both
internal and overseas telegrams may be dictated over the
telephone. **Post:** The Italian postal system tends to be
subject to delays. Letters between Italy and other
European countries usually take a week to ten days to
arrive. Letters intended for *Poste Restante* collection

should be addressed to Fermo Posta and the town.
Stamps are sold in post offices and tobacconists. Post
office hours: 0800/0830-1200/1230 and 1400/1430-
1730/1800 Monday to Friday; Saturday mornings only.
Press: The main towns publish a weekly booklet with
entertainment programmes, sports events, restaurants,
nightclubs, etc. A daily English-language newspaper,
Daily American, is published in Rome. Among the most
important Italian dailies are *La Stampa* (Turin), *Corriere
della Sera* (Milan), *La Repubblica* (Rome), *Il
Messaggero* (Rome), *Il Giorno* (Milan) and *Il Giornale*
(Milan).
**BBC World Service and Voice of America
frequencies:** From time to time these change. See the
section *How to Use this Book* for more information.
BBC:

MHz	17.64	12.09	9.410	7.325

Voice of America:

MHz	15.20	9.760	6.040	5.995

PASSPORT/VISA

Regulations and requirements may be subject to change at short notice, and you are advised to contact the appropriate diplomatic or consular authority before finalising travel arrangements. Details of these may be found at the head of this country's entry. Any numbers in the chart refer to the footnotes below.

	Passport Required?	Visa Required?	Return Ticket Required?
Full British	1	No	No
BVP	Valid	-	-
Australian	Yes	No	No
Canadian	Yes	No	No
USA	Yes	No	No
Other EU (As of 31/12/94)	1	No	No
Japanese	Yes	No	No

Note: The regulations stated below also apply to San
Marino and the Vatican City.
PASSPORTS: Valid passport required by all except:
(a) **[1]** nationals of Belgium, France, Germany, Greece,
Luxembourg, The Netherlands, Portugal and Spain with a
valid national ID card, and the UK with a British Visitors
Passport;
(b) nationals of Andorra, Austria, Liechtenstein, Monaco,
San Marino and Switzerland if carrying valid national ID
cards.
British Visitors Passport: A British Visitors Passport
can be used for holidays or unpaid business trips of up to
3 months to Italy.
VISAS: Required by all except:
(a) nationals of countries referred to in the chart above
for stays not exceeding 3 months;
(b) nationals of Andorra, Argentina, Austria, Bermuda,
Bolivia, Brazil, Chile, Colombia, Costa Rica, Croatia,
Cyprus, Czech Republic, Ecuador, El Salvador, Finland,
Guatemala, Honduras, Hong Kong (British nationals),
Hungary, Iceland, Jamaica, Kenya, South Korea,
Liechtenstein, Malaysia, Malta, Mexico, Monaco, New
Zealand, Norway, Paraguay, Poland, San Marino,
Singapore, Slovak Republic, Slovenia, Sweden,
Switzerland, Uruguay, Vatican City and Yugoslavia
(Serbia and Montenegro) for stays not exceeding 3
months;
(c) nationals of Venezuela for visits not exceeding 2 months;
(d) nationals of Israel for stays not exceeding 1 month.
Transit visas: Not required by those continuing their
journey to a third country by the same or connecting
aircraft, or by those who continue their journey to a third
country within 48 hours from the same airport at which
they arrive. Tickets with reserved seats and valid
documents for onward travel must be held. This facility
is not available to stateless persons and nationals of
Afghanistan, Algeria, Angola, Bangladesh, Cape Verde,
Eritrea, Ethiopia, Ghana, Guinea-Bissau, India, Iran,
Morocco, North Korea, Mongolia, Mozambique, Nigeria,
Pakistan, São Tomé e Princípe, Senegal, Somalia, Sri
Lanka, Taiwan (China), Vietnam and Zimbabwe.
Types of visa: *Transit:* applicants must present their

Timatic

Health
GALILEO/WORLDSPAN: **TI-DFT/ROM/HE**
SABRE: **TIDFT/ROM/HE**

Visa
GALILEO/WORLDSPAN: **TI-DFT/ROM/VI**
SABRE: **TIDFT/ROM/VI**

For more information on Timatic codes refer to Contents.

Exploring Italy by train

The following range of special railcards will enable you to see Italy by train and save money:

Tourist Travel Pass (BTLC – "Biglietti Turistici di Libera Circolazione")

These are 1st- or 2nd-class tickets for customers not resident in Italy.
They allow either 8, 15, 21 or 30 days unlimited travel during the period for which they are valid on the entire network of the Italian State Railways.
With the *Tourist Travel Pass* tickets, the holder is entitled to unlimited travel on any train without paying the supplement for Intercity or Eurocity, except for ETR "Pendolino" (ETR 450) high-speed trains for which there is a small extra charge.
It can also be purchased from FS Italian Tourist Company Agencies, CIT.

Italy Flexi Railcard (IFR)

These are "flexible" 1st- or 2nd-class tickets for customers residing outside Europe and allow unlimited travel for either 4, 8 or 12 days, within 9, 21 or 30 days respectively from the date of validity.
With the *Italy Flexi Railcard* it is possible to enjoy unlimited travel on all trains without paying the IC and EC supplements, except on ETR Pendolino trains for which the same terms apply as for the *Tourist Travel Pass.*
These can also be purchased abroad from FS Italian Tourist Company Agencies (CIT).

Kilometric Cards (Biglietti Chilometrici)

About 15% discount.
This entitles the holder to make single journeys up to a maximum distance of 3000km.
It can also be used by more than one person at a time up to a maximum of five.
For children aged between 4 and 12, half of the kilometres travelled are counted.
These cards are valid for two months from the date they are first stamped and can also be purchased abroad from CIT or licensed travel agencies.

Group Cards (Biglietti per Comitive)

20% discount for groups of 6 to 24 ticket holders.
For every ten persons, one person can travel free.
30% discount for groups of over 25 ticket holders.
For every 15 persons in groups of 25-50, one person may travel free and for every 10 persons in groups exceeding 50 persons. The maximum number of people travelling free may not exceed 5.

No discounts are given on travel during peak seasons (Easter, Christmas and summer). The tickets are valid for one month.

Book of Reduced Rate Tickets (Carnet di Biglietti a Tariffa Ridotta)

This can be held by one person only and is in the holder's name. It is issued for a minimum of 4 tickets, for 1st- and 2nd-class travel and for distances of more than 70 kilometres.
Discounts are as follows:
10% on journeys of up to 350km.
20% on journeys of more than 350km.
It may be used up to a month after the date it is issued.

Travel Card (Tessere di Autorizzazione)

This allows you to purchase single or return tickets with a discount of about 40%. It is valid for a month, three months, six months or a year depending and falls into four categories:
• Category A for 1st- and 2nd-class tickets.
• Category B for 2nd-class tickets only.
• Category A/IC for 1st- and 2nd-class tickets with exemption from payment of Intercity supplement.
• Category B/IC for 2nd-class tickets with exemption from payment of Intercity supplement.

Green Card (Carta Verde)

This is in the holder's name, valid for a year and costs Lire 40,000. It is issued to young people between 12 and 26 years of age and entitles the holder to a discount of 20% on 1st- or 2nd-class tickets .

Silver Card (Carta d'Argento)

This is non-transferable and is valid for one year. It costs Lire 40,000 and is issued to persons who are at least 60 years old. It includes 1st- or 2nd-class tickets with a discount of 20%.

Ferrovie Dello Stato SpA
Area Trasporto
Passenger Division

---

passports endorsed with the visa of the countries beyond Italy which they intend to visit and rail/air tickets as evidence of the continuation of their journey. *Entry visa:* tourist or business. Details from the Italian Consulate. No visas for multiple entries can be issued.
Cost: £12.
Validity: 2 months from date of issue with some exceptions.
Application to: Consulate (or Consular section at Embassy). For addresses, see top of entry. Postal applications are not acceptable.
Application requirements: (a) Passport which has been valid for at least 5 months. (b) Completed application form. (c) Return ticket. (d) 2 passport-size photographs. (e) Proof of financial means. (f) Where applicable, a letter from sponsoring company in Italy; a work reference; a letter from school, college or university. (g) Where applicable, marriage certificate showing proof of marriage to an EU national.
Stateless persons and holders of travel documents must present 4 forms and 4 photographs.
Working days required: 1.
Note: In the UK, current visa requirements are held on an automatic 'dial & listen' service. Tel: (0171) 259 6322.

MONEY

Currency: Italian Lira (Lit). Notes are in denominations of Lit100,000, 50,000, 20,000, 10,000, 5000, 2000 and 1000. Coins are in denominations of Lit1000, 500, 200, 100, 50 and 20. There is a plan to introduce a 'new Lira' worth 1000 times the present currency, but no firm date has been established for this at the time of writing.
Currency exchange: Travellers cheques, cheques and foreign money can be changed at banks, railway stations

and airports, and very often at main hotels (generally at a less convenient rate). Many UK banks offer differing exchange rates depending on the denominations of Italian currency being bought or sold. Check with banks for details and current rates.
Credit cards: Access/Mastercard, Diners Club and Visa are widely accepted. Check with your credit card company for merchant acceptability and other facilities which may be available.
Travellers cheques are accepted almost everywhere.
Exchange rate indicators: The following figures are included as a guide to the movements of the Lira against Sterling and the US Dollar:

Date:	Oct '92	Sep '93	Jan '94	Jan '95
£1.00=	2108	2380	2532	2538
$1.00=	1329	1559	1712	1622

Currency restrictions: Check with the bank before departure. Import and export of both foreign and local currency is limited to Lit20,000,000. If it is intended to import or export amounts greater than this, the amount imported should be declared and validated on form V2 on arrival.
Banking hours: These vary from city to city but, in general, 0830-1330 and 1530-1930 Monday to Friday.

DUTY FREE

The following goods may be imported into Italy without incurring customs duty by:
(a) Residents of European countries travelling from the EU:
200 cigarettes or 50 cigars or 100 cigarillos or 250g of tobacco; 1 litre of spirits (over 22% proof) or 2 litres of fortified or sparkling wine; 50g of perfume and 250ml of eau de toilette; 1000g of coffee or 400g of coffee extract; 200g of tea or 80g of tea extract; goods to the value of

Lit594,360 (if over 15 years of age), to the value of Lit152,400 (if under 15 years of age).
(b) Residents of European countries travelling from a non-EU country:
200 cigarettes or 50 cigars or 100 cigarillos or 250g of tobacco; 750ml of spirits (over 22% proof) or 2 litres of alcoholic beverages (not over 22% proof); 50g (60cc/2fl oz) of perfume and 250ml of eau de toilette; 500g of coffee or 200g of coffee extract; 100g of tea or 40g of tea extract; goods to the value of Lit68,580 (if over 15 years of age), to the value of Lit35,052 (if under 15 years of age).
(c) *Passengers over 17 years of age arriving from EU countries with duty-paid goods:
800 cigarettes and 400 cigarillos and 200 cigars and 1kg of tobacco; 90 litres of wine (including up to 60 litres of sparkling wine); 10 litres of spirits; 20 litres of intermediate products (such as fortified wine); 110 litres of beer.
(d) Other passengers:
400 cigarettes or 100 cigars or 200 cigarillos or 500g of tobacco; goods to the value of Lit67,000; alcohol and other allowances are as for passengers travelling from non-EU countries above.
Note [*]: Although there are now no legal limits imposed on importing duty-paid tobacco and alcoholic products from one EU country to another, travellers may be questioned at customs if they exceed the above amounts and may be asked to prove that the goods are for personal use only.

PUBLIC HOLIDAYS

Jan 1 '95 New Year's Day. **Jan 6** Epiphany. **Apr 17** Easter Monday. **Apr 25** Liberation Day. **May 1** Labour Day. **Aug 15** Assumption. **Nov 1** All Saints' Day. **Nov 5** National Unity Day. **Dec 8** Immaculate Conception. **Dec**

---

25 Christmas Day. **Dec 26** St Stephen's Day. **Jan 1 '96** New Year's Day. **Jan 6** Epiphany. **Apr 8** Easter Monday. **Apr 25** Liberation Day.

In addition, local feast days are held in honour of town patron saints, generally without closure of shops and offices. These include:

Turin/Genoa/Florence: Jun 24 (St John the Baptist). **Milan:** Dec 7 (St Ambrose). **Siena:** Palio Horserace. **Venice:** Apr 25 (St Mark). **Bologna:** Oct 4 (St Petronius). **Naples:** Sep 19 (St Gennaro). **Bari:** Dec 6 (St Nicholas). **Palermo:** Jul 15 (St Rosalia). **Rome:** Jun 29 (St Peter).

HEALTH

Regulations and requirements may be subject to change at short notice, and you are advised to contact your doctor well in advance of your intended date of departure. Any numbers in the chart refer to the footnotes below.

	Special Precautions?	Certificate Required?
Yellow Fever	No	No
Cholera	No	No
Typhoid & Polio	No	-
Malaria	No	-
Food & Drink	1	-

[1]: Tap water is generally safe to drink. Bottled water is available. The inscription 'Acqua Non Potabile' means water is not drinkable. Milk is pasteurised and dairy products are safe for consumption. Local meat, poultry, seafood, fruit and vegetables are considered safe to eat. *Rabies* is present. For those at high risk, vaccination before arrival should be considered. If you are bitten abroad, seek medical advice without delay. For more information consult the *Health* section at the back of the book.

Health care: A Reciprocal Health Agreement with the rest of the EU allows free dental and medical (including hospital) treatment on presentation of form E111; prescribed medicines must be paid for. Insurance is advised for specialist treatment. Italy is well endowed with health spas, some famous as far back as the Roman era. The most important and best-equipped health resorts in Italy are Abano Terme and Montegrotto Terme (Veneto), Acqui Terme (Piemonte), Chianciano and Montecatini Terme (Tuscany), Fiuggi (Lazio), Porretta Terme and Salsomaggiore Terme (Emilia-Romagna), Sciacca (Sicily) and Sirmione (Lombardia). At Merano (Alto Adige) it is possible to have a special grape-diet treatment.

TRAVEL - International

AIR: Italy's national airline is *Alitalia (AZ)*.
For free advice on air travel, call the Air Travel Advisory Bureau in the UK on (0171) 636 5000 (London) *or* (0161) 832 2000 (Manchester).
Approximate flight times: From Rome to *London* is 2 hours 30 minutes, to *Los Angeles* is 15 hours 35 minutes, to *New York* is 9 hours 45 minutes, to *Singapore* is 13 hours 55 minutes and to *Sydney* is 24 hours 50 minutes.
International airports: Rome *(ROM)* (Leonardo da Vinci or Fiumicino), 35km (22 miles) southwest of the city (travel time – 50 minutes). Airport facilities include outgoing duty-free shop (0800-2230), car hire (0700-2200), bank/bureau de change (0700-2200) and bar/restaurant (0700-2230). There is a direct rail link to Termini Station. Taxis are also available to the city.
Rome *(ROM)* (Ciampino), 32km (20 miles) from the city (travel time – 60 minutes). Airport facilities include a bank/bureau de change, duty-free shop and souvenir shop and café. Buses are available to the underground station Anagnina. Taxis are also available.
Bologna *(BLQ)* (Borgo Panigale), 6km (4 miles) northwest of the city (travel time – 20 minutes). Good airport facilities. Buses are available to the city.
Catania *(CTA)* (Fontanarossa), 7km (4.5 miles) from the city.
Genoa *(GOA)* (Cristoforo Colombo, Sestri), 7km (4.5 miles) west of the city (travel time – 25 minutes). Duty-free facilities. Buses are available to the city.
Milan *(MIL)* (Linate), 10km (6 miles) east of the city (travel time – 25 minutes). Airport facilities include outgoing duty-free facilities, car hire, bank/bureau de change and bar/restaurant. Taxis and buses are available to the city.
Milan *(MIL)* (Malpensa), 46km (29 miles) northwest of the city (travel time – 80 minutes). Duty-free facilities.
Naples *(NAP)* (Capodichino), 7km (4.5 miles) north of the city (travel time – 35 minutes). Duty-free facilities.
Pisa *(PSA)* (Galileo Galilei), 2km (1.5 miles) south of the city (travel time – 10 minutes). Duty-free facilities.
Note: People travelling to Florence can fly to Pisa and then take the new train service directly from Pisa Airport

to Florence, which takes one hour. The rail station in Pisa is practically inside the airport. Rail services connect with arrivals and departures of all international flights and major domestic services.
Palermo *(PMO)* (Punta Raisi), 32km (20 miles) west of the city (travel time – 25 minutes).
Turin *(TRN)* (Caselle), 16km (10 miles) northwest of the city (travel time – 35 minutes).
Venice *(VCE)* (Marco Polo), 13km (8 miles) northwest of the city (travel time – 20 minutes).
SEA: International sailings to Italy run from Greece, Libya, South America, the Far East, Malta, Spain, France and Tunisia. For details, contact shipping agents direct or consult the *Travellers' Handbook*, available from the Italian State Tourist Office.
RAIL: The main rail connections from London (Victoria) and Paris to Italy are:
Palatino (Paris/Rome). Couchettes and sleeping cars only.
Naples Express (Paris, Turin, Genoa, Pisa, Rome, Naples).
Simplon Express (Paris, Lausanne, Brigue, Domodossola, Milan, Venice, Trieste).
Italia Express (Calais, Lille, Strasbourg, Basle, Milan, Bologna, Florence, Rome).
Many other European trains have through-coaches to the main Italian cities.
ROAD: Road routes from the UK to Italy run through France, Austria, Switzerland and Slovenia and most routes use the tunnels under the Alps and Appennines.
Coach: *Eurolines* run coach services from the UK to the following destinations: Turin, Milan, Bologna, Florence and Rome throughout the year; and Verona, Vicenza, Padua and Venice in summer only. For information on timetables, call *Eurolines*. Tel: (0171) 730 8235 (reservations). **Car:** Italian Railways run regular daily services called 'autotreno' to convey cars, especially during the summer holiday season:
Milan–Genoa–Naples–Villa San Giovanni; Bologna–Naples–Villa San Giovanni. These services operate from special railway stations and are generally bookable at the departure station. Owners must travel on the same train. The documents required are the log-book, valid driving licence with Italian translation, Green Card insurance and national identity plate fixed to the rear of the vehicle. For information on routes, contact the Italian State Tourist Office.
See below for information on required **documentation** and **traffic regulations.**

TRAVEL - Internal

AIR: *Alitalia (AZ)* and other airlines run services to all the major cities. There are over 30 airports. For details, contact the airlines or the Italian State Tourist Office.
SEA: Italy's principal ports are Venice, Genoa, La Spezia, Civitavecchia, Naples, Messina, Cagliari, Bari, Pescara, Ancona, Trieste, Palermo, Catania, Livorno and Brindisi. A number of car and passenger ferries operate throughout the year linking Italian ports. **Ferries:** Regular boat and hydrofoil services run to the islands of Capri, Elba, Giglio, Sardegna (Sardinia), Sicilia (Sicily) and the Aeolian Islands. There are also some links along the coast.
RAIL: There are over 20,000km (12,400 miles) of track in the country, of which slightly over half is electrified. The *Italian State Railways (FS)* run a nationwide network at very reasonable fares, calculated on the distance travelled, and there are a number of excellent reductions. These include the *Tourist Travel Pass* and the *Italy Flexi Railcard* tickets which give almost unlimited travel on all rail services including TEE and 'Rapido' trains, without payment of the supplementary charges which normally apply (however, a supplement *is* payable on high-speed *Pendolino* trains). Tickets on express trains should be booked in advance. Children aged between 4-11 years of age pay half the adult rate. First- and second-class travel is available on most services. Regional timetables (including some bus links) are generally on sale at station bookstalls. For further information, contact Italian State Railways (FS). Tel: (6) 47301 (head office) *or* 487 1270 (information and reservations). Fax: (6) 44 24 16 46. Telex: 622345.
In addition to *FS*, there are also several local railway companies, most of whom run short-distance trains on narrow-gauge track. On Sicily, frequent services run from Palermo and Catania/Siracusa to mainland destinations via the Messina train ferries. There are also local trains which run from Palermo to Agrigento and Catania. On Sardinia, several daily trains run from Cagliari to Porto Torres and Olbia.
ROAD: There are nearly 300,000km (185,500 miles) of roads in Italy, including 6000km (3700 miles) of motorway which link all parts of the country. Tolls are charged at varying distances and scales, except for the Salerno–Reggio Calabria stretch which is toll-free.

Secondary roads are also excellent and require no tolls. Road signs are international. Many petrol stations are closed 1200-1500. Visitors are advised to check locally about exact opening times.
Traffic regulations: Traffic drives on the right. Speed limits are 50kmph (30mph) in urban areas, 80/90kmph (50/60mph) on country roads, 130kmph (80mph) on motorways. Undipped headlights are prohibited in towns and cities, but are compulsory when passing through tunnels. All vehicles must carry a red warning triangle, available at border posts. **Note:** Fines for speeding and other driving offences are on-the-spot and particularly heavy.
Breakdown service: In case of breakdown on any Italian road, dial 116 at the nearest telephone box. Tell the operator where you are, your plate number and type of car and the nearest *ACI Office* will be informed for immediate assistance.
Customs regulations: Visitors must carry their log-book, which must either be in their name as owner or must have the owner's written permission to drive the vehicle. Customs documents for the temporary importation of motor vehicles (also aircraft and pleasure-boats) have been abolished.
Bus: Good coach services run between towns and cities and there are also extensive local buses, including good services on Sicily and Sardinia. In more remote areas, buses will usually connect with rail services.
Taxi: Services are available in and between all cities.
Car hire: Self-drive hire is available in most cities and resorts. Many international and Italian firms operate this service with different rates and conditions. With the larger firms it is possible to book from other countries through the car hire companies, their agents or through the air companies. Generally, small local firms offer cheaper rates, but cars can only be booked locally. Many car rental agencies have booths at the airport or information in hotels. *Avis* has offices in Rome at Via Sardegna (tel: (6) 470 1288) or Via Tiburtina (tel: (6) 413 1414 *or* 412 5429), *Hertz* are at Ciampino Airport (tel: (6) 79 34 06 16), and *Europcar* at Via Lombardia 7 (tel: (6) 48 71 27 41 *or* 487 162). Many special-rate fly/drive deals are available for Italy.
Documentation: Visitors must either carry an international Green Card for their car or motor vehicle (also for boats) or other insurance. A UK driving licence is valid in Italy but green-coloured licences must be accompanied by a translation obtainable free of charge from the RAC, AA, ACI frontier and provincial offices or the Italian State Tourist Office. Motorcycles no longer require customs documents, but refer to the customs regulations above. A driving licence or a motorcycle driving licence is required for motorcycles over 50cc. Passengers are required by law to wear seat belts.
URBAN: All the big towns and cities (Rome, Milan, Naples, Turin, Genoa, Venice) have good public transport networks.
Metro: In Rome there are two underground lines – Metropolitana A from Via Ottaviano via Termini station to Via Anagnina, and Metropolitana B between Termini Station and Exhibition City (EUR) (Via Laurentina). Both day and monthly passes are available. Milan also has a metro service, with tickets usable on both metro and bus, and there are plans to construct one in Turin.
Tram: There is a 28km (17-mile) network consisting of eight routes in Rome; Milan, Naples and Turin also have tram services.
Bus: Services operate in all main cities and towns; in Rome, the network is extensive and complements the metro and tram systems. The fare structure is integrated between the various modes. Buy a flat-fare ticket or a weekly pass in advance from a roadside or station machine. Information is available from the ATAC booth in front of the Termini station. Trolleybuses also run in a number of other towns. In larger cities, fares are generally pre-purchased from machines or shops. Bus fares – generally at a standard rate per run – can be bought in packets of five or multiples and are fed into a stamping machine on boarding the bus.
Taxi: Available in most towns and cities. In Rome they are relatively expensive, with extra charges for night service, luggage and taxis called by telephone. All charges are listed on a rate card displayed in the cab with an English translation. Taxis can only be hailed at strategically located stands or by telephone. Avoid taxis that are not metered. An 8-10% tip is expected by taxi drivers and this is sometimes added to the fare for foreigners.
City tours: *Rome:* Run by many travel agencies, these tours allow first-time visitors to get a general impression of the main sights and enables them to plan further sightseeing. Information is available from the local tourist office. Horse carriages are available in Rome. Charges are high. In *Venice*, privately hired boats and gondolas are available, as well as a public ferry service.
JOURNEY TIMES: The following chart gives approximate journey times (in hours and minutes) from

Rome to other major cities/towns in Italy.

	Air	Road	Rail
Florence	0.45	2.30	2.30
Milan	0.65	6.00	6.00
Venice	0.65	6.00	6.30
Naples	0.45	2.00	2.30
Palermo	0.60	10.00	14.30
Cagliari	0.55	-	-

ACCOMMODATION

HOTELS: There are about 40,000 hotels throughout the country. Every hotel has its fixed charges agreed with the provincial tourist board. Charges vary according to class, season, services available and locality. The Italian State Tourist Office publishes every year the offical list of all Italian hotels and pensions (*Annuario Alberghi*) which can be consulted through one's travel agent or the Italian State Tourist Office. In all hotels and pensions, service charges are included in the rates. VAT (IVA in Italy) operates in all hotels at 10% (19% in deluxe hotels) on room charges only.

Visitors are now required by law to obtain an official receipt when staying at hotels. Rome is well provided with hotels, but it is advisable to book in advance. Rates are high with added extras. To obtain complete prices, ask for quotations of inclusive rates. Cheap hotels, which usually provide basic board (room plus shower), offer an economical form of accommodation throughout Italy, and there is a wide choice in the cities. Again, especially in the main cities, it is wise to book in advance (bookings should always be made through travel agents or hotel representatives). There are many regional hotel associations in Italy; the principal national organisation is FAIAT (Federazione delle Associazioni Italiane Alberghi e Turismo), Via Toscana 1, 00187 Rome. Tel: (6) 474 1151/2/3. Fax: (6) 487 1197. Telex: 613116. **Grading:** Hotels are graded on a scale of **1** to **5 stars**.

MOTELS: Located on motorways and main roads. The biggest chain is AGIP.

FARMHOUSE HOLIDAYS: These are organised in the UK through International Chapters Ltd. (tel: (0171) 722 9560) or Interhome (tel: (0181) 891 1294).

SELF-CATERING: Villas, flats and chalets are available for rent at most Italian resorts. Information is available through daily newspapers and agencies in the UK and from the Italian State Tourist Office or Tourist Office *(Azienda Autonoma di Soggiorno)* of the locality concerned. The latter are also able to advise about boarding with Italian families.

TOURIST VILLAGES: These consist of bungalows and apartments, usually built in or near popular resorts. The bungalows vary in size, but usually accommodate four people and have restaurant facilities.

CAMPING/CARAVANNING: Camping is very popular in Italy. The local Tourist Office in the nearest town will give information and particulars of the most suitable sites. On the larger campsites it is possible to rent tents/caravans. There are over 1600 campsites and full details of the sites can be obtained in the publication *Campeggi e Villaggi Turistici In Italia*, published by the Touring Club Italiano and Federcampeggio. An abridged list of sites with location map, *Carta d'Italia Parchi Campeggio*, can be obtained free of charge by writing to Centro Internazionale Prenotazione, Federcampeggio, Casella Postale 23, 50041 Calenzano (Firenze). Tel: (55) 882 391. Telex: 570397. The Italian State Tourist Office may also be able to supply information.

The tariffs at Italian campsites vary according to the area and the type of campsite. There are discounts for members of the AIT, FICC and FIA. Usually there is no charge for children under three years of age. The Touring Club Italiano offers campsites already equipped with fixed tents, restaurants, etc. For details write to TCI, Corso Italia 10, 20122 Milano. Tel: (2) 85261. Fax: (2) 852 6362. Telex: 321160. To book places in advance on campsites belonging to the International Campsite Booking Centre, it is necessary to write to Centro Internazionale Prenotazioni Campeggio, Casella Postale 23, 50041 Calenzano (Firenze), asking for the list of the campsites with the booking form.

YOUTH HOSTELS: There are 52 youth hostels run by the Italian Youth Hostels Association (*Associazione Italiana Alberghi per la Gioventù*) throughout Italy. Listing and opening dates can be obtained from the Italian State Tourist Office, Via Marghera 2, 00185 Rome, Italy. Tel: (6) 49711. Fax: (6) 496 3379. During the summer season, in the major cities, reservations are essential and must be applied for direct to the hostel at least 15 days in advance, specifying dates and numbers. There are also student hostels in several towns.

RESORTS & EXCURSIONS

For ease and speed of reference, the country has been divided into the following areas: Northern Italy

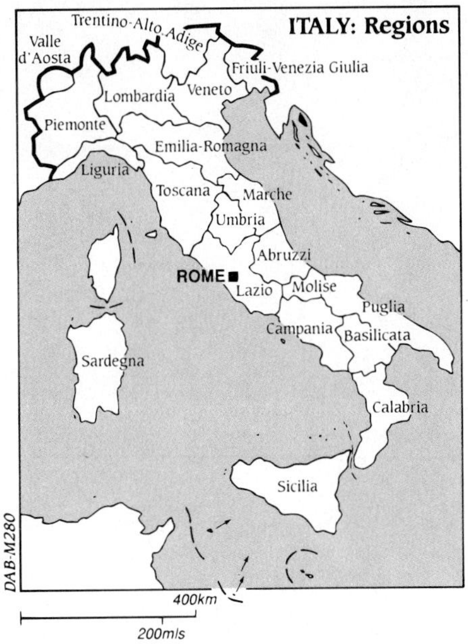

(including the cities of Turin, Milan, Venice, Bologna, Genoa, Trieste and Vicenza); Central Italy (including the cities of Florence, Pisa, Ancona, Perugia, Rome, Pescara and Campobasso); Southern Italy (including the cities of Naples, Bari, Potenza and Catanzaro, as well as the resort towns in the Bay of Naples); and The Islands (Sicily and Sardinia). Main holiday resorts are included in each section, as well as important religious sites, business centres and a brief mention of the region's art history.

Northern Italy

(Administrative *Regioni:* Valle d'Aosta, Piemonte, Lombardy, Liguria, Trentino-Alto Adige, Veneto, Emilia-Romagna and Friuli-Venezia Giulia.)

VALLE D'AOSTA: A ruggedly scenic region at the foot of Europe's highest mountains – Mont Blanc, Monte Rosa, Cervino (Matterhorn) and Gran Paradiso – bordering France and Switzerland. Valle d'Aosta is politically autonomous and to some extent culturally distinct from the rest of Italy; French is spoken as a first language by most of the inhabitants. The picturesque ruins of countless castles and other fortifications testify to the region's immense strategic significance before the era of air travel, it being the gateway to two of the most important routes through the Alps, the Little and Great St Bernard Passes. Tourism, wine-growing, pasturing and iron-working are the major industries.

Aosta, the principal city, has many well-preserved Roman and medieval buildings. It was founded in the first century by the Emperor Augustus as a settlement *(colonia)* for discharged soldiers of the elite Pretorian Guard. The massive Roman city walls are almost complete and, within them, the old town retains the grid-iron street plan characteristic of all such military townships. Two impressive gateways, the *Porta Pretoria,* formed the main entrance into the old Roman town and a medieval noble family lived in its tower, which now houses temporary exhibitions. Further ancient Roman sites include the *Teatro Romano,* where theatrical presentations are still shown on a platform overlooking the old theatre; *Arco di Augusto,* erected in 25BC to honour the Emperor Augustus (for whom the city is named – Aosta being a corruption of Augustus); the *Forum* and the still well-intact *Roman Bridge,* which once arched gracefully over the River Buthier, now entirely dried up.

There are several fine ski resorts in the area (see below under *Ski Resorts*), most notably **Courmayeur** and **Breuil-Cervinia**.

Ibexes may be seen in the **Gran Paradiso National Park**, a popular destination for hill-walkers and climbers. The *Mont Blanc Tunnel* has largely superseded the St Bernard Passes as a major overland freight route.

PIEMONTE: The densely populated Upper Po Basin is the site of Italy's most important heavy industries, a vast plain pinned to the earth by gargantuan factories and held flat by a harness of motorways. By contrast, the mountains to the west, on the border with France, are sparsely populated and have a wholly pastoral economy. To the north is *Lake Maggiore*, the most elegant of the north Italian lakes and popular since Roman times as a retreat for city-dwellers.

The best-known **wines** of this region are *Barolo*, Italy's most celebrated red, and *Asti Spumante*, a sparkling white. *Barolo* wine is produced in the hills surrounding the town of **Alba,** where there are a number of wine museums. Alba itself is one of the region's most interesting towns, with medieval towers, Baroque and Renaissance architecture, and cobbled streets full of specialist delicatessens and shops. The most exciting time to visit is during the month of October, when the *October Festival* (involving a donkey race and displays of medieval pageantry) and the *Truffle Festival* are celebrated. *Asti Spumante* is produced just outside the town of **Asti,** a normally quiet little town, except during the month of September when it holds its annual *Palio* and comes suddenly alive with street banquets, medieval markets, an historic 14th-century parade and a bare-backed horse race around the arena of *Campo del Palio.*

Torino (Turin) is the largest city in the region and the fourth-largest in the country. For the first few decades of this century, it was the automobile capital of the world. It was here that the Futurists became so excited with the potential of mechanised transport that they declared Time dead – henceforth, they naïvely declared, everything would be measured in terms of speed alone. The city remains the focus of Italy's automobile industry. *Fiat* offer guided tours of their headquarters, where a full-scale test track may be found on the roof. Turin does, of course, add up to far more than an infatuation with motor- cars. The inhabitants boast that, with its broad, tree-lined avenues flanked by tall, handsome townhouses, it is *La Parigi d'Italia*, the Italian Paris. Uptown Turin is centred on the main shopping street, *Via Roma,* which links the city's favourite square, the *Piazza San Carlo,* with its most dramatic building, the baroque *Palazzo Madama,* which houses the *Museum of Ancient Art,* one of several nationally important museums in the city. The *Turin Shroud* may be viewed in the 15th-century white marble *Cathedral*.

LOMBARDIA: A prosperous region with fertile soil, a temperate climate and, for the tourist, the spectacular lakes *Como, Garda, Maggiore* (shared with Piemonte) and *Lugano.* As in Piemonte, the *Po Valley* is the site of much heavy industry. High mountains in the north, marking Italy's frontier with Switzerland, provide excellent skiing and climbing. Lombardia's most famous culinary inventions are *minestrone* soup and *osso buco* – literally ox knuckles.

Milan is Italy's most sophisticated city, a financial and commercial centre of world importance and a rival to Paris in the spheres of modern art and fashion. Its international character is marked by a concentration of skyscrapers found nowhere else in Italy, contrasting and competing with the landmarks of historic Milan, but built in the same boastful spirit of civic pride that, 500 years ago, gave the city its splendid Gothic *Duomo.* Even today, this is the world's second-largest church, yet despite its size, it creates an impression of delicate and ethereal beauty due to its pale colour and the fine intricate carving that covers its exterior. The whole fabric of the city – its many palaces, piazzas and churches – speaks of centuries of continuous prosperity. The *Castello Sforzesco*, in the west of the city, is a massive fortified castle, begun by the Viscontis and finished by the Sforzas. It was the political and social bastion of the ruling Sforzas during Milan's peak as a political/cultural centre and many of the Renaissance elite were entertained in its luxurious domains. Its court artists included Leonardo da Vinci and Bramante and it now houses a number of museums. Leonardo da Vinci's famous fresco, *The Last Supper,* may be viewed at the convent of *Santa Maria della Grazie*. The *Teatro della Scala* remains the undisputed world capital of opera and is well worth viewing for its magnificent opulence.

Just south of Milan is the town of **Pavia**, the ancient capital known as 'the city of 100 towers'. One of these, the *Torre Civica*, suddenly collapsed in 1989, killing four people. The town also has many interesting churches, including the Renaissance *Duomo,* thought to have been worked on by Bramante and da Vinci; the Romanesque *San Michele,* with an elaborately carved façade; and the 12th-century *San Pietro in Ciel d'Oro,* with a magnificent 14th-century altarpiece. The *Broletto,* Pavia's medieval town hall, and the 14th-century *Castello,* housing an art gallery, archaeology museum and sculpture museum, are also worth visiting. Though sedate and resting in an air of dusty elegance by day, Pavia bursts into life at night when its people come out for their evening promenade and the streets seem to buzz with activity. The *Certosa di Pavia,* 10km (6 miles) outside of town, is a monastery famous for its lavish design. Originating as the family mausoleum of the Visconti family, it was later finished by the Sforzas and became the dwellings for a Carthusian order of monks sworn to deep contemplation and for whom speech is forbidden. However, a chosen few are allowed to give visitors a guided tour and tell the story behind their palatial surroundings.

Cremona, the birthplace of the Stradivarius violin, is a

Your Clients will take pleasure in being our Customer.

Hertz. Your holiday car hire company for Italy

Hertz rents Fords and other fine cars.

To get to know a country, you need a car. A car gives you that special freedom to travel and explore, which gives you a range of options to suit your holiday moods and tastes.

With four wheels, you see more and experience more - which is what holidays are all about. And with a Hertz car, you get the extra benefits of guaranteed quality and flexibility for even greater enjoyment.

Italy offers so much more than pastas and piazzas. It's a country full of style, elegance and culture - a diverse land with olive groves and vineyards, lakes and volcanoes. But you need to discover it - by car.

You can experience the true taste of Italy by letting Hertz put you in the driving seat. In fact, Hertz has been leading the world in car rental for more than 75 years. Wherever we are in the world, we adhere to the principles that have made us successful - excellent service and efficient organisation.

Why? Because we want you to enjoy your holiday - free from worry, free from constraint. It's as simple as that.

charming haven of historic architecture. A walk around the medieval *Piazza del Comune* offers various architectural treats: the *Torazzo*, one of Italy's tallest medieval towers; the *Duomo*, with its magnificent astrological clock; and the *Loggia dei Militia*, the former headquarters of the town's medieval army. There are also two interesting museums: the *Museo Strativariano*, housing a wealth of Stradivarius musical instruments, and the *Museo Civico*, with more Stadivari and some interesting bits and pieces belonging to Garibaldi.
Mantua was another Lombardia bastion of the ruling dynasties of the Viscontis and Sforzas. It is also the birthplace of a number of renowned Italians, ranging from Virgil (a statue of whom overlooks the square facing the *Broletto*, the medieval town hall) to Tazio Nuvolone, one of Italy's most famous racing drivers (for whom there is a small museum dedicated to his accomplishments). Its churches, *Sant'Andrea* (designed by Alberti and the burial place of Mantua's famous court painter, Mantegna) and the Baroque *Duomo* in the *Piazza Sordello* are both important works of architecture. However, the most famous sites of Mantua are its two palaces: the *Palazzo Ducale* and the *Palazzo del Te*. The Palazzo Ducale, once the largest in Europe, was the home of the Gonzagas family, and has a number of impressive paintings by artists such as Rubens and Mantegna. The Palazzo del Te was built as a Renaissance pleasure palace for Frederico Gonzaga (known as a playboy) and his mistress, Isabella. The decorations by Giulio Romano are outstanding and well worth viewing.
Bergamo, nestled at the foot of the Bergamese Alps, is made up of two cities – the old and once Venetian-ruled *Bergamo Alta* (upper Bergamo) and the modern *Bergamo Bassa* (lower Bergamo). The old city is well appreciated for its ancient Venetian fortifications, palaces, towers and churches, including the 12th-century *Palazzo della Ragione*, the *Torre del Comune*, the *Duomo* of Bergamo, *Colleoni Chapel* and the *Church of Santa Maria Maggiore*. The modern city's main attraction is the *Accademia Carrara*, one of Italy's largest art collections, with paintings by Canaletto, Botticelli, Mantegna, Carpaccio, Bellini and Lotto, amongst others. The two cities are connected by a funicular railway.
The great northern **lakes** lie in a series of long, deep valleys running down onto the plains from the Alps. Lake Garda is perhaps the wildest and most spectacular, Como the most attractive and Maggiore the most elegant (and populous). Lake Lugano lies for the most part in Switzerland.
Resorts on *Lake Maggiore* include: Pallanza (where the Villa Taranto has a fine botanical garden), Stresa, Arona, Intra and Orta; on *Lake Como:* Cadenabbia, Cernobbio, Bellagio, Tremezzo and Menaggio; and on *Lake Garda:* Limone, Sirmione, Desenzano and Gardone.
The major **mountain resorts**, winter and summer, are Livigno (duty-free area), Madesimo, Stelvio, Santa Caterina Valfurva, Bormio, Aprica and Chiesa.
LIGURIA: 320km (200 miles) of rocky, wooded coastline running from France to Tuscany, where the Italian 'boot' begins. This is the *Riviera*, Italy's answer to the Côte d'Azur, and there are ample facilities for tourists even in the smallest of ports. The coastal hills are less developed.
Genoa, capital of Liguria, has long been an important commercial and military port. The medieval district of the city holds many treasures, such as the *Porta Soprana* (the old stone entrance gate to the city), the *Church of Sant'Agostino* (next to the *Museo dell'Architectura e Scultura Ligure),* the beautiful *Church of San Donato*, the 12th-century *Church of Santa Maria di Castello* and the Gothic *Cattedrale di San Lorenzo*. Outside the medieval district, *Via Garibaldi*, where many of the city's richest inhabitants built their palaces, is a beautiful walk, with *Palazzo Podesta*, *Palazzo Bianco* (now an art gallery with paintings by Van Dyck and Rubens) and the magnificently decorated *Palazzo Rosso* (adjacent to Palazzo Bianco and housing paintings by Titian, Caravaggio and Dürer). A tour (once daily in the afternoon) around the Genoa harbour is available, and the city is also recommended for its excellent shopping opportunities.
Ligurian **resorts** are very popular with holidaymakers.
Portofino is one of the best known, with its small picturesque harbour full of sleek pleasure yachts, luxury clothes shops, its romantic villas owned by the rich and famous perched on the hillside and the *Castello di San Giorgio*, sitting high up on a promontory with magnificent views of the Portofino harbour and bay. The beach at **Santa Margherita Ligure**, just 5km (3 miles) south of Portofino, is an excellent place to swim, with an almost fairytale swimmer's-eye view of the surrounding cliffs and villas from the warm and crystal-clear aquamarine water. Nearby **Rapallo**, 8km (5 miles) south of Portofino, is a less fashionable but more reasonable town to stay in and is recommended for those seeking a more lively alternative to the quieter and more exclusive

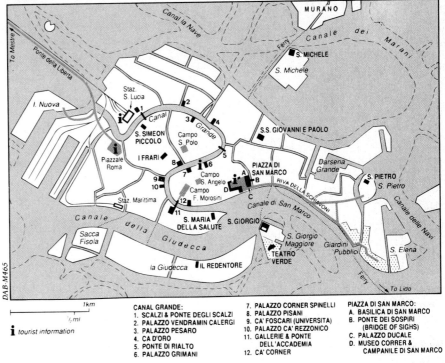

VENICE

CANAL GRANDE:
1. SCALZI & PONTE DEGLI SCALZI
2. PALAZZO VENDRAMIN CALERGI
3. PALAZZO PESARO
4. CA D'ORO
5. PONTE DI RIALTO
6. PALAZZO GRIMANI
7. PALAZZO CORNER SPINELLI
8. PALAZZO PISANI
9. CA' FOSCARI (UNIVERSITA)
10. PALAZZO CA' REZZONICO
11. GALLERIE & PONTE DELL'ACCADEMIA
12. CA' CORNER
PIAZZA DI SAN MARCO:
A. BASILICA DI SAN MARCO
B. PONTE DEI SOSPIRI (BRIDGE OF SIGHS)
C. PALAZZO DUCALE
D. MUSEO CORRER & CAMPANILE DI SAN MARCO

1km
1/2 mi
i *tourist information*

resorts of Portofino and Santa Margherita. Other resorts in this region include Ventimiglia, San Remo, Diano Marina, Alassio, Pietra Ligure, Spotorno, Sestri Levante, Lerici and the Cinque Terre, five relatively unspoilt fishing villages.
TRENTINO & ALTO ADIGE: These wholly mountainous regions on the Swiss border straddle the valley of the River Isarco, which flows from the *Brenner Pass* down into Lake Garda. Germanic and Italian cultures blend here to the extent that, towards the north, German is increasingly found as the first language. *The Dolomites* to the east are a range of distinctively craggy mountains, isolated to such an extent from both Italy and Switzerland that in the more remote valleys the inhabitants speak Ladin, an ancient Romance language not much different from Latin.
Trento is the principal town of Trentino and is worth visiting for its wealth of art works, gathered by the dynasty of princes who ruled the area from the 10th-18th centuries. Many of these artistic acquisitions are viewable in the town's museums, which include the *Castello di Buonconsiglio, Museo Provinciale d'Arte* and the *Museo Diocesano Trentino.*
Bolzano is the principal town of Alto Aldige, further north. A somewhat austere commercial town, it appears as an unlikely portal to one of the most extraordinary panoramic drives in Italy – the mountain route through the Dolomites to Cortina d'Ampezzo called *La Grande Strada delle Dolomiti*. Upon entering the *Val d'Ega*, at the beginning of the route, the scenery is suddenly lush with foliage and rocks as the light seeps through the forest trees. About 20km (12 miles) from the beginning of the route is *Lake Carezza*, a beautiful limpid pool of bright green water reflecting the trees and mountains around it. This is just the beginning of an awe-inspiring passage through the Dolomites and its small alpine towns, ski resorts and endless panoramas of craggy peaks and tree-clad mountainsides.
One of the most famous mountain resorts and the second largest town in this region is **Merano**, 28km (17 miles) north of Bolzano. Popular for its spas, thermal waters and moderate climate (the temperature tends to remain above freezing all winter, despite its close proximity to a range of snow-laden ski slopes), it is also visually rewarding, with extensive landscaped gardens and a charming mixture of architectural styles from Gothic to Art Nouveau. Other **mountain resorts** in the region include Solda, Selva di Val Gardena, Santa Cristina, Oritsei, Corvara, Bressanone, Brunico, Vipiteno, Madonna di Campiglio, Canazei, Moena, Pozza di Fassa, San Martino di Castrozza and Riva, which lies at the top of Lake Garda.
VENETO: The *Lower Po Valley*, the eastern bank of Lake Garda and the eastern Dolomites, occupying what was once the Republic of Venice.
Venezia (Venice) stands on an island in a lagoon at the northern end of the Adriatic Sea, a position which gave it

unique economic and defensive advantages over its trading rivals. Much of the wealth generated was, of course, invested in the construction of monuments to the glory of both God and the merchants, and Venice must be counted as one of the highlights of any tour of Italy. The city's main monuments – the *Doge's Palace, St Mark's Square* and the *Bridge of Sighs* – have gained fame through the innumerable paintings representing them, not least by such artists as Canaletto, but the whole city is in many ways a work of art. Away from the main thoroughfares, it is characterised by little canals, small squares (often containing remarkable Gothic churches) and above all, since it contains no motor traffic, by serenity – the city's ancient name was 'La Serenissima'. One of the most evocative representations of Venice must be in Thomas Mann's book, *Death in Venice.*
Note: The causeway linking the city with the mainland can become very clogged with traffic. Although there is a large car park on the island, it is often easier to park at one of several near the north end of the causeway and continue by foot, bus or taxi; there are also trains connecting with boats.
The Venetian aristocracy built many villas in the surrounding countryside; some, including the *Villa Pisani* at *Stra* and the *Villa Valmarana* at **Vicenza,** are open to the public.
Popular **Adriatic resorts** include Lido di Iesolo, Bibione and Caorle.
The city of **Padua** is famous for the great *Basilica of St Antony;* St Antony himself was buried here and it is an important pilgrimage site. The city also contains works by Giotto (Scrovegni Chapel frescoes) and Donatello. Nearby, **Abano** and **Montegrotto** provide fully equipped thermal establishments for the treatment of many rheumatic complaints.
Vicenza is the birthplace of Andrea Palladio, whose published analyses of ancient architecture did much to spread the Renaissance throughout Europe. His buildings here include the *Basilica Palladiana* and the *Palazzo Chiericatai.*
Verona, historically associated, among other things, with Shakespeare (*Romeo and Juliet* and *The Two Gentlemen of Verona*) contains a well-preserved *Roman Arena* (operas are staged there in summer), and the lovely but austere *Church of San Zeno*. This graceful city is surrounded by a river and there are many beautiful bridges, as well as churches, squares and markets.
Cortina d'Ampezzo is Italy's best-known (but not most challenging) ski resort. The Winter Olympics were held here in 1956. It makes a fine base for exploring the Dolomites in summer.
EMILIA-ROMAGNA: A region of gentle hills between the *River Po* and the *Appennines*. As elsewhere in the Po Basin, intensive agriculture is pursued alongside heavy industry.
Bologna is one of the oldest cities in Italy and the site of Europe's oldest university. Often overlooked as a tourist

destination, it nevertheless possesses a distinctive charm, due largely to the imaginative use of brickwork. Arcades flanking many of the streets add to the appeal. Notable buildings include the *Cathedral of San Pietro,* the huge Gothic *Church of San Petronio,* numerous palaces and the *Leaning Towers* of the *Piazza di Porta Ravegnana.* The city is also the home of Bolognese meat sauce and the Bologna sausage.

Parma boasts a fine Romanesque cathedral and baptistry, and an opera house with strong connections with Verdi, who lived at nearby **Sant'Agata.**

Italy's most celebrated poet, Dante, is buried at **Ravenna**, the ancient capital of the western Roman Empire during its decline under Gothic and Byzantine domination. The city's former importance is marked by the profusion of extravagant mosaics found in its many Romanesque buildings. The *International School of Mosaics* at Ravenna is open to foreigners.

Faenza (known to the French as 'Faience') is famed for its majolica pottery. This craft has enjoyed a resurgence in recent years under the direction of the *Faenza International Institute of Ceramics.*

Other cities in Emilia-Romagna include **Modena** and **Ferrara**, both with many fine palaces associated with the Este family; and **Reggio**, the old provincial capital.

Adriatic resorts include: Rimini, Riccione, Cattolica, Milano, Marittima and Cesenatico, all within easy reach of the tiny Republic of San Marino (see the entry on *San Marino* later in this book).

FRIULI-VENEZIA GIULIA: A region in the northeastern corner of Italy bordering Austria and Slovenia. It has changed hands many times over the centuries and Friulian society is a complex mix of cultures. Half of the population speak Friulian, a language closely allied to ancient Latin.

In the 18th century, the Austrian Emperors commissioned the construction of a deep-water port at **Trieste** and so ended Venice's long domination of the Adriatic Sea. The port has remained the most important in the area and, following the collapse of the Austro-Hungarian Empire after the First World War, was ceded to Italy. This arrangement was not finally formalised until 1962, when a long-running border dispute with the then Yugoslavia was settled with the aid of the United Nations. Although there are several Roman remains (most notably the 2nd-century theatre), the most prominent buildings are no older than the port.

The coast west of Trieste has some excellent **beach resorts**. Sistiana, Duino, Lignano and Grado are among the most popular.

Inland are **Udine** and **Pordenone**, agricultural centres on the fertile Friuli plain. Further north are the foothills of the eastern *Dolomites* and the *Julian Alps* (part of Slovenia) where ski resorts are now being developed. The road from Udine to Villach in Austria is an important overland freight route; it winds up the dramatic valley of the *Isonzo,* a river rendered an astonishing shade of blue by minerals leached from the Julian Alps.

SKI RESORTS: The majority of the Italian ski resorts are in the Alps and in the Dolomites, although there are also a few in the Appennines and it is possible to ski along the slopes of *Mount Etna* in Sicily (see relevant sections below). The following examples all have hotels, boarding houses and/or self-catering and are equipped with first-class lift systems. For further details, contact the Italian State Tourist Office in London, tour operators or travel agents.

Valle d'Aosta: Cervinia, Courmayeur, Chamois, Gressoney, La Thuille, Pila, Valtournenche.

Piemonte: Bardonecchia, Claviere, Limone-Piemonte, Macugnaga, Sauze d'Oulx, Sestriere, Sportinia.

Lombardia: Aprica, Bormio, Chiesa di Valmalenco, Foppolo, Livigno, Madesimo, Ponte di Legno, Santa Caterina di Valfurva, Tonale.

Trentino: Andalo, Canazei, Madonna di Campiglio, Marilleva, Pozza di Fassa, San Martino di Castrozza.

Alto Adige (Südtirol): Alpi di Siusi (Seiseralm), Campo Tures (Sand in Taufers), Colfosco (Kolfuschg), Corvara in Badia (Kurfar), Crontour area (ten localities), including Brunico (Bruneck) and San Vigilio di Marebbe (St Vigil in Enneberg), Dobbiaco (Toblach), Nova Levante (Welschnofen), Ortisei (St Ulrich), Passo Stelvio (Stilfserjoch) (only summer skiing), Renon (Ritten), San Candido (Innichen), Santa Cristina Valgardena (St Christina), Selva di Val Gardena (Wolkenstein), Val Senales (Schnalstal).

Friuli-Venezia Giulia: Piancavallo, Sella Nevea.

Veneto: Alleghe, Arabba, Ravascletto, Cortina d'Ampezzo, Falcade.

Central Italy

(Administrative *Regioni:* Tuscany, Marche, Umbria, Abruzzi, Molise and Lazio.)

TUSCANY: This fertile region lies between the northern Appennines and the Mediterranean Sea. The landscape of Tuscany is, typically, one of vine-covered hills, cypress woods, fields of sunflowers and remote hilltop villages. *Chianti,* the best-known Italian wine, is made here. There are a number of **volcanic spas**, most notably *Montecatini, Bagni di Lucca, Casciana Terme* and *Chianciano.*

Florence (Firenze), the principal Tuscan city, is the world's most celebrated storehouse of Renaissance art and architecture. Set on the banks of the *Arno* below the wooded foothills of the Appennines, this beautiful city has long been the focus of Italian arts and letters. Dante, Boccaccio, Petrarch, Giotto, Leonardo da Vinci, Michelangelo, Brunelleschi, Alberti, Masaccio, Donatello, Botticelli, Vasari and Fra Angelico are among the many associated with establishing the pre-eminence of the city. Brunelleschi's revolutionary design for the dome of the *Cathedral of Santa Maria del Fiore* is

FLORENCE

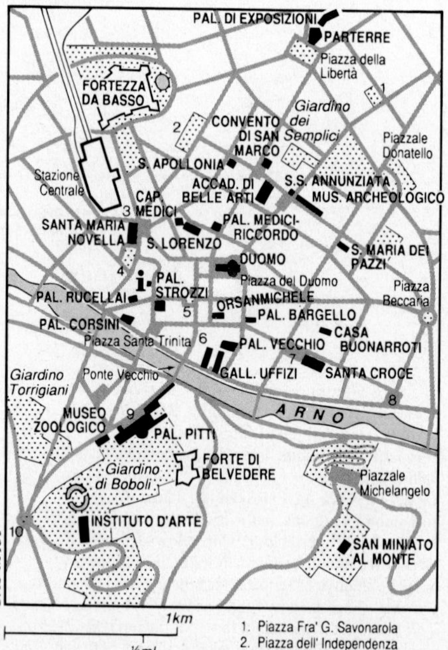

i tourist information

1. Piazza Fra' G. Savonarola
2. Piazza dell' Independenza
3. Piazza della Stazione
4. Piazza Santa Maria Novella
5. Piazza della Repubblica
6. Piazza della Signoria
7. Piazza Santa Croce
8. Piazza Piave 9. Piazza de' Pitti
10. Piazzale della Porta Romana

generally accepted as the first expression of Renaissance ideas in architecture. This dome still dominates the city's roofscape, just as the great *Piazza del Duomo* at its feet dominates life at street level. The square is ringed with cafés and is a popular meeting point. Between there and the river are many of the best-loved palaces – including *Palazzo Strozzi, Palazzo Corsini, Palazzo Rucellai, Palazzo Vecchio* and the *Uffizi Gallery* – whilst close by to the north are the churches of *Santa Maria Novella* and *San Lorenzo* (by Brunelleschi, Michelangelo and others), and the *Palazzo Medici-Ricccordi.* The *Palazzo Pitti* and the *Boboli Gardens* are just across the river (via the Ponte Vecchio).

The *Uffizi Gallery* houses a celebrated art collection – indeed it claims to hold the finest collections of paintings anywhere in the world. Examples of work start from the transition period when Europe was emerging from the Middle Ages, largely represented by religious paintings and icons (notably by Lorenzo Monaco, Giottino and Gentile da Fabriano), through the highpoint of the Renaissance to the early 18th century. Some of the most famous paintings of each period are in the Uffizi, such as Botticelli's *Birth Of Venus,* Leonardo da Vinci's *Annunciation,* Michelangelo's *Holy Family,* Titian's *Urbino Venus* and Caravaggio's *Young Bacchus.* One of the most striking paintings is the *Medusa* by Caravaggio. Michelangelo's famous statue of *David* may be viewed at the *Accademia di Belle Arti* near the University.

Siena's most prosperous era pre-dated the Renaissance and consequently much of the fabric of the city is in the older Gothic and Romanesque styles. There is a fine Gothic and Romanesque *Cathedral* built in stunning black and white marble with a magnificent interior (visitors dressed inappropriately, ie in short skirts, shorts or skimpy shirts, will be denied entry). The *Piazza del Campo,* overlooked by the giant *campanile* of the *Palazzo Pubblico,* is possibly the most complete Gothic piazza in Italy. The city is an important religious centre, being the birthplace of St Catherine, and there is a church here devoted to her worship. The 700-year-old university holds a summer school in Italian. Siena is probably most famous for its *Palios,* bare-backed horse races which take place every year on July 2 and August 16 around the huge *Campo* in the centre of Siena. It has been a special event since the 14th century and attracts crowds from all over the world.

Pisa, north of Siena, is famous for its *Leaning Tower,* a free-standing *campanile* or bell tower associated with the 11th-century Gothic *Cathedral* nearby. Near the *Quadrilateral* is the *Campo Santo Cemetery.* Built in the 13th century to enclose earth brought from Jerusalem, it is a unique collonaded quadrangle in the Tuscan Gothic style.

Other towns of note in Tuscany include **Lucca**, famous for its one hundred churches and robust city walls; **San Gimignano,** known as the 'city of beautiful towers' and one of the best-preserved medieval towns in Italy; **Volterra,** another beautifully preserved medieval town perched on a hilltop; **Livorno** (Leghorn), the principal commercial port; and **Carrara**, where high-grade white marble has been quarried since Etruscan times.

The coast of Tuscany offers many sandy beaches. Popular **beach resorts** include Viareggio, Forte dei Marmi, Lido di Camaiore, Marina di Pietrasanta, Marina di Massa, Tirrenia, Castiglione della Pescaia, San Vincenzo, Castiglioncello, Quercianella, Porto Santo Stefano, Porto Ercole, Ansedonia and Talamone.

The **Tuscan Archipelago** is a group of scattered islands lying between Tuscany and Corsica. The best known are Elba and Giglio. There are regular hydrofoil and ferry links with mainland ports. **Elba** is 17.5km (28 miles) long and 7.5km (12 miles) wide, and can be reached by steamer or hydrofoil from *Piombino.* Famous as the place where Napoleon was briefly exiled before his final defeat at Waterloo, it has lovely beaches and campsites shaded by pines. Napoleon's two homes can be visited: one, the *Palazzina Napoleonica dei Mulini,* which he created out of two windmills, situated near the *Forte della Stella,* **Portoferraio** and the other, 6km (4 miles) away, the *Villa Napoleonica di San Martino,* which he set up as his country seat. Near to this villa is the *Pinacoteca Foresiana,* a neo-classical art gallery built in 1851.

MARCHE: A mountainous agricultural region on the central Adriatic coast south of San Marino.

Ancona, the regional capital and largest town in the region, is an important naval and commercial port with several well-preserved Roman remains such as the *Arco di Traiano* and the *Resti di Anfiteatro Romano.*

Urbino was once Italy's greatest seat of learning and is now a pleasant Renaissance hilltown, its skyline a soaring vista of domes and towers. Also the birthplace of Raphael, several of his works may be viewed in the art gallery at the *Ducal Palace,* along with works by Piero della Francesca and Titian. Raphael's childhood home is also open for viewing.

Loreto is said to be the site of the house of the Virgin Mary and attracts many pilgrims from around the world. According to legend, the house was moved from Nazareth in the 13th century to protect it from marauding Muslims. Angels carried it first to the Balkans then on to Loreto; the journey took four years. The house is enclosed in the elaborate Gothic *Sanctuaria della Santa Casa.* The *Madonna of Loreto* was elected patron saint of airmen in 1920.

Popular **beach resorts** include: Gabicce, Pesaro (Rossini's birthplace), Fano, Senigallia, Civitanova, San Benedetto del Tronto, Porto Recanati and Porto Potenza Picena. As elsewhere on the Adriatic coast, beach resorts tend to be highly organised, with tables and sun loungers laid out in neat lines (often very close together). More informal beaches may be found below the spectacular Costa Conero cliffs a few miles south of Ancona.

UMBRIA: A mountainous inland region between Tuscany and Marche. There is very little industry here and few towns of any great size. The principal agricultural products are corn, olives, sugar beet, tobacco, wine and wool.

Perugia, the region's capital, has been continuously inhabited for more than 25 centuries and contains many Etruscan and Roman remains, with well-preserved buildings reflecting every era in the subsequent development of Italian architecture. Particularly notable are the ancient Etruscan city walls. *L'Università per Stranieri* offers courses for foreigners wishing to study Italian language and civilisation.

Assisi is a picturesque medieval hilltown to the east of Perugia. Famous as the home of St Francis, founder of the Franciscan Order of monks, it attracts many tourists. The life of St Francis is commemorated in 28 frescoes by Giotto in the *Basilica di San Francesco,* Italy's earliest Gothic church.

Arezzo, set on a hillside, has both a strong modern and

medieval aspect. The *Medici Fortress* and the *Cathedral,* built in the 13th-16th centuries, stand majestically on the hilltop overlooking the modern part of town which sits on the plain below. The *Piazza Grande* is a wonderful medieval square with an old well in the centre, surrounded by impressive historic buildings on all sides: the *Palazzetto della Fraternità,* the *Church of Santa Maria della Pieve* and *Loggiato del Vasari* (once the residence of Vasari, art historian and patron of many of Italy's most famous painters). The *Basilica di San Francesco* contains the famous frescoes of Piero della Francesca, *Story of the Cross.* Amidst all this history, the city still thrives today and is now the centre of the antique trade.

Other important Umbrian towns include **Spoleto**, host to an annual festival of music, drama and dance; **Orvieto**, perched on a volcanic outcrop rising from the Umbrian lowlands; and **Città di Castello**, mountain stronghold of the Vitelli family.

ABRUZZI: This region encompasses the highest parts of the great Appennine chain. The northern mountains are generally too desolate for agriculture and much of the land is sparsely populated. A **ski resort** has been built in the limestone massif of **Gran Sasso**. The southern uplands are covered with a great forest of beech, which has been designated a national park. Marsican brown bears (unique to Italy), wolves, chamois and eagles may be seen here. **L'Aquila**, the principal city, contains an imposing castle. **Celano** is an interesting town, dominated by a turreted castle whose fortified walls provide a walkway around the castle offering picturesque views over the surrounding hilly countryside. The rest of the town appears to be thriving with active and trendy young people, which projects a surprising contrast to the staid medieval architecture.

Tagliocozzo, named after the Greek muse of Theatre, appears at first sight to be just like any other town until one discovers the old Renaissance square with its 14th-15th-century houses and lantern-lit alleys twisting around behind it. A stroll through this area at night is a remarkable experience.

The main **Adriatic resorts** are Giulianova, Silvi Marina, Francavilla and Montesilvano. Pescara is, as its name implies, primarily a fishing port.

MOLISE: One of the poorest parts of mainland Italy, this area is mountainous with poor soil and a scattered population. It does, however, possess its own rugged beauty. The Matese mountain range is still the haven of wolves and various birds of prey. It also offers some excellent skiing resorts and tends not to be as overcrowded as some of Italy's other skiing areas. The winter sports centre of **Campitello Matese** is well recommended and for those looking for a quiet place to retreat after a day's skiing, the town of **San Massimo** is an excellent place to stay, with its peaceful lamplit streets and hospitable people. The largest cities in the region are the industrial towns of **Isernia** and **Campobasso**. The only Adriatic resort of any size is **Vasto**.

LAZIO: On the western side of the Italian 'boot', this is a region of volcanic hills, lakes and fine beaches.

Rome, the 'eternal city', exerts an enduring fascination over its countless visitors. Capital of Italy and the country's largest city, it is littered with the relics of over 2000 years of history. Only in very few places in the world is the visitor confronted with the past in such an immediate and forceful way. It has a unique atmosphere. The monuments of ancient times and the splendours of the Baroque are the backdrop to the hectic buzz of swarming scooters, bellowing motorists and animated street cafés.

The streets contain reminders of all the eras in Rome's rich history – the *Colosseum* and the *Forum* are the most famous from the classical period, ancient basilicas bear witness to the early Christian era. As the major city of the Counter Reformation, it is not surprising that Rome is also infused with the feel of the Baroque. It is, indeed, the influence of the 17th century which defines the city through the work of architects such as Bernini, Maderno and Borromini. The magnificent squares and flamboyant façades mask a wealth of painting and sculpture by some of the greatest high-Rennaisance and Baroque artists – Michelangelo, Bernini, Caravaggio, Caracci and Raphael to name but a few.

The *Via del Corso*, Rome's main thoroughfare, cuts through the length of the city centre from the *Piazza Venezia* in the south with the vast marble *Vittorio Emanuele Monument* (erected in the late 19th century to honour Italy's first king and to commemorate the unification of Italy), to emerge in the *Piazza del Popolo* in the north, beyond which lies the cool green refuge of the *Villa Borghese*. To the east of the *Via del Corso* lie the elegant shopping streets including the *Via Condotti* and the *Via Borgognona* which lead up to the *Piazza di Spagna* and the famous *Spanish Steps*. At the nearby *Trevi Fountain* visitors guarantee their return to Rome by throwing a coin into the waters. To the west of the *Via*

del Corso a maze of narrow streets wind their way down to the Tiber River. It is here, in the historic centre of Rome, that the most complete ancient Roman structure is found. *The Pantheon,* on *Piazza della Rotonda,* was the work of Emperor Hadrian and was finished in AD125. Monumental in scale, the dimensions of the dome and its height are precisely equal while the building's interior is illuminated by the sunlight entering through the 9m (30ft) hole in the dome's roof. Just beyond the Pantheon lies the *Piazza Navona*. It is a long thin square, on a classical site, but rebuilt in the 17th century at the behest of Pope Innocent X in the high-Baroque style. It is almost entirely enclosed and thronged with people night and day. It is here that the crowds come on a warm summer's evening to sit late into the night on one of the many café terraces and to watch the passing scene. Moving across to the right (west) bank of the Tiber, the Vatican City is an independent sovereign state and has its own chapter later in *The World Travel Guide*. On the way to the Vatican the visitor will pass the circular hulk of the *Castel Sant'Angelo,* burial place of the Emperor Hadrian and in later times the papal city's main fortified defence. Moving south, the district of *Trastevere* is the city's alternative focus and is home to numerous bars, restaurants and nightclubs. The life-long inhabitants of Trastevere regard their home as separate from Rome across the river, an independence that is celebrated every year in July with its *Festa Noiantri*.

Inland from Rome are the hill towns known as the *Castelli Romani,* which are popular for excursions. **Tivoli**, just 40km (25 miles) east of Rome, was once the haven of the rich, first in Roman times and later during the Renaissance. It is well-known for its magnificent villas and gardens, such as the *Villa d'Este, Villa Gregoriana* and, just outside of Tivoli, the *Villa Adriana*. **Frascati**, only 20km (12.5 miles) south of Rome, is famous for its *Frascati* wine, a light, delicate, dry white wine which has an international reputation. The town itself is also very pleasant. Many of the town's restaurants specialise in the local wine and it is widely available in all local shops. Other hill resorts include **Genzano, Castel Gandolfo** and **Rocca di Papa.**

The presence of malarial mosquitoes in the coastal marshes that once stretched the length of Lazio prevented settlement on any scale. The marshes have been drained and this quiet, gentle coastline can now be enjoyed without risk. **Ostia**, the ancient port of Rome, is now a well-organised beach resort. **Terracina**, further south, is a resort with miles of soft, white sand beach. The nearby town has a modern quarter offering plenty of shops, cafés and restaurants. The crumbling but lively old part of town is higher up on the hill. The *Duomo* is appealing, as is the Roman *Temple of Jupiter Anxurus,* believed to have been built in the 1st century BC. On the very top of the hill overlooking the sea, it is a perfect place, either by day or night, to view the town of Terracina and, indeed, the entire bay spread out on either side.

One of the most popular resorts among the locals is **Sperlonga**, south of Terracina. The beach there is among the most beautiful in the region and the town itself is reminiscent of a Greek island village. Getting around town can be hard work. Seemingly endless steps wind up and around through white arches and vaulted ceilings only to suddenly open up with spectacular views of the sea and cliffs. Down below, on the far end of the beach, is a romantic-looking grotto beside the remains of the *Villa of Tiberius*. 30km (20 miles) offshore is the unspoilt island of **Ponza**.

Other resorts in the area include Anzio (site of the Allied Second World War landing), Sabaudia and San Felice Circeo.

Civitavecchia is an important naval and merchant port; there are also regular sailings to Sardinia.

Southern Italy

(Administrative *Regioni:* Campania, Puglia, Basilicata, Calabria.)

CAMPANIA: Called *Campania Felix* ('blessed country') by the Romans because of its fertile soil, mild climate and (by southern Italian standards) plentiful water. Wine, citrus fruits, tobacco, wheat and vegetables are grown.

Naples, the third-largest Italian city, occupies one of the most beautiful natural settings of any city in Europe. Above it is the bare cone of *Mount Vesuvius*, an active volcano, and beside it the broad sweep of the *Bay of Naples* and the *Tyrrhennian Sea*. The city itself is a mad jumble of tenements and traffic, street vendors and crumbling palaces.

A toll road leads most of the way up to the summit of **Vesuvius** (it is the local Lover's Lane); the final few hundred yards involve an energetic scramble up a bare pumice track. The viewing platform is right on the rim of the caldera and provides a dizzying view of both the steam-filled abyss and the whole of the Bay of Naples.

Nearby, the remains of **Pompeii** and **Herculaneum**, engulfed in the great eruption of AD79, are a unique record of how ordinary 1st-century Romans lived their daily lives. Moulds of people and animals found well-preserved, buried under the burning ash, can be seen at Pompeii, and the decoration in some of the excavated villas is amazingly intact, including numerous wall paintings of gods and humans in scenes ranging from the heroic to the erotic.

The city of **Caserta** was the country seat of the Kings of Naples. The Baroque *Royal Palace* owes much to Versailles. There are imposing Greek temples at **Paestum**.

The peninsula just south of Naples is one of the most popular regions in Italy for holidaymakers, especially those in search of sun and sand. But the added bonus for many is the extraordinary beauty of the region: sheer craggy cliffs rise over the shimmering blue-green Mediterranean waters, and everywhere there are views of hills and sea. History and culture are also present in abundance and it is easy to understand the persistent attraction of the area for visitors.

Sorrento, located on the north side of the peninsula, has attracted artists for centuries. Wagner, Nietzsche and Gorky have spent some time here and Ibsen wrote *The Ghosts* while in Sorrento (the town does possess a somewhat haunted quality at night, with dimly but artistically lit ruins just visible in the depths of its plunging forested gorges). The *Museo Correale* in Sorrento has Roman relics and some furniture, paintings and porcelain belonging to the Correale family, but the outside part of the museum is by far the more interesting, with a walk through gardens and vineyards to a promontory overlooking the bay offering a spectacular view of the harbour and the surrounding towns and cliffs. Sorrento is also the closest link to the island of **Capri**, just off the coast (links are also available from Positano, Amalfi and Naples). Ferries and hydrofoils leave from the harbour throughout the day, arriving at the *Marina Grande*. Boats are then available from here to Capri's main tourist attraction, the *Blue Grotto*. Other sites worth seeing include the *Villa Tiberio*, built as the Roman Emperor Tiberius's retirement villa on the island and notorious for the pursuit of various pleasures which took place inside its once luxurious walls. Now reduced to an organised rubble of stones, it takes some imagining, but the views are superb and almost worth the strenuous 45-minute walk up the hill. The *Garden of Augustus,* south of the town of Capri, is pretty, but often crowded with tourists. From here there is access to a 'beach' down a winding road where visitors are permitted to swim off the rocks of this wild shore.

Ischia, another island in the Bay of Naples, is easily accessible from Sorrento or from Naples. Although larger than Capri, it is not quite so popular with tourists, but well-visited by the locals who appreciate it more for its calm and scenic beauty.

Amalfi, situated in the middle of the south side of the peninsula, is perhaps the most well-known of the region's resort towns. However, the town still has an authentic air about it, despite its popularity with tourists. The mostly Romanesque *Duomo* with its 13th-century bell tower, located in the main square, looks entirely untouched by the contemporary hustle and bustle around it. The *Cloister of Paradise,* just to the right of the cathedral, also makes good viewing. There are some excellent restaurants and the local wine, *Sammarco,* bottled in Amalfi, is superb and surprisingly inexpensive. Perched high above Amalfi, 'closer to the sky than the seashore', as André Gide wrote, is the former independent republic of **Ravello**. From here, the most spectacular views of the Amalfi Coast can be had, above all from the *Villa Cimbrone* where marble statues line a belvedere that is perched on the very edge of the cliff 335m (1100ft) up.

Positano, about 25km (16 miles) along the coast from Amalfi, is a small exclusive resort of great beauty. Heaped high above the coast, its brightly painted houses and bougainvillea have inspired a thousand picture postcards and draw crowds of visitors every summer. Other Campanian resorts include: Maiori, Vietri sul Mare and Palinuro.

PUGLIA (Apulia): A southeastern region encompassing the forested crags of the *Gargano spur,* the mostly flat *Salentine peninsula* (the 'heel' of Italy) and, between them, the *Murge,* a limestone plateau riddled with caves (notably at **Castellana**). With the exception of **Bari** and **Taranto**, both large industrial ports, the Apulian economy is wholly agricultural. The main products are tobacco, grapes, vegetables, almonds and olives. Puglia was important in Roman times as the gateway to the eastern Mediterranean. The port of **Brindisi**, now eclipsed by Bari in commercial terms, was the terminus of the *Via Appia*, along which Eastern produce was conveyed to Rome and beyond. The *Museo Archeologico Provinciale* houses many relics from this prosperous era.

ROME

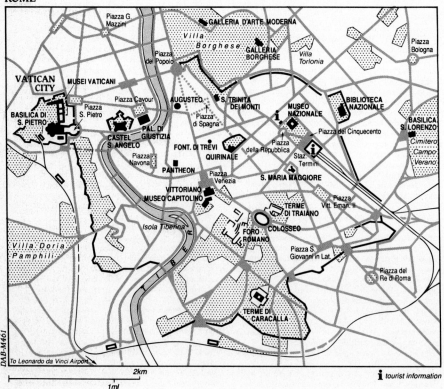

Piazza G. Mazzini
Villa Borghese
GALLERIA D'ARTE MODERNA
GALLERIA BORGHESE
Villa Torlonia
Piazza Bologna
Piazza del Popolo
VATICAN CITY
MUSEI VATICANI
Piazza Cavour
AUGUSTEO
S. TRINITA DEI MONTI
Piazza di Spagna
MUSEO NAZIONALE
BIBLIOTECA NAZIONALE
BASILICA DI S. PIETRO
Piazza S. Pietro
PAL. DI GIUSTIZIA
CASTEL S. ANGELO
Piazza del Cinquecento
BASILICA S. LORENZO
Cimitero Campo Verano
Piazza Navona
FONT. DI TREVI
FON. DI TREVI
QUIRINALE
Piazza della Repubblica
Staz. Termini
PANTHEON
Piazza Venezia
Piazza della Republica
VITTORIANO
MUSEO CAPITOLINO
S. MARIA MAGGIORE
Isola Tiberina
TERME DI TRAIANO
Piazza Vitt. Eman. II
Villa Doria Pamphili
FORO ROMANO
COLOSSEO
Piazza S. Giovanni in Lat.
Piazza del Re di Roma
TERME DI CARACALLA
DAB-M461
To Leonardo da Vinci Airport
2km
1ml
i tourist information

Virgil died in Brindisi in 19BC.
On the *Murge* plateau between **Alberobello** and **Selva di Fasano,** the countryside is littered with thousands of extraordinary stone dwellings known as *trulli*. Circular with conical roofs (also of stone), they are similar to the more famous *nuraghi* of Sardinia.
At the northern end of the plateau is a unique octagonal castle, the *Castella del Monte*, built as a hunting lodge in the 13th century by the Holy Roman Emperor Frederick II (the self-styled *Stupor Mundi*, 'Wonder of the World'). Nearby, at **Canosa di Puglia,** are the extensive remains of the important Roman town of *Canusium*.
The convent of *Santa Maria delle Grazie* in **San Giovanni Rotondo** is an important pilgrimage site because of its connections with Padre Pio da Petralcina. There are fine **beaches** on the Adriatic coast between Barletta and Bari.
BASILICATA (Lucania): A remote and mainly mountainous region between Puglia and Calabria. It is heavily forested in the north around *Monte Vulture*, a large extinct volcano; elsewhere, the hills are flinty and barren. Many rivers flow down from the southern Appennines into the *Gulf of Taranto*, irrigating the fertile coastal plain behind **Metaponto** (birthplace of Pythagoras). The population is small.
The principal town, **Potenza**, was almost entirely rebuilt after a severe earthquake in 1857, only to suffer a similar scale of destruction in the Second World War.
CALABRIA: The toe of the 'boot', a spectacularly beautiful region of high mountains, dense forests and relatively empty beaches. Chestnut, beech, oak and pine cover almost half of Calabria and are a rich hunting ground for mushroom enthusiasts. *Porcini* (boletus edulis), fresh, dried and pickled, therefore adorn the shelves of all the speciality shops of the region. Higher up in the mountains the land only sustains light grazing, but the meadows are abloom with a multitude of wild flowers each spring. It is only on isolated patches of reclaimed land on the marshy coast that agriculture is possible and consequently the inhabitants are amongst the poorest in Italy. They are further tormented by frequent earthquakes. Some wolves still survive in the mountains, particularly in the central Sila Massifs.
Catanzaro, Cotenza and **Reggio,** on the straits of Messina, are the major towns. The best beaches are on the west coast. A typical and especially picturesque little town is **Tropea,** built on the rocks above the Tyrrhenian Sea, with a high street that is at its most busy in the evening and ends abruptly at a panorama platform above the beach. A multitude of shy cats slink through the cobbled alleys undisturbed at siesta time; and secluded sandy coves among outcrops of rock alternate with long stretches of beach as far as the eye can see. The beaches on the east coast of Calabria are rockier and more rugged

but even better for undisturbed beach adventures – especially during the often already very warm months of May and June.

The Islands

(Sicily and Sardinia.)
SICILIA: Strategically situated between Italy and north Africa and with fertile soil and rich coastal fishing grounds, Sicily has suffered an almost continuous round of invasion for as long as history has been recorded. The Greeks, Carthaginians, Romans, Byzantines, Arabs, Normans, Angevins, Aragonese, Bourbons and, most recently, the Germans (and the Allies) during the Second World War – all have left their mark on this unique island, the most populous in the Mediterranean. The economy is based on the production of citrus fruit, almonds, olives, vegetables, wine (including *Marsala),* wheat and beans, together with mining, fishing (anchovies, tuna, cuttlefish and swordfish) and the raising of sheep and goats.
The capital, **Palermo,** is a splendid city in a grand style, opulent, vital, full of remarkable architecture, particularly Norman and Baroque. Notable buildings include the *Martorana, Santa Maria di Gesu, San Giuseppe dei Teatini* and *San Cataldo* churches, the *Cathedral* and the *Palazzo dei Normanni.* The catacombs at the *Capuchin Monastery* contain thousands of mummified bodies.
Syracuse is said to possess the best natural harbour in

Italy. The old town stands on a small island just off the coast and contains many historic buildings. Archimedes lived and died here.
Catania is a spacious city dating mostly from the 18th century, having been rebuilt following a succession of earthquakes. Europe's largest and most active volcano, **Mount Etna,** stands nearby and with its fine beaches the city attracts many tourists.
Taormina, further up the coast, is an immensely picturesque resort town. Perched on a cliff within sight of Mount Etna, it has fine beaches, a well-preserved Greek theatre, a castle and a cathedral.
Messina, a busy port with a deep natural harbour, was almost entirely destroyed by an earthquake in 1908. The *Cathedral* is an exact replica of that destroyed in the 1908 calamity, which was built in the 11th century by King Roger.
Sicily is littered with the remains of successive invading cultures and a full listing of important sites is beyond the scope of this book. The following is a representative selection of sites and buildings: the Norman *Cathedral* at **Monreale,** containing an acre and a half of dazzling mosaics; the numerous Greek remains at **Agrigénto,** said to be better preserved than any in Greece itself; the Greek theatre at **Syracuse;** the vast *Temple of Apollo* at **Selinunte;** and the Byzantine cliff dwellings at *Cava d'Ispica* near **Modica.**
Popular **seaside resorts** include Cefalù (near Palermo), Mondello, Acitrezza, Acireale, Taormina (see above) and Tindari. There are extensive sandy beaches on the southern coast.
Many attractive small islands surround Sicily, offering excellent facilities for **underwater fishing.**
Accommodation is generally simple (although there are some excellent hotels). These islands are the **Lipari Group** (*Lipari* itself, *Vulcano, Panarea* and *Stromboli), Ustica, Favignana, Levanzo, Marettimo, Pantelleria* and *Lampedusa.*
SARDINIA (Sardegna): This is the second-largest island in the Mediterranean. Much of Sardinia away from the coasts is an almost lunar landscape of crags and chasms and is largely uninhabited. In recent years, there has been much investment in tourist infrastructure, particularly in the northern area known as the *Costa Smeralda* and on the west coast near Alghera. This is the only region in Italy without motorways. The Sardinian language is closer to Latin than is modern Italian.
Cagliari, the capital, stands in a marshy valley at the south of the island. It was founded by the Phoenicians and subsequently expanded by the Romans, who knew it as *Carales.* It is today a busy commercial port and site of most of the island's heavy industry.
The only other towns of any size are **Sassari,** in the northwest near the resort area around Alghero; **Nuoro,** an agricultural town on the edge of the central massif, a good base from which to explore the interior; and **Olbia,** a fishing port and car-ferry terminus on the edge of the *Costa Smeralda.*
There are numerous Bronze Age remains throughout the islands, the best known being the *nuraghi* – circular

Tyrrhenian Sea
Stromboli
• Ustica
I. Lipari
Lipari
Palermo
Bagheria
Messina
I. Egadi
Trápani
Taormina
Str. di Messina
Segesta
Corleone
Etna 3323m △
Catania
Marsala
Platani
SICILY
Caltanissetta
Salso
Agrigénto
Gela
Syracuse
Pantelleria
Ragusa
Sicilian Channel
Malta Channel
100km
50mls
DAB-M289
DAB-M288
□ international airport

Corsica (France)
Strait of Bonifacio
La Maddalena
Santa Teresa
I. Asinara
Golfo dell' Asinara
Costa Smeralda
Olbia
Sassari
Alghero
Macomer
Nuoro
Golfo di Orosei
SARDINIA
Tirso
P. la Marmora 1834m △
Arbatax
Oristano
Campidano Plain
Iglesias
Cagliari
I. di S. Pietro
Flumendosa
Carbonia
Golfo di Cagliari
Capo Carbonara
I. di S. Antioco
Capo Teulada
Mediterranean Sea
100km
50mls
□ airport

(sometimes conical) stone dwellings. The largest collection of these may be found at **Su Nuraxi**, about 80km (50 miles) north of Cagliari.
Beach resorts include: Santa Margherita di Pula, Alghero, Santa Teresa, Porto Cervo, Capo Boi and the island of La Maddalena.
POPULAR ITINERARIES: 5-day: Venice–Padua–Verona–Mantua–Venice. **7-day:** (a) Turin–Milan–Verona–Padua–Venice. (b) Florence–Lucca–Pisa–St Gimignano–Siena–Arezzo–Florence. (c) Rome–Ostia–Terracina–Ponza–Sperlonga–Tivoli–Frascati–Rome. (d) Naples–Pompeii–Sorrento–Capri–Positano–Amalfi–Ravello–Herculaneum.

SOCIAL PROFILE

FOOD & DRINK: Table service is most common in restaurants and bars. There are no licensing laws.
Pasta plays a substantial part in Italian recipes, but nearly all regions have developed their own special dishes. Examples of dishes from each region are listed below. Italy has over 20 major wine regions, from Val d'Aosta on the French border to Sicily and Sardinia in the south.
Drink: Wines are named after grape varieties or after their village or area of origin. The most widespread is the *Chianti* group of vineyards, governed by the *Chianti Classico* quality controls (denoted by a black cockerel on the neck of each bottle). The Chianti area is the only area in Italy with such quality controls. *Denominazione di origine controllata* wines come from officially recognised wine-growing areas (similar to Appellation Controllé in France), while wines designated *Denominazione controllata e garantita* are wines of fine quality. Vermouths from Piemonte vary from dry and light pink to dark-coloured and sweet. Aperitifs such as *Campari* and *Punt e Mes* are excellent appetisers, while Italian liqueurs include *Strega, Galliano, Amaretto* and *Sambuca.* Examples of wine from each region are listed below.
Rome: **Food:** *abbacchio* (suckling lamb in white wine flavoured with rosemary), *cannelloni* (pasta stuffed with meat, calves' brains, spinach, egg and cheese), *broccoli romani* (broccoli in white wine), *salsa romana* (sweet-sour brown sauce with raisins, chestnut and lentil purée served with game) and *gnocchi alla romana* (semolina dumplings). Of Rome's cheeses the best include *mozzarella, caciotta romana* (semi-hard, sweet sheep cheese), *pecorino* (hard, sharp sheep's milk cheese) and *gorgonzola.* **Wines:** Frascati, Albano, Grottaferrata, Velletri, Montefiascone, and Marino (whites); Marino, Cesanese and Piglio (reds).
Piemonte and Val d'Aosta: **Food:** *fonduta* (a hot dip with Fontina cheese, milk and egg yolks sprinkled with truffles and white pepper), *lepre piemontese* (hare cooked in Barbera wine and sprinkled with herbs and bitter chocolate), *zabaglione* (hot dessert with beaten egg and Marsala wine). **Wines:** Barolo, Barbera, Barbaresco, Gattinara and Grignolino.
Lombardia: **Food:** *risotto alla milanese* (rice with saffron and white wine), *zuppa pavese* (tasty clear soup with poached eggs), *minestrone* (thick soup with chopped vegetables), *osso buco* (shin of veal cooked in tomato sauce served with rice), *panettone* (Christmas cake with sultanas and candied fruit). **Wines:** Valtellina, Sassella, Grumello and Inferno.
Trentino and Alto Adige: **Food:** some excellent sausages and hams come from these regions. **Wines:** Lago di Caldaro and Santa Maddalena.
Veneto: **Food:** *fegato alla ceneziana* (calves' liver thinly sliced and cooked in butter with onions), *baccalà alla vicentina* (salt cod simmered in milk), *radicchio rosso di treviso* (wild red chicory with a bitter taste). **Wines:** Soave, Bardolino and Valpolicella.
Friuli-Venezia Giulia: **Food:** *pasta e fagioli* (pasta and beans), *prosciutto di San Daniele* (raw ham). **Wines:** Tokai, Malvasia, Pinot Bianco and Pinot Grigio (whites); Merlot, Cabernet and Pinot Nero (reds).
Liguria: **Food:** *pesto* (sauce made of basil, garlic, pine nuts and *pecorino* cheese with pasta), *cima genovese* (cold veal stuffed with calves' brains, onions and herbs), *pandolce* (sweet cake with orange flavour). **Wine:** Sciacchettra.
Emilia-Romagna: **Food:** *parmigiano* (parmesan cheese), *prosciutto di Parma* (Parma ham), *pasta con salsa bolognese* (sauce of meat, cheese and tomato served with pasta), *vitello alla bolognese* (veal cutlet cooked with Parma ham and cheese), *cotechino e zampone* (pigs' trotters stuffed with pork and sausages). **Wines:** Lambrusco, Albana, Trebbiano and Sangiovese.
Tuscany: **Food:** *bistecca alla fiorentina* (thick T-bone steak grilled over charcoal, sprinkled with freshly ground black pepper and olive oil), *minestrone alla fiorentina* (tasty vegetable soup with slices of country bread), *pappardelle alla lepre* (pasta with hare sauce), *tortina di carciofi* (baked artichoke pie), *cinghiale di maremma* (wild boar from Maremma region near Grosseto) with dishes of ham, sausages and steaks. Sweets include *panforte di Siena* (confection of honey, candied fruits, almonds and cloves), *castagnaccio* (chestnut cake with nuts and sultanas) and *ricciarelli* (delicate biscuit of honey and almonds from Siena). **Wines:** Chianti, Vernaccia, Aleatico and Brunello di Montalcino.
Marche: **Food:** *brodetto* (many varieties of fish on toast, garnished with carrot, celery, tomato, laurel tips and white wine), *pasticciata* (pasta baked in oven, a method preferred by Marches). **Wine:** Verdicchio.
Abruzzo-Molise: **Food:** the favourite pasta in this region is known as *maccheroni alla chitarra* because it is cut in thin strips. Desserts include *parrozzo* (rich chocolate cake) and *zeppole* (sweetened pasta). **Wines:** Cerasolo di Abruzzo, Montepulciano (reds); Trebbiano (dry white). The district is also home of a strong liqueur known as *Centerbe.*
Umbria: **Food:** Truffles, spaghetti, *porchetta alla perugina* (suckling pig), *carne ai capperi e acciughe* (veal with caper and herb sauce) and good-quality local sausages, salami and *prosciutto* famous throughout Italy. **Wine:** Orvieto (white, sweet or dry).
Campania: **Food:** *pizza* (the culinary pride of Campania) served in a great variety of recipes, *bistecca alla pizzaiola* (steak with sauce made from tomatoes, garlic and oregano), *sfogliatelle* (sweet ricotta cheese turnovers) and *mozzarella* cheese (originally made with buffalo milk). **Wines** come from the islands of Capri and Ischia.
Puglia: **Food:** *coniglio ai capperi* (rabbit cooked with capers) and *ostriche* (fresh oysters baked with bread crumbs). **Wines:** Sansevero, Santo Stefano, Aleatico di Puglia.
Calabria and Basilicata: **Food:** *sagne chine* (lasagne with artichoke and meat balls), *zuppa di cipolle* (onion soup with Italian brandy), *sarde* (fresh sardines with olive oil and oregano), *alici al limone* (fresh anchovies baked with lemon juice), *melanzane Sott'Olio* (pickled aubergines), *mostaccioli* (chocolate biscuits) or *cannariculi* (fried honey biscuits). **Wines:** Agliatico and Cirò.
Sicily: **Food:** *pesce spada* (swordfish stuffed with brandy, mozzarella and herbs, grilled on charcoal), *pasta con le sarde* (pasta with fresh sardines), *caponata* (rich dish of olives, anchovies and aubergines), *pizza siciliana* (pizza with olives and capers) and *triglie alla siciliana* (grilled mullet with orange peel and white wine). Excellent sweets are *cassata* (ice cream of various flavours with candied fruit and bitter chocolate) and *frutti di marturana* (marzipan fruits). **Wines:** Regaleali, Corvo di Salaparuta (both red and white, a highly aromatic wine ideal for fish), Marsala.
Sardinia: **Food:** the coastline offers a wide selection of fish, including lobster which is served in soup, stews and grills. Main dishes include *burrida* (fish stew with dogfish and skate) and *calamaretti alla sarda* (stuffed baby squid). **Wines:** Vernaccia, Cannonau, Piani, Oliena and Malvasia.
NIGHTLIFE: Nightclubs, discos, restaurants and bars with floorshows and dancing can be found in most major towns and tourist resorts. In the capital, English-language films can be found at the Pasquine Cinema, *Vicolo della Paglia,* just off Santa Maria in Trastevere. Restaurants and cafés throughout Italy will invariably have tables outside: in Rome the *Massimo D'Azeglio* is a hotel restaurant famous for its classic food. Open-air concerts in summer are organised by the *Opera House* and the *Academy of St Cecilia,* while there is open-air theatre at the *Baths of Caracalla.* Jazz, rock, folk and country music can all be heard at various venues.
SHOPPING: Many Italian products are world-famous for their style and quality. Care should be taken when buying antiques since Italy is renowned for skilled imitators. Prices are generally fixed and bargaining is not general practice, although a discount may be given on a large purchase. Florence, Milan and Rome are famous as important fashion centres, but smaller towns also offer good scope for shopping. It is advisable to avoid hawkers or sellers on the beaches. Some places are known for particular products, eg Como (Lombardia) for silk, Prato (Tuscany) for textiles, Empoli (Tuscany) for the production of bottles and glasses in green glass, Deruta (Umbria) and Faenza (Emilia-Romagna) for pottery, Carrara (Tuscany) for marble. Torre Annunziata (Campania) and Alghero (Sardinia) are centres for handicraft products in coral, and in several parts of Sardinia business cards and writing paper made of cork are produced. Cremona (Valle d'Aosta) is famous for its handmade violins. Castelfidardo (Marche) is famous for its accordion factories, and for its production of guitars and organs. Two small towns concentrate on producing their speciality: Valenza (Piemonte), which has a large number of goldsmith artisans, and Sulmona (Abruzzo), which produces 'confetti', sugar-coated almonds used all over Italy for wedding celebrations. Vietri sul Mare (Campania) is one of the most important centres of ceramic paving-tiles, and Ravenna (Emilia-Romagna) is famous for mosaics. Main shopping areas are listed below.
Rome offers a wide choice of shops and markets. Every shop in the fashionable Via Condotti–Via Sistina area offers a choice of styles, colours and designs rarely matched, but at very high prices. Equally expensive are shops along Via Vittorio Veneto, a street famous for its outdoor cafés. Old books and prints can be bought from bookstalls of Piazza Borghese. Rome's flea market is at Porta Portese in Trastevere on Sunday mornings, selling everything from second-hand shoes to 'genuine antiques'.
Milan's industrial wealth is reflected in the chic, elegant shops of Via Montenapoleone. Prices tend to be higher than in other major cities.
Venice is still famous for its glassware, and there is a great deal of both good and bad glass; that made on the island of Murano, where there are also art dealers and skilful goldsmiths, has a reputation for quality. Venetian lace is also exquisite and expensive; however, most of the lace sold is no longer made locally (only lace made on the island of Burano may properly be called Venetian lace).
Florence boasts some of the finest goldsmiths, selling from shops largely concentrated along both sides of the Ponte Vecchio bridge. Florentine jewellery has a particular quality of satin finish called *satinato.* Much filigree jewellery can also be found. Cameos are another speciality of Florence, carved from exotic shells.
Southern Italy: In the south there are still families hand-making the same local products as their ancestors: pottery and carpets in each region; filigree jewellery and products of wrought iron and brass in Abruzzo; products in wood in Calabria; corals and cameos in Campania; a variety of textiles, including tablecloths, in Sicily and Sardinia. In Cagliari it is possible to find artistic copies of bronze statuettes from the Nuraghe period of the Sardinian Bronze Age. In the larger towns such as Naples, Bari, Reggio, Calabria, Palermo and Cagliari there are elegant shops with a whole range of Italian products. Many smaller towns have outdoor markets, but souvenirs sold there are sometimes of very low quality, probably mass-produced elsewhere.
Shopping hours: 0900-1300 and 1600-1930 Monday to Saturday, with some variations in northern Italy where the lunch break is shorter and the shops close earlier. Food shops are often closed Wednesday afternoon.
SPORT: Football is the most popular spectator sport (the national team won the World Cup in 1934, 1938 and 1982 and hosted the 1990 event, in which they finished third). Other popular sports are **cycling** (the *Giro d'Italia* is the most famous cycling race through Italy); **motor racing**, held at the Monza autodrome near Milan (Lombardia); **sailing, motorboat racing** and **riding. Golf:** There are first-class golf courses all over Italy, from Lombardia and Trentino in the north, through Tuscany (near Florence) and Lazio (near Rome), down to Calabria and Sardinia where the golf season is very long due to the mild climate. There are thousands of **tennis** courts (both covered and in the open-air) in the big towns and tourist resorts. Bocce **bowls** is as traditional in Italy as it is in France, especially in small villages where it is played Sunday after High Mass. **Fishing** can be enjoyed in the rivers in northern Italy or in the open sea, where it is possible to rent a boat with or without fishermen. Divers and underwater fishermen will find their paradise in Sardinia and Sicily, around the Tremiti Islands (Puglia) in the Adriatic, or along the coasts of Tuscany and Liguria, where equipment can be hired. The **winter sports** resorts are expanding throughout, in the Alpine regions in places such as Cervinia and Courmayeur in Val d'Aosta, Claviere and Sauze d'Oulx in Piemonte, Aprica and Bormio in Lombardia, Alpi di Siusi, Cortina d'Ampezzo, Marilleva and Selva di Valgardena in the Dolomites (Trentino–Alto Adige–Veneto), and in Central Italy, in resorts such as Abetone (Tuscany), Campo Imperatore in Lazio, and in several places in Abruzzo, down to Mount Etna in Sicily. **Equestrian:** One of Rome's most prestigious events is its international horse show held in May. There is also flat racing starting in February at the Capanelle track. Each of the three seasons lasts two months, the second starting in May and the third in September. Trotting races take place at the Villa Gloria track in February, June to November. Genoa has frequent **yachting** regattas, as does Santa Margherita Ligura, where a canoe and small boat regatta is also held in July.
SPECIAL EVENTS: Traditional festivals are celebrated in most towns and villages in commemoration of local historical or religious events, the most notable and spectacular being the following:
Agrigento: Folklore. Almond Blossom Festival (February).
Ascoli Piceno: Joust of the Quintana. Historical pageant with over 1000 people (annually the first Sunday in August).
Arezzo: Joust of the Saracen with armoured knights, dating from the 13th century (annually the first Sunday in September).
Assisi: Celebration of the Holy Week (Easter Week). Music and Song contest (annually the first Saturday and Sunday in May).
Bari: 'Sagra di San Nicola', historical procession in costume (May).
Cagliari: 'Sagra di Sant'Efisio', one of the biggest and

host colourful processions in the world (May 1).
Florence: 'Scoppio del Carro', Explosion of the Cart in the Cathedral Square, annually on Easter Sunday; and 'Gioco del Calcio', 16th-century football match in medieval costumes (June 24 and 28).
Foligno: Revival of a 17th-century joust with 600 knights in costumes (second Sunday in September).
Gubbio: 'Festa dei Ceri', procession of local costumes (May 15).
Lucca: 'Luminaria di Santa Croce'. Illuminations and procession (September 14).
Marostica: Human Chess Game (every year in September).
Naples: 'Festa di San'Gennaro', gathering in the Cathedral to pray for the liquefaction of the saint's blood.
Nuoro: Festival of the Redeemer (last week in August).
Oristano: 'Sa Sartiglia', medieval procession and jousting (Carnival Time).
Piana Degli Albanesi (Palermo): Celebration of Epiphany according to Byzantine rite (January 6). Also Easter celebrations (Easter Sunday).
Pisa: Historical regatta and illuminations (June 16-17).
Rome: Epiphany Fair (January 6). 'Festa de'Noantri' (July 16-24).
Sansepolcro (Arezzo): 'Palio dei Balestrieri', medieval contest (second Sunday in September).
Sassari: Traditional procession of over 3,000 people, the Cavalcata Sarda (annually the first Sunday in May).
Siena: Bare-back horserace (July 2 and August 16).
Venice: 'Carnevale' (February). Procession of gondolas (July 16-17). 'Il Redentore', historical regatta (annually the first Sunday in September).
Viareggio: 'Carnevale' (February).
Viterbo: Procession of the 'Macchina di Santa Rosa', commemorating the transport of the saint's body to the Church of Santa Rosa (September 3).
SOCIAL CONVENTIONS: The social structure is heavily influenced by the Roman Catholic church and, generally speaking, family ties are stronger than in most other countries in Western Europe. Normal social courtesies should be observed. Dress is casual in most places, though beachwear should be confined to the beach. Conservative clothes are expected when visiting religious buildings and smaller, traditional communities. Formal wear is usually indicated on invitations. Smoking is prohibited in some public buildings, transport and cinemas. Visitors are warned to take precautions against theft, particularly in the cities. **Tipping:** Service charges and state taxes are included in all hotel bills. It is customary to give 10% in addition.

BUSINESS PROFILE

ECONOMY: The Italian economy performed well during the late 1980s, to the point where Italy claimed *il sorpasso*, the overtaking of Britain in per capita gross domestic product. Entering the 1990s, there are signs of significant economic difficulties, exemplified by the Government's inability to control the vast public sector deficit. Traditionally agricultural, Italy industrialised rapidly after 1945, particularly in manufacturing and engineering, to the point where only 12% of the population is now engaged in agriculture. The majority of these live in the south of Italy, which is substantially poorer than the centre and north of the country. The role of a group of large state holding companies was vital in ensuring economic growth, although it is now widely felt that these have outlived their usefulness and should be broken up. (The collapse of one of these, Efim, in July 1992, has badly dented financial confidence.) However, it is the decline of the dynamic small- and medium-sized business sector that is causing most concern amongst · economic analysts. The 'Clean Hands' campaign which was effective in galvinising opposition to the corruption and ineffectiveness of the former political class has, so far, failed to provide a viable alternative. The government of Silvio Berlusconi descended into a welter of confusion as a result of conflicts within the coalition and the suspect behaviour of Berlusconi himself. At the time of writing Berlusconi's government has fallen and a new Prime Minister has yet to be appointed. This has had a short-term effect on business confidence. Nonetheless, Italy's achievements have been remarkable, all the more so given the lack of any natural resources. All the country's oil and many of its raw materials must be imported. The economy thus relies heavily on the export of manufactured goods to pay for these, particularly of industrial machinery, vehicles, aircraft, chemicals, electronics, textiles and clothing. The tourism industry has also steadily grown in importance. Main trading partners are EU countries, Latin America, the USA, Canada, Saudi Arabia, the CIS and Libya.
BUSINESS: A knowledge of Italian is a distinct advantage. Prior appointments are essential. Remember that ministries and most public offices close at 1345 and, except by special appointment, it is not possible to see

officials in the afternoon. Milan, Turin and Genoa form the industrial triangle of Italy; Bologna, Florence, Padua, Rome, Verona and Vicenza also have important business centres. In all the above cities major trade fairs take place throughout the year. See under the relevant city sections in *Resorts & Excursions*. **Office hours:** 0900-1300 and 1400-1800 Monday to Friday.
COMMERCIAL INFORMATION: The following organisation can offer advice: Unione Italiana delle Camere di Commercio, Industria, Artigianato e Agricoltura (Italian Union of Chambers of Commerce, Industry, Crafts and Agriculture), Piazza Sallustio 21, 00187 Rome. Tel: (6) 47041. Telex: 622327.
CONFERENCES/CONVENTIONS: There are many hotels with facilities. Further information can be obtained from the national conference organisation ItalCongressi, Largo Virgilio Testa 23, 00144 Rome. Tel: (6) 592 2574. Fax: (6) 592 2649. Telex: 624688.

CLIMATE

Summer is hot, especially in the south. Spring and autumn are mild with fine, sunny weather. Winter in the south is much drier and warmer than in northern and central areas. Mountain regions are colder with heavy winter snowfalls.
Required clothing: Lightweight cottons and linens are worn during the summer, except in the mountains. Lightweight to mediumweights are worn in the south during winter, while warmer clothes are worn elsewhere. Alpine wear is advised for winter mountain resorts.

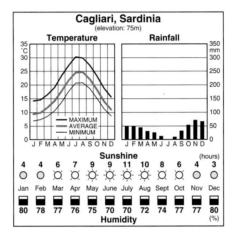

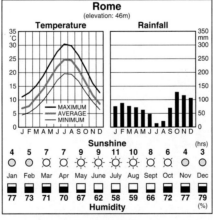

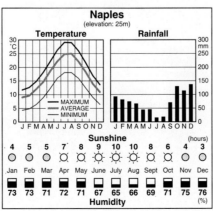

Jamaica

Location: Caribbean.

Jamaica Tourist Board (JTB)
2 St Lucia Avenue, Kingston 5, Jamaica
Tel: 929 9200. Fax: 929 9375. Telex: 2140.
Jamaica High Commission
1-2 Prince Consort Road, London SW7 2BZ
Tel: (0171) 823 9911. Fax: (0171) 589 5154. Telex: 263304.
Jamaica Tourist Board
Address as above
Tel: (0171) 224 0505 *or* 0800 445 566. Fax: (0171) 224 0551. Telex: 295510. Opening hours: 0930-1730 Monday to Friday.
British High Commission
PO Box 575, Trafalgar Road, Kingston 10, Jamaica
Tel: 926 9050. Fax: 929 7869. Telex: 2110 (a/b UKREPKIN JA).
Jamaican Embassy
1520 New Hampshire Avenue, NW, Washington, DC 20036
Tel: (202) 452 0660. Fax: (202) 452 0081.
Jamaican Consulate General
2nd Floor, 767 Third Avenue, New York, NY 10017
Tel: (212) 935 9000. Fax: (212) 935 7507.
Jamaica Tourist Board
20th Floor, 801 Second Avenue, New York, NY 10017
Tel: (212) 856 9727. Fax: (212) 856 9730.
Embassy of the United States of America
3rd Floor, Jamaica Mutual Life Center, 2 Oxford Road, Kingston 5, Jamaica
Tel: 929 4850/9. Fax: 926 6743.
Jamaica High Commission
Suite 800, 275 Slater Street, Ottawa, Ontario K1P 5H9
Tel: (613) 233 9311 *or* 233 9314. Fax: (613) 233 0611.
Consulates in: St Albert, Toronto and Winnipeg.
Jamaica Tourist Board
Suite 616, One Eglinton Avenue, Toronto, Ontario M4P 3A1
Tel: (416) 482 7850. Fax: (416) 482 1730.
Canadian High Commission
PO Box 1500, Mutual Security Bank Building, 30-36 Knutsford Boulevard, Kingston 5, Jamaica
Tel: 926 1500/7. Fax: 926 1702. Telex: 2130 (a/b BEAVER JA).

AREA: 10,991 sq km (4244 sq miles).
POPULATION: 2,374,193 (1991 estimate).
POPULATION DENSITY: 216 per sq km.
CAPITAL: Kingston. **Population:** 661,600 (1989 estimate).
GEOGRAPHY: Jamaica is the third-largest island in the West Indies, a narrow outcrop of a submerged mountain range. The island is crossed by a range of mountains reaching 2256m (7402ft) at the Blue Mountain Peak in the east and descending towards the west with a series of spurs and forested gullies running north and south. Most of the best beaches are on the north and west coasts. The island's luxuriant tropical and subtropical vegetation is probably unsurpassed anywhere in the Caribbean.
LANGUAGE: Official language is English. Local *patois* is also spoken.
RELIGION: Protestant majority (Anglican, Baptist and Methodist) with Roman Catholic, Jewish, Muslim, Hindu

You can please all your clients all the time.

Because with 5 unique, Super-Inclusive resorts we have a vacation that's perfect for each and every one of your clients.

Hedonism II, for an uninhibited search for pleasure. Jamaica Jamaica, for serious sports, including a tennis and golf school and a championship course right on the property. Boscobel Beach, a tropical adventure for the whole family and the only Caribbean Super-Inclusive where children under 14 can stay, play and eat free. And our two spectacular Super-Inclusive Lido resorts; Grand Lido, luxurious, laid back elegance in a surrounding of architectural splendor. And the newest member of the SuperClubs family, Sans Souci Lido, offering the splendor and charm of tropical

elegance with natural mineral springs, soothing massages and impeccable service.

The Super-Inclusive Difference

When it's Super-Inclusive it's not just a meal, it's a feast in your client's choice of a variety of award winning restaurants. It's not just cocktails, it's top shelf. It's not just a show, it's the hottest live entertainment on the island. It's not just comfortable, it's lavish, luxurious and romantic. And if it's SuperClubs, it's not just another booking, it's satisfied clients, enthusiastic referrals and repeat business.

To give your clients the perfect Super-Inclusive tropical vacation, you need to look no further than SuperClubs.

SuperClubs®

The Caribbean's Only Super-Inclusive℠ Resorts.

For rates, reservations or information call SuperClubs in the U.K. at **0749 677200.**

Boscobel Beach

Sans Souci L I D O.

Grand L I D O.

JAMAICA JAMAICA

HEDONISM II.

and Bahai communities. Rastafarianism, a religion based on belief in the divinity of the late Emperor of Ethiopia, Haile Selassie (Ras Tafari), is also widely practised.
TIME: GMT - 5.
ELECTRICITY: 110 volts AC, 50Hz, single phase. American 2-pin plugs are standard, but many hotels offer, in addition, 220 volts AC, 50Hz, single phase, from 3-pin sockets.
COMMUNICATIONS: Telephone: Full IDD is available. Country code: 1 809. There are no area codes. Outgoing international code: 011. **Fax:** This service is available from 0700-1000 daily at the *Jamintel* office in Kingston. Widely available in most hotels and offices. **Telex/telegram:** Facilities for sending telex and telegrams are widely available. Telex facilities at the British High Commission may be used in emergencies.
Post: Airmail to Europe takes up to four days. Post office hours: 0830-1630 Monday to Friday. **Press:** Daily papers are *The Daily Gleaner, The Star* and *The Jamaica Herald.*
BBC World Service and Voice of America frequencies: From time to time these change. See the section *How to Use this Book* for more information.
BBC:

MHz	17.84	15.22	9.915	6.195

Voice of America:

MHz	15.21	11.70	6.130	5.995

PASSPORT/VISA

Regulations and requirements may be subject to change at short notice, and you are advised to contact the appropriate diplomatic or consular authority before finalising travel arrangements. Details of these may be found at the head of this country's entry. Any numbers in the chart refer to the footnotes below.

	Passport Required?	Visa Required?	Return Ticket Required?
Full British	Yes	No	Yes
BVP	Not valid/2	-	-
Australian	Yes	No	Yes
Canadian	1	No	Yes
USA	1	No	Yes
Other EU (As of 31/12/94)	Yes	No	Yes
Japanese	Yes	No	Yes

PASSPORTS: [1] Valid passport required by all except for residents and nationals of the USA and Canada entering Jamaica from either the USA or Canada who hold a valid national ID. If entering from other countries, they *do* require a passport.
British Visitors Passports: [2] Not accepted. Although the immigration authorities of this country may in certain circumstances accept British Visitors Passports for persons arriving for holidays or unpaid business trips of up to 3 months, travellers are reminded that no formal agreement exists to this effect and the situation may, therefore, change at short notice. In addition, UK nationals using a BVP and returning to the UK from a country with which no such formal agreement exists may be subject to delays and interrogation by UK immigration.
VISAS: Required by all except:
(a) nationals of EU countries (nationals of the UK and Ireland for a period of 6 months; nationals of Denmark, Italy, Luxembourg, The Netherlands, Belgium and Germany for a period not exceeding 3 months; nationals of France, Greece, Portugal and Spain for a period not exceeding 30 days);
(b) nationals of Commonwealth countries;
(c) nationals of the USA (including Virgin Islands and Puerto Rico) for stays not exceeding 6 months;
(d) nationals of Austria, Finland, Iceland, Israel, Liechtenstein, Mexico, Norway, San Marino, Sweden, Switzerland and Turkey for stays not exceeding 3 months;
(e) nationals of Argentina, Brazil, Chile, Costa Rica, Ecuador, Japan and Uruguay for stays not exceeding 30 days;
(f) nationals of Venezuela for stays not exceeding 14 days.
All the above *must* have a valid passport, evidence of sufficient funds and a return or outward-bound ticket for their next destination.
Note: Except for persons in certain categories, a Work Permit is required for a business visit. The Consulate (or Consular section at Embassy or High Commission) can advise.
Types of visa: Entry and Transit. Cost of visas vary – enquire on application.
Application to: Consulate (or Consular section at Embassy or High Commission). For addresses, see top of entry.
Application requirements: (a) 2 passport-size photos.

(b) Valid passport. (c) Completed application form(s). (d) Fee.
Working days required: 48 hours, but some applications are referred to Immigration authorities in Kingston, for which time should be allowed when applying for visa.
Temporary residence: Enquire at Embassy.

MONEY

Currency: Jamaican Dollar (J$) = 100 cents. Notes are in denominations of J$100, 50, 20, 10, 5, 2 and 1. Coins are in denominations of J$1, and 50, 25, 20, 10, 5 and 1 cents.
Currency exchange: Visitors should change money only at airport bureaux, banks or hotels.
Credit cards: Access/Mastercard, American Express, Diners Club and Visa are all widely accepted. Check with your credit card company for details of merchant acceptability and other services which may be available.
Travellers cheques: US Dollar cheques are recommended.
Eurocheques are now accepted by all commercial banks.
Exchange rate indicators: The following figures are included as a guide to the movements of the Jamaican Dollar against Sterling and the US Dollar:

Date:	Oct '92	Sep '93	Jan '94	Jan '95
£1.00=	35.07	37.49	42.10	49.95
$1.00=	22.10	24.55	28.45	31.93

Currency restrictions: Free import and export of foreign currency is allowed, subject to declaration.
Banking hours: 0900-1400 Monday to Thursday and 0900-1500 Friday.

DUTY FREE

The following goods may be imported into Jamaica without incurring customs duty:
200 cigarettes or 25 cigars or 250g tobacco; 1 pint of spirits (excluding rum); 1 litre of wine; 340ml of eau de toilette; 150g of perfume; gifts to the value of J$1000 during each 6-month period.
Prohibited items: Explosives, firearms, dangerous drugs (including marijuana), meat, fresh fruit, coffee, honey or vegetables cannot be brought into Jamaica. Cats and dogs are also prohibited unless arriving directly from the UK, having been born and bred there, carrying a certificate from the Ministry of Agriculture, Fisheries and Food (Hook Rise, Tolworth, Surbiton, Surrey) and if a permit for their import has been obtained from the Ministry of Agriculture, Hope Gardens, Kingston 6.

PUBLIC HOLIDAYS

Jan 2 '95 For New Year's Day. **Mar 1** Ash Wednesday. **Apr 14** Good Friday. **Apr 17** Easter Monday. **May 23** Labour Day. **Aug 7** Independence Day. **Oct 16** National Heroes' Day. **Dec 25-26** Christmas. **Jan 1 '96** New Year's Day. **Feb 21** Ash Wednesday. **Apr 5** Good Friday. **Apr 8** Easter Monday.

HEALTH

Regulations and requirements may be subject to change at short notice, and you are advised to contact your doctor well in advance of your intended date of departure. Any numbers in the chart refer to the footnotes below.

	Special Precautions?	Certificate Required?
Yellow Fever	No	1
Cholera	No	No
Typhoid & Polio	Yes	-
Malaria	No	-
Food & Drink	2	-

[1]: A yellow fever vaccination certificate is required from travellers over one year of age coming from infected areas.
[2]: Mains water is normally chlorinated, and whilst relatively safe may cause mild abdominal upsets. Bottled water is available. Milk is pasteurised and dairy products are safe for consumption. Local meat, poultry, seafood, fruit and vegetables are generally considered safe to eat.
Health care: Health insurance is recommended. There are 30 government-controlled hospitals.

TRAVEL - International

AIR: Jamaica's national airline is *Air Jamaica (JM)*. For free advice on air travel, call the Air Travel Advisory

Bureau in the UK on (0171) 636 5000 (London) *or* (0161) 832 2000 (Manchester).
Approximate flight times: From Kingston or Montego Bay to *London* is 10 hours (direct flight), to *Los Angeles* is 8 hours 40 minutes, to *New York* is 5 hours and to *Singapore* is 33 hours.
International airports: *Norman Manley International (KIN)* (Kingston) is 17.5km (11 miles) southeast of the city. Coach, bus and taxis depart to the city. Duty-free facilities are available.
Montego Bay (MBJ) (International) is 3km (2 miles) north of the city. Duty-free facilities are available.
Trans Jamaica Airlines (JQ) runs shuttle services between the airports.
Departure tax: J$400 for all passengers over two years of age. Transit passengers are exempt.
SEA: Both Montego Bay and Ocho Rios are ports of call for the following cruise lines: *Royal Viking, Royal Caribbean, Norwegian Caribbean, Carnival Cruise, Costa Lines, Sun Line* and *Holland America.* Two ships, the *Regent Sea* and the *Britanis*, start their cruises from Montego Bay. Other passenger/freight lines *(Geest)* sail from North, South and Central American ports. *Lauro Lines* sail to Kingston from the Mediterranean.

TRAVEL - Internal

AIR: *Trans Jamaica Airlines (JQ)* runs services to and from Kingston, Montego Bay, Port Antonio, Mandeville, Ocho Rios and Negril. During the winter season there are frequent daily flights, as well as shuttle flights between the two major airports.
SEA: There are a number of local operators running yacht tours around the island, as well as cruises. Boats and yachts can also be hired on a daily or weekly basis. Contact the Tourist Board for details.
RAIL: A diesel service runs twice daily between Kingston and Montego Bay. The total network extends to almost 340km (211 miles) and is an enjoyable way to see the interior of the island.
Note: Since 1994, the service has been suspended with no immediate plans to resume daily scheduled runs.
ROAD: There is a 17,000km (11,000-mile) road network, one-third tarred. Traffic in Jamaica drives on the left. **Bus:** Reliable service in Kingston and Montego Bay; less reliable for trans-island travel. Coach and minibus tours are bookable at most hotels. **Taxi:** Not all taxis are metered, so it is best to check standard charges prior to embarkation on journey. 10% tip is usual. **Car hire:** Most major towns, as well as airports, have rental facilities, both local and international. Rental can also be arranged via hotels. **Documentation:** A full UK driving licence is valid for up to a year.
URBAN: Kingston's public conventional bus services have deteriorated due to operational and engineering problems, and most transport in the capital is now by private minibus.
JOURNEY TIMES: The following chart gives approximate journey times (in hours and minutes) from Montego Bay to other major cities/towns in Jamaica.

	Air	Road	Rail
Kingston	0.30	3.00	4.00
Negril	0.20	1.30	-
Ocho Rios	0.30	2.00	-
Port Antonio	0.40	4.30	-

ACCOMMODATION

HOTELS: There are over 144 hotels and guest-houses throughout the island; all are subject to 12.5% general consumption tax. 90% of all hotels belong to the Jamaica Hotel & Tourist Association, 2 Ardene Road, Kingston 10. Tel: 926 3635/6. Fax: 929 1054.
Grading: Hotels are government-controlled in four categories: **A, B, C** and **D.** The categories are based on rates charged. Many of the hotels offer accommodation according to one of a number of 'Plans' widely used in the Caribbean; these include *Modified American Plan* (MAP), which consists of room, breakfast and dinner, and *European Plan* (EP), which consists of room only.

Health	
GALILEO/WORLDSPAN:	**TI-DFT/KIN/HE**
SABRE:	**TIDFT/KIN/HE**
Visa	
GALILEO/WORLDSPAN:	**TI-DFT/KIN/VI**
SABRE:	**TIDFT/KIN/VI**

For more information on Timatic codes refer to Contents.

Timatic

SELF-CATERING: There are over 837 cottages for rent on the island. Information is available from the Jamaica Tourist Board. The properties range from small apartments to houses with several bedrooms. Some tour operators can arrange villa accommodation including car rental and tours, as well as travel to and from the villa. Information is also available from the Jamaican Association of Villas & Apartments Ltd (JAVA), PO Box 298, Pineapple Place, Ocho Rios, St Ann. Tel: 974 2508.
CAMPING/CARAVANNING: The island has many campsites, including the well-known Strawberry Fields, which offers all types of facilities, including the hiring of tents and ancillary equipment.

RESORTS & EXCURSIONS

Jamaica is a tropical island of lush green vegetation, waterfalls and dazzling white beaches. Columbus was in the habit of declaring that each new island he chanced upon was more beautiful than the last, but he seems to have maintained a lifelong enthusiasm for the beauty of Jamaica, despite having been marooned there for a year on his last voyage. One of the larger islands of the Caribbean, it offers excellent tourist facilities and superb beaches and scenery. For the purposes of this guide the main resorts in Jamaica have been divided into the following sections: Montego Bay (including the northwest coast resort of Negril); the North Coast Resorts (including Falmouth, Ocho Rios and Port Antonio); and Kingston and the South (including Mandeville and Spanish Town).

Montego Bay

One of the world's great seaside resorts, **Montego Bay** (or Mo'Bay, as it is more colloquially called) is the capital of Jamaican tourism and market town for a large part of western Jamaica. Dating back to 1492, Montego Bay is Jamaica's second-largest city and one of the most modern in the Caribbean. From *Gloucester* and *Kent Avenues* there is a superb view onto the clear Caribbean waters – the main tourist attraction – and the long reef protecting the bay. Most of the hotels are found on a strip of coastline about a mile and a half long. There are three main beaches: *Doctor's Cave Beach* (so named because it was once owned by a Dr McCatty and had a cave that has since eroded away) which has beautiful white sand, and where the exceptionally clear water is believed to be fed by mineral springs; *Walter Fletcher Beach,* nearest the centre and a short walk from the Upper Deck Hotel; and *Cornwall Beach,* which is a few yards from the local Tourist Board Office. A short way inland from the Bay is *Rose Hall,* a restored Great House on a sugar plantation.
Rocklands Feeding Station is home to some of the most exotic birds in the world, such as the mango hummingbird, orange quit and the national bird of Jamaica, the Doctor Bird. Visitors are allowed to feed the birds at certain times of the day.
The *Governor's Coach* is a 65km (40-mile) diesel train ride through thick mountain forests into the interior, passing through banana and coconut plantations and *Ipswich Caves* (a series of deep limestone recesses) to the sugar estate of the famous *Appleton Rum Factory* and **Catadupa**, where shirts and dresses are made to measure.
Negril is 80km (50 miles) west of Montego Bay and has a beach stretching for 11km (7 miles) which offers sailing, water-skiing, deep-sea fishing, scuba diving, parasailing and windsurfing. First coming to attention as an artists' centre and, later, as a focus of 'alternative' culture in the 1960s, it is becoming increasingly popular as a holiday destination which, perhaps untypically, seems likely to preserve much of its original character – indeed, the law requires all buildings to be of modest proportions. Along the street, entrepreneurial Jamaicans sell a variety of craft goods from the many shanty-like shops in Negril. There is also a hectic nightlife in the many clubs that have, over the years, proliferated along the beach. *Rick's Café* is a favourite haunt both for Jamaicans and visitors; located at **West Point**, which is as far west as Jamaica goes, it is famous as the place from which to observe the sun going down.

North Coast Resorts

Falmouth: A delightful harbour resort, 42km (26 miles) from Montego Bay. From here one can visit **Rafters Village** for rafting on the *Martha Brae,* and a fascinating crocodile farm called *Jamaica Swamp Safaris*. There is also a plantation mansion, *Greenwood Great House*, once owned by the Barrett Brownings. The *Church of St Paul* offers Sunday services, where visitors can listen to the choir singing.
Ocho Rios lies roughly 108km (67 miles) east of Montego Bay. The name is said to have come from the old Spanish word for *roaring river* or, in modern Spanish, *eight rivers.* Ocho Rios was once a sleepy fishing village, and although there are now resort facilities, international hotels and restaurants offering a variety of cuisines, the town has kept something of the sleepy atmosphere of small-town Jamaica. One of the most stunning sights in Jamaica is *Dunn's River Falls,* a crystal water stairway which leads to the nearby botanical gardens. Ocho Rios is known as the garden-lover's paradise, and the *Shaw Park Botanical Gardens* exhibit the fascinating variety of the area's exotic flora, for which the town is celebrated. Not surprisingly, two of the most popular tours available are to working plantations at *Brimmer Hall* and *Prospect* where sugar, bananas and spices are still grown and harvested, using many of the traditional skills handed down through generations. Any sightseeing itinerary should include a drive along *Fern Gully,* a road running along an old riverbed that winds through a 6.5km (4-mile) valley of ferns. Another tour is the *Jamaica Night on the White River,* a canoe ride up the torchlit river to the sound of drums. Dinner and open bar is available on the riverbank (Sunday evenings). *Columbus Park,* at **Discovery Bay**, commemorates Columbus' arrival in Jamaica with a museum and 24-hour open-air park exhibiting relics of Jamaican history. Other tours include *Runaway Bay,* which has fine beaches, excellent scuba diving and horseriding; and the *Runaway Caves* nearby, which offer a boat ride 35m (120ft) below ground on a lake in the limestone *Green Grotto.*
Port Antonio, one of the Caribbean's most beautiful bays, is surrounded by the *Blue Mountains.* The town dates back to the 16th century, and sights include *Mitchell's Folly,* a 2-storey mansion built by the American millionaire Dan Mitchell in 1905, and the ruins of a 60-room *Great House.* The surrounding sea is rich in game fish, with blue marlin as the great prize (there is an annual Blue Marlin Tournament run alongside the Jamaican International Fishing Tournament in Port Antonio every autumn); there are also kingfish, yellowtail, wahoo and bonito. The island's most palatial homes are nestled in the foothills. Rafting is available on the *Rio Grande,* comprising 2-hour trips on 2-passenger bamboo rafts, which begin high in the *Blue Mountains* at **Berrydale,** sail past plantations of bananas and sugar cane, and end up at *Rafter's Rest* restaurant at *Margaret's Bay.* The scenic *Somerset Falls* nearby are a popular picnic spot. Beaches in the Port Antonio area include *San San* and *Boston* (where the Jamaican 'jerk pork' is found), while the *Blue Lagoon* is a salt-water cove offering fishing, swimming and water-skiing and is considered one of the finest coves in the Caribbean.

Kingston and the South

Kingston is Jamaica's capital city and cultural centre. With the largest natural harbour in the Caribbean (and seventh largest in the world), Kingston is also an industrial centre where Georgian architecture mixes with modern office blocks while, on the outskirts, spreading suburbs house the hundreds of thousands who increasingly work in the city. Although most tourists head for the beaches and resorts, Kingston has much to offer in the way of sightseeing.
The *National Gallery of Art* has a colourful display of modern art and is recommended. *Hope Botanical Gardens* contain a wide variety of trees and plants, and are particularly famous for orchids. A band plays here on Sunday afternoons. There is a *Crafts Market* on King Street and the *Port Royal,* on top of the peninsula bordering *Kingston Harbour*, is a museum to the time when Kingston was known as the 'richest and wickedest city on earth' under the domination of Captain Morgan and his buccaneers. The *White Marl Arawak Museum* is also worth visiting; here one can see artefacts and relics of the ancient culture of the Arawak Indians. The grounds of the *University of the West Indies*, built on what was once a sugar plantation, are open to the public. *Caymanas Park* is a popular racetrack, where one can bet on the horses every Wednesday and Saturday and public holidays. The *Caymanas Golf Course* hosts the Jamaica Open and Pro-Am, held every November. Polo is played nearby every weekend.
Spanish Town, a short drive to the west of Kingston, is the former capital of Jamaica. The *Spanish Town Square* is said to be one of the finest examples of Georgian architecture in the Western hemisphere. The Spanish *Cathedral of St Jago de la Vega* is the oldest in the West Indies.
Mandeville: Summer capital amid beautiful gardens and fruits, Mandeville is in the middle of Jamaica's citrus industry, 600m (2000ft) above sea level and the highest town on the island. Mandeville offers cool relief from the heat of the coast, and has a golf course and tennis and horseriding facilities. The town is the centre of the bauxite industry, and as such is a good starting point for trips to the surrounding areas.
On the south coast are *Milk River Spa,* the world's most radioactive mineral bath with waters at a temperature of 33°C; *Lover's Leap* in the Santa Cruz Mountains, a sheer 18m (60ft) cliff overhanging the sea; *Treasure Beach* and the resort of *Bluefields.*

SOCIAL PROFILE

FOOD & DRINK: Jamaican food is full of fire and spice, taking advantage of pungent spices and peppers. Jamaican dishes include 'rice and peas', a tasty dish with no peas at all but with kidney beans, white rice, coconut milk, scallions (spring onions) and coconut oil. Another dish is salt fish (dried cod) and *ackee* (the exotic cooked fruit of the ackee tree), curried goat and rice (spicy and strong), Jamaican pepperpot soup (salt pork, salt beef, *okra* and Indian kale known as *callaloo),* chicken fricassé Jamaican-style (a rich chicken stew with carrots, scallions, yams, onions, tomatoes and peppers prepared in unrefined coconut oil) and roast suckling pig (a 3-month-old piglet which is boned and stuffed with rice, peppers, diced yam and thyme mixed with shredded coconut and corn meal). *Patties* are the staple snack of Jamaica (pastries filled with ground beef and bread-crumbs) and can be found everywhere, but vary in price and filling. Waiter service is usually available in catering establishments.
Drink: Jamaican rum is world-famous, especially *Gold Label* and *Appleton. Rumona* is a delicious rum cordial. *Red Stripe* beer is excellent, as is *Tia Maria* (a Blue Mountain coffee and chocolate liqueur). Fresh fruit juice is also recommended, as is Blue Mountain coffee, an excellent variety. Bars have table and/or counter service. There are no licensing hours and alcohol can be bought all day.
NIGHTLIFE: At larger resort hotels small bands and occasional guitar-carrying *calypso* singers can be heard. Folkloric shows are held and steel bands often play. At least once a week there is a torchlit, steel-band show with limbo dancing and fire-eating demonstrations. There are also discotheques, nightclubs and jazz music. Native to Jamaica is *Reggae* music and dancing. The Jamaica Tourist Board arranges 'Meet the People' evenings in various scenic locations through the island. Contact the Tourist Office in Kingston, Montego Bay, Port Antonio or Ocho Rios.
SHOPPING: Special purchases are locally made items and duty-free bargains. Crafts include hand-loomed fabrics, embroidery, silk screening, woodcarvings, oil paintings, woven straw items and sandalmaking. Custom-made rugs and reproductions of pewter and china from the ruins of the ancient submerged city of Port Royal can be bought in the In-Craft workshop. At *Highgate Village* in the mountains, Quakers run a workshop specialising in wicker and wood furniture, floor mats and other tropical furnishings. Jamaican rum, the *Rumona* liqueur (the world's only rum-based liqueur, hard to find outside the island) and *Ian Sangsters Rum Cream* are unique purchases. Other local specialities are *Pepper Jellies,* jams and spices. There are shops offering facilities for 'in-bond' shopping which allows visitors to purchase a range of international goods free of tax or duty at very competitive prices. These goods are sealed (hence the 'bond') and because goods are tax- or duty-free can only be opened once away from Jamaican waters or territory. All goods must be paid for in Jamaican currency. **Shopping hours:** 0900-1700 Monday to Friday. Some shops close half day Wednesday in Kingston, and Thursday in the rest of the island.
SPORT: Watersports: Many hotels have **swimming** pools and beaches. The best beaches for bathing are mainly on the northern coast. **Surfing** is also best on the north coast, east of Port Antonio, where long lines of breakers roll into Boston Bay. Clear waters, coral reefs, shipwrecks, sponge forests, submerged caves and fish offer interesting underwater exploring. **Diving** shops are equipped for rentals and offer guided **snorkel** and **scuba** trips. There are also a number of clubs and centres offering instruction and equipment. Most beach hotels have sunfish, sailfish and/or windsurfboards for hire. To charter larger boats contact the Royal Jamaica Yacht Club. Facilities for **water-skiing** are offered at most beach hotels and at the Kingston Ski Club at Morgan's Harbour. **Fishing:** Fresh- and sea-water fishing are popular. Mountain mullet, hognose mullet, drummer and small snook are caught in rivers. **Deep-sea fishing** charters can be arranged through hotels in main resorts. **Spearfishing** is permitted among the reefs. No licence is needed. Entry forms are available

Dragon Bay
PORT ANTONIO

The best kept secret . . .

. . . situated in an area of pristine natural beauty adjacent to the Blue Lagoon, Dragon Bay is the setting for one of the most beautiful hotels in the Caribbean. This picturesque resort captures so much of the true essence of Jamaica and was the location for the filming of movies such as **Cocktail and Club Paradise**.

Overlooking a spectacular sandy bay and surrounded by tropical gardens, Dragon Bay offers for the active, diving, snorkelling and sailing by day, and dining under the tropical stars to the rhythms of live reggae and calypso music by night. For those who seek a private and relaxing holiday, Dragon Bay is a special hideaway which can be enjoyed from the privacy of our luxurious, newly-refurbished, air-conditioned villas or rooms, each with its own private facilities and panoramic views of a turquoise Caribbean sea.

For the adventurous there is a wide range of local attractions and activities to choose from, including rafting on the Rio Grande river made famous by Errol Flynn; swimming in the cool clear waters of Reach Falls; hiking or cycling amidst the unique fauna and flora of the Blue Mountains or exploring the Nonsuch Caves with their impressive stalactite and stalagmite formations, to name but a few.

Tennis courts, volley ball and a fresh water swimming pool as well as 2 bars and 2 restaurants serving both traditional Jamaican and exquisite international cuisine are available for your enjoyment.

With the skillful and friendly management of Abela Hotels & Resorts, and our long tradition of hospitality, Dragon Bay offers you an unparalleled Jamaican Experience.

TOP COMMISSION PAID TO AGENTS

ABELA HOTELS & RESORTS
Tradition of Hospitality

For information or reservations call:
Dragon Bay, PO Box 176, Port Antonio, Parish of Portland, Jamaica WI. Tel: 1-809 993 3281/3. Fax: 1-809 993 3284.
UK, J A Marketing Services, 21 Embassy Court, Wellington Road, London NW8 9SX, UK. Tel/Fax: (071) 586 3814. **USA**, Robert Reid Associates. Tel: (402) 398 3218, Fax: (402) 398 5484.
Italy, Abela Hotels. Tel: (2) 669 83899. Fax:(2) 669 82022. **Germany**, Abela Hotels. Tel: (49) 0381 5460. Fax: (49) 0381 54023. **France**, Abela Hotels. Tel: (1) 47 58 89 98. Fax: (1) 47 58 09 65.
Individual Reservations: Worldwide UTELL International. Tel: (0171) 413 8877. Fax: (0171) 413 8883.

for the Blue Marlin Tournament competition held in Port Antonio during September. **Tennis:** There are plenty of courts and most hotels without their own court have access to those nearby. **Golf:** Jamaica has developed some of the Caribbean's most beautiful and challenging golf courses. Montego Bay is the best area and it is not necessary to be resident at a hotel to play on its three courses. **Horse-riding:** Some stables for horseriding are open all year, others run schedules during the winter season and most arrangements can be made through hotels. The Chukka Cove Riding Centre at Runaway Bay offers tuition, polo and accommodation. **Cricket** is the national pastime and matches are played from January to August in Sabina Park, Kingston and other locations throughout the island. Probably the second most popular sport is **football**, which is played throughout the year. **Polo** has a tradition going back over a century; matches are played all year round in Kingston. Matches at Kingston and at Drax Hall, near Ocho Rios, are played every week. **Horseraces** are held at Caymanas Race Track, Kingston.

SPECIAL EVENTS: The following is a selection of the major festivals and other special events celebrated annually in Jamaica during 1995/96. For a complete list, contact the Jamaica Tourist Board.
Mar '95 *JAMI Awards* (local music industry awards), Kingston. **Apr** *Carnival,* Kingston; *The Annual Red Stripe International Horse Show & Gymkhana,* Ocho Rios. **May** *Jamaica International Hot Air Balloon Festival and Air Show,* Montpelier. **Jun** *Ikebana International Show* (exhibition). **Jul** *Jamaica Festival Contest and Exhibition Finals.* **Aug** *Reggae Sunsplash* (world's leading reggae stars perform in concerts and at special beach parties), Montego Bay. **Aug 2** *Jamaica Festival Grand Gala,* Kingston. **Sep** *Montego Bay Blue Marlin Tournament.* **Oct** *Port Antonio Blue Marlin Tournament.* **Nov** *Harmony Hall Art Exhibiton,* Ocho Rios. **Dec** *Johnnie Walker World Championships of Golf,* Montego Bay. **Feb 6 '96** *Bob Marley's Birthday Bash,* Kingston.
Throughout the year there are also fishing, equestrian, golf, tennis, fashion, musical and horticultural events.
SOCIAL CONVENTIONS: Handshaking is the customary form of greeting. Normal codes of practice should be observed when visiting someone's home. Jamaicans are generally very hospitable and guests will usually be encouraged to stay for a meal. In these instances a small gift is appreciated. Casual wear is suitable during the day, but shorts and swimsuits must be confined to beaches and poolsides. Evening dress varies from very casual in Negril to quite formal during the season in other resorts, where some hotels and restaurants require men to wear jackets and ties at dinner. In the summer people dress up less. As tourism is a major industry in Jamaica, the visitor is well catered for, and hotel and restaurant staff are generally friendly and efficient. Outside Kingston the pace of life is relaxed and people are welcoming and hospitable. Music and African culture are very apparent, as are old British colonial influences. Signs can be seen on the island claiming 'Jah lives', Jah being the name given to God by the Rastafarians. Possession of marijuana may lead to imprisonment and deportation. Above all the visitor must not try to smuggle it out of the country since the authorities are aware of all the tricks.
Tipping: Most Jamaican hotels and restaurants add a service charge of 10%; otherwise 10-15% is expected. Chambermaids, waiters, hotel bellboys and airport porters all expect tips. Taxi drivers receive 10% of the fare.

BUSINESS PROFILE

ECONOMY: Jamaica is the world's largest producer of bauxite and alumina, and the economy has suffered during the 1980s as a result of the low world price and falling demand for the ores. Decisions by the mines' owners, a group of American multinationals, to scale down the level of operations precipitated a major row with the Government which subsequently took control of one of the mines and re-opened it. Tourism has become the major source of foreign exchange and has grown rapidly despite the impact of several hurricanes. Agriculture (principally sugar cane, bananas, coffee and cocoa) has maintained a steady position in the economy, and improved efficiency and production methods offset by climatic conditions and the state of the world markets. Manufacturing is expanding steadily, with cement, textiles, tobacco and other consumer goods among the products. The Manley government embarked on a familiar course of privatisation of state-owned enterprises and tight budgetary controls implemented with IMF support. His successor and former deputy, P J Patterson, has

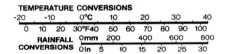

continued with the same policy package. The USA dominates Jamaica's trade, providing half the country's imports and taking over 30% of exports.
BUSINESS: Business people should wear a 'shirtjac' (bush jacket without a tie), also known locally as a *kareba.* Usual formalities are required and appointments and business cards are normal. All trade samples now need an import licence which can be obtained from the Trade Administration Department, PO Box 25, The Office Centre, 12 Ocean Boulevard, Kingston. Tel: 922 1840. Samples of non-commercial value are allowed into the country without a licence prior to arrival, although it may still be necessary to visit the office of the Trade Administrator to exchange the licence copy for a clearance copy which the customs authorities demand before clearing the goods. **Office hours:** 0830-1630/1700 Monday to Friday.
COMMERCIAL INFORMATION: The following organisation can offer advice: Jamaica Chamber of Commerce *and* Associated Chambers of Commerce of Jamaica, PO Box 172, 7-8 East Parade, Kingston. Tel: 922 0150. Fax: 924 9056.
CONFERENCES/CONVENTIONS: The Jamaican Conference Centre in Kingston was opened by HM Queen Elizabeth II in 1983. There are also several hotels in Jamaica with dedicated conference facilities. Seating is available for up to 1000 persons at some centres. The Jamaican Tourist Board (address at top of entry) can supply information.

CLIMATE

Tropical all year. The rainy months are May and October, but showers may occur at any time. Cooler evenings.
Required clothing: Lightweight cottons and linens; light woollens are advised for evenings. Avoid synthetics.

TEMPERATURE CONVERSIONS
```
-20    -10      0°C      10       20       30       40
 0   10   20  30°F40   50   60   70   80   90  100
      RAINFALL  0mm    200      400      600      800
   CONVERSIONS  0In   5    10    15    20    25    30
```

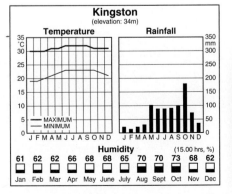

Kingston
(elevation: 34m)
Temperature / Rainfall
```
Humidity                        (15.00 hrs, %)
61   62   62   66   68   68   65   70   70   73   68   62
Jan  Feb  Mar  Apr  May June July Aug Sept Oct  Nov  Dec
```

□ *international airport*
800km
400mls

C.I.S.
CHINA
CHINA
C.I.S.
Sakhalin
Hokkaido
Sapporo
Islands occupied by Russia since WW2
D.P.R. OF KOREA
Sea of Japan
Sado I.
Sendai
REPUBLIC OF KOREA
Honshu
JAPAN
TOKYO
Fujisan 3776m
Fukuoka
Shikoku
PACIFIC OCEAN
Nagasaki
Kyushu
East China Sea
1 Yokohama
2 Nagoya
3 Kyoto
4 Osaka
5 Kobe
6 Hiroshima
Ryukyu Is.
Okinawa
Bonin Is.
Volcano Is. · Iwo Jima

Location: Far East.

Japan National Tourist Organisation
Tokyo Kotsu Kaikan Building, 2-10-1 Yuraku-cho, Chiyoda-ku, Tokyo, Japan
Tel: (3) 32 16 19 01. Fax: (3) 32 14 76 80.
Embassy of Japan
101-104 Piccadilly, London W1V 9FN
Tel: (0171) 465 6500. Fax: (0171) 491 9348. Opening hours: 0930-1230 and 1430-1630 Monday to Friday.
Consulate in: Edinburgh (tel: (0131) 225 4777; fax: (0131) 225 4828).
JETRO (Japan External Trade Organisation)
Leconfield House, Curzon Street, London W1Y 8LQ
Tel: (0171) 493 7226. Fax: (0171) 491 7570.
Japan National Tourist Organisation
167 Regent Street, London W1R 7FD
Tel: (0171) 734 9638. Fax: (0171) 734 4290. Opening hours: 0930-1730 Monday to Friday.
British Embassy
No 1 Ichiban-cho, Chiyoda-ku, Tokyo 102, Japan
Tel: (3) 32 65 55 11. Fax: (3) 52 75 31 64. Telex: 22755 (a/b PRODROME J).
Consulates in: Osaka, Hiroshima, Fukuoka and Nagoya.
Embassy of Japan
2520 Massachusetts Avenue, NW, Washington, DC 20008
Tel: (202) 939 6700. Fax: (202) 328 2184.
Consulates in: Agaña, Anchorage, Atlanta, Boston, Chicago, Honolulu, Houston, Kansas City, Los Angeles, New Orleans, New York (tel: (212) 371 8222), Portland, Saipan, San Francisco and Seattle.
Japan Information and Culture Center
Lafayette Center III, 1115 21st Street, NW, Washington, DC 20036
Tel: (202) 939 6900. Fax: (202) 822 6524.
Embassy of the United States of America
PO Box 258, Unit 45004, 10-1, Akasaka 1-chome, Minato-ku, Tokyo 107, Japan
Tel: (3) 32 24 50 00. Fax: (3) 35 05 18 62.
Consulates in: Okinawa, Osaka-Kobe, Sapporo and Fukuoka.
Embassy of Japan
255 Sussex Drive, Ottawa, Ontario K1N 9E6
Tel: (613) 236 8541. Fax: (613) 563 9047.
Consulates in: Edmonton, Halifax, Montréal, Regina, St

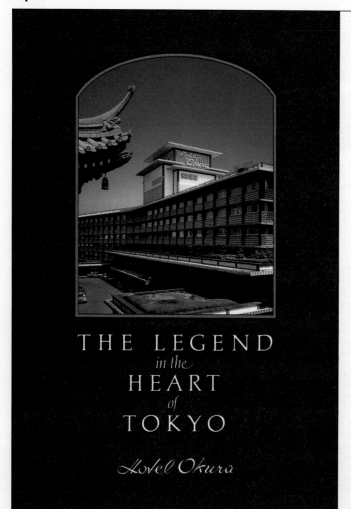

THE LEGEND
in the
HEART
of
TOKYO

Hotel Okura

John's, Toronto, Vancouver and Winnipeg.
Japan National Tourist Organisation
165 University Avenue, Toronto, Ontario M5H 3B8
Tel: (416) 366 7140. Fax: (416) 366 4530.
Canadian Embassy
3-38 Akasaka 7-chome, Minato-ku, Tokyo 107, Japan
Tel: (3) 34 08 21 01. Fax: (3) 34 79 53 20. Telex: 22218
(a/b DOMCAN J).
Consulates in: Fukuoka, Nagoya and Osaka.

AREA: 377,815 sq km (145,875 sq miles).
POPULATION: 123,587,297 (1992).
POPULATION DENSITY: 332 per sq km.
CAPITAL: Tokyo. **Population:** 11,633,582 (1992).
GEOGRAPHY: Japan is separated from the Asian mainland by 160km (100 miles) of sea. About 70% of the country is covered by hills and mountains, a number of which are active or inactive volcanoes. A series of mountain ranges run from northern Hokkaido to southern Kyushu. The Japanese Alps (the most prominent range) run in a north–south direction through central Honshu. The highest mountain is Mount Fuji at 3776m (12,388ft). Lowlands and plains are small and scattered, mostly lying along the coast and composed of alluvial lowlands and diluvial uplands. Largest is Kanto Plain in the Tokyo Bay region. The coastline is very long in relation to the land area, and has very varied features. The deeply indented bays with good natural harbours tend to be adjacent to mountainous terrain.
LANGUAGE: Japanese. Some English is spoken in major cities.
RELIGION: Shintoist and Buddhist (most Japanese follow both religions) with a Christian minority.
TIME: GMT + 9.
ELECTRICITY: 100 volts AC, 60Hz in the west (Osaka). 100 volts AC, 50Hz in eastern Japan and Tokyo. Plugs are flat 2-pin and light bulbs are screw-type.
COMMUNICATIONS: Telephone: Full IDD service. Country code: 81. Outgoing international code: 001. International calls can be made from the KDD (International Telephone and Telegraph Centre), 3-2-5 Kasumigaseki, Chiyoda-ku. International calls can also be placed from hotels.
Fax: Sending and receiving can be arranged at any hour at major hotels. KDD (Kokusai Denshin Denwa Co Ltd) offers facilities in Tokyo, Osaka, Yokohama and Nagoya. **Telex/telegram:** Telex booths are

available at main post offices and main offices of Kokusai Denshin Denwa Co Ltd and Nippon Denshin Denwa Kaisha. Telegrams can be sent from the main hotels and from the above companies, also from larger post offices in major cities. Two rates are available. Overseas telegrams can also be sent from the Central Post Office in Tokyo until midnight. **Post:** Letters can be taken to the Central Post Office in front of Tokyo Station or the International Post Office, near exit A-2 Otemachi subway station, which provide English-speaking personnel. Airmail to Europe takes four to six days to arrive. All main post offices have *Poste Restante* facilities and will hold mail for up to ten days. Post office hours: 0900-1700 Monday to Friday, 0900-1200 Saturday. The International Post Office and Central Post Office are open weekdays until 1900 and until 1700 Saturday. **Press:** The English-language daily newspapers in Tokyo include *The Asahi Evening News, The Daily Yomiuri, The Japan Times* and *The Mainichi Daily News.*
BBC World Service and Voice of America frequencies: From time to time these change. See the section *How to Use this Book* for more information.
BBC:

| MHz | 21.72 | 17.83 | 15.28 | 9.740 |

Voice of America:

| MHz | 15.43 | 11.72 | 5.985 | 1.143 |

PASSPORT/VISA

Regulations and requirements may be subject to change at short notice, and you are advised to contact the appropriate diplomatic or consular authority before finalising travel arrangements. Details of these may be found at the head of this country's entry. Any numbers in the chart refer to the footnotes below.

	Passport Required?	Visa Required?	Return Ticket Required?
Full British	Yes	No/1	Yes
BVP	Not valid	-	-
Australian	Yes	Yes	Yes
Canadian	Yes	No/3	Yes
USA	Yes	No/3	Yes
Other EU (As of 31/12/94)	Yes	No/1/2	Yes
Japanese	-	-	-

PASSPORTS: Valid passport required by all.
Note: The Japanese authorities do not recognise passports of: (a) Chinese residents of Taiwan (China); (b) Andorra (nationals of Andorra must hold a passport issued by the French or Spanish authorities); (c) the Democratic People's Republic of Korea; (d) collective passports issued to groups of passengers (other than those issued to a family travelling together); (e) tourists, whether or not they hold a visa, who do not possess visible means of support for tourism, onward or return tickets and other documents for their next destination. Such people may be refused entry.
British Visitors Passport: Not accepted.
VISAS: Required by all except:
(a) **[1]** nationals of Germany, Republic of Ireland and the UK* for a stay not exceeding 6 months;
(b) **[2]** nationals of Belgium, Denmark, France, Greece, Italy, Luxembourg, The Netherlands, Portugal (persons whose passport was originally issued in present or former Portuguese colonial territories *do* require a visa) and Spain for a stay not exceeding 3 months;
(c) **[3]** nationals of Canada and the USA for a stay not exceeding 3 months;
(d) nationals of Argentina, Bahamas, Barbados, Chile, Colombia, Costa Rica, Croatia, Cyprus, Dominican Republic, El Salvador, Finland, Guatemala, Honduras, Iceland, Israel, Lesotho, Malta, Mauritius, New Zealand, Norway, Peru, San Marino, Singapore, Slovenia, Suriname, Sweden, Tunisia, Turkey, Uruguay and Yugoslavia (Serbia and Montenegro) for stays not exceeding 3 months;
(e) nationals of Austria, Liechtenstein, Mexico (diplomatic passport holders *do* need a visa) and Switzerland for a stay not

exceeding 6 months;
(f) nationals of Brunei for a stay not exceeding 14 days.
Note [*]: All UK passports with the endorsement 'Holder is subject to control under the Commonwealth Immigration Act' *do* require a visa.
Types of visa: *Business* (cost varies); *Tourist*: prices depend on nature of intended visit: for example, UK and Irish nationals would not normally require a visa, but for long stays or for working visits UK nationals pay £7.10, Indian nationals £5.20; visas for all other nationals usually cost £19.00. Contact the Consulate (or Consular section at Embassy) for further details.
Validity: Depends on a variety of conditions, including nationality and purpose of visit. Enquire at the Consulate (or Consular section at Embassy) for further details.
Application to: Consulate (or Consular section at Embassy). For addresses, see top of entry.
Application requirements: (a) Passport. (b) *1-2 completed application forms. (c) *1-2 passport-size photographs. (d) Return air/sea ticket or copy. (e) A letter of introduction for Business visas.
Note [*]: Nationals of Communist and Middle Eastern countries must always submit 2 completed visa application forms and 2 photos. Requirements for other nationals vary – check with the Consulate (or Consular section at Embassy) for more detailed information.
Working days required: 7 days in most cases.

MONEY

Currency: Japanese Yen (¥). Notes are in denominations of ¥10,000, 5000 and 1000. Coins are in denominations of ¥500, 100, 50, 10, 5 and 1.
Currency exchange: All money must be exchanged at an authorised bank or money changer.
Credit cards: Visa, Diners Club, American Express, Access/Mastercard and other major credit cards are widely used. Check with your credit card company for merchant acceptability.
Travellers cheques: These can be exchanged at major banks and larger hotels.
Exchange rate indicators: The following figures are included as a guide to the movements of the Japanese Yen against Sterling and the US Dollar:

Date:	**Oct '92**	**Sep '93**	**Jan '94**	**Jan '95**
£1.00=	**193.50**	**159.00**	**165.12**	**156.09**
$1.00=	**121.93**	**104.13**	**111.60**	**99.77**

Currency restrictions: Import of local currency is unrestricted; export is limited to ¥5,000,000. There are no restrictions on the import or export of foreign currency.
Banking hours: 0900-1500 Monday to Friday.

DUTY FREE

The following goods may be imported into Japan without incurring customs duty:
400 cigarettes or 100 cigars or 500g of tobacco; 3 bottles (approximately 760cc each) of spirits; 57ml of perfume; gifts up to the value of ¥200,000.
Note: Tobacco and alcohol allowances are for those aged 20 or over. Oral declaration is necessary on arrival at Customs.
Prohibited items: Guns, pornography and narcotic drugs.

PUBLIC HOLIDAYS

Jan 1 '95 New Year's Day. **Jan 15** Coming of Age Day. **Feb 11** National Foundation Day. **Mar 21** Vernal Equinox Day. **Apr 29** Greenery Day. **May 3** Constitution Memorial Day. **May 5** Children's Day. **Sep 15** Respect for the Aged Day. **Sep 23** Autumnal Equinox Day. **Oct 10** Health Sports Day. **Nov 3** Culture Day. **Nov 23** Labour Thanksgiving Day. **Dec 23** Birthday of the Emperor. **Jan 1 '96** New Year's Day. **Jan 15** Coming of Age Day. **Feb 11** National Foundation Day. **Mar 21** Vernal Equinox Day. **Apr 29** Greenery Day.
Note: (a) If a holiday falls on a Sunday, the following day is treated as a holiday. (b) Over the New Year, almost all shops are closed January 1-3.

HEALTH

Regulations and requirements may be subject to change at short notice, and you are advised to contact your doctor well in advance of your intended date of departure. Any numbers in the chart refer to the footnotes below.

	Special Precautions?	Certificate Required?
Yellow Fever	No	No
Cholera	No	No
Typhoid & Polio	Yes	-
Malaria	No	-
Food & Drink	No	-

Health care: Health insurance is strongly recommended. The International Association for Medical Assistance to Travellers provides English-speaking doctors. There are hospitals in major cities such as Tokyo, Osaka, Kyoto, Kobe, Hiroshima and Okinawa.

TRAVEL - International

AIR: Japan's largest international airline is *Japan Air Lines (JL).*
For free advice on air travel, call the Air Travel Advisory Bureau in the UK on (0171) 636 5000 (London) *or* (0161) 832 2000 (Manchester).
Approximate flight times: From *Hong Kong* to Osaka is 3 hours. From *London* to Tokyo is 11 hours 30 minutes on a non-stop flight (stopover can add a further 5 or 6 hours) and to Osaka is 15 hours. From *New York* to Tokyo is 14 hours. From *Los Angeles* to Tokyo is 10 hours. From *Singapore* to Tokyo is 7 hours 30 minutes. From *Sydney* to Tokyo is 10 hours.
International airports: *New Tokyo International Airport (TYO)* (Narita City) is 66km (41 miles) northeast of Tokyo (travel time – 1 hour 10 minutes). Airport facilities include an outgoing duty-free shop, bank/bureau de change (0900-2400) and car hire *(Nippon Rent-a-Car)*. There is a bus to the City Air Terminal every 10 minutes from 0700-2400, then taxi to hotels (bus tickets are bought in the terminal). The journey from Tokyo City Air Terminal, located at Hakozaki, Nihombashi, to Tokyo Central Station takes 15 minutes by bus or taxi. There is a coach to major hotels every 20-50 minutes, 0700-2100. JR Narita Express line runs from Narita station terminal located beneath the airport to Tokyo station (travel time – 53 minutes), Shinjuku (travel time – 80 minutes) and Yokohama (travel time – 90 minutes) every hour and every half-hour at busy periods from 0745-2145. Keisei 'Skyliner Train' also runs from the airport terminal to Keisei Ueno Station (travel time – 60 minutes) from 0920-2200. There are taxis to the city, with a surcharge after 2200 (travel time – 60-70 minutes).
A second terminal opened on December 6, 1992, with its own Japan Railways and Keisei Line station in the basement. There is also a free shuttle bus connecting both terminals every 10-15 minutes (travel time – 10 minutes). The terminal itself consists of a main and a satellite building connected by a fully-automated shuttle.
Osaka International (OSA) (Itami) is 20km (12 miles) northwest of Osaka. Airport facilities include an outgoing duty-free shop, car hire, bank/bureau de change and bar/restaurant. There is a bus to the city every 20 minutes from 0800-2120 (travel time – 30 minutes). Return is from the coach terminal, Umeda, and there are pick-ups at major hotels from 0620-2020. A train goes to the city every 15 minutes from 0432-2350. Return is from Hankyu railway station, Umeda (train to Hotarugaike station) from 0500-0007. There are buses to the city every 20 minutes from 0808-2130. Return is from Osaka bus station, Maru Building, every 10 minutes from 0612-2012. Taxis to the city impose a surcharge after 2200.
Fukuoka International (FUK) is 25 minutes travel time from Fukuoka City. Airport facilities include an outgoing duty-free shop, car hire, bank/bureau de change and bar/restaurant.
Nagoya International (NGO) has flights to 29 international destinations including: Hong Kong, Seoul, Bangkok, Singapore, Honolulu, Taipei, Brisbane, Melbourne and Sydney, Frankfurt/M and Paris.
Departure tax: ¥2000 is levied at *New Tokyo International Airport* (none at other airports).
SEA: Japan is easily accessible by sea, and passenger ships include the major ports on their schedules. The *Royal Viking Line's* world cruise puts in at Kobe and there are also cruises between the Japanese islands en route to Shanghai and Hong Kong. The *Pearl of Scandinavia* leaves from Kobe on a cruise along the coast of China.
RAIL: The Trans-Siberian route to Japan is an interesting and very well-organised, if lengthy, trip. Connections can be made daily from London (Liverpool Street) via Harwich or London (Victoria) and via Dover through Europe to Moscow. There are sleeping cars four times a week from Hook of Holland to Moscow, and twice a week from Ostend to Moscow. The route from Moscow can be either by air, train and boat or train and boat via Khabarovsk and Nakhodka (a port east of Vladivostok) to Yokohama, or from Vladivostok by ferry to Niigata.

TRAVEL - Internal

AIR: Services are run by *Japan Airlines (JL), All Nippon Airways (NH)* and *TOA Domestic Airlines (JD). Japanese Airlines* provide English-speaking hostesses and ground staff and link major cities, whereas the others serve similar routes and smaller towns.
Tokyo's domestic airport is *Haneda*. A monorail service runs from Hamamatsu-cho to Haneda. One international airline, *China Airlines*, serves Haneda. Other international flights to and from Haneda are made via *Tokyo, Osaka, Fukuoka* or *Nagoya,* Main routes are Tokyo–Sapporo; Tokyo–Fukuoka; Tokyo–Osaka; and Tokyo–Naha.
Tickets can be purchased at automatic machines at *Tokyo International Airport's* domestic departure counter and at *Osaka International Airport.*
RAIL: Japan's rail network is one of the best in the world, and is widely used for both business and pleasure. Very frequent services run on the main routes. *Shinkansen,* the 'Bullet Trains', are the fastest, with compartments for wheelchair passengers, diners and buffet cars. Supplements are payable on the three classes of express train and in 'Green' (first-class) cars of principal trains, for which reservations must be made.
Japan Rail Pass: An economical pass for foreign tourists, which must be purchased before arrival in Japan, can be obtained from *Japan Airlines* (*JL* users only), Japan Travel Bureau, Miki Travel, Nippon Travel Agency, Tokyu Travel Europe and Kintetsu International Express. It can also be used on Japan Rail buses and Japan Rail ferries. See the *Japan Rail Pass* brochure available from the Tourist Board. Express and 'limited express' trains are best for intercity.
ROAD: Driving in Japan is complicated for those who cannot read the language as it will be a problem to understand the road signs. Traffic in cities is often congested. Traffic drives on the left. The Keiyo Highway, Tohoku Expressway, Tomei Expressway and the Meishin Expressway link Japan's major Pacific coastal cities, passing through excellent scenery.
Documentation: An International Driving Permit is required.
URBAN: Public transport is well developed, efficient and crowded. The **underground** systems and privately-run suburban rail services, which serve all the main cities, are very convenient, but best avoided in rush hours. **Bus:** These can be confusing and are best used with someone who knows the system. Otherwise visitors should get exact details of their destination from the hotel. Fares systems are highly automated, particularly rail and underground, but passes may be available. On buses, payment may be made on leaving. Tokyo has a very large public transport network of buses, tramways, two underground systems and half a dozen private railways. The underground, tramway and bus services, run by the Tokyo Transportation Bureau, have a flat central area fare and stage fares elsewhere. Books of tickets can be bought. The Eidan underground is a bigger 7-line system. **Taxi:** There is a minimum charge for the first 2km (1.2 miles) and there is a time charge in slow traffic. It is advisable for visitors to have prepared in advance the name and address of their destination in Japanese writing, together with the name of some nearby landmark; a map may also help. Hotels can provide this service.
JOURNEY TIMES: The following chart gives approximate journey times (in hours and minutes) from Tokyo to other major cities/towns in Japan.

	Air	Road	Rail	Sea
Nagoya	-	4.00	2.00	-
Kagoshima	1.50	26.00	10.00	48.00
Fukuoka	1.45	13.00	6.30	-
Nagasaki	1.40	18.00	9.00	-
Okinawa	2.30	-	-	60.00
Osaka	1.00	6.00	3.15	-
Sapporo	1.25	-	14.00	-

ACCOMMODATION

HOTELS: Hotels are 'Western' or 'Japanese' style, sometimes both. Western is much like any modern American or European hotel. Japanese style is comfortable and provides an exciting new experience; for instance, in some hotels the Japanese tea ceremony is demonstrated. Many non-obligatory extras are available. Service charges of 10-15% and taxes of 3% (6% if hotel charge exceeds ¥15,000 per night) are added to the bill.
Grading: No accommodation grading system operates in Japan. For further information contact the Japan Hotel Association, Shin Otemachi Building, 2-2-1 Otemachi, Chiyoda-ku, Toyko 100. Tel: (3) 32 79 27 06. Fax: (3) 32 74 53 75; or The Japan Tourist Hotel Association, Kokusai Kanko Kaikan, 8-3 Marunouchi 1-chrome, Chiyoda-ku, Toyko 100. Tel: (3) 32 31 53 30. Fax: (3) 32 01 55 68.
GUEST-HOUSES: Staying at a *ryokan*, a traditional inn, is one of the real delights of Japan. Japanese-style inns are rarely cheaper than their Western-style equivalents; usually, however, breakfast and dinner – generally Japanese dishes – are included in the overnight rates. Full facilities are provided. No shoes are worn in the house as slippers are provided. Small gifts or 5% may be given with the bill.
YOUTH HOSTELS: There are many Youth Hostels throughout Japan. Contact Japan Youth Hostels Inc, Hoken Kaikan, 1-2 Sadohara-cho, 1-Chome, Ichigaya, Shinjuku, Tokyo 162. Tel: (3) 32 69 58 31.

RESORTS & EXCURSIONS

Japan is a chain of mountainous islands lying off the coasts of China and, in the far north of Hokkaido, Russia. Much of the land is unsuitable for agriculture and remains as forest. The coastline is indented with numerous bays and inlets.
Tokyo: There is much to see in the capital: the *Imperial Palace* with its grounds set out as a park; *Ginza*, the shopping and entertainment area; *Shinjuku*, the western quarter with a national park, the *Botanical Garden* and the *Meiji Shrine*. There is a thriving nightlife with clubs, theatres, music and food from all over the world.
From Tokyo visitors can go to see the *Boso Peninsula* and **Shirahama** with its fine beaches; **Narita**, a pilgrimage centre; **Mito**, particularly in February when it is covered with plum blossoms; **Mashiko**, the pottery centre; *Bonsai Village* at Omiya; *Ogawa-machi*, the home of paper-making; and most of all **Nikko** which, set in a national park, and with splendid temples and mausoleums, is one of the most visited sites in the country.

Kamakura, one hour south of Tokyo by train, was once the seat of the 12th-century feudal government. Surrounded by forested mountains on three sides, and Sagami Bay on the other, it is known for its many old temples and shrines, as well as its well-preserved historical sites. Highlights include the *Great Bronze Statue of Buddha*, the colourful *Tsurugaoka Hachimangu Shrine*, the *Kamakura Museum*, the *Modern Art Museum*, *Tokeiji Temple*, *Hase Kannon Temple* and picturesque **Enoshima Island**, with its shrine and aquarium, connected to the mainland by the *Benten Bridge*.
Fuji-Hakone-Izu: This area, which contains *Mount Fuji*, Japan's highest mountain, is one of great appeal to the visitor. Attractions include *Fuji Five Lakes* and a hot spring resort, **Hakone**; swimming and boating and facilities for skating, hiking, fishing and camping are available.
Japanese Alps: These mountains, in the centre of **Honshu Island**, are popular with both native and foreign climbers. **Matsumoto**, the main gateway to the Japanese Alps, has the imposing *Matsumoto Castle*, the oldest remaining castle in Japan. **Takayama**, situated in the valley surrounding the Alps, has preserved a 17th-century townscape with its old houses and shops.
Kanazawa, on the western coast, is well-known for its *Kenrokuen Garden* and its silk-dying and porcelain.
Nagoya is one of the major industrial cities, as well as being a centre for traditional handicrafts. It is within easy reach of the Alps and the **Ise-Shima National Park**, which includes the towns of **Toba**, famed for its cultured pearl farms, and **Ise**, with its *Grand Shrine*.
Kyoto was founded in AD794 as a ceremonial capital built in the classical Chinese style. It is best seen on foot. Visitors can stroll round the temples, palaces and shrines, see the Zen headquarters and walk through the quiet streets with their workshops of the textile weavers.
Nara dates back from the earliest days of the Japanese people. It draws a million visitors a year to see its traditional house, the 5-storey pagoda of *Kofuku-ji*, its ancient statues and ceremonial buildings, and its famous *Great Buddha Hall* – the largest wooden structure in the world – and the world's largest bronze statue, that of Buddha.
Nagasaki is said to be Japan's first international city. There is the *Peace Park* to see, as well as *Glover House* (the site of 'Madame Butterfly'), the *Chinese Temple*, the *Spectacles Bridge*, the *Suwa Shrine*, the hot springs and *Mount Aso*, the largest active volcano in the world.
North of Tokyo are some other interesting towns and tourist sites. **Aizu-Wakamatsu**, famous for its lacquerware, has *Tsurugaoka Castle* and *Aizu Buke-yashiki*, a large complex of restored samurai houses and museums. Nearby **Bandai-Kogen Plateau** is a popular mountain resort with many beautiful lakes and terns. Further north, **Sendai**, surrounded by picturesque wooded hills, is the home of the famous *Tanabata Star Festival* in August. Proceeding even further north is **Hiraizumi**, an historical town housing the *Chusonji* and *Motsuji* temples. *Lake Towada*, in the far north, is a beautiful crater lake at the centre of the scenic **Towada-Hachimantai National Park**. In *Oirase Valley*, extending 14km (9 miles) from the eastern shore of the lake, there are waterfalls, rapids and rocks nestled amid the lush greenery. **Akita**, facing the northwest coast, is a

modern city, but still possesses some interesting historical sites and the famous *Kanto Lantern-balancing Festival* takes place there in early August.
POPULAR ITINERARIES: 5-day: (a) Tokyo–Kamakura–Hakone–Kyoto–Nara– Tokyo. (b) Tokyo–Matsumoto–Takayama–Kanazawa–Kyoto–Tokyo. **7-day:** (a) Tokyo–Hakone–Toba–Ise–Kyoto–Nara–Kyoto–Nikko–Tokyo. (b) Tokyo–Matsumoto–Takayama–Kanazawa–Kyoto–Tokyo. (c) Tokyo–Sendai–Hiraizumi–Lake Towada–Akita–Bandai-Kogen Plateau–Aizu-Wakamatsu–Tokyo.

SOCIAL PROFILE

FOOD & DRINK: Japanese cuisine, now popular in the West, involves very sensitive flavours, fresh crisp vegetables and an absence of richness. Specialities include *teriyaki* (marinated beef/chicken/fish seared on a hot plate), *sukiyaki* (thin slices of beef, bean curd and vegetables cooked in soy sauce and then dipped in egg), *tempura* (deep fried seafood and vegetables), *sushi* (slices of raw seafood placed on lightly-vinegared rice balls – very tasty and refreshing), and *sashimi* (slices of raw seafood dipped in soy sauce). The best place to try sushi is a *Kaiten* Sushi Bar, where many varieties pass the customer on a conveyor belt allowing complete choice over which delicacies to try, at more reasonable prices than a traditional Sushi Bar. Fine Oriental food (Korean – very hot – and Chinese) is served in restaurants. An amazing number and variety of international restaurants are also available, which cater for every possible taste and budget, from French and Italian to Chinese, Indian and Thai. Western dishes in expensive places are good, but cheaper restaurants may be disappointing. Restaurants have table service and in some places it is customary to remove footwear. **Drink:** *Sake*, hot rice wine, is strong and distinctively fresh-tasting. *Shochu*, a strong aquavit, is an acquired taste. Japanese wines are worth trying once, and beer – similar to lager – is recommended. Popular brands are *Kirin*, *Sapporo*, *Suntory* and *Asahi*. Waiter service is common in bars. The Japanese are very fond of original Scotch Whisky, but this is both very expensive and highly sought after; therefore Japanese versions of this drink are often consumed. There are no licensing hours. Drinking is subject to long-standing rituals of politeness. The hostess will pour a drink for the visitor, and will insist on the visitor's glass being full. It is also appreciated if the visitor pours drinks for the host, but it is bad manners for a visitor to pour one for himself.
NIGHTLIFE: Tokyo has an abundance of cinemas, theatres, bars, coffee shops, discos and nightclubs. A wide range of bars is available, from the posh and stylish to cheap street stalls. In the summer, rooftop beer gardens are popular. Some clubs have hostesses who expect to be bought drinks and snacks. In bigger nightclubs and bars, a basic hostess charge is levied. However, there are thousands of other bars and clubs. In Tokyo there are concerts almost every night ranging from classical to rock. Foreign opera companies, ballet companies, orchestras and rock/pop stars visit Japan all year round. Some live jazz houses are also available. For those who

would like to try the traditional Japanese performing arts, there is *Kabuki* and *Noh* theatre in Tokyo. *Play Guide* ticket offices are situated in major department stores. It is advisable to purchase the tickets in advance because shows are quickly sold out. *Karaoke* bars are a very popular form of entertainment in Japan.

SHOPPING: A blend of Oriental goods and Western sales techniques confront the shopper, particularly at the big department stores, which are more like exhibitions than shops. Playgrounds for children are available. Special purchases include *kimonos, mingei* (local crafts including kites and folk toys); *Kyoto* silks, fans, screens, dolls; religious articles such as Shinto and Buddhist artefacts; paper lanterns; hi-fi equipment, cameras, televisions and other electronic equipment. **Tax exemptions** are available on presentation of passport. Bargaining is not usual. **Shopping hours:** 1000-1900.

SPORT: A great variety of sports are available. **Sumo,** ceremonial wrestling, and **judo** are Japan's national sports, drawing huge crowds. There are opportunities for the visitor to purchase a costume and learn some of the techniques. Classes are for men and women and in most large schools English is spoken. **Kendo,** Japanese fencing, is spectacular and practised in numerous clubs and college halls. **Baseball** is the favourite team sport with the season lasting almost all year round. There are day and night games and tickets are reasonably priced and widely available. **Golf** is very popular with businessmen and there are excellent courses in and around Tokyo. It is expensive, as in most countries, and there are some courses where membership is required or it is only possible to play by invitation. **Football** is just beginning to take off in a big way in Japan with the introduction of the Japanese soccer J-League. **Skiing** is very popular and there are many good ski slopes especially in the Japanese Alps and on the northern island of Hokkaido.

SPECIAL EVENTS: A large number of festivals are celebrated in Japan throughout the year in different parts of the country. Some are hugely spectacular, others are religiously orientated. The following are a selection of annual events and festivals. For full details of events in 1995/96, contact the Japan National Tourist Organisation.
Mar 12-26 '95 *Sumo Tournaments,* Osaka. **Apr 8** *'Kamakura Matsuri' of Tsurugaoke Hachimangu Shrine,* Kamakura, Kanagawa. **May 7-21** *Sumo Tournaments,* Tokyo. **May 15** *'Aoi Matsuri' or Hollyhock Festival of Shimogamo and Kamigamo shrines,* Kyoto. **May 17-18** *Grand Festival of Toshogu Shrine,* Tochigi. **Jul 7** *'Tansbata' or Star Festival,* throughout Japan. **Jul 17** *'Gion Matsuri' of Yasaka Shrine,* Kyoto. **Jul 24-25** *'Tenjin Matsuri' of Temmangu Shrine,* Osaka. **Jul 29** *Fireworks display on the Sumida River,* Asakura. **Aug 1-7** *'Nebuta Matsuri' in Aomori and 'Neputa Matsuri',* Hirosaki Aomori. **Aug 6** *Peace Ceremony,* Hiroshima. **Aug 12-15** *'Awa Odori' at Tokushima,* Tokushima. **Aug 16** *'Daimonji' Bonfire on Mt Nyoigadake,* Kyoto. **Sep 28-31** *World Judo Championships,* Chiba. **Oct 2-9** *'Takayama Matsuri' of Hachiman Shrine,* Takayama. **Oct 22** *'Jidal Matsuri' or Festival of Eras, Heian Shrine,* Kyoto. **Nov 15** *'Shichi-go-san' or Children's Shrine Visiting Day,* throughout Japan. **Dec** *'Chichibu Yo-Matsuri' or all-night festival,* Chichubu City, Saltama. **Dec 17-19** *'Hagoita Ichi' or battle-dore Fair,* Asakusa, Tokyo.

SOCIAL CONVENTIONS: Japanese manners and customs are vastly different from those of Western people. A strict code of behaviour and politeness is recognised and followed by almost all Japanese. However, they are aware of the difference between themselves and the West and therefore do not expect visitors to be familiar with all their customs but expect them to behave formally and politely. A straightforward refusal does not form part of Japanese etiquette. A vague 'yes' does not really mean 'yes' but the visitor may be comforted to know that confusion caused by non-committal replies occurs between the Japanese themselves. Entertaining guests at home is not as customary as in the West, as it is an enterprise not taken lightly and the full red-carpet treatment is given. Japanese men are also sensitive lest their wives be embarrassed and feel that their hospitality is inadequate by Western standards; for instance, by the inconvenience to a foreign guest of the custom of sitting on the floor. Bowing is the customary greeting but handshaking is becoming more common for business meetings with Westerners. The suffix *san* should be used when addressing all men and women; for instance Mr Yamada would be addressed as Yamada-san. When entering a Japanese home or restaurant it is customary to remove shoes. Table manners are very important, although the Japanese host will be very tolerant towards a visitor. However, it is best if visitors familiarise themselves with basic table etiquette and use chopsticks. It is customary for a guest to bring a small gift when visiting someone's

home. Exchange of gifts is also a common business practice and may take the form of souvenir items such as company pens, ties or high-quality spirits. Smoking is only restricted where notified. **Tipping:** Tips are never expected; where a visitor wishes to show particular appreciation of a service, money should not be given in the form of loose change but rather as a small financial gift. Special printed envelopes can be bought for financial gifts of this type.

BUSINESS PROFILE

ECONOMY: Japan is the economic phenomenon of the late 20th century: Japan's gross national product ranks second in the world after the United States. A variety of factors have contributed to the country's current prevailing success. A wholly modern economy built up following the devastation of the Second World War was not hampered, in the manner of the American and some European economies, by a large defence commitment. Judicious application of import controls is coupled with a uniquely aggressive export drive orchestrated by the powerful Ministry of International Trade and Industry (MITI), while an exceptionally high savings ratio in proportion to net earnings has fuelled a consistently high level of industrial investment in manufacturing industries which have honed the process of cutting overheads down to a fine art. Finally, the structure of the Japanese domestic economy revolves around a series of large multi-product corporations serviced with components and raw materials by a plethora of small firms with low overheads and labour costs (a function increasingly met by the 'Tiger' economies of the Pacific Basin: Singapore, South Korea, Taiwan (China) and Hong Kong), and using a distribution system which foreign companies complain is especially restrictive. The result is a US$3000-billion gross national product and an annual trade surplus of US$100 billion. Manufactured goods are the strongest sector, particularly vehicles and electronic goods, although traditional industries such as coal mining, shipbuilding and steel are also profitable. The only sector which does not measure up to Western standards at present is agriculture which is inefficient and heavily protected by the Government, partly as a result of the vagaries of the Japanese electoral system. Rice farming, for instance, is one of a variety of issues behind the apparently serious trade row between Japan and the United States: the USA alleges rice imports are being unfairly restricted to protect Japanese farmers. Conversely, there have been many occasions of Western nations complaining about the 'dumping' of cheap Japanese goods in already saturated markets. The newest and fastest growing sector of the Japanese economy is financial services – despite the sharp decline since 1990, the Tokyo Stock Exchange is the largest in the world in terms of the value of shares traded – and, here again, American and European companies complain of discrimination (such as the exclusion of British market-makers from the Tokyo market). These routine allegations cannot disguise the massive success of the post-war Japanese economy, especially given the almost total lack of raw materials (particularly oil). The USA has a 20% share of Japan's import market, followed by Korea and Indonesia (5.5%), Australia, China, Taiwan (China) and Saudi Arabia (5%). The emphasis in Japanese trade is slowly switching from manufactured goods to exports of services and 'invisibles' (such as finance and insurance). Overseas investments are growing rapidly, particularly in property. Within Japan itself, property reached astronomical levels at the beginning of the 1990s, triggering a crash in 1991 which was a major contributor to the economic slowdown which followed in 1992. While such notions are relative – Japan's trade surplus continues to set new records – there is no doubt that the 'slump' caused a major rethink among Japanese policy-makers, themselves affected by major political realignments since the turn of the 1990s. The new buzz word is *kyosei* ('symbiosis'), which is intended to reflect the new policy objective of co-existence with major trading partners rather than the unalloyed pursuit of ever greater trade surpluses. In January 1995, the industrial area including Kobe and its surroundings was hit by a major earthquake. Despite the devastation, the Japanese economy should not be severely affected in the long term.

BUSINESS: A large supply of visiting cards printed in English and Japanese is essential. Cards can be quickly printed on arrival with Japanese translation on the reverse side. Appointments should be made in advance, and, because of the formality, visits should consist of more than a few days. Punctuality is important. Business discussions are often preceded by tea and are usually very formal. **Office hours:** 0900-1700 Monday to Friday.

COMMERCIAL INFORMATION: The following organisations can offer advice: JETRO (Japan External Trade Organisation) (for address see top of entry); *or*

Japanese Chamber of Commerce, 2nd Floor, Salisbury House, 29 Finsbury Circus, London EC2M 5QQ. Tel: (0171) 628 0069. Fax: (0171) 628 0248; *or* Nippon Shoko Kaigi-sho (Japan Chamber of Commerce and Industry), 3-2-2, Marunouchi, Chiyoda-ku, Tokyo. Tel: (3) 32 83 78 51; *or* JETRO (Japan External Trade Organisation), 2-2-5 Toranomon, Minato-ku, Tokyo 105. Tel: (3) 35 82 55 22. Fax: (3) 35 87 02 19.

CONFERENCES/CONVENTIONS: The Japan Convention Bureau is a division of the Japan National Tourist Organisation (address at top of entry); its *Convention Planner's Guide to Japan* lists 35 cities with conference facilities including Tokyo, Kyoto, Osaka, Yokohama, Hiroshima and Nagasaki. In 1992 there were 1389 international meetings in Japan. During that year, Kyoto proved to be the favourite meeting destination for the third consecutive year, hosting 182 conventions. For further information, contact the Japan Convention Bureau, 2-10-1 Yurakucho, Chiyoda-ku, Toyko 100. Tel: (3) 32 16 29 05. Fax: (3) 32 14 76 80.

CLIMATE

Except for the Hokkaido area and the subtropical Okinawa region, the weather is in general mostly temperate, with four seasons. Winters are cool and sunny in the south, cold and sunny around Tokyo (which occasionally has snow), and very cold around Hokkaido, which is covered in snow for up to four months a year. Summer, between June and September, ranges from warm to very hot, while spring and autumn are generally mild throughout the country. Rain falls throughout the year but June and early July is the main rainy season. Hokkaido, however, is much drier than the Tokyo area. Rainfall is intermittent with sunshine. Typhoons are only likely to occur in September or October but rarely last more than a day.

Required clothing: Lightweight cottons and linens are required throughout summer in most areas. There is much less rainfall than in Western Europe. Light- to medium-weights during spring and autumn; medium- to heavy-weights for winter months, according to region. Much warmer clothes will be needed in the mountains all year round.

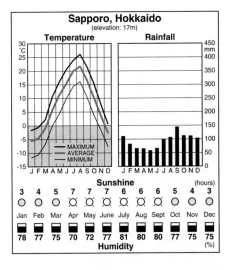

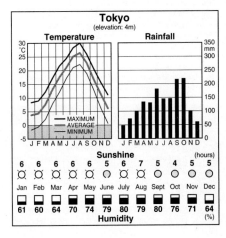

Jersey

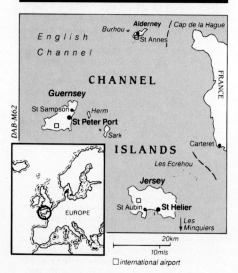

Location: English Channel (off the north French coast).

Jersey Tourism
Liberation Square, St Helier, Jersey JE1 1BB
Tel: 500 800. Fax: 500 808.

Jersey Tourism (Information and Public Relations Office)
Wordsmith Marketing and Public Relations
38 Dover Street, London W1X 3RB
Tel: (0171) 493 5278. Fax: (0171) 491 1565. Opening
hours: 0930-1730 Monday to Friday.

AREA: 116.2 sq km (44.8 sq miles).
POPULATION: 84,082 (1991).
POPULATION DENSITY: 724 per sq km.
CAPITAL: St Helier. **Population:** 28,123 (1991).
GEOGRAPHY: Jersey is the largest of the Channel
Islands, lying approximately 170km (100 miles) south of
the coast of England and 23km (14 miles) from the coast
of Normandy in France. The island is roughly 14.5km (9
miles) by 8km (5 miles). It slopes down from north to south
and often appears to visitors to be largely composed of
pink granite. Jersey has over 20 bays, many small
harbours and magnificent beaches bathed by the warm
waters of the Gulf Stream. The sunshine record for the
British Isles has been held by Jersey for the past 30 years,
with an average of over 1900 hours.
LANGUAGE: English is commonly used. A dialect of
Norman-French is still spoken by some people.
RELIGION: Each of Jersey's parishes has its own
Anglican church, but some parishes, particularly St
Helier, have been subdivided to provide more than one
centre for Church of England worship. There are 12
Roman Catholic and 18 Methodist churches, as well as a
wide range of free churches.
TIME: GMT (GMT + 1 March to October).
ELECTRICITY: 240 volts AC, 50Hz.
COMMUNICATIONS: Telephone: STD code to
Jersey from the UK is 01534, from elsewhere dial UK
code, followed by 1534. Outgoing international code: 00.
Note: In April 1995 local 5-digit telephone numbers
starting with a '7' will be prefixed with an '8'. **Fax:**
Facilities are available for business guests in a few hotels
and at fax bureaux in St Helier. **Telex:** Facilities are
available at larger hotels. **Post:** There is a standard one-
price rate to the UK, which is in general as good as first-
class UK service, although the prices are lower than UK

second class. There is also one rate for internal mail. UK
stamps are not valid in Jersey. The main post office is in
Broad Street, St Helier. Post office hours: 0900-1730
Monday to Friday, 0900-1230 Saturday. **Press:**
Newspapers published in Jersey are the *Freestyle Weekly*,
Jersey Evening Post and *Jersey Weekly Post*.

PASSPORT/VISA

The regulations for Tourist and Business visas are the
same as for the UK (see the *Passport/Visa* section for the
United Kingdom later in the book).

MONEY

Currency: Pound Sterling (£) = 100 pence. Notes are in
denominations of £50, 20, 10, 5 and 1. Coins are in
denominations of £1, and 50, 20, 10, 5, 2 and 1 pence. In
1992, a new 10-pence coin was introduced; the old 10-
pence piece is no longer legal tender. In 1990 a new
smaller 5-pence coin came into circulation; the old 5-
pence piece is no longer legal tender. All UK notes and
coins are legal tender, and circulate with the Channel
Islands issue.
Note: Channel Islands notes and coins are not accepted
in the UK, although notes can be reconverted at parity in
UK banks.
Currency exchange: Money can be exchanged at
bureaux de change, in banks and at many hotels.
Credit cards: Access/Mastercard, American Express,
Diners Club and Visa are all widely accepted. Check
with your credit card company for details of merchant
acceptability and other services which may be available.
Travellers cheques: These are widely accepted.
Exchange rates: The following is included as a guide to
the movement of Sterling against the US Dollar:

Date:	Oct '92	Sep '93	Jan '94	Jan '95
$1.00=	0.63	0.65	0.65	0.64

Currency restrictions: There are no currency
restrictions.
Banking hours: 0930-1530 Monday to Friday. Some
banks are open on Saturday morning.

DUTY FREE

The Channel Islands are a low-duty zone. The following
goods may be imported into Jersey by persons over 17
years of age without incurring customs duty:
*200 cigarettes or 50 cigars or 100 cigarillos or 250g of
tobacco; 2 litres of still table wine; 1 litre of spirits or 2
litres of alcoholic beverages (under 22%) or 2 litres of
sparkling wine; 50g (2 fl oz) perfume and 250ml eau de
toilette; other goods to a value of *£136.*
Note: (a) [*] No limit for goods brought in from an EU
country. (b) There is a total ban on the importation of
animals other than from the UK or other Channel Islands.

PUBLIC HOLIDAYS

Jan 1 '95 New Year's Day. **Apr 14** Good Friday. **Apr 17**
Easter Monday. **May 8** May Day Holiday. **May 9**
Liberation Day. **May 29** Spring Bank Holiday. **Aug 28**
Summer Bank Holiday. **Dec 25** Christmas Day. **Dec 26**
Boxing Day. **Jan 1 '96** New Year's Day. **Apr 5** Good
Friday. **Apr 8** Easter Monday.

HEALTH

Regulations and requirements may be subject to change at short notice, and you are advised to contact your doctor well in advance of your intended date of departure. Any numbers in the chart refer to the footnotes below.		
	Special Precautions?	**Certificate Required?**
Yellow Fever	No	No
Cholera	No	No
Typhoid & Polio	No	-
Malaria	No	-
Food & Drink	No	-

Health care: There is a Reciprocal Health Agreement
with the UK. On presenting proof of UK residence
(driving licence, NHS card, etc) free in- and out-patient
treatment is available at the General Hospital, Gloucester
Street, St Helier (tel: 59000). The agreement does not
cover the costs of medical treatment at a doctor's surgery
(but there is a free GP-style surgery most mornings at the
General Hospital), prescribed medicines, or dental
treatment, but travel by ambulance is free. Despite the
agreement, private medical insurance is advised for UK
residents on long visits in case emergency repatriation is
necessary and to cover the cost of prescribed medicines
and dental treatment. All visitors should bring the name
and address of their family doctor in the event of a
serious accident or illness.

TRAVEL

AIR: Approximate flight time: From London to Jersey
is 40 minutes.
For free advice on air travel, call the Air Travel Advisory
Bureau in the UK on (0171) 636 5000 (London) *or*
(0161) 832 2000 (Manchester).
International airport: *St Peters'* *(JER)* is 8km (5 miles)
from St Helier. Facilities include bureau de change, low-
tariff shopping, restaurant and bar, and provision for the
disabled. Taxis are available and the local bus leaves for
the city centre every 15 minutes.
SEA: From the UK: There are night and daytime
car/passenger ferry sailing from Weymouth and a night-
only winter schedule. There are two *Condor* hydrofoils
offering a daily service from Weymouth during the
tourist season, taking 3 hours and 30 minutes.
From France: St Malo: Car-only crossing is provided by
Commodore Travel/Morvan Fils, car/passenger ferries by
Emeraude Ferries, hydrofoil crossing by *Condor/Morvan
Fils*, and crossing by 'vedettes' (200-capacity ferries) by
Vedettes Blanches and *Vedettes Armoricaines*. From
Granville, Port Bail and Carteret, passenger ferries are
provided by *Vedettes Vertes Granvillaises, Vedettes
Armoricaines, SMCJ, Nord Sud Voyages, Jersey Ferries*
and *Vedettes Blanches*.
Visitors bringing speedboats, surfboards or sailboards
into Jersey *must* register at the Harbour Office on arrival.
Third Party insurance is required.
ROAD: Traffic drives on the left. There are over 800km
(500 miles) of roads and lanes crisscrossing the island.
There is a speed limit of 40kmph (25mph) or 30kmph
(19mph) in built-up areas, which is reduced in some
places to 20kmph (12mph). **Bus:** These operate
throughout the island; the network centres on the bus and
coach station at Weighbridge, St Helier. **Car hire:** This
is generally very cheap, and so is petrol. There are over
35 car hire firms, mostly in St Helier. Persons wishing to
hire a car must: (a) be over 20 years of age; (b) have had
a full licence for at least one year; and (c) have a valid
full licence with no endorsements or disqualifications for
dangerous driving or driving over the alcohol limit within
the previous five years. **Bicycle hire** is available from
eight firms in St Helier, one in St Ouen and one in
Millbrook. **Motorcycles** and **mopeds** can also be hired –
there are ten firms in St Helier. Crash helmets must be
worn. Addresses and telephone numbers of all these
companies can be obtained from the tourist office (for
address, see top of entry). **Documentation:** Visitors who
wish to bring their own car must have a valid certificate
of insurance or an international Green Card, and a valid
driving licence. Nationality plates must be displayed.
Motor caravans and **trailers** may *not* be imported.

ACCOMMODATION

The booklet *Jersey 1995*, available from the tourist office
(addresses at top of entry), gives comprehensive
information on all forms of accommodation on the island.
Short-break and longer-stay holidays are available
throughout the year. The most popular season is from
May until September.
HOTELS: The official accommodation list is obtainable
from the Jersey Hotel and Guest House Association, 60
Stopford Road, St Helier, Jersey JR2 4LB. Tel: 21421.
Fax: 22496. **Grading:** Jersey has its own hotel and guest-
house grading scheme. Hotels are graded from **1** to **5
suns** and guest-houses are graded from **1** to **3 diamonds**.
The greater the number of suns or diamonds, the higher
the grade achieved. All hotels are inspected and graded
annually. *Disabled Visitors:* The Maison des Landes, St
Ouen, Jersey JE3 2AE (tel: 481 683) offers
accommodation for up to 40 disabled visitors and
family/friends. It is open between early April and late
October.
GUEST-HOUSES: There are over 230 guest-houses on
the island, some offering bed, breakfast and evening
meals, others just bed & breakfast. Despite the large
number of establishments, advance booking is
recommended as many guest-houses are not open
throughout the whole year. **Grading:** See *Hotels* above.
HOLIDAY VILLAGES: There are two holiday villages
on the island: Jersey Holiday Village, Portelet Bay. Tel:
45555 *or* 47302 and Pontins Ltd, Holiday Village,
Plémont Bay, St Ouen, Jersey JE3 2BD. Tel: 481 873 (no
facilities for children under three).
SELF-CATERING: There is limited self-catering
accommodation registered with the Tourism Department.
Premises taking less than six people do not have to
register and are not inspected. This type of
accommodation is available through a number of
handling agents. Furnished flats, bungalows, chalets and
villas are not generally available, owing to the acute
shortage of housing for permanent residents. Some units
do, however, become available at various times and
advertisements can be placed in the local newspaper.

Contact the *Jersey Evening Post*, Advertisement Department, PO Box 582, Five Oaks, St Saviour, Jersey JE4 8XQ. Tel: 783 333. Fax: 879 681.
CAMPING: Camping is only permitted on recognised campsites, of which there are six. Due to limited capacity, advance booking is essential. There are no caravan sites on Jersey.

RESORTS & EXCURSIONS

St Helier, the capital and by far the biggest town on the island, is overlooked by two fortifications. *Elizabeth Castle* is built on an island on the bay, and can be reached at low tide. This fortress withstood the army of Oliver Cromwell for seven weeks in 1651, and was used by the occupying Germans during the last war. *Fort Regent* is built on an outcrop above the town. It has recently been converted into a leisure complex with sports and conference facilities. There is an aquarium, a postal museum, a funfair, swimming pools and a wide variety of indoor sporting facilities, while the castle's ramparts give excellent views across the town and the bay. Also worth a visit is the *Jersey Museum* at Pier Road.
The best shopping area in the town is in the King Street–Queen Street precinct area. Most luxury goods are less expensive than in the UK, as Jersey, although not tax free, has low duties on items such as alcohol, cigarettes, perfume, cosmetics and electrical goods.
The North (St Mary, St John, Trinity): The main beaches in this region are those at *Plémont,* with a sheltered bay, rock pools and caves; *Grde Lecq,* reached by a road that runs through a wooded valley; *Bonne Nuit Bay,* a peaceful harbour with a small beach nestling behind a huge headland; *Bouley Bay,* particularly popular with sub-aqua enthusiasts and anglers; and *Rozel,* on the northeast coast, a fishing harbour with an old fort and a small sandy beach. The coast of France can be seen on a clear day.
The *Jersey Zoological Park,* in **Trinity,** is the headquarters of the Jersey Wildlife Preservation Trust, founded by Gerald Durrell. The Trust is a sanctuary for many endangered species of animals, and a visit to the zoo is strongly recommended. More wildlife can be encountered at the *Carnation Nursery and Butterfly Farm* in **St Mary,** home of hundreds of rare and exotic butterflies. *La Mare Vineyards,* close to **Devil's Hole**, has vineyards set in the grounds of an 18th-century farmhouse. There are displays from the local cider industry and homemade products are on sale.
The West (St Ouen, St Peter, St Brelade): The west coast consists almost entirely of one 8km (5-mile) beach on *St Ouen's Bay.* The area is very good for surfers, but is only suitable for strong swimmers.
There are many traditional crafts practised in this part of the island, and many of the workshops can be visited and the products purchased; these include decorative candles at *Portinfer* (St Ouen), local pottery and leatherwork at *L'Etacq* (St Ouen) and stone-ground flour from locally grown corn at *Le Moulin de Quetival,* St Peter's Valley. The grounds of the fine old *St Ouen Manor* are occasionally open to the public. In **St Peter's Village** is a motor museum, adjoining an old German bunker, which houses a collection of veteran and vintage cars, motorcycles, military vehicles and a Jersey steam railway exhibition. There is also a museum in **St Ouen,** displaying floats entered in the well-known *Battle of the Flowers,* a local festival held each year on the second Thursday in August.
The South (St Brelade, St Peter, St Lawrence, St Helier, St Saviour, St Clement): The main beaches in this region are those at *St Clement's Bay,* with several rock pools and sandy gullies; *St Aubin's Bay,* a 5km (3-mile) stretch of sand curving round from St Aubin to the capital; *Portelet,* a secluded sandy bay; *St Brelade's Bay,* widely regarded as one of the most beautiful beaches on the island, ideal for windsurfing and water-skiing; and *Beauport,* a small bay to the west of St Brelade flanked by towering rocks of pink granite.
Howard Davies Park in **St Saviour** is one of the most attractive of Jersey's public gardens with many subtropical trees and shrubs which flourish in the mild climate. In the **St Lawrence** parish, St Peter's Valley, is the *German Military Underground Hospital,* which has several reminders of Jersey's occupation during the Second World War. There are many displays of photographs and documents, and a collection of firearms, daggers and memorabilia.
The East (St Martin, Grouville): The two main beaches in this region cover almost the whole of the eastern coast, and are separated by the promontory of Petit Portelet. To the north of this is *St Catherine's Bay,* popular with anglers, and the tiny village of **Anne Port.** Further south is the *Royal Bay of Grouville* dominated by a magnificent castle, *Mont Orgueil,* which overlooks the small port of **Gorey.** The town is famous for its pottery and visits around the workshop can be arranged.

ST HELIER

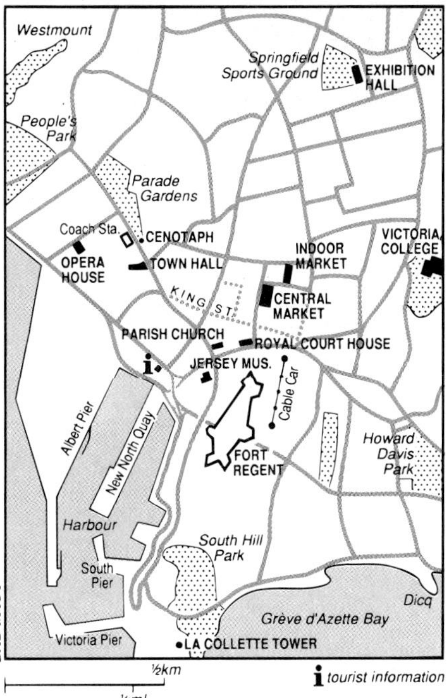

Inland, at *La Hougue Bie* in Grouville, a museum housed in a massive neolithic tomb dating back 5000 years has exhibitions on the agriculture, archaeology, geology and history of the island.
Probably the best way of seeing the island is to walk or cycle round it. The north has the highest land and the most rugged scenery, but gentler walks are possible inland and in the south. One suggested route follows the line of the old Jersey Railway – now a traffic-free public path – which runs from St Aubin to the lighthouse at **Corbière** on the island's southwestern tip.

SOCIAL PROFILE

FOOD & DRINK: Jersey has an excellent range of restaurants to cater for every taste. Seafood is very popular and a wide selection of home-grown produce is available. The island has an enviable reputation for good cuisine whether in small pubs, wine bars or high-class restaurants. **Licensing hours:** 0900-2300 Monday to Saturday, 1100-1300 and 1630-2300 Sunday.
SHOPPING: The island is a low-duty area and there is no VAT. As well as St Helier (where there are two covered markets), there are shopping areas such as Red Houses, St Brelade and Gorey, St Martin. Luxury items such as spirits, cigarettes, jewellery and perfumes are popular buys. Local products such as knitwear, pottery, woodcrafts and even flowers are good value. **Shopping hours:** 0930-1730 Monday to Saturday; some shops close early Thursday afternoon.
SPORT: There are facilities for most sports, particularly watersports such as surfing, windsurfing, water-skiing, fishing, sailing and sub-aqua. **Swimming** is a popular leisure activity, and there are many bays and beaches offering excellent bathing (see *Resorts & Excursions* above). Bathers should beware, however, as Jersey has some of the largest tidal movements in the world, with as much as 12m (40ft) between low and high tide, causing very strong currents. Some beaches are patrolled by beach guards and have safe areas marked with warning flags. On the western coast (St Ouen's Bay), the strong waves can also prove hazardous. There are open-air swimming pools at Havre de Pas and West Park, and two at Fort Regent. **Surfing:** The best area is around St Ouen Bay. There are surfing schools and equipment-hire facilities at the Watersplash and the Sands and year-round professional tuition at El Tico. **Sub aqua:** The waters around the island support a rich and varied marine life and there are good facilities for divers. **Boat dives, skindiving** and equipment hire are available from Watersports or the Underwater Centre at Bouley Bay. **Windsurfing** races are held every Sunday during the summer, and there are several schools including the Jersey Wind & Water Windsurfer Schools at St Aubin and St Brelade's Bay, Longbeach Windsurfing & Boating Centre, the Sands and the Watersplash. **Water-skiing:** Facilities and tuition are available at La Haule, St Aubin's Bay and St Brelade's Bay. **Yachting:** There are two sailing clubs on the island: The Royal Channel Islands Yacht Club, St Aubin, and The St Helier Yacht Club. There is also a **canoeing** school in St Helier. There are two 18-hole **golf** courses: La Moye, St Brelade and Royal Jersey, plus two 9-hole courses, one at Grd'Azette and the other at Five Mile Road, St Ouen. Booking is advisable. Jersey holds its own Open Championship every year which is attended by many well-known European professional golfers. **Tennis:** There are courts at Caesarean Tennis Club and at Grd'Azette. **Horseriding:** Several schools provide tuition and escorted hacks. **Squash:** Temporary membership of the island's two clubs is available; contact Jersey Squash Club and the Lido Squash and Social Club. There are also courts at the Fort Regent Leisure Centre. **Angling** is very popular, particularly during the summer, and there are a number of sea-fishing clubs which run shore and boat festivals during the summer. Boating and fishing trips operate from St Helier. *Warning:* Fishing from rocks should not be attempted until the visitor has obtained information about local tides, currents and weather conditions. Fly fishing is available at the Val de la Mer and the St Catherine Reservoirs; temporary membership can be obtained.
SPECIAL EVENTS: The following is a selection of the major festivals and other special events celebrated in Jersey in 1995/96. For a complete list, contact the Tourist Office.
1995 *50th Anniversary of the Liberation of Jersey.* **Apr 10-Oct 1 '95** *Occupation of Jersey Exhibition.* **Apr 19-23** *Jersey Jazz Festival.* **Apr 28-May 8** *Official EBU Jersey Festival of Bridge.* **May 4-10** *Liberation of Jersey 50th Anniversary.* **May 5-7** *Jersey International Air Rally.* **May 9** *The Occupation Tapestry Official Opening.* **May 15-29** *Jersey International Festival.* **May 27-28** *Helier Morris Men Spring Ale.* **Jun 1-4** *Jersey Good Food Festival.* **Jun 19-24** *Jersey Irish Festival Week.* **Jun 23-26** *Yacht Club de St Lunaire Raid Breitling.* **Jul 10-16** *Jersey Floral Festival.* **Jul 28-30** *1995 Jersey Open Boat Bass Festival.* **Aug 10** *Jersey Battle of Flowers.* **Sep 14-18** *1995 Jersey World Music Festival.* **Oct 10 '95-Jan '96** *The View from the Bunker exhibition.*
SOCIAL CONVENTIONS: Similar to the rest of the UK, with French influences. **Tipping:** In general, this follows UK practice.

BUSINESS PROFILE

ECONOMY: Although agriculture is still important as a source of employment and prestige – Jersey cows are renowned throughout the world – offshore banking and tourism produce more for the economy: the former because of the island's exemption from the UK tax system and the latter through continental influence and a friendly climate.
BUSINESS: Business people are generally expected to dress smartly (suits are usual). Appointments should be made and the exchange of business cards is customary. A knowledge of English is essential. **Office hours:** 0900/0930-1700/1730 Monday to Friday.
COMMERCIAL INFORMATION: The following organisation can offer advice: Jersey Chamber of Commerce, 19 Royal Square, St Helier, Jersey JE2 4WA. Tel: 24536. Fax: 34942.
CONFERENCES/CONVENTIONS: Jersey plays host each year to a large number of conferences; the main period is from October to May. For further information, contact the Conference Executive, Jersey Tourism, Liberation Square, St Helier, Jersey JE1 1BB. Tel: 878 000. Fax: 35569.

CLIMATE

The most popular holiday season is from May until the end of September, with temperatures averaging 20-21°C. Rainfall averages 33 inches a year, most of which falls during the cooler months. Sea temperatures average over 17°C in deep water during the summer.
Required clothing: Normal beach and holiday wear for summer, with a jersey or similar as there are often sea breezes. Warm winterwear and rainwear are advised.

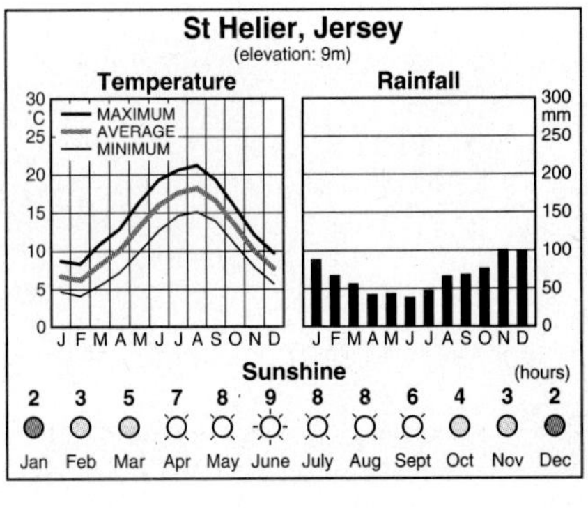

Location: Middle East.

Ministry of Tourism
PO Box 224, Amman, Jordan
Tel: (6) 642 311. Fax: (6) 648 465. Telex: 21741 (a/b TOURIS JO).

Embassy of the Hashemite Kingdom of Jordan
6 Upper Phillimore Gardens, London W8 7HB
Tel: (0171) 937 3685. Fax: (0171) 937 8795. Telex: 923187. Opening hours: 0915-1500 Monday to Friday.

Jordan Information Bureau
11/12 Buckingham Gate, London SW1E 6LB
Tel: (0171) 630 9277. Fax: (0171) 233 7520.

Royal Jordanian Airlines/Tourist Information
211 Regent Street, London W1R 7DD
Tel: (0171) 437 9465. Fax: (0171) 494 0433. Telex: 24330.

British Embassy
PO Box 87, Abdoun, Amman, Jordan
Tel: (6) 823 100. Fax: (6) 813 759. Telex: 22209 (a/b PRODRM JO).

Embassy of the Hashemite Kingdom of Jordan
Consular Section: 3504 International Drive, NW, Washington, DC 20008
Tel: (202) 966 2664. Fax: (202) 966 3110.

Jordan Information Bureau
2319 Wyoming Avenue, NW, Washington, DC 20008
Tel: (202) 265 1606. Fax: (202) 667 0777.

Royal Jordanian Airlines
18th Floor, 535 Fifth Avenue, New York, NY 10017
Tel: (212) 949 0060. Fax: (212) 949 0488.

Embassy of the United States of America
PO Box 354, Jabal, Amman 11118, Jordan
Tel: (6) 820 101. Fax: (6) 820 146.

Embassy of the Hashemite Kingdom of Jordan
Suite 701, 100 Bronson Avenue, Ottawa, Ontario K1R 6G8
Tel: (613) 238 8090. Fax: (613) 232 3341.

Jordan Tourist Information Office
c/o Royal Jordanian Airlines, Suite 738, 1801 McGill College, Montréal, Québec H3A 2N4
Tel: (514) 288 1655. Fax: (514) 288 7572.

Canadian Embassy
PO Box 815403, Pearl of Shmeisani Building, Shmeisani, Amman, Jordan
Tel: (6) 666 124/5/6. Fax: (6) 689 227. Telex: 23080 (a/b CANAD JO).

AREA: 97,740 sq km (37,738 sq miles).
POPULATION: 4,145,000 (1991 estimate). Of these, an estimated 3,888,000 live on the East Bank of the River Jordan (1991 estimate), the remainder live on the West Bank which is occupied by Israel. About half a million people in East Jordan are classified as Palestinian refugees and are maintained by the United Nations Relief and Works Agency. Another quarter of a million people are reckoned to have been displaced by the events of the 1967 Middle East war.
POPULATION DENSITY: 42.4 per sq km.
CAPITAL: Amman. **Population:** 965,000 (1991).
GEOGRAPHY: Jordan shares borders with Israel, Syria, Iraq and Saudi Arabia. The Dead Sea is to the northwest and the Gulf of Aqaba to the southwest. A high plateau extends 324km (201 miles) from Syria to Ras en Naqab in the south with the capital of Amman at a height of 800m (2625ft). Northwest of the capital are undulating hills, some forested, others cultivated. The Dead Sea depression, 400m (1300ft) below sea level in the west, is the lowest point on earth. The River Jordan connects the Dead Sea with Lake Tiberias (Israel). To the west of the Jordan is the occupied West Bank. The

Late Roman/Byzantine remains, Pella

JORDAN OFFERS MORE...

Hot baths in mineral rich thermal springs first used by the Romans – or a soothing soak in the warm buoyant waters of the Dead Sea, the lowest spot on Earth.

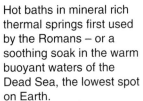

Breathtaking Petra, where the Nabataean Arabs carved a capital city from the rose-red cliffs, around the time of Christ.

Sun, sea, sand and water sports at warm Aqaba on the Red Sea, with world-renowned corals and marine life.

Early Islamic desert castles, lodges and baths with fine Ummayyad architecture and rare painted frescoes.

Mountain climbing, camel riding and desert trekking among the pink sand expanses and towering cliffs of Wadi Rum.

...MUCH MORE THAN YOU HAVE EVER DREAMED OF

For more information please contact:
Ministry of Tourism
PO Box 224
Amman 11118, Jordan
Tel: (962 6) 642 311/4. Telex: 21741 Touris Jo
Fax: (962 6) 648 465
or contact your nearest Royal Jordanian Airline Office

east of the country is mainly desert. Jordan has a tiny stretch of Red Sea coast, centred on Aqaba.

LANGUAGE: Arabic is the official language. English and some French are also spoken.

RELIGION: Over 80% Sunni Muslim, with Christian and Shi'ite Muslim minorities.

TIME: GMT + 2 (GMT + 3 from April to September).

ELECTRICITY: 220 volts AC, 50Hz. Lamp sockets are screw-type, and there is a wide range of wall sockets.

COMMUNICATIONS: Telephone: IDD service is available within cities, with direct dialling to most countries. Country code: 962 (followed by 6 for Amman). Outgoing international code: 00. There are now telephone and facsimile connections to Israel from Jordan. **Fax:** The use of fax is increasing. Most good hotels have facilities. **Telex/telegram:** Public telex facilities are available at leading hotels. The overseas telegram service is reasonably good. Telegrams may be sent from the Central Telegraph Office; Post Office, 1st Circle, Jebel Amman; Post Office, Jordan Intercontinental, Jebel Amman; or from major hotels and post offices. **Post:** Packages should be left opened for customs officials. Airmail to Western Europe takes three to five days. For a higher charge, there is a rapid service guaranteeing delivery within 24 hours to around 22 countries. Post office opening hours: 0800-1800 Saturday to Thursday, closed Friday (except for the downtown post office on Prince Mohammed Street in Amman which is open Friday). **Press:** The English-language newspapers are *The Jordan Times* (daily) and *The Star* (weekly).

BBC World Service and Voice of America frequencies: From time to time these change. See the section *How to Use this Book* for more information.

BBC:

MHz	11.76	6.195	1.413	1.323

Voice of America:

MHz	15.44	11.96	9.700	7.205

PASSPORT/VISA

Regulations and requirements may be subject to change at short notice, and you are advised to contact the appropriate diplomatic or consular authority before finalising travel arrangements. Details of these may be found at the head of this country's entry. Any numbers in the chart refer to the footnotes below.

	Passport Required?	Visa Required?	Return Ticket Required?
Full British	Yes	Yes	No
BVP	Not valid	-	-
Australian	Yes	Yes	No
Canadian	Yes	Yes	No
USA	Yes	Yes	No
Other EU (As of 31/12/94)	Yes	Yes	No
Japanese	Yes	Yes	No

Restricted entry and transit: Entry will be refused to nationals of Bangladesh, Bahamas, India, Pakistan, Sri Lanka and all African countries with the exception of Egypt and South Africa if they have not obtained prior approval from the Ministry of the Interior in Amman.

PASSPORTS: Valid passport required by all.

British Visitors Passport: Not acceptable.

VISAS: Required by all except nationals of Bahrain, Egypt, Iraq, Kuwait, Oman, Qatar, Saudi Arabia, Syria and the United Arab Emirates. Nationals of certain countries – including all Western European countries, the USA, Canada, Australia, New Zealand and Japan – can obtain visas on arrival at the airport in Jordan. Those arriving in Jordan overland directly from occupied territories must hold a visa for Jordan. This must be obtained from a Jordanian representation abroad. (Not applicable to nationals of Bangladesh, Bahamas, India, Pakistan and Sri Lanka, who are required to seek prior approval from the Ministry of the Interior, as well as holding a visa.)

Types of visa: The price of visas is determined on a reciprocal basis. For UK nationals – *Single-entry* valid for 3 months: £27; *Double-entry* valid for 3 months: £48.

Visa fees are not payable by groups of 5 people or more whose journey has been arranged through a travel agent and who intend to stay in Jordan for at least 4 nights.

Validity: Validity varies according to nationality. For UK, US, Canadian and Australian nationals visas are valid for: *Tourist:* 3 months (single-entry); *Business:* 3 months.

Application to: Consulate (or Consular section of Embassy). For addresses, see top of entry.

Application requirements: (a) Completed application form. (b) Passport valid for at least 6 months. (c) 1 passport-size photo. (d) Stamped, self-addressed

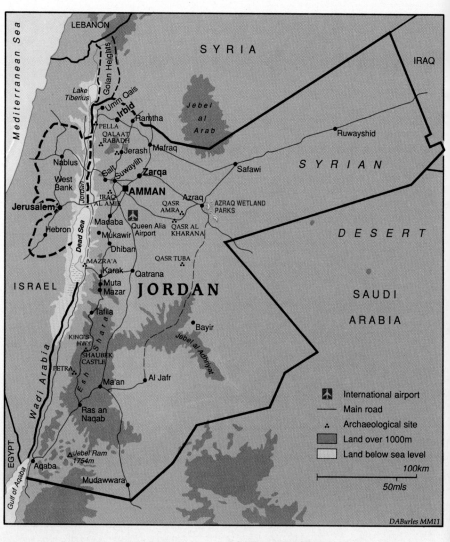

DABurles MM11

envelope if applying by post. (e) Fee (only cash or postal orders are accepted). (f) Company letter for Business visa.

Working days required: 2 days, if applying in person. Allow a few days for postal applications.

Temporary residence: Apply to Embassy.

MONEY

Currency: Dinar (JD) = 1000 fils. Notes are in denominations of JD20, 10, 5 and 1, and 500 fils. Coins are in denominations of 500, 250, 100, 50, 25, 20, 10 and 5 fils.

Credit cards: American Express and Visa are widely accepted, whilst Access/Mastercard and Diners Club have more limited use. Check with your credit card company for details of merchant acceptability and other services which may be available.

Travellers cheques: Those issued by UK banks are accepted by licensed banks and bureaux de change.

Exchange rate indicators: The following figures are included as a guide to the movements of the Dinar against Sterling and the US Dollar:

Date:	Oct '92	Sep '93	Jan '94	Jan '95
£1.00=	1.09	1.06	1.04	1.10
$1.00=	0.68	0.68	0.69	0.70

Currency restrictions: The import of both local and foreign currency is unrestricted provided that it is declared. Export of local currency is limited to JD300. Export of foreign currency is limited to the amount imported and declared on arrival. Israeli currency is prohibited.

Banking hours: 0830-1230 and 1530-1730 Saturday to Thursday. Hours during Ramadan are from 0830-1000, although some banks open in the afternoon.

DUTY FREE

The following goods may be imported into Jordan without incurring customs duty:
200 cigarettes or 25 cigars or 200g of tobacco; 1 bottle of wine or 1 bottle of spirits; a reasonable amount of perfume for personal use; gifts up to the value of JD250 or the equivalent to US$320.

PUBLIC HOLIDAYS

Jan 15 '95 Arbour Day. **Mar 3** Eid al-Fitr (End of Ramadan). **Mar 22** Arab League Day. **May 10** Eid al-Adha (Feast of the Sacrifice). **May 25** Independence Day. **May 31** Islamic New Year. **Aug 9** Mouloud (Prophet's Birthday). **Aug 11** King Hussein's Accession. **Nov 14** King Hussein's Birthday. **Dec 20** Leilat al-Meiraj. **Jan 15 '96** Arbour Day. **Feb 22** Eid al-Fitr (End of Ramadan). **Mar 22** Arab League Day. **Apr 29** Eid al-Adha (Feast of the Sacrifice).

Note: (a) Christmas and Easter holidays are only observed by Christian business establishments. (b) Muslim festivals are timed according to local sightings of various phases of the Moon and the dates given above are approximations. During the lunar month of Ramadan that precedes Eid al-Fitr, Muslims fast during the day and feast at night and normal business patterns may be interrupted. Many restaurants are closed during the day and there may be restrictions on smoking and drinking. Some disruption may continue into Eid al-Fitr itself. Eid al-Fitr and Eid al-Adha may last anything from two to ten days, depending on the region. For more information see the section *World of Islam* at the back of the book.

HEALTH

Regulations and requirements may be subject to change at short notice, and you are advised to contact your doctor well in advance of your intended date of departure. Any numbers in the chart refer to the footnotes below.

	Special Precautions?	Certificate Required?
Yellow Fever	No	1
Cholera	Yes	2
Typhoid & Polio	Yes	-
Malaria	No	-
Food & Drink	3	-

[1]: A yellow fever vaccination certificate is required from travellers over one year of age coming from infected areas.

[2]: Following WHO guidelines issued in 1973, a cholera

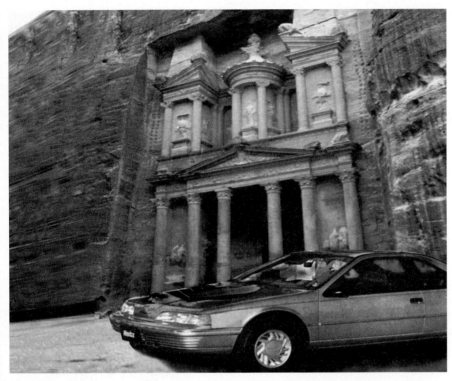

vaccination certificate is not a condition of entry to Jordan. However, cholera is a risk in this country and precautions are essential. Up-to-date advice should be sought before deciding whether these precautions should include a vaccination as medical opinion is divided over its effectiveness. See the *Health* section at the back of the book.

[3]: Water that is not bottled should never be drunk unless it has first been boiled or otherwise sterilised. Milk should not be consumed unless bought in a container stating that it has been pasteurised. Avoid dairy products which are likely to have been made from unboiled milk. Food and water in rural areas may carry increased risk. Only eat well-cooked meat and fish, preferably served hot. Salad and mayonnaise may carry increased risk. Vegetables should be cooked and fruit peeled.

Rabies is present. For those at high risk, vaccination before arrival should be considered. If you are bitten abroad, seek medical advice without delay. For more information consult the *Health* section at the back of the book.

Health care: Health insurance is recommended. There are excellent hospitals in large towns and cities, with clinics in many villages.

TRAVEL - International

AIR: The national airline is *Royal Jordanian Airlines (RJ)*.

Approximate flight time: From London to Amman is 5 hours 30 minutes.

International airport: *Queen Alia International (AMM)*

Health
GALILEO/WORLDSPAN: **TI-DFT/AMM/HE**
SABRE: **TIDFT/AMM/HE**
Visa
GALILEO/WORLDSPAN: **TI-DFT/AMM/VI**
SABRE: **TIDFT/AMM/VI**
For more information on Timatic codes refer to Contents.

is 32km (20 miles) southeast of the capital, to which it is connected by a good highway (travel time – 30 minutes). There is a regular bus service, and taxis are also available. There are duty-free facilities.

The previous international airport, situated 5km (3 miles) northeast of the city, is now only used for charter flights.

Departure tax: JD10 for individual tourists, JD25 for Jordanian nationals on international departures. Transit passengers are exempt.

SEA: The only port is Aqaba, which is on the cruise itineraries for *Neptune, Royal Viking Sea* and *Navarino. Fayez* sails from Saudi Arabia and Egypt.

Sea tax: JD6.

Car and passenger ferries: Aqaba to Suez and Aqaba to Nueibe. There is a weekly passenger service to Suez and Jeddah. Contact *Telestar Maritime Agency*.

RAIL: No scheduled international services, but there are tracks to Syria.

ROAD: Routes are via Syria and Turkey through Ramtha, 115km (70 miles) north of Amman (driving time from Damascus is four hours, plus up to three hours delay at the frontier). There is a shared taxi service from Amman to Damascus. Multiple-entry visas may be needed. A coach service runs from Damascus to Irbid or Amman. Public buses and coaches run from Amman to Damascus and Baghdad daily, as well as to Allenby Bridge for the crossing to the occupied West Bank. To cross, permission is required – apply to the Ministry of the Interior, Amman. The granting of permission is usually routine, but allow three full working days.

Road tax: JD4.

TRAVEL - Internal

AIR: *Royal Jordanian Airlines* operate regular flights to Aqaba. It is also possible to hire executive jets and helicopters.

RAIL: There is no longer a reliable public railway service.

ROAD: Main roads are good (there are nearly 3000km/1900 miles of paved roads in the country), but desert tracks should be avoided. It is important to make sure that the vehicle is in good repair if travelling on minor roads or tracks. Take plenty of water and follow local advice carefully. In case of breakdown, contact the Automobile Association. Traffic drives on the right. **Bus:** Services are efficient and cheap. *JETT* bus company (tel:

(6) 664 146) operates services from Amman to other towns and cities in the country. There are daily services to Aqaba and Petra. **Taxi:** Shared taxi service to all towns on fixed routes, also available for private hire. Shared taxis to Petra should be booked in advance owing to demand. **Car hire:** *Avis* and four national companies operate services, available also from hotels and travel agents. Drivers are available for the day.

Documentation: An International Driving Permit is required. Visitors are not allowed to drive a vehicle with normal Jordanian plates unless they have a Jordanian driving licence.

Note: When using routes which go near the Israeli border (and even when sailing or swimming in the Red Sea without a guide) the traveller should always have all papers in order and within reach.

URBAN: There are conventional buses and extensive fixed-route 'Servis' (shared taxis) in Amman. The 'Servis' are licensed, with a standard fare scale, but there are no fixed pick-up or set-down points. Vehicles often fill up at central or outer terminal points and then run non-stop.

ACCOMMODATION

There are several high-standard hotels in Amman and Aqaba where alcoholic drinks can be served at all times. Hotels are fully booked during business periods so reservations are advised. Winter and summer rates are the same. All rates are subject to 20% tax and service.

Grading: Hotels are graded from **5-** to **1-star**. 5- and 4-star hotels have discotheques and nightclubs with live music, but no elaborate floorshows.

RESORTS & EXCURSIONS

Due to Jordan's small size any destination within the country may be reached by road from the capital, Amman, in a day.

Amman

Amman, the capital since 1921, contains about a third of the population. It was formerly the Ammonite capital of Rabbath-Ammon and later the Graeco-Roman city of Philadelphia. Amman, often referred to as the 'white city', was originally, like Rome, built on seven hills

The Obelisk Monument, Petra

which still form its natural focal points. With extensive modern building projects, Amman is now very well equipped with excellent hotels and tourist facilities, especially in the *Jabal* (hill) areas. The central *souk* is lively and interesting and provides a taste of a more traditional city. Remains from Roman, Greek and Ottoman Turk occupations are dotted around the city, the main attraction being the Roman amphitheatre from the 2nd century AD in the centre of the city. There is also the *Jebel el Qalat* (citadel) which houses the *Archaeological Museum;* the *National Gallery of Fine Arts* and *Popular Museum of Costume and Jewellery.* Amman is very well placed for excursions to the other parts of the country.

North of Amman

Jerash is less than one hour's drive from Amman through the picturesque hills of ancient **Gilead**. A magnificent Graeco-Roman city on an ancient site, beautifully preserved by the desert sands, Jerash is justly famous for the *Triumphal Arch,* the *Hippodrome,* the great elliptical forum, the theatres, baths and gateways, the Roman bridge and the wide street of columns which leads to the *Temple of Artemis*. *Son et lumière* programmes run in four different languages (French, English, German and Arabic). Other languages can be catered for upon request (cost: JD1 per person). For information on festivals in Jerash, see *Special Events* in the *Social Profile* section below.
Irbid, which is 77km (49 miles) from Amman, is a city of Roman tombs and statues, and narrow streets with close-packed shops and arched entrances. **Umm Qais** in the far north of the country, the Biblical *'Gadara'*, dominates the area round *Lake Tiberias* (Sea of Galilee). Once a city favoured by the Romans for its hot springs and theatres, it had declined to a small village by the time of the Islamic conquests. Its ruins, however, are still impressive: the *Acropolis* built in 218BC, the forum, the colonnaded street with still-visible chariot tracks and the *Nymphaeum* and remains of a large basilica. Returning along the northwest border from Umm Qais to Jerash through the lush scenery of the *Jordan River Valley*, one can visit the town of **Al Hammeh**, in sight of the Israeli-occupied *Golan Heights*, a town known for its hot springs and mineral waters; and **Pella**, once a city of the *Roman Decapolis*, now being excavated, and the hilltop castle of *Qalaat al-Rabadh* built by the Arabs in defence against the crusaders. The scenery in this surprisingly fertile part of Jordan is often very beautiful, especially in the spring when the Jordan Valley and surrounding area is covered in flowers.

East of Amman

Towards **Azraq** and beyond is the vast desert which makes up so much of Jordan. Within this arid landscape are the fertile oases of the *Shaumari* and *Azraq Wetland Parks,* now run with the help of the World Wildlife Fund. Wild animals once native to Jordan, such as the oryx and gazelle, are being re-introduced, while the wetlands are visited by thousands of migratory birds each year. The *Shaumari* was opened in October 1983 in an attempt to protect the country's dwindling oryx population. There are plans to open a further ten wildlife reserves which will cover more than 4100 sq km (1580 sq miles). The project is being organised by the Jordanian Royal Society for the Conservation of Nature, a body which has recently stepped up its efforts to protect the country's wildlife and to prevent pollution affecting the very busy port of Aqaba. Severe fines are imposed on anyone contravening Jordan's strict laws on these matters.
Also in the east are the desert *Umayyad castles* (Qasr) of *Amra* and *Al-Kharanah*. Built as hunting lodges and to protect caravan routes, they are well preserved with frescoes and beautiful vaulted rooms.

West of Amman

Salt, once the Biblical 'Gilead', is a now a small town set in a fertile landscape, retaining much of its old character as a former leading city of *Transjordan*. Filled with the character, sights, sounds and aromas of an old Arab town with its narrow *souk,* its innumerable flights of steps, and its donkeys and coffee houses, it has a tolerant, friendly, oriental atmosphere. 24km (15 miles) from Amman is *Iraq al-Amir*, the only Hellenistic palace still to be seen in the Middle East.

South of Amman

The **Dead Sea**, 392m (1286ft) below sea level and the lowest point on earth, glistens by day and night in an eerie, dry landscape. The Biblical cities of Sodom and Gomorrah are thought to be beneath its waters. Supporting no life and having no outlet, even the non-swimmer can float freely in the rich salt water. The Dead Sea at the end of the *River Jordan* is the natural barrier between Jordan and the occupied West Bank.

Jordan Valley

There are three routes from Amman to Aqaba, the most picturesque being *The King's Highway,* the whole length of which is dotted with places of interest. **Madaba** and nearby *Mount Nebo,* where Moses is said to have struck the rock, were both flourishing Byzantine towns and have churches and well-preserved mosaics. In Madaba there are also ancient maps of 6th-century Palestine, a museum and an old family carpet-making industry which uses ancient looms. Off the Highway is **Mukawir**, a small village near the ruins of *Machaerus of Herod Antipas,* where Salome danced. From the summit of nearby *Qasr al-Meshneque,* where St John was beheaded, is a magnificent view of the Dead Sea, and sometimes even of Jerusalem and the *Mount of Olives.* Nearby *Zarqa Main* has hot mineral-water springs. Rugged scenery characterises this area; deep gorges, waterfalls, white rocks, small oases, birds and wild flowers. Further south on the Highway is **Kerak**, a beautiful medieval town surrounded by high walls and with a castle. Other places of historical, scenic or religious interest along the route before Petra include **Mutah** and **Mazar**, **Tafila**, **Edomite Qasr Buseirah** and the magnificent crusader hill fortress, *Shaubek Castle.*
Petra is one of the wonders of the Middle-Eastern world: a gigantic natural amphitheatre hidden in the rocks out of which a delicately coloured city with immense façades

has been carved; it was lost for hundreds of years and only rediscovered in 1812. The temples and caves of Petra rest high up above a chasm, with huge white rocks forming the *Bab,* or gate, of the *Siq,* the narrow entrance which towers over 21m (70ft) high. Until recently the rock caves were still inhabited by Bedouins. Most of this unique city was built by the Nabatean Arabs in the 5th and 6th centuries BC as an important link in the caravan routes. It was added to by the Romans who carved out a huge theatre and, possibly, the spectacular classical façade of the *Khazneh* (treasury). Away from the road, it is only possible to reach Petra on horseback. This city of rock stairs, rock streets, rock-carved tombs and dwellings and temples has among its other attractions the *Qasr al-Bint* castle shrine and the *Al-Habis* caves and museums; while a short distance away from the more commercialised site of Petra is *Al-Barid* where a number of tombs lie in solitude and tranquillity among the rocks. There is a rest house in Petra built against the rock wall near the beginning of the *Siq,* where it is advisable to book early in season, but is bitterly cold in winter. A variety of hotels offer accommodation. The last stop south before Aqaba is *Wadi Rum,* about five hours from Amman by road. A Beau Geste-type fort run by the colourful Desert Patrol (Camel Corps), it was built to defend the valley in a great plain of escarpments and desert wilderness, and is a place

Mosaic floor, Jerash

Scuba diving at Aqaba, on the shores of the Gulf of Aqaba (Red Sea)

strongly associated with T E Lawrence (Lawrence of Arabia). Many Bedouins, of a tribe thought to be descended from Mohammed, still live in the valley in tents. Some tours will arrange trips into the desert to stay with a Bedouin tribe or camping in the valley, a round trip being 97km (60 miles).

Aqaba: At the northeast end of the *Gulf of Aqaba* is Jordan's only port, and can be reached from Amman by road or air. It has grown considerably over the past few years, both as a port and as a tourist centre, due in part to its excellent beach and watersports facilities, and its low humidity and hot climate. The town has a variety of small shops and several good restaurants, and it leaves most of the other tourist facilities to be provided for by the hotels. These include windsurfing, scuba diving, sailing and fishing. Most hotels have swimming pools, and will offer continental and some traditional cuisine. Some provide business and conference facilities and excursions to Amman, Petra and Wadi Rum. A year-round resort, Aqaba boasts some of the best coral-reef diving and snorkelling sites in the world, often very close to shore, in a water temperature which rarely falls below 20°C.

SOCIAL PROFILE

FOOD & DRINK: The cuisine varies although most restaurants have a mixed menu which includes both Arabic and European dishes. Dishes include *meze* (small

starters such as *humus, fool, kube* and *tabouleh*); a variety of *kebabs; Mahshi Waraq 'inab* (vine leaves stuffed with rice, minced meat and spices); *musakhan* (chicken in olive oil and onion sauce roasted on Arab bread); and the Jordanian speciality *mensaf* (stewed lamb in a yogurt sauce served on a bed of rice), a dish which is normally eaten with the hand. **Drink:** Drinking Arabic coffee is a ritual. Local beer and wine are available, as are imported beverages. There are no licensing laws. During Ramadan drinking and smoking in public is forbidden between sunrise and sunset.

NIGHTLIFE: There are nightclubs, theatres and cinemas in Amman, while some other major towns have cinemas.

SHOPPING: Every town will have a *souk* (market), and there are also many good craft and jewellery shops. There is a particularly good gold and jewellery market in Amman. Special items include: Hebron glass, mother-of-pearl boxes, pottery, backgammon sets, embroidered table cloths, jewelled rosaries and worry beads, nativity sets made of olive wood, leather hassocks, old and new brass and copper items, kaftans hand-embroidered with silver and gold thread. **Shopping hours:** 0900-1300 and 1530-1830 Sunday to Thursday (closed Friday).

SPORT: Aqaba, on the shores of the Gulf of Aqaba (Red Sea), offers **swimming, boating, scuba diving** and **water-skiing**. There is a diving centre at Aqaba, but diving is limited to experienced divers with licences. It is forbidden to remove coral or shells, or to use harpoon

guns and fishing spears. There are public swimming pools at the Hussein Youth City and various hotels in Amman. The Dead Sea is another popular area. In Amman, the Hussein Youth City has **tennis** courts, as does the YMCA and several hotels. **Football** and **squash** are also available in Amman.

SPECIAL EVENTS: There are two major festivals every year in Jordan: the *Jerash Festival for Culture and Arts* takes place every August during a 2-week period and includes daily performances by Jordanian, Arab and international folklore troupes and performing artists. There is also the *Aqaba Water Sports Festival* in mid-November which includes international-class competition in water-skiing and other aquatic sports.

SOCIAL CONVENTIONS: Handshaking is the customary form of greeting. Jordanians are proud of their Arab culture, and hospitality here is a matter of great importance. Visitors are made to feel very welcome and Jordanians are happy to act as hosts and guides, and keen to inform the tourists about their traditions and culture. Islam always plays an important role in society and it is essential that Muslim beliefs are respected (see *World of Islam* at the back of the book). Arabic coffee will normally be served continuously during social occasions. To signal that no more is wanted, slightly tilt the cup when handing it back, otherwise it will be refilled. A small gift is quite acceptable in return for hospitality. Women are expected to dress modestly and beachwear must only be worn on the beach or poolside.

Photography: It is polite to ask permission to take photographs of people and livestock, in some places photography is forbidden. **Tipping:** 10-12% service charge is generally added in hotels and restaurants and extra tips are discretionary. Porters' and drivers' tips are about 8%.

BUSINESS PROFILE

ECONOMY: Jordan's agricultural sector has never recovered from the loss of the West Bank after the 1967 Middle East war, which deprived Jordan of 80% of its fruit-growing area and a proportionate amount of export revenue. Tomatoes, citrus fruit, cucumbers, water melons, aubergines and wheat are the principal commodities grown in the remaining, mostly desert area. The country's political stability – an unusual asset in the volatile Middle East – has ensured Jordan a steady flow of foreign aid which now underpins the economy. Industry, mostly light, has grown steadily along with tourism. The main industries are phosphate mining and potash extraction from the Dead Sea area. Other commercial enterprises include paints, plastics and cement. The ongoing search for exploitable oil deposits, unsuccessful thus far, continues.

BUSINESS: English is widely spoken in business circles. Avoid Friday appointments. A good supply of visiting cards is essential. Formality in dress is important and for men a suit and tie should be worn for business meetings. **Office hours:** 0900-1700 Saturday, Wednesday and Thursday. **Government office hours:** 0800-1400 Saturday to Thursday.

COMMERCIAL INFORMATION: The following organisation can offer advice: Amman Chamber of Commerce, PO Box 287, Amman. Tel: (6) 666 151. Telex: 21543.

CLIMATE

Hot and dry summers with cool evenings. The Jordan Valley below sea level is warm during winter and extremely hot in summer. Rain falls between November and March, while colder weather conditions occur in December/January.

Required clothing: Lightweight cottons and linens are advised between May and September. Warmer clothes are necessary for winter and cool summer evenings. Rainwear is needed from November to April.

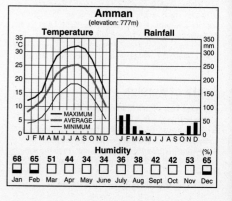

Kazakhstan

□ international airport

1000km
500mls

Location: Central Asia, north of Iran.

Ministry of Tourism, Physical Culture and Sports of the Republic of Kazakhstan
48 Abai Avenue, Almaty, Kazakhstan
Tel: (3272) 673 986. Fax: (3272) 675 088. Telex: 2251347 (a/b TREK SU).

National Company for Foreign Tourism 'Intourist Kazakhstan'
48 Abai Avenue, 480072 Almaty, Kazakhstan
Tel: (3272) 677 024 or 677 866. Fax: (3272) 636 634 or 631 207. Telex: 251232 (a/b PTB SU).

Kazakh Council for Tourism and Travel
5 Mitina Street, Almaty, Kazakhstan
Tel: (3272) 648 858.

Intourist
219 Marsh Wall, Isle of Dogs, London E14 9FJ
Tel: (0171) 538 8600. Fax: (0171) 538 5967.

British Embassy
173 Furmanov Street, Almaty, Kazakhstan
Tel: (3272) 506 191. Fax: (3272) 506 260. Telex: 613398 (a/b SMAIL SU).

Embassy of the Republic of Kazakhstan
3421 Massachusetts Avenue, NW, Washington, DC 20007
Tel: (202) 333 4504 (information) or 333 4507 (Consular section). Fax: (202) 333 4509. Telex: 49616772 (a/b REP KAZ).

Fair Winds Trading Company
Suite 1610, 5151 E. Broadway Boulevard, Tucson, AZ 85711
Tel: (520) 748 1288. Fax: (520) 748 1347. Telex: 6507151271 (a/b MCI UW).

Embassy of the United States of America
99 Furmanov Street, Almaty, Kazakhstan
Tel: (3272) 632 426. Fax: (3272) 633 883. Telex: 251375 (a/b IMIMB SU).

The Canadian Embassy
Hotel Kazakhstan, Rooms 912 and 914, 52 Lenina Street, 480110, Almaty, Kazakhstan
Tel: (3272) 619 107.

Russian Travel Information Office
Suite 630, 1801 McGill College Avenue, Montréal, Québec H3A 2N4
Tel: (514) 849 6394. Fax: (514) 849 6743.
Can provide information on Kazakhstan.

AREA: 2,717,300 sq km (1,049,150 sq miles).
POPULATION: 16,900,000 (1993 estimate).
POPULATION DENSITY: 6.2 per sq km.
CAPITAL: Almaty (Alma-Ata). **Population:** 1,200,000 (1993 estimate).
GEOGRAPHY: Five times the size of France and half the size of the United States, Kazakhstan is the second largest state in the Commonwealth of Independent States, and is bordered by the Russian Federation to the north and west, the Caspian Sea, Turkmenistan and Uzbekistan to the southwest, Kyrgyzstan to the south and China to the southeast. 90% of the country is made up of steppe, the sand massives of the Kara Kum and the vast desert of Kizilkum, while in the southeast of the country the mountains of the Tien Shan and the Altai form a great natural frontier with tens of thousands of lakes and rivers. The Aral Sea and Lake Balkhash are the country's largest expanses of water.
LANGUAGE: The official language is Kazakh, a Turkic language closely related to Uzbek, Kyrgyz, Turkmen and Turkish. The Government has undertaken to replace the Russian Cyrillic alphabet with the Turkish version of the Roman alphabet by 1995. Meanwhile the Cyrillic alphabet is in general use and most people in the cities can speak Russian, whereas country people tend to only speak Kazakh. English is usually spoken by those involved in tourism. Uygur and other regional languages and dialects are also spoken.
RELIGION: Mainly Sunni Muslim. There are Russian Orthodox and Jewish minorities. There are ten independent denominations of Christianity. The Kazakhs do not express their religious feelings fervently – Kazakhstan is an outlying district of the Muslim world and a meeting point of Russian, Chinese and Central Asian civilisations. Islam plays a minor role in policy and there are no significant Islamic political organisations in the country.
TIME: GMT + 6 (GMT + 7 from last Sunday in March to Saturday before last Sunday in September).
ELECTRICITY: 220 volts AC, 50Hz. Round 2-pin continental plugs are standard.

COMMUNICATIONS: Telephone: Country code: 7 (3272 for Almaty). International calls can be made at a reduced rate from 2000-0800 local time. International calls should be made from a telephone office; these are usually attached to post offices. Hotel Dostyk in Almaty has IDD by satellite for residents only. Its Business Centre offers a range of telecommunications services. The Hotel Otrar has an Urgent International Call Booth which is reliable, if more expensive than the normal service. Generally payphones are no longer in operation since inflation has rendered coins worthless. **Telex:** Available in main hotels (for residents only). **Telegram:** Facilities available from any post office. **Post:** Full postal facilities are available at main post offices in the cities, which are open 24 hours a day, 7 days a week. The Main Post Office in Almaty is located on Ulitsa Kurmangazy. International postal communication is undertaken by the firm *Blitz-Pochta*. Delivery within the republic takes three to five days. Post to Western Europe and the USA takes between two and three weeks. Mail addresses should be laid out in the following order: country, postcode, city, street, house number and lastly the person's name. Post office hours: 0900-1800 Monday to Friday. Visitors can also use post offices located within major *Intourist* hotels. **Press:** There are 70 newspapers and 50 magazines in Kazakh, Russian, German, Uygur and Korean published in the country. The most popular are *Egemen Kazakhstan, Kazakhstan Pravda, Panorama, Express K* and the international newspaper *Asia*.
BBC World Service and Voice of America frequencies and wavelengths: From time to time these change. See the section *How to Use this Book* for more information.
BBC:

MHz	17.64	15.07	9.410	6.180

Voice of America:

MHz	9.670	6.040	5.995	1.197

PASSPORT/VISA

Regulations and requirements may be subject to change at short notice, and you are advised to contact the appropriate diplomatic or consular authority before finalising travel arrangements. Details of these may be found at the head of this country's entry. Any numbers in the chart refer to the footnotes below.

	Passport Required?	Visa Required?	Return Ticket Required?
Full British	Yes*	Yes*	Yes*
BVP	Not valid	-	-
Australian	Yes*	Yes*	Yes*
Canadian	Yes*	Yes*	Yes*
USA	Yes*	Yes*	Yes*
Other EU (As of 31/12/94)	Yes*	Yes*	Yes*
Japanese	Yes*	Yes*	Yes*

Note [*]: Visa regulations within the CIS are currently liable to change. Prospective travellers are advised to contact *Intourist Travel Ltd* who offer a comprehensive visa service for all of the republics within the CIS. Tel: (0171) 538 5902 in the UK; (212) 757 3884 in the USA.
PASSPORTS: Valid passport required by all.
British Visitors Passport: Not acceptable.
VISAS: Required by all except nationals of CIS, Cuba, North Korea, Vietnam and Eastern European countries travelling direct from their own countries.
Note: Foreign visitors entering Kazakhstan from territories of the former USSR illegally (ie without proper Entry visas) will be fined US$250.
Types of visa: 7-day Entry/Exit visa; 14-day Entry/Exit visa; 1-month Entry/Exit visa; Over 1-month Entry/Exit visa; 1-year Multiple-entry visa; 2-year Multiple-entry visa; Transit visa. Visas are also divided into Business, Tourist, Student, Medical and Resident.
Cost: Varies according to notice given by applicant: US$30 with 1 week's notice, US$60 with 3 working days' notice, US$100 with one working day's notice. Multiple-entry visas cost US$120.
Application to: Russian embassies will issue visas for Kazakhstan, but only if they receive confirmation from the Kazakh Foreign Office that they have authorisation to do so. Obtaining a visa before travel may involve a lengthy, bureaucratic application process. Visas are available on arrival in Kazakhstan for US$180. Although this may be simpler and quicker, visas obtained before travel are considerably cheaper.
Application Requirements: (a) Completed application form. (b) Valid passport. (c) 1 passport-size photo. (d) Copy of confirmation telex from hotel in Kazakhstan. (e) Covering letter from travel agency in country of origin. (f) Letter of invitation from host organisation in Kazakhstan for Business visa. (g) Stamped self-addressed envelope. (h) Fee.

MONEY

Currency: Kazakhstan's new currency, the Tenge, was introduced on November 15, 1993. 1 Tenge = 100 tiyin. Notes are in denominations of 100, 50, 20, 10, 5, 2 and 1 Tenge, and 20, 10, 5, 3 and 1 tigin. All Kazakh currency is in notes only – there are no coins. Kazakhstan no longer uses the Rouble.
Currency exchange: Foreign currency should only be exchanged at official bureaux and all transactions must be recorded on the currency declaration form which is issued on arrival. It is wise to retain all exchange receipts, although they are seldom inspected these days. Unless travelling with *Intourist*, in which case accommodation, transport and meals are paid before departure, money should be brought in US Dollars cash and exchanged when necessary. However, payment is generally preferred in US currency rather than the local currency.
Credit cards: Major European and international credit cards, including Visa and Diners Club, are accepted in the larger hotels in Almaty (Hotel Otrar and Hotel Dostyk). There are no faciliites for credit-card cash withdrawals in Kazakhstan.
Travellers cheques: American Express travellers cheques in US Dollars are the most widely accepted.
Exchange rate indicators: The national currency, the Tenge, may only be obtained within Kazakhstan. Conversion of the Tenge back into hard currency may prove difficult, if not impossible. Official exchange rates available in January 1994 were: £1.00 = 11.06 Tenge; US$1.00 = 7.52 Tenge. The commercial rate was somewhat higher, ie £1 = 13.5 Tenge; and US$1 = 9.35 Tenge.

Timatic	Health
	GALILEO/WORLDSPAN: **TI-DFT/ALA/HE**
	SABRE: **TIDFT/ALA/HE**
	Visa
	GALILEO/WORLDSPAN: **TI-DFT/ALA/VI**
	SABRE: **TIDFT/ALA/VI**
	For more information on Timatic codes refer to Contents.

Currency restrictions: The import and export of local currency is prohibited for foreigners. The import of foreign currency is unlimited, subject to declaration. The export of foreign currency is limited to the amount declared on arrival.
Banking hours: 0930-1730 Monday to Friday. Banks close for lunch 1300-1400. All banks are closed Saturday and Sunday.

DUTY FREE

The following goods may be imported into Kazakhstan without incurring customs duty:
250 cigarettes or 250g of tobacco products; 1 litre of spirits; 2 litres of wine; a reasonable quantity of perfume for personal use; gifts up to the equivalent value of Rub1000.
Note: On entering the country, tourists must complete a customs declaration form which must be retained until departure. This allows the import of articles intended for personal use, including currency and valuables which must be registered on the declaration form. Customs inspection can be long and detailed.
Prohibited imports: Military weapons and ammunition, narcotics and drug paraphernalia, pornography, loose pearls and anything owned by a third party that is to be carried in for that third party.
Prohibited exports: As prohibited imports, as well as annulled securities, state loan certificates, lottery tickets, works of art and antiques (unless permission has been granted by the Ministry of Culture), saiga horns, Siberian stag, punctuate and red deer antlers (unless on organised hunting trip), and punctuate deer skins.

PUBLIC HOLIDAYS

Jan 1 '95 New Year. **Jan 28** Constitution Day. **Mar 8** International Women's Day. **Mar 22** Nauriz Meyrami (Kazakh New Year). **May 1** Labour Day. **May 9** Victory Day. **Dec 16** Republic Day. **Jan 1 '96** New Year. **Jan 27** Constitution Day. **Mar 8** International Women's Day. **Mar 22** Nauriz Meyrami (Kazakh New Year).

HEALTH

Regulations and requirements may be subject to change at short notice, and you are advised to contact your doctor well in advance of your intended date of departure. Any numbers in the chart refer to the footnotes below.

	Special Precautions?	Certificate Required?
Yellow Fever	No	No
Cholera	No	No
Typhoid & Polio	Yes	-
Malaria	No	-
Food & Drink	1	-

[1]: All water should be regarded as being a potential health risk. Water used for drinking, brushing teeth or making ice should have first been boiled or otherwise sterilised. Milk is pasteurised and dairy products are safe for consumption. Only eat well-cooked meat and fish, preferably served hot. Pork, salad and mayonnaise may carry increased risk. Vegetables should be cooked and fruit peeled.
Rabies is present. For those at high risk, vaccination before arrival should be considered. If you are bitten abroad seek medical advice without delay. For more information, consult the *Health* section at the back of the book.
Health care: There is a large network of hospitals, emergency centres and pharmacies. The largest include the Central Hospital, the Maternity and Childhood Institute Clinic and the Medical Teaching Institute Clinic in Almaty, and the Spinal Centre and Hospital of Rehabilitation Treatment in Karaganda. If a tourist falls ill whilst in Kazakhstan, emergency treatment is available at any public medical institution free of charge. However, medical insurance is strongly recommended.

TRAVEL - International

AIR: Kazakhstan's national airline is *Kazakhstan Airlines.* Almaty is rapidly gaining importance as an international hub. It has air links with 63 cities in the CIS. *Kazakhstan Airlines* fly to Almaty from Frankfurt/M on Wednesdays and Saturdays and from Vienna (via Ataran on the Caspian) on Mondays. From London the best connections are via Tashkent on *Uzbekistan Airways*; from Frankfurt/M on *Lufthansa* (twice a week); from Moscow on *British Airways* or *Aeroflot*; and from Istanbul on *Turkish Airways* or *Aeroflot.* There are no direct flights from the USA or Australia. Further connections are offered by *CAAC* and *Aeroflot* from Almaty to Urumchi in China, from where there are connections to Beijing. Charter flights are also available to Cairo and Alexandria in Egypt; Dubai in the UAE; Islamabad and Karachi in Pakistan; Delhi and Bombay in India; and Tehran in Iran. There are also flights to Novosibirsk and Irkutsk in the Russian Federation, Bishkek in Kyrgyzstan, Ashkhabad in Turkmenistan and Samarkand in Uzbekistan. New direct routes from Almaty to Tehran, Delhi and Tel Aviv are planned.
Approximate flight times: From *London* to Almaty (via Moscow) is 8 hours, not including stopover time in Moscow; from *Istanbul* is 5 hours 30 minutes, from *Ulgi* (Mongolia) is 4 hours and from *Hannover* and *Frankfurt/M* is 7 hours.
International airports: *Almaty (ALA)* is located 10km (6 miles) north of the city. Bus no. 92 connects the airport with the city centre (travel time – 20 minutes). Taxis are also available at the airport for transport into the city centre. Airport facilities include *Hertz* rent-a-car, restaurant and post office.
SEA: Freight is carried on the Caspian Sea to Russia and Iran.
RAIL: There are international rail connections with the Russian Federation, Uzbekistan, Tajikistan, Turkmenistan and China. Services run from Almaty to Urumchi in China twice-weekly and daily to Moscow (the journey takes three days) and connect with the entire Russian Federation railway network. Trains leave Almaty, Bishkek and Tashkent twice a day for Moscow. The Tashkent–Novosibirsk express passes through Almaty each day in both directions. The lines from Almaty in the north connect with the *Trans-Siberian Railway* running west to Chimkent and finally to Orenburg in the Russian Federation. A new rail line is being built to connect Kazakhstan to Iran and Turkey.
ROAD: There are good road connections into Russia, the other Central Asian states and China. **Bus:** Buses leave Chimkent for Tashkent every 25 minutes 0700-1925. The journey is 160km (100 miles) and takes three hours. There are also buses from Chimkent to Bishkek.

TRAVEL - Internal

AIR: There are frequent flights from Almaty to Chimkent (four times a day), Dzhambul, Karaganda, Akmola, Pavlodar, Kzil-Orda, Semipalatinsk and Ust-Kamenogorsk. Flights also leave Chimkent for Almaty, Semipalatinsk and Karaganda.
Domestic airports: *Chimkent* has an airport offering mostly domestic flights. However, there are also services to Moscow (four a week) and Novosibirsk in the Russian Federation, and to Tashkent in Uzbekistan (daily). Bus no. 12 runs from the city centre to the airport.
Semipalatinsk has a domestic airport with flights to Almaty, Dzhambul, Chimkent, Karaganda and Ust-Kamenogorsk. However, it also receives flights from Moscow (four a week), Tashkent, Krasnoyarsk, Omsk, Tomsk and Bishkek.
The airport at *Ust-Kamenogorsk* receives flights from Almaty and a few other Kazakh cities, as well as from Moscow, Novosibirsk and a few other Siberian cities. Bus no. 12 runs to the Hotel Ust-Kamenogorsk in the city centre.
RIVER: River trips can be taken in Semipalatinsk on the River Irtysh.
RAIL: There are two *TurkSib* trains leaving Chimkent daily, one to Tashkent in Uzbekistan and the other to Novosibirsk in the Russian Federation, stopping at destinations in between. The cost of rail travel in Kazakhstan is minimal in comparison with Western Europe and there are regular connections between all the main centres. Queues at stations to buy a ticket can be long and passengers should bring their own food and drink on any train journey.
ROAD: Traffic drives on the right. There is a reasonable network of roads in Kazakhstan connecting all the towns and regional centres. Petrol supplies are reasonably reliable in comparison with other Central Asian republics. **Bus:** There are regular bus connections between all the main cities of Kazakhstan. **Taxi:** These are available in all Kazakh cities. **Car hire:** *Hertz* has offices at Almaty International Airport and at the business centre opposite the Hotel Kazakhstan in the city centre. Tel: (3272) 622 515. Tel/Fax: (3272) 631 832. Telex: 251477 (a/b HERTZ SU). **Documentation:** An international driving licence is required.
URBAN: Almaty is served by trolleybuses and buses.

ACCOMMODATION

HOTELS: There are 13 tourist hotels in Kazakhstan. Most towns in Kazakhstan have a limited supply of reasonable accommodation. It is advisable to make reservations in advance, either directly or through a travel agency. All *Intourist* hotels demand hard currency from foreigners, which will work out more expensive than paying in Roubles but does guarantee a basic level of comfort, although Western standards should not be expected. **Grading**: Hotels in Almaty are classified as follows: The Dostyk Hotel is *super class A*, the Otrar, Medeo and Kazakhstan hotels are of *super class B*, the Alatau Hotel is *first class*. The other hotels in Almaty, as well as those in Karaganda, Chimkent, Akmola, Kokshetau and Kostanai, are second class. The Dostyk Hotel boasts two restaurants serving Continental and American cuisine, a well-stocked bar and pleasant beer garden, as well as a business centre. Accommodation at the hotel may be booked in advance through *Fair Winds Trading Company*, who can also arrange accommodation in other towns in Kazakhstan (for contact details, see top of entry). Hotels in Chimkent include the Voskhod, Chimkent and Druzhba. The Hotel Interkosmos in Leninsk is stylish but expensive. The Hotel Taraz in Dzhambul is good value for money. Classification of tourist hotels and campsites is carried out by the Ministry of Tourism, Physical Culture and Sports of the Republic of Kazakhstan; classification of other forms of accommodation is carried out by the local authorities.
Turbazas: These 'tourist bases' are an alternative to hotel accommodation. For a dollar or two in local currency visitors have access to basic bungalow accommodation and three meals a day.
CAMPING: The only designated campsites are the permanent base camps from which the high peaks of Kazakhstan are climbed. Travellers pitch their tents in other localities at their own risk, although there are no regulations against it.

RESORTS & EXCURSIONS

90% of Kazakhstan is made up of steppe. For centuries these vast plains were home only to nomads and they are still virtually empty. Most settlements are concentrated in the southeast and the east of the republic where the plains give way to the mountains of the *Altai* and the *Tien Shan.*

The South

South Kazakhstan is a focus of Central Asian history and culture and there are many famous monuments in the region. It is a scenically diverse region in which all four seasons can be experienced in the space of a day as the snow-capped peaks, lakes and glaciers of the *Tien Shan* range give way to steppe and desert land which stretches for thousands of kilometres. The mountains serve as a centre for mountaineering and skiing and there are resorts offering a wide variety of winter sports. The desert is home to the *Singing Barkhan* – a sand dune 80m (260ft) high and 3km (2 miles) long, which, as it crumbles and shifts, produces a peculiar sound reminiscent of loud singing.
Almaty (formerly – *Alma Ata*) is the capital of the newly independent republic of Kazakhstan and enjoys a beautiful setting between mountains and plains. It is a city of modern architecture, wide streets, cool fountains, parks and squares and spectacular mountain views and, particularly in spring and autumn, is an attractive place despite the inevitable legacy of Soviet architecture. Attractions in the city include the *Panfilov Park* which is dominated by one of the world's tallest wooden buildings, the *Zenkov Cathedral.* This served in Soviet times as a concert and exhibition hall, but is currently standing empty, whilst the Christians of Almaty worship at *St Nicholas Cathedral.* Almaty boasts several fine museums including the *Museum of Kazakh National Instruments*, the *Central State Museum* and the *State Art Museum* which has amongst its exhibits traditional Kazakh rugs, jewellery and clothing. The *Arasan baths,* in the western area of Panfilov Park, have Eastern, Finnish and Russian saunas. The 4000m-high (1310ft) *Alatau Mountains* near Almaty offer numerous opportunities all year round for sports and recreation. There are large areas of unspoilt nature among the mountains which attract many walkers and climbers to the region in summer and skiers in the winter.
The *Tien Shan Mountains* in the southeast of Kazakhstan stretch for more than 1500km (932 miles). The highest peaks are *Pobeda Peak* (7439m/24,406ft) and *Khan-Tengri Peak* (7010m/23,000ft), a snow-white marble-like pyramid. The huge *Inylchek Glacier,* reaching almost 60km (37 miles) in length, splits the summits and at its centre lies the beautiful *Mertzbakher Lake.* The *Khan-Tengri International Mountaineering Camp* provides experienced mountain guides to take visitors on organised climbing and trekking programmes. Other facilities include horseriding, souvenir shop and bar. For further information, contact Kazakhstan International Mountaineering Camp 'Khan-Tengri', 48 Abai Avenue, 480072 Almaty. Tel: (3272) 677 024 *or* 677 866. Fax: (3272) 636 634 *or* 631 207. Telex: 251232 (a/b PTB SU).
The city of **Chimkent** is an industrial city, producing the largest amount of lead in the CIS. 160km (100 miles) away (travel time – 2 hours 30 minutes) is the 14th-century *Kodja Ahmed Yasavi Mausoleum* in **Turkestan;** built under Tamerlane, this mausoleum has the largest dome in Central Asia. **Dzhambul**, too, is an industrial city in the region with some reproductions of ancient remains

from when it was known as *Taraz* – these are housed in the *Karakhan* and the *Daudbek Shahmansur Mausoleums*. The nearby village of **Golovachovka**, 18km (11 miles) to the west, has authentic remains from Taraz, including the 11th-century *Babadzi-Khatun Mausoleum* and the 12th-century *Mausoleum Aisha Bibi*. Another ancient historical centre is **Taldikorgan**. Much of this region was crossed by the 124km (77-mile) *Great Silk Road*.

The West

West Kazakhstan marks the southern convergence of Europe and Asia in the basin of the Caspian Sea. The region's *Karagie Depression,* 132m (433ft) below sea level, is the lowest point in the world after the Dead Sea in Sinai. There are many architectural heritage sites in this region, including the subterranean cross-shaped *Shakpak-Ata Mosque* (12th-14th century) which is hewn out of rock.

The North

The nature reserve of *Kurgaldjino* in the north of Kazakhstan houses the most northerly settlement of pink flamingoes in the world, while another nature reserve, *Naurzum*, offers a rich landscape of geographical contrasts – salt lakes ringed by forests, the remains of ancient pines strewn amongst sand dunes, pine forests growing out of salt-marsh beds, vast meadows, and rare animals such as hisser swans and grave eagles.

The Centre

Central Kazakhstan has one of the largest lakes in the world. The unique *Lake Balkhash* is one-half saline, one-half fresh water. Some archaeological and ethnographical sites have been preserved in central Kazakhstan. There are Bronze Age and Early Iron Age sites and New Stone Age and Bronze Age settlements in the *Karkarala Oasis*. The *Bayan-Aul National Park* has rock drawings, stone sculptures, clean, sparkling lakes and pines clinging to the rocks. The **Baikonur Cosmodrome**, located 5km (3 miles) from the garrison city of **Leninsk** and 230km (143 miles) from **Kzil-Orda**, is the Central Asian answer to *Cape Canaveral* – tours are available during which visitors can witness space launches. It was from here, on April 12, 1961, that Yuri Gagarin, the first world cosmonaut, took off and it is still a point of departure for space launches. For information on group tours of the Cosmodrome, contact Intourist in Almaty, Hotel Otrar, Gogol Street 73, 480126 Almaty (tel: (3272) 330 045) *or* Kramds Mountain Company, Ulitsa Mira 115, 480091 Almaty. Tel: (3272) 447 530.

The East

East Kazakhstan offers a colourful landscape of snow-capped mountain peaks, plunging forested canyons and picturesque cedar forests. *Lake Marakol* rivals Baikal in beauty. It is 35km (22 miles) long and 19km (12 miles) wide and lies 1449m (4754ft) above sea level. The city of **Semipalatinsk**, 30km (19 miles) from Siberia, was a Russian place of exile; Dostoyevsky was exiled here from 1857-1859 and his house is preserved as a museum – exhibits include notes for *Crime and Punishment* and *The Idiot*. Other museums in the city include the *Abai Kununbaev Museum*, commemorating the Kazakh poet, and the *History Museum*. Nuclear tests were carried out southwest of Semipalatinsk until 1990, although today background radiation is easily within reach of internationally accepted levels. The town of **Ust-Kamenogorsk** is a mining and smelting town and is the gateway to the *Altai Mountains*. Occupying the central point of the continent, these gentle mountains are covered with meadows and woods and stretch for a thousand kilometres into Mongolia. **Rakhmanovski** in the Altai Mountains offers a *turbaza* (see *Accommodation*) and is renowned for its cross-country skiing.

The Spas

Kazakhstan has a wide range of spas offering various treatments. There are 98 sanatoria holiday hotels and 115 preventative medicine sanatoria. Most are located in areas with much to interest the tourist, such as sports, cultural events, historical and archaeological sites, and offer developed excursion facilities. The most internationally renowned resorts include **Sari Agach** (in the south), **Mujaldi** (in the Pavlodar region), **Arasan-Kapal** (in the Taldikorgan region), **Jani-Kurgan** (in the Kzil-Orda region), **Kokshetau** and **Zerenda** (in the Kokshetau region) and those located in **Zaili Alatau**.

Nature Reserves

Aksu-Jabagli: Located in southern Kazakhstan, 1000-4000m (3280-13,120ft) above sea level, and home to 238 species of birds, 42 species of animals and 1300 species of plants.
Almaty: Located in the southern Tien Shan Mountains and home to snow leopards, jeirans, gazelles, arkhars and the unique Tjan-Shan fir tree.
Barsa Kelmes: Translated as 'the land of no return', this island, off the northwestern Aral Sea coast, is the home of the rarest hoofed animal in the world – the kulan.
The West-Altai: Located in the Altai Mountains and home to 16 types of forest, 30 species of mammals and 120 species of birds.
Kurgaldjino: Located in central Kazakhstan, this A-class nature reserve is of international importance, and its feather-grass steppe is home to 300 types of plant and the most northerly settlement of flamingoes in the world.
Marakol: Located in the southern foothills of the Altai Mountains and home to 232 species of bird, 50 species of animal and 1000 types of plant.
Naurzum: Located in northern Kazakhstan and home to such rare animals as white herons, jack-bustards, hisser swans and grave eagles.
Ustiurt: Located in west Kazakhstan in the Karagie Depression, 132m (433ft) below sea level, this chalk-cliffed reserve is the largest in the country.
Bayan-Aul National Nature Park: Located in central Kazakhstan and known as 'the museum of nature'.

SOCIAL PROFILE

FOOD & DRINK: Kazakh dishes include *kazi, chuzhuk, suret* and *besbarmak* (made from horse meat or mutton). *Shashlyk* (skewered chunks of mutton barbecued over charcoal) and *lepeshka* (round unleavened bread) are often sold on street corners and make an appetizing meal. *Plov* is made up of scraps of mutton, shredded yellow turnip and rice and is a staple dish in all the Central Asian republics. Other mutton dishes such as *laghman* and *beshbermak* include long thick noodles garnished with a spicy meat sauce. *Manty* (boiled noodle sacks of meat and vegetables), *samsa* (samosas) and *chiburekki* (deep-fried dough cakes) are all popular as snacks. Almaty is renowned for its apples – indeed the city was named after them. **Drink:** Kazakh tea or *chai* is very popular and there are national cafés called *Chai-Khana* (tea-rooms) where visitors may sip this Kazakh speciality. It is drunk very strong with cream. Beer, vodka, brandy and sparkling wine are available in many restaurants. The national speciality is *kumis*, fermented mare's milk. Cafés where this can be ordered are called *Kumis-Khana*. Refusing it when offered may cause offence. In the steppe and desert regions where camels are bred, the camel's milk, called *shubat*, is offered to guests.
NIGHTLIFE: There are a number of nightclubs and casinos in Almaty and several other cities. Many restaurants play music after 2000, although this often consists of highly synthesised cover versions of Turkish and Russian hits which will not be everyone's cup of *chai*.
SHOPPING: Located north of Panfilov Park, Almaty has a bazaar, where a diverse range of items can be bought.
SPORT: All the regional centres boast sport complexes, **swimming** pools and training halls. Near Almaty, 12km (7 miles) from the city centre surrounded by mountains, the Medeo **ice-skating** rink is the largest speed-skating rink in the world and is very popular with all the inhabitants of the capital. A comfortable hotel, restaurant, café and modern ski resort are located nearby. **Ice hockey** games can be viewed at the rink in Ust-Kamenogorsk. On a spur of Zaili Alatau, 7km (4 miles) to the south, the **winter sports** complex of Chimbulak offers some of the finest **skiing** in the CIS and many ski competitions take place here. Skis and boots can be hired, but they are not up to Western European or American standards. Costs are minimal. **Horseriding** is also popular in Kazakhstan. Visitors may either take part in or view competitions of the many Kazakh equestrian sports, such as *baiga, kiz-kuu* and *kokpar*.
SPECIAL EVENTS: The Medeo complex (see *Sport* above) is the venue for the International Song Festival, *The Voice of Asia*, which is held annually at the end of July/beginning of August and attracts participants from Asia, Europe and the USA. In August, folk festivals in Almaty attract people from all over the south of the country during which national music, songs, dance, sports, national costumes and dishes can be experienced.
SOCIAL CONVENTIONS: Kazakhs are very hospitable. When greeting a guest the host gives him both hands as if showing that he is unarmed. When addressing a guest or elder, a Kazakh may address him with a shortened form of the guest's or elder's name and the suffix 'ke'. For example, Abkhan may be called Abeke, Nurslutan can be called Nureke. This should be regarded as indicating a high level of respect for the visitor. At a Kazakh home the most honoured guest, usually the oldest, is traditionally offered a boiled sheep's head on a beautiful dish as a further sign of respect. National customs forbid young people whose parents are still alive from cutting the sheep's head. They must pass the dish to the other guests for cutting. Inside mosques women observe their own ritual in a separate room, and must cover their heads and their arms (see *World of Islam* at the back of the book for more information). Formal dress is often required when visiting the theatre, or attending a dinner party. Shorts should not be worn except on the sports ground. **Tipping** is not customary at restaurants and cafés. A service charge is included in hotel and restaurant bills. There is also a fixed charge in taxi and railway transport.

BUSINESS PROFILE

ECONOMY: Kazakhstan has large natural deposits – iron, nickel, zinc, mangan, coal, chromium, copper, lead, gold and silver are presently being mined. Stones such as marble and granite also exist in great quantity. However, most consumer goods have to be imported from other republics of the CIS. Therefore, the Government lays priority on the expansion of the manufacturing industry. Agriculture is also important; principal commodities include wheat, meat products and wool. Trade with neighbouring countries has increased rapidly, especially South Korea and China. The irrigation demands on rivers in Kazakhstan and Uzbekistan to feed cotton fields caused the Aral Sea, into which the rivers flow, to shrink by one-third in the space of 20 years – this may qualify as the world's greatest single ecological disaster. Two large oil fields are presently being exploited in an American joint venture and a gas field in a US$1-billion project with British Gas, and there are growing indications that Kazakhstan may boast the largest unexploited oil and gas fields in the world. Kazakhstan has followed the course of most other former Soviet republics by relaxing central state control over day-to-day management of the economy while maintaining overall strategic direction. Some parts of the economy have been transferred to the private sector (presently about 10%) while the Kazakh exchequer took the decision in mid-1993 to introduce a new currency, the tenge, as a better option than the original decision to stay in the Rouble Zone. Kazakhstan is a member of the Central Asian Economic Union – ECO, the European Bank for Reconstruction and Development and, since 1992, of the World Bank and the IMF.
COMMERCIAL INFORMATION: The following organisation can offer advice: Ministry of External Economic Relations, pr. Ablaikhana 77, Almaty. Tel: (3272) 624 057; *or*
Ministry of Trade, pr. Ablaikhana 93/95, Almaty. Tel: (3272) 604 040 *or* 623 812; *or*
Chamber of Commerce and Industry of Kazakhstan, pr. Ablaikhana 93/95, 480091 Almaty. Tel: (3272) 621 446. Fax: (3272) 620 594. Telex: 251228 (a/b KAZINSU).
CONFERENCES/CONVENTIONS: Many international business events by such organisations as UNESCO, ICF and others are held in the Alatau Winter Resort near Almaty. There is an annual International Exhibition Fair called Karkara held at the Exhibition Complex of the Business Cooperation Centre in Almaty every September. Businessmen and company directors from all over the world meet here to make contacts and conclude business contracts. Other large industrial towns such as Karaganda, Pavlodar and Chimkent have conference and convention facilities and other industrial exhibitions and fairs are held here.

CLIMATE

Continental climate with cold winters and hot summers. The south receives about 3000 hours of sunshine annually, and the north receives 2000 hours. The hottest month is usually July (August in the mountain regions).

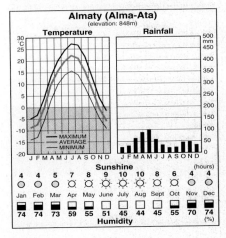

Almaty (Alma-Ata)
(elevation: 848m)

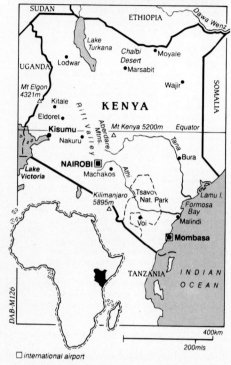

□ *international airport*

Location: East Africa.

Kenya Tourist Development Corporation
PO Box 42013, Utalii House, Uhuru Highway, Nairobi,
Kenya
Tel: (2) 330 820. Fax: (2) 227 815. Telex: 23009.
Kenya High Commission
45 Portland Place, London W1N 4AS
Tel: (0171) 636 2371/5. Fax: (0171) 323 6717. Telex:
262551. Opening hours: 0900-1300 and 1400-1700
Monday to Friday.
Kenya Tourist Office
25 Brook's Mews, off Davies Street, Mayfair, London
W1Y 1LG
Tel: (0171) 355 3144. Fax: (0171) 495 8656. Opening
hours: 0900-1700 Monday to Friday.
British High Commission
PO Box 30465, Bruce House, Standard Street, Nairobi,
Kenya
Tel: (2) 335 944. Fax: (2) 333 196. Telex: 22219 (a/b
UKREP).
Consulates in: Mombasa and Malindi.
Kenya Embassy
2249 R Street, NW, Washington, DC 20008
Tel: (202) 387 6101. Fax: (202) 462 3829.
Kenya Tourist Office
424 Madison Avenue, New York, NY 10017
Tel: (212) 486 1300. Fax: (212) 688 0911.
Embassy of the United States of America
PO Box 30137, Unit 64100, corner of Moi and Hailé
Sélassie Avenues, Nairobi, Kenya
Tel: (2) 334 141. Fax: (2) 340 838. Telex: 22964.
Kenya High Commission
415 Laurier Avenue East, Ottawa, Ontario K1N 6R4

Tel: (613) 563 1773/6. Fax: (613) 235 6599.
Canadian High Commission
PO Box 30481, Comcraft House, Hailé Sélassie Avenue,
Nairobi, Kenya
Tel: (2) 214 804. Fax: (2) 216 485. Telex: 22198 (a/b
DOMCAN).

AREA: 580,367 sq km (224,0181 sq miles).
POPULATION: 25,905,000 (1989 estimate).
POPULATION DENSITY: 44.7 per sq km.
CAPITAL: Nairobi. **Population:** 1,162,189 (1985
estimate).
GEOGRAPHY: Kenya shares borders with Ethiopia in
the north, Sudan in the northwest, Uganda in the west,
Tanzania in the south, and Somalia in the northeast. To
the east lies the Indian Ocean. The country is divided into
four regions: the arid deserts of the north, the savannah
lands of the south, the fertile lowlands along the coast
and around the shores of Lake Victoria, and highlands in
the west, where the capital Nairobi is situated. Northwest
of Nairobi runs the Rift Valley, containing the town of
Nakuru and Aberdare National Park, overlooked by
Mount Kenya (5200m/17,000ft), which also has a
national park. In the far northwest is Lake Turkana
(formerly Lake Rudolph). Kenya is a multi-tribal society
and has a diverse pattern of tribes; in the north live
Somalis and the nomadic Hamitic peoples (Turkana,
Rendille and Samburu), in the south and eastern lowlands
are Kamba and Masai cattle herders and the Nilotic Luo
live around Lake Victoria. The largest tribe is the Kikuyu
who live in the central highlands and have traditionally
been the dominant tribe in commerce and politics,
although this is now shifting. There are many other
smaller tribes and although Kenya emphasises
nationalism, tribal and cultural identity is evident. A
small European settler population remains in the
highlands, involved in farming and commerce.
LANGUAGE: Kiswahili is the national and English the
official language.
RELIGION: Mostly traditional, and about 25%
Christian, 6% Muslim.
TIME: GMT + 3.
ELECTRICITY: 220/240 volts AC, 50Hz. Plugs are
UK-type round 2-pin or flat 3-pin. Bayonet-type light
sockets exist in Kenya.
COMMUNICATIONS: Telephone: IDD service is
available to the main cities. Country code: 254 (followed
by 2 for Nairobi, 11 for Mombasa and 37 for Nakuru).
Outgoing international code: 000. **Fax:** This service is
available to the public at the Main Post Office and the
Kenyatta International Conference Centre in Nairobi, and
at some major hotels in Nairobi and Mombasa.
Telex/telegram: Telex facilities are available at Nairobi
General Post Office. Most hotels have facilities for their
guests. Overseas telegrams can be sent from all post and
telegraphic offices and private telephones. Nairobi GPO
is open 24 hours. **Post:** Airmail to Western Europe takes
up to four days, and the service is generally reliable. Post
offices are open 0800-1700 Monday to Friday; 0800-
1300 Saturday. **Press:** The main dailies include *Daily
Nation, The Weekly Review, Kenya Times* and *The
Standard.* Nairobi is the main publishing centre.
**BBC World Service and Voice of America
frequencies:** From time to time these change. See the
section *How to Use this Book* for more information.
BBC:

MHz	21.47	17.88	15.42	9.630

Voice of America:

MHz	21.49	15.60	9.525	6.035

PASSPORT/VISA

Regulations and requirements may be subject to change at short notice, and you are advised to contact the appropriate diplomatic or consular authority before finalising travel arrangements. Details of these may be found at the head of this country's entry. Any numbers in the chart refer to the footnotes below.

	Passport Required?	Visa Required?	Return Ticket Required?
Full British	Yes	No	Yes
BVP	Not valid	-	-
Australian	Yes	Yes	Yes
Canadian	Yes	Yes	Yes
USA	Yes	Yes	Yes
Other EU (As of 31/12/94)	Yes	1	Yes
Japanese	Yes	Yes	Yes

PASSPORTS: Valid passport required by all.
British Visitors Passport: Not acceptable.
VISAS: Required by all except:
(a) nationals of the UK;

(b) [1] nationals of Denmark, Germany, Ireland, Italy and
Spain (all other EU nationals *do* require a visa);
(c) nationals of Ethiopia, Finland, Norway, San Marino,
Sweden, Turkey and Uruguay;
(d) nationals of the following Commonwealth countries:
Bahamas, Bangladesh, Barbados, Belize, Brunei,
Botswana, Cyprus, Eritrea (provided holding valid UK
passport), Fiji, Gambia, Ghana, Grenada, Jamaica,
Kiribati, Lesotho, Malawi, Malaysia, Maldives, Malta,
Mauritius, Namibia, Nauru, Papua New Guinea, Norway,
St Lucia, St Vincent & the Grenadines, Seychelles, Sierra
Leone, Singapore, Solomon Islands, Swaziland,
Tanzania, Tonga, Trinidad & Tobago, Tuvalu, Uganda,
Vanuatu, Western Samoa, Zambia and Zimbabwe;
(e) those visitors travelling to a third destination and
holding valid onward or return tickets provided they do
not leave the airport.
Note: Travellers needing a visa are advised to acquire
one before their journey; a visitor's pass is available to
those without a visa on arrival, but a deposit of £250
refundable upon departure may be required before a pass
is issued. A return or onward air ticket to a country
outside East Africa is required for all nationals with
visas.
Types of visa: Entry and Transit. Cost – £18 for most
nationals for standard visas.
Validity: Up to 3 months. Renewals or extensions can be
made at Immigration in Nyayo House, Uhuru Highway,
Nairobi.
Application to: Consulate (or Consular section at
Embassy or High Commission). For addresses, see top of
entry.
Application requirements: (a) Valid passport. (b)
Completed application form. (c) Fee. (d) 2 passport-size
photos for referrable visas only.
Working days required: Consult Embassy or High
Commission. The length of time it takes to process the
application depends on whether or not it has to be
referred to Nairobi; otherwise 24 hours.
Temporary residence: Apply to Principal Immigration
Officer, PO Box 30191, Nairobi.

MONEY

Currency: Kenyan Shilling (KSh) = 100 cents. Notes are
in denominations of KSh500, 200, 100, 50, 20 and 10.
Coins are in denominations of KSh5 and 1, and 50, 10
and 5 cents.
Currency exchange: Currency can be exchanged at the
major banks, some of which are more cooperative than
others. Black market transactions are common, but
inadvisable.
Credit cards: Access/Mastercard, American Express,
Diners Club and Visa are all widely accepted. Check
with your credit card company for details of merchant
acceptability and other services which may be available.
Travellers cheques: These can be changed at banks.
Note: Tanzanian and Ugandan currencies are only
negotiable if in the form of travellers cheques.
Exchange rate indicators: The following figures are
included as a guide to the movements of the Kenyan
Shilling against Sterling and the US Dollar:

Date:	Oct '92	Sep '93	Jan '94	Jan '95
£1.00=	55.12	99.83	100.75	70.16
$1.00=	34.73	65.38	68.10	44.85

Currency restrictions: The import and export of local
currency is prohibited. Free import of foreign currency is
allowed provided it is declared. Foreign currency may be
exported up to either the equivalent of KhS5000 or the
amount declared on arrival. There is no limit placed on
travellers cheques and letters of credit.
Banking hours: 0900-1400 Monday to Friday; 0900-
1100 on the first and last Saturday of each month. The
airport banks are open until midnight every day. Banks
on the coast close half an hour earlier. National and
international banks have branches in Mombasa, Nairobi,
Kisumu, Thika, Eldoret, Kericho, Nyeri and in most
other major towns.

DUTY FREE

The following goods may be imported into Kenya by
passengers over 16 years of age without incurring
customs duty:
*200 cigarettes or 225g of tobacco; 1 bottle of spirits or
wine; 1 pint of perfume.*
Note: Firearms and ammunition require a police permit.
Gold, diamonds and wildlife skins or game trophies not
from the authorised Kenyan government department are
prohibited.

PUBLIC HOLIDAYS

Jan 1 '95 New Year's Day. **Mar 3** Eid al-Fitr (End of
Ramadan). **Apr 14** Good Friday. **Apr 17** Easter Monday.

May 1 Labour Day. **May 10** Eid al-Adha (Feast of the Sacrifice). **Jun 1** Madaraka Day. **Oct 20** Kenyatta Day. **Dec 12** Jamhuri Day. **Dec 25-26** Christmas. **Jan 1 '96** New Year's Day. **Feb 22** Eid al-Fitr (End of Ramadan). **Apr 5** Good Friday. **Apr 8** Easter Monday.

Note: (a) Holidays falling on a Sunday are observed the following Monday. (b) Muslim festivals are timed according to local sightings of various phases of the Moon and the dates given above are approximations. During the lunar month of Ramadan that precedes Eid al-Fitr, Muslims fast during the day and feast at night and normal business patterns may be interrupted. Many restaurants are closed during the day and there may be restrictions on smoking and drinking. Some disruption may continue into Eid al-Fitr itself. Eid al-Fitr and Eid al-Adha may last anything from two to ten days, depending on the region. For more information, see the section *World of Islam* at the back of the book.

HEALTH

Regulations and requirements may be subject to change at short notice, and you are advised to contact your doctor well in advance of your intended date of departure. Any numbers in the chart refer to the footnotes below.

	Special Precautions?	Certificate Required?
Yellow Fever	Yes	1
Cholera	Yes	2
Typhoid & Polio	Yes	-
Malaria	3	-
Food & Drink	4	-

[1]: A yellow fever vaccination certificate is required from travellers over one year of age arriving from infected areas; those countries formerly classified as endemic zones are considered to be still infected by the Kenyan authorities. Travellers arriving from non-endemic zones shold note that vaccination is strongly recommended for travel outside the urban areas, even if an outbreak of the disease has not been reported and they would normally not require a vaccination certificate to enter the country.

[2]: Following WHO guidelines issued in 1973, a cholera vaccination certificate is no longer a condition of entry to Kenya. However, cholera is a serious risk in this country and precautions are essential. Up-to-date advice should be sought before deciding whether these precautions should include vaccination, as medical opinion is divided over its effectiveness. See the *Health* section at the back of the book.

[3]: Malaria risk exists throughout the year in the whole country. There is usually less risk in Nairobi and in the highlands (above 2500m/8200ft) of the Central, Rift Valley, Eastern Nyanza and Western Provinces. The predominant *falciparum* strain has been reported as 'highly resistant' to chloroquine and 'resistant' to sulfadoxine/pyrimethamine.

[4]: Mains water is normally chlorinated, and whilst relatively safe may cause mild abdominal upsets. Bottled water is available and is advised for the first few weeks of the stay. Drinking water outside main cities and towns is likely to be contaminated and sterilisation is considered essential. Milk is pasteurised and dairy products are safe for consumption. Local meat, poultry, seafood, fruit and vegetables are generally considered safe to eat.

Meningitis is a risk depending on the area visited and time of year.

Rabies is present. For those at high risk, vaccination before arrival should be considered. If you are bitten abroad, seek medical advice without delay. For more information, consult the *Health* section at the back of the book.

Bilharzia (schistosomiasis) is present. Avoid swimming and paddling in fresh water. Swimming pools which are well-chlorinated and maintained are safe.

Note: There is a risk of contracting *AIDS* if the necessary precautions are not taken. It is advisable to take a kit of sterilised needles for any possible injections needed.

Health care: Health insurance is essential. *East African Flying Doctor Services* have introduced special Tourist Membership which guarantees that any member injured or ill while on safari can call on a flying doctor for free air transport.

TRAVEL - International

AIR: Kenya's national airline is *Kenya Airways (KQ)*. For free advice on air travel, call the Air Travel Advisory Bureau in the UK on (0171) 636 5000 (London) *or* (0161) 832 2000 (Manchester).

Approximate flight times: From Nairobi to *London* is 8 hours; to *New York* is 17 hours 30 minutes; to *Los Angeles* is 20 hours; to *Singapore* is 13 hours and to *Sydney* is 25 hours.

International airports: *Nairobi (NBO)* (Jomo Kenyatta International) is 13km (8 miles) southeast of the city. Bus no. 34 runs every 30 minutes from 0630-2100 (travel time – 30 minutes). Taxis are also available to the city. Airport facilities include an outgoing duty-free shop, 24-hour bank/bureau de change, post office (0800-1700 Monday to Friday), restaurant/bar and car hire from a range of international companies.

Mombasa (MBA) (Moi International) is 13km (8 miles) west of the city. There is a regular bus service by *Kenya Airways* to their city centre office in Mombasa (travel time – 15 minutes). Taxis are available. Airport facilities include an outgoing duty-free shop, bank (0500-1400), restaurant/bar, 24-hour tourist information and car hire from a range of international companies.

Note: Immigration procedures in Kenyan airports are likely to be extremely slow, so it is advisable to arrive early.

Departure tax: US$20.

SEA/LAKE: A regular international passenger service operates between Mombasa, the Seychelles and Bombay. Short-distance ships sail between Mombasa, Dar-es-Salaam and Zanzibar. The ports in the Lake Victoria passenger service include Port Victoria/Kisumu, Homa Bay and Mfangano. Passenger and cruise lines that run to Kenya are as follows: *TFC Tours, Polish Ocean, Hellenic Lines* (from the USA and Red Sea), *Moore/McCormack (USA), Lykes Lines* and *Norwegian American.*

Ferries in Lake Victoria connect Kisumu in Kenya to Mwanza, Musoma and Bukoba in Tanzania. Fares are paid for in the port of embarkation currency. It is also possible to get ferries from Mombasa to Pemba and Zanzibar in Tanzania, and also to Chiamboni in Somalia. Enquire locally for details.

RAIL: The through train services to Uganda and Tanzania are currently suspended, but a thrice-weekly train runs to the frontier from where there are onward connections by taxi.

ROAD: Kenya can be entered by road from all neighbouring countries, *although some routes may be inadvisable due to uncertain political conditions.* Check with the Foreign Office if in doubt.

Travel from Somalia is generally via Liboi, where a change of bus will be required. The route from Sudan is currently not recommended due to the civil war in the south. The main crossing points from Tanzania are at Namanga and Lunga Lunga, with smaller posts at Isebania and Taveta. Some direct coach services operate. From Uganda there are crossing points at Malaba and Buisa. Note that at Malaba the Kenyan and Ugandan customs posts are about 1km (0.6 miles) apart and no transport between them is available. For all road frontier crossings, it is advisable to contact the Kenya AA (PO Box 40087, Nairobi) prior to departure from country of origin for up-to-date information concerning insurance requirements and conditions.

Note: For their own safety when travelling overland through the northeastern province of Kenya, travellers are advised to contact the Tourist Development Corporation for advice. Four-wheel-drive vehicles are recommended for travel in this region.

TRAVEL - Internal

AIR: *Kenya Airways* operates an extensive network of flights, which includes scheduled services to Mombasa, Malindi, Lamu Island, Kisumu (on the shore of Lake Victoria) and inclusive tours to the game parks and the coast from Nairobi. There are also private airlines such as *Caspair* operating light aircraft to small air strips. Planes can also be chartered and are useful for transportation into game parks.

Departure tax: KSh100 on all domestic flights.

SEA: Local ferries run between Mombasa, Malindi and Lamu. For details, contact local authorities and tour operators.

RAIL: *Kenya Railways Corporation* runs passenger trains between Mombasa and Nairobi; trains generally leave in the evening and arrive the following morning after a journey of about 13-14 hours. There are also branches connecting Taveta and Kisumu to the passenger network. There is a daily train in each direction on the Nairobi–Kisumu route, and also an overnight service (travel time – approx. 14 hours). Trains are sometimes delayed, but most of the rolling stock is modern and comfortable, and most trains have restaurant cars. There are three classes: first class is excellent, with 2-berth compartments, wardrobe, etc; second class is more basic but comfortable; third is basic. The dining-car service on the Nairobi–Mombasa route is very highly regarded. Sleeping compartments should be booked in advance. Children under 3 years of age travel free. Children between 3-15 years of age pay half-fare.

ROAD: Traffic drives on the left. All major roads are now tarred and many of the others have been improved, particularly in the southwest, although vast areas of the north still suffer from very poor communications. Care should be taken when leaving trunk roads as the surfaces of the lesser roads vary greatly in quality, particularly during the rainy season. There are petrol stations on most highways. The Kilifi Bridge linking Mombasa to Malindi has opened, serving as an alternative to the Kilifi ferry, and easing traffic flows to the northern circuit. **Bus:** There is a network of regular buses and shared minibuses *(Matatu);* the fares do not vary greatly, but buses tend to be the safer method of transport. All bus companies are privately run. In some towns the different bus services and the *Matatu* share the same terminus. **Taxi:** Kenya is very well served by long-distance taxis, carrying up to seven passengers. The best services are between the capital and Mombasa and Nakuru. Taxis and minibuses are a convenient method of travel on the coast. **Car hire:** Self-drive and chauffeur-driven cars may be hired from a number of travel agents in Nairobi, Mombasa and Malindi. This can be expensive, and rates – particularly the mileage charges – can vary a good deal. Only 4-wheel-drive cars should be considered. **Tours and safaris:** Many tour companies in Nairobi offer package arrangements for visits to the game parks and other attractions. *Rhino Safaris* offer a fleet of over 100 safari vehicles to all the game parks and reserves. Before booking it is very important to know exactly what the all-in price provides. **Documentation:** UK or foreign driving licences are accepted for up to 90 days, but this must be endorsed in Kenya at a local police station. Visitors bringing in vehicles with registration other than Ugandan or Tanzanian must obtain an 'International Circulation Permit' from the Licensing Officer in Nairobi. This will be issued free of charge on production of a permit of customs duty receipt and a certificate of insurance. An International Driving Permit is strongly recommended, although it is not legally required. For further details, apply to the Registrar of Motor Vehicles in Nairobi.

URBAN: Bus: Nairobi and Mombasa have efficient bus systems. Only single tickets are sold (by conductors). There are also unregulated *Mátatu,* 12- to 25-seat light pick-ups and minibuses. These are often severely overloaded and recklessly driven and therefore should be used with caution. **Taxi:** *Kenatco* runs a fleet of taxis and these are usually very reliable. The older yellow-band taxis do not have meters, so fares should be agreed in advance. A 10% tip is expected. Taxis cannot be hailed in the street.

JOURNEY TIMES: The following chart gives approximate journey times (in hours and minutes) from Nairobi to other major cities/towns in Kenya.

	Air	Road	Rail
Kisumu	1.05	7.00	14.00
Malindi	0.45	8.00	-
Mombasa	1.00	6.00	14.00
Lamu	1.30	13.00	-
Diani	1.30	7.00	-
Nakuru	0.30	3.00	5.00
Eldoret	1.15	7.00	9.00
Masai Mara	0.30	5.00	-
Amboseli	0.30	3.00	-

ACCOMMODATION

HOTELS: Many of Nairobi's hotels are up to top international standards, and some of them are very much in the colonial style. Cheaper hotels are also available. Hotel bills must be paid in foreign currency, or in Kenyan Shillings drawn from an external, a shipping or an airline account. **Grading:** Accommodation in Kenya is divided into groups: town hotels, vacation hotels, lodges and country hotels. Within each group, grading is according to amenities and variety of facilities. The rating is subject to the fulfilment of strict requirements concerning technical equipment, comfort, services, sanitation and security. For further information, contact the Kenya Association of Hotel Keepers & Caterers, PO Box 46406, Nairobi. Tel: (2) 330 868.

CAMPING/CARAVANNING: There are no restrictions on camping in Kenya. Visitors should be aware that camping in remote regions can be dangerous due to wild animals and to *shifta* (armed bandits); the latter are a hazard particularly in the far north. A list of licensed tented camps is available from the Tourist Office or the press section of the High Commission.

YOUTH HOSTELS: There are youth hostels in all major towns. For further information, contact the Youth Office, PO Box 48661, Nairobi. Tel: (2) 723 012. Fax: (2) 721 735.

RESORTS & EXCURSIONS

For the purpose of this guide, Kenya has been divided into three regions: Central Highlands, The Coast and National Parks.

Central Highlands

Nairobi: The 'Green City in the Sun' is an attractive city with wide tree-lined streets and spacious parkland suburbs. Its pleasant nature together with judicious investment in facilities such as the *Kenyatta Conference Centre* have made Nairobi an important centre for international business and conference activities. However, despite the capital's appearance, urban crime (as in most big cities) is on the increase and visitors are advised to take such precautions as they would take in any other cosmopolitan centre in the world (this would include avoiding certain areas, especially at night – some travellers advise against walking alone through *Uhuru Park* at any time). There is a full range of shopping opportunities, from purpose-built American-style malls to rickety African markets, and a variety of restaurants and nightclubs. The *African Heritage Café*, Banda Street, serves traditional African meals. The *Thorn Tree Café* at the New Stanley Hotel is an open-air café and a good place to meet fellow visitors. The *New Supreme* and *Minar* serve top-quality Indian food and there is a good choice of international food at all hotels. The *Carnivore* serves barbecued wild game. There are open-air swimming pools at the Serena, Boulevard and Jacaranda hotels – non-residents may pay to swim. Other places of interest in or near Nairobi include: *Bomas of Kenya*, a short distance outside the city centre, where displays of traditional dancing are put on for visitors; *Kenya National Museum* with its particularly good ethnographic exhibits; *Snake Park*, opposite the museum, houses snakes indigenous to East Africa and a few from other parts of the world; adjacent to the Snake Park is a collection of traditional mud and thatch huts and granaries containing tools characteristic of different tribes. *Nairobi National Park* is just 8km (5 miles) from Nairobi city centre yet still seems a savage and lonely place during the week (carloads of city-dwellers invade at the weekend). It was Kenya's first national park and today still looks much as it did in the early photographs – wild, undulating pasture dotted with every kind of East African plain-dwelling animal except elephants. Visits can be arranged through the Hilton Hotel. At the gates to the park is the *Animal Orphanage* where young, sick and wounded animals are cared for.

Lake Naivasha is an hour's drive from the capital. It is known for the abundance and variety of its birdlife and spectacular views. There are opportunities for rock climbing.

Nanyuki, at the foot of *Mount Kenya*, provides a starting point both for climbers and safaris.

Nakuru is situated in the *Rift Valley* about 230km (140 miles) west of Nairobi. It has the feel of a frontier town. *Lake Nakuru National Park* was once said to be home to half the world's total population of pink flamingoes, and even today visitors in winter will encounter these ungainly birds in large numbers. Many less spectacular birds can also be seen. Baboons are often to be seen on the lake's western cliffs. *Menengai Crater*, an extinct volcano, stands nearby. 50km (30 miles) to the north of Nakuru, along a fairly good road, is *Lake Baringo*, smaller than Lake Nakuru, but with the same variety of birdlife. There is a permanent tented camp on the island at its centre, where boats may be hired to cruise through the reeds at the lake's northern end, a habitat rich in water fowl, egrets, giant herons and fishing eagles.

Kisumu on *Lake Victoria* is a commercial centre linked by road to the capital. Visits can be made to *Mount Elgon National Park*, famous for its mountain flora and fauna.

The Coast

Mombasa: The second largest city in Kenya, 500km (300 miles) from Nairobi. Until the ascendancy of the Western powers in the Indian Ocean, Mombasa was second only to Zanzibar as a centre for trade with Arabia, India and the Far East – slaves and ivory were exchanged for spices and small goods, and later for gold dollars. Mombasa is still an important port, prospering from its position at the head of the only railway into the Kenyan interior, but visitors are likely to find the rakish grey forms of foreign warships to be more typical of modern Mombasa than the flotillas of Arab dhows that still collect in the *Old Harbour*. Mombasa is the headquarters for Kenya's coastal tourist trade, but has none of the fine beaches to be found to the north and south. There are, however, several places of interest: The *Old Town* retains a strongly Arab flavour, with narrow, crowded streets and street vendors selling all manner of local and imported craftwork; *Fort Jesus*, built by the Portuguese in 1593 and taken by the Omani Arabs in 1698 after a 33-month seige, is now a museum and worth visiting (0830-1830 every day of the year); *Biashara Street* is probably the best place to go to buy kikoi and khanga cloths; the *Old Harbour* is an interesting place for early morning and late afternoon strolls, and is often filled with sailing dhows from the Yemen and Persian Gulf; *The Ivory Room* off Treasury Square is now permanently closed. The *Tourist Office* is on Moi Avenue near the Giant Tusks (0800-1200 and 1400-1630 Monday to Friday; 0800-1200 Saturday). Staff are very helpful.

Malindi, 125km (80 miles) north of Mombasa, contains the *Malindi and Watamu Marine National Parks* where one can see fish through a glass-bottomed boat or take part in snorkelling or skindiving. Close to Watamu is a ruined city (now the *Gedi National Park*) which dates from the 13th century and is very well preserved. The little village of **Mambrui**, north of Malindi, is also worth a visit.

Lamu Island, 200km (125 miles) north of Malindi, is an exceptionally beautiful place with fine white sandy beaches, sailing dhows and a fascinating town. No motorised vehicles are allowed on the island and the streets are so narrow that donkeys and hand-carts are the only vehicles that can negotiate them. There are many mosques and fine old Arab houses with impressive carved wooden doors. Other attractions in the city include the *Hindu Temple* in Mwagogo Road, off Treasury Square, and the bazaars. Fishing trips may be taken by dhow and day trips to the 14th- and 15th-century ruins on the nearby islands of **Pate** and **Manda** can be arranged with local boat owners. On the Prophet's Birthday there is a week-long festival, with dancing, singing and other celebrations. Many Muslims come to Lamu from all along the coast to enjoy this celebration. The best time to visit the island is outside the main tourist season (April-November).

The South Coast, protected by its coral reef, is famous for its beautiful and safe beaches. Resorts include Likoni, Tiwi, Diani Beach and Shimoni.

The North Coast is famous for such resorts as Bamburi Beach, Kenya Beach, Watamu Beach and Casuarina Beach.

National Parks

Kenya's national parks and game reserves have long been famous for their variety and wealth of flora and fauna. That they have remained Africa's foremost areas of accessible wilderness is due to a vigorous campaign of preservation and management mounted since the 1960s with increasing success by the Kenyan government. Whilst drought and overgrazing have destroyed some regions and there is still conflict between tribal interests and wildlife preservation, the Government fully recognises that Kenya's future prosperity may depend on maintaining its remarkable natural heritage.

One-tenth of all land in Kenya is designated as national parkland. Forty parks and reserves cover all habitats from desert to mountain forest, and there are even two marine parks in the Indian Ocean. Tourist facilities are extremely good. There are many organised safaris, but those with the time and money may choose to hire their own vehicle and camping equipment. Day trips by balloon are becoming a very popular way to view game, especially in the Masai Mara Game Reserve, and it is advisable to book well in advance.

Some smaller parks are described in the preceding sections covering the Central Highlands and the Coast. The following is a selection of the better-known parks.

Aberdare National Park: A densely wooded mountain range rising to over 4000m (13,000ft), adjacent to Mount Kenya. It is possible to see **elephants, rhinos,** rare forest **antelopes** such as the **bongo** and **dik-dik, leopards, lions** and **monkeys.** However, the thick vegetation and misty alpine climate hides most wildlife from the inexpert observer, the exceptions being **giant forest pigs, baboons** and **buffaloes,** which often sleep or feed beside the many dirt tracks. Most visitors prefer to watch for animals from the comfort of the park's two lodges, *Treetops* and the *Ark,* both built on platforms overlooking clearings which are floodlit at night. On the higher slopes, giant alpine plants sprout from an almost perpetual fog. There are many waterfalls, the greatest being *Guru Falls* which drops over 300m (1000ft).

Amboseli National Park: A small park by Kenyan standards, covering just under 400 sq km (155 sq miles) at the centre of the border with Tanzania, 220km (140 miles) from Nairobi. The fine view it affords of snow-capped *Mount Kilimanjaro,* Africa's highest mountain (5895m/19,340ft), brings many visitors, but the park itself has seen better days. The once-lush savannah is now largely a dust-bowl and most animals have retreated into areas of scrub forest and marshland.

Masai Mara National Reserve: 390km (240 miles) from Nairobi in the southwest corner of the country, this reserve is a slice of Africa as seen by Hollywood – a vast rolling plain beneath the Mara escarpment striped black once a year by millions of **wildebeeste** and **zebra** migrating north from the Serengeti plains in neighbouring Tanzania. Continually harried by predators, thick columns of exhausted animals eventually converge at one spot on the *Mara River* and wait nervously to cross. A panic anywhere within the herd is transmitted flank-to-flank until it reaches those by the river, who fall 6m (20ft) into water already bloodied and bobbing with bloated carcasses. The inelegant beasts must swim past **crocodiles, hippos** and flapping **vultures** to join the sparse but growing herd on the other side. The stench of corruption is unimaginable and this spectacle is probable best seen from one of three balloons operating from *Grosvenor's Camp.* During the migration season (July/August), the reserve's resident **lions** lounge prominently in the sun, fat and seemingly placid, and apparently indifferent to tourists. Other animals to be seen, at any time of the year, include **elephants, cheetahs, baboons, gazelles, giraffes, jackals, hyenas, water buffaloes, ostriches** and several types of **antelope**. There are 13 tented camps and two lodges *(Mara Serena Lodge* and *Keekorok Lodge)* in the reserve. Grosvenor's Camp, with its own airstrip, is the largest and best-equipped. A luxury hotel stands on the escarpment just outside the reserve and gives fine views over the plain. Masai tribespeople live on the reserve's fringes. They are often keen to sell traditional bead necklaces and decorated gourds to tourists, or to pose for tourist cameras in return for a small fee.

Meru National Park: 400km (250 miles) from Nairobi, this features Kenya's only colony of **white rhinos.** It remains one of the more unspoilt parks.

Mount Kenya National Park: 600 sq km (230 sq miles) of forest and bare rock straddling the equator, all above 1800m (6000ft), rising to over 5000m (17,000ft) in the year-round snow fields at the mountain's peak. The ascent is very beautiful and may be climbed without special equipment, but it is advisable to take time so as to avoid altitude sickness. Climbers should be accompanied by a guide. Porters are also available and there are huts to stay in along the way. Plenty of warm clothes are required as well as one's own food supplies. A *Rockclimber's Guide to Mount Kenya and Mount Kilimanjaro* can be bought from the Mountain Club of Kenya, PO Box 45741, Nairobi (tel: (2) 501 747). The mountain is one of the last haunts of the **black leopard** and the **black and white colobus monkey**. Lord Baden-Powell is buried nearby in **Nyeri.**

Samburu Game Park: An area of semi-desert halfway between Nairobi and *Lake Turkana* that provides a rare chance to see the **oryx, gerenuk, reticulated giraffe** and **Grevy's zebra. Ostriches** and **elephants** are easily spotted in this open habitat. There are two lodges, *Samburu Lodge* and *River Lodge,* both of which hang out bait to attract **leopards** for the guests to study whilst sitting at the bar. The park takes its name from the Samburu people, distantly related to the Masai.

Tsavo National Park: At 21,000 sq km (8,000 sq miles), it is Kenya's largest park by far, but much of it is closed to the public. Despite a drastic fall in the **elephant** population in the 1970s (caused by over-stocking), there are still many large herds. Much of the land is open savannah and bush woodland inhabited by **buffaloes,** a few **rhinos, lions, antelopes, gazelles, giraffes** and **zebras. Crocodiles** and **hippos** can be seen at *Mzima Springs* in the west of the park.

Lake Turkana (formerly Lake Rudolph): There are several parks and reserves in the far north of Kenya, gathered around Lake Turkana. This extraordinary lake, running for several hundred miles through windswept and largely uninhabited deserts, contains many unique species of fish and marine plants and has recently gained a reputation as a fishing resort. Several lodges have sprung up on the eastern shore to cater for this trade and consequently general tourism is expected to increase. Despite the harsh climate, many of Kenya's better-known animals manage to survive here, as do the tiny people of the El Molo tribe, who fish the eastern waters. There are two large volcanic islands in the lake. The flooded crater of the southernmost island has a resident population of unnaturally **large crocodiles**. The lake is subject to violent storms, which disturb algae to produce remarkable colour changes in the water.

SOCIAL PROFILE

FOOD & DRINK: Kenya's national dishes appear on most hotel menus. The country's beef, chicken, lamb and pork are outstandingly good, as are the wide variety of tropical fruits. Local trout, Nile perch and lobster, shrimps and Mombasa oysters are included on menus in season. Indian and Middle Eastern food is available in most areas. Some game-park lodges serve game, including buffalo steaks marinaded in local liqueurs and berries, often garnished with wild honey and cream. Most Kenyans eat maize, beans and maize meal. At the small 'hotelis', *chai* (tea boiled with milk and sugar) and *mandazi* (doughnuts) are popular. There is a wide range of restaurants in Nairobi and Mombasa, otherwise hotels in smaller towns offer restaurant service. **Drink:** Locally brewed beer (*Tusker* and *White Cap*) and bottled sodas may be found throughout the country. *Kenya Cane* (spirit distilled from sugar cane) and *Kenya Gold* (a coffee liqueur) are produced in Kenya. Traditional beer made with honey *uki* and locally made spirit distilled from maize (*changaa*) may sometimes be found.

NIGHTLIFE: Most of the major hotels in Nairobi and the tourist resorts have dancing with live bands or discotheques each evening. There are also a few nightclubs with an African flavour. There is a large selection of cinemas in Nairobi which show mainly American, British and European films.

SHOPPING: *Khanga, kitenge* and *kikoi* cloths may be bought in markets and the Bishara Streets of Nairobi and Mombasa. There is a particularly good cooperative shop in Machakos which sells *kiondos*, bags dyed with natural dyes and with strong leather straps. *Makonde* carvings are sold throughout the country, and young Kamba and Masai men sell carvings and necklaces on the beaches of the south coast. **Shopping hours:** 0830-1230 and 1400-1630 Monday to Saturday. **Note:** The sale of souvenirs made of wildlife skins (this includes reptiles) is forbidden.

SPORT: Tennis, squash, bowls, horseriding and **polo** are all popular sports. Kenya also has good **athletics** facilities and the Kenyans have a fine record in world competitions. Sports clubs accept visitors.

Watersports: Sailing, water-skiing, swimming and surfing are popular in the coastal resorts both north and south of Mombasa; these include Malindi, Nyali, Bamburi, Shanzu, Kikambala and Kilifi. These resorts have fine sandy beaches and there are several coral reefs. Trout **fishing** in the lakes is particularly good between November and March.

SPECIAL EVENTS: The following is a selection of special events celebrated annually in Kenya. For a complete list, contact the Tourist Office.
Apr (Easter Period) *Kenya Safari Rally.* **Apr** *Kenya Domestic Tourism Exhibition.* **May** *Kenya International Tourism Exhibition.* **May/Jun** *Kenya Schools Music Festival.* **Sep** *Mombasa National Show.* **Sep/Oct** *Nairobi International Show* (organised by the Agricultural Society of Kenya, featuring all aspects of Kenyan business and industry).

SOCIAL CONVENTIONS: Western European habits prevail throughout Kenya as a result of British influences in the country. Kenyans are generally very friendly. Dress is informal, and casual lightweight clothes are accepted for all but the smartest social occasions. **Tipping:** A KSh10 tip is usual except where a service charge has been made, in which case any additional amount is at the visitor's discretion.

BUSINESS PROFILE

ECONOMY: The Kenyan economy is largely agricultural: 85% of the population work on the land. The main cash crops are tea and coffee, both of which were severely affected by the droughts of the 1980s. Kenya is one of the few African countries with a significant dairy industry. Apart from tea and coffee, petroleum products are Kenya's main export, although the country is also a major importer of crude oil. Manufactured goods account for the rest of Kenya's imports, which come mostly from the UK, Germany and Japan. The UK and Germany, along with neighbouring Uganda, are Kenya's main export markets. Kenya is the third-largest recipient of British aid in the world and the largest in Africa. Much of this is direct financial assistance to ease Kenya's short-term balance of payments problems. Kenya has reached agreement with the IMF on a Structural Adjustment Programme (similar to many negotiated in the Third World) that should increase commercial opportunities in the country. Kenya has been one of Africa's strongest economies, with average growth of 5% in the late 1980s, and the economic outlook is fairly good provided the problems of an overweight public sector, rising inflation and unemployment are tackled. A speedy resolution of the current political uncertainty is also necessary.
BUSINESS: Lightweight suits are recommended for all occasions. Prior appointments are necessary. Although Kiswahili is the national language, English is the official language and is widely spoken. **Office hours:** 0800-1300 and 1400-1700 Monday to Friday, 0830-1200 Saturday.

In Mombasa, offices usually open and close half an hour earlier.
COMMERCIAL INFORMATION: The following organisations can offer advice: Kenya National Chamber of Commerce and Industry, PO Box 47024, Ufanisi House, Haïlé Sélassie Avenue, Nairobi. Tel: (2) 334 413; *or* Investment Promotion Centre, PO Box 55704, 8th Floor, National Bank Building, Harambee Avenue, Nairobi. Tel: (2) 221 401. Fax: (2) 336 663. Telex: 25460.
CONFERENCES/CONVENTIONS: The Kenyatta International Conference Centre is in Nairobi. For further information, contact the Kenyatta International Conference Centre, PO Box 30746, Nairobi. Tel: (2) 332 383.

CLIMATE

The coastal areas are tropical, but tempered by monsoon winds. The lowlands are hot but mainly dry, while the highlands are more temperate with four seasons. Nairobi has a very pleasant climate throughout the year due to its altitude. Near Lake Victoria the temperatures are much higher and rainfall can be heavy.
Required clothing: Lightweight cottons and linens with rainwear are advised for the coast and lakeside. Warmer clothing is needed in June and July and for the cooler mornings on the coast. Lightweights are needed for much of the year in the highlands. Rainwear is advisable between March and June and October and December.

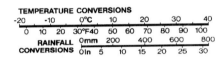

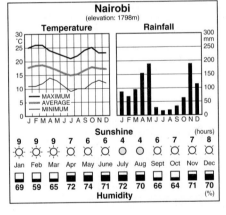

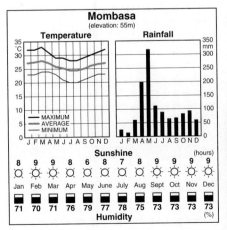

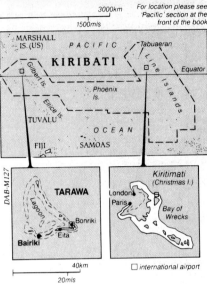

Location: South Pacific, Micronesia.

Kiribati Visitors Bureau
PO Box 261, Bikenibeu, Bairiki, Tarawa, Kiribati
Tel: 28288. Fax: 26193. Telex: 77022.
Consulate of Kiribati
Faith House, 7 Tufton Street, London SW1P 3QN
Tel: (0171) 222 6952. Fax: (0171) 976 7180.
Honorary Consul of Kiribati
8 Brookhouse Street, Leicester LE2 05D
Tel: (01162) 543 781. Fax: (01162) 471 690.
Commonwealth Information Centre
Commonwealth Institute
230 Kensington High Street, London W8 6NQ
Tel: (0171) 603 4535. Fax: (0171) 602 7374.
Provides general information on Kiribati.
British High Commission
PO Box 61, Bairiki, Tarawa, Kiribati
Tel: 21327. Fax: 21488. Telex: 77050 (a/b UKREP KI).
Consulate of Kiribati
Suite 503, 850 Richards Street, Honolulu, HI 96813
Tel: (808) 521 7703. Fax: (808) 521 8304.
The Canadian High Commission in Wellington deals with enquiries relating to Kiribati (see *New Zealand* later in this book).

AREA: 861 sq km (332 sq miles).
POPULATION: 72,298 (1990).
POPULATION DENSITY: 89.2 per sq km.
CAPITAL: Tarawa. **Population:** 28,802 (1990).
GEOGRAPHY: Kiribati (pronounced 'Kiribass', formerly the Gilbert Islands) consists of three groups in the central Pacific: Kiribati (including Banaba, formerly Ocean Island), the Line Islands and the Phoenix Islands. The 33 islands, scattered across two million square miles of the central Pacific, are low-lying coral atolls with coastal lagoons. The exception is Banaba, which is a coral formation rising to 80m (265ft). The soil is generally poor, apart from Banaba, and rainfall is variable. Coconut palms and pandanus trees comprise the main vegetation. There are no hills or streams throughout the group. Water is obtained from storage tanks or wells.
LANGUAGE: I-Kiribati and English.
RELIGION: Gilbert Islands Protestant Church and Roman Catholic.
TIME: GMT + 12, except as follows:

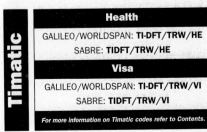

Health		
GALILEO/WORLDSPAN:	**TI-DFT/TRW/HE**	
SABRE:	**TIDFT/TRW/HE**	
Visa		
GALILEO/WORLDSPAN:	**TI-DFT/TRW/VI**	
SABRE:	**TIDFT/TRW/VI**	

For more information on Timatic codes refer to Contents.

Canton Island, Enderbury Island: GMT - 11; **Christmas Island:** GMT - 10.
ELECTRICITY: 240 volts AC, 50Hz.
COMMUNICATIONS: The Government provides radio and postal services to all inhabited islands.
Telephone: IDD is available throughout urban Tarawa. Country code: 686. Radio telephone calls can be arranged to most outer islands. All international calls from Kiribati have to go through the operator. **Fax:** This is available at the local Telecoms Office. **Telex/telegram:** Available in Betio 0800-1900 daily and on outer islands 0800-1600 Monday to Friday. Telegrams may take several days to reach Europe. **Post:** Airmail to Western Europe takes up to two weeks. There is a weekly postal service for overseas mail. Post office hours: 0800-1230 and 1330-1615 Monday to Friday. **Press:** The weekly paper is *Te Uekera,* published in English and I-Kiribati.
BBC World Service and Voice of America frequencies: From time to time these change. See the section *How to Use this Book* for more information.

BBC:				
MHz	**17.83**	**15.34**	**11.95**	**9.640**
Voice of America:				
MHz	**18.82**	**15.18**	**9.525**	**1.735**

PASSPORT/VISA

Regulations and requirements may be subject to change at short notice, and you are advised to contact the appropriate diplomatic or consular authority before finalising travel arrangements. Details of these may be found at the head of this country's entry. Any numbers in the chart refer to the footnotes below.

	Passport Required?	Visa Required?	Return Ticket Required?
Full British	Yes	1	Yes
BVP	Not valid	-	-
Australian	Yes	Yes	Yes
Canadian	Yes	No	Yes
USA	Yes	Yes	Yes
Other EU (As of 31/12/94)	Yes	1	Yes
Japanese	Yes	Yes	Yes

PASSPORTS: Required by all.
British Visitors Passport: Not accepted.
VISAS: Required by all except:
(a) **[1]** nationals of Denmark, Spain and the UK (excluding Northern Ireland). All other EU nationals *do* require a visa;
(b) nationals of Antigua & Barbuda, Bahamas, Barbados, Bermuda, Botswana, British Virgin Islands, Canada, Cayman Islands, Cook Islands, Cyprus, Ecuador, Falkland Islands, Fiji, Gibraltar, Grenada, Guam, Guyana, Hong Kong, Iceland, Malaysia, Malta, Montserrat, New Zealand, Niue, Norway, The Philippines, St Kitts & Nevis, St Lucia, Samoa (American), Western Samoa, San Marino, Seychelles, Sierra Leone, Singapore, Solomon Islands, Sweden, Switzerland, Tonga, Trinidad & Tobago, Trust Territories, Tunisia, Turks & Caicos Islands, Tuvalu, Uruguay, Vanuatu and Zimbabwe.
Note: (a) Maximum period of stay without a visa for nationals of the above list varies from country to country. Enquire at Consulate for details. (b) Nationals of some countries require references along with their visas. Check details with the Consulate (or the Consular section at the Embassy or High Commission).
Types of visa: *Transit:* not required by travellers holding valid documents and confirmed tickets for return or onward travel, and providing they do not leave the airport. *Business and Tourist visas:* £8 plus £3 referral fee.
Application to: Principal Immigration Officer, Ministry of Home Affairs and Rural Development, PO Box 75, Bairiki, Tarawa (fax: 686 21133); or any Kiribati or British Consulate. For addresses, see top of this entry.
Application requirements: Completed forms and appropriate letters from company/sponsors if on business.
Temporary residence: Apply to Office of the President, PO Box 68, Bairiki, Tarawa, Kiribati.

MONEY

Currency: Australian Dollar (A$) = 100 cents. Notes are in denominations of A$100, 50, 20, 10, 5 and 2. Coins are in denominations of A$1, and 50, 20, 10, 5, 2 and 1 cents.
Currency exchange: US Dollars may be exchanged for local currency at the Bank of Kiribati Ltd or local hotels.
Credit cards: Not accepted.
Travellers cheques: Accepted in hotels, some shops and at the Bank of Kiribati Ltd.
Exchange rate indicators: The following figures are included as a guide to the movements of the Australian Dollar against Sterling and the US Dollar:

Date:	**Oct '92**	**Sep '93**	**Jan '94**	**Jan '95**
£1.00=	2.22	2.36	2.18	2.02
$1.00=	1.40	1.55	1.47	1.29

Currency restrictions: There are no restrictions on the import or export of either foreign or local currency.
Banking hours: 0900-1500 Monday to Friday.

DUTY FREE

The following goods may be imported into Kiribati without incurring customs duty:
200 cigarettes or 50 cigars or 225g tobacco; 1 litre of spirits and 1 litre of wine (for persons over 21 years of age); a reasonable amount of perfume for personal use.

PUBLIC HOLIDAYS

Jan 1 '95 New Year's Day. **Apr 14-17** Easter. **Jul 12** Independence Day. **Aug 4** Youth Day. **Dec 25-26** Christmas. **Jan 1 '96** New Year's Day. **Apr 5-8** Easter.

HEALTH

Regulations and requirements may be subject to change at short notice, and you are advised to contact your doctor well in advance of your intended date of departure. Any numbers in the chart refer to the footnotes below.

	Special Precautions?	Certificate Required?
Yellow Fever	No	1
Cholera	No	No
Typhoid & Polio	Yes	-
Malaria	No	-
Food & Drink	2	-

[1]: A yellow fever vaccination certificate is required from travellers over one year of age coming from infected areas.
[2]: All water should be regarded as a potential health risk. Water used for drinking, brushing teeth or making ice should have first been boiled or otherwise sterilised. Only eat well-cooked meat and fish, preferably served hot. Pork, salad and mayonnaise may carry increased risk. Vegetables should be cooked and fruit peeled.
Health care: Health insurance is recommended. Tungaru Central Hospital on Tarawa provides medical service to all the islands. Government dispensaries on all islands are equipped to handle minor ailments and injuries.

TRAVEL - International

AIR: Kiribati is mainly served by *Air Nauru (ON)* and *Air Marshall Islands.* The national airline, *Air Tungaru (VK),* flies to Hawaii (Honolulu) and Fiji.
Approximate flight time: From London to Tarawa via Sydney and Nauru is 30 hours 30 minutes (excluding stopover time).
International airports: *Tarawa (TRW)* and *Christmas Island (CXI).*
Departure Tax: A$10.
SEA: International ports are Tarawa, Banaba and Christmas Island, all served by the following cargo lines: *Pacific Forum Line, Bank Line, Daiwa Line, Tanker Ship (McDonald Hamilton)* and *China Navigation Co.*

TRAVEL - Internal

AIR: *Air Tungaru (VK)* operates an internal scheduled service to nearly all outer islands linking them with Tarawa.
ROAD: Traffic drives on the left. All-weather roads are limited to urban Tarawa and Christmas Island. **Buses** and **taxis** are available on urban Tarawa only. **Car hire:** Available on urban Tarawa and Christmas Island only.
Documentation: International Driving Permit required.

ACCOMMODATION

HOTELS: There are four hotels in Kiribati, on Tarawa, Christmas Island and Abemama.
REST HOUSES: Inexpensive rest houses can be found on all the other islands, for example Otintai, Tarawa; Robert Louis Stevenson, Abemama; Captain Cook, Christmas Island. However, cooking facilities are limited and visitors should take what they need with them. Prices for accommodation in rest houses vary considerably.

RESORTS & EXCURSIONS

There are few tours available in Kiribati. However, visits to Second World War battlegrounds and natural history expeditions with studies of the local birdlife (large colonies of which live on **Christmas Island**) are available. There are also trips to see outrigger canoe races and dancing contests. Excellent facilities exist in Kiribati for snorkelling and deep-sea fishing or simply sunbathing on one of the many beaches. Visitors are always welcome in the *maneaba,* a traditional community meeting house, where they may enjoy traditional dancing, singing and storytelling – local culture is still the dominant influence in these islands.

SOCIAL PROFILE

FOOD & DRINK: There are few restaurants in Kiribati as tourism has not yet become a main source of income. They are mainly situated in the larger towns and include the M'Aneaba restaurant at Aantebuku and the Otintai Hotel dining room, both on Tarawa. Local specialities in the southern islands of Kiribati include the boiled fruit of *pandanus* (screwpine), sliced thinly and spread with coconut cream. A Kiribati delicacy is *palu sami,* which is coconut cream with sliced onion and curry powder, wrapped in taro leaves and pressure cooked in an earth-oven packed with seaweed. It can be eaten on its own or served with roast pork or chicken. As in many of the islands of the South Pacific, there is a tendency amongst local people to regard imported canned products as luxuries.
NIGHTLIFE: There are 'Island Nights' which feature traditional Polynesian music and dancing, film shows and feasts in *maneabas* (local meeting houses) which can be found throughout the islands.
SHOPPING: Handicrafts include baskets, table mats, fans and cups made from pandanus leaves, coconut leaves, coconut shells and sea shells. Sea-shell necklaces are popular, as are models of Gilbertese canoes and houses. A prized item is the Kiribati shark-tooth sword made of polished coconut wood with shark teeth, filed to razor sharpness, lashed to the two edges. These days, most examples are modern reproductions. **Shopping hours:** 0700-1200 and 1400-1900 Monday to Friday 0800-1200 Saturday.
SPORT: Hotels offer **canoeing, fishing** and **snorkelling** facilities. **Birdwatching** is popular, especially on Christmas Island where millions of birds swarm everywhere. Game fishing on Christmas Island is also becoming popular. A fishing licence is unnecessary and charters are easily available. **Swimming:** Numerous beaches offer safe bathing.
SOCIAL CONVENTIONS: Like the other Pacific islanders, the people are very friendly and hospitable and retain much of their traditional culture and lifestyle. In this casual atmosphere European customs still prevail alongside local traditions. Although in official correspondence the Western convention of signing names with initials is adopted, it is more polite (and customary) to address people by their first name. Bikinis should not be worn except on the beach. **Tipping:** Not expected.

BUSINESS PROFILE

ECONOMY: The end of phosphate mining in Kiribati had a devastating effect on the economy given that the commodity was the major export earner (accounting for 85% of revenue). Coconuts are the principal agricultural product: agriculture as a whole is limited by the poor quality of the soil. Fishing, especially tuna, is the other major economic activity. Despite reasonable earnings from all these, Kiribati is heavily dependent on foreign aid to meet an annual balance of payments deficit approaching A$20 million. Most trade takes place with Australia, New Zealand, the UK, Japan, the USA, Papua New Guinea and Fiji.
BUSINESS: Shirt and smart trousers or skirt will suffice most of the time; ties need only be worn for formal occasions. **Office hours:** 0800-1230 and 1330-1615 Monday to Friday.

CLIMATE

Maritime equatorial in the central islands of the group. The islands to the north and south are more tropical. The trade winds blow between March and October, making this the most pleasant time of the year, while the highest rainfall (December to March) is concentrated on the northern islands. November to February is more wet and humid than the rest of the year.

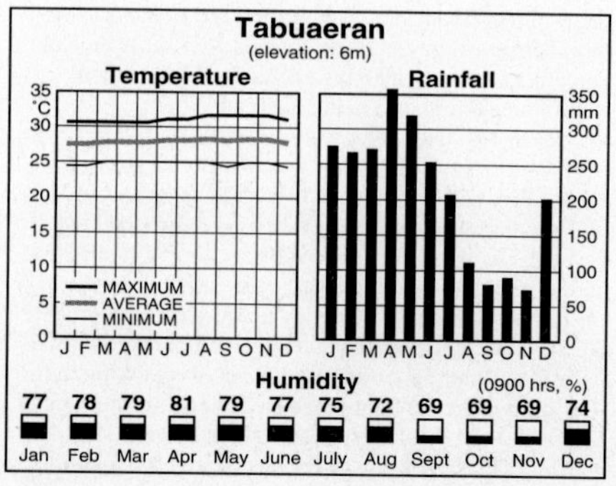
Tabuaeran
(elevation: 6m)
Temperature
Rainfall
35 °C 30 25 20 15 10 5 0
350 mm 300 250 200 150 100 50 0
MAXIMUM
AVERAGE
MINIMUM
J F M A M J J A S O N D
J F M A M J J A S O N D
Humidity
(0900 hrs, %)
77 78 79 81 79 77 75 72 69 69 69 74
Jan Feb Mar Apr May June July Aug Sept Oct Nov Dec

Democratic People's Republic of Korea

□ international airport

200km

100mls

C.I.S.

C.I.S.

CHINA

CHINA

Changbai Shan

Yalu

Chongjin

DEMOCRATIC
PEOPLE'S
REPUBLIC OF KOREA

Kimchaek

Sinuiju
Hamhung

Hungnam

PYONGYANG Wonsan

Yellow
Sea

Nampo

Sea of
Japan

Imjin

Kaesong

Demilitarized
zone

SEOUL

REPUBLIC OF KOREA

Location: Far East.

Ryohaengsa (Korea International Travel Company)
Central District, Pyongyang, DPR Korea
Tel: (2) 817 201. Fax: (2) 817 607. Telex: 5998 (a/b RHS KP).
Kumgangsan International Tourist Company
Pyonchon District, Pyongyang, DPR Korea
Tel: (2) 814 284. Fax: (2) 814 622.
General Delegation of the DPR of Korea
104 boulevard Bineau, 92200 Neuilly-sur-Seine, France
Tel: (1) 47 45 17 97. Fax: (1) 47 38 12 50. Telex: 615021F.

AREA: 120,538 sq km (46,540 sq miles).
POPULATION: 22,193,000 (1992 estimate).
POPULATION DENSITY: 184.1 per sq km.
CAPITAL: Pyongyang. **Population:** 2,000,000 (1986 estimate).
GEOGRAPHY: The Democratic People's Republic of Korea shares borders in the north with China, in the east with the Sea of Japan, in the west with the Yellow Sea and in the south with the demilitarised zone (separating it from the Republic of Korea). Most of the land consists of hills and low mountains and only a small area is cultivable. Intensive water and soil conservation programmes, including land reclamation from the sea, are given high priority. The eastern coast is rocky and steep with mountains rising from the water and this area contains most of the river waterways.
LANGUAGE: Korean.
RELIGION: There is no official religion, but Buddhism is practised by a sizeable minority and there are also Christian and Chundo Kyo minorities.
TIME: GMT + 9.
ELECTRICITY: 110/220 volts AC, 60Hz.
COMMUNICATIONS: Telephone: IDD to the country is available, although there is a very sparse internal network. Country code: 850. International calls from the country have to go through the operator. **Telex/telegram:** Services are available in all Pyongyang hotels. **Post:** Services are extremely slow and limited outside the capital. Airmail takes about ten days to reach Western Europe. Post office hours: 0900-2100 daily. **Press:** Major

daily newspapers include *Rodong Shinmun, Minju Choson* and *Pyongyang Shinmun.* The *Pyongyang Times* is published weekly in English. There are also several monthly English-language magazines.
BBC World Service and Voice of America frequencies: From time to time these change. See the section *How to Use this Book* for more information.
BBC:

MHz	21.71	17.83	15.28	9.740

Voice of America:

MHz	15.43	11.72	5.985	1.143

PASSPORT/VISA

Regulations and requirements may be subject to change at short notice, and you are advised to contact the appropriate diplomatic or consular authority before finalising travel arrangements. Details of these may be found at the head of this country's entry. Any numbers in the chart refer to the footnotes below.

	Passport Required?	Visa Required?	Return Ticket Required?
Full British	Yes	Yes	Yes
BVP	Not valid	-	-
Australian	Yes	Yes	Yes
Canadian	Yes	Yes	Yes
USA	Yes	Yes	Yes
Other EU (As of 31/12/'94)	Yes	Yes	Yes
Japanese	Yes	Yes	Yes

PASSPORTS: Valid passport required by all.
British Visitors Passport: Not accepted.
VISAS: Required by all.
Applications to: Consular section of the General Delegation of the DPR Korea in France. Applications should be made well in advance. Tourists can generally only enter as part of a group sanctioned by the Korean Tourist Bureau. It is only possible to travel as an individual if the whole tour itinerary is pre-booked.

MONEY

Currency: Won (NKW) = 100 jon. Notes are in denominations of NKW100, 50, 10, 5 and 1. Coins are in denominations of 50, 10, 5 and 1 jon.
Exchange rate indicators: The following figures are included as a guide to the movements of the Won against Sterling and the US Dollar:

Date:	Oct '92	Sep '93	Jan '94	Jan '95
£1.00=	3.40	3.29	3.18	3.36
$1.00=	2.14	2.15	2.15	2.15

Currency restrictions: Import and export of local currency is prohibited. There are no restrictions on foreign currency, but the amount must be declared.

DUTY FREE

The following goods may be imported into the Democratic People's Republic of Korea without incurring customs duty:
A reasonable amount of tobacco and alcoholic beverages.
Prohibited items: Binoculars, wireless sets, arms, ammunition, explosives, drugs, plants and seeds. Animals and all groceries require valid certificates of entry.

PUBLIC HOLIDAYS

Jan 1 '95 New Year's Day. **Feb 16** Kim Jong Il's Birthday. **Mar 8** International Women's Day. **Apr 15** Kim Il Sung's Birthday. **May 1** May Day. **Jun 1** International Children's Day. **Aug 15** Anniversary of Liberation. **Sep 9** Independence Day. **Oct 10** Anniversary of the Foundation of the Korean Workers' Party. **Dec 27** Anniversary of the Constitution. **Jan 1 '96** New Year's Day. **Feb 16** Kim Jong Il's Birthday. **Mar 8** International Women's Day. **Apr 15** Kim Il Sung's Birthday.

HEALTH

Regulations and requirements may be subject to change at short notice, and you are advised to contact your doctor well in advance of your intended date of departure. Any numbers in the chart refer to the footnotes below.

	Special Precautions?	Certificate Required?
Yellow Fever	No	No
Cholera	Yes	1
Typhoid & Polio	Yes	-
Malaria	No	-
Food & Drink	2	-

[1]: Following WHO guidelines issued in 1973, a cholera vaccination certificate is not a condition of entry to the Democratic People's Republic of Korea. However, cholera is a risk in this country and precautions are essential. Up-to-date advice should be sought before deciding whether these precautions should include a vaccination, as medical opinion is divided over its effectiveness. See the *Health* section at the back of the book.
[2]: All water should be regarded as a potential health risk. Water used for drinking, brushing teeth or making ice should have first been boiled or otherwise sterilised. Milk is unpasteurised and should be boiled. Powdered or tinned milk is available and is advised, but make sure that it is reconstituted with pure water. Avoid dairy products which are likely to have been made from unboiled milk. Only eat well-cooked meat and fish, preferably served hot. Pork, salad and mayonnaise may carry increased risk. Vegetables should be cooked and fruit peeled.
Rabies is present. For those at high risk, vaccination before arrival should be considered. If you are bitten abroad, seek medical advice without delay. For more information, consult the *Health* section at the back of the book.
Health care: Health insurance is essential.

TRAVEL - International

AIR: The main airlines serving the Democratic People's Republic of Korea are *Civil Aviation Company (JS), Aeroflot Russian International Airlines (SU)* and *Civil Aviation Administration of China* (CA). Connecting flights to North Korea are available from Moscow, Khabarovsk (Russian Federation) and Beijing (China).
Approximate flight time: From London to Pyongyang is 16 hours.
International airport: *Pyongyang (FNJ)* (Sunan) is 30km (18.5 miles) from the city (travel time – 45 minutes).
SEA: Main international ports are Chongjin, Hungnam, Haeju, Najin, Wonsan and Nampo, the port of Pyongyang.
RAIL: A through-train from Pyongyang to Beijing runs four times a week and there is also a thrice-weekly sleeping car through to Moscow via Khabarovsk. There are no routes to the Republic of Korea.
ROAD: There are roads from Dandong, Lu-ta, Liaoyang, Jilin and Changchun in China and Vladivostock in the Russian Federation, but foreigners are only permitted to enter the country by rail or by air.

TRAVEL - Internal

AIR: There are flights from Pyongyang, Hamhung and Chongjin, although foreigners are not allowed to use these.
RAIL: The extensive rail network built by the Japanese during the Second World War has been broken by the separation of north and south Korea, but the main passenger routes run from Pyongyang to Sinuiju, Haeju and Chongjin. Service, however, is slow.
ROAD: Traffic drives on the right. The quality of major roads is good; many are dual carriageways. There are no buses between cities.
URBAN: Pyongyang has a 4-line metro and regular bus services.
JOURNEY TIMES: The following chart gives approximate journey times (in hours and minutes) from Pyongyang to other major cities/towns in the Democratic People's Republic of Korea.

	Road	Rail
Diamond Mt	10.00	-
Kaesong	8.00	6.00
Nampo	1.30	8.00

ACCOMMODATION

Pyongyang has five first-class hotels where foreigners stay, although groups cannot know in advance which one will be used. All other towns have one first-class hotel for use by groups.

RESORTS & EXCURSIONS

Pyongyang was completely rebuilt after the Korean War as a city of wide avenues, neatly designed parks and enormous marble public buildings. The *Palace of Culture*, the *Grand Theatre*, the *Juche Tower* and the *Ongrui Restaurant* epitomise the Korean variant of Communist architecture. The *Gates of Pyongyang* are worth seeing, and *Morangborg Park* and *Taesongsan Recreation Ground* (with its fairground attractions) offer relaxation. For the (mainly communist) 13th World Festival of Youth and Students in 1989, a 150,000-seat stadium was built in Pyongyang. **Mangyongdae**, Kim Il

City sights of Pyongyang

silver and tungsten. Since the main industrial infrastructure was developed in the 1950s, development resources have gradually been shifted to light industry and latterly concentrated on automation and modernisation. Most trade is conducted with the CIS, Japan and China, where a number of joint industrial ventures have been set up. Trade with the West is low but is slowly rising (Western Europe in total accounts for about 5%). Korea has yet to adopt any of the political or economic reforms which have swept Eastern Europe, nor does it seem likely to do so as long as the current leadership retains power. However, the North faces severe economic difficulties in the short-term, following the loss of a large number of key export markets, particularly parts of the CIS, which will compound what has been an almost total lack of growth. This is now starting to affect key sectors of the economy: there have been recent unconfirmed reports of food and energy shortages. Trade has also been hit by the insistence of North Korea's trading partners that convertible currencies should be used in all transactions, exacerbating the North's already severe lack of foreign exchange. The North's economic planners will inevitably start to look to the South, which long ago outstripped the North on economic performance (despite a dearth of raw materials, the South's GDP, with twice the population, is six to eight times that of the North). The crisis led in 1993 to a unique official admission that certain targets specified in the 1987 Five Year Plan had not been met. Economic preoccupations also lay behind Pyongyang's agreement with the US on nuclear inspections. The effect of a change at the helm — with the Dear Leader replacing his father, the Great Leader — may not be immediately apparent, but some opening up to the world by the hermit-like North Koreans is inevitable and, indeed, starting to take place.

BUSINESS: Suits are required. Business transactions will take place outside the office, generally in the evening, as visitors are not allowed to enter offices.

COMMERCIAL INFORMATION: The following organisation can offer advice: Korean Committee for the Promotion of International Trade Central District, Pyongyang.

CLIMATE

Moderate with four distinct seasons. The hottest time is July to August, which is also the rainy season; coldest is from December to January. Spring and autumn are mild and mainly dry.

Required clothing: Lightweight cottons and linens are worn during the summer. Light- to medium-weights are advised in the spring and autumn, and medium- to heavy-weights in the winter. Waterproofing is advisable during the rainy season.

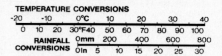

Sung's birthplace, is a national shrine. His family's thatched cottage, now a museum, overlooks the *Taedong River* and the capital. Many ancient buildings in **Kaesong** (six hours from the capital by train), bear witness to Korea's 500-year imperial history. The town is surrounded by beautiful pine-clad hills. **Kumgangsan** is the country's largest national park, consisting of a range of mountains along the east coast of the country. Its unspoilt, diverse environment is popular with birdwatchers, photographers and botanists. **Myoyangsan,** whose name means 'exotic fragrant mountain', offers pleasant walks and climbs through a contrasting scenery of waterfalls, woods and Buddhist pagodas, just 120km (75 miles) northeast of the capital. The *Exhibition Centre*, with its imposing 4-ton bronze doors, houses thousands of gifts presented by foreigners to Kim Il Sung and his son.

POPULAR ITINERARIES: 7-day: Pyongyang–Mangyongdae–Myoyangsan–Kaesong–Pyongyang.

SOCIAL PROFILE

FOOD & DRINK: Reasonable restaurants can be found in the main towns and cooking is usually based on the staple food, rice. In hotels and restaurants it is better to stick to the Korean, Chinese or Japanese items on the menu as experience of Western and Russian cooking is

limited. Eating out is arranged by the guide. Those drinking alcohol should be discreet.

NIGHTLIFE: A night at the revolutionary opera provides a unique experience. There are also circuses and musical events of a high quality.

SPORT: As mentioned in *Resorts & Excursions* above, in 1989 the country hosted the 13th World Festival of Youth and Students with a consequent expansion of sports facilities around the capital.

SPECIAL EVENTS: The following is a selection of the major festivals and other special events celebrated in the Democratic People's Republic of Korea in 1995/96. For a complete list, contact the Korea International Travel Company.

Apr 13 '95 *April Spring Art Festival,* Pyongyang. **Jul 8** *Kim Il Sung's memorial celebrations.* **Apr '96** *April Spring Art Festival,* Pyongyang.

SOCIAL CONVENTIONS: Discretion and a low political profile are advised. **Tipping:** Not practised.

BUSINESS PROFILE

ECONOMY: The Democratic People's Republic of Korea has a Soviet-style command economy based on heavy industry. The country has rich mineral deposits, including most of the major base metals, as well as gold,

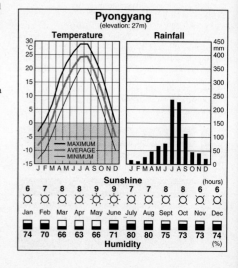

Korea (Republic of)

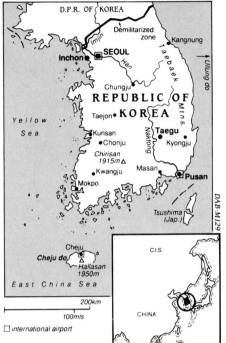

□ international airport

Location: Far East.

Korea National Tourism Corporation
PO Box 903, KNTC Building, 10 Ta-dong, Chung-gu, Seoul 100, Republic of Korea
Tel: (2) 757 6030 *or* 757 0086. Fax: (2) 757 5997. Telex: 28555.
Korea Tourist Association
12th Floor, Tourism Centre Building, 10 Ta-Dong, Chung-gu, Seoul 100, Republic of Korea
Tel: (2) 757 2345. Fax: (2) 757 9756. Telex: 25151.
Korea Association of Travel Agents
132-4 Pongnae-dong 1GA, Chung-gu, Seoul, Republic of Korea
Tel: (2) 752 8692. Fax: (2) 752 8694.
Embassy of the Republic of Korea
4 Palace Gate, London W8 5NF
Tel: (0171) 581 0247 *or* 581 3330 (visas). Fax: (0171) 581 8076. Opening hours: 0930-1730 Monday to Friday; 1000-1200 and 1400-1600 Monday to Friday (Visa section).
Korea National Tourism Corporation
20 St George Street, London W1R 9RE
Tel: (0171) 409 2100 *or* 408 1591. Fax: (0171) 491 2302.
The KNTC can also offer advice and information on conference facilities in the Republic of Korea.
British Embassy
4 Chung-dong, Chung-gu, Seoul 100, Republic of Korea
Tel: (2) 735 7341/3. Fax: (2) 725 1738 *or* 736 6241.
Telex: 27320 (a/b PRODROM K).
Consulate in: Pusan (tel: (51) 463 0041 *or* 463 4630; fax: (51) 462 5933).
Embassy of the Republic of Korea
2450 Massachusetts Avenue, NW, Washington, DC 20008
Tel: (202) 939 5600. Fax: (202) 797 0595.

Korean Consulate General
5th Floor, 460 Park Avenue, 57th Street, New York, NY 10022
Tel: (212) 752 1700. Fax: (212) 888 6320.
Korea National Tourism Corporation
Suite 750, 7th Floor, 2 Executive Drive, Fort Lee, NJ 07024
Tel: (201) 585 0909. Fax: (201) 585 9041.
Embassy of the United States of America
Unit 15550, 82 Sejong-Ro, Chongro-ku, Seoul 96205-0001, Republic of Korea
Tel: (2) 397 4114. Fax: (2) 738 8845.
Consulate in: Pusan (tel: (51) 246 7791; fax: (51) 246 8859).
Embassy of the Republic of Korea
5th Floor, 151 Slater Street, Ottawa, Ontario K1P 5H3
Tel: (613) 232 1715-7. Fax: (613) 232 0928.
Consulates in: Montréal, Toronto and Vancouver.
Korea National Tourism Corporation
Suite 406, 480 University Avenue, Toronto, Ontario M5G 1V2
Tel: (416) 348 9056. Fax: (416) 348 9058.
Canadian Embassy
PO Box 6299, 10th Floor, Kolon Building, 45 Mugyo-dong, Chung-gu, Seoul 100-662, Republic of Korea
Tel: (2) 753 2605/8 *or* 753 7290/3. Fax: (2) 755 0686.

AREA: 99,299 sq km (38,340 sq miles), excluding demilitarised zone.
POPULATION: 43,663,405 (1992 estimate).

POPULATION DENSITY: 439.7 per sq km.
CAPITAL: Seoul. **Population:** 10,612,577 (1990).
GEOGRAPHY: The Republic of Korea (South Korea) shares borders to the north with the demilitarised zone (separating it from the Democratic People's Republic of Korea), to the east with the Sea of Japan, to the south with the Korea Strait (separating it from Japan) and to the west with the Yellow Sea. There are many islands, bays and peninsulas in the Korea Strait. The volcanic island of Cheju do lies off the southwest coast. Most of the country consists of hills and mountains and the 30% of flat plain contain the majority of the population and cultivation. Most rivers rise in the mountains to the east, flowing west and south to the Yellow Sea. The Naktong River flows into the Korea Strait near the southern port of Pusan. The eastern coast is rocky and steep with mountains rising from the sea.
LANGUAGE: Korean.
RELIGION: Mahayana Buddhism with a large Christian minority. Also Confucianism, Daoism and Chundo Kyo.
TIME: GMT + 9.
ELECTRICITY: 110/220 volts AC, 60Hz. Policy is to phase out the 110-volt supply.
COMMUNICATIONS: Telephone: IDD is available to Seoul and other major cities. Country code: 82. Outgoing international code: 001. **Fax:** This service is available at major hotels and business centres. **Telex/telegram:** There is a service at all main hotels. Korea International Telecommunications Services at 1, Choong-ro, Chung-gu, Seoul provide a 24-hour public service. **Post:** Airmail to Western Europe takes up to ten days. Post offices open 0900-1700 Monday to Friday; 0900-1300 Saturday. **Press:** English-language national dailies are *The Korea Herald, The Korea Economic Journal, Korea Newsreview* and *The Korea Times.*
BBC World Service and Voice of America frequencies: From time to time these change. See the section *How to Use this Book* for more information.

Seoul by night

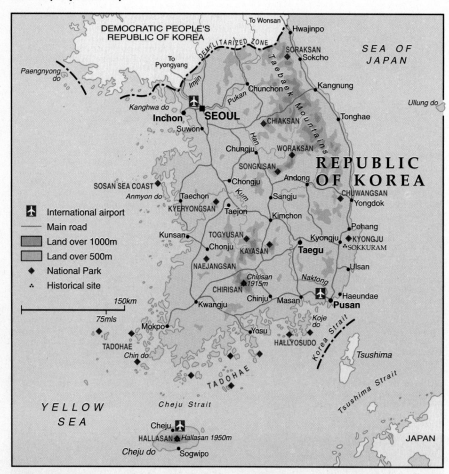

DEMOCRATIC PEOPLE'S REPUBLIC OF KOREA

To Wonsan
Hwajinpo
To Pyongyang
SORAKSAN
Sokcho
SEA OF JAPAN
Paengnyong do
Imjin
Pukan
Chunchon
Kangnung
Kanghwa do
SEOUL
Inchon
Suwon
CHIAKSAN
Tonghae
Ullung do
Chungju
WORAKSAN
Han
SONGNISAN
REPUBLIC OF KOREA
Chongju
Andong
SOSAN SEA COAST
Kum
Anmyon do
Taechon
KYERYONGSAN
Taejon
Sangju
CHUWANGSAN
Yongdok
Kunsan
TOGYUSAN
Kimchon
Kyongju
KYONGJU
Chonju
KAYASAN
Taegu
SOKKURAM
NAEJANGSAN
Ulsan
Chirisan 1915m
Naktong
CHIRISAN
Chinju
Masan
Haeundae
Kwangju
Pusan
Koje do
Mokpo
Yosu
HALLYOSUDO
Korea Strait
TADOHAE
Chin do
Tsushima
TADOHAE
Tsushima Strait
YELLOW SEA
Cheju Strait
JAPAN
Cheju
HALLASAN Hallasan 1950m
Cheju do
Sogwipo

- ✈ International airport
- —— Main road
- ▨ Land over 1000m
- ▨ Land over 500m
- ◆ National Park
- ∴ Historical site

150km
75mls

Date:	Oct '92	Sep '93	Jan '94	Jan '95
£1.00=	1265	1235	1194	1233
$1.00=	797	808	807	788

Currency restrictions: There are restrictions on the import of both local and foreign currency; check with the Embassy for current allowances. If the amount of foreign currency is greater than US$5000, it must be registered on arrival. Export of local currency (Korean Won) is limited to SKW500,000. Export of foreign currency is limited to to the amount declared on arrival.
Banking hours: 0930-1630 Monday to Friday; 0930-1330 Saturday.

DUTY FREE

The following goods may be imported into the Republic of Korea without incurring customs duty:
200 cigarettes or 50 cigars or 200g pipe tobacco (total quantity not exceeding 500g); 1 litre bottle of alcohol; 2oz of perfume; gifts up to SKW300,000.
Note: It is prohibited to bring the following articles into the country: any printed material, films, or phonograph records considered by the authorities to be subversive or harmful to national security or public interests; any firearms, explosives or other weapons; textile fabrics in excess of 5 sq m (6 sq yards); more than five foreign phonograph records; radio equipment and any animals or plants prohibited by the relevant regulations. Approval is required for the export of Korean antiques or valuable cultural items from the Seoul Metropolitan Government, Art & Antique Assessment Office, Seoul, tel: (2) 664 8997; or in Kimpo, tel: (2) 662 0106.

PUBLIC HOLIDAYS

Jan 1-2 '95 New Year. **Jan 30-Feb 1** Lunar New Year. **Mar 1** Independence Day. **Apr 5** Arbor Day. **May 5** Children's Day. **May 7** Buddha's Birthday. **Jun 6** Memorial Day. **Jul 17** Constitution Day. **Aug 15** Liberation Day. **Sep 8-10** Thanksgiving Day. **Oct 3** National Foundation Day. **Dec 25** Christmas Day. **Jan 1-2 '96** New Year. **Feb 18-20** Lunar New Year. **Mar 1** Independence Day. **Apr 5** Arbor Day.

HEALTH

Regulations and requirements may be subject to change at short notice, and you are advised to contact your doctor well in advance of your intended date of departure. Any numbers in the chart refer to the footnotes below.

	Special Precautions?	Certificate Required?
Yellow Fever	No	-
Cholera	Yes/1	-
Typhoid & Polio	Yes	
Malaria	No	-
Food & Drink	2	-

[1]: Following WHO guidelines issued in 1973, a cholera vaccination certificate is not a condition of entry to the Republic of Korea. However, cholera is a risk in this country and precautions are essential. Up-to-date advice should be sought before deciding whether these precautions should include a vaccination, as medical opinion is divided over its effectiveness. See the *Health* section at the back of the book.
[2]: Mains water is normally chlorinated, and whilst relatively safe may cause mild abdominal upsets. Bottled water is available and is advised for the first few weeks of the stay. Milk is unpasteurised and should be boiled. Powdered or tinned milk is available and is advised, but make sure that it is reconstituted with pure water. Avoid dairy products which are likely to have been made from unboiled milk. Only eat well-cooked meat and fish, preferably served hot. Pork, salad and mayonnaise may carry increased risk. Vegetables should be cooked and fruit peeled.
Japanese encephalitis and dengue fever are transmitted by mosquitoes between June and the end of October in rural areas. A vaccine is available, and travellers are advised to consult their doctor prior to departure. Other prevalent diseases include *clonorchiasis* (oriental liver fluke) and *paragonimiasis* (oriental lung fluke).
HIV/AIDS: People wishing to stay in the Republic of Korea for more than three months must supply a certificate showing they have tested HIV negative, issued within one month before their arrival.
Health care: Health insurance is recommended. There are facilities in all tourist areas, and hotels will recommend a local doctor.

TRAVEL - International

AIR: The Republic of Korea's national airline is *Korean Air (KE).*

BBC:

MHz	21.71	15.28	9.740	7.180

Voice of America:

MHz	15.43	11.72	5.985	1.143

PASSPORT/VISA

Regulations and requirements may be subject to change at short notice, and you are advised to contact the appropriate diplomatic or consular authority before finalising travel arrangements. Details of these may be found at the head of this country's entry. Any numbers in the chart refer to the footnotes below.

	Passport Required?	Visa Required?	Return Ticket Required?
Full British	Yes	1	No
BVP	Not valid	-	-
Australian	Yes	2	Yes
Canadian	Yes	No	Yes
USA	Yes	No	Yes
Other EU (As of 31/12/94)	Yes	1	Yes
Japanese	Yes	2	Yes

Restricted entry: Holders of passports containing valid or expired visas for North Korea or any other evidence of having visited that country must receive special permission from the authorities in Seoul and should apply for a visa at least a month in advance.
PASSPORTS: Valid passport required by all.
British Visitors Passport: Not acceptable.
VISAS: Required by all except:
(a) nationals of the Korea Republic;
(b) **[1]** nationals of Belgium, Denmark, France, Germany, Greece, Ireland, Luxembourg, The Netherlands, Spain and the UK for stays of up to 3 months; nationals of Italy and Portugal for stays of up to 2 months;
(c) nationals of Austria, Bahamas, Bangladesh, Barbados, Canada, Colombia, Costa Rica, Dominica, Finland, Grenada, Haiti, Hungary, Iceland, Jamaica, Liberia, Malaysia, Malta, Mexico, Morocco, Norway, Pakistan, Peru, Poland, Singapore, Suriname, Sweden, Switzerland, Thailand and Turkey for stays of up to 3 months;
(d) nationals of Lesotho for stays of up to 2 months;
(e) nationals of Tunisia for stays of up to 1 month;
(f) **[2]** nationals of all other countries are allowed to stay for a maximum of 15 days without a visa for touristic purposes only if they hold a confirmed onward ticket, with the exception of Albania, CIS (ie former USSR),

Cambodia, China, Cuba, Croatia, Czech Republic, Estonia, Hong Kong, Laos, Latvia, Lithuania, Former Yugoslav Republic of Macedonia, Mongolia, Romania, Slovak Republic, Vietnam and Yugoslavia (Serbia and Montenegro).
Note: There are visa exemptions for the following categories: business, touristic visits, meetings, medical treatment, lectures, games and contests, performances, location shots and cultural exchange. For full details, contact the Embassy (or Consular section at Embassy).
Types of visa: Tourist, Transit and Business; cost – £13.50.
Validity: Up to 3 months from the date of issue.
Application to: Consulate (or Consular section at Embassy). For addresses, see top of entry.
Application requirements: (a) Passport with at least 6 months remaining validity. (b) Completed application form. (c) Passport-size photo. (d) £13.50 fee, payable by company cheque or postal order only. (e) Business visas require a letter of invitation from company in the Korea Republic and a recommendation letter from own company. (f) Copy of green card if US permanent resident. (g) Stamped, self-addressed envelope if applying by post. Allow a further week for return of documents.
Working days required: 2-3 days (short stay); 4-8 weeks (work and residence).
Temporary residence: Applications for a residence certificate or for a stay of more than 90 days should be made to the Immigration Office in Seoul. Tel: (2) 503 7010.

MONEY

Currency: Won (SKW) = 100 chon. Notes are in denominations of SKW10,000, 5000 amd 1000. Coins are in denominations of SKW500, 100, 50, 10, 5 and 1. A larger denomination, the Chon *(jeon)*, valued at SKW1000, is also in use, but only on cheques, banker's orders, etc.
Credit cards: Diners Club, Visa, American Express and Access/Mastercard are widely accepted, but check with your credit card company for details of merchant acceptability and other services which may be available.
Travellers cheques: Accepted, but may be difficult to change in smaller towns.
Exchange rate indicators: The following figures are included as a guide to the movements of the Won against Sterling and the US Dollar:

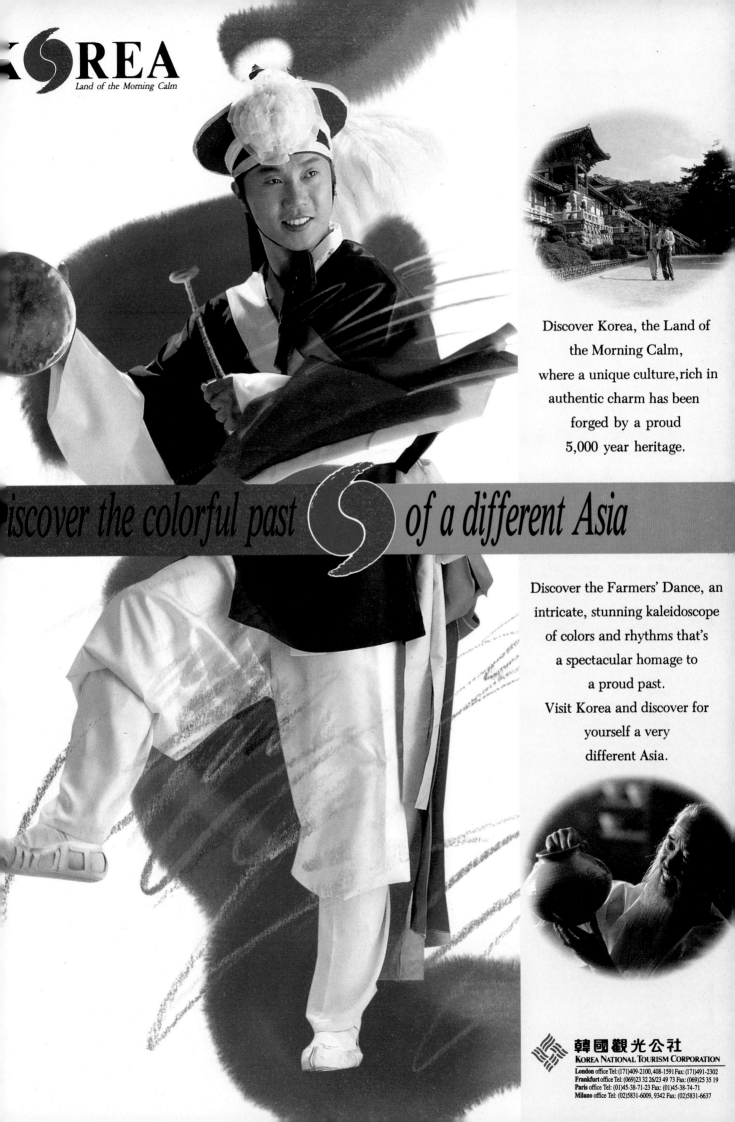

KOREA
Land of the Morning Calm

iscover the colorful past of a different Asia

Discover Korea, the Land of
the Morning Calm,
where a unique culture, rich in
authentic charm has been
forged by a proud
5,000 year heritage.

Discover the Farmers' Dance, an
intricate, stunning kaleidoscope
of colors and rhythms that's
a spectacular homage to
a proud past.
Visit Korea and discover for
yourself a very
different Asia.

韓國觀光公社
KOREA NATIONAL TOURISM CORPORATION

London office Tel: (171)409-2100, 408-1591 Fax: (171)491-2302
Frankfurt office Tel: (069)23 32 26/23 49 73 Fax: (069)25 35 19
Paris office Tel: (01)45-38-71-23 Fax: (01)45-38-74-71
Milano office Tel: (02)5831-6009, 9342 Fax: (02)5831-6637

Approximate flight times: From *London* to Seoul is 12 hours; add 1 hour if flying to any other main city. From *New York* to Seoul is 17 hours 40 minutes (including stopover in Anchorage), from *Los Angeles* is 10 hours 30 minutes and from *Sydney* is 9 hours.

International airports: *Seoul (SEL)* (Kimpo) is 26km (16 miles) from the city. Coaches depart to the city every 8 minutes from 0530-2140 (travel time – 50 minutes). Buses depart every 5 minutes. Taxis to the city are also available. Airport facilities include: currency exchange, pharmacy, children's restroom, post office, gift shop, duty-free shop, car hire, local products shop and restaurant.

Pusan (PUS) (Kim Hae) is 27km (17 miles) from Pusan in the far south. The airport receives flights from Tokyo, Osaka and Fukuoka. There are bus, coach and taxi services to the town. Airport facilities include: currency exchange, post office, duty-free shop, snack bar, gift shop, restaurant, travel information service and car hire.

Cheju (CJU) (Cheju). Buses and coaches are available to the town. Airport facilities include: currency exchange, post office, duty-free shop, snack bar, gift shop and travel information service.

Departure tax: SKW8000, payable at the airport.

SEA: International ports are Pusan (in the far south) and Inchon (due west of Seoul). Passenger lines are *Pukwan Ferry* and *Orient Overseas Lines.* Cargo/passenger lines include *American Mail* and *American President.* Crossings from Japan can be made via *Pukwan* ferry (Pusan–Shimonoseki). Three weekly trips from the USA are offered by *Lykes Lines* and *American President Lines. Knutsen Lines* run services from Australia.

RAIL/ROAD: There are no rail or road links with the Democratic People's Republic of Korea across the Republic of Korea's only land frontier. However, this may change in the near future as the border is to be opened gradually, starting with foreign visitors travelling in organised groups.

TRAVEL - Internal

AIR: *Korean Air (KE)* and *Asiana Air* run frequent services between Seoul and Pusan, Taegu, Cheju, Ulsan and Kwangju.

Departure tax: SKW1000 payable for domestic flights.

SEA: A steamer service runs along the scenic south coast between Mokpo and Pusan twice daily. A hydrofoil service links Pusan and Yosu via Ch'ungmu, five times a day *(Angel Line).* Ferries connect Pusan with Cheju do Island once a day. Car ferries run three times a week.

RAIL: *Korean National Railroads* connect major destinations. Super-express trains operate on Seoul–Mokpo, Seoul–Pusan (twice weekly), Seoul–Chungju–Yosu (fully air-conditioned), Seoul–Inchon (particularly scenic) and Seoul–Onyang (second-class only) routes. Some have air-conditioning and restaurant cars. A supplement is payable for better-quality accommodation on some trains. Station signs in English are common and English translations of timetables are usually available. Children under six travel free and children 6-12 pay half fare.

ROAD: The network extends over more than 50,000km (32,000 miles) of roads; half of it is paved. Excellent motorways link all major cities, but minor roads are often badly maintained. Traffic drives on the right. **Bus:** Local and express buses are inexpensive, though local buses within cities are often crowded and make no allowances for English-speakers. Air-conditioned super-express buses, operating in competition with trains, connect major cities and are to be recommended for their comfort, while towns and villages are linked by local bus services. **Taxi:** Cheap and a good way to travel. **Car hire:** Available from some hotels and travel agents. *Hertz* in Seoul operates 200 cars. *Cheju Rent-a-Car* operates 30 cars. **Documentation:** International Driving Permit required.

URBAN: Seoul has underground and suburban railways and well-developed bus services, all of which are very crowded. Taxis are widely available. Good bus services also operate in other cities.

JOURNEY TIMES: The following chart gives approximate journey times (in hours and minutes) from Seoul to other major cities/towns in the Republic of Korea.

	Air	Road	Rail
Pusan	0.50	5.30	4.10
Taegu	0.40	3.50	4.10
Kwangju	0.50	3.55	6.00
Ulsan	0.50	4.40	4.00
Chonju	1.10	5.20	6.30
Cheju	0.55	-	-
Kyongju		4.40	3.30

Additional times: From Pusan to Cheju by sea is 11 hours. From Mokpo to Cheju by sea is 5 hours 30 minutes. From Pusan to Kyongju is 1 hour by road and 40 minutes by rail.

Top picture: Mt Hallasan, Cheju Do. Above: Kum San Temple.

ACCOMMODATION

HOTELS: There are many modern tourist hotels in the major cities and tourist areas. All of these are registered with the Government. Most rooms have private baths as well as heating and cooling systems. Facilities in most tourist hotels include dining rooms, convention halls, bars, souvenir shops, cocktail lounges, barber and beauty shops and recreation areas. **Grading:** All registered hotels are classified according to their standard and quality of service. The *Rose of Sharon,* the national flower of Korea, is used as a symbol of quality and hotels range from 5 Sharons (deluxe) to 2 Sharons (third class). For further information, contact the Korea Tourist Association. For addresses, see top of entry.

YOGWANS: These are Korean inns, very reasonable and considered by many travellers as the 'only place to stay'. Sleeping arrangements consist of a small mattress and a firm pillow on the *ondol,* the hot floor-heating system which is traditional in Korea. There are also Western-style rooms. For further information, contact Korea Hotels & Accommodation Association, c/o Korea Tourist Association, PO Box 1130, Seoul, Korea. Tel: (2) 556 2356. Fax: (2) 556 3818.

SELF-CATERING: Cottages are available for rent at seaside resorts, but fees are high and few services are provided.

CAMPING: Campsites are located throughout the country. Contact the Tourist Association for details.

YOUTH HOSTELS: At present there are 20 youth hostels in Korea, mainly located in Seoul, Kyongju, Pusan, Puyo, Sokcho and vicinities. For more information and reservations, contact the Korean Youth Hostel Association, Room 409, Chokson Hyundai Building, 80 Chokson-dong, Chongno-gu, Seoul. Tel: (2) 725 3031.

RESORTS & EXCURSIONS

Most visitors to Korea start their tours in **Seoul,** the capital, which has recovered from the devastation of the Korean War to become a bustling and sophisticated commercial centre. There are, however, still many glimpses of its past, including royal palaces, markets,

Top picture: Olympic Complex. Above: Silk market, Seoul

museums and traces of the ancient walls. Seoul has been the nation's capital since 1394 and is still laid out in the traditional square pattern adopted by many Chinese cities. The city was encircled by 16km (10 miles) of high walls, and when it was threatened all nine gates were closed. Four of the gates still remain.

A whole-day tour of ancient and modern Seoul includes a visit to *Changdokkung Palace,* which has been used for royal functions since the 17th century. The main gate to the palace is believed to be the oldest in Seoul. Adjoining the palace are the *Secret Gardens,* a picturesque area of lakes and woodland which was once a retreat for members of the royal family.

Toksukung Palace was once a royal villa, but is now a *Museum of Modern Arts,* while *Kyongbokkung Palace,* which dates back to 1394, was burned during the Japanese invasion of 1592 and was left in ruins until 1868, when it was rebuilt. The grounds house many of Korea's most historic stone pagodas and monuments. The *Great South Gate of Seoul,* called Namdaemun, is regarded as Korea's foremost national treasure. It was built in 1448, but had to be repaired after the Korean War.

Seoul's *Pagoda Park* commemorates the spot where the Korean Declaration of Independence was proclaimed in 1919; the park was designed as a setting for the huge *Wongak-sa Pagoda,* built of marble and granite. A good viewpoint is *Namsan Mountain* in the middle of the city. On the top is the *Seoul Tower,* a new TV transmitter with an observation deck which has spectacular views extending west to Inchon. Other spots for city sightseeing include the *Octagonal Pagoda,* built in 1348, and the *East Gate Market Place.*

On the border with North Korea, about an hour from Seoul, is **Panmunjom.** It was here where the armistice negotiations took place. A truce village is situated here and peace negotiations are still held here sometimes. 50km (30 miles) south of Seoul is the Korean Folk Village of **Suwon.** The village is a real, live and functioning rural community out of a past era where artefacts and dress are authentic, where craftsmen can be observed at their trades and where folk dances and other traditional Korean entertainments and customs are performed daily.

Another popular touring area is centred on **Kyongju** on the southeast coast about 320km (200 miles) from Seoul. It is an area rich with the relics of Korea's history and culture and was named by UNESCO as one of the world's ten most important historic city sites. It was the capital of the Shilla Dynasty from 57BC to AD935 and at that time was one of the six largest cities in the world. Kyongju is Korea's best-known centre of ancient history and crafts and the city has many temples, royal tombs and monuments and what is regarded as the finest pre-modern astronomic observatory in Asia, probably one of the oldest structures of its kind in the world. The local branch of the *National Museum* has thousands of relics of the Shilla era, including gold crowns and girdles, jewellery, ceramics and weapons. Just outside the town is the *Pulguksa Temple,* one of Korea's most important Buddhist sites. Many of the structures here date back to AD751, but some of the wooden buildings have been rebuilt many times over the centuries. Nearby is the *Sokkuram Grotto,* with its huge granite Buddha. The *Onung* or Five Tombs complex is believed to be the burial place of the first Shilla king, his queen and three later monarchs. Within easy reach of Kyongju is the *Pomun Lake Resort,* a complex of hotels, a convention centre, golf course, marina and shopping centre.

Also in this area is the **Kayasan National Park**. It is known as the home of Korea's best-known temple, the *Haeinsa Temple.* Built in 802AD, it houses a number of historic and artistic treasures. It is famous for the *Tripitaka Koreana,* a set of over 80,000 wooden printing blocks. These blocks are engraved with one of the most extensive collection of Buddhist scriptures found throughout Asia. They can still be used today although they were completed in 1252 after 16 years of work.

In the south of Korea is **Pusan,** the country's largest seaport. The area has two important beach resorts, *Haeundae* and *Songjong. Haeundae* is probably the most popular resort in the area and has a long, sandy beach with a good range of hotels and restaurants. There are also medicinal hot springs. Another hot-spring resort is *Tongnae;* nearby is *Kumgang Park* which boasts some unusual rock formations and historic relics, including a pagoda and several temples.

An up-and-coming tourist area is **Cheju do Island**, a 1-hour flight from Seoul and only 40 minutes from Pusan. Different in many ways from the Korean mainland, its volcanic origin gives a distinct landscape dominated by *Mount Halla,* Korea's highest mountain at 1950m (6400ft). Striking contrasts in scenery are part of any tour on Cheju do Island, which might include visits to *Samsonghyol Caves,* the *Grotto of the Serpent* and the *Dragon Pool.* A full-day tour of the island takes in visits to tangerine orchards, the *Chongbang Waterfalls,* a model farm village and *Songsanilchulbong Park.* The mountainous terrain of Korea's **East Coast** provides breathtaking scenery, a blaze of colour in autumn and the setting for winter sports with a modern, fully-equipped ski centre. There are plenty of touring opportunities along this 390km (240-mile) stretch of coastline, from the popular beach of *Hwajinpo* down to Pusan in the south. The mountains run down to the sea, but are interspersed by a series of long, sandy beaches, harbours and small fishing villages. Three national parks – **Mount Soraksan**, **Mount Odaesan** and **Mount Chuwangsan** – have been designated and all are accessible from a new coastal highway opened in 1978. In the Soraksan National Park, **Sorakdong Village** has been developed as a tourist resort village and is the starting point for climbing trails; nearby is the *Sinhung-sa Temple,* first built in AD645, but reconstructed in the 17th century. A cable car runs between Sorakdong Village and the *Kwongumsong Fortress,* parts of which date back to 57BC. *Mount Soraksan* (1708m/5604ft) is regarded as the most beautiful mountain in Korea. In the same area is the city of **Sokcho**, a major fishing port, and nearby is the newly developed *Choksan Hot Springs* resort. Another interesting national park is **Mount Songnisan National Park**. Situated in it is the famous *Popchusa Temple* which was built in 553AD. It houses several renowned works of art.

POPULAR ITINERARIES: 5-day: Seoul–Pusan–Kyongju–Mt Songnisan National Park–Korean Folk Village–Panmunjom–Seoul. **7-day:** Seoul–Mt Soraksan National Park–Kyongju–Haeinsa Temple–Pusan–Cheju do Island–Seoul.

SOCIAL PROFILE

FOOD & DRINK: Korea has its own cuisine, quite different from Chinese or Japanese. Rice is the staple food and a typical Korean meal consists of rice, soup, rice water and 8-20 side dishes of vegetables, fish, poultry, eggs, bean-curd and sea plants. Most Korean soups and side dishes are heavily laced with red pepper. Dishes include *kimchi* (highly spiced pickle of Chinese cabbage or white radish with turnips, onions, salt, fish,

Do Dam Sam Bong

chestnuts and red pepper), soups (based on beef, pork, oxtail, other meat, fish, chicken and cabbage, almost all spiced), *pulgogi* (marinated, charcoal-broiled beef barbecue), *Genghis Khan* (thin slices of beef and vegetables boiled at the table) or *sinsollo* (meat, fish, eggs and vegetables such as chestnuts and pinenuts cooked in a brazier chafing dish at the table). Other examples of local cuisine are *sanjok* (strips of steak with onions and mushrooms), *kalbichim* (steamed beef ribs), fresh abalone and shrimps (from Cheju do Island, served with mustard, soy or chilli sauces) and Korean seaweed (prized throughout the Far East). There is waiter as well as counter service. Most major hotels will offer a selection of restaurants, serving Korean, Japanese and Chinese cuisine or more Western-style food. **Drink:** Local drinks are mostly made from fermented rice or wheat and include *jungjong* (expensive variant of rice wine), *soju* (like vodka and made from potatoes or grain) or *yakju/takju* (cloudy and light tan-coloured) known together as *makkoli*. Korean beers are *Crown* and *OB*. *Ginseng* wine is strong and sweet, similar to brandy, but varies in taste according to the basic ingredient used. The most common type of drinking establishment is the *Suljip* (wine bar), but there are also beer houses serving well-known European brands.
NIGHTLIFE: Seoul has a growing number of nightclubs, cabarets, restaurants, theatres and beer halls. There are also many cinemas. Operas, concerts and recitals can be seen at the National Theatre and performances of Korean classical music, dances and plays can be seen at Korea House and the Drama Centre. For daily listings of events, consult Korea's English-language papers. Licensed casinos operate at various locations throughout the country.
SHOPPING: Favourite buys to look for are hand-tailored clothes, sweaters (plain, embroidered or beaded), silks, brocades, handbags, leatherwork, gold jewellery, topaz, amethyst, amber, jade and silver, ginseng, paintings, costume dolls, musical instruments, brassware, lacquerware, wood carvings, baskets, scrolls and screens. Prices are fixed in department stores, but may be negotiated in arcades and markets. Major cities have 'Foreigners' duty-free shops where people can use foreign currency with a valid passport. Hotels will be able to tell guests the location. **Shopping hours:** 1030-1930 Monday to Friday. Smaller shops open earlier and close late.
SPORT: Climbing: The Korea National Park has excellent climbs at Mount Pukhan, Seoul, Mount Sorak on the East Coast and Mount Halla and Cheju do Island. **Shooting:** There is pheasant shooting on Cheju do Island between November and February. **Skiing:** Principle resorts are the Yongpyong Ski Resort (Dragon Valley International Ski Resort) at Tackwallyong Area and Chonmasan Ski Resort near Seoul. Modern facilities, lifts, accommodation and equipment are available in several areas. **Swimming:** Major hotels have swimming pools and there are fine beaches along the coast and lakes in the resorts. There are large outdoor pools at Walker

Hill Resort. **Horseracing:** The horseracing season in Seoul starts in June at Tuksom Track, 13km (8 miles) from the downtown area. **Fishing** is regarded as a major leisure activity, as Korea is surrounded by sea on three sides and has many reservoirs and streams. **T'aekwondo** is the main martial art practised in Korea.
SPECIAL EVENTS: Korea celebrates many annual festivals throughout the year. The most significant festival is Buddha's Birthday in which the 'Feast of Lanterns' is performed in Korea's streets. Of great importance are the annual village rituals which are nationally recognised. At these festivals, mountain spirits, great generals and royalty of the past are remembered and celebrated, as well as festivals that mark the changing seasons and festivals of prayer for a good harvest. All festivals are characterised by processions, by masked and costumed local people, music, dancing, battles and sports, to recreate the original historic event or to conjure up good spirits. Some of the major festivals and events for 1995/96 are listed below, but contact the Korea National Tourism Corporation for more details and exact dates.
Mar '95 *Sŏkchŏnje*, Seoul. **Apr** *King Tanjong Festival*, Yongwol; *Cherry Blossom Festival*, Chinae; *Chindo Yongdung Festival (Korea's Moses Miracle)*, Chin do Island. **May** *Royal Shrine Rites*, Seoul; *Chinnam Festival*, Yosu; *Miryang Arang Festival; Ch'un-Hyang Festival*, Namwon. **Jun** *Tano Festival*, Kangnung; *Andong Folk Festival*, Andong. **Oct** *National Folk Arts Competition; Sejong Cultural Festival*, Yosu; *Paekche Cultural Festival*, Puyo; *Halla Cultural Festival*, Cheju do Island; *Shilla Cultural Festival*, Kyongju. **Nov** *Kaech'on Art Festival*, Chinju. **Feb '96** *Samil Folk Festival*, Ch'angnyŏng-gun. **Mar** *Sŏkchŏnje*, Seoul.
SOCIAL CONVENTIONS: Shoes should be removed before entering a Korean home. Entertainment is usually lavish and Koreans may sometimes be offended if their hospitality is refused. Customs are similar to those in the West. Small gifts are customary and, again, traditional etiquette requires the use of the right hand for giving and receiving. Dress should be casual and practical clothes are suitable. The rural population wear traditional costume. For men it is the *hanbok*, a short jacket, loose trousers and *kat* – a tall, dark hat with round brim. Women wear a *chima-jeogon*, a very loose, unfitted dress of silk with a *chogori*, a small jacket resembling a bolero with long sleeves. **Tipping:** Though not a Korean custom, most hotels and other tourist facilities add a 10% service charge to bills. Taxi drivers are not tipped unless they help with the luggage.

BUSINESS PROFILE

ECONOMY: Korea is one of the so-called 'Tiger economies' of the Pacific Rim, which have undergone rapid growth and industrialisation since the 1960s and have forged a major presence in world export markets. Korea's strength lies in four areas: shipbuilding, steel, consumer electronics (of which Korea is the world's

eighth-largest producer) and construction. Korean companies have established a major presence in the world construction industry, providing a major source of 'invisible earnings'. This has produced one of the world's highest economic growth rates during the last decade. The early 1990s have brought worries about overheating, and as inflation and the trade deficit have increased rapidly, the Government is hoping to engineer a gradual slowdown. An important economic issue in the 1990s will be whether the family-owned commercial groups, the *chaebol* who are the heart and soul of the Korean economy, will be able to reform themselves to adjust to the demands of a mature industrial economy. Furthermore, pressure will grow on the Korean government to liberalise its trading and financial systems to allow greater foreign involvement in the economy. Compared with the North, which has extensive coal and mineral deposits, the South is relatively poor in natural resources, although there have been recent offshore discoveries of natural gas which should help to reduce South Korea's dependence on imported energy. Economic factors have played a central role in the evolving political situation in the region, underpinning the rapprochement between Seoul and Moscow, and may be decisive in the future of divided Korea itself. The USA and Japan are South Korea's main trading partners, but export growth during the 1990s is likely to be driven by the country's newer trading relationships, in particular the CIS and the People's Republic of China.
BUSINESS: Businessmen are expected to wear a suit and tie. English is widely spoken in commercial and official circles. Prior appointments are necessary and business cards are widely used. The use of the right hand when giving and receiving particularly applies to business cards. Best months for business visits are February to June. **Office hours:** 0830-1800 Monday to Friday; 0900-1300 Saturday.
COMMERCIAL INFORMATION: The following organisations can offer advice: Korean Chamber of Commerce and Industry (KCCI), PO Box 25, 45 4-ka, Namdaemun-no, Chung-gu, Seoul 100. Tel: (2) 316 3114. Fax: (2) 757 9475; *or* Korea Trade Centre, 5th Floor, 39 St James Street, London SW1A 1JD. Tel: (0171) 491 8057. Fax: (0171) 491 7913. Telex: 22375 (a/b KOTRA).
CONFERENCES/CONVENTIONS: The new Korea Exhibition Centre (KOEX) in Seoul opened in 1988, forming part of the World Trade Centre, 159 Samsong-dong, Kangnam-gu, Seoul 135-731. Tel: (2) 551 1141. Fax: (2) 551 1311. Between 1981 and 1990 the average annual growth rate of the Korean convention industry registered about 11% in terms of events and 33% in participants. In 1990, 220 international events were held throughout the country. The Korea Convention and Co-ordinating Committee (c/o Korea National Tourism Corporation, 10 Ta-dong, Chung-gu, Seoul; tel: (2) 757 6030; fax: (2) 757 5997) can also offer advice and information on meeting facilities in the Republic of Korea.

CLIMATE

Moderate climate with four seasons. The hottest part of the year is during the rainy season between July and August, and the coldest is December and January. Spring and autumn are mild and mainly dry.
Required clothing: Lightweight cottons and linens are worn during summer, with light- to medium-weights in spring and autumn. Medium- to heavy-weights are advised during the winter.

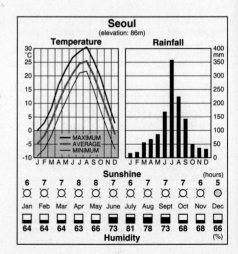

Seoul (elevation: 86m)

Temperature / Rainfall / Sunshine (hours) / Humidity (%)

	Jan	Feb	Mar	Apr	May	June	July	Aug	Sept	Oct	Nov	Dec
Sunshine	6	7	7	8	7	6	7	6	7	7	6	5
Humidity	64	64	64	63	66	73	81	78	73	68	68	66

Kuwait

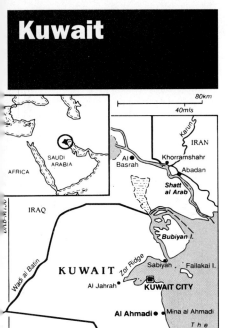

☐ *international airport*

Location: Middle East.

Note: Travel to and near the Iraq-Kuwait border is hazardous. In the past, persons found near the border were detained by Iraqi security forces, and were endangered by occasional exchanges of fire in the demilitarised zone near Iraq. Unexploded bombs, mines, booby traps and other items remain in open areas and beaches throughout Kuwait. In the past three years, there have been approximately six fire bombing incidents and a shooting. No serious casualties resulted from these incidents. The crime rate in Kuwait is moderate. However, weapons left over from the 1991 Gulf War remain in the hands of the populace and shooting incidents have occured. The occasional terrorist bombings and shootings over the past three years have usually been directed against Kuwaiti targets. Both verbal and physical harrassment of women is a continuing problem.
Source: US State Department – September 20, 1994.

Department of Tourism
Ministry of Information PO Box 193, 13002 Safat, Kuwait City, Kuwait
Tel: 243 6644. Fax: 242 9758. Telex: 44041.
Touristic Enterprises Company of Kuwait
PO Box 23310, 13094 Safat, Kuwait City, Kuwait
Tel: 565 2775. Fax: 565 7594. Telex: 22801.
Embassy of the State of Kuwait
45-46 Queen's Gate, London SW7 5HR
Tel: (0171) 589 4533 (ask for Press Office for tourist information). Fax: (0171) 589 2978. Telex: 261017.
Opening hours: 0930-1300 and 1400-1600 Monday to Friday; 0930-1230 Monday to Friday (Visa section).
British Embassy
PO Box 2, Arabian Gulf Street, 13001 Safat, Kuwait City, Kuwait
Tel: 2432 0461/71/81/9 *or* 240 3324-7. Fax: 240 7395.
Telex: 44614 (a/b PRODROM KT).
Embassy of the State of Kuwait
2940 Tilden Street, NW, Washington, DC 20008
Tel: (202) 966 0702. Fax: (202) 966 0517.
Embassy of the United States of America
PO Box 77, Arabian Gulf Street, 13001 Safat, Kuwait City, Kuwait

Tel: 242 4151/9. Fax: 244 2855. Telex: 2039 (a/b HILTELS KT).
Embassy of the State of Kuwait
80 Elgin Street, Ottawa, Ontario K1P 1C6
Tel: (613) 780 9999. Fax: (613) 780 9905.
Canadian Embassy
PO Box 25281, Block 4, House No 24, Al-Mutawakel, 13113 Safat, Kuwait City, Kuwait
Tel: 256 3025. Fax: 256 4167.

AREA: 17,818 sq km (6880 sq miles).
POPULATION: 1,350,000 (1992 estimate).
POPULATION DENSITY: 120.3 per sq km.
CAPITAL: Kuwait City. **Population:** 44,335 (1985).
GEOGRAPHY: Kuwait shares borders with Iraq and Saudi Arabia. To the southeast lies the Persian Gulf, where Kuwait has sovereignty over nine small islands. The landscape is predominantly desert plateau with a lower, more fertile coastal belt.
LANGUAGE: Arabic, but English is widely understood, especially in commerce and industry.
RELIGION: 95% Muslim, with Christian and Hindu minorities.
TIME: GMT + 3.
ELECTRICITY: 240 volts AC, 50Hz; single phase. UK-type flat 3-pin plugs are used.
COMMUNICATIONS: Telephone: Full IDD is available. Country code: 965. Outgoing international code: 00. **Fax:** Several hotels have facilities.
Telex/telegram: Telex facilities are available at main hotels or the central post office (24 hours). 24-hour telegram services are available at the Ministry of Post and Telegraph Offices, Abdullah Al Salem Square, Kuwait City, but must be handed to the post office (opening hours: 0700-2359 Saturday to Wednesday; 0700-1200 Thursday). **Post:** Airmail to Western Europe takes about five days. **Press:** The English-language newspapers are the *Arab Times* and the *Kuwait Times*. Although remaining loyal to the Royal family, the press enjoys a fair degree of freedom.
BBC World Service frequencies: From time to time these change. See the section *How to Use this Book* for more information.
BBC:

MHz	21.47	15.07	11.76	9.410

A service is also available on 1413kHz and 702kHz (0100-0500 GMT).

PASSPORT/VISA

Regulations and requirements may be subject to change at short notice, and you are advised to contact the appropriate diplomatic or consular authority before finalising travel arrangements. Details of these may be found at the head of this country's entry. Any numbers in the chart refer to the footnotes below.

	Passport Required?	Visa Required?	Return Ticket Required?
Full British	Yes	Yes	No
BVP	Not valid	-	-
Australian	Yes	Yes	No
Canadian	Yes	Yes	No
USA	Yes	Yes	No
Other EU (As of 31/12/94)	Yes	Yes	No
Japanese	Yes	Yes	No

Restricted entry: Holders of Israeli passports and holders of passports containing valid or expired visas for Israel or any other evidence of having visited the country will be refused entry or transit permission.
PASSPORTS: Valid passport required by all.
British Visitors Passport: Not acceptable.
VISAS: Required by all except nationals of Bahrain, Oman, Qatar, Saudi Arabia and the United Arab Emirates.
Types of visa: Ordinary visa and Transit visa; Entry Permit. Transit visas are not required if passengers hold onward tickets and do not leave the airport. Full visas are generally only required by those intending (and invited) to take up employment. UK nationals visiting for up to a month will, usually, only need an Entry Permit (effectively a short-stay visa). However, it is advisable to check with the Embassy well in advance if an Entry Permit will be sufficient as applications for full visas can take some time. Entry Permits are issued free of charge.
Cost: The fee for a full visa depends on the applicant's nationality (nationals of Italy, Norway, Sweden, Turkey, the UK and the USA are exempt).
Note: Visas and Entry Permits are only issued to business visitors on the invitation of a contact in Kuwait.
Validity: *Entry Permit:* 1 month from date of entry. *Visa:* Enquire at Consulate (or Consular section at Embassy).
Application to: Consulate (or Consular section at Embassy). For addresses, see top of entry.
Application requirements: *Entry Permit:* (a) Valid passport. (b) 2 completed application forms (originals, not

photocopies). (c) 2 passport-size photos. (d) Covering letter from visitor's company. (e) Fax or other confirmation from sponsor/contact in Kuwait. (f) Registered, self-addressed envelope. *Visa:* As above, plus: (g) 'No Objection Certificate (NOC)' from the Kuwaiti Ministry of the Interior (must be obtained before application can proceed). (h) Fee (where applicable).
Working days required: 24 hours (plus, for Visa applications, up to a month for obtaining the NOC).
Temporary residence: Enquire at Embassy. Note that 'British Citizens' who wish to take up employment will require instead (or eventually) a *Residence Permit*. This must be obtained before arrival in Kuwait as it is not possible to transfer status from 'visitor' to 'temporary resident' without first returning to the UK.

MONEY

Currency: Kuwait Dinar (KD) = 1000 fils. Notes are in denominations of KD20, 10, 5 and 1, and 500 and 250 fils. Coins are in denominations of 100, 50, 20, 10, 5 and 1 fils.
Credit cards: Access/Mastercard, Diners Club, Visa and American Express are accepted. Check with your credit card company for details of merchant acceptability and other services which may be available.
Travellers cheques: Widely accepted.
Exchange rate indicators: The following figures are included as a guide to the movements of the Kuwait Dinar against Sterling and the US Dollar:

Date:	Oct '92	Sep '93	Jan '94	Jan '95
£1.00=	0.47	0.46	0.44	0.47
$1.00=	0.30	0.30	0.30	0.30

Currency restrictions: There are no restrictions on import or export apart from gold bullion, which must be declared.
Banking hours: 0800-1200 Saturday to Thursday.

DUTY FREE

The following goods may be imported into Kuwait without incurring customs duty:
500 cigarettes or 907g of tobacco.
Prohibited items: All alcoholic or narcotic imports are strictly prohibited; also, pork products and goods of Israeli or South African origin. Penalties for attempting to smuggle restricted items are severe.

PUBLIC HOLIDAYS

Jan 1 '95 New Year's Day. **Feb 2** Start of Ramadan. **Feb 25** Kuwaiti National Day. **Mar 2** Eid al-Fitr (End of Ramadan). **May 10** Eid al-Adha (Feast of the Sacrifice). **May 31** Islamic New Year. **Aug 9** Mouloud (Prophet's Birthday). **Dec 20** Leilat al-Meiraj. **Jan 1 '96** New Year's Day. **Jan 22** Start of Ramadan. **Feb 25** Kuwaiti National Day. **Feb 22** Eid al-Fitr (End of Ramadan).
Note: Muslim festivals are timed according to local sightings of various phases of the Moon and the dates given above are approximations. During the lunar month of Ramadan that precedes Eid al-Fitr, Muslims fast during the day and feast at night and normal business patterns may be interrupted. Many restaurants are closed during the day and there may be restrictions on smoking and drinking. Some disruption may continue into Eid al-Fitr itself. Eid al-Fitr and Eid al-Adha may last anything from two to ten days, depending on the region. For more information see the section *World of Islam* at the back of the book.

HEALTH

Regulations and requirements may be subject to change at short notice, and you are advised to contact your doctor well in advance of your intended date of departure. Any numbers in the chart refer to the footnotes below.

	Special Precautions?	Certificate Required?
Yellow Fever	No	No
Cholera	Yes	1
Typhoid & Polio	Yes	-
Malaria	No	-
Food & Drink	2	

[1]: Following WHO guidelines issued in 1973, a cholera vaccination certificate is no longer a condition of entry to Kuwait. However, cholera is a risk in this country and precautions are essential. Up-to-date advice should be sought before deciding whether these precautions should include vaccination as medical opinion is divided over its effectiveness. See the *Health* section at the back of the book.
[2]: Mains water is normally chlorinated, and whilst relatively safe may cause mild abdominal upsets. Bottled water is available and is advised for the first few weeks of the stay. Milk is pasteurised and dairy products are

safe for consumption. Local meat, poultry, seafood, fruit and vegetables are generally considered safe to eat.
Health care: Medical insurance is essential. Both private and government health services are available.

TRAVEL - International

AIR: Kuwait's national airline is *Kuwait Airways (KU)*.
Approximate flight times: From Kuwait to *London* is 6 hours, to *New York* is 13 hours, to *Los Angeles* is 19 hours, to *Singapore* is 11 hours 30 minutes and to *Sydney* is 17 hours.
International airport: *Kuwait (KWI)*, 16km (10 miles) south of Kuwait City (travel time – 25 minutes). Reliable transport to and from the city, including bus (travel time – 30 minutes) departing every 45 minutes 0600-2300 and taxi service. Tel: 433 4499 (24-hour flight information). Facilities include restaurants, shops, cafeteria, bank/bureau de change, car rental (*Al Mulla, Avis, Budget* and *Europcar*), conference room and post office.
Departure tax: KD2 for international departures.
SEA: More than 30 shipping lines call regularly at Kuwait City, Kuwait's major port. Most traffic is commercial.
ROAD: Note: Due to the current political and military situation in both Lebanon and southern Iraq, it is wise to check with the Embassy before selecting a route. There are excellent road links with Saudi Arabia and Iraq and hence on to Syria and Jordan. There are two preferred routes from the Mediterranean: Tripoli–Homs–Baghdad–Basra–Kuwait, and Beirut–Damascus–Amman–Kuwait. The latter route follows the Trans-Arabian Pipeline (TAP line) through Saudi Arabia; the former runs across the Syrian desert.

TRAVEL - Internal

SEA: Dhows and other small craft may be chartered for trips to the offshore islands.
ROAD: There is a good road network only between cities. **Bus:** *Kuwait Transport Company* operates a nationwide service which is both reliable and inexpensive. **Taxi:** These are recognisable by red licence plates and may be hired by the day, in which case fares should be agreed beforehand. Shared taxis are also available. Taxis can be phoned and this service is popular and reliable. A standard rate is applicable in most taxis, but those at hotel ranks are more expensive. Tipping is not expected. **Car hire:** Self-drive is available. If you produce an International Driving Permit, the rental company, within five days, will produce a temporary local licence, valid for one month. **Documentation:** International Driving Permit required. A temporary driving licence is available from local authorities on presentation of a valid British or Northern Ireland driving licence. Insurance must be arranged with the Gulf Insurance Company or the Kuwait Insurance Company.

ACCOMMODATION

Note: Many hotels suffered damage and looting during the Gulf War, but Kuwait has been busy making reparations and most establishments, including the main hotels, have now re-opened. Accommodation is generally expensive. All rates are subject to a 15% service charge.

RESORTS & EXCURSIONS

Kuwait City is a bustling metropolis of high-rise office buildings, luxury hotels, wide boulevards and well-tended parks and gardens. Its seaport is used by oil tankers, cargo ships and many pleasure craft. Its most dominant landmark is *Kuwait Towers,* and its oldest is *Seif Palace,* built in 1896, whose interior has a lot of original Islamic mosaic tilework, though these suffered badly during the Iraqi occupation. The *Kuwait Museum* was also stripped of many artefacts and has not yet re-opened.
Excursions: Failakai Island: A port with many old dhows which can be reached by boat. There are also some Bronze Age and Greek archaeological sites well worth viewing. **Al Jahrah:** Traditional-style *Boums* and *Sambuks* (boats) are still built here, although nowadays vessels are destined to work as pleasure boats rather than pearl fishing or trading vessels. **Mina Al Ahmadi:** Oil port with immense jetties for supertanker traffic.

SOCIAL PROFILE

FOOD & DRINK: There is a good choice of restaurants serving a wide choice of international and Arab cuisine and prices are reasonable.
Note: Alcohol is totally prohibited in Kuwait.
NIGHTLIFE: Several cinemas in Kuwait City show recent films. Two theatres often put on very good amateur produc-tions. There is also a selection of nightclubs.
SHOPPING: All the basic and most luxury goods are available in boutiques or small general stores in Kuwait

City. **Shopping hours:** 0830-1230 Saturday to Thursday; 1530-2030 Friday.
SPORT: Swimming, sailing and **scuba diving** are available. **Powerboating** is a Kuwaiti passion. **Horseriding** clubs flourish in the winter. There are numerous **tennis** courts in the capital, usually owned by hotels. **Football** is popular.
SOCIAL CONVENTIONS: Handshaking is the customary form of greeting. It is unlikely that a visitor will be invited to a Kuwaiti's home, as entertaining is usually conducted in a hotel or restaurant. A small gift promoting the company, or representing one's native country, is always welcome. The visitor will notice that Kuwaitis wear the national dress of long white *dishdashes* and white headcloths, and that most women wear *yashmaks*. It is important for women to dress modestly according to Islamic law. It is not acceptable for men to wear shorts in public or to go shirtless. All other Islamic rules and customs must be respected. Any user of narcotics can expect to receive a sentence of up to five years imprisonment, plus a heavy fine if caught. 'No Smoking' signs are posted in many shops. It is greatly appreciated if visitors learn at least a few words of Arabic. **Tipping:** A service charge of 15% is usually added to bills in hotels, restaurants and clubs. Otherwise 10% is acceptable.

BUSINESS PROFILE

ECONOMY: Kuwait's considerable wealth is the result of the country's vast oil deposits: Kuwait possesses between 15-20% of the world's total known reserves. Oil now accounts for about 70% of domestic output, reflecting the Government's strategy of diversifying the economy as far as possible since oil production has steadily declined from its peak in 1972. The Government has eschewed heavy industrial projects in favour of light manufacturing industries such as paper and cement. There is a small fishing industry and some agriculture. Before the Gulf War, transit trade with Iraq was also an important source of income. The most important non-petroleum sector, however, is overseas investment. This is controlled by the somewhat secretive Kuwait Invest-ment Office (KIO), which has acquired major holdings in a number of large Western corporations (including British Petroleum, which the Kuwaitis were controversially forced to reduce in 1987 on instructions from the British government). The yearly income from KIO investments is at least as large as the country's US$6-billion annual receipts from oil. 90% of Kuwait's export earnings are derived from oil, with Japan, The Netherlands and Italy as the main markets. The principal exporters to Kuwait are, in descending order of value: Japan, the USA, Germany and the UK, which have cornered about 10% of the market. Reconstruction contracts have temporarily boosted the volume of trade between Kuwait and the West.
BUSINESS: Men are expected to wear suits and ties for business and formal social occasions. English is widely spoken in business circles although a few words or phrases of Arabic are always well received. Visiting cards are widely used. Some of the bigger hotels have translation and bilingual secretarial services. **Office hours:** 0800-1300 and 1600-2000 Saturday to Thursday (winter); 0800-1300 and 1500-1900 Saturday to Wednesday (summer).
COMMERCIAL INFORMATION: The following organisation can offer advice: Kuwait Chamber of Commerce and Industry, PO Box 775, Chamber's Building, Ali as-Salem Street, 13008 Safat, Kuwait City. Tel: 243 3864 *or* 246 3600. Fax: 240 4110.

CLIMATE

Kuwait shares European weather patterns but is hotter and drier. Summers (April to October) are hot and humid with very little rain. Winters (November to March) are cool with limited rain. Springs are cool and pleasant.

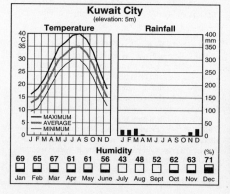

Kuwait City
(elevation: 5m)

	Temperature		Rainfall	

MAXIMUM
AVERAGE
MINIMUM

Humidity

												(%)
69	65	67	61	61	56	43	48	52	62	63	71	
Jan	Feb	Mar	Apr	May	June	July	Aug	Sept	Oct	Nov	Dec	

Kyrgyzstan

□ *international airport*

Location: Central Asia, north of Afghanistan and Tajikistan.

Kyrgyzintourist
Ala-Too Hotel, Erkindik Prospekt 1, 720041 Bishkek, Kyrgyzstan
Tel: (3312) 226 442. Fax: (3312) 223 942.
Ministry of Tourism
ul Sovietskaya 4A, 720023 Bishkek, Kyrgyzstan
Tel: (3312) 410 356. Fax: (3312) 415 554. Telex: 245111 (a/b ALATO SU).
Ministry of Foreign Affairs
ul Abdumomuntov 205, 720003 Bishkek, Kyrgyzstan
Tel: (3312) 225 914 *or* 220 545 *or* 220 552. Fax: (3312) 225 735.
Intourist
219 Marsh Wall, Isle of Dogs, London E14 9FJ
Tel: (0171) 538 8600. Fax: (0171) 538 5967.
Embassy of the Republic of Kyrgyzstan
Suite 706, 1511 K Street, NW, Washington, DC 20005
Tel: (202) 347 3732 *or* 628 0433 (visa enquiries). Fax: (202) 347 3718.
Also deals with enquiries from Canada.
Fair Winds Trading Compnay
Suite 1610, 5151 E. Broadway Boulevard, Tucson, AZ 85711
Tel: (520) 748 1288. Fax: (520) 748 1347. Telex: 6507151271 (a/b MCI UW).
Embassy of the United States of America
Erkindik Prospekt 66, 720002 Bishkek, Kyrgyzstan
Tel: (3312) 222 777 *or* 222 920 *or* 225 358 (after hours). Fax: (3312) 223 210. Telex: 245133 (a/b AMEMB SU).
Russian Travel Information Office
Suite 630, 1801 McGill College Avenue, Montréal, Québec H3A 2N4
Tel: (514) 849 6394. Fax: (514) 849 6743.
Can provide information on Kyrgyzstan.
The Canadian Embassy in Almaty deals with enquiries relating to Kyrgyzstan (see *Kazakhstan* earlier in this book).

AREA: 198,500 sq km (76,640 sq miles).
POPULATION: 4,421,000 (1991 estimate).
POPULATION DENSITY: 22.3 per sq km.
CAPITAL: Bishkek (Frunze). **Population:** 625,000 (1990).
GEOGRAPHY: Kyrgyzstan is bordered by Kazakhstan,

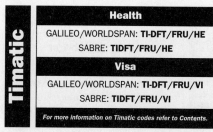

Uzbekistan, Tajikistan and China. The majestic Tien Shan (Heavenly Mountains) range occupies the greater part of the area. Its highest peak is Pik Pobedy at 7439m (24,406ft).

LANGUAGE: The official language is Kyrgyz, a Turkic language closely related to Uzbek, Kazakh, Turkmen and Turkish. Any attempt by a foreigner to speak Kyrgyz will be greatly appreciated. In deference to the large Russian population of Kyrgyzstan, Russian is also protected under law. However, the Government has undertaken to replace the Russian Cyrillic Alphabet currently in use with the Turkish version of the Roman alphabet by 1995. Meanwhile most people can speak Russian, albeit often reluctantly. English is widely spoken by those involved in tourism. Uzbek, Kazakh, Tajik and various other regional languages and dialects are also spoken.

RELIGION: Predominantly Sunni Muslim with a Russian Orthodox minority.

TIME: GMT + 5 (GMT + 6 from second Sunday in April to Saturday before last Sunday in September).

ELECTRICITY: 220 volts AC, 50Hz. Round 2-pin continental plugs are standard.

COMMUNICATIONS: **Telephone:** Country code: 7 (3312 for Bishkek). International calls should be made from a telephone office which will usually be found attached to a post office; they can also be made from some hotels by asking at reception. All international calls from Kyrgyzstan have to go through the operator. Local calls (within the city) are free of charge if made from private telephones; hotels sometimes levy a small charge. Direct-dial calls within the former USSR are obtained by dialling 8 and waiting for another dial tone and then dialling the city code followed by the number. **Fax:** Services are available in main hotels for residents only. **Telex/telegram:** Telegram and telex services (the latter with dual Cyrillic and Latin keyboards; impractical except in emergencies) are available from post offices in large towns. Telex is also available in the main hotels (for residents only). **Post:** Post to and from Western Europe and the USA can take anything between two weeks and two months. Stamped envelopes can be bought from post offices. Mail to recipients within Kyrgyzstan should be addressed in the following order: country, postcode, city, street, house number and lastly the person's name. Visitors can also use post offices located within major *Intourist* hotels. Post office hours: 0900-1800 Monday to Friday. **Press:** The Kyrgyz press is among the most free in Central Asia. The main dailies are published in Bishkek and include *Bishkek Shamy*, *Kyrgyz Tuusu* (both in Kyrgyz) and *Vecherny Bishkek*, *Respublica* and *Slova Kyrgyzstana* (in Russian). There is also an English-language weekly, the *Kyrgyzstan Chronicle*.

BBC World Service and Voice of America frequencies and wavelengths: From time to time these change. See the section *How to Use this Book* for more information.

BBC:				
MHz	**17.64**	**15.57**	**11.76**	**7.160**
Voice of America:				
MHz	**9.670**	**6.040**	**5.995**	**1.260**

PASSPORT/VISA

Regulations and requirements may be subject to change at short notice, and you are advised to contact the appropriate diplomatic or consular authority before finalising travel arrangements. Details of these may be found at the head of this country's entry. Any numbers in the chart refer to the footnotes below.

	Passport Required?	Visa Required?	Return Ticket Required?
Full British	Yes*	Yes*	No*
BVP	Not valid	-	-
Australian	Yes*	Yes*	No*
Canadian	Yes*	Yes*	No*
USA	Yes*	Yes*	No*
Other EU (As of 31/12/94)	Yes*	Yes*	No*
Japanese	Yes*	Yes*	No*

Note [*]: Visa regulations are liable to change. Prospective travellers are advised to contact *Intourist Travel Ltd* who offer a comprehensive visa service for all of the republics within the CIS. Tel: (0171) 538 5902 in the UK; (212) 757 3884 in the USA.

PASSPORTS: Valid passport required by all.

British Visitors Passport: Not acceptable.

VISAS: Required by all except nationals of Bulgaria, China, CIS, Cuba, Czech Republic, Hungary, Poland, Romania and Slovak Republic. A visa for any CIS member state is valid for 3-day transit through Kyrgyzstan. Those with a CIS visa wishing to stay longer should apply in person to the Foreign Ministry on arrival. It is no longer necessary to have visas for each town to be visited. For those wishing to continue on to China, Chinese visas should be obtained before departure for Kyrgyzstan.

Types of visa: Business (Multiple-entry) and Tourist (Single-entry, Double-entry and Multiple-entry).

Cost: *Single-entry:* varies according to notice given by applicant: US$30 with 5 working days' notice, US$50 with 3 working days' notice, US$80 with one working day's notice. *Double-entry:* US$70. *Multiple-entry:* US$100.

Validity: 60 days from date of issue.

Application to: Ministry of Foreign Affairs in Bishkek (address at top of entry) or Russian Federation Embassy (see *Russian Federation* later in the book). Nationals of the USA and Canada should apply to the Kyrgyz Embassy in Washington. There is Kyrgyz consular representation in the Russian Federation embassies in Brussels and in Vienna, both of which will shortly start issuing visas.

Application requirements: (a) Completed application form. (b) 2 identical passport-size photos. (c) Valid passport. (d) Letter summarising purpose of business visit and planned itinerary† from applicant's head of department for Business visa. (e) Letter of invitation for business visits exceeding 60 days. (f) Letter with planned itinerary† from tourist applicants. (g) Stamped self-addressed envelope. (h) Fee.

Note [†]: There are no internal travel restrictions within Kyrgyzstan.

Working days required: 7-15 days. A same-day visa is sometimes available for the price of approximately US$80.

Temporary residence: Temporary residence permits come under the same regulations as Business visas, but may take longer to obtain.

MONEY

Currency: Kyrgyzstan was the first country in the CIS to leave the Rouble Zone, launching the Som in May 1993 on the back of a US$80-million credit from the International Monetary Fund (IMF). 1 Som = 100 tyn. Notes are in denominations of 20, 5 and 1 Som, and 50, 10 and 1 tyn. All new Kyrgyz currency is in notes – there are no coins. Neighbouring republics have been unwilling to accept the new currency, leading to a fall in Kyrgyzstan's exports. The Som is supported by loans from Western agencies such as the IMF and the World Bank but, despite this, there has been a rapid drop in value since its introduction. The preferred hard currency is US Dollars, although Russian Roubles are also acceptable. There is little divergence between the official and unofficial exchange rates.

Currency exchange: All bills are normally settled in cash. Intourist tours are usually fully paid for before departure. Due to a shortage of change, travellers are advised to carry plenty of small notes. Currency exchange receipts are not necessary.

Credit cards: Credit cards are accepted in some of the larger hotels in Bishkek. Check with your credit card company for merchant acceptability and other services which may be available.

Travellers cheques: These are accepted in one bank in Bishkek; commission charges are high. Cash is recommended.

Eurocheques: These are not accepted.

Exchange rate indicators: Exchange rates for the Som were £1.00 = 6.00, US$1.00 = 4.00 in May 1993; and £1.00 = 15.75, US$1 = 10.50 in January 1994.

Currency restrictions: The import and export of foreign and national currency is unrestricted.

Banking hours: Usually 0800-1700 Monday to Friday. However, all financial transactions must be completed before 1300.

DUTY FREE

The following goods may be imported into Kyrgyzstan without incurring customs duty:

250 cigarettes or 250g of tobacco products; 1 litre of spirits; 2 litres of wine; a reasonable quantity of perfume for personal use; gifts up to an equivalent value of Rub1000.

Note: On entering the country, tourists must complete a customs declaration form which must be retained until departure. This allows the import of articles intended for personal use, including currency and valuables which must be registered on the declaration form. Customs inspection can be long and detailed.

Prohibited imports: Military weapons and ammunition, narcotics and drug paraphernalia, pornography, loose pearls and anything owned by a third party that is to be carried in for that third party. If you have any query regarding items that may be imported, an information sheet is available on request from Intourist.

Prohibited exports: As prohibited imports, as well as annulled securities, state loan certificates, lottery tickets, works of art and antiques (unless permission has been granted by the Ministry of Culture), saiga horns, Siberian stag, punctuate and red deer antlers (unless on organised hunting trip), and punctuate deer skins.

PUBLIC HOLIDAYS

Jan 1 '95 New Year's Day. **Jan 7** Russian Orthodox Christmas. **Mar** Naurus (Lunar New Year). **Mar 8** International Women's Day. **May 1** Labour Day. **May 5** Constitution Day. **May 9** Victory Day. **Jun 13** Kurban Ait (Day of Remembrance). **Aug 31** Independence Day. **Jan 1 '96** New Year's Day. **Jan 7** Russian Orthodox Christmas. **Mar** Naurus (Lunar New Year). **Mar 8** International Women's Day.

HEALTH

Regulations and requirements may be subject to change at short notice, and you are advised to contact your doctor well in advance of your intended date of departure. Any numbers in the chart refer to the footnotes below.

	Special Precautions?	Certificate Required?
Yellow Fever	No	No
Cholera	No	No
Typhoid & Polio	No	-
Malaria	No	-
Food & Drink	1	-

[1]: The water has been tested by the US-based Center for Diseases Control and found to be generally bacteria-free; however, it does have a high metal content. Milk is pasteurised and dairy products are safe for consumption. Only eat well-cooked meat and fish, preferably served hot. Pork, salad and mayonnaise may carry increased risk. Vegetables should be cooked and fruit peeled. Due to the difficulty of obtaining a balanced diet in some parts of Kyrgyzstan, visitors are recommended to take vitamin supplements.

Rabies is present. For those at high risk, vaccination before arrival should be considered. If you are bitten abroad seek medical advice without delay. For more information, consult the *Health* section at the back of the book.

Health care: Medical services offered to foreigners, except emergency care, require immediate cash payment and are somewhat limited. There is a severe shortage of basic medical supplies, including disposable needles, anesthetics and antibiotics, and travellers are advised to bring any necessary medication or equipment. Elderly travellers and those with existing health problems may be at risk due to inadequate medical facilities. The US Embassy maintains a list of English-speaking physicians in the area. Medical insurance is strongly recommended.

TRAVEL - International

AIR: The national airline is *Kyrgyz Air*. It offers a weekly connection from Istanbul. The airport is subject to fuel shortages and is periodically shut. When it is open, connections from Europe and the USA are via Moscow or Almaty (see entry for *Kazakhstan* earlier in this book). There are direct flights to Bishkek from Hannover and Stuttgart. Discussions are underway to open direct flights to India and Pakistan.

Approximate flight times: From *London* to Almati in Kazakhstan (via Moscow) is 8 hours, excluding stopover in Moscow; from *Istanbul* is 5 hours 30 minutes and from *Frankfurt/M* is 7 hours. There then follows a 4-hour bus journey to Bishkek.

International airport: *Manas Airport (FRU)* is 20km (12.5 miles) north of Bishkek. There is a minibus shuttle service to the city centre (when the airport is functioning).

RAIL: There are rail connections with the Russian Federation (the journey to Moscow takes three days) and with the other Central Asian republics.

ROAD: The main international road links are with Kazakhstan and there are also two crossing points into China. There are regular **bus** links from Bishkek to Tashkent (10-12 hours) and Almaty (4 hours); use the long-distance (*zapadni*) bus station in Bishkek. There is a direct service to Osh from Tashkent via the Fergana Valley (see the entry for *Uzbekistan* later in the book).

TRAVEL - Internal

AIR: Subject to fuel availability there are internal connections from Bishkek to Cholpan-Ata, Kara-Kol, Naryn and Osh. Access to the Central Tien-Shan region is via helicopter, which ferries climbers up the Inylchek Valley.

RAIL: The only internal rail line in Kyrgyzstan runs from Bishkek to Balikchi at the western end of Lake Issyk-Kul. Osh, in the south of the country, can be

reached by rail via Tashkent (Uzbekistan).
ROAD: Kyrgyzstan has 25,000km (15,625 miles) of roads. **Bus/coach:** There are regular bus and coach connections to all parts of Kyrgyzstan, but they are crowded. **Taxi:** Taxis or cars for hire can be found in all major towns. Many are unlicensed, and fares should be agreed in advance. As many of the street names, particularly in the capital, have changed since independence, visitors are advised to ask for both the old and the new names when seeking directions. **Car hire** is not available. It is possible to hire cars with drivers for long-distance journeys, but because of the shortage of petrol, it is generally an expensive option. Foreigners are generally expected to pay in US Dollars.
Documentation: An International Driving Licence and two photos are required. Licenses for long-stay residents intending to buy or import a car can be obtained from the Protocol Department of the Foreign Ministry.
URBAN: There are bus and trolleybus services around the capital.
JOURNEY TIMES: The following chart gives approximate journey times from Bishkek (in hours and minutes) to other towns in Kyrgyzstan.

	Road
Osh	12.00
Tokmak	1.00
Balikchi	2.30
Kara-Kol	5.30

ACCOMMODATION

HOTELS: There are no restrictions on where foreigners may stay, but accommodation is limited outside the capital, Bishkek, and visitors should not expect Western standards of comfort, although hotels are generally clean. Tourists will be charged a special tourist rate, which is payable in US Dollars and can be as much as ten times what the locals pay. Accommodation at the Dostuk Hotel may be booked in advance through *Fair Winds Trading Company* (for contact details, see top of entry) or directly with the hotel (tel: (3312) 284 218 *or* 284 226; fax: (3312) 284 466). Other hotels in Bishkek include the Ala-Too (tel: (3312) 226 041), the Bishkek (tel: (3312) 220 321) and the Issyk-Kul (tel: (3312) 445 509). Some hotels outside Bishkek are still wary of accepting foreigners travelling independently. In Osh there is the Hotel Osh (tel: (33222) 24717).
Turbazas: These 'tourist bases' are an alternative to hotel accommodation. For a dollar or two in local currency visitors have access to basic bungalow accommodation and three meals a day.
Sanatoria: Since the break-up of the Soviet Union, the sanatoria on the shores of Lake Issyk-Kul – originally built by cooperatives and trade unions for fatigued workers – have started to take in tourists, but the atmosphere may not be to everyone's taste.
Mountaineering camps: *Kyrgyzintourist* and *Dostuk Trekking* run a number of camps for mountaineers attempting to climb the many peaks in Kyrgyzstan's mountains.

RESORTS & EXCURSIONS

The main attraction of Kyrgyzstan lies in the breathtaking landscape of mountains, glaciers and lakes; their isolation ensures that they have been almost forgotten by the crowds. The lakes and mountainous terrain provide opportunities for trekking, skiing, climbing, sailing and swimming.
The capital **Bishkek** was founded in 1878 on the site of a clay fort built by the Khan of Kokand and destroyed by the Russians, and sits at the foot of the Tien Shan mountain range. A largely Soviet-built city, it has a similar spacious atmosphere to its Kazakh neighbour, Almaty. *Ulitsa Sovietskaya*, the broad tree-lined road between the railway station and the city centre, houses the *Kyrgyz State Opera and Ballet Theatre,* the *Chernyshevsky Public Library* and the *State Art Museum.* Other attractions include the *History Museum* in the Old Square *(Stary Ploshad),* the *Lenin Museum,* the *Zoological Museum* and the *Kyrgyz Drama Theatre.* The Government plans to redevelop the former *General Frunze Museum* on Frunze Street – which commemorated the Kyrgyz-born Russian general who subdued Central Asia for the Bolsheviks – into a celebration of the ethnic diversity that is found in Kyrgyzstan. A section on Jewish culture has already been opened.
Less than an hour's drive from Bishkek the **Ala-Archa Nature Reserve** offers spectacular scenery for trekking and skiing. Less than an hour's drive east from the city, the *Burana Tower* is a 25m-high (82ft) minaret which dates from the 11th century and is all that remains of the ancient city of *Balasagun.*
Still further east lies the jewel in the crown of the newly independent republic. Lying 1600m (5249ft) above sea level, the saltwater *Lake Issyk-Kul* was closed to foreigners during the Soviet era. Both its Kyrgyz name and Chinese name (Ze-Hai) mean warm sea, as it never freezes over, despite the altitude. Surrounded by snow-capped mountains and ringed with sandy beaches, the lake has a pristine and outstanding beauty. On the north shore, the town of **Cholpan-Alta** is a spa town which was a former retreat for the Communist Party elite. The resort of Issyk-kul is now open to Anyone, although it is very busy during the summer season and visitors are advised to book in advance. In the *Kungay Ala-Too Mountains* behind it, four trekking routes start, leading eventually to *Medeo*, outside *Almaty* (Kazakhstan), 4-6 days away. For scuba-diving enthusiasts, there is spectacularly clear water and a 12th-century town that lies 2-3m (6-10ft) below the surface of the lake near **Ulan**, 18km (11 miles) from Balikchi.
At the southeast end of the lake is the town of **Kara-Kol,** with its attractive houses and tree-lined streets, and behind it are the *Terskay Ala-Too Mountains*, an unspoilt wilderness populated only by nomadic shepherds, and only then during the summer. There are few roads and no hotels. 16km (10 miles) outside Kara-Kol is the health resort of **Ak-Soo** with hot mineral springs.
For more ambitous travellers it is possible to follow the route of the old *Silk Road* to Kashgar in China, crossing the border at the *Torugart Pass*, near *Lake Chatyr-Kul.* Trekking and skiing in the mountains can be organised by *Dostuk Trekking* (tel: (3312) 427 471; fax: (3312) 419 129). Trekking tours are also offered by *Exodus Travel* (tel: (0181) 675 5550; fax: (0181) 673 0779). Tours are also offered by *Tien Shan Travel* (tel: (3312) 272 885; fax: (3312) 270 576).
Osh, Kyrgyzstan's second city, is in the south on the Uzbek border. Although it is 2500 years old, few traces of its ancient history remain. Since the 10th century pilgrims have come to visit the *Suleiman Gora*, a hill in the middle of the city where legend has it that the Prophet once prayed. Childless women come here in the hope that they may conceive (the hill is supposed to look like a pregnant woman lying on her back). Other attractions include the *Museum of Local Studies* and the bazaar. North of Osh is the town of **Uzgen** where there is a mausoleum that is supposed to have contained the body of the Kyrgyz hero Manas. East of Osh is the **Sary-Chelek Nature Reserve**, which includes the stunning *Lake Sary-Chelek.*
Kyrgyzstan also offers mountaineering camps: the *Ala-Archa camp*, 40km (25 miles) from Bishkek, offers over 160 routes and is the base for attempts to climb the Kyrgyz range (highest point: 4876m/15,997ft). In the south, the *Pamir camp* offers opportunities on the peaks of the *Pamir Mountains*, such as *Pik Lenina* and *Pik Communism*, both over 7000m (22,966ft).
Dostuk Trekking and *Tien Shan Travel* run package and itineraries to suit individual tastes. *Dostuk Trekking* can arrange visas into China and runs an itinerary from Beijing to Almati, as well as sightseeing and more ambitious walking, mountaineering and heli-skiing tours in Kyrgyzstan and the neighbouring republics. *Kyrgyzintourist* offers a series of standard packages of camping, hiking, horseriding, skiing, white-water rafting and visits to sites of interest en route. These include the Issyk-Kul tour: 11 days travelling along the shores of Lake Issyk-Kul staying in campsites, and includes swimming, boating, horseriding, fishing, a yacht cruise, a sample of Kyrgyz national cuisine and visits to the Burana Tower and museums in Bishkek. For the more adventurous, there is a 17-day, 140km (87.5-mile) trek along the northern slopes of the Terskay Ala-Too which involves crossing four mountain passes. They also offer heli-skiing holidays; visitors stay in hotels in Bishkek and are ferried to the Kyrgyz mountain range in helicopters to ski the 'virgin snow-capped slopes'. *Kyrgyzintourist* also offer a white-water rafting itinerary down some of the many Kyrgyz mountain rivers.

SOCIAL PROFILE

FOOD & DRINK: Kyrgyz food shows the effect of its location and history: befitting a nation descended from nomadic herdsmen, mutton is the staple meat, enlivened with Chinese influences. *Shashlyk* (skewered chunks of mutton barbecued over charcoal) and *lipioshka* (round unleavened bread) are often sold on street corners. *Plov* is a Central Asian staple: rice fried with shredded turnip and scraps of mutton, served with bread. *Laghman* is a noodle soup with mutton and vegetables that was originally imported from Chinese Turkestan. *Beshbarmak* is noodles with shredded, boiled meat in bouillon. Around Lake Issyk-Kul, the noodles are sometimes served with jellied potato starch rather than meat. *Shorpur* is a meat soup with potatoes and other vegetables. *Manty* (steamed noodle sacks of meat and vegetables), *samsa* (samosas) and *chiburekki* (deep-fried dough cakes) are all popular as snacks. The Kyrgyz and the Kazakhs are almost alone among Central Asian peoples in eating horse meat; only young mares are used and they are fed on the Alpine grasses, which are thought to impart a particularly good flavour. Restaurants in the capital tend to stop serving at 2200.
Drink: Black or green tea is the most popular drink. *Koumys* (fermented mares' milk) is mildly alcoholic and can still be found in the countryside; refusing an offer of *koumys* may cause offence. Other local specialities include *dzarma* (fermented barley flour) and *boso* (fermented millet, resembling beer). During the summer, *chai khanas* (open-air tea houses) are popular. Beer, vodka and local brandy are all widely available in resturants.
NIGHTLIFE: There are performances of both Russian and European operas and ballets in the State Opera House in Bishkek. Local music and theatre has enjoyed a strong revival since independence and excerpts from the *Manas*, the Kyrgyz national epic about the eponymous warrior that runs to some 500,000 lines, play to packed houses. The Manas was originally handed down orally, but was written down in the early part of this century.
SHOPPING: In Bishkek, Osh and Al-Medin bazaars are popular for food and handicrafts. There is also a shop in the Art Gallery that sells paintings and traditional Kyrgyz products. Particularly popular are embroidered Kyrgyz felt hats (*kalpak*), felt carpets and chess sets with traditional Kyrgyz figures.
SPORT: Equestrian: The national sports reflect the importance of the horse in Kyrgyz culture. *Ulak Tartysh* is a team game in which the two mounted teams attempt to deliver the carcass of a goat weighing 30-40kg over the opposition's goal line. Players are allowed to wrestle the goat from an opponent, but physical assault is frowned upon. Each game is 15 minutes long. *Aht Chabysh* are horse races held over distances varying between 4-50km (2.5-31 miles). Competitors under 13 year of age are barred from entering. *Udarysh* is a competition on horseback in which two riders or two teams of riders attempt to wrestle each other, and frequently their mounts, to the ground. Other sports such as **football**, **skiing** and **swimming** are also popular.
SPECIAL EVENTS: *Naurus* and *Independence Day* are both colourful festivals.
SOCIAL CONVENTIONS: Tipping: Not expected but greatly appreciated.

BUSINESS PROFILE

ECONOMY: Similar to the other Central Asian States, the Government of Kyrgyzstan inherited an imbalanced and disfunctional economy from the Soviet Union. It has chosen a policy of rapid change, including privatisation and a freely floating currency, to try to cure its economic ills. Some of the more grotesque Soviet-era follies, such as the sugar mill that imported sugar cane from Cuba, have been closed down, and others are restructuring. Agriculture is still the largest employer, occupying 33% of the population (1993) despite the relatively small productive area of the republic. 48% of the irrigated agricultural land is devoted to growing fodder for livestock. Other agricultural products include grain, potatoes, fruit and vegetables, cotton and tobacco. Average wages were US$180 per annum in 1993. Unemployment is rising as unprofitable industries are closed. Hopes for the future rest on tourism and Kyrgyzstan's mineral resources. Tourism is potentially a strong foreign exchange earner, but the country lacks much of the basic infrastructure and this will take time to create. Kyrgyzstan has deposits of iron ore, copper, lead, zinc, mercury, antimony, tin, bismuth, vanadium, bauxite, molybdenum, manganese, silver and gold. Irregularities concerning the exploitation of the gold resources have led to the downfall of a number of government officials. There are also large amounts of decorative construction materials, such as marble, granite and limestone. The economy is still shrinking rapidly and there are few signs of its recovery in the short term, the continued support of Western agencies such as the IMF and the World Bank notwithstanding. In the long term, the agreement signed in January 1994 with the neighbouring states of Uzbekistan and Kazakhstan, which abolishes border tariffs and puts into place a number of other measures that should improve trade, may, together with Western credits and technology, make for a rosier picture, but it will take time. Like the other republics of Soviet Central Asia, Kyrgyzstan has suffered from the emigration of ethnic Russians, with their technical skills, since the break-up of the Soviet Union. Kyrgyzstan is a member of the World Bank, the

IMF, the European Bank for Reconstruction and Development and the Asian Development Bank.

BUSINESS: Kyrgyzstan is actively seeking overseas partners to modernise its industry and introduce new technology. To this end it has enacted a number of laws to encourage and protect foreign investors: the law on property extends to all foreign investors the rights granted to Kyrgyz citizens with respect to ownership; foreigners are allowed to purchase businesses and buildings to carry out their activities, but the Government reserves the exclusive right to own land, natural resources, water, agriculture and livestock. There are significant tax holidays for foreign investors. In order to invest in Kyrgyzstan, foreigners must be registered with the Ministry of Economy and Finance. Applications to set up in Kyrgyzstan should be sent in the first instance to the State Committee on Foreign Investments and Economic Assistance (Goskominvest). The Government is particularly interested in encouraging investment in mining, industry – including electronics, light agricultural machinery and pharmaceuticals – petroleum, hydro-electricity and agriculture. **Business hours:** 0900-1730 Monday to Friday.

COMMERCIAL INFORMATION: The following organisations can offer advice: State Committee on Foreign Investment, ul Kievskaya 96, 720002 Bishkek. Tel: (3312) 220 363. Fax: (3312) 226 391; *or* Ministry of Economy and Finance, ul Erkindik 58, 720874 Bishkek. Tel: (3312) 228 922. Fax: (3312) 227 404; *or* Kyrgyz Chamber of Commerce and Industry, Abdumomunova 205, 720300 Bishkek. Tel: (3312) 264 942. Fax: (3312) 225 358. Telex: 251239; *or* International Fund for the Promotion of Entrepreneurship and Foreign Investments, ul Sovietskaya 152-116, 720000 Bishkek. Tel: (3312) 414 566. Fax: (3312) 414 572.

Information can also be obtained from the US Department of Commerce Business Information Service for the Newly Independent States, Room 7413, US Department of Commerce, Washington, DC 20230. Tel: (202) 482 4655. Fax: (202) 482 2293.

CLIMATE

Kyrgyzstan has a continental climate with relatively little rainfall. It averages 247 sunny days a year. In the summer in the mountains the mornings are generally fine and the afternoons hazy with occasional rain. In the lowlands the temperature ranges from -4°/-6°C in January to 16°/24°C in July. In the highlands the temperatures range from -14°/-20°C in January to 8°/12°C in July. There are heavy snowfalls in the winter.

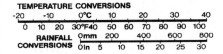
TEMPERATURE CONVERSIONS

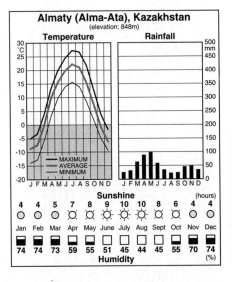

Location: South-East Asia.

National Tourism Department
Ministry of Trade and Tourism, BP 3556, Vientiane, Laos
Tel: (21) 3254. Fax: (21) 5025.

Embassy of the Lao People's Democratic Republic
74 avenue Raymond Poincaré, 75116 Paris, France
Tel: (1) 45 53 02 98. Fax: (1) 47 27 57 89. Telex: 610711.
Opening hours: 0900-1230 and 1400-1700 Monday to Friday; 0900-1230 Monday to Friday (Visa section).

Orbitours Pty Ltd
GPO Box 3309, 7th Floor, Dymocks Building, 428 George Street, Sydney, NSW 2001, Australia
Tel: (2) 221 7322. Fax: (2) 221 7425. Telex: AA127081.
The British Embassy in Bangkok deals with enquiries relating to Laos (see *Thailand* later in this book).

Embassy of the Lao People's Democratic Republic
2222 S Street, NW, Washington, DC 20008
Tel: (202) 332 6416/7. Fax: (202) 332 4923.
Also deals with enquiries from Canada.

Embassy of the United States of America
BP 114, rue Bartholomie, Vientiane, Laos
Tel: (21) 212 581/2/3. Fax: (21) 212 854.

The Canadian Embassy in Bangkok deals with enquiries relating to Laos (see *Thailand* later in this book).

AREA: 236,800 sq km (91,400 sq miles).
POPULATION: 4,170,000 (1990 estimate).
POPULATION DENSITY: 17.6 per sq km.
CAPITAL: Vientiane. **Population:** 442,000 (1990 estimate).
GEOGRAPHY: Laos is a landlocked country bordered to the north by China, to the east by Vietnam, to the

---

south by Cambodia and to the west by Thailand and Myanmar. Apart from the Mekong River plains along the border of Thailand, the country is mountainous, particularly in the north, and in places is densely forested.

LANGUAGE: Lao. French, Vietnamese and some English are also spoken. Tribal languages, such as Meo, are also spoken.

RELIGION: The Laos-Lum (Valley Laos) people follow the Hinayana (Theravada) form of Buddhism. The religion of the Laos-Theung (Laos of the mountain tops) ranges from traditional Confucianism to Animism and Christianity.

TIME: GMT + 7.

ELECTRICITY: 220 volts AC, 50Hz.

COMMUNICATIONS: Telephone: Restricted IDD available. Country code: 856 (followed by 21 for Vientiane). Telephone links exist with Bangkok. **Press:** English-language dailies in Laos include the *Vientiane May*.

BBC World Service and Voice of America frequencies: From time to time these change. See the section *How to Use this Book* for more information.

BBC:
MHz	17.79	11.75	9.740	6.195

Voice of America:
MHz	15.43	11.72	5.985	1.143

PASSPORT/VISA

Regulations and requirements may be subject to change at short notice, and you are advised to contact the appropriate diplomatic or consular authority before finalising travel arrangements. Details of these may be found at the head of this country's entry. Any numbers in the chart refer to the footnotes below.

	Passport Required?	Visa Required?	Return Ticket Required?
Full British	Yes	Yes	Yes
BVP	Not valid	-	-
Australian	Yes	Yes	Yes
Canadian	Yes	Yes	Yes
USA	Yes	Yes	Yes
Other EU (As of 31/12/94)	Yes	Yes	Yes
Japanese	Yes	Yes	Yes

PASSPORTS: Required by all.
British Visitors Passport: Not accepted.
VISAS: Required by all. Transit visas are not required for passengers who continue their onward journey by the same aircraft. The same ticket and visa requirements for entry to the next destination apply. This facility applies to all nationals.
Note: Business visas require an invitation from a corresponding organisation in Laos.
Validity: Enquire at the nearest consular representative.
Application to: Consulate (or Consular section at Embassy). For addresses, see top of entry.
Note: A visa valid for Laos can easily be obtained from local travel agencies in Bangkok (Thailand).
Application requirements: (a) 2 passport-size photos. (b) 2 forms. (c) Letter from sponsor for business application.
Working days required: Applications should be made as far in advance as possible.

MONEY

Currency: Laotian New Kip (Kp) = 100 cents. Notes are in denominations of Kp500, 100, 20 and 10.
Currency exchange: Thai and US currency is widely accepted in shops, markets and hotels in Vientiane and Luang Prabang.
Credit cards: Limited acceptance.
Travellers cheques: Limited acceptance.
Exchange rate indicators: The following figures are included as a guide to the movements of the Laotian New Kip against Sterling and the US Dollar:

Date:	Oct '92	Sep '93	Jan '94	Jan '95
£1.00=	1131	1102	1063	1127
$1.00=	712	722	719	720

Currency restrictions: No restrictions on the import or export of foreign currency, although banks will only accept Thai Bahts, Pounds Sterling or US Dollars. The import and export of local currency is prohibited.
Banking hours: 0830-1130 and 1400-1500 Monday to Saturday (winter); 0800-1200 and 1330-1630 Monday to Saturday (summer, Mar 1-Sep 30).

DUTY FREE

The following goods may be imported into Laos **from countries not bordering Laos** without incurring

---

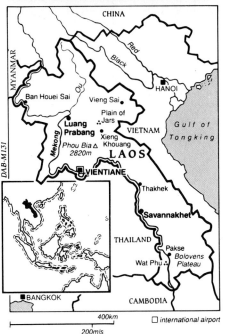

customs duty:
500 cigarettes or 100 cigars or 500g of tobacco; 1 bottle of spirits; 2 bottles of wine; perfume for personal use.

PUBLIC HOLIDAYS

Jan 24 '95 Army Day. **Apr 13-15** Lao New Year (Water Festival). **May 1** Labour Day. **Dec 2** National Day. **Jan 24 '96** Army Day. **Apr 13-15** Lao New Year (Water Festival).

HEALTH

Regulations and requirements may be subject to change at short notice, and you are advised to contact your doctor well in advance of your intended date of departure. Any numbers in the chart refer to the footnotes below.

	Special Precautions?	Certificate Required?
Yellow Fever	No	1
Cholera	Yes	2
Typhoid & Polio	Yes	-
Malaria	Yes/3	-
Food & Drink	Yes/4	-

[1]: A yellow fever vaccination certificate is required from travellers coming from infected areas.
[2]: Following WHO guidelines issued in 1973, a cholera vaccination certificate is not a condition of entry to Laos. However, cholera is a serious risk in this country and precautions are essential. Up-to-date advice should be sought before deciding whether these precautions should include vaccination, as medical opinion is divided over its effectiveness. See the *Health* section at the back of the book.
[3]: Malaria risk exists throughout the year in the whole country, except Vientiane. The malignant *falciparum* form is prevalent and is reported to be 'highly resistant' to chloroquine.
[4]: All water should be regarded as being potentially contaminated. Water used for drinking, brushing teeth or making ice should have first been boiled or otherwise sterilised. Milk is unpasteurised and should be boiled. Powdered or tinned milk is available and is advised, but make sure that it is reconstituted with pure water. Avoid dairy products which are likely to have been made from unboiled milk. Only eat well-cooked meat and fish, preferably served hot. Pork, salad and mayonnaise may carry increased risk. Vegetables should be cooked and fruit peeled.
Rabies is present. For those at high risk, vaccination before arrival should be considered. If you are bitten abroad seek medical advice without delay. For more information consult the *Health* section at the back of the book.
Health care: Any treatment must generally be paid for in cash. Health insurance is essential.

TRAVEL - International

AIR: The national airline of Laos is *Lao International (QV). Del Chang*, a US-owned company, joined with *Lao Aviation* in 1991 to form *Lao International* and now has international routes from Vientiane to Hanoi, Bangkok, Phnom Penh and Ho Chi Minh City.
International airport: *Vientiane (VTE)* (Wattay) is 4km (2.5 miles) from the city (travel time – 20 minutes).
Departure tax: US$5; children under two years are exempt.
RAIL: There are no railways in Laos, but the Thai system stretches from Bangkok via Nakhon Ratchasima to Nong Khai on the Laos/Thailand border. A ferry and a bridge links the Lao side of the Mekong, 19km (12 miles) east of Vientiane.
ROAD: It is possible to enter Laos from Thailand at Nong Khai either by ferry or over the Friendship Bridge. It is possible to enter Laos by road from Vietnam.

TRAVEL - Internal

AIR: Domestic air services run from Vientiane to Luang Prabang, Pakse and Savannakhet.
RIVER: The Mekong and other rivers are a vital part of the country's transportation system.
ROAD: Many of the roads have been paved in recent years, including the main highway from the Thai border at Savannakhet to the Vietnamese border. However, few main roads are suitable for all-weather driving. In the north of the country there is a road link between Vientiane and Luang Prabang, and from Vientiane to Nam Dong and Tran Ninh. **Bus:** Services link only a few

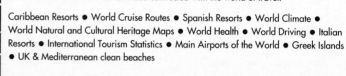
major towns. **Car hire:** Arrangements can be made through hotels. **Documentation:** International Driving Permit recommended, although it is not legally required.
URBAN: Taxis are available in Vientiane, but only operate along fixed routes similar to those of the urban buses.

ACCOMMODATION

HOTELS: There are hotels in Vientiane, but facilities are sparse elsewhere. Local village hostels are available, but with few amenities. For more details of prices and location, contact the Embassy.
CAMPING: There are no facilities for camping in Laos.

RESORTS & EXCURSIONS

Until 1988, when 500 visitors arrived, Western tourists were not allowed access to Laos, but the country has recently opened up and it is perfectly feasible to travel independently all over the country. Most Laotian monuments are Buddhist, but many structures show the influence of the French upon the country, not least the *Monument des Morts* in **Vientiane** which bears a striking, if somewhat rococo, similarity to the Arc de Triomphe in Paris. Visitors will find Vientiane to be an extremely relaxed city for a national capital. 25km (15 miles) from the capital is the stone garden of *Xieng Khuane*. In the royal palace at **Luang Prabang**, the former capital of Laos, there is fine artwork, and the visitor can see gifts made to former kings. Nearby, the *Phousi* in the town centre is a huge rock which visitors can ascend for a panoramic view of the river. Several interesting excursions along the *Mekong River* are possible from Luang Prabang, including a visit to the *Pak Ou Caves* where a there are a great many statues of Buddha. **Wat Xieng Khwan**, in Vientiane province near the ferry port to Thailand, has an extraordinary temple.

SOCIAL PROFILE

FOOD & DRINK: Rice, especially sticky rice, is the staple food and dishes will be Indo-Chinese in flavour and presentation. Lao food can be found on the stalls in the markets. There are several fairly good French restaurants in Vientiane, catering mainly for the diplomatic community. Baguettes and croissants are normally eaten for breakfast. **Drink:** Rice whisky *lao lao* is popular and there are two brands available. The beer is also good.
SHOPPING: The markets in Vientiane and Luang Prabang (about 40 minutes by air from Vientiane) are good. Silk, silver jewellery and handmade shirts are good buys. Although the majority of shops have fixed prices, bartering is still advisable for antiques and other art objects. **Shopping hours:** 0800-1200 and 1400-1700 Monday to Friday; 0800-1200 Saturday.
SPECIAL EVENTS: The majority of festivals are linked to Buddhist holidays. The following occur annually:
Apr '95 *Pi Mai* (celebrations for the new lunar year). **May** *Visakha Bu-saa* (Buddha's birth, enlightenment and death). **Aug/Sep** *Haw Khao Padap Din* (Festival of the Dead); *Boat Races*, Luang Prabang. **Nov** *That Luang Festival* (processions of monks receiving alms and floral votives; fireworks and music), Vientiane. **Dec/Jan '96** *Bun Pha Wet* (the life of Prince Vessantara is recited). **Feb** *Magha Puja* (anniversary of a speech held by Buddha); *Tet* and *Chinese New Year*.
SOCIAL CONVENTIONS: Religious beliefs should be

respected. Lao people should not be touched on the head. Handshaking is not that usual, Lao people greet each other with their palms together and a slight bowing of the head. Avoid all topics of politics and related subjects in conversation. **Tipping:** Practised modestly in hotels and restaurants.

BUSINESS PROFILE

ECONOMY: Laos is one of the world's poorest countries, and its predominantly agricultural economy has been unable to operate at much above subsistence level since the mid-1970s. The country has considerable, though largely untapped, reserves of tin, lead and zinc, as well as iron ore, coal and timber. Laos has a large balance of payments deficit, once financed by the USA but now supported by the CIS. The Laotian economy, whose problems are compounded by a shortage of skilled labour and foreign exchange, depends also on East European and Vietnamese support and lately from certain Western countries, principally Sweden and Japan. Rice, both highland and lowland varieties, is the main crop grown, but others include maize, cassava, pulses, groundnuts, fruits, sugar cane and tobacco. The small-scale manufacturing industries include beer and cigarette production. The CIS is Laos' largest trading partner by a considerable margin.
BUSINESS: Punctuality is appreciated. Lightweight suits, shirt and tie should be worn. English is not spoken by all officials and a knowledge of French will be useful. Business cards should have a Laotian translation on the reverse. Best time to visit is during the dry season, from November to April. **Office hours:** 0800-1200 and 1400-1700 Monday to Friday; 0800-1200 Saturday.
COMMERCIAL INFORMATION: The following organisations can offer advice: Lao National Chamber of Commerce and Industry, BP 4596, rue Phonsay, Vientiane. Tel: (21) 7184. Fax: (21) 9045; *or* Société Lao Import-Export (SOLIMPEX), BP 278, 43-47 avenue Lane Xang, Vientiane. Tel: (21) 2944. Fax: (21) 5753. Telex: 4318.

CLIMATE

Throughout most of the country the climate is hot and tropical, with the rainy season between May and October when temperatures are at their highest. The dry season runs from November to April.

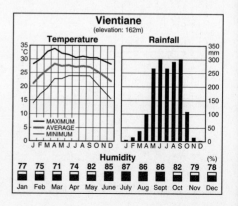

Vientiane
(elevation: 162m)

Temperature — Rainfall

35 °C / 30 / 25 / 20 / 15 / 10 / 5 / 0
MAXIMUM / AVERAGE / MINIMUM
J F M A M J J A S O N D

350 mm / 300 / 250 / 200 / 150 / 100 / 50 / 0
J F M A M J J A S O N D

Humidity (%)

Jan	Feb	Mar	Apr	May	June	July	Aug	Sept	Oct	Nov	Dec
77	75	71	74	82	85	87	86	86	82	79	78

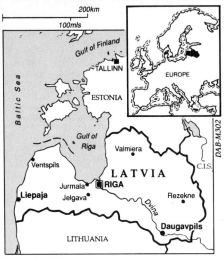

□ *international airport*

Location: Northern Europe.

National Tourist Board of Latvia
Ministry of Transport, Pils Laukums 4, Riga LV 1050,
Latvia
Tel: (2) 229 945. Fax: (2) 217 180 *or* 217 169.
Latvian Embassy
45 Nottingham Place, London W1M 3FE
Tel: (0171) 312 0040. Fax: (0171) 312 0042. Opening
hours: 1100-1300 Monday to Friday (Visa section).
British Embassy
3rd Floor, Elizabetes Iela 2, LV-1340 Riga, Latvia
Tel: (2) 320 737 *or* 325 592. Fax: (2) 322 973.
Latvian Embassy
4325 17th Street, NW, Washington, DC 20011
Tel: (202) 726 8213/4. Fax: (202) 726 6785.
Embassy of the United States of America
Raina bulvaris 7, LV-1050 Riga, Latvia
Tel: (2) 210 005 *or* 220 367 *or* (35849) 311 348 (cellular
link). Fax: (2) 226 530 *or* (35849) 314 665 (cellular link).
Consulate General of Latvia
230 Clemow Avenue, Ottawa, Ontario K1S 2B6
Tel: (613) 238 6868. Fax: (613) 238 7044.
Canadian Embassy
Elizabetes 45-47, LV-1010 Riga, Latvia.
Tel: (88) 30141. Fax: (88) 30140.

AREA: 64,589 sq km (24,938 sq miles).
POPULATION: 2,606,176 (1993 estimate).
POPULATION DENSITY: 40.4 per sq km.
CAPITAL: Riga. **Population:** 897,078 (1991 estimate).
GEOGRAPHY: Latvia is situated on the Baltic coast
and borders Estonia in the north, Lithuania in the south,
the Russian Federation in the east and Belarus in the
southeast. The coastal plain is mostly flat, but inland to
the east the land is hilly with forests and lakes. There are
about 12,000 rivers in Latvia, the biggest being the River
Dvina. The ports of Riga and Ventspils never freeze over
during the winter.
LANGUAGE: Latvian is the official language. It is an
Indo-European, non-Slavic and non-Germanic language
and is similar only to Lithuanian. Russian and,
increasingly, English are widely spoken. German and
Swedish may also be understood.
RELIGION: Predominantly Protestant (Lutheran) with

Roman Catholics in the east of the country. There is also
a Russian Orthodox minority.
TIME: GMT + 2 (GMT + 3 from last Sunday in March
to Saturday before last Sunday in September).
ELECTRICITY: 220 volts AC, 50Hz. European-style
2-pin plugs are in use.
COMMUNICATIONS: Telephone: IDD is available.
Country code: 371. Outgoing international code: 810.
Directory enquiries: 09. Two American telecommunications companies and *Swedish Telecom* are currently
competing for the contract to update the Latvian
telephone system. **Fax/telex:** Facilities are available in
the Main Post Office in Riga (for address, see below).
Telegram: For services from public phones, dial 06.
There is also a service at the hotel service bureau. **Post:**
The Main Post Office is at Brivibas bulvaris 21. Tel: (2)
224 155. Fax: (2) 331 920. Airmail to Western Europe
takes up to six days. **Press:** Newspapers are published in
Latvian and Russian. *Atmoda* (Awakening) appears once
a month in English and *Baltija* magazine appears three
times a year in English, Russian, German and Latvian.
The Baltic Observer is an English-language paper
published weekly.
**BBC World Service and Voice of America
frequencies:** From time to time these change. See the
section *How to Use this Book* for more information.
BBC:

| MHz | 15.07 | 12.09 | 9.410 | 6.195 |

Voice of America:

| MHz | 11.97 | 9.670 | 6.040 | 5.995 |

PASSPORT/VISA

	Passport Required?	Visa Required?	Return Ticket Required?
Full British	Yes	No	Yes
BVP	Not valid	-	-
Australian	Yes	Yes	Yes
Canadian	Yes	Yes	Yes
USA	Yes	Yes/1	Yes
Other EU (As of 31/12/94)	Yes	Yes/1	Yes
Japanese	Yes	Yes	Yes

PASSPORT: Required by all.
British Visitors Passport: Not accepted.
VISAS: Required by all except nationals of the Czech
Republic, Estonia, Hungary, Lithuania, Poland, Slovak
Republic and the UK.
[1] Visas can be obtained at the airport and the sea
passenger port in Riga by US and most European
nationals, but it is advisable to get them in advance from
the Embassy. A Latvian visa is also valid for the other
Baltic republics.
Note: Visa regulations are liable to change. It is
advisable to contact the Latvian Embassy (addresses at
top of entry) at least three weeks before travelling for the
latest information.
Types of visa: Business and Tourist. Cost: £7 if applying
in person, £10 by post (with the exception of US
nationals for whom visas are free).
Validity: *Business:* 6 months. *Tourist:* 3 months. Specify
Single- or Multiple-entry on application.
Application to: Consulate (or Consular section of
Embassy). For addresses, see top of entry.
Application requirements: (a) Valid passport. (b) 1
completed application form. (c) 2 passport-size photos.
(d) A letter from sponsoring company/organisation in
Latvia is helpful for Business visas, but not essential.
Notice required: 3 working days.

MONEY

Currency: 1 Latvian Lat (Ls) = 100 santimi. Notes are in
denominations of Ls500, 200, 50, 20, 10 and 5. Coins are
in denominations of Ls2 and 1, and 50, 20, 10, 5, 2 and 1
santimi.
Currency exchange: The banking system is presently
being developed, but several bureaux de change have
opened in hotels, post offices and train stations. These
tend to close at 1600. The most convenient currencies to
change are the German DM and US Dollars in small
denominations.
Credit cards: Only accepted on a very limited basis by
hotels and some petrol stations. Check with your credit
card company for details of merchant acceptability and
other services which may be available.
Exchange rate indicators: The following figures are
included as a guide to the movements of the Latvian Lat
against Sterling and the US Dollar:

Date:	Sep '93	Jan '94	Jan '95
£1.00=	0.94	0.89	0.86
$1.00=	0.61	0.60	0.55

Currency restrictions: There are no restrictions on the
import and export of both local and foreign currency.
Banking hours: 1000-1400 and 1500-1800 Monday to
Friday.

DUTY FREE

The following goods may be imported into Latvia
without incurring customs duty by travellers of 16 years
or older:
*250 cigarettes or 250g tobacco; 1 litre of spirits and 2
litres of wine.*

PUBLIC HOLIDAYS

Jan 1 '95 New Year's Day. **Apr 14** Good Friday. **May 1**
Labour Day. **Jun 23** Ligo Festival. **Jun 24** Midsummer
Festival. **Nov 18** National Day (Proclamation of the
Republic). **Dec 25-26** Christmas. **Dec 31** New Year's
Eve. **Jan 1 '96** New Year's Day. **Apr 5** Good Friday.

HEALTH

	Special Precautions?	Certificate Required?
Yellow Fever	No	No
Cholera	No	No
Typhoid & Polio	No	-
Malaria	No	-
Food & Drink	1	-

[1]: All tap water should be regarded as potentially
contaminated, particularly in Riga. Water used for
drinking, brushing teeth or making ice should have first
been boiled or otherwise sterilised.
Rabies is present. For those at high risk, vaccination
before arrival should be considered. If you are bitten
abroad, seek medical advice without delay. For more
information, consult the *Health* section at the back of the
book.
Health care: The dentist surgery at 9 Stabu St has an
emergency service from 2000-0800 (tel: (2) 274 546) and
the reception of the City Clinical Hospital No 1 (8
Bruninieku St, tel: (2) 276 787) is open 24 hours. Health
insurance is advised. Ordinary first-aid essentials such as
plasters, aspirin, etc are practically unavailable, therefore
it is wise to buy these before travelling.

TRAVEL - International

AIR: Latvia's national airline is *Baltic International
Airlines* and offers twice-weekly flights from Düsseldorf
via Frankfurt/M to Riga. Other airlines to serve Riga are
Austrian Airlines, SAS and *Lufthansa*. There are indirect
flights to the Latvian capital via Moscow, Copenhagen,
Stockholm and Helsinki from all major European cities.
Lufthansa has a direct service from Frankfurt/M to Riga
five times a week. *Aeroflot Russian International
Airlines (RIA)* offers connections twice-weekly to
Vienna, as well as connections to Zurich (either via
Copenhagen or Moscow).
Approximate flight times: From *Frankfurt/M* to Riga is
2 hours 10 minutes; from *London* to Riga is 3 hours 10
minutes (via Helsinki); from *New York* to Riga is
approximately 14 hours (via Helsinki).
International airport: *Riga (RIX)* (Spilva), 7km (4
miles) from the city (travel time – 15-20 minutes). Tel:
(2) 207 009 *or* 223 305. Airport facilities include duty-
free shop, bank (0600-2400), bureau de change (0630-
2330), car hire (*Avis, Europcar and Hertz*), restaurant
(1200-2000), bar/café (0700-2300) and post office (0800-
1300, 1330-1900). Bus no. 22 runs every 20-30 minutes
to the city centre from 0550-2315. An express bus
service goes to various hotels in the city. Taxis are also
available in the city.
SEA: There are ferry connections from Riga to Rostock
and Kiel, as well as from Stockholm with the *Baltic
Express Line*. Several shipping lines run cruises on the
Baltic Sea calling at Riga.
RAIL: Latvia has links with neighbouring Belarus and
with Estonia to the north and Lithuania to the south. The
main route into Western Europe runs from Riga to Berlin
via Warsaw and Vilnius.
ROAD: The road network is relatively well-developed

and there are good routes through to Belarus and to the neighbouring two Baltic Republics. Entry by car is possible from Finland, the Russian Federation, Poland, Belarus or Lithuania. Border posts between Poland and Lithuania: Ogrodniki–Lazdijai; between Poland and Belarus: Terespol–Brest. Recent changes in Eastern Europe have opened a new highway through the Baltic countries, known as the *Via Baltica*. To drive along the Via Baltica is to discover places that were closed to Western tourists for decades. Services along this highly attractive route are improving all the time. Both the road network and signposting are being modernised; the service station network is represented by both local and foreign companies.

TRAVEL - Internal

RAIL: Latvia's reasonably well-developed rail network includes routes from Riga to all other major towns in the country. The railway terminal is Stacijas lauk. For information about trains, dial 007.
ROAD: There are good connections to all parts of the country from Riga. Traffic drives on the right. Since independence, petrol shortages have dramatically increased and drivers should expect delays at the petrol pumps. Diesel and normal 4-star petrol are readily available, though lead-free petrol can only be obtained at two petrol stations in Riga (Pernavas Iela 28 and Brivibas Iela 386) and at one station at the M12 near Panevezvys. **Bus:** A better form of transport than trains in Latvia. The Central Bus Station is at Pragas Iela 1. **Car hire:** Available through hotels, reservations recommended. Drivers can also be hired. **Traffic regulations:** Seat belts must be worn. Speed limits on country lanes are 80kmph (50mph) and in cities 50kmph (32mph). **Documentation:** European nationals should be in possession of the new European Driving Licence.
URBAN: Public transport in Riga runs from 0530-2400. Taxis in Riga are cheap, but prices are rising due to petrol shortages. The state-run taxis generally have cheaper fares than privately-run ones. There is a surcharge at night. All parts of the city can also be reached by bus. A 3-zone fare system is used in the city, tickets should be punched in the appropriate machine when entering the particular form of transport. Fines for fare dodging are common. Tickets for buses, trams and trolleybuses can be bought in advance from kiosks.

ACCOMMODATION

HOTELS: Due to the present level of bed-capacity, early reservation is absolutely necessary. Since independence, there has been a scramble from Western firms to turn the old state-run hotels into modern Western-standard enterprises. Five of the 13 main hotels in Riga are currently already being renovated in joint ventures with Western firms. In December 1991, the only first-class hotel in Latvia, the Hotel de Rome, opened offering high levels of comfort in its 90 rooms with mini-bar, colour TV, radio and telephone. It also has several shops and conference rooms. Many more such joint ventures with firms from all over Western Europe and the United States will ensure that the standard of accommodation in Latvia rapidly reaches Western European levels. Outside Riga, which for the time being is the main location of the current expansion in hotel accommodation, Latvia enjoys a good range of modest accommodation, left over from the pre-independence days, including large hotels and smaller pension-type establishments. **Grading:** A star-grading system is to be introduced at some time in the future. For more details contact the Latvian Embassy or the Tourist office (for addresses, see top of entry).

Riga

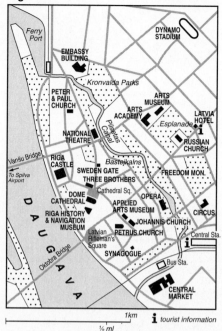

1km
½ ml   **i** *tourist information*

RURAL ACCOMMODATION: Advice on farm holidays, bed & breakfast and self-catering cottages may be obtained from Lauku celotajs (Country Traveller), 2 Republikas sq 2, 1119 Riga, LV-1981. Tel: (2) 327 629. Fax: (2) 325 433.
CAMPING: Most of Latvia's campsites are located along main highways and the Riga Gulf, especially the resort of Jurmala. For more details, contact the Latvian Embassy or the Tourist office (for addresses, see top of entry).
YOUTH HOSTELS: Information on youth accommodation is available from the Latvian Youth Tourism Centre, 2 Kr Barona Street, Riga, LV-1050. Tel: (2) 225 307 *or* 224 494.

RESORTS & EXCURSIONS

According to legend, once in a hundred years the devil rears his head from the waters of the Dvina River and asks whether Riga is 'ready' yet. If the answer were 'yes', the now nearly 900-year-old city would be doomed to sink into the Dvina.
Riga, situated on a sandy plain 15km (9 miles) from the mouth of the River Dvina, is the capital of Latvia and is one of the most beautiful of the Baltic cities. The Latvian capital is a major tourist attraction, and has excellent air, train and road connections. It is rich in history and culture with buildings of remarkable Gothic, Baroque, Classical and Art Nouveau splendour. *Old Riga* contains a remarkable diversity of architectural styles, perhaps best epitomised by the *Dome Cathedral*. Begun in 1211, the building has been added to throughout the centuries, resulting in a fascinating blend of Romanesque, Gothic, Renaissance, Baroque and Classical styles. The cathedral's organ, with nearly 7000 pipes, is recognised as one of the world's greatest musical instruments and concerts are regularly performed here. The numerous other historical buildings in Riga bear witness to Latvia's chequered history. Since its restoration after the First World War, the old quarter of the city has been a protected area. The one surviving town gate is the so-called *Sweden Gate*, whilst the symbol of Riga, the 137m (450ft) high tower of *St Peter's Church*, towers above the city. The *St John's Church* of the former Dominican monastery was built in the 14th century and is one of several interesting churches in this former episcopal seat. Most of the structure dates back to the 15th century and was constructed in a mixture of Romanesque and Gothic styles. The Catholic *St Jacob's Church* was built in 1226 and is a fine example of Gothic architecture. The delightful *Viestura Garden* is ideal for relaxation. Its foundations were laid by Peter the Great who planted the first tree, an event commemorated by a flagstone in the park. *Alexander Gate*, the entrance to the park, was erected to mark the Russian victory over Napoleon's army. It was in this park that the first Latvian Song Festival was held in 1873. At the end of the 18th century, Katharina II built the *Peter and Paul Church*

north of the castle. Merchants' houses from the Middle Ages such as the *Three Brothers* and the 24 warehouses in the old quarter are also picturesque examples of Latvian architecture. The residence of Peter I near the Cathedral has been dramatically altered and rebuilt. Riga has several museums including the *Historical Museum of Latvia* (founded in 1896), housed in the castle, and the *Latvian Museum of Medicine,* as well as two art galleries – the *Museum of Foreign Art,* which contains Flemish masterpieces, and the state *Art Gallery of Latvia*. The *Riga Motor Museum* displays the history of motor-car engineering, with veteran cars including rarities such as Stalin's and Brezhnev's private cars. In central Riga the *Freedom Monument (Brivibas Piemineklis)* is a very significant site for Latvians. Built in 1935, the monument is a striking obelisk crowned by a female figure with upstretched arms holding three stars which represent the three historic regions of Latvia: Kurzeme, Vidzeme and Latgale. Reminiscent of the famous Statue of Liberty in New York, though much smaller at 42m (138ft), the statue ranks among the most distinguished monuments in Europe. In the newer part of the city is the *Warriors' Cemetery* which was designed by the sculptor Zale, the architect Birznieks and the landscape gardener Zeidaks. Approximately 2000 graves from World War I are divided into three sections.
Not far from the city is the open-air *Latvian Ethnographic Museum*. With buildings from all over the country, ranging from wooden churches to windmills, it covers traditional rural architecture from the 16th-19th centuries.
17km (11 miles) from the Latvian capital, the Baltic resort of **Jurmala** – consisting of 12 small villages – extends over 30km (19 miles) along the *Gulf of Riga* at the mouth of the River Lielupe. Fresh pine forest-scented air, sun and endless sandy beaches make this stretch of coast a particularly attractive holiday destination for all age groups. Drivers entering Jurmala need to purchase a special ticket; the fee is used to sponsor ecological programmes in the area. The area is connected by roads and the commuter railway which takes about 15 minutes from Riga. Another Latvian health resort is **Sigulda**, about 53km (33 miles) from Riga. Situated on the picturesque banks of the *River Gauja,* the town has been established since the 13th century and attractions here include the ruins of the castle and local caves. In the *National Park* that is situated here, *Turaida Castle* (13th century) and its museum can be visited, as well as a sculpture park where Latvian folk poetry has been captured in stone. There is good downhill skiing in winter, and in summer Sigulda is a popular boating spot. The most important Baroque building is the *Palace* in *Pilsrundale*, about 77km (48 miles) south of Riga, near the Lithuanian border. This fine summer residence of the Dukes of Courland was designed by the Italian architect Rastrelli who also designed the Winter Palace in St Petersburg – an outstanding blend of Baroque architecture and Rococo decorative art, with gardens modelled on those of Versailles. The surrounding park is excellent for long walks. Nature enthusiasts will enjoy the rich flora and fauna in the regions of *Kurzeme, Vidzeme* and *Latgale,* which are also a favourite with hikers. Throughout the country, the landscape is dotted with picturesque villages such as **Cesis, Kolka, Talsi** and **Bauska,** where life generally follows a very relaxed pace amidst beautiful countryside. Nearby **Kuldiga,** situated on the banks of the River Venta, is Latvia's highest waterfall and a favourite picnic spot.
POPULAR ITINERARIES: 5-day: Riga–Sigulda–Pilsrundale–Riga. **7-day:** Riga–Jurmala–Kolka–Kuldiga–Cesis–Bauska Region–Riga.

SOCIAL PROFILE

FOOD & DRINK: Hors d'oeuvres are very good and often the best part of the meal. Local specialities include *kotletes* (meat patties), *skabu kapostu zupa* (cabbage soup), *Alexander Torte* (raspberry- or cranberry-filled pastry strips), smoked fish, including salmon and trout, sweet-bread soup with dried fruit, *piragi* (pastry filled with bacon and onions) and sorrel soup with boiled pork, onions, potatoes and barley. Potatoes feature regularly on the menu prepared in a variety of ways. There is also a large selection of excellent dairy products on offer such as *smetana* (a blend between sour cream and yoghurt). **Drink:** Riga's *Black Balsam* is a thick, black alcoholic liquid which has been produced since 1700. The exact recipe is a closely guarded secret, but some of the ingredients include ginger, oak bark, bitter orange peel and cognac. It is drunk either with coffee or mixed with vodka. There are several good local beers including the dark beer *Bauskas Tumsais* and the pale *Gaisais*. *Kvass* is a

refreshing summer drink.

NIGHTLIFE: Riga has a range of restaurants, bars and cafés.

SHOPPING: Amber is of high quality and a good buy in all three Baltic Republics. Other purchases include folk art, wickerwork and earthenware. **Shopping hours:** 0900/1000-1800/1900 Monday to Friday, 0900/1000-1600/1700 Saturday. Most shops close 1400-1500 for lunch. Food shops open 0800/0900-2000/2100.

SPECIAL EVENTS: *John's Night,* the summer solstice on June 23-24, is the main festival celebrated in Latvia. Beer is brewed specially for the event and a special cheese is prepared. People wear wreaths of flowers and greenery and spend the night around the bonfire where summer solstice songs are sung. Other events celebrated in 1995 include:
Mar '95 *Riga Cathedral* (international boys' choir festival). **Apr** *Baltic Theatre Spring*; *Symposium of Documentaries of the Baltics*, Riga. **Jul** *23rd Latvian Singer Festival* and *13th Latvian Dance Festival.*
For a complete list, contact the Embassy (for addresses, see beginning of entry).

SOCIAL CONVENTIONS: Handshaking is customary. Normal courtesies should be observed. Western cigarettes are a welcome gift to Latvian smokers. The Latvians are somewhat reserved and formal, but nevertheless very hospitable. They are proud of their culture and their national heritage and visitors should take care to respect this sense of national identity. **Tipping:** Taxi fares and restaurant bills include a tip. Tipping is usually expected, but it is wise to maintain a sense of proportion, bearing in mind that the value of US$1 is equivalent to about one-third of one month's salary (see *Money* above).

BUSINESS PROFILE

ECONOMY: The Latvian economy before the Second World War was dominated by light industry. After 1945, heavy industry was introduced leaving a legacy of extensive pollution which the Latvians are committed to cleaning up. With few raw materials, Latvia is dependent on producing manufactured goods from imported materials. Key industries include vehicle and

railway rolling stock manufacture, electronics, fertilisers and chemicals, timber and light machinery. Dairy farming, fishing and timber are important in the agricultural sector. The infrastructure is, in common with the other Baltic States, comparatively well-developed. Latvia faces a major problem with electricity supply. It is hoping to buy one billion kW/h from Lithuania, which has the only nuclear power plant in the Baltics. Estonia announced last year that it will provide only 40% of the electricity supplied to Latvia last year. Latvia currently produces 50% of its consumption; about 60% of its domestic production comes from three hydroelectric plants on the River Dvina. Together, energy imports account for one-third of Latvia's total import bill. The Government has initiated economic reforms to bring in a market economy and encourage foreign investment despite serious short-term difficulties arising from lack of raw materials, particularly oil, and the disruption of old trading links with the former Soviet Union. Latvia was admitted to the European Bank for Reconstruction and Development in December 1991. The following year it took up membership of the World Bank and IMF. In March 1993, Latvia introduced its own currency, the Lat, running initially parallel with the Latvian Rouble at an exchange rate of Ls1 to 200 Latvian Roubles.

BUSINESS: Business cards are exchanged. Appointments should be arranged in advance. In general, business is conducted in a fairly formal manner and old Soviet ways persist. **Office hours:** 0830-1730 Monday to Friday.

COMMERCIAL INFORMATION: The following organisations can offer advice: Latvian Chamber of Commerce and Industry, Brivibas bulvaris 21, Riga LV 1849. Tel: (2) 225 595. Fax: (2) 332 276. Telex: 161100; *or*
Latvia International Commerce Centre, Tirgonu Iela 8, Riga. Tel: (2) 211 602. Fax: (93) 48836. Telex: 161176.

CLIMATE

Temperate climate, but with considerable temperature variations. Summer is warm with relatively mild weather in spring and autumn. Winter, which lasts from November to mid-March, can be very cold. Rainfall is

distributed throughout the year with the heaviest rainfall in August. Snowfall is common in the winter months.
Required clothing: Light- to medium-weights are worn during summer months. Medium- to heavy-weights are needed during winter. Rainwear is advisable all year.

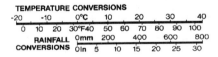

TEMPERATURE CONVERSIONS						
-20	-10	0°C	10	20	30	40
0	10 20	30°F40	50 60	70 80	90 100	

RAINFALL CONVERSIONS					
0mm	200	400	600	800	
0In 5	10	15	20	25	30

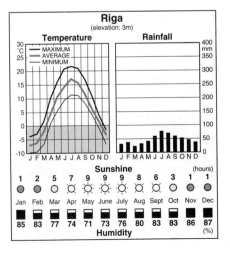

Riga
(elevation: 3m)

Location: Middle East.

Note: Lebanon is now much calmer than it was during the civil war, but travel outside the main towns on a purely personal basis is still inadvisable. Arrangements, such as meeting at the airport, internal travel and accommodation, are best organised beforehand. Visitors are advised to avoid the southern suburbs of Beirut, South Lebanon and the north and west of the Bekaa Valley, particularly the area around Baalbeck and Hermel. Visitors are strongly advised to register with their Embassy on arrival.
Source: FCO Travel Advice Unit – December 1, 1994.

National Council of Tourism in Lebanon (CNTL)
PO Box 11-5344, rue Banque de Liban, Beirut, Lebanon
Tel: (1) 864 532. Telex: 20898.
Embassy of the Republic of Lebanon
21 Kensington Palace Gardens, London W8 4QM
Tel: (0171) 229 7265. Fax: (0171) 243 1699. Telex: 262048. Opening hours: 0900-1230 Monday to Friday.
Lebanese Consular Section
15 Palace Gardens Mews, London W8 4QQ
Tel: (0171) 727 6696. Fax: (0171) 243 1699. Telex: 262048. Opening hours: 0930-1230 Monday to Friday.
British Embassy
East Beirut:
PO Box 60180, Middle East Airlines Building, Tripoli Autostrade, Jal el Dib, East Beirut, Lebanon
Tel: (1) 417 007 *or* 410 596 *or* 416 112. Telex: 44104 (a/b PRODROM LE).
West Beirut:
Shamma Building, Raouché, Ras Beirut, Lebanon
Tel: (1) 812 849 *or* 812 851 *or* 804 929. Telex: 20465 (a/b PRODROM LE).
Consulate in: Tripoli.
Embassy of the Republic of Lebanon
2560 28th Street, NW, Washington, DC 20008
Tel: (202) 939 6300. Fax: (202) 939 6324.

Lebanese Consulate
9 East 76th Street, New York, NY 10021
Tel: (212) 744 7905. Fax: (212) 749 1510.
Embassy of the United States of America
PO Box 70-840, Antelias, Beirut, Lebanon
Tel: (1) 417 774 *or* 402 200 *or* 403 300. Fax: (1) 407 112.
Embassy of Lebanon
640 Lyon Street, Ottawa, Ontario K1S 3Z5
Tel: (613) 236 5825 *or* 236 5855. Fax: (613) 232 1609.
Consulate in: Montréal (tel: (514) 276 2638).
The Canadian Embassy in Damascus deals with enquiries relating to Lebanon (see *Syria* later in this book).

AREA: 10,452 sq km (4036 sq miles).
POPULATION: 2,745,000 (1991 estimate).
POPULATION DENSITY: 262.6 per sq km.
CAPITAL: Beirut. **Population:** 1,500,000 (1991).
GEOGRAPHY: Lebanon shares borders to the north and east with Syria, and to the south with Israel, while to the west lies the Mediterranean. It is a mountainous country and between the two parallel mountain ranges of Jebel Liban and Jebel esh Sharqi lies the fertile Bekaa Valley. Approximately half of the country lies at an altitude of over 900m (3000ft). Into this small country is packed such a variety of scenery that there are few places to equal it in beauty and choice. The famous cedar trees grow high in the mountains, while the lower slopes bear grapes, apricots, plums, peaches, figs, olives and barley, often on terraces painstakingly cut out from the mountainsides. On the coastal plain, citrus fruit, bananas and vegetables are cultivated, with radishes and beans grown in tiny patches.
LANGUAGE: The official language is Arabic. French is the second most commonly used language and English is also spoken, especially in business circles. Kurdish and Armenian are spoken by a small percentage of the population.
RELIGION: 57% Muslim (Shia majority), 42% Christian (mostly Roman Catholic) and 1% others including Jewish.
TIME: GMT + 2 (GMT + 3 from March to September).
ELECTRICITY: 110/220 volts AC, 50Hz. Subject to fluctuation and blackouts.
COMMUNICATIONS: Telephone: IDD is available. Country code: 961. Outgoing international code: 00. **Telex:** International facilities available. Contact Embassy for details. **Post:** Service to Europe usually takes four days, to the USA five or six days. **Press:** There are a number of English-language dailies. Most newspapers are in Arabic or French. The papers tend to have strong political affiliations.
BBC World Service and Voice of America frequencies: From time to time these change. See the section *How to Use this Book* for more information.
BBC:
| MHz | 21.47 | 15.57 | 9.410 | 1.323 |
Voice of America:
| MHz | 9.670 | 6.040 | 5.995 | 1.260 |

PASSPORT/VISA

Regulations and requirements may be subject to change at short notice, and you are advised to contact the appropriate diplomatic or consular authority before finalising your travel arrangements. Details of these may be found at the head of this country's entry. Any numbers in the chart refer to the footnotes below.

	Passport Required?	Visa Required?	Return Ticket Required?
Full British	Yes	Yes	Yes
BVP	Not valid	-	-
Australian	Yes	Yes	Yes
Canadian	Yes	Yes	Yes
USA	Yes	Yes	Yes
Other EU (As of 31/12/94)	Yes	Yes	Yes
Japanese	Yes	Yes	Yes

Restricted entry: Passports containing a visa for Israel, valid or expired, used or unused, are not valid for travel to Lebanon.
PASSPORTS: Valid passport required by all except nationals of Syria arriving from their country with a valid national ID. Passports must be valid for at least 6 months beyond the estimated duration of stay in Lebanon.
British Visitors Passport: Not acceptable.
VISAS: Required by all except nationals of Bahrain, Kuwait, Oman, Qatar, Saudi Arabia, Syria and United Arab Emirates.
Types of visa: Transit, Visitor and Business; *Single-entry* – £12, *Multiple-entry* – £24. Employment visas are not being issued by the Embassy unless agreed by both the Ministry of Labour and the Sûreté Générale in Beirut.
Validity: Visitor visas are generally valid for between 2

weeks and 3 months and are renewable on request when in the country. Transit visas are valid for between 24 hours and 2 weeks.
Application to: Consulate (or Consular section at Embassy). It is necessary for visitors to apply in person if resident in London, unless they are applying as part of a group. For addresses, see top of entry.
Application requirements: *Business visas:* (a) Valid passport. (b) Invitation telex from Lebanese company host to Embassy in London. (c) Letter from applicant's company in the UK. (d) 2 completed application forms. (e) 2 passport-size photos. (f) Fee.
Working days required: 48 hours.
Temporary residence: Formalities for temporary residence will be arranged in Lebanon.

MONEY

Currency: Lebanese Pound (L£) = 100 piastres. Notes are in denominations of L£1000, 500, 250, 100, 50, 25, 10, 5 and 1. Coins are in denominations of L£1, and 50, 25, 10, 5, 2.5 and 1 piastres.
Credit cards: Limited acceptance of Access/Mastercard, Diners Club and Visa. Check with your credit card company for details of merchant acceptability and other services which may be available.
Travellers cheques: Limited acceptance.
Exchange rate indicators: The following figures are included as a guide to the movements of the Lebanese Pound against Sterling and the US Dollar:
Date:	Oct '92	Sep '93	Jan '94	Jan '95
£1.00=	3189.6	2637.5	2531.4	2576.7
$1.00=	2009.8	1727.3	1711	1647
Currency restrictions: There are no restrictions on the import or export of foreign or local currency.
Banking hours: 0830-1230 Monday to Saturday.

DUTY FREE

The following goods may be imported into Lebanon without incurring customs duty:
* 200 cigarettes or 200g cigars or 200g of tobacco; 1 litre of alcohol; 60g of perfume.
Note [*]: From June to October some visitors may be allowed *500 cigarettes or 500g of tobacco.* A valid import licence is required for any arms or ammunition.

PUBLIC HOLIDAYS

Jan 1 '95 New Year's Day. **Feb 9** Feast of St Marron. **Mar 3** Eid al-Fitr (End of Ramadan). **Mar 22** Arab League Anniversary. **Apr 17** Easter Monday (Western Church). **Apr 21-24** Easter (Eastern Church). **May 10** Eid al-Adha (Feast of the Sacrifice). **May 25** Ascension Day (Western Church). **May 31** Islamic New Year. **Jun 9** Ashoura. **Aug 9** Mouloud (Prophet's Birthday). **Aug 15** Assumption Day. **Nov 1** All Saints' Day. **Nov 22** Independence Day. **Dec 20** Leilat al-Meiraj (Ascension of the Prophet). **Dec 25** Christmas Day. **Dec 31** Evacuation Day. **Jan 1 '96** New Year's Day. **Feb 9** Feast of St Marron. **Feb 22** Eid al-Fitr (End of Ramadan). **Mar 22** Arab League Anniversary. **Apr 8** Easter Monday (Western Church). **Apr 12-15** Easter (Eastern Church).
Note: Muslim festivals are timed according to local sightings of various phases of the Moon and the dates given above are approximations. During the lunar month of Ramadan that precedes Eid al-Fitr, Muslims fast during the day and feast at night and normal business patterns may be interrupted. Many restaurants are closed during the day and there may be restrictions on smoking and drinking. Some disruption may continue into Eid al-Fitr itself. Eid al-Fitr and Eid al-Adha may last anything from two to ten days, depending on the region. For more information see the section *World of Islam* at the back of the book.

HEALTH

Regulations and requirements may be subject to change at short notice, and you are advised to contact your doctor well in advance of your intended date of departure. Any numbers in the chart refer to the footnotes below.

	Special Precautions?	Certificate Required?
Yellow Fever	No	1
Cholera	Yes	2
Typhoid & Polio	Yes	-
Malaria	No	-
Food & Drink	3	-

[1]: A yellow fever vaccination certificate is required from travellers arriving from infected areas.
[2]: Following WHO guidelines issued in 1973, a cholera vaccination certificate is not a condition of entry to Lebanon. However, cholera is a risk in this country and

precautions are essential. Up-to-date advice should be sought before deciding whether these precautions should include vaccination, as medical opinion is divided over its effectiveness. See the *Health* section at the back of the book.
[3]: Mains water is normally chlorinated, and whilst relatively safe may cause mild abdominal upsets. Bottled water is available and is advised for the first few weeks of the stay. Drinking water outside main towns and cities is likely to be contaminated and sterilisation is considered essential. Milk is pasteurised and dairy products are safe for consumption. Local meat, poultry, seafood, fruit and vegetables are generally considered safe to eat.
Rabies is present. For those at high risk, vaccination before arrival should be considered. If you are bitten abroad, seek medical advice without delay. For more information, consult the *Health* section at the back of the book.
Health care: Health insurance is essential.

TRAVEL - International

AIR: The national airline is *Middle East Airlines – Air Liban (ME).*
Approximate flight time: From London to Beirut is 5 hours 5 minutes.
International airport: *Beirut International (BEY)* (Khaldeh) is 16km (10 miles) south of the city (travel time – 20 minutes). Duty-free facilities are available. Bus and yellow taxi services are available to the city.
SEA: Main international ports are Beirut, Tripoli, Jounieh, Tyre and Sidon. No cruise ships put in at any of the Lebanese ports.
RAIL: There are no passenger services operating at present.
ROAD: Best international routes are via Turkey and Aleppo–Homs and Lattaguieh in Syria along the north–south coastal road, and also the Beirut–Damascus trunk road. Bus services are available from Europe. For details, contact the Embassy. Communications are often disrupted due to the unstable political situation. Refer to the Embassy for travel advice.

TRAVEL - Internal

AIR: *Middle East Airlines – Air Liban (ME)* run internal flights to major cities.
SEA: Ports are served by coastal passenger ferries. For details, contact the Embassy.
ROAD: Traffic drives on the right. **Bus:** Intercity buses run by private companies are cheap and efficient, but not comfortable. Services can be disrupted. **Taxi:** Intercity taxis operate throughout Beirut and Lebanon. Travel is normally shared. Prices are negotiated in advance. Town taxis have red licence plates, and an official tariff. There is a surcharge of 50% after 2200. **Car hire:** Self-drive cars are available, but chauffeur-driven vehicles are recommended. Check with the National Council of Tourism. **Documentation:** An International Driving Permit is recommended, although it is not legally required. A temporary licence to drive is available from local authorities on presentation of a valid British or Northern Ireland driving licence. Green Card insurance is required. **Note:** Road travel can be dangerous due to the political situation.
URBAN: In Beirut, private shared taxis have provided the only public transport since normal bus services were suspended in 1975. They only operate during daylight hours.

ACCOMMODATION

HOTELS: Hotels are available to suit all budgets, but the availability of accommodation is unpredictable due to the unstable political situation within Lebanon, with many hotels closed. Check reservations very carefully through Lebanese representatives at home before departing. Winter and summer rates are the same. The volatile situation means that all rates may be subject to considerable variation. All accommodation rates are subject to a 15% service charge. **Grading:** Hotels are classified from **1** to **4 stars** (**A** and **B** within each class).
GUEST-HOUSES: Local hostels are available in coastal villages with reasonable prices.
SELF-CATERING: Furnished and other apartments are available for rent.
CAMPING/YOUTH HOSTELS: There are youth hostels in major towns. Youth Centre (part of the National Tourism Council) provides information on campsites, cheap rooms, youth hostels and work camps.

RESORTS & EXCURSIONS

Beirut is at the crossing of three continents. It is a city of many sects, a fact which has contributed to the country's recent tragic history of violence. Despite this, life in many parts of the city continues in a surprisingly calm fashion, with shoppers in the streets and sunbathers on beaches. The city is deeply divided; the most obvious manifestation of this is the 'Green Line' which separates Muslim West Beirut from the Christian East. The city is, at present, in a process of reconstruction. There is still a huge amount of rebuilding to do but, if peace holds, it may once again become a popular destination for tourists and holidaymakers. Its seafront location boasts beaches, clifftops, restaurants and, until recently, theatres and a dazzling variety of shopping possibilities.
Tripoli, the country's second city, still retains much of its provincial charm. There are two parts – the port area and the city proper – which are divided by acres of fragrant orange plantations.
Sidon is a city with a sea castle built of stones from Roman remains and it offers well-stocked markets.
Tyre is out of bounds to ordinary citizens, but it is well worth persisting with the local authorities to see the remains of the ancient city which are immense and very impressive. The chariot-racing arena has been perfectly preserved.
Byblos is reputed to be the oldest town in the world, with Phoenician, Egyptian and Byzantine influences much apparent. Fishing boats and pleasure craft ply the harbour.
Beiteddine, in the *Chouf Mountains,* is the site of the palace built by the Amir Bishir in the 19th century. The courtyard and state rooms are well worth a visit.
Baalbek contains one of the best-preserved temple areas of the Roman world still in existence. It is, in fact, a complex of several temples behind which soar the columns of the *Temple of Jupiter.*

SOCIAL PROFILE

FOOD & DRINK: In Beirut there is every kind of restaurant: French, Italian, German, Austrian, Scandinavian, Greek, Chinese, Japanese, American, Indian, Malaysian, Spanish and Filipino. Good Arab food is available everywhere. A dish unique to Lebanon is *kibbe,* made of lamb or fish pounded to a fine paste, with burghol or cracked wheat, and served raw or baked in flat trays or rolled into balls and fried. Also recommended is the traditional Lebanese *maza,* a range of up to 40 small dishes served as hors d'oeuvres with *arak.* Main courses are likely to include Lebanese staple ingredients of vegetables, rice and mutton. *Lahm mishwi* (pieces of mutton with onions, peppers and tomato) is popular. Other typical dishes are *tabbouli, houmos* and *mtabbal.* Lebanese palates also favour pastries with local varieties of baked doughs flavoured with nuts, cream and syrup. A meal is always concluded with a wide range of fruits including melon, apples, oranges, persimmon, tangerines, cactus fruit, grapes and figs. Table service is the norm in restaurants. **Drink:** Bars have table and/or counter service. Although many Lebanese are Muslim, alcohol is not prohibited.
NIGHTLIFE: Nightclubs spice the evenings in Beirut (although many have now been closed) and mountain resorts. Entertainment ranges from solo guitarists to orchestras and floor shows. Some British-type pubs can be found in Beirut. There are many cinemas presenting the latest films from all over the world. The Casino du Liban in Maameltain earns its international reputation with its lavish gambling halls, luxurious restaurants and cabaret.
SHOPPING: Lebanon's traditional *souks* or markets are found all over the country offering decorative and precious handmade items at very low prices. Special purchases include traditional pottery and glassware, as well as cutlery made of tempered steel or copper with ram or buffalo bone handles shaped in the form of beautiful and colourful birds' heads. Brass and copper goods include braziers, bowls, fluted jugs, ashtrays, swords and doorstops, all attractively designed and hand-engraved. Cloth, silk and wool kaftans, *abayas* (embroidered nightwear) and table linen are popular, as are handworked gold and silver. Shops sell the latest Western goods including clothes, cosmetics, furniture and electrical appliances.
SPORT: Watersports: The Mediterranean coast offers **swimming, scuba diving, snorkelling, water-skiing** and **sailing** all year. Many beaches offer full facilities and most have guest memberships and freshwater pools to supplement the sea. Boats may be rented by **anglers** along the coast, but most local anglers prefer to fish in the deep waters by the shore. **Winter sports:** Mountain resorts such as The Lebanon Cedars, Farayam, Laklouk and Karrat Bakish offer excellent accommodation and winter sports facilities. **Golf:** The Golf Club of Lebanon has a 9-hole (par 72) course available to visitors on application for guest membership (details from hotel or Tourist Police). **Tennis:** There is a wide selection of tennis courts in major towns and resorts. **Horseriding:** Lebanon's Equestrian Federation now includes six riding clubs with excellent Arab horses available. **Spectator sports:** Numerous local clubs play **football** all year, ranging from small playing fields to national competitions.
SOCIAL CONVENTIONS: Handshaking is the normal form of greeting. Many Lebanese are Muslim and their traditions and customs should be respected. It is acceptable to give a small gift, particularly if invited home for a meal. As far as dress is concerned, casual dress is suitable for daytime wear, except in main towns where dress tends to be rather formal. Smarter hotels and restaurants often require guests to dress for dinner. Smoking is common and acceptable unless specified otherwise. **Tipping:** Service is generally included in hotel and restaurant bills and it is not necessary to tip taxi-drivers.

BUSINESS PROFILE

ECONOMY: Before the onset of the ruinous civil war in the mid-1970s, Beirut was the major financial and commercial centre for the Middle East. However, 17 years of civil war almost completely destroyed the Lebanese economy. The physical destruction wrought by the fighting was exacerbated by the fragmentation of the country into a patchwork of warring fiefdoms. Now, following the end of the civil war, Lebanon is only just beginning to re-emerge as a properly functioning society and economy. Reconstruction financed by expatriate capital and international aid and investment is under way but the task is a vast one, beginning with the restoration of the most basic amenities, and it will be many years before it is completed. In the meantime, Lebanon's agricultural economy, which accounted for about a quarter of pre-war GDP, is growing quickly with citrus fruit, olives and cereals as the main products. Some light industries, including textiles, processed foods and industrial machinery, are showing signs of recovery. There are no significant mineral resources. It is the future of the services sector, which dominated the pre-war Lebanese economy, which will prove decisive in the long term. The banking industry, which showed amazing resilience throughout the fighting, has recovered well, as has transit trade, which was all but wiped out. Further grounds for optimism can be found in the performance of basic economic indicators such as inflation, budget deficit and currency stability, which have benfited from reasonably sound fiscal management. Saudi Arabia is the principal market for Lebanese exports, while the EU countries – particularly Italy and France – are the main suppliers of the country's imports.
BUSINESS: Business people usually wear a jacket and tie. English is spoken by many local business people and normal courtesies are observed. Appointments and business cards are used. Best months for business visits are October to December and February to June. **Office hours:** *June to October:* 0800-1300 Monday to Saturday. *November to May:* 0830-1230 and 1500-1800 Monday to Friday, 0830-1230 Saturday.
COMMERCIAL INFORMATION: The following organisation can offer advice: Beirut Chamber of Commerce and Industry, PO Box 11-1801, Sanayeh, Beirut. Tel: (1) 349 530. Fax: (1) 865 802. Telex: 22269.

CLIMATE

There are four seasons. Summer (June to September) is hot on the coast and cooler in the mountains. Spring and autumn are warm and pleasant. Winter (December to mid-March) is mostly rainy, with snow in the mountains.

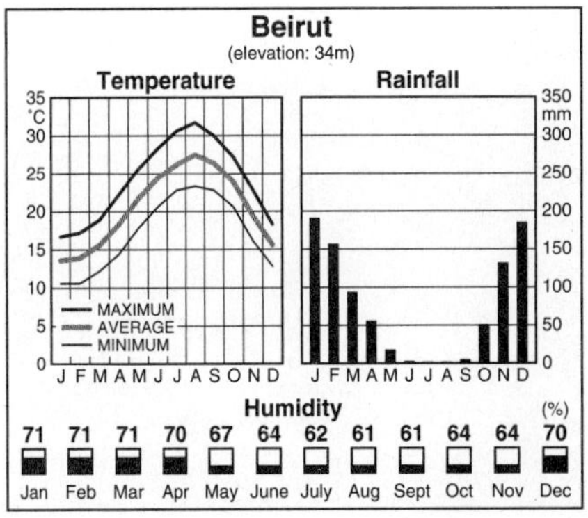
Beirut
(elevation: 34m)
Temperature
Rainfall
35 °C 30 25 20 15 10 5 0
350 mm 300 250 200 150 100 50 0
MAXIMUM
AVERAGE
MINIMUM
J F M A M J J A S O N D
J F M A M J J A S O N D
Humidity
(%)
71 71 71 70 67 64 62 61 61 64 64 70
Jan Feb Mar Apr May June July Aug Sept Oct Nov Dec

Lesotho

□ international airport

Location: Southern Africa.

Lesotho Tourist Board
PO Box 1378, Maseru 100, Lesotho
Tel: 313 760 *or* 312 896 (information). Fax: 310 108.
Telex: 4280 (a/b LO).

High Commission for the Kingdom of Lesotho
7 Chesham Place, Belgravia, London SW1 8HN
Tel: (0171) 235 5686. Fax: (0171) 235 5023. Telex:
262995. Opening hours: 0900-1600 Monday to Friday.

British High Commission
PO Box Ms 521, Maseru 100, Lesotho
Tel: 313 961. Fax: 310 120. Telex: 4343 (a/b LO).

Embassy of the Kingdom of Lesotho
2511 Massachusetts Avenue, NW, Washington, DC
20008
Tel: (202) 797 5533/4/5/6. Fax: (202) 234 6815.

Embassy of the United States of America
PO Box 333, Maseru 100, Lesotho
Tel: 312 666. Fax: 310 116. Telex: 4506 (a/b LO).

High Commission for the Kingdom of Lesotho
202 Clemow Avenue, Ottawa, Ontario K1S 2B4
Tel: (613) 236 9449 *or* 236 0960. Fax: (613) 238 3341.
Consulates in: Montréal and Vancouver.
**The Canadian Embassy in Pretoria deals with
enquiries relating to Lesotho (see *South Africa* later in
this book).**

Embassy of the Kingdom of Lesotho
Godeesberger Alle 53175 Bonn 50, Federal Republic of
Germany
Tel: (228) 376 868/9. Fax: (228) 379 947.

AREA: 30,355 sq km (11,720 sq miles).
POPULATION: 1,700,000 (1989 estimate).
POPULATION DENSITY: 56 per sq km.
CAPITAL: Maseru. **Population:** 109,000 (1986).
GEOGRAPHY: Lesotho is a landlocked country
surrounded on all sides by South Africa. It is a
mountainous kingdom situated at the highest part of the
Drakensberg escarpment on the eastern rim of the South
African plateau. Its mountainous terrain is cut by
countless valleys and ravines making it a country of great
beauty. To the west the land descends through a foothill
zone of rolling hills to a lowland belt along the border
where two-thirds of the population live. Three large
rivers, the Orange, the Caledon and the Tugela, rise in the
mountains.
LANGUAGE: Sesotho and English.
RELIGION: 39% Catholic, 24% Lesotho Evangelical.
The remainder belong to other denominations.
TIME: GMT + 2.
ELECTRICITY: 220-240 volts AC, 50Hz.
COMMUNICATIONS: Telephone: IDD is available to
some cities. Country code: 266 (no area codes). Outgoing
international code: 00. There is a limited internal
telephone network. **Telex/telegram:** Limited facilities
exist in main post offices and hotels. For charges contact
the High Commission or Embassy. **Post:** Post offices are
generally open 0800-1300 and 1400-1630 Monday to
Friday, 0800-1200 Saturday. **Press:** *Lesotho Today* is the
major English language newspaper. The *Mirror* is also
published in English.
**BBC World Service and Voice of America
frequencies:** From time to time these change. See the

section *How to Use this Book* for more information.
BBC:

MHz	1.97			

A service is also available on 90.2FM.
Voice of America:

MHz	21.49	15.60	9.525	6.035

PASSPORT/VISA

Regulations and requirements may be subject to change at short notice, and you are advised to contact the appropriate diplomatic or consular authority before finalising travel arrangements. Details of these may be found at the head of this country's entry. Any numbers in the chart refer to the footnotes below.

	Passport Required?	Visa Required?	Return Ticket Required?
Full British	Yes	No/1	Yes
BVP	Not valid	-	-
Australian	Yes	Yes	Yes
Canadian	Yes	Yes	Yes
USA	Yes	Yes	Yes
Other EU (As of 31/12/94)	Yes	Yes/1	Yes
Japanese	Yes	Yes	Yes

Note: Visitors travelling via South Africa will need to
comply with South African passport/visa regulations.
PASSPORTS: Required by all.

PHOTO CREDIT: DI JONES

SOUTH AFRICA

To Bethlehem

Mont-aux-
Sources
3282m △

Oxbow

Butha-
Buthe

Hlotse

*Thaba
Phatsoa* △

Lejone

Teyateyaneng

To Bloemfontein

■MASERU
Thaba Bosiu
HA KHOTSO
✈ God Help
Roma Me Pass
*Thaba Putsoa
Pass*

Bokong

Mokhotlong

Thabana-
Ntlenyana
3482m △

To Durban

Marakabei

Linakeng

LESOTHO

Ramabanta

Semonkong

Mafeteng

*Maletsunyane
Falls*

Qabane

Nkau

Patlong

SEHLABATHEBE
NATIONAL PARK

Mohales
Hoek

Mphaki

Qacha's Nek

To Kokstad/Durban

PAUL KRUGER
INSCRIPTION

Moyeni

Orange

To
Aliwal North

SOUTH AFRICA

✈ International
airport

— Main road

⬥ Historical site

Land over 3000m

Land over 2000m

Land over 1000m

100km
50mls

British Visitors Passport: Not accepted.
VISAS: Required by all except the following for visits of up to 30 days:
(a) **[1]** holders of British passports in which they are described as British subjects being 'Citizen of the United Kingdom and Colonies';
(b) nationals of all Commonwealth countries (except nationals of Australia, Canada, Ghana, India and Nigeria who *do* need visas);
(c) nationals of Iceland, Israel, Madagascar, Norway, Sweden and Switzerland.
Note: At the time of writing visa regulations for Lesotho are under review and therefore might be subject to change. Check with nearest Embassy for up-to-date information.
Types of visa: Tourist, Business and Transit. Cost: *Single-entry* – £5, *Multiple-entry* – £10.
Validity: Up to 3 months (Single-entry) or 6 months (Multiple-entry).
Application to: Consulate (or Consular section at Embassy or High Commission). For addresses, see top of entry.
Application requirements: (a) 2 application forms. (b) 2 passport-size photos. (c) Return ticket. (d) Business sponsor's letter for Business visa.
Working days required: 1.
Temporary residence: Apply to the Ministry of Home Affairs, Maseru. Enquire at Embassy for details.

MONEY

Currency: Loti (Lo) = 100 lisente. Notes are in denominations of Lo50, 20, 10, 5 and 2. Coins are in denominations of Lo1, and 50, 25, 10, 5, 2 and 1 lisente. The plural of 'loti' is 'maloti' and the singular of 'lisente' is 'sente'. The South African Rand is accepted as legal currency on a par with the Loti.
Credit cards: Limited acceptance of Visa, Access/

Mastercard and Diners Club. Check with your credit card company for details of merchant acceptability and other services which may be available.
Travellers cheques: Limited use outside the capital.
Exchange rate indicators: The following figures are included as a guide to the movements of the Loti against Sterling and the US Dollar:

Date:	Oct '92	Sep '93	Jan '94	Jan '95
£1.00=	4.68	5.16	5.03	5.55
$1.00=	2.95	3.38	3.40	3.54

Currency restrictions: The import and export of currency is not restricted, but must be done in consultation with a bank.
Banking hours: 0830-1530 Monday, Tuesday, Thursday and Friday, 0830-1300 Wednesday and 0830-1100 Saturday.

DUTY FREE

The following goods may be imported into Lesotho without incurring customs duty:
400 cigarettes and 50 cigars and 250g of tobacco; 1 litre of alcohol; perfume not exceeding 300ml.
Note: No alcohol may be imported by nationals of South Africa. Sporting equipment may be imported as part of passenger's luggage.

PUBLIC HOLIDAYS

Jan 1 '95 New Year's Day. **Mar 12** Moshoeshoe's Day. **Mar 21** Tree Planting Day. **Apr 14-17** Easter. **May 25** Ascension Day. **Jul 3** Family Day. **Jul 17** King's Birthday. **Oct 2** National Sports Day. **Oct 4** Independence Day. **Dec 25** Christmas Day. **Dec 26** Boxing Day. **Jan 1 '96** New Year's Day. **Mar 12** Moshoeshoe's Day. **Apr 5-8** Easter.

HEALTH

Regulations and requirements may be subject to change at short notice, and you are advised to contact your doctor well in advance of your intended date of departure. Any numbers in the chart refer to the footnotes below.	Special Precautions?	Certificate Required?
Yellow Fever	Yes	1
Cholera	Yes	-
Typhoid & Polio	Yes	-
Malaria	No	-
Food & Drink	2	-

[1]: Yellow fever vaccination certificate required of travellers arriving from infected areas.
[2]: Tap water is considered safe to drink. However, drinking water outside main cities and towns may be contaminated and sterilisation is advisable. Milk is pasteurised and dairy products are safe for consumption. Local meat, poultry, seafood, fruit and vegetables are generally considered safe to eat.
Lesotho is free of *bilharzia* (schistosomiasis) and people may swim in fresh water without danger.
Health care: Health insurance is recommended.
Note: Since the most practical way to reach Lesotho is to go through South Africa, it will also be necessary to conform to South African health regulations.

TRAVEL - International

AIR: Lesotho's national airline is *Lesotho Airways Corporation.*
Approximate flight time: From London to Maseru is 14 hours (including 2 hours for stopover).
International airport: *Maseru (MSU)* (Moshoeshoe I International) is 18km (11 miles) south of Maseru. Buses go to the city (travel time – 35 minutes). Airport facilities include bank (1200-1400), bureau de change (0700-1800 Tuesday and Friday), bar, restaurant and flight information (all open 0700-1800 in winter, 0730-1730 in summer) and car rental (*Avis* and *Budget*).
Departure tax: Lo20. Transit passengers and children under five years of age are exempt.
ROAD: Routes exist to the west and south from South Africa. There are three major road links to South Africa: at Maseru Bridge (0600-2200), at Ficksburg Bridge in the north (open 24 hours) and at Van Rooyen's Gate in the south (0600-2000). Other crossing points exist, but the road surfaces are less good. All of these are open by 0800, but some close as early as 1600.

TRAVEL - Internal

AIR: Charter flights are available within Lesotho providing connections to the main towns.
ROAD: Traffic drives on the left. The road system is underdeveloped, and few roads are paved. The main road which runs through the towns around the western and southern borders is tarred, but other roads can be impassable during the rainy season. There are **minibuses** in the lowlands. **Documentation:** International Driving Permit recommended. National driving licences are normally valid, providing that they are either in English or accompanied by a certified translation. Enquire at the High Commission or Embassy for details.
JOURNEY TIMES: The following chart gives journey times (in hours and minutes) from Maseru to other towns in Lesotho.

	Air	Road
Teyateyaneng	-	0.20
Leribe	0.20	1.00
Butha-Buthe	-	1.30
Mokhotlong	0.35	7.00
Qachas Nek	0.45	8.00
Thabatseka	0.25	5.00
Mohales Hoek	0.20	1.30
Quthing	0.30	3.00
Mafeteng	0.15	1.00

ACCOMMODATION

HOTELS: There are hotels of varying quality in the main towns and mountain lodges giving access to the wilder regions. There are several hotels in Maseru of international standard. Further information can be obtained from the Lesotho Hotels & Hospitality Association, PO Box 1072, Maseru 100, Lesotho. Tel: 325 800.
LODGES: Commercial concerns have built several lodges providing bungalow accommodation.
YOUTH HOSTELS: Current information can be obtained from the Youth Hostel Association, PO Box 970, Maseru. Tel: 332 900.

RESORTS & EXCURSIONS

Maseru is the obvious stepping-off point for a holiday. There are local highlights to visit such as the historical cemetery and the fascinating architecture of the *King's Palace* and the *Prime Minister's Residence*. From Maseru you can take many day trips, either independently or by luxury coach, visiting surrounding points of interest.
Near Maseru, the *Ha Khotso bushmen rock paintings* make an interesting visit. Also nearby is *Thaba Bosiu*, a flat-topped hill where the Basotho made a last heroic

stand against the Boers. Many of their chiefs are buried here.

The *Outward Bound Centre* in Lesotho is situated at **Thaba Phatsoa** in the foothills of the *Malutis*. Half a million Rand have been spent on the camp, equipment and transport. The staff are skilled instructors using teaching techniques perfected in the Outward Bound's 33 centres throughout the world. Outward Bound is a concept of providing young people with the opportunity of encountering the more rugged aspects of nature and extending their own physical and mental capacities. Courses include rock-climbing, mountaineering, canoeing, sailing, camping and riding. For more information contact the Outward Bound Association, PO Box 367, Leribe 300, Lesotho. Tel: (11) 659 0524 (in Johannesburg).

Pony trekking: At the moment three treks are offered, two of them covering the great falls at *Ribaneng, Ketane* and *Maletsunyane*, the latter being particularly noteworthy as it is the highest single-drop fall in southern Africa. There is a choice of return, once **Semonkong** has been reached, between going back to Maseru by road on the fourth day or continuing the pony ride for another two days to the *Ha Ramabanta*, where motor transport will be available for the return to Maseru. The other route is the *Molimo Nthuse* circular trip, starting at the *Molimo Nthuse* ('God Help Me') *Centre* (the actual base for the *Basotho Pony Trekking Centre*) and going over *Thaba Putsoa* ('Blue Mountain') *Pass* to reach *Ha Marakabei-Senqunyane Lodge* on the second day. The return trip via **Molikaliko** and **Qiloane Falls** reaches Molimo Nthuse from a different direction on the fifth day. Unlike the three falls of the first trip, Qiloane is a wide fall with several smaller drops. Overnight stops are usually made in the rural areas in the huts of the remote Basotho where a taste of real Basotho life is experienced. All the routes pass through magnificent countryside.

The South: The southern region of Lesotho is being promoted for tourism, with hotels at **Moyeni, Mohales Hoek** and the new building of the *Orange River Hotel* which has facilities for swimming, horseriding, mountain climbing and hiking. Worth visiting in the district are the *Motlejoeng Caves*, 2km (1.2 miles) south of Mahale's Hoek; the dinosaur footprints at **Maphutseng** and **Moyeni**; the *Masitise Cave House* and the petrified forest on the mountain of *Thaba-Ts'oeu*. In the southeast, in the region bordering South Africa, is one of the most beautiful parts of Lesotho, if not southern Africa. It is ideal for trekking. Places of most interest include **Ramanbanta, Semonkong** (where the *Maletsunyane Waterfalls* are to be found) and the **Sehlabathebe National Park.**

SOCIAL PROFILE

FOOD & DRINK: The main hotels in Maseru serve international food, but there are also some interesting places to dine in the main towns. Hotels and restaurants in Lesotho cater for all nationalities. There are *halal* foods and seafood. Cooking styles include French, Italian and Continental, with Chinese dishes at the China Garden Restaurant in Maseru. Much food has to be imported from South Africa, but freshwater fish is in abundant supply. **Drink:** Good beer is widely available and better establishments will have a good choice of beers, spirits and wines.

NIGHTLIFE: Some hotels and restaurants have live entertainment. There are also several cinemas in Maseru and there are casinos at the two major international hotels.

SHOPPING: There are many handicraft shops and centres selling items including Lesotho's famous conical hats; grass-woven articles (mats, brooms and baskets); pottery; wool and mohair rugs; tapestries and other textiles; rock painting reproductions; traditional seed, clay bead and porcupine quill jewellery; silver and gold items; copper work (particularly chess sets of African design) and ebony items. **Shopping hours:** 0800-1700 Monday to Friday; 0800-1300 Saturday.

SPORT: Fishing: Lesotho's dams and rivers contain local and imported fish. Brown and rainbow trout and carp provide satisfying sport for anglers.

Hiking/climbing: Pony trekking and mountain climbing are popular and ideal ways of seeing the rugged beauty of the land. **Birdwatching:** As many as 279 species of birds have been recorded and keen birdwatchers should take a trip along the Mountain Road to see birds rare to southern Africa. **Swimming:** Bilharzia-free rivers and lakes and hotel pools are available for bathing. **Tennis:** Maseru has high-standard tennis courts. **Golf:** There is a 9-hole golf course. **Spectator sports: Horseracing** is a popular sport and meetings take place throughout the country. **Football** is Lesotho's national game and matches are played most Saturdays and Sundays.

SOCIAL CONVENTIONS: If spending some time in

PHOTO CREDIT: DI JONES

PHOTO CREDIT: PETER MILLIN

rural villages, it is polite to inform the Head Chief. It is likely that he will be very helpful. Normal social courtesies and a friendly, warm approach will be greatly appreciated. Dress should be practical and casual but local customs should be respected (including those regarding modesty in dress). Religion plays an important part in daily life. **Photography:** Photographs must not be taken of the following: the palace, police establishments, government offices, the airport or monetary authority buildings. **Tipping:** It is customary in restaurants and hotels to give a tip as a reward for good service.

BUSINESS PROFILE

ECONOMY: 80% of the population are engaged in agriculture; farming maize, wheat and other crops. Nonetheless, over half the country's food must be imported from South Africa. Wool, mohair and hides are important exports. Prospects for the embryonic diamond industry were dashed by the slump in world demand in the early 1980s. Since then, tourism has become the country's principal source of foreign exchange. While Lesotho's government has regularly sought both foreign aid – particularly for infrastructure programmes – and, more recently, capital investment from the Far East which Lesotho hopes to attract by promoting the country as a source of cheap labour and an export platform for the region. South Africa, which exercises something of a stranglehold over the economy, is Lesotho's major trading partner: the Southern African Customs Union provides over 95% of the country's imports. The first phase of the Lesotho Highlands Water Project to deliver water to South Africa and provide 60% of Lesotho's electricity supply will begin in 1996. The Katse Dam will improve Lesotho's economic position, as well as providing a boost for the tourism industry with the offering of sailing, canoeing and other watersports on the ensuing 35.8-sq-km (13.8 sq-mile) lake.
BUSINESS: Lightweight suit, shirt and tie should be worn for business meetings. English will be spoken by most business people. Usual business formalities should be observed, but expect a casual atmosphere and pace.
Office hours: 0800-1300 and 1400-1630 Monday to Friday; 0800-1300 Saturday. **Government office hours:** 0800-1245 and 1400-1630 Monday to Friday; 0800-1300 Saturday.
COMMERCIAL INFORMATION: The following organisations can offer advice: Ministry of Trade and Industry, PO Box 747, Maseru 100. Tel: 322 802. Fax: 310 121. Telex: 4384; *or*
Lesotho National Development Corporation, Private Bag A96, Development House, First Floor, Kingsway Road, Maseru 100. Tel: 312 012. Fax: 311 008. Telex: 4341; *or*
Lesotho Chamber of Commerce and Industry, PO Box 79, Maseru 100. Tel: 323 482.
CONFERENCES/CONVENTIONS: The Lesotho Tourist Board can provide advice (for address see top of entry).

CLIMATE

Temperate climate with well-marked seasons. Summer is the rainy season. 85% of rainfall occurs from October to April, especially in the mountains. Snow occurs in the highlands from May to September. The hottest period is from January to February. Lesotho is a land of clear blue skies and more than 300 days of sunshine.
Required clothing: During the summer, lightweight cottons with warmer wear for the evenings is needed. In winter, medium- to heavy-weight clothes are advised. Waterproofing is necessary during the rainy season.

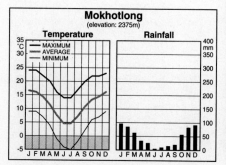

Mokhotlong
(elevation: 2375m)
Temperature　　Rainfall

PHOTO CREDIT: IVOR MIGDOLL

PHOTO CREDIT: PETER MILLIN

Liberia

□ *international airport*

Location: West Africa.

Note: Visitors are warned against travel to Liberia due to continued fighting and unsettled conditions in many areas, despite a peace accord signed in 1993 and subsequent efforts to reach an implementation agreement in September 1994. Although a safety buffer exists around Monrovia, roads outside the capital are not open for regular travel, and are heavily mined. Travellers to the interior of Liberia may be in danger of being detained, harassed, delayed, injured or killed. Monrovia's crime rate is extremely high. Foreigners have been targets of street crime and violent robbery in their homes. The police are ill-equipped and largely incapable of providing effective protection.
Source: US State Department – October 27, 1994.

Bureau of Tourism
Sinkor, Monrovia, Liberia.
Embassy of the Republic of Liberia
2 Pembridge Place, London W2 4XB
Tel: (0171) 221 1036. Opening hours: 0900-1530 Monday to Friday.
The British High Commission in Abidjan deals with enquiries relating to Liberia (see *Côte d'Ivoire* earlier in this book).
Embassy of the Republic of Liberia
5303 Colorado Avenue NW, Washington, DC 20011
Tel: (202) 723 0437-40.
Also deals with enquiries from Canada.
Embassy of the United States of America
PO Box 10-0098, 111 United Nations Drive, Mamba Point, Monrovia, Liberia
Tel: 222 991-4 *or* 226 370. Fax: 223 710 *or* 226 148.
Consulate of the Republic of Liberia

Suite 1720, 1080 Beaver Hall Hill, Montréal, Québec H22 1S8
Tel: (514) 871 4741. Fax: (514) 397 0816.
Consulate also in: Rexdale.
The Canadian Embassy in Accra deals with enquiries relating to Liberia (see *Ghana* earlier in this book).

AREA: 97,754 sq km (37,743 sq miles)
POPULATION: 2,520,000 (1991 estimate).
POPULATION DENSITY: 25.8 per sq km.
CAPITAL: Monrovia. **Population:** 421,058 (1984).
GEOGRAPHY: Liberia borders Sierra Leone, Guinea Republic and Côte d'Ivoire. The Atlantic coastline to the west is 560km (348 miles) long, of which over half is sandy beach. Lying parallel to the shore are three distinct belts. The low coastal belt is well watered by shallow lagoons, tidal creeks and mangrove swamps, behind which rises a gently undulating plateau, 500-800m (1640-2625ft) high, partly covered with dense forests. Inland and to the north is the mountain region which includes Mount Nimba at 1752m (5748ft) and Waulo Mountain at 1400m (4593ft). About half the country's population are rural dwellers.
LANGUAGE: English is the official language. The main African languages are Bassa, Kpelle and Kru.
RELIGION: Officially a Christian state; Islam is practised in the north and traditional beliefs exist throughout the country.
TIME: GMT.
ELECTRICITY: 110 volts AC, 60Hz.
COMMUNICATIONS: Telephone: IDD service to some cities. Country code: 231 (no area codes). Outgoing international code: 00. The internal network in Monrovia is gradually being extended over the country. **Telex/telegram:** Cable communication exists with Europe and USA via Dakar, but not with West Africa. **Post:** Airmail to Europe takes 5-12 days. **Press:** The Liberian press is in the English-language, with four main papers: *The Daily Observer, Mirror, Sunday Express* and *The New Liberian.*
BBC World Service and Voice of America frequencies: From time to time these change. See the section *How to Use this Book* for more information.

BBC:

MHz	17.79	15.40	15.07	12.09
Voice of America:				
MHz	11.97	9.670	6.040	5.995

PASSPORT/VISA

Regulations and requirements may be subject to change at short notice, and you are advised to contact the appropriate diplomatic or consular authority before finalising travel arrangements. Details of these may be found at the head of this country's entry. Any numbers in the chart refer to the footnotes below.

	Passport Required?	Visa Required?	Return Ticket Required?
Full British	Yes	Yes	Yes
BVP	Not valid	-	-
Australian	Yes	Yes	Yes
Canadian	Yes	Yes	Yes
USA	Yes	Yes	Yes
Other EU (As of 31/12/94)	Yes	Yes	Yes
Japanese	Yes	Yes	Yes

PASSPORTS: Valid passport required by all.
British Visitors Passport: Not acceptable.
VISAS: Required by all except:
(a) nationals of Benin, Burkina Faso, Cape Verde, Côte d'Ivoire, Gambia, Ghana, Guinea Republic, Guinea-Bissau, South Korea, Mali, Mauritania, Niger, Nigeria, Senegal, Sierra Leone and Togo;
(b) those continuing their journey to a third country within 48 hours on the next available flight, provided they hold confirmed onward tickets.
Types of visa: Tourist, Business and Resident.
Validity: Valid for 60 days from date of issue.
Application to: Consulate (or Consular section at Embassy). For addresses, see top of entry.
Application requirements: (a) Completed application form in duplicate, with a passport-size photo attached to each form. (b) Valid passport. (c) Onward ticket. (d) International yellow fever inoculation certificate.
Working days required: 1.
Temporary residence: Application should be made prior to arrival to the Ministry of Foreign Affairs, Monrovia.
Note: All visitors holding a visa issued abroad and intending to stay in Liberia for more than 15 days must report within 48 hours of their arrival to the Immigration Office, Broad Street, Monrovia. Two passport-size photos must be submitted.

MONEY

Currency: Liberian Dollar (L$) = 100 cents. The currency is pegged to the US Dollar (L$1 = US$1) and US Dollar notes are in circulation in the following denominations: US$100, 50, 20, 10, 5, 2 and 1 as legal tender, and L$5. Coins are in denominations of L$5 and 1, and 50, 25, 10, 5 and 1 cents.
Credit cards: The use of Access/Mastercard and Diners Club is limited. Check with credit card company for details of merchant acceptability and other services which may be available.
Exchange rate indicators: The following figures are included as a guide to the movements of the Liberian Dollar against Sterling and the US Dollar:

Date:	Oct '92	Sep '93	Jan '94	Jan '95
£1.00=	1.59	1.53	1.47	1.56
$1.00=	1.00	1.00	1.00	1.00

Currency restrictions: There are no restrictions on import or export of local or foreign currency.
Banking hours: 0900-1200 Monday to Thursday, 0800-1400 Friday. The Bank of Monrovia, Trubman Boulevard, Sinkor, is also open 0800-1100 Saturday.

DUTY FREE

The following goods may be imported into Liberia without incurring customs duty:
200 cigarettes or 25 cigars or 250g tobacco products; 1 litre of alcoholic beverage; 100g (4 fl oz) of perfume; goods to the value of US$125.

PUBLIC HOLIDAYS

Jan 1 '95 New Year's Day. **Feb 11** Armed Forces Day. **Mar 12** Decoration Day. **Mar 15** J J Robert's Birthday. **Apr 11** Fast and Prayer Day. **Apr 12** National Redemption Day. **Apr 14** Good Friday. **May 14** National Unification Day. **Jul 26** Independence Day. **Aug 24** Flag Day. **Nov 6** Thanksgiving Day. **Nov 12** National Memorial Day. **Nov 29** President Trubman's Birthday. **Dec 25** Christmas Day. **Jan 1 '96** New Year's Day. **Feb 11** Armed Forces Day. **Mar 12** Decoration Day. **Mar 15** J J Robert's Birthday. **Apr 5** Good Friday. **Apr 11** Fast and Prayer Day. **Apr 12** National Redemption Day.

HEALTH

Regulations and requirements may be subject to change at short notice, and you are advised to contact your doctor well in advance of your intended date of departure. Any numbers in the chart refer to the footnotes below.

	Special Precautions?	Certificate Required?
Yellow Fever	Yes	1
Cholera	Yes	2
Typhoid & Polio	Yes	-
Malaria	3	-
Food & Drink	4	-

[1]: A yellow fever vaccination certificate is required from all travellers over one year of age. Note that the certificate must be presented with all visa applications.
[2]: Following WHO guidelines issued in 1973, a cholera vaccination certificate is not a condition of entry to Liberia. However, cholera is a serious risk in this country and precautions are essential. Up-to-date advice should be sought before deciding whether these precautions should include vaccination, as medical opinion is divided over its effectiveness. See the *Health* section at the back of the book.
[3]: Malaria risk, predominantly in the malignant *falciparum* form, exists all year throughout the country. High resistance to chloroquine and resistance to sulfadoxine-pyrimethamine has been reported.
[4]: All water should be regarded as being potentially contaminated. Water used for drinking, brushing teeth or making ice should have first been boiled or otherwise sterilised. Milk is unpasteurised and should be boiled. Powdered or tinned milk is available and is advised, but make sure that it is reconstituted with pure water. Avoid dairy products which are likely to have been made from unboiled milk. Only eat well-cooked meat and fish, preferably served hot. Pork, salad and mayonnaise may carry increased risk. Vegetables should be cooked and fruit peeled.
Meningitis is a risk, depending on the area visited and time of year.
Rabies is present. For those at high risk, vaccination before arrival should be considered. If you are bitten abroad seek medical advice without delay. For more information, consult the *Health* section at the back of

the book.

Bilharzia (schistosomiasis) is present. Avoid swimming and paddling in fresh water. Swimming pools which are well-chlorinated and maintained are safe.

Health care: Chemists are well supplied with European and American medicines. There are good private physicians as well as clinics and hospitals. Medical insurance is essential.

TRAVEL - International

AIR: Liberia's national airline is *Air Liberia (NL)*. Other main airlines servicing Liberia include *Ethiopian Airlines, Aeroflot* and *Zambia Airways*.

Approximate flight time: From London to Monrovia is 9 hours 40 minutes.

International airport: *Monrovia (MLW)* (Robertsfield International) is 60km (38 miles) southeast of the city. There are bus services and taxis to and from the city. Airport facilities include restaurant, bar, duty-free shop, post office and gift shops. Some West African airlines land at *Spriggs Payne Airport* which is in the city itself.

Departure tax: US$20 must be paid by all passengers embarking for destinations abroad, except children under 12 years and those transiting within 48 hours.

SEA: There are unscheduled freighter services with passenger accommodation from European ports. The main Liberian ports are Monrovia, Buchanan, Greenville, Harper and Robertsport. The port in Monrovia is presently being expanded.

ROAD: Best routes to Liberia are through Guinea Republic, Sierra Leone and Côte d'Ivoire, but they are impassable during the rainy season. The northeastern route to Sierra Leone (via Kolahun and Kailahun) is currently closed.

TRAVEL - Internal

AIR: *Air Liberia (NL)* operates regular services from Monrovia to major towns. There are 60 airfields for small aircraft.

SEA/RIVER: There is a passenger service between Monrovia and Buchanan. Unscheduled coastal steamers may sometimes take passengers. Small craft are used for local transportation on Liberia's many rivers.

Canoe safaris: Between December and March, the Liberian Forest Development Authority arranges canoe trips upriver from Greenville, a small seaport 200km (125 miles) southeast of Monrovia.

RAIL: Three lines run inland from the coast. All are primarily used for the transport of mining produce from the interior, but the privately-owned *LAMCO* line operates a daily passenger/freight service from Buchanan to Yekepa, near the border with Côte d'Ivoire and Guinea.

ROAD: Traffic drives on the right. Difficulties in bypassing lagoons and bridging river estuaries often result in long detours and delays along the coast. Main roads are from Monrovia to Buchanan and from Monrovia to Sanniquellie with branches to Ganta and Harper. Many of the smaller roads are still untarred. Vehicle transport is limited. **Bus:** Primitive bus services between main towns may be available. **Car hire:** Self-drive or chauffeured cars may be hired from Monrovia. **Documentation:** An International Driving Permit is recommended, although it is not legally required. A temporary licence to drive is available from local authorities on presentation of a valid British or Northern Ireland driving licence and is valid for up to 30 days.

URBAN: A minibus service operates in Monrovia. Taxis are available and tipping is unnecessary.

ACCOMMODATION

HOTELS: Hotel accommodation can be quite expensive, but not extortionate by international standards. It is advisable to book well in advance, whatever the category of accommodation. There are a few air-conditioned hotels of international standard and a range of inexpensive hotels and motels. The top hotels charge from US$60 a night. Hotels in the mid-range charge from US$25-35 and tend to provide the bare minimum of necessities.

GUEST-HOUSES: There are several mission guest-houses with both cooking and laundry facilities about 4km (2 miles) from the city centre. Prices are from L$10 a night.

CAMPING: There are no official sites; camping is free. Use caution.

YOUTH HOSTELS: The YMCA is cheap, but often full, and is located on the corner of Broad and McDonald streets.

RESORTS & EXCURSIONS

Monrovia, the capital, is a sprawling city on the coast divided by inlets, lagoons and rocky headlands. The city has several nightclubs, restaurants and bars, centred on the area around Gurley Street. There are several good sandy beaches near the capital.

Providence Island, where the first settlers from the USA arrived in the early 19th century, has a museum which records both this event and the indigenous arts and crafts of the region. 80km (50 miles) from the capital is *Lake Piso*, ideal for swimming, fishing and watersports. Conducted tours of the *Firestone Rubber Plantation*, one of the largest in the world, make an interesting day excursion, situated only 50km (30 miles) from Monrovia. There are several museums and cultural centres outside the capital; contact the Embassy information department for further details. Some of the country's most beautiful beaches can be found at **Robertsport**.

The most evocative description of Liberia can be found in Graham Greene's *Journey without Maps*, an account of his overland trip across the country in 1935. Although it can now hardly pretend to be an up-to-date guide book, the descriptions and the atmosphere of the country it creates – particularly when dealing with the mysterious and jungle-rich interior – make the book a valuable and entertaining introduction for anyone planning to visit the country.

SOCIAL PROFILE

FOOD & DRINK: Liberia's hotels, motels and restaurants serve a variety of American, European, Asian and African dishes, as well as the more predictable fare of hotel dining rooms. Here, as well as in the smaller towns of the north and east, the visitor should enjoy sampling some of the more unusual West African foods in 'Cookhouses' which serve rice with traditional Liberian dishes. **Drink:** Liberia produces a lot of its own brands of alcoholic drink, which are readily available – some of the beers are excellent; wines and imported beverages are also available.

NIGHTLIFE: In Monrovia, nightlife is extensive with dozens of crowded nightclubs, discotheques and bars open until the early hours. Most of the nightlife centres are on Gurley Street. Providence Island has a bandstand and an amphitheatre where performances of traditional African music and dance are staged.

SHOPPING: Monrovia's sidestreets are crowded with tailors selling brightly coloured tie-dyed and embroidered cloth which they will make up immediately into African or European styles. Monrovia offers the shopper elegant boutiques and shops as well as modern, air-conditioned supermarkets which compete with old-fashioned stores. Liberian handicrafts include carvings in sapwood, camwood, ebony and mahogany, stone items, soapstone carvings (such as fertility symbols from the Kissi), ritual masks, metal jewellery and figurines and reed dolls of the Loma. **Shopping hours:** 0800-1300 and 1500-1800 Monday to Saturday.

SPORT: Swimming and **boating** are popular at the many sandy beaches. These include Bernard's Beach, Elwa Beach, Kenema Beach, Kendaje Beach, Sugar Beach, Cedar Beach, Cooper's Beach and Caesar's Beach, all of which charge a small entrance fee. Lake Piso is also ideal for swimming and other watersports. **Skindiving:** Season from December to May, when the sea is at its clearest. **Angling:** There is good fishing in the Saint Paul and Mesurado rivers, along the coast and at Lake Piso, where there are traditional fishing villages. **Tennis** and **golf:** There are various private clubs. **Horseriding:** There is a riding club in Monrovia. **Football** is the Liberian national sport.

SOCIAL CONVENTIONS: In Muslim areas the visitor should respect the conventions of dress and the food laws, since failure to do so will be taken as an insult. Dress is casual and must be practical, but smarter dress will be expected in hotel dining rooms and for important social functions. The visitor should be aware that the cost of living is high. Sending flowers or chocolates to hosts is inappropriate; a letter of thanks is all that is required. **Tipping:** There is no need to tip taxi drivers, but other tips are normally 50 cents.

BUSINESS PROFILE

ECONOMY: Liberia's economic development was fuelled by substantial American investment, with the result that much of the economy is under US control. 70% of the population work the land, producing rice as the staple food and palm oil, coffee and cocoa as cash

crops. Rubber, however, is the major agricultural earner. The country's major trading commodity is iron ore, which was at one time responsible for 75% of export earnings, but has since declined to about 50% with the fall in world demand for steel. The Government's efforts during the 1980s to diversify Liberia's economic base did attract some light manufacturing concerns, producing cement and other building materials, soap, shoes, umbrellas and other consumer products. Germany, Korea and Italy are Liberia's main foreign customers; Norway, Korea and Singapore are the leading importers into the country. The civil war has, however, inflicted considerable damage on Liberia's economy and trade volumes have fallen drastically. The country will take many years to recover.

BUSINESS: Business dress is informal – normally a safari suit or a shirt and tie is acceptable. The language used in business circles is English. **Office hours:** 0800-1200 and 1400-1600 Monday to Friday.

COMMERCIAL INFORMATION: The following organisation can offer advice: Liberia Chamber of Commerce, PO Box 92, Monrovia. Tel: 223 738 *or* 222 040. Telex: 44211.

CLIMATE

Hot, tropical climate with little variation in temperature. The wet season runs from May to October. The dry *Harmattan* wind blows from December to March, making the coastal belt particularly arid.

Required clothing: Lightweight cottons and linens are worn throughout the year, with waterproofing advised during the wet season.

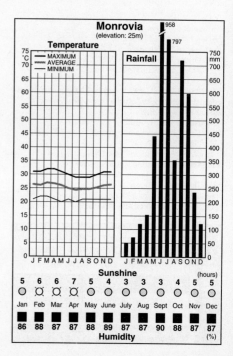

Monrovia
(elevation: 25m)

Temperature — MAXIMUM, AVERAGE, MINIMUM. Rainfall 958, 797.

Sunshine (hours): Jan 5, Feb 6, Mar 6, Apr 7, May 5, June 4, July 3, Aug 3, Sept 3, Oct 4, Nov 5, Dec 5.

Humidity (%): Jan 86, Feb 88, Mar 87, Apr 87, May 88, June 89, July 87, Aug 87, Sept 90, Oct 88, Nov 87, Dec 87.

Libya

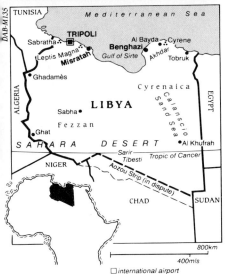

DAB-M135

International airport

Location: North Africa.

Note: The Socialist People's Libyan Arab Great Jamahirya does not currently maintain embassies in the United States of America or in the United Kingdom and it is generally very difficult to get a visa as a tourist. This situation is not likely to change in the immediate future. Since April 1992, UN Security Council sanctions have included a ban on flights to and from Libya making speedy evacuation from Libya for medical or other emergencies difficult. There have been recent incidents of criminal violence against foreign residents and tourists. It is unwise to use or carry cameras. Harsh penalties are imposed for the possession or use of alcohol and for criticising the country, its leadership or religion. *Source: Travel Advice Unit, Foreign and Commonwealth Office, London – January 5, 1995.*

Department of Tourism and Fairs
PO Box 891, Sharia Omar Mukhtar, Tripoli, Libya
Tel: (21) 32255. Telex: 20179.

Libyan Interests Section
c/o Royal Embassy of Saudi Arabia
119 Harley Street, London W1
Tel: (0171) 486 8387. Fax: (0171) 224 6349. Telex: 266767.

Libyan People's Bureau
2 rue Charles Lamoureux, 75116 Paris, France
Tel: (1) 47 04 71 60. Telex: 620643. Opening hours:
0900-1500 Monday to Friday.

British Interests Section
c/o Embassy of the Italian Republic
PO Box 4206, Sharia Uahran 1, Tripoli, Libya
Tel: (21) 31191. Fax: (21) 45753. Telex: 20296 (a/b BRITEMB LY).

Embassy of the Socialist People's Libyan Arab Jamahiriya
c/o Permanent Mission of the Socialist People's Libyan Arab Jamahiriya to the United Nations
309-315 East 48th Street, New York, NY 10017
Tel: (212) 752 5775.

AREA: 1,775,500 sq km (685,524 sq miles).
POPULATION: 3,773,000 (1988 estimate).
POPULATION DENSITY: 2.1 per sq km.
CAPITAL: Tripoli. **Population:** 481,295 (1973).
GEOGRAPHY: Libya consists mostly of huge areas of desert. It shares borders with Tunisia and Algeria in the west, and Egypt in the east, while the Sahara extends

across the southern frontiers with Niger, Chad and the Sudan. There are almost 2000km (1250 miles) of Mediterranean coast, with a low plain extending from the Tunisian border to the Jebel Akhdar (Green Mountain) area in the east. Inland the terrain becomes more hilly. Agriculture has developed mainly on the coast between Zuara and Misratah in the west and from Marsa Susa to Benghazi in the east. In the uplands of the old province of Cyrenaica and on Jebel Akhdar the vegetation is more lush. With the exception of the 'Sand Sea' of the Sarir Calanscio, and the Saharan mountains of the Sarir Tibesti, there are oases scattered throughout the country.
LANGUAGE: Arabic (which must be used for all official purposes), with some English or Italian. English is normally understood by people working in hotels, restaurants and shops.
RELIGION: Sunni Muslim.
TIME: GMT + 2.
ELECTRICITY: 150/220 volts AC, 50Hz. All services may be intermittently disrupted by power cuts.
COMMUNICATIONS: Telephone: IDD service is available. Country code: 218. Outgoing international code: 00. **Telex:** Services are available at the larger hotels. **Post:** Postal services are available in all main towns, but services are generally poor and erratic, and mail may be subject to censorship. Airmail to Europe takes approximately two weeks. **Press:** There are several newspapers and periodicals, but none is published in English. The main dailies are *Arraid* and *El Balag.*
BBC World Service and Voice of America frequencies: From time to time these change. See the section *How to Use this Book* for more information.

BBC:

MHz	21.47	17.64	15.07	9.410

Voice of America:

MHz	11.97	9.670	6.040	5.995

PASSPORT/VISA

Regulations and requirements may be subject to change at short notice, and you are advised to contact the appropriate diplomatic or consular authority before finalising travel arrangements. Details of these may be found at the head of this country's entry. Any numbers in the chart refer to the footnotes below.

	Passport Required?	Visa Required?	Return Ticket Required?
Full British	Yes	Yes	Yes
BVP	Not valid	-	-
Australian	Yes	Yes	Yes
Canadian	Yes	Yes/1	Yes
USA	Yes	Yes	Yes
Other EU (As of 31/12/94)	Yes	Yes/2	Yes
Japanese	Yes	Yes	Yes

Restricted entry and transit: Holders of Israeli passports, or holders of passports containing a valid or expired visa for Israel, will be refused entry or transit. All passports are formally inspected.
PASSPORTS: Valid passport required by all except holders of Palestinian Identity Documents and national ID cards issued to nationals of the following countries: Algeria, Bahrain, Egypt, Iraq, Jordan, Kuwait, Lebanon, Mauritania, Morocco, Oman, Qatar, Saudi Arabia, Somalia, Sudan, Syria, Tunisia, United Arab Emirates and Yemen.
British Visitors Passport: Not accepted.
VISAS: Required by all except nationals of Algeria, Bahrain, Egypt, Iraq, Jordan, Kuwait, Lebanon, Malta, Mauritania, Morocco, Oman, Qatar, Saudi Arabia, Somalia, Sudan, Syria, Tunisia, United Arab Emirates and Yemen who must hold a *No Objection Certificate* or return tickets.
Types of visa: *Work visa* (cost – £50); *Business visa* (cost – £20); *Short-stay visa* (cost – £20).
Application requirements: (a) Two completed, typed visa application forms. (b) Two recent, passport-size photos. (c) Visa authorisation telex/invitation with reference number. (d) The passport details must be translated into Arabic. A rubber stamp for this can be obtained from the passport office in the relevant country. (e) The passport must contain at least six months' validity.
Note: (a) Enquiries for visa applications should generally be addressed to any of Libya's diplomatic representatives in the relevant country or abroad (such as the Libyan Interests Section in London; address at top of entry). (b) Business visitors should be sponsored by a Libyan company who will organise the issue of a Business visa for them. (c) All travellers in possession of a Visitor's visa will be refused entry if they do not possess at least US$500 or equivalent. (d) **[1]** US nationals and their families do not require a visa if sponsered by a Libyan company. (e) **[2]** Nationals of Germany must obtain their visas in Bonn. (f) Pakistani nationals must have both a re-entry and a permanent visa.

MONEY

Currency: Libyan Dinar (LD) = 1000 dirhams. Notes are in denominations of LD10, 5 and 1, and 500 and 250 dirhams. Coins are in denominations of 100, 50, 20, 10, 5 and 1 dirhams.
Credit cards: Limited acceptance of Diners Club and Visa. Check with credit card company for details of merchant acceptability and other services which may be available.
Travellers cheques: Use of these is common.
Exchange rate indicators: The following figures are included as a guide to the movements of the Libyan Dinar against Sterling and the US Dollar:

Date:	Oct '92	Sep '93	Jan '94	Jan '95
£1.00=	0.44	0.45	0.45	0.56
$1.00=	0.28	0.30	0.30	0.36

Currency restrictions: Free import of foreign currency, subject to declaration. Export of foreign currency limited to the amount declared on import. The import and export of local currency is limited to LD20.
Banking hours: 0800-1200 Saturday to Wednesday (winter); 0800-1200 Saturday to Thursday and 1600-1700 Saturday and Wednesday (summer).

DUTY FREE

The following goods may be imported into Libya without incurring customs duty:
200 cigarettes or 250g of tobacco or 25 cigars; a reasonable amount of perfume.
Prohibited items: All alcohol is prohibited, as is the import of any kind of food. All goods made in Israel or manufactured by companies that do business with Israel are prohibited. For a full list of prohibited items contact the nearest Libyan diplomatic representative.

PUBLIC HOLIDAYS

Feb 1 '95 Start of Ramadan. **Mar 2** Eid al-Fitr (End of Ramadan). **Mar 28** British Evacuation Day. **May 10** Eid al-Adha (Feast of the Sacrifice). **May 31** Islamic New Year. **Jun 11** Evacuation Day. **Jun 9** Ashoura. **Aug 9** Mouloud (Prophet's Birthday). **Sep 1** Revolution Day. **Oct 7** Evacuation Day. **Dec 20** Leilat al-Meiraj. **Jan 22 '96** Start of Ramadan. **Feb 22** Eid al-Fitr (End of Ramadan). **Mar 28** British Evacuation Day.
Note: Muslim festivals are timed according to local sightings of various phases of the Moon and the dates given above are approximations. During the lunar month of Ramadan that precedes Eid al-Fitr, Muslims fast during the day and feast at night and normal business patterns may be interrupted. Many restaurants are closed during the day and there may be restrictions on smoking and drinking. Some disruption may continue into Eid al-Fitr itself. Eid al-Fitr and Eid al-Adha may last anything from two to ten days, depending on the region. For more information see the section *World of Islam* at the back of the book.

HEALTH

Regulations and requirements may be subject to change at short notice, and you are advised to contact your doctor well in advance of your intended date of departure. Any numbers in the chart refer to the footnotes below.

	Special Precautions?	Certificate Required?
Yellow Fever	Yes	1
Cholera	Yes	2
Typhoid & Polio	Yes	-
Malaria	3	-
Food & Drink	4	-

[1]: A yellow fever vaccination certificate is required from travellers over one year of age arriving from infected areas.
[2]: Following WHO guidelines issued in 1973, a cholera vaccination certificate is not a condition of entry to Libya. However, cholera is a risk in this country and precautions are essential. Up-to-date advice should be sought before deciding whether these precautions should include vaccination, as medical opinion is divided over its effectiveness. See the *Health* section at the back of the book.
[3]: A very limited malaria risk exists in two small areas in the southwest of the country from February to August.
[4]: Mains water is normally chlorinated, and whilst relatively safe may cause mild abdominal upsets. Bottled water is available and is advised for the first few weeks of the stay. Drinking water outside main cities and towns is likely to be contaminated and sterilisation is considered essential. Milk is unpasteurised and should be boiled. Powdered or tinned milk is available and is advised, but make sure that it is reconstituted with pure water. Avoid dairy products which are likely to have been made from unboiled milk. Only eat well-cooked

meat and fish, preferably served hot. Salad and
mayonnaise may carry increased risk. Vegetables should
be cooked and fruit peeled.
Rabies is present. For those at high risk, vaccination before
arrival should be considered. If you are bitten abroad seek
medical advice without delay. For more information,
consult the *Health* section at the back of the book.
Bilharzia (schistosomiasis) is present. Avoid swimming
and paddling in fresh water. Swimming pools which are
well-chlorinated and maintained are safe.
Health care: Medical facilities outside the main cities
are limited. Full health insurance is recommended.

TRAVEL - International

AIR: Libya's national airline is *Jamahiriya Libyan Arab
Airlines (LN)*.
Approximate flight time: From London to Tripoli is 6
hours (including stopover time).
International airports: *Tripoli International (TIP)* is
35km (21 miles) south of the city (travel time – 40
minutes). Bus and taxi services are available to the city.
Benina International (BEN) is 29km (18 miles) from
Benghazi city centre.
Sabha (SEB) is 11km (7 miles) from the town.
SEA: The main ports are as-Sider, Benghazi, Mersa
Brega, Misratah and Tripoli. A new port is presently
being built at Darna. Several shipping lines operate
services from Europe to Libya. A car ferry operated by
the Libyan government shipping line sails regularly from
Tripoli to Malta and several Italian ports. Italian lines of
Grimaldi and *Tirrenia* run similar services from Genoa
and Naples to Tripoli and Benghazi.
RAIL: There is no passenger rail system.
ROAD: Main routes to Libya are from Tunisia, Algeria,
Niger, Chad and Egypt. The border with Egypt has been
re-opened, although the most used route is via Tunisia.

TRAVEL - Internal

AIR: *Jamahiriya Libyan Arab Airlines (LN)* provide fast
and frequent internal services between Tripoli, Benghazi,
Sabha, Al Bayda, Mersa Brega, Tobruk, Misratah,
Ghadamès and Al Khufrah. They also offer an hourly
shuttle between Tripoli and Benghazi.
ROAD: The main through road follows the coast from
west to east. Main roads are Al Qaddahia–Sabha,
Sabha–Ghat, Tripoli–Sabha, Agedabia–Al Khufrah,
Garian–Jefren, Tarhouna–Homs, Mersa Susa–Ras,
Hilal–Derna and Tobruk–Jaghboub. Since 1969,
signposts other than Arabic script have been
prohibited; signs and house numbers are, in any case, rare
outside the main towns. Petrol is available throughout
Libya, and is currently about half the price of that in
Britain. There are no reliable town maps. Spare parts are
often difficult to obtain: in particular, automatic
transmissions can prove almost impossible to repair. The
quality of servicing is generally poor by European
standards, as is the standard of driving. Traffic drives on
the right. **Bus & taxi:** There is a bus service between
Tripoli and Benghazi. A minibus service operates from
Benghazi to Tobruk. Taxi fares should be agreed in
advance. **Car rental:** Self-drive cars are available in
Tripoli and Benghazi. **Documentation:** National driving
licence valid for three months. Afterwards, a Libyan
licence must be obtained.
URBAN: A substantial publicly-owned bus system
operates in Tripoli. Fares are charged on a 3-zone basis.
There is a similar system in operation in Benghazi.
Services are generally irregular and overcrowded.

ACCOMMODATION

Tripoli and Benghazi have comfortable modern hotels,
such as the Grand, Kasr Libya, Libya Palace and Marhaba
in Tripoli, and the Kasr al Jazeera and Omar Khayam in
Benghazi. There are hotels in Al Bayda, Cyrene (Shahat),
Ghadamès, Homs, Sabha, Tobruk and Derna.

RESORTS & EXCURSIONS

The old city in **Tripoli** is a typically picturesque north
African jumble of narrow alleyways; photographers are
advised not to take pictures of the port. Other historical
towns include **Leptis Magna** which is 120km (75 miles)
east of Tripoli, **Cyrene** which is 245km (150 miles) east
of Benghazi, **Sabratha** which is 75km (45 miles) west of
Tripoli and **Ghadamès**, the 'Pearl of the Desert', which
is 800km (500 miles) south of Tripoli, connected by air.

SOCIAL PROFILE

FOOD & DRINK: Since alcohol was banned by the
Government in 1969 many restaurants have closed, and
those remaining are very expensive. Hotel restaurants,
although not particularly good, are therefore often the

only eating places. Most restaurants have table service,
and although food is traditionally eaten with the right
hand only, knives and forks will generally be available.
There are no bars.
NIGHTLIFE: All nightclubs have been closed. There
are several cinemas in major towns, some showing
foreign films. There are no theatres or concert halls.
SHOPPING: *Souks* in the main towns are the
workplaces of many weavers, copper-, gold- and silversmiths and leatherworkers. There are numerous other
stalls selling a variety of items including spices, metal
engravings and various pieces of jewellery.
SPORT: There are good beaches for **swimming** away
from the municipal beaches of Tripoli and Benghazi.
Facilities for **tennis, golf** and **10-pin bowling** are
available in the major cities. Spectator sports include
football and **horseracing**.
SOCIAL CONVENTIONS: Life in Libya is regulated
fairly strictly along socialist/Islamic principles; in
general, Arab courtesies and social customs prevail and
should be respected. Women do not generally attend
typical Arab gatherings. See also the *World of Islam*
section at the back of the book. In religious buildings and
small towns women should dress modestly. Beachwear
must only be worn on the beach. Smoking is common
and codes of practice concerning smoking are the same
as in Europe. **Photography:** It is unwise to use or carry
cameras. **Tipping:** A tip of 10-20% is usually included in
hotel and restaurant bills.

BUSINESS PROFILE

ECONOMY: 95% of Libya's export earnings come from
oil, which has enabled the Qathafi government to finance
substantial military expenditure and build up the country's
economic infrastructure. The fluctuations in oil prices are
thus a major problem for the state's economic planners,
who are uncertain as to what revenues will be available
from one year to the next. Revenues in 1973 were around
US$4 billion, rising to US$21 billion in 1980, but falling to
US$5 billion by 1987. Libya now has a substantial external
debt, the servicing of which imposes further demands on
finance. The domestic economy, previously buoyant, is
now showing signs of strain. Nonetheless, sufficient funds
were found to complete a major irrigation project in 1991 –
the largest of its type in the world – which will bring water
to previously arid areas. The Government has relaxed the
previously tight restrictions on private ownership and
foreign investment in an effort to stimulate the economy.
Libya was a prime mover behind the formation of the
Union of the Arab Maghreb. Qathafi has tried similar
alliances in the past, mostly out of a desire to promote Pan-
Arabism, but on this occasion, economic considerations
seem to be more important. Italy and Germany are Libya's
major trading partners. UN economic sanctions, related to
the Lockerbie dispute, have so far had little effect on the
country beyond mild inconvenience.
BUSINESS: Shirt sleeves are acceptable business wear in
hot weather. Suits and ties are worn for more formal
occasions. Most business dealings take place with state
organisations and English is often understood. It is, however,
government policy for official documents to be in Arabic (or
translated into Arabic) and for official business to be
conducted in Arabic. Business visitors need to be fully
prepared for this. Appointments are necessary and business
cards are useful, though not widely used. Hours for
businesses and government offices fluctuate, but the working
day starts early. **Office hours:** Generally 0700-1400.
COMMERCIAL INFORMATION: The following
organisation can offer advice: Tripoli Chamber of
Commerce, Industry and Agriculture, PO Box 2321, Sharia
al-Fatah September, Tripoli. Tel: (21) 33755. Telex: 20181.

CLIMATE

Summers are hot and winters mild with cooler evenings.
The desert has hot days and cold nights.

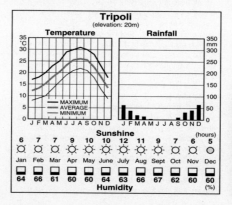

Tripoli
(elevation: 20m)

Liechtenstein

Location: Western Europe.

Note: Liechtenstein maintains very few overseas
missions and is generally represented by Switzerland.
Addresses of Swiss missions may be found in the
Switzerland entry later in this book.

Liechtenstein National Tourist Office
Postfach 139, Kirchstrasse 10, FL-9490 Vaduz,
Liechtenstein
Tel: 392 1111. Fax: 392 1618. Telex: 889488.
Swiss National Tourist Office (SNTO)
Swiss Centre, Swiss Court, London W1V 8EE
Tel: (0171) 734 1921 (general enquiries) *or* 734 4577
(trade only). Fax: (0171) 734 4577. Opening hours:
0900-1700 Monday to Friday.
British Consulate General
Dufourstrasse 56, CH-8008 Zurich, Switzerland
Tel: (1) 261 1520-6. Fax: (1) 252 8351. Telex: 816467
(a/b UKZH CH).
Deals with enquiries relating to Liechtenstein.
Consulate General of the United States of America
Zollikerstrasse 141, CH-8008 Zurich, Switzerland
Tel: (1) 422 2566. Fax: (1) 383 9814.
Deals with enquiries relating to Liechtenstein.
**The Canadian Embassy in Bern deals with enquiries
relating to Liechtenstein (see *Switzerland* later in this
book).**

AREA: 160 sq km (61.8 sq miles).
POPULATION: 29,386 (1992 estimate).
POPULATION DENSITY: 183.7 per sq km.
CAPITAL: Vaduz. **Population:** 4887 (1991).
GEOGRAPHY: Liechtenstein shares borders with
Austria and Switzerland and lies between the upper
reaches of the Rhine Valley and the Austrian Alps. The

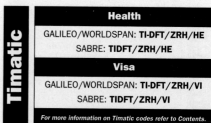

Health	
GALILEO/WORLDSPAN: **TI-DFT/ZRH/HE**	
SABRE: **TIDFT/ZRH/HE**	

Visa	
GALILEO/WORLDSPAN: **TI-DFT/ZRH/VI**	
SABRE: **TIDFT/ZRH/VI**	

For more information on Timatic codes refer to Contents.

principality is noted for its fine vineyards.
LANGUAGE: German; a dialect of Alemannish is widely spoken. English is also spoken.
RELIGION: Christian, predominantly Roman Catholic.
TIME: GMT + 1 (GMT + 2 from last Sunday in March to Saturday before last Sunday in September).
ELECTRICITY: 220 volts AC, 50Hz.
COMMUNICATIONS: Telephone: Full IDD service. Country code: 41 75. Outgoing international code: 00.
Fax: Most hotels have facilities. **Telex/telegram:** Telecommunications are available from post offices and hotels. Service is reliable and efficient. **Post:** Post office opening hours: 0800-1200 and 1400-1800 Monday to Friday, 0800-1200 Saturday (0800-1800 Monday to Friday, 0800-1100 Saturday in Vaduz). No extra charge is made for letters sent by airmail within Europe. Post to European destinations takes three to four days. **Press:** There are two daily newspapers, *Liechtensteiner Vaterland* and *Liechtensteiner Volksblatt*. Neither is printed in English.
BBC World Service and Voice of America frequencies: From time to time these change. See the section *How to Use this Book* for more information.
BBC:

| MHz | 15.07 | 12.09 | 9.750 | 3.955 |

A service is also available on 648kHz and 198kHz (0100-0500 GMT).
Voice of America:

| MHz | 9.670 | 6.040 | 5.995 | 1.197 |

PASSPORT/VISA

The passport and visa requirements for persons visiting Liechtenstein are the same as for Switzerland. For further details, see the entry for *Switzerland* later in the book.

MONEY

Currency: Swiss Franc (SFr) = 100 centimes. Notes are in denominations of SFr1000, 500, 100, 50, 20 and 10. Coins are in denominations of SFr5, 2 and 1, and 50, 20, 10 and 5 centimes. The principality of Liechtenstein belongs to the Swiss monetary area.
Credit cards: All major credit cards are accepted, American Express being particularly useful.
Travellers cheques: Widely accepted.
Exchange rate indicators: The following figures are included as a guide to the movements of the Swiss Franc against Sterling and the US Dollar:

Date:	Oct '92	Sep '93	Jan '94	Jan '95
£1.00=	2.17	2.17	2.20	2.05
$1.00=	1.37	1.42	1.50	1.31

Currency restrictions: There are no restrictions on the import and export of either local or foreign currency.
Banking hours: 0800-1200 and 1330-1630 Monday to Friday.

DUTY FREE

The customs regulations for persons visiting Liechtenstein are the same as for Switzerland. For further details, see the entry for *Switzerland* later in this book.

PUBLIC HOLIDAYS

Jan 1 '95 New Year's Day. **Jan 6** Epiphany. **Mar 19** St Joseph's Day. **Apr 14** Good Friday. **Apr 17** Easter Monday. **May 1** Labour Day. **May 25** Ascension. **Jun 5** Whit Monday. **Jun 15** Corpus Christi. **Aug 15** Assumption and National Holiday. **Sep 8** Nativity of the Virgin Mary. **Nov 1** All Saints' Day. **Dec 8** Immaculate Conception. **Dec 25** Christmas. **Dec 26** St Stephen's Day. **Jan 1 '96** New Year's Day. **Jan 6** Epiphany. **Mar 19** St Joseph's Day. **Apr 5** Good Friday. **Apr 8** Easter Monday.

HEALTH

Regulations and requirements may be subject to change at short notice, and you are advised to contact your doctor well in advance of your intended date of departure. Any numbers in the chart refer to the footnotes below.		
	Special Precautions?	**Certificate Required?**
Yellow Fever	No	No
Cholera	No	No
Typhoid & Polio	No	-
Malaria	No	-
Food & Drink	No	-

Rabies is present. For those at high risk, vaccination before arrival should be considered. If you are bitten abroad seek medical advice without delay. For more information, consult the *Health* section at the back of the book.
Health care: Health insurance is recommended. Medical facilities are scarce, but of a high standard.

TRAVEL

AIR: Approximate flight time: From London to Zurich is 1 hour 30 minutes. For further details, see the entry for *Switzerland*.
International airport: The nearest international airport (and the most convenient for travel from the UK) is *Zurich (Kloten)*, at a distance of approximately 120km (73 miles). Travel to Liechtenstein can then be continued by rail, bus or road. An autoroute connects Zurich with Liechtenstein (first exit: Balzers). Cars can be hired through agencies at the airport for this journey, and in Liechtenstein.
RAIL: The best rail access is via the Swiss border stations at Buchs (SG) or Sargans (easier and closer when coming from Zurich) or the Austrian station at Feldkirch. All are well served by express trains and connected with Vaduz by bus. From Buchs it takes only 15 minutes by bus or 10 minutes by taxi.
ROAD: An autoroute (N13) runs along Liechtenstein's Rhine frontier to Lake Constance, Austria and Germany in the north, and southwards past Chur towards St Moritz. To the west there are autoroutes to Zurich, Bern and Basel. Traffic drives on the right. **Bus:** Local buses operate between all 11 villages, and to the Liechtenstein alpine area. **Documentation:** A national driving licence is sufficient.
JOURNEY TIMES: The following chart gives approximate journey times (in hours and minutes) from Vaduz to major cities in Europe.

	Road	Rail
Zurich	1.30	1.30
Geneva	4.00	6.00
Munich	3.00	4.30
Frankfurt/M	5.30	7.30
Milan	3.30	5.00
Paris	10.00	9.00

ACCOMMODATION

HOTELS/GUEST-HOUSES: Until recently, with few notable exceptions, the best hotels (although none of deluxe standard) were in or near Vaduz, but new establishments have now been built along the Rhine Valley and among the mountains. There are 46 hotels and guest-houses in Liechtenstein, with approximately 1400 beds in total. Eight hotels have an indoor swimming pool. In the alpine region, there are around 50 chalets and other self-catering establishments. About 150 establishments belong to the Liechtensteiner Gastgewerbeverband, Hotel Kulm, Dorfzentrum, FL-9497 Triesenberg. Tel: 262 8777. Fax: 268 2861.
INNS: A Liechtenstein speciality is the mountain inn. All are at least 1200m (4000ft) up, but easily accessible by car. They are ideal for those seeking peace and quiet and clean air. Some of these inns have recently been enlarged and modernised.
ALPINE HUTS: There are alpine huts at Gafadura, 1428m (4284ft) high, which accommodates 50, and at Bettlerjoch Pfälzer-Hütte, 2111m (6333ft) high, which accommodates 100.
CAMPING: Campsites exist at Mittagspitze, FL-9495 Triesen (tel: 392 3677 *or* 392 2686; fax: 392 3680) and Bendern, FL-9487 Bendern (tel: 373 1211).
HOLIDAY APARTMENTS/CHALETS: Contact the local tourist office in Malbun, Triesenberg or Vaduz for information.
YOUTH HOSTELS: Liechtenstein's only youth hostel is between Schaan and Vaduz, 500m (1640ft) away from the main road. It has sleeping accommodation for 96 (12 rooms with six beds, four rooms with four beds and four rooms with two beds).

RESORTS & EXCURSIONS

The Principality of Liechtenstein covers both lowlands – including part of the fertile Rhine Valley and the steep western slope of the Three Sisters massif – and mountains. The latter are in the eastern part of the country and are accessible through three high valleys, the best known being that of Malbun, Liechtenstein's premier ski resort (see below).
RESORTS: Vaduz, Triesen, Balzers, Triesenberg, Planken, Schaan, Eschen, Mauren, Gamprin, Schellenberg, Ruggell and Malbun Steg.

UK STD CODES

As of 16 April 1995, the UK STD codes will change. Insert a 1 after the first zero in the old STD code, eg. 071 becomes 0171.

There are five exceptions:

CITY	NEW CODE	+ PREFIX
Bristol	0117	9
Leicester	0116	2
Leeds	0113	2
Nottingham	0115	9
Sheffield	0114	2

The **winter sports** area is concentrated around **Malbun** at 1600m (5250ft) and **Steg** at 1300m (4250ft). At Malbun there are two chair lifts, four ski lifts and a natural ice rink. Steg has become famous for its popular cross-country skiing loop with three distances – 4km (2.5 miles), 6km (4 miles), 10.5km (7 miles) – which is also equipped for use at night. Steg also has a ski lift and sledge-run.
EXCURSIONS: In summer, hikers and ramblers may wish to explore Liechtenstein's vineyards, forests and nature reserves. The principality's mountains attract climbers of all abilities. For the less energetic, there are several sites of interest to the tourist. In the capital, **Vaduz**, visit the *Art Collection of the Principality, Postage Stamp Museum* and the *National Library*. The *National Museum* in Vaduz is temporarily closed for renovation, but may re-open by the beginning of 1997. There are local museums in **Triesenberg, Balzers** and Schaan. Also worth a visit are the *St Maria zum Trost Chapel* in Schaan; in **Schaan**; the *Gutenberg Castle* and *St Peter's Chapel* at Balzers; the *St Mamerten* and *Maria Chapels* and the old part of the village in **Triesen**; the *Chapel of St Joseph* in **Planken**; Roman excavations at **Eschen-Nendeln**; parish churches in **Mauren, Bendern** and **Ruggell**; and the ruins of the upper and lower **Burg Schellenberg**.

SOCIAL PROFILE

FOOD & DRINK: The cuisine is Swiss with Austrian overtones and there are a good number of restaurants. **Drink:** Some extremely good wines are produced in Liechtenstein, particularly *Vaduzer* (red wine). All internationally known beverages are obtainable. There are strict laws against drinking and driving.
NIGHTLIFE: There are cinemas in Vaduz and Balzers. Dancers congregate at the Maschlina-Bar in Triesen; Tiffany in Eschen; Derby in Schaanwald; Roxy, Trailer and Römerkeller at Balzers and Turna in Malbun.
SHOPPING: Prices and the range of goods are the same as Switzerland. Apart from the usual souvenirs, there are attractive dolls in local costumes, handmade ceramics, pottery, and Liechtenstein postage stamps. **Shopping hours:** Generally 0800-1200 and 1330-1630 Monday to Friday; 0800-1600 Saturday. From April to October souvenir stores in Vaduz are open Sunday and holidays.
SPORT: Several hotels have indoor **swimming** pools. **Bowling** is a popular sport, catered for in several hotels. **Winter sports:** Excellent facilities. Main resorts include Malbun and Steg. Malbun is gaining popularity on the international **skiing** circuit for its varied facilities, and is a particularly good resort for beginners. Steg has particularly good **cross-country** skiing. In the summer, all the resorts are good starting points for **walking** tours. Gaflei at 1500m (4920ft) is the starting point for the *Fürstensteig*, a path along the high ridge dividing the Rhine and Samina valleys.
SPECIAL EVENTS: The following is the most important special event to be celebrated in Liechtenstein in 1995. For a list of all festivals scheduled for 1995/96, contact the Swiss Tourist Board.
Aug 15 '95 *National Holiday Celebrations* (with fireworks), Vaduz.
SOCIAL CONVENTIONS: These are the same as those for the rest of northwest Europe. Regulations concerning smoking are becoming increasingly strict. **Tipping:** 15% service charge will be included in most bills, but additional tips for extra services are expected. Taxis will indicate if service has not been included.

Tipping of servants in private houses is expected.

BUSINESS PROFILE

ECONOMY: Manufacturing industry has developed rapidly since the Second World War, before which the economy was predominantly agricultural. Metals, machine tools and precision instruments form the bulk of Liechtenstein's exports. These used to be sent out through Switzerland, which handles Liechtenstein's external interests on behalf of the Government, but an increasing number of firms are now exporting directly from Liechtenstein. The fastest-growing sector of the economy is in financial services: 25,000 foreign corporations have taken advantage of the strict laws on banking secrecy to establish nominee companies which pay no tax on either incomes or profits. The country's authorities have realised, however, that they will need to introduce monitoring mechanisms in the near future to bring Liechtenstein into line with other Western European states, including Switzerland. With a very small domestic market, Liechtenstein has a large balance of payments surplus. Liechtenstein joined the European Free Trade Area (EFTA) in 1991, and the European Economic Area in 1992. In April the same year, Liechtenstein joined the European Bank for Reconstruction and Development. Exports are divided between other EFTA members, the EU and other countries.
BUSINESS: Personal visits and the following of all business formalities are very important. Times to avoid business visits are over Easter, the second half of July and August, and the week before Christmas. **Office hours:** Generally 0800-1200 and 1400-1800 Monday to Friday. Often, however, lunchtime is shorter and closing is therefore earlier.
COMMERCIAL INFORMATION: The following organisation can offer advice: Liechtenstein Industrie- und Handelskammer (Chamber of Industry and Commerce), Postfach 232, Josef Rheinberger-Strasse 11, FL-9490 Vaduz. Tel: 232 2744. Fax: 233 1503.
CONFERENCES/CONVENTIONS: Although there is no conference asssociation in Liechtenstein a number of hotels have conference facilities and can organise conventions: Löwen and Schlössle in Vaduz, Meierhof in Triesen, Kulm in Triesenberg, Gorfion and Malbuner-Hof in Malbun/Triesenberg.

CLIMATE

The climate is temperate, with warm, wet summers and cool to cold winters.
Required clothing: Mediumweights with some lightweight clothing is advised for summer. Warmer heavyweights are worn in winter. Waterproofing is needed throughout the year.

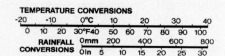

TEMPERATURE CONVERSIONS

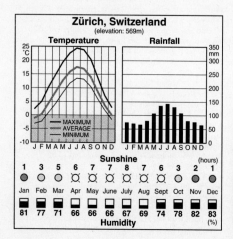

Zürich, Switzerland
(elevation: 569m)

□ *international airport*

Location: Northern Europe.

Lithuanian State Tourism Department
Gedimino pr. 30/1, 2695 Vilnius, Lithuania
Tel: (2) 226 706 *or* 622 610. Fax: (2) 226 819.
Embassy of the Republic of Lithuania
17 Essex Villas, London W8 7BP
Tel: (0171) 938 2481. Fax: (0171) 938 3329. Opening hours: 1400-1700 Monday, Wednesday and Friday.
Visa section: 1000-1300 Monday and Friday; 1400-1700 Wednesday.
British Embassy
PO Box 863, Antakalnio 2, 2600 Vilnius, Lithuania
Tel: (2) 222 070/1. Fax: (2) 357 579.
Embassy of the Republic of Lithuania
2622 16th Street, NW, Washington, DC 20009
Tel: (202) 234 5860 *or* 234 2639. Fax: (202) 328 0466.
Consulates in: Chicago, Los Angeles and New York (212) 354 7849).
Embassy of the United States of America
Akmenu 6, 2600 Vilnius, Lithuania
Tel: (2) 223 031. Fax: (2) 222 779.
Honorary Consulate of the Republic of Lithuania
Suite 502, 235 Yorkland Boulevard, Willowdale, Ontario M2J 4Y8
Tel: (416) 494 8313. Fax: (416) 494 4382.
Canadian Embassy
Didzioji g. 8-5, 2001 Vilnius, Lithuania
Tel: (2) 220 898. Fax: (2) 220 884.

AREA: 65,200 sq km (25,170 sq miles).
POPULATION: 3,751,000 (1993 estimate).
POPULATION DENSITY: 57.1 per sq km.
CAPITAL: Vilnius. **Population:** 590,100 (1993).
GEOGRAPHY: Lithuania is situated on the eastern Baltic coast and borders Latvia in the north, the Kaliningrad region of the Russian Federation and Poland in the southwest and Belarus in the southwest and east. The geometrical centre of Europe lies in eastern Lithuania near the village of Bernotai, 25km (16 miles) north of Vilnius. The landscape alternates between lowland plains and hilly uplands and has a dense, intricate network of rivers, including the Nemunas and the Neris. 1.5% of the country's territory is made up of lakes of which there are over 2800. The majority of these

lie in the east of the country and include Lake Druksiai and Lake Tauragnas.
LANGUAGE: Lithuanian is the official language. Lithuanian has a large number of dialects for such a small territory, including High Lithuanian (*Aukstaiciai*) and Low Lithuanian (*Zemaiciai*).
RELIGION: Predominantly Roman Catholic with a minority of Evangelical Lutheran, Evangelical Reformist and Russian Orthodox.
TIME: GMT + 2 (GMT + 3 from last Sunday in March to Saturday before last Sunday in September).
ELECTRICITY: 220 volts AC, 50Hz. European 2-pin plugs are in use.
COMMUNICATIONS: Telephone: IDD is available. Country code: 370 (2 for Vilnius, 7 for Kaunas, 61 for Klaipeda, 36 for Palanga). Outgoing international code: 810. **Fax:** Services in Vilnius are available at the Telegraph Centre (Universiteto 14. Tel: (2) 619 913), open 24 hours a day; at the Hotel Lietuva (Ukmerges 20); and at the Comliet Office (Architektu 146. Tel: (2) 290 011). **Post:** Post to Western Europe takes up to six days. The Central Post Office is at Gedimino pr. 7, 2000 Vilnius. Tel: (2) 616 614. Urgent correspondence is handled by *Express Mail Service* at Vokieciu 7, 2024 Vilnius. Tel: (2) 628 024. **Press:** Newspapers are published in Lithuanian and some in Russian or Polish. The major dailies are *Lietuvos Rytas*, *Respublika*, *Lietuvos Aidas* and *Valstieciu Laikrastis*. The weekly papers *The Baltic Independent*, *Lithuanian Weekly*, *The Baltic Observer* and *The Baltic News* are published in English. *The Baltic Independent* covers Estonia, Latvia and Lithuania. For subscriptions, write to: 150 Cranbrook Road, Parkstone, Poole, Dorset BH12 3JB. Tel: (01202) 741 727. Fax: (01202) 715 066. **Radio/television:** There are several television companies in Lithuania, including: *Lithuanian State Television*, *Tele-3* (broadcasts many foreign programmes with Lithuanian subtitles), *Baltic TV* and *LitPoliinter*. All broadcasts are in Lithuanian.
BBC World Service and Voice of America frequencies: From time to time these change. See the section *How to Use this Book* for more information.
BBC:

| MHz | 12.10 | 9.140 | 7.120 | 3.955 |

English-language news are also broadcast on 666kHz at 2000 and 2430.
Voice of America:

| MHz | 11.97 | 9.670 | 6.040 | 5.995 |

PASSPORT/VISA

Regulations and requirements may be subject to change at short notice, and you are advised to contact the appropriate diplomatic or consular authority before finalising travel arrangements. Details of these may be found at the head of this country's entry. Any numbers in the chart refer to the footnotes below.

	Passport Required?	Visa Required?	Return Ticket Required?
Full British	Yes	No	No
BVP	Not Valid	-	-
Australian	Yes	No	No
Canadian	Yes	Yes	No
USA	Yes	No	No
Other EU (As of 31/12/94)	Yes	1	No
Japanese	Yes	No	No

PASSPORT: Required by all.
British Visitors Passport: Not valid.
VISA: The situation is still changing regarding visa requirements. At present, a visa is required by all except:
(a) **[1]** nationals of Denmark, Italy and the UK (other EU nationals *do* need a visa);
(b) nationals of Bulgaria, Czech Republic, Estonia, Hungary, Iceland, Latvia, Liechtenstein, Norway, Poland, Slovak Republic and Switzerland.
Visas issued for Lithuania are also valid for Estonia and Latvia in most cases. For the latest information, contact the Embassy *at least 3 weeks* before travelling.
Note: Nationals or permanent residents of countries where Lithuania as yet has no diplomatic representation can obtain a visa on arrival at an extra cost of £7.
Types of visa: *Single-entry visa* – £17. *Multiple-entry visa* – £43. *Single-entry Transit visa* – £10. *Multiple-entry Transit visa* – £17.
Validity: Single- and Multiple-entry visas are valid for up to 90 days. Transit visas are valid for 2 days.
Application to: Consulate (or Consular section of Embassy). For addresses, see top of entry.
Application requirements: (a) Passport. (b) 1 passport-size photo. (c) 1 completed application form. (d) Fee. (e) If applying by post, enclose payment for registered return postage (£3).
Working days required: 5 days. Visas can be obtained in 1 day at an additional charge of £7.

Your Travel Guide in the Baltic States
All the service you need - all the comfort you want!

DELTA tourism agency
Group incoming tourism

✉ P.O.Box 1153
Laisvės al.85-4 LT-3000 Kaunas
tel.: 00 370-7 / 20 58 96
fax: 00 370-7 / 22 94 71

Touristik information
individual tourism / outgoing programmes

✉ P.O.Box 1153
Laisvės al.88 LT-3000 Kaunas
tel.: 00 370-7 / 20 49 11
fax: 00 370-7 / 20 06 21

MONEY

Currency: The Litas, Lithuania's new permanent currency, was introduced in July 1993. Lita = 100 centas. Notes are in denominations of 100, 50, 20, 10, 5, 2 and 1 Litas. Coins are in denominations of 5, 2 and 1 Litas, and 50, 20 and 10 centas.
Currency exchange: Currency can be exchanged at the Hotel Lietuva, Ukmerges 20, Vilnius (tel: (2) 356 074), where daily exchange rates are posted. Currency can also be exchanged in Kaunas and Klaipeda.
Exchange rate indicators: The following figures are included as a guide to the movements of the Lita against Sterling and the US Dollar:

Date:	Jan '94	Jan '95
£1.00=	5.76	6.25
$1.00=	3.89	4.00

Currency restrictions: The import of local and foreign currency is unlimited, but must be declared on arrival. The export is limited to the amount declared.

DUTY FREE

The following goods may be imported into Lithuania without incurring customs duty:
250 cigarettes or 50 cigars or 250g tobacco; 1 litre of spirits or 2 litres of wine.

PUBLIC HOLIDAYS

Jan 1 '95 New Year's Day. **Feb 16** Independence Day. **Apr 14** Good Friday. **Apr 17**. Easter Monday. **May 7** Mother's Day. **Jul 6** Anniversary of the Coronation of Grand Duke Mindaugas. **Nov 1** All Saints' Day. **Dec 25-26** Christmas. **Jan 1 '96** New Year's Day. **Apr 5** Good Friday. **Apr 8** Easter Monday.

HEALTH

Regulations and requirements may be subject to change at short notice, and you are advised to contact your doctor well in advance of your intended date of departure. Any numbers in the chart refer to the footnotes below.

	Special Precautions?	Certificate Required?
Yellow Fever	No	No
Cholera	No	No
Typhoid & Polio	No	-
Malaria	No	-
Food & Drink	No	-

Rabies is present. For those at high risk, vaccination before arrival should be considered. If you are bitten abroad seek medical advice without delay. For more information, consult the *Health* section at the back of the book.
Health care: Health insurance is recommended. Although emergency treatment for foreign tourists is provided free of charge, all other medical services incur a charge.

TRAVEL - International

AIR: The national airline is *Lithuanian Airlines (LAL)* flies from Vilnius to Amsterdam, Copenhagen, Berlin, Frankfurt/M, London, Paris, Moscow and Warsaw. *Air Lithuania* offers flights from Vilnius, Kaunas and Palanga to Helsinki, Prague, Oslo, Hamburg and Kristianstad. Other airlines offering connections to Vilnius are *Aeroflot, Austrian Airlines, Estonian Air, LOT, Lufthansa, Malev, SAS, Swiss Air* and *Taffo*. For further information, contact *Lithuanian Airlines (LAL)* in the UK on tel: (01293) 551 737; fax: (01293) 553 321 or

Air Lithuania in Kaunas on (7) 229 706.
Approximate flight times: From *London* to Vilnius is 3 hours, from *Copenhagen* is 1 hour 30 minutes and from *Berlin* is 1 hour 20 minutes.
International airports: *Vilnius Airport (VNO)* is situated approximately 10km (6 miles) from the city centre. Tel: (2) 630 201. There are taxi and bus services to the city. There are also international airports in Kaunas (tel: (7) 541 400) and Palanga (tel: (36) 52236); the latter serves the whole of the Baltic coast.
SEA: Klaipeda is the only natural ice-free port of the Baltic countries connected by trade routes with 200 foreign ports. There are ferry services:
Klaipeda—Mukran (Island of Rügen, Germany), daily, taking 18 hours (in Klaipeda tel: (61) 56375 17825 *or* 55052; fax: (61) 57377 or in Sassnitz, Germany tel: (38392) 33135 *or* 33179); Klapeida–Kiel (Germany), twice-weekly, taking 30 hours (in Klapeida tel: (61) 56116 *or* 99420 *or* 56188; fax: (61) 18479 *or* 57849 *or* 55549 or in Hamburg, Germany contact Schneider Reisen tel: (40) 38 02 06 81); Klapeida–Ahus (Sweden), Wednesdays, taking 18 hours (tel: (61) 54354 *or* 56116);
Klapeida–Federicija (Denmark), Mondays and Thursdays (tel: (61) 56415; fax: (61) 56405).
RAIL: Lithuania has a well-developed rail network and Vilnius is the focal point for rail connections in the region. Major routes go to Klaipeda, Riga (Latvia), Warsaw (Poland), Minsk (Belarus), Moscow and Kaliningrad (Russian Federation). Vilnius has passenger train connections with Warsaw, Berlin, Budapest, Prague, Sofia through Belarus and a direct connection with Suwalki (Poland).
ROAD: Lithuania has a good network of roads connecting the country with all neighbouring states. The crossing points on the Lithuanian-Polish border are Ogrodniki (Poland)–Lazdijai (Lithuania) and for trucks at Kalvarija (Lithuania). There are numerous crossing points with Latvia, Belarus and the Kaliningrad region of the Russian Federation. The international road *Via Baltica* will go from Tallinn to Warsaw through Latvia and Lithuania, thus connecting Scandanavia with Western Europe. **Coach:** There are passenger coaches from Vilnius to Copenhagen, Warsaw, Gdansk, Riga, Tallinn, Minsk and Kaliningrad. Charter buses go to all Western European countries.

TRAVEL - Internal

AIR: There are domestic airports at Kaunas, Palanga and Siauliai. There are not many domestic flights.
RAIL: There are good connections from Vilnius to Kaunas, Klaipeda and Siauliai. Twice-daily passenger trains (including a sleeper train) connect Vilnius with the Baltic coast. Though the train does not stop in Palanga, the major resort on the Baltic coast, passengers to Palanga usually get off at Kretinga station or in Klaipeda, and then reach Palanga by bus. Passengers to Neringa (Nida, Juodkrante) can go to Klaipeda by train, and then take a bus. Suburban trains going to Ignalina connect Vilnius with the popular lake district of the National Park. The ancient Trakai Castle can be reached by taking the suburban train going to Trakai. For further information, contact the domestic ticket offices in Vilnius (tel: (2) 626 956).
ROAD: There is a good network of roads within the country. Modern 4-lane motorways connect Vilnius with Kaunas, Klaipeda and Panevezys. **Bus:** Generally, buses are more frequent and quicker than domestic trains and serve almost every town and village. For reservations, contact Vilnius Bus Terminal on tel: (2) 262 977. **Car hire:** *Balticar* (tel: (2) 227 025), *Eva Rent* (tel: (2) 643 419) and *Neca* (tel: (7) 200 258) can provide chauffeur-driven or self-drive cars. **Traffic regulations:** Seat belts must be worn. The speed limit is 110kmph (68mph) on motorways, 90kmph (56mph) on country lanes and 60kmph (38mph) inside towns. Traffic drives on the right. **Documentation:** European nationals should be in possession of the new European driving licence. Otherwise, a national driving licence is sufficient.
URBAN: Public transport in urban districts includes **buses** and **trolleybuses**, which usually run from 0600-0100. Transport coupons are bought at news kiosks before boarding either the bus or trolleybus. **Taxi:** These display illuminated *Taksi* signs and can be hailed in the street, found at taxi ranks or ordered by phone.

ACCOMMODATION

HOTELS: Since independence, Western-style hotels and motels are being built in Lithuania in cooperation with foreign firms. Modernisation and renovation programmes are generally concentrated in the capital. The 3-star 23-storey Hotel Lietuva, with 350 rooms, is the largest and is situated near the city centre (tel: (2) 356 016). Other major hotels are Neringa, Astorija, Vilnius, Karolina, Turistas and the Sarunas. The modern Villon Hotel is 19km (12 miles) from Vilnius, on the road to Riga. All major hotels (Baltija, Lietuva, Nemunas and Neris) in Kaunas are concentrated in the centre of the town. The main hotels in Klaipeda are Klaipeda Pamarys, Prusija and Vetrunge. Meanwhile Vilnius and the other major centres in the country enjoy an adequate range of good accommodation including large hotels and smaller pensions. A star grading system is in force. For further details, contact the Lithuanian State Tourism Department (see address at the beginning of this entry) *or* the Lithuanian National Hotel Association (LIETUVA), 20 Ukmerges Street, 2600 Vilnius. Tel: (2) 356 010. Fax: (2) 356 270. Telex: 261929.
PRIVATE ROOMS: Travel agencies can arrange rental of rooms in private homes as well as houses. This is especially popular in resort regions.
CAMPING: Campsites are not numerous. The majority of them are located in the most picturesques regions: Palanga (on the shore of the Baltic Sea), Trakai (lake district) and near larger towns. There are three sites in close proximity to Vilnius. Pitching a tent is permitted at the majority of Lithuanian lakes and rivers (including the National Park) for a small fee, but almost no other facilities are provided at these sites.
YOUTH HOSTELS: For further information, contact the Youth Hostels Information Center, Kauno 1A-510, Vilnius (tel: (2) 260 606) or in Pazanga, Sauletekio 39A, Vilnius. Tel: (2) 764 483.

RESORTS & EXCURSIONS

The historic city of **Vilnius** (founded 1323) is the capital of Lithuania. Surrounded on three sides by wooded hills and situated in a picturesque valley formed by the rivers *Neris* and *Vilnia*, the ancient and modern centre of the city lies on the southern or left bank of the river. Unlike Tallinn and Riga in the other Baltic Republics, Vilnius is not of Germanic origin, although like these other cities it has a large old quarter which is gradually being restored. Almost all major European architectural styles are represented although ultimately it was the Baroque which came to dominate. The heart of the capital is the beautiful and spacious *Gediminas Square*, the main feature of which is the *Cathedral* built in the Classical style. Other interesting churches are the Gothic *St Ann's Church* and the *St Peter and St Paul Church,* which houses the body of St Casimieras, one of the most revered of Lithuania's dukes. It also includes some fine sculptures. Any itinerary of the city should include the historic *University of Vilnius,* which was granted its charter in 1579, the Golden Age in the city's history. The university is among the oldest universities in Central Europe and has a distinctly Renaissance feel with its inner courtyards and arcades. To enjoy a view of the whole city visitors should climb the tower of *Gediminas Castle*. High on a hill in the centre of the city it rises above Vilnius and is the symbol of the Lithuanian capital.
About 25km (18 miles) from Vilnius lies **Trakai**, an ancient capital of Lithuania. Situated on the shore of the picturesque *Lake Galve,* on which boat rides are available, the city has a castle dating from the 14th century. Further to the west is the spa of **Birstonas**, renowned for its mineral waters and tranquility. To the west of Vilnius lies the industrial and cultural centre of **Kaunas**, Lithuania's second city. Also known as the 'city of museums' it boasts, amongst others, the *Museum of Devil's Sculptures* and a memorial to those who suffered during the Nazi occupation. The most famous museum is dedicated to the works of the Lithuanian painter Ciurlionis. Kaunas also numbers three theatres, some 11th-century castle ruins and the old *City Hall* among its attractions. Other places of interest in Lithuania include the small riverside spa resort of **Druskininkai,** situated 135km (84 miles) from Vilnius, and the small town of **Rumsiskes**, 80km (50 miles) from Vilnius and 20km (12.5 miles) from Kaunas, with its open-air museum of wooden architecture exhibiting farmhouses from all the various regions of the country. Popular seaside resorts include **Palanga** and **Kursiu Nerija** (with the settlements of Nida and Juodkrante), which are famous for their clean white sand beaches, natural sand dunes and pine forests. **Nida** is the last village on the Lithuanian half of the spit surrounded by endless stretches of clean white sand. A lighthouse from 1874 can be visited here, and the *Thomas Mann Museum*, situated in the house where the German writer spent his holidays between 1930-32. Palanga also boasts the *Amber Museum* and an interesting botanical park. To the south lies the city of **Klaipeda**, an important seaport as well as the main centre for ferry connections from Lithuania. The two main towns in the north of the country are **Siauliai**, an important industrial centre with the famous *Hill of Crosses* about 10km (6 miles) from the city, and **Panevezys** with its famous *Drama Theatre*.
POPULAR ITINERARIES: 5-day: (a) Vilnius–Kaunas–Rumsiskes–Vilnius. (b) Vilnius–Palanga–Klaipeda–Nida–Vilnius. (c) Vilnius–Trakai–Birstonas–Vilnius.

SOCIAL PROFILE

FOOD & DRINK: Local specialities include *skilandis* (smoked meat), *salti barsciai* (cold soup), *cepelinai* (made from grated potatoes with a minced meat filling), *vedarai* (potato sausage) and *bulviniai blynai* (potato dumplings). Smoked eel is a famous Baltic delicacy. Waiter service is the norm in restaurants and cafés, but self-service restaurants, bistros and snack bars are numerous. **Drink:** Local brands of beer and imported drinks are popular. A famous Lithuanian spirit is *midus,* a mild alcoholic beverage made from honey.
NIGHTLIFE: Cinemas can be found in all towns. Lithuanian theatres, most of which are concentrated in the capital, are also renowned. The Jaunimo *teatras* in Vilnius are famous throughout the country. Opera and ballet are staged in the city at the Vilnius Opera Theatre and Kaunas has a Musical Theatre. Puppet shows are staged for children in Vilnius and Kaunas. There are restaurants with live music as well as numerous discotheques and nightclubs with variety shows in the larger towns.
SHOPPING: Amber, linen goods and local crafts are good buys. National artists sell their works in specialised art galleries in major towns.
SPORT: Lithuania has extensive sporting facilities including the 15,000-seat *Zalgiris* stadium in Vilnius and facilities for **swimming, football, handball, basketball** (the most popular sport), **tennis** and **ice hockey**. **Sailing** and **wind-surfing** are popular on the lakes near Trakai, at Kursiu marios (a lagoon at the Baltic) and at Kauno marios near Kaunas.
SPECIAL EVENTS: The following are some of the main festivals in Lithuania during 1995. For full details, contact the Lithuanian State Tourism Department.
Apr 1-2 '95 *International Handball Games,* Kaunas. **Apr 1-23** *The 13th International Church Music Festival,* Siauliai. **May 3** *Final Concert of the Cycle 'All W.A. Mozart's piano concertos'*. **May 17-21** *Lithuanian International Theatre Festival,* Vilnius. **May 25-28** *International Folklore Festival 'Skamba, Skamba Kankliai'*. **Jun 24-5** *International Amber Rowing Regatta,* Trakai. **Jul 1-12** *Summer Music Festival,* Vilnius. **Jul 30-Aug 5** *The 5th World Lithuanian Sport Games.* **Sep 27-Oct 5** *International Piano and Organ Competition,* Vilnius. **Oct 13** *Celebration of the 225th anniversary of the birth of Beethoven,* Vilnius. **Feb-May '96** *International Ballet Project,* Vilnius. **Mar** *21st Klaipeda Music Spring,* Klaipeda. **Apr** *The 14th International Church Music Festival,* Siauliai.
SOCIAL CONVENTIONS: Handshaking is customary. Normal courtesies should be observed. The Lithuanians are proud of their culture and their national heritage and visitors should take care to respect this sense of national identity. **Tipping:** Taxi fares and restaurant bills include a tip. Otherwise, tips are discretionary.

BUSINESS PROFILE

ECONOMY: Lithuania has historically been the least developed of the Baltic republics with a smaller industrial base and greater dependence on agriculture. Electrical, electronic and optical goods and light machinery are the main industrial products. Food-processing is also an important industry, with an ample supply of agricultural products from Lithuania's own farming and fisheries sector. Lacking raw materials, Lithuania is totally dependent on supplies of Russian fuels and metals. Lithuania's other economic asset is the Baltic's only naturally ice-free port (other than Kaliningrad). Lithuania has agreed, along with nine other countries bordering on the Baltic, to establish a regional cooperation organisation, the Council of Baltic Sea States. The Government has embarked on a series of reforms to introduce a market economy and liberalise foreign trade, although in the early stages, extensive government intervention is likely to be needed to ensure the supply of essential goods and maintain economic stability. The major obstacles met by the programme of privatisation, which began in 1990, concern the restitution of agricultural land ownership and privatisation of large, unprofitable state-owned enterprises that need fundamental technological renovation. Also, the bulk of the country's trade remains with the former republics of the CIS.
BUSINESS: Business is conducted in a fairly formal manner and a smart appearance is important. Appointments should be made in advance. English is used for international commerce. A knowledge of German, Russian or Polish may also be useful. **Office hours:** 0900-1300 and 1400-1800 Monday to Friday.
COMMERCIAL INFORMATION: The following organisations can offer advice: Association of Lithuanian Chambers of Commerce and Industry, Kudirkos 18, 2600 Vilnius. Tel: (2) 222 617 *or* 222 630. Fax: (2) 222 621;
or
Ministry of Trade and Industry, J. Tumo-Vaizganto 8A/2, 2739 Vilnius. Tel: (2) 628 230. Fax: (2) 225 967 *or* 620 638.
CONFERENCES/CONVENTIONS: Although there is no conference association in Lithuania, a number of hotels in Vilnius have conference facilities and can organise conventions. Some rest homes in Palanga also provide facilities during the low season. For further information, contact the Lithuanian State Tourism Department (for address, see top of entry) or the Lithuanian National Hotel Association (for address see *Accommodation* section).

CLIMATE

Temperate climate, but with considerable temperature variations. Summer is warm with relatively mild weather in spring and autumn. Winter, which lasts from November to mid-March, can be very cold. Rainfall is distributed throughout the year with the heaviest rainfall in August. Heavy snowfalls are common in the winter months.

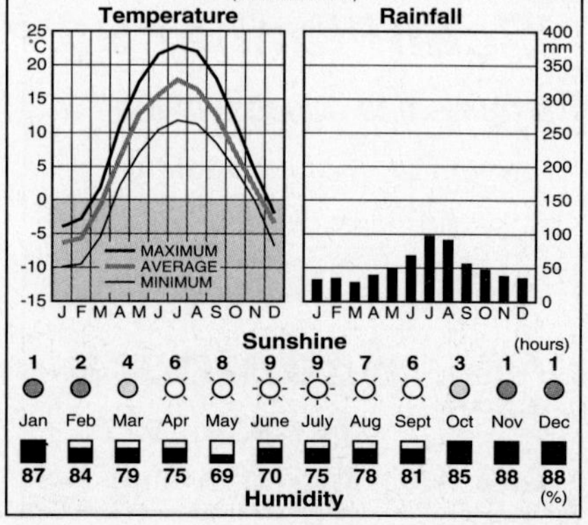

Luxembourg

30km
15mls

BELGIUM

Clervaux

Wiltz

D i e k i r c h

Süre

Diekirch

Ettelbrück

Echternach

Redange

L U X E M B O U R G

Grevenmacher

Radio
Luxembourg

L u x e m b o u r g

■ LUXEMBOURG-
VILLE

Differdange

● Esch-sur-Alzette

●Dudelange

FRANCE

FEDERAL
REPUBLIC OF
GERMANY

DAB-M137

□ *international airport*

Location: Western Europe.

Office National du Tourisme
BP 1001, 77 rue d'Anvers, L-1010 Luxembourg-Ville,
Luxembourg
Tel: 400 808. Fax: 404 748. Telex: 2715 (a/b ONTOUR).
Embassy of the Grand Duchy of Luxembourg
27 Wilton Crescent, London SW1X 8SD
Tel: (0171) 235 6961. Fax: (0171) 235 9734. Telex:
28120 (a/b AMBLUX). Opening hours: 0900-1300 and
1400-1700 Monday to Friday. *Visa section:* 1000-1200
Monday to Friday.
Luxembourg Tourist Office
122 Regent Street, London W1R 5FE
Tel: (0171) 434 2800. Fax: (0171) 734 1205. Telex:
94016933 (a/b LUXT). Opening hours: 0900-1700
Monday to Friday.
British Embassy
14 boulevard Roosevelt, L-2450 Luxembourg-Ville,
Luxembourg
Tel: 229 864/5/6. Fax: 229 867. Telex: 3443 (a/b
PRODROLU).
Embassy of the Grand Duchy of Luxembourg
2200 Massachusetts Avenue, NW, Washington, DC
20008
Tel: (202) 265 4171. Fax: (202) 328 8270. Telex: 64130.
Consulates in: Atlanta, Chicago, Fort Worth, Kansas
City (Missouri), Los Angeles, Miami, Middletown, New
Orleans, New York, Mountain View, Pittsburgh, San
Francisco, Seattle and Youngstown.
Luxembourg National Tourist Office
17 Beekman Place, New York, NY 10022
Tel: (212) 935 8888. Fax: (212) 935 5896. Telex:
620241.
Embassy of the United States of America
22 boulevard Emmanuel-Servais, L-2535 Luxembourg-
Ville, Luxembourg
Tel: 460 123. Fax: 461 401.

Luxembourg Consulate
3877 Draper Avenue, Montréal, Québec H4A 2N9
Tel: (514) 489 6052.
Consulates also in: Calgary and Vancouver.
Consulate of Canada
c/o Price Waterhouse and Co., PO Box 1443, avenue de
la Liberté, L-1930 Luxembourg-Ville, Luxembourg
Tel: 402 420. Fax: 402 455, ext 600. Telex: 1231.

AREA: 2586 sq km (999 sq miles).
POPULATION: 389,800 (1992 estimate).
POPULATION DENSITY: 150.7 per sq km.
CAPITAL: Luxembourg-Ville. **Population:** 75,377
(1991 estimate).
GEOGRAPHY: Luxembourg shares borders to the
north and west with Belgium, to the south with France
and to the east with Germany. One-third of the country is
made up of the hills and forests of the Ardennes, while
the rest is wooded farmland. In the southeast is the rich
wine-growing valley of Moselle.
LANGUAGE: The official languages are French and
German. The local vernacular is Letzeburgesch, a
German-Moselle-Frankish dialect. Many Luxembourgers
also speak English.
RELIGION: 97% Roman Catholic, 1.2% Protestant,
1.8% others.
TIME: GMT + 1 (GMT + 2 from last Sunday in March
to Saturday before last Sunday in September).
ELECTRICITY: 220 volts AC, 50Hz.
COMMUNICATIONS: Telephone: Full IDD is
available. Country code: 352 (no area codes). Outgoing
international code: 00. International phones have a
yellow sign showing a telephone dial with a receiver in
the centre. **Fax:** There is a fax booth at the Luxembourg-
Ville main post office. Faxes may be sent to a central
number (491 175) for delivery by express mail within
Luxembourg. **Telegram/telex:** There are facilities at the
post office at 25 rue Aldringen, Luxembourg-Ville, and
in all major towns. Hotels often allow guests to use their
facilities. **Post:** Post to other European destinations takes
two to four days. There are *Poste Restante* facilities
throughout the country. Prospective recipients must first
register for a PO Box. Mail will be held for up to one
month. Post office hours are generally 0800-1200 and
1330-1700 Monday to Friday. The Luxembourg-Ville
main office is open 0700-1900. Smaller offices may open
for only a few hours. Telephone 49911 for details. **Press:**
The daily with the highest circulation is the *Luxemburger
Wort – La Voix du Luxembourg.* There is one English-
language newspaper, *The Luxembourg News.*
**BBC World Service and Voice of America
frequencies:** From time to time these change. See the
section *How to Use this Book* for more information.
BBC:

| MHz | 12.09 | 9.750 | 6.195 | 3.955 |

A service is also available on 648kHz and 198kHz
(0100-0500 GMT).
Voice of America:

| MHz | 11.97 | 9.670 | 6.040 | 5.995 |

PASSPORT/VISA

*Regulations and requirements may be subject to change at short notice, and you
are advised to contact the appropriate diplomatic or consular authority before
finalising travel arrangements. Details of these may be found at the head of this
country's entry. Any numbers in the chart refer to the footnotes below.*

	Passport Required?	Visa Required?	Return Ticket Required?
Full British	1	No	Yes
BVP	Valid	-	-
Australian	Yes	No	Yes
Canadian	Yes	No	Yes
USA	Yes	No	Yes
Other EU (As of 31/12/94)	1	No	Yes
Japanese	Yes	No	Yes

Note: Proof of adequate finances and return or onward
ticket (and visa for country of next destination if needed)
are required for all visitors.
PASSPORTS: A valid passport is required by all except:
(a) **[1]** nationals of EU countries who hold a valid
national ID card or, if UK citizens, a BVP;
(b) nationals of Andorra, Austria, Liechtenstein, Malta,
Monaco, San Marino and Switzerland, providing they
hold a valid national ID card.
British Visitors Passport: A British Visitors Passport is
valid for holidays or unpaid business trips to
Luxembourg; children under 16 cannot, however, go on
their brother's or sister's passport. For further
information, see the *Passport/Visa* section of *How to use
this Book* at the beginning of the book.
Note: 60-hour ID cards are *not* acceptable; in certain

circumstances (enquire at Consulate) expired passports
may be acceptable as ID cards; and where full national
passports are required, they must be valid for at least 3
months after the last day of the intended visit.
VISAS: Required by all except:
(a) nationals of countries referred to in the above chart;
(b) nationals of those countries listed under passport
exemptions above;
(c) nationals of Argentina, Brazil, Brunei, Chile, Costa
Rica, Cyprus, Czech Republic, Ecuador, El Salvador,
Finland, Guatemala, Honduras, Hungary, Iceland, Israel,
Jamaica, South Korea, Malawi, Malaysia, Mexico, New
Zealand, Nicaragua, Norway, Panama, Paraguay, Poland,
Singapore, Slovak Republic, Slovenia, Sweden, Uruguay,
Vatican City and Venezuela.
Types of visa: Tourist and Transit.
Cost and validity: *Tourist visa:* £21 for a stay of up to 1
month; £28 for a stay of up to 3 months; £34 for a stay of
up to 12 months or multiple visits. *Transit visa:* £9.
Transit visas are valid only for such stops as are
necessary for transit; 3 days maximum stay.
Note: As visas will normally be valid for all three
Benelux countries (Belgium, The Netherlands and
Luxembourg), passports or travel documents must also
be valid for all 3 countries.
Application to: Consulate (or Consular section at
Embassy) of the Benelux country which the applicant
will enter first.
Application requirements: (a) Completed application
form. (b) Registered self-addressed envelope for return of
visas. (c) 1 passport-size photo. (d) Relevant passport or
travel document. (e) Fee. (f) Signed declaration stating
that visa holder agrees to abide by terms of visa.
Note: In some cases, 5 forms and 3 photos will be
required. Enquire at Consulate (or Consular section at
Embassy) for further details.
Working days required: Usually within 24 hours or by
return of post. Some applications can take up to 3 weeks,
including Arab, Chinese, Ghanaian, Mauritian, Pakistani,
South African and Sri Lankan, all republics of former
Yugoslavia (except Slovenia) and non-resident Indians
and Bangladeshis.
Temporary residence: Enquire about special application
procedures at Embassy.

MONEY

Currency: Luxembourg Franc (LFr) = 100 centimes.
Notes are in denominations of LFr5000, 1000, 500 and
100. LFr50 and 20 notes have been taken out of
circulation. Coins are in denominations of LFr50, 20, 5
and 1, and 50 centimes. The Luxembourg Franc is on a
par with the Belgian Franc. However, Luxembourg
Francs are not always legal tender in Belgium, whereas
Belgian Francs are always accepted in Luxembourg.
Credit cards: Access/Mastercard, American Express,
Visa and Diners Club are all widely accepted. Check
with your credit card company for details of merchant
acceptability and other services which may be available.
Travellers cheques: Widely accepted.
Exchange rate indicators: The following figures are
included as a guide to the movements of the Luxembourg
Franc against Sterling and the US Dollar:

Date:	Oct '92	Sep '93	Jan '94	Jan '95
£1.00=	50.20	53.25	53.50	49.80
$1.00=	31.63	34.88	36.15	31.83

Currency restrictions: There are no restrictions on the
import and export of either local or foreign currency.
Banking hours: Generally 0900-1200 and 1330-1630
Monday to Friday, but may vary greatly.

DUTY FREE

The following goods may be imported into Luxembourg
without incurring customs duty by:
(a) travellers arriving from EU countries:
*300 cigarettes or 75 cigars or 150 cigarillos or 400g of
tobacco products; *1.5 litres of alcohol over 22% proof
or 3 litres of alcohol not over 22% proof or 3 litres of
sparkling wine; *5 litres of table wine; 1000g of coffee or
400g of coffee extract/essence; 200g of tea or 80g of tea
extract/essence; 75g of perfume and 375ml of eau de
toilette; other goods to the value of LFr25,000 (LFr6400
for passengers under 15 years of age).*
(b) travellers arriving from other European countries and
from outside Europe:
*200 cigarettes or 50 cigars or 100 cigarillos or 250g of
tobacco products; *1 litre of alcohol over 22% proof or 2
litres of alcohol not over 22% proof or 2 litres of
sparkling wine; *2 litres of table wine; 50g of perfume
and 250ml of eau de toilette; 500g of coffee or 200g of
coffee extract/essence; 100g of tea or 40g of tea
extract/essence; other goods to the value of LFr2000
(LFr1000 for passengers under 15 years of age).*

(c) travellers over 17 years of age arriving from EU countries with duty-paid goods:
800 cigarettes and 400 cigarillos and 200 cigars and 1kg of tobacco; 90 litres of wine (including up to 60 litres of sparkling wine); 10 litres of spirits over 22% proof or 20 litres of alcohol not over 22% proof; 110 litres of beer.
Note: (a) [*] Alcohol and tobacco products are only available to passengers of 17 years of age or over. (b) Although there are now no legal limits imposed on importing *duty-paid* tobacco and alcoholic products from one EU country to another, travellers may be questioned if they exceed the above amounts and may be asked to prove that the goods are for personal use only.

PUBLIC HOLIDAYS

Jan 1 '95 New Year's Day. **Feb 27** Carnival. **Apr 17** Easter Monday. **May 1** Labour Day. **May 25** Ascension Day. **Jun 5** Whit Monday. **Jun 23** National Day. **Aug 15** Assumption Day. **Sep 4** Luxembourg City Kermesse. **Nov 1** All Saints' Day. **Dec 25** Christmas Day. **Dec 26** St Stephen's Day. **Jan 1 '96** New Year's Day. **Feb 19** Carnival. **Apr 8** Easter Monday.
Note: A maximum of two official public holidays falling on a Sunday may be deferred to the following Monday. Confirm with the National Tourist Office.

HEALTH

Regulations and requirements may be subject to change at short notice, and you are advised to contact your doctor well in advance of your intended date of departure. Any numbers in the chart refer to the footnotes below.

	Special Precautions?	Certificate Required?
Yellow Fever	No	No
Cholera	No	No
Typhoid & Polio	No	-
Malaria	No	-
Food & Drink	1	-

[1]: Tap water is considered safe to drink. Milk is pasteurised and dairy products are safe for consumption. Local meat, poultry, seafood, fruit and vegetables are generally considered safe to eat.
Rabies is present. For those at high risk, vaccination before arrival should be considered. If you are bitten abroad seek medical advice without delay. For more information, consult the *Health* section at the back of the book.
Health care: There are Reciprocal Health Agreements with all other EU member states. UK citizens should obtain form E111 from the Department of Health before travelling. This entitles them to free hospital treatment and a partial refund of other medical and dental treatments. Refunds are paid by the *Caisse National d'Assurance Maladie des Ouvriers.*

TRAVEL - International

AIR: Luxembourg's national airline is *Luxair (LG).* For free advice on air travel, call the Air Travel Advisory Bureau in the UK on (0171) 636 5000 *or* (0161) 832 2000 (Manchester).
Approximate flight time: From London to Luxembourg is 1 hour.
International airport: *Luxembourg (LUX)* (Findel) is 7km (4.5 miles) northeast of the city. Airport facilities include an outgoing duty-free shop, car hire (0800-1900), bank/bureau de change (0800-1230 and 1330-1900) and a tourist information office (1000-1800). Travel time from the airport to the city centre is approximately 20 minutes. Coaches depart for the city every 50 minutes from 0605-2245; returning coaches depart from the city's air terminus at platform 5, place de la Gare, from 0535-2230. Bus no. 9 departs for the city every 40 minutes from 0520-2312; returning buses depart from Neudorf bus station, place de la Gare, from 0503-2250. Taxis are available.
RAIL: The direct daily rail connection *London* (Victoria)–*Ostend*–*Brussels*–*Luxembourg* takes about 11 hours if the crossing is by ferry; if the crossing is by jetfoil, the journey takes 8 hours 30 minutes. There are direct train links with principal cities in neighbouring countries. Inter-Rail and Eurailpass are valid.
ROAD: Luxembourg is easily reached from the UK via Belgium or France within a day. Luxembourg-Ville is about 320km (200 miles) from Ostend, and 420km (260 miles) from Boulogne or Calais. Either way, the quickest route is to take the motorway to Brussels then head south through Namur along the E411.

TRAVEL - Internal

RAIL: The efficient rail service is run by *CFL* and is fully integrated with the bus network. Reductions are offered for weekend and holiday return tickets. *CFL* rail services and *CFL/CRL* buses in Luxembourg are covered by the *Benelux Tourrail* rail pass covering Belgium, The Netherlands and Luxembourg. This gives unlimited travel on any five days within a 17-day period throughout the year. There are also single-day tickets which give unlimited travel on all trains/buses, which cost LFr120, and concessions for old-age pensioners. *Rail/Coach Rover Tickets* are valid for both networks.
ROAD: As in the rest of Western Europe, there is an excellent network of roads and motorways in Luxembourg. Traffic drives on the right. **Bus:** Cross-country buses are punctual and operate between all major towns. **Taxi:** These are metered. There is a minimum charge and a 10% surcharge is applied from 2200-0600. Taxis are plentiful but cannot be hailed in the street. A 15% tip is usual for taxi drivers. **Car hire:** All the main agencies operate in Luxembourg. **Traffic regulations:** The minimum age for driving is 17. It is obligatory to carry LFr600 at all times for the payment of fines; there are stiff drinking/driving spot fines. The wearing of seat belts is compulsory in the front seat and in the back, where seat belts are fitted. Children under 10 years of age must travel on back seats. Motorcyclists must use a dipped beam even by day. The speed limit is 60kmph (37mph) in built-up areas, 90kmph (56mph) outside built-up areas, and 120kmph (74mph) on motorways. For more details, contact Automobile Club du Grand-Duché de Luxembourg, 54 route de Longwy, Bertrange, Luxembourg-Helfenterbruck. Tel: 450 045.
Documentation: Third Party insurance is necessary. A Green Card is not obligatory but is *strongly recommended.* Without it, visitors have only the minimum legal cover in Luxembourg (if they have motor insurance at home). The Green Card tops this up to the level of cover provided by the visitor's domestic policy. A valid national driving licence is sufficient.
URBAN: Luxembourg-Ville has municipal bus services, for which single-journey flat-fare tickets may be purchased; 10-journey tickets are also available, but must be purchased in advance.
JOURNEY TIMES: The following chart gives approximate journey times (in hours and minutes) from Luxembourg-Ville to other major cities/towns in Europe.

	Air	Road	Rail
Amsterdam	0.45	5.30	6.30
Brussels	0.45	2.00	2.30
Frankfurt/M	0.50	2.30	3.30
Paris	1.00	4.00	4.00
London	1.00	*8.00	**8.00
Zurich	1.20	5.00	5.00

Note: [*] Including ferry crossing (via Calais); [**] jetfoil crossing via Ostend.

ACCOMMODATION

HOTELS: For information on hotels in Luxembourg, contact the Luxembourg National Tourist Office (which can supply a free national guide) *or* the National Hotel Association, Horesca (to which all hotels in the Grand Duchy belong) at 9 rue des Trévires, L-2628 Luxembourg. Tel: 487 165. Fax: 487 156. **Grading:** Luxembourg has a wide range of hotels and has recently adopted the *Benelux* system of classification, in which the standard of the accommodation is indicated by a row of 3-pointed stars from the highest (five stars) to the minimum (one star). However, membership of this scheme is voluntary, and at present, only approximately a quarter of hotels have been classified. There may be first-class hotels, therefore, which do not have a classification. *Benelux* star ratings comply with the following criteria:
5-star (H5): This is a new category signifying luxury hotel. There are two establishments in this category.
4-star (H4): First-class hotels. 80% of rooms have a private bath. Other amenities include night reception and room service. 15% of graded hotels in Luxembourg belong to this category. There are 32 in this category.
3-star (H3): Half of the rooms have private bath. Other amenities include day reception. 29% of graded hotels in Luxembourg belong to this category. There are 49 in this category.
2-star (H2): A quarter of rooms have private bath. Other amenities include a bar. 9% of graded hotels in Luxembourg belong to this category. There are 29 hotels in this grouping.
1-star (H1): Simple hotel. No private baths, but hot and cold water in rooms. Breakfast available. 12% of graded hotels in Luxembourg belong to this category.
HOLIDAY APARTMENTS: A number of holiday flats and chalets are available throughout the country. A free pamphlet giving location and facilities is published by the National Tourist Office.
CAMPING: There are over 120 campsites throughout the country. According to government regulations, campsites are ranged in three different categories and the tariff in each camp is shown at the entrance. The National Tourist Office publishes a free, comprehensive brochure giving all relevant information concerning campsites.
YOUTH HOSTELS: There are youth hostels at Beaufort, Bourglinster, Echternach, Ettelbruck, Grevenmacher, Hollenfels, Lultzhausen, Luxembourg-Ville, Vianden and Wiltz. A *Youth Hostel Guide* may be obtained free of charge from the National Tourist Office in London or the Luxembourg Youth Hostels Association, 2 rue du Fort Olisy, L-2261 Luxembourg-Ville. Tel: 226 889. Fax: 223 360.

RESORTS & EXCURSIONS

Resorts: Luxembourg, Clervaux, Diekirch, Echternach, Esch-sur-Sûre, Remich, Vianden, Wiltz and Mondorf-les-Bains (which has recently been completely revamped with a sports and leisure centre).
Excursions: Museum of Natural History and the Museum of History and Art in *Luxembourg State Museum;* tumulus at **Bill/Mersch**; Roman palace at **Echternach**; *Trevirian Oppidum* (1st century) at **Titelberg**; Gallo-Roman rural sanctuary at **Steinsel**; *Gallo-Roman Villa* at **Mersch**; castles at **Beaufort, Larochette, Bourscheid** and **Vianden**; chair lift, castle and wild boar sanctuary at Vianden; and the **Germano-Luxembourg Natural Park** (daily tours by coach from Luxembourg-Ville bus station).

SOCIAL PROFILE

FOOD & DRINK: Luxembourg cooking combines German heartiness with Franco-Belgian finesse. Local dishes include *carré de porc fumé* (smoked pork and broad beans or sauerkraut – of Teutonic origin), *cochon de lait en gelée* (jellied suckling pig), and *jambon d'Ardennes* (famous smoked Ardennes ham). The preparation of trout, pike and crayfish is excellent, as are the pastries and cakes. *Tarte aux quetsches* is recommended. Delicious desserts are prepared with local liqueurs and some restaurants will make *omelette soufflée au kirsch.* A dash of *quetsch, mirabelle* or *kirsch* will be added to babas or fruit cups. Most aspects of restaurants and bars are similar to the rest of Europe.
Drink: Luxembourg's white Moselle wines resemble those of the Rhine, but are drier than the fruitier wines of the French Moselle. Beer is another speciality and is a traditional industry. Best-known brands are *Mousel, Bofferding, Diekirch, Funck* and *Simon.* There are also many local liqueurs and strong spirits such as *Eau de vie* (45-50% alcohol). The minimum age for drinking in bars is 17, and anyone younger than 17 must be accompanied by an adult to cafés and bars. Hours are generally from 0700-2400 (weekdays) and until 0300 (weekends and public holidays). Nightclubs are generally open until 0300.
SHOPPING: Special purchases include beautiful porcelain and crystal. Villeroy and Boch crystal factories in Septfontaines are open to visitors. A regional speciality is earthenware pottery from Nospelt, where in August there is a fortnight's exhibition of local work.
Shopping hours: 0900-1200 and 1400-1800 (closed Monday morning). Some shops open during lunch.
SPORT: Although small, Luxembourg offers the tourist opportunities for **walking tours, riding, tennis** and **golf,** and some **rock climbing, boating** and **water-skiing.** **Hunting** permits, valid for five days only, are granted to foreigners non-resident in the Grand Duchy and **fishing** licences are issued by the District Commissioners of Luxembourg, Diekirch and Grevenmacher, as well as by different communal administrations.
SPECIAL EVENTS: Luxembourg is European City of Culture in 1995. For a list of associated events throughout the year, contact the National Tourist Office. **May 29-Jun 3 '95** *Olympic Games of the Small Nations.*
SOCIAL CONVENTIONS: Handshaking is the normal greeting. The code of practice for visiting someone's home is similar to other Western European countries: it is acceptable to give gifts if invited for a meal. Casual dress is widely acceptable, but some dining rooms, clubs and social functions will demand formal attire. Evening wear, black tie (for men) is usually specified on invitation if required. Smoking is prohibited where notified and is becoming increasingly unacceptable. **Tipping:** Bills generally include service, but a rounding up is often given. Taxi drivers expect 15% of meter charge.

BUSINESS PROFILE

ECONOMY: Even by Western European standards, Luxembourg is a prosperous country with a high standard of living and virtually no unemployment. Two very different industries – banking and steel – are the mainstays of the economy. Domestically produced iron ore was used for the steel industry until 1981, when mining ceased, since when the steel industry has relied on imported raw materials; nonetheless, having weathered the global downturn in demand for steel and other crises in the industry, this is likely to remain an important economic sector for the time being. Banking is less important as an employer, but more valuable now in its contribution to GNP. The Government is coming under international pressure, however, to relax its strict laws on banking secrecy which have proved so valuable in attracting bankers to the country. The Government will act on this in order to harmonise Luxembourg practice with the rest of the EU, but it has also reinforced a general perception within Luxembourg that the country has replaced over-dependence on steel with over-dependence on financial services (Luxembourg is a major insurance centre as well). With this in mind, the Government is encouraging new industries to set up or develop indigenously in Luxembourg: construction and audio-visual equipment are the most promising candidates at present. Chemicals have performed steadily. Luxembourg also has a healthy agricultural sector which produces potatoes, barley, oats, wheat and fruit. The economy has long been linked with that of Belgium through the Belgo-Luxembourg Economic Union, established in 1921, through a 1958 Treaty of Economic Union, and latterly through the European Union, with whom Luxembourg conducts most of its foreign trade.

BUSINESS: Business persons are expected to wear suits. It is advisable to make prior appointments and business cards are often used. Avoid business visits during Christmas and New Year, Easter week and July and August. **Office hours:** Generally 0830-1200 and 1400-1800 Monday to Friday.

COMMERCIAL INFORMATION: The following organisations can offer advice: Belgium/Luxembourg Chamber of Commerce, 8 John Street, London WC1N 2ES. Tel: (0171) 831 3508. Fax: (0171) 831 9151; *or* Chamber of Commerce, 7 rue Alcide de Gasperi, L-2981 Luxembourg-Kirchberg. Tel: 435 853. Fax: 438 326. Telex: 60174.

CONFERENCES/CONVENTIONS: The location of the Grand Duchy of Luxembourg at the heart of the EU ensures its status as one of the most popular destinations for conferences and conventions in Western Europe. The number of nights spent in Luxembourg for meetings purposes exceeded 5500 in 1988 and this figure is likely to increase steadily in years to come. For further information, contact Luxembourg Congrès, PO Box 840, L-2018 Luxembourg. Tel: 463 434. Fax: 474 011.

CLIMATE

Warm weather from May to September and snow likely during winter months. The north, the Ardennes region, tends to be wetter than the south.

Required clothing: European; waterproofs are advisable at all times of the year.

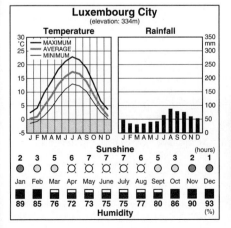

Luxembourg City
(elevation: 334m)

Temperature	Rainfall

Sunshine (hours)

Jan	Feb	Mar	Apr	May	June	July	Aug	Sept	Oct	Nov	Dec
2	3	5	6	7	7	7	6	5	3	2	1

Humidity (%)

| 89 | 85 | 76 | 72 | 73 | 75 | 75 | 77 | 80 | 86 | 90 | 93 |

Macau

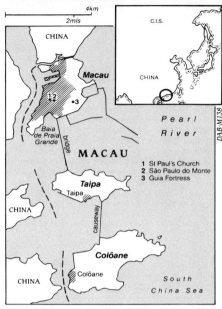

1 St Paul's Church
2 São Paulo do Monte
3 Guia Fortress

Location: South China coast.

Direcção dos Serviços de Turismo (Macau Government Tourist Office)
CP 3006, Edificio Ritz, Largo do Senado 9, Macau
Tel: 388 644. Fax: 510 104. Telex: 88338 (a/b TURIS OM).

Embassy of the Portuguese Republic
11 Belgrave Square, London SW1X 8PP
Tel: (0171) 235 5331/4. Fax: (0171) 245 1287. Telex: 28484. Opening hours: 1000-1300 and 1400-1700 Monday to Friday.

Portuguese Consulate General
Silver City House, 62 Brompton Road, London SW3 1BJ
Tel: (0171) 581 8722/4. Fax: (0171) 581 3085. Opening hours: 0900-1330 Monday to Friday.

Macau Tourist Information Bureau
6 Sherlock Mews, Paddington Street, London W1M 3RH
Tel: (0171) 224 3390. Fax: (0171) 224 0601. Opening hours: 1030-1730 Monday to Friday.

The British Trade Commission in Hong Kong serves as the nearest British Government Representative and deals with enquiries relating to Macau (see *Hong Kong* **earlier in this book).**

Embassy of the Portuguese Republic
2125 Kalorama Road, NW, Washington, DC 20008
Tel: (202) 328 8610. Fax: (202) 462 3726.
Consulate Generals in: Boston, Honolulu, Houston, Los Angeles, Miami, Newark, New Bedford, New Orleans, New York (tel: (212) 246 4580), Philadelphia, Providence, San Francisco and Waterbury.

Macau Tourist Information Bureau
Suite 316, 70A Greenwich Avenue, New York, NY 10011
Tel: (212) 206 6828. Fax: (212) 924 0882.

Macau Tourist Information Bureau
PO Box 1860, 3133 Lake Hollywood Drive, Los Angeles, CA 90068
Tel: (213) 851 3402. Fax: (213) 851 3684. Telex: 910-3214604.

The General Consulate of the United States of America in Hong Kong deals with enquiries relating to Macau (see *Hong Kong* **earlier in this book).**

Embassy of the Portuguese Republic
645 Island Park Drive, Ottawa, Ontario K1Y 0B8
Tel: (613) 729 0883 *or* 729 2922. Fax: (613) 729 4236.

Health

GALILEO/WORLDSPAN: **TI-DFT/QMP/HE**
SABRE: **TIDFT/QMP/HE**

Visa

GALILEO/WORLDSPAN: **TI-DFT/QMP/VI**
SABRE: **TIDFT/QMP/VI**

For more information on Timatic codes refer to Contents.

Consulates in: Edmonton, Halifax, Montréal, Québec, St John's, Toronto, Vancouver and Winnipeg.

Macau Tourist Information Bureau
Western Canada:
10551 Shellbridge Way, Street 157, Richmond, British Columbia V6X 2W9
Tel: (604) 231 9040. Fax: (604) 231 9031.
Eastern Canada:
5059 Yonge Street, North York, Ontario M2N 5P2
Tel: (416) 466 6552. Fax: (416) 221 5227.

The Canadian Commission in Hong Kong deals with enquiries relating to Macau (see *Hong Kong* **earlier in the book).**

AREA: 18 sq km (6.95 sq miles).
POPULATION: 355,693 (1991).
POPULATION DENSITY: 19,761 per sq km.
CAPITAL: Macau.
GEOGRAPHY: Macau is situated on a tiny peninsula at the mouth of the Pearl River and is linked to mainland China by a narrow isthmus, the Ferreira do Amaral. The territory also includes the islands of Taipa and Colôane, which are linked to the peninsula by a causeway and a bridge. The landscape is essentially flat, with seven small hills.
LANGUAGE: The official languages are Portuguese and Chinese (Cantonese). English is widely spoken by those engaged in trade, tourism and commerce.
RELIGION: Roman Catholic, Buddhism, Daoism and Confucianism.
TIME: GMT + 8.
ELECTRICITY: Usually 220 volts AC; older establishments use 110 volts AC, 50Hz.
COMMUNICATIONS: Telephone: IDD service is available. Country code: 853. Outgoing international code: 00. International facilities are available at the General Post Office at Leal Senado Square, Macau City, and the Central Post Offices in Taipa and Colôane. **Fax:** Hotels have fax facilities. **Telex/telegram:** Services available at larger hotels and telecommunication offices, as well as all pay-phones. **Post:** Airmail to Europe takes three to five days. **Press:** Newspapers are in Portuguese or Chinese. The English-language papers are *The Standard, The South China Morning Post*, the monthly *Macau Travel Talk* and the biennial *Macau Image*.
BBC World Service and Voice of America frequencies: From time to time these change. See the section *How to Use this Book* for more information.

BBC:

MHz	0.675		

Voice of America:

MHz	17.74	15.15	11.76	7.275

PASSPORT/VISA

Regulations and requirements may be subject to change at short notice, and you are advised to contact the appropriate diplomatic or consular authority before finalising travel arrangements. Details of these may be found at the head of this country's entry. Any numbers in the chart refer to the footnotes below.

	Passport Required?	Visa Required?	Return Ticket Required?
Full British	Yes	No	No
BVP	Not valid	-	-
Australian	Yes	No	No
Canadian	Yes	No	No
USA	Yes	No	No
Other EU (As of 31/12/94)	Yes	No	No
Japanese	Yes	No	No

PASSPORTS: Valid passport required by all.
British Visitors Passport: Not acceptable.
VISAS: Visas may be obtained on arrival in Macau. However, nationals of countries which do not maintain diplomatic relations with Portugal *must* obtain their visas in advance from Portuguese Consulates overseas, and may not obtain them on arrival in Macau. Visas are required by all except:
(a) nationals of countries listed in the chart above for stays not exceeding 20 days*;
(b) nationals of Austria, Brazil, Finland, India, South Korea, Malaysia, New Zealand, Norway, Philippines, Singapore, South Africa, Sweden, Switzerland and Thailand;
(c) residents of Hong Kong who are British and Commonwealth subjects, for a stay not exceeding 20 days; residents of Hong Kong who are nationals of other countries do not require visas if staying less than 3 days;
(d) Chinese residents holding Hong Kong identity cards or re-entry permits, or holders of a British passport endorsed 'British subject' are allowed a 3-month stay.
Note [*]: Visas *will* be required if intending to stay more than 20 days.

Types of visa: Tourist and Business. Cost: *Individual* – HK$190; *Family* – HK$380; HK$95 for children under 12; *Group* – HK$95 per person for bona fide groups of 15 persons or more.

Validity: 20 days. Can be extended by 1 month at no charge on application to the immigration office.

Application to: Consulate (or Consular section at Embassy). For addresses, see top of entry.

Application requirements: (a) 2 application forms. (b) 2 passport-size photos. (c) Valid passport. (d) Return or onward ticket. (e) Alien Registration or Green Card. (f) Company letter of responsibility for those travelling on business.

Working days required: Visas can normally be issued the same day.

Temporary residence: Enquire at Information Bureau.

MONEY

Currency: Pataca (MOP) = 100 avos. Notes are in denominations of MOP1000, 500, 100, 50, 10 and 5. Coins are in denominations of MOP5 and 1, and 50, 20 and 10 avos.

Credit cards: Access/Mastercard and Visa are accepted. Check with your credit card company for details of merchant acceptability and other services which may be available.

Travellers cheques: These may be exchanged at banks, bureaux de change and at many hotels.

Exchange rate indicators: The following figures are included as a guide to the movements of the Pataca against Sterling and the US Dollar:

Date:	Oct '92	Sep '93	Jan '94	Jan '95
£1.00=	12.63	12.25	11.78	12.50
$1.00=	7.96	8.02	7.97	7.99

Note: The Pataca is loosely pegged to the Hong Kong Dollar.

Currency restrictions: There are no restrictions on the import or export of either local or foreign currency.

Banking hours: 0930-1600 Monday to Friday, 0930-1200 Saturday.

DUTY FREE

The following goods may be imported into Macau without incurring customs duty:
A reasonable amount of tobacco, alcohol and perfume for personal use.

Prohibited items: Drugs and firearms.

Note: There is a 5% duty on the import of electrical appliances and equipment. There are no export duties, but as travel is almost invariably via Hong Kong, the relevant Hong Kong import/export regulations must be observed. See the *Hong Kong* entry earlier in the *book*.

PUBLIC HOLIDAYS

Jan 1 '95 New Year's Day. **Jan 31-Feb 2** Chinese New Year. **Apr 5** Ching Ming Festival. **Apr 14-16** Easter. **Apr 25** Anniversary of the Portuguese Revolution. **May 1** Labour Day. **Jun 10** Camões/Portuguese Communities Day. **Jun 13** Dragon Boat Festival. **Jun 24** Feast of St John the Baptist. **Sep 20** Day following Chinese Mid-Autumn Festival. **Oct 1** National Day of the People's Republic of China. **Oct 5** Portuguese Republic Day. **Nov 1** Festival of Ancestors. **Nov 2** All Souls' Day. **Dec 1** Restoration of Independence. **Dec 8** Feast of the Immaculate Conception. **Dec 22** Winter Solstice. **Dec 24-25** Christmas. **Jan 1 '96** New Year's Day. **Feb 19-21** Chinese New Year. **Apr 5** Ching Ming Festival. **Apr 5-8** Easter. **Apr 25** Anniversary of the Portuguese Revolution.

HEALTH

Regulations and requirements may be subject to change at short notice, and you are advised to contact your doctor well in advance of your intended date of departure. Any numbers in the chart refer to the footnotes below.

	Special Precautions?	Certificate Required?
Yellow Fever	No	No
Cholera	No	No
Typhoid & Polio	No	-
Malaria	No	-
Food & Drink	1	-

[1]: All water should be regarded as a potential health risk. Water used for drinking, brushing teeth or making ice should have first been boiled or otherwise sterilised. Milk is unpasteurised and should be boiled. Powdered or tinned milk is available and is advised, but make sure that it is reconstituted with pure water. Avoid dairy products which are likely to have been made from unboiled milk. Only eat well-cooked meat and fish, preferably served hot. Pork, salad and mayonnaise may carry increased

risk. Vegetables should be cooked and fruit peeled.

Health care: Health insurance is recommended. There are good medical facilities, and religious orders or hotels will also give assistance.

TRAVEL - International

AIR: An airport is currently under construction in Macau. The airport is planned to open on July 18, 1995. There are also plans for a national airline named *Air Macau* which will begin services in November. At present, most transport is via Hong Kong.

Approximate flight time: From London to Hong Kong is 18 hours; for other flight times, see *Hong Kong* entry.

Helicopter services: *East Asia Airlines* operate daily flights in two 8-seat Bell 222 helicopters (travel time – 20 minutes). Cost: HK$900 (weekdays), HK$1000 (weekends and public holidays).

Departure tax: Passengers embarking at Hong Kong for Macau must pay HK$26 per person. Departure tax from Macau is HK$22 per person.

SEA: A ferry service operates 24 hours a day between Macau and Kaohsiung, Taiwan (China). The *Macmosa* departs from Macau each Tuesday and Saturday morning arriving 24 hours later; departure from Kaohsiung is Sunday and Wednesday afternoon. Onward travel to China can be arranged. The journey time to Hong Kong by jumbo-catamaran is about 70 minutes and by high-speed ferry is 90 minutes. Further information is available from: *Hong Kong Ferries* (formerly Sealink), Central Harbour Services Pier, Pier Road, Central, Hong Kong. Tel: 542 3081. Fax: 854 3847. Telex: 81340 (a/b HYFCO HX); *or*
Hong Kong Hi-Speed Ferries Limited, 13th Floor, V Heun Building, 138 Queen's Road, Central, Hong Kong. Tel: 815 3043. Fax: 543 0324. Telex: 89846 (a/b HKFPF HX). The **baggage allowance** is currently 20kg per person on high-speed ferries. In general, luggage is limited to hand-carried items. Tour operators can arrange luggage-handling where required.

Jetfoils operate a 24-hour service and take about 55 minutes from Hong Kong. Bookings for groups can be made directly by contacting any of the following: *Far East Hydrofoil Co Ltd.* Tel: 859 3333. Fax: 858 1014. Telex: 74200 (a/b SEDAM HX); *or*
Hong Kong Macau Hydrofoil Co Ltd. Tel: 559 9255 *or* 521 8302. Fax: 810 0952. Telex: 74493 (a/b HMHCO HX).

TRAVEL - Internal

ROAD: Traffic drives on the left. There is a bridge to Taipa Island, with plans to construct a second bridge carrying a 4-lane highway from the international airport (currently under construction in the Pearl River estuary) to the Macau–China border at Gongbei. **Bus:** There are five bus routes in the city. No. 3 runs from the ferry terminal to the city centre. Bus services operate daily to the islands. First buses run from about 0700, the last at about midnight (but the last to the islands leaves at about 2300). **Car hire:** For information and bookings contact: *Macau Mokes Group Ltd,* Avenida Marciano Baptista. Tel: 378 851. Fax: 555 433. Telex: 88251 (a/b MBC OM); *or Avis Rent-A-Car,* Mandarin Oriental. Tel: 336 789 *or* 567 888 ext. 3004. Fax: 314 112. **Taxi:** Most taxis are black with a cream-coloured top. *Rickshaws* and *pedicabs,* bicycles with a 2-seater section at the back, are also available for hire. Prices should be agreed in advance. It is worth remembering that many of the attractions in Macau are located on hilltops, beyond the reach of even the strongest-legged pedicab driver. Chauffeur-driven limousines are also available.

Documentation: An International Driving Permit is not required for drivers from the UK.

ACCOMMODATION

There are various types of accommodation, with the full range from first-class to economy-class hotels, plus inns, villa-apartments housed in new buildings and older colonial hotels. At weekends the hotels, villas and inns are usually full, so it is wise to make a reservation. There are presently about 6000 hotel rooms in Macau. Most hotels are air-conditioned and have a private bath. A 10% service charge is added to hotel bills plus a 5% government tax. For further information, contact the Macau Hotels Association, c/o Mr B Williams (General Manager), Mandarin Oriental Hotel, Avenida de Amiizode. Tel: 567 888. Fax: 320 595.

RESORTS & EXCURSIONS

MACAU: The most famous sight in Macau is probably the ruins of the *Church of St Paul's,* originally built in 1602 and rebuilt in 1835 after a disastrous typhoon. The Jesuit citadel of *São Paulo do Monte* is almost directly in

the centre of Macau. It forms the strong central point of the old city wall, and was instrumental in preventing the Dutch from conquering the city in 1622. The 17th-century *Guia Fortress* stands on the highest point in Macau; its lighthouse is the oldest on the China coast. The complex of temples known as *Kun Iam Tong* dates from the time of the Ming Dynasty, about 400 years ago, and contains, amongst other works of art, a small statue of Marco Polo. The oldest Chinese temple in the country is that of the *Goddess A-Ma,* and dates back at least six centuries. It has some excellent multi-coloured bas-relief stone carvings. The finest expression of Portuguese architecture is probably the *Leal Senado,* the Senate Chamber. The *Public Library,* off the main staircase, and the main chamber itself are well worth a visit. The *Sun Yat Sen Memorial Home,* the former residence of the Revolutionary leader who overthrew the Ching Dynasty in 1910, is now a museum. It is open every day except Tuesday between 1000 and 1300, and also between 1500 and 1700 at weekends. *São Domingo's Church,* built in the 17th century, is one of the most beautiful religious buildings in Macau. Other churches of interest include those of *Santo Agostinho, São Jose* and *S Lourenco. Monuments* of note in the country include those in honour of Jorge Alvares and Vasco da Gama. The *Chinese Garden of Lou Lim Ioc* offers a relaxing alternative.

TAIPA: The island of Taipa is known for its firework factories. It also contains several small Buddhist temples and some old Portuguese buildings.

COLOANE: Colôane has several beaches, as well as woods and hills. It has interesting Chinese temples, the *Chapel of St Francis Xavier* and a traditional junk-building yard near the village.

SOCIAL PROFILE

FOOD & DRINK: Most restaurants have table service. Hotels, inns and restaurants offer a wide variety of food. They specialise in Portuguese dishes, but also offer cuisine from China, Japan, Korea and Indonesia. Local Macau food is spicy, a unique combination of Chinese and Portuguese cooking methods. Dishes include *bacalhau* (cod served baked, grilled, stewed or boiled), *caldo verde* and *sopa a alentejana* (rich soups with vegetables, meat and olive oil), 'African chicken' (grilled with hot spices), *galinha a portuguesa* (chicken baked with potatoes, onions, eggs and saffron – the appearance of curry without the spice), *minche* (minced meat with fried potato and onion), Macau sole (fried fish is usually served with salad) and *feijoados* (from Brazil, stews of kidney beans, pork, potatoes, cabbage and spicy sausage). The speciality of *dim sum* (Chinese savoury snacks steamed and served in bamboo baskets on trollies) includes *cha siu bao* (steamed pork dumplings), *har gau* (steamed shrimp dumplings) and *shui mai* (steamed and minced pork with shrimp). **Drink:** Alcohol is easily obtainable. There are no licensing laws. All restaurants offer a variety of Portuguese red and white wines and sparkling *vinho verde,* as well as port and brandy, all at low prices.

NIGHTLIFE: Most of the nightlife is centred on the hotels, many of which have nightclubs with cabaret, Portuguese folk dancing, lively dance bands, discotheques, international menus and bars. In summer there are several open-air *esplanadas* serving soft drinks around the square in front of Hotel Lisboa. Gambling is a big attraction for visitors to Macau and the casinos are open 24 hours, providing famous entertainers, baccarat, blackjack, roulette and Chinese games like *fantan* and *dai-siu* (big and small). There are also *keno* and one-armed bandits (called 'hungry tigers' in Macau).

SHOPPING: Macau's most popular buys remain jewellery (particularly gold), Chinese antiques, porcelain, pottery, electric gadgetry, cameras, watches and beading work. They are available at duty-free prices because Macau is a free port and no sales tax is charged. Bargaining is expected on many items. Other popular buys are Chinese herbs and medicines, dried seafood (such as sharks' fins), abalone, Chinese and Macau pastries, and locally made knitwear from stalls. When purchasing antiques, gold and jewellery, it is advisable to patronise shops recommended by the Goldsmiths' and Jewellers' Association and the Macau Government Tourist Office (who publish a shopping guide). A warranty and a receipt should be asked for when buying jewellery, gold, cameras, watches and electrical goods. **Shopping hours:** Generally 1000-2000 Monday to Saturday. Some shops may be closed on the first of every month.

SPORT: Greyhound *racing* takes place at the Canidrome on Avenida General Castelo Branco on Tuesday, Thursday, weekends and Hong Kong public holidays from 2000. The Macau Jockey Club organises flat races at its track on the island of Taipa. The Far East's gala motorcycle and Formula III car racing event, the Macau Grand Prix, is held during the third week in November. Courts and equipment are available for **badminton** and **tennis** on request in advance from the Macau Government

Tourist Office. A **bowling** centre with four lanes is located on the ground floor of Hotel Lisboa. **Squash** courts are available at the Oriental Macau and Royal hotels. **Swimming** pools are found in major hotels like the Hyatt Regency, Lisboa, Pousada de S Tiago, Pousada de Colôane, Royal, Oriental Macau and Estoril. Public pools are also in Macau and Colôane Island.

SPECIAL EVENTS: The Macau Tourist Information Bureau and Government Tourist Office can supply details of the many festivals celebrated in Macau. Some of the 1995 events are listed below. Festivals which are also official public holidays are listed in the *Public Holidays* section above.

May 7 '95 *Feast of the Bathing of Lord Buddha; Feast of the Drunken Dragon; Tam Kong Festival.* **May 13** *Procession of Our Lady of Fatima.* **Jun 2** *International Dragon Boat Festival.* **Sep/Oct** *International Fireworks Festival.* **Sep 9** *Mid-Autumn Festival.* **Oct/Nov** *Macau International Music Festival.* **Nov 18-19** *Macau Grand Prix.* **Dec 3** *Macau Marathon.*

SOCIAL CONVENTIONS: Entertaining generally takes place in restaurants and public places. It is rare to be invited to a private home, unless the person is wealthy. Spirits are standard gifts in return for hospitality. Apart from the most formal occasions in restaurants and nightclubs, casual wear is acceptable. **Tipping:** A 10% service charge will be added to most hotel and restaurant bills, but a small tip should also be left.

BUSINESS PROFILE

ECONOMY: Macau has long been an important international distribution outlet for many Chinese products and in this way is fairly similar to Hong Kong. Its overall economic development has been hindered, however, by a lack of infrastructure. It has an active manufacturing and exporting sector whose main products are textiles, toys, optics, rubber, china, furniture and footwear. Macau is increasingly famous for its gambling facilities and tourism has now developed as a major source of income. China, Hong Kong and the USA are the territory's major trading partners. On December 20, 1999, Macau will become a Special Administrative Region of the People's Republic of China, thus sharing the same status that Hong Kong will achieve in 1997. The Sino-Portuguese agreement guarantees the continuation of Macau's free capitalist economy for 50 years.

BUSINESS: Business people are expected to dress smartly. Calling cards are essential, appointments should be made in advance and punctuality is appreciated. The Macau Business Centre (PO Box 138, Ground Floor, Edificio Ribeiro. Tel: 373 379 *or* 511 631 *or* 323 598. Fax: 511 631. Telex: 88251 MBC OM) offers secretarial and supporting services, meeting rooms, microphones, tape recorders, video tape and telex.

COMMERCIAL INFORMATION: The following organisation can offer advice: Associação Comercial de Macau, 5th Floor, Edificio ACM, Rua de Xangai 175. Tel: 572 042. Fax: 594 513. Telex: 88229.

CONFERENCES/CONVENTIONS: There are three major meetings venues: the Jai Alai Stadium (with seating for up to 5000), the Forum (a multi-purpose complex with seating for up to 4000) and the University of Macau conference centre (with seating for up to 764). Several hotels also have facilities, and support services can be provided by the Macau Business Centre (see above). For further information, contact the Macau Tourist Information Bureau in London (for address, see top of entry).

CLIMATE

Subtropical climate with very hot summers and a rainy period during the summer months. Most rain occurs in the afternoon. Winds can reach gale force, and typhoons are not unknown.

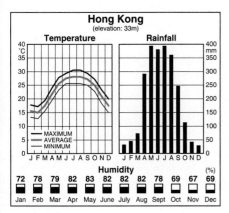

Hong Kong
(elevation: 33m)

Humidity												(%)
72	78	79	82	83	82	82	82	78	69	67	69	
Jan	Feb	Mar	Apr	May	June	July	Aug	Sept	Oct	Nov	Dec	

Macedonia
(Former Yugoslav Republic of)

☐ *international airport*

Location: Ex-Yugoslav republic; southeastern Europe.

Note: In deference to Greek sensibilities the United Nations and other international organisations have recognised Macedonia under the interim name of 'The Former Yugoslav Republic of Macedonia' (FYRM).

Ministry of Foreign Relations
Dame Gruev bb, 91000 Skopje, Former Yugoslav Republic of Macedonia
Tel: (91) 236 311.
ECGD (Country Policy Desk)
Tel: (0171) 512 7000.
Foreign and Commonwealth Office
Tel: (0171) 270 3000 (switchboard) *or* 270 4129 (travel advice). Opening hours: 0930-1600 Monday to Friday.
Embassy of the Former Yugoslav Republic of Macedonia
10 Harcourt House, 19A Cavendish Square, London W1M 9AD
Tel: (0171) 499 2864. Fax: (0171) 499 2864. Opening hours: 0900-1700 Monday to Friday.
Office of the British Government Representative
Ul Veljko Vlahovic 26, 91000 Skopje, Former Yugoslav Republic of Macedonia
Tel: (91) 117 799. Fax: (91) 220 119. Telex: 51516 (a/b AA SKOPMA).
Representative Office of the Former Yugoslav Republic of Macedonia
Suite 402, 1015 15th Street, NW, Washington, DC 20005
Tel: (202) 682 0519.
Macedonian World Congress
PO Box 2826, Ormond Beach, FL 32175-2826
Tel: (904) 676 2466. Fax: (904) 676 2462.
Embassy of the United States
c/o USAID, Ul Veljko Vlahovic 26, 91000 Skopje, Former Yugoslav Republic of Macedonia
Tel: (91) 117 2121. Fax: (91) 118 105.

AREA: 25,713 sq km (9928 sq miles), or 10% of the territory of the former Yugoslav federation (its fourth-

---

largest republic).

Note: The ex-Yugoslav republic of 'Macedonia' is only one of three areas of the historical region of 'Macedonia', which includes Pirin Macedonia (Bulgaria) and Aegean Macedonia (Greece), with a total area of 66,600 sq km (25,700 sq miles), most of which is in Greece.
POPULATION: 2,033,964 (1991), or 9% of the total population of the former Yugoslav federation (its fourth most populous republic).
Note: FYRM contains the majority of people claiming to be 'Macedonians', whose existence as a separate nation is denied in both Bulgaria and Greece (similarly in Albania and Serbia).
POPULATION DENSITY: 79.1 per sq km.
CAPITAL: Skopje. **Population:** 563,301 (1991).
GEOGRAPHY: Roughly rectangular in shape, and on the strategic Vardar Valley north–south communications route, FYRM is landlocked, bordering Serbia to the north, Albania to the west, Greece to the south and Bulgaria to the east.
LANGUAGE: Under the new unitary constitution of November 1991, Macedonian is the official language (using the Cyrillic alphabet and being akin to Bulgarian). Albanian, Turkish, Roma and Serbo-Croat are also used by ethnic groups.
RELIGION: Eastern Orthodox Macedonians approximately 64.6%, Muslim Albanians 21%, Muslim Turks 5% and Serbian Orthodox Serbs 2.1%. As elsewhere in the former Yugoslav federation, local politics are now strongly divided along national confessional lines.
Note: As the Albanians did not cooperate with the 1991 census, the figure given for their share of the population is a contested estimate, with the true figure more like 30% of the total.
TIME: GMT + 1 (GMT + 2 from last Sunday in March to Saturday before last Sunday in September).
ELECTRICITY: 220 volts AC, 50Hz.
COMMUNICATIONS: Telecommunications/Post: IDD is available. Country code: 389. Outgoing international code: 99. All telecommunications services, as well as the post, are generally working normally, although uncertainty still surrounds all future international connections via Serbia and Greece, whose respective authorities subjected FYRM to an economic blockade in 1992. **Press:** The two main daily newspapers, both printed in Skopje, are *Nova Makedonija* and *Vecer*. **TV/Radio:** The state TV-radio station, *RTS*, broadcasts in Macedonian, Albanian and Turkish. The Ministry of Information acts as the state news agency, periodically producing material in English for international distribution.
BBC World Service and Voice of America frequencies: From time to time these change. See the section *How to Use this Book* for more information.
BBC:

MHz	17.64	12.09	9.410	6.180

Voice of America:

MHz	9.670	6.040	5.995	1.260

PASSPORT/VISA

Regulations and requirements may be subject to change at short notice, and you are advised to contact the appropriate diplomatic or consular authority before finalising travel arrangements. Details of these may be found at the head of this country's entry. Any numbers in the chart refer to footnotes below.

	Passport Required?	Visa Required?	Return Ticket Required?
Full British	Yes	No	No
BVP	Not valid	-	-
Australian	Yes	Yes/1	Yes
Canadian	Yes	Yes/1	Yes
USA	Yes	Yes/1	No
Other EU (As of 31/12/94)	Yes	No/2	No
Japanese	Yes	No	No

PASSPORTS: Valid passport required by all.
British Visitors Passport: Not accepted.
VISAS: Required by all except:
(a) nationals of Argentina, Austria, Bolivia, Bulgaria, Costa Rica, Chile, Cuba, Czech Republic, Finland, Iceland, Israel, Hungary, Malta, Mexico, Monaco, Norway, Poland, Romania, Russian Federation, San Marino, Slovenia, Sweden, Switzerland, Turkey and Yugoslavia (Serbia and Montenegro);
(b) **[2]** nationals of EU countries (except nationals of Greece who *do* need a visa);
(c) nationals of Japan.
Note [1]: Nationals of Australia, Canada, South Korea and USA can obtain a visa at the point of arrival.
Types of visa: *Single-entry:* US$10, *Double-entry:* US$20, *Multiple-entry:* US$30. A *Business visa* costs

US$30 unless in a group when there is a charge of US$4 per person. Children under 14 years pay half the normal price.

Validity: Where they are required, visas are valid for 3 or 6 months.

Application to: Nearest Diplomatic or Consular mission (for addresses, see above).

Application requirements: (a) Application form. (b) Valid passport. (c) Self-addressed, postage-paid, registered envelope for return of passport and documents. (d) Fee payable in cash or by postal order (cheques will only be accepted from travel agencies, firms and companies).

Note: Nationals who require visas may, on entry, be expected to state that they have at least US$150 per person per day for their intended stay in the FYRM, and may be asked to produce a return ticket.

Working days required: Visas are issued immediately to personal callers. Postal applications take 7 days.

MONEY

Currency: The Former Yugoslav Republic of Macedonia declared monetary independence in April 1992. It introduced its own currency in the form of coupons, the Macedonian Denar (1 denar = 100 deni).

Currency exchange: As elsewhere in the ex-Yugoslav republics, the only true repositories of value and real mediums of exchange locally are the Deutschmark and the US Dollar (Sterling is rarely used or seen in the republic). *Emigré* hard currency remittances are reportedly of considerable local importance, although few of these resources ever enter the official banking system. The local currency is non-convertible.

PUBLIC HOLIDAYS

Jan 1 '95 New Year's Day. **May 1-2** Labour Days. **Jul 4** Veterans' Day. **Aug 2** Bank Holiday. **Oct 11** Bank Holiday. **Nov 29-30** Republic Days. **Jan 1 '96** New Year's Day.

HEALTH

Regulations and requirements may be subject to change at short notice, and you are advised to contact your doctor well in advance of your intended date of departure. Any numbers in the chart refer to the footnotes below.

	Special Precautions?	Certificate Required?
Yellow Fever	No	No
Cholera	No	No
Typhoid & Polio	No	-
Malaria	No	-
Food & Drink	1	-

[1]: Mains water is normally chlorinated, and whilst relatively safe may cause mild abdominal upsets. Bottled water is available and is advised for the first few weeks of the stay. Milk is pasteurised and dairy products are safe for consumption. Local meat, poultry, seafood, fruit and vegetables are generally considered safe to eat. *Rabies* is present. For those at high risk, vaccination before arrival should be considered. If you are bitten abroad seek medical advice without delay. For more information, consult the *Health* section at the back of the book.

Health care: Prescribed medicines must be paid for. Health insurance with emergency repatriation is strongly recommended.

TRAVEL - International

AIR: The national airline is *Palair Macedonian Airlines,* based in Skopje. It offers connections to the USA, Canada and Australia.

Note: Because of the unstable political situation in this region, normal use of the main north–south road and rail routes through and beyond FYRM may be difficult if not impossible with extensive delays on borders with both Serbia and Greece. The main routes to Albania and Bulgaria are operating more or less normally.

TRAVEL - Internal

AIR: The Belgrade–Skopje–Ohrid air service, formerly run by *JAT,* is no longer operating at present. *Palair Macedonian Airlines* run domestic services.

RAIL/ROAD: All the main internal road and rail services are operating normally, with links from Skopje

to Kumanovo in the north, to Teluvo in the west, to Stip in the east and to Tilov, Velco, Prilep and Bitola in the south.

Note: The local situation is very changeable and the advice of the FCO's travel advice unit should be sought prior to any visit.

ACCOMMODATION

FYRM has no deluxe/A-class hotels. There are B-class hotels in Skopje and the Ohrid Lake tourist area on the border with Albania and Greece.

RESORTS & EXCURSIONS

The Former Yugoslav Republic of Macedonia is a mountainous land right at the heart of the Balkans. Its churches and mosques contain many fine examples of art and architecture from the Byzantine and Ottoman periods. **Skopje**, Macedonia's capital, is largely new due to an earthquake in 1963. There is, however, plenty to see. *Skopje Old Town* is the most attractive quarter of the city. It is full of shops and restaurants. Here also is the *Church of the Holy Saviour* with its intricately carved iconostasis (a screen in orthodox churches on which icons are hung). Also to be found in the Old Town are the *Kursumli Ani* (16th century) and the *Suli An* (15th century) caravanserais and the *Daut Pasha Baths* with its two large and seven small domes. It now houses the *Art Gallery.* There are also a number of mosques dating from the Ottoman period, particularly the 15th-century *Mustafa Pasha Mosque* as well as the old 10th-century *Kale Fortress* and a magnificent foot bridge spanning the *River Varda.* Near Skopje is the *Nerezi Monastery* with the accompanying 12th-century *Church of St Pantelejmon* housing magnificent Byzantine frescoes.

Bitola, 5km (3 miles) from the Greek border, is the second-largest town in Macedonia. It was an important centre of Ottoman rule and also has the nearby ruins of the Greek city of *Heraclea.* **Ohrid** on *Lake Ohrid* is probably the most attractive town in Macedonia. Here St Clement of Ohrid laid the foundations of the first Slav university. In the 10th and 11th centuries Ohrid became the capital of the Macedonian Tsar Samuil. The walls of his fortress still survive and now provide a venue for summer concerts, operas and plays. Near the old fortress are the remains of a Classical theatre. Dotted around this beautiful town are a number of ancient churches, particularly the Cathedral of *St Sophia* containing some magnificent 10th-century frescoes.

SOCIAL PROFILE

FOOD & DRINK: Macedonian dishes show big Turkish and Greek influences. Different varieties of kebabs can be found almost everywhere as can dishes such as *musaka* (aubergines and potatoes baked in layers with minced meat). National specialities are *gravce na tavce* (beans in a skillet) and the delicious Ohrid trout.

SPECIAL EVENTS: The *Ohrid Folklore Festival* is celebrated annually during July and August.

SOCIAL CONVENTIONS: Handshaking is the common practice on introduction. Local business protocol is fairly informal, but things go very slowly or not at all due to the local bureaucracy and the more recent general socio-economic collapse in the republic.

BUSINESS PROFILE

ECONOMY: The poorest and least economically developed of the former Yugoslav republics, FYRM accounted for 5.6% of Yugoslavia's GDP in 1990/91 (around US$3 billion), with a GDP per capita of around US$1400 (US$1200 less than the all-Yugoslav average). A predominantly agricultural economy with few natural resources, it was formerly the most dependent of the poorer Yugoslav republics on federal subsidies from the richer north for its economic development. These ended in 1991, when the old Yugoslav market also disappeared, thereby bringing about a virtual collapse of the local industrial sector, which consisted mainly of capital goods. In addition, local attempts to bring about an internationally recognised independence prompted the Belgrade government to renounce responsibility for the former republic's foreign debt, which is a problem that remains an obstacle to the receipt of further World Bank aid. This was followed, in 1992, by a devastating Greek and Serbian economic blockade, which brought the republic to the point of complete socio-economic collapse. Even with recognition and some help from official

government and multilateral agency sources, the republic has very poor future economic prospects. The only substantive local economic asset is tobacco, but its largely high-tar classification had made it increasingly unviable in EU markets, even before foreign blockades made such exports impossible. More promising in the longer term are the hard currency remittances of the 150,000 or more *émigré* Macedonians in Western Europe and North America (plus another 200,000 in Australia), but even here, chronic political uncertainty is preventing anything but the most minimal repatriation of the considerable resources reportedly involved.

BUSINESS: Suits and ties are correct attire for men, with skirt, blouse and tights the accepted attire for women. Compared to the northern ex-Yugoslav republics, English and German are not so widely used as second languages. **Office hours:** 0700/0800-1500/1600 Monday to Friday.

COMMERCIAL INFORMATION: The following organisations can offer advice: National Bank of Macedonia, Kompleks Banki bb, 91000 Skopje. Tel: (91) 112 177. Fax: (91) 111 161. Telex: 51415; *or* Economic Chamber of Macedonia, PO Box 324, Dimitrie Cupovski 13, 91000 Skopje. Tel: (91) 111 088. Fax: (91) 116 210. Telex: 51438.

CLIMATE

Mostly a landlocked country, FYRM has a pronounced continental climate, with very cold winters and hot summers.

Required clothing: Mediumweight clothing and warm overcoats in winter; lightweight clothing and raincoats required for the summer.

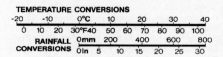

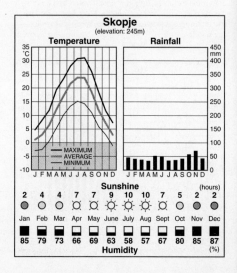

Madagascar

□ *international airport*

Location: Indian Ocean, 500km (300 miles) off the coast of Mozambique.

Maison de Tourisme de Madagascar
BP 610, Tsimbazaza, 101 Antananarivo, Madagascar
Tel: (2) 26298. Fax: (2) 26719. Telex: 26298.
Consulate of the Republic of Madagascar
16 Lanark Mansions, Pennard Road, London W12 8DT
Tel: (0181) 746 0133. Fax: (0181) 746 0134. Opening hours: 0930-1300 Monday to Friday.
British Embassy
BP 167, Première Etage, Immeuble 'Ny Havana', Cité de 67 Ha, 101 Antananarivo, Madagascar
Tel: (2) 27749 *or* 27370 *or* 33765. Fax: (2) 26690. Telex: 22459 (a/b PRODRO MG).
Embassy of the Republic of Madagascar
2374 Massachusetts Avenue, NW, Washington, DC 20008
Tel: (202) 265 5525/6. Fax: (202) 483 7603.
Embassy of the United States of America
BP 620, 14-16 rue Rainitovo, Antsahavola, 101 Antananarivo, Madagascar
Tel: (2) 21257 *or* 20089 *or* 20718. Fax: (2) 34539. Telex: 22202.
Embassy of the Republic of Madagascar
282 Somerset Street West, Ottawa, Ontario K2P 0J6
Tel: (613) 563 2506 *or* 563 2438. Fax: (613) 231 3261.
The Canadian Embassy in Dar-es-Salaam deals with enquiries relating to Madagascar (see *Tanzania* later in this book).

AREA: 587,041 sq km (226,658 sq miles).
POPULATION: 12,660,000 (1992 estimate).
POPULATION DENSITY: 21.6 per sq km.
CAPITAL: Antananarivo (formerly Tananarive).
Population: 1,000,000 (1992).
GEOGRAPHY: Madagascar, the fourth-largest island in

the world, lies in the Indian Ocean off the coast of Mozambique. It includes several much smaller islands. A central chain of high mountains, the Hauts Plateaux, occupies more than half of the main island and is responsible for the marked differences – ethnically, climatically and scenically – between the east and west coasts. The narrow strip of lowlands on the east coast, settled from the 6th century by Polynesian seafarers, is largely covered by dense rainforests, whereas the broader west coast landscape, once covered by dry deciduous forests, is now mostly savannah. The east coast receives the monsoon and, on both coasts, the climate is wetter towards the north. The southern tip of the island is semi-desert, with great forests of cactus-like plants. The capital, Antananarivo, is high up in the Hauts Plateaux near the island's centre. Much of Madagascar's flora and fauna is unique to the island. There are 3000 endemic species of butterfly; the many endemic species of lemurs fill the niches occupied elsewhere by animals as varied as racoons, monkeys, marmots, bush babies, sloths and even (though this variant is now extinct) bears; there is a similar diversity of reptiles, amphibians and birds (especially ducks), and also at all levels of plant life.
LANGUAGE: The official languages are Malagasy (which is related to Indonesian) and French. Local dialects are also spoken. Very little English is spoken.
RELIGION: 51% follow Animist beliefs, about 43% Christian; remainder Muslim.
TIME: GMT + 3.
ELECTRICITY: Mostly 220 volts AC, also 110/380 volts AC; 50Hz. Plugs are generally 2-pin.
COMMUNICATIONS: Telephone: IDD is available to major towns. Country code: 261. Outgoing international code: 16. **Telex/telegram:** Telex services are available at the telecommunications centre and the Colbert and Hilton hotels in the capital. The main post office (*PTT*) in Antananarivo offers a 24-hour telegram transmission service. **Post:** The *Poste Restante* facilities at main post offices are the most reliable option. Airmail to Europe takes at least seven days and surface mail three to four months. **Press:** There are no English-language newspapers; five dailies are published in French and/or Malagasy.
BBC World Service and Voice of America frequencies: From time to time these change. See the section *How to Use this Book* for more information.
BBC:

MHz	21.47	11.94	6.005	3.255

Voice of America:

MHz	21.49	15.60	9.525	6.035

PASSPORT/VISA

Regulations and requirements may be subject to change at short notice, and you are advised to contact the appropriate diplomatic or consular authority before finalising travel arrangements. Details of these may be found at the head of this country's entry. Any numbers in the chart refer to the footnotes below.

	Passport Required?	Visa Required?	Return Ticket Required?
Full British	Yes	Yes	Yes
BVP	Not valid	-	-
Australian	Yes	Yes	Yes
Canadian	Yes	Yes	Yes
USA	Yes	Yes	Yes
Other EU (As of 31/12/94)	Yes	Yes	Yes
Japanese	Yes	Yes	Yes

PASSPORTS: Valid passport required by all.
British Visitors Passport: Not acceptable.
VISAS: Required by all.
Types of visa: Business and Tourist. A Transit visa is not required by those who continue their journey to a third country by the same or first connecting aircraft within 24 hours, provided that tickets and documents are held for their onward journey and they do not leave the airport. Business visas cost £50 (2 entries – £60). Tourist visas cost £35 (2 entries – £45).
Validity: Visas are issued for the duration of 30 or 90 days (no difference in cost) and are valid for 6 months from date of issue.
Application to: Consulate (or Consular section at Embassy). For addresses, see top of entry.
Application requirements: (a) Passport. (b) 1 application form. (c) 4 passport-size photos. (d) Letter of recommendation on company headed notepaper if requesting Business visa. (e) Return ticket or confirmation of booking from travel agent. (f) Add £1 for recorded postage per passport to visa fees if applying by post.
Note: Independent travellers on a tourist visa are required to spend a minimum of FFr2000 (£250) during their stay in Madagascar.
Working days required: In person – same day; post – 7 days.

MONEY

Currency: Malagasy Franc (MGFr) = 100 centimes. Notes are in denominations of MGFr10,000, 5000, 1000 and 500. Coins are in denominations of MGFr100, 50, 20, 10, 5, 2 and 1.
Credit cards: Visa, American Express, Access/Mastercard and Diners Club are accepted at the capital's Colbert and Hilton hotels. These and other cards have limited use elsewhere in the country. Check with your credit card company for details of merchant acceptability and other services which may be available.
Travellers cheques: These can be exchanged in banks and major hotels.
Exchange rate indicators: The following figures are included as a guide to the movements of the Malagasy Franc against Sterling and the US Dollar:

Date	Oct '92	Sep '93	Jan '94	Jan '95
£1.00=	2726	2789	2732	5691
$1.00=	1718	1827	1846	3638

Note: The Malagasy Franc began floating on the international money market in March 1994.
Currency restrictions: Foreign currencies are unrestricted provided they are declared on import and the exported amounts do not exceed the declaration. The maximum amount of local currency that may be imported and exported is MGFr25,000. These regulations are for foreign tourists; businessmen should enquire at a Malagasy Consulate.
Banking hours: 0800-1100 and 1400-1600 Monday to Friday.

DUTY FREE

The following goods can be imported into Madagascar without incurring customs duty:
500 cigarettes or 25 cigars or 500g of tobacco; 1 bottle of alcoholic beverage.

PUBLIC HOLIDAYS

Jan 1 '95 New Year's Day. **Mar 29** Commemoration of the 1947 Rebellion. **Apr 14** Good Friday. **Apr 17** Easter Monday. **May 1** Labour Day. **May 25** Ascension. **Jun 5** Whitsun. **Jun 26** Independence Day. **Nov 1** All Saints' Day. **Dec 25** Christmas. **Dec 30** Anniversary of the Republic of Madagascar. **Jan 1 '96** New Year's Day. **Mar 29** Commemoration of the 1947 Rebellion. **Apr 5** Good Friday. **Apr 8** Easter Monday.

HEALTH

Regulations and requirements may be subject to change at short notice, and you are advised to contact your doctor well in advance of your intended date of departure. Any numbers in the chart refer to the footnotes below.

	Special Precautions?	Certificate Required?
Yellow Fever	Yes	1
Cholera	Yes	2
Typhoid & Polio	Yes	-
Malaria	3	-
Food & Drink	4	-

[1]: A yellow fever vaccination certificate is required from travellers arriving from, or having passed through, an area considered by the Malagasy authorities to be infected; enquire at Embassy.
[2]: A cholera vaccination certificate is recommended for travellers arriving from, or having passed through, an area considered by the Malagasy authorities to be infected; enquire at Embassy. See the *Health* section at the back of the book.
[3]: Malaria risk, predominantly in the malignant *falciparum* form, exists all year throughout the country and is highest in coastal areas. Resistance to chloroquine has been reported.
[4]: All water should be regarded as being potentially contaminated. Water used for drinking, brushing teeth or making ice should have first been boiled or otherwise sterilised. Milk is unpasteurised and should be boiled. Powdered or tinned milk is available and is advised, but make sure that it is reconstituted with pure water. Avoid dairy products which are likely to have been made from unboiled milk. Only eat well-cooked meat and fish, preferably served hot. Pork, salad and mayonnaise may carry increased risk. Vegetables should be cooked and fruit peeled.
Rabies is present. For those at high risk, vaccination before arrival should be considered. If you are bitten abroad seek medical advice without delay. For more information consult the *Health* section at the back of the book.
Bilharzia (schistosomiasis) is present. Avoid swimming and paddling in fresh water. Swimming pools which are

well-chlorinated and maintained are safe.
Hepatitis is endemic and precautions are advised.
Health care: Health insurance is strongly recommended; it should include cover for emergency repatriation. It is highly recommended that visitors bring medication for stomach upset.

TRAVEL - International

AIR: Madagascar's national airline is *Air Madagascar (MD).*
Approximate flight time: From London to Antananarivo is 13 hours 50 minutes (including connection in Paris). There are regular flights from Madagascar to Réunion, Mauritius, Kenya, Tanzania, the Comoro Islands and the Seychelles.
International airports: *Antananarivo (TNR),* 17km (11 miles) from the city. Airport facilities include restaurant and bureau de change. It is linked by a regular bus service to the *Air Madagascar* office and the Hilton Hotel (the centre for Madagascar Airtours). Taxis asking special higher rates are also available at the airport.
Further airports are at *Nosy Bé* (links with the Seychelles), *Mahajanga* (East Africa and the Comoro Islands), *Toamasina* (Mauritius and Réunion islands); and *Arivonimamo* (international standby airport), 45km (28 miles) from the capital.
Departure tax: MGFr66,000 on most international flights; MGFr6600 for flights within the region. Transit passengers are exempt.
SEA: International tour operators promote Madagascar as a stopping place on extended cruises of the Indian and western Pacific Oceans. Expensive private cruises can be arranged from the USA and Europe. Toamasina is the main port.

TRAVEL - Internal

AIR: Most of Madagascar can be reached by air (there are more than 100 airfields), the exceptions being a few towns in the central highlands. *Air Madagascar's* 'Air Tourist Pass' is available and allows unlimited travel for certain periods.
Departure tax: MGFr6000 for domestic flights.
SEA/RIVER/CANAL: Madagascar has a strong maritime tradition and there are many coastal transport services. Rapids render many of the rivers unnavigable; the *Maison de Tourisme* can organise small-boat safaris on the Betsiboka and the Tsiribihina. The Pangalanes Canal runs for almost 600km (370 miles) along the east coast. Much of it is currently too clogged with silt for commercial traffic; the *Maison de Tourisme* can arrange sailing holidays.
RAIL: There are passenger rail services from the east coast port of Toamasina via Antananarivo to Antsirabe (branch line to Lake Alaotra); and from Manakara, also on the east coast, to Fianarantsoa. The northern line is to be extended. The southern line passes through spectacular rainforests. First-class carriages are air-conditioned. Light refreshments are sometimes available. One or two trains run daily on each route. Children under 4 travel free. Children aged 4-6 pay half fare.
ROAD: The road network is in need of repair. Tarred roads of varying quality link the main towns in the central highlands and continue to the most populous parts of the east and northwest coasts. There are three main routes, from Antananarivo to Majungo (RN4), to Toamasina (RN2) and to Fianarantsoa (RN7). There are isolated sections of tarred road elsewhere, but dirt tracks are more normal. Many roads are impassable in the rainy season (November to March). In 1988, the World Bank approved a US$140-million loan to rehabilitate the network. Traffic drives on the right. **Bus:** A flat fare is charged, irrespective of the distance travelled. Services can be unreliable. **Taxi:** Flat fares apply except in Antananarivo and Fianarantsoa, where fare is calculated according to whether the ride is confined to the 'lower town' or goes on to the 'upper town'. There are two types of taxi: the *Taxi-be,* which is quick and comfortable, and the *Taxi-brousse* (bush taxi), which is cheaper, slower, makes more stops and generally operates on cross-country routes. Fares should be agreed in advance and tipping is unnecessary. **Rickshaw:** The *pousse-pousse* takes passengers except where traffic or gradient makes it impractical. Prices are not controlled and vary according to distance. **Stagecoach:** A few covered wagons continue to take passengers in Antananarivo. **Car hire:** This is not widespread and car-hire agencies can only be found in the main tourist towns. It is advisable to make enquiries in advance about insurance requirements for car hire. **Motorbike hire:** Available through Club Double M, Androhibe, BP 1398, 101 Antananarivo. Tel: (2) 42392. Telex: 22577 (a/b CLUB MM MG). **Documentation:** A national driving licence is all that is required.

ACCOMMODATION

Since hotel development is in its early stages, some areas are better served than others, notably the capital Antananarivo, Nosy Bé and Toamasina. However, recent projects aimed at increasing the number of international-standard establishments have led to the opening of national tourism centres where good- to medium-standard accommodation is now available at moderate prices. As well as classified or classifiable accommodation, group and youth lodging is available. European-style accommodation is scarce outside the larger towns, and those visiting remote areas should travel with an open mind. Enquiries should be addressed to the Tourism Office in Antananarivo or *Air Madagascar* agencies. The *Guide to Madagascar* by Hilary Bradt provides excellent information on hotels and is available through the Madagascan Consulate in the UK or through bookshops. **Grading:** Hotels are classified from **1** to **5 stars** (5-star being equivalent to an international standard of about 3 stars); a secondary system of **ravinala** (travellers' palms) is used for more 'rustic' accommodation. More information is available from the Groupement des Associations et des Syndicats du Tourisme de Madagascar (GAST), BP 465, 41 Lalana Ratsimilaho, Ambatonakanga, Antananarivo. Tel: (2) 22230 *or* 27680. Fax: (2) 34901. Telex: 22478.

RESORTS & EXCURSIONS

The *Maison de Tourisme* (address at top of entry) offers a wide range of tours, some lasting as long as a month.
Note: Those who intend to make their own arrangements should be aware that bandits operate in certain highland regions and that the terrain and climate make surface travel exceedingly difficult (and often impossible) throughout much of the country for much of the year.

The Central Highlands

The capital and several other important towns are situated in the central section of the *Hauts Plateaux*, the chain of rugged, ravine-riven mountains that run from north to south down the centre of Madagascar.
Antananarivo, often abbreviated to *Tana*, is built on three levels. Dominating the city is the *Queen's Palace* and associated Royal Village or *Rova*. Now a national monument (opening: 0900-1200 and 1400-1700), it was once the residency of the Merina Dynasty which, in the 19th century, united all Madagascar for the first time. On the lowest level is the market of Analakely. The *Zuma Market,* claimed to be the second-largest in the world and certainly worth a visit, is busiest Friday. The *Tsimbazaza Zoological and Botanical Garden* is open 0800-1100 and 1400-1700 Thursday, Sunday and holidays. The Tourist Information Office is nearby. It is wise not to wander too far after dark.
Ambohimanga, the birthplace of the Malagasy state, is 20km (12 miles) from the capital. Known variously as 'the blue city', 'the holy city' and 'the forbidden city', it is surrounded by forests. The citadel was an important Merina stronghold and retains several structures associated with their ceremonies. Its main gate is an enormous stone disc; 40 men were needed to roll it into position. Ancestor worship may be witnessed Sunday.
Mantasoa, 80km (50 miles) from the capital, is a popular spot for picnics. The area was landscaped for the Merina Queens by a shipwrecked Frenchman and includes an artificial lake, pine forests and Madagascar's first industrial park.
Ampefy, 90km (60 miles) from the capital, is a volcanic region with spectacular waterfalls and geysers. Dams are used here to catch eels.
Perinet, 140km (90 miles) from the capital, is a nature reserve, home of the *indri* (a tail-less lemur) and many species of orchid. Also known as *Andasibe*.
Antsirabe, 170km (110 miles) from the capital, is a thermal spa and Madagascar's main industrial centre. The volcanic hills surrounding the town are dotted with crater lakes. Madagascar's second-highest mountain, *Tsiafajovona,* may be seen to the west of the road from Antananarivo.

The North

The lush north is dominated by two great mountains. *Tsarantanana,* at 2880m (9450ft) the island's highest, is covered with the giant ferns and lichens peculiar to high altitude rainforests. *Montagne d'Arbre* (1500m/4900ft) is a national park and is famous for its orchids and lemurs. The monsoon falls in the north between December and March.
Mahajanga, a provincial capital, stands at the mouth of Madagascar's largest river, the *Betsiboka.* The road to the capital is open between July and October. Boats depart for Nosy Bé and several other islands. The beach here is said to be free of sharks. The island's finest grottoes are at **Anjohibe**, 90km (60 miles) inland. There is a nature reserve at **Ankarafantsika**.
Nosy Bé is Madagascar's most important holiday resort. An island surrounded by smaller islands lying off the northwest coast, it is one hour by air from the capital. Exotic perfume plants such as ylang-ylang, vanilla (Madagascar is the world's largest producer), lemon grass and patchouli are grown here. The main town is **Hell-Ville**. Nearby, there is a ruined 17th-century Indian village.
Antseranana (formerly Diégo Suarez) is a cosmopolitan seaport overlooking a beautiful gulf at the northernmost tip of the island. It is a provincial capital. There are many lakes, waterfalls and grottoes in the rainforests above the port. Wildlife includes lemurs, crocodiles and orchids. Permission to visit the national park at Montagne d'Arbre nearby must be obtained from the *Ministère des Eaux et Forêts,* which has an office in the town. Boats may be taken to Nosy Bé. There is a good sandy beach at **Ramena**, but sharks may be a problem. The road southwards to the capital is only open between July and October.
Ile Ste-Marie (Nosy Boraha) lies off the east coast, 150km (90 miles) north of Toamasina. Its dense vegetation and the difficulty of navigating the lagoons which surround it made it an ideal base for pirates and, later, a colony for convicts. There are many clove plantations and several historic sites, including Madagascar's oldest Catholic church.
Toamasina, on the northeast coast, is the country's main port and a provincial capital. It is an 8-hour drive from Antananarivo and, like the capital, it has several busy markets, including the *Bazaar Be.* 11km (7 miles) north of the town are the *Ivolina Gardens,* containing every kind of vegetable species from the eastern forests and many varieties of animal life.
Vatomandry, further south, is a very popular beach resort even though the sharks prevent swimming.

The South

The arid south is noted for its many remarkable species of cactus- and baobab-like plants and for the highly developed funerary art of its inhabitants, past and present.
Fianarantsoa, a provincial capital, is an important centre for wine and rice production and a good base for exploring the southern highlands. Places to visit in the surrounding mountains include **Amabalavao**, said to be the 'home of the departed', where *antemore* paper and *lamba aridrano* silk are made; nearby **Ambondrome** and **Ifandana** crags, where the revered bones of exhumed ancestors may be seen (the latter was the site of a mass suicide in 1811); **Ambositra** and the neighbouring **Zafimaniny** villages, where intricate marquetry products are made; the **Isalo National Park**, situated in a chain of sandstone mountains (camping is possible but it can only be reached by 4-wheel-drive vehicle or on foot with a guide); and **Ranomafana**, a thermal spa.
Mananjary is a popular beach resort on the east coast (but not for sea-bathing because of sharks).
Taolanaro (formerly Fort Dauphin), in the southeast corner of the island, is the site of the first French settlement. Parts of the 17th-century fort remain. The city and surrounding area are famous for its seafood and for its orchids and carnivorous pitcher plants, which can be seen at the *Mandona Agricultural Centre* at **Sainte-Luce Bay**.

The West

Western Madagascar was once covered with deciduous forests, but is now mostly savannah. The economy is based around the *zebu*, a species of ox introduced to the island in the 8th century by settlers from South-East Asia.
Toliara, a provincial capital on the southwest coast, has excellent bathing beaches and opportunities for skindiving, fishing, sailing and other watersports.

SOCIAL PROFILE

FOOD & DRINK: In Madagascar eating well means eating a lot. Malagasy cooking is based on a large serving of rice with a dressing of sauces, meat, vegetables and seasoning. Dishes include *ro* (a mixture of herbs and leaves with rice); beef and pork marinaded in vinegar, water and oil, then cooked with leaves and vegetables, onion and pickles and seasoned with pimento; *ravitoto* (meat and leaves cooked together); *ramazava* (leaves, pieces of beef and pork browned in oil); *vary amid 'anana* (rice, leaves or herbs, meat and sometimes shrimps) often eaten with *kitoza* (long slices of smoked, cured or fried meat). The people of Madagascar enjoy very hot food and often serve dishes with hot peppers. **Drink:** The choice of beverages is limited. The national wine is acceptable. Malagasy drinks include *litchel* (an aperitif made from litchis), *betsa* (fermented alcohol) and *toaka gasy* (distilled from cane sugar and rice) and 'Three Horseshoes' lager. Non-alcoholic drinks include *ranon 'apango* or *rano vda* (made from burnt rice) and local mineral waters.

NIGHTLIFE: There are a few discotheques, sometimes with bands and solo musicians. Casinos can be found at Antananarivo, Toamasina and on Nosy Bé. Most main towns have cinemas and theatres, and touring theatre groups perform local plays throughout the country. Traditional dance troupes can also be seen.

SHOPPING: Handicrafts include *lamba* (traditional squares of cloth in various designs and woven materials); *zafimaniny* marquetry, which is applied to furniture, chessboards and boxes; silverwork such as *mahafaly* crosses and *vangavanga* bracelets; jewellery made from shells and precious stones; items woven from reeds, raffia and straw; *antemore* paper decorated with dried flowers; and embroidery. All products incorporating Malagasy flora or fauna (including dried flowers) require export permits. Shoppers should make sure that they obtain this at the time of purchase; they should also be aware that many items on sale (including tortoise-shell products) have been manufactured illegally and may not be taken out of the country, with or without a permit. **Shopping hours:** 0800-1200 and 1400-1800 Monday to Saturday.

SPORT: Tennis: There are courts in most main towns. **Golf:** Facilities at Tana. **Watersports:** Many towns have municipal pools. Sea-bathing along the east coast is not advised due to sharks. Main **diving** centres are Nosy Bé (with its neighbouring islands Tanikely, Nosy Mitsio and Nosy Radama), Nosy Lava, Toliara and Ile Ste-Marie (Nosy Boraha). **Water-skiing** and **sailing** centres are located at Ambohibao (Lake Mantasoa), Antsiralse (on Andraikiba Lake) and Ramona. **Trekking:** The *Maison de Tourisme* can organise a variety of trekking and hiking trips in many different parts of the country. They are generally designed to cater for specific interest groups – speleologists, mineralogists, ethnologists, ornithologists, those who wish to see rare orchids or lemurs, etc. Pony-trekking is also possible. **Spectator sports:** There are numerous **football** pitches and during the dry season it has been known to use rice fields as pitches. **Basketball** and **volleyball** are very popular and covered stadiums have been built.

SPECIAL EVENTS: There are many customary events and celebrations (see *Social Conventions* below), especially in rural areas. *Mphira gasy* (Malagasy singers) sing and dance theatrically in groups recounting a story and presenting its moral; typically a performance lasts from 30 minutes to an hour. The rice harvest is celebrated in many places.

SOCIAL CONVENTIONS: Visitors to Madagascar remark on the welcoming nature of the people, though some unprepared Westerners may be irritated by their relaxed attitude to time (public forms of transport, for example, will not generally move until they're full – no matter how long it takes to fill the last seat). Dress is casual, except for the very smartest hotel and restaurant functions. Entertaining is done in restaurants and bars, and a good degree of acquaintance is necessary before being invited to a family home. Outside major towns, the people are poor but very hospitable. However, to offer money for lodging could be construed as an insult, therefore it is advisable to offer a contribution to the host towards the next family or village festival, which should be warmly received. It is also advisable to give a certain amount to the village headman. Respect should be paid to the many local taboos (*fady*) – but as these vary from region to region this is not easy and very often the best that a traveller can do is show that his intentions are honourable; however, it is clear that advice should be sought before approaching tombs and graves. It remains the practice in some regions (though it is becoming increasingly rare due to the enormous cost) to invite an ancestor to a village celebration, disinterring the body so that the ancestor may attend physically, and later re-interring the body with new shrouds; this traditional observance (known as *famadihana*) amply demonstrates the continuing hold of traditional beliefs. Visitors invited to such an occasion should consider it a great honour.

Photography: Do not photograph military or police establishments. **Tipping:** Not customary, although waiters expect 10% of the bill. In European-style hotels and restaurants the French system of tipping is followed. One should also tip in Chinese and Vietnamese establishments.

BUSINESS PROFILE

ECONOMY: Madagascar's overwhelmingly agricultural economy relies heavily on coffee production to earn foreign exchange. Vanilla, cloves, sisal, cocoa and butter beans are the island's other important cash crops exported in quantity. Rice and cassava are produced primarily for domestic staple consumption.

Fishing is one industry underdeveloped thus far: the Government, which exercises extensive control over the economy, is hoping to improve its performance. The country has appreciable mineral deposits of chromium ore and other materials, including uranium and bauxite, but these are scattered and fairly inaccessible, and the Government has found exploitation to be uneconomic. About 17% of the gross national product derives from the manufacturing industry, mainly textiles and food-processing. Madagascar's once dire balance of payments problem was alleviated during the 1980s under IMF tutelage, but the country still depends on loans and aid from the EU (especially France) and the World Bank. France accounts for about 30% of all Madagascar's trade; the USA and the CIS are other important trading partners. More recently, the Government has been looking at ways of exploiting Madagascar's other prominent asset: its abundance of exotic wildlife. Tourism has obvious development potential, but there is also the possibility of devising some kind of 'debt for nature' scheme analogous to the support programmes set up in South America to protect the rainforests.

BUSINESS: Tropical lightweight suits are appropriate wear. If arranged far enough in advance, the Embassy can arrange interpreters for business meetings.

COMMERCIAL INFORMATION: The following organisation can offer advice: Fédération des Chambres de Commerce, d'Industrie et d'Agriculture de Madagascar, BP 166, 20 rue Colbert, 101 Antananarivo. Tel: (2) 21567.

CLIMATE

Hot and subtropical climate, colder in the mountains. Rainy season: November to March. Dry season: April to October. The south and west regions are hot and dry. Monsoons bring storms and cyclones to the east and north from December to March. The mountains, including Antananarivo, are warm and thundery from November to April and dry, cool and windy the rest of the year.

Required clothing: Lightweights are worn during the summer on high central plateaux and throughout the year in the north and south. Warmer clothes are advised during evenings and winter in mountainous areas. Rainwear is advisable.

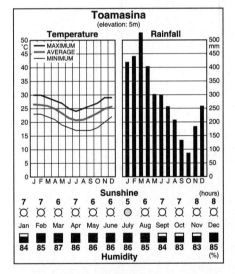

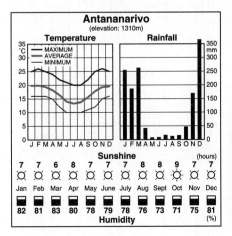

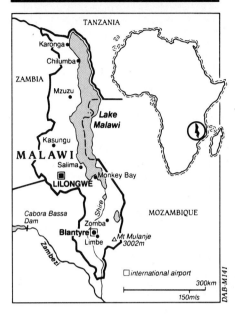

Location: Southeast Africa.

Department of Tourism
PO Box 402, Blantyre, Malawi
Tel: 620 300. Fax: 620 947. Telex: 44645.

High Commission for the Republic of Malawi *and* **Tourist Office**
33 Grosvenor Street, London W1X 0DE
Tel: (0171) 491 4172/7. Fax: (0171) 491 9916. Telex: 263308. Opening hours: 0930-1300 and 1400-1700 Monday to Friday.

British High Commission
PO Box 30042, Lingadzi House, Lilongwe 3, Malawi
Tel: 782 400. Fax: 782 657. Telex: 44727 (a/b UK REPLI MI).

Embassy of the Republic of Malawi
2408 Massachusetts Avenue, NW, Washington, DC 20008
Tel: (202) 797 1007. Fax: (202) 265 0976.

Embassy of the United States of America
PO Box 30016, Area 40, Flat 18, Lilongwe 3, Malawi
Tel: 783 166. Fax: 780 471. Telex: 44627.

High Commission for the Republic of Malawi
7 Clemow Avenue, Ottawa, Ontario K1S 2A9
Tel: (613) 236 8931. Fax: (613) 236 1054.
Consulates in: Montréal and Toronto.

The Canadian High Commission in Luska deals with enquiries relating to Malawi (see *Zambia* later in the book).

AREA: 118,484 sq km (45,747 sq miles).
POPULATION: 8,556,000 (1991 estimate).
POPULATION DENSITY: 72.2 per sq km.
CAPITAL: Lilongwe. **Population:** 233,973 (1987, including suburbs). Blantyre, with a population of 331,588 (1987), is the largest city in the country.
GEOGRAPHY: Malawi shares borders to the north and northeast with Tanzania, to the south, east and southwest with Mozambique and to the west and northwest with Zambia. Lake Malawi, the third-largest lake in Africa, is the dominant feature of the country, forming the eastern boundary with Tanzania and Mozambique. The scenery varies in the different regions: the Northern Region is

mountainous, the highest peaks reaching to over 3000m (9843ft), with the rolling Nyika Plateau, rugged escarpments, valleys and the thickly forested slopes of the Viphya Plateau. The Central Region is mainly a plateau, over 1000m (3300ft) high, with fine upland scenery. This is the country's main agricultural area. The Southern Region is low-lying with the 2100m-high (6890ft) Zomba Plateau south of Lake Malawi and the huge, isolated Mulanje Massif in the southeast. The variety of landscape, and the wildlife it supports, makes this relatively unspoilt country particularly attractive to visitors.

LANGUAGE: The official language is English. Chichewa is widely spoken and is regarded as the national language especially by Malawi's largest single ethnic group, the Chewa, who live along the lakeshore and on the plains. The Tonga live mainly in the Northern Region, as far as Usisya, and speak Chi Tonga. The Tumbuka-Henga live mostly between Mzimba and Karonga, while even further north live the Ngonde, who also have their own language.

RELIGION: Animist with Christian, Hindu and Muslim minorities. Along the southern lakeshore the Yao culture groups, a number of whom are Muslim, predominate (they are also found at Salima and Nkhotakota in the Central Region along with the Ngoni – the *Ngoma* is their spectacular war dance). The Ngonde are a predominantly Christian group.

TIME: GMT + 2.

ELECTRICITY: 230/240 volts AC, 50Hz. A variety of plugs are in use, most modern buildings using square 3-pin plugs.

COMMUNICATIONS: Telephone: IDD is available. Country code: 265 (no area codes). Outgoing international code: 101. **Fax:** Bureaux offering public fax services have recently opened in Blantyre and Zomba. **Telex/telegram:** Bureaux offering public telex services have recently opened in Blantyre and Zomba. Public facilities for sending telegrams exist at the Main Post Office. **Post:** Letters take about ten days to reach Europe by airmail. Post offices are generally open 0730-1200 and 1300-1700 Monday to Friday. Post offices in some of the larger towns may be open 0900-1000 Sunday, but only to sell stamps or to accept telegrams. **Press:** The two main newspapers are *The Daily Times* (Monday to Friday) and *The Malawi News* (Saturday). There are a number of independent newpapers most of which are either weekly or come out every other two days including: *The Monitor, The Enquirer, The Independent, The New Voice, The Democrat, The Herald, The Michiru Sun, The Nation* and *The Express.*

BBC World Service and Voice of America frequencies: From time to time these change. See the section *How to Use this Book* for more information.

BBC:

MHz	21.47	11.94	6.190	3.255

Voice of America:

MHz	21.49	15.60	9.525	6.035

PASSPORT/VISA

Regulations and requirements may be subject to change at short notice, and you are advised to contact the appropriate diplomatic or consular authority before finalising travel arrangements. Details of these may be found at the head of this country's entry. Any numbers in the chart refer to the footnotes below.

	Passport Required?	Visa Required?	Return Ticket Required?
Full British	Yes	No	Yes
BVP	Not valid	-	-
Australian	Yes	No	Yes
Canadian	Yes	No	Yes
USA	Yes	No	Yes
Other EU (As of 31/12/94)	Yes	1	Yes
Japanese	Yes	Yes	Yes

PASSPORTS: Valid passport required by all.
British Visitors Passport: Not acceptable.
VISAS: Required by all except:
(a) nationals of countries shown in the chart above;
(b) [1] nationals of Belgium, Denmark, Germany, Ireland, Luxembourg, The Netherlands and Portugal (nationals of other EU countries *do* need visas);
(c) nationals of Antigua & Barbuda, Bahamas, Bangladesh, Barbados, Belize, Botswana, Brunei, Cyprus, Dominica, Fiji, Finland, Gambia, Ghana, Grenada, Guyana, Iceland, Israel, Jamaica, Kenya, Kiribati, Lesotho, Madagascar, Maldives, Malta, Mauritius, Mozambique, Namibia, Nauru, New Zealand, Nigeria, Norway, Papua New Guinea, San Marino, Seychelles, Sierra Leone, Singapore, Solomon Islands, South Africa, Sri Lanka, St Kitts & Nevis, St Lucia, St Vincent & the Grenadines, Swaziland, Sweden, Tanzania, Tonga, Trinidad & Tobago, Tuvalu, Uganda,

Vanuatu, Western Samoa, Zambia and Zimbabwe.
Types of visa: Tourist (3-, 6- and 12-month) and Transit. Cost varies according to nationality of visitor and the exchange rate of the Kwacha. Transit visas are valid for 3 days, but are not usually required of Western or Commonwealth visitors.
Validity: Upon entry into Malawi a 3-month Tourist visa is granted, subject to certain conditions. Extensions will not normally be granted in Malawi.
Application to: Consulate (or Consular section at Embassy or High Commission). For addresses, see top of entry. Alternatively, contact the Deputy Chief Immigration Officer at the address below.
Application requirements: (a) 2 application forms. (b) 2 passport-size photos. (c) Fee (variable). (d) Valid passport. (e) Onward ticket. (f) Proof of means of support during residence in country. (g) Letter from company/sponsor where required.
Working days required: 5 days.
Temporary residence: Application should be made prior to arrival. Contact the Controller of Immigration Services, PO Box 331, Blantyre, Malawi.

MONEY

Currency: Kwache (Mk) = 100 tambala. Notes are in denominations of Mk100. 50, 20, 10, 5 and 1. Coins are in denominations of Mk1, and 50, 20, 10, 5, 2 and 1 tambala.
Currency exchange: Lesser-known currencies will be difficult to exchange in Malawi.
Credit cards: Acceptance of credit cards is limited, but in the capital and main hotels Access/Mastercard, Diners Club and American Express can be used. Check with your credit card company for details of merchant acceptability and other services which may be available.
Travellers cheques: These and major currencies, including US Dollars and Sterling, can be exchanged in banks, hotels and other institutions. In remote areas, the Treasury Office of Local District Commissioners offices will cash cheques.
Exchange rate indicators: The following figures are included as a guide to the movements of the Kwacha against Sterling and the US Dollar:

Date:	Oct '92	Sep '93	Jan '94	Jan '95
£1.00=	6.51	6.63	6.61	24.08
$1.00=	4.10	4.34	4.46	15.39

Currency restrictions: Import and export of local currency up to Mk200 is allowed. Import of foreign currency is unlimited if declared. Export of foreign currency is allowed up to the amount declared on entry.
Banking hours: 0800-1300 Monday to Friday.

DUTY FREE

The following goods may be imported into Malawi without incurring customs duty:
*200 cigarettes or 250g of tobacco in any form; *1 litre of spirits; *1 litre of beer or 1 litre of wine; 250ml of eau de toilette; 50g of perfume.*
Note [*]: Alcoholic goods are only available to passengers 16 years of age or older.
Prohibited items: The import of firearms is prohibited unless a permit has been bought in advance from the Registrar of Firearms, Box 41, Zomba.

PUBLIC HOLIDAYS

Jan 1 '95 New Year's Day. **Mar 3** Martyrs' Day. **Apr 14-17** Easter. **May 14** Kamuzu Day. **Jul 6** Republic Day. **Oct 17** Mothers' Day. **Dec 21** National Tree Planting Day. **Dec 25** Christmas Day. **Dec 26** Boxing Day. **Jan 1 '96** New Year's Day. **Mar 3** Martyrs' Day. **Apr 5-8** Easter.
Note: If a public holiday falls on a Saturday, the previous day will be a holiday; if on a Sunday the next day will be the holiday. *Ad hoc* public holidays or extensions may also be declared, sometimes at short notice.

HEALTH

Regulations and requirements may be subject to change at short notice, and you are advised to contact your doctor well in advance of your intended date of departure. Any numbers in the chart refer to the footnotes below.

	Special Precautions?	Certificate Required?
Yellow Fever	No	1
Cholera	Yes	2
Typhoid & Polio	Yes	-
Malaria	3	-
Food & Drink	4	-

[1]: A yellow fever vaccination certificate is required from travellers arriving from infected areas.
[2]: Following WHO guidelines issued in 1973, a cholera vaccination certificate is not a condition of entry to Malawi. However, cholera is a risk in this country and precautions are essential. Up-to-date advice should be sought before deciding whether these precautions should include vaccination, as medical opinion is divided over its effectiveness. See the *Health* section at the back of the book.
[3]: Malaria risk exists all year throughout the country. The predominant malignant *falciparum* strain is reported to be 'highly resistant' to chloroquine and 'resistant' to sulfadoxine/pyrimethamine.
[4]: All water should be regarded as being potentially contaminated. Water used for drinking, brushing teeth or making ice should have first been boiled or otherwise sterilised. Milk is unpasteurised and should be boiled. Powdered or tinned milk is available and is advised, but make sure that it is reconstituted with pure water. Avoid dairy products which are likely to have been made from unboiled milk. Only eat well-cooked meat and fish, preferably served hot. Pork, salad and mayonnaise may carry increased risk. Vegetables should be cooked and fruit peeled.
Rabies is present. For those at high risk, vaccination before arrival should be considered. If you are bitten abroad seek medical advice without delay. For more information consult the *Health* section at the back of the book.
Bilharzia (schistosomiasis) is present, but Lake Malawi is entirely safe. Avoid swimming and paddling in slow-moving fresh water elsewhere. Swimming pools which are well-chlorinated and maintained are safe.
Health care: Health insurance is essential. It is advisable to take personal medical supplies.

TRAVEL - International

AIR: Malawi's national airline is *Air Malawi (QM).* There are connections from Amsterdam to Lilongwe on *KLM* and from Paris with *Air France.* There are also connections between Malawi and Kenya, Mauritius, South Africa and Zimbabwe.
Approximate flight time: From London to Lilongwe is 12 hours 10 minutes (including 1 hour in Harare).
International airports: *Lilongwe (LLW)* (Kamuzu International) is 22km (14 miles) from the city. Taxi services are available to the city from the airport. Airport facilities include a duty-free shop, post office, car hire (*Avis* and *SS Rent-a-Car*), bank/bureau de change (0730-2100), restaurant (0600-2200) and bar (0730-2200).
Blantyre (BLZ) (Chileka) is 18km (11 miles) from the city. There is a coach service to the city. Airport facilities include car hire (*Avis* and *SS Rent-a-Car*), restaurant and bar (0730-2000).
Departure tax: A passenger service charge of US$20 (payable in US currency) is levied on all international flights. Malawi passport holders can pay in local currency (Mk40).

TRAVEL - Internal

AIR: The air network *Air Malawi* links Blantyre and Lilongwe with local airports at Mzuzu and Karonga. In addition, planes are available for charter, thereby giving access to the many small airports in the country; contact *Capital Air Services Ltd.*
SEA: Cruises on Lake Malawi's shores are run by local steamer services. Food and cabins are available. For details contact the local authorities. *Malawi Railways* operate boat services on the lake from the railhead at Chipoka.
RAIL: *Malawi Railways* operate the lines in the country. The main route (see map) connects Mchinji, Lilongwe, Salima, Chipoka, Blantyre, Limbe and Nsanje to the Mozambique port of Beira. The connection between Chipoka and Beira on this line has been suspended since 1985. The other line connects Lilongwe–Salima–Blantyre.
For further information, contact Malawi Railways, PO Box 5144, Limbe. Tel: 640 844. Fax: 640 683. Telex: 44810.
ROAD: Traffic drives on the left. There are over 11,500km (7200 miles) of roads in the country. All major and most secondary roads are all-weather. The main north–south highway to Karonga is now sealed. **Bus:** There is a good bus system, including an express service, connecting main towns. The journey from Mzuzu to Karonga is particularly spectacular. Luxury coaches operate Blantyre–Mzuzu–Lilongwe. **Car hire:** This is available in major towns. Cars should be reserved well in advance as they are in big demand.

Kasungu National Park

Chauffeur-driven cars are also available.
Documentation: Nationals of certain countries, including the UK, do not require an International Driving Permit. A national driving licence is sufficient.
URBAN: Bus: Double-decker buses are available in Blantyre and Lilongwe and there is a regular bus service in all major cities. **Taxi:** These are in short supply and cannot be hailed on the street. For taxi services in Blantyre, tel: 636 402. Taxi drivers expect a 30-tambala tip.
JOURNEY TIMES: The following chart gives approximate average journey times (in hours and minutes) from Lilongwe to other major cities/towns in Malawi.

	Air	Road
Blantyre	0.40	4.30
Mzuzu	1.00	5.00
Zomba	-	4.00
Karonga	1.30	6.30
Salima	-	1.00
Mangochi	1.00	4.30

ACCOMMODATION

HOTELS: In the main centres there are excellent hotels, the most sophisticated being in Blantyre and Lilongwe. In addition, there are some excellent lodge-style hotels in the main tourist resorts.
REST HOUSES: Clean and comfortable rest houses are operated by the Department of Tourism. All have bathrooms and cooking facilities, although guests generally have to provide their own food.
CAMPING: There are a few developed sites, some of which offer superb lake or mountain views. Campsites can be found throughout the country. The camping season is a long one with the dry weather lasting from April to November. Facilities at all the sites include water, toilets and shade.

RESORTS & EXCURSIONS

For convenience, the country has been divided into four sections: North, Central, South and Lake Malawi. There is also a section giving information on the Wildlife Reserves and National Parks in Malawi.

The Northern Region

The road from **Kasungu** to Mzuzu, the least visited centre of the northern region, crosses the rolling grasslands of the Viphya Plateau. Further north towards the *Livingstonia Mission* is the Livingstonia escarpment and the *Manchewe Falls,* which are approached along the escarpment road made up of '22 hairpin bends. The Manchewe Falls are a spectacular sight, set amidst magnificent scenery. There is a museum in Livingstonia. The region has recently become more popular with visitors, and there is now a first-class hotel at **Mzuzu,** which caters for visitors to local beauty spots such as *Nyika National Park* and *Nkhata Bay.*

Lake Malawi

Stretching from the northeastern-most tip of Malawi to **Mangochi** in the south is the massive **Lake Malawi**. The surface area of the lake covers nearly 24,000 sq km (15,000 sq miles), and lies in the deep, trough-like rift valley which runs the length of the country. The shores of the lake are generally sandy, and the water itself is free of bilharzia. Crocodiles (the scourge of African lakes) have been effectively eliminated from main resort areas. There are no tides or currents. Most of the hotels provide pleasure craft enabling visitors to enjoy water-skiing, sailing, fishing or windsurfing. For tropical fish enthusiasts and snorkellers, Lake Malawi is an underwater paradise. It is now known to contain more species of fish than any other lake in the world; over 350 at the latest count. Some of the rarest tropical fish in the world are unique to the lake, which is also

the home of fish eagles, black eagles, several varieties of kingfishers, terns and many other birds.
Likoma Island in the middle of the lake is worth a visit – there are excellent swimming facilities off the beaches and a very interesting *Anglican Cathedral* up the hill.
One of the best ways of seeing Lake Malawi is to cruise in the 630-ton *Ilala II,* the lake's mini-liner which travels between *Monkey Bay* (north of Club Makokola) and **Karonga** in the north of the country. The 1052km (654-mile) voyage gives the passenger the opportunity to visit lake ports and to view the spectacular mountain scenery. March to May are the calmest months for the 'Lake Cruise', and regular scheduled voyages are made from Friday to the Wednesday of the following week. The heavy demand for cabins on the *Ilala II* during the holiday season means that advanced payment and bookings are essential.
Cape Maclear, near Monkey Bay, is worth a visit – there is a sandy beach and warm lakewater to swim in.
Thumbi Island is a nature reserve offshore from the bay. *Nkhata Bay* is quiet and deserted.
Nkhotakota was once the centre of the slave trade in southern Africa. It is also one of Africa's oldest market towns.

The Central Region

Salima is the main lakeshore resort of the central region, offering excellent tourist facilities and a campsite.
Lizard Island, near Salima, is a nature reserve, and home to many varieties of lizard and eagle.
Due west of Salima, across a large fertile plain, is the new capital city of **Lilongwe**. Situated on the crossroads of the agriculturally rich central region, Lilongwe replaced Zomba as Malawi's capital. It is a modern city of imaginative architecture in an unspoiled garden setting. North of the capital is the 2000 sq km (770 sq

miles) **Kasungu National Park** – a vast area of undulating woods and grassland teeming with wildlife (see below). Northwest of Lilongwe is the country's main tobacco-growing area.

The Southern Region

Blantyre, the commercial centre of the southern region, was established at the end of the last century. It is really two cities; Blantyre and Limbe, about 7km (4 miles) apart, and separated by an industrial zone. The *National Museum* is halfway between Blantyre and Limbe, off the main road.

Southwest of Blantyre is **Lengwe**, the smallest of the country's national parks (see below). 60km (35 miles) north of Blantyre is the university town of **Zomba**, the country's former capital, which has an excellent market. Nearby is *Zomba Mountain*, sparkling with waterfalls and trout streams, pine plantations and rare plants, particularly orchids. Its foothills shelter one of Africa's most picturesque golf courses, situated among streams, tiny waterfalls, trees and rock formations. Also in the region is *Chingwe's Hole*, reputed to be too deep to measure.

To the southeast are large tea estates, out of which rises the magnificent **Mulanje Massif**, a huge block of mountains of more than 640 sq km (250 sq miles) rising to over 3000m (9850ft) at its highest point at **Sapitwa**. For the tourist, Mulanje offers a wide scope of activities, from rock climbing and mountain walking, to the more leisurely pursuit of trout fishing. Most areas of the massif are accessible by either paths or firebreaks. A number of well-tended forestry huts provide suitable bases for exploring the grassy uplands, forests and numerous summits. The normal time for visiting Mulanje is from April to December, although many visitors enjoy the dramatic effects of the heavy rains which fall for the rest of the year.

Woodcarving from local cedar is available in the villages at the base of the massif.

National Parks

Malawi has five main National Parks open to visitors:
Nyika National Park is situated in the north of the northern region and is open to visitors throughout the year. It covers most of the Nyika Plateau, which lies at an altitude of 2000-3000m (6562-9843ft). The rolling grassland is broken by deep valleys and occasional patches of evergreen, natural forest and bubbling streams. Nyika is known to sustain many rare birds, butterflies, game and a multitude of flowers. *Chelinda Camp*, set high up on the edge of a pine forest and overlooking a trout-filled dam, provides accommodation in comfortable cottages with log fires. The *Chowo Forest*, located near *Chelinda*, is excellent for walking. It is one of the last areas of natural forest left in the park.

Kasungu National Park, situated in the northwest of the central region, 112km (68 miles) from Lilongwe, consists of some 2000 sq km (770 sq miles) of woodland. The park is best known for its elephants, which appear in the early morning and evening to drink from *dambos* or river channels. The grasslands support large herds of buffalo, and occasionally rhino appear. Less common are the elusive cheetahs, leopards and lions, which occasionally appear for a few days. Other animals include the sable antelope, zebra, kudu and reedbuck. Kasungu is usually open from the beginning of May until the end of December. Accommodation is available at the *Lifupa Wildlife Lodge*, a complex of thatched rondavel cottages with a restaurant, day camp, swimming pool and basic provisions.

Lengwe National Park, in the southwest corner of the southern region, is only 130 sq km (80 sq miles). This park has the distinction of being the farthest place north where the rare, shy Nyala antelope is found. This beautiful animal may be seen, often in large numbers, together with Livingstone's Suni, one of the smallest species of antelope, and the equally rare Blue or Samango monkey. Other game include bushbuck, kudu, hartebeest, impala, warthog and duiker. Visitors may view game at close quarters from concealed hides. The best time of day for this is first thing in the morning. Limited accommodation is available at *Lengwe Game Camp*.

Liwonde National Park, situated on the flat plain of the Shire Valley, stretches from *Lake Malombe* in the north to Liwonde township in the south. Boats are available for trips through reed swamps, where hippo, elephants and waterbuck come to drink. When travelling by road, woodland and grassland animals such as sable antelope, kudu, duiker and baboon can also be seen. An aquatic bird sanctuary has been developed, home to a variety of birdlife including egrets, herons, ducks, geese, kingfishers and nesting

cormorants. The park is closed from November to May. Camping and catering facilities at *Mvuu Camp* run by Wilderness Safaris is also available. There are also plans for the introduction of boat trips from one of the hotels on the southern tip of Lake Malawi to Liwonde Barrage and back. Enquire at the Tourist Office for up-to-date details of these developments.

Lake Malawi National Park, on the southern and central parts of the lake, is the most recent of Malawi's parks, established in 1980. Tropical fish, which can be viewed with the use of scuba equipment and masks, are a speciality of the park, while further inland klipspringer, bushbuck and vervet monkeys may be seen. Access to the park is easy throughout the year. There are camping facilities and plans to build other accommodation, including a modern hotel, in the near future. There are also good hotels at *Nkopola Lodge, Mulangeri, Boadzulu Resorts, Sun and Sun, Palm Beach* and *Club Makokola*. Enquire at the Tourist Office for further details.

In addition to the National Parks there are a number of other reserves, sanctuaries and protected areas where there are no facilities at present for visitors. The **Majete Game Reserve**, about 65km (40 miles) to the north of Lengwe, is less accessible and less well provided for, but has a large number of animals including hippos, elephants and big cats. Southeast of Lengwe is the **Mwabvi Game Reserve**, which has a small number of black rhino, impala, zebra and sable. Others include the **Nkhotakota Game Reserve** in the Central Region, **Lizard Island** near Salima, **Lilongwe Nature Sanctuary** in the capital itself, and **Michiru Mountain Park** near Blantyre, which offers some of the best birdwatching in the area.

SOCIAL PROFILE

FOOD & DRINK: Fresh fish from Lake Malawi is the country's speciality, *chambo* (Tilapia fish) being the main lake delicacy. There are trout from streams on the Zomba, Mulanje and Nyika plateaux. Hotel restaurants and many of those in the cities are of a very high standard. They offer a wide choice of excellent food including *haute cuisine*, the unique *Lake Malawi* dishes and the best Malawi beef. Poultry and dairy produce are plentiful and tropical fruits are abundant in season. The local beer is very good and imported beer and soft drinks are widely available. Wine is imported from major wine-producing countries.

SHOPPING: Malawi produces a variety of colourful arts and crafts. Items are invariably handmade and there is no mass production of curios aimed specifically at the tourist market. Purchases include woodcarvings, wood and cane furniture, soapstone carvings, decorated wooden articles, colourful textiles, pottery, beadwork, cane and raffia items. Traditional musical instruments are also sold throughout Malawi.
Shopping hours: 0800-1700 Monday to Saturday.
SPORT: Fishing: Lake Malawi offers excellent fishing, particularly on the southern shores in April when anglers take part in the tackle tournament organised by the Angling Society. A popular collecting point for anglers is Mangochi, roughly 190km (120 miles) from Blantyre, while Boadzulu Island, Nkopola Lodge and White Rock are also good spots. Boats should be arranged in advance from lakeshore hotels. Catches include lake yellow fish, lake salmon and lake tiger. River mouths in the Salima area, the Kapichira Falls on the Shire, and Nyika and Zomba Plateaux are also excellent bases for fishermen. Visitors should contact the Angling Society at PO Box 744, Blantyre, for further information.
Mountaineering: *Mount Mulanje*, rising to a height of 3000m (9850ft), is the highest mountain in central Africa and has proven to be an irresistible lure to climbers. The mountain includes the longest sheer rock face in Africa, as well as some less challenging trekking along mountain paths. A 2- to 6-day tour is recommended, and there are huts available for hire. *Dedza* in the Central Region offers challenging slopes, as do *Michiru Ndirande* and *Chiradzulu* near Blantyre. In the north, 1- to 6-day wilderness trails are available to walkers along the grassland of the *Nyika Plateau*. Guides and porters are available; visitors must, however, supply their own camping equipment. **Golf:** There are seven golf courses in Malawi, most are 9-hole courses with alternate tees to provide 18 holes. Green and caddy fees are very reasonable.
Watersports: Swimming, water-skiing and sailing are all popular in Lake Malawi. **Horseriding** is also available.
SPECIAL EVENTS: Dance plays a part in most ceremonies in Malawi, an important dance being the *Gule Wamkulu* with its heavily carved masks, feathers

and skin paint. It is performed by the Chewa and Mang'anja, and this and other national dances can be seen at *Kamuzu Day Celebrations* on May 14, or at the annual *Malawi Republic Day* celebrations on July 6.

BUSINESS PROFILE

ECONOMY: The economy is almost entirely agricultural, with both subsistence and cash crops including tobacco, sugar, tea and maize being farmed. Despite being self-sufficient in food, Malawi ran up a vast balance of payments deficit during the 1980s and is now heavily dependent on foreign aid, both bilateral and from the World Bank. The situation has now been made worse by the drought currently affecting the country (Malawi had largely escaped the effects of previous spells). Manufacturing industry is small as yet and concentrated in light industrial import substitution projects such as textiles, agricultural implements and processed foodstuffs. The UK is Malawi's most important trading partner, taking one-third of the country's exports and providing 15% of Malawi's imports. South Africa, Japan, Germany and the Netherlands are Malawi's other important trading partners.
BUSINESS: Suits or a jacket and tie are suitable for business meetings in cities. Similar to the European system, appointments should generally be made and business cards are used. Offices tend to open early in Malawi. Best months for business visits are May to July and September to November. **Office hours:** 0730-1700 Monday to Friday.
COMMERCIAL INFORMATION: The following organisation can offer advice: The Associated Chambers of Commerce and Industry of Malawi, PO Box 258, Chichiri Trade Fair Grounds, Blantyre. Tel: 671 988. Fax: 671 147. Telex: 43992.
CONFERENCES/CONVENTIONS: Malawi's only dedicated conference centre is the Kwacha International Conference Centre in Blantyre, with seating for up to 500 persons. Details of this and hotels with conference facilities can be obtained from the Department of Tourism. For address, see top of entry.

CLIMATE

Varies from cool in the highlands to warm around Lake Malawi. Winter (May to July) is dry and nights can be cold, particularly in the highlands. The rainy season runs from November to March. Around Lake Malawi the climate is particularly dry with cooling breezes.
Required clothing: Lightweights are worn all year around Lake Malawi, with warmer clothes advised in the mountains, particularly during winter and on chilly evenings elsewhere. Waterproofing is advisable.

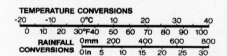

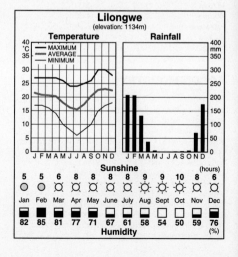

Malaysia

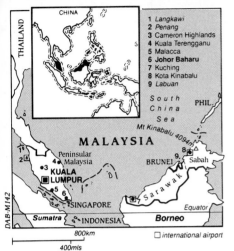

Location: South-East Asia.

Malaysia Tourism Promotion Board
24-27th Floors, Menara Dato' Onn, Putra World Trade Centre, 45 Jalan Tun Ismail, 50480 Kuala Lumpur, Malaysia
Tel: (3) 293 5188. Fax: (3) 293 5884. Telex: 30093 (a/b MTDCKL MA).
Malaysian High Commission
45 Belgrave Square, London SW1X 8QT
Tel: (0171) 235 8033. Fax: (0171) 235 5161

(information) *or* 235 5162 (immigration). Telex: 262550.
Opening hours: 0900-1700 Monday to Friday;
0915-1215 Monday to Friday (Consular section).
Malaysia Tourism Promotion Board
57 Trafalgar Square, London WC2N 5DU
Tel: (0171) 930 7932. Fax: (0171) 930 9015. Telex: 299659. Opening hours: 0900-1700 Monday to Friday.
Malaysian Trade Commission
17 Curzon Street, London W1Y 7FE
Tel: (0171) 499 7388. Fax: (0171) 493 8804. Opening hours: 0900-1700 Monday to Friday.
British High Commission
PO Box 11030, 185 Jalan Ampang, 50732 Kuala Lumpur, Malaysia
Tel: (3) 248 2122 *or* 248 7122 (Consular section). Fax: (3) 248 0880.
Honorary British Representatives in: Johor Baharu, Kuching, Kota Kinabalu, Miri and Penang.
Embassy of the Federation of Malaysia (Visa section)
2401 Massachusetts Avenue, NW, Washington, DC 20008
Tel: (202) 328 2738. Fax: (202) 483 7661.
Malaysia Tourism Promotion Board
Suite 804, 818 West Seventh Street, Los Angeles, CA 90017
Tel: (213) 689 9702. Fax: (213) 689 1530. Telex: 6714719 (a/b MTIC UW).
Embassy of the United States of America
PO Box 10035, 376 Jalan Tun Razak, 50700 Kuala Lumpur, Malaysia
Tel: (3) 248 9011. Fax: (3) 242 2207.
High Commission for the Federation of Malaysia
60 Boteler Street, Ottawa, Ontario K1N 8Y7
Tel: (613) 241 5182. Fax: (613) 241 5214.
Consulate in: Toronto.

Malaysia Tourist Information Centre
830 Burrard Street, Vancouver, British Columbia V6Z 2K4
Tel: (604) 689 8899. Fax: (604) 689 8804.
Canadian High Commission
PO Box 10990, 7th Floor, Plaza MBF, 172 Jalan Ampang, 50732 Kuala Lumpur, Malaysia
Tel: (3) 261 2000. Fax: (3) 261 3428. Telex: 30269 (a/b DOMCAN MA).

AREA: 329,758 sq km (127,320 sq miles).
POPULATION: 18,606,300 (1992).
POPULATION DENSITY: 56.4 per sq km.
CAPITAL: Kuala Lumpur. **Population:** 1,158,200 (1991).
GEOGRAPHY: Malaysia is situated in central South-East Asia, bordering on Thailand in the north, with Singapore and Indonesia to the south and the Philippines to the east. It is composed of Peninsular Malaysia and the states of Sabah and Sarawak on the north coast of the island of Borneo, 650-950km (404-600 miles) across the South China Sea. Peninsular Malaysia is an area of forested mountain ranges running north–south, on either side of which are low-lying coastal plains. The coastline extends some 1900km (1200 miles). The west coast consists of mangrove swamps and mudflats which separate into bays and inlets. In the west, the plains have been cleared and cultivated, while the unsheltered east coast consists of tranquil beaches backed by dense jungle. Sarawak has alluvial and, in places, swampy coastal plains with rivers penetrating the jungle-covered hills and mountains of the interior. Sabah has a narrow coastal plain which gives way to mountains and jungle. Mount Kinabalu, at 4094m (13,432ft), is the highest peak in Malaysia. The major islands are Langkawi (a group of 99 islands), Penang and Pangkor off the west coast; and Tioman, Redang, Kapas, Perhentian and Rawa off the east coast.
LANGUAGE: Bahasa Malaysia is the national and official language, but English is widely spoken. Other languages are Chinese (Mandarin), Iban and Tamil.
RELIGION: 53% Muslim, 19% Buddhist. The remainder are Taoist, Confucianist, Hindu and Animist.
TIME: GMT + 8.
ELECTRICITY: 220 volts AC, 50Hz. Square 3-pin plugs and bayonet-type light fittings are generally used.

Tropical Malaysian island

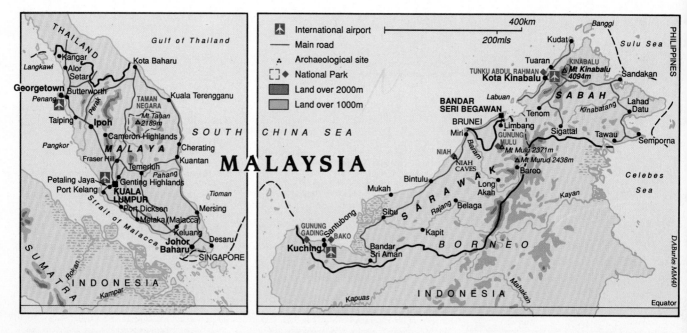

COMMUNICATIONS: Telephone:

Telephone: IDD service is available. Country code: 60. Outgoing international code: 00. Public coin-operated phones can be found in many areas, such as supermarkets and post offices. Local calls cost 10 sen. Telephone Card public phones can be found throughout the country. These can be purchased at airports, petrol stations and some shops for amounts ranging from R3-50. There are presently two types – *Kadfon* and *Unicard* – and these can only be used in their appropriate marked phonebooths. **Fax:** Centres for public use are located in the main post offices of all large towns. Most main hotels also have facilities. **Telegram/telex:** Public telex facilities are available 24 hours at Telegraph Office, Jalan Raja Chulan, Kuala Lumpur, and most main hotels. Telegrams can be sent from any telegraph office. **Post:** There are post offices in the commercial centre of all towns, open 0800-1700 Monday to Saturday. **Press:** The English-language dailies printed in Peninsular Malaysia are the *National Echo, Business Times, Malay Mail, New Straits Times* and *The Star*. There are also several English-language Sunday newspapers and periodicals. *The Borneo Bulletin*, published in Brunei, also circulates. There are many printed in other languages and several in two or three languages.
BBC World Service frequencies: From time to time these change. See the section *How to Use this Book* for more information.

BBC:				
MHz	15.31	11.95	6.195	3.915
Voice of America:				
MHz	15.42	11.76	9.770	7.120

PASSPORT/VISA

Regulations and requirements may be subject to change at short notice, and you are advised to contact the appropriate diplomatic or consular authority before finalising travel arrangements. Details of these may be found at the head of this country's entry. Any numbers in the chart refer to the footnotes below.

	Passport Required?	Visa Required?	Return Ticket Required?
Full British	Yes	No/1	Yes
BVP	Not valid	-	-
Australian	Yes	No/1	Yes
Canadian	Yes	No/1	Yes
USA	Yes	No/1	Yes
Other EU (As of 31/12/94)	Yes	No/1	Yes
Japanese	Yes	No/1	Yes

Restricted entry: Nationals of Israel and Yugoslavia (Serbia and Montenegro), women who are in an advanced state of pregnancy (6 months or over) and those of scruffy appearance will be denied entry. Passports issued by Taiwan (China) are not recognised unless accompanied by a document in lieu of a passport with an entry visa. All visitors to Malaysia must have proof of sufficient funds for their length of stay and a return or onward ticket.
PASSPORTS: A valid passport or other travel document recognised by the Malaysian government is required by all. The former should be valid for at least 6 months beyond the intended stay in Malaysia and the latter should be endorsed with a valid re-entry permit. All visitors must also have proof of adequate funds and an onward or return sea or air ticket.
British Visitors Passport: Refer to the Malaysian High Commission before travelling regarding up-to-date acceptability of the British Visitors' Passport.
VISAS: Most visitors (including all nationals of countries listed in the chart) do not require a visa to enter Malaysia if the period is less than a month and the purpose of the visit is business or social (see below for more detailed requirements). However, **[1]** all visitors require a **Visit Pass**. This will be issued at the port of entry if the visitor is travelling for business or tourism, or for a social visit; those travelling for other purposes should apply in advance of their visit. The length of stay granted by the Visit Pass is at the discretion of the Immigration authorities. Those issued with a Visit Pass for tourism or a social visit are not allowed to take up any employment or engage in any business or professional activity during their stay in Malaysia.
In addition to the Visit Pass, **visas** are required at all times by holders of any Certificate of Identity, Titre de Voyage or passport for nationals of Bangladesh, Bhutan, Cuba, India, North Korea, Mongolia, Myanmar, Nepal, Pakistan, People's Republic of China, Sri Lanka, Taiwan (China), Vietnam and by all others except:
(a) holders of full British passports and Commonwealth and British Protected Persons (other than holders of Bangladeshi, Indian, Pakistani and Sri Lankan passports who *do* need a visa for any length of stay) visiting Malaysia for any purpose and who can prove that they will return to their country of origin;
(b) nationals of Liechtenstein, The Netherlands, San Marino and Switzerland for whatever purpose for a period of 2 months;
(c) nationals with full passports issued by Austria, Belgium, Czech Republic, Denmark, Finland, Germany, Hungary, Iceland, Italy, Japan, South Korea, Luxembourg, Norway, Slovak Republic, Sweden and the USA do not require a visa for a social/business visit for a period of 3 months;
(d) nationals of Algeria, Bahrain, Egypt, Jordan, Kuwait, Lebanon, Morocco, Oman, Qatar, Saudi Arabia, Tunisia, Turkey, UAE and Yemen for a business/social visit for a period of 3 months;
(e) nationals of Australia and New Zealand for a period of 2 months;
(f) members of ASEAN countries, ie Brunei, Indonesia, Philippines, Thailand and Singapore, for a 1-month visit for purposes of business or tourism only;
(g) nationals of Afghanistan, Iran, Iraq, Libya and Syria for a visit of 2 weeks for purposes of business or

tourism only;
(h) nationals of Albania, Bulgaria, Romania and the CIS for 1 week for purposes of business or tourism only.
Validity: The permitted length of stay is entered on the Visit Pass at the time it is issued and is at the discretion of the issuer. Extensions are possible.
Cost: The cost of visas varies according to nationality.
Application and inquiries to: Immigration section at Malaysian High Commission. For address, see top of entry.
Application requirements: (a) Passport-size photo. (b) Fee. (c) Completed form. (d) Proof of sufficient funds. (e) Onward or return ticket.
Working days: 2.
Temporary residence: Contact the Immigration Attaché at the Malaysian High Commission. Those wishing to take up employment should have their prospective employers contact the Immigration Department in Malaysia, Block I, Level 1-7, Jalan Damansara, Damansar Height, 50550 Kuala Lumpur. Tel: (3) 255 5077. Fax: (3) 256 2340.

MONEY

Currency: Ringgit (R) = 100 sen. Notes are in denominations of R1000, 500, 100, 50, 20, 10, 5 and 1. Coins are in denominations of R1, and 50, 20, 10, 5 and 1 sen. There are also a large number of commemorative coins in various denominations which are legal tender. The Ringgit is often referred to as the Malaysian Dollar.
Credit cards: Visa, Access/Mastercard, Diners Club and American Express are accepted. Check with your credit card company for details of merchant acceptability and other services which may be available.
Travellers cheques: Accepted by all banks, hotels and large department stores.
Exchange rate indicators: The following figures are included as a guide to the movements of the Ringgit against Sterling and the US Dollar:

Date:	Oct '92	Sep '93	Jan '94	Jan '95
£1.00=	4.98	3.90	3.99	3.99
$1.00=	2.50	2.55	2.69	2.55

Currency restrictions: There are no restrictions on the import or export of either local or foreign currency by visitors (except Israeli currency).
Banking hours: Banks are open by 1000 (by 0800 in Sabah), and close at 1500. Banks in Sabah generally break for lunch (1200-1400). Saturday opening times are usually 0930-1130.

DUTY FREE

The following goods may be imported into Malaysia without incurring customs duty:
200 cigarettes or 50 cigars or 225g of tobacco; 1 litre of spirits or wine or malt liquor; perfumes in opened bottles to the value of R200; gifts and souvenirs not exceeding a total value of R200.
Controlled & prohibited items: Visitors must declare valuables and may have to pay a deposit. It is prohibited to import any goods from Israel. Non-prescribed drugs, weapons, pornography and any cloth bearing the imprint or reproduction of any verses of the Koran are prohibited. Drug-smuggling carries the death penalty.

Plan A Convention Where The Tea Breaks Get Longer And Longer

...ring and after a ...nvention, you need ...me out'. Longer tea ...eaks mean more time ... see all the fascinating ...aces in and around ...uala Lumpur. A longer ... break also gives you ...e chance to sample ...eh Tarik', a delicious ...p of 'pulled tea' that ... truly a sight to see! ...here are more than a ...w nice surprises about ...uala Lumpur. Besides ...pacious, comfortable, ...tate-of-the-art business ...nd accommodation ...acilities, there are

KUALA LUMPUR

Tea, anyone? Teh Tarik literally means 'Pulled Tea'. The 'pulling' is to cool the tea.

cultural sights and opportunities for great bargain shopping and indeed mountain resorts, hill resorts, virgin jungle for trekking, golf resorts and beach resorts just a short drive away. So take your time planning your next convention. Just fix the destination first for Kuala Lumpur, Malaysia!

MALAYSIA FASCINATING DESTINATIONS

Other convention destinations in Malaysia.

Langkawi- A Legendary Island with the Bluest of Waters.

Malacca-One of the Most Famous, Historical Cities in Asia.

Sarawak-Convention Centres and resorts nestled in natural surroundings.

PUBLIC HOLIDAYS

Jan 1 '95 New Year's Day [1]. **Jan 17** Thaipusam [2]. **Jan 22** Birthday of D.Y.M.M. Sultan of Kedah [3]. **Jan 31-Feb 1** Chinese New Year. **Feb 1** Federal Territory Day (Wilayah Persekutuan, Kuala Lumpur and Labuan only); Awal Ramadhan (Johor and Malacca only). **Feb 17** Hari Nuzul al-Quran [4]. **Mar 3-4** Hari Raya Puasa (End of Ramadan). **Mar 11** Birthday of D.Y.M.M. Sultan of Selangor [5]. **Mar 21** Anniversary of the Coronation of D.Y.M.M. Sultan of Terengganu [6]. **Mar 30-31** Birthday of D.Y.M.M. Sultan of Kelantan [7]. **Apr 8** Birthday of D.Y.M.M. Sultan of Johor [8]. **Apr 14** Good Friday [9]. **Apr 15** Proclamation Day of Malacca as a Historical City [10]. **Apr 19** Birthday of D.Y.M.M. Sultan of Perak [11]. **Apr 29** Birthday of D.Y.M.M. Sultan of Terengganu [12]. **May 1** Labour Day. **May 7** Hari Hol Negeri Pahang [13]. **May 10** Hari Raya Qurban (Feast of the Sacrifice). **May 11** Second Day of Hari Raya Qurban [14]. **May 14** Wesak Day. **May 30-31** Ka'amatan Festival [15]. **May 31** Awal Muharram. **Jun 1-2** Gawai Dayak [16]. **Jun 3** Official Birthday of HM the Yang di-Pertuan Agong. **Jul 1** Birthday of D.Y.M.M. Tuanku Raja Perlis [17]. **Jul 8** Birthday of T.Y.T. Yang Di Pertua Negeri of Penang [18]. **Jul 19** Birthday of D.Y.M.M. Yang Di-Pertuan Besar of Negeri Sembilan [19]. **Aug 9** Mouloud (Prophet's Birthday). **Aug 31** National Day. **Sep 9** Birthday of T.Y.T. Yang Di-Pertua Negeri Sarawak [16]. **Sep 16** Birthday of T.Y.T. Yang Di-Pertua Negeri Sabah. [20]. **Oct 14** Birthday of T.Y.T. Yang Di-Pertua Negeri of Malacca [10]. **Oct 23** Deepavali [21]. **Oct 24** Birthday of D.Y.M.M. Sultan of Pahang [22]. **Nov 29** Hari Hol Almarhum Sultan Ismail [8]. **Dec 20** Israk and Mikraj 1416 [23]. **Dec 25** Christmas. **Jan '96** Thaipusam [2]. **Jan 1** New Year's Day [1]. **Jan 22** Birthday of D.Y.M.M. Sultan of Kedah [3]. **Jan/Feb** Awal Ramadhan (Johor and Malacca only). **Feb** Hari Nuzul al-Quran [4]. **Feb 1** Federal Territory Day (Wilayah Persekutuan, Kuala Lumpur and Labuan only). **Feb 19-21** Chinese New Year. **Feb 22** Hari Raya Puasa (End of Ramadan). **Mar 11** Birthday of D.Y.M.M. Sultan of Selangor [5]. **Mar 21** Anniversary of the Coronation of D.Y.M.M. Sultan of Terengganu [6]. **Mar 30-31** Birthday of D.Y.M.M. Sultan of Kelantan [7]. **Apr 8** Birthday of D.Y.M.M. Sultan of Johor [8]. **Apr 5** Good Friday [9]. **Apr 15** Proclamation Day of Malacca as a Historical City [10]. **Apr 19** Birthday of D.Y.M.M. Sultan of Perak [11]. **Apr 29** Birthday of D.Y.M.M. Sultan of Terengganu [12]; Hari Raya Qurban (Feast of the Sacrifice). **Notes:** (a) [1] Except Perlis, Kedah, Johor, Kelantan and Terengganu. [2] Johor, Negeri Semblian, Perak, Penang and Selangor only. [3] Kedah only. [4] Kelantan, Pahang, Perak, Perlis, Selangor and Terengganu only. [5] Selangor only. [6] Terengganu only. [7] Kelantan only. [8] Johor only. [9] Sabah and Sarawak only. [10] Malacca only. [11] Perak only. [12] Terengganu only. [13] Pahang only. [14] Kedah, Kelantan, Perlis and Terengganu only. [15] Sabah and Federal Territory Labuan only. [16] Sarawak only. [17] Perlis only. [18] Penang only. [19] Negeri Sembilan only. [20] Sabah only. [21] Except Sabah and Sarawak. [22] Pahang only. [23] Kedah and Negeri Sembilan only. (b) Should a holiday fall on a Sunday, or a declared public holiday, it will be observed on the next working day. (c) Muslim festivals are not widely celebrated in Sabah, Sarawak or Labuan Federal Territory. Elsewhere, they are timed according to local sightings of various phases of the Moon and the dates given above (for Hari Raya Puasa, Hari Raya Qurban and Mouloud) are approximations. During the lunar month of Ramadan that precedes Hari Raya Puasa (Eid al-Fitr), Muslims fast during the day and feast at night and normal business patterns may be interrupted. Many restaurants are closed during the day and there may be restrictions on smoking and drinking. Some disruption may continue into Hari Raya Puasa itself. Hari Raya Puasa and Hari Raya Qurban (Eid al-Adha) may last anything from two to ten days, depending on the region. For more information see the section *World of Islam* at the back of the book. (d) Hindu festivals are declared according to local astronomical observations and it is only possible to forecast the month of their occurrence. They are not widely celebrated in Sabah or Sarawak.

HEALTH

Regulations and requirements may be subject to change at short notice, and you are advised to contact your doctor well in advance of your intended date of departure. Any numbers in the chart refer to the footnotes below.

	Special Precautions?	Certificate Required?
Yellow Fever	No	1
Cholera	Yes	2
Typhoid & Polio	Yes	-
Malaria	Yes/3	-
Food & Drink	4	-

Note: A valid Smallpox vaccination certificate is required of all travellers over six months of age having visited one of the smallpox-infected countries of South America or Africa within the previous 2 weeks. Countries considered to be infected are those listed in the *WHO/Weekly Epidemiological Record.*

[1]: A yellow fever vaccination certificate is required from travellers over one year of age coming from infected areas. Those countries formerly classified as endemic are considered by the Malaysian authorities to be infected areas.

[2]: Following WHO guidelines issued in 1973, a cholera vaccination certificate is not a condition of entry to Malaysia. However, cholera is a risk in this country and precautions are essential. Up-to-date advice should be sought before deciding whether these precautions should include vaccination, as medical opinion is divided over its effectiveness. See the *Health* section at the back of the book.

[3]: Malaria risk exists only in small foci in isolated inland regions below 1700m (5577ft). Urban and coastal areas are generally safe, the exception being Sabah where there is a risk, predominantly in the malignant *falciparum* form, throughout the year. The *falciparum* strain is reported to be 'highly resistant' to chloroquine and 'resistant' to sulfadoxine/pyrimethamine.

[4]: All water should be regarded as being potentially contaminated. Water used for drinking, brushing teeth or making ice should have first been boiled or otherwise sterilised. Milk is unpasteurised and should be boiled. Powdered or tinned milk is available and is advised, but make sure that it is reconstituted with pure water. Avoid dairy products which are likely to have been made from unboiled milk. Only eat well-cooked meat and fish, preferably served hot. Pork, salad and mayonnaise may carry increased risk. Vegetables should be cooked and fruit peeled.

Note: It is generally considered safe to drink water straight from the tap; however, as no authority is absolutely clear on this matter the above advice is included as it reflects the necessity for caution for visitors who are unused to the Malaysian way of life.

Rabies is present. For those at high risk, vaccination before arrival should be considered. If you are bitten abroad seek medical advice without delay. For more information, consult the *Health* section at the back of the book.

Health care: Health insurance is recommended. Hospitals are found in all the main cities and can deal with all major needs. Smaller towns and rural areas have travelling dispensaries. In an emergency, dial 999.

TRAVEL - International

AIR: The national airline is *Malaysia Airlines (MH).* For free advice on air travel, call the Air Travel Advisory Bureau on (0171) 636 5000 (London) *or* (0161) 832 2000 (Manchester).

Approximate flight time: From London to Kuala Lumpur is 12 hours.

International airports: *Kuala Lumpur* (Subang International) (KUL) is 22.5km (14 miles) west of the city (travel time – 35 minutes). A bus goes to the city (Jalan Sultan Mohammed Bus Terminal) every 30 minutes. A taxi to the city centre is available. Fare coupons are available from a counter in the terminal. Airport facilities include an incoming and outgoing duty-free shop, bank/bureau de change, post office, restaurant and bar, and several car-hire firms, all open 0900-2300. *Penang* (Bayan Lepas) (PEN) is 16km (10 miles) from Georgetown, capital of this small island off the northwest coast of the peninsula. Though not receiving as many international flights as Kuala Lumpur, there are connections from the UK via Hong Kong, Singapore or Bangkok. Airport facilities include an incoming and outgoing duty-free shop, restaurant and bar, bank and exchange, and several car hire firms, all open 0900-2200. *Kota Kinabalu (BKI)* is 6.5km (4 miles) from the city. Situated on the northern coast of Sabah state (the northeastern part of Borneo Island), this airport is the international gateway to East Malaysia (Sabah and Sarawak) and receives international flights from all over the world. Connections from the UK go via Singapore, Hong Kong and Kuala Lumpur. Airport facilities include bank/bureau de change facilities, restaurant and bar, all open 0900-2200. *Kuching (KCH)* is 11km (7 miles) from the city. Situated in the west of Sarawak on the island of Borneo, the airport receives a limited number of international flights.

Departure tax: R20 for international departures, including to Brunei and Singapore.

SEA: The major international ports are Georgetown (Penang), Port Kelang (for Kuala Lumpur) and, in East Malaysia (for Sabah and Sarawak), Kota Kinabalu, Lahad Dato, Sandakan, Tawau, Labuan Island and Kuching. There are two new ports under development in Sarawak: Bintulu and Pending Point. Shipping lines with passenger services to Malaysia include *Blue Funnel, P&O* and *Straits Shipping.* Cargo/passenger lines are *Austasia, Knutsen, Lykes, Neptune Orient, Orient Overseas* and *Straits Shipping.*

RAIL: Through services operate to and from Singapore via Kuala Lumpur and between Butterworth and Bangkok daily.

ROAD: Peninsular Malaysia is linked by good roads to Thailand and (via a causeway) to Singapore. Road connections between the two eastern states, Sarawak and Sabah, and their neighbours on Borneo, Brunei and the Indonesian state of Kalimantan are fairly good.

TRAVEL - Internal

AIR: *Malaysia Airlines (MH)* serves numerous commercial airports in Peninsular Malaysia. In East Malaysia, *MH*, backed by *Pelangi Air*, crisscross both Sabah and Sarawak and also fly to Brunei. *Singapore Airlines, Royal Brunei* and *Thai International* operate flights to certain Malaysian destinations. Plans are underway for the further development of several airports, including Kuala Lumpur. There are many other small airstrips also in use.

Departure tax: R5.

SEA/RIVER: Coastal ferries sail frequently between Penang and Butterworth and there is a scheduled passenger service linking Port Kelang with both Sarawak and Sabah. Small rivercraft often provide the most practical means of getting about in East Malaysia, even in the towns, and they are the only way to reach the more isolated settlements (unless one has access to a helicopter). Boats may easily be chartered and river buses and taxis are plentiful.

RAIL: *Malayan Railways* operate nearly 2092km (1300 miles) of line. There are three classes of train: De Luxe or First Class (with upholstered seats), Eksekutif or Second Class (with padded leather seats) and Ekonomi or Third Class (with cushioned plastic seats). The fast daytime 'Express Rakyat' runs from Singapore to Butterworth. Express trains are modern, and some have sleeping berths and buffet cars. Some trains are air-conditioned. East Malaysia has one railway line; it runs along the coast from Kota Kinabalu (Sabah), then inland up a steep jungle valley to the small town of Tenom. Other than this line, there are two main lines operated for a passenger service. One runs along the west coast and from Singapore which runs northwards to Kuala Lumpur and Butterworth, meeting the Thai railways at the border. The other line separates from the west coast line at the town of Gemas and takes a northeastern route to Kota Baharu and Tenom. There is also a passenger service to two of Malaysia's seaports – Penang and Padang Besar on the west coast. There are no rail services in Sarawak.

Cheap fares: Children under four travel free; children 4-11 pay half fare.

Special tickets: The *Malayan Railway Pass* is available in 10- and 30-day tickets, giving unlimited travel on all trains through Peninsular Malaysia and Singapore except the 'Express Rakyat' and the 'Mesra Express'. The pass can be purchased from train stations in Butterworth, Johor Baharu, Kuala Lumpur, Padang Besar, Port Kelang, Rantau Panjang, Wakaf Baharu and Singapore. However, reservations must be made in advance for seats in First Class air-conditioned trains and a supplement is charged. Reservations may be made up to three months in advance from the Director of Commerce, Malayan Railway, Jalan Sultan Hishamuddin, Kuala Lumpur. Enquire at the Malaysia Tourism Promotion Board for further details.

ROAD: Traffic drives on the left. Most roads in the Peninsular states are paved and signs leading to the various destinations are well placed and clear. The north–south highway, spanning 890km (553 miles) from Bukit Kayu Hitam (on the Kedah-Thailand border) to Johor Baharu is now fully open to traffic since the Sultan opened the last stretch between Tapah and Gopeng. The dual carriageway will provide shorter travel times between towns. **Bus:** Local bus networks are extensive; there are almost 1000 routes, with regular services in and between all principal cities. Four-wheel-drive buses are used in rural areas of Sabah and Sarawak. **Minibus:** Available in the city areas. **Trishaw:** These are inexpensive for short trips. Pre-arrange the price. **Taxi:** Shared and normal taxis are a fast means of inter-town travel, but delays may be encountered whilst drivers get their passenger load before moving off. There is a 50% surcharge for fares between 2400-0600 and an extra R1 is charged for taxis booked by phone. Taxi coupons providing fixed prices to specific destinations can be purchased at the Kuala Lumpur railway station and the airport. **Car hire:** This is available through several agencies. Some agencies provide cars on an unlimited-mileage basis. Cars with driver are also available. **Documentation:** An International Driving Licence is

ASSUNTA HOSPITAL

JALAN TEMPLER
46990 PETALING JAYA
WEST MALAYSIA
TEL NO: 603-7923433
FAX NO: 603-7914933

Assunta Hospital is situated in the modern township of Petaling Jaya in the city of Kuala Lumpur, the capital of Malaysia. It is about 15 minutes' drive from the International Airport of Subang and about 30 minutes from the capital city, Kuala Lumpur. Petaling Jaya Hilton, an international hotel, is also situated very near the hospital.

Assunta Hospital has 344 beds and a staff of 700. Our medical specialists and nurses and other health personnel speak English. Translation for Mandarin-, Japanese-, German- and French-speaking clients is available.

The hospital has a complete range of services for outpatient and inpatient care. At present, there are 77 specialists, 11 full-time consultants and 66 visiting consultants covering various specialities.

Assunta Hospital offers 24-hour services for:
Ambulance Service • Accident & Emergency Care • Outpatient Treatment • Operating Theatre • Blood Bank • Laboratories • X-ray & C T Scanner • Angiography • Mammography • Pharmacy

Other facilities include:
 Surgery • Laparoscopic Surgery • Obstetrics & Gynaecology • Paediatrics • Orthopaedics • Eye, Ear, Nose & Throat • Dermatology • Plastic Surgery • Urology • Neurosurgery • Oncology • Physiotherapy

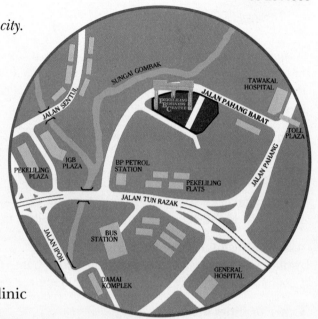
required. A national driving licence is sufficient for UK nationals, but has to be endorsed by the Registrar of Motor Vehicles in Malaysia.

URBAN: Parking in the centre of Kuala Lumpur and other towns is restricted to spaces for which a charge is made and a receipt is given. Public transport services in Kuala Lumpur are provided by conventional buses and by 'Bas Mini' fixed-route minibuses, taxis and pedi-cabs (trishaws) licensed by the Government. Bus fares vary, but the 'Bas Mini' rates are flat. These are used for shorter journeys, and tend to be crowded. A monorail system in Kuala Lumpur was completed in 1992.

JOURNEY TIMES: The following chart gives approximate journey times (in hours and minutes) from Kuala Lumpur to other major centres in Malaysia.

	Air	Road	Rail
Ipoh	0.30	3.00	4.30
Penang	0.45	6.00	9.30
Alur Setar	0.45	7.00	7.30
Kuantan	0.35	4.00	-
Johor Baharu	0.35	5.00	6.00
Singapore	0.45	6.00	7.00

ACCOMMODATION

HOTELS: Malaysia has many hotels of luxury and economy class. Two new hotels have recently been built in Kuala Lumpur – the Swiss Inn Kuala Lumpur and the 515-room Marriott International. It is necessary to book well in advance, especially during school and public holidays when the Malaysians take their holidays in the popular resorts, notably Penang, Langkawi and the highlands. The more basic hotels have little in the way of modern washing or bathing facilities, often only a water trough instead of a bath or shower. There is no formal classification system. Government tax of 5% and service charge of 10% are added to bills. Tips are only expected (on the basis of good service) for room service and porterage. Laundry service is available in most hotels. For further information, contact the Malaysian Association of Hotels, c/o Malaysia Tourist Information Complex, 109 Jalan Ampang, 50450 Kuala Lumpur. Tel: (3) 242 0516. Fax: (3) 248 8059.

GOVERNMENT REST HOUSES: These are subsidised, moderately priced hotels. They are basic, but always clean and comfortable, with full facilities and usually good restaurants. As they are primarily travelling

inns they tend to fill up quickly, so it is advisable to telephone and reserve a room.

CAMPING: There are camping facilities in the Taman Negara or national park. Here jungle lodges provide tents, camp beds, pressure lamps and mosquito nets for trips into the rainforests.

YOUTH HOSTELS: There are not many of these, but they are very cheap. Accommodation is in dormitories and meals can be arranged. Visitors must register at the hostel from 1700-2000. Hostels are to be found in Cameron Highlands, Kuala Lumpur, Kuantan, Malacca, Penang and Port Dickson. The Kuala Lumpur International Youth Hostel is at 21 Jalan Kampung Attap, 50460 Kuala Lumpur. Further details can be obtained from the Youth Hostel Association or the Malaysian Tourism Promotion Board.

RESORTS & EXCURSIONS

For the purpose of this section the country has been divided into five regions: Kuala Lumpur, Malacca and the Southwest; Penang, Langkawi & Pangkor; the Hill Resorts; the East Coast; and Sabah & Sarawak.

Kuala Lumpur, Malacca and the Southwest

This is the most developed and densely populated region of the country. This is also where the most important historical remains are found.

Malaysia's capital city and main international gateway, **Kuala Lumpur**, was founded in the 1890s, and its architecture reflects a cosmopolitan mix of Malay, Chinese, Indian and European cultures. Primarily a business and commercial centre, the city has much to offer the leisure visitor. The *Tasek Perdana Lake Gardens* are one of the city's most well-known natural landmarks, a popular spot for picnics and walking. Boats may be hired. Within the gardens are *Parliament House* and the *National Monument*. Close by is the *National Museum* which houses many historical exhibits. Near the railway station is the *National Mosque* surrounded by lawns ornamented with fountains. Nearby is the old Chinese temple of *Chan See Yuen* and the colourful Indian temple of *Sri Mahamariaman*. At the recently developed 50-year-old *Central Market*, local craftsmen can be seen at work, local food savoured at hawker stalls, and cultural and musical performances enjoyed. The *Batu Caves* lie a few miles to the north of the city. These large natural caves, reached by 272 steps, house the Hindu shrine of Lord Subramaniam. Nearby is the *Museum Cave,* a fascinating display of brightly coloured statues and murals from Hindu mythology. *Templar Park,* 22km (14 miles) north of Kuala Lumpur, is a well-preserved tract of primary rainforest which is rich in scenic beauty. Jungle paths, swimming lagoons and waterfalls all lie within the park boundaries. Malaysia's latest agricultural park, located at Cherakah in Shah Alam, Selangor, has a large playing area with premises for skateboarders and rollerskaters.

Petaling Jaya, midway between the airport and Kuala Lumpur, was intended as a dormitory town, but has now become a major centre in its own right. It has international hotels, restaurants and nightlife and is close to four excellent golf courses.

Port Dickson is on the coast, about one and a half hour's travelling time from Kuala Lumpur. Malaysians flock here from the city at weekends, but with 18km (11 miles) of beach there is always plenty of room. The bays are ideal for all kinds of watersports and fishing and there are facilities for water-skiing, motor cruising and deep-sea fishing.

Port Kelang, further to the north, is Malaysia's main port, famous for its fish restaurants specialising in steamed crabs, fried prawns and shark's fins.

The city of **Malacca** is two hours by road from Kuala Lumpur. Founded in the early 15th century, Malacca remains predominantly a Chinese community, although there are many reminders of periods under Portuguese, Dutch and British rule; some of these can be seen in the Malacca museum. Architectural remains include the *Cheng Hoon Teng Temple* in the centre of the city, the gateway of the *A Formosa* Portuguese fortress, *St Paul's Church* with the grave of St Xavier, the *Stadthuys,* the Dutch *Christ Church* and the *Tranquerah Mosque,* one of the oldest in the country. There are several international hotels in Malacca, augmented by a fully-equipped resort complex 12km (7 miles) outside the city.

The journey south from Malacca to Johor Baharu and on to Singapore passes through **Muar** and **Batu Pahat.**

Penang, Langkawi & Pangkor

The island of **Penang**, described as the 'Pearl of the Orient', lies just off the northwest coast of Peninsular Malaysia. Recently a network of expanded tourist facilities has been created. As well as being a particularly beautiful tropical island of palm trees and sandy beaches, it is also the main international gateway to northern Malaysia. It was the natural harbour which first attracted the British to Penang in the late 18th century, and the port is still one of the most important in the country. There is a regular ferry service between the island and the town of Butterworth on the mainland. The third-longest bridge in the world links Penang to the mainland.

Georgetown, the island's one town, is made up of Malay, Chinese, Thai, Indian and European cultures. The main shopping is on Campbell Street and Canarvon Street. Worth visiting are *Khoo Kongsi,* an old Chinese clan house, *Fort Cornwallis,* a British 18th-century fortress, *Penang Museum and Art Gallery* and the many churches, temples and mosques found throughout the town.

For those who want a single-centre holiday, Penang is a good choice, enabling the visitor to see something of Malaysian life in the town and small villages, as well as offering some of the most beautiful beaches in the country. Some of the most attractive beaches are situated along *Batu Feringgi* on the north coast. The island's main hotels are along this strip, although new international hotels have recently appeared close to the airport and also in Georgetown.

Penang has more than just beaches; one of the most unusual attractions is the *Snake Temple,* which swarms with venomous snakes, but visitors will be relieved to know that they are heavily drugged with incense. In the centre of the island is *Penang Hill;* the 700m (2300ft) summit, where there is a delightful small hotel which is gained by a funicular railway and offers splendid views and leisure walks.

More than 100km (60 miles) north of Penang lie the 99 islands, many of which are just outcrops of coral, that make up **Langkawi.** The largest, Langkawi Island, is the only one with sophisticated tourist facilities (it has been declared a free port and duty-free shopping is available). It is currently enjoying something of a building boom, with several international hotels under construction. There is already a fully-equipped resort complex. The island's many coves, lagoons and inlets make it ideal for all kinds of watersports such as swimming, sailing, fishing and scuba diving. Horseriding and golf are also available. Travel to Langkawi is by air from Kuala Lumpur, Penang and Alur Setar or by road and sea.

Unspoilt, seldom-visited **Pangkor Island,** about 100km (60 miles) south of Penang (and half an hour by ferry from Lumut), has recently gained popularity as a result of two new international hotels. Innumerable bays boast excellent sandy beaches and all kinds of watersports. Pangkor has no air links.

The Hill Resorts

Dotted about the mountain range which runs down the spine of Malaysia are several hill resorts. All are situated more than 1400m (4500ft) above sea level and offer cool, pleasant weather after the humidity of the plain and the cities.

Less than one hour by road from Kuala Lumpur is **Genting Highlands,** which boasts Malaysia's only casino (passports required). Genting Highlands can also be reached by regular helicopter service from Kuala

Top picture: Minarets. Above: Malaysian shutters.

Terengganu

Bordering Thailand in the north is the state of Kelantan, whose capital **Kota Baharu** is a colourful, vibrant city. The beaches here are clean and unspoilt and the sea ideal for swimming, diving and fishing. The state is renowned for its many cultural festivals, some of which are unique to the region. *Puja Umur* (the birthday of the Sultan) is celebrated with a week-long festival, beginning with a parade in Kota Baharu. A form of art unique to Kelantan is the *Ma'yong*, a combination of ballet, opera, romantic drama and comedy, originally a form of court entertainment. Shadow play, top-spinning and kite flying are also to be seen.

Johor Baharu, in the southern state of Johor, is Malaysia's southernmost gateway, and also the road and rail gateway from Singapore via a 1.5km (1-mile) causeway that connects the island to Peninsular Malaysia. Places of interest include *Johor Lama,* the seat of the Johor Sultanate after eviction from Malacca; the *Kota Tinggi Waterfalls;* the *Ayer Hitam* ceramic works; *Muar,* famous throughout the country for its ghazal music and trance-inducing Kuda Kepang dances; the rubber and palm-oil plantations; and **Desaru,** Johor's newest beach resort. Desaru boasts unspoilt beaches and jungle. All kinds of sports are played here, from swimming, canoeing and snorkelling to pony riding and jungle trekking. There are also plans to develop a second 18-hole golf course. Accommodation is in Malaysian-style chalets and hotels, and campers are also welcome.

Sabah & Sarawak

Despite being separated from Peninsular Malaysia (Sabah by 950km/600 miles and Sarawak by 650km/404 miles) by the South China Sea, Sabah and Sarawak can be reached by direct flights from Kuala Lumpur and Singapore.

Sabah, known as 'The Land Below The Wind', is home of the world's oldest jungles and one of South-East Asia's highest peaks, *Mount Kinabalu.* A large part of the ascent can be made by road, but the final part must be climbed by foot. The region also offers excellent opportunities for expeditions and technical rock climbing. Contact the Park Warden, PO Box 626, Kota Kinabalu. Tel: (88) 211 881. The **Mount Kinabalu National Park** is famous for containing over 500 species of birds and over 800 species of orchids. Overnight accommodation is available.

Lumpur. Facilities include four hotels, golf courses with a magnificent clubhouse, an artificial lake, a health and sports centre, and an indoor swimming pool. **Fraser Hill,** set in lush jungle 100km (60 miles) north of Kuala Lumpur, is popular with both holidaymakers and golf enthusiasts. A wide range of other sports are available. There is also a self-contained township, self-catering bungalows and an international standard hotel. A daily shuttle service operates between the Merlin Hotel and Fraser Hill.

Still further north, about four hours from Kuala Lumpur, are the **Cameron Highlands.** These are one of the best-known mountain resorts in Asia, and consist of three separate townships: **Brinchang, Tanah Rata** and **Ringlet.** An international-standard hotel and many bungalows are set around a golf course in lush green surroundings. Tennis, squash, badminton, jungle walks and swimming are available. From here you can visit **Gunung Brinchang** at 2064m (6773ft) above sea level, the highest inhabited point in Peninsular Malaysia and therefore a magnificent viewpoint.

The East Coast

This part of the country contains many of the finest beaches, including some of the least spoilt in southern Asia. In effect, the whole east coast is one huge beach, backed by jungle. The region, which covers two-thirds of Peninsular Malaysia, comprises the states of Kelantan, Terengganu, Pahang and Johor, as well as the islands of Tioman and Rawa. It is served by daily *MH* services from Kuala Lumpur into Kota Baharu, Kuantan and Kuala Terengganu and from Penang into Kota Baharu. Air-conditioned coaches connect from most major towns in the country to the east coast resorts, though clients should be reminded that travel by road is

sometimes impossible during the monsoons.

Kuantan, the state capital of Pahang, is fast gaining popularity as a beach resort. The region around Kuantan is also well known for village festivals and for the craft of weaving pandanus leaves into mats, hats and baskets. Woodcarving and batik are also traditional crafts in this part of the country.

Asia's first Club Mediterranée holiday village is in **Cherating**, about 45km (30 miles) north of Kuantan. Also in the region is Malaysia's answer to Loch Ness, *Lake Chini,* in whose waters mythological monsters are said to lurk, guarding the entrance to a legendary sunken city.

In the north of the state is Malaysia's largest national park, **Taman Negara.** Surrounded by the world's oldest tropical forest (supposedly 130 million years old), the park has remained virtually untouched and is a favourite haunt for outdoor enthusiasts, especially bird-watchers. The journey to the park headquarters involves travel by train, road and a 3-hour boat ride. Accommodation is modest and limited, and clients are advised to make early reservations.

The island of **Tioman,** in the South China Sea off the coast of Pahang, will be familiar to fans of the film 'South Pacific', as it was here that the film-makers found their mythical Bali Hai. Tioman is the largest of a group of 64 volcanic islands and a must for deep-sea diving enthusiasts. The islands are accessible by boat from Mersing or by helicopter or light aircraft from Mersing, Kuala Lumpur or Singapore.

The state of **Terengganu** has 225km (140 miles) of white sandy beaches. Swimming and all forms of watersports are favourite pastimes. There are several turtle-breeding beaches; at *Rantau Abang,* the Visitor Centre can arrange for guests to watch giant turtles laying their eggs.

Kota Kinabalu, the capital and main gateway, is a new city built upon the ruins of Jesselton, which was badly damaged during the Second World War, and designed around the gold-domed *State Mosque.* From *Signal Hill* there is a good view of the city.

Just south of Kota Kinabalu is the resort of **Tanjung Aru,** where the recently opened beach complex has been designed with both business traveller and holidaymaker in mind. As well as conference and meeting facilities, there is also a ferry-shuttle service into the town.

Tuaran is half an hour's drive from Kota Kinabalu. The road runs through lush valleys, forested hills and rubber plantations. The town has a good *'Tamu'* (market).

Sandakan, nearly 400km (250 miles) from Kota Kinabalu, is the old capital of Borneo. 24km (15 miles) from the town is the *Sepilok Sanctuary,* home of the 'wild men of Borneo', the world's largest orang-utan population.

The **Tenom** region can be reached from Kota Kinabalu by Sabah's only railway line. A spectacular and thrilling experience, it follows the *Padas River* up through narrow jungle gorges in the *Crocker Range.* Tenom town is renowned for its style of longhouse building, unchanged in centuries, and for the traditional songs and dances performed there.

The state of **Sarawak** occupies the northwest coastal region of the island of Borneo. Most people who live in Sarawak use the intricate network of waterways to get about. Visitors are encouraged to do so too, although taxis and hire cars are available in the larger towns for those who prefer more conventional means of transport.

Kuching, on the banks of the River Sarawak, is the financial and commercial centre of the state, as well as being a gateway to a huge area of dense tropical rainforest and mountain ranges. Villages on stilts still cling precariously to the river banks. A visit to the *Sarawak Museum* affords valuable insights into the history, wildlife and anthropology of Borneo.

Overnight excursions can be made up the *Skrang River,* with accommodation provided in longhouses. There are also downriver trips to **Santubong,** an ancient trading post on the coast.

The **Bako National Park,** covering an area of approximately 26 sq km (10 sq miles), has interesting wildlife and vegetation, including carnivorous plants, long-nosed monkeys and Sambar deer. Excursions are organised from Kuching.

Other excursions, often via **Miri,** can be made to the *Niah Caves,* which show evidence of human existence dating back to 5000BC. The caves are also valued for their guano and bird's nests, the latter being used to make soup. Many of the caves – and some are more easily accessible than others – may be visited with a guide. Excursions to the independent Sultanate of **Brunei** can also be made (see the separate country entry above).

POPULAR ITINERARIES: 5-day: (a) Kuala Lumpur–Genting Highlands–Fraser Hill–Cameron Highlands–Penang–Kuala Lumpur. (b) Kuala Lumpur–Penang–Langkawi–Georgetown–Kuala Lumpur.

SOCIAL PROFILE

FOOD & DRINK: In multi-racial Malaysia, every type of cooking from South-East Asia can be tasted. Malay food concentrates on subtleties of taste using a blend of spices, ginger, coconut milk and peanuts. *Sambals* (a paste of ground chilli, onion and tamarind) is often used as a side dish. *Blachan* (a dried shrimp paste) is used in many dishes and *ikan bilis* (tiny sun-dried fish) are eaten with drinks. Popular Malay dishes include *satay* which consists of a variety of meats, especially chicken, barbecued on small skewers with a dipping sauce of spicy peanuts and a salad of cucumber, onion and compressed rice cakes. The best sauce often takes several hours to prepare to attain its subtle flavour. *Gula Malacca* (a firm sago pudding in palm sugar sauce) is also served in restaurants. There are many regional types of Chinese cooking including Cantonese, Peking, Hakka, Sichuan and Taiwanese. Indian food is also popular, with curries ranging from mild to very hot indeed. Vegetarian food, chutneys and Indian breads are also available. Indonesian cuisine also combines the use of dried seafoods and spiced vegetables with the Japanese method of preparation with fresh ingredients cooked to retain the natural flavour. Japanese-style seafood such as *siakaiu beef* (grilled at the table), *tempura* (deep-fried seafood) and *sashimi* (raw fish with salad) are excellent. Korean and Thai food are available in restaurants. Amongst Malaysia's exotic fruits are starfruit, durian, guavas, mangos, mangosteen and pomelos. Western food is served throughout the country, particularly in major hotels which have continental menus and international coffee shops. Table service is normal, and in Chinese restaurants chopsticks are customary. Indian and Malay food is eaten with the fingers. **Drink:** Although the country is largely Islamic, alcohol is available. Local beers such as *Tiger* and *Anchor* are recommended and also the famous *Singapore Gin Sling.*

NIGHTLIFE: Kuala Lumpur has a selection of reputable nightclubs and discotheques, most belonging to the big hotels. Penang is also lively at night, larger hotels having cocktail lounges, dining, dancing and cultural shows. There are night markets in most towns, including both Kuala Lumpur and Penang Chinatown. Malay and Chinese films often have English subtitles and there are also English films. The national lottery and Malaysia's only casino at Genting Highlands are government approved and visitors are not supposed to gamble elsewhere. *Keno* and Chinese *Tai Sai,* roulette, baccarat, french bull and blackjack are played at the casino. Dress is relatively formal and visitors must be over 21.

SHOPPING: Shopping in Malaysia ranges from exclusive department stores to street markets. Bargaining is expected in the markets, unless fixed prices are displayed. The islands of Labuan and Langkawi are duty-free zones. Cameras, pens, watches, cosmetics, perfume and electronic goods are available duty-free throughout Malaysia. Malaysian speciality goods include pewterware, silverware and brassware; batik; jewellery; pottery and *songket.* Enquire at Malaysian Royal Customs and Excise about claiming cashback on duty free. **Shopping hours:** Most shops keep their own opening hours, usually within the range of 0900-2200.

SPORT: Malaysia has many unusual sports, including **Gasing-top spinning** (called *Main Gasing*) using tops fashioned from hardwood and delicately balanced with lead. **Wau-kite flying** is a traditional pastime. **Sepak Takraw** is a game like volleyball, played with a ball made of rattan strips. Players may use their heads, knees and feet but not their hands. **Car racing:** Held at Batu Tiga track near Kuala Lumpur. **Golf:** There are more than 40 golf clubs. The Malaysian Open Golf Championships, held each March, attract top professionals. **Horseracing:** Held in Ipoh, Kuala Lumpur and Penang. **Hunting:** Big-game hunting is regulated by Federal Game Wardens who issue necessary licenses. Guides, trackers and porters must be recruited locally. The importation of arms must be arranged through the Malaysia Police Department. For further information write to Chief Game Warden, MATIC, 109 Jalan Ampang, 50450 Kuala Lumpur. Tel: (3) 243 4929. **Karate:** More than 150 karate training centres offer regular training sessions under black-belt instructors six days a week. Visitors are welcome to receive free karate training for one week in any of the centres. A list can be obtained from the Chief Instructor, Karate Budokan International, Jalan Jubilee, Kuala Lumpur. **Yacht races:** These are held every Sunday at Port Dickson, about 95km (60 miles) from Kuala Lumpur. **Golf:** There are a number of excellent golf courses, such as the Glenmarie Golf and Country Club near Kuala Lumpur and its international airport. A new golf resort is being developed at Kuala Terengganu.

SPECIAL EVENTS: Some of the strangest and most colourful festivals in the world are held in Malaysia, many of which are linked with state or regional public holidays. *Chinese New Year* is a major festival wherein the Lion Dance is performed, gifts are exchanged, visits to the temples are made and 'open houses' are held for the welcoming of friends and relatives. Children are given *ang-pows* – money placed in bright red envelopes. The following is a selection of major festivals and other special events celebrated annually in Malaysia.
Mar 19 '95 *Regatta Lipa-Lipa,* Semporna (Sabah). **Apr 19-23** *Water Sports Festival,* Kuala Kangsar (Perak). **Apr 27-29** *Kertok Festival,* Rantau Panjang (Kelantan). **Apr 29-30** *Castrol Motorcross,* Kangar (Perlis). **May 1-**

Rebanc drummers

Kite flyer

31 *Keamatan Festival,* Kota Kinabalu (Sabah). **May 13-14** *Sabah International Fishing Competition.* **May 20-29** *Sabah Fest,* Kota Kinabalu. **May 25-29** *Malaysian International Kite Festival,* Pantai Sri Tujuh Tumpat (Kelantan). **May 27-30** *International Orchid Festival and Ipoh City Day Celebrations,* Ipoh (Perak). **May 27-Jun 4** *Malacca Tourism Week,* Bandar Hilir (Melaka). **May 30-Jun 2** *Gawai Dayak Festival,* Sarawak. **Jun 3-4** *Fraser's Hill International Bird Race,* Fraser's Hill. **Jun 4** *Malacca Dragon Boat Race,* Klebang Beach (Melakaa). **Jun 3-6** *Kuching Waterfront Carnival.* **Jun 3-7** *Orchid and Flower Week,* Kangar (Perlis). **Jun 26-27** *Rompin Beach Festival,* Rompin Beach (Pahang). **Jun 27-29** *Silat Festival,* Tanah Merah (Kelantan); *St Pedro Festival,* Bandar Hilir (Melaka). **Jul 1-31** *July Fest (National Park),* Taman Negara Pahang (Jerantut). **Jul 2-9** *Flora Festival,* Kuala Lumpur. **Jul 13-18** *Perlis Handicraft Week* and *Kuala Perlis Water Sports,* Kuala (Perlis). **Jul 27-31** *Kelantan International Drum Festival,* State Stadium Kota Baharu, Kelantan. **Aug 1-31** *Kuching Festival 1995.* **Aug 11-20** *Durian Festival,* Tapah (Perak). **Aug 13-31** *Lumut Festival.* **Aug 19-31** *Johor Carnival '95.* **Aug 20-24** *Cameron Highlands Flower Fest.* **Sep 3** *Kuantan Beach Run,* Telok Chempedak Cherating (Kuantan Pahang). **Sep 8-10** *Tioman International Regatta,* Tioman Island. **Sep 9-23** *Malaysia Fest,* Kuala Lumpur. **Sep 24** *Pangkor Half Marathon,* Pangkor Island. **Oct 3-5** *Kelantan Top-Spinning Competition,* Padang Merdeka Pasir Puteh. **Oct 12-15** *Johor Master Golf.* **Oct 15-30** *Shopping Carnival,* Kuala Lumpur. **Oct 21-24** *Tasik Melati Festival,* Perlis. **Oct 22-31** *Borneo Safari,* Sabah. **Oct 24** *Total Eclipse of the Sun,* Kudat (Sabah). **Oct 29-30** *Kuantan River Festival,* Explanade Garden, Kuantan. **Oct/Nov** *Deepavali* or the 'Festival of Lights', celebrated by the Indian population. Hindu homes are decorated with candles and oil lamps for 'open house'. **Nov 1-13** *Penang Festival.* **Nov 11** *Meveka Carnival,* Air Keroh. **Nov 11-12** *Treasure Hunt,* Kangar (Perlis). **Nov 11-25** *Cultural Fest Negeri Sembilan,* Taman Seni Budaya, Seremban and Negeri Sembilan. **Nov 17-20** *Melaka Sea Carnival,* Klebang Beach, Kota Belud Tamu Besar (Sabah). **Nov 24-30** *Perlis Cultural Fest,* Kangar. In November the Chinese celebrate the *Nine Emperor God's Festival,* in which volunteers are put into a trance before their cheeks are pierced by long skewers. The Indian population holds a similar event in February. Both festivals are held in towns where there is a sizeable Indian or Chinese community. For a full list of special events for 1995/96 contact the Malaysia Tourism Promotion Board.
SOCIAL CONVENTIONS: Malaysia's population is a mixture of diverse cultures and characters. In general, the racial groups integrate, but keep to their individual traditions and lifestyles. Malays still form more than half of the total population and lead a calm life governed by the authority of elders and a strong sense of respect and etiquette. The Indian, Pakistani and Sri Lankan members of the population originally came to Malaysia to take up positions in the civil service, police and local government departments, as well as in the new rubber plantations, but many are now among the professional classes. European influences (Dutch, British and Portuguese in particular)

are also very marked in Malaysia, although the European section of the population is now small. As far as greetings are concerned, the Malaysian equivalent of 'hello' is the Muslim 'peace be with you'. Malay men are addressed *Encik* (pronounced Enchik) with or without the name; Malay women should be called *Cik* (pronounced Che) if they are single and *Puan* if they are married. Chinese and Indians usually use Western forms of address. Hospitality is always warm, lavish and informal. Visitors should follow Malaysian example and respect religious beliefs, such as taking off footwear at the door and wearing appropriate clothing. Dress should be informal, but not over-casual. Within towns, smoking has now become the subject of government disapproval and fines are levied in a number of public places, such as cinemas, theatres and libraries. **Tipping:** 10% service charge and 5% government tax are commonly included in bills. Taxi drivers are not tipped.

BUSINESS PROFILE

ECONOMY: The Malaysian economy is centred on the production of a number of key commodities: crude oil, palm oil, tin and rubber, of which Malaysia is the world's largest producer. These four items account for over 65% of Malaysia's export earnings. Despite the spectacular decline in the prices of tin and oil during the 1980s, Malaysia coped unusually well with the global recession of the late 1980s. Timber production, another important industry, has also been cut back through conservation measures. The Government has embarked upon an economic development strategy which has targeted particular industries for development: as well as those which are dependent on the country's natural resources, electronics, transport equipment, machinery, steel and textiles have been selected to broaden Malaysia's economic base. Manufacturing now accounts for over a quarter of the gross national product. Japan, which exchanges finished products for raw materials – particularly oil and gas – is Malaysia's largest trading partner, followed by the USA and Singapore. The rapid growth of the 1980s, averaging 7-8% per annum, will have to be curtailed somewhat during the early 1990s to avoid 'overheating' in the form of high inflation and an explosion of the country's current account deficit.
BUSINESS: Suits or safari suits are acceptable for business meetings. Business visitors should remember that the Malay population is predominantly Muslim and religious customs should be respected and normal courtesies observed, eg appointments, punctuality and calling cards. **Office hours** vary between Peninsular Malaysia and East Malaysia. In general most offices are open by 0830 and close between 1600 and 1730. Almost all close for an hour between 1200 and 1400. Most close at 1200 Saturday.
COMMERCIAL INFORMATION: The following organisations can offer advice: National Chamber of Commerce and Industry of Malaysia, 37 Jalan Kia Peng, 50450 Kuala Lumpur. Tel: (3) 241 9600 *or* 442 9871 *or* 442 7624. Fax: (3) 241 3775 *or* 441 6043. Telex: 33642; *or*
Malaysian International Chamber of Commerce and

Industry (MICCI), PO Box 12921, Wisma Damansara, 10th Floor, Jalan Semantan, 50792 Kuala Lumpur. Tel: (3) 254 2677. Fax: (3) 255 4946.
CONFERENCES/CONVENTIONS: Many conferences and conventions are held in Malaysia each year. Apart from the dedicated facilities at the Putra World Trade Centre in Kuala Lumpur, many hotels have facilities. Further information can be obtained from the Malaysia Tourism Promotion Board, Convention Promotion Division, 24th-27th Floor, Menara Dato' Onn, Putra World Trade Centre, 45 Jalan Tun Ismail, 50480 Kuala Lumpur. Tel: (3) 293 5188. Fax: (3) 293 5884.

CLIMATE

Tropical without extremely high temperatures. Days are very warm, while nights are fairly cool. The main rainy season in the east runs between November and February, while August is the wettest period on the west coast. East Malaysia has heavy rains (November to February) in Sabah and in Sarawak. However, it is difficult to standardise the country's climate, as rainfall differs on the east and west coasts according to the prevailing monsoon winds (northeast or southwest).
Required clothing: Lightweight cottons and linens are worn throughout the year. Waterproofing is advisable all year.

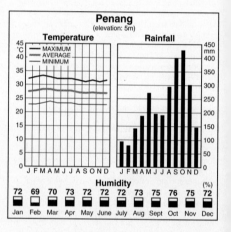

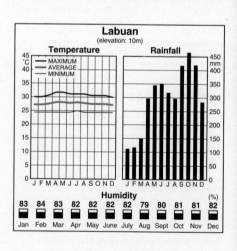

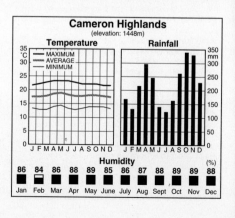

Maldives Republic

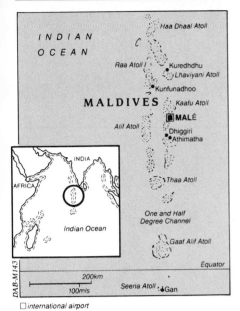

□ *international airport*

Location: A group of islands in the Indian Ocean, 500km (300 miles) southwest of the southern tip of India.

Ministry of Tourism
Boduthaku/Rufaanu Magu, Malé 20-05, Maldives
Tel: 323 224/8. Fax: 322 512. Telex: 66019 (a/b TOURISM MF).

Ministry of Trade and Industries
Ghaazee Building, Ameer Ahmed Magu, Malé 20-05, Maldives
Tel: 323 668. Fax: 323 756. Telex: 77076.

Honorary Tourism Representative for the Maldives Republic in the UK
Maldive Travel, 3 Esher House, 11 Edith Terrace, London SW10 0TH
Tel: (0171) 352 2246 *or* 351 9351. Fax: (0171) 351 3382. Telex: 9413686 (a/b MAGIC G).

The British High Commission in Colombo deals with enquiries relating to the Maldives (see *Sri Lanka* later in this book).

Maldives Mission to the United Nations
Suite 800C, 820 Second Avenue, New York, NY 10017
Tel: (212) 599 6194. Fax: (212) 972 3970. Telex: 0960945 (a/b UNSOPAC NYK).

The Embassy of the United States in Colombo deals with enquiries relating to the Maldives (see *Sri Lanka* later in this book).

The Canadian High Commission in Colombo deals with enquiries relating to the Maldives (see *Sri Lanka* later in this book).

AREA: 298 sq km (115 sq miles).
POPULATION: 238,363 (1993 estimate).

POPULATION DENSITY: 799.8 per sq km.
CAPITAL: Malé. **Population:** 70,105 (1994 estimate).
GEOGRAPHY: The Maldives Republic is located 500km (300 miles) southwest of the southern tip of India and consists of about 1190 low-lying coral islands, of which only 200 are inhabited. Most of the inhabited islands are covered by lush tropical vegetation and palm trees, while the numerous uninhabited islands, some of which are mere sand spits or coral tips, are covered in shrubs. Each island is surrounded by a reef enclosing a shallow lagoon. Hundreds of these islands together with other coral growth form an atoll, surrounding a lagoon. All the islands are low-lying, none more than 2m (7ft) above sea level. The majority of the indigenous population do not mix with the tourist visitors, with the exception of those involved with tourism in the resorts and Malé.
LANGUAGE: The national language is Dhivehi. English is spoken on Malé and resort islands.
RELIGION: The indigenous population is almost entirely Sunni Muslim.
TIME: GMT + 5.
ELECTRICITY: 220 volts AC, 50Hz. Round-pin plugs are used, although square-pin plugs are now becoming more common.
COMMUNICATIONS: Telephone: IDD is available. Country code: 960. Outgoing international code: 00. **Fax:** Services are available in Malé and the resorts. **Telex/telegram:** Telecommunications in the Maldives are good – telex and telegram services are available to and from anywhere in the world from the Telecommunications Company in Malé, Dhiraagu and the resorts. **Post:** Airmail to Western Europe takes about a week. Post office hours: 0730-1330 and 1600-1750 Saturday to Thursday. **Press:** The Dhivehi dailies *Haveeru* and *Aafathis* have English sections. Information about local events is widely available on all the resort islands.
BBC World Service frequencies: From time to time these change. See the section *How to Use this Book* for more information.

Bandos Resort

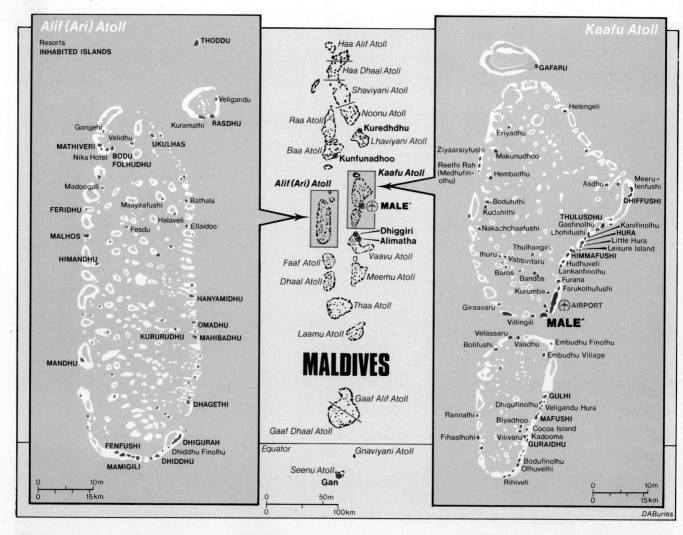

DABurles

BBC:

| MHz | 17.79 | 15.31 | 11.96 | 9.740 |

A service is also available on 1413kHz.

Voice of America:

| MHz | 15.18 | 6.110 | 15.42 | 9.760 |

PASSPORT/VISA

Regulations and requirements may be subject to change at short notice, and you are advised to contact the appropriate diplomatic or consular authority before finalising travel arrangements. Details of these may be found at the head of this country's entry. Any numbers in the chart refer to the footnotes below.

	Passport Required?	Visa Required?	Return Ticket Required?
Full British	Yes	1	Yes
BVP	Not valid	-	-
Australian	Yes	1	Yes
Canadian	Yes	1	Yes
USA	Yes	1	Yes
Other EU (As of 31/12/94)	Yes	1	Yes
Japanese	Yes	1	Yes

PASSPORTS: Valid passport required by all.
British Visitors Passport: Not accepted.
VISAS: [1] Required by all. Visas are valid for 30 days and will be issued on arrival at Malé airport free of charge. Visas may be extended on payment of a small fee.
Note: Foreigners who enter the Maldives must be in possession of US$25 per day of stay. This does not include those entering through a tourist agency or on recruitment.

MONEY

Currency: Maldivian Rufiya (MRF) = 100 laris. Notes are in denominations of MRF500, 100, 50, 20, 10, 5 and 2. Coins are in denominations of MRF1, and 50, 25, 10, 5, 2 and 1 laris.
Credit cards: Most major island resorts will accept American Express, Visa, Mastercard, Eurocard and Diners Club. Arrangements vary from island to island, and it is advisable to check with your credit card company for details of merchant acceptability and other facilities which may be available.
Exchange rate indicators: The following figures are included as a guide to the movement of the Maldivian Rufiya against Sterling and the US Dollar:

Date:	Oct '92	Sep '93	Jan '94	Jan '95
£1.00=	18.21	18.33	17.68	18.40
$1.00=	11.48	12.00	11.95	11.76

Currency restrictions: There are no restrictions on import or export. Transactions in resorts and hotels can be made in most hard currencies.
Banking hours: 0900-1300 Sunday to Thursday.

DUTY FREE

The following goods may be imported into the Maldives Republic without incurring customs duty:
200 cigarettes or 50 cigars or 250g of tobacco; a reasonable number of gifts.
Note: Alcoholic beverages, pornographic literature, idols of worship or drugs may not be imported. The export of black coral and tortoiseshell, except in the form of ornaments, is forbidden (the Government has banned the killing of turtles).

PUBLIC HOLIDAYS

Jan 2 '95 Martyr's Day. **Mar 3** Eid al-Fitr (End of Ramadan). **May 10** Eid al-Adha (Feast of the Sacrifice). **May 31** Islamic New Year. **Jul 26** Independence Day. **Aug 9** Mouloud (Prophet's Birthday). **Nov 3** Victory Day. **Nov 11** Republic Day. **Jan 2 '96** Martyr's Day. **Note:** (a) Some holidays are celebrated according to the Islamic calendar and others are public or government holidays. (b) Muslim festivals are timed according to local sightings of various phases of the Moon and the

dates given above are approximations. During the lunar month of Ramadan that precedes Eid al-Fitr, Muslims fast during the day and feast at night and normal business patterns may be interrupted. Many restaurants are closed during the day and there may be restrictions on drinking. Some disruption may continue into Eid al-Fitr itself, although this is generally unlikely to affect life on the resort islands. Eid al-Fitr and Eid al-Adha may last anything from two to ten days, depending on the region. For more information see the section *World of Islam* at the back of the book.

HEALTH

Regulations and requirements may be subject to change at short notice, and you are advised to contact your doctor well in advance of your intended date of departure. Any numbers in the chart refer to the footnotes below.

	Special Precautions?	Certificate Required?
Yellow Fever	No	1
Cholera	Yes	2
Typhoid & Polio	Yes	-
Malaria	3	-
Food & Drink	4	-

[1]: A yellow fever vaccination certificate is required from travellers arriving from infected areas.
[2]: Following WHO guidelines issued in 1973, a cholera vaccination certificate is not a condition of entry to the Maldives. However, cholera is a risk in this country and precautions are essential. Up-to-date advice should be sought before deciding whether these precautions should include vaccination as medical opinion is divided over its effectiveness. See the *Health* section at the back of the book.
[3]: Malaria is disappearing; the last two indigenous cases were reported in 1983.
[4]: The water provided in the resort areas is generally safe to drink. In other areas water of uncertain origin used for drinking, brushing teeth or making ice should have first been boiled or otherwise sterilised.
Rabies is present. For those at high risk, vaccination before arrival should be considered. If you are bitten abroad seek medical advice without delay. For more

NO NEWS ... NO SHOES ...

Blend with nature

Sail our pristine seas

Get into our under sea world

Enjoy!
MALDIVES
Where we teach you the art of doing nothing.

For further information:
Ministry of Tourism, Ghazee Building, Malé, 20-05, Republic of Maldives.
Tel: (960) 323 224. Fax: (960) 322 512. Telex: 66019 TOURISM MF.

Holiday Island
...the remnants of virgin nature

Location: This island is the ideal retreat for those who deserve and desire a holiday away from the rush of the mainstream. Located just 30 minutes by helicopter, or two hours by speedboat from Malé International Airport, this truly beautiful island is right on the tip of the South Ari Atoll.

Accommodation: *Holiday Island* has 142 luxury beach-front guest rooms, all with air-conditioning, IDD telephone in both bedroom and bathroom, minibar, channel music, 21" colour television with in-house video network plus round-the-world news via satellite. The bathrooms have hot and cold fresh water, bath tubs, bidets and hair dryers.

Food and Drink: The main restaurant offers rich buffets, delighting gourmets with both Western and Oriental cuisine. The Coffee House serves an à la carte menu with surprising variety. The Holiday Bar stocks a formidable selection of alcoholic and non-alcoholic beverages, with special pride taken in the presentation of very special cocktails with enticing names such as "The Maldive Lady" and the "Turtle Rider" which must be tried in the Piano Bar.

Sports & Leisure Facilities: *Holiday Island* offer a wide range of activities for the enthusiast. Snorkelling, scuba diving, windsurfing, water-skiing, parasailing, cat-boat sailing, banana riding, canoeing, billiards, table tennis, volleyball, tennis and basketball. Gym and sauna facilities are also available.

In the Evening: *Holiday Island* has its own discotheque, with live bands performing once a week. Cultural shows and Karaoke will add further new dimensions to your evening.

If you are looking for an ideal holiday, do come to *Holiday Island* where our first priority is your comfort and pleasure.

Dhiffushi, PO Box 2073, South Ari-Atoll, Republic of Maldives
Tel: 450011, Fax: 450022, Tlx: 66033 HOLISLE MF

VILLA Group of Resorts: Fun Island, Paradise Island, Holiday Island, Sun Island.
Head Office: Villa Building, Ibrahim Hassan Didi Magu.
PO Box 2073, Male 20-02, Republic of Maldives.
Tel: 325194, Fax: 325177, Telex: 66090 VILLA MF

Paradise Island
...something special for the Romantic and the Dreamer

Location: This enchanting island is located on the eastern edge of North Malé Atoll. A mere 10-minute speedboat ride will take you to this delightful destination – **Paradise Island.**

Accommodation: 140 attractively designed, elegantly furnished guest rooms, including 40 waterside bungalows with private terrace and 100 beachfront rooms with open-air shower and access to a private garden. All rooms have air-conditioning, satellite TV with in-house video network, channel music, minibar, IDD telephone in the bedroom as well as in the en suite bathroom, which has hot and cold water shower, bath, bidet and hairdryer.

Restaurants and Bars: Western and Oriental restaurants, including Sun Rise, Sun Set, Japanese Speciality, and the 24-hour coffee shop, provide the ultimate in delicious cuisine of your choice and the well-stocked Paradise Bar.

Conference and Meeting Rooms: An elegant Conference/Banquet room equipped with audio-visual facilities, fax, telex, photocopying and computers.

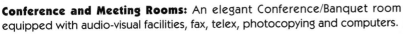

Recreational Facilities: A swimming pool for adults and kids, sauna, steam bath, gym, karaoke and a Piano Bar.

Sports & Leisure facilities: A wide range of water sports activities – scuba diving, windsurfing, cat sailing, canoeing, banana riding and water-skiing. Other sports include football, volleyball, badminton, table tennis, billiards and also a floodlit tennis court.

Night Entertainment: A discotheque to warm up the night with exciting live music, cultural shows and many other surprises . . .

Lankanfinolhu, PO Box 2073, North Malé Atoll, Republic of Maldives
Tel: 440011, Fax: 440022, Telex: 77088 PARAISLE MF

VILLA Group of Resorts:
Fun Island, Paradise Island, Holiday Island, Sun Island.
Head Office: Villa Building, Ibrahim Hassan Didi Magu.
PO Box 2073, Male 20-02, Republic of Maldives.
Tel: 325194, Fax: 325177, Telex: 66090 VILLA MF

information, consult the *Health* section at the back of the book.

Health care: There is a hospital on Malé and first-aid facilities are available on all resort islands. Health insurance is recommended.

TRAVEL - International

AIR: The national airline is *Air Maldives*, although it does not operate international services. Direct flights are operated from a number of countries in the region (such as India, Singapore, Sri Lanka and the United Arab Emirates) and also from Europe.

Approximate flight time: From London to Malé is 11 hours (excluding stopover).

International airport: *Malé International (MLE)* on Hulhule Island is 2km (1.2 miles) from the capital (travel time – 15 minutes). Boats from the various island resorts meet each arriving plane to take visitors to their respective accommodation. If an advance booking has been made, representatives of the resorts will receive tourists at the airport and will take care of all onward transport arrangements. Airport facilities include left luggage, first aid, bank, duty-free shops, snack bar, post office and restaurant.

Departure tax: US$10.

TRAVEL - Internal

AIR: Internal air services are operated by *Air Maldives*, linking Malé with Kaadedhdhoo and Gan. There are also services to Hanimaadhoo in the north, although these islands will not be on most visitors' itineraries.

A number of companies operate helicopter service around the Maldives. Twin-otter and float planes are also available. The transfer from the airport to the resort islands may be an optional extra on the tour. These services are also available for trips around the islands. For further information, contact Hummingbird Helicopters (tel: 325 708; fax: 323 161); *or* Maldivian Air Taxi Pte. Ltd. (tel: 315 201/2/3; fax: 315 203); *or* Seagull Airways (tel: 315 124/5; fax: 315 123); *or* Maldives Air Services Ltd. (tel: 314 808; fax: 325 058).

SEA: Visitors generally remain on their resort island for the duration of their stay, although island-hopping trips by ferries are widely available. Local charter boats are also easily available for hire. Mega-speed catamarans meet arrivals at the airport, although they do not have scheduled departures. The catamarans connect the airport with Ari Atoll and some outlying islands. The indigenous inhabitants, however, live a parochial life and tend to visit only Malé, and even then irregularly.

ROAD: Travel on individual islands does not present any problem since few of them take longer than half an hour to cross on foot.

ACCOMMODATION

HOTELS: There are three hotels on Malé and one on Gan; there are also 43 guest-houses on Malé and rooms in private homes, although most visitors stay on resort islands. There are no **guest-houses** or **self-catering** facilities on any of the resort islands. For more information, contact the Maldives Association of Tourism Industry (MATI), H Deens Villa, Meheli Goalhi, Malé. Tel: 326 640. Fax: 326 641.

RESORTS: There are 70 resorts which vary from extravagantly luxurious to fairly simple. Accommodation almost invariably consists of thatch-roofed coral cabanas with ensuite facilities. The rooms are fan-cooled although some have air-conditioning and/or a refrigerator. Many resort groups have recently installed desalination plants to provide clean tap water. The resorts are fully integral communities with sport and leisure facilities, restaurants and bars and, in some cases, a shop and/or disco. No island has more than one resort and these range in size from 6-250 units with most having between 30-50 units. Different islands tend to attract different nationalities.

RESORTS & EXCURSIONS

For a long time, the Maldives Republic was one of the best-kept secrets in the world; a beautiful string of low-lying coral islands in the Indian Ocean, a paradise for scuba divers, watersport enthusiasts and sunseekers alike. All of these attractions are still very much in evidence, but in recent years the tourism potential of the country has been developed in the form of a large number of island resorts. Several tour operators have added the Maldives to their programmes, and since the introduction of direct flights from Europe the islands have become an increasingly popular longhaul destination.

The Maldives consist of 19 atolls, about 1190 islands in all, most of them uninhabited. Most of the resorts are to be found in **Malé (Kaafu) Atoll**. A few are found in

Vaavu, **Baa** and **Lhaviyani**. **Alifu (Ari) Atoll** has been declared the new Tourism Zone of the Maldives and work to upgrade and build new resorts is progressing in this area. All resorts offer night-fishing trips, superb snorkelling and windsurfing, and most have facilities for scuba diving, dhoni sailing, water-skiing and volleyball.

Some offer other sporting facilities, including badminton and tennis.

The following section describes some of the major resort islands in the Maldives; further information can be obtained from the UK Tourism Representative (see top of entry for address), from tour operators or by contacting

the island resort direct.

The capital of the Maldives is **Malé**, situated close to the airport on the southern point of the North Malé Atoll. Although accommodation is available, very few foreign visitors stay in the capital; even those doing business normally stay in one of the nearby resort islands and travel to Malé by boat. Most islands provide boat services to the capital at least once a week (a small charge is usually made). The capital also has several shops which sell examples of local handicrafts and imported goods. Other attractions include the *National Museum*, the fish and fruit markets, the beautiful 17th-century *Hukuru (or Friday) Mosque* and the *Grand Mosque*, with its magnificent gold-domed minaret.

Kaafu Atoll – North

The following section describes some of the major resorts in the Kaafu Atoll (also known as the North and South Malé Atolls). See the map for location.

Baros is about 450m (1500ft) long and 180m (600ft) wide, and this oval-shaped island is located approximately one hour by boat from the airport. One side of the island is full of corals, within 3-6m (10-20ft) of the shallow beach, perfect for snorkelling and diving lessons, whilst the other side is a superb beach ideal for swimming and water-skiing.

East of Baros is the island of **Bandos**, one of the larger resorts whose accommodation consists of well-furnished beach houses. There is a particularly good diving school; one of the attractions is a dive down to the aptly-named *Shark Point*.

The island of **Vaadhu**, on the north tip of the South Malé Atoll and about 45 minutes by boat from the airport, also has a fully-equipped diving school. There are 31 cabana-style rooms whose features include freshwater showers, and which reflect the high level of capital investment which has been made in the resort.

Hudhuveli, situated on the east side of the North Malé Atoll is, like Bandos and Vaadhu, operated by Deen's Orchid Agency. It is a modern beach resort with single-unit bungalows with straw roofing and freshwater showers.

Ihuru is a small island, exceedingly beautiful and much photographed. The accommodation consists of simple bungalows with a total of 45 beds.

Kurumba: This tiny island covers an area of half a square mile and is 20 minutes by boat from the airport and 30 minutes from Malé. There are conference facilities, swimming pools, gymnasiums and jacuzzis, as well as a number of restaurants. Most watersports can be arranged, including scuba diving; the colourful fish in the lagoon will eat out of your hand.

Nakatchafushi boasts the country's largest lagoon, and is perhaps one of the most photographed of all the islands. Located on the western side of the Malé Atoll, it is 24km (15 miles) from the airport, a travel time of approximately 90 minutes. The lagoon is perfect for watersports and a long strip of sand at the western end of the island is a haven for beachcombers.

Full Moon (Furana) is a resort which can be reached in 20 minutes from the airport. The resort's deep lagoon makes it a favourite base for visiting yachts. It also boasts a gymnasium and a business centre.

Makunudhoo: It is a 2-hour voyage from the airport to this island, one of the most expensive resorts and one which is renowned for its food. The Maldivian-run island probably provides the best anchorage of any resort and always has yachts for charter. It is protected on all sides by a beautiful lagoon. The accommodation consists of individual thatched bungalows situated in coconut groves leading down to the beach.

Kanifinolhu (Kani) is on the eastern edge of the atoll. The seas around the island boast some of the best inside reefs in the country, and the protection provided by the external reef makes diving possible even in the roughest conditions. The style of the accommodation is influenced by local and oriental design and some rooms have air-conditioning. The island has a desalination plant for fresh water.

Farukolhufushi and **Thulhaagiri** have superb facilities for watersports. Thulhagiri has a swimming pool and one windsurfing board for every twin-bedded room.

Other highly regarded north Malé resorts are **Boduhithi** and the neighbouring **Kudahithi** and, closer to the airport, **Lhohifushi**, which has a beautiful lagoon and a wide range of watersport facilities. Kudahithi, one of the most expensive resort in the Maldives, has only six units – excellent for small, private groups.

Kaafu Atoll – South

Still in the Malé (Kaafu) Atoll, but to the south of the airport, are a further score of resorts. Notable among these are **Biyadhoo** and **Villivaru** which are 30km (20 miles) from the airport. Both are owned and managed by

the Taj group from India. The nearby **Cocoa Island** has only eight 2-storey thatched huts, all of which are beautifully furnished. Private groups can rent the entire resort.

To the south of Cocoa Island are the 'twin' islands of **Veligandu Huraa (Palm Tree Island)** and **Dhigufinolhu**, connected by a causeway across the lagoon. The latter is the more lively of the two, with more rooms and more in the way of entertainment: Veligandu Huraa has individual bungalows and a more intimate atmosphere. They are only a gentle stroll away from each other should one feel the need for a change of mood.

North of Cocoa Island is **Kadooma**, where flowering shrubs surround chalet-style accommodation. Trips can be arranged to the nearby fishing village.

Bodufinolhu (Fun Island) is located on the eastern reef of the South Malé Atoll. It is ringed with a massive lagoon and connected to two uninhabited islets which can be reached on foot at low tide. All rooms are on the beachfront with en-suite bathrooms, air-conditioning, IDD telephones and hot and cold desalinated water.

Other Atolls

Most of the resorts are to be found in the North and South Malé Atolls, but there are also several others, most in the northern island groups (see map).

Resorts in the **Alifu (Ari) Atoll**, which is to the west of Malé, include **Kuramathi**, a relatively large island which has first-class facilities and offers an excellent beach, superb diving, windsurfing, water-skiing, parasailing and night fishing. **Nika Island** is a small, away-from-it-all, up-market, 26-room resort offering clients some of the most comfortable boats in the Maldives. **Fesdu** is situated in the heart of the atoll rather than on the periphery. Accommodation consists of 50 thatched round-houses, all of which are close to the beach. **Angaga**, also in Ari Atoll, is small and impressively constructed in traditional Maldivian style and with air-conditioned rooms and fresh hot and cold water. Among other resorts are **Halaveli**, **Bathala**, **Ellaidoo**, **Machchafushi**, **Gangehi**, **Madoogali** and **Maayaafushi**. Several others are under construction or have recently opened and there are now 23 resorts in the Ari Atoll.

To the south is the **Vaavu Atoll** with some of the best diving in the entire archipelago. A well-established, long-popular resort, especially among visiting Italians, is the 70-bungalow **Alimatha**.

To the north is **Lhaviyani Atoll** with the fairly simple 250-bungalow **Kuredhdhu** resort, essentially a spot for the besotted diver.

The **Baa Atoll** is about 130km (80 miles) northwest of the capital, one of the few places where traditional arts and crafts are still practised. The atoll has one resort, **Kunfunadhoo**, with 50 beds. It is temporarily closed for redevelopment at the moment.

Most tourism is in the northern atolls, but **Seenu**, the

southernmost atoll of the archipelago (situated south of the equator), is known to many as the site of a former RAF staging post in **Gan**. It provides tourist accommodation at the Ocean Reef Club. There is a regular, heavily-booked domestic flight between Malé and Gan operated by *Air Maldives*. Helicopter services are also available. Check locally for more information.

SOCIAL PROFILE

FOOD & DRINK: Malé, the capital, has a few simple restaurants which serve local and international food. On the other islands there are no restaurants other than those run by the resort. Cuisine is international, with all foodstuffs other than seafood imported. The fish is magnificent. Curries and oriental buffets are widely available. **Drink:** There is a good range of alcoholic and non-alcoholic drink available at the resorts, reflecting the demands of the visitors. There are a few local cocktails, including *The Maldive Lady*, a powerful and delicious concoction, the composition varying from bar to bar and island to island.
Note: All bars are situated in tourist resorts (no alcohol is available on Malé). All accept cash, but normally add orders onto the total bill. Locals do not drink at all.
NIGHTLIFE: There is little or no organised nightlife, though most resorts have informal discotheques around the bar areas, sometimes featuring live bands playing either traditional or Western music. Beach parties and barbecues are also popular. On some evenings many resorts have cultural shows and some show videos.
SHOPPING: Local purchases include sea shells (only when bought in official shops; they may *not* be removed from the beach or from the sea), lacquered wooden boxes and reed mats. There are strict prohibitions against the export of any type of coral. **Shopping hours:** 0800-2300 Saturday to Thursday. Shops officially shut for 15 minutes five times a day in deference to Muslim prayer times; however, this rule is not always strictly adhered to in the tourist areas away from the capital.
SPORT: Scuba diving and **windsurfing** facilities with fully qualified multilingual instructors are available at all resorts. Night **dives** are arranged. The underwater life is rated among the best in the world. Most resorts have glass-bottomed boats and **water-skiing** facilities and some have catamarans for hire. **Fishing** trips, either by day or by night, are popular and readily arranged. Those at night will usually end with a barbecue at the resort with the day's catch being cooked and eaten. Some resorts have facilities for sports such as **tennis**, **football**, **volleyball** and **badminton**.
SOCIAL CONVENTIONS: Dress is informal, but locals, who are Muslim, will be offended by nudity or scanty clothing in public places, and the Government rigidly enforces these standards. Handshaking is the most common form of greeting. The indigenous population not involved in the tourist trade lives in isolated island communities maintaining almost total privacy. A large

number of locals smoke, but smoking and eating during Ramadan is discouraged. **Tipping:** This is officially discouraged.

BUSINESS PROFILE

ECONOMY: Tourism is now the most important part of the economy (17% of GDP in 1992). There is very little cultivable land. Fishing and shipping and, to a lesser extent, agriculture, are the other economic mainstays for the Maldives. Many of the 70 resort islands currently in operation have in recent years made considerable investment in infrastructure such as desalination plants, refurbished accommodation, generators and air-conditioning, and there is every sign that this sector of the economy will continue to thrive in the forseeable future.
BUSINESS: Since the islands import almost everything, business potential is high, but only on Malé. Most business takes place during the morning. **Office hours:** 0730-1330 Saturday to Thursday. Friday is the official rest day.
COMMERCIAL INFORMATION: The following organisation can offer advice: State Trading Organisation, STO Building, 7 Haveeree Higun, Malé 20-02. Tel: 325 485 *or* 323 279. Fax: 325 218. Telex: 66006 (a/b STO MF).

CLIMATE

The Maldives have a hot tropical climate. There are two monsoons, the southwest monsoon from May to October and the northeast monsoon from November to April. Generally the southwest monsoon brings more wind and rain in June and July. The temperature rarely falls below 25°C, even during the night. The best time to visit is November to Easter.
Required clothing: Lightweight cottons and linens throughout the year. Light rainwear is advisable during the monsoon season.

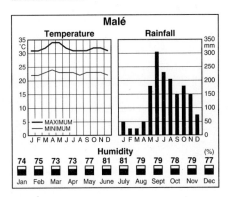

☐ *international airport*

600km

300mls

W. SAH.

Tropic of Cancer

SAHARA DESERT

ALGERIA

MAURITANIA

Adrar des Iforas

MALI

Timbuktu Niger

Gao

Macina Marches

SENEGAL

Kayes

Mopti Bandiagara

Ségou Djenne

BAMAKO Niger Bani

NIGER

BURKINA FASO

GUINEA

Sikasso

BENIN

GHANA T.

C.D'IV.

DAB-M144

Location: Central West Africa.

Note: Banditry and insurgent attacks continue to occur in many parts of northern Mali. Foreigners have been victims of armed robbery and could become victims of insurgent attacks in the areas of Mopti, Timbuktu, Gao and the Kidal regions. Those travelling in the Gourma area northwest of Douentza as well as those travelling by riverboat north of Mopti are open to this risk as well. The Mauritanian border zone in the Kayes and the Koulikoro regions are also considered unsafe. Armed robbery and banditry occur, though, less frequently in downtown Bamako, along major travel routes and near principal cities.
Source: US State Department – December 9, 1994.

Ministry of Handicrafts and Tourism
BP 234, Koulouba, Bamako, Mali
Tel: 225 687. Telex: 2559.
Société Malienne d'Exploitation des Ressources Touristiques (SMERT)
BP 222, place de la République, Bamako, Mali
Tel: 225 942. Telex: 2433.
Embassy of the Republic of Mali
487 avenue Molière, B-1060 Brussels, Belgium
Tel: (2) 345 7432 *or* 345 7589. Fax: (2) 344 5700. Telex: 22508. Opening hours: 0900-1330 and 1400-1630 Monday to Friday.
British Consulate
BP 1598, Plan International, Bamako, Mali
Tel: 230 583. Fax: 222 878.
Embassy of the Republic of Mali
2130 R Street, NW, Washington, DC 20008
Tel: (202) 332 2249 *or* 939 8950. Fax: (202) 332 6603.
Embassy of the United States of America
BP 34, rue Rochester NY et rue Mohamed V, Bamako, Mali
Tel: 225 663 *or* 225 470. Fax: 223 712 *or* 223 933. Telex: 2248 (a/b AMEMB MJ).
Embassy of the Republic of Mali
50 Goulburn Avenue, Ottawa, Ontario K1N 8C8
Tel: (613) 232 1501 *or* 232 3264. Fax: (613) 232 7429.
Consulates in: Montréal and Toronto.
Canadian Embassy
PO Box 198, Bamako, Mali
Tel: 222 236. Fax: 224 362. Telex: 2530.

Health	
GALILEO/WORLDSPAN: **TI-DFT/BKO/HE**	
SABRE: **TIDFT/BKO/HE**	
Visa	
GALILEO/WORLDSPAN: **TI-DFT/BKO/VI**	
SABRE: **TIDFT/BKO/VI**	

Timatic

For more information on Timatic codes refer to Contents.

AREA: 1,240,192 sq km (478,841 sq miles).
POPULATION: 8,461,000 (1990 estimate).
POPULATION DENSITY: 6.8 per sq km.
CAPITAL: Bamako. **Population:** 740,000 (1984).
GEOGRAPHY: Mali is a landlocked republic, sharing borders with Mauritania, Algeria, Burkina Faso, Côte d'Ivoire, Guinea, Niger and Senegal. It is a vast land of flat plains fed by two major rivers, the Senegal on its western edge and the great River Niger. On its journey north the Niger converges with the River Bani, and forms a rich inland delta, the marshlands of the Macina, stretching for some 450km (280 miles) along the river's length, in some places 200km (124 miles) wide. The central part of the country is arid grazing land, called the Sahel, which has suffered great drought. At Timbuktu the Niger reaches the desert and here it turns first to the east, then to the southeast at Bourem, where it heads for the ocean. In the desert, near the Algerian and Niger borders in the northeast, the Adrar des Iforas massif rises 800m (2625ft). The north of the country is true desert except for the few oases along the ancient trans-Sahara camel routes. Tuaregs still live around these oases and camel routes. Further south live the Peulh cattle-raising nomads. The majority of the population lives in the savannah region in the south. The peoples of this region comprise Songhai, Malinke, Senoufou, Dogon and the Bambara (the largest ethnic group).
LANGUAGE: The official language is French. Local languages include Bambara, Senoufou, Sarakolle, Tuareg and Arabic.
RELIGION: Muslim, with Christian and Animist minorities.
TIME: GMT.
ELECTRICITY: 220 volts AC, 50Hz in Bamako. Larger towns in Mali have their own locally-generated supply.
COMMUNICATIONS: Telephone: Limited IDD service. Country code: 223. Outgong international code: 00. There are manual exchanges and operator service in the provinces, which can prove unreliable. International calls are expensive and collect calls cannot be made from Mali. **Telex:** These can be sent from the Central Telex Office in Bamako and main hotels. **Post:** International post limited is to main towns and the central post office. Airmail to Europe takes approximately two weeks. For further details, contact the Embassy. **Press:** There are no English-language newspapers. The only daily, *L'Essor,* is published in French.
BBC World Service and Voice of America frequencies: From time to time these change. See the section *How to Use this Book* for more information.
BBC:

MHz	17.79	15.40	15.07	9.410

Voice of America:

MHz	21.49	15.60	9.525	6.035

PASSPORT/VISA

Regulations and requirements may be subject to change at short notice, and you are advised to contact the appropriate diplomatic or consular authority before finalising travel arrangements. Details of these may be found at the head of this country's entry. Any numbers in the chart refer to the footnotes below.

	Passport Required?	Visa Required?	Return Ticket Required?
Full British	Yes	Yes	Yes
BVP	Not valid	-	-
Australian	Yes	Yes	Yes
Canadian	Yes	Yes	Yes
USA	Yes	Yes	Yes
Other EU (As of 31/12/94)	Yes	Yes	Yes
Japanese	Yes	Yes	Yes

PASSPORTS: Valid passport required by all except nationals of Algeria, Benin, Burkina Faso, Cameroon, Chad, Côte d'Ivoire, Gambia, Guinea, Mauritania, Morocco, Niger, Nigeria, Senegal, Togo and Tunisia in possession of valid ID or a passport expired for not more than 5 years.
British Visitors Passport: Not acceptable.
VISAS: Required by all except nationals of the countries referred to under passport exemptions above.
Types of visa: Tourist, Transit and Business. Cost: BFr1132 per person plus BFr200 postal charges.
Validity: 1 month from the date of entry, although visas can be extended in Mali, either in Bamako at the Immigration Service or at any police station. Visas may be obtained up to 6 months in advance of travelling to Mali.
Application to: Consulate (or Consular section at Embassy). For addresses, see top of entry.
Application requirements: (a) 2 application forms. (b) 2 passport-size photos. (c) Stamped, self-addressed envelope. (d) If application is for Business visa, 2

documents of attestation. (e) Applications must be sent by registered post. (f) Fee payment must be made in cash.
Working days required: 5.
Temporary residence: Enquire at Embassy.

MONEY

Currency: CFA Franc (CFA Fr) = 100 centimes. Notes are in denominations of CFA Fr10,000, 5000, 2500, 1000 and 500. Coins are in denominations of CFA Fr500, 250, 100, 50, 25, 10, 5, 2 and 1. Mali is part of the French Franc zone and the CFA Franc is pegged to the French Franc at fixed parity.
Note: At the beginning of 1994, the CFA Franc was devalued against the French Franc.
Currency exchange: Possible at main banks in Bamako, but plenty of time should be allowed, as changing money at a bank can be a slow process and exchange rates are often out-of-date. French Franc notes are sometimes accepted in cash transactions.
Credit cards: Visa, Diners Club and Access/Mastercard are accepted in two hotels in Bamako. Cash advances on credit cards is available at only one bank in Mali, the BMCD Bank in Bamako, and only with a Visa credit card. Check with your credit card company for details of merchant acceptability and other services which may be available.
Travellers cheques: Can be exchanged at banks.
Exchange rate indicators: The following figures are included as a guide to the movements of the CFA Franc against Sterling and the US Dollar:

Date:	Oct '92	Sep '93	Jan '94	Jan '95
£1.00=	413.75	433.87	436.78	834.94
$1.00=	260.71	284.13	295.22	553.68

Currency restrictions: The import and export of local currency is unlimited. The import of foreign currency is unlimited provided it is declared, whilst export is limited to bank notes up to a value of CFA Fr25,000.
Banking hours: 0730-1200 and 1315-1500 Monday to Thursday, 0730-1230 Friday.

DUTY FREE

The following items may be imported into Mali without incurring customs duty:
1000 cigarettes or 250 cigars or 2kg of tobacco; a reasonable amount of alcoholic beverage and perfume in open bottles for personal use.
Note: Cameras and films must be declared.

PUBLIC HOLIDAYS

Jan 1 '95 New Year's Day. **Jan 20** Armed Forces Day. **Mar 2** Korité (End of Ramadan). **Apr 17** Easter Monday. **May 1** Labour Day. **May 10** Tabaski (Feast of the Sacrifice). **May 25** Africa Day. **Aug 9** Mouloud (Prophet's Birthday). **Sep 8** Baptism of the Prophet. **Sep 22** Independence Day. **Nov 19** Anniversary of the 1968 Coup. **Dec 25** Christmas Day. **Jan 1 '96** New Year's Day. **Feb 22** Korité (End of Ramadan). **Apr 5** Easter Monday.
Note: Muslim festivals are timed according to local sightings of various phases of the Moon and the dates given above are approximations. During the lunar month of Ramadan that precedes Korité (Eid al-Fitr), Muslims fast during the day and feast at night and normal business patterns may be interrupted. Many restaurants are closed during the day and there may be restrictions on smoking and drinking. Some disruption may continue into Korité itself. Korité and Tabaski (Eid al-Adha) may last anything from two to ten days, depending on the region. For more information see the section *World of Islam* at the back of the book.

HEALTH

Regulations and requirements may be subject to change at short notice, and you are advised to contact your doctor well in advance of your intended date of departure. Any numbers in the chart refer to the footnotes below.

	Special Precautions?	Certificate Required?
Yellow Fever	Yes	1
Cholera	Yes	2
Typhoid & Polio	Yes	-
Malaria	3	-
Food & Drink	4	-

[1]: A yellow fever vaccination certificate is required by all travellers over one year of age arriving from all countries.
[2]: Following WHO guidelines issued in 1973, a cholera vaccination certificate is not a condition of entry to Mali. However, cholera is a serious risk in this country and precautions are essential. Up-to-date advice should be

sought before deciding whether these precautions should include vaccination, as medical opinion is divided over its effectiveness. See the *Health* section at the back of the book.
[3]: Malaria, mainly in the malignant *falciparum* form, is present all year throughout the country. Resistance to chloroquine has been reported.
[4]: All water should be regarded as being potentially contaminated. Water used for drinking, brushing teeth or making ice should have first been boiled or otherwise sterilised. Milk is unpasteurised and should be boiled. Powdered or tinned milk is available and is advised, but make sure that it is reconstituted with pure water. Avoid dairy products which are likely to have been made from unboiled milk. Only eat well-cooked meat and fish, preferably served hot. Pork, salad and mayonnaise may carry increased risk. Vegetables should be cooked and fruit peeled.
Rabies is present. For those at high risk, vaccination before arrival should be considered. If you are bitten abroad seek medical advice without delay. For more information, consult the *Health* section at the back of the book.
Bilharzia (schistosomiasis) is present. Avoid swimming and paddling in fresh water. Swimming pools which are well-chlorinated and maintained are safe.
Health care: Health insurance is essential. There are 3500 hospital beds and one doctor for every 26,000 inhabitants. Many medicines are unavailable and doctors and hospitals expect immediate cash payment for health care services.

TRAVEL - International

AIR: Mali's national airline is *Air Mali (MY)*. Mali also has a share in the multinational airline, *Air Afrique*.
Approximate flight time: From London to Bamako is 11 hours (including stopover in Brussels or Paris).
International airport: *Bamako (BKO)* is 15km (9 miles) from the city (travel time – 20 minutes). A bus service into the city is available.
Departure tax: CFA Fr3500; for destinations in Africa CFA Fr2500.
RAIL: There is a twice-weekly service from Bamako to Dakar (Senegal) which has air-conditioning, sleeper facilities and restaurant cars. It will also carry cars. There are plans to extend rail links into Guinea.
ROAD: The best road connections are from Côte d'Ivoire and Burkina Faso. The remote and desolate trans-Saharan route from Algeria is hazardous. There are also road links with Senegal and Guinea. The all-weather road follows the Niger as far as Niamey (Niger). **Bus:** Services operate from Kankan (Güinea) to Bamako, as well as from Bobo Dioulasso (Burkina Faso) to Ségou and Mopti, and Niamey (Niger) to Gao.

TRAVEL - Internal

AIR: Some domestic flights are provided by *Tombouctou Air Service* and light aircraft can be chartered from the *Société des Transports Aériens (STA)*.
RIVER: Between July and December there are weekly services between Bamako and Gao via Timbuktu along the River Niger. However, because of drought in the Sahel desert, services are sometimes suspended. The journey is approximately 1300km (800 miles) and takes five or six days. Between December and March travel is only possible between Mopti and Gao. Food is available on the boats and first-class cabins can be booked in advance. Motorised and non-motorised *pirogues* are available for hire between Timbuktu and Mopti. Following the completion of the Manantali Dam in 1988, work is continuing to improve the navigability of the River Senegal.
RAIL: There is a daily service from Bamako to Kayes, en route to Dakar on the Senegal coast. There are two trains, one Malian and one Senegalese – the Senegalese train is far superior, with air-conditioning and buffet car. The railway line is Mali's most important method of transport, over and above the road link. There is also a daily service from Bamako to Koulikoro.
ROAD: Traffic drives on the right. Roads in Mali range from moderate to very bad. The main road runs from Sikasso in the south to Bamako, and to Mopti and Gao. The roads from Bamako to Mopti, Douentza, Koutiala, Sikasso and Bougouni, along with a few other roads, are paved. Between Mopti and Gao travel can be difficult during the rainy season (mid-June to mid-September) when the Niger, at its confluence with the Bani, splits into a network of channels, and floods its banks to form the marshlands of the Macina. Stops at customs and police checkpoints are frequent on major roads and driving is particularly hazardous after dark. **Bus:** Services run between the main towns. **Documentation:** International Driving Permit recommended, although not legally required.
Note: Off the main roads visitors should travel in convoy and take a complete set of spare parts.
URBAN: Taxi: Collective taxis in cities are very cheap. The taxis charge standard fare regardless of the distance travelled. Tipping is not expected.

ACCOMMODATION

HOTELS: Only Bamako has hotels that meet international standards, but other main towns have hotels of an adequate standard and some have air-conditioning. Accommodation tends to be expensive and difficult to obtain at short notice – advance booking is recommended. Further information can be obtained from Hotel Sofitel (Bamako l'Amitié), PO Box 1720, Bamako. Tel: 224 321 *or* 224 395. Fax: 224 385.
LODGES: There are a number of *campements* in the National Park of La Boucle du Baoule. The reserve is 120km (75 miles) from Bamako.

RESORTS & EXCURSIONS

Bamako, the capital, is a modern town which is the educational and cultural centre of Mali. The main places of interest are the markets, the *Botanical Gardens,* the zoo and the craft centre.
Djenne is known as the 'Jewel of the Niger'. Founded in 1250, it has a beautiful mosque and it is one of the oldest trading towns along the trans-Saharan caravan routes.
Old Djenne was founded around 250BC and is located about 5km (3 miles) from Djenne.
Mopti is at the confluence of the Bani and the Niger and is built on three islands joined by dykes. There is another fine mosque here.
Southeast of Mopti is the **Bandiagara** country, peopled by the Dogons, whose ancient beliefs have been largely untouched by Islam. Visitors should treat villagers with respect.
Timbuktu is a name which has passed into English vernacular as a byword for inaccessibility and remoteness. It is, however, neither of these things due to the magnificent camel caravans (some of them comprised of over 3000 animals) which arrive every year from the Taoudenni salt mines to distribute their produce throughout the Sahel. By the 15th century, Timbuktu was the centre of a lucrative trade in salt and gold, straddling the trans-Saharan caravan routes, as well as being a great centre of Islamic learning. Much of this ancient city is in decay, but it is the site of many beautiful mosques *(Djingerebur, Sankore* and *Sidi Yahaya* for example) and tombs, some dating back to the 14th century.
Gao is another ancient city which had its heyday in the 15th century. Gao houses the mosque of *Kankan Moussa* and the tombs of the Askia Dynasty. There are also two excellent markets. The city has recently undergone much urban development.
San and **Ségou** are both interesting towns.
The **National Park of La Boucle de Baoule** contains an array of southern Sahelian species of wildlife, including giraffe, leopard, lion, elephant, buffalo and hippo.

SOCIAL PROFILE

FOOD & DRINK: Several of the hotels, notably the Hôtel de l'Amitié, have restaurant and bar facilities of international standard, serving international cuisine, and most towns have small restaurants serving local and north African dishes. Hotel restaurants are open to non-residents. A particular Malian speciality is *La Capitaine Sangha*, a kind of Nile perch served with hot chilli sauce, whole fried bananas and rice. There is a limited choice of restaurants. **Drink:** Alcohol is available in bars (with very late opening hours), but since the majority are Muslim there is a good range of fresh fruit juices. Most people tend to drink fruit juice rather than alcohol. Malian tamarind and guava juices are delicious.
NIGHTLIFE: Bamako has a good selection of nightclubs with music and dancing.
SHOPPING: Traditional crafts range from the striking masks of the Bambara, Dogon and Malinko peoples, to woodcarvings, woven cloth and mats, gold and silver jewellery and copperware. Excellent pottery is made in the Ségou region, while Timbuktu is a good centre for iron and copper articles, including swords, daggers and traditional household utensils.
SPORT: In Bamako, Omni-Sport, a Soviet-built sports complex, has a **swimming** pool and good facilities for a large number of sports.
SOCIAL CONVENTIONS: Proud of their glorious past, these people consider their poverty less important than their rich traditions. They are dignified and reserved and though they may appear aloof and distant, they are not hostile and will gracefully welcome visitors into their homes. Visitors must remember that this is a Muslim country and the religious customs and beliefs of the people should be respected. Modesty in dress, particularly for women, is essential. **Photography:** This is no longer restricted, except for military subjects. However, interpretation of what is considered off limits tends to vary. Other subjects may be considered sensitive from a cultural or religious point of view and it is advisable to obtain permission before taking photographs in Mali. **Tipping:** A 10% tip is customary in restaurants and bars, but is not normal for taxi drivers. Porters receive CFA Fr100 per piece of luggage.

BUSINESS PROFILE

ECONOMY: The economy of Mali, one of the poorest countries in the world, is almost entirely agricultural even though less than 2% of the land is, or indeed can be, cultivated. The people are engaged in raising livestock and growing subsistence crops such as millet, sorghum, maize and, increasingly, rice. In a good season, enough is produced for some export business. Otherwise, exports rely on cash crops, principally cotton and groundnuts; fruit and vegetables are exported to Europe. Indeed, despite poor rainfall, Mali has produced agricultural surpluses two years running. There is no significant industry and virtually all non-agricultural products have to be imported. Large aid grants and loans assist Mali to balance its budget and develop aspects of its economy. The new government has introduced decentralising and liberalisation measures as conditions for international support. It is also hoping to develop the tourist industry, as well as mining to exploit recently discovered deposits of phosphates, bauxite, manganese and uranium to add to the growing quantities of salt, limestone and gold. France is Mali's major trading partner, providing a quarter of imports and taking a similar proportion of exports. Mali is a member of ECOWAS and a variety of other West African multinational economic organisations.
BUSINESS: The forms of address are those of France, eg *Monsieur le Directeur.* Lightweight or tropical suit and tie are advised for only the smartest meetings. Otherwise, a light, open-neck shirt is worn. It is essential to be able to speak French for business purposes. **Office hours:** 0730-1230 and 1300-1600 Monday to Thursday, 0730-1230 and 1430-1730 Friday.
COMMERCIAL INFORMATION: The following organisation can offer advice: Chambre de Commerce et d'Industrie du Mali, BP 46, place de la Liberté, Bamako. Tel: 225 036. Fax: 221 120. Telex: 2435.
CONFERENCES/CONVENTIONS: Information can be obtained from the Ministry of Foreign Affairs (Protocol Section). Tel: 225 489. Fax: 223 359.

CLIMATE

Three main seasons which vary according to latitude. Rainy season runs between June and October, diminishing further north. The cooler season (October to February) is followed by extremely hot, dry weather until June.
Required clothing: Lightweight cottons and linens are worn throughout most of the year, though warmer clothing is needed between November and February. Waterproofing is advised during the rainy season.

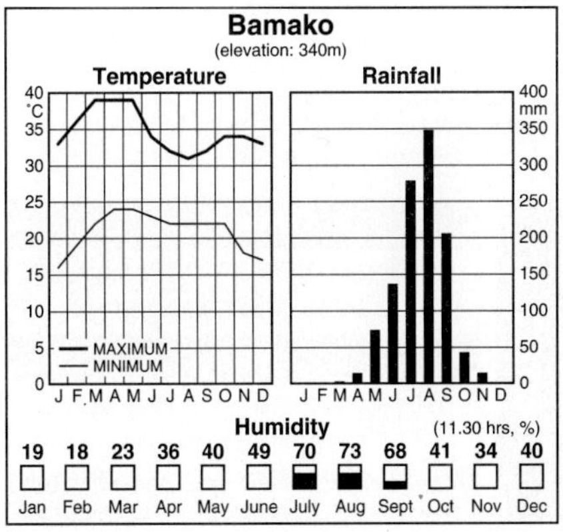
Bamako
(elevation: 340m)
Temperature
Rainfall
40 °C 35 30 25 20 15 10 5 0
400 mm 350 300 250 200 150 100 50 0
MAXIMUM
MINIMUM
J F M A M J J A S O N D
J F M A M J J A S O N D
Humidity
(11.30 hrs, %)
19 18 23 36 40 49 70 73 68 41 34 40
Jan Feb Mar Apr May June July Aug Sept Oct Nov Dec

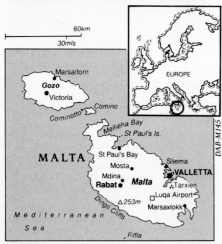

Location: Mediterranean, south of Sicily.

National Tourism Organisation – Malta (NTOM)
280 Republic Street, Valletta CMR 02, Malta
Tel: 238 282. Fax: 224 001. Telex: 1105.
High Commission for the Republic of Malta
16 Kensington Square, London W8 5HH
Tel: (0171) 938 1712. Fax: (0171) 937 8664 *or* 937 0979.
Telex: 261102 (a/b MLTLDN G). Opening hours: 0900-
1300 and 1400-1700 Monday to Friday; 1000-1300 and
1400-1600 (Consular section).
Malta National Tourist Office
Suite 300, Mappin House, 4 Winsley Street, London
W1N 7AR
Tel: (0171) 323 0506. Fax: (0171) 323 9154.
British High Commission
PO Box 506, 7 St Anne Street, Floriana, Valletta VLT
15, Malta
Tel: 233 1347. Fax: 622 001. Telex: 1249 (a/b UKREP
MW).
Embassy of the Republic of Malta
2017 Connecticut Avenue, NW, Washington, DC 20008
Tel: (202) 462 3611/2. Fax: (202) 387 5470. Telex:
62431.
Consulates in: Carnegie, Detroit, Houston,
Independence, Los Angeles, St Paul, St Louis and San
Francisco.
Embassy of the United States of America
PO Box 535, 2nd Floor, Development House, St Anne
Street, Floriana, Valletta, Malta
Tel: 235 960. Fax: 243 229.
Consulate General of the Republic of Malta
Suite 305, 1 St John's Road, Toronto, Ontario M6P 4C7
Tel: (416) 767 4902 *or* 767 2901. Fax: (416) 767 0563.
Telex: 06984767.
Consulates also in: Montréal, St John's and Vancouver.
Consulate of Canada
Demajo House, 103 Archbishop Street, Valletta, Malta
Tel: 233 121/6. Fax: 235 145. Telex: 1278 (a/b OJAMED
MW).

AREA: 316 sq km (122 sq miles).
POPULATION: 359,543 (1991 estimate).
POPULATION DENSITY: 1139 per sq km.
CAPITAL: Valletta. **Population:** 9183 (1991 estimate).
GEOGRAPHY: The Maltese archipelago is situated in
the middle of the Mediterranean, with the largest
inhabited island, Malta, lying 93km (58 miles) south of

	Health
	GALILEO/WORLDSPAN: TI-DFT/MLA/HE
	SABRE: TIDFT/MLA/HE
	Visa
	GALILEO/WORLDSPAN: TI-DFT/MLA/VI
	SABRE: TIDFT/MLA/VI

For more information on Timatic codes refer to Contents.

Sicily and 290km (180 miles) from North Africa. Gozo
and Comino are the only other inhabited islands. The
landscape of all three is characterised by low hills with
terraced fields. Malta has no mountains or rivers. Its
coastline is indented with harbours, bays, creeks, sandy
beaches and rocky coves. Gozo is connected to Malta by
ferry and is more thickly vegetated, with many flat-
topped hills and craggy cliffs. Comino, the smallest
island, is connected to Malta and Gozo by ferry and is
very sparsely populated.
LANGUAGE: Maltese (a Semitic language) and English
are the official languages. Italian is also widely spoken.
RELIGION: Roman Catholic.
TIME: GMT + 1 (GMT + 2 from last Sunday in March
to Saturday before last Sunday in September).
ELECTRICITY: 240 volts AC, 50Hz. There is no
standardisation of electrical fittings, although the 13-amp
square-pin socket and plug seem to be gaining in
popularity.
COMMUNICATIONS: Telephone: IDD is available
from the following locations: Main Telegraph Office, St
Georges Road, St Julian's (24-hour service); branch
office, South Street, Valletta (0800-1900 Monday to
Saturday); Luqa Airport (0700-1900 daily); Bisazza
Street, Sliema (0800-1300 Monday to Friday in summer,
0800-1200 and 1300-1600 rest of the year); Gozo (0730-
2100 daily). Country code: 356. There are no area codes.
Outgoing international code: 00. Local calls can be made
from numerous red phone-boxes located all over the
island. **Fax:** *Telemalta Corporation* provides an
international service through its offices and branches.
Telex/telegram: Both can be sent from *Telemalta
Corporation*, St Georges Road, St Julian's. **Post:** Good
postal services exist within the island. **Press:** The two
Maltese dailies are *L'Orizzont* and *In-Nazzjon Taghna*.
The daily English-language newspapers published on the
island are *The Independent* and *The Times of Malta*.
**BBC World Service and Voice of America
frequencies:** From time to time these change. See the
section *How to Use this Book* for more information.
BBC:

MHz	17.70	15.07	12.09	9.410
Voice of America:				
MHz	11.97	9.670	6.040	5.995

PASSPORT/VISA

Regulations and requirements may be subject to change at short notice, and you are advised to contact the appropriate diplomatic or consular authority before finalising travel arrangements. Details of these may be found at the head of this country's entry. Any numbers in the chart refer to the footnotes below.

	Passport Required?	Visa Required?	Return Ticket Required?
Full British	1	No	Yes
BVP	Valid	-	-
Australian	Yes	No	Yes
Canadian	Yes	No	Yes
USA	Yes	No	Yes
Other EU (As of 31/12/94)	1	No	Yes
Japanese	Yes	No	Yes

PASSPORTS: Valid passport required by all except:
(a) [1] nationals of EU countries in possession of valid
national ID card or, the case of the UK, a BVP, who are
visiting as tourists for no more than 3 months;
(b) nationals of Austria, Cyprus, Iceland, Liechtenstein,
Norway, Sweden, Switzerland and Turkey in possession
of a national ID card.
British Visitors Passport: Valid for stays of up to 3
months for holidays or unpaid business trips.
VISAS: Required by all except:
(a) nationals of countries listed in the chart above;
(b) nationals of Commonwealth countries (except
nationals of Bangladesh, Ghana, India, Nigeria and Sri
Lanka who *do* need a visa to enter Malta);
(c) nationals of Algeria, Argentina, Austria, Chile,
Croatia, Cyprus, Czech Republic, Egypt, Finland,
Iceland, Indonesia, Israel, South Korea, Kuwait, Libya,
Liechtenstein, Monaco, Morocco, Norway, Poland, San
Marino, Saudi Arabia, Slovak Republic, Slovenia,
Sweden, Switzerland, Tunisia, Turkey, Uruguay and
Vatican City;
(d) holders of Hungarian passports, who may stay for up
to 30 days.
Types of visa: Single-entry and Transit visas are
available from Maltese Embassies, High Commissions
and Consulates. A Single-entry visa costs £18; Transit
visa, £9. Multiple-entry visas for one year are issued only
by the Immigration Police in Malta.
Validity: *Single-entry visa* – 3 months; *Transit visa* – 24
hours. For renewal or extension, apply to the High
Commission or Embassy.
Application to: Consulate (or Consular section at

Embassy or High Commission). For addresses, see top of
entry.
Application requirements: (a) 3 application forms. (b) 2
passport-size photos. These can be handed in at the High
Commission or Embassy.
Working days required: 15 days, by post or in person.
Temporary residence: Apply to Principal Immigration
Officer, Immigration Office, Police Headquarters,
Floriana, Malta.

MONEY

Currency: Maltese Lira (M£) = 100 cents = 1000 mils.
Notes are in denominations of M£20, 10, 5 and 2. Coins
are in denominations of M£1, and 50, 25, 10, 5, 2 and 1
cents, and 5, 3 and 2 mils. A number of gold and silver
coins are also minted.
Currency exchange: Money can be changed at banks,
some hotels, and larger shops and restaurants.
Credit cards: Access/Mastercard, American Express,
Diners Club and Visa are accepted. Check with your
credit card company for details of merchant acceptability
and other services which may be available.
Travellers cheques: Exchanged in the normal authorised
institutions.
Exchange rate indicators: The following figures are
included as a guide to the movements of the Maltese Lira
against Sterling and the US Dollar:

Date:	Oct '92	Sep '93	Jan '94	Jan '95
£1.00=	0.51	0.58	0.58	0.58
$1.00=	0.32	0.38	0.39	0.37

Currency restrictions: The import of local currency is
limited to M£50. Import and export of foreign currency,
up to the amount declared on import, is free subject to
declaration. The export of local currency is limited to
M£25.
Banking hours: 0800-1200 Monday to Thursday; 0800-
1200 and 1430-1600 Friday; 0800-1130 Saturday.

DUTY FREE

The following items may be imported into Malta without
incurring customs duty:
*200 cigarettes or 50 cigars or 100 cigarillos or 250g
tobacco; 1 litre of spirits; 1 litre of wine; 10ml perfume;
125ml eau de toilette; gifts up to the value of M£50.*
Note: It is advisable to declare any larger or unusual
items of electrical equipment brought into the island
(such as video cameras, portable televisions or video
recorders), as this will prevent duty being levied on these
items when leaving the country.
Restricted entry: Pets are not allowed into Malta
without prior approval of the Director of Agriculture and
Fisheries. Pets imported from the UK have to go into
quarantine for 3 weeks. All dogs and cats must be
vaccinated against rabies at least 20 days before they are
imported.

PUBLIC HOLIDAYS

Jan 1 '95 New Year's Day. **Feb 10** St Paul's Shipwreck.
Mar 19 St Joseph's Day. **Mar 31** Freedom Day. **Apr 14**
Good Friday. **May 1** Workers' Day. **Jun 7**
Commemoration of 1919 Riot. **Jun 29** Feast of St Peter
and St Paul. **Aug 15** Feast of the Assumption. **Sep 8**
Feast of our Lady of Victories. **Sep 21** Independence
Day. **Dec 8** Feast of the Immaculate Conception. **Dec 13**
Republic Day. **Dec 25** Christmas Day. **Jan 1 '96** New
Year's Day. **Feb 10** St Paul's Shipwreck. **Mar 19** St
Joseph's Day. **Mar 31** Freedom Day. **Apr 5** Good
Friday.

HEALTH

Regulations and requirements may be subject to change at short notice, and you are advised to contact your doctor well in advance of your intended date of departure. Any numbers in the chart refer to the footnotes below.

	Special Precautions?	Certificate Required?
Yellow Fever	No	1
Cholera	No	2
Typhoid & Polio	No	-
Malaria	No	-
Food & Drink	3	-

[1]: A yellow fever vaccination certificate is required
from travellers over nine months of age arriving from
infected areas. If indicated on epidemiological grounds,
infants under nine months of age are subject to isolation
or surveillance if arriving from an infected area.
[2]: A cholera vaccination certificate may be required
from travellers arriving from infected areas.

Dive into the clear blue waters of Gozo

St. Andrew's Divers Cove is superbly located in the picturesque fishing village of Xlendi just 20 metres from the bay.

◆ Renowned for its professional and friendly service, it has, in its five years of existence, grown to become one of the most frequented centres in the Maltese Islands, offering diving around Gozo and Comino.

◆ Self-catering apartments are all within 250 metres of the centre and the 4-star sea front St. Patrick's Hotel is only 45 metres away.

◆ It caters fully for both beginners and professional divers and all levels in between.

It is recognised by five diving federations: **C.M.A.S., P.A.D.I., S.S.I., S.A.A.** and **I.D.D.**

◆ Courses can be provided in a variety of languages including English, German, Italian, French and Maltese.

◆ A fully stocked dive shop enables the visitor to obtain some fantastic bargains, as prices for diving equipment are at least 30% cheaper in Malta than in the rest of Europe.

Now also announcing a second and larger centre at Mgarr Harbour, just across the waterfront. All the same services will be available within walking distance of the L'Imgarr Hotel (5 star).

St. Andrew's Divers Cove, St. Simon Street, Xlendi Bay, Island of Gozo, Malta.
Tel: +356 55 13 01. Fax: +356 56 15 48.

---

[3]: Mains water is normally chlorinated and, whilst safe, may cause mild abdominal upsets. Bottled water is available and is advised for the first few weeks of the stay. Milk is pasteurised and dairy products are safe for consumption. Local meat, poultry, seafood, fruit and vegetables are generally considered safe to eat.
Health care: UK passport-holders staying less than 30 days will receive emergency hospital treatment only at a state-run hospital. The principal hospitals are St Luke's, Gwardamanga in Malta and Craig Hospital in Gozo. Health insurance is advised.

TRAVEL - International

AIR: Malta's national airline is *Air Malta (KM).*
Approximate flight time: From London to Luqa is 3 hours.
International airport: *Luqa,* 8km (5 miles) southeast of Valletta (travel time – 15 minutes). Airport facilities include incoming and outgoing duty-free shops, car hire, bank, bureau de change and restaurant/bar. All facilities are open 24 hours. Buses 32, 33, 34 and 35 go every 30 minutes from 0600-2100 to and from Valletta City Gate. There is a full taxi service to all parts of Malta, with fares regulated by meter. The new terminal, opened in February 1992, has an annual capacity of 2.5 million passengers.
SEA: The main ports are Grand Harbour, Marsaxlokk and Mgarr/Gozo. The *Gozo Channel Company* operates a service between Malta and Catania (Sicily) from April to September. There are links at Catania with Tripoli and Benghazi.
A new high-speed (45 knots) **catamaran** service now operates between Malta and Sicily twice a week. The service operates to several Sicilian ports.

TRAVEL - Internal

AIR: There is a helicopter service operating all year round between Malta and Gozo. A quick alternative to the ferry service, it runs eight times a day and takes only ten minutes.
SEA: A passenger car ferry operates several times daily between Cirkewwa in Malta and Mgarr in Gozo, with connections to Comino. Crossing time is about 20 minutes. For further information, contact the *Gozo Channel Company,* Hay Wharf, Sa Maison in Malta.

In addition, a new hovercraft service is now in operation between Malta and Gozo. The first boat leaves Gozo at 0700 and the last one leaves Malta at 2030. This service is for passengers only.
ROAD: Driving is on the left. Speed limit is 64kmph (39mph). **Bus:** Good local services operate from Luqa, Valletta, Sa Maison and Victoria (Gozo) to all towns.
Taxi: Identifiable by their all-white livery and red number plates. Taxis are under meter charge at government-controlled prices. **Car hire:** A number of car hire firms offer self-drive cars. Both *Hertz* and *Avis* have desks at the airport. Rates on Malta are among the cheapest in Europe. **Documentation:** Full national driving licence is needed.

ACCOMMODATION

Accommodation in Malta is provided in hotels, holiday complexes, guest-houses, hostels or self-catering flats. Many hotels offer substantial reductions, particularly during the off season. For further information, contact the Hotel and Restaurants Association, Flat 1, 66 Tower Road, Sliema SLM 16, Malta. Tel: 318 133/4. Fax: 336 477.
Grading: There is a star classification standard for all hotels in the Maltese islands, introduced by the Secretariat for Tourism and the Hotels and Catering Establishments Board. All classified hotels are thoroughly inspected before their star grading is allocated and are regularly inspected to ensure that standards are maintained. Gradings range from **1** to **5 stars,** indicating the level of standards, facilities and services offered by the hotel. Gradings are as follows:
5-star: Superior standard, fully air-conditioned accommodation; all rooms with private bath and shower, telephone, radio and TV; room service on a 24-hour basis; bar; restaurant and coffee shop; lounge area; dancing facilities; pool and sports facilities; 24-hour reception; laundry, pressing and dry-cleaning; shops and hairdresser.
4-star: High standard, fully air-conditioned accommodation; all rooms with private bath or shower and internal or external telephone and radio; room service from breakfast time to midnight; bar; restaurant; pool or service beach facilities; 24-hour reception; laundry, pressing and dry-cleaning; lounge; shops,

including hairdresser.
3-star: Good accommodation; all rooms with private bath or shower and internal or external telephone; bar and restaurant facilities; lounge area; 24-hour reception; laundry, pressing and dry-cleaning service.
2-star: Modest accommodation; at least 20% of rooms have private bath or shower; all rooms with washbasin and mirror; at least breakfast facilities are offered; telephone or service bell in all rooms; front office service during the day and at least porter service during the night.
1-star: Small hotel with simple accommodation; at least common bath and toilet facilities are available; all rooms with washbasin and mirror; at least breakfast facilities are offered; front office service during the day and at least porter service during the night.

RESORTS & EXCURSIONS

The Maltese islands, situated almost at the centre of the Mediterranean, offer the attraction of clear blue waters, secluded bays and sandy beaches while, in the towns, medieval walled citadels and splendid baroque churches and palaces reflect the rich history of the islands.

Gozo

Gozo is the sister island and the second-largest of the archipelago. The landscape consists of flat-topped hills, steep valleys and rugged cliffs and villas that nestle among peach, lemon, olive and orange groves. In spring the island comes ablaze with the flowering hibiscus, oleander, mimosa and bougainvillaea. Some of the local crafts (lace and knitwear) are sold from the doorways of houses and on the street.
The capital of Gozo is **Victoria** (formerly Rabat), built by the Arabs on *Castle Hill,* which offers the visitor panoramic views of the whole island. The cathedral has no dome, but inside a *trompe l'oeil* painting on its ceiling gives the illusion of a dome. There is also a cathedral museum.
The *Museum of Archaeology* contains Roman remains from a shipwreck on the island and items excavated from the neolithic temple at **Ggantija.**
Other places of interest on Gozo include the *Citadel* ('Gran Castello'), with its historic bastions and old

houses (one of them set up as a folk museum). There are alabaster caves at **Xaghra**, with stalactites and stalagmites. These underground caves are known as *Xerri's Grotto* and *Ninu's Grotto*. The basilica at *Ta'Pinu*, near the village of **Gharb**, is one of the most beautiful of Maltese churches and an official Vatican place of pilgrimage. **Xewkija** is a small town with a beautiful new church, built round the old parish *Church of St John the Baptist.*

The waters surrounding the island are unpolluted and crystal clear. The most important beaches are *I-Qawra* (better known as the inland sea, with a secluded pebbly bathing pool, crystal clear water and sheer cliffs), an unspoilt sandy beach known as *Ir-Ramla I-Hamra* and *Xlendi Bay*. In summer there are numerous festivals with fireworks and horseracing in the streets. **Marsalforn** is a fishing village on the north coast which has become one of Gozo's most popular seaside resorts.

Malta

Valletta: The town was built at the end of the 16th century by the Knights of St John as the island's new capital and, more importantly, as a fortress commanding an impregnable position over the peninsula. The city developed around what is now Republic Street, Old Bakery Street and Merchants Street, the latter containing some of the finest examples of Maltese-style Baroque architecture in the islands. The *Co-Cathedral of St John's* has an austere exterior, but the interior is a sumptuous mixture of gilded tracery, marble mosaic floors and a lapis lazuli altar behind which is a remarkable marble group of the Baptism of Christ. The painting by Caravaggio of the beheading of St John is in the Oratory. The *Grand Master's Palace* in Republic Street was built 500 years ago as the abode of the Grand Master of the Order of St John, and contains a series of paintings depicting the great siege of 1565, painted by a pupil of Michelangelo, and a group of tapestries originally designed for Louis XIV. The palace also houses an armoury which has one of the best collections in existence. The *Manoel Theatre*, named after one of the most popular Grand Masters, is the second-oldest theatre in Europe and stages performances of opera, theatre, music and ballet between October and May. The *National Museum of Fine Art*, housed in an 18th-century palace, has a collection of furniture, paintings and

treasures connected with the Knights of St John. The *Church of Our Lady of Victories*, built in 1566, is the oldest church in Valletta and was built to commemorate the victory over the Turks. At the nearby Auberge de Provence is the *National Museum of Archaeology,* which has exhibits from the area dating back to prehistory. The town also has a bustling market in the Floriana suburb on Sunday mornings and another one in Merchants Street from Monday to Saturday.

Within close proximity to Paola are the archaeological sites of *Tarxien*, with its neolithic temple; *Hypogeum*, a complex of ancient underground burial chambers on three levels dating back 3000 years; and *Ghar Dalam* (Dark Cave) where the remains of now extinct birds and animals such as dwarf hippos and elephants were found.

Sliema lies on the *Grand Harbour* facing Valletta. It is a large, modern cosmopolitan town bustling with hotels, shops, cafés, cinemas, restaurants, bars, clubs and discos. The shoreline here is rocky, but is nevertheless good for bathing.

Mdina is perched on a high plateau towering over the rest of the island. It was once Malta's capital and the citadel is one of the finest surviving examples of a medieval walled city. The town is entered by a stone drawbridge which leads to a maze of narrow streets, lined with churches, monasteries and palaces, connected by tiny piazzas. Of particular interest is the Norman-style *Palazzo Faisan* which has a collection of antique weapons and pottery, a cathedral, and a museum that still houses a magnificent collection of art treasures, survivals from the sacking which the town suffered at the hands of the French in the 18th century. From *Bastion Square* the visitor has a breathtaking view of the surrounding fields and villages, and also of *St Paul's Bay*.

Rabat has many fine Baroque churches, *St Paul's* and *St Agatha's catacombs* and the *Roman Villa*. There are many interesting walks within close proximity to the town, such as the *Chadwick Lake, Dingli Cliffs* and *Verdala Castle* overlooking *Buskett Gardens*, the only wooded area in Malta.

On the southwest shore is the *Blue Grotto* where, legend reports, sirens bewitched seafarers with their songs. Four caves reflect the brilliant colours of the corals and minerals in the limestone. The most spectacular is the Blue Grotto itself, which is best viewed in the early morning with a calm sea. Buses run to the caves from

Valletta.

Marsaxlokk, **Birzebbugia** and **Marsacala** are typical Maltese fishing communities, sprawled along the coves and inlets at the southernmost tip of Malta. Fishing nets and colourfully painted boats crowd the waterfronts, and each day's fresh catch can be eaten at the family-run tavernas. Also at Marsaxlokk is the recently discovered *Temple of Juno* which was originally used by the Greeks as a place of worship to the goddess of fertility.

The most popular beach area is along the north coast where sandy beaches are plentiful and the clear waters here are ideal for sailing, skindiving and water-skiing. The best beaches are at *Paradise Bay, Golden Bay, Mellieha Bay, Armier Bay* and *Ghajn Tuffieha Bay*, all of which are very popular during the summer and pleasantly quiet during spring.

Comino

The island of **Comino**, thick with wild herbs (particularly cumin), lies between Malta and Gozo and is inhabited by probably no more than a dozen farmers. Paths which wind through the unusual rock formations provide the only communication links and the island is ideal for anyone seeking a very quiet holiday. A few sandy coves and small bays, such as *Blue Lagoon,* are the main attractions.

SOCIAL PROFILE

FOOD & DRINK: There is a very good choice of restaurants and cafés from deluxe to fast food (hamburgers and fish & chips) including Chinese, fish and beachside tavernas and bars. Table service is normal, but many bars and cafés have table and/or counter service. Local dishes include *lampuki pie, bragoli* and *fenek* (rabbit cooked in wine). Pork and fish dishes are recommended and vegetables are excellent. The best Maltese fruits are oranges and grapes; also delicious are strawberries, melons, mulberries, tangerines, pomegranates and figs. **Drink:** Maltese beer is excellent, and foreign beers are also available. There is a wide variety of good and inexpensive Maltese wine and foreign wines and spirits. Licensing hours of bars, restaurants and cafés are usually 0900-0100 and beyond, although alcohol can only be bought before 0100. Most hotel bars close between 1300 and 1600 and then reopen after 1800.

NIGHTLIFE: There are several discotheques. Roulette, baccarat, black jack and boule can be played at the palatial 'Dragonara' casino, St Julian's. The Manoel Theatre is one of the oldest in Europe. Cinemas show many English and American films.

SHOPPING: Special purchases include Malta weave, pottery, glass, ceramics, dolls, copper and brass items. Malta is renowned for its gold and silver filigree work and handmade lace. **Shopping hours:** 0900-1300 and 1600-1900 Monday to Saturday.

SPORT: Rowing regattas are held frequently from April to November; these take place in the Grand Harbour during April and September. The Valletta Yacht Club is at Couvre Port, Manoel Island, in Marsamxetto Harbour (temporary members accepted). **Golf:** There is an 18-hole golf course at the Marsa Sports Club which also has facilities for **tennis, squash, cricket, polo** and **horseracing. Underwater sports** meetings are organised by the Federation of Underwater Activities. Ideal conditions exist in Malta for scuba diving and snorkelling. **Bowling:** There is a 10-pin bowling centre at St George's Bay, St Julian's. **Swimming:** Most large hotels have their own swimming pool and bathing is safe everywhere around the islands. **Windsurfing** has become a very popular sport and many hotels and beach establishments offer equipment. **Spectator sports: Football** is very popular and matches are played at the Stadium, Ta'Qali and at the Marsa Stadium from September to June. **Water polo:** National water polo competitions are held during summer. Matches are played at the National Swimming Pool, Marsascala. A summer league takes place at various water-polo clubs. **Horseraces** are held all Sunday afternoons at the Marsa National Racecourse from the end of October to the middle of May. **Clay Pigeon/Skeet shooting:** This is a popular sport in Malta with regular practice-sessions and competitions on Sunday mornings.

SPECIAL EVENTS: The Malta National Tourist Office can supply full details of events taking place in Malta in 1995/96. The following list is a selection of events:
Mar 1-5 '95 *Antiques Fair,* Valletta. **Mar 5** *Cultural Tour around Malta.* **Mar 9-12** *Food and Drink Fair,* Valletta. **Mar 10-19** *The Second Malta International Boat Show,* Valletta. **Mar 18** *Malta Open Judo Championship.* **Apr 7-16** *Holy Week processions,* throughout Malta. **Mid-Apr** *Europa '95 Yacht Race.* **Apr 21-22** *International Archery Tournament.* **May 8** *ATP 'Senior Tour' Tennis Tournament,* Marsa. **May 27** *10th International Malta-Sicily Windsurf Race.* **Jun 1-3** *The Maltese Cross – New Opera, 'Il-Bandu',* Mdina and Rabat. **Jun 23-25** *Mdina Pageant,* Mdina. **Jun 29** *Mnarja,* Rabat. **Jul 19-23** *Farsons Food and Beer Festival.* **End of Jul** *The Malta Jazz Festival.* **Jul-Aug** *Maltafest.* **Aug 6** *'Lejla Mgarrija'.* **Aug 18-21** *First Sportsman Travel International Snorkelling 'Challenge'.* **Aug 22-23** *'Lampuki Bonanza'.* **Sep 7** *September Pageant.* **Sep 23-24** *Malta International Air Show,* Luqa Airport. **Oct 5-8** *3rd Sportsman Travel International Cricket Challenge; Birgu Festival.* **Oct 11** *Malta vs Holland (European Football Championships),* Ta' Qali. **Oct 25-29** *Festival of Baroque Culture.* **Nov 5-10** *7th International Choir Festival.* **Nov 6-11** *9th Blue Dolphin of Malta International Photographic Competition.* **Nov 12** *Malta vs Belarus (European Football Championships),* Ta' Qali. **Nov 27-Dec 2** *Rothmans Grand Prix Professional Snooker Tournament.*
SOCIAL CONVENTIONS: The usual European courtesies are expected, but the visitor should also bear in mind the tremendous importance of Roman Catholicism; if visiting a church, for instance, modest dress covering the shoulders and legs will be expected. Smoking is

prohibited on public transport and in some public buildings, including cinemas. **Tipping:** 10% is expected in hotels and restaurants when not included in the bill. Taxi drivers are tipped 10%.

BUSINESS PROFILE

ECONOMY: For many years the British naval dockyards were the mainstay of the Maltese economy. Their closure in 1979 forced the Government to devise a comprehensive economic policy for the islands. The docks were nationalised and converted to operate as a commercial shipyard, engaged in both shipbuilding and repair, which remains a key source of income despite the recent world recession in merchant shipping. The light industry sector began to develop from the early 1960s onwards and now boasts such varied industries as textiles and clothing (the most important), plastics, printing, electronic components and electrical equipment. Agriculture has maintained a steady and important role in the economy, with grapes, potatoes and onions the principal products, many of which are exported. Tourism is a valuable source of foreign exchange. Lacking significant raw materials, Malta must import most of its requirements, particularly oil, the bulk of which comes from Libya, leaving the country with a continuous balance of payments deficit. Italy is the largest trading partner, followed by Germany and the United Kingdom.
BUSINESS: English is widely spoken in business circles and, on the whole, Maltese business people have a conservative approach to business protocol. Punctuality is expected and appreciated and dress must be smart. The best months for business visits are October to May.
Office hours: 0830-1245 and 1430-1730 Monday to Friday, 0830-1200 Saturday. Some smaller offices close 1300-1600, opening again later.
COMMERCIAL INFORMATION: The following organisations can offer advice: Office of the Deputy Prime Minister and of the Minister of Foreign Affairs, Palazzo Parisio, Merchants Street, Valletta. Tel: 242 191. Fax: 237 822. Telex: 1497; *or*
Malta International Business Authority (MIBA), PO Box 29, Palazzo Spinola, St Julian's STJ 01. Tel: 344 230. Fax: 344 334. Telex: 1692; *or*
Malta Chamber of Commerce, Exchange Buildings, Republic Street, Valletta VLT 05. Tel: 247 233. Fax: 245 223.
CONFERENCES/CONVENTIONS: The Malta National Tourist Office can loan a free promotional video to conference and incentive organisers and is happy to assist with all initial enquiries. For further information, contact the Conference and Incentive Travel Executive at the National Tourism Organisation of Malta (see above).

CLIMATE

Warm most of the year. The hottest months are between July and September, but the heat is tempered by cooling sea breezes. Rain falls for very short periods, mainly in the cooler winter months.
Required clothing: Lightweight cottons and linens are worn between March and September, although warmer clothes may occasionally be necessary in spring and autumn and on cooler evenings. A light raincoat is advisable for winter.

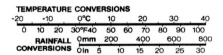

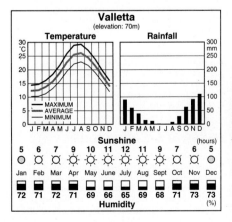

Martinique

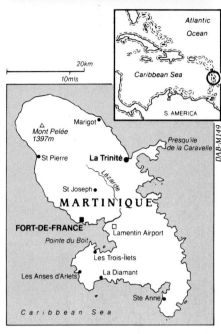

Location: Caribbean; northernmost of the Windward group of islands.

Diplomatic representation: Martinique is an Overseas Department of the Republic of France. Addresses of French Embassies, Consulates and Tourist Offices may be found in the *France* entry earlier in the *World Travel Guide.* The following may be contacted for further information.

Office du Tourisme
BP 520, Pavillon du Tourisme, boulevard Alfassa, 97206 Fort-de-France, Martinique
Tel: 637 960. Fax: 736 693. Telex: 912678.
Délégation Regionale au Tourisme
41 rue Gabriel Péri, 97200 Fort-de-France, Martinique
Tel: 631 861.
French West Indies Tourist Office
178 Piccadilly, London W1V 0AL
Tel: (0171) 629 2869. Fax: (0171) 493 6594. Telex: 21902. Opening hours: 0900-1700 Monday to Friday.
British Consulate
Route du Phare, 97200 Fort-de-France, Martinique
Tel: 615 630. Fax: 613 389. Telex: 912729 (a/b SERGIO MR).
Martinique Tourist Office
Suite 480, 1981 McGill College Avenue, Montréal, Québec H3A 2W9
Tel: (514) 844 8566. Fax: (514) 844 8901.

AREA: 1100 sq km (424.7 sq miles).
POPULATION: 359,572 (1990).
POPULATION DENSITY: 326.9 per sq km.
CAPITAL: Fort-de-France. **Population:** 101,540 (1990).
GEOGRAPHY: The French Overseas Department of Martinique, a volcanic and picturesque island, is the northernmost of the Windward Caribbean group. The

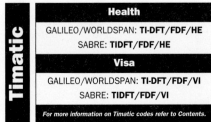

island is noticeably more rocky than those of the Leeward group, with beaches (of fine black or white or peppered sand) surrounded by sugar, palm, banana and pineapple plantations. Christopher Columbus called it 'the most beautiful country in the world' and before he named it in honour of St Martin, it was called *Madidina* ('island of flowers') by the native population.
LANGUAGE: The official language is French; the main local dialect is Creole.
RELIGION: The majority of the population are Roman Catholic.
TIME: GMT - 4.
ELECTRICITY: 220/380 volts AC, 50Hz.
COMMUNICATIONS: Telephone: IDD is available. Country code: 596. Outgoing international code: 19. Other islands can only be reached through the international operator. There are both payphones and cardphones on the island. *Télécartes* (phonecards) are sold at the PTT Office in rue Antoine Siger, Fort-de-France. There are only cardphones at the airport. **Telex:** There are reasonable public telex facilities available in the main hotels. **Post:** Letters to Europe must be sent by airmail from the main post offices and take about a week to reach Europe. Post offices are open 0700-1800 Monday to Friday, and Saturday mornings. **Press:** Newspapers are in French and vary in their political bias. The main daily is *France Antilles.*
BBC World Service and Voice of America frequencies: From time to time these change. See the section *How to Use this Book* for more information.

BBC:				
MHz	**17.84**	**15.22**	**9.915**	**5.975**
Voice of America:				
MHz	**15.21**	**11.70**	**6.130**	**0.930**

PASSPORT/VISA

The regulations for Tourist and Business visas are the same as for France (see the *Passport/Visa* section for France above). Visitors should specify that they wish to visit Martinique when they make their application.

MONEY

Currency: French Franc (FFr) = 100 centimes. Notes are in denominations of FFr500, 200, 100, 50 and 20. Coins are in denominations of FFr20, 10, 5, 2 and 1, and 50, 20, 10 and 5 centimes.
Currency exchange: US and Canadian dollars are widely accepted.
Credit cards: Diners Club, American Express and Visa are accepted. Access/Mastercard has limited acceptance. Check with your credit card company for details of merchant acceptability and other services which may be available.
Travellers cheques: Accepted in most places, and may qualify for discounts on luxury items.
Exchange rate indicators: The following figures are included as a guide to the movements of the French Franc against Sterling and the US Dollar:

Date:	**Oct '92**	**Sep '93**	**Jan '94**	**Jan '95**
£1.00=	**8.28**	**8.67**	**8.74**	**8.35**
$1.00=	**5.21**	**5.68**	**5.90**	**5.34**

Currency restrictions: As for France.

DUTY FREE

The island of Martinique is an Overseas Department of France, and therefore duty-free allowances are the same as those for France.

PUBLIC HOLIDAYS

Jan 1 '95 New Year's Day. **Apr 14-17** Easter. **May 1** Labour Day. **May 8** Victory Day. **May 25** Ascension Day. **Jun 5** Whit Monday. **Jul 14** National Day. **Aug 15** Assumption. **Nov 1** All Saints' Day. **Nov 11** Armistice Day. **Dec 25** Christmas Day. **Jan 1 '96** New Year's Day. **Apr 5-8** Easter.

HEALTH

Regulations and requirements may be subject to change at short notice, and you are advised to contact your doctor well in advance of your intended date of departure. Any numbers in the chart refer to the footnotes below.

	Special Precautions?	Certificate Required?
Yellow Fever	No	1
Cholera	No	No
Typhoid & Polio	Yes	-
Malaria	No	-
Food & Drink	2	-

[1]: A yellow fever vaccination certificate is required from travellers over one year of age arriving from infected areas.
[2]: Mains water is normally chlorinated, and whilst relatively safe may cause mild abdominal upsets. Bottled water is available and is advised for the first few weeks of the stay. Drinking water outside main cities and towns may be contaminated and sterilisation is advisable. Milk is pasteurised and dairy products are safe for consumption. Local meat, poultry, seafood, fruit and vegetables are generally considered safe to eat.
Bilharzia (schistosomiasis) is present. Avoid swimming and paddling in fresh water. Swimming pools which are well-chlorinated and maintained are safe.
Tuberculosis is still present in Martinique. Consult your doctor for advice on inoculation before departure.
Health care: A Reciprocal Health Agreement exists between France and the UK. However, the benefits which go with this agreement may not be fully available in Martinique. Check with your doctor before departure. Martinique has 14 hospitals.

TRAVEL - International

AIR: Martinique's national airline is *Air Martinique (NN).*
Approximate flight times: From *London* to Martinique is 12 hours (including an average stopover time of 1 hour in Paris); from *Los Angeles* is 9 hours; from *New York* is 6 hours and from *Singapore* is 33 hours.
International airport: *Fort-de-France* (FDF) (Lamentin) is 15km (9 miles) from the city. Airport facilities include restaurant, shops and car hire. *LIAT, Air Antilles, Air Guadeloupe, BWIA* and *Air France* offer flights from Fort-de-France to many other Caribbean islands.
Departure tax: FFr75.
SEA: Martinique is a point of call for the following international cruise lines: *Chandris, Holland America, Royal Caribbean, Cunard, Sun Line, Sitmar, TUI Cruises* and *Princess Cruises.* There are ships plying the Caribbean between Martinique and Guadeloupe and others sail from Miami and San Juan. There are also regular ferry services around the islands.

TRAVEL - Internal

AIR: Aeroplanes and helicopters may be chartered from *Air Martinique.*
SEA: Scheduled ferries ply between Fort-de-France, Pointe du Boit and Anse Mitan.
ROAD: Traffic drives on the right. The road system is well-developed and surfaced. **Bus:** A limited service is provided. **Taxi:** Government-controlled, plentiful and reasonably cheap if shared. There is a surcharge at night. Martinique has a system of communal taxis. **Car hire:** The island has excellent car-rental facilities. 50cc **mopeds** do not need a licence and can be hired from TS Auto, 38 route de Ste Thérèse, Fort-de-France. Tel: 633 305. **Bicycles** can also be hired. **Documentation:** An International Driving Permit is recommended, but a national driving licence is sufficient, provided the driver has at least one year's experience.

ACCOMMODATION

HOTELS: There is a good selection of hotels on Martinique. 10% service is charged, sometimes with other government taxes added. There is a *Relais de la Martinique,* an association of small hotels and guest-houses offering special reservation and tour facilities. Hotels range from deluxe, to medium- and low-priced. For further information, contact the tourist office. For further information contact Chambre Syndicale des Hôtels de Tourisme de la Martinique, Entrée Montgéralde, Route de Chateauboeuf, Fort-de-France. Tel: 702 780.
SELF-CATERING: *Gîtes* (furnished apartments or bungalows) are widely available. For rental, contact the Association pour le Tourisme en Espace Rural, Relais des Gîtes de France, BP 1122, Maison du Tourisme Vert, 9 boulevard du Général-de-Gaulle, 97248 Fort-de-France Cédex. Tel: 634 869.

RESORTS & EXCURSIONS

The terrain of Martinique varies from the high mountains of the north and centre to the rolling hills around Fort-de-France and the safe, sheltered harbours of the lower west coast. **Mont Pelée,** the 1430m (4700ft) volcanic mountain in the north, last erupted in 1902 (in a unique explosion which literally ripped the summit off), destroying the city of St Pierre and its entire 30,000 population. (Only a prisoner, Auguste Ciparis, survived – who was subsequently pardoned and ended his days as a fairground exhibit in America.) The remains of St Pierre are now a tourist attraction. Photomurals are on display in the *Musée Volcanologique.*
The region is being developed as a natural park and leisure area. Near **Carbet,** where Columbus landed on his fourth voyage in 1502, is the restored plantation of **Leyritz,** which is now visited by many tourists. The *Centre d'Art Paul Gauguin* may be found in Carbet itself. North of this region is **Pointe du Boit,** Martinique's major resort area.
Fort-de-France, the island's capital, is a town of winding streets and colourful markets. In the centre of the town is the park of *La Savanne.* A statue in La Savanne square commemorates Napoleon's Empress Josephine, a native of Martinique, whose home, *La Pagerie,* is one of the main tourist attractions. **Les Trois-Ilets** (Josephine's birthplace) is situated across the bay from Fort-de-France.
The *Musée Departmental* has remains of the predominantly Arawak and Carib Indian prehistory of the island. There is an interesting *Caribbean Arts Centre.* Martinique has ten small museums celebrating aspects of the island's culture and history including the Empress Josephine's connection with the island, the eruption of Pelée, the rum trade and dolls made from local materials.
Ste Anne, La Diamant and **Les Anses d'Arlets** have some of the island's best bathing beaches. *HMS Diamond Rock,* 4km (2.5 miles) off Diamant, is a rock which was designated a man-of-war by the British during the Napoleonic wars and rates a 12-gun salute from passing British warships.

SOCIAL PROFILE

FOOD & DRINK: French influences and seafood includes lobster, turtle, red snapper, conch and sea urchin. Island specialities include stuffed crab, stewed conch, roast wild goat, jugged rabbit and broiled local dove. *Colombo* is goat, chicken, pork or lamb in a thick curry sauce. Creole cuisine is also widely available and is an original combination of French, Indian and African traditions seasoned with exotic spices. Meals are ended with exotic fruit. **Drink:** There is a great supply of French wines, champagne, liqueurs and local rum. Local specialities are *ti punch*, a brew of rum, lime juice, bitters and syrup, *shrub*, a Christmas liqueur consisting of rum and orange peel, and *planteur*, made from rum and fruit juice. Guava, soursop, passionfruit, mandarin and sugar cane juice are all common. There are no licensing restrictions.
NIGHTLIFE: There are plenty of restaurants, bars, discotheques, and displays of local dancing and music. The *Ballet Martiniquais* is one of the world's most prestigious traditional ballet companies. Limbo dancers and steel bands are often laid on at hotels in the evenings. The local guide, *Choubouloute,* contains information on local entertainment and is sold at newsagents for FFr5.
SHOPPING: French imports are worthwhile purchases, especially wines, liqueurs and Lalique crystal. Local items include rum, straw goods, bamboo hats, voodoo dolls, baskets and objects of aromatic vetiver roots. A discount of 20% is given if payment is made by travellers cheques in some tourist shops. **Shopping hours:** 0830-1300 and 1500-1800 Monday to Friday.
SPORT: Watersports: Swimming, water-skiing, smallboat sailing, snorkelling and spearfishing are available at many coastal resorts. **Tennis:** There are courts at many large hotels. Visitors can obtain temporary membership and play at night as well as during the day. For further information, contact Club de Tennis de Martinique, Petit Manoir, Lamentin. Tel: 510 800. **Horseriding** is a very enjoyable way to see Martinique's lovely countryside. **Golf:** There is an 18-hole golf course at Trois-Ilets. There is also **horseracing** at the Carère track at Lamentin. **Hiking** and **mountain-climbing** are also catered for.
SPECIAL EVENTS: From January 1 to Lent every weekend is celebrated by a carnival, culminating in the festivities on *Ash Wednesday*. The main carnival takes place in the beginning of February for *Mardi Gras*, when everyone dresses up in fantastic costumes and parades the streets. On Ash Wednesday, 'devils' clad in black and white form a procession, lamenting the death of Vaval. At *Easter*, children fly coloured kites. Dances originating in Africa are a feature of these events. The *Béguine* is a famous dance from this part of the world. *Gommier races* (with enormous rectangular sailing boats with colourful sails and teams of oarsmen) are a wonderful sight at festivals from July to January.

SOCIAL CONVENTIONS: The atmosphere is generally relaxed and informal. Casual dress is acceptable everywhere, but formal attire is needed for dining out and nightclubs. **Tipping:** 10% is acceptable.

BUSINESS PROFILE

ECONOMY: The economy relies almost exclusively on tourism and agriculture. Sugar cane and bananas are the main crops, both of which have suffered severely from the series of hurricanes which devastated much of the Caribbean during the 1980s and also seriously affected the tourist infrastructure. Tourism has been in decline due to global recession and political instability on the island. The Government is trying to encourage diversification in the economy, by promoting other crops among farmers on the one hand and providing incentives for small businesses and light industry on the other. These have yet to fill the gaps left by the decline of traditional economic sectors, however. France accounts for over 75% of Martinique's foreign trade, with the remainder of the import market captured by the major EU economies and the United States. There is considerable trepidation on the island about the long-term effects of the Single European Market and the fierce economic competition which this is likely to bring.
BUSINESS: Lightweight suits and safari suits are recommended. The best time to visit is January to March and June to September. A command of French is useful, as much of the island's business is connected with France. **Office hours:** 0800-1700 Monday to Friday, 0800-1200 Saturday.
COMMERCIAL INFORMATION: The following organisation can offer advice: Chambre de Commerce et d'Industrie de la Martinique, 50-56 rue Ernest Deproge, Fort-de-France. Tel: 552 800. Fax: 606 668. Telex: 912633.

CLIMATE

Warm weather throughout the year, with the main rainy season occurring in the autumn. However, showers can occur at any time, but they are usually brief. Cooler in the upland areas.
Required clothing: Lightweight, with waterproof wear advised for the rainy season.

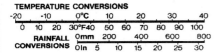

TEMPERATURE CONVERSIONS
-20   -10   0°C   10   20   30   40
0 10 20 30°F40 50 60 70 80 90 100
RAINFALL   0mm   200   400   600   800
CONVERSIONS   0In   5   10   15   20   25   30

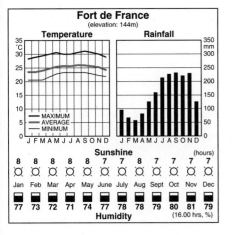

Fort de France
(elevation: 144m)

□ international airport

600km
300mls

ALGERIA

WESTERN SAHARA (Incorporated into Morocco)
• Bir Moghrein
Tropic of Cancer
SAHARA DESERT
• Fdérik
Adrar
■ Nouadhibou
Atar • • Chinguetti
MAURITANIA
• Tidjikdja
■ NOUAKCHOTT
• Boutilimit
Hodh
Rosso
• Kaédi
Afollé
• Néma
SENEGAL
MALI
Senegal
ATLANTIC OCEAN
DAB-M1150

Location: West Africa.

Société Mauritanienne de Tourisme et d'Hôtellerie (SMTH)
BP 552, Nouakchott, Mauritania
Tel: 53351.
Honorary Consulate of the Islamic Republic of Mauritania
140 Bow Common Lane, London E3 4BH
Tel: (0181) 980 4382. Fax: (0181) 556 6032.
Embassy of the Islamic Republic of Mauritania
5 rue de Montévidéo, 75116 Paris, France
Tel: (1) 45 04 88 54.
Consulate of the Islamic Republic of Mauritania
89 rue Cherche Midi, 75006 Paris, France
Tel: (1) 45 48 23 88. Fax: (1) 45 48 14 18.
The British Embassy in Rabat deals with enquiries relating to Mauritania (see *Morocco* later in this book).
Embassy of the Islamic Republic of Mauritania
2129 Leroy Place, NW, Washington, DC 20008
Tel: (202) 232 5700. Fax: (202) 319 2623.
Embassy of the United States of America
BP 222, Nouakchott, Mauritania
Tel: 52660/3. Fax: 51592. Telex: 5558.
Embassy of the Islamic Republic of Mauritania
249 McLeod Street, Ottawa, Ontario K2P 1A1
Tel: (613) 237 3283/4/5. Fax: (613) 237 3287.
The Canadian Embassy in Dakar deals with enquiries relating to Mauritania (see *Senegal* later in this book).

AREA: 1,030,700 sq km (397,950 sq miles).
POPULATION: 2,036,000 (1990 estimate).
POPULATION DENSITY: 2 per sq km.
CAPITAL: Nouakchott. **Population:** 450,000 (1986).
GEOGRAPHY: Mauritania is bordered by Algeria, Mali, Western Sahara (Sahrawi Arab Democratic Republic) and Senegal. To the west lies the Atlantic Ocean. Mauritania consists mainly of the vast Saharan plain of sand and scrub. Most of this area is a sea of sand dunes, but in places the land rises to rocky plateaux with deep ravines leaving isolated peaks. The Adrar plateau in the central region rises to 500m (1640ft) and the Tagant further south to 600m (1970ft). The area is scattered with towns, small villages and oases. The northern bank of the Senegal River, which forms the country's southern border, is the only area in the country with any degree of permanent vegetation and it supports a wide variety of wildlife.
LANGUAGE: The official languages are Arabic and

French. The Moors of Arab/Berber stock, speaking Hassaniya dialects of Arabic, comprise the majority of the people. Other dialects include Soninke, Pulaar and Wolof. English is rarely spoken.
RELIGION: Islam is the official religion. Despite ethnic and cultural differences among Mauritanians, they are all bound by a common Muslim attachment to the Malekite sect.
TIME: GMT.
ELECTRICITY: 127/220 volts AC, 50Hz. Round 2-pin plugs are normal.
COMMUNICATIONS: Telephone: IDD is available in Nouakchott and Nouadhibou. Country code: 222 (no area codes). Outgoing international calls must go through the operator. **Telex:** Nouakchott and Nouadhibou have telex facilities. **Post:** International postal facilities are limited to main cities. Airmail to Europe takes approximately two weeks. **Press:** Newspapers are in French and Arabic. The only daily is *Ach-Chaab*.
BBC World Service and Voice of America frequencies: From time to time these change. See the section *How to Use this Book* for more information.

BBC:				
MHz	17.79	15.40	15.07	9.410
Voice of America:				
MHz	21.49	15.60	9.525	6.035

PASSPORT/VISA

Regulations and requirements may be subject to change at short notice, and you are advised to contact the appropriate diplomatic or consular authority before finalising travel arrangements. Details of these may be found at the head of this country's entry. Any numbers in the chart refer to the footnotes below.

	Passport Required?	Visa Required?	Return Ticket Required?
Full British	Yes	Yes	Yes
BVP	Not valid	-	-
Australian	Yes	Yes	Yes
Canadian	Yes	Yes	Yes
USA	Yes	Yes	Yes
Other EU (As of 31/12/94)	Yes	1	Yes
Japanese	Yes	Yes	Yes

PASSPORTS: Valid passports required by all except nationals of Burkina Faso, Cameroon, Central African Republic, Chad, Congo, Côte d'Ivoire, Gabon, Gambia, Guinea Republic, Madagascar, Mali, Niger, Senegal and Sierra Leone, who may enter on a national identity card or passport which has expired no longer than 5 years.
British Visitors Passport: Not accepted.
VISAS: Required by all except:
(a) **[1]** nationals of France (all other EU nationals *do* need a visa);
(b) nationals of Benin, Burkina Faso, Cameroon, Cape Verde, Central African Republic, Chad, Congo, Côte d'Ivoire, Gabon, Gambia, Ghana, Guinea, Guinea-Bissau, Liberia, Madagascar, Mali, Niger, Nigeria, Romania, Senegal, Sierra Leone, Togo and Tunisia;
(c) members of the League of Arab States (except nationals of Morocco who *do* need a visa). For a full list of the League of Arab States, see *International Organisations* at the beginning of this book.
Types of visa: Tourist or Business (valid for 1 month). Cost: 112FFr. Visitors intending to stay for more than one month should apply to the local immigration office on arrival.
Transit: A visa is not required for passengers arriving by air and continuing to a third country within 24 hours, by the same or connecting aircraft, provided they hold tickets with reserved seats, and other documents for their onward journey, and do not leave the airport.
Application to: Consulate (or Consular section at Embassy). For addresses, see top of entry. The Honorary Consulate in London does *not* issue visas.
Application requirements: (a) 3 application forms. (b) 3 passport-size photos. (c) Fee. (d) Yellow fever vaccination certificate. (e) Evidence of return ticket *or* sufficient currency for the length of stay. (f) Company

Health		
GALILEO/WORLDSPAN: **TI-DFT/NKC/HE**		
SABRE: **TIDFT/NKC/HE**		
Visa		
GALILEO/WORLDSPAN: **TI-DFT/NKC/VI**		
SABRE: **TIDFT/NKC/VI**		

For more information on Timatic codes refer to Contents.

Timatic

letter for Business visas. (g) Stamped, self-addressed envelope if applying by post.
Working days required: 3.

MONEY

Currency: Mauritanian Ougiya (U) = 5 khoums. Notes are in denominations of U1000, 500, 200 and 100. Coins are in denominations of U20, 10, 5 and 1, and 1 khoum.
Credit cards: Generally not accepted. American Express is accepted in a few hotels in Nouakchott and Nouadhibou.
Travellers cheques: Limited use.
Exchange rate indicators: The following figures are included as a guide to the movements of the Ougiya against Sterling and the US Dollar:

Date:	Oct '92	Sep '93	Jan '94	Jan '95
£1.00=	168.22	174.20	181.95	190.75
$1.00=	105.99	114.08	122.98	121.92

Currency restrictions: The import and export of local currency is prohibited. There is no restriction on the import of foreign currency provided the amount is declared on arrival. The balance of foreign currency not spent but declared on entry may be exported, but the import declaration must be produced.
Banking hours: 0700-1500 Sunday to Thursday.

DUTY FREE

The following items can be imported into Mauritania by persons over 18 years of age without incurring customs duty:
200 cigarettes or 25 cigars or 450g of tobacco (females – cigarettes only); 50g of perfume.
Prohibited items: Alcohol.

PUBLIC HOLIDAYS

Jan 1 '95 New Year's Day. **Mar 3** Korité (End of Ramadan). **May 1** Labour Day. **May 10** Tabaski (Feast of the Sacrifice). **May 25** African Liberation Day (Anniversary of the OAU's Foundation). **May 31** Islamic New Year. **Aug 9** Mouloud (Prophet's Birthday). **Nov 28** National Day. **Dec 20** Leilat al-Meiraj. **Jan 1 '96** New Year's Day. **Feb 22** Korité (End of Ramadan).
Note: Muslim festivals are timed according to local sightings of various phases of the Moon and the dates given above are approximations. During the lunar month of Ramadan that precedes Korité (Eid al-Fitr), Muslims fast during the day and feast at night and normal business patterns may be interrupted. Many restaurants are closed during the day and there may be restrictions on smoking and drinking. Some disruption may continue into Korité itself. Korité and Tabaski (Eid al-Adha) may last anything from two to ten days, depending on the region. For more information see the section *World of Islam* at the back of the book.

HEALTH

Regulations and requirements may be subject to change at short notice, and you are advised to contact your doctor well in advance of your intended date of departure. Any numbers in the chart refer to the footnotes below.

	Special Precautions?	Certificate Required?
Yellow Fever	Yes	1
Cholera	Yes	2
Typhoid & Polio	Yes	-
Malaria	3	-
Food & Drink	4	-

[1]: A yellow fever vaccination certificate is required from all travellers over one year of age, except travellers arriving from a non-infected area and staying less than two weeks in the country.
[2]: Following WHO guidelines issued in 1973, a cholera vaccination certificate is not a condition of entry to Mauritania. However, cholera is a serious risk in this country and precautions are essential. Up-to-date advice should be sought before deciding whether these precautions should include vaccination, as medical opinion is divided over its effectiveness. See the *Health* section at the back of the book.
[3]: Malaria risk, mainly in the malignant *falciparum* form, exists throughout the year except in the following northern areas: Dakhlet-Nouadhibou, Inchiri, Adrar and Tiris-Zemour.
[4]: All water should be regarded as being potentially contaminated. Water used for drinking, brushing teeth or making ice should have first been boiled or otherwise sterilised. Milk is unpasteurised and should be boiled. Powdered or tinned milk is available and is

advised, but make sure it is reconstituted with pure water. Avoid dairy products which are likely to have been made from unboiled milk. Only eat well-cooked meat and fish, preferably served hot. Pork, salad and mayonnaise may carry increased risk. Vegetables should be cooked and fruit peeled.
Rabies is present. For those at high risk, vaccination before arrival should be considered. If you are bitten abroad, seek medical advice without delay. For more information, consult the *Health* section at the back of the book.
Bilharzia (schistosomiasis) is present. Avoid swimming and paddling in fresh water. Swimming pools which are well-chlorinated and maintained are safe.
Health care: Medical facilities are very limited. The hospital in the capital has 450 beds; there are fewer than 100 other beds elsewhere. Health insurance, to include cover for emergency repatriation, is essential.

TRAVEL - International

AIR: Mauritania's national airline is *Air Mauritanie (MR)*.
Approximate flight time: From London to Nouakchott is 7 hours (via Paris).
International airports: *Nouakchott (NKC)* is 4km (2.5 miles) east of the city (travel time – 20 minutes). Taxis are available to the city.
Nouadhibou (NDB) is 4km (2.5 miles) from the city. Taxis are available to the city.
SEA: The principal port is Nouadhibou and there is a small port at Nouakchott, while St Louis in Senegal also serves Mauritania.
RAIL: A line from Nouadhibou to Fderik is primarily for hauling iron ore for export. The ore trains do, however, include a passenger coach which provides a daily return service.
ROAD: The most reliable way into Mauritania overland is from Senegal. From Dakar, the journey to Nouakchott is along a 575km (360-mile) tarred road. The River Senegal has to be crossed by ferry at Rosso. A service operates 0730-1200 and 1500-1800 daily. There is also a paved road from Mali. Travellers intending to drive into Mauritania from the north should contact the nearest Mauritanian diplomatic mission for an assessment of political conditions in the Western Sahara; the *Route de Mauritanie* via Algeria and Senegal is out of service.

TRAVEL - Internal

AIR: *Air Mauritanie (MR)* operates internal flights between Nouakchott and the main towns. At present there are two daily connecting flights between Nouadhibou and Nouakchott.
RAIL: The only line runs between Nouadhibou and Zouerate and serves the ore mines. Services are free but journeys are long and arduous and not recommended.
ROAD: There are adequate roads linking Nouakchott with Rosso in the south of the country, Néma in the southeast and Akjoujt in the north. A paved highway, namely *La Route de l'Espoir*, runs east from Nouakchott to Mali. All other routes are sand tracks necessitating the use of 4-wheel-drive vehicles. In some regions during and after the rainy season roads may become impassable. Similarly, in the dry season tracks can be obscured by drifting sand; a guide is highly recommended if not essential. **Car hire:** Available in Nouakchott, Nouadhibou and Atar. Four-wheel-drive vehicles with a driver can be hired and are recommended, but they are very expensive. **Documentation:** An International Driving Permit is recommended, although it is not legally required.
Note: Never attempt any desert journey without a full set of spare parts and essential safety equipment. The *Ministère du Commerce de l'Artisanat et du Tourisme* in Nouakchott can give further information and advice on road travel. Tel: 52805. Fax: 56886.
URBAN: Taxis are very expensive in the towns (Nouakchott and Nouadhibou) but plentiful. Fares are set, not metered, and a small tip is expected.

ACCOMMODATION

HOTELS: Hotel accommodation is very limited in Mauritania and visitors are advised to book well in advance. The larger hotels in Nouakchott are very comfortable and have air-conditioning, but even in the capital accommodation is limited and expensive. Bills normally include service and local tax. For more information, contact the Société Mauritanienne de Tourisme et d'Hôtellerie (address at beginning of entry).
REST HOUSES: There are numerous government rest

houses throughout the country, bookable through the *Ministère du Commerce de l'Artisanat et du Tourisme* (see contact details under Road in the Travel Internal section).

RESORTS & EXCURSIONS

Much of the land is dry and inhospitable. There are also political and military impediments to travel, mainly concerning the Moroccan adventure in Western Sahara.
Nouakchott: The capital of Mauritania is a new city created in 1960. It lies near the sea in a flat landscape of low dunes scattered with thorn bushes, on a site adjoining an old Moorish settlement, the *Ksar*. The modern buildings maintain the traditional Berber style of architecture. The following places are worth visiting: the *Plage du Wharf,* the mosque, the Ksar and its market, the African market and the camel market, the crafts centre, the *Maison de la Culture* and the carpet factory.
Nouadhibou: A growing port and centre of the fishing industry, Nouadhibou is situated on a peninsula at the northern end of the *Bay of Levrier*. Inland, the landscape is empty desert.
The Coast: Mauritania's coast is essentially an 800km-long (500-mile) sandy beach, all but devoid of vegetation, but supporting an astonishingly large and varied population of birds. The waters are equally rich in fish and consequently, despite the shortage of fresh water, some coastal stretches are inhabited by man. One tribe, halfway between Nouakchott and Nouadhibou, survives through a symbiotic relationship with wild dolphins: the marine mammals drive fish towards the shore, the tribesmen swim out with nets, and both get their share. Foreign trawlers are rapidly depleting offshore fish stocks.
Adrar Region: It is important to check on conditions for travel before setting out for this region as government permission may be necessary. The Adrar is a spectacular massif of pink and brown plateaux gilded with dunes and intersected by deep canyons sheltering palm groves. It lies in the north central part of the country, and begins about 320km (200 miles) northeast of Nouakchott. Atar, capital of the region, is an oasis lying on the route of salt caravans. It is the market centre for the nomads of northern Mauritania and has an old quarter, the *Ksar*, with flat-roofed houses and a fine palm grove. The oasis of *Azoughui* was the *Almoravid* capital in the 11th and 12th centuries, and remains of fortified buildings from this period can still be seen. A whole day excursion from Atar leads over the breathtaking mountain pass of *Homogjar* to **Chinguetti**, a holy city of Islam, founded in the 13th century, which has a medieval mosque and a library housing ancient manuscripts. Much of the old town is disappearing under the encroaching drifts of sand.
Affolé and Assaba: It is worth making a tour of the Affolé and Assaba regions, south and southeast of the Tagant, via **Kiffa, Tamchakett** and **Ayoun el Atrous,** to the wild plateaux of **El Agher.** The interesting archaeological sites include *Koumbi Saleh*, once capital of the Ghana Empire, 70km (45 miles) from Timbedra along a good track. Near Tamchakett is **Tagdawst**, which has been identified as *Aoudaghost*, ancient capital of a Berber empire. **Oualata** lies 100km (60 miles) from **Néma** at the end of a desert track, and was at one time one of the greatest caravan entrepôts of the Sahara. A fortified medieval town built in terraces up a rocky peak, it has for centuries been a place of refuge for scholars and has a fine library. The Muslim cemetery of **Tirzet** is nearby.

SOCIAL PROFILE

FOOD & DRINK: A limited number of hotel restaurants in the capital serve Western food, but restaurants serve more traditional fare; the local dishes, based on millet, can be delicious and inexpensive. Mauritanian food includes *mechoui* (whole roast lamb), dates, spiced fish and rice with vegetables, fish balls, dried fish, dried meat and *couscous*. **Drink:** Consumption of alcohol is prohibited by the Islamic faith, but alcoholic beverages may be found in hotel bars. *Zrig* (camel's milk) is a common drink, as is sweet mint tea.
SHOPPING: Handicrafts such as dyed leather cushions and some engraved silver items, rugs and woodcarvings can be bought on the open market. A fine selection of silver jewellery, daggers, wood and silver chests and carpets can be bought in the crafts centre in Nouakchott. Unique to the Tagant region are neolithic arrowheads, awls and pottery, while at Boutilimit in the south is a Marabout centre (Institute of High Islamic Studies) where fine carpets of goat and camel hair are made.
Shopping hours: 0800-1200 and 1400-1900 Saturday to Thursday; 0800-1200 and 1530/1600-1900 during

hivernage (the rainy season from June to November).
SOCIAL CONVENTIONS: Islam has been the major influence in this country since the 7th and 8th centuries and visitors should respect the religious laws and customs. Dress for women should be uncompromisingly modest. Nearly all the population have traditionally been nomadic herdsmen. The bulk of the population is divided into the Bidan (55%) and the Harattin (20%), with negroes concentrated in the Senegal River area. Class and tribal differences tend to be contiguous. **Tipping:** 12-15% is normal.

BUSINESS PROFILE

ECONOMY: Successive years of drought have turned once fertile land to desert, and heavy losses of livestock have led most of the nomadic population to find employment in the towns. Agricultural production takes place mainly in the south on the Senegal River where the land is irrigated. Vegetables, millet, rice and dates are the main crops, and the Government is concentrating its resources on improving the agricultural produce in this area. The most important industry is the exploitation of iron ore in the north of the country which is undergoing a major expansion. Copper mining has been suspended due to lack of competitiveness (a result of the low world price), but may resume in the near future. Mauritania, which remains an exceptionally poor country, relies on a great deal of foreign aid, most of which comes from the Arab countries. Japan and the southern EU countries are Mauritania's main export markets, while the major exporters to the country are France (30%) and Spain (26%), followed by Germany, The Netherlands and the USA. The present government has embarked on an IMF-supervised structural adjustment programme which seeks to foster private enterprise and reform state-owned commercial concerns, especially the banking system which was close to disintegration. Mauritania is a member of the Economic Community of West African States (ECOWAS) and the Union of the Arab Maghreb.
BUSINESS: Use forms of address as for France, eg *Monsieur le Directeur.* It is essential that businessmen have a sound knowledge of French, as very few executives speak English. **Office hours:** 0800-1500 Saturday to Wednesday, 0800-1300 Thursday.
COMMERCIAL INFORMATION: The following organisation can offer advice: Chambre de Commerce, d'Agriculture, d'Elevage, d'Industrie et des Mines de Mauritanie, BP 215, Nouakchott. Tel: 52214. Telex: 581.

CLIMATE

Most of the country is hot and dry with practically no rain. In the south, however, rainfall is higher with a rainy season which runs from July to September. The coast is tempered by trade winds and is mild with the exception of the hot Nouakchott region (where the rainy season begins a month later). Deserts are cooler and windy in March and April.
Required clothing: Lightweight cottons and linens, with a warm wrap for cool evenings. Waterproofing is necessary for the rainy season.

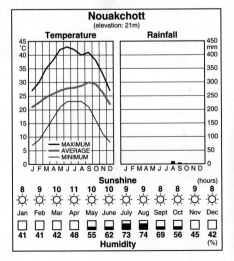

Nouakchott (elevation: 21m)												
Sunshine (hours)												
	8	9	10	11	10	10	9	9	8	8	9	8
	Jan	Feb	Mar	Apr	May	June	July	Aug	Sept	Oct	Nov	Dec
Humidity (%)	41	41	42	48	55	62	73	74	69	56	45	42

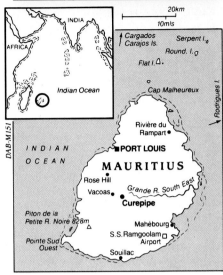

Mauritius

Location: Indian Ocean, off southeast coast of Africa; due east of Madagascar.

Mauritius Government Tourist Office
Emmanuel Anquetil Building, Sir Seewoosagur Ramgoolam Street, Port Louis, Mauritius
Tel: 201 1703. Fax: 212 5142. Telex: 4249.
Mauritius High Commission
32/33 Elvaston Place, London SW7 5NW
Tel: (0171) 581 0294. Fax: (0171) 823 8437. Telex: 917772. Opening hours: 0930-1300 and 1400-1700 Monday to Friday; 0930-1200 Monday to Friday (Consular section).
Mauritius Government Tourist Office
32 Elvaston Place, London SW7 5NW
Tel: (0171) 584 3666. Fax: (0171) 225 1135. Opening hours: 0930-1700 Monday to Thursday and 0930-1630 Friday.
British High Commission
PO Box 186, Curepipe, King George V Avenue, Floréal, Mauritius
Tel: 686 5795/6/7/8. Fax: 686 5792. Telex: 4266 (a/b UKREP IW).
Embassy of Mauritius
Suite 441, 4301 Connecticut Avenue, NW, Washington, DC 20008
Tel: (202) 244 1491. Fax: (202) 966 0983.
Also deals with enquiries from Canada.
Mauritius Tourist Information Service
Suite 227, Court Executive Building, 8 Haven Avenue, Port Washington, NY 11050
Tel: (516) 944 3737. Fax: (516) 944 8458.
Embassy of the United States of America
4th Floor, Rogers House, President John F Kennedy Street, Port Louis, Mauritius
Tel: 208 9763/4/5/6/7. Fax: 208 9534.
Honorary Consulate of Mauritius
Suite 200, 606 Cathcart Street, H3B 1K9
Tel: (514) 393 9500. Fax: (514) 393 9324.
The Canadian High Commission in Dar-es-Salaam deals with enquiries relating to Mauritius (see *Tanzania* **later in this book).**

AREA: 2040 sq km (788 sq miles).
POPULATION: 1,058,775 (1990).
POPULATION DENSITY: 519 per sq km.
CAPITAL: Port Louis. **Population:** 142,087 (1991 estimate).

	Health
GALILEO/WORLDSPAN:	**TI-DFT/MRU/HE**
SABRE:	**TIDFT/MRU/HE**
	Visa
GALILEO/WORLDSPAN:	**TI-DFT/MRU/VI**
SABRE:	**TIDFT/MRU/VI**

For more information on Timatic codes refer to Contents.

GEOGRAPHY: Mauritius is in the Indian Ocean 2000km (1200 miles) off the southeastern coast of Africa, due east of Madagascar. The island-state stands on what was once a land bridge between Asia and Africa called the Mascarene Archipelago. From the coast the land rises to form a broad fertile plain on which sugar cane flourishes. Some 500km (300 miles) east is Rodrigues Island, while northeast is Cargados Carajos Shoals and 900km (560 miles) to the north is Agalega.
LANGUAGE: English is the official language. The most widely spoken languages are Creole, Hindi and Bhojpuri. French, Urdu and Chinese are also spoken. In the 1983 census 13 different language groups were specifically identified, with Creole and Hindi speakers accounting for about half the population.
RELIGION: 51% Hindu, 31% Christian, 16% Muslim.
TIME: GMT + 4.
ELECTRICITY: 220/240 volts AC, 50Hz. UK-type 3-pin plugs are commonly used in hotels.
COMMUNICATIONS: Telephone: IDD is available. Country code: 230. There are no area codes. Outgoing international code: 00. There are a limited number of public telephone booths, mainly at the airport and in major hotels. **Fax:** Most hotels have facilities.
Telex/telegram: Messages can be sent from the Mauritius Telecommunications Service offices at Cassis and Port Louis. There are also public facilities at Overseas Telecoms Services Ltd, Rogers House, President John F Kennedy Street, Port Louis. **Post:** Airmail to Western Europe usually takes five days, four to six weeks by sea. Post office hours: Generally 0900-1100 and 1200-1600 Monday to Friday; 0800-1100 Saturday. **Press:** Of the seven daily newspapers, two are published in Chinese and the remainder in French and English. *L'Express* and *Le Mauricien* have the highest circulation.
BBC World Service and Voice of America frequencies: From time to time these change. See the section *How to Use this Book* for more information.
BBC:

MHz	21.47	11.94	6.190	3.255

Voice of America:

MHz	21.49	15.60	9.525	6.035

PASSPORT/VISA

Regulations and requirements may be subject to change at short notice, and you are advised to contact the appropriate diplomatic or consular authority before finalising travel arrangements. Details of these may be found at the head of this country's entry. Any numbers in the chart refer to the footnotes below.

	Passport Required?	Visa Required?	Return Ticket Required?
Full British	Yes	No	Yes
BVP	Not valid	-	-
Australian	Yes	No	Yes
Canadian	Yes	No	Yes
USA	Yes	No	Yes
Other EU (As of 31/12/94)	Yes	No	Yes
Japanese	Yes	No	Yes

PASSPORTS: Required by all. The passport has to be valid for at least six months.
British Visitors Passport: Not acceptable.
VISAS: Required by all except:
(a) nationals referred to in the chart above;
(b) nationals of Commonwealth countries for stays of up to 3 months (except nationals of Sri Lanka, India, Pakistan, Nepal and Bangladesh who *do* require a visa);
(c) nationals of Austria, Bahrain, Cyprus, Finland, Iceland, Israel, Kuwait, Monaco, Norway, Qatar, San Marino, Saudi Arabia, Sweden, Switzerland, Tunisia, Turkey, United Arab Emirates and Vatican City for stays of up to 3 months;
(d) nationals of Albania, Bulgaria, CIS, the Comores, Czech Republic, Fiji, Hungary, Madagascar, Poland, Romania and Slovak Republic can obtain a visa on arrival for a stay of up to 15 days.
Types of visa: Tourist and Business; both are obtainable free of charge. Visas are not required by passengers in transit providing they continue their journey to a third country within 72 hours.
Validity: Tourist and Business visas are normally valid for up to 3 months. Applications for extension should be made to the relevant authority (see below).
Application to: Consulate (or Consular section at Embassy or High Commission). For addresses, see top of entry.
Application requirements: (a) Valid passport. (b) Passport-size photo. (c) Proof of means of support during stay.
Working days required: Varies according to nationality of applicant.
Temporary residence: Residence permits are issued by the Passport and Immigration Officer, Passport and

Immigration Office, Line Barracks, Port Louis. Work permits are necessary for those taking up employment.

MONEY

Currency: Mauritian Rupee (MRe) = 100 cents. Notes are in denominations of MRe1000, 500, 200, 100, 50, 20, 10 and 5. Coins are in denominations of MRe5 and 1, and 50, 25, 10, 5, 2 and 1 cents.
Credit cards: Access/Mastercard, Visa, Diners Club and American Express are widely accepted. Check with your credit card company for details of merchant acceptability and other services which may be available.
Travellers cheques: May be exchanged at banks, hotels and authorised dealers.
Exchange rate indicators: The following figures are included as a guide to the movements of the Mauritian Rupee against Sterling and the US Dollar:

Date:	Oct '92	Sep '93	Jan '94	Jan '95
£1.00=	26.97	27.54	27.35	28.24
$1.00=	15.73	18.03	18.49	18.05

Currency restrictions: Import of foreign currency is unlimited, subject to declaration, whilst export is limited to the amount declared on import. Import of local currency is limited to MRe700, export to MRe350.
Banking hours: 0930-1430 Monday to Friday, 0930-1130 Saturday (except for Bank of Mauritius).

DUTY FREE

The following goods may be imported into Mauritius by persons over 16 years of age without incurring customs duty:
250g of tobacco products; 2 litres of wine, ale or beer and 1 litre of spirits; 250ml of eau de toilette and up to 100ml of perfume for personal use.

PUBLIC HOLIDAYS

Jan 1-2 '95 New Year. **Jan 30** Chinese Spring Festival. **Mar 3** Eid al-Fitr (End of Ramadam). **Mar 12** Independence Day. **Apr 11** Ougadi. **Apr 14** Good Friday. **May 1** Labour Day. **Aug 15** Assumption. **Nov 1** All Saints' Day. **Nov 3** Divali. **Dec 25** Christmas Day. **Jan 1-2 '96** New Year. **Feb 22** Eid al-Fitr (End of Ramadan). **Mar 12** Independence Day. **Apr 5** Good Friday. **Apr *Ougadi.
Note: [*] Enquire at the Tourist Office for exact date. (a) There is a diversity of cultures in Mauritius, each with its own holidays. (b) Muslim festivals are timed according to local sightings of various phases of the Moon and the dates given above are approximations. During the lunar month of Ramadan that precedes Eid al-Fitr, Muslims fast during the day and feast at night and normal business patterns may be interrupted. Some disruption may continue into Eid al-Fitr itself. Eid al-Fitr and Eid al-Adha may last anything from two to ten days, depending on the town or region. For more information, see the section *World of Islam* at the back of the book. (c) Hindu and Chinese festivals are declared according to local astronomical observations and it is often only possible to forecast the approximate time of their occurrence.

HEALTH

Regulations and requirements may be subject to change at short notice, and you are advised to contact your doctor well in advance of your intended date of departure. Any numbers in the chart refer to the footnotes below.

	Special Precautions?	Certificate Required?
Yellow Fever	No	1
Cholera	No	No
Typhoid & Polio	No	-
Malaria	2	-
Food & Drink	3	-

[1]: A yellow fever vaccination certificate is required of travellers over one year of age arriving from infected areas. The Mauritius government considers those countries and areas classified as yellow fever endemic to be infected.
[2]: Malaria risk, exclusively in the benign *vivax* form, exists throughout the year in northern rural areas apart from Rodrigues Island.
[3]: Water used for drinking should have first been boiled or otherwise sterilised. Bottled water is readily available. Milk is unpasteurised and should be boiled. Powdered or tinned milk is available and is advised, but make sure that it is reconstituted with pure water. Avoid dairy products which are likely to have been made from unboiled milk. Vegetables should be cooked and fruit peeled. *Bilharzia* (schistosomiasis) is present. Avoid swimming and paddling in fresh water. Swimming pools which are well-chlorinated and maintained are safe.
Health care: Public medical facilities are numerous and of a high standard and there are several private clinics. All treatment at state-run hospitals is free for Mauritians and certain minor treatment may be free for visitors (check with Embassy or High Commission). Nonetheless, health insurance is advised.

TRAVEL - International

AIR: The national airline of Mauritius is *Air Mauritius (MK).*
Approximate flight time: From London to Mauritius is 11 hours 30 minutes (nonstop).
International airport: *Mauritius (MRU)* (Sir Seewoosagur Ramgoolam) is 48km (30 miles) southeast of Port Louis (travel time – 40 minutes). Airport facilities include duty-free shopping, banking facilities, snack bar, post office, shops and car hire (*Avis, Europcar* and *Hertz*). There are taxi services to the city.
Departure tax: MRe100. Passengers transiting within 48 hours and children under two years of age are exempt.
SEA: Port Louis is the main port. It is primarily commercial (sugar exports, general imports) but there is a limited passenger service to Réunion and Rodrigues Island.

TRAVEL - Internal

AIR: *Air Mauritius* operates daily flights connecting Plaisance Airport and Rodrigues Island.
SEA: Regular sailings go to Rodrigues Island from Port Louis. Contact *Rogers & Co,* PO Box 60, President John F Kennedy Street, Port Louis. Tel: 208 6801. Telex: 4312.
ROAD: There is a good network of paved roads covering the island. Traffic drives on the left. **Bus:** There are excellent and numerous bus services to all parts of the island. **Taxi:** These have white registration plates with black figures. Taxis are metered. Taxi drivers do not expect a tip. **Car hire:** There are numerous car-hire firms.
Documentation: International Driving Permit recommended, although a foreign licence is accepted. A temporary driving licence is available from local authorities on presentation of a valid British or Northern Ireland driving licence.
URBAN: Bus and taxi services are available in urban areas.
JOURNEY TIMES: The following chart gives approximate journey times (in hours and minutes) from Port Louis to other major cities/towns in Mauritius.

	Road
Curepipe	0.20
Plaisance	1.00
Grand Bay	0.30
St Geran	1.00
Touessrok	1.00
Souillac	1.00

ACCOMMODATION

There is an abundance of hotels throughout the island and a number of smaller family holiday bungalows. From June to September and during the Christmas season, reservations should be made in advance. For more information, contact the Tourist Office at the address above or the Association des Hôteliers et Restaurateurs Ile Maurice, Grand Bay. Tel: 263 8971. Fax: 263 7907.

RESORTS & EXCURSIONS

Port Louis: Capital and main port of Mauritius, the city was founded by the French Governor, Mahé de Labourdonnais, in 1736. The harbour is sheltered by a semi-circle of mountains. The city has plenty of character, and in some quarters, signs of its past elegance are still evident. Off the main square, the palm-lined *Place d'Armes,* there are some particularly fine French colonial buildings, especially *Government House* (18th century) and the *Municipal Theatre,* built around the same time. There are two cathedrals, Protestant and Catholic, a fine *Supreme Court Building,* some 18th-century barracks and the *Natural History Museum* (exhibiting Mauritius's most famous bird, the extinct Dodo). On the outskirts of the city, at the foot of the mountains, is the *Champ de Mars,* originally laid out by the French for military parades, and now a race-course. The best views of the race-course, city and harbour are from a splendid boulevard called *Edward VII Avenue,* and from *Fort Adelaide,* a citadel fortified in the time of William IV. South of Port Louis is *Le Reduit,* the French colonial residence of the President of Mauritius, set in magnificent gardens. Other places of interest include the *Jummah Mosque* in Royal Street and the *Chinese Pagoda.*
Curepipe: The island's main residential town provides good shops and restaurants. Between Curepipe and Vacoas is the spectacular *Trou aux Cerfs,* an extinct crater 85m (280ft) deep and more than 180m (600ft) wide, from the rim of which an extensive view of the island can be seen.
Pamplemousses Gardens: The gardens are known to naturalists throughout the world for their large collection of indigenous and exotic plants, including the *Giant Victoria Regia* lily and many species of palm trees. Of particular interest is the talipot palm, which is said to flower once every 100 years and then die. There are also tortoises here, some of them over 100 years old.
Rochester Falls: Water cascades over spectacular rock formations. Spectacular joints have been formed by the contraction of lava due to sudden cooling. The falls are near **Souillac** and can be reached by a road which crosses a sugar plantation that is open to visitors.
Grand Bassin: Within a short distance of *Mare Longue* and resting in the crater of an extinct volcano, this is one of the island's two natural lakes. It is a place of pilgrimage for a large number of Mauritians of the Hindu faith.
Plaine Champagne: The highest part of the central plateau (740m/2430ft), from where there is a superb view of the *Rivière Noire Mountains* and the sea lining the horizon. The forest-clad slopes of Rivière Noire contain some fine specimens of indigenous timber and interesting plants peculiar to the island. For the keen birdwatcher, the mountains are the habitat of most of the remaining indigenous species.
Chamarel: A twisting tarred road leads from *Case Noyale* village to Chamarel. This is a mound of undulating land of contrasting layers of colour, and the patches of blue, green, red and yellow earth are believed to be the result of weathering. The nearby *Chamarel Waterfall* emerges from the moors and primeval vegetation and is very beautiful.
Casela Bird Park: This park, set in the district of Rivière Noire, stretches over 20 acres of land and contains more than 140 varieties, amounting to 2500 birds. Specimens from the five continents may be seen there, but the main attraction is the Mauritian Pink Pigeon, which is one of the rarest birds in the world. Other attractions are the fish ponds, tortoises, monkeys, orchids (seasonal), and the scenery which has a peaceful atmosphere created by the trees, streams and small cascades.
Aquarium: Facing the calm water of the lagoon between *Pointe aux Piments* and *Trou aux Biches* is the Aquarium populated by 200 species of fish, invertebrates, live coral and sponges, all originating from the waters around the island. An open-circuit sea-water cycle of one million litres runs through the 36 tanks everyday. The Aquarium offers a unique opportunity to admire the colourful treasures of the Indian Ocean.
La Vanille Crocodile Park: Near *Rivière des Anguilles,* in the wild south, this is a farm breeding Nile crocodiles imported from Madagascar. The site offers a vast park with a nature walk through luxuriant forest studded with freshwater springs. A small zoo of animals found in the wild in Mauritius is also located here.
Domaine des Grands Bois: On the 2000 acres of this magnificent park visitors can watch the rich fauna in a lush exotic setting. Ebony, eucalyptus, palm trees and wild orchids provide the backdrop for stags, deer, monkeys and other wildlife.
Domaine Les Pailles: This nature park nestling at the foot of a mountain range covers an area of 3000 acres. Among the attractions are a replica of a sugar mill and an old rum distillery as well as interesting animal life. Drives through the park in Land-Rovers or horse-drawn carriges are also possible.

Beaches

Tamarin: Lying in the shadow of the Rivière Mountains, Tamarin has a fine lagoon which is split in two by the Rivière Noire estuary. The bathing at this point is a big attraction and amenities are provided for exciting surfing in the big ocean swells.
Grand Baie: The northern coastline beyond *Baie du Tombeau* has many delightful beaches: *Pointe aux Piments,* famous for its underwater scenery; *Trou aux Biches,* with its fringe of *filaos* (casuarina) and coconut palms and its splendid Hindu temple; then further up the coast *Choisy,* one of the most popular beaches on the island, offering facilities for safe bathing, sailing, windsurfing and water-skiing; and finally the coastline curves into Grand Baie itself, the main centre for yachting, water-skiing, windsurfing and many other sports.
Péreybère: This delightful little cove is midway on the coast road between Grand Baie and Cap Malheureux. The deep clear, blue water makes it one of the very best bathing places on the whole island.
Cap Malheureux: This is a fishing village in the extreme north with a magnificent view of *Flat Island, Round Island* and *Gunner's Quoin,* islands of volcanic origin, rising from the sparkling light-green sea.
Grand Gaube: Further along the coast is another charming fishing village where fishermen have earned a well-deserved reputation for their skill in the making of sailing craft and of deep-sea fishing.

Paradise Cove is the ultimate in intimate hideaways.

Superbly located in ten acres of unspoilt landscape, this private and secluded cove is the ideal place to relax and enjoy the peace and tranquillity or explore the private setting of the small beaches.

• This superb hotel has 64 air-conditioned rooms, all sea-facing with terraces or balconies giving direct access to the beach. These beautiful rooms are superbly appointed with mini-bars, TVs including video channels, IDD telephones and bathrooms with separate showers. There are special facilities for children.

• Our two restaurants, beach bar and poolside bar offer a choice of formal and informal dining with the emphasis on fresh produce and seafood.

• Guests can enjoy a vast range of sporting activities free of charge including water-skiing, glass-bottom boat, snorkelling, kayaks, tennis, archery, volleyball, mountain bikes and kite-flying. Deep-sea fishing, cruising aboard the hotel's catamaran and scuba diving (CMAS) can also be arranged for a nominal fee.

• Discover the cultural aspects of our magical island through our nightly entertainment; from the evocative traditional dance and music of the Séga, to the graciousness of the Indian classical dance.

Attention to detail makes staying at Paradise Cove an unforgettable experience.

PARADISE COVE HOTEL, ANSE LA RAIE, MAURITIUS. TEL: (230) 262 7983. FAX: (230) 262 7736.

Roches Noires/Poste Lafayette: These are both favoured seaside resorts, especially in the hotter months, because of the fresh prevailing winds that blow almost all the year round from the sea.
Belle Mare: A beautiful white sandy beach with fine bathing. The coast, with its white sweep of sands at *Palmar* and *Trou d'Eau Douce,* stretches out lazily to **Grand Port**, a quaint little village by the sea. There the beach narrows and the road follows the coastline closely to **Mahébourg**. *Pointe d'Esny*, the adjoining white sandy beach with its string of bungalows, leads to Blue Bay.
Blue Bay: In a semi-circle of *filao* trees lies one of the finest bathing spots on the island. Situated on the southeast coast, not far from Mahébourg, Blue Bay offers a fine stretch of white sandy beach, and a deep, clear, light-blue bathing pool. There is also scope for yachting and windsurfing.

SOCIAL PROFILE

FOOD & DRINK: Waiter service is normal in restaurants and bars. Standards of cuisine, whether French, Creole, Indian, Chinese or English, are generally very high but fruit, meat, vegetables and even fresh seafood are often in short supply and restaurants must often depend on imports. Specialities include venison (in season), *camarons* (freshwater prawns) in hot sauces, octopus, creole fish, fresh pineapple with chilli sauce, and rice with curry.
Drink: Rum and beer are staple beverages for Mauritians but there is good imported wine, mineral water, *alouda* (almond drink) and fresh coconut milk.
NIGHTLIFE: In some towns and in Grand Bay there are discotheques and nightclubs with music and dancing. Rivière Noire is a Creole fishermen's district where *sega* dancing is especially lively on Saturday nights. *Sega* troupes give performances at most hotels. Gamblers are lavishly catered for; casinos in the island's hotels are amongst the island's attractions.
SHOPPING: The Central Market in Port Louis is full of beautifully displayed goods, including fruit, vegetables, spices, fish, meat and handicrafts. Island crafts include jewellery, Chinese and Indian jade, silks, basketry and pottery. There is no duty on textile products. Shop signs may be in English, French or Chinese. **Shopping hours:** *Port Louis:* 0900-1700 Monday to Friday, 0900-1200 Saturday. *Curepipe, Rose Hill, Quatre Bornes:* 0900-1800 Monday to Wednesday, Friday and Saturday; 0900-1200

Thursday and Sunday.
SPORT: Swimming: Beaches, lagoons and inlets around the coast offer plenty of opportunity for safe bathing (see above under *Resorts & Excursions*), supplemented by hotel swimming pools. **Skindiving:** Grand Baie, north of Pamplemousses Gardens, is a popular beach for skindiving. **Fishing:** There is good coastal and inland fishing around the island. **Horseracing:** The Hippodrome at the Champ de Mars has meetings at the weekends between May and October.
SPECIAL EVENTS: With origins in three continents and three major religions there is a great diversity of religious and cultural festivals. The following is only a selection. For a complete list and for exact dates of the following in 1995, enquire at the Government Tourist Office.
Apr '95 *Cavadee, Sword Climbing Ceremony,* Bambous, Médine. **May** *Fire Walking Ceremony,* Rose Hill. **Aug 30** *Ganesh Chaturthi.* **Sep** *Mid-Autumn Festival.* **Oct 23** *Divali.*
SOCIAL CONVENTIONS: Handshaking is the customary form of greeting. Visitors should respect the traditions of their hosts, particularly when visiting a private house. The type of hospitality the visitor receives is determined by the religion and social customs of the host, which are closely related. It is appropriate to give a gift as a small token of appreciation if invited for a meal. Dress is normally informal although men will need to wear a suit for particularly formal occasions. **Tipping:** 10% is usual in most hotels and restaurants.

BUSINESS PROFILE

ECONOMY: Until recently, the Mauritian economy was based on the production and export of sugar. The only other cash crops of any significance are tobacco and tea. During the late 1970s, the economy experienced considerable difficulties owing to a combination of poor sugar harvests and low world prices for the commodity, aggravated by the general effects of world recession. Earlier in the decade, Mauritius had established an Export Processing Zone, which produced manufactured goods specifically for export, using large quantities of raw materials by attracting foreign investment into the country on favourable terms. With the sugar price failing to recover in the 1980s, this strategy began to pay off as Mauritius' balance of payments improved. Textiles are the key industry in the Export Processing Zone, although

there has been recent diversification into other manufactured goods such as consumer electronics and electrical devices. France, the United States, Hong Kong, the UK and South Africa are the country's largest trading partners. The Government's latest initiative proposes the establishment of offshore financial and banking facilities on the island. As there is hardly a small island nation worldwide which does not try to do the same, it remains to be seen how Mauritius fares against the myriad competition. Mauritius is a member of the Indian Ocean Commission, which seeks to promote regional economic cooperation.
BUSINESS: Safari suits are often worn in business circles. Appointments should be made. English is widely understood in the business community. **Office hours:** 0900-1600 Monday to Friday; 0900-1200 Saturday (some offices only).
COMMERCIAL INFORMATION: The following organisation can offer advice: Mauritius Chamber of Commerce and Industry, 3 Royal Street, Port Louis. Tel: 208 3301. Fax: 208 0076. Telex: 4277.

CLIMATE

Warm coastal climate (particularly January to April). Temperatures are slightly lower with more rain inland on the plateau around Curepipe. Tropical storms are likely in the cyclone season which runs from December to March. Sea breezes blow all year, especially on the east coast.

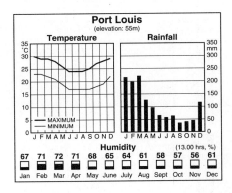

Mexico

□ *international airport*

1000km

500mis

Location: Southern North America.

Fondo Nacional de Fomento al Turismo (FONATUR)
17th Floor, Insurgentes Sur 800, Colonia del Valle,
03100 México DF, Mexico
Tel: (5) 687 2697. Telex: 1777636.

Embassy of the United Mexican States
42 Hertford Street, Mayfair, London W1Y 7TF
Tel: (0171) 499 8586. Fax: (0171) 495 4035.

Consular Section of the Embassy of the United Mexican States
8 Halkin Street, London SW1X 7DW
Tel: (0171) 235 6393. Fax: (0171) 235 5480 (visa information). Opening hours: 0930-1300 and 1500-1730 Monday to Friday (0900-1400 Monday to Friday during August); recorded information outside these hours.

Mexican Ministry of Tourism
3rd Floor, 60-61 Trafalgar Square, London WC2N 5DS
Tel: (0171) 734 1058. Opening hours: 1000-1300 and 1500-1730 Monday to Friday.

British Embassy
Apartado 96 bis, Río Lerma 71, Colonia Cuauhtémoc, 06500 México DF, Mexico
Tel: (5) 207 2089 or 207 2149 or 207 2449 or 207 2509. Fax: (5) 207 7672. Telex: 1773093 (a/b UKEMME).
Consulates in: Mexico City, Acapulco, Ciudad Juárez, Guadalajara, Mérida, Monterrey, Tampico and Veracruz.

Embassy of the United Mexican States
1911 Pennsylvania Avenue, NW, Washington, DC 20006
Tel: (202) 728 1600. Fax: (202) 728 1659.

Mexican Government Tourism Office
Suite 10002, 405 Park Avenue, New York, NY 10022
Tel: (212) 755 7261 or 838 2949.
Offices also in: Chicago, Houston, Los Angeles, Miami and Washington, DC.

Embassy of the United States of America
Paseo de la Reforma 305, Colonia Cuauhtémoc, 06500 México DF, Mexico
Tel: (5) 211 0042. Fax: (5) 511 9980 or 208 3373.
Consulates in: Ciudad Juárez, Guadalajara, Monterrey, Tijuana, Hermosillo, Matamoros, Mazatlán, Mérida and Nuevo Larido.

Embassy of the United Mexican States
Suite 1800, 130 Albert Street, Ottawa, Ontario K1P 5G4
Tel: (613) 233 8988 or 233 9272 or 233 9917. Fax: (613) 235 9123.
Consulates in: Calgary, Montréal, Québec, Toronto and Vancouver.

Mexican Government Tourism Office
Suite 1801, 2 Bloor Street West, Toronto, Ontario M4W 3E2
Tel: (416) 925 0704. Fax: (416) 925 6061.
Office also in: Montréal.

Canadian Embassy
Apartado Postal 105-05, Calle Schiller 529 (Rincon del Bosque), Colonia Polanco, 11560 México DF, Mexico
Tel: (5) 724 7900. Fax: (5) 724 7980 (administration) or

724 7981 (public affairs) or 724 7982 (trade). Telex: 1771191.
Consulates in: Acapulco, Cancún, Guadalajara, Mazatlán, Monterry, Oaxaca, Puerto Vallarta and Tijuana.

AREA: 1,958,201 sq km (756,066 sq miles).
POPULATION: 85,000,000 (1993).
POPULATION DENSITY: 41.5 per sq km.
CAPITAL: Mexico City. **Population:** 18,000,000 (1993).
GEOGRAPHY: Mexico is at the southern extremity of North America and is bounded in the north by the USA, northwest by the Gulf of California, west by the Pacific, south by Guatemala and Belize, and east by the Gulf of Mexico and the Caribbean. Mexico's geographical features range from swamp to desert, and from tropical lowland jungle to high alpine vegetation. Over half the country has an altitude above 1000m (3300ft). The central land mass is a plateau flanked by ranges of mountains to the east and west that lie roughly parallel to the coast. The northern area of this plateau is arid and thinly populated, and occupies 40% of the total area of Mexico. The southern area is crossed by a range of volcanic mountains running from Cape Corrientes in the west through the Valley of Mexico to Veracruz in the east, and includes the magnificent volcanoes of Orizaba, Popocatépetl, Ixtaccíhuatl, Nevado de Toluca, Matlalcueyetl and Cofre de Perote. This is the heart of Mexico and where almost half of the population lives. To the south the land falls away to the sparsely populated Isthmus of Tehuantepec whose slopes and flatlands support both commercial and subsistence agriculture. In the east the Gulf Coast and the Yucatán peninsula are flat and receive over 75% of Mexico's rain. The most productive agricultural region in Mexico is the northwest, while the Gulf Coast produces most of Mexico's oil and sulphur. Along the northwest coast, opposite the peninsula of Baja California, and to the southeast along the coast of Bahía de Campeche and the Yucatán peninsula, the lowlands are swampy with coastal lagoons.
LANGUAGE: Spanish is the official language. English is widely spoken.
RELIGION: 97% Roman Catholic.
TIME: Mexico spans three different time zones:
South, Central and Eastern Mexico: GMT - 6 (Central Standard Time).
Nayarit, Sonora, Sinaloa and Baja California Sur: GMT - 7 (Mountain Time).
Baja California Norte (Pacific Time): GMT - 8 (GMT - 7 from first Sunday in April to Saturday before last Sunday in October).
Daylight saving is operated during summer months; clocks are put forward by one hour.
ELECTRICITY: 110 volts AC, 60Hz. US 2-pin (flat) plugs are usual.
COMMUNICATIONS: Telephone: IDD is available. Country code: 52. Outgoing international code: 98. Long-distance calls are very expensive. **Fax:** Major hotels have facilities. **Telex/telegram:** International telex facilities are available at a number of hotels in Mexico City and in Acapulco, Chihuahua, Guadalajara, Mérida, Monterrey, Puebla, Tampico and Veracruz. The telegraphic system is run by *Telegrafos Nacionales* and telegrams should be handed in to their offices. In Mexico the main office for international telegrams is at Balderas y Colón, México 1 DF. **Post:** Airmail to Europe takes about six days. Surface mail is slow. Within the capital there is an immediate delivery *(Entrega Inmediata)* service, which usually takes two or three days. **Press:** The major daily newspapers published in Spanish are *Excélsior, La Universal, La Journada, Uno Más Uno* and *El Día.* The English-language daily is *The News.*
BBC World Service and Voice of America frequencies: From time to time these change. See the section *How to Use this Book* for more information.
BBC:

MHz	17.84	15.22	9.590	5.975
Voice of America:				
MHz	15.20	11.91	9.775	6.130

Timatic

Health	
GALILEO/WORLDSPAN:	**TI-DFT/MEX/HE**
SABRE:	**TIDFT/MEX/HE**

Visa	
GALILEO/WORLDSPAN:	**TI-DFT/MEX/VI**
SABRE:	**TIDFT/MEX/VI**

For more information on Timatic codes refer to Contents.

PASSPORT/VISA

Regulations and requirements may be subject to change at short notice, and you are advised to contact the appropriate diplomatic or consular authority before finalising travel arrangements. Details of these may be found at the head of this country's entry. Any numbers in the chart refer to the footnotes below.

	Passport Required?	Visa Required?	Return Ticket Required?
Full British	Yes	No/3	No
BVP	Not valid	-	-
Australian	Yes	2/3	No
Canadian	No/1	2/3	No
USA	No/1	2/3	No
Other EU (As of 31/12/94)	Yes	2/3	No
Japanese	No/1	2/3	No

Note: No brief account of the complex Mexican Passport/Visa regulations is likely to be fully successful. Readers are advised to use the following for general guidance, but to check on the requirements that specifically apply to them with the appropriate Consulate (or Consular section at Embassy). Non-compliance with visa regulations will result in fines and transportation (at the carrier's expense) to the visitor's country of origin.
PASSPORTS: Valid passport required by all except **[1]** US, Japanese and Canadian citizens who can present a birth certificate or other acceptable national ID with a photograph.
British Visitors Passport: Not accepted.
Note: Minors (ie under 18 years of age) of any nationality travelling with one parent or *unaccompanied* to Mexico require both parents' consent certified by a public notary or an authorisation signed by the parents at the Mexican Consulate in person, identifying themselves with their passports. It is necessary that the non-travelling parents sign or provide such authorisation along with 2 passport-size photos of their child.
TOURIST CARDS: Available *only* to people entering Mexico on holiday, for reasons of health, or to engage in scientific, artistic or sporting activities which are neither remunerative nor lucrative. The card is a single-entry document and is issued free of charge. *The Consular office retains the right to request further evidence of the applicant's intention to visit Mexico as a tourist whenever such intention has not been established to the Consul's satisfaction. The same right applies with regard to evidence of the applicant's financial means to sustain him/herself while in Mexico.*
Note: (a) Visitors travelling without minors (see note above) and eligible for Tourist Cards (see below) can be issued with Tourist Cards on board the plane or at the point of entry in Mexico. (b) *Tourist Cards must be kept by the visitor during the entire length of stay as they will have to be presented and stamped on leaving.*
Nationals of the following countries are eligible for a Tourist Card:
(a) **[2]** EU countries for stays of up to 6 months (except nationals of France who *do* need a visa);
(b) **[2]** Australia, Canada, Japan and the USA for stays of up to 6 months;
(c) Argentina, Austria, Chile, Costa Rica, Finland, Iceland, Israel, South Korea, Liechtenstein, Monaco, New Zealand, Norway, San Marino, Singapore, Sweden, Switzerland, Uruguay for stays of up to 6 months;
(d) Venezuela for stays of up to 30 days.
For requirements and regulations relevant to other nationalities, contact the Mexican Embassy.
Application to: Consulate (or Consular section at Embassy). For addresses, see top of entry.
Application requirements: *Tourist Cards:* (a) Passport with a minimum of 6 months' validity. (b) If applying by post, a covering letter with date of entry and departure. (c) Postal applications have to be accompanied by a stamped, self-addressed envelope for recorded or registered delivery. (d) International Certificate of Vaccination against Cholera is required for travellers arriving within 2 weeks of visiting an infected area.
In some cases a personal application may be required.
Cost: Tourist Cards are issued free of charge.
VISAS: Available for all except holders of a Tourist Card or visa-replacing document. Applications should be accompanied by submission of the following to the Embassy: (a) Passport with minimum of 6 months' validity. (b) Application form. (c) 1 passport-size photo. (d) Original return ticket. (e) Fee (payable in cash only). (f) Proof of sufficient funds to cover length of stay. (g) Postal applications have to be accompanied by a stamped, self-addressed envelope for recorded or registered delivery. (h) If applying by post, a covering

MEXICO

Someone thought about your trip to Mexico long before you did.
American Express® is here to help.

American Express can provide you with the best travel arrangements in Mexico's most fascinating destinations. Contact us for programs of the highest quality and value to best suit your needs:

1. Costumized itineraries for individuals or groups.
2. Ground services.
3. Excursions, Sightseeing Tours and City Packages.
4. Meetings and Conventions.
5. Special affinity groups.
6. Incentive groups.

American Express Destination Services has offices in all Mexico's key cities and resorts, including:
Mexico City, Acapulco, Cancun, Ixtapa and Puerto Vallarta.

For further information please call:
Mexico City
Phone: (525) 326-28-31
Fax: (525) 611-11-13

letter with date of entry and departure.
In some cases a personal application may be required.
Notes: (a) **[3]** If intending to undertake business or work of a technical nature, normal visa regulations *do not* apply. It may be necessary to obtain a Business Card or a Technician Card. It is vital to contact the local Mexican consular representative well in advance of intended date of departure in order to secure the necessary authorisation (for addresses, see top of entry).
(b) Nationals of Afghanistan, Bangladesh, Cambodia, China, Iraq, Iran, Jordan, North Korea, Lebanon, Libya, Pakistan, Sri Lanka, Syria, Taiwan (China), Turkey and Vietnam will only be issued a visa if the Home Office in Mexico grants a permit. This process takes approximately 2-3 weeks.
Application to: Consulate (or Consular section at Embassy). For addresses, see top of entry.
Cost: Visa prices vary according to the exchange rate.
Working days required: In person – 2 days; by post – 1 week: Applications should not be made more than 3 months before date of departure.
Temporary residence: Apply to Mexican Embassy.

MONEY

Currency: Nuevo Peso (N$) = 100 cents. Notes are in denominations of N$100, 50, 20 and 10. Coins are in denominations of N$10, 5, 2 and 1, and 50, 20, 10 and 5 cents.
Note: The Nuevo Peso was introduced on January 1, 1993. It is equivalent to 1000 former Pesos. There was a dual exchange rate system in effect between December 1982 and November 1991.
Currency exchange: The exchange rate of the Mexican Peso against Sterling and other hard currencies has, in recent years, been subject to considerable fluctuation (see table below).
Credit cards: American Express, Diners Club, Visa and Access/Mastercard are widely accepted. Check with your credit card company for details of merchant acceptability and other services which may be available.
Travellers cheques: Travellers cheques or letters of credit in US Dollars issued by well-known banks or travel organisations are readily negotiable in banks and hotels. Sterling travellers cheques are not readily negotiable except at head offices of banks in the capital, and may be subject to a considerable discount.

Exchange rate indicators: The following figures are included as a guide to the movements of the Mexican Peso against Sterling and the US Dollar (free-market rates). The figures after Oct 1992 refer to the Nuevo Peso introduced in January 1993:

Date:	Oct '92	Sep '93	Jan '94	Jan '95
£1.00=	4922	4.76	4.60	7.71
$1.00=	101	3.12	3.11	4.92

Currency restrictions: Local currency may be imported up to N$5000; the import of foreign currency is unlimited provided declared. Foreign currency may be exported up to the amount imported and declared; local currency may be exported up to N$5000. The export of gold coins is prohibited.
Banking hours: 0900-1330 Monday to Friday; some banks are open Saturday afternoon.

DUTY FREE

The following goods may be imported into Mexico by persons over 18 years of age without incurring customs duty:
400 cigarettes or 50 cigars or 250g of pipe tobacco; 3 litres of wine or spirits; a reasonable amount of perfume or eau de toilette; 1 stills camera, 1 portable film or video camera and up to 12 unexposed rolls of film or video cassettes for each camera; a reasonable amount of personal and electrical goods; various objects with the value of up to US$300 or equivalent.

PUBLIC HOLIDAYS

Jan 1 '95 New Year's Day. **Feb 5** Constitution Day. **Mar 21** Birth of Benito Juaréz. **Apr 14-17** Easter. **May 1** Labour Day. **May 5** *Anniversary of Battle of Puebla. **Sep 16** Independence Day. **Oct 12** Discovery of America. **Nov 1** *All Saints' Day. **Nov 2** *All Souls' Day. **Nov 20** Anniversary of the Mexican Revolution of 1910. **Dec 12** *Day of Our Lady of Guadalupe. **Dec 25** Christmas. **Jan 1 '96** New Year's Day. **Feb 5** Constitution Day. **Mar 21** Birth of Benito Juárez. **Apr 5-8** Easter.
Note: (a) [*] Not official holidays, but widely celebrated.
(b) In addition there are many local holidays. For details, contact the Mexican Tourist Office.

HEALTH

Regulations and requirements may be subject to change at short notice, and you are advised to contact your doctor well in advance of your intended date of departure. Any numbers in the chart refer to the footnotes below.

	Special Precautions?	Certificate Required?
Yellow Fever	No	1
Cholera	Yes	2
Typhoid & Polio	Yes	-
Malaria	3	-
Food & Drink	4	-

[1]: Yellow fever vaccination certificate is required from travellers over six months of age arriving from infected areas.
[2]: An International Certificate of Vaccination against Cholera is required of all travellers arriving within two weeks of having visited an infected area. Cholera is a serious risk in this country and precautions are essential. Up-to-date advice should be sought before deciding whether these precautions should include vaccination, as medical opinion is divided over its effectiveness. See the *Health* section at the back of the book.
[3]: Malaria risk, predominantly in the benign *vivax* form, exists in rural areas of the following states (in decreasing order of importance): Oaxaca, Chiapas, Guerrero, Campeche, Quintana Roo, Sinaloa, Michoacán, Nayarit, Colima and Tabasco. Foci of the *falciparum* strain exist mainly in Chiapas.
[4]: Water supplied in bottles and from taps marked 'drinking/sterilised water' in hotels can be drunk without precautions. All other water should be regarded as being potentially contaminated. Water used for drinking, brushing teeth or making ice should have first been boiled or otherwise sterilised. Milk in major cities, hotels and resorts is pasteurised. Otherwise, milk is unpasteurised and should first be boiled. Powdered or tinned milk is available and is advised, but make sure that it is reconstituted with pure water. Avoid dairy products which are likely to have been made from unboiled milk. Only eat well-cooked meat and fish, preferably served hot. Pork, salad and mayonnaise may carry increased risk. Vegetables should be cooked and fruit peeled. *Rabies* is present. For those at high risk, vaccination

before arrival should be considered. If you are bitten abroad seek medical advice without delay. For more information consult the *Health* section at the back of the book.

Health care: Health insurance is recommended. Medical facilities are very good and there are both private and state-organised hospitals, doctors, clinics and chemists. Medicines are often available without prescriptions and pharmacists are permitted to diagnose and treat minor ailments. Due to the high altitude of Mexico City, visitors may take some time to acclimatise to the atmosphere, particularly since its geographical location results in an accumulation of smog. The levels of pollution in Mexico City are extremely high, and are considered a health threat, so caution should be taken.

TRAVEL - International

AIR: Mexico's national airlines are *Aerovias de Mexico (AM)* and *Mexicana (MX).*
For free advice on air travel, call the Air Travel Advisory Bureau in the UK on (0171) 636 5000 (London) *or* (0161) 832 2000 (Manchester).

Approximate flight times: From Mexico City to *London* is 10 hours; to *Los Angeles* is 5 hours 20 minutes; to *New York* is 5 hours; to *Singapore* is 22 hours 45 minutes and to *Sydney* is 19 hours.

International airports: *Mexico City (MEX)* (Benito Juárez) is 15km (8 miles) south of the city. Airport facilities include duty-free facilities (0600-2400), restaurants (0700-2400), 24-hour bank/bureau de change, 24-hour bar, 24-hour snack bar, chemist (0500-2200), 24-hour shops, tourist information (0600-2300), 24-hour left luggage, post office (0800-1900), first aid (with vaccinations for cholera and yellow fever available) and car rental *(Avis, Dollar* and *National).* Buses run to the city every 15 minutes from 0600-2200 for a fare of Mex$3 (travel time – 35 minutes). Return is from Camino Real Hotel, Reforma Street from 0600-2200. Metro trains depart to the city every 20 minutes. The airport metro station is 20 minutes walk from the airport terminal. Hotel courtesy coach is available to the Airport Holiday Inn. Taxis are also available for approximately Mex$10 (travel time – 20 minutes).

Guadalajara (GDL) (Miguel Hidalgo) is 20km (12 miles) southeast of the city (travel time – 30 minutes). Airport facilities include restaurant, bar, snack bar, bank, post office and shops. Coaches depart to the city every 10 minutes (0500-2400). Hotel courtesy coaches are available to Camino Real, El Tapatio, Holiday Inn and Sheraton hotels.

Acapulco (ACA) (General Juan N Alvarez) is 26km (16 miles) southeast of the city (travel time – 30 minutes). Airport facilities include restaurant, bank, post office and car hire. Coaches run to the city. Return is from Las Hamacas Hotel. Taxi services are available to the city, with a surcharge after 2200.

Monterrey (MRY) (General Mariano Escobero) is 24km (15 miles) northeast of the city (travel time – 45 minutes). Airport facilities include restaurant, bar, bank, post office, shops and car hire. Coach and taxi services run to the city.

Departure tax: Approximately US$11 for international flights.

SEA: The major cruise ports in Mexico are Cozumel, Acapulco, Tampico, Zihuatanejo/Ixtapa, Manzanillo, Puerto Vallarta and Mazatlán. Regular passenger ships run from the USA, South America and Australia. Principal shipping lines are *Polish Ocean Lines, P&O* and *Fred Olsen Lines.*

RAIL: Railway connections with Mexico can be made from any city in the USA or Canada. All trains are provided with pullman sleepers, restaurant cars, lounge observation and club cars. Most trains are air-conditioned.

ROAD: Main points of entry from the USA are Mexicali from San Diego; Nogales from Phoenix/Tucson; El Paso/Ciudad Juárez from Tucson and Alberquerque; Eagle Pass/Piedras Negras from Del Río, San Angelo and El Paso; Laredo/Nuevo Laredo from Houston, San Antonia and Del Río; and Brownsville/Matamoros from Houston and Galveston. From Guatemala there are two main roads into Mexico. The Pan American Highway crosses into Mexico from Guatemala and continues through Central America and South America.

TRAVEL - Internal

AIR: There is an excellent network of daily scheduled services between principal commercial centres operated by *Aerovias de México* and *Mexicana.* Many of these smaller airports will also have capacity for large planes and some international flights. Flights between Mexico City and Guadalajara take about 55 minutes and Mexico City to Monterrey about 75 minutes.

Departure tax: Approximately US$9 for domestic flights.

SEA: Steamer ferries operate regularly between Mazatlán and La Paz (Baja California) daily; between Guaymas and Santa Rosalia, across the Gulf of California; between La Paz and Topolobampo three or four times weekly; and from Puerto Vallarta to Cabo San Lucas twice-weekly. Some west coast cruises include Pacific ports such as Mazatlán, Puerto Vallarta and Acapulco.

RAIL: Mexico has a good railway network and trains link all the main towns in the country. However, most people travel by bus since it is considerably faster and provides a more extensive service. Children under five travel free, provided they are accompanied by a parent. Children aged 5-11 pay half-fare.

ROAD: Traffic drives on the right. Mexico's road network extends to almost 235,000km (146,000 miles), of which slightly less than half is paved. A toll is charged for use of the expressways, which are managed by *Caminos y Puentes Federales de Ingresos y Servicios Conexos.* Rest areas at toll sites also provide ambulance and breakdown services. An organisation known as 'Angeles Verdes' (Green Angels) provides breakdown assistance to tourists on the highways free of charge except for petrol, oil and spare parts. **Bus:** Mexico is linked by an excellent and very economical bus system. There are first-class and deluxe coaches as well as ordinary buses. Central bus terminals in major cities provide service and information on fares and schedules. **Car hire:** Self-drive cars are available at airports, city centres and resorts. **Documentation:** Foreign driving licence or International Driving Permit accepted. It is suggested that visitors insure their vehicle; there are some short-term policies available at very reasonable rates in Mexico.

URBAN: There is an excellent and cheap metro system in Mexico City with frequent trains and flat fares. However, it is often crowded and some familiarity with the city is necessary to use it successfully. The metro opens at 0500 Monday to Saturday and 0700 Sunday. There is also a small tramway network, and extensive bus and trolleybus services. The latter system has recently been modernised, and also has a flat fare. There is a state-run bus and trolleybus service in Guadalajara, with trolleybuses running in tunnels, and also extensive private bus services. **Taxi:** Four different types of taxi operate in Mexico City. Yellow and white taxis (usually Volkswagens) are metered, as are orange taxis *(Sitio),* which are available at taxi-stands. These charge slightly more, and it is advisable to agree the fare before starting the journey. *Turismo* taxis with English-speaking drivers are available outside main hotels. They are not metered and fares should be agreed before starting journey. *Peseros* (green and white) are shared taxis travelling on fixed routes, for which fares are charged according to the distance travelled. Tipping is not compulsory for any of the taxi services.

JOURNEY TIMES: The following chart gives approximate journey times (in hours and minutes) from Mexico City to other major cities/towns in Mexico.

	Air	Road	Rail
Acapulco	0.35	3.30	-
Cancún	2.15	30.00	-
Oaxaca	0.15	10.00	12.00
Chihuahua	2.15	34.00	40.00
Puerto Vallarta	1.55	14.00	-
Guadalajara	0.55	7.00	12.00
Tijuana	2.45	36.00	-

ACCOMMODATION

HOTELS: The enormous growth of tourism in Mexico is reflected in the wide range of hotels from the modern, elegant and expensive to the clean and modest. There are a variety of chain hotels throughout Mexico as well as 'dude' ranches, thermal spas and resorts that feature specific facilities. Reservations should be confirmed by hotels in writing at the time of booking as hotel tariffs are liable to alteration at any time; it is especially important to make reservations when travelling in the high season. There is a wide range of prices with plenty of choice throughout the country; every hotel is required to display officially approved rate schedules, but the visitor should note that most rates do not include meals. There are also a number of more modest **guest-houses** (*casas de huespedes*). Information can be obtained from the Mexican Hotel and Motel Association, CP 11590, Thiers 83, Colonia Anzures, México DF. Tel: (5) 203 9988 *or* 203 6946. **Grading:** Mexico operates a 5-star grading system similar to that in Europe, with an additional *Gran Turismo* category. All hotels are covered. The criteria for inclusion in each of the six grades are as follows:

Gran Turismo: 108 criteria including central air-conditioning, satellite dish and minimum floor area of 32 sq metres (105 sq ft). Shopping area and additional quality services are also required.

5-star: 96-101 criteria including room service 16 hours a day and minimum floor area of 28 sq metres (92 sq ft). Restaurant, cafeteria, nightclub, commercial areas, good hygiene and security are also required.

4-star: 71-76 criteria including adequate furniture and minimum floor area of 25 sq metres (82 sq ft). Some commercial areas and a good standard of maintenance are also required.

3-star: 47-52 criteria including adequate furniture and minimum floor area of 21.5 sq metres (71 sq ft). Restaurant, cafeteria, ceiling fan and some complimentary service are required.

2-star: 33-37 criteria including adequate furniture and minimum floor area of 19 sq metres (62 sq ft). Standards for hygiene and security should be met. First-aid facilities are required.

1-star: 24-27 criteria including adequate furniture and minimum floor area of 15 sq metres (49 sq ft). Standards for guests' comfort should be met.

CAMPING/CARAVANNING: The national parks in Mexico are officially the only areas where no permits or fees are required for camping and hiking. Camping is allowed anywhere within the park areas. Further information can be obtained from the Ministry of Tourism or the National Park Headquarters, Nezahualcoyotl 109, México 1 DF. Tel: (5) 352 8249. Most camping, however, is outside national parks, the most popular regions being the west coast and Baja California. The western Pacific coast has excellent caravan 'hookups' while Baja California is far more informal and isolated. The number of caravan parks along Mexico's major motorways is growing, and there is no difficulty in locating places to park.

RESORTS & EXCURSIONS

Mexico, rich in reminders of ancient civilisations, is also a modern developing nation. Temples and cathedrals contrast with futuristic buildings, motorways and fully-equipped beach resorts. Mexico City, one of the world's largest cities, has one of the world's largest universities. Elsewhere, elements of the ancient and colonial cultures persist in aspects of rural life. Fetes and festivals are celebrated with enthusiasm, and the markets in towns and villages are lively and colourful.

Mexico City

The capital of Mexico stands at an altitude of 2240m (7350ft) beneath two snow-capped volcanoes, *Popocatépetl* and *Ixtaccíhuatl.* It is a huge rambling city with a distinctly colonial feel. Many of the buildings are in the exuberant Latin American Baroque style. In the centre of town is *The Zócalo.* It was begun in 1573 and

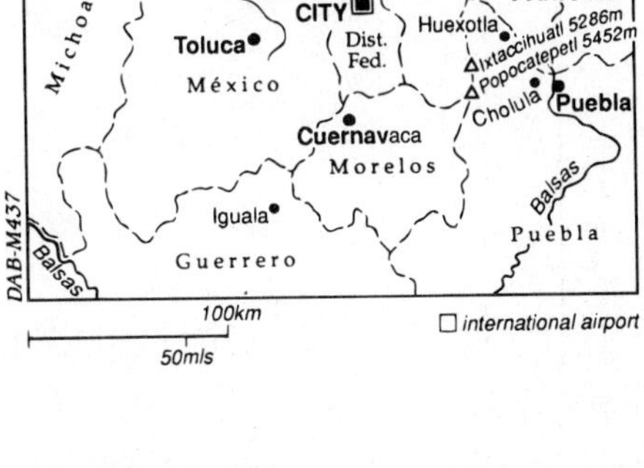

EXPERIENCE THE LUXURY OF MEXICO CITY'S FINEST HOTEL

◆ The Fiesta Americana Reforma Mexico City is located 12 miles, (30 minutes) from Mexico International Airport, on the Paseo de la Reforma, in the business and cultural heart of Mexico City.

◆ The 363 king and 247 double rooms are all equipped with individual climate controls, colour TV with Cablevision, direct line telephones, service-bars, bathrooms with tub and shower.

◆ 20 suites with bedroom and living room, fully furnished dining room, visitors restroom.

◆ Non-smoking floor.

◆ 3 floors dedicated to the up-market traveller with express check-in, concierge service, an exclusive lounge with reading room, evening cocktails, complementary morning newspaper and continental breakfast.

◆ Garage parking, babysitting, beauty shops, purified water, handicapped facilities, wake-up service.

◆ Health club with exercise facilites and sauna.

◆ Restaurants and clubs.

◆ 24-hour room service.

FIESTA AMERICANA
REFOMA MR
H O T E L

For more information contact: Reforma #80, 06600 Mexico, D.F. Tel: (905) 705 1515. Fax: (905) 705 1313.

completed in the 19th century and is enormous. Only the Red Square in Moscow is larger. The *National Palace,* built in 1692 on the ruins of the Palace of Montezuma, is now the office of the President of the Republic. *Plaza de las Tres Culturas* celebrates the three major cultures that have shaped Mexico: there are Aztec ruins, a 17th-century colonial church built in the Baroque style and several fine late 20th-century buildings. The *Basilica of Nuestra Señora De Guadalupe*, a shrine built on a spot where the Virgin is said to have appeared to the Indian Juan Diego in 1531, is a major pilgrimage site. Built in 1976, it has a capacity of 10,000 inside plus another 25,000 outside when the 70 surrounding portals are opened. *Chapultepec Park* is the site of a castle that houses the *National Museum of History* and the *National Museum of Anthropology,* which holds an enormous and absolutely fascinating collection of Pre-Columbian artefacts. The floating gardens of *Xochimilco* are an amazing piece of Aztec engineering. Bands of 'Mariachis' (so-named because 'mariachi' was often used at weddings) ply their trade from small boats. They play a very emotional music form with guitars and trumpets and sentimental singing. The Mariachis themselves are usually dressed in ornate clothes and giant sombreros. It is a good afternoon visit, as is the *Plaza Garibaldi* where musicians from all over Mexico play for the public. The *Polyforum de Siqueiros,* built to an exciting design by David Alfaro Siqueiros, is a huge exhibition centre with plenty of space for dancing and theatrical performances. The *Ciudad Universitaria,* located in *Pedregal Square,* is another fine example of modern Mexican architecture. The complex includes a stadium with capacity for 100,000 spectators.

DAY EXCURSIONS FROM MEXICO CITY:

Teotihuacan, the 'City of the Gods', 48km (30 miles) northeast of Mexico City, was built about 2000 years ago. Here are the *Pyramids of the Sun and Moon*, the Citadel with the *Temple of Quetzacoatl* (the plumed serpent) and the *Palace of Quetzalpapalotl* (the plumed butterfly), all found in a mile-long stretch called the Avenue of the Dead.

Tula, 95km (59 miles) north of Mexico City, is the former capital of the Toltec empire. It is renowned for its *Atlantes*, several high columns depicting warriors, and its attractive squares and flower gardens. Other places of interest include the *Palacio de Cortés* and a 16th-century church.

Cuernavaca, 85km (53 miles) from the capital, is built around two large squares. On one stands the *Palacio de Cortés* (built in 1538), now a museum containing frescoes by Diego Rivera. The Cathedral dates from the 16th century. The town also contains the 18th-century *Borda Gardens* and the Indian market which sells *huaraches* (sandals) and leather goods. Articles made of straw are sold too. **Xochicalco,** 40km (25 miles) south of Cuernavaca, is one of the country's most interesting ceremonial centres, especially noted for its *Building of the Plumed Serpent.*

Tepotzotlán, 43km (27 miles) from the capital, is notable for its Churrigueresque Baroque church, the façade of which is decorated with more than 300 sculptures. The convent, dating from the 16th century, has monumental buttresses. On a hill nearby, there is an Aztec shrine dedicated to the god of feasting and drinking where annually, on September 8, a fete is held which features Aztec dancing and the performance of an Aztec play. In the town itself, in the third week of December, a different kind of performance takes place. The experiences of Mexican pilgrims en route to Bethlehem are enacted in *pastorellas.*

Toluca, 66km (41 miles) from the capital, lies in a valley dominated by the snow-capped *Nevado de Toluca,* an extinct volcano (its two craters are known as the Sun and the Moon). As well as a fine market, the town has two interesting museums, dedicated to archaeology and to folk art. Nearby are the Indian villages of *Tenancingo, Metepec* and *Chiconcuac.* 8km (5 miles) north of Toluca is *Calixtlahuaca*, an Aztec site of archaeological interest where a circular pyramid is dedicated to the god of wind.

Taxco, 160km (100 miles) from Mexico City, has also been classed as a national monument. The town's fortune was made from the silver mines. The selling of silverware and jewellery is a thriving local trade. As well as numerous interesting narrow cobbled streets, the *Church of Santa Prisca* is a jewel of Baroque architecture, with a *reredos* decorated with gold leaf and a wealth of statues and ornaments. Residences of the colonial period include the *Casa Humboldt, Casa de Borda* and *Casa de Figueroa.* The *Cacahuamilpa Caves* are to the north of Taxco.

Nestling in the foothills of the Sierra Madre is **Puebla.** Capital of the state of the same name, it can be reached by a 96km (60-mile) drive southwest from Mexico City. It is famous for its colonial architecture with glazed tiles, which cover most of the church domes and house walls, and for the skilled craftsmen who produce them. Sights include the *Cathedral* (one of the largest and oldest in Mexico), the *Church of Santo Domingo* and the *Chapel of the Rosary.* The Cathedral has 14 chapels and is built of blue-grey stone, whilst a feature of the Church of Santo Domingo is its goldleaf ornamentation. The *Casa del Alfenique* displays craftware and regional costumes. From Puebla it is possible to see the volcanoes of *Popocatépetl, Ixtaccíhuatl* and *Pico de Orizaba.*

Acolman, 39km (24 miles) north of the capital on the road to Teotihuacan, is gathered about a convent founded in the 16th century by an Augustinian order.

Cholula, 124km (77 miles) from Mexico City, is a pre-Hispanic religious centre containing more than 400 shrines and temples; today there are over 350 churches, many built on the ruins of former places of worship. The *Pyramid of Tepanapa* is the largest of all Mexican pyramids; on the top of it stands the *Sanctuary of Nuestra Señora de los Remedios.* The 49 domes of the *Capilla Real* (Royal Chapel) give it the appearance of a mosque. Also worth a visit is *San Francisco Acatepec*, a church 6km (3.5 miles) from Cholula. The town is noted for its fiestas which include Moor and Christian dances on August 15 and Indian dances on September 8, the fete of the *Virgen de los Remedios.*

Ixtapan de la Sal, 80km (50 miles) from Toluca, is a picturesque village with excellent hot springs and spa facilities. **Valle de Bravo,** 80km (50 miles) southwest of Toluca, is a resort town at an elevation of 1869m (6135ft) set amid pines on a large lake.

Central Mexico and Colonial Cities

The central highlands, benefitting from a milder climate, constitute the most populous region of Mexico. Many of the colonial cities include a unique blend of indigenous and Spanish culture; these historic centres have remained virtually intact since the time of the conquest. The conquistadores built very Spanish-looking villages near the silver mines. Today, the main attractions of this region are the architecture, the views, and some very good local cooking.

One of the most popular circuits is the one following the so-called *Independence Route*, starting from Mexico City, going north, towards Querétaro, San Miguel Allende, Guanajuato, Morelia, Patzcuaro and Guadalajara. Another circuit starts in Guadalajara, again going north, to Aguascalientes, Zacatecas and San Luis Potosi.

Guadalajara, capital of Jalisco, still has a Spanish colonial atmosphere, despite being the agricultural, commercial and industrial centre of the western highlands. The *Cathedral* has 11 altars, 30 columns and a big art collection. There are also a lot of parks: the *Parque Agua Azul* ('Blue Water') is noteworthy for its forest-like atmosphere; the *Parque des las Armas* is where the boys and girls of the town serenade each other. Around the Cathedral there are two parks, the *Parque de los Laureles* and the *Parque de la Revolución*. The *Plaza de Rotunda* contains columns and statues in honour of Jalisco's past heroes; the *Plaza Libertad* has a market with a wide range of locally produced goods. During the annual October Festival, horsemanship and bullfighting can be seen at the *charreada* (rodeo). The famous 'Mexican Hat Dance' originated in this area, locally it is called *'Jarabe Tapati'*.

Guanajuato is on Mexico's famous 'Independence Route', a road 1400km (875 miles) in length, along which can be traced Mexico's historic struggle for independence. The town preserves a colonial charm in places such as *Hidalgo*, an underground street, the *Governor's Palace*, the *Juarez Theatre*, the *University*, the *Basilica of Nuestra Señora de Guanajuato* and the *Valenciana Church.* The parish *Church of Dolores Hidalgo* is of great significance, being the place where, in 1810, Father Miguel Hidalgo raised the 'Grito de Dolore', the cry of rebellion against the Spanish when, with 80,000 armed supporters, he commenced the independence struggle.

The aristocrat among the colonial cities is **Morelia,** a city halfway between the capital and Guadalajara. Apart from a few modern buildings, the city retains an atmosphere of the old Spain. The *Plaza de los Martires* forms the centre of the city, flanked on one side by the *Cathedral*, bearing an unusual pink stone façade, with its 61m-high (200ft) tower. Other sights include the *College of San Nicolas* (founded 1540), the *Church of Santa Rosa* and the impressive *Aqueduct* built in 1790 to carry water into the city. Between November and February, visitors should go to the *Monarch Butterfly Refuge* near Angangueo, near Morelia. Each year these butterflies migrate from Canada and the USA to a mountain bordering the state of Michoacan in Mexico.

Patzcuaro, situated in the Tarascan Indian country, is best known for butterfly net fishing for whitefish. Every Friday morning the plaza is covered with numerous market stalls, offering ceramics, woodcarvings, copper and woven goods, laquerware and even furniture for sale. The Day of the Dead on November 2 is celebrated in **Janitzio** as nowhere else in Mexico.

Querétaro is where the Emperor Maximilian was captured, tried and executed and where the present Mexican constitution was drawn up in 1917. A former San Franciscan monastery is now a local museum, whilst the San Agustin monastery has become the *Federal Palace.* The mansion of the Marquis Villa del Aguila, who ordered the building of the town's aqueduct, is in the *Plaza de la Independencia.* The town has excellent hotels and restaurants.

San Miguel de Allende, founded by a Franciscan friar in 1542, is now classed as a national monument. It is a place of narrow, cobbled streets and squares lined with trees. The houses and patios have elegant colonial architecture and the town is a fitting location for the *Allende Institute*, a school of fine arts named after a hero of the revolution whose name was also added to the name of the town. In 1880 the Indian master mason, Ceferino Gutierez, applied the tools of his trade to the architecture of the *Parroquia de San Miguel.* Its Franciscan starkness was transformed into Gothic. The *Casa de los Perros* (House of Dogs) has sculptured dogs on its balcony. The annual *Posadas* at Christmas-time is one of the fiestas for which the town is noted.

Aguascalientes has belonged to the Kingdom of Nueva Galicia since 1535. It was a stopping place for travellers on the silver route during the 18th century. Many of the Baroque buildings from this period still remain; the most interesting are the temples of Guadalupe, Encino, San Marcos, San Diego and San José de la Merced; also worth visiting are the government and municipal palaces, the *House of Culture* and *Excedra*, and the Ionian column marking the centre of Mexico.

The state capital of **San Luis Potosi**, 351km (218 miles) northeast of Guadalajara, is the centre of a rich mining and agricultural area. Featured throughout the city are colourful, glazed tiles found on churches, plazas and streets. Good examples are the *Church of San Francisco* with its blue-and-white tiled dome and a suspended glass boat in the transept and *Carmen*, at the Plaza Morelos, with a tiled dome and intricate façade and *Iglesia de San Miguelito* in the old part of the city. Other sites include the *Palacio de Gobierno* (1770), housing paintings of former governors, and the colonial treasury, the *Antigua Caja Real* (1767).

Zacatecas was founded by the Spanish in 1546; at that time the nearby silver mines were among the richest in the country. Much of the revenue was sent to Spain, but much remained to finance the fine cathedrals and palaces. The *Convent of Guadalupe* houses one of the largest art collections of the Americas and is also an important place for pilgrimages.

Northern Mexico

The north is mostly desert, a vast, high, windswept plateau flanked by the Occidental and Oriental chains of the *Sierra Madre.* Most of the population is gathered in several large cities and on the coasts; parts of the plateau are used for agriculture, but much of the north bears little trace of man.

Chihuahua, capital of the state of the same name (Mexico's largest), is an important industrial and commercial centre. There are many edifices dating from the colonial era, including the 18th-century *Cathedral,* the *Government Palace,* the *City Hall* and *Quinta Luz,* which is the *Villa Museum* (containing Pancho Villa memorabilia). There is a monument to the *División del Norte of Doroteo Arango* (Pancho Villa in the unfamiliar guise of his real name). Entertainments include bullfights, dog and horseraces, nightclubs and restaurants.

In the state of Chihuahua, **Ciudad Juárez** has a commercial and cultural centre with modern buildings based on traditional styles of architecture. The handicrafts section includes *sarapes* (blankets) and glassware. There are bullfights, and horse and greyhound racing, along with a good nightlife. Restaurants serve international and Mexican food.

The remarkable *Copper Canyon Railway* passes through Chihuahua on its way from Ojinaga on the Rio Grande to the Gulf of California. It is an engineering miracle in itself and also provides a good way of seeing the canyons, mesas and bare peaks of the Sierra Madre Occidental. The view at the *Barranca del Cobre*, where the *Urique River* has cut a 3660m-deep (12,000ft) chasm through the mountains, rivals the Grand Canyon. The journey lasts about 13 hours.

Monterrey is Mexico's industrial powerhouse, standing beneath the highest peaks of the Sierra Madre Oriental in a setting of great natural beauty. The remnants of Monterrey's more tranquil past (the *Cathedral*, the *Palacio del Gobierno*, the *Obispado*) compete with its present-day preoccupations.

Tijuana claims to be 'the world's most visited city', receiving more than 20 million visitors every year, many of them day-trippers from California. With San Diego just a few miles away across the border, it is the land gateway to and from the USA, thriving on the sale of souvenirs.

Baja California

Baja California is a peninsula 1100km (700 miles) long that extends south from Tijuana into the Pacific Ocean. It comprises two states, Baja California Norte and Baja California Sur. The enclosed Gulf is rich in marine life and offers excellent opportunities for experienced divers and anglers (although the currents are treacherous). The estuary of the *Colorado River* lies at the top of the Gulf; only a trickle of fresh water now reaches the sea, most having been diverted for agriculture far upstream. The Pacific coast of the peninsula is an important breeding ground for whales. The interior is mountainous desert, for the most part waterless and inhabited by only the hardiest plants and animals.

Cabo San Lucas and **San Jose del Cabo** are the main tourist destinations, offering miles of excellent beaches. At Cabo San Lucas on the tip of the peninsula, 260km (162 miles) from La Paz, seals may often be seen.

Mexicali is the capital of Baja California Norte. It provides a base for those who wish to explore the surrounding mountains and countryside of Rumorosa.

La Paz, the capital of Baja California Sur, is in a bay on the Gulf of California. Watersports and deep-sea angling are well catered for. The beaches of *Las Hamacas, Palmeira, El Coromuel* and *Puerto Balandra* provide excellent bases for swimmers and skindivers; the waters are calm and clear. Fish and seafood figure prominently on local menus.

Southern Mexico

The states of **Guerrero, Oaxaca, Chiapas** and **Tabasco** form the junction between North and Central America. Here is where the two Sierra Madre chains merge before continuing south towards the Andes, the deserts give way to highland forests and lowland jungles, and the mean annual temperature is 21°C and more. Acapulco attracts the most visitors (see below), but there is much else to satisfy the more adventurous tourist. As elsewhere in Mexico, there are many picturesque and charming hilltop towns. There are lagoons on both coasts and many beautiful lakes high up in the mountains.

Oaxaca, or the 'Jade City', features pleasant gardens, an archaeological museum, arcade-fringed squares and several fine churches, including the fortress-like *Santo Domingo* which dates back to the 17th century. The inside of the church is decorated with a profusion of colourful Baroque ornaments, statues and altars. Next to the Santo Domingo is a monastery. In the central, cafe-lined square, an orchestra gives free concerts twice a week. The Cathedral in this square was commenced in the 16th century and completed two centuries later. Hand-woven and hand-embroidered clothing, gold jewellery and shiny black pottery can be bought at the market on Saturdays. The *Archaeological Museum* has a collection of Zapotec and Mixtec artefacts in gold, jade, silver, turquoise and quartz. In the *Church of la Soledad* there is the statue of the Virgin of la Soledad, patron saint of the town to whom many miracles are ascribed.

Mitla, 45km (28 miles) from Oaxaca, features numerous Mixtec remains, including the *Hall of Columns* and the *Column of Life* which visitors are invited to grasp if they wish to determine how long they will live. The *Frisel Museum* is in Mitla.

Monte Albán, 14km (9 miles) from Oaxaca, was a sacred city in prehistoric times and the religious centre of the Zapotec culture, which flourished 2000 years ago. The remarkable *Central Plaza,* the *Ball Court* and many of the tombs are open to the public. It is an amazing complex situated on a levelled mountain top. Aldous Huxley wrote that 'Monte Albán is the work of men who knew their architectural business consummately well'. The town covers an area of 38 sq km (15 sq miles). Day trips by bus are available at Oaxaca.

Tuxlta Gutierrez is the state capital of Chiapas and the home of Mexico's famed *marimba* music. Set in a thriving coffee-growing region, it is a good base to explore the nearby villages where life has changed little since pre-hispanic times. A short drive away is the impressive **Sumidero Canyon**. Mountain peaks surround the 1829m (6000ft) drop along the 42km (26-mile) rift and are an impressive sight.

San Cristobal de las Casas was founded in 1528 by Diego de Mazariegos as the colonial capital of the region. At an altitude of 2195m (7200ft), the 2-hour drive from Tuxlta Gutierrez involves a rapid temperature change. It is a cool, white washed town with an almost alpine atmosphere. During the year, several festivals are held here, making it an important gathering spot for the local craftsmen. In the near vicinity are a number of indigenous villages populated by Tzeltzal, Tzotzil and Chamula people. These can be visited, but the visitor should respect local traditions and sensitivities, especially when taking photographs. San Cristobal is also known as a centre for writers, musicians and poets.

The capital of Yucatán State is **Mérida**, the 'White City', founded in 1542 on the site of an ancient Mayan town. It has an air of elegant, faded grandeur, a legacy of its once worldwide importance as a centre of *henequén* (sisal used in the manufacture of rope) production. It is still reckoned to be one of the best places in Latin America to buy fine quality cotton hammocks. There is much to keep the tourist here, including a fine cathedral, the *Casa de Montejo*, and a museum of archaeology, but above all it is a good base for excursions.

Mayan World

More than 3000 years ago in the diverse landscape of what is now Guatemala, Belize, western Honduras and part of El Salvador as well as the Mexican states of Yucatán, Quintana Roo, Campeche, Chiapas and Tabasco, there emerged a highly sophisticated civilisation, the Mayas.

This variety of landscape was also matched by the abundance of flora and fauna unrivalled anywhere else in the continent. Birdlife, especially, seems to abound, including toucans, parrots and macaws, hummingbirds and others. The lowland rainforest of Chiapas, Campeche and Quintana Roo is home to such exotic wildlife as ocelots, margays, whitetail deer, anteaters, peccaries, tapirs, howler and spider monkeys and jaguars, the largest wildcats in the Americas. The upland cloud-forests are home to the multicoloured guacamayas as well as the resplendent and elusive quetzal, an emerald-coloured bird with trailing feathers once considered sacred by the ancient Mayas. The coast also supports a wealth of birdlife, as well as alligators and manatee, a rare aquatic animal distantly related to the elephant, which can be found in the coastal lagoons. The Wildlife Reserve of Contoy Island is the resting and nesting place for hundreds of migrant and resident birds. Even the underwater world can offer a richness of species such as marlin, snapper, grouper, bonito, wahoo, shrimp, lobster, octopus and sailfish, and the beaches are important nesting places for sea turtles during the summer months.

At the height of their development (AD250-900) the Mayans built extraordinary temples and ceremonial centres, many of which are now engulfed by the rainforest. Among the most important archaeological sites to be found in this region are Palenque and Bonampak (Chiapas); La Venta and Comacalco (Tabasco); Edzna, Chicanna and Becan (Campeche); Chichén-Itzá and Uxmal (Yucatán) and Tulum and Coba (Quintana Roo).

Nestled in the foothills at the edge of the Chiapas rainforest lies **Palenque**. This small but important Mayan site is one of the most aesthetically appealing sites of the Mayan world, with its exquisite stucco façades. The *Temple of Inscriptions* (above the crypt of a Maya king), the *Multileveled Palace* and the *Temple of the Count* are exquisite. It is easily reached in a couple of hours drive from Villahermosa or San Cristobal de las Casas.

The site of **Bonampak**, 150km (90 miles) southeast of Palenque, is famous for the finest Mayan murals ever to be discovered. Housed in the *Temple of Frescoes*, the multicoloured murals depict scenes of Mayan warfare, sacrifice and celebration.

The museum park of **Parque-Museo La Venta** not only boasts one of the few extensive collections of Olmec artefacts, but it is also the only archaeological site ever to be completely transplanted. The original Olmec city of La Venta (15,000BC) was situated on the island of Tonala and featured, among other exceptional sculptures, the colossal human heads that now characterise the Olmec civilisation. Originally evacuated in 1925, it was moved to **Villahermosa** in the 1970s due to the fear that nearby oil drilling would damage the site. The museum park contains 30 Olmec sculptures set in a botanical garden.

About 67km (42 miles) from Villahermosa is **Comacalco**. This archaeological site of the Maya civilisation dates back to the late classic period (AD500-900). Some of the structures resemble those at Palenque though they are still unique in the region. All the buildings here are made from bricks rather than the stone used elsewhere. In fact, Comacalco means 'in the house of bricks'. Sights are the *Great Acropolis* with its detailed stucco masks and the small museum.

Edzna, 65km (40 miles) southeast of Campeche, dates back to 300BC. Besides the Chenes-style architecture, visitors can also see an extensive network of canals, reservoirs and waterholes. Attractions include the *Great Acropolis*, the *Small Acropolis*, the *Platform of the Knives*, the *Ball Court*, the *Temple of Stone Masks* and the *Nohochna*.

The famous archaeological and World Heritage site of **Chichén-Itzá**, 120km (75 miles) east of Mérida, contains the *Pyramid of Kukulcan (El Castillo),* where one can find the 'Red tiger with jade eyes'. During the spring and autumn equinox (March 21-22 and September 21-22), huge crowds gather to see a unique spectacle, when shadows create the illusion of a serpent descending the northern staircase. Of interest are also the snaking columns of the *Temple of the Warriors*, a ball court in perfect condition, *El Caracol* (the observatory), the *Caves of Balankanche* and the *Sacred Cenote* (where bejewelled young girls were thrown into the well as sacrifices to the rain god Chac).

The elaborate stucco work and detailed façades of **Uxmal**, 80km (50 miles) south of Mérida, have led to a comparison of the city with Rome. Among the fine stonework are the entwined serpents in the *Nun's Quadrangle*, the *House of Pigeons* and the *Ball Court*. Other attractions include the *Pyramid of the Magician* and the *Governor's Palace*.

The walled fortress of **Tulum**, 131km (78 miles) south of Cancún, has been described as one of the most dramatic sites of the pre-hispanic world. Perched atop rugged cliffs on the coast, this last outpost of the Maya civilisation commands a breathtaking view of the Caribbean. Settlement here dates from AD900-1500 and sights include the *Temple of the Descending God, El Castillo* and the *Temple of the Frescoes*.

Coba, 38km (24 miles) north of Tulum, is possibly the largest archaeological site on the Yucatán peninsula. This town, set amongst dense jungle and marshlands and including four lakes, dates from the classical period and is believed to have been occupied during the time of the conquest. The most significant groupings of sites are the *Coba Group*, *Las Pinturas*, the *Macanxoc Group*, the *Crossroad Pyramid* and the *Chumuc Mul Group*. It also houses the tallest structure in Yucatán, the *Nohoch Mul Pyramid*.

Beach Resorts

PACIFIC COAST: Acapulco, situated on Acapulco Bay, is probably the most famous beach resort in Mexico. The town stretches for over 16km (10 miles) round the bay. It has many beaches as well as numerous top-class hotels. The *malecón* (seaside promenade) runs along the beaches. There is a square in the centre of the old town to the west of the Bay. This lively and fashionable resort offers skindiving, angling, parachute sailing, water-skiing, golf, tennis, riding and the unique spectacle of the Quebrada divers. The waters of the Bay are famous for their calmness and safety, though the beach of *La Condesa* has rougher waters and a good surf for those who want it. The two beaches nearest the centre of the town are *Playa Caleta* and *Playa Caletilla*; the sun on these is considered to be at its best in the morning. The late afternoon sun is thought to be best on *Playa Hornos*, which is further around the bay to the east. Scuba-diving lessons can be arranged on request. Nearby is **Roqueta Island**, visited regularly by glass-bottomed boats from which the underwater image of the Virgin of Guadelupe can be seen. The island itself is popular for family trips.

Fort San Diego, in the middle of the town, is where the last battle of the Mexican War of Independence was fought. Admission is free but it is closed Thursday.

Behind the town of Acapulco rise the *Sierra Madre Mountains*, a favourite location for photographers who relish the verdant greenery, the rocky cliffs and the breathtaking views over the bay.

16km (10 miles) away is **Pie de la Costa** which has a lagoon and several large beaches. The surf is risky.

Ixtapa-Zihuatanejo, to the north of Acapulco, is a new resort complex with moorings for yachts and a golf course.

Manzanillo, a major seaport, has recently become an important resort. The emphasis is on watersports, but the spacious beaches afford good swimming. Fishing is of a world-class standard.

Mazatlán, famed as an angling centre, also has numerous beaches and facilities for surfing, skindiving, tennis, golf, riding and shooting. The name of the town means 'Place of the Stag' in the Nahuatl language, an indication of the town's longstanding association with sporting activities. The *malecón*, which runs along the beachfront, is disguised by a variety of names, being named Avenida Camaron in the north and then proceeding through a number of name changes till it becomes Olas Atlas in the south. In the evening strollers promenade along this beachfront among the *arañas* (covered carts), 4-wheeled carriages and 3-wheeled taxis. The *Mirador* is a tower on the *malecón* from

which divers give a spectacular display twice a day. 'El Faro' on the promontory of Cerro del Creston is one of the highest lighthouses in the world. There are direct flights from Los Angeles as well as from numerous Mexican cities and a ferry crosses regularly from La Paz in Baja California. The island of *Mexcaltitan* nearby is said to be the original home of the Aztecs. **Puerto Vallarta** is the largest town in the immense Bahía de Banderas resort area (1 hour 10 minutes by air from Mexico City). It is situated on the *Bahía de Banderos Bay*, which is the largest natural bay in Mexico. There are a hundred miles of coastline with many sandy beaches and facilities for parasailing, shooting, scuba diving, sailboarding, fishing, golf and tennis. Boat trips provide opportunities to explore the coast. For the visitor who would relish the experience of journeying in a dugout canoe there is the chance to visit **Yelapa**, a Polynesian-style village which cannot be visited in any other way. The mountains behind the bay may be explored on horseback. *Charreadas*, uniquely Mexican rodeos, are held at certain times of the year. Amongst the smaller resorts are **San Blas, Barra de Navidad, Zihuatanejo, Puerto Escondido** and **Puerto Angel**.
CARIBBEAN COAST: Cozumel, Cancún and **Isla Mujeres** are island resorts off the Yucatán Peninsula. Only recently developed for tourism, they offer sun, sand and sea in a wild and beautiful tropical setting. The seafood is particularly good. Giant turtles come ashore to breed on Isla Mujeres.
Veracruz is a lively seaport, with excellent seafood cuisine – the visitor will particularly enjoy carnival time in this easy-going city.
POPULAR ITINERARIES: 5-day: (a) México DF–San Miguel de Allende–Guanajuato–Guadalajara–Morelia–México DF. (b) Cancún–Chitchén-Itzá–Mérida–Uxmal–Tulum–Cancún. **7-day:** (a) México DF–Oaxaca–Tuxtla Gutierrez–San Cristobal de las Casas–Palenque–Mérida–México DF. (b) México DF–Oaxaca–Puerto Angel–Acapulco–Cuernavaca–México DF.

SOCIAL PROFILE

FOOD & DRINK: Self-service (fast food) is available but table-service is usual. Bars have table- and/or counter-service. There are laws relating to minors and licensing on civic holidays. Mexican cuisine is delicious and varied; there are many specialities, such as *turkey mole*, a sauce containing a score of ingredients including several sorts of chilli, tomatoes, peanuts, chocolate, almonds, onions and garlic. Another sauce, *guacamole*, incorporates avocado pears, red peppers, onions and tomatoes, and often accompanies turkey, chicken, with *tortillas* (pancakes made with maize). There are also *enchiladas, tacos* (maize pancakes served with pork, chicken, vegetables or cheese and chilli) and *tamales*. Every region of Mexico has its own cuisine. International cuisine is available at most hotels in the larger cities, and at most restaurants. There is a wide variety of exotic fruits such as papayas, mangoes, guavas, *zapotes*, pineapples, *mameyes* and *tunas* (juicy prickly pears, fruit of the cactus). **Drink:** Imported spirits are expensive, local spirits probably give better value for money; the best buys are rum and gin. European aperitifs are produced in Mexico and are of excellent quality; and, of course, there is *tequila* (made from *maguey*, a variety of cactus). It is traditionally drunk neat with a pinch of salt and a bite of lemon, and makes excellent cocktails. Mexico's coffee liqueur, *kahlúa*, is world famous. *Hidalgo, Domecq* and *Derrasola* are good Mexican white wines, whilst *Los Reyes* and *Calafia* are excellent reds. Mexico is a producer of excellent beer; both the dark beers and the light beers are worth sampling. All the big supermarkets sell spirits, beer and wine.
NIGHTLIFE: With a range of settings from panoramic restaurants to intimate bars, Mexico City offers excellent music and assorted cuisine, with some of the best bars and restaurants located in hotels. Nightlife is very vibrant and exciting and features a large variety of top-name entertainers, international shows, jazz groups, rock groups, traditional Mexican music and dancing, Spanish flamenco dancers and gypsy violins. Worth seeing is the impressive light show, with accompanying sound show at the archaeological site of Teotihuacan. The history and mythology of this ancient civilisation are re-created through a gorgeous display of coloured lights, poetic dialogue and music. The season runs from October to May.
SHOPPING: Good buys include silverware, ceramics and locally made pottery, woven wool blankets (*sarapes*), brightly coloured scarves in wool or silk (*rebozos*), richly embroidered charro hats, straw work, blown glass, embossed leather, hard and semi-precious stones, gold and silver jewellery, finely pleated men's shirts in cotton voile (*guayaberas*), white dresses

embroidered with multi-coloured flowers (*huipiles*), which are sold in the markets, and hammocks. The best shopping is in Mexico City, Cuernavaca, Taxco, San Miguel de Allende, Acapulco, Guadalajara, Oaxaca, Mérida and Campeche. **Shopping hours:** 0900-2000 Monday to Saturday (Mexico City) and 0900-1400 and 1600-2000 Monday to Friday (rest of the country).
SPORTS: Horseriding: Horses and professional guides are available in major towns and resorts. **Tennis:** Almost all major resorts have tennis courts and there are complexes which include luxury accommodation at Cancún on the Caribbean coast and at Manzanillo, Ixtapa and Puerto Vallarta on the Pacific coast. Acapulco, however, remains the tennis capital, with almost perfect weather from October through to June. **Golf:** Although many of Mexico's best golf courses are part of private clubs or resort hotel complexes, some of them allow visitors, particularly in the tourist resorts. **Swimming:** Major city hotels and most hotel resorts have swimming pools and some towns have public baths. Both seaboards have warm waters ideal for bathing and there are many resorts, the most famous of which is Acapulco. **Water-skiing:** Acapulco has particularly good facilities, but other resorts also have equipment for hire, including speedboats. **Surfing/parasailing:** Surfing can be enjoyed on the pacific breakers and parasailing is another exciting sport. **Scuba diving/snorkelling:** Diving is particularly popular in the clear waters of Cozumel and Cancún, although equipment can be hired in most major coastal resorts. **Sailing/windsurfing:** The Gulf, Caribbean and Pacific coasts and mountain lakes offer excellent sailing. Most resort hotels will rent small sailing boats to guests. Windsurfing has become extremely popular. For further information write to the Mexican Sailing Federation, 13th Floor, Balderas 36, Mexico City. **Fishing:** Mexico's coast offers some of the best deep-sea fishing in the world. Every major port has charter boats and fishing gear for hire and even the smallest fishing village is likely to have at least one fishing boat for hire. Freshwater fishing is also allowed in lakes, lagoons, dams and rivers. Regulations vary according to season. A Mexican fishing permit is obtainable, free of charge, from the local game or fish warden, the office of the Captain of the Port, or any local office of the Secretary of Commerce. Anglers may request more information from the Secretaría de Pesca, Permisos de Pesca Deportiva, Baja California 252, 06100 México DF. **Spectator sports: Football** is played every Sunday at noon and Thursday night throughout the year at the Aztec Stadium in Mexico City and at other locations throughout the country. The Mexican **baseball** league begins in April and in the capital games can be seen almost daily since there are two home teams. **Jai alai** is a very fast game of Basque *pelota* played with a small ball and straw rackets and can be watched at Fronton courts in Acapulco, Tijuana and Mexico City. **Horseraces** are held four times a week at The Hippodrome de las Americanas in Mexico City and Tijuana (October and September).
SPECIAL EVENTS: Mexicans celebrate more than 120 fetes and festivals in a year, some of them religious, others secular, national or local. Most provide occasion for music, dancing, processions and fireworks. The following is a selection of the major festivals and other special events celebrated annually in Mexico. For a complete list, contact the Mexican Tourist Office.
Apr '95 *International Horse Fair,* Texcoco. **Apr-May** *San Marcos National Fair,* Aquascalientes. **May** *Holy Cross Day* (celebrated by construction workers), nationwide. **Jun** *Corpus Christi* (special events varying regionally), nationwide. **Jul (last two Mondays)** *Guelaguetza* (votive cultural event dating back to pre-Columbian times), Oaxaca. **Aug** *Eve of the Feast of the Assumption of the Virgin Mary* (streets carpeted in designs of flower-petals and coloured sawdust, and a midnight procession), Huamantla (Tlaxcala). **Sep-Oct** *Coronation of the Regional Festivities Queen* (and several other celebrations), San Miguel de Allende (Guanajuato). **Oct** *October Festivals,* Guadalajara. **Dec** *National Silver Fair,* Taxco; *Festival of the Radishes* (local farmers compete to produce the best or biggest radish, others make radish carvings and exhibit them), Oaxaca. **Jan 6 '95** *Feast of the Epiphany* (the 'Three Kings' bring gifts to Mexican children), nationwide. **Feb (third week)** *Mardi Gras,* nationwide. **Mar** *Fair* (in celebration of Benito Juárez's birthday), Gelatao (Oaxaca).
SOCIAL CONVENTIONS: Handshaking is the most common form of greeting. Casual sportswear is acceptable for daytime dress throughout the country. At beach resorts, dress is very informal for men and women and nowhere are men expected to wear ties. In Mexico City, however, dress tends to be smart in elegant restaurants and hotel dining rooms. Smoking is unrestricted except where notified. Mexicans regard relationships and friendships as the most important thing in life next to religion and they are not afraid to show

their emotions. A large Mexican family always seems to find room for one more and a visitor who becomes friends with a Mexican will invariably be made part of the family. Visitors should always remember that local customs and traditions are important. **Tipping:** Service charges are rarely added to hotel, restaurant or bar bills and many of the staff depend on tips for their livelihood. 15% is expected and 20% if the service has been very good. Airport porterage is charged at the equivalent of US$1 per bag.

BUSINESS PROFILE

ECONOMY: Agriculture is the main economic sector although it is relatively weak in terms of efficiency and productivity. The main crops produced for export are coffee, tomatoes, fruit and vegetables. Although practically anything can be grown in Mexico, only one-sixth of the land is suitable for cultivation. Improving the efficiency of Mexican farming is a high priority for the Government. The source of most of Mexico's wealth in recent years is its considerable oil deposits. Mexico is the world's fourth-largest producer of crude oil, and oil products now account for one-third of total export earnings. Other mineral deposits include silver, bismuth, arsenic and antimony and smaller deposits of sulphur, lead, zinc and cadmium. Production has been limited over the years, however, by inadequate investment. The country's oil revenues have for the most part been used to finance a successful industrialisation programme. Car assembly, steel, textiles, food-processing and breweries are the main industries, all of which have developed rapidly since the 1960s so that Mexico is now self-sufficient in almost all semi-manufactured goods. The USA dominate Mexico's trade, providing 70% of the country's imports (US$14.5 billion) and taking slightly under 70% (US$18 billion) of its exports. The Mexican economy is expected to receive a powerful boost following the signing of the North American Free Trade Area (NAFTA) agreement with the USA and Canada. The deal, finally signed at the end of November 1993 after more than two years of complex negotiations, arose from an initiative by Mexico's President Salinas. Despite the apparent imbalance of bringing together two members of G7 with a Third World economy, the prospects for the new common market, which rivals the EU in population and net output, are almost unanimously thought to be good for all parties, but especially Mexico. Forecasts were uniformly optimistic, but in 1994, just as NAFTA was about to come into force, the Mexican government suddenly faced major political problems in the form of an armed rebellion in the south of the country and large-scale civil discontent at the corruption of the ruling Partido Revolucionario Institucional (PRI), which had just won its umpteenth successive presidential election. The result, on the economic front, was a sudden collapse in the value of the Mexican Peso and entreaties to Washington for American support to prevent total currency collapse. Short-term prospects are uncertain. Outside the American continent, Japan, Germany and Spain are Mexico's other important trading partners. Britain is the largest foreign investor in Mexico after the USA.
BUSINESS: English is widely spoken in business circles although it is preferable for the visitor to be able to speak Spanish. Letters written in Spanish should be replied to in Spanish. Business wear is formal. Mexicans attach much importance to courtesy and the use of titles. Prior appointments are necessary and if in doubt about a correct title it is advisable to use *licenciado* in place of *señor.* Best months for business visits are January to June and September to November. Avoid the two weeks before and after Christmas and Easter. **Office hours:** Vary considerably; usually 0800-1500 Monday to Friday.
COMMERCIAL INFORMATION: The following organisation can offer advice: Confederacíon de Cámaras Nacionales de Comercio, Servicios y Turismo (CONCANACO), Apartado 113 bis, 2° y 3°, Balderas 144, Centro Cuauhtémoc, 06079 México DF. Tel: (5) 709 1559. Fax: (5) 709 1152. Telex: 1777318.
CONFERENCES/CONVENTIONS: The meetings, conventions, exhibitions and incentives planner's kit issued by the Mexican Ministry of Tourism lists over 70 convention venues in Mexico City, Acapulco, Taxco, Morelia, Puerto Vallarta, Ixtapa, Guadalajara, Mazatlán, Cancún and Mérida. Taxco, Acapulco, Morelia and Cancún have dedicated centres, the largest of which, in Acapulco, can seat up to 8000 people.

CLIMATE

Climate varies according to altitude. Coastal areas and lowlands (*tierra caliente*) are hot and steamy with high humidity, while the central plateau is temperate even in winter. The climate of the inland highlands is mostly mild, but sharp changes in temperatures occur between day and night. The cold lands (*tierra fría*) lie above 2000m (6600ft). Rainfall varies greatly from region to region. Only the Sierra Madre Oriental, the Isthmus of Tehuantepec and the state of Chiapas in the far south receive any appreciable amount of rain during the year, with the wet season running between June and September. All other areas have rainless seasons, while the northern and central areas of the central plateau are dry and arid. There is some snow in the north in winter. The dry season runs from October to May.

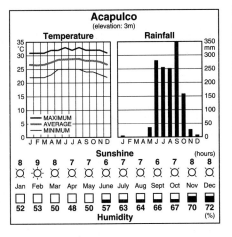

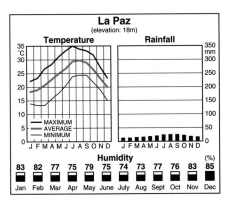

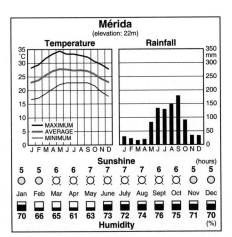

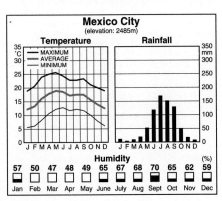

Moldova

□ *international airport*

100km

50mls

Location: Southeastern Europe.

Note: Travellers are advised that only essential travel should be undertaken into or through the Transdniestria region, where there are frequent checkpoints manned by armed, young and inexperienced paramilitary units who are not under the control of the Moldovan government and whose members rarely understand English. Tourists and truckers may be subject to extortion or robbery at checkpoints.
Source: US State Department – August 24, 1994.

Ministry of Foreign Affairs
1 Piata Marii Adunări Nationale, Chisinău 277033, Moldova
Tel: (2) 233 940 *or* 233 338. Fax: (2) 232 302. Telex: 163130.
Moldova-Tur
Hotel National, 4 Stefan cel Mare, 277058 Chisinău, Moldova
Tel: (2) 266 679 *or* 266 646. Fax: (2) 262 586. Telex: 162112 (a/b INTUR SU).
Intourist
219 Marsh Wall, Isle of Dogs, London E14 9PD
Tel: (0171) 538 8600. Fax: (0171) 538 5967. Opening hours: 0900-1700 Monday to Friday.
The British Embassy in Moscow deals with enquiries relating to Moldova (see *Russian Federation* later in this book).
Embassy of Moldova
1511 K Street, NW, Washington, DC 20005
Tel: (202) 783 3012 *or* 783 4218 (Consular section). Fax: (202) 783 3342.
Intourist USA Inc
Suite 603, 610 Fifth Avenue, New York, NY 10020
Tel: (212) 757 3884. Fax: (212) 459 0031.
Embassy of the United States of America
Strada Alexei Mateevici 103, Chisinău, Moldova
Tel: (2) 233 772 *or* 237 345 (after hours). Fax: (2) 232 494.
Intourist
Suite 630, 1801 McGill College Avenue, Montréal, Québec H3A 2N4
Tel: (514) 849 6394. Fax: (514) 849 6743.
Embassy of Moldova
Al. Alexandru 40, Sector 1, Bucharest, Romania
Tel/Fax: (40) 312 9790. Telex: 10910.
Embassy of Moldova
18 Kuznetsky Most, Moscow, Russian Federation
Tel: (095) 928 5405.

The Canadian Embassy in Bucharest deals with enquiries relating to Moldova (see *Romania* later in this book).

AREA: 33,700 sq km (13,000 sq miles).
POPULATION: 4,394,000 (1992).
POPULATION DENSITY: 130.4 per sq km.
CAPITAL: Chisinău. **Population:** 753,500 (1991).
GEOGRAPHY: Moldova is a small landlocked state in southeastern Europe – one of the most highly populated republics of the former USSR. To the north, east and south Moldova is bound by Ukraine; to the west by Romania. The River Prut constitutes the border with Romania. The country has rich pastures and wooded slopes, ideal for wine-growing.
LANGUAGE: Romanian. In 1940, after Soviet annexation, the Cyrillic script was introduced as another measure in the creation of a separate 'Soviet Moldavian National Identity'. Between 1940 and 1989 the language was referred to as Moldavian. In 1989 the Latin alphabet was gradually reintroduced but, as a result of 45 years of forced 'Russification', many people find it difficult to speak proper Romanian. Russian is still the most widely spoken language in Moldova. The ethnic and linguistic make-up of Moldova is as follows: Moldovans 64.5%, Ukrainians 13.8%, Russians 13.0%, Gagauz 3.5%, Bulgarians 1.5%, Others 1.7%.
RELIGION: Mostly Eastern Orthodox Christian and other Christian denominations. About 2% of the population are Jewish. There are more than 850 churches, 11 Christian Orthodox monasteries, two Armenian churches and more than 60 churches of the Seventh Day Adventists. There is one synagogue (in Chisinău).
TIME: GMT + 2 (GMT + 3 from last Sunday in March to Saturday before last Sunday in September).
ELECTRICITY: 220 volts AC, 50Hz.
COMMUNICATIONS: Telephone: IDD is available to major towns. Country code: 373. Outgoing international calls must generally go through the operator. **Post:** All mail to and from Moldova is subject to long delays, sometimes up to six weeks. Letters should be sent recorded delivery to avoid loss. The postal and telecommunication systems are in need of modernisation. The Main Post Office is at 73 Stefan cel Mare, 277012 Chisinău. Post office hours: 0900-2000 Monday to Sunday. **Press:** The press is generally uncensored. There are more than a dozen daily newspapers in Moldova, the most popular being *Moldova Suveraná* published in Romanian (circulation 103,080). The Russian-language *Nezavisimaia Moldova* has a circulation of 60,692. Most of the papers are either pro-independence or pro-unification. Romanian and, to a lesser extent, Russian newspapers are available in Moldova. English-language publications can sometimes be found at major hotels in Chisinău. Western press deliveries are erratic. **Media:** The news agency, Moldovan Information Agency Moldovapres, can be contacted at str. Pushkin 22, 277012 Chisinău. Tel: (2) 234 519 *or* 233 428. Fax: (2) 234 371. Telex: 163140. **Radio/TV:** Radio Chisinău broadcasts in both Romanian and Russian and is located at str. Miorita 1, 277028 Chisinău. Tel: (2) 721 077. Radio Chisinău also occasionally broadcasts in Gagauzian and Yiddish. Chisinău Television can be found at str. Hincesti 64, 277028 Chisinău. TV special projects include programmes in Ukrainian, Gagauzian, Bulgarian, Hebrew and Yiddish.
BBC World Service frequencies: From time to time these change. See the section *How to Use this Book* for more information.
BBC:

MHz	15.07	11.78	9.410	6.195

Services in Romanian, Russian and English are also available on 68.48MHz (0600-0800 and 1800-2200 local time).

PASSPORT/VISA

Regulations and requirements may be subject to change at short notice, and you are advised to contact the appropriate diplomatic or consular authority before finalising travel arrangements. Details of these may be found at the head of this country's entry. Any numbers in the chart refer to the footnotes below.

	Passport Required?	Visa Required?	Return Ticket Required?
Full British	Yes*	Yes*	No*
BVP	Not valid*	-	-
Australian	Yes*	Yes*	No*
Canadian	Yes*	Yes*	No*
USA	Yes*	Yes*	No*
Other EU (As of 31/12/94)	Yes*	Yes*	No*
Japanese	Yes*	Yes*	No*

Note [*]: Regulations and requirements may be subject

to change. It is advisable to contact the appropriate diplomatic or consular authority before finalising travel arrangements.
PASSPORT: Required by all.
British Visitors Passport: Not acceptable.
VISA: Required by all except nationals of CIS and Romania.
Types of visa: Business, Tourist and Transit, single-double- or multiple-entry. Cost: *Single-entry in 1-month period* – US$30 for nationals of Germany, Italy and the USA; US$40 for other nationals. *Double-entry in 1-month period* – US$60. *Multiple-entry in 1-month period* – US$80. *Multiple-entry in 3-month period* – US$120. *Multiple-entry in 6-month period* – US$180. *Multiple-entry in 1-year period* – US$270. *Transit* – US$25 (single); US$50 (double). Same-day visas cost US$20 extra for each type of visa. Single-entry Tourist visas are available for US$50 at Chisinău airport.
Note: Certain nationals may be charged more for each type of visa.
Validity: Duration of the visa is individually specified for each visit.
Application to: Consulate (or Consular section at Embassy). For addresses, see top of entry.
Application requirements: (a) Valid passport. (b) Application form (c) 1 passport-size photo. (d) For Business visa, letters from company and from sponsor etc.† (e) Visa or voucher from the tourist agency and itinerary for Tourist visa. (f) Fee. (g) Pre-paid, Express Mail, self-addressed return envelope for postal applications.
Note [†]: Nationals of Germany, Italy and the USA do not need letters of invitation from Moldova.
Working days required: 5 days (same day for urgent visas with surcharge of US$20).
Temporary residence: Application to the Foreign Ministry in Moldova.

MONEY

Currency: On November 29, 1993 a new currency, the Leu (plural Lay), replaced the Rouble. 1 Leu (L) = 100 bani. The new banknotes depict Moldova's medieval founder, Stefan the Great. The exchange rate at the time of the introduction was US$1 = L3.85.
Currency exchange: Foreign currencies can be exchanged in hotels or bureaux de change. Moldova is essentially a cash-only economy.
Credit cards: Credit cards are rarely accepted. Check with your credit card company for details of merchant acceptability and other services which may be available.
Travellers cheques: Rarely accepted.
Currency restrictions: The import and export of local currency is prohibited, except for residents of Moldova who may import up to the amount they declared on departure and export up to the equivalent of Rbl500,000 if declared on departure. The import of foreign currency is unlimited if declared. The export of foreign currency is limited to the amount declared on arrival, except for residents who may only export the equivalent of up to US$500, provided it is declared on departure.

DUTY FREE

There are no established rules or guidelines as yet regarding duty-free items brought into Moldova.

PUBLIC HOLIDAYS

Jan 7 '95 Moldovan Christmas. **First week in Mar** Mertsishor (Spring Festival). **Mar 8** International Women's Day. **Apr 21** Good Friday. **Apr 24** Easter Monday. **May 9** Commemoration Day. **Aug 27** Independence Day. **Aug 31** Limba Noastra (Our Language Day). **Jan 7 '96** Moldovan Christmas. **First week in Mar** Mertsishor (Spring Festival). **Mar 8** International Women's Day. **Apr 12** Good Friday. **Apr 15** Easter Monday.

Timatic

Health
GALILEO/WORLDSPAN: **TI-DFT/KIV/HE**
SABRE: **TIDFT/KIV/HE**

Visa
GALILEO/WORLDSPAN: **TI-DFT/KIV/VI**
SABRE: **TIDFT/KIV/VI**

For more information on Timatic codes refer to Contents.

HEALTH

Regulations and requirements may be subject to change at short notice, and you are advised to contact your doctor well in advance of your intended date of departure. Any numbers in the chart refer to the footnotes below.

	Special Precautions?	Certificate Required?
Yellow Fever	No	No
Cholera	No	No
Typhoid & Polio	Yes	-
Malaria	No	-
Food & Drink	1	-

[1]: Mains water is normally chlorinated but bottled water is available and advised. Local meat, poultry, fruit and vegetables are generally considered safe to eat.
Rabies is present and casual exposure to stray dogs is common throughout Chisinău. Vaccination before arrival should be considered. If you are bitten abroad, seek medical advice without delay. For more information consult the *Health* section at the back of the book.
Hepatitis B is also prevalent in Moldova.
Health care: In case of emergency, contact the Emergency Unit at Suite 401, 4th Floor at the Hotel National. The First City Out-Patient Clinic provides 24-hour assistance as well. The US Embassy maintains a list of English-speaking physicians. There is a shortage of basic medical supplies, including disposable needles, anesthetics, antibiotics and vaccines. Elderly travellers and those with existing health problems may be at risk due to inadequate medical facilities. All services and prescriptions are charged for and doctors and hospitals often expect immediate cash payment; medical insurance is strongly recommended.

TRAVEL - International

AIR: Moldova's national airline is *Air Moldova*. Only *Air Moldova* and *Tarom* (Romania's national airline) fly regularly to Moldova. There are also charter airlines operating between Chisinău and some major destinations in the CIS, Romania, Turkey, Germany and Israel.
Approximate flight times: From *Moscow* to Chisinău is 2 hours, from *Kiev* is 1 hour 30 minutes and from *St Petersburg* is 3 hours.
International airport: *Chisinău International* is 14.5km (9 miles) from the city centre (travel time – 25 minutes). There is a regular bus service to the city. Taxis are also available. *Moldova-Tur* offers a courtesy pick-up by prior arrangement.
RAIL: Moscow (22 hours) and Kiev (10 hours) connect three times a day with Chisinău. Further routes are to Odessa (3 hours) and Benderi (Tighina) (1 hour). There is also a regular rail link with Bucharest (Romania) and Sofia (Bulgaria) via Ungheni. The journey takes 11 hours 30 minutes and 23 hours respectively.
ROAD: Moldova can be entered from Ukraine and also from Romania via the border crossing at Leusheni. From Chisinău to Odessa is 183km (114 miles).

TRAVEL - Internal

RAIL: There are over 1200km (750 miles) of railway track in use in Moldova.
ROAD: The road network covers 10,000km (6250 miles). **Taxi:** These can be found in front of the main hotels housing foreigners. Fares should be negotiated in advance, though drivers prefer to charge per hour. The going rate is L30 per hour. Taxis run mainly on liquid gas. Butane bottles are installed in the boots; hence there is relatively little room for luggage. **Car hire:** Self-drive cars can be obtained through *Moldova-Tur*. Prices are L78 per day or L10 per hour plus L0.15 per kilometre.
Documentation: An International Driving Permit is required.
URBAN: Buses and trolleybuses are cheap but notoriously crowded and unreliable. A bus ride costs 6 bani and for trolleybuses it is 5 bani.

ACCOMMODATION

HOTELS: There is a small selection of hotels in the capital Chisinău, with the Hotel Intourist (2 Stefan cel Mare; tel: (2) 266 083) at the top end of the market. Its location is fairly central, close to the railway station and about 6km (4 miles) from the airport. The Motel Strugurash (230 Kotovsky Shosse; tel: (2) 226 000) is located approximately 8km (5 miles) from the city centre, in close proximity to the Ialovenu vineyard.

RESORTS & EXCURSIONS

The Moldovan capital of **Chisinău** (formerly Kishinev) stands on the banks of the small river Byk. The city was founded around 1470 and the history and life of Moldova through the centuries is best presented in the *History and Regional Lore Museum*, a beautiful Turkish-style complex at 82 Pirogov Street. A branch of the art museum is housed in a former 19th-century *Cathedral*, one of the city's finest historical monuments. The *Fine Arts Museum*, 115 Stefan cel Mare, houses good examples of Russian, West European and Moldovan paintings, sculpture and applied arts. The *Pushkin House* at Antonovskaya Street is the place where the great Russian poet spent his days in exile between 1820-23. The museum is famous as the place where Pushkin began working on his epic poem *Eugene Onegin*. There are also two old cemeteries in Chisinău, the *Armenian Cemetery* is at the top of Armenian str. and the *Jewish Cemetery* at Zelenaya str., Novie Boyukany. The latter is famous as the burial place for the victims of the Chisinău Pogrom in 1903; in the 1960s the lower part of the cemetery was deliberately razed by the authorities. Due to massive Jewish emigration from Moldova during the 1980s and beginning of the 1990s the state of the cemetery has significantly deteriorated. The only working synagogue in Chisinău is situated not far from the city centre, off Armyanskaya str. The former Chisinău Choral Synagogue today houses the *Chekhov Drama Theatre* (28 June Street). The *Monument of Stefan cel Mare* (Stefan the Great) is situated at the entrance to the well-tended Pushkin Park. He was Moldova's Gospodar (ruler) between 1457-1504 during a time of brief independence, thus securing him a special place in Moldova's history. The monument by the sculptor Plamadeala was unveiled in 1927. In 1990-91 the monument was the focal point of meetings and violent clashes between Moldova's Nationalists and pro-Soviet supporters. Just outside the park is an impressive building housing the largest cinema *Patria* (Motherland) which was built in 1947 by German POWs.
Picturesque bathing beaches line the man-made *Chisinău Lake* (formerly Komsomol Lake). Boats can also be hired. There are two parts to the complex: the *Exhibition of Achievements* and the open-air *Green Theatre* with a seating capacity of 7000. Trolleybus nos. 4, 5, 7, 8 and 12 connect with the city centre.
Situated 70km (44 miles) from Chisinău is **Tiraspol,** founded in 1792 on the then Russian border. It now has a population of 200,000 and is one of the main industrial centres of the country. It is also the capital of the self-proclaimed Transdniestria. Local industry is centred around food-processing and silk mills.
Benderi (Tighina) is one of the oldest towns in Moldova. Its beautiful 17th-century fortress, as well as the town itself, were seriously damaged during the recent fighting.
Bălti, 150km (94 miles) from the capital, is a major industrial centre north of Chisinău. The main products from this area are sugar, vegetable oils and fur coats. Approximately 160km (100 miles) south of Chisinău is **Cahul.** The town is famous for its thermal spas and mud treatments and there is a small hotel in the town. There is also a good local theatre. **Hirjauca** is also a renowned spa in the area.
Moldova is a wine-growing country and the vineyards and wine-cellars of **Mileshti** and **Krikova-Veki** are famous throughout.

SOCIAL PROFILE

FOOD & DRINK: There are plenty of small restaurants and coffee shops. The service tends to be slow, but the cuisine is delicious. Local specialities include *mititeyi* (small grilled sausages with onion and pepper) and *mamaliga* (thick, sticky maize pie) which is served with *brinza* (feta cheese). *Tocana* (pork stew) should be tried with sweet-and-sour watermelons and apples. **Drink:** There are more than 100 varieties of excellent wines produced in Moldova. White wines include *Reisling, Gligote* and *Semilion. Moldovan Cabernet* and *Bordeaux* are noteworthy reds. *Nistru* or *Doina* brandy is an ideal accompaniment with desserts.
NIGHTLIFE: In Chisinău there is a good selection of theatres and concerts halls. The Opera is situated at 79 Stefan cel Mare, next to Organ Hall. The Pushkin Music and Drama Theatre, also at 79 Stefan cel Mare, specialises in Romanian productions, as does the Youth Theatre Luceafărul (Poetic Star) in 7 Fontanny Lane. All performances in the Chekhov Drama Theatre (28 June Street) are exclusively in Russian (the building used to be the Chisinău Choral Synagogue). The Philarmonia Concert Hall, 78 25 October str., houses Moldova's

Symphony Orchestra. It is also the base for the folklore Doina Choir, the internationally renowned Zhok National Dance Ensemble and the Fluerash Orchestra of National Music. Russian and Romanian productions can be seen in the puppet theatre Licurici (Glow-worm) at 121 Kievskaya str.

SHOPPING: Good buys are the vividly coloured costumes, hand-made carpets and locally produced wines and brandies. **Shopping hours:** Larger shops open 0800-2000.

SOCIAL CONVENTIONS: Dress should be casual but conservative. For official engagements men should wear a jacket and tie. A small gift such as cigarettes, perfume or coffee are generally appreciated. The country is famous for its tradition of folk arts and there are many vivacious musical groups (*Tarafs*), which play a variety of rare folk instruments including the *tsambal* (not unlike a dulcimer), *cimpoi* (bagpipe), *fluier* and *nai*.

Tipping: 5-10% will be gladly accepted.

BUSINESS PROFILE

ECONOMY: Moldova's economy is dominated by agriculture, food-processing and related industries. Some 85% of the country's terrain is cultivated. The republic was formerly the largest wine region in the Soviet Union and continues to rely on this for revenue. Moldovan wines have won several prizes in international competitions. In addition to wine grapes, Moldova is also a major grower of fruit, vegetables, tobacco and grain. Although Moldova's wine industry suffered serious set-backs when some of the vineyards were uprooted during Gorbachev's anti-alcohol campaign in the mid-1980s, the industry has since considerably recovered and has been providing the national economy with a steady trickle of hard currency revenue. After the demise of the Soviet Union a significant number of skilled personnel lost their jobs at Moldova's electronic factories, whose production was mostly under contract to the Soviet Defence and Space industries. These factories are now seeking new partners in the West. Moldova's intended transition to a market economy has been hampered by the war in Transdniestria and the fall-off in trade with the other former Soviet republics. In pursuit of international support for its economy, Moldova joined the IMF, World Bank and European Bank for Reconstruction and Development.

COMMERCIAL INFORMATION: The following organisation can offer advice: Chamber of Commerce and Industry of the Republic of Moldova, 28 Emineskou, 277012 Chisinău. Tel: (2) 221 552. Fax: (2) 233 810.

CLIMATE

Very mild and pleasant. Temperate with warm summers 20-23°C, crisp, sunny autumns and cold, sometimes snowy, winters.

Required clothing: Mediumweights, heavy topcoat and overshoes for winter; lightweights for summer. A light raincoat is useful.

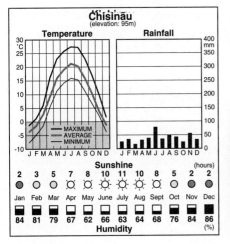

Chisinău
(elevation: 95m)

Location: Western Europe.

Direction du Tourisme et des Congrès de la Principauté de Monaco
2a boulevard des Moulins, Monte Carlo, MC-98030 Monaco
Tel: 92 16 61 16 (administration) *or* 92 16 61 66 (information). Fax: 92 16 60 00. Telex: 469760 (a/b MC).

Monaco Embassy *and* **Consulate General**
4 Cromwell Place, London SW7 2JE
Tel: (0171) 225 2679. Fax: (0171) 581 8161. Opening hours: 1000-1230 and 1400-1700 Monday to Friday.

Monaco Government Tourist & Convention Office
3/18 Chelsea Garden Market, Chelsea Harbour, London SW10 0XE
Tel: (0171) 352 9962. Fax: (0171) 352 2103. Opening hours: 0930-1730 Monday to Friday.

British Consulate General
BP 265, 33 boulevard Princesse Charlotte, Monte Carlo, MC-98005 Monaco
Tel: 93 50 99 66. Fax: 93 50 14 47. Telex: 420307 (a/b BRITAIN MARSL).

Consulate General of the Principality of Monaco *and* **Monaco Government Tourist & Convention Office**
19th Floor, 845 Third Avenue, New York, NY 10022
Tel: (212) 759 5227. Fax: (212) 754 9320.
Consulates in: Boston, Chicago, Dallas, Palm Beach, Los Angeles, New Orleans, Philadelphia, San Francisco and Washington, DC.

Consulate General of the United States of America
31 rue Maréchal Joffre, 06000 Nice, France
Tel: 93 88 89 55. Fax: 93 87 07 38.

Consulate General of the Principality of Monaco
Suite 1500, 1115 Sherbrooke Street, Montréal, Québec H3A 2W1
Tel: (514) 849 0589. Fax: (514) 631 2771.
Consulate in: Vancouver.

The Canadian Embassy in Paris deals with enquiries relating to Monaco (see *France* **earlier in the book).**

AREA: 1.95 sq km (0.75 sq mile).
POPULATION: 29,876 (1990).
POPULATION DENSITY: 15,321 per sq km.
CAPITAL: Monaco-Ville.
GEOGRAPHY: Monaco is second only to the Vatican as the smallest independent state in Europe. Set on the Mediterranean coast of France just a few miles from the Italian border, the principality is a constitutional monarchy and relies largely on foreign currency for an

economic base. Its principal industry is tourism. The country is a narrow ribbon of coastline backed by the Alpes-Maritimes foothills, creating a natural amphitheatre overlooking the sea, with the population centred in four districts. Monaco-Ville is set on a rocky promontory dominating the coast. The Palace is the home of the Grimaldi family, the oldest ruling house in Europe. Monaco-Ville also boasts a fine Romanesque cathedral among its other attractions. La Condamine is the area around the Port, while Monte Carlo is the main centre for business and entertainment. Fontvieille has been set aside as an area for new light industrial and residential development.

LANGUAGE: French. Monégasque (a mixture of French Provençal and Italian Ligurian), English and Italian are also spoken. Native Monégasques make up only a minority of Monaco's population (5070 according to the 1990 census).

RELIGION: Roman Catholic (Monaco has a Catholic Bishop) with Anglican minorities.

TIME: GMT + 1 (GMT + 2 from last Sunday in March to Saturday before last Sunday in September).

ELECTRICITY: 220 volts AC, 50Hz. Round 2-pin plugs are in use.

COMMUNICATIONS: Telephone: Full IDD is available. As with France, the country code is 33. The area code (either 92 or 93) prefixes telephone numbers and must also be dialled within Monaco. Outgoing international code: 19. **Fax:** Some hotels have facilities. **Telex/telegram:** Available at hotels and post offices. Telephones and telegraphic services are open 0800-2100 daily at the main post office (see below). **Post:** Same rates as France. The Main Post Office is at The Scala Palace, Beaumarchais Square. Opening hours: 0800-1900 Monday to Friday and 0800-1200 Saturday. There are special Monégasque stamps. **Press:** The main daily is *Nice-Matin*. The *Journal de Monaco* is published weekly. French newspapers are widely available, as are English books and magazines.

BBC World Service and Voice of America frequencies: From time to time these change. See the section *How to Use this Book* for more information.

BBC:				
MHz	12.09	9.760	9.410	0.648
Voice of America:				
MHz	11.97	9.670	6.040	5.995

PASSPORT/VISA

The passport and visa requirements for persons visiting Monaco as a tourist are the same as for France. For further details, see the earlier entry for *France*. Monaco is not a member of the EU, however, so residency and long-stay requirements differ and are liable to changes. For further details, contact any French Consulate.

MONEY

Currency: French Franc. See the entry for *France* for details of exchange rate, currency restrictions, etc.
Credit cards: Access/Mastercard, American Express, Crédit Agricole, Diners Club and Visa are widely accepted. Check with your credit card company for details of merchant acceptability and other services which may be available.
Banking hours: 0900-1200 and 1400-1630 Monday to Friday.

PUBLIC HOLIDAYS

Jan 2 '95 For New Year's Day. **Jan 27** St Devote's Day. **Feb 28** Shrove Tuesday (half day). **Apr 17** Easter Monday. **May 1** Labour Day. **May 25** Ascension Day. **Jun 5** Whit Monday. **Aug 15** Assumption. **Nov 1** All Saints' Day. **Nov 19** Monaco National Commemoration Day. **Dec 8** Immaculate Conception. **Dec 25** Christmas Day. **Jan 1 '96** New Year's Day. **Jan 27** St Devote's Day. **Feb 20** Shrove Tuesday (half day).

HEALTH

Regulations and requirements may be subject to change at short notice, and you are advised to contact your doctor well in advance of your intended date of departure. Any numbers in the chart refer to the footnotes below.

	Special Precautions?	Certificate Required?
Yellow Fever	No	No
Cholera	No	No
Typhoid & Polio	No	-
Malaria	No	-
Food & Drink	1	-

[1]: Mains water is normally chlorinated, and safe to drink. Milk is pasteurised and dairy products are safe for

consumption. Local meat, poultry, seafood, fruit and vegetables are generally considered safe to eat.
Rabies is present. For those at high risk, vaccination before arrival should be considered. If you are bitten abroad seek medical advice without delay. For more information, consult the *Health* section at the back of the book.
Health care: Health insurance is recommended. There are high standards of medical care.

TRAVEL

AIR: There is no airport in Monaco. Helicopter services run by *Héli-Air Monaco* link the principality with the nearest airport, *Nice* (Nice-Cote d'Azur), 22km (14 miles) from Monaco. The journey takes 6 minutes. *Héli-Air* also serves points along the Côte d'Azur and in Italy. Taxis or special buses are available from place d'Armes, place du Casino, Tourist Office, Hotel Mirabeau and Hotel Beach Plaza. For more information, contact Héli-Air Monaco, Monaco Heliport, Quartier de Fontvieille, MC-98000 Monaco. Tel: 92 05 00 50. Fax: 92 05 76 17. Telex: 479343 (a/b ELIAIR).
RAIL: An extensive train service runs through the principality to all neighbouring towns, with connections at Marseille onto high-speed *TGV* trains to Paris. There are also daily and overnight through trains. The *SNCF Métrazur* summer service runs every 30 minutes, stopping at all towns on the Côte d'Azur between Cannes and the Italian frontier at Menton, including Monaco. For passenger information, tel: 93 25 54 54.
ROAD: Cannes and Nice are 50km (31 miles) and 18km (11 miles) west of Monaco. The French/Italian border and Menton are 12km (7 miles) and 9km (6 miles) east of Monaco. No formalities are required to cross the frontier between France and the Principality of Monaco.
Coach: There is a direct service connecting Nice airport with Monaco. For passenger information, tel: 93 21 30 83.
Bus: There are good connections with the surrounding areas, with the following regular services:
Nice: Seaside route with stops at Cap d'Ail, Eze-sur-Mer, Beaulieu-sur-Mer and Villefranche-sur-Mer. Service from 0600-2100 approximately every 30 minutes. Middle Corniche route with stops at Cap d'Ail, Eze-Village and Col de Villefranche. Services from 0600-1815 (2000 Saturday and Sunday) approximately every hour.
Menton: Seaside route with stops in Roquebrune and Cap-Martin (service from 0530-2100) approximately every 30 minutes.
Service to Saint Roman/Rocher de Monaco, Jardin Exotique/Rocher de Monaco, Gare SNCF/Larvotto Beach and Rocher de Monaco/Parking Touristique Fontvieille. Buses run approximately every five minutes between Monaco-Ville and the Casino, every ten minutes towards St Roman or the Jardin Exotique and between the Railway Station and beaches (Larvotto).
Taxi: Available from Casino Square, Monaco-Monte Carlo Railway Station and avenue Princesse Grace. Surcharge after 2200. **Documentation:** As for France, a national driving licence will suffice.
JOURNEY TIMES: The following chart gives approximate journey times (in hours and minutes) from Monaco to a selection of other cities in Europe.

	Air	Road	Rail	Sea
London	1.45	-	-	-
Paris	1.15	-	-	-
Nice	*0.06	0.45	0.30	0.20
Menton	-	0.35	0.25	-
Geneva	0.50	3.30	4.00	-
Rome	1.00	-	-	-

Note [*]: Time by helicopter – see above under *Air*.

ACCOMMODATION

HOTELS: Some of the most luxurious hotels and conference facilities are centred in Monaco, and all are equipped with extensive modern amenities. In 1993 there were 601,111 overnight visitors in the principality and from January to May 1994 there were 237,941. For further information contact the Association de l'Industrie Hôtelière Monégasque, 20 avenue de Fontvieille, Monte Carlo, MC-98000 Monaco. Tel: 92 05 35 20. **Grading:** Hotels in Monaco are graded in a **1-**, **2-**, **3-**, **4-** and **4-star deluxe** system. The principality has 18 hotels, one of which is in the 4-star deluxe category and six of which are in the 4-star category.
SELF-CATERING: Apartments are available to let. For further details contact Utoring Diffusion, 44 boulevard d'Italie, Monte Carlo. Tel: 93 30 30 79.

RESORTS & EXCURSIONS

Monaco forms an enclave into the French Département of the Alpes Maritimes. The narrow ribbon of coastline is backed by the mountains, which form a natural protective barrier. This area creates a natural amphitheatre. From the heights of the *Tête de Chien* or Mont Agel, or from lower down from the Moyenne-Corniche at the level of the entrance to the *Jardin Exotique,* there are a number of panoramic viewpoints looking out over exceptional scenery. The ancestral Rocher and the promontory of Spélugues border the harbour where pleasure boats are moored. The rock of Monaco has a medieval air. It is a city of bright, clean streets which converge on the *Prince's Palace Square,* where there are museums, boutiques and restaurants.
Monaco-Ville: *The Prince's Palace and State Apartment*: Daily 0930-1830 June to September and 1000-1700 during October, an admission fee is charged. *Place du Palais:* Changing of the Guard daily at 1155, admission is free. *Museum of Napoleonic Souvenirs and Collection of the Palace's Historic Archives*: Daily (except Monday) 1030-1230 and 1400-1700 December to May; 0930-1830 June to Spetember; 1000-1700 October. An admission fee is charged. *Oceanographic Museum and Aquarium*: Daily 0930-1900 October and March; 0900-1900 April, May and September; 0900-2000 June to August; 1000-1800 November to February. An admission fee is charged. *Wax Museum of the Princes of Monaco*: Daily 1030-1700 November to January; 0930-1900 February to October. An admission fee is charged. *Monte-Carlo Story* (multivision show): Daily 1100-1700 March to October; 1400-1700 November to February (closed Dec 1-25); 1100-1800 July and August. An admission fee is charged. *Azur Express Tourist Train* (commentaries in French, Italian, German and English): Daily 1030-1200 and 1400-1800 February to October. Two tours are available, a fee is charged.
Monaco: *Exotic Garden and Observatory Caves – Museum of Prehistoric Anthropology*: Daily 0900-1900 May 15 to September 15; 0900-1800/nightfall May 14 to September 16. An admission fee is charged. *Zoological Gardens*: Daily 1000-1200 and 1400-1700 October to February; 1000-1200 and 1400-1800 March to May; 0900-1200 and 1400-1900 June to September. An admission fee is charged.
Monte Carlo: *National Museum of Dolls and Clockwork Exhibits of Yesteryear:* Daily 1000-1215 and 1430-1830 October to Easter; 1000-1830 Easter to September. An admission fee is charged. *Casino* (minimum age for entrance is 21): Gambling rooms, daily from 1200. Private gambling rooms, daily from 1500 November to April and 1600 May to October. An admission fee is charged. *Sun Casino – Hôtel Loews* (minimum age for entrance is 21): Gambling rooms, from 1700 Monday to Thursday and 1600 Friday to Sunday and public holidays. Admission is free.
Monte Carlo Bord de Mer (Larvotto): The creation of this new district was made possible by re-routing railway tracks underground. The development has a beach, restaurants, snack bar and shops.
This part of Monaco also has extensive sporting facilities at the prestigious Monte Carlo Sporting and Sea Clubs where there are restaurants and an Olympic-sized swimming pool.
Note: For a description of the area of France surrounding Monaco, see the *Southeast* section of the entry for *France* earlier in the *World Travel Guide*.

SOCIAL PROFILE

FOOD & DRINK: Restaurants in Monaco offer a wide choice of food. Service and standards are excellent. Cuisine is similar to France, with some delicious local specialities. There are many restaurants and bars with late opening hours. Specialities include: *barbaguian*, a type of pastry filled with rice and pumpkin; *fougasse*, fragrant orange flower water pastries decorated with nuts, almonds and aniseed; *socca*, chickpea flour pancakes; *stocafi*, dried cod cooked in a tomato sauce.
NIGHTLIFE: The world-famous Monte Carlo Casino is a perennial attraction. The building also houses the Casino Cabaret and the *Salle Garnier,* the delightful gilded Opera House offering a winter season of ballet, opera and music. There are further gambling venues in the Loews Monte Carlo Hotel, the Café de Paris and the Monte Carlo Sporting Club. There are also numerous nightclubs, cinemas, discotheques and variety shows.
SHOPPING: Monégasque products include perfume, chocolates, anchovies, ceramics, clothing, hosiery, shoes, books, jewellery and embroidery. Handcrafted items are sold at Boutique du Rocher, a charity of the late Princess Grace. Monégasque stamps are highly prized by collectors. **Shopping hours:** 0900-1200 and 1500-1900 Monday to Saturday.
SPORT: Golf: The Monte Carlo Golf Club has an undulating course where tournaments are regularly staged. There is also a miniature golf course.
Tennis/squash: The Monte Carlo Country Club has excellent tennis and squash facilities, and is the venue for international tennis championships which attract big-name tennis stars. **Swimming:** Bathing in the sea is safe (if often crowded), and in addition to hotel swimming pools there are several heated seawater pools open throughout the year. **Sailing:** The Yacht Club de Monaco offers sailing lessons during July and August and the harbour also has facilities. **Water-sports:** Monaco has facilities for water-skiing, skindiving, parasailing and windsurfing. **Spectator sports:** In late May the famous *Monaco Grand Prix Formula One* race takes place through the narrow winding streets. In addition to the above, there are also a number of health spas and beauty centres in Monaco.
SPECIAL EVENTS: The following is a selection of festivals and events taking place in Monaco in 1995. In addition to the following, there are musical events throughout the year. For further information concerning events and festivals, contact the Government Tourist & Convention Office (addresses at the top of this entry).
Apr 6-9 '95 *11th Monte Carlo Grand Prix of Magic.* **Apr 15-May 14** *Monte Carlo Spring Arts Festival.* **Apr 15-Sep 30** *5th Biennial of Contemporary Sculpture.* **Apr 22-30** *Monte Carlo International Tennis Championships.* **May 3** *Monte Carlo World Music Awards.* **May 6-7** *28th International Floral Contest.* **May 10-Jun 5** *International Contemporary Art Award Exhibition.* **May 25-28** *Monte Carlo Automobile Grand Prix.* **May 28** *53rd Monaco F1 Grand Prix.* **Jun 3-5** *Monaco Expo Cactus.* **Jun 9-11** *3rd International Bonzai Exhibition.* **Jul 18, 22 & 25** *30th International Fireworks Festival.* **Jul 29-Aug 15** *11th International Biennial of Antique Dealers, Jewellers and Art Galleries.* **Aug 4** *Monégasque Red Cross Gala.* **Aug 5 & 8** *30th International Fireworks Festival.* **Oct 13-15** *14th Mini Grand Prix of radio-controlled cars.* **Oct 16-20** *13th Baroque Music Week.*
SOCIAL CONVENTIONS: Casual wear is acceptable for daytime and dress is the same as for the rest of the French Riviera. Smart restaurants, dining rooms, clubs and the Casino's private rooms require more formal attire. Smoking during meals is frowned upon. Handshaking and, more familiarly, kissing both cheeks, are accepted forms of greeting. **Tipping:** Hotel and restaurant bills generally include a 15% service charge; however, where this is not added it is customary to leave a 15% tip. Taxi drivers are usually tipped 15% of the fare.

BUSINESS PROFILE

ECONOMY: The heart of the economy is banking, insurance and tourism. The financial sector accounts for just over one-third of non-industrial turnover. The property business is also thriving after a downturn early in the 1980s which coincided with the global recession. Construction and light industry – pharmaceuticals, plastics and electronics – are the other important productive sectors. Almost all the principality's external trade is conducted with France. 'Offshore banking' has been hampered by French restrictions on foreign exchange movements, but these should have been eased by the introduction of EU regulations at the end of 1992.
BUSINESS: A suit should be worn and prior appointments are necessary. Business meetings are formal. It is considered impolite to begin a conversation in French and then revert to English. **Office hours:** 0800-1200 and 1400-1800 Monday to Friday.
COMMERCIAL INFORMATION: The following organisation can offer advice: Conseil Economique (consultative organisation dealing with all aspects of the national economy), 8 rue Louis Notari, Monte Carlo, MC-98000 Monaco. Tel: 93 30 20 82. Fax: 93 50 05 96.
CONFERENCES/CONVENTIONS: There is a full range of facilities at the Convention Centre and Auditorium (built at the very edge of the sea), including technical support and exhibition areas. The International Conference Centre (with a capacity for up to 450 persons) also has support facilities. Six other venues are listed in the Monte Carlo brochure. A new Cultural and Exhibition Centre is planned for 1998. From 1978 to 1994 Monaco hosted over 3000 events, with 461 held in 1990; during this 16-year period the number per annum more than doubled. Further information can be obtained from the Direction du Tourisme et des Congrès de la Principauté de Monaco (see top of entry for address).

CLIMATE

Monaco has a mild climate throughout the year, the hottest months being July and August, and the coolest being January and February. Rain mostly falls during the cooler winter months and there is an average of only 60 days' rain per year.
Required clothing: Lightweights are worn, with a warm wrap for cooler summer evenings. Light- to medium-weights are advised for winter. For Climate Chart see the entry for France earlier in the book.

Mongolia

□ *international airport*

Location: Central Asia.

Mongolian Tourism Federation
Shuren Company, Suhbaatar Square, Soyolyn tov orgoo, Ulan Bator, Mongolia.
Juulchin (Mongolian Foreign Tourism Corporation)
Chinggis Khan Avenue 5B, Ulan Bator 210543, Mongolia
Tel: (1) 328 428. Fax: (1) 320 246.
Mongolian Embassy
7 Kensington Court, London W8 5DL
Tel: (0171) 937 0150. Fax: (0171) 937 1117. Telex: 28844. Opening hours:1100-1230 Monday to Friday.
Mongolia Tourist Information Service
Dudenstrasse 78, D-10905 Berlin, Germany
Tel: (30) 786 5056. Fax: (30) 786 5596.
British Embassy
PO Box 703, 30 Enkh Taivny Gudamzh, Ulan Bator 13, Mongolia
Tel: (1) 358 133. Fax: (873) 144 5143. Telex: 79261 (a/b UKREP MH).
Embassy of Mongolia
2833 M Street, NW, Washington, DC 20007
Tel: (202) 333 7117. Fax: (202) 298 9227.
Also deals with enquiries from Canada.
The US Embassy in Beijing deals with enquiries relating to Mongolia (see *China* **earlier in this book). The Canadian Embassy in Beijing deals with enquiries relating to Mongolia (see** *China* **earlier in this book).**

AREA: 1,565,000 sq km (604,250 sq miles).
POPULATION: 2,200,000 (1993 estimate).
POPULATION DENSITY: 1.4 per sq km.
CAPITAL: Ulan Bator. **Population:** 600,900 (1992).
GEOGRAPH: Mongolia has a 3000km (1864-mile) border with the Russian Federation in the north and a 4670km (2901-mile) border with China in the south. From north to south it can be divided into four areas: mountain-forest steppe, mountain steppe and, in the extreme south, semi-desert and desert (the latter being about 3% of the entire territory). The majority of the country has a high elevation, with the principal mountains concentrated in the west. The highest point is peak Nairamdal in the Altai Mountains at 4370m (14,337ft). The lowest point, Lake Khoch Nuur in the east, lies at 560m (1820ft). There are several hundred lakes in the country and numerous rivers, of which the

Zabkhan is the longest at 1300km (800 miles).
LANGUAGE: Mongolian Khalkha is the official language. There are also many Mongolian dialects.
RELIGION: Buddhist Lamaism is the main religion. Also Shamanism.
TIME: GMT + 8 (GMT + 9 from last Sunday in March to Saturday before last Sunday in September).
ELECTRICITY: 220 volts AC, 60Hz.
COMMUNICATIONS: Telephone: In August 1994 an Asiasat Earth station was put into operation which has facilitated a vast improvement in international telecommunications with Mongolia. Country code: 976. Area codes: Ulan Bator: 1, Darhan: 37, Erdenet: 35, Hovd: 43. **Fax:** Service began in December 1990. **Telex:** Limited facilities available in Ulan Bator. **Post:** Airmail to Europe takes up to two weeks. There is a DHL service in Ulan Bator. **Press:** The main newspapers include *Ardyn Erkh*, *Ardchilal* and *Ug*. The English-language papers published in Mongolia are *The Mongol Messenger* and *The Independent*.
BBC World Service and Voice of America frequencies: From time to time these change. See the section *How to Use this Book* for more information.

BBC:

MHz	21.72	15.36	11.82	7.180
Voice of America:				
MHz	17.74	11.76	7.275	1.575

PASSPORT/VISA

Regulations and requirements may be subject to change at short notice, and you are advised to contact the appropriate diplomatic or consular authority before finalising travel arrangements. Details of these may be found at the head of this country's entry. Any numbers in the chart refer to the footnotes below.

	Passport Required?	Visa Required?	Return Ticket Required?
Full British	Yes	Yes	No
BVP	Not valid	-	-
Australian	Yes	Yes	No
Canadian	Yes	Yes	No
USA	Yes	Yes	No
Other EU (As of 31/12/94)	Yes	Yes	No
Japanese	Yes	Yes	No

PASSPORTS: Valid passport required by all except nationals of Bulgaria, China, CIS, Cuba, Czech Republic, Hungary, North Korea, Poland, Romania, Slovak Republic, Vietnam and Yugoslavia (Serbia and Montenegro) holding a valid national ID.
British Visitors Passport: Not accepted.
VISAS: Required by all except those mentioned under passports.
Types of visa: Tourist or Business. Visas should be obtained through tourism companies or travel agencies. A group visa in the name of the tour leader is valid for all tourists on the list attached – providing relevant details (nationality, sex, date of birth, passport numbers, and dates of issue and expiry) are given at the time of application (a group consists of 6-25 persons). Tourist and Business visas cost £17 in the UK. Tourist visas are also required for stopovers.
Validity: Any length of time is considered.
Application to: Travel agencies arranging visits to Mongolia, or from Mongolian Embassies in London, New York, Washington, New Delhi, Tokyo, Paris, Geneva, Brussels and Bonn.
Application requirements: (a) Valid passport. (b) 1 passport-size photo. (c) Confirmation and approval for the intended visit from the appropriate travel company. (d) A registered, stamped and self-addressed envelope is required for postal applications.
Working days required: 7 days. In urgent cases a visa can be issued on the day of application. Transit visas can be issued in 2 days.
Temporary residence/work permit: Enquire at the Mongolian Embassy.

MONEY

Currency: Tugrik (Tug) = 100 mongos. Notes are in denominations of Tug5000, 1000, 500, 100, 50, 20, 10, 5, 3 and 1. Coins are in denominations of Tug200, 100, 50 and 20, and 50, 20 and 10 mongos.
Currency exchange: Official organisations authorised to exchange foreign currency include commercial banks in Ulan Bator and bureaux de change at certain hotels.
Credit cards: Accepted by main commercial banks and large hotels.
Travellers cheques: Midland Bank and Thomas Cook (UK) travellers cheques are accepted.
Exchange rate indicators: The following figures are included as a guide to the movements of the Tugrik against Sterling and the US Dollar:

Date:	Oct '92	Sep '93	Jan '94	Jan '95
£1.00=	632.6	612.2	590.8	641.71
$1.00=	398.6	400.9	399.3	410.17

Currency restrictions: The import of local currency is up to Tug500, provided a bank certificate is held and the amount is declared on arrival. Export is allowed up to the amount declared on arrival. Import of foreign currency is unlimited. Export is limited to the amount declared on arrival.
Banking hours:1000-1500 Monday to Friday.

DUTY FREE

The following goods may be imported into Mongolia without incurring customs duty:
600 cigarettes; 2 litres of alcoholic beverages; a reasonable amount of perfume.
Prohibited items: Guns, weapons and ammunition without special permission; explosive items; radioactive substances; narcotics; pornographic publications; any publication, records, films and drawings against Mongolia; research materials; paleontological and archaeological findings; collections of various plants and their seeds; birds and wild or domestic animals; wool, raw skins, hides and furs without permission from the appropriate authorities.
Note: (a) Every tourist must fill in a customs declaration which should be retained until departure. This allows for the free import and re-export of articles intended for personal use for the duration of stay. (b) Goods to the value of Tug20,000 are allowed to be exported from Mongolia.

PUBLIC HOLIDAYS

Jan 1 '95 New Year's Day. **Feb 1-2** Tsagaan Sar (Lunar New Year). **Mar 8** International Women's Day. **Jul 11-13** National Independence Day. **Nov 26** Republic Day. **Jan 1 '96** New Year's Day. **Jan/Feb** Tsagaan Sar (Lunar New Year). **Mar 8** International Women's Day.

HEALTH

Regulations and requirements may be subject to change at short notice, and you are advised to contact your doctor well in advance of your intended date of departure. Any numbers in the chart refer to the footnotes below.

	Special Precautions?	Certificate Required?
Yellow Fever	No	-
Cholera	No	-
Typhoid & Polio	Yes	-
Malaria	No	-
Food & Drink	1	-

[1]: All water should be regarded as being potentially contaminated. Water used for drinking, brushing teeth or making ice should have first been boiled or otherwise sterilised. Milk is unpasteurised and should be boiled. Powdered or tinned milk is available and is advised, but make sure that it is reconstituted with pure water. Avoid dairy products which are likely to have been made from unboiled milk. Only eat well-cooked meat and fish, preferably served hot. Pork, salad and mayonnaise may carry increased risk. Vegetables should be cooked and fruit peeled.
Rabies is present. For those at high risk, vaccination before arrival should be considered. If you are bitten abroad seek medical advice without delay. For more information consult the *Health* section at the back of the book.
Health care: There are almost 23,000 hospital beds and more than 5000 doctors in Mongolia. Health insurance is recommended.

TRAVEL - International

AIR: Mongolia's national airline is *Air Mongol (Mongolian Civil Air Transport or MIAT) (OM)*.
Approximate flight time: From London to Ulan Bator is 14 hours including stopovers.
International airport: *Ulan Bator (ULN)* (Buyant Ukha) is 15km (9 miles) from the city.
RAIL: Ulan Bator is linked to Russia and China by the *Trans-Mongolian Railway*. An express train runs once a week between Moscow, Ulan Bator and Beijing. Trains on international routes have sleeping and restaurant cars. There are also two other weekly trains from Ulan Bator to Beijing as well as one to Moscow.
ROAD: There are several international road links; the principal route is via Irkutsk (East Siberia) to Ulan Bator.

TRAVEL - Internal

AIR: Internal flights are operated by *Air Mongol*. This is the recommended means of travelling to remote areas.

RAIL: There are 1600km (1000 miles) of track. The main line runs from north to south: Sühbaatar–Darhan–Ulan Bator–Saynshand. Branch lines serve the principal industrial regions.

ROAD: Paved roads are to be found only in or near major cities. **Bus:** There are bus services between towns, but the roads are mostly unpaved. **Car hire:** Available through tourism companies. Jeeps, camels or horses are available for hunters, trekkers and special interest travellers.

JOURNEY TIMES: The following chart gives approximate journey times (in hours and minutes) from Ulan Bator to other major cities/towns in Mongolia.

	Air	Road
Erdenet	1.30	-
Gobi Desert	1.30	-
Gurran Naur	1.30	-
Khujurt	0.45	-
Karkorum	1.00	-
Terelj	-	1.00

ACCOMMODATION

HOTELS: There are hotels in most major centres, particularly in Ulan Bator, Erdenet and Darhan. These provide full board, daily excursions and entrance fees to museums and the services of a guide or interpreter. Accommodation can be arranged through tourism companies or directly with the hotels. **Grading:** Deluxe, semi-deluxe, first-class and tourist are the four categories of Mongolian hotels.

RESORT SPAS: There is limited accommodation for visitors. Prices are available on request.

CAMPING: At Terelj, Undur Dov and Chinggisiin Urguu there are tourist camps where visitors try living in a Mongolian *yurt* for a while. There are also country tourist camps at Khujirt which are open from May to October.

RESORTS & EXCURSIONS

The capital **Ulan Bator** is the country's political, commercial and cultural centre. There are a number of museums in the city, the largest being the *State Central Museum.* The paleontological section has a magnificent display of the skeletons of giant dinosaurs. Others include the *Fine Arts Museum* and the *Museum of Revolution.* There are also several Buddhist temple museums and the still-functioning *Gandan Monastery* is an interesting visit. Ulan Bator also has several theatres and theatre groups, such as the *State Opera and Ballet Theatre,* the *State Drama Theatre* and the *Folk Song and Dance Ensemble.* The Ulan Bator *State Public Library* has a unique collection of 11th-century Sanskrit manuscripts.

Travel outside the capital must usually be by prior arrangement. Every province has its own museums containing examples of local culture. The most popular tour takes the visitor to the **Gobi Desert,** the habitat of several rare animals, including Bactrian wild camels, snow leopards, Przhevalsky horses and Gobi bears. Coaches take parties to the country's tourist camps. The nearest to Ulan Bator is **Terelj,** 85km (50 miles) from the capital, where the *Gorki Mountains,* the *Tortoise Rock* and the *Terelj River* may be seen. **Khangal** is a mountainous region with 40 hot-water springs renowned for their curing properties. Another therapeutic spring can be found in **Khujirt,** where the ruins of the world-renowned *Kharkhorin,* capital of the Great Mongolian Empire of the 13th century, can also be found

SOCIAL PROFILE

FOOD & DRINK: Meat is the basis of the diet, primarily beef and mutton. The local cooking is quite distinctive. One local speciality is 'Boodog'. This is the whole carcass of a goat roasted from the inside with the entrails and bones being taken out through the throat; the carcass is filled with burning hot stones and the neck tied tightly. Thus the goat is cooked from the inside to the outside. Fish is also beginning to be widely available.

Drink: Mongolian vodka is excellent, as is the beer (though expensive). However, hot and cold beverages are included with all meals, with liquors available at an additional cost.

NIGHTLIFE: There are evening performances at the State Opera and Ballet Theatre, State Drama Theatre and Puppet Theatre; the Folk Song and Dance Ensemble and People's Army Song and Dance Ensemble are in the capital. Other major towns also have theatres. Circus entertainment is also very popular.

SHOPPING: In Ulan Bator there are many duty-free shops where convertible currencies are accepted. In all other shops, local currency must be used. The best buys include wines, cashmere garments, camel-wool blankets, national costumes, boots, jewellery, carpets, books and

records.

SPORT: An increasing number of sports facilities are being developed and most major towns have organised sporting events. Traditional sports include **horseracing, wrestling** and **archery,** which are all ancient and highly skilled contests with complex traditional rules.

SPECIAL EVENTS: For full details of events in 1995/96 contact the Mongolian National Tourism Organisation.

SOCIAL CONVENTIONS: Religious customs should be respected. **Tipping:** Not customary.

BUSINESS PROFILE

ECONOMY: The vast bulk of the working population is engaged in animal herding. Industrial activity is dominated by food, hides and wool processing, and is concentrated around Ulan Bator. Coal mining takes place mostly at the major fields of Darhan and Choybalsan; there are other important mineral deposits of flouspar, tungsten, tin, gold and lead. Textiles and light engineering complete Mongolia's main economic activities. A deterioration in relations with China since the early 1970s led to a downturn in the economy, but in recent years both industrial output and grain production have risen somewhat. The Government is seeking to develop the economy by concentrating on the infrastructure and the introduction of a new metal-working sector. In 1984 some 80% of Mongolia's trade was with the former USSR, and most of the remainder was with other Eastern European countries. From 1990 onwards, in common with its fellow members of COMECON, the Soviet bloc economic and trading union, Mongolia entered a period of major political and economic liberalisation. In particular, the Government introduced a crash programme of privatisation which aims to transfer 80% of the economy into private hands through a scheme under which the people are allocated vouchers which they convert into stocks of their choice as enterprises come on to the market. The upheaval in the Soviet Union caused great concern in Mongolia; relations with the former superpower have deteriorated seriously and the new government has so far proved unable to reach agreement with Moscow on future trade relations. This has led to severe shortages of raw materials and a consequent decline in output as well as a loss of traditional markets. Industrial production is between 50-80% below 1990 levels; exports were halved in 1991. As for future prospects, the Japanese and other East Asian nations are better placed to exploit any new opportunities. However, remote and impoverished as Mongolia is, it faces an uphill struggle to improve its economic prospects and will, in the forseeable future, be heavily dependent on multilateral aid.

BUSINESS: Suits are recommended; mediumweight for summer, and heavyweight for winter. Translator services should be arranged prior to departure to Mongolia. **Office hours:** 0900-1800 Monday to Friday; 0900-1500 Saturday.

COMMERCIAL INFORMATION: The following organisation can offer advice: Mongolian Chamber of Commerce and Industry, Sambuugiyn Gudamj, Ulan Bator 11. Tel: (1) 324 620. Telex: 79336.

CONFERENCES/CONVENTIONS: For further information contact the Chamber of Commerce and Industry (for address, see above).

CLIMATE

A cool climate with short, mild summers and long, severe winters (October to April). Some rain falls during summer and there is snow during winter.

Required clothing: Mediumweights are worn during summer, with very warm heavyweights advised for winter.

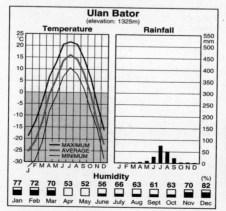

Montserrat

Location: Leeward Islands, Caribbean.

Montserrat Tourist Board
PO Box 7, Marine Road, Plymouth, Montserrat
Tel: 2230. Fax: 7430.

UK Passport Office
Visas to British Dependent Territories
Room 203, Clive House, 70 Petty France, London SW1H 9HD
Tel: (0171) 271 8616. Opening hours: 0900-1600 Monday to Friday.

Anguilla Tourist Office
3 Epirus Road, London SW6 7UJ
Tel: (0171) 730 7144. Fax: (0171) 938 4793. Opening hours: 0930-1700 Monday to Friday.
Also deals with enquiries for Montserrat.

Caribbean Tourism Association
20 East 46th Street, New York, NY 10017
Tel: (212) 682 0435. Fax: (212) 697 4258.
Also deals with enquiries from Canada.

High Commission for the Countries of the Organisation of Eastern Caribbean States
Suite 1610, Tower B, 112 Kent Street, Place de Ville, Ottawa, Ontario K1P 5P2
Tel: (613) 236 8952. Fax: (613) 236 3042.

AREA: 102 sq km (39.5 sq miles).
POPULATION: 11,900 (1987 estimate).
POPULATION DENSITY: 116.7 per sq km.
CAPITAL: Plymouth. **Population:** 1478 (1980).
GEOGRAPHY: Montserrat is one of the Leeward Islands group in the Caribbean. It is a volcanic island with black sandy beaches and lush tropical vegetation. There are three main volcanic mountains on the island and Chance's Peak is its highest point at 915m (3002ft). The crater of Galways Soufrière can be reached by road and the more energetic can see the hot springs and high mountain pools. The Great Alps Waterfall is one of the most spectacular sights in the West Indies.
LANGUAGE: English.

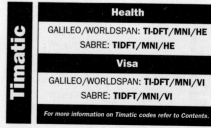

Timatic	Health		
	GALILEO/WORLDSPAN: **TI-DFT/MNI/HE**		
	SABRE: **TIDFT/MNI/HE**		
	Visa		
	GALILEO/WORLDSPAN: **TI-DFT/MNI/VI**		
	SABRE: **TIDFT/MNI/VI**		
	For more information on Timatic codes refer to Contents.		

Ulan Bator
(elevation: 1325m)

	Jan	Feb	Mar	Apr	May	June	July	Aug	Sept	Oct	Nov	Dec
Humidity (%)	77	72	70	53	52	56	66	63	61	63	70	82

RELIGION: Roman Catholic, Anglicans, Methodist and other Christian denominations.

TIME: GMT - 4.

ELECTRICITY: 120/220 volts AC, 60Hz.

COMMUNICATIONS: Telephone: Full IDD is available. Country code: 1 809 followed by 491. Outgoing international code: 011. **Fax/telex/telegram:** Cable & Wireless (WI) Ltd runs international links from Plymouth. **Post:** The Main Post Office in Plymouth is open 0815-1555 Monday, Tuesday, Thursday and Friday, and 0815-1125 Wednesday and Saturday. **Press:** All newspapers are in English and are published weekly or twice-weekly.

BBC World Service and Voice of America frequencies: From time to time these change. See the section *How to Use this Book* for more information.

BBC:

MHz	17.84	15.22	9.915	5.975

Voice of America:

MHz	15.21	11.70	6.130	0.930

PASSPORT/VISA

Regulations and requirements may be subject to change at short notice, and you are advised to contact the appropriate diplomatic or consular authority before finalising travel arrangements. Details of these may be found at the head of this country's entry. Any numbers in the chart refer to the footnotes below.

	Passport Required?	Visa Required?	Return Ticket Required?
Full British	No/1	No	Yes
BVP	Not valid	-	-
Australian	No/2	No	Yes
Canadian	No/1	No	Yes
USA	No/1	No	Yes
Other EU (As of 31/12/94)	No/2	No/3	Yes
Japanese	No/2	No	Yes

PASSPORTS: Valid passports are required by all except:

(a) **[1]** nationals of Canada, the USA and the UK may enter as tourists with a valid national ID card or other form of identity for a maximum stay of 6 months;

(b) **[2]** all other nationals referred to in the above chart provided they enter as tourists for a maximum stay of 14 days.

British Visitors Passport: Not accepted. Although the immigration authorities of this country may in certain circumstances accept British Visitors Passports for persons arriving for holidays or unpaid business trips of up to 3 months, travellers are reminded that no formal agreement exists to this effect and the situation may, therefore, change at short notice. In addition, UK nationals using a BVP and returning to the UK from a country with which no such formal agreement exists may be subject to delays and interrogation by UK immigration.

VISAS: Required by all except:

(a) nationals of countries mentioned in the chart above;

(b) nationals of Commonwealth countries;

(c) **[3]** nationals of EU countries (except nationals of Ireland and Portugal who *do* require visas if their stay exceeds 14 days and if entering on business);

(d) nationals of Fiji, Iceland, Liechtenstein, Norway, San Marino, Sweden and Tunisia.

Note: Other nationals do not require a passport or visa provided they enter as tourists and continue their journey to a third country within 14 days. This facility does not extend to nationals of Afghanistan, Albania, Angola, Argentina, Bosnia-Hercegovina, Bulgaria, China, CIS, Croatia, Cuba, Czech Republic, Hungary, North Korea, Former Yugoslav Republic of Macedonia, Mongolia, Romania, Slovak Republic, Slovenia, Syria, Vietnam and Yugoslavia (Serbia and Montenegro) who *do* need a visa and a passport at all times.

Types of visa: Tourist and Transit (cost depends on nationality).

Validity: Depends on nationality.

Application to: Consulate (or Consular section at High Commission). For addresses, see top of entry.

Application requirements: Enquiries to The Chief Immigration Officer, Government Head Office, Plymouth, Montserrat.

Working days required: Enquire at High Commission.

Note: All passengers must hold a return or onward ticket to a country to which they have a legal right of entry and sufficient funds to cover the period of their stay. Passengers not in possession of a return or onward ticket may be required to leave a deposit on arrival. Passengers not complying with any of the entry regulations listed above may be deported.

Temporary residence: Enquire at High Commission.

MONEY

Currency: East Caribbean Dollar (EC$) = 100 cents. Notes are in denominations of EC$100, 20, 10, 5 and 1. Coins are in denominations of 50, 25, 10, 5, 2 and 1 cents.

Currency exchange: There are three banks in Montserrat.

Credit cards: Visa is widely accepted. Check with your credit card company for details of merchant acceptability and other services which may be available.

Travellers cheques: Accepted in tourist areas and by selected merchants.

Exchange rate indicators: The following figures are included as a guide to the movements of the East Caribbean Dollar against Sterling and the US Dollar:

Date:	Oct '92	Sep '93	Jan '94	Jan '95
£1.00=	4.27	4.13	3.99	4.22
$1.00=	*2.70	*2.71	*2.70	*2.70

Note [*]: The Eastern Caribbean Dollar is tied to the US Dollar.

Currency restrictions: There are no restrictions on the import of local or foreign currency if declared. Export of local and foreign currency is limited to the amount imported and declared. Any foreign currency exported is subject to a 1.75% levy.

Banking hours: 0800-1500 Monday, Tuesday and Thursday; 0800-1300 Wednesday; 0800-1700 Friday.

DUTY FREE

The following goods may be imported into Montserrat without incurring customs duty:

*200 cigarettes or 50 cigars; *wines and spirits not exceeding 1.14 litres; 168g (6oz) of perfume; gifts up to a value of EC$250.*

Note [*]: Tobacco products and alcoholic beverages are only available to passengers 17 years of age or over.

Prohibited items: The importation of all firearms is strictly prohibited.

PUBLIC HOLIDAYS

Jan 1 '95 New Year's Day. **Mar 17** St Patrick's Day. **Apr 14** Good Friday. **Apr 17** Easter Monday. **May 1** Labour Day. **Jun 5** Whit Monday. **Jun 12** Queen's Official Birthday. **Aug 7** August Monday. **Nov 23** Liberation Day. **Dec 25-26** Christmas. **Dec 31** Festival Day. **Jan 1 '96** New Year's Day. **Mar 17** St Patrick's Day. **Apr 5** Good Friday. **Apr 8** Easter Monday.

HEALTH

Regulations and requirements may be subject to change at short notice, and you are advised to contact your doctor well in advance of your intended date of departure. Any numbers in the chart refer to the footnotes below.

	Special Precautions?	Certificate Required?
Yellow Fever	No	1
Cholera	No	-
Typhoid & Polio	Yes	-
Malaria	No	-
Food & Drink	2	

[1]: A yellow fever vaccination certificate is required of travellers over one year of age coming from infected areas.

[2]: Mains water is normally chlorinated, and whilst relatively safe may cause mild abdominal upsets. Bottled water is available and is advised for the first few weeks of the stay. Milk is pasteurised and dairy products are safe for consumption. Local meat, poultry, seafood, fruit and vegetables are generally considered safe to eat. *Bilharzia* (schistosomiasis) is present. Avoid swimming and paddling in fresh water. Swimming pools which are well-chlorinated and maintained are safe.

Health care: The general hospital has 70 beds and there are eight doctors on the island. There is a Reciprocal Health Agreement with the UK, but it is of a limited nature. On presentation of proof of UK residence, free treatment is available at the general hospital and at state-run clinics to those aged over 65 and under 16. Dental treatment is also free for school-age children. Private health insurance is recommended.

TRAVEL - International

AIR: The nearest international gateway is Antigua.

Approximate flight times: From *London* to Montserrat is 8.5 hours, including an hour's stopover in Antigua; from *Los Angeles* is 9 hours; from *New York* is 6 hours and from *Singapore* is 33 hours.

International airport: *Plymouth (PLH)* (Blackburne) is 17km (11 miles) from the city (travel time – 20 minutes). Airport facilities include restaurant, bar and shops. Taxis run to Plymouth (costing about US$11) and resort hotels.

Departure tax: EC$25. Passengers transiting within 24 hours pay EC$5. Children under 12 years of age are exempt.

SEA: *Holland America* runs cruises from Miami to Montserrat.

TRAVEL - Internal

SEA: Charter yachts are available. The main harbour is at Plymouth. A new jetty has recently been constructed. For visiting craft there is a yacht club and several marinas.

ROAD: Traffic drives on the left. There are good road networks to all towns. Montserrat has 185km (115 miles) of well-paved roads, but driving can be difficult for those not used to winding mountain roads. **Bus:** There are many sightseeing buses. Scheduled buses come hourly. **Taxi:** There are fixed rates for standard journeys. Drivers can act as guides and a number of different tours can be arranged. **Car hire:** This is available at the airport, in Plymouth, or via hotel. A car (with or without driver) is often included in the price of accommodation. **Documentation:** A valid foreign licence can be used to purchase a temporary licence at either the airport or Plymouth police station.

ACCOMMODATION

HOTELS: Hotels are generally small, with personal service. Rates are more expensive in the winter than in the summer. Some hotels have cottages as well as a selection of rooms. Maid, babysitting and laundry services can be arranged. A 7% government tax, usually with a 10% service charge, is added to all bills.

Grading: There are too few hotels for any grading system to be very significant. Hotels in Montserrat, like many others in the Caribbean, offer accommodation according to one of a number of plans:

FAP (Full American Plan): Room with all meals (including afternoon tea, supper, etc).

AP (American Plan): Room with three meals.

MAP (Modified American Plan): Breakfast and dinner included with the price of the room plus, in some places, British-style afternoon tea.

CP (Continental Plan): Room and breakfast only.

EP (European Plan): Room only.

SELF-CATERING: Villas and apartments are available throughout the island, bookable direct or through the Montserrat Tourist Board. All accommodation booking must be confirmed with a 20% deposit. A service charge of 10% is added on all accommodation bills.

RESORTS & EXCURSIONS

When Irish settlers arrived in Montserrat during the 17th-18th centuries (from other islands in the Caribbean, from the colony of Virginia and as prisoners of Oliver Cromwell) they nicknamed it *The Emerald Isle* because of the lush green giant ferns and forests climbing the sides of Montserrat's two volcanoes. Place names like *Galway Estates, Cork Hill* and *St Patrick's* (not to mention *Potato Hill*) still bear witness to the Irish influence. For the purposes of this guide Montserrat has been divided into two regions: The Coast (where most towns and resorts are to be found) and Inland (where the volcanic natural features of the island can be explored).

The Coast

The capital, **Plymouth**, is a small settlement of about 3500 people which still has a very 'British' atmosphere. Places of interest include the *Government House* and the 18th-century Anglican *Church of St Anthony*. 300m (1000ft) above the town is the 18th-century *Old Fort* on St George's Hill. The *Dutchers Studio* in *Olveston* is worth a visit. There are also the *Galway Estates* ruins with artefacts of the old sugar industry, and the *Bransby Point* fortifications with restored cannons. *Rendezvous Bay* contains the only white (coral) sand beach in Montserrat; sand in the other bays is of volcanic origin and may be grey or black. Several bays offer excellent opportunities for snorkelling and a variety of watersports; others are totally undeveloped (though plans for some of them exist, and those who like their scenery untouched should make the most of current opportunities). *Sport* in the *Social Profile* section gives further information about

watersports and sports in general.
Montserrat's national bird, the *icterus oberi* (a species of oriole), can be seen at *Woodlands* or *Bamboo Forest* areas.

Inland

The interior of Montserrat has several places of interest, though they are not always easy to get to and a pair of good walking shoes is recommended; however, those energetic enough to trek past sulphurous springs and vents to get to a waterfall (and some warm bathing beneath it), climb mountains and scramble down into dormant volcanoes will be amply rewarded by the scenery en route and the magnificent views.

The best view of the island is from the summit of the 900m (3000ft) *Chance Peak;* reaching it involves a stiff 1- to 2-hour climb; there are steps along the way to help the traveller. The small lake at the summit may or may not contain a mermaid, but only those who get there will have any chance of finding out. If she is there, legend says that whoever grabs her comb and makes it down to the sea before being caught by her companion, the diamond serpent, gets her treasure. Taking children (but not the very young) to some other places is easier, but it is often advisable to take a guide, as paths are not smooth and assistance will be appreciated along some of the rougher stretches.

A quarter of an hour's drive from the capital the route to the *Great Alps Waterfall* commences; after leaving the cars, visitors take a path (following roughly the course of the White River, crossing it a few times) through the underbrush (called 'land of the prickly bush' for a good reason) and into lush green woods where a stream plummets from 20m (70ft) down into a pool.

An expedition into the mouth of *Galways Soufrière* is a must for those fascinated by the sulphurous hubbling and bubbling of a volcano. Those who get to the car park and want to try something else can take a walk to the *Bamboo Forest* (three hours there and back).

SOCIAL PROFILE

FOOD & DRINK: There are restaurants in the main towns, as well as hotel dining rooms. The island specialities are fresh seafood and *mountain chicken* – not actually chicken, but the leg from a local species of large frog (Dominica is the only other island where these frogs can be found). Barbecues are popular and other local dishes include pumpkin soup, goat water, aubergine patties, salt fish, crêpes and dishes made from abundant local fruits. *Dasheen* and other local vegetables are served in most hotels. Waiter service is normal. **Drink:** Most bars serve imported beers, spirits and wines. Rum is the local drink often served in punch or cocktails. The local rum punch liqueur is *Perks Punch.*

NIGHTLIFE: Some hotels arrange live entertainment with local music and dance. Barbecues are very popular. Further information can usually be found in hotels.

SHOPPING: Locally made items include jewellery, needlework, ceramics, glassware and some interesting artefacts made from coconut. Clothing, tablecovers and soft items may be purchased from a government-run boutique. Plymouth really comes alive on market days, with hawkers of tropical produce and handmade items.
Shopping hours: 0800-1200 and 1300-1600 Monday, Tuesday and Thursday; 0800-1200 Wednesday and Saturday; 0800-1200 and 1300-1700 Friday.

SPORT: Golf: Visitors can play at the 11-hole Belham River Valley course, which is arranged to be playable as two 9-hole golf courses. **Hiking:** A popular destination for hikers is Galways Soufrière. **Swimming:** Most hotels and villas have their own swimming pools. Beaches are of 'black' volcanic sand. East coast beaches are picturesque, but dangerous for swimmers.
Scuba diving/snorkelling: The surrounding waters are excellent for scuba diving. Equipment may be rented or purchased on the island. Snorkelling equipment is available at the Vue Pointe Hotel. Hotels can arrange professional instruction. **Sailing:** Montserrat has a yacht club. **Tennis:** The Vue Pointe Hotel has tennis courts open to visitors. **Fishing:** Sea-fishing trips can be organised through hotels. **Cricket** is popular and matches are played from February to June.

SPECIAL EVENTS: Carnival celebrations take place at Christmas and up to the New Year. *St Patrick's Day* is particularly celebrated in St Patrick's village. Other events for 1995 include:
Mar '95 *Montserrat Open Golf Tournament.* **Mar 17** *St Patrick's Day.* **May 1** *Regional Fishing Tournament.*
May 6-7 *Around the Island Boat Race.* **Aug** *Montserrat Annual Pilgrimage.* **Oct 29-30** *3rd Annual Mountain Bike Meet.*

SOCIAL CONVENTIONS: Casual clothes are acceptable. Beachwear should be confined to the beach or poolside. The lifestyle is generally peaceful, combining many English influences with West Indian. The people are usually friendly and relaxed. All visitors are made welcome. **Tipping:** Service charge and government tax is added to restaurant and hotel bills.

BUSINESS PROFILE

ECONOMY: The island's main economic activity is agriculture, which performs well below its potential, though its output is perfectly adequate and reasonably efficient. The main crops are cotton, and fruit and vegetables including peppers and limes. The Government is aiming for eventual self-sufficiency in agricultural produce: the emphasis has been on livestock in recent years which has shown promising development. Tourism is the other important economic sector, contributing about one-quarter of the gross national product. There is little industry apart from food-processing and textiles whose export performance has improved sharply with increased access to North American markets. 'Offshore' financial services, an increasingly common feature of small Caribbean economies, are expected to grow over the next few years. The Government is hoping that the recent clean-up and introduction of stricter regulations will improve Montserrat's tarnished image. The island's main trading partner is the USA, which take 90% of Montserrat's exports and provide 30% of imports. The rest of Montserrat's trade takes place with fellow members of CARICOM, the Caribbean trading bloc, and the UK.
BUSINESS: A short- or long-sleeved shirt or safari suit is suitable for most business visits. **Office hours:** 0800-1200 and 1300-1600 Monday to Friday.
COMMERCIAL INFORMATION: The following organisation can offer advice: Montserrat Chamber of Commerce and Industry, PO Box 384, Marine Drive,

Plymouth. Tel: 3640. Fax: 4660.
CONFERENCES/CONVENTIONS: Up to 125 persons can be seated at the largest venue, where extra rooms and back-up facilities are available. Contact the Montserrat Tourist Board for further details (for address, see top of entry).

CLIMATE

The climate is subtropical, tempered by trade winds. There is little climatic variation throughout the year. The heaviest rainfall occurs during the summer months; however, the heavy cloudbursts serve to refresh the atmosphere and once they are over the sun reappears.
Required clothing: Tropical lightweights are worn, with light woollens for cooler evenings. A light raincoat or an umbrella is useful.

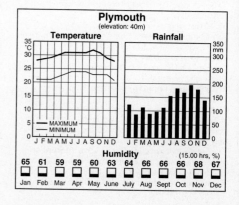

Morocco

1 Gibraltar (Brit.)
2 Ceuta (Sp.)
3 Melilla (Sp.)

ATLANTIC OCEAN

PORTUGAL   SPAIN

Tangier

RABAT   Fés
Casablanca   Meknes
Madeira (Port.)

MOROCCO

Marrakech

Jebel Toubkal 4165m △
Agadir
Canary Is. (Sp.)   Ifni

Laayoune

ALGERIA

Dakhla   Tropic of Cancer

MALI

MAURITANIA

600km
300mls

☐ international airport

DAB-M158

Location: North Africa.

Office National Marocain de Tourisme
31 angle avenue Al Abtal, Zankat Oued Fes, Rabat, Morocco
Tel: (7) 775 171. Fax: (7) 777 437. Telex: 31933.

Embassy of the Kingdom of Morocco
49 Queen's Gate Gardens, London SW7 5NE
Tel: (0171) 581 5001. Fax: (0171) 225 3862. Telex: 28389. Opening hours: 1000-1700 Monday to Friday.
Moroccan Consulate
Diamond House, 97-99 Praed Street, London W2 1NT
Tel: (0171) 724 0719. Opening hours: 1000-1300 Monday to Friday.
Moroccan National Tourist Office
205 Regent Street, London W1R 7DE
Tel: (0171) 437 0073. Fax: (0171) 734 8172. Opening hours: 0930-1730 Monday to Friday.
British Embassy
BP 45, 17 boulevard de la Tour Hassan, Rabat, Morocco
Tel: (7) 720 905 or 209 0516 or 314 0314. Fax: (7) 704 531 or 720 906. Telex: 31022 (a/b PRODROME).
Consulates in: Casablanca, Tangier and Agadir.
Embassy of the Kingdom of Morocco
1601 21st Street, NW, Washington, DC 20009
Tel: (202) 462 7979/82. Fax: (202) 265 0161.
Moroccan National Tourist Office
Suite 1201, 20 East 46th Street, New York, NY 10017
Tel: (212) 557 2520. Fax: (212) 949 8148.
Office also in: Orlando.
Embassy of the United States of America
BP 003, 2 avenue de Marrakech, Rabat, Morocco
Tel: (7) 762 265. Fax: (7) 765 661. Telex: 31005 (a/b M).
Consulate in: Casablanca.
Embassy of the Kingdom of Morocco
38 Range Road, Ottawa, Ontario K1N 8J4
Tel: (613) 236 7391/2. Fax: (613) 236 6164.
Consulates in: Montréal and Vancouver.
Moroccan National Tourist Office
Suite 1460, 2001 rue Université, Montréal, Québec H3A 2A6
Tel: (514) 842 8111/2. Fax: (514) 842 5316.

Canadian Embassy
CP 709, 13 bis, rue Jaafar As-Sadik, Rabat-Agdal, Morocco
Tel: (7) 672 134 or 672 880. Fax: (7) 672 187. Telex: 31964 (a/b CDARABAT M).

AREA: 710,850 sq km (274,461 sq miles).
POPULATION: 24,487,000 (1991).
POPULATION DENSITY: 34.4 per sq km (excluding Western Sahara).
CAPITAL: Rabat. **Population:** 1,472,000 (1990).
GEOGRAPHY: Morocco is located on the westernmost tip of north Africa, bordering Algeria to the east and Mauritania to the southeast. Running through the middle of the country is the Atlas mountain range, which leads to the fertile plains and sandy beaches of the Atlantic coast. The Middle Atlas range sweeps up from the south, rising to over 3000m (9850ft), covered with woodlands of pine, oak and cedar, open pastureland and small lakes. The Rif Mountains run along the north coast. The ports of Ceuta (Sebta) and Melilla on the north coast are administered by Spain.
LANGUAGE: The official language is Arabic, but some Berber is spoken. French is widely spoken throughout the country, except in the northern regions where Spanish is more predominant. English is also understood, particularly in the north and around Agadir.
RELIGION: Predominantly Muslim with Jewish and Christian minorities. Morocco's population and culture stems from a cross section of origins, including Berbers, Arabs, Moors and Jews.
TIME: GMT.
ELECTRICITY: 110-127 volts AC, 50Hz is most common, but 220 volts is standard for new installations. 2-pin round plugs are used.
COMMUNICATIONS: Telephone: IDD is available. Country code: 212. Outgoing international code: 00.
Fax: This is available in major hotels. **Telex/telegram:** There are telex facilities available in most of Morocco's major hotels. Telegram facilities are available throughout the country at main post offices. **Post:** Airmail to Europe takes up to one week and can be unreliable. **Press:** Daily newspapers are published in French and Arabic. The main publications are Le Matin, L'Opinion and Al Alam.
BBC World Service and Voice of America frequencies: From time to time these change. See the section How to Use this Book for more information.

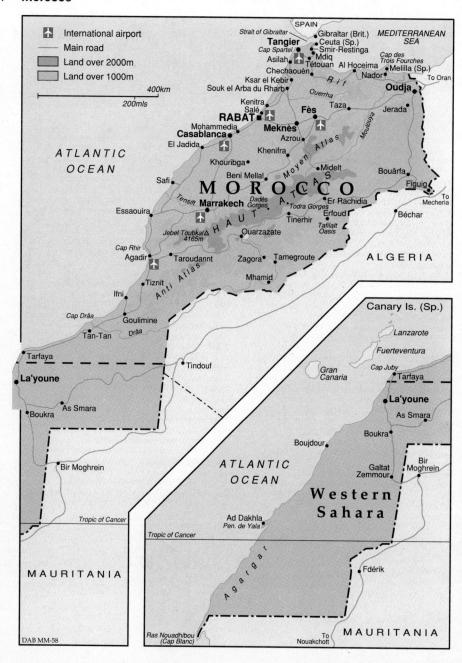

International airport
— Main road
▨ Land over 2000m
▨ Land over 1000m

400km
200mls

SPAIN
Strait of Gibraltar
Tangier
Gibraltar (Brit.)
MEDITERRANEAN SEA
Cap Spartel
Ceuta (Sp.)
Smir-Restinga
Asilah
Mdiq
Chechaouèn
Tétouan
Al Hoceima
Cap des Trois Fourches
Melilla (Sp.)
To Oran
Ksar el Kebir
Nador
Souk el Arba du Rharb
Ouerrha
Rif
Kenitra
Salé
RABAT
Fès
Taza
Jerada
Oudja
Mohammedia
Meknès
Casablanca
Azrou
El Jadida
ATLANTIC OCEAN
Khenifra
Moulouya
Khouribga
Moyen Atlas
Midelt
Bouârfa
Safi
Beni Mellal
Figuig
MOROCCO
To Mecheria
Essaouira
Tensift
Marrakech
Dadès Gorges
Todra Gorges
Er Rachidia
HAUT ATLAS
Tinerhir
Erfoud
Béchar
Cap Rhir
Jebel Toubkal△ 4165m
Ouarzazate
Tafilalt Oasis
Agadir
Taroudannt
Zagora
Tamegroute
ALGERIA
Tiznit
Anti Atlas
Mhamid
Ifni
Cap Drâa
Goulimine
Drâa
Tan-Tan
Tindouf
Canary Is. (Sp.)
Tarfaya
Lanzarote
Fuerteventura
La'youne
Cap Juby
Tarfaya
As Smara
Gran Canaria
La'youne
Boukra
As Smara
Boujdour
Boukra
Bir Moghrein
ATLANTIC OCEAN
Galtat Zemmour
Bir Moghrein
Tropic of Cancer
Western Sahara
Tropic of Cancer
Ad Dakhla
Pen. de Yala
MAURITANIA
Agargar
Fdérik
Ras Nouadhibou (Cap Blanc)
To Nouakchott
MAURITANIA

DAB MM-58

BBC:

| MHz | 17.70 | 15.07 | 12.09 | 9.410 |

Voice of America:

| MHz | 11.86 | 9.670 | 6.040 | 5.995 |

PASSPORT/VISA

Regulations and requirements may be subject to change at short notice, and you are advised to contact the appropriate diplomatic or consular authority before finalising travel arrangements. Details of these may be found at the head of this country's entry. Any numbers in the chart refer to the footnotes below.

	Passport Required?	Visa Required?	Return Ticket Required?
Full British	Yes	No	Yes
BVP	Not valid	-	-
Australian	Yes	No	Yes
Canadian	Yes	No	Yes
USA	Yes	No	Yes
Other EU (As of 31/12/94)	Yes/1	2	Yes
Japanese	Yes	No	Yes

Note: Visa requirements vary and are subject to change. It is advisable to contact the Embassy or Consulate for up-to-date information.
Restricted entry: Israeli passport holders are prohibited from entering Morocco. Those of scruffy appearance will be prevented from entering Morocco.
PASSPORTS: Valid passport required by all except:
(a) **[1]** nationals of Denmark, France, Germany and Spain who travel as an organised group can enter with their

national ID cards or other passport-replacing documents (all other EU nationals *do* need a passport);
(b) nationals of Austria, Finland, Iceland, Norway, Sweden and Switzerland who travel as an organised group can also enter with their national ID cards or other passport-replacing documents.
British Visitors Passport: Not accepted.
Note: Children 16 and under may travel on their parents' passport, but must have photographs included in these passports. Children over 16 must have their own passports.
VISAS: Required by all except:
(a) nationals of countries as shown in the chart;
(b) **[2]** nationals of EU countries (except nationals of Belgium, Luxembourg and The Netherlands who *do* require a visa);
(c) nationals of Commonwealth countries;
(d) nationals of Andorra, Argentina, Austria, Bahrain, Brazil, Chile, Congo, Côte d'Ivoire, Finland, Guinea, Iceland, Indonesia, South Korea, Libya, Liechtenstein,

Mali, Malta, Mexico, Monaco, New Zealand, Niger, Norway, Oman, Peru, Philippines, Qatar, Romania, Saudi Arabia, Senegal, Sweden, Switzerland, Tunisia, Turkey, United Arab Emirates and Venezuela.
Note: In order to get a visa, nationals of Algeria, Angola, Benin, Bosnia-Hercegovina, Burundi, Croatia, Egypt, Ethopia, Guinea-Bissau, India, Iraq, Iran, Jordan, Lebanon, Liberia, Former Yugoslav Republic of Macedonia, Madagascar, Kuwait, Malawi, Mozambique, Pakistan, Rwanda, Slovak Republic, Slovenia, Sudan, Syria, Togo, Yugoslavia (Serbia and Montenegro) and Zimbawe must have a letter of recommendation from their country's embassy or wait for their application to be approved by the relevant authorities in Rabat.
Types of visa: *Single-entry visa* – £5; *Double-entry visa* – £8 (these prices may fluctuate in accordance with the Moroccan Dirham/Pound Sterling exchange rate). Transit visa is free of charge.
Validity: Entry visas are valid for 3 months; visitors wishing to stay longer should apply to the police within 15 days of arrival (except nationals of France and Spain who may stay for an unlimited period provided they report to the police within 3 months). For other visa enquiries, contact the Embassy.
Application to: Consulate (or Consular section at Embassy). For addresses, see top of entry.
Application requirements: (a) 4 completed application forms. (b) 4 passport-size photos. (c) Valid passport (valid for more than 6 months on date of entry into Morocco). (d) Fee. (e) Sufficient funds for length of stay.
Working days required: Application forms are sent to Morocco for clearance and so it is advisable to apply well in advance of intended travel date.

MONEY

Currency: Moroccan Dirham (DH) = 100 centimes. Notes are in denominations of DH200, 100, 50 and 10. Coins are in denominations of DH5 and 1, and 50, 20, 10 and 5 centimes.
Credit cards: Some credit cards are accepted. Check with your credit card company for details of merchant acceptability and other services which may be available.
Exchange rate indicators: The following figures are included as a guide to the movement of the Moroccan Dirham against Sterling and the US Dollar:

Date:	Oct '92	Sep '93	Jan '94	Jan '95
£1.00=	13.22	13.96	13.98	13.94
$1.00=	8.33	9.14	9.45	8.91

Currency restrictions: The import and export of local currency is prohibited; all local currency must be reconverted prior to departure. The import and export of foreign currency is unlimited. Upon production of bank vouchers, half the Moroccan currency purchased during a visitor's stay may be re-exchanged for foreign currency (subject to some limitations).
Banking hours: 0830-1100 and 1430-1630 Monday to Friday (winter); 0800-1400 Monday to Friday (summer). These hours may vary during Ramadan.

DUTY FREE

The following goods may be imported into Morocco without incurring customs duty:
200 cigarettes or 50 cigars or 400g of tobacco; 1 litre of spirits and 1 litre of wine; 250ml of perfume.
Restricted items: A special permit is required for sporting guns and ammunition which is obtainable upon arrival from the Police authorities for passenger holding a permit from their country of origin.

PUBLIC HOLIDAYS

Jan 1 '95 New Year's Day. **Jan 11** Manifesto of Independence. **Mar 2-3** Eid al-Fitr. **Mar 3** Feast of the Throne. **May 1** Labour Day. **May 9-10** Eid al-Adha. **May 23** National Feast. **May 30-31** Muslim New Year. **Jun 9-10** Achoura. **Jul 9** Youth Day (King's Birthday). **Aug 14** Allegiance of Oued ed-Dahab. **Aug 9-10** Prophet's Birthday. **Nov 6** Green March Anniversary. **Nov 18** Independence Day. **Jan 1 '96** New Year's Day. **Jan 11** Manifesto of Independence. **Feb 22** Eid al-Fitr. **Mar 3** Feast of the Throne.
Note: Muslim festivals are timed according to local sightings of various phases of the Moon and the dates given above are approximations. During the lunar month of Ramadan that precedes Eid al-Fitr, Muslims fast during the day and feast at night and normal business patterns may be interrupted. Some disruption may continue into Eid al-Fitr itself. Eid al-Fitr and Eid al-Adha may last anything from two to ten days, depending on the region. For more information, see the section *World of Islam* at the back of the book.

Timatic

Health	
GALILEO/WORLDSPAN:	**TI-DFT/RBA/HE**
SABRE:	**TIDFT/RBA/HE**

Visa	
GALILEO/WORLDSPAN:	**TI-DFT/RBA/VI**
SABRE:	**TIDFT/RBA/VI**

For more information on Timatic codes refer to Contents.

MOROCCO

royal air maroc

More than you imagined

GOLF • FISHING • CONVENTION • TREKKING

Morocco's strong golfing tradition, which dates back to the opening of the first major course in Tangier in 1917, is but one of the many pleasant surprises the country has in store for the visitor. There is a wide variety of well designed, beautifully laid-out courses, all with club houses of an equally high standard. With a fine climate allowing play all year round and with reasonable green fees for less than those of southern Europe, the 3 hour flight from London is certainly worth making for beginners and experts alike. First-class accommodation is available within easy reach of all the major courses.

King Hassan II and his family are great golfing enthusiasts which has led to a greater awareness of the game in the country. Many tour operators have included golfing holidays in their schedule, making ready-made packages easy to find.

AGADIR ROYAL GOLF CLUB *9 holes*
Architect: M. Wilson & Colonel Kamili
Address: km 12 route Ait Melloul, BP246, Inezgane
Tel: 08-241278 & 831278 & 241278
Fax: 08-844380
Length: 3600m Par 36

ANFA ROYAL GOLF CLUB *9 holes*
Address: Rampe d'Anfa, Casablanca
Tel: 02-361026 & 365355 Fax: 02-393374
Tlx: 22938 rgam
Length: 2710m Par 35
Green Fees: 250 DHS
Caddies: 60DHS

DAR ES-SALAM ROYAL GOLF CLUB *45 holes*
Architect: Robert Trent Jones SR
Address: Route des Zaers, Rabat
Tel: 07-755 864/65 Fax: 07-757671
Telex: 32963 rgrdes
Length: RED 6702m Par 73 (18 holes)
6205m Par 72 (18 holes) GREEN 2170m Par 32 (9 holes)
Green Fees: 375 DHS

EL-JADIDA ROYAL GOLF CLUB *18 holes*
Architect Cabell B. Robinson
Address: km7, Route de Casablanca, El-Jadida
Tel: 03-352251 & 352252 Fax: 03-344360
Length: 6274m Par 72
Green Fees: 250 DHS

FEZ ROYAL GOLF CLUB *9 holes*
Address: route d'Ifrane-Imouzzer, ain-cheggag, Fez
Tel: 07-763849
Length: 3168m Par 37

MARRAKESH ROYAL GOLF CLUB *18 holes*
Address: route d'Ouarzazate BP 634, Marrakesh
Tel: 04-444341 & 444705 & 400084
Fax: 04-430084
Length: 6200m Par 72
Green Fees 250 DHS (weekend 300DHS)
Caddies: 60 DHS

MEKNES ROYAL GOLF CLUB *9 holes*
Address: babBelkari.jnan Lbahraoui, Meknes
Tel: 05 530753 Fax: 05-550504
Length: 2707m Par 36
Green Fees: 200DHS
Caddies: 40 DHS

MOHAMMEDIA ROYAL GOLF CLUB *18 holes*
Architect: Pierre Uruguayen
Address: BP12, Mohamedia
Tel: 03-324656/324666/322052
Fax: 03-321102
Length: 5917m Par 72
Green Fees: 300 DHS

OUARZAZATE ROYAL GOLF CLUB *9 holes*
Architect: Cabell B. Robinson
Address: BP83, Ouarzazate
Tel: 04-882653 Fax: 04-883344
Length: 3150m Par 36

TANGIER ROYAL GOLF CLUB *18 holes*
Architect: Cotton & Frank Pennink
Address: BP 41, Tangier
Tel: 09-944484 & 939429 Fax: 09-945450
Length: 5545m Par 70
Green Fees: 200DHS

THE DUNES GOLF CLUB *27 holes*
Architect: Cabell B. Robinson
Address: Club Med golf course, secteur balnéaire, Agadir
Tel: 08-834690 & 834648 Fax: 08-834649
Length: Oued 3050m Par 36 (9 holes)
Eucalyptus 3174m Par 36 (9 holes) Tamaris 3204m
Green Fees: 530 DHS (18 holes) 320 DHS (9 holes)

THE PALMERAIE GOLF CLUB *18 holes*
Architect: Robert Trent Jones SR
Address circuit de la palmeraie BP 1488, Marrakesh
Tel: 04- 302045 & 301010 Fax: 04-306685 & 302020 Tlx: 72729 & 72749 & 72844
Length: 6214m Par 72
Green fees: 350 DHS (18 holes) 200DHS (9 holes)

CABO-NEGRO ROYAL GOLF CLUB *9 holes*
Architect: Hawtree & Sons, revised by Cabell B. Robinson
Address: BP696G, Tetouan
Tel: 978303 & 978141 Fax: 09-978305
Length: 3087m Par 36
Green Fees: 620 DHS
Caddies: 50DHS

BENSLIMANE ROYAL GOLF CLUB *9 holes*
Architect: David Coen
Address: ave. des Far, BP83, Benslimane
Tel:03-328793 Fax: 03-291933
Length: 3100m Par 36

Photograph by Royal Air Maroc

GOLF FA

CILITIES *95*

Every form of fishing is available in Morocco, from deep-sea fishing and surf casting on the Atlantic and Mediterranean coasts to freshwater angling in rivers and lakes.

Known as 'the fishing paradise' by surf casting aficionados, *Dakhla* is situated on the southernmost Atlantic shore 660 miles south of Agadir. Surrounded as it is by the desert, *Dakhla* benefits from the reliable Saharan climate. The village is small and clean its captivating harbour teeming with fish. It is not uncommon to take half a dozen bass in a day, either by casting or jigging. Hundred-pound corbine are not uncommon.

The rocky inlets of the Mediterranean coast are rich with many species of fish. The much longer Atlantic coast experiences greater climatic variation and this, coupled with a unique confluence of ocean currents, accounts for the presence of both cold-water and tropical fish along the Moroccan coast. In the region of *Rabat*, the largest catch is the tarpon, while further south skate, umbrine, sea perch, mullet and conger-eels can be taken.

The Mediterranean waters off Morocco are comparatively unfrequented, the warm waters are rich in a wide variety of marine life, ideal for scuba diving and spear-fishing alike.

There are highly active spear-fishing clubs in all the main coastal resorts from Melilla to the Straits of Gibraltar.

Excellent trout fishing is available in the clear sparkling mountain streams of the *Middle Atlas*, particularly in the area of Azron and the less accessible region around Khenifra. Pike and trout lakes may be found throughout the country, from the valleys of the Rif to Immouzer, close to Agadir on the Atlantic coast.

An artificial dam, *Lake Moulay Youssef (Aitadl)*, is situated in stunning surroundings at the foot of the Atlas Mountains 80km east of Marrakesh. In addition to black bass, one can also take barbel, sun perch and a large number of sizeable carp. The lake can be fished from the shore; alternatively boats can easily be hired for fishing the deeper waters.

Fishing guides in Morocco are very knowledgeable about fishing areas and can be relied on to offer all the help and advice you are likely to need. Permits may be required: enquire locally for details.

FISHING 98

Morocco - the perfect destination for your conference or incentive trip. Moroccan hotels offer a sophisticated range of facilities for international meetings with a diversity of environments, making them an ideal destination for all. Nowhere is the legendary hospitality more evident than in the quality, style and courtesy of the major venues for both meeting and incentive travellers. Every wish is catered for. Sports and leisure facilities at the major hotels are unrivalled. International golf courses, flying clubs, equestrian centres, ski resorts and sun-drenched beaches are often only a short journey away. Hunting, shooting and fishing acquire a new meaning when you are stalking wild boar in the Atlas Mountains, or casting for trout in sparkling mountain streams. And for the truly adventurous, expeditions to the deep south can easily be arranged. The following hotels offer the highest standard in conference facilities and activities for business travellers.

Marrakesh
La Mamounia
Hotel Es Saadi
Hotel Mansour Eddahbi
Imperial Borj
Palais de Congrés
Hotel Atlas Ansi
Hotel Tichka
Palmeraie Golf Palace

Fez
Palais Jamai
Jnane Hotel

Casablanca
Royal Mansour
Sheraton
Hyatt Regency

Rabat
Hyatt Regency

Agadir
Europa hotel Safir
Hotel Amadil
Medina Palace Hotel
Safari Hotel

Photograph by Chris Lawrence. 01380 828533

VENTION '95

Morocco is, above all, a land of mountains, most famously the *Atlas* chain and the *Rif* ranges. Perhaps the most celebrated is *Le Deren* in the High Atlas, the 'mountain of mountains', known to the Phoenicians and ancient Greeks as the realm of legendary Atlas who supported the world on his shoulders.

Of all the mountain sports practised in Morocco, trekking (on foot or by ski) is the best adapted to the natural and human potential of the *High Atlas* and other mountain ranges: this vast and little-frequented area is waiting for you to discover it. An exceptional network of mule tracks traverses this dramatic and varied scenery, crowned with towering but easily accessible summits. The region has an incomparable climate with hours of sunshine and everlasting snow, but no glaciers. In addition, trekking allows contact with a proud and hospitable population which has kept its ancestral traditions, particularly in the fields of architecture, dress and dance.

To visit the *High Atlas* in the summer months is to enter a land of magic. The towering mountains, plunging gorges and high plateaux are home to a sparse and nomadic population. Occasional Berber villages adorn this spectacular landscape, as do secluded caves decorated with etchings depicting the fierce battles of antiquity.

In winter and early spring there is a chance to ski and cross-country trek using the 'ski-mule' which allows for comfortable descents on virgin snow. The *Middle Atlas* limestone plateau is rich in forest and moorlands, and the gently undulating slopes shelter small mountain lakes, making the range ideal for walking. Also of note is the region of *Taza*, equally rich in caves and remarkable abysses such as the renowned *Friuato*. Given good snow conditions, this area also offers an incomparable region for cross-country skiing.

The pre-Sahara massifs of the *Sirwa* and *Sarho* is a region of almost eerie mystery. Treks can be arranged through the very heart of this strange and jagged landscape.

ROYAL AIR

Created in 1953 of the merger between Air Atlas and Air Maroc, the airline became Royal Air Maroc in June 1957.
Although run with an autonomous management, the Government holds 93% of Royal Air Maroc shares.
RAM's main subsidiaries are the "Societe Touristique de Royal Air Maroc", their caterers at Mohammed V International Airport, as well as the Amadil and Atlas Hotels in Agadir and the Atlas Hotel in Marrakech, and Royal Air Inter, the domestic airline.
Royal Air Maroc, through its cargo activities, aids the promotion of Moroccan exports, it currently transports over 20,000 tons of freight and this figure will increase throughout 1994.
In October 1983, RAM's aeronautical workshops attained their FAA accreditation, testifying an equivalent standard to the USA. This is due to the highly qualified personnel of whom 750 are specialised technicians and to a sophisticated infrastructure.
RAM has a professional training centre and pilot school with highly qualified teaching staff and the latest technology. The school's fleet of 12 aircraft is available to the pilots and technicians of other airlines.

The destinations catered for by Royal Air Maroc has expan rapidly over the years. It currently serves 61 destinations ir countries. North and Equatorial Africa, Montréal, New York Rio de Janeiro; most major European and Middle East ci connect with the major Moroccan destinations.
As the network expands so does the number of craft required, from an initial fleet of 8 DCs and 1 Constellation in 1957 airline has expanded rapidly and now has one of the most mod fleets in service. It has shown a continued commitmen updating its fleet and this year alone will add 11 new Boe 737s to its fleet of Boeing 747s, 757s and existing 737 combined total of 40 planes. The order demonstrates the airlir continuing commitment to fleet renewal on medium-rar airplanes and underlines RAMs confidence in the future tra growth between Europe and Morocco.Services from Lonc Heathrow to Tangier, Casablanca, Agadir and Marrakech are c daily basis with four non-stop flights to Casablanca and three n stop flights to Tangier with easy connections to up to 18 ci throughout Morocco.

HEALTH

	Special Precautions?	Certificate Required?
Yellow Fever	No	No
Cholera	No	No
Typhoid & Polio	Yes	-
Malaria	Yes/1	-
Food & Drink	2	-

Regulations and requirements may be subject to change at short notice, and you are advised to contact your doctor well in advance of your intended date of departure. Any numbers in the chart refer to the footnotes below.

[1]: A minimal malaria risk, exclusively in the benign *vivax* form, exists from May to October in rural areas of the following provinces: Beni Mellal, Chefchaouèn, Larache, Khouribga, Settat, Khénifra, Khémisset and Taza.

[2]: Bottled water is available and is advised for the first few weeks of the stay. Drinking water outside main cities and towns may be contaminated and sterilisation is advisable. Milk is unpasteurised and should be boiled. Powdered or tinned milk is available and is advised, but make sure that it is reconstituted with pure water. Avoid dairy products which are likely to have been made from unboiled milk. Only eat well-cooked meat and fish, preferably served hot. Salad and mayonnaise may carry increased risk. Vegetables should be cooked and fruit peeled.

Rabies is present. For those at high risk, vaccination before arrival should be considered. If you are bitten abroad seek medical advice without delay. For more information, consult the *Health* section at the back of the book.

Bilharzia (schistosomiasis) is present in small foci. Avoid swimming and paddling in fresh water. Swimming pools which are well-chlorinated and maintained are safe.

Health care: There are good medical facilities in all main cities, including emergency pharmacies (sometimes in the Town Hall) outside normal opening hours. Government hospitals provide free or minimal charge emergency treatment. Full health insurance is essential.

TRAVEL - International

AIR: Morocco's national airline is *Royal Air Maroc (AT)*.
For free information on air travel, call the Air Travel

Advisory Bureau in the UK on (0171) 636 5000 (London) *or* (0161) 832 2000 (Manchester).
Approximate flight times: From London to *Rabat* is 3 hours and to *Tangier* is 2 hours 30 minutes.
International airports: *Casablanca (CAS)* (Mohammed V) is 30km (19 miles) south of the city (travel time – 35 minutes). Airport facilities include outgoing duty-free shop (closed after last arrival), post office, banking and currency exchange facilities (open for arrival and departure of planes), restaurant and bar (0800-2300) and car hire (*Avis, Hertz, Europcar, Intercar* and *Locoto*). There are bus and taxi services into Casablanca and coach services available to Rabat.
Rabat (RBA) (Salé) is 10km (6 miles) northeast of the city (travel time – 15 minutes). Airport facilities include restaurant, snack bar, bank, post office, shops and car hire. Taxi service is available to the city.
Tangier (TNG) (Boukhalef Souahel) is 12km (7.5 miles) from the city (travel time – 20 minutes). Airport facilities include outgoing duty-free shop, banking and currency exchange facilities, restaurant and bar (0900-2100), car hire facilities (*Avis, Omnium, Starc-Hertz* and *Moroccan Holidays*). Bus and taxi services are available into Tangier.
Agadir (AGA) (Al Massira) is 28km (17.5 miles) from the city (travel time – 30 minutes). Airport facilities include banking and currency exchange, bar and car hire (*Europcar, Hertz* and *Africa Car*). Bus and taxi services go into the town.
Fès (FEZ) (Saïs) is 10km (6 miles) from the city (travel time – 10 minutes). Taxi service is available to the city.
Marrakech (RAK) (Menara) is 6km (4 miles) from the city. There are banking facilities at the airport. Taxi and bus services are available to the city.
SEA: Principal ports are Tangier, Casablanca and Ceuta. Lines serving these ports are *Transtour, Compañía Trasmediterránea, Limadet, Bland Line* (from Spain and Gibraltar), *Polish Ocean Lines* and *Nautilus* (from Spain and the USA), and *Comanav*.
Car/passenger ferries: There are cheap and regular car- and passenger-ferry links between southern Spain and Tangier and the Spanish enclaves on the north Moroccan coast. Most links are roll-on, roll-off car ferries except where shown. The routes are from Algeciras to Ceuta (Sebta) (car ferry); Algeciras to Tangier (hydrofoil and car ferry); Tarifa to Tangier (hydrofoil only); Gibraltar to Tangier (hydrofoil and car ferry); Almería to Melilla (car ferry) and Málaga to Melilla (car ferry).
There are also car ferries between Sète on the French coast (between Béziers and Montpellier on the Golfe du

Lyon) and Tangier run by *Compagnie Marocaine de Navigation*.
RAIL: At the time of writing (November 1994), rail links between Morocco and Algeria were suspended. The main international routes are from Oujda to Algiers or from Oran to Algiers.
ROAD: The best road link is from southern Spain or France via passenger/car ferries (see above under *Sea*). There is also a road link on the north Algerian border.

TRAVEL - Internal

AIR: *Royal Air Maroc (AT)* operates regular services from Casablanca airport to Agadir, Al Hoceima, Dakhla, Fès, Marrakech, Ouarzazate, Oujda, Rabat, Tangier and Tetouan. There are discounts for those under 26 years of age of up to 40%.
RAIL: The Moroccan rail system is all standard gauge and, though limited, provides regular and cheap services with first-class travel available. Rail fares are amongst the cheapest in the world, although a supplement must be paid for air-conditioned trains. Sleeping cars and restaurant cars are available. The network runs from Oujda in the northeast to Casablanca on the west coast, Tangier on the north coast and Marrakech in the interior. The main routes include Marrakech–Casablanca–Rabat–Meknes–Fès–Oujda, Marrakech–Casablanca–Rabat, Marrakech–Casablanca–Meknes–Fès and Casablanca–Rabat–Tangier. The most useful route is from Fès to Rabat and Casablanca, with five daily and two overnight trains. There are also two daily trains and one overnight train (without sleepers) which run from Casablanca to Marrakech.
Cheap fares: Children under 4 travel free and children from 4-10 may travel for half fare. The European Inter-Rail pass (for those under 26 years of age) is valid in Morocco; holders may be entitled to a discount on the fare of a ferry ticket – check with the company concerned for details. Discounts of up to 30% are available for groups of more than ten. First- and second-class seats can be reserved in advance. Trains can also be chartered.
ROAD: Traffic drives on the right. The major Moroccan roads, particularly those covering the north and northwest of the country, are all-weather highways. In the interior, south of the High Atlas Mountains, road travel becomes much more difficult, especially across the Atlas Mountains in winter. **Coach:** The main centres are connected by a wide variety of coach services, many of which are privately run. The two largest firms are *CTM*

(covering the whole country) and *SATAS* (between Casablanca, Agadir and south of Agadir). **Bus:** Connections between most major towns and villages are regular and frequent, although buses can be very crowded and it may be wise to buy tickets in advance and arrive well before departure to secure a seat. The price of tickets is very low, especially with some of the smaller local bus companies. It is customary to tip the guard for loading luggage. For charter purposes, air-conditioned motor coaches are available from several companies. **Taxi:** Those available in major towns, the *petits taxis,* are metered (see below under *Urban*). Other larger taxis, usually Mercedes cars, are used for travel to areas outside towns. These can be shared, but fares should be agreed before departure. **Car hire:** *Avis* and *Hertz* can deliver cars to Gibraltar or Tangier from London. Major hire companies have offices in Tangier, Casablanca and Agadir. Car hire is generally expensive. **Documentation:** Foreign driving licences are accepted, as well as International Driving Licences. Third Party insurance is required. A Green Card is also necessary. Insurance can be arranged locally.
URBAN: There are extensive bus services in Casablanca and other main towns. Pre-purchase tickets are sold. Urban area *petits taxis* are plentiful and have metered fares. Taxi drivers expect a 10% tip.
JOURNEY TIMES: The following chart gives approximate journey times (in hours and minutes) from Casablanca to other major cities/towns in Morocco.

	Air	Road	Rail
Rabat	0.30	1.30	1.00
Marrakech	*0.40	4.00	4.00
Agadir	*0.55	9.00	-
Fès	*0.40	5.00	5.00
Meknès	-	2.30	3.30
Tangier	*0.50	7.00	6.00
Oujda	*1.05	12.00	12.00
Laayoune	1.30	20.00	-
Er Rachidia	1.35	12.00	-

Note [*]: These represent times by the main air link from Casablanca.

ACCOMMODATION

HOTELS: Morocco has 100,000 hotel beds. In all sizeable centres there is quite a wide choice. The upper end of the market is represented by internationally known hotels in most main towns. For more information contact the Fédération Nationale de l'Industrie Hôtelière, 11 rue du Caporal Beaux, Casablanca. Tel: (2) 319 083. Fax: (2) 317 425. Telex: 21857. **Grading:** Hotels are rated from **1** to **5 stars.**
SELF-CATERING: Self-catering apartments are available in Agadir, Marrakech and Tangier. Full details are available from the National Tourist Office.
CAMPING/CARAVANNING: There are established campsites with good facilities in many parts of Morocco. Full details are available in a brochure from the National Tourist Office.
YOUTH HOSTELS: There are hostels in Asni, Azrou, Casablanca, Fès, Ifrane, Meknes and Rabat. Up-to-date information is available from the Union Marocaine des Auberges de Jeunesse, 6 place Amiral Phillibert, Casablanca. Tel: (2) 220 551.

RESORTS & EXCURSIONS

For the purpose of this guide Morocco has been divided into three parts: Imperial Cities, The Coast and The South.

Imperial Cities

Fès, Marrakech, Meknès and Rabat are known as the Imperial Cities, each having been the country's capital at some time during its history.
Rabat, the present capital of Morocco, was founded in the 12th century. It is a town of trees and flowers, and many monumental gateways, including the *Gate of the Ambassadors* and the *Oudaias Kasbah Gate.* There is a good selection of hotels and numerous pavement cafés. The nearby Mamora forest and the many beaches are popular tourist attractions, particularly during the summer.
Other attractions include *Tour Hassan,* the grandiose minaret of a vast, uncompleted 12th-century mosque; the *Mohammed V Mausoleum,* an outstanding example of traditional Moroccan architecture; the *Royal Palace;* the *Chellah,* with superb monuments, delightful gardens and Roman ruins; the *Oudaias;* the *National Museum of Handicrafts* and the antique Moorish café. The battlements surrounding the old town, and part of the new city, date from the mid-12th century. Also worth a visit is **Salé,** Rabat's twin city, at the opposite side of the river, believed to have been founded in the 11th century.
Meknès is protected by 16km (25 miles) of battlements, flanked by towers and bastions. The city reflects the power and the constructive genius of King Moulay Ismail, a contemporary of Louis XIV, who ruled the country for 55 years. The *Michlifen* and *Djebel Habri* are two ski resorts above Meknès. The city boasts a wonderful *souk* (market).
Fès is the most ancient and impressive of the imperial cities. Built in the 8th century it has more history and mystery than anywhere else in Morocco. Officially encompassing two cities – El Bali and Jadid – Fès is famous for the *Nejjarine Square* and *Fountain,* the *Er Rsif* and *Andalous* mosques, the *Royal Palace,* the *Kasbah* and *Karaouine University,* which is older than Oxford University. The old part of the city – Fès El Bali – still retains the magical, bustling atmosphere of an ancient time. It is a huge maze of winding streets and covered bazaars where, if one is not careful (it is a good idea to hire an official guide), it is easy to become lost. There are magnificent examples of Hispano-Arabic architecture as well as numerous opportunities to see traditional craftsmen at work. The *medina* (market) in Fès El Bali is one of the largest in the world. Here one can buy almost anything. It is particularly good for carpets, rugs and ornate metal work. Here, as in all of Morocco, business is conducted in a leisurely, although deadly earnest, way with the accompaniment of endless glasses of sweet mint tea. Fès is, perhaps, one of the most fascinating cities anywhere in the Middle East or north Africa.
The valley of *Ouergha* to the north is famed for its *souks* and Morocco's most celebrated gathering of riders, which is said to have been attended by Pope Sylvester II prior to his accession in AD999 and resulted in him introducing Arab mathematics to Europe. Other attractions are the *Karaouine Mosque* and *Mesbahai Medersa,* an old school, remarkable for its traditional architecture and late afternoon auctions in the *Kissaria,* the shopping area.
Founded in 1062, **Marrakech** was once the capital of an empire which stretched from Toledo to Senegal. Called the 'Pink City' because of the colour of the local earth used in its construction, it is a city of labyrinthine alleyways, secluded palaces, museums, mosques and markets. The city's gardens are still supplied with water from 11th-century underground irrigation canals. The *Djemmaa-el-Fna* (Place of the Dead), the city square, comes alive after nightfall; thronged with dancers, fortunetellers, musicians, acrobats, storytellers and snake charmers, it is an exciting and occasionally bewildering place – an exotic spectacle that is striking and endlessly surprising. *Koutoubia,* the 12th-century minaret, is as tall as the towers of Nôtre Dame and dominates the Marrakech skyline. The *Ben Youssef Medersa,* with its mosaics, marbles and carved woodwork, is the largest theological site in the Mahgreb. Other interesting places to see are the sumptuous *Bahia Palace;* the beautiful *Saadian Tombs* housing the remains of rulers of the Saadian Dynasty; the *Menara and Aquedal gardens* and the famed camel market.
An hour's drive from Marrakech is **Oukaimeden,** Morocco's best ski resort. This trip can be combined with a visit to **Ourika** (which has a donkey market) and **Asni**. The latter is an excellent base for visiting *Mount Toubkai,* Morocco's highest mountain, set in spectacular countryside.

The Coast

The Mediterranean coast between Tangier and Nador has a string of creeks, bays, sheltered beaches and cliffs along the Mediterranean shore, ideal for swimming, boating and fishing. *Al Hoceima, MDiq, Taifor* and *Smir-Restinga* are all new resorts, offering a wide variety of accommodation, from luxury hotels to well-situated bungalows.

PHOTO CREDIT: CHRIS LAWRENCE

The Atlantic coast is often rocky, with some long stretches of fine sand and calm bays.

Tangier, gateway to Africa, is the country's most cosmopolitan town, a place where – surviving from the days when Tangier was a free port – the street signs are in three languages; in fact, no less than 12 nations have occupied the city at one time or another since the 5th century. The city has a picturesque and active market called the *Grand Socco*. Other places worth visiting include the *Mendoubia Gardens, the Sidi Bounabib Mosque*, the *Moulay Ismail Mosque* and the *Merinid College*. Excursions in the region include visits to the mountain town of **Chechaouen**, the fishing village of **Asilah** and the *Caves of Hercules* at **Cape Spartel**. Also on the Atlantic coast is the newer city of **Casablanca**. Founded at the beginning of the century, it is the country's principal commercial town, the second-largest town in Africa and one of the continent's biggest ports. Here stands the *Hassan II Mosque*, the world's largest mosque with one of the world's tallest minarets. Just south of Casablanca is **Azemmour**, in a picturesque location along the banks of the Oum er-Rbia, with its abundance of violet bougainvillea and its purple ramparts (which visitors may walk along after agreeing a fee for the guardian to unlock them). Slightly further south is **El Jadida** which has a remarkable Portuguese fortress and one of the most beautiful beaches on the Atlantic coast. It also boasts the *Church of Assumption*, and enormous underground *Cistern* and the 'Gate on the Sea' and fortifications. Travelling further south along the coast brings visitors to **Safi**, a fishing port with a Portuguese palace, pottery shops and a medina.

Agadir is a modern holiday city with superb beaches, excellent resort hotels and self-catering accommodation, which offers all types of sports activities. From here there are excursions to the towns of **Taroudant, Tiznit, Tafraout, Goulimine, Essaouira** and, of course, the famous Marrakech.

Mohammedia is another popular resort in this region.

The South

The South is a region rich in folklore and spectacular scenery, dotted with small oasis villages and quiet towns surrounded by orchards and olive groves. **Erfoud** is the centre for excursions to the oasis of *Tafilalt,* kept green and fertile by the underground waters of the Ziz and the Rheris. **Er Rachidia** is the provincial capital of the Tafilalt region, and has a bustling market on the main square. On the road between Er Rachidia and Erfoud are the 'Blue Springs' at **Meski** and the natural amphitheatre of *Cirque de Jaffar* near **Midelt. Tinerhir**, once a garrison of the French Foreign Legion, is worth visiting for its kasbahs. Near Tinerhir is the outstanding scenery of the *Dades* and *Todra* gorges.

Ouarzazate: Of particular interest is the kasbah of *Taourirt*, the *Museum of Arts and Crafts* and the *Carpet Weavers' Cooperative Shop*.

Zagora: From the top of the Djebel Zagora there is a spectacular view of the *Draa Valley* and desert. 18km (11 miles) away from Zagora is the oasis of **Tamergroute** which has a library containing some of the earliest Arabic manuscripts, written nine centuries ago on gazelle skins. They are on display at the *Zaouia Nasseria*. Nearby, **Mhamid** and its palm groves are at the gates of the great sand desert. South of Agadir, the pink kasbahs of **Tafraoute** perch on spurs of rock, their façades often painted with strange designs in white or ochre.

Goulimine is the site of the *Blue Men's souk,* held each weekend. A camel market also takes place once a week, on Saturday.

POPULAR ITINERARIES: 5-day: (a) Tangier–Meknès–Fès–Chechaouen–Tangier. (b) Agadir–Tiznit–Goulimine–Agadir. (c) Agadir–Essaouira–Marrakech–Agadir. **7-day:** (a) Tangier–Meknès–Fès–Marrakech–Rabat–Tangier. (b) Agadir–Marrakech–Ouarzazate–Zagora–Marrakech.

SOCIAL PROFILE

FOOD & DRINK: Morocco's traditional *haute cuisine* dishes are excellent and good value for money. They are often exceedingly elaborate, based on a diet of meat and sweet pastries. Typical specialities include: *harira,* a rich soup, and *bastilla,* a pigeon-meat pastry made from dozens of different layers of thick flaky dough. *Couscous,* a dish based on savoury semolina that can be combined with egg, chicken, lamb or vegetables, is a staple Moroccan dish. *Touajen* are stews, often rich and fragrant, using marinaded lamb or chicken. *Hout* is a fish version of the same stew, while *djaja mahamara* is chicken stuffed with almonds, semolina and raisins. Also popular are *mchoui,* pit-roasted mutton, and *kab-el-ghzal,* almond pastries. Hotel restaurants usually serve French cuisine. Restaurants offer a good selection of food,

including typical Moroccan dishes, French, Italian or Spanish meals. The 3-course fixed menus are not expensive. Many of the souks have stalls selling kebabs *(brochettes)* often served with a spicy sauce. Most restaurants have waiter service. **Drink:** The national drink is mint tea made with green tea, fresh mint and sugar. It is very refreshing and its consumption is an integral part of Moroccan social courtesy. Coffee is made very strong, except at breakfast. Bars can have either waiter or counter service. Laws on alcohol are fairly liberal (for non-Muslim visitors) and bars in most tourist areas stay open late. Wines, beers and spirits are widely available. Locally produced wines, beers and mineral waters are excellent and good value, but imported drinks tend to be expensive.

NIGHTLIFE: Morocco offers a variety of entertainment from casinos, discotheques, restaurants and nightclubs, often with belly dancing. There are modern nightclubs in all the cities and resorts around the country. There are casinos in Marrakech and Mohammedia. Traditional Moroccan entertainment, such as folk dancing, can be seen in every town.

SHOPPING: The cooperative shops of Moroccan craftsmen, *coopartim,* operate under state control selling local handicrafts at fixed prices and issue an authenticity receipt or a certificate of origin for customs when exporting. *Souks* are also worthwhile places to visit for local products. Special buys are leather, tanned and dyed in Fès; copperware; silver; silk or cotton garments; and wool rugs, carpets and blankets. Bargaining is essential, and good buys generally work out at around a third of asking price. In the south there are Berber carpet auctions, especially in Marrakech, Taroudannt and Tiznit. Visitors will need a guide to make the best of these occasions. **Shopping hours:** Generally 0830-1230 and 1400-1830 Monday to Saturday (0830-1200 and 1400-1900 Monday to Saturday in Tangier), but some shops in medinas *(souks)* may open Sunday and many shops close Friday.

SPORT: Swimming: Sandy beaches offer safe bathing, although the Atlantic can be cold even in summer. Mohammedia, Agadir, El Jadida, Oualidia, Safi and Essaouira are all good bathing resorts. The Mediterranean coast is now being developed and newly-built resort villages offer superb swimming and diving. **Fishing** permits are necessary for trout streams, lakes and pike lakes, and are issued by the Waters and Forests Department or local clubs. Sea-fishing trips can also be organised. **Hunting:** The Arboaua area offers wild boar, partridge, hare, mallard, quail and snipe during the season, which lasts from October to March. Hunting permits are available from the National Tourist Office, and a permit for the importation of hunting rifles can be issued on production of a valid national shooting permit and three photographs. **Golf:** There are courses at the Dar es Salaam Club in Rabat, Mohammedia, Tangier Country Club, Casablanca's Royal Golf Anfa, Cabo Negro, Agadir and Marrakech. **Winter sports:** Ifrane in the Middle Atlas and Oukaimeder in the High Atlas offer skiing facilities. Mount Tidiquin in the Ketama district and Djebel Bou Volane in the Middle Atlas are popular areas for expedition-type skiing and walking trips (with few amenities). **Horseriding:** There are horseriding clubs in all major towns, notably Casablanca, Rabat, Marrakech, Agadir and Fès. Several clubs organise pony treks in the Middle Atlas.

SPECIAL EVENTS: Festivals and special events are largely organised at the last minute and often depend on the lunar calendar. For further information contact the Moroccan National Tourist Office (for addresses, see top of entry).

SOCIAL CONVENTIONS: Handshaking is the customary form of greeting. Many of the manners and social customs emulate French manners, particularly amongst the middle class. The visitor may find, in some social situations, that patience and firmness will pay dividends. Often visitors may find themselves the centre of unsolicited attention. In towns, young boys after money will be eager to point out the way, sell goods or simply charge for a photograph, while unofficial guides will always be offering advice or services. The visitor should be courteous but wary of the latter. Normal social courtesies should be observed in someone's home. Casual wear is widely acceptable, although swimsuits and shorts should be confined to the beach or poolside. Smoking is widespread and it is customary to offer cigarettes. **Tipping:** Service charges are usually included in hotel bills; it is customary to tip hairdressers, cinema usherettes and waiters between DH1-2.

BUSINESS PROFILE

ECONOMY: Agriculture employs most of the working population, the principal crops being cereals, citrus fruits and vegetables. Morocco is the world's largest

exporter of phosphate rock and has other considerable mineral assets, including iron ore, coal, lead, zinc, cobalt, copper, silver and manganese. The main components of the manufacturing sector are food-processing, textiles and leather goods production. Tourism and remittances from Moroccan workers abroad are other major sources of revenue. The economy ran into some difficulty during the early 1980s due to the high cost of imported oil – Morocco has no deposits of its own – and of servicing its external debt. Debt rescheduling, falling oil prices and better harvests have since improved its economic position and Morocco is starting to benefit from one of the best infrastructures on the African continent. The country's economic performance is still vulnerable to the effects of a high birth rate, unemployment and an inefficient public sector, although the settlement of the war in the Western Sahara should lift some of the public expenditure burden. The Government has introduced a series of IMF-sponsored reforms, including trade liberalisation and public expenditure cuts in exchange for successive assistance programmes. The King has expressed his desire for Morocco to join the European Union, but this is a somewhat fanciful notion and the country must be content with membership of the Union of the Arab Maghreb. Morocco's main trading partner is France, followed by other EU countries. Spain, Germany and the USA are Morocco's main import suppliers.

BUSINESS: Business people should be of a smart appearance, although a suit is not necessary in very hot weather. Appointments should be made in advance. Negotiations often involve a great deal of bargaining and a visitor should expect to deal with a number of people. **Office hours:** *Winter* (September to July, except Ramadan): 0830-1200 and 1430-1800 or later; *Ramadan:* 0900-1500/1600; *Summer* (July to early September): 0800-1500/1600, though many revert to winter hours.

COMMERCIAL INFORMATION: The following organisation can offer advice: La Fédération des Chambres de Commerce et d'Industrie du Maroc, 6 rue d'Erfoud, Rabat-Agdal. Tel: (7) 767 078. Fax: (7) 767 076. Telex: 36662.

CONFERENCES/CONVENTIONS: The Pullman Conference Centre in Marrakech provides meeting facilities for up to 5000 people. Further information can be obtained from Pullman Hotels in London at Resinter, c/o Novotel Hotel, 1 Shortlands, London W6 8DR. Tel: (0171) 724 1000.

CLIMATE

The climate varies from area to area. The coast has a warm, Mediterranean climate tempered on the eastern coast by southwest trade winds. Inland areas have a hotter, drier, continental climate. In the south of the country the weather is very hot and dry throughout most of the year, with the nights coolest in the months of December and January. Rain falls from November to March in coastal areas. Mostly dry with high temperatures in summer. Cooler climate in the mountains. Marrakech and Agadir enjoy an average temperature of 21°C in the winter.

Required clothing: Lightweight cottons and linens are worn during summer, with warm mediumweights for the evenings during winter and in the mountains. Waterproofing is advisable in the wet season, particularly on the coast and in the mountains.

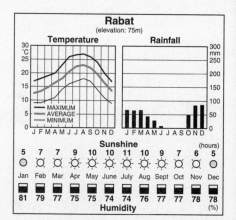

Mozambique

☐ *international airport*

Location: Southeast Africa.

Note: There is a danger of banditry on roads and local advice should be taken before travelling overland. There is still a risk from unexploded mines. Journeys, during daylight hours only, should be limited to the roads linking Maputo/Xai-Xai, Maputo/Swaziland (Namaacha border post), Beira/Zimbabwe and Beira/Malawi (via the Tete corridor). Where possible travel in groups/convoys. It is strongly advised not to use the main Maputo/Ressano Garcia road to South Africa. It is better to travel there via Swaziland. There have been violent incidents, sometimes involving firearms and resulting in death, in central Maputo after dark. Visitors should be careful.
Source: FCO Travel Advice Unit – December 20, 1994.

Empresa Nacional de Turismo (ENT) (Mozambique National Tourism Company)
CP 614, Avda 25 de Setembro 1211, Maputo, Mozambique.
Tel: 25011. Telex: 6303.
Embassy of the Republic of Mozambique
21 Fitzroy Square, London W1P 5HJ
Tel: (0171) 383 3800. Fax: (0171) 383 3801. Telex: 263481 (a/b MOZEM G). Opening hours: 0900-1700 Monday to Friday; 0930-1300 Monday to Friday (Consular section).
British Embassy
Caixa Postal 55, Avenida Vladimir I Lénine 310, Maputo, Mozambique.
Tel: (1) 420 111/2/5/6/7. Fax: (1) 421 666. Telex: 6265 (a/b PROMO MO).
Embassy of the Republic of Mozambique
Suite 570, 1990 M Street, NW, Washington, DC 20036
Tel: (202) 293 7146. Fax: (202) 835 0245. Telex: 248530.
Also deals with enquiries from Canada.
Embassy of the United States of America
Caixa Postal 783, Avenida Kenneth Kaunda 193,

Maputo, Mozambique
Tel: (1) 492 797. Fax: (1) 490 114. Telex: 6143 (a/b AMEMB MO).
Canadian Embassy
PO Box 1578, rue Tomas Nduda, 1345, Maputo, Mozambique
Tel: (1) 492 623. Fax: (1) 492 667. Telex: 6684 (a/b ACDI MO).

AREA: 799,380 sq km (308,641 sq miles).
POPULATION: 15,730,900 (1990 estimate).
POPULATION DENSITY: 19.7 per sq km.
CAPITAL: Maputo. **Population:** 1,006,765 (1987 estimate).
GEOGRAPHY: Mozambique borders Tanzania to the north, Zambia to the northwest, Zimbabwe to the west, and South Africa and Swaziland to the south. To the east lies the Indian Ocean and a coastline of nearly 2500km (1550 miles) with beaches bordered by lagoons, coral reefs and strings of islands. Behind the coastline a vast low plateau rising towards mountains in the west and north accounts for nearly half the area of Mozambique. The landscape of the plateau is savannah – more or less dry and open woodlands with tracts of short grass steppe. The western and northern highlands are patched with forest. The Zambezi is the largest and most important of the 25 main rivers which flow through Mozambique into the Indian Ocean. The major concentrations of population (comprising many different tribal groups) are along the coast and in the fertile and relatively productive river valleys, notably in Zambezia and Gaza provinces. The Makua-Lomwe, who belong to the Central Bantu, live mainly in the area north of Zambezia, Nampula, Niassa and Cabo Delgado provinces. The Thonga, who are the predominant race in the southern lowlands, provide a great deal of the labour for the South African mines. In the Inhambane coastal district are the Chopi and Tonga, while in the central area are the Shona. The Makonde inhabit the far north. Mestizos and Asians live in the main populated area along the coast and in the more fertile river valleys.
LANGUAGE: Portuguese is the official language. Many local African languages, such as Shangaan, Ronga and Muchope, are also spoken.
RELIGION: Christian (mainly Roman Catholic), Muslim and Hindu. Many also follow traditional beliefs.
TIME: GMT + 2.
ELECTRICITY: 220 volts AC, 50Hz.
COMMUNICATIONS: Telephone: IDD is available. Country code: 258. Outgoing international calls must go through the operator. **Telex/telegram:** Connections are via South Africa to international telecommunications network. There is a reliable telex service in Maputo and Beira. Internal communications exist between most major towns. **Post:** Postal services are available in main centres. Airmail to Europe usually takes five to seven days, but sometimes longer. **Press:** There are no English-language newspapers published in Mozambique. The daily papers are *Notícias* and *Diário de Mozambique*.
BBC World Service and Voice of America frequencies: From time to time these change. See the section *How to Use this Book* for more information.
BBC:

| MHz | 21.47 | 11.94 | 6.190 | 3.255 |

Voice of America:

| MHz | 21.49 | 15.60 | 9.525 | 6.035 |

PASSPORT/VISA

Regulations and requirements may be subject to change at short notice, and you are advised to contact the appropriate diplomatic or consular authority before finalising travel arrangements. Details of these may be found at the head of this country's entry. Any numbers in the chart refer to the footnotes below.

	Passport Required?	Visa Required?	Return Ticket Required?
Full British	Yes	Yes	Yes
BVP	Not valid	-	-
Australian	Yes	Yes	Yes
Canadian	Yes	Yes	Yes
USA	Yes	Yes	Yes
Other EU (As of 31/12/94)	Yes	Yes	Yes
Japanese	Yes	Yes	Yes

PASSPORTS: Valid passport required by all. Passports must have a minimum validity of six months.
British Visitors Passport: Not accepted.
VISAS: Required by all.
Types of visa: Tourist, Transit or Business; cost £20 (Single-entry Tourist visa), £40 (Multiple-entry Business visa, valid for 90 days).
Validity: 1 month (extendable in Mozambique); 3 months for Business visas.
Application to: Mozambique Embassies or Consulates

or
Ministerio de Negocias Estrangeiros, CP 290, Maputo. Telex: 6418; *or*
Direccão de Nacional de Migraco, Avenue Ho Chi Minh, Maputo. Telex: 6254; *or*
Empresa Nacional de Turismo (see top of entry).
Note: A visa can sometimes be obtained through a contact living in Mozambique.
Application requirements: (a) Official application form. (b) 3 passport-size photos. (c) Passport. (d) A letter of invitation to Mozambique and/or introduction from an official or business institution. (e) Fee (cheques should be made out to the Mozambique Embassy). (f) Stamped, self-addressed envelope for postal applications.
Working days required: 5. Visas can be processed in 24 hours for a 75% fee increase or in 72 hours for a 50% fee increase.
Temporary residence: Apply to the Embassy (for addresses, see above).

MONEY

Currency: Mozambique Metical (M) = 100 centavos. Notes are in denominations of M10,000, 5000, 1000, 500, 100 and 50. Coins are in denominations of M20, 10, 5, 2.5 and 1, and 50 centavos.
Exchange rate indicators: The following figures are included as a guide to the movements of the Metical against Sterling and the US Dollar:

Date:	Oct '92	Sep '93	Jan '94	Jan '95
£1.00=	4310.43	6632.05	7810.30	10,099.40
$1.00=	2716.09	4343.19	5279.01	6455.35

Currency restrictions: Import and export of local currency is prohibited. Free import of foreign currency is allowed, subject to declaration. Export of foreign currency is limited to the amount declared on import.
Banking hours: 0745-1145 Monday to Friday.

DUTY FREE

The following goods may be imported into Mozambique without incurring customs duty:
200 cigarettes or 250g of tobacco; 500ml of spirits; a reasonable quantity of perfume (opened).
Controlled items: Narcotics are prohibited. Firearms require a permit.

PUBLIC HOLIDAYS

Jan 1 '95 New Year's Day. **Feb 3** Heroes' Day. **Apr 7** Women's Day. **May 1** Labour Day. **Jun 25** Independence and Foundation of FRELIMO Day. **Sep 7** Victory Day. **Sep 25** Armed Forces Day. **Dec 25** Family Day. **Jan 1 '96** New Year's Day. **Feb 3** Heroes' Day. **Apr 7** Women's Day.

HEALTH

Regulations and requirements may be subject to change at short notice, and you are advised to contact your doctor well in advance of your intended date of departure. Any numbers in the chart refer to the footnotes below.

	Special Precautions?	Certificate Required?
Yellow Fever	No	1
Cholera	Yes	2
Typhoid & Polio	Yes	-
Malaria	3	
Food & Drink	4	

[1]: A yellow fever vaccination certificate is required of travellers over one year of age coming from infected areas.
[2]: Following WHO guidelines issued in 1973, a cholera vaccination certificate is not a condition of entry to Mozambique. However, cholera is a serious risk in this country and precautions are essential. Up-to-date advice should be sought before deciding whether these precautions should include vaccination, as medical opinion is divided over its effectiveness. See the *Health* section at the back of the book.
[3]: Malaria risk exists throughout the year in the whole country. The predominant *falciparum* strain is reported to be 'highly resistant' to chloroquine.
[4]: All water should be regarded as being potentially contaminated. Water used for drinking, brushing teeth or making ice should have first been boiled or otherwise sterilised. Milk is unpasteurised and should be boiled. Powdered or tinned milk is available and is advised, but make sure that it is reconstituted with pure water. Avoid dairy products which are likely to have been made from unboiled milk. Only eat well-cooked meat and fish, preferably served hot. Pork, salad and mayonnaise may carry increased risk. Vegetables should be cooked and fruit peeled.

Rabies is present. For those at high risk, vaccination before arrival should be considered. If you are bitten abroad seek medical advice without delay. For more information, consult the *Health* section at the back of the book. *Bilharzia* (schistosomiasis) is present. Avoid swimming and paddling in fresh water. Swimming pools which are well-chlorinated and maintained are safe.

Health care: Full health insurance is essential. Medical facilities are scarce and of a poor standard. Many rural health centres were forced to close during the conflict with the MNR rebels. There is one doctor per 44,000 inhabitants.

TRAVEL - International

AIR: Mozambique's national airline is *LAM-Linhas Aéreas de Moçambique (TM)*.
Approximate flight time: From London to Maputo is 14 hours, including stopover in Johannesburg.
International airports: *Maputo (MPM)* (Mavalane) is 8km (5 miles) north of the city (travel time – 20 minutes). Airport facilities include restaurant, bar, snack bar and post office. Taxis are rarely available at the airport and the visitor should arrange for someone to meet them if possible.
Beira (BEW) is 13km (8 miles) from the city (travel time – 15 minutes). Beira only receives flights from Continental Europe, other African countries and America. Airport facilities include restaurant, shops and a post office.
Departure tax: US$20 or US$10 if within Africa.
SEA: British, European, American, Japanese and South African cargo vessels call at Maputo and Beira, but there are no regular passenger services.
RAIL: A train runs six times a week from Johannesburg to the Mozambique border at Komatipoort where there is a connection (not guaranteed) to Maputo. There are no connections at present between Harare and Beira or Harare and Maputo, as the border crossings are closed; railway connections to Zimbabwe are being rehabilitated. There are connections from Malawi to Beira (though the border may still have to be crossed on foot) and to Nacala.
Note: Rail services are sporadic and unreliable.
ROAD: There are good road links with all neighbouring countries except Tanzania. For entry requirements and routes for border crossing, contact the Embassy.

TRAVEL - Internal

AIR: There are flights linking Maputo with Blantyre (Malawi), Inhambane, Beira, Quelimane, Tete, Lichinga, Nampula and Pemba. Flights depart from Maputo between 0500 and 0730 and are subject to seasonal alterations. Air-taxi services are also available, and are the safest means of transport outside the main cities due to the fighting within the country.
Departure tax: US$10.
RAIL: There is no rail connection between Maputo and Beira. There is a rail link between Beira and Tete and lines from the towns of Moçambique and Nacala, via the junction at Monapo, to Nampula and Lichinga. Trains also run from Maputo to Goba and Ressano Garcia, and northwards on the line to Zimbabwe. Most trains have three classes, but there are few sleepers and no dining or air-conditioned cars. For seats and sleepers it is necessary to book in advance. All train services are subject to disruption.
ROAD: Tarred roads connect Maputo with Beira and Beira with Tete. Traffic drives on the left. **Bus:** There are regular services covering most of the country. It is essential to carry food and water on long journeys. There are frequent controls on the roads to check papers, especially in the north and near the border with Zimbabwe. Bus travel is the cheapest form of transport in the country. **Taxi:** Rarely available outside Maputo. **Car hire:** There are only one or two car-hire firms and consequently rental cars are very difficult to obtain. Only hard currency is accepted. **Documentation:** International Driving Permit required.
Note: Owing to fighting within Mozambique, travel by road outside the capital is currently inadvisable.
URBAN: Bus services in Maputo are being improved with the introduction of new vehicles, and there are now fairly extensive services. Taxis are metered but hard to find. Taxi drivers expect a 10% tip.

ACCOMMODATION

HOTELS: Hotels of international standard are found in the cities of Maputo and Beira, and accommodation is adequate in smaller towns. Prices are available on request.
GUEST-HOUSES: It is possible to rent holiday cottages, bungalows and *rondavels* cheaply.
CAMPING/CARAVANNING: There are campsites along the beaches, and a rest camp with a restaurant in

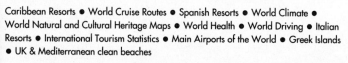
Gorongosa Game Park. Camping is also permitted at various Catholic and Protestant missions in the country.

RESORTS & EXCURSIONS

The country is opening to tourism, but so far only package tours are permitted. Individual visitors are not allowed.
Beira has lovely beaches and is the base for trips to *Gorongosa National Park*. Other beaches are at *Ponta do Ouro, Malagane* (in the south), **Inhaca Island** (near Maputo), **Inhambane** with its beach resort of *Tofo* (about 400km/250 miles north of the capital), **Xai-Xai**, *San Martino do Bilene* and *Chonguene*. The museum in **Maputo** houses paintings and sculptures by well-known local artists. The gallery in the Ministry of Labour building is also worth a visit, as is the market.
Moçambique is a fascinating town, full of 17th- and 18th-century buildings, many of them from the colonial Portuguese period. There are also some interesting mosques dating from that period.
Regions that are being developed as tourist resorts include the **Bazaruto Archipelago**, an excellent game-fishing area, and the islands of **Santa Carolina** and **Zalala**, north of Beira.
NATIONAL PARKS: There are three good national parks in Mozambique. The **Gorongosa National Park** is open from the beginning of May to the end of October. Visits can be booked through the LAM office in Maputo. Access is provided by an airstrip at Chitengo. Guides and cars are available inside the park. The **Maputo Elephant Park** is on the right bank of the Maputo River. The **Marromeu National Park** is at the mouth of the Zambesi River.

SOCIAL PROFILE

FOOD & DRINK: The cuisine is mainly Portuguese with Far Eastern influences. Specialities are *piri-piri* chicken, shellfish, including Delagoa Bay prawns (which are grilled and served with *piri-piri* sauce), *matapa* (sauce of ground peanuts and cassava leaves) with rice or *wusa* (stiff maize porridge). Restaurants are to be found in main towns, as well as hotel dining rooms.
NIGHTLIFE: There are a number of nightclubs in Maputo which offer music and dancing. The style of music varies from typical Mozambican ballads to Western pop music. Most major towns have cinemas.
SHOPPING: Special purchases include basketwork, reed mats, woodcarvings, masks, printed cloth and leather articles. **Shopping hours:** 0830-1300 and 1500-1830 Tuesday to Saturday. Shops are closed Monday morning and open 1400-1830 in the afternoon.
SPORT: Fishing: There is good fishing for marlin, barracuda, sailfish and swordfish. Notable resorts are Inhaca Island near Maputo, the Bazaruto Archipelago and Mozambique Island. **Swimming:** There are many safe beaches and lagoons with safe bathing; however, there is a danger of occasional sharks in the warm Indian Ocean. Many hotels have pools. **Skindiving:** Some resorts have facilities and excellent clear waters full of underwater sights for the skindiver to explore. Zavora's coral reef is outstanding.
SPECIAL EVENTS: For details of special events in 1995/96, contact the Mozambique National Tourism Company.
SOCIAL CONVENTIONS: Shaking hands is the customary form of greeting. The courtesies and modes of address customary in Portugal and other Latin countries are still observed. Casual wear is acceptable. Formal dress is seldom required. **Tipping:** 10% is customary, although it is discouraged in hotels.

BUSINESS PROFILE

ECONOMY: The departure of Portuguese personnel, who made up most of the skilled workforce immediately after independence, and the subsequent debilitating civil war has devastated the Mozambiquan economy. The industrial base, which has never been extensive, is very weak. Those light industries still functioning include food-processing, textiles, brewing, cement and fertilizer production. Heavy industry and mining have the potential for major development but demand a more substantial infrastructure than the Government can sustain. Agriculture, which employs 90% of the working population, contributes little beyond subsistence level, and during the 1980s was further worsened by recurrent drought. Cash crops include cashew nuts, tea, sugar, sisal, cotton, copra, oil seeds and some citrus fruit. Mozambique consequently depends heavily on large injections of foreign aid. The generally parlous state of the economy has shown some signs of improvement, as the Economic Recovery Plan instituted in 1987 starts to take effect. The USA, Singapore and Zimbabwe are Mozambique's most important trading partners. The political settlement reached in 1992 will allow the long task of reconstruction to begin. The all-important Beira and Limpopo rail corridors have been open for some months under a local ceasefire agreement and foreign investment has been picking up.
BUSINESS: Safari suits are advised for the hot season, while lightweight suits or jackets should be worn for the rest of the year. Prior appointments are recommended. There are few translation facilities available in Maputo, though it is usually possible to find someone in business circles who can help. January is the main holiday month, so this should be avoided for business trips. **Office hours:** 0730-1200 and 1400-1730 Monday to Friday, 0800-1200 Saturday.
COMMERCIAL INFORMATION: The following organisation can offer advice: Câmara de Comércio de Moçambique, CP 1836, Rua Mateus Sansão Mutemba 452, Maputo. Tel: (1) 491 970. Telex: 6498.

CLIMATE

Climate varies according to area. Inland is cooler than the coast and rainfall higher as the land rises, with most rain between January and March. Hottest and wettest season is October to March. From April to September the coast has warm, mainly dry weather tempered by sea breezes.

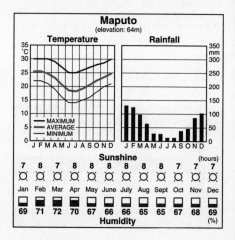

Maputo
(elevation: 64m)

	Jan	Feb	Mar	Apr	May	June	July	Aug	Sept	Oct	Nov	Dec
Sunshine (hours)	7	8	7	8	8	8	8	8	8	7	7	7
Humidity (%)	69	71	72	70	67	66	66	65	65	67	68	69

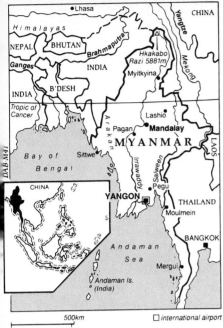

500km
300mls
☐ *international airport*

Location: South-East Asia.

Note: The Union of Myanmar, the name adopted by Burma in 1989, is now in general use. The old name continues to be used, but should not be used in official communications.
Care should be taken when travelling to the southern Shan State, as well as the Thai-Myanmar border. Both are areas of potentially active conflict. Special care should be taken not to cross the border into Myanmar inadvertently. The only legal border crossing to the area is at Tachilek.
Source: US State Department – October 24, 1994.

Myanmar Hotels and Tourism Services
PO Box 1398, 77-91 Sule Pagoda Road, Yangon 11141, Myanmar
Tel: (1) 83363. Fax: (1) 89588. Telex: 21330 (a/b HOTOCO BM).

Myanmar Travel and Tours
PO Box 559, 77-79 Sule Pagoda Road, Yangon 11141, Myanmar
Tel: (1) 75828. Fax: (1) 89588. Telex: 21330.

Embassy of the Union of Myanmar
19a Charles Street, Berkeley Square, London W1X 8ER
Tel: (0171) 629 6966 *or* 499 8841 (Visa section). Fax: (0171) 629 4169. Telex: 267609 (a/b MYANMA G).
Opening hours: 0930-1630 Monday to Friday; 1000-1300 Monday to Friday (Consular section).

British Embassy
PO Box 638, 80 Strand Road, Yangon, Myanmar
Tel: (1) 81700/3. Fax: (1) 85929 Telex: 21216 (a/b PRODRM BM).

Embassy of the Union of Myanmar
2300 S Street, NW, Washington, DC 20008
Tel: (202) 332 9044/5. Fax: (202) 332 9046. Telex: 248310.

Embassy of the United States of America
581 Merchant Street, Yangon, Myanmar
Tel: (1) 82055 *or* 82182. Fax: (1) 80409. Telex: 21230 (a/b AMBYGN BM).

Embassy of the Union of Myanmar
Suite 902, The Sandringham Apartments, 85 Range Road, Ottawa, Ontario K1N 8J6
Tel: (613) 232 6434/5 *or* 232 6446. Fax: (613) 232 6435.
The Canadian Embassy in Bangkok deals with enquiries relating to Myanmar (see *Thailand* **later in this book).**

AREA: 676,552 sq km (261,218 sq miles).
POPULATION: 41,550,000 (1988 estimate).
POPULATION DENSITY: 61.4 per sq km.
CAPITAL: Yangon (Rangoon). **Population:** 2,513,023 (1983).
GEOGRAPHY: Myanmar is a diamond-shaped country extending 925km (575 miles) from east to west and 2100km (1300 miles) from north to south. It is bounded by China, Laos and Thailand in the east, and by Bangladesh, India and the Indian Ocean in the south and west. The Irrawaddy River runs through the centre of the country and fans out to form a delta on the south coast; Yangon stands beside one of its many mouths. North of the delta lies the Irrawaddy basin and central Myanmar, which is protected by a horseshoe of mountains rising to over 3000m (10,000ft), creating profound climatic effects. To the west are the Arakan, Chin and Naga mountains and the Patkai Hills; the Kachin Hills are to the north; to the east lies the Shan Plateau, which extends to the Tenasserim coastal ranges. Intensive irrigated farming is practised throughout central Myanmar, and fruit, vegetables and citrus crops thrive on the Shan Plateau, but much of the land and mountains are covered by subtropical forest.
LANGUAGE: The official language is Burmese. There are over 100 distinct languages and dialects spoken in Myanmar. English is spoken in business circles.
RELIGION: 85% Theravada Buddhist. The remainder are Hindu, Muslim, Christian and Animist.
TIME: GMT + 6.30.
ELECTRICITY: 220/230 volts AC, 50Hz.
COMMUNICATIONS: Telephone: IDD is available to the main cities. Country code: 95. Outgoing international code: 0. There is a limited public internal service.
Telex/telegram: Telegrams may be sent from the Central Telegraph Office on Maha Bandoola Street and there are further facilities at the Post and Telecommunications Corporation in Yangon. Telex facilities are available to businessmen at main hotels but not to the public. **Post:** Service to Europe takes up to a week and letter forms are quicker than ordinary letters. To ensure despatch it is advisable to go to the post office personally to obtain a certificate of posting, for which a small fee is charged.
Press: The English-language newspaper is *The Working People's Daily.*
BBC World Service and Voice of America frequencies: From time to time these change. See the section *How to Use this Book* for more information.

BBC:				
MHz	17.79	11.75	9.740	3.915
Voice of America:				
MHz	17.74	15.40	11.71	7.125

PASSPORT/VISA

Regulations and requirements may be subject to change at short notice, and you are advised to contact the appropriate diplomatic or consular authority before finalising travel arrangements. Details of these may be found at the head of this country's entry. Any numbers in the chart refer to the footnotes below.

	Passport Required?	Visa Required?	Return Ticket Required?
Full British	Yes	Yes	Yes
BVP	Not valid	-	-
Australian	Yes	Yes	Yes
Canadian	Yes	Yes	Yes
USA	Yes	Yes	Yes
Other EU (As of 31/12/94)	Yes	Yes	Yes
Japanese	Yes	Yes	Yes

Restricted entry: Holders of passports issued by North Korea are refused admission.
PASSPORTS: Valid passport required by all.
British Visitors Passport: Not accepted.
VISAS: Required by all. A separate visa is required for each child over 7 years of age even if travelling on their parent's passport.
Types of visa: Tourist visa and Business visa. Cost: £12. for Tourist visa; £20 for Business visa.
Validity: Tourist visas are granted for a *maximum of 28 days stay* in Myanmar, but are valid for 3 months from the date of issue. Business visas can be extended once in Myanmar.
Application to: Consulate (or Consular section at Embassy). For addresses, see top of entry.
Application requirements: *Tourist visa:* (a) 3 passport-

size photos. (b) 2 application forms. (c) Air ticket to Myanmar or a letter from airline or travel agency concerned giving details of flights in and out of Yangon (land entry into Myanmar is not allowed). (d) Valid passport.
Business visa: (a) 3 application forms. (b) 3 passport-size photos. (c) Letter from sponsoring body, firm or department stating detailed reasons for the applicant's visit and the name of the Myanmar government department, corporation or agency to be contacted; the letter must state the precise nature of the business to be conducted and indicate the financial status of the applicant. (d) Valid passport.
Working days required: 24 hours (provided the Government's letter of permission has been submitted).
Exit permits: A *Report of Departure Form D* is required by all persons holding Entry or Transit visas for stays exceeding 30 days. The permit must be acquired before booking passage.

MONEY

Currency: Kyat (Kt) = 100 pyas. Notes are in denominations of Kt200, 90, 45, 15, 10, 5 and 1. Coins are in denominations of Kt1, and 50, 25, 10, 5 and 1 pyas. Kt100,000 is known as a *lakh*, and Kt10 million as a *crore*. Kyat is pronounced like the English word 'chat'. To combat the black market and limit the financial power of dissident groups, currency denominations are occasionally declared invalid without prior notice. Limited refunds are usually allowed for certain sectors of the population.
Credit cards: These are not generally accepted, but check with your credit card company for details of merchant acceptability and other services which may be available.
Travellers cheques: Accepted.
Exchange rate indicators: The following figures are included as a guide to the movements of the Kyat against Sterling and the US Dollar:

Date:	Oct '92	Sep '93	Jan '94	Jan '95
£1.00=	11.31	9.48	9.48	9.19
$1.00=	7.13	6.20	6.40	5.87

Currency restrictions: The import and export of local currency is prohibited. There are no import limits on foreign currencies, but the amounts must be declared on entry and the declaration certificate kept safe – on departure, foreign currencies are checked with the amounts declared on entry. A minimum equivalent to US$300 must be exchanged on entry. Only a quarter of the foreign currency converted to Kyats during stay in Myanmar will be allowed to be re-converted on exit. There are regular customs checks at Yangon airport, aimed at curbing black-market activities; this makes it essential to keep all receipts in order to account for money spent while in the country.
Banking hours: 1000-1400 Monday to Friday.

DUTY FREE

The following goods may be taken into Myanmar by persons over 17 years of age without incurring customs duty:
400 cigarettes or 100 cigars or 250g tobacco; 1.136 litres of alcohol; 500ml of perfume or eau de cologne.
Prohibited items: Playing cards, gambling equipment and pornography.
Note: Travellers must obtain a permit from the Exchange Control Department to take jewellery totalling more than Kt250 in value out of Myanmar. All jewellery (including wedding rings) should be declared; failure to do so may result in visitors being refused permission to export it on departure.

PUBLIC HOLIDAYS

Jan 4 '95 Independence Day. **Feb 12** Union Day. **Mar** Full Moon of Tabaung. **Mar 2** Peasants' Day. **Mar 27** Armed Forces Day. **Apr** Maha Thingyan (Water Festival). **Apr 17** Myanmar New Year. **May 1** Workers' Day. **May 10** Eid al-Adha (Feast of the Sacrifice). **May** Full Moon of Kason. **Jul 19** Martyrs' Day. **Jul/Aug** Full Moon of Waso. **Oct** Full Moon of Thadingyut. **Oct** Diwali. **Nov** Tazaungdaing Festival. **Dec 3** National Day. **Dec 25** Christmas Day. **Jan 4 '96** Independence Day. **Feb 12** Union Day. **Mar** Full Moon of Tabaung. **Mar 2** Peasants' Day. **Mar 27** Armed Forces Day. **Apr** Maha Thingyan (Water Festival). **Apr 17** Myanmar New Year.
Note: Buddhist holidays are determined according to lunar sightings, and dates given here are approximations only. Other festivals celebrated by minorities include the Hindu Devali festival in November; Islamic observance

of Bakri Idd in late November; Christmas and Easter; and the Karen New Year in early January. For further information on holidays in 1995/96, contact the Embassy.

HEALTH

Regulations and requirements may be subject to change at short notice, and you are advised to contact your doctor well in advance of your intended date of departure. Any numbers in the chart refer to the footnotes below.

	Special Precautions?	Certificate Required?
Yellow Fever	Yes	1
Cholera	Yes	2
Typhoid & Polio	Yes	-
Malaria	3	-
Food & Drink	4	-

[1]: A yellow fever vaccination certificate is required from all travellers arriving from infected areas. Nationals and residents of Myanmar are required to possess certificates of vaccination on their departure to an infected area.

[2]: Following WHO guidelines issued in 1973, a cholera vaccination certificate is no longer a condition of entry to Myanmar. However, cholera is a serious risk in this country and precautions are essential. Up-to-date advice should be sought before deciding whether these precautions should include vaccination, as medical opinion is divided over its effectiveness. See the *Health* section at the back of the book.

[3]: Malaria risk (predominantly in the malignant *falciparum* form) exists below 1000m in the following areas: (a) throughout the year in Karen State; (b) from March to December in Chin, Kachin, Kayah, Mon, Rakhine and Shan States, in Pegu Division, and in Hlegu, Hmawbi and Taikkyi townships of Yangon; (c) from April to December in rural areas of Tenasserim Division; (d) from May to December in Irrawaddy Division and rural areas of Mandalay Division; (e) from June to November in rural areas of Magwe Division and in Sagaing Division. The *falciparum* strain is reported to be 'highly resistant' to chloroquine and 'resistant' to sulfadoxine/pyrimethamine.

[4]: All water should be regarded as being potentially contaminated. Water used for drinking, brushing teeth or making ice should have first been boiled or otherwise sterilised. Milk is unpasteurised and should be boiled. Powdered or tinned milk is available and is advised, but make sure that it is reconstituted with pure water. Avoid dairy products which are likely to have been made from unboiled milk. Only eat well-cooked meat and fish, preferably served hot. Pork, salad and mayonnaise may carry increased risk. Vegetables should be cooked and fruit peeled.

The WHO advises that foci of *plague* are present in Myanmar. Further information should be sought from the Department of Health or from any of the hospitals specialising in tropical diseases listed in the *Health* section at the back of the book.

Japanese encephalitis may be caught via mosquito bites, particularly in rural areas between June and October. A vaccine is available, and travellers are advised to consult their doctor prior to departure.

Rabies is present. For those at high risk, vaccination before arrival should be considered. If you are bitten abroad seek medical advice without delay. For more information, consult the *Health* section at the back of the book.

Health care: Health insurance is strongly recommended. There are hospitals and clinics in cities and larger towns, and regional health centres in outlying areas. It is advisable to carry a remedy against minor enteric upsets.

TRAVEL - International

AIR: Myanmar's national airline is *Myanmar Airways (UB).*

International airport: Yangon (YGN) (Mingaladon) is 19km (12 miles) from the city. Airport facilities include restaurant, bar, snack bar, bank, post office, duty-free shop and tourist information. Travel to the city is by taxi (not always available) or by bus no. 9, departing every 15 minutes (travel time – 30 minutes). Bus no. 9 returns from Merchant Street.

Departure tax: US$6 or Kt15 is levied; children under 18 years of age and passengers in direct transit are exempt.

Note: Air travel is the only reliable means of access into Myanmar.

TRAVEL - Internal

AIR: Air travel is the most efficient way of moving within Myanmar, but there is a rather limited schedule of

flights. Internal security can restrict ease of movement. There are daily flights to most towns; charter flights are also available. There are over 50 airstrips in the country. For tickets and information, contact Myanmar Hotels and Tourism Services (address at top of entry).

Internal flight times: From Yangon to *Mandalay* is 2 hours 10 minutes; to *Pagan* is 1 hour 30 minutes; and to *Heho* is 1 hour 25 minutes.

SEA/RIVER: The best way of seeing Myanmar is by boat, particularly between Bhamo–Mandalay and Mandalay–Pagan. Myanmar has about 8000km (5000 miles) of navigable rivers. Local travel agents can arrange trips. It is generally necessary to provide one's own food.

Note: Delays are frequent, so allow plenty of time for boat travel.

RAIL: *Myanmar Railways* provide services on several routes, the principal line being Yangon to Mandalay (travel time – 12-14 hours). Overnight trains have sleeping cars. There is also a good service from Mandalay–Lashio–Myitkyina. The state-run railway has 4300km (2700 miles) of track and serves most of Myanmar. First class is available but, with the exception of the Yangon to Mandalay line, services are regularly afflicted with delays caused by climatic, technical and bureaucratic difficulties. Tickets must be purchased through Myanmar Hotels and Tourism Services, 24 hours in advance if possible; it is also worth travelling first class if possible. There are regular services from Yangon to Mandalay and from Yangon to Thazi. Combined rail/bus tickets are obtainable.

ROAD: Traffic drives on the right. There are long-

distance **buses,** but these are not recommended due to their condition and the condition of the roads. There has been some modernisation of Myanmar's once antiquated vehicles. Japanese pick-up trucks run unscheduled services between large towns. **Bicycles** are available for hire. **Documentation:** An International Driving Permit is required. This must be presented to the police, who will endorse it or issue a visitor's licence.

URBAN: Yangon has a circular rail service. There is also an antiquated and overcrowded bus service in all cities. Yangon has blue government taxis with set fares. Unmetered 3- and 4-wheel taxis are available in cities, as are rickshaws; it is wise to pre-arrange fares.

ACCOMMODATION

Bookings should be made well in advance. Yangon only has 400 hotel beds. Contact the Myanmar Hotels and Tourism Services. There are also hotels at the resorts of Sandoway, Taunggyi and Pagan. In general, advance booking is advisable, particularly from November to March. **Grading:** There is an increasing number of hotels, divided into three categories: luxury, first class and lower.

Visitors travelling away from the normal tourist routes should carry sleeping bags or blankets, as pagodas, temples and monasteries will usually only accommodate visitors for a night or two. Although reserved for state officials in many towns, inns will often accommodate travellers who have been granted official permission.

RESORTS & EXCURSIONS

Much of Upper and Lower Myanmar is out of bounds, owing to the civil war. Few coastal resorts have been opened to tourists, but Sunday round-trip flights are arranged by the Tourist Corporation to Napali and Sandoway beaches during the dry season.

For the purpose of this guide, Myanmar has been divided into four regions: The South (including Yangon); Central Myanmar (including Pagan and Mandalay); The East and The Northwest.

The South

Yangon (or *Rangoon*), the capital, is a city of Buddhist temples, open-air markets, food stalls and ill-repaired colonial architecture. It has a population of over two million. Although most of the city has been built in the last hundred years, and although it suffered considerable damage during the Second World War, there are still several examples of a more ancient culture. These include the golden *Shwe Dagon Pagoda,* one of the most spectacular Buddhist shrines in Asia and reputedly 2500 years old (although rebuilt in 1769); the *Sule Pagoda*; the *Botataung Pagoda*, hollow inside with a mirrored maze; and the *Maha Pasan Guha* or 'Great Cave'.

Outside the capital, places worth visiting include the *Naga-Yone* enclosure near **Myinkaba**, with a Buddha figure entwined and protected by a huge cobra – a combination of Buddhism and Brahman astrology; *Kyaik Tyo* and its 'Golden Rock Pagoda', an 5.5m (18ft) shrine built on a gold-plated boulder atop a cliff; and **Pegu**, founded in 1573, with its golden *Shwemawdaw Pagoda* and market. Just northeast of Pegu is the *Shwethalyaung Buddha,* revered as one of the most beautiful and lifelike of reclining Buddhas, which was lost and totally overgrown by jungle after the destruction of Pegu in 1757. It was rediscovered in the British era, during the construction of the railway line.

Central Myanmar

Pagan is one of the greatest historical areas in the country. It is best seen at sunrise or sunset. More than 13,000 pagodas were once spread over this dry plain during the golden age of the 11 great kings (roughly 1044-1287); this came to an end with the threat of invasion by Kublai Khan from China, and this extraordinary area was abandoned. Now there are fewer than 3000 pagodas. The actual village of Pagan has a museum, market and places to eat and stay; within walking distance of Pagan, there are lacquerware workshops and an attractive temple. There are dozens of open temples in the Pagan area (about 40 sq km), but places of special interest include the *Shwegugyi Temple*, built in 1311 and noted for its fine stucco carvings; the *Gawdawpalin Temple*, badly damaged in the 1975 earthquake, but still one of the most impressive of the Pagan temples; and the *Thatbyinnyu Temple,* which is the highest in Pagan.

Mandalay, the old royal city, is rich in palaces, stupas, temples and pagodas (although the city has suffered several bad fires which have destroyed some buildings), and is the main centre of Buddhism and Burmese arts. There are some excellent craft markets and there are thriving stone-carving workshops and gold-leaf industries. Taking its name from *Mandalay Hill* (rising about 240m/787ft to the northeast of the palace), the city was founded by King Mindon in 1857, the old wooden palace buildings at Amarapura being moved and reconstructed. Sights of interest include the huge *Shweyattaw Buddha*, close to the hill, with its outstretched finger pointing towards the city; the *Eindawya Pagoda*, built in 1847 and covered in gold leaf; the *Shwekyimyint Pagoda* containing the original Buddha image consecrated by Prince Minshinzaw during the Pagan period; and the *Mahumuni Pagoda* or 'Great Pagoda', housing the famous and revered Mahumuni image. Covered in gold leaf over the years by devout Buddhists, this image was brought from Arakan in 1784, although it is thought to be much older. The base, moat and huge walls are virtually all that remain of the once stupendous *Mandalay Palace*, which was an immense walled city (mostly of timber construction) rather than a palace. It was burnt down in 1942. A large-scale model gives an indication of what it must have been like. The *Shwenandaw Kyaung Monastery* was at one time part of the palace complex and was used as an apartment by King Mindon and his chief queen. Like the palace, the wooden building was once beautifully gilded. There are some extraordinary carved panels inside and also a photograph of the *Atumashi Kyaung Monastery*, destroyed by fire in 1890. The ruins can be seen to the south of the *Kuthodaw Pagoda*, called 'the world's biggest book' because of the 729 marble slabs that surround the central pagoda – they are inscribed with the entire Buddhist canon.

The area around Mandalay contains several older, abandoned capital cities. **Sagaing** is easily accessible to the visitor, and contains interesting pagodas at *Tupayon, Aungmyelawka* and *Kaunghmudaw*. Sagaing was for a time the capital of an independent Shan Kingdom. In the 15th century, **Ava** was chosen as the kingdom's new capital and it remained so until well into the 19th century, when the kingdom vanished; the old city walls can still be traced. **Mingun** (a pleasant river trip from Mandalay) possesses the famous *Mingun Bell*, supposedly the largest uncracked, hung bell in the world. It was cast in 1790 by King Bodawpaya to be hung in his giant pagoda, which was never finished, due to the king's death in 1819. The base of the pagoda alone is about 50m (165ft) high. **Amarapura**, south of Mandalay, was founded by Bodawpaya in 1783 and the city is famous for its cotton and silk weaving.

The East

This region of the country offers the visitor opportunities for walking and rock-climbing, and the various hill stations, such as *Kalaw,* provide a pine-forested escape from the heat and humidity of Yangon. The caves and lake at **Pindaya** are famous; the caves contain thousands of Buddha images. Near the village of **Yengan** are the *Padah-Lin Caves,* containing prehistoric paintings. *Inle Lake* on the Shan Plateau is famous for its floating gardens and leg-rowing fishermen. *Maymyo* is a charming British hill station further north, with attractive waterfalls and a pleasant climate because of its high altitude.

The Northwest

Difficult communications usually prevent tourists from visiting this largely tribal region. Many of Myanmar's minority peoples live here.

SOCIAL PROFILE

FOOD & DRINK: The regional food is hot and spicy. Fish, rice, noodles and vegetables spiced with onions, ginger, garlic and chillies are the common local ingredients. Local dishes include *lethok son* (a sort of spicy vegetarian rice salad), *mohinga* (fish soup with noodles) and *oh-no khauk swe* (rice noodles, chicken and coconut milk). The avocados by Inle Lake are very good. Delicious fruits are available in the markets and food stalls appear on the corners of most large towns. Chinese and Indian cuisine is offered in many hotels and restaurants. **Drink:** Tea is a popular drink; the spices which are added to it can make the tongue turn bright red. Locally produced soft drinks are generally of poor quality and rather expensive. Coffee is not common. Locally produced beer, rum, whisky and gin are generally available.

NIGHTLIFE: Western-style nightlife is non-existent, although there are occasional performances in Yangon's three theatres. Cinemas are popular and seven of Yangon's 50 cinemas regularly show English-language films.

SPORT: Many Western sports are played. **Football** can be seen at Aung San Stadium in Yangon and on small fields throughout the country. The national game is **Chinglone;** its object is to keep a cane ball in the air for as long as possible using only feet and knees with teams of six players. Burmese **boxing** is another popular sport; it can appear extremely vicious to the uninitiated spectator.

SPECIAL EVENTS: The Buddhist calendar is full of festivals, many timed to coincide with the full moon. Any visitor would be unlucky not to be able to enjoy at least one during any stay. The Myanmar New Year, *Maha Thingyan,* takes place in mid-April and lasts for at least three days. Two other major festivals are *Thadingyut,* at the October full moon, and *Tazaungdaing,* in early November. The Buddhist Lent (July to October) is marked by three months' fasting and other religious observances.

SOCIAL CONVENTIONS: Handshaking is the normal form of greeting. Full names are used, preceded by *U* (pronounced *oo*) in the case of an older or well-respected man's name, *Aung* for younger men and *Ko* for adult males; a woman's name is preceded by *Daw.* Courtesy and respect for tradition and religion is expected; for instance, shoes and socks must be removed before entering any religious building and it is customary to remove shoes before entering a traditional home (in most modern residences this is no longer observed except in bedrooms). When sitting, avoid displaying the soles of the feet, as this is considered offensive. Small presents are acceptable and appreciated, although never expected. Shorts and mini-skirts should not be worn. **Tipping:** It is usual to give 5-10% on hotel and restaurant bills. Taxi drivers do not expect a tip.

BUSINESS PROFILE

ECONOMY: A potentially rich country, Myanmar has all but stood still economically under the brutal maladministration of the Burma Socialist Programme Party (now the National Unity Party). A major part of the country's GDP is spent on arms which are then used against its own minorities. Agriculture, mainly livestock and fishing, is the largest single sector but continues to rely on traditional non-mechanised methods. Rice, generally the principal export earner, has diminished in importance in line with the continually depressed state of the world market. Teak is the country's other main export. Other crops include oil-seeds, sugar cane, cotton, jute and rubber. Myanmar has significant deposits of oil, tin, copper and coal, but has failed to exploit them fully, although there are current plans to institute major redevelopment of this sector. A wide range of manufactured goods are assembled locally but the majority are imported ready-made. Myanmar's economic development will continue to be stunted as long as its chronic foreign exchange problems continue: this has forced the Government and state-controlled trading agencies to arrange awkward barter deals. China, Japan and the 'Tiger' economies of the Pacific Basin (notably Singapore) are Myanmar's main trading partners. With changes in Vietnam and Laos highlighting a vast potential earner of hard currency, the Government of Myanmar has announced its intention to boost tourism, designating 1996 as 'The Year of Myanmar'. More disturbingly there have been verified reports that the authorities are using forced labour to renovate potential tourist sites and develop infrastructure improvements. There have also been reports of villages being forcibly cleared to make way for new facilities. It remains to be seen whether large scale tourism can take off in a country with such an appalling human rights record.

BUSINESS: Lightweight suits are recommended during the day; jackets needed for top-level meetings. Most commercial business transactions will be conducted in English. Business cards in Burmese script can be useful. The best time to visit is October to February. **Office hours:** 0930-1630 Monday to Friday.

COMMERCIAL INFORMATION: There are over 20 Government Corporations dealing with all aspects of business. The Inspection and Agency Corporation in Yangon promotes business with foreign companies. For further information, contact the Myanmar Foreign Trade Bank, PO Box 203, 80-86 Maha Bandoola Garden Street, Yangon. Tel: (1) 84911. Fax: (1) 89585. Telex: 21300.

CLIMATE

A monsoon climate with three main seasons. The hottest period is between February and May, with little or no rain. Rainy season exists from May to October and dry, cooler weather from October to February.

Required clothing: Lightweight cottons and linens throughout most of the year are required. Light raincoat or umbrella needed during rainy season. Warmer clothes are advised for coolest period and some evenings.

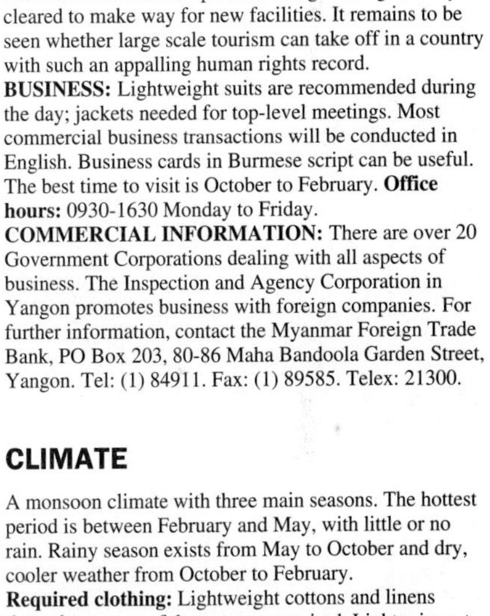

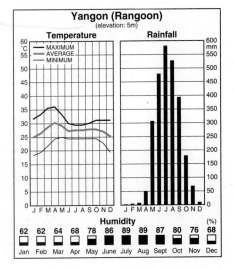

Namibia

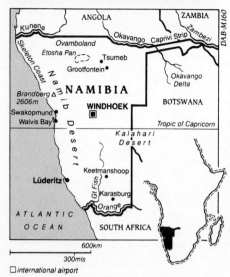

Location: Southwest Africa.

Namibia Tourism
Private Bag 13346, Windhoek, Namibia
Tel: (61) 284 9111. Fax: (61) 221 1930.

Ministry of Environment & Tourism
Private Bag 13346, Windhoek, Namibia
Tel: (61) 284 2360. Fax: (61) 221 1930.
High Commission for the Republic of Namibia
6 Chandos Street, London W1M 0LQ
Tel: (0171) 636 6244. Fax: (0171) 637 5694. Opening
hours: 0900-1300 and 1400-1700 Monday to Friday.
Namibia Tourism
Address as High Commission.
Tel: (0171) 636 2924. Fax: (0171) 636 2969. Opening
hours: 0900-1300 and 1400-1700 Monday to Friday.
British High Commission
116 Robert Mugabe Avenue, Windhoek, Namibia
Tel: (61) 223 022. Fax: (61) 228 895.
Embassy of the Republic of Namibia
1605 New Hampshire Avenue, NW, Washington, DC
20009
Tel: (202) 986 0540. Fax: (202) 986 0443.
Also deals with enquiries from Canada.
Embassy of the United States of America
Private Bag 12029, Ausspannplatz, 14 Lossen Street,
Windhoek, Namibia
Tel: (61) 221 601 *or* 222 675 *or* 222 680. Fax: (61) 229
792.
**The Canadian Embassy in Pretoria deals with
enquiries relating to Namibia (see the entry on** *South
Africa* **later in the book).**

AREA: 824,268 sq km (318,250 sq miles).
POPULATION: 1,426,711 (1991 estimate).
POPULATION DENSITY: 1.7 per sq km.
CAPITAL: Windhoek. **Population:** 142,000 (1991
estimate).

GEOGRAPHY: Namibia is in southwest Africa. It is a
large and mainly barren country sharing borders with
Angola to the north, Botswana to the east, South Africa
to the south and, in the Caprivi Strip, a narrow
panhandle of Namibian territory jutting from the
northeast corner of the country, with Zambia and
Zimbabwe. To the west is 1280km (795 miles) of some
of the most desolate and lonely coastline in the world.
The port of Walvis Bay, situated roughly halfway down
Namibia's coast, was returned by South Africa to
Namibian jurisdiction in February 1994. Along its entire
length, the vast shifting sand dunes of the Namib Desert
spread inland for 80-130km (50-80 miles). In the
interior, the escarpment of a north–south plateau slopes
away to the east and north into the vast interior sand
basin of the Kalahari. In the far northwest the 66,000 sq
km (25,500 sq miles) of the Kaokoland mountains run
along the coast, while further inland lies the Etosha Pan
(a dried-out saline lake), surrounded by grasslands and
bush which support a large and varied wildlife. The
Etosha National Park & Game Reserve is one of the
finest in Africa, in that it remains, to a large extent, free
of man's influence.
LANGUAGE: English is the official language.
Afrikaans, German, Herero and Owambo, amongst a
variety of tongues, are also spoken.
RELIGION: Christian majority.
TIME: GMT + 1 (GMT + 2 from September to April).
ELECTRICITY: 220/240 volts AC. Outlets are of the
3-pin type.
COMMUNICATIONS: Telephone: IDD is available.
Country code: 264. Outgoing international code: 09. **Fax:**
Some hotels have facilities. **Telex/telegram:** Good
facilities to all major centres. A telegraph service is
available in every town. **Post:** Good postal service.
Airmail to Europe takes from approximately four days to
two weeks. **Press:** Newspapers are printed Monday to
Friday. English-language dailies include *The Windhoek
Advertiser* and *The Namibian.*
**BBC World Service and Voice of America
frequencies:** From time to time these change. See the
section *How to Use this Book* for more information.
BBC:

MHz	21.66	17.88	6.190	3.255

Voice of America:

MHz	21.49	15.60	9.525	6.035

PASSPORT/VISA

Regulations and requirements may be subject to change at short notice, and you
are advised to contact the appropriate diplomatic or consular authority before
finalising travel arrangements. Details of these may be found at the head of this
country's entry. Any numbers in the chart refer to the footnotes below.

	Passport Required?	Visa Required?	Return Ticket Required?
Full British	Yes	No	Yes
BVP	Not valid	-	-
Australian	Yes	No	Yes
Canadian	Yes	No	Yes
USA	Yes	No	Yes
Other EU (As of 31/12/94)	Yes	1	Yes
Japanese	Yes	No	Yes

PASSPORTS: Valid passport required by all. Passports
must be valid for a minimum of 6 months after the date
of the intended visit.
British Visitors Passport: Not accepted.
VISAS: Required by all except:
(a) **[1]** nationals of EU countries (except nationals of
Greece who *do* require a visa) for a stay up to 3 months;
(b) nationals of Austria, CIS, Finland, Iceland,
Liechtenstein, Norway, Sweden and Switzerland for a
stay up to 3 months;
(c) nationals of Australia, Canada, Japan and the USA for
a stay up to 3 months;
(d) nationals of Angola, Botswana, Brazil, Cuba, Kenya,
Lesotho, Mozambique, New Zealand, Singapore,
Swaziland, South Africa, Tanzania, Zambia and
Zimbabwe for a stay up to 3 months.
Types of visa: Tourist, Business and Transit. Cost:

Health		
GALILEO/WORLDSPAN: **TI-DFT/WDH/HE**		
SABRE: **TIDFT/WDH/HE**		
Visa		
GALILEO/WORLDSPAN: **TI-DFT/WDH/VI**		
SABRE: **TIDFT/WDH/VI**		

Timatic

For more information on Timatic codes refer to Contents.

PHOTO CREDIT: PAUL GOLDSTEIN

Oryx, Damaraland

Namibia

A VAST DIFFERENCE

Namibia Tourism:

Private Bag 13346, Windhoek, Namibia. Tel: (010 26461) 284 2360. Fax: 22 1930.
Or: Namibia Verkehrsbüro, Postfach 2041, 61209 Bad Homburg 3, Germany.
Tel: (06172) 406650. Fax: (06172) 406690.
Namibia Tourism, 6 Chandos Street, London W1M. Tel: (0171) 636 2924/2928. Fax: (1071) 636 2969.

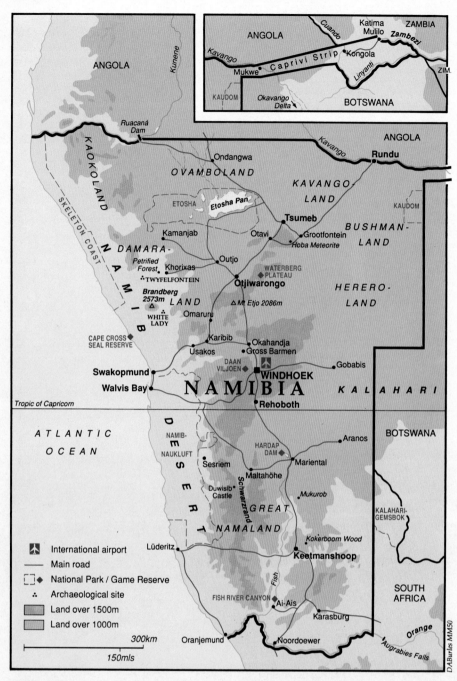

HEALTH

Regulations and requirements may be subject to change at short notice, and you are advised to contact your doctor well in advance of your intended date of departure. Any numbers in the chart refer to the footnotes below.

	Special Precautions?	Certificate Required?
Yellow Fever	Yes	1
Cholera	No	No
Typhoid & Polio	Yes	-
Malaria	2	-
Food & Drink	3	-

[1]: A yellow fever vaccination certificate is required from travellers arriving from infected areas. Those countries or parts of countries that were included in the former endemic zone in Africa and South America are regarded by the Namibian authorities as infected. Travellers with scheduled airlines whose flights have originated outside areas regarded as infected but have passed through such areas in transit are not required to possess a certificate provided they have remained at the scheduled airport or in the adjacent town during transit. All passengers with unscheduled airlines whose flights originated or passed in transit through an infected area are required to possess a certificate. The certificate is not insisted upon in the case of children under one year of age, but such infants may be subject to surveillance and they will not be allowed to proceed to Natal or to the Lowveld of the Transvaal in South Africa within six days of leaving any place or port within an infected area.
[2]: Malaria risk exists in the northern rural regions from November to May/June and along the Kavango River throughout the year. The predominant *falciparum* strain is reported to be 'highly resistant' to chloroquine. A weekly dose of 300mg of chloroquine plus a daily dose of 200mg of proguanil is the recommended prophylaxis.
[3]: Mains water is normally chlorinated, and whilst relatively safe may cause mild abdominal upsets. Bottled water is available and is advised for the first few weeks of the stay. Drinking water outside main cities and towns may be contaminated and sterilisation is advisable. Milk is pasteurised and dairy products are safe for consumption. Local meat, poultry, seafood, fruit and vegetables are generally considered safe to eat.
Rabies is present. For those at high risk, vaccination before arrival should be considered. If you are bitten abroad, seek medical advice without delay. For more information, consult the *Health* section at the back of the book.
Bilharzia (schistosomiasis) is present in Kavango and the Caprivi Strip. Avoid swimming and paddling in fresh water in these regions (also because of the presence of crocodiles). Swimming pools which are well chlorinated and maintained are safe.
Health care: Anti-bite serums for snakes and scorpions are advised. Health insurance is essential.

TRAVEL - International

AIR: Namibia's national airline is *Air Namibia (SW)*, which provides thrice-weekly direct flights to Windhoek, all three via Frankfurt/M. *SAA* also has landing rights.
Approximate flight time: From London to Windhoek is 12 hours (including a stopover of 2 hours and 35 minutes in Frankfurt/M).
International airport: *Windhoek (WDH)* (J G Strijdom) is 42km (20 miles) from the city (travel time – 35 minutes). Airport facilities include restaurant, bar, snack bar, post office, currency exchange and car hire. A bus service to the city meets all flight arrivals. Return is from the *SAA* terminus at the corner of Independence Avenue and Peter Müller Street, 90 minutes before flight departure, with pick-ups at Eros Airport and Safari Motel.
SEA: There is a modern deep-water harbour at Walvis Bay. There is also a small port at Lüderitz.
RAIL: There are two train routes from South Africa to Namibia: Johannesburg–De Aar–Keetmanshoop–Windhoek and Cape Town–De Aar–Windhoek.
ROAD: A tarred road runs from the south through Upington in South Africa to Grünau, where it connects with the tarred road from Cape Town. The untarred road from the east from Botswana to Gobabis is currently being upgraded as part of a new trans-Kalahari highway. The road from Luanda in Angola through Namibia to South Africa is tarred.

TRAVEL - Internal

AIR: Flying is the quickest and often the most economical way to travel around the country. *Air Namibia* links all of the major towns in the territory.

Single – N$20 (approx. UK£5); *Multiple* – N$50; *Transit* – N$20.
Validity: 3 months. Extensions for a further 3 months are available from the Ministry of Home Affairs in Windhoek.
Application to: Consulate (or Consular section at High Commission). For addresses, see top of entry.
Application requirements: (a) Valid passport. (b) Completed application form. (c) 2 passport-size photos. (d) Return ticket. (e) Company letter if on business.
Working days required: 2 working days.
Temporary residence: Apply to the High Commission or Embassy (addresses at top of entry).

MONEY

Currency: The Namibian Dollar (N$) has now been introduced, in note denominations of N$100, 50 and 10. Coins were also introduced in 1994 in denominations of N$5 and 1. It is linked to the South African Rand on a 1:1 basis (South African Rand = 100 cents). The South African Rand is also acceptable as currency in Namibia.
Credit cards: Access/Mastercard, Diners Club, American Express and Visa are accepted. Check with your credit card company for details of merchant acceptability and other services which may be available.
Exchange rate indicators: The following figures are included as a guide to the movements of the Rand against Sterling and the US Dollar:

Date:	Oct '92	Sep '93	Jan '94	Jan '95
£1.00=	4.68	5.16	5.02	5.54
$1.00=	2.95	3.38	3.39	3.54

Currency restrictions: All currency must be declared at port of entry. The import and export of local currency is limited to N$500. The import of foreign currency is unlimited. Export is limited to the amount imported and declared on arrival.
Banking hours: 0900-1530 Monday to Friday, 0830-1100 Saturday.

DUTY FREE

The following may be imported into Namibia by persons over 16 years of age without incurring customs duty:
400 cigarettes or 50 cigars or 250g of tobacco; 2 litres of wine and 1 litre of spirits; 50ml of perfume and 250ml of eau de toilette; gifts to the value of N$500, but including value of imported duty-free items.
Controlled items: Hunting rifles need a permit which should be issued by customs when entering the country. Handguns are not allowed.

PUBLIC HOLIDAYS

Jan 1 '95 New Year's Day. **Mar 21** Independence Day. **Apr 14-17** Easter. **May 1** Workers' Day. **May 4** Casinga Day. **May 25** Ascension Day and Africa Day, Anniversary of the OAU's Foundation. **Aug 26** Heroes' Day. **Oct 7** Day of Goodwill. **Dec 10** Human Rights Day. **Dec 25-26** Christmas. **Jan 1 '96** New Year's Day. **Mar 21** Independence Day. **Apr 5-8** Easter.

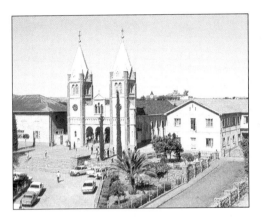

PHOTO CREDIT: PAUL GOLDSTEIN

PHOTO CREDIT: PAUL GOLDSTEIN

Top picture: Quiver Tree. Above: Kunene.

RAIL: The main rail routes in Namibia are
Windhoek–Keetmanshoop–De Aar, Walvis Bay–
Swakopmund–Windhoek–Tsumeb and Lüderitz–
Keetmanshoop. First- and second-class carriages are
available on these routes. Light refreshments are offered
on some services. On overnight voyages, seats in first-
class compartments convert to four couchettes and those
in second-class to six couchettes. Local passenger and
goods trains run daily. Children under two years of age
travel free and children 2-11 pay half fare.
ROAD: Traffic drives on the right. Roads are generally
fairly well maintained. There are 37,000km (23,000
miles) of gravel and 4400km (2700 miles) of all-weather
roads. **Bus:** Services are not well developed and there is
no transport except **taxis** in Windhoek. A luxury bus
service exists between Windhoek and all major centres in
Namibia and South Africa. **Car hire:** Self-drive cars are
available at the airport and Windhoek city centre.
Documentation: An International Driving Permit is
required.

ACCOMMODATION

HOTELS: There are good quality hotels both in
Windhoek and Swakopmund, and some scattered
throughout the country. In Windhoek there is the 4-star
Kalahari Sands Hotel. 3-star hotels include the Safari
Hotel in Windhoek, the Hansa Hotel in Swakopmund, the
Mokuti Lodge at Etosha and the Canyon Hotel in
Keetmanshoop. Hotel accommodation is limited and
visitors are advised to book well in advance. For further
information, contact Han-Hotel Association, PO Box
2862, Windhoek. **Grading:** Hotels are classified on a
scale of **1** to **5 stars.**
LODGES: In the Etosha National Park and other game
reserves there are well-equipped rest camps with
comfortable accommodation. Further information is
available from the Han-Hotel Association (address
above).
CAMPING: Some of the national parks have camping
facilities, notably the Etosha National Park & Game
Reserve. There is also camping at Ai-Ais, a hot-spring
area towards the South African border, Hardap Dam in
the south, Gross Barmen near Okahandja, and Popa Falls
in Kavango and at various places along the coast.

RESORTS & EXCURSIONS

Windhoek is the attractive capital of the country and
surrounded by mountains. Like other towns in the
country, it has several examples of German colonial
architecture, including the *Christuskirche*, the *Alte Feste*
and the *Tintenpalast* (Ink Palace), the former colonial
administrative building.
The delightful little seaside resort of **Swakopmund** is
situated in the middle of Namibia's coastline. It is
surrounded by desert and sea, and has several interesting
buildings which date back to the time when Namibia was
a German colony. **Lüderitz** is a small port in the
southern Namib region, with much charm and
atmosphere from bygone days of diamond prospecting.
Ai-Ais and **Gross Barmen** are hot-spring resorts and
there are spectacular falls at **Augrabies** (South African
Parks Board). The **Brandberg/Twyfelfontein** area has
some very ancient rock engravings and paintings of
which the *White Lady of the Brandberg* is the most well
known. The petrified forest and the *Welwitschia mirabilis*
plant are other attractions.
Namibia's many attractions include ten national parks,
under the control of the Ministry of Environment and
Tourism. Some of them are listed below.
The **Etosha National Park** is certainly one of the most
famous game sanctuaries in the world and remains
largely free of human influence. Its 22,270 sq km (8599
sq miles) are located in the north around the Etosha Pan.
This depression is 1065m (3494ft) above sea level,
forming a huge, salty hollow which is only occasionally
filled with water and surrounded by grasslands and bush.
There are vast stocks of wildlife, particularly elephants,
lions, zebras, giraffes, springboks, kudus, gemsboks or
oryxes, hyenas, jackals, leopards and cheetahs. It is open
throughout the year. There are well-equipped camps with
comfortable rondavel (grass hut) accommodation and
camping facilities. **Waterberg Plateau Park,** Namibia's
only mountain resort with its striking red sandstone cliffs,
is home to many rare and endangered species of game
and is a popular stopover for visitors on their way to
Etosha National Park. There are good facilities here for
game viewing and a number of hiking trails. Also en
route to Etosha is **Lake Otjikoto,** 24km (15 miles)
northeast of the mining town of **Tsumeb.** Once fabled to
be bottomless, it is now known to be 55m-deep (140ft)
and contains some rare fish. Northeast of here is
Kaudom Game Reserve in Kavango, where there are
two camping areas and blue wildebeest, elephant, lion,

A Step in the Right Direction

A step taken together is a step in the right direction.

With determination, planning and co-ordination any obstacle can be overcome.

Namibia Development Corporation's experienced team of multi-disciplinary professionals provides vital services to smooth your path. The right venture partner for instance. Or raising additional finance.

Naturally, our extensive data base helps you stay a step ahead. Whether you wish to identify a project, assess its viability or make contact with the right managerial skills, the Namibia Development Corporation has the information to keep you moving forward.

Contact the Namibia Development Corporation and take a step in the right direction.

N·D·C
Developing Solutions.

The Manager: Corporate Communication and Marketing.
Call +264-61-206911. Fax +264-61-223854. Telex 0908-800 WK.

Stocks

Hotels and Resorts Namibia

Where the Skeleton Coast comes to life

Swakopmund Hotel & Entertainment Centre

Swakopmund is Namibia's premier holiday resort and is a lively, delightful place which still retains much of its German character. This is an oasis after the desolation of the desert regions one has to cross to get here; green lawns, gardens full of colourful flowers, shops and restaurants welcome you into this very continental town.

The Swakopmund Hotel & Entertainment Centre is an exceptional facility built in and around the historical old station building. It offers the very best in 4-star luxury and has 90 tastefully decorated rooms and 2 luxury suites all with private facilities.

The hotel boasts a casino with 250 slot machines, blackjack and roulette. The Entertainment Centre has 2 cinemas, a video games arcade, speciality shopping, a restaurant, action bar and fast food outlets. These are also conference facilities for up to 350 people. In addition to all this, the following attractions can also be arranged: gym and aerobics, tennis, horse-riding, camel riding excursions and golf at the Rossyn Golf Course, one of the only 4 desert courses in the world.

Safe swimming and wonderful white beaches make Swakopmund the perfect seaside resort, and the proximity to the desert and its unusual and beautiful dunes make it a unique holiday destination.

The Windhoek Country Club Resort

Scheduled to open in May 1995, the Windhoek Country Club Resort is set to revolutionise the Namibian tourist and conference trade. It is located 4 minutes' drive from Eros Airport, and just 42km from Windhoek Airport.

The Windhoek Country Club Resort has been designed and built to the highest international standards. Breathtakingly beautiful, the hotel makes the most of its desert setting, using sandstone and Namibian quartzite to create a strikingly unique oasis.

This 5-star hotel has 150 rooms, and 2 magnificent luxury Presidential suites. A full service restaurant is linked to the hotel and swimming pool, while the entertainment centre boasts an exciting, top-class action bar and speciality shopping. The casino, built along a grotto theme, has slot machines, gaming tables and a superb bar. A championship 18-hole golf course, tennis and lawn bowls are also offered. The hotel has superb conference facilities and can cater for up to 650 people, with audio-visual and other necessary equipment on hand. For further information, contact:

Marketing and Sales Division
Stocks Hotels and Resorts
3rd Floor, TC Watermeyer
Corner 10th Avenue/Rivonia Boulevard
PO Box 1091, Rivonia 2128, Namibia
Tel: (27 11) 806-4192/3. (International)
Tel: (011) 806-4192/3. (National)
Fax: (27 11)806-4105 (International)
Fax: (011)806-4108 (National)

Swakopmund Hotel &
Entertainment Centre
2 Bahnhof Street
Swakopmund
PO Box 616
Swakopmund
Tel: (0641) 63330
Fax: (0641) 63344

NAMIBIA RESORTS INTERNATIONAL
FOUR UNIQUE DESTINATIONS COMBINE THE ULTIMATE AFRICAN ADVENTURE WITH INTERNATIONAL COMFORT

Namibia. Seasonal sanctuary to over a quarter-of-a-million of Africa's most beautiful birds. Home to large herds of roaming game. Haven for southern Africa's largest White Rhino population. And at every turn, waiting to pamper you and introduce you to Africa at its absolute best, is Namibia Resorts International – part of the Ohlthaver and List group, one of Namibia's oldest and largest industrial groups. As indigenous as the land itself, Namibia Resorts International operates the most extensive hotel group in Namibia. From stop over accommodation in the major centres, to four unforgettable resorts in the untamed reaches of Namibia, each as remarkable and unique as its surroundings – yet as sophisticated as its guests.

MOKUTI LODGE ★★★★ T YYY

The last word in luxury and relaxed hospitality, with a 4 star international rating, Mokuti Lodge is Africa at its absolute best, situated as it is on the edge of the famed Etosha National Park. Here, visitors can enjoy a thrilling day of game-viewing, or wild trail-blazing on foot or horseback. To complete the day the visitor can come home to all the comforts of luxury thatched accommodation, fine dining in two restaurants or under a clear African sky around a fire in the boma. Mokuti is set in exotic gardens, with a swimming pool and a host of other amenities of international standard. Mokuti has its own registered air strip and one of southern Africa's most comprehensive and sophisticated conference centres.

STRAND HOTEL

Situated right on the beach itself, in the charming, historic town of Swakopmund, the Strand Hotel offers beach lazing, sun bathing, continental kitchen, comfortable accommodation and a host of sporting activities for the energetic. It's also a wonderful base from which to explore the romantic Skeleton Coast, the nearby Namib Park which is a natural desert reserve featuring a petrified forest of fossilised Welwitschia plants, desert camel rides or just to enjoy the seaside atmosphere. Bordered by the mighty South Atlantic on the one side and a formidable desert on the other, it is possible for the visitor to pick up the famous Namibian semi-precious stones that dot the desert sands.

MIDGARD RESORT

Midgard Resort nestled in the Otjihavera Mountains is a luxurious bush haven offering charming hospitality, sumptuous buffets of wholesome, home-grown farm fare, pure spring waters and serene and uplifting surroundings. Mountain drives, relaxing evenings, game viewing and perhaps a visit to the resident stud farm plus a great deal of pampering all contribute to the revitalising effect of Midgard. A state-of-the-art conference centre offers solace for the city-weary executive.

OTJIWA GAME RANCH

Otjiwa offers the ultimate African adventure for those who want to rough it – just a little. Home to a large variety of game and one of the largest private collections of White Rhino in southern Africa, Otjiwa is a must for hunting enthusiasts and a vertitable paradise for fishermen. In addition to self-catering accommodation, building is soon to begin on what will assuredly be Namibia's most exotic venue with thatched accommodation on stilts on the expansive Ranch Dam.

So when planning your visit to Namibia, one of Africa's unspoilt, yet progressive peaceful countries, let the locals host and guide you in style – Namibia Resorts International.

NAMIBIA RESORTS International

Namibia Resorts International.
As unique as the land it occupies. As international as its visitors.

For further information ask your travel agent or complete coupon and post to:
Namibia Resorts International, P.O. Box 2862, WINDHOEK, NAMIBIA, OR
Tel. (061) 233145, Fax (061) 234512.

Name ....

Company ....

Address ....

....

....

MEDDER & ASSOCIATES 2176

cheetah, leopard and various species of antelope wander. Further northeast, the *Popa Falls* rest camp, where crocodiles and hippos bask in the water, is a popular haven on the banks of the **Okavango River.** About 12km (7 miles) to the south is **Mahango Game Reserve,** catering to day visitors only, with elephants, buffalo and lechwe. Heading still further northeast is **East Caprivi,** bordered by the Kwando, Linyanti, Chobe and Zambezi Rivers. This region of swamps and flood plains has several safari lodges and offers fishing, hiking and game viewing, particularly in the **Mudumu** and **Mamili National Parks.** The town of **Katima Mulilo,** on the banks of the **Zambezi River,** has an *Arts Centre* where visitors may purchase various handicrafts such as baskets, bracelets, malachite and soapstone carvings. There are also game-viewing cruises down the Zambezi River on the *Zambesi Queen,* a 56m (142ft) riverboat which departs from Zambesi Lodge. Flights to Victoria Falls, less than an hour's flight away, are available from Katima Mulilo.

Fish River Canyon is in the south of the country and only second in dimensions to the Grand Canyon. Situated between Seeheim and Ai-Ais, the gigantic cleft stretches for 150km (17 miles) and is up to 27km (93 miles) wide and up to 550m (1804ft) deep in parts. Trips are best arranged from **Keetsmanshoop.** Situated on the Fish River is **Hardap Dam.** The **Kokerboom (Quiver Tree) Forest,** located 14km (9 miles) northeast of Keetmanshoop on Gariganus Farm, features aloes *(kokerbooms)* which grow up to 8 metres and were often used by the Bush people to make quivers for their arrows (thus 'quiver trees'). The trees create a bizarrely elegant effect and are now a protected plant in Namibia.

The Namib Desert appears more like the surface of the moon with its towering sand dunes (some of them 300m/1000ft high), and is believed to be the oldest desert in the world. **Namib Naukluft Park,** at 49,768 sq km (19,215 sq miles), is the fourth-largest conservation area in the world. There are campsites in the Namib Desert at **Sesriem,** where the Tsauchab River disappears down a deep gorge in the plain leaving pools of water where many animals feed, and in the Naukluft. The nearby **Sossusvlei** area is an ocean of sand dunes up to 300m (762ft) high, stretching as far as the eye can see and is home to countless water birds in the rainy season and oryx, springbok and ostriches during the dry season.

The Skeleton Coast is a strange desert shoreline with massive dunes and treacherous rocks, the name relating to the number of ships wrecked and lost in the vicinity. The cold Benguela current keeps the coastline cool, damp and rain-free for most of the year, with a thick coastal fog.

Namibia has ample opportunities for the self-drive tourist and many local tour operators and travel consultants offer interesting packages or arrange tailor-made tours covering a variety of areas. More information on tours and excursions can be obtained from the Namibia Tourism Office (address at top of entry) or the Tasa-Tourism and Safari Association of Namibia, PO Box 6850, Windhoek.

POPULAR ITINERARIES: 5-day: Windhoek–Sesriem–Swakopmund–Etosha–Windhoek. **7-day:** (a) *South:* Windhoek–Quiver Tree Forest–Fish River Canyon–Ai-Ais–Lüderitz–Sesriem–Sossusvlei. (b) *Northwest:* Windhoek–Swakopmund–Skeleton Coast–Twyfelfontein–Etosha–Otjikoto Lake–Waterberg. (c) *Remote Northwest (fly-drive):* Windhoek–Northern Skeleton Coast–Kunene River. **10-day:** *Northeast:* Windhoek–Etosha–Okavango River–Mahango Game Reserve–Caprivi–Mudumu and Mamili National Parks–Katima Mulilo–Zambezi River–Victoria Falls.

SOCIAL PROFILE

FOOD & DRINK: Restaurants and cafés reflect the German influence on Namibia and most dining rooms offer a reasonable choice of local and continental cuisine. They are found mainly in the major cities. A speciality of Namibia is game in all variations; worth a try are *biltong* (air-dried meat) and *Rauchfleisch* (smoked meat).

NIGHTLIFE: In the central area of Windhoek there are restaurants, cafés, a cinema and a theatre.

SHOPPING: Windhoek has a selection of fashionable shops. Local crafts can be bought in some specialised shops and at the Windhoek Street Market, held every second Saturday. Good buys include diamonds and semi-precious stones, Herero dolls, hand-carved wooden objects, jewellery, *karosse* rugs, liqueur chocolates made in Windhoek and Swakara garments. **Shopping hours:** 0830-1700 Monday to Friday, 0830-1300 Saturday. Some bigger supermarkets are also open 1100-1300 and 1600-1900 Sunday.

SPORT: Northwest of Usakos, rising out of the Namib, is the 2000m (6562ft) Spitzkoppe where there is good **mountaineering.** Some of the coastal and river areas provide good opportunities for **fishing.** There are several

PHOTO CREDIT: PAUL GOLDSTEIN

hiking trails in the Fish River Canyon, the Waterberg Plateau Park, the Naukluft Mountains and the Ugab River.

SPECIAL EVENTS: The following is a selection of festivals celebrated in Namibia during 1995: **Mar 21 '95** *Orange River Canoe Race.* **Apr 16-17** *Golf Tournament,* Windhoek. **Apr 19-23** *Namibia International Trade Fair,* Windhoek. **Apr 19-May 1** *Windhoek Carnival.* **Apr 22-May 22** *Miss Universe.* **May 1-4** *Canoe National Championship,* Okavango River; *Raft Carnival,* Rundu. **May 14-15** *Namibian Open Championship* (golf), Windhoek. **Aug 28-Sep 3** *Fistball World Championship.* **Sep 3-4** *J&B Gold Cup,* Windhoek. **Oct** *Motor Cross Rally,* Swakopmund (Country Club). **Nov 12-13** *Windhoek Open Championship* (golf). **Dec 3-4** *Rössmund Open Championship* (golf), Swakopmund.

SOCIAL CONVENTIONS: Western customs prevail; normal courtesies should be shown when visiting someone's home. **Tipping:** 10% is customary.

BUSINESS PROFILE

ECONOMY: The newly independent Namibia has bright economic prospects. Mining has been the mainstay of the economy under South African control. Namibian mines produce diamonds, copper, lead, zinc and uranium – the Rossing uranium mine is the world's largest; the sector contributes about 35% of the national product. A smaller but nonetheless valuable proportion comes from agriculture and fisheries. Livestock dominates the agricultural sector, although a sizeable proportion of the population is engaged in subsistence farming of crops such as wheat, maize and millet. Agriculture is becoming

increasingly difficult as the years pass and the desert encroaches on previously fertile soil. It has also been seriously damaged during the early 1990s by the drought afflicting the whole region. Namibia enjoys some of the richest fishing grounds in the world, although catches of pilchard – the main species in the area – have been depleted by excessive fishing. Commercial shipping, a potentially lucrative business, may receive a boost now that South Africa has returned Walvis Bay, the best deep-water port in Africa on the Atlantic side, to the Namibians. The problem facing the new government in managing the economy is how to meet the expectations of the poorer black population while not alienating the white-run multinational companies which control most of Namibian business. Most of the country's trade is with South Africa: raw materials are exported in exchange for manufactured goods. This pattern is likely to continue for the forseeable future although there will be some growth in trading links with other countries.

BUSINESS: Suits should be worn in winter, safari suits in summer. Prior appointments are necessary. English is widely spoken in business circles. The best times to visit are February to May and September to November. **Office hours:** 0730-1630/1700 Monday to Friday.

COMMERCIAL INFORMATION: The following organisation can offer advice: Namibia National Chamber of Commerce and Industry, PO Box 9355, Windhoek. Tel: (61) 228 809. Fax: (61) 228 009.

CLIMATE

The cold Benguela current keeps the coast of the Namib Desert cool, damp and rain-free for most of the year with thick coastal fog. Inland all the rain falls in

summer (October to April). Summer temperatures are high while the altitude means that nights are cool and winters are fairly cold.

Required clothing: Light cottons, with slightly heavier cottons or light woollens for evening. In inland areas, shoes are essential during the day as the ground is so hot.

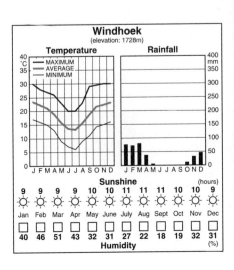

Top left: Dune 45, Sossusvlei. Top right: Alluvial Fan, Damaraland. Above: Fish River Canyon.

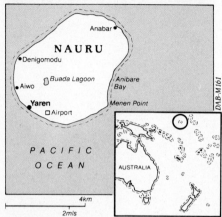

Location: South Pacific.

Nauru Government Office
3 Chesham Street, London SW1X 8ND
Tel: (0171) 235 6911. Fax: (0171) 235 7423. Opening
hours: 0930-1700 Monday to Friday.
**The British Embassy in Suva deals with enquiries
relating to Nauru (see *Fiji* earlier in this book).**

AREA: 21.3 sq km (8.2 sq miles).
POPULATION: 9350 (1989 estimate).
POPULATION DENSITY: 439 per sq km.
CAPITAL: Yaren District.
GEOGRAPHY: Nauru is an oval-shaped outcrop,
situated in the South Pacific west of Kiribati, surrounded
by a reef, which is exposed at low tide. There is no deep-
water harbour on the island but offshore moorings are
reputedly the deepest in the world. The island's beaches,
interspersed by coral pinnacles, are bordered inland by a
fertile coastal strip encircling the island. On the inner
side of the fertile section there is a coral cliff which rises
to a height of 60m (200ft). Above the cliff is an extensive
plateau bearing high-grade phosphate which is infertile
and unpopulated, with the exception of a small fringe
around a shallow lagoon and a few bush-like trees.
Mining operations, which have gutted the island, will
probably cease by 1995 when the phosphates are
exhausted and the island will have to be re-landscaped
due to the disruption caused. A case before the
International Court of Justice in The Hague bought by
Nauru against Australia has recently been settled with
Australia agreeing to pay Nauru over A$100 million
towards costs incurred.
LANGUAGE: Nauruan and English.
RELIGION: Christian, mostly Nauruan Protestant
Church.
TIME: GMT + 12.
ELECTRICITY: 110/240 volts AC, 50Hz.
COMMUNICATIONS: Telephone: IDD is available.
Country code: 674. Outgoing international calls must be
made through the operator. **Telex/telegram:** Facilities at
Nauru Government Communications Office. **Post:**
Airmail to Europe takes up to a week. **Press:** The main
newspaper is *The Bulletin*, published fortnightly in
Nauruan and English.
**BBC World Service and Voice of America
frequencies:** From time to time these change. See the
section *How to Use this Book* for more information.
BBC:

MHz	17.83	11.95	9.740	6.195

Voice of America:

MHz	18.82	15.18	9.525	1.735

PASSPORT/VISA

Regulations and requirements may be subject to change at short notice, and you are advised to contact the appropriate diplomatic or consular authority before finalising travel arrangements. Details of these may be found at the head of this country's entry. Any numbers in the chart refer to the footnotes below.

	Passport Required?	Visa Required?	Return Ticket Required?
Full British	Yes	Yes	Yes
BVP	Not valid	-	-
Australian	Yes	Yes	Yes
Canadian	Yes	Yes	Yes
USA	Yes	Yes	Yes
Other EU (As of 31/12/94)	Yes	Yes	Yes
Japanese	Yes	Yes	Yes

PASSPORTS: Valid passport required by all.
British Visitors Passport: Not accepted.
VISAS: Required by all except those in transit who
continue their journey to a third country by the same or
first connecting aircraft, provided they hold tickets with
reserved seats and other documents for onward travel.
Types of visa: Visitor and Business. Both are free of
charge.
Validity: Visas are limited to a maximum of 4 months
validity, but can be extended by applying to the Principal
Immigration Officer in Nauru.
Application to: Principal Immigration Officer, Alf
Itsimaera, Immigration Department. Tel: 444 3161. Fax:
444 3189.
Application requirements: There are no application
forms. Write giving full name, date of birth, marital
status, occupation, country of birth and nationality, name
of country issuing passport, passport number and date of
issue, purpose of visit, duration of intended stay, and
means of arrival and departure with approximate dates.
Applicants for Business visas require a letter from their
sponsoring company.
Working days required: Applications have to be sent to
Nauru so plenty of time should be allowed.
Temporary residence: Contact the Principal
Immigration Officer in Nauru.

MONEY

Currency: Australian Dollar (A$) = 100 cents. Notes are in
denominations of A$100, 50, 20, 10, 5, 2 and 1. Coins are in
denominations of A$1, and 50, 20, 10, 5, 2 and 1 cents.
Credit cards: American Express, Diners Club and Visa
are accepted. Check with your credit card company for
details of merchant acceptability and other services
which may be available.
Exchange rate indicators: The following figures are
included as a guide to the movements of the Australian
Dollar against Sterling and the US Dollar:

Date:	Oct '92	Sep '93	Jan '94	Jan '95
£1.00=	2.22	2.36	2.18	2.02
$1.00=	1.40	1.55	1.47	1.29

Currency restrictions: There are no restrictions on the
import or export of either local or foreign currency.

DUTY FREE

The following goods may be imported into Nauru
without incurring customs duty:
*400 cigarettes or 50 cigars or 450g of tobacco; 3 bottles
of alcoholic beverage (if visitor is over 21 years of age);
a reasonable amount of perfume.*
Prohibited items: Narcotics and firearms.
Note: Nauruan artefacts may not be exported without a
licence.

PUBLIC HOLIDAYS

Jan 1 '95 New Year's Day. **Jan 31** Independence Day.
Apr 14-17 Easter. **May 17** Constitution Day. **Oct 26**
Angam Day. **Dec 25-26** Christmas. **Jan 1 '96** New
Year's Day. **Jan 31** Independence Day. **Apr 5-8** Easter.

HEALTH

Regulations and requirements may be subject to change at short notice, and you are advised to contact your doctor well in advance of your intended date of departure. Any numbers in the chart refer to the footnotes below.

	Special Precautions?	Certificate Required?
Yellow Fever	No	1
Cholera	No	No
Typhoid & Polio	Yes	-
Malaria	No	-
Food & Drink	2	

[1]: A yellow fever vaccination certificate is required
from travellers over one year of age coming from
infected areas.
[2]: Mains water is normally chlorinated, and whilst
relatively safe may cause mild abdominal upsets. Bottled
water is available and is advised for the first few weeks
of the stay. Drinking water outside main cities and towns
may be contaminated and sterilisation is advisable. Local
meat, poultry, seafood, fruit and vegetables are generally
considered safe to eat.
Health care: Health insurance is recommended.
Standards of health care are high.

TRAVEL - International

AIR: Nauru's national airline is *Air Nauru (ON)*.
Approximate flight time: From London to Nauru Island
is 31 hours, including stopovers in Hong Kong, Manila,
Koror and Guam.
International airport: *Nauru Island (INU)*. Airport
facilities include restaurant, snack bar, bar, shops and
tourist information. There are buses to the town available
after every arriving flight costing approximately A$1.
Taxis are also available.
Departure tax: A$10 per person on departure.
Passengers in transit and those under 12 years of age are
exempt.
SEA: The international port is Nauru, served by *Nauru
Pacific Line, Royal Shipping Co.* and *Daiwa Navigation
Co.* Main sealinks are with Australia, New Zealand and
Japan. Coastal hazards force commercial vessels to moor
some way offshore at what are reputed to be the deepest
permanent anchorages in the world.

TRAVEL - Internal

RAIL: There are just over 5km (3 miles) of railway to
serve the phosphate area.
ROAD: A sealed road, 19km (12 miles) long, circles the
island and there are several miles of road running inland
to Buada and the phosphate areas. Traffic drives on the
left. **Buses** provide public transport. **Car hire** is
available. **Documentation:** A national driving licence
will suffice.

RESORTS & EXCURIONS

Since the extensive phosphate fields were found in the
1900s, the island is still mainly used for the exploration
of the natural fertilizer. The *Nauru Phosphate
Corporation* is the largest employer. The population lives
mainly at the coasts or on the shore of *Buada Lagoon*, the
remainder of the island being used for phosphor
extraction. Nauru is not a major tourist destination and
there are only two hotels. One is situated on the west
coast, with restaurants and shops nearby. The other is at
Anibare Bay, on the sparsely populated east coast.

SOCIAL PROFILE

FOOD & DRINK: Most of the available food is canned,
refined and imported. Fresh food is limited to a small
amount of fish, and very occasionally beef. There are no
local fruit or vegetables. The island is very well served
with restaurants with a wide range of international dishes,
but little is fresh. Most international brands of alcohol are
available.
NIGHTLIFE: This mostly revolves around the dining
rooms and bars. There is one cinema located in the
southern part of the island.
SHOPPING: Service and goods at government shops
tend to be of poor quality. The range of goods and

UK STD CODES

As of 16 April 1995, the UK STD codes will change. Insert a 1 after the first zero in the old STD code, eg. 071 becomes 0171.

There are five exceptions:

CITY	NEW CODE	+ PREFIX
Bristol	0117	9
Leicester	0116	2
Leeds	0113	2
Nottingham	0115	9
Sheffield	0114	2

standards at Chinese shops is better, but Nauru is not a shopper's paradise. Visitors should buy essential goods in advance. The absence of taxes means that electrical goods, cigarettes and alcohol are cheaper.

SPORT: The national game is Australian-rules **football**, which is played all through Saturday on the sports field just north of Buada Lagoon (on the western side of the island); there is no charge for spectators. Nearby are **tennis** and **volleyball** courts. **Snooker** is at the *East End Club*.

SOCIAL CONVENTIONS: The island has a casual atmosphere in which diplomacy and tact are always preferable to confrontation; European customs continue alongside local traditions. **Tipping:** Not generally practised.

BUSINESS PROFILE

ECONOMY: Nauru's economy depends almost entirely on the extraction and sale of phosphates, of which the Nauru Phosphate Corporation has a monopoly. Much of the revenue has been invested in long-term economic development programmes, anticipating the eventual exhaustion of the phosphate deposits, which is expected in the mid-1990s. The island is, however, becoming increasingly important as a centre for offshore banking. There is some agriculture but it is limited by the lack of fertile land. There is no tourist industry. Almost all the island's revenue derives from phosphates; most imports of foodstuffs, consumer and capital goods come from New Zealand and Australia.

BUSINESS: Shirt and smart trousers or skirt will suffice; more formal wear needed only for very special occasions. English and French are widely spoken. The best time to visit is May to October.

COMMERCIAL INFORMATION: The following organisation can offer advice: Central Bank of Nauru, PO Box 289, Nauru. Tel: 444 3238. Fax: 444 3203. Telex: 33085.

CLIMATE

A maritime, equatorial climate tempered by northeast trade winds from March to October. The wettest period is from December to March.

Required clothing: Lightweight cottons and linens with waterproofing all year.

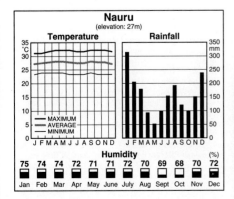

Nauru
(elevation: 27m)

Humidity											(%)
75	74	74	72	71	71	72	70	69	68	70	72
Jan	Feb	Mar	Apr	May	June	July	Aug	Sept	Oct	Nov	Dec

Nepal

☐ *international airport*

400km
200mls

Location: Indian sub-continent.

Department of Tourism
HM Government of Nepal, Patan Dhoka, Lalitpur, Kathmandu, Nepal
Tel: (1) 523 692. Fax: (1) 527 852. Telex: 2693.

Royal Nepalese Embassy
12a Kensington Palace Gardens, London W8 4QU
Tel: (0171) 229 1594 *or* 229 6231. Fax: (0171) 792 9861. Telex: 261072. Opening hours: 0900-1300 and 1400-1730 Monday to Friday.

British Embassy
PO Box 106, Lainchaur, Kathmandu, Nepal
Tel: (1) 410 583 *or* 411 281. Fax: (1) 411 789. Telex: 2343 (a/b BRITEM NP).

Royal Nepalese Embassy
2131 Leroy Place, NW, Washington, DC 20008
Tel: (202) 667 4550. Fax: (202) 667 5534. Telex: 440085 (a/b EVER UI).

Nepalese Consulate General
Suite 202, 820 2nd Avenue, New York, NY 10017
Tel: (212) 370 4188. Fax: (212) 953 2038.

Embassy of the United States of America
Pani Pokhari, Kathmandu, Nepal
Tel: (1) 411 179. Fax: (1) 419 963. Telex: 2381.

Nepalese Consulate General
PO Box 33, BDO Dunwoody Ward Mallette, Royal Bank Plaza, Toronto, Ontario M5J 2J9
Tel: (416) 865 0210. Fax: (416) 865 0904.

The Canadian High Commission in New Delhi deals with enquiries relating to Nepal (see *India* **earlier in this book).**

AREA: 147,181 sq km (56,827 sq miles).
POPULATION: 18,462,0181 (1991).
POPULATION DENSITY: 125.4 per sq km.
CAPITAL: Kathmandu. **Population:** 235,160 (1981).
GEOGRAPHY: Nepal is a landlocked kingdom sharing borders with Tibet to the north and northwest, and India to the west, south and east. The country can be divided into five zones: the Terai, the Siwaliks, the Mahabharat Lekh, the Midlands or Pahar and the Himalayas. The greater part of the country lies on the southern slope of the Himalayas extending down from the highest peaks

Timatic

Health
GALILEO/WORLDSPAN: **TI-DFT/KTM/HE**
SABRE: **TIDFT/KTM/HE**

Visa
GALILEO/WORLDSPAN: **TI-DFT/KTM/VI**
SABRE: **TIDFT/KTM/VI**

For more information on Timatic codes refer to Contents.

through hill country to the upper edge of the Ganges Plain. The hilly central area is crossed by the Lower Himalayas where there are eight of the highest peaks in the world, leading up to Mount Everest. Wildlife in Nepal includes tigers, leopards, gaur, elephants, buffalo and deer.

LANGUAGE: The official language is Nepali. There are many other languages including Maithir and Bhojpuri.

RELIGION: Mainly Hindu and Buddhist with a small Muslim minority.

TIME: GMT + 5.45.

ELECTRICITY: 220 volts AC, 50Hz. There are frequent power cuts.

COMMUNICATIONS: Telephone: IDD is available to Kathmandu only. All other calls go through the operator. Country code: 977. Outgoing international code: 00. The Telecommunication Office, Tripureshnawar, deals with telephone calls, cables and telexes. The International Telephone Office is open 1000-1700 Sunday to Friday, but international telephone connections are very difficult. **Fax:** Many travel agents and a few hotels have fax services. The Nepal Telecommunications Corporation booth at the airport has fax services. **Telex/telegram:** The Central Telegraph Office offers a 24-hour international telephone and telegram service seven days a week. **Post:** Postal services are available in most centres. Make sure that letters are hand cancelled at the post office (post boxes should not be used for important communications). Main hotels will also handle mail. Post office hours: the General Post Office in Kathmandu is open 1000-1700 (1600 in winter) Sunday to Friday. **Press:** English-language dailies available in Nepal are *The Commoner*, *The Motherland* and *The Rising Nepal*. *The Independent* is published weekly. *The International Herald Tribune*, *Time* and *Newsweek* can all be found in Kathmandu. *Himal* is a magazine published six times a year, devoted to environmental issues throughout the Himalayas. At certain times of day there are radio and television news broadcasts in English.

BBC World Service and Voice of America frequencies: From time to time these change. See the section *How to Use this Book* for more information.

BBC:

MHz	17.79	15.31	11.75	9.740

A service is also available on 1413kHz.

Voice of America:

MHz	21.49	15.60	9.525	6.035

PASSPORT/VISA

Regulations and requirements may be subject to change at short notice, and you are advised to contact the appropriate diplomatic or consular authority before finalising travel arrangements. Details of these may be found at the head of this country's entry. Any numbers in the chart refer to the footnotes below.

	Passport Required?	Visa Required?	Return Ticket Required?
Full British	Yes	Yes	No
BVP	Not valid	-	-
Australian	Yes	Yes	No
Canadian	Yes	Yes	No
USA	Yes	Yes	No
Other EU (As of 31/12/94)	Yes	Yes	No
Japanese	Yes	Yes	No

PASSPORTS: Valid passport required by all except nationals of India.

British Visitors Passport: Not acceptable.

VISAS: Required by all except nationals of India.

Types of visa: Tourist – £20 per person. A 30-day visa can be obtained for US$25 plus a 25% surcharge at the airport. Business can be conducted on a Tourist visa.

Validity: Entry valid up to 6 months maximum (and with visa extension of no more than 4 months in one year), and valid for 30 days after entry. For full conditions on visa extension (including charges and conditions), contact the Consulate (or Consular section at Embassy). Visas can be extended in Nepal for the second month, provided visitors have proof that they have exchanged US$1 per day of extension.

Application to: Consulate (or Consular section at Embassy). For addresses, see top of entry.

Application requirements: (a) 1 completed application form. (b) Valid passport. (c) 1 passport-size photo. (d) Fee.

Working days required: 1.

MONEY

Currency: Nepalese Rupee (Rs) = 100 paisa. Notes are in denominations of Rs1000, 500, 100, 50, 20, 10, 5, 2 and 1. Coins are in denominations of Rs1, and 50, 25, 10 and 5 paisa.

Currency exchange: It is illegal to exchange your currency with persons other than authorised dealers in foreign exchange. Obtain Foreign Exchange Encashment Receipts when changing currency and keep them, as these will help in many transactions, including getting visa extensions and trekking permits.

Credit cards: American Express is widely accepted, while Access/Mastercard and Visa have more limited use. Check with your credit card company for details of merchant acceptability and other services which may be available.

Travellers cheques: Accepted at banks and major hotels. If trekking, it is important to bear in mind that cash is necessary.

Exchange rate indicators: The following figures are included as a guide to the movements of the Nepalese Rupee against Sterling and the US Dollar:

Date:	Oct '92	Sep '93	Jan '94	Jan '95
£1.00=	73.74	69.90	68.50	77.24
$1.00=	46.47	45.78	46.30	49.37

Currency restrictions: Import of local and Indian currency is prohibited. Foreign currency must be declared. Export of local currency is prohibited. Only 15% of the amount exchanged into local currency will be reconverted into foreign currency on departure and exchange receipts must be presented.

Banking hours: 1000-1450 Sunday to Thursday; 1000-1250 Friday. The Nepal Rastra Bank Exchange Counters at New Road, Kathmandu, are open 0800-2000.

DUTY FREE

The following goods may be imported into Nepal without incurring customs duty:

200 cigarettes or 50 cigars; 1 litre of alcoholic beverage or 12 cans of beer; a reasonable amount of perfume.
Note: (a) All baggage must be declared on arrival and departure. (b) There are limits on the importation of certain goods including cameras, videos and electronic goods. (c) Objects of archaeological or historical interest may not be exported; certain antique articles must be referred to the Department of Archaeology before export.

PUBLIC HOLIDAYS

Jan 11 '95 National Unity Day. **Jan 30** Martyrs' Day. **Feb/Mar** Shivaratri. **Feb 18** Tribhuvan Jayanti (King Tribhuvan's Birthday); Rashtriya Prajatantra Divas (Democracy Day). **Mar 8** Nepalese Women's Day. **Mar 17** Holi. **Apr 9** Birthday of Lord Ram. **Apr 14** Navabarsha (New Year's Day). **Apr/May** Baishakh Purnima (Birthday of Lord Buddha). **Sep** Indra Jatra (Festival of Rain God). **Oct (one week)** Dasain. **Oct/Nov (three days)** Deepawali (Festival of Lights). **Nov 8** Queen Aishworya's Birthday. **Nov 9** Constitution Day. **Dec 29** King Birendra's Birthday. **Jan 11 '96** National Unity Day. **Jan 30** Martyrs' Day. **Feb/Mar** Shivaratri. **Feb 18** Tribhuvan Jayanti (King Tribhuvan's Birthday); Rashtriya Prajatantra Divas (Democracy Day). **Mar 8** Nepalese Women's Day. **Mar** Holi. **Apr 9** Birthday of Lord Ram. **Apr 14** Navabarsha (New Year's Day). **Apr/May** Baishakh Purnima (Birthday of Lord Buddha).

HEALTH

Regulations and requirements may be subject to change at short notice, and you are advised to contact your doctor well in advance of your intended date of departure. Any numbers in the chart refer to the footnotes below.		
	Special Precautions?	Certificate Required?
Yellow Fever	No	1
Cholera	Yes	2
Typhoid & Polio	Yes	-
Malaria	3	-
Food & Drink	4	-

[1]: A yellow fever vaccination certificate is required of travellers coming from infected areas.
[2]: Following WHO guidelines issued in 1973, a cholera vaccination certificate is not a condition of entry to Nepal. However, cholera is a serious risk in this country and precautions are essential. Up-to-date advice should be sought before deciding whether these precautions should include vaccination, as medical opinion is divided over its effectiveness. See the *Health* section at the back of the book.
[3]: Malaria risk, mainly in the benign *vivax* form, exists throughout the year in rural areas of the Terai districts of

Dhanukha, Mahotari, Sarlahi, Rautahat, Bara, Parsa, Rupendehi, Kapilvastu and especially along the Indian border. The malignant *falciparum* form has been reported to be 'resistant' to chloroquine.
[4]: All water should be regarded as being potentially contaminated. Water used for drinking, brushing teeth or making ice should have first been boiled or otherwise sterilised. Milk is unpasteurised and should be boiled. Powdered or tinned milk is available and is advised, but make sure that it is reconstituted with pure water. Avoid dairy products which are likely to have been made from unboiled milk. Only eat well-cooked meat and fish, preferably served hot. Pork, salad and mayonnaise may carry increased risk. Vegetables should be cooked and fruit peeled.

Rabies is present. For those at high risk, vaccination before arrival should be considered. If you are bitten abroad seek medical advice without delay. For more information consult the *Health* section at the back of the book.

Japanese encephalitis exists particularly in rural areas between June and October. A vaccine is available, and travellers are advised to consult their doctor prior to departure. It is transmitted by mosquitoes.

High altitude sickness is a hazard for trekkers, so it is important to be in good health before travelling. Advice can be obtained from the Himalayan Rescue Association near the Kathmandu Guest House, Thamel.

Health care: The most convenient hospital for visitor care is Patan Hospital in Lagankhel. Most hospitals have English-speaking staff and big hotels have doctors. Pharmacies in Kathmandu, mainly along New Road, offer a wide range of Western drugs at low prices. In Kathmandu you can get certain vaccinations free of charge at the Infectious Diseases Clinic. Full medical insurance is essential.

TRAVEL - International

AIR: Nepal's national airline is *Royal Air Nepal (RA)*.
Approximate flight time: From London to Kathmandu is 10 hours 15 minutes (not including stopover time).
International airport: *Kathmandu (KTM)* (Tribhuvan) is 6.5km (4 miles) east of the city (travel time – 20 minutes). There are full duty-free facilities at Kathmandu airport. A coach to the city meets all flight arrivals (0600-1800). Taxis are available.
Departure tax: Rs700 for international flights.
RAIL: Two stretches of the Indian Railway Line run to the border with Nepal, where cycle-rickshaws are available for onward journeys.
ROAD: There are 12 possible points of entry. New roads have been built linking Kathmandu with India and Tibet.

TRAVEL - Internal

AIR: There is a network of domestic flights linking major towns, radiating from Kathmandu. Many of these offer spectacular views across the mountains. Helicopters can be chartered from the *Royal Nepal Airlines Corporation*.
RAIL: There are light- and narrow-gauge railways in Nepal.
ROAD: The road system is of unpredictable quality. Traffic drives on the left. **Bus:** There are services operated by the *Transport Corporation of Nepal* and also by private operators. **Car hire:** Cars can be hired from the *Hertz* representative and *Gorkha Travels*, or from the *Avis* representative and *Yeti Travels*, both in Kathmandu. Chauffeur-driven cars can only be hired in the Kathmandu Valley. **Documentation:** An International Driving Permit is valid in Nepal for 15 days. The minimum driving age is 18. A temporary licence to drive is available from local authorities on presentation of a valid national driving licence.
URBAN: There are bus services in the populous areas around Kathmandu, which include the neighbouring cities of Patan and Bhaktapur. A trolleybus route provides frequent journeys over the 11km (7-mile) Kathmandu–Bhaktapur road. Private minibuses feed the trolleybus route from nearby villages. On buses and trolleybuses belonging to the *Transport Corporation of Nepal* a 4-stage fare system applies, with colour-coded tickets issued by conductors. **Taxi:** Metered taxis are plentiful in Kathmandu; at night the meter reading plus 50% is standard. Private taxis are more expensive and fares should be agreed before departure. **Tempos:** These are metered 3-wheel scooters, which work out slightly cheaper than taxis. **Rickshaws:** These operate throughout the city. Fares should be negotiated in advance. **Bicycles and motorcycles:** These can be hired from bike-shops or hotels by the hour or by the day. Motorcyclists require

a driving licence. Bicyclists should make sure they have a working bell.

ACCOMMODATION

HOTELS: Kathmandu has an increasing number of international-class hotels which are particularly busy during spring and autumn, when it is advisable to book well in advance. Comfortable hotels can also be found in Pokhara, and the Royal Chitwan National Park in the Terai Jungle. A government tax is added to bills, which varies according to the star rating of the hotel. For more information, contact the Hotel Association of Nepal, Hattisar, Kathmandu. Tel: (1) 220 707.
LODGES: Besides the officially recognised hotels, there are a number of lodges or hostels which in Kathmandu are located in the old part of the town, in the streets around the Durbar Square or in the Thamel district. The *Lukla Sherpa Cooperative* offers lodging to mountaineers in Sherpa country (PO Box 1338, Kathmandu), and accommodation at Paplu in the Sagarmatha zone can be provided by the *Hostellerier des Sherpas,* who can be contacted through *Great Himalaya Adventure,* Kantipath, Kathmandu.

RESORTS & EXCURSIONS

Nepal is known as the abode of the gods. For many years a secret, unknown country, it was, in the 1950s, faced with making a leap from the 11th century to modern times. Visited first by mountaineers and trekkers, it later became the haunt of hippies. In 1989 restrictions barring several areas to tourists were lifted.

Kathmandu

The capital is a magical place. In the centre is *Durbar Square* where there is a wonderful collection of temples and shrines, both Buddhist and Hindu. They are generally built in the pagoda style with a mass of intricate exterior carving. The old *Royal Palace* is in the square, as is the *Statue of Hanuman the Monkey-God,* clad in a red cloak. Here also is the house of the living goddess – the Kumari. Climbing upwards from the city one can reach the famous *Monkey Temple*. There are a great many steps leading up to the temple frequented by an even greater number of monkeys. The monkeys should be treated with some caution since their behaviour can be unpredictable. A few kilometres from Kathmandu is *Bodnath Stupa*. It has become a centre of Tibetan exile culture and is a good place to buy Tibetan handicrafts and artefacts. It is a hugely impressive stupa. There are also a number of monasteries. Respect should be shown for local sensitivities when visiting religious sites or temples. Just 5km (3 miles) west of the city, below the **Nagarjun Forest,** are the *Balaju Water Gardens,* with a reclining statue of Lord Vishnu and a 22-headed seadragon fountain. 19km (12 miles) south of Kathmandu, and accessible by taxi, are the *Godavari Royal Botanical Gardens* housing trees, shrubs and beautiful orchids in an idyllic setting.

The Kathmandu Valley

Kathmandu was once one of three equal cities, the other two being **Patan** and **Bhaktapur**. The *National Art Museum* in Bhaktapur, located in the old *Malla Palace* has unusual, colourful animal paintings on the second floor which are worth a look. Other museums in Bhaktapur are the *National Woodworking Museum,* showing fine examples of Newari woodcarving, and the *National Brass and Bronze Museum,* both in Dattatreya Square. Patan has the *Jawalakhel Zoo,* housing exotic South Asian animals.
West of Kathmandu is the amazing Buddhist *stupa* of *Swayambhunath,* with its large staring eyes. There are shrines for every purpose in the valley, such as the *Shrine of Ganesh the Elephant-God,* reputed to bring good luck. There are four Ganesh temples in the valley, each a masterpiece of Nepalese architecture – one in Kathmandu's Durbar Square, one in **Chabahil,** one in **Chobar** and one near Bhaktapur. **Lumbini,** being the birthplace of Lord Buddha, is one of the world's most important pilgrimage sites.
The nearby **Royal Chitwan National Park** is a jungle overflowing with wildlife. There are many lodges here offering visitor accommodation, canoeing, white-water rafting and elephant rides. **Nagarkot Village,** situated on rice steppes in magnificent countryside, provides spectacular views of Mount Everest, mist permitting. The hill town of **Gorkha** is the ancestral home of the Shah Dynasty and residence of the original Gurkha soldiers. There is a lively bazaar and the *Royal Trek to Pokhara* begins here. The secluded town of **Pokhara** lies 200km

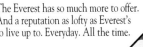

(125 miles) west of Kathmandu in the centre of Nepal on *Lake Phewa*. No other place in the world commands such a view of the Himalayas. It is a starting point for mountaineers and trekkers, and was at one time the home of JRR Tolkein.

The Mountains

One of the principal reasons for visiting Nepal must be either to see or to climb the mountains, especially **Mount Everest**. A number of local agents can arrange trips with guides into the mountains for a day. Climbing and mountain treks can also be arranged. Trekking permits are necessary for travel beyond Kathmandu and Pokhara and are issued by the Central Immigration Office. The trekking season is generally from September to May, but the best periods are October to December and March to April. The countryside is generally rugged and the trails are loose but, with a *qualified* guide (eg one obtained through a reputable agency) and other sensible precautions, trekking is normally a perfectly safe activity, offering by far the best way of viewing the spectacular countryside. Some agents can arrange flights in light aircraft over Mount Everest. Flights are also available from Jomosom and other locations west of the capital, flying over the spectacular *Annapurna* range.

SOCIAL PROFILE

FOOD & DRINK: Despite its isolation and the variety of its local produce, Nepal has not developed a distinctive style of cooking. It is, more often than not, Dal Bhat – lentils and rice. An exception is *Newar* cuisine, which can be very elaborate and spicy. Most dishes here are regional Indian. Rice is the staple food. Dishes include *dal* (lentil soup), spiced vegetables, *chapatis* and *tsampa* (eaten by the hill people), which is a raw grain, ground and mixed with milk, tea or water. Sweets and spicy snacks include *jelabi, laddus* and *mukdals*. Regional dishes include *gurr*, a Sherpa dish of raw potatoes, pounded with spices, then grilled like pancakes on a hot, flat stone. Tibetan cooking includes *thukba* (thick soup) and *momos* (fried or boiled, stuffed ravioli). Meat includes goat, pork, chicken or buffalo, but beef is forbidden. There is a wide selection of restaurants in Kathmandu, although elsewhere the choice is limited. A 12% government tax is added to bills. **Drink:** The national drink is *chiya* (tea brewed with milk, sugar and spices; in the mountains it is salted with yak butter). Another popular mountain drink is *chang* (beer made from fermented barley, maize, rye or millet). *Arak* (potato alcohol) and *raksi* (wheat or rice spirit) are also drunk. Nepalese beer is available, as is good quality local rum, vodka and gin. Local whisky is not so palatable, but imported varieties are widely available.

NIGHTLIFE: Kathmandu has a few cinemas featuring mainly Indian films. For Western films, see the programmes of the European and American cultural centres. Most people are asleep by 2200. Nightlife is fairly limited; a few temples and restaurants offer entertainment and some tourist hotels stage Nepalese folk dances and musical shows. There is a casino with baccarat, chemin de fer and roulette, open 24 hours a day, every day, at the Soaltee Oberoi Hotel.

SHOPPING: There are bargains for those careful to avoid fakes and the badly made souvenirs sold by unscrupulous traders. Popular buys include locally made clothes such as lopsided *topi* (caps), knitted mittens and socks, Tibetan dresses, woven shawls, Tibetan multicoloured jackets and men's diagonally fastened shirts; and *pashmin* (fine goat's-wool blankets), *khukri* (the national knife), *saranghi* (a small, 4-stringed viola played with a horse-hair bow), Tibetan tea bowls, *papier mâché* dance masks, Buddhist statuettes and filigree ornaments, bamboo flutes and other folk objects. **Shopping hours:** 1000-1900 Sunday to Friday (some stay open on Saturday and holidays).

SPORT: Golf: The Royal Golf Club has a 9-hole course open to member-sponsored guests. **Tennis:** Several of Kathmandu's hotels have tennis courts open to non-residents for a small fee. Alternatively, contact the Tennis (HIT) Centre. **Fishing:** Terai rivers and valley lakes are often good fishing grounds for *asla* (snow trout) and *masheer*. The best months are February, March, October and November. Permits can be obtained from the National Parks and Wildlife Conservation Department in Banswar. **Swimming:** Several hotels in Kathmandu have pools open to non-residents. Caution is needed when swimming in mountain rivers; the larger lowland rivers are safer, but bathers should be wary of the occasional crocodile.

Horseriding: Must be arranged in advance. The Nepal National Health & Sports Council will be able to provide information on a wide range of sporting activities available in the country.

SPECIAL EVENTS: Nepalese festivals fall into several categories. Most are performed in honour of the gods and goddesses, some mark the seasons or agricultural cycles, and others are simply family celebrations. The usual form of celebration is to take ritual baths in rivers or lakes, visit temples to offer worship, and feasting and ritual fasting. The festivals in Kathmandu Valley are the most rich and spectacular. For a list of special events and festivals in Nepal, send a stamped, self-addressed envelope to the Embassy.

SOCIAL CONVENTIONS: Superstition and religion merge into one. As a foreigner, all visitors are 'polluted' and there are several customs associated with this attitude: never step over the feet of a person, always walk round; never offer food and drink which is 'polluted', in other words, food that you have tasted or bitten; never offer or accept anything with the left hand, use the right or both hands. It is rude to point at a person or statue with a finger (or even with a foot). Shoes and footwear should be removed when entering houses or shrines. Kitchens and eating areas of houses should also not be entered with footwear, as the hearth of a home is sacred. Do not stand in front of a person who is eating as this means your feet will be next to his food; squat or sit by his side. Local *Chorten* are built to pacify local demons or dead persons and should be passed by in a clockwise direction, as should temples; the earth and universe revolve in this direction. Small flat stones with inscriptions and supplications next to the *Chorten* should not be removed as souvenirs; this is considered as sacrilege by the Nepalese. Avoid touching a Nepalese dressed all in white; his dress signifies a death in the family. Shaking hands is not a common form of greeting; the normal greeting is to press the palms together in a prayer-like gesture. A gift given to a host or hostess will probably be laid aside unopened; to open a parcel in the presence of a guest is considered uncivil. Casual wear is suitable except for the most formal meetings or social occasions. Bikinis, shorts, bare shoulders and backs may not be appreciated. Men only remove their shirts when bathing. Overt public displays of affection, especially near religious places, are inappropriate. Nepalese cities are generally safe, but take sensible precautions with personal possessions. **Photography:** Always ask permission first. In general it is allowed outside temples and at festivals, but not at religious ceremonies or inside temples; however, there is no hard and fast rule and the only way to be sure of not giving offence is to ask first and accept the answer. **Tipping:** Only usual in tourist hotels and restaurants. Taxi drivers need only be tipped when they have been particularly helpful. 10% is sufficient for all three services. Elsewhere tipping should be avoided.

BUSINESS PROFILE

ECONOMY: Nepal is one of the world's least developed countries, with the tenth-lowest per capita GNP (according to World Bank figures). Although most of the land is uncultivable, 90% of the working population find employment in agriculture and forestry. Foodstuffs and live animals provide about 30% of Nepal's export earnings. The manufacturing sector is very small and concentrated in light industries such as construction materials, carpet-making and food-processing. The country has a considerable hydroelectric potential which would save Nepal from having to import much of its energy requirements, but it is as yet highly underdeveloped. The Government has a cherished hope of exporting hydroelectric power to northern India, where energy is in short supply, but the project is fraught with political difficulties. There is some mining of mica and small quantities of lignite, copper, coal and iron ore. The country runs a large trade deficit and relies on extensive amounts of foreign aid, especially food aid. India is the main trading partner, and the 15-month dispute resolved in June 1990 caused considerable damage to the Nepalese economy. The frontier with China has recently been opened and a trade agreement signed with the Chinese government. The election of an avowedly Marxist government in 1994 is likely to see attempts to redress the imbalances in the distribution of wealth in this relatively poor nation. Tourism remains the biggest earner of foreign exchange.
BUSINESS: Tropical-weight suits or shirt and tie are recommended. Best time to visit is October to May.
Office hours: 1000-1700 Sunday to Friday (summer); 1000-1600 Sunday to Friday (winter).
COMMERCIAL INFORMATION: The following organisations can offer advice: Nepal Chamber of Commerce, PO Box 198, Chamber Bhavan, Kantipath, Kathmandu. Tel: (1) 222 890. Fax: (1) 229 998. Telex: 2349; *or*
Federation of Nepalese Chambers of Commerce and Industry, PO Box 269, Tripureshor, Kathmandu. Tel: (1) 475 032. Fax: (1) 474 051. Telex: 2786.

CLIMATE

Nepal's weather is generally predictable and pleasant. Summer and monsoon are from June to October. The remainder of the year is dry. Spring and autumn are the most pleasant seasons; winter temperatures drop to freezing with a high level of snowfall in the mountains.
Required clothing: Lightweight and tropical clothes with umbrella are advised for June to August. Between October and March lightweight clothes are worn in Kathmandu, with a coat for evenings and warm clothing for the mountains.

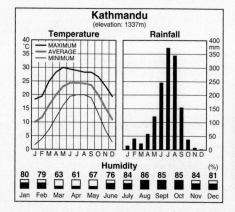

Kathmandu
(elevation: 1337m)

Temperature	Rainfall
MAXIMUM / AVERAGE / MINIMUM	

Humidity

	Jan	Feb	Mar	Apr	May	June	July	Aug	Sept	Oct	Nov	Dec
(%)	80	79	63	61	67	76	84	86	85	85	84	81

The Netherlands

☐ *international airport*

100km
50mls

Location: Northwest Europe.

Nederlands Bureau voor Toerisme
PO Box 458, 2260 MG Leidschendam, The Netherlands
Tel: (70) 370 5705. Fax: (70) 320 1654. Telex: 32588.
Royal Netherlands Embassy
38 Hyde Park Gate, London SW7 5DP
Tel: (0171) 584 5040. Fax: (0171) 581 3450. Telex: 28812 (a/b NETEMB G). *Consular section:* Tel: (0171) 589 2280. Opening hours: 1000-1330 Monday to Friday.
Netherlands Board of Tourism
PO Box 523, London SW1E 6NT
Tel: (0891) 200 277 (calls are charged at the higher rate of 39/49p per minute). Fax: (0171) 828 7941. Telex: 269005.
British Embassy
Lange Voorhout 10, 2514 ED The Hague, The Netherlands
Tel: (70) 364 5800. Fax: (70) 360 3839. Telex: 31600 (a/b BEMB NL).
Royal Netherlands Embassy
4200 Linnean Avenue, NW, Washington, DC 20008
Tel: (202) 244 5300. Fax: (202) 362 3430.
Consulate General of The Netherlands
11th Floor, 1 Rockefeller Plaza, New York, NY 10020-2094
Tel: (212) 246 1429. Fax: (212) 333 3603.
Netherlands Board of Tourism
21st Floor, 355 Lexington Avenue, New York, NY 10017
Tel: (212) 370 7360. Fax: (212) 370 9507.
Embassy of the United States of America
Lange Voorhout 102, 2514 EJ The Hague, The Netherlands
Tel: (70) 310 9209. Fax: (70) 361 4688. Telex: 31016.
Royal Netherlands Embassy
3rd Floor, 350 Albert Street, Ottawa, Ontario K1R 1A4
Tel: (613) 237 5030. Fax: (613) 237 6471.
Consulates in: Calgary, Edmonton, Halifax, Kingston,

London, Montréal, Québec, Regina, St John, St John's, Thunder Bay, Toronto, Vancouver and Winnipeg.
Netherlands Board of Tourism
Suite 710, 25 Adelaide Street East, Toronto, Ontario M5C 1Y2
Tel: (416) 363 1577. Fax: (416) 363 1470.
Canadian Embassy
Sophialaan 7, The Hague, The Netherlands
Tel: (70) 361 4111. Fax: (70) 356 1111. Telex: 31270.

AREA: 33,938 sq km (13,104 sq miles).
POPULATION: 1L5,200,000 (1993).
POPULATION DENSITY: 447 per sq km.
CAPITAL: Amsterdam. **Population:** 713,407 (1992).
SEAT OF GOVERNMENT: The Hague. **Population:** 445,287 (1992).
GEOGRAPHY: The Netherlands shares borders to the south with Belgium and the east with Germany, while the North Sea lies to the north and west. Large areas of The Netherlands have been reclaimed from the sea and consequently one-fifth of the country lies below sea level. The country is flat and level and is criss-crossed by rivers and canals. Areas reclaimed from the sea, known as *polders*, are extremely fertile. The landscape is broken by the forest of Arnhem, the bulb fields in the west, the lakes of central and northern areas, and coastal dunes which are among the most impressive in Europe.
LANGUAGE: Dutch. English is widely spoken and understood. French and German are also spoken.
RELIGION: 38% Roman Catholic, 30% Protestant; 26% do not profess any religion.
TIME: GMT + 1 (GMT + 2 from last Sunday in March to Saturday before last Sunday in September).
ELECTRICITY: 220 volts AC, 50Hz.
COMMUNICATIONS: Telephone: Full IDD is available. Country code: 31 (followed by 20 for Amsterdam, 10 for Rotterdam and 70 for The Hague). Outgoing international code: 09. Telephone information is given in French, English and German. The cheap rate is from 1800-0800 Monday to Friday and at the weekend. Calls can be made from public booths or post offices. Booths accept 25 cents, Gld1 and Gld2.5 coins or cards. These can be bought at post offices, VVV offices, and shops displaying the *PTT-telephone card* poster. **Fax:** Services are widely available and are also provided by some hotels. **Telex/telegram:** There are no major public telex offices, but there are facilities in main hotels. Telegram facilities are available at all main post offices; telegrams can also be sent directly from telephone kiosks. **Post:** Stamps are available from all post offices as well as from tobacconists and kiosks selling postcards and souvenirs. Mail within Europe takes approximately five days. Post offices are open 0830-1700 Monday to Friday. Some major post offices are open 0830-1200 Saturday. There are all-night post offices in Amsterdam (Niedwezijds Voorburgwal, behind the Royal Palace) and Rotterdam (Coolsingel). **Press:** The main dailies are *De Telegraaf, Algemeen Dagblad* and *De Volkskrant*. Foreign newspapers are widely available.
BBC World Service and Voice of America frequencies: From time to time these change. See the section *How to Use this Book* for more information.
BBC:

MHz	9.750	6.180	3.955	0.648

A service is also available on 648kHz/463m and 198kHz/1515m (0100-0500 GMT).
Voice of America:

MHz	11.97	9.670	6.040	5.995

PASSPORT/VISA

Regulations and requirements may be subject to change at short notice, and you are advised to contact the appropriate diplomatic or consular authority before finalising travel arrangements. Details of these may be found at the head of this country's entry. Any numbers in the chart refer to the footnotes below.

	Passport Required?	Visa Required?	Return Ticket Required?
Full British	1	No	No/2
BVP	Valid	No	No/2
Australian	Yes	No	No/2
Canadian	Yes	No	No/2
USA	Yes	No	No/2
Other EU (As of 31/12/94)	1	No	No/2
Japanese	Yes	No	No/2

PASSPORTS: Valid passport required by all except:
(a) **[1]** nationals of EU countries who hold a valid national ID card or, if UK citizens, a BVP;
(b) nationals of Andorra, Austria, Liechtenstein, Malta, Monaco, San Marino and Switzerland with a valid national ID card.
Where national passports are required, they must be valid for at least 3 months after the last day of the intended visit.

Note: [2] It is advisable to have a return ticket, but not obligatory. If a visitor is not in possession of a return ticket, proof of sufficient means of support may be required.

British Visitors Passport: A BVP is valid for holidays or unpaid business trips of up to 3 months. Children under 16 years of age travelling to The Netherlands, Luxembourg or Belgium *cannot* do so on their brother's or sister's passport.

VISAS: Required by all except:
(a) nationals of countries referred to in the chart;
(b) nationals of Andorra, Argentina, Austria, Bermuda, Brazil, Brunei, Burkina Faso, Chile, Costa Rica, Cyprus, Czech Republic, Ecuador, El Salvador, Finland, Guatemala, Honduras, Hong Kong (British Passport holders only), Hungary, Iceland, Israel, Jamaica, South Korea, Liechtenstein, Malawi, Malaysia, Malta, Mexico, Monaco, New Zealand, Nicaragua, Norway, Panama, Paraguay, Poland, San Marino, Singapore, Slovak Republic, Slovenia, Sweden, Switzerland, Turkey (if resident in an EU country), Uruguay, Vatican City and Venezuela.
All visa exemptions are for stays of up to 3 months. Nationals of all other countries require a visa.

Types of visa: Transit, Travel and Sojourn (for tourist or business purposes). Enquire at Consulate General for further details.

Benelux Visas can be issued by the Belgium, Luxembourg or Netherlands embassies abroad, valid for entry into all three countries. The visa number must begin with the letters BE, NE or LUX. Passengers with this type of visa are strongly advised to be holding onward or return tickets, or proof of means of support.

Validity: Transit: 24 hours. Travel and Sojourn visas depend on duration of visit(s).

Application to: Consulate (or Consular section at Embassy). For addresses, see top of entry.

Application requirements: (a) Completed application forms. (b) Valid passport (must be valid for at least 3 months after date of departure from The Netherlands). (c) Fee where applicable (payable in cash). (d) Passport-size photos (not needed for Transit visas).
The number of forms and photos required is dependent on the nationality of the applicant.

Working days required: Often within 24 hours, but can take up to 6 weeks for certain nationals (see entry for *Luxembourg* earlier in the book).

Temporary residence: Work permit and residence permit required if other than EU member. Enquire at the Embassy.

MONEY

Currency: Guilder (Gld) = 100 cents. Notes are in denominations of Gld1000, 250, 100, 50, 25, 10 and 5. Coins are in denominations of Gld5, 2.5 and 1, and 25, 10 and 5 cents.

Currency exchange: Exchange offices are indicated by the letters GWK.

Credit cards: Access/Mastercard, American Express, Diners Club and Visa are accepted. Check with your credit card company for details of merchant acceptability and other services which may be available.

Travellers cheques: The easiest form of currency to exchange.

Exchange rate indicators: The following figures are included as a guide to the movements of the Guilder against Sterling and the US Dollar:

Date:	Oct '92	Sep '93	Jan '94	Jan '95
£1.00=	2.74	2.76	2.87	2.71
$1.00=	1.73	1.81	1.94	1.74

Currency restrictions: There are no restrictions on the import and export of either local or foreign currency.

Banking hours: 0900-1600 Monday to Friday; 1700-2000 Thursday evening.

DUTY FREE

The following goods may be imported into The Netherlands without incurring customs duty:
(a) Travellers arriving from EU countries with duty-paid goods:
*800 cigarettes and 400 cigarillos and 200 cigars and 1kg tobacco; *90 litres of wine including up to 60 litres of sparkling wine; *10 litres of spirits and 20 litres of fortified wine and 110 litres of beer.*
(b) Travellers from non-EU European countries or bought duty free within the EU:
*200 cigarettes or 50 cigars or 100 cigarillos or 250g of tobacco; *1 litre of alcoholic beverages stronger than 22° proof or 2 litres less than 22° proof or 2 litres of fortified wine; *2 litres of wine; *8 litres of non-sparkling Luxembourg wine; *50g of perfume and 250ml of eau de toilette; *other goods to the value of Gld125.*
(c) Travellers originating from outside Europe:
*400 cigarettes or 100 cigars or 500g tobacco; *wine,*

*spirits and perfume same as for non-EU European countries; *other goods to the value of Gld125.*
Note: (a) [*] These allowances are only for travellers aged 17 years and above. (b) Although there are now no legal limits imposed on importing duty-paid tobacco and alcoholic products from one EU country to another, travellers may be questioned at customs if they exceed the above amounts and may be asked to prove that the goods are for personal use only. (c) Enquiries concerning current import regulations should be made to the Royal Netherlands Embassy in the country of departure, or to the national Chamber of Commerce. (d) Cats and dogs imported into The Netherlands from any countries other than Belgium or Luxembourg require a health certificate and a rabies certificate. The importation of psittacine birds (parrots or parrot-like birds) is limited to two per family, and a health certificate is required for each bird. The importation of monkeys is prohibited. For more information, contact the Agricultural Department at the Royal Netherlands Embassy.

PUBLIC HOLIDAYS

Jan 1 '95 New Year's Day. **Apr 14** Good Friday. **Apr 17** Easter Monday. **Apr 30** Queen's Day. **May 5** National Liberation Day. **May 25** Ascension Day. **Jun 5** Whit Monday. **Dec 25-26** Christmas. **Jan 1 '96** New Year's Day. **Apr 5** Good Friday. **Apr 8** Easter Monday. **Apr 30** Queen's Day.

HEALTH

Regulations and requirements may be subject to change at short notice, and you are advised to contact your doctor well in advance of your intended date of departure. Any numbers in the chart refer to the footnotes below.

	Special Precautions?	Certificate Required?
Yellow Fever	No	No
Cholera	No	No
Typhoid & Polio	No	-
Malaria	No	-
Food & Drink	No	-

Rabies is present. For those at high risk, vaccination before arrival should be considered. If you are bitten abroad seek medical advice without delay. For more information, consult the *Health* section at the back of the book.

Health care: The standard of health care (and other social services) is very high in The Netherlands. There is a Reciprocal Health Agreement with all other EU countries. On presentation of form E111 by UK residents (available from post offices or the Department of Health), all medical treatment, including hospital treatment, is free; prescribed medicines and dental treatment must, however, be paid for. For police, fire or ambulance emergencies, dial 06-11 anywhere in the country.

TRAVEL - International

AIR: The Netherlands' national airline is *Royal Dutch Airlines (KLM).*
For free advice on air travel, call the Air Travel Advisory Bureau in the UK on (0171) 636 5000 (London) *or* (0161) 832 2000 (Manchester).
Approximate flight times: From Amsterdam to *Belfast* is 1 hour 5 minutes; to *London* is 1 hour; to *Manchester* is 1 hour 5 minutes and to *New York* is 9 hours 45 minutes (including stopover in London).
International airports: Principally Amsterdam, with a number of international flights also operated from Rotterdam, Eindhoven and Maastricht.
Amsterdam (AMS) (Schiphol) is 15km (9 miles) southwest of the city (travel time by train – 20 minutes). Airport facilities: restaurants, outgoing duty-free shop, banks, car rental. *KLM* buses provide a daily service from 0600-2400 departing every 30 minutes and stopping at the following hotels: Hotel Ibis; Amsterdam Hilton; Golden Tulip Barbizon; Centraal; Park Hotel and Apollo Hotel, and return to Schiphol. Trains to Zuid station (Amsterdam South) run every 15 minutes from 0525-0015; return is from Zuid station, Parnassusweg/ Minervalaan (via tram no. 5 from the city centre) from 0545-0040. There is now a direct rail link between the airport and Amsterdam Central Station, with trains every 15 minutes and an all-night service. There is a service to the RAI Congress Centre every 15 minutes from 0525-0012. Return is from RAI station (via tram no. 4 from the city centre) from 0545-0040. Plentiful taxis are available to the city.

Rotterdam (RTM) (Zestienhoven) is 9km (5.5 miles) northwest of the city (travel time – 15 minutes). Airport facilities: restaurant, bank, outgoing duty-free shop and car rental. 24-hour flight information: (10) 446 0814. Bus no. 33 departs every 30 minutes from 0700-1900. Return is from Central Station, Knisplein, from 0630-1830. Taxis to the city are also available.
Eindhoven (EIN) (Welschap) airport is 8km (5 miles) from the city. Airport facilities: car rental and outgoing duty-free shop. Flight information: (40) 516 142. Coaches run every 15 minutes and taxis to the city are also available.
Maastricht (MST) (Beek) airport is 8km (5 miles) from the city. Airport facilities: outgoing duty-free shop.
Groningen (GRQ) (Elede) airport is 9km (6 miles) from the city.
Enschede (ENS) (Twente) airport is 8km (5 miles) from the city.
SEA: Regular car and passenger ferries are operated from the UK to The Netherlands via the following routes and shipping lines:
North Sea Ferries: Hull to Rotterdam (Europoort); travel time – 14 hours; 1 sailing nightly.
Olau Line UK Ltd: Sheerness to Flushing (Vlissingen); travel time – 7 hours (day), 8 hours 30 mins (night); 2 sailings daily.
Stena-Sealink: Harwich to Hook of Holland; travel time – 7 hours 30 mins (day), 8 hours (night); 2 sailings daily.
Hoverspeed UK Ltd: coach/hovercraft service from London to Amsterdam; travel time – 10 hours; 2 or 3 services daily.
Note: *North Sea Ferries* and *P&O* run services to The Netherlands via Belgium.
RAIL: Rail connections from London via either Harwich and Hook of Holland, or Dover and Ostend (boat or jetfoil). Information is available in the UK from any British Rail Travel Centre. There are direct links from Amsterdam to Paris, Brussels, Zurich, Frankfurt/M, Copenhagen and Luxembourg.
ROAD: The Netherlands are connected to the rest of Europe by a superb network of motorways. Although frontier formalities between The Netherlands and Germany and Belgium have now all but vanished, motorists – particularly on smaller roads – should be prepared to stop when asked to do so by a customs official.

TRAVEL - Internal

AIR: *KLM Cityhopper (HN)* operates between Amsterdam, Rotterdam, Groningen, Enschede, Maastricht and Eindhoven. Enquire at *KLM* offices or at the Board of Tourism for further information.
SEA: Ferry service to the Wadden Islands across the Ijsselmeer (former Zuyder Sea) and Schelde Estuary. There is also a service to the Frisian Islands across the Waddenzee. *Boat Tours* run excursions from Amsterdam, Rotterdam, Utrecht, Arnhem, Groningen, Giethoorn, Delft and Maastricht.
RAIL: The highly developed rail network is efficient and cheap, and connects all towns. Both Intercity and local trains run at least half-hourly on all principal routes. Rail and bus timetables are integrated, and there is a common fare structure throughout the country.
Cheap fares: *Rail Rovers* are available for one or seven days. UK prices are as follows:

	1st Class	2nd Class
1 day:	£35.00	£23.50
7 days:	£84.00	£56.00

Public Transport Link Rovers are issued in conjunction with *Rail Rovers*. These cover unlimited travel on all public transport buses and trams in town and country, and on the metro system in Amsterdam and Rotterdam. *Euro Domino* tickets are available for travel in The Netherlands, Belgium and Luxembourg. 3-, 5- and 10-day passes are available. The *Benelux Tourrail Card* allows unlimited travel for any five days within a 1 month period. Other deals include *Multi-Rovers, Family Rovers* and *Teenage Rovers*. Children under four years of age travel free on all journeys within The Netherlands. Children between 4-11 years travelling unaccompanied are entitled to a 40% reduction on the adult single or day-return fare. Those accompanied by an adult travel for Gld1. On international journeys, children aged 4-11 pay half of the adult fare on the Dutch rail section of the trip. Even greater savings are available on the *Child's Railrunner* tickets for children aged 4-11 years travelling with a fare-paying adult (19 years or older), and includes up to three children travelling with any one adult. Contact the Railway Authority of any of the participating countries for prices and further information.
Inter-Rail passes are also valid in The Netherlands. Any enquiries about rail travel, the purchase of *Rail Rover* tickets, etc in the UK should be addressed to: Holland Rail, Gilbert Street, Ropley, Hampshire SO2 4BY. Tel: (01962) 773 646. Fax: (01962) 773 6255.

ROAD: There is an excellent road system. Visitors to The Netherlands may use credit cards when obtaining petrol. The motoring association in The Netherlands is the ANWB (Koninklijke Nederlandsche Toeristenbond), PO Box 93200, Wassenaarseweg 220, The Hague. Tel: (70) 314 1420. **Bus:** Extensive regional bus networks exist. Long-distance coaches also operate between the cities, but costs are generally on a par with trains. **Taxi:** It is less usual to hail a taxi in the street in Holland. Taxis have an illuminated sign 'taxi' on the roof and there are taxi ranks at railway stations and at various other points in the cities. Taxis can also be phoned. Usually there are meters in the taxi showing the fare, including the tip. **Car hire:** Available from airports and main hotels. All European car-hire companies are represented. **Bicycle hire:** Bikes can be hired from all main railway stations, but must be returned to the station from which they are hired. A returnable deposit is required. **Regulations:** Driving is on the right. Drivers should be particularly aware of cyclists; often there are special cycle lanes. There is a chronic shortage of parking space in central Amsterdam, and the rush hours (0700-0900 and 1700-1900) should be avoided throughout the whole country. Parking fines are severe. Headlights should be dipped in built-up areas, but it is prohibited to use sidelights only. Children under 12 should not travel in the front seat. Seat belts are compulsory. Speed limits are 80kmph (50mph) on major roads, 120kmph (75mph) on motorways and 50kmph (30mph) in towns. **Documentation:** An International Driving Licence is not required, as long as a driving licence from the country of origin is held. Trailers and caravans are allowed in without documents. A Green Card is advisable, but not compulsory. Without it, drivers with motor insurance policies in their home country are granted only the minimum legal cover in The Netherlands; the Green Card tops this up to the level of cover provided by the driver's own policy.
URBAN: Public transport is very well developed in the cities and large towns. A *strippenkaart* national fares system exists. Strips of 15 tickets each are widely available at railway stations, post offices and some tourist offices. These are accepted anywhere in payment of standard zonal fares. There are also individual and multi-day tickets for the cities. For more detailed information on travel within Amsterdam, Rotterdam and The Hague, see below. All the towns and cities are well served by bus services; in addition, Utrecht has a tram service, and there are trolleybuses in Arnhem. **Amsterdam:** Information: VVV (Amsterdam Tourist Office), Stationsplein 10 (opposite Central Station). Tel: (6) 34 03 40 66. Opening hours: 0700-2230 Monday to Sunday (summer); normal office hours (winter). Amsterdam has an extensive network of buses, trams and metro *(GVB)*, with frequent services from early morning to about midnight. There are less frequent services throughout the night at a higher fare. Full information on services (including a map), day tickets and *strippenkaart* (strip-tickets) can be obtained from the GVB office in front of the Central Station (0700-2230 daily) or the GVB Central Office at Prins Hendrikkade 108-114. The GVB is easy to use, and the tram system can be very useful, since it is not only good value (as are the buses and metro) but also enables reasonably quick travel even during the busiest periods of the day. *RAI Trade Fair Centre:* A 45-minute walk, a taxi ride, or tram no. 4 from the city centre. **Taxi:** Taxis are not generally hailed, but found at a limited number of ranks in the city centre. They can also be ordered by phone. *Car hire:* The major European firms, including *Hertz* and *Avis,* are represented. Cars can also be hired through most hotels.
Rotterdam: The city has excellent bus and tram services and a 2-line metro network. These work on a zonal system. Information is available from the Central Station. *Taxi:* Available from ranks or by phone. *Car hire:* The major European firms, including *Avis* and *Hertz,* are represented.
The Hague: The Hague has bus and tram services. Information is available from the Central Station, Koningin Julianaplein. *Taxi:* Available from ranks or by phone. *Car hire:* Avis and Hertz are represented.
JOURNEY TIMES: The following chart gives approximate journey times (in hours and minutes) from Amsterdam to other major cities in The Netherlands.

	Air	Road	Rail
The Hague	-	0.40	0.44
Rotterdam	-	1.00	1.00
Utrecht	-	0.25	0.30
Groningen	-	2.00	2.20
Arnhem	-	1.10	1.10
Maastricht	0.40	2.30	2.30
Vlissingen	-	2.00	2.45
Eindhoven	0.30	1.30	1.25
Breda	-	1.30	1.50

ACCOMMODATION

HOTELS: The Netherlands has a wide range of accommodation, from luxury hotels in big towns to modern motels along motorways. The Netherlands Reserverings Centrum (NRC) can make reservations throughout the country: Postbus 404, 2260 AK Leidschendam. Tel: (70) 320 2611. Telex: 33755.
Grading: The Netherlands Board of Tourism issues a shield to all approved hotels by which they can be recognised. This must be affixed to the front of the hotel in a conspicuous position. Hotels which display this sign conform to the official standards set by Dutch law on hotels and it protects the tourist and guarantees certain standards of quality. Some hotels are also graded according to the *Benelux* system in which standard is indicated by a row of 3-pointed stars from the highest (5-star) to the minimum (1-star). However, membership of this scheme is voluntary, and there may be first-class hotels which are not classified in this way. *Benelux* star ratings adhere to the following criteria:
5-star (H5): This is a new category signifying luxury hotel.
4-star (H4): First-class hotels. 80% of rooms have a private bath. Other amenities include night reception and room service.
3-star (H3): Half of the rooms have a private bath. Other amenities include day reception.
2-star (H2): A quarter of rooms have a private bath. Other amenities include a bar.
1-star (H1): Simple hotel. No private baths, but hot and cold water in rooms. Breakfast available.
Cat H: Hotel with minimal comfort.
Cat O: Simple accommodation.
For further information contact: Bedrijfschap HORECA, Postbus 121, Baron de Coubertinlaan 6, 2700 Zoetermeer. Tel: (70) 317 1171.
GUEST-HOUSES: These are called *pensions* and rates vary. Book through local tourist offices.
SELF-CATERING: Farmhouses for groups can be booked months in advance via the local tourist offices. Holiday chalets, especially in the relatively unknown parts of Zeeland, can be booked through the local tourist office. Bungalow parks throughout the country can be booked through The Netherlands Reservation Centre; see above.
CAMPING/CARAVANNING: There are some 2500 registered campsites in Holland. Only 500 offer advanced booking, the others operate on a first-come, first-served basis. Off-site camping is not permitted. Prices are fairly high and it is often far better value to stay more than one night. A list is available from the Board of Tourism.
YOUTH HOSTELS: Over 50 in various towns and villages. Information is available from Stiching Nederlandse Jeugdherberg Centrale, Prof. Tulpstraat 2-6, Amsterdam.

RESORTS & EXCURSIONS

For the purpose of this survey, the country has been divided into seven regions: *Amsterdam* (including the province of Noord-Holland); *Rotterdam; The Hague* (including the province of Zuid-Holland); *Utrecht; The North* (the provinces of Friesland, Groningen and Drenthe); *The East* (the provinces of Flevoland, Overijssel and Gelderland); and *The South* (the provinces

AMSTERDAM

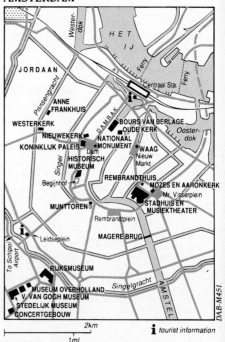

2km
1ml
i *tourist information*

of Noord-Brabant, Zeeland and Limburg). There is also a brief section devoted to coastal resorts.

Amsterdam

Tourist Office: Tel: (6) 34 03 40 66. Opening hours: 0900-1700 Monday to Friday.
Amsterdam, the capital of The Netherlands though not the seat of government, is built around a concentric network of canals spanned by over 1000 bridges (one of the most attractive ways of viewing the city is on a canal tour). Many of the city's houses date back to Holland's golden age in the 17th century. These narrow fronted merchant's houses are characterised by the traditionally Dutch ornamented gables. Amsterdam has long been a centre of diamond cutting and it is still possible to see diamond cutters at work. The city boasts 53 museums, 61 art galleries, 12 concert halls and 20 theatres; a special canal boat links 16 of the major museums. In the local countryside it is still possible to see working windmills. There are annual events such as the Amsterdam Art Weeks and the Holland Festival.
It is possible to book a VVV-approved guide/hostess in Amsterdam by contacting Guidor, c/o The Netherlands Reservation Centre (address in the *Accommodation* section above).
SIGHTSEEING: A selection of some of the most popular sights is as follows:
Rijksmuseum: National museum with Dutch paintings dating from the 16th-19th century, including *The Nightwatch* by Rembrandt. It is situated at Stadhouderskade 42. Opening hours: 1000-1700 Tuesday to Saturday, 1300-1700 Sunday and holidays, closed Monday, January 1 and April 30.
Anne Frank's House: Prinsengracht 263. Opening hours: 0900-1700 Monday to Saturday and 1000-1700 Sunday (winter); 0900-1900 Monday to Saturday and 1000-1900 Sunday (summer). Closed December 25, New Year's Day and Yom Kippur.
Van Gogh Museum: Paulus Potterstraat 7. Opening hours: 1000-1700 Monday to Saturday, 1300-1700 Sunday and holidays, closed New Year's Day.
Museum Het Rembrandthuis: Jodenbreestraat 4-6. Opening hours: 1000-1700 Monday to Saturday, 1300-1700 Sunday and holidays, closed New Year's Day.
Stedelijk Museum (Museum of Modern Art): Paulus Potterstraat 13. Opening hours: 1100-1700 Monday to Sunday, closed New Year's Day.
Other interesting places to visit include: The *Royal Palace;* the *Nieuwe Kerk;* the *Martelwerktuigenmuseum* (the Torture Museum); the *Munt Tower,* which looms over the floating flower market on the Singel canal; the open-air market at *Waterlooplein;* the *Begijnhof* (14th-century almshouses around a quiet courtyard); and bookshops in the *Oudemanhuispoort.*
NIGHTLIFE: Many of the nightclubs are concentrated

Travel Holland by Rail

Holland has the densest railway network in Europe. As a result, all business centers and tourist attractions are easy to reach by train. Dutch trains are super comfortable and can take you wherever you want to go: from the bulb fields to the World Trade Center in Amsterdam; from the beaches to the largest port in the world, Rotterdam. Moreover, from Schiphol Airport the country's southern border is only three hours away, its northernmost point two and half hours, and Amsterdam a mere fifteen minutes. So, why not travel the way the Dutch do. After all, the train is fast, comfortable, safe and economical. Train tickets can now be purchased outside Holland so that when you arrive at Schiphol Airport you can travel on to your next destination without delay.

For more information or our free brochure:

Great Britain	**USA/Canada**	**Other countries**
Holland Rail	Netherlands Board of Tourism	N.V. Nederlandse Spoorwegen
Gilbert Street	225 N. Michigan Avenue,	Buro Aktie Service
Ropley	Suite 326	Postbus 2398
Hampshire SO24 OBY	Chicago, IL 60601	3500 GJ Utrecht
Tel. 01962 773646	Tel. (312) 819-0300	

in the Rembrantsplein–Leidseplein area. There is a weekly magazine, 'Amsterdam This Week', which will give visitors a good idea of the week's events and clubs worth visiting. *Walletjes*, the notorious 'red-light' district of the city, is on the east side of Damrak. Here and around Leidseplein are any number of bars and clubs, many with live music, from cabaret to modern jazz.
Concert halls/theatres: *Stadsschouwburg* (opera) and *Concertgebouw* (classical music, opera, ballet). Enquiries can be made through the VVV Theatre Booking Office situated on Stationsplein 10, Amsterdam, open 1000-1600 Monday to Saturday.
NOORD-HOLLAND: Tourist Office: As for Amsterdam (above).
The Amsterdam VVV publishes a booklet outlining over 15 excursions which highlight the Dutch image abroad (ie clogs, tulips, cheese and windmills). Day trips are available to **Alkmaar**, where there is a famous cheese market at Waagplein open 1000-1200 from mid-April to mid-September every Friday; a frequent train service runs from Central Station. There is also a good bus service from Central Station to **Volendam** and **Marken**, both old fishing villages, largely built of wood. The former is predominantly Catholic, the latter Protestant.
Haarlem (20km/12 miles west of Amsterdam) is a centre of Dutch tulip-growing and the surrounding countryside affords a fine view of the bulb fields from the end of March to mid-May. The town itself has a fine museum. Nearby are **Hoorn** and **Enkhuizen**, which are well known watersports centres. The casino at **Zandvoort** (5km/3 miles west of Haarlem), also the site of the *Dutch Grand Prix;* and the *National Zuyder Zee Museum,* Wierdijk 18, Enkhuizen, an outdoor museum with ships and reconstructed houses, open from early April to late October, 1000-1700 Monday to Sunday (closed January 1 and December 25-26). There is a famous *Flower Auction* in **Aalsmeer**, Legmeerdijk 313; open 0730-1130 Monday to Friday. Near **Lisse**, 8km (5 miles) south of Haarlem, are the *Keukenhof Gardens,* which have a lily show in the last week; open March 24-May 25, 0800-1930 Monday to Sunday. The *Frans Roozen Nurseries & Tulip Show* and the bulb fields can be visited at Vogelenzangweg 49; 0800-1800 Monday to Sunday (March 25-May 27) and 0900-1700 Monday to Sunday (July to September). **Broek op Langedijk**

has Europe's oldest vegetable auction hall with a large and interesting exhibition of the land reclamation of the surrounding area; open April 4-October 1, 1200-1700 Monday to Friday, 1200-1600 Sunday by appointment only.

The Hague

Tourist Office: Tel: (6) 34 03 50 51. Telex: 31490. The Hague (Den Haag, officially 's-Gravenhage) is a cosmopolitan city which has over 60 foreign embassies and is the seat of the International Court of Justice, as well as being the capital of the province of Zuid-Holland. Although The Hague is the seat of government of The Netherlands, it is not the country's capital. The central part of the Old Town is the *Binnenhof,* an irregular group of buildings surrounding an open space. The seaside resort of **Scheveningen** (which has the country's only pier) is a nearby suburb.
SIGHTSEEING: A selection of some of the most popular sights is as follows:
Madurodam Miniature Town: Haringkade 175. Opening hours: 0900-2300 Monday to Sunday (March to May); 0900-2300 (June to August); 0900-2130 (September); 0900-1800 (October to January) (illuminated after dark).
Panorama Mesdag: Zeestraat 65B. Largest panoramic circular painting in the world, created by the artist Mesdag and others, famous for its perfect optical illusion. Opening hours: 1000-1700 Monday to Saturday, 1200-1700 Sunday and holidays, closed December 25.
Antique Walk: VVV route including most of the 150 antique shops in The Hague – the detailed description and map are printed on the back of a reproduction 1614 print and are available from VVV information offices.
Parliament Buildings and Knight's Hall: Tel: (70) 364 6144. 13th-century buildings with regular tours and slide shows explaining the history of the Binnenhof. Opening hours: 1000-1600 Monday to Saturday (last guided tour 1555).
Royal Cabinet of Paintings: In the Mauritshuis at Korte Vijverberg 8. Tel: (70) 365 4779. Collection includes the *Anatomical Lesson of Dr Tulp* by Rembrandt, and other 17th-century Dutch works. Opening hours: 1000-1700 Tuesday to Saturday, 1100-1700 Sunday and holidays, closed January 1, April 30

and December 25.
Other interesting places to visit include: The *Huis ten Bosch Palace,* the *Puppet Museum,* the antique market at the *Lange Voorhout,* the *Duinoord* district built in the style of old Dutch architecture, the *Haagse Bos* wooded park, the 17th-century *Nieuwe Kerk* and the *Royal Library.*
ZUID-HOLLAND: Tourist Office: Tel: (15) 126 100. 22km (14 miles) southeast of Rotterdam and about 45km (28 miles) southeast of The Hague is **Kinderdijk**, near **Alblasserdam**, a good place to see windmills. They can be visited during the week. **Delft**, centre of the Dutch pottery industry and world famous for its blue hand-painted ceramics, is roughly midway between Rotterdam and The Hague. **Gouda**, 20km (12 miles) southeast of Rotterdam, is famous for its cheese market and the *Candlelight Festival* in December. The town centre is dominated by the massive late-Gothic *Town Hall.* Nearby is the pretty old town of **Oudewater**, noted for its beautiful 17th-century, gabled houses. 12km (7 miles) northwest of Gouda is the town of **Boskoop**, renowned for its fruit trees; a visit during the blossom season is a delightful experience. **Dordrecht**, 15km (9 miles) southeast of Rotterdam and about 37km (23 miles) southeast of The Hague, was an important port until a flood in 1421 reduced the economic importance of the town. The museum in the city has a good collection of paintings from the 17th, 18th and 19th centuries, while the most striking building is probably the *Grote Kerk,* begun in about 1305. **Leiden** (20km/12 miles northeast of The Hague, 40km/25 miles north of Rotterdam), the birthplace of Rembrandt, was a famous weaving town during the Middle Ages, and played a large part in the wars of independence against Spain in the 16th century. The university was founded by William the Silent in 1575 in return for the city's loyalty. The Pilgrim Fathers lived here for ten years (1610-1620) and *The Pilgrim Fathers' Documentation Centre* in **Boisotkade** (Vliet 45) has many artefacts, records and paintings dating from the period of their stay in the city.
There are many **beach resorts** in this region of the country. Some of the major ones include Scheveningen, Katwijk aan Zee, Noordwijk aan Zee, Monster, Wassenaar, 's-Gravenzande, Wassenaar and Ter Heijde.

Rotterdam

Tourist Office: Tel: (10) 402 3200. Fax: (10) 413 0124. Telex: 21228.

Rotterdam is the world's largest port and is the hub of the Dutch economy. Much of the city was obliterated during the Second World War, and only small parts of the old city remain. Historically, the city has been an important manufacturing centre since the 14th century, but its pre-eminence as a port dates only from the early 19th century.

SIGHTSEEING: A selection of some of the most popular sights is as follows:

Euromast & Space Tower: Parkhaven 20. The Observation Tower at 185m (605ft) is the highest point in Holland. Opening hours: Euromast – 1000-1900 daily (winter); 1000-2100 (summer). Space Tower – 1100-1600 daily (1000-1800 Saturday and Sunday January-February).

Museumschip 'De Buffel': Leuvehaven. This is now part of the Maritime Museum. Tel: (10) 413 2680.

Museum Boymans van Beuningen: Mathenesserlaan 18-20. Tel: (10) 441 9400. A unique collection of paintings, sculptures and objets d'art. Opening hours: 1000-1700 Tuesday to Saturday, 1100-1700 Sunday and holidays, closed January 1 and April 30.

Harbour tours: Willemsplein. Tel: (10) 413 5400. Boat tours *(Spido)* through the harbour of Rotterdam are available throughout the year. In the summer there are excursions to Europoort, the Delta Project and evening tours. There are also luxury motor cruisers for hire. A drive through the harbour of Rotterdam is also possible. The journey is one of between 100-150km (60-90 miles), and takes in almost every aspect of this massive harbour. The route passes wharves and warehouses, futuristic grain silos and unloading equipment, cranes and bridges, oil refineries, power stations and lighthouses, all of which create a skyline of awesome beauty, particularly at sunset. The docks, waterways, canals and ports-within-ports are interspersed with some surprising and apparently incongruous features; at one point the route passes a garden city built for shipyard workers, while further on there is a village and, at the harbour's westernmost point, a beach. A visit to Rotterdam harbour is recommended, even for someone with no interest in or knowledge of the arcana of grain silos or crude-oil terminals.

Blijdorp Zoo: Van Aersenlaan 49. Tel: (10) 443 1431. An open-plan zoo, beautifully laid out, with a restaurant. Opening hours: 0900-1700 Monday to Sunday.

Museums: The municipal museums are open 1000-1700 Monday to Saturday, 1100-1700 Sunday and holidays. They are closed on January 1 and April 30.

Other interesting places to visit include: 17th-century houses in the *Delfshaven* quarter of the city; the *Pilgrimskerk;* collections of maps and seacharts at the *Delfshaven Old Town Hall;* many traditional workshops for pottery, watchmaking and woodturning.

NIGHTLIFE: The major concert venue is the *De Doelen Concert Hall* (classical music, plays), which has 2000 seats.

Utrecht

Tourist Office: Vredenburg 90, 3511 BD Utrecht. Tel: (6) 34 03 40 85. Fax: (30) 331 417.

The province of Utrecht, in the very heart of The Netherlands, contains numerous country houses, estates and castles set in landscaped parks and beautiful woods. The city of Utrecht – the fourth largest in The Netherlands – is set on a slightly elevated tract of land (the *Geest),* a fact which, in a country vulnerable to flooding, has greatly aided the city's commercial development. It is one of the oldest cities in the country, the site first having been being settled by the Romans. During the Middle Ages, Utrecht was often an imperial residence, and the city's bishops regularly played an important role in the secular affairs of Europe. The city's prosperity allowed the construction of several beautiful churches, particularly the *Cathedral of St Michael* (13th century), *St Pieterskerk* and *St Janskerk* (both 11th century) and *St Jacobkerk* (12th century). Other buildings of note include the *House of the Teutonic Order,* the 14th-century *Huys Oudaen,* the *Hospice of St Bartholomew* and the *Neudeflat,* a more modern construction (built in the 1960s), but one which affords from its 15th-floor restaurant a superb view across the city. The city also has several museums, including the *Central Museum* (which has an excellent Department of Modern Art), the *Archepiscopal Museum,* the *Railway Museum,* the *Archaeological Collection* and the *Municipal Museum.*

The countryside around Utrecht is very fertile and seems like one large garden. The town makes a convenient base for excursions into the Veluwe region in the province of Gelderland (see below under *The East*).

25km (16 miles) to the northeast of Utrecht is the town of **Amersfoort**, set in a region of heathland and forest. The old town is well preserved, one of the most attractive buildings being the *Church of St George.* 8km (5 miles) away is the town of **Soestdijk**, containing the *Royal Palace* and the beautiful parklands of the Queen Mother. Between Soestdijk and Hilversum is **Baarn**, a favourite summer resort among the Dutch.

The North

Tourist Offices: *Friesland* (tel: (6) 32 02 40 60); *Groningen* (tel: (63) 202 3050); *Drenthe* (tel: (5920) 14324).

FRIESLAND: The province of Friesland in the northwest of the country has its own language and its own distinct culture. A large part of the marshlands along the North Sea coast have been reclaimed from the sea. Friesian cattle are among the most famous inhabitants of the area. The Friesian lake district in the southern part of the state centres on the town of **Sneek**. It is a good place for watersports, particularly yachting. Near Sneek is the small town of **Bolsward,** which has a magnificent Renaissance *Town Hall.* **Leeuwarden**, the capital of Friesland, has several old buildings and the *Friesian Museum,* probably the most important provincial museum in the country. 6km (4 miles) to the west is the village of **Marssum**, which has a 16th-century manor house. There are daily ferry connections with four of the Friesian Islands and a chain of museums on the *Aldfaer's Erf Route.* The Hollandse and Friesian Islands (Texel, Vlieland, Terschelling, Ameland and Schiermonnikoog), on which there are bird sanctuaries and areas of outstanding natural beauty, lie north of the mainland. Accommodation and campsites are available.

GRONINGEN: The agricultural province of Groningen is known for its fortified country houses dating back to the 14th century. The provincial capital, **Groningen** is commercially the most important town in the north of The Netherlands, as well as being a major cultural centre. The city suffered considerable damage during the Second World War, but many of the 16th-18th century buildings have now been restored.

DRENTHE: This is a province of extensive cycle paths, prehistoric monuments (particularly in the area of the village of **Havelte**) and Saxon villages. The region is almost entirely agricultural, much of the land being drained by the system of *venns* and *weiks.* The main town, **Assen**, set in an area of woodlands, was an insignificant village until the middle of the last century, and has no historical monuments. The *Provincial Museum* is, however, worth a visit. There are also several Megalithic tombs to be found south and southwest of the town.

The East

Tourist Offices: *Overijssel* (tel: (546) 818 767); *Gelderland* (tel: (63) 202 4075); *Flevoland* (tel: (3200) 43444).

The wooded east consists of the provinces of Overijssel, Gelderland and Flevoland.

OVERIJSSEL: The province of Overijssel is a region of great variety. In the little town of **Giethoorn**, small canals take the place of streets, and all transport is by boat. At **Wanneperveen** there is a well-equipped watersports centre. The old Hanseatic towns of **Zwolle** and **Kampen** have splendid quays and historic buildings. There are bird sanctuaries along the *Ijsselmeer.*

GELDERLAND: This is The Netherland's most extensive province, stretching from the rivers of the south to the sand dunes of the north. Gelderland is often referred to as 'the back garden of the west'. **Arnhem** is the major city. It was heavily damaged in the Second World War; indeed, its important position on the Rhine has led to it being captured, stormed and occupied on many occasions during its long history. The old part of the town has, however, been artfully rebuilt. There is a large open-air museum near Arnhem showing a collection of old farms, mills, houses and workshops, all of which have been brought together to form a splendid park. Not far from the town centre there is a zoo and a safari park.

Nearby is the **Hoge Veluwe National Park**, an extensive sandy region and a popular tourist area, which contains a game reserve (in the south), and the *Kroller-Muller Art Gallery and Museum,* with many modern sculptures and paintings (including a Van Gogh collection). One ticket enables the visitor to see all of this, and there are free bicycles available to cycle round the park. Gallery and museum opening hours: 1000-1700 Tuesday to Saturday, 1100-1700 Sunday and holidays (April to October); 1300-1700 daily (November

to March). Sculpture park opening hours: 1000-1630 Tuesday to Saturday, 1100-1630 Sunday and holidays (April to October).

Almost all the old traditional villages have been converted into holiday resorts. There are no towns of any size in the Veluwe region.

FLEVOLAND: Much of Flevoland was drained for the first time in the 1950s and 1960s, and is in many ways a museum of geography; the southern part of the province is not yet completely ready for cultivation, and visitors can witness the various stages of agricultural preparation. **Lelystad** is the main town of the region, built to a controversial design in the 1960s. Part of the province has also been designated as an overspill area for Randstad Holland. Flevoland's 1100 sq km (425 sq miles) of land include many large bungalow parks.

The South

Tourist Offices: *North Brabant* (tel: (76) 222 444); *Limburg* (tel: (4406) 13364); *Zeeland* (tel: (1180) 33000).

NORTH BRABANT: This province consists mainly of a plain, rarely more than 30m (100ft) above sea level, and is mostly agricultural. The region is known for its carnival days in February and the *Oude Stijl Jazz Festival.* The capital of the province is the city of **'s-Hertogenbosch** (non-Dutch speaking visitors will welcome the use of 'Den Bosch' as a widely accepted abbreviation) situated at the centre of a region of flat pasture land which floods each winter. *St Jan's Cathedral* is the largest in the country; the provincial museum is also interesting. Other major cities in this large and comparatively densely populated province include **Eindhoven**, an industrial centre which has grown in the last 100 years; **Breda**, an old city with many medieval buildings – it was here that the declaration was signed in 1566 which marked the start of the Dutch War of Independence; and **Tilburg**, an industrial centre which also has a large amusement and recreation park (to the north of the city) whose attractions include a haunted castle.

At **Europaweg, Kaatsheuvel,** is the *De Efteling Recreation and Adventure Park,* with approximately 50 attractions, including a large fairytale wood and a big dipper; open 1000-1800 Monday to Saturday from the end of March to mid-October.

At Museumpark 1, **Overloon,** is the *Dutch National War & Recreation Museum,* which includes displays of heavy armament in a park setting and other exhibits devoted to the history of the Second World War. Open 1000-1700 Monday to Sunday (early April to September); 1000-1800 Monday to Sunday (June to August); closed January 1, December 24-26 and December 31.

At Beekse Bergen 1, **Hilvarenbeek,** is the *De Beekse Bergen Safari Park.* Safari buses are available (continuous journey). Opening hours: 1000-1800 April to September; 1000-1630 October.

LIMBURG: The province of Limburg, the most southerly in the country, is bordered by both Belgium and Germany. The rolling hills covered with footpaths make this a good place for walking holidays. It is also famous for its cuisine. In the extreme south of the province is the city of **Maastricht**, and its position at the crossroads of three countries makes it ideal for excursions to such nearby cities as Aachen over the border in the Federal Republic of Germany. Maastricht itself is one of the oldest towns in the country, and its *Church of St Servatius* is the oldest in The Netherlands. The church treasury is particularly interesting. Further north is the town of **Roermond**, an important cultural and artistic centre dominated by the superb *Munsterkerk.*

ZEELAND: The province of Zeeland has several medieval harbour towns where some of the best seafood in Europe can be found. Most of the province lies below sea level and has been reclaimed from the sea. The region also includes several islands and peninsulas in the southwest Netherlands (Walcheren, Goeree-Overflakkee, Schouwen-Duiveland, Tholen, St Filipsland and North and South Beveland). The province has become renowned for a massive engineering project of flood barriers designed to protect the mainland and the results of reclamation from the devastating floods which periodically sweep the coastline. The countryside is intensively farmed. The capital of the province is **Middelburg**, a town which has been important since medieval times. The *Town Hall* is widely regarded as being one of the most attractive non-religious Gothic buildings in Europe. 8km (5 miles) to the north is the small town of **Veere** which retains many buildings from its golden age in the early 16th century. The North Sea port of **Flushing** (Vlissingen) is, for many British travellers arriving by boat, their first sight of The Netherlands. It is also the country's first town in another sense; in 1572 it became the first place to fly the free Dutch flag during the War of Independence.

The Coast

There are 280km (175 miles) of beaches and over 50 resorts in The Netherlands, almost all of which are easily accessible from Rotterdam, Amsterdam and The Hague. Large areas have been specially allocated for naturists and the beaches themselves are broad, sandy and gently sloping. There is surf along the coast, and those who wish to swim must be strong enough to withstand the hidden currents. Swimmers should obtain and follow local advice. In the high season, life guards are on duty along the more dangerous stretches of the coast.

SOCIAL PROFILE

FOOD & DRINK: There are few dishes which can be described as quintessentially Dutch, and those that do fall into this category are a far cry from the elaborate creations of French or Italian cuisine. Almost every large town, however, has a wide range of restaurants specialising in their own brands of international dishes including Chinese, Italian, French, Balkan, Spanish, German, American and British. Indonesian cuisine, a result of the Dutch colonisation of the East Indies, with its use of spices and exotic ingredients, is particularly delicious. A typical Dutch breakfast usually consists of several varieties of bread, thin slices of Dutch cheese, prepared meats and sausage, butter and jam or honey and often a boiled egg. A working lunch would be *koffietafel,* once again with breads, various cold cuts, cheese and conserves. There will often be a side dish of omelette, cottage pie or salad.
The most common daytime snack are *broodjes* (sandwiches) and are served in the ubiquitous sandwich bars – *broodjeswinkels.* Filled pancakes are also popular. Lightly salted 'green' herring can be bought from street stalls (they are held by the tail and slipped down into the throat). More substantial dishes are generally reserved for the Dutch themselves for the evening meal: *erwtensoep* (thick pea soup served with smoked sausage, cubes of bacon, pig's knuckle and brown or white bread), *groentensoep* (clear consommé with vegetables, vermicelli and meatballs), *hutspot* (potatoes, carrots and onions), *klapstuk* (an accompaniment of stewed lean beef), and *boerenkool met rookworst* (frost-crisped kale and potatoes served with smoked sausage). Seafood dishes are often excellent, particularly in Amsterdam or Rotterdam, and include *gebakken zeetong* (fried sole), *lekkerbekjes* (fried whiting), royal imperial oysters, shrimps, mussels, lobster and eel (smoked, filleted and served on toast or stewed or fried). Favourite Dutch desserts include *flensjes* or *pannekoeken* (25 varieties of Dutch pancake), *wafels met slagroom* (waffles with whipped cream), *poffertje* (small dough balls fried and dusted with sugar) and *spekkoek* (alternate layers of heavy buttered sponge and spices from Indonesia), which translated means 'bacon cake'. Coffee, tea, chocolate and fruit juice are drunk at breakfast. Restaurants usually have table service. Bars and cafés generally have the same, though some are self-service. **Drink:** The local spirit is *jenever* (Dutch gin), normally taken straight and chilled as a chaser with a glass of beer, but it is sometimes drunk with cola or vermouth; it comes in many varieties depending on the spices used. Favoured brands are *Bols, Bokma, De Kuyper* and *Claeryn.* Dutch beer is excellent. It is a light, gassy *pils* type beer, always served chilled, generally in small (slightly under half-pint) glasses. The most popular brand in Amsterdam is *Amstel.* Imported beers are also available, as are many other alcoholic beverages. Dutch liqueurs are excellent and include *Curaçao, Triple Sec* (similar to Cointreau), *Parfait d'Amour* and Dutch-made versions of crème de menthe, apricot brandy and anisette. There are no licensing laws and drink can be bought all day. Bars open later and stay open until the early hours of the morning at weekends.
NIGHTLIFE: Large cities have sophisticated nightclubs and discos, but late opening bars and cafés are just as popular as in provincial towns. There are theatres and cinemas in all major towns. Amsterdam is a cosmopolitan city, with some of the liveliest nightlife in Europe. There are legal casinos in Amsterdam, Breda, Eindhoven, Den Haag, Groningen, Nymegen, Rotterdam, Zandvoort, Valkenburg and Scheveningen (which claims to have the largest in Europe); all have an age limit of 'over 18' (passports must be shown).
SHOPPING: Special purchases include Delft (between The Hague and Rotterdam) blue pottery and pottery from Makkum and Workum, costume dolls, silverware

from Schoonhoven, glass and crystal from Leerdam and diamonds from Amsterdam. **Shopping hours:** 0900-1800 Monday-Friday; 1900-2100 Thursday; 0900-1700 Saturday. In the smaller towns shops are open Friday night.
Note: Bulbs and plants may not be exported except by commercial growers, or by individuals with a health certificate from the Plant Disease Service.
SPORT: Football, athletics and **cycling** are the most popular national sports. **Tennis** courts and **golf** courses are available. For local information, contact the Board of Tourism. **Sailing** on Loosdrechtse Plassen (south of Amsterdam), Friesland Lakes, Veerse Meer and the Ijsselmeer. Boats can be hired without difficulty in most places. Touring Holland's canals and rivers is popular. **Water-skiing** is not permitted on inland lakes. **Fishing** is popular throughout the country, but while no licence is needed for sea fishing, inland fishing licences are required and are available at local post offices.
SPECIAL EVENTS: The following list gives a selection of the major festivals and special events in The Netherlands during 1995:
Mar-Apr '95 *Mondrian Exhibition,* The Hague. **Mar 11-19** *The European Fine Art Fair,* Maastricht. **Mar 23-May 25** *Spring Garden of Europe,* Keukenhof. **Jun 1-30** *Holland Festival,* Amsterdam. **Jul 14-16** *North Sea Jazz Festival,* The Hague. **Jul 18-21** *Four Day March,* Nijmegen. **Aug 1-11** *World Scout Jamboree,* Dronten. **Aug 10-14** *Aug Sail '95,* Amsterdam. **Sep 8-10** *World Harbour Days,* Rotterdam.
For more information on events and festivals held in The Netherlands in 1995, contact the Press and Public Relations Officer at the Royal Netherlands Embassy, or The Netherlands Board of Tourism.
SOCIAL CONVENTIONS: It is customary to shake hands. English is spoken as a second language by many and is willingly used; many Dutch people will also speak German and French. Hospitality is very much the same as for the rest of Europe and America. It is customary to take a small gift if invited for a meal. Casual wear is widely acceptable. Men are expected to wear a suit for business and social functions. Formal wear may be required for smart restaurants, bars and clubs. Evening dress (black tie for men) is generally specified on invitation. **Tipping:** All hotels and restaurants include 15% service and VAT. It is customary to leave small change when paying a bill. Gld1-2 is usual for porters, doormen and taxi drivers. Hairdressers and barbers have inclusive service prices.

BUSINESS PROFILE

ECONOMY: The Netherlands has few natural resources other than natural gas and it relies mainly on exports of manufactured goods and agricultural products. After the USA, The Netherlands is the world's largest exporter of farm produce. Dairy products, meat, vegetables and flowers are the main products. Industry is well-developed with all kinds of heavy engineering, production of petrochemicals and plastics, pharmaceuticals, synthetic fibres and steel. There is a wide range of light industries, including the manufacturing of electronic goods, although the traditionally strong textiles sector is in decline. Most of The Netherlands' industry is concentrated in the Randstad, a small region – 5% of the total land area – bounded by the three main cities of Amsterdam, Rotterdam and The Hague. The country's economic prospects are good and The Netherlands has weathered the recession of the early 1990s well. The country has a strong base in new technological industries of computing, telecommunications and biotechnology. The main black spot on the economic front is the continuing excessive budget deficit, which the Government must act to arrest before it damages future economic development. The bulk of The Netherlands' trade takes place inside the European Union. Germany is the largest single trading partner, responsible for about 25% of The Netherlands' imports and exports. Belgium/Luxembourg, France and the UK follow.
BUSINESS: Appointments are necessary and visiting cards are exchanged. The Dutch expect a certain standard of dress for business occasions. Best months for business visits are March to May and September to November. Practical information can be obtained from the Economic Information Service in The Hague (tel: (70) 379 8933). The majority of Dutch business people speak extremely good English, and promotional literature can be disseminated in English. However, interpreters can be booked through the Director of Congress Interpreters, at Prinsegracht 993 in Amsterdam. Tel: (20) 625 2535. Fax: (20) 626 5642. Translators can be booked through the United Dutch Translation Office, Keizersgracht 560-2, 1017 EM Amsterdam. Tel: (20) 626 5889. Fax: (20) 622 2371.

Alternatively, through The Netherlands Chamber of Commerce in the country of departure. (There are Netherlands-British Chambers of Commerce in London, Manchester and The Hague, and Netherlands-US Chambers of Commerce in New York and Chicago.) There are also many secretarial agencies in The Netherlands, such as International Secretaries, who will be able to supply short-term help to visiting business travellers. The principal venue for trade fairs is the RAI Exhibition Centre in Amsterdam. **Office hours:** 0830-1700 Monday to Friday.
COMMERCIAL INFORMATION: The following organisations can offer advice: The Hague Chamber of Commerce and Industry, Konigskade 30, 2596 AA The Hague. Tel: (70) 379 5795. Fax: (70) 324 0684. Telex: 33003; *or* Amsterdam Chamber of Commerce and Industry, De Ruyterkade 5, 1013 AA Amsterdam. Tel: (20) 523 6600. Fax: (20) 523 6677.
CONFERENCES/CONVENTIONS: The largest conference and exhibition centres are RAI in Amsterdam and the Jaarbeurs in Utrecht. There are smaller centres in The Hague, Rotterdam and Maastricht, as well as many hotels with facilities. The fourth-largest conference centre in The Netherlands is Noordwijk, where the largest hotel has a helipad; this small seaside town has won prizes for its clean beaches. Amsterdam and The Hague both have business centres. For further information, contact The Netherlands Convention Bureau, Amsteldijk 166, 1079 LH Amsterdam. Tel: (20) 646 2580. Fax: (20) 644 5935. (See above for details of support services.)

CLIMATE

Mild, maritime climate. Summers are generally warm with changeable periods, but excessively hot weather is rare. Winters can be fairly cold with the possibility of some snow. Rainfall is prevalent all year.
Required clothing: European according to season with light- to medium-weights worn in warmer months and medium- to heavy-weights in winter. Rainwear is advisable all year.

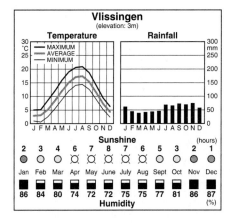

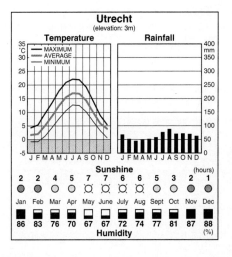

New Caledonia

200km
100mls

AUSTRALIA

Huon
Récifs
d'Entrecasteaux

Grand Récif
de Cook

NEW
CALEDONIA

Koumac
Mt Panié 1628m
Hienghène

Ouvéa
Lifou

Thio

Bourail

Maré

Coral
Sea

NOUMEA

I. des Pins
I. Walpole

Loyalty Islands

DAB-M165

☐ international airport

Location: South Pacific.

Diplomatic representation: New Caledonia is a French Overseas Territory; addresses of French Embassies, Consulates and Tourist Offices may be found in the *France* section above.

GIE Destination Nouvelle-Calédonie
BP 688, Immeuble Manhattan, 39-41 rue de Verdun, Nouméa, New Caledonia
Tel: 272 632. Fax: 274 623.

AREA: 19,103 sq km (7376 sq miles).
POPULATION: 164,173 (1989).
POPULATION DENSITY: 8.6 per sq km.
CAPITAL: Nouméa. **Population:** 65,110 (1989).
GEOGRAPHY: New Caledonia (which has been a French Overseas Territory since 1958) is an island group approximately 20,000km (12,428 miles) off the northeast coast of Australia. Mountains run the entire length of the main island. On the western side the land is relatively flat and forested by gum trees. The east coast is more mountainous with beautiful seashores fringed by tropical plants. Crystalline serpentine rock covers more than half the island. About 48km (30 miles) southeastwards lies Ile des Pins (Kunie), an island famed for its caves and grottoes containing stalactites and stalagmites. The Loyalty Group lies to the east of New Caledonia, the main islands being Ouvéa, Lifou and Maré. The remaining islands are the Chesterfield Group, Hinter, Huon Group, Matthew and Walpole.
LANGUAGE: French is the official language, but Polynesian and Melanesian are also spoken. English is also widely spoken.
RELIGION: Roman Catholic, Protestant.
TIME: GMT + 11.
ELECTRICITY: 220 volts AC, 50Hz.
COMMUNICATIONS: Telephone: IDD is available. Country code: 687. Outgoing international code: 00. There is a 24-hour service for international calls.

Timatic

Health

GALILEO/WORLDSPAN: **TI-DFT/NOU/HE**
SABRE: **TIDFT/NOU/HE**

Visa

GALILEO/WORLDSPAN: **TI-DFT/NOU/VI**
SABRE: **TIDFT/NOU/VI**

For more information on Timatic codes refer to Contents.

International calls are bookable at the Post Office (0730-1800) or through hotels. **Telex/telegram:** Telex facilities are available in most businesses and hotels. The central telex/telegram agency is at rue Eugène Porcheron, Nouméa. **Post:** Airmail to Western Europe takes up to a week. The Post Office, located on rue Eugène Porcheron, is open 0715-1115 and 1200-1800. **Press:** Newspapers are published in French and include *Les Nouvelles Calédoniennes*.
BBC World Service and Voice of America frequencies: From time to time these change. See the section *How to Use this Book* for more information.
BBC:

MHz	17.83	15.34	11.95	9.740

Voice of America:

MHz	18.82	15.18	9.525	1.735

PASSPORT/VISA

Regulations and requirements may be subject to change at short notice, and you are advised to contact the appropriate diplomatic or consular authority before finalising travel arrangements. Details of these may be found at the head of this country's entry. Any numbers in the chart refer to the footnotes below.

	Passport Required?	Visa Required?	Return Ticket Required?
Full British	Yes	No	Yes
BVP	Not valid	-	-
Australian	Yes	Yes	Yes
Canadian	Yes	No/2	Yes
USA	Yes	No/2	Yes
Other EU (As of 31/12/94)	Yes/1	No	Yes
Japanese	Yes	No/2	Yes

PASSPORTS: Valid passport required by all except [1] nationals of France carrying a valid national ID card or passport expired a maximum of five years.
British Visitors Passport: Not accepted.
VISAS: Required by all except:
(a) nationals of France for an unlimited period, other EU nationals for a stay not exceeding 3 months;
(b) nationals of Andorra, Austria, Iceland, Monaco, Norway, San Marino, Sweden, Switzerland and Vatican City for a stay not exceeding 3 months;
(c) nationals of Brunei, Cyprus, Czech Republic, Finland, Hungary, South Korea, Liechtenstein, Malta, New Zealand, Poland, Singapore, Slovak Republic and Slovenia for a stay not exceeding 1 month;
(d) [2] nationals of Canada, Japan and the USA for a stay not exceeding 1 month.
Note: Visa requirements for other nationals wishing to visit New Caledonia are subject to frequent change at short notice and travellers should contact the French Consulate General for up-to-date information.
Types of visa: Tourist and Transit (cost and validity on application).
Application to: French Consulate General. For addresses, see top of *France* entry.
Application requirements: (a) 3 completed application forms. (b) 3 passport-size photos. (c) Onward ticket.
Working days required: Usually 1 day, although up to 1 month depending on nationality of applicant.
Temporary residence: Contact French Consulate General (or Consular section at Embassy).

MONEY

Currency: French Pacific Franc (CFP Fr) = 100 centimes. Notes are in denominations of CFP Fr10,000, 5000, 1000 and 500. Coins are in denominations of CFP Fr100, 50, 20, 10, 5, 2 and 1, and 50 centimes. New Caledonia is part of the French Monetary Area.
Currency exchange: Exchange facilities are available at the airport and at trade banks.
Credit cards: American Express and Visa are widely accepted; Access/Mastercard and Diners Club have more limited use. Check with your credit card company for details of merchant acceptability and other services which may be available.
Exchange rate indicators: The following figures are included as a guide to the movement of the French Pacific Franc against Sterling and the US Dollar:

Date:	Oct '92	Sep '93	Jan '94	Jan '95
£1.00=	150.0	156.25	158.00	152.40
$1.00=	94.52	102.32	106.79	97.41

Currency restrictions: Import and export restrictions for currency are the same as those for France (see *Money* in the *France* entry above).
Banking hours: 0730-1545 Monday to Friday.

DUTY FREE

The following goods may be imported into New Caledonia without incurring customs duty:
200 cigarettes or 50 cigars or 250g of tobacco; 1 bottle of alcoholic beverage; a reasonable amount of perfume for personal use.

PUBLIC HOLIDAYS

Jan 1 '95 New Year's Day. **Apr 17** Easter Monday. **May 1** Labour Day. **May 8** Liberation Day. **May 25** Ascension Day. **Jun 5** Whit Monday. **Jul 14** Fall of the Bastille. **Nov 11** Armistice Day. **Dec 25** Christmas Day. **Jan 1 '96** New Year's Day. **Apr 8** Easter Monday.

HEALTH

Regulations and requirements may be subject to change at short notice, and you are advised to contact your doctor well in advance of your intended date of departure. Any numbers in the chart refer to the footnotes below.

	Special Precautions?	Certificate Required?
Yellow Fever	No	1
Cholera	No	2
Typhoid & Polio	Yes	-
Malaria	No	-
Food & Drink	3	-

[1]: A yellow fever vaccination certificate is required from travellers over one year of age arriving from infected areas.
[2]: Travellers arriving from infected areas do not require cholera vaccination and will not be given chemoprophylaxis. They are required, however, to fill out a form for use by the Health Service.
[3]: Mains water is normally chlorinated, and whilst relatively safe may cause mild abdominal upsets. Bottled water is available and is advised for the first few weeks of the stay. Drinking water outside main cities and towns may be contaminated and sterilisation is advisable. Milk is pasteurised and dairy products are safe for consumption. Local meat, poultry, seafood, fruit and vegetables are generally considered safe to eat.
Health care: Nouméa has one public hospital, three private clinics and an adequate selection of chemists. Hotels can generally recommend an English-speaking doctor or dentist. Health insurance is recommended.

TRAVEL - International

AIR: New Caledonia's national airline is *Air Calédonie International (SB)*.
Approximate flight time: From London to Nouméa is 26 hours, including three stopovers, but this may increase to 30 hours, depending on the day of travel.
International airport: *Nouméa (NOU)* (La Tontouta), 48km (30 miles) from the city (travel time – 60 minutes). Airport facilities include post office (0700-1100 and 1200-1600), bureau de change, duty-free shops (available for scheduled flights), bar, restaurant and car rental (*Avis* and *Hertz*). Taxi and coach services are available to the city.
SEA: International port is Nouméa, served by the following shipping lines: *Chandris, CTC, P&O, Princess Cruises, Sitmar* and *Polish Ocean Lines*.

TRAVEL - Internal

AIR: Domestic flights run by *Air Caledonie (TY)*, maintaining regular services from Nouméa to airfields on the island, and the other smaller islands. The principal local airport is *Magenta Airport*, 6km (4 miles) from Nouméa city centre. From here *Air Caledonie* operates regular flights to Touhó (east coast), Koné, Koumac, Belep (west coast), and to the neighbouring Ile des Pins and the Loyalty Islands: Maré, Ouvéa, Lifou and Tiga.
Charter flights: Light aircraft are available from *Air Caledonie* for charter; for further details, contact *Air Caledonie, Aviazur*.
Approximate flight times: From Nouméa to *Kunie* (Ile des Pins) is 30 minutes; to *Lifou* is 50 minutes; to *Maré* is 50 minutes; to *Ouvéa* is 45 minutes; to *Tiga* is 45 minutes; to *Koné* is 35 minutes; to *Touhó* is 1 hour 5 minutes; to *Koumac* is 1 hour 40 minutes and to *Belep* is 2 hours 35 minutes.
SEA: There are regular sea links to the other smaller islands from Grande Terre (for further details, contact the local authorities).
ROAD: The road system is limited. Traffic drives on the right. **Bus:** These are available throughout the island. A mail bus makes a round trip of the island. **Taxi:** Charges are for time and distance. There is a surcharge after 1900 and on Sundays. **Car hire:** *Avis, Budget, Hertz* and *AB*

WORLD TRAVEL ATLAS

As well as a complete set of conventional plates, the World Travel Atlas contains a wealth of specialist maps and charts designed specifically for use by the travel trade and students of travel and tourism.
The only atlas of its kind, the World Travel Atlas has quickly established itself as an essential reference work for all those connected with the world of travel.

Caribbean Resorts ● World Cruise Routes ● Spanish Resorts ● World Climate ● World Natural and Cultural Heritage Maps ● World Health ● World Driving ● Italian Resorts ● International Tourism Statistics ● Main Airports of the World ● Greek Islands ● UK & Mediterranean clean beaches

COLUMBUS PRESS

Call Columbus Press for further details on (0171) 417 0700 or fax (0171) 417 0710.

Location and local *Mencar* all have representatives in the capital. Special vehicles (called 'Baby Cars') are available for hire 0600-1930. **Documentation:** International or national driving permit is required. **JOURNEY TIMES:** The following chart gives approximate journey times (in hours and minutes) from Nouméa to other major cities/towns in New Caledonia.

	Air	Road
Bourail	-	2.10
Hienghene	-	5.10
Koné	0.35	3.30
Poindimie	-	4.10
Thio	-	2.00
Tontouta	-	0.45
Touhó	1.05	4.40

ACCOMMODATION

There is a very good selection of accommodation available with hotels, country inns and rural lodgings.
HOTELS: Hotels are mostly small and intimate. Prices range from moderate to expensive. Modern hotels have been built at Anse Vata and the Baie des Citrons and there is also new bungalow-style accommodation in remoter parts of the main island and in the outer islands. For further information, contact Union de l'Hôtellerie Touristique de Nouvelle Caledonie, c/o Kuendi Beach Motel, BP 404, Nouméa. Tel: 278 989. Fax: 276 033.
CAMPING: Permission should be sought from landowners before setting up camp.
YOUTH HOSTELS: Situated outside the city is a hostel with dormitories and communal facilities at reasonable rates. Non-YHA members are also accommodated.

RESORTS & EXCURSIONS

Grande Terre – Nouméa

Nouméa, the capital, overlooks one of the world's largest sheltered natural harbours. It is a busy little city with a population composed of many racial groups: French, Melanesian and Indonesian amongst others. Minibuses and *Le Petit Train* are probably the best ways of seeing the city and its suburbs. The centre of the network is the bus depot on the *Baie de la Moselle.*
Attractions in the city include *St Joseph's Cathedral,* the *Berheim Library,* the market, many old colonial houses and the *Aquarium,* one of the world's leading centres of marine scientific research. Nearby, the *South Pacific Commission Building* houses a collection of native handicrafts from all over the South Seas. The *New Caledonia Museum* is open Tuesday to Saturday, and also contains many local handicrafts and ornaments. 4km (2.5 miles) from the capital is the *Botanical Park,* the home of over 700 species of animals.
Near Nouméa is the *Amedée Lighthouse,* constructed in Paris during the reign of Napoleon III and shipped to New Caledonia in pieces. It is situated in a coral reef 18km (11 miles) from the capital. There are excellent opportunities for swimming and scuba diving in the lagoon.
East of the capital is *Mont-Doré,* a mountain surrounded by magnificent coastal scenery. On the way, stops can be made at the Melanesian village of **St Louis,** and the *Plum Lookout* for a spectacular view across the surrounding reef.

The Coast

The West Coast: 170km (105 miles) from Nouméa is **Bourail,** where there are many elaborate and beautiful caves and rock formations shaped by the Pacific breakers. Further north is the ancient site of *Koné,* where decorated pottery dating back to the 10th century BC has been discovered. From the town of **Koumac,** a new road has been constructed which loops round the top of the island. The scenery consists of pure white sand beaches and offshore atolls, backed by dense rainforest.
The East Coast: The new road takes one to *Hienghéne,* which has a lagoon surrounded by 120m-high (400ft) black cliffs. **Poindimié,** the main town of the east coast, is further south. Nearby is **Touhó,** overlooked by a 500m (1640ft) peak. The region is dotted with churches and Melanesian villages, forests, coconut palms and beautiful beaches. At the southern point of this coast is **Yaté,** a town surrounded by lakes, waterfalls and rich wooded countryside. Day trips are available from the capital.

Ile des Pins

Discovered and named the Isle of Pines by Captain Cook in 1774, the Ile des Pins lies some 70km (45 miles) off the southeast coast of Grande Terre. This exceedingly beautiful island has many white sand beaches and turquoise lagoons and is lush with rainforests, pines, orchids and ferns. For ancient man it was also clearly an attractive home: archaeological excavations have revealed settlements over 4000 years old. The island was also briefly used as a convict settlement during the 19th century following the Paris Commune. The giant ruins of the jail can still be seen, though now half-strangled by the dense vegetation. There are many rural lodges on the island which offer simple but excellent accommodation on or near the beaches. Day trips are available from Nouméa to **Vao,** the main town on Ile des Pins.

The Loyalty Islands

This archipelago lies 100km (60 miles) off the east coast of New Caledonia, and is widely regarded as being superb for scuba diving and spear-fishing.
Maré Island, the furthest south, has an area of 650 sq km (250 sq miles). Most of the population live in the town of **Tadine.**
Lifou Island, the largest of the three with 1150 sq km (445 sq miles), has over 7000 inhabitants. The main town is **Chépénétié.**
Ouvéa Island is 130 sq km (50 sq miles), but is rarely more than 3 or 4km (2 or 2.5 miles) wide. The lagoon is particularly rich in fish. Almost all of the population live in **Fayavé.**

SOCIAL PROFILE

FOOD & DRINK: The choice of eating-places and food on New Caledonia is excellent; costs vary from moderate to expensive. Fine food is a passion and *Cordon Bleu* cuisine is widely available. Gourmet restaurants and bistros serve French, Italian, Spanish, Indonesian, African and Chinese cooking. Dishes include Pacific spiny lobsters, prawns, crabs or mangrove oysters and salads of raw fish (marinated in lime juice). An island speciality is *bougna;* roast pig, fish or chicken wrapped in banana leaves and cooked on hot stones covered with sand. First-class delicatessens and grocers in Nouméa and at Anse Vata Beach provide a wide choice of picnic fare. Wine is imported from France and there is a very good selection.
NIGHTLIFE: There are plenty of discos and also a casino, the only one in the South Pacific, situated at Anse Beach. Nightclubs in Nouméa are lively with both European and local floorshows. There are also several cinemas which show French films.

SHOPPING: In Nouméa boutiques sell fashionable French clothes, mainly casual but sometimes *haute couture.* Further purchases include luxury French goods such as perfume, jewellery and footwear, and silk scarves, sandals and handbags from Italy can also be found. Duty-free items are also sold. Local items include curios made of shells, coral, woodcarving, ceramics, hand-painted materials, aloha shirts, tapa cloth and records of Polynesian music. Discounts may be obtained in duty-free shops. **Shopping hours:** 0730-1100 and 1400-1800 Monday to Friday; 0730-1100 Saturday.
SPORT: Watersports: Scuba diving and **snorkelling** facilities provide compressors, tanks, wet suits, regulators and qualified instructors. For further details, contact the Nauti Club, Kuto, Ile des Pins and the Amédeé Diving Club. Special facilities for **fishing** are available on Turtle Island. The coral barrier reef off the shore of Nouméa is excellent for underwater spearfishing. For further details, contact The Spear Fishing Club in Nouméa. Fine beaches throughout the islands are supplemented by hotel pools and the Olympic-size **swimming** pool behind the Château Royal Casino is open daily. **Tennis:** On presentation of a tourist card, visitors can play tennis on the courts at Mont Coffyn Tennis Club; there are also courts at Château Royal Casino at Anse Vata beach. **Squash:** The new club at the Baie des Pêcheurs welcomes visitors. Equipment is available on the premises. **Horseriding:** Horses are kept at Club d'Etrier where visitors must be introduced by a member. Melanesian men and women wearing bright clothes play weekend **cricket** in the squares. Arrangements can be made in the capital for **hiking** trips into the interior.
SOCIAL CONVENTIONS: There is a casual atmosphere, and local traditions still prevail alongside European customs. Casual wear is the norm, but smart restaurants require a less casual style of dress. Long trousers are required for men at night in restaurants and clubs. Only the casino requires a jacket and tie. **Tipping:** There is absolutely no tipping.

BUSINESS PROFILE

ECONOMY: The mainstays of the country's economy are mining, fishing, tourism, forestry and agriculture. A certain amount of light industry is currently being developed. After Canada and the USA, New Caledonia is the world's largest producer of nickel. The economy is relatively prosperous, although recent economic growth has been inhibited by the low world price for nickel, which accounts for nearly 90% of export revenue. Standards of living are nonetheless fairly high. The agricultural sector produces cereals, fruit and vegetables, as well as copra and coffee for export. The country is an Associate Member of the EU. France is the largest trading partner, responsible for approximately half of all imports and exports.
BUSINESS: Appointments should be made. Business people generally work long hours and take long lunch breaks, but business lunches are rare as most businessmen go home at lunchtime. Prices should be quoted in French or French Pacific Francs. Best time to visit is May to October. **Office hours:** 0730-1130 and 1330-1730 Monday to Friday; 0730-1130 Saturday.
COMMERCIAL INFORMATION: The following organisation can offer advice: Chambre de Commerce et d'Industrie, BP M3, Nouméa Cédex. Tel: 272 551. Fax: 278 114.

CLIMATE

Warm, subtropical climate. The cool season is from June to September and the hottest period from October to May. The main rains are between January and March. The seasons are less defined on the east coast than the west. Climate is tempered by trade winds.

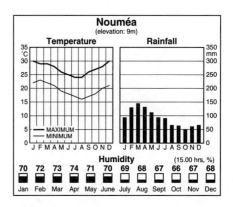

New Zealand

300km
150mls

North Cape

Whangarei

Auckland □ **North Island**

Hamilton

Rotorua Lake

Mt Egmont 2518m ▲ L. Taupo

Wanganui • Napier

Cook Strait

Palmerston North

□ **WELLINGTON**

T a s m a n S e a

Nelson

NEW ZEALAND

Mt Cook 3764m ▲ □ **Christchurch**

Southern Alps

Canterbury Plain

Timaru

South Island

Queenstown

Dunedin

SOUTH PACIFIC OCEAN

Invercargill

Stewart I.

← Chatham I

DAB-M166

AUSTRALIA

□ *international airport*

Location: South Pacific.

New Zealand Tourism Board
PO Box 95, 256 Lambton Quay, Wellington, New Zealand
Tel: (4) 472 8860. Fax: (4) 478 1736.
New Zealand High Commission
New Zealand House, 80 Haymarket, London SW1Y 4TQ
Tel: (0171) 930 8422 *or* (0891) 200 288 (recorded visa information; calls are charged at the higher rate of 39/49p per minute). Fax: (0171) 839 4580. Telex: 24368.
Opening hours: 1000-1200 and 1400-1600 Monday to Friday.
New Zealand Tourism Board
New Zealand House, 80 Haymarket, London SW1Y 4TQ
Tel: (0839) 300 900. (Recorded information line; calls are charged at the higher rate of 39/49p per minute).
Opening hours: 0900-1700 Monday to Friday.
British High Commission
PO Box 1812, 44 Hill Street, Wellington 1, New Zealand
Tel: (4) 472 6049. Fax: (4) 471 1974. Telex: 3325 (a/b UKREP NZ).
Consulates in: Auckland and Christchurch.
New Zealand Embassy
37 Observatory Circle, NW, Washington, DC 20008
Tel: (202) 328 4800. Fax: (202) 667 5227.
Consulate General in: Los Angeles (tel: (310) 477 8241).
New Zealand Tourist Board
Suite 300, 501 Santa Monica Boulevard, Santa Monica, CA 90401
Tel: (310) 395 7480. Fax: (310) 395 5453.
Embassy of the United States of America
PO Box 1190, 29 Fitzherbert Terrace, Thorndon, Wellington, New Zealand
Tel: (4) 472 2068. Fax: (4) 471 2380 *or* 723 3537.
New Zealand High Commission
Suite 727, Metropolitan House, 99 Bank Street, Ottawa, Ontario K1P 5G4
Tel: (613) 238 5991. Fax: (613) 238 5707.
New Zealand Tourism Board
Suite 1200, 888 Dunsmuir Street, Vancouver, British Columbia V6C 3K4
Tel: (604) 684 2117. Fax: (604) 684 1265.
Canadian High Commission
PO Box 12049, 61 Molesworth Street, Thorndon, Wellington 1, New Zealand
Tel: (4) 473 9577. Fax: (4) 471 2082.
Consulate in: Auckland.

AREA: 270,534 sq km (104,454 sq miles).
POPULATION: 3,454,900 (1992 estimate).
POPULATION DENSITY: 12.8 per sq km.

CAPITAL: Wellington. **Population:** 325,682 (1991 estimate). Auckland, with a population of 885,571 (1991 estimate), is the largest city in the country.
GEOGRAPHY: New Zealand is 1930km (1200 miles) southeast of Australia and consists of two major islands, the North Island (114,470 sq km/44,197 sq miles) and the South Island (150,660 sq km/58,170 sq miles) which are separated by Cook Strait. Stewart Island (1750 sq km/676 sq miles) is located immediately south of the South Island, and the Chatham Islands lie 675km (420 miles) to the southeast of the North Island. Going from north to south temperatures decrease. Compared to its huge neighbour Australia, New Zealand's three islands make up a country that is relatively small (about 20% more land mass than the British Isles). Two-thirds of the country is mountainous, a region of swift flowing rivers, deep alpine lakes and dense subtropical forest known as 'bush'. The country's largest city, Auckland, is situated on the peninsula which forms the northern part of North Island. The southern part of North Island is characterised by fertile coastal plains rising up to volcanic peaks. Around Rotorua, 240km (149 miles) south of Auckland, there is violent thermal activity in the form of geysers, pools of boiling mud, springs of hot mineral water, silica terraces, coloured craters and hissing fumaroles which make Rotorua a world-famous tourist attraction. The South Island is larger, although only about one-third of the population live there. The Southern Alps extend the whole length of the island, culminating in Mount Cook, the country's highest peak. In the same region are the Franz Josef and Fox glaciers.
There are also four Associated Territories: The **Cook Islands**, about 3500km (2175 miles) northeast of New Zealand; **Niue**, 920km (570 miles) west of the Cook Islands (area 260 sq km/100 sq miles); **Tokelau**, three atolls about 960km (600 miles) northwest of Niue (area 12 sq km/4 sq miles); and the **Ross Dependency**, which consists of over 700,000 sq km (270,270 sq miles) of the Antarctic.
Note: For further information on the **Cook Islands** and **Niue**, see their individual entries.
LANGUAGE: The official languages are English and Maori.
RELIGION: 27% Anglican, 14% Roman Catholic; and other Christian denominations.
TIME: GMT + 12 (GMT + 13 from the last week in March to the first week in October).
ELECTRICITY: 230 volts AC, 50Hz. Most hotels provide 110-volt AC sockets (rated at 20 watts) for electric razors only.
COMMUNICATIONS: Telephone: IDD is available. Country code: 64. Outgoing international code: 00. **Fax:** Many hotels provide facilities. **Telegram/telex:** Telegrams can be sent from all post offices or telephoned through at any time. All main post offices and some hotels have public telex facilities. **Post:** Post offices are open 0900-1700 Monday to Friday. Airmail to Western Europe takes four to five days and to the USA three to ten days. **Press:** The English-language daily newspapers with the highest circulation include *New Zealand Herald, The Press* and *Evening Post.*
BBC World Service and Voice of America frequencies: From time to time these change. See the section *How to Use this Book* for more information.
BBC:

MHz	17.83	15.34	11.95	9.740

Voice of America:

MHz	11.72	9.525	5.985	1.735

PASSPORT/VISA

Regulations and requirements may be subject to change at short notice, and you are advised to contact the appropriate diplomatic or consular authority before finalising travel arrangements. Details of these may be found at the head of this country's entry. Any numbers in the chart refer to the footnotes below.

	Passport Required?	Visa Required?	Return Ticket Required?
Full British	Yes	No	Yes
BVP	Not valid	-	-
Australian	Yes	No	No
Canadian	Yes	No	Yes
USA	Yes	No	Yes
Other EU (As of 31/12/94)	Yes	No/1	Yes
Japanese	Yes	No	Yes

PASSPORTS: Valid passport required by all. Citizens of countries whose governments are not recognised by New Zealand should check that their documentation is acceptable. Passports should be valid for at least 3 months beyond the intended period of stay.
British Visitors Passport: Not acceptable.
VISAS: Required by all except:

(a) nationals of the UK and other British passport holders for visits of up to 6 months providing they have evidence of the right of abode;
(b) nationals of EU countries for visits up to 3 months, but note **[1]** that Portuguese nationals *must* have right of residence in Portugal and French nationals *must* be residing in France (see *(d)* below);
(c) nationals of Austria, Brunei, Canada, Finland, Iceland, Indonesia, Japan, South Korea, Kiribati, Liechtenstein, Malaysia, Malta, Monaco, Nauru, Norway, Singapore, Sweden, Switzerland, Thailand, Tuvalu and the USA (except US Samoans, who *do* require a visa) for visits of up to 3 months;
(d) French citizens residing in Tahiti or New Caledonia for visits of up to 30 days;
(e) nationals of Australia and New Zealand Associated Territories: Cook Islands, Niue and Tokelau.
Types of visa: Visitors (£25), Work (£50) and Residents (£275).
Validity: Variable.
Application to: Consulate (or Consular section at Embassy or Immigration Service at High Commission). For addresses, see top of entry.
Application requirements: (a) Application form(s). (b) 1 passport-size photo. (c) Valid passport. (d) Sufficient funds for duration of stay – NZ$1000 for each person for every month or NZ$400 if the accommodation is already paid for. (e) Onward ticket. (f) Company/sponsor letter for Business visas. (g) Fee.
Working days required: 21.
Temporary residence: Maximum 6 months stay without a visa, 12 months with visa.

MONEY

Currency: New Zealand Dollar (NZ$) = 100 cents. Notes are in denominations of NZ$100, 50, 20, 10 and 5. Coins are in denominations of NZ$2 and 1, and 50, 20, 10 and 5 cents.
Currency exchange: Exchange facilities are available throughout New Zealand.
Credit cards: Access/Mastercard, American Express, Diners Club and Visa are accepted. Check with your credit card company for details of merchant acceptability and other services which may be available.
Travellers cheques: Can be exchanged at official rates at trading banks and large hotels.
Exchange rate indicators: The following figures are included as a guide to the movements of the New Zealand Dollar against Sterling and the US Dollar:

Date:	Oct '92	Sep '93	Jan '94	Jan '95
£1.00=	2.94	2.81	2.65	2.44
$1.00=	1.85	1.84	1.79	1.56

Currency restrictions: There are no restrictions on the import and export of foreign or local currency.
Banking hours: 1000-1600 Monday to Friday.

DUTY FREE

The following items may be imported into New Zealand without incurring customs duty:
*200 cigarettes or 50 cigars or 250g tobacco or a mixture of up to 250g; *4.5 litres of wine or beer; *1.125 litres or 40oz spirits or liqueurs; *a reasonable amount of perfume for personal use; goods to a total value of NZ$700.
Note [*]: Only for persons over 17 years of age.
Prohibited items: The New Zealand government publishes a full list of personal items allowed for import without incurring duty such as jewellery and photographic or sporting equipment (firearms, however, require a police permit). Visitors are advised not to take fruit or plant material with them.

PUBLIC HOLIDAYS

Jan 1-3 '95 New Year. **Feb 6** Waitangi Day. **Apr 14-17** Easter. **Apr 25** ANZAC Day. **Jun 5** Queen's Birthday. **Oct 23** Labour Day. **Dec 25-26** Christmas. **Jan 1-2 '96** New Year. **Feb 6** Waitangi Day. **Apr 5-8** Easter. **Apr 25** ANZAC Day.

Health	
GALILEO/WORLDSPAN: **TI-DFT/WLG/HE**	
SABRE: **TIDFT/WLG/HE**	

Visa	
GALILEO/WORLDSPAN: **TI-DFT/WLG/VI**	
SABRE: **TIDFT/WLG/VI**	

Timatic

For more information on Timatic codes refer to Contents.

Note: Each province also observes its particular anniversary day as a holiday.

HEALTH

Regulations and requirements may be subject to change at short notice, and you are advised to contact your doctor well in advance of your intended date of departure. Any numbers in the chart refer to the footnotes below.

	Special Precautions?	Certificate Required?
Yellow Fever	No	No
Cholera	No	No
Typhoid & Polio	No	-
Malaria	No	-
Food & Drink	1	-

[1]: Tap water is considered safe to drink. Milk is pasteurised and dairy products are safe for consumption. Local meat, poultry, seafood, fruit and vegetables are generally considered safe to eat.
Health care: Medical facilities, both public and private, are of a high standard. There are no snakes or dangerous wild animals in New Zealand. Sandflies are prevalent in some cases, but these can be effectively countered with insect repellent. The only poisonous creature is the very rare Katipo spider. Should visitors need drugs or pharmaceutical supplies outside normal shopping hours they should refer to 'Urgent Pharmacies' in the local telephone directory for the location of the nearest pharmacy or check with their hotel. Medical insurance is advised.

TRAVEL - International

AIR: New Zealand's national airline is *Air New Zealand (NZ)*.
For free advice on air travel, call the Air Travel Advisory Bureau on (0171) 636 5000 (London) *or* (0161) 832 2000 (Manchester).
Approximate flight times: From *London* to Auckland is 28 hours, to Wellington 30 hours and to Christchurch 30 hours 30 minutes.
From *Los Angeles* to Auckland is 12 hours 45 minutes.

From *New York* to Auckland is 17 hours 45 minutes.
From *Singapore* to Auckland is 11 hours 15 minutes.
From *Sydney* to Auckland is 3 hours 20 minutes.
International airports: *Auckland (AKL)* (Mangere), 22.5km (14 miles) south of the city (travel time – 40 minutes). Airport facilities include outgoing duty-free shop with a full range of items, car hire *(Avis, Budget* and *Hertz)* and bank/currency exchange facilities open to cover the times of all international flights. A coach service runs every 30 minutes on the hour and half-hour 0700-2300 to the downtown terminal. Taxis are available to the city with a surcharge after 2200 and at weekends.
Christchurch (CHC) airport, 10km (6 miles) northwest of the city (travel time – 20 minutes). Airport facilities include outgoing duty-free shop with a full range of items, car hire *(Avis, Budget* and *Hertz)* and bank/currency exchange facilities open to cover the times of all international flights. Bus no. 24 runs every 30 minutes 0630-2200. Taxis are available to the city with a surcharge after 2200.
Wellington (WLG) (Rongotai), 8km (5 miles) southeast of the city (travel time – 30 minutes). Airport facilities include an outgoing duty-free shop with a full range of items, car hire *(Avis* and *Hertz)* and bank/currency exchange facilities open to cover the times of all international flights. A coach service runs every 20 minutes 0600-2200. Taxis are available to the city with a surcharge after 2200.
Departure tax: NZ$20 on all departures. Transit passengers and children under two years of age are exempt.
SEA: The principal ports are Auckland, Wellington, Lyttleton, Dunedin, Picton and Opua, which are served by the following shipping lines: *Ben Shipping, CTC, Port Royal Interocean, P&O* and *Sitmar. Polish Ocean Lines* sail from Europe, and *Farrell Lines* from the USA. Inter-island rail ferry service is available between Wellington and Picton several times daily.

TRAVEL - Internal

AIR: *Air New Zealand (NZ), Mount Cook Airlines (NM)* and *Ansett New Zealand (ZQ)* operate domestic flights between the major airports (see above), as well as *Palmerston North, Dunedin, Napier, Queenstown, Rotorua* and 27 other airports throughout the two islands.

RAIL: There is a reliable but limited rail service on 5000km (3106 miles) of railway with many routes of great scenic attraction. Express services run between Auckland and Wellington (daytime and overnight), Christchurch and Invercargill, Christchurch and Picton, Christchurch and Greymouth, Auckland and Rotorua, Auckland and Tauranga and Wellington and Napier. There are dining cars on some trains, but there are no sleeping cars on overnight services. All services are one-class travel only.
Travel passes: Allow unlimited travel on *New Zealand Railways'* train, coach and ferry services.
ROAD: There are 96,000km (59,650 miles) of roads. Traffic drives on the left. **Coach:** Modern coaches operate scheduled services throughout the country. It is advisable to make reservations for seats. Contact an Intercity Travel Centre for details. A *Kiwi Coach Pass* is available for use on *Mt Cook Landliner Services* and other principal operators' services. *Newmans Coachlines* run a flexipass. It is advisable to make reservations for seats. Contact the Tourism Board for details. **Bus:** There are regional bus networks which serve most parts of the country. **Taxi:** There are metered taxis throughout the country. **Car hire:** Major international firms and local firms have offices at airports and most major cities and towns. The minimum age for driving a rented car is 21.
Documentation: Domestic permits are accepted from the following states: Australia, Canada, Germany, Fiji, Namibia, The Netherlands, South Africa, Switzerland, the UK and the USA. Otherwise an International Driving Permit is required.
URBAN: Good local bus services are provided in the main towns; there are also trolleybuses in Wellington. Both Auckland and Wellington have zonal fares with pre-purchase tickets and day passes.
JOURNEY TIMES: The following chart gives approximate journey times (in hours and minutes) from Wellington to other major cities/towns in New Zealand.

	Air	Road	Rail	Sea
Auckland	1.00	9.00	10.00	-
Rotorua	1.15	3.30	6.00	-
Napier	1.00	6.30	6.00	-
N. Plymouth	1.00	8.30	-	-
Palmerston N.	0.30	2.30	2.30	-
Picton	0.30	-	-	3.00
Christchurch	0.45	*7.20	*5.20	-
Dunedin	1.20	*12.20	*11.20	-

Queenstown	2.05	*15.40	-	-
Bay of Islands	2.00	14.00	-	-
Nelson	0.20	6.00	-	-
Mt Cook	2.00	10.00	-	-
Glaciers (west coast)	§1.45	8.20	-	-

Notes: [*] Plus ferry crossing of 3 hours. [§] Plus 2.30 hours by road.

ACCOMMODATION

MOTELS & HOTELS: New Zealand has hotels and motels of international standard, moderately priced modern hotels, private hotels and guest-houses. Rates on the whole are cheaper in rural areas, while every city and town has low-cost motels or hotels. Low-cost motels have grown greatly in popularity in recent years, and most have a wide range of facilities; they offer self-catering, and account for 75% of the accommodation. Most belong to the Motel Association of New Zealand (Inc), PO Box 1697, Wellington. Tel: (4) 385 8011. Fax: (4) 385 8026. Some establishments belong to the Hotel Association of New Zealand, PO Box 503, 8th Floor, Education House, 178-182 Willis Street, Wellington. Tel: (4) 385 1369. Fax: (4) 384 8044. **Disabled travellers:** The Tourist Department can supply a publication, *New Zealand Access: Guide for the Less Mobile Traveller,* which lists suitable accommodation and facilities.
Grading: Hotels are graded from 1-4 stars. Motels are graded on a separate scale of 1-5 stars.
CAMPING/CARAVANNING: There are many campsites throughout New Zealand. Rates and facilities vary considerably. It is advisable to make advance reservations from December to Easter. *New Zealand Motor Camps* offer communal washing, cooking and other facilities at main resorts. Visitors are required to provide their own tents and equipment at these camps, but equipment can be hired from a number of companies. Occupants are usually required to supply their own linen, blankets and cutlery. A number of companies can arrange motor camper rentals, with a range of fully equipped vehicles; full details can be obtained from the New Zealand Tourism Board.
FARM HOLIDAYS: Many farms offer accommodation to visitors.
YOUTH HOSTELS: The Youth Hostel Association runs hostels throughout the country and in most towns, and reservations can be made in advance from December to March. The association's address is PO Box 68149, Auckland. Tel: (9) 309 2802. Fax: (9) 373 5083. In the major cities there are alternative cheap forms of accommodation, for example backpackers' hostels, which are located all over the country.

RESORTS & EXCURSIONS

In order to simplify this section, the two main islands are described separately. However, North and South Islands may easily be incorporated into a single visit, as travel between the two, either by boat or plane, is quite straightforward (see the *Travel – Internal* section above). For information on Niue, an island associated with New Zealand almost midway between Tonga and Samoa, please refer to the separate entry later in the *World Travel Guide.*

North Island

The visitor is most likely to arrive in New Zealand at its largest city, the business centre of **Auckland**. The city's low-rise buildings spread over the neighbouring low hills, and there is a fine harbour to explore. Recent developments include new restaurants along Parnell and Ponsonby Road. The city offers good shopping and has a handsome university section, while an exploration of its suburbs is recommended – the beach and town of **Takapuna** just across the water, for example. Public transport is swift and cheap with a flat-fare system. The driver will often provide useful information.
The beaches of **Northland**, the peninsula stretching away from Auckland, are particularly popular with swimmers and sunbathers. There are many small beach settlements throughout the country, ideal for a quiet and relaxing holiday.
Wellington, the capital city, has its buildings grouped along a series of steep hillsides overlooking a deep harbour. A compact city, it has many good shops and pedestrian streets, while several of its restaurants and hotels offer splendid views across to the nearby South Island. Wellington is the terminus for ferries and for trips to the islands in the straits.
Since the country is scattered with volcanoes, mostly extinct, it would be a great pity to miss the famous **Rotorua** which, along with the glow-worm caves of *Waitomo,* is probably one of the best-known tourist attractions in the country. Rotorua presents a good base for exploring the geysers and the large thermal zone of the North Island. There are also other areas of geyser activity in the region – one such is *Orakei Korako,* about 30 minutes from Rotorua. Rotorua is also a major centre of Maori culture and there is an arts centre where young Maoris continue the tradition of carving wood and stone. Souvenirs can be purchased, and visitors might also see the shy, nocturnal kiwi.
Besides Rotorua, four active volcanoes may also be visited in the North Island and other extinct volcanoes, such as *Mount Egmont* on the west coast, add a unique note of exotic distinction to the country's scenery. Unspoilt regions such as the *Coromandel Peninsula* will also appeal to lovers of wild beauty. *Lake Taupo,* in the very middle of the North Island, offers much sport for fishing enthusiasts, and in the northeast coastal towns there are also good facilities for deep-sea fishing.

South Island

At **Nelson**, a small city on the coast, the visitor will find a garden town with spectacular beaches and a growing arts community. There is an excellent choice of routes for exploring the natural beauty of the South Island and to take in such attractive towns as **Dunedin** and **Invercargill**, both having strong Scottish roots and still retaining a Celtic flavour.
On the edge of the Canterbury Plains is the 'Garden City' of **Christchurch**, which has some very English characteristics. The *River Avon* flows through the centre of the city, flanked by many old stone buildings and stately homes. The neo-Gothic Cathedral and its surrounding square are the nucleus of the city, and other places of interest include the *Old Canterbury University,* the *Canterbury Museum*, the *Chamber of Commerce Building, Riccarton House* and the *Provincial Council Buildings.* There are also many parks, gardens, galleries and museums.
The mountain resort of **Queenstown** is a major centre for ski enthusiasts from all over the world. At warmer times of the year it is a wonderful place for hiking, a pastime well catered for all over the South Island, with plenty of tracks provided. The scenery of the South Island is extraordinary and much can be accomplished in a short time, but it would be a pity not to linger in such attractive small towns as **Arthur's Pass,** reached through a rainforest along narrow roads and past gushing waterfalls, or to view the mass of **Mount Cook**, and the exhilarating ski-plane rides.
There are also a number of national parks covering a total of 5.25 million acres, with scenery that includes forests, valleys, thermal areas, lakes, mountains, glaciers and coastal bays. Most have good facilities for the visitor. One of these is the **Abel Tasman Park** in the northwest which can be reached on foot, or better still by boat from the small town of **Kaiteriteri.** For nature enthusiasts such parks offer a rare opportunity to observe the wildlife, increasingly rare in the more populated areas where imported species, particularly birds, have driven out local creatures. Once the flat plains surrounding Christchurch were dotted with many species of the ostrich-like moas, but now they have been replaced with sheep, while the nation's symbol, the kiwi, is rarely seen in daylight and it is unlikely the visitor will see one outside a zoo. Nevertheless, the keen ornithologist will still be able to find many species in their natural habitat. New Zealand is also a haven for many rare plants, particularly ferns and heathers.
POPULAR ITINERIES: 5-day: Auckland–Waitomo–Rotorua–Lake Taupo–Wellington. **7-day:** (a) Nelson–Christchurch–Dunedin–Invercargill–Queenstown–Mount Cook–Kaiteriteri. (b) Auckland–Waitomo–Rotorua–Queenstown–Mount Cook–Christchurch.

SOCIAL PROFILE

FOOD & DRINK: New Zealand has a reputation as a leading producer of meat and dairy produce with lamb, beef and pork on most menus. Venison is also widely available as deer farming increases. Locally produced vegetables, such as *kumara* (a natural sweet potato), are good. There is also a wide range of fish available including snapper, grouper, John Dory and trout. Seasonal delicacies such as whitebait, oysters, crayfish, scallops and game birds are recommended. New Zealand's traditional dessert is *pavlova,* a large round cake with a meringue base, topped with fruit and cream. Many picnic areas with barbecue facilities are provided at roadside sites. Restaurants are usually informal except for very exclusive ones. Waiter service is normal, but self-service and fast-food chains are also available. Many restaurants invite the customer to 'BYO' (bring your own liquor). **Drink:** New Zealand boasts an excellent range of domestic wines and beers, some of which have won international awards. A wide range of domestic and imported wines, spirits and beers is available from hotel bars, 'bottle stores', wholesalers and wine shops. Bars have counter service and public bars are very informal. Lounge bars and 'house bars' (for hotel guests only) are sometimes more formal and occasionally have table service. The minimum drinking age in a bar is 18 if escorted by an adult, otherwise 21. There is some variation in licensing hours in major cities and some hotel bars open Sunday, providing a meal is eaten. In most hotels and taverns, licensing hours are 1100-2300 except Sunday.
NIGHTLIFE: New Zealand has an active and varied entertainment industry. Theatres offer good entertainment ranging from drama, comedy and musicals to pop concerts and shows. In large cities there are often professional performers or guest artists from overseas. Visitors should check 'What's On' in local papers when touring. There are also cinemas and a small selection of nightclubs in larger cities.
SHOPPING: Special purchases include distinctive jewellery made from New Zealand *greenstone* (a kind of jade) and from the beautiful translucent *paua* shell. Maori arts and crafts are reflected in a number of items such as the carved greenstone *tiki* (a unique Maori charm) and intricate woodcarvings often inlaid with paua shell. Other items of note include woollen goods, travel rugs, lambswool rugs, leather and skin products. **Shopping hours:** Nearly all stores and shops are open 0900-1730 Monday to Friday and 1000-1300 Saturday. Some shops open until 2100 Thursday/Friday and some open Sunday. There are invariably extended hours in resort areas.
SPORT: Rugby and **netball** are the national sports, while **football, soccer** and **cricket** are also played. New Zealand enjoys a unique reputation as a country with virtually unlimited scope for outdoor recreation. There are many **golf** courses. **Skiing:** A major winter sport that is well catered for on the slopes of Mount Ruapehu in the North Island and the ski fields of Coronet Peak, Treble Cone and Mount Hutt in the South Island. **Hiking** tours are available throughout New Zealand, examples being the Milford Track, Routeburn Track, Hollyford Valley and Fjordland National Park. **Fishing:** The lakes and rivers of the Taupo and Rotorua districts are known for excellent trout fishing. Deep-sea fishing is good off the coastline of Northland (the peninsula north of Auckland in the North Island). The South Island offers good trout and salmon fishing. Tourists can buy special 1-month licences through the Tourism Board. **Lawn bowls:** A popular national sport played from September to April; most towns have greens. **Tennis:** Most towns and resorts have courts. **Swimming:** There are municipal and hotel swimming pools plus miles of safe coastline. **Other sports:** There is also **motor-racing, greyhound-racing, horseracing** (trotting, pacing and gallops), **athletics** and **sheep dog trials.** Details of all events appear in local papers.
SPECIAL EVENTS: The following are the main special events for 1995/96. For further details, contact the New Zealand Tourism Board.
Feb 17-Mar 12 '95 *Wellington Fringe Festival.* **Mar** *Trans-Tasman Air Race,* Palm North; *Inter Dominion Trotting Championships,* Addington. **Mar 3-25** *Taranaki Festival and Searchlight Tattoo,* New Plymouth. **Mar 4-5** *National Highland Games,* Tauranga. **Mar 9-12** *World Kite Festival,* Napier. **Mar 11-12** *Pasifika Festival,* Auckland. **Mar 11-15** *Sri Lanka v New Zealand (1st Test),* Napier. **Mar 17-26** *Bluff Festival.* **Mar 18-22** *Sri Lanka v New Zealand (2nd Test),* Dunedin. **Mar 18-26** *Scottish Week,* Dunedin. **Mar 26-Apr 2** *Amateur Golf Championships,* Palm North. **Apr** *Great New Zealand Wine and Food Festival,* Hamilton. **Apr 1-9** *Festival of New Zealand Writing,* Dunedin. **Apr 9** *Family Bush Festival,* Waitakere. **Apr 12-15** *Air Balloon Fiesta,* Hamilton. **Apr 14-17** *Queenstown Easter Sports Festival.* **May** *National Woolcraft Festival,* Invercargill. **May 5-7** *NZ Made Extravaganza,* ASB Stadium, Auckland. **May 10-14** *Brass Band Championships,* Rotorua. **May 25-28** *Home Interiors,* Wellington. **Jun** *Taranaki Rhododendron Festival.* **Jun 2-5** *Craft Fair,* Taupo. **Jun 7-15** *Indoor Bowls Championships,* Palm North. **Sep 10-16** *World Golf Festival,* Canterbury. **Sep 29-Oct 1** *The Great New Zealand Craft Show,* Dunedin Stadium. **Oct 22** *Auckland International Marathon.* **Oct 23-24** *Henderson Spring Wine Festival.* **Jan 10 '96** *Edwin Fox Sailing Ship Centenary,* Picton. **Feb 10** *Air NZ Marlborough Wine and Food Festival,* Blenheim. **Feb 13-21** *Dunedin Festival.* **Mar** *World Championship Golden Shears,* Masterton. **Mar 1-24** *International Festival of the Arts,* Wellington.
SOCIAL CONVENTIONS: Should a visitor be invited to a formal Maori occasion, the *hongi* (pressing of noses) is common. Casual dress is widely acceptable. New Zealanders are generally very relaxed and hospitable. Stiff formality is rarely appreciated and after introductions first names are generally used. Smoking is restricted where notified. **Tipping:** Service charges and

taxes are not added to hotel or restaurant bills. Tips are not expected.

BUSINESS PROFILE

ECONOMY: Although New Zealand is primarily thought of as an agricultural country, this sector employs less than 10% of the workforce and contributes just 8% of GNP. Nonetheless, it remains an important source of export earnings, particularly from wool, meat and dairy products. There are significant natural resources, of which the energy-related, notably natural gas and coal, have been developed. There are some promising mineral deposits of titanium, gold, silver and sulphur which have yet to be exploited. From the late 1970s a new generation of industrial enterprises centred on these resources were established to replace the traditional industries (textiles, agricultural machinery and fertilisers) which were declining. From the mid-1980s to date, New Zealand has undergone the most radical economic transformation of any Western industrialised country, with extensive privatisation, the dismantling of many welfare systems, abolition of subsidies and tariff barriers and a plethora of corporate regulations. The strengthening of the economy has been reflected in the achievement of an increasingly healthy decrease in inflation. Australia is New Zealand's largest trading partner, and the two governments have worked on establishing a completely free trading regime between them. Japan, the United States and the UK are the other major trading partners. The EU is the largest single overseas market. There is some worry in New Zealand that the increasing exclusivity of European trade spells potential problems for the future of New Zealand's agricultural exports.
BUSINESS: Business wear is generally conservative and both sexes tend toward tailored suits. Some businessmen dress in shorts and knee-length socks during summer, particularly in the North Island, but a suit is preferable for visitors. Appointments are necessary and punctuality is appreciated. Calling cards are usually exchanged. The business approach is fairly conservative and visitors should avoid the period from Christmas to the end of January. The best months for business visits are February to April and October to November. **Office hours:** 0900-1700 Monday to Friday.
COMMERCIAL INFORMATION: The following organisation can offer advice: New Zealand Chambers of Commerce and Industry, PO Box 1590, 9th Floor, 109 Featherston Street, Wellington. Tel: (4) 472 3376. Fax: (4) 471 1767.
CONFERENCES/CONVENTIONS: The largest centres are in Auckland, Wellington and Christchurch. Many hotels also have facilities. There are over 20 regional convention bureaux in New Zealand, most of which are members of NZ Convention Association (Inc), PO Box 33-1202, Suite 3, Level 1, 15 Huron Street, Takapuna, Auckland. Tel: (9) 486 4128. Fax: (9) 486 4126. The organisation is also known as Conventions New Zealand.

CLIMATE

Subtropical in the North Island, temperate in the South Island. The North has no extremes of heat or cold, but winter can be quite cool in the South with snow in the mountains. Rainfall is distributed throughout the year.
Required clothing: Lightweight cottons and linens are worn in the North Island most of the year and in summer in the South Island. Mediumweights are worn during winter in the South Island. Rainwear is advisable throughout the year, and essential if visiting the rainforest areas in the South Island.

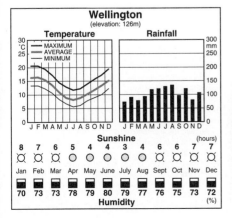

Wellington (elevation: 126m) — Temperature, Rainfall, Sunshine, Humidity

Nicaragua

□ *international airport*

Location: Central America.

Note: Due to occasional flare ups of armed violence, some areas of the North continue to be dangerous. Do not travel at night and take local advice before deviating from the main Pan-American Highway. Travel by road between Nicaragua and Honduras, even on main roads, is potentially dangerous. Beacause of land mines in certain rural areas, it can be hazardous to venture off main roads. Street crime is prevalent in Managua. Long-term visitors are advised to notify their consular representative of their presence on arrival in Nicaragua and ask for up-to-date information.
Source: FCO Travel Advice Unit – December 1, 1994.

Instituto Nicaragüense de Turismo (Inturismo)
Apartado 122, Avenida Bolívar Sur, Managua, Nicaragua
Tel: (2) 25436. Fax: (2) 25314. Telex: 1299.
Embassy of the Republic of Nicaragua
8 Gloucester Road, London SW7 4PP
Tel: (0171) 584 4365 *or* 584 3231 (Consular section). Fax: (0171) 823 8790. Opening hours: 1000-1300 Monday to Friday.
British Embassy
Apartado A-169, El Reparto 'Los Robles', Primera Etapa, Entrada principal de la Carretera a Masaya, 4a Casa a Mano Derecha, Managua, Nicaragua
Tel: (2) 780 014 *or* 780 887 *or* 674 050. Fax: (2) 784 085. Telex: 2166 (a/b PRODROME NK).
Embassy of the Republic of Nicaragua
1627 New Hampshire Avenue, NW, Washington, DC 20009
Tel: (202) 939 6570. Fax: (202) 939 6542.
Embassy of the United States of America
Apartado 327, Km 4.5, Carretera Sur, Managua, Nicaragua
Tel: (2) 666 010 *or* 666 015/8. Fax: (2) 666 046.
Embassy of the Republic of Nicaragua
Suite 407, 130 Albert Street, Ottawa, Ontario K1P 5G4
Tel: (613) 234 9361/2. Fax: (613) 238 7666.
Honorary Consulate of Canada
Apartado 514, 208 Calle del Triunfo, Frente Plazoleta Telcor Central, Managua, Nicaragua.
Tel: (2) 627 574 *or* 621 304. Fax: (2) 624 923.

Timatic

Health	
GALILEO/WORLDSPAN:	TI-DFT/MGA/HE
SABRE:	TIDFT/MGA/HE
Visa	
GALILEO/WORLDSPAN:	TI-DFT/MGA/VI
SABRE:	TIDFT/MGA/VI

For more information on Timatic codes refer to Contents.

AREA: 120,254 sq km (46,430 sq miles).
POPULATION: 4,264,845 (1993 estimate).
POPULATION DENSITY: 33.3 per sq km.
CAPITAL: Managua. **Population:** 819,679 (1981 estimate).
GEOGRAPHY: Nicaragua borders Honduras to the north and Costa Rica to the south. To the east lies the Caribbean, and to the west the Pacific. In the north are the Isabella Mountains, while the country's main feature in the southwest is Lake Nicaragua, 148km (92 miles) long and about 55km (34 miles) at its widest. The island of Ometepe is the largest of the 310 islands on the lake. These islands have a reputation for great beauty, and are one of the country's main tourist attractions. Lake Managua is situated to the north. Volcanoes, including the famous Momotombo, protrude from the surrounding lowlands northwest of the lakes. The country's main rivers are the San Juan, the lower reaches of which form the border with Costa Rica, and the Rio Grande. The Corn Islands *(Islas del Maiz)* in the Caribbean are two small beautiful islands fringed with white coral and palms. They are very popular as holiday resorts with both Nicaraguans and tourists. The majority of Nicaragua's population live and work in the lowland between the Pacific and western shores of Lake Nicaragua, the southwestern shore of Lake Managua and the southwestern sides of the range of volcanoes. It is only in recent years that settlers have taken to coffee growing and cattle farming in the highlands around Matagalpa and Jinotega.
LANGUAGE: Spanish. Along the Mosquito Coast *(Costa de Mosquito)* there are English-speaking communities in which African or mixed African and indigenous Indians predominate.
RELIGION: 85% Roman Catholic.
TIME: GMT - 5.
ELECTRICITY: 110 volts AC, 60Hz.
COMMUNICATIONS: Telephone: IDD is available. Country code: 505. Outgoing international code: 00. **Telex/telegram:** Facilities in Managua. **Post:** Airmail to Europe takes up to two weeks. *Poste Restante* services are available in Managua. Post offices are open 0900-1730 Monday to Saturday. **Press:** All newspapers are in Spanish. The main publications are *Barricada, La Prensa, La Tribuna* and *El Nuevo Diario.*
BBC World Service and Voice of America frequencies: From time to time these change. See the section *How to Use this Book* for more information.

BBC:				
MHz	17.84	15.22	9.915	5.975
Voice of America:				
MHz	15.21	11.74	9.815	6.030

PASSPORT/VISA

Regulations and requirements may be subject to change at short notice, and you are advised to contact the appropriate diplomatic or consular authority before finalising travel arrangements. Details of these may be found at the head of this country's entry. Any numbers in the chart refer to the footnotes below.

	Passport Required?	Visa Required?	Return Ticket Required?
Full British	Yes	No/1	Yes
BVP	Not valid	-	-
Australian	Yes	Yes	Yes
Canadian	Yes	Yes	Yes
USA	Yes	No	Yes
Other EU (As of 31/12/94)	Yes	1	Yes
Japanese	Yes	Yes	Yes

PASSPORTS: Valid passport, at least 6 months old (with a further 6 months to run), required by all.
British Visitors Passport: Not acceptable.
VISAS: Required by all except:
(a) [1] nationals of Belgium, Denmark, Greece, Ireland, Luxembourg, The Netherlands, Spain and the UK for stays of up to 90 days (all other EU nationals *do* need a visa);
(b) nationals of Argentina, Bolivia, Chile, Finland, Guatemala, El Salvador, Hungary, Honduras, Liechtenstein, Norway, Sweden, Switzerland and the USA for stays of up to 90 days.
Types of visa: Tourist and Business. Cost: £18.00 or US$25.
Validity: Most Tourist visas are valid for 1 month.
Application to: Consulate (or Consular section at Embassy). For addresses, see top of entry.
Note: Applications from nationals of the following countries have to be referred to Managua: Afghanistan, Albania, Algeria, Colombia, People's Republic of China, Cuba, Dominican Republic, Ecuador, Ethiopia, Haiti, Hong Kong, India, Iraq, Pakistan, Peru, Somalia and Sri Lanka.
Application requirements: (a) Valid passport. (b)

Completed application form. (c) 2 passport-size photos. (d) Fee of US$25. (e) Onward or return ticket. (f) Evidence of sufficient means (at least US$500) to cover expenses during stay.
Working days required: 48 hours. Applications which have to be referred to Managua can take up to two weeks.
Temporary residence: Enquire at Embassy.

MONEY

Currency: Nicaraguan Gold Córdoba (C) = 100 centavos. Notes are in denominations of C100, 50, 20, 10, 5 and 1, and 50 centavos.
Credit cards: Access/Mastercard, Visa, American Express and Diners Club are accepted on a limited basis. Check with your credit card company for details of merchant acceptability and other services which may be available.
Travellers cheques: Accepted in a number of places, though it is advisable to have them in US Dollars.
Exchange rate indicators: The following figures are included as a guide to the movement of the Nicaraguan Gold Córdoba against Sterling and the US Dollar:

Date:	Oct '92	Sep '93	Jan '94	Jan '95
£1.00=	8.58	9.48	9.38	11.05
$1.00=	5.41	6.21	6.34	7.06

Note: Frequent adjustments to the traded value of the Córdoba and the various exchange systems that have been used make it impossible to make meaningful comparative assessments over successive years. The figures above represent the exchange rate for the Córdoba.
Currency restrictions: There are no restrictions on the import or export of currency.
Banking hours: 0830-1200 and 1400-1630 Monday to Friday, 0830-1130 Saturday.

DUTY FREE

The following items can be imported into Nicaragua without incurring customs duty:
200 cigarettes or 500g tobacco; 3 litres of spirits or wine; 1 bottle perfume or eau de cologne.
Prohibited imports: Canned meats and dairy products; medicines without an accompanying prescription; military uniforms; and firearms not covered by the regulations governing the importation of firearms for sporting purposes. Contact the Embassy for details (for addresses, see top of entry).
Prohibited exports: Archaeological items, artefacts of historic or monetary value, food, and medicines not accompanied by a prescription.

PUBLIC HOLIDAYS

Jan 1 '95 New Year's Day. **Apr 13** Maundy Thursday. **Apr 14** Good Friday. **May 1** Labour Day. **Jul 19** Liberation Day. **Aug 10** Managua Local Holiday. **Sep 14** Battle of San Jacinto. **Sep 15** Independence Day. **Nov 2** All Souls' Day. **Dec 25** Christmas Day. **Jan 1 '96** New Year's Day. **Apr 4** Maundy Thursday. **Apr 5** Good Friday.
Note: A considerable number of local holidays are also observed.

HEALTH

Regulations and requirements may be subject to change at short notice, and you are advised to contact your doctor well in advance of your intended date of departure. Any numbers in the chart refer to the footnotes below.

	Special Precautions?	Certificate Required?
Yellow Fever	No	1
Cholera	No	No
Typhoid & Polio	Yes	-
Malaria	2	-
Food & Drink	3	-

[1]: A yellow fever vaccination certificate is required from all travellers aged one year and over arriving from infected areas.
[2]: Major risk of malaria, predominantly in the benign *vivax* form, exists from June to December in rural areas as well as in the outskirts of the towns of Bluefields, Bonanza, Chinandega, Jinotega, León, Matagalpa, Puerto Cabezas, Rosita and Siuna.
[3]: All water should be regarded as being potentially contaminated. Water used for drinking, brushing teeth or making ice should have first been boiled or otherwise sterilised. Milk is unpasteurised and should be boiled. Powdered or tinned milk is available and is advised, but make sure that it is reconstituted with pure water. Avoid dairy products which are likely to have been made from unboiled milk. Only eat well-cooked meat and fish, preferably served hot. Pork, salad and mayonnaise may carry increased risk. Vegetables should be cooked and fruit peeled.
Rabies is present. For those at high risk, vaccination before arrival should be considered. If you are bitten abroad seek medical advice without delay. For more information, consult the *Health* section at the back of the book.
Health care: Medical insurance is essential.

TRAVEL - International

AIR: Nicaragua's national airline is *Nica.*
Approximate flight time: From London to Managua is 20 hours 30 minutes including stopovers in Madrid and Havana.
International airport: *Managua (MGA)* (Augusto Cesar Sandino) is 9km (5.5 miles) from the city (travel time – 15 minutes). Full duty-free facilities are available. There is a bus every 10 minutes 0500-2200. A taxi service runs to the city.
Departure tax: US$10 on all departures.
SEA: Major ports are Corinto, Puerto Sandino, El Bluff and Puerto Cabezas which are served by shipping lines from Nicaragua, as well as Central American, North American and European countries.
ROAD: The Pan-American Highway runs through Nicaragua via Esteli and Managua. **Bus:** There are daily bus services *(Ticabus)* between Managua and most Central American capitals. Tickets are sold up to five days in advance, and all border documentation must be completed before the ticket is issued.

TRAVEL - Internal

SEA: A twice-weekly boat service runs between Bluefields and the Corn Islands. It is also possible to visit the 300 or so islands on Lake Nicaragua, which are very beautiful.
RAIL: There is only one railway, the *Ferro-Carril del Pacifico*, 349km (245 miles) long. A diesel service has increased both speed and comfort. Trains from Managua run two or three times daily to León, and four times daily to Granada. There is also a service between León and Rio Grande. Children under 4 years travel free. Children aged 4-10 pay half fare.
ROAD: Traffic drives on the right. **Bus:** There is a service to most large towns. Booking seats in Managua in advance is advisable. **Taxi:** Available at airport or in Managua. Prices should be agreed before departure. A map of each area in the city determines taxi prices. **Car hire:** Available in Managua or at the airport. This is the best way of travelling, as public transport is slow and overcrowded. Tarred roads exist to San Juan del Sur and Corinto. **Documentation:** National licences are only valid for 30 days.
URBAN: The bus and minibus services in Managua are cheap, but they can be both crowded and confusing.
JOURNEY TIMES: The following chart gives approximate journey times (in hours and minutes) from Managua to other major cities/towns in Nicaragua.

	Road
Granada	1.00
Masaya	0.30
Esteli	2.15
Chinandega	1.30
Matagalpa	1.45
Jinotega	2.30
Rivas	1.30

ACCOMMODATION

Many of the hotels were destroyed in the earthquake of 1972, although new hotels are gradually being opened in Managua. Several have been built along the highway that bypasses the old part of the city, but there is still a shortage. A 10% tax is levied on all hotel bills. There are *motels* along the Pan-American Highway and modern resort hotels along the west coast, offering a good standard of accommodation. **Grading:** Hotels in Managua have been divided into three categories: upper, middle and lower, to provide an indication of price and standard.

RESORTS & EXCURSIONS

The Towns

Managua: The centre of the capital was completely destroyed by an earthquake in December 1972, and there was further severe damage during the civil wars of 1978-1979. The Government has now decided that it will rebuild the old centre, adding parks and recreational facilities. In the old centre of Managua one can still see examples of colonial architecture in the *National Palace* and the *Cathedral.*
Places of Interest: There are several volcanic crater lagoons in the environs of Managua, some of which have become centres of watersports and residential development and also have attractive boating, fishing and picnicking facilities. *Laguna de Xiloa* is the most popular of these lagoons. Boats can be hired on the shores of *Lake Managua* for visiting the still-smoking *Momotombo volcano* and the shore villages. A recreation centre has recently been built on the shores of the nearby *Tiscapa Lagoon.*
León: The 'intellectual' capital of Nicaragua, with a university, religious colleges, the largest cathedral in Central America and several colonial churches. There was heavy fighting here during the civil wars of 1978-1979 and much of it was damaged.
Granada: The third city of the country lies at the foot of the *Mombacho volcano*. It has many beautiful buildings and has faithfully preserved its Castilian traditions. The cathedral has been rebuilt in neo-Classical style. Also of interest are the *Church of La Merced,* the *Church of Jalteva* and the fortress-church of *San Francisco*.

The Beaches

There are several beaches on the Pacific coast about an hour's drive from Managua. The nearest are *Pochomil* and *Masachapa*. Adjacent to the latter is *Montelimar Beach Resort,* the largest of its kind in Central America. A visit to the *El Velero* beach, where the sea is ideal for both surfing and swimming, is recommended. On the Caribbean coast there are a number of small ports, the most important of which is **Bluefields**. From here one can get a boat to the beautiful, coral-fringed **Corn Islands (Islas del Maiz)**, the larger of which is a popular Nicaraguan holiday resort with surfing and bathing facilities that make it ideal for tourists.

SOCIAL PROFILE

FOOD & DRINK: Restaurants, particularly in Managua, serve a variety of cooking styles including Spanish, Italian, French, Latin American and Chinese. Local dishes include *gallapinto* (fried rice and pinto beans) and *mondongo* (tripe soup). Plantain is used in many dishes and *papas a la crema* (potatoes in cream) is a popular side dish. Food is often scooped up in *tortillas* instead of using cutlery. Roast corn on the cob is sold on the streets. Seafood is available as are imported beverages. Shortages occur in some areas. **Drink:** There are a number of cheap but good restaurants/bars *(coreders)* where beer, often the cheap local brand, is available. Multi-coloured fruit drinks made from fresh tropical fruit are superior to bottled soft drinks. At the other end of the scale, the few plush hotels have sophisticated restaurant/bars with a choice of international cuisine and beverages.
NIGHTLIFE: Managua has several nightclubs, some offering live music. There are also cinemas with French, Spanish and English films. Tipitapa, a tourist resort on the shore of Lake Managua, has a casino.
SHOPPING: Local items include goldwork, embroidery, shoes and paintings. Traditional crafts are available, particularly in Masaya, at the handicrafts market.
Shopping hours: 0800-1800 Monday to Friday and 0800-1200 Saturday.
SPORT: Watersports: Beaches on the Pacific coast offer safe **swimming** as do those on the Caribbean, including the popular Corn Islands. Often the better beaches have a small entrance charge. Many of the better hotels have pools open to non-residents. In the volcanic crater lagoons there is also safe swimming. Bathing in Lake Managua and Lake Nicaragua should be avoided due to contamination. Bathing is possible in the Laguna de Tiscapa. El Velero beach or Pochomil on the Pacific coast are ideal for **surfing** as are a number of other beaches along the west coast. **Other sports:** There are a number of good **fishing** spots on the country's waterways and sea shores. **Baseball** is the national game.
SPECIAL EVENTS: The following is a selection of festivals and other special events celebrated annually in Nicaragua. For a complete list of events in 1995/96, contact the Tourist Office.
Easter *Fiesta,* Granada; *Holy Week Ceremonies,* León. **Aug** *Festival of Santo Domingo,* Managua; *Assumption of the Virgin (fiesta),* Granada. **Dec** *Christmas Mummers and Masques Festival*, Granada. **Jan** *Masaya* (indigenous celebration), Catarina.
SOCIAL CONVENTIONS: Dress is informal.

Photography: Avoid photographing military sites or personnel. **Tipping:** 10% of the bill is customary in hotels and restaurants. No tip is necessary for taxi drivers but porters expect a small tip.

BUSINESS PROFILE

ECONOMY: Agriculture is the main economic activity, with cotton, coffee, sugar, bananas and meat as the principal exports. The greater proportion of the economy is in private hands, especially now that the Chamorro government has returned the confiscated properties to its original owners. In 1991 the Nicaraguan economy underwent an intense process of economic and institutional reforms, and the implementation of the third stage of a stabilisation programme which succeeded in stopping the chronic hyperinflation process. It has been possible to stop the continuous fall of economic activities, and to revert this process and achieve a considerable growth. The main reason for this has been the economic liberalisation at all levels, starting from the access of foreign exchange, elimination of state monopolies, tax reduction, access to new markets and the privatisation programme. The large volume of credits and external assistance has helped to maintain the added demand and increase it while state consumption was reduced. Mexico, Japan and other Central American countries are now Nicaragua's largest trading partners.
BUSINESS: Businessmen often wear sports shirts in hot weather but never shorts. A knowledge of Spanish is an advantage, though some business people speak English. Enquire at Embassy for interpreter services. Best time to visit is November to March. **Office hours:** 0800-1200 and 1430-1730 Monday to Friday, 0800-1300 Saturday.
COMMERCIAL INFORMATION: The following organisations can offer advice: Cámara de Comercio de Nicaragua, Apartado 135, Frente a Lotería Popular, C C Managua JR. Tel: (2) 670 718; *or* Centro de Información Comercial, Ministry of Economy and Development, Apartado Postal 8, Km 6, Carretera a Masaya, Managua. Tel: (2) 71269.

CLIMATE

Tropical climate for most of the country. The dry season is from December to May, and the rainy season is from June to November. The northern mountain regions have a much cooler climate.
Required clothing: Lightweight cottons and linens are required throughout the year. Waterproofing is advisable particularly during the rainy season. Warmer clothes are advised for the northern mountains.

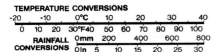

TEMPERATURE CONVERSIONS

-20	-10	0°C	10	20	30	40

0	10	20	30°F40	50	60	70	80	90	100

RAINFALL CONVERSIONS

0mm	200	400	600	800

0In	5	10	15	20	25	30

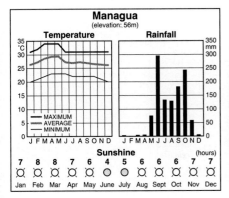

Managua
(elevation: 56m)

□ *international airport*

Location: Central Africa.

Office National du Tourisme (ONT)
BP 612, avenue du Président H Luebke, Niamey, Niger
Tel: 732 447. Telex: 5467.
Embassy of the Republic of Niger
154 rue du Longchamp, 75116 Paris, France
Tel: (1) 45 04 80 60. Fax: (1) 45 04 62 26. Telex: 611080. Opening hours: 0900-1230 (for applications) and 1430-1800 Monday to Friday.
Honorary British Vice-Consulate
BP 11168, Niamey, Niger
Tel: 732 015 *or* 732 539.
Embassy of the Republic of Niger
2204 R Street, NW, Washington, DC 20008
Tel: (202) 483 4224/5/6/7.
Embassy of the United States of America
BP 11201, rue des Ambassades, Niamey, Niger
Tel: 722 661/2/3/4. Fax: 733 167. Telex: 5444 (a/b NI).
Embassy of the Republic of Niger
38 Blackburn Avenue, Ottawa, Ontario K1N 8A2
Tel: (613) 232 4291/2/3. Fax: (613) 230 9808.
Canadian Embassy
PO Box 362, Sonara II Building, avenue du Premier Pont, Niamey, Niger
Tel: 733 686/7 *or* 733 758. Fax: 735 064. Telex: 5264 (a/b DOMCAN NI).

AREA: 1,267,000 sq km (489,191 sq miles).
POPULATION: 7,984,000 (1991 estimate).
POPULATION DENSITY: 6.3 per sq km.
CAPITAL: Niamey. **Population:** 360,000 (1981 estimate).
GEOGRAPHY: Niger has borders with Libya and Algeria to the north, Chad to the east, Nigeria and Benin to the south, and Mali and Burkina Faso to the west. The capital, Niamey, stands on the north bank of the Niger River, and has long been a major trading centre on this important navigable waterway. The river meanders for 500km (300 miles) through the southwestern corner of the country. To the east is a band of semi-arid bush country along the border with Nigeria, shrinking by 20km (12 miles) every year as over-grazing claims more land for the *Ténéré Desert*, which already occupies over half of Niger. This desert is divided by a range of low mountains, *Aïr ou Azbine*, in the eastern foothills of which lies the city of Agadez. Surrounded by green valleys and hot springs amid semi-desert, this regional capital is still a major terminus for Saharan caravans. The desert to the west of the mountains is a stoney plain hosting seasonal pastures; to the north and west are mostly vast expanses of sand. There is arable land beside Lake Chad in the extreme southeastern corner of the country. The Hausa people live along the border with Nigeria and most are farmers. The Songhai and Djerma people live in the Niger valley and exist by farming and fishing. The nomadic Fulani, who are a tall, fine-featured people, have spread all over the Sahel. The robed and veiled Tuaregs once dominated the southern cities; the few who remain are camel herders and caravanners on the Saharan routes. The Manga (or Kanun) live near Lake Chad and are well known for their colourful ceremonies in which pipes and drums accompany slow, stately dancing.
LANGUAGE: The official language is French. Also spoken are Hausa (by 60% of the population), Djerma, Manga, Zarma and Tuareg dialects.
RELIGION: 95% Muslim, 0.5% Christian, remainder Animist.
TIME: GMT + 1.
ELECTRICITY: 220/380 volts AC, 50Hz.
COMMUNICATIONS: Telephone: IDD is available. Country code: 227 (no area codes). Outgoing international code: 00. **Telex/telegram:** Services are available from the Chief Telegraph Office, Niamey, some hotels and other telegraph offices. There are three rates of charge. **Post:** Airmail to Western Europe takes up to two weeks. Post offices are generally open 0730-1230 and 1530-1800. **Press:** All newspapers are published in French.
BBC World Service and Voice of America frequencies: From time to time these change. See the section *How to Use this Book* for more information.
BBC:

MHz	17.79	15.40	15.07	9.410

Voice of America:

MHz	21.49	15.60	9.525	6.035

PASSPORT/VISA

Regulations and requirements may be subject to change at short notice, and you are advised to contact the appropriate diplomatic or consular authority before finalising travel arrangements. Details of these may be found at the head of this country's entry. Any numbers in the chart refer to the footnotes below.

	Passport Required?	Visa Required?	Return Ticket Required?
Full British	Yes	No	Yes
BVP	Not valid	-	-
Australian	Yes	Yes	Yes
Canadian	Yes	Yes	Yes
USA	Yes	Yes	Yes
Other EU (As of 31/12/94)	Yes	1	Yes
Japanese	Yes	Yes	Yes

PASSPORTS: Valid passport required by all.
British Visitors Passport: Not accepted.
VISAS: Required by all except:
(a) **[1]** nationals of EU countries (except nationals of Belgium, France, Greece, Italy, Luxembourg, Spain and Portugal who *do* require visas);
(b) nationals of Benin, Burkina Faso, Cameroon, Cape Verde, Central African Republic, Chad, Congo, Côte d'Ivoire, Finland, Gabon, Gambia, Ghana, Guinea, Guinea-Bissau, Liberia, Mali, Mauritania, Morocco, Nigeria, Norway, Senegal, Sierra Leone, Sweden, Togo, Tunisia and Yugoslavia (Serbia and Montenegro).
Note: Citizens of the newly independent states of former Yugoslavia should contact the nearest Embassy of Niger in order to obtain information on their eligibility for visa exemption.
All exemptions are for stays of up to 3 months only.
Application to: Consulate (or Consular section at Embassy). For addresses, see top of entry.
Application requirements: (a) 3 completed application forms. (b) 3 passport-size photos. (c) A return ticket or proof of sufficient funds to cover repatriation costs. (d) Visitors entering by road: bank letter guaranteeing to cover repatriation costs and proof of car insurance. (e) Letter of assurance pledging that the visitor will not take up employment while in Niger. (f) Postal applications should be accompanied by a stamped, self-addressed envelope. (g) Fee of FFr300 or its equivalent depending on place of application.
Working days required: 24 hours.
Exit permit: Must be obtained from the Immigration Department in Niamey before departure.
Note: Passports must be presented to the police in each town where an overnight stay is intended. Passports are

Health

GALILEO/WORLDSPAN:	**TI-DFT/NIM/HE**
SABRE:	**TIDFT/NIM/HE**

Visa

GALILEO/WORLDSPAN:	**TI-DFT/NIM/VI**
SABRE:	**TIDFT/NIM/VI**

For more information on Timatic codes refer to Contents.

stamped at each town, so blank pages will be required. It is prohibited to travel by any route other than that stamped in the passport by the police.

MONEY

Currency: CFA Franc (CFA Fr) = 100 centimes. Notes are in denominations of CFA Fr10,000, 5000, 1000 and 500. Coins are in denominations of CFA Fr500, 100, 50, 25, 10, 5, 2 and 1.
Note: At the beginning of 1994, the CFA Franc was devalued against the French Franc.
Credit cards: Access/Mastercard and Diners Club are both accepted on a limited basis. Check with your credit card company for details of merchant acceptability and other services which may be available.
Travellers cheques: Accepted by hotels, restaurants, most shops and airline offices.
Exchange rate indicators: The following figures are included as a guide to the movements of the CFA Franc against Sterling and the US Dollar:

Date:	Oct '92	Sep '93	Jan '94	Jan '95
£1.00=	431.75	433.87	436.79	834.94
$1.00=	260.71	284.13	295.22	533.68

Currency restrictions: The import and export of foreign currency is unlimited. The import of local currency is unrestricted. Export of local currency is limited to CFA Fr25,000.
Banking hours: 0800-1100 and 1600-1700 Monday to Friday.

DUTY FREE

The following items may be imported into Niger by passengers of 15 years of age or older without incurring customs duty:
200 cigarettes or 100 cigarillos or 25 cigars or 250g of tobacco; 1 litre of spirits.
Note: (a) A licence is required for sporting guns. Customs must authorise their temporary admission. (b) Digging up or attempting to export ancient artefacts is prohibited. (c) Pornography is prohibited. (d) Apparatus for transmission or reception needs special authorisation (as does photographic equipment, see *Photography* under *Social Conventions*). (e) Selling cars without permission is prohibited.

PUBLIC HOLIDAYS

Jan 1 '95 New Year's Day. **Mar 2** Eid al-Fitr (End of Ramadan). **Apr 15** Anniversary of the 1974 coup. **Apr 17** Easter Monday. **May 1** Labour Day. **May 10** Eid al-Adha (Feast of the Sacrifice). **May 31** Islamic New Year. **Aug 3** Independence Day. **Aug 9** Mouloud (Prophet's Birthday). **Dec 18** Republic Day. **Dec 25** Christmas Day. **Jan 1 '96** New Year's Day. **Feb 22** Eid al-Fitr (End of Ramadan). **Apr 15** Anniversary of the 1974 coup. **Apr 8** Easter Monday.
Note: (a) Muslim festivals are timed according to local sightings of various phases of the Moon and the dates given above are approximations. During the lunar month of Ramadan that precedes Eid al-Fitr, Muslims fast during the day and feast at night and normal business patterns may be interrupted. Many restaurants are closed during the day and there may be restrictions on smoking and drinking. Some disruption may continue into Eid al-Fitr itself. Eid al-Fitr and Eid al-Adha may last anything from two to ten days, depending on the region. For more information see the section *World of Islam* at the back of the book. (b) Niger's small Christian community also observes Easter, Whitsun, Ascension, Assumption, All Saints' Day and Christmas.

HEALTH

Regulations and requirements may be subject to change at short notice, and you are advised to contact your doctor well in advance of your intended date of departure. Any numbers in the chart refer to the footnotes below.

	Special Precautions?	Certificate Required?
Yellow Fever	Yes	1
Cholera	Yes	2
Typhoid & Polio	Yes	-
Malaria	3	-
Food & Drink	4	-

[1]: A yellow fever vaccination certificate is required of all travellers over one year of age arriving from all countries: it is also recommended for all travellers leaving Niger.
[2]: Following WHO guidelines issued in 1973, a cholera vaccination certificate is not a condition of entry to Niger. However, cholera is a serious risk in this country and precautions are essential. Up-to-date advice should be sought before deciding whether these precautions should include vaccination as medical opinion is divided over its effectiveness. See the *Health* section at the back of the book.
[3]: Malaria risk, predominantly in the malignant *falciparum* form, exists all year throughout the country. Chloroquine-resistance has been reported.
[4]: All water should be regarded as being potentially contaminated. Water used for drinking, brushing teeth or making ice should have first been boiled or otherwise sterilised. Milk is unpasteurised and should be boiled. Powdered or tinned milk is available and is advised, but make sure that it is reconstituted with pure water. Avoid dairy products which are likely to have been made from unboiled milk. Only eat well-cooked meat and fish, preferably served hot. Pork, salad and mayonnaise may carry increased risk. Vegetables should be cooked and fruit peeled.
Rabies is present. For those at high risk, vaccination before arrival should be considered. If you are bitten abroad seek medical advice without delay. For more information, consult the *Health* section at the back of the book.
Bilharzia (schistosomiasis) is present. Avoid swimming and paddling in fresh water. Swimming pools which are well-chlorinated and maintained are safe.
Health care: The two main hospitals are in Niamey and Zinder. Only the main centres have reasonable medical facilities. Personal medicines should be brought in as these can be difficult or impossible to obtain in Niger. Full health insurance is essential, and this should include cover for emergency repatriation.

TRAVEL - International

AIR: The national airline is *Air Niger (AW)*. Most international flights, however, are operated by *Air Afrique (RK)* and *UTA (UT)*. (There are no direct flights to Niger from the UK.)
Approximate flight time: From London to Niamey is 6 hours excluding stopover time in Paris.
International airport: *Niamey (NIM)*, 12km (7.5 miles) southeast of the city (travel time – 25 minutes). Airport facilities include bar, shops, post office, currency exchange and car hire. There are no duty-free facilities at Niamey airport. Taxi services are available to the city. Hotels have their own vehicles and provide free transport for their clients between the hotel and the airport.
ROAD: There are main roads from Kano (Nigeria) to Zinder, and from Benin, Burkina Faso and Mali. The principal trans-Sahara desert track runs from Algiers to Asamakka and Arlit, with a paved road to Agadez. Desert driving can be difficult, marker beacons may not always be visible, and petrol is not always available. **Bus:** Services operate from Burkina Faso, Benin and Mali.

TRAVEL - Internal

Note: It is essential that all visitors report to the police station in any town where they are making an overnight stop; see above under *Passport/Visa.*
AIR: *Air Niger* runs services from Niamey to Agadez, Tahoua, Zinder, Arlit and Maradi. Charter flights can be arranged; contact *Air Niger* or *Transniger* in Niamey.
ROAD: Traffic drives on the right. There are over 1500km (930 miles) of roads which are passable at all times. Principal internal roads are from Niamey to Zinder, Tahoua, Arlit and Gaya. Many tracks are impassable during heavy rain. The best season for road travel is from December to March. Petrol stations are infrequent and garages are extremely expensive. It is prohibited to travel by a different route than the one entered in the passport by the police at the previous town. **Bus:** There are reasonable services between the main centres, now that many roads have been sealed. Coach services operate from Niamey to Zinder, Agadez, N'guemi and Tera. Elsewhere, it is common practice to pay for rides in cross-country lorries; note that this can be an extremely slow and uncomfortable means of transport and that extra payment is expected of those who wish to ride in the cab. **Car hire:** Self-drive and chauffeur-driven cars are available, the latter being compulsory outside the capital. **Note:** Much of the country requires 4-wheel-drive vehicles, guides and full equipment.
Documentation: An International Driving Permit and a Carnet de Passage are required. Minimum age is 23. Two photos are required.
JOURNEY TIMES: The following chart gives approximate journey times (in hours and minutes) from Niamey to other major cities and towns in Niger.

	Air	Road
Zinder	0.45	12.00
Maradi	-	9.00
Tahoua	-	7.00
Dosso	-	1.00
Tillabéri	-	4.50
Agadez	-	17.00

ACCOMMODATION

Hotel accommodation is difficult to obtain and reservations for major international hotels should be booked overseas. All reservations should be made well in advance. There are good hotels in Niamey, Zinder, Ayorou, La Tapoa, Maradi and Agadez. There are also 'Encampments' in Agadez, Boubon, Namaro and Tillabéri. Local hotels are available on a first-come, first-served basis. For further information, contact the Société Nigérienne d'Hôtellerie (SONHOTEL), BP 11040, Niamey. Tel: 732 387. Telex: 5239 (a/b TOUROTEL NI).

RESORTS & EXCURSIONS

Niamey, spread along the northern bank of the *River Niger*, is a sprawling city with a modern centre and shanty towns on the outskirts. The two markets, the Small and Great markets, are of interest to the visitor. Other places of interest include the *Great Mosque*, the *National Museum* (including a large park with botanical gardens and a zoo, and an artisan/crafts area), the *Franco-Nigerian Cultural Centre* and the *Hippodrome* where horse and camel races often take place Sunday. Tours of the city are available.
Outside Niamey is the famous **'W' National Park,** with its abundant wildlife including buffalos, elephants, lions, hyenas, jackals and baboons. The birdlife is also proliferous.
Agadez is a beautiful old Tuareg capital which is still a caravan trading city: it also now has a thriving tourist trade. Beautiful silver and leather work can be bought in the back streets and the minaret of the mosque can be climbed at sunset for a spectacular view of the town. Expeditions can be arranged through the mountains to the springs at **Igouloulef** and **Tafadek** or the prehistoric site at **Iferouane** and beyond the *Ténéré Desert* and the *Djado Mountain.*
The town of **Zinder** was the capital of Niger until 1927. The old part of the town is a compact maze of alleyways, typical of a Hausa town. Near the centre is the *Sultan's Palace* and the mosque, which offers a good view from the minaret. The part of the town known as *Zengou* was formerly a caravan encampment. There is an excellent market here Thursday, selling beautiful leatherwork.
On the route from Zinder is the town of **Dosso,** founded in the 13th century by the Zarmas after the fall of Gao. It has an exceptional palace, a lively village square and celebrates many festivals with parades and official ceremonies. Niger's economic centre is **Maradi** where the people are engaged in various activities from agriculture to diverse crafts. The *Sultanate* and the *Mosque* there are well worth viewing.
The **Ayorou** region on the Mali frontier is an old trading station where a market is held every Sunday. In the region around **Tillabéri** giraffes are often encountered, often in quite large numbers. Two-day tours are available from the capital.
The *Aïr Mountains*, north of Agadez, enjoy slightly more rain than the surrounding semi-desert lowlands and were, until recently, home to many species of animals not generally seen at this latitude – leopards, lions and giraffes for example. However, the drought has even taken hold here and the stranded populations are dwindling rapidly. Special permission may be required to visit the region.

SOCIAL PROFILE

FOOD & DRINK: European, Asian and African dishes are served using local fish, meat and vegetables. There is a good selection of imported beverages. Shortages of locally produced foodstuffs are, however, common due to drought. There are a few good restaurants in the main cities and in hotel dining rooms. Alcohol is available, but there are restrictions due to Muslim beliefs.
NIGHTLIFE: In Niamey there are several nightclubs with music and dancing. There are also three open-air cinemas in the capital.
SHOPPING: Markets in the main towns, notably Niamey and Agadez, sell a range of local artefacts. The Centre des Métiers d'Art de Niger, close to the National Museum, is worth visiting, as a wide range of local goods can be bought there. Courteous bargaining is expected and items include multi-coloured blankets, leather goods, engraved calabashes, silver jewellery, swords and knives.
Shopping hours: 0800-1200 and 1600-1900 Monday to Friday, 0800-1200 Saturday.
SPORT: Visitors can take **canoes** or **motorboats** along

the Niger river to the Mali border of the 'W' game park. There are several **swimming** pools in Niamey and Agadez, but it is not advisable to swim in the lakes or rivers. There are two **riding** centres in the capital. **Fishing** is possible throughout the year, the main season being from April to September. Big-game **hunting** has been outlawed.

SPECIAL EVENTS: The following festivals are celebrated annually. The Peulh people celebrate the end of the rainy season with a lively festival. Also of interest is the *Cure salée*, when the nomads gather their cattle to lead them to the new pastures. The yearly wrestling championships are held in the traditional style and the *Agricultural Fair* draws crowds with the included art exhibition.

SOCIAL CONVENTIONS: Handshaking is customary. Casual wear is widely suitable. Women should avoid wearing revealing clothes. Traditional beliefs and Muslim customs should be respected. **Photography:** Permits are required for photography and filming, these can be obtained from police stations. Tour operators and tourist bureaux are often able to make arrangements. Film is expensive and local facilities for processing film are not always good. Ask local people for permission before taking their photographs. Military installations, airports and administrative buildings (including the Presidential Palace) should not be photographed.

Tipping: Expected for most services, usually 10%. Most hotels add a 10-15% service charge.

BUSINESS PROFILE

ECONOMY: Niger is one of the world's poorest countries. 90% of the country's inhabitants are employed on the land, although less than 5% of the actual land area is cultivated. An already difficult situation is exacerbated by the ever-expanding desert, drought and problems with pest control. Less than one-tenth of the crops grown are cash crops – cotton and groundnuts – while the rest are grown for domestic consumption. Even so, Niger needs external aid to feed the population. The country's most valuable commodity is its deposits of uranium, of which Niger is the fifth-largest non-communist producer, although world demand has been low of late following Chernobyl and the general downturn in the nuclear power industry. France buys most of Niger's uranium at a subsidised price. Otherwise Nigeria and Côte d'Ivoire are the country's main trading partners.

BUSINESS: A lightweight suit and tie are generally acceptable. A knowledge of French is essential, as interpreters are not readily available and executives seldom speak English. **Office hours:** 0730-1230 and 1530-1830 Monday to Friday, 0730-1230 Saturday.

COMMERCIAL INFORMATION: The following organisations can offer advice: Conseil National de Développement, c/o Ministry of Planning, Niamey. Tel: 722 233. Telex: 5214; *or* Chambre de Commerce, d'Agriculture, d'Industrie et d'Artisanat du Niger, BP 209, place de la Concertation, Niamey. Tel: 732 210. Telex: 5242.

CLIMATE

Summers are extremely hot. The dry season is from October to May. Heavy rains with high temperatures are common in July and August.

Required clothing: Lightweight cottons and linens are required most of the year. Warmer clothes during the cool evenings, especially in the north, are essential. Rainwear is advisable.

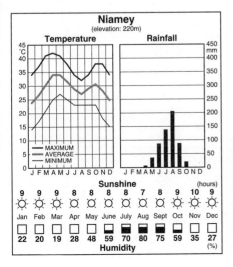

Niamey
(elevation: 220m)

Nigeria

□ *international airport*

Location: West Africa.

Note: Nigeria experiences civil unrest and violence from time to time, but causes and locations vary. Some of the locations where outbreaks of violence have occurred include the Lagos area, southwestern Nigeria and parts of Delta, Rivers, Plateau and Kaduna States. In addition, Chadian troop incursions have reportedly occurred at the border area in the far northwest, near Lake Chad. Strikes by oil workers and other union workers have seriously disrupted production and distribution of fuel throughout Nigeria, with the greatest impact experienced in Lagos, where electricity, water facilities and transportation have been disrupted.
Source: US State Department – July 20, 1994.

Nigerian Tourist Board
PO Box 2944, Trade Fair Complex, Badagry Expressway, Lagos, Nigeria
Tel: (1) 618 665.
Nigerian Tourism Development Corporation
Private Mail Bag 167, Block 2, Sefadu Street, Zone 4, Wuse, Garki, Abuja, Nigeria
Tel: (9) 523 0418. Fax: (9) 523 0962.
High Commission for the Federal Republic of Nigeria
Nigeria House, 9 Northumberland Avenue, London WC2N 5BX
Tel: (0171) 839 1244. Fax: (0171) 839 8746. Telex: 23665 *or* 916814.
Nigerian Consular Section
56-57 Fleet Street, London EC4Y 1BT
Tel: (0171) 353 3776. Fax: (0171) 353 4352. Opening hours: 0930-1300 Monday to Friday.
British High Commission
Private Mail Bag 12136, 11 Eleke Crescent, Victoria Island, Lagos, Nigeria
Tel: (1) 619 531 *or* 619 537. Fax: (1) 666 909 (Visa section). Telex: 21247 (a/b UKREP NG).
Deputy High Commission in: Kaduna.
Embassy of the Federal Republic of Nigeria
1333 16th Street, NW, Washington, DC 20036
Tel: (202) 986 8400. Fax: (202) 775 1385.
Nigerian Consulate General
828 2nd Avenue, New York, NY 10017
Tel: (212) 808 0301.

Timatic

Health
GALILEO/WORLDSPAN: **TI-DFT/LOS/HE**
SABRE: **TIDFT/LOS/HE**

Visa
GALILEO/WORLDSPAN: **TI-DFT/LOS/VI**
SABRE: **TIDFT/LOS/VI**

For more information on Timatic codes refer to Contents.

Embassy of the United States of America
PO Box 554, 2 Eleke Crescent, Victoria Island, Lagos, · Nigeria
Tel: (1) 261 0097 *or* 261 0050. Fax: (1) 261 0257. Telex: 23616 (a/b AMEMLA NG).
Consulate in: Abuja.
High Commission for the Federal Republic of Nigeria
295 Metcalfe Street, Ottawa, Ontario K2P 1R9
Tel: (613) 236 0521. Fax: (613) 236 0529.
Canadian High Commission
PO Box 54506, Ikoyi Station, Committee of Vice-Chancellors Building, Plot 8A, 4 Idowu-Taylor Street, Victoria Island, Lagos, Nigeria
Tel: (1) 269 2915/8. Fax: (1) 269 2919. Telex: 21275 (a/b DOMCAN NG).

AREA: 923,768 sq km (356,669 sq miles).
POPULATION: 88,514,501 (1991).
POPULATION DENSITY: 95.8 per sq km.
CAPITAL: Abuja (1991). Formerly Lagos. **Population:** Lagos – 1,060,848 (1975). Foreign diplomats will continue to be accredited to Lagos for up to five years because of shortage of houses and offices.
GEOGRAPHY: Nigeria has borders with Niger to the north, Chad (across Lake Chad) to the northeast, Cameroon to the east and Benin to the west. To the south, the Gulf of Guinea is indented by the Bight of Benin and the Bight of Biafra. The country's topography and vegetation vary considerably. The coastal region is a low-lying area of lagoons, sandy beaches and mangrove swamps which merges into an area of rainforest where palm trees grow to over 30m (100ft). From here the landscape changes to savannah and open woodland, rising to the Central Jos Plateau at 1800m (6000ft). The northern part of the country is desert and semi-desert, marking the southern extent of the Sahara.
LANGUAGE: The official language is English. There are over 250 local languages, the principal ones being Hausa (north), Yoruba (southwest) and Ibo (southeast).
RELIGION: Islamic majority, particularly in the north and west of the country, with a Christian minority (who make up a majority in the south). There are many local religions.
TIME: GMT + 1.
ELECTRICITY: 210/250 volts AC, 50Hz. Single phase.
COMMUNICATIONS: Telephone: Full IDD is available. Country code: 234. Outgoing international code: 009. **Telex/telegram:** International telegraph and telex services are operated by Nigerian Telecommunications Limited (NITEL) in all large cities. **Post:** Airmail to Europe is unreliable and takes up to three weeks. Delivery may be more reliable through international couriers who are represented in major towns. **Press:** English-language newspapers include the *Chronicle*, the *Concord*, the *Daily Sketch*, the *Daily Star*, the *Daily Times*, *The Guardian*, the *New Nigerian*, the *Nigerian Herald*, the *Nigerian Tribune* and the *Observer*.
BBC World Service and Voice of America frequencies: From time to time these change. See the section *How to Use this Book* for more information.

BBC:				
MHz	17.79	15.40	15.07	9.410
Voice of America:				
MHz	21.49	15.60	9.525	6.035

PASSPORT/VISA

Regulations and requirements may be subject to change at short notice, and you are advised to contact the appropriate diplomatic or consular authority before finalising travel arrangements. Details of these may be found at the head of this country's entry. Any numbers in the chart refer to the footnotes below.

	Passport Required?	Visa Required?	Return Ticket Required?
Full British	Yes	Yes	Yes
BVP	Not valid	-	-
Australian	Yes	Yes	Yes
Canadian	Yes	Yes	Yes
USA	Yes	Yes	Yes
Other EU (As of 31/12/94)	Yes	Yes	Yes
Japanese	Yes	Yes	Yes

PASSPORTS: Valid passport required by all.
British Visitors Passport: Not accepted.
VISAS: Required by all except:
(a) nationals of ECOWAS countries (Benin, Burkina Faso, Cape Verde, Côte d'Ivoire, Gambia, Ghana, Guinea, Guinea-Bissau, Liberia, Mali, Mauritania, Niger, Senegal, Sierra Leone and Togo) for stays of up to 90 days;
(b) nationals of Cameroon and Chad for stays of up to 90 days.

Note: Children under 16 years of age accompanying their parents residing in Nigeria (provided the name of such a child is entered in the passport of one of the parents) do not require visas, but must, however, complete one application form accompanied by a photo. All children holding their own passport must have separate visas or re-entry permits.
Types of visa: Tourist, Transit and Business (employment/temporary work). Cost depends on nationality; UK nationals pay £30.
Transit visas: Not required by:
(a) those noted under visa exemptions above;
(b) those continuing their journey to a third country by the same aircraft and not leaving the airport;
(c) those who transit Nigeria within 48 hours, provided they hold tickets with confirmed reservations and documents valid for a third country beyond Nigeria (they will be permitted to leave the airport, but passports will normally be retained by the immigration authorities; hotel accommodation is available near Lagos airport.)
Re-entry permits: Required by all residents who are not nationals of Nigeria. Permit must be obtained before departure.
Application to: Consulate (or Consular section at Embassy or High Commission). For addresses, see top of entry.
Application requirements: (a) Completed application form. (b) Passport. (c) 1 passport-size photo. (d) Letter of introduction from a company or a resident of Nigeria, accepting immigration responsibility for applicant; any Nigerian inviting a visitor must attach photocopies of pages 1-5 of his own passport, while a resident must enclose a copy of his residence permit. (e) Onward or return ticket for Tourist visas.
Working days required: 2 days.

MONEY

Currency: Naira (N) = 100 kobo. Notes are in denominations of N50, 20, 10 and 5, and 50 kobo. Coins are in denominations of N1, and 50, 25, 10, 5 and 1 kobo.
Currency exchange: The Government of Nigeria has fixed an artificially high rate for local currency (the Naira) in terms of its value in exchange for foreign currencies. However, trading on the black market is extremely dangerous and could lead to arrest. Therefore, visitors are advised to exchange currency at the official rate and at approved exchange facilities, which often include major hotels. Inter-bank transfers are frequently difficult, if not impossible, to accomplish.
Credit cards: American Express, Access/Mastercard, Diners Club and Visa are rarely accepted in Nigeria and, because of the prevalance of credit card fraud, their use is ill-advised.
Travellers cheques: Accepted.
Exchange rate indicators: The following figures are included as a guide to the movements of the Nigerian Naira against Sterling and the US Dollar:

Date:	Oct '92	Sep '93	Jan '94	Jan '95
£1.00=	30.76	45.91	32.39	34.42
$1.00=	8.45	30.07	21.89	22.00

Currency restrictions: Import of foreign currency is unlimited, but it must be declared on arrival; export is limited to the amount declared. Import and export of local currency is restricted to N50 in notes. Penalties for black market transactions are severe.
Banking hours: 0800-1500 Monday; 0800-1330 Tuesday to Friday. There are over 80 commercial banks. The Government owns 60% of all foreign banks.

DUTY FREE

The following goods may be imported into Nigeria by persons over 18 years of age without incurring customs duty:
200 cigarettes or 50 cigars or 200g of tobacco; 1 litre of spirits; a small amount of perfume; gifts to the value of N300.
Note: (a) If more than each of the above is imported, duty will be levied on the whole quantity. Heavy duty will be levied on luxury items such as cameras or radios unless the visitor's stay is temporary. (b) The import of champagne or sparkling wine will result in heavy fines or imprisonment. (c) It is forbidden to buy or sell antiques from or to anyone other than the Director of Antiquities or an accredited agent; visitors should obtain a clearance permit from one of the above before presenting antiques, artefacts or curios at the airport.

PUBLIC HOLIDAYS

Jan 1 '95 New Year's Day. **Mar 2** Eid al-Fitr (End of Ramadan). **Apr 14-17** Easter. **May 1** May Day. **May 10** Eid al-Kabir (Feast of the Sacrifice). **Aug 9** Mouloud (Prophet's Birthday). **Oct 1** National Day. **Dec 25-26** Christmas. **Jan 1 '96** New Year's Day. **Feb 22** Eid al-Fitr (End of Ramadan). **Apr 5-8** Easter.
Note: Muslim festivals are timed according to local sightings of various phases of the Moon and the dates given above are approximations. During the lunar month of Ramadan that precedes Eid al-Fitr, Muslims fast during the day and feast at night and normal business patterns may be interrupted. Many restaurants are closed during the day and there may be restrictions on smoking and drinking. Some disruption may continue into Eid al-Fitr itself. Eid al-Fitr and Eid al-Kabir (Eid al-Adha) may last anything from two to ten days, depending on the region. For more information see the section *World of Islam* at the back of the book.

HEALTH

Regulations and requirements may be subject to change at short notice, and you are advised to contact your doctor well in advance of your intended date of departure. Any numbers in the chart refer to the footnotes below.

	Special Precautions?	Certificate Required?
Yellow Fever	Yes	1
Cholera	Yes	2
Typhoid & Polio	Yes	-
Malaria	3	-
Food & Drink	4	-

[1]: A yellow fever vaccination certificate is required of travellers over one year of age arriving from infected areas. Travellers arriving from non-endemic zones should note that vaccination is strongly recommended for travel outside the urban areas, even if an outbreak of the disease has not been reported and they would normally not require a vaccination certificate to enter the country. The risk of contracting yellow fever is highest in Lagos and Kaduna states.
[2]: Following WHO guidelines issued in 1973, a cholera vaccination certificate is not a condition of entry to Nigeria. However, evidence of cholera vaccination is required by certain nationals before they may enter the country (check with the nearest Nigerian Embassy) and vaccination is therefore advised. Cholera is a serious risk in this country and precautions are essential. Up-to-date advice should be sought before deciding whether these precautions should include vaccination, as medical opinion is divided over its effectiveness. See the *Health* section at the back of the book.
[3]: Malaria risk exists all year throughout the country. The predominant *falciparum* strain has been reported to be 'resistant' to chloroquine.
[4]: All water should be regarded as being potentially contaminated. Water used for drinking, brushing teeth or making ice should have first been boiled or otherwise sterilised. Milk is unpasteurised and should be boiled. Powdered or tinned milk is available and is advised, but make sure that it is reconstituted with pure water. Avoid dairy products which are likely to have been made from unboiled milk. Only eat well-cooked meat and fish, preferably served hot. Pork, salad and mayonnaise may carry increased risk. Vegetables should be cooked and fruit peeled.
Rabies is present. For those at high risk, vaccination before arrival should be considered. If you are bitten abroad, seek medical advice without delay. For more information, consult the *Health* section at the back of the book.
Bilharzia (schistosomiasis) is present. Avoid swimming and paddling in fresh water. Swimming pools which are well-chlorinated and maintained are safe.
Health care: It is advisable to take a sufficient supply of drugs or medication to meet personal needs, as there are often shortages of such items in Nigeria. Doctors and hospitals often expect immediate cash payment for health services. Medical insurance is essential.

TRAVEL - International

AIR: Nigeria's national airline is *Nigeria Airways (WT)*. For free advice on air travel, call the Air Travel Advisory Bureau in the UK on (0171) 636 5000 (London) *or* (0161) 832 2000 (Manchester).
Approximate flight times: From Lagos to *London* is 7 hours 40 minutes and to *New York* is 12 hours 10 minutes.
International airports: *Lagos (LOS)* (Murtala Muhammed) is 22km (13 miles) north of Lagos (travel time – 40 minutes). Airport facilities include restaurant, bar, snack bar, bank, post office and car hire. There is a free coach service every 10 minutes. Taxis to the city are available.
Note: Pickpockets and confidence artists, some posing as local immigration and other government officials, are especially common at Murtala Muhammed Airport.
Kano (KAN) is 8km (5 miles) north of Kano (travel time – 25 minutes). Airport facilities include restaurant, bank, post office, duty-free shop and car hire. Buses leave for the city every 10 minutes 0600-2200, and taxis are available.
Abuja (ABV) is 35km (22 miles) from the city.
Departure tax: US$35 (nationals of Nigeria and alien residents with work permit N600 included). Transit passengers and children under two years old are exempt.
SEA: Services to Lagos, Port Harcourt and Calabar sail from London, Liverpool and other European ports.
ROAD: Links are with Benin, Niger, Chad and Cameroon. The principal trans-Saharan routes pass through Nigeria from Niger. The principal link with Benin is via the Idoroko border point along the good coast road to Lagos. All land borders, with the exception of the border with Chad, which was closed in May 1984, have now been re-opened.

TRAVEL - Internal

AIR: *Nigeria Airways* operate between Lagos, Ibadan, Benin City, Port Harcourt, Enugu, Calabar, Kaduna, Kano, Jos, Sokoto, Maiduguri and Yola. Charter facilities are available in Lagos from *Aero Contractors, Pan-African Airlines* and *Delta Air Charter.* It is advisable to book internal flights well in advance. There is often considerable delay in internal air services. Lack of fuel sometimes disrupts internal commercial air travel.
Departure tax: N50.
SEA: Ferry services operate along the south coast and along the Niger and Benue rivers. For timetables and prices, enquire locally.
RAIL: The two main routes are from Lagos to Kano (via Ibadan–Oyo–Ogbombosho–Kaduna–Zaria); and from Port Harcourt to Maiduguri (via Aba–Enugu–Makurdi–Jos). These two lines link up Kaduna and Kafanchan. There is also a branch line from Zaria to Gusau and Kaura Namoda. A daily service runs on both main routes. Sleeping cars are available, which must be booked in advance. There are three classes and some trains have restaurant cars and air-conditioning. Trains are generally slower than buses, but cheaper.
ROAD: Traffic drives on the right. The national road system links all the main centres, although in some areas secondary roads become impassable during the rains. Reports of armed robberies in broad daylight on rural roads in the northern half of Nigeria have been reported and appear to be increasing. **Buses** and **taxis** (in the shape of Ford Transit vans) run between the main towns. **Car hire** is not difficult to obtain in Lagos and Abuja, but it is best to go through hotels. Chaffeur-driven cars are advised. **Documentation:** An International Driving Permit is required, accompanied by two passport-size photos.
URBAN: Public transport in Lagos operates in rather chaotic conditions. The city suffers from chronic traffic congestion, which makes it impossible for buses and taxis to operate efficiently, especially during the rush hours. There are *Lagos State Corporation* buses, two private bus companies and several thousand private minibuses. Taxis in Lagos are yellow and both fares and tip should be agreed in advance. A ferry service runs to Lagos Island.

ACCOMMODATION

HOTELS: There are first-class hotels in Lagos and in the major towns, but they are heavily booked and advance reservation is essential. Lagos is one of the most congested cities in Africa, and the majority of good hotels are on Lagos Island. Hotels are generally very expensive, but there is a variety of alternative accommodation. Further information can be obtained from the Hotel and Personal Services Employers Association of Nigeria, Ahmadu Bello Way, Victoria Island. Tel: (1) 617 937.
OTHER ACCOMMODATION: Government-run **catering rest-houses** are scattered throughout the country and offer accommodation in colonial-style rest houses. In many towns, **Christian missions** are able to offer good basic accommodation at a reasonable price. The universities have **guest-houses** for visiting academics, but may be able to accommodate other visitors. Most of the big towns have **sporting clubs** which offer cheap accommodation and eating facilities, and can be used by visitors who take temporary membership. Port Harcourt is the centre of the national oil industry and offers a large selection of accommodation to the industry, which is also available to tourists.

RESORTS & EXCURSIONS

Nigeria is the most populated and prosperous of the West African nations; if the Sahel countries are excluded, it is also by far the largest. For the purpose of this section (which only covers major tourist destinations), it has been divided into regions which do not necessarily reflect cultural or administrative boundaries.

The Southwest

Lagos is a busy and overcrowded city and reputed to be the most expensive city in the world. Its commercial and administrative centre is on Lagos Island at the heart of the city, linked to the mainland by two road bridges. **Ikoyi** and **Victoria** islands are also connected to **Lagos Island**, and both have wealthy residential areas and beautiful gardens. The *National Museum* at **Onikan** on Lagos Island houses numerous exhibits of Nigeria's ancient civilisations and has a craft centre which sells examples of Nigerian craft at fixed prices. In the *Jankara Market* on Lagos Island one can bargain for locally dyed cotton and handwoven cloth, herbs and leather goods. **Ibadan** is famous for its university and its market (one of the biggest in Nigeria). It is a convenient base for trips to the other, more traditional, old towns of the Western State.

The large, traditional town of **Oyo** has some old Portuguese-style houses and is the site of the capital of the old Yoruba Empire.

Oshogbo is the founding centre of the internationally-renowned school of Oshogbo art and home of the shrines and grove of Oshun, the Yoruba goddess of fertility. The famous *Oshun shrine* is to be found here. The *Oshun Festival* takes place towards the end of August each year. *Ile-Ife*, the ancient name of the town of **Ife**, is the cradle of Yoruba culture, and includes the *Ife Museum*, which has many fine bronze and terracotta sculptures dating back to the 13th century. The university here is a centre for batik-dying.

Akure is a good base from which to explore the seven *Olumirin Waterfalls*.

The Mouth of the Niger

Modern **Benin City** is a rapidly developing metropolis, but there are a few reminders of its long Yoruba history. The old city's moat and wall survive in places and the *National Museum* houses an interesting collection of Benin royal art. The *Oba's Palace* is worth visiting, although permission needs to be obtained in Lagos. Many of the villages in **Cross River State** are of interest for their handicrafts and traditions of magic, but may only be accessible by foot or canoe. *Sapoba*, *Abaraka*, *Sapele*, *Warri* and *Auchi*, however, can be reached by road. **Calabar** is a pleasant town in a beautiful setting, high on a hill above the *Calabar River*. **Ikot Ekepne** is the centre for beautiful baskets and carvings, and at **Oron** there is a museum renowned for its exhibits of Ibibio and Efik carvings. **Ikom**, on the road to Cameroon, has curious carved monoliths set in circles.

Port Harcourt has long been an important merchant port and is today the centre of Nigeria's oil industry.

The North

Kaduna is a government town laid out by the British and has fine buildings and modern amenities. The ancient walled city of **Zaria** to the north retains much of its old character and has a fine mosque and *Emir's Palace*. Outside **Katsina**, on the border with Niger, are some old Hausa burial mounds and the city is the site of spectacular Sallah festivals (see below under *Special Events*).

Kano was the largest of the ancient Hausa cities and is today Nigeria's third-largest city. The walled old town still remains and gives the city a medieval atmosphere, although the city was founded at least 1000 years ago, being of strategic importance on the trans-Saharan trade routes. *Kurmi Market* has many tourist souvenirs, including the richly embroidered Fulani horse blankets and decorations used at festivals. The famous dye pits *(Kofar Mata)*, still in use and apparently some of the oldest in Africa, are interesting, as is the *Grand Mosque*. The *Emir's Palace* is an outstanding example of Hausa architecture. The city has many colonial-style sporting clubs and good restaurants and nightlife.

Jos is a favourite holiday centre on account of its location (1200m/3900ft above sea level) and pleasant climate. The *Jos Museum* has a large collection of pottery from all over the country, and the nearby *Museum of Traditional Nigerian Architecture* holds a collection of full-size replicas representing different styles of Nigerian architecture, including *Katsina Palace*, *Zaria Mosque* and the *Kano Wall*. There is also a small zoo and easy access to such sights as the *Assob Falls*.

At **Maiduguri**, the Sallah festival is held three months after the festival of Eid al-Fitr, during which Borno horsemen demonstrate their equestrian prowess. The town also has a palace, park, zoo and museum. The area around *Lake Chad* is flat and prone to flooding during and after the rains. The whole region is of special

interest to the ornithologist and nature enthusiast. In contrast, some of the most striking and fascinating mountain scenery can be enjoyed around **Biu** and towards the Cameroon border.

Abuja, the new federal capital (set up in December 1991), is as yet undeveloped for tourism. It has a beautiful setting which gives magnificent views across the savannah.

SOCIAL PROFILE

FOOD & DRINK: There are restaurants of all varieties in Lagos and the major towns. European and Oriental food is readily available. Although there are self-service cafés, mainly in department stores, most restaurants have table service. Nigerian food is typical of that found throughout West Africa, and meals will often include yam, sweet potatoes, plantain and pepper soup, with regional variations. In the north, meat is more popular than in other areas; specialities are *suya* (barbecued liver and beef on sticks) and *kilishi* (spiced dried meat), in the east *egussi soup* (stew of meat, dried fish and melon seeds), and in the south goat meat and bush meat, particularly antelope, which is considered a delicacy. **Drink:** There are many brands of locally brewed and bottled beer which are very good. Spirits are expensive. Larger hotels and clubs have bars and cocktail lounges.

NIGHTLIFE: There are nightclubs in many of the hotels in Lagos and in the Surulere district. Some clubs have live entertainment, details of which are given in the local newspapers. North of Oyo in Ogbomosho there is a lively market, particularly in the evenings. Local festivals which generally take place in the summer months provide a good opportunity to see dancing, music and traditional costumes.

SHOPPING: Markets are the most interesting places to shop. Special purchases include *adire* (patterned, indigo-dyed cloth), batiks and pottery from the southwest, leatherwork and *kaduna* cotton from the north and carvings from the east. Designs vary greatly, many towns having their own distinctive style. Other purchases include herbs, beadwork, basketry and ceremonial masks such as those of the Ekpo. **Shopping hours:** 0800-1700 Monday to Friday; 0800-1630 Saturday.

SPORT: Swimming: The numerous beaches offer bathing, although many have strong currents and bathers should not swim far from the shore, especially in Lagos. Many of the better hotels have pools. **Tennis/squash:** Various clubs in major towns have courts where visitors are welcome to apply for temporary membership. **Golf:** Courses are attached to local sports and social clubs in many of the larger towns. **Fishing:** Good river and sea angling is available throughout the country.

SPECIAL EVENTS: In the predominantly Muslim north the most important festival is *Sallah,* celebrated three months after the feast of Eid al-Fitr, particularly in the towns of Katsina, Kano and Zaria. Every family is required to slaughter a ram and festivities last for several days, with horseback processions, musicians and dancers. Featured also in northern communities are *Durbars,* long lines of horsemen led by a band, the horses in quilted armour with the riders wearing quilted coats and wielding ceremonial swords. In the south there are masquerades and festivals marking events in local religions. At Oshogbo, the *Oshun* festival is held at the end of the rainy season (August to September), attracting thousands of childless women who seek the help of the Yoruba goddess of fertility. Festivals in the western states include masquerades in June, the *Oro* festival in July and the *Shango* festival in August. Other festivals are held in February, July and August in the northern town of Ogbomosho.

SOCIAL CONVENTIONS: Shaking hands with everyone is customary on meeting and departing. In Yorubaland it is a sign of respect to curtsy when introduced, and to enquire after relations, even if this is a first meeting. Unless the visitor knows someone well it is unusual to be invited to a Nigerian's home. Most entertaining, particularly in Lagos, takes place in clubs or restaurants and social customs are British oriented. A small gift of appreciation is always welcome and business souvenirs bearing the company logo are also acceptable. Casual wear is suitable and a lightweight suit and tie are only necessary for businessmen on formal meetings; on most other occasions men will not need to wear a jacket, although a tie might be expected. Women should dress modestly, and respect local customs regarding dress, particularly in the Muslim north. It is inadvisable for women to wear trousers. There are over 250 tribes in Nigeria, the principal groups being the Hausa in the north, the Ibo in the southeast and the Yoruba in the southwest. The larger of the minor groups are the Fulani, Tiv, Kanuri, Igala, Idoma, Igbirra and Nupe in the north; the Ibibio, Efik, Ekoi and Ijaw in the east; and the Edo, Urhobo, Itsekiri and Ijaw in the west. A result of this ethnic variety is the diversity of art, dance

forms, language, music, customs and crafts. Nigerians have a very strong sense of ethnic allegiance. **Tipping:** Unless a service charge has been included, 10% is expected for most services. Note that for taxi drivers the fare including a tip should be agreed before the journey. Airport porters should be tipped per case.

BUSINESS PROFILE

ECONOMY: The economy is heavily dependent on oil, which accounts for over 90% of the foreign exchange revenues, and although Nigeria is a member of the OPEC cartel, its earnings are still vulnerable to fluctuations on the world market. The low world price since 1986 cut Nigeria's foreign earnings by a considerable margin. The country also has vast untapped reserves of natural gas and coal. Agriculture still occupies well over half of the population, but there is a steady drift of labour towards the towns. Government policy is concerned with reducing the reliance on oil, increasing agricultural yields, which have suffered from drought and under-investment, and increasing the standard of living of the rural population. Nevertheless, successive governments have not succeeded in restoring Nigeria's one-time self-sufficiency in food. Exports of cash crops, mostly groundnuts, cocoa and palm oil, have remained steady but are now completely overshadowed as export earners by oil. Nigeria has some minerals other than oil and gas, including tin, coal, iron ore, zinc and some uranium. The oil boom is now coming to an end, however, and Nigeria needs to diversify and boost other parts of its economy. Most major manufacturing industries have been established, but all have suffered from the world recession during the 1980s and some from a lack of spare parts caused by the shortage of foreign exchange. Nigeria now faces something of a fiscal crisis and urgently needs to reschedule its foreign debt and cut its budget deficit. Unfortunately, the present military government seems to have little conception of how to do this, or anything else. However, the military's evident reluctance to cede power to civilians under any circumstances will limit the extent of international support for the Nigerian economy: major creditors and multinational institutions are already running short of patience. At home, the Abacha regime has had no more success than any of its predecessors in tackling the chronic mismanagement and corruption that has sadly dogged Nigeria for many years. The UK remains the largest single exporter to the country, although export credit premiums are rising steeply. Germany, France, the USA and, increasingly, Brazil are other principal sources of imports. The bulk of Nigeria's exports are sold to the USA, Germany, France, Italy and Brazil.

BUSINESS: English is spoken in business circles. It is common for business meetings to take place without a prior appointment, although these should be made for government visits. Business deals will often progress at a slower pace than is common in Europe. **Office hours:** 0730-1530 Monday to Friday.

COMMERCIAL INFORMATION: The following organisation can offer advice: The Nigerian Association of Chambers of Commerce, Industry, Mines and Agriculture, Private Mail Bag 12816, 15a Ikorodu Road, Maryland, Lagos. Tel: (1) 964 737. Telex: 21368.

CLIMATE

Varies from area to area. The southern coast is hot and humid with a rainy season from March to November. During the dry season, the *Harmattan* wind blows from the Sahara. The north's rainy season is from April to September. Nights can be cold in December and January. **Required clothing:** Lightweight cottons and linens are worn, with a warm wrap advisable in the north. Rainwear is essential during the rainy season.

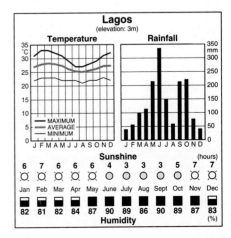

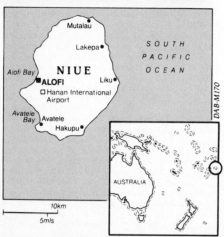

DAB-M170

Location: South Pacific.

Niue Tourism Section
PO Box 42, Planning & Development Department, Alofi, Niue
Tel: 4126 or 4018. Fax: 4232.
Destination Marketing
375 Upper Richmond Road West, East Sheen, London SW14 7NX
Tel: (0181) 392 1838. Fax: (0181) 878 0998.
Niue Airlines (NAL)
Hanan International Airport, Alofi, Niue
Tel: 4115 or 4183. Fax: 4216.
Niue Consulate
PO Box 68541, Newton, Auckland, New Zealand
Tel: (649) 774 081. Fax: (649) 389 720. Telex: NZ60175.
Niue has no national tourist offices overseas, but the Niue Consulate in New Zealand deals with enquiries on tourism and trade.

AREA: 259 sq km (100 sq miles).
POPULATION: 2239 (1991).
POPULATION DENSITY: 8.6 per sq km.
CAPITAL: Alofi.
GEOGRAPHY: Niue is an isolated island located 480km (298 miles) east of Tonga, 560km (348 miles) southeast of Western Samoa and 980km (609 miles) west of Rarotonga. Niue offers visitors many natural wonders and a superb climate. It has 2500 hectares of the most undisturbed forests in the world, designated *tapu* areas by the locals, where no humans were allowed to set foot for centuries. Now all the *tapu* forests, except the one controlled by *Hakupu* village, are penetrable. These forests are full of lush undergrowth, coconut palms and some of the oldest ebony trees known. Light and scattered forest covers approximately 14,000 hectares. At the edge of the forest, the coast gives way to extraordinary coral outcrops.
LANGUAGE: Niuean and English.
RELIGION: Mostly Ekalesai Niue, a Protestant denomination; also Latter Day Saints, Jehovah's Witnesses, Roman Catholic and Seventh Day Adventist.
TIME: GMT - 11.
ELECTRICITY: 240 volts AC, 50Hz. Plugs are the standard 3-pin type.
COMMUNICATIONS: Telephone: IDD and local facilities are available. Country code: 683. There are telephones in hotels, motels and guest-houses. Services are run by the Telecommunications Department located at the Central Administration Building in Alofi, which also provides **fax** and **telex** facilities, and is open 24

hours a day. The following are local emergency telephone numbers: Police – 999. Fire – 4133. Hospital – 998. **Post:** The Niue Post Office is open 0800-1500 Monday to Friday. **Press:** There are no English-language papers published in Niue. **Television:** Programmes are broadcast 1730-2300 Monday to Saturday only. **BBC World Service frequencies:** From time to time these change. See the section *How to Use this Book* for more information.
BBC:

MHz	17.83	15.34	11.95	9.740

PASSPORT/VISA

Regulations and requirements may be subject to change at short notice, and you are advised to contact the appropriate diplomatic or consular authority before finalising travel arrangements. Details of these may be found at the head of this country's entry. Any numbers in the chart refer to the footnotes below.

	Passport Required?	Visa Required?	Return Ticket Required?
Full British	Yes	No/1	Yes
BVP	Not valid	-	-
Australian	Yes	No/2	Yes
Canadian	Yes	No/1	Yes
USA	Yes	No/1	Yes
Other EU (As of 31/12/94)	Yes	No/1	Yes
Japanese	Yes	No/1	Yes

PASSPORTS: Required by all.
British Visitors Passport: Not accepted.
VISAS: Not required by bona fide tourists staying less than 30 days with return or onward tickets and sufficient funds for length of stay. **[1]** However, an Entry Permit is required by all nationals, which is granted on arrival (**[2]** except to nationals of New Zealand and Australia who *only* require a passport). Visas *are* required for all nationals staying over 30 days except nationals of New Zealand.
Types of visa: Ordinary and Transit. Transit visas are not required by nationals of New Zealand or by other nationals continuing their journey by the same or first connecting aircraft.
Validity: Entry Permit – 30 days. Extensions are available from the Immigration Office, PO Box 67, Administration Blocks, Alofi, Niue *or* the Secretary to the Government's Office, PO Box 42, Alofi, Niue. Tel: 4224. Fax: 4232. Telex: 67014.
Application to: Consulate (for address, see top of entry).
Temporary residence: Check with the Immigration Office (address above).

MONEY

Currency: The New Zealand Dollar is legal tender (for further information, see the entry on *New Zealand* earlier in the book). Niue sometimes produces commemorative coins which, when available, may be obtained at the Westpac Bank or the Philatelic Bureau.
Currency exchange: The Westpac Bank in Alofi can exchange currency.
Credit cards: American Express, Diners Club, Mastercard and Visa are accepted at the Niue Hotel. Mastercard and American Express are accepted by most tour agencies and Sails Restaurant accepts American Express, Diners Club and Mastercard. Contact your credit card company for details of merchant acceptability and other services which may be available.
Exchange rate indicators: See the entry on *New Zealand* earlier in the book.
Currency restrictions: There are no restrictions on the import or export of local or foreign currency. However, there are restrictions on postal notes, money orders, cheques or promissory notes in New Zealand currency, which must be declared to the Westpac Banking Corporation in Niue.
Banking hours: 0900-1400 Monday to Thursday; 0830-1400 Friday.

DUTY FREE

The following items can be imported into Niue by persons of 17 years of age or older without incurring customs duty:
1 bottle of spirits; 1 bottle of wine; 200 cigarettes or 227g of tobacco or 50 cigars; goods to the value of NZ$50.
Restricted imports: Visitors are allowed to import only one radio, one cassette player, one record player, one tape recorder, one typewriter, one pair of binoculars, one camera and one movie camera or video. Firearms and ammunition are prohibited unless permission is received from the Chief Officer of Police at the Police Department of Niue. Visitors wishing to import animals, animal

products, plant or plant material or goods must complete a baggage declaration form.
Restricted exports: Artefacts, coral and valuable shells.

PUBLIC HOLIDAYS

Jan 1 '95 New Year's Day. **Jan 2** Commission Holiday. **Feb 6** Waitangi Day. **Apr 14** Good Friday. **Apr 17** Easter Monday. **Apr 25** ANZAC Day. **Jun 10** Queen's Official Birthday. **Oct 9-10** Constitution Day. **Oct 16** Peniamina's Day. **Dec 25** Christmas Day. **Dec 26** Boxing Day. **Jan 1 '96** New Year's Day. **Feb 6** Waitangi Day. **Apr 5-8** Easter.

HEALTH

Regulations and requirements may be subject to change at short notice, and you are advised to contact your doctor well in advance of your intended date of departure. Any numbers in the chart refer to the footnotes below.

	Special Precautions?	Certificate Required?
Yellow Fever	No	1
Cholera	No	No
Typhoid & Polio	Yes	-
Malaria	No	-
Food & Drink	2	-

[1]: A yellow fever certificate is required from all travellers over one year of age arriving from an infected area.
[2]: Drinking water is from natural spring and rainwater and is considered safe to drink.
Health care: The Lord Liverpool Hospital offers medical and dental treatment and has three health clinics around the island. There is a 24-hour on-call emergency service (see *Communications* above for emergency telephone numbers).

TRAVEL - International

AIR: *Samoa Air* provides weekly flights to Niue from Pago Pago, American Samoa. *Niue Airlines* operates fortnightly services every Saturday (arriving Friday) from Auckland, New Zealand, and *Air Nauru* now also operates a weekly service from Auckland. *Polynesian Airlines* also serve the island.
International airport: *Niue International (IUE)* (Hanan) is 7km (4 miles) north of Alofi. There are some shops at the airport open for scheduled flights. Tour buses and taxis are available from the airport to all tourist destinations.
Departure tax: NZ$20. Children under five years of age are exempt.
SEA: It is possible to visit Niue by yacht, but weekday arrivals are preferred. Moorings and buoys are available.

TRAVEL - Internal

ROAD: There are 123km (76 miles) of paved roads in Niue. The road network was badly damaged by a cyclone in February 1990. Driving is on the left. There is no organised public transport on Niue. **Car hire:** Cars can be hired on the island although it is best to make reservations before arrival. Car hire companies include *Ama's Rental* (tel: 4054; fax: 4180) and *Maile Rentals* (tel: 4027 or 4088; fax: 4131). Bicycles, motorbikes, motorscooters and vans can also be hired on the island.
Documentation: Along with their national driving licence, visitors must obtain a local licence from the Niue Police Department.

ACCOMMODATION

HOTELS: The Niue Hotel is the largest hotel on the island and has a swimming pool, restaurant and bar. The Niue Island Lodge nearby offers more budget-conscious accommodation, suitable for school or diving groups, and guests can use the facilities at the Niue Hotel.
MOTELS: There are two motels on the island, both offering fully-equipped kitchens for cooking – Damiana's Holiday Motel in Vavatele Village in Alofi and Esther's Village Motel, 7km (4 miles) from the city centre and 15 minutes from Avatele Beach.
GUEST-HOUSES: Peleni's Guest-house in Alofi offers guests the choice of having their meals served or cooked by themselves in the kitchen provided.
CAMPING: There are no camping facilities in Niue.

RESORTS & EXCURSIONS

Recommended sites in **Alofi** include the *Niue Cultural Centre*, exhibiting unique Niuean artefacts; the *Huanaki Museum*, located next to the hospital and housing an interesting collection of artefacts and historical records; the

Womens' Club Town Hall, with a craftshop featuring various handicrafts for sale; and *Alofi Market,* open Friday. 5km (3 miles) north of Alofi, near **Makapu Point,** *Peniamina's Grave,* the Niuean who first brought Christianity to the island, can be found in a small clearing on the left side of the road. The *Experimental Farm,* a centre for animal husbandry and plant testing, is another popular destination for visitors. *Opaahi* is the site of Captain Cook's landing where he received a hostile reception by the natives and was almost hit by a spear. Another interesting excursion is the deserted village of *Fatiau Tuai,* 1600m (5249ft) from the main road on the seaward side of **Vaiea Village.** The original inhabitants suffered from an eye disease and the entire population was moved by the Government to Vaiea. The coastline here is stunning for its rough surf crashing against the shore and shooting up through blowholes.

Chasms are another of Niue's natural wonders. The amazing *Vaikona Chasm* can be reached by the Namuke sea track from the main road about 4km (2.5 miles) south of **Liku.** *Togo Chasm* is also popular. Located on the eastern side of the island, 4km (2.5 miles) north of **Hakupu,** it is one of Niue's most magnificent scenic areas with a tropical rainforest, towering coral pinnacles and an oasis of white sand, coconut palms and a pond hidden beneath overhanging cliffs (guide recommended). *Matapa Chasm* is another well-known scenic attraction, reached by road from the foot of **Hikutavake Hill.** *Vaotoi Pool,* 3km (2 miles) north of Hakupu, is the scene of the wreck of a Japan-ese fishing vessel which was beached during a storm in 1967. However, access to many of the chasms and pools are along difficult paths and an experienced guide is usually considered necessary.

There are good swimming holes at *Vaitafe,* 800m (2625ft) south of **Fulala** and 2.5km (1.5 miles) north of **Lakepa,** at *Avaiki,* and at *Limu,* perhaps the most beautiful on the north coast with its colourful coral and its wide variety of marine life (thatched cottages and a barbecue area can also be found here). **Avatele Bay** is another excellent location for swimming and snorkel-ling and visitors may watch the many fisherman in their canoes and dinghies who fish the bay's waters for tuna, wahoo and marlin, as well as the spectacular sunsets that set over the bay.

There are also hundreds of caves which are excellent for land explorations or dive sites. *Talava – The Arches* are a group of extraordinary arches and caverns, many containing stalactites and stalagmites, which may be visited at low tide. Other caves known for their spectacular formations are *Ulupaka Cave,* reached by a track 800m (2625ft) south of Lakepa, and *Palaha Caves,* 180m (591ft) north of Palaha. *Anatoloa Cave,* 1600m (5249ft) north of Lakepa and a 5-minute walk from the main road, is hard to find but is well worth the effort. It was once the home of a dangerous god and human bones can be found in it. There are also some national and maritime parks which are well worth visiting.

SOCIAL PROFILE

FOOD & DRINK: Many ceremonies and social events stem from the processing of food. One community ritual is based on the extraction of *nu pia* starch from arrowroot, which is used in traditional dishes and soups and often given as a gift. Another ritualised ceremony surrounds *ti* root, which is made into a sweet drink or eaten as a sweet with coconuts. The *luku* fern is another indigenous plant used in Niuean cooking and is boiled, stir-fried or baked in an earth oven with coconut cream and chicken or corned beef. Other popular foods include taro, kumara, coconuts, pawpaw, bananas, tomatoes, capsicum and many varieties of yam. In addition to the Niue Hotel Restaurant, open all day and evening, seven days a week, there are only two other fully fledged restaurants in Niue. Sails Restaurant, in Makapu Point, specialises in steak and seafood, and is open for lunch and dinner Tuesday to Saturday; reservations are essential. Jena's de la Cuisine in Alofi is open for lunch and dinner Monday to Saturday. Lunch only is available at Gabe's, Niue Trading, RR Rex & Sons and the South Seas Snack Bar. Restaurants do not have service charge or tax.

NIGHTLIFE: The Niue Sports Club provides regular entertainment on weekends, from bar/discos to nights of village dances. The Niue Hotel is the centre of Niue's nightlife with cultural shows, dine and dance and specialty food nights. Sails Restaurant features *Fiafia* nights on Friday.

SHOPPING: Niuean women are especially regarded for the quality of their weaving, producing hats, baskets, handbags and mats from indigenous plants, such as pandanus, which make excellent buys for the visitor. These are available to visitors at the Niue Handicraft Shop in Alofi and Hinapoto Handcrafts at the Cultural Centre. Other recommended purchases include T-shirts, stamps and coins. **Shopping hours:** 0830-1600 Monday

to Friday. Village shops and roadside dairies are open later and at weekends.

SPORT: At Niue Sport Club, there is a 9-hole **golf** course, with balls, clubs and trundlers for hire, and two **tennis** courts. Traditional Niuean **cricket** is the most popular spectator sport and can be seen in Hakupu. **Forest walking, swimming** and **scuba diving/ snorkelling,** along with various types of **fishing,** are visitors' favourite pastimes. The waters surrounding Niue are crystal clear and unpolluted. Limu is a popular diving site. Because of the sheer drops from reefs into deep ocean, land-based game fishing is a unique experience here. Red bass, wahoo, tuna, sailfish and marlin abound. Traditional outrigger canoes can be arranged for line-fishing expeditions. For information, contact the Niue Tourism Section (see address at top of entry). Twin-hulled dive boats, scuba and snorkelling gear and PADI certification courses are available at Niue Adventures Ltd, PO Box 141, Niue. Tel: 4102. Fax: 4010. Telex: 67913 (a/b TCOB).

SPECIAL EVENTS: The major festivals on the island are *Prayer Week* and *Takai Week,* celebrated in the first week of January, and the *Constitutional Celebrations* in October.

SOCIAL CONVENTIONS: Exchanges of money and food through the community's children form a major ritual, once a rite of passage expressing the power of the father through his skill in fishing and planting crops. Niuean children are bestowed with gifts of money or handmade mats and cloths from their relatives upon coming of age. Girls also have their ears pierced and boys receive their first haircut. It is polite to ask permission before entering private land. Niueans consider Sunday as a serious day of rest and most attend church both in the morning and afternoon. Certain activities, such as boating and fishing, are not allowed on Sunday. For further information on Sunday restrictions and protocol, contact the Niue Tourism Section (for address, see top of entry). Clothing is usually casual, cool and comfortable but women often wear a hat and cover their shoulders for church and men wear long trousers. Swimming attire is not acceptable in towns or villages. **Tipping:** Not encouraged.

BUSINESS PROFILE

ECONOMY: The Niue economy is dependent on subsistence agriculture and small-scale industry. Coconut cream was the largest export until the closure of the factory in 1989. Handicrafts, footballs, honey, taro and limes are now the leading export products, with New Zealand by far the largest recipient. Tourism, although a major industry for the island, was seriously damaged by the suspension of air transport in 1989 and the cyclone of the following year destroyed the island's only hotel. The island's future economic development depends largely on rehabilitation of this sector. The Government has also taken measures to stem the wave of emigration which has resulted in three times as many islanders living in New Zealand as at home. Niue depends heavily on foreign aid.

BUSINESS: Shaking hands is the usual form of greeting and leaving. Lightweight or tropical suits are recommended for business. Official invitations will always state the dress code required: 'formal' means a jacket and tie for men and 'fiafia' means casual dress is acceptable. **Office hours:** 0730-1500 Monday to Thursday; 0730-1600 Friday.

CONFERENCES/CONVENTIONS: Facilities for small meetings of approximately 15-25 persons are available.

CLIMATE

Tropical climate bathed by southeast trade winds, Niue has warm days and pleasantly cool nights.
Required clothing: Cotton shorts and shirts (or cotton dresses for women) with a wrap for the evenings.

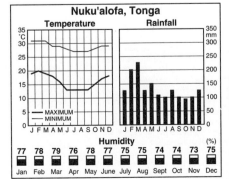

Nuku'alofa, Tonga

Norway

Location: Northern Europe, Scandinavia.

NORTRA (Norwegian Tourist Board)
PO Box 499, Sentrum, 0105 Oslo 1, Norway
Tel: (22) 427 044. Fax: (22) 336 998. Telex: 78582.
Travel and Tourism Section
Ministry of Industry, PO Box 8014 Dep, Plønsgate 8, 0030 Oslo 1, Norway
Tel: (22) 349 090. Fax: (22) 349 525. Telex: 21428.
Royal Norwegian Embassy
25 Belgrave Square, London SW1X 8QD
Tel: (0171) 235 7151. Fax: (0171) 245 6993. Telex: 22321. Opening hours: 0900-1600 Monday to Friday (general enquiries); 1000-1230 Monday to Friday (Visa section).
Consulates in: Edinburgh and Newcastle-upon-Tyne.
Norwegian Tourist Board
Charles House, 5-11 Lower Regent Street, London SW1Y 4LR
Tel: (0171) 839 6255. Fax: (0171) 839 6014. Opening hours: 0900-1300 and 1400-1630 Monday to Friday (general enquiries).
British Embassy
Thomas Heftyesgate 8, 0244 Oslo 2, Norway
Tel: (22) 552 400. Fax: (22) 434 005.
Consulates in: Ålesund, Bergen, Harstad, Haugesund, Kristiansund (N), Kristiansund (S), Stavanger, Tromsø and Trondheim.
Royal Norwegian Embassy
2720 34th Street, NW, Washington, DC 20008
Tel: (202) 333 6000. Fax: (202) 337 0870.
Consulate Generals in: Houston, Los Angeles, Minneapolis, Miami, New York (tel: (212) 421 7333) and San Francisco.
Scandinavian Tourist Board
18th Floor, 655 Third Avenue, New York, NY 10017-5617
Tel: (212) 949 2333. Fax: (212) 983 5260.

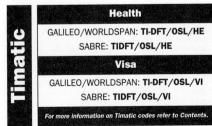

Health	
GALILEO/WORLDSPAN: **TI-DFT/OSL/HE**	
SABRE: **TIDFT/OSL/HE**	
Visa	
GALILEO/WORLDSPAN: **TI-DFT/OSL/VI**	
SABRE: **TIDFT/OSL/VI**	

For more information on Timatic codes refer to Contents.

Timatic

Embassy of the United States of America
Drammensveien 18, 0244 Oslo 2, Norway
Tel: (22) 448 550. Fax: (22) 430 777.
Royal Norwegian Embassy
Suite 532, Royal Bank Centre, 90 Sparks Street, Ottawa,
Ontario K1P 5B4
Tel: (613) 238 6571. Fax: (613) 238 2765.
Consulates in: Calgary, Dartmouth, Edmonton,
Mississauga, Montréal, Québec, Regina, St John, St
John's, Vancouver, Victoria, Ville de la Baie and
Winnipeg.
Canadian Embassy
Oscar's Gate 20, 0244 Oslo, Norway
Tel: (22) 466 955/9. Fax: (22) 693 467.

AREA: 323,877 sq km (125,050 sq miles).
POPULATION: 4,274,030 (1992 estimate)
POPULATION DENSITY: 13.1 per sq km.
CAPITAL: Oslo. **Population:** 467,090 (1992).
GEOGRAPHY: Norway is bordered to the north by the
Arctic Ocean, to the east by the CIS, Finland and
Sweden, to the south by the Skagerrak (which separates it
from Denmark) and to the west by the North Sea. The
coastline is 2735km (1700 miles) long, its most
outstanding feature being the fjords. Most of them are
between 80-160km long (50-100 miles), and are often
very deep and surrounded by towering mountains. Much
of northern Norway lies beyond the Arctic Circle and the
landscape is stark. In the south the landscape consists of
forests with many lakes and rivers.
LANGUAGE: Norwegian (Bokmål and Nynorsk).
Lappish is spoken by the Sami population in the north.
English is widely spoken.
RELIGION: 92% Evangelical Lutherans; plus other
Christian denominations.
TIME: Norway Mainland: GMT + 1 (GMT + 2 last
Sunday in March to Saturday before last Sunday in
September).
Jan Mayen Islands, Svalbard: GMT + 1.
ELECTRICITY: 220 volts AC, 50Hz. Plugs are of the
Continental round 2-pin type.
COMMUNICATIONS: Telephone: IDD is available.
Country code: 47. Outgoing international code: 095. **Fax:**
This service is available at major hotels. **Telex/telegram:**
Televerket's headquarters are at Teledirektoratet,
Universitetsgt 2. It is easiest to send telegrams by
telephone or telex. The telephone directories give
instructions in English on page 16. **Post:** Hotel
receptions, shops and kiosks selling postcards will sell
stamps. Airmail within Europe takes two to four days.
There are *Poste Restante* facilities at post offices in all
major cities. Post office hours: 0900-1700 Monday to
Friday, 0900-1300 Saturday. **Press:** The national
newspapers published in Oslo are *Aftenposten, Verdens
Gang, Arbeiderbladet* and *Dagbladet*. There are no
English-language newspapers.
**BBC World Service and Voice of America
frequencies:** From time to time these change. See the
section *How to Use this Book* for more information.
BBC:

| MHz | 12.09 | 9.410 | 6.195 | 3.955 |

A service is also available on 648kHz and 198kHz (0100-
0500 GMT).
Voice of America:

| MHz | 15.20 | 9.760 | 6.040 | 5.995 |

PASSPORT/VISA

	Passport Required?	Visa Required?	Return Ticket Required?
Full British	1	No	No
BVP	Valid	-	-
Australian	Yes	No	No
Canadian	Yes	No	No
USA	Yes	No	No
Other EU (As of 31/12/94)	1	No	No
Japanese	Yes	No	No

PASSPORTS: Valid passport required by all except:
(a) **[1]** EU nationals if holding a national ID card or, in
the case of the UK, a BVP;
(b) nationals of Austria, Finland, Iceland, Liechtenstein,
Sweden and Switzerland if holding a national ID card.
Note: Passports must be valid for at least 2 months
beyond the intended period of stay. Expired passports can
in no way be considered as valid travel documents.
British Visitors Passport: BVPs are valid for holidays
or unpaid business trips of up to 3 months. The sum
duration of such visits to Denmark, Finland, Iceland,

Norway and Sweden must add up to less than 3 months
in any 9-month period.
VISAS: Required by all except:
(a) nationals of the countries referred to in the chart
above;
(b) nationals of Andorra, Argentina, Austria, Bahamas,
Barbados, Belize, Bermuda, Bolivia, Botswana, Brazil,
Brunei, Chile, Colombia, Costa Rica, Côte d'Ivoire,
Croatia, Cuba, Cyprus, Czech Republic, Dominica,
Dominican Republic, Ecuador, El Salvador, Fiji, Finland,
Grenada, Guatemala, Guyana, Haiti, Honduras, Hungary,
Iceland, Israel, Jamaica, Japan, Kenya, Kiribati, South
Korea, Lesotho, Liechtenstein, Lithuania (for tourism
only), Macau, Malawi, Malaysia, Malta, Mauritius,
Mexico, Monaco, Namibia, New Zealand, Nicaragua,
Niger, Panama, Paraguay, Peru, Poland, San Marino,
Seychelles, Singapore, Slovak Republic, Slovenia,
Solomon Islands, St Kitts & Nevis, St Lucia, St Vincent
& the Grenadines, Suriname, Swaziland, Sweden,
Switzerland, Tanzania, Thailand, Trinidad & Tobago,
Tuvalu, Uganda, Uruguay, Vatican City, Venezuela,
Zambia and Zimbabwe.
Types of visa: Tourist/Entry visas: £14.
Validity: Up to 3 months. For renewal or extension
apply to Embassy.
Application to: Consulate (or Consular section at
Embassy). For addresses, see top of entry.
Application requirements: (a) Valid passport. (b) 2
application forms. (c) 2 passport-size photos.
Working days required: 3-6 weeks by post or in person.
Temporary residence: Apply to Embassy for residence
and work permit if the stay exceeds 3 months.

MONEY

Currency: Norwegian Krone (NKr) = 100 øre. Notes are
in denominations of NKr1000, 500, 100 and 50. Coins
are in denominations of NKr10, 5 and 1, and 50 and 10
øre.
Currency exchange: Eurocheque cards allow
encashment of personal cheques.
Credit cards: Access/Mastercard, American Express,
Diners Club and Visa are accepted. Check with your
credit card company for details of merchant acceptability
and other services which may be available.
Travellers cheques: Accepted in banks, hotels, shops
and by airlines.
Exchange rate indicators: The following figures are
included as a guide to the movements of the Krone
against Sterling and the US Dollar:

Date:	Oct '92	Sep '93	Jan '94	Jan '95
£1.00=	9.97	10.70	11.13	10.58
$1.00=	6.28	7.01	7.52	6.76

Currency restrictions: The import and export of local
currency is limited to NKr25,000. Export of foreign
currency is limited to the amount declared on import. No
restrictions on travellers cheques.
Banking hours: 0815/0900-1700 Monday to Thursday
in major cities and 0900-1530 Friday.

DUTY FREE

The following items can be imported into Norway
without incurring customs duty by:
(a) Residents of European countries:
*200 cigarettes or 250g of tobacco products and 200
leaves of cigarette paper (arrivals over 16 years of age
only); 1 litre of spirits and 1 litre of wine or 2 litres of
wine and 2 litres of beer (arrivals over 20 years of age
only); other goods to the value of NKr1200.*
(b) Residents of non-European countries:
*400 cigarettes or 500g of tobacco products and 200
leaves of cigarette paper (arrivals over 16 years of age
only); 1 litre of spirits and 1 litre of wine or 2 litres of
wine and 2 litres of beer (arrivals over 20 years of age
only); other goods to the value of NKr1200.*

Prohibited items: Spirits over 60% volume (120° proof)
and wine over 22% volume, certain foodstuffs (including
eggs, potatoes, meat, meat products, dairy products and
poultry), mammals, birds, exotic animals, narcotics,
medicines, poisons and firearms, ammunitions and
explosives.

PUBLIC HOLIDAYS

Jan 1 '95 New Year's Day. **Apr 13** Maundy Thursday.
Apr 14 Good Friday. **Apr 17** Easter Monday. **May 1**
May Day. **May 17** National Independence Day. **May 25**
Ascension. **Jun 4-5** Whitsun. **Dec 25** Christmas. **Dec 26**
Boxing Day. **Jan 1 '96** New Year's Day. **Apr 4** Maundy
Thursday. **Apr 5** Good Friday. **Apr 8** Easter Monday.

HEALTH

	Special Precautions?	Certificate Required?
Yellow Fever	No	No
Cholera	No	No
Typhoid & Polio	No	-
Malaria	No	-
Food & Drink	No	-

Rabies is only present on the islands of Svalbard.
Health care: There are Reciprocal Health Agreements
with most European countries. That with the UK allows
free hospital in-patient treatment and ambulance travel on
presentation of a UK passport. The cost of other
treatment (including tooth extractions) may be partially
refunded under the Norwegian social insurance scheme.
Before leaving Norway, receipts should be presented at
the social insurance office ('Trygdekasse') of the district
where treatment was carried out. Chemists are called
'Apotek'. Standards of health care are high.

TRAVEL - International

AIR: Norwegian air travel is served by *Wideroe Norsk
Air, Norway Airlines, Braathens SAFE* and *Scandinavian
Airlines System (SAS)*, a Scandinavian airline. *British
Airways* and *Air UK* also operate services to Norway.
For free advice on air travel, call the Air Travel Advisory
Bureau on (0171) 636 5000 (London) *or* (0161) 832 2000
(Manchester).
Approximate flight times: From *London* to Oslo is 1
hour 45 minutes, to Bergen is 1 hour 40 minutes and to
Stavanger is 1 hour 30 minutes.
From *New York* to Oslo is 10 hours 45 minutes
(including stopover in London).
International airports: *Oslo (OSL)* (Fornebu) is 8km (5
miles) from the city (travel time – 25 minutes). Airport
facilities include banks/bureaux de change (0630-2000),
duty-free shops (0600-2200), bar (1300-2200), restaurant
(1230-2000), snack bar (0630-2100), chemist (0630-
2100), various shops (0630-2200), left luggage (0600-
2330), post office (0700-1730 Monday to Thursday,
0700-1830 Friday and 0830-1330 Saturday) and car
rental *(Avis, Budget, Hertz* and *Tradecar)*. A coach goes
to the city every 20 minutes 0750-2230. Bus no. 31 goes
every 30 minutes 0338-0008. Taxis are available to the
city. There is a surcharge after 2200.
Stavanger (SVG) (Sola) is 14.5km (9 miles) southwest of
the city (travel time – 20 minutes). Airport facilities
include duty-free shops, bar (1200-2000), restaurant
(1000-2000 Monday to Friday, 1000-1700 Saturday),
snack bar (0615-2100 Monday to Saturday, 0800-2200
Sunday), many shops, 24-hour tourist information, post
office (0830-1600 Monday to Friday, 0830-1200
Saturday), banks/bureaux de change (0745-1730 Monday
to Friday, 0745-1630 Saturday and 1100-1630 Sunday),
left luggage (0800-2200), 24-hour lockers and car hire
(Avis, Budget, Hertz and *InterRent/Europcar)*. There is a
coach to the Royal Atlantic Hotel, Jembaneveien 1. Bus
no. 40 goes every 20 minutes 0620-2400 for a fare of
approximately NKr19 (travel time – 30 minutes). Taxi
services are available to the city with a surcharge after
2200 (travel time – 15 minutes).
Bergen (BGO) (Flesland) is 19km (12 miles) southwest
of the city (travel time – 30 minutes). Airport facilities
include left luggage (0730-2400), lockers (0600-2400),
banks (0730-1530; until 1730 in summer), bureaux de
change, post office (0830-1630 Monday to Friday, 0900-
1300 Saturday), duty-free shops, bar (1200-2200), cafés,
shops, tourist information (0900-1800 Monday to Friday,
1100-1800 Saturday to Sunday), nursery (0600-2400)

and car rental (*Avis, Budget, Hertz, InterRent, Europcar* and *Thrifty*). There is a coach to the city which returns from Flyterminalen Bus Station 60 minutes before flight departure. Bus (Flyplassen) service goes every 60 minutes 0645-2130. Return is from Flyterminalen. Taxi services are available to the city for a fare of approximately NKr170 with a surcharge after 2200 (travel time – 25 minutes).

SEA: The main passenger ports are Oslo, Narvik, Stavanger, Kristiansund and Bergen. The main sea routes from the UK are operated by the *Color Line*, are from Newcastle to Bergen (travel time – 18 hours 30 minutes) and to Stavanger (travel time – 22 hours).

RAIL: Connections from the UK are from London via Dover/Ostend (via The Netherlands, Germany, Denmark and Sweden) or Harwich/Hook of Holland, or from Newcastle to Bergen via Stavanger. There are two principal routes to Sweden, with daytime and overnight trains from Malmö and Stockholm.

Cheap fares: Reduced fares on rail services have vastly increased the use and range of internal services. *Nordturist* tickets, also known as *Scanrail* cards, allow 21 days' unlimited travel in Denmark, Sweden, Norway and Finland on railways and selected ferries, and a 50% reduction on other ferry services. *Inter-Rail* tickets are valid in Norway.

ROAD: The only routes are from Sweden or Finland in the far north. Camping trailers up to 2.3m (7ft 6 inches) wide, with number plates, are permitted on holiday visits.

TRAVEL - Internal

AIR: Domestic flights are run by *Scandinavian Airlines System (SAS), Braathen's SAFE (BU)* and *Widerøes Air Transport Company (WF)*. Fifty airports with scheduled services exist in the fjord country of western Norway and along the remaining coast. Charter sea or land planes are available at most destinations. There is an internal service from Oslo to all towns and cities via *SAS* and *BU*. Coastal links are by *WF, SAS* and *BU*. Reduced airfare tickets are available for families, children under 12 years (who pay half price), groups and pensioners. For further information, contact Widerøe Flyveselskap A/S, PO Box 82, Mustadsvei 1, Lilleaker, 0216 Oslo 2. Tel: (22) 736 500. Fax: (22) 736 590.

SEA: All coastal towns are served by ferries, catamarans and hydrofoils. The Hurtigrute (express) from Bergen to Kirkenes (near the Russian border) takes about 11 days round trip, leaving daily and stopping at 35 ports on the west coast. Various ferry trips are available (half price in spring and autumn). It is possible to embark at Trondheim, Bodø or Tromsø.

RAIL: All services are run by *NSR Travel* (Norwegian State Railways). The main internal rail routes are: Oslo–Trondheim (*Dovre Line*); Trondheim–Bodø (*Nordland Railway*); Oslo–Bergen (*Bergen Railway*); and Oslo–Stavanger (*Sorland Railway*). There are also services to Charlottenburg (Stockholm) and Halden (Malmö) on routes to Sweden. Seats on express trains must be reserved. There are buffet/restaurant cars on some trains, and sleepers on long-distance overnight services. Heavy luggage may be sent in advance. Children under 4 years of age travel free; children 4-14 years pay half-fare only. The *ScanRail Pass*, valid for all of Scandinavia, offers a substantial reduction. For further information contact Norwegian State Railways, Persontrafikk, Gernbametorhet 1, 0048 Oslo. Tel: (22) 171 400. Fax: (22) 366 458; *or* Norwegian State Railways Travel Bureau, Norway House, 21-24 Cockspur Street, London SW1Y 5DA. Tel: (0171) 930 6666. Fax: (0171) 321 0624. Telex: 28380.

ROAD: Traffic drives on the right. The road system is of variable quality (especially under freezing winter conditions in the north), but supplemented by numerous car ferries across the fjords. **Bus:** Principal long-distance internal bus routes are from Bo (in Telemark) to Haugesund (8 hours); from Ålesund–Molde–Kristiansund to Trondheim (8 hours); and from Fauske to Kirkenes (4 days) with links to the Bo line in the north. Inter-Nordic runs from Trondheim to Stockholm. There are also extensive regional local bus services, some of which are operated by companies with interests in the ferries. The official 'Rutehefte' is a must for anyone using public transport, and gives extensive

timetable information and maps of all bus, train, ferry and air routes. **Taxi:** In most cases fares are metered. Taxis can be found at ranks or booked by telephone. **Car hire:** Available in airports and most towns, but costly; in general, problems of cost and parking make public transport more practical and convenient. It is also possible to hire bicycles. **Regulations:** The minimum age for driving is 18. There are severe penalties for drunken driving and illegal parking. Seat belts are compulsory. Children under 12 must travel in the back of the car. *It is obligatory for all vehicles to drive with dipped headlights at all times,* even on the brightest summer day. This includes motorcycles and mopeds. Carrying spare headlight bulbs is recommended. Speed limits are 80-90kmph (49-56mph) outside built-up areas, and 50kmph (31mph) in built-up areas. Snow chains or studded winter tyres are advised during the winter. Petrol stations are numerous, although tourists are only able to purchase petrol with credit cards in some of them. The contact for AIT (Alliance Internationale de Tourisme) is the Norwegian Automobile Association (NAF), Storgt 2, 1055 Oslo 2. Tel: (22) 341 400. Fax: (22) 331 373. **Documentation:** International Driving Permit or national driving licence and log book are required. A Green Card is strongly recommended (for those with more than Third Party cover on their domestic policy). Without it, visitors with motor insurance in their own countries are allowed the minimum legal cover in Norway; the Green Card tops this up to the level of cover provided by the visitor's own policy.

URBAN: Good public transport systems operate in the main towns. Oslo has bus, rail, metro and tramway services. Tickets are pre-purchased and self-cancelled, and there is one hour's free transfer between any of the modes. Meters on taxis are obligatory.

JOURNEY TIMES: The following chart gives approximate journey times (in hours and minutes) from Oslo to other major cities/towns in Norway.

	Air	Road	Rail
Bergen	0.35	9.00	8.00
Kristiansund	0.30	5.00	5.00
Lillehammer	0.20	3.00	2.30
Stavanger	0.35	7.00	8.00
Tromsø	1.40	20.00	-
Trondheim	0.40	10.00	9.00

ACCOMMODATION

HOTELS: First-class hotels are to be found all over the country. Facilities in all establishments are classified, as hotels must come up to official high standards; for example, there must be a reception service, dining room, and a minimum of 30 rooms, each with full bath and shower. Many hotels are still family-run establishments. Full *en pension* terms are available to guests staying at the same establishment for at least three to five days. Hotels usually allow a reduction on the same *en pension* rate for children according to age. This reduction may only apply when the child concerned occupies an extra bed in the parents' room. There are several schemes which offer visitors reduced rates in selected hotels. A **Fjord Pass** (which covers two adults with special concessions for children under 15) is accepted by 300 hotels in the period May 1-September 30; reductions of 20% or more are possible. The **Nordic Passepartout** is a pan-Scandinavian card accepted by over 50 hotels in Norway in the main summer period and at weekends; the visitor's fifth night is free. A **Scandinavian Bonus Pass** (which covers two adults with special concessions for children under 16) is accepted by 45 hotels in Norway between May 15-September 1 and at weekends during winter; a Scanrail railway pass will also be accepted. **Scandinavian Hotel Express** is a travel club which enables visitors to have reductions of 50% in certain hotels. Roughly 50% of establishments belong to Norsk Hotell og Resturantforbund, Essendrupsgt 6, 0368 Oslo. Tel: (22) 965 080. Fax: (22) 569 620. **Grading:** There is no grading system, but establishments designated *turisthotel* or *høyfjellshotell* must meet specified standards.

GUEST-HOUSES & MOUNTAIN LODGES: Guest-houses (*pensjonat*) and mountain lodges are generally smaller in size and offer less elaborate facilities than hotels, although many establishments can offer the same standard as those officially listed as hotels.

FARMHOUSE HOLIDAYS: Farms selected are working farms and anyone who wants to can join in the work, but guests are at liberty to plan their own day, and the hosts will generally be able to suggest tours, excursions and other activities. Contact the tourist office for further information. The tour operator Troll Park offers many farmhouse holidays and a programme printed in Norwegian, German and English is available from Troll Park A/S, Postboks 373, 2600 Lillehammer.

SELF-CATERING: Chalets, log cabins and apartments are available for rent by groups and will generally work out less expensive per head than other kinds of holiday. Most chalets have electric lighting, heating and hot plates; some have kerosene lamps, calor gas for cooking and wood fires, while water will often have to be fetched from a nearby well or stream. Chalets are grouped near a central building which may contain such facilities as a cafeteria, lounges, TV rooms, sauna, a grocer's shop, and in some cases a swimming pool. All chalets and apartments are regularly inspected by responsible rental firms. Bookings can be made by writing to various firms. *Den Norske Hytteformidling A/S*, Box 3404 Bgulsen, Oslo 0406 (tel: (22) 356 710; fax: (22) 719 413) organises chalet holidays all over Norway, with full board or self-catering.

Rorbu holidays: A *Rorbu* is a hut or shelter used by fishermen during the winter cod-fishing season. Equipped with all the necessary facilities, these are leased to holidaymakers during the summer, providing an inexpensive form of accommodation. They will often be actually over the water. Catching your own fish will further reduce the cost of the holiday. For more information on Rorbu holidays, contact *Destinasjon Lofoten*, Boks 210, 8301 Svolvær. Tel: (760) 73000. Fax: (760) 73001.

CAMPING/CARAVANNING: Offsite camping is permitted in uninhabited areas (not lay-bys), but fires are illegal in field or woodland areas between April 15-September 15. Farmers must be asked for permission for farmland camping. The Tourist Board publishes a list of 'Camp Sites in Norway'. Further details and a manual are available from the Norwegian Automobile Association (NAF), Storgt 2, 0155 Oslo 2. **Grading:** There are over 1000 authorised sites in Norway, classified according to standards and amenities from **1-** to **5-star** camps, with charges varying accordingly. Notice of available amenities is posted in each camp.

YOUTH HOSTELS: There are some 100 youth hostels spread all over Norway, some of which are open all year round. Others are in apartment houses attached to schools or universities and are open only during the summer season. Sleeping bags can be hired if necessary. Groups must always make advance bookings. All are welcome, but members of the Norwegian Youth Hostel Association (NUH), or similar associations in other countries, have priority. International membership cards can be bought at most youth hostels. Hostels vary from **1-** to **3-star** establishments. Breakfast is usually NKr50-60. Detailed information can be obtained from the Tourist Board's Camping/YH list, or direct from *Norske Vandrerhjem*, Dronningensgt 26, 0154 Oslo 1. Tel: (22) 421 410. Fax: (22) 424 476.

RESORTS & EXCURSIONS

For the purpose of clarity this section has been divided into several sub-sections. These do not necessarily reflect cultural or administrative boundaries.

The Oslo Fjord

The region surrounding the 110km-long (70-mile) Oslo Fjord is the most popular in Norway. The coast is fringed with islands, while the interior is criss-crossed with rivers and dotted with lakes. Its a good place to go boating or bathing. There are many traces of early civilisation: rock carvings, burial mounds, ships' graves, stone churches, manor farms and fortresses.

Oslo, the capital, is Norway's most important industrial, commercial and shipping centre. Of the city's total land area, some 12% has been developed while the remainder is a network of woodland trails, islands and countless lakes offering good fishing and bathing. Oslo is also the focus of national art and culture, with major collections, maritime museums, theatres, opera, concerts and restaurants of every category.

SIGHTSEEING/EXCURSIONS: Oslo: *Akershus Castle; Munch Museum;* **Holmenkollen** ski jump, museum and restaurant; *Norwegian Folk Museum;* the Viking ships; *Fram Museum; Kon-Tiki Museum; Norwegian Maritime Museum, Vigeland's Park and museum* and sightseeing boat trips on the fjord.

Further afield: The *Tertitten* narrow gauge railway at **Sorumsand**, open-air zoo at **Ski**, 17th-century fortress town and *Kongsten Fortress* at **Fredrikstad**, Vansjo

inland waterway system and recreational centre, the *Road of the Ancients* between Fredrikstad and **Skjeberg** (Bronze Age rock carvings and Viking burial mounds), the *Naval Museum* at **Horten** and the *Whaling Museum* at **Sandefjord**.

RESORTS: Holmestrand, Horten, Tonsberg, Sandefjord, Larvik, Oslo, Sarpsborg, Fredrikstad and Halden.

The Eastern Valleys

This part of Norway comprises several of the largest and most picturesque valleys in the whole country. This is a typical inland region, bordered to the north, west and south by the mighty massifs of the Rondane, Dovrefjell and Jotunheimen ranges and the Hardanger plateau. Further south the country slopes down to the lakes. This area is notable for its stable climate.

Hedmark is a county of extensive forests and has Norway's longest river, the *Glåma*. There are several major tourist resorts in this area, often placed close to recreational facilities and offering varied and up-to-date accommodation. Mountain hikes, riding, glacier rambles, summer ski racing, canoeing and fishing are popular activities and larger resorts offer varied programmes of amusements.

SIGHTSEEING/EXCURSIONS: Paddle steamer trip across *Lake Mjosa; Railway Museum* at **Hamar**; 17th-century *Kongsvinger Castle; Norwegian Forestry Museum* at **Elverum**; boat excursions on *Lake Femund*; north Europe's biggest open-air museum at **Lillehammer**; *Norwegian Historical Vehicles Museum* and glassworks at **Gjovik** and **Jevnaker**; 12th-century stave churches at **Valdres**; summer skiing on *Veslejuvbreen* near **Juvasshytta**; *Blue Dye Works* at **Modum**; *Folk Museum* at **Hallingal**; and the chair lift to *Geilohøgda* at **Geilo**.

RESORTS: Winter & Summer: Geilo, Gjovik, Fagernes, Lillehammer, Otta, Dombas and Tynset.
Summer only: Rena, Elverum, Hamar, Kongsvinger, Honefoss, Drammen and Kongsberg.

Telemark and the South Coast

This region comprises the coastal strip running from Oslo Fjord round the southern tip of Norway, a region of skerries, bathing beaches, sheltered anchorages, picturesque little harbours and villages. Further inland the country is wooded, intersected here and there by valleys running up to extensive moors and mountain ranges which have marked trails and tourist lodges for those wishing to tour on foot. This area is renowned for its cultural crafts including silverware. The *Telemark Waterway* links **Skien** on the coast with the interior by a system of locks and canals which can be negotiated by boat.

SIGHTSEEING/EXCURSIONS: The *Victoria*, sailing from Skien to **Dalen** through 18 locks and canals; canoeing on lakes and canals; *Lakeland Amusement Park* in **Skien**; *Berg-Kragero Museum* and excursions among the islands at **Kragero**; stave church from 1240 at **Heddal**; *Krosso* cable railway at **Rjukan**; old town at **Arendal**; *Ibsen Museum* at **Grimstad**; silverworks at **Setesdal**; skerry excursions, *Christiansholm Fortress* and the zoo at **Kristiansund**; *Maritime Museum* at **Mandal**; museum at **Farsund**; and ancient monuments, rock carvings and burial mounds at **Litalandet**.

RESORTS: Winter & Summer: Bykle, Dalen, Hovden and Rjukan.
Summer only: Skien, Porsgrunn, Kragero, Risor, Arendal, Grimstad, Lillesand, Kristiansund, Mandal, Farsund, Flekkefjord and Evje.

The Western Fjords

The fjord country covers the area from Stavanger in the south to Kristiansund in the north, and from the North Sea in the west to the mountain ranges in the east. Many of the fjords are only 100m (330ft) wide in places, with vertical cliffs rising over 1000m (3300ft) on either side. The longest, Sognefjord, runs for over 200km (124 miles) into the interior. Others include the Ryfylke Fjords, Hardanger Fjord, Sunn Fjord, Nord Fjord, Geiranger Fjord and Romsdal Fjord. In the mountain region of west Norway, the glaciers often reach right down to the bottom of the adjacent valley. The whole region offers excellent river and lake fishing, as well as hiking, boat and cycling tours.

SIGHTSEEING/EXCURSIONS: There is a cathedral, an Iron Age farm and boat excursions on the fjord at **Stavanger**; daily fishing trips, an annual cultural festival (May/June), a museum and an aquarium at **Bergen**; a cable-car ride to **Fløyfjell** from Bergen town centre; daily excursions to the *Hardanger Fjord* and the *Vøringfoss Falls* at **Mabodalen**; *Borgund Ståve Church* (AD1150) at **Laerdal**; the Flam railway line, dropping 900m (2952ft) in 20km (12 miles); *Sunnmøre Museum* at

☐ airport

200km
100mls

EUROPE

Ålesund; and the *Romsdal Museum* and jazz festival at **Molde**.

RESORTS: Winter & Summer: Voss.
Summer only: Egersund, Stavanger, Haugesund, Bergen, Sogndal, Floro, Ålesund, Andalsnes, Molde and Kristiansund.

North Norway

In the extreme north of Norway there are majestic mountains, rolling moors, deep fertile valleys, sheltered fjords and thousands of islands. There is also continuous daylight from April to August. Due to the Gulf Stream which sweeps up the coastline, the climate is exceptionally temperate. Fishing, often combined with farming, is still the main source of livelihood. The main attraction in north Norway is the scenery, but there is also very good sea fishing, salmon rivers and thousands of lakes and rivers well stocked with trout.

SIGHTSEEING/EXCURSIONS: *Tromsø Museum, Tromsø Marine Aquarium* and *Polar Museum* in **Tromsø**; North Norway and International Deep-Sea Fishing Festivals (June/July) in **Harstad**; *Tromsø War Museum* in **Bardu**; rock carvings (2500-4500 years old) in **Blasfjord**; primeval pine forests, cliffs and waterfalls in **Reisadalen**; *Cathedral* and sea fishing excursions in **Bodø**; the *Glom Fjord*; the *Grønnli Grotto* (stalactite cave with a subterranean waterfall); cable-car to *Fagernesfjell Bird Colony* at **Røst** and **Vørøy**; Samic

STAVANGER

½km
¼ml

i tourist information

RESO HOTELS
- always in the heart!

RESO HOTELS - with six hotels in Norway, centrally located
in the five largest cities. With us you will stay first-class, in the
heart of the city, near everything you wish to see and experience.
You will be a short trip away from beautiful natural surroundings
and have the sea virtually at your door. Each hotel is an experience
in itself, with its own history and unique personality. Regardless which
Reso hotel you choose, you can be sure that you will have a first-class stay!

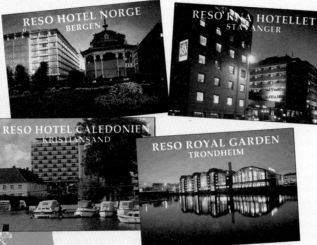

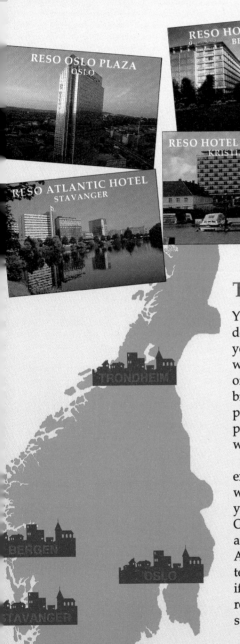

The land of fairytales

You can think of Norway as a small kingdom or a big country, depending on how
you choose to look at it. In Norway, you
will find all the opportunities and variety
of activities you would expect to find in a
bigger country, and at the same time, the
pleasant, friendly atmosphere of a smaller
place. And Norway is an easy country in
which to find your way around.

Oslo, the capital, offers a wide range of
exciting things to see and do, no matter
what your interest. Oslo is cosmopolitan,
yet less crowded than most capital cities.
Only half a million inhabitants share an
area about the size of cities like Los
Angeles and Paris. Oslo is also less polluted and safer than most capitals. And few -
if any - capitals in the world can boast finer
recreational facilities, right on their doorstep.

You deserve a bit of luxury

It is nice to stay at a hotel and really
unwind. Treat yourself a little, without
spending a lot. At Reso Hotels you can
relax and sleep as long as you want. In
the mornings you will find a plentiful
breakfast buffet waiting for you, with
fresh coffee and homemade bread. Or
perhaps you prefer the peace and quiet
of breakfast in bed.

We have special weekend rates year-
round and holiday-friendly rates during
the summer months. For further information, ring Reso ReservationService at
22 17 17 00, or directly to one of our fine
Reso hotels.

Welcome to Reso experience!

SIMPLY THE BEST · RESO·HOTELS · PLACE TO STAY!

RESO OSLO PLAZA TEL: (47) 22 17 10 00 FAX: (47) 22 17 73 00
RESO ATLANTIC HOTEL TEL: (47) 51 52 75 20 FAX: (47) 51 56 10 75
RESO KNA HOTELLET TEL: (47) 51 52 85 00 FAX: (47) 51 53 59 97

RESO ROYAL GARDEN TEL: (47) 73 52 11 00 FAX: (47) 73 53 17 66
RESO HOTEL CALEDONIEN TEL: (47) 38 02 91 00 FAX: (47) 38 02 59 90
RESO HOTEL NORGE TEL: (47) 55 21 01 00 FAX: (47) 55 21 02 99

RESO RESERVATIONSERVICE TEL: (47) 22 17 17 00 FAX: (47) 22 10 52

collections at **Karasjok;** riverboats to **Sauvtso;** church and Meridian stone at **Hammerfest;** *North Cape* (viewpoint in the extreme north of Norway); and the *King Oscar* and *St George's chapels* at **Kirkenes.**
RESORTS: Winter & Summer: Harstad, Narvik and Svolvær.
Summer only: Rana, Mosjøen, Bodø, Finnsnes, Tromsø, Kautokeino, Karasjok, Alta, Kirkenes, Vadsø, Hammerfest, Vardø and Nordkapp.

Trøndelag

The Trøndelag counties are bordered to the west by the Norwegian Sea and a screen of islands and skerries, past which the Trondheim Fjord passes into rich farmland and the interior. To the east there are extensive moors dotted with well-stocked lakes, while to the south and southeast the mountain massifs of Trollheimen and Sylene dominate the scene. A number of rivers flow through rolling farm country. The region offers most outdoors activities with a special emphasis on sea and freshwater fishing, in particular salmon fishing. The climate is mild and warm enough for bathing.
SIGHTSEEING/EXCURSIONS: *Nidaros Cathedral,* 12th-century *Archbishop's Palace,* and *Ringve Musical Museum* in **Trondheim;** *Trollheimen range* with marked trails, pony trekking, salmon and trout fishing and riding camps; *Kongsvold Botanical Mountain Garden* at **Oppdal og Orkdalen;** *Rein Abbey* in **Rissa;** good fishing in the sea or rivers everywhere; prehistoric monuments including burial mounds, monoliths and stone circles at **Eggekvammen** and **Tingvoll;** *Helge Farm* at **Byafossen;** the Olav drama at **Stiklestad;** fortress ruins from 1525 at **Steinviksholm;** rock carvings and burial mounds at **Skogn, Hell, Leirfall** and **Lekaøya.**
RESORTS: Winter & Summer: Røros and Oppdal.
Summer only: Orkanger, Trondheim, Stjørdal Levanger, Verdal Steinkjer, Namsos and Rorvik.

SOCIAL PROFILE

FOOD & DRINK: Breakfasts are often enormous with a variety of fish, meat, cheese and bread served from a cold buffet with coffee and boiled or fried eggs. Many hotels and restaurants serve lunch from a *koldtbord* (cold table), with smoked salmon, fresh lobster, shrimp and hot dishes. Open sandwiches are topped with meat, fish, cheese and salads. Other dishes include roast venison, ptarmigan in cream sauce, wild cranberries, *multer* (a berry with a unique flavour), *lutefisk* (a hot, highly flavoured cod fish) and herring prepared in various ways.
Drink: *Aquavit* (schnapps) is a popular drink, but in general alcohol is limited and expensive, although beer and wine are generally served in restaurants. Bars have table and counter service. Licensing laws are strict and alcohol is sold only by the state through special monopoly. Licensing hours are also enforced and only wine and beer are served Sunday.
NIGHTLIFE: Several hotels and restaurants in Oslo stage cabaret programmes and floor shows. Venues change so it is best to check in the local newspaper. Theatres, cinemas, nightclubs and discotheques are located in major centres. Resorts have dance music, and folk dancing is popular.
SHOPPING: Most towns and resorts have a shop where typical Norwegian handicrafts are on sale. Silversmiths and potteries are numerous and worth visiting. Traditional items include furs, printed textiles, woven articles, knitwear, woodcarving, silver, enamel, pewter, glass and porcelain. Tax-free cheques can be obtained from any of the 2500 shops carrying the sticker 'Tax free for tourists'. These shops save visitors 10-15% of the price paid by residents. VAT refunds are paid in cash at airports, ferries, cruise ships and border crossings.
Shopping hours: 0900-1700/1800 Monday to Friday; 0900-1500/1600 Saturday. One late night opening a week is usual, in Oslo this is Thursday.
SPORT: Tennis: A number of resort hotels have their own courts. **Golf:** Oslo (Bogstad links) and Stokke (between Tønsberg and Sandefjord) all have 18-hole golf courses, and there are shorter courses in Bergen, Sarpsborg, Hamar, Kristiansund and Trondheim. Most clubs are open to visitors. **Horseriding:** Riding holidays are becoming more popular. There are riding schools and clubs throughout the country with horses for hire and instruction provided, also a number of hotels keep horses.
Skiing: Summer skiing June/July at some central resorts. Winter sports from December to April. **Fishing:** Angling is popular on Norway's many inland waters and surrounding sea. There are over 100 salmon rivers flowing into the fjords where reasonably priced sport is offered. A national fishing licence is necessary, obtainable from post offices. A permit is required for freshwater fishing. **Boating:** A number of hotels,

campsites and chalets have boats for use by visitors on the coast and inland waters. **Windsurfing/water-skiing:** Hotels and campsites located near stretches of water often hire out equipment for windsurfing or water-skiing and offer instruction. **Swimming:** Norway's coast and inland waters are ideal for bathing in warm months. There are several specially designated beaches for naturists. Many resort hotels have pools.
SPECIAL EVENTS: The following is a selection of major festivals and other special events celebrated in Norway. For a complete list of events in 1995/96 contact the Tourist Board.
Apr '95 *Vossajazz,* Voss. **May 17** *Constitution Day Processions,* throughout Norway. **May 24** *International Music Festival,* Bergen. **Jun** *Night Jazz Festival,* Bergen; *Norwegian Short Film Festival,* Grimstad; *Edvard Grieg Festival,* Lofthus/Hardangar. **Jun 23** *Midsummer Night Celebrations,* throughout Norway. **Jul** *International Jazz Festival,* Kongsberg; *International Seafishing Festival,* Harstad. **Aug** *St Olav Days,* Trondheim; *Chamber Music Festival,* Oslo; *Seafood Festival,* Mandal; *Norwegian Film Festival,* Haugesund. **Aug 27** *Norwegian Food Festival,* Ålesund. **Sep** *Oslo Marathon.* **Dec 10** *Nobel Peace Prize Ceremony,* Oslo.
SOCIAL CONVENTIONS: Normal courtesies should be observed. It is customary for the guest to refrain from drinking until the host toasts their health. Casual dress is normal. The main meal of the day, lunch, may take place late in the afternoon (often as late as 1700); however, if invited out Norwegians will generally be happy to dine in the evening. If invited to the home the visitor should bring flowers for the hostess. Punctuality is expected. Smoking is prohibited in some public buildings and on public transport. **Tipping:** It is not customary to tip taxi drivers. Waiters expect a tip of no more than 5% of the bill, porters at airports and railway stations charge per piece of luggage. Hotel porters are tipped NKr5-10 according to the number of pieces of luggage.

BUSINESS PROFILE

ECONOMY: There is little cultivatable land in Norway, but many farmers, the majority of whom breed livestock, combine this with tree-felling to supply Norway's numerous sawmills. Wood products and paper are consequently both strong industries. Offshore fishing has been in decline for some time, but a large number of fish-farms have been established, making Norway by far the world's largest supplier of salmon. Economic development immediately after the Second World War was concentrated in heavy engineering industries such as shipbuilding. These have also declined since the mid-1970s, but Norway has sustained its economic prosperity through development of an exceptionally strong energy sector: the country has abundant resources for hydroelectric power which have allowed much-reduced overheads for larger industries, such as aluminium production, which has established factories near power stations. In addition, from the mid-1970s Norway has, like Britain, been a major oil exporter, having discovered large deposits in the North Sea. Some advanced technological industries of world standard have developed in recent years, but the best prospects for exporters to Norway are in service industries. Britain, Germany and Sweden are the biggest importers to the country. These three countries are also Norway's largest export markets. Norway is a member of the European Free Trade Association, having decided in 1973 not to join the EU, although it enjoys wholly liberalised trade with the Union in all sectors apart from agriculture, which in Norway remains heavily protected. Moreover, EFTA established a free trade zone with the EU, known as the European Economic Area, in 1991. Another referendum was held in 1994 on the question of entry into the EU. On this occasion, there was the added incentive that both its land neighbours, Sweden and Finland, were scheduled to join the EU. Nevertheless, the Norwegians once again rejected membership by a narrow margin, and thus failed to join their Scandinavian neighbours entering the EU at the beginning of 1995.
BUSINESS: Business people are expected to dress smartly. Prior appointments are necessary. Norwegian business people tend to be reserved and formal. English is widely spoken. Punctuality is essential. Calling cards are common. The best months for business visits are February to May and October to December. **Office hours:** 0800-1600 Monday to Friday.
COMMERCIAL INFORMATION: The following organisation can offer advice: Norwegian Trade Council, Drammensveien 40, 0243 Oslo. Tel: (22) 926 300. Fax: (22) 926 400. Telex: 78532.
CONFERENCES/CONVENTIONS: Information is available from The Representation Business, Charter House, 96/98 Church Street, Croydon CR0 1RD. Tel: (0181) 867 0266. Fax: (0181) 688 9331.

CLIMATE

Coastal areas have a moderate climate due to the Gulf Stream and North Atlantic Drift. Inland temperatures are more extreme with hot summers and cold winters (November to March). In general, the lowlands of the south experience colder winters and warmer summers than the coastal areas. Rain is distributed throughout the year with frequent inland snowfalls during the winter. The northern part of the country inside the Arctic Circle has continuous daylight at midsummer, and twilight all day during winter.
Required clothing: European according to the season. Light- to medium-weights are worn in summer. Warmer weights are worn during the winter. Waterproofing is advisable throughout the year.

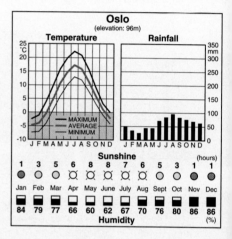

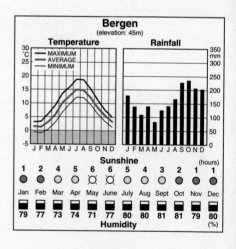

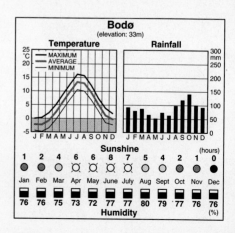

Oman

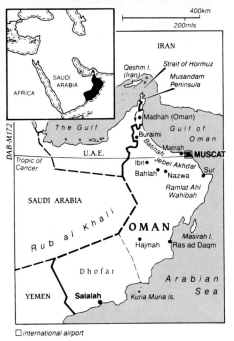

☐ *international airport*

Location: Middle East, southeastern tip of Arabian Peninsula.

Directorate General of Tourism
PO Box 550, Muscat, Code 113, Oman
Tel: 799 500. Fax: 794 213 *or* 794 239.

Embassy of the Sultanate of Oman
167 Queen's Gate, South Kensington, London SW7 5HE
Tel: (0171) 225 0001. Fax: (0171) 589 2505. Telex: 918775. Opening hours: 0900-1530 Monday to Friday.

British Embassy
PO Box 300, Muscat, Code 113, Oman
Tel: 738 501/5. Fax: 736 040. Telex: 5216 (a/b PRODROME ON).

Embassy of the Sultanate of Oman
2535 Belmont Road, NW, Washington, DC 20008
Tel: (202) 387 1980/2. Fax: (202) 745 4933.
Also deals with enquiries from Canada.

Embassy of the United States of America
PO Box 202, Madinat Qaboos, 115 Muscat, Oman
Tel: 698 989. Fax: 699 779.

Canadian Consulate
PO Box 8275, Muttrah, Flat 310, Building 477, Way 2907, Moosa Abdul Rahman Hassan Building, Al-Noor Street, Ruwi, Muscat, Oman
Tel: 791 738. Fax: 791 740.

AREA: 300,000 sq km (120,000 sq miles).
POPULATION: 2,017,000 (1994 estimate). In addition there were an estimated 350,000 expatriate workers in 1992.
POPULATION DENSITY: 6.7 per sq km (excluding expatriates).
CAPITAL: Muscat. **Population:** 450,000 (1990 estimate).
GEOGRAPHY: Oman is bordered to the west by the United Arab Emirates, Saudi Arabia and the Republic of Yemen. The Musandam Peninsula forms a coastal

Timatic	Health
	GALILEO/WORLDSPAN: **TI-DFT/MCT/HE**
	SABRE: **TIDFT/MCT/HE**
	Visa
	GALILEO/WORLDSPAN: **TI-DFT/MCT/VI**
	SABRE: **TIDFT/MCT/VI**
	For more information on Timatic codes refer to Contents.

enclave on the Strait of Hormuz. The 2700km (1700 miles) of coastline are surrounded by the Arabian and Indian Seas. The Hajir Mountains divide the land stretching from the Musandam Peninsula to the southeast. To the west lies the fertile narrow plain of the Batinah coast dominated by the Jebel Akhdar. Dhofar in the south, which is divided from the north by a desert, has a coastal plain beyond which are mountains. Out to sea are the Kuria Muria Islands. The Batinah coast is inhabited by descendants of Asian merchants, Baluchi traders and other Arab nationals, who are more aware of the outside world than the tribesmen of the interior and mountains. Along the coast at Muscat and Matrah, Arab traditions remain strong despite increasing Western influence. In the southern capital of Salalah are many black Omanis descended mainly from former slaves, whereas the interior is populated by the nomadic *Bedus* (Bedouin).

LANGUAGE: Arabic and English.
RELIGION: Ibadi Muslim, with Sunni and Shia Muslim minorities.
TIME: GMT + 4.
ELECTRICITY: 220/240 volts AC, 50Hz.
COMMUNICATIONS: Telephone: IDD is available. Country code: 968. Outgoing international code: 00.
Fax: Services are available from GTO. Some hotels provide facilities. **Telex/telegram:** Services are available at the counter in the GTO office, Muscat. In case of difficulty, book calls through the international operator.
Post: Airmail to Western Europe takes up to two weeks.
Press: English-language newspapers include *The Times of Oman* and *The Oman Daily Observer.*
BBC World Service and Voice of America frequencies: From time to time these change. See the section *How to Use this Book* for more information.
BBC:

MHz			
21.47	15.07	12.09	7.160

A service is also available on 1413kHz and 702kHz (0100-0500 GMT).
Voice of America:

MHz			
11.97	9.670	6.040	5.995

PASSPORT/VISA

Regulations and requirements may be subject to change at short notice, and you are advised to contact the appropriate diplomatic or consular authority before finalising travel arrangements. Details of these may be found at the head of this country's entry. Any numbers in the chart refer to the footnotes below.

	Passport Required?	Visa Required?	Return Ticket Required?
Full British	Yes	Yes	Yes
BVP	Not valid	-	-
Australian	Yes	Yes	Yes
Canadian	Yes	Yes	Yes
USA	Yes	Yes	Yes
Other EU (As of 31/12/94)	Yes	Yes	Yes
Japanese	Yes	Yes	Yes

Restricted entry: Holders of Israeli passports or visas, or anyone showing any evidence of having visited Israel, will be refused entry.
PASSPORTS: Valid passport required by all.
British Visitors Passport: Not accepted.
VISAS: Tourist and Business visas are required by all except nationals of Bahrain, Kuwait, Qatar, Saudi Arabia and the United Arab Emirates.
Note: Any visitor arriving in Oman without a visa or 'No Objection Certificate' (NOC) will be refused entry. Visitors are not allowed to enter Oman by road unless their visa or NOC states such validity and a designated point of entry.
Validity: Visas are valid for a visit of up to 3 weeks beginning any time during a month from the date of issue.
Application to: Consulate (or Consular section at Embassy). For addresses, see top of entry. Applications are referred to Muscat by fax.
Application requirements: (a) 1 typed application form, completed and signed. (b) 2 recent passport-size photos. (c) A full valid passport must be presented so that visas can be stamped into them. (d) Business letter or employer's certificate. (e) Fee (for UK nationals – £45; other EU nationals – £21. All others should contact the Embassy for up-to-date details).
Passengers who have a new passport, but whose visa is entered in a previous passport, should also carry their previous passport. Passengers who have a new passport, but whose 'No Objection Certificate' (NOC) is entered in a previous passport, should also carry their previous passport. Passports must have spare pages.
Working days required: Approximately 7 days. Postal applications take longer.

MONEY

Currency: Omani Rial (OR) = 1000 baiza. Notes are in denominations of OR50, 20, 10, 5 and 1, and 500, 250, 200 and 100 baiza. Coins are in denominations of 500, 250, 200, 100, 50, 25, 10 and 5 baiza.
Credit cards: American Express is accepted, as are other major credit cards, although Access/Mastercard and Visa may have more limited acceptance. Check with your credit card company for details of merchant acceptability and other services which may be available.
Travellers cheques: Easily exchanged.
Exchange rate indicators: The following figures are included as a guide to the movements of the Omani Rial against Sterling and the US Dollar:

Date:	Oct '92	Sep '93	Jan '94	Jan '95
£1.00=	0.62	0.59	0.57	0.60
$1.00=	0.39	0.38	0.38	0.38

Currency restrictions: There are no restrictions on the import or export of local or foreign currency. Israeli currency is prohibited.
Banking hours: 0800-1200 Saturday to Wednesday and 0800-1130 Thursday.

DUTY FREE

The following items may be imported into Oman without incurring customs duty:
A reasonable quantity of tobacco products; 227ml perfume and eau de cologne.
Prohibited items: Alcohol, narcotics, fresh foods, firearms (including toys and replicas) and pornographic films/literature.

PUBLIC HOLIDAYS

Feb 1 '95 Start of Ramadan. **Mar 3** Eid al-Fitr (End of Ramadan). **May 10** Eid al-Adha (Feast of the Sacrifice). **May 31** Muharram (Islamic New Year). **Jun 9** Ashoura. **Aug 9** Mouloud (Prophet's Birthday). **Nov 18** National Day. **Nov 19** Sultan's Birthday. **Dec 20** Leilat al-Meiraj (Ascension of the Prophet). **Jan 22 '96** Start of Ramadan. **Feb 22** Eid al-Fitr (End of Ramadan). **Apr 29** Eid al-Adha (Feast of the Sacrifice).
Note: Muslim festivals are timed according to local sightings of various phases of the Moon and the dates given above are approximations. During the lunar month of Ramadan that precedes Eid al-Fitr, Muslims fast during the day and feast at night and normal business patterns may be interrupted. Many restaurants are closed during the day and there may be restrictions on smoking and drinking. Some disruption may continue into Eid al-Fitr itself. Eid al-Fitr and Eid al-Adha may last anything from two to ten days, depending on the region. For more information, see the section *World of Islam* at the back of the book.

HEALTH

Regulations and requirements may be subject to change at short notice, and you are advised to contact your doctor well in advance of your intended date of departure. Any numbers in the chart refer to the footnotes below.

	Special Precautions?	Certificate Required?
Yellow Fever	No	1
Cholera	Yes	2
Typhoid & Polio	Yes	-
Malaria	3	-
Food & Drink	4	-

[1]: A yellow fever vaccination certificate is required from travellers arriving from infected areas.
[2]: Following WHO guidelines issued in 1973, a cholera vaccination certificate is not a condition of entry to Oman. However, cholera is a risk in this country and precautions are essential. Up-to-date advice should be sought before deciding whether these precautions should include vaccination, as medical opinion is divided over its effectiveness. See the *Health* section at the back of the book.
[3]: Malaria risk, predominantly in the malignant *falciparum* form, exists throughout the year in the whole country. Chloroquine resistance has been reported.
[4]: All water outside the capital area should be regarded as being potentially contaminated. Water used for drinking, brushing teeth or making ice should have first been boiled or otherwise sterilised. Bottled water is available and, it is advised, is safe throughout Oman. Food bought in the main supermarkets can be regarded as safe. Outside the capital area, milk may be unpasteurised and if so, should be boiled. Powdered or tinned milk is available and is advised, but make sure that it is reconstituted with pure water. Avoid dairy products which are likely to have been made from unboiled milk.

Only eat well-cooked meat and fish, preferably served hot. Salad and mayonnaise may carry increased risk. Vegetables should be cooked and fruit peeled.
Rabies is present. For those at high risk, vaccination before arrival should be considered. If you are bitten abroad, seek medical advice without delay. For more information, consult the *Health* section at the back of the book.
Health care: Oman has an extensive public health service (free to Omani nationals), with approximately 50 hospitals, 80 health centres and 90 preventative health centres. However, costs are high for foreigners and health insurance is essential.

TRAVEL - International

AIR: Oman has two national airlines, *Oman Air* and *Oman Aviation*, and jointly owns *Gulf Air* with the governments of Abu Dhabi, Bahrain and Qatar.
Approximate flight times: From Muscat to *London* is 8 hours 10 minutes; to *Singapore* 6 hours 30 minutes and to *Sydney* 16 hours.
International airport: *Muscat (MCT)* (Seeb International), 40km (25 miles) west of the city (travel time – 30 minutes). Airport facilities include 24-hour bank/bureau de change, 24-hour duty-free shops, 24-hour bar, restaurant (1200-1500 and 1900-0100) and car hire *(Avis, Budget* and *Almadar).* Taxis and buses to the city are available.
Departure tax: OR3 for all departures. Transit passengers and children under 12 years old are exempt.
SEA: The main ports are Mina Qaboos and Mina Raysut. Traffic is mainly commercial.
ROAD: Travel into Oman by land is only possible with prior government permission. The best route is the north–south road from Muscat to Salalah, a journey of some 10-12 hours. Road travel through Saudi Arabia and the United Arab Emirates is extremely limited.

TRAVEL - Internal

AIR: *Gulf Air (GFA)* runs domestic flights to Salalah from Seeb airport; the approximate flight time is two hours. Tickets for internal air travel can be obtained from travel agencies in Muscat. Permission is required from the Ministry of Information.
ROAD: Traffic drives on the right. Principal routes run from north to south. **Bus:** *The Oman National Transport Company* has been developing a network of services in Muscat and north Oman using modern vehicles. There is competition from taxis and pick-up trucks converted for passenger service. **Taxi:** Prices are high and fares should be agreed in advance. Shared taxis are also available. **Car hire:** Available from *Zubair Travel* in Muscat, and from *Budget* and *Avis*, who have offices at hotels throughout the country.
Regulations: Visitors are not allowed to travel into the interior further up the coast than Seeb, 50km (30 miles) from Muscat, without written permission from the Ministry of the Interior. Heavy penalties are imposed for drinking and driving. It is also forbidden to drive on the beaches. **Documentation:** Holders of Tourist visas can use their national driving licence for up to seven days. For those on business, or where the stay exceeds seven days, a local licence must be obtained from the Police on presentation of their national driving licence or International Driving Permit.

ACCOMMODATION

There are about a dozen modern hotels. Smaller hotels are cheaper but facilities are limited. There are very few hotels in provincial areas but a large hotel-building programme has been initiated. Booking well in advance is strongly recommended. All rates are subject to a 15% service charge.

RESORTS & EXCURSIONS

Muscat: This old walled town is dominated by two well-preserved 16th-century Portuguese forts, *Jelali* and *Mirani.* The town consists of old houses, narrow streets and three beautifully carved original gates. The *Ali Mosque*, the *New Mosque* and the *Sultan's Palace* are well worth visiting.
Salalah is the capital of the southern region. It is a city set amongst coconut groves and banana plantations, sprawled along sandy beaches that run the length of its plain. The lush vegetation makes Salalah seem almost tropical.
Sur is situated in the northeastern province of Sharqiya. It is a seafaring town, a fishing village and a trading port all rolled into one. Famous for its traditional ship building, Sur started trading along the African coast as early as the 6th century. It is an old town with winding streets, carved wooden doors and old arabesque buildings.
Sohar: There is a very large and functional *souk* (market) here full of tailors, fruit-sellers and fishermen. An imposing 4-storey fort with six towers overlooks the bay.
Matrah-Muscat: Archaeological excavation of the tumuli at the site of *Souks Bausharios* is fascinating.
Nazwa is the main town in the interior province. It was the capital in the 6th and 7th centuries. The town's immense palm oasis stretches for 13km (8 miles) along the course of two wadis. It is famous for its fort and its gold and silver handicrafts.
Jabrin: The 17th-century fortified palace situated here is notable for its painted wooden ceilings and the splendid view across the desert to the mountains.
Bahlah: This ancient town, known for its pottery, has a good *souk* and nearby is the picturesque village of **Al Hamra.**
Jebel Akhdar: Literally 'The Green Mountain', noted for its picturesque terraced villages.
Al Hazm: On the northern slopes of the Jebel Akhdar is the fortress of *Al Hazm Fort,* built in 1708, and the oasis town of **Rustag**.
Qurum: Encapsulates Oman's archaeology, history and culture. The *National Museum* has a collection of silver, jewellery, weapons and ancient stone artefacts. From here *dhows* cruise along the palm-fringed coast and there are excellent fishing grounds and beaches.
Note: A permit to visit forts must be obtained from the Department of Castles and Forts, Ministry of National Heritage and Culture.

SOCIAL PROFILE

FOOD & DRINK: A number of restaurants have opened in recent years, but many people retain the habit of dining at hotels. There is a wide variety of cuisine on offer, including Arabic, Indian, Oriental, European and international dishes. Coffee houses are popular. Waiter service is usual. **Drink:** Muslim law forbids alcohol, but most hotel bars and restaurants serve alcohol. Visitors are only allowed to drink alcohol in licensed hotels and restaurants. To buy alcohol for home consumption, Western nationals must obtain a licence from their Embassy.
NIGHTLIFE: There are a few nightclubs and bars in Muscat, mostly in the hotels. There are three air-conditioned cinemas in Ruwi and an open-air cinema at the Al Falaj Hotel showing Arab, Indian and English films.
SHOPPING: The modern shops are mostly in Ruwi and Qurum. The two main *souks* are located in Matrah and Muscat. Traditional crafts include silver and gold jewellery, *khanjars* (Omani daggers), handwoven textiles, carpets and baskets. Antique Khanjars (over 50 years old) may not be exported. It is wise to check with the Ministry of National Heritage and Culture for the neccesary documentation before purchasing. **Shopping hours:** 0800-1300 and 1600-2000 Saturday to Thursday. *Souks* open 0800-1100 and 1600-1900. Many shops close on Friday. Opening hours are one hour later during Ramadan.
SPORT: There are many beaches offering good **bathing, skindiving** and **sailing** facilities. Many hotels have pools. There are also three private sports clubs with **water-skiing** and **fishing** facilities. A fishing permit is required from the Directorate General of Fisheries, and spearfishing is strictly prohibited. In the southern region, fishing is restricted to between Mughsayl and Taqah. Hunting is completely forbidden. There are many sports clubs based in Muscat offering facilities for **tennis** and **squash**. Several **golf** clubs are open to visitors. **Hockey, football, volleyball** and **basketball** are popular spectator sports and matches are staged at the Wattayah Stadium. **Camel** and **horseraces** are held on Fridays and public holidays at a variety of locations.
SOCIAL CONVENTIONS: Shaking hands is the usual form of greeting. A small gift, either promoting your company or country, is well received. As far as dress is concerned, it is important that women dress modestly; ie long skirts or dresses (below the knee) with long sleeves. Tight-fitting clothes must be avoided and although this is not strictly followed by Westerners, it is far better to adopt this practice and avoid causing offence. Shorts should never be worn in public and beachwear is prohibited anywhere except the beach. Collecting sea shells, abalones corals, crayfish and turtle eggs is also prohibited. Littering is forbidden. It is polite not to smoke in public, but generally no-smoking signs are posted where appropriate. **Photography:** Visitors should ask permission before attempting to photograph people or their property. 'No Photography' signs exist in certain places and must be observed.
Tipping: Becoming more common and 10-15% should be given.

BUSINESS PROFILE

ECONOMY: Oman was acutely underdeveloped until the discovery of oil in the early 1970s. Exports of the product now account for over 90% of the GDP and almost all of the country's export earnings. Although Oman is not a member of OPEC (Organisation of Petroleum Exporting Countries), its pricing policy tends to follow that of OPEC closely. The Government has used some of its oil money to develop indigenous industries such as construction, mining, fishing and agriculture. The latter, due to Oman's desert land, is confined to the coastal plain and a few irrigated areas in the interior. Dates, limes and alfalfa are the main products; some livestock is also bred. There are also mineral deposits of copper, chromite, marble, gypsum and limestone which are being exploited. February 1991 saw the launch of Oman's fourth 5-year economic development plan. Among the sectors which will receive particular emphasis are oil and gas, mining, agriculture and fisheries, health care, power generation, education, telecommunications, transport and construction. Industrial production (apart from oil-related industry) has increased rapidly since the early 1980s, averaging 10-15% annual growth, but still accounts for less than 10% of economic output. Japan is the country's largest trading partner, exchanging oil for manufactured goods. One deal of particular note in 1992 has been signed with the CIS-member Kazakhstan. Worth perhaps US$1.5 billion, it covers the creation of an Omani-Kazakh consortium to build an oil pipeline from Kazakhstan's Tengiz field (in whose development British Gas is involved) to a suitable port. Eight possible routes have been identified, but some lengthy diplomacy will be needed before a route can finally be agreed. The UK and the United Arab Emirates are the other important sources of Omani imports.
BUSINESS: Men should wear suits and ties for business and formal occasions. English is usually spoken in business circles, but a few words or phrases of Arabic will be useful and welcome. Appointments are essential and punctuality is gradually becoming more important in business circles. Visiting cards are widely used. **Office hours:** 0830-1300 and 1600-1900 Saturday to Wednesday; 0800-1300 Thursday. Many will also open 1600-1900 Saturday to Wednesday. **Government office hours:** 0730-1430 Saturday to Wednesday. All offices are closed Friday. Office hours open and close one hour later during Ramadan.
COMMERCIAL INFORMATION: The following organisations can offer advice: Ministry of Commerce and Industry, PO Box 550, Muscat 113. Tel: 799 500. Fax: 794 213 *or* 794 239. Telex: 3665; *or*
Oman Chamber of Commerce and Industry, PO Box 1400, 112 Ruwi. Tel: 707 674. Fax: 708 497. Telex: 3389.

CLIMATE

The months of June and July are particularly hot. Rainfall varies according to the region. During the period June to September there is a light monsoon rain in Salalah.
Required clothing: Lightweights are worn throughout the year, with a warm wrap for cooler winter evenings. Light rainwear is advisable.

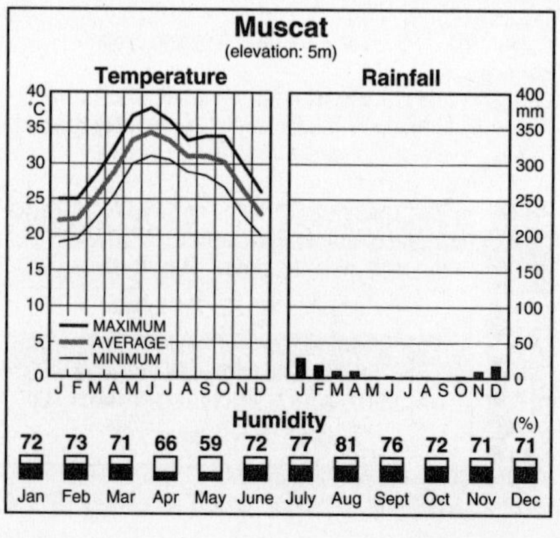
Muscat
(elevation: 5m)
Temperature
Rainfall
40 °C 35 30 25 20 15 10 5 0
400 mm 350 300 250 200 150 100 50 0
MAXIMUM
AVERAGE
MINIMUM
J F M A M J J A S O N D
J F M A M J J A S O N D
Humidity
(%)
72 73 71 66 59 72 77 81 76 72 71 71
Jan Feb Mar Apr May June July Aug Sept Oct Nov Dec

The Pacific

Most of the countries in the Pacific have their own entries elsewhere; consult the *Contents* pages.

PACIFIC OVERVIEW

The vast, sparsely populated region of the Pacific Ocean, which covers a quarter of the earth's surface, has been the subject of growing interest in the last few years. It is neither easy, nor especially useful, to make generalisations about the area and the myriad of small islands peppered across it. All have unique features of geography, economy and, not least, of political history: some are newly independent; others are designated as Trust Territories; yet others are straightforward colonies. There are, nevertheless, global political and economic trends which are certain to create a substantial impact throughout the Pacific.

One significant trend of the last two decades, which will probably now be arrested, has been the growing militarisation of the Pacific. As well as the better-known nuclear testing complexes operated by France and the USA, the region saw a proliferation of intelligence-gathering, early-warning and other 'support' facilities during the 1970s and 1980s. With the end of the Cold War, however, communist expansionism no longer provides a pretext for the strategic exploitation of the Pacific. For the Pacific islands themselves, this reduces the threat to their own autonomy from being swept up in the global superpower conflict. One by-product of this is that the major powers no longer have the same degree of incentive to underwrite the economies of those islands in which they previously took an interest. The islands must develop their own economic systems and have focused on three principal areas in which they hope to progress.

One of these is tourism. Much of the region is currently within reach of the North American traveller, but further exploitation of its tourism potential is dependent either on the development of cheaper, faster and, perhaps, less-polluting forms of long-distance transport to bring the Pacific within reach of Europe; or on a substantial increase in the disposable incomes of the populations of Asia and South America. Neither of these are likely to be realised in the short term.

Another economic asset which may produce more immediate dividends is the Pacific's awe-inspiring wealth of natural resources. Commercial fishing, notably by Japan, has long been carried out on a huge scale, but has yet to make any real impact on the ocean's deep-sea fish stocks. The region also has enormous mineral potential: much attention has been given to developing commercially viable methods of harvesting the mineral-rich manganese nodules that cover much of the ocean's abyssal plains, but there are believed to be other mineral deposits of great value. Additionally, the whole Pacific Rim has great potential as an energy source, initially from geothermal installations, later perhaps from deep-sea tidal and temperature gradient devices.

Many Pacific nations are just a few score square kilometres of land, but their boundaries enclose hundreds of thousands of square kilometre of ocean. Finally, the islands stand to benefit from the rapidly growing Pacific trade axis as Japan and the fast-growing economies of other Pacific Rim countries link up with the west coast of the Americas. This offers opportunities for developing transit facilities for shipping and 'offshore' financial services of the type which have long been offered by, for example, Jersey and the Cayman Islands: Nauru, Vanuatu and Tonga are likely candidates. The islands will need more than this type of business to sustain a healthy economy, and it remains to be seen whether they are able to develop their undoubted assets without becoming excessively dominated by foreign commercial interests.

On a darker note, one problem which has arisen in the last few years, and is worrying several Pacific governments, concerns the possible consequences of global warming on sea levels. A number of islands face serious threats to their land mass; some, such as Nauru, could disappear altogether. The Pacific islands are consequently an increasingly vocal presence at international fora discussing global environmental questions.

The Pacific Islands of Micronesia

(Islands formerly comprising the US-administered Pacific Trust Territory.)

Location: South Pacific, Micronesia.

Note: This region was administered by the USA on behalf of the United Nations until 1990. It includes the *Federated States of Micronesia,* the *Republic of the Marshall Islands,* the *Northern Mariana Islands* and the *Republic of Palau.* The Northern Marianas have had US Commonwealth status since 1986. Under the terms of the Compacts of Free Association between the USA and the other former territories, each is a sovereign self-governing State pursuing its foreign policy along agreed guidelines, with the USA retaining responsibility for defence in exchange for economic aid. However, the position of Palau will remain effectively unaltered until it can muster a sufficiently large majority to vote for new arrangements. The *Federated States of Micronesia* and the *Republic of the Marshall Islands* became members of the United Nations in 1991.

AREA: 20,124,000 sq km (7,770,000 sq miles) of which 2159 sq km (833.6 sq miles) is land.
POPULATION: See individual entries.
GEOGRAPHY: Micronesia comprises four archipelagos: the Federated States of Micronesia (Caroline Islands), the Republic of the Marshall Islands, the Northern Mariana Islands and the Republic of Palau. Each archipelago is composed of hundreds of island groups, within which there are many islands varying widely in topography. A more detailed description is given under the individual entry for each country below. There are three distinct population groups: Malayans who passed through Indonesia and the Philippines; Melanesians coming from the islands of the southwest Pacific; and Polynesians who inhabited the South Pacific.
LANGUAGE: English, Japanese and nine local languages.
RELIGION: Roman Catholic and Protestant with Mormon and Bahai minorities.
TIME: See individual entries.
ELECTRICITY: 110/120 volts AC, 60Hz. Plugs are the American flat 2-pin type.
COMMUNICATIONS: Telephone: IDD is available to any of the islands. See individual entries for country code. **Fax:** Available in Palau and the Northern Marianas. **Telex/telegram:** 24-hour service available in some areas. **Post:** Airmail to Europe takes at least ten days. Post offices are located in the centre of each state. **Press:** The English-language newspapers are *Pacific Daily News* (Guam), which is the only daily newspaper in the region and is distributed throughout all the islands, *Marshall Islands Journal* (Marshall Islands), *Marianas Review* (Northern Marianas), *Marianas Variety News* (Northern Marianas) and *Palau Weekly* (Palau).
Note: Further information is provided under individual entries.
BBC World Service and Voice of America frequencies: From time to time these change. See the section *How to Use this Book* for more information.

BBC:				
MHz	**15.36**	**9.915**	**7.150**	**5.975**
Voice of America:				
MHz	**18.82**	**15.18**	**9.525**	**1.735**

PASSPORT/VISA

Note: (a) Each of the four constitutional governments is responsible for its own tourism policies, and regulations may be subject to change. (b) On many islands, especially the remoter ones, it is not the possession of documents (necessary though they are) that secures access, but the consent of the islanders.
For more details, see the individual entries below.

MONEY

Currency: US Dollar (US$) = 100 cents. Notes are in denominations of US$100, 50, 20, 10, 5, 2 and 1. Coins are in denominations of US$1, and 50, 25, 10, 5 and 1 cents.
Currency exchange: Foreign exchange services are limited.
Credit cards: Access/Mastercard, American Express and Visa are accepted in most urban areas. Check with your credit card company for details of merchant acceptability and other services which may be available.
Travellers cheques: US Dollar travellers cheques are advised.
Exchange rate indicators: The following figures are included as a guide to the movements of the US Dollar against Sterling:

Date:	**Oct '92**	**Sep '93**	**Jan '94**	**Jan '95**
£1.00=	**1.59**	**1.53**	**1.49**	**1.56**

Currency restrictions: No limit on the amount of foreign or local currency to be imported or exported. Any amount can be reconverted.
Banking hours: 1000-1500 Monday to Thursday; 1000-1800 Friday.

PUBLIC HOLIDAYS

Some US public holidays are observed in addition to regional public holidays, though there are variations from island to island. See individual entries for main holidays in each region.

HEALTH

Regulations and requirements may be subject to change at short notice, and you are advised to contact your doctor well in advance of your intended date of departure. Any numbers in the chart refer to the footnotes below.

	Special Precautions?	Certificate Required?
Yellow Fever	1	No
Cholera	2	No
Typhoid & Polio	3	-
Malaria	No	-
Food & Drink	4	-

[1]: Risk of yellow fever infection still exists and vaccinations are recommended for all.
[2]: Following WHO guidelines issued in 1973, a cholera vaccination is no longer a condition of entry. However, risk of cholera infection still exists in the Marshall Islands and precautions are recommended. Up-to-date advice should be sought before deciding whether these precautions should include vaccination as medical opinion is divided over its effectiveness. See the *Health* section at the end of the book.
[3]: Smallpox, typhoid, para-typhoid and tetanus vaccinations are strongly recommended.
[4]: Mains water is normally chlorinated, and whilst relatively safe may cause mild abdominal upsets. Drinking water outside main cities and towns may be contaminated and sterilisation is advisable. Bottled water is available and is advised for the first few weeks of the stay. Milk is pasteurised and dairy products are safe for consumption. Local meat, poultry, seafood, fruit and vegetables are generally considered safe to eat.
Health care: Health insurance is recommended. There are nine hospitals in the region, with a total of 629 beds and 55 doctors.

TRAVEL - International

AIR: The region's major airline is *Air Micronesia.*
Approximate flight times: Flight durations from London to destinations in the Pacific vary considerably depending on the route taken. The most common route would include a stopover in Los Angeles and Honolulu; eg the flight time from London to Honolulu is 19 hours 30 minutes and from Honolulu to the Marshall Islands 4 hours 30 minutes.
International airports: *Saipan (SPN), Guam (GUM)* and *Palau* when entering from the north and west, *Pohnpei (PNI)* from the south and *Majuro (MAJ)* from the south and east.
Regional airlines: Scheduled inter-island travel, charters and sightseeing are offered by several local airlines. There is excellent provision for travelling from Guam and Majuro to the various islands. Flights between the islands tend to be rarer. Airlines include:
Air Marshall Islands (AMI): This government-owned airline runs charters, sightseeing tours and point-to-point flights between Majuro and other islands in the Marshalls; also international flights to Honolulu, Fiji, Kiribati and Tuvalu.
Air Micronesia (CO): Operates between islands in all four groups, and to Hawaii, Guam, the Philippines, Australia, Papua New Guinea, South Korea, Taiwan and Japan.
Several smaller airlines fly to Guam.
SEA: The major ports are Pohnpei, Majuro, Saipan, Tuik, Yap and Karor. The following cargo/passenger lines serve the islands: *Nauru Pacific, Royal Shipping Co, Daiwa Navigation Co, Oceania Line Inc, P&O,*

Saipan Shipping Co and *Tiger Line*.
There are numerous boats for touring, ranging from small speed boats to large glass-bottomed boats for fishing, sightseeing, sunset cruising, scuba diving and short-distance travel. A ferry provides service between Saipan and Tinian. Inter-island vessels provide limited and irregular service between Saipan and the smaller islands. Requests for reservations should be directed to the Office of the Government of the following: Saipan, Commonwealth of the Northern Marianas; Office of Transportation in Majuro, Marshall Islands; Konor, Palau; Kolonia, Pohnpei; Moen, Chuuk; and Colonia, Yap.
Cabin space is limited, and passengers may be required to sleep on deck (bring own mat). The field trip ships are leased by the governments to private firms, and rates are subject to change.
Cruise lines: *Princess, Royal Viking* and *Norwegian American* currently offer cruises to the islands.

TRAVEL - Internal

ROAD: Good roads are limited to the major island centres. **Bus:** There are no local bus systems other than tourist services. However, public transport is widely available in all the Micronesia district centres in the form of sedans, pickups and *jeepneys*. **Taxi:** Inexpensive taxis are available throughout Micronesia. **Car hire:** Each major centre offers rental cars, either through international or local agents. **Documentation:** A valid national driving licence is required.

ACCOMMODATION

Accommodation is extremely varied. Rooms are scarce in some districts and single guests may be required to share twin-bedded rooms with other single guests.

SOCIAL PROFILE

FOOD & DRINK: Most hotels serve Continental, Japanese, Chinese, Western-style and local cuisine. On some remote islands the arrival of a stranger calls for a feast of fish, clams, octopus, langusta, sea cucumber and eels. Breadfruit (pounded, boiled, baked or fried), taro, rice and cassava (tapioca) are popular staples. Among the regional delicacies are coconut crabs and mangrove clams. Although some dining rooms serve buffet-style fare, table service is usual and operates at a leisurely pace. See individual entries.
NIGHTLIFE: Some hotels have cocktail lounges with live entertainment. In Saipan there are nightclubs featuring music and dancing. Throughout Micronesia there are cinemas in major areas. However, tourists seek their own entertainment for the most part. See individual entries.
SPORT: There is excellent **fishing, hiking** and **watersports.** The islands are particularly appealing for skindivers, as the surrounding waters offer unsurpassed underwater scenery and marine life. See individual entries.
SPECIAL EVENTS: See individual entries.
SOCIAL CONVENTIONS: The Western understanding of private property is alien to many parts of Micronesia and personal possessions should be well looked after, though not necessarily under lock and key; outside main tourist areas, where normal precautions apply, it is usually sufficient just to keep items out of sight. All land, however, does have an owner and before using it, protocol in many areas demands that permission is sought; in places this includes use of footpaths as there is not necessarily immediate right of way. A clearly expressed desire to be courteous will usually see the visitor through. See individual entries.

BUSINESS PROFILE

ECONOMY: In all four territories subsistence agriculture is a key employer. Copra, coconuts, cassava and sweet potatoes are the major crops: yields are sufficient in some cases to sustain export markets. Fishing is similarly important. The Marshalls and Palau have developed small-scale light industries engaged in food-processing, boatbuilding and the like. Tourism is growing but is generally hindered by the lack of facilities and the difficulty of access: Micronesia and the Northern Marianas have gone furthest in efforts to overcome these obstacles and develop tourist industries, relying principally on aid and foreign investment from the USA and Japan.
BUSINESS: Lightweight suits or shirt and tie are usually worn. Appointments should be made and calling cards

are exchanged. Best time to visit is May to October.
Office hours: 0800-1700 Monday to Friday.
Government office hours: 0730-1130 and 1230-1630 Monday to Friday.

CLIMATE

With 2000 islands spread over 7.8 million sq km (3 million sq miles) of the Pacific Ocean, the islands have a variety of weather. The period from autumn to winter (November to April) is the most pleasant time, while May to October is the wet season. The climate can generally be described as tropical in this part of the world, but the cooling sea breezes prevent really extreme temperatures and humidity. For regional climate charts see under the individual entries below.
Required clothing: Lightweight cottons and linens and rainwear.

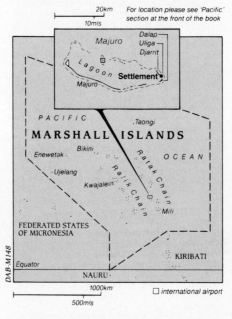

Marshall Islands

20km / 10mls   For location please see 'Pacific' section at the front of the book

Location: Western Pacific Ocean.

Marshall Islands Visitors Authority
PO Box 1727, Ministry of Resources and Development, Majuro, Marshall Islands 96960
Tel: 625 3206. Fax: 625 3218.
Embassy of the Republic of the Marshall Islands
2433 Massachusetts Avenue, NW, Washington, DC 20008
Tel: (202) 234 5414 *or* 232 3218. Fax: (202) 232 3236.
Embassy of the United States of America
PO Box1379, Majuro, Marshall Islands 96960-1379
Tel: 247 40115. Fax: 247 4012.

AREA: 180 sq km (191 sq miles).
POPULATION: 43,355 (1988).
POPULATION DENSITY: 240.9 per sq km.
CAPITAL: Majuro. **Population:** 19,605.
GEOGRAPHY: The Marshall Islands consist of two almost parallel chains of atolls and islands and lie west of the International Date Line. Majuro atoll is 2285km (1428 miles) west of Honolulu, 1624km (1015 miles) east of Guam and 2625km (1641 miles) southeast of Toyko. The eastern *Ratak* (Sunrise) Chain consists of 15 atolls and islands, and the western *Ralik* (Sunset) Chain consists of 16 atolls and islands. Together these two chains comprise 1152 islands and islets dispersed over more than 1,900,000 sq km (500,000 sq miles) of the central Pacific.
LANGUAGE: Marshallese is the offical language. English is widely understood.
RELIGION: 80% of the population belong to the independant Protestant Christian Church of the Marshall Islands.
TIME: There are two time zones:

Marshall Islands: GMT + 12.
Ebon Atoll: GMT - 12.
ELECTRICITY: 110 volts AC, 60Hz. Plugs are American 2-pin style.
COMMUNICATIONS: Telephone: IDD is available. Country code: 692. There are international satellite links. In Majuro dial 625 3399 *or* 625 3355 for the hospital; 625 3183 for the fire services; 625 3666 for police; and 411 for general information. Outgoing international calls must be made through the operator. **Telex/telegram:** 24-hour telex and telegram facilities are available in Majuro, near the High School in Rita, and in Ebeye. Opening hours: 0800-1200 and 1300-1700 Monday to Friday.
Post: A US post office is located in Majuro. Post office hours: 1000-1530 Monday to Friday; 0800-1200 Saturday. **Press:** The English-language newspaper is the *Marshall Islands Journal*.

PASSPORT/VISA

Regulations and requirements may be subject to change at short notice, and you are advised to contact the appropriate diplomatic or consular authority before finalising travel arrangements. Details of these may be found at the head of this country's entry. Any numbers in the chart refer to the footnotes below.

	Passport Required?	Visa Required?	Return Ticket Required?
Full British	Yes	Yes	Yes
BVP	Not valid	-	-
Australian	Yes	Yes	Yes
Canadian	Yes	Yes	Yes
USA	Yes	No	Yes
Other EU (As of 31/12/94)	Yes	Yes	Yes
Japanese	Yes	Yes	Yes

PASSPORTS: Valid passports are required by all.
British Visitors Passport: Not accepted.
VISAS: Required by all except US citizens who have a valid passport, return or onward ticket and sufficient funds for duration of stay.
Types of visa: Various.
Validity: 90 days; extensions are available.
Application to: Immigration Controller, Ministry of Foreign Affairs, Republic of the Marshall Islands, Majuro 96960. Tel: 625 3181. Fax: 625 3685. Telex: 0927 (a/b FRN AFS).
Application requirements: (a) Proof of adequate funds. (b) Return ticket.
Working days required: By post: applications are dealt with on receipt.
Temporary residence: Apply to Immigration Controller (address above).

PUBLIC HOLIDAYS

Jan 1 '95 New Year's Day. **Mar 1** Memorial and Nuclear Victims' Remembrance Day. **May 1** Constitution Day. **Jul 1** Fisherman's Day. **Sep 5** Dri Jerbal (Labour) Day. **Sep 30** Manit (Cultural) Day. **Oct 21** Independence Day. **Nov 17** President's Day. **Dec 4** Kamolo Day (Thanksgiving). **Dec 25** Christmas Day. **Jan 1 '96** New Year's Day. **Mar 1** Memorial and Nuclear Victims' Remembrance Day.
Note: Variations occur from island to island.

HEALTH

Health care: The Marshall Islands have two main hospitals, one in Majuro and one in Ebeye. A medical facility also exists in Kwajalein.

DUTY FREE

The following items may be imported into the Marshall Islands by passengers over 18 years of age without incurring customs duty:
600 cigarettes or 454g of cigars or tobacco; 2 litres of alcoholic beverage.
Prohibited items: Firearms, ammunition, drugs and pornographic materials are not permitted. Birds, animals, fruit and plants need certification from the Quarantine Division of the Ministry of Resources and Development. Coral, turtle shells and certain other natural resources cannot be exported. Any artefacts or objects of historical value cannot be taken out of the country.

TRAVEL

AIR: The *Airline of the Marshall Islands (AMI)* provides regular scheduled internal flights to ten of the atolls in the Marshall Islands and has planes available for charter. Flights are available between Honolulu and the Marshall Islands and to Fiji via Kiribati and Tuvalu. *Air Micronesia* stops in Majuro and Kwajalein on its island-

hopper service between Guam and Honolulu.
International airport: *Majuro International Airport (MAJ).* There are buses, taxis and hotel transport from the airport to downtown.
Departure tax: US$15 on international flights. Travellers under 18 years of age are exempt.
SEA: The international port is Majuro. Shipping lines servicing the Marshalls include *Matson Lines, Daiwa Lines, Tiger Lines, Nauru Pacific Line* and *Philippine, Micronesia & Orient Line.*
Four government-owned field ships connect the islands within the Marshalls on a regular schedule. Comfortable passenger cabins are available on these ships and arrangements can be made for charter trips. **Cruise:** *Royal Viking Line* sometimes calls at Majuro port, but not on a regular basis. Inter-island cruises are available. Boats can be rented from one of eight boat rental companies on the islands for sightseeing, diving tours, picnics, game fishing, snorkelling, water-skiing and other boating activities.
ROAD: All the main roads are paved. Driving is on the left. The minimum age is 18. **Bus:** Services run to and from Laura daily except Sunday. **Taxi:** Plentiful and cheap. Generally used on a seat-sharing basis. **Car hire:** These are usually Japanese sedans. Companies include *Martina* (tel: 625 3104), *Deluxe* (tel: 625 3665) and *Coral* (tel: 625 3724). **Documentation:** A national driving licence is valid for 30 days.

ACCOMMODATION

There are currently about 130 hotels in Majuro and some islands have guest-houses. Hotel space is expected to triple in the next two years to 400 rooms. **Camping** facilities are available on Majuro and various other islands. For further information, contact the Visitors Authority (address at top of entry).

RESORTS & EXCURSIONS

Many of the atolls are dotted with Flame of the Forest, hibiscus and different-coloured plumeria flowers. There are also at least 160 species of coral surrounding the islands. The uninhabited atolls are noted for their coconut and papaya plantations and for pandanus and breadfruit trees. The first stop in the Marshall Islands should be either **Majuro** or **Ebeye**, although visits to outer islands can be arranged. There are Sunday day-trips to **Mili** or **Maloelap** atolls where there are opportunities to snorkel over Second World War wrecks, eat local food and watch cultural dancing. There are also many historic sites and buildings. The *Alele Museum* and Visitors Authority can provide information on various sites.

SOCIAL PROFILE

FOOD & DRINK: There are several restaurants in Majuro, serving American, Western, Chinese and Marshallese specialities. Consumption of alcohol is forbidden on some of the islands.
NIGHTLIFE: There are several nightclubs on Majuro and Ebeye and some hotels offer traditional dancing.
SHOPPING: Special purchases include *kili* handbags woven by former residents of Bikini, stick charts (once used to navigate long distances between the region's scattered islands), plaited floor mats, fans, purses, shell necklaces and baskets. There is a 3% sales tax in Majuro.
Shopping hours: 0800-2000 Monday to Thursday, 0800-2200 Friday to Saturday and 0800-1800 Sunday.
SPORT: Diving opportunities include drop-offs, coral heads, black coral and Second World War wrecks. **Fishing** expeditions can be arranged by local hotels or the Marshalls Billfish Club. **Basketball, volleyball, softball** and **tennis** are the favourite sports. Children play many indigenous games using local materials.
SPECIAL EVENTS: The following is a selection of the festivals and other special events celebrated annually in the Marshall Islands.
Mid-Jun *Billfish Tournament.* **Jul 1-2 (weekend)** *Marshall Islands' Fishing Tournament.* **Aug** *Folk Art Festival,* Alele Museum.
SOCIAL CONVENTIONS: Informal dress is usual for both business and social occasions. Scanty clothing (including topless bathing) is considered offensive. Use of islands, paths, beaches, etc may require permission in many areas; it is best to check locally. **Tipping:** Unnecessary.

BUSINESS PROFILE

COMMERCIAL INFORMATION: For further information contact the Majuro Chamber of Commerce, Majuro 96960. Tel: 625 3051. Fax: 625 3343.

CLIMATE

Tropical, with cooling sea breezes and frequent rain. Tradewinds blow steadily from the northeast from December through March. Wettest months are usually October to November. The average temperature is 27°C, with a daily variation of 12 degrees.

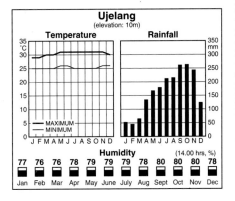

Humidity												(14.00 hrs, %)
77	76	76	78	79	79	79	78	80	80	80	78
Jan	Feb	Mar	Apr	May	June	July	Aug	Sept	Oct	Nov	Dec

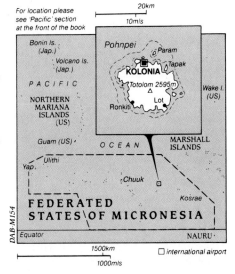

Federated States of Micronesia

For location please see 'Pacific' section at the front of the book

Including Yap, Pohnpei, Kosrae and Chuuk (formerly Truk).

Location: Western Pacific Ocean.

Resources and Development Department
Pohnpei 96941, Federated States of Micronesia
Tel: 320 5133.
Resources and Development Department
Chuuk 96942, Federated States of Micronesia
Tel: 330 2552. Fax: 330 4194.
Embassy of the Federated States of Micronesia
1725 N Street, NW, Washington, DC 20036
Tel: (202) 223 4383. Fax: (202) 223 4391.
Embassy of the United States of America
PO Box 1286, Kolonia, Pohnpei 96941, Federated States of Micronesia
Tel: 320 2187. Fax: 320 2186.

AREA: Kosrae (5 islands) – 110 sq km (42 sq miles); **Pohnpei** (163 islands) – 344 sq km (133 sq miles); **Chuuk (formerly Truk)** (294 islands) – 127 sq km (49 sq miles); **Yap** (145 islands) – 119 sq km (46 sq miles). **Total:** 700 sq km (270 sq miles).
POPULATION: 100,000 (1988 estimate).
POPULATION DENSITY: 143 per sq km.
CAPITAL: Pohnpei. **Population:** 31,000 (1988).
GEOGRAPHY: The Federated States of Micronesia lie 3680km (2300 miles) north of Australia and 4000km

(2500 miles) west of Hawaii. They comprise 607 islands scattered over 1.6 million sq km (617,761 sq miles), the most widely spread Pacific Islands group. Yap's uplands are covered by dry meadows and scrub growth. Chuuk lagoon is circled by one of the largest barrier reefs in the world, while Pohnpei has mountains rising to over 600m (2000ft).
LANGUAGE: English; Micronesian Japanese is widely spoken (Kosrean, Ponapean, Chuukese and Yorese).
RELIGION: Mostly Roman Catholic with other Christian denominations.
TIME: Due to the vast area covered by the islands, Micronesia spans two time zones:
Chuuk and Yap: GMT + 10.
Kosrae and Pohnpei: GMT + 11.
COMMUNICATIONS: Telephone: IDD is available. Country code: 691. Outgoing international calls must be made through the operator. **Telex/telegram:** Facilities at island capitals and main hotels. **Post:** Post offices are located in Kolonia for Pohnpei, Moen for Chuuk, Lelu for Kosrae and Colonia for Yap. Opening hours: 0830-1630 Monday to Friday; 1000-1200 Saturday. **Press:** See main entry above.

PASSPORT/VISA

Regulations and requirements may be subject to change at short notice, and you are advised to contact the appropriate diplomatic or consular authority before finalising travel arrangements. Details of these may be found at the head of this country's entry. Any numbers in the chart refer to the footnotes below.

	Passport Required?	Visa Required?	Return Ticket Required?
Full British	Yes	No/2	Yes
BVP	Not valid	-	-
Australian	Yes	No/2	Yes
Canadian	Yes	No/2	Yes
USA	No	No	Yes
Other EU (As of 31/12/94)	Yes	No/2	Yes
Japanese	1	No/2	Yes

PASSPORTS: Valid passports are required by all except:
(a) nationals of the USA with acceptable documentation;
(b) [1] nationals of Japan with a re-entry permit issued for touristic purposes.
British Visitors Passport: Not accepted.
VISAS: [2] Not required for visits of less than 30 days; entry permits are issued on arrival. For longer stays, advance permission is required.
Types of visa: Various. Cost on application.
Validity: Various.
Application to: Division of Immigration, Office of the Attorney General, Central Office, PO Box PS 106, Palikir, Pohnpei 96941. Tel: 320 2606.
Application requirements: (a) Proof of adequate funds. (b) Return or onward ticket.
Working days required: Must apply by post; applications are dealt with on receipt.
Temporary residence: Apply to Division of Immigration (address above).
Note: Foreign-owned vessels or aircraft are required to have entry permits (visas) applied for and in their possession prior to entering Micronesia.

MONEY

Currency: Giant stone money remains in use on Yap, but not for ordinary transactions or any that are likely to involve visitors. Coins weigh up to 4500kg (4.5 tons) with diameters of up to 3.5m (12ft). For information on convertible currency, see *Money* in the introductory section above.

DUTY FREE

The following items may be imported into the Federated States of Micronesia without incurring customs duty:
*600 cigarettes or 454g of cigars or tobacco; *8 litres of beer; *4.5 litres of wine; *2.7 litres of alcoholic beverage.*
Note [*]: For passengers over 21 years of age.
Prohibited items: Firearms and ammunition. Plants and animals must be declared and will be subject to restrictions.

PUBLIC HOLIDAYS

Jan 1 '95 New Year's Day. **Mar 1** Yap State Day. **May 10** Federation Day. **Sep 8** Kosrae State Day. **Sep 11** Pohnpei State Liberation Day. **Sep 23** Chuuk State Charter Day. **Nov 3** Independence Day. **Nov 8** Pohnpei Constitution Day. **Dec 24** Yap Constitution Day. **Dec 25** Christmas Day. **Jan 1 '96** New Year's Day. **Mar 1** Yap

State Day.
Note: Variations occur from island to island.

HEALTH

Health care: All the Federated States have good government hospitals in the main cities. There are also good dental services and chemists.

TRAVEL

AIR: *Air Micronesia (CO)* flights link the major islands with Guam, Tokyo, Manila and Honolulu. *Air Nauru* provides services twice a week from Kosrae, Pohnpei, Chuuk and Guam. Flights also run daily between Pohnpei and Kosrae on *Pacific Missionary Aviation* aircraft.
Approximate flight times: See main entry above.
International airport: *Pohnpei* is 1.5km (1 mile) from Kolonia.
Departure tax: US$5 for domestic and international departures.
SEA: International ports are Pohnpei, Chuuk and Yap. *Nauru Pacific Shipping Lines* provide passenger sailings from Honolulu to Pohnpei and Chuuk. Inter-island trading ships based in Pohnpei, Yap and Chuuk visit the outlying islands.
ROAD: There are good roads in and around major island centres. **Bus:** No service. **Taxi:** Available throughout the Federated States and inexpensive. **Car hire:** Self-drive cars are available in major towns. **Documentation:** National driving licence or International Driving Permit required.

ACCOMMODATION

There are hotels in the various island capitals. Parts of Chuuk, Pohnpei and Kosrae are being developed into beach resorts. There are no official **camping** grounds, but private arrangements can be made with local landowners.

RESORTS & EXCURSIONS

The most important historical sites include *The Spanish Wall* and *Catholic Bell Tower* in **Pohnpei**, the *Japanese Wartime Communication Centre* at Xavier High School in **Chuuk** and the ruins of *INSARU* in **Kosrae**. There are also small museums in Kosrae and Chuuk. The *Chuuk Lagoon* is one of the largest in the world and holds more than 60 warships. The *Enpein Marine Park* and ancient ruins of *Nan Madol* in Pohnpei are well worth visiting. All States have beautiful white sandy beaches.

SOCIAL PROFILE

FOOD & DRINK: Local specialities include breadfruit (Chuuk) and thin slices of raw fish dipped in a peppery sauce. *Sakau*, as it is known on Pohnpei, or *kava*, as it is known throughout the rest of Polynesia, is made from the root of a shrub which yields a mildly narcotic substance when squeezed through hibiscus bark. There are several *sakau* bars where visitors can sample it and watch it being made. Although some dining rooms serve buffet-style fare, table service is usual and operates at a leisurely pace. Pohnpeians have over 100 words for yams and grow them to massive proportions (it may take several men to carry one); yams occupy a central position in local culture. Alcohol is prohibited on Chuuk (with the consequence that nearby islands are often used as picnic resorts).
NIGHTLIFE: There are good restaurants and a few cinemas in major island centres. Locals and visitors alike enjoy making their own entertainment. *Sakau* drinking is the most frequent evening activity on Pohnpei. Cultural dances can be arranged through tourist offices or hotels. Most hotels have music, dancing and discos.
SHOPPING: Favourite purchases on Chuuk include love sticks and war clubs. Yap people produce colourful grass skirts, *lava-lavas* woven from hibiscus bark, woven baby cradles, betel-nut pouches and stone money. On Pohnpei there are elaborate, carefully scaled model canoes and woven items. **Shopping hours:** 0800-1900. Some stores open 1200-1700 Sunday.
SPORT: There are facilities available for fishing, snorkelling, scuba diving, hiking, windsurfing, tennis, canoeing, football, basketball, volleyball and baseball.
SPECIAL EVENTS: In Yap, *mitmits* are feasts. accompanied by dancing and exchanges of gifts which are given by villages reciprocally, often after a period of years has elapsed. *Liberation Day* (Sep 11) in Pohnpei is preceded by a week of sports and traditional events, including canoe racing. Also in Pohnpei funeral feasts are important events lasting several days. In Kosrae a notice at the airport invites visitors to participate in Sunday church services.
SOCIAL CONVENTIONS: There are considerable

variations of custom and belief. 95% of Kosreans are Congregationalists with a deeply held respect for Sunday as a day of rest. Pre-European influences are stronger elsewhere and nowhere more so than in Yap where visitors are only allowed with prior permission. Use of islands, paths, beaches, etc may also require permission in many areas; it is best to check beforehand.
Photography: Permission should always be sought. Though the people are friendly, and usually accommodating, not to seek prior permission before taking pictures is considered an insult, especially on some of the remoter islands.

CLIMATE

Tropical with year-round high humidity.

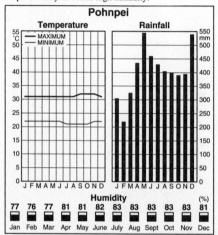

Northern Mariana Islands

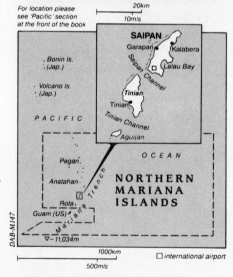

Including Saipan, Tinian and Rota (formerly the Marianas).
Location: Western Pacific Ocean.

Marianas Visitors' Bureau
PO Box 861, Saipan 96950, Northern Mariana Islands
Tel: 234 8327. Fax: 234 3596.
Immigration and Naturalisation Office
Commonwealth of the Northern Mariana Islands, Saipan 96950, Northern Mariana Islands
Tel: 234 7787.
Embassy of the United States of America
For address in the UK see top of USA entry.

AREA: 457 sq km (176.5 sq miles).
POPULATION: 31,563 (1987 estimate).
POPULATION DENSITY: 69.1 per sq km.
CAPITAL: Saipan. **Population:** 19,200 (1990).
GEOGRAPHY: Located to the south of Japan and to the north of Guam, the Northern Mariana Islands comprise 14 islands, the main ones being Saipan, Tinian and Rota. The group is compact, consisting of a single chain 650km (400 miles) long. The islands have high volcanic cones.

LANGUAGE: English. Chamorro and Carolinian are the native tongues. Japanese is widely spoken.
RELIGION: Mostly Roman Catholic.
TIME: GMT + 10.
COMMUNICATIONS: Telephone: IDD is available. Country code: 670. Outgoing international calls must be made through the operator. There are payphones in Saipan and most hotels; restaurants and other public facilities have telephones which visitors can use. **Fax:** A service is available. **Telex/telegram:** Telexes and telegrams can be sent from Micronesia Telecommunications, PO Box 306, Saipan. Tel: 234 6100. Opening hours: 0730-1930. **Post:** The post office in Saipan is open 0900-1600. **Press:** The English-language newspapers are the *Marianas Review* and the *Marianas Variety News*.

PASSPORT/VISA

Regulations and requirements may be subject to change at short notice, and you are advised to contact the appropriate diplomatic or consular authority before finalising travel arrangements. Details of these may be found at the head of this country's entry. Any numbers in the chart refer to the footnotes below.

	Passport Required?	Visa Required?	Return Ticket Required?
Full British	Yes	No/2	Yes
BVP	Not valid	-	-
Australian	Yes	No/2	Yes
Canadian	Yes	No/2	Yes
USA	No	No	Yes
Other EU (As of 31/12/94)	Yes	No/2	Yes
Japanese	Yes	No/2	Yes

PASSPORTS: Valid passports are required by all except nationals of the USA with acceptable documentation.
British Visitors Passport: Not accepted.
VISAS: [2] Not required for visits of less than 30 days; entry permits are issued on arrival. For longer stays, advance permission is required.
Types of visa: Various.
Validity: Various.
Application to: Immigration and Naturalisation Office (for address, see top of entry).
Application requirements: (a) Proof of adequate funds. (b) Return or onward ticket.
Working days required: By post: applications are dealt with on receipt. In person: 10-15 minutes.
Temporary residence: Apply to Immigration and Naturalisation Office (for address see top of entry).

DUTY FREE

The following goods may be imported into the Northern Mariana Islands without incurring customs duty:
*3 cartons of cigarettes or 454g of cigars or tobacco; *2 litres of alcoholic beverage.*
Note [*]: For passengers over 21 years of age.

PUBLIC HOLIDAYS

Jan 1 '95 New Year's Day. **Jan 3** Commonwealth Day. **Feb 14** George Washington's Birthday celebrations. **May 23** Memorial Day. **Jul 4** US Independence Day. **Sep 5** Labour Day. **Nov 25** Thanksgiving Day. **Dec 25** Christmas Day. **Jan 1 '96** New Year's Day. **Jan 3** Commonwealth Day. **Feb 14** George Washington's Birthday celebrations.
Note: Variations occur from island to island.

TRAVEL

AIR: See the main entry for the region above.
International airport: Saipan (SPN).
SEA: The international port of the Northern Mariana Islands is Saipan. The following lines sail there: *Nauru Pacific Line, Royal Shipping Co* (PO Box 238, Saipan), *Daiwa Navigation Co, Oceania Line Inc, P&O, Saipan Shipping Co* and *Tiger Line*.
ROAD: There are good roads in and around major island centres. **Bus:** There is a public bus service. **Taxi:** Available in all main centres. **Car hire:** Self-drive cars are available in major towns. **Documentation:** International Driving Permit or national licence accepted.

ACCOMMODATION

Hotels in the Northern Mariana Islands vary in standard from luxury to basic. They cater mainly for a Japanese market.

SOCIAL PROFILE

FOOD & DRINK: Local specialities include *kelaguin*, a chewy mixture of diced chicken and shredded coconut

and thin slices of raw coconut dipped in a peppery sauce.

NIGHTLIFE: There are several popular bars in Garapan and a few nightclubs and discos.

SHOPPING: Special purchases here include wishing dolls, coconut masks, coconut-crab decorations and woodcarvings, plus numerous duty-free items. **Shopping hours:** 0800-2100 Monday to Friday.

SPORT: Watersports are popular with many suitable **diving** and **snorkelling** locations; **windsurfing** is popular on Saipan. Local **fishing** competitions are held in several places. San Jose has a **bowling** alley and there are 9- and 18-hole **golf** courses.

SPECIAL EVENTS: Village fiestas in honour of local patron saints are among the principal annual celebrations. The *Flame Tree Festival*, which celebrates the American liberation of the islands, takes place during the two weeks preceding July 4; it consists of a variety of entertainments and coincides with the flowering of the orange-red blossoms of the royal poinciana trees, hence its name. On Rota, the second weekend in October sees the largest annual event in the islands in honour of San Francisco do Borja, patron saint of Songsong village; it is a revelrous extravaganza of feasting, drinking, music, dancing and processions which attracts visitors from many neighbouring Micronesian islands. Accommodation during this period is hard to find. For further information on special events in the Northern Marianas contact the Mariana Islands Visitors' Bureau (address at top of entry), which produces an annual listing.

SOCIAL CONVENTIONS: The Chamorro culture of the original inhabitants can still be traced, although it is overlaid by strong American influences. Western conventions are well understood.

BUSINESS PROFILE

COMMERCIAL INFORMATION: For further information contact the Saipan Chamber of Commerce, PO Box 806, Chalan Kanoa, Saipan 96950. Tel: 234 6132. Fax: 234 7151.

CLIMATE

The rainy season is July to November.

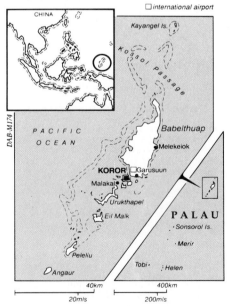

Republic of Palau

(Formerly part of the Caroline Islands.)
Location: Western Pacific Ocean.

Palau Visitors Authority
PO Box 256, Koror, Palau 96940
Tel: 488 2793 *or* 488 1930. Fax: 488 1725 *or* 488 1453.
Liaison Office of the United States of America
PO Box 6028, Koror, Palau 96940
Tel: 488 2920. Fax: 488 2911.

AREA: 508 sq km (196 sq miles); Babelthuap Island: 409 sq km (160 sq miles).

POPULATION: 15,105 (1990 estimate).

POPULATION DENSITY: 29.7 per sq km.

CAPITAL: Koror. **Population:** 10,486 (1990 estimate).

GEOGRAPHY: Palau, the westernmost cluster of the six major island groups that make up the Caroline Islands, lies 1000km (600 miles) east of the Philippines. The archipelago stretches over 650km (400 miles) from the atoll of Kayangel to the islet of Tobi. The Palau islands include more than 200 islands, of which only eight are inhabited. With three exceptions, all of the islands are located within a single barrier reef and represent two geological formations. The largest are volcanic and rugged with interior jungle and large areas of grassed terraces. The Rock Islands, now known as the Floating Garden Islands, are of limestone formation, while Kayangel, at the northernmost tip, is a classic coral atoll.

LANGUAGE: English and Palauan.

RELIGION: Roman Catholic majority.

TIME: GMT + 9.

COMMUNICATIONS: Telephone: Country code: 680. Outgoing international code: 011. **Fax:** Some hotels have facilities. **Telex/telegram:** Both services are available in Koror. **Post:** Post office located in Koror. Opening hours: 0730-1600. **Press:** The English-language newspaper is the *Tia Belau*, published twice-weekly.

PASSPORT/VISA

Regulations and requirements may be subject to change at short notice, and you are advised to contact the appropriate diplomatic or consular authority before finalising travel arrangements. Details of these may be found at the head of this country's entry. Any numbers in the chart refer to the footnotes below.

	Passport Required?	Visa Required?	Return Ticket Required?
Full British	Yes	No/2	Yes
BVP	Not valid	-	-
Australian	Yes	No/2	Yes
Canadian	Yes	No/2	Yes
USA	No	No	Yes
Other EU (As of 31/12/94)	Yes	No/2	Yes
Japanese	1	No/2	Yes

PASSPORTS: Valid passports are required by all except:
(a) nationals of the USA with acceptable documentation;
(b) [1] nationals of Japan with a re-entry permit for touristic purposes.
British Visitors Passport: Not accepted.
VISAS: [2] Not required for visits of less than 30 days; entry permits are issued on arrival. For longer stays, advance permission is required.
Types of visa: Various. Cost on application.
Validity: Various.
Application to: Division of Immigration, Bureau of Legal Affairs, Ministry of Justice, PO Box 100, Koror 96940. Tel: 488 9655. Fax: 488 9649.
Application requirements: (a) Proof of adequate funds. (b) Return ticket.
Working days required: Postal applications are dealt with on receipt.
Temporary residence: Apply to Division of Immigration (address above).

DUTY FREE

The following goods may be imported into the Republic of Palau without incurring customs duty:
*200 cigarettes or 454g of cigars or tobacco; *2litres of alcoholic beverage.*
Note [*]: For passengers over 21 years of age only.

PUBLIC HOLIDAYS

Jan 1 '95 New Year's Day. **Mar 15** Youth Day. **May 5** Senior Citizens' Day. **Jun 1** President's Day. **Jul 9** Constitution Day. **Sep 5** Labour Day. **Oct 24** UN Day. **Nov 24** Thanksgiving Day. **Dec 25** Christmas Day. **Jan 1 '96** New Year's Day. **Mar 15** Youth Day.
Note: Variations occur from island to island.

TRAVEL

AIR: *Palau Paradise Air* operates flights twice-daily (except Saturday) between Babelthuap–Peleliu, Peleliu–Angaur and Babelthuap–Angaur.
International airport: *Palau International*, on Babelthuap Island, which is near Koror Island.
Departure tax: US$10.
SEA: International cruise lines seldom call at Palau

ports. Visitors who sail privately to Palau will find Naval Oceanographic charts to be most useful. US Naval Chart HO 5500 covers the entire region of Micronesia. Unscheduled inter-island boat services to Babelthuap, Kayangel and Peleliu are available at boat docks around Koror.
ROAD: The road network is being extended but there is little central planning, and many routes are inaccessible to ordinary traffic. **Taxi:** There are many taxis in Koror offering comfortable travel. However, they are not metered and fares are not controlled, so it is advisable to agree on the fare in advance.

SOCIAL PROFILE

FOOD & DRINK: Several restaurants serve American and Japanese food. On request they will generally serve local specialities including mangrove crab and lobster-like langusta. Fresh fish and fruits are especially delicious here.
NIGHTLIFE: Many restaurants have a bar. A few places offer evening entertainment. The Visitors Authority or agents can arrange dance shows (for address, see top of entry).
SHOPPING: Palau's best-known art form is the *storyboard*. These are carvings on various lengths of wood, sometimes shaped into crocodiles, turtles or fish and painted. The storyboards depict Palauan stories taken from about 30 popular legends or recorded events. In addition to the storyboards, models of *bais* (houses), canoes and sculptured figurines called *dilukai* are also carved. Other gifts include jewellery, etchings, turtleshell trays (a form of Palauan women's money) and baskets, purses, hats and mats woven from pandanas and palm.
Shopping hours: 0800-2100 Monday to Saturday.
SPORT: Palau has some of the world's most spectacular **diving** locations. For example, Jellyfish Lake offers the weird experience of **snorkelling** through a dense population of innocuous jellyfish; elsewhere the waters contain many vertical drops. Rock Island is considered to be the finest location.
SPECIAL EVENTS: The following list gives a selection of the major festivals and special events in Palau during 1995/96:
Mar 15 '95 *Youth Day Fair.* **May 5** *Senior Citizen's Fair.* **Jul 9** *Palau Arts Festival; Tourism Week; Annual Sportfishing.*

SOCIAL CONVENTIONS: Traditional Palauan society was a complex matriarchal system. The people are now amongst the most enterprising in the region, though a version of traditional beliefs, *Modekngei*, exists alongside the imported Christian beliefs. The political system is modeled on that of the USA, and Western culture is being assimilated – not least because of the many Palauans who continue their education abroad.
Tipping: Optional.

BUSINESS PROFILE

COMMERCIAL INFORMATION: For further information contact the Palau Chamber of Commerce, Koror 96940.
CONFERENCES/CONVENTIONS: The Airai View Hotel in Koror can provide facilities for up to 150 delegates. For more information, contact the Airai View Hotel, PO Box 37, Koror 96940. Tel: 587 3485. Fax: 488 1027.

CLIMATE

Tends to be wet and hot throughout the year, creating a humid environment.

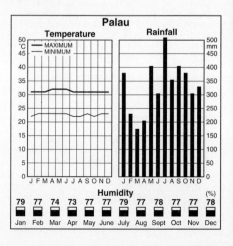

Pakistan

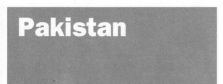

□ *international airport*

Location: Indian subcontinent.

Ministry of Culture, Sports & Tourism
Tourism Wing, Government of Pakistan, 13-T/U College Road, Commercial Area, Markaz F-7, Islamabad, Pakistan
Tel: (51) 211 790 or 213 121. Fax: (51) 815 767. Telex: 34318 (a/b TOUR PAK).

Pakistan Tourism Development Corporation
House No 2, Street 61, F-7/4 Islamabad, Pakistan
Tel: (51) 811 001/4 or 222 290. Fax: (51) 824 173.
Telex: 54356 (a/b PTDC P).

High Commission of the Islamic Republic of Pakistan
35-36 Lowndes Square, London SW1X 9JN
Tel: (0171) 235 2044. Telex: 290226. Opening hours: 0930-1730 Monday to Friday; *Visa section:* 1000-1300 for applications, 1630-1715 for collections.

British High Commission
PO Box 1122, Diplomatic Enclave, Ramna 5, Islamabad, Pakistan
Tel: (51) 822 131/5. Fax: (51) 823 439. Telex: 54122 (a/b UKEMBPK).
Consulates in: Karachi and Lahore.

Embassy of the Islamic Republic of Pakistan
2315 Massachusetts Avenue, NW, Washington, DC 20008
Tel: (202) 939 6200. Fax: (202) 387 0484.

Consulate General of the Islamic Republic of Pakistan
12 East 65th Street, New York, NY 10021
Tel: (212) 879 5800. Fax: (212) 517 6987.

Embassy of the United States of America
PO Box 1048, Unit 6220, Diplomatic Enclave, Ramna 5, Islamabad, Pakistan
Tel: (51) 826 161/79. Fax: (51) 214 222. Telex: 825864 (a/b AEISL PK).
Consulates in: Karachi, Lahore and Peshawar.

High Commission of the Islamic Republic of Pakistan
Suite 608, Burnside Building, 151 Slater Street, Ottawa, Ontario K1P 5H3
Tel: (613) 238 7881. Fax: (613) 238 7296.
Consulates in: Montréal and Toronto.

PTDC Vester
Farimagsgade 3, 1606 Copenhagen V, Denmark

Tel: 331 2118 or 33 39 44 55. Fax: 33 93 97 99.
Representatives for the Pakistan Tourism Development Corporation.

Canadian High Commission
PO Box 1042, Diplomatic Enclave, Sector G-5, Islamabad, Pakistan
Tel: (51) 211 101. Fax: (51) 211 540. Telex: 5700 (a/b DOCAN PK).
Consulate in: Karachi.

AREA: 803,950 sq km (502,469 sq miles).
POPULATION: 120,840,000 (1993 estimate).
POPULATION DENSITY: 151.8 per sq km.
CAPITAL: Islamabad. **Population:** 400,000 (1993).
GEOGRAPHY: Pakistan has borders to the north with Afghanistan, to the east with India and to the west with Iran; the Arabian Sea lies to the south. In the far northwest is the disputed territory of Jammu and Kashmir, bounded by Afghanistan, China and India. Pakistan comprises distinct regions. The northern highlands – the Hindu Kush – are rugged and mountainous; the Indus Valley is a flat, alluvial plain with five major rivers dominating the upper region, eventually joining the Indus River flowing south to the Makran coast; Sindh is bounded east by the Thar Desert and the Rann of Kutch, and on the west by the Kirthar Range; the Baluchistan Plateau is an arid tableland encircled by mountains.
LANGUAGE: Urdu and English with regional languages of Sindhi, Baluchi, Punjabi and Pashtu. There are numerous local dialects.
RELIGION: 97% Muslims, 2% Hindu, 1% Christian.
TIME: GMT + 5.
ELECTRICITY: 220 volts AC, 50Hz. Round 2- or 3-pin plugs are in use.
COMMUNICATIONS: Telephone: IDD is available. Country code: 92. Outgoing international code: 00. **Fax:** A service was introduced in 1986 by the Pakistan telephone and telegraph department. **Telex/telegram:** There are services at post offices, telegraph offices and main hotels. The Central Telegraph Offices provide a 24-hour service. **Post:** Airmail takes four to five days to reach Western Europe. There are *Poste Restante* facilities in Lahore, Karachi and Rawalpindi. General Post Offices in major cities offer 24-hour services. Important letters

Chaukundi tombs near Karachi

International airport
Main road
Land over 3000m
Land over 1000m
Land over 200m
Historical site

400km
200mls

should be registered or insured. **Press:** The English-language press enjoys a great deal of influence in business circles but most publications are in Urdu. Dailies include *Baluchistan Times, The Financial Post, The Leader, The Pakistan Observer, The Star, The Nation, The News, The Frontier Post* and *The Dawn*. **BBC World Service and Voice of America frequencies:** From time to time these change. See the section *How to Use this Book* for more information.

BBC:

| MHz | 17.79 | 15.31 | 9.740 | 1.413 |

A service is also available on 1413kHz.

Voice of America:

| MHz | 21.49 | 15.60 | 9.525 | 6.035 |

PASSPORT/VISA

Regulations and requirements may be subject to change at short notice, and you are advised to contact the appropriate diplomatic or consular authority before finalising travel arrangements. Details of these may be found at the head of this country's entry. Any numbers in the chart refer to the footnotes below.

	Passport Required?	Visa Required?	Return Ticket Required?
Full British	Yes	Yes	Yes
BVP	Not valid	-	-
Australian	Yes	Yes	Yes
Canadian	Yes	Yes	Yes
USA	Yes	Yes	Yes
Other EU (As of 31/12/94)	Yes	Yes	Yes
Japanese	Yes	Yes	Yes

Note: Visa requirements for Pakistan are liable to change at short notice. Consult the nearest consular representative of Pakistan well in advance of travel. **Restricted entry and transit:** The Government of Pakistan refuses entry to: (a) nationals of Israel, even for transit; (b) holders of passports issued by the Government of Taiwan (China), except for transit or to change aircraft without leaving the airport. **PASSPORTS:** Valid passport required by all.

British Visitors Passport: Not accepted. **VISAS:** Required by all. **Types of visa:** Single-entry and Double-entry generally for a maximum stay of 3 months. A Multiple-entry visa is also available allowing six journeys in a total period not exceeding one year, maximum 3-month stay at any one time. Visas must be used within 6 months of the date of issue. Price of visa varies according to nationality (*Single-entry* – £24; *Double-entry* – £48; *Multiple-entry* – £72 for UK nationals). Certain nationals are issued with visas free of charge, but they must be obtained prior to travel. For further information, consult the High Commission or Embassy. **Application to:** Consulate (or Consular section at Embassy or High Commission). For addresses, see top of entry. **Application requirements:** (a) Valid passport. (b) 1 application form. (c) 1 passport-size photo. (d) Confirmed return/onward ticket.

MONEY

Currency: Pakistani Rupee (Re, singular; Rs, plural) = 100 paisa. Notes are in denominations of Rs1000, 500, 100, 50, 10, 5, 2 and 1. Coins are in denominations of Rs1, and 50, 25, 10 and 5 paisa. **Credit cards:** American Express is the most widely

accepted card. Access/Mastercard, Diners Club and Visa have more limited use. Check with your credit card company for details of merchant acceptability and other services which may be available.

Travellers cheques: Generally accepted at most banks, 4- and 5-star hotels and major shops.

Exchange rate indicators: The following figures are included as a guide to the movements of the Pakistani Rupee against Sterling and the US Dollar:

Date:	Oct '92	Sep '93	Jan '94	Jan '95
£1.00=	37.00	45.62	44.52	48.14
$1.00=	23.31	29.88	30.09	30.77

Currency restrictions: The import and export of local currency is limited to Rs300. Unlimited import and export of foreign currency is allowed.

Banking hours: 0900-1300 and 1500-2000 Sunday to Thursday, closed Friday. Some banks open on Saturday.

DUTY FREE

The following items may be imported into Pakistan without incurring customs duty:
200 cigarettes or 50 cigars or 500g tobacco; 250ml of perfume and eau de toilette (opened); still and/or movie camera with film.
Note: (a) The import of alcohol, matches, plants, fruit and vegetables is prohibited. However, if a visitor imports alcohol by mistake or with the intention of taking it out of Pakistan, it will be held by customs and returned on departure. (b) Precious stones and jewellery can be *exported* up to a value of Rs10,000 (Rs5000 for nationals of Afghanistan, the Gulf States, Iran and Nepal) and carpets to the value of Rs25,000, if accompanied by an export permit. All items are subject to proof of having been purchased in foreign currency. The export of antiques is prohibited.

PUBLIC HOLIDAYS

Feb 1 '95 Beginning of Ramadan. **Mar 2** Eid al-Fitr (End of Ramadan). **Mar 23** Pakistan Day. **May 1** Labour Day. **May 12** Eid ul-Azha (Feast of the Sacrifice). **May 31** Muharram (Islamic New Year). **Jun 9** Ashoura. **Jul 1** Bank Holiday. **Aug 9** Eid-i-Milad-un-Nabi (Prophet's Birthday). **Aug 14** Independence Day. **Sep 6** Defence of Pakistan Day. **Sep 11** Anniversary of the Death of Quaid-i-Azam. **Nov 9** Iqbal Day. **Dec 25** Quaid-i-Azam's Birthday and Christmas Day. **Dec 31** Bank Holiday. **Jan 22 '96** Beginning of Ramadan. **Feb 22** Eid al-Fitr (End of Ramadan). **Mar 23** Pakistan Day. **Apr 29** Eid ul-Azha (Feast of the Sacrifice).
Note: (a) Muslim festivals are timed according to local sightings of various phases of the Moon and the dates given above are approximations. During the lunar month of Ramadan that precedes Eid al-Fitr, Muslims fast during the day and feast at night and normal business patterns may be interrupted. Most restaurants are closed during the day and there is a restriction on smoking and drinking in public places. Eid al-Fitr and Eid ul-Azha may last anything from two to four days, depending on the region. For more information see the section *World of Islam* at the back of the book. (b) Christian holidays are taken by the Christian community only.

HEALTH

Regulations and requirements may be subject to change at short notice, and you are advised to contact your doctor well in advance of your intended date of departure. Any numbers in the chart refer to the footnotes below.

	Special Precautions?	Certificate Required?
Yellow Fever	No	1
Cholera	Yes	2
Typhoid & Polio	Yes	-
Malaria	3	-
Food & Drink	4	-

[1]: Yellow fever vaccination certificate is required of all travellers coming from any part of a country in which yellow fever is endemic. Infants under six months of age are exempt if the mother's vaccination certificate shows her to have been vaccinated prior to the child's birth.
[2]: Following WHO guidelines issued in 1973, a cholera vaccination certificate is no longer a condition of entry to Pakistan. However, cholera is a serious risk in this country and precautions are essential. Up-to-date advice should be sought before deciding whether these precautions should include vaccination as medical opinion is divided over its effectiveness. See the *Health* section at the back of the book.
[3]: Malaria risk exists throughout the year in all areas

The King Priest form Moenjodaro, the centre of 5000-year-old Indus Valley civilisation

below 2000m. The malignant *falciparum* strain is present and has been reported as chloroquine-resistant.
[4]: All water should be regarded as being potentially contaminated. Water used for drinking, brushing teeth or making ice should have first been boiled or otherwise sterilised. Milk is unpasteurised and should be boiled. Powdered or tinned milk is available and is advised, but make sure that it is reconstituted with pure water. Avoid dairy products which are likely to have been made from unboiled milk. Only eat well-cooked meat and fish, preferably served hot. Salad and mayonnaise may carry increased risk. Vegetables should be cooked and fruit peeled.
Rabies is present. For those at high risk, vaccination before arrival should be considered. If you are bitten abroad seek medical advice without delay. For more information, consult the *Health* section at the back of the book.
Health care: Full health insurance is essential.

TRAVEL - International

AIR: Pakistan's national airline is *Pakistan International Airlines (PK)*, linking Pakistan with 47 destinations around the world.
Approximate flight times: From Karachi to *London* is 11 hours 50 minutes, to *Los Angeles* is 22 hours 30 minutes, to *New York* is 21 hours 40 minutes, to *Riyadh* is 3 hours 35 minutes and to *Singapore* is 6 hours 55 minutes.
International airports: *Karachi (KHI)* (Civil), 12km (8 miles) east of the city (travel time – 25 minutes). Good airport facilities exist, including duty-free shops, bar/restaurant, post office, bank and shops. Coaches to the city meet all arrivals. A bus runs from

dusk to dawn every 30 minutes. Taxi services to the city are available.
Lahore (LHE), 11km (7 miles) southeast of the city (travel time – 20 minutes). Airport facilities include car hire, bank, restaurant and shops. Coaches leave every 20 minutes for the city. Buses go every 10 minutes. Taxi services to the city are also available.
Islamabad (ISB) (International), 15km (9 miles) east of the city (travel time – 20 minutes). There are full duty-free facilities. Coach and taxi services to the city are available.
Peshawar (PEW), 4km (2.5 miles) from the city (travel time – 10 minutes). Full bus and taxi services to the city are available.
Departure tax: Rs400 for passengers travelling first class, Rs300 for club class and Rs200 for economy class. There is also an additional Foreign Travel Tax of Rs700 on tickets issued within Pakistan. Transit passengers and children under two years of age are exempt.
SEA: The major port is Karachi (Kemari). There are a number of shipping lines serving Karachi from Europe. It is both Pakistan's and Afghanistan's port for goods, together with Port Qasim.
RAIL: The only rail link to India is a train from Lahore to Amritsar which leaves daily at 1100. Passengers have to be at the station by 0900 for customs and immigration procedures. A rail link also extends over the Iranian border to Zahedan; the Express train leaves every Friday at 1050; and the Passenger train, which travels as far as Taftan, leaves every Tuesday at 1045 from Quetta.
ROAD: Road links from China, Iran, India and Afghanistan. The main road link is between Karachi and Lahore. There is a road from Kabul (Afghanistan) to Rawalpindi. Another road runs from Karachi to

Verdant dales in the Hunza Valley

Quetta and to the border with Iran. Visitors exiting Pakistan by land routes are subject to a road toll of Rs2.

TRAVEL - Internal

AIR: Most domestic services are operated by *PIA*. Other airlines are *Aero Asia* and *Shaheen*. There are many daily flights from Karachi to Lahore, Rawalpindi and other commercial centres. Air transport is the quickest and most efficient means of travel.
Departure tax: Rs20 for internal flights.
RIVER: Traffic along the Indus River is almost exclusively commercial and many goods are carried to Punjab and the north.
RAIL: A legacy of British rule is an extensive rail network, based on the main line from Karachi to Lahore, Rawalpindi and Peshawar, which has several daytime and overnight trains. Most other routes have several daily trains. Even first-class compartments can be hot and crowded. Travel in air-conditioned coaches is advised, as are reservations on long-distance journeys and overnight service. Children under 3 years of age travel free. Children aged 3-11 years pay half fare.
Pakistan Railways offer concessions for tourists (on presentation of a certificate issued by PTDC), excluding Indian nationals travelling by rail. A discount of 25% is offered to individuals and groups, and 50% for students. Vehicles owned by foreign tourists or hired locally are also eligible to 25% discount in freight charges when transported by rail. Details are available from railway offices in Pakistan.
Approximate rail times: *Karachi* to Lahore is 16 hours, to Rawalpindi is 28 hours and to Peshawar is 32 hours; and *Lahore* to Rawalpindi is 6 hours.
ROAD: Traffic drives on the left. The highway network between cities is well made and maintained. **Bus:** Regular services run between most towns and villages. Lahore–Rawalpindi–Peshawar has an hourly service. Air-conditioned coaches/buses are recommended for long distances. Advance booking is advised. **Car hire:** Available in major cities as well as at Karachi, Lahore and Rawalpindi airports. Most hotels can book cars for guests. **Documentation:** An International Driving Permit will be issued on presentation of visitor's national driving licence.
URBAN: Extensive **bus** and **minibus** services operate in Lahore, Karachi and other towns, although services can be crowded. **Taxi:** Reasonably priced and widely available, they are by far the most efficient means of urban travel. Note that they may not operate after sunset during Ramadan. **Auto-rickshaws** are also available.

ACCOMMODATION

HOTELS: Pakistan offers a wide range of accommodation. Modern well-equipped hotels are to be found in most major towns and offer excellent facilities such as swimming pools and sports facilities. There are also cottages, Dak bungalows and rest houses in all principal hill stations and health resorts. A government room tax of 15% is added to the cost of accommodation. In all cases it is advisable to book well in advance and check reservations. For further information contact the Pakistan Hotel Association, PO Box 7448, Shafi Court, Merewether Road, Civil Lines, Karachi 75530. Tel: (21) 568 6407. Telex: 516408.
PTDC HOTELS & MOTELS: The Pakistan Tourism Development Corporation operates four hotels located at Lahore, Rawalpindi, Murree and Peshawar. PTDC also runs well-furnished and moderately-priced motels at 15 different tourist locations throughout the country. For reservation of accommodation in motels, contact PTDC Motels Reservation Office, Block 4-B, Markaz F-7, Bhitai Road, Islamabad 44000. Tel: (51) 819 384. Fax: (51) 218 233. Telex: 54356 (a/b PTDC PK).
YOUTH HOSTELS: The Pakistan Youth Hostel Association has nine hostels throughout the country available to members of affiliated organisations. Details can be obtained from the Pakistan Youth Hostel Association, 110 Firdous Market, Gurberg 111, Lahore.

RESORTS & EXCURSIONS

KARACHI: The largest city in Pakistan, formerly the capital, is situated on the shores of the Arabian Sea near the mouth of the Indus. The capital of Sindh Province, it is now a modern industrial city and Pakistan's major port. Though not strictly a tourist centre there are a number of attractions, such as the fish wharf where brightly-coloured boats bring in seafood, one of the country's major foreign exchange earners. The hundreds of street restaurants, tea houses, samosa and juice stalls are pretty lively. Boats can be hired to sail out of the harbour. There are architectural reminders of the former British Imperial presence, especially in the clubs. The most magnificent building, however, is the *Quaid-i-Azam's Mazar*, the mausoleum of the founder of Pakistan, made entirely of white marble with impressive north African arches and magnificent Chinese crystal chandeliers. The changing of the guards, which takes place three times a day, is the best time to visit. Other places to visit are the *National Museum,* parks, zoo and a beach at **Clifton.**
SINDH: A region known for the remarkable quality of its light, with two main places of interest: **Mohenjodaro,** a settlement dating back 5000 years, and **Thatta,** notable for its mausoleums and mosques. There are sporting facilities on *Lake Haleji,* 14km (9 miles) away.
THE PUNJAB: Lahore is a historic, bustling city with buildings of pink and white marble. There is plenty to see: bazaars, the *Badshahi Mosque* – one of the largest mosques in the whole world and an example of Moghul architecture rivalled only by the Taj Mahal, the beautiful *Shalimar Gardens*, the *National Museum of Archaeology* and the *Gate of Chauburji*. Near **Taxila** are two interesting excavated sites, **Sirkap** and **Jaulian**, dating back to the Buddhist Gandhara period.
Other towns in the Punjab include **Faisalabad** (formerly Lyallpur), **Attock, Harappa, Multan** and **Bahawalpur. Islamabad,** the capital of Pakistan since 1963, and **Rawalpindi,** are both located on the *Pothowar Plain*. The decision to build a new capital city in this area transformed the sleepy town of Rawalpindi into an important twin to Islamabad. Now Rawalpindi houses many of the civil servants working in the government district. The old part of the town boasts fine examples of local architecture and bazaars crammed into the narrow streets with craftsmen still using the traditional methods. As a planned capital Islamabad lacks some of the regional flair of other cities but it houses an interesting variety of modern buildings especially in the part designated for government offices. The city itself has an air of spaciousness with parks, gardens and fountains below the silhouette of the *Margalla Hills*. In the midst of these lies *Daman-e-Koh*, a terraced garden with an excellent view over the city. Also in Islamabad is the *Shah Faisal Masjid* (mosque) which can accommodate 100,000 worshippers. The majestic white building comprises four 88m (288ft) minarets and a desert tent-like structure, the main prayer chamber. About 8km (5 miles) from the city is *Rawal Lake* with an abundance of leisure facilities including watersports and a picnic area. North of Rawalpindi is the beautiful *Swat Valley*. This is an area of wild mountains and fantastic alpine scenery. It was, in ancient times, the home of the famous Gandhara school of sculpture, a manifestation of Greek influenced Buddhist forms. The ruins of great Buddhist stupas, monasteries and statues are found all over Swat. It is now the home to the Swat Pathans and also boasts popular mountain retreats such as **Mingora, Kalam, Miandam, Behrain,** etc.
KASHMIR: In this province are some of the highest mountains in the world, one of the most famous being *Nanga Parbat*. Here too is the second highest mountain in the world, *K2,* also known as Mount Godwin-Austen. The **Baltoro Glacier** and the **Batura Glacier** are the largest outside the Polar region. The settlements of **Gilgit** and **Skardu** are well-known stop-offs on the mountaineering trail. It is now possible to follow the **Karakoram Highway** all the way through from Gilgit to **Hunza,** over the *Khunjerab Pass* and on to Kashgar in the Xinjiang Province of China. This is the ancient Silk Road and must rank as one of the most spectacular journeys on Earth.
PESHAWAR: The capital of the North West Frontier Province, this is the area of the Pashtuns or Pathans as they have come to be known in more recent times. **Peshawar City** is surrounded by high walls with 20 gates

Camel riding on the beach at Karachi

leading into it. There is evidence in the lawns and parks of the former colonial days. Much of the surrounding area is still under the jurisdiction of tribal law. These areas can be visited only if one has a permit from the relevant authorities. Many of the tribesmen carry firearms, the normal adornment for a Pathan warrior. In the land of the Afridis is the *Khyber Pass,* a 1200m-high (3960ft) sheer rock wall separating Pakistan and Afghanistan. North of Peshawar in the Hindu Kush Mountains is the wild and beautiful area of **Chitral**, famous for the Kalash people, last of the pagan tribes of Kafiristan. This valley is noted for its hot springs and trout-filled rivers.

SOCIAL PROFILE

FOOD & DRINK: There are three types of cuisine in Pakistan: Pakistani, Western and Chinese. Local cuisine is based on curry or *masala* (hot and spicy) sauces accompanying chicken, mutton, shrimps and a wide choice of vegetables. Specialities include *brain masala, biryani* (seasoned rice with mutton, chicken and yoghurt), *pilao* (similar but less spicy) and *sag gosht* (spinach and lamb curry). Lahore is the centre for Mogul-style cuisine known as *moghlai.* Specialities include *chicken tandoori, shish kebabs* (charcoal-grilled meat on skewers), *shami-kebabs* (patties of chopped meat fried in *ghee* or butter), *tikka-kebabs* (grilled mutton or beef seasoned and spiced) and *chicken tikka* (highly seasoned chicken quarters, charcoal-grilled). Desserts include pastries, *shahi tukray* (slices of fried bread cooked in milk or cream, sweetened with syrup and topped with nuts and saffron), *halwa* (sweetmeat made with eggs, carrots, maize cream, *sooji* and nuts) and *firni* (similar to vanilla custard). **Drink:** The national drink is tea, drunk strong with milk and often very sweet. Alcohol may be bought at major hotels by visitors who have been issued a Liquor Permit from the Excise and Taxation Office. Wine is expensive and only available in top restaurants. Pakistani-brewed beer is widely available, as are canned carbonated drinks. There are no bars since there are strict laws concerning alcohol, and it is illegal to drink in public. Waiter service is provided in the larger hotels and restaurants.
NIGHTLIFE: Top hotels have bars and dancing but there is little Western-style nightlife. Cinemas in the large cities show international as well as Pakistani films. Cultural programmes of traditional music and dance can be seen and the Pakistani Arts Academy performs at various times during the year. Festivals and annual celebrations are well worth seeing.
SHOPPING: Special purchases include carved wooden tables, trays, screens, silver trinkets, pottery, camel-skin

lamps, bamboo decorations, brassware, cane items, conch-shell ornaments, glass bangles, gold ornaments, hand-embroidered shawls, rugs and carpets, silks, cashmere shawls and *saleem shahi* shoes with upturned toes. While some of the major towns have craft centres where handicrafts from different regions are sold, bazaars often provide the most interesting shopping. It is expected that the customer should bargain for goods.
Shopping hours: 0930-1300 and 1500-2000 Saturday to Thursday. Bazaars stay open longer.
SPORT: Golf: Clubs are located in the large cities and visitors are generally allowed to play a course on the introduction of a member or by acquiring temporary membership. **Tennis:** Clubs in the large cities have courts and visitors must be introduced by a member or can often obtain temporary membership through the Pakistan Tourism Development Corporation.
Watersports: In addition to the beaches, **swimming** pools can be found in various clubs in large towns and in major hotels. Kemari sail or motorboats can be hired at a previously agreed price. Deep-sea night **fishing** is particularly good. There are also freshwater lakes with good fishing. **Spectator sports: Cricket,** the national sport, can be watched in most major towns at many different levels. Pakistan are the current world champions of the one day game. **Football** and **hockey** are fast becoming popular national sports and regular matches can be seen in the stadium at Karachi and at other sportsfields all over the country. **Polo** matches can be seen in major cities and most notably in the northern towns of Gilgit and Chitral and **horseracing** takes place in winter in Karachi and Lahore.
SPECIAL EVENTS: The following is a list of some of the special events taking place in Pakistan during 1995/96:
May 14-15 '95 *Joshi or Chilimjusht,* Chitral. **Jul 25** *Shandur Pass Polo Tournament,* Chitral. **Mid-Jul** *Utchal (Kalash Festival),* Chitral. **Mid-Sep** *Jashan-e-Khyber,* Peshawar. **Oct** *Lok Mela,* Islamabad; *Lok Mela (Folk Festival),* Chitral. **Mid-Oct** *Jashan-e-Gilgit,* Gilgit. **Feb '96** *Sibi Festival,* Sibi (Balochistan); *Basant Kite Flying Festival,* Lahore. **Feb (last week)** *National Horse and Cattle Show,* Lahore. **Mar (last week)** *Mela Chiraghan (Festival of Lamps),* Lahore.
SOCIAL CONVENTIONS: Shaking hands is the usual form of greeting. Mutual hospitality and courtesy are of great importance at all levels, whatever the social standing of the host. Visitors must remember that most Pakistanis are Muslim and should respect their customs and beliefs. Smoking is prohibited in some public places and it is polite to ask permission before lighting a cigarette. It is common for visiting business people to be

entertained in hotels and restaurants. If invited to a private home, a gift or national souvenir is welcome. Informal dress is acceptable for most occasions. Women should avoid wearing tight clothing and should ensure that their arms and legs are covered. Pakistani society is divided into classes and within each group there is a subtle social grading. The Quoran is the law for Muslims and it influences every aspect of daily life. See the section *World of Islam* at the back of the book for more information.
Tipping: Most high-class hotels and restaurants add 10% service charge. Other tipping is discretionary.

BUSINESS PROFILE

ECONOMY: About half of the Pakistani labour force works in agriculture with wheat, rice, sugar cane and cotton as the main products. Poor weather and underdevelopment have hindered significant growth in this sector in recent years and the Government is attempting to stimulate other parts of the economy. Mining has considerable potential, given that deposits have been positively identified but little investment has been made in their exploitation. Oil production began during the 1980s, but remains on a small scale by world standards. Pakistan has reserves of graphite and limestone, as well as copper and coal. Established manufacturing industries include textiles, food-processing and building materials. Pakistan's lack of prosperity entitles the country to considerable foreign aid which has been more forthcoming since Pakistan managed to improve its rate of repayment – with the exception of the USA which recently cut its aid provision drastically due to Pakistan's refusal to curtail its nuclear programme. Despite this, Pakistan has recently made a great deal of economic progress: trade barriers and exchange controls have been largely removed (boosting foreign exchange accounts by US$1 billion as remittances from abroad resumed after the Gulf War); the budget deficit has been cut; and government coffers have been swelled by the proceeds of the privatisation of nearly 100 banks, industrial concerns, transport and communications organisations. Foreign investment has risen sharply, assisted by a new foreign investment law: for this reason, the Government is worried about the effect of Islamisation upon the economy. Japan is the country's largest trading partner, providing 16% of the country's imports and buying 10% of its exports. The USA, Saudi Arabia, Germany and the UK are the other principal trading partners.
BUSINESS: Ties should be worn for important business appointments. English is commonly used. Appointments should be made, remembering that businesses are usually closed Friday and Muslim holidays. Visiting cards should be used. **Office hours:** 0900-1700 Saturday to Thursday.
Government office hours: 0900-1700 Sunday to Thursday.
COMMERCIAL INFORMATION: The following organisation can offer advice: Overseas Investors' Chamber of Commerce and Industry, PO Box 4833, Talpur Road, Karachi. Tel: (21) 222 557. Fax: (21) 242 7315. Telex: 2870.

CLIMATE

Three seasons: winter (November-March) is warm and cooled by sea breezes on the coast, summer (April-July) has extreme temperatures, the monsoon season (July-September) has the highest rainfall on the hills. Karachi has little rain. The best time to visit the south is between November and March, when the days are cool and clear. The best time to visit northern Pakistan is from April to October.

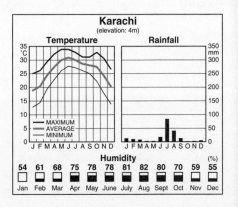

View of Gasherbrum-I Peak (8068m)

Panama

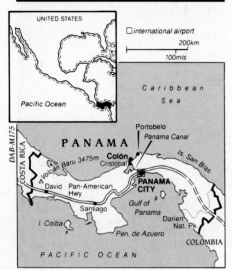

Location: Central America.

Note: The Darien area is known to be frequented by Colombian guerrillas and smugglers. Travel south of Yavza to the Colombian border is only possible by foot and is risky for individual travellers or small groups. Occasional flare-ups of armed violence continue to occur in metropolitan areas of Panama, where there have also been occasional and random bombings in public places. *Source: US State Department – September 2, 1994.*

Instituto Panameño de Turismo (IPAT)
Apartado 4421, Centro de Convenciones ATLAPA, Vía Israel, Panamá 5, Republic of Panama
Tel: 267 000. Fax: 263 483. Telex: 3359.
Embassy & Consulate of the Republic of Panama *and* **Information & Tourist Affairs**
48 Park Street, London W1Y 3PD
Tel: (0171) 493 4646. Fax: (0171) 493 4499. Telex: 8812982 (a/b PANCON G). Opening hours: 1000-1200 and 1400-1600 Monday to Friday.
British Embassy
Apartado 889, Zona 1, 4th & 5th Floors, Torre Banco Sur, Calle 53 Este, Panamá 1, Republic of Panama
Tel: 690 866. Fax: 230 730. Telex: 3620 (a/b PROPANA PG).
Embassy of the Republic of Panama
2862 McGill Terrace, NW, Washington, DC 20008
Tel: (202) 483 1407. Fax: (202) 483 8413.
Embassy of the United States of America
Apartado 6959, Avenida Balboa, Entre Calle 37 y 38, Panamá 5, Republic of Panama
Tel: 271 777. Fax: 271 964. Telex: 3583.
Consulate in: Cristobal (tel: 412 440 *or* 412 2478).
Consulate of Panama
Suite 210, 2788 Bathurst Street, Toronto, Ontario L3R 3E9
Tel: (416) 787 2122 *or* 787 2724.
Consulates in: Halifax, Montréal and Vancouver.
Canadian Consulate
Aero Peru Piso 5B, Calle Manuel y Caza, Edificio Proconsa, Campo Alegre, Panamá, Republic of Panama
Tel: 647 014 *or* 642 325. Fax: 235 470.

AREA: 75,517 sq km (29,157 sq miles).
POPULATION: 2,514,586 (1992 estimate).

Health

GALILEO/WORLDSPAN:	**TI-DFT/PTY/HE**
SABRE:	**TIDFT/PTY/HE**

Visa

GALILEO/WORLDSPAN:	**TI-DFT/PTY/VI**
SABRE:	**TIDFT/PTY/VI**

For more information on Timatic codes refer to Contents.

POPULATION DENSITY: 33.3 per sq km.
CAPITAL: Panama City. **Population:** 413,505 (1990).
GEOGRAPHY: Panama forms the land link between the North and South American continents. Panama borders Colombia to the east, Costa Rica to the west, and the Caribbean and the Pacific Ocean to the north and south. The country forms an S-shaped isthmus which runs east–west over a total length of 772km (480 miles) and is 60-177km (37-110 miles) wide. The landscape is mountainous with lowlands on both coastlines cut by streams, wooded slopes and a wide area of savannah-covered plains and rolling hills called *El Interior* between the Azuero peninsula and the Central Mountains. The Caribbean and the Pacific Ocean are linked by the man-made Panama Canal, cut into a gap between the Cordillera de Talamanca and the San Blas mountain range and stretching for over 65km (40 miles); the length of the Canal is often referred to as 80km (50 miles) as this is the distance between deep-water points of entry. Only about a quarter of the country is inhabited. The majority of the population live either around the Canal and main cities of Panama City and Colón or in the Pacific lowlands and the adjacent mountains. (40% of the population are concentrated in the two cities which control the entrance and exit of the Canal.)
LANGUAGE: The official language is Spanish, but English is widely spoken.
RELIGION: 98% Roman Catholic.
TIME: GMT - 5.
ELECTRICITY: 120 volts AC, 60Hz. Plugs are the flat 2-pin American type.
COMMUNICATIONS: Telephone: IDD is available. Country code: 507. There are no area codes. Outgoing international code: 00. **Fax:** Main post offices and some hotels have facilities. **Telex:** Facilities in Panama City and major hotels. A tax of US$1 is levied against each call. **Telegram:** Facilities exist in main post offices of Panama City and other major cities and hotels. A tax of 50 cents is levied against each telegram. **Post:** Airmail to Western Europe takes five to ten days. Main post offices have *Poste Restante* and EMS (Express Mail Services) facilities. Post office hours: 0630-1745 Monday to Friday, 0700-1700 Saturday. **Press:** *El Panamá América* and *Crítica Libre* (both in Spanish) are the largest daily newspapers. *Colón News* is a weekly paper published in both English and Spanish and the US Army publishes a daily newspaper in English, *Tropic Times.*
BBC World Service and Voice of America frequencies: From time to time these change. See the section *How to Use this Book* for more information.
BBC:

MHz	17.84	15.22	9.590	0.930

Voice of America:

MHz	15.21	11.74	9.815	6.030

PASSPORT/VISA

Regulations and requirements may be subject to change at short notice, and you are advised to contact the appropriate diplomatic or consular authority before finalising travel arrangements. Details of these may be found at the head of this country's entry. Any numbers in the chart refer to the footnotes below.

	Passport Required?	Visa Required?	Return Ticket Required?
Full British	Yes	1/2	Yes
BVP	Not valid	-	-
Australian	Yes	Yes	Yes
Canadian	Yes	Yes	Yes
USA	Yes	Yes	Yes
Other EU (As of 31/12/94)	Yes	1/2	Yes
Japanese	Yes	Yes	Yes

Note: (a) No brief account of the complex Panamanian Visa regulations is likely to be fully successful. Readers are advised to use the following for general guidance, but to check on the requirements that specifically apply to them with the appropriate Consulate (or Consular section at Embassy). (b) Panamanian immigration procedures are rigidly enforced and non-compliance with the regulations may result in transportation at carrier's expense to country of origin. Visitors who do not comply with the regulations *may* be permitted to enter Panama at the Immigration official's discretion, but must show evidence of sufficent funds to cover their stay. Passport and visa regulations are liable to change at short notice and visitors are advised to consult the Panamanian Consul before travelling. (c) Nationals of the following countries must have authorisation from the immigration authorities in Panama before attempting to enter: Afghanistan, Albania, Algeria, Andorra, Angola, Bahrain, Bangladesh, Benin, Bhutan, Bosnia-Hercegovina, Botswana, Bulgaria, Burkina Faso, Burundi, Cambodia, Cameroon, Central African Republic, People's Republic of China, CIS, Congo,

Croatia, Cuba, Czech Republic, Ethiopia, Fiji, Gabon, Gambia, Ghana, Haiti, Hong Kong, Hungary, India, Indonesia, Iran, Iraq, Jordan, Kenya, Kiribati, Kuwait, Laos, Lesotho, Lebanon, Liberia, Libya, Former Yugoslav Republic of Macedonia, Madagascar, Malawi, Malaysia, Maldives, Mali, Mauritania, Mauritius, Morocco, Myanmar, Mongolia, Mozambique, Nauru, Nepal, Niger, Nigeria, North Korea, Oman, Pakistan, Papua New Guinea, Poland, Qatar, Romania, Rwanda, Saudi Arabia, Senegal, Sierra Leone, Slovak Republic, Slovenia, Somalia, South Africa, Sri Lanka, Sudan, Syria, Tanzania, Togo, Tonga, Tunisia, Turkey, Tuvalu, Uganda, United Arab Emirates, Vanuatu, Vietnam, Yemen, Yugoslavia (Montenegro and Serbia), Zaïre, Zambia and Zimbabwe.
PASSPORTS: Valid passport required by all.
British Visitors Passport: Not accepted.
Tourist Card: Nationals of those countries whose applications must be referred to Panama *cannot* be issued with a Tourist Card (see list above). The Tourist Card is required by all other nationalities, except those nationalities who enjoy visa exemption (see list below). The Tourist Card will be issued either on the flight or from the travel agent.
Cost: Free if acquired in advance of travel; US$5 if acquired at the airport or on the flight.
VISAS: Required by all except:
(a) **[1]** nationals of Germany, Spain and the UK (all other EU nationals *do* require visas);
(b) nationals of Austria, Chile, Costa Rica, El Salvador, Finland, Honduras, Switzerland and Uruguay.
Note: [2] All business visitors need a Business visa.
Types of visa: Tourist and Business.
Cost: £10. Visas are issued free to nationals of Columbia, Denmark, Mexico, The Netherlands, Norway and the USA.
Validity: Validity of a Tourist or Business visa is 30 days from the date of entry, to be used within a 3-month period from date of issue (extendable to 90 days when in Panama).
Application to: Consulate (or Consular section at Embassy). For addresses, see top of entry.
Application requirements: (a) Valid passport. (b) 2 passport-size photos. (c) 2 completed application forms. (d) Return ticket. (e) Fee (for some nationalities). (f) For Business visa, a letter from the sponsor in the UK stating nature of business, and evidence of funds to cover expenses whilst in Panama.
Working days required: 24 hours when applying in person.

MONEY

Currency: Balboa (Ba) = 100 centésimos. There is no Panamanian paper currency; coins exist in denominations of Ba100 and 1, and 50, 25, 10, 5 and 1 centésimos. US currency circulates freely: Ba1 = US$1.
Currency exchange: Banks and *cambios* are available for changing currency.
Credit cards: Visa and American Express are the most commonly used, but Access/Mastercard and Diners Club are also accepted. Check with your credit card company for details of merchant acceptability and other services which may be available.
Exchange rate indicators: The following figures are included as a guide to the movements of the Balboa against Sterling:

Date:	Oct '92	Sep '93	Jan '94	Jan '95
£1.00=	1.59	1.53	1.48	1.56

Currency restrictions: There are no restrictions on the import and export of either foreign or local currency. Visitors must have a minimum of US$150 when entering Panama (or US$10 per day for stays exceeding 15 days).
Banking hours: 0800-1330 Monday to Friday.

DUTY FREE

The following items may be imported into Panama without incurring customs duty:
500 cigarettes or 50 cigars or 500g tobacco; 3 bottles of alcohol; perfume and eau de cologne in opened bottles for personal use.
Prohibited items: Fruit, vegetable and animal products.

PUBLIC HOLIDAYS

Jan 1 '95 New Year's Day. **Jan 9** National Martyrs' Day. **Feb 28** Shrove Tuesday. **Apr 14** Good Friday. **May 1** Labour Day. **Aug 15** Foundation of Panama City (capital only). **Oct 11** Revolution Day. **Nov 1** National Anthem Day. **Nov 2** All Souls' Day. **Nov 3** Independence from Colombia (1903). **Nov 4** National Flag Day. **Nov 6** For Independence Day (Colón only). **Nov 10** First Call of Independence. **Nov 28** Independence from Spain. **Dec 8** Mothers' Day, Immaculate Conception. **Dec 25**

Christmas Day. **Jan 1 '96** New Year's Day. **Jan 9** National Martyrs' Day. **Feb 20** Shrove Tuesday. **Apr 5** Good Friday.

HEALTH

Regulations and requirements may be subject to change at short notice, and you are advised to contact your doctor well in advance of your intended date of departure. Any numbers in the chart refer to the footnotes below.

	Special Precautions?	Certificate Required?
Yellow Fever	Yes	1
Cholera	2	No
Typhoid & Polio	3	-
Malaria	4	-
Food & Drink	5	-

[1]: A certificate is required for travellers over one year of age coming from an infected area. Travellers arriving from non-endemic zones should note that vaccination is strongly recommended for travel outside the urban areas, even if an outbreak of the disease has not been reported and they would normally not require a vaccination certificate to enter the country.
[2]: There is only a small risk of contracting cholera in Panama, but travellers may want to take precautions.
[3]: Typhoid fevers are common, but polio is not present.
[4]: Malaria risk, predominantly in the benign *vivax* form, exists throughout the year in rural areas surrounding Lakes Boyana and Gatún; in Alto Chucunaque and Darien areas; and in the continental areas adjacent to the San Blas archipelago. The malignant *falciparum* form is reported to be 'resistant' to chloroquine.
[5]: Mains water is normally chlorinated, and whilst relatively safe, may cause mild abdominal upsets. Bottled water is available and is advised for the first few weeks of the stay. Drinking water outside main cities and towns is likely to be contaminated and sterilisation is considered essential. Milk is pasteurised and dairy products are safe for consumption. Local meat, poultry, seafood, fruit and vegetables are generally considered safe to eat.
Rabies is present. For those at high risk, vaccination before arrival should be considered. If you are bitten abroad seek medical advice without delay. For more information, consult the *Health* section at the back of the book.
Health care: Medical facilities are of a high standard, although those outside the capital are limited. There are approximately 7000 hospital beds and 2000 doctors in the country. Medical charges are high and health insurance is essential.

TRAVEL - International

AIR: Panama's national airline is *Air Panama International (OP)*.
Approximate flight times: From Panama City to *London* is 14 hours and to *Miami* is 2 hours 45 minutes.
International airport: *Panama City (PAC)* (Tocumen) is 27km (17 miles) northeast of the city (travel time – 25 minutes). Airport services include a bank, car hire, restaurant and full duty-free facilities. Buses and taxis go to the city.
Departure tax: US$20.
SEA: The Panama Canal is the major route from the Atlantic to the Pacific Ocean, and Panama (Balboa) is a port of call for many cruise lines and ocean vessels for both passenger and freight. Cruise lines include *Sitmar, Cunard, Royal Viking, Princess, Delta, Norwegian American* and *P&O*.
RAIL: There is an international link from Costa Rica (Puerto Cortés) to David and Bajo Baquete in the north of Panama.
ROAD: The principal route to Panama is the Pan-American Highway from Costa Rica to Panama City. The rainy season causes adverse conditions on the route south to Colombia. The Trans-Isthman Highway links Panama City and Colón.

TRAVEL - Internal

AIR: Smaller airports for internal flights are: *Aeropuerto Marcos A. Gelabert* in Paitilla and *Enrique Maleck* in David, Chiriquí. Internal air services are operated by *Cia Panameña de Aviación (COPA), Aeroperlas SANSAPA* and *Alas Chiricanas* which link Panama City with all centres in the interior.
RAIL: The *Ferrocarril de Panamá* operates a passenger and freight train service between Panama City and Colón which runs seven or eight times daily. This route offers splendid views of the jungle and the canal. There is also a railway operated by the *United Fruit Subsidiary* serving its plantations in Bocas del Toro and Puerto Armuelles. Trains are one class; air-conditioned accommodation is available on payment of a supplement to adult and child fares. Children under 5 travel free. Children aged 5-14 pay half fare.
ROAD: Bus: Traffic drives on the right. There are services between most large towns, but they can be very slow. **Taxi:** Not metered, prices vary considerably. Fares should be agreed in advance. **Car hire:** Available in city centres and airport. **Documentation:** A national driving licence will be sufficient.
URBAN: Extensive bus and minibus services run in Panama City. There is a flat fare with coin-operated turnstiles at the entrances of most buses.
JOURNEY TIMES: The following chart gives approximate journey times (in hours and minutes) from Panama City to other major cities in Panama.

	Air	Road
Chiriquí	0.45	6.00
Santiago	0.30	3.00
Chitre	0.30	3.10

ACCOMMODATION

HOTELS: Panama is in the middle of an extensive hotel expansion programme, not only in Panama City, but also in the countryside and in mountain and seaside areas. Accommodation ranges from international standard to inexpensive country inns, very simple hotels and new resort-style hotels. There is a 10% government tax added to hotel bills. For further information, contact Instituto Panameña de Turismo (IPAT), Centro de convenciones ATLAPA, Apartado 4421, Vía Israel, Panamá 5. Tel: 267 000. Fax: 263 483.
CAMPING: There are no official campsites, but it is possible to camp on some beaches, and also along parts of the Pan-American Highway.

RESORTS & EXCURSIONS

Panama offers a wide variety of tourist attractions, including excellent shopping. Its position as a crossing point between the Atlantic and the Pacific has naturally made it a major commercial route. Panama City's Central Avenue, Colón's Front Street and the newer shopping sectors around the hotels, and Tocumen's duty-free stores have grown because of this trade.
Panama City: The capital is a curious blend of old Spain, modern America and the bazaar atmosphere of the East. In the old part of the city with its narrow, cobblestoned streets and colonial buildings, most of the interesting sights are to be found. These include the *Plaza de Francia,* the *Court of Justice Building,* the *Paseo de las Bóvedas* along the massive stone wall, *San José Church* with its magnificent golden Baroque altar and the *Santo Domingo Church,* next to which is the *Museum of Colonial Religious Art.* Overlooking the bay is the *President's Palace*, the most impressive building in the city; further along the waterfront is the colourful public market. The most interesting museum in town is the *Museum of the Panamanian Man* north of the market and near the shopping centres. A worthwhile excursion from the city is a visit to **Panamá Viejo** and its ruins including the square tower of the old cathedral, 6km (4 miles) away. This is the original Panama City which – like Fort San Lorenzo – was, in 1671, sacked and looted by Henry Morgan. The **Panama Canal** to the west of the city itself naturally attracts many visitors; recommended is a train or bus ride alongside or a boat trip on the canal – the scenery is beautiful, and the mechanics of the canal equally fascinating. The canal was opened in 1914, and an average transit takes eight hours to complete.
Balboa: A rather Americanised suburb between the Canal quays and *Ancón Hill.* An hour's launch ride away is the island of **Taboga,** where fine beaches and quality hotels abound. The main method of transport is water taxis, known locally as *pangas.* A longer trip by launch is necessary to get to the **Pearl Islands,** which are visited mainly by sea-anglers.
Colón: The second-biggest city in Panama lies on the Caribbean end of the Canal, visitors should see the cathedral and the statues on the promenade known as the *Paseo Centenario.* Front Street is famous as a shopping centre for duty-free luxuries, though it is now rather run down. The city is bustling and quite rough – most visitors just pass through rather than spending a lot of time here.
San Blas Islands: An interesting trip can be made from Colón to the San Blas archipelago which comprises 365 islands. It is the home of the Cuna Indians, the most sophisticated and politically organised of the Indians in Panama.
Portobelo: 48km (30 miles) east of Colón, a Spanish garrison town for two centuries with three large stone forts facing the entrance to the harbour. Also in the town are an old Spanish cannon, and the treasure house where

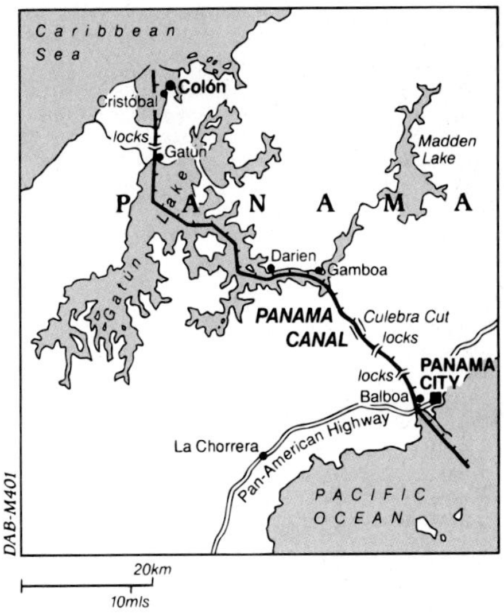

gold and silver from Peru and Bolivia were stored before being shipped to Spain.
Azuero Peninsula: Much more relaxed and peaceful than Panama's cities is the Pacific Peninsula de Azuero, where charming small colonial towns, quiet villages and near-empty beaches await visitors who do not expect to find big hotels.
Note: The *Fiestas* in the various cities are all worth attending, particularly the one at Panama City during the Carnival. This is held on the four days before Ash Wednesday. Others are held to celebrate local patron saints. *Las Balserías*, a Guaymí Indian celebration held in Chiriquí Province every February, includes feasts and a contest in which the young men toss Balsa logs at one another; those who emerge undamaged may choose their mates.

SOCIAL PROFILE

FOOD & DRINK: French, Spanish and American food is available in all restaurants and hotels in Panama City and Colón. There is a huge selection of excellent restaurants in Panama City, as well as other main cities. There are also several Oriental restaurants. Native cooking is reminiscent of creole cuisine, hot and spicy. Dishes include *ceviche* (fish marinated in lime juice, onions and peppers), *palacones de plátano* (fried plantain), *sancocho* (Panamanian stew with chicken, meat and vegetables), *tamales* (seasoned pie wrapped in banana leaves), *carimañolas* and *empanadas* (turnovers filled with meat, chicken or cheese). Waiter service is the norm. The choice and availability of wines, spirits and beers in hotels, restaurants and bars is unlimited.
NIGHTLIFE: Panama City in particular, has a wide range of nightlife from nightclubs and casinos to cockfights, folk ballet, belly dancing and classical theatre. There are floor shows and dancing in all the big hotels, as well as many other clubs. Other large towns and resorts have music, dancing, casinos and cinemas. Further details can be found in local papers.
SHOPPING: Panama is a duty-free haven and luxury goods from all over the world can be bought at a saving of at least one-third. Local items include leatherware, patterned, beaded necklaces made by Guaymí Indians, native costumes, handicrafts of carved wood, ceramics, *papier mâché* artefacts, macramé and mahogany bowls.
Shopping hours: 0800-1800 Monday to Saturday.
SPORT: Fishing: Fish are abundant in the Panamanian waters of the Pacific and the Caribbean. Locations include Piñas Bay, Coiba Island, Contadora Island and Taboga on the Pacific side and the San Blas Islands and the Chiriquí Lagoon off the archipelago of Bocas Del Toro in the Caribbean. **Watersports: Surfing** and **water-skiing** are popular on Pacific beaches such as Santa Clara, Nuevo Gogona and San Carlos and on the San Blas Islands. Surfing is good at Río Mar. **Golf:** There are six golf courses on the isthmus. Panama Country Club, Summit and Fort Amador's courses are all open to tourists. Guest cards are needed to play the 18-hole course at Coronado Beach Country Club.
SPECIAL EVENTS: The following is a selection of better-known festivals and events held throughout Panama. For further information contact the Tourist Office.
Late Apr '95 *Azuero Fair.* **Jul** *Boat Races,* Taboga Island. **Sep** *Agricultural Fair,* Bocas Del Toro. **Feb '96** *Mardi Gras* (carnival), Panama City and Las Tablas. **Mid-Feb** *Las Balserías* (Guaymí Indian celebration – see *Resorts & Excursions* above), Chiriquí Province.
SOCIAL CONVENTIONS: Handshaking is the normal

form of greeting and dress should be casual. The culture is a vibrant mixture of Spanish and American lifestyles. The Mestizo majority, which is largely rural, shares many of the characteristics of Mestizo culture found throughout Central America. Only three indigenous Indian tribes have retained their individuality and traditional lifestyles as a result of withdrawing into virtually inaccessible areas. **Tipping:** 10% is customary in hotels and restaurants. Taxi drivers do not expect tips and rates should be arranged before the trip.

BUSINESS PROFILE

ECONOMY: Until the political upheaval of the late 1980s, Panama enjoyed a relatively prosperous economy based on agriculture, light industry, revenues from the Panama Canal and the service sector. Over half the land area is given over to agriculture: the main cash crops are sugar cane, coffee and bananas, while the main food crops are rice, maize and beans. The country has significant reserves of timber, particularly mahogany, and good fishing stocks, amongst which shrimps are a major and valuable export earner. Local industries include food-processing, clothing, paper and building materials. Panama also exports petroleum refined from imported crude oil. Further revenues are obtained from tolls levied on ships passing through the Panama Canal, which is due to come under full Panamanian control by the end of the century, and from registration fees for a plethora of 'offshore' companies exploiting Panama's strict banking and commercial secrecy laws. In mid-1990 the Endara government announced the introduction of a 'Strategy of Development and Economic Modernisation' in anticipation of a large aid injection from the USA: although receipts from this quarter have not reached Panamanian expectations, many aspects of the 'Strategy' plan have been implemented, including privatisation of state enterprises, reform of the tax and social security systems and the removal of price controls and import tariffs. About 40% of both-way trade is with the USA and Japan; Costa Rica and Germany are the country's other important trading partners. About 30% of all trade passes through the Colón freeport. Panama is attracting growing interest from Hong Kong business enterprises – there are historic links between Panama and China dating back to the building of the Canal – which may provide a much needed, if somewhat unexpected, source of investment in the country.
BUSINESS: Punctuality is appreciated and the exchange of business cards is normal. Suits are necessary for business meetings. **Office hours:** 0800-1200 and 1400-1700 Monday to Friday.
COMMERCIAL INFORMATION: The following organisation can offer advice: Cámara de Comercio, Industrias y Agricultura de Panamá (Chamber of Commerce), Apartado 74, Avenida Samuel Lewis, Edificio Comosa, Planta Baja, Panamá 1. Tel: 648 498. Fax: 274 186. Telex: 2434.

CLIMATE

Temperatures are high across the whole country throughout the year, though cooler at high altitudes. The rainy season lasts from May to September. Rainfall is twice as heavy on the Pacific coast as it is on the lowlands of the Caribbean coast.
Required clothing: Lightweight cottons and linens are worn, with rainwear advisable, particularly in the rainy season. Warmer clothes are needed in the highlands.

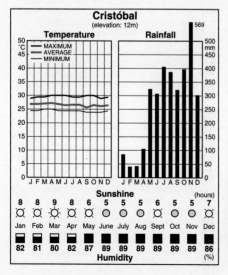

Papua New Guinea

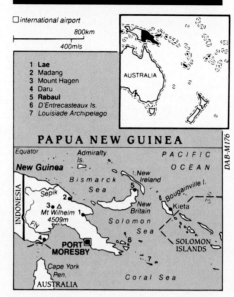

☐ international airport

1	**Lae**
2	**Madang**
3	**Mount Hagen**
4	**Daru**
5	**Rabaul**
6	*D'Entrecasteaux Is.*
7	*Louisiade Archipelago*

Location: South Pacific.

Note: The government of Papua New Guinea does not allow travel to Bougainville, the largest island in the North Solomons Province, because of an active armed insurgency. Along the largely inaccessible Papua New Guinea/Indonesia border, an Indonesian secessionist group remains active. As a result of volcanic eruptions in September 1994, visits to the town of Rabaul are temporarily limited to 3 days. Travellers to Rabaul are advised to seek up-to-date information on travel restrictions to the area before travelling.
Source: US State Department – November 17, 1994.

Tourism Promotion Authority
PO Box 7144, Boroko, Papua New Guinea
Tel: 272 521. Fax: 259 119.
Papua New Guinea High Commission
14 Waterloo Place, London SW1Y 4AR
Tel: (0171) 930 0922/7. Fax: (0171) 930 0828. Telex: 25827 (a/b KUNDU G). Opening hours for visa applications: 0900-1300 Monday to Friday.
British High Commission
PO Box 4778, Kiroki Street, Waigani, Boroko, Papua New Guinea
Tel: 251 677 *or* 251 643 *or* 251 645. Fax: 253 547. Telex: 22142 (a/b UKREP NE).
Papua New Guinea Embassy
3rd Floor, 1615 New Hampshire Avenue, NW, Washington, DC 20009
Tel: (202) 745 3680. Fax: (202) 745 3679.
Papua New Guinea Tourism Office
Suite 3000, 5000 Birch Street, Newport Beach, CA 92660
Tel: (714) 752 5440. Fax: (714) 476 3741.
Embassy of the United States of America
PO Box 1492, Armit Street, Port Moresby, Papua New Guinea
Tel: 211 455 *or* 211 594 *or* 211 654. Fax: 213 423. Telex: 22189 (a/b USAEMB).
Papua New Guinea Consulate
Suite 2001, 22 St Clair Avenue East, Toronto, Ontario M4T 2S3
Tel: (416) 926 1400.

Canadian Consulate
PO Box 851, 2nd Floor, The Lodge, Brampton Street, Port Moresby, Papua New Guinea
Tel: 213 599. Fax: 213 612.

AREA: 462,840 sq km (178,840 sq miles).
POPULATION: 3,772,000 (1991 estimate).
POPULATION DENSITY: 8.1 per sq km.
CAPITAL: Port Moresby. **Population:** 145,300 (1987 estimate).
GEOGRAPHY: Papua New Guinea consists of over 600 islands and lies in the middle of the long chain of islands stretching from mainland South-East Asia. It lies in the South Pacific, 160km (100 miles) north of Australia. The country occupies the eastern half of the second-largest non-continental island in the world, as well as the smaller islands of the Bismarck Archipelago (New Britain, New Ireland, Bougainville and Admiralty Island), the D'Entrecasteaux Island group and the three islands of the Louisiade Archipelago. The main island shares a land border with Irian Jaya, a province of Indonesia. The mainland and larger islands are mountainous and rugged, divided by large fertile upland valleys. Fast-flowing rivers from the highlands descend to the coastal plains. A line of active volcanoes stretches along the north coast of the mainland and continues on the island of New Britain. To the north and south of this central mountain range on the main island lie vast stretches of mangrove swamps and coastal river deltas. Volcanoes and thermal pools are also found in the southeast of other islands. Papua New Guinea also offers the greatest variety of terrestrial ecosystems in the South Pacific, including five types of lowland rainforest, 13 types of montane rainforest, five varieties of palm and swamp forest and three different mangrove forests. Two-thirds of the entire world's species of orchids come from Papua New Guinea. Birds include 38 species of the bird-of-paradise, and the megapode and cassowary. Marsupials and mammals include cuscus, tree kangaroos, wallabies, bandicoots, spiny ant-eaters and, in the coastal waters, the dugong. There are between 170 and 200 species of frog and 450 species of butterfly.
LANGUAGE: The official language is English, which is widely used in business and government circles. Pidgin English and Hiri Motu are more commonly used (700 other languages and dialects are also spoken).
RELIGION: 90% Christian.
TIME: GMT + 10.
ELECTRICITY: 240 volts AC, 50Hz. Australian-style 3-pin plugs are in use. Some hotels provide 110-volt outlets in guest-rooms.
COMMUNICATIONS: Telephone: IDD is available. Country code: 675. Outgoing international code: 05. There are no area codes in Papua New Guinea. **Fax:** Services are available at all major companies and government departments. **Telex/telegram:** Hotels and large businesses will have telex machines. Telegram facilities are available in main centres. **Post:** Airmail to Europe takes seven to ten days. Post office hours: 0800-1600 Monday to Friday; 0900-1200 Saturday. **Press:** The dailies include the *Niugini News* and the *Papua New Guinea Post Courier*. The latter is published in English.
BBC World Service and Voice of America frequencies: From time to time these change. See the section *How to Use this Book* for more information.
BBC:

MHz	17.83	11.95	9.740	6.195
Voice of America:				
MHz	18.82	15.18	9.525	1.735

PASSPORT/VISA

Regulations and requirements may be subject to change at short notice, and you are advised to contact the appropriate diplomatic or consular authority before finalising travel arrangements. Details of these may be found at the head of this country's entry. Any numbers in the chart refer to the footnotes below.

	Passport Required?	Visa Required?	Return Ticket Required?
Full British	Yes	Yes	Yes
BVP	Not valid	-	-
Australian	Yes	Yes	Yes
Canadian	Yes	Yes	Yes
USA	Yes	Yes	Yes
Other EU (As of 31/12/94)	Yes	Yes	Yes
Japanese	Yes	Yes	Yes

Note: On receipt of a stamped, self-addressed envelope, the High Commission can supply information sheets on how to apply for visas for Papua New Guinea. The information below should be considered as a guide, as visa requirements may be subject to change at short notice.
PASSPORTS: Valid passport required by all. Passports

Cristóbal
(elevation: 12m)

Temperature

- MAXIMUM
- AVERAGE
- MINIMUM

Rainfall

J F M A M J J A S O N D

Sunshine (hours)

8	8	9	8	6	5	5	5	6	5	5	7
Jan	Feb	Mar	Apr	May	June	July	Aug	Sept	Oct	Nov	Dec
82	81	80	82	87	89	89	89	89	89	89	86

Humidity (%)

Timatic

Health

GALILEO/WORLDSPAN: TI-DFT/POM/HE
SABRE: TIDFT/POM/HE

Visa

GALILEO/WORLDSPAN: TI-DFT/POM/VI
SABRE: TIDFT/POM/VI

For more information on Timatic codes refer to Contents.

should be valid for 1 year after entry.
British Visitors Passport: Not acceptable.
VISAS: Required by all nationals.
Types of visa: *Tourist:* £7. *Business:* £7 (Single-entry), £105 (Multiple-entry). There are different charges for certain special categories of visitors (including yachtsmen and those engaged in medical, research or expedition activities). There will also be charges for extensions and costs incurred in processing documents.
Note: 30-day Tourist visas and 21-day Business visas can be obtained at Jackson Field airport in Port Moresby on arrival. However, visitors are advised by the High Commission/Embassy that visas should be held before entering Papua New Guinea.
Validity: *Tourist:* 2 months. *Business:* (a) periods of not more than 4 weeks for Single-entry; *or* (b) 12 months with a maximum length of 2 months per stay for Multiple-entry. Details of renewals or extensions are available from the Embassy or High Commission.
Application to: Consulate (or Consular section at Embassy or High Commission). For addresses, see top of entry.
Application requirements: *Tourist:* (a) Completed application form (1 per passport submitted). (b) Passport with minimum 1 year remaining validity. (c) Return ticket. (d) Postal applications should be accompanied by a self-addressed, recorded delivery envelope. (e) Fee (postal order or bank drafts only).
Business: (a)-(e) as for Tourist visa, plus: (f) Itinerary of travel from firm. (g) For Multiple-entry Business visa, a detailed letter in support of application covering: curriculum vitae, confirmation of ongoing project in Papua New Guinea, parent company's annual report and confirming possession of onward/return ticket. (h) For visas issued at the airport, a letter of guarantee from sponsor must have been sent in advance to the Director of Immigration at the airport.
Working days required: 48 hours minimum for Business and Tourist visas. Temporary residence visas take up to 6 weeks or more. It is advisable for visa applications to be made a week or more before departure date.
Temporary residence: Available for those entering for employment purposes, usually professional persons or those undertaking research, journalism, consultancy, film-making, etc. Clearance is by the Director General, Migration Division, Department of Foreign Affairs, Post Office, PO Box 422, Waigani, Port Moresby. Fax: 255 206. Telex: 22377 (a/b NE).

MONEY

Currency: Kina (Ka) = 100 toea (T). Notes are in denominations of Ka50, 20, 10, 5 and 2. Coins are in denominations of Ka1, and T20, 10, 5, 2 and 1.
Credit cards: Exchange facilities are available through trade banks. American Express is the most widely accepted credit card. Holders of this and other cards should check with their credit card company for details of merchant acceptability and other services which may be available.
Travellers cheques: Accepted by most shops and hotels.
Exchange rate indicators: The following figures are included as a guide to the movements of the Kina against Sterling and the US Dollar:

Date:	Oct '92	Sep '93	Jan '94	Jan '95
£1.00=	1.54	1.51	1.44	1.84
$1.00=	0.97	0.99	0.97	1.18

Currency restrictions: There are no restrictions on the import of either local or foreign currency. Export is limited to the amount imported.
Banking hours: 0900-1400 Monday to Thursday; 0900-1700 Friday.

DUTY FREE

The following may be imported into Papua New Guinea by persons over 18 years of age without incurring customs duty:
200 cigarettes or 50 cigars or 250g tobacco; 1 litre of spirits, wine or beer; a reasonable quantity of perfume; goods up to a value of Ka200 (Ka100 for persons under 18 years of age) excluding radios, tape recorders, television sets, video cameras, video tapes, record players, souvenirs and gifts.
Prohibited items: Plants and soil.

PUBLIC HOLIDAYS

Jan 1 '95 New Year's Day. **Apr 14-17** Easter. **Jun 7** Queen's Official Birthday. **Jul 23** Remembrance Day. **Sep 16** Independence Day and Constitution Day. **Dec 25** Christmas Day. **Dec 26** Boxing Day. **Jan 1 '96** New Year's Day. **Apr 5-8** Easter.
Note: In addition, there are various regional festivals throughout the year.

HEALTH

Regulations and requirements may be subject to change at short notice, and you are advised to contact your doctor well in advance of your intended date of departure. Any numbers in the chart refer to the footnotes below.

	Special Precautions?	Certificate Required?
Yellow Fever	No	1
Cholera	Yes	2
Typhoid & Polio	Yes	-
Malaria	3	-
Food & Drink	4	-

[1]: A yellow fever vaccination certificate is required of travellers over one year of age arriving from infected areas.
[2]: Following WHO guidelines issued in 1973, a cholera vaccination certificate is not a condition of entry to Papua New Guinea. However, cholera is a serious risk in this country and precautions are essential. Up-to-date advice should be sought before deciding whether these precautions should include vaccination, as medical opinion is divided over its effectiveness. See the *Health* section at the back of the book.
[3]: Malaria risk exists all year throughout the country below 1800m. The predominant *falciparum* strain is reported to be 'highly resistant' to chloroquine and 'resistant' to sulfadoxine/pyrimethamine.
[4]: All water should be regarded as being potentially contaminated. Water used for drinking, brushing teeth or making ice should have first been boiled or otherwise sterilised. Milk is pasteurised and dairy products are safe for consumption. Only eat well-cooked meat and fish, preferably served hot. Pork, salad and mayonnaise may carry increased risk. Vegetables should be cooked and fruit peeled.
Hepatitis A is endemic.
Health care: The main hospitals are Port Moresby General (Papuan region), Goroka Base (Highlands) and Angau Memorial. There are 16 others and 460 health centres throughout the country. Christian missions also provide some health services and there are private doctors in the main towns. Doctors and hospitals often expect immediate payment for medical services. Sudden shortages of common medications can sometimes occur and travellers who may need ongoing or routine medical treatment are advised to obtain visas for Australia, where medical facilities are more reliable, before leaving their country of origin. Health insurance is essential.

TRAVEL - International

AIR: Papua New Guinea's national airline is *Air Niugini (PX).*
Approximate flight time: The total flying time from London to Port Moresby is up to 30 hours (using current services and routes), but the journey takes at least two days to complete.
International airport: *Port Moresby (POM)* (Jackson Field), 8km (5 miles) from the city. There are duty-free and banking facilities at the airport. Buses are available to the city (travel time – 20 minutes).
Departure tax: Ka15 is levied on international flights. Children under two years of age and passengers not leaving the airport are exempt.
SEA: The international ports are Lae, Madang, Port Moresby, Wewak (Sepik), Rabaul (New Britain), Kieta (North Solomons) and Momote (Manus).
Passenger/cruise lines running regular services are *CTC, Lindblad, P&O* and *Sitmar.* Cargo/passenger lines are *Austasia, Australia/West Pacific* and *Bank Line.*

TRAVEL - Internal

AIR: Services are run by *Talair, Air Niugini* and *Douglas Airways* to all main centres, but are expensive. Internal services should be booked between November and February. *Air Niugini* flies to over 100 airstrips throughout the country and operates regular services to the 20 major urban centres of the country. *Air Niugini* also offers reductions for pre-booking excursions. Charter services are also in operation. The Government sometimes declares a state of emergency in Port Moresby as a result of the increase in violent crime. Travellers should make enquiries about curfew arrangements.
SEA: Cruises and excursions are available lasting 3-16 days. These go mainly to the islands and some otherwise inaccessible places on the coast. Cargo/passenger services between Madang and Lae are run by *Lutheran Shipping* with facilities including passenger cabins, accommodation and meals.
RIVER: For the local people in some regions of the country, rivers, particularly the Sepik, provide the main thoroughfares. In these areas it is possible to hire motorised canoes or obtain passage on a trading boat though, apart from cruises, there are no regular public transport operators on the rivers. See *Resorts & Excursions* section below.
ROAD: Driving is on the left. Due to the rugged terrain of Papua New Guinea, road development of the interior has been slow. The network, currently 4900km (3062 miles), is being extended. There is a network of roads that connect the northern coast towns of Madang and Lae with the major urban centres in the Highlands region. There are few roads connecting the various provinces, however, due to the mountainous terrain. **Bus:** PMVs (public motor vehicles) operate in the main centres from bus shelters or they can be hailed. **Taxi:** Available in district centres but expensive. Although operated on a metred basis, fares can be negotiated. **Car hire:** *Avis, Budget* and the *Travelodge Hotel Cars Service* are available in principal towns. **Documentation:** A national driving licence is sufficient.

ACCOMMODATION

Adequate and comfortable accommodation is available throughout Papua New Guinea. Generally it is more expensive than in most Australasian states.
HOTELS: There are hotels of international standard in Port Moresby, Lae, Madang and most major centres. Many motels also offer good value accommodation.
LODGES: There is a developing tourist industry and tourist accommodation is increasing in many hitherto inaccessible areas. There are lodges in the Highlands and on the Sepik River, many of which can only be reached by air or river. Generally they consist of bungalows constructed of local materials.

RESORTS & EXCURSIONS

The tribal diversity of a country with over 700 languages cannot easily be summarised, though in Papua New Guinea it is the tribal life that is most fascinating to the visitor.
Some of the excursions in Papua New Guinea are interestingly different to those offered elsewhere; for example tourists can be taken to one of the many wrecks of Second World War aircrafts that lie in the jungle.
Haus Tambarans ('Spirit Houses') are a feature of many towns and villages in the country, especially in the area of the *Sepik River,* so only a few of them can be given specific mention. Only initiated men of a tribe can enter (though in places this rule is relaxed for foreigners). They are built in a variety of styles, with massive carved wooden supports being a major feature. Other carvings and masks inside represent spirits. The orator's stools in these places are not used for sitting on; bunches of leaves are slapped down on the stools as the orator makes his points.

Port Moresby

Port Moresby, the capital, is situated on the magnificent *Fairfax Harbour.* It houses the *National Parliament,* the *National Museum,* which contains exhibits of pottery from all the provinces, the *Botanical Gardens* and the *Catholic Cathedral* (which is built in the *Haus Tambaran* style). The National Museum contains a historical record stretching back over 50,000 years. There are many sporting facilities in Port Moresby, including scuba diving, windsurfing, sailing, game fishing, water-skiing, golf, tennis and squash.
There are several interesting things to see in the Port Moresby area. These include:
The Kokoda Trail and Sogeri: The Kokoda Trail is a 40km (24-mile) drive from Port Moresby. The Sogeri road offers many magnificent views and winds through rubber plantations.
Village Arts: Situated at **Six Mile**, near the airport, this is a government-owned artefacts shop with the best artefact collection in the country.
Other places of interest near Port Moresby include: the *Wairiata National Park; Moitaka Crocodile Farm; Loloata Island* and the *Sea Park Oceanarium.*

Lae and the Morobe Province

Lae is Papua New Guinea's second city and an important commercial centre and seaport. The *Botanical Gardens* are among the best in the country. *Mount Lunaman* in the centre of the town was used by the Germans and the Japanese as a lookout point. It gives a magnificent view over the *Huon Gulf* and the *Markham Valley*.

Outside Lae is **Wau**, formerly a gold-mining centre. The *Wau Ecology Institute*, a privately funded organisation, has a small museum and zoo. Visitors can see cassowaries, tree kangaroos, crocodiles, birds of paradise, native butterflies and rhododendrons. Sights near Wau are *McAdam National Park* and *Mount Kaindi*, **Finschhafen** (a very pretty coastal town) and the **Tami Islands,** whose people are renowned for their carved wooden bowls. **Sialum** is an attractive area of coastline known for its coral terraces. White-water rafting on the *Watut River* is an attraction for the adventurous.

Madang

Madang, the capital of Madang Province, is an ideal starting place for many of the tours round the islands and up the Sepik River (see below). It has a variety of shops, hotels, restaurants and markets, where storyboards depicting myths and legends can be bought. In nearby **Yabobs** and **Bilbils**, traditional pottery-making can be seen.

There are four main population groupings in the province: island, coastal, river and mountain, each with its own diet, traditions and customs. The **Manam** islanders make houses out of sago trees and toddy palms with leaves and leaf stems tied into each other. The *Ramu River* people make similar houses, but on stilts, and have a tradition of carving influenced by the cultures of the Sepik River. The mountain people are smaller in stature; they grow crops that would be familiar to an English gardener: lettuce, radishes, cabbages and potatoes. The families of the coastal population place a special value on dog's teeth necklaces, tambu shell headbands and pig tusk amulets. These items are sometimes still used as currency in tribal transactions.

The Sepik River

The Sepik River is the longest river in Papua New Guinea and has been for many centuries the trade route into the interior. It winds down from the mountains near the border with Irian Jaya, draining immense tracts of scarcely explored jungle, swamp and grassland until it meets the sea, where it is more than a mile wide. It abounds with meandering waterways, oxbow lakes, tributaries and backwaters, swamps, lagoons, lakes and channels cut by man to short-cut its looping journey. Unusually though, for a great river, it has no delta system and its waters spew directly into the sea with enormous force. From the many villages along its banks come highly-prized examples of primitive art. The *Haus Tambaran* at **Angoram** possesses a display of art from almost the entire length of the river. At **Kambaramba** village, and elsewhere, houses are built on stilts as a protection against flooding and the dugout canoe is still the main local means of transport. (The visitor, however, has the option of taking a cruise.) Woodcarving is one of the main local crafts and its architectural use in gables and posts in houses is a noteworthy feature. This can be seen at the village of **Tambanum**.

In **Timbunke** village, further examples of construction techniques, including bridge-building, can be seen. Around the *Chambri Lakes* there are some of the many species of birds for which Papua New Guinea is famous. These include egrets, pied herons, brahminee kites, whistling kites, jacanas, darters, cormorants and kingfishers. Also in the Chambri area can be found a unique pottery-making village, **Aibom**, where clay fireplaces, storage and cooking pots are made by the coil method and fired in the open-air by women.

At **Kanganaman**, the slow rebuilding is taking place of a *Haus Tambaran* of national cultural importance. The rebuilding provides an excellent opportunity to see clearly the carvings on the immense Haus Posts. **Korogo** is famous for its '*Mei Masks*'.

In the upper reaches of the Sepik, insect totems dominate clan representation and artforms, using praying mantis and rhinoceros-beetle motifs and featuring distinctive insect eyes. Canoe prows are extremely elaborate, as are the tops of stepladders leading into dwellings. At **Waskusk**, the ceiling of the *Haus Tambaran* depicts the dream of a leader, but conditions on the river sometimes make this village inaccessible. At **Yigei**, Upper Sepik-style *Garamut Drums* ('Slit Gongs') can be seen (and heard); and there are dramatic designs in white and yellow along the waterway in **Swagap Village**, which also has simple, elegant pottery and fireplaces, and often very fine examples of the canoe-builders craft.

The birds round Chambri Lake have already been mentioned, but the varied wildlife of the river and its tributaries is itself a constant source of fascination. Islands of tangled vegetation and the debris of fallen trees float down the river to the Bismarck Sea. Salt and freshwater crocodiles can be seen at night, using spotlights. Along the river, great areas of swamp and grassland provide a home for waders, herons, fish-eagles and many other wildfowl. Sometimes it is possible to go on a night or early morning excursion into the jungle and experience a unique world of sound as the birds prepare for the day's hunting.

Tours along the river have a flexible itinerary in order to take advantage of river conditions and the many local customs and events which visitors may be interested in.

The Highlands

The majority of the country's population live in this least accessible part of Papua New Guinea.

The **Eastern Highlands** have the longest history of contact with the West. **Kainantu** is reached from Lae through the *Kassim Pass*. It has a large cultural centre, selling traditional artefacts; it also provides training in print-making and weaving. The largest town is **Goroka**. It is an agricultural and commercial centre for the entire Highlands region. The *J K McCarthy Museum* has a comprehensive display of regional artefacts; the Leahy wing contains photographs taken by early explorers. In the town centre the *Raun Raun Theatre* company provides contemporary performances of traditional stories and legends. **Bena Bena Village**, 10km (6 miles) from Goroka, is the largest handweaving organisation in the Highlands. Also nearby is **Asaro**, where the men coat themselves with grey mud and re-enact for visitors their historic revenge on a neighbouring village. The legend has it that, having been defeated in battle, the resourceful villagers covered themselves in mud and paid their opponents a visit. This successfully frightened the opposition, who ran away under the impression that they were being visited by ghosts.

Kundiawa, a small town, is the capital of Simbu Province. Some of the local caves are used as burial places; others are popular with cavers. Rafting down the *Wahgi* and *Purari* rivers is also exciting. *Mount Wilhelm*, 4509m (1480ft), is in Simbu Province and is the highest mountain in Papua New Guinea.

In some ways **Mount Hagen** in the **Western Highlands** resembles a town from the Wild West. Its expansion is only recent and the local population will organise a *sing-sing* (celebration) to mark a diverse variety of events; anything from payment of a bride-price to the opening of a new road. There is also a cultural centre in the town. The *Baiyer River Wildlife Sanctuary* lies 55km (34 miles) north of Mount Hagen and is one of the best places to see the famous *birds of paradise*. Possums, tree kangaroos, parrots and cassowaries may also be seen.

The **Mendi Valley** of the **Southern Highlands** is noted for its spectacular scenery and limestone caves. It is home to the *Huli Wigmen* who wear red and yellow face-paint and elaborately decorated wigs of human hair. **Wabang** in **Enga Province** has a large cultural centre with an art gallery and a museum. Young artists can be seen working on sand paintings. War shields, wigs, weapons and other artefacts from all over Papua New Guinea are on display. Enga is the most primitive of the Highland Provinces.

The Islands

The main islands are **New Britain**, New Ireland and the Manus group (together comprising the Bismarck Archipelago), the northernmost Solomon Islands of Bougainville and Buka, and an eastern group of islands including the Trobriand and D'Entrecasteaux Islands. Rabaul on New Britain is the capital of the island and offers several hotels, clubs, restaurants, dances and other forms of entertainment. There are also sporting facilities including a golf course, though the main sporting interest is likely to centre on the various watersports on offer, which include diving, snorkelling, boating, fishing, sailing and windsurfing. For the sightseer Rabaul offers *Gunantabu* (the remains of Queen Emma's residence) with her private cemetery; the remains of the *German Government House* on Namanula Hill; a 576km (360-mile) underground tunnel system left by the Japanese; the *Admirals Bunker*, now a museum; an orchid park; and *Rabaul Market*, which is famous throughout the South Pacific. *Malmaluan* and *Namanula Lookouts* offer panoramic views, whilst really enthusiastic climbers may like to try out the extinct and active volcanoes on the island.

The **New Ireland** and the **Manus** group of islands are off the general tourist trail. In the Northern Western islands of the latter group there are no trees. The islanders have a tradition of making sea-going canoes out of logs that floated down the Sepik into the surrounding ocean. **Bougainville** and **Buka** are separated by a narrow channel of islets. Before Bougainville was closed to visitors, tourists were well catered for and local dancers would regularly visit the hotels, retelling stories from the history of their clans. Activities included scuba diving, snorkelling, game fishing and swimming. Bushwalking and caving expeditions could also be arranged. Ranging from a 6-hour downhill hike from **Panguna** to **Arawa** to a 3-day jungle trek to the summit of *Mount Balbi,* a dormant volcano. Visitors had to contact the Tourism Officer before undertaking a trek, as permission is required to enter villages en route. Arawa has a 9-hole golf course for those who like to do their walking in more sedate surroundings. Near Arawa there is the *Butterfly Farm* in **Kerei Village** where the Wildlife Officer could arrange a visit. Another popular, albeit unlikely, stopping place for tourists was the Bougainville copper mine (now closed), a vast enterprise which dwarfed the visitor. Visits could be arranged through the Bougainville Copper Limited Visitors Liaison Officer.

Relics of Japanese and German occupation abound throughout Papua New Guinea and the visitor will have no trouble finding them. However, the wreck of Admiral Yamamoto's plane in the rainforest of **Buin** may be of particular interest.

The islands offshore to Bougainville have many white sandy beaches.

The **Trobriands** are the most accessible of the groups of islands in **Milne Bay Province**. As elsewhere in the islands, swimming and snorkelling enthusiasts are well catered for. The harvesting of yams from May to September is accompanied by extended rituals and celebrations which peak in the months of July and August.

The **D'Entrecasteaux Islands** rise mountainously out of the sea. In the centre of **Goodenough Island** there is a large stone decorated with mysterious paintings.

SOCIAL PROFILE

FOOD & DRINK: Hotel dining rooms cater for most visitors and menus in main centres are fairly extensive. The more remote the area, the more likely it is that the food will be basic and the menus simple. However, increasing use is made of fresh local meat, fish, vegetables and fruit, including pineapples, pawpaws, mangoes, passion fruit and bananas. Traditional cuisine of Papua New Guinea is confined to root crops such as taro, kaukau and yams, sago and pig (cooked in the earth on traditional feasts). The number of European, Chinese and Indonesian restaurants is rising. Waiter service is usual. Alcohol is readily available and includes Australian and Filipino beers.

NIGHTLIFE: Several hotels in Port Moresby have dancing in the evenings and some organise live entertainment. There are two cinemas and one drive-in cinema. The Arts Theatre stages regular performances. The local newspaper advertises programmes. *Sing-sings*, tribal events on a smaller scale than the biannual festival, are sometimes held.

SHOPPING: A wide range of crafts is available in shops; alternatively the visitor can buy direct from villagers. Favourite buys include local carvings of ceremonial masks and statuettes from Angoram and the Sepik, *Buka* basketry, arrows, bows and decorated axes, crocodile carvings from the Trobriands, pottery and local art. The many butterfly farms send specimens of unusual species throughout the world. Shopping hours: 0900-1700 Monday to Friday; 0900-1200 Saturday (some open longer and/or Sunday).

SPORT: Fishing: Game fish are plentiful in Port Moresby, Lae, Madang, Rabaul and Wewak. Information is available from Moresby Game Fishing Club, Box 5028, Boroko. **Golf:** Port Moresby Golf Club has one of the oldest courses in Papua New Guinea, which is open to visitors. Other clubs are at Lae, Madang, Rabaul, Wau and Minj. **Horseriding:** Visitors are welcome to ride horses at Illimo Farm, Port Moresby, where instruction is available in the afternoons and at weekends. **Sailing:** The Royal Papua Yacht Club makes its extensive facilities available to visitors; the season begins in late April. **Diving:** Skindiving facilities and qualified instructors are available. Port Moresby, Rabaul and Madang offer a wide variety of dives ranging from wrecks to reefs. Diving holidays can also be arranged at locations such as Loloaka and Wuvulu Island. There is an underwater club in Port Moresby which is open to visitors. **Squash:** Courts and equipment are available in major centres. **Hiking:** Back packing/hiking tours are on offer, ranging from simple bush walks to extended tours through the rugged interior.

SPECIAL EVENTS: National Independence Day and (in some towns) the Chinese New Year are major occasions of celebration. However, the visitor to the island should not turn down any chances to go to a *sing-sing*, a colourful tribal gathering where there is dancing, singing and chanting. There are also some very impressive flower festivals and traditional feasts. The

following is a selection of events celebrated annually:
May/Jun *Kula Festival*. **Jun** *Port Moresby Show*. **Late Jul** *Mount Hagen Festival*. **Mid-Aug** *Goroka Show*. **Sep** *Hiri Maole Festival; Maborosa Festival*. **Oct** *Morobe Show*. **Oct/Nov** *Tolai Warwagira*, Rabaul. **Dec** *New Ireland Kula Festival*.

SOCIAL CONVENTIONS: Papua New Guinea's culture includes areas of society that are relatively primitive in lifestyle. There are universities at Lae (which is a University of Technology with a liberal infusion of Europeans and North Americans) and at Port Moresby. Casual clothes are recommended. Informality is the order of the day and although shorts are quite acceptable, beachwear is always best confined to the beach. In the evenings some hotels expect men to wear long trousers but ties are rare. A long dress is appropriate for women on formal occasions. **Tipping:** Not customary and discouraged.

BUSINESS PROFILE

ECONOMY: Most of the population is engaged in subsistence agriculture. The most important commercial cash crops are copra, coffee, cocoa, timber, palm oil, rubber, tea, sugar and peanuts. In recent years the economy has been transformed by the discovery of significant mineral deposits. Papua New Guinea boasts the largest known supply of low-grade copper, the entire production is exported to Western Europe and Japan under long-term contract. Other identified mineral deposits include gold and chromite. Traces of oil and natural gas have also been located. Earnings from gold and copper should keep the economy in a buoyant state well into the next century. The closure of the Bougainville mines threw the country into recession but a recovery has been under way, fuelled by new mineral discoveries elsewhere. Light industry has grown steadily, mostly to meet consumer demands: the construction industry, printing, brewing, bottling and packaging are among these. At present, the economy is still heavily dependent on financial aid from Australia, although this support is due to cease in the near future. The largest importers are Australia, with 50% of the market, followed by Japan, Singapore and the USA.

BUSINESS: Business affairs tend to be conducted in a very informal fashion. A conventional suit will not be required – shirt and tie or safari suit are sufficient. **Office hours:** 0800-1700 Monday to Friday.

COMMERCIAL INFORMATION: The following organisation can offer advice: Papua New Guinea Chamber of Commerce and Industry, PO Box 1621, Port Moresby. Tel: 213 057. Fax: 214 203.

CONFERENCES/CONVENTIONS: Some hotels provide facilities.

CLIMATE

Hot, tropical climate at sea level, cooling towards the highlands which also cause climatic variation from one area to another, affecting the southeast trade winds and the northwest monsoons. The majority of the rain falls between December and March due to the northwest monsoon, although Port Moresby enjoys a dry season at this time. Frost and occasional snow falls on the highest mountain peaks.

Required clothing: Tropical, lightweights and cottons are recommended. In the highlands, warmer clothing is needed. Rainwear is advised for the monsoon season (December to March).

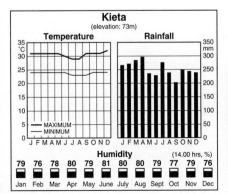

Paraguay

☐ *international airport*

Location: Central South America.

Dirección General de Turismo
Ministerio de Obras Públicas y Communicaciones, Palma 468, Asunción, Paraguay
Tel: (21) 440 793. Fax: (21) 441 530.
Embassy of the Republic of Paraguay
Braemar Lodge, Cornwall Gardens, London SW7 4AQ
Tel: (0171) 937 1253 *or* 937 6629 (Visa section). Fax: (0171) 937 5687. Opening hours: 1000-1500 Monday to Friday.
British Embassy
Casilla 404, Calle Presidente Franco 706, Asunción, Paraguay
Tel: (21) 44472 *or* 49146. Fax: (21) 446 385. Telex: 44023 (a/b PRODROME PY).
Embassy of the Republic of Paraguay
2400 Massachusetts Avenue, NW, Washington, DC 20008
Tel: (202) 483 6960/1. Fax: (202) 234 4508.
Consulate Generals in: Coral Gables (Florida), Dallas, Huntington Beach (California), New Orleans, New York and San Francisco.
Embassy of the United States of America
Casilla 402, Avenida Mariscal López 1776, Asunción, Paraguay
Tel: (21) 213 715. Fax: (21) 213 728.
Embassy of Paraguay
151 Slater Street, Suite 401, Ottawa, Ontario, K1P 5H3
Tel: (613) 567 1283. Fax: (613) 567 1679.
Canadian Consulate
Casilla 2577, El Paraguayo Independiente 995, Entrepiso, Oficianas 1 y 2, Asunción, Paraguay
Tel: (21) 449 505 *or* 491 730. Fax: (21) 449 506. Telex: 652.

AREA: 406,752 sq km (157,048 sq miles).
POPULATION: 4,397,306 (1991 estimate).
POPULATION DENSITY: 10.8 per sq km.
CAPITAL: Asunción. **Population:** 454,881 (1982).
GEOGRAPHY: Paraguay is a landlocked country surrounded by Argentina, Bolivia and Brazil, lying some 1440km (900 miles) up the River Paraná from the

Atlantic. The River Paraguay, a tributary of the Paraná, divides the country into two sharply contrasting regions. The *Oriental* zone, which covers 159,800 sq km (61,700 sq miles), consists of undulating country intersected by chains of hills rising to about 600m (2000ft), merging into the Mato Grosso Plateau in the north; the Paraná crosses the area in the east and south. East and southeast of Asunción lie the oldest centres of settlement inhabited by the greater part of the population. This area is bordered to the west by rolling pastures, and to the south by thick primeval forests. The *Occidental* zone, or Paraguayan Chaco, covers 246,827 sq km (95,300 sq miles). It is a flat alluvial plain, composed mainly of grey clay, which is marked by large areas of permanent swamp in the southern and eastern regions. Apart from a few small settlements, it is sparsely populated.
LANGUAGE: The official language is Spanish. Guaraní is widely spoken. Most Paraguayans are bilingual, but prefer to speak Guaraní outside Asunción.
RELIGION: Roman Catholic.
TIME: GMT - 4 (GMT - 3 from October to February).
ELECTRICITY: 220 volts AC, 50Hz.
COMMUNICATIONS: Telephone: IDD is available. Country code: 595. Limited internal network apart from the main cities. **Fax:** Some hotels provide facilities. **Telex/telegram:** Many hotels have telex facilities. Services are also available at *Antelco* (Administración Nacional de Telecommunicaciones) from where telegrams can also be sent. **Post:** Airmail to Europe takes five days. **Press:** The main newspapers are *El Diario*, *ABC Color*, *Ultima Hora* and *Hoy*. American newspapers are available.
BBC World Service and Voice of America frequencies: From time to time these change. See the section *How to Use this Book* for more information.
BBC:

MHz	15.26	15.19	11.75	9.915

Voice of America:

MHz	15.21	11.58	9.775	5.995

PASSPORT/VISA

Regulations and requirements may be subject to change at short notice, and you are advised to contact the appropriate diplomatic or consular authority before finalising travel arrangements. Details of these may be found at the head of this country's entry. Any numbers in the chart refer to the footnotes below.

	Passport Required?	Visa Required?	Return Ticket Required?
Full British	Yes	No	Yes
BVP	Not valid	-	-
Australian	Yes	Yes	Yes
Canadian	Yes	No	Yes
USA	Yes	No	Yes
Other EU (As of 31/12/94)	Yes	1	Yes
Japanese	Yes	No	Yes

PASSPORTS: Valid passport required by all except nationals of Argentina, Brazil, Chile and Uruguay with valid ID cards entering as tourists direct from their own country.
British Visitors Passport: Not accepted.
VISAS: Required by all except the following entering as tourists for stays of up to 90 days:
(a) nationals of those countries mentioned in the chart above;
(b) [1] nationals of EU countries (except France and Portugal who *do* require visas);
(c) nationals of Argentina, Austria, Bolivia, Brazil, Colombia, Costa Rica, Ecuador, Finland, Norway, Peru, Sweden, Switzerland and Uruguay.
Types of visa: Tourist, Business and Transit.
Validity: 1-3 months.
Application to: Consulate (or Consular section at Embassy). For addresses, see top of entry.
Application requirements: (a) Valid passport. (b) Completed application form. (c) Tourists require a letter from tour operator giving details of bookings and itinerary. (d) Business visitors require a covering letter from employer including name of contact in Paraguay. (e) 1 passport-size photo. (f) Stamped, self-addressed envelope for those applying by post.
Working days required: 7 days maximum.
Temporary residence: Apply to immigration section of the Ministry for the Interior.

MONEY

Currency: Guaraní (G). Notes are in denominations of G50,000, 10,000, 5000, 1000 and 500. Coins are in denominations of G50, 10, 5 and 1.
Currency exchange: Travellers cheques, currency and

all commercial transactions must be conducted at the free market rate. Many cheap hotels will neither accept credit cards nor exchange travellers cheques. US Dollars, which are more easily negotiable than Sterling, are widely accepted throughout the country.

Credit cards: Access/Mastercard, American Express and Visa are widely accepted, while Diners Club has more limited use. Check with your credit card company for details of merchant acceptability and other services which may be available.

Travellers cheques: Banks will not cash travellers cheques in anything other than Guaranís. *Cambios* will, however, give US Dollars. There are no facilities for exchanging travellers cheques at the airport.

Exchange rate indicators: The following figures are included as a guide to the movements of the Guaraní against Sterling and the US Dollar:

Date:	Oct '92	Sep '93	Jan '94	Jan '95
£1.00=	2459.2	2678.4	2655.7	2994.1
$1.00=	1549.6	1754.0	1795.0	1913.8

Currency restrictions: There are no import or export restrictions on local or foreign currency.
Banking hours: 0830-1215 Monday to Friday.

DUTY FREE

The following items may be imported into Paraguay without incurring customs duty:
A reasonable quantity of tobacco and alcoholic beverages; a reasonable quantity of perfume for personal use.

PUBLIC HOLIDAYS

Jan 1 '95 New Year's Day. **Feb 3** San Blás (National Saint). **Mar 1** Heroes' Day. **Apr 13** Maundy Thursday. **Apr 14** Good Friday. **May 1** Labour Day. **May 14-15** National Independence Day. **May 25** Ascension Day. **Jun 12** Peace of Chaco. **Jun 15** Corpus Christi. **Aug 15** Founding of Asunción. **Aug 25** Constitution Day. **Sep 29** Battle of Boquerón. **Oct 12** Columbus Day. **Nov 1** All Saints' Day. **Dec 8** Immaculate Conception. **Dec 25** Christmas Day. **Jan 1 '96** New Year's Day. **Feb 3** San Blás (National Saint). **Mar 1** Heroes' Day. **Apr 4** Maundy Thursday. **Apr 5** Good Friday.

HEALTH

Regulations and requirements may be subject to change at short notice, and you are advised to contact your doctor well in advance of your intended date of departure. Any numbers in the chart refer to the footnotes below.

	Special Precautions?	Certificate Required?
Yellow Fever	No	1
Cholera	No	No
Typhoid & Polio	Yes	-
Malaria	2	-
Food & Drink	3	-

[1]: A yellow fever vaccination certificate is required from travellers leaving Paraguay to go to endemic areas. A certificate is also required from travellers arriving in the country from endemic areas.
[2]: Malaria risk, predominantly in the benign *vivax* form, exists from October to May in some rural areas of Alto Paraná, Amambay, Caaguazú, Canendiyú and San Pedro Departments.
[3]: Mains water is normally chlorinated, and whilst relatively safe may cause mild abdominal upsets. Bottled water is available and is advised for the first few weeks of the stay. Drinking water outside main cities and towns is likely to be contaminated and sterilisation is considered essential. Milk is unpasteurised and should be boiled. Powdered or tinned milk is available and is advised, but make sure that it is reconstituted with pure water. Avoid dairy products which are likely to have been made from unboiled milk. Only eat well-cooked meat and fish, preferably served hot. Pork, salad and mayonnaise may carry increased risk. Vegetables should be cooked and fruit peeled.
Rabies is present. For those at high risk, vaccination before arrival should be considered. If you are bitten abroad seek medical advice without delay. For more information, consult the *Health* section at the back of the book.
Health care: Health insurance is essential.

TRAVEL - International

AIR: Paraguay's national airline is *Líneas Aéreas Paraguyayas (LAP).*
Approximate flight time: From London to Paraguay is

15-19 hours, depending on the route taken.
International airport: *Asunción (ASU)* (Silvio Pettirossi) is 16km (10 miles) from the city (travel time - 20 minutes). A coach and taxi service runs to the city.
Departure tax: US$15 is levied on all international departures. Transit passengers and children under two years of age are exempt.
SEA: A ferry between Posadas (Argentina) and Encarnación offers an alternative to travelling to Buenos Aires, about 321km (200 miles) longer, by way of the Argentine provinces of Missiones and Corrientes and then across the new bridge over the Paraná River to Resistencia. Those who prefer to continue along the left bank of the Paraná River will have to travel to Paraná, provincial capital of Entre Rios, crossing under the Paraná River in the tunnel between the cities of Paraná and Santa Fé.
RAIL: There is no through service to Argentina, but a weekly train from Asunción serves Posadas in Argentina by means of a train-ferry, with connections to Concordia and Buenos Aires. The rail services are very slow.
ROAD: The roads from Rio and São Paulo to Asunción (via the Iguazú Falls) are paved and generally good, as is the one from Buenos Aires. **Bus:** There are daily services from São Paulo and Rio de Janeiro (Brazil), Santa Fé, Rosario, Córdoba, Buenos Aires (Argentina) and Montevideo (Uruguay).

TRAVEL - Internal

AIR: Air service is run by *LAP, TAM (Transportes Aero Militar), LATN (Lineas Aéreas de Transporte Nacional), Aeronorte* and *Aerosur.* The most popular visitors' flight is to the Iguazú Falls from Asunción with *Varig Airways.* Air-taxis are popular with those wishing to discover the trackless Gran Chaco (see *Geography* above). Travel agencies offer daily city tours, but services suffer from frequent upsets by weather conditions.
RAIL: A weekly service links Asunción and Encarnación – which are 431km (268 miles) apart – using original steam locomotives. There is also a twice-weekly service from San Salvador to Abay. Services are often unreliable, however, and whole routes may be abandoned for months at a time.
ROAD: Traffic drives on the right. Roads serving the main centres are in good condition. However, unsurfaced roads may be closed in bad weather. Approximately 10% of roads are surfaced. A highway links Asunción with Iguazú Falls, a drive of up to six hours. **Bus:** Often the best and cheapest method of transport within Paraguay. For longer distances, advance booking may be necessary. There are express links to major centres. **Car hire:** Cars can be hired through local tourist agencies.
Documentation: National driving licence or International Driving Permit are both accepted.
URBAN: Bus and minibus services are provided by private companies in Asunción, with 2-zone fares collected by conductors. There also remain two routes of the government-operated tramway.
JOURNEY TIMES: The following chart gives approximate journey times (in hours and minutes) from Asunción to other major cities in Paraguay.

	Air	Road	Rail	River
PJ Caballero	1.15	11.00	-	13.00
Concepción	1.00	12.00	-	14.00
C. del Este	1.05	5.00	-	-
Valle Mí	1.30	-	-	15.00
Encarnación	1.10	5.00	14.00	9.00

ACCOMMODATION

Outside the capital, accommodation is limited. All accommodation must be booked in writing well in advance; details of current prices are available from the Embassy (see top of entry for address). All hotels in Asunción are likely to be fully booked throughout the tourist season (July and August). Visitors are advised to consult a reputable travel agent for up-to-date information, or to ascertain the rates with hotels when making reservations. For further information contact: Dirección General de Turismo (see top of entry for address).

RESORTS & EXCURSIONS

A popular tourist itinerary is the 'Central Circuit', a route of some 200km (125 miles) that takes in some of the country's most interesting sites.
Asunción: The capital city is situated on the *Bay of Asunción,* an inlet off the Paraguay River. Planned on a colonial Spanish grid system, it has many parks and plazas. On the way to the waterfront the visitor enters the old part of town, an area of architectural variety. A good view of the city can be had from the *Parque Carlos*

Antonio Lopez high above Asunción. The *Botanical Gardens* are situated in a former estate of the Lopez family on the Paraguay River. There is also a golf-course and a small zoo. The *Lopez Residence* has been converted into a natural history museum and library. Package trips can be booked to see the *Iguazú Falls* and the *Salto Crystal Falls,* and river trips to **Villeta** or up the *Pilcomayo River* to the *Chaco.* **Luque,** near the capital, is the home of the famous Paraguayan harps.
San Lorenzo: Founded in 1775, the town is the site of the university halls of residence and an interesting Gothic-style church.
Ita: Founded in 1539 by Domingo Martinez, its main speciality is the handpainted Gallinita hens made of black clay.
Yaguarón: The city is set in an orange-growing district and played a part during the Spanish conquest as a base for the Franciscan missions. Their churches date back to 1775.
Paraguarí: Situated in the foothills of the **Cordillera des Altos,** this is a historic village with several old buildings in colonial style.
Chololo: A holiday centre where tourist facilities include bars, restaurants and bungalows for rent.
Piribebuy: The scene of bloody fighting during the war of the triple alliance. The Encaje-yú spindle lace, the 'sixty stripe' Paraní poncho and other handmade goods are produced here. It is also famous as a place of worship of the 'Virgin of Miracles'.
San Bernadino: Situated on *Lake Ypacarai,* the town is a holiday resort and very popular during the summer months. It has a beach, good hotels, bars and restaurants.
Ciudad Del Este is the fastest-growing town in the country and offers extensive shopping facilities. The *Monday Falls* are 10km (6 miles) from the town.
Encarnación has many colonial buildings and a sleepy waterfront area complete with *gauchos* and sandy streets.
The Paraguyan Chaco: This vast scarcely populated area consists mainly of empty plains and forests. The drive from Asunción leads through the Low Chaco, a land of palm forests and marshes, and reaches the Middle Chaco with its capital **Filadelfia.** Here Mennonites of German descent have set up farms and other agricultural outlets as well as their own schools. Therefore they are considered to be the only organised community in the whole of the Chaco region.

SOCIAL PROFILE

FOOD & DRINK: Typical local dishes include *chipas* (maize bread flavoured with egg and cheese), *sopa Paraguaya* (soup of mashed corn, cheese, milk and onions), *soo-yosopy* (a soup of cornmeal and ground beef), *albondiga* (meatball soup) and *boríborí* (another soup of diced meat, vegetables and small balls of maize mixed with cheese). *Palmitos* (palm hearts), *surubí* (a fish found in the Paraná) and the local beef are excellent. There is a wide choice of restaurants in Asunción, most with table service. **Drink:** The national drink is *cana,* distilled from sugarcane and honey. Sugar cane juice, known as *mosto,* and the national red wine are worth trying, as is *yerba maté,* a refreshing drink popular with nearly all Paraguayans. There are no strict licensing hours and alcohol is widely available.
NIGHTLIFE: In Asunción there are a number of bars, casinos and discotheques. The *parrilladas* or open-air restaurants offer by far the best atmosphere, especially in Asunción. There is a casino at the border towns of Ciudad Del Este and Encarnación.
SHOPPING: Special purchases include *nandutí* lace, made by the women of Itagua, and *aho poí* sports shirts, made in a variety of colours and designs. Other items include leather goods, wood handicrafts, silver *yerba maté* cups and native jewellery. **Shopping hours:** 0800-2000 Monday to Friday; 0730-1200 Saturday.
SPORT: Football is the national sport. There are **tennis** facilities at hotels and in Asunción. The Asunción Golf Club has an 18-hole **golf** course. **Water-skiing** facilities are available at one hotel on the River Paraguay. Some large hotels have **swimming** pools. **Fishing** is a special attraction. The *dorado,* found in the Paraguay, Paraná and Tebicuary rivers, can weigh up to 29kg (65 pounds). International fishing contests are held near Asunción. There are many other smaller fish that are peculiar to Paraguay such as the *surubi, pati, pacu, manguruyus, armados, moncholos* and *bagres.* There are also small lakes with trout and local varieties of fish.
SPECIAL EVENTS: Annual festivals of note in Paraguay are as follows (check with the Embassy for exact dates):
Apr '95 *Semana Santa* (week-long Easter festival). **May 15** *Día de la Independencia* (Independence Day parades and festivities). **Jun 24** *Verbena de San Juan* (traditional fiesta, including walking on hot embers). **Jul** *Festival del Nanduti* (traditional music and crafts festival with parade

of floats), Itaugua. **Aug 15** *Día de la Virgen de la Asunción* and *Aniversario de la Fundación de Asunción* (religious and cultural celebrations). **Sep** *Festival de la Alfalfa,* Sapucai. **Oct** *Encuentro Internacional de Coros* (choir festival), Encarnación. **Nov** *Festival del Poyvi* (arts, crafts and music fair), Carapeguá. **Dec** *Apertura de Temporada* (opening of the tourism season), San Bernadino. **Feb '96** *San Blás Fiesta.*
SOCIAL CONVENTIONS: Shaking hands is the usual form of greeting. Normal codes of behaviour should be observed. Smoking is not allowed in cinemas and theatres. Dress tends to be informal and sportswear is popular. **Photography:** Avoid sensitive subjects, eg military installations. **Tipping:** 10-15% is normally included in hotel, restaurant and bar bills.

BUSINESS PROFILE

ECONOMY: Paraguay's agriculture plays an important part in its economy, supplying nearly one-third of the GNP and almost all the country's export earnings. Production of Paraguay's principal cash crops, cotton and soya, expanded rapidly during the late 1980s with the best prospects for the future in increased growth of these and other commodities. The country's agricultural potential is, in principle, immense. Recently completed hydroelectric projects, undertaken as joint projects with Brazil and including the world's largest hydroelectric dam at Itaipú, have given Paraguay self-sufficiency in energy. The economy has now recovered from the recession of the early 1980s and is one of the fastest-

growing in Latin America. Unlike many other countries on the continent, it is without an excessive foreign debt. Indigenous industry has grown quickly, but there are still considerable opportunities for exports of manufactured goods. Paraguay is a member of the 11-strong Associación Latinoamericana de Integración, which seeks to promote free trade and economic development within Latin America. Paraguay, alongside Bolivia, enjoys special tariff concessions, which may in the near future see the country develop as an export market for the rest of the continent. Brazil, the USA and Argentina are the largest trading partners. Admission to the Mercosur group of southern Latin American countries will further assist trade growth and economic development.
BUSINESS: For formal occasions or business affairs men should wear lightweight suits and ties or a dinner jacket in the evening. Most business people are able to conduct a conversation in English, but a knowledge of Spanish will be useful. Appointments and normal business courtesies apply. Best time to visit is from May to September. **Office hours:** 0800-1200 and 1500-1730/1900 Monday to Friday; 0800-1200 Saturday.
COMMERCIAL INFORMATION: The following organisation can offer advice: Cámara y Bolsa de Comercio, Estrella 540, Asunción. Tel: (21) 493 321. Fax: (21) 440 817.

CLIMATE

Subtropical with rapid changes in temperature throughout the year. Summer (December to March) can be very hot.

Winter (June to September) is mild with few cold days. Rainfall is heaviest from December to March.
Required clothing: Lightweight cottons and linens are worn in warmer months, with some warm clothes for spring and autumn. Mediumweights are best for winter. Rainwear is advisable throughout the year.

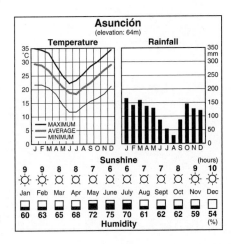

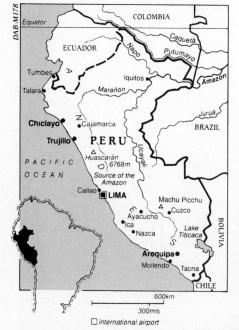

□ international airport

Location: Western South America.

Fondo de Promoción Turística del Perú (FOPTUR)
Calle Uno S/N Urb Corpác, Piso 14, Mitinci, San Isidro, Lima, Peru
Tel: (14) 440 8333 or 442 9407 or 440 7120, ext. 269. Fax: (14) 442 9280 or 440 6119.

Embassy of the Republic of Peru
52 Sloane Street, London SW1X 9SP
Tel: (0171) 235 1917 or 235 6867 (Visa section). Fax: (0171) 235 4463. Telex: 917888. Opening hours: 0930-1630 Monday to Friday; 0900-1330 and 1430-1600 Monday to Friday (Visa section).

British Embassy
Casilla 854, Edificio El Pacífico 11°, Plaza Washington, Natalio Sanchez 125, Lima 100, Peru
Tel: (14) 433 4839. Fax: (14) 433 4735. Telex: 25230 (a/b PU PRODROME).
Consulates in: Arequipa, Piura, Trujillo, Iquitos and Cuzco.

Embassy of the Republic of Peru
1700 Massachusetts Avenue, NW, Washington, DC 20036
Tel: (202) 833 9860/9. Fax: (202) 659 8124.

Embassy of the United States of America
Apartado 1995, Avenida Garcilaso de la Vega 1400, Lima 100, Peru
Tel: (14) 433 8000. Fax: (14) 431 6682. Telex: 25212.

Embassy of the Republic of Peru
Suite 1901, 130 Albert Street, Ottawa, Ontario K1P 5G4
Tel: (613) 238 1777. Fax: (613) 232 3062.
Consulate in: Montréal.

Canadian Embassy
Casilla 18-1126, Frederico Gerdes 130, Miraflores, Lima, Peru
Tel: (14) 444 4015 or 444 3841 or 444 3893. Fax: (14) 444 4347. Telex: 25323 (a/b PE DOMCAN).

AREA: 1,285,216 sq km (496,225 sq miles).
POPULATION: 23,878,670 (1993 estimate).
POPULATION DENSITY: 18.5 per sq km.
CAPITAL: Lima. **Population:** 6,386,308 (1993 estimate).
GEOGRAPHY: Peru is a large, mountainous country straddling the equator on the Pacific coast of South America. It has borders with Ecuador and Colombia to the north, Brazil and Bolivia to the east, and Chile to the south. The Pacific Ocean lies to the west. There are three natural zones, running roughly north to south: Costa, Sierra and Selva. The *Costa* region, which contains Lima, the capital, is a narrow coastal plain consisting of large tracts of desert broken by fertile valleys. The cotton and sugar plantations and most of the so far exploited oilfields lie in this area. The *Sierra* contains the Andes, with peaks of over 6000m (20,000ft), most of the country's mineral resources and the greater part of its livestock. The bulk of the Indian population live in this area. The *Selva*, an area of fertile, subtropical uplands, lies between the Andes and the jungles of eastern Peru. As yet, it is largely undeveloped. Sections of a proposed international highway are at present being built through it, with some sections already in use. The Amazonian jungle of eastern Peru has vast natural resources. The absence of land communications, however, left the area largely uncharted until full-scale oil exploration began in 1973. The population is largely Indian and Mestizos with a noticeable influence from European (mainly Spanish), Chinese and African settlers.
LANGUAGE: Spanish and Quechua. Aymará is spoken in the department of Puno. Many other dialects exist in the jungle regions. English is spoken in major tourist areas.
RELIGION: 99% Roman Catholic.
TIME: GMT - 5.
ELECTRICITY: 220 volts AC, 60Hz.
COMMUNICATIONS: Telephone: IDD is available. Country code: 51. Outgoing international code: 00. City code for Lima: 14. **Fax:** ENTEL PERU offers a fax service throughout the country. The main hotels also have facilities. **Telex/telegram:** Facilities are available at Lima and main hotels, with services run by ENTEL PERU. These close in the evenings and during holidays, although ENTEL PERU run 24-hour offices at Av. Bolivia 347 and Jr. Cusco 303, Lima. These offices are open every day of the year. Telex services exist at Bolivar, Crillon and Sheraton hotels and at public booths. Country code is PE. **Post:** Airmail to Western Europe takes up to two weeks. Postal facilities are limited outside Lima. First-class airmail from the UK addressed to PO boxes in Peru usually takes four days, but may be subject to delay. The main post office is near the Plaza de Armas and opens 0800-2000 Monday to Saturday; 0800-1400 Sunday. **Press:** Newspapers are in Spanish. Morning dailies include *La República, La Nación, Expreso, Ojo, Gestión, El Peruano, El Mundo* and *El Comercio*. The English-language weekly newspaper is *The Lima Times*.
BBC World Service and Voice of America frequencies: From time to time these change. See the section *How to Use this Book* for more information.

BBC:

MHz	17.84	15.26	15.22	9.915

Voice of America:

MHz	15.21	11.58	9.775	5.995

PASSPORT/VISA

Regulations and requirements may be subject to change at short notice, and you are advised to contact the appropriate diplomatic or consular authority before finalising travel arrangements. Details of these may be found at the head of this country's entry. Any numbers in the chart refer to the footnotes below.

	Passport Required?	Visa Required?	Return Ticket Required?
Full British	Yes	1/3	Yes
BVP	Not valid	-	-
Australian	Yes	Yes	Yes
Canadian	Yes	2/3	Yes
USA	Yes	2/3	Yes
Other EU (As of 31/12/94)	Yes	1/3	Yes
Japanese	Yes	2/3	Yes

PASSPORTS: Valid passport required by all.
British Visitors Passport: Not accepted.
VISAS: Required by all except:
(a) **[1]** EU nationals travelling as tourists for stays of up

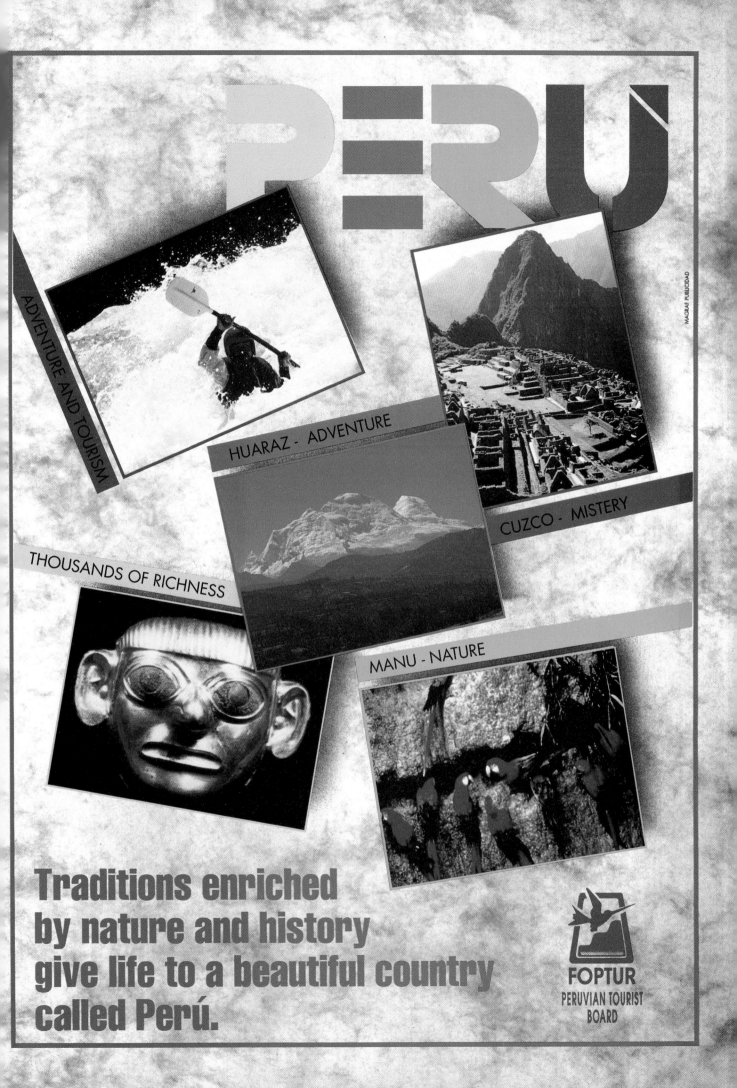

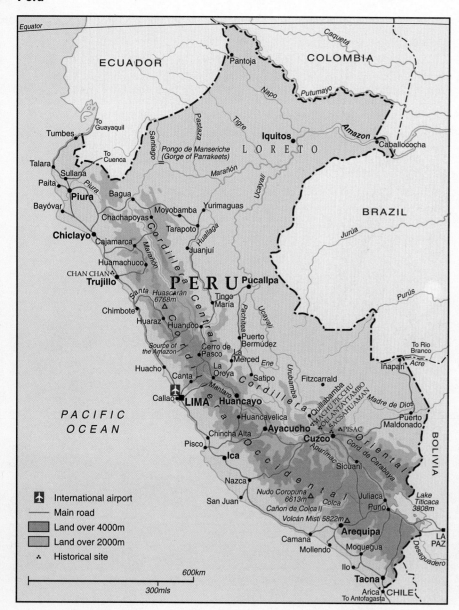

- International airport
- Main road
- Land over 4000m
- Land over 2000m
- Historical site

currency. *Casas de Cambios* are recommended for their good rates, speed and honesty.

Credit cards: American Express, Access/Mastercard, Diners Club and Visa are all accepted, but usage facilities may be limited outside Lima. Check with your credit card company for details of merchant acceptability and other services which may be available.

Travellers cheques: American Express state that they will sell travellers cheques and give out emergency money, but only at the Lima Tours Office in Lima (Belén 1040). The *Casas de Cambios* charge 2% commission for changing travellers cheques. Outside Lima, changing travellers cheques is a slow and laborious process.

Exchange rate indicators: The following figures are included as a guide to the movements of the Nuevo Sol against Sterling and the US Dollar:

Date:	Oct '92	Sep '93	Jan '94	Jan '95
£1.00=	2.52	3.12	3.19	3.41
$1.00=	1.59	2.04	2.15	2.18

Currency restrictions: There are no restrictions on the import and export of local currency. Export of foreign currency is limited to the amount imported. Exchange receipts must be kept for reconversion of Nuevo Sol into foreign currency.

Banking hours: 0815-1130 Monday to Friday (January to March); 0915-1245 Monday to Friday (April to December). Some banks may open in the afternoon.

DUTY FREE

The following items may be imported into Peru without incurring customs duty:
400 cigarettes or 50 cigars or 250g of tobacco; 3 litres of spirits or 3 litres of wine; a reasonable amount of perfume for personal use.

PUBLIC HOLIDAYS

Jan 1 '95 New Year's Day. **Mar 13** Maundy Thursday. **Apr 14** Good Friday. **May 1** Labour Day. **Jun 29** St Peter and St Paul. **Jul 28-29** Independence Day. **Aug 30** St Rosa of Lima. **Oct 8** Battle of Angamos. **Nov 1** All Saints' Day. **Dec 8** Immaculate Conception. **Dec 25** Christmas Day. **Jan 1 '96** New Year's Day. **Apr 4** Maundy Thursday. **Apr 5** Good Friday.

HEALTH

Regulations and requirements may be subject to change at short notice, and you are advised to contact your doctor well in advance of your intended date of departure. Any numbers in the chart refer to the footnotes below.

	Special Precautions?	Certificate Required?
Yellow Fever	Yes	1
Cholera	No	No
Typhoid & Polio	Yes	-
Malaria	2	-
Food & Drink	3	-

[1]: A yellow fever vaccination certificate is required of travellers over six months of age arriving from infected areas. Travellers arriving from non-endemic zones should note that vaccination is strongly recommended for travel outside the urban ares, even if an outbreak has not been reported and they would normally not require a vaccination certificate to enter the country.

[2]: Malaria risk, almost exclusively in the benign *vivax* form, exists throughout the year in rural areas below 1500m (4922ft). *Falciparum* malaria occurs sporadically in areas bordering Bolivia (Madre de Dios River), Brazil (Yavari and Acre River), Colombia (Putumayo River), Ecuador (Napo River) and in Zarumilla Province (Tumbes Dep.) and in areas where petroleum deposits are being exploited. Resistance to chloroquine and sulfadoxine/pyrimethamine of the *falciparum* strain has been reported.

[3]: Mains water is normally chlorinated, and whilst relatively safe may cause mild abdominal upsets. Bottled water is available. Drinking water outside main cities and towns is likely to be contaminated and sterilisation is considered essential. Milk is unpasteurised and should be boiled. Powdered or tinned milk is available and is advised, but make sure that it is reconstituted with pure water. Avoid dairy products which are likely to have been made from unboiled milk. Only eat well-cooked meat and fish, preferably served hot. Pork, salad and mayonnaise may carry increased risk. Vegetables should be cooked and fruit peeled.
Rabies is present. For those at high risk, vaccination before arrival should be considered. If you are bitten abroad, seek medical advice without delay. For more information,

to 3 months (except nationals of Spain who *do* require a visa);
(b) [2] nationals of countries shown in the chart above travelling as tourists for stays of up to 3 months;
(c) nationals of Argentina, Austria, Brazil, Czech Republic, Costa Rica, Ecuador, El Salvador, Finland, Guatemala, Honduras, South Korea, Liechtenstein, Mexico, Nicaragua, Norway, Panama, Paraguay, Sweden, Switzerland, Uruguay and Venezuela travelling as tourists for stays of up to 3 months;
(d) nationals of Bolivia, Chile, Colombia and Dominican Republic travelling as tourists for stays of up to 2 months (an extension to 3 months is available);
(e) nationals of Caribbean countries travelling as tourists for stays of up to 3 months (except nationals of Cuba who *do* require a visa);
(f) visitors on an *approved* organised trip.
Note: Those exempted under (a) and (b) must be in possession of a yellow *Cedula 'C'* along with documents for onward travel. The Cedula 'C' is usually issued free of charge by the carrier.
Types of visa: Visitors and Business. Transit visas are not required by those who continue their journey to a

third country within 24 hours by the same or first connecting flight, provided that they hold tickets with reserved seats and other documents for their onward journey and do not leave the transit area of the airport.
Cost: US$20.
Note for business travellers: [3] Visitors of nationalities exempted above who are not going to receive money from Peruvian sources do not require a Business visa. Upon arrival in Peru the Business visa holder must register at the Dirección General de Constribuciones for taxation purposes. Business visa holders can remain in Peru for 90 days. If wishing to extend the visit, an application must be lodged with the Direccion General de Migraciones.
Application to: Consulate (or Consular section at Embassy). For addresses, see top of entry.
Application requirements: (a) Valid passport. (b) Open or through ticket to show the visitor will be leaving Peru. (c) 2 colour passport-size photographs. (d) Fee. (e) 2 completed visa application forms. (f) For Business visas, a company letter specifying the reason for the trip.
Note: All nationals are advised to check with the Peruvian Consulate prior to departure to obtain current details of any documentation which might be required.
Working days required: Usually 24 hours.

MONEY

Currency: Nuevo Sol = 100 céntimos. Neuvo Sol notes are in denominations of 100, 50, 10 and 5.
Currency exchange: Changing currencies other than the US Dollar can be both difficult and, in terms of the high commission rates charged, expensive. Banco de la Nación is the only institution regularly authorised to deal in foreign exchange. The main hotels and *Casas de Cambios* are, however, allowed to exchange foreign

Health

GALILEO/WORLDSPAN: **TI-DFT/LIM/HE**
SABRE: **TIDFT/LIM/HE**

Visa

GALILEO/WORLDSPAN: **TI-DFT/LIM/VI**
SABRE: **TIDFT/LIM/VI**

For more information on Timatic codes refer to Contents.

PERU – AN HISTORICAL OVERVIEW

HISTORY: The indigenous Inca civilisation of what is now Peru was conquered by Spain in the early 16th century. The city of Lima was founded in 1535 and became the effective capital of the viceroyalty of Peru, established seven years later. Spain ruled the country until the early 19th century, using the rich silver reserves to finance its costly imperialist struggles with France, England and The Netherlands. The wars of independence, which expelled the Spanish from virtually the entire South American continent, reached Peru in the early 1820s. After the 1821 declaration of independence, Peru was challenged by the royalists. The new Government appealed to the revolutionary leader Simon Bolívar for assistance. Arriving from Colombia, Bolívar defeated the royalists at the Battle of Ayacucho in December 1824, after which he became Head of State. Relations between Peru and its neighbours were difficult in the early years of independence. There were border disputes with Brazil and Ecuador (which have not been settled to this day) and with Chile. The War of the Pacific, which broke out between Peru, supported by Bolivia, and Chile in 1879 ended after five years with a complete victory for Chile and the loss to Peru of some southern territories. Internal problems dominated the agenda for the next 30 years as a series of governments struggled to keep the economy, which was almost completely destroyed as a result of the Pacific War, from disintegrating. The first of Peru's many military coups was in 1914. The junta lasted five years before giving way to the civilian government of Augusto Leguía. Between 1919 and 1930, despite rampant corruption, Leguía instituted important reforms in education and social services. His tenure ended with another military takeover. While the military have always been a powerful force in Peruvian politics, their principal opponent and the country's largest political party for much of the 20th century has been the Alianza Popular Revolucionaria Americana (APRA), founded by Dr Victor Raúl Haya de la Torre in 1924 as a continent-wide anti-imperialist movement, but increasingly moderate and Peruvian-centred in its appeal. APRA has nevertheless been illegal for much of its history. Civilian administrations from 1963-67 and 1980-85 were headed by the right-wing President Belaunde Terry of the Acción Popular Party, although APRA was usually the largest party in the Chamber of Deputies. Under Alan Garcia, APRA took power for the first time in 1985. Garcia's administration was a failure on both the political and economic front. Garcia decided to suspend repayment on Peru's large foreign debt accumulated during the 1970s and increase state control of the economy, particularly the financial and banking sectors. Massive capital flight followed before exchange controls were introduced; investment dropped to near-zero; loans dried up and the Government's attempts to maintain living standards resulted in hyperinflation running to thousands of per cent per annum. On the political front, Garcia was faced with the continuing growth of the Maoist guerrilla movement Sendero Luminoso (Shining Path), which benefited substantially from the deteriorating economic situation; the Government declared states of emergency in ten of Peru's two dozen provinces, giving the military a virtually free hand in operations against the guerrillas. By the end of the 1980s, amid rumours of a possible military coup, it was clear that Garcia's days were numbered. Local elections in November 1989 brought victory for the Democratic Front coalition, defeating a socialist grouping into second and pushing the ruling APRA into third. This pattern was expected to be repeated in the presidential elections the following year. However, these elections, held in April 1990, developed into a two-way race between Mario Vargas Llosa, the world-renowned author who led the Democratic Front coalition, and the comparatively unknown independent centrist candidate, Alberto Fujimori, an agricultural engineer of Japanese extraction, who was the surprise landslide winner. The new government followed the trend on the Latin American continent for economic shock treatment. Most price controls and government subsidies were abolished at a stroke in August 1990, producing excessive inflation for that month. Since then, the rate has dropped to a more manageable 10% monthly, heralding what the Government hopes is the start of an economic recovery. It is, however, extremely fragile: the currency has been highly unstable; agricultural and manufacturing production levels are at best, stable. The Government is relying on creating a sound fiscal environment to stimulate commercial prosperity. The strategy may be undermined by continuing capital flight (exchange controls having been lifted) and the distorting effects of the illegal cocaine economy. The Bush administration, which was concerned about cocaine production for different reasons, signed a number of agreements with the Peruvians during 1991 to increase anti-trafficking operations. As US aid to countries supposedly involved in the global narcotics industry is now conditional on the implementation of counter-measures by the recipient government, the Peruvians had little choice other than to cooperate. Peru's foreign policy under Fujimori has been devoted to economic matters – trade agreements and aid commitments – and the resolution of border disputes. The disagreement with Ecuador over access to the Amazonian river system is one of the most difficult on the continent. Several military clashes have occurred since a brief war over the issue in 1942, the most recent in 1981. The foreign policy priority remains, however, the need for economic support from the international community. Foreign investors were already reluctant to commit assets to Peru because of the escalating political violence, for which Sendero Luminoso has been principally responsible. Towards the end of 1991, Fujimori issued a series of decrees which made Peru the most economically liberal country in Latin America. On April 5, 1992, with the backing of the security forces, Fujimori staged a constitutional coup; congress was suspended indefinitely and the entire judiciary sent on leave pending 'reorganisation' while Fujimori ruled by decree. There was no immediate improvement in any aspect of Peruvian life and, as the months passed, Fujimori's days seemed increasingly to be numbered. Then, in September 1992, the security forces made a major breakthrough by capturing Sendero leader Abimael Guzman and his deputy and partner Elena Iparraguirre. This was just part of the major reversal in Sendero's fortunes which has since occurred. At the time of writing, most of the movement's central committee have been detained and the majority of Sendero's hard core have been killed or arrested. Sendero has been driven out of many of its urban strongholds and now relies on its territory in the coca-growing regions. Sendero's weakness became strikingly apparent in September 1993 when, a year after his capture, Guzman issued a plea from jail to his former comrades-in-arms to open negotiations with the Government, a course of action which Sendero had vigorously rejected in the past. The recent successes in the campaign against the guerrillas has boosted Fujimori's political fortunes; he now stands a reasonable chance of re-election in 1995, should he choose to stand.

GOVERNMENT: Under the 1980 constitution, executive power lay with the elected President, with a bicameral legislature consisting of a Senate and a Chamber of Deputies. In 1992, general elections were held to elect members of the Congreso Constituyente Democrático (CCD), the Democratic Constituent Assembly, which comprises just 80 members who work in different commissions. In October 1993, as a result of a national referendum, the present constitution was approved and promulgated at the end of the year.

Mascara Senor de Sipan

consult the *Health* section at the back of the book.
Health care: There are approximately 455 hospitals
(30,000 beds) and 28,000 doctors. Medical insurance is
recommended.

TRAVEL - International

AIR: Peru's national airlines are *Aeroperu (PL)* and
Faucett (CF).
Approximate flight times: From Lima to *London* is 19
hours (including stopover in Miami), to *Los Angeles* is 9
hours, to *Miami* is 6 hours and to *New York* is 9 hours 30
minutes. Direct flights from Europe take 14 hours.
International airport: *Lima (LIM)* (Jorge Chávez
International) is 16km (10 miles) northwest of the city
(travel time – 35 minutes). Taxis to the city are available.
Airport facilities include a duty-free and handicraft shop,
bank, coffee shops, restaurants and gambling machines.
Departure tax: US$17.70 is levied on all international
departures. Transit passengers and children under two
years are exempt.
SEA: Some international cruises occasionally call at
Callao, the main seaport.
RAIL: There are two daily trains from Tacna to Arica

Convent Santa Catalina

(Chile).
ROAD: The main international highway is the Pan-
American Highway running north–south through the
coastal desert of Peru. *TEPSA* and *Ormeño* operate buses
from Ecuador, through Peru to Chile.

TRAVEL - Internal

AIR: There are approximately eight airlines. *Aeroperu*,
Americana and *Faucett* handle virtually all domestic air
traffic, linking Lima to Arequipa, Ayacucho, Cuzco,
Iquitos, Piura, Pucallpa, Talara, Trujillo, Tumbes,
Yurimagnas, Tacna, Chiclayo and other cities.
Departure tax: Passengers departing from Lima to
Cuzco, Iquitos, Arequipa and other cities must pay an
airport tax of US$4.
RIVER: Transportation is available between
Pucallpa–Iquitos (approximately 5 days) and from
Iquitos to the border (2.5 days, about three times a week).
RAIL: There are two main rail networks, which do not
intersect. In addition, a number of short tracks have been
constructed by mining interests and there is a short spur
from the Chilean network reaching as far as Tacna. There
are no connections between Lima and Cuzco. Fast and

comfortable electric *autovagons* are operated on some
routes. Visitors should be aware that railway stations and
trains are the haunts of thieves at night and they are
advised to travel only by day.
The *Central Railroad* links Lima, La Oroya, Huancayo
and Huancavelica. At 4781m (15,686ft), the section from
La Oroya to Huancayo is the highest standard-gauge
railroad in the world. Unfortunately this spectacular
journey is no longer available to passengers; the line is
now only used for the transportation of minerals.
The *Southern Railroad* runs from Arequipa through
Juliaca to Puno on Lake Titicaca. There is a daytime
connection from Puno and Juliaca to Cuzco four times a
week. From Cuzco there is a daily train to Machu Picchu,
which takes approximately 4 hours. Always check for
revised schedules.
ROAD: The Central Highway connects Lima with La
Oroya and Huancayo. From La Oroya there is a road
connecting Cerro de Pasco, Huánuco, Tingo María and
Pucallpa on the Ucayali River. Few roads in Peru are
paved. Landslides are frequent in the rainy season
(December-March) and road surfaces are very rough,
making for slow travel and frequent breakdowns. The
Peruvian Touring Club prepares itineraries and sells
maps. Traffic drives on the right. All foreign vehicles
must display a 'Customs Duty Payment Voucher'. **Bus:**
Operated extensively, providing a very cheap means of
travel. Greyhound-type buses are operated by *Ormeño*,
Cruz del Sur, *Oltursa* and *TEPSA* along the Pan-
American Highway. **Taxi:** Stationed at hotels and at
airports. **Car hire:** *Hertz, Avis, National, Budget, Dollar,
First, Lady's Car, Gentle, Inka's* and *Limousine Service*
have rental agencies in Lima and principal cities.
Documentation: An international driving licence is
required.
URBAN: Public transport in Lima is provided by
conventional buses and by minibuses (*colectivos*). The
minimum rate is US$0.30. Taxis do not have meters and
fares should be agreed before departure, though they are
relatively inexpensive.
JOURNEY TIMES: The following chart gives
approximate journey times (in hours and minutes) from
Lima to other major cities/towns in Peru.

	Air	Road
Arequipa	1.10	18.00
Cajamarca	1.20	16.00
Chiclayo	1.00	12.00
Cuzco	1.00	30.00
Huaraz	-	8.00
Ica	-	5.00
Iquitos	1.30	-
Juliaca	2.00	28.00
Nazca	-	8.00
Pucallpa	0.50	22.00
P. M'nado	2.00	-
Tacna	1.40	24.00
Trujillo	1.00	8.00
Tumbes	1.40	24.00

ACCOMMODATION

HOTELS: Lima has the largest choice of hotels in Peru,
and only here can hotels of international standard be
found. In many towns the government-run *Hoteles de
Turistas* are available. Although these hotels are in many
cases modern, they are frequently converted estate
houses. Throughout Lima and in most major towns, there
are many economical *pensiones* to be found. Hotel prices
in the provinces are lower than in the capital. **Grading:**
The standard of the state tourist hotels (*Hoteles de
Turistas)* in the provincial cities varies considerably, but
they frequently offer good accommodation. Hotels are
classified by the star system, the highest and most
luxurious being 5 stars. The level of comfort, quality of
service and general infrastructure are the criteria for
inclusion in each grade. All accommodation prices are
subject to 18% tax (IGV). Hotels of the higher categories
might also add 13% service charges. Under a new
regulation, all places that provide accommodation must
have a plaque outside bearing the letters **H** (Hotel), **HR**
(Hotel Residencial), **HS** (Hostal Residencial) or **P**
(Pension). Prices vary accordingly. For further
information, contact the Asociación de Hoteles,
Restaurantes y Afines (AHORA), Of 306, Avenida José
Pardo 620, Miraflores, Lima 18. Tel: (14) 446 8773.
CAMPING/CARAVANNING: There are very few
official camping areas anywhere in South America and
no formal arrangements exist in Peru.
YOUTH HOSTELS: There are 28 youth hostels in the
country with dormitory, single or twin rooms. They
usually have a bar or cafeteria and a kitchen. A variety
of sporting facilities is on offer: some have swimming
pools, trekking, skiing and many watersports facilities.
For information contact Youth Tourist Hostels – Lima,
Casimiro Ulloa 328, San Antonio, Lima 18. Tel: (14)
446 5488.

RESORTS & EXCURSIONS

To indicate to visitors something of the flavour of Peru, a selection of towns and notable areas is included below. These are described from south to north, and are situated in fertile plains and valleys, barren deserts, on the towering peaks of the Andes or deep in the Amazonian jungle.

Tacna: A frontier town on the Chilean border, containing a *Cathedral* designed by Eiffel. The *Railway Museum* is worth visiting. The Alianza Field, site of the monument to the fallen in the Battle of the Pacific War (1880) is situated 8km (5 miles) from the town. Excursions to the traditional towns of *Pocollay, Pachía, Calana* and *Tarata* are recommended.

Situated 2359m (7740ft) above sea level on the slopes of Misti, **Arequipa** is known as the *'White City'*. Both Spanish colonial and Andalusian influences are visible everywhere. Sites of interest include the *Santa Catalina Convent* – a beautiful 'city within a city', the *Casa del Moral* mansion and the *Goyeneche Palace*. The suburbs of **Yanahuara** and **Cayma** are worth visiting for their churches. Beautiful countryside dotted with attractive villages surrounds Arequipa. The nearby *Colca Canyon* is considered to be one of the deepest in the Americas.

Puno is situated on the Callao plateau over 3800m (12,467ft) above sea level. Spaniards were lured to the region by the vast mineral wealth, and the area is dotted with colonial churches and pre-Colombian remains. Puno is the greatest centre of the Peruvian folklore tradition. Beautiful *alpaca* wool textiles, as well as *Torito de Pucara*, local pottery and silver artefacts are available.

Lake Titicaca is described as the highest navigable lake in the world. The local Uros people are descendants of the original inhabitants, and continue to dwell around and make their living from the lake. The islands of **Taquille** and **Amantani** are of great social, ethnical and archaeological importance, and can be visited by motorboat.

Situated 3360m (11,024ft) above sea level, **Cuzco** became the capital of the Inca Empire. Remains of granite stone walls of the Inca palaces and temples can still be seen, the most notable of which is the *Koricancha*, or Sun Temple. Of the several churches, the 17th-century *La Merced* and its monastery, *San Francisco Belén de los Reyes, Santa Clara* and *San Blas* are the most interesting, and represent a blend of colonial and Indian architecture. The Cuzco market is also an attraction of the area. Overlooking Cuzco is the immense ruined fortress of **Sacsayhuaman.** Also easily accessible are the Inca sites of *Kenko, Puca Pucara, Tambomachay, Pisac, Ollantaytambo* – and *Machu Picchu.*

The visitor can reach **Machu Picchu** from Cuzco by train, by foot on the Inca Trail or by a combination of both. There are three types of train: local, tourist and the faster *autovagons*. The journey takes approximately 4 hours. Those wishing to walk the *Inca Trail* usually catch a local train to Kilometre 88. From there it is just over 35km (22 miles) to the ruins, but due to the difficulty of the terrain, trekkers should allow at least three days to complete the journey. The stone ruins of palaces, towers, temples, staircases and other remains are currently being restored. Best viewed at dawn or dusk, Machu Picchu is an unforgettable experience.

Ica and Nazca: Both cities have treasure houses containing pre-Inca primitive objects. In the arid terrain surrounding Nazca are great drawings, which depict images reminiscent of modern airport runways and have caused much speculation among archaeologists. There are daily flights over the Nazca region.

Ayacucho: Known as the 'town of a hundred churches'; indeed, from some aspects it seems as though there are more churches than houses. It is famous as a source of handicrafts including pottery, leatherwork, textiles and jewellery.

Lima, the capital, is an ancient Spanish city founded by Francisco Pizarro in 1535 and known as the 'City of Kings'. The city's splendid museums, galleries and monuments live side by side with modern suburbs containing the new banks and businesses of a burgeoning economy. Bullfighting is a passion for many Peruvians; in October and November the famous bullfighting festival takes place at the *Plaza de Acho* bullring.

Trujillo is known as 'the City of the Eternal Spring'. Its mansions and archaeological areas are well worth visiting.

Chan-Chan is the largest clay city in the world.

Chiclayo is a northern city with a hot and sunny climate. Chiclayo and other towns in northern Peru are centres of witchcraft. Among the places of archaeological interest around Chiclayo are *Túcume, Bátan Grande* and *Huaca Rajada,* where a royal Moche mausoleum was found in 1987. Five clay chambers were discovered under pyramids. It is thought that these pyramids were positioned to gather the sun's energy. The greatest discovery was the tomb of the *Señor de Sipán*, whose funeral clothes were adorned with gold, silver and jewels. He held a golden sceptre in his left hand and a golden child's rattle

representing the A-Apayec divinity was placed on his pelvis. Researchers have ascertained that he was a royal ruler 1600 years ago and that he was about 30 years old when he died. He was probably revered as a demigod. However, the *Señor de Sipán* is still enshrouded in mystery: his precise identity and cause of death is unknown. The bodies of two women, a priest, a high official and a dog (thought to be a guide and protector on the journey to the after-life) were also found in the tomb. Apparently, they died in a self-sacrificial ritual. A half-hourly minibus service from the intersection of Amazonas and Sáenz Peña Avenues in Chiclayo takes visitors to the burial site. The priceless funereal artefacts unearthed from the tomb can be viewed at the Brüning Museum in **Lambayeque,** 11km (7 miles) north of Chiclayo. There is a regular coach service from Chiclayo's Main Square to Lambayeque.

The most northerly Peruvian town, **Tumbes** is a major sporting and deep-sea fishing centre.

In the northern Highlands, **Cajamarca** is famed for its traditionally-styled churches. The town is surrounded by beautiful countryside.

The Jungle: The Amazon Basin covers more than half of Peru, but it is mostly inaccessible to tourists. It is possible to take a boat from Pucallpa to Iquitos on the *Ucayali River*, but many of the Amazonian cities, such as Iquitos, Pucallpa and Puerto Maldonado, capital of the Madre de Dios Department, are best reached by air. National Reserves and Parks exist within the jungle region, with a variety of plants, trees and animals. Launches regularly take visitors to areas inhabited by Amazonian Indian tribes.

SOCIAL PROFILE

FOOD & DRINK: The hot and flavoursome nature of Peruvian food, created by *ají* and *ajo* (hot pepper and garlic), has become celebrated at home and abroad. Peruvians enjoy a wide variety of vegetables; there are over 2000 kinds of indigenous and cultivated potatoes alone. Tropical fruits are abundant, as are avocados. *Ceviche* is a local speciality (uncooked fish marinated in lemon juice and hot pepper, served with corn-on-the-cob, potatoes and onions). *Escabeche* is a cooked fish appetiser eaten cold, served with peppers and onions. *Corvina* is sea bass prepared in several ways and is always an excellent choice. Scallops *(conchitas)* are excellent, as are mussels *(choros)* and shrimps

(camarones), which are plentiful and delicious. *Chupe de camarones* is a chowder-type soup made with shrimp, milk, eggs, potatoes and peppers. Other specialities include *sopa criolla* (spicy soup with beef and noodles), *ají de gallina* (shredded chicken in a piquant cream sauce), *anticuchos* (strips of beef or fish marinated in vinegar and spices, then barbecued on skewers) and *lomo saltado* (morsels of beef sautéed with onions and peppers, served with fried potatoes and rice). Rice and potatoes accompany virtually every dish. Traditional desserts are *arroz con leche* (rice pudding), *mazamorra morada* (rich, fruity, purple pudding), *suspiro* and *manjar blanco*, both made from sweetened condensed milk and *picarones* (free-form doughnuts served with syrup). Table service is the norm in hotels and restaurants. **Drink:** Peruvian beers are excellent and national wines are good. The most famous drink is *pisco sour*, made from a potent grape brandy. Other pisco-based drinks are *algar-robina* (pisco and carob syrup), *chilcano* (pisco and ginger ale) or *capitán* (pisco and vermouth). *Chicha de jora* (fermented) and *chicha morada* (non-alcoholic) are popular drinks dating from Inca times.
NIGHTLIFE: Traditional Peruvian social life, for the most part, takes place at home among the family, but there are nevertheless many good bars, pubs, discotheques and casinos in the major towns and tourist resorts. *Peñas* are places of traditional Peruvian nightlife. *Peñas* always serve snacks and some serve full meals. Here one can enjoy *criolla* or folk music, especially at the weekend.
SHOPPING: There are many attractive Peruvian handicrafts such as *alpaca* wool sweaters, *alpaca* and *llama* rugs, Indian masks, weaving, reproduction jewellery and much more. Galleries and handicraft shops abound in the Miraflores, San Isidro and Pueblo Libre districts of Lima. The Indian market in La Marina

Avenue (8th-10th blocks), Pueblo Libre, is worth a visit. *Aresanías del Perú*, the state-run handicraft shops, are located in San Isidro and at the airport. **Shopping hours:** 1030-1300 and 1600-1900 Monday to Saturday.
SPORT: Golf and tennis: In Lima and suburbs. Some private clubs will make their facilities available to tourists. **Horseriding:** Central highlands and in the horse-breeding areas south as far as Ica.
Mountaineering: There are many peaks over 6000m (19,686ft) in the Andean Range, and many of them are unconquered. **Exploring:** Contact South American Explorers Club. **Watersports:** Many watersports are available on the coast and **surfing** is a particular favourite as the beaches of Lima rank alongside the best in Hawaii or California. Boards may be hired. **Fishing:** Good sea fishing and trout is found in lakes such as Titicaca and Conococha.
SPECIAL EVENTS: The following is a selection of the major festivals held throughout Peru. Check with the Embassy for details:
Apr '95 *Easter Week* (celebrated across the country, but particularly in Ayacucho). **Apr (third week)** *National Contest of Paso Horses*, Mamacona, near Lima. **May (beginning)** *Festival of the Cross.* **Jun** *Corpus Christi and Folklore Festival*, Cuzco; *Festival of the Virgin of Perpetual Help*, Piura; *Raqchui Folklore Festival*, Sicuani; *Inti Raymi* or *Festival of the Sun*, Cuzco. **Jul** *Festival of the Virgin of Carmen*, Paucartambo and many other cities. **Sep** *Festival of the Virgin of Cocharcas*, Huancayo. **Sep (last week)** *International Spring Festival*, Trujillo. **Oct (whole month)** *Lord of Miracles Festivities*, Lima; *Bullfighting Festival*, Lima. **Oct** *Wine Festival*, Ica. **Nov (weekends)** *Bullfighting season*, Lima. **Nov** *Folklore Week*, Puno. **Dec 24** *Santuranticuy* (Christmas Eve), Cuzco. **Jan 6 '96** *Epiphany.* **Feb** *Virgen de la Candelaria*, Puno. **Feb-Mar** *Carnival* (the beginning of Lent is celebrated throughout the country,

but particularly in Cajamarca, Puno, Ayacucho and Iquitos); *Festival de la Marinera*, Trujillo. **Mar** *La Vendimia* (wine festival), Ica.
SOCIAL CONVENTIONS: Shaking hands is the customary form of greeting. Visitors should follow normal social courtesies and the atmosphere is generally informal. A small gift from a company or home country is sufficient. Dress is usually informal, although for some social occasions men wear a jacket and tie. Many local businessmen wear an open-necked shirt called a *guayaberas* during the summer. Shorts and beach attire should only be worn in summer resorts. Life is conducted at a leisurely pace and Peruvians laughingly speak of *la hora Peruana* when referring to their tendency to arrive late for everything. **Tipping:** Service charges of 18% are added to all bills. Additional tips of 5% are expected. Taxi drivers do not generally expect tips.

BUSINESS PROFILE

ECONOMY: Peru has abundant mineral resources which produce most of the country's foreign earnings. Agriculture, which is more important for the numbers employed than for its contribution to national wealth, produces sugar cane, potatoes, maize, rice, cereals, cotton and coffee. Peru is also the world's largest producer of coca, although the Government has an agreement with the USA to try and eliminate the crop. Fishing is also important – Peru's catch was devastated in the early 1980s by climatic changes, but in recent years has recovered its former position as the world's leading producer. Peru has some oil reserves, but these are not large and the country has fluctuated between being a net exporter and net importer during the last decade. Other mineral deposits, which are thought to be considerable, include copper, silver, gold, iron ore, coal and phosphates. The mining sector has been badly affected, however, by low world prices and industrial problems. Peru has formidable overseas debt problems, with total external borrowings of around US$22 billion (1993). The Government has recently negotiated a novel debt-for-exports deal with the USA which should help to lift the burden. Financial aid from the USA and other donors was cut in 1992. There are signs that donors may relent in view of the seriousness of the situation. Gross National Product grew by 6.5% per annum during 1992-93. Peru is a member of the Andean Treaty and of the 11-member Asociación Latinoamericana de Integración which seeks to promote free trade and economic development in Latin America. Peru's major trading partners are the USA, Japan and Germany.
BUSINESS: Some business people will speak English, but the majority speak Spanish and a business visitor to Peru who does not speak the language should arrange for an interpreter. Appointments should be made and confirmed and although Peruvians can be late, visitors are expected to arrive on time. Visiting cards are used. **Office hours:** 0900-1700 Monday to Friday.
COMMERCIAL INFORMATION: The following organisation can offer advice: Confederación de Cámaras de Comercio y Producción del Perú, Avenida Gregorio Escobedo 398, Lima 11. Tel: (14) 463 3434. Fax: (14) 463 2820.
CONFERENCES/CONVENTIONS: For further information contact: Fondo de Promoción Turistica (FOPTUR) (for address, see top of entry); *or* Cámara Nacional de Turismo (CANATUR), Calle Santander 170, Miraflores, Lima 18. Tel: (14) 446 8775. Fax: (14) 444 3294.

CLIMATE

Varies according to area. On the coast winter lasts from June to September. During this period, the mountainous areas are often sunny. Heavy rains in the mountains and jungle last from December to April.
Required clothing: Lightweights during summer with warmer clothes worn in upland areas. Mediumweights are advised during cooler months.

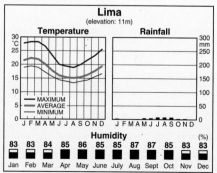

Lima
(elevation: 11m)

	Temperature	Rainfall

MAXIMUM
AVERAGE
MINIMUM

Humidity (%)

Jan	Feb	Mar	Apr	May	June	July	Aug	Sept	Oct	Nov	Dec
83	83	84	85	86	85	85	87	87	85	83	83

Philippines

The Visayas:
1 Panay
2 Masbate
3 Samar
4 Negros
5 Cebu
6 Bohol
7 Leyte

□ *international airport*

Location: South-East Asia.

Philippine Department of Tourism
Department of Tourism Building, Teodoro Valencia

Circle, Rizal Park, Ermita, Manila, Philippines
Tel: (2) 599 031. Fax: (2) 501 567. Telex: 66412 (a/b MOTPM).

Philippine Convention and Visitors Corporation
4th Floor, Legaspi Towers, 300 Roxas Boulevard, Metro Manila, Philippines
Tel: (2) 575 031. Fax: (2) 521 6165. Telex: 40604 (a/b PCVC PM).

Embassy of the Republic of the Philippines
9a Palace Green, London W8 4QE
Tel: (0171) 937 1600. Fax: (0171) 937 2925. Telex: 24411 (a/b AMPHIL G). Opening hours: 0900-1300 and 1400-1700 Monday to Friday.

Philippine Department of Tourism
17 Albemarle Street, London W1X 4LE
Tel: (0171) 499 5443 (general enquiries) *or* 499 5652 (incentive travel). Fax: (0171) 499 5772. Opening hours: 0900-1700 Monday to Friday.

British Embassy
15th-17th Floors, LV Locsin Building, 6752 Ayala Avenue, Makati, Metro Manila 3116, Philippines
Tel: (2) 816 7116 (general) *or* 816 7348/9 (Consular) *or* 816 7271 (visas). Fax: (2) 819 7206 *or* 810 2745 (Consular/visa) *or* 815 6233 (commercial). Telex: 63282 (a/b PRODME PN).

Embassy of the Republic of the Philippines
1600 Massachusetts Avenue, NW, Washington, DC 20036
Tel: (202) 467 9300. Fax: (202) 328 7614.
Consulate Generals in: New York (tel: (212) 764 1330; fax: (212) 382 1146; *Also deals with enquiries from Canada*), Chicago (tel: (312) 332 6458), San Francisco (tel: (415) 433 6666) and Los Angeles (tel: (213) 387 5321).

Embassy of the United States of America
1201 Roxas Boulevard, Ermita Manila 1000, Philippines

Tel: (2) 521 7116. Fax: (2) 522 4361. Telex: 72227366.
Embassy of the Republic of the Philippines
Suite 606, 130 Albert Street, Ottawa, Ontario K1P 5G4
Tel: (613) 233 1121/3. Fax: (613) 233 4165.
Canadian Embassy
PO Box 2168, 9th-11th Floors, Allied Bank Center, 6754 Ayala Avenue, 1261 Makati, Metro Manila, Philippines
Tel: (2) 810 8861. Fax: (2) 810 8839 *or* 810 4299. Telex: 63676 (a/b DOMCAN PN).

AREA: 300,000 sq km (115,831 sq miles).
POPULATION: 65,000,000 (1994 estimate).
POPULATION DENSITY: 202 per sq km.
CAPITAL: Manila. **Population:** 12,000,000 (1994 estimate).
GEOGRAPHY: The Philippines lie off the southeast coast of Asia between Taiwan and Borneo in the Pacific Ocean and South China Sea. They are composed of 7107 islands and islets. The two largest islands, Luzon in the north and Mindanao in the south, account for 65% of the total land area and contain 60% of the country's population. Between the two lie the Visayas Islands.
LANGUAGE: Filipino, based on Tagalog, is the national language. English is widely spoken, Spanish less so. The Philippines is the third-largest English-speaking country in the world. There are over 111 cultural and racial groups, each with its own language or dialect.
RELIGION: 85% Roman Catholic; the rest are made up mostly of Muslims, other Christian denominations, Buddhists and Taoists.
TIME: GMT + 8.
ELECTRICITY: 220 volts (110 volts in Baguio) AC,

Timatic

Health	
GALILEO/WORLDSPAN: **TI-DFT/MNL/HE**	
SABRE: **TIDFT/MNL/HE**	
Visa	
GALILEO/WORLDSPAN: **TI-DFT/MNL/VI**	
SABRE: **TIDFT/MNL/VI**	

For more information on Timatic codes refer to Contents.

Lechon Festival

| | International airport |
| Land over 2000m |
| Land over 1000m |

300km

150mls

PASSPORTS: Passport valid for at least six months beyond intended length of stay required by all, except holders of a Hong Kong Identity Card issued to residents of Hong Kong or a Taiwan (China) Certificate of Identity.

British Visitors Passport: Not acceptable.

Note: All children of Philippine nationality must hold individual passports. Children of other nationalities up to the age of 21 are not permitted entry unless accompanied by their parents or met by their parents at the airport.

VISAS: Required by all except:

(a) transit passengers;

(b) **[1]** bona fide foreign tourists (including business persons), provided stay does not exceed 21 days and they have passports valid for at least 6 months and onward tickets (those who wish to stay for more than 21 days require a visa*);

(c) nationals of Brazil, Gibraltar, Israel, Romania and Sri Lanka for entry into the Philippines for a period of not more than 59 days;

(d) passengers of Chinese origin holding a British passport issued in Hong Kong for a stay of 7 days.

Note [*]: Nationals of Albania, Bosnia-Hercegovina, Cambodia, CIS, China, Croatia, Iran, Laos, Libya, North Korea, the Former Yugoslav Republic of Macedonia (FYR), Slovenia, Vietnam, and Serbia and Montenegro *do* require a visa to enter the Philippines for any purpose. In addition, nationals of North Korea must have their applications approved by the authorities in Manila before visas can be issued.

Types of visa: Tourist and Business.

Cost: Usually £18 for stays of between 21 and 59 days.

Validity: Tourist and Business visas are valid for up to 59 days after entry. Refer to Commission on Immigration and Deportation for extension procedure. Visa extensions are not possible for nationals of Bulgaria, Czech Republic, Hungary, Mongolia, Poland and Slovak Republic.

Application to: Consular section at Embassy. For addresses, see top of entry.

Application requirements: (a) 1 application form. (b) 1 passport-size photograph. (c) Passport valid for at least 6 months. (d) Proof of means of support during stay. (e) Fee.

Application for a non-immigrant visa should be made in person.

Working days required: 1.

MONEY

Currency: Philippine Peso (PP) = 100 centavos. Notes are in denominations of PP1000, 500, 100, 50, 20, 10, 5 and 2. Coins are in denominations of PP1, and 50, 25, 10, 5 and 1 centavos.

Currency exchange: Travellers cheques and major foreign currency may be cashed in large commercial banks and Central Bank dealers in Metro Manila. They are also accepted in most hotels, restaurants and shops. Always use authorised money-changers or banks in Metro Manila. Outside the capital there is a shortage of facilities for changing foreign currency, and rates may get progressively worse further from the city. It is advisable to carry a sufficient amount of Philippine Pesos when travelling to other provinces.

Credit cards: American Express, Diners Club, Access/Mastercard and Visa are widely accepted in major establishments throughout the big cities of the Philippines. Check with your credit card company for details of merchant acceptability and other services which may be available.

Travellers cheques: See *Currency exchange* above.

Exchange rate indicators: The following figures are included as a guide to the movements of the Philippine Peso against Sterling and the US Dollar:

Date:	Oct '92	Sep '93	Jan '94	Jan '95
£1.00=	35.00	42.24	40.91	38.17
$1.00=	22.05	27.66	27.65	24.40

Currency restrictions: The import and export of local currency is limited to PP5000 unless authorised by the Central Bank. Free import of foreign currency.

Banking hours: 0900-1600 Monday to Friday.

DUTY FREE

The following items may be imported into the Philippines without incurring customs duty:

400 cigarettes or 50 cigars or 250g tobacco; 2 litres of alcoholic beverage; a reasonable amount of clothing and shoes, jewellery and perfume for personal use.

Prohibited items: Firearms, explosives, pornographic material, seditious or subversive material, narcotics and other internationally prohibited drugs (unless accompanied by a medical prescription).

60Hz. 110 volts is available in most hotels. Flat and round 2- and 3-pin plugs are in use.

COMMUNICATIONS: Telephone: IDD is available to main towns. Country code: 63. International calls to the smaller towns must be booked through the operator. Outgoing international code: 00. **Fax:** All 3- to 5-star hotels, most government offices and most businesses have facsimile services. **Telex/telegram:** Telegrams can be sent from Eastern Telecommunications Philippines Incorporated offices. Public telex booths are operated by the same company, along with Globe-Mackay Cable and Radio Corporation and RCA Communications. **Post:** Airmail to Europe takes at least 5 days. Post office hours: 0800-1700 Monday to Friday. **Press:** There are about 20 daily newspapers. English-language daily newspapers include the *Philippine Star, Malaya, Manila Times, Philippine Journal, Business World, News Today, Business Star* and *People's Journal*.

BBC World Service and Voice of America frequencies: From time to time these change. See the section *How to Use this Book* for more information.

BBC:

| MHz | 17.83 | 15.36 | 11.95 | 9.740 |
| Voice of America: |
| MHz | 15.43 | 11.76 | 9.770 | 7.120 |

PASSPORT/VISA

Regulations and requirements may be subject to change at short notice, and you are advised to contact the appropriate diplomatic or consular authority before finalising travel arrangements. Details of these may be found at the head of this country's entry. Any numbers in the chart refer to the footnotes below.

	Passport Required?	Visa Required?	Return Ticket Required?
Full British	Yes	1	Yes
BVP	Not valid	-	-
Australian	Yes	1	Yes
Canadian	Yes	1	Yes
USA	Yes	1	Yes
Other EU (As of 31/12/94)	Yes	1	Yes
Japanese	Yes	1	Yes

Greens 5,000 ft. above sea level.

The magical seascapes of Anilao, Batangas. Sculptured stretches of coral reef. Perpendicular submarine cliffs. Neon fish. Giant tuna. Secret shoals. All within a few hours from Manila's International Airport.

The challenge of Camp John Hay lies high in the cool mountains of Baguio. Drive through hills. Putter through valleys. And enjoy the freshness of pine-scented air as you play.

Go for a round or take a dive! The minute you're out of the airport, golf or scuba could be just an hour away!

When in Manila, there are 11 courses to choose from. Elsewhere in our islands, you have a choice from over 40 courses and clubs. Try the championship course of Iloilo, the oldest in the islands. Or a course nestled in the heart of a sugar cane plantation in Negros Occidental. A course that goes around the historic walled city of Intramuros. Or a course overlooking the azure seascapes of Cavite. Whichever you choose, there'll be plenty of sunshine, lots of fresh air, many friendly and experienced caddies — a total golf holiday packaged in very affordable prices. That 's the Philippines... for beginners as well as pros, a golfer's haven.

Landing to tee-off could be just two hours apart. There are lots of courses within the city, all of which are reasonably priced.

What if you're in for the dive? Then a colorful welcome awaits you deep down in any of our numerous diving spots. Nearest Manila about 2 hours away is Batangas, replete with corals and glorious underwater architecture. For the more experienced and

Rainbows 50 ft. below.

adventurous, there's the Apo Reef of Mindoro with its mysterious shipwrecks. Relatively unexplored but teeming with marine life is Tubbataha Reef in Palawan. Many divers have found Cebu favorable because of the luxurious accommodations and diving facilities it offers. While the rest of the Visayas remain popular because the gentle slopes and underwater walls provide excellent photographic possibilities.

Go ahead. Dive or drive. Swim or sail. Go fishing. Or go head for the tennis courts. The more activities you ask for, the more you'll find that our Islands Philippines is the perfect choice for you.

What a catch! Cast a line and a marlin might just be your prize.

Life's a beach... here in our Islands Philippines. Here you can wrestle with the wind or walk on water as you try your hand at windsurfing.

Our islands have it!

Islands PHILIPPINES

DEPARTMENT OF TOURISM, Department of Tourism Bldg., T.M. Kalaw St.,Rizal Park, Manila, Philippines, P.O. Box 3451, Manila Phils., Tel. 59-90-31 • Cable: DEPTOUR , • Telex: 40183 Deptour PM 66412 MOTPN, 40435 BT PROM PM • PHILIPPINE CONVENTION & VISITORS CORPORATION Fourth Floor, Suite 10-17, Legaspi Towers 300, Roxas Blvd., Metro Manila, Philippines, P.O. Box EA-459, Tel. 575-031 • Telex 40604 Cable-MNL Fax: (632) 5216165

Embassy of the Philippines, Philippine Department of Tourism, 17 Albemarle Street, London, W1X & 7HA , Tel: (071) 499 5443 • Fax:(071) 499 5772 • Tlx: . 265115 PTOELP G

PUBLIC HOLIDAYS

Jan 1 '95 New Year's Day. **Feb 25** Edsa Revolution Anniversary. **Apr 9** Araw Ng Kagitingan (Day of Valour). **Apr 13** Maundy Thursday. **Apr 14** Good Friday. **May 1** Labour Day. **Jun 12** Independence Day. **Aug 28** National Heroes Day. **Nov 1** All Saints' Day. **Nov 30** Bonifacio Day. **Dec 25** Christmas. **Dec 30** Rizal Day. **Dec 31** Special Public Holiday. **Jan 1 '96** New Year's Day. **Feb 25** Edsa Revolution Anniversary. **Apr 4** Maundy Thursday. **Apr 5** Good Friday. **Apr 8** Easter Monday. **Note:** Easter is a major holiday in the Philippines and travel may be disrupted.

HEALTH

Regulations and requirements may be subject to change at short notice, and you are advised to contact your doctor well in advance of your intended date of departure. Any numbers in the chart refer to the footnotes below.

	Special Precautions?	Certificate Required?
Yellow Fever	No	1
Cholera	Yes	2
Typhoid & Polio	Yes	-
Malaria	Yes/3	-
Food & Drink	4	-

[1]: A yellow fever certificate is required from travellers arriving within 6 days from infected areas, except children under one year of age, who may, however, be subject to isolation or surveillance.

[2]: Following WHO guidelines issued in 1973, a cholera vaccination certificate is not a condition of entry to the Philippines. However, cholera is a serious risk in this country and precautions are essential. Up-to-date advice should be sought before deciding whether these precautions should include vaccination, as medical opinion is divided over its effectiveness. See the *Health* section at the back of the book.

[3]: Malaria risk exists throughout the year in areas below 600m, except in the Provinces of Bohol, Catanduanes, Cebu and Leyte. No risk is considered to exist in urban areas or in the plains. The malignant *falciparum* strain is present and is reported to be 'highly resistant' to chloroquine.

[4]: Water used for drinking, brushing teeth or making ice should have first been boiled or otherwise sterilised. Milk is unpasteurised and should be boiled. Powdered or tinned milk is available and is advised, but make sure that it is reconstituted with pure water. Avoid dairy products which are likely to have been made from unboiled milk. Only eat well-cooked meat and fish, preferably served hot. Pork, salad and mayonnaise may carry increased risk. Vegetables should be cooked and fruit peeled.
Rabies is present. For those at high risk, vaccination before arrival should be considered. If you are bitten abroad, seek medical advice without delay. For more information, consult the *Health* section at the back of the book.
Bilharzia (schistosomiasis) is present. Avoid swimming and paddling in stagnant fresh water. Swimming pools which are well-chlorinated and maintained are safe.
Health care: Health insurance is highly recommended. There are approximately 1600 hospitals, three-quarters of which are private.

TRAVEL - International

AIR: The Philippines' national airline is *Philippine Airlines (PR)*.
Note: The period over Easter, from Good Friday to the following Bank holiday (and sometimes beyond), is a major holiday in the Philippines as is Christmas and New Year. There may be some difficulty booking a flight during these periods.
Approximate flight times: From Manila to *London* is 18 hours; to *Paris* is 21 hours 15 minutes; to *Los Angeles* is 16 hours 55 minutes; to *New York* is 25 hours 20 minutes; to *Singapore* is 3 hours 10 minutes; to *Hong Kong* is 1 hour 50 minutes; to *Bangkok* is 3 hours 50 minutes; to *Tokyo* is 4 hours 15 minutes and to *Sydney* is 8 hours 50 minutes.
International airport: *Ninoy Aquino (MNL)*, 12km (7.5 miles) southeast of Manila. Airport facilities include banks, post office, medical clinic, baggage deposit area, duty-free shops and car hire. Bus and taxi services are available to the city (travel time – 35 minutes).
Departure tax: PP500 for international departures. Children under two years of age and transit passengers are exempt.
SEA: Manila is a major seaport, a crossroads of trade in the Asia-Pacific region. Shipping lines which call at Manila include *American President Lines, Anline, Ben Line Container Ltd, Everett Lines, Hapag-Lloyd, 'K'*

Main picture: Beach scenery. Above: Philippine Eagle. Above right: Carabao Festival of Pulilan.

Line, Knutsen Line, Lykes Orient Line, Orient Overseas
Container Line, Scandutch, Sealand, United States Line
and the *Waterman Line*. Schedules and rates are listed in
the shipping pages of daily newspapers.

TRAVEL - Internal

AIR: *Philippine Airlines* offer comprehensive internal
services with a wide range of discount fares. Demand is
heavy, so flights should be booked in advance. Privately-
owned airlines also operate.
Departure tax: PP50 on domestic flights.
SEA: Inter-island ships with first-class accommodation
connect the major island ports. For details, contact local
shipping lines.
RAIL: The only railway is on Luzon Island, from Manila
to San Fernando and south from Manila to Camalig
(operated by *Philippine National Railways*). This
network runs three trains daily to and from Manila, one
overnight with couchettes and dining car. There is also
some air-conditioned accommodation. Children under
three travel free of charge and children aged three to nine
pay half fare.
ROAD: There are 160,632.76 km (100,395.47m) of
roads spread among the islands, with highways on the
Mindanao, Visayas and Luzon island groups. Traffic
drives on the right. **Bus:** There are bus services between
the towns and also widely available 'jeepneys'. These are
shared taxis using jeep-derived vehicles equipped to
carry up to 14 passengers on bench seats. Fares are
similar to buses. **Taxi:** Taxis are available in the cities
and in large towns. Make sure meters are used, as some
taxi drivers will set an exorbitant and arbitrary rate. **Car
hire:** Car rentals, with or without driver, are available in
Manila and in major cities. The minimum age is 18.
Documentation: International Driving Permit required,
together with a national driving licence.
URBAN: A number of bus routes are operated by *Metro
Manila Transport* using conventional vehicles, including
double-deckers, and Manila's air-conditioned *Love Bus*
which has become part of the city's attractions, besides
providing a comfortable ride on specially designated
routes. Most journeys, however, are made by *jeepneys*, of
which there are an estimated 30,000 in Manila alone. The
Metro, a light rail transit link, opened in 1984 and is now
fully operational. 15km (9 miles) in length, it runs from
Baclaran terminal in the south to Caloocan terminal in
the north.
JOURNEY TIMES: The following chart gives
approximate journey times (in hours and minutes) from
Manila to other major cities/towns in the Philippines.

	Air	Road	Sea
Baguio	0.50	4.00	-
Banaue	*0.50	4.00	-
Batangas	-	2.00	-
Cebu	1.10	-	24.00
Cagayan de Oro	1.25	-	48.00
Davao	1.30	-	48.00
Iloilo	1.00	-	24.00
Laoag	1.25	7.00	-
Palawan	1.10		24.00

Note [*]: As far as Baguio City and then another 4 hours
by road.

ACCOMMODATION

HOTELS: In Manila there are some 10,000 first-class
hotel rooms. There are numerous smaller hotels, inns,
hostels and pensions. Prices are often quoted both in
Philippine Pesos and US Dollars. A complete directory
of hotels is available from the Department of Tourism.
The majority of establishments belong to the Hotel and
Restaurant Association of the Philippines (HRAP),
Room 205, Regina Building, Trasiera, corner of
Aguirre Street, Legaspi Village, Makati, Metro Manila.
Tel: (2) 815 4659 *or* 815 4661. Fax: (2) 815 4663. In
addition, most regions have their own associations.
Grading: Hotels are graded in the following categories
based on standards set by the Office of Tourism
Services, Department of Tourism, Manila: Economy
(43% of all establishments are in this grade), Standard
(39%), First class (9%) and Deluxe (9%).
SELF-CATERING: 'Apartels' are available for
minimum stays of a week.
HOMESTAY: The National Homestay Programme
provides travellers with comfortable accommodation in
Filipino family homes throughout the islands.
Adequate lighting, ventilation, bath and toilet are
provided; home-cooked meals are usually also
available. There are various regional Homestay
Associations. For further information contact the
Department of Tourism.
CAMPING/CARAVANNING: Offered only in a very
limited number of places.

RESORTS & EXCURSIONS

The Philippines are composed of 7107 islands, with a total coastline longer than that of the USA. The warm tropical waters offer the attractions of sunbathing and swimming, while divers can explore coral gardens and dramatic drop-offs on the sea bed. Charter planes can be hired for reaching some of the more remote islands. Inland, the rich history and culture of the Filipino people, the dramatic landscapes and thriving cities will fascinate the visitor. For the purposes of this guide, this section has been divided into three areas, with the main tourist attractions listed under Luzon, the Visayas, and Mindanao and the South.

Luzon

Luzon is the largest and most northerly of the main islands. The spectacular landscape is made up of mountainous regions in the north, the flat vistas of the central plain, lakes and volcanoes in the southern peninsula, and a coastline dotted with caves and sandy-beached islands.

Manila, capital and hub of the nation, is situated on the east coast. Manila has been a port for hundreds of years, founded in 1571 on the ruins of a Muslim settlement. The oldest part of the city, the *Intramuros* or Walled City, was protected by a massive wall, some of which still remains today despite savage fighting staged here in the Second World War. Places of interest include *San Augustin Church, American Cemetery, Coconut Palace, Manila Cathedral,* from which there is an excellent view of the 2072 sq km (800 sq miles) of the harbour, and the ruins of *Fort Santiago.* Outside the Intramuros is *Chinatown,* a market in the district of Binondo, crowded with shops, stalls and restaurants. *Luneta National Park* contains the *Rizal Monument,* a memorial to the execution of this great Filipino intellectual of the late 19th century.

Manila is a good base from which to make excursions, for instance to **Las Piñas,** situated a little way outside the city, where the famous Bamboo Organ is and the *Sarao Jeepney factory,* where people are allowed to wander around free of charge.

About an hour's drive away from Manila through coconut plantations, *Tagaytay Ridge* in **Cavite** overlooks a lake that contains *Taal Volcano,* which contains another lake. Tagaytay is a popular destination in summer when all kinds of festivities are celebrated and roadside stalls overflow with flowering plants and fruits in season.

Laguna, a short distance from Manila, is a province famous for hot sulphur springs. The 'Towns of Baths', **Pansol, Los Baños** and **Cuyab,** are situated here. The series of mineral springs of *Hidden Valley* lie secreted in a 90m (300ft) deep crater in **Alaminos**, enclosed by rich forests. The pools vary in temperature from warm to cold, and the lush trails end up at a gorge with a waterfall.

Villa Escudero, an 800-hectare coconut plantation in **Laguna Province** less than two hours by road from Manila, is part of an actual working plantation, yielding rare glimpses into rural life. Guests are taken on a tour of a typical village on a cart drawn by a *carabao,* or water buffalo.

Corregidor Island, 'The Rock', a famous memorial to those who fell during the Japanese invasion, is accessible by hydrofoil. Day tours include refreshments and guide.

A day trip to the town of **Pagsanjan**, 63km (39 miles) southeast of Manila, includes dug-out canoe rides down the jungle-bordered river to the *Pagsanjan Falls.* These were the location for the filming of 'Apocalypse Now', and are a popular excursion.

250km (150 miles) north of Manila is **Baguio**, 1525m (5000ft) above sea level, a cool haven from the summer heat. It is accessible both by air and land, though the drive up the zigzagging *Kennon Road* is more popular as it offers spectacular views of the countryside. Baguio has a good variety of restaurants, mountain views and walking excursions. Main attractions include *The Mansion,* summer residence of the Philippine president; *Bell Church*; *Baguio Cathedral*; and the *Crystal Caves,* composed of crystalline metamorphic rocks and once an ancient burial site.

Banaue is four hours' bus ride north of Baguio. A remote mountainous community lives here, and tourists can visit their settlements. The beautiful rice terraces are the main attraction of this area. A breathtaking sight, they rise majestically to an altitude of 1525m (5000ft), and encompass an area of 10,360 sq km (4000 sq miles). The terraces were hand-carved some 2000 years ago using crude tools cutting into once barren rock, each ledge completely encompassing the mountain. Banaue has a tourist hotel and many good pensions.

Hundred Islands lies off the coast of **Pangasinan,** 400 islets surrounded by white sand beaches. This area is ideal for skindiving, swimming and fishing. Hundred Islands is the second-largest marine reservation in the world, teeming with over 2000 species of aquatic life. The caves and domes of **Marcos Island** and the *Devil's Kitchen* are worth exploring.

The entire province of **Palawan** is a remarkable terrain for adventure and exploration, with its primeval rainforests, *St Paul's Underground River* and *Tubbattaha Reef.*

Mindoro island, reached by ferry from Batangas pier and south of Manila, is a place where the stunning scenery includes *Mount Halcon,* 2695m (8841ft) high, *Naujan Lake* and the *Tamarao Falls* – with a pool at their base surrounded by a thick wall of vegetation. **La Union,** situated on the northwest coast of Luzon, has some of the best beach-resort facilities on the island. There are regular buses to La Union from Manila and Baguio.

Bicol Region, situated in the east, offers beaches, hotels and sights such as the *Mayon Volcano,* a nearly perfect cone, *Tiwi Hotsprings, Naglambong Boiling Lake* and *Kalayukay Beach Resort.*

The Visayas

The Visayas is a group of islands between Luzon and Mindanao. The main islands are **Samar, Panay, Negros, Cebu** and **Leyte,** famous as the island first sighted by the Spanish explorer Ferdinand Magellan in the 16th century and as the landing point for the American liberation forces in 1944. Samar and Leyte are linked by the *San Juanico Bridge,* the longest in the country.

Cebu City is the main resort of the Visayas. Cebu is the most densely populated island, a commercial centre with an international harbour, and the Philippines' second city. City sights include *Magellan's Cross*, a wooden cross planted by Magellan himself over 450 years ago to commemorate the baptism into the Christian faith of Rajah Humabon and his wife Juana with 800 followers, and *Fort San Pedro*, the oldest and smallest Spanish fort in the country.

Carcar town, south of Cebu City, has many preserved Castillian houses, gardens and churches. The *Chapel of the Last Supper* features hand-carved life-size statues of Christ and his apostles dating back to Spanish times. The *Magellan Monument* on **Mactan Island** was raised in 1886 to mark the spot where Magellan died, felled by the fierce chieftain, Datu Lapu-Lapu, who refused to submit to the Spanish conquerors. There is also a monument to Datu Lapu-Lapu honouring him as the first Filipino patriot. **Maribago** is the centre of the region's guitar-making industry. As well as many historical sites there are popular hotels, beach clubs and resorts.

Iloilo on Panay is an agricultural province producing root crops, vegetables, cacao, coffee and numerous tropical fruits. The attractions include beach resorts and, in **Iloilo City,** the 18th-century *Miagao Church,* a unique piece of Baroque colonial architecture with a facade decorated with impressions of coconut and papaya trees. **Sicogon Island** is a haven for scuba divers, and has mountains and virgin forests to explore. **Boracay Island** is another such island paradise, accessible by air via Kalibo, followed by a bus or jeepney ride to Caticlan, and finally by ferry or pumpboat to Boracay. A BMW survey considered its powdery-fine white-sand beach to be amongst the best in the world.

Bohol Island, just across the straits from Cebu in Central Visayas, is the site of some of the country's most fascinating natural wonders; hundreds of limestone hills, some 30m (100ft) high, that in summer, look like oversized chocolate drops, earning them the name '*Chocolate Hills*'. They are situated about 55km (34 miles) northeast of **Tagbilaran City**, the island's capital. Bohol also offers handsome white-sand beaches and pretty secluded coves, accessible via good roads. The island is a coconut-growing area and its local handicrafts are mostly of woven materials: grass mats, hats and baskets. *Baclayon Church* merits a visit, as it is probably the oldest stone church in the Philippines, dating back to 1595. The island can be reached by plane or ferry. The air journey from Cebu to Tagbilaran takes 20 minutes. Ferries go from Cebu to Tagbilaran or Tubigon, another port north of the capital.

Mindanao & the South

Mindanao is the second-largest and the most southerly island, with a very different feel from the rest of the country. A variety of Muslim ethnic groups live here, now concentrated around *Lake Lanao* and **Jolo** in the southernmost islands.

In the southwestern tip of Mindanao is **Zamboanga City,** considered by some as the most romantic place in the Philippines and a favourite resort amongst tourists. The city is noted for its seashells, unspoiled tropical scenery and magnificent flowers. Zamboanga was founded by the Spanish, and the 17th-century walls of *Fort Pilar,* built to protect the Spanish and Christian Filipinos from Muslim onslaughts, are still standing. The city has a number of hotels, cars for hire, good public transport and *vintas* (small boats), often with colourful sails, available to take visitors round the city bay. The *flea market* sells Muslim pottery, clothes and brassware. About 2km (1.2 miles) from Fort Pilar are the houses of the Badjaos, which are stilted constructions on the water. Water gypsies live in boats in this area, moving to wherever the fishing is best. *Plaza Pershing* and *Pasonanca Park* are worth visiting.

Sta Cruz Island has a sand beach which turns pink when the corals from the sea are washed ashore, and is ideal for bathing, snorkelling and scuba diving. There is also an old Muslim burial ground here.

Davao province is the industrial centre of Mindanao, renowned for its pearl and banana exports, as well as its wonderful beaches. **Davao City** is one of the most progressive industrial cities in the country. The province is the site of *Mount Apo,* the highest peak in the country, while the *Apo Range* has spectacular waterfalls, rapids, forests, springs and mountain lakes.

Cagayan de Oro, on the northern coast of Mindanao, is the gateway to some of the most beautiful provinces in the Philippines. By way of contrast, in *Bukidnon* there are huge cattle ranches and the famous Del Monte pineapple fields, and *Iligan City* is the site of the hydroelectric complex driven by the *Maria Cristina Falls.*

Lanao del Sur is the province where Muslim people, known as the Maranaos, live by the shores of *Lake Lanao*. Other attractions include *Signal Hill; Sacred Mountain;* the native market, *Torongan;* homes of the Maranao royalty; the various Muslim mosques on the shores of the lake; and examples of the famous brassware industry centred in *Tugaua.*

SOCIAL PROFILE

FOOD & DRINK: Unlike a lot of Asian cooking, Filipino cuisine is distinguished by its moderate use of spices. Chinese, Malay, Spanish, Japanese and American influences have all left their mark in a subtle blending of cultures and flavours. Naturally, seafoods feature strongly, freshly harvested and often simply grilled, boiled, fried or steamed and served with *kalamansi* (the local lemon), *bagoong* (a fish paste) or vinegar with *labuyo* (the fiery native pepper). Restaurants specialising in seafoods abound, offering crabs, lobsters, prawns, oysters, tuna, freshwater fish, *bangus* (the bony but prized milkfish) and the sweet *maliputo*, found in deep-water lakes. The *lechon* (roasted whole pig) is prepared for fiestas and family celebrations. Other delightful specialities include *kare-kare* (an oxtail stew in peanut sauce served with bagoong), *sinigang* (meat or fish in a pleasantly sour broth) and *adobo* (braised pork and chicken, in tangy soy sauce, vinegar and garlic). Among the regional dishes, the Ilocos region's *pinakbet* (vegetables sauteed with pork and bagoong), Central Luzon's *relleno* (boned and stuffed chicken or fish) and the Visayas' *kinilaw* (raw fish marinated in a spicy vinegar dressing) top the list. Rice is a staple substance of the Filipino cuisine. Fruit is plentiful with mangoes, papayas, bananas, chicos, lanzones, guavas and rambutans. Philippine food preserves like *atsara* (a chutney-like vegetable preserve) and the numerous native desserts like the *pili nut brittle* (a crunchy sweet made with the luscious pili nuts found only in the Bicol region) can be purchased in local markets. All the regional dishes are available in Manila's excellent restaurants which, like the restaurants of all the main towns, offer a varied cuisine. For the less adventurous, there are also European-style restaurants and American fast food. Restaurants are generally informal, with table service.

Drink: Alcoholic drinks include locally brewed beer and the delicious Philippine rum. The local San Miguel beer is considered one of the best in the world. Waiter service is common in bars. There are no strict regulations regarding the sale of alcohol.

NIGHTLIFE: The choice of entertainment in Manila displays the Filipino's affinity for music. 5-star hotels offer everything from high-tech discos to lavish cultural songs and dances, as well as superb pop singers and performers, trios, show bands and classical string ensembles. On most evenings there are cultural performances by local artists or foreign groups at the many other venues for the performing arts. Free concerts are offered by several parks every week, and occasionally by banks and other corporations. The Philippines also have some unusual musical groups like the Pangwat Kawayan bamboo orchestra, which uses bamboo musical instruments, and the Rondalla group which uses tiny guitars like the ukelele. Casinos are located in Manila, Cebu, Zamboanga, Iloilo and Davao.

SHOPPING: The Philippines are a haven for shoppers. Countless bargain opportunities for the handicrafts of the different regions are found in the numerous

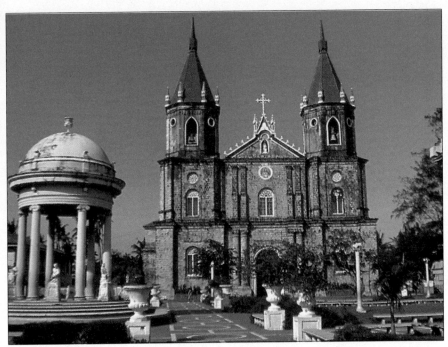

Molo Church, Iloilo City

Jeepney

shopping complexes, which range from sleek air-conditioned department stores and malls to open-air bazaars. The chain stores offer everything from the famous *barong tagalong* (hand-embroidered dress shirts for men in delicate *jusi* material) to Tiffany lamps made with capiz shells. But for local colour there's nothing like going to the flea markets where shoppers can find all kinds of cloth weaves, brassware from the south, woodcarvings and other local crafts, as well as rare seashells and other souvenirs. Some particularly good buys are the silver jewellery from Baguio, coral trinket boxes, rattan furniture, baskets in different designs, woven grass mats (*banig*), antique wooden figurines of saints, ready-to-wear clothes, garments embroidered with the traditional callado, Filipino dresses for women (usually made from banana and pineapple fibres), cigars and *abaca* placemats. Handicraft stores are found everywhere in the country, especially in cities. Large department stores sell both local and foreign manufactured goods. **Shopping hours:** 0900-1930 Monday to Saturday. Most department stores and supermarkets are open Sunday.
SPORT: Golf: Golf is popular in larger cities. There is a municipal golf course and driving range in Manila and also a miniature golf course. Most golf courses are designed by world-renowned golf architects and are equipped with amenities not just for golfers, but for non-golfers as well. Country clubs usually allow visitors to play on invitation from members; alternatively hotel staff can make arrangements. **Scuba & snorkelling:** The Philippines' crystal clear waters, tropical climate, colourful coral reefs, marine life and hospitable islands make it a rare diver's paradise, with adventures ranging from resort-based to extended trips on luxury vessels to unexplored areas. The islands of Batangas, Cebu, Mindoro (particularly Apo Reef Marine Park) and Palawan offer some of the best diving sites in the country. **Boating:** *Bancas* (canoes) can be rented at all beaches. **Swimming:** Beaches and pools are ubiquitous. **Tennis:** Courts are available in most major cities and resorts. **Fishing:** The Philippines' warm waters, measuring almost 2,000,000 sq km (772,200 sq miles) of fishing grounds, rank 12th in worldwide fish production. These grounds are inhabited by some 2400 fish species, including many game fish such as giant tuna, tanguingue, king mackerel, great barracuda, swordfish and marlins. Local tour operators in Manila will help with excursions. Game fishing is best from December to August. **Spectator sports:** **Basketball** is popular all year round. **Horseracing, football, American baseball, cock-fighting** and **boxing** are also popular. A unique game is **Sipa**, played with a small wicker ball, which the visitor can watch in Manila at the Rizal Court.
SPECIAL EVENTS: Dozens of colourful festivals are celebrated in the Philippines each year. A comprehensive listing, including all important Muslim festivals and Catholic feast days in honour of patron saints etc, may be obtained from the Department of Tourism. The following is a list of some of the major events in the Philippines:
Mar '95 *Holy Week Lenten Rituals* (nationwide);

Moriones (street drama festival), Boac, Mogpop, Gasan and Marinduque. **Apr** *Turumba* (flower festival), Pakil and Laguna. **May** *Santacruzan and Flores de Mayo Festival* (nationwide); *Carabao Festival,* Pulilan and Bulacan; *Pahiyas* (parades and flower decorations), Lucban and Sariaya; *Obando Fertility Rites,* Obando and Bulacan. **Jun** *Parada Ng Lechon* (roast pig feast), Balayan and Batangas. **Jul** *Pagoda Sa Wawa* (water parade), Balayan and Batangas. **Aug** *Kadayawan Sa Dabaw* (street dancing and tribal shows), Davao City. **Sep** *Nuestra Señora de Penafrancia* (religious parade), Naga City and Camarines Sur. **Oct** *Masskara Festival,* Bacolod City and Negros Occidental. **Nov** *All Saints' Day* (nationwide). **Dec** *Simbang Gabi* (Dawn masses); *Giant Lantern Festival,* San Fernando and Pampanga. **Jan '96** *Ati-Atihan Carnival,* Kalibo; *Sinulog Festival,* Cebu; *Nazareno* (religious festival), Quiapo and Metro Manila. **Feb** *Paraw Regatta,* Iloilo.
SOCIAL CONVENTIONS: Government officials are addressed by their titles such as Senator, Congressman or Director. Otherwise, usual modes of address and levels of politeness are expected. Casual dress is acceptable in most places, but in Muslim areas the visitor should cover up. Filipino men may wear an embroidered long-sleeved shirt or a plain white barong tagalog with black trousers for formal occasions. The Philippines are, in many respects, more Westernised than any other Asian country, but there is a rich underlay of Malaysian culture. **Tipping:** Usually 10% of the bill. Hotels generally have a 15% service charge.

BUSINESS PROFILE

ECONOMY: The Philippine economy is basically agricultural, with rice, corn, coconut including copra, sugar cane and bananas as the main crops. But the country is fast moving towards industrialisation with the Government providing the stimulus through an ever-improving package of fiscal incentives. Five government export processing zones and 23 private sector industrial estates are in operation. On top of that, Subic, which had once been an important base for the US Navy, is now being converted into a special economic zone. Manufacturing is increasingly geared towards production for export and the country's growing presence in the world markets is seen in its exports of semi-conductors, garments, furniture, giftware and food products, among a host of others. The Government's main economic concern has been to reschedule repayment of the country's considerable foreign debt. The Philippines has a trade surplus with most of its major trading partners, including the USA, the UK, The Netherlands, Japan and Taiwan (China)615. Drilling for oil is underway, and it is estimated that the country's oil production, which is now about 14,000 barrels a day, could leap to 270,000 barrels a day by the year 2000.
BUSINESS: The weather is almost uniformly warm and humid and so short-sleeved shirts, preferably with a tie, can be worn for business visits. However, with most offices being air-conditioned, it is best to wear safari

suits or a long-sleeved Filipino *barong tagalog* when visiting top business officials and executives. Prior appointments are necessary and it is customary to exchange business cards. Filipinos have an American business style and English is widely spoken. Best months for business visits are October to November and January to May. Unless one has urgent business matters to attend to, business visits during December (ie Christmas) are not recommended as delays tend to be unavoidable. **Office hours:** These vary. Usually 0800-1200 and 1300-1700 Monday to Friday. Some private sector offices are open 0800-1200 Saturday.
COMMERCIAL INFORMATION: The following organisations can offer advice: Philippine Trade and Investment Promotion Office, 1A Cumberland House, Kensington Court, London W8 5NX. Tel: (0171) 937 1898. Fax: (0171) 937 2747; *or*
Philippine Chamber of Commerce and Industry, Ground Floor, CCP Complex, Roxas Boulevard, Makati, Metro Manila 2801. Tel: (2) 833 8591 *or* 832 0309. Fax: (2) 816 1946. Telex: 62042.
CONFERENCES/CONVENTIONS: 102 establishments belong to the Philippine Convention and Visitors Corporation (PCVC). It has US offices in New York, as well as in Sydney and Tokyo. For further general information, contact the Philippine Convention and Visitors Corporation (for address, see top of entry).

CLIMATE

Tropical climate tempered by constant sea breezes. There are three distinct seasons: the rainy season (June to September), cool and dry (October to February), and hot and mainly dry (March to May). Evenings are cooler. Typhoons occasionally occur from June to September.
Required clothing: Lightweight cottons and linens are worn throughout most of the year, with warmer clothes useful on cooler evenings. Rainwear or umbrellas are advisable for the rainy season.

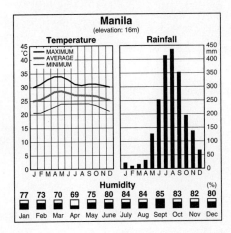

Manila
(elevation: 16m)

	Jan	Feb	Mar	Apr	May	June	July	Aug	Sept	Oct	Nov	Dec
Humidity (%)	77	73	70	69	75	80	84	84	85	83	82	80

☐ *international airport*

St Mary's Street, Gdansk

Location: Central Europe.

State, Sports and Tourism Administration
12 Swietokrzyska Street, 00-916 Warsaw, Poland
Tel: (22) 263 787 *or* 694 4433. Fax: (2) 694 5176. Telex: 816560.

Embassy of the Republic of Poland
47 Portland Place, London W1N 3AG
Tel: (0171) 580 4324/9. Fax: (0171) 323 4018. Telex: 265691 (a/b POLAMB G). Opening hours: 0830-1630 Monday to Friday.

Consulate General of the Republic of Poland
73 New Cavendish Street, London W1M 7RB
Tel: (0171) 580 0476. Fax: (0171) 323 2320. Opening hours: 1000-1400 Monday to Friday, except Wednesday 1000-1200. Telephone enquiries: 0830-1630 Monday to Friday.

Polish National Tourist Office
First Floor, Remo House, 310-312 Regent Street, London W1R 5AJ
Tel: (0171) 580 8811. Fax: (0171) 580 8866. Opening hours: 1000-1700 Monday to Friday.

LOT – Polish Airlines
313 Regent Street, London W1R 7PE
Tel: (0171) 580 5037. Fax: (0171) 323 0774.

British Embassy
Aleja Róz 1, 00-556 Warsaw, Poland
Tel: (2) 628 1001/2/3/4/5. Fax: (22) 217 161. Telex: 813694 (a/b PROD PL).

Embassy of the Republic of Poland
2640 16th Street, NW, Washington, DC 20009
Tel: (202) 234 3800/1/2. Fax: (202) 328 6271.

Polish National Tourist Office
Suite 224, 333 North Michigan Avenue, Chicago, IL 60601

Tel: (312) 236 9013. Fax: (312) 236 1125.
or
Suite 1711, 275 Madison Avenue, New York, NY 10016
Tel: (212) 338 9412. Fax: (212) 338 9283.
Also deals with enquiries from Canada.
Embassy of the United States of America
PO Box 5010, Aleja Ujazdowskie 29/31, 00-540 Warsaw, Poland
Tel: (2) 628 3041. Fax: (2) 628 8298. Telex: 817771 (a/b EMUSA PL).
Consulates in: Kraków and Poznan.
Embassy of the Republic of Poland
443 Daly Avenue, Ottawa, Ontario K1N 6H3
Tel: (613) 789 0468 *or* 789 3376/7. Fax: (613) 789 1218.
Consulates in: Montréal, Toronto and Vancouver.
Canadian Embassy
Ulica Matejki 1/5, 00-481 Warsaw, Poland
Tel: (22) 298 051. Fax: (22) 296 457.

AREA: 312,685 sq km (120,728 sq miles).
POPULATION: 38,418,100 (1992 estimate).
POPULATION DENSITY: 122.9 per sq km.
CAPITAL: Warsaw. **Population:** 1,644,500 (1992 estimate).
GEOGRAPHY: Poland shares borders to the north with the Baltic Sea, to the east with the Russian Federation, Belarus, Ukraine and Lithuania, to the south with the Czech Republic and the Slovak Republic and to the west with Germany. The Baltic coast provides over 500km (300 miles) of sandy beaches, bays, steep cliffs and dunes. Northern Poland is dominated by lakes, islands and wooded hills joined by many rivers and canals. The Mazurian Lake District to the northeast is particularly beautiful. Lake Hancza, the deepest lake in Poland, is located in this district. The River Vistula has cut a wide valley from Gdansk on the Baltic coast to Warsaw in the heart of the country. The rest of the country rises slowly to the Sudety Mountains which run along the border with the Czech Republic. To the west, the River Oder, with Szczecin at its mouth, forms the northwest border with Germany.
LANGUAGE: Polish is the official language. Many foreign languages are also spoken.
RELIGION: 95% Roman Catholic; other religions include Greek Orthodox, Russian Orthodox, Protestant, Jewish and Muslim.
TIME: GMT + 1 (GMT + 2 from last Sunday in March to Saturday before last Sunday in September).
ELECTRICITY: 220 volts AC, 50Hz; Continental sockets.
COMMUNICATIONS: Telephone: Full IDD is available. Country code: 48. Outgoing international code: 00. Cheap rate on long-distance calls is available from 1600-0600. Tokens can be purchased from post offices for local calls. **Telex/telegram:** Telex services are available at *Foreign Trade Enterprises* and *Urzad Pocztowy* in Warsaw, 24 hours a day. *Orbis* hotels also provide services. Telegram services are provided at all main post offices and by phone. **Post:** Service to Western Europe takes up to four days. *Poste Restante* facilities are available at post offices throughout the country. Post office hours: 0800-1800 Monday to Friday. **Press:** Independent publications are flourishing following the changes in the political system; about 100 newspapers are now available. The principal dailies are *Gazeta Wyborcza, Rzeczpospolita* and *Zycie Warszawy.*
BBC World Service and Voice of America frequencies: From time to time these change. See the section *How to Use this Book* for more information.
BBC:

MHz:	15.07	12.09	6.195	3.955
Voice of America:				
MHz	9.670	6.040	5.995	1.197

PASSPORT/VISA

Regulations and requirements may be subject to change at short notice, and you are advised to contact the appropriate diplomatic or consular authority before finalising travel arrangements. Details of these may be found at the head of this country's entry. Any numbers in the chart refer to the footnotes below.

	Passport Required?	Visa Required?	Return Ticket Required?
Full British	Yes	No/1	No
BVP	Not valid	-	-
Australian	Yes	Yes	No
Canadian	Yes	Yes	No
USA	Yes	No	No
Other EU (As of 31/12/94)	Yes	No/2	No
Japanese	Yes	Yes	No

PASSPORTS: Valid passport required by all.
British Visitors Passport: Not accepted.

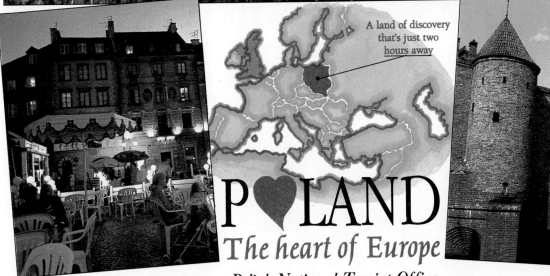

VISAS: Required by all except:
(a) **[1]** nationals of the UK for tourist or business visits not exceeding 6 months;
(b) **[2]** nationals of Belgium, Denmark, France, Germany, Italy, Luxembourg, The Netherlands, Ireland, Portugal and Spain for visits not exceeding 3 months (except nationals of Greece who *do* require a visa);
(c) nationals of Andorra, Argentina, Austria, Costa Rica, Croatia, Cyprus, Czech Republic, Finland, Iceland, Liechtenstein, Latvia, Lithuania, South Korea, Malta, Monaco, Norway, San Marino, Slovak Republic, Slovenia, Switzerland, Sweden, Uruguay and the USA for visits not exceeding 3 months;
(d) nationals of Bulgaria, Cuba, Estonia, Hungary, Macedonia (FYROM), Mongolia and Romania for visits not exceeding 1 month;
(e) nationals of Hong Kong holding British passports for visits not exceeding 14 days.
Types of visa: *Entry:* £21-37; *Transit:* £10-15 (both Single-entry). Prices vary according to the applicant's

nationality.
Validity: Entry visa valid up to 6 months. Extensions can be arranged in Poland through the district passport office. Transit visas are valid for up to 48 hours.
Application to: Consulate (or Consular section at Embassy). For addresses, see top of entry.
Note: Visas may be obtained on arrival in Poland by nationals of Singapore and Taiwan (China).
Application requirements: (a) Valid passport. (b) Completed application form. (c) 2 passport-size photos. (d) Company letter (where applicable).
Applications for visas not including these requirements will not be considered by the Consular offices and will be returned to the applicant.
Working days required: 7 (tourist); 2 (business).
Temporary residence: Apply to Consulate.

MONEY

Currency: Zloty (Zl) = 100 groszy. On January 1, 1995 the Zloty was devalued by a factor of 10,000. From January 1, 1995, new notes and coins are in operation. The new notes are in denominations of Zl200, 100, 50, 20 and 10. The new coins are in denominations of Zl5, 2 and 1, and 50, 20, 10, 5, 2 and 1 groszy. The old notes (valid until the end of 1997) are in denominations of Zl2,000,000, 1,000,000, 500,000, 100,000, 50,000, 20,000, 10,000, 5000, 2000, 1000, 500, 200 and 100.
Note: Prices in stores will be displayed in both the old and new denominations for the next two years.
Currency exchange: Foreign currency can be exchanged at all border crossing points, hotels and bureaux de change, some of which are open 24 hours. Cash can be

obtained from Visa credit cards from banks.
Credit cards: American Express, Access/Mastercard, Visa and Diners Club are accepted in large establishments. Check with your credit card company for details of merchant acceptability and other services which may be available.
Travellers cheques: Readily exchanged (*but see above*).
Exchange rate indicators: The following figures are included as a guide to the movements of the Zloty against Sterling and the US Dollar:

Date:	Oct '92	Sep '93	Jan '94	Jan '95
£1.00=	23,773	29,553	31,578	*3.80
$1.00=	14,980	19,353	21,344	*2.42

Note [*]: These figures refer to the new Zloty.
Currency restrictions: The import and export of local currency is prohibited. The import of foreign currency is unlimited, provided it is declared on arrival. The export of foreign currency is limited to the balance of amounts declared on arrival.
Banking hours: 0800-1800 Monday to Friday.

DUTY FREE

The following items may be imported into Poland by persons over 18 years of age without incurring customs duty:
250 cigarettes or 50 cigars or 250g tobacco; 2 litres of wine and half a litre of other alcoholic beverage.
Note: (a) Fur, leather and gold articles are subject to customs duty. (b) The export of antiques, works of art and certain other items from Poland is prohibited. (c) A customs declaration must be presented at the border. (d) Firearms and narcotics are prohibited. (e) Duty-free

Cracow – City of Culture and History

Cracow is a medieval treasure, fortunate to have survived the various turmoils of the twentieth century comparatively unscathed. This was officially recognised in 1978 when its historic centre was added to the UNESCO list of World Cultural Heritage Sites. The city also recognises its responsibility for maintaining and restoring what has not withstood the passage of time, and the complex task of renovating the city began some years ago. Currently Kazimierz, the old Jewish quarter, is being renovated to a standard which will enable it to host numerous meetings, cultural events and scientific seminars in the future.

Cracow – a Spiritual and Political Capital

Cracow was the political capital of Poland until the 17th century, and its spiritual capital after Poland was deprived of independence. *Wawel*, the old residence of kings where coronations took place and the site of the royal necropolis, exemplifies both these powerful civic traditions. Wawel Hill was the end of the Royal Road through the city; the marvellous Renaissance *Royal Castle* and the *Cathedral* located on the Hill were central to the nation's political and spiritual life. Most of the Polish monarchs were crowned at the Cathedral which also, from the 14th century, became the final resting place of the Polish kings; after the loss of independence in the 18th century it became a burial place for national heroes such as Tadeusz Koscluszko and Prince Józef Poniatowski; great Romantic national poets such as Adam Mickiewicz and Julisz Slowacki; and military leaders including Marshal Jósef Pilsudski and General Wladyslaw Sikorski. The relics of St Stanislaus, the patron saint of Poland and the Cracow archdiocese, are also entombed here. All in all, the Cathedral has long been a national sanctuary, a symbol of spiritual identity and of national survival despite often overwhelming odds. It is impossible to visit this magnificent building without sharing something of this feeling. The Cathedral also houses the *Sigismund Chapel,* one of the pearls of the northern Renaissance.

A visit to the *Royal Castle* is, likewise, to make a journey back through history, enabling the visitor to experience, layer by layer, successive epochs and their different cultural styles. From its origins as a small Romanesque castle, it was extensively enlarged in the 14th century as a fine Gothic residence; after a serious fire, construction of a Renaissance palace followed with many eminent Italian architects working on the construction. The impressive courtyard with its pillars and arcades was completed in 1536. *Wawel Hill* is undoubtedly something more than just a group of valuable monuments and the site of national culture. Perhaps the word that springs to mind would be 'mystical'. It is believed that under the *Church of St Gereon* there is a sacred stone, *Chakram,* one of the seven sacred stones of the earth, which causes exceptional magnetic activity around the ruins of this Romanesque church.

Cracow also has a rich prehistory, and the grave-mounds of the legendary rulers Krakus and Wanda bear witness to this ancient heritage.

Excavations have revealed the prehistory of the medieval city, the oldest remnants of which date back 100,000 years. The *Chakram* is probably connected with a legendary epoch and its pagan cults.

Cracow – a Journey Through History

The first description of Cracow is to be found in the merchant Ibrahim-Ibn-Jacob's 10th-century account. The town belonged to the Czechs at that time, but it was soon annexed to the Polish state, then ruled by the first Piasts. Cracow later acquired the new function of a capital in the reign of Casimir the Restorer. After the conflict between King Boleslaus the Bold and Bishop Stanislaus Szczepanowski – which ended, in true early medieval style with a martyrdom – the king was forced to flee the country.

In the 11th century the second *Romanesque Cathedral* was built at the foot of Wawel Hill in a settlement called the Circle which constituted the first circle of the future Cracow. Within its borders the Romanesque churches of *St Andrew, St Martin* and *Mary Magdalene* were built. In the 12th century, the churches of *St Adalbert, St Florian* and *St Nicholas* were erected outside the borders of the Circle; while, in the area of the later *Kazimierz* district, the churches of *St Michael Archangel* on the Skalka Hill, *St Jacob* and *St Warzyniec* were constructed. This Romanesque Cracow was destroyed during the Tartar invasion of 1241, an event commemorated every hour of the day by the bugle-call from the tower of *St Mary's Church.*

Medieval Splendour

Cracow gained its civic rights in 1257; the regular pattern of city streets – which largely survives to this day – developed from around that time. The result is a chequered plan of streets centring on the 40,000-square-metre *Market Square,* the largest of its kind in Europe. *Sukiennice,* the medieval Cloth Hall, is situated in its centre and still performs its original commercial function. *St Mary's Church,* with its unique towers, also borders the square. The wonderful Gothic Franciscan and Dominican churches also date from this period.

The unification of Poland by Ladislaus the Short in the 14th century gave fresh impetus to Cracow's cultural development, not least because Wawel became the venue for royal coronations. King Casimir the Great, a noted patron of the arts, founded the satellite towns of *Kazimierz* and *Stradom.* At this time Master Wit Stwosz (Veit Stoss), the Nuremberg craftsman, created a unique masterpiece, the main altar in St Mary's Church, one of the most remarkable achievements of medieval art. The city was encircled by walls with seven gates and 47 towers, fortifications which survived until the 19th century when the Austrian authorities decided to demolish them. *Planty,* the city gardens, were established in their place and they encircle the historic part of the city today, although the *Barbican, St Florian's Gate* and a section of the city walls still survive. The Barbican is one of the gems of European architecture: a circular Gothic structure with seven turrets and battlements for artillery, unconquered until the 19th century when it fell victim to new developments in siege warfare.

Medieval Spiritual Life – *Alma Mater Cracoviensis*

In 1364 Casimir the Great founded *Cracow University,* after Prague the oldest university in Central Europe. The founding college of the Academy is the *Collegium Maius* with a Gothic quadrangle courtyard and galleries. Intellectual life in the University flourished in the 15th century, especially in the fields of mathematics and astronomy: noted teachers included Pawel Wlodkowic, Wojciech of Brudzewo and Nicolaus Copernicus, the creator of the heliocentric theory, who heralded a radical change in the study of science and philosophy.

The Golden Age of Cracow

In 1386, when Ladislaus Jagiello was crowned king of Poland, Cracow became the capital of a state which included ethnic Polish lands as well as much of modern-day Russia and Lithuania.

The royal court played a significant role in shaping cultural and artistic life and in the 15th century the city was the centre of an artistic movement supported by patronage accorded both by King Casimir Jagiellonczyk and the rich urban middle class. Philip Buonaccorsi, an Italian humanist known as Kallimach, and Conrad Celtis, an itinerant philosopher, lived in Cracow at that time. Cracow was indeed a cosmopolitan town with thriving German and Italian communities, as well as many Jews fleeing persecution in Bohemia and Spain.

Italian influence was particularly strong during the reigns of Sigismund the Old and Sigismund Augustus, the last Jagiellonians. Francis of Florence, who supervised the construction of the Renaissance *Royal Castle,* was one of many craftsmen from Italy working in Cracow. The *Sigismund Chapel* also dates from this time.

Cracow the Baroque

With the demise of the Jagiellonian dynasty in 1572, the monarchy became an elective office. Some of the kings thus chosen were not even Polish, a development which allowed ever-more cosmopolitan influences to take root. One such was the flowering of the Baroque. Eminent Italian architects and sculptors moved to Cracow and were responsible for the construction of the *Church of St Peter and St Paul* and the refurbishment of the *Wawel Cathedral.* At the same time the Gothic churches of *Corpus Christi* and *St Mary's* acquired a more Baroque form. The Cracovian Baroque is a fascinating variant of the Roman example of this style.

Nevertheless, the period culminated with the sad – from Cracow's point of view – decision of King Sigismund III to abandon the city as his capital in favour of Warsaw.

Classicist Peace and the Romantic Sturm und Drang

The Cracovian Academy was reformed as a result of the 18th-century Enlightenment, a period which, in turn, left its mark on the architecture of the city. Cultural life continued to thrive. Due to the partitions of the late 18th century the city fell under the control of Austria, remaining a Habsburg possession until 1918. During this period Cracow became the spiritual capital of Poland, assuming an almost mystic role as a focus for national identity, culture and art. At that time Wawel became the burial place for national heroes, and in the Paulite Church, situated on Skalka Hill, the National Pantheon was created in the 19th century. The tombs of such national figures as J. Dlugosz, S. Wyspianski, J. Malczewski and K. Szymanowski can be found here.

Cracow under the Influence of Modernism

Despite falling under Austrian control, the city enjoyed considerable freedom and, together with the Galicia Region to which it belonged, acquired autonomy. The links between Cracow and Vienna were to prove to be exceptionally significant, due in part to the short distance between these two cultural centres. Cracow was able to embrace a revolution in art which disentangled itself from the influence of the past to strike out in new directions. Impressionism, expressionism and naturalism left their marks on the works of art of that period.

The Second World War – A Struggle for Survival

The Second World War, though it did not destroy the historic structure of the city, nevertheless caused great devastation and disruption – and not only to the buildings. Human life paid a vastly more terrible toll. From 1939 many people, including professors of the Jagiellonian University and the most eminent members of the intellectual élite of the city, were sent to the concentration camps of Sachsenhausen and Auschwitz.

The brunt of the hardships of this time fell on the inhabitants of the Jewish Quarter of *Kazimierz*, a district with an architectural and cultural tradition as rich as any in the city.

Kazimierz – The Mystical District of Cracow

In 1335 the area of Kazimierz, which had been laid out beyond the Vistula River on the site of an old medieval settlement, was granted civic rights by King Casimir the Great. The period of prosperity for Kazimerz lasted till the middle of the 16th century. After Cracow, it was the second richest town in Poland. In 1494 the king ordained that the Jews were to leave the area of the city and move to Kazimierz, on the pretext of their having caused the great fire. The persecutions of Jews in Europe led to Kazimierz becoming a dwelling area for Jews from all over the continent. In the 16th century a significant cultural centre emerged here; later, an *oppidum Iudaecorum*

was included in the Cracow district of Kazimierz. The oldest synagogue in Poland, dating from the 15th century, can still be seen in Józefa Street. The main hall of prayers within part of the 16th century structure has been preserved. Nowadays the Old Synagogue houses the Jewish Museum. The Poper's Baroque Synagogue stands in Szeroka Street and the Remuh Synagogue opposite: the adjacent Remuh Cemetery was founded in 1553. Szeroka Street, once called Great Street, was the central street of Kazimierz, and here the Old Synagogue and the Landaus House are to be found. The action of Steven Spielberg's Oscar-winning film Schindler's List takes place in Cracow and was shot in the Cracovian Kazimierz. Spielberg decided to reconstruct the Cracow Ghetto in Szeroka and adjacent streets, and to present the lives of Cracow Jews in the actual ghetto (built in the Podgórze district in 1941), and its tragic destruction in 1943, as a result of which the centuries-old Jewish community was almost totally exterminated.

ECOS is a revitalisation programme for Kazimierz and is being carried out in co-operation with Berlin and Edinburgh with the objective of enhancing the infrastructure and standard of accommodation while simultaneously improving the historic urban structure of the district. The City Council also works closely with the Jewish community to revitalise the area.

Treasures of the Past

Cracow is a city housing several unique museum collections, a treasure-house of numerous gems of both Polish and foreign cultures. The *State Art Collection* at Wawel Castle contains a collection of precious national treasures and works of art which are exhibited in the Royal Chambers, the Royal Treasury and the Armoury. One of its most precious exhibits is a collection of 136 16th-century Flemish tapestries commissioned by Sigismund Augustus, the last Jagiellonian monarch. Priceless paintings of Italian, Dutch and Flemish masters are exhibited in the Renaissance chambers of the Royal Castle. Other displays include a rare collection of 17th-century Turkish tents and gold artefacts. The *Szczerbiec*, the coronation sword of the Polish kings, provides the crowning touch to the exhibition.

The origins of the *Museum of the Jagiellonian University* date back to the year 1400 when gifts from Queen Jadwiga initiated the collection. The renovated interiors of the *Cracow Academy* house a fascinating collection of astronomical instruments including a 15th-century globe probably used by Nicolaus Copernicus during his studies at the Jagiellonian University, as well as a collection of sceptres and the insignia of the rectors of the Jagiellonian University.

The exhibition *History and Culture of Cracow* in the *Historic Museum of the City of Cracow* at the *Krzysztofory Palace* provides valuable insights into the city's rich past. There is a branch of the museum in the *Kazimierz Synagogue*, which specialises in the history of the Cracow Jews, while the 15th-century *House at the Cross* in Szczepanska Street concerns itself with the history of the Cracow theatre.

The *National Museum* has one of the largest art collections in Poland. The exhibits are shown in several branches of the museum: 1) *The Main*

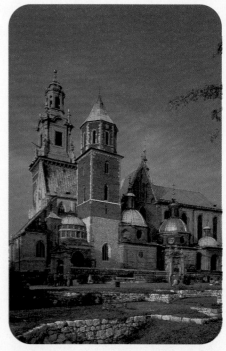

Building: Polish art and culture from the Middle Ages to the 19th century, with a gallery of the Polish art of the 20th century. 2) *The Cloth Hall* in the Main Market Square: a gallery of Polish 19th-century paintings, including works by Jan Matejko such as *The Ceremony of the Grand Master of the Teutonic Order Swearing Allegiance to King Sigismund the Old of Poland* and *The Battle of Grunwald*. 3) *The House of Jan Matejko* in Florianska Street and the *Stanislaw Wyspiánski Museum* in 9 Kanonicza Street. In the *Czartoryski Museum* in 19 Jana Street is a collection which includes Leonardo da Vinci's *Lady with an Ermine* and Rembrandt's *Landscape with a Good Samaritan*. Recently Cracow posseses a unique collection of Eastern art – almost five thousand wood-block prints, Japanese and Chinese paintings, tapestries, clothing and military accessories – as a result of a donation made in 1903 by Feliks Mangha Jasinski, an art expert and collector. Only recently the collection was properly exhibited at the *Centre of Japanese Art*. Andrzej Wajda allocated his Kyoto prize for the creation of the *Kyoto-Cracow Foundation*, the objective of which was opening the Centre of Japanese Art.

Contemporary Artistic Life in the City of Tradition and History

The city hosts numerous international events, including: The Days of Organ Music; Tyniec Organ Recitals; The International Festival of Organ Music; Music in Old Cracow; The Festival of Guitar Music; Jazz Juniors; Shanties; The Cracow Theatre Reminiscences; The International Triennial of Graphics; The Festival of Jewish Culture; The International Festival of Short Films. Notable events in 1994 included The Matejko Days; The Centenary of the Slowacki Theatre and the Krzysztof Penderecki Days of Music.

June sees the festival of culture known as The Days of Cracow which keeps many medieval traditions alive. This magical spectacle, full of lights and fireworks, ends with the sight of wreaths being floated down the Vistula at the foot of Wawel Hill.

Lajkonik is a Cracovian festivity commemorating the defeat of the invading Tartars in the 13th century which partially destroyed the city. The procession goes from the *Norbertine Convent* in the *Zwierzyniec* district to the *Main Market Square* and commemorates the deeds of the rafter of Zwierzyniec who killed a Tartar commander and entered the city in his attire. The Cracovian Christmas cribs are a unique curiosity of the city, and can be seen in December at the foot of the *Adam Mickiewcz Monument* in the Main Market Square. The May Procession of Corpus Christi between Wawel Cathedral and the Church at *Skalka* is also an exceptionally picturesque ceremony. The whole episcopate and a group of believers, some in their regional costume, take part.

The first public performance at the *Cracow Opera* took place in 1792. Many eminent singers have graced its stage, including Ada Sari, Adam Didur and Jan Kiepura. Teresa Zylis-Gara and Wieslaw Ochman began their careers here.

A group of notable contemporary Polish composers, often referred to as the Cracow School, is connected with the Academy of Music. Krzysztof Penderecki is one of its most celebrated representatives.

There are four large classical orchestras. *The Cracow Philharmonic* is world-famous and has featured a number of equally world-famous soloists including Witold Malcuzynski, Swiatoslaw Richter, Arthur Rubinstein and Isaac Stern. Krzysztof Penderecki, the outstanding Polish composer and conductor, has performed with the orchestra. The *Orchestra of the Polish Radio in Cracow,* established in 1947, performs symphonic and chamber concerts. Two more recent additions to the musical life of the city is the *Capella Cracoviensis*, founded in 1970 by Stanislaw Galonski; and the *Sinfonietta Cracovia*, founded in 1993.

The following are the most important of the City's numerous theatres:

The *Old (Stary) Theatre,* established in 1799, is one of the oldest in the country. The 19th century was its heyday, when it promoted a revolutionary style of acting with performances by such noted thespians as Helena Modrzejewska. After the war it became one of the best theatres in Poland, staging work by Jerzy Grotowski, Jerzy Jarocki and Lidia Zamkow amongst others. In the 1960s three great directors – Jarocki, Konrad Swinarski and Andrzej Wajda – began their major contributions to the Cracow stage. Since then, a new generation of talent has emerged with the likes of Krystian Lupa, Krzysztof Babicki and Tadeusz Bradecki.

The magnificent building of the *Slowacki Theatre* was inspired by the Paris Opera House: it has recently been completely restored. The theatre, which was opened in 1893, was regarded as a national stage and remarkable actors such as Ludwik Solski have performed here. The theatre has always striven to blend tradition with innovation. The personality most closely associated with the avant-garde theatre

was the director and writer Tadeusz Kantor many of whose performances were staged in the cellars at Kanonicza Street. His world-famous *Cricot 2* company explored new techniques and philosophies though his visionary blending of fantasy and reality.

The *Stu Theatre* represents, to some extent, a new type of repertory theatre. The theatre stages musicals, mini-operas and performances based on ritual customs, and also has a unique collection of paintings. The Stu Theatre initiates many artistic events on the borders of different categories of art. To complete this varied picture one should also mention the *KTO Theatre*, noted for its street performances. These may often be seen in the *Main Market Square.* Street entertainment of a less formal kind is to be found throughout the city, from mime artists and jugglers to itinerant musicians and traditional folk dancers.

Cracow has also its 'underground', a vast network of historic cellars many of which have been converted to play host to a veritable cultural labyrinth of night life. Jazz, theatres, cabarets, satirical revues, folk music – all this and more can be found beneath the ancient city streets. Perhaps the most famous is the *Rams Cellar*, where Ewa Demarczyk – the 'Black Angel of Polish Song' – began her career. Such noted contemporary Polish composers as Zygmunt Konieczny, Zbigniew Preisner and Zbigniew Raj began their great careers in these cellars. The 'Cracow underground' is also the scene of many cultural events of a more historical nature, such as the ceremony commemorating the Grand Master of the tutonic Order swearing allegiance to King Sigismund the Old of Poland, enacted in authentic Renaissance dress.

Towards the Future

Cracow is in every way well placed to regain its position as one of the principal cities of Central Europe. In addition to its intellectual, historical and cultural traditions the city is also seeking to carve out a new role for itself, that of a modern international meeting-place. During the next decade Cracow hopes to have established itself as the seat of several pan-national organisations such as the Eastern Europe Section of the European Community. The city is already a member of many international bodies, including the League of European Cities, Eurocities and the revitalised Hanseatic League (an association of over 100 towns in the Baltic and Black Sea area, echoing the medieval trading union of that name). Recent major international events hosted in Cracow include the Symposium of the Conference on Security and European Co-operation in 1991 and the Month of European Culture in 1992. 1996 will see the city welcome delegates at the 5th International Conference of Historic Cities, while hopes are high that the millenium year 2000 will be celebrated with Cracow being designated the City of European Culture.

These two events can stand as a symbol of the different perspectives the city of Cracow enjoys, looking equally towards the past, the present and the future. Cracow is a city aware of, but not trapped by, its rich past. The present is one of excitement and vitality. As for the future, to the end of the century and beyond – who can tell? Without doubt it promises to be a time of prosperity and achievement. Whatever the reason for your visit, we look forward to your being able to share this future with us!

By Joanna Trzos, Promotion and Offers Bureau, Municipality of Cracow

Promotion and Offers Bureau, Municipality of Cracow, Mr. Jacek Kowalski PL Wszystkich Swietych 3/4, 31-004, Cracow. Tel: 48-12 161-526/7. Tel/fax: 48-12 22-55-31.

shops are located at border crossing points. Payment for purchases can be made either in foreign or local currency, travellers cheques or credit cards.

PUBLIC HOLIDAYS

Jan 1 '95 New Year's Day. **Apr 17** Easter Monday. **May 1** Labour Day. **May 3** Polish National Day. **May 9** Victory Day. **Jun 15** Corpus Christi. **Aug 15** Assumption. **Nov 1** All Saints' Day. **Nov 11** Independence Day. **Dec 25-26** Christmas. **Jan 1 '96** New Year's Day. **Apr 8** Easter Monday.

HEALTH

Regulations and requirements may be subject to change at short notice, and you are advised to contact your doctor well in advance of your intended date of departure. Any numbers in the chart refer to the footnotes below.

	Special Precautions?	Certificate Required?
Yellow Fever	No	No
Cholera	No	No
Typhoid & Polio	No	-
Malaria	No	-
Food & Drink	1	-

[1]: Mains water is normally chlorinated, and whilst relatively safe may cause mild abdominal upsets. Bottled water is available and is advised for the first few weeks of the stay. Milk is pasteurised and dairy products are safe for consumption. Local meat, poultry, seafood, fruit and vegetables are generally considered safe to eat. *Rabies* is present. For those at high risk, vaccination before arrival should be considered. If you are bitten abroad seek medical advice without delay. For more information, consult the *Health* section at the back of the book.
Health care: There are Reciprocal Health Agreements with most European countries for hospital treatment and medical expenses. The Agreement with the UK allows free medical treatment (including hospital treatment) and some free dental treatment on presentation of an NHS card. UK citizens must, however, pay a call-out charge as well as 30% of the cost of prescribed medicines obtained at a public pharmacy.

TRAVEL - International

AIR: Poland's national airline is *LOT Polish Airlines (LOT).*
Approximate flight times: From Warsaw to *London* is 2 hours 30 minutes, to *Frankfurt/M* is 1 hour 50 minutes, and to *Prague* is 1 hour 10 minutes.
International airports: *Warsaw (WAW)* (Okecie) is 10km (6 miles) southwest of the city (travel time – 40 minutes by bus; 15 minutes by taxi). Full duty-free facilities are available. Airport facilities include bureaux de change (0800-2000), tourist information and car rental (*Avis* and *Orbis*). Taxis are available. A bus departs every 25 minutes from 0500-2300.
Cracow (KRK) (Balice) is 18km (10 miles) from the city centre. Buses and taxis are available. There are no duty-free facilities.
Wroclaw (WRO) (Strachowice) is 8km (5 miles) from the city centre. Buses and taxis are available. Duty-free facilities are also available. There is a daily connection to Frankfurt/M and twice-weekly (Thursday and Sunday) to Düsseldorf.
SEA: *Polish Ocean Lines* operates from Europe, South America, Middle East, North Africa and South East Asia to Gdynia. For further information, telephone (0171) 251 3389 (UK) *or* (514) 393 9100 (Canada).
RAIL: All services from Western Europe to Poland pass through Germany, the Czech Republic or the Slovak Republic. Main routes are Berlin–Warsaw–Moscow; Paris–Warsaw; and from Vienna, Budapest and Prague to Warsaw. There is a car-sleeper service from the Hook of Holland to Poznan/Warsaw (see below). Since May 31 1993, EuroCity trains have started running from Berlin to Warsaw.
ROAD: Poland is best reached from Germany and the Czech Republic or the car-sleeper rail service from the Hook of Holland to Poznan/Warsaw. There are extensive **bus** and **coach** services.

TRAVEL - Internal

AIR: All internal airlines are operated by *LOT (Polish Airlines)* and there is a comprehensive network linking all major cities. For details of routes and fares contact *LOT* offices (see top of entry).
RAIL: *Polish State Railway (PKP)* services link all parts of the country in a network radiating from Warsaw.

Top picture: Mazurian Lakes. Above: The Royal Kazienki Palace.

On the warmer side of the Baltic

at the point where the hills drop gently into the sea, surrounded by forests so beautiful as to be compared only with the wilderness of Canada, located between Gdańsk and Gdynia you will find the town of Sopot. This is where one hundred years ago the German Rilke fell in love. In a remote manor house Schopenhauer wrote his works. People from all over Germany travelled to the Wagner festivals held in the Opera located in the depths of

the forest. The crowned heads and the world's richest organized horse races, tennis tournaments, yachting races, convalesced and won fortunes in the casinos.

Klaus Kinski, a man who never stopped challenging the world, was born here.

Nowadays you and your friends can also holiday here in Sopot, without spending a fortune, any time of the year.

Sopot – the most beautiful turn-of-the-century resort in Northern Europe

SOPOT

45 thousand inhabitants, the longest wooden pier in Europe (512m): a 4 km long sandy beach; over 3,000 accommodation places, a rock and pop music festival in August; a casino; numerous restaurants, cafes, pubs, night clubs and bars; 6 galleries, 3 theatres, 2 cinemas; mineral water health spas, a tennis court complex, a stud farm,

SOPOT

a horse racing course, a covered horse arena; water sports equipment for hire, a 110 m high hill and ski lift, 42 km of marked footpaths located in the forested hilly moraine, numerous cultural (concerts), sporting and entertainment events, 20 minutes ride by taxi from the airport terminal, 25 minutes from the ferry terminal.

Sopot Town Council, ul. Kościuszki 25/27, Tel. +48 (0) 58 51 23 22, 51 11 78, fax 51 26 87

There are two classes of travel. Reservations are required on express trains. The 'Polrailpass' is available for 8, 15, 21 or 30 days. This pass is available from Polorbis, travel agents and international rail ticket outlets, as well as from railway stations and travel agents within Poland. Intercity express trains are cheap and efficient. Children under four years of age travel free. Children aged 4-10 pay half fare.

ROAD: Traffic drives on the right. Unleaded petrol is available in all major cities and a full list of filling stations can be obtained from the Polish National Tourist Office. The Polish motoring club *Polski Zwiazek Motorowy (PZM)* can be called on 981 nationwide for assistance. For further information, contact Polski Zwiazek Motorowy, Ulica Kazimierzowska 66, 02-518 Warsaw. Tel: (22) 499 361. **Bus:** There are good regional bus and coach services operated by *Polish Motor Communications (PKS)* connecting most towns. **Car hire:** Self-drive cars are available at the airport or through various car rental offices in town centres. The minimum age is 21. Charges are usually based on a daily rate plus a kilometre charge. **Regulations:** The speed limit is 60kmph (38mph) in built-up areas, 90kmph (57mph) on major roads and 110kmph (69mph) on motorways. Seat belts and warning triangles are compulsory. Trams have the right of way.

Documentation: Tourists travelling in their own cars should have car registration cards, their national driving licence and valid Green Card motor insurance. An International Driving Permit is recommended, although not legally required.

URBAN: Bus: There are good services in all towns, with additional trams and trolleybuses operating in a dozen of the larger urban areas. Warsaw has bus, tramway and rail services. A flat fare is charged and there are pre-purchase tickets and passes. **Tram:** 7-day tourist tickets can be purchased. In 1983, trolleybuses were reintroduced on one route and construction was begun on a metro. Most public transport operates from 0530-2300. **Taxi:** These are available in all main towns. They are usually found at ranks or phoned. There is a surcharge from 2300-0500 and for journeys out of town as well as for weekends. Taxi drivers may insist on payment in hard currency. **Tipping** is not necessary.

JOURNEY TIMES: The following chart gives approximate journey times (in hours and minutes) from Warsaw to other major cities/towns in Poland.

	Air	Road	Rail
Cracόw	1.40	4.00	4.00
Poznan	1.00	4.00	3.00
Wroclaw	1.15	6.00	6.00
Gdansk	1.00	6.00	5.00
Szczecin	2.00	8.00	6.45
Katowice	1.30	4.30	4.00
Lódz	-	2.00	2.00

ACCOMMODATION

HOTELS: Hotels in Poland are run by Forte, Intercontinental, Marriott, Novotel, Holiday Inn and Orbis, amongst others. International Student Hotels offer better facilities than youth hostels and are inexpensive, comfortable and pleasant. **Grading:** Hotels in Poland are graded in five categories: luxury, 4-star, 3-star, 2-star and 1-star. In addition there are tourist hotels, boarding houses and motels, each graded into three or four categories.

GUEST-HOUSES: Three categories are available in all towns and run by regional tourist boards. Reservations can be made from local offices.

CAMPING/CARAVANNING: There are over 200 campsites in Poland, nearly 75% of which are fitted with 220-volt powerpoints and several with 24-volt points for caravans. Facilities also include washrooms, canteens and nearby restaurants and food kiosks. The main camping season is Jun/Jul-end of August. Holders of a international camping card (FICC) qualify for a 10% rebate on rates. **Grading:** There are two categories. Category I sites cover an area of 100 sq m (10,764 sq ft) and have 24-hour reception and lighting.

YOUTH HOSTELS: There are about 1200 hostels in Poland. Addresses can be found in the *Youth Hostel Handbook* published by Youth Hostels Federation (*Almatur*), 15 Copernika Street, 00-359 Warsaw.

RESORTS & EXCURSIONS

The following is an outline of the attractions to be encountered in a circular tour of seven of Poland's major cities. A brief description of Zakopane, Poland's premier ski resort, is also included.

WARSAW: The *River Vistula* runs through the middle of this modern capital. Warsaw was completely destroyed during the Second World War, but now the

Old Town has been rebuilt. The *Wilanów Palace*, one of the reconstructed buildings, has a rare collection of old paintings and furniture, and in the *Orangerie* is the *Museum of Posters*. The reconstructed *Royal Castle* is well worth seeing, as is the *Palace of Culture and Science*, with its views over the whole city. The *Lazienki Palace* is set in a lovely park with an open-air Greek theatre and a monument to Chopin.

Excursions: *Zelazowa Wola*, 53km (32 miles) west of Warsaw, an attractive park in which stands the manor house where Chopin was born; *Kampinos National Park*, 340 sq km (130 sq miles) of forest, marsh and sand where it is possible to see wild boars and elks; *Bialowieza National Park*, 1250 sq km (480 sq miles) of

WARSAW

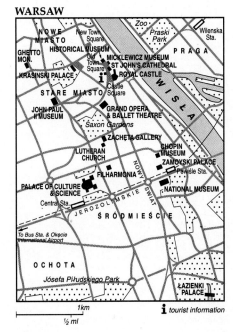
tourist information

Mazurian Lake

primeval forest straddling the border with Belarus, the last major refuge of the European bison, also inhabited by lynx, moose, wild forest ponies and other rare forest-dwellers. **Lublin**, a charming medieval city with five universities, is 164km (102 miles) southeast of Warsaw.

CRACOW: Poland's second city also stands on the banks of the River Vistula but far to the south in the wooded foothills of the *Tatra Mountains*. It still retains its charming medieval air, having largely escaped destruction during the Second World War. In the centre is the *Cloth Hall* built in the 14th century. Opposite is *St Mary's Church* with its world-famous wooden altar carved by Wit Stwosz. The *Jagiellonian University* founded in 1364 is one of the oldest in Europe. Here Copernicus studied and visitors may see the astronomical instruments he used. Overlooking Craców is the *Royal Castle* with its marvellous 16th-century tapestries. Next to the Castle is the *Royal Cathedral* where many of the Polish kings are buried as Craców was Poland's capital until 1596. *Czartoryski Museum* contains ancient art, European paintings, and crafts.

Excursions: At **Wieliczka**, 13km (8 miles) from Craców, cathedral-like salt mines are open to visitors. The route spans 4.5km leading to the oldest part of the mine through 14th- and 15th-century chapels and crystal caves. 70km (43 miles) from Craców lies the site of **Oswiecim (Auschwitz)** concentration camp in which 4 million people were killed. The camp area has been designated as a Monument to the Victims of Oswiecim. There is a *Museum of Martyrdom* on the site. Other excursions include the *Bledowska Desert*, perhaps the only true desert in Europe; **Wadowice**, birthplace of Pope John Paul II; and the portrait of the Madonna in the huge monastery complex at **Czestochowa**, 100km (60 miles) north of Craców, reputed to have been painted by St Luke.

ZAKOPANE: About 112km (70 miles) south of

Craców, this charming resort and winter sports centre lies in the heart of the Tatra Mountains. There is a fairytale atmosphere here – 'gingerbread' wooden cottages and people still in national dress.

Excursions: Organised trips are available to *Dunajec Rapids; Koscieliska Valley,* through beautiful countryside; *Kasprowy Wierch,* by means of a cable car offering spectacular views; and to *Morskie Oko,* a mountain lake.

WROCLAW: The principal city of southwest Poland and capital of Lower Silesia can claim to be the cradle of the Polish state: it was here that the Polanie tribe built their first fortified settlement (on Ostrow Tumski Island). During the 14th century, it fell under the rule of the Bohemians, in the 16th century the Habsburgs, the Prussians and then the German Reich. At the end of the Second World War the town was used as the 'Festung Breslau', a Nazi stronghold. The modern city is threaded with 90km (56 miles) of canals and tributaries of the River Oder and there are more than a hundred bridges. Sights include the *Town Hall* and the *Cathedral* on **Ostrow Tumski Island** (Ostrow Tumski means 'Cathedral Island').

Excursions: The spas and health resorts of the *Klódzko Valley;* the rugged *Stolowe Mountains;* ski resorts in the *Karkonosze Mountains* on the border with the Czech Republic; and the many picturesque medieval (and earlier) towns in the region, such as **Swidnica**, **Bolslawiec** and **Paczkow**.

POZNAN: This sedate city stands beside the *River Warta* in the middle of the flatlands of western Poland. More than half of the city was destroyed during the Second World War but much has been restored. Sights include the Italianate town hall in the *Old Market Square,* the *Gorki Palace,* the *Dzyalinski Mansion* (now a hotel), the 12th-century *Church of St John* and *Przemyslaw Castle,* once seat of the Grand Dukes of Poland. Of more recent interest is the huge monument in memory of the

workers killed in *Plac Mickiewicza* by the police during disturbances in 1956. Watersports can be enjoyed in and on the many lakes in the woods surrounding the city. The *Poznan International Trade Fair* is held here every year in June.

Excursions: Gniezno also claims to be the birthplace of the Polish state. Three brothers, Lech, Czech and Rus, are said to have been the founders of the Slavic nations. Lech was supposed to have settled at Gniezno on finding white eagles nesting there. The white eagle later became the symbol of Poland. At **Biskupin** nearby, there is a large and well-preserved prehistoric settlement.

SZCZECIN: Standing 60km (37 miles) upstream from the mouth of the *River Oder*, this is none the less the largest port on the Baltic Sea. Formerly known as Stettin, it was the capital of Pomerania and sights include the Pomeranian princes' 14th-century chateau and the 12th-century cathedral. The city was largely rebuilt in the last century, taking Paris as a model, and has a spacious feel to it, with many wide, tree-lined boulevards.

Excursions: The beach resorts of the Pomeranian coast, such as *Kolobrzeg* (large and fashionable) or *Leba* (a quiet resort with a beach of fabulous white sand); and the beech woods of the *Wolin National Park,* home of the rare European sea eagle.

GDANSK: Formerly known as Danzig, this important Baltic port has had a troubled history. The Order of Teutonic Knights took it from the Poles in the 14th century and later lost it to the Prussians. In the 20th century, it was the first city to be attacked by Nazi Germany in 1939 and its Lenin Shipyards were the birthplace of *Solidarinosc* (Solidarity) and thus of today's democratic Poland. Almost the entire city was destroyed in the Second World War, but was restored to its former beauty. The city is now a provincial capital at the mouth of the Vistula and Motlawa and a commercial, industrial and scientific centre. Sights include the *Town Hall,* restored Renaissance-style houses, the 17th-century *Golden Gate* and the largest Gothic Church in Poland, the *Church of the Virgin Mary*. The beach resort at nearby **Sopot** has Europe's longest pier (500m/1640ft).

Excursions: The forested *Hel Peninsula;* the *Kashubian Lakeland;* the narrow-gauge railway that runs along the *Vistula Spit;* the Teutonic castles at **Malbork** (Marienburg), **Gniew** and elsewhere; and the *Nicolaus Copernicus Museum* at **Torun**, his birthplace. Further east is **Mazuria**, a huge, thinly populated area of lakes, dense forests and swamps. It is rich in wildlife, including wild bison and Europe's largest herd of elks, and offers every form of outdoor pursuit – mushroom-collecting, sailing, canoeing, camping, etc. In the heart of a Mazurian forest, at **Ketrzyn** (Rastenburg), is the site of *Hitler's 'Eagle's Nest',* the concrete bunker where members of his High Staff tried to assassinate him in August 1944.

POPULAR ITINERARIES: 5-day: Gdansk–Torun–Mazuria–Warsaw–Poznan. **7-day:** Warsaw–Craców–Zakopane–Czestochowa–Poznan–Szczecin–Gdansk.

SOCIAL PROFILE

FOOD & DRINK: Poland has a distinctive cuisine, with typical ingredients being dill, marjoram, caraway seeds, wild mushrooms and sour cream, which is frequently added to soups, sauces and braised meats. The national dish of Poland is *bigos,* made with sauerkraut, fresh cabbage, onions and any variety of leftover meat. Polish meals start with *przekaski* (starters), such as pike in aspic, marinated fish in sour cream, salted and rolled herring fillets with pickles and onions, *kulebiak* (a large mushroom and cabbage pasty) or Polish sausages such as the long, thin and highly spiced *kabanos* or the hunters' sausage *(mysliwska)* made with pork and game. Soups play an important part at mealtimes and are usually rich and very thick. Soups such as *barszcz* (beetroot soup, excellent with sour cream) or *rosol* (beef or chicken boullion) are often served in cups with small hot pasties stuffed with meat or cabbage. Popular dishes include *zrazy zawijane* (mushroom-stuffed beefsteak rolls in sour cream) served with boiled *kasha* (buckwheat) and pig's knuckles. Poland is also a good country for fish *(ryba)* such as carp served in sweet-and-sour jellied sauce, and poached pike with horseradish in cream. Herring *(sledz)* is particularly popular and is served up in countless different ways. Pastries *(ciastka)* are also very good. Table service is the norm in restaurants. **Drink:** Vodka *(wódka),* the national drink, is drunk chilled. *Wyborowa* is considered the best standard vodka, but there are many flavoured varieties such as *zubrowka* (bison grass), *tarniowka* (sloe plum), *sliwowica* (prune) and *pieprzowka* (vodka with ground white pepper). Western drinks, such as whisky, gin or brandy, can be obtained in most bars but are expensive. Wine is available but, again, is imported and expensive. The best bottled beer is *zywiec*, a fairly strong lager-type beer. Bars have table and/or counter service. Coffee shops are very popular in Poland and are the favourite places for social meetings from early morning to late at night. They do not close during the day and have the same function as do pubs in the United Kingdom. Alcoholic drinks are available throughout the day.

NIGHTLIFE: Warsaw also reflects the strong theatrical and musical traditions of Poland, with about 17 theatres, and three opera companies. Cinemas in Poland show both Polish and foreign films. There are some discos in Poland, as well as a few nightclubs and music clubs in Warsaw.

SHOPPING: Special purchases: glass and enamelware, handwoven rugs, silverware, handmade jewellery with amber and silver, dolls in regional costumes, woodcarvings and clay and metal sculptures. **Shopping hours:** 1000-1900 Monday to Friday.

SPORT: Tour operators can arrange special-interest recreation stays in Poland for sports clubs, youth organisations and school children, such as **yachting** and other **watersports** on the Mazurian Lakes, **horseriding** and winter sports holidays. **Winter sports:** The most popular resorts are Zakopane in the Tatra Mountains and Krynica in the Beskidy Mountains. **Skiing** runs from November through to May. Another winter sport is **ice-boating** on Poland's frozen waterways. **Fishing:** For angling, tourists need to buy a fishing licence for about £11 which is valid for 7 days. **Sailing:** The main sailing regions are the Mazurian Lakes and the Suwalki and Augustow Lakes. **Swimming:** There are swimming pools in most cities and beaches along the Baltic coast. Swimming is also particularly good in the Mazurian Lakes. There is, however, fairly high pollution in rivers and so it is not a good idea to swim in them. **Racing:** The main horseracing tracks are Warsaw (Sluzewiec), Sopot, Raculka (near Zielona Gora), Bialy Bor (near Slupsk) and Ksiaz (near Walbrzych). **Train spotting** is a popular pastime in Poland and special holidays for rail enthusiasts are available from certain tour operators.

SPECIAL EVENTS: The following series of events are highlights in the Polish calendar. For further details of events in 1995/96, contact the Polish National Tourist Office (address at top of entry).
Mar '95 *INFATOUR-MAZURY '95* (international tourism fair), Olsztyn. **Mar 23-26** *20th Alternative Theatre Festival*, Craców. **Apr 21-29** *30th Organ Music Festival*, Craców. **Apr 29-May 4** *5th International of Sacral Music*, Czestochowa. **May 17-22** *International Book Fair*, Warsaw. **May 30-Jun 3** *International Festival of Short Films*, Craców. **Jun/Jul** *International Theatre Festival*, Poznan. **Jun-Aug** *International Festival of Chamber and Organ Music*, Kamien Pomorski. **Jun 14-Jul 25** *Mozart Festival*, Warsaw. **Jul 29-Aug 6** *Week of Culture*, Bielsko-Biala. **Aug** *Dominikanski Fair*, Gdansk; *International Festival of Street Theatre*, Jelenia Gora; *International Chopin Festival*, Duszniki-Zdroj. **Sep** *TT Warsaw Tour & Travel '95*. **Oct 1-22** *Chopin International Piano Competition* (held every five years), Warsaw. **Oct (second half)** *Jazz Jamboree '95*, Warsaw.

SOCIAL CONVENTIONS: Poles are friendly, industrious people and foreigners are usually made very welcome. There are vast contrasts between urban and rural life and the Polish peasantry is very religious and conservative, maintaining a traditional lifestyle. Roman Catholicism plays an important role in daily life and criticism or jokes about religion are not appreciated, despite the general good humour of the people. Music and art are also important aspects of Polish culture. Shaking hands is the normal form of greeting. Normal courtesies are observed when visiting private homes and it is customary to bring flowers. Fairly conservative casual wear is the most suitable attire, but dress should be formal when specified for entertaining in the evening or in a smart restaurant. Smoking is restricted in some public buildings. **Photography:** Military installations such as bridges, ports, airports, border points, etc should not be photographed. **Tipping:** A service charge is usually added to restaurant bills.

BUSINESS PROFILE

ECONOMY: The working population is divided roughly in half between agriculture and industry. Although some productive land is under state control, there have long been numerous private farms which are responsible for the bulk of Polish produce. Livestock is particularly important and Polish meat is a major export earner. Rye, wheat, oats, sugar beet and potatoes are the main crops. The main industries are shipbuilding, textiles, steel, cement, chemicals and foodstuffs. After a period of rapid growth during the 1970s, financed by relatively easy credit from the West, Polish industry has undergone severe recession, particularly in the heavier

industries, and although there has been some recovery since the introduction of market reforms, the problems are still considerable. Since the fall of Communism, the old facets of the Soviet-style command economy have for the most part been removed. Price controls and other financial restrictions have been dropped and Poland has embarked on a major programme of privatisation, using a voucher-based system similar to that introduced in the former Czechoslovakia. The Zloty is now convertible while the tax and fiscal system is undergoing a complete restructuring. Inflation has been brought down from nearly 700% to around 40% per annum (3% per month). Poland has signed an association agreement with the European Union and expects to seek membership around the turn of the century. A trade agreement with EFTA (the European Free Trade Association) is, however, being held up by disagreements over import tariff reductions. Poland's main trading partners are Germany and the CIS.
BUSINESS: Men are expected to wear a suit and tie at business meetings. In Poland a formal approach is favoured and it is therefore advisable to give plenty of notice of an intended visit. Employees in state organisations do not take a lunch break; they have their main meal after 1500. **Office hours:** 0700-1600 Monday to Friday.
COMMERCIAL INFORMATION: The following organisation can offer advice: Krajowa Izba Gospodarcza (Polish Chamber of Commerce), PO Box 361, Trebacka 4, 00-074 Warsaw. Tel: (22) 260 221. Fax: (22) 274 673. Telex: 814361.
CONFERENCES/CONVENTIONS: The most popular conference venues are in Warsaw. Events are also hosted in Craców, whereas Wroclaw, Gdansk and other towns are used occasionally. A comprehensive range of support facilities is provided by ORBIS SA, PO Box 146, 00-950 Warsaw. Tel: (22) 261 658. Fax: (22) 261 297.

The Town Hall, Poznan

CLIMATE

Temperate with warm summers, crisp, sunny autumns and cold winters. Snow covers the mountainous area in the south of Poland (mid-December to April). Rain falls throughout the year.
Required clothing: Light- to medium-weights are worn during warmer months. Medium- to heavy-weights are needed during winter. Rainwear is advisable all year.

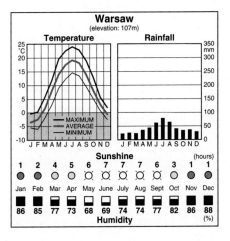

Portugal

□ international airport

Location: Western Europe.

ICEP/Turismo
Avenida Conde Valbom 30, 4° & 5°, 1016 Lisbon, Portugal
Tel: (1) 352 5810.

Embassy of the Portuguese Republic
11 Belgrave Square, London SW1X 8PP
Tel: (0171) 235 5331/4. Fax: (0171) 245 1287. Telex: 28484. Opening hours: 1000-1300 and 1400-1700 Monday to Friday.

Portuguese Consulate
Silver City House, 62 Brompton Road, London SW3 1BJ
Tel: (0171) 581 8722/3/4. Fax: (0171) 581 3085.
Opening hours: 0900-1330 Monday to Friday.

ICEP/Investment Trade and Tourism of Portugal
(National Tourism Office)
2nd Floor, 22-25a Sackville Street, London W1X 1DE
Tel: (0171) 494 1441. Fax: (0171) 494 1868. Telex: 265653. Opening hours: 0930-1730 Monday to Friday.

British Embassy
Rua de S Domingos à Lapa 35-37, 37 1200 Lisbon, Portugal
Tel: (1) 396 1191 *or* 396 1147 *or* 396 3181. Fax: (1) 397 6768.
Consulates in: Funchal (Madeira), Oporto, Ribeira Grande (Azores) and Portimão.

Embassy of the Portuguese Republic
2125 Kalorama Road, NW, Washington, DC 20008
Tel: (202) 328 8610. Fax: (202) 462 3726.
Consulate Generals in: Boston, Honolulu, Houston, Los Angeles, Miami, Newark, New Bedford, New York (tel: (212) 246 4580), Philadelphia, Providence, San Francisco and Waterbury.

ICEP/Portuguese National Tourist Office
4th Floor, 590 Fifth Avenue, New York, NY 10036-4704

Tel: (212) 354 4403. Fax: (212) 764 6137. Telex: 2341401 (a/b CTPA UR).

Embassy of the United States of America
Avenida das Forças Armadas, 1600 Lisbon Cedex, Portugal
Tel: (1) 726 6600 *or* 726 6659 *or* 726 8670. Fax: (1) 726 9109.
Consulate in: Ponta Delgada (Azores).

Embassy of the Portuguese Republic
645 Island Park Drive, Ottawa, Ontario K1Y 0B8
Tel: (613) 729 0883 *or* 729 2922. Fax: (613) 729 4236.
Consulates in: Edmonton, Halifax, Montréal, Québec, St John's, Toronto, Vancouver and Winnipeg.

ICEP/Portuguese National Tourist Office
Suite 1005, 60 Bloor Street W, Toronto, Ontario M4W 3B8
Tel: (416) 921 7376. Fax: (416) 921 1353.

Canadian Embassy
4th Floor, Avenida da Liberdade 144/56, 1200 Lisbon, Portugal
Tel: (1) 347 4892. Fax: (1) 347 6466. Telex: 12377 (a/b DOMCAN P).
Consulate in: Faro.

AREA: 92,389 sq km (35,672 sq miles).
POPULATION: 9,858,600 (1991).
POPULATION DENSITY: 106.7 per sq km.
CAPITAL: Lisbon. **Population:** 2,048,200 (1992).
GEOGRAPHY: Portugal occupies the southwest part of the Iberian Peninsula and shares borders in the north and the east with Spain, while to the south and west lies the Atlantic Ocean. The country is divided into various provinces, including the Atlantic islands of Madeira and the Azores; the latter lying some 1220km (760 miles) due west of Lisbon. The Douro, Tagus and Guadiana rivers flow across the border from Spain. North Portugal is mountainous, the highest part being the *Serra da Estrela*, a popular area for skiing. South of Lisbon stretch the vast plains of the *Alentejo* region. A range of mountains divides the *Alentejo* from the Algarve, which runs along the south coast, and is one of the most popular resort areas with wide sandy beaches and attractive bays.
LANGUAGE: Portuguese.
RELIGION: Roman Catholic.
TIME: GMT + 1 (GMT + 2 from last Sunday in March to Saturday before last Sunday in September).
ELECTRICITY: 220 volts AC, 50Hz. 110 volts in some areas and 220 DC in parts of the south. Continental 2-pin plugs are in use.
COMMUNICATIONS: Telephone: IDD is available. Country code: 351. Outgoing international code: 00. There are call boxes in most villages and all towns, also public phones in many cafés and bars from which international calls may be made. **Fax:** This service is available to the public at bureaux and large hotels in major cities. **Telex/telegram:** There are telegram and telex facilities at most major hotels. The public telex office at Praca D Luis 30-1, Lisbon is open 0900-1800 Monday to Friday. **Post:** Airmail to European destinations from Continental Portugal and the Azores takes three days; from Madeira up to five days. There are *Poste Restante* facilities at post offices throughout the country. **Press:** There is only one English-language newspaper, the weekly *Anglo Portuguese News.*
BBC World Service and Voice of America frequencies: From time to time these change. See the section *How to Use this Book* for more information.
BBC:

MHz	17.70	12.09	9.410	6.195

Voice of America:

MHz	11.97	9.670	6.040	5.995

PASSPORT/VISA

Regulations and requirements may be subject to change at short notice, and you are advised to contact the appropriate diplomatic or consular authority before finalising travel arrangements. Details of these may be found at the head of this country's entry. Any numbers in the chart refer to the footnotes below.

	Passport Required?	Visa Required?	Return Ticket Required?
Full British	1	No/2	No
BVP	Valid	No	No
Australian	Yes	No/3	No
Canadian	Yes	No/4	No
USA	Yes	No/4	No
Other EU (As of 31/12/94)	1	No/2	No
Japanese	Yes	No/3	No

PASSPORTS: Valid passport required by all except:
(a) **[1]** nationals of Belgium, Denmark, France, Germany, Greece, Ireland, Italy, Luxembourg, The Netherlands and Spain holding national ID cards, or BVP in the case of UK citizens;

(b) nationals of Austria, Finland, Liechtenstein, Malta, Norway, Sweden and Switzerland holding national ID cards.
British Visitors Passport: Accepted.
VISAS: Required by all except:
(a) **[2]** nationals of EU countries for stays of up to 3 months;
(b) **[3]** nationals of Australia and Japan for stays of up to 3 months;
(c) **[4]** nationals of Canada and the USA for stays of up to 2 months;
(d) nationals of Andorra, Argentina, Austria, Bermuda, Chile, Costa Rica, Croatia, Cyprus, Czech Republic, Finland, Hungary, Israel, Liechtenstein, Malta, Mexico, Monaco, New Zealand, Norway, Poland, San Marino, Slovak Republic, Slovenia, Switzerland and Uruguay for stays of up to 3 months;
(e) nationals of Ecuador, Iceland, South Korea, Malawi, Seychelles and Sweden for stays of up to 2 months;
(f) nationals of Brazil for stays of up to 6 months.
Nationals of other countries should consult the Portuguese Consulate for further information.
Types of visa: Entry visa: cost £21.55.
Validity: Visas are valid for 120 days after the date of issue, and up to 60 days from date of entry.
Application to: Consulate (or Consular section at Embassy). For addresses, see top of entry.
Application requirements: (a) Valid passport. (b) Application form. (c) Passport-size photo. (d) Letter from employer if travelling on business.
Working days required: Normally 48 hours, longer if the application has to be referred to Portugal. Applications by post should be accompanied by a large stamped, self-addressed envelope.
Temporary residence: Applications for residence visa must be accompanied by a declaration of interest (explanation of reasons, intentions and statement of financial capacity). Contact the Consulate for further details.
Note: Usually it is sufficient for visitors to Madeira and the Azores to satisfy the entry conditions for Portugal. Exceptions are noted in the sections below on Madeira and the Azores.

MONEY

Currency: Escudo (Esc) = 100 centavos. Notes are in denominations of Esc10,000, 5000, 1000 and 500. The Esc1000 note is known as a *conto*. Coins are in denominations of Esc200, 100, 50, 20, 10 and 5.
Currency exchange: Many UK banks offer differing exchange rates depending on the denominations of Portuguese currency being bought or sold. It is common practice for banks to charge 0.5% commission with a minimum charge of Esc2000 (approximately £9.00). However, some banks do not charge any commission on transactions of less than Esc5000. Check with banks for details and current rates.
Credit cards: Access/Mastercard, American Express and Visa are widely accepted. Check with your credit card company for details of merchant acceptability and other services which may be available.
Travellers cheques: Readily exchanged. *Eurocheques* may be used at many banks in conjunction with appropriate encashment cards.
Exchange rate indicators: The following figures are included as a guide to the movements of the Escudo against Sterling and the US Dollar:

Date:	Oct '92	Sep '93	Jan '94	Jan '95
£1.00=	217.70	253.30	261.43	249.07
$1.00=	137.18	165.88	176.70	159.20

Currency restrictions: The import of local or foreign currency in cash or travellers cheques is unlimited. The personal export allowance is Esc100,000 cash or (local) travellers cheques, or the equivalent of Esc1,000,000 in foreign currency. This limit may be exceeded on presentation of proof that the same or a larger amount was imported. There is no limit on the movement of credit cards, cheques, or travellers cheques issued outside Portugal in the name of the visitor. The export of gold, silver, jewellery and other valuables is limited to a value of Esc30,000 and subject to special conditions. For details, contact the Embassy (see top of entry for addresses).
Banking hours: Generally, 0830-1500 Monday to Friday. Certain banks in Lisbon are open 1800-2300 Monday to Friday. In the Algarve, the bank in the Vilamoura Marina Shopping Centre is open daily from 0900-2100.

DUTY FREE

(a) The following goods may be imported into Portugal by visitors over 17 years of age from non-EU countries without incurring customs duty or government tax:
200 cigarettes or 100 cigarillos or 50 cigars or 250g of

Tourism and Portuguese Airports

With its mild climate and warm hospitable people, Portugal is one of the most pleasant tourist destinations in Europe.

The **1994 ASTA Congress** was held in Lisboa, the capital of a country with a history stretching back eight centuries.

Lisboa International Airport: the area of expansion due to be completed in 1998 is shown in pale pink.

WELCOME

About 7000 representatives participated in the event and were able to experience at first hand the country and its travel, hotel, restaurant and entertainment facilities at local and national levels.

The first to greet the participants on arrival, and the last to bid them farewell at departure, was Lisboa International Airport, while the respective authority – **ANA, E.P.*** – was one of the five major sponsors of the ASTA Congress.

In four years' time, the Portuguese capital will be the site of **EXPO '98.**

Lisboa Airport is pursuing its own modernization programme and preparing for this world event by doubling its present capacity to 12 million passengers a year.

This premier aerial gateway to Portugal is being superbly equipped to suit the needs of passengers, customers and non-travelling visitors alike.

The same policy is being carried out by **ANA, E.P.** regarding other Portuguese international airports: *Sá Carneiro* (Porto) in the North, *Faro* (Algarve) in the South, *Funchal* in the Madeira Archipelago and *Ponta Delgada* in the Azores Archipelago.

Uma calorosa saudação portuguesa de **boas-vindas** ou de **despedida** para si ao **aterrar** ou **descolar** nos nossos aeroportos ou enquanto estiver a voar no vasto espaço aéreo que controlamos.

Desenvolvemos e **gerimos** aeroportos e serviços de tráfego aéreo em Portugal.

A traditional warm portuguese **welcome** or **farewell** to you on **landing** or **taking-off** at our airports or while flying in the vast air space controlled by us.

We **develop** and **manage** airports and air traffic services in Portugal.

***ANA, E.P.** is a public corporation responsible for the development and management of airport and air navigation infrastructure in Portugal. It renders Air Traffic Services in two Flight Information Regions, one of them comprising a vast oceanic area of the North Atlantic.

ana

aeroportos e navegação aérea · e.p.

tobacco; 1 litre of spirits over 22% or 2 litres of spirits up to 22%; 2 litres of wine; 50g of perfume and 250ml of eau de toilette; 500g of coffee or 200g of coffee extract; 100g of tea or 40g of tea extract; further goods up to Esc7500.

(b) Visitors over 17 years of age from EU countries may import goods in the following quantities without incurring customs duty or government tax:

300 cigarettes or 150 cigarillos or 75 cigars or 400g of tobacco; 1.5 litres of spirits over 22 % or 3 litres of spirits up to 22%; 5 litres of wine; 75g of perfume and 375ml of eau de toilette; 1kg of coffee or 400g of coffee extract; 200g of tea or 80g of tea extract; further goods up to Esc60,000.

(c) Visitors over 17 years of age arriving from EU countries with duty-paid goods:

800 cigarettes and 400 cigarillos and 200 cigars and 1kg of tobacco; 90 litres of wine (including up to 60 litres of sparkling wine); 10 litres of spirits; 20 litres of intermediate products (such as fortified wine); 110 litres of beer.

Note: Although there are now no legal limits imposed on importing duty-paid tobacco and alcoholic products from one EU country to another, travellers may be questioned at customs if they exceed the above amounts and may be asked to prove that the goods are for personal use only.

PUBLIC HOLIDAYS

Jan 1 '95 New Year's Day. **Feb 28** Carnival. **Apr 14** Easter Friday. **Apr 25** National Day. **May 1** Labour Day. **Jun 10** Portugal Day. **Jun 15** Corpus Christi. **Aug 15** Assumption. **Oct 5** Republic Day. **Nov 1** All Saints' Day. **Dec 1** Independence Day. **Dec 8** Immaculate Conception. **Dec 25** Christmas. **Jan 1 '96** New Year's Day. **Feb 18** Carnival. **Apr 5** Easter Friday. **Apr 25** National Day.

Note: The Tourist Office brochure *Portugal – Fairs, Festivals and Folk Pilgrimages* gives details of local holidays.

HEALTH

Regulations and requirements may be subject to change at short notice, and you are advised to contact your doctor well in advance of your intended date of departure. Any numbers in the chart refer to the footnotes below.

	Special Precautions?	Certificate Required?
Yellow Fever	No	1
Cholera	No	No
Typhoid & Polio	No	-
Malaria	No	-
Food & Drink	2	-

[1]: A yellow fever vaccination certificate is required from travellers over one year of age arriving in or destined for the Azores or Madeira if coming from infected areas. No certificate is, however, required from transit passengers at Funchal, Porto Santo and Santa Maria.

[2]: Mains water is normally chlorinated, and whilst relatively safe may cause mild abdominal upsets. Bottled water is available and is advised for the first few weeks of the stay. Drinking water outside main cities and towns may be contaminated and sterilisation is advisable. Milk is pasteurised and dairy products are safe for consumption. Local meat, poultry, seafood, fruit and vegetables are generally considered safe to eat.

Health care: There are Reciprocal Health Agreements with most European countries. The agreement with the UK allows free in-patient treatment in general wards of official hospitals to those presenting UK passports (other EU nationals must present form E111). Other medical treatment, all dental treatment and prescribed medicines must be paid for. This Agreement is also effective in Madeira and the Azores. Those wishing to take advantage of it should inform the doctor prior to treatment that they wish to be treated under EU social security arrangements. Medical fees paid whilst in Portugal cannot be reimbursed by the British NHS.

TRAVEL - International

AIR: Portugal's national airline is *TAP Air Portugal (TP).*

For free advice on air travel, call the Air Travel Advisory Bureau on (0171) 636 5000 (London) *or* (0161) 832 2000 (Manchester).

Approximate flight times: From Lisbon to *London* is 2 hours 30 minutes and to *New York* is 8 hours.

International airports: *Lisbon (LIS)* (Portela de Sacavem), 7km (4.5 miles) north of the city (travel time – 30 minutes). Greenline Bus, nos. 44, 45 and 83, run every 10 minutes from 0530-0100 to the city centre and main railway station. A special 'Airbus' departs to the city centre every 20 minutes. Taxi services to the city are available, with a surcharge after 2200. Airport facilities include 24-hour bureau de change, tourist information (0600-0200), duty-free shops (0700-0130) and car rental (*Avis, Eurodollar, Inter-Rent* and *Hertz*).

Faro (FAO), 4km (3 miles) west of the city (travel time – 25 minutes). Bus nos. 17 and 18 go to the city; taxis are available.

Oporto (OPO) (Oporto Sá Carneiro), 11km (about 7 miles) from the city. Taxis to the city are available.

Lisbon, Faro and *Oporto* airports all have the following airport facilities: outgoing duty-free shop; bank/bureau de change (open normal banking hours); car hire, including *Hertz, Avis, Eurodollar* (in Lisbon only) and *Inter-Rent*; and a restaurant/bar.

SEA: The principal ports for international passengers are Lisbon, Leixões (Oporto), Funchal (Madeira) and Portimão (Algarve), served by *P&O, Union Castle, Olympia, Linea C, Cunard* and *Italia.* For details contact shipping lines.

RAIL: There is a daily service between London, Paris and Lisbon, taking approximately 26 hours. The 'Sud-Express' runs between Paris and Lisbon, offering first- and second-class seats, sleepers and a restaurant car.

ROAD: The only land border is shared with Spain, and there are seven frontier posts in the north and six on the western and southern border. Border posts are usually open 0700-2400, but close earlier in winter. Ferries from the UK (Plymouth) to Santander in northern Spain obviate the need to drive through France. Cars can be imported for up to six months. See below for information on **documentation** and **regulations**.

TRAVEL - Internal

AIR: *Air Portugal (TP)* and *Portugalia* run services between Lisbon, Faro, Madeira, Porto Santo, Oporto and the Azores. The airline for the Azores is *SATA (Sociedade Acoriana de Transportes Aereos) (SP),* which operates between the various islands. Charter flights are also available.

SEA/RIVER: Internal transport is available from all coastal ports and along the major rivers. For details, contact local ports.

RAIL: *Portuguese Railways (CP)* provide a rail service to every town. The tourist areas of Cascais and Sintra are connected to Lisbon by frequent express trains.

Cheap fares: On 'Blue Days', usually Monday afternoon to Thursday, special rates are available. There are also special fares (with 20-30% reductions) for groups of ten or more *(Bilhete de Grupo)*, minimum distance 75km/47 miles (single journey) and 150km/94 miles (return journey). Application should be made four days in advance by the group leader. Tourist Tickets (*Bilhete Turisticos*) for 7, 14 or 21 days of unlimited travel are also available. The Rail Cheque *(Cheque Trem)*, obtainable in four different values, can be in one name or a company's name and has no time limit; it gives a reduction of 15% and can be used both for purchasing tickets and many other railway services.

An International Youth Ticket *(BIJ)* entitles those aged between 12 and 26 to a discount subject to certain conditions in 24 countries including Portugal.

Senior citizens are entitled to 50% reduction on production of proof of age. Children under 4 travel free. Children aged 4-11 pay half fare.

Family Card, Inter-Rail Card, Rail Inclusive Tours and *Special Tourist Trips* are amongst other offers from *Portuguese Railways,* Cáminhos de Ferro Portugueses, Éstaçao Santa Apólonia, Lisbon 1200. Tel: (1) 367 848 *or* 886 0236. Telex: 15813 (a/b MARPOL P) (reservations). Rail information is also available from the National Tourist Office.

ROAD: Traffic drives on the right. Every town and village can be reached by an adequate system of roads. Petrol stations are open 0700-2400. Travel by motorway is subject to a toll according to distance covered and type of vehicle. A small tax may be added to petrol bought with a credit card. **Taxi:** Charges are according to distance and they are all metered. **Car hire:** Available from main towns and airports, with or without driver.

Regulations: Minimum age for driving is 18. Cars may be imported for up to six months. Traffic signs are international. Headlights should be dipped in built-up areas and side lights used when parking in badly-lit areas. Children should not travel in the front seat. Seat belts should be worn. Warning triangles are compulsory. It is forbidden to carry cans of petrol in vehicles. Speed limits are 50kmph (30mph) in built-up areas, 90kmph (56mph) outside built-up areas and 120kmph (70mph) on motorways. Visitors who have passed their driving test for less than one year must display a yellow disc with '90' on it on the rear of their vehicle and must not go faster than 90kmph (56mph) (or lower where appropriate). Permitted speeds will vary if trailers are being used. **Documentation:** International Driving Permits or foreign driving licences are accepted. Third Party insurance is compulsory and a Green Card must be obtained. A Carnet de Passage is needed for a van.

JOURNEY TIMES: The following chart gives approximate journey times (in hours and minutes) from Lisbon to other major cities/towns in Portugal.

	Air	Road	Rail
Faro	0.35	4.00	5.00
Oporto	0.45	5.00	3.00
Funchal	1.30	-	-

ACCOMMODATION

There is a wide range of accommodation available all over the country, ranging from luxury hotels, pensions, boarding houses and inns to simple guest-houses, manor houses, campsites and youth hostels. The government-run *pousadas* offer very good value and are often situated in places of scenic beauty in converted castles, palaces or old inns.

HOTELS: Most hotels have a private swimming pool and serve international cuisine as well as some typically Portuguese dishes. During the low season, hotels normally grant substantial reductions. There should be an officially authorised list of prices displayed in every bedroom, and children under eight years of age are entitled to a reduction of 50% on the price of full meals and 50% on the price of an extra bed – if sharing parents' room or apartment. Further information can be obtained from the Associação dos Hõteis de Portugal, Avenida Santos Dumont, 52 – 2°/Esq, 1000 Lisbon (tel: (1) 793 1141; fax: (1) 793 3504); *or* Associação da Industria Hoteleira e Similare, Avenida Duque d'Avila 75, 1000 Lisbon. Tel: (1) 352 0979. Fax: (1) 352 0979. **Grading:** Classification of hotels is according to the international **1-** to **5-star** system and their prices are officially approved. Apartment hotels are classified from 2- to 4-star, motels from 2- to 3-star and boarding houses from 1- to 4-star; there are also 4-star *albergarias.*

POUSADAS: The *pousadas* are a network of inns operated by the Government, and housed in historic buildings, castles, palaces and convents, or sometimes built especially for the purpose. They have often been geographically sited in regions not on the usual tourist itinerary to give people the opportunity to visit the whole country. The architecture and design of the *pousadas* has been carefully studied in order to give visitors a better knowledge of the cultural traditions of the various regions of the country, with particular attention paid to handicrafts, cooking and wines. A guide to *pousadas* can be obtained from the National Tourist Office.

PRIVATE HOUSES: Rooms are available in private houses and on farms all over Portugal. Some of the old manor houses are now open to visitors and provide good opportunities for the tourist to make contact with Portuguese customs and people. For further information, contact the National Tourist Office or local travel agents.

SELF-CATERING: There is self-catering tourist accommodation in deluxe, first- and second-class tourist villages and tourist apartments, particularly on the Algarve. Tour operators can arrange a wide variety of villas for self-catering parties.

YOUTH HOSTELS: Youth hostels are located to give young people the opportunity of visiting towns, countryside, mountains and coastal areas. Tourists from 14-40 years of age can obtain accommodation and meals. For further information contact MOVIJOVEM, Avenida Duque d'Avila 137, 1000 Lisbon. Tel: (1) 355 9081. Fax: (1) 352 8621.

CAMPING/CARAVANNING: Portugal provides camping and caravan parks near beaches and in thickly wooded areas. Some have model installations including swimming pools, games fields, supermarkets and restaurants. A guide published by the Directorate-General gives the names of existing parks and details of their classification, equipment and capacity. For further information, contact Federação Portuguesa de Campismo, Avenida 5 de Outubro 15, 30°, 1000 Lisbon. Tel: (1) 522 715.

TOURISM POLICY

Investment Trade and Tourism of Portugal (ICEP) has drawn the general outlines for a new development plan aimed at creating conditions to allow a sustained growth in the tourism sector for both medium- and long-term. This strategy will ensure an increase in the number of tourists, leading to a progressive growth rate of the daily expenditure and to a better balance in the occupancy rates throughout the year.

ICEP's policy is also geared to the diversification of products through encouraging the private sector into a more competitive attitude towards the prospective client and, thus, broadening the prospective offer.

To achieve this, goals investment will be stimulated in areas such as sport and leisure, namely golf and nautical activities, shooting and hunting, cultural and historical heritage attractions, rural tourism, spas, congresses and incentives, along with the sun and sea, Portugal's traditional product.

RESORTS & EXCURSIONS

There are six major tourist regions in Portugal. These are, from north to south: the coastal regions of the Costa Verde, the Costa de Prata, the Costa de Lisboa (including the Costa do Estoril, Costa Azul, Costa Alentejana) and the Algarve and, inland, the Montanhas and the agricultural region of the Planícies.

Costa Verde

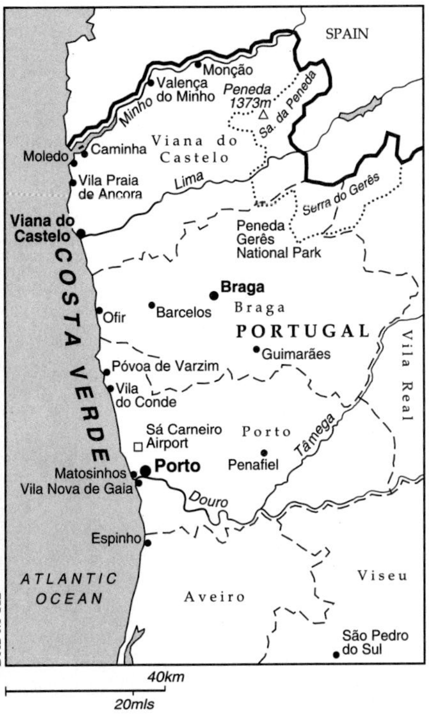

The Costa Verde is the region occupying the northwest corner of Portugal, starting at the northern border with Spain and stretching south of Oporto and as far east as Vila Real. It encompasses the rivers *Minho, Lima* and *Douro* together with the *Peneda-Gerês National Park*. Some places have become somewhat 'touristy', but along the coast and in the countryside you can still find quiet areas. The vicinity of Oporto is the home of the famous Port wine. There are also natural spas in this area. The coastal area is well covered by maritime pine forests. There are good beaches in many of the resorts between Espinho and the mouth of the Minho River. Away from the beaches, through the Minho and Douro Valley, there is plenty of interesting local life to see.

Oporto (Porto) is the second-largest city in Portugal and the major town in Costa Verde. Oporto prospered under the Romans and was the birthplace of Prince Henry the Navigator, a driving force behind the great maritime discoveries of the 15th and 16th centuries. A trading agreement with England in 1703 bought wealth to the town and saw the start of the famous Port wine trade. At the wine lodges in the area, visitors are always welcome.

Póvoa de Varzim, north of Porto, is an elegant sea resort. Here traditional industries such as fisheries and silversmiths exist next to thriving tourist institutions.

Other towns of interest in the area include: **Espinho**, a modern beach resort; **Vila do Conde**, a quiet fishing resort famous for its traditional crafts such as 'bone lace', chocolate-making and fishing boats; **Ofir**, a vast expanse of sandy beach fringed by pinewoods; **Barcelos**, famous for its handicrafts, particularly ceramics; **Viana do Castelo**, a fortress town noted for Renaissance and Manueline architecture and local products such as ceramics, embroidery, jewellery and filigree; **Valença**, a 13th-century border town; **Monção**, home of Alvarinho vinho verde; **Braga**, which has a 12th-century cathedral; **Peneda-Gerês National Park**, 170,000 acres of mountain countryside and wildlife; and **Guimarães**, the first medieval capital. There are *spas* at Caldelas, Gerez, Vizela and Monção.

Resorts in the area include: Aboinha, Afife, Alem do Rio, Amarante, Arcos de Valdevez, Aver-o-Mar, Baião, Barcelos, Bom Jesus do Monte, Braga, Caldas de Canavezes, Caldas das Taipas, Caldas de Vizela, Caldelas, Canicada, Castro de Laboreiro, Entre-os-Rios, Ermesinde, Espinho, Esposende, Fafe, Felgueiras, Gerez, Granja, Guardeiras, Guimaraes, Gulpilhares, Leça do Bailio, Leça da Palmeira, Lousada, Marco de Canavezes, Matosinhos, Melgaco, Moledo do Minho, Monção, Monte Faro, Monte de São Felix, Novelas, Ofir, Pacos de Ferreira, Paredes, Penha, Ponte da Barca, Ponte de Lima, Porto, Póvoa de Varzim, Praia de Miramar, Riba de Ave, Rio Caldo, Santa Marta, Santo Tirso, São Bento de Porta Aberta, São Martinho do Campo, São Tiago, São Vicente, Seixas, Serra do Marão, Terras do Bouro, Torre, Valenca, Valongo, Viana do Castelo, Vieira do Minho, Vila do Conde, Vila Nova de Cerveira, Vila Nova de Famalicao and Vila Praia de Ãncora.

Costa de Prata

The Costa de Prata forms a long narrow strip which stretches along the coastline between the south of the Costa Verde and the north of the Costa de Lisboa regions. In the north is Espinho, and in the south, Ericeira. The region embraces Coimbra, the shrine of Fatima, and the caves of Santo Antonio and Alvados. Here there are long beaches, pinewoods and the **Berlengas Islands**, where there is good sea fishing. There are spas at Luso and Curia and a casino at Figueira da Foz. Like the Costa Verde, this region has its fair share of monuments, temples, castles, palaces, monasteries and museums and it also boasts modern tourist resorts with good beaches. All this makes the area popular with sightseers the whole year round.

Coimbra is Portugal's third-largest city. It is an ancient university town, famous for its twisting streets, terraced houses and a particular style of *Fado,* the melancholy but moving music which is distinctive to the Portuguese. Worth visiting are the 12th-century *Sé Cathedral*, the *Art Museum* housed in a former Bishop's Palace, the *Church and Monastery of the Holy Cross,* and the *University*, one of the oldest in Europe.

Other towns of interest in the area include: **Aveiro**, the 'Venice of Portugal', surrounded by salt flats, beaches and lagoons and dominated by the central canal; **Torreira**, a typical fishing village between ocean and lagoon which can be reached by boat from Aveiro; **Anadia**, the centre of the wine-growing region of Bairrada with visits to wine cellars; **Conimbriga**, where fine Roman remains dating from AD1 can be seen; **Bussaco**, famous for its National Park founded by Carmelite friars, and for its 'enchanted forest'; **Figueira da Foz,** a modern resort with a fine beach and a casino; **Pinhal do Rei**, a beautiful pine forest; **Fatima**, centre for pilgrimages celebrating the appearance of the Virgin Mary there in 1917 (special ceremonies take place here on the 13th of each month between May and October); **Batalha**, where the *Battle Abbey* (more properly the Mosteiro de Santa Maria) commemorates the 1386 signing of the alliance between England and Portugal (the oldest alliance in Europe); the caves of **Santo António e Alvados**; the fishing village of **Nazaré; Alcobaça**, a quiet town with narrow streets and open-air market; and **Obidos**, a medieval walled town. An annual fair takes place at the end of March at **Leiria**, a quiet country town situated between Lisbon and Oporto and dominated by a 12th-century castle built on a plateau high above the town. There are *spas* at **Caldas da Rainha**, **Curia, Luso, Vimeiro** and **Cucos**.

Resorts in the area include: Abrantes, Agueda, Albergaria-a-Velha, Alcobaca, Aljubarrota, Anadia, Arouca, Aveiro, Avelar, Batalha, Bombarral, Buarcos, Bussaco, Cacia, Caldas da Rainha, Caldas de São Jorge, Cantanhede, Castelo de Bode, Coimbra, Cucos, Curia, Esmoriz-Barrinhas, Estarreja, Etroncamento, Fatima, Fermentelos, Ferreira do Zêzere, Figueira de Foz, Figueiro dos Vinhos, Forte da Barra, Foz do Arelho, Ilha do Lombo, Ilhavo, Leiria, Luso, Marinha Grande, Mealhada, Minde, Mira de Aire, Monte Real, Murtosa, Nazaré, Obidos, Oliveira de Azeméis, Oliveira do Bairro, Peniche, Piedade, Pombal, Porto de Barcas, Praia da Areia Branca, Praia da Barra, Praia do Furadouro, Praia de Mira, Praia de Pedrogao, Praia do Porto Novo, Praia de Santa Cruz, Rossio ao Sul do Tejo, Sangalhos, Santa Luzia, São Joao da Madeira, São Martinho do Porto, São Pedro de Muel, Seixal da Lourinha, Serém, Sever do Vouga, Sobrado de Paiva, Tomar, Torres Novas, Torres Vedras, Torreira, Vale de Cambra, Vale Gracioso, Vale do Grou, Vale da Mó, Vieira de Leiria, Vila Nova da Barquinha, Vila Nova de Ourem and Vimeiro.

Montanhas

The mountainous region in the northeast of Portugal is an unspoiled area of rugged countryside with castles perched on hilltops, forests, rivers and spas. There are vineyards, old mansions, mountain climbing and walks, and trout fishing.

Resorts in the area include: Alfândega da Fé, Alijo, Alpedrinha, Alto do Caçador, Arganil, Armamar, Belmonte, Bragança, Caldas de Alcafache, Caldas de Aregos, Caldas da Cavaca, Caldas da Felgueira, Caldas de São Gemil, Caramulo, Carvalhelhos, Castelo Branco, Castro de Aire, Catraia de São Romao, Celorico da Beira, Cernache do Bonjardim, Chaves, Cinfães, Coja, Covilhã, Escalhão, Figueira de Castelo Rodrigo, Fornos de Algodres, Fundão, Gândara de Espariz, Gouveia, Guarda, Lamego, Lousa, Luga do Torrao, Macedo de Cavaleiros, Mangualde, Manteigas, Miranda do Douro, Mirandela, Mogadouro, Moimenta da Beira, Monfortinho, Nelas, Oliveira de Frades, Oliveira do Hospital Orvalho, Pedras Salgadas, Penacova, Penhas da Saude, Peso da Regua, Pinhao, Pinheiro de Lafoes, Pinhel, Povoa das Quartas, Resende, Rio Torto, Sabagal, São Joao de Pesqueira, São Pedro do Sul, Seia, Serra da Estrela, Serta, Torre de Moncorvo, Urgeirica, Vidago, Vila Flor, Vila Nova de Poiares, Vila Real, Vilar Formoso, Vimioso, Vinhais, Viseu and Vouzela.

Costa de Lisboa

This area comprises Lisbon, the Estoril coast, Costa Azul, and the Costa Alentejana to the south. Lisbon, the capital of Portugal, lies on seven low hills at the estuary of the River Tagus (Tejo), 10km (6 miles) from the Atlantic Ocean on the west coast, with the Algarve to the south and Costa de Prata and Costa Verde to the north. The Estoril coast runs along the mouth of the Tagus Estuary on to the Atlantic as far as Ericeira. Here there are long Atlantic beaches, pleasant countryside, castles, palaces and parks around Lisbon and also the international life of the Costa de Estoril, where there is a casino, varied nightlife, restaurants, watersports, golf, shopping and riding.

Lisbon is a lively, international city. In the centre of the city is the medieval *Castle of São Jorge,* which stands with its ten towers on the hill where the original colony was situated in Phoenician times. Nearby is *Alfama,* the old Moorish quarter, which has narrow winding streets and whitewashed houses, and the *Bairro Alto,* centre of *Fado* (the traditional folksongs of Lisbon).

Nearby is **Belem**, from where the ships of Vasco da Gama, Alvares Cabral and other famous explorers were launched; the town has a famous tower and the *Hieronymite Monastery*. Other points of interest include the 12th-century *Lisbon Cathedral*, the *Coach Museum*, the *Gulbenkian Museum*, the 2.5km-long (1.5-mile) suspension bridge over the Tagus, and the beautiful *azulejos,* the traditional blue and white tiles which adorn so many of the city's churches.

The beach resorts of **Estoril** and **Cascais** are a few miles away from the capital. The former is adjusting well to the demands of tourism and is maintaining the high standards of its hotels, which fringe the glorious *Tamariz Beach.* Cascais has changed even more quickly, from a small fishing village with good but empty beaches to a lively resort with bars, nightclubs and cheap, high-quality restaurants.

Other towns in the area include: **Sintra**, a town in the mountains 25km (15 miles) from Lisbon, with a summer palace, the Monserrate gardens and twice-monthly antique market; **Colares**, a small village famous for its red wines; **Queluz**, with the 18th-century pink rococo palace; **Mafra**, home of the Baroque monastery built in 1717; **Ericeira**, a small fishing village; **Sesimbra**, a busy fishing village with good beaches and brightly painted boats, famous for its seafood and an old Moorish castle overlooking the village; **Troia**, a modern tourist complex on a peninsula parallel to the town of Setubal with good beaches, hotels, restaurants, supermarket, swimming pools, nightclubs, golf course and nautical sports centre; **Setubal**, 39km (24 miles) south of Lisbon; and the village of **Palmela,** with its 12th-century castle and old monastery (which is now a *pousada* – see *Accommodation* above).

Resorts in the area include: Lisbon, Caparica, Palmela, Azeitao, Arrabida, Setubal, Troia, Sesimbra, Carcavelos, Estoril, Cascais, Guincho, Colares, Sintra, São Pedro de Sintra, Queluz, Ericeira, Praia das Macas, Praia Grande and Parede.

Planícies

This large inland area includes the regions of the Cova da Beira, Ribatejo and Alentejo, Monsarraz, Marvao, Moura, Monsanto. Throughout the area there are many typical Portuguese villages set in rich arable landscape. The Planícies is the country's granary, and also the source of much of its cork. Attractions include shooting and reservoir fishing, a wealth of local folklore which finds expression in the countless local festivals, and easy access to the Costa Alentejana with the quiet beaches of Alentejo. The area is known for its local cuisine, particularly seafood, and its handicrafts.

Resorts in the area include: Alcacer do Sal, Alter do

Chao, Beja, Benavente, Campo Maior, Castanheira, Castelo de Vide, Caxarias, Charneca do Infantado, Coruche, Elvas, Estremoz, Evora, Ferreira do Alentejo, Grandola, Lagoa de Santo Andre, Marvao, Minde, Monsaraz, Monte das Flores, Montemor-o-Novo, Moura Ponte do Sor, Portalegre, Rio Maior, Santa Clara-a-Velha, Santarem, Santiago do Cacem, Serpa, Sines, Tomar, Torrao, Costa Alentejana from Troia to Algarve; Sines and Vila Nove de Milfontes.

The Algarve

The Algarve is located in the far south of Portugal, bordered by the Atlantic on two sides, by the mountains in the north and Spain in the east. It stretches from the Spanish border westwards to Cabo de São Vicente (Cape St Vincent). The area is well geared to provide for tourists and it has become a favourite package destination with good beaches and and well equipped sports facilities
Faro, the capital of the Algarve, was destroyed by an earthquake in 1755, and only part of the old town remains. **Loulé** is a market town famous for crafts such as leather and copper. **Albufeira** is a busy market town with a Moorish atmosphere. **Armação de Pêra** is a fishing village with one of the biggest beaches on the Algarve. **Silves** is an old walled city with a 12th-century cathedral. **Carvoeiro** is an old fishing village with a picturesque harbour. **Portimão** is one of the largest towns and fishing ports in the Algarve, known for its furniture and wickerwork. **Monchique** is set high in the mountains and has a spa. **Lagos** has historical shipyards. **Sagres** is the centre of the lobster fishing industry, with a 17th-century fortress. **Cape St Vincent** is the most southwesterly point of mainland Europe.
Resorts in the area include: Albufeira, Armação de Pêra, Lagos, Portimão, Praia da Rocha, Silves, Tavira, Vila Real de Santo Antonio, Olhao, Quarteira, Carvoeiro Loule, Sagres, Vilamoura, Monte Gordo, S. Bras de Alportel, Aljezur and Monchique.
POPULAR ITINERARIES: 5-day: (a) Oporto–Braga–Guimarães–Amarante. (b) Faro–Silves–Serra de Monchique–Lagos–Sagres. (c) Évora–Estremoz–Portalegre–Castelo de Vide–Marvao. **7-day:** (a) Lisbon–Queluz–Sintra–Mafra–Cascais–Estoril. (b) Coimbra–Leiria–Batalha–Alcobaça–Nazaré–S. Martinho do Porto–Caldas da Rainha–Óbidos.

SOCIAL PROFILE

FOOD & DRINK: Seafood is popular, especially in Lisbon, but can be expensive. Soup is a main dish. Typical Portuguese dishes include *sopa de marisco* (shellfish soup cooked and served with wine), *caldo verde* (green soup), made with finely shredded green kale leaves in broth, and *bacalhau*, dried cod, cooked in over 100 different ways. *Caldeirada* is a fish stew with as many as nine kinds of fish, cooked with onions and tomatoes. Also typical is *carne de porco a Alentejana,* in which bits of fried pork are covered with a sauce of clams stewed with tomato and onions. Puddings include *arroz doce* (rice pudding), Madeira pudding and *nuvens* (egg custard). Carrot jam is worth a try. Table service is normal. **Drink:** Portuguese table wines are good value. The most popular regional names are *Dao* and *Serradayres* for red wines and *Bucelas* and *Colares* for white wines. Sparkling rosé wines are mostly produced for export. *Mateus Rosé* is a famous lightweight rosé. Portuguese brandies are also good; the best are produced around Oporto where Port wines come from. There are no licensing hours.
NIGHTLIFE: The large towns offer every kind of entertainment. There are many nightclubs, theatres, cinemas, stage shows, folk dancing and music performances. Portugal offers bullfights on horseback. The traditional *Fado* can be heard in many restaurants and performances begin at about 2200. The theatre season is from October to May. Gambling is authorised and Estoril, Figueira da Foz, Espinho, Alvor, Vilamoura and Monte Gordo have casinos. The elegant Casino Monumental in Póvoa de Varzim is the most renowned.
SHOPPING: Items include leather goods, copper, ceramics, handcrafted silver and gold, embroidery and tapestry, woodcarving, cork products, porcelain and china, crystal and glassware. **Shopping hours:** Generally 0900-1300 and 1500-1900 Monday to Friday; 0900-1300 Saturday (December also 1500-1900). Shopping centres are usually open 1000-2400 Monday to Sunday.
SPORT: The National Tourist Office has brochures listing the hotels and centres which offer amenities for a wide range of sports. **Golf:** There are championship golf courses in most major centres where visitors can arrange to play. **Tennis:** Most resorts and cities have tennis courts available. **Horseriding:** Horses and

instruction are available in many resorts. **Watersports:** Skindiving, swimming, offshore fishing, deep-sea fishing, water-skiing, sailing and windsurfing are popular. The Algarve offers watersports all year round, although the tides can be strong in the winter.
Spectator sports: The Portugal Golf and Portugal Tennis Opens. **Other sports:** These include **clay pigeon shooting** and **squash.**
SPECIAL EVENTS: June is one of the best months for festivals in Portugal, and the festivals of St Anthony, St John and St Peter, held in Lisbon, are central events. Also of note are the *Gulbenkian Festival of Music* in winter, the *Santiago Fair* in Setubal, the *Wine Harvest Festival* at Palmela in September, the *Algarve Song and Dance Festival* in September and the world-famous *Our Lady of Fatima* pilgrimages during May and October. There are many other religious and *Lady Saint* festivals. There are carnivals throughout the country in the days leading up to Shrove Tuesday.
For a full list of local festivals, contact the National Tourist Office.
SOCIAL CONVENTIONS: The Portuguese way of life is leisurely, and old-fashioned politeness is essential. Warm, Latin hospitality is the norm. The country has a deeply individual national character, although each province has its own traditions and folklore. Casual wear is widely acceptable, although beachwear should not be worn in towns. In restaurants it is usual to smoke only at the end of the meal. Smoking is prohibited in cinemas, theatres and on buses. **Tipping:** Generally 10-15%. Taxi drivers are tipped 10%.

BUSINESS PROFILE

ECONOMY: Portugal has a traditionally agrarian economy that has industrialised extensively in recent years. Agriculture still employs over 25% of the workforce, producing wheat, maize, tomatoes, potatoes and grapes. Production has undergone a relative decline so that Portugal now imports a sizeable proportion of its foodstuffs after having long been self-sufficient. The manufacturing sector is dominated by the textile industry, in which there has been major investment, and both it and the footwear industry are vital export earners. Other significant products are paper, cork and other wood products, electrical appliances, chemicals and ceramics. Portugal has grown rapidly since joining the European Community in 1986. Both foreign and internal investment have been high and the country's infrastructure has been extensively modernised. There remain problems: at 6%, inflation is high by EU standards; the large agricultural sector remains very inefficient; and the disparity between the relatively prosperous north and the poorer south continues. Although Britain has historically been Portugal's main trading partner, the growth of bilateral trade has failed to keep pace with that of Portugal's other trading partners, particularly Germany, France, Spain and Italy.
BUSINESS: Business people are expected to dress smartly and formal attire is expected in some dining rooms and for important social functions. English is widely spoken in business circles, although when visiting a small family business it is best to check in advance. Visiting cards are generally only exchanged by more senior members of a company. July and August are best avoided. **Office hours:** 0900-1300 and 1500-1900 Monday to Friday.
COMMERCIAL INFORMATION: The following organisations can offer advice: Associação Comercial de Lisboa, Câmara de Comércio e Indústria Portuguesa, Rua das Portas de Santo Antão 89, 1194 Lisbon. Tel: (1) 342 7179. Fax: (1) 342 4304. Telex: 13441; *or* Confederação do Comércio Português (CPP), Rua dos Correeiros 79, 1° Andar, 1100 Lisbon. Tel: (1) 347 7430. Fax: (1) 347 8638. Telex: 14829.
CONFERENCES/CONVENTIONS: Lisbon is the main centre for conventions, with venues that can seat up to 1500 persons: in 1987 the Lisbon Convention Bureau was founded and in 1989 a major Congress Centre opened, fully integrated with the Lisbon International Fair's exhibition facilities. The Fair is a department of the Portuguese Industrial Association which promotes trade fairs, exhibitions and meetings. The Bureau is a non profit-making association of companies providing support services to conference organisers. Its *Services Directory* includes details of the Congress Centre and hotels with conference facilities. For information, contact the Lisbon Convention Bureau, Rua Jardim do Regedor 50, 1100 Lisbon. Tel: (1) 342 5527. Fax: (1) 346 3521. Lisbon opened the Belem Cultural Centre in 1992 to coincide with Portugal's EU presidency, featuring high-quality technical equipment and facilities for meetings of up to

1400 delegates. For further information, contact the Belem Cultural Centre, Rua Dom Lourenço de Almeida 6, 1400 Lisbon. Tel: (01) 362 1475/82. Fax: (1) 362 1474. Telex: 60766 (a/b CECBEL P).

CLIMATE

The northwest has mild winters with high levels of rainfall and fairly short summers. The northeast has longer winters and hot summers. In the south, summers (March to October) are warm with very little rain except in early spring and autumn. High temperatures are moderated by a permanent breeze in Estoril (July to August).
Required clothing: Light- to medium-weights and rainwear are advised.

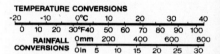

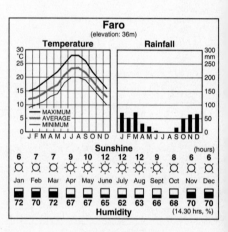

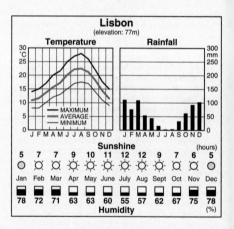

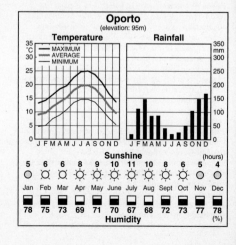

Madeira

Location: Atlantic Ocean, 535 nautical miles southwest of Lisbon.

AREA: 794 sq km (314 sq miles).
POPULATION: 253,000 (1991).
POPULATION DENSITY: 318.7 per sq km.
CAPITAL: Funchal. **Population:** 120,000 (1991).
GEOGRAPHY: The group comprises the main island of Madeira, the smaller island of Porto Santo and the three uninhabited islets of Ilheu Chao, Deserta Grande and Ilheu de Bugio. The islands are hilly and of volcanic origin and the coast of Madeira is steep and rocky with deep eroded lava gorges running down to the sea. These are particularly impressive on the north coast of Madeira island. The largest of a group of five islands formed by volcanic eruption, Madeira is in fact the summit of a mountain range rising 6.5km (4 miles) from the sea bed. Its volcanic origin can be clearly seen in its mountainous interior and in the lava streams which break up the line of cliffs on its coast. At Cabo Girão, west of the capital of Funchal, is the second-highest cliff in the world. Inland, Pico Ruivo is the island's highest point (1862m/6109ft) with the slightly lower Pico de Arieiro (1810m/5940ft) nearby. Both are destinations for sightseeing tours, commanding fine views of the surrounding mountains. Madeira's volcanic origin means that it has no sandy beaches, although there is a small beach, Prainha, near the whaling village of Canical on the extreme east of the island. Madeira itself is 58km (36 miles) long and 23km (14 miles) wide. Porto Santo is much smaller, only 14km (9 miles) long and 5km (3 miles) wide, with a long, golden sandy beach, complementing Madeira.
TIME: GMT (GMT + 1 from last Sunday in March to Saturday before last Sunday in September).
ELECTRICITY: 220 volts AC, 50Hz. 2-pin round plugs are in use.
COMMUNICATIONS: Services are similar to those offered on the mainland.
BBC World Service and Voice of America frequencies: From time to time these change. See the section *How to Use this Book* for more information.
BBC:

MHz	17.70	15.07	12.09	9.410
Voice of America:				
MHz	11.97	9.670	6.040	5.995

PASSPORT/VISA

The passport and visa requirements are the same as for visiting mainland Portugal.

HEALTH

As for mainland Portugal; see above.

TRAVEL

AIR: The airline serving Madeira is *Air Portugal TAP (TP).*
Approximate flight time: From London to Funchal is 3 hours 40 minutes.
International airports: *Funchal (FNC),* 23km (14 miles) from the city, and *Porto Santo (PXO),* which is served by flights from Funchal and Lisbon.
SEA: The main passenger port is Funchal, served by *BI, CTC, P&O, Fred Olsen, Cunard, Polish Ocean,*

Norwegian American, Norwegian Cruises/Union Lloyd, Costa and *Lauro.* Ferry services from Madeira to Porto Santo take three hours.

ACCOMMODATION

There are many luxury hotels on the island along the coast. These tend to be fully booked during the summer and over the Christmas period, therefore early booking is advisable. Most of the hotels compensate for the lack of beaches on the island of Madeira by providing swimming pools.

RESORTS & EXCURSIONS

Much of Madeira's appeal comes from the fact that it is a spectacularly beautiful island, lush with woods, vineyards and rich farmland, pitted with valleys and with a coastline consisting mainly of sheer cliffs. It is described by the locals as a 'floating garden', reflecting the efforts of centuries of intensive cultivation. There are beautiful walks following the routes on the *levadas* (irrigation channels) which cover the island. As well as travelling around the island to see the countryside, one should visit the *Botanical Gardens* in Funchal, beautifully laid out in the grounds of an old country house. There are extravagant terraces of tropical flowers and other more delicate varieties grown in greenhouses. Open from 1000-1700, admission to the gardens is free; there is also a superb view across the harbour.
Although a number of excursions are available on Madeira, one which should be singled out is the toboggan run down to Funchal from the villages of *Monte* or *Terreiro da Luta.* Before motor vehicles, the toboggan was commonly used in Madeira and a number of special 'runs' were constructed. Today the toboggans carry tourists with two men using ropes to control the wide 'carro', a large wicker basket mounted on wooden runners.
Madeira is an island whose success is based on providing quality service and a high standard of holidaymaking. It is nevertheless unlikely ever to be overrun by groups of conference delegates, for hoteliers are well aware of their obligations to individuals who choose to take their holiday on Madeira. It is, if nothing else, an island for the independently minded.
Funchal: There are several regular sightseeing bus tours which take in many of the town's attractions. These include the *Mercado dos Lavradores* (the lively flower and vegetable market), the *Botanical Gardens,* the *Sé* (the 15th-century cathedral), the *Quinta das Cruzes* and the *Museu de Arte Sacra* (Museum of Sacred Art), a large villa containing many European works of art. A visit to the wine lodge is recommended; there one may taste and buy various Madeira wines. The lodge is conveniently situated next door to the Madeira Tourist Office in Avenida Arriaga, which can provide information on all aspects of excursions on the island.
Baia de Zarco is the new name given by the Madeira Tourist Office to a key tourist area located 24km (15 miles) from Funchal. The principal villages are **Agua de Pera, Machico, Canical, Portela, Porto da Cruz, Santa de Serra** and **Santa Cruz.** The area offers a wide variety of watersports, golf and tennis, and has a selection of hotels and holiday villas. **Prainha,** near the island's eastern tip, has Madeira's best sand beach.
The coast: Most coastal towns offer a wide variety of watersports; these can be reached from Funchal by means of a road network which offers spectacular views. Many of the towns have fine churches and other examples of Portuguese colonial architecture. The main centres on the more accessible southern coast include the fishing village of **Camara de Lobos,** a favourite spot of Winston Churchill's, 8km (5 miles) west of Funchal; **Calheta;** and **Porta do Sol,** which is situated on both sides of a deep ravine. The roads are often rough, but the sea views are magnificent. The scenery in the north is wilder and even more spectacular, and the area contains many of the island's best vineyards and colonial architecture. **Porto do Moniz, São Vincente** and **Santana** are the main towns.
Inland Madeira: The moutainous interior is served by a network of twisting roads, many of which go up to the summits of some of the highest peaks. Good places to visit include **Camacha,** centre of the wickerwork industry; **Eira do Serrado,** the crater of an extinct volcano inside which lies the hidden village of **Curral das Freiras;** and *Pico Ruivo,* the island's highest point. The return journey to Funchal from **Monte** or **Terreiro da Luta** can be made by means of the toboggan run. **Porto Santo** is 15 minutes from Funchal by plane (advance booking essential). The terrain is flatter and has more sandy beaches than Madeira. Day-trips from Madeira can be organised. The tiny capital, **Vila Baleira,** contains the house where Christopher Columbus once lived.

SOCIAL PROFILE

FOOD & DRINK: Regional dishes include *sopa de tomate e cebola* (tomato and onion soup), *caldeirada* (fish soup), *bife de atum e milho frito* (tuna steak and fried maize), *carne em vinha d'alho* (pickled pork and garlic), *espetada* (fresh black scabbard fish) and *bolo de mel* (Madeira honey cake). **Drink:** Popular wines of Madeira are *malmsey* (Malvasia), a sweet dessert wine, *bual* and the dry *serceal.* Wines, spirits and beers imported from mainland Portugal and Europe are also available. *Galão,* a glass of milky coffee and *bica,* a small cup of very black coffee, are also popular.
NIGHTLIFE: Some hotels have excellent nightclubs with music for dancing and international cabaret entertainment. Folk entertainment is also included in the weekly programme of these hotels and in most cases non-residents are welcome.
SHOPPING: In Funchal there is a wide variety of shops selling everyday goods, as well as many souvenirs. Special purchases include Madeira folk art such as embroidery, tapestry and wickerwork. Madeira wine is a popular gift.
SPORT: Golf: Madeira Golf course and Palheiro Golf Course are the two new 18-hole courses on the island. Clubs, buggies and trolleys are available for hire. The courses are located within 29km (18 miles) of Funchal. Many hotels have their own **tennis** courts and some allow non-residents to use them. **Watersports:** As well as the sea, there are many **swimming** pools, some on hotel rooftops and others along the seafront. There is also a Lido, large enough for 2000 people, with pools, shops and restaurants. Arrangements for watersports, including **water-skiing, windsurfing, snorkelling, scuba diving** and **fishing,** can be made through some hotels.
SPECIAL EVENTS: Throughout the year numerous events take place on Madeira and it is a good idea to visit at the time of a specific festival. Around Christmas and New Year, for example, there are some really spectacular celebrations. Cruise ships often stop the night of December 31 in Funchal Harbour so that passengers can appreciate the firework displays, accompanied by church bells and ships' sirens, which herald the New Year. The *Flower Festival* in April, the *Wine Festival* in September, *Carnival* in February and the *Saint Silvester Festival* in December are just a few of the events that can add a memorable highlight to a holiday.

CLIMATE

Mild subtropical climate with warm summers and extremely mild winters.
Required clothing: Mid-seasonal wear (as for the Azores).

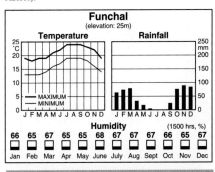

Azores

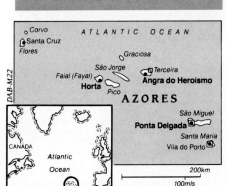

Location: Atlantic, 1220km (760 miles) due west of Portugal.

AREA: 2247 sq km (868 sq miles).
POPULATION: 237,800 (1991).
POPULATION DENSITY: 108.3 per sq km.
CAPITAL: São Miguel: Ponta Delgada; **Faial:** Horta; **Terceira:** Angra do Heroismo.
GEOGRAPHY: The Azores are a widely separated group of nine islands in the Atlantic, due west of mainland Portugal. Principal groups of islands are São Miguel and Santa Maria, Terceira, Graciosa, São Jorge, Pico, Faial, Flores and Corvo. The islands are mountainous in the interior and forested, leading down to long beaches and fishing harbours. There are several hot springs and spas.
TIME: GMT - 1 (GMT from last Sunday in March to last Saturday in September).
ELECTRICITY: 220/110 volts. 2-pin round plugs are in use.
COMMUNICATIONS: Services are similar to, but less extensive than, those offered on the mainland.
BBC World Service and Voice of America frequencies: From time to time these change. See the section *How to Use this Book* for more information.
BBC:

MHz	17.70	15.07	12.09	6.195

Voice of America:

MHz	11.97	9.670	6.040	5.995

PASSPORT/VISA

The passport and visa requirements are the same as for visiting mainland Portugal.

HEALTH

As for mainland Portugal; see above.

TRAVEL

AIR: The Azores' local airline is *SATA (SP),* which runs inter-connecting flights between the islands.
Approximate flight time: From London to the Azores is 3 hours 10 minutes, plus stopover time in Lisbon of 2-12 hours.
International airports: *Ponta Delgada (PDL)* (São Miguel), *Santa Maria (SMX)* (Vila do Porto), and *Terceira (TER)* (Terceira).
SEA: *CTC* and *P&O* run cruises to the main port of Ponta Delgada.

ACCOMMODATION

The main islands have a reasonably good selection of hotel accommodation, and hotels are rarely full, so although it is a good safeguard, it is not vital to book in advance.

RESORTS & EXCURSIONS

During the last 500 years the Azores have remained almost completely unspoilt. There are no hotel blocks and not too many people. There is some good scenery. Volcanic craters form lakes, and there are high cliffs, gentle valleys, unusual flowers amid lush vegetation, geysers, mineral-water springs and secluded coves. Inland the countryside is speckled with whitewashed cottages.
Santa Maria was the first island to be discovered and contains vineyards, green fields, palm trees and windmills. There are two excellent beaches with soft sand at São Lourenco and Praia. There is also a 15th-century parish church and the town hall is located in a former 16th-century convent. The island is ideal for underwater fishing and water-skiing.
São Miguel is the largest island in the group and perhaps the most beautiful. Certainly one of the most spectacular sights on any of the islands is São Miguel's *Sete Cidades* – a 40-sq-km (15 sq miles) extinct crater with two lakes, one of deep blue and the other emerald green. At *Furnas* you can bathe in the volcanic streams and therapeutic sulphurous springs. Embroideries and pineapple products are the main souvenirs of this island.
Terceira: Called the 'Lilac Isle' because of the distinctive colouring of its sunsets, this gently rural island is the home of unique rope bullfights. This island, too, is covered with an abundance of hydrangeas and azaleas and along the highways are gaily coloured little stands that serve as altar stations for the Whitsun Festival of the Holy Spirit – also celebrated throughout the Azores.

Graciosa contains the geological curiosity of *Furna de Enxofre*, a small, warm sulphur lake in a grotto beneath a crater, access to which is via a spiral staircase 80m (270ft) down. The island also boasts the black, underground *Lake Caldeira*, and the hot springs with bathhouse of *Carapacho*. Here many of the islands' typical windmills are scattered amongst the fields. Vineyards form a major part of the island's economy. *Santa Cruz*, the capital, is a village with 18th-century houses.
São Jorge is surrounded by sheer, black rock cliffs and a profusion of vegetation that covers the steep slopes down to the sea. Cedar woods surround the island's capital of *Velas*, which has old buildings and a 17th-century church. São Jorge is the centre for the Azore's dairy produce.
Fayal: The name means 'beech tree', but the islands' main trees are now the strawberry trees or *arbutus*. Blue hydrangea hedges line the fields. The coast is indented with sheltered bays, and there are pines and exotic trees from Japan and elsewhere. *Horta* is the islands' main port, an ideal harbour for yachts and a meeting point for yachtsmen who cross the ocean, as well as a place where large cruise liners dock. *Caldeira* is an immense crater carpeted with greenery and has breathtaking views.
Pico gets its name from the mountain at its centre, which is Portugal's highest peak (2351m/7720ft). The snow-capped cone's hues vary constantly in the different lights during the day from the grey sunrise to the fiery colours of the sunset. The island is renowned for its vineyards that grow the famous 'verdelho' wine of Pico. This harsh and rocky island is also a centre for the Azores whaling industry.
Flores was named after its profusion of flowers. It is often regarded as the prettiest of the islands, with its rugged terrain, flowers growing in the deep canyons, and waterfalls casting hues of blue and green as they splash down into the sea. The island is ideal for watersports.
Corvo, the smallest island, has only one village and its few hundred inhabitants are related to one another. Nobody ever locks their front door and there is no jail or courthouse. Corvo has the living traditions of a pastoral and fishing community.

SOCIAL PROFILE

FOOD & DRINK: Generally the food is Portuguese; crayfish and rabbit are specialities. Locally produced wines are recommended, as are the brandies distilled on the islands.
SHOPPING: Locally made linens and woollen goods, lace and pottery make good buys.
SPORT: Watersports, including deep-sea **fishing,** are catered for at many coastal resorts, particularly on São Miguel where tourist facilities are more developed. Some hotels have **tennis** courts, and **golf** is available.

CLIMATE

Subtropical due to the Gulf Stream. Very equable and slightly humid climate. The rainy season is from November to March.
Required clothing: Mid-season clothes are best; the temperatures are mild at all times of the year.

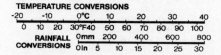

```
TEMPERATURE CONVERSIONS
-20        -10       0°C       10       20       30       40
   0   10   20  30°F40   50   60   70   80   90  100
RAINFALL   0mm   200       400       600       800
CONVERSIONS 0In  5    10    15    20    25    30
```

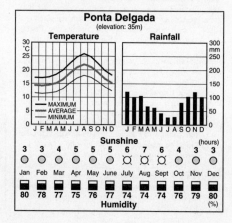

Ponta Delgada
(elevation: 35m)

Temperature / Rainfall

Sunshine (hours)
Jan	Feb	Mar	Apr	May	June	July	Aug	Sept	Oct	Nov	Dec
3	3	4	5	5	6	7	6	4	3	3	3
80	78	77	75	76	77	74	74	74	76	79	80

Humidity (%)

Puerto Rico

Location: Caribbean.

Diplomatic representation: As an *estado libre asociado* (a 'commonwealth state') of the USA, Puerto Rico manages its own affairs, but is represented abroad by US Embassies and Consulates. Addresses of these and of US Tourist Offices may be found in the *United States of America* entry later in the *World Travel Guide*. Tourist information may also be obtained from:

Puerto Rico Hotel and Tourism Association
Suite 702, Plaza Center, 954 Ponce de León Avenue, Miramar, Santurce 00907, Puerto Rico
Tel: 725 2902. Fax: 725 2913.
Commonwealth of Puerto Rico Tourism Company
PO Box 4435, Old San Juan Station, 301 San Justo Street, San Juan 00905, Puerto Rico
Tel: 721 2400. Fax: 725 4417. Telex: 3450158.
British Consulate
American Airline Buildings 1101, 1509 Lopez Landron Street, Santurce 00911, Puerto Rico
Tel: 721 5193 *or* 728 6366. Telex: 3454325.
Commonwealth of Puerto Rico Tourism Company
23rd Floor, 575 Fifth Avenue, New York, NY 10017
Tel: (212) 599 6262. Fax: (212) 818 1866.
Government of Puerto Rico Tourism Company
Suite 300, 43 Colborne Street, Toronto, Ontario M5E 1E3
Tel: (416) 368 9025. Fax: (416) 368 5350.

AREA: 8959 sq km (3459 sq miles).
POPULATION: 3,551,000 (1991).
POPULATION DENSITY: 396.4 per sq km.
CAPITAL: San Juan. **Population:** 434,849 (1980).
GEOGRAPHY: Puerto Rico is an island east of the Dominican Republic and west of the British Virgin Islands. Also included are several smaller islands, such as Culebra, Mona and Vieques. The island is comparatively small, 8959 sq km (3459 sq miles), with a central mountain range reaching an altitude of 1338m (4390ft) at Cerro de Punta, and surrounded by low coastal plains. The capital is on the northeast shore. Much of the natural forest has been cleared for agriculture, but the trees in the northeast are protected as a national park. The other main towns are Ponce, Bayamón and Caguas.
LANGUAGE: Spanish is the official language; English is widely spoken.
RELIGION: 85% Roman Catholic; the remainder are other Christian denominations and Jews.
TIME: GMT - 4. The island does not observe Daylight

Health		
GALILEO/WORLDSPAN: **TI-DFT/SJU/HE**		
SABRE: **TIDFT/SJU/HE**		
Visa		
GALILEO/WORLDSPAN: **TI-DFT/SJU/VI**		
SABRE: **TIDFT/SJU/VI**		

For more information on Timatic codes refer to Contents.

Timatic

Saving Time.

ELECTRICITY: 120 volts AC, 60Hz.

COMMUNICATIONS: Telephone: IDD service is available. Country code: 1 809. Outgoing international code: 135 or 011 depending on the area. **Telex:** Facilities are available in the capital and in main hotels. **Post:** Airmail to Western Europe takes up to a week. **Press:** The English-language newspaper published in Puerto Rico is *The San Juan Star;* others include *El Vocero de Puerto Rico, El Nuevo Dia* and *El Mundo.*

BBC World Service and Voice of America frequencies: From time to time these change. See the section *How to Use this Book* for more information.

BBC:

MHz	17.84	15.22	9.915	5.975

Voice of America:

MHz	15.21	11.70	6.130	0.930

PASSPORT/VISA

The passport and visa requirements for entering Puerto Rico are the same as for entering the USA. See the *Passport/Visa* section in the *United States of America* entry later in the book.

MONEY

Currency: US Dollar (US$) = 100 cents. For denominations, see the *Money* section of the general *USA* entry later in the book.

Credit cards: All international credit cards are accepted. **Travellers cheques:** Cheques in various currencies are accepted, but US Dollar cheques are preferred.

Currency restrictions: Refer to the *USA* entry.

Banking hours: 0900-1430 Monday to Thursday; 0900-1430 and 1530-1700 Friday.

DUTY FREE

As for the USA; see later in the *World Travel Guide.*

PUBLIC HOLIDAYS

Jan 1 '95 New Year's Day. **Jan 6** Epiphany. **Jan 11** Birthday of Eugenio María de Hostos. **Jan 15** Martin Luther King Day. **Feb 20** Washington-Lincoln Day. **Mar 22** Emancipation of the Slaves. **Apr 14** Good Friday. **Apr**

17 José de Diego's Birthday. **May 29** Memorial Day. **Jun 24** Feast of St John the Baptist. **Jul 4** US Independence Day. **Jul 17** Luis Muñoz Rivera's Birthday. **Jul 26** Constitution Day. **Jul 27** José Celso Barbosa's Birthday. **Sep 4** Labour Day. **Oct 9** Columbus Day. **Nov 11** Veterans' Day. **Nov 20** For Discovery of Puerto Rico Day. **Nov 23** Thanksgiving Day. **Dec 25** Christmas Day. **Jan 1 '96** New Year's Day. **Jan 6** Epiphany. **Jan 11** Birthday of Eugenio María de Hostos. **Jan 15** Martin Luther King Day. **Feb** Washington-Lincoln Day. **Mar 22** Emancipation of the Slaves. **Apr 5** Good Friday.

HEALTH

Regulations and requirements may be subject to change at short notice, and you are advised to contact your doctor well in advance of your intended date of departure. Any numbers in the chart refer to the footnotes below.

	Special Precautions?	Certificate Required?
Yellow Fever	No	No
Cholera	No	No
Typhoid & Polio	Yes	-
Malaria	No	-
Food & Drink	1	-

[1]: Water is purified in main areas, although bottled water may be preferable. Tap water is considered safe to drink. Milk is pasteurised and dairy products are safe for consumption. Local meat, poultry, seafood, fruit and vegetables are generally considered safe to eat.

Rabies is present. For those at high risk, vaccination before arrival should be considered. If you are bitten abroad, seek medical advice without delay. For more information, consult the *Health* section at the back of the book.

Bilharzia (schistosomiasis) is present. Avoid swimming and paddling in fresh water. Swimming pools which are well-chlorinated and maintained are safe.

Health care: Health services are good but costly; health insurance is recommended.

TRAVEL - International

AIR: There is no local airline, but frequent flights connect Puerto Rico with other islands and cities in the Caribbean.

Approximate flight times: From Puerto Rico to *Chicago* is 5 hours 40 minutes, to *London* is 8 hours (direct), to *Los Angeles* is 10 hours 45 minutes, to *Miami* is 2 hours 35 minutes, to *New York* is 4 hours and to *Washington DC* is 3 hours 50 minutes.

International airport: *Luis Muñoz Marin (SJU)* is 14km (9 miles) east of San Juan. Airport facilities include a restaurant, bar, bank, post office, hotel reservations, a duty-free shop and car hire. Bus T2 runs every 30 minutes from 0600-2300. Taxis are available.

SEA: The main passenger port is San Juan. The following cruise lines run services to San Juan: *NCL, Commodore, Royal Caribbean, Costa, Cunard, Chandris, Astor United Cruises, Sitmar, Home Lines, Norwegian Viking* and *Princess Cruises.*

TRAVEL - Internal

AIR: *Prinair (PQ)* run high-frequency commuter services to Ponce and Mayagüez.

ROAD: Taxi: A special service called a *linea* will pick up and drop off passengers where they wish. They operate between San Juan and most towns, at a fixed rate. **Car hire:** Available at the airport and city agencies. Rental companies include: *AAA, Afro, Atlantic, Avis, Budget* and *Discount.* Traffic drives on the right. **Documentation:** International Driving Licence.

URBAN: Bus: San Juan has local bus services *(Guaguas)* and there are bus terminals in Bayamón, Catano, Country Club and Rio Piedras, as well as the capital. Buses usually tend not to run after 2100. There are also coach and bus companies offering sightseeing trips. These include: *American Sightseeing/Travel Service Inc, Gray Line Sightseeing Tours, Normandie Tours, Rico Sun Tours, Taino Tours Inc* and *Will Rey Tours.* **Taxi:** *Publicos* (shared taxis) have P or PD at the end of licence plate numbers and run regular routes between established points. They usually operate only during daylight hours and depart from the main *plaza* (central square) of a town. *Publicos* must be insured by law and the Public Service Commission fixes their routes and reasonable rates. Conventional taxis are hired by the hour, and charges are metered except in charter trips outside the usual taxi zones. They can be hailed in the street, or called by telephone. They are available at the airport and at stands at most hotels. Taxi drivers expect a 15% tip.

JOURNEY TIMES: The following chart gives approximate journey times (in hours and minutes) from San Juan to other major cities and resorts in Puerto Rico.

	Air	Road	Sea
Ponce	0.30	1.30	-
Mayagüez	0.30	2.30	-
Vieques	0.30	*0.45	2.00
Fajardo	-	0.45	-
Dorado	-	0.35	-
Humacao-Palmas -	0.45	-	

Note [*]: To Fajardo.

ACCOMMODATION

HOTELS: San Juan has modern Americanised hotels and there is similar lodging in Ponce. *Paradores* (Government-sponsored inns) are less modern, but of a good standard. For further information, contact the Puerto Rico Hotel and Tourism Association (for address, see top of entry).
APARTMENTS & CONDOMINIUMS: Available from a number of companies specialising in renting this type of accommodation. See under *Accommodation* in the general introduction to the *United States of America* later in this book. Condominiums and flats are best around Luquillo Beach to the northeast.

RESORTS & EXCURSIONS

The capital city of **San Juan** is divided into the old and the new. The old part was founded in 1521 and is now officially declared a National Historic Zone, and many 16th- and 17th-century buildings have been restored and refurbished in the original Spanish style. The city boasts many shops, restaurants, art galleries and museums. The *Pablo Casals Museum* has manuscripts and photographs relating to the work of the famous cellist. Videotapes of performances from past Casals festivals (held every June) can be viewed on request. *Casa de los Contrafuertes* houses the *Latin American Graphic Arts Museum* and the *Pharmacy Museum*, with its recreated apothecary shop. *Casa del Callejon* is a traditional Spanish-style home, which holds the *Museum of Colonial Architecture* and the *Museum of the Puerto Rican Family*. *Casa del Libro* holds a rare collection of early manuscripts and books, some dating back to the 15th century. The *San Juan Museum of Art & History* was built in 1855 as a market and restored in 1979 as a cultural centre where the patio is often used for concerts. *Plaza de San José*, at the 'top' of old San Juan and marked by a statue of Juan Ponce de León, is a cosy area of small museums and pleasant cafés. Other places of interest in Old San Juan include *El Morro* (a 16th-century Spanish fortress) and the 18th-century fort of *San Cristobal*, built in 1771. Both buildings are perched on clifftops at the tip of a peninsula. El Morro, in particular, has many exhibits documenting Puerto Rico's role in the discovery of the New World and was instrumental in the defence of San Juan in the 16th century and its continuing survival. *Casa Blanca*, dating from 1523, was built as a home for Ponce de León, and the *Dominican convent* (also started in 1523) now houses the *Instituto de Cultura Puertorriquena*. *La Fortaleza*, completed in 1540, is now the Governor's residence – the oldest of its kind in the Western hemisphere. The old *San Juan City Wall*, dating from the 1630s, was built by the Spanish and it follows the peninsula contour, providing picturesque vantage points for viewing Old San Juan and the sea. *San Juan Cathedral*, originally built in the 1520s, was completely restored in 1977. *San José Church* is the second-oldest church in the Western hemisphere – Ponce de León's body was interred here until the early 20th century. The *Alcaldia*, or City Hall, was built between 1604-1789. The *Casino* (not to be confused with gambling clubs) is a beautiful building dating from 1917. Recently refurbished, the rich interior boasts marble floors, exquisite plasterwork and 4.7m (12ft) chandeliers.
New San Juan is connected to the old town by a narrow neck of land, and modern architecture has flourished in recent years. There are *Botanical Gardens* and a *Museum of Anthropology* for the leisurely visitor. Bay cruises are also available, which offer excellent views of the city.
El Yunque, east of the capital, is a 27,000-acre rainforest (with over 240 species of trees) and bird sanctuary, which can be visited by narrow-gauge train or road. It is the only tropical rainforest in the US National Forest System and is located in the *Luquillo Mountains.*
The beautiful town of **Ponce**, on the southern side of the island and connected to the capital by a toll road, is situated near many excellent beaches. It hosts an *Indian Ceremonial Park* and also has several buildings of interest, including a sugar mill and rum museum. The *Museum of Art* there contains more than 1000 paintings and 400 sculptures, ranging from ancient classical to contemporary art. Its collection of 19th-century Pre-Raphaelite paintings is among the best in the Americas.
The Arroyo to Ponce train stops at **Guayama,** where the station has been restored as a crafts centre.
The *Tibes Indian Ceremonial Centre,* a short drive from Ponce, is an ancient Indian burial ground. A replica of a Taino Indian village has been built near the small museum, reception area and exhibition hall. The museum is open 0900-1600 Tuesday to Sunday.
The *Phosphorescent Bay,* near **La Parguera** in the southwest of the island, is a major attraction. Here, marine life, microscopic in size, lights up when disturbed by fish, boats or any movement. The phenomenon – especially vivid on moonless nights – is rarely found elsewhere. Boat trips are available at night. There is another phosphorescent bay in **Vieques.**
The *Camuy Caves,* near **Arecibo** on the north coast, is the third-largest cave system in the world. There are well-paved access roads, a reception area, and electric trains to the entrance of the caves. The *Arecibo Observatory* is the site of the largest radar/radio telescope in the world. Located in the unusual karst country of Puerto Rico, the 20-acre dish is best seen from a small airplane flight between San Juan and Mayagüez. Visitors are welcome 1400-1630 Sundays.
The *Caguana Indian Ceremonial Park,* south of the Arecibo Observatory, was built by Taino Indians as a site for recreation and worship 800 years ago. There is another Ceremonial Park in Ponce.
There are old colonial towns at **San German** and **Mayagüez** and a *Tropical Agricultural Research Station* near the Mayagüez division of the University of Puerto Rico, with cuttings of hundreds of tropical plants; visitors are allowed in the gardens 0730-1200 and 1300-1630 Monday to Friday.
Many of the drives through the centre of the island take in spectacular scenery and are to be recommended. The **Espirito Santo** is a navigable river that flows from the Luquillo Mountains to the Atlantic, and has 24-passenger launches available for river tours along 8km (5 miles) of the route. Special arrangements can be made for groups and the boat ride usually takes about two hours.

SOCIAL PROFILE

FOOD & DRINK: Puerto Rico (and especially San Juan) abounds with good restaurants, catering for all tastes from Spanish to Chinese, Italian, French and Greek. The island cuisine is Spanish-based, with rice and beans as the staple diet. *Paella*, chicken dishes, black bean soup, *sacocho* (beef stew), *jueyes* (land crabs) and *pan de agua* (native bread) are all excellent, as is the delicately seasoned *langosta*. Island rums such as *barrilito* are not to be missed.
NIGHTLIFE: Abundant, ranging from spectacular shows in large hotels to jazz recitals, classical concerts and discos. There is also gambling in San Juan, with casinos at the *Carib Inn, Caribe Hilton, Concha, Condado Plaza, Sands* and *Ramada* hotels, to name a few. Some casinos do require formal wear after 2000.
SHOPPING: Special purchases are cigars, hammocks, straw weaving, sculpture, *santos* (carved religious figures), coconut devil masks and stringed musical instruments. **Shopping hours:** 0900-1700 Monday to Saturday. Some shops open on Sunday if cruise liners are in port.
SPORT: There is **horseracing** at Rio Pedras (El Comandante) all year round. **Horseriding** is available from various ranches on the island, such as Rancho Borinquen, Rancho Criollo and Rancho Guayama. There are eight **baseball** teams in the league and the San Juan-Santurce stadium seats close to 25,000 people. There are other ball parks at Arecibo, Caguas, Mayagüez and Ponce. There are many **golf** courses, including *Punto Borinquen* at Aguadillo (18 holes), and the *Dorado Del Mar Country Club* (18 holes – there are four 18-hole courses at Dorado). **Tennis** courts are available all over the island, especially at major hotels. In addition, play is available on 17 floodlit public courts in San Juan's Central Park, which is open daily. There are also six courts available at the *Dorado Del Mar Country Club* at Dorado. Deep-sea **fishing** is available, with blue and white marlin, sailfish, wahoo, Allison tuna, mackerel, dolphin, tarpon and snook to be found. Fully equipped boats with crew are available for charter all over the island. Palmas del Mar rents small- to medium-sized boats for day **sailing** and the resort is headquarters for the annual *Copa del Palmas*, the major 1-design regatta in Puerto Rico. Motorboats and rowing boats are also available. Puerto Rico's shoreline has many areas protected by beautiful coral reefs and keys, and **snorkelling** in shallow reef waters and mangrove areas is an excellent way of seeing the beautiful and colourful underworld of the sea. **Scuba diving** instruction and equipment rental are available at watersports offices of major hotels and resorts. Many beaches cater for **surfing** and **windsurfing,** for example Pine Grove and Condado beaches.
SPECIAL EVENTS: The following is a selection of the special events which take place annually in Puerto Rico: **Apr '95** *Puerto Rico Orchid Show,* Hato Rey; *Mavi Festival* (costumes, floats, arts & crafts shows and mavi drinking – a local drink made from sassafras), Juana Diaz. **May** *Semana de la Danza* (a week-long celebration of a national dance form – *la danza*), Old San Juan; *Pineapple Festival,* Lajas. **Jun** *San Juan Bautista Day* (begins a week of festivities celebrating San Juan's patron saint), San Juan. **Jul** *Barranquitas Artisans Fair,* Barranquitas. **Sep** *Inter-American Festival of the Arts,* San Juan. **Oct** *National Plantain Festival,* Corozal. **Nov** *Arts & Crafts Fair,* Mayagüez and Cabo Rojo; *Jayuya Indian Festival,* Jayuya. **Nov-Dec** *Fiesta de la Musica Puertorriquena* (annual classical and folk music concerts), Old San Juan; *Festival of Typical Dishes,* Luquillo Beach. **Dec-Jan** *Navidades* (island-wide Christmas festivities). **Dec 24-28** *Hatillo Festival of the Masks,* Hatillo. **Jan '96** *San Sebastian Street Festival,* Old San Juan.
'Fiestas Patronales' celebrations are held in each town's plaza to honour the area's patron saint. These fiestas usually last for ten days and include religious processions, games, local food and dance. For further details, contact the Commonwealth of Puerto Rico Tourism Company.
SOCIAL CONVENTIONS: Handshaking is the customary form of greeting. Casual dress is acceptable, but shorts should not be worn in hotel dining rooms or casinos, where formal dress is required after 2000. Spanish and American manners and conventions exist side by side on the island. Some hotels require formal dress. **Tipping:** Generally 15-20% if not included on the bill.

BUSINESS PROFILE

ECONOMY: Puerto Rico has few natural resources, although some nickel and copper has been located. Manufacturing has overtaken agriculture as the main source of income following an intensive programme of industrialisation by the Government. Pharmaceuticals, electrical and electronic equipment, processed food, textiles, clothing, rum, petrochemicals and refined oil are the main industries. In the agricultural sector, dairy and livestock produce is now more important than sugar cane, the island's main crop. Fresh fruit and vegetables are increasingly grown for export. Tourism is the main service industry. The USA and American corporations dominate the economy and Puerto Rican trade patterns, although the country has important trading links with Japan, the Dominican Republic and Venezuela.
BUSINESS: A knowledge of Spanish (the official language) is very useful, although English is widely spoken; most people in the tourist industry and the greater metropolitan areas are bilingual. Lightweight suits are advised for business meetings. **Office hours:** 0830-1630 Monday to Friday.
COMMERCIAL INFORMATION: The following organisation can offer advice: Chamber of Commerce of Puerto Rico, Chamber of Commerce Buildings, PO Box S-3789, Tetuán 100, San Juan 00904. Tel: 721 6060. Fax: 723 1891.

CLIMATE

Hot tropical climate. The temperature varies little throughout the year. Cooler in the upland areas.
Required clothing: Lightweight tropical clothes.

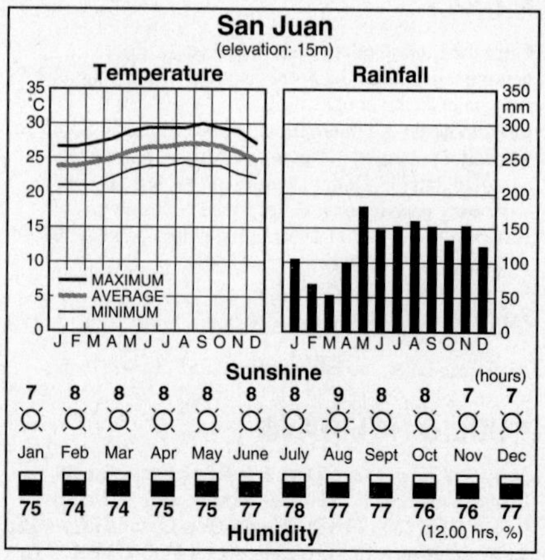

Qatar

Location: Middle East, Gulf Coast.

Ministry of Information and Culture
PO Box 1836, Doha, Qatar
Tel: 831 333. Fax: 831 518. Telex: 4229.
Embassy of the State of Qatar
1 South Audley Streeet, London W1Y 5DQ
Tel: (0171) 493 2200. Fax: (0171) 235 754. Telex: 28469
(a/b QAT EMB). Opening hours: 0930-1600 Monday to
Friday.
British Embassy
PO Box 3, Doha, Qatar
Tel: 421 991. Fax: 438 692. Telex: 4205 (a/b PRODRO
DH).
Embassy of the State of Qatar
Suite 1180, 600 New Hampshire Avenue, NW,
Washington, DC 20037
Tel: (202) 338 0111. Fax: (202) 342 9895.
Also deals with enquiries from Canada.
Embassy of the United States of America
PO Box 2399, 149 Ali Bin Ahmed Street, Farig Bin
Omran, Doha, Qatar
Tel: 864 701/2/3. Fax: 861 669.
**The Canadian Embassy in Kuwait City deals with
enquiries relating to Qatar (see** *Kuwait* **earlier in the
book).**

AREA: 11,437 sq km (4416 sq miles).
POPULATION: 486,000 (1990 estimate).
POPULATION DENSITY: 42.5 per sq km.
CAPITAL: Doha. **Population:** 217,294 (1986).
GEOGRAPHY: Qatar is an oil-rich peninsula jutting
out into the Gulf between Bahrain and the United Arab
Emirates. There are hills in the northwest, but the rest of
the country consists of sand dunes and salt flats, with
scattered vegetation towards the north.
LANGUAGE: Arabic is the official language. Some
English is spoken.

Health

| GALILEO/WORLDSPAN: **TI-DFT/DOH/HE** |
| SABRE: **TIDFT/DOH/HE** |

Visa

| GALILEO/WORLDSPAN: **TI-DFT/DOH/VI** |
| SABRE: **TIDFT/DOH/VI** |

For more information on Timatic codes refer to Contents.

RELIGION: Muslim.
TIME: GMT + 3.
ELECTRICITY: 240/415 volts AC, 50Hz.
COMMUNICATIONS: Telephone: IDD is available.
Country code: 974. There are no area codes. Outgoing
international code: 0. **Fax:** Available at some major
hotels. **Telex/telegram:** The Cable and Wireless Office
in Doha (open 0600-2300) and major hotels provide
these services. **Post:** Airmail to Europe takes up to a
week. **Press:** The main dailies are *Al-Arrayah*, *Al-Arab*
and *Al-Asharq*. English-language newspapers include
The Gulf Times.
**BBC World Service and Voice of America
frequencies:** From time to time these change. See the
section *How to Use this Book* for more information.
BBC:

| MHz | 21.47 | 15.57 | 11.76 | 9.145 |

A service is also available on 1413kHz and 702kHz
(0100-0500 GMT).
Voice of America:

| MHz | 11.97 | 9.670 | 6.040 | 5.995 |

PASSPORT/VISA

*Regulations and requirements may be subject to change at short notice, and you
are advised to contact the appropriate diplomatic or consular authority before
finalising travel arrangements. Details of these may be found at the head of this
country's entry. Any numbers in the chart refer to the footnotes below.*

	Passport Required?	Visa Required?	Return Ticket Required?
Full British	Yes	No/1	Yes
BVP	Not valid	-	-
Australian	Yes	Yes	Yes
Canadian	Yes	Yes	Yes
USA	Yes	Yes	Yes
Other EU (As of 31/12/94)	Yes	Yes	Yes
Japanese	Yes	Yes	Yes

Restricted entry: The Government refuses entry and
transit to holders of passports issued by Israel, or to those
with stamps issued by Israel in their passports.
PASSPORTS: Valid passport required by all.
British Visitors Passport: Not accepted.
VISAS: Required by all except:
(a) **[1]** nationals of the UK and Dependencies with right
of abode in the UK for a stay not exceeding 30 days;
(b) nationals of Bahrain, Kuwait, Oman, Saudi Arabia
and the United Arab Emirates.
Types of visa: Entry visa and 72-hour visa. Entry visas
are valid for two weeks. A 72-hour visa can be granted at
Doha Airport if the traveller has a valid passport, an
onward ticket, proof of being a representative of a
commercial company and is met at Doha Airport by a
recognised commercial company representative in Qatar.
Application to: Consulate (or Consular section at
Embassy). For addresses, see top of entry.
An Entry visa valid for two weeks can be obtained by
applying to the Qatar National Hotels Company. If there
is no objection, the concerned authorities will in turn
inform the appropriate hotel of their approval who will
notify the applicant accordingly. The approval remains
valid for one month from the date of issue.
For longer-period visas apply to the Immigration
Department, Ministry of Interior, PO Box 2433, Doha.
Tel: 822 822.
Application requirements: (a) Completed visa
application form. (b) 3 passport-size photos. (c) Fee of
£24 for Single-entry; £44 for up to 6 months Multiple-
entry and £84 for up to 12 months Multiple-entry. (d)
Health certificates (see note under *Health*).
Working days required: 24 hours, although
applications should be made well in advance of the
intended departure date.

MONEY

Currency: Qatar Riyal (QR) = 100 dirhams. Notes are in
denominations of QR500, 100, 50, 10, 5 and 1. Coins are
in denominations of 50, 25, 10 and 5 dirhams.
Credit cards: Access/Mastercard, American Express,
Diners Club and Visa are widely accepted. Check with
your credit card company for details of merchant
acceptability and other services which may be available.
Travellers cheques: Widely accepted.
Exchange rate indicators: The following figures are
included as a guide to the movements of the Riyal against
Sterling and the US Dollar:

Date:	Oct '92	Sep '93	Jan '94	Jan '95
£1.00=	5.88	5.57	5.38	5.69
$1.00=	3.70	3.65	3.63	3.64

Currency restrictions: There are no restrictions on the

import or export of either local or foreign currency.
Israeli currency is prohibited.
Banking hours: 0730-1130 Saturday to Thursday.

DUTY FREE

The following goods may be imported into Qatar without
incurring customs duty:
454g of tobacco; perfume to the value of QR1000.
Prohibited items: All alcohol is prohibited to those who
do not hold a licence. Firearms can only be imported
with a licence obtained in advance from the Ministry of
Defence, Government of Qatar.

PUBLIC HOLIDAYS

Feb 22 '95 Anniversary of The Amir's Accession. **Mar 3**
Eid al-Fitr (End of Ramadan). **May 10** Eid al-Adha
(Feast of the Sacrifice). **May 31** Islamic New Year. **Sep
3** National Day. **Dec 20** Leilat al-Meiraj (Ascension of
the Prophet). **Feb 22 '96** Anniversary of The Amir's
Accession and Eid al-Fitr (End of Ramadan).
Note: Muslim festivals are timed according to local
sightings of various phases of the Moon and the dates
given above are approximations. During the lunar month
of Ramadan that precedes Eid al-Fitr, Muslims fast
during the day and feast at night and normal business
patterns may be interrupted. Many restaurants are closed
during the day and there may be restrictions on smoking
and drinking. Some disruption may continue into Eid al-
Fitr itself. Eid al-Fitr and Eid al-Adha may last anything
from two to ten days, depending on the region. For more
information see the section *World of Islam* at the back of
the book.

HEALTH

*Regulations and requirements may be subject to change at short notice, and
you are advised to contact your doctor well in advance of your intended date of
departure. Any numbers in the chart refer to the footnotes below.*

	Special Precautions?	Certificate Required?
Yellow Fever	No	1
Cholera	Yes	-
Typhoid & Polio	Yes	-
Malaria	No	-
Food & Drink	2	-

[1]: A yellow fever vaccination certificate is required
from travellers over one year of age arriving from
infected areas.
[2]: All water should be regarded as being potentially
contaminated. Water used for drinking, brushing teeth or
making ice should have first been boiled or otherwise
sterilised. Milk is unpasteurised and should be boiled.
Powdered or tinned milk is available and is advised, but
make sure that it is reconstituted with pure water. Avoid
dairy products which are likely to have been made from
unboiled milk. Only eat well-cooked meat and fish,
preferably served hot. Salad and mayonnaise may carry
increased risk. Vegetables should be cooked and fruit
peeled.
Rabies is present. For those at high risk, vaccination
before arrival should be considered. If you are bitten
abroad, seek medical advice without delay. For more
information, consult the *Health* section at the back of the
book.
Note: Certificates proving the visitor to be HIV negative
and free of tuberculosis, syphilis, leprosy and hepatitis B
are required.
Health care: There are several hospitals in Qatar, the
most recent and modern being the Hamad General
Hospital. The Poly Clinic has good dentists. Charges are
high and health insurance is essential. Due to the intense
heat, visitors should maintain a high salt and fluid intake.

TRAVEL - International

AIR: *Gulf Air (GF)* and *Qatar Airways* are the major
airlines serving Qatar.
Approximate flight time: From Doha to London is 7
hours 15 minutes.
International airport: *Doha (DOH)* is 8km (5 miles)
southeast of the city (travel time – 25 minutes). Facilities
include car hire, bank, restaurant and a duty-free shop.
Taxis are available to the city with official rates
displayed.
SEA: The main international ports are Doha and Umm
Said. The traffic is mostly commercial, but some
passenger lines call at Doha.

ROAD: Access is possible via both the UAE and Saudi Arabia, but the main international route from Saudi Arabia is unreliable and often impassable during the rainy season.

TRAVEL - Internal

ROAD: The road system is fair, but conditions are poor during the wet season. Driving is on the right. **Bus:** No organised public bus service. **Taxi:** These have black and yellow number plates and are metered. Taxis can be hired on an hourly basis. **Car hire:** Available from local companies at the airport and hotels. **Documentation:** A 90-day Temporary Driving Permit will be granted at The Traffic and Licence Office on presentation of a national driving licence or an International Driving Permit. Applicants will be required to pass an oral highway code test and should be accompanied by someone who knows the procedure. A renewal at the end of the 90-day period is possible. Third Party insurance is necessary.

ACCOMMODATION

Recent building ensures that Qatar is well served by first-class hotels. There are also a number of 3- or 4-star hotels offering reasonable accommodation. Advanced booking is strongly advised. All rates are subject to a 15% service charge. For more information contact the Qatar National Hotels Company, PO Box 2977, Doha. Tel: 426 414. Fax: 431 223.

RESORTS & EXCURSIONS

DOHA: The city is a rich mixture of traditional Arabic and modern architecture. The *Grand Mosque* with its many domes and the *Abu Bakir al-Siddiq Mosque* are particularly interesting. There is an excellent *National Museum* in Doha tracing the country's development. The modern town clusters around the Grand Mosque, the *New Amir's Palace* and the *Clock Tower.*

THE NORTH: This area contains most of the historic sites, including **Umm Salal Mohammed,** a relatively large village dominated by the ruins of a 19th-century fort. At **Zubara** is the *Qalit Marir Fortress.* **Al Khor** is the second-largest city, situated around a natural shallow harbour. **Gharya** has a golden sandy beach stretching for miles. **Ruwais** boasts a harbour, from where there is an occasional *dhow* service to Bahrain. There are also good beaches at **Fuwairat,** on the northeast coast, and **Ras Abruk,** opposite Hawar Island.

THE WEST COAST: There are beaches at **Umm Bab** ('The Palm Tree Beach'), **Dukhan** and **Salwah,** near the Saudi border.

THE SOUTH: This is a region of sand dunes and beaches, offering opportunities to go pearl hunting, or to practise any of a number of watersports. The 'inland sea' of **Khor al-Odeid** is the centre of a region of outstanding natural beauty, surrounded by the *Sandi Hills,* accessible only to 4-wheel-drive vehicles.

SOCIAL PROFILE

FOOD & DRINK: While the best food is generally found in hotels, Western, Chinese, Indian and American cuisine is also available. All the major hotels have good public restaurants and most offer outside catering of high quality; waiters, crockery and cutlery will be provided on request. There are a reasonable number of places to eat in Doha, including snack bars serving fast foods, as well as the traditional Levantine *shawarma* and Egyptian *foul* and *taamiyeh.* Restaurants are scarce outside the capital. Alcohol is prohibited.

NIGHTLIFE: Public entertainment is rather limited. Doha has a cinema showing English-language films and the National Theatre. Live entertainment is infrequent, but some international artistes do perform in Qatar.

SPORT: Football is the national sport. Doha boasts several marinas, sub-aqua clubs and **sailing** facilities as well as a number of sports clubs which are open to visitors. There are several **camel race** tracks, the main one just off the road to Dukhan, but spectators need a 4-wheel-drive vehicle to follow the race. The graded track is 18km (11 miles) long through the desert and sometimes more than 250 camels take part with big money prizes and prestige at stake.

SOCIAL CONVENTIONS: The visitor should be fully aware of Muslim religious laws and customs. Women should always dress modestly. Also observe that it is acceptable to cross legs, whereas showing the sole of the foot or unknowingly pointing it at a person is considered an insult. At business and social functions, the traditional Qatari coffee, in tiny handleless cups, will invariably be served. This is a ritual of welcome with strict rules: guests are served in order of seniority – a few drops at first, then, after three or four others have been served, the server returns to fill the first cup; always hold the cup in the right hand; two cups are polite, but never take only one or more than three. It is also worth noting that catering staff are treated with the same respect as other employees. See the section *World of Islam* at the back of the book for further information. **Tipping:** Taxi drivers do not expect a tip. A service charge is often added to bills in hotels and most restaurants, otherwise 10% is appropriate.

BUSINESS PROFILE

ECONOMY: Oil transformed Qatar from an impoverished outcrop on the Arabian peninsula into one of the richest countries in the world in terms of per capita income. Crude petroleum, which is of a very high grade, provides virtually all the country's income. Revenues are dictated by world prices and the requirements of OPEC, of which Qatar is a member, and although prices and production have fallen from their peak in the 1970s, Qatar continues to enjoy a healthy trade surplus. Part of the revenues have been used to develop indigenous industry, mainly based on petrochemicals and refining but also including a steel plant and flour mill. Industrial development is likely to increase sharply during the next few years, observers believe, following the appointment of a new Industry and Works Minister. Agriculture is necessarily limited by the climate and the nature of the country's water resources, although the Government has established a number of experimental projects with artificial resources. The most important economic development in Qatar in recent years has been the discovery of the North Dome gas field, now confirmed as the world's largest. Most of Qatar's oil is sold to Japan and Italy, with whom Qatar signed a 5-year economic and technical cooperation agreement in January 1992. EU countries, Japan and the USA share most of the country's trade.

BUSINESS: Politeness and patience in business dealings are needed. **Office hours:** 0730-1200 and 1500-1800 Saturday to Thursday.

COMMERCIAL INFORMATION: The following organisation can offer advice: Qatar Chamber of Commerce, PO Box 402, Doha. Tel: 425 131. Fax: 324 338. Telex: 4078 (a/b TIJARA DH).

CONFERENCES/CONVENTIONS: Several of Doha's largest hotels provide facilities with extensive support services, including simultaneous translation systems and full audio-visual capability. Contact individual hotels for more information.

CLIMATE

Summer (June to September) is very hot with low rainfall. Winter is cooler with occasional rainfall. Spring and autumn are warm and pleasant.

Required clothing: Lightweight cottons and linens are worn during summer months, with warm clothes for cooler evenings and during the winter. Rainwear is advisable during winter.

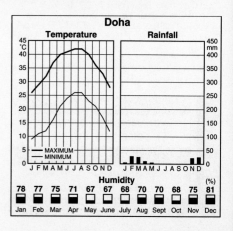

Doha

Temperature / Rainfall / Humidity chart for Doha

	Jan	Feb	Mar	Apr	May	June	July	Aug	Sept	Oct	Nov	Dec
Humidity (%)	78	77	75	71	67	67	68	70	70	68	75	81

Location: Due east of Madagascar, in the Indian Ocean.

Diplomatic Representation: Réunion is an Overseas Département of the Republic of France; addresses of French Embassies, Consulates and Tourist Offices may be found in the *France* section earlier in the *World Travel Guide*. Tourist information may also be obtained from:

Comité du Tourisme de la Réunion
BP 1119, 97482 Saint-Denis Cedex, Réunion
Tel: 418 441. Fax: 202 593. Telex: 916068.

Office du Tourisme
48 rue Saint-Marie, 97400 Saint-Denis, Réunion
Tel: 418 300. Fax: 213 776. Telex: 916822.

Comité du Tourisme de la Réunion
90 rue la Boétie, 75008 Paris, France
Tel: (1) 40 75 02 79. Fax: (1) 40 75 02 73.

British Consulate
136 Chemin Neuf, 97417 La Montagne, Réunion
Tel: 210 619. Telex: 916104 (a/b MARYL RE).

AREA: 2512 sq km (970 sq miles).
POPULATION: 597,828 (1990).
POPULATION DENSITY: 238 per sq km.
CAPITAL: Saint-Denis. **Population:** 121,952 (1990).
GEOGRAPHY: Réunion lies 760km (407 miles) due east of Madagascar in the Indian Ocean. Running diagonally across the island is a chain of volcanic peaks, separating a green humid eastern zone *(Le Vent)* from a dry, sheltered south and west *(Sous le Vent)*. The majority of the population lives along the coast. Sugar cane production accounts for over half the arable land in a country where many basic foodstuffs are imported. Five smaller islands, with a total area of less than 50 sq km (20 sq miles), are all uninhabited.
LANGUAGE: French is the official language. Local Creole *patois* is also spoken.
RELIGION: The majority of the population is Roman Catholic with a Muslim minority.
TIME: GMT + 4.
ELECTRICITY: 220 volts AC, 50Hz.
COMMUNICATIONS: Telephone: IDD is available. Country code: 262. There are no area codes. Outgoing international code: 19. **Telex/telegram:** Facilities are available in Saint-Denis. **Post:** Airmail to Western Europe takes up to three weeks. *Poste Restante* facilities are available in Saint-Denis. **Press:** The two biggest dailies are the *Quotidien de la Réunion* and the *Journal de l'Ile de la Réunion*. Other titles are *Témoignages* and *le*

Réunionnais. There are no English-language dailies.
BBC World Service and Voice of America frequencies: From time to time these change. See the section *How to Use this Book* for more information.
BBC:

MHz	21.47	11.94	6.190	3.255

Voice of America:

MHz	21.49	15.60	9.525	6.035

PASSPORT/VISA

The regulations for tourist and Business visas are the same as for France (see the *Passport/Visa* section for *France* earlier in this book). Visitors should specify that they wish to visit Réunion when they make their application.

MONEY

Currency: French Franc (FFr) = 100 centimes. Notes are in denominations of FFr500, 200, 100, 50 and 20. Coins are in denominations of FFr20, 10, 5, 2 and 1, and 50, 20, 10 and 5 centimes.
Credit cards: American Express, Diners Club and Visa are widely accepted. Access/Mastercard has more limited use. Check with your credit card company for details of merchant acceptability and other services which may be available.
Travellers cheques: Accepted in all the usual institutions.
Exchange rate indicators: The following figures are included as a guide to the movements of the French Franc against Sterling and the US Dollar:

Date:	Oct '92	Sep '93	Jan '94	Jan '95
£1.00=	8.27	8.68	8.74	8.35
$1.00=	5.21	5.68	5.90	5.34

Currency restrictions: Restrictions on the import and export of both foreign and local currency are the same as those for France. See the entry for *France* earlier in the book.
Banking hours: 0800-1600 Monday to Friday.

DUTY FREE

(a) The following goods may be imported into Réunion without incurring customs duty:
200 cigarettes or 100 cigarillos or 50 cigars or 250g of tobacco; 1 litre of spirits over 22% proof or 2 litres of spirits; 2 litres of sparkling wine of less than 22% proof; 50g of perfume and 250ml of eau de toilette; other goods to the value of FFr300.
(b) For passengers arriving from Mauritius:
200 cigarettes or 50 cigars or 250g tobacco.

PUBLIC HOLIDAYS

Public holidays celebrated in Réunion are the same as in France (see the entry for *France* earlier in the *World Travel Guide*) with the following date also observed:
Dec 20 '95 Abolition of Slavery.

HEALTH

Regulations and requirements may be subject to change at short notice, and you are advised to contact your doctor well in advance of your intended date of departure. Any numbers in the chart refer to the footnotes below.

	Special Precautions?	Certificate Required?
Yellow Fever	No	1
Cholera	No	-
Typhoid & Polio	2	-
Malaria	No	-
Food & Drink	3	-

[1]: A yellow fever vaccination certificate is required from travellers over one year of age arriving from infected areas.
[2]: There is a risk of typhoid, but not of polio.
[3]: All water should be regarded as being potentially contaminated. Water used for drinking, brushing teeth or making ice should have first been boiled or otherwise sterilised. Milk is unpasteurised and should be boiled. Powdered or tinned milk is available and is advised, but make sure that it is reconstituted with pure water. Avoid dairy products which are likely to have been made from unboiled milk. Only eat well-cooked meat and fish, preferably served hot. Pork, salad and mayonnaise may carry increased risk. Vegetables should be cooked and fruit peeled. *Rabies* is present. For those at high risk, vaccination before arrival should be considered. If you are bitten abroad seek medical advice without delay. For more information, consult the *Health* section at the back of the book.
Health care: There are 19 hospitals and there is an out-patient clinic in each town or village. The French national health scheme is in force and there is a Reciprocal Health Agreement with the UK; see the entry for *France*. Facilities are limited and full health insurance is advised.

TRAVEL - International

AIR: The main airline to serve Réunion is *Air France (AF)*.
Approximate flight time: From London to Réunion is 14 hours 40 minutes.
International airport: *Saint-Denis (RUN)* (Gillot) is 5.5km (3.5 miles) from the town (travel time – 20 minutes).
SEA: Both freight and passenger lines (a large number are French) put in at Pointe-des-Galets.

TRAVEL - Internal

AIR: Aero-clubs at Gillot Airport hire planes for flights over the island, which are well worth the price.
SEA: Four shipping lines run services around the island.
ROAD: Roads are fair and over 2975km (1850 miles) of highway are tarred. Speed limits are the same as in France. The main road runs on a north–south axis. The island can be easily crossed by bus, taxi or hired car. **Bus:** Services are excellent and luxurious, with very comfortable vehicles. Buses stop by request. **Car hire:** Available from the airport and from rental firms in Saint-Denis.
Documentation: An International Driving Permit is recommended, though not legally required.

ACCOMMODATION

There is a good range of hotels, inns, lodges and *pensions*. Prices are high (and plumbing somewhat basic), but the food is often excellent. Tariffs usually include bed and breakfast, tax and service charges. For further information, contact the Association Réunionnaise des Centres de Vacances et de Loisirs (tel: 281 847); *or* the Relais Départemental de Gîtes Ruraux, 10 place Sarda Garriga, 97400 Saint-Denis (tel: 907 890; fax: 418 429); *or* Chambre Syndicale de l'Industrie Hôtelière de la Réunion, Lieu dit 'Tamatave', 97435 Saint-Gilles-les-Hautes (tel: 553 730; fax: 553 729). **Grading:** Hotels range from **1** to **4 stars.**

RESORTS & EXCURSIONS

Saint-Denis, the capital, has several places of interest, including the *Natural History Museum* and the *Leon Dierx Art Gallery* with its collection of French Impressionist paintings. There are various temples, a mosque and a cathedral, a sign of the cultural and religious variety of the island population. Around town a good trip to take is the *Plaine d'Affouches* in **La Montagne** which is lined by lush tamarind trees and *calumets*, a type of wild fig tree. From **Brûlé** a footpath leads to the *Roche-Ecrite*, a 2227m-high (7306ft) summit which overlooks the whole of the northern part of the island and slopes down to the cirques of Malfate and Salazie.
There are over 600km (370 miles) of footpaths leading through the island. A special feature on Réunion are the so-called *cirques* – large volcanic valleys surrounded by mountains, creating a natural amphitheatre of about 10km (6 miles) in diameter. Day-long sightseeing trips to the cirques may be arranged with travel agents in Saint-Denis.
Cilaos, once infamous as a refuge for escaped slaves, is a lovely mountain area rising to about 1220m (4000ft) with impressive views from *Le Bras Sec* and *Ilet à Cordres*. The most beautiful cirque is probably **Salazie,** with its magnificent waterfalls, especially those known as *Le Voile de la Mariée* (The Bride's Veil) near **Hell-Bourg.** There is a day trip to **Grand-Ilet,** taking in some spectacularly rugged scenery. *Piton des Neiges* is the highest point on the island and is an enjoyable hike from Hell-Bourg. **Mafate** is the most secluded of the valleys, unconnected by any road with the outside world. In the valley is the historic town of **St Paul,** Réunion's original capital, and birthplace of Leconte de Lisle. There are tours to the island's still-active volcano, *La Fournaise*.
Nez-de-Boeuf ('ox's nose') affords a splendid view over the *Rivière des Remparts*, 1000m (3300ft) below, the *Plaine des Sables* and the *Belle Combe* pass. The *Enclos Fouque* crater and the highest peak of the 2631m (8632ft) *Fournaise* can both be explored on foot. The still active *Bory* and *Brûlant* craters are also interesting excursions. Réunion abounds with tropical flowers, trees and fruit and there are tours which aim to show the visitor some of the many species on the island, before returning to the *Botanical Gardens* at Saint-Denis.
Beaches: Réunion does not have extensive beaches, but those on the Leeward west coast are beautiful with yellow, black or white sands. Some of the best beaches are to be found at *Saint-Gilles, Saint-Leu* and *Etang-Sale*. These are mostly shallow coral, running out to the reef. The *Corail Turtle Farm* near Saint-Leu is an interesting place.

SOCIAL PROFILE

FOOD & DRINK: A variety of excellent restaurants, some run by hotels, offer good French cuisine and Creole specialities, notably *rougail* (seafood with sauces) and many different unique curries – these include duck, eel and octopus curry (*zourite*). Worth trying is *bredes*, a delicious local vegetable rather like spinach. Traditional spicy Indian cuisine also appears on the menu, under the heading *massalés*. There are about ten good first-class restaurants in Saint-Denis. Seaside restaurants in particular serve authentic local cuisine – a mixture of Chinese, African and Indian cooking. **Drink:** Arab coffee (*café Bourbon*), French wine and liqueurs, and good local rum such as *rhum arrange* (white rum with vanilla, orchids, aniseed and cinnamon). Local beer and wine are also very good. A full range of alcoholic drinks is available. Licensing hours are largely unrestricted.

SHOPPING: Local handicrafts include lace and embroidery, coral jewellery and basketwork. Tamarind wood, olive wood and ironwood provide the material for furniture in the traditional 'colonial' style, and are used by sculptors and other craftsmen. Rum, vanilla and extracts of vetiver, geranium and ylang-ylang are also recommended purchases. In Saint-Denis the main shopping streets are rue du Maréchal-Leclerc, rue Jean-Chatel and rue Juliette-Dodu. **Shopping hours:** 0830-1200 and 1430-1800 Monday to Saturday.

SPORT: Watersports: Good swimming and other activities are to be found along the *Sous le Vent* coast, especially at Saint-Gilles-des-Bains, which has a reef-protected lagoon. On the more remote beaches, sharks may be a danger, so it is best to enquire locally.
Walking/trekking: There are excellent walking opportunities in the mountains. **Mountaineering:** Good climbing is to be had among the volcanic peaks. **Spas:** Rest cures are available in mountain resorts, such as Cilaos, which is a mountain spa. **Fishing:** Trout fishing is to be found at the Takamaka Falls.
SPECIAL EVENTS: May '95 *Fête du chouchou*, Hell-Bourg, Salazie. **Jun** *Fête de la Musique*, throughout Réunion. **Jul** *Guava Festival*. **Aug** *Fête du Safran*, St Joseph; *Surfing Competition*, St-Leu. **Sep** *Tour de l'île cycling race*. **Oct** *Fête du Vétiver*, St Joseph. **Nov** *Fête des lentilles*, Cilaos.
SOCIAL CONVENTIONS: The islanders follow French fashion. Normal social courtesies should be observed. The immigrants from India, Pakistan and Europe have retained their cultural identities. **Tipping:** Widely practiced and 10% is normal.

BUSINESS PROFILE

ECONOMY: Sugar cane is the principal crop and export earner in this mainly agricultural economy. Other crops grown, given that the soil is mostly of volcanic origin, include vanilla, tobacco, vetiver and ylang-ylang, the last two of which are used in tropical essences. The only industries are those for processing sugar and making rum. Réunion is thus far from self-sufficient in food or anything else and relies on large injections of French aid to cover its trade and budgetary deficits. Apart from France, Réunion trades with Germany, Italy, South Africa and Bahrain.
BUSINESS: The atmosphere is relaxed and friendly; suits will only be required for the most formal of meetings. A sound knowledge of the French language will be useful, since there are no formal interpreter services available. Prices should be quoted in French Francs, and all trade literature should be in French. **Office hours:** 0800-1200 and 1400-1800 Monday to Friday.
COMMERCIAL INFORMATION: The following organisations can offer advice: Chambre de Commerce et d'Industrie de la Réunion, BP 120, 5 bis rue de Paris, 97463 Saint-Denis Cedex. Tel: 215 366. Fax: 418 034. Telex: 916278; *or*
Délégation Régionale au Commerce, à l'Artisanat et au Tourisme, Préfecture de la Réunion, 97400 Saint-Denis. Tel: 407 758. Fax: 407 701. Telex: 916111.

CLIMATE

Hot tropical climate. Temperatures are cooler in the hills, occasionally dropping to freezing point in the mountains at night. The cyclone season (January to March) is hot and wet.

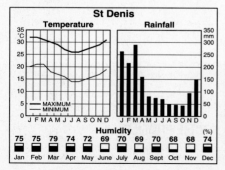

Romania

□ *international airport*

200km
100mls

Location: Eastern Europe.

National Tourist Office (Carpati)
Boulevard Magheru 7, Bucharest 70161, Romania
Tel: (1) 614 5160. Fax: (1) 312 2594. Telex: 11270.
Embassy of Romania
Arundel House, 4 Palace Green, London W8 4QD
Tel: (0171) 937 9666/8. Fax: (0171) 937 8069. Opening hours: 0900-1700 Monday to Friday. *Visa section:* Tel: (0171) 937 9667 (recorded information). Opening hours: 1000-1200 and 1400-1500 (for collections only) Monday to Friday.
Romanian National Tourist Office (Carpati)
83A Marylebone High Street, London W1M 3DE
Tel/Fax: (0171) 224 3692. Telex: 262107. Opening hours: 1000-1700 Monday to Friday (telephone enquiries only).
British Embassy
Strada Jules Michelet 24, 70154 Bucharest, Romania
Tel: (1) 120 303/4/5/6. Fax: (1) 120 229. Telex: 011295 (a/b PRODM R).
Embassy of Romania
1607 23rd Street, NW, Washington, DC 20008
Tel: (202) 332 4848 *or* 232 4747 (Consular section). Fax: (202) 232 4748.
Consulate in: New York (tel: (212) 682 9120).
Romanian National Tourist Office
Suite 210, 342 Madison Avenue, New York, NY 10173
Tel: (212) 697 6971. Fax: (212) 697 6972. Telex: 422990 (a/b RNTONYC).
Embassy of the United States of America
Strada Tudor Arghezi 7-9, Bucharest, Romania
Tel: (1) 210 0149 *or* 210 4042 (Consular section) *or* 210 6384 (after hours). Fax: (1) 312 5567 *or* 211 3360 (Consular section). Telex: 11416.
Embassy of Romania
655 Rideau Street, Ottawa, Ontario K1N 6A3
Tel: (613) 789 5345 *or* 789 3709. Fax: (613) 789 4365.
Consulates in: Montréal and Toronto.
Canadian Embassy
PO Box 117, Post Office No. 22, 36 Nicolae Iorga, 71118 Bucharest, Romania
Tel: (1) 312 8345 *or* 312 0365. Fax: (1) 312 0366. Telex: 10690 (a/b CANAD R).

Timatic

Health
GALILEO/WORLDSPAN: **TI-DFT/BUH/HE**
SABRE: **TIDFT/BUH/HE**

Visa
GALILEO/WORLDSPAN: **TI-DFT/BUH/VI**
SABRE: **TIDFT/BUH/VI**

For more information on Timatic codes refer to Contents.

AREA: 237,500 sq km (91,699 sq miles).
POPULATION: 22,760,449 (1992).
POPULATION DENSITY: 95.8 per sq km.
CAPITAL: Bucharest. **Population:** 2,064,474 (1992 estimate).
GEOGRAPHY: Romania is bordered to the north and east by Moldova and Ukraine, the southeast by the Black Sea, the south by Bulgaria, the southwest and west by Yugoslavia (Serbia and Montenegro) and in the west by Hungary. The country is divided into four geographical areas. Transylvania (a belt of Alpine massifs and forests) and Moldavia compose the northern half of the country, which is divided down the middle by the north–south strip of the Carpathian Mountains. South of the east–west line of the Carpathians lies the flat Danube plain of Walachia with the capital Bucharest, its border with Bulgaria being defined by the course of the Danube. Romania's coastline is along the Black Sea, incorporating the Black Sea port of Constanta and the Danube Delta.
LANGUAGE: Romanian is the official language. Some Hungarian and German are spoken in border areas, while mainly French and some English are spoken by those connected with the tourist industry.
RELIGION: 87% Romanian Orthodox, with Roman Catholic (5%), Reformed/Lutheran (3%) and Unitarian (1%). The remainder are Protestant, Muslim and Jewish.
TIME: GMT + 2 (GMT + 3 from last Sunday in March to Saturday before last Sunday in September).
ELECTRICITY: 220 volts AC, 50Hz. Plugs are of the 2-pin type.
COMMUNICATIONS: Telephone: IDD is available. Country code: 40. Most outgoing calls are made through the operator – dial 991 for internal collect calls and 971 for international operator assistance. However, direct-dial national and international services are becoming increasingly available. Outgoing international code: 00. Public telephones are widely available. Hotels often impose a high service charge for long-distance calls, but usually do not charge for local calls. It can be difficult to call abroad, and attempts have been known to take days rather than hours. **Fax:** Facilities are available at most large hotels. **Telex/telegram:** Facilities at post offices and a night telegram service (2000-0700) are available in Bucharest. Telex facilities are available at large hotels. Telegrams are an inexpensive and efficient form of international communication from Romania. **Post:** Airmail to Western Europe takes up to two weeks. Post offices are open daily, including Saturday mornings. **Press:** There are a great number of daily and weekly newspapers published in Romanian, Hungarian and German. There are no English-language dailies.
BBC World Service and Voice of America frequencies: From time to time these change. See the section *How to Use this Book* for more information.
BBC:

MHz	17.64	15.07	9.410	6.180
Voice of America:				
MHz	9.670	6.040	5.995	1.197

PASSPORT/VISA

Regulations and requirements may be subject to change at short notice, and you are advised to contact the appropriate diplomatic or consular authority before finalising travel arrangements. Details of these may be found at the head of this country's entry. Any numbers in the chart refer to the footnotes below.

	Passport Required?	Visa Required?	Return Ticket Required?
Full British	Yes	Yes	Yes
BVP	Not valid	-	-
Australian	Yes	Yes	Yes
Canadian	Yes	Yes	Yes
USA	Yes	Yes	Yes
Other EU (As of 31/12/94)	Yes	Yes	Yes
Japanese	Yes	Yes	Yes

PASSPORTS: Valid passport with a minimum validity of 3 months after return required by all, except nationals of Moldova who may enter with a national ID.
British Visitors Passport: Not acceptable.
VISAS: Required by all except:
(a) nationals of Bulgaria, Central African Republic, CIS, Croatia, Czech Republic, Hungary, Moldova, Mongolia, Poland, Slovak Republic, Slovenia and Yugoslavia (Serbia and Montenegro);
(b) nationals of Turkey for a stay of up to 2 months;
(c) nationals of Cyprus, Equatorial Guinea, Mauritania, Morocco, San Marino, São Tomé e Príncipe, Tanzania, Tunisia and Zambia for stays of up to 90 days;
(d) nationals of Congo and Cuba for stays of up to 30 days;
(e) nationals of Mexico for stays of up to 6 months.
Special requirements: Nationals of Afghanistan,

Distinctly Bucharest
Uniquely Inter·Continental

As the first international in Romania, Bucharest InterContinental has catered for some of Eastern Europe's most discerning travellers. Located in the heart of the city, the Bucharest InterContinental is just minutes from business, shopping, sightseeing and entertainment. The hotel also houses three restaurants and lounges, a modern nightclub, a wide range of function rooms, a ballroom equipped for 500, and one of Eastern Europe's best casinos.

HOTEL
INTER·CONTINENTAL
BUCHAREST

Rooms: 423 air-conditioned and centrally heated guestrooms.

DINING AND ENTERTAINMENT:

Balada Restaurant – fine dining on the 21st floor with a panoramic view over the city.

Madrigal Restaurant – lobby-level restaurant serving international cuisine.

Corso Brasserie – informal meals and snacks.

Belvedere – quiet club to chat over a cocktail.

Luna Bar – cocktail lounge adjoining the Balada Restaurant.

Night Club – Meals and entertainment.

Casino.

4 Nicolae Balcescu Boulevard, 70121 Bucharest, Romania.
Tel: 40 1 210 73 30. Fax: 40 1 312 04 86, 312 10 17.
Telex: 11541 INTER R. Cable: INTERCONTBUC.

Albania, Angola, Bangladesh, China, Ethiopia, Ghana, India, Iran, Iraq, Jordan, Lebanon, Mali, Nigeria, Pakistan, Philippines, Sierra Leone, Somalia, Sri Lanka, Sudan, Syria, Vietnam and Zaïre need an official notarised invitation from a company or individual in Romania in order to obtain a visa. The invitation is telexed to the Police Inspectorate in Bucharest for approval. This process takes at least 10 days and costs a further £5.

Types of visa: Business, Tourist and Transit (Single-entry and Double-entry) visas are available, as well as a reduced Tourist visa for all-inclusive package tours.

Cost: *Business and Tourist visas* – £26 for UK nationals; £25 for other nationals; *Tourist visas for Package Tourists* – £1; *Transit visas* – £26 for UK nationals; £17 for other nationals. Transit visas are required of all nationals except those listed under visa exemptions above and those continuing their journey without leaving the airport.

Note: Visa fees fluctuate according to the exchange rate of the Pound Sterling against the US Dollar. Contact the Consulate in advance regarding fees.

Validity: Business visas are valid for a stay of up to 30 days; Transit visa for 3 days (Single-entry) and 6 days (Double-entry) within 3 months of the date of issue. Transit visas are obtainable at any border crossing or airport.

Application to: Consulate (or Consular section at Embassy). For addresses, see top of entry. For those with prepaid accommodation, visas can also be granted at any border point, including airports, for a fee of US$33.

Application requirements: (a) Valid passport (due to expire no less than 3 months after return from Romania). (b) 1 application form. (c) 1 passport-size photo. (d) Letter indicating date of departure and length of stay (Business visa applications should also include the name of the sponsoring Romanian company). (e) Fee (paid in cash or by postal order only). (f) For reduced package-tour visas a copy of invoice from travel agent. (g) Postal applications should be accompanied by a stamped, self-addressed envelope. (h) Proof of means of support or sufficient funds for length of stay.

All nationals are advised to check with the Romanian consulate prior to departure to obtain current details of any documentation which might be required.

Working days required: Non-urgent standard 3-month visas are issued within a minimum of 7 or more working days. Visas can be processed within 24 hours for an extra cost of £5.

Temporary residence: Enquire at Embassy.

MONEY

Currency: Leu (plural Lei) = 100 bani. Notes are in denominations of 5000, 1000, 500 and 200 Lei. Coins are in denominations of 100, 50, 20, 10, 5 and 1 Lei.

Currency exchange: It is recommended that visitors bring hard currency, particularly US Dollars, as this can be easily and even eagerly exchanged by shops, restaurants and hotels. Sterling can be easily exchanged in most resorts. All hard foreign currencies can be exchanged at banks and authorised exchange offices. Rates can vary from one place to another, so visitors are advised to shop around for the best rate of exchange. Exchanges on the black market are frequently made, but visitors are advised to exchange money through proper exchange channels and to receive a currency exchange receipt, as certain services require visitors to show the receipt as proof of having made at least one financial transaction. The receipt for currency exchange has to be presented to settle hotel bills, unless the payment is made by voucher, credit card or travellers cheque.

Credit cards: Access/Mastercard, American Express, Diners Club and Visa are accepted in large hotels only. Check with your credit card company for details of merchant acceptability and other services which may be available.

Travellers cheques: Like credit cards, these will only be useful in hotels and for obtaining cash at the Tourist Office.

Exchange rate indicators: The following figures are included as a guide to the movements of the Leu against Sterling and the US Dollar:

Date:	Oct '92	Sep '93	Jan '94	Jan '95
£1.00=	677.79	1253.33	1918.72	2776.00
$1.00=	27.09	820.78	1296.87	1774.37

Currency restrictions: The import or export of local currency is prohibited. There are no restrictions on the import of foreign currency. Foreigners may export up to the unused amount.

Banking hours: 0900-1200 Monday to Friday.

DUTY FREE

The following items may be imported into Romania without incurring customs duty:

200 cigarettes or 300g of tobacco; 2 litres of of spirits; 4 litres of wine or beer; gifts up to a value of 2000 Lei.

Prohibited imports: Ammunition, explosives, narcotics and pornographic material.

Prohibited exports: Articles of cultural, historical or artistic value.

Note: Valuable goods, such as jewellery, and foreign currency over the value of US$1000 per person must be declared on entry. Endorsed customs declarations must be kept, as they must be shown on leaving the country.

PUBLIC HOLIDAYS

Jan 1-2 '95 New Year. **Apr 23** Orthodox Easter Holiday. **May 1** International Labour Day. **Dec 1** National Day. **Dec 25-26** Christmas. **Jan 1-2 '96** New Year. **Apr 15** Orthodox Easter Holiday.

HEALTH

Regulations and requirements may be subject to change at short notice, and you are advised to contact your doctor well in advance of your intended date of departure. Any numbers in the chart refer to the footnotes below.

	Special Precautions?	Certificate Required?
Yellow Fever	No	No
Cholera	1	No
Typhoid & Polio	Yes	-
Malaria	No	-
Food & Drink	2	-

[1]: There have been a number of confirmed cases of cholera, mainly in the Constanta region, and travellers may want to take precautions.

[2]: Mains water is normally chlorinated, and whilst relatively safe may cause mild abdominal upsets. Bottled water is available and is advised for the first few days of the stay. Milk is pasteurised and dairy products are safe for consumption. Local meat, poultry, seafood, fruit and vegetables are generally considered safe to eat. Toilet paper is usually like coarse crepe paper, so visitors are advised to take their own supply.

Note: Romania has currently been experiencing water shortages and visitors may find that tap water is only available during certain hours. This is particularly true around Bucharest and other large towns. Visitors in the mountain areas will find it less of a problem as the water is supplied by local mountain springs and is full of natural minerals and very safe.

Hepatitis A and *B* exist in Romania.

Rabies is present. For those at high risk, vaccination before arrival should be considered. If you are bitten abroad seek medical advice without delay. For more information, consult the *Health* section at the back of the book.

Health care: Medical care in Romania is limited and there is a serious shortage of basic medical supplies. There is a Reciprocal Health Agreement with the UK. Those presenting a UK passport and a driver's licence or NHS card are entitled to free treatment in hospitals and some free medical and dental treatment elsewhere. Charges are made for medicine supplied by a public chemist. Other nationals should contact a Romanian Embassy for details of other agreements. Nationals of countries who do not have a Reciprocal Health Agreement with Romania are expected to pay immediate cash for health services.

TRAVEL - International

AIR: Romania's national airline is *Tarom (RO)*. Other airlines that fly to Bucharest include *Delta, Air France, Lufthansa, Alitalia* and *Swissair.*

Approximate flight time: From London to Bucharest is 2 hours 55 minutes.

International airport: *Bucharest (BUH)* (Otopeni) is 16km (10 miles) north of the city (travel time – 35 minutes). The airport has been greatly modernised in the past few years, but some visitors may find it relatively limited compared to Western European or American standards. A bar, snack bar, restaurant, 24-hour left luggage, 24-hour first aid, post office, car rental and full duty-free facilities are available. A 24-hour coach service runs hourly. Return is from Tarom Agency, 10 Brezoianu Street. Bus no. 49 runs every 20 minutes from 0530-2350. Return is from Scinteia House, Press Square. Taxis are also available.

There are also international airports at *Constanta* (Mihail Kogalniceanu) and *Timisoara.*

SEA: The main international passenger ports are Constanta and Sulina on the Black Sea. There is a ferry service on the Danube, starting from Orsova, to Bulgaria. Passenger boats also operate on the new European riverway from Rotterdam to Constanta, via the Romanian Danube Canal and the Black Sea. **River cruises:** Sailing from Vienna to the Black Sea along the Danube, these stop at various places of interest, including Bratislava, Budapest, Belgrade, Bazias, Giurgiu, Calafat and Bucharest. The cruises incorporate varied itineraries: historic towns, museums, art collections, monasteries, spas, archaeological sites, folk evenings, nature reserves and of course, the dramatic scenery of Eastern Europe, including Transylvania. For further information, contact the National Tourist Office (address at top of entry).

RAIL: Main international trains from Western Europe to Romania (Bucharest) are the *Orient Express* and the *Wiener Waltzer.* The *Orient Express* departs from Paris Gare de l'Est at 2315, reaching Bucharest at 1220 two days later (total travel time – about 38 hours). Sleeping cars from Paris run four times a week in winter only. All have first- and second-class carriages. The *Wiener Waltzer* runs to Bucharest in summer only (June to September) and includes two nights travel from Basel, arriving in Bucharest two days later at 0815. There are no through carriages from Basel, which means moving to the Bucharest coaches in Vienna. As well as day carriages, there are sleeping cars from Vienna to both Bucharest and Constanta on the Black Sea coast. There are also through trains from other Eastern European cities.

ROAD: The most direct international routes to Romania are via Germany, Austria and Hungary. The best route from Hungary is the E64 from Budapest to Szeged through Arad, Brasov, Campina and Ploiesti. There is also a route from Szeged to Timisoara. A more frequently used route from Hungary to Germany is through Oradea (E60).

See below for information on **documentation**.

TRAVEL - Internal

AIR: The main airport for internal flights is *Baneasa* (travel time – 20 minutes to Otopeni). *Tarom (RO)* operates regular services from there to Constanta, Arad, Bacau, Caransebes, Baia Mare, Cluj-Napoca, Iasi, Satu Mare, Timisoara, Oradea, Tirgu Mures, Sibiu, Suceava and Tulcea.

RAIL: Bucharest's main station is the Gare du Nord on Calea Grivitei. *Romanian State Railways* run efficient and cheap services, some with sleeping and restaurant cars. Supplements are payable on rapide and express trains, for which seats must be reserved in advance. Express routes run from Bucharest to Timisoara, Cluj-Napoca, Iasi, Constanta and Brasov. Rail Inclusive Tour tickets include transport and hotel accommodation. There are no platforms of any great height in Romania, making entering and alighting a little difficult for the elderly or infirm. There is a discount of 10-15% for non-express trains.

ROAD: Traffic drives on the right. The *Romanian Automobile Club* (ACR) has its headquarters in Bucharest and offers services through all its branches to *AA* and *RAC* members. The petrol coupon system has been abandoned. Speed limits are 60kmph (37mph) in built-up areas and up to 90kmph (57mph) on main roads. Driving under alcohol influence is forbidden. For further information, contact the national car association, *Automobil Clubul Román (ACR),* Strada Take Ionescu 27, 70154 Bucharest. Tel: 927 in Bucharest (or 12345 if elsewhere in the country). **Coach:** Local services operate to most towns and villages. The main coach stations in Bucharest are at 164 Soseaua Alexandriei, 1 Ion Ionescu de la Brad Boulevard, 1 Piata Gării Filarest, 221 Soseaua Chitilei, 141 Pacii Boulevard and 3 Gării Obor Boulevard. **Taxi:** Metered taxis can be hailed in the street or called from hotels. Prices are relatively low, but drivers expect a 10% tip. **Car hire:** Available at hotels and at Bucharest Airport. Driving is very erratic, so it might be advisable to hire a car with a driver.

Documentation: National driving licence or International Driving Permit and Green Card insurance are required.

URBAN: Good public transport facilities are provided in the main centres. Bucharest has a good bus and tram system and a metro. Tickets are pre-purchased from agents, and there are stamping machines on board buses and trains. There are are also daily, weekly and fortnightly passes. A separate 18-route minibus network is operated.

ACCOMMODATION

HOTELS: Visitors are advised to purchase prepaid vouchers for accommodation through a travel agency which has contract links with the National Tourist Office. Bookings will be confirmed by telex (any booking not confirmed may not be honoured). Room prices are very reasonable compared to Western European prices. For further information, contact ANAT, 1-7 Dorobanti Street, Hotel Dorobanti, First Floor, Bucharest 1. Tel: (1) 211

Bravo Investments SA (Bravo Tours).
Piata Unirii 1, Bucharest, Romania.
Tel: +40 1 614 5882. Fax: +40 1 312 5439

5450/9. Telex: 11170. **Grading:** Hotels are classified from **1** to **4 stars**.

BED & BREAKFAST: Accommodation of this type is very plentiful in Romania. For further information, contact the Romanian National Tourist Board (Carpati) (see addresses at top of entry).

SELF-CATERING: Addresses of private accommodation and self-catering establishments are available from local tourist offices.

CAMPING/CARAVANNING: There are around 100 campsites in Romania. Prepaid tourist coupons valid from May to September are available from specialised travel agencies.

YOUTH HOSTELS: Hostels (Strada Onesti) are open in July and August. Information is available from the Youth Tourist Bureau, Strada Onesti 4-6, Bucharest, or through a travel agent specialising in Balkan travel.

RESORTS & EXCURSIONS

Romania's main resort areas are the Black Sea Coast, the Danube Delta, the Carpathian Mountains, Bukovina and Transylvania.

BLACK SEA COAST: This coastline is the principal tourist area of Romania and ideal for family holidays. Its 70km (43 miles) of fine white sandy beaches boast many resorts, the main ones being **Mamaia, Eforie Nord, Techirghiol, Eforie Sud, Costinesti, Neptun-Olimp, Jupiter, Venus-Aurora, Saturn** and **Mangalia.** There are ten boating centres for watersports on the sea and lakes, and both daytime and evening cruises from the Dobrudja region to other resorts. The curative properties of the salt waters and the mud from *Lake Techirghiol* (whose thermal springs have a year-round temperature of 24°C), Mangalia, Eforie and Neptun, make the Romanian Riviera popular with those seeking spa treatments, especially for rheumatism. The Greek/Byzantine port of **Constanta,** founded in the 6th century BC, merits a visit, and inland there are interesting archaeological sites including the ancient Greek city ruins of *Histria, Tomis* and *Callatis.* The area is inhabited by foxes, otters, wildcats and boars and in the migratory periods one can see over 300 species of birds.

DANUBE DELTA: A vast expanse of protected watery wilderness in the north of the Romanian Black Sea coast, comprised by the three main arms of the Danube with numerous little waterways, wetlands, small patches of forest and a rich and varied wildlife including over 300 species of birds. The backwaters can be explored by fishing boat or floating hotel, and several hotels and campsites welcome visitors. The main town of the Delta is **Tulcea** with its excellent *Danube Delta Museum.*

CARPATHIAN MOUNTAINS: This beautiful and densely forested mountainous area lends itself to many sporting and leisure activities such as skiing, bob-sleighing, horseriding and tennis. Situated in picturesque valleys and on mountain slopes are many health and winter resorts, open all year round and well equipped with ski-hire facilities etc. The major resorts are: **Sinaia** (bob-sleigh tracks); **Busteni; Predeal** and **Poiana Brasov** (illuminated ski slopes); **Semenic; Paltinis; Bilea; Borsa** and **Durau.**

All are equipped to cater for a long winter sports season running from December to April. Spectacular mountain lakes are found in the *Fagaras* and *Retezat* ranges, and caves in the *Apuseni, Mehedinti* and *Bihor* regions.

BUKOVINA: An area in the northern Carpathian foothills which have unique churches and monasteries with exceptional frescoes dating back 500 years. **Sucevita** is the home of a monastery with the largest number of frescoes in the region. 29km (18 miles) west of Sucevita is **Moldovita,** renowned for its spectacular paintings. The Moldavian region has 48 monasteries in total, nearly all of them built to celebrate victories over the Turks in the 14th and 15th centuries.

TRANSYLVANIA: Since Roman times Romanian spas have been known for their miraculous healing powers. Transylvania holds many well-equipped spa towns, such as **Baile Felix, Baile Herculane, Sovata** and **Covasana,** some of which have facilities offering acupuncture, acupressure and slimming cures. It is here that the myth of Dracula, immortalised in Bram Stoker's famous novel, originated. The original Dracula was a medieval King of unpleasant habits known as 'Vlad the Impaler'. One of Vlad's original abodes, *Bran Castle,* set in a commanding position, with its thick walls and peaked tower, offers a dramatic view and a chilling atmosphere. (Tours are available to Bran Castle from the mountain resort of Poiana Brasov, where it is possible to ski in winter and do mountain climbing and walking in summer.) From here one can travel to **Sibiu** which has a great market.

SOCIAL PROFILE

FOOD & DRINK: Although there are some regional differences between the provinces, there is a definite national culinary tradition. Dishes include *ciorba de perisoare* (soup with meatballs), *ciorba tanancasca* (meat with vegetables), lamb *bors,* giblet soup and a variety of fish soups. The Romanians excel in full-bodied soups, some of the best being cream of mushroom, chicken, 'ping pong' (or meatball soup with cream), beef vegetable and bean soup. Sour cream or eggs are often added to soups. *Mamaliga* (a staple of mashed cornmeal) is served in many ways. Other national specialities include *tocana* (pork, beef or mutton stew seasoned with onions and served with *mamaliga*), *ghiveci* (over 20 vegetables cooked in oil and served cold), Moldavian *parjoale* (flat meat patties, highly spiced and served with garnishes), *sarmale* (pork balls in cabbage leaves), *mititei* (a variety of highly-seasoned charcoal-grilled meat) and *patricieni* (charcoal-grilled sausages similar to Frankfurters). Fish dishes include *nisetru la gratar* (grilled Black Sea sturgeon), *raci* (crayfish) and *scrumbii la gratar* (grilled herring). Desserts include *placinte cu poale in briu* (rolled cheese pies), Moldavian *cozonac* (brioche) and *pasca* (a sweet cheesecake). Pancakes, served with jam, and donuts, topped with sour cream or jam, are also popular desserts. Breakfasts almost always include eggs, either soft-boiled, hard-boiled, fried or scrambled. Omelettes, filled with either cheese, ham or mushrooms, are also frequently served. Vegetarians may have difficulties, as most local specialities are meat-based. Fresh vegetables can be hard to find but fruit can be bought in the markets. Sugar and salt are rationed to the Romanians and are in short supply in hotels. Fresh milk is almost unobtainable, although powdered milk can be purchased fairly easily (in 3-5kg bags). It might be advisable, therefore, for visitors to take their own supplies. Although there are inexpensive self-service snack bars, table service is the norm. **Drink:** A traditional drink with entrées is *tzuica* (plum brandy) which varies in strength, dryness and smell according to locality. *Tzuica de Bihor* is the strongest and generally known as *palinca.* Romanian wines have won international prizes and include *pinot noir, cabernet sauvignon* and *chardonnay* from the Murfatlar vineyards. *Grasa* and *feteasa* from Moldavia's Cotnari vineyards are also recommended. Many Romanian wines are taken with soda water and hot wine is also popular. Romanian beers are excellent. Romanian sparkling wines, or *methode champagnoise,* are very good and superb value. *Gluhwein* (mulled wine) is another popular Romanian drink. There are no licensing hours, but the legal age for drinking in a bar is 18.

NIGHTLIFE: Bucharest has a growing number of discotheques and nightspots with entertainment and live dancing. Restaurants at most major hotels double as nightclubs with floor shows and there are also several Parisian-style cafés. A new casino has opened in the Calea Victoriei. Opera is performed at the Romanian Opera House and the Romanian Athenaeum has two symphony orchestras. Folk entertainment is performed at the Rapsodia Romana Artistic Ensemble Hall and there are a number of theatres.

SHOPPING: Specialist purchases include embroideries, pottery, porcelain, silverware, carpets, fabrics, wool jumpers, woodcarvings, metal, leather goods, rugs, glass paintings and silk dresses. **Shopping hours:** 0800-1800 Monday to Saturday for small local shops, while larger stores and department stores are open until 2000. Some shops open 0600-1200 Sunday, although these vary according to season.

SPORT: Tennis: There are lawn tennis courts in seaside and mountain resorts and in many towns. The Ile Nastase Sports and Fitness Club, situated in the Primavera suburb of Bucharest, may accept temporary membership. **Horseriding:** Centres at Izvin (Banat), Mangalia (the sea coast), Radauti (northern Moldavia) and Simbata de Jos (near Fagaras). The state race-course is at Ploiesti. **Winter sports:** There are numerous facilities. Ski pistes of varying degrees of difficulty are found in almost all mountain resorts, the majority of which are equipped with cable cars. National and international **skiing** and **bob-sleighing** competitions are organised in the main winter sports resorts (Sinaia, Predeal and Poiana Brasov). **Sledging** tracks, **skating** and **ice hockey** are available at most mountain resorts. **Fishing:** Romania has many easily accessible places for fishing such as the Danube Delta (where there are over 160 fish species including sturgeon, wel, pike and carp) and on lake shores around big cities. **Watersports:** Beautiful beaches and luxury resorts line the Black Sea coast. The sea is clean and tideless and a full range of facilities is available.

SPECIAL EVENTS: Folk festivals include dances, music and displays of traditional art. Contact the National Tourist Office for full details of events. The following are of special interest:
Apr *International and National Festival of Dance Sports,* Timisoara. **May** *Tanjaua de pe Marna (National Festival of Spring Agriculture Customs),* Hoteni; *The Feast of Narcisses,* Vlãhita; *International Jazz Festival,* Brasov. **Jul-Aug** *The National Festival of Light Music of Mamaia.* **Sep** *The Golden Stag (International Light Music Festival),* Brasov.

SOCIAL CONVENTIONS: Romanians are very Latin in their behaviour. Handshaking is the most common form of greeting, but it is customary for men to kiss a woman's hand when being introduced. Visitors should follow normal European courtesies on social occasions. Dress tends to be rather conservative but casual wear is suitable. Beachwear should not be worn away from the beach or poolside. Smoking is prohibited on public transport, in cinemas and theatres. Many Romanians are smokers and gifts of Western cigarettes are greatly appreciated. Other well-appreciated gifts include toiletries and Western clothing. **Photography:** Sensitive installations of military importance should not be photographed. Some tourist attractions require visitors to pay a fee of approximately 2000 Lei for taking photographs. **Tipping:** A 12% service charge is added in most restaurants. Porters, chambermaids and taxi drivers expect tips.

BUSINESS PROFILE

ECONOMY: Agriculture was a key sector of the economy employing nearly one-third of the workforce, but the recent decrease in trade relations with former trading partners has severely cut the amount of agricultural revenue. The country is an important producer of wheat and maize, but it also grows vegetables, fruit, sugar-beet and vegetable oil seeds; many farms also breed livestock. The sector as a whole has suffered from lack of investment due to economic policies which have favoured heavy industry. Forestry is being developed under a long-term programme. Romanian industry produces industrial and transport equipment, metals, furniture, chemical products and manufactured consumer goods, but the most important sector is oil, natural gas and oil-derived products (petrochemicals, paints and varnishes). The development of the sector has been unsteady and despite its oil deposits and other energy schemes, including hydroelectric and nuclear, Romanians have suffered

severe power shortages. Similarly, the food supply situation deteriorated during the 1980s. Part of the reason was the Ceausescu government's overriding desire to eliminate its foreign debt which meant that every conceivable product was assigned for export even to the detriment of the population. The bulk of Romania's imports during the 1980s comprised machinery, equipment and raw materials in accordance with industrial development plans; consumer goods were given a very low priority. The National Salvation Front government has concentrated upon turning Romania into a market economy. Substantial progress has been made: the Leu is now directly convertible; price controls have been removed; and the National Privatisation Agency distributed over 4 million share certificates preparatory to the sale of state assets, 30% of which were allocated to the general public. The de-collectivisation programme has seen 46% of farmland turned over to its original owners. For all that, Romania's current economic health is poor: inflation is high, unemployment is rising and economic output is falling. Romania has recently signed a trade agreement with the European Free Trade Association, an economic cooperation agreement with the European Union, and has access to loans from the European Bank for Reconstruction and Development. In 1992, along with 10 other counties, Romania founded the Black Sea Economic Co-Operation Group with the aim of helping to coordinate regional economic and infrastructure improvements. The CIS is the largest trading partner, followed by Egypt, Italy and Germany. It is as yet unclear whether there will be any significant change in Romanian trade patterns although agriculture and tourism are two areas of potential growth.
BUSINESS: A suit is essential at all business meetings and only on very hot days are shirt-sleeves acceptable. English, German and French are used in business circles. Appointments are necessary and punctuality expected. Business cards are widely used. **Office hours:** 0700-1530 Monday to Friday; 0700-1230 Saturday.
COMMERCIAL INFORMATION: The following organisations can offer advice: Ministry of Commerce, Str. Apolodor 17, 70663 Bucharest. Tel: (1) 141 141. Fax: (1) 312 2342. Telex: 10564; *or* Chamber of Commerce and Industry of Romania, Boulevard Nicolae Balcescu 22, 79502 Bucharest. Tel: (1) 615 4703. Fax: (1) 312 2091. Telex: 11374; *or* Chamber of Commerce and Industry Bacau, Str.

Libertati, nr. 1, Bacau 5500. Tel: (34) 146 262 *or* 146 233 *or* 130 564 *or* 135 732 *or* 135 859 *or* 144 735 *or* 136 839 *or* 145 621. Fax: (34) 171 070/8 *or* 136 839.
CONFERENCES/CONVENTIONS: The Hotel Intercontinental and the Bucharest in Bucharest, and the Aro in Brasov have facilities for conferences.

CLIMATE

Summer temperatures are moderated on the coast by sea breezes while inland at sea level it is hot. Winters are coldest in the Carpathian Mountains where there is snow from December through to April. Snow also falls throughout most of the country. Winters are mildest on the coast.
Required clothing: Lightweights are worn in summer on the coast and in low inland areas. Warmer clothes are needed in winter and throughout the year in the uplands. Rainwear is recommended in the spring and autumn.

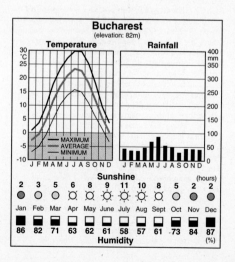

Russian Federation

Location: Eastern Europe/Asia.

Note: At the time of writing, travellers are strongly advised not to enter Chechnya (also known as Chechenia or the Chechen Republic). The political situation remains particularly unsettled in Russia's Caucasus area. Travel restrictions remain in force in those areas of North Ossetia and Ingushetia where a state of emergency applies. For up-to-date information, contact the FCO Travel Advice Unit. Tel: (0171) 270 4129.
Sources: US State Department – December 16, 1994, and FCO Travel Advice Unit – January 25, 1995.

Vao Intourist
ul. Mokhovaya 13, 103009 Moscow, Russian Federation
Tel: (095) 292 2260. Fax: (095) 230 6305. Telex: 411211.

Embassy of the Russian Federation
13 Kensington Palace Gardens, London W8 4QX
Tel: (0171) 229 3628. Fax: (0171) 727 8625. Opening hours: 0830-1200 and 1400-1800 Monday to Friday.

Consular Section
5 Kensington Palace Gardens, London W8 4QS
Tel: (0171) 229 8027. Fax: (0171) 229 3215. Opening hours: 1000-1230 Monday to Friday (closed

Wednesday).

Intourist Travel Limited
Intourist House, 219 Marsh Wall, Meridian Gate II, Isle of Dogs, London E14 9FJ
Tel: (0171) 538 8600 (general enquiries) *or* 538 5902 (visas) *or* 538 3202 (reservations) *or* 538 3203 (sales). Fax: (0171) 538 5967. Telex: 27232.

British Embassy
Sofiyskaya Naberezhnaya 14, Moscow 72, Russian Federation
Tel: (095) 230 6333 (8 lines). Fax: (095) 249 4636. Telex: 413341 (a/b BEMOS SU).

British Consulate General
c/o Grand Hotel Europe, Rooms 252/292, St Petersburg,

Sergiyev Posad (formerly Zagorsk)

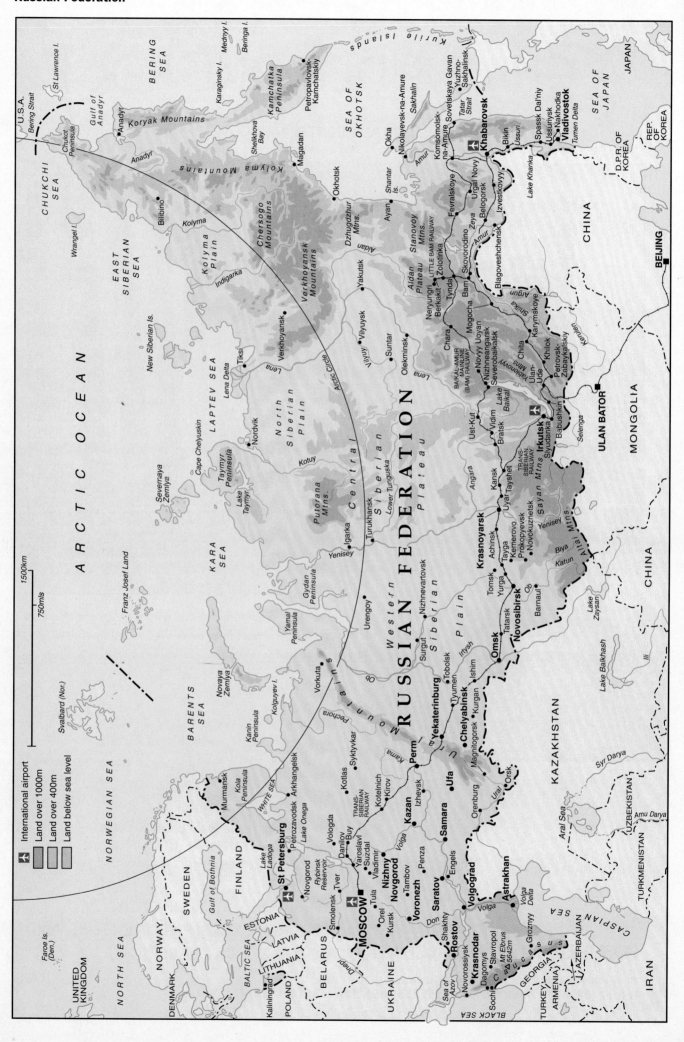

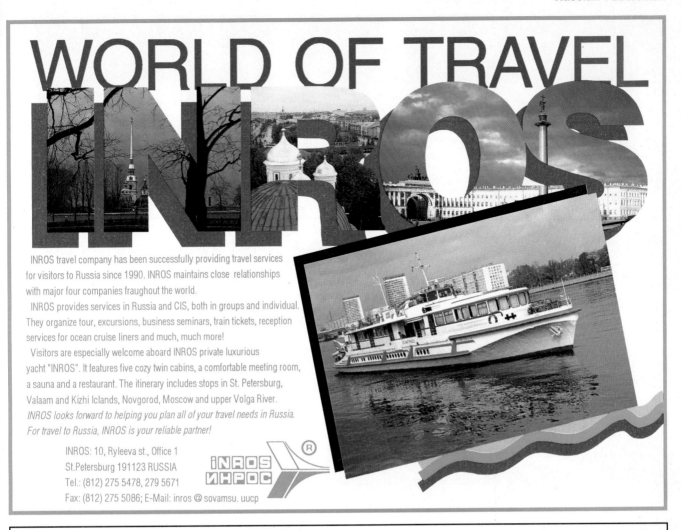

Russian Federation
Tel: (0812) 119 6036. Fax: (0812) 119 6037.
Embassy of the Russian Federation
1125 16th Street, NW, Washington, DC 20036
Tel: (202) 628 7551 *or* 628 8548.
Intourist
Suite 603, 610 Fifth Avenue, New York, NY 10020
Tel: (212) 757 3884. Fax: (212) 459 0031.
Embassy of the United States of America
Novinskiy Bulvar 19/23, Moscow, Russian Federation
Tel: (095) 252 2451/9 *or* 252 1898 (after hours duty officer). Fax: (095) 956 4261. Telex: 413160 (a/b USGSO SU).
US Consulate General
ul. Furshtatskaya 15, St Petersburg 191028, Russian Federation
Tel: (0812) 275 1701 *or* 850 4170 *or* 274 8692 (after hours duty officer). Fax: (0812) 850 1473. Telex: 64-121527.
Embassy of the Russian Federation
285 Charlotte Street, Ottawa, Ontario K1N 8L5
Tel: (613) 235 4341. Fax: (613) 236 6342.
Russian Consular Section
52 Range Road, Ottawa, Ontario K1N 8J5
Tel: (613) 236 7220 *or* 236 6215. Fax: (613) 238 6158.
Consulate in: Montréal.
Russian Travel Information Office
Suite 630, 1801 McGill College Avenue, Montréal, Québec H3A 2N4
Tel: (514) 849 6394. Fax: (514) 849 6743. Telex: 055-62018.
Canadian Embassy
23 Starokonyushenny Pereulok, 121002 Moscow, Russian Federation
Tel: (095) 241 1111 *or* 241 5070. Fax: (095) 241 4400 *or* 241 4232 (nightline). Telex: 413401 (a/b DMCAN SU).
Consulate in: St Petersburg.

AREA: 17,075,400 sq km (6,592,850 sq miles).
POPULATION: 148,485,000 (1991 estimate).
POPULATION DENSITY: 8.7 per sq km.
CAPITAL: Moscow. **Population:** 8,801,000 (1990).
GEOGRAPHY: The Russian Federation covers almost twice the area of the United States of America, and

reaches from Moscow in the west over the Urals and the vast Siberian plains to the Sea of Okhotsk in the east. The border between European Russia and Siberia (Asia) is formed by the Ural Mountains, the Ural River and the Manych Depression. European Russia extends from the North Polar Sea across the Central Russian Uplands to the Black Sea, the Northern Caucasus and the Caspian Sea. Siberia stretches from the West Siberian Plain across the Central Siberian Plateau between Yenisey and Lena, including the Sayan, Yablonovy and Stanovoy ranges in the south to the East Siberian mountains between Lena and the Pacific coast including the Chukotskiy and Kamchatka peninsulas.
The following republics are part of the Russian Federation. Population figures were drawn up in 1990 unless stated otherwise.

Republic	Area (sq km)	Population	Capital
Adygheya	7600	436,000	Maikop
Bashkortostan	143,600	3,964,000	Ufa
Buryatia	351,300	1,049,000	Ulan-Ude
Chechnya	-	-	Grozny
Chuvashia	18,300	-	Cheboksary
Daghestan	50,300	1,823,000	Makhachkala
Gorno-Altai	92,600	194,000	Gorno-Altaisk
Ingushetia	-	-	Nazran
Kabardino-Balkaria	12,500	768,000	Nalchik
Kalmykia	76,100	325,000	Elista
Karachayevo-Cherkess	14,100	422,000	Cherkessk
Karelia	172,400	796,000	Petrozavodsk
Khakassia	61,900	573,000	Abakan
Komi	415,900	1,265,000	Syktyvkar
Mari El	23,200	-	Yoshkar-Ola
Mordovia	26,200	964,000	Saransk
Northern Ossetia	8000	638,000	Vladikavkaz
Sakha (Yakutia)	3,103,200	*1,077,000	Yakutsk
Tatarstan	68,000	3,658,000	Kazan
Tuva	170,500	314,000	Kyzyl
Udmurtia	42,100	1,619,000	Izhevsk

Note [*]: 1992 figure.
LANGUAGE: Russian. English, French or German are spoken by some people.
RELIGION: Mainly Christian with the Russian Orthodox Church being the largest Christian community. Muslim, Buddhist and Jewish minorities also exist.

TIME: Kaliningrad: GMT + 2 (GMT + 3 from last Sunday in March to Saturday before last Sunday in September).
Moscow, St Petersburg: GMT + 3 (GMT + 4 from last Sunday in March to Saturday before last Sunday in September).
Volgograd: GMT + 4 (GMT + 5 from last Sunday in March to Saturday before last Sunday in September).
Irkutsk: GMT + 8 (GMT + 9 from last Sunday in March to Saturday before last Sunday in September).
Tiksi, Yakutsk: GMT + 9 (GMT + 10 from last Sunday in March to Saturday before last Sunday in September).
Khabarovsk, Okhotsk, Vladivostok: GMT + 10 (GMT + 11 from last Sunday in March to Saturday before last Sunday in September).
Magadan, Sakhalin Island: GMT + 11 (GMT + 12 from last Sunday in March to Saturday before last Sunday in September).
Anadyr, Petropavlosk: GMT + 12 (GMT + 13 from last Sunday in March to Saturday before last Sunday in September).
ELECTRICITY: 220 volts AC, 50Hz.
COMMUNICATIONS: Telephone: IDD is available. Country Code: 7. When dialling the Russian Federation from abroad, the 0 of the area code must *not* be omitted. Outgoing international code: 810. Most international calls made from the cities of Moscow, St Petersburg and Nizhny Novgorod can be dialled directly, but in smaller cities and towns it may be necessary to go through the international operator and these should be booked well in advance. Telephone booths for international phone calls

INTOURBANK is one of the most dynamic and progressive entities in the financial services sector in the Russian Federation.

Igor Obozintsev, Chairman of the Board of Directors

INTOURBANK began its operations three years ago and today is a commercial bank for the development of foreign tourism, whose principal task is to offer assistance, from funding and banking services on a commercial basis to programmes committed to the development of foreign tourism within the Russian Federation.

The bank's strategy focuses on crediting and attracting capital to support programmes promoting the infrastructure of foreign tourism, settling accounts between hotels, transport companies, tour operators and other businesses servicing the tourist industry.

INTOURBANK pursues a policy of expanding its own network of branches and sections in Russia's biggest tourist centres.

INTOURBANK is always open to new business. .opportunities.

INTOURBANK

Commercial Bank for the Development of Foreign Tourism

OUR ADDRESS: 11 DOLGORUKOVSKAYA STREET, BLD 2, MOSCOW 103055, RUSSIAN FEDERATION
TEL: (095) 973 22 73, 973 22 66. FAX: (095) 973 22 59, 973 22 66 OR 7-511 017 3193.

are available at main post offices. International calls can be booked by dialling 8194 or, if the call is booked from a hotel, 333 4101. Some Moscow hotels have telephone booths with IDD. Local calls cost Rub40 for 3 minutes. The emergency services can be reached as follows: fire – 01; police – 02; ambulance – 03. For enquiries regarding Moscow private telephone numbers, dial 09; for businesses, 927 0009. For national directory enquiries regarding the Russian Federation and the CIS, dial 927 0009. **Fax:** Services are available in numerous business centres and hotels, although the latter option is more expensive. **Telex/telegram:** Telex services are available in most cities and at the offices of the Commercial Department of the British Embassy, Kutuzovsky Prospekt 7/4, 12148 Moscow. Telegrams may be sent from hotels. **Post:** Airmail to Western Europe takes over ten days. There are mailboxes and post offices in every hotel. *Poste Restante* facilities are available at the larger hotels. Inland surface mail is often slow. Post office hours: 0900-1900. **Media:** The state information agency, *Informatsionnoye Telegrafnoye Agentstvo Rossii-Telegrafnoye Agentstvo Suverennykh Stran (ITAR-TASS),* can be contacted in London on (0171) 580 5543 or in Moscow at Tverskoy bul. 10-12. Tel: (095) 229 7925. Fax: (095) 203 3080. *Rossiyskoye Informatsionnoye Agentstvo-Novosti (RIA – Novosti)* has contacts with foreign press in 110 countries and can be contacted in London on (0171) 370 1873. Its Moscow branch is located at Zubovsky bul. 4, Moscow. Tel: (095) 201 2424. Fax: (095) 201 2119. Telex: 411323. *Interfax* and *Postfactum* are independent news agencies, both located in Moscow. **Press:** The main dailies in the Russian Federation are *Pravda* and *Izvestiya,* both published in Moscow. Newspapers and magazines are published in some 25 languages. Multi-lingual editions of the *Moscow News* and the *New Times* are available weekly. *Commersant, Moscow Times, Moscow Tribune* and *Financial and Business News* are published in English. St Petersburg titles published in English include the *St Petersburg Press, Neva News* and *St Petersburg Today.* **BBC World Service and Voice of America frequencies:** From time to time these change. See the section *How to Use this Book* for more information.

BBC:

| MHz | 17.64 | 15.07 | 9.415 | 6.195 |

Voice of America:

| MHz | 15.20 | 9.765 | 6.040 | 5.995 |

PASSPORT/VISA

Regulations and requirements may be subject to change at short notice, and you are advised to contact the appropriate diplomatic or consular authority before finalising travel arrangements. Details of these may be found at the head of this country's entry. Any numbers in the chart refer to the footnotes below.

	Passport Required?	Visa Required?	Return Ticket Required?
Full British	Yes	Yes	Yes
BVP	Not valid	-	-
Australian	Yes	Yes	Yes
Canadian	Yes	Yes	Yes
USA	Yes	Yes	Yes
Other EU (As of 31/12/94)	Yes	Yes	Yes
Japanese	Yes	Yes	Yes

Note: Passport and Visa regulations for all the CIS states are liable to change at short notice. If there is no Consular representative of a CIS state in a particular country, the Embassy of the Russian Federation may be empowered to issue visas for that state. In the absence of a specific Consular representative issuing visas for a destination, contact the nearest Consular representative of the Russian Federation well in advance of travel.
PASSPORTS: Valid passport required by all. British passports must be valid for 10 years and for at least 3 months after returning from the CIS.
Note: Whilst in the country, visitors must carry ID at all times. Rather than carry orginal documents, it is advisable to carry photocopies of passports and visas, which will facilitate replacement should either be stolen.
British Visitors Passport: Not accepted.
VISAS: Required by all.
Note: Passengers without valid visas arriving in the Russian Federation from Ukraine or Belarus are charged a penalty for illegal entry at the rate of US$250 per person.
Types of visa: Entry/exit Tourist; Business (for business or educational visits, trade fairs and exhibitions); and Transit (see below). Cost: £10 for UK nationals, other nationals may be charged more – check with the Consulate. Tour operators charge £10 plus VAT for obtaining visas for their clients. Generally, all visa types need proof of accommodation. *Transit visas:* Travellers with Transit visas are allowed a maximum of 72 hours to transit provided they are in possession of confirmed onward travel

documentation and valid entry requirement for the onward destination. Passengers may leave the airport under certain conditions on a Transit visa, but anyone intending independent excursions must obtain a full visa.
It is possible for passengers arriving in the Russian Federation without a Transit visa to obtain it at the Moscow Sheremetyevo Airport, but this is risky and inadvisable, as it is far more costly and passengers may be refused entry and sent back. Cost: 1 day – US$72; up to 2 days – US$90 and up to 3 days – US$110.
Application to: Consulate (or Consular section at Embassy). For addresses, see top of entry.
Application requirements: *Tourist visa:* (a) Completed application form. (b) 3 recent identical passport-size photos. (c) Photocopy of the first 5 pages of a valid passport, trimmed to actual size (if British visitors hold a new EC-format passport, pages 32 and 33 must also be photocopied). (d) A copy of a voucher (exchange order) issued by an authorised travel company with indication of reference number, names, dates of entry and exit, itinerary, means of transportation, class of services and amount of money paid by a client. (e) Fee.
Business visa: (a) Completed application form. (b) 3 recent identical passport-size photos. (c) Photocopy of first 5 pages (plus 32 and 33 if EC-format) of a valid passport. (d) An introductory letter from company or firm indicating the purpose, itinerary, organisation to be visited, period of stay and exact departure dates of flights. (e) An invitation from the organisation, department or institution to be visited in the CIS. (f) Fee. (g) Postal applications must be accompanied by a large, stamped, self-addressed envelope. Those who are travelling in groups (standard Intourist tours, coach tours, international competitions, package tours, cruises) should submit all documentation to the tour operator making the travel arrangements. Applications should be made directly to the nearest Intourist office. For visits to relatives/friends in the CIS, enquire at the Consulate for details of application procedures.
Working days required: Applications for visas may not be made earlier than 3 months before departure, and in no case later than 14 working days before departure, whether by post or personal visit.

MONEY

Currency: Rouble (Rub) = 100 kopeks. Notes are in denominations of Rub100,000, 50,000, 10,000, 5000,

Khabarovsk is the main economic and cultural centre of the Far East. It is also the administrative centre of the Khabarovsk Territory which consists of 825,000 square kilometres.

The area of the city is 400 square kilometres which is half the size of Moscow. The city is has a population of more than 600,000 people.

Khabarovsk was founded in 1858 as a military outpost for defence of the Russian/Chinese border. Its first inhabitants were Cossacks of the 13th Batallion, under the leadership of Captain Dyachenko. In 1880 the military settlement received city status and adopted in 1893 the name of one of the first Russian explorers of the 17th century, Yerofei Khabarov.Historical wooden and brick houses preserved from the time of the city's founding give Khabarovsk an unmistakable charm.

Joint-stock company "Intour-Khabarovsk" with more than 30 years' experience is one of the biggest and most reliable travel agencies in the Far East and Siberia. We employ 650 professional staff and have a turnover of more than US 15 million a year. We have a strong partnership with travel agencies in Japan, Germany, USA, South Korea, Australia, Singapore, China and several other countries. Our company caters for group and individual travel, organising astounding specialist tours. We can arrange tours across Russia, including business trips, hunting tours, fishing tours, mountaineering and visits to major cities of Siberia, Yakutia, Sakhalin, Primorjye and Amur Territory. Our company "Intour-Khabarovsk" wishes you a warm welcome to Russia!

The main feature of the city is the great Amur River, which provides one of the borders of the city. The Amur is one of the ten largest rivers in the world, graced with its great water supply and vast variety of fish.

Khabarovsk has one of the largest airports in the entire country, uniting the city with other Pacific Rim countries: Japan (Niigata), South Korea (Seoul), North Korea (Pyongyang), China (Harbin), the USA (Anchorage and San Francisco), and Singapore.

The Far East composes the easternmost territory of the country and is situated in the continental climate zone which is characterized by both summer and winter monsoon winds. The average temperature in the summer is 25-30°C while in the winter temperatures can fall to -25 and -30°C.

Every year, more than 30,000 tourists from abroad stay at the 4-star Hotel "Intourist" in Khabarovsk. The 10-storey complex for 515 guests, located in the centre of the city, contains 25 single rooms, 232 double rooms and 13 suites. Hotel "Intourist" provides experienced guides, business centre, post office, shopping arcade, barber/beauty parlour, bar and restaurants serving Japanese, Western and Russian cuisines. Modern means of communication make it possible to connect with any part of the world from the hotel rooms.

There is a great variety of natural riches in the territory. For this reason the Tsar's government took such an enormous interest in the Far East and began to develop it in the 17th century.

The Far East's natural surroundings attract numerous tourists who are enraptured by the untouched beauty of the Ussuri Taiga whose flora and fauna represent a most natural combination of north and south.

Hotel "Intourist" is only 14 km from the international airport, and close to the railway station (7km) and port (3km). The people of Khabarovsk are very proud of their city and are always happy to welcome guests.

BAROVSK"
welcome to Russia!

Khabarovsk Intourist Offers the following tours

Cruises on the Amur River on the comfortable vessel
"Erofey Khabarov"

Train rides along the Baikal-Amur Railroad
sightseeing tours of the cities of Siberia, Yakutia, Sakhalin
and Amur Territory
Specialised tours for hunters, fishermen ornothologists and
lovers of scuba diving, snorkelling and canoe trips
Russian language seminars
Train rides on the Trans-Siberian Railroad
Meeting with Khabarovsk artists with visits to Art Galleries
and studios

We also offer the following services in Khabarovsk:
Boat rides on the Amur River
Visits to the Nanai village of Sikachi-Alyan
Helicopter excursions
Entertainment such as folk music concerts, theatre visits,
circuses and Russian tea parties
Excursion to botanical garden
Out of town excursions to the Ussuri taiga sanctuary
Visits to families in Khabarovsk
One day boat trips to Fooyan, China
Visits to schools, kindergartens and industrial complexes
One day trip to Vladivostok
Excursion to Russian/Chinese border
Welcome to Khabarovsk! Hope to see you soon!

Our address: Intourist Sales Dept.
2 Amurski Blvd.
Khabarovsk, 680065, Russia

Tel: 33-87-74, 39-90-44
Fax: 1-509-689-3295-42-2251, 1-509-689-3295-42-2111
Tlx. 141194 FIRMA SU

Intourist
Khabarovsk

It's also completely new on the inside...

It's not only on the outside that
Aeroflot Russian International Airlines have changed.
Along with our new fleet of A310 Airbuses, comes a new
standard in service and quality.
If you fly to Eastern Europe or the Far East,
our daily flights direct to Moscow, Tokyo, Bangkok
and Hong Kong offer the shortest routes,
and the keenest prices.
You'll also find the latest in-flight video
entertainment on first class, business class and economy.
Get the inside information on our new
range of services, and call the number below.

AEROFLOT
Russian International Airlines

70 Piccadilly London W1V 9HH
Office Tel: 071-491 1764 Bookings and Information Tel: 071-355 2233 Telex: 21704 Fax: 071-355 2323

Medincentre

MEDINCENTRE FOR SERVICES TO THE DIPLOMATIC AND CORRESPONDENTS CORPS

Travel Safely

MOSCOW

4th Dobryninsky per. 4,
Moscow-117049, Russia

MEDINCENTRE offers many specialist services for diplomats and business people visiting Moscow who wish to ensure that they have the security of knowing that MEDINCENTRE can be relied upon to provide for their needs should they fall ill or suffer injury during their stay. Medicentre is staffed by fully trained experts in their field many trained in Japan and Europe. They offer assistance 24-hours a day.
Remember MEDINCENTRE and ensure that your health is not one of your worries on your trip to Moscow.

24-hour Telephone
095 945-79-82
095 237-39-04 First-aid
095 237-53-95   Clinic

Information Telephone
095 237-59-33 - Reception
095 236-31-16 - Secretary

Fax: 7 502 222 1556

1000, 500, 200, 100, 50, 25, 10, 5, 3 and 1. Coins are in denominations of Rub1, and 50, 20, 15, 10, 5, 3, 2 and 1 kopeks, though they are rarely used due to very high inflation. There are also Soviet Olympic coins dated 1977-1980 in denominations of Rub150, 100, 10, 5 and 1.
Currency exchange: Foreign currency should only be exchanged at official bureaux and all transactions must be recorded on the currency declaration form which is issued on arrival. It is wise to retain all exchange receipts. Bureaux de change are numerous and easy to locate. Large shops offer their own exchange facilities.
Credit cards: Major European and international credit cards, including American Express, Visa and Diners Club, are accepted in the larger hotels and at foreign currency shops and restaurants.
Eurocheques up to Rub300 can be cashed in banks.
Travellers cheques are preferable to cash, but visitors to Moscow would be wise to take some hard currency for purchases.
Exchange rate indicators: The following figures are included as a guide to the movements of the Rouble against Sterling and the US Dollar:

Date:	Oct '92	Sep '93	Jan '94	Jan '95
£1.00=	0.95	*0.86	*0.86	*1.04
$1.00=	*0.60	*0.56	*0.58	*0.67

Note [*]: Official rate. The true market rate differs immensely (£1 = Rub5612, US$1 = Rub3587 according to the *Financial Times*, January 1995). A single exchange rate is established for the Rouble by the Central Bank of Russia twice a week.
Currency restrictions: The import and export of local currency is prohibited. All remaining local currency must be reconverted at the point of departure. The import of foreign currency is unlimited, subject to declaration. The export of foreign currency is limited to the amount declared on arrival.
Banking hours: 0930-1730 Monday to Friday.

DUTY FREE

Duty-free regulations within the CIS are liable to change at short notice. The following goods may be imported into the Russian Federation without incurring customs duty:
200 cigarettes or 100 cigars or cigarillos or 250g of tobacco; 1 litre of spirits; 2 litres of still wine and 2 litres of sparkling wine; a reasonable quantity of perfume for personal use; gifts up to a value of Rub1000.

Note: On entering the country, tourists must complete a customs declaration form which must be retained until departure. This allows the import of articles intended for personal use, including currency and valuables which must be registered on the declaration form. Cameras, jewellery, computers and musical instruments should all be declared. Customs inspection can be long and detailed. It is advisable when shopping to ask for a certificate from the shop which states that goods have been paid for in hard currency. Presentation of such certificates should speed up customs formalities.
Prohibited imports: Military weapons and ammunition, narcotics and drug paraphernalia, pornography, loose pearls and anything owned by a third party that is to be carried in for that third party. If you have any query regarding items that may be imported, an information sheet is available on request from Intourist.
Prohibited exports: As prohibited imports, as well as annulled securities, state loan certificates, lottery tickets, works of art and antiques (unless permission has been granted by the Ministry of Culture), saiga horns, Siberian stag, punctuate and red deer antlers (unless on organised hunting trip), and punctuate deer skins.

PUBLIC HOLIDAYS

Jan 1-2 '95 New Year. **Mar 8** International Women's Day. **Apr 23** Russian Orthodox Easter. **May 9** Victory in Europe Day. **Jun 12** Russian Independence Day. **Nov 7** Constitution Day. **Dec 31** New Year's Eve. **Jan 1 '96** New Year's Day. **Mar 8** International Women's Day. **Apr 15** Russian Orthodox Easter.

HEALTH

Regulations and requirements may be subject to change at short notice, and you are advised to contact your doctor well in advance of your intended date of departure. Any numbers in the chart refer to the footnotes below.

	Special Precautions?	Certificate Required?
Yellow Fever	No	No
Cholera	1	No
Typhoid & Polio	2	-
Malaria	No	-
Food & Drink	3	-

[1]: Cholera has been reported in Daghestan. Up-to-date advice should be sought before deciding wheter precautions should include vaccination, as medical opinion is divided over its effectiveness. See *Health* section at the back of the book. Sensible personal hygiene and diet are advised for visitors to the region.
[2]: There is a risk of typhoid and other tick-borne diseases in east and central Siberia.
[3]: All water should be regarded as being a potential health risk. Water used for drinking, brushing teeth or making ice should have first been boiled or otherwise sterilised. Milk is pasteurised and dairy products are safe for consumption. Only eat well-cooked meat and fish, preferably served hot. Pork, salad and mayonnaise may carry increased risk. Vegetables should be cooked and fruit peeled.
Rabies is present. For those at high risk, vaccination before arrival should be considered. If you are bitten abroad, seek medical advice without delay. For more information consult the *Health* section at the back of the book.
Widespread outbreaks of *diptheria* have been reported. Consult a doctor regarding inoculation before travelling to Russia.
Health care: The highly developed health service provides free medical treatment for all citizens. If a traveller becomes ill during a booked tour in the CIS, emergency treatment is free, with small sums to be paid for medicines and hospital treatment. If a longer stay than originally planned becomes necessary because of the illness, the visitor has to pay for all further treatment – travel insurance is therefore recommended for all travellers. It is advisable to take a supply of those medicines that are likely to be required (but check first that they may be legally imported) as medicines can prove difficult to get hold of.

TRAVEL - International

Note: At the time of writing, Russia had temporarily closed its borders with Georgia and Azerbaijan, suspending all flights, road and sea traffic between the North Caucasus and these two countries.
AIR: The national airline is *Aeroflot Russian International Airlines (SU)*.
For free advice on air travel, call the Air Travel Advisory

Bureau in the UK on (0171) 636 5000 (London) *or* (0161) 832 2000 (Manchester).

Approximate flight times: From *London* to Moscow or St Petersburg is 3 hours 45 minutes.

From Moscow to *Almaty* is 4 hours 15 minutes, to *Baku* is 3 hours, to *Bukhara* is 3 hours 45 minutes, to *Dzhambul* is 3 hours 45 minutes, to *Kiev* is 1 hour 30 minutes, to *Minsk* is 1 hour 30 minutes, to *Odessa* is 2 hours, to *Samarkand* is 3 hours 45 minutes and to *Yerevan* is 4 hours 30 minutes,

International airports: *Moscow (SVO)* (Sheremetyevo) is 29km (18 miles) northwest of the city. Airport facilities include outgoing duty-free shops, banks/bureaux de change, restaurants and first aid. Coaches depart for the airport from the Central Air Terminal in Moscow, 37 Leningradsky Prospekt (travel time – 35 minutes for domestic flights, 50 minutes for international flights). Taxis are available at the airport to the city centre for approx. US$50 (travel time – 40 minutes). Moscow also has three primarily domestic airports: see *Travel – Internal* below.

St Petersburg (LED) (Pulkovo) is 17km (10.5 miles) south of the city (travel time – 45 minutes). Airport facilities include 24-hour banks/bureaux de change, 24-hour tourist information, 24-hour duty-free shops, restaurant (0900-2300), bar (1000-2000), 24-hour snack bar, 24-hour left luggage and 24-hour first aid. Buses are available to the city centre (travel time – 45 minutes). Taxis are available for approx. US$20 (travel time – 20 minutes).

Intourist offers stopover facilities in Moscow (not exceeding two nights) to transit passengers at special reduced rates including transport, accommodation, full board and guided tour. Four weeks' notice is required.

SEA: Cruise holidays can be arranged by the Russian shipping line *CTC Limited*. UK address: 1 Regent Street, London SW1Y 4NN. Tel: (0171) 896 8888. Fax: (0171) 839 2483. Round-trip cruises include St Petersburg on the Baltic and travel from Tilbury to destinations in Scandinavia (during May, July and August).

RAIL: There are various connections from London. The sleeper coach to Moscow takes about 53 hours. The main routes are:

Harwich–Hook of Holland–Berlin–Warsaw–*Moscow*.
Dover–Ostend–Berlin–Warsaw–*Moscow*.

Services from Harwich are daily, with the train leaving at 0925 from London Liverpool Street Station and the ferry at 1130 from Harwich Docks. Services from Dover are also daily, with the train leaving at 0730 from London Victoria Station and the ferry at 1000 from Dover Docks. There are through trains or coaches from other Western and Eastern European cities and from Turkey, Iran, Mongolia and China.

ROAD: Foreign tourists may drive their own cars or may hire cars from Intourist (see *Travel – Internal* below). The following crossing points between Finland and the Russian Federation are available: Vaalima–Torfianovska; Nuijamaa–Brusnichnoye and Rajajooseppi–Lotta. There are also crossing points between the Russian Federation and Hungary, Poland, Romania and the Slovak Republic. Those entering by car should have their visas registered at the hotel, motel or campsite where they will stay for the first night; are advised to insure their vehicle with *Ingosstrakh*, which has offices at all crossing points and in most major cities; and should also purchase Intourist service coupons at the border. For information on the documentation required temporarily to import a car, contact Intourist. It should be noted that, once in the CIS, foreigners would be wise to only drive on routes agreed beforehand with Intourist (see below). Although motorcyclists can enter Russia, cyclists wishing to cross the Russian border should find out whether this is permissible from the Russian Embassy or their travel agent before departure.

Note: A road tax is payable upon entry to the Russian Federation.

TRAVEL - Internal

AIR: The internal network radiates from Moscow's four airports. *Aeroflot* runs services from Moscow to most major cities. All-inclusive tours are available from Intourist.

Domestic airports: *Vnukovo Airport (VKO)* is 29.5km (18 miles) southwest of Moscow. Coaches go to the airport from the Central Air Terminal (travel time – 75 minutes). Outgoing duty-free facilities are available at the airport. Taxis are available to the city.

Domodedovo (DME) is 40km (25 miles) from Moscow. A coach goes from the Central Air Terminal to the airport (travel time – 1 hour 20 minutes).

Bykovo Airport (BKA) is the smallest of Moscow's airports. Coaches go to the airport from the Central Air Terminal.

Approximate flight times: From Moscow to *Bratsk* is 6 hours 45 minutes, to *Donetsk* is 1 hour 30 minutes, to *Irkutsk* is 7 hours, to *Khabarovsk* is 7 hours 30 minutes, to *Kharkov* is 1 hour 15 minutes, to *St Petersburg* is 1 hour, to *Lvov* is 2 hours 15 minutes, to *Volgograd* is 1 hour 30 minutes and to *Yalta* is 2 hours 15 minutes.

SEA: Due to its geographical placement, the Russian Federation has ports on its Pacific and Baltic shores and in the south on the Black Sea. The most important eastern ports are Vladivostok, Magadan, Nakhodka and Petropavlovsk; the most important western ports are St Petersburg and Kaliningrad on the Baltic. The only link to the Atlantic is the port of Murmansk on the Kola peninsula, which never freezes over. Major harbours on the Black Sea are Novorossiysk and Sochi. There are plans to build an extension to the St Petersburg harbour at Ust-Luga. Upgrading of facilities at Kaliningrad and Vyborg is also planned. Sea cruises on the Black Sea and the Baltic are popular.

RIVER: Cruises and excursions are available on the Volga, Lena, Irtysh, Ob, Yenisey, Don and Amur rivers. Many companies (including Mir Tesen and Orthodox Cruise Company) offer cruises on board comfortable, modern boats. The Volga towns, the Golden Ring and Moscow–St Petersburg are popular routes.

RAIL: The 87,090km (54,432 miles) of track are a vital part of the infrastructure due to the poor road system. The largest and busiest rail network in the world is predominantly for freight traffic. Only a few long-distance routes are open for travel by tourists, and reservations must be made on all journeys. Children under 5 travel free. Children aged 5-9 pay half fare. Rail travellers are advised to store valuables in the compartment under the bed or seat and not to leave the compartment unattended.

The *Trans-Siberian Express,* probably the most famous train journey in the world, is one of the best ways of seeing the interior of the country. It runs from Moscow to the Pacific coast of Siberia and on to Japan. There is a daily service, but the steamer from Nakhodka to Yokohama only sails approximately once a week. The through journey from Moscow to Yokohama takes ten days. It is the world's longest continuous train journey, crossing seven time zones and 9745km (5778 miles) from Europe to the Pacific, with 91 stops from Vladivostok to Moscow. Bed linen and towels are provided in the 'Soft Class' (first class) berths, and there is a toilet and wash basin at the end of each carriage. An attendant serves tea from the samovar for a small charge and there is a restaurant car on every train where meals can be purchased with Roubles. (However, no alcohol is available on the train, so passengers are advised to bring their own if desired.) Another epic journey may be made on the *Trans-Mongolian Railway.* It runs from Moscow to Irkutsk (Siberia), skirting Lake Baikal and then entering Mongolia. The journey to the Mongolian capital, Ulan Bator, is remarkable for its dramatic scenery. The journey concludes in Beijing. For further information on both train holidays, contact Intourist.

ROAD: The European part of the Russian Federation depends heavily on its road network, which totals 854,000km (533,750 miles) throughout the Federation. Of these, 624,100km (390,063 miles) are paved. Generally, the few roads in Siberia and further east are impassable during the winter. It is a good idea to arrange motoring holidays through Intourist or another reputable agency. It is also a good idea to pre-plan the itinerary and accommodation requirements. On the majority of Intourist routes, signposts are also written in the Latin alphabet. Some Russian phrase books such as the Penguin edition contain useful vocabulary related to driving. Travellers can take their own car (see *Travel – International* above) or hire a vehicle through Intourist; tariffs include the cost of insurance. Intourist can arrange to have hire cars waiting at authorised border crossings. Chauffeured cars are available in major cities. Sample distances: Moscow to St Petersburg: 692km (432 miles); Moscow to Minsk: 690km (429 miles); Moscow to Rostov-on-Don: 1198km (744 miles); Moscow to Kiev: 858km (533 miles); Moscow to Odessa: 1347km (837 miles). A motoring guide is available from Intourist.

Bus: Long-distance coach services operate but they are generally not available for tourist travel. **Traffic regulations:** Traffic drives on the right. Speeds are limited to 60kmph (37mph) in built-up areas and 90kmph (55mph) elsewhere. Hooting the horn is forbidden except when to do so might prevent an accident. Motorists should avoid driving at night if possible. It is forbidden to carry unauthorised passengers or pick up hitch-hikers. Driving under the influence of drugs or alcohol is forbidden. Every car must display registration plates and stickers denoting the country of registration and be fitted with seat belts, a first-aid kit, a fire extinguisher and an emergency sign (triangle) or red light. In case of an accident, contact the nearest traffic inspection officer or Intourist office and make sure all participants fill in written statements, to be witnessed by a militia inspector.

All repairs will be at the foreign motorist's expense. **Documentation:** An international or national driving licence with an authorised translation is necessary. Visitors travelling in their own cars must also possess the following documents at all times: passport and visa; service vouchers issued by Intourist; itinerary card bearing visitor's name and citizenship, car registration number and full details of itinerary presented upon entry to the the Russian Federation relating to the route to be taken and the date and place of stopovers; a chart of Intourist's routes; form provided by Customs on arrival guaranteeing that the car will be taken out of the Russian Federation on departure; petrol vouchers purchased at the border; and insurance cover documents. Contact Intourist for full details. A road tax is payable upon entry to the country (see end of *Travel – International* above). Motor insurance for travel within the Russian Federation can be arranged prior to departure through Black Sea and Baltic Insurance Company Limited, 65 Fenchurch Street, London EC3 M4EY (tel: (0171) 709 9202; fax: (0171) 702 3557), or upon entry to the Russian Federation at the offices of Ingosstrakh, the Russian Federation foreign insurance agency.

URBAN: Public transport in the cities is comprehensive and cheap. Many services are electric traction (metro, tramway, trolleybus). Stations on the Moscow and St Petersburg metros are always elegant and often palatial. Fares are standard for the various modes. Taxis are also available; they can be hailed in the street, hired at a rank or booked by telephone. It is safer to use officially marked taxis which should not be shared with strangers.

JOURNEY TIMES: The following chart gives approximate journey times (in hours and minutes) from Moscow to other major cities/towns in the Russian Federation.

	Air	Rail	Sea
Khabarovsk	7.30	-	-
St Petersburg	1.00	9.00	-
Irkutsk	7.00	88.00	-
Nakhodka	-	-	141.00
Volgograd	1.45	-	-

ACCOMMODATION

HOTELS: There are approximately 2500 hotels in the Russian Federation, of which around 100 specialise in accommodating foreign guests. Some hotels meet international standards, whereas others are very basic. Direct reservations by clients are on the increase. Several new hotels have been opened in Moscow and St Petersburg, partly as joint-ventures, ie the Aerostar (4-star), the Olympic-Penta (all rooms with bathroom, air-conditioning, radio, TV, IDD) and the Novotel at the Moscow airport. The Pullman Iris also offers 4-star comfort. St Petersburg's Grand Hotel Europe is one of the first 5-star hotels in the Russian Federation. The Hotel Helen is a Russian-Finnish joint-venture, 20km (12.5 miles) from the St Petersburg airport. **BED & BREAKFAST:** Several companies provide bed & breakfast accommodation with English-speaking families in Moscow, St Petersburg and other cities. **CAMPING/CARAVANNING:** Camping holidays are now offered by a number of independent companies.

RESORTS & EXCURSIONS

Moscow

The capital was founded in 1147, but there is evidence that there has been a settlement here since Neolithic times. The focal point of the city is *Red Square*, on one side of which is the *Kremlin* surrounded by a thick red fortress wall containing 20 towers in all, at intervals. The *Sobakina Tower,* designed to withstand sieges, contains a secret escape passage. The *Tainitskaya Tower* translates as the 'Tower of Secrets', because it also had a secret subterranean passage leading to the river. The *Trinity Gate* is the tallest of the towers. The *Water-Hoist Tower* conveyed water to the Kremlin. The *Nabatnaya Tower* contained an alarm bell that was rung in times of danger. In the Kremlin grounds, the *Uspensky Cathedral* (1475-79), designed by the Italian architect Aristotle Fioravanti, contains three of the oldest Russian icons. The tsars were crowned here; Ivan the Terrible's throne is situated near the entrance. Also within the Kremlin stand the 14th-century *Grand Kremlin Palace* and the golden-domed *Belfry of Ivan the Great. St Basil's Cathedral* (built 1555-60), at another end of the square, is famous for its brightly-coloured domes. As the story goes, Ivan the Terrible was so overwhelmed by its beauty that he blinded the architect so that he could never create another building as impressive as this. Opposite St Basil's, the *Spassky (Redeemer's) Gate* is the main entrance to the Kremlin, built in 1491 by Pietro Antonio Solario. The

YOUR ARMCHAIR VIEW OF MOSCOW

Hotel Ukraina is situated on the banks of the Moskva River and offers a beautiful panoramic view of Moscow city centre: the White House of the Russian Parliament, the Town Hall and Novy Arbat Street, as well as the Kremlin. The hotel's location in the administrative and economic heart of Moscow is popular with both tourists and business travellers.

The hotel has over 1010 well-appointed rooms with first-class fittings and all facilities. A large number of shops and kiosks are situated within the building, and our guests are treated to delicious cuisine specialities of the Ukraine, Russia and Europe.

Hotel Ukraina's Executive Centre offers a comprehensive service for business travellers, including facilities for conferences and seminars. Our Administration Department organises sightseeing tours, museum and theatre visits and can arrange your car rental or flight reservation.

UKRAINA
Hotel
Complex

2/1 Kutuzovsky Prospekt, 12149 Moscow
Tel: (010-7) 095 243-3030 **Enquiries** / 243-2596 **Reservations**
Fax: (010-7) 095 243-2896/243-3092

Blagoveshchensky (Annunciation) Cathedral was built for Ivan III. It is extravagantly decorated, from its copper domes to its agate- and jasper-tiled floors. It contains 16th-century frescoes and a precious collection of icons. *Our Lady of Kazan Cathedral* has recently been reconstructed and rededicated. The superb murals in the *Faceted Chamber* date from the late 15th century. Sadly the Chamber is not open to the public. The *State Historical Museum* is also located in Red Square. Although there is talk of finally burying Lenin's embalmed body, *Lenin's Mausoleum* is still open to the public on certain days. However, the changing of the guards in front of the Mausoleum, a ritual which used to attract many sightseers, was discontinued in 1993. *Tverskaya Street* near Red Square is one of the main shopping streets. *Arbat Street* is the main thoroughfare of a traditionally bohemian quarter. Today it is a pedestrian zone with crafts and artists' stalls and street performers. The area known as *Kitai-Gorod* lies east of the Kremlin, and is notable for its 16th- and 17th-century churches, especially the 5-domed *Cathedral of the Sign,* with its amazing acoustic properties. The splendid *English Estate* dates from the same period, a remnant of the area's former importance as a diplomatic and commercial centre. The nearby *Romanov Apartments* are now a museum. *Zayauzie* is a quiet, attractive district, with its handsome merchants' mansions. The world-famous *Bolshoi Opera and Ballet Theatre* at Teatralnaya Square dates from 1824 and has an interior colour scheme of red and gold. *Moscow University* is situated on the southwestern periphery of the city in the *Vorobyevi Hills.* The lookout tower in the park in front of the University complex offers excellent views over the city and the vast *Luzhniki Stadium. Novodevichy Convent* near Sportivnaya metro station houses a museum of rare and ancient Russian art, and is one of the finest examples of 16th- and 17th-century architecture in the city. The neighbouring *Ostozhenka* and *Prechistenka Streets* feature urban mansions and estates associated with many classic Russian authors including Tolstoy. The dancer Isadora Duncan shared her studio with her husband, the poet Sergei Yesenin, in the classically-designed estate of the millionaire Ushkov in Prechistenka Street. *Herzen Street* is one of the oldest in Moscow. It contains the *Moscow State University,* the grand *Tchaikovsky Conservatoire* and the ornate *Mayakovsky Academic Theatre.* The area around *Kuznetzky Most* and *Petrovka Street* is a hub of social and cultural activity, with its popular theatres, fashion shops and business community. One of the most popular new, but macabre attractions is the *KGB Museum* housed in the sinister *Lubyanka* building. The well-preserved *Zamoskvorechye* district was originally a mercantile and artisans' quarter. Many of its churches, warehouses, shops and houses survive. The area is home to the *Tretyakov Gallery,* containing the work of Russian artists and an extensive collection of icons, among them the 'Trinity' by Andrei Rublyov. Other places of interest are: the *Pushkin Museum of Fine Arts* with its cosmopolitan collection; the *Moscow Circus,* the old with animal acts and clowns and the new with more technical wonders; *Izmailovo Park,* formerly the Tsar's estate and the elegant *Tsaritsino* landscaped park; the *Exhibition of Economic Achievements,* where on a large site in the northwest of the city all aspects of Russian life are displayed – agriculture, industry, culture and science. The site also contains a zoo and a circus and there is skating and skiing. The nearby *Ostankino TV Tower* is the tallest in Europe, with a revolving restaurant at the top. The *Space Conquerors' Monument,* representing the trajectory of a rocket launch, also dominates the area. The local *Museum of Serf Art* is a reminder of the past. The *Metro* system is a tourist attraction in itself, as well as a cheap and convenient means of travelling around the city. Many stations are sumptously decorated with marble, glittering chandeliers and works of art. A boat tour on the *Moskva River* is a pleasant way of discovering the city. Excursions start at the *Kutuzovskaya Pier,* accessible from Kutuzovskaya Metro. The river is a superb vantage point to view the *White House* (the Parliament Building), scene of the dramatic siege of 1993, as well as many of the sights listed above.

Excursions: The *State Museum of Ceramics* in **Kuskovo,** 10km (6 miles) from the centre of Moscow, has a fascinating collection of Russian china, porcelain and glass. *Arkhangelskoye Estate,* a museum housed in a palace 16km (10 miles) from Moscow, exhibits European paintings and sculptures, but the main attraction is the grounds which are laid out in the French style. **Zhostovo,** 30km (19 miles) from Moscow, is a centre renowned for its lacquered trays, and **Fedoskino,** 35km (22 miles) from Moscow, produces lacquer miniatures, brooches and other handicrafts. *Yasnaya Polyana* is historically significant as the author Leo Tolstoy's estate. It is located near the town of **Tula,** which is over 160km (100 miles) from the capital. The author of *War and Peace* and *Anna Karenina* is buried here. His house, surrounded by landscaped parkland, is now a museum open to the public. Tchaikovsky's home at **Klin,** 90km (56 miles) from Moscow, and Boris Pasternak's home at **Peredelkino** (30 minutes' drive from the capital), are also museums. **Tver,** situated 160km (100 miles) from Moscow on the upper Volga, is where Catherine II built a palace in order to take a rest en route from Moscow to St Petersburg. The *Putyevoi Dvorets* (Route Palace) was built by Kazakov in 1763-75. The palace overlooks the river, a convenient location for the tsarina to disembark. The town is also notable for its star-shaped square.

The Golden Ring

Several ancient towns of great historical, architectural and spiritual significance make up the 'Golden Ring', extending northeast from Moscow. They are a rich collection of kremlins (citadels), monasteries, cathedrals and fortresses. All are within easy reach of the capital. Since many were founded on river banks, a cruise is a pleasant way of discovering the region. Modern boats plying the Volga afford comfortable accommodation. As some major sites such as Vladimir and Suzdal are not located near the Volga, a minibus tour with hotel accommodation is a better option for visitors whose primary interest is the region's architectural heritage.

Sergiyev Posad (formerly Zagorsk), a small town situated on two rivers, is the centre of the handmade toy industry; the *Toy Museum* has a collection beginning in the Bronze Age. The *Trinity Monastery of St Sergius* dates from the Middle Ages and is a major pilgrimage centre. Its *Cathedral of the Dormition* has wonderful blue domes decorated with gold stars. The museum contains examples of Russian ecclesiastical art and crafts. In nearby **Sofrin,** the *Icon Workshops* produce ecclesiastical ware. Also near Sergiyev Posad, the literary and artistic museum of *Abramtsevo* houses paintings by Repin, Serov and Vrubel. The museum is surrounded by parkland and birch woods. Ornate traditional Russian huts are dotted around the estate. **Rostov Veliky,** founded in the 9th century, has a beautiful *Kremlin* and the *Cathedral of the Dormition.* The town overlooks the shores of the Nero lake, and is surrounded by ancient monasteries. Neighbouring **Yaroslavl** lies on the banks of the Volga, and contains a host of ancient churches, most notably the *Transfiguration of the Saviour Cathedral,* built in the early 16th century. **Kostroma** stands at the confluence of the Volga and the River Kostroma. It is a renowned cheese-making centre. Its most outstanding building is the *Ipatievski Monastery-Fortress.* Built during the first half of the 14th century, it became the Romanov's residence three centuries later. The open-air museum features a collection of traditional Russian buildings, including wooden churches, log cabins and windmills brought from all over Russia. East of Moscow is **Suzdal,** perhaps the most important town in the Golden Ring. It boasts 50 well-preserved examples of ancient architecture contained within a relatively small area, providing a wonderfully coherent vision of its past. Historically it was a political and religious centre, and is now a major tourist attraction. The wives of tsars and boyars were exiled to the *Blessed Virgin Convent.* Less than 32km (20 miles) away is **Vladimir,** which played a prominent part in the rise of the Russian state. The city's two magnificent cathedrals date from the 12th century. Another notable monument is the *Golden Gate,* a unique example of old Russian engineering skills. The nearby village of **Bogolyubovo** features a 12th-century fortress and *Church of the Protecting Veil.* **Uglich,** another beautiful town on the banks of the Volga, is notable for its *Kremlin* and the *Chambers of Prince Dmitry.* Ivan the Terrible's son and heir died here.

Karelia

Bounded by Finland and the White Sea, Karelia's landscape is a patchwork of lakes, marshes and forests, whose canopies shade abundant mushrooms and berries. The region's capital, **Petrozavodsk,** is a staging post for a variety of holiday activities in the region. The small island of **Kizhi** within **Lake Onega** is easily accessible by hydrofoil from here. The island was an early pagan centre. Its surviving heritage features the 22-domed 18th-century *Church of the Transfiguration,* whose wooden structure was built without a single nail. The open-air museum is a collection of Russian and Karel wooden buildings from the 14th-19th centuries. The region is ideal for adventure holidays on the *Shuya, Suna* and *Vama-Vodla* rivers. Tranquil waters offering spectacular views of the countryside are suddenly interrupted by rapids cascading over glacial boulders. The white waters may be negotiated by kayak or cataraft. The Suna is excellent for fishing. The *Kivach Waterfall* along its path is especially beautiful. Karel pies called *kalitkas* may be sampled in the local hamlets, often no more than a cluster of sturdy wooden cottages. A real sauna followed by a plunge into a river or lake is an ideal way to unwind at the end of an adventure-packed day.

Murmansk

Almost due north of St Petersburg, this is the largest city within the Arctic Circle. This important port on the shores of *Kola Bay* is warmed by the waters of the Gulf Stream and is free of ice throughout the year. It was built with British assistance during the First World War. The northern lights are seen here in November and December and in March the *Sports Festival of the Peoples of the North* is held.

Arkhangelsk, the largest city in the White Sea area, was only opened to tourists in 1990. Before the founding of St Petersburg it was the first and only seaport in Russia. From here, visitors may travel to the nearby village of *Mali Kareli* to view Russian white stone and wooden architecture.

Novgorod

South of St Petersburg, Nizhny Novgorod was founded over 1100 years ago and was one of the most important towns of ancient Russia. Novgorod was the founding city of Rus, the nucleus of modern Russia, although Kiev later became the capital. The dissident scientist Andrei Sakharov and the author Alexander Solzhenitsyn were exiled here during the Soviet era, when the town was known as Gorky. Picturesquely located on the banks of the River Volkhov, the city is a treasure trove of ancient architecture, with 39 cathedrals and churches. Within the walls of the *Kremlin, St Sophia's Cathedral* (mid-11th century) is the oldest stone structure of Russia.

St Petersburg

The Federation's second largest city, 715km (444 miles) northwest of Moscow, is known both as a cultural centre and for its elegant buildings. The city is spread over 42 islands in the delta of the River Neva. In comparison to Moscow, which tended to orientate itself to the East, it has always retained a European flair and was intended as a 'Window to the West'. It was built by Peter the Great in 1703 and remained the capital for 200 years of Tsarist Russia. Known as Petrograd after the civil war, and Leningrad during the Soviet period, the city reverted to its original name in 1991 by popular demand. Wide boulevards, slow flowing canals, bridges and some of the best examples of tsarist architecture made the city known as the Venice of the North. Though badly damaged in World War II, much of it is now reconstructed. In June and July the city has famous White Nights, when darkness recedes to a brief twilight, when it takes on an unusual aura. Many of the most interesting sites, especially those on the left bank of the River Neva, can be explored on foot. The *Palace Square* and the *Winter Palace* are the most popular attractions for followers of Russian history. Troops fired on demonstrators there in 1905 and the Palace witnessed the capitulation of the provisional government, allowing the Bolsheviks to take the country into eight decades of Communist rule. The

Hermitage houses the vast private collection of the tsars. The *Museum of the History of the City* gives a comprehensive picture of St Petersburg's history. Exploring the city the visitor will inevitably see the *Alexandrovskaya Column*. *St Isaac's Cathedral* is one of the biggest dome buildings of the world and, like the *Kazansky Cathedral*, houses a museum. Also worth a visit is the *St Peter and Paul Fortress,* a former prison that is now a popular museum. Members of the Romanov Dynasty are buried in the Cathedral of the same name. The gorgeously-decorated *Yusupov Mansion* was built for the aristocratic family of the same name. Its rooms are sumptuously decorated in mid-19th century style. The mansion's concert hall is now a venue for recitals, theatrical productions, opera and ballet. A waxwork exhibition commemorates Rasputin, who died in the building. The grand *Nevsky Prospekt*, dominated by the spire of the *Admiralty Building*, is one of the city's main thoroughfares and is lined by opulent buildings. These include the *Kazan Cathedral* and the *Church of the Resurrection*. The collection at the *Russian Museum* covers nearly a thousand years of Russian art history. Nevsky Prospect crosses the Fontanka River at Anichkov Bridge, and continues to Palace Square. Further sights are the *Cathedral of St Nicholas* (Russian Baroque), still a working church; the *Alexander Nevsky Monastery,* the main religious centre in St Petersburg; and the *Museums of Ethnography* and *Russian Art*. The homes of Dostoyevsky, Pushkin, Anna Akhmatova and Rimsky-Korsakov serve as museums dedicated to their former occupants. The cruiser *Aurora* is berthed on the Neva. A blank shot was fired from her bow to give a signal to start the assault on the Winter Palace in 1917. Lenin also announced the victory of the revolution from here.
Excursions: The following palaces beyond the outskirts of St Petersburg are collectively known as the *Summer Palaces*. *Petrodvorets* is a former summer palace of Tsar Peter the Great and is known for its beautiful cascades and fountains. It is located 34km (21 miles) from St Petersburg on the southern shore of the Gulf of Finland. He designed the initial plans himself, and he appointed European and Russian architects to realise his grand project which was intended to rival Versailles. *Oranienbaum* was built as the summer residence of Alexander Menshikov, Peter the Great's associate. From here, he oversaw the construction of the *Kronstadt* naval fortress on the nearby **Kotlin Island.** Thankfully, the

palace and its parkland escaped damage during the Second World War. Its *Chinese* and *Sliding Hill Pavilions* are exceptionally beautiful. The *Grand Catherine Palace* at **Tsarskoye Selo** was built for Peter the Great's wife. The Scottish architect Charles Cameron designed some of the interiors, though a greater number by Bartholomeo Rastrelli survive. Pushkin spent his formative years in the town. Cameron also designed the subtle buildings at nearby **Pavlovsk,** which were designed to complement the parkland's beauty. The park itself, designed by the Italian Gonzago, is one of the finest landscaped parks in Europe. The estate was originally part of Tsarskoye Selo, but Catherine II gave it to her son Paul. Although she commissioned Cameron to design the estate, Paul, whose relationship with his mother was strained, decided to redecorate the palace.
Lake Ladoga, a vast and often turbulent lake, is linked to St Petersburg by the River Neva. Of the islands in the lake's northern archipelago, **Valaam** is the most significant because of its ancient monastery. Its golden domes suddenly rise from the mist that frequently shrouds visiting cruise ships. The founding religious community frequently suffered Swedish and Viking attacks during the Middle Ages. The present buildings date from the late 18th century. As well as being an important pilgrimage centre, the monastery was a noted centre for innovations in crafts and agriculture. Its missionaries brought Orthodox Christianity to the shores of Alaska. A religious community was re-established on the island in 1989, and restoration of the monastery is already under way. Despite years of neglect, Valaam still retains a mysterious air.

River Volga

The mighty Volga provides an additional road into Russia. Travelling by river from Kazan to Rostov-on-Don makes a pleasant tour.
Kazan: The cultural centre of the Tartars, this city boasts a *Kremlin* dating from the 16th century which, with its towers and churches, is fascinating to visit. The *Tartar State Museum* and the 18th-century *Mosque* are also of interest.
Ulyanovsk: Lenin's birthplace; his parents' house here used to be a popular museum.
Samara: A major space centre, the city was founded in the 16th century around a fortress surveying the Volga

and Samara rivers. The *Old Town* is notable for its fine turn-of-the-century buildings. The Volga shoreline and the nature reserves of the *Zhiguli Hills* are accessible from Samara.
Volgograd: Formerly Stalingrad, the *Victory Museum*

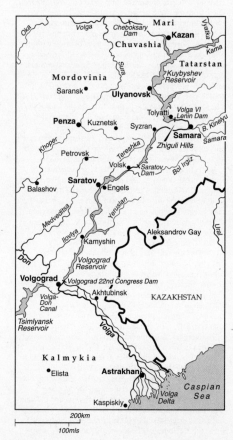

Located in the historical city centre (30 minutes from the airport by taxi), THE ASTORIA offers traditional Russian hospitality. One of the most famous hotels in St Petersburg and the whole of Russia, THE ASTORIA opened in 1912. After years of service, it was closed for restoration to its original charm and re-opened in 1991.

RESTAURANTS

The Winter Garden, Astoria and Angleterre serve the widest selection of international and traditional Russian cuisine.

ACCOMMODATION

The Astoria boasts 308 double rooms, 72 single rooms, 53 suites and 3 apartments. All rooms are air-conditioned and have private bath, telephone, colour TV, radio and refrigerator.

OTHER FACILITIES

Shops, beauty parlour and hairdresser's, fitness centre with sauna, indoor swimming pool and solarium, business centre and service bureau.

Major European and other convertible currencies are accepted, as well as American Express, Diner's Club, Mastercard and VISA credit cards.

ASTORIA HOTEL
39 Bolshaya Morskaya Street
St Petersburg, 190000 Russia
Tel: (812) 2105010, 2105009.
Fax: (812) 3159668.

celebrates the victory over the Nazis, and the whole city is a monument to the year-long battle that took place there. Tours to the battlefields are available. The town stands at the confluence of the Volga and Don rivers. Boat trips and fishing tours taking in both rivers are possible on both. Visits to outlying Cossack and Volga-German villages provide a glimpse of the region's history.

Kaliningrad

The tract of land sandwiched between Lithuania and Poland on the Baltic shoreline is an annexe of the Russian Federation. Its principal town is now called Kaliningrad, although it was known as Königsberg when it was the centre of German Eastern Prussia. The area was ceded to the erstwhile Soviet Union following the Second World War. The territory's future prosperity depends on the Government's plans to give it special economic status. Architectural remnants which survived the war mark the city's German heritage, such as the *Dome Cathedral.* The philosopher Immanuel Kant, the town's most famous son, is buried near here, and his memory is honoured by the *Kant Museum*. The *Amber Museum,* housed in a restored German fortress tower, glorifies this local precious stone. The town has many attractive parks and gardens, as well as a zoo. Nearby, **Svetlogorsk** is a verdant coastal spa resort which has lost none of its charm. The *Kurshe Spit* is a beautiful sand peninsula extending nearly 100km (63 miles) along the coast, and is a rich habitat for plants and animals.

Black Sea

Rostov-on-Don: Once an Armenian town, its low buildings still show Armenian influences. Especially interesting is the *Cathedral of Resurrection*. There are several parks, four theatres, an orchestra, a race-course and a beach. Rostov is the gateway to the Caucasus.
Sochi: A popular resort with a subtropical climate, and a famous health spa, it is situated on the Black Sea's eastern coast beneath the dramatic *Caucasus Mountains.* An observation tower on *Mt Bolshoi Akhun,* 23km (14 miles) from the town, provides a spectacular view of the town, almost all of the Caucasian Riviera and the surrounding mountains. There is a large *Riviera Park* with many tourist facilities and a *Botanical Garden,* founded during the last century, with beautiful, interesting trees and shrubs from all over the world. Boat and hovercraft trips on the Black Sea are available from the town's port.
Dagomys: For those who want a resort-based holiday, this new holiday centre lying to the north of Sochi is ideal. Overlooking the Black Sea, it is beautifully located amongst thickly wooded hills and subtropical greenery. The new Intourist complex has a hotel, several restaurants, coffee shops and bars and sports facilities. An esplanade connects the complex with the beach where there are boats and pedaloes for hire. A visit to the Panorama Bar on the top floor of the Dagomys Hotel is recommended. Nearby is the *Dagomys State Tea Farm* where visitors can sample the fragrant Krasnodar tea accompanied by the delicious local pastries, jams, fruits and nuts whilst enjoying the spectacular mountain scenery.

The Urals, Siberia and the Far East

Yekaterinburg is the birthplace of Russian President Boris Yeltsin. The city is also historically important as the last resting place of the Romanov royal family, assassinated during the Bolshevik revolution.
Siberia covers an area of over 12,800,000 sq km (4,000,000 sq miles) and contains unimaginably vast stretches of forest and taiga. This 'sleeping land', the literal translation of its name, possesses a million lakes, 53,000 rivers and an enormous wealth of natural resources. Although the temperature in winter falls well below freezing point, the weather in summer can be very warm. Tourism is less well-developed than elsewhere in Russia and some parts are still not accessible to international curiosity. However, much of the region has been opened up recently, including **Sakhalin Island** and the **Chukchi Peninsula** just across the Bering Strait from Alaska. The taiga is within easy reach of many of the region's cities. Air-hopping is one way of discovering the wilderness. A famous alternative is the *Trans-Siberian Railway*, the longest continuous railway in the world, a journey which is one of the greatest travel adventures. The line cuts through an area bigger than Western Europe, crossing a landscape which includes arctic wastes, tundra and steppes. The most scenic part of the journey is between Khabarovsk and Irkutsk.
Khabarovsk on the Amur is the largest industrial centre of eastern Siberia and an important transport junction. The town (founded in 1858) was named after the scientist Khabarov. The red brick houses in the centre have curious roofs shaped like pine needles, and are intermingled with the constructivist architecture of the 1930s. Worth a visit is the regional museum which offers an insight into the different cultures of the Amur people. Among its 100 or so different goods for export are such exotic items as ginseng and Ussuri tigers.
Irkutsk is over 300 years old and owes much of its development to its location at the tradeways to Mongolia and China. At the end of the last century the city began to take on the aspect of a 'boom town' where trade in gold, fur and diamonds had suddenly created new wealth. It was to Irkutsk that many 19th-century revolutionaries, such as the Decembrists, were exiled. The *University of Irkutsk* was the first establishment of higher education in eastern Siberia. In former times, as well as today, this important Siberian city is one of the world's biggest suppliers of fur.
The town lies on the banks of the Angara, the only outflowing river from **Lake Baikal.** The lake is accessible from Irkutsk by hydrofoil during the summer. Statistics about Baikal are astounding; with a depth of 1637m (5371ft) it is the world's deepest lake. Its surface area equals that of The Netherlands and Belgium put together. It is 25 million years old, and it would take three months to walk around its 2000km (1243-mile) shoreline. The purity of its water is maintained by millions of tiny crayfish, providing a habitat for a wide variety of fish, including sturgeon, loach, grayling and *omul* (a type of salmon), one of many species unique to Baikal. Its shores are a feeding ground for wildfowl and the occasional bear. Freshwater seal colonies are found around the **Ushkan Islands** in the centre of the lake. **Olkhon Island** is the site of primitive rock drawings and a unique necropolis of an ancient Siberian tribe whose members are thought to have been ancestors of indigenous North Americans. The local climate is often harsh; the surface of the entire lake often freezes over in winter (trains were moved across the ice during the Russo-Japanese war). The *sarma* wind can sink boats and rip the roofs off buildings. While the human race now dominates the lake, it remains to be seen whether it will be a responsible custodian of the region's flora and fauna.
Many of the inhabitants of the Buryat Republic are Buddhists. Dozens of picturesque temples (*datsans)* sprang up round Lake Baikal after Empress Elizabeth, Peter the Great's daughter, recognised the Buddhist religion in Russia. Although most *datsans* were destroyed during the 1930s, many of their treasures were preserved in the Russian Orthodox church in **Ulan Ude,** the capital. The *Sandalwood Buddha,* on display in the town's *Exhibition Hall,* is said to have been made with the Buddha himself sitting as a model.
Yakutsk was founded as a garrison town, and is capital of the vast Sakha (Yakutia) Autonomous Republic. Today it is a major scientific centre for permafrost research. The republic's landscapes range from Alpine meadows to moss-covered tundra, with sandy deserts close to the Arctic zone. This is pioneer country, complete with gold-mining settlements.
Vladivostok, a military and naval port, was opened to foreign visitors in 1990. As a gateway to the Pacific and the East, the town has enormous commercial potential. It is within easy reach of the **Ussuriysk taiga**, a unique habitat for plants of the pre-glacial period, as well as tigers, leopard, bison, boar and bears.

Adventure Holidays in Russia

A few years ago it was an adventure just to get past the immigration formalities in the Soviet Union. Only a privileged few saw the beautiful secrets locked away from the world in the one-sixth of the globe's land mass that made up the largest country in the world. But in a freer, and more open Russia, the veil is coming off the country's great adventure possibilities and they are almost limitless.
Groups are venturing into the great Russian expanses, some being the first Western feet to walk the once-secret landscapes. They can be seen from the opulence of a railway carriage once built for Communist Party leaders, or close up; clinging to a rock face in the Pamir Mountains or rambling through flower-carpeted Siberian valleys and forests. There are a number of opportunities on offer. For those who like it soft there are railway holidays, and for those who like it tough, the options include mountaineering, skiing, river rafting, mountain biking and trekking.
The Russians have also quickly developed some high-tech offerings despite not yet having had time to develop a Disney World or a Universal Studios. It is possible to fly in a MIG-29 aircraft, a fighter capable of more than twice the speed of sound, that was once part of the formidable Soviet Air Force. The flight is with an air-force pilot and should the passenger hold a pilot's licence they get the extra thrill of being allowed hands-on control.
Other military hardware now available as part of the Russian theme park are tanks. A tour operator now offers drives on the bone-crunching terrain of a former Soviet Army tank training course.
Those interested in Russia's achievements in the field of space travel should visit Star City, just outside Moscow, which is a cosmonaut training complex open to visitors.
The increase in tour operators offering Russia from Europe now means a wide choice for potential visitors. A bias towards tailor-made holidays has brought added activities and adventures to the traveller's scope. There is a large potential to develop independent adventure tourism, but it will probably be a 2-decade venture, as adventure in Russia is currently a group market.
Specialist tour operators offer a range of options as well as Intourist, the former state tourist organisation that has become a tour operator and travel agent. Its London general manager, Roger Figg, said "It is a reactive market at the moment in which we respond to what people ask for. Russia adventure is most affordable in groups of about 8-16. It is not yet a holiday for the individual. While, technically, people can go anywhere in Russia, the adventure market is concentrated in three mains areas – southern Siberia, Central Asia and the Caucasus. The opportunities are huge but will take some time to develop. We get people come to us with dreams of traversing the Urals by bicycle but we have to tell them how difficult these things are to arrange."
Russia's severe winters, the sort that helped defeat Napoleon and Hitler, do not put off tourists. And with cities like Moscow having 164 days of snow a year on average, visitors get plenty of opportunity to join locals in the popular art of skating.
The major cities offer some sport, but their attractions are their historic buildings and a rich cultural heritage. The real sporting challenges are hundreds, if not thousands, of miles from Russia's main population centres. In a country that spans 11 time zones it is an endless playground for groups to tackle hard adventure in regions where accommodation is basic but good.
The softest adventure is by the *Bolshoi Express* train – the Orient Express of the north. This shows how former Communist Party officials of the 1950s enjoyed their luxury. Its itineraries, offered by operators like Steppes East and Cox & Kings, include Moscow, St Petersburg, Volgograd and Siberia. Instone Holidays also feature holiday by Russian rail including the famed Trans-Siberian route to the Far East and Vladivostock.
Downhill skiing enjoys a shorter season in Russia and generally lasts from January to March in areas like Dombai, Tsakhadzor and Elbrus. Skiing in Russia calls for much fitness and skill, more than the average skier takes with them each year to Zermatt, Igls or Courchavel, and facilities in general will take some years to equal those of Europe's luxury alpine resorts.
However, heli-skiing is now available in the Caucasus where, it is claimed, the powder snow rivals that of Colorado and there is a guarantee of snow throughout the short season. Amid the wilds of Karelia, north of St Petersburg, cross-country skiing is routed through the taiga forest and over a terrain of frozen rivers and lakes including Onega and Ladoga. Winter camping, in tents with heating, is also an option for the hardy. Mr Figg, of Intourist, says "Cross-country skiing is widely available, but downhill skiing has no infrastructure, so the way to do it is heli-skiing. But that means Russia is mostly open

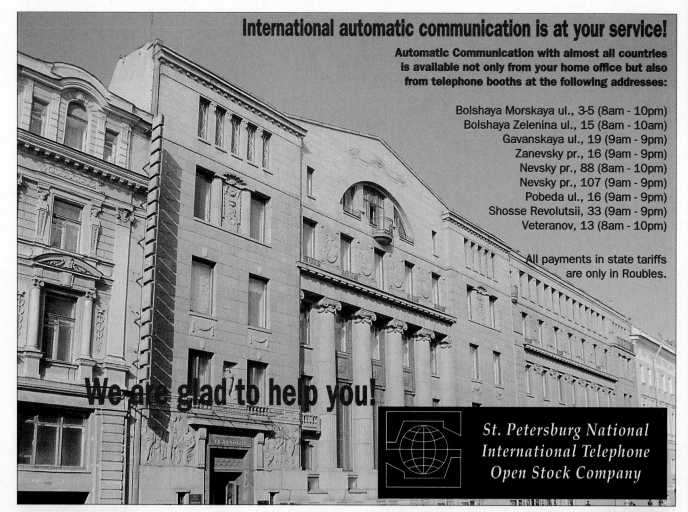

to very good skiers. Twenty years will see many, many more opportunities."

Treks go up to 3200m (10,499ft) in altitude and on the way the landscape changes from alpine meadows of red poppies to snow-capped peaks and scenic plateaux. Tour operators, as Russia gives up its secrets, continue to investigate new opportunities in new areas for backpackers and adventure seekers. Until recently, previously unexploited areas of the Fan Mountains, known as Matcha, had never been trodden by Western feet. Specialist Steppes East is pioneering trekking/camping itineraries this year.

Perm in the Middle Ural Mountains is home to some of the more rare birds of prey. The Baseguy National Reserve has been created on the Kama River Basin and ornithologists can get glimpses of eagle owls, great grey owls, Ural owls and golden eagles.

The Caucasus Mountains, which stretch from the Black Sea to the Caspian Sea, separate Russia from Georgia and Armenia. Dominating the range is Mount Elbrus, at 5642m (18,510ft) the highest peak in Europe. And it is hardly surprising that it should attract the attention of adventure fans. The jagged peaks overlook a vast vegetation range from palm trees to deciduous forest and flower-carpeted valleys. For the sport enthusiast, Elbrus has skiing or offers a strenuous, though non-technical, climb to its summit. Trekking, again strenuous, is in the beautiful scenery of the peak and it neighbours. Available are 6-day Elbrus trekking circuits and 3-summit climbs in the Adyl-Su Valley including the Elbrus peak.

Siberia used to be associated with salt mines and permafrost. Now all can be revealed; the Altai region of southern Siberia rivals Switzerland for rolling hills, snowy peaks, flowers and pine forests. Undiscovered areas of Siberia, on the borders of Kazakhstan and Mongolia where summer temperatures hit 22°C, are heady with the scents of its flowers, herbs and trees. Mount Belukha rises to 4506m (14,784ft) over a few scattered villages in an area where the bear population outnumbers the human species.

Not unsurprisingly, among tours offered are botany itineraries through June and July with safari camp accommodation. There are also horseriding holidays, with routes through the Alpine meadows and coniferous forests of the Sayano Altai Mountains, which also include opportunities for botany,

birdwatching and river rafting.

Central Asia's Lake Baikal – dubbed the Blue Eye of Siberia – offers canoeing and camping holidays for groups. It is reputed to be the oldest lake in the world and is, by far, the deepest at 1637m (5371ft).

The Kamchatka River in Russia's Far East has some stiff river-raft tests as well as canoeing. Wilderness treks are also available in a remote area which is of great geological interest because of its range of extinct volcanoes.

Getting around the Pacific peninsula, reminiscent of Alaska just across the Bering Sea, can be done by flying, on all-terrain vehicles or on two sturdily-shod feet.

Those who seek adventure in the Russian Federation are the 20th-century pioneers with the spirit and wherewithal to open up a country that would take centuries to explore fully.

POPULAR ITINERARIES: 5-day: (a) Moscow–Suzdal–Sergiev Posad–Rostov Veliky–Kostroma–Moscow. (b) St Petersburg–Tsarskoye Selo–Valaam–Petrozavodsk–Kizhi–St Petersburg. **7-day:** (a) Tula–Moscow–Tver–St Petersburg. (b) Vladivostok–Khabarovsk–Ulan Ude–Lake Baikal–Irkutsk. (c) Novgorod–Kazan–Ulyanovsk–Samara–Volgograd–Rostov-on-Don–Sochi.

SOCIAL PROFILE

FOOD & DRINK: The kind of food visitors will eat from day to day depends on which city they are visiting and the time of year. Breakfast is often similar to the Scandinavian, with cold meats, boiled eggs and bread served with Russian tea. *Kasha* (porridge) is a staple breakfast dish, made with milk and oats, buckwheat or semolina. For the midday and evening meal the food is often more traditional, again depending on the region. One of the more famous Russian dishes is *borshch*, a beetroot soup served hot with sour cream, and the sister dish of *akroshka*, a kvas soup served cold. Several dishes which are now often seen as international but find their origin in Russia are *beef stroganov* (beef stewed in sour cream with fried potatoes), *bliny* (small pancakes filled with caviar, fish, melted butter or sour cream), *aladyi* (crumpets with the same filling and jam) and especially *ikra* or *krasnaya ikra* (black and red caviar). The local *chicken kiev* should not be confused with Western imitations. *Tsipleonok tabaka* is another

chicken dish: the meat is roast on a spit. *Whole roast suckling pig* and *roast goose stuffed with buckwheat, roast duck stuffed with apples* and *shashlik* (shish kebab) are served at parties and for special occasions. A vegetable variant of *shashlik* also exists. Local dishes well worth trying include *kotlyety po Pozharsky* (chicken cutlets), *pirozhky* (fried rolls with different fillings, usually meat), *prostakvasha* (yoghurt), *pelmeni* (meat dumplings), *rossolnik* (hot soup, usually made of pickled vegetables) and *shchi* (cabbage soup). *Stuffed cabbage leaves* and *sweet peppers* are filled with boiled rice and minced meat. *Mushrooms in sour cream* are very popular. The great variety of salads available include *winter salad* and *vinegret* (made of diced vegetables). Desserts include *morozhenoye* (ice cream), *ponchiki* (hot sugared doughnuts) and *vareniki* (dumplings containing fresh berries, cherries or jam). Intourist meal vouchers are widely acceptable and an increasing number of hotels and restaurants in Moscow accept foreign currency, as do some bars.

Drink: One of the most popular drinks is *chai* (tea served without milk). Coffee is generally available with meals and in cafés, although standards vary. Soft drinks, fruit juices and mineral waters are widely available. Vodka is often flavoured and coloured with herbs and spices such as *zubrovka* (a kind of grass), *ryabinovka* (steeped with rowan-tree berries), *starka* (dark, smooth, aged vodka) and *pertsovka* (with hot pepper). *Posolskaya, Stolichnaya* and *Rossiskaya* are popular brands. *Krushon* is a highly-recommended cold 'punch'; champagne, brandy and summer fruit are poured into a hollowed watermelon and chilled for several hours. This delicious cocktail is traditionally served from a crystal bowl. White wine and cucumber are used to make a drier variant. *Nastoika* is a fortified wine made of herbs, leaves, flowers, fruit and roots of plants with medicinal properties. *Nalivka* is a sweet liqueur made with fruit or berries. The cherry and strawberry flavours are highly recommended. *Ryabin Cognac* ('Ryabina na Konyakye') is made from rowan-tree berries.

Russian champagne is surprisingly good and reasonably priced. Imported wines from Georgia, Ukraine and Moldova and Armenian Cognac are excellent (for further information, see the separate entries on these countries). *Kvas* is a refreshing and unusual drink, made from a fermented mixture of rye bread, jam, yeast and water, and should be tried on a hot day. Drinks are ordered by

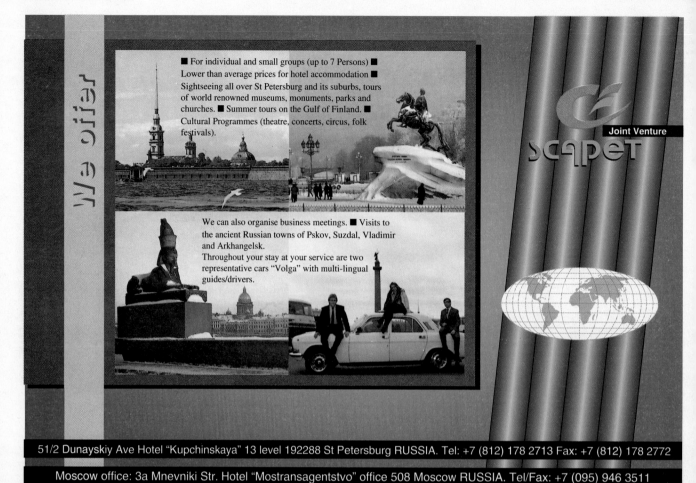

grams or by the bottle. City-centre bars close around midnight.

NIGHTLIFE: Theatre, circus, concert and variety performances are the main evening entertainments. Tickets are available in advance or from ticket booths immediately before performances. The repertoire of theatres provides a change of programme almost nightly. In the course of one month, 30 different productions may be presented by the Bolshoi Opera and Ballet Company. Details of performances can be obtained on arrival. Visitors should apply to the service bureau of their hotel. Dancing takes place in many of the Intourist restaurants and night bars, as well as in the main local restaurants. Moscow alone boasts 69 casinos, including the Cherry Casino and Gabriella. Discotheques include Night Flight and Arlekino, which also has a restaurant. The Russkaya Troika restaurant in the Orlenok Hotel has a cabaret show. All of these establishments are open from 2200-0600.

SHOPPING: Most tourist centres have foreign currency shops, and most consumer goods are now available in Moscow and St Petersburg. A wide range of goods such as watches, cameras, wines and spirits, furs, ceramics and glass, jewellery and toys may be bought for foreign currency only (cash or travellers cheques) at favourable prices. Although a few ordinary shops accept hard currency, most take payment in Roubles only. A system of queueing is used in local shops for choosing goods, for payment and for collection, so allow some time for souvenir hunting. *Palekh* and *Kholui* lacquered boxes make attractive souvenirs. Traditional and satirical *Matryoshka* dolls (wooden dolls within dolls) are widely available. *Khokhloma* wooden cups, saucers and spoons are painted gold, red and black. *Dymkovskaya Igrushka* are pottery figurines based on popular folklore characters. Engraved amber, *Gzhel* porcelain, *Vologda* lace and *Fabergé* eggs and jewellery are highly sought-after. Most tourist shops are closed Sunday, but food shops are usually open every day. Antiquities, valuables, works of art and manuscripts other than those offered for sale in souvenir shops may not be taken out of the CIS without an export licence. **Shopping hours:** 0900-1900. Department stores and supermarkets are open throughout lunchtime. Stores which are open 24 hours a day are becoming more common.

Hiking trips are available in the Caucasus, at Teberda-Dombay (west) and at Baksan Elbrus (north). **Skiing:** There is skiing in the same areas. As for the big cities, Moscow has a ski jump in the Vorobyevi Hills and Intourist can organise days of cross-country skiing, with poles and boots provided, at Suzdal. Cross-country skiing is available outside the city at Olgino on the Gulf of Finland. **Skating:** Many towns and cities have artificial ice rinks for the summer but during the hard winters frozen lakes and rivers ensure plenty of room for Russians and visitors to skate side by side. St Petersburg's Central Recreation Park is a favourite among skaters and it also has a ski centre. **Horseriding:** An equestrian sports centre has been laid out at Bitsa Forest Park and there is also riding at Sokolniki, Moscow and a cycle track at Krylatskoye to the northwest of the city. **Fishing:** The Veselovskaye Reservoir in the Rostov-on-Don region is noted for pike, perch, carp, bream, gudgeon, bullhead and roach. **Spectator sports:** Almost every provincial city has a football team and larger cities have several clubs organised within factories, unions and government offices. International events include the *Kremlin Cup* tennis tournament and the *Izvestia Hockey Prize*. Russia's ethnic diversity is reflected in the wide variety of local traditional sports. Martial arts are a recent import and are steadily gaining popularity.

SPORT: For more detailed information about sports activities, refer to the *Adventure Holidays in Russia* feature.

SPECIAL EVENTS: The following is a selection of some of the main events in 1995/96:
May 5-13 '95 *Moscow Stars Music & Dance Festival*, Moscow. **Jun (last two weeks)** *'White Nights' Art Festival*, St Petersburg. **Autumn** *Red Carnation International Song Festival*. **Jan 7 '96** *Russian Orthodox Christmas*.

SOCIAL CONVENTIONS: It is customary to shake hands when greeting someone. Visits to homes and cities can be organised by Intourist and visitors will find that, although the people vary from region to region and from city to city, they are welcoming and hospitable. Company or business gifts are well received. Each region has its own characteristic mode of dress, some quite unlike Western styles, and visitors should be aware of this contrast. Conservative wear is suitable for most places and the seasonal weather should always be borne in mind. Smoking is acceptable unless stated otherwise. Avoid ostentatious displays of wealth; it is advisable to keep expensive jewellery, watches and cameras out of

sight and take precautions against pickpocketing.
Tipping: Hotels in Moscow and other large cities include a 10-15% service charge. Otherwise 10% is customary.

BUSINESS PROFILE

ECONOMY: The Russian economy has long been hampered by an unwieldy system of economic management under which all production and pricing was centrally administered under the diktats of The Five Year Plan produced by the State Planning Committee (Gosplan). The key advantage enjoyed by the Russian Federation is an enormous abundance of natural resources of every description. Energy resources include oil, gas, coal, nuclear fuels and hydroelectric resources. There are deposits of almost every mineral, many of them known to be the world's largest deposits, while countless others have yet to be discovered. There are vast areas of fertile land, forest and fresh water. The fact that the former Soviet Union was ultimately unable to feed itself without large imports of grain from the USA, Canada and Argentina is perhaps the most damning indictment of the Soviet economic regime. Much of the blame must be laid at the door of the collective farm system, but an equally important factor was the inadequate infrastructure. Roads and railways are still sparse and in poor condition; the telephone system is antique. On top of that, there is a shortage of working transport equipment to exploit what transport systems do exist, leading to poor distribution and consequent shortages and waste. The economy is also paying the price of its past obsession with heavy industry, initiated by Stalin and continued by his successors, and its consistently high defence spending during the Cold War. The industrial economy is thus extensive, particularly in steel, heavy engineering and chemicals. Light industry, and notably consumer products, are comparatively weak. The consumer sector and agriculture are the areas the Russian Federation is most keen to promote. The economic community agreement reached between the CIS republics in the Kazakh capital Almaty in October 1991 allows for coordinated policies in energy, transport, the finance and banking systems, customs and tariffs and foreign economic relations and declares that 'private ownership, free enterprise and competition [will] form the basis for economic recovery'. If the Russian Federation is to make the transition to capitalism successfully, there will also need to be a root and branch reform of the financial system. The Rouble is now desperately weak, and needs substantial international support. A large disparity persists between the nominal official and real (black) market rates. Among the consequences of the financial instability are rocketing inflation – driven up further by the unfreezing of prices at the end of 1991 – capital flight and a shortage of paper money. Foreign trade patterns are being re-organised after the dissolution of the Council for Mutual Economic Assistance (COMECON) in April 1991. Yeltsin has instituted a policy of deregulated foreign trade for the Russian Federation, transferring responsibility from designated government ministries to individual producers; the other CIS republics will probably follow this pattern. The barter system which provided the basis of much of the Soviet Union's foreign trade, particularly inside COMECON, has been replaced by hard-currency deals. Within the Russian Federation, however, barter remains a common means of conducting transactions. At the heart of the problems facing the Russian government is whether it can sustain social stability for a sufficient period to allow the economy to recover, assuming that it does. An enormous increase in organised crime, wide disparities between the mass of poor people and the 'nouveau riche' who have benefited from Russia's primitive form of capitalism, and – most threatening of all – pressures for independence in many of Russia's autonomous regions, exemplified by the 1994/95 war between Moscow and Chechnya are the Russian Federation's most pressing threats to its stability. The international community has a key role to play here in providing much of the investment capital, financial support, technological and managerial expertise that Russia needs so badly. Membership of international institutions including the IMF, World Bank and European Bank for Reconstruction and Development have produced some gains, notably a US$24-billion package of aid and soft loans. However, there are increasingly sharp disagreements within the Russian government about the extent to which important economic decisions should pass into the hands of foreigners.
BUSINESS: As a result of recent economic changes which have taken place in the Russian Federation, there are now several dozens of thousand of private companies in operation and international business relations have become active. The main business centres are Moscow,

St Petersburg, Novgorod, Novosibirsk and Vladivostock.
Office hours: 0900-1800/1900 Monday to Friday.
COMMERCIAL INFORMATION: The following organisations can offer advice: The Trade Delegation of the Russian Federation, 32/3 Highgate, West Hill, London N6 6NL. Tel: (0181) 340 4492. Fax: (0181) 348 0112; *or*
BSCC *(formerly the British Soviet Chamber of Commerce)*, 42 Southwark Street, London SE1 1UN. Tel: (0171) 403 1706. Fax: (0171) 403 1245. Moscow Office: BSCC, Business Centre, Suite 102, Ground Floor, Bolshoi Strochenovsky per 22/25, 113054 Moscow. Tel: (095) 230 6120. Fax: (095) 230 6124. Telex: 413523 (a/b BRISSU). *(Information supplied to members only); or*
Ministry of External Economic Relations, Smolenskaya-Sennaya pl. 32/34, 121200 Moscow. Tel: (095) 244 1258; *or*
Chamber of Commerce and Industry of the Russian Federation, ul. Ilynka 6, 103684 Moscow. Tel: (095) 298 3231. Fax: (095) 230 2455. Telex: 411126; *or*
Commercial and Scientific Departments, Kutuzovsky Prospekt 7/4, 121248 Moscow. Tel: (7503) 956 6052/3 (international satellite line) *or* (095) 248 2001 (domestic line). Fax: (095) 249 4636. Telex: 413341 (a/b BEMOS SU); *or*
Overseas Marketing Corporation, Room 947, Hotel Mezhdynarodnaya II, Krasnopresnenskaya Nab. 12, Moscow. Tel: (095) 253 1701. Fax: (095) 253 9487. Telex: 413627.
For further information, refer to the *Partnership in Action* section below.
CONFERENCES/CONVENTIONS: With every passing year an increasing number of conferences, seminars and symposia (including some for the tourist industry) take place in the Russian Federation. The Conference and Incentives Manager at Intourist (London) can offer information (see top of entry for address).

PARTNERSHIP IN ACTION
by Richard Cawthorne

Times have changed – bureaucracy and Cold War politics are no longer barriers for Western companies seeking to forge commercial relationships with their Russian counterparts.
The whole process of dealing with what was the Soviet Union has been so fraught for so long that many people are finding it hard to adjust. Nevertheless, if you want to do it, you now can. Just remember the golden rule – be careful.
"There are plenty of business opportunities out there, but people are wary," said Jane Belova, of the Confederation of British Industry's (CBI) East and Central Europe Department.
"Development is fairly slow, which is understandable – things are still a bit rocky, with legislation not in place or being changed, especially in the areas of property rights and who owns what, which makes it difficult when you are wanting to set up and buy things out there. "You do have to be careful and people are being very cautious. It is a matter of the authorities sorting these things out."
At its most basic level, Western business people can now make contact with like-minded companies in Russia and establish a joint venture. The make-up of the new operation is a matter for the commercial judgment of the partners, not for the Russian government.
Companies looking for partners can consult lists of interested parties supplied by the Russian Federation to organisations like the East European Trade Council, a Department of Trade and Industry (DTI) offshoot, or the CBI, while the Russo-British Chamber of Commerce has a bulletin in which Russian companies advertise and maintains a Moscow office with a business centre for members' use only.
The CBI also organises missions to the Former Soviet

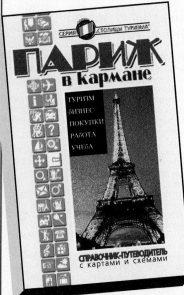

Union (although not recently) and meetings for Russian delegations to the UK wishing to contact business people in their sectors, and is planning a series of seminars during 1995 focusing on the Russian Federation.

The Department of Trade and Industry produces several paid publications listing contacts and runs a Russia Desk to handle inquiries.

"The country is now very much more open than it was, but regulations vary according to what you want to do and what the business is," said a spokesman. "The short answer to anyone considering trying to set up links with Russian companies is to contact us and ask for the Russia Desk.

"It is a complicated area and still a difficult one for British businesses to get into, but certainly one that is opening up very quickly."

One man involved in the recent history of Russia more than most is Michael Hall, executive director of BSCC, once the British-Soviet Chamber of Commerce. BSCC is now a holding company which incorporates the Russo-British Chamber and other organisations concerned with the 15 countries that made up the Former Soviet Union (FSU).

"Any business person who decides that a market has potential in terms of the possibility of placing useful sale – or purchase – orders will need to visit it more than once to understand it sufficiently to do business there, and to develop the mutual understanding with a suitable partner enough to discuss the real potential," he said.

"It is a sad truism that while there are a great many new entrepreneurs in the FSU, there are also those who have had no experience in foreign trade, as this was an area that was completely centralised under the old system.

"All trade was transacted through one of 120 or so Foreign Trade Organisations, usually based in Moscow, whose staff were trained specifically in matters related to buying and selling overseas. Such experience was thinly spread, and as a result the challenges of doing such trade are often underestimated.

"Nothing can substitute for an in-depth study. The economy, the political situation, geography, internal and international communications, telecommunications and a host of other considerations must all be researched. A number of visits will be necessary to build up relationships."

Hall said opportunities throughout the FSU were 'numerous', but competition, especially from mainland Europe, was strong.

Things are even more complicated in the travel industry, according to Instone Travel managing director Des McGuinness, who was Intourist's commercial director in the UK before the Russian state tourism company was broken up.

"Two years ago, there were maybe two ground handlers – Intourist and Mosintour. Now there are 2000 in Moscow alone, which of course have no history," he said.

"It comes down to who you know. Not all ground-handling companies can provide a full tourist service in Russia, and the trick is knowing which ones can and paying their price, because obviously they are more expensive than the rest."

Instone Travel itself is a joint venture between McGuinness and Mosintour, formerly the Moscow division of Intourist, which was granted independence by Boris Yeltsin. "It is just between me and them," said McGuinness. "There were no special regulations or legislation to worry about."

He agreed that the number of emerging companies in Russia meant there was a lot of opportunity in the market – but it was a volatile market.

Another travel company with big business to the FSU is Peltours, where Eastern European Department manager Elias Demetriou highlighted a familiar problem.

"The largest difficulty with Russia is the visas," he said. "Many of the FSU republics now have embassies in the UK, and to enter many of these countries British passport holders no longer need visas, but for Russia it is a nightmare. People should leave plenty of time to get them."

Despite such lingering difficulties, companies like Instone, Intourist and Peltours with their specialist knowledge say they are doing well in the Russian market. Other successful 'joint venturers' include department store company Littlewoods, which has been operating in St Petersburg for about three years; financial giant Coopers and Lybrand, and communications conglomerate Cable and Wireless.

"Once you have found a partner and you are prepared to work together, it is getting easier because other people have paved the way. You are not the first any more," said CBI's Jane Belova.

"It is a matter of trust between individuals. People are wary about how things are going to be paid for, the problem of whether your opposite number has enough hard currency to pay for things, that sort of thing. But it

has become a lot more straightforward."

Charting new territory has always entailed risks and challenges. Provided they exercise caution and common sense, those pioneering Western businesses that do business in the Russian Federation could well find golden opportunities.

Further information:
BSCC (incorporating Russo-British Chamber of Commerce). Tel: (0171) 403 1706.
Confederation of British Industry, East European Department. Tel: (0171) 379 7400.
Department of Trade and Industry. Tel: (0171) 215 5000.
East European Trade Council. Tel: (0171) 222 7622.
Foreign and Commonwealth Office (for visa updates). Tel: (0171) 270 3000.
Guild of Business Travel Agents. Tel: (0171) 222 2744.
Instone Travel. Tel: (0181) 983 0204.
Intourist Travel. Tel: (0171) 538 8600.
Peltours. Tel: (0181) 346 9144.
Russian Trade Delegation. Tel: (0181) 340 4491.
Advice and assistance on the ground is also readily available from the British Embassy in Moscow.
For further contact addresses, refer to *Commercial Information* within the *Business Profile* above.

CLIMATE

Northern & Central European Russia: The most varied climate; mildest areas are along the Baltic coast. Summer sunshine may be nine hours a day, but winters can be very cold.
Siberia: Very cold winters, but summers can be pleasant, although they tend to be short and wet. There is considerable seasonal temperature variation.
Southern European Russia: Winter is shorter than in the north. Steppes (in the southeast) have hot, dry summers and very cold winters. The north and northeastern Black Sea has mild winters, but heavy rainfall all the year round.

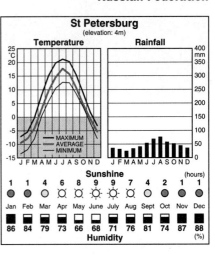

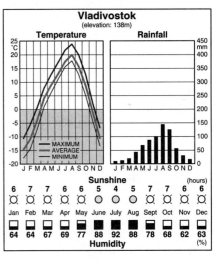

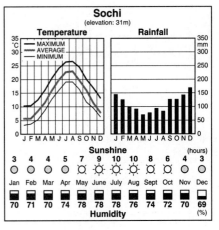

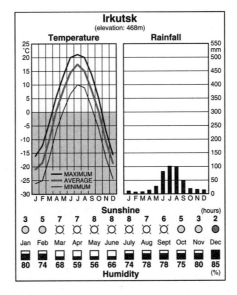

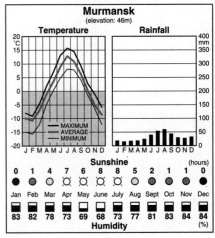

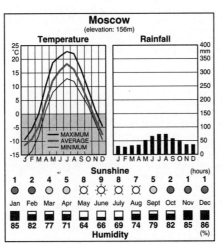

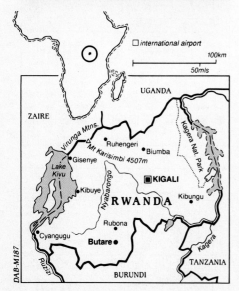

Rwanda

Location: Central Africa.

Note: At the time of writing, the US Department of State and the British Foreign and Commonwealth Office advise against travel to Rwanda. Although fighting inside Rwanda has largely ceased, the situation is very volatile, and there is high potential for new outbreaks of ethnic violence. Border areas, especially adjacent to Zaïre and Burundi, are particularly unstable. Violence is not directed at foreigners, but there is a danger of being caught in the middle of fighting. No civilian police force exists. Looting, robbery and revenge killings continue throughout the country. Water and fuel are scarce, and electricity and telephone services are not functioning.
Telephone and fax numbers listed below were accurate before services were suspended.
Sources: US State Department – August 4, 1994 and FCO Travel Advice Unit – January 28, 1995.

Office rwandais du tourisme et des parcs nationaux (ORTPN)
BP 905, Kigali, Rwanda
Tel: 76514. Fax: 76512.
Embassy of the Republic of Rwanda
1 avenue des Fleurs, Woluwe St Pierre, B-1150 Brussels, Belgium
Tel: (2) 763 0702/5 *or* 763 0721. Fax: (2) 763 0753.
Telex: 26653.
Consulate in: Antwerp.
The British Embassy in Kampala deals with enquiries relating to Rwanda (see *Uganda* later in this book).
Embassy of the Republic of Rwanda
1714 New Hampshire Avenue, NW, Washington, DC 20009
Tel: (202) 232 2882. Fax: (202) 232 4544.
Embassy of the United States of America
BP 28, boulevard de la Révolution, Kigali, Rwanda
Tel: 75601/2/3. Fax: 72128.
Emergency Consular services only.

Timatic

Health
GALILEO/WORLDSPAN: **TI-DFT/KGL/HE**
SABRE: **TIDFT/KGL/HE**

Visa
GALILEO/WORLDSPAN: **TI-DFT/KGL/VI**
SABRE: **TIDFT/KGL/VI**

For more information on Timatic codes refer to Contents.

Embassy of the Republic of Rwanda
121 Sherwood Drive, Ottawa, Ontario K1Y 3V1
Tel: (613) 722 5835 *or* 722 7921. Fax: (613) 729 3291.
Honorary Consulates in: Montréal and Toronto.
Canadian Embassy
PO Box 1177, rue Akagera, Kigali, Rwanda
Tel: 73210 *or* 73278 *or* 73787. Fax: 72719. Telex: 22592 (a/b DOMCAN RW).

AREA: 26,338 sq km (10,169 sq miles).
POPULATION: 7,164,994 (1991).
POPULATION DENSITY: 272 per sq km.
CAPITAL: Kigali. **Population:** 232,733 (1990).
GEOGRAPHY: Rwanda is a small mountainous country in central Africa, bordered to the north by Uganda, to the east by Tanzania, to the south by Burundi and to the west by Zaïre. The country is divided by great peaks of up to 3000m (9842ft) which run across the country from north to south. The Birunga volcanoes, rising steeply from Lake Kivu in the west, slope down first to a hilly central plateau and further eastwards to an area of marshy lakes around the upper reaches of the Kagera River, where the Kagera National Park is situated.
LANGUAGE: The official languages are Kinyarwanda and French. Kiswahili is used for trade and commerce.
RELIGION: Christian (mostly Roman Catholic) with Islamic and Animist minorities.
TIME: GMT + 2.
ELECTRICITY: 220 volts AC, 50Hz. There is no electricity supply at present. Some hotels have their own generators.
COMMUNICATIONS: Telephone: At present there is no telephone service in Rwanda. Country code: 250. There are no area codes. When the service is operating, outgoing international calls must go through the operator. **Telex/telegram:** Facilities are available in Kigali and main hotels. **Post:** In Kigali post offices open 0800-1200 and 1400-1700 Monday to Friday; 0800-1200 Saturday. Airmail to Western Europe takes approximately two weeks. **Press:** There are no English-language newspapers. Publications are in French or Kinyarwanda and are weekly or quarterly.
BBC World Service and Voice of America frequencies: From time to time these change. See the section *How to Use this Book* for more information.
BBC:

MHz	21.47	17.88	15.42	9.630
Voice of America:				
MHz	21.49	15.60	9.525	6.035

PASSPORT/VISA

Regulations and requirements may be subject to change at short notice, and you are advised to contact the appropriate diplomatic or consular authority before finalising travel arrangements. Details of these may be found at the head of this country's entry. Any numbers in the chart refer to the footnotes below.

	Passport Required?	Visa Required?	Return Ticket Required?
Full British	Yes	Yes	Yes
BVP	Not valid	-	-
Australian	Yes	Yes	Yes
Canadian	Yes	Yes	Yes
USA	Yes	Yes	Yes
Other EU (As of 31/12/94)	Yes	Yes	Yes
Japanese	Yes	Yes	Yes

Restricted entry: The Government refuses admission and transit to nationals of Burundi without a regular visa. Visa-free transit by nationals of Burundi is only permitted by the same flight without leaving the airport.
PASSPORTS: Valid passport required by all.
British Visitors Passport: Not accepted.
VISAS: Required by all nationalities.
Validity: Generally 3 months.
Types of visa: Entry. Cost: BFr1500, plus BFr250 if the passport is to be returned by registered mail. Transit visas are not required by those who continue their journey to a third country on the same day, without leaving the airport.
Application to: Representatives of Rwanda in Addis Ababa, Beijing, Bern, Bonn, Brussels, Bujumbura, Cairo, Dar es Salaam, Hamburg, Kampala, Kinshasa, Mainz, Mombasa, Montréal, Moscow, Munich, Nairobi, New York, Ottawa, Paris, Pretoria, Stuttgart, Tokyo, Toronto or Washington.
Application requirements: (a) Valid passport. (b) 2 passport-size photos. (c) Yellow fever vaccination certificate. (d) 2 completed application forms. (e) Company letters or guarantee. (f) Fee.
Temporary residence: Visas can be extended at the Immigration Office in Kigali.

MONEY

Currency: Rwanda Franc (Rw Fr) = 100 centimes. Notes are in denominations of Rw Fr5000, 1000, 500 and 100. Coins are in denominations of Rw Fr50, 20, 10, 5, 2 and 1.
Credit cards: Access/Mastercard is most widely accepted, with more limited use of Diners Club. Check with your credit card company for details of merchant acceptability and other services which may be available.
Exchange rate indicators: The following figures are included as a guide to the movements of the Rwanda Franc against Sterling and the US Dollar:

Date:	Oct '92	Sep '93	Jan '94	Jan '95
£1.00=	234.60	216.10	211.30	216.50
$1.00=	147.83	141.52	142.82	138.38

Currency restrictions: The import and export of local currency is limited to Rw Fr5000. The import of foreign currency is unlimited, subject to declaration. The export is limited to the amount declared.
Banking hours: 0800-1200 and 1400-1800 Monday to Friday; 0800-1300 Saturday.

DUTY FREE

The following items may be imported into Rwanda by persons over 16 years of age without incurring customs duty:
200 cigarettes or 50 cigars or 454g tobacco; 2 bottles of spirits or wine (opened); a reasonable amount of perfume.

PUBLIC HOLIDAYS

Jan 1 '95 New Year's Day. **Jan 28** Democracy Day. **Apr 17** Easter Monday. **May 1** Labour Day. **May 25** Ascension Day. **Jun 5** Whit Monday. **Jul 1** Anniversary of Independence. **Jul 5** National Peace and Unity Day. **Aug 4** Peace and Reconciliation Day. **Aug 15** Assumption. **Sep 25** Kamarampaka Day. **Oct 26** Armed Forces Day. **Nov 1** All Saints' Day. **Dec 25-26** Christmas. **Jan 1 '96** New Year's Day. **Jan 28** Democracy Day. **Apr 8** Easter Monday.

HEALTH

Regulations and requirements may be subject to change at short notice, and you are advised to contact your doctor well in advance of your intended date of departure. Any numbers in the chart refer to the footnotes below.

	Special Precautions?	Certificate Required?
Yellow Fever	Yes	1
Cholera	Yes	2
Typhoid & Polio	Yes	-
Malaria	3	-
Food & Drink	4	-

Note: There is a constant danger of disease due to the lack of sanitation. The risk of epidemics is high.
[1]: A yellow fever vaccination certificate is required from all travellers over one year of age.
[2]: Following WHO guidelines issued in 1973, a cholera vaccination certificate is not a condition of entry to Rwanda. However, cholera is a serious risk in this country and precautions are essential. Up-to-date advice should be sought before deciding whether these precautions should include vaccination, as medical opinion is divided over its effectiveness. See the *Health* section at the back of the book.
[3]: Malaria risk exists all year throughout the country. The predominant, malignant *falciparum* strain is reported to be 'highly resistant' to chloroquine and 'resistant' to sulfadoxine-pyrimethamine.
[4]: Visitors are advised to bring their own supplies of food, bottled water and vitamins. Clean water is scarce, and all water should be regarded as being potentially contaminated. Water used for drinking, brushing teeth or making ice should have first been boiled or otherwise sterilised. Milk is unpasteurised and should be boiled. Powdered or tinned milk is available and is advised, but make sure that it is reconstituted with pure water. Avoid dairy products which are likely to have been made from unboiled milk. Only eat well-cooked meat and fish, preferably served hot. Pork, salad and mayonnaise may carry increased risk. Vegetables should be cooked and fruit peeled.
Rabies is present. For those at high risk, vaccination before arrival should be considered. If you are bitten abroad seek medical advice without delay. For more information, consult the *Health* section at the back of

the book.

Bilharzia (schistosomiasis) is present. Avoid swimming and paddling in fresh water. Swimming pools which are well-chlorinated and maintained are safe.

Health care: Medical facilities are severely limited and extremely overburdened. Almost all medical facilities in Kigali were destroyed during the civil war. Medical insurance, including cover for emergency repatriation, is essential. Visitors are advised to bring their own personal medications.

TRAVEL - International

AIR: There is no commercial air service to Rwanda at present. Rwanda's national airline *Air Rwanda (NR)* does not operate international services, except to Entebbe in Uganda and Bujumbura in Burundi. *Air France* is the general sales agent in the United Kingdom, representing *Air Burundi (PB)*, the local airline running services in the region. Normally flights operate via Paris and there are two flights a week.

Approximate flight time: From London to Kigali is 13 hours, including stopovers.

International airport: *Kigali (KGL)* (Kanombe), 12km (7.5 miles) east of Kigali (travel time – 25 minutes). Airport facilities include bar, duty-free shop, post office and currency exchange. Coach and taxi services are available.

ROAD: International routes are available from the surrounding countries of Zaïre, Uganda and Tanzania.
Bus: There is a regular twice-weekly service from Kampala in Uganda to Kigali Wednesday and Saturday.

TRAVEL - Internal

AIR: *Air Rwanda (NR)* runs internal services to the main towns. Chartered planes are also available though expensive.

Departure tax: Rw Fr300 for all domestic flights.
ROAD: Traffic drives on the right. The network is sparse and most roads are in bad condition, although the roads linking the capital with Butare, Bugarana and the frontier posts are of better quality. **Bus:** Services are operated by *L'Office National des Transports en Commun* and are classified into three groups: Urban (route numbers prefixed by A, B or C); Suburban (D routes); and Interurban. A timetable and tariff booklet is available in Rwanda. **Taxi:** Available in Kigali and other large towns. Fares should be agreed in advance. Tipping is not expected. **Car hire:** Limited facilities in Rwanda. There are no international car hire firms operating, but there are local companies in Kigali. **Documentation:** An International Driving Permit is required.

ACCOMMODATION

HOTELS: Found mostly in Kigali; they are expensive. Missions with dormitory accommodation are recommended, particularly in remote districts and smaller towns. Ruhengeri and Gisenye mission station hotels are excellent.

GUEST-HOUSES: Outside the main towns there are guest-houses which are generally cheaper than hotels. There is a guest-house at the edge of the Kagera National Park at Biumba in the northeast of the country.

CAMPING: This is now forbidden. Rest huts are available on the expedition route in the Virunga Volcanoes.

RESORTS & EXCURSIONS

Rwanda is a mountainous land in the heart of Africa, split by the Rift Valley, and dominated by a mountain range which traverses the country from north to south. The three areas of principal interest are the Virunga Volcanoes, the Kagera National Park and the region around Lake Kivu. The capital city of **Kigali** is mainly a commercial and administrative centre and has little in the way of tourist attractions.

Kibungu, in the east of the country, is in the centre of a region of lakes and waterfalls, including *Lake Mungesera* and the *Rusumo Falls*. It is also close to the southern tip of the **Kagera National Park**, which covers over 2500 sq km (1000 sq miles) of savannah to the west of the *Kagera River* (the frontier with Tanzania). The park has a variety of wildlife and is a habitat for over 500 species of birds. There are accommodation facilities on the edge of the park at **Gabiro**, 100km (60 miles) to the north. Reservations should be made in advance. In the rainy season (December, March and April) many of the routes become impassable.

West of Kagera is the **Parc des Volcans**, one of the last sanctuaries of the mountain gorilla. The ORTPN-bureau in Kigali can organise guided tours of the park for small parties; it is advisable to book well in advance. This region is composed of volcanic mountains of which two, across the frontier in Zaïre, are still active.

Gisenye is the main centre for excursions in the Parc des Volcans. Plane trips can be made from here to view the craters. Situated on the north of *Lake Kivu*, it also offers many opportunities for water sports or for excursions on the lake. **Kibuye**, further south, is another lakeside resort. Near **Cyangugu**, on the southern shores of the lake, are the spectacular grottoes of *Kaboza* and *Nyenji*, and the thermal waters at **Nyakabuye**. Nearby, the *Rugege Forest* is the home of many rare species of wildlife.

East of Cyangugu is **Butare**, the intellectual capital of the country. It boasts an interesting museum, craft shops and a botanical garden. North of Butare is **Gitarama**, which has a good art museum; nearby is the cathedral town of **Kabgayi**; and at **Mushubati** the grottoes of *Bihongori*.

ORTPN in Kigali will be able to give up-to-date information about tours and excursions in the country. For address, see top of entry.

SOCIAL PROFILE

FOOD & DRINK: Hotels generally serve a reasonable choice of European dishes while restaurants serve Franco-Belgian cuisine and some African dishes.
Drink: A fairly good selection of beers, spirits and wines is available. Beer is also brewed locally.

NIGHTLIFE: Apart from the many small bars, there is little in the way of nightlife. There are a few cinemas in Kigali. The Rwanda National Ballet is famous for its traditional dancing and singing and can be seen either at national ceremonies or sometimes on request in the villages.

SHOPPING: Special purchases include woven baskets with pointed lids, native clay statuettes, masks, charms and knives called *pangas* or *umuhoro*, with blades shaped like a question mark. Do not buy souvenir gorilla skulls or hands; if they are offered, report the trader to the police. **Shopping hours:** Dawn to dusk.

SPORT: Safaris: Kagera National Park at Gabiro, accessible by air or road, is devoted to game preservation and has lions, zebras, antelopes, hippos, buffalo, leopards, apes, impala, crested herons, fish eagles and cormorants. **Climbing/expeditions:** The Virunga Volcanoes between Ruhengeri and Gisenye are popular with climbers. Nyiragongo in Zaïre is the most commonly climbed from Gisenye. Rwandan guides are available for 2- or 3-day expeditions to view the craters. **Watersports:** There is a sandy beach at Gisenye and **swimming** is safe in Lake Kivu. **Water-skiing** is also possible.

SOCIAL CONVENTIONS: The traditional way of life is based on agriculture and cattle. The Rwandans settle in the fertile areas, but they do not form villages, each family being surrounded by its own fields. The majority of the population belong to the Hutu tribe. There is a significant minority (15%) Tutsi population and a smaller minority of Twa, a mixed race of pygmies and probably the country's first inhabitants, traditionally potters and hunters. After internal unrest

---

in the past, a degree of tolerance between the various groups now exists. Normal social courtesies apply.
Tipping: 10% is normal.

BUSINESS PROFILE

ECONOMY: Subsistence agriculture is the core of the Rwandan economy. During the last decade the Government has tried to redirect the agricultural sector towards the production of cash crops such as tea and coffee, of which the latter is a particularly important export earner. Rice and sugar plantations have also been developed. Rwanda has some mineral deposits, mainly tin but also several rare ores which are in heavy demand in the world market. However, exploitation has not always been worthwhile: tungsten mining ceased in 1987 when it proved uneconomic. One bright prospect for the future is the discovery of natural gas deposits which may be among the world's largest. Before the civil war, Rwanda's economic indicators were good by African standards, although the collapse of the world coffee price during 1990 darkened the outlook. All that was before the appalling massacres of 1994 which have left a complete political, economic and social vacuum in Rwanda. The new government, dominated by the Rwandan Patriotic Front, barely has the means to govern; there is next to no money and almost all the skilled administrators were murdered. As long as the Hutu militias, now in exile but armed and organised, pose a potential threat to the new government and large numbers of people refuse to return home, there is no prospect of reconstruction. The short- and medium-term outlook is extremely bleak. Rwanda will need to rely on its long-term contacts with the European Union, particularly Belgium and Germany, which have guaranteed a steady flow of development aid. Outside the EU, Kenya, Uganda and the USA are Rwanda's main trading partners. Trade with Britain is worth less than £10 million per annum, with a large surplus in Britain's favour.

BUSINESS: Lightweight suits are advised and appointments are necessary. Best time to visit is from April to October or December to January. A knowledge of French is useful as only few executives speak English. **Office hours:** 0800-1600 Monday to Friday; 0800-1200 Saturday.

COMMERCIAL INFORMATION: The following organisation can offer advice: Chambre de Commerce et d'Industrie du Rwanda, BP 319, Kigali. Tel: 83537. Fax: 83532. Telex: 22662.

CLIMATE

Despite its proximity to the Equator the climate in Rwanda is cooled by the high altitude. It is warm throughout most of the country but cooler in the mountains. There are two rainy seasons: mid-January to April and mid-October to mid-December.
Required clothing: Lightweights are required for most of the year with warmer clothes for cooler upland evenings. Rainwear is advisable.

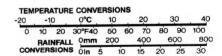

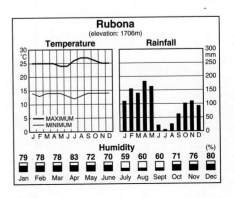

Location: Eastern Caribbean, Windward Islands.

Diplomatic representation: Although the Netherlands Antilles are part of the Kingdom of the Netherlands, they are not formally represented by Royal Netherlands Embassies. Information and advice may be obtained at the addresses below.

Saba Tourist Bureau
PO Box 527, Windwardside, Saba
Tel: (4) 62231. Fax: (4) 62350. Telex: 8006.
Office of the Minister Plenipotentiary of the Netherlands Antilles
Antillenhuis, Badhuisweg 173-175, 2597 JP The Hague, The Netherlands
Tel: (70) 351 2811. Fax: (70) 351 2722. Telex: 31161.
Also deals with tourism enquiries for Saba.
The British Consulate in Willemstad deals with enquiries relating to Saba (see *Curaçao* earlier in the book).
The Consulate of the United States of America in Willemstad deals with enquiries relating to Saba (see *Curaçao* earlier in the book).
Saba Tourist Bureau
c/o New Concepts-Canada
Suite 70, 2455 Cawthra Road, Mississauga, Ontario L5A 3P1
Tel: (416) 803 0131. Fax: (416) 803 0132.
The Canadian Consulate in Willemstad deals with enquiries relating to Saba (see *Curaçao* earlier in the book).

AREA: 13 sq km (5 sq miles).
POPULATION: 1116 (1991 estimate).
POPULATION DENSITY: 85.8 per sq km.
CAPITAL: The Bottom. **NA capital:** Willemstad, Curaçao.
GEOGRAPHY: Saba is one of three Windward Islands in the Netherlands Antilles, although geographically it is part of the Leeward Group of the Lesser Antilles, lying 265km (165 miles) east of Puerto Rico, 44km (27 miles) south of St Maarten and 21km (13 miles) west of St Eustatius. Saba is the peak of a submerged extinct volcano. Mount Scenery is thick with forest and rises to almost 900m (3000ft) in less than 2km (1.2 miles). There are four villages, until recently connected only by

thousands of steps cut from the rock. A road now links the airport with The Bottom.
LANGUAGE: Popularly English, but Dutch (the official language of the Netherlands Antilles) is used for legal documents and taught in schools.
RELIGION: Roman Catholic majority; also Anglican and Wesleyan.
TIME: GMT - 4.
ELECTRICITY: 110 volts AC, 60Hz.
COMMUNICATIONS: Telephone: Fully automatic system with good IDD. Country code: 599. Outgoing international code: 00. Calls made through the operator are more expensive and include a 15% tax. The exchange is located in The Bottom. **Telegram:** Services operated by *Lands Radio Dienst* and *All American Cables*. **Post:** The Post Office is in The Bottom. Airmail to Europe takes four to six days, surface mail four to six weeks.
Press: The *Saba Herald* is published monthly in English.
BBC World Service and Voice of America frequencies: From time to time these change. See the section *How to Use this Book* for more information.
BBC:

MHz	17.84	15.22	9.915	5.975

Voice of America:

MHz	15.21	11.70	6.130	0.930

PASSPORT/VISA

Regulations and requirements may be subject to change at short notice, and you are advised to contact the appropriate diplomatic or consular authority before finalising travel arrangements. Details of these may be found at the head of this country's entry. Any numbers in the chart refer to the footnotes below.

	Passport Required?	Visa Required?	Return Ticket Required?
Full British	Yes	No	Yes
BVP	Valid/1	-	-
Australian	Yes	4	Yes
Canadian	2	4	Yes
USA	3	4	Yes
Other EU (As of 31/12/94)	1	4/5	Yes
Japanese	Yes	4	Yes

PASSPORTS: Valid passport required by all except:
(a) **[1]** nationals of Belgium, Luxembourg and The Netherlands holding a *toeristkaart*, nationals of Germany holding a valid national ID card and UK nationals holding a British Visitors Passport;
(b) **[2]** nationals of Canada holding birth certificate or proof of citizenship;
(c) **[3]** nationals of the USA holding valid photo ID plus a voter's registration card or birth certificate, and alien residents of the USA with acceptable documentation;
(d) nationals of San Marino holding a national ID card;
(e) nationals and alien residents of Venezuela, and travellers in Venezuela visiting the Netherlands Antilles, holding a valid national ID card;
(f) nationals of Brazil, Mexico and Trinidad & Tobago entering for tourism only holding a valid national ID card.
British Visitors Passport: Acceptable.
VISAS: [4] Visas are only required for nationals of the Dominican Republic and Haiti resident there. All other nationals are allowed to stay in Saba for 14 days without a visa (but might need a Temporary Certificate of Admission, see below) provided they have a return or onward ticket. All visitors staying more than 90 days require a visa. Transit passengers staying no longer than 24 hours holding confirmed tickets and valid passports do not require visas or Certificates of Admission.
For stays of between 14 and 28 days a **Temporary Certificate of Admission** is required, which in the case of the following countries will be issued by the Immigration authorities on arrival in Saba:
(a) **[5]** Belgium, Germany, Luxembourg, The Netherlands, Spain and the UK;
(b) Bolivia, Burkina Faso, Chile, Colombia, Costa Rica, Czech Republic, Ecuador, Hungary, Israel, Jamaica, South Korea, Malawi, Mauritius, Niger, Philippines, Poland, San Marino, Slovak Republic, Swaziland and Togo.
The following must apply in writing at least 1 month in advance *before* entering the country even for tourist purposes for a Certificate of Admission: nationals of Albania, Bosnia-Hercegovina, Bulgaria, Cambodia, China, CIS, Croatia, Cuba, Estonia, Former Yugoslav Republic of Macedonia, North Korea, Latvia, Libya, Lithuania, Romania, Vietnam, Yugoslavia (Serbia and Montenegro) and holders of Zimbabwe passports issued on or after November 11, 1965.
All other nationals have to apply for the Certificate after 14 days of stay.
Further information about visa requirements may be

obtained from the Office of the Minister Plenipotentiary of the Netherlands Antilles; and whilst Royal Netherlands Embassies do not formally represent the Netherlands Antilles in any way, they might also be able to offer limited advice and information. For addresses, see top of this entry and top of *The Netherlands* entry above.
Temporary residence: Enquire at the Office of the Minister Plenipotentiary of the Netherlands Antilles.

MONEY

Currency: Netherlands Antilles Guilder or Florin (NAG) = 100 cents. Notes are in denominations of NAG500, 250, 100, 50, 25, 10 and 5. Coins are in denominations of NAG2.50 and 1, and 50, 25, 10, 5 and 1 cents. The currency is tied to the US Dollar.
Credit cards: Access/Mastercard and Visa are accepted in large establishments. Check with your credit card company for details of merchant acceptability and other services which may be available.
Exchange rate indicators: The following figures are included as a guide to the movement of the Netherlands Antilles Florin against Sterling and the US Dollar:

Date:	Oct '92	Sep '93	Jan '94	Jan '95
£1.00=	2.83	2.74	2.64	2.80
$1.00=	*1.79	*1.79	*1.79	*1.79

Note [*]: The NAG is linked to the US Dollar.
Currency restrictions: The import and export of local currency is limited to NAG200. There is no limit on foreign currency. The import of Dutch or Suriname silver coins is prohibited.
Banking hours: 0830-1200 and 1330-1630 Monday to Friday.

DUTY FREE

The following items may be imported into Saba by tourists over 15 years of age only without incurring customs duty:
400 cigarettes or 50 cigars or 250g tobacco; 2 litres of alcoholic beverages; 250ml of perfume (entire amount will be dutiable if more is imported); gifts to a value of NAG100.
Prohibited items: It is forbidden to import parrots and parakeets, dogs and cats from Central and South America. The import of souvenirs and leather goods from Haiti is not advisable.

PUBLIC HOLIDAYS

Jan 1 '95 New Year's Day. **Apr 14-17** Easter. **Apr 30** Queen's Birthday. **May 1** Labour Day. **May 25** Ascension. **Jun 5** Whit Monday. **Dec 6** Saba Day. **Dec 25-26** Christmas. **Jan 1 '96** New Year's Day. **Apr 5-8** Easter. **Apr 30** Queen's Birthday.

HEALTH

Regulations and requirements may be subject to change at short notice, and you are advised to contact your doctor well in advance of your intended date of departure. Any numbers in the chart refer to the footnotes below.

	Special Precautions?	Certificate Required?
Yellow Fever	No	1
Cholera	No	No
Typhoid & Polio	Yes	-
Malaria	No	-
Food & Drink	2	-

[1]: A yellow fever certificate is required from travellers over six months of age arriving from infected areas.
[2]: Water on the island is considered safe to drink. Bottled mineral water is widely available. Milk is pasteurised and dairy products are safe for consumption. Local meat, poultry, seafood, fruit and vegetables are generally considered safe to eat.
Health care: There is a hospital in The Bottom. Medical insurance is essential.

TRAVEL - International

AIR: The national airline of the Netherlands Antilles is *ALM (LM)*.
Approximate flight times: From Saba to *London* is 13 hours, to *Los Angeles* is 10 hours, to *New York* is 6 hours and to *Singapore* is 34 hours (all depending on connections).
International airport: *Juancho Yrausquin (SAB)* at

Cove Bay. The runway, at 400m (1300ft), is one of the shortest in the world. There are daily STOL turboprop flights to St Eustatius and St Kitts (and thus the airport may be classified as 'international') and thrice-daily to St Maarten.

Departure tax: US$2 to other Netherland Antilles and Aruba, US$5 for all other destinations.

SEA: Small boats operate from the Leo A Chance Pier at Fort Baai. There is a regular ferry service to St Maarten and a weekly cargo boat brings groceries and other supplies from St Maarten. Cruise ships call occasionally.

TRAVEL - Internal

ROAD: Saba has one road, 15km (9.5 miles) long, bisecting the island from the airport to Fort Baai. Taxis are available. Traffic drives on the right. Self-drive cars may be hired at Douglas Johnson's *The Square Nickel.*

ACCOMMODATION

There are five guest-houses – Captain's Quarters, Cranston's Antique Inn, Scout's Inn, Juliana's Apartments and Sharon's Ocean View – with a total of 50 rooms. Each has its own restaurant and bar.

RESORTS & EXCURSIONS

Mount Scenery is an extinct volcano rising from the floor of the Caribbean; the 250m (820ft) above sea level are known as Saba. There is only one road and with a population of just over 1000, Saba is the most unspoilt of the Netherlands Antilles; the inhabitants will claim that visitors are so few that each one is something of a celebrity. The island's four villages are mere clusters of ornate timber cottages dangling on the flanks of the mountain. Vegetation becomes increasingly lush towards the summit and the crater itself holds a tropical rainforest splattered with exotic flowers – begonias, giant heliconias and orchids. Tours may be taken by taxi from the airport or pier, or on foot via the forest trails and thousands of stone-cut steps linking the villages. The *Harry L Johnson Memorial Museum* in **Windwardside** is the restored home of a Dutch sea captain; visitors are offered a plate of pork, freshly cooked in the kitchen's rock oven. Windwardside also contains the *Tourist Office,* the island's two largest guest-houses and most of its shops. The island's capital, **The Bottom,** is situated 250m (820ft) above the ocean on a plateau surrounded by volcanic domes. Here, the *Artisan Foundation* exhibits early examples of Saba Lace; intricate embroidery on linen that resembles lace. The climate is milder than neighbouring St Eustatius (21km/13 miles away), but the island is subject to sudden downpours.

SOCIAL PROFILE

FOOD & DRINK: Fine local cuisine is offered at the island's guest-houses and there are several public restaurants, including the *Saba Chinese Restaurant* and *Guido's Italian Restaurant.* Local specialities include *calaloo* soup, curried goat, breadfruit, soursop ice cream and exotic fruit grown on the island – mangoes, papayas, figs, bananas and bitter mangoes. Restaurants and bars are usually closed by midnight. **Drink:** Most well-known brands of drink are available and Saba has its own brand of rum – *Saba Spice,* a blend of rum, aniseed, cinnamon, orange peel, cloves, nutmeg, spice bush and brown sugar. **NIGHTLIFE:** There are few visitors to the island and generally evenings are quiet, but Friday and Saturday nights there is dancing at *Guido's Italian Restaurant* and at *Lime Time.* The *Captain's Quarters* and *Scout's Place* guest-houses have lively bars.

SHOPPING: By the middle of the last century, the decline in the world's demand for sugar and indigo had left Saba looking at a very bleak future; the plantations, the only source of employment, reverted to forest. Undaunted, the men built boats and became fishermen, the women stayed at home and embroidered napkins and table cloths using a technique remembered by Mary Gertrude Johnson from her days in a Venezuelan convent. The fishing industry is now marginal but the embroidery has become Saba's chief claim to fame. *The Saba Artisans' Foundation* (founded in 1972 with money from the United Nations' Development Programme) in The Bottom promotes local lacework, silk-screened fabrics and garments printed and handmade by Sabans, as does the *Island Craft Shop* in Windwardside. *Saba Spice,* a 150-proof rum of local manufacture, is an acquired taste – a good gift to take home for friends and relatives. **Shopping hours:** 0800-1200 and 1400-1800 Monday to Saturday.

SPORT: There are few facilities for organised sport on the island. There is a concrete **tennis** court at the Sunny

Valley Youth Centre in The Bottom and a **swimming** pool at the Captain's Quarters and at Scout's Place. There are no beaches. **Hiking** to the summit of Mount Scenery is popular with visitors – Bernard Johnson offers guided tours – but Saba's greatest sporting potential is in **scuba diving.** The waters around the island have been declared a protected marine park in recognition of the unique opportunities for wall diving they present to experienced divers. Visibility varies from 20-30m (75-100ft) with a water temperature of 30°C in summer, whilst in winter visibility is up to 40m (125ft) with a water temperature of 24°C. The fragile coral reefs clinging to the submerged mountain slopes are teeming with colourful grazing fish, preyed on by sharks and barracuda. Giant sea turtles and humpback whales are seasonal visitors. There are already two dive shops on the island, *Saba Deep* in Fort Baai and *Sea Saba* in Windwardside. Both have their own boats and diving equipment (beginners are confined to the shallow waters of Fort Baai) and qualified divemasters, such as *Sea Saba*'s Greg Johnson, can provide tuition at all levels. **SPECIAL EVENTS:** *Saba Days* are celebrated on the first weekend in December with donkey racing, dancing and parties. The *Carnival* is held every July with colourful costumes, dancing and Caribbean music. **SOCIAL CONVENTIONS:** Dutch customs are still important throughout the Netherlands Antilles, but tourism on neighbouring St Maarten has brought some US influence to Saba (several businesses are US-owned). Dress is casual and lightweight cottons are advised. **Tipping:** A surcharge of 15% is usually added to guest-house and restaurant bills to cover government and utility taxes. Elsewhere 10-15% is appreciated but never expected.

BUSINESS PROFILE

ECONOMY: Falling oil prices and the recent trend towards transhipment have badly affected the Netherlands Antilles, once regarded as among the most affluent islands in the Caribbean, but as oil-related industries are confined to Curaçao and to a lesser extent, Bonaire, the Windward Islands – of which Saba is one – probably have less to lose. Saba continues to earn a modest income from fishing and handmade textiles. Tourism has, as is the case elsewhere in the island group, become of increasing importance.
BUSINESS: Business is fairly formal and visitors should wear a tropical suit. Appointments should be made and always kept as it is very discourteous to be late. **Office hours:** 0800-1200 and 1330-1630 Monday to Friday.
COMMERCIAL INFORMATION: The following organisations can offer advice: Curaçao Chamber of Commerce and Industry, PO Box 10, Kaya Junior Salas 1, Willemstad, Curaçao. Tel: (9) 611 455. Fax: (9) 615 652; *or*
St Maarten Chamber of Commerce and Industry, PO Box 454, W.J.A. Nisbeth Road, Philipsburg, St Maarten. Tel: (6) 23590. Fax: (5) 23512. Telex: 8063.

CLIMATE

Hot, but tempered by cooling trade winds. The annual mean temperature is 27°C, varying by no more than two or three degrees throughout the year; average rainfall is 1667mm. The temperature can drop to 16°C on winter evenings. When climbing Mount Scenery, the temperature will drop by approximately 0.2°C for each 100m (330ft) gained in altitude.
Required clothing: Tropicals and cottons are worn throughout the year. Umbrellas or light waterproofs are needed for the rainy season.

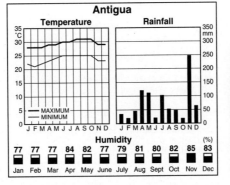

Location: Eastern Caribbean, Windward Islands.

Diplomatic representation: Although the Netherlands Antilles are part of the Kingdom of the Netherlands, they are not formally represented by Royal Netherlands Embassies. Information and advice may be obtained at the addresses below.

St Eustatius Tourist Bureau
Fort Oranjestad z/n, Oranjestad, St Eustatius
Tel: (3) 82433. Fax: (3) 82433. Telex: 8080.
Office of the Minister Plenipotentiary of the Netherlands Antilles
Antillenhuis, Badhuisweg 173-175, 2597 JP The Hague, The Netherlands
Tel: (70) 351 2811. Fax: (70) 351 2722. Telex: 31161.
Caribbean Tourism
Vigilant House, 120 Wilton Road, London SW1V 1JZ
Tel: (0171) 233 8382. Fax: (0171) 873 8551. Opening hours: 0900-1730 Monday to Friday.
The British Consulate in Willemstad deals with enquiries relating to St Eustatius (see *Curaçao* earlier in the book).
The Consulate of the United States of America in Willemstad deals with enquiries relating to St Eustatius (see *Curaçao* earlier in the book).
The Canadian Consulate in Willemstad deals with enquiries relating to St Eustatius (see *Curaçao* earlier in the book).

AREA: 21 sq km (8 sq miles).
POPULATION: 1781 (1991 estimate).
POPULATION DENSITY: 84.8 per sq km.
CAPITAL: Oranjestad. **NA capital:** Willemstad, Curaçao.
GEOGRAPHY: Politically, St Eustatius is one of three Windward Islands in the Netherlands Antilles; geographically it is part of the Leeward Group of the Lesser Antilles. It lies 286km (178 miles) east of Puerto Rico, 171km (106 miles) east of St Croix, 56km (35 miles) due south of St Maarten and 14km (9 miles) northwest of St Kitts. On the south end of the island is an extinct volcano called The Quill, which has a lush rainforest in the crater. Twice a year, sea turtles clamber up onto the black volcanic sands that rim the island to lay

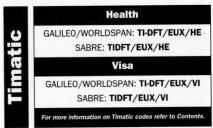

their eggs; giant land crabs hunt on the beaches every night.

LANGUAGE: English is the official language of the Windward Islands. Papiamento (a local *patois*), French and Spanish may also be spoken.

RELIGION: The majority are Protestant with a Roman Catholic minority.

TIME: GMT - 4.

ELECTRICITY: 110/220 volts AC, 60Hz.

COMMUNICATIONS: Telephone: Fully automatic system with good IDD connections. Country code: 599. Outgoing international code: 00. Calls made through the operator are more expensive and include a 15% tax. **Telegram:** Services operated by *Lands Radio Dienst* and *All American Cables*. **Post:** Airmail to Europe takes four to six days, surface mail four to six weeks. **Press:** No newspapers are published on St Eustatius, but an English-language daily, *The News*, is published on Curaçao. All other newspapers in the Netherlands Antilles are published in Dutch or Papiamento.

BBC World Service and Voice of America frequencies: From time to time these change. See the section *How to Use this Book* for more information.

BBC:

| MHz | 17.84 | 15.22 | 9.915 | 5.975 |

Voice of America:

| MHz | 15.21 | 11.70 | 6.130 | 0.930 |

PASSPORT/VISA

Regulations and requirements may be subject to change at short notice, and you are advised to contact the appropriate diplomatic or consular authority before finalising travel arrangements. Details of these may be found at the head of this country's entry. Any numbers in the chart refer to the footnotes below.

	Passport Required?	Visa Required?	Return Ticket Required?
Full British	Yes	No	Yes
BVP	Valid/1	-	-
Australian	Yes	4	Yes
Canadian	3	4	Yes
USA	2	4	Yes
Other EU (As of 31/12/94)	1	4/5	Yes
Japanese	Yes	4	Yes

PASSPORTS: Valid passport required by all except:
(a) **[1]** nationals of Belgium, Luxembourg and The Netherlands holding a *toeristkaart*, nationals of Germany holding a valid national ID card and UK nationals holding a British Visitors Passport;
(b) **[2]** nationals of the USA holding valid photo ID plus a voter's registration card or birth certificate, and alien residents of the USA with acceptable documentation;
(c) **[3]** nationals of Canada with a birth certificate or proof of citizenship;
(d) nationals of San Marino holding a valid national ID card;
(e) nationals and alien residents of Venezuela, and travellers in Venezuela visiting the Netherlands Antilles, holding a valid national ID card;
(f) nationals of Brazil, Mexico and Trinidad & Tobago entering for tourism only holding a valid national ID card.
British Visitors Passport: Acceptable.
VISAS: [4] Visas are only required for nationals of the Dominican Republic and Haiti resident there. All other nationals are allowed to stay in St Eustatius for 14 days without a visa (but might need a Temporary Certificate of Admission, see below) provided they have a return or onward ticket. All visitors staying more than 90 days require a visa. Transit passengers staying no longer than 24 hours holding confirmed tickets and valid passports do not require visas or Certificates of Admission.
For stays of between 14 and 28 days a **Temporary Certificate of Admission** is required, which in the case of the following countries will be issued by the Immigration authorities on arrival in St Eustatius:
(a) **[5]** Belgium, Germany, Luxembourg, The Netherlands, Spain and the UK;
(b) Bolivia, Burkina Faso, Chile, Colombia, Costa Rica, Czech Republic, Ecuador, Hungary, Israel, Jamaica, Malawi, Mauritius, Niger, Philippines, Poland, San Marino, Slovak Republic, South Korea, Swaziland and Togo;
(c) Estonia, Latvia and Lithuania only if resident in an EU country.
The following must apply in writing at least 1 month in advance, *before* entering the country even for tourist purposes for a Certificate of Admission: nationals of Albania, Bosnia-Hercegovina, Bulgaria, Cambodia, China, CIS, Croatia, Cuba, Estonia, Former Yugoslav Republic of Macedonia, Latvia, Libya, Lithuania, North Korea, Romania, Vietnam, Yugoslavia (Serbia and Montenegro) and holders of Zimbabwe passports issued

on or after November 11, 1965.
All other nationals have to apply for the Certificate after 14 days of stay.
Further information about visa requirements may be obtained from the Office of the Minister Plenipotentiary of the Netherlands Antilles; and whilst Royal Netherlands Embassies do not formally represent the Netherlands Antilles in any way, they might also be able to offer limited advice and information. For addresses, see top of this entry and top of *The Netherlands* entry above.
Temporary residence: Enquire at the Office of the Minister Plenipotentiary of the Netherlands Antilles.

MONEY

Currency: Netherlands Antilles Guilder or Florin (NAG) = 100 cents. Notes are in denominations of NAG500, 250, 100, 50, 25, 10 and 5. Coins are in denominations of NAG2.5 and 1, and 50, 25, 10, 5 and 1 cents. The currency is tied to the US Dollar.
Credit cards: Access/Mastercard and Visa are accepted in large establishments. Check with your credit card company for details of merchant acceptability and other services which may be available.
Exchange rate indicators: The following figures are included as a guide to the movement of the Netherlands Antilles Florin against Sterling and the US Dollar:

Date:	Oct '92	Sep '93	Jan '94	Jan '95
£1.00=	2.83	2.74	2.64	2.80
$1.00=	1.79	*1.79	*1.79	*1.79

Note [*]: The NAG is linked to the US Dollar.
Currency restrictions: The import and export of local currency is limited to NAG200. The import and export of foreign currency is unlimited. The import of Dutch or Suriname silver coins is prohibited.
Banking hours: 0830-1200 and 1330-1630 Monday to Friday.

DUTY FREE

The following may be imported into St Eustatius by tourists over 15 years of age only without incurring customs duty:
400 cigarettes or 50 cigars or 250g tobacco; 2 litres of alcoholic beverages; 250ml perfume (entire amount will be dutiable if more is imported); gifts to a value of NAG100.
Prohibited items: It is forbidden to import parrots and parakeets, dogs and cats from Central and South America. The import of souvenirs and leather goods from Haiti is not advisable.

PUBLIC HOLIDAYS

Jan 1 '95 New Year's Day. **Apr 14-17** Easter. **Apr 30** Queen's Day. **May 1** Labour Day. **May 25** Ascension Day. **Jun 5** Whit Monday. **Nov 16** St Eustatius Day. **Dec 25** Christmas Day. **Dec 26** Boxing Day. **Jan 1 '96** New Year's Day. **Apr 5-8** Easter. **Apr 30** Queen's Day.

HEALTH

Regulations and requirements may be subject to change at short notice, and you are advised to contact your doctor well in advance of your intended date of departure. Any numbers in the chart refer to the footnotes below.

	Special Precautions?	Certificate Required?
Yellow Fever	No	1
Cholera	No	No
Typhoid & Polio	Yes	-
Malaria	No	-
Food & Drink	2	-

[1]: A yellow fever certificate is required from travellers over six months of age arriving from infected areas.
[2]: Water on the island is considered safe to drink. Bottled mineral water is widely available. Milk is pasteurised and dairy products are safe for consumption. Local meat, poultry, seafood, fruit and vegetables are generally considered safe to eat.
Health care: There is one hospital on St Eustatius. Health insurance is advised.

TRAVEL - International

AIR: The national airline of the Netherlands Antilles is *ALM (LM)*.
Approximate flight times: From St Eustatius to *London* is 12 hours, to *Los Angeles* is 9 hours, to *New York* is 5 hours and to *Singapore* is 33 hours (these will vary

considerably, depending on connections).
International airport: *F D Roosevelt (EUX)*, 1km (0.6 miles) from Oranjestad, is served by daily scheduled flights from St Kitts & Nevis, from St Maarten four times daily (flight time – 30 minutes) and from Saba. The runway is too small for jets.
Departure tax: US$10 for international departures.
SEA: A 900m-long (3000ft) deep-water pier at Oranjestad can accommodate ocean liners. Small boats operate to the other islands in the Leeward Group; the 21km (13-mile) trip to Saba takes about two hours.

TRAVEL - Internal

ROAD: St Eustatius is a very small island and consequently has very few roads; a road of sorts runs right around the coast and a track leads up to the rim of *The Quill,* an extinct volcano in the south. The entire system can be walked in a few hours, but there are 15 **car hire** and **taxi** companies in Oranjestad. Traffic drives on the right. There are an equal number of cars and donkeys on the island; the latter may also be hired.
Documentation: A national driving licence is acceptable.

ACCOMMODATION

There are three small hotels – Golden Era, La Maison Sur La Plage and The Old Gin House – offering a total of 50 beds, and several guest-houses. There are also several fully-equipped apartments available for weekly rental. Advance booking is advised.

RESORTS & EXCURSIONS

St Eustatius, popularly known as 'Statia', was a thriving transhipment port during the 17th and 18th centuries, becoming known throughout the Caribbean as 'The Golden Rock'. The subsequent decline of the island has only recently been halted by a moderate influx of tourists. Statia is quiet and unhurried, with reminders of its bustling commercial past surviving only in the ruins of old warehouses, the weed-choked *Jewish Cemetery* (attached to the second-oldest synagogue in the New World), colonial houses, *Fort Amsterdam* above the town, and the foundations of the Dutch sea walls, now sunk beneath the clear waters of the bay. Many of the submerged ruins can be seen by scuba divers or snorkellers; equipment can be hired and trips organised by the *Happy Hooker Watersports Centre* in the lower town, next to the small tourist complex known as 'The Inns of Gallows Bay', and at *Surfside Statia* near The Old Gin House. Other attractions of the island include walking up *The Quill,* a forested dormant volcano; donkey rides along the black sand beach to *Forte de Windt;* surfing off the northeast coast; and fishing trips. Contact the Tourist Office for details.

SOCIAL PROFILE

FOOD & DRINK: Despite the island's small size, it has nine restaurants offering nine different blends of imported and local cuisine. The hotel restaurants are probably the best – indeed the Mooshay Bay Dining Room at The Old Gin House, where Continental food is served on old pewter plates, has been given a 5-star rating by Gourmet Magazine – but the local Creole-style cooking is particularly suited for seafood dishes: pickled conch shell meat, grilled spicy fish and lobster, and turtle dishes are recommended. The Chinese Restaurant offers authentic Cantonese cuisine; other restaurants also offer Cantonese dishes, together with American, French and local specialities. **Drink:** There are no licensing hours on the island (although most restaurants and bars are usually closed by midnight), and alcohol is virtually tax free. Most well-known brand names are available; a 'greenie' is a Heineken.
NIGHTLIFE: Centred on the main hotels and restaurants, including dancing to both taped Western music and live local bands, who may play one of the two different indigenous blends of reggae and calypso – 'Pim Pim' and 'Hippy'.
SHOPPING: The reductions on duty-free imports make the purchase of some perfume, jewellery or alcohol well worthwhile. **Shopping hours:** 0800-1200 and 1400-1800 Monday to Saturday.
SPORT: Watersports predominate, and for almost every visitor will form the central part of any holiday. **Snorkelling, windsurfing** and **water-skiing** are all available with facilities and tuition as necessary, but the island is perhaps becoming best-known as a centre for **scuba diving**. Many wrecks lie on the black sand amid

coral reefs and the submerged old port just off Oranjestad have long attracted a staggering variety of marine life; since the opening of Surfside Statia, a large and modern scuba centre adjacent to The Old Gin House, the fish have been joined by increasing numbers of expert divers, drawn by a unique combination of first-rate facilities, with warm and clear water, countless wrecks, coral, and – onshore – comfortable hotels and excellent cuisine. The centre has two air compressors, 60 tanks, and two dive boats; training is available for beginners. The Happy Hooker Watersports Centre in the lower town also hires out equipment.

SPECIAL EVENTS: The *Carnival* sweeps back and forth through the island every year during the month of July; this is of course a popular time to visit and advance booking is essential.

SOCIAL CONVENTIONS: Dutch customs are still important throughout the Netherlands Antilles, but American influences from the Virgin Islands nearby are dominant on St Eustatius. Dress is casual and lightweight cottons are advised. Bathing suits should be confined to the beach and poolside areas only. It is common to dress up in the evening. **Tipping:** Hotels add a 5-10% government tax and 10-15% service charge. Doormen and waiters expect a 10% tip, but taxi drivers are not usually tipped.

BUSINESS PROFILE

ECONOMY: Falling oil prices and the trend towards transhipment at sea in recent years have badly affected the Netherlands Antilles, once regarded as among the most affluent island groups in the Caribbean, but as oil-related industries are confined to Curaçao and, to a lesser extent, Bonaire (Aruba is no longer part of the Netherlands Antilles), the Windward Islands perhaps had less to lose. St Eustatius earns a modest income from agriculture and from a major petroleum transhipment installation, but it is tourism which dominates the economy. There have been some efforts to develop the fishing industry but, for the time being, government employment (in the administration for the Netherlands Antilles group) is the most important source of regular employment.

BUSINESS: Office hours: 0800-1200 and 1330-1630 Monday to Friday.

COMMERCIAL INFORMATION: The following organisation can offer advice: St Maarten Chamber of Commerce and Industry, PO Box 454, Walter Nisbeth Road, Philipsburg, St Maarten. Tel: (5) 23595. Fax: (5) 23512.

CLIMATE

Hot, but tempered by cooling trade winds. The annual mean temperature is 27°C, varying by no more than two or three degrees throughout the year; the average rainfall is 1771mm.

Required clothing: Tropicals and lightweight cottons are worn throughout the year. Umbrellas or light waterproofs are also advisable.

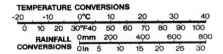

TEMPERATURE CONVERSIONS

-20	-10	0°C	10	20	30	40
0	10	20	30°F 40	50	60	70	80	90	100

RAINFALL CONVERSIONS

| 0mm | 200 | 400 | 600 | 800 |
| 0in | 5 | 10 | 15 | 20 | 25 | 30 |

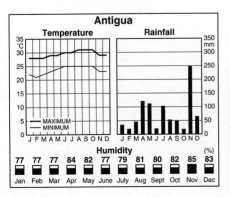

Antigua

Temperature / Rainfall

Humidity (%)

Jan	Feb	Mar	Apr	May	June	July	Aug	Sept	Oct	Nov	Dec
77	77	77	84	82	77	79	81	80	82	85	83

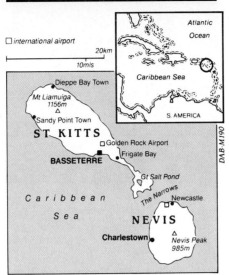

St Kitts & Nevis

□ *international airport*

20km
10mls

Atlantic Ocean

Caribbean Sea

S. AMERICA

DAB-M190

Dieppe Bay Town

Mt Liamuiga 1156m △

Sandy Point Town

ST KITTS

□ Golden Rock Airport

Frigate Bay

BASSETERRE ■

Gt Salt Pond

Caribbean Sea

The Narrows

Newcastle

NEVIS

Charlestown ● Nevis Peak 985m

Location: Eastern Caribbean, Leeward Islands.

St Kitts & Nevis Department of Tourism
PO Box 132, Bay Road, Basseterre, St Kitts
Tel: 465 2620 *or* 465 4040. Fax: 465 8794.
or
Main Street, Charlestown, Nevis
Tel: 469 1042. Fax: 469 1066.

High Commission for Eastern Caribbean States
10 Kensington Court, London W8 5DL
Tel: (0171) 937 9522. Fax: (0171) 937 5514. Telex: 913047 (a/b ECACOM G). Opening hours: 0930-1730 Monday to Friday.

St Kitts & Nevis Tourism Office
Address as for High Commission
Tel: (0171) 376 0881. Fax: (0171) 937 3611. Opening hours: 0930-1730 Monday to Friday.

The British High Commission in St John's deals with enquiries relating to St Kitts & Nevis (see *Antigua* earlier in this book).

Embassy of St Kitts & Nevis
Suite 608, 2100 M Street, NW, Washington, DC 20037
Tel: (202) 833 3550. Fax: (202) 833 3553.

St Kitts & Nevis Tourist Office
414 East 75th Street, New York, NY 10021
Tel: (212) 535 1234. Fax: (212) 734 6511.
Offices also in: Chicago.

Honorary Consulate of St Kitts & Nevis
602 CLL Group Building, 2695 Dutch Village Road, Halifax, Nova Scotia B3J 4T9
Tel: (902) 455 9090. Fax: (902) 455 1993.

St Kitts & Nevis Tourist Board
Suite 508, 11 Yorkville Avenue, Toronto, Ontario M4W 1L3
Tel: (416) 921 7717 *or* 921 7558. Fax: (416) 921 7997.

The Canadian High Commission in Bridgetown deals with enquiries relating to St Kitts & Nevis (see *Barbados* earlier in this book).

AREA: St Kitts: 168.4 sq km (65.1 sq miles). **Nevis:** 93.2 sq km (36 sq miles). **Total:** 261.6 sq km (101.1 sq miles).
POPULATION: 44,000 (1988 estimate).
POPULATION DENSITY: 168.2 per sq km.

	Health
	GALILEO/WORLDSPAN: **TI-DFT/SKB/HE**
	SABRE: **TIDFT/SKB/HE**

	Visa
	GALILEO/WORLDSPAN: **TI-DFT/SKB/VI**
	SABRE: **TIDFT/SKB/VI**

For more information on Timatic codes refer to Contents.

Timatic

CAPITAL: Basseterre. **Population:** 14,725 (1983).
GEOGRAPHY: St Kitts (officially known as St Christopher) lies in the northern part of the Leeward Islands in the eastern Caribbean. The high central body of the island is made up of three groups of rugged volcanic peaks split by deep ravines. The vegetation on the central mountain range is rainforest, thinning higher up to dense bushy cover. From here the island's volcanic crater, Mount Liamuiga, rises to almost 1200m (4000ft). The foothills, particularly to the north, form a gently rolling landscape of sugar-cane plantations and grassland, while uncultivated lowland slopes are covered with thick tropical woodland and exotic fruits such as papaya, mangoes, avocados, bananas and breadfruit. To the southeast of the island, a low-lying peninsula, on which there are many excellent beaches, stretches towards Nevis.
3km (2 miles) to the south and only minutes away by air or ferry across The Narrows channel is the smaller island of **Nevis**, which is almost circular in shape. The island is skirted by miles of silver-sand beaches, golden coconut groves and a calm, turquoise sea in which great brown pelicans dive for the rich harvest of fish. The central peak of the island, Nevis Peak, is 985m (3000ft) high and its tip is usually capped with white clouds. The mountain is flanked on the north and south sides by two lesser mountains, Saddle Hill and Hurricane Hill, which once served as look-out posts for Nelson's fleet. Hurricane Hill on the north side commands a view of St Kitts and Barbuda. On the island's west side massed rows of palm trees form a coconut forest. There are pleasant coral beaches on the island's north and west coasts.
LANGUAGE: The official language is English.
RELIGION: Anglican Communion Church and other Christian denominations.
TIME: GMT - 4.
ELECTRICITY: 230 volts AC, 60Hz (110 volts available in some hotels).
COMMUNICATIONS: Telephone: IDD is available to St Kitts & Nevis. Country code: 1 809. Outgoing international code: 1 (Caribbean, Canada and USA); 011 (elsewhere). **Fax:** This service is available to the public at the offices of *SKANTEL* (see below) and at some hotels. **Telex/telegram:** Facilities available at main hotels and at the offices of *SKANTEL* at Cayon Street, Basseterre and Main Street, Charlestown. Opening hours: 0700-1900 Monday to Friday, 0700-1400 and 1900-2000 Saturday and 0800-1000 and 1900-2000 Sundays and public holidays. **Post:** Airmail to Western Europe takes five to seven days. Post offices are open 0800-1500 Monday to Friday and Saturday, 0800-1100 Thursday.
Press: There are two newspapers, both published in English – the weekly *Democrat* and the twice-weekly *Labour Spokesman*.

BBC World Service and Voice of America frequencies: From time to time these change. See the section *How to Use this Book* for more information.

BBC:				
MHz	17.84	15.22	9.915	5.975
Voice of America:				
MHz	15.21	11.70	6.130	0.930

PASSPORT/VISA

Regulations and requirements may be subject to change at short notice, and you are advised to contact the appropriate diplomatic or consular authority before finalising travel arrangements. Details of these may be found at the head of this country's entry. Any numbers in the chart refer to the footnotes below.

	Passport Required?	Visa Required?	Return Ticket Required?
Full British	Yes	No	Yes
BVP	Not valid/2	-	-
Australian	Yes	No	Yes
Canadian	No/1	No	Yes
USA	No/1	No	Yes
Other EU (As of 31/12/94)	Yes	3	Yes
Japanese	Yes	No	Yes

PASSPORTS: Valid passport required by all **[1]** except nationals of Canada and the USA with valid ID (for up to 6 months).
British Visitors Passport: [2] Not officially accepted. Although the immigration authorities of this country may in certain circumstances accept British Visitors Passports for persons arriving for holidays or unpaid business trips of up to 3 months, travellers are reminded that no formal agreement exists to this effect and the situation may, therefore, change at short notice. In addition, UK nationals using a BVP and returning to the UK from a country with which no such formal agreement exists may be subject to delays and interrogation by UK immigration.
VISAS: Required by all except:

(a) nationals of those countries shown in the chart above;
(b) **[3]** nationals of most EU countries (except nationals of Portugal who *do* require visas);
(c) nationals of Commonwealth countries;
(d) nationals of Argentina, Austria, Bahrain, Bolivia, Chile, China, Colombia, Costa Rica, Ecuador, Egypt, El Salvador, Fiji, Finland, Guatemala, Honduras, Iceland, Israel, Jordan, South Korea, Kuwait, Liechtenstein, Mexico, Monaco, Netherlands Antilles, Nicaragua, Norway, Oman, Panama, Paraguay, Peru, Puerto Rico, Qatar, Saudi Arabia, Sweden, Switzerland, Taiwan (China), Turkey, United Arab Emirates, Uruguay, US Virgin Islands and Venezuela;
(e) visitors continuing their journey to a third country within 14 days. This is not available for nationals of Albania, Bosnia-Hercegovina, Bulgaria, CIS, Croatia, Czech Republic, Haiti, Hungary, North Korea, Former Yugoslav Republic of Macedonia, Mongolia, Poland, Romania, Slovak Republic, Slovenia, Vietnam and Yugoslavia (Serbia and Montenegro).
Types of visa: Ordinary. Cost depends on nationality of applicant.
Validity: Usually up to 6 months.
Application to: Consulate (or Consular section at Embassy or High Commission) or Tourist Board. For addresses, see top of entry.
Working days required: 2-3 days.
Temporary residence: Apply to the Ministry of Home Affairs, Basseterre, St Kitts.

MONEY

Currency: Eastern Caribbean Dollar (EC$) = 100 cents. Notes are in denominations of EC$100, 20, 10, 5 and 1. Coins are in denominations of EC$1, and 25, 10, 5, 2 and 1 cents. The Eastern Caribbean Dollar is pegged to the US Dollar and US Dollars are also legal tender on the islands.
Credit cards: Visa and American Express are widely accepted, Access/Mastercard and Diners Club have more limited acceptance. Check with your credit card company for details of merchant acceptability and other services which may be available.
Exchange rate indicators: The following figures are included as a guide to the movements of the Eastern Caribbean Dollar against Sterling and the US Dollar:

Date:	Oct '92	Sep '93	Jan '94	Jan '95
£1.00=	4.27	4.13	4.00	4.22
$1.00=	*2.70	*2.70	*2.70	*2.70

Note [*]: The Eastern Caribbean Dollar is tied to the US Dollar.
Currency restrictions: There are no restrictions on the import or export of local currency. There is free import of foreign currency, subject to declaration. Export of foreign currency is limited to the amount imported and declared.
Banking hours: 0800-1300 Monday to Thursday, 0800-1500/1700 Friday and 0830-1130 Saturday.

DUTY FREE

The following goods may be imported into St Kitts & Nevis without incurring customs duty:
200 cigarettes or 50 cigars or 225g of tobacco; 1.136 litres of wine or spirits; 150g perfume.
Note: There are several duty-free shops, selling a range of goods, including perfumes, textiles, clothing, porcelain, crystal and jewellery.

PUBLIC HOLIDAYS

Jan 1 '95 New Year's Day/Carnival Day. **Apr 14** Good Friday. **Apr 17** Easter Monday. **May 1** Labour Day. **Jun 5** Whit Monday. **Aug 7** August Monday. **Sep 19** Independence Day. **Dec 25** Christmas Day. **Dec 26** Boxing Day. **Jan 1 '96** New Year's Day/Carnival Day. **Apr 5** Good Friday. **Apr 8** Easter Monday.

HEALTH

Regulations and requirements may be subject to change at short notice, and you are advised to contact your doctor well in advance of your intended date of departure. Any numbers in the chart refer to the footnotes below.

	Special Precautions?	Certificate Required?
Yellow Fever	No	1
Cholera	No	No
Typhoid & Polio	Yes	-
Malaria	No	-
Food & Drink	2	-

[1]: A yellow fever vaccination certificate is required from travellers over one year of age arriving from infected areas.
[2]: Mains water is normally chlorinated, and whilst

relatively safe may cause mild abdominal upsets. Bottled water is available and is advised for the first few weeks of the stay. Drinking water outside main cities and towns may be contaminated and sterilisation is advisable. Milk is pasteurised and dairy products are safe for consumption. Local meat, poultry, seafood, fruit and vegetables are generally considered safe to eat.
Health care: There are large general hospitals in Basseterre and Charlestown, and a smaller public hospital at Sandy Point, St Kitts. There are no private hospitals, but several doctors and dentists are in private practice. Health insurance is advised.

TRAVEL - International

AIR: *LIAT (LI)* runs six flights a week from Antigua and offers day-trip charters to Montserrat, St Maarten (for duty-free shopping) and Antigua & Barbuda. Other airlines serving the islands include *Air BVI, American Eagle* and *Windward Islands Airways.*
Approximate flight times: From *London* to St Kitts is 10 hours, including stopover in Antigua. From *New York* to St Kitts is 5 hours.
International airports: *St Kitts (SKB)* (Golden Rock) is 3.2km (2 miles) from Basseterre on St Kitts. Airport facilities include restaurant and duty-free shop. There are at present no currency exchange facilities at the airport. Taxi fares are regulated; fares from the airport to Basseterre are approximately EC$13-16 (50 cents is charged on each additional piece of luggage over one). *Newcastle Airfield (NEV)* is 11km (7 miles) from Charlestown on Nevis.
Departure tax: EC$20 (US$8).
SEA: Basseterre is a deep-water port capable of berthing ships up to 120m (400ft) and is regularly visited by cruise liners operated by *Cunard, Ocean Cruise, Regency Cruise, Royal Caribbean Cruises, Regency Cruise, Pacquet Cruise* and *P&O.*

TRAVEL - Internal

AIR: The local airline, *LIAT (LI)*, runs five flights daily between St Kitts and the island of Nevis.
SEA: There is a regular passenger ferry service between Basseterre (St Kitts) and Charlestown (Nevis) with four sailings daily except Thursday and Sunday (travel time – 40 minutes). For information, contact the General Manager, St Kitts & Nevis Port Authority, Basseterre.
ROAD: A good road network on both islands makes any area accessible within minutes. Driving is on the left. **Bus:** There are privately-run bus services, which are comfortable and make regular but unscheduled runs between villages. **Taxi:** Services on both islands have set rates. A schedule of taxi rates is obtainable at the government headquarters. On St Kitts, there is a 25% surcharge between 2300-0600. On Nevis, there is a 50% surcharge between 2200-0600. Taxi drivers expect a 10% tip. **Car & moped hire:** A selection of cars and mopeds can be hired from several companies. It is best to book cars through the airline well in advance.
Documentation: Before driving any vehicle, including motorcycles, a local Temporary Driver's Licence must be obtained from the Police Traffic Department. This is readily issued on presentation of an International Driving Permit or national driving licence and a fee of EC$30, and is valid for one year.
JOURNEY TIMES: The following chart gives journey times from Basseterre, St Kitts (in hours and minutes) to other major towns on the islands.

	Air	Road	Sea
Newcastle, Nevis	0.05	-	-
Charlestown, Nevis	-	-	0.45
Sandy Point	-	0.20	-
Brimstone Hill	-	0.35	-
Frigate Bay	-	0.10	-
Cockleshell Bay	-	0.35	-

ACCOMMODATION

In general, prices are considerably lower in the low season (mid-April to mid-December). Group discounts and package rates are offered by most hotels on request. A government tax of 7% is levied on all hotel bills and the hotels themselves add 10% service charge.
HOTELS: There are over 20 hotels on the two islands, the majority being on St Kitts; most are small and owner-managed, offering a high standard of facilities and comfort. Many are converted from the great houses and sugar mills on the old estates. Further development on St Kitts will add 200 more beds. A full list of hotels can be obtained from the Embassy, High Commission or Tourist Board. The majority of hotels belong to the St Kitts & Nevis Hotel & Tourism Association (HTA), PO Box 438, Basseterre, St Kitts. Tel: 465 5304. Fax: 465 7746.
Grading: Though not a grading structure, many hotels in the Caribbean offer accommodation according to one of a number of plans: **FAP** is **Full American Plan**: room with all meals (including afternoon tea, supper, etc); **AP** is **American Plan**: room with three meals; **MAP** is **Modified American Plan**: breakfast and dinner included with the price of the room plus, in some places, British-style afternoon tea; **CP** is **Continental Plan**: room and breakfast only; **EP** is **European Plan**: room only.
GUEST-HOUSES: There are several guest-houses on both islands. A list is available from the Tourist Board.
SELF-CATERING: There are villas and apartments available. A list and full details are available from the Tourist Board.

RESORTS & EXCURSIONS

St Kitts

Basseterre: The capital retains the flavour of both French and British occupation, and there are many Georgian buildings surrounding *Independence Square.* A deep-water harbour for cruise ships has recently been completed. Sights in or near the capital include: *The Circus, Independence Square,* the market, *St George's Church, Craft House, Brimstone Hill Fortress, Black Rocks, Caribelle Batik Factory* (considered to be the most beautiful factory in the world), the *Primate Research Centre, Frigate Bay Development,* the southeastern peninsula and *Mount Liamuiga's* volcanic crater.
Brimstone Hill: One of the most impressive New World forts, built on the peak of a sulphuric prominence, known as 'The Gibraltar of the West Indies'. It commands the southern approach to what were the sugar mill plains, and commands a view of the nearby islands of Saba and St Eustatius. Built in 1690, it was the scene of a number of Franco/British battles during the 18th century.
Frigate Bay: This is the main resort area on the island and has been designated a Tourist Area by the Government. It boasts two fine beaches, hotels, a golf course and a casino.
Day trip charter flights to neighbouring islands depart regularly from Golden Rock.

Nevis

Since the 18th century, Nevis has been known as the 'Queen of the Caribbean', and over the last 100 years the island has become one of the world's most exclusive resorts and spas. Most of the original plantation owners lived on the island and it became renowned as a centre of elegant and gracious living. Although Nevis has lived through an earthquake and a tidal wave which is claimed to have buried the former capital, the island is still dotted, as is St Kitts, with fascinating old buildings and historic sites.

Charlestown: The capital is a delightful town, with weathered wooden buildings decorated like delicate gingerbread and great arches of brilliantly coloured bougainvillaea. The town contains several reminders of Nevisian history, such as the *Cotton Ginnery,* Alexander Hamilton's birthplace and museum, the *Court House,* the *War Memorial,* the *Alexandra Hospital* and the *Jewish Cemetery.* Some of the plantation houses have now been transformed into superb hotels, such as the famous *Nisbet.* Other sights in or near Charlestown include: *Nevis Philatelic Bureau, Public Library,* the market, *Bath House* (one of the oldest hotels in the Leeward Islands), Eva Wilkin's studio, Eden Brown's Great House, *Fig Tree Church, Nelson Museum, Bath Hot Springs* and *Newcastle Pottery.*

Elsewhere: North of Charlestown is *Pinney's Beach,* one of the best on the island, an expanse of silver sand, backed by palm trees. Further north still, *Black Sand Beach* and *Hurricane Hill* offer an excellent view of both St Kitts and Barbuda.

SOCIAL PROFILE

FOOD & DRINK: St Kitts & Nevis has built up a widely established reputation for fine food, a reputation which the local restaurateurs guard zealously. Restaurants specialise in West Indian, Creole, Continental, Indian, Chinese and French cuisine. Most restaurants in St Kitts offer a continental menu with island variations. Local dishes include roast suckling pig, spiny lobster, crab back or curries. Restaurants that cater more for locals also offer conch (curried, soused or in salad), turtle stews, rice and peas and goat's water (mutton stew). Christophine, yams, breadfruit and papaya are also served. Nevis is less grand and Charlestown's small restaurants cater more to Nevisians than visitors. Local specialities are native vegetable soup, lobster, mutton, beef and turtle stews. Fruit, including mangoes, papayas and bananas, is sold at the waterfront market. **Drink:** The locally produced *CSR* (cane spirit), belonging to the Baron Rothschild family, is excellent. A wide range of imported drinks is available.

NIGHTLIFE: Very low key. A number of hotels and inns have string or steel bands to dance to on Saturday nights in the peak season, and there is a disco called J's Place at the foot of the Brimstone Hill Fortress in St Kitts. Reflections Night Club, also in St Kitts, is open until the small hours, as is the Cotton Club. St Kitts has a casino at the Royal St Kitts, complete with slot machines, roulette wheels and blackjack tables. In Nevis the Club Trenim is recommended. Otherwise entertainment centres around the pleasant bars of the inns and hotels.

SHOPPING: Local crafts include carvings, batik, wall hangings, leather art and coconut work. Local textiles and designs are also available. Stamp collectors should note the excellent Philatelic Bureau in Basseterre. Duty-free shopping is relatively new to St Kitts and, as yet, only a few shops feature imported merchandise at substantial savings. Nevis' hot pepper sauce, ranked among the Caribbean's best, is a good take-home item and can be bought at the Main Street grocery in Charlestown. **Shopping hours:** 0800-1600 Monday to Wednesday and Friday, 0800-1200 Thursday; 0800-1800 Saturday.

SPORT: Swimming is excellent; most hotels have freshwater pools and some have their own beaches. **Scuba** and **snorkelling** are catered for and beach hotels generally have equipment. Several Basseterre skippers are equipped to take scuba parties. **Sailing** boats can be hired from beach hotels, although Nevis has very limited facilities. Fast boats and **water-skiing** equipment are available for hire. **Fishing** trips can be organised. Deep-sea fishing is a speciality. An 18-hole international **golf** championship course is at Frigate Bay and a 9-hole course at Golden Rock, both on St Kitts. There is also an 18-hole championship golf course on Nevis. A number of **tennis** courts are available on both islands, and clubs welcome visitors. Many of the hotels have their own (mainly hard) tennis courts.

Other sports include **mountaineering, hiking, cricket, football** and **horseriding.**

SPECIAL EVENTS: Festivals in St Kitts & Nevis have a special atmosphere and visitors are encouraged to take part in the parades, pageants and parties. The following is a selection of special events celebrated during 1995/96:
Apr 15-17 '95 *Australia v Leeward Islands* (cricket), St Kitts. **May 18-21** *Annual Golf Tournament,* Frigate Bay Golf Club, St Kitts. **May 27-28** *St Kitts Horticultural Society Show.* **Jun** *St Kitts/Nevis Regatta; Guavaburry Caribbean Offshore Regatta.* **Aug 2-8** *Culturama,* Nevis. **Sep 12-19** *Independence Week of Activities.* **Oct 29-Nov 5** *Tourism Week,* St Kitts. **Oct 29** *Oceanfest,* St Kitts. **Dec 24 '95-Jan 2 '96** *National Carnival,* St Kitts/Nevis.

SOCIAL CONVENTIONS: Commercialisation has not yet taken over and the easy-going, quiet way of life of the local people remains almost unspoiled. All visitors to the islands are cordially welcomed; marriages are valid after two day's residence. Islanders maintain traditions of calypso dancing and music and this can be seen particularly during the summer months. Dress is informal at most hotels. It is suggested that visitors be suitably attired when in town and in places of business. For more formal occasions and functions, a lightweight suit and tie is recommended. **Tipping:** 10% service charge is added to hotel bills. In restaurants leave 10-15% and tip taxi drivers 10% of the fare.

BUSINESS PROFILE

ECONOMY: St Kitts & Nevis has an agricultural economy, the mainstay of which is the sugar industry. As the world sugar price has been very low in the past few years, St Kitts & Nevis has come to rely on regular injections of foreign aid to prevent economic collapse. The Government is trying to broaden the range of the islands' manufacturing industry, which was taken into state ownership in 1975. One notable result of this policy has been the establishment of a thriving electronics and data processing sector. Tourism is also seen as a promising growth area and is developing rapidly, especially on Nevis, though political uncertainties have hampered infrastructure development. The UK and the USA are the islands' main trading partners.

BUSINESS: Business wear for men usually consists of a short- or long-sleeved shirt and tie, or open-neck tunic-shirt or alternatively, safari-type suits. **Office hours:** 0800-1200 and 1300-1600 Monday to Saturday; early closing Thursday.

COMMERCIAL INFORMATION: The following organisation can offer advice: St Kitts & Nevis Chamber of Industry and Commerce, PO Box 332, South Square Street, Basseterre. Tel: 465 2980. Fax: 465 4490. Telex: 6822.

CONFERENCES/CONVENTIONS: For further information on conferences and convention possibilities, contact the St Kitts & Nevis Hotel & Tourism Association (for address, see *Accommodation* above).

CLIMATE

Hot and tropical climate tempered by trade winds throughout most of the year. The driest period is from January to April and there is increased rainfall in summer and towards the end of the year. The volume of rain varies according to altitude; rain showers can occur throughout the year. The average annual rainfall is about 125cm (50 inches) to 200cm (80 inches) with a wetter season from May to October. Like the other Leeward Islands, St Kitts lies in the track of violent tropical hurricanes which are most likely to develop between August and October.

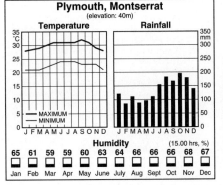

Plymouth, Montserrat
(elevation: 40m)
Temperature / Rainfall

Humidity (15.00 hrs, %)
Jan	Feb	Mar	Apr	May	June	July	Aug	Sept	Oct	Nov	Dec
65	61	59	59	60	63	64	66	66	66	68	67

St Lucia

Location: Eastern Caribbean, Windward Islands.

St Lucia Tourist Board
PO Box 221, Pointe Seraphine, Castries, St Lucia
Tel: 25968. Fax: 31121.
High Commission for Eastern Caribbean States
10 Kensington Court, London W8 5DL
Tel: (0171) 937 9522. Fax: (0171) 937 5514. Telex: 913047 (a/b ECACOM G). Opening hours: 0930-1730 Monday to Friday.
St Lucia Tourist Board
421A Finchley Road, London NW3 6HJ
Tel: (0171) 431 3675. Fax: (0171) 431 7920. Opening hours: 0930-1800 Monday to Friday.
British High Commission
PO Box 227, Columbus Square, Castries, St Lucia
Tel: 22484. Fax: 31543. Telex: 6314 (a/b UKREP SLC LC).
Embassy of St Lucia
Suite 309, 2100 M Street, NW, Washington, DC 20037
Tel: (202) 463 7378/9. Fax: (202) 887 5746.
Consulate in: New York (tel: (212) 697 9360).
St Lucia Tourist Board
9th Floor, 820 Second Avenue, New York, NY 10017
Tel: (212) 867 2950/1. Fax: (212) 370 7867. Telex: 666762.
High Commission for Eastern Caribbean States
Suite 1610, Tower B, Place de Ville, 112 Kent Street, Ottawa, Ontario K1P 5P2
Tel: (613) 236 8952. Fax: (613) 236 3042. Telex: 0534476.
St Lucia Tourist Board
Suite 457, 4975 Dundas Street West, Islington, Ontario M4A 4X4
Tel: (416) 236 0936. Fax: (416) 236 0937.
The Canadian High Commission in Bridgetown deals with enquiries relating to St Lucia (see *Barbados* earlier in this book).

AREA: 616.3 sq km (238 sq miles).
POPULATION: 151,300 (1993).
POPULATION DENSITY: 245.5 per sq km.
CAPITAL: Castries. **Population:** 57,322 (1993).
GEOGRAPHY: St Lucia is the second largest of the Windward Islands. It has some of the finest mountain

Health	
GALILEO/WORLDSPAN:	TI-DFT/SLU/HE
SABRE:	TIDFT/SLU/HE
Visa	
GALILEO/WORLDSPAN:	TI-DFT/V/VI
SABRE:	TIDFT/SLU/VI

For more information on Timatic codes refer to Contents.

Timatic

scenery in the West Indies, rich with tropical vegetation. For so small an island, 43km (27 miles) by 23km (14 miles), St Lucia has a great variety of plant and animal life. Orchids and exotic plants of the genus *anthurium* grow wild in the rainforests and the roadsides are covered with many colourful and aromatic tropical flowers. Flamboyant trees spread shade and blossom everywhere. Indigenous wildlife includes a species of ground lizard unique to St Lucia, and the *agouti* and the *manicou*, two rabbit-like animals, common throughout the island. The Amazon versicolor parrot is another, though more elusive, inhabitant of the deep interior rainforest. The highest peak is Mount Gimie, 950m (3117ft). Most spectacular are Gros Piton and Petit Piton, ancient, volcanic forest-covered cones which rise out of the sea on the west coast. *Soufri* (vents in a volcano which exude hydrogen sulphide, steam and other gases) and boiling waterpools can be seen here. The mountains are intersected by short rivers which in some areas form broad fertile valleys. The island has excellent beaches and is surrounded by a clear, warm sea.

LANGUAGE: English and local French *patois*.
RELIGION: 82% Roman Catholic, also Anglican, Methodist, Seventh Day Adventist and Baptist.
TIME: GMT - 4.
ELECTRICITY: 220 volts AC, 50Hz.
COMMUNICATIONS: Telephone: IDD is available. Country code: 1 809 45. Outgoing international code: 011. **Fax:** Available to the public in Castries at the offices of *Cable & Wireless* (tel: 23301) and at some hotels. **Telex/telegram:** Facilities limited to main towns and hotels and the public telex booth at Cable & Wireless. **Post:** Airmail to Western Europe takes up to a week. *Poste Restante* mail will only be released on presentation of suitable identification. Post office hours: 0800-1630 Monday to Friday, 0900-1330 Saturday. **Press:** The main newspapers are *The Voice of St Lucia* and *The Crusader*.
BBC World Service and Voice of America frequencies: From time to time these change. See the section *How to Use this Book* for more information.

BBC:

| MHz | 17.84 | 15.22 | 9.915 | 5.975 |

Voice of America:

| MHz | 15.21 | 11.70 | 6.130 | 0.930 |

PASSPORT/VISA

Regulations and requirements may be subject to change at short notice, and you are advised to contact the appropriate diplomatic or consular authority before finalising travel arrangements. Details of these may be found at the head of this country's entry. Any numbers in the chart refer to the footnotes below.

	Passport Required?	Visa Required?	Return Ticket Required?
Full British	1	No	Yes
BVP	Not valid/2	-	-
Australian	Yes	No	Yes
Canadian	1	No	Yes
USA	1	No	Yes
Other EU (As of 31/12/94)	Yes	No	Yes
Japanese	Yes	No	Yes

PASSPORTS: Valid passports are required by all except [1] nationals of Canada, the UK and the USA with valid proof of identity (for visits of up to 6 weeks).
British Visitors Passport: [2] Not officially accepted. Although the immigration authorities of this country may in certain circumstances accept British Visitors Passports for persons arriving for holidays or unpaid business trips of up to 3 months, travellers are reminded that no formal agreement exists to this effect and the situation may, therefore, change at short notice. In addition, UK nationals using a BVP and returning to the UK from a country with which no such formal agreement exists may be subject to delays and interrogation by UK immigration.
VISAS: Required by all except:
(a) nationals of countries as shown in the chart above;
(b) nationals of Commonwealth countries;
(c) nationals of Argentina, Austria, Bolivia, Brazil, Costa Rica, Dominican Republic, Ecuador, El Salvador, Fiji, Finland, Guatemala, Haiti, Honduras, Iceland, Indonesia, South Korea, Kuwait, Liechtenstein, Mexico, Nicaragua, Norway, Panama, Peru, Philippines, San Marino, Suriname, Sweden, Switzerland, Taiwan (China), Turkey, Uruguay and Venezuela;
(d) nationals of most African countries (except nationals of Libya and South Africa who *do* need visas).
Transit: Transit passengers who continue their journey within 14 days do not require a Transit visa. This does not apply for nationals of Cuba and Eastern European countries.
Types of visa: Single-entry; cost depends on nationality of the applicant, but usually about £20.

Validity: Up to 6 weeks. Extensions to visas can be made at the Immigration Department in St Lucia.
Application to: Consulate (or Consular section at Embassy or High Commission). For addresses, see top of entry.
Application requirements: (a) Valid passport. (b) Completed application form(s). (c) Passport-size photo(s). (d) Sufficient funds to cover duration of stay. (e) Fee (approx. £20, payable by postal order or cash).
Working days required: Dependent upon nationality of applicant, normally 2-3 days.
Temporary residence: Refer applications or enquiries to Consulate, Embassy or High Commission. Processed through the Ministry of Foreign Affairs, Castries.

MONEY

Currency: Eastern Caribbean Dollar (EC$) = 100 cents. Notes are in denominations of EC$100, 20, 10, 5 and 1. Coins are in denominations of EC$1, and 50, 25, 10, 5, 2 and 1 cents. US Dollars are also accepted as legal tender.
Currency exchange: US Dollars ensure a better exchange rate.
Credit cards: Access/Mastercard, American Express, Diners Club and Visa are all widely accepted. Check with your credit card company for details of merchant acceptability and other services which may be available.
Travellers cheques: Accepted. US Dollar cheques preferred.
Exchange rate indicators: The following figures are included as a guide to the movements of the Eastern Caribbean Dollar against Sterling and the US Dollar:

Date:	Oct '92	Sep '93	Jan '94	Jan '95
£1.00=	4.27	4.13	4.00	4.22
$1.00=	*2.70	*2.70	*2.70	*2.70

Note [*]: The Eastern Caribbean Dollar is tied to the US Dollar.
Currency restrictions: Free import of local currency, subject to declaration. Export of local currency is limited to the amount declared on import. There are no restrictions on the import or export of foreign currency.
Banking hours: Generally 0800-1500 Monday to Thursday, 0800-1700 Friday. Some banks open 0800-1200 Saturday.

DUTY FREE

The following items may be imported into St Lucia without incurring customs duty:
200 cigarettes or 250g tobacco products; 1 litre of alcoholic beverage.

PUBLIC HOLIDAYS

Jan 1-2 '95 New Year. **Feb 22** Independence Day. **Feb 27-28** Carnival. **Apr 14** Good Friday. **Apr 17** Easter Monday. **May 1** Labour Day. **Jun 5** Whit Monday. **Jun 15** Corpus Christi. **Aug 7** Emancipation Day. **Oct 2** Thanksgiving Day. **Dec 13** St Lucia Day. **Dec 25-26** Christmas. **Jan 1-2 '96** New Year. **Feb** Carnival. **Feb 22** Independence Day. **Apr 5** Good Friday. **Apr 8** Easter Monday.

HEALTH

Regulations and requirements may be subject to change at short notice, and you are advised to contact your doctor well in advance of your intended date of departure. Any numbers in the chart refer to the footnotes below.

	Special Precautions?	Certificate Required?
Yellow Fever	No	1
Cholera	No	No
Typhoid & Polio	Yes	-
Malaria	No	-
Food & Drink	2	-

[1]: A yellow fever vaccination certificate is required from travellers over one year of age arriving from infected areas.
[2]: Mains water is normally chlorinated, and whilst relatively safe may cause mild abdominal upsets. Bottled water is available and is advised for the first few weeks of the stay. Milk is pasteurised and dairy products are safe for consumption. Local meat, poultry, seafood, fruit and vegetables are generally considered safe to eat. *Bilharzia* (schistosomiasis) is present. Avoid swimming and paddling in fresh water. Swimming pools which are well-chlorinated and maintained are safe.
Health care: Costs of health care are high and full health insurance is essential.

TRAVEL - International

AIR: St Lucia is served direct by *British Airways (BA)* and by *British West Indian Airways (BW)*.

Approximate flight times: From Castries to *London* is 8 hours 25 minutes (via Barbados), to *Barbados* is 30 minutes, to *Los Angeles* is 9 hours, to *New York* is 5 hours and to *Singapore* is 33 hours.
International airports: *Vigie (SLU)* and *Hewanorra (UVF)*, 3km (2 miles) and 67km (42 miles) from Castries respectively. Taxis or buses are available from airports to Castries. Both runways are equipped for jets. Airport facilities at Vigie include a bar/restaurant and car hire; at Hewanorra there is a bar/restaurant, left luggage and lockers (0800-1600), shops, tourist information, outgoing duty-free shop and car hire (*Avis, Budget, Dollar, Hertz* and *National*).
Departure tax: EC$27 on all international departures and EC$20 for Caribbean destinations. Transit passengers and children under two years are exempt.
SEA: St Lucia is served by a number of cruise lines as well as local passenger/freight lines. Lines include *Cunard, Costa, P&O* and *Sun Line*. The main ports are Castries, Vieux Fort and Soufrière. The duty-free port at Pointe Seraphine offers 2-berth cruise ship facilities, duty-free shopping, restaurants and bars; it may be visited by any tourist holding a current passport (further information in the *Shopping* section below). Work on the construction of a third berth for cruise ships began in 1989.

TRAVEL - Internal

AIR: It is possible to charter planes. Charter flights operate between Vigie and Hewanorra airports. The regional airline *LIAT* offers flights to neighbouring islands.
SEA: Boat charters are easily available at Castries, Marigot Bay and Rodney Bay.
ROAD: All major centres are served by a reasonably good road network. The main cross-island route runs from Vieux Fort in the south of the island to Castries in the north. Traffic drives on the left. **Bus:** Services connect rural areas with the capital. There is a good service from Castries to Gros Islet in the north of the island with buses departing every 30 minutes during the day. **Taxi:** Hiring a taxi is easy and cheap, with standard trips having fixed rates. Tipping is unnecessary. **Car hire:** Cars can be obtained either in Castries, Soufrière and Vieux Fort, or through hotels. Mini-mokes are particularly popular. Hotels and local tour operators run coach trips for groups. **Documentation:** On presentation of a national driving licence or International Driving Permit a local licence will be issued.

ACCOMMODATION

HOTELS: St Lucia has a range of accommodation to suit every taste and every budget, from deluxe hotels to self-catering apartments. All-inclusive holidays are also proving very popular and several hotels now offer this option. Most hotels provide some form of entertainment in the evening, from calypso music to the ever-popular limbo dancing. Details are available from hotels' reservation desks. A government tax of 8% and service charge of 10-15% are added to bills. A leaflet giving hotel and guest-house rates is produced by the St Lucia Hotel and Tourism Association, PO Box 545, Vide Boutielle, Castries. Tel: 25978. Fax: 27967. **Grading:** Though not a grading structure, many hotels in the Caribbean offer accommodation according to one of a number of plans: **AP** is **American Plan**: room with three meals; **MAP** is **Modified American Plan**: breakfast and dinner included with the price of the room plus, in some places, British-style afternoon tea; **CP** is **Continental Plan**: room and breakfast only; **EP** is **European Plan**: room only. Hotels in St Lucia are also graded on a scale from **3** to **5 stars**.
GUEST-HOUSES: A range of accommodation is available, some of which offers self-catering facilities.

RESORTS & EXCURSIONS

St Lucia is a beautiful volcanic island with green jungles, undulating agricultural land and dazzling beaches. It is an island of contrasts, and the visitor can stroll for hours along unspoiled beaches, enjoy the tropical splendour of the lush rainforests in its interior, marvel at the hot springs in the world's only 'drive-in' volcano, go horseriding on rugged mountain trails, play golf or simply sunbathe; all among some of the most varied scenery in the Caribbean. Considerable French influence is still felt throughout the island.

Castries and the North

Castries is one of the most beautifully situated Caribbean cities. Surrounded by hills, its large, safe, land-locked harbour at the head of a wide bay is a constant hive of activity. Castries is a major port of call for cruise ships, which dock at Pointe Seraphine. The spacious *Columbus Square* boasts tropical scenery and the 19th-century *Catholic Cathedral* (where the art of gospel singing is very much alive). There is also a colourful, bustling market.

Morne Fortune, 'the hill of good luck', affords the visitor the chance to inspect the fortification which defends Castries. It also provides a magnificent panorama of the city and the surrounding area.

Gros Islet, on the northwest coast of the island, stages an 'impromptu' street party every Friday. Nearby **Pigeon Point** has a small museum telling the history of the island. It was from here that Admiral Rodney set sail in 1782 and destroyed the French Fleet in one of the most decisive engagements in European history. This end of the island is now being developed as a centre for tourism.

Anse La Raye, on the west coast south of Castries, is a vividly coloured fishing village where locals make boats from gum trees and sails from chicken feathers. **Marigot Bay**, also on the west coast, is a secluded and idyllic palm-fringed yachtsman's paradise. Above Marigot Bay lies **Cul de Sac**, an area of three large banana plantations. From above, they look like gently moving oceans of green leaves. It was here that 'Dr Doolittle' was filmed.

Soufrière and the South

Soufrière is the second-largest settlement on the island. This deep-water port stands at the foot of two extinct volcanoes, the **Pitons**. Rising to 798m (2619ft) above sea level, these are probably St Lucia's most famous attractions. The town itself is typically West Indian, a cluster of brightly painted arcaded buildings set hard against the jungle.

The road between Soufrière and Fond St Jacques runs eastwards through rainforest; here are the *Diamond Waterfalls* and *Sulphur Springs*.

The picturesque little villages of **Choiseul** and **Laborie** are surrounded by splendid vegetation.

On the east of the island, the headlands project into the ocean; a visit to **Dennery** and **Micoud** is highly recommended.

Coastal Excursions

There are several boat trips which offer the visitor an exhilarating day viewing the island from the sea and possibly weighing anchor to picnic at an exciting location. Alternative means of transport include brigs, catamarans and private yachts.

SOCIAL PROFILE

FOOD & DRINK: Most hotels have restaurants, in addition to a wide range in the major towns serving many different types of food. Waiter service is the norm. Local dishes include *langouste* (local lobster) cooked in a variety of ways, *lambi* (conch) and other fresh seafood, breadfruit and other local fruit and vegetables. *Pepper pot* and fried plantain are two local specialities worth trying. In general the food is a combination of Creole with West Indian and French influences. **Drink:** Many imported spirits are available, but the local drink is rum, often served in punch and cocktails. Caribbean beer and plenty of delicious fresh fruit juices are also available.

NIGHTLIFE: Centres mainly in hotels, particularly the St Lucian, Halcyon and Le Sport hotels. During summer there is little nightlife, but during the winter the resorts are lively, with plenty of local music and dance.

SHOPPING: Special purchases include unique batik and silkscreen designs made into shifts, sports shirts, table mats, cocktail napkins and shopping bags produced at a studio on the road between Castries and La Toc. Other craft outlets sell locally made bowls, beads, straw hats, flour-sack shirts, sisal rugs, bags, sandals and woodwork. Work began in 1989 on the expansion of the recently opened duty-free port at Pointe Seraphine, which already has 23 duty-free shops, bars and restaurants placed around an open piazza. Duty-free shopping is available to all visitors, provided they present their passport or airline ticket when purchasing goods. **Shopping hours:** 0800-1800 Monday to Friday, 0800-1200 Saturday.

SPORT: Watersports: St Lucia is one of the world's breeziest places, where the trade winds blow in from the sea to the southern shore. The sandy beach of Anse de Sable offers ideal windsurfing conditions for both novice and expert. The west coast, too, offers a selection of resorts and hotels geared to the special needs of the active watersports enthusiast, while elsewhere on the island guests can enjoy water-skiing or scuba diving. Enthusiasts' equipment can be accommodated by *British Airways* and *BWIA*, with windsurfers' boards carried as excess baggage and charged according to size. Hotels hire out hobbycats, dinghies and small speedboats by the hour or half-day. From Marigot Bay and Rodney Bay the more experienced sailor can hire a variety of craft from comparatively basic, small yachts to larger 12m (40ft) and 18m (60ft) vessels, with crew if required. Tour operators

can also arrange for stays of a week or more on the island to be coupled with a 'free floating' holiday on board a chartered yacht visiting the neighbouring islands. All west coast beaches have good swimming. The Atlantic coast has rugged surf and is not recommended to anyone with little experience and ability, and even an extremely proficient swimmer should not go unaccompanied. Many of the sports facilities are available free of charge.

Walking: Tours to Mount du Cap and Pigeon Point can be arranged at Le Sport Hotel. Tours into the rainforest, plantations and the Pitons can be arranged through Anse Chastenet. **Golf:** There are courses at Cap Estate, the northern tip of the island, and at La Toc. **Tennis:** All the main hotels have courts and arrangements can be made through hotels to play at St Lucia Tennis Club. **Fishing:** Sea trips are possible, fishing for barracuda, mackerel, kingfish, etc. **Climbing:** Local guides are available to help climbers tackle the Pitons. **Horseriding:** There are stables at Cap Estate.

SPECIAL EVENTS: The following are important events which take place annually on St Lucia:

Mar 28 '95 *West Indies President's Eleven Cricket Match.* **May 11-14** *St Lucia Jazz Festival.* **Aug 30** *Feast of St Rose of Lima* (flower festival and street parade). **Oct** *Feast of Le Marguerite* (flower festival and street parade); *St Lucia Game Fishing Tournament.* **Nov 22** *St Cecilia's Day* (Feast of the Musicians). **Dec 4** *Atlantic Rally for Cruisers.* **Dec 13** *National Day* (cultural and sporting activities throughout the island in celebration of the island's patron saint – St Lucia). **Feb '96** *Carnival.*

SOCIAL CONVENTIONS: Some French influences still remain alongside the West Indian style of life. The people are friendly and hospitable and encourage visitors to relax and enjoy their leisurely lifestyle. The *madras* and *foulards* are not often seen in towns, but are sometimes worn at festivals such as the *Feast of St Rose of Lima* in August. Casual wear is acceptable, although some hotels and restaurants encourage guests to dress for dinner. Beachwear should not be worn in towns. **Tipping:** 10-15% is added to bills. Taxi drivers do not expect tips.

BUSINESS PROFILE

ECONOMY: Although the economy still relies heavily on agriculture (the main exports are bananas, coconuts and cocoa), tourism is an increasingly important source of income. There is a small, light industrial sector producing plastic, textiles and industrial gases, and assembling electronic components. Foreign investment has been slow in arriving but has grown steadily since the early 1980s. The industrial development programme has gradually reduced the economy's dependency on agriculture. The late 1980s saw a construction and consumer spending boom which threatened to overheat the economy, despite the damage wrought by Hurricane Hugo in late 1989, but the Government has managed to avoid serious recession. The USA and the UK are the main trading partners; the USA for imports and the UK for exports.

BUSINESS: Short- or long-sleeved shirt and tie or a safari suit are suitable for most business visits. **Office hours:** 0800-1600 Monday to Friday.

COMMERCIAL INFORMATION: The following organisation can offer advice: St Lucia Chamber of Commerce, Industry and Agriculture, PO Box 482, Micoud Street, Castries. Tel: 23165. Fax: 36907.

CONFERENCES/CONVENTIONS: Some hotels offer conference and back-up facilities, with seating for up to 200 persons. For further information, contact Conference and Incentive Services Ltd, Laborie Street, Castries. Tel: 27058.

CLIMATE

Hot, tropical climate tempered by trade winds throughout most of the year. The driest period is from January to April and there is increased rainfall in summer and towards the end of the year.

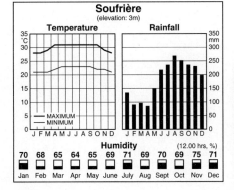

Soufrière
(elevation: 3m)

Location: Eastern Caribbean, Windward Islands.

Diplomatic representation: Although the Netherlands Antilles are part of the Kingdom of the Netherlands, they are not formally represented by Royal Netherlands Embassies. Information and advice may be obtained at the addresses below.

St Maarten Tourist Board
23 Walter Nisbeth Road, Imperial Building, Philipsburg, St Maarten
Tel: (5) 22337. Fax: (5) 22734.
Office of the Minister Plenipotentiary of the Netherlands Antilles
Antillenhuis, Badhuisweg 173-175, 2597 JP The Hague, The Netherlands
Tel: (70) 351 2811. Fax: (70) 351 2722. Telex: 31161.
Caribbean Tourism
Vigilant House, 120 Wilton Road, London SW1V 1JZ
Tel: (0171) 233 8382. Fax: (0171) 873 8551. Opening hours: 0900-1730 Monday to Friday.
The British Consulate in Willemstad deals with enquiries relating to St Maarten (see *Curaçao* earlier in the book).
St Maarten Tourist Information Office
675 3rd Avenue, New York, NY 10017
Tel: (212) 953 2084. Fax: (212) 242 0001.
The Consulate of the United States of America in Willemstad deals with enquiries relating to St Maarten (see *Curaçao* earlier in the book).
St Maarten Government Tourist Information Office
243 Ellerslie Avenue, Willowdale, Ontario M2N 1M8
Tel: (416) 223 3501. Fax: (416) 223 6887.
The Canadian Consulate in Willemstad deals with enquiries relating to St Maarten (see *Curaçao* earlier in the book).

AREA: 41 sq km (16 sq miles).
POPULATION: 36,408 (1993 estimate).
POPULATION DENSITY: 888 per sq km.
CAPITAL: Philipsburg. **NA capital:** Willemstad, Curaçao.
GEOGRAPHY: Politically, St Maarten is one of three Windward Islands in the Netherlands Antilles, although geographically it is part of the Leeward Group of the Lesser Antilles, and not strictly an island – it occupies just one-third of an island otherwise under French control

(the French sector is called St Martin), lying 8km (5 miles) south of Anguilla, 232km (144 miles) east of Puerto Rico and 56km (35 miles) due north of St Eustatius. St Maarten is the southern sector, an area of wooded mountains rising from white sandy beaches. To the west, the mountains give way to lagoons and salt flats.

Note: For information on the French sector (St Martin), see the *Guadeloupe* entry earlier in this book.

LANGUAGE: Mainly English although Dutch (the official language of the Netherlands Antilles) is used for legal documents and taught in schools. Papiamento is the local *patois*; French may also be spoken.

RELIGION: Protestant, with Roman Catholic and Jewish minorities.

TIME: GMT - 4.

ELECTRICITY: 110/220 volts AC, 60Hz.

COMMUNICATIONS: Telephone: Fully automatic system with good IDD. Country code: 599. Outgoing international code: 00. Calls made through the operator are more expensive and include a 15% tax. **Fax:** Some hotels provide facilities. **Telegram:** Services operated by *Lands Radio Dienst* and *All American Cables.* **Post:** Airmail to Western Europe takes four to six days, surface mail takes four to six weeks. **Press:** No newspapers are published on St Maarten, but an English-language daily, *The News,* is published on Curaçao. All other newspapers in the Netherlands Antilles are published in Dutch or Papiamento.

BBC World Service and Voice of America frequencies: From time to time these change. See the section *How to Use this Book* for more information.

BBC:

MHz	17.84	15.22	9.915	5.975

Voice of America:

MHz	15.21	11.70	6.130	0.930

PASSPORT/VISA

Regulations and requirements may be subject to change at short notice, and you are advised to contact the appropriate diplomatic or consular authority before finalising travel arrangements. Details of these may be found at the head of this country's entry. Any numbers in the chart refer to the footnotes below.

	Passport Required?	Visa Required?	Return Ticket Required?
Full British	Yes	No	Yes
BVP	Valid/1	-	-
Australian	Yes	4	Yes
Canadian	3	4	Yes
USA	2	4	Yes
Other EU (As of 31/12/94)	1	4/5	Yes
Japanese	Yes	4	Yes

PASSPORTS: Valid passport required by all except:
(a) **[1]** nationals of Belgium, Luxembourg and The Netherlands holding a *toeristkaart,* nationals of Germany holding a valid national ID card and UK nationals holding a British Visitors Passport;
(b) **[2]** nationals of the USA holding valid photo ID plus a voter's registration card or birth certificate, and alien residents of the USA with acceptable documentation;
(c) **[3]** nationals of Canada with a birth certificate or proof of citizenship;
(d) nationals of San Marino holding a national ID card;
(e) nationals and alien residents of Venezuela, and travellers in Venezuela visiting the Netherlands Antilles, holding a valid national ID card;
(f) nationals of Brazil, Mexico and Trinidad & Tobago entering for tourism only holding a valid national ID card.
British Visitors Passport: Acceptable.

VISAS: [4] Visas are only required for nationals of the Dominican Republic and Haiti resident there. All other nationals are allowed to stay in St Maarten for 14 days without a visa (but might need a Temporary Certificate of Admission, see below) provided they have a return or onward ticket. All visitors staying more than 90 days require a visa. Transit passengers staying no longer than 24 hours holding confirmed tickets and valid passports do not require visas or Certificates of Admission.
For stays of between 14 and 28 days a **Temporary Certificate of Admission** is required, which in the case of the following countries will be issued by the Immigration authorities on arrival in St Maarten:
(a) **[5]** Belgium, Germany, Luxembourg, The Netherlands, Spain and the UK;
(b) Bolivia, Burkina Faso, Chile, Colombia, Costa Rica, Czech Republic, Ecuador, Hungary, Israel, Jamaica, South Korea, Malawi, Mauritius, Niger, Philippines, Poland, San Marino, Slovak Republic, Swaziland and Togo;
(c) Estonia, Latvia and Lithuania only if resident in an EU country.
The following must apply in writing at least 1 month in advance *before* entering the country even for tourist

purposes for a Temporary Certificate of Admission: nationals of Albania, Bosnia-Hercegovina, Bulgaria, Cambodia, China, CIS, Croatia, Cuba, Estonia, Former Yugoslav Republic of Macedonia, Latvia, Libya, Lithuania, North Korea, Romania, Vietnam, Yugoslavia (Serbia and Montenegro) and holders of Zimbabwe passports issued on or after November 11, 1965. All other nationals have to apply for the Certificate after 14 days of stay.
Further information about visa requirements may be obtained from the Office of the Minister Plenipotentiary of the Netherlands Antilles; and whilst Royal Netherlands Embassies do not formally represent the Netherlands Antilles in any way, they might also be able to offer limited advice and information. For addresses, see top of this entry and top of *The Netherlands* entry above.

Temporary residence: Enquire at the Office of the Minister Plenipotentiary of the Netherlands Antilles.

MONEY

Currency: Netherlands Antilles Guilder or Florin (NAG) = 100 cents. Notes are in denominations of NAG500, 250, 100, 50, 25, 10 and 5. Coins are in denominations of NAG2.5 and 1, and 50, 25, 10, 5 and 1 cents. There are also a large number of commemorative coins which are legal tender. The currency is tied to the US Dollar.

Credit cards: Access/Mastercard and Visa are accepted in large establishments. Check with your credit card company for details of merchant acceptability and other services which may be available.

Exchange rate indicators: The following figures are included as a guide to the movement of the Netherlands Antilles Florin against Sterling and the US Dollar:

Date:	Oct '92	Sep '93	Jan '94	Jan '95
£1.00=	2.83	2.74	2.64	2.80
$1.00=	*1.79	*1.79	*1.79	*1.79

Note [*]: The NAG is linked to the US Dollar.
Currency restrictions: The import and export of local currency is limited to NAG200. There are no restrictions on the import and export of foreign currency. The import of Dutch or Suriname silver coins is prohibited.
Banking hours: 0830-1530 Monday to Friday.

DUTY FREE

The following items may be imported into St Maarten by visitors over 15 years of age without incurring customs duty:
400 cigarettes or 50 cigars or 250g tobacco; 2 litres of alcoholic beverages; 250ml of perfume (entire amount will be dutiable if more is imported); gifts to a value of NAG100.
Prohibited items: It is forbidden to import parrots, parakeets, dogs and cats from Central and South America. The import of souvenirs and leather goods from Haiti is not advisable.

PUBLIC HOLIDAYS

Jan 1 '95 New Year's Day. **Apr 14-17** Easter. **Apr 30** Queen's Birthday. **May 1** Labour Day. **May 25** Ascension Day. **Jun 5** Whit Monday. **Nov 11** St Maarten Day. **Dec 25-26** Christmas. **Jan 1 '96** New Year's Day. **Apr 5-8** Easter. **Apr 30** Queen's Birthday.

HEALTH

Regulations and requirements may be subject to change at short notice, and you are advised to contact your doctor well in advance of your intended date of departure. Any numbers in the chart refer to the footnotes below.

	Special Precautions?	Certificate Required?
Yellow Fever	No	1
Cholera	No	No
Typhoid & Polio	Yes	-
Malaria	No	-
Food & Drink	2	-

[1]: A yellow fever certificate is required from travellers over six months of age arriving from infected areas.
[2]: Water on the island is considered safe to drink. Bottled mineral water is widely available. Milk is pasteurised and dairy products are safe for consumption. Local meat, poultry, seafood, fruit and vegetables are generally considered safe to eat.
Health care: There is one general hospital, the St Rose Hospital in Philipsburg. Medical insurance is advised.

TRAVEL - International

AIR: The national airline of the Netherlands Antilles is *ALM (LM).* The government-owned *Windward Islands*

Airways International (WIA – Winair), based at *Juliana Airport,* has scheduled flights to the Lesser Antilles, as well as charter flights to destinations throughout the Eastern Caribbean.
Approximate flight times: From St Maarten to *London* is 12-14 hours, to *Los Angeles* is 9 hours, to *New York* is 4 hours 10 minutes, to *St Croix* is 45 minutes and to *Singapore* is 33 hours (all depending on connections).
International airports: *Juliana (SXM),* 15km (9.5 miles) west of Philipsburg, receives regular scheduled flights from other Caribbean islands, the USA and Europe. There are good bus services to Philipsburg and taxis are available.
Esperance (SFG) in the French sector is smaller and not equipped for jets.
Departure tax: US$10 for all international departures. US$5 for flights within the Caribbean islands. Transit passengers and children under two years of age are exempt.
SEA: St Maarten is a leading port of call for cruise liners. Cruises operated by *Holland America, Cunard, Prince's Cruise* and *Royal Viking* regularly stop at Philipsburg.

TRAVEL - Internal

SEA: Small boats may be chartered for fishing trips, scuba diving, water-skiing or visits to neighbouring islands.
ROAD: Most roads are good. Traffic drives on the right.
Taxi: There are good services on the island running from the airport, main hotels and towns. **Car hire:** There are plenty of car hire firms in the city and at the airport. Chauffeur-driven cars are also available.
Documentation: A national driving licence is acceptable.

ACCOMMODATION

HOTELS: St Maarten has long been a popular holiday destination and is well prepared for the year-round onrush, with over 40 hotels offering a total of nearly 9000 beds – more than 500 to be found in one hotel, the Mullet Bay Resort by the airport. This and other luxury hotels are equipped with everything a visitor could ever need, from casinos to beauty parlours, and have extensive watersports facilities on the premises; even modest beachside establishments usually have their own swimming pool, restaurant and a few skis to lend. A government tax of 5% is levied on all hotel bills and many hotels add a 10-15% service charge. Some even add a further 10% as an energy surcharge. Further information about hotels is available from the St Maarten Hotel & Tourism Association, PO Box 486, Promenade 14, Philipsburg. Tel: (5) 23133. Telex: 8014.
GUEST-HOUSES: Several guest-houses cater for the less demanding; apartments may be rented.

RESORTS & EXCURSIONS

The most prominent physical feature in St Maarten is the thickly wooded *Mt Flagstaff,* an extinct volcano, but the most important is undoubtedly the excellent beach that follows the south and west coasts. Beach activities and shopping at duty-free centres satisfy most tourists but there are several places of interest for the more enterprising visitor.
Philipsburg, the only town of any size, is situated on a sand bar that separates *Great Salt Pond,* an *étang* or salt marsh, from the ocean. The entire town consists of two streets, Voorstraat (Front Street) and Achterstraat (Back Street), running the length of the isthmus and joined by short, narrow alleys. Land has been reclaimed from the marsh for the construction of a ring road; local wits have suggested that this should be called Nieuwstraat (New Street) to preserve a Dutch feel of the place. Indeed, many buildings do date back to the early colonial era, and despite the multitude of duty-free shops, Philipsburg retains a predominantly colonial atmosphere. Worth seeing are its nine shingled churches and the *Queen Wilhelmina Golden Jubilee Monument.* Nearby is *Fort Amsterdam,* dating from the time of the earliest settlers. Inland are the picturesque ruins of several plantation mansions, set in the wooded hills around Mount Flagstaff, and the *Border Monument,* celebrating 300 years of cooperation between the French and the Dutch. Across the border (no passports are required) is the charming market town of **Marigot.**
EXCURSIONS: Small boats are available for various watersports and fishing.

SOCIAL PROFILE

FOOD & DRINK: St Maarten's cuisine is as varied as its history, combining Dutch, French, English, Creole and, more recently, international, influences. Seafood is,

of course, a speciality. **Drink:** Duty on alcohol (and other goods) is low and prices in St Maarten are as cheap as duty-free havens elsewhere. Most well-known brands are available.

NIGHTLIFE: Many of the restaurants and bars have live entertainment and dancing until the early hours. All the large hotels have casinos.

SHOPPING: There is a good range of high quality duty-free shopping available in Philipsburg. **Shopping hours:** 0800-1200 and 1400-1800 Monday to Saturday.

SPORT: Most large hotels have equipment for the full range of **watersports** – snorkelling, scuba diving, water-skiing, windsurfing and sailing – and most have their own swimming pools and **tennis** courts. There is a **golf** course at the Sheraton Mullet Bay Resort.

SPECIAL EVENTS: *Carnival*, which commences in mid-April, lasts for three weeks, and finishes spectacularly with the burning of King Moui-Moui. Light-hearted races for prizes take place monthly, and each year there is a relay race in which the tussle for the island between the French and the Dutch is re-enacted. In February each year a regatta is held.

SOCIAL CONVENTIONS: Dutch customs are still important throughout the Netherlands Antilles, but tourism has brought increasing American influences and St Maarten is perhaps more easy-going than the southern islands. Dress is casual and lightweight cottons are advised, but it is common to dress up in the evening. **Tipping:** Hotel bills always include a government tax of 5% and often a service charge of 10-15%. Elsewhere, 10-15% is acceptable for doormen, waiters and bar staff. Taxi drivers do not expect a tip.

BUSINESS PROFILE

ECONOMY: During its time as a Dutch colony, sugar-cane and livestock were the major products, despite the fact that the poor soil and lack of rain made these

activities somewhat unprofitable. With the end of slavery in 1863, resulting in the breakdown of the plantation system, these activities declined as many ex-slaves left the island to look for other work. The island had a brief period as a major exporter of salt to the USA and neighbouring islands from the rich deposits found in the Great Salt Pond near Philipsburg, but by 1949 this industry had also ended and a further exodus of the population took place. Since then the island has resorted to subsistence farming and fishing, making tourism its major emphasis. It now totally dominates the economy: 70% of all visitors to the Netherlands Antilles visit St Maarten, resulting in over 900,000 tourists annually. Further investment in tourist infrastructure is planned, including a new major port capable of docking eight cruise ships simultaneously. Government service provides one of the few alternative sources of employment.

BUSINESS: Formality in business is expected in most of the Netherlands Antilles and lightweight tropical suits should be worn. Appointments should be made in advance and punctuality is taken very seriously. **Office hours:** 0800-1200 and 1330-1630 Monday to Friday.

COMMERCIAL INFORMATION: The following organisation can offer advice: St Maarten Chamber of Commerce and Industry, PO Box 454, Walter Nisbeth Road, Philipsburg. Tel: (5) 23590. Fax: (5) 23512. Telex: 8063.

CLIMATE

Hot but tempered by cooling trade winds. The annual mean temperature is 27°C, varying by no more than two or three degrees throughout the year; average rainfall is 1772mm.

Required clothing: Tropicals and cottons are worn throughout the year. Umbrellas or light waterproofs are advisable.

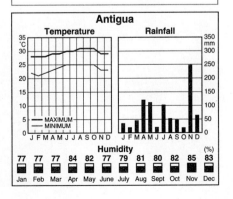

Antigua — Temperature / Rainfall / Humidity

	Jan	Feb	Mar	Apr	May	June	July	Aug	Sept	Oct	Nov	Dec
Humidity (%)	77	77	77	84	82	77	79	81	80	82	85	83

St Vincent & The Grenadines

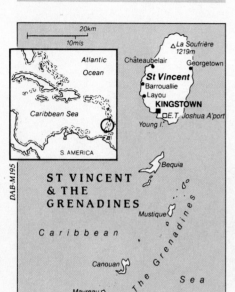

Yacht chartering in St Vincent & The Grenadines

Location: Eastern Caribbean, Windward Islands.

St Vincent & the Grenadines Department of Tourism
PO Box 834, Bay Street, Kingstown, St Vincent
Tel: (45) 71502. Fax: (45) 62610.
High Commission for Eastern Caribbean States
10 Kensington Court, London W8 5DL
Tel: (0171) 937 9522. Fax: (0171) 937 5514.
Opening hours: 0930-1730 Monday to Friday. *Visa Section*: 0930-1300 and 1400-1530 Monday to Thursday, 0930-1300 and 1400-1500 Friday.
St Vincent & the Grenadines Tourist Office
Address as for High Commission
Tel: (0171) 937 6570. Fax: (0171) 937 3611. Opening hours: 1000-1730 Monday to Friday.
British High Commission
PO Box 132, Granby Street, Kingstown, St Vincent
Tel: (45) 71701/2. Fax: (45) 62750. Telex: 7516 (a/b UKREP SVT VQ).
Embassy of St Vincent & the Grenadines
Suite 102, 1717 Massachusetts Avenue, NW, Washington, DC 20036
Tel: (202) 462 7806 *or* 462 7846. Fax: (202) 462 7807.
St Vincent & the Grenadines Tourist Office
21st Floor, 801 Second Avenue, New York, NY 10017
Tel: (212) 687 4981. Fax: (212) 949 5946.
St Vincent & the Grenadines Consulate
210 Shephard Avenue East, Willowdale, Ontario, M2N 3A9
Tel: (416) 222 0745. Fax: (416) 222 3830.

St Vincent & the Grenadines Tourism Office
32 Park Road, Toronto, Ontario N4W 2N4
Tel: (416) 924 5796. Fax: (416) 924 5844.
The Canadian High Commission in Bridgetown deals with enquiries relating to St Vincent & the Grenadines (see *Barbados* earlier in this book).

AREA: St Vincent: 344 sq km (133 sq miles).
Grenadines: 45.3 sq km (16.7 sq miles). **Total:** 389.3 sq km (150.3 sq miles).
POPULATION: 107,598 (1991).
POPULATION DENSITY: 312.8 per sq km.
CAPITAL: Kingstown. **Population:** 15,670 (1991).
GEOGRAPHY: St Vincent & the Grenadines make up part of the Windward Islands and lie south of St Lucia. St Vincent, like all the Windwards, is volcanic and mountainous with luxuriant vegetation and black sand beaches. The highest peak of St Vincent, *La Soufrière* (1219m/4000ft), is volcanic, and deep down in the crater is a lake. The 'tail' of the Comet of St Vincent (the Grenadines) is a string of islands and cays that splays south from Bequia (pronounced Beck-Way), Petit Nevis, Isle à Quatre and Pigeon Island to Battowia, Baliceaux, Mustique, Petit Mustique, Savan, Canouan, Petit Canouan, Mayreau and the Tobago Cays, Union Island, Palm Island and Petit St Vincent. All of the Grenadines are famous for their white beaches, clear waters and verdant scenery.
LANGUAGE: English.
RELIGION: Roman Catholic, Anglican, Methodist and other Christian denominations.
TIME: GMT - 4.
ELECTRICITY: 220/240 volts AC, 50Hz.
COMMUNICATIONS: Telephone: IDD is available. Country code: 1 809. Outgoing international code: 0.
Fax: Faxes can be sent from most hotels.
Telex/telegram: Facilities are limited to main towns and hotels. **Post:** Airmail to Western Europe takes up to two weeks. Post office hours: 0830-1500 Monday to Friday, 0830-1130 Saturday. **Press:** All newspapers are in

English and are published weekly. The most popular
papers are *The Vincentian* and *The News*.
**BBC World Service and Voice of America
frequencies:** From time to time these change. See the
section *How to Use this Book* for more information.
BBC:

MHz	17.84	15.22	9.915	5.975

Voice of America:

MHz	15.12	11.60	9.455	6.130

PASSPORT/VISA

Regulations and requirements may be subject to change at short notice, and you are advised to contact the appropriate diplomatic or consular authority before finalising travel arrangements. Details of these may be found at the head of this country's entry. Any numbers in the chart refer to the footnotes below.

	Passport Required?	Visa Required?	Return Ticket Required?
Full British	Yes	No	Yes
BVP	Not valid/2	-	-
Australian	Yes	No	Yes
Canadian	Yes	No	Yes
USA	1	No	Yes
Other EU (As of 31/12/94)	Yes	No	Yes
Japanese	Yes	No	Yes

PASSPORTS: Valid passports required by all **[1]** except
nationals of the USA holding proof of identity with
photograph for a stay not exceeding 6 months.
British Visitors Passport: [2] Although the immigration
authorities of this country may in certain circumstances
accept British Visitors Passports for persons arriving for
holidays or unpaid business trips of up to 3 months,
travellers are reminded that no formal agreement exists
and the situation may, therefore, change at short notice.
In addition, UK nationals using a BVP and returning to
the UK from a country with which no such formal
agreement exists may be subject to delays and
interrogation by UK immigration.
VISAS: Not required. Length of stay is determined by
immigration authority on arrival, if necessary.
Temporary residence: Refer applications or enquiries to
the Tourism Department, Embassy or High Commission
(addresses at top of entry) or to the Prime Minister's
Office in Kingstown.

MONEY

Currency: Eastern Caribbean Dollar (EC$) = 100 cents.
Notes are in denominations of EC$100, 50, 20, 10, 5 and
1. Coins are in denominations of EC$1, and 50, 25, 10, 5,
2 and 1 cents.
Credit cards: All major credit cards are widely accepted.
Check with your credit card company for details of
merchant acceptability and other services which may be
available.
Exchange rate indicators: The following figures are
included as a guide to the movements of the Eastern
Caribbean Dollar against Sterling and the US Dollar:

Date:	Oct '92	Sep '93	Jan '94	Jan '95
£1.00=	4.27	4.13	4.00	4.22
$1.00=	*2.70	*2.70	*2.70	*2.70

Note [*]: The Eastern Caribbean Dollar is tied to the US
Dollar.
Currency restrictions: There are no currency
restrictions. The import and export of travellers cheques
and other currencies is unlimited. Free import of local
currency is subject to declaration.
Banking hours: 0800-1300/1500 Monday to Friday. The
bank at *E T Joshua Airport* opens 0700-1700 Monday to
Saturday with additional extensions during the major
festivals.

DUTY FREE

The following items may be imported into St Vincent &
the Grenadines without incurring customs duty:

200 cigarettes or 50 cigars or 225g of tobacco; 1.136
litres of alcoholic beverage.

PUBLIC HOLIDAYS

Jan 1 '95 New Year's Day. **Jan 22** St Vincent & the
Grenadines Day. **Apr 14** Good Friday. **Apr 17** Easter
Monday. **May 1** Labour Day/Fisherman's Day. **Jun 5**
Whit Monday. **Jul 10** CARICOM Day. **Jul 11** Carnival
Tuesday. **Aug 7** August Monday. **Oct 27** Independence
Day. **Dec 25** Christmas Day. **Dec 26** Boxing Day. **Jan 1
'96** New Year's Day. **Jan 22** St Vincent & the
Grenadines Day. **Apr 5** Good Friday. **Apr 8** Easter
Monday.

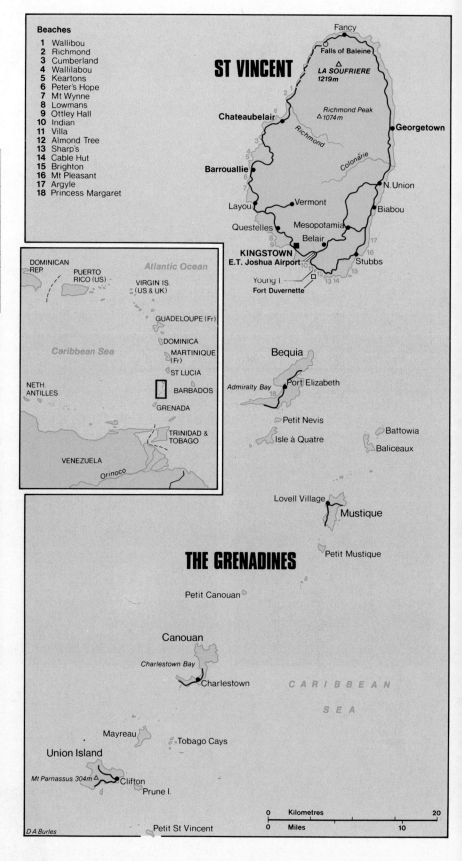

Beaches
1. Wallibou
2. Richmond
3. Cumberland
4. Wallilabou
5. Keartons
6. Peter's Hope
7. Mt Wynne
8. Lowmans
9. Ottley Hall
10. Indian
11. Villa
12. Almond Tree
13. Sharp's
14. Cable Hut
15. Brighton
16. Mt Pleasant
17. Argyle
18. Princess Margaret

HEALTH

Regulations and requirements may be subject to change at short notice, and you are advised to contact your doctor well in advance of your intended date of departure. Any numbers in the chart refer to the footnotes below.

	Special Precautions?	Certificate Required?
Yellow Fever	No	1
Cholera	No	No
Typhoid & Polio	Yes	-
Malaria	No	-
Food & Drink		2

[1]: A yellow fever vaccination certificate is required from travellers over one year of age arriving from infected areas.

[2]: Mains water is normally chlorinated, and whilst relatively safe, may cause mild abdominal upsets. Bottled water is available. Milk is pasteurised and dairy products are safe for consumption. Local meat, poultry, seafood, fruit and vegetables are generally considered safe to eat. **Health care:** Health insurance is recommended. There is one large hospital, the Kingstown General Hospital, augmented by a further 30 or so state-run clinics and dispensaries.

TRAVEL - International

AIR: The main airline to serve St Vincent & the Grenadines is *LIAT (LI)* (handled by *British Airways*). *Mustique Airways* and *Aero Services* run services from Barbados and *Air Martinique* runs from the French West Indies.

Approximate flight times: From St Vincent to *London* (via Barbados) is 9 hours, to *Los Angeles* is 9 hours, to *New York* is 5 hours and to *Singapore* is 33 hours.

International airport: *E T Joshua (SVD)* is 3km (2 miles) from Kingstown. Buses and taxis go from the airport to the city. There are standard fares to a number of major hotels throughout the island. There are also small airports on Bequia, Union Island, Canouan and Mustique for light aircraft.

Departure tax: EC$20 on all international departures.

SEA: Kingstown and some of the Grenadines are ports of call for a number of cruise lines: *CIC, Epirotiki, Paquet Cruises, Hapag Lloyd* and *Princess Cruises,* for example. Some lines also put in at one or other of the Grenadine Islands. Smaller boats ply between the islands, especially to and from Barbados.

TRAVEL - Internal

AIR: Local and charter services are available. Small planes can be chartered for inter-island travel. *Aero Services, Mustique Air* and *Air Martinique* run regular services to Mustique, Canouan and Union Island.

SEA: Yacht chartering is easily arranged and one of the best ways to explore the Grenadines. Yachts can be hired locally, with or without crew. There is a regular service to Bequia, Mustique, Canouan and Union Island from St Vincent. A mail boat runs twice-weekly through the Grenadines. The Tourist Office can help with all details.

ROAD: Traffic drives on the left. **Bus:** Services run regularly throughout St Vincent. The buses are open-air and brightly coloured. Small minibuses run a shared *route-taxi* service with a standard fare anywhere along the route. Public transport is crowded but cheap. **Taxi:** These are shared and charge standard rates (fixed by the Government). A list is available from the Tourist Board. **Car hire:** Easily arranged through a number of national and international firms. **Documentation:** A local driving licence is essential and can be obtained on presentation of a valid national or international licence either at the airport or at the police station in Bay Street, Kingstown, or at the Licensing Authority in Halifax Street, Kingstown (opening hours: 0900-1500 Monday to Friday). Fee: EC$40.

ACCOMMODATION

From casual and economical to elegant and exclusive, lodgings in St Vincent & the Grenadines offer something for every taste and budget. The choice ranges from a rustic cottage on the beach or a historic country hotel in the mountains, to a luxury resort with an island to itself. Young Island, a small island off the south coast of St Vincent, with a cottage community of separate huts including all modern facilities, is widely considered to be the closest place to paradise in the whole of the Caribbean. All hotels are small and stress personal service. A list of rates is available from the St Vincent Department of Tourism and all its overseas offices. All rooms are subject to a 7% hotel tax.

Grading: Many hotels in the Caribbean offer accommodation according to one of a number of plans: **FAP** (Full American Plan): room and all meals supplied (including afternoon tea, supper, etc); **AP** (American Plan): room and three meals supplied; **MAP** (Modified American Plan): breakfast and dinner included with the price of the room plus, in some places, British-style afternoon tea; **CP** (Continental Plan): room and breakfast only; **EP** (European Plan): room only. For further information regarding accommodation, contact the St Vincent & the Grenadines Hotel Association, PO Box 834, Kingstown. Tel: (45) 71072. Fax: (45) 74174.

A natural mooring spot

RESORTS & EXCURSIONS

St Vincent

St Vincent is a lush, volcanic island of steep mountain ridges, valleys and waterfalls. The rugged eastern coast is lined with cliffs and rocky shores, while the western coastline dips sharply down to black- and gold-sand beaches. To the north, *La Soufrière,* St Vincent's volcano, rises to 1219m (4000ft). St Vincent has frequent rains and rich volcanic soil, which produces an abundance of fruit, vegetables and spices. The interior flatlands and valleys are thickly planted with coconuts, bananas, breadfruit, nutmeg and arrowroot.

Kingstown, capital of St Vincent, is a lively port and market town on the southern coast. The town contains 12 small blocks with a variety of shops and a busy dock area which is the centre of commerce for the islands. The Saturday morning market, comprising many stalls piled high with fresh fruit and vegetables, brings everyone to town. In the centre of Kingstown, *St Mary's Roman Catholic Cathedral,* built of grey stone, is a graceful combination of several European architectural styles displaying Romanesque arches, Gothic spires and Moorish ornamentation. The ruins of *Fort Charlotte* overlook a 180m (590ft) ridge north of town and offer a magnificent southward view of the Grenadines. The oldest *Botanical Gardens* in the Western hemisphere occupy 20 acres to the north of Kingstown and contain a display of tropical trees, blossoms and plants, including a breadfruit tree descended from the original one brought to the island in 1765 by Captain Bligh. Within the gardens there is also an extensive collection of ancient stone artefacts.

The *Falls of Baleine,* at the northern tip of St Vincent, are accessible only by boat. The 18m (59ft) freshwater falls stream from volcanic slopes and form a series of shallow pools at the base. A challenging hike for the more adventurous is the just over 5km (3 miles) journey up *La Soufrière,* St Vincent's northern volcano which affords a wonderful bird's-eye view of the crater and its islands, all of St Vincent and the Caribbean.

Strung along the western coast are the fishing villages of **Questelles, Layou, Barrouallie** and **Châteaubelair,** all of which have charming pastel-coloured cottages and excellent black-sand beaches from which fishermen set out daily in small brightly painted boats.

Young Island: Only 180m (590ft) off St Vincent, Young Island rises from the sea, a 25-acre mountain blanketed with tropical foliage and blossoms. Young Island provides an excellent view of the procession of yachts sailing into the harbour of St Vincent. The entire island comprises one resort called 'Young Island Resort', which consists of 29 rustic cottages set on the beaches and

wide shallows and coral. The island stretches over 11 sq km (7.9 sq miles) and has two hotels: the *Tamarind Beach Hotel* and *Canouan Beach Hotel*. There are also two guest-houses: *Villa Le Bijou* and the *Anchor Inn*.

Tobago Cays: South of Canouan are the Tobago Cays, numerous islets and coves guarded by some of the most spectacular coral reefs in the world. Visitors can sail, snorkel and beachcomb in complete seclusion. The only way to get here is by chartered yacht.

Mayreau: East of the Cays is Mayreau, one of the smaller Grenadines, which is a privately-owned island with few residents. *Salt Whistle Bay Resort*, the only hotel, welcomes guests and can be reached by boat from Union Island.

Union Island: *Mount Parnassus* on Union Island soars 275m (900ft) from the sea – guarding the entrance to the southern Grenadines. The 2100-acre mountainous island is fringed by superb beaches and is the stopping-off point for yachtsmen and visitors heading to some of the smaller Grenadines. *Clifton Harbour*, the main town, is small and commercial. There are several beachfront inns with a relaxed atmosphere.

Palm Island: The 110-acre flat Palm Island acquired its name due to the graceful coconut palms that line the beaches – 8000 in all. This private island has been turned into a resort; the *Palm Island Beach Club*, made up of 20 beachfront stone cottages. Here it is possible to dine in the open air and all watersports take place off the wide, white shores.

Petit St Vincent: The southernmost Grenadine governed by St Vincent is Petit St Vincent, a 113-acre resort set on beaches. The luxuriant foliage and the 22 villas of Petit St Vincent offer guests the ultimate luxury and seclusion, including private patios and seaside vistas. Visitors gather for meals in beachfront pavilions and the ambience is carefree and festive.

SOCIAL PROFILE

FOOD & DRINK: St Vincent is one of the few islands where good West Indian cuisine can almost always be enjoyed in hotels. Specialities include *red snapper*, kingfish, *lambi* (a sea shellfish), *calaloo* soup, *souse* (a sauce made from pigs' foot) and sea-moss drink. In addition there is plenty of fresh fruit, vegetables and seafoods on offer. Lobster is available in season. **Drink:** Vincentian beer and rum, a major ingredient in punch and cocktails, are the local drinks, as are a wide variety of local exotic fruit juices.

NIGHTLIFE: Most evening events take place in hotels and it is best to ask at individual hotels for a calendar of events. The Aquatic Club is now operated by Stilson ('Stilly') Fraser as a nightclub. The Attic in Kingstown features a wide variety of music during the week and live entertainment on weekends. There is one casino on the island, at Peniston, on the Leeward side.

SHOPPING: Designs on sea-island cottons can be bought and made up into clothes within two or three days at a number of shops. Handicrafts and all varieties of straw-made items, grass rugs and other souvenirs can be bought at a number of workshops and giftshops. **Shopping hours:** 0800-1200 and 1300-1600 Monday to Friday, 0800-1200 Saturday.

SPORT: Sailing and all kinds of **watersports** are a major pastime. Various boats head south regularly through the Grenadines. For the novice, professionals are available to handle the sails. Visitors can, of course, bring their own yacht, or charter one, either with or without crew. Yachts are available for charter from The Lagoon Marina and Hotel (tel: (45) 84308; fax: (45) 74716 or 89255) and Frangipani Yacht Services (tel: (45) 83244; fax: (45) 83824). Other watersports, particularly **scuba diving**, can be arranged through some hotels. **Fishing:** Deep-sea fishing excursions are available. **Spectator sports:** Cricket and football are very popular. **Tennis:** Courts are available at Kingstown Tennis Club and facilities may also be arranged through hotels. **Horseriding:** Can be arranged by certain hotels.

SPECIAL EVENTS: The following major events occur annually in St Vincent & the Grenadines:
Mar '95 *National Music Festival*. **Mar 13-19** *National Heroes Week*. **May 22-28** *National Heritage Week*. **Apr 13-17** *Easter Regatta Bequia/Easterval*, Union Island. **Apr 29-30** *Texaco National Championship*. **May 22-28** *National Trust Heritage Week*. **May 30** *Guiness Half Marathon/10k Road Race*. **Jun 31-Jul 11** *Carnival Period* **[1]**. **Aug 1-7** *Canouan Regatta* **[2]**. **Sep 1-30** *National Dance Festival*. **Sep 17** *Kentucky Fried Chicken Round-D-Town Relay*. **Oct 1-31** *National Drama Festival*. **Nov 1-31** *Schools Drama Festival*. **Dec 14-24** *Nine Mornings Festival* **[3]**.
Notes: **[1]** *St Vincent & the Grenadines Carnival* (first week in July) is one of the largest in the West Indies and lasts for at least ten days, ending with the Street Parade. The Festival exposes the islands' artistic talents in music, brass bands, steel and calypso bands, costume design,

hillsides. There is a freshwater pool and tennis courts hidden in the hilltop trees. Adjoining Young Island is the 18th-century *Fort Duvernette,* sculpted from an enormous rock, towering 60m (200ft) above the sea. A ferry, a smaller version of the *African Queen,* runs regularly between Young Island and St Vincent.

The Grenadines

Bequia: This island lies 14km (9 miles) south of St Vincent and is the largest of the Grenadines, measuring 18 sq km (7 sq miles). Little changed by time, it is an island on which life is completely oriented to the sea. It can be reached by boat, although an airport, *J F Mitchell,* was opened in May 1992. Its seclusion has ensured it retained its age-old traditions of boat building and fishing. In the marine park, spearfishing, snares and nets are prohibited. The islanders themselves are the world's last hand-harpooners and their activities do not affect marine stocks, unlike the mechanised fishing of some fleets. The centre of the island is hilly and forested, providing a dramatic backdrop to the bays and beaches. *Admiralty Bay,* the island's natural harbour, is a favourite anchoring spot for yachtsmen from all over the world, and here visitors can watch men building their boats by hand on the shores. The attractive region around *Lower Bay* has good opportunities for swimming and other watersports.

The quaint waterfront of **Port Elizabeth** is lined with bars, restaurants and craft shops. Bequia is encircled by gold-sand beaches, many of which disappear into coves, excellent for sailing, scuba diving and snorkelling. Lodgings vary from luxurious resort cottages to small, simple West Indian inns. Much of the nightlife centres on the hotels and beachside barbecues, invariably accompanied by a steel band.

Mustique: Heading south, the next port of call is Mustique, a gem in the ocean only taking up 4.5 sq km (2 sq miles). Mustique is privately owned, with a landscape as gentle as its lifestyle – verdent hills roll into soft white-sand beaches and turquoise waters. This island has long been a hiding place for the rich and famous, including Princess Margaret and other members of the British Royal Family. A sprawling 18th-century plantation house has been converted into the island's only resort. Elegant accommodation is available in several stone houses, widely separated for seclusion. The public rooms of the *Main House* are beautifully decorated with antiques and afternoon tea is served daily on the veranda. There is a hilltop swimming pool with a magnificent panorama, as well as tennis, horseriding, motorcycling and all watersports.

Canouan: The island claims some of the best beaches in the Caribbean – long stretches of powder-white sands,

folk dances and calypso dances. The street parades, featuring costumed bands with as many as ten sections, depict scenes from mythology and folklore, as well as contemporary and futuristic themes. A Carnival King and Queen as well as a Calypso King will be chosen. The greatest experience is *playing mas* (participating in one of the costumed bands). **[2]** *Canouan Annual Yacht Races* (beginning of August) – activities include a fishing competition, a cricket match, 'Greasy Pig', donkey relay races, a Queen and Calypso competition, crab races and various regattas. **[3]** *Nine Mornings* (December) – nine mornings before Christmas people parade through the streets of Kingstown long before dawn. The most recent addition to St Vincent's unique Christmas celebration is the organised dances held in St Vincent's dance halls on each of the nine mornings.

SOCIAL CONVENTIONS: The Vincentians are fun-loving and easy-going people, and the informal and relaxed lifestyle combines many English influences with West Indian. The Saturday market in Kingstown is bustling with life seemingly involving all islanders. All visitors are made welcome and casual wear is widely acceptable. Refrain, however, from wearing beachwear or mini shorts on the streets or while shopping. **Tipping:** 10-15% service added to the bill. Taxi drivers do not expect tips.

BUSINESS PROFILE

ECONOMY: St Vincent is poor by eastern Caribbean standards, with agriculture being the main source of income and export earnings. Bananas are the main crop and St Vincent is also the world's leading producer of arrowroot; other exotic fruit, vegetables and root crops also make a contribution to the economy. The Single European Market, introduced in 1992, is regarded as a potentially serious threat to St Vincent's export markets. Fishing has also been revitalised and a processing complex built. Tourism is little-developed by regional standards and its growth has been hampered by the lack of suitable infrastructure. Apart from the USA and the UK, St Vincent has important trade links with Trinidad & Tobago, Barbados and St Lucia.

BUSINESS: Short- or long-sleeved shirt and tie or a safari suit are suitable for most business visits.

Government office hours: These vary from department to department but generally 0800-1615 Monday to Friday, with some opening for a few hours Saturday morning.

COMMERCIAL INFORMATION: The following organisation can offer advice: St Vincent & The Grenadines Chamber of Industry and Commerce, PO Box 134, Halifax Street, Kingstown. Tel: (45) 71464. Fax: (45) 62944.

CONFERENCE/CONVENTIONS: For information, contact the St Vincent & the Grenadines Department of Tourism (for address, see top of entry).

CLIMATE

Tropical, with trade winds tempering the hottest months, June and July.

Required clothing: Lightweights and waterproofs.

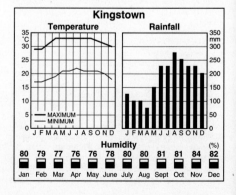

San Marino

Location: Western Europe; northeastern part of the Italian peninsula.

Ufficio di Stato per il Turismo
Palazzo del Turismo, Contrada Omagnano 20, 47031
Republicca di San Marino
Tel: 882 400. Fax: 990 388. Telex: 282.
Secretariat of State for Foreign and Political Affairs
Palazzo Begni, Republicca di San Marino
Tel: 882 209. Fax: 992 018.
British Consulate
Palazzo Castelbarco, Lungarno Corsini 2, 50123
Florence, Italy
Tel: (55) 212 594 *or* 284 133. Fax: (55) 219 112.
The Canadian Embassy in Rome deals with enquiries relating to San Marino (see *Italy* earlier in this book).
Consulate General of San Marino
27 McNider Avenue, Montréal, Québec H2V 3X4
Tel: (514) 871 3838. Fax: (514) 876 4217.
Consulate in: Toronto.

AREA: 60.5 sq km (23.4 sq miles).
POPULATION: 23,719 (1992).
POPULATION DENSITY: 392 per sq km.
CAPITAL: San Marino. **Population:** 4185 (1990 estimate).
GEOGRAPHY: San Marino is a tiny state bordered by the Italian regions of Emilia-Romagna to the north and east and Marche to the south and west. The landscape is for the most part green with rolling hills, dominated by the three peaks of Mount Titano. Within San Marino lie the capital of the same name and eight villages.
LANGUAGE: Italian.
RELIGION: Roman Catholic.
TIME: GMT + 1 (GMT + 2 from last Sunday in March to Saturday before last Sunday in September).
ELECTRICITY: 220 volts AC, 50Hz.
COMMUNICATIONS: Telephone: IDD is available. Country code: 39 549. There are no area codes. Outgoing international code: 00. **Telex/telegram:** Telex country code: 505 1 SO. Facilities are available in main hotels. **Post:** Good postal service. Airmail to European destinations takes approximately four days. *Poste Restante* facilities are available at all post offices. **Press:** No daily newspapers are published in San Marino; Italian

newspapers are widely available.
BBC World Service and Voice of America frequencies: From time to time these change. See the section *How to Use this Book* for more information.
BBC:

MHz	17.64	15.07	12.09	7.325

A service is also available on 648kHz and 198kHz (0100-0500 GMT).
Voice of America:

MHz	11.97	9.670	6.040	5.995

PASSPORT/VISA

Travellers will necessarily enter San Marino from Italy. As there are no frontier formalities imposed, any person visiting San Marino must comply with Italian passport/visa regulations; refer to the *Passport/Visa* section in the *Italy* entry, earlier in this book.

MONEY

Currency: Italian Lira (Lit). Notes are in denominations of Lit500,000, 100,000, 50,000, 20,000, 10,000, 5000, 2000 and 1000. Coins are in denominations of Lit1000, 500, 200, 100, 50, 20, 10 and 5.
Currency exchange: Many UK banks offer differing exchange rates depending on the denominations of Italian currency being bought or sold. Check with banks for details and current rates.
Exchange rate indicators: The following figures are included as a guide to the movements of the Lira against Sterling and the US Dollar:

Date:	Oct '92	Sep '93	Jan '94	Jan '95
£1.00=	2108	2380	2533	2538
$1.00=	1329	1559	1712	1622

Note: For further information, see the *Money* section in the *Italy* entry earlier in this book.

DUTY FREE

Visitors must comply with Italian customs regulations; see the relevant *Italy* section in the *World Travel Guide*.

PUBLIC HOLIDAYS

Jan 1 '95 New Year's Day. **Jan 6** Epiphany. **Feb 5** Liberation and St Agatha's Day. **Mar 25** Anniversary of the Arengo. **Apr 1** Captains Regent Investiture. **Apr 17** Easter Monday. **May 1** Labour Day. **Jun 15** Corpus Christi. **Jul 28** Anniversary of the Fall of Fascism. **Aug 15** Assumption. **Sep 3** San Marino Day and Republic Day. **Oct 1** Captains-Regent Investiture. **Nov 1** All Saints' Day. **Nov 2** Commemoration of the Dead. **Dec 8** Immaculate Conception. **Dec 25** Christmas. **Dec 26** St Stephen's Day. **Jan 1 '96** New Year's Day. **Jan 6** Epiphany. **Feb 5** Liberation and St Agatha's Day. **Mar 25** Anniversary of the Arengo. **Apr 1** Captain-Regent Investiture. **Apr 8** Easter Monday.

HEALTH

The health regulations and recommendations are the same as for Italy. See the *Health* section in the entry for *Italy*, earlier in this book.

TRAVEL

AIR: The Italian national airline is *Alitalia (AZ)*.
Approximate flight time: From London to Bologna/Rimini is 2 hours 30 minutes.
International airports: *Bologna (BLQ)* is 125km (78 miles) from San Marino and *Rimini (RMI)* is 27km (17 miles) from San Marino. Good bus services are available to San Marino.
RAIL: The nearest railhead is at Rimini. A funicular serves the capital and Borgo Maggiore. There are no internal railways.

ACCOMMODATION

All hotels in San Marino are comfortable and of a good standard. Every hotel allows special reductions for groups, children and large families. Full- and half-board arrangements are also available. For more information, contact the Ufficio di Stato per il Turismo (address at beginning of entry). **Grading:** Hotels in San Marino are classified in four categories, with 1/A category hotels at the luxury end of the market, 1/B category hotels being slightly more modest, and 2 and 3 category hotels for budget travellers.

RESORTS & EXCURSIONS

The whole of the centre of the city of San Marino is a perfectly preserved medieval square and there are also museums, galleries and various churches. The lower

cliffs of *Mount Titano* are capped with three fortified towers, linked by a system of walls and pathways that are accessible from the city below. The city itself is enclosed by three walls with numerous gateways, towers, ramparts, churches and medieval houses. Other places worth visiting are the *Government Palace;* the *Basilica;* the *State Museum* and *Art Gallery; St Francis' Church,* which also has a museum and art gallery; the *Capuccin Friars Church of St Quirino;* and the *Exhibition of San Marino Handicrafts.*
Eight villages are scattered around the countryside outside the capital. Places of interest include *Malatesta Castle* at **Serravalle;** the modern church and the stamp and coin museum at **Borgo Maggiore;** the church and convent at **Valdragone;** and the fort at **Pennarossa.** Ancient ruins can be seen throughout the Republic. Attractions outside the city and villages include *Mount Titano,* pine woods, springs, streams, lakes and hunting and fishing reserves. There is easy access to Italian beaches on the Adriatic coast nearby.

SOCIAL PROFILE

FOOD & DRINK: Italian cuisine is widely available. Popular first courses include *tortellini, passatelle* (broth), *tagliatelle, lasagne, ravioli, cannelloni* and *arbalester's passaduri* (a local speciality). Main dishes include roast rabbit with fennel, devilled chicken, quails, veal escalopes, Bolognese veal cutlets, assorted 'mouthfuls' (three types of tender meat) and Roman veal escalopes. San Marino tart and *caccietello* (similar to crême caramel) may be ordered for desert. There is a wide selection of restaurants, both in the capital and in the outlying villages. Table service is customary, although a few are self-service. **Drink:** San Marino muscat, *briancele, albana* and *sangiovese* are all good quality wines produced locally. *Mistra* is the local liqueur.
NIGHTLIFE: Reviews, festivals and theatrical productions are popular.
SHOPPING: Special purchases include locally-made ceramics; stamps and coins bought from the State Numismatic & Philatelic Office, local wines and liqueurs, local jewellery, playing cards and cigarettes. **Shopping hours:** 0830-1300 and 1530-1930 Monday to Saturday.
SPORT: There are facilities for **tennis, roller skating, basketball, gymnastics, hunting, fishing, swimming** and **bowls.** There is a sports club at Serraville with modern equipment and there are numerous tennis courts and **football** pitches throughout the Republic.
SOCIAL CONVENTIONS: Normal European courtesies and codes of conduct should be observed.
Tipping: Service charges are generally included in hotel bills. An extra tip is usual.

BUSINESS PROFILE

ECONOMY: The only agricultural product exported is wine. The other principal crops are wheat, barley, maize and olive oil. Other exports include woollen goods, furniture and ceramics. Tourism provides most of the Republic's income, with approximately three million visitors each year accounting for over 60% of the national income. An unusual source of revenue is postage stamps, which are produced several times a year, sold almost entirely to collectors and bring in 10% of the national income. Details of San Marino's external trade are included with those of Italy, with whom San Marino maintains a customs union.
BUSINESS: A suit is recommended and prior appointments are absolutely essential. Avoid making appointments early in the morning or straight after lunch. A knowledge of Italian is useful.

CLIMATE

Temperate. Moderate snow in winter, some brief showers in summer. The atmosphere is clean, typical of low mountain and hill country with sea breezes.
Required clothing: Light- to medium-weights and rainwear are required.

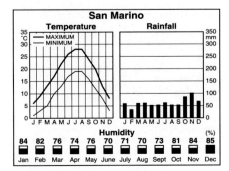

São Tomé e Príncipe

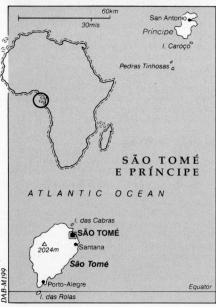

60km
30mis

San Antonio
Príncipe

I. Caroço

Pedras Tinhosas

SÃO TOMÉ
E PRÍNCIPE

ATLANTIC OCEAN

I. das Cabras
■ SÃO TOMÉ
Santana
2024m
São Tomé
Porto-Alegre
Equator
I. das Rolas

□ *international airport*

Location: West Africa, Gulf of Guinea.

Ministry of Foreign Affairs and Cooperation
CP 111, São Tomé, São Tomé e Príncipe
Tel: 21077. Fax: 22597. Telex: 211.
Honorary Consulate of the Democratic Republic of São Tomé e Príncipe
42 North Audley Street, London W1A 4PY
Tel: (0171) 499 1995. Fax: (0171) 629 6460. Telex:
262513. Opening hours: 0900-1730 Monday to Friday.
Embassy of the Democratic Republic of São Tomé e Príncipe
42 avenue Brugmann, B-1060 Brussels, Belgium
Tel: (2) 347 5375. Fax: (2) 347 5408. Telex: 65313.
British Consulate
c/o Hull Blythe (Angola) Ltd, BP 15, São Tomé, São Tomé e Príncipe
Telex: 220 (a/b HBALTD ST).
Embassy of the Democratic Republic of São Tomé e Príncipe
c/o The Permanent Mission of São Tomé e Príncipe to the United Nations, Suite 1504, 801 Second Avenue, New York, NY 10017
Tel: (212) 697 4211/2. Fax: (212) 687 8389 *or* 787 1173.
Consulate of the Democratic Republic of São Tomé e Príncipe
4068 Beaconsfield Avenue, Montréal, Québec H4A 2H3
Tel: (514) 484 2706.
The Canadian Embassy in Libreville deals with enquiries relating to São Tomé e Príncipe (see *Gabon* earlier in this book).

AREA: 1001 sq km (386.5 sq miles).
POPULATION: 117,504 (1991 estimate).
POPULATION DENSITY: 117.4 per sq km.
CAPITAL: São Tomé.
GEOGRAPHY: São Tomé e Príncipe comprises two main islands (São Tomé and Príncipe) and the islets Cabras, Gago Coutinho, Pedras Tinhosas and Rolas. These lie approximately 200km (120 miles) off the west coast of Gabon, in the Gulf of Guinea. The country is rugged and has a great deal of forest cover and few natural resources.
LANGUAGE: Portuguese and native dialects (Fôrro and Angolares). Some English is spoken, but French is more common.
RELIGION: Roman Catholic majority.
TIME: GMT.
ELECTRICITY: 220 volts AC.
COMMUNICATIONS: Telephone: Very limited IDD is available. Country code: 239. There are no area codes. All international calls must be booked through the operator. 45% of all local calls are placed through automatic exchanges. **Telex/telegram:** Facilities are available in the capital and main hotels. The telex code is ST. **Post:** Airmail to Europe takes up to two weeks.

Press: Newspapers are printed in Portuguese.
BBC World Service and Voice of America frequencies: From time to time these change. See the section *How to Use this Book* for more information.
BBC:

MHz	21.66	17.88	15.40	9.600

Voice of America:

MHz	21.49	15.60	9.525	6.035

PASSPORT/VISA

Regulations and requirements may be subject to change at short notice, and you are advised to contact the appropriate diplomatic or consular authority before finalising travel arrangements. Details of these may be found at the head of this country's entry. Any numbers in the chart refer to the footnotes below.

	Passport Required?	Visa Required?	Return Ticket Required?
Full British	Yes	Yes	Yes
BVP	Not valid	-	-
Australian	Yes	Yes	Yes
Canadian	Yes	Yes	Yes
USA	Yes	Yes	Yes
Other EU (As of 31/12/94)	Yes	Yes	Yes
Japanese	Yes	Yes	Yes

PASSPORTS: Valid passport required by all.
British Visitors Passport: Not accepted.
VISAS: Required by all. *Transit* visas are not required by those holding tickets with reserved seats and other documents for onward or return travel on the same day.
Validity: Enquire at Embassy.
Application requirements: (a) Fee of £35. (b) Cost of postage. (c) 2 passport-size photos.
Applications to: Consulate (or Consular section at Embassy). For addresses, see top of entry.
Working days required: 1.
Temporary residence: Enquire at Embassy.

MONEY

Currency: Dobra (Db) = 100 cêntimos. Notes are in denominations of Db1000, 500, 100 and 50. Coins are in denominations of Db20, 10, 5, 2 and 1, and 50 cêntimos.
Exchange rate indicators: The following figures are included as a guide to the movements of the Dobra against Sterling and the US Dollar:

Date:	Oct '92	Sep '93	Jan '94	Jan '95
£1.00=	379.56	367.30	354.48	1485.14
$1.00=	239.17	240.54	239.59	949.27

Currency restrictions: Free import and export of local and foreign currency, subject to declaration.
Banking hours: 0730-1130 Monday to Friday.

DUTY FREE

The following may be imported into São Tomé e Príncipe without incurring customs duty:
Reasonable quantities of tobacco products, alcohol (opened) and perfume (opened).

PUBLIC HOLIDAYS

Jan 1 '95 New Year's Day. **Feb 3** Commemoration of the 1953 Massacre. **Feb 28** Shrove Tuesday. **Apr 14** Good Friday. **Apr 17** Easter Monday. **May 1** Workers' Day. **May 25** Ascension. **Jun 15** Corpus Christi. **Jul 12** Independence Day. **Aug 15** Assumption. **Sep 30** Agricultural Nationalisation Day. **Nov 1** All Saints' Day. **Dec 21** Peoples' Popular Power Day. **Dec 25-26** Christmas. **Jan 1 '96** New Year's Day. **Feb 3** Commemoration of the 1953 Massacre. **Feb 20** Shrove Tuesday. **Apr 5** Good Friday. **Apr 8** Easter Monday.

HEALTH

Regulations and requirements may be subject to change at short notice, and you are advised to contact your doctor well in advance of your intended date of departure. Any numbers in the chart refer to the footnotes below.

	Special Precautions?	Certificate Required?
Yellow Fever	No	1
Cholera	Yes	2
Typhoid & Polio	Yes	-
Malaria	3	-
Food & Drink	4	-

[1]: A yellow fever vaccination certificate is required from travellers over one year of age arriving from all countries, except travellers arriving from a non-infected area and staying less than two weeks in the country. Travellers arriving from non-

endemic zones should note that vaccination is strongly recommended for travel outside the urban areas, even if an outbreak of the disease has not been reported and they would normally not require a vaccination certificate to enter the country.
[2]: Following WHO guidelines issued in 1973, a cholera vaccination certificate is not a condition of entry to São Tomé e Príncipe. However, cholera is a risk in this country and precautions are essential. Up-to-date advice should be sought before deciding whether these precautions should include vaccination, as medical opinion is divided over its effectiveness. See the *Health* section at the back of the book.
[3]: Malaria risk exists all year throughout the country. Chloroquine-resistance of the *falciparum* strain has been reported.
[4]: All water should be regarded as being potentially contaminated. Water used for drinking, brushing teeth or making ice should have first been boiled or otherwise sterilised. Milk is unpasteurised and should be boiled. Powdered or tinned milk is available and is advised, but make sure that it is reconstituted with pure water. Avoid dairy products which are likely to have been made from unboiled milk. Only eat well-cooked meat and fish, preferably served hot. Pork, salad and mayonnaise may carry increased risk. Vegetables should be cooked and fruit peeled.
Rabies is present. For those at high risk, vaccination before arrival should be considered. If you are bitten abroad, seek medical advice without delay. For more information, consult the *Health* section at the back of the book.
Bilharzia (schistosomiasis) is present. Avoid swimming and paddling in fresh water. Swimming pools which are well-chlorinated and maintained are safe.
Health care: Health insurance is essential. There are 16 hospitals and clinics and approximately 40 doctors.

TRAVEL - International

AIR: The national airline is *Air São Tomé*. It operates six flights weekly (except Wednesday) between São Tomé and Libreville (Gabon), where they connect with ingoing or outgoing long-haul flights to or from Europe. There are also scheduled flights from Portugal and Angola.
Approximate flight time: From London to São Tomé is 10 hours.
International airport: *São Tomé (TMS)*, 5.5km (3.5 miles) from the town.
Departure tax: US$20 per adult, payable in cash on departure for all international flights. US$10 must be paid for children and US$2 for infants.
SEA: The main port is São Tomé, but this is not deep-water and few international cruise lines or other passenger ships call there.

TRAVEL - Internal

AIR/SEA: There are three flights a week from São Tomé to Príncipe (flight time – 50 minutes) and a limited ferry service.
ROAD: Traffic drives on the right. There are over 280km (175 miles) of roads, although in general these are deteriorating. Some of them are asphalted around São Tomé town, but 4-wheel-drive vehicles are necessary to get further afield. There is a **bus** network, and **taxis** are also in operation. **Car hire** can be arranged through the Miramar Hotel (see below). **Documentation:** An International Driving Permit is required.

ACCOMMODATION

There are currently about ten hotels in the country, including the 50-room luxury establishment Miramar Hotel in the capital São Tomé, opened in 1986 to coincide with a campaign initiative to promote tourism. It has restaurants, a coffee shop, snack bar, swimming pool, duty-free shop, two bars, a swimming pool, tennis and squash courts, a snooker table, in-house video and satellite TV, a marina with facilities for watersports (including scuba diving) and fishing, as well as conference facilities for up to 200 delegates. The new Marlin Beach hotel is situated on one of the most beautiful beaches of São Tomé. It offers standard and first-class accommodation as well as a restaurant and a swimming pool. The Bom Bom Island Resort on the northern coast of Príncipe offers 25 first-class bungalows. Apart from the hotels there is also a chain of state-run inns, operated at more modest levels of comfort.

RESORTS & EXCURSIONS

The islands lie on an alignment of once-active volcanoes, with rugged landscapes, dense forests and virgin palm-fringed beaches. Still almost totally undiscovered by the tourist trade, indeed only open to tourists since 1987, these islands provide unspoiled beauty and isolation from the world now rarely found anywhere else. The history of the islands is dominated by the slave trade and slave-worked plantations. These plantations, now mostly nationalised, still remain a major feature of the landscape. The town of **São Tomé** is picturesque, with colonial Portuguese architecture and attractive parks. Excursions by car or boat and watersports can usually be arranged at the hotel.

SOCIAL PROFILE

FOOD & DRINK: There are several restaurants in the capital, augmented by a considerable number of more informal eating establishments patronised by the inhabitants. Reservations are nearly always required, even at the higher profile restaurants, not for lack of space but to allow the proprietor to obtain sufficient food in advance. Grilled fish and chicken are popular. Most dishes are highly spiced.
SOCIAL CONVENTIONS: The Portuguese influence is very strong. The people are friendly and courteous. Every greeting is accompanied by a handshake. Normal social courtesies should be observed. Alcohol is available and smoking is acceptable. **Tipping:** Not always welcomed.

BUSINESS PROFILE

ECONOMY: The economy is based on the export of agricultural products, mainly cocoa, palm oil, bananas, coffee and coconuts. This concentration on cash crops, most of which are exported, means the country has to import the bulk of its food requirements. Efforts to develop the fishing industry have not been particularly successful, as local fishers have had to compete against 'factory ships' from the CIS and Australia. The Government therefore decided to sell fishing rights in São Tomé's territorial waters to the countries which operate the big fleets. There is virtually no manufacturing industry apart from some food-processing plants and factories producing consumer items such as soap, textiles and beer. Portugal and Angola have a significant corner of the import market, while many exports are bought by The Netherlands.
BUSINESS: Bush jackets or safari suits are commonly worn and appointments are advised. Generally an informal atmosphere prevails. Business is conducted in Portuguese; a knowledge of French is also useful. **COMMERCIAL INFORMATION:** The Ministry of Foreign Affairs and Cooperation can offer advice (see address at top of entry).

CLIMATE

An equatorial climate with heavy rainfall, high temperatures and humidity. The south of the main island, being mountainous, is wetter than the north. The main dry season is from early June to late September. There is another dry season, the 'Pequenha Gravana', from the end of December to the start of February.
Required clothing: Tropicals and lightweight cottons throughout the year. Umbrellas or light waterproofs for the rainy season are advised.

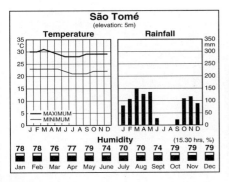

São Tomé
(elevation: 5m)

Temperature   Rainfall

Humidity   (15.30 hrs, %)

Jan	Feb	Mar	Apr	May	June	July	Aug	Sept	Oct	Nov	Dec
78	78	76	77	79	74	70	70	74	79	79	79

Saudi Arabia

□ *international airport*

1000km
500mls

Location: Middle East.

Saudi Hotels and Resort Areas Co (SHARACO)
PO Box 5500, Riyadh 11422, Saudi Arabia
Tel: (1) 465 7177. Fax: (1) 465 7172. Telex: 400366.
Saudi Arabian Ministry of Foreign Affairs
Nasseriya Street, Riyadh 11124, Saudi Arabia
Tel: (1) 405 5000. Telex: 405000.
Royal Embassy of Saudi Arabia
30 Charles Street, London W1X 7PM
Tel: (0171) 917 3000. Opening hours: 0900-1500 Monday to Friday. *Consular section:* 0900-1130 (visa applications), 1400-1530 (passport collection) Monday to Friday.
Saudi Arabian Information Centre
Cavendish House, 18 Cavendish Square, London W1M 0AQ
Tel: (0171) 629 8803. Fax: (0171) 629 0374. Telex: 266065 (a/b SAINFC G).
British Embassy
PO Box 94351, Riyadh 11693, Saudi Arabia
Tel: (1) 488 0077 *or* 488 0088 (Commercial enquiries). Fax: (1) 488 2373. Telex: 406488 (a/b BRITEM SJ).
Consulates in: Jeddah and Al Khobar.
Royal Embassy of Saudi Arabia
601 New Hampshire Avenue, NW, Washington, DC 20037
Tel: (202) 342 3800.
Consulates in: Houston, Los Angeles and New York (tel: (212) 752 2740).
Embassy of the United States of America
PO Box 94309, Collector Road M, Diplomatic Quarter, Riyadh 11693
Tel: (1) 488 3800. Fax: (1) 488 7360. Telex: 401363 (a/b USFCS SJ).
Royal Embassy of Saudi Arabia
Suite 901, 99 Bank Street, Ottawa, Ontario K1P 6B9
Tel: (613) 237 4100/1/2/3 *or* 237 41004/5 (Consular section). Fax: (613) 237 0567. Telex: 0534285.
Canadian Embassy
PO Box 94321, Diplomatic Quarter, Riyadh 11693, Saudi Arabia
Tel: (1) 488 2288 *or* 488 0292 *or* 488 0275. Fax: (1) 488 1997. Telex: 404893 (a/b DOMCAN SJ).

Timatic

Health
GALILEO/WORLDSPAN: TI-DFT/RUH/HE
SABRE: TIDFT/RUH/HE

Visa
GALILEO/WORLDSPAN: TI-DFT/RUH/VI
SABRE: TIDFT/RUH/VI

For more information on Timatic codes refer to Contents.

AREA: 2,240,000 sq km (864,869 sq miles).
POPULATION: 14,870,000 (1990 estimate).
POPULATION DENSITY: 6.6 per sq km.
CAPITAL: Riyadh. **Population:** 2,000,000 (1989).
GEOGRAPHY: Saudi Arabia occupies four-fifths of the Arabian peninsula. It is bordered to the northwest by Jordan, to the north by Iraq and Kuwait, to the east by the Gulf of Oman, Qatar, the United Arab Emirates and Oman, and to the south by Yemen. To the west lies the Red Sea. Along the Red Sea coast is a narrow coastal strip *(Tihama)* which becomes relatively hotter and more humid towards the south and has areas of extensive tidal flats and lava fields. Behind this coastal plain is a series of plateaus reaching up to 2000m (6560ft). The southern part of this range, *Asir,* has some peaks of over 3000m (9840ft). North of these mountains, in the far north, is *An Nafud,* a sand sea, and further south the landscape rises to *Najd,* a semi-desert area scattered with oases. Still further south the land falls away, levelling out to unremitting desert, the uninhabited 'Empty Quarter' or *Rub al Khali.* Along the Gulf coast is a low fertile plain giving way to limestone ridges inland.
LANGUAGE: Arabic. English is spoken in business circles.
RELIGION: The majority of Saudi Arabians are Sunni Muslim, but Shi'ites predominate in the Eastern Province.
TIME: GMT + 3.
ELECTRICITY: 125/215 volts AC, 50/60Hz.
COMMUNICATIONS: Telephone: A sophisticated telecommunications network and satellite, microwave and cable systems span the country. Full IDD is available. Country code: 966. Outgoing international code: 00. **Fax:** Major hotels provide facilities.
Telex/telegram: Telegrams can be sent from all post offices. All major hotels have telex facilities. **Post:** Internal and international services available from the Central Post Office. Post is delivered to box numbers. Airmail to Europe takes up to a week. Surface mail takes up to five months. **Press:** The main newspapers include *Al-Riyadh* and *Al-Jizirah.* English-language dailies include *Arab News, Saudi Gazette* and *Riyadh Daily.*
BBC World Service and Voice of America frequencies: From time to time these change. See the section *How to Use this Book* for more information.
BBC:

MHz	21.47	15.57	11.76	1.413

A service is also available on 1413kHz and 702kHz (0100-0500 GMT).
Voice of America:

MHz	15.44	11.96	9.705	6.060

PASSPORT/VISA

Regulations and requirements may be subject to change at short notice, and you are advised to contact the appropriate diplomatic or consular authority before finalising travel arrangements. Details of these may be found at the head of this country's entry. Any numbers in the chart refer to the footnotes below.

	Passport Required?	Visa Required?	Return Ticket Required?
Full British	Yes	Yes	Yes
BVP	Not valid	-	-
Australian	Yes	Yes	Yes
Canadian	Yes	Yes	Yes
USA	Yes	Yes	Yes
Other EU (As of 31/12/94)	Yes	Yes	Yes
Japanese	Yes	Yes	Yes

Restricted entry: (a) Holders of an Israeli passport or passports with Israeli stamps in them are denied entry. Saudi Arabia also refuses entry to those of the Jewish faith. (b) Passengers not complying with Saudi conventions of dress and behaviour, including those who appear to be in a state of intoxication, will be refused entry (see *Social Conventions* below).
Note: (a) Unaccompanied women must be met at the airport by their sponsor or husband or have confirmed onward reservations as far as their final destination in Saudi Arabia. If met by a sponsor, it is worth noting that there are restrictions on women travelling by car with men who are not related by blood or marriage: enquire at the Information Centre or Embassy. (b) No foreign passenger who is working as a domestic servant in Saudi Arabia should be transported to Saudi Arabia unless holding a valid non-refundable return ticket.
PASSPORTS: A valid passport is required by all except Muslim pilgrims holding 'Pilgrim Passes', tickets and other documents for their onward or return journey and entering the country via Jeddah or Dhahran. All passports must be valid for at least 6 months beyond the estimated stay in Saudi Arabia.
British Visitors Passport: Not accepted.

VISAS: Required by all except nationals of Bahrain, Kuwait, Oman, Qatar and the United Arab Emirates and holders of re-entry permits and 'Landing Permits' issued by the Saudi Arabian Ministry of Foreign Affairs (address above).

Note: Visa requirements are liable to change. For up-to-date information contact the nearest Embassy.

Types of visa: Business, Transit and Single- or Multiple-entry (the latter are *not* Tourist visas and are meant only for those visiting relatives etc). Transit visas are not required by passengers proceeding to a third country if in possession of confirmed tickets and other onward travel documentation. Travellers must not leave the airport confines and must continue their journey by the same or next connecting flight (maximum 12 hours stay permitted at Dhahran and Jeddah).

Application to: Consulate (or Consular section at Embassy). For addresses, see top of entry.

Cost: The equivalent of SA R50 in local currency at the current exchange rate (£8-9).

Application requirements: For a Business visa, a letter endorsed by the Saudi Minister of Foreign Affairs is required, together with a valid passport, completed application form and 2 passport-size photos.

MONEY

Currency: Saudi Arabian Riyal (SA R) = 100 halalah; 5 halalah = 20 qurush. Notes are in denominations of SA R500, 100, 50, 10, 5 and 1. Coins are in denominations of 50, 25, 10, 5 and 1 halalah.

Credit cards: Access/Mastercard, American Express, Diners Club and Visa are all widely accepted. Check with your credit card company for details of merchant acceptability and other services which may be available.

Exchange rate indicators: The following figures are included as a guide to the movements of the Riyal against Sterling and the US Dollar:

Date:	Oct '92	Sep '93	Jan '94	Jan '95
£1.00=	6.06	5.75	5.55	5.87
$1.00=	3.82	3.76	3.75	3.75

Currency restrictions: Free import and export of both local and foreign currency. Israeli currency is prohibited.

Banking hours: 0830-1200 and 1700-1900 Saturday to Wednesday; 0830-1200 Thursday.

DUTY FREE

The following items may be imported into Saudi Arabia without incurring customs duty:

600 cigarettes or 100 cigars or 500g tobacco; perfume for personal use.

Note: Duty is levied on cameras and typewriters, but if these articles are re-exported within 90 days the customs charges may be refunded. It is advisable not to put film in the camera.

Prohibited items: Alcohol, pornography, pork, contraceptives, firearms, pearls, children's dolls, jewellery or statues shaped in the form of an animal or human, musical instruments and items listed as prohibited by the Arab League (copy available from the Embassy).

PUBLIC HOLIDAYS

Mar 2 '95 Eid al-Fitr (End of Ramadan). **May 9** Eid al-Adha (Feast of the Sacrifice). **Feb 22 '96** Eid al-Fitr (End of Ramadan). **Apr 28** Eid al-Adha (Feast of the Sacrifice).

Note: Muslim festivals are timed according to local sightings of various phases of the Moon and the dates given above are approximations. During the lunar month of Ramadan that precedes Eid al-Fitr, Muslims fast during the day and feast at night and normal business patterns may be interrupted. Some disruption may continue into Eid al-Fitr itself. Eid al-Fitr and Eid al-Adha may last anything from two to ten days, depending on the region. During Hajj (when pilgrims visit Mecca) all government establishments and some businesses will be closed for five to ten days. For more information see the section *World of Islam* at the back of the book.

HEALTH

Regulations and requirements may be subject to change at short notice, and you are advised to contact your doctor well in advance of your intended date of departure. Any numbers in the chart refer to the footnotes below.

	Special Precautions?	Certificate Required?
Yellow Fever	No	1
Cholera	Yes	2
Typhoid & Polio	Yes	-
Malaria	3	-
Food & Drink	4	-

[1]: A yellow fever vaccination certificate is required from all travellers arriving from countries of which any parts are infected.

[2]: Following WHO guidelines issued in 1973, a cholera vaccination certificate is not a condition of entry to Saudi Arabia, except perhaps for certain pilgrims arriving during Hajj. However, cholera is a risk in this country and precautions are essential. Up-to-date advice should be sought before deciding whether these precautions should include vaccination, as medical opinion is divided over its effectiveness. See the *Health* section at the back of the book.

[3]: Malaria risk, predominantly in the malignant *falciparum* form, exists throughout the year in areas other than the Eastern, Northern and Central Provinces, the high altitude areas of Asir Province, and the urban areas of the Western Province (Jeddah, Mecca, Medina and Taif). Resistance to chloroquine has been reported.

[4]: All water should be regarded as being potentially contaminated. Water used for drinking, brushing teeth or making ice should have first been boiled or otherwise sterilised. Milk is unpasteurised and should be boiled. Powdered or tinned milk is available and is advised, but make sure that it is reconstituted with pure water. Avoid dairy products which are likely to have been made from unboiled milk. Only eat well-cooked meat and fish, preferably served hot. Salad and mayonnaise may carry increased risk. Vegetables should be cooked and fruit peeled.

Note: During the Hajj (annual pilgrimage to Mecca), Saudi Arabia requires vaccination of pilgrims against *meningococcal meningitis*. Although this applies mainly to pilgrims, other travellers may find themselves affected, especially during the month of August.

Rabies is present. For those at high risk, vaccination before arrival should be considered. If you are bitten abroad, seek medical advice without delay. For more information, consult the *Health* section at the back of the book.

Bilharzia (schistosomiasis) is present. Avoid swimming and paddling in fresh water. Swimming pools which are well-chlorinated and maintained are safe.

Health care: Medical facilities are generally of a high standard, but treatment is expensive. Health insurance is essential.

TRAVEL - International

AIR: Saudi Arabia's national airline is *Saudia (SV)*. For free advice on air travel, call the Air Travel Advisory Bureau in the UK on (0171) 636 5000 (London) *or* (0161) 832 2000 (Manchester).

Approximate flight times: From *London* to Dhahran is 6 hours 25 minutes, to Jeddah is 5 hours 50 minutes and to Riyadh is 6 hours 25 minutes.

From *Los Angeles* to Jeddah is 18 hours 45 minutes and to Riyadh is 21 hours 15 minutes.

From *New York* to Jeddah is 12 hours 5 minutes and to Riyadh is 15 hours 45 minutes.

From *Singapore* to Jeddah is 11 hours 55 minutes.

International airports: *Riyadh (RUH)* (King Khalid International) airport, 35km (22 miles) north of the city. Good bus and taxi services.

Dhahran (DHA) (Al Khobar) airport, 8km (5 miles) southeast of the complex (travel time – 20 minutes). Taxis are available.

Jeddah (JED) (King Abdul Aziz) airport, 18km (11 miles) north of the city (travel time – 40 minutes). Buses leave every 30 minutes (24-hour service) for Jeddah and there are also buses for Mecca, Medina and Taif. Taxis are available. This airport occupies the largest area in the world.

SEA: The main international passenger ports are Dammam (Gulf) and Jeddah and Yanbu (Red Sea).

ROAD: The principal international routes from Jordan are Amman to Dammam, Medina and Jeddah. There are also roads to Yemen (from Jeddah), Kuwait, Qatar and the United Arab Emirates. A causeway has recently been opened to link Al Khobar with Bahrain.

TRAVEL - Internal

AIR: There are 19 domestic airports and air travel is by far the most convenient form of travelling around the country. *Saudia* connects all main centres. 'Arabian Express' economy class (75 minutes) connects Jeddah with Riyadh and Riyadh with Dhahran (no advance reservations). Get a boarding pass the evening before departure. There are special flights for pilgrims arriving at or departing from Jeddah during Hajj.

SEA: Dhows may be chartered for outings on both coasts.

RAIL: Children under four travel free. Children aged 4-11 pay half fare. The only functioning railway is the Riyadh–Dammam line, which is via Dhahran, Abqaiq, Hofuf, Harad and Al Yamamah. There is a daily service in air-conditioned trains with dining car. The service does not run on Thursdays. The railway on the west coast made famous by Lawrence's raid has long since been abandoned to the desert.

ROAD: Traffic drives on the right. There are 25,000km (15,000 miles) of roads linking the main towns and rural areas. The network is constantly being upgraded and expanded (most recently, an expressway has been built from Jeddah to Medina and the trans-peninsula road from Jeddah to Dammam has been upgraded) and on the main routes, much of it is of the highest standard. The corniche that winds down the escarpment between Taif and Mecca is as spectacular a feature of engineering as may be seen anywhere. However, standards of driving are erratic, particularly in the Eastern Province, where it is not unknown for lorry drivers to equip their vehicles with hub-knives similar to those seen in the film 'Ben Hur'. Criteria for apportioning blame after traffic accidents are also erratic and many driving offences carry an automatic prison sentence. As foreigners are tolerated rather than welcomed in Saudi Arabia, it is best to drive with extreme caution at all times. Women are not allowed to drive vehicles or ride bicycles on public roads. Non-Muslims may not enter Mecca or the immediate area; police are stationed to ensure that they turn off onto a specially-built ring road, known amongst expatriates as the 'Christian Bypass'. **Bus:** Services have recently been developed by SAPTCO to serve inter-urban and local needs. Modern vehicles have been acquired, including air-conditioned double-deckers. All buses must have a screened-off section for the exclusive use of female passengers. **Taxi:** Available in all cities, but often very expensive. Few have meters, and fares should be negotiated in advance. **Car hire:** The major international car rental agencies have offices in Saudi Arabia. The minimum age is 25. **Documentation:** A national driving licence is valid for up to three months if accompanied by an officially-sanctioned translation into Arabic. An International Driving Permit (with translation) is recommended, but not required by law. There are restrictions on women travelling by car with men who are not related by blood or marriage.

ACCOMMODATION

There is a good range of hotel accommodation throughout the country. Accommodation is generally easy to find, except during the pilgrim season when advance reservations are recommended. Service charges are fixed at 15% for deluxe and first-category hotels and at 10% for all others. Hotel charges double in Mecca and Medina during the pilgrimage season, and increase by 25% during the summer months in resort areas such as Taif, Abha, Kamis Mushait and Al-Baha. **Grading:** There are seven grades of hotel in Saudi Arabia: deluxe, first-class A and B, second-class A and B, and third-class A and B.

RESORTS & EXCURSIONS

For the purpose of this section, the country has been divided into four sections: The Najd, The Hejaz, Hasa and The Asir. This does not necessarily represent tribal or administrative boundaries.

The Najd (Central Region)

The Najd is a stony desert plateau at the heart of Saudi Arabia, somewhat isolated from the rest of the peninsula. It was from here that Ibn Saud led his tribe of nomads out to create a new kingdom through conquest. Despite oil wealth, some Najdis still lead a semi-nomadic life, tending camels and sheep, but many have settled in the same towns they once milked for tribute with threats of violence. Watchtowers, standing guard on all the high points in Najd, are a reminder of this age-old conflict between nomad and farmer.

Riyadh (Ryad), the royal capital, is a modern city built on the site of the first town captured by Ibn Saud, when he stormed the *Musmat Fort* in 1902 (a spearhead embedded in the main door is said to be the one with which Ibn Saud killed the Turkish governor). Apart from the fort and a few traditional Najdi palaces near Deera Square, little trace of the old town remains. The *King's Camel Races* are held near the city in April or May. Other places of interest in Najd are **Diriya, Wadi Hanifa, Shaib Awsat, Shaib Laha, Al-Hair, Wadi-al-Jafi, Tumair, Towqr, Aneyzah, Qassim** and **Hail**.

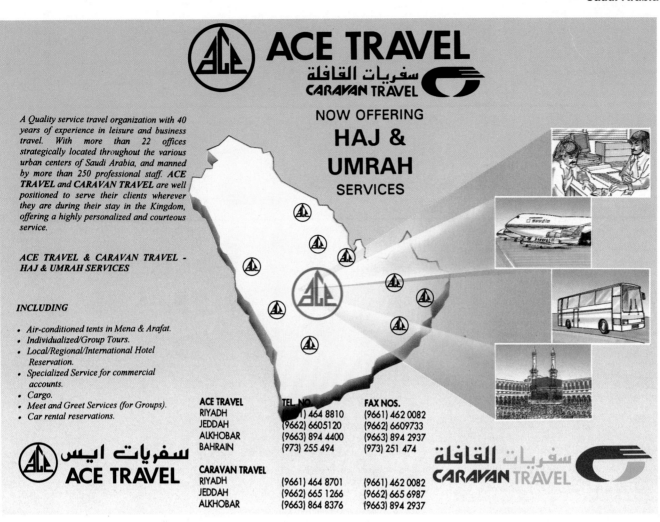
The Hejaz (Western Region)

The west coast is a centre for trade, but of equal importance is the concentration of Islamic holy cities, including Mecca and Medina, which attract pilgrims from all over the world. The region also includes the city of Jeddah, which was until recently Saudi Arabia's diplomatic capital and remains the most important commercial and cultural gateway to the country.
Mecca: The spiritual centre of the Islamic world, forbidden to non-Muslims. Places of significance to Muslims include the *Kaabah Enclosure*, the *Mountain of Light*, the *Plain of Arafat* and the *House of Abdullah Bin Abdul Muttalib*, where Mohammed was born.
Medina: The second-holiest city in Islam and also forbidden to non-Muslims.
Jeddah: Although the city has grown phenomenally, priority is being given to the preservation of the ancient city. The ragged, coral-coloured Ottoman buildings are currently being renovated. Leisure facilities have increased and the corniche has a 'Brighton' feel about it. There is an amusement park and a wonderful creek allowing both sailing and snorkelling. Its hotels and restaurants are cosmopolitan and there are good fish and meat markets.
Taif: Perched on top of a 900m (3000ft) cliff at the edge of the plateau above Mecca, this resort town enjoys a milder climate than much of the country and was for a long time the official summer capital. It is noted for its pink palaces and for the astounding modern corniche road that winds down the sheer cliffs of the Taif escarpment to the hot coastal plain.
Other important towns in the Hejaz include **Usta, Wadi Fatima, Hanakiyah, Khaybar** and **Yanbu.**

Hasa (Eastern Region)

Fertile lowland coastal plains inhabited by the kingdom's Shia minority, who have traditionally lived by fishing, diving for pearls, raising date palms and trading abroad and with the interior. All of Saudi Arabia's vast stocks of oil lie under Hasa or beneath the Gulf and the locals are now out-numbered by foreign oil-workers from all over the World.
Places retaining some flavour of old Hasa include **Hofuf,** a lively oasis with Turkish influence and a camel market; **Jebel-al-Qara,** where the potteries have been worked by eight generations of the same family; **Abqaiq,** which has

a 5000-year-old saltmine, still in operation; the ruined customs house at **Uqair,** once an important Portuguese port and caravan terminus; and **Tarut Island,** site of the oldest town on the peninsula, now a picturesque settlement of fishermen and weavers.

The Asir (South Region)

A range of coastal mountains and the only part of the kingdom where there is significant wild vegetation, mostly palms and evergreen bushes. Millet, wheat and dates are grown using largely traditional methods. The inhabitants are darker than other Saudis, being in part descended from African slaves. Baboons, gazelles, leopards, honey badgers, mongooses and other 'African' animals inhabit remoter areas. Unique to Asir are the ancient *gasaba* towers, phallus-shaped and of unknown purpose.
Places to visit include the ancient caravan city of **Qaryat-al-Fau,** currently being excavated; the great dam and temple at **Najran;** and nearby, amidst orchards of pomegranates, limes and bananas, the ornate ruins of the ancient cities of **Timna** and **Shiban.**

SOCIAL PROFILE

FOOD & DRINK: Local food is often strongly flavoured and spicy. The staple diet is *pitta* bread (flat, unleavened bread) which accompanies every dish. Rice, lentils, chick peas *(hummus)* and cracked wheat *(burghul)* are also common. The most common meats are lamb and chicken. Beef is rare and pork is proscribed under Islamic law. The main meat meal of the day is lunch, either *kultra* (meat on skewers) or *kebabs* served with soup and vegetables. Arabic cakes, cream desserts and rice pudding *(muhalabia)* also feature in the diet. *Mezzeh,* the equivalent of hôrs d'oeuvres, may include up to 40 dishes. Foreign cooking is on offer in larger towns and the whole range of international cuisine, including fast food, is available in the oil-producing Eastern Province and in Jeddah. Restaurants have table service.
Drink: There are no bars. Alcohol is forbidden by law, and there are severe penalties for infringement; it is important to note that this applies to all nationals regardless of religion. Arabic coffee and fruit drinks are popular alternatives. Alcohol-free beers and cocktails are

served in hotel bars.
NIGHTLIFE: Apart from restaurants and hotels there is no nightlife in the Western sense.
SHOPPING: *Souks* (markets) sell incense and incense burners, jewellery, bronze and brassware, richly decorated daggers and swords, and in the Eastern Province, huge brass-bonded chests. Bargaining is often expected, even for modern goods such as cameras and electrical equipment (which can be very good value).
Shopping hours: 0900-1300 and 1630-2000 Saturday to Thursday (Ramadan 2000-0100). These hours differ in various parts of the country.
SPORT: Obhir Creek, 50km (30 miles) north of Jeddah, has good facilities for **swimming, water-skiing, fishing** and **sailing,** and there are similar beaches on the Gulf coast south of Al Khobar. Elsewhere, hotels have swimming pools. The British and US embassies have men-only health clubs as well as swimming pools, **golf** clubs and **squash** and **tennis** facilities. Most companies employing foreign workers also have some sports facilities. The desert terrain provides great opportunities for off-road **motorcycling** but this sport is prohibited from time to time. **Football** is popular and most large towns have modern stadia.
SOCIAL CONVENTIONS: Saudi culture is based on Islam and the perfection of the Arabic language. The Saudi form of Islam is conservative and fundamentalist, based on the 18th-century revivalist movement of the Najdi leader Shaikh Mohammed Ibn Abdel-Wahhab. This still has a great effect on Saudi society, especially on the position of women, who do not generally go out without being totally covered in black robes *(abaya)* and masks, although there are regional variations of dress. The Najd and other remote areas remain true to Wahhabi tradition, but throughout the country this way of life is being threatened by modernisation and rapid development. For more information see *World of Islam* at the back of the book. Shaking hands is the customary form of greeting. Invitations to private homes are unusual. Entertaining is usually in hotels or restaurants and although the custom of eating with the right hand persists, it is more likely that knives and forks will be used. A small gift either promoting the company or representing your country will generally be well received. Women are expected to dress modestly and it is best to do so to avoid offence. Men should not wear shorts in public or go without a shirt. The norms for

public behaviour are extremely conservative and religious police, known as Mutawwa'in, are charged with enforcing these standards. Customs regarding smoking are the same as in Europe and non-smoking areas are indicated. During Ramadan, Muslims are not allowed to eat, smoke or drink during the day and it is illegal for a foreign visitor to do so in public. **Tipping:** The practice of tipping is becoming much more common and waiters, hotel porters and taxi drivers should be given 10-15%.

BUSINESS PROFILE

ECONOMY: Oil and natural gas products account for all but a tiny fraction of Saudi exports (representing two-thirds of GNP and 90% of exports). Saudi Arabia is the world's third-largest producer of oil (after the CIS and the USA) and it dominates the economy; its discovery transformed a barren and impoverished desert state into a wealthy and increasingly modern economy. Revenues have fluctuated with the price of oil on the world market and the production quotas imposed by OPEC: they were therefore relatively depressed during the 1980s. Although economic activity has slowed somewhat as a result, Saudi Arabia has vast reserves – the largest known in the world – and few long-term worries. The remainder of the economy is engaged in agriculture and newly developed industries. Agriculture supports one-sixth of the workforce, producing wheat, fruit, vegetables, barley, eggs and poultry, in most of which the kingdom is now self-sufficient. Considerable effort has been put into ensuring adequate irrigation in a country with miniscule rainfall. The industrial sector produces petrochemicals, steel, engineering products and a wide range of consumer goods. Construction is also a key industry. Service industries such as finance and business services, consultancies and property are the fastest-growing sectors at present. Japan and the USA are the largest exporters to Saudi Arabia, while most of the kingdom's oil is sold to Germany, Italy, France and South Korea. Britain is also an important and long-established trading partner, and the country's principal supplier of armaments, of which the Saudis buy a very great deal. The Al Yamamah Contract signed in 1986 is, at £20 billion over ten years, the largest weapons contract in history.
BUSINESS: Appointments are necessary. Visiting cards printed in English with an Arab translation are usually exchanged. Men should wear suits for business meetings and formal social occasions. Thursday and Friday are official holidays. **Office hours:** 0900-1300 and 1630-2000 Saturday to Thursday (Ramadan 2000-0100), with some regional variation (eg Dhahran offices: 0700-1130 and 1300-1630 Saturday to Wednesday). **Government office hours:** 0730-1430 Saturday to Wednesday.
COMMERCIAL INFORMATION: The following organisation can offer advice: Council of Saudi Arabian Chambers of Commerce and Industry, PO Box 16683, Riyadh 11474. Tel: (1) 405 3200. Fax: (1) 402 4747. Telex: 405808.
CONFERENCES/CONVENTIONS: Information can be obtained from: Riyadh Exhibitions Company Ltd, PO Box 56010, Riyadh 11554. Tel: (1) 454 1448. Fax: (1) 454 4846. Telex: 406359.

CLIMATE

Saudi Arabia has a desert climate. In Jeddah it is warm for most of the year. Riyadh, which is inland, is hotter in summer and colder in winter, when occasional heavy rainstorms occur. The Rub al Khali seldom receives rain, making Saudi Arabia one of the driest countries in the world.
Required clothing: Tropical or lightweight clothing.

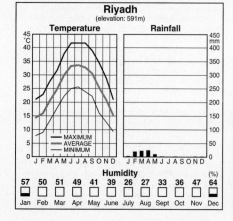

Riyadh
(elevation: 591m)

Senegal

□ *international airport*

Location: West Africa.

Note: Sporadic violence has been reported in the Ziguinchor region of western Casamance (in southern Senegal) connected with separatist activity. Although violence is not directed at foreigners, it is advisable to avoid travel in this region. Several incidents have occurred near popular resort areas.
Source: US State Department – February 18, 1994.

Ministry of Tourism and Air Transport
BP 4049, 23 rue Calmette, Dakar
Tel: 236 502. Fax: 229 413.
Embassy of the Republic of Senegal
11 Phillimore Gardens, London W8 7QG
Tel: (0171) 937 0925/6. Telex: 917119 (a/b AMBSEN G). Opening hours: 0900-1530 Monday to Friday; 0900-1200 (visa applications).
British Embassy
BP 6025, 20 rue du Docteur Guillet, Dakar, Senegal
Tel: 237 392 *or* 239 971. Fax: 232 766. Telex: 21690 (a/b PRODOME SG).
Embassy of the Republic of Senegal
2112 Wyoming Avenue, NW, Washington, DC 20008
Tel: (202) 234 0540/1.
Embassy of the United States of America
BP 49, avenue Jean XXIII, Dakar, Senegal
Tel: 234 296 *or* 233 424. Fax: 222 991. Telex: 21793 (a/b AMEMB SG).
Embassy of the Republic of Senegal
57 Malborough Avenue, Ottawa, Ontario K1N 8E8
Tel: (613) 238 6392. Fax: (613) 238 2695. Telex: 0534531.
Honorary consulates in: Montréal, Toronto and Vancouver.
Canadian Embassy
PO Box 3373, Immeuble Daniel Sorano, 45 avenue de la République, Dakar, Senegal
Tel: 239 290. Fax: 238 749. Telex: 51632 (a/b DOMCAN SG).

AREA: 196,722 sq km (75,955 sq miles).
POPULATION: 6,881,919 (1988 estimate).
POPULATION DENSITY: 35 per sq km.
CAPITAL: Dakar. **Population:** 850,000 (1979 estimate).
GEOGRAPHY: Senegal is bordered by Guinea Republic and Guinea-Bissau to the south, Mali to the east and Mauritania to the north, and encloses the confederated state of The Gambia. To the west lies the Atlantic Ocean. Most land is less than 100m (330ft) above sea level, except for the Fouta Djallon foothills in the southeast and the Bambouk Mountains on the Mali

border. On the coast between Dakar and St Louis is a strip of shifting dunes. South of Dakar there are shallow estuaries along the coastline, which is fringed by palm trees. In the northern part of the country, south of the Senegal Basin, lies the arid Fouta Ferlo, a hot dry Sahelian plain with little vegetation.
LANGUAGE: The official language is French. There are many local languages, the principal one being Wolof. Other groups include Senegalo-Guinean, Mandé and Peulh.
RELIGION: 90% Muslim, 5% Roman Catholic and Protestant, and a minority of traditional beliefs.
TIME: GMT.
ELECTRICITY: 220 volts AC, 50Hz.
COMMUNICATIONS: Telephone: IDD is available. Country code: 221. Outgoing international code: 00. **Fax:** SONATEL (responsible for all telecommunications) has a fax machine. Some hotels also have facilities. **Telex/telegram:** There are facilities at main post offices and several hotels. **Post:** Airmail to Europe takes between seven and ten days, and surface mail between two and six weeks. **Press:** All newspapers are in French and nearly all are controlled directly by political parties.
BBC World Service and Voice of America frequencies: From time to time these change. See the section *How to Use this Book* for more information.
BBC:

MHz	17.79	15.40	15.07	9.410

Voice of America:

MHz	21.49	15.60	9.525	6.035

PASSPORT/VISA

Regulations and requirements may be subject to change at short notice, and you are advised to contact the appropriate diplomatic or consular authority before finalising travel arrangements. Details of these may be found at the head of this country's entry. Any numbers in the chart refer to the footnotes below.

	Passport Required?	Visa Required?	Return Ticket Required?
Full British	Yes	No	Yes
BVP	Not valid	-	-
Australian	Yes	Yes	Yes
Canadian	Yes	No	Yes
USA	Yes	No	Yes
Other EU (As of 31/12/94)	Yes	No	Yes
Japanese	Yes	Yes	Yes

PASSPORTS: Valid passport required by all.
British Visitors Passport: Not accepted.
VISAS: Required by all except:
(a) nationals of those countries listed in the chart above;
(b) nationals of Algeria, Benin, Burkina Faso, Cape Verde, Central African Republic, Congo, Côte d'Ivoire, Gabon, Gambia, Ghana, Guinea, Guinea-Bissau, Liberia, Mali, Mauritania, Mauritius, Morocco, Niger, Nigeria, Rwanda, Sierra Leone, Togo and Tunisia.
Types of visa: *Entry visa* (tourist and business): £8.05 (for stays of up to 1 month) and £3.50 (for stays between 1 and 3 months). *Transit visa:* £3.50. Transit visas are required by all except those nationals referred to above in visa exemptions, and passengers holding confirmed reservation and travel documents for onward journey by same or next connecting flight.
Validity: 3 months from the date of issue.
Application to: Consulate (or Consular section at Embassy). For addresses, see top of entry.
Application requirements: (a) Valid passport. (b) 2 passport-size photos. (c) Company letter for Business visa.
Working days required: 1 (use registered post for postal applications).
Note: Applications from nationals of Israel must be referred to the authorities in Dakar, and will therefore take longer.

MONEY

Currency: CFA Franc (CFA Fr) = 100 centimes. Notes are in denominations of CFA Fr10,000, 5000, 1000 and 500. Coins are in denominations of CFA Fr500, 100, 50, 25, 10, 5, 2 and 1. The notes are also legal tender in the republics which formerly comprised French West Africa, ie Benin, Burkina Faso, Côte d'Ivoire, Mali, Niger and Togo. Senegal is part of the French Monetary Area.
Note: At the beginning of 1994, the CFA Franc was devalued against the French Franc.
Credit cards: American Express is the most widely accepted, although Access/Mastercard, Diners Club and Visa have limited use. Check with your credit card company for details of merchant acceptability and other services which may be available.
Exchange rate indicators: The following figures are included as a guide to the movements of the CFA Franc against Sterling and the US Dollar:

Date:	Oct '92	Sep '93	Jan '94	Jan '95
£1.00=	413.75	433.88	436.78	834.94
$1.00=	260.71	284.79	295.23	533.68

Currency restrictions: Import of both foreign and local currency is unlimited, subject to declaration. Export of local currency is restricted to CFA Fr20,000. Export of foreign currency equivalent to more than CFA Fr50,000 is limited to the amount declared on arrival and a detailed list of all exchanges must be shown.

Banking hours: 0800-1115 and 1430-1630 Monday to Friday.

DUTY FREE

The following may be imported into Senegal by persons over 18 years of age without incurring customs duty:
200 cigarettes or 50 cigars or 250g tobacco; a reasonable quantity of perfume for personal use.
Note: There is no free import of alcoholic beverages.

PUBLIC HOLIDAYS

Jan 1 '95 New Year's Day. **Mar 2** Korité (End of Ramadan). **Apr 14** Good Friday. **Apr 17** Easter Monday. **May 1** Labour Day. **May 10** Tabaski (Feast of the Sacrifice). **May 25** Ascension Day. **Jun 5** Whit Monday. **Jul 15** Day of Association. **Aug 9** Mouloud (Prophet's Birthday). **Aug 15** Assumption. **Nov 1** All Saints' Day. **Dec 25** Christmas. **Jan 1 '96** New Year's Day. **Feb 22** Korité (End of Ramadan). **Apr 5** Good Friday. **Apr 8** Easter Monday.
Note: Muslim festivals are timed according to local sightings of various phases of the Moon and the dates given above are approximations. During the lunar month of Ramadan that precedes Korité (Eid al-Fitr), Muslims fast during the day and feast at night and normal business patterns may be interrupted. Many restaurants are closed during the day and there may be restrictions on smoking and drinking. Some disruption may continue into Korité itself. Korité and Tabaski (Eid al-Adha) may last anything from two to ten days, depending on the region. For more information see the section *World of Islam* at the back of the book.

HEALTH

Regulations and requirements may be subject to change at short notice, and you are advised to contact your doctor well in advance of your intended date of departure. Any numbers in the chart refer to the footnotes below.

	Special Precautions?	Certificate Required?
Yellow Fever	Yes	1
Cholera	Yes	2
Typhoid & Polio	Yes	-
Malaria	3	-
Food & Drink	4	-

[1]: A yellow fever vaccination certificate is required from all travellers over one year of age.
[2]: Following WHO guidelines issued in 1973, a cholera vaccination certificate is not a condition of entry to Senegal. However, cholera is a risk in this country and precautions are essential. Up-to-date advice should be sought before deciding whether these precautions should include vaccination, as medical opinion is divided over its effectiveness. See the *Health* section at the back of the book.
[3]: Malaria risk, predominantly in the malignant *falciparum* form, exists all year throughout the country; there is a lower risk in the Cap Vert region from January to June. Resistance to chloroquine has been reported.
[4]: All water should be regarded as being potentially contaminated. Water used for drinking, brushing teeth or making ice should first be boiled or otherwise sterilised. Milk is unpasteurised and should be boiled. Powdered or tinned milk is available and is advised, but make sure that it is reconstituted with pure water. Avoid dairy products which are likely to have been made from unboiled milk. Only eat well-cooked meat and fish, preferably served hot. Pork, salad and mayonnaise may carry increased risk. Vegetables should be cooked and fruit peeled.
Rabies is present. For those at high risk, vaccination before arrival should be considered. If you are bitten abroad, seek medical advice without delay. For more information, consult the *Health* section at the back of the book.
Bilharzia (schistosomiasis) is present. Avoid swimming and paddling in fresh water. Swimming pools which are well-chlorinated and maintained are safe.
Meningitis risk exists, depending on area visited and time of year.
Health care: In Dakar, doctors are plentiful and most medicines are available. Up-country, however, facilities are minimal. Health insurance is essential.

TRAVEL - International

AIR: Senegal's national airline is *Air Sénégal/SONATRA (DS).*
Approximate flight times: From Dakar to *London* is 6 hours 10 minutes, to *New York* is 8 hours 10 minutes and to *Paris* is 7 hours.
International airport: *Dakar (DKR)* (Dakar-Yoff) is 17km (10.5 miles) northwest of the city (travel time – 25 minutes). Airport facilities include duty-free shop, bar/restaurant, bank, post office and car hire. Regular coach and bus services go to and from Dakar. Metered taxis are available.
Departure tax: CFA Fr5000 for international flights and CFA Fr4000 for flights within Africa.
SEA: There are regular sailings from France, the Canary Islands, Morocco, Spain and several South American and West African ports. Fares tend to be expensive. The main port is Dakar.
RAIL: There are two passenger trains (one Senegalese and one Malian) with restaurant and sleeping cars, running from Bamako, Mali, twice a week. The journey can take 30-36 hours. It is advisable to travel on the Senegalese train (well up to Western standards), rather than the Malian train (very basic indeed).
ROADS: Roads from Mauritania are tarred and in good condition; the best place to cross the border is at Rosso. Roads from Guinea-Bissau are not yet tarred; there is a border crossing at São Domingo. There is a route from Senegal to Mali via Tambacounda. There is access across the Sahara by a 5500km (2120-mile) road that runs from Algeria via Mali. The trans-Gambian highway crosses the River Gambia by ferry. There is a good network of **buses** and **taxis** running across the major borders.

TRAVEL - Internal

AIR: *Air Senegal* runs services to all the main towns in Senegal. *Gambia Air Shuttle* offers flights from Dakar to Banjul (Gambia) twice-daily.
Departure tax: CFA Fr2000 for all internal flights.
SEA: A boat operating on a weekly basis runs from Dakar to Ziguinchor.
RAIL: The country has a network of about 1034km (643 miles) of rail track. Trains run from Dakar to towns en route for Mali. There is also a service between Dakar and St Louis. There is an ongoing programme of upgrading and expansion. Children under 3 travel free. Children aged 3-9 pay half fare.
ROAD: There are approximately 2951km (1834 miles) of asphalt roads linking the major towns and in the coastal region. The network of roads in the interior are rough (about 10,400km/6460 miles in all) and may become impassable during the rainy season. There are often police checkpoints at the entrance and exit to villages to enforce speed restrictions; fines are paid on the spot. Traffic drives on the right. **Bus:** Long-distance services operate subject to demand only. **Taxi:** Available in most towns and fares are metered. It is cheaper to hail a taxi in the street than arrange to be collected from the hotel. Bush taxis and estate cars are good for journeys into the interior. **Car hire:** Companies are found in Dakar and the main towns. **Documentation:** A French or International Driving Permit is required.
URBAN: Bus and minibus services operate in Dakar.

ACCOMMODATION

HOTELS: The government-controlled expansion of tourism has lead to an increasing number of hotels. There are a number which are of international standard, and more development is under way, including a number of hotels on the Petite Côte (the stretch of beaches between Dakar and Joal). In Casamance some luxury resorts like the Club Méditerranée have been built. It is advisable to book accommodation in advance, particularly in Dakar where there is an increased demand during the tourist season, which lasts from December to May. Hotels in Dakar generally have air-conditioning but tend to be expensive. An establishment in its own class is the Bou el Mogdad, the River Region floating hotel, which has comfortable cabins and a lively shipboard life.
CAMPING: Government campsites *(campements)* provide a few beds, but no bedding. There are basic facilities for the traveller who prefers to wander from the beaten track, although camping independently is strongly discouraged. Sometimes bungalows or grass huts are available; visitors must otherwise provide their own tents.
MISSIONS: Catholic missions will accommodate tourists only in cases of real need.
VILLAGE HUTS: A village will sometimes courteously offer a stranger one of the local huts as living accommodation, but it is necessary for visitors to provide their own bedding.

RESORTS & EXCURSIONS

Dakar is a bustling modern city and major port with good restaurants and shops and a lively nightlife. There is an enjoyable boat ride to **Gorée Island**, an old fortified slaving station and one of the first French settlements on the continent. There is a very interesting museum on the island, along with a zoo, colonial mansions and slaves' houses. Dakar's markets include the *Sandaga* and the *Kermel*, the former being famous for its silverworking. There is a pleasant trip from Dakar to the beach at **N'Gor**, near the airport.
St Louis is another old French fortified settlement, from the days of slave-trading. There are good beaches. A cruise lasting several days can be made up the Senegal River from here.
Ziguinchor is a good base for visiting the **Basse Casamance** region, with mangrove swamps and palm trees.
On the island of **Karaban** the ruins of a *Breton church* and a colonial settlement can be seen.
There are a number of national parks in Senegal, particularly rich in birdlife. The best time for viewing is usually winter: *Niokolo Koba, Basse Casamance, Langue de Barbarie* and *Djoudi* are especially recommended. All these parks have some type of basic accommodation, mostly in the form of *campements*. The *Lac de Guiers* is the home of a wide variety of birds.
The area around the source of the *River Saloum* is rich in archaeological remains – relics of an ancient civilisation about which little is known.

SOCIAL PROFILE

FOOD & DRINK: Senegalese food is considered among the best in Africa. The basis of many dishes is chicken or fish, but the distinctive taste is due to ingredients not found outside Africa. This food is served in many restaurants in Dakar. Provincial rest houses serve less sophisticated but delicious variations. Dishes include *chicken au yassa* (chicken with lemon, pimento and onions), *tiebou dienne* (rice and fish), *dem à la St Louis* (stuffed mullet), *maffe* (chicken or mutton in peanut sauce) and *accras* (a kind of fritter). Suckling pig is popular in the Casamance region. **Drink:** There are bars in some hotels and clubs. Although predominantly a Muslim country, alcohol is available. The traditional drink is mint tea, the first cup drunk slightly bitter, the second with more sugar and the third very sweet. The Casamance drink is palm wine, which is drunk either fresh or fermented. *Toufam* (a kind of yoghurt thinned with sugared water) is served in Toucouleur villages. A unique drink is home-roasted coffee with pimento.
NIGHTLIFE: Traditional Senegalese festivals are held throughout the year. There are several nightclubs in Dakar and a casino on the route to N'Gor. There are many cinemas showing the latest French films.
SHOPPING: Bargaining is customary. At Soumbe-dionne, on the Corniche de Fann, is a craft village where the visitor can watch craftsmen at work and buy their handicrafts. Purchases include woodcarving in the form of African gaming boards, masks and statues; musical instruments; and metalwork, including copper pendants, bowls and statuettes. Most markets and centres sell traditional fabric, embroidery and costume, pottery, necklaces of clay beads and costume jewellery of wood or various seeds. **Shopping hours:** Generally 0800-1200 and 1430-1800 Monday to Saturday. Some shops open Sunday morning, others are closed Monday.
SPORT: Swimming: There are swimming pools in many hotels and at the Dakar Lido. There is good bathing at N'Gor Beach, Hann Bay, Petite Côte and Casamance. The coast from Cap Vert to St Louis is not suitable for swimming. **Water-skiing:** Facilities are available at Dakar alongside the 'Children's Beach' on the lagoon between N'Gor and its island and at the Hanns Bay marinas.
Fishing: The Centre de Pêche Sportive at Dakar port and the Hann Bay marinas have fully-equipped deep-sea fishing boats for hire. **Skindiving:** Underwater enthusiasts will find good diving waters all around the Cap Vert Peninsula. **Horseriding:** Horses are available for riding in the Cap Vert area. **Tennis:** Courts are at N'Gor, Nianing, Dakar and Cap Skirring. **Golf:** There is a 9-hole golf course at Camberene and miniature golf at Dakar-Yoff.
Spectator sports: Senegalese are keen **footballers** and followers of African **wrestling**. There are matches every Sunday at the Fass arena and in the suburbs or at the Iba Mar Diop Stadium near the Great Mosque.
SOCIAL CONVENTIONS: Greetings are appropriate when coming across local people, especially in the bush, and the visitor should make the effort to learn these in one of the local dialects. Handshaking on meeting, regardless of how many times a day one meets the person, is normal. When visiting a village it is polite to call upon the village headman or schoolteacher to explain that you want to spend the night there or visit the area. They will often act

as interpreter and will be helpful guides to the customs of
the village and also in terms of money, ensuring that a
traveller does not find himself in the embarrassing
position of paying for hospitality that was given in
friendship. Return hospitality with a gift of medicines,
food or money for the community. It is not advisable to
give money indiscriminately as tourists have encouraged
the practice of begging. Casual wear is widely acceptable.
Scanty swimwear should be reserved for the beach.
Smoking is prohibited in some public places (especially
mosques). **Tipping:** A service charge of 10-15% is
included in all hotel and restaurant bills. Taxi drivers are
not normally given a tip.

BUSINESS PROFILE

ECONOMY: In a good year, Senegal is the world's
leading producer of groundnuts, which are the country's
key export commodity. The country's finances are
therefore hostage to the volume of the groundnut harvest
and price levels. In recent years, both have been
unfavourable and Senegal has consequently had to appeal
for foreign aid to purchase necessary imported
foodstuffs. Other agricultural produce – rice, sugar and
cotton – are being successfully cultivated and have been
introduced in pursuit of diversification, which has
occurred, but slowly. There is plentiful fishing with a
wide range of species suitable for export, although the
accessible area is small. Currently exploitable mineral
deposits are limited to phosphates (the chemical industry
draws on sizeable deposits of lime phosphate and
aluminium phosphate within Senegal); some iron ore has
been identified and there is thought to be oil inland.
Senegal is the most industrialised country in French West
Africa after Côte d'Ivoire. The main industries are
involved in the processing of agricultural products and
phosphates, milling, textiles, commercial vehicle
assembly, food and drink, farming materials
(implements, fertilisers, etc), paint, asbestos, cement,
printing and boat-building. The country remains
nonetheless heavily dependent on foreign aid and its
finances remain weak. The IMF has had one of its
longest Structural Adjustment Programmes in operation
in Senegal but the results have been mediocre and the
Fund appears to view some of the problems as virtually
insoluble. Senegal is a member of the CFA Franc Zone.
France is the major trading partner, followed by Côte
d'Ivoire, Mali, Spain and the USA.
BUSINESS: A lightweight suit is acceptable for
business. French will generally be needed for meetings.
Appointments should be made and punctuality is
expected, despite the fact that a customer may be slightly
late. Visiting cards are essential, preferably in French and
English. The period from July to October should be
avoided for business visits, as many people are on
holiday. **Office hours:** 0800-1200 and 1430-1800
Monday to Friday; 0800-1200 Saturday. During
Ramadan some offices open 0730-1430.
COMMERCIAL INFORMATION: The following
organisations can offer advice: Chambre de Commerce et
d'Industrie et d'Agriculture de la Région de Dakar, BP
118, 1 place de l'Indépendance, Dakar. Tel: 237 189.
Telex: 61112; *or*
Syndicat des Commerçants Importateurs et Exportateurs
de la République du Sénégal (SCIMPEX), BP 806, 12-14
avenue Albert Sarraut, Dakar. Tel: 213 662.

CLIMATE

The dry season runs from December through to May with
cool trade winds in coastal areas. Throughout the rest of
the year a hot monsoon wind blows from the south
bringing the rainy season and hot, humid weather.
Rainfall is heavy in Casamance and in the southeast and
slight in the Sahelian region in the north and northeast,
where temperatures tend to be higher.

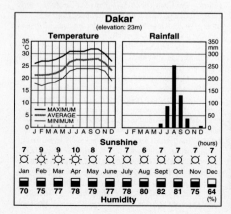

Dakar
(elevation: 23m)

Temperature / Rainfall / Sunshine (hours) / Humidity (%)

	Jan	Feb	Mar	Apr	May	June	July	Aug	Sept	Oct	Nov	Dec
Sunshine	7	9	9	10	8	7	6	7	7	7	7	7
Humidity	70	75	77	78	79	77	78	80	82	81	75	64

Seychelles

80km
40mls

• Bird I.
• Denis I.

Seychelles Group

Praslin
La Digue   □ *international airport*

◇ Silhouette

▷VICTORIA
Mahé

Amirante Is.

SEYCHELLES   Desroches   Coëtivy

INDIAN OCEAN

Aldabra Is.
◦ Cosmoledo Atoll

Farquhar Atoll

400km
200mls

INDIA
AFRICA
Indian Ocean

DAB-M202

Location: Indian Ocean, 1600km (990 miles) east of Kenya.

Seychelles Tourist Board
PO Box 92, Independence House, Victoria, Mahé,
Seychelles
Tel: 225 333. Telex: 2275 (a/b SEYTOB SZ).
High Commission for the Republic of the Seychelles
PO Box 4PE, 2nd Floor, Eros House, 111 Baker Street,
London W1M 1FE
Tel: (0171) 224 1660. Fax: (0171) 487 5756. Telex:
281446. Opening hours: 0900-1630 Monday to Thursday
and 0900-1200 Friday.
Seychelles Tourist Office
Address as above
Tel: (0171) 224 1670. Fax: (0171) 487 5756. Opening
hours: 1000-1600 Monday to Friday.
British High Commission
PO Box 161, 3rd Floor, Victoria House, Victoria, Mahé,
Seychelles
Tel: 225 225 *or* 225 356. Fax: 225 127. Telex: 2269 (a/b
UKREP SZ).
Embassy of the Republic of the Seychelles *and* **Tourist
Office**
Suite 900F, 820 Second Avenue, New York, NY 10017
Tel: (212) 687 9766/7. Fax: (212) 922 9177.
Also deals with enquiries from Canada.
Embassy of the United States of America
PO Box 251, Victoria House, Victoria, Mahé, Seychelles
Tel: 225 256. Fax: 225 189.
**The Canadian High Commission in Dar-es-Salaam
deals with enquiries relating to the Seychelles (see**
Tanzania **later in this book).**

AREA: 454 sq km (175 sq miles).
POPULATION: 68,000 (1990).
POPULATION DENSITY: 149.8 per sq km.
CAPITAL: Victoria (Mahé). **Population:** 24,325 (1987).
GEOGRAPHY: The Seychelles Archipelago occupies
400,000 sq km (150,000 sq miles) of the Indian Ocean
northeast of Madagascar and contains 115 islands and
islets. These fall into two groups of markedly different
appearance, stemming from their distinct geologies:
Granitic: A dense cluster of 42 islands, unique in being
the only mid-ocean group in the world with a granite rock
formation. Their lush green vegetation is tropical in
character, with a profusion of coconut palms, bananas,

Timatic

Health
GALILEO/WORLDSPAN: **TI-DFT/SEZ/HE**
SABRE: **TIDFT/SEZ/HE**

Visa
GALILEO/WORLDSPAN: **TI-DFT/SEZ/VI**
SABRE: **TIDFT/SEZ/VI**

For more information on Timatic codes refer to Contents.

---

mangoes, yams, breadfruit and other tropical fruit.
Indigenous forest exists on the higher slopes where
cinnamon and tea are planted. All, including the second
largest, Praslin, are less than 65km (40 miles) from Mahé.
Coralline: Isolated coral outcrops speckling a vast area of
the Indian Ocean to the southwest of the granitic group.
They rise only a few feet above sea level but are covered
with rich and dense vegetation due to fertilisation by
copious amounts of guano. There is no permanent
population. Aldabra, the largest atoll in the world, contains
one-third of all Seychellois land and is a UNESCO-
designated World Heritage Site. The largest island in either
group is **Mahé**, lying 4°S of the equator. It is 27km (17
miles) long by 8km (5 miles) wide and contains Victoria,
the capital and main port, and 90% of the population. Mahé
is typical of the granitic islands, being mountainous and
covered with jungle vegetation. Its highest point, indeed the
highest point in the Seychelles, is Morne Seychellois
(905m/2970ft). The isolated nature of the Seychelles has
given rise to the evolution of many unique species of flora
and fauna, including the coco-de-mer palm and unique
varieties of orchid, giant tortoise, gecko, chameleon and
'flying fox' (fruitbat). National parks and reserves have
been set up to protect this heritage. The Seychellois are
born out of a mixture of French and British landowners,
freed African slaves and a small number of Indian and
Chinese immigrants, creating a unique culture.
LANGUAGE: The official language is Creole, but
English and French are widely spoken.
RELIGION: 92% Roman Catholic with Anglican,
Seventh Day Adventist, Muslim and other minorities.
TIME: GMT + 4.
ELECTRICITY: 240 volts AC, 50Hz. British 3-pin plugs
are in use.
COMMUNICATIONS: Telecommunications:
SEYTELS offers a 24-hour service for telexes, telegrams,
telephones and faxes via SEYTELS/Cable & Wireless Ltd,
Francis Rachel Street, Victoria, Mahé. Phonecards were
introduced in 1988. IDD is available. Country code: 248.
Outgoing international calls must be made through the
operator. **Post:** The main post office is in Victoria. Airmail
collections are at 1500 weekdays and 1200 Saturdays;
airmail to Western Europe normally takes up to a week.
Post office hours: 0800-1200 and 1300-1600 Monday to
Friday; 0800-1200 Saturday. **Press:** English-language
newspapers include *The Seychelles Nation* (morning daily)
and the *Seychelles Weekend Nation, The People* (monthly,
published by the Seychelles Progressive Front) and
Seychelles Today (monthly news review).
BBC World Service and Voice of America frequencies:
From time to time these change. See the section *How to
Use this Book* for more information.
BBC:

MHz	21.47	17.88	15.42	9.630

Voice of America:

MHz	21.49	15.60	9.525	6.035

Radio Television Seychelles broadcasts a full news bulletin
in English at 1900 daily on 1368kHz; headlines are
broadcast in English at 0700 and 1300.

PASSPORT/VISA

*Regulations and requirements may be subject to change at short notice, and you
are advised to contact the appropriate diplomatic or consular authority before
finalising travel arrangements. Details of these may be found at the head of this
country's entry. Any numbers in the chart refer to the footnotes below.*

	Passport Required?	Visa Required?	Return Ticket Required?
Full British	Yes	No	Yes
BVP	Not valid	-	-
Australian	Yes	No	Yes
Canadian	Yes	No	Yes
USA	Yes	No	Yes
Other EU (As of 31/12/94)	Yes	No	Yes
Japanese	Yes	No	Yes

PASSPORTS: Valid passport required by all.
British Visitors Passport: Not accepted.
VISAS: Not required. A visitor's permit, valid initially for
4 weeks, is issued on arrival, subject to possession of a
return or onward ticket, booked accommodation and
sufficient funds to cover the duration of stay; alternatively
a deposit may be made by 'security' bond in lieu. The pass
may be renewed for up to three months for a fee of S
Rs200. For further information, contact the nearest
Seychelles Tourist Office.
Transit: Passengers in transit must have tickets with
reserved seats for their onward journey.
Temporary residence: Enquire at the High Commission.

MONEY

Currency: Seychelles Rupee (S Re: singular; S Rs: plural)

= 100 cents. Notes are in denominations of S Rs100, 50, 25 and 10. Coins are in denominations of S Rs5 and 1, and 25, 10 and 5 cents. A number of gold and silver coins are also minted (with face values as high as S Rs1500), but these are not in general circulation.

Currency exchange: Exchange facilities are available at the airport banks, which are open for all flight departures and arrivals. The following banks have branches in the Seychelles and will exchange travellers cheques and foreign currency: *Barclays Bank International Limited, Bank of Baroda, Banque Française Commerciale, Development Bank of Seychelles, Habib Bank Limited* and *Standard Chartered Bank Plc.*

Credit cards: American Express and Visa are widely accepted; Access/Mastercard and Diners Club have more limited use. Check with your credit card company for details of merchant acceptability and other services which may be available.

Travellers cheques: Accepted in most hotels, guest-houses, restaurants and shops.

Exchange rate indicators: The following figures are included as a guide to the movements of the Seychelles Rupee against Sterling and the US Dollar:

Date:	Oct '92	Sep '93	Jan '94	Jan '95
£1.00=	7.85	7.80	7.86	7.77
$1.00=	4.95	5.11	5.31	4.97

Currency restrictions: There are no restrictions on the import and export of foreign currency. The import of local currency is unlimited; export is restricted to S Rs100 in notes and S Rs10 in coins. **Banking hours:** 0830-1300 Monday to Friday; 0830-1100 Saturday.

DUTY FREE

The following items may be imported into the Seychelles without incurring customs duty:
200 cigarettes or 50 cigars or 250g of tobacco; 1 litre of spirits; 1 litre of wine; 200cc of perfume and 200cc eau de toilette; other dutiable goods to a total not exceeding S Rs1000 (S Rs500 for children).

Prohibited items: The import of non-prescribed drugs and all firearms, including air pistols, air rifles and spearfishing guns, is prohibited. The import of animals and food and other agricultural produce is strictly controlled and subject to licensing. No pets are admitted without written permission from the Chief Veterinary Officer, Seychelles. There is a 15-day quarantine period on arrival.

PUBLIC HOLIDAYS

Jan 2 '95 For New Year's Day. **Apr 14-15** Easter. **May 1** Labour Day. **Jun 5** Liberation Day. **Jun 15** Corpus Christi. **Jun 29** Independence Day. **Aug 15** Assumption. **Nov 1** All Saints' Day. **Dec 8** Immaculate Conception. **Dec 25** Christmas Day. **Jan 1 '96** New Year's Day. **Apr 5-8** Easter.

HEALTH

Regulations and requirements may be subject to change at short notice, and you are advised to contact your doctor well in advance of your intended date of departure. Any numbers in the chart refer to the footnotes below.

	Special Precautions?	Certificate Required?
Yellow Fever	No	Yes/1
Cholera	No	No
Typhoid & Polio	Yes	- -
Malaria	No	-
Food & Drink	2	-

[1]: A yellow fever vaccination certificate is required by all visitors arriving from affected areas.

[2]: Mains water is normally chlorinated, and whilst relatively safe may cause mild abdominal upsets. Bottled water is available and is advised for the first few weeks of the stay. Milk is pasteurised and dairy products are safe for consumption. Local meat, poultry, seafood, fruit and vegetables are generally considered safe to eat.

Rabies may be present in certain areas. For those at high risk, vaccination before arrival should be considered. If you are bitten abroad, seek medical advice without delay. For more information, consult the *Health* section at the back of the book.

Health care: There is a large general hospital in Victoria and there are clinics elsewhere on Mahé, Praslin and La Digue. Visitors may obtain emergency treatment for a basic consultancy fee of S Rs75. Additional medical insurance is advised.

TRAVEL - International

AIR: The Seychelles' national airline is *Air Seychelles* (*HM*). Other airlines flying to the Seychelles include *British Airways, Air France, Kenya Airways, Air India,* *Somali Airways* and *Aeroflot.*

Approximate flight times: From *London* to Mahé is 11 hours 30 minutes (15 hours via Nairobi) and from *New York* is 24 hours (via London).

International airport: *Mahé Island (SEZ)* (Seychelles International) is 10km (16 miles) southeast from Victoria (travel time – 20 minutes). Some coach services are provided by agents and taxis are available. Airport facilities include an outgoing duty-free shop, banking and currency exchange facilities (0830-1230 Monday to Friday; 0830-1200 Saturday), car hire and restaurant/bar (0800 until the last flight).

SEA: Cruise and cargo ships call at Mahé but there are no scheduled services.

TRAVEL - Internal

AIR: *Air Seychelles* provides an efficient network of scheduled and chartered services from Mahé to Praslin, Denis, Bird, Frégate and Desroches islands.

SEA: Privately-owned schooners provide regular inter-island connections between Mahé, Praslin and La Digue. Government-run ferries also operate on some routes.

ROAD: Traffic drives on the left. There are paved roads only on the two largest islands, Mahé and Praslin; elsewhere the roads are sandy tracks. **Bus:** *SPTC* buses run on a regular basis on Mahé between the rural areas and Victoria, the main town. A bus service also operates on Praslin from 0530-1900 and on La Digue. There are a number of 18-seater coaches for airport transfers and excursions. Prices for buses and coaches are very reasonable. **Taxi:** There are about 135 taxis on Mahé and Praslin with government-controlled rates. Rates on Praslin are 25% higher and there is a surcharge between 2000-0600 on both islands. **Car hire:** There are over 550 cars for hire on Mahé, and a limited number on Praslin. It is advisable to make advance reservations, especially in the high season. Conditions of hire and insurance should be carefully checked. Hire is on an unlimited-mileage basis and the price includes Third Party insurance and tax. Minimum age is 21. Petrol is approximately 30% more expensive than in Europe. **Bicycles** may be hired on Praslin and La Digue. **Traffic regulations:** There is a speed limit of 65kmph (40mph) on the open road, decreasing to 40kmph (25mph) in built-up areas and throughout Praslin. **Documentation:** A national driving licence is sufficient.

JOURNEY TIMES: The following chart gives approximate journey times (in hours and minutes) from Mahé to other islands in the Seychelles.

	Air	Sea
Praslin	0.15	2.30
La Digue	-	3.15
Bird Is.	0.30	7.00
Denis Is.	0.30	6.00
Round Is.	-	0.30
Frégate Is.	0.15	2.00
Moyenne	-	0.30
Desroches	1.00	-

Note: The ferry from Praslin to La Digue takes approximately 30 minutes.

ACCOMMODATION

Although the Seychelles have been a popular tourist destination for more than ten years and now offer the full range of accommodation from self-catering apartments to luxury hotels, careful planning has ensured that the islands have retained the astonishing beauty and quiet charm that attracted the first tourists. Right from the start, the Government decreed that no new building could be higher than the surrounding palm trees, with the result that big-city levels of comfort and convenience have been achieved in thoroughly Seychellois settings. There are about 4500 hotel beds on the islands and it is advisable to confirm reservations with a deposit, particularly during the high season from December to January and in August. For further information, contact the Compagnie Seychelloise de Promotion Hôtelière Ltd, PO Box 683, Victoria, Mahé. Tel: 224 694. Fax: 225 291. Telex: 2407.

HOTELS & GUEST-HOUSES: All recently-built hotels come well up to international standards and there are a number of large resort hotels equipped with air-conditioning, private bathrooms, swimming pools and full sporting facilities. Older hotels and guest-houses on the smaller islands may lack some sophistication, but their charming seclusion has long recommended them to those seeking complete peace and privacy: the late Somerset Maugham once sought out the quietest so that he could write a novel without interruption. Many are former plantation houses modestly modernised and run by the resident owner. Thatched-roof chalets and guest-houses, built in the local style, are to be found mainly on outlying islands. The Seychelles Hotel Association comprises ten hotels on the islands. More information is available from the Association at PO Box 595, Victoria, Mahé. There are no youth hostels and camping is not permitted. For up-to-date prices, contact the Tourist Office.

SELF-CATERING: Self-catering units are available on the main islands. For details, contact the Tourist Office.

RESORTS & EXCURSIONS

Granitic Islands

Mahé: Surrounded by coral reefs, this is the largest of the islands, and houses the international airport, the port and capital (Victoria), the majority of the population and most of the hotels. It is an island of powdery white sands (there are almost 70 beaches on Mahé alone) and lush vegetation, rising through plantations of coconut palms and cinnamon to forested peaks that afford unparalleled views of neighbouring islands. Excursions can be made in glass-bottomed boats from Victoria to nearby *St Anne Marine National Park,* which encloses the islands of St Anne, Cerf, Long, Round and Moyenne; or by coach, taking in such attractions as the market, the *Botanical Gardens* (with coco-de-mer, giant tortoises and orchids), and a replica of London's *Vauxhall Bridge Tower* in Victoria, before setting off around the island to visit Colonial-style mansions in graceful decline, old plantations of cinnamon and vanilla, and everywhere the greenest of vibrant green jungles. Tourists may also visit the *Morne Seychellois National Park,* occupying the highest part of the island. The *National Museum* in Victoria celebrates Seychellois history, folklore and music, and has particularly fine displays depicting the history of spice cultivation.

Praslin: The second largest island is two to three hours by boat or 15 minutes by air (20 scheduled flights per day) from Mahé. It is famous for the *Vallée de Mai,* which contains the double-nutted coco-de-mer palm. Regular excursions are available to smaller islands such as Cousin, Aride, Curieuse and La Digue.

La Digue: Three to three and a half hours by schooner from Mahé or half an hour from Praslin, this beautiful island is the breeding ground of the rare Black Paradise Flycatcher. There are very few cars and the ox-cart remains the principal means of transport (although bicycles may be hired). There are beautiful old plantation houses, such as *Chateau Saint-Cloud,* as well as a vanilla plantation, copra factories and superb beaches.

Frégate: The most easterly and isolated of the granitic islands, Frégate is associated with pirates (Ian Fleming was obsessed with the notion that a pirate's hoard was buried here). It is also the home of the almost extinct magpie robin. Frégate is 15 minutes by air from Mahé.

Thérèse: Notable for its rock-pools and tortoise colony.

Cousin: Two hours by boat from Mahé, Cousin was bought (in 1968) by the International Council for Bird Protection, who operate it as a nature reserve. Amongst the rare bird species thus protected are the brush warbler, the Seychelles toc-toc and the fairy tern. The best time to visit is April or May, when a quarter of a million birds nest on the island. All visits to the island must be made as part of an organised tour. Local rangers act as guides; a full tour of the island takes between one and two hours. Local operators can arrange these trips, usually in conjunction with visits to other islands.

Aride: Two hours from Mahé, Aride is the most northerly of the granitic islands. Home to vast colonies of seabirds, in 1973 it was bought by Christopher Cadbury, President of the Royal Society for Nature Conservation. It is open to visitors from October to the end of April.

Curieuse: Approximately 3km (2 miles) long, Curieuse is covered by lush vegetation and huge takamaka trees. It has been designated a reserve for giant tortoises (imported from Aldabra). Day trips may be arranged from Praslin.

Silhouette: Thought to have been home to one of the Indian Ocean's most notorious pirates, Hodoul, this island may be seen from Beau Vallon Beach on Mahé. It has a population of about 200. Sights include an old plantation house of traditional Seychellois timber construction.

Coralline Islands

Denis: Five to seven hours by boat or 30 minutes by air from Mahé, Denis is also on the edge of the continental shelf and attracts many deep-sea fishermen. Marlin may be caught from October to December. The island's seabird population has, over the years, left rich deposits of guano, which has encouraged the growth of lush vegetation. The minimum stay is two days.

Bird: Six to eight hours by boat or 30 minutes by plane from Mahé, this island is famous for the millions of sooty terns who migrate here to breed between May and September. Its location at the edge of the Seychelles continental shelf (the sea floor drops rapidly to 2000m/5000ft) also makes it a favoured destination for fishermen. Another claim to fame is Esmeralda, said to be 150 years old and the largest tortoise in the world.

Desroches: The largest of the Amirantes archipelago, Desroches is 193km (120 miles) southwest of Mahé (one hour by air). The surrounding coral reef keeps the coastal waters calm and makes it an ideal destination for those seeking watersports. Although Desroches was only recently developed as a resort, there are facilities for water-skiing, windsurfing, sailing, fishing and scuba diving; water scooters may also be hired. The diving is particularly good: there are sea cliffs, tunnels and caves – and, of course, multitudes of fish of many different species. Lessons are available. Visibility is best from September to May. Accommodation is in 20 chalets set amongst casuarina trees and coconut palms.

Plants and Wildlife

As a result of their extraordinary, isolated history, the Seychelles are rich in rare plants which flourish nowhere else on the planet. 81 species are unique survivors from the luxuriant tropical forests which covered the islands until man's belated arrival two centuries ago. Outstanding amongst these is the coco-de-mer (sea coconut), native to Praslin, which grows in the Vallée de Mai. Its seed is the largest in nature, and gave rise to many legends when it was washed ashore on the coasts of Africa, India and Indonesia. Since the islands were unknown, the nuts were thought to have grown under the sea – hence the name. Among the many orchids is the vanilla, once widely cultivated for the essence produced from its aromatic pods. Its ornate leaves and lovely flowers make a wonderful display. It is not, however, necessary to travel the length and breadth of the islands to see interesting plants, as many of them can be viewed in Victoria's Botanical Gardens. The Seychelles are also a major attraction for birdwatchers. Millions of terns nest on some of the islands – among them that most beautiful of seabirds, the fairy tern. Up to two million sooty terns nest on Bird Island, and on Aride can be found the world's largest colonies of lesser noddies, roseate terns and other tropical birds. Some species, on the other hand, are less well represented and are rare almost to the point of extinction. The paradise flycatcher has dwindled to some 30 pairs on one island, La Digue. The Seychelles magpie robin is confined to Frégate, the black parrot to Praslin and the melodious brush warbler to Cousin.

It was only some 20 years ago that active conservation of endangered species began in the Seychelles. Since then, with the establishment of island sanctuaries and nature reserves, much has been done to make the Seychelles a paradise for birds – and for those who love to watch them.

SOCIAL PROFILE

FOOD & DRINK: Seychellois Creole cuisine is influenced by French, African, Chinese, Indian and English traditions. The careful blending of spices is a major feature and much use is made of coconut milk and breadfruit. Local specialities include *kat-kat banane,* coconut curries, *chatini requin, bourgeois grillé, soupe de tectec, bouillon brède, chauve-souris* (fruit bat), *cari bernique, salade de palmiste* (made from the 'heart' of the coconut palm and sometimes known as 'millionaire's salad') and *la daube* (made from breadfruit, yams, cassavas and bananas). Breadfruit is prepared in similar ways to the potato (mashed, chipped, roasted, etc) but has a slightly sweeter taste. Other locally produced fruits and vegetables include aubergines, calabashes, choux choutes, patoles, paw-paws (papaya), bananas, mangoes, avocados, jackfruits, grapefruits, guavas, lychees, pineapples, melons, limes and golden apples. Lobster, octopus, pork and chicken are used more frequently than beef or lamb, which must be imported. Most restaurants offer a few items of what is termed 'international' cuisine, generally with a bias towards preparations of fresh fish and shellfish, as well as the Creole delicacies mentioned above. There are Italian and Chinese restaurants on Mahé. Some of the main hotels have bakeries and home-baked bread is also a feature of some of the small guest-houses and lodges. Waiter service is the norm. All restaurants which are members of the *Seychelles Restaurateurs' Association* quote an average price per person for a 3-course meal inclusive of two glasses of wine and coffee. Prior notice should be given in restaurants for groups of four or more and advance bookings should be made for restaurants on Round and Cerf and for *La Réserve* restaurant on Praslin.

Drink: A wide range of wines, spirits and other alcoholic beverages is available in the Seychelles. *Seybrew,* a German style lager, is made locally. The same company also produces *Guinness* under licence and soft drinks. Local tea is also popular – see below under *Shopping*. A hotel licence permits hotel residents to drink at any time. Alcohol can be sold to anyone between 1400-1800 Monday to Friday; 0800-1200 and 1400-1800 Saturday. Other bars open 1130-1500 and 1800-2200. It is illegal to drink alcohol on any road or in public.

NIGHTLIFE: Largely undeveloped and unsophisticated. There is, however, much to be enjoyed in the evenings, and a speciality is the local *camtolet* music, often accompanied by dancers. Several hotels have evening barbecues and dinner dances. Theatre productions are often staged (in Creole, French and English) and there are cinemas in Victoria and casinos at *Beau Vallon Bay Hotel* and the *Plantation Club.*

SHOPPING: Local handicrafts include work with textiles (such as batik), fibres (such as basketwares, table-mats and hats) and wood (such as traditional furniture, ornaments and model boats). Pottery and paintings may also be bought. Special souvenirs might include a coco-de-mer or jewellery made from green snail shells. Tea-growing and manufacturing in the Seychelles is done on a small scale. Local tea can be bought in the shops or when visiting the tea factory on Mahé, where many blends of tea may be sampled at the *Tea Tavern.* Vanilla is cultivated as a climbing plant around the base of trees as pollination can be done by hand. Pods can be bought in shops and used as flavouring. Cinnamon grows wild on all the islands. It can be bought as oil or in quills made from dried bark which can be freshly grated before use. **Shopping hours:** 0800-1700 Monday to Friday; 0800-1200 Saturday. Some shops close 1200-1300 weekdays.

SPORT: Golf: The *Reef Hotel* has a 9-hole golf course at Anse Aux Pins, on Mahé, and visitors can arrange temporary membership at the clubhouse, as well as hire equipment. **Fishing:** Game fishing is a comparatively new sport in the Seychelles, but the abundance of fish has already made the islands popular with enthusiasts. Fishing seasons are governed by weather conditions: from May to September, the trade winds blow from the southeast; and from November to February, from the northwest. Black, blue and striped marlin, sailfish, yellowfish and dogtooth tuna, wahoo and barracuda are just a few of the game fish found in these tropical waters. **Boat charters:** Power boats, cabin cruisers and yachts are available for charter for anglers and others wishing to explore the islands at their own pace. Vessels may be booked in advance by the day, week or month. Reservations may be made at local agents or through *The Marine Charter Association,* PO Box 469, Victoria, Mahé. Tel: 322 126. Telex: 2359 (a/b MCA SZ). **Diving:** Coral reef diving is perhaps the main sporting attraction in the Seychelles. Spearfishing is forbidden and, perhaps as a consequence, the fish are not afraid of people. The clear water makes conditions perfect for underwater photography. The coastal waters are a haven for 100 species of coral and over 900 species of fish.

The *Seychelles Underwater Centre* is run by professional divers and is affiliated to the *British Sub Aqua Club*. The address is PO Box 384, Victoria, Mahé. Tel: 247 357.
Watersports: Windsurfers, canoes, sailing dinghies, etc may be hired on the more popular beaches, such as Beau Vallon Bay on Mahé, and water-skiing and paragliding are available at many other resort areas. Equipment may be hired. **Other:** There are also opportunities for **squash, tennis** and **badminton.**
SPECIAL EVENTS: The following events are celebrated annually in the Seychelles:
Apr *SUBIO, Festival of Underwater Images.* **End Sep** *La Fête La Digue Annual Regatta.* **End Oct** *Creole Festival.* **Nov** *Annual Fishing Competition.*
SOCIAL CONVENTIONS: The people live a simple and unsophisticated island life and tourism is carefully controlled to protect the unspoilt charm of the islands. Before the international airport opened in 1971, the islands could be reached only by sea, and since they are miles from anywhere, visitors were few and far between and the people were little influenced by the outside world. They developed their own language and culture which – like so many things on the islands – are unique. Shaking hands is the customary form of greeting. The Seychellois are very hospitable and welcome guests into their homes. When visiting someone's home, a gift is acceptable. A mixture of imperial and metric systems operates. For example, petrol is dispensed in litres, whilst bars sell bottled and draught beer in half-pint measures. Casual wear is essential and formal clothes are only worn by church-goers. Swimwear should only be worn on the beaches. **Tipping:** Tips in restaurants, hotels, taxi drivers, porters, etc are usually 5-10% of the bill or fare. All hotel and restaurant tariffs include a service charge, but payment is not obligatory.

BUSINESS PROFILE

ECONOMY: During the early 1970s, tourism overtook agriculture as the largest sector in the Seychelles economy and now accounts for approximately 20% of domestic economic activity and draws 90% of Seychelles' foreign exchange earnings. The rapid overall growth the economy experienced during the 1970s as a result of the tourist boom has faltered in the 1980s, undermined by high fares, insufficient routes and internal political uncertainty. Shaken by the prospect of economic decline so soon after the advent of prosperity, the Government is seeking to diversify the economy. The fishing fleet is to be modernised and expanded and a 200-mile exclusion zone has been declared. Local industry is concentrated in brewing and tobacco, plastics, soap and detergent; there is also some small-scale manufacturing. The National Oil Corporation was set up to develop exploration after gas was discovered offshore in 1980. Fish, copra and cinnamon are the main exports while food, fuel, manufactured goods and transport equipment are the main imports. The Seychelles' geographical position allows for a thriving re-export business.
BUSINESS: Businessmen do not wear suits and ties, although a smart appearance is advised. Most executives speak English and/or French. **Office hours:** 0800-1200 and 1300-1600 Monday to Friday.
COMMERCIAL INFORMATION: The following organisation can offer advice: Seychelles Chamber of Commerce and Industry, PO Box 443, 38 Premier Building, Victoria, Mahé. Tel: 223 812 *or* 221 422.

CLIMATE

The islands lie outside the cyclone belt but receive monsoon rains from November to February with the northwest trade winds. This hot and humid season gives way to a period of cooler weather though the temperature rarely falls below 24°C and rougher seas when the trade winds blow from the southeast (May to September).

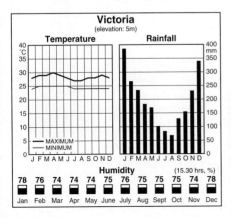

Victoria
(elevation: 5m)

Temperature — **Rainfall**

MAXIMUM / MINIMUM

J F M A M J J A S O N D J F M A M J J A S O N D

Humidity (15.30 hrs, %)

78	76	74	74	74	75	76	75	75	75	74	78
Jan	Feb	Mar	Apr	May	June	July	Aug	Sept	Oct	Nov	Dec

Sierra Leone

200km
100mls

GUINEA

CONAKRY
Kabala
Gt. Scarcies
Niger
Rokel
Loma Mtns.
Makeni
Lunsar
Sefadu
ATLANTIC OCEAN
SIERRA LEONE
FREETOWN
Yawri Bay
Bo
Sewa
Kenema
Sherbro I.
Bonthe
Pujehun
Mano
Turner's Pen.
LIBERIA

DAB-M203

□ *international airport*

Location: West Africa.

Note: The security situation in Sierra Leone is deteriorating. Rebel forces have taken several expatriate hostages, including six Britons, in the past three months. It is strongly advised not to travel to or through Sierra Leone. *Source: FCO Travel Advice Unit – January 26, 1995.*

National Tourist Board of Sierra Leone
PO Box 1435, International Conference Centre, Aberdeen Hill, Freetown, Sierra Leone
Tel: 272 520 *or* 272 396. Fax: 272 197.
High Commission for the Republic of Sierra Leone
33 Portland Place, London W1N 3AG
Tel: (0171) 636 6483/6. Fax: (0171) 927 8130. Opening hours: 1000-1300 and 1430-1530 Monday to Friday.
National Tourist Board of Sierra Leone
375 Upper Richmond Road West, London SW14 7NX
Tel: (0181) 392 9188. Fax: (0181) 392 1318. Opening hours: 0900-1800 Monday to Friday.
British High Commission
Standard Chartered Bank Building of Sierra Leone Ltd, Lightfoot Boston Street, Freetown, Sierra Leone
Tel: 223 961/5. Telex: 3235 (a/b 3235 UKREP SL).
Embassy of the Republic of Sierra Leone
1701 19th Street, NW, Washington, DC 20009
Tel: (202) 939 9261.
Also deals with enquiries from Canada.
Embassy of the United States of America
Corner of Walpole and Siaka Stevens Streets, Freetown, Sierra Leone
Tel: 226 481/5 *or* 226 155. Fax: 225 471.
The Canadian High Commission in Accra deals with enquiries relating to Sierra Leone (see *Ghana* earlier in the book).

AREA: 71,740 sq km (27,699 sq miles).
POPULATION: 4,260,000 (1991 estimate).
POPULATION DENSITY: 59.4 per sq km.
CAPITAL: Freetown. **Population:** 469,776 (1985).
GEOGRAPHY: Sierra Leone is bordered to the northwest, north and northeast by Guinea Republic, and to the southeast by Liberia. To the south and southwest lies the Atlantic Ocean. A flat plain up to 110km (70 miles) wide stretches the length of the coast except for the Freetown peninsula, where the Sierra Lyoa Mountains rise to 1000m (3280ft). In some coastal areas, sand bars have formed that stretch out as far as 112km (70 miles). Behind the coastal plain is the central forested area,

drained by eight principal rivers, which has been cleared for agriculture. The land rises in altitude towards the east to the Guinea Highlands, a high plateau with peaks rising to over 1830m (6000ft) in the Loma Mountains and Tingi Hills area. The Mende tribe is prominent in the south and the Temne in the west and central areas.
LANGUAGE: The official language is English. Krio is more widely spoken. Local dialects are Mende and Temne.
RELIGION: Principally Animist with Muslim and Christian minorities.
TIME: GMT.
ELECTRICITY: 230/240 volts AC, 50Hz. Supply subject to fluctuations.
COMMUNICATIONS: Telephone: IDD is available. Country code: 232. Outgoing international calls must go through the operator. **Telex/telegram:** Facilities at Slecom House, 7 Wallace Johnson Street, Freetown. **Post:** Airmail to Western Europe takes about five days. **Press:** Sierra Leone's English-language daily is *The Daily Mail*. Other newspapers are the *New Shaft, Citizen* and *Vision*.
BBC World Service and Voice of America frequencies: From time to time these change. See the section *How to Use this Book* for more information.

BBC:

MHz	17.79	15.40	15.07	9.600

Voice of America:

MHz	21.49	15.60	9.525	6.035

PASSPORT/VISA

Regulations and requirements may be subject to change at short notice, and you are advised to contact the appropriate diplomatic or consular authority before finalising travel arrangements. Details of these may be found at the head of this country's entry. Any numbers in the chart refer to the footnotes below.

	Passport Required?	Visa Required?	Return Ticket Required?
Full British	Yes	Yes	Yes
BVP	Not valid	-	-
Australian	Yes	Yes	Yes
Canadian	Yes	Yes	Yes
USA	Yes	Yes	Yes
Other EU (As of 31/12/94)	Yes	Yes	Yes
Japanese	Yes	Yes	Yes

Restricted entry: Nationals of Liberia should check with the High Commission, since visa applications are judged individually.
PASSPORTS: Valid passport required by all.
British Visitors Passport: Not accepted.
VISAS: Required by all except:
(a) nationals of Benin, Burkina Faso, Cape Verde, Côte d'Ivoire, Gambia, Ghana, Guinea Republic, Guinea-Bissau, Mali, Mauritania, Niger, Nigeria, Senegal and Togo (a return ticket is required by these nationals for visits of less than 90 days);
(b) holders of a re-entry permit.
Types of visa: Tourist and Business. Cost: *Tourist* – £35; *Business* – £45.
Validity: Entry Permits and visas generally allow a stay of 1 week extendable up to 6 months in Sierra Leone.
Application to: Consulate (or Consular section at Embassy or High Commission). For addresses, see top of entry.
Application requirements: (a) Completed application form. (b) 1 passport-size photo. (c) Passport. (d) Company letter for Business visa.
Working days required: 3 days. Several weeks where referral to authorities in Sierra Leone is necessary.

MONEY

Currency: Leone (Le) = 100 cents. Notes are in denominations of Le100, 50, 20, 10, 5 and 2. Coins are in denominations of Le1, and 50, 20, 10, 5, 1 and 0.5 cents. In June 1986, a system of 'floating' exchange rates was introduced to correct persistent over-valuation of the Leone.
Credit cards: American Express is widely accepted and Access/Mastercard, Diners Club and Visa have limited acceptance. Check with your credit card company for details of merchant acceptability and other facilities which might be available.
Exchange rate indicators: The following figures are included as a guide to the movements of the Leone against Sterling and the US Dollar:

Date:	Oct '92	Sep '93	Jan '94	Jan '95
£1.00=	798.85	841.75	812.35	930.28
$1.00=	503.37	551.24	549.07	594.62

Currency restriction: The import and export of local currency is limited to Le50,000. Export of foreign currency up to US$5000 (larger amounts must be authorised by the National Bank of Sierra Leone) is permitted if declared on entry.
Banking hours: 0800-1330 Monday to Thursday; 0800-1400 Friday.

Timatic

Health
GALILEO/WORLDSPAN: **TI-DFT/FNA/HE**
SABRE: **TIDFT/FNA/HE**

Visa
GALILEO/WORLDSPAN: **TI-DFT/FNA/VI**
SABRE: **TIDFT/FNA/VI**

For more information on Timatic codes refer to Contents.

DUTY FREE

The following may be imported into Sierra Leone without incurring customs duty: *200 cigarettes or 225g tobacco; 1.136 litres of wine or spirits; 1.136 litres of perfume.*

PUBLIC HOLIDAYS

Jan 1 '95 New Year's Day. **Mar 2** Eid al-Fitr (End of Ramadan). **Apr 14-17** Easter. **Apr 27** Independence Day. **May 10** Eid al-Adha (Feast of the Sacrifice). **Aug 9** Mouloud (Prophet's Birthday). **Dec 25-26** Christmas. **Jan 1 '96** New Year's Day. **Feb 22** Eid al-Fitr (End of Ramadan). **Apr 5-8** Easter.
Note: Muslim festivals are timed according to local sightings of various phases of the Moon and the dates given above are approximations. During the lunar month of Ramadan that precedes Eid al-Fitr, Muslims fast during the day and feast at night and normal business patterns may be interrupted. Many restaurants are closed during the day and there may be restrictions on smoking and drinking. Some disruption may continue into Eid al-Fitr itself. Eid al-Fitr and Eid al-Adha may last anything from two to ten days, depending on the region. For more information see the section *World of Islam* at the back of the book.

HEALTH

Regulations and requirements may be subject to change at short notice, and you are advised to contact your doctor well in advance of your intended date of departure. Any numbers in the chart refer to the footnotes below.

	Special Precautions?	Certificate Required?
Yellow Fever	Yes	1
Cholera	Yes	2
Typhoid & Polio	Yes	-
Malaria	3	-
Food & Drink	4	-

[1]: A yellow fever certificate is required of travellers arriving from infected areas. Travellers arriving from non-endemic zones should note that vaccination is strongly recommended for travel outside the urban areas, even if an outbreak of the disease has not been reported and they would normally not require a vaccination certificate to enter the country.
[2]: Following WHO guidelines issued in 1973, a cholera vaccination certificate is not a condition of entry to Sierra Leone. However, cholera is a serious risk in this country and precautions are essential. Up-to-date advice should be sought before deciding whether these precautions should include vaccination, as medical opinion is divided over its effectiveness. See the *Health* section later the book.
[3]: Malaria risk exists, predominantly in the malignant *falciparum* form, all year throughout the country. Resistance to chloroquine has been reported.
[4]: All water should be regarded as being potentially contaminated. Water used for drinking, brushing teeth or making ice should have first been boiled or otherwise sterilised. Milk is unpasteurised and should be boiled. Powdered or tinned milk is available and is advised, but make sure that it is reconstituted with pure water. Avoid dairy products which are likely to have been made from unboiled milk. Only eat well-cooked meat and fish, preferably served hot. Pork, salad and mayonnaise may carry increased risk. Vegetables should be cooked and fruit peeled.
Rabies is present. For those at high risk, vaccination before arrival should be considered. If you are bitten abroad seek medical advice without delay. For more information, consult the *Health* section at the back of the book.
Bilharzia (schistosomiasis) is present. Avoid swimming and paddling in fresh water. Swimming pools which are well-chlorinated and maintained are safe.
Health care: Medical facilities are extremely limited and are, if anything, continuing to decline. According to UN estimates, Sierra Leone has the highest death rate and the second-highest infant mortality rate (200 out of every 1000 infants die within a year of birth). Missions and foreign aid organisations provide some medical facilities. Health insurance is strongly recommended. It is advisable to take personal medical supplies.

TRAVEL - International

AIR: Sierra Leone's national airline is *Sierra National Airlines.* It currently only operates flights between Freetown and Paris. Other airlines serving Sierra Leone are *Air Gambia, KLM* and *UTA*.
Approximate flight time: From London to Freetown is 6 hours 30 minutes (direct flight).
International airport: *Freetown (FNA)* (Lungi), is 24km (18 miles) north of the city (travel time – 2 hours). There is a catamaran/ferry link as well as taxi and bus services to the city. Airport facilities include a post office, bar, shops and currency exchange.
Departure tax: Le5000 on international departures. Transit passengers are exempt.
SEA: The principal port is Freetown which has services to Liberia and Guinea Republic.
RAIL: There are no passenger services at present.
ROAD: There are routes from Guinea Republic and Liberia, but access depends on the prevailing political situation. Contact the Embassy or High Commission for up-to-date information.

TRAVEL - Internal

AIR: *Sierra National Airlines* run flights to Hastings, Kenema, Bo, Gbangbatoke, Yengema and Bonthe.
SEA: Ferries connect all coastal ports. For details, contact local authorities.
ROAD: Traffic drives on the right. Sierra Leone has over 6440km (4000 miles) of roads. Although the principal highways have a tarred surface, the secondary roads are poorly maintained and often impassable during the rainy season. There are some roadblocks at night on major roads near centres of population. **Bus:** Local and long-distance bus services are operated by the *Sierra Leone Road Transport Corporation.* Buses are fast and cheap and connect all the major centres. **Documentation:** An International Driving Permit is required.
URBAN: Limited bus services in Freetown are operated by the *Road Transport Corporation,* though a substantial part of the city's public transport is provided by minibuses and shared taxis.

ACCOMMODATION

There are several hotels in Freetown of international standard with air-conditioning and swimming pools. It is always advisable to make reservations in advance. Additionally, there are three luxury hotels located on the peninsula at Lakka and Tokay. The YMCA in Freetown offers clean, cheap accommodation with shared bathroom and kitchen facilities at a reasonable rate. Hotels in the interior are rare, although in Bo there is now the Hotel Sir Milton which is of international standard. There are also rest houses, for which application must be made to the Ministry of the Interior; guests must bring their own linen.

RESORTS & EXCURSIONS

The most accessible part of Sierra Leone is the **Freetown Peninsula**. From *Leicester Peak* superb views of the city between the sea and the mountains unfold below, and a narrow, steep road through the mountains leads to the old Creole Villages (dating from 1800) of **Leicester, Gloucester** and **Regent**. The area was chosen as a resettlement area for liberated slaves who built the villages of **Sussex**, **York**, **Kent**, **Waterloo**, **Hastings** and **Wellington**. **Freetown** itself, surrounded by thickly vegetated hills, is both a colourful and historic port. Attractions include a 500-year-old cotton tree; the museum; the *De Ruyter Stone*; *Government Wharf* and *'King's Yard'* (where freed slaves waited to be given land); *Fourah Bay College,* the oldest university in West Africa; *Marcon's Church,* built in 1820; and the *City Hotel,* immortalised in Graham Greene's novel 'The Heart of the Matter'. The *King Jimmy Market* and the bazaars offer a colourful spectacle and interesting shopping. A boat trip up the *Rokel River* to **Bunce Island,** one of the first slave trading stations of West Africa, makes an interesting excursion.
GAME PARKS: Permits, obtainable from the Ministry of Agriculture and Forestry in Freetown, are necessary for visits to Reserves, and a guide is provided. For hunting, a special pass is required (48 hours notice is needed).
The Outamba-Kilimi National Park in northern Sierra Leone, which can be reached from Freetown by road or air, offers varied and spectacular scenery and, at this and other reserves, there are game animals such as elephants, chimpanzees and pigmy hippos. The **Sakanbiarwa** plant reserve has an extensive collection of orchids, which are at their best early in the year.

SOCIAL PROFILE

FOOD & DRINK: Restaurants in the capital serve English, French, Armenian and Lebanese food. African food is served in hotels; local dishes include excellent fish, lobster and prawns, exotic fruit and vegetables.
NIGHTLIFE: Freetown has nightclubs and two casinos and there is music, dancing and local entertainment arranged by the hotels along Lumley Beach in the Cape Sierra district. A beachside club has the country's top pop groups playing on its terrace.
SHOPPING: Opening hours: 0800-1200 and 1400-1700 Monday to Saturday.
SPORT: The tourist resorts in Cape Sierra, Lakka and Tokay have good beaches with safe **swimming** and facilities for **windsurfing, yachting** and game **fishing**. The coral in the clear waters off York and Lumley beaches are an added attraction for **divers**. There is also a first-class **golf** course. In Freetown, the Siaka stadium and sports complex has facilities for **football,** swimming, diving, **basketball, gymnastics** and **athletics.** Domestic league football matches can be seen here.
SOCIAL CONVENTIONS: The majority of people in Sierra Leone still live a traditional, agricultural way of life, with ruling chiefs, religions which preserve social stability as well as local music, dance, customs and traditions. Handshaking is the normal form of greeting. It is usual to be entertained in a hotel or restaurant, particularly for business visitors. Small tokens of appreciation are always welcome. Casual wear is suitable everywhere. Men are rarely expected to wear suits and ties. **Tipping:** Most hotels and restaurants include a service charge of 10-15%. Taxi drivers do not expect tips.

BUSINESS PROFILE

ECONOMY: One of Africa's poorest countries, agriculture employs over two-thirds of the workforce in Sierra Leone, growing coffee, cocoa, palm kernels, nuts, ginger and cassava. Fishing is also significant. Industry is confined to light manufacturing, mostly of consumer goods such as textiles, furniture and suitcases. The mainstay of the economy is mining, which supplies the bulk of the country's foreign exchange: diamonds are the main commodity, with gold (which is growing in importance), bauxite and titanium ore making up the balance. Titanium is the most lucrative of these products and production is likely to increase rapidly following the discovery of new deposits. Sierra Leone has had problems, however, with its oil industry; although deposits have been identified they are proving difficult to develop and Sierra Leone has had to buy most of its needs on the world market using up much precious foreign exchange. In 1986 a barter arrangement was reached with Britain which eased the pressure. Since then, Sierra Leone has entered into several agreements with the IMF, all of which have been aborted because of the Government's failure to curb expenditure and reduce its debt. A creeping insurgency against Captain Strasser's military government sustained by Foday Sankohh's Revolutionary United Front (which appears to consist largely of disaffected soldiery) with the backing of Charles Taylor, the rebel Liberian leader, has reached a point of gruesome crisis. If an agreement is not reached, the situation could, potentially, develop into anarchic chaos on a scale to match that in Somalia or Liberia. This would spell disaster for an already fragile economy.
BUSINESS: English is the most common language in business circles. Appointments and punctuality are expected. Visiting cards are essential. September to June are the best months for business visits. **Office hours:** 0800-1200 and 1400-1645 Monday to Friday.
COMMERCIAL INFORMATION: The following organisation can offer advice: Sierra Leone Chamber of Commerce, Industry and Agriculture, PO Box 502, 5th Floor, Guma Building, Lamina, Sankoh Street, Freetown. Tel: 226 305. Fax: 228 005. Telex: 3712.

CLIMATE

Tropical and humid all year. Between November and April the coastal areas are cooled by sea breezes. In December and January the dry dusty *Harmattan* wind blows from the Sahara. During the rainy season between May and November rainfall can be torrential.

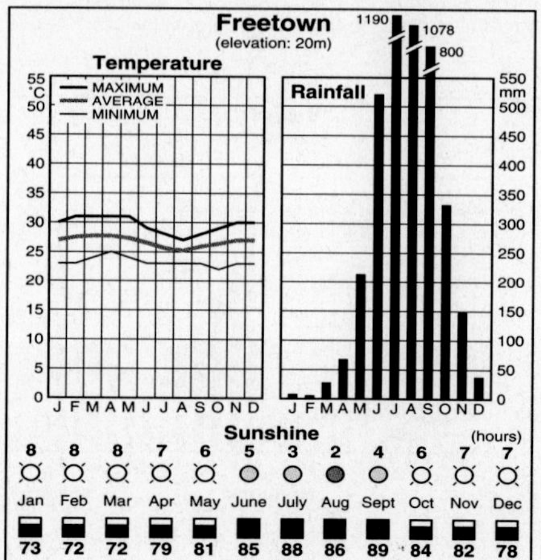
Freetown
(elevation: 20m)
Temperature
MAXIMUM
AVERAGE
MINIMUM
°C
55 50 45 40 35 30 25 20 15 10 5 0
J F M A M J J A S O N D
Rainfall
mm
550 500 450 400 350 300 250 200 150 100 50 0
1190
1078
800
J F M A M J J A S O N D
Sunshine
(hours)
8 8 8 7 6 5 3 2 4 6 7 7
Jan Feb Mar Apr May June July Aug Sept Oct Nov Dec
73 72 72 79 81 85 88 86 89 84 82 78
Humidity
(%)

Singapore

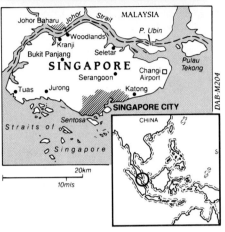

Location: South-East Asia.

Singapore Tourist Promotion Board
Raffles City Tower #36-04, 250 North Bridge Road,
Singapore 0617
Tel: 339 6622. Fax: 339 9423. Telex: 33375.
High Commission for the Republic of Singapore
9 Wilton Crescent, London SW1X 8SA
Tel: (0171) 235 8315 *or* 235 5441 (Visa section). Fax:
(0171) 245 6583. Telex: 262564. Opening hours: 1000-
1230 and 1400-1600 Monday to Friday.
Singapore Tourist Promotion Board
1st Floor, Carrington House, 126-130 Regent Street,
London W1R 5FE
Tel: (0171) 437 0033. Fax: (0171) 734 2191. Opening
hours: 0900-1700 Monday to Friday.
British High Commission
Tanglin Road, Singapore 1024
Tel: 473 9333. Fax: 475 2320 *or* 474 0468.
Embassy of the Republic of Singapore
3501 International Place, NW, Washington, DC 20008
Tel: (202) 537 3100. Fax: (202) 537 0876.
Singapore Tourist Promotion Board
NBR, 12th Floor, 590 Fifth Avenue, New York, NY
10036
Tel: (212) 302 4861. Fax: (212) 302 4801.
Office also in: Chicago.
Embassy of the United States of America
30 Hill Street, Singapore 0617
Tel: 338 0251. Fax: 338 4550.
Consulate of the Republic of Singapore
Suite 1305, 999 West Hastings Street, Vancouver, British
Columbia V6C 2W2
Tel: (604) 669 5115. Fax: (604) 669 5153.
Singapore Tourist Promotion Board
Suite 1000, 121 King Street West, Toronto, Ontario M5H
3T9
Tel: (416) 323 9139. Fax: (416) 363 5752.
Canadian High Commission
PO Box 845, 14th & 15th Floors, IBM Towers, 80 Anson
Road, Singapore 9016
Tel: 225 6363. Fax: 225 2450. Telex: 21277 (a/b
DOMCAN RS).

AREA: 626.4 sq km (241.9 sq miles).
POPULATION: 2,818,200 (1992 estimate).
POPULATION DENSITY: 4499.1 per sq km.
GEOGRAPHY: The island of Singapore is situated off
the southern extremity of the Malay Peninsula, to which
it is joined by a causeway carrying a road, railway and
waterpipe. The Johor Strait between the island and the

	Health
GALILEO/WORLDSPAN: **TI-DFT/SIN/HE**	
SABRE: **TIDFT/SIN/HE**	
	Visa
GALILEO/WORLDSPAN: **TI-DFT/SIN/VI**	
SABRE: **TIDFT/SIN/VI**	

For more information on Timatic codes refer to Contents.

mainland is about 1km (0.8 miles) wide. The Republic of
Singapore includes some 58 islets. It is a mainly flat
country with low hills, the highest being Bukit Timah at
163m (545ft). In the northeast the island large areas
have been reclaimed, and much of the original jungle and
swamp covering the low-lying areas has been cleared.
LANGUAGE: Chinese (Mandarin), English, Malay and
Tamil. Most Singaporeans are bilingual and speak
English, which is used for business and administration.
RELIGION: Confucian, Taoist, Buddhist, Christian,
Hindu and Muslim.
TIME: GMT + 8.
ELECTRICITY: 220/240 volts AC, 50Hz. Plug fittings
of the 3-pin square type are in use. Many hotels have
110-volt outlets.
COMMUNICATIONS: Telephone: Full IDD is
available. Country code: 65. Outgoing international code:
005. **Fax:** There are services at many major hotels and at
the Telecoms buildings in Robinson Road and Exeter
Road. **Telex/telegram:** Telegrams can be sent from post
offices, hotels, the Central Telegraph Office at 35
Robinson Road and the Comcentre near Orchard Road.
Outgoing telexes can be sent from public telex booths,
Telecoms service counters and at many hotels. Incoming
international telexes are accepted only when replying to
an outgoing telex from Singapore and when the sender is
present. **Post:** Airmail to Europe takes up to a week.
There are limited postal facilities at many hotels. Post
office hours: 0900-1700 Monday to Friday, and until
2100 on Wednesday. The airport and Orchard Point
branches are open 0800-2000 daily. **Press:** The local
English-language newspapers are *The Business Times,
The Straits Times* and *The New Paper.*
**BBC World Service and Voice of America
frequencies:** From time to time these change. See the
section *How to Use this Book* for more information.

BBC:				
MHz	17.83	15.31	11.95	6.195
Voice of America:				
MHz	15.43	15.18	9.770	7.120

PASSPORT/VISA

*Regulations and requirements may be subject to change at short notice, and you
are advised to contact the appropriate diplomatic or consular authority before
finalising travel arrangements. Details of these may be found at the head of this
country's entry. Any numbers in the chart refer to the footnotes below.*

	Passport Required?	Visa Required?	Return Ticket Required?
Full British	Yes	No/1	Yes
BVP	Not valid	-	-
Australian	Yes	No/1	Yes
Canadian	Yes	No/1	Yes
USA	Yes	No/1	Yes
Other EU (As of 31/12/94)	Yes	No/1	Yes
Japanese	Yes	No/1	Yes

Note: (a) Women in an advanced state of pregnancy
must obtain a Social Visit Pass prior to arrival; apply at
the High Commission or Embassy. (b) Severe penalties
are imposed on those found in possession of narcotics;
the death penalty is in force for those convicted of
trafficking in heroin or morphine.
PASSPORTS: Valid passport required by all.
British Visitors Passport: Not acceptable.
VISAS: Required only by the following:
(a) nationals of Afghanistan, Algeria, Azerbaijan,
Cambodia, China, CIS, India, Iraq, Jordan, Laos,
Lebanon, Libya, Syria, Tunisia, Vietnam and Yemen;
(b) those holding Refugee Travel Documents issued by
Middle East countries to refugees from Palestine, Hong
Kong ID cards or travel documents of Arab countries.
Visitors from Thailand and the Philippines need a visa if
their stay exceeds 14 days.
[1] All other nationals require a 14-day Social Visit Pass,
which is issued on arrival, provided the traveller holds a
valid national passport, confirmed onward or return
travel documentation, and sufficient funds to cover
expenses for duration of stay. For a stay of up to 2 weeks
or longer, the passport has to be valid for 6 months after
departure from Singapore.The Social Visit Pass can be
extended to a maximum of 3 months (in one calendar
year) on application to the Singapore Immigration
Department in Singapore, subject to the entry
requirements being met and at the discretion of the
Immigration official in Singapore.
Types of visa: *Visa* (enquire at High Commission or
Embassy for costs), *Social Visit/Student Pass* (cost
dependent on nationality of applicant; for UK passport
holders approximately £6.50, payable in cash or by postal
order) and *Professional Visit Pass* (cost: Sing$25, to be
paid on arrival in local currency). *Transit visas* are not
normally required if the visitor has confirmed onward

travel documents and leaves Singapore within 14 days.
This facility is not, however, available to nationals listed
under (a) and (b) above who require visas in *all* cases.
Note: Holders of valid passports from the republics of
the former USSR or China *may* visit for a maximum of
36 hours in transit without visas provided they hold
confirmed onward/return bookings.
Validity: *Social Visit/Student Pass:* Maximum of 3
months. *Professional Visit Pass:* Up to 6 months. *Visa:*
Enquire at High Commission or Embassy.
Application to: Consulate (or Consular section at High
Commission or Embassy). For addresses, see top of
entry.
Application requirements: *For Social Visit Pass:* (a)
Valid travel documents. (b) Sufficient funds. (c) 1
passport-size photo. (d) 2 completed application forms.
For Student Pass: (a) Valid travel documents. (b) 2
passport-size photos. (c) 2 copies of acceptance letter
from college/university in Singapore. (d) 2 completed
application forms.
For Professional Visit Pass: (a) Valid travel documents
(photocopy of passport will suffice). (b) 2 passport-size
photos. (c) 2 copies respectively of letters from own and
sponsoring company. (d) 2 copies of letter stating the
reason for visit. (e) 2 completed application forms.
For Visa: (a) Valid passport. (b) 2 completed application
forms. (c) 2 passport-size photos. (d) 2 copies of letter
stating reason for visit. (e) 2 copies of a letter from local
sponsor in Singapore.
Working days required: 6-8 weeks.
Temporary residence: Apply to Consulate (or Consular
section of High Commission or Embassy), who will
forward application to the authorities in Singapore.

MONEY

Currency: Singapore Dollar (Sing$) = 100 cents. Notes
are in denominations of Sing$10,000, 1000, 500, 100, 50,
20, 10, 5, 2 and 1. Coins are in denominations of Sing$1,
and 50, 20, 10, 5 and 1 cents.
The currency of Brunei is also legal tender; 1 Brunei
Dollar = 1 Singapore Dollar.
Credit cards: Access/Mastercard, American Express,
Diners Club and Visa are widely accepted. Check with
your credit card company for details of merchant
acceptability and other facilities which may be available.
Exchange rate indicators: The following figures are
included as a guide to the movements of the Singapore
Dollar against Sterling and the US Dollar:

Date:	Oct '92	Sep '93	Jan '94	Jan '95
£1.00=	2.57	2.45	2.38	2.28
$1.00=	1.62	1.61	1.61	1.46

Currency restrictions: There is no restriction on the
import and export of local or foreign currency.
Banking hours: 1000-1500 Monday to Friday; 1100-
1600 Saturday. Branches of certain major banks on
Orchard Road open 0930-1500 Sunday.

DUTY FREE

The following goods may be imported into Singapore
without incurring customs duty:
*1 litre of spirits; 1 litre of wine and 1 litre of beer; food
items not exceeding the value of Sing$50.*
Note: These allowances do not apply if arriving from
Malaysia.
Prohibited items: Firearms, non-prescribed drugs, all
pornographic films and literature. There are severe
penalties for possession of narcotics. Export permits are
required for arms, ammunition, explosives, animals,
precious metals and stones, drugs and poisons.

PUBLIC HOLIDAYS

Jan 2 '95 For New Year's Day. **Jan 31-Feb 2** Chinese
New Year. **Mar 3** Hari Raya Puasa (End of Ramadan).
Apr 14 Good Friday. **May 1** Labour Day. **May 10** Hari
Raya Haji (Feast of the Sacrifice). **May 15** Vesak Day.
Aug 9 National Day. **Oct 23** Deepavali (Festival of
Lights). **Dec 25** Christmas Day. **Jan 1 '96** New Year's
Day. **Feb 19-21** Chinese New Year. **Feb 22** Hari Raya
Puasa (End of Ramadan). **Apr 5** Good Friday.
Note: (a) Not all Muslim festivals listed above are
national holidays, but all will affect Muslim businesses.
Muslim festivals are timed according to local sightings of
various phases of the Moon and the dates given above are
approximations. During the lunar month of Ramadan that
precedes Hari Raya Puasa (Eid al-Fitr), Muslims fast
during the day and feast at night and normal business
patterns may be interrupted. Many restaurants are closed
during the day and there may be restrictions on smoking
and drinking. Some disruption may continue into Hari
Raya Puasa itself. Hari Raya Puasa and Hari Raya Haji

(Eid al-Adha) may last anything from two to ten days, depending on the town. For more information see the section *World of Islam* at the back of the book. (b) Hindu festivals are declared according to local astronomical observations and it is only possible to forecast the month of their occurrence.

HEALTH

Regulations and requirements may be subject to change at short notice, and you are advised to contact your doctor well in advance of your intended date of departure. Any numbers in the chart refer to the footnotes below.

	Special Precautions?	Certificate Required?
Yellow Fever	No	1
Cholera	Yes	-
Typhoid & Polio	2	-
Malaria	No	-
Food & Drink	3	-

[1]: A yellow fever certificate of vaccination is required from persons over one year of age who have been in or passed through any country classified either partly or wholly as a yellow fever endemic zone within the previous six days. The countries formerly classified as endemic zones are considered by the Singapore authorities to be still infected.
[2]: Polio has been eliminated, but there may be a risk of typhoid.
[3]: Mains water is normally chlorinated, and whilst relatively safe may cause mild abdominal upsets. Bottled water is available and is advised for the first few weeks of the stay. Milk is pasteurised and dairy products are safe for consumption. Local meat, poultry, seafood, fruit and vegetables are generally considered safe to eat.
Health care: Singapore General Hospital receives emergency cases and health care is exceptionally good. There is a large private sector. Health insurance is recommended.

TRAVEL - International

AIR: Singapore's national airline is *Singapore Airlines (SQ).*
For free advice on air travel, call the Air Travel Advisory Bureau on (0171) 636 5000 (London) *or* (0161) 832 2000 (Manchester).
Approximate flight times: From *London* to Singapore is 13 hours, from *Los Angeles* is 20 hours 25 minutes, from *New York* is 21 hours 55 minutes and from *Sydney* is 9 hours 15 minutes.
International airport: *Changi (SIN)*, 20km (12 miles) east of the city (travel time – 30 minutes). Airport facilities include duty-free shops, shops, restaurant, banks, car hire and hotel reservation service. Buses run to the city every 10 minutes 0700-2330 (not recommended for the elderly or those with baggage). Full taxi service to the city is available by metered cabs, with surcharge of Sing$3 for taxis from the airport and 50% surcharge for fares 2400-0600.
Departure tax: Sing$15 levied on all international flights. Transit passengers and children under two years of age are exempt.
SEA: The international port is Singapore itself, the second-busiest in the world.
RAIL: Trains run to Kuala Lumpur and Butterworth (Malaysia) on a route which extends to Bangkok. There are five trains daily between Singapore and Kuala Lumpur, some of which offer air-conditioning and dining cars. There are also overnight trains with sleepers.
ROAD: Singapore is connected to Malaysia and the mainland of Asia by a causeway which crosses the Johor Strait; bus and coach services operate to the Malaysian town of Johor Baharu and beyond.

TRAVEL - Internal

AIR: Sightseeing flights can be arranged locally through the *Republic of Singapore Flying Club.*
SEA: A ferry leaves the World Trade Centre for Sentosa every 15 minutes from 0730, seven days a week. There are also cruises of the harbour and islands and cruises in junks.
ROAD: Bus: There is a well-developed system of local services run by two main companies. The service is cheap and efficient. There are additional peak-hours-only shuttle and minibus services. A flat fare system operates on the one-man routes. A timetable and route map are available from bookstores. Traffic drives on the left. **Car hire:** There are several car hire/self-drive firms with offices at the airport and in hotels. **Documentation:** International Driving Permit required.
URBAN: Taxi: These are numerous and relatively cheap. They can be picked up from outside hotels and official ranks or flagged down in the streets. Taxis are often scarce during the rush hours (0700-1015 and 1600-1800) and during heavy rain storms. Fares are metered and only this fare must be paid but there are a number of surcharges: 50 cents on the metered fare for each passenger if more than two adults (three children under 12 count as two adults); Sing$1 for all luggage placed in the boot; 50% on the metered fare for journeys 2400-0600; Sing$3 for all journeys starting at the airport; Sing$2 for all taxis booked by telephone; Sing$3 if booked more than half an hour in advance; Sing$1 for all trips starting in the Central Business District 1600-1900 Monday to Friday and 1200-1500 Saturday. It is possible to negotiate hourly rates for round-island tours. **Metro:** Singapore has one of the most advanced metro systems in the world. When complete, the network of two lines will serve 42 stations over 67km (42 miles) of track. The trains operate 0600-2400 with stations being served on average every six minutes. Fares range from 50 cents to Sing$1.10. **Central Business District (CBD):** To reduce congestion, no car or taxi may enter the CBD carrying less than four persons (including the driver) from 0730-1015 and 1630-1830 Monday to Saturday unless an area licence sticker is displayed on the windscreen. These may be purchased for Sing$3 from kiosks on the main roads into the area.

ACCOMMODATION

HOTELS: There is a wide variety of accommodation, characterised by new, high-class hotels (over 60 hotels in Singapore have more than 50 rooms). These have extensive facilities including swimming pools, health clubs, several restaurants, full business services and shopping arcades. It is advisable to make advance reservations. All rooms are subject to 4% tax and 10% service charge. For further information on accommodation in Singapore, contact the Singapore Tourist Promotion Board (address at beginning of entry) who can supply the *Singapore Hotels* brochure. The following organisation also offers information: Singapore Hotel Association, 37 Duxton Hill, Singapore 0208. Tel: 227 7577. Fax: 227 9085. **Grading:** Some hotels are designated as being 'International Standard' with all modern conveniences such as swimming pools and air-conditioning and prices range from Sing$100 a night.

RESORTS & EXCURSIONS

Singapore is truly cosmopolitan, a fascinating mixture of people and culture: Chinese, Indian, Japanese, Arab, European and Malay to name but a few. The Singapore Tourist Promotion Board publishes a wide range of brochures and booklets giving information on every aspect of the country. Below are listed some of the main attractions in Singapore City itself, including the several parks and gardens, and descriptions of the most popular outlying islands.

Singapore City

Singapore City was founded in 1819 by Sir Stamford Raffles of the British East India Company, who recommended that different areas of the town be set aside for the various ethnic groups. Although there has been some cultural assimilation, there are still fascinating pockets where traditional cultures exist, principally in Chinatown, Arab Street, Serangoon Road (focus of the Indian community) and Padang Square with very strong colonial associations. The best way to experience the remarkable diversity of the city is on foot: the traditional architecture, customs and cuisine of the various ethnic areas are, in turn, in fascinating contrast to the lavish, space-age shopping centres of Orchard Road and Raffles City.
Arab Street is the centre of the Arabian quarter of Singapore. Other streets with excellent shopping opportunities are *Baghdad Street* and *Bussorah Street,* while *Sultan Plaza* is a centre for cloth traders. The golden dome of the *Sultan Mosque* dominates the area; nearby are two historic Muslim burial grounds.
Chinatown is a bustling and colourful area with shops and restaurants, and also several temples such as the *Fuk Tak Ch'i* in Telok Ayer Street and the *Temple of the Calm Sea.* Ancient crafts of calligraphy, paper-making and fortune-telling are practised, and a wide range of traditional goods and foodstuffs can be bought.
Serangoon Road is the centre of the Indian quarter. Apart from the shops and restaurants, attractions in the area include the *Sri Veeramakalimman Temple,* the *Mahatma Gandhi Memorial Hall* in Race Course Lane and *Farrer Park.*
No trip to Singapore would be complete without a visit to *Raffles,* one of the most famous hotels in the world. A Singapore Sling in the *Long Bar* is almost *de rigeur*; alternatively, drop into the *Writer's Bar* which provided inspiration for, amongst others, Noel Coward, Somerset Maugham and Joseph Conrad. A statue of the man himself – Sir Stamford Raffles – has been erected on the banks of the Singapore River on the spot where he is believed to have first set foot in Singapore. Nearby is the *Parliament House,* the oldest government building in the country, the core of which dates back to the 1820s.
Not far from Raffles Hotel is the beautiful *Armenian Church* in Hill Street, the oldest church in Singapore. This building is also a reminder of another nationality who contributed much to the development of this cosmopolitan city.
Nowhere is a culture's personality more strongly expressed than in its religious architecture and Singapore provides fascinating examples of this. Buddhist temples, mosques, Catholic and Anglican cathedrals and Hindu temples are all likely to be encountered during a comparatively brief walk around some of the central areas of Singapore. *St Andrew's Cathedral,* the *Cathedral of the Good Shepherd,* the *Al-Abrar Mosque,* the *Kong Meng Sang Phor Kark See Temple Complex,* the *Chettiar Hindu Temple* and the *Sri Mariamman Temple* are only a few of these. The *Singapore Official Guide* (a handy pocket-sized publication) gives further information on these and other religious buildings in Singapore.
The *Singapore Science Centre* in Jurong is a remarkable complex which includes many hundreds of exhibits (many of which are 'hands-on'), the Aviation Gallery which traces the history of flight and the Omnitheatre, a cinema with a planetarium-like screen. It is open 1000-1800 Tuesday to Sunday.
The *New Ming Village* in Pandan Road is certainly the place to visit for Chinese porcelain. Craftsmen produce almost indistinguishable imitations of ancient masterpieces of Ming and Qing culture, and many of the items are available for purchase. Opening hours: 0900-1730 daily.
Other interesting attractions in Singapore City include the *National Museum & Art Gallery, Merlion Park,* the *Thong Chai Medical Institution, The Singapore Mint Coin Gallery, The Singapore Crocodilarium* (feeding time at 1100, crocodile wrestling at 1315 and 1615), the informal *bird singing contest* every Sunday at 0800 at the corner of Tiong Bahru and Seng Poh Roads, and the *Van Kleef Aquarium* in River Valley Road, with over 6000 species of freshwater and marine animals.

Parks & Gardens

The **Botanic Gardens,** over 47 hectares of landscaped parkland and primary jungle, are situated to the west of the city (Napier/Cluny Roads), and are home to a wide range of animal and plant life. The gardens are open 0500-2300 Monday to Friday and until midnight at weekends and public holidays. Admission is free.
The **Bukit Timah Reserve**, northwest of the Botanic Gardens on Bukit Timah Road, consists of tropical vegetation with clearly marked trails which lead up to the highest hill in Singapore, Bukit Timah. Admission is free.
Fort Canning Park, on Fort Canning Rise, was once an ancient fort of the Malay kings covering seven acres. The ruins still survive, as does a 19th-century Christian cemetery.
Haw Par Villa (The Tiger Balm Gardens) in Pasir Panjang Road are a monument to Chinese mythology, with many stone statues offering fascinating glimpses into ancient beliefs and superstitions. The Gardens are open 0800-1800 daily.
The **Chinese and Japanese Gardens** are to be found west of the centre. The two are linked by a 65m (200ft) ornamental bridge, and are superb examples of the master skills of oriental landscape gardeners, with thousands of varieties of flowers, shrubs and trees. The gardens are open 0900-1900 Monday to Saturday and 0830-1900 Sunday and public holidays. An admission fee is charged.
The **Mandai Orchid Garden** is a commercial orchid farm with a hillside of exotic orchids of many different species and a spectacular water garden. Opening hours: 0900-1730 daily. A small admission fee is charged.
The **Jurong Bird Park** on Jurong Hill (near the Chinese and Japanese Gardens) covers more than 20 hectares and is home to an incomparable collection of South-East Asian birds. There is also the world's largest walk-in aviary, a nocturnal house and several spectacular bird shows. The park is open 0900-1800 daily.
The **Singapore Zoological Gardens**, towards the north of the island of Singapore, are largely an 'open' zoo, using natural barriers rather than iron bars. Over 170 animals live here, including many which are rare or endangered, such as orang-utans, Sumatran tigers, Komodo dragons and clouded leopards. Daily attractions include breakfast or tea with an orang-utan (0900, 1500 respectively) and Animal Showtime (1030, 1130, 1430 and 1530). The zoo is open daily 0830-1800.

The Islands

Sentosa is the largest and best known of Singapore's offshore islands, and also one of the closest to the mainland. It is a multi-million dollar pleasure resort

offering a wide range of activities and attractions. These include the *Butterfly Park,* with over 50 species; the *Maritime Museum,* which traces Singapore's remarkable history as a port; the *Rare Stone Museum;* the *Garden Plaza;* the *Rasa Sentosa Food Centre; The New Food Centre* and the *Pasar Malam Night Bazaar.*
Sentosa's beaches are among its most popular attractions and a wide range of watersports are available.
How to get there: Sentosa is linked to Singapore by regular ferry services (every 15 minutes 0730-2245) and a cable car (1000-2100 Monday to Saturday, 0900-2100 Sunday and public holidays). There is also a causeway with regular bus services linking Sentosa to the city centre. An admission fee for entry to the island is charged and composite tickets can also be bought which give admission to some of the attractions; enquire locally for details.
St John's Island is large, hilly and tree-shaded with several excellent beaches. There are also several walking trails.
How to get there: There is a regular ferry service from the World Trade Centre which takes about one hour.
Kusu Island is noted for two landmarks: the *Keramat* (a Muslim shrine) and the Chinese *Tua Pekong Temple.*
How to get there: There is a regular ferry service from the World Trade Centre which takes about 30 minutes.
Pulau Hantu, Pulau Sekeng and the **Sisters islands** (the latter being part of the group of Southern Islands) are ideal for fishing, snorkelling and swimming enthusiasts.
How to get there: There are no regular ferry services but boats can be chartered; enquire locally for information.
Malaysia: The east coast of the Malaysian Peninsula is a popular resort area, particularly Desaru. For more information, see the entry on *Malaysia* above.

SOCIAL PROFILE

FOOD & DRINK: Singapore is a gourmet's paradise, ranging from humble street stalls to 5-star restaurants. There are over 30 different cooking styles, including various regional styles of Chinese cuisine, Indian, Malay, Indonesian, Japanese, Korean, Italian, Swiss, American, Russian, French and English. Malay cuisine is a favourite, famed for its use of spices and coconut milk. *Satay* (skewers of marinated chicken cooked over charcoal) served with peanut sauce, cucumber, onion and rice is popular. Hot, spicy or sweet Indonesian cuisine includes *beef rendang* (coconut milk curry), *chicken sambal* and *gado gado* (a fruit and vegetable salad in peanut sauce). One of the best ways to eat in Singapore is in the open, at one of the 8000 street foodstalls. Some are quiet and casual while others are in areas bustling with activity. All have a vast selection of cheap, mouthwatering food. Newton Circus and Rasa Singapura are food centres where all types of Asian food can be sampled cheaply. Although there are many self-service establishments, waiter service is more common in restaurants. **Drink:** Bars/cocktail lounges often have table and counter service. There are no licensing hours. 'Happy hours' with discounts on drinks are usually from 1700-1900.
NIGHTLIFE: There are cultural shows, street operas, special types of street theatre, fine theatres and international films providing inexpensive entertainment. Most hotels have bars or cocktail lounges which stay open until the early hours of the morning. Nightclubs have international entertainers and generally serve a wide range of food.
SHOPPING: The vast range of available goods and competitive prices have led to Singapore rightly being known as a shopper's paradise. Special purchases include Chinese, Indian, Malay, Balinese and Filipino antiques; batiks; cameras; Chinese, Persian and Indian carpets; imported or tailored clothing; jewellery and specialised items made of reptile and snake skins, including shoes, briefcases, handbags and wallets. Silks, perfumes, silverware and wigs are other favourite buys. The herding of shop owners from 'Chinatown' into multi-storey complexes lost some of the exciting shopping atmosphere, although these huge centres do provide an air-conditioned environment. Orchard Road is the main shopping street, although many of the large hotel complexes, such as Marina Square, have shopping centres attached. Although most outlets operate Western-style fixed pricing, bargains can in some places still be made but generally only after good research and shrewd negotiating. Electrical equipment of all types can be bought at Sungei Road, but caution is advised as there are many imitation products around. For more information on shopping in Singapore, see the *Singapore Shopping* brochure published by the Singapore Tourist Promotion Board. **Shopping hours:** 0930-2100 daily.
SPORT: Many sports associations and clubs welcome visitors. **Badminton** is almost a national sport played all year round. **Cricket** is also played in Singapore, the Singapore Cricket Club being one of the oldest sporting associations in the world. It has a sports ground where

cricket, soccer, tennis, hockey and rugby are played.
Bowling is also very popular with several lanes catering
for the enthusiast. The Singapore Island Country Golf
Club, the Keppel Club and Sentosa Island have 18-hole
golf courses. Night-time driving, pitching and putting are
available until 2100 at the country club. The Singapore
Turf Club is responsible for all **horseracing** meetings.
Polo matches are played regularly at the Singapore Polo
Club. **Fishing** is a year-round sport. Boats and
equipment, inexpensive to hire, are available at the
Jardine Steps, Changi Park. **Canoeing** and **windsurfing**
faculties are found at Sentosa Island and windsurfing at
East Coast Park. Many Singaporeans drive over to
Malaysia to enjoy the **watersports** off the East coast. For
further information, see the *Malaysia* entry above.
SPECIAL EVENTS: The cosmopolitan character of
Singapore means that a great number of festivals and
special events are regularly celebrated; visitors staying
for more than a few days would be unlucky not to catch
at least one. The following is a selection of the main
festivals taking place during 1995/96. For more
information and for exact dates, see the *Singapore
Calender of Festivals* leaflet published by the Singapore
Tourist Promotion Board.
Feb 11-Mar 12 '95 *Hari Raya Puasa.* **Apr 15-30**
Singapore International Film Festival. **May 28** *Birthday
of the Third Prince.* **Jul 1-31** *Singapore Food Festival.*
Jul 27-Aug 25 *Festival of Hungry Ghosts.* **Aug 9**
National Day. **Sep 9** *Mooncake Festival.* **Oct** *Navarathiv.*
Nov *Thimithi; Deepavali.* **Jan '96** *Pongal.* **Jan/Feb**
Thaipusam. **Feb 19-21** *Chinese New Year.*
SOCIAL CONVENTIONS: Handshaking is the usual
form of greeting, regardless of race. Social courtesies are
often fairly formal. When invited to a private home a gift
is appreciated and if on business a company souvenir is
appropriate. Dress is informal. Most first-class
restaurants and some hotel dining rooms expect men to
wear a jacket and tie in the evenings; a smart appearance
is expected for business meetings. Evening dress for local
men and women is unusual. Each of the diverse racial
groups in Singapore has retained its own cultural and
religious identity while developing as an integral part of
the Singapore community. Over 50% of the population is
under 20 years of age. Laws relating to jaywalking and
littering are strictly enforced in the urban areas. Smoking
is widely discouraged and illegal in enclosed public
places (including restaurants). Dropping a cigarette end

in the street or smoking illegally can lead to an
immediate fine of up to Sing$500. **Tipping:** Officially
discouraged in restaurants, hotels and the airport. A 10%
service charge is included in restaurant bills.

BUSINESS PROFILE

ECONOMY: Singapore's fortunes rely on entrepôt trade,
shipbuilding and repairing, oil refining, electronics,
banking and, to a slightly lesser extent, tourism. From the
late 1970s, the Government initiated a strategy of
upgrading the economy by establishing export-oriented
and service industries with the intention of making
Singapore an economic fulcrum of the region. High-
technology manufacturing, particularly computer and
telecommunications equipment, and financial services,
mainly banking and insurance, have performed particularly
well and gone some way to fulfilling the Government's
intentions. The state has also started to benefit from the
political situation in Hong Kong with many companies in
the region deciding to relocate their operations to
Singapore: corporate telecommunications is one striking
example, with Singapore now the most important hub in
South-East Asia. The vibrant economic activity more than
compensates for Singapore's lack of natural resources. All
foodstuffs and raw materials have to be imported. The
only important natural resource is the superb natural
harbour which, with the exception of Rotterdam's, is the
busiest in the world. The per capita income is second in the
region only to that of Japan. The largest exporters to
Singapore are Japan, the USA and Malaysia, who between
them collect nearly half of Singapore's US$70-billion
annual import bill. The same three countries are also
Singapore's principal overseas markets.
BUSINESS: English is widely spoken in business
circles. Appointments should be made and punctuality is
important. Chinese people should be addressed with their
surnames first, while Malays do not have surnames but
use the initial of their father's name before their own.
Visiting cards are essential, although it is policy for
government officials not to use them.
COMMERCIAL INFORMATION: The following
organisations can offer advice: Singapore Federation of
Chambers of Commerce and Industry, #03-01 Chinese
Chamber of Commerce Building, 47 Hill Street,
Singapore 0617. Tel: 338 9761. Fax: 339 5630; *or*
Singapore International Chamber of Commerce, #10-001

John Hancock Tower, 6 Raffles Quay, Singapore 0104.
Tel: 224 1255. Fax: 224 2785.
CONFERENCES/CONVENTIONS: Singapore is the
top convention city in Asia and ranks among the top ten
meetings destinations in the world. There are many hotels
with extensive conference facilities, including the latest
audio-visual equipment, secretarial services, translation
and simultaneous interpretation systems, whilst Raffles
City, a brand new and completely self-contained
convention city, can accommodate up to 6000 delegates
under one roof. Full information on Singapore as a
conference destination can be obtained from the
Singapore Convention Bureau, #36-04 Raffles City
Tower, 250 North Bridge Road, Singapore 0617. Tel:
339 6622. Fax: 339 9423. The Bureau, a division within
the Singapore Tourist Promotion Board, is a non-
profitmaking organisation with the dual objectives of
marketing Singapore as an international exhibition and
convention city and of assisting with the planning and
staging of individual events.

CLIMATE

Warm and humid through most of the year. There is no
distinct wet/dry season. Most rain falls during the
northeast monsoon (November to January) and showers
are usually sudden and heavy.
Required clothing: Lightweight cottons and linens. An
umbrella or light raincoat is recommended.

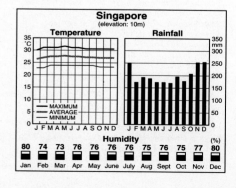

Singapore
(elevation: 10m)

Temperature   **Rainfall**

MAXIMUM
AVERAGE
MINIMUM

	Jan	Feb	Mar	Apr	May	June	July	Aug	Sept	Oct	Nov	Dec
Humidity (%)	80	74	73	76	76	76	76	75	76	75	77	80

Slovak Republic

Location: Central Europe.

Ministry of Economy
Tourism Section
Mierova 19, 827 15 Bratislava, Slovak Republic
Tel: (7) 234 984 *or* 299 8747 *or* 299 8746. Fax: (7) 237 827.

Lake Strbske Pleso and Gerlachovsky Mountains

SATUR (Tourist Office)
Mileticova 1, 824 72 Bratislava, Slovak Republic
Tel: (7) 212 205. Fax: (7) 212 664.

Embassy of the Slovak Republic
25 Kensington Palace Gardens, London W8 4QY
Tel: (0171) 243 0803. Fax: (0171) 727 5824. Opening
hours: 0900-1700 Monday to Friday; *Consular section*:
1000-1230 Monday to Friday.

British Embassy
Gröslingova 35, 811 09 Bratislava, Slovak Republic
Tel: (7) 364 420. Fax: (7) 364 396.

Embassy of the Slovak Republic
Suite 380, 2201 Wisconsin Avenue, NW, Washington,
DC 20007
Tel: (202) 965 5160 *or* 965 5161. Fax: (202) 965 5166.

Slovakia Travel Service
Suite 3601, 10 East 40th Street, New York, NY 10016
Tel: (212) 213 3865 *or* 213 3862. Fax: (212) 213 4461 *or*
684 7646.
Also deals with enquiries from Canada.

Embassy of the United States of America
Hviezdoslavovo námestie 4, 811 02 Bratislava, Slovak
Republic
Tel: (7) 330 861 *or* 333 338. Fax: (7) 330 096.

Embassy of the Slovak Republic
50 Rideau Terrace, Ottawa, Ontario K1M 2A1
Tel: (613) 749 2496 *or* 749 0568 *or* 749 4442 *or* 741
3778. Fax: (613) 749 4989.

**The Canadian Embassy in Prague deals with
enquiries relating to the Slovak Republic (see *Czech
Republic* earlier in the book).**

AREA: 49,035 sq km (18,932 sq miles).
POPULATION: 5,289,608 (1991 estimate).
POPULATION DENSITY: 108 per sq km.
CAPITAL: Bratislava. **Population:** 442,197 (1991).
GEOGRAPHY: The Slovak Republic is situated in
Central Europe, sharing frontiers with the Czech
Republic, Austria, Poland, Hungary and Ukraine. The
republic is hilly and picturesque, with historic castles,
forests, pure mountain streams, romantic valleys and
lakes, as well as excellent facilities to 'take the waters' at
one of the famous spas or to ski and hike in the
mountains. The Tatra range and the foothills of the
Carpathians descend to the huge and fertile Danube
Plain, located in the southwest near Bratislava. The
famous Danube River flows through the southeast of the
Slovak Republic and into Hungary. The Slovak Republic
was once under Hungarian rule and this is reflected in its
music, food and architecture, especially in the south.
LANGUAGE: The official language is Slovak. Czech,
Hungarian, German and English are also spoken.
RELIGION: The majority are Roman Catholic.
Protestant churches comprise the remainder with
Reformed, Lutheran, Methodist, Moravian and Baptist
denominations. There is also a Jewish minority.
TIME: GMT + 1 (GMT + 2 from last Sunday in March
to Saturday before last Sunday in September).
ELECTRICITY: Generally 220 volts AC, 50Hz. Most
major hotels have standard international 2-pin razor
plugs. Lamp fittings are normally of the screw type.
COMMUNICATIONS: Telephone: IDD is available.
Country code: 42. Outgoing international code: 00. There
are public telephone booths, including special kiosks for

The Bratislava Triangle

offers special opportunities and reasons to visit.

Three other capitals can easily be reached from here: Prague by air, Vienna and Budapest by boat on the Danube. Three unique cultures are yours to discover in local museums, galleries and opera houses.

Three different cuisines to be enjoyed – beer and dumplings, wine and wiener-schnitzel and good Halászlé (fish soup) or Goulash, bryndzové halušky and many other local specialities.

Discover the Secrets of Slovakia

SLOVENSKO

Slovakia forms the beautiful link between Austria, the Czech Republic, Poland, Ukraine and Hungary. Ideal for those people in search of history, scenery and affordable prices, Slovakia offers a unique opportunity to enjoy and escape to the High Tatra Mountains with their gentle valleys, health spas, deep forests and the lovely churches scattered throughout the Republic.

More than a thousand years of history, from Stone Age settlements and Roman ruins to over 100 hilltop castles are waiting to be explored.

A friendly, welcoming spirit awaits you in villages and cities, in cottages and private family accommodation as well as in good hotels. Relaxing in peaceful surroundings, hiking, shopping for hand-made crafts, skiing or visiting out-of-the-way historical sites, all of your activities are enhanced by the undiscovered beauty of Slovakia.

international calls. Surcharges can be quite high on long-distance calls from hotels. Local calls cost Sk2.
Telex/telegram: Facilities are available at all main towns and hotels. Services are available 24 hours at Kollárska 12 (centre of Bratislava) and next to the main railway station on Dimitrovovo námestie. **Post:** *Poste Restante* services are available. Post office hours: 0800-1800 Monday to Friday. **Press:** There are no English-language newspapers published.
BBC World Service and Voice of America frequencies: From time to time these change. See the section *How to Use this Book* for more information.
BBC:

MHz	15.07	12.09	9.410	6.195
Voice of America:				
MHz	15.20	9.760	6.040	3.980

PASSPORT/VISA

Regulations and requirements may be subject to change at short notice, and you are advised to contact the appropriate diplomatic or consular authority before finalising travel arrangements. Details of these may be found at the head of this country's entry. Any numbers in the chart refer to the footnotes below.

	Passport Required?	Visa Required?	Return Ticket Required?
Full British	Yes	No	No
BVP	Not valid	-	-
Australian	Yes	Yes	No
Canadian	Yes	Yes	No
USA	Yes	No	No
Other EU (As of 31/12/94)	Yes/1	No	No
Japanese	Yes	Yes	No

PASSPORTS: Valid passport required by all except **[1]** nationals of Germany who can enter with a valid national ID card. Passports must be valid for at least 8 months at the time of application.
British Visitors Passport: Not accepted.
VISAS: Required by all except:
(a) nationals of EU countries for stays of up to 3 months (except nationals of the UK for stays of up to 6 months and nationals of Italy for up to 30 days);
(b) nationals of Andorra, Aruba, Estonia, Finland, Hungary, Iceland, Latvia, Liechtenstein, Lithuania, Malaysia, Malta, Monaco, Norway, Poland, Slovenia, Sweden and Switzerland for up to 3 months;
(c) nationals of Austria, Bulgaria, Croatia, Cuba, Cyprus, French Overseas Departments, San Marino, USA and Vatican City for up to 30 days;
(d) nationals of the Czech Republic for an unspecified amount of time;
(e) nationals of the Russian Federation and Ukraine with

an authorised invitation or proof of pre-paid package tour for an unspecified amount of time;
(f) nationals of Romania with proof of sufficient funds for 30 days (at least US$15 per day).
Types of visa: Tourist, Transit and Double Transit. Cost depends on nationality and ranges from £2-£60. Tourist visas are generally £14-£30. Children aged 15 or under do not have to pay for a visa, although a handling charge of £2 may be levied in certain cases.
Validity: *Transit:* 48 hours. *Tourist:* 6 months from date of issue for 30-day visit.
Note: No fee is charged for nationals of Afghanistan, Albania, Bolivia (tourist visa), China (tourist visa), Costa Rica, Ecuador, India, Pakistan, Seychelles and South Africa (tourist visa). Canadian passport holders are charged £30 for single- and double-entry visas.
Application to: Consular section at Embassy. For addresses, see top of entry.
Note: Single-entry visas for a maximum stay of up to 30 days can also be issued at the border crossing Bratislava–Petrzalka/Berg (Austria). This facility is not available to nationals of all African states (except South Africa), Afghanistan, Albania, Armenia, Azerbaijan, Bangladesh, Bosnia-Hercegovina, Cambodia, China, Georgia, India, Iran, Iraq, Kazakhstan, Kyrgyzstan, Laos, Lebanon, Former Yugoslav Republic of Macedonia, Mauritius, Moldova, Mongolia, Pakistan, Philippines, Sri Lanka, Syria, Tadjikistan, Tunisia, Turkey, Turkmenistan, Uzbekistan, Vietnam, Yemen and Yugoslavia (Serbia and Montenegro).
Application requirements: (a) Completed application form (2 forms for double transit). (b) 2 passport-size photos. (c) Passport valid for at least 8 months, with one blank page. (d) Fee (cash or postal orders only).
Working days required: Same day in most cases if application is received before 1230.
Temporary residence: Special application form required. Enquire at Embassy.

MONEY

Currency: Koruna (Sk) or Slovak Crown – Slovenská koruna = 100 halierov (singular: heller). Notes are in denominations of Sk1000, 500, 100, 50, 20 and 10. Coins are in denominations of Sk10, 5, 2 and 1, and 50, 20, 10 and 5 halierov.
Currency exchange: Foreign currency (including travellers cheques) can be exchanged at exchange offices, *SATUR* offices, main hotels, *Tuzex* stores and road border crossings, as well as post offices and some travel agencies.
Credit cards: Major cards such as American Express, Diners Club, Visa and Access/Mastercard may be used to exchange currency and are also accepted in better hotels, restaurants and shops. Check with your credit card company for details of merchant acceptability and other services which may be available.
Travellers cheques: These are widely accepted (see *Currency exchange* above).
Eurocheque: These can be cashed up to a maximum of Sk6500 per day.
Exchange rate indicators: The following figures are included as a guide to the movements of the Koruna against Sterling and the US Dollar:

Date:	Sep '93	Jan '94	Nov '94	Jan '95
£1.00=	48.61	49.15	48.19	48.62
$1.00=	31.83	33.22	30.16	31.07

Currency restrictions: The import and export of local

currency is not permitted. There is no restriction on foreign currency.
Banking hours: Generally 0800-1700 Monday to Friday.

DUTY FREE

The following goods may be imported into the Slovak Republic by visitors 18 years of age or older without incurring customs duty:
200 cigarettes or 100 cigarillos or 50 cigars or 250g of tobacco products; 1 litre of spirits; 2 litres of wine; 500ml of perfume or 2550ml eau de toilette; gifts up to Sk1000; all goods bought at Tuzex shops by tourists.
Prohibited items: All forms of pornographic literature. All items of value, such as cameras and tents, must be declared at Customs on entry to enable export clearance on departure.

PUBLIC HOLIDAYS

Jan 1 '95 New Year's Day; Independence Day of the Slovak Republic. **Jan 6** Epiphany. **Apr 14** Good Friday. **Apr 17** Easter Monday. **May 1** Labour Day. **Jul 5** Day of the Apostles St Cyril and St Methodius. **Aug 29** Anniversary of the Slovak National Uprising. **Sep 1** Day of Constitution of the Slovak Republic. **Sep 15** Our Lady of the Seven Sorrows. **Nov 1** All Saints' Day. **Dec 24-26** Christmas. **Jan 1 '96** New Year's Day; Independence Day of the Slovak Republic. **Jan 6** Epiphany. **Apr 5** Good Friday. **Apr 8** Easter Monday.

HEALTH

Regulations and requirements may be subject to change at short notice, and you are advised to contact your doctor well in advance of your intended date of departure. Any numbers in the chart refer to the footnotes below.

	Special Precautions?	Certificate Required?
Yellow Fever	No	No
Cholera	No	No
Typhoid & Polio	No	-
Malaria	No	-
Food & Drink	1	-

[1]: Mains water is normally chlorinated, and whilst relatively safe may cause mild abdominal upsets. Bottled water is available and is advised for the first few weeks of the stay. Milk is pasteurised and dairy products are safe for consumption. Local meat, poultry, seafood, fruit and vegetables are generally considered safe to eat.
Health care: There is a Reciprocal Health Agreement with the UK. On production of a UK passport, hospital and other medical care will be provided free of charge should visitors fall ill or have an accident while on holiday. Prescribed medicine will be charged for.

TRAVEL - International

AIR: The Slovak Republic is served by *Czechoslovak Airlines (OK)*, *Hamus Air Bulgaria*, *Eurowings*, *Tatra Air* and *Aeroflot*.
Approximate flight time: From London to Bratislava is 1 hour 45 minutes.
International airports: *Bratislava (BTS)* (Ivánká), 10km (6 miles) from the city centre, is served from Continental Europe only. Bus no 24 runs to the city, stopping en route, for Sk5 (travel time – 30 minutes). Taxis are also available (travel time – 15 minutes). Airport facilities include duty-free shops (0700-1900 Monday to Friday), bank (0800-1430 Monday to Friday), post office (0700-1500 Monday to Friday), restaurant (until 1900), bar (0700-1900), snack bar (0700-1900), 24-hour flight information, 24-hour left luggage, 24-hour tourist information, 24-hour first aid, disabled facilities and car hire *(Budget, Europcar, Hertz* and *Univox)*.
Poprad-Tatry is 5km (2.5 miles) from the city.
Vienna International Airport (Schwechat) is 50km (31 miles) from Bratislava and can be used as a gateway for inter-continental travellers.
Departure tax: US$5.98.
RIVER: International connections from Austria are possible on the Danube which is also linked with the Rhine and Main. Services run as follows: Bratislava–Vienna–Bratislava; Bratislava–Hainburg–Bratislava; and Vienna–Bratislava–Budapest, both ways.
RAIL: The most convenient route to the Slovak Republic from Western Europe is via Vienna or Prague. There are also routes from Budapest and Kiev (Ukraine).
ROAD: The Slovak Republic can be entered via the Czech Republic, Poland, the CIS, Hungary or Austria. There is a motorway from Bratislava via Brno to Prague. Petrol coupons must be purchased before entering the country and are available at border crossings.

Slovakia's Rich Natural and Cultural Heritage

SLOVAKIA'S CULTURAL HERITAGE

Much of Europe's history has been acted out across Slovakia's physical and cultural boundaries. Every age has left its unique mark on the country's character. Today, visitors can find Romanesque rotundas, Gothic cathedrals, Baroque manor houses and Renaissance palaces within the boundaries of a single city.

The Slovak Republic has designated 16 towns as Historic Monument Preservation Areas to maintain their architectural treasures: Bratislava, Bardejov, Nitra, Irnava, Banská Štiavnica, Kežmarok, Košice, Levoča, Spišská Sobota, Spišské Podhradic and Prešov, Trenčin, Banská Bystrica, Kremnica and Žillina. Each one has its own points of interest.

Bratislava, the capital of Slovakia, is the republic's political, economic and cultural centre. It was a Celtic settlement in the first century BC and the Romans later established forts here. During the Great Moravian period (7th-9th century) a fort and a church stood on the site now occupied by Bratislava's castle. The settlement was granted town status in 1291 by Andrew III.

A centre of production, most notably in the wine trade, the town grew in importance and influence over the centuries. In 1465 Hungary's first university was established here. In 1536 King Ferdinand I proclaimed it Hungary's capital, a role it fulfilled for 250 years.

Listed buildings in the city's Monument Preservation Area date from the thirteenth century. Most are open to the public.

Bardejov is a mediaeval city, standing within 14th-century walls and reached by one of four city gates. The 15th-century St Egydius church, the 16th-century town hall and the Gothic burgher houses are of particular architectural interest.

Nitra is closely linked with the earliest history of the Slovak nation with its fortified settlements dating back to the 6th century. In the 9th-century the town became the centre of the Principality of Nitra.

Trnava, established as a Royal Town in 1230, was a centre of Hungarian Church administration for 250 years from the 16th century. Its university was established in 1635.

Banská Štiavnica, a 13th-century mining town, later rebuilt in the Renaissance style, is the home of Europe's first mining school dating from 1763. Within seven years the status of the school was raised to that of a Mining Academy.

Kežmarok was proclaimed a Free Royal Town in 1442. It has many points of interest, including a 15th-century town hall and a magnificent-18th century lyceum.

Kremnica, originally a mining town, was granted the privilege of a mint in 1328 and its architecture echoes these royal associations. The castle dates from 14th century, and there is also a large complex of Gothic and Renaissance buildings.

The region of **Spiš** contains many well-preserved mediaeval towns and villages. Prominent amongst these is **Levoča** (now a Historic Monument Preservation Area) a town with an eventful past.

In 1271 Levoća became the capital of the Union of Spis Saxons. It was dominated by German merchants and famous for its goldsmiths, copper engravers and carver's workshops. The often-rebuilt 14th-century St James' church contains what is, at 18.6m, the highest Gothic altar in the world.

Spišské Podradie (Spišská Kapitula) has been the seat of provosts and bishops since the 13th-century, developing as an ecclesiastic village round the site of a 12th-century church.

Košice, the capital of Eastern Slovakia, also has a rich history and its citizens are justly proud of its monumental St Elisabeth's Cathedral.

FOLK ART

The preservation of Slovakia's historical past is not restricted to the maintenance of monumental architecture. Evidence of the cultural history of ordinary people is also of great interest. For this reason many Folk Monument Preservation Areas have been established. These comprise preservation areas containing traditional country residences, characterised by wooden walled houses and outbuildings complemented by village churches. The rock dwellings and 3-roomed houses of Brhlovce are particularly interesting, as are the Anabaptist courts attached to houses of prayer in the **Velké Leváre** and **Plaveký Štvrtok** areas.

Log houses with white-painted ornaments can be seen in **Cičmany, Vlkolinec, Ždiar, Podbiel** and **Špania dolina.** **Osturńa** contains fine examples of log structures and outbuildings enclosed into single units with colourfully painted façades. There are also open-air museums in which many traditional structures have been reconstructed. The two central museums are the Slovak Village Museum in **Martin-Jahonicke háje** and the open-air Mining Museum in **Banská Štiavnica.** Five regional museums exhibit collections of folk architecture: the Orava Village Museum in **Zuberec,** the Kysuce Village Museum in **Vychylovka,** the Liptov Village Museum in **Pribylina** and the Folk Architecture Museum in **Bardejov** and **Svidnik.**

SPA RESORTS

The following spa resorts enjoy an international reputation. Visitors can choose residential or out-patient treatment.

1. Bardejovské kúpele - Therapeutic procedures make use of hydrocarbonated chloride-sodium water from six springs. Suitable for the treatment of digestive and respiratory complaints.

2. Dudince – Hydrocarbonated chloride-sodium-calcium-sulphur-carbon-hyptonic water, rich in salts. Suitable for treatment of nervous diseases and rheumatism.

3. Piešťany – Hot spring (69.5°c) hydrogen sulphide-radioactive water. Suitable for treatment of rheumatism and nervous disorders.

4. Sliač – Carbonic-calcium magnesium water. Highly regarded spa for the treatment of cardio-vascular diseases.

5. Irenčianske Teplice – Sulphuric springs specialises in treatment of rheumatic and nervous problems.

NATURAL FEATURES:

A Starting Point for Tourism Development

Despite its small size, the Republic of Slovakia's geography is varied, ranging from the lowlands of the south, through the central massives, to the towering Tatra range in the north. The landscape itself represents a good basis for the development of tourism; new mountain resorts, for example, can adapt to the needs of both winter and summer visitors. Slovakia has a strong network of protected areas comprising unspoiled tracts of its varied countryside. Fifteen protected landscape areas and five National Parks have been established. Among the National Parks presently attracting the largest number of visitors are:

1. The Low Tatras National Park (811 sq km) set in the second highest mountain range in the Western Carpathians.

The core of the range is made up of granite and crystallic slate. The northern part is mainly limestone and dolomite. The Demänová Caves are located in this area.

Tourist resorts are not evenly distributed. The majority of those with first-class technical equipment are located on either side of the Chopok peak, in the area of the Demänová Valley and **Tále.** Other major resorts are at crossing-points of the range: **Donovaly,** with ski-lifts, a hotel and a trailer camp; and **Certovica** with excellent ski areas, mountain hotels and accommodation facilities in the picturesque village of **Vyšná Boca.**

The Demänová Valley, with several established tourism complexes, runs over a length of 15km. New facilities have been built in several of its resorts.

2. The Tatra National Park (769 sq km) is the oldest National Park in Slovakia, encompassing the High Tatras, the Belianske Tatras and the eastern edge of the Western Tatras. The area has an abundance of wildlife including brown bears, chamois and marmot.

The Tatras contain several resorts. The most important tourism centres (**Štrbské Pleso, Smokovce, Tatranská** and **Lomnica**) are well-equipped with facilities, including ski-tows and cable cars to the high peaks. All resorts are easily accessible via road and rail systems connected to the airport. The High Tatras attract 4.5 million visitors annually.

Štrbské Pleso, skirting a lake of the same name, is the highest settlement in the Tatras. For many tourists it serves as a starting point for hikes into the valleys and high-mountain ascents. It has high-standard modern hotels, restaurants, shopping and sports facilities. It is well-known to sportsmen, and in 1970 played host to the World Championship Nordic ski event.

The Smokovce Settlements – Starý (Old), Nový (New), Horný (Upper) and Dolný (Lower) – are the administrative, tourist and social centre of the High Tatras. **Starý Smokovce** is the core settlement. It has nine hotels and several sanitoria. Excellent climatic conditions make it an effective centre for the treatment of non-specific diseases of the respiratory tract.

Tatranská Lomnica – founded in 1892 as a state spa – is the starting point for tours into the eastern High Tatras. A skytram takes visitors up to the Skalnate Pleso (1750m) which boasts the best downhill ski-runs in the range. Nearby, on the second highest peak in the Tatras – Lomnicky stit (2632m) – stands an observatory and meteorological station, accessible via chairlift.

The **Western Tatras (Roháče)** deserve a special mention. The tour along the range's principle ridge is a thrilling experience. The striking peaks, deep valleys, terraced tarns and plateaus abounding in high-altitude flora will take the breath of even the most experienced visitors. The tourist centres of Zuberec and Zverovka lie within this area, as do Oravice and Pribylina which both have established motor camps.

3. Picniny National Park (21 sq km) is a bilateral National Park shared with the Polish Republic. The park lies 30km northeast of the High Tatras. This park fulfils the role of a 'quiet zone'.

A picturesque region, set around the Dunajec River canyon, this site offers a unique opportunity for river rafting. The secluded mediaeval Red Monastery complex stands close to the river.

4. The Little Fatra National Park (200 sq km) is suitable for year-round hiking tours. The winter tourism centre, **Vrátna,** with its well-established base for downhill skiing, attracts a huge number of visitors each year.

5. The Slovensky Raj National Park (Slovak Paradise) (142 sq km) lies to the east of the Low Tatras. This park's most famous features are its many canyons, which cut through to depths of up to 200 m, with huge waterfalls and rushing rivers.

PROTECTED LANDSCAPE REGIONS

These regions cover much wider areas than the above-mentioned National Parks. There are 15 such regions across Slovakia all of which have their natural beauty unspoiled by human activity.

FOOD AND DRINK

Since time immemorial, good food and congenial hospitality have formed an intrinsic part of Slovak culture. This tradition is continued today in *koliba* or *salàs* (shepherd huts), cosy wine cellars, popular taverns and alehouses. Each region of Slovakia has its own atmosphere and customs and cuisine. Although the Slovakian national dish is generally acknowledged to be bryndzove halusky (potato pasta with ewe's cheese and diced fried bacon), in southern Slovakia baked goose is the local speciality, while in eastern Slovakia mushroom and sour cream soup with black bread is considered a delicacy.

Wine and beer are both popular drinks in Slovakia. There are eight established wine-producing regions. The most popular liquors are borovička (juniper brandy), the finely scented marhulovica (apricot brandy) and the well-known slivovica (plum brandy). All are renowned – naturally! – for their medicinal properties.

Tatranska Lomnica, High Tatra

Railways of the Slovak Republic (ŽSR)

Slovakia's network provides direct connections with Hamburg, Berlin, Warsaw, Krakow, Vienna, Budapest, Bucarest, Moskow, L'vov, Vilnius and St Petersburg.

There are through trains which run to the High Tatras the most popular area of the country. From Vienna, changing at Bratislava there are 3 trains daily, from Budapest there are also 3 trains, changing at Bratislava. The fare from Poprad-High Tatras to Vienna is **27.54 ECU** (2nd class), **41.31 ECU** (1st class), to Budapest is **33.05 ECU** (2nd class) and **49.58 ECU** (1st class).

Higher quality trains also run on ŽSR lines: a supplement must be paid on tickets for these services:
Budapest – Bratislava – Hamburg international train EC 174/175 - HUNGARIA,
Budapest – Žilina – Warszawa international train IC 130/131 - POLÓNIA.
There are also domestic IC trains 510/511 TATRAN, 512/513 KRIVÁŇ, which connects the capital of the Slovak Republic with Košice, capital of east Slovakia.
The internal IC trains require compulsory seat reservation.
Attractive rates are available with the sale of EURO DOMINO, RAIL EUROPS, EURO MINI-GRUPPE, BIJ, INTER RAIL tickets.

For information and seat reservations please contact:
Booking Office ŽSR
Railwa station   Fax: +42-7-496 701
Bratislava hl. st.
Predstaničné nám. č. 1   Telex: 42-7-911 231
810 02 Bratislava

TRAVEL - Internal

AIR: *Czechoslovak Airlines* operate an extensive domestic network that includes flights from Bratislava to most major cities including Poprad, Presov, Piestany, Banská Bystrica and Kosice. The domestic airline *Slov Air* operates scheduled and chartered flights from Ivánká Airport, Bratislava. Tel: (7) 236 720.
RIVER: The network of navigable waterways amounts to 2372km (1482 miles). The Danube is the main artery for transport by ship which is operated by Slovenská plavba dunajská (Slovak Danube Sailing Company). Cruises covering historic and tourist interests are also operated. Further information is available from The Blue Danube Travel, Fajnorovo nábr. 2, 811 02 Bratislava. Tel: (7) 366 515 *or* 333 905. Fax: (7) 333 905.
RAIL: The rail network is operated by *Railways of the Slovak Republic*. There are several daily express trains between Bratislava and main cities and resorts. For details on train schedules, telephone (7) 204 4484 *or* 204 1111. Reservations should be made in advance on major routes. Fares are low, but supplements are charged for travel by express trains. Further details can be obtained from Cedok in London or from SATUR.
ROAD: Traffic drives on the right. The major routes run from Bratislava to Presov, via Nitra, Banská Bystrica and Poprad, and via Trencin, Zilina, Kralovany and Poprad.
Bus: The extensive network covers areas not accessible by rail, and is efficient and comfortable. **Car hire:** Self-drive cars may be pre-booked through the tourist office in main towns and resorts. Otherwise, hire cars can be obtained from *Hertz* (tel: (7) 291 481), *Magnum* (tel: (7) 832 195), *Favorit Car* (tel: (7) 284 152) or *Auto Danubius* (tel: (7) 213 096). Seat belts are compulsory and drinking is absolutely prohibited. Filling stations tend to be closed in the evenings. **Documentation:** A valid national driving licence is sufficient for car hire.
URBAN: Buses, trolleybuses and tramways exist in Bratislava and several other towns. Most services run from 0430-2400. All the cities operate flat-fare systems and pre-purchased passes are available. Tickets should be punched in the appropriate machine on entering the tram or bus. A separate ticket is usually required when changing routes. There is a fine for fare evasion. Blue badges on tram and bus stops indicate an all-night service. **Taxi:** These are available in all the main towns and are metered and cheap; higher fares are charged at night.

JOURNEY TIMES: The following chart gives approximate journey times from Bratislava (in hours and minutes) to other major towns in the Slovak Republic.

	Air	Road	Rail
Poprad	0.45	4.00	4.30
Kosice	1.00	5.30	7.00
B. Bystrica	-	2.30	4.10
Piestany Spa	-	0.50	0.50

ACCOMMODATION

Accommodation facilities in the Slovak Republic have until now comprised both commercial and non-commercial capacities. The majority was social tourism accommodation, which accounted for roughly 77,000 beds (of which 11,000 belonged to Slovak spas, 4000 to holiday homes for trade union recreation, while 62,000 were in plant-owned recreational facilities). Commercial tourism accounted for 62,000 beds. These figures demonstrate the short supply of beds within the commercial sphere, further evidence of which is a small number of permanent beds per 1000 inhabitants, amounting in 1990 to 7500. Newly arisen social and economic conditions and the transition to a market economy have now created further opportunities for developing commercial tourism. The survey below depicts the network of accommodation facilities in the sphere of commercial tourism (data from 1990):

SR regions	No. of acc. facilities	No. of permanent beds
West Slovakia	199	17,195
Central Slovakia	371	22,166
East Slovakia	320	22,633
SR in total	**890**	**61,994**

The predominance of facilities in the central and eastern parts of the country is explained by the concentration of important tourist centres within these regions, such as Low Tatras, High Tatras, Velká Matra and Malá Fatra. At present, accommodation facilities are being classified according to the branch standard no. 735412/1991, issued by the Ministry of Trade and Tourism of the Slovak Republic, wherein principles were set for labelling and dividing accommodation facilities into respective categories. Facilities are divided by type (hotels, hostels, etc) and, within each type, into classes, depending on the level of equipment and services, marked by a specific number of stars. The survey below shows the structure of the various establishments within the sphere of

commercial tourism and number of beds in the Slovak Republic:

	No. of acc. facilities	No. of permanent beds
Total SR	890	61,994
Hotels, motels, floating hotels	379	26,617
of which: 5-star	1	103
4-star	11	2426
3-star	87	9519
2-star	145	7907
1-star	135	6662
Estates of cottages	144	11,956
Boarding houses	68	2030
Hostels	201	7841
Campsites	98	3345
Beds in private houses	-	10,205

It can be seen that most establishments fall into categories at the lower end of the market (such as hostels, estates of cottages, campsites). These represent a substantial supply for less demanding younger tourists.
HOTELS: Prices compare very favourably with Western hotels, though services and facilities are often more limited. There is a shortage of accommodation in the peak seasons (May to October, but especially during July and August), and it is wise to pre-book. Hotel accommodation accounts for the largest share (approximately 43% of the overall capacity of commercial tourism establishments). As yet, a relatively small portion of the hotel network is made up of intermediate and upper classes. At present, higher-standard hotels are to be found primarily in Bratislava, in regional towns (such as Banská Bystrica and Kosice), in spas of national and international significance and in major tourist resorts (such as the High Tatras). Future development and investment will result in upward reclassification of many establishments. Two examples of hotels suitable for the international business market are the new Hotel Forum Bratislava, which has recently been built in the city centre with 200 rooms, a number of restaurants and conference facilities; and the 4-star Hotel Danube and the Hotel Perugia, particularly recommended for business travellers. For further information, contact the Union of Hotels and Restaurants of the Slovak Republic, Hotel Lux, Nám. Slobody 2, 97400 Banská Bystrica. Tel/Fax: (8) 753 853. **Grading:** The international 5-star system has recently been introduced for hotel classification, but the old **ABC** system may still be encountered in remote areas. The present system is: **5-**

star (formerly **A+** or **Deluxe**), **4-star** (formerly **A**), **3-star** (formerly **B+**), **2-star** (formerly **B**), and **1-star** (formerly **C**). You can expect rooms with private bath or shower in hotels classified 3-star (or B+) and upwards.
MOTELS: Motels are split into two categories.
Grading: In **B motels** every room is provided with central heating and a wash-basin with hot and cold water; on every floor there is a separate bathroom and WC for men and women. **A motels** are provided with the following extras: a lift, a bathroom or shower with every room, a radio receiver and in some cases a TV set. Car parking facilities are available in both types.
PRIVATE HOUSES: Cedok (London) Ltd can arrange stays in private houses in the Slovak Republic throughout the year.
SELF-CATERING: Chalet Communities in many parts of the country are available in two categories. **Grading: B chalets** offer drinking water, WC and heating in winter. Some may provide meals. **A chalets** have the following extras: electric lighting, flushing WC, washroom with running water, washing and ironing facilities and a sports ground. For further information, contact Cedok (London) Ltd.
CAMPING/CARAVANNING: Campsites have all the regular facilities such as showers, cooking amenities, shops and, in some cases, caravans for hire. For further information, contact the Camping and Caravanning Federation of Slovakia, Junácka 6, 832 80 Bratislava. Tel: (7) 279 0223 *or* 279 0224. Fax: (7) 279 0569. **Car camps:** In the **B** category these have a car park, fenced-in campsite, day and night service, washroom, WC, drinking water and a roofed structure with cookers and washing-up equipment. Car camps in the **A** category are provided with the following extras: sale of refreshments, showers with hot and cold water, flushing WC, washing and ironing facilities, a reception office, a social room, sale of toiletries and souvenirs.

RESORTS & EXCURSIONS

Every historical period and century has left behind monuments in the Slovak Republic which are admired by the world. Alongside castles, manors, chateaux and historical buildings, visitors to the Slovak Republic will also find great natural beauty: towering mountain peaks and quiet valleys, rivers, mountain lakes with crystal-clear waters and extensive cave systems.
The capital of the Slovak Republic, **Bratislava**, is the political, economic and cultural centre of the country. Its history is inextricably linked with the Celtic and Roman periods; there is also archaeological evidence dating back to the Great Moravian period. The fortified settlement grew in importance over the years and was granted town privileges in 1291. Matthias Corvinus established the first university, the *Academia Istropolitana*, in 1465. After the Battle of Mohácz in 1536, Bratislava became the capital and coronation town of Hungary and remained so for 250 years. The city contains palaces bearing the architectural style of almost every age: Rococo, Baroque, Classical and Renaissance. The *Devín Castle*, recently renovated, dominates the city. Other sights include the 13th-century *Old Town Hall*, the *Primate's Palace* (1777), *Michael's Tower* (14th-15th centuries), *St*

BRATISLAVA

Map labels:
Kalvária, Vinohrady, Filiáka Sta., Hlavní Stanica Sta., SLAVIN MONUMENT, Slavin Hill, Slobody Square, PARLIAMENT, STARE MESTO, OBCHODNÁ, NIVY, MICHAEL'S TOWER, PHARMACEUTICAL MUSEUM, ACAD. ISTROPOLITANA, PRIMATE'S PALACE, NATIONAL THEATRE, DEVÍN CASTLE, REDUTA THEATRE, NATIONAL MUSEUM, SNP Bridge, NATIONAL GALLERY, Hydrofoil Terminal, ČA Bridge, DANUBE, Janko Král'Park, To Bus Sta. & Ivanka Airport

1km
½ ml
i *tourist information*

1. ST MARTIN CATHEDRAL
2. Hviedoslavo Square
3. Hlavné Square
4. Františkankie Square
5. Kamenné Square

Martin's Cathedral (14th and 15th centuries), *Segner's Mansion* (1648) and *Roland's Fountain* (1573). On a walk through the Kapitulská, Klariská, Laurinská and Nálepkova streets, visitors will pass especially fine parish houses. Throughout the city are numerous examples of sacral buildings such as cloisters and churches. There are fine views of the Danube and the elegant modern bridge leading to Austria. Its theatres and concert halls are outstanding. The most important art museum is *The Slovak National Gallery*. Also interesting is the *Municipal Museum* which is housed in the old Town Hall on Hlavné Námestie (Main Square). There is also a *Pharmaceutical Museum* and a *zoo*.
The medieval town of **Bardejov** centres around an oblong square lined with fine examples of Gothic *burgher houses* with additions made during the Renaissance period. The 16th-century *Town Hall* also combines aspects of Gothic and Renaissance styles and should not be missed. The town can only be accessed through the four gates in the 14th-century *city walls*, circling the centre. The 15th-century *St Egydius Church* also merits a visit.
Nitra, the centre of the principality of the same name, is an old Slavonic fortified settlement which developed between the 6th and 9th centuries. It is renowned for the *castle complex*, the *monastery*, the *Franciscan Church*

(1624), the *Provost's Palace* (1779), the *Old Administration Building* (1874) and *Our Lady's Column* (1739).
The history of **Trnava** dates back as far as the Neolithic Age and the Great Moravian Period. In 1238 it became a royal town and was the centre for church administration for Hungary for 250 years from 1541 onwards. The city offers fine examples of 17th- and 18th-century architecture in the *university* buildings (founded 1635).
The mining tradition of **Banská Stiavnica** can be traced back to the 13th century. Renaissance-style *burgher houses* can be found in the city centre; other sights include the *old castle* (1548), several sacral buildings and the 11 buildings of the *Mining and Forestry Academy* dating from the 18th and 19th centuries.
Kezmarok was proclaimed a free royal town in 1442. Well worth a visit is the 15th-century Gothic *chateau* with its 17th-century chapel. Throughout the city are the remnants of the town and castle walls dating from the 14th and 16th centuries. Also of interest are the *Lyceum* (1755) and the *Belfry* (1586).
Mining and coin-minting (granted in 1328) played an important role in the history of **Kremnica**. Historic buildings include the *Town Castle* (14th-19th centuries) with an extensive complex of Gothic and Renaissance buildings, the *St Trinity Pest Column* (1767-72) and the

Strbské Pleso

the country, housing large numbers of wildlife (including chamois and marmot) and alpine plants (13,000 species). This is due to the great difference in elevation covering a range from 900-2655m (2953-8710ft). Within the area of the High Tatras are more than 90 mountain lakes, the largest being *Great Hincovo Lake* (20ha) at 1946m (6429ft) above sea level. The park caters for all needs of recreation with a good selection of accommodation and sporting facilities (mountaineering and hiking). 225km (141 miles) of marked hiking trails and three state spas can be found here. An ideal starting point for tours into the eastern part of the High Tatras is **Tatranská Lomnica**. Founded in 1892 as a State climatic spa, it nestles in the foothills of *Skalnaté Pleso* (1751m/5745ft) which boasts the best downhill ski track in the Tatras. The town offers extensive skiing facilities such as a ski-tow, two ski-jumps and a bobsleigh track. Trips to the astronomical observatory can be arranged. A skytram goes up to *Lomnicky stít*, the second highest peak in the Tatras (2632m/8635ft). The picturesque Goral village of **Zdiar** lies at the divide of the *Belianske Tatry* and the *Spisská Magura* mountain ranges. Several ski-tows and excellent ski terrains are suitable for beginners in particular.

The **Pieniny National Park** is a bilateral national park shared with Poland, 30km (19 miles) northeast of the High Tatras.

The **Little Fatra National Park** (200 sq km/99 sq miles) is renowned for the scenic beauty of its valleys and gorges and its abundant wildlife. It is a favourite with hikers in both winter and summer.

Canyons, up to 200m (656ft) deep, cut through the **Slovensky raj (Slovak Paradise) National Park**. The area is riddled with basins and waterfalls in a rugged landscape. *Hrabusice-Podlesok* is an ideal starting point for extensive hiking tours.

SPAS: The country offers a great wealth of curative springs, thermal spas, climatic health resorts and natural mineral waters which are renowned throughout the world.

Bardejovské kúpele was already established as a health resort in the 13th century; **Dudince's** spring is rated among the best in the area due to its mineral composition; the world-famous thermal health resort of **Piestany** specialises in rheumatic treatment; **Sliac** was first mentioned in 1244 and is the most important spa for the treatment of cardio-vascular disorders; and **Trencianske Teplice**, known since 1488, is situated near a sulphuric spring and is suitable for the treatment of nervous disorders.

SOCIAL PROFILE

FOOD & DRINK: Food is often based on Austro-Hungarian dishes; *wiener schnitzel* and sauerkraut, dumplings and pork are very popular. The national speciality is *bryndzove halusky* (potato pasta with ewe-cheese and small pieces of fried bacon) and in the east visitors should sample the gruel made of mushrooms and sour cream, served with black rye bread. The mountainous region of the Slovak Republic is renowned for different varieties of roast mutton, whereas the southern part of the country serves geese, baked in charcoal ovens. Western-style fresh vegetables are often unavailable. There is a wide selection of restaurants, beer taverns and wine cellars with counter service, but table service is often available. **Drink:** Popular beverages include fresh fruit juices, liqueurs and wines. A particular speciality is *borovicka* (strong gin) and the aromatic *marhulovica* (apricot brandy). Beers, *slivovica* (plum brandy) and sparkling wine from the Bratislava region are also famous. There are no rigid licensing hours.

NIGHTLIFE: Theatre and opera are of a high standard all over Eastern Europe. Much of the nightlife takes place in hotels, although nightclubs are to be found in major cities.

SHOPPING: Souvenirs include pottery, porcelain, wooden carvings, hand-embroidered clothing and food items. As well as *Tuzex* outlets, of which a current list can be obtained from SATUR and Cedok offices, there are a number of excellent shops specialising in glass and crystal, while various associations of regional artists and craftsmen run their own retail outlets (pay in local currency). Other special purchases include folk ceramics from the eastern part of the Slovak Republic and woodcarvings from Spisska Bela. **Shopping hours:** 0900-1800/1900 Monday to Friday, 0900-1200 Saturday. Some shops open Sunday morning. Smaller shops may close 1200-1400 for lunch.

SPORT: Football, volleyball, tennis and ice hockey are popular. There is a very good network of marked trails in all mountain areas, and it is possible to plan a walking tour in advance. **Hunting** is available.

Winter sports tours can be arranged through the tourist office; check for details. The many and varied rivers and lakes provide excellent opportunities for watersports –

miners' small *gallery houses* (18th-19th centuries). The region of **Spis** is dotted with numerous historic medieval towns, hamlets and other settlements. The most important is **Levoca**, which has an eventful history. In 1271 it became the capital of the Union of Spis Saxons and in 1323 it was declared a free royal town. This is reflected in the repeated alterations to *St James Church*, which originally dates from the 14th century. It houses the highest Gothic altar in the world (18.6m/61ft high and 6m/12ft wide) built by Master Pavol and complemented by 12 side altars. Also of importance is the town square flanked by the Renaissance *Town Hall*, the *Building of Town Weights* and over 50 *burgher houses*. **Spisská Kapitula** has been the seat of provosts and later bishops since the 13th century. Developing around a 12th-century church is a city reminiscent of a medieval town. It houses such ecclesiastic buildings as the *Cloister of the Brothers of Mercy* and a fine Baroque church.

Kosice is the capital of the eastern Slovak region and bears significant reminders of its rich history, with its numerous Gothic buildings. Towering over the city is the monumental *St Elisabeth Cathedral*.

WINTER SPORTS: The mountains, forests and lakes are enchanting and ideal for outdoor holidaying as well as winter sports. There are popular winter sports centres

in 30 mountain regions, of which the *Tatra Mountains* are the best. In this region alone are over 40 ski tows and funiculars. Other popular mountain areas include the *Slovensky raj* range, with its deep canyons, and the *Malá Fatra* range with its neighbouring *Vratna Dolina Valley*. There are also numerous lakes and rivers amidst the glacial landscape, offering excellent fishing, canoeing, boating and freshwater swimming. The primary watersports areas are at **Orava**, **Liptovská Mara** and **Zemplínska Sírava**.

NATIONAL PARKS: There are five national parks and 15 protected landscape areas in the Slovak Republic. Protected landscape areas are to a large extent untouched by human hand. The countryside is dotted with varied natural formations and numerous species of flora and fauna.

The **Low Tatras National Park** covers the second highest mountain range within the western Carpathians. Within the boundaries of the national park are several ski and recreation resorts, the most renowned lying in the foothills of the *Chopok* (2024m/6640ft). Also situated in the park is the *Demänová Valley*, running over a length of 15km (9 miles), with an extensive cave system. The *Demänová Cave of Liberty* and the *Demänová Ice Cave* are open to the public.

The **Tatra National Park** is the oldest national park in

Traditional Farm House, Zdiar, High Tatra

canoeing, sailing, water-skiing, fishing, etc (see *Resorts & Excursions* above).
SPECIAL EVENTS: Most towns have their own folk festivals, with dancing, local costumes and food. These tend to be in the summer months leading up to the harvest festivals in September. The following is a selection of special events celebrated during 1995 in the Slovak Republic.
Feb '95 *International Ski race,* Interhotel Tatry, Stary Smokovec. **Feb 1-4** *Slovakiatour* (tourism trade fair), Bratislava. **Mar** *Downhill European Cup (Women),* Lomnické Sedlo; *European Cup Ski Alpinism,* Vysoké Tatry. **Mar-Sep** *Davis Cup,* Bratislava. **Mar 16-19** *Expotour Slovakia '95* (tourism trade fair), Zilina. **Apr 24-30** *Middle European Festival of Concert Art,* Zilina. **May** *Grand Prix of Slovakia* (yachts), Piestany; *47th International Tatra Slalom,* Liptovsky Mikulás; *International Tatra Water Slalom,* Liptovsky Mikulás; *Danubian Cup '95,* Bratislava; *50th Anniversary of Slovakia,* Svidník/Dukla. **May 14** *World Championship Motorbike Races,* Zarnovica. **Jun** *Slovnaft Meeting* (athletics), Bratislava; *World Horse Drill Cup,* Sal'a; *Prix of Danube* (festival of children's TV programmes), Bratislava; *Art Film* (film festival), Trencianske Teplice; *Culture Summer '95,* Bratislava; *Myjava Folklore Festival '95; Kosice International Folklore Festival '95.* **Jun 16-18** *19th Zamagurie Folk Festival,* Cerveny Klástor. **Jun 22-25** *Rock Pop Bratislava.* **Jun 22-26** *Eurofolklore 1995* (international folklore festival), Banská Bystrica. **Jul** *Slovak Cup* (yachts), Piestany. **Jul 7-9** *Folklore Festival under Polana,* Detva; *41st Vychodná Folklore Festival.* **Jul 8-9** *Zemplín Festival* (international folklore festival), Hrádok/Michalovce. **Aug 3-6** *Rysy 95,* Tatranská Lomnica. **Aug 4-6** *20th Podrohdche Folklore Festival,* Zuberec; *Jánosik's Days* (folklore festival), Terchová. **Aug 21-27** *Dobro Fest '95,* Trnava. **Sep** *World Championship in Grass Skiing,* Bezovec/Kálnica; *Organ Festival,* Kosice. **Sep-Oct** *15th BIB* (exhibition of illustrations for children), Bratislava. **Sep 2-3** *42nd International Pieniny Slalom,* Dunajec and Cerveny Klástor. **Sep 29-Oct 13** *Bratislava Music Festival.* **Oct** *Ascent on 101 Castles and Palaces,* Spisská Nová Ves and Povazsky Inovec. **Oct 11-15** *3rd International Festival of Mountain Films,* Poprad. **Oct 20-22** *Bratislava Jazz Days.* **Nov** *International Festival of Greek-Orthodox Choirs,* Kosice. **Dec** *World Cup Ski Jumping,* Strbské Pleso.
For further details of special events, contact the Tourist Office, which also arranges music festival tours.
SOCIAL CONVENTIONS: Dress should be casual, but conservative, except at formal dinners and at quality hotels or restaurants. **Photography:** Areas where there are military installations should not be photographed.
Tipping: A 5-10% tip will be discreetly accepted; some

alteration in customs is to be expected in the wake of political and social changes.

BUSINESS PROFILE

ECONOMY: Of all the Soviet bloc economies, the former Czechoslovakia experienced the highest degree of state control, without even the small-scale private enterprise that existed to some extent in all Eastern European economies. Under central planning, and particularly in the aftermath of the 'Prague Spring', economic development concentrated on heavy industry at the expense of traditional strengths in light and craft-based industries, such as textiles, clothing, glass and ceramics (though these continue to remain significant). These inefficient and, in some cases, redundant industrial monoliths are now a considerable millstone around the neck of the economy, particularly in the Slovak Republic. The other problem is a dearth of natural resources – the country had hitherto relied heavily on the former Soviet Union for most of its raw materials, particularly oil, supplies of which have been cut to one-third and payment required in hard currency. The oil shortage reached crisis proportions at the end of 1990 and was resolved satisfactorily only after urgent personal discussions between Presidents Havel and Gorbachev. The following year, the Government embarked on an ambitious programme of privatisation as the cornerstone of its declared policy of introducing a market economy. This has happened at breakneck speed despite the misgivings of observers from across the political spectrum. Questions have been raised concerning the lack of financial infrastructure, the possible consequences of extensive foreign ownership, and the use of an untried voucher scheme which gives equity stakes in industrial enterprises to any individuals who apply. The autumn of 1991 saw 1700 enterprises denationalised in the space of just two weeks. This was the first part of a two-phase plan, beginning in May 1992 and ending in December of that year, which placed most of the industry and agriculture in private hands. There has also been extensive fiscal and budgetary reform, with the aim of creating a fully-fledged capitalist financial system with strong safeguards against inflation. Limited currency convertibility has been introduced as a necessary step towards promoting foreign investment. This is being keenly sought. The Slovak Republic has changed its approach towards privatisation methods, introducing direct sales, tenders and auctions. Priortiy areas are machinery industries, chemical industries, textiles, leather, shoes, glass, electronics, nuclear energy and car manufacturing. Agriculture is particularly important as an export sector (beer and timber are much in demand). For the time being, the majority of trade is conducted with

former members of COMECON, the defunct Soviet bloc economic union, but the focus at present is on developing links with Western Europe. The former Czechoslovakia negotiated associate membership with the European Community. Since the split, the negotiations have continued with both republics, thus acknowledging their separate status. Furture trade patterns are likely to see the Slovak Republic improve its links with Poland, Ukraine and Hungary, while also establishing new ones with countries such as Germany, France, Austria and the USA.
BUSINESS: Businessmen wear suits. A knowledge of German or Hungarian is useful as English is not widely spoken. Long business lunches are usual. Avoid visits during July and August as many businesses close for holidays. **Office hours:** 0800-1600 Monday to Friday.
COMMERCIAL INFORMATION: The following organisation can offer advice: Slovenská obchodná a priemyselná komora (Slovak Chamber of Commerce and Industry), Gorkého 9, 816 03 Bratislava. Tel: (7) 316 402 *or* 333 272. Fax: (7) 330 754 *or* 333 291.
CONFERENCES/CONVENTIONS: Information can be obtained from the Slovak Chamber of Commerce and Industry (for address, see above).

CLIMATE

Cold winters, mild summers.
Required clothing: Mediumweights, heavy topcoat and overshoes for winter; lightweights for summer. Rainwear is advisable throughout the year.

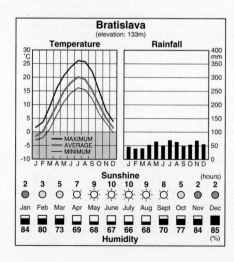

Slovenia

☐ *international airport*

Location: Southern Central Europe.

Centre of Tourist and Economic Promotion
Igriska 5, 61000 Ljubljana, Slovenia
Tel: (61) 125 6306 *or* 125 6172. Fax: (61) 125 7323.
Embassy of the Republic of Slovenia
Suite 1, Cavendish Court, 11-15 Wigmore Street, London
W1H 9LA
Tel: (0171) 495 7775. Fax: (0171) 495 7776. Opening
hours: 0900-1700 Monday to Friday; 0900-1200 Monday
to Friday (Visa section).
Slovenian Tourist Office
2 Canfield Place, London NW6 3BT
Tel: (0171) 372 3844. Fax: (0171) 372 3763. Opening
hours: 0900-1700 Monday to Friday.
British Embassy
4th Floor, Trg Republike 3, 61000 Ljubljana, Slovenia
Tel: (61) 157 191. Fax: (61) 150 174.
Embassy of the Republic of Slovenia
1525 New Hampshire Avenue, NW, Washington, DC
20036
Tel: (202) 667 5363. Fax: (202) 667 4563.
Consulate in: New York (tel: (212) 370 3006).
Slovenian Tourist Office
Suite 3006, 122 East 42nd Street, New York, NY 10168-
0072
Tel: (212) 682 5896. Fax: (212) 661 2469.
Embassy of the United States of America
Prazakova 4, 61000 Ljubljana, Slovenia
Tel: (61) 301 427 *or* 301 472 *or* 301 485. Fax: (61) 301
401.
Embassy of the Republic of Slovenia
Suite 2101, 150 Metcalfe Street, Ottawa, Ontario K2P
1P1
Tel: (613) 565 5781/2. Fax: (613) 565 5783.
**The Canadian Embassy in Budapest deals with
enquiries relating to Slovenia (see *Hungary* earlier in
this book).**

AREA: 20,254 sq km (7820 sq miles).
POPULATION: 1,965,986 (1991).
POPULATION DENSITY: 97.1 per sq km.

CAPITAL: Ljubljana. **Population:** 276,133 (1991).
GEOGRAPHY: This compact and strategically
important country is dominated by mountains, rivers
and major north–south and east–west transit routes.
Slovenia borders Italy to the west, Austria to the north,
Hungary to the northeast and Croatia to the southeast,
plus a 47km (30-mile) Adriatic Sea coastline, where the
main port is Koper.
LANGUAGE: Slovene (Latinate alphabet) which is
closely related to the Serbo-Croat (or Croato-Serb) of
the ex-Yugoslav republics to the southeast.
RELIGION: 90% Roman Catholic, 3% Eastern
Orthodox, plus smaller ethnic Italian and Hungarian
minorities.
TIME: GMT + 1 (GMT + 2 from last Sunday in March
to Saturday before last Sunday in September).
ELECTRICITY: 220 volts AC, 50Hz.
COMMUNICATIONS: The telecommunications
system is presently undergoing restructuring concerning
individual telephone numbers. **Telephone:** IDD is
available. Telephone lines between Ljubljana and
Belgrade have been indefinitely cut, although services
to and from Zagreb are generally available. Country
code: 386. Outgoing international code: 00. Calls can be
made either with tokens or phonecards. **Fax:** Available
to and from Western Europe. **Telex/telegram:** Telex
facilities are limited. **Post:** Reasonable internal service.
Stamps can be bought at bookstalls. Post office hours:
0800-1900 Monday to Friday; 0800-1300 Saturday. The
post office at Cigaletova 5 is open 24 hours. **Press:** The
main local newspaper is *Delo* (Ljubljana). The state
news agency, *STA*, produces material in English for
international distribution on a daily basis. English-
language publications include *Ars Vivendi, Flaneur,
MM Slovenia, Slovenian Business Report, Slovenija* and
Slovenia Weekly. The state TV and radio station *RTS*
produces regular news and other broadcasts in English
and other West European languages during the tourist
season.
**BBC World Service and Voice of America
frequencies:** From time to time these change. See the
section *How to Use this Book* for more information.
BBC:

MHz	15.07	12.09	9.410	6.195

Voice of America:

MHz	9.6706.040	5.995	1.260

PASSPORT/VISA

*Regulations and requirements may be subject to change at short notice, and you
are advised to contact the appropriate diplomatic or consular authority before
finalising travel arrangements. Details of these may be found at the head of this
country's entry. Any numbers in the chart refer to the footnotes below.*

	Passport Required?	Visa Required?	Return Ticket Required?
Full British	1	No	Yes
BVP	Valid/2	-	-
Australian	Yes	No	Yes
Canadian	Yes	No	Yes
USA	Yes	No	Yes
Other EU (As of 31/12/94)	1	No	Yes
Japanese	Yes	No	Yes

PASSPORTS: Valid passports required by all except **[1]**
nationals of EU countries entering with a valid national
ID card or, in the case of UK citizens, a BVP for
touristic purposes only.
British Visitors Passport: [2] A BVP is acceptable for
UK nationals if travelling for tourist purposes only.
VISAS: These can be issued at border points and are
required by all except:
(a) nationals of those countries listed in the chart above;
(b) nationals of Algeria, Argentina, Austria, Bosnia-
Hercegovina, Chile, Croatia, Cyprus, Czech Republic,
Finland, Hungary, Iceland, Iran, Israel, South Korea,
Liechtenstein, Former Yugoslav Republic of
Macedonia, Malta, Monaco, New Zealand, Norway,
Poland, San Marino, Sweden, Switzerland, Tunisia,
Turkey, Vatican City and Uruguay for stays of up to 90
days;
(c) nationals of Bulgaria, Romania and Slovak Republic
for stays of up to 30 days;
(d) nationals of Singapore for stays of up to 14 days;
(e) nationals of the Russian Federation with an
invitation or a letter of guarantee covering expenses or
on an organised package tour for up to 90 days.
Types of visa: *Single-entry:* £21; *Multiple-entry:* £42.
Validity: *Single-* and *Multiple-entry:* up to 3 months.
Application to: Consulate (or Consulate section at
Embassy). For addresses, see top of entry.
Application requirements: (a) Valid passport. (b)
Application form. (c) Fee.

Note: Applications for visas *must* be made in person.
Working days required: 1-2.

MONEY

Currency: Slovene Tolar (SIT) = 100 stotins. Notes are
in denominations of SIT5000, 1000, 500, 200, 100, 50,
20 and 10. Coins are in denominations of SIT5, 2 and 1,
and 50, 20 and 10 stotins. The Tolar replaced the
Yugoslav Dinar in October 1991.
Currency exchange: The Slovenian Tolar is internally
fully convertible.
Travellers cheques: Widely accepted.
Exchange rate indicators: The following figures are
included as a guide to the exchange rate of the Slovene
Tolar against Sterling and the US Dollar:

Date:	Oct '92	Sep '93	Jan '94	Jan '95
£1.00=	143.31	180.20	194.95	200.35
$1.00=	90.30	118.00	131.77	128.06

Currency restrictions: The import and export of local
currency is limited to SIT5000. There is unrestricted
import and export of foreign currency subject to amount
declared on arrival.
Banking hours: 0900-1200 and 1400-1700 Monday to
Friday. Some branches are open 0730-1200 Saturday for
payments and withdrawals.

DUTY FREE

The following goods can be imported into Slovenia
without incurring customs duty:
*200 cigarettes or 50 cigars or 250g of tobacco; 1 litre of
wine; 1 litre of spirits; 50ml perfume; 250ml eau de
toilette; gifts up to a value of DM100.*

PUBLIC HOLIDAYS

Jan 1-2 '95 New Year. **Feb 8** Culture Day. **Apr 17**
Easter Monday. **Apr 27** Resistance Day. **May 1-2**
Labour Days. **Jun 4** Whit Sunday. **Jun 25** National Day.
Aug 15 Assumption. **Oct 31** Reformation Day. **Nov 1**
Remembrance Day. **Dec 25** Christmas Day. **Dec 26**
Independence Day. **Jan 1-2 '96** New Year. **Feb 8**
Culture Day. **Apr 8** Easter Monday. **Apr 27** Resistance
Day.

HEALTH

*Regulations and requirements may be subject to change at short notice, and
you are advised to contact your doctor well in advance of your intended date of
departure. Any numbers in the chart refer to the footnotes below.*

	Special Precautions?	Certificate Required?
Yellow Fever	No	No
Cholera	No	No
Typhoid & Polio	No	-
Malaria	No	-
Food & Drink	1	-

[1]: Mains water is normally chlorinated, and whilst
relatively safe may cause mild abdominal upsets. Bottled
water is available and is advised for the first few weeks
of the stay. Milk is pasteurised and dairy products are
safe for consumption. Local meat, poultry, seafood, fruit
and vegetables are generally considered safe to eat.
Rabies is present. For those at high risk, vaccination
before arrival should be considered. If you are bitten
abroad seek medical advice without delay. For more
information, consult the *Health* section at the back of the
book.
Health care: There is a Reciprocal Health Agreement
with the UK, allowing free hospital and other medical
treatment and some free dental treatment to those
presenting a UK passport. Prescribed medicines must be
paid for.

TRAVEL - International

AIR: The national airline is *Adria Airways* which
operates direct flights from London to Ljubljana.
Approximate flight time: From London to Ljubljana is
2 hours.
International airports: *Ljubljana (LJU)* (Brnik) is 25km
(15 miles) from the city. Airport facilities include bank
(0900-1200 and 1430-1730), post office (0700-1800
Monday to Friday, 0700-1200 Saturday), duty-free shop
(0700-2100), bar (0730-2000), restaurant (0800-1900),
snack bar (0730-2000), shops (0800-1900) and car hire
(*Hertz* and *Budget*). Buses are available to Kranj (travel
time – 15 minutes) and to Ljubljana (travel time – 45

minutes). Taxis are also available.

Maribor also has some international connections.

SEA: Ferries link the Adriatic coast with Italian ports.

RAIL: Connections and through coaches are available from principal Eastern and Western European cities. There are other links, particularly via Venice and Vienna. International trains have couchette coaches as well as bar and dining cars. On some lines transport for cars is provided.

ROAD: The following frontier posts are open for road traffic:

From **Italy:** San Bartolomeo–Lazaret; Albaro Veskova–Skofije; Pesse–Kozina; Fernetti–Fernetici (Sezana); Gorizia–Nova Gorica; Stupizza–Robic; Uccea–Uceja; Passo del Predil–Predel; and Fusine Laghi–Ratece.

From **Austria:** Wurzenpass (Villach)–Korensko sedlo; Loibltunnel–Ljubelj; Seebergsattel–Jezersko; Grablach–Holmec; Rabenstein–Vic; Eibiswald–Radlji od Dravi; Langegg–Jurij; Spielfeld–Sentilj; Mureck–Trate; Sicheldorf–Gederovci; Radkersburg–Gornja Radgona; and Bonisdorf–Kuzma.

From **Hungary:** Bajansenye–Hodos.

Nearly all the border passings mentioned above are open 24 hours a day.

See below for information regarding **documentation** and **traffic regulations**.

TRAVEL - Internal

AIR: There are domestic airports at Maribor in the east of the country and on the Adriatic Coast at Portoroz.

SEA: Slovenia has ports at Koper, Izola and Piran.

ROAD: There is a good network of high-quality roads in Slovenia. However, due to the war, they now effectively stop at Zagreb. There are extensive detours via Hungary for traffic going to and coming from Belgrade further south. Traffic drives on the right. For further information, contact the national automobile club *Auto-Moto Zveza Slovenije (AMZS)*, Dunajska 128, 61000 Ljubljana. Tel: (61) 168 1111. **Speed limits:** 120kmph (75mph) on motorways, 100kmph (62mph) on other roads. In cities it is 60kmph (38mph). School buses cannot be overtaken. The alcohol limit is 0.5‰. **Documentation:** Full national driving licences are accepted. No customs documents are required, but car log books and Third Party insurance are necessary. A Green Card is also advisable.

URBAN: Ljubljana has bus services and taxis are widely available.

JOURNEY TIMES: The following chart gives approximate journey times from Ljubljana (in hours and minutes) to other major cities/towns in Slovenia.

	Road	Rail
Portoroz	1.30	2.30
Maribor	2.00	2.30
Lipica	1.00	-
Bled	0.45	1.15
Murska Sobota	3.00	3.30
Postojna	0.45	1.00
Novo Mesto	1.00	1.30

ACCOMMODATION

HOTELS: Slovenia has over 75,000 beds in hotels throughout the country. Standards are high and accommodation is classified from Deluxe to A, B, C and D class. Further hotel information is available from the Tourism and Catering Association of the Chamber of Economy of Slovenia, Slovenska 54, 61000 Ljubljana. Tel: (61) 132 8218. Fax: (61) 302 983; *or* the Centre of Tourist and Economic Promotion (for address, see top of entry).

RESORTS & EXCURSIONS

The Slovene capital, **Ljubljana**, stretches along the banks of the Ljubljanca River. The old part of the town is particularly picturesque. There are three bridges crossing the river, one leading directly to the *Town Hall* (1718) with its Baroque fountain and two open courtyards. Towering over the city are the twin towers of *Ljubljana Cathedral* (1708) which house some impressive frescoes. The *Castle*, situated on a hill, overlooks the river. The Castle is currently undergoing repairs and only part of it is open to the public. The tower offers a splendid view of the city. On the eastern bank of the river is the *Town Museum* with an extensive collection of Roman artefacts. Near to the *University* is the *Ursuline Church* (1726) with an altar by Robba. The *National Museum*, the *National Gallery*, the *Municipal Gallery* and the *Modern Art Gallery* with the quiet *Tivoli Gardens* are all interesting. The **Julian Alps** are a popular skiing area in the winter, particularly the resorts

of **Kranjska Gora** and **Bovec. Podkoren** is situated in the mountains near the Austrian border. The fashionable mountain resort of **Bled** is set on the idyllic *Lake Bled*, where skating and curling take place in winter, and swimming and rowing in summer. The trout and carp fishing is also very good. Sights include the neo-Gothic *Parish Church* (1904) with its interesting frescoes and *Bled Castle*, the former seat of the bishops of Brixen. Perching above a 100m (328ft) drop, the castle offers magnificent views over the city and lake. **Ptuj** contains Roman remains, a medieval centre and is the scene of traditional carnivals. **Portoroz** is the largest and best-known resort in Slovenia. The port of **Koper** still retains an Italian atmosphere. The old town, entered through *Muda Gate,* is particularly worth exploring. Passing the *Bridge Fountain*, the street widens onto the city's central square. In general, the sights are clustered around the *Town Tower* (1480) which dominates the skyline. Fine examples of the Venetian Gothic style are the 15th-century *Cathedral*, the *loggia* and the *Praetor's Palace*; also of interest is the Romanesque *Carmin Rotunda* (1317). Well worth a visit is the excellent *Provincial Museum* which houses old maps of the area.

SOCIAL PROFILE

FOOD & DRINK: Slovenia's national cuisine shows an Austro-German influence with sauerkraut, grilled sausage and apple strudel often appearing on menus.

SHOPPING: Shopping hours: 0800-1900 Monday to Friday.

NIGHTLIFE: There is a good selection of theatres, cinemas and clubs in the larger towns. Ljubljana also has a good opera house and the symphony orchestra plays regularly in the Big Hall of the Cultural and Congress Centre.

SPORT: Skiing and **spa resorts** exist in all regions, but particularly Bled, Bohinj and Vogel. **Fishing** permits are available from hotels or local authorities. Fishing on the Adriatic coast is unrestricted, but freshwater angling and fishing with equipment require a permit. 'Fish-linking' with a local small craft owner is popular. **Sailing** is popular along the coast. Berths and boats can be hired at all ports. Permits are needed for boats brought into the country. **Spectator sports: Football** is very popular.

SPECIAL EVENTS: The following is a selection of the major festivals and other special events celebrated in Slovenia during 1995/96. For a complete list, contact the Tourist Board.

Jun 17-Sep '95 *21st International Biennial of Graphic Art*, Ljubljana. **Jul-Aug** *43rd International Summer Festival*, Ljubljana. **Aug 28-Sep 3** *41st International Wine Fair*, Ljubljana. **Jan 6-7 '96** *Golden Fox World Cup Women's Slalom and Giant Slalom*, Maribor. **Feb 3-4** *Kompas Holidays Cup Men's Slalom and Giant Slalom*, Kranjska Gora.

SOCIAL CONVENTIONS: Shaking hands is the normal form of greeting. Usual European social conventions apply and informal dress is widely acceptable. Smoking is prohibited on public transport, in cinemas, theatres, public offices and in waiting rooms.

Tipping: 10% is generally expected in hotels, restaurants and for taxis.

BUSINESS PROFILE

ECONOMY: By far the richest and most economically developed of the former Yugoslav republics, Slovenia accounted for 20% of Yugoslavia's GDP (around US$10.7 billion) and industrial output, and 30% of its exports (60% of which went to Western convertible currency markets) in 1990-91, with a GDP per capita of around US$5000 in the same year (double the Yugoslav average, but only a third of that then prevailing in Austria). A highly industrialised economy with a foodstuffs deficit and no natural resources, Slovenia was seriously affected by the various adverse consequences of the civil war (notably the collapse of the old Yugoslav market) in 1991, when the GDP fell by 15%. Export performances declined in 1991, mainly due to the destruction of internal Yugoslavian markets. Foreign economic assistance and investment has been forthcoming, with recently acquired IMF membership expediting its arrival, but not on the large scale envisaged by the Government. As of June 1992, when the Bank of Slovenia had foreign exchange reserves of around US$500 million, Slovenia was unique among the ex-Yugoslav republics in repaying its foreign debt share more or less according to schedule (US$1.8 billion, plus around 20% of unallocated federal debt, or around 20% of the total Yugoslav foreign debt). Prior to the imposition of UN economic sanctions against Serbia and Montenegro in June 1992, Slovenia

accounted for around 25% of bilateral UK trade with Yugoslavia in 1991 (the Serbian share of such trade was around 65%), when British creditor interests also held around 8% of Slovenia's foreign debt. In 1993 the Slovenian trade deficit stood at US$136.8 million, with a balance of payments surplus of US$196 million. Although still high, the inflation rate is falling and the signing of agreements with EFTA and the EU can only boost exports. Slovenia's main trading partners are Germany, Italy, Croatia and Austria. Sustained growth will depend on the stability of the other former Yugoslav republics and the efficiency of the Government in the continuation of its privatisation programme and its efforts to combat rising unemployment.

BUSINESS: Smart dress is advised. Appointments are usual and visitors should be punctual. Visiting cards are essential. Slovenia is the most efficient and reliable of the ex-Yugoslav republics, being in many respects comparable to Austria and Germany. Executives will generally have a good knowledge of German, English and sometimes Italian. There is a well-developed network of local agents, advisers, consultants and lawyers willing to act for foreign companies. **Office hours:** 0700-1500 Monday to Friday.

COMMERCIAL INFORMATION: The following organisation can offer advice: Chamber of Economy of Slovenia, Slovenska 41, 61000 Ljubljana. Tel: (61) 125 0122. Fax: (61) 218 242.

CONFERENCES/CONVENTIONS: Slovenia's tradition as a meeting place goes back to 1821, when it played host to the Congress of the Holy Alliance. The main conference locations are Ljubljana, Bled, Portoroz, Radenci and Rogaska Slatina, where there are meeting facilities for up to 2000 participants. For more information, contact the Chamber of Economy of Slovenia, Conferences and Conventions Department, Slovenska 41, 61000 Ljubljana. Tel: (61) 125 6306. Fax: (61) 219 536; *or* Cankarjev dom, Congress and Cultural Center, Presernova 10, 61000 Ljubljana. Tel: (61) 223 841. Fax: (61) 217 431.

CLIMATE

Continental. Climate with warm summers and cold winters (snowfalls in the Alps). Mediterranean climate on the coast.

Required clothing: Mediumweight clothing and heavy overcoats in winter; lightweight clothing and raincoats for the summer, particularly for the higher Alpine north.

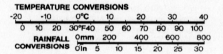

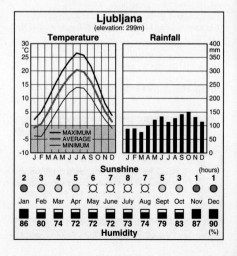

Solomon Islands

□ *international airport*

600km

300mls

PACIFIC

P.N.G.

Ontong
Java Atoll

Kieta

Choiseul

Santa Isabel

New
Georgia

Malaita

OCEAN

HONIARA

Guadalcanal

San Cristóbal

Santa
Cruz Is.

SOLOMON

ISLANDS

Rennell I.

VANUATU

AUSTRALIA

DAB-M205

Location: Southwestern Pacific.

Solomon Islands Tourist Authority
PO Box 321, Honiara, Solomon Islands
Tel: 22442. Fax: 23986.
Solomon Islands Honorary Consulate
19 Springfield Road, London SW19 7AL
Tel: (0181) 296 0232. Fax: (0181) 946 1744.
Embassy of the Solomon Islands
BP 3, avenue de l'Yser 13, B-1040 Brussels, Belgium
Tel: (2) 732 7085. Fax: (2) 732 6885.
British High Commission
PO Box 676, Telekom House, Mendana Avenue,
Honiara, Solomon Islands
Tel: 21705/6. Fax: 20765. Telex: 66324 (a/b UKREP
HQ).
Solomon Islands Tourist Authority
c/o The Permanent Mission to the United Nations,
Suite 800B, 820 Second Avenue, New York, NY 10017
Tel: (212) 599 6194. Fax: (212) 661 8925.
Also deals with enquiries from Canada.
**The Canadian High Commission in Canberra deals
with enquiries relating to the Solomon Islands (see
Australia earlier in the book).**

AREA: 27,566 sq km (10,639 sq miles).
POPULATION: 318,707 (1990 estimate).
POPULATION DENSITY: 11.6 per sq km.
CAPITAL: Honiara. **Population:** 35,288 (1990
estimate).
GEOGRAPHY: The Solomon Islands Archipelago is
scattered in the southwestern Pacific, east of Papua New
Guinea. The group comprises most of the Solomon
Islands (those in the northwest are part of Papua New
Guinea), the Ontong Java Islands, Rennell Island and the
Santa Cruz Islands, which lie further to the east. The
larger of the islands are 145-193km (90-120 miles) in
length, while the smallest are no more than coral
outcrops. The terrain is generally quite rugged, with
foothills that rise gently to a peak and then fall away
steeply to the sea on the other side. The capital Honiara is
situated on Guadalcanal Island which also has the highest
mountain, Mount Makarakombu, at 2447m (8028ft).
There are a number of dormant volcanoes scattered
throughout the archipelago.
LANGUAGE: English is the official language. Pidgin
English and over 87 different local dialects are also
spoken.
RELIGION: More than 95% of the population are

Christian.
TIME: GMT + 11.
ELECTRICITY: 240 volts AC, 50Hz. Australian-type
flat 3-pin plugs are in use.
COMMUNICATIONS: Telephone: IDD is available.
Country code: 677. Outgoing international code: 00.
There are no area codes. **Fax:** *Solomon Telekom* provides
services at its offices in Honiara, though introduction
elsewhere has been gradual and only some hotels have
facilities. Address: Solomon Telekom, PO Box 148,
Honiara, Guadalcanal. Tel: 21576. Fax: 23110. Telex:
66301. **Telex/telegram:** Services available 24 hours a
day administered by Solomon Telekom (address above).
Post: Airmail to Europe takes approximately seven days.
The Main Post Office in Honiara opens 0900-1630
Monday to Friday; 0900-1100 Saturday. Other post
office opening hours are 0800-1630 Monday to Friday;
0800-1200 Saturday. **Press:** The main newspaper is the
weekly *The Solomon Star*.
**BBC World Service and Voice of America
frequencies:** From time to time these change. See the
section *How to Use this Book* for more information.
BBC:

MHz	17.83	11.95	9.740	6.195

Voice of America:

MHz	18.82	15.18	9.525	1.735

PASSPORT/VISA

*Regulations and requirements may be subject to change at short notice, and you
are advised to contact the appropriate diplomatic or consular authority before
finalising travel arrangements. Details of these may be found at the head of this
country's entry. Any numbers in the chart refer to the footnotes below.*

	Passport Required?	Visa Required?	Return Ticket Required?
Full British	Yes	No	Yes
BVP	Not valid	-	-
Australian	Yes	No	Yes
Canadian	Yes	No	Yes
USA	Yes	No	Yes
Other EU (As of 31/12/94)	Yes	No	Yes
Japanese	Yes	No	Yes

PASSPORTS: Valid passport required by all.
British Visitors Passport: Not accepted.
VISAS: Visas are not required for a stay of up to 3
months except for nationals of Bangladesh, India,
Pakistan and Sri Lanka who *do* require a visa. A Visitors
Permit is required by all other nationals and will be
issued on arrival at the airport.
Application to: Principal Immigration Officer, Ministry
of Commerce, Employment and Trade, PO Box G26,
Honiara. Tel: 21140. Telex: 66311.
Application requirements: Enquire at Immigration
Division, Ministry of Commerce and Primary Industries.
Working days required: Apply well in advance.
Temporary residence: Ministry of Commerce and
Primary Industries.

MONEY

Currency: Solomon Islands Dollar (SI$) = 100 cents.
Notes are in denominations of SI$50, 20, 10, 5 and 2.
Coins are in denominations of SI$1, and 50, 20, 10, 5, 2
and 1 cents.
Credit cards: Diners Club is accepted on a limited basis.
Check with your credit card company for details of
merchant acceptability and other facilities which may be
available.
Travellers cheques: Can be exchanged at banks.
Exchange rate indicators: The following figures are
included as a guide to the movements of the Solomon
Islands Dollar against Sterling and the US Dollar:

Date:	Oct '92	Sep '93	Jan '94	Jan '95
£1.00=	4.72	4.85	4.72	5.14
$1.00=	2.97	3.17	3.19	3.29

Currency restrictions: Free import of foreign currency,
subject to declaration; export limited to amount declared
on arrival. Free import of local currency, export limited
to SI$250.
Banking hours: 0830-1500 Monday to Friday.

DUTY FREE

The following items may be imported into the Solomon
Islands without incurring customs duty:
*200 cigarettes or 250g cigars or 250g of tobacco; 2 litres
of wine/spirits; other dutiable goods to a total value of
SI$40.*
Prohibited items: Unlicensed firearms or other weapons.

PUBLIC HOLIDAYS

Jan 1 '95 New Year's Day. **Apr 14-17** Easter. **Jun 5**
Whit Monday. **Jun 10** Queen's Official Birthday. **Jul 7**
Independence Day. **Dec 25-26** Christmas. **Jan 1 '96** New
Year's Day. **Apr 14-17** Easter.

HEALTH

*Regulations and requirements may be subject to change at short notice, and
you are advised to contact your doctor well in advance of your intended date of
departure. Any numbers in the chart refer to the footnotes below.*

	Special Precautions?	Certificate Required?
Yellow Fever	No	1
Cholera	No	No
Typhoid & Polio	Yes	-
Malaria	2	-
Food & Drink	3	-

[1]: A yellow fever vaccination certificate is required by
travellers arriving from infected areas.
[2]: Malaria risk exists throughout the year except in
some outlying islets in the east and south. The malignant
falciparum strain is present and is reported to be
'resistant' to chloroquine.
[3]: All water should be regarded as being a potential
health risk. Water used for drinking, brushing teeth or
making ice should first be boiled or otherwise sterilised.
Milk is unpasteurised and should be boiled. Powdered or
tinned milk is available and is advised, but make sure
that it is reconstituted with pure water. Avoid dairy
products which are likely to have been made from
unboiled milk. Only eat well-cooked meat and fish,
preferably served hot. Pork, salad and mayonnaise may
carry increased risk. Vegetables should be cooked and
fruit peeled.
Health care: There are eight hospitals, the largest being
the Central Hospital in Honiara, Guadalcanal. Church
missions provide medical facilities on outlying islands.
Health insurance is essential.

TRAVEL - International

AIR: The national airline is *Solomon Island Airways
(IE)*.
Approximate flight time: From London to Honiara is 29
hours 45 minutes, excluding stopover time in Brisbane.
International airport: *Honiara (HIR)* (Henderson Field)
on Guadalcanal Island, 20km (8 miles) from Honiara
(travel time – 20 minutes). Bus and taxi services are
available.
Departure tax: SI$30 for all departures. Transit
passengers and children under two years are exempt.
SEA: International ports are Honiara (Guadalcanal
Island) and Yandina (Rennell Island). Plans are in hand
to build a new deep-sea harbour at Noro on New
Georgia, which will replace the port at Gizo. The two
principal passenger lines with services to the Solomons
are *P&O* and *Sitmar*.

TRAVEL - Internal

AIR: Domestic scheduled and charter services are run by
Solomon Island Airways (IE) from Henderson Field to
most main islands and towns in the Solomons.
Flightseeing tours can be arranged.
SEA: Large and small ships provide the best means of
travelling between islands. Services are run by the
Government and by a host of private operators; some of
the Christian missions even have their own fleets.
ROAD: Traffic drives on the left. There are over
1300km (800 miles) of roads throughout the islands.
About 455km (280 miles) are main roads and a further
800km (500 miles) are privately maintained roads for
plantation use. Road maintenance is limited and the
general condition of the roads is poor. **Taxi:** Available in
Honiara and Auki. It is advisable to agree the fare
beforehand. **Car hire:** This is available through hotels in
Honiara. **Documentation:** A national driving licence will
suffice.

ACCOMMODATION

HOTELS: There are only six hotels in Honiara. Visitors
are advised to make advance reservations. The
Tavanipupu Island Resort in the Marau Sound
(Guadalcanal) is accessible by air and sea.
Accommodation is also available in the Reef Islands,
Western Solomons and Malaita. A number of lodges and

resorts on the islands offer a variety of leisure activities.
A full list of accommodation and rates is available from
the Solomon Islands Tourist Authority (address at top of
entry).
CAMPING: Camping is rare and is best confined to
remoter areas. Permission should always be obtained
from the landowner, usually the village chief, before
pitching a tent.

RESORTS & EXCURSIONS

**Guadalcanal, Malaita, Choiseul, New Georgia, San
Cristobal** and **Santa Isabel** are the main islands. They
are up to 200km (120 miles) long and up to 50km (30
miles) wide. The wildlife on the islands is of great
interest, consisting of a mixture of introduced and
indigenous species. Most islands are populated with a
range of reptiles (including turtles), as well as marsupials
including 'flying foxes' (fruit bats), phalangers and
opossums. Later introductions include pigs and chickens.
Europeans brought cats, horses, cattle and goats. Hawks,
cuckoos, waders and other often colourful birds exhibit
the diversity of behaviour typical of island creatures. The
buff-headed coucal is the world's largest cuckoo. The
ubiquitous ants, beetles, spiders, moths, butterflies and
frogs also come in a variety of forms. The ocean around
the islands is crammed with exotic creatures, though
visitors would be well advised to be cautious of some of
them.
Honiara, the capital on **Guadalcanal,** has a museum,
botanical gardens and *Chinatown.* There are relics of
World War II in and around the town and noticeboards
indicate major battles and incidents that took place
during the battle for Guadalcanal. Villages and scenic
drives are within easy reach.
Three travel agencies can arrange excursions around
Guadalcanal and other islands. Popular tours include the
battlefields of World War II, the *Betikama* carving
centre, *Chapura* and *Tambea* villages on Guadalcanal,
and *Laulasi* and *Alite* villages on the island of **Malaita,**
where shells are broken, rounded and, after further
working, strung together. They are used to denote status
and as gifts and items of barter in inter-tribal deals. The
strings of shells can be worn as bracelets, necklaces, belts
and earrings. They may also include animal and fish
teeth, and, in times past, the teeth of murderers.
Collectively, these items are known as 'shell money'.
Carvings for the tourist trade are made on **Rennell** and
Bellona. Miniature daggers, spears and clubs are very
popular. Other carvings show scenes from life on the
Solomon Islands, both human and animal.
Tourists can easily organise their own excursions, with
timetables and information provided by the tourist
authority and travel agents.

SOCIAL PROFILE

FOOD & DRINK: Local recipes include *tapioca*
pudding and *taro* roots with *taro* leaves. There are a few
restaurants outside the hotels in Honaria. Both Asian and
European food is served and the cuisine is generally
good. There are two Chinese restaurants in Honiara
which are quite popular. Spirits, wine and beer are
available. Table service is normal.
NIGHTLIFE: Honiara is a comparatively quiet town,
although there are a few clubs with music and dancing,
the occasional film show and snooker and darts. The
clubs offer temporary membership to visitors.
SHOPPING: Local purchases include mother-of-pearl
items, walking sticks, carved and inlaid wood, copper
murals, conch shells and rare varieties of cowrie. New
Georgia in the western district is known for carved fish,
turtles and birds. Carvings in ebony, inlaid with shell, are
unique. Duty-free shopping is available at a number of
stores in Honiara. **Shopping hours:** 0800-1700 Monday
to Friday, 0800-1230 Saturday.
SPORT: Surrounding waters have good **fishing** potential
and enquiries may be made at the Point Cruz Yacht Club,
which welcomes visitors. A number of resorts now offer
a broad variety of sea and other sports. **Swimming** is not
recommended in the sea around Honiara because of
sharks. In any case, swimmers should beware of sea
urchins, bristle-worms, stinging corals, crown of thorn
starfish and further exotic sealife. There are a number of
swimming pools. **Tennis** courts are at the Guadalcanal
Club and arrangements can be made through the hotels.
Dives are arranged most weekends by the Skin Diver
Association which can be contacted through the Solomon
Islands Tourist Authority. There is a 9-hole **golf** course
outside Honiara and local tourist agents will make
arrangements. The Tamba Village Resort west of
Honiara has a miniature golf course.
SPECIAL EVENTS: Each part of the Solomon Islands
has its own *Province Day.* These are listed below:
Jun 8 '95 Temotu. **Jun 29** Central. **Jul 8** Isabel. **Jul 31**

Guadalcanal. **Aug 3** Makira. **Aug 14** Malaita. **Dec 7**
Western.
SOCIAL CONVENTIONS: A casual atmosphere
prevails and European customs exist alongside local
traditions. Informal wear is widely suitable although
women often wear long dresses for evening functions.
Men need never wear ties. It is customary to cover
thighs. Visitors are discouraged from wearing beachwear
and shorts around towns and villages. **Tipping:** There is
no tipping on the Solomon Islands and visitors are
requested to honour this local custom.

BUSINESS PROFILE

ECONOMY: The economy continues to depend on
subsistence agriculture, employing about 90% of the
population in producing coconuts, sweet potatoes,
cassava, fruit and vegetables, although fish and related
products have been the most important exports since
1984. A great deal of copra continues to be produced, but
the world price has in recent years been steadily
declining and government economic policy is concerned
with increasing foreign investment and commercial
development. New agricultural products included cocoa
and palm oil while an indigenous timber industry was
successfully developed and some rich mineral deposits
have been located. The latter include phosphates, bauxite
and asbestos and there is a possibility of gold, silver and
copper. Tourism is relatively minor as yet but may
develop significantly in the future. The Solomon Islands
also enjoy substantial overseas aid. Australia and Japan
are the main trading partners. The islands' total trade in
1987 was US$130 million.
BUSINESS: Shirt and smart trousers or skirt will suffice.
English and French are widely spoken. The best time to
visit is May to October. **Office hours:** 0800-1200 and
1300-1630 Monday to Friday, 0730-1200 Saturday.
COMMERCIAL INFORMATION: The following
organisations can offer advice: Ministry of Foreign
Affairs, PO Box G10, Honiara. Tel: 22223. Telex:
66311; *or*
Solomon Islands Chamber of Commerce, PO Box 64,
Honiara. Tel: 22960. Telex: 66448.

CLIMATE

Semi-tropical, mainly hot and humid, with little annual
variation in temperature. The wet season (November to
April) can bring severe tropical storms.
Required clothing: Tropical, lightweights and cottons
are recommended. Rainwear from November to April.

□ *international airport*

Location: East Africa.

Note: Looting, banditry and all forms of violent crime
are common in Somalia, particularly in the capital city of
Mogadishu. While banditry and inter-clan tension are
major problems in many areas of Somalia, these
difficulties are less severe in the northern parts of the
country. There is no functioning national government,
and embassies have been withdrawn. The following
information largely represents the situation before the
current ruinous civil war, and is presented in the hope
that it will again prove useful.
Source: US State Department – September 22, 1994.

Embassy of the Somali Democratic Republic
60 Portland Place, London W1N 3DG
Tel: (0171) 580 7148. Telex: 267672 (a/b SOMDIP).
Opening hours: 1000-1530 Monday to Friday.
Presently closed.
British Embassy
PO Box 1036, Hassan Geedi Abtow, Mogadishu,
Somalia
Tel: (1) 20288/9. Telex: 3617.
All staff presently withdrawn.
Embassy of the Somali Democratic Republic
Suite 710, 600 New Hampshire Avenue, NW,
Washington, DC 20037
Presently closed.
**The Canadian Embassy in Nairobi deals with
enquiries relating to Somalia (see *Kenya* earlier in the
book).**

AREA: 637,657 sq km (246,201 sq miles).
POPULATION: 7,691,000 (1991 estimate).
POPULATION DENSITY: 12.1 per sq km.
CAPITAL: Mogadishu. **Population:** 500,000 (1981).
GEOGRAPHY: Somalia is bounded to the north by the
Gulf of Aden, to the south and west by Kenya, to the
west by Ethiopia and to the northwest by Djibouti. To the
east lies the Indian Ocean. Somalia is an arid country and

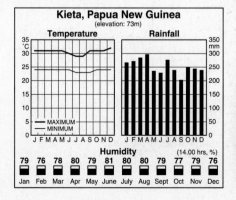

Kieta, Papua New Guinea
(elevation: 73m)

Temperature   Rainfall

Humidity												(14.00 hrs, %)
79	76	78	80	79	81	80	80	79	77	79	76	
Jan	Feb	Mar	Apr	May	June	July	Aug	Sept	Oct	Nov	Dec	

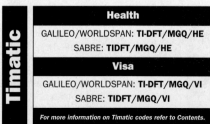

the scenery includes mountains in the north, the flat semi-desert plains in the interior and the subtropical region in the south. Separated from the sea by a narrow coastal plain, the mountains slope south and west to the central, almost waterless plateau which makes up most of the country. The beaches are protected by a coral reef that runs from Mogadishu to the Kenyan border in the south. They are among the longest in the world. There are only two rivers, the Jubba and the Shabeelle, and both rise in the Ogaden region of Ethiopia. Along their banks is most of the country's agricultural land. The Somali population is concentrated in the coastal towns, in the wetter, northern areas and in the south near the two rivers. A large nomadic population is scattered over the interior, although drought in recent years has led to many settling as farmers or fishermen in newly formed communities.

LANGUAGE: Somali and Arabic are the official languages. Swahili is spoken, particularly in the south. Some English and Italian are also spoken.

RELIGION: 90% Muslim, with a Christian (mostly Roman Catholic) minority.

TIME: GMT + 3.

ELECTRICITY: 220 volts AC, 50Hz.

COMMUNICATIONS: Telephone: IDD is available. Country code: 252. Outgoing international calls must go through the operator. **Telex/telegram:** There are limited facilities in the capital, but the main Post Office in Mogadishu, opposite the Hotel Juba, offers services. **Post:** Airmail to Europe takes up to two weeks. **Press:** No English-language dailies are published.

BBC World Service and Voice of America frequencies: From time to time these change. See the section *How to Use this Book* for more information.

BBC:

| MHz | 21.47 | 17.64 | 15.42 | 6.005 |

A service is also available on 1413kHz (0100-0500 GMT).

Voice of America:

| MHz | 21.49 | 15.60 | 9.525 | 6.035 |

PASSPORT/VISA

Regulations and requirements may be subject to change at short notice, and you are advised to contact the appropriate diplomatic or consular authority before finalising travel arrangements. Details of these may be found at the head of this country's entry. Any numbers in the chart refer to the footnotes below.

	Passport Required?	Visa Required?	Return Ticket Required?
Full British	Yes	Yes	Yes
BVP	Not valid	-	-
Australian	Yes	Yes	Yes
Canadian	Yes	Yes	Yes
USA	Yes	Yes	Yes
Other EU (As of 31/12/94)	Yes	Yes	Yes
Japanese	Yes	Yes	Yes

Note: The Somali Embassy is currently closed due to civil war in Somalia. Contact the Foreign Office (tel: (0171) 270 2894) for any information regarding entry into Somalia.

PASSPORTS: Valid passport required by all.

British Visitors Passport: Not accepted.

VISAS: Required by all. Transit visas are not required by visitors with reserved seats and documents for onward travel who continue their journey to a third country by the same aircraft on the day of arrival without leaving the airport.

Types of visa: Tourist and Business, cost £10; Transit.

Validity: Depends on nationality.

Application to: Consulate (or Consular section at Embassy). For addresses, see top of entry.

Application requirements: (a) 2 completed application forms. (b) 2 passport-size photos. (c) Fee. (d) For Business visa, confirmation telex from sponsor in Somalia. (e) For Business visa, letter from sponsor.

Working days required: 1 month.

Temporary residence: Apply to Embassy.

MONEY

Currency: Somali Shilling (SoSh) = 100 cents. Notes are in denominations of SoSh1000, 500, 100, 20, 10 and 5. Coins are in denominations of SoSh1, and 50, 10, 5 and 1 cents.

Credit cards: Diners Club has limited acceptability. Check with your credit card company for details of merchant acceptability and other facilities which may be available.

Travellers cheques: US travellers cheques are preferred. These can be cashed at banks and some hotels.

Exchange rate indicators: The following figures are included as a guide to the movements of the Somali

Shilling against Sterling and the US Dollar:

Date:	Oct '92	Sep '93	Jan '94	Jan '95
£1.00=	3985.38	4009.9	3869.7	4096.4
$1.00=	2511.27	2626.0	2615.6	2618.3

Note: The Shilling has been devalued a number of times in recent years.

Currency restrictions: The import and export of local currency is limited to SoSh200. Free import of foreign currency, subject to declaration on arrival and exchange at the national banks within five days. Export of foreign currency limited to the amount declared on import. All foreign exchange transactions should be recorded on the official currency form which may be required prior to departure from Somalia.

Banking hours: 0800-1130 Saturday to Thursday.

DUTY FREE

The following goods may be imported into Somalia without incurring customs duty:
400 cigarettes or 400g of tobacco; 1 bottle of wine or spirits; a reasonable amount of perfume for personal use.

PUBLIC HOLIDAYS

Jan 1 '95 New Year's Day. **Mar 3** Eid al-Fitr (End of Ramadan). **May 1** Labour Day. **May 10** Eid al-Adha (Feast of the Sacrifice). **Jun 9** Ashoura. **Jun 26** Independence Day. **Jul 1** Foundation of the Republic. **Aug 9** Mouloud (Prophet's Birthday). **Jan 1 '96** New Year's Day. **Feb 22** Eid al-Fitr (End of Ramadan). **Apr 29** Eid al-Adha (Feast of the Sacrifice).

Note: Muslim festivals are timed according to local sightings of various phases of the Moon and the dates given above are approximations. During the lunar month of Ramadan that precedes Eid al-Fitr, Muslims fast during the day and feast at night and normal business patterns may be interrupted. Many restaurants are closed during the day and there may be restrictions on smoking and drinking. Some disruption may continue into Eid al-Fitr itself. Eid al-Fitr and Eid al-Adha may last anything from two to ten days, depending on the region. For more information see the section *World of Islam* at the back of the book.

HEALTH

Regulations and requirements may be subject to change at short notice, and you are advised to contact your doctor well in advance of your intended date of departure. Any numbers in the chart refer to the footnotes below.

	Special Precautions?	Certificate Required?
Yellow Fever	Yes	1
Cholera	Yes	2
Typhoid & Polio	Yes	-
Malaria	3	-
Food & Drink	4	-

[1]: A yellow fever vaccination certificate is required from travellers arriving from infected areas. Travellers arriving from non-endemic zones should note that vaccination is strongly recommended for travel outside the urban areas, even if an outbreak of the disease has not been reported and they would normally not require a vaccination certificate to enter the country.

[2]: A cholera vaccination certificate is required from all travellers.

[3]: Malaria risk, predominantly in the malignant *falciparum* form, exists all year throughout the country. Resistance to chloroquine has been reported.

[4]: Mains water is normally chlorinated, and whilst relatively safe may cause mild abdominal upsets. Bottled water is available and is advised for the first few weeks of stay. Drinking water outside main cities and towns is likely to be contaminated and sterilisation is considered essential. Milk is unpasteurised and should be boiled. Powdered or tinned milk is available and is advised, but make sure that it is reconstituted with pure water. Avoid dairy products which are likely to have been made from unboiled milk. Only eat well-cooked meat and fish, preferably served hot. Pork, salad and mayonnaise may carry increased risk. Vegetables should be cooked and fruit peeled.

Rabies is present. For those at high risk, vaccination before arrival should be considered. If you are bitten abroad seek medical advice without delay. For more information, consult the *Health* section at the back of the book.

Bilharzia (schistosomiasis) is present. Avoid swimming and paddling in fresh water. Swimming pools which are well-chlorinated and maintained are safe.

Health care: Health insurance is essential. Medical treatment at government-run hospitals and dispensaries is free for Somalians and may sometimes be free for visitors.

TRAVEL - International

AIR: Somalia's national airline is *Somali Airlines (HH)*.

Approximate flight time: From London to Mogadishu is 11 hours 35 minutes, excluding stopover time in Rome.

International airport: *Mogadishu (MGQ)* is 6km (4 miles) west of the city. There is a taxi service to the city centre.

Departure tax: The equivalent of US$20 is levied on all international departures. Transit passengers and children under two years are exempt.

SEA: The principal ports are Mogadishu, Kismayu, Berbera and Marka. The *Norwegian American Line* operates a passenger service to Mogadishu.

ROAD: There are routes to Somalia from Djibouti and Kenya. There is no border crossing with Ethiopia at present. Roads are underdeveloped, and travel requires suitable 4-wheel-drive desert vehicles.

TRAVEL - Internal

AIR: *Somali Airlines (HH)* run regular services to all major towns.

SEA: Modern Somalia is essentially a broad strip of coastal desert. Roads are poor and consequently, coastal shipping is an important form of transport, both socially and economically.

ROAD: Traffic drives on the right. It is difficult to travel outside Mogadishu by car. Existing roads run from the capital to Burao and Baidoa and there are sealed roads between Mogadishu and Kismayu and Mogadishu and Hargeysa. Passenger transport is restricted almost entirely to road haulage. There are few cars and buses although there are reasonable bus services between the major centres in the south. **Taxi:** These are available in large towns. **Car hire:** Available in Mogadishu. **Documentation:** An International Driving Permit is required.

URBAN: Minibuses and shared taxi-type services run in Mogadishu, but availability may be restricted outside normal working hours (0700-1400 Saturday to Thursday).

ACCOMMODATION

HOTELS: In the main cities of Mogadishu and Hargeysa there are international standard hotels. There are also hotels in Afgoi, Berbera, Borama, Burao, Kismayu and Marka. The latter boasts the best hotel in Somalia, set in attractive parkland offering ethnic accommodation in chalets.

REST HOUSES: Government-run rest houses are located in many places with dormitory accommodation for four to ten people.

LODGES: There are tourist and hunting lodges in national parks at Lac Badana and Bush-Bush as well as in other areas.

RESORTS & EXCURSIONS

Kismayu National Park, in the southwest, contains many common and a few rare East African species. **Hargeysa** in the north contains rarer species. A third park has recently opened outside Mogadishu and there are ten game reserves.

SOCIAL PROFILE

FOOD & DRINK: In peacetime, restaurants in the major cities serve European, Chinese, Italian and Somali food. Local food includes lobster, prawn, squid, crab, fresh tuna, Somali bananas, mangoes and papaya. A traditional Somali meal is roast kid and spiced rice.

NIGHTLIFE: Local bands playing European and African music perform at nightclubs. There are frequent traditional feasts with ritualistic and recreational dance, music and folk songs.

SHOPPING: Traditional crafts include gold, silver jewellery, woven cloth and baskets from the Benadir region, meerschaum and wood carvings. **Shopping hours:** 0800/0900-1230 and 1630-1900 Saturday to Thursday.

SPORT: Miles of sandy beaches offer safe **bathing**, protected from sharks by the coral reef. Some hotels have swimming pools. The **golf** club and Anglo-American Beach Club in Mogadishu are both open to non-

members. There is some good **fishing**, particularly along the northeast coast, which is believed to be among the richest fishing grounds in the world.
SOCIAL CONVENTIONS: Traditional dance, music, song and craftsmanship flourish despite gradual modern development. Informal wear is acceptable and there is no objection to bikinis on the beach. **Tipping:** 10-15% is normal in hotels and restaurants.

BUSINESS PROFILE

ECONOMY: Somalia's economy has been almost completely dislocated by years of military action and political strife which, together with the severe East African drought, have caused an acute refugee problem which has strained the country's already limited resources. The present phase of civil strife has set the country back yet further, to the point where it now ranks amongst the most deprived countries in the world. Subsistence agriculture and livestock rearing occupy most of the working population, although any improvements have been hampered by primitive techniques, poor soil and climatic conditions, and a chronic shortage of skilled labour. Exports of livestock, hide and skins provided about 80% of the country's export earnings although revenue was seriously affected by a ban on purchases of Somali animals imposed by the main buyer, Saudi Arabia, on health grounds. Cash crops can be grown in some areas where there is adequate irrigation: bananas are grown for export; cotton, maize, sorghum and other crops are produced for domestic consumption. Plans to develop the fishing industry have been formulated but have yet to be implemented. Similarly, port facilities have potential but have not been developed to any degree, except by the superpowers for their own strategic purposes. There is no industry to speak of, but Somalia does have considerable potential as a source of minerals. However, no deposits have been found that would prove to be both commercially viable and practicable in terms of investment, labour and political stability. The main suppliers of imported goods to Somalia are Italy, the USA, Germany, Saudi Arabia and the UK. Somalia has a large foreign debt, which only large aid packages have rendered manageable. In recent years, aid provision to the country has been more often determined by geopolitical considerations than economic requirements. The current civil war has had catastrophic results for future economic development.
BUSINESS: For business, wear lightweight suits or safari-style jackets without a tie in hot weather. The best time to visit is October to May. **Office hours:** 0800-1230 and 1630-1900 Saturday to Thursday. **Government office hours:** 0800-1400 Saturday to Thursday.
COMMERCIAL INFORMATION: The following organisation can offer advice: Chamber of Commerce, Industry and Agriculture, PO Box 27, Via Asha, Mogadishu. Tel: (1) 3209.

CLIMATE

There are four seasons. The *Jilal* starts around January and is the harshest period, hot and very dry. *Gu* is the first rainy season lasting from March to June. *Hagaa*, during August, is a time of dry monsoon winds and dust clouds. The second rainy season is from September to December and is called *Dayr*.
Required clothing: Lightweights and rainwear.

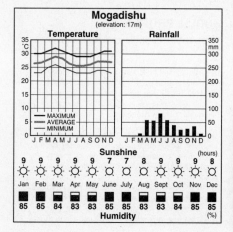

Mogadishu
(elevation: 17m)

South Africa

Location: Southern Africa.

South African Tourism Board (SATOUR)
Private Bag X164, 442 Rigel Avenue South, Frasmusrand, Pretoria 0001, South Africa
Tel: (12) 347 0600. Fax: (12) 454 889.
High Commission of the Republic of South Africa
South Africa House, Trafalgar Square, London WC2N 5DP
Tel: (0171) 930 4488. Fax: (0171) 321 0835. Telex: 8952626. Opening hours: 1000-1200 and 1400-1600 Monday to Friday.
South African Consulate
Address as for High Commission
Tel: (0891) 441 100 (Visa, immigration and health information line; calls are charged at the higher rate of 39/49p per minute). Fax: (0171) 925 0367. Opening hours (personal applications only): 1000-1200 and 1400-1600 Monday to Friday.
South African Tourism Board (SATOUR)
5-6 Alt Grove, London SW19 4DZ
Tel: (0181) 944 8080. Fax: (0181) 944 6705. Opening hours: 0930-1700 Monday to Friday.
British High Commission
Approximately July-December
255 Hill Street, Arcadia, Pretoria 0002, South Africa
Tel: (12) 433 121. Fax: (12) 433 277. Telex: 31323 (a/b BREMB SA).
(Until new Parliamentary dates are finalised, route all material via Pretoria.)
Exact dates pending
91 Parliament Street, Cape Town 8001, South Africa
Tel: (21) 461 7220. Fax: (21) 461 0017.
Consulates in: Cape Town, Johannesburg, East London, Port Elizabeth and Durban.
Embassy of the Republic of South Africa
3051 Massachusetts Avenue, NW, Washington, DC 20008
Tel: (202) 232 4400. Fax: (202) 265 1607. Telex: 248364.
Consulates in: Chicago, Los Angeles and New York (tel: (212) 213 4880).

Timatic	Health		
	GALILEO/WORLDSPAN: **TI-DFT/DUR/HE**		
	SABRE: **TIDFT/DUR/HE**		
	Visa		
	GALILEO/WORLDSPAN: **TI-DFT/DUR/VI**		
	SABRE: **TIDFT/DUR/VI**		

For more information on Timatic codes refer to Contents.

South African Tourism Board (SATOUR)
Suite 2040, 500 Fifth Avenue, New York, NY 10110
Tel: (212) 730 2929 *or* (800) 822 5368. Fax: (212) 764 1980.
Office also in: Los Angeles.
Embassy of the United States of America
PO Box 9536, 877 Pretorius Street, Pretoria, South Africa
Tel: (12) 342 1048. Fax: (12) 342 2244.
Consulates in: Cape Town, Durban and Johannesburg.
High Commission of the Republic of South Africa
15 Sussex Drive, Ottawa, Ontario K1M 1M8
Tel: (613) 744 0330. Fax: (613) 741 1639. Telex: 0534185.
Consulates in: Montréal and Toronto.
South African Tourism Board
Suite 205, 4117 Lawrence Avenue East, Scarborough, Ontario M1E 2S2
Tel: (416) 283 0563. Fax: (416) 283 5465.
Canadian High Commission
PO Box 26006, Arcadia, Pretoria 0007, South Africa
Tel: (12) 324 3970. Fax: (12) 323 1564. Telex: 5322112 (a/b CANAD SA).

AREA: 1,221,037 sq km (471,445 sq miles).
POPULATION: 40,284,634 (1994 estimate).
POPULATION DENSITY: 32.9 per sq km.
CAPITAL: Pretoria (administrative). **Population:** 1,025,790 (1993).
Cape Town (legislative). **Population:** 1,869,144 (1993).
Bloemfontein (judicial). **Population:** 300,150 (1993).
GEOGRAPHY: The Republic of South Africa lies at the southern end of the African continent. It is bounded by the Indian Ocean to the east and the Atlantic Ocean to the west, and is bordered to the north by Namibia, Botswana, Zimbabwe, Mozambique and Swaziland and totally encloses Lesotho. South Africa has three major geographical regions, namely plateau, mountains and the coastal belt. The high plateau has sharp escarpments which rise above the plains, or *veld*. The vegetation is open grassland, changing to bush in the Northern Transvaal, and the Thornveld in the arid southwest. Despite two major river systems, the Limpopo and the Orange, most of the plateau lacks surface water. Along the coastline are sandy beaches and rocky coves, and the vegetation is shrublike. The mountainous regions which run along the coastline from the Cape of Good Hope to the Limpopo Valley in the northeast of the country are split into the Drakensberg, Nuweveldberg and Stormberg ranges.
Following the 1994 elections, South Africa was organised into nine regions. These comprise the Western Cape with its state and national capital of Cape Town, the Eastern Cape with its state capital of King William's Town, the Northern Cape with its state capital Kimberley, KwaZulu/Natal with its state capital Pietermaritzburg, the Orange Free State with its state capital of Bloemfontein, the North West with its state capital Mmabatho, the Northern Transvaal with its state capital Pietersburg, the Eastern Transvaal with its state capital of Nelspruit, and PWV (Pretoria and Witwatersrand Vereeniging) with its state capital of Johannesburg.
LANGUAGE: The official languages at national level are Afrikaans, English, isiNdebele, Sesotho sa Leboa, Sesotho, siSwati, Xitsonga, Setswana, Tshivenda, isiXhosa and isiZulu.
RELIGION: Dutch Reformed Church, Nederduitsch Hervormde, Church of England, Roman Catholic, Congregational, Methodist, Lutheran and other Christian groups. There are also Jews, independent black church movements, Hindus and Muslims.
TIME: GMT + 2.
ELECTRICITY: 250 volts AC (Pretoria) and 220/230 volts AC elsewhere, 50Hz.
COMMUNICATIONS: Telephone: IDD is available. Country code: 27. Outgoing international code: 09. **Fax:** Most main hotels have this service. **Telex/telegram:** Telegraph services are available in all towns. Public telex facilities are available in Cape Town, Durban, Johannesburg (24-hour service) and Pretoria post offices. **Post:** Airmail to Europe takes up to seven days. Post office hours: Generally 0800-1630 Monday to Friday, 0800-1200 Saturday. Some transactions may not be carried out after 1530 Monday to Friday or after 1100 Saturday. The smaller post offices close for lunch 1300-1400. *Poste Restante* services are available throughout the country. **Press:** The main newspapers are in English and Afrikaans, and include *Business Day, Cape Times, The Argus, The Citizen, The Star, Sowetan Citizen* and *Natal Mercury*.
BBC World Service and Voice of America frequencies: From time to time these change. See the section *How to Use this Book* for more information.
BBC:

MHz	21.66	11.97	6.190	3.255

The incredible journey. South Africa by steam.

ORDER YOUR "DREAM OF STEAM" GUIDES FOR FULL DETAILS OF SAFARIS FROM CAPE TOWN.

It's the unforgettable Dream of Steam. A bit of nostalgia, a lot of fun, a wonderful way to discover the beauty of the country. You'll travel in comfort in an authentically restored vintage coach. At night, your four-berth compartment (for two persons) or two berth coupé (for one) becomes a comfortable bedroom with a wash basin.

For the comfort-conscious traveller, a Union Limited Steam Safari must be one of the best value-for-money ways of discovering South Africa. For those of us who need a relaxing change of pace, Union Limited offers good old-fashioned service, meals reminiscent of the old South African Railways' famous fare and a variety of routes of different durations.

Every day is different, every minute offers new sights as we steam through some of the most beautiful parts of the country. You'll take in magnificent views through the windows of "Protea"- the dining car which was built in 1933 for the exclusive use of The Union Limited, the forerunner of today's luxury Blue Train.

Tours range from Day Rambles to extended 15 day Safaris and even a four hour meal on board the Roving Diner. Our day-by-day information guides tell you more about these relaxing and fun filled trips.

Call or write to order yours now!

THE UNION LIMITED · TRANSNET · AUTHENTIC STEAM RAIL TOURS

STEAM SAFARIS
• 5-day Golden Thread
• 9-day Round-in-Nine
• 15-day Zambezi
• Other safaris

DAY RAMBLES FROM CAPE TOWN

DINNER ON THE ROVING DINER EX CAPE TOWN

PLEASE WRITE TO: UNION LIMITED STEAM RAILTOURS, PO BOX 4325, CAPE TOWN, 8000, REPUBLIC OF SOUTH AFRICA. OR FAX TO: (27) 21 405-4395. OR CALL (27) 21 405-4391.

The Unforgettable Dream of Steam.

Voice of America:

MHz	21.49	15.60	9.525	6.035

PASSPORT/VISA

Regulations and requirements may be subject to change at short notice, and you are advised to contact the appropriate diplomatic or consular authority before finalising travel arrangements. Details of these may be found at the head of this country's entry. Any numbers in the chart refer to the footnotes below.

	Passport Required?	Visa Required?	Return Ticket Required?
Full British	Yes	No	Yes
BVP	Not valid	-	-
Australian	Yes	No	Yes
Canadian	Yes	No	Yes
USA	Yes	No	Yes
Other EU (As of 31/12/94)	Yes	No	Yes
Japanese	Yes	No	-

PASSPORTS: Valid passport required by all. The passport must be valid for at least 6 months beyond the date of departure from South Africa.
British Visitors Passport: Not accepted.
VISAS: Required by all except:
(a) nationals of countries referred to in the chart above;
(b) nationals of Andorra, Argentina, Austria, Bahrain, Bolivia, Botswana, Brazil, Chile, Cape Verde, Costa Rica, Ecuador, Finland, Iceland, Israel, Lesotho, Liechtenstein, Monaco, Namibia, New Zealand, Norway, Paraguay, St Helena, Singapore, Swaziland, Sweden, Switzerland and Uruguay for business, tourist or transit purposes of up to 90 days;
(c) nationals of all other South and Central American countries (except nationals of Colombia), Barbados, Benin, Burundi, Comoro Islands, Czech Republic, Côte d'Ivoire, Congo, Cyprus, Egypt, Gabon, Hong Kong, Hungary, Jordan, Kenya, South Korea, Kuwait, Madagascar, Malawi, Malaysia, Mali, Malta, Morocco, Mauritius, Mexico, Nicaragua, Oman, Poland, Qatar, Saudi Arabia, Senegal, Seychelles, Slovak Republic, Taiwan (China), Thailand, Tunisia, Turkey, United Arab Emirates and Zambia for business, tourist or transit purposes of up to 30 days.
Note: Holders of Visitors' visas are not allowed to take up employment in South Africa.
Types of visas: Transit, Visitor's (which, subject to certain conditions, may be used for business purposes) and Study and Employment visas (longer term). All visas are issued free of charge.
Application to: Consulate (or Consular section at Embassy). For addresses, see top of entry. Applicants in countries where South Africa is not represented may send their applications direct to the Director-General for Home Affairs, Private Bag X114, Civitas, Struben Street, Pretoria 0001. Tel: (12) 314 8911. Fax: (12) 326 4571. Telex: 3668 or 3664.
Application requirements: (a) Valid passport. (b) 2 passport-size photos. (c) 1 application form correctly filled out (failure to complete the application fully and in detail may result in visa being delayed or refused). (d) Sufficient funds to cover expenses of visit. (e) Onward/return ticket (or sufficient funds to pay for one) and, if in transit, proof of sufficient documentation for admission to the country of destination. (f) No criminal record. (g) Visitors should be of sound mind and body. (h) Applications for employment or study must be accompanied by completed medical forms IM10 and IM13 if stay is for over one year. (i) In the case of failure to comply with any regulations, visitors may be required to leave a deposit with the Immigration Officer.
Working days required: Applications should be made well in advance. Although the minimum time taken is 2 days, nationals requiring a visa applying from the UK are advised to apply up to 10 weeks beforehand.
Temporary residence: Temporary residence permits are available at the airport on arrival, valid for a period of 3 months. Extensions must be applied for to the Director-General for Home Affairs in Pretoria (address above) or its nearest regional office, or at a police station if none of the former are available.

MONEY

Currency: Rand (R) = 100 cents. Notes are in denominations of R50, 20, 10 and 5. Coins are in denominations of R2 and 1, and 50, 20, 10, 5, 2 and 1 cents.
Credit cards: Access/Mastercard, American Express, Diners Club and Visa are widely accepted. Check with your credit card company for details of merchant acceptability and other facilities which may be available.

Travellers cheques: Valid at banks, hotels, restaurants and shops.
Exchange rate indicators: The following figures are included as a guide to the movements of the Rand against Sterling and the US Dollar:

Date:	Oct '92	Sep '93	Jan '94	Jan '95
£1.00=	*4.68	*5.16	*5.03	5.54
$1.00=	2.95	*3.38	*3.40	3.54

Note [*]: Commercial rate.
Currency restrictions: The import and export of SA Reserve Bank notes is limited to R500. There is free import of foreign currency, subject to declaration. The export of foreign currency is limited to the amount declared on arrival.
Banking hours: 0830-1530 Monday to Friday, 0800-1130 Saturday.

DUTY FREE

The following goods may be imported into South Africa by passengers over 18 years of age without incurring customs duty:
400 cigarettes and 50 cigars and 250g of tobacco; 1 litre of spirits and 2 litres of wine; 50ml of perfume and 250ml eau de toilette; gifts up to a value of R500 per person.
Note: There is a flat-rate duty of 20% on gifts in excess of R500 and up to R10,000.

PUBLIC HOLIDAYS

Jan 1 '95 New Year's Day. **Apr 14** Good Friday. **Apr 17** Family Day. **Apr 27** Constitution Day. **May 1** Workers' Day. **Jun 16** Youth Day. **Aug 9** National Women's Day. **Sep 24** Heritage Day. **Dec 16** Day of Reconciliation. **Dec 25** Christmas. Day. **Dec 26** Day of Goodwill. **Jan 1 '96** New Year's Day. **Apr** Family Day. **Apr 5** Good Friday.

HEALTH

Regulations and requirements may be subject to change at short notice, and you are advised to contact your doctor well in advance of your intended date of departure. Any numbers in the chart refer to the footnotes below.

	Special Precautions?	Certificate Required?
Yellow Fever	No	1
Cholera	Yes	2
Typhoid & Polio	Yes	-
Malaria	3	-
Food & Drink	4	-

[1]: A yellow fever vaccination certificate is required from travellers over one year of age arriving from infected areas. African countries formerly classified as endemic zones are considered by the South African authorities to be infected areas. Travellers arriving on flights with scheduled airlines that originated outside an infected area, and passengers who transited through an infected area but remained at the scheduled airport or in the adjacent town during transit, do not require a certificate. Passengers arriving by unscheduled flights at airports other than those used by scheduled airlines must possess a certificate. Infants under one year of age without a certificate may be subject to surveillance and will not be allowed into Natal or to the Lowveld of the Transvaal within six days of leaving an infected area.
[2]: Following WHO guidelines issued in 1973, a cholera vaccination certificate is not a condition of entry to South Africa. However, cholera is a risk in parts of this country, particularly in rural areas, and precautions are recommended for those likely to be at risk. Up-to-date advice should be sought before deciding whether these precautions should include vaccination, as medical opinion is divided over its effectiveness. See the *Health* section at the back of the book.
[3]: Malaria risk, predominantly in the malignant *falciparum* form, exists throughout the year in Northern Transvaal (including the Kruger National Park), Eastern Lowveld and Northern Natal. Resistance to chloroquine has been reported. It is strongly recommended that visitors to these areas take anti-malaria tablets before entering these zones (tablets are available from pharmacies without prescription).
[4]: Tap water is considered safe to drink in urban areas but may be contaminated elsewhere and sterilisation is advisable. Milk is pasteurised and dairy products are safe for consumption. Local meat, poultry, seafood, fruit and vegetables are generally considered safe to eat. *Rabies* is present. For those at high risk, vaccination before arrival should be considered. If you are bitten abroad seek medical advice without delay. For more information, consult the *Health* section at the back of

the book.
Bilharzia (schistosomiasis) is common in the north and east and may be present elsewhere. Avoid swimming and paddling in fresh water. Swimming pools which are well-chlorinated and maintained are safe.
Health care: Medical facilities are excellent. Health insurance is recommended.
A leaflet on health precautions is available from the South African High Commission.

TRAVEL - International

AIR: South Africa's national airline is *South African Airways (SAA)*.
For free advice on air travel, call the Air Travel Advisory Bureau on (0171) 636 5000 (London) or (0161) 832 2000 (Manchester).
Approximate flight times: From *London* to Cape Town is 11 hours 35 minutes, to Durban 12 hours 55 minutes and to Johannesburg is 10 hours 50 minutes.
From *Los Angeles* to Johannesburg is 23 hours 5 minutes (no direct flight available).
International airports: *D F Malan Airport (CPT)* (Cape Town), 22km (14 miles) southeast of the city (travel time – 25 minutes). Tel: (21) 934 0407. Airport facilities include outgoing duty-free shop, car rental (0600-0305), bank/bureau de change (0830-1630 Monday to Friday, 0830-1200 Saturday) and restaurant/bar (0600-0305). *Inter-Cape* buses meet all inward and outgoing flights. Courtesy buses are operated by some hotels. Taxis are available, with a surcharge after 2300.
Louis Botha Airport (DUR) (Durban), 16km (10 miles) southwest of the city (travel time – 20 minutes). Tel: (31) 426 111 or 426 145. Airport facilities include outgoing duty-free shop, car rental (0600-1330), bank/bureau de change (0830-1630 Monday to Friday, 0830-1200 Saturday) and bar/restaurant (0600-1330). Coaches meet all arrivals 0800-2200. Taxis are available.
Jan Smuts International Airport (JNB) (Johannesburg), 24km (15 miles) east of the city (travel time – 30 minutes). Airport facilities include incoming and outgoing duty-free shops, post office, car rental, bank/bureau de change (24 hours), restaurant (0700-2200) and bar (1000-2400). Bus services to Pretoria and Johannesburg are available 0500-2200. Trains link Kempton Park with Johannesburg. Taxis are available. Courtesy coaches are operated by some major hotels.
SEA: The main ports are Cape Town, Durban, Port Elizabeth and East London. *St Helena Shipping Co Ltd* runs a regular passenger service from Avonmouth to Cape Town. The *Royal Viking Line* includes South Africa on its southern Africa cruise. Cruises are offered by various companies between South Africa and the Indian Ocean Islands. Cruise lines include *P&O* and *Cunard*.
RAIL: The main routes are from South Africa to Zimbabwe, Botswana and Mozambique. Contact *South African Railways (TRANSNET)*.
ROAD: There are two main routes into South Africa: from Zimbabwe (via Beit Bridge) and Botswana (via Ramatlabama).

TRAVEL - Internal

AIR: Daily flights link Cape Town, Durban, Pretoria, Port Elizabeth, East London, Kimberley and Bloemfontein with other connecting flights to provincial towns. *South African Airways (SAA)* operate on the principal routes.
Discounts: An 'Africa Explorer' fare is available to foreign visitors entering South Africa with an IATA airline. It offers a significant saving for anyone planning to use *SAA's* internal network. The fare is valid for a minimum of seven days and a maximum of one month: travel may originate and terminate at any point within South Africa which is served by the airline. Travel is not permitted more than once in the same direction over any given sector. There is also a 30% reduction on some standby fares. *SAA* has various other discount domestic fares including Apex, Slumber, Supersaver and Saver fares. Contact *SAA* for details.
SEA: *Starlight Cruises* offer links between major ports.
RAIL: The principal intercity services are as follows: the **Blue Train** (luxury express) between Pretoria, Johannesburg and Cape Town (every other day); the **Trans-Oranje** between Cape Town and Durban via Kimberley and Bloemfontein (weekly); the **Trans-Natal Express** between Durban and Johannesburg (daily); *Rovos Rail* offer luxury steam safaris to the eastern Transvaal. The *Transnet Museum* also offers various steam safaris around South Africa and Zimbabwe; and the **Trans-Karoo Express** between Cape Town, Johannesburg and Pretoria (four times a week). All long-distance trains are equipped with sleeping compartments, included in fares, and most have restaurant cars.

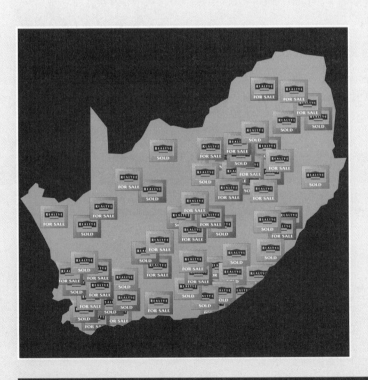

Visiting Southern Africa, purchase Standard Bank South African Rand Travellers Cheques. Obtainable in denominations of R20, R50, R100, R200, and R500, Standard Bank South African Rand Travellers Cheques are acceptable as cash by hotels, shops and restaurants in South Africa and are generally acceptable in Botswana, Malawi, Zimbabwe, Mauritius, Swaziland and the Seychelles.

South African Rand travellers cheques for your convenience

Lost and stolen travellers cheques are replaced within 24 hours subject to certain conditions.

For further information and the name of your nearest distributor, contact The Manager, Retail Foreign Exchange, Standard Bank of South Africa Limited, Foreign Trade Services Department, P.O. Box 8288 Johannesburg 2000 RSA. Tel: (2711) 636-5054. Fax: (2711) 636-2439.

Standard Bank

With us you can go so much further.

SOUTH AFRICA...
A BUDDING DESTINATION

A CURIOUS ENIGMA, UNSPOILT AND UNEXPLORED
NOW... SOUTHERN AFRICA BECKONS YOU

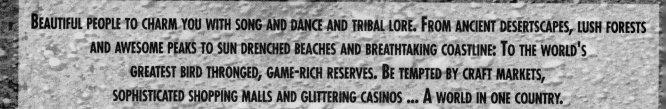

BEAUTIFUL PEOPLE TO CHARM YOU WITH SONG AND DANCE AND TRIBAL LORE. FROM ANCIENT DESERTSCAPES, LUSH FORESTS AND AWESOME PEAKS TO SUN DRENCHED BEACHES AND BREATHTAKING COASTLINE: TO THE WORLD'S GREATEST BIRD THRONGED, GAME-RICH RESERVES. BE TEMPTED BY CRAFT MARKETS, SOPHISTICATED SHOPPING MALLS AND GLITTERING CASINOS ... A WORLD IN ONE COUNTRY.

FOR GROUPS, ECOTOURISTS, CONFERENCES AND BUSINESS GATHERINGS THERE ARE OPTIONS FOR EVERY INTEREST. RESERVATIONS HOTLINE CONFIRM ALL ARRANGEMENTS FOR YOU FROM INITIAL TAKE OFF TO FINAL FAREWELL. CONTACT: P.O. BOX 782902, SANDTON, 2146, SOUTH AFRICA. TEL: 27 11 886 2472 FAX: 27 11 886 2769

RESERVATIONS
HOTLINE
Innovative Destination Management

IATA   SAACI SAGK

Picture this . . .

Set in the pleasant country atmosphere of Halfway House in Johannesburg, the Eskom Conference and Exhibition Centre is probably the most sophisticated and modern conference facility in Southern Africa. The Centre boasts 22 lecture rooms, 4 medium-sized conference rooms, 2 auditoriums and an executive boardroom. The combined delegate capacity is an impressive 1252.

The complex also has comprehensive sports and recreational facilities, including a fully equipped gymnasium, squash courts, an olympic size swimming pool, table tennis and a snooker room.

In addition the centre provides a shuttle service to and from Jan Smuts and Grand Central Airports, 24 hour security, a convenience shop, safes for valuables and a full in house catering service including an á la carte restaurant. Car hire can also be arranged.

Extensive accommodation facilities are available at the centre, ranging from student accommodation to air-conditioned standard and de luxe rooms with bathrooms en suite, the latter with TV and telephone. Total number of rooms: 703

For additional information phone us in Johannesburg: (011) 313-7131 or 313-7165

The conference venues are equipped with state of the art audiovisual aids and equipment, including a barco system, push-button microphones and simultaneous translation facilities.

ESKOM
Conference & Exhibition Centre

A total of 648 square metres of indoor exhibition space is available. This space is a combination of open floor space for larger exhibits and semi permanent cubicle facilities.

Reservations Johannesburg (011) 313-7340
Private Bag X13 Halfway House 1685
Johannesburg, South Africa

Reservations are recommended for principal trains and all overnight journeys. There are frequent local trains in the Cape Town and Pretoria/Johannesburg urban areas. All trains have first- and second-class accommodation. Children under 2 years of age travel free. Children aged 2-11 pay half fare.
ROAD: There is a well-maintained network of roads and motorways in populous regions. 30% of roads are paved (with all major roads tarred to a high standard). Traffic drives on the left. Fines for speeding are very heavy. It is illegal to carry petrol other than in built-in petrol tanks. Petrol stations are usually open all week 0700-1900. Some are open 24 hours. **Bus/coach:** Various operators, such as *Greyhound* and *Translux,* run intercity express links using modern air-conditioned coaches. Courier/drivers supervise the tours. On many of the intercity tours passengers may break their journey at any scheduled stop en route by prior arrangement at time of booking and continue on a subsequent coach at no extra cost other than for additional accommodation. **Taxi:** Available throughout the country, at all towns, hotels and airports, with rates for distance and time. For long-distance travel, a quotation should be sought. **Car hire:** Self-drive and chauffeur-driven cars are available at most airports and in major city centres. *Avis, Imperial* and *Budget* are represented nationwide. **Documentation:** An International Driving Permit is required. British visitors who are planning to drive in South Africa should check with the *AA* or *RAC* prior to departure that they have all the correct documentation.
URBAN: There are good bus and suburban rail networks in all the main towns, with trolleybuses in Johannesburg. Fares in Cape Town and Johannesburg are zonal, with payment in cash or with 10-ride pre-purchase 'clipcards' from kiosks. In Pretoria there are various pre-purchase ticket systems, including a cheap pass for off-peak travel only. In Durban, conventional buses face stiff competition from minibuses and combi-taxis (both legal and illegal), which are also found in other South African towns. These should be used with care. For ordinary taxis, fares within the city areas are more expensive than long distances. Taxis do not cruise and must be called from a rank. Taxi drivers expect a 10% tip.
JOURNEY TIMES: The following chart gives approximate journey times (in hours and minutes) from Cape Town to other major cities/towns in South Africa.

	Air	Road	Rail
Johannesburg	2.00	15.00	25.00
Durban	2.00	18.00	38.00
Pretoria	2.00	16.00	26.00
Port Elizabeth	1.00	7.00	-
Bloemfontein	1.30	10.00	21.00

ACCOMMODATION

South Africa offers a wide range of accommodation from luxury 5-star hotels to thatched huts *(rondavels)* in game reserves. 'Time-sharing condominiums' are developing in popular resorts. Comprehensive accommodation guides giving details of facilities, including provision for the handicapped, are available at all SATOUR offices and from tourism board regional offices. Information covers hotels, motels, game park rest camps, caravan and campsites and supplementary accommodation such as beach cottages, holiday flats and bungalows. Rates should always be confirmed at time of booking. It is forbidden by law to levy service charges, although phone calls may be charged for.
HOTELS: All hotels are registered with the South African Tourism Board, which controls standards. For further information, contact SATOUR Standards Department, Private Bag X164, Pretoria 0001. Tel: (12) 347 0600. Fax: (12) 454 768. Telex: 320457. 800 hotels are members of the Federated Hotel Association of South

Africa (FEDHASA), PO Box 514, Rivonia 2128. Tel: (11) 444 8982. Fax: (11) 444 8987. FEDHASA has regional offices throughout the country. **Grading:** The National Grading and Classification Scheme was introduced in 1994. Participation is voluntary. Hotels are graded **1** to **5 stars** according to the range of facilities on offer plus an optional classification band grading the level of services and hospitality. The classification band is colour-coded as follows:

Burgundy – Acceptable standard of services and hospitality in addition to the required facilities.
Silver – Superior services, hospitality, quality and ambience.
Each hotel taking part in the scheme will display a plaque indicating the star-rating and the classification band.
SELF-CATERING: Holiday flats, guest farms, resorts and health spas are available along main routes.
Grading: The Accreditation and Classification Programme for self-catering accommodation is part of the National Grading and Classification Scheme which was introduced in 1994. Self-catering accommodation is graded **1** to **5 stars** according to the facilities available and the level of services and hospitality. The classification band is split into three levels.
CAMPING/CARAVANNING: Caravan parks are to be found along all the tourist routes in South Africa, particularly at places favoured for recreation and sightseeing. The standard is usually high. Many caravan parks have campsites. A number of companies can arrange motor camper rentals, with a range of fully equipped vehicles. Full details can be obtained from SATOUR. **Grading:** Camp- and caravan-sites are classed as self-catering accommodation (see above).
GAME RESERVES: Game reserve rest camps are protected enclosures within the confines of the park. Accommodation is usually in thatched huts known as *rondavels,* or in small cottages. Some camps have air-conditioned accommodation. Most *rondavels* and cottages are self-contained, with private baths and showers, and sometimes kitchens. Some camps have luxury air-conditioned accommodation.

RESORTS & EXCURSIONS

South Africa was organised into nine regions in 1994 (see *Geography* above).

However, for the purpose of this section, South Africa has been divided up into the following regions: The Southern Transvaal; The Eastern Transvaal; The Northern Cape; The Eastern Cape & The Garden Route; The Western & Southern Cape; and the Natal Coast & the Drakensberg.

The Southern Transvaal

Nicknamed 'Witwatersrand' (Ridge of White Waters) by 19th-century prospectors, the area contains the richest gold reef in the world. The man-made lakes scattered along the reef provide facilities for boating, fishing and birdwatching, and the area is rich in parks, nature reserves and gardens.
JOHANNESBURG: The discovery of gold near Johannesburg in 1886 turned a small shanty town into the bustling modern city which is today the centre of the world's gold-mining industry and the commercial nucleus of South Africa.
Sightseeing: *Carlton Panorama* is 202m (663ft) high, providing stunning views over Johannesburg, along with a sound and light show. *Northcliff Ridge* is the highest natural point in Johannesburg, affording a panoramic view of the city. *Gold Reef City* is a living replica of early Johannesburg, complete with hotels, bars, shops and theatres. *Johannesburg Art Gallery* has a fine collection of English, Dutch, French and South African art. *The Planetarium* makes an interesting visit, as are the craft markets at *Zoo Lake* and *Hillbrow. The Florence Bloom Bird Sanctuary,* within Delta Park, is home for a large variety of birds, as is the *Melrose Bird Sanctuary. The Harvey Wild Flower Reserve* at **Linksfield** has stunning views over Johannesburg and Magaliesberg. *The Zoological Gardens* have a wide variety of animals and *The Botanic Gardens* contain exotic trees, over 4000 species of roses, and a herb garden.
Museums: Johannesburg has numerous museums. *The Adler Museum of the History of Medicine* includes an African herbarium and a witch doctor's premises; *The Afrikana Museum* contains exhibitions of early Johannesburg memorabilia in their settlement of the Cape; *The Africana Museum* contains a vast ethnological collection; *The Bensusan Museum of Photography* has early equipment and a history of photography; *The Bernberg Museum of Costume* houses 18th- and 19th-century period costumes; and *The Jewish Museum* has

displays of ceremonial art and a history of South African Judaism from the 1920s to the present day.
PRETORIA: Named after the Voortrekker leader Andries Pretorius, Pretoria is the administrative capital of the country with many parks and gardens. The city is known as the 'Jacaranda City' because of the flowering trees lining its streets in late spring. Its indigenous flora include protea, aloe, cycad, acacia, wild fig and fever trees.
Sightseeing: *Church Street* is 26km (16 miles) long and one of the world's longest straight streets. There are many museums, including *The Fort Klapperkop Military Museum, The Museum of Geological Survey* (with its collection of fossils and precious/semi-precious stones), *The Pretoria Art Museum* and *The Transvaal Museum of Natural History. The State Theatre* has facilities for all the performing arts. *The Austin Roberts Bird Sanctuary* features a variety of waterbirds. Other nature sanctuaries include *Derdepoort Regional Park, Fountains Valley Nature Reserve, Wonderboom Nature Reserve, The National Botanical Garden* and *Meyers Park Nature Reserve.*
EXCURSIONS: The Southern Transvaal's many attractions include dozens of nature reserves. The beautiful *Magaliesberg* mountain range, named after Magali, chief of the Po tribe, has abundant flora and fauna in private game and nature reserves, providing a nesting ground for the endangered Cape vulture. The area boasts the *Hartbeespoort Dam,* a popular recreational spot, complete with watersports, fishing, hiking and camping facilities. *The Aquarium,* 3km (2 miles) from the dam, has indigenous and exotic fish, as well as crocodiles and performing seals. There is a zoo and snake park and a nature reserve.
Near **Krugersdorp,** the *Sterkfontein Caves* contain a one-million-year-old female skull.

The Eastern Transvaal

The high and virtually treeless grassland plateau of the Transvaal stretches for hundreds of kilometres until it reaches the Drakensberg range of mountains, plunging into a beautiful subtropical woodland known as the *Lowveld.* Vast numbers of animals can be found here.
EXCURSIONS: The **Kruger National Park** comprises about 2,000,000 hectares and has a variety of animal species unequalled elsewhere on the African continent.

THE CONSERVATION CORPORATION

FOR EXCLUSIVE WILDLIFE EXPERIENCES

Species include zebra, giraffe, wildebeest, elephant, impala, leopard, cheetah, rhino, buffalo, cicada, ostrich, lilac-breasted roller, hornbill and fish eagle. There is excellent accommodation in the park.

Manyeleti Game Reserve, to the east of the Kruger, houses two trail camps, *Khoka Moya* and *Honey Guide,* who cater particularly for those preferring game-viewing on foot. Open-vehicle game drives take place in the evening. Khoka Moya comprises four double en suite cabins and separate dining, lounge and bar areas. Honey Guide accommodates a maximum of 12 in six large East African tents. Two- and three-day package safaris are a speciality.

The western border of the Kruger National Park has seen the development of several private game reserves, to provide sanctuaries for the Lowveld flora and fauna. The **Sabi Sabi Private Game Reserve** offers excellent wildlife game-viewing of giraffe, antelope, warthog, lion, elephant, rhino, buffalo, leopard, hyena, zebra and bountiful birdlife. Thatched bungalows and a variety of activities are also available to visitors. Other game reserves in this region include the *Klaserie, Timbavati* and the *Umbabat Nature Reserve.*

There are many panoramic routes which can be taken through this area, but one of the most famous is the **Summit Route.** This takes in *Long Tom Pass,* 2150m (7050ft) above sea level; *Sabie,* situated against the backdrop of Mauchsberg and Mount Anderson with an abundance of waterfalls and wild flowers; *Graskop,* a forestry village perched on a spur of the Drakensberg escarpment; *Pilgrim's Rest,* a gold-rush town with many historic buildings; *Mount Sheba Nature Reserve,* embracing 1500 hectares of ravines and waterfalls; *Pinnacle Rock,* a massive, free-standing granite column; *God's Window,* a spectacular viewing point over the Lowveld 1000m (3300ft) below; *Lisbon Falls* and *Berlin Falls; Bourke's Luck Potholes,* formed by the swirling action of pebble-laden flood water over the course of time; *Blyde River Canyon* and the *Blyderivierspoort Nature Reserve,* an immense ravine containing a multitude of flora and fauna and with spectacular viewing points; *F H Odendaal Camp,* with good vantage points and accommodation facilities; *Sybrand Van Nierkerk (Swadini Camp),* dominated by Mariepskop and the cliffs of Swadini buttress, with a reptile park just outside the nature reserve; *The Museum of Man* containing rock paintings and archaeological excavations; the *Echo Caves* at the head of the *Molopong Valley,* with their Stone and Iron Age tools; and the *Abel Erasmus Pass* and *J G Strijdom Tunnel,* rising 335m (1100ft) above the *Ohrigstad River* before descending more than 700m (2300ft) to the beautiful *Olifants River.* **Nelspruit** is a good base for seeing the famous *Sudwala Caves.* The caves (extending far into the Mankelekele Mountain) are of immense interest to scientists as well as tourists and comprise a linked series of chambers adorned with stalactites and stalagmites. Some of the chambers are vast, such as the *PR Owen Hall,* a subterranean amphitheatre with acoustics so good that concerts have been held there. Guided tours are available. There is a *Dinosaur Park* near the caves containing life-size replicas of the kind of prehistoric reptiles that roamed South Africa 250 million years ago.

The Northern Cape

This area, a vast (and often barren) wilderness, is watered by the *Orange River* and is home to large numbers of animals, many of them protected species. The discovery of vast diamond deposits in the northern Cape helped to create its principal town, Kimberley. In Namaqualand in the west, the discovery of copper as well as precious and semi-precious stones has continued since the 1850s. The area is also famous for its Bushmen rock-art.

KIMBERLEY: In 1866 a boy found a shiny 'pebble' at *Hopetown,* 128km (80 miles) south of Kimberley, allowing a primitive and sparsely populated settlement to become what is now the diamond capital of the world. Today, Kimberley is an attractive city with broad tree-lined streets and good shopping centres. Its attractions include *The Big Hole,* which is the largest man-made excavation in the world, and *The Kimberley Mine Museum,* with its replicas of 19th-century Kimberley at the height of the gold rush. *The De Beers Hall Museum* houses a display of cut and uncut diamonds; here can be seen the famous '616' – at 616 carats, the largest uncut diamond in the world – and the 'Eureka' diamond, the first to be discovered in South Africa. *The William Humphreys Art Gallery* has one of the finest collections of South African art, along with French, English, Dutch and Flemish contributions.

EXCURSIONS: Nooitgedacht, near Kimberley, has pavements of Ventersdorp lava, over 2500 million years old, polished by slow-moving glaciers during an ice age 250 million years ago. The area also has some very fine examples of Bushmen, or *San,* art, in the form of rock

paintings. The paintings are scattered over an area stretching from the Cape to the Zambezi and from the east coast lowlands to the southwest. The engravings are usually 'pecked' into the rock with flint and similar sharp implements, and are characterised by a boldness and simplicity of design combined with extremely accurate draughtsmanship and limited use of colour. They are believed to be about 10,000 years old.

Olifantshoek has rock engravings and is known as the *Gateway to the White and Roaring Sands at Witsand,* 70km (45 miles) away. Any disturbance of the 100m (330ft) high sands, particularly in hot weather, produces a strange moaning noise.

The national park at **Vaalbos** has eland, kudu, giraffe, red hartebeest and springbok.

There are ancient and extensive mines on the southern slopes of the *Gatkopies,* near **Postmasburg.** Archaeological findings indicate that Hottentots mined here for specularite from AD700.

Augrabies is a Hottentot name for 'place of great noise', which accurately describes the falls plummeting 56m (184ft) into a 20m (66ft) wide ravine, 120km (75 miles) west of **Upington.** There are spectacular rapids as the river drops a further 35m (115ft) along the ravine's 18km (11-mile) length. The area is a national park, and is home to many animal species, including baboons, vervet monkeys, rhino and antelope.

The **Kalahari Gemsbok National Park** shares a common boundary with the Botswana National Park, a staggering area of 127,135 sq km (79,000 sq miles). It is the largest nature conservation area in southern Africa and one of the largest unspoilt ecosystems in the world, supporting fauna and flora in bewildering variety.

Namaqualand is a vast area of seemingly barren semi-desert, harbouring a treasure-house of floral beauty, appearing after sufficient winter rains: daisies, aloes, lilies, perennial herbs and many other flower species. The rich deposits of copper in the region had been used for centuries by the Nama tribe of Hottentots before the advent of white settlers in the 17th century; in 1685 the Governor of the Cape, Simon van der Stel, led an expedition to the 'Copper Mountain', near to the present town of **Springbok.** The copper boom finally began in earnest in the 19th century.

The Eastern Cape & The Garden Route

The eastern Cape has an extraordinary variety of scenic beauty, ranging from the vast and arid Great Karoo to the Knysna forest, the fertile agricultural lands of the Little Karoo and the Long Kloof. Two of the country's major seaports (East London and Port Elizabeth) are located in this area.

PORT ELIZABETH: This city has a thriving cultural life. The Cape Performing Arts Board presents ballet, opera, music and drama productions in the newly restored *Opera House* and there are productions of Shakespeare in *The Mannville Open Air Theatre* in St George's Park. The city boasts excellent shops and amenities, including extensive parks and public gardens. Plans are underway to 'reclaim' the city's beaches along the sheltered warm water bay, where all sorts of watersports can be enjoyed.

Sightseeing: Tourist attractions include the *Apple Express,* one of the few remaining narrow-gauge steam trains, in operation since 1906 and running from Port Elizabeth to Loerie in the Long Kloof. The *City Hall* and *Market Square* are worth a visit, with a replica of the *Dias Cross,* a memorial to the Portuguese navigator Bartholomeo Dias. There is also a memorial to Prester John here.

The Oceanarium, Snake Park and *Tropical House* are on the seafront at Humewood. *The King George IV Art Gallery & Fine Arts Hall* has an excellent collection of 19th- and 20th-century art. *Settler's Park Nature Reserve* at How Avenue abounds with indigenous flora and *St George's Park* has open-air exhibitions and craft fairs, as well as theatrical productions.

EXCURSIONS: The **Addo Elephant National Park,** 72km (45 miles) north of Port Elizabeth, was created in 1931 to protect the last of the eastern Cape elephants. There are also black rhino, buffalo and antelope and more than 170 species of birds.

The **Zuurberg National Park** is situated in the *Winterhoek Mountains* and contains a large variety of flora and fauna, including the *Alexandria Forest,* an evergreen coastal high forest, where black eagles breed.

East London is situated on the magnificent coastline of the eastern seaboard, part of the 'Romantic Coast'. There are excellent beaches at *Eastern Beach, Nahoon Beach* and *Orient Beach.* The city has very good amenities. The museum contains a fine natural history collection.

The **Karoo** is a vast and beautiful upland area with spectacular sunsets. The novelist Olive Schreiner made the area famous and her house at *Cradock* has been

restored. The *Mountain Zebra National Park* is worth a visit, on the northern slopes of the Bankberg range. The town of **Graaff-Reinet** is situated in the heart of the *Karoo Nature Reserve,* at the foot of the *Sneeuberg Mountains.* It has many attractive 18th- and 19th-century buildings, as well as parks and museums, and is an excellent centre for exploring the area.

The **Garden Route** encompasses about 200km (124 miles) and includes the *Outeniqua Mountains* inland, the arid plains of the *Little Karoo,* the *Tsitsikamma Coastal National Park* and the *Swartberg Mountains* with their immense subterranean *Cango Caves.* There is a spectacular variety of flora, including the protected red 'George' lily. *Jeffrey's Bay* offers spectacular surfing. *St Francis Bay* has wide, unspoilt beaches and is a shell-collector's paradise, while *Mossel Bay* is famous for its mussels. The lagoon at *Paradise Beach* is a sanctuary for many birds, including flamingo and swans. **Knysna** is situated between lush inland forests and the Knysna lagoon and is a popular tourist resort. The lagoon is a National Park area, stretching from *Buffels Bay* to *Noetzie,* both with beautiful beaches. *The Wilderness National Lakes* area, with its ferns, lakes and tidal rivers, lies between Knysna and **George.** The latter town is known as the 'Garden City' because of its magnificent yellowwood and stinkwood trees. **Oudtshoorn** is famous for its ostrich farms.

The Western & Southern Cape

An area of outstanding natural and floral beauty, stretching from the remote rocky outcrops beyond Lambert's Bay in the west to the mountains of the southern peninsula. The area is famous for its wines.

CAPE TOWN: South Africa's administrative capital is situated at the foot of *Table Mountain* looking out onto the Atlantic Ocean. Places of interest include *The Castle of Good Hope* in Darling Street, built in 1666; *The Cultural History Museum;* the Malay quarter; *The Nico Malan Theatre Complex;* and *The Old Townhouse* on Greenmarket Square, housing a permanent collection of 17th-century Dutch and Flemish paintings. *The Victoria & Alfred Waterfront,* the old Victorian harbour which has been restored, offers free entertainment, a variety of shops, taverns and restaurants has become a major attraction. There are excellent sporting and shopping facilities.

EXCURSIONS: The **Cape of Good Hope Nature Reserve** covers the southern tip of the Cape peninsula, with a profusion of flowers, birds and animals. There are many fishing villages and holiday resorts around the bay, including *Llandudno, Hout Bay, Kommetjie* and *Fish Hoek; Chapman's Peak* has a spectacular scenic drive from Hout Bay, traversing *Chapman's Peak Mountain.* **Stellenbosch,** centre for wine production, has many attractive buildings, including the *Village Museum* and the *Dutch Reform Church.* **Franschhoek** is also a wine production centre, which originally hosted refugee Huguenots from France, many of them involved in wine-growing, who brought their skills to South Africa.

The **Franschhoek Pass** is a spectacular mountain pass. The *Drakenstein Valley* has picturesque vineyards, orchards and farms and there are many 'wine routes' which can be followed. The **Bontebok National Park,** near Swellendam, has many varieties of game.

The fertility of the southern Cape region gradually gives way to the rugged and beautiful **West Coast,** which has abundant shellfish.

The Natal Coast and the Drakensberg

DURBAN is a holiday resort situated beside the Indian Ocean. It is a cosmopolitan city, with a blend of Zulu, Western and Asian cultures. From palm-shaded, seafront promenades and modern skyscrapers, to temples, bazaars and mosques, Durban is a city of contrast. Because of its subtropical climate, it is possible to swim and sunbathe all year round. Sailing, windsurfing and diving are all popular activities, and Durban's sandy beaches make it popular with families. *Durban Harbour* is also a good starting point for pleasure cruises. Places of interest in the city include the *Indian Bazaar, Victoria Street Market, Marine World* and *Durban Art Gallery.* The *City Hall* is a gem of Edwardian architecture and also houses the *Natural Science Museum.* Durban is the natural place from which to visit the Zulu homelands, historic battlefields and game and nature reserves. The *Natal Coast* offers a choice of resorts, such as *Scottburgh, Margate* and *Southbroom,* with excellent beaches, fishing and golf. Northeast of Durban, the *Dolphin Coast* is a 90km (56-mile) stretch of beaches studded with coves and rock pools. Surfing, diving, sailing and snorkelling are all on offer here. The *Hawaan Nature Reserve* and the *Lagoon Trail* near **Umhlanga** are of interest to tree enthusiasts and bird lovers respectively.

Lud's Island – your own private paradise

Imagine you are on an island paradise with its beautiful indigenous forest that spreads down to the beach and the clear waters that surround this heavenly place.

You are on Lud's Island! Private, personal and unique. The only privately-owned island on the entire South African coast. Completely unspoilt, it is only eight minutes' drive from the country's most exclusive resort of Plettenberg Bay – rated as one of the world's finest. The island, situated in the estuary of the Keurbooms River, offers you the time of your life. Safe swimming, windsailing, boating, canoeing, fishing, flying, trail walks, forest exploring, diving and waterskiing. Or simply just relaxing in its unbeatable climate! Laze in the magnificent sunshine and relax in the tranquillity of nature. Nature lovers will never forget a stroll through the forest with its amazing bird life, the Blue Cranes, variety of wild geese or the first glance of the shy little Grysbok, the legendary Springbuck, the dainty Klipspringer or beautiful, rare Bontebok. Stroll along the golden beaches, collect fascinating shells or take the ever-popular sunset cruise on the picturesque Keurbooms River.

Perhaps you would enjoy the thrill and excitement of the most beautiful flight in Africa. Fly over the great Knysna Lakes and majestic heads that form the entrance to the historic old port. Look down on the romantic Wilderness and the spectacular Robberg Peninsula Reserve at Plettenberg Bay. Your stay on Lud's Island will be a most comfortable one. This exclusive 60-acre nature reserve caters for a limited number of guests in truly superb, heavy-beamed lodges – so typical of Africa. The lovely en suite bedrooms are completely private and unique in comfort and design. The main lodge, famous for its high-roofed thatch design, elegant restaurant, fine cellar and impressive fireplace, is one of the most beautiful found anywhere.

Delicious island cuisine is served in front of a crackling fire in cosy surroundings providing an unbeatable ambience. Outdoor breakfasts and fish grills in the African-style Boma (enclosure) looking out across the tranquillity of the slow-moving river are a truly unforgettable experience. the island also has its own 1000m airstrip and a small, private harbour.

Besides catering for a limited number of guests on a bed & breakfast basis, small conferences of up to 18 people can be accommodated.

So, if it's something unique you are looking for, look at Lud's Island – the unforgettable experience of a lifetime.

For further information, contact:

LUD'S ISLAND

SOUTH AFRICA
TEL: + (27 4457) 9442. FAX: + (27 4457) 9393

all play and no work

Marina Palms offers you so much. Luxury holiday accommodation in picturesque surroundings and an ideal climate. An Olympic-size swimming pool with kiddies' pool, poolbar and *braai* (barbeque) facilities, children's play area and fully-equipped games room.

You're within strolling distance of Margate's cinema, amusement park, Waterworld and main fishing pier.

You will find some of the most popular golf courses on the South Coast. For the nature lover – take a drive to Oribi Gorge, the birdpark or crocodile farm. For the more adventurous, the Wild Casino is only a half hour's drive away for golf, 10-pin bowling or to play your hand with Lady Luck.

The design of the complex displays great perception, allowing users a wide range of holiday accommodation, ranging from single suites, one-bedroom and even units which comfortably accommodate eight people. All luxury suites are equipped with ceiling fans, private kitchen, colour TV, telephone and M Net.

All service and maintenance headaches are a thing of the past, Every suite is fully serviced daily (incl. bedding and towels). Same-day laundry service.

MARINA PALMS
MARGATE

Marine Drive
P.O. Box 27 Margate 4275, South Africa
Tel: +27 (03931) 72636 *or* 72627
Fax: +27 (03931) 71109
Comp/mpy. reg. 62/01422/07

A RATHER UNCONVENTIONAL CONVENTION CENTRE

IF YOU'RE USED TO LAST MINUTE PANIC AND THINGS GOING WRONG YOU WILL FIND OUR APPROACH RATHER UNCONVENTIONAL:

TOTAL INVOLVEMENT IS THE KEY NOTE

OUR GOAL IS TO DELIVER QUALITY CUSTOMER SERVICE

WHETHER YOU ARE PLANNING A CONFERENCE OR FUNCTION EVENT, THE COMBINED CONFERENCE AND HOSPITALITY INDUSTRY KNOWLEDGE AND EXPERIENCE OF OUR TEAM WILL ASSIST YOU IN IDENTIFYING THE NEEDS AND RESOURCES THAT WILL SATISFY THE ORGANISERS AND PARTICIPANTS!

THE CENTRE, LOCATED IN THE EASTERN SUBURBS OF PRETORIA WITH EASY ACCESS TO HIGHWAYS AND MAJOR AIRPORTS, OFFERS FACILITIES FOR GROUPS OF 10 TO 450, WHILST UP TO 700 PEOPLE CAN BE CATERED FOR IN PARALLEL SESSIONS.

THIS IDEAL SETTING FOR YOUR NEXT EVENT HAS SATISFIED CRITICAL INTERNATIONAL SCRUTINY.
SO BEFORE YOUR NEXT CONFERENCE OR FUNCTION, TRY SOMETHING A LITTLE UNCONVENTIONAL.

 CSIR   FOR RESERVATIONS AND INFORMATION PLEASE CONTACT CENTRAL RESERVATIONS
P.O. BOX 395 PRETORIA 0001 SOUTH AFRICA – TEL: 09 27 12 841 3809 / 841 3822 – FAX: 09 27 12 841 3827

Between Natal's coast and the mountains, there is an area of gentle pastoral beauty known as the **Natal Midlands.** This region is characterised by undulating wooded hills and grassy plains with scattered villages and lush farmland. There are a number of game reserves with a huge variety of animal and bird life in the Midlands and the foothills of the Drakensberg. The rivers flowing through the foothills offer excellent fishing.
Pietermaritzburg is the largest city in the area. Although founded by the Voortrekkers, the town's architectural heritage is mostly Victorian. The city is particularly attractive in September, when the azaleas are in bloom. The *Botanic Gardens* enable visitors to look at a range of indigenous flora. Within easy reach of Pietermaritzburg are the *Howick Falls*, the *Karkloof Falls* and the *Albert Falls Public Resort and Nature Reserve.*
The **Drakensberg** is South Africa's largest mountain range. Its name means 'Dragon Mountain' and stems from the fossilised remains of dinosaurs found in the region. It is a refreshing place with cold mountain streams shaded by ferns and ancient yellowwood trees. The mountains are capped with snow in winter. The area provides good climbing and is the realm of eagles and bearded vultures. Popular climbs include *Champagne Castle, Cathkin Peak* and *Cathedral Peak.* There are nature trails for walkers and those on horseback. Hotels and leisure resorts (such as the Drakensberg Gardens and Sani Pass Hotel) have excellent facilities for other sports. In the nearby caves are good examples of the rock art of the Bushmen who, until a century ago, inhabited the area. The Main Caves situated in the **Giant's Castle Game Reserve** boast more than 500 rock paintings in a single shelter. The reserve is dominated by a massive basalt wall incorporating the peaks of *Giant's Castle* (3314m/10,873ft) and *Injasuti* (3459m/11,349ft). The reserve, which flanks the border with Lesotho, is home to the eland, other antelope and a variety of birds, including lammergeyer, Cape vulture, jackal buzzard, black eagle and lanner falcon. The **Royal Natal National Park** plugs a niche between Lesotho and the Orange Free State. It is one of Natal's most stunning reserves. Its dramatic scenery includes the *Amphitheatre*, an 8km-long (5mile) crescent-shaped curve in the main basalt wall. It is flanked by two impressive peaks, the *Sentinel* (3165m/10,384ft) and the *Eastern Buttress* (3047m/9997ft). Even higher is *Mont-aux-Sources* at 3284m (10,775ft). It is the source of the Tugela River

which plummets 2000m (6562ft) over the edge of the plateau. Hikers should enjoy following the spectacular *Tugela Gorge.*
POPULAR ITINERARIES: 5-day: Kruger National Park–Blyde River Canyon Nature Reserve. **7-day:** (a) Springbok–Augrabies Falls–Upington–Kalahari Gemsbok National Park. (b) Mossel Bay–Oudtshoorn–George–Knytsna–Wilderness National Lakes Park–Isitsikamma Coastal National Park.

SOCIAL PROFILE

FOOD & DRINK: A thriving agricultural sector yields excellent fresh produce, meat, fruit and wines. Typical South African dishes include *sosaties* (a type of kebab), *bobotie* (a curried mince dish), *bredies* (meat, tomato and vegetable casseroles), crayfish (or rock lobster) and many other seafood dishes traditional to the Western Cape Province. Curries and chutneys are excellent. *Biltong* (dried meat) is a savoury speciality. Although there is a wide choice of self-service restaurants, most have table service. **Drink:** There are excellent local red and white wines, and sherries. Beer is also very good. Bars/cocktail lounges have bartender service. 'Liquor stores' are open 0900-1700 weekdays and close at 1300 Saturday.
NIGHTLIFE: Cinemas show a variety of international films. In the large cities there are regular plays, operas and symphony concerts. There are a number of nightclubs and discotheques open until late. The large hotels usually have live music or cabaret.
SHOPPING: Stores are generally modern. Special purchases include Swakara coats, gold, diamond and semi-precious stone jewellery, leather, suede and fur goods, ceramics and African handicrafts, safari suits and feathers. **Shopping hours:** 0830-1700 Monday to Friday, 0830-1300 Saturday. Some shops are open Sunday.
SPORT: South Africans are ardent sports enthusiasts. Visitors are made welcome at many venues. **Golf:** Played on more than 400 courses. Visitors can play on weekdays. Fees are not exorbitant and equipment and caddies can be hired. **Tennis/squash:** Many hotels can arrange tennis and squash facilities. Details are available from SATOUR. **Sailing:** Hotels on the coast will arrange sailing and yachting. **Swimming:** Hotels in coastal areas will give advice on the best sea bathing and surfing locations. Most hotels have swimming pools.
Fishing: Sea fishing is particularly popular off the Indian

Ocean coast.
SPECIAL EVENTS: The following is a selection of events and festivals celebrated in South Africa during 1995/96. For further details, contact SATOUR (for addresses, see top of entry).
Mar/Apr '95 *Durban Point Easter Festival.* **Apr** *Ohlsson's Two Oceans Marathon (Road Race),* Cape Peninsula. **Apr 1-17** *Rand Easter Show,* Johannesburg. **May/Jun** *Rugby World Cup Tournament.* **Jun** *Comrades Marathon,* Pietermaritzburg to Durban. **Jul** *Standard Bank National Arts Festival,* Grahamstown. **Jul 1** *Rothmans July Handicap,* Durban. **Aug/Sep** *Namaqualand Flower Season.* **Sep** *Johannesburg All Africa International Athletics Meeting.* **Sep 29-Oct 7** *International Eisteddfod of South Africa,* Roodepoort. **Oct** *Jacaranda Time in Pretoria.* **Oct 25-28** *Stellenbosch Food and Wine Festival.* **Nov** *Ficksburg Cherry Festival.* **Dec** *Million Dollar Golf Challenge,* Sun City.
SOCIAL CONVENTIONS: Handshaking is the usual form of greeting. Normal courtesies should be shown when visiting someone's home. Casual wear is widely acceptable. Formal social functions often call for a dinner jacket and black tie for men and full-length dresses for women; this will be specified on the invitation. Smoking is prohibited during cinema and theatre performances.
Tipping: Normally 10% if service is not included. It is customary to tip porters, waiters, taxi drivers, caddies and room service. Porters and room service are usually given a R2 tip. By law, hotel rates do not include a service charge.

BUSINESS PROFILE

ECONOMY: South Africa has one of the world's largest economies and completely dominates the southern part of the African continent. Agriculture is strong enough to allow South Africa virtual self-sufficiency in foodstuffs: livestock is widespread and sugar, maize and cereals are produced in large quantities. The foundation of the modern South African economy, however, is mining. The country has considerable deposits of common minerals such as coal, but also of valuable ores which are in high demand but are scarce outside the CIS: chromium, manganese, vanadium and platinum appear in the largest concentrations anywhere in the world. Its most valuable minerals, however, are gold and diamonds, and South

Africa has long been the world's largest producer and exporter of both. Despite the importance of mining, manufacturing is the largest sector of the economy. Metal industries include steel and heavy engineering, producing machinery and transport equipment. Advanced technological and service industries have emerged in recent years, but have yet to compete in scale or sophistication with their counterparts in Europe, North America or Japan. The only key mineral that South Africa lacks is oil and during apartheid rule the South African government went to considerable and elaborate lengths to procure it. South Africa was also the target of an embargo on the sale of armaments. Pretoria's response has been the creation of an indigenous defence manufacturing industry which has been successful enough to become an important exporter in its own right. (South African products of all descriptions were generally disguised before or during export to deceive or reassure purchasers as to the origin.) Despite managing to avoid serious damage from economic sanctions, South Africa effectively spent most of the 1980s in recession. This stemmed from excessive government spending compounded by a sharp fall in foreign investment and, in some cases, outright withdrawal. High inflation and foreign debt, plus a weak currency, forced the Government into unprecedented debt rescheduling in 1989. This had immense political consequences which ultimately led to the demise of apartheid and the dawn of genuinely representative government. The future of the economy is a key item on the political agenda: both domestic and foreign business interests are hoping for a stable political transition and an operating environment relatively free of control and regulation. The short- and medium-term outlook is mixed however, as recessionary forces continue to depress the economy into the 1990s. The improved political situation will hopefully stimulate

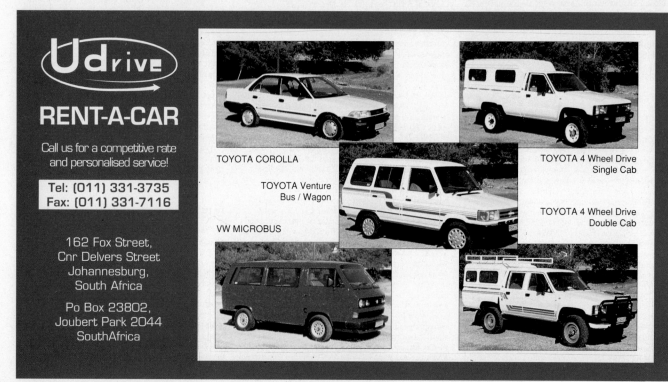

a return of foreign investment and a rapid growth in trade. The Mandela government has an ambitious domestic programme of major housing and infrastructure projects whose success is essential to its long-term political survival. Severe drought has badly affected the agricultural sector. The USA, the UK, Germany, Japan, Italy and Switzerland have historically been South Africa's main trading partners, but the country's trading patterns can be expected to have changed significantly by the turn of the century.

BUSINESS: Suits are generally expected to be worn for meetings, safari-style suits are often suitable for summer. Appointments are generally necessary and punctuality is expected. Visiting cards are widely used. **Office hours:** 0830-1630 Monday to Friday.

COMMERCIAL INFORMATION: The following organisations can offer advice: South African Chamber of Business (SACOB), PO Box 91267, Auckland Park 2006. Tel: (11) 482 2524. Fax: (11) 726 1344; *or* South African Foreign Trade Organisation (SAFTO), PO Box 782706, Sandton 2146. Tel: (11) 883 3737. Fax: (11) 883 6569. Telex: 424111.

CONFERENCES/CONVENTIONS: There are roughly 815 conference venues in South Africa of which 326 are in the Transvaal, 226 in the Cape, 155 in Natal and 39 in the Orange Free State. The main conference venues are in Pretoria and Johannesburg though facilities exist in all other major towns, provided mainly by hotels and universities. The Conference and Incentive Promotions Division of SATOUR exists to promote South African venues and to ensure high standards of service and facilities for the conference organiser. Contact SATOUR Conference and Incentive Division, Private Bag X164, Pretoria 0001. Tel: (12) 347 0600. Fax: (12) 451419. Telex: 3204575 (a/b SA).

CLIMATE

South Africa's climate is generally sunny and pleasant. Winters are usually mild, although snow falls on the mountain ranges of the Cape and Natal and occasionally in lower-lying areas, when a brief cold spell can be expected throughout the country. Since South Africa lies south of the Equator, the seasons are the reverse of those in the northern hemisphere.

Required clothing: Lightweight cottons and linens and rainwear. Warmer clothes are needed for winter.

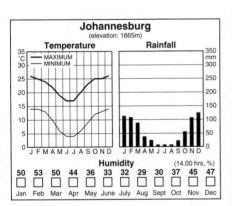

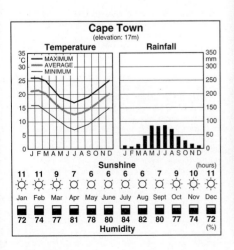

Top picture: Farm cottage, Swellendam. Above: Zebra, Burchells

Location: Western Europe.

Secretaría Gerneral de Turismo
María de Molina 50, 28006 Madrid, Spain
Tel: (1) 411 4014. Fax: (1) 411 4232. Telex: 23100.
Embassy of the Kingdom of Spain
24 Belgrave Square, London SW1X 8SB
Tel: (0171) 235 5555/6/7. Fax: (0171) 235 9905. Telex: 21110 *or* 261333.
Spanish Consulate
20 Draycott Place, London SW3 2RZ
Tel: (0171) 589 8989 *or* (0891) 600 123 (Recorded visa information; calls are charged at the higher rate of 39/49p per minute). Fax: (0171) 581 7888. Opening hours: 0930-1200 Monday to Friday (closed Spanish national holidays).
Consulates in: Manchester and Edinburgh.
Instituto Cervantes
23 Manchester Square, London W1M 5AP
Tel: (0171) 235 3317. Fax: (0171) 235 4115.
Information on language courses in Spain etc.
Spanish Labour Office
20 Peel Street, London W8 7PD
Tel: (0171) 221 0098. Fax: (0171) 229 7270.
Information on working and free health care in Spain.
Spanish National Tourist Office
Metro House, 57-58 St James's Street, London SW1A 1LD
Tel: (0171) 499 0901 (general information) *or* 499 4593 (travel agents & promotional material) *or* 499 9237 (customer services) *or* 499 1243 (exhibitions) *or* 499 3257 (PR). Fax: (0171) 629 4257. Opening hours: 0915-1615 Monday to Friday.

British Embassy
Calle de Fernando el Santo 16, 28010 Madrid, Spain
Tel: (1) 319 0200. Fax: (1) 319 0423. Telex: 27656 (a/b INGLA E).
Consulates in: Seville, Alicante, Barcelona, Tarragona, Bilbao, Lanzarote, Las Palmas (Grand Canary), Santa Cruz de Tenerife (Canary Islands), Málaga, Palma, Ibiza, Santander, Menorca and Vigo.
Embassy of the Kingdom of Spain
2375 Pennsylvania Avenue, NW, Washington, DC 20037
Tel: (202) 452 0100 *or* 728 2340. Fax: (202) 728 2317.
Consulates in: Boston, Chicago, Houston, Los Angeles, Miami, New Orleans, New York (tel: (212) 355 4090), Puerto Rico and San Francisco.
Spanish National Tourist Office
665 Fifth Avenue, New York, NY 10022
Tel: (212) 759 8822. Fax: (212) 980 1053. Telex: 426782 (a/b SNTO UI).
Offices also in: Chicago, Los Angeles and Miami.
Embassy of the United States of America
Serrano 75, 28006 Madrid, Spain
Tel: (1) 577 4000. Fax: (1) 577 5735. Telex: 27763.
Embassy of the Kingdom of Spain
Suite 802, 350 Sparks Street, Ottawa, Ontario K1R 7S8
Tel: (613) 237 2193/4. Fax: (613) 236 9246.
Consulates in: Burnaby, Calgary, Halifax, Montréal, Québec, St John's, Toronto and Winnipeg.
Spanish National Tourist Office
Suite 1400, 102 Bloor Street West, Toronto, Ontario M5S 1M8
Tel: (416) 961 3131. Fax: (416) 961 1992. Telex: 06-218206.
Canadian Embassy
Edificio Goya, Calle Nunez de Balboa 35, 28080 Madrid, Spain
Tel: (1) 431 4300. Fax: (1) 431 2367. Telex: 27347 (a/b DOMCAN E).
Consulates in: Barcelona, Málaga and Seville.

AREA: 504,782 sq km (194,897 sq miles).
POPULATION: 38,872,268 (1991).
POPULATION DENSITY: 77 per sq km.
CAPITAL: Madrid. **Population**: 3,010,492 (1991).
GEOGRAPHY: Spain shares the Iberian peninsula with Portugal and is bounded to the north by the Pyrénées, which separate Spain from France. The Balearic Islands (Mallorca, Menorca, Ibiza and Formentera), 193km (120 miles) southeast of Barcelona, and the Canary Islands off the west coast of Africa are part of Spain, as are the tiny enclaves of Ceuta and Melilla on the north African mainland. With the exception of Switzerland, mainland Spain is the highest and most mountainous country in Europe, with an average height of 610m (2000ft). The Pyrénées stretch roughly 400km (249 miles) from the Basque Country in the west to the Mediterranean Sea; at times the peaks rise to over 1524m (5000ft), the highest point being 3404m (11,169ft). The main physical feature of Spain is the vast central plateau, or *Meseta*, divided by several chains of sierras. The higher northern area includes Castile and León, the southern section comprises Castile/La Mancha and Extremadura. In the south the plateau drops abruptly at the Sierra Morena, beyond which lies the valley of Guadalquivir. Southeast of Granada is the Sierra Nevada, part of the Betic Cordillera, which runs parallel to the Mediterranean, rising to 3481m (11,420ft) and the highest point on the Spanish peninsula (the Pico del Teide on Tenerife in the Canaries is the highest peak in Spain). The Mediterranean coastal area reaches from the French frontier in the northeast down to the Straits of Gibraltar, the narrow strip of water linking the Mediterranean with the Atlantic and separating Spain from North Africa.
LANGUAGE: Spanish (Castilian), Catalan, Galician and Basque.
RELIGION: Roman Catholic majority.
TIME: Mainland Spain/Balearics: GMT + 1 (GMT + 2 from last Sunday in March to Saturday before last Sunday in September).
The Canary Islands: GMT (GMT + 1 from last Sunday in March to Saturday before last Sunday in September).
ELECTRICITY: 220 volts AC (110/125 volts in some older buildings), 50Hz. Generally, round 2-pin plugs and screw-type lamp fittings are in use.
COMMUNICATIONS: Telephone: IDD is available. Country code: 34. Outgoing international code: 07. Area codes for a selection of major centres: Madrid 1, Alicante 65, Balearic Islands 71, Barcelona 3, Benidorm 65, Bilbao 4, Granada 58, Las Palmas 28, Málaga and Torremolinos 5, Santander 42, Seville 5, Tenerife 22 and Valencia 6. For calls made from within Spain, dial 9 before the above numbers. **Fax:** This is generally available at 4- and 5-star hotels, especially those catering for the business and conference traveller.
Telex/telegram: Facilities are available at main post offices. A 24-hour service is available in Madrid at Plaza de la Cibeles; in Barcelona at Plaza Antonio Lopez; in Bilbao at 15 Calle Alameda Urquijo. There are also

Church of the Trinity, Atienza, Guadalajara

Carmona. Cantabria.

One of the less popular views of Spain.

Northern Spain comes as an unexpected bonus to travellers who thought they'd seen everything Spain had to offer. • In the regions of Galicia, Asturias, Cantabria and the Basque Country, first-time visitors will find a pleasant surprise around almost every corner. • As you can see, the terrain doesn't conform to most people's perception of Spain. Villages nestle in deep, lush valleys against a perpetual backdrop of mountains. • But that's the real beauty of "Green" Spain. The daily discovery of hidden gems, be it prehistoric caves at Altamira, the small fishing port of Vivero, a night in Charles I's castle at Hondarribia or the uncannily orange sunset in Naranjo de Bulnes. • Should you pine for the occasional glimpse of the ocean, simply take the nearest wooded valley to the coast and walk the deserted sands or watch the fishing boats returning with your supper. • It's at times like these you'll see Northern Spain in its real colours.

ESPAÑA

**Passion
for life.**

For further information please contact your travel agent. The Spanish Tourist Office, 57 St. James's Street, London SW1A 1LD.
Fax 071-629-4257. For replies please send legible address label.

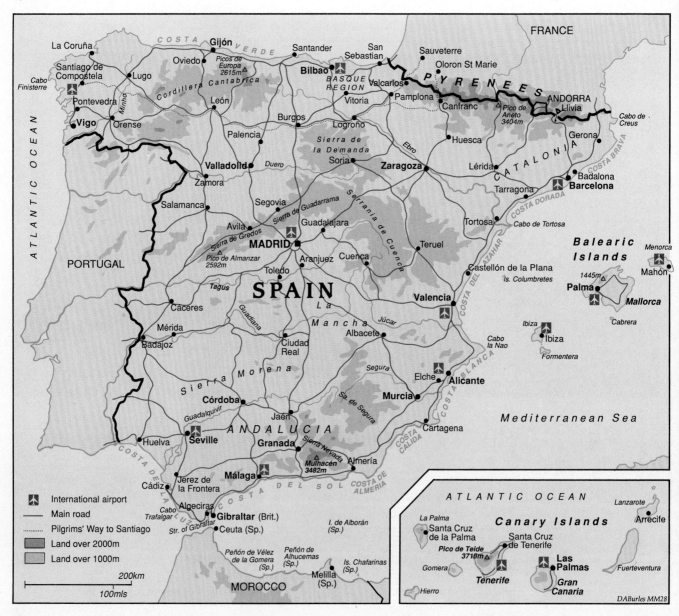

facilities in major hotels. Charges for automatically connected telex transmissions are by the minute, with a one-minute minimum charge. Transmissions through the operator are at the same rate, with a 3-minute minimum charge. Urgent business transmissions to Britain can be made from the British Embassy in Madrid, the British Consulates General at Barcelona and Bilbao, and the British Consulates at Seville and the Canary Islands. There is a surcharge of 90% of the cost during normal working hours. **Post:** There are efficient internal and international postal services to all countries. Airmail within Europe usually takes about five days. *Poste Restante* facilities are available at main post offices. **Press:** The English-language daily is *The Iberian Daily Sun. Guidepost* is Spain's American weekly newspaper. Local newspapers published in English include the *Majorca Daily Bulletin, Costa Blanca News, Ibiza Now* and the English-language edition of *Sur.* Spanish dailies with large circulations include *ABC, Diario 16, El Pais* and *El Mundo.*
BBC World Service and Voice of America frequencies: From time to time these change. See the section *How to Use this Book* for more information.
BBC:

| MHz | 17.70 | 15.07 | 12.09 | 6.195 |

Timatic	**Health**
	GALILEO/WORLDSPAN: **TI-DFT/MAD/HE**
	SABRE: **TIDFT/MAD/HE**
	Visa
	GALILEO/WORLDSPAN: **TI-DFT/MAD/VI**
	SABRE: **TIDFT/MAD/VI**
	For more information on Timatic codes refer to Contents.

A service is also available on 648kHz and 198kHz (0100-0500 GMT).
Voice of America:

| MHz | 15.20 | 9.760 | 6.040 | 5.995 |

PASSPORT/VISA

Regulations and requirements may be subject to change at short notice, and you are advised to contact the appropriate diplomatic or consular authority before finalising travel arrangements. Details of these may be found at the head of this country's entry. Any numbers in the chart refer to the footnotes below.

	Passport Required?	Visa Required?	Return Ticket Required?
Full British	1	No	No
BVP	2	No	No
Australian	Yes	Yes	Yes
Canadian	Yes	No	Yes
USA	Yes	No	Yes
Other EU (As of 31/12/94)	1	No	No
Japanese	Yes	No	Yes

PASSPORTS: Valid passport required by all except:
(a) **[1]** nationals of EU countries with valid national ID cards (BVPs if UK nationals); and nationals of Belgium, France, Luxembourg, The Netherlands and Portugal with passports expired less than a max. of 5 years; nationals of Germany and the UK with passports expired less than a max. of 1 year (nationals of Ireland *do* require passports); (b) nationals of Andorra, Austria, Liechtenstein, Malta, Monaco and Switzerland holding valid national ID cards or expired passports (maximum of 5 years).
British Visitors Passport: [2] A BVP is valid for holidays or unpaid business trips of up to 3 months. They will not however be valid for any visits after September 30, 1995.
VISAS: Required by all except:

(a) nationals of EU countries for visits not exceeding 90 days;
(b) nationals of Canada and the USA for stays not exceeding 90 days;
(c) nationals of Andorra, Argentina, Austria, Bolivia, Brazil, Chile, Colombia, Costa Rica, Croatia, Cyprus, Czech Republic, Ecuador, El Salvador, Finland, Guatemala, Honduras, Hungary, Iceland, Japan, Kenya, South Korea, Liechtenstein, Malta, Mexico, Monaco, New Zealand, Nicaragua, Norway, Panama, Paraguay, San Marino, Singapore, Slovak Republic, Slovenia, Sweden, Switzerland, Uruguay, Vatican City and Venezuela for stays not exceeding 90 days;
(d) nationals of Algeria, Morocco, Tunisia and Turkey for one entry not exceeding 30 days per year provided they have 'leave to stay or remain in the UK or an EU country for an indefinite period' (nationals of Morocco on business *do* require visas);
(e) children of any nationality under 14 years of age holding valid passports and accompanied by an adult.
Note: Visas are required by nationals of all countries not exempted above and are generally valid for stays of up to 30 days or 5 days transit. For further information, contact the Consulate (for addresses, see top of entry).
Types of visa: Special, Tourist and Business; UK prices: £14.40, £28.80 and £43.20 respectively. Transit visas are not required by those not needing Tourist visas.
Validity: Visas are normally valid for between 30 and 90 days (but see above). Visitors wishing to stay longer should make an application for a Special visa.
Application to: Consulate (or Consular section at Embassy). For addresses, see top of entry.
Application requirements: (a) 3 application forms. (b) 3 passport-size photos. (c) Valid passport. (d) Closed travel tickets. (e) Confirmed accommodation. (f) For Business visa, written invitation from company or organisation in Spain, or proof of trade/professional interest in Spain. (g) A stamped, self-addressed envelope if applying by post. (h) Proof of means of support to cover the intended stay

TOURISM FOR THE FUTURE

Viajes Barceló

INCOMING OFFICES - SPAIN

ALICANTE
- Alicante
- Benidorm

ANDALUCÍA
- Sevilla
- Torremolinos

BALEARIC ISLANDS
- Ibiza
- Majorca
- Menorca

CATALONIA
- Barcelona
- Lloret de Mar
- Salou

FUERTEVENTURA
- Puerto del Rosario

LANZAROTE
- Puerto del Carmen

LAS PALMAS
- Playa del Inglés
- San Fernando de Maspalomas

MADRID

MURCIA
- La Manga del Mar Menor

TENERIFE
- Playa de las Américas
- Puerto de la Cruz

Feliz viaje. vía

INTERNATIONAL INCOMING OFFICES

- **ARGENTINA**
- **BOLIVIA**
- **COLOMBIA**
- **COSTA RICA**
- **CHILE**
- **DOMINICAN REPUBLIC**
- **ECUADOR**
- **GUATEMALA**
- **MEXICO**
- **NICARAGUA**
- **PARAGUAY**
- **PERU**
- **USA**

Viajes Barceló

HEAD OFFICE
C/ José Rover Motta, 27
07006 PALMA DE MALLORCA
BALEARIC ISLANDS. SPAIN
Tel.: (34 - 71) 46 97 63
Fax: (34 - 71) 46 95 81

Feliz viaje. vía

**HEAD OFFICE
PALMA DE MALLORCA**
C/ José Rover Motta, 27
07006 PALMA DE MALLORCA
BALEARIC ISLANDS. SPAIN
Tel.: (34 - 71) 46 66 11
Fax: (34 - 71) 46 50 39

**HEAD OFFICE
MADRID**
C/ Vizconde de Matamala, 1
28028 MADRID
Tel.: (34 - 1) 726 - 47 00 / 46 07
Fax: (34 - 1) 725 - 69 15 / 46 00
Telex: 45.402

may be requested by the Passport Control Authorities upon arrival in Spain.

Note: Requirements for visas vary according to nationality, passport, travel document used and the purpose and duration of the trip. For further information, contact the Consulate (for addresses, see above).

Working days required: Between 1 day and 6 weeks, depending on nationality.

Temporary residence: Refer enquiries to Consulate.

MONEY

Currency: Peseta (Pta). Notes are in denominations of Pta10,000, 5000, 2000, 1000 and 500. Coins are in denominations of Pta500, 200, 100, 50, 25, 10, 5 and 1.

Currency exchange: Money can be changed in any bank and most travel agencies. National Girobank Postcheques may be used to withdraw cash from UK accounts at main Spanish post offices. If buying Pesetas in advance, note that rates of exchange at many UK banks depend on the denominations of Spanish currency being bought or sold. Check with banks for details and current rates.

Credit cards: Access/Mastercard, American Express, Diners Club and Visa are widely accepted. Check with your credit card company for details of merchant acceptability and other facilities which may be available.

Travellers cheques: International travellers cheques and Eurocheques are widely accepted.

Exchange rate indicators: The following figures are included as a guide to the movements of the Peseta against Sterling and the US Dollar:

Date:	Oct '92	Sep '93	Jan '94	Jan '95
£1.00=	172.65	201.05	211.46	205.93
$1.00=	108.79	131.66	142.92	131.63

Currency restrictions: The import and export of local currency is subject to declaration if the amount exceeds Pta1,000,000 and the amount exported must not exceed the amount declared on arrival. The import and export of foreign currency is unlimited, but should be declared if the quantity exceeds Pta500,000 per person per journey, to avoid difficulties on leaving Spain.

Banking hours: 0830-1630 Monday to Thursday, 0830-1400 Friday and 0830-1300 Saturday (October to May); 0830-1400 Monday to Friday (June to September).

DUTY FREE

(a) The following items may be imported into Spain by passengers of 15 years or older from Europe and the Mediterranean countries of Asia and Africa without incurring customs duty:

200 cigarettes or 100 cigarillos or 50 cigars or 250g tobacco [1]; *1 litre of spirits if exceeding 22% volume or 2 litres of alcoholic beverage not exceeding 22% volume; 2 litres of wine; 250ml eau de toilette and 50g of perfume; gifts to the value of Pta5000 (Pta2000 for children under 15 years of age).*

(b) Visitors over 17 years of age arriving from EU countries with duty-paid goods:

800 cigarettes and 400 cigarillos and 200 cigars and 1kg of tobacco; 90 litres of wine (including up to 60 litres of sparkling wine); 10 litres of spirits; 20 litres of intermediate products (such as fortified wine); 110 litres of beer.

Notes: (a) **[1]** The allowance on tobacco products is doubled for all other nationals. (b) Although there are now no legal limits imposed on importing duty-paid tobacco and alcoholic products from one EU country to another, travellers may be questioned at customs if they exceed the above amounts and may be asked to prove that the goods are for personal use only. (c) There are no import restrictions for the Canary Islands (except for gifts valued at more than Pta8000).

PUBLIC HOLIDAYS

The following public holidays are celebrated throughout Spain:

Jan 1 '95 New Year's Day. **Jan 6** Epiphany. **Apr 14** Good Friday. **May 1** St Joseph the Workman. **Aug 15** Assumption. **Oct 12** National Day. **Nov 1** All Saints' Day. **Dec 6** Constitution Day. **Dec 8** Immaculate Conception. **Dec 25** Christmas Day. **Jan 1 '96** New Year's Day. **Jan 6** Epiphany. **Apr 5** Good Friday.

The following dates are also celebrated as regional public holidays (may vary from year to year):

Jan 2 '95 Andalucia, Aragon, Asturias, Canary Islands and Extremadura. **Feb 28** Andalucia. **Mar 20** Cantabria, Castile/La Mancha, Castile León and Madrid. **Apr 13** Maundy Thursday: every region *except* Canary Islands, Cantabria and Catalonia. **Apr 17** Easter Monday: Catalonia, Valencia, Navarre, Basque Country and La Rioja. **May 2** Madrid. **May 17** Galicia. **May 30** Canary Islands. **May 31** Castile/La Mancha. **Jun 9** La Rioja and Murcia. **Jul 25** Aragon, Balearic Islands, Canary Islands, Castile León, Galicia, Murcia, Navarre and Basque Country. **Jul 28** Cantabria. **Sep 8** Extremadura and

Asturias. **Sep 11** Catalonia. **Sep 15** Cantabria. **Oct 9** Valencia. **Dec 26** Catalonia and Balearic Islands.

HEALTH

Regulations and requirements may be subject to change at short notice, and you are advised to contact your doctor well in advance of your intended date of departure. Any numbers in the chart refer to the footnotes below.

	Special Precautions?	Certificate Required?
Yellow Fever	No	No
Cholera	No	No
Typhoid & Polio	No	-
Malaria	No	-
Food & Drink	1	-

[1]: Mains water is normally chlorinated, and whilst relatively safe may cause mild abdominal upsets. Bottled water is available and is advised for the first few weeks of the stay. Milk is pasteurised and dairy products are safe for consumption. Local meat, poultry, seafood, fruit and vegetables are generally considered safe to eat.

Health care: There is a Reciprocal Health Agreement with the UK. Medical treatment provided by state scheme doctors at state scheme hospitals and health centres (*ambulatorios*) is free to UK citizens if in possession of form E111. This Agreement is, however, implemented to a limited degree in most holiday resorts and health insurance is *strongly advised.* Prescribed medicines and dental treatment must be paid for by all visitors. Further information is available from the Labour Office (for address, see top of entry).

TRAVEL - International

Note: For information on travel to and within the **Canary Islands** and the **Balearic Islands** see the respective entries below.

AIR: Spain's national airline is *IBERIA (IB).*
For free advice on air travel, call the Air Travel Advisory Bureau on (0171) 636 5000 (London) *or* (0161) 832 2000 (Manchester).

Approximate flight times: From *London* to Barcelona is 2 hours; to Ibiza is 2 hours 20 minutes; to Madrid is 2 hours and to Málaga is 2 hours 20 minutes.
From *Los Angeles* to Madrid is 13 hours.
From *New York* to Madrid is 7 hours 25 minutes.
From *Sydney* to Madrid is 29 hours 5 minutes.

International airports: *Alicante (ALC)* (Altet), 15km (9 miles) southwest of the city. Airport facilities include a duty-free shop, bank, exchange office, car rental desk and restaurant. Coach service runs every 60 minutes to the city from 0730-2330. A taxi service is available to the city. There is a taxi connection between Alicante and Valencia Airport.

Barcelona (BCN) (del Prat), 15km (9 miles) southwest of the city. Airport facilities include a 24-hour bank, restaurant, bar, several car rental companies, hotel reservation and tourist information desks and a duty-free shop. Bus service to the city departs every 30 minutes from 0630-2300. Rail service is every 30 minutes from 0613-43. Taxi service to the city is available.

Bilbao (BIO), 10km (6 miles) north of the city. Taxi service to the city is available. Airport facilities include a restaurant, duty-free shop, tourist information desk and car rental offices.

Madrid (MAD) (Barajas), 16km (10 miles) east of the city. Airport facilities include restaurants and bars (0700-2400), 24-hour bank, several car rental offices, hotel reservation and tourist information desks and outgoing duty-free shop. Coach service departs to the city every 15 minutes from 0545-0015. Taxi service is available.

Málaga (AGP), 10km (6 miles) southwest of the city. Airport facilities include duty-free shop, bank, restaurant and car hire firms. Bus runs every 30 minutes from 0600-2310. Train service runs every 30 minutes from 0715-2345. Taxi service to the city is available.

Santiago de Compostela (SCQ), 10km (6 miles) northeast of the city. Bus service from 0715-2215. Taxis are available to the city centre.

Seville (SVQ), 8km (5 miles) from the city. Taxis are available to the city centre.

Valencia (VLC) (Manises), 18km (11 miles) from the city. Airport facilities include several car hire firms, 24-hour bank, restaurant, bar and duty-free shop. Taxis are available to the city centre.

SEA: *Brittany Ferries* operate a service to Santander (on the north coast) from Plymouth, taking 24 hours. An additional service is provided by *P&O* from Portsmouth to Bilbao.

RAIL: There are direct trains between Madrid–Paris and Madrid–Lisbon, as well as Barcelona–Paris, Barcelona–Zürich–Milan and Barcelona–Geneva. These services are called *Talgo, Estrella* or *Train-Hotel.* On other

international services to and from Spain, a change of train is necessary.

ROAD: The main route from the UK is via France. The main autoroutes to Spain from France are via Bordeaux or Toulouse to Bilbao (north Spain) and via Marseille or Toulouse to Barcelona (east Spain). A number of coach operators offer services to Spain. In the UK, *Eurolines,* departing from Victoria Coach Station in London, serve more than 20 destinations in Spain. For further information, contact Eurolines, 23 Crawley Road, Luton LU1 1HX. Tel: (01582) 404 511. Fax: (01582) 400 694. See below for information on **documentation** and **traffic regulations**.

TRAVEL - Internal

AIR: Domestic flights are run by *Iberia (IB), Aviaco (AO)* and *Air Europa* (AEA).
Scheduled flights connect all main towns as well as to the Balearic and Canary Islands and enclaves in North Africa. Air taxis are available at most airports. Reservations should be made well in advance.

SEA: There are regular hydrofoil and car and passenger ferry sailings from Algeciras to Ceuta (North African enclave); Málaga and Almeria to Melilla (North African enclave); Barcelona, Valencia and Alicante to the Balearic Islands; and Cádiz to the Canary Islands. There are also inter-island services.

RAIL: The state-owned company RENFE operates a railway network connecting all the regions on the Iberian peninsula. It is mainly a radial network, with connections between Madrid and all the major cities. There are also some transversal services connecting the northwest coast with the Mediterranean coast, as well as services from the French border down the Mediterranean coast. Principal trains are air-conditioned, and many have restaurant or buffet service. A Spanish Railways timetable can be purchased in the UK through European Rail Timetables, 39 Kilton Glade, Worksop, Notts S81 0PX. Tel: (01909) 485 855. Reservations for passenger services in Spain may be made in the UK through Ultima Travel (tel: (0151) 339 6171) or E. Raymond & Co. Ltd. (tel: (0151) 236 2960).

Discount Rail Travel: The Spanish rail system is one of the cheapest in Europe. A discount of 10% applies to standard return tickets and 20% to day returns. Groups of eight or more qualify for up to 50% discount on advance bookings. Children under 4 years travel free, and children aged 4-11 years pay half fare. Travellers can also enjoy savings by using any one of the European passes available, such as the *Euro Domino Freedom Pass,* which enables holders to make flexible travel arrangements. The Euro Domino Freedom Pass is available in 19 European countries, but must be bought in the country of residence for which a valid passport or other form of ID has to be shown. In the UK, this pass is available from British Rail International. The tickets are valid for 3, 5 or 10 days within a month. Also available from British Rail International, the *Inter-Rail Pass* entitles UK residents under 26 to unlimited rail travel for one month. The *Rail Europe Senior (RES)* card entitles senior citizens to 40% discount on rail travel throughout Spain even during peak hours. The card is available from all British Rail stations.

Note: Seat reservations are required on all intercity trains. This ruling applies to the passes and cards mentioned above.

High-Speed Trains: The *Ave* service connects Madrid and Seville in under three hours, with 12 services each way via Córdoba. Some services also stop at Ciudad Real and Puerto Llano (La Mancha). The *Talgo 200* connects Madrid and Malaga thrice-daily in less than five hours. Holders of the cards and passes mentioned above qualify for discounts, albeit less substantial than the rates quoted above. Further information and reservations may be made on tel: (1) 563 0202; fax: (1) 527 7428.

Motorail: Services are operated on night trains. Although not all routes are bookable outside Spain, reservations *can* be made in the UK for the following routes: Barcelona–Málaga, Bilbao–Málaga, Bilbao–Cádiz and Bilbao–Alicante. For further information and reservations, contact Rail Shop. Tel: (0345) 300 003.

Tourist Trains: The *Transcantabrico* and *Andalus Express* offer a pleasant way of discovering their respective regions. There are also a number of privately-run *narrow-gauge* railways in Spain, located mainly in the north of Spain as well as the Mediterranean coast and the Balearic Islands, which run at a leisurely pace through picturesque scenery. For more information on tourist trains, contact the Spanish National Tourist Office.

ROAD: There are more than 150,000km (95,000 miles) of roads. Motorways are well-maintained and connect Spain north–south. Tolls are in operation on some sections and have to be paid in Pesetas. Trunk roads between major cities are generally fast and well-maintained. Rural roads are of differing quality. **Bus:** There are bus lines which are efficient and cheap, operating between cities and towns. Departures are generally from a central terminal at which the operators will have individual booths selling tickets. Most places have a bus link of some kind, even the more remote villages. **Car hire:** All major car hire companies are represented in major cities. Minimum age for car hire is 21 years. **Motorcycles:** No person under 18 may hire or ride a vehicle over 75cc. Crash helmets must be worn. **Traffic regulations:** Traffic drives on the right. Side lights must be used at night in built-up areas. Spare bulbs and red hazard triangles must be kept in all vehicles. Traffic lights: green for go, amber, then red for stop; two red lights mean 'No Entry'. Seat belts to be worn by travellers of any age on the front seats; seat belts have to be worn in the back where fitted. The speed limit for motorways is 120kmph (75mph) in general, but for buses and lorries the limit is 100kmph (60mph); in built-up areas the limit is 50kmph (30mph); for other roads it is 90kmph (56mph). **Documentation:** An International Driving Permit is required or a translation of the national driving licence (available from the Consulate), or a new EU-format driving licence (3-part pink document). Third Party insurance is also required and a Green Card is strongly recommended.

URBAN: Traffic in Spanish cities is normally heavy, and urban driving takes some time to adjust to. City public transport facilities are generally good. Barcelona and Madrid have metros as well as buses. Pre-purchase multi-journey tickets are sold. Other towns and resorts are well served by local buses. Metered taxis are available in most major cities and taxi drivers expect a 2-3% tip.

JOURNEY TIMES: The following chart gives approximate journey times (in hours and minutes) from Madrid to other major cities/towns in Spain.

	Air	Road	Rail
Barcelona	1.00	8.00	8.00
Bilbao	0.50	5.00	6.00
Canary Is.	2.30	-	-
Málaga	1.00	8.30	7.00
Mallorca	1.00	-	* -
Palma	1.10	*6.00	*5.00
Santander	0.50	5.00	6.00
Seville	0.55	6.00	7.00
Valencia	0.50	5.00	4.00

Note [*]: Plus 9 hours by boat.

ACCOMMODATION

HOTELS & HOSTELS: A variety of hotel-type accommodation is available including apartment-hotels, hotel-residencias and motels. The term *residencia* denotes an establishment where dining-room facilities are not provided, although there must be provisions for the serving of breakfast and a cafeteria. Detailed information is available from Federación Española de Hoteles, Orense 32, 28020 Madrid. Tel: (1) 556 7112 *or* 556 7202. Fax: (1) 556 7361; *or* ZONTUR, Gremio Toneleros 24, Polígono San Castelló, 07009 Palma de Mallorca. Tel: (71) 430 483. Fax: (71) 759 155.

Grading: Most accommodation in Spain is provided in hotels, classified from **1** to **5** stars (the few exceptions have a Grande De Luxe category); or hostels or *pensiones*, classified from **1** to **3 stars**.

The following is an outline of the facilities available in the hotel and hostel categories.

5-star hotels: Air-conditioning in all public rooms and bedrooms, central heating, two or more lifts, lounges, bar, garage (within towns), hairdressers, all bedrooms with en-suite bathrooms and telephone, some suites with sitting rooms, and laundry and ironing service.

4-star hotels: Air-conditioning in every room, unless climatic conditions require central heating or refrigeration only, the minimum of two hotel lounges, 75% of the bedrooms with en-suite bathroom and the rest with shower, washbasin, WC and hot and cold running water, laundry and ironing service, telephone in every room, garage parking (in towns), lift and bar.

3-star hotels: Permanently installed heating or air-conditioning according to climate, lounge, lift, bar, 50% of the bedrooms have en-suite bathrooms, 50% have shower, washbasin, WC and hot and cold running water, laundry and ironing service, telephone in every room.

2-star hotels: Permanently installed heating or air-conditioning according to climate, lounge, lift in buildings of two or more storeys, bar, 15% of rooms with en-suite bathrooms, 45% with shower, washbasin and WC and the rest with shower, washbasin and hot and cold running water, one common bathroom to every six rooms, laundry and ironing service, telephone in every room.

1-star hotels: Permanently installed heating, lift in buildings of more than four storeys, lounge, 25% of bedrooms with shower, washbasin and WC, 25% with shower and washbasin, the rest have washbasin and hot and cold running water, one common bathroom every

SPAIN: Autonomous communities
Galicia
Castile and León
Aragón
Catalonia
MADRID
Extremadura
Castile-La Mancha
Comunidad Valenciana
Islas Baleares
Andalucia
Región de Murcia
Canarias
Ceuta
Melilla
DAB-M282
1 Principado de Asturias
2 Cantabria
3 Pais Vasco
4 Comunidad Foral de Navarra
5 La Rioja
6 Comunidad de Madrid
400km
200mls

seven rooms, laundry and ironing service, telephone on every floor.

3-star hostels: Permanently installed heating, lift in buildings of more than four storeys, lounge, 5% of bedrooms with en-suite bathroom, 10% with shower, washbasin and WC, 85% with shower and washbasin and hot and cold running water, one common bathroom to every eight rooms, laundry and ironing service, telephone in every room.

2-star hostels: Permanently installed heating, lift in buildings of five storeys or more, lounge or comfortable lobby, one common bathroom to every ten rooms, all bedrooms with washbasin and hot and cold water, general telephone.

1-star hostels: All rooms with washbasins and cold running water; one bathroom for every 12 rooms; general telephone.

It is always advisable to book accommodation well in advance, particularly during festivals or at popular resorts on the coast from late spring to October. Reservations may be made by writing direct to the hotels, lists of which may be obtained from the Spanish National Tourist Office (SNTO), or through travel agents or certain hotel booking services. Letters to 5-, 4- or 3-star hotels may be written in English, but it is advisable to write in Spanish to lower categories.

GOVERNMENT LODGES: A chain of lodging places has been set up by the Ministry of Tourism in places of special interest or remote locations. These include attractive modern buildings and ancient monuments of historic interest, such as monasteries, convents, old palaces and castles. Standards are uniformly high, but not at the expense of individual charm and character. Below is a brief description of each type of lodging:

Paradores (National Tourist Inns): Each *Parador* is a hotel with all modern amenities including rooms with private bathroom, hot and cold running water, central heating, telephone in every room, public sitting rooms, garages and complementary services. Advance booking is advised. For further information, contact Central De Reservas De España, Calle Requena 3, Madrid 28013. Tel: (1) 559 0069 (20 lines). Fax: (1) 559 3233. Telex: 41461 *or* 44607. Alternatively, contact the UK representative, Keytel International, 402 Edgware Road, London W2 1ED. Tel: (0171) 402 8182. Fax: (0171) 724 9503. Telex: 21780 (a/b KEYTEL G).

Hosterias (traditional restaurants): These are typical restaurants, decorated in the style of the region in which they are situated and serve excellent meals.

GUEST-HOUSES: *Pensiones* are common throughout Spain and vary in quality from austere to relatively luxurious. They are usually run by the family on the premises and provide bed and board only.

CAMPING/CARAVANNING: There are numerous campsites throughout the country, again covering a wide quality and price range. Permission from the local police and landowner is essential for off-site camping provided there are not more than three tents/caravans or ten campers in any one place. Regulations demand that off-site camping is in isolated areas only. The Spanish Federation of Camping has recently opened a new booking centre. For further information, contact ANCE, General Oraa 52, 2°, 28006 Madrid. Tel: (1) 562 9994. Fax: (1) 563 7094. Telex: 42066 (a/b FCCV E).

RESORTS & EXCURSIONS

The Kingdom of Spain occupies four-fifths of the Iberian peninsula and is a land of great geographical and cultural diversity with much to offer the tourist. Spain's beach

resorts on the south and northwest Mediterranean coasts continue to attract sunseekers, but increasingly tourists are discovering the fascinations of an ancient and beautiful Spain away from the beaches. There is a huge variety of landscape in Spain: dense deciduous and coniferous forests, endless arid plains, lush salt marshes, picturesque rocky bays, mist-shrouded mountain tops, broad sandy beaches, uniquely Spanish medieval cities, ancient rivers meandering through orchards and clear mountain streams plunging through chasms, and everywhere castles, palaces and other reminders of Spain's incomparably rich history.

The wide range of influences on Spanish **architecture** through the ages makes it difficult to isolate a style and define it as typically Spanish; major influences include Roman, Visigoth, Romanesque, Moorish, Byzantine, Medieval, Renaissance, Baroque and Art Nouveau styles. Throughout Spain a sense of the historical traditions that have shaped the country is reflected in the castles, churches, monuments and houses.

Certain examples defining the pure style of these influences can be seen: Roman remains at Italica, Sagunto, Tarragona, Mérida (theatre and amphitheatre), Segovia (aqueduct) and Alcudia; Moorish architecture at Córdoba (the Great Mosque), Seville (the Alcázar, the Giralda tower) and, above all, at Granada (the Alhambra). The Mudejar style, developed from the interaction of Christian and Muslim ideas, can be seen in the finely detailed ceramic work at Teruel. Gothic churches from the early, middle and late periods can be found at Burgos, Toledo, León, Barcelona, Girona, Pamplona, Segovia and Seville, and fine examples of the Baroque style at Salamanca and Valladolid.

The majority of castles adopted as the standard image of the country date from the 15th century. The 16th, 17th and 18th centuries saw the construction of many beautiful palaces and religious and civic buildings, adding to an already rich architectural heritage. The 19th and early 20th centuries added only moderately to this heritage, although the work of Antonio Gaudí stands out as being exceptional (see *Barcelona* below).

Spanish **wildlife** is also enormously diverse. Amongst the more exotic mammals are: bears, ibexes and chamois in the foothills of the great northern mountains; wild boars, lynxes, mongooses and even wild camels amidst the marshes and sand dunes of the Coto de Doñana (also home to chameleons, tarantulas, scorpions, tortoises and terrapins); and wolves in Murcia and perhaps elsewhere. There are resident populations of flamingoes, ibises, spoonbills, bee-eaters and golden orioles in the Coto de Doñana; hoopoes, bustards, owls and eagles may be seen throughout the country; vultures inhabit the highest peaks, including, in the Pyrénées, rare lammergeiers – large, shy birds that drop scavenged bones from a great height onto rocks to break them open and release the nutritious marrow. Several major migration routes cross Spain and, at the right time of year, the skies are filled with millions of birds of many different species heading north from Africa. The white stork is amongst those that stop to breed, and in spring and summer almost every church tower seems to be capped by a large, shaggy nest. There are excellent opportunities for sea and river fishing. Salmon abound in the inlets along the northwest coast and most rivers and streams have healthy populations of trout.

Spain's 52 provinces have, since 1983, been administered as 17 Autonomous Communities, each with a degree of self-government. For the purpose of this section, however, the country has been divided into eight regions, which do not necessarily reflect political or cultural boundaries: **Andalucia, Ceuta & Melilla,** *including the Costa de Almería, the Costa del Sol and the Costa de la Luz;* **Castile/La Mancha & Extremadura; Madrid; Castile/León & La Rioja; The Northern Region,** *including the Basque Country, Cantabria, Asturias and Galicia;* **Navarre & Aragón; Catalonia,** *including the Costa Brava and the Costa Dorada;* and **Valencia & Murcia,** *including the Costa del Azahar, Costa Blanca and the Costa Calida.*

The regional map below gives the frontiers of these regions; the dotted lines denote Autonomous

Daily scheduled flights from European airports to Spain

Alicante

Amsterdam

Brussels

Dublin

Edinburgh

Frankfurt

Geneva

Gran Canaria

Helsinki

London

Madrid

Malaga

Palma

Paris

Zurich

viva air
IBERIA GROUP

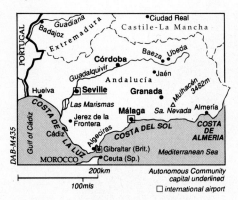

Communities. There is also a separate section on Spain's **Ski Resorts.**

Information on **The Balearic Islands** and **The Canary Islands**, both integral parts of the Kingdom of Spain, may be found in the separate entries immediately following Spain's *Climate* section.

Andalucia, Ceuta & Melilla

Including the **Costa de Almería**, the **Costa del Sol** and the **Costa de la Luz.**
Andalucia is a mountainous region in the far south of Spain, rich in minerals and an important centre for the production of olives, grapes, oranges and lemons.
INLAND: The regional capital is **Seville,** one of the largest cities in Spain, and one bearing numerous traces of the 500 years of Moorish occupation. Seville is the romantic heart of the country, the city of Carmen and Don Juan; its cathedral is the largest Gothic building in the world and has a superb collection of art and period stonework. Christopher Columbus and St Ferdinand are buried here. Of great importance also is the *Alcázar*, the palace-fortress of the Arab kings, together with *Giralda* and *Torre de Oro*, reputedly once covered in gold leaf, and the *River Guadalquivir*. Holy Week in Seville embodies the religious fervour of the Spanish, and is one of the most interesting festivals in the country. Early

booking for accommodation at festival time is essential. Holy Week is followed closely by the famous April Fair, during which couples parade the fairground mounted on fine Andalucian horses, dressed in the traditional flamenco costume. Drinking, eating, song and dance are the order of the day for the whole week and the fairground with its coloured lanterns and *casetas* bordering the streets is a continuous movement of colour.
Córdoba to the northeast has further relics of the Moorish Empire, the most spectacular being the 8th-century mosque with painted columns and arches. The building is so magnificent that it has been preserved through the changes of religion.
Granada contains probably the greatest tribute to the Moorish Empire in Spain, the *Alhambra*. This fortress palace, home of the Moorish kings, defies accurate description for its sumptuous elegance and beauty. It is surrounded by the exquisite gardens of the *Generalife*, whose ponds and fountains help to cool the hot summer air. The Alhambra is possibly the single most splendid building in a country bearing relics of numerous epochs and civilisations. Granada's magnificent cathedral houses the tombs of King Ferdinand and Queen Isabella.
South of Granada, and only about 40km (25 miles) from the coast, is the upland area of the **Sierra Nevada**, a mountain range running roughly east to west. It contains the highest peaks in Iberia; one of these, the Pico de Veleta (over 3400m/11,155ft) is accessible for most of its height by road, and coach trips are available. The region offers the unique opportunity to combine a holiday of winter sports with coastal sunshine and watersports in the Mediterranean (see below). Mountain resorts include *Capileira* (south of the Pico de Veleta), *Borreguiles* and *Pradollano* (both in the Solynieve region).
Jaén, capital of the northwestern Sierra Nevada, is an ancient town rich in historic buildings and art treasures; the *Provincial Museum*, the *Cathedral* and the *Castle of Santa Catalina* are among them. **Baeza**, 48km (30 miles) from Jaén, displays architectural styles which span Romanesque to Renaissance. Baeza as a whole has an air of nobility and strength; the aristocratic design and countless nobles' mansions are enhanced in appearance by the prevailing golden hue of the stone.
Barely 10km (6 miles) from Baeza and 58km (36 miles) from Jaén lies **Ubeda**, with Renaissance palaces to be seen on all sides.
COSTA DE ALMERIA: To the east of the Costa del

SEVILLE

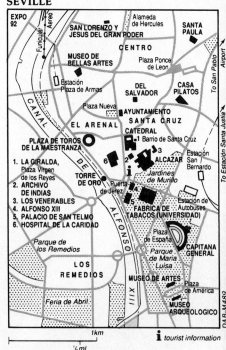

Sol is the province of **Almería.** The capital of the same name is a Roman port with many Moorish-style houses, dominated by two castles. It is surrounded by subtropical vegetation and hills and is situated within a wide bay. Attractions in the town include the 16th-century *Cathedral*, the *Church of Santiago el Viejo* and the Moorish *Alcazaba*.
Resorts on the Costa de Almería: Adra, Roquetas, Cabo de Gata, Aguadulce, Mojácar and San José.
COSTA DEL SOL: This extends along almost all of the

Mediterranean coast of Andalucía from the Costa de Almería to Tarifa in the south. The Costa del Sol is a densely populated tourist area mainly because of the fine beaches and picturesque towns.

The main city of this area, **Málaga,** lies only a few miles from the famous tourist resorts of **Marbella** and **Torremolinos.** Over 160km (100 miles) of coastline ensure that, despite its popularity, it is still possible to find a relatively uncrowded beach. In the same province is **Nerja,** known as the 'Balcony of Europe' on account of its having a promontory look-out which is perched high above the sea with commanding views of the Mediterranean. It is also the home of well-preserved prehistoric caves. An excursion can be made from Málaga into the hinterland to the old Spanish mountain town of **Ronda,** spectacularly situated on a gorge in the *Sierra de Ronda.*

Resorts on the Costa del Sol: Calahonda, Torre del Mar, El Palo, Málaga, Nerja, Torremolinos, Benalmádena Costa, Fuengirola/Mijas, Marbella, San Pedro de Alcántara and Estepona.

COSTA DE LA LUZ: This runs along the southern Atlantic coast of Spain between Tarifa and the Portuguese border, featuring long sandy beaches and unspoilt sand dunes.

From **Algeciras** ferries run to Tangier and Ceuta on the north African coast, as well as to the Canary Islands. Taking the road from Algeciras to **Cádiz** is one of the most enjoyable drives in the country, offering spectacular views of the Straits of Gibraltar, the North African coastline and the Atlas Mountains. Cádiz is characterised by palm trees, look-out towers and white-fronted houses. It is one of the oldest towns in Iberia, founded by the Phoenicians around 1000BC. Less than half an hour away is the sherry town of **Jerez,** housing the great *bodegas* whose product has linked the town with England

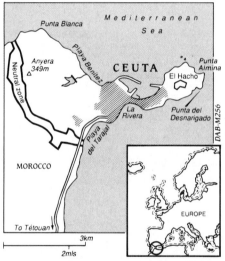

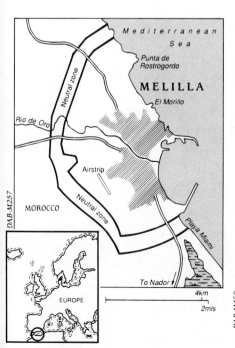

since importation of 'sherris-sack' into this country began in the 16th century.

In the province of Huelva is the town of **El Rocío** where one of the most important Spanish festivals is held, that of the *Virgin of El Rocío.* Also of interest are the beautiful stalactite caves of *Gruta de las Maravillas* in **Aracena** in the north of Huelva province and the national park, *Coto de Doñana* (see the general introduction above).

Resorts on the Costa de la Luz: Barbate, Algeciras, Tarifa, Conil de la Frontera, Chiclana de la Frontera, Cádiz, El Puerto de Santa María, Rota, Chipiona, Sanlúcar de Barrameda, Torre la Higuera, Mazagón, Punta Umbría, El Rompido, La Antilla and Isla Cristina.

THE AFRICAN ENCLAVES: Ceuta is a free port on the north coast of Africa. The city is dominated by the *Plaza de Africa* in the town centre, and by the cathedral. The promontory has the remains of the old fortress. Bus services are available into Morocco, and there are regular car-ferry sailings from Algeciras.

Melilla is also a free port on the north coast of Africa, and is served by car ferries from Málaga and Almería. The town is mainly modern, but there are several older buildings, including a 16th-century church.

Balearic & Canary Islands

See separate entries below.

Castile/La Mancha & Extremadura

This inland region lies between Madrid and Andalucia. Bordered by mountains to the north, east and south, it is irrigated by two large rivers, the Tajo and the Guadiana, both of which flow westwards to Portugal and thence to the Atlantic. Castile/La Mancha, the higher, western part of the region, is also known as *Castila La Nueva* (New Castile).

CASTILE/LA MANCHA: To the south of Madrid is the ancient Spanish capital of **Toledo.** Rising above the plains and a gorge of the River Tajo, the city is dominated by the magnificent cathedral and *Alcazar.* The town seems tortured by streets as narrow as the steel blades for which it is famous. Toledo is justly proud of its collection of paintings by El Greco, who lived and painted here. El Greco's most famous painting, 'The Burial of the Conde Orgaz', is preserved in the *Santo Tome Church.*

Guadalajara, capital of the province of the same name, is situated northeast of the capital, on the Rio Henares. Sights include the 15th-century *Palacio del Infantado* and the *Church of San Gines.*

The provincial capital of **Ciudad Real** is the chief town in the La Mancha region, the home of Don Quixote. There are many places in the surrounding area associated with Don Quixote, including *Campo de Criptana,* believed to be the setting for his fight with the windmills.

Cuenca, also a provincial capital, is famous for its hanging houses. It is one of the most attractive of Spain's medieval towns, and the Gothic cathedral is particularly richly decorated. The nearby countryside includes woods, lakes,

spectacular caves, towering mountains and valleys, many with fortified towns and villages clinging to their sides.

Albacete is the centre of a wine-producing region. The town witnessed two exceptionally bloody battles during the *Reconquista,* but the considerable rebuilding of the town has left few reminders of its history. More evidence, however, is scattered in the surrounding countryside, where such places as the Moorish castle at **Almansa** and the old fortified towns of **Chinchilla de Monte Aragón** and **Villena** reflect the area's stormy past.

EXTREMADURA: This region consists of the provinces of Cáceres and Badajoz. **Cáceres** was founded in the 1st century BC by the Romans, and was later destroyed by the Visigoths and rebuilt by the Moors. There are traces of all the stages of the city's history, although most of the buildings date from Cáceres' Golden Age during the 16th century. Nearby is the beautiful village of **Arroyo de la Luz.** 48km (30 miles) away is the town of **Trujillo,** the birthplace of Pizarro. Also in this province is **Plasencia,** founded in the 12th century, which has a beautiful medieval aqueduct and a cathedral.

The ancient fortified town of **Badajoz** (in the province of the same name), is situated very close to the Portuguese frontier, and was founded by the Romans. The *Alcazaba,* the Moorish part of the town, is on a hill in the northeast of the town. Not far away is the town of **Alburquerque,** which has the ruins of a massive castle and a large Gothic church. In the same province is the town of **Mérida,** famous for ancient Roman ruins; the remains are housed in the *Museum of Archaeology.* A few kilometres away is **Medellín,** where Cortés was born in 1485.

Madrid

The capital city **Madrid,** in the region of the same name, is a cosmopolitan metropolis with many theatres, cinemas and opera houses, and over 50 museums and art galleries. These include the *Prado,* one of the most celebrated and comprehensive art galleries in the world (see below), and the *Royal Palace,* set in a luxurious 18th-century garden, housing paintings, tapestries, carpets, armour, and an outstanding collection of clocks. The popular centre of Madrid is the *Puerta del Sol,* from which ten streets radiate. To its south is the site of 'Kilometre Zero', a stone slab from which all distances are measured in Spain. A short walk southwest of the Puerta del Sol leads to the *Plaza Mayor,* a spacious square surrounded by arcades sheltering small shops. From here one can explore an area which still has some of the flavour of Old Madrid.

The Prado Museum has one of the most remarkable art collections in the world, including many supreme works of art acquired by Spanish monarchs. Works by El Greco, Murillo, Goya, Velazquez, Titian, Raphael, Botticelli, Veronese, Tintoretto, Breughel and Bosch can be found here. Plans are being made to assemble a collection by Spain's most famous 20th-century artist, Pablo Picasso. 'Guernica', one of his greatest masterpieces – a monument to the people's suffering

MADRID

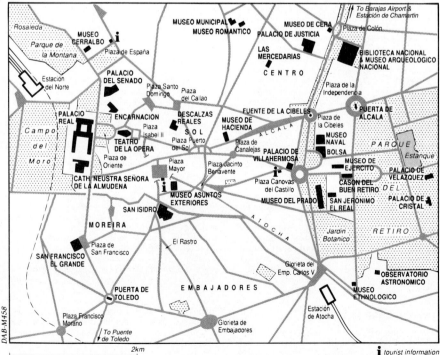

i *tourist information*

View from the bridge, Alicante

during the Civil War – has now been returned to Spain and hangs in the *Centro Cultural Reina Sofía*. The *Thyssen-Bornemisza Museum* housed in the *Villahermosa Palace* opposite the Prado Museum is, with its 800 works of art, one of the largest private collections in the world.
EXCURSIONS: There are many places of interest within easy reach of the city. The great *Monastery of San Lorenzo del Escorial* is situated about 40km (25 miles) north of Madrid, and includes a church, a royal palace, a monastery, a mausoleum and a famous library. The Escorial was built in 1563-84 by Philip II, and is now a burial place of Spanish kings and queens. 9km (6 miles) from the Escorial is the *Valle de los Caídos* (Valley of the Fallen), a huge crypt cut into the mountainside surmounted by a stone cross reaching 152m (500ft) into the sky. Franco conceived this dramatic monument as a tribute to those who died in the Civil War, and is buried here. **Alcalá de Henares** is the birthplace of Cervantes and Catherine of Aragón. **Aranjuez** is famous for its summer palace and the *Casita del Labrador*, situated near the banks of the cooling *River Tagus*, on whose fertile soil are grown the asparagus and strawberries for which the town is also renowned.
September sees the *Ferias Mayores* (Great Fairs) and the Easter processions of Semana Santa, both typically extravagant and colourful affairs. Several special tours are available, including the 'Castles in Spain Tour', run by Viajes Marsans for three days, departing from Madrid. The *Guadarrama* region offers winter sports. For further information see the *Ski Resorts* section below.

Castile/León & La Rioja

The inland region of Castile and León lies to the north and northwest of Madrid and occupies the northern part of the Meseta Central, the plateau that covers much of

central Spain. As with the previous region, Castile and León is hemmed in by high mountains to the north, east and south and is the catchment area for a large river, the Douro, which flows westward into Portugal. Hot and dry throughout much of the year, the region's extensive plains nonetheless make it an important agricultural asset for a country as mountainous as Spain.
CASTILE LA VIEJA: Avila is the highest provincial capital in the country, its medieval quality retained and enhanced by the magnificence of its surrounding walls. The celebrated *Convent of St Therese the Mystic* is here. **Segovia** has a working Roman aqueduct, one of the best preserved structures of its kind in the world. There are many unspoilt Romanesque churches, dominated by the cathedral and by the Arab *Alcazar*. The turrets soaring from its rocky outcrop are said to be the inspiration for Walt Disney's fairytale castles.
The province of **Soria** has a large number of archaeological remains of the Celtiberian and Roman civilisations, and many of these may be seen in the *Museo Numantino* in the provincial capital of the same name. 9km (6 miles) north of the town is the site of *Numancia*, a fortified Celtiberian town. Attractions in the town of Soria include the 13th-century *Church of San Juan de Duero*, the *Cathedral of San Pedro* and the *Renaissance Palacio de los Condes de Gómara*.
La Rioja is a province famous for its vineyards. The capital, **Logroño**, is in the centre of the province. It is a district with a great historical past; the origins of poetry in the Castilian language lie here, and it contains the channel of a European stream of culture – the *Road to Santiago*.
Burgos was the birthplace of the great knight El Cid, the embodiment of a strong, romantic tradition of chivalry and honour. His tomb can be seen at Valladolid (see below).
Palencia, the capital of the province of the same name, was the one-time residence of the Kings of Castile and

seat of the Cortes of Castile. The cathedral is one of the finest late-Gothic buildings in the country. The city has several other late-medieval buildings and an archaeological museum.
The city of **Valladolid** is the capital of a province rich in castles and other ancient buildings. It is famous for its lush gardens, which provide such a refreshing contrast to the aridity of much of the surrounding landscape, and also for its *Ferias Mayores* (Great Fairs) in September, and its Easter Procession. Book early if a visit is planned at either of these times. The city is also associated with four of the most famous names in the history of the Iberian peninsula: Columbus (although not a Spaniard) died here in 1506, and his house can be visited; so too can the old home of Cervantes, which has now been turned into a museum; and Ferdinand and Isabella were married here in 1469, bringing together the crowns of Castile and Aragón. The city also has a beautiful medieval cathedral and a university.
LEON: The city of **León** was recaptured from the Moors in 850, and the architecture reflects its long history under Christian rule. The cathedral is one of the finest examples of the Gothic style in the country. There are several places of interest within easy reach of León, including the spectacular **Puerto de Pajares, Benavente** and the attractive region around **Astorga**, a town which, like other towns in the region, was a stopping point on the *Way of St James* (see the section on Santiago de Compostela in the *Northern Region* below).
South of León is the province of **Zamora**; the provincial capital of the same name was the scene of many fierce struggles between the Moors and the Christians during the Reconquista, in which the Spanish hero El Cid figured prominently. The town has a Romanesque cathedral and several 12th-century churches. 19km (12 miles) northwest of the town is an artificial lake, created in 1931; on the shores of the lake, in **El Campillo**, is a Visigoth church dating from the 7th century, which was moved when its original site was flooded by the new reservoir.
The southernmost province of León, **Salamanca**, has as its capital the ancient university town of the same name. It is situated on the swiftly flowing *Tormes River*, and has many superb old buildings, weathered to a golden-brown hue. The most famous of these is the *Cathedral*, built between the early-16th and the mid-18th centuries, and reflecting the styles of architecture prevalent during the various stages of its construction. The university buildings and the fine houses around the *Plaza Mayor* are also particularly striking. The fiesta in September is very popular, and bookings should be made well in advance.

The Northern Region

Including the **Basque Country, Cantabria, Asturias** and **Galicia.**
This region consists of the northwestern part of the country and the northern coastal region stretching to the French frontier. The eastern coastal area adjacent to the French border is now made up of fashionable tourist beaches and picturesque small towns.
THE BASQUE COUNTRY: The provinces of **Guipúzcoa, Vizcaya** and **Alava** form the Basque provinces, occupying a coastal position in the eastern part of the *Cantabrian Mountains*. The economy of this fertile region is strongly based on agricultural produce, although recently the area has also become one of Spain's foremost industrial areas. The Basques themselves are a very ancient pre-Indo-European race, and the origins of their language have baffled etymologists for centuries. The area managed to maintain a considerable degree of independence until the 19th century.
The main city of the region is **Bilbao**, founded in the early 14th century. The *Old Town* has a Gothic cathedral, and an attractive town hall. The provincial capital of **San Sebastián**, situated very close to the French frontier, is one of the most fashionable and popular Spanish seaside resorts. 7km (4 miles) west of the town is *Monte Ulía*, which offers superb views across the countryside and the *Bay of Biscay*. The art treasures found in San Sebastián and Bilbao and in the 13th-century *Castle of Butron*, near Bilbao, are also worthy of note.
The third provincial capital of the Basque region, and also the regional capital, is **Vitoria**, famous as being the site of a British victory during the Peninsula War, an event commemorated in various places in the city.
Vitoria is remarkable for having two cathedrals; one was completed in the 15th century, whilst the other, on which work commenced in 1907, has yet to be finished.
CANTABRIA: Although the province of Cantabria is historically in Old Castile, owing to its position on the coast, it has been included in this section. The historical capital of **Santander** is set in a beautiful bay ringed with hills. The Gothic cathedral was destroyed by fire in 1941, but has been carefully restored. The *Municipal Museum* contains a fine collection of paintings by many 17th- and

18th-century artists. Nearby are the fine beaches of *El Sardinero* and *Magdalena*. The latter makes a convenient base for expeditions to the highest of the *Cantabrian Mountains*, the vulture-haunted *Picos de Europa* (actually in Asturias), several attractive beach resorts such as **Comillas** and **San Vincente,** and the *Caves of Altamira*, with detailed wall paintings dating back 13,000 years. Admission is now very limited and must be applied for. **Solares** is a town in this region noted for the therapeutic qualities of its mineral waters. There are several pleasant resorts, including **Santillana del Mar,** a completely preserved medieval town.

ASTURIAS: This formerly independent principality contains two towns of note; Oviedo, the capital, and the port and industrial centre of Gijón. The chief interest in **Oviedo** is the small, old central area, dominated by the cathedral. The port of **Gijón** has a large and very popular beach and there are others nearby.

GALICIA: Comprising the provinces of La Coruña, Lugo, Orense and Pontevedra, Galicia is a mountainous region with large tracts of heathland broken by gorges and fast-flowing rivers. The coastline has many sandy bays, often backed with forests of fir and eucalyptus, and deep fjord-like estuaries (*rías*) which cut into the land at the river-mouths. The dominant building material is granite.

La Coruña (Corunna) is the largest town in this region, and was possibly founded by the Phoenicians. Since then it has enjoyed a tempestuous history. Its most attractive feature is the *Ciudad Vega* on the north spur of the harbour. The famous pilgrimage town of **Santiago de Compostela** is also in the province; for further information, see below under the section on *The Way of St James*. The Roman town of **Lugo** is noted for having one of the finest surviving examples of Roman walls.

Orense first attracted the Romans on account of its therapeutic waters. The 13th-century cathedral was built on the site of one dating from the 6th century.

Pontevedra, the region's fourth provincial capital, is a granite town with arcaded streets and many ancient buildings. Further south is the important port of **Vigo,** the centre of a region of attractive countryside. A good view of the town and the bay can be had from the *Castillo del Castro.*

THE WAY OF ST JAMES: During the Middle Ages, the tomb of St James at Santiago de Compostela was regarded as one of the most holy sites in Christendom and thousands of pilgrims travelled through Spain each year to visit the shrine. This route, the *Way of St James,* was lined with monasteries, religious houses, chapels and hospices to cater for the pilgrims. Many of these buildings still survive, and any traveller following the route today will find it an uplifting introduction to the religious architecture of medieval Spain. The route began in Navarre, at Canfranc or Valcarlos; from there, travelling west, the main stopping places were Pamplona, Santo Domingo de la Calzada, Logroño, Burgos, León, Astorga and Santiago de Compostela. The Saint's feast day, July 25 (the term 'day' is a misnomer since the festival runs for a full week) is celebrated in vigorous style in Santiago de Compostela, and accommodation should be booked well in advance. There are several specialist books on the subject of this and other old pilgrim routes which may be followed, both in Spain and elsewhere in Europe.

NORTH ATLANTIC COASTAL RESORTS: The region's coastline – stretching from the French frontier along the Cantabrian coast to Cap Finisterre, and then southwards to the border with Portugal – has many fine beaches which are as yet largely undiscovered. This is at least partly due to the climate being slightly harsher than in the south of the country. The beaches are mostly of fine sand, often surrounded by cliffs and crags. Much of

Oviedo, Asturias

the hinterland is lush, earning the coast of Asturias the title of Costa Verde. In Galicia the rivers have fjord-like estuaries called *rías.*

Resorts on the North Atlantic Coast: Fuenterrabia, San Sebastián, Orio, Zaraúz, Guetaria, Zumaya, Deva, Motrico, Ondarroa, Lequeitio, Ibarranguelua, Pedernales, Mundaca, Baquio, Gorliz, Plencia, Sopelana, Algorta, Las Arenas, Abanto y Ciervana, Castro Urdiales, Laredo, Isla, Ajo, Somo, Santander, Santa Cruz de Bezana, Liencres, Miengo, Suances, Cobreces, Comillas, San Vicente de la Barquera, Pechón, Colombres, Llanes, Ribadesella, Colunga, Villaviciosa, Gijón, Luanco, Salinas, Cudillero, Luarca, Tapia de Casariego,

Castropol, Ribadeo, Barreiros, Foz, Ceruo, Jove, Vivero, Vicedo, El Barquero, Ortiguerira, Cedeira, Valdovino, San Martin de Covas, El Ferrol del Caudillo, Cabanas, Mino, Sada, Mera, Santa Cruz, Santa Cristina, La Coruña, Cayon, Malpica, Lage, Camarinas, Finisterre, Curcubion, Carnota, Muros, Noya, Puerto del Son, Santa Eugenia de Ribera, Puebla del Caraminal, Rianjo, Villagarcía de Arosa, Villanueva de Arosa, Cambados, El Grove, La Toja, Sangenjo, Poyo, Pontevedra, Marín, Bueu, Cangas de Morrazo, Redondela, Vigo, Nigran, Bayona and La Guardia.

MOUNTAIN RESORTS: The *Cantabrian Range* stretches between the *Cantabrian Corniche* and the *Rías Gallegas*. The highest peaks are the Picos de Europa (2615m/8579ft), favoured by walkers, climbers and wildlife enthusiasts. Parts of the Cantabrian Range are suitable for winter sports. For more information, see the *Ski Resorts* section below.

Navarre & Aragón

These two former medieval Iberian kingdoms lie southwest of the French border, with the Pyrenees to the northeast. The landscape offers spectacular views from the mountains contrasting with the lush valleys of the lower ground.

NAVARRE: The approximate frontiers of the old strategically placed Kingdom of Navarre still survive in this region of dry, dusty uplands and rich, fertile valleys. Both Navarre and Aragón have been largely ignored by visitors, with a few notable exceptions: one such is **Pamplona**, once the capital of the Kingdom of Navarre, and now the regional capital. It is famous for the *Corrida*, the 'running of the bulls', at the festival of *San Fermín* (July). On these days the young men of the town and anyone else who feels sufficiently brave can prove

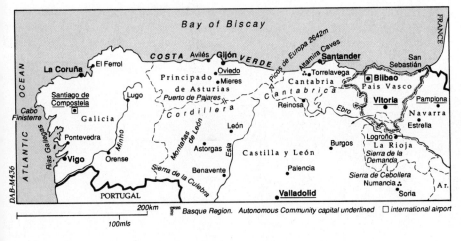

themselves by running in front of a large herd of bulls that virtually stampede through the closed streets of the town. The town was the spiritual home of Ernest Hemingway and is now a very popular tourist attraction. Book early and expect relatively high prices.

ARAGON: Another old Iberian kingdom, Aragón is geographically a fairly featureless region, with many remote plains. The kingdom rose to prominence in the late 15th century. Many of the kings resided at **Zaragoza** (Saragossa), now the regional capital. Like most settlements of any size in Aragón, the town is situated in a *huerta,* a narrow oasis following the course of a river. Zaragoza is a university town, with a medieval cathedral and an excellent museum. In the surrounding countryside there are several areas noted for their wine production, such as **Borja** and **Cariñena,** and several castles. **Huesca,** situated in the foothills of the Pyrenees, is an important market town. There are several attractions within easy reach, including the *Parque Nacional de Ordesa,* excellent walking and climbing country; the popular summer holiday resort of **Arguis** in the *Puerto de Monrepós* region; the spa town of **Balneario de Panticosa;** and the high-altitude resort and frontier town of **Canfranc.**

The third and southernmost province of Aragón is **Teruel.** The provincial capital is on a hill surrounded by the gorges of the Rio Turia. It has a very strong Moorish influence (the last mosque was not closed until ten years after the end of the Reconquista in 1492), and there are several architectural survivals from its Islamic period. Nearby is the small episcopal city of **Sergobe,** spectacularly situated between two castle-crowned hills. **THE PYRENEES:** There are several mountain resorts in Navarre and Aragón, some of which offer excellent skiing, sometimes for up to six months of the year. For more information, see the *Ski Resorts* section below.

Valencia/Murcia

Including the **Costa del Azahar,** the **Costa Blanca** and the **Costa Calida.**
VALENCIA: The city of Valencia is famous for its orange groves and is a popular tourist resort with two main beaches, both a short bus ride from the town. It has a 13th-century church which also claims possession of the Holy Grail. The chief attraction is the *Fallas* (March 19), a festival culminating in the burning of papier-mâché effigies satirising famous Spanish figures. There is also a magnificent fireworks display.
THE COSTA DEL AZAHAR: This extends from Vinaroz along the coast of Castellón province and the Gulf of Valencia to beyond Denia. The region has expansive beaches, but its most outstanding feature is, perhaps, the ancient fortress town of **Peñiscola,** a dramatic sight when viewed from a distance. Other places of interest are the ruined castle of **Chisvert,** inland from Peñiscola; the 16th-century *Torre del Rey* at **Oropesa;** and the Carmelite monastery at the *Desierto de las Palmas.* North of Valencia is the attractive provincial capital of Castellón, **Castellón de la Plana.** It is situated on a fertile plain, and is the centre of a thriving trade in citrus fruits.
Resorts along the Costa del Azahar: Vinaroz, Benicarlo, Peñiscola, Alcosebre, Oropesa, Benicasim, Valencia, Cullera, Gandia and Oliva.
ALICANTE & THE COSTA BLANCA: Further south along the coast is **Alicante,** situated centrally on the

Costa Blanca (the White Coast). The town is dominated by the vast Moorish castle of *Santa Barbara,* which offers superb views of the city. Excursions from Alicante include a run inland to **Guadalest,** a village perched like an eagle's eyrie high in the mountains and accessible in the last stages only by donkey or on foot. Also of great interest are several historical sites, including castles at **Elda** and **Villena,** and **Elche,** where there is a forest of over a million palm trees, *Botanical Gardens* and the *Basilica,* where the medieval 'Mystery' passion play takes place every August.
The region of the **Costa Blanca** has expanded rapidly in recent years and has developed most of the coastal towns between the Peñón de Ifach and Alicante as tourist resorts. Being further south, temperatures are hotter than the Costa Brava and in general the beaches are larger, particularly the beautiful twin bays of **Benidorm,** the largest and most popular resort. All resorts are very busy during the summer.
One of the many places to visit here is the *Peñón de Ifach* (Ifach Rock), 5km (3 miles) off the main road past the walled town of **Calpe.** 1.5km (1 mile) further on is the 300m (1000ft) monolith of *Peñón,* surrounded by legend and accessible through a tunnel.
Resorts on the Costa Blanca: Denia, Javea, Moraira, Calpe, Benidorm, Villajoyosa, Alicante, Los Arenales del Sol, Santa Pola, Guardamar del Segura, Torrevieja, Campoamor, Santiago de la Ribera, La Manga del Mar Menor, Puerto de Mazarrón and Aguilas.
MURCIA & THE COSTA CALIDA: This region lies to the south of Valencia and Alicante and is thinly populated except in the areas around the river valleys. The mountains of Andalucía reach right down to the sea. **Murcia,** the town, has both a university and a cathedral. In summer the temperatures can be almost unbearably hot. The most impressive festivals are in Holy Week, and during the spring when there is a 'Battle of the Flowers'. The coastal region of Murcia, the **Costa** (which is often regarded as being part of the Costa Blanca), has a few resorts. These include *Mar Menor, La Unión, Carboneras, Puerto de Mazarrón, Aguilas* and the area's main coastal town, **Cartagena,** founded, as its name implies, by the Carthaginians in 221BC. The museum here has a good collection of Roman and pre-Roman artefacts.

Catalonia

Including the **Costa Brava** and the **Costa Dorada.**
Catalonia is a hilly coastal region in Spain's northwest

corner, bordering France. It has an ancient culture distinct from those of neighbouring regions and many of the inhabitants speak Catalan, a Romance language. The environs of Barcelona are Spain's industrial and commercial powerhouse, but inland and up the coast, the rocky, forested landscape is largely unspoilt and Catalonia attracts many tourists, mainly to seaside resorts on the Costa Brava and Costa Dorada. Despite its energetic bustle, tourists are also drawn to Barcelona itself, a city of great charm, many fine buildings and a vibrant nightlife. The region is also an important centre for the production of olive oil, wine, almonds and fruit. **Note:** The names of cities and sites described in this section are given in Catalan. Where the Spanish (Castilian) name is very different it appears in brackets after the Catalan version.
BARCELONA: This, the second-largest city in the country, is Spain's major commercial and industrial centre and one of the most important Mediterranean ports. The *Barri Gótic* (old town) near the railway station has a museum with a fine collection of Picasso's early sketches. The old cathedral, the *Episcopal Palace,* the

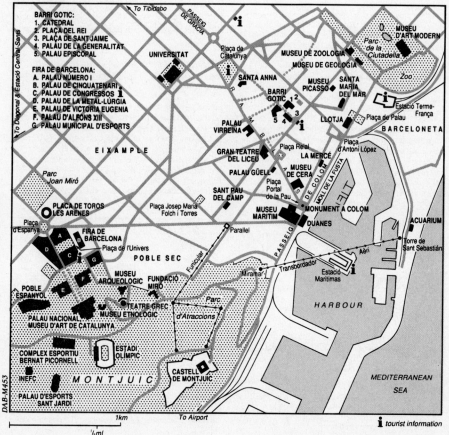

IF THE QUESTION IS

Where?

THE ANSWER IS

Catalonia

Catalunya

Catalonia Tourist Board
Passeig de Gràcia 112, 2n.
Tel. 34-3-415 16 17*. Fax 34-3-415 14 34.
08008 **BARCELONA**. SPAIN

Hermandad de las Palmas, Almonte, Huelva

Palau de la Generalitat and the *Plaça del Rei* have architecture to rival the Baroque splendours of central Europe. The *Ramblas,* originally the site of the ancient city walls, is now the major promenade area of the city, where one goes to see and be seen. Proceeding from the port towards *Plaça Catalunya* (the principal square), the atmosphere becomes more sophisticated. The Ramblas are home to food, flower and bird markets and are lined by bookstalls. Beyond Plaça Catalunya, the *Eixample* (Ensanche), whose name means extension, boasts a wealth of Art Nouveau and Art Deco architecture. *Gràcia* is a particularly attractive neighbourhood. Museums worth visiting include the *Picasso Museum,* the *Museum of Catalan Art,* the *Maritime Museum,* the *Peldralbes Monastery* housing a Thyssen collection and the *Zoological Museum.* Like most towns and cities in Catalonia, Barcelona is famous for its excellent Romanesque art; and of course it contains the most famous examples of the work of the visionary Catalan architect, Antonio Gaudí (see below). The funicular to Tibidabo, the highest of the peaks that enclose Barcelona, and the cable car to *Montjuic* in the southern suburbs,

Convento de las Duenãs, Salamanca

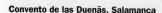

offer spectacular views over the city. Fun fairs are located on both peaks.
Gaudí was born in the 1850s, and began work at the age of 32 on what is now one of the world's most extraordinary churches, the *Sagrada Familia* in Barcelona. Statues portraying biblical scenes are sculpted into the walls of the building, surrounded by stone palm leaves, strange viney branches and fungus-like vegetation. George Orwell described the church as 'one of the most hideous buildings in the world', and although unfinished (Gaudí died while work was still in progress) the people of Barcelona are intensely proud of it. Now a century old, construction still continues. Recent structures added to Gaudí's own work have provoked lively local debate. Other examples of his work are the *Casa Battlló* (with mask-shaped balconies and an undulating blue roof) and the *Casa Mila* (an apartment block taking the form of a dragon perched precariously on a melting slab of cheese). Overlooking the city and the port, *Parc Güell* was conceived as a garden city. It was never completed, but the park features exquisite tiled pavilions and fountains. The walkways stand on curious

sculpted pillars, and are flanked by throne-like stone seats.
THE COSTA BRAVA: This coast, which begins 65km (40 miles) northeast of Barcelona, is a stretch of spectacular pine-clad rocky coastline interspersed with fine sandy bays, and is one of the most famous resort areas in the country. Some places (such as Tossa de Mar) remain relatively unspoilt by the massive influx of holidaymakers and retain the small-town flavour of the original town; others (such as Lloret de Mar), have an intensely developed tourist industry. Summer is very crowded everywhere, but with persistence and a short walk relatively isolated beaches can be found. Coastal ferries operate between most resorts on the Costa Brava. Although most visitors come to the Costa Brava for a relaxing holiday of sun and sea rather than serious sightseeing, there are nevertheless certain points of cultural interest in the area. These include **Girona** (Gerona), one of Catalonia's oldest cities with a well-preserved *Jewish quarter;* **Figueres,** home of the *Salvador Dali Museum;* **Cadaquès,** an enchanting fishing village nestling on the coast about 30 minutes bus drive from Figueres, where Dali lived for many years; and **Empúries** (Ampurias) with its impressive Graeco-Roman remains.
Resorts on the Costa Brava: Roses, San Pedro Pescador, San Martín d'Empúries, La Escala, Estartit, Bagur, Palafrugell, Palamós, Platja d'Aro, S'Agaro, Sant Feliú de Guixols (the market is worth a visit), Tossa de Mar, Lloret de Mar and Blanes.
THE COSTA DORADA: This extends south from Barcelona to Tarragona, with fine sandy beaches that are often separated by the road or railway from the interior. The lively and cosmopolitan resort town of **Sitges** on the Costa Dorada has several museums, in particular the *Cav-Ferrat* which houses two paintings by El Greco. Off the A2 motorway towards Lleida are two monasteries, the Cistercian *Monastery of Santa Cruz* dating back to 1159 and, near the ancient medieval town of **Montblanc,** the *Santa María* at **Poblet. Lleida** (Lérida) itself is the capital of a province that includes the wildest, most mountainous area of the Pyrénées. Its wealth of scenery and monuments make it one of the most interesting and attractive areas in Spain. The coastal city of **Tarragona** is one of the finest examples of a Roman city in existence, virtually built on the Roman plan. The amphitheatre overlooking the sea is well preserved and atmospheric; in addition there is an aqueduct. Just along the coast, **Salou** boasts the *Port-Aventura Theme Park,* inaugurated in spring 1995. The town of **Manresa** has a 14th-century church noted for its stained glass. 60km (37 miles) northwest of Barcelona is **Montserrat,** the site of a world-famous monastery, the legendary home of the Holy Grail, and the actual home of the famous Black Madonna. Founded in 880, it is set in the 'serrated mountain' landscape 1135m (3725ft) above the *Llobregat River* valley. There are inspiring views from the monastery and on the mountain walk from the *Hermitage of San Jeronimo.*
Resorts on the Costa Dorada: Calella de la Costa, Arenys de Mar, Castelldefels, Sitges, Calafell, Comarruga, Torredembarra, Tarragona, Salou, Cambrils, Miami Playa, Hospital del Infante and San Carlos de la Rapita.
THE PYRENEES: There are several mountain resorts in Catalonia, some of which offer excellent skiing for up to six months of the year. For more information, see the *Ski Resorts* section below.

Ski Resorts

Spain offers many possibilities for a winter sports holiday, and in many regions (particularly in the Penibetic Chain) there is a unique opportunity to combine winter sports with coastal sunshine. There are many natural ski-runs and many winter resorts, equipped with modern facilities, all blessed with the promise of warm sun and blue skies. There is also a wide range of hotels, inns and refuges from which to choose.
There are five main skiing regions in Spain; these are the Pyrenean Range, the Cantabrian Range, the Iberian Chain, the Central Chain and the Penibetic Chain. These ranges have diverse characteristics, and all are attractive for mountaineering in general and in particular for winter sports. A brief description of these regions, together with a list of major resorts, is given below. More detailed information may be found by consulting the many booklets and leaflets published or distributed by the Spanish National Tourist Office, in particular the trilingual (English-Spanish-French) book entitled *Guide to Winter & Mountain Resorts* and the English-language booklet *Winter Sports – Spain.* These publications provide invaluable information on individual resorts, accommodation available, transport, etc in greater detail than is possible here.
In the following section, each resort is listed in **bold,**

Each year, 60 million people come to get to know Spain.

But only a few succeed.

Only by travelling with **RACC TRAVEL** can one get to know Spain as well as the Spaniards. Or better. Because it suggests exclusive, personalized itineraries, so that its clients don´t just stick with the typical visits, but get to know the real Spain and its fantastic possibilities for tourism.
RACC TRAVEL organizes group travel and conventions, and specializes in the most important motor events (F1, rallies, motorcycle racing...), because **RACC** is the largest motoring club in Spain.
It also organizes complete itineraries to travel around Spain and the "Get to know Catalonia by car" programme. So that its clients know where to go, how to get there and what to visit, and have all their hotel rooms booked.
Contact **RACC TRAVEL** and check out all the possibilites it offers. You'll discover another way of travelling. And get to know Spain better than anyone.

RACC TRAVEL Balmes,49 3° Tel. 3-454 80 08 - Fax.3-451 56 98   08007 - BARCELONA.

followed by the province in which it is situated. The nearest airport, the range of altitudes and the area of snow are given afterwards in *italics.*

Most resorts offer rental or sale of equipment; nightclub; bars; hospital; nursery; a Catholic church; and accommodation either at the resort or within 30km (19 miles). Some offer facilities such as a heated pool; tennis; mini-golf; riding; skeet shooting and bowling. All have ski lifts (apart from the Nordic skiing centres), many have baby lifts and chair lifts, and some also have cabin lifts, cable cars or funiculars. Further details may be found by consulting either of the publications referred to above.

THE PYRENEAN RANGE: A region of high valleys allowing steep descents, with most of the resorts concentrated in the Catalonian area. The Aragónese Pyrenees contain the highest altitudes in the range; some are over 3400m (11,155ft). The Navarran Pyrenees have no mountain resorts, and are notable for their gentle slopes and superb forests.

Catalonian Pyrenees

Vallter 2000, Girona. *Airport:* Girona 90km (55 miles). Barcelona 150km (93 miles). *Alt:* 2000-2650m (6560-8400ft). *Snow area:* 50 sq km (20 sq miles).

Nuria, Girona. *Airport:* Girona 110km (68 miles). Barcelona 135km (84 miles). *Alt:* 1960-2920m (6430-9580ft). *Snow area:* 79 sq km (30 sq miles).

La Molina-Supermolina, Girona. *Airport:* Girona 140km (87 miles). Barcelona 160km (99 miles). *Alt:* 1436-2540m (4711-8333ft). *Snow area:* 70 sq km (27 sq miles).

Masella, Girona. *Airport:* Girona 160km (99 miles). Barcelona 175km (108 miles). *Alt:* 1600-2530m (5249-8300ft). *Snow area:* 43 sq km (16 sq miles).

Rasos de Peguera, Barcelona. *Airport:* Barcelona 135km (83 miles). *Alt:* 1800-2050m (5903-6725ft). *Snow area:* 15 sq km (6 sq miles).

Port de Comte, Lleida. *Airport:* Barcelona 160km (99 miles). *Alt:* 1700-2380m (5577-7808ft). *Snow area:* 80 sq km (30 sq miles).

San Juan de l'Erm, Lleida (Nordic skiing). *Airport:* Cerdaña (light aircraft). *Alt:* 1600-2150m (5249-7053ft). *Snow area:* 40 sq km (15 sq miles).

Lles, Lleida (Nordic skiing). *Airport:* Cerdaña (light aircraft). *Alt:* 1900-2300m (6233-7545ft). *Snow area:* 30 sq km (11 sq miles).

Llessúy, Lleida. *Airport:* Barcelona 258km (160 miles). *Alt:* 1280-2900m (4199-9514ft). *Snow area:* 30 sq km (11 sq miles).

Super Espot, Lleida. *Airport:* Barcelona 270km (167 miles). *Alt:* 1480-2320m (4855-7611ft).

Baqueira Beret, Lleida (the largest resort). *Airport:* Barcelona 309km (192 miles). *Alt:* 1520-2470m (4986-8103ft). *Snow area:* 40 sq km (15 sq miles).

Tuca-Betrén, Lleida. *Airport:* Barcelona 295km (183 miles). *Alt:* 1050-2250m (3444-6381ft). *Snow area:* 15 sq km (5 sq miles).

Aragónese Pyrenees

Cerler, Huesca. *Airport:* Zaragoza 227km (141 miles). Barcelona 300km (186 miles). *Alt:* 1500-2850m (4921-1770ft). *Snow area:* 24 sq km (9 sq miles).

Panticosa, Huesca. *Airport:* Zaragoza 168km (104 miles). *Alt:* 1165-2100m (3822-6889ft).

El Formigal, Huesca. *Airport:* Zaragoza 167km (103 miles). *Alt:* 1500-2350m (4921-7709ft). *Snow area:* 38 sq km (14 sq miles).

Candanchú, Huesca. *Airport:* Zaragoza 180km (111 miles). *Alt:* 1450-2400m (4757-7874ft). *Snow area:* 18 sq km (7 sq miles).

Astún, Huesca. *Airport:* Zaragoza 180km (111 miles). *Alt:* 1420-2400m (4658-7874ft). *Snow area:* 40 sq km (15 sq miles).

In addition to the above-mentioned resorts, there are throughout the Pyrenees other places which are highly suitable for skiing in which modern facilities will soon be installed to make best use of their excellent natural advantages. Enquire at the Spanish National Tourist Office for up-to-date details of the facilities available. Of these, the main resorts/areas are:

Tossa de Das, Barcelona; *Camprodon,* Girona; *Valle de Farreras,* Lleida; *Bosost,* Lleida; *La Maladeta,* Huesca; *Val de Broto,* Huesca; *Bielsa,* Huesca; *Isaba,* Navarra; and *Burguete,* Navarra.

THE CANTABRIAN RANGE: Situated in the north of the country, the Cantabrian Range drops sharply towards the Atlantic, but falls away more gently to the south. It is more rugged at its eastern end than in Galicia and has a number of important ski centres. The Enol Lakes are also a major attraction.

Alto Campo, Santander. *Airport:* Cantabria 99km (61 miles). *Alt:* 1515-2150m (4970-7053ft). *Snow area:* 20 sq km (7 sq miles).

Valgrande-Pajares, Asturias & León. *Airport:* Oviedo 100km (62 miles). *Alt:* 1350-1834m (4429-6017ft). *Snow area:* 75 sq km (28 sq miles).

San Isidro, León & Asturias. *Airport:* Oviedo 70km (43 miles). *Alt:* 1500-1955m (4921-6414ft). *Snow area:* 60 sq km (23 sq miles).

Cabeza de Manzaneda, Orense. *Airport:* Santiago de Compostela 190km (118 miles). *Alt:* 1450-1760m (4757-5774ft). *Snow area:* 20 sq km (7 sq miles).

Other winter sports centres in this region include *Riaño-Maraña* on the slopes of Mampodre; *San Emiliano* in the northwestern part of the region; and *Leitariegos* in the western part of the range.

IBERIAN SYSTEM: This extends northwest from the Demanda Range in Burgos to the Alcaraz Range on the Mediterranean. Many of the slopes are pine-forested. The highest point in the system is the Moncayo summit at 2313m (7588ft).

Valdezcaray, Logroño. *Airport*: Villafía (Burgos) for light aircraft 100km (62 miles). *Alt:* 1550-1860m (5085-2821ft). *Snow area*: 8 sq km (3 sq miles).

Lunada-Espinosa, Burgos. *Airport*: Villafía (Burgos) for light aircraft 100km (62 miles).

Valle del Sol, Burgos. *Airport*: Villafía (Burgos) for light aircraft 100km (62 miles). *Alt:* 1500-1700m (4921-5577ft). *Snow area:* 15 sq km (5 sq miles).

Sierra de Gudar, Teruel. *Airport:* Valencia 135 km (83 miles). *Alt:* 1600-2025m (5249-6643ft). *Snow area:* 15 sq km (5 sq miles).

CENTRAL SYSTEM: This is also known as the Carpetan Range and runs from northeast to southwest dividing the central Meseta into two parts, although there are several passes which allow lines of communication. The Guadarrama and Gredos ranges are found within this system. The highest peak rises to over 2500m (8202ft). The region is within easy reach of Madrid.

La Pinilla, Segovia. *Airport:* Madrid 112km (69 miles). *Alt:* 1500-2270m (4921-7447ft). *Snow area:* 15 sq km (5 sq miles).

Valcotos, Madrid. *Airport:* Madrid 82km (50 miles). *Alt:* 1785-2270m (5856-7447ft). *Snow area:* 30 sq km (11 sq miles).

Valdesqui, Madrid. *Airport:* Madrid 85km (52 miles). *Alt:* 1876-2260m (6154-7414ft). *Snow area:* 20 sq km (7 sq miles).

Puerto de Navacerrada, Madrid. *Airport:* 75km (46 miles). *Alt:* 1700-2200m (5577-7217ft). *Snow area:* 42 sq km (16 sq miles).

PENIBETIC SYSTEM: This is in the south of the country, and the range is broken by a fault line dividing it into a northern and a southern block. The southern block contains the main skiing areas, and also the highest peaks in the Spanish mainland (Sierra Nevada), reaching to over 3440m. The effect of river erosion has opened deep gorges leading to meadows and beaches on the Mediterranean coast. Some of the ski runs are less than 35km (21 miles) from the famous city of Granada.

Solynieve, Granada. *Airport:* Granada 34km (21 miles). *Alt:* 2100-3470m (6889-11384ft). *Snow area:* 40 sq km (10 sq miles).

POPULAR ITINERARIES: 5-day: (a) Madrid–Toledo–Aranjuez–Alcalá de Henares–Guadalajara–Segovia–Avila–San Lorenzo del Escorial–Madrid. (b) Málaga–Marbella–Algeciras–Cádiz–Coto de Doñana–Jerez–Aracena–Seville–Málaga. (c) San Sebastián–Bilbao–Santander–Santillana del Mar–San Vicente–Picos de Europa–Oviedo.

7-day: (a) Seville–Cordoba–Ubeda–Baeza–Jaén–Granada–Sierra Nevada–Almería. (b) Seville–Badajoz–Mérida–Cáceres–Salamanca–Zamora–Astorga–León–Oviedo–Gijón. (c) Madrid–Alcalá de Henares–Guadalajara–Cuenca–Teruel–Albacete–Cuidad Real–Toledo–Aranjuez–Madrid. (d) Madrid–San Lorenzo del Escorial–Avila–Segovia–Valladolid–Salamanca–Plasencia–Cáceres–Badajoz–Trujillo–Madrid. (e) Figueres–Empúries–Girona–Cadaquès–Barcelona–Montserrat–Sitges–Tarragona. (f) Valcarlos–Pamplona–Santo Domingo de la Calzada–Logroño–Burgos/León–Astorga–Santiago de Compostela.

SOCIAL PROFILE

FOOD & DRINK: Eating out in Spain is often cheap and meals are substantial rather than gourmet. One of the best ways to sample Spanish food is to try *tapas,* or snacks, which are served at any time of day in local bars. These range from cheese and olives to squid or meat delicacies, and are priced accordingly. Many of the specialities of Spanish cuisine are based on seafood, although regional specialities are easier to find inland than along the coast. In the northern Basque provinces, there is cod *vizcaina* or cod *pil-pil; angulas,* the tasty baby eels from Aguinaga; bream and squid. Asturias has its bean soup, *fabada,* cheeses and the best cider in Spain, and in Galicia there are shellfish, especially good in casseroles, and a number of regional seafood dishes such as *hake à la Gallega.*

In the eastern regions the *paella* has a well-deserved reputation. It can be prepared in many ways, based on meat or seafood. Catalonia offers, among its outstanding specialities, lobster Catalan, *butifarra* sausage stewed with beans, and partridge with cabbage. *Pan amb tomaquet,* bread rubbed with olive oil and tomato, is a delicious accompaniment to local ham and cheese.

The Castile area specialises in roast meats, mainly lamb, beef, veal and suckling pig, but there are also stews, sausages, country ham and partridges. Andalucía is noted for its cooking (which shows a strong Arab influence), especially *gazpacho,* a delicious cold vegetable soup, a variety of fried fish including fresh anchovies, *jabugo* ham from Huelva and many dishes based on the fish which the coast provides in such abundance. Restaurants are classified by the Government and many offer tourist menus *(menu del día).* Restaurants and cafés have table service.

Drink: Spain is essentially a wine-drinking country, with sherry being one of the principal export products. Its English name is the anglicised version of the producing town Jerez (pronounced *kherez),* from which the wine was first shipped to England. Today, Britain buys about 75% of all sherry exports. There are four main types: *fino* (very pale and very dry), *amontillado* (dry, richer in body and darker in colour), *oloroso* (medium, full-bodied, fragrant and golden) and *dulce* (sweet). Sanlúcar de Barrameda and Puerto de Santa María are other towns famous for their sherry and well-worth visiting. Tourists are able to visit one of the *bodegas* (above-ground wine stores) in Jerez. In the Basque Country a favourite is *chacolí,* a 'green' wine, slightly sparkling and a little sour, rather than dry.

The principal table wines are the *riojas* and *valdepenas,* named after the regions in which they are produced. In general, *rioja,* from the region around Logroño in the northeast, resembles the French Bordeaux, though it is less delicate. *Valdepenas* is a rougher wine, but pleasant and hearty. It will be found at its best in the region where it is grown, midway between Madrid and Cordóba. In Catalonia the *ampurdán* and *perelada* wines tend to be heavy and those that are not rather sweet are harsh, with the exception of the magnificent full-bodied Burgundy-type *penedés* wines. Alicante wine, dry and strong, is really a light aperitif. Nearby, the Murcia region produces excellent wine. Often it makes a pleasant change to try the unbottled wines of the house *(vino de la casa).* It is much cheaper than the bottled wines and even in small places is usually good. Similarly inexpensive supermarket wine is very acceptable. Among the many brands of sparkling wines known locally as *cava,* the most popular are *Codorniú* and *Freixenet,* dry or semi-dry. The majority of Spanish sparkling wines are sweet and fruity.

Spanish brandy is as different from French as Scotch whisky is from Irish. It is relatively cheap and pleasant, although most brandy drinkers find it a little sweet.

Spain has several good mineral waters. A popular brand is *Lanjarón* which comes from the town of the same name. It can be still or fizzy. *Vichy Catalan* is almost exactly like French Vichy. *Malavella* is slightly effervescent and *Font Vella* is still. Cocktail lounges have table and/or counter service. There are no licensing hours.

NIGHTLIFE: Spaniards often start the evening with *el paseo,* a leisurely stroll through the main streets, wearing their most fashionable clothes. A café terrace is an excellent vantage point to observe this tradition, or enjoy street theatre in the larger cities. The atmosphere is especially vibrant at fiesta time, or when the local football team has won, when celebrations are marked by a cacophony of car horns, firecrackers and a sea of flags and team regalia. *Tapas* bars offer delicious snacks in a relaxed, enjoyable setting and it is fun to try out several bars in one night. The nightclubs of Ibiza, Barcelona and Madrid have attracted the attention of the international media, but the variety on offer caters for most tastes. Things work up to *la marcha* (good fun) relatively late and it is possible to dance literally until dawn. Flamenco or other regional dancing displays provide an alternative for those who prefer to watch dancing.

SHOPPING: In Spain the shopper can find items of high quality at a fair price, not only in the cities, but in the small towns as well. In Madrid the Rastro Market is recommended, particularly Sunday. Half of the market takes place in the open air and half in more permanent galleries, and has a character all its own. Catalonian textiles are world famous and there are mills throughout the region. Spanish leather goods are prized throughout the world, offering high-fashion originals at reasonable prices. Of note are the suede coats and jackets. The furriers of Spain are also outstanding. In general, all leather goods, particularly those of Andalucía, combine excellent craftsmanship with high-quality design. Fine, handcrafted wooden furniture is one of the outstanding products. Valencia is especially important in this field, and has a yearly international furniture fair. Alicante is

Mojacar, Almerica

an important centre for toy manufacturing. Shoe manufacturing is also of an especially high quality; the production centres are in Alicante and the Balearics. Fine rugs and carpets are made in Cáceres, Granada

Cedeira, La Coruña

and Murcia. The numerous excellent sherries, wines and spirits produced in Spain make good souvenirs to take home.

Shopping hours: 0930/1000-1300/1330 and 1630/1730-1930/2000 Monday to Saturday. Department stores open 0930/1000-2000 Monday to Saturday.

SPORTS: There are excellent facilities for **tennis**, **sailing**, **racing** and other sports in most major cities and throughout the islands. Climatic conditions in southern Spain make outdoor sporting activities possible throughout the year. **Golf** is becoming increasingly popular; at present Spain has nearly 200 golf courses. **Watersports:** Water-skiing, swimming, sailing, sea fishing and windsurfing facilities can be found at all seaside resorts on the Costa del Sol, Costa Brava and Costa Blanca. These can be busy in the summer months. Windsurfing world championships are held in Tarifa, near Cádiz. **Winter sports:** Spain offers ideal conditions for winter sports and climbing; see the *Ski Resorts* section above for further information. **Spectator sports:** A typical and spectacular sport is *pelota vasca*, or *jai-alai*. In the principal northern Spanish cities are courts where there are daily matches from October to June. In the towns and cities of the Basque regions the game is played in summer as well. **Football** is probably the most popular spectator sport, with clubs such as Real Madrid and Barcelona being among the most famous in the world; first-class matches are usually played Sunday. International matches are also staged from time to time. **Horseracing:** There is a magnificent track in Madrid with meetings in the autumn and spring; there is racing in San Sebastián in the summer and in Seville in winter. Palma de Mallorca has a track for trotting races. **SPECIAL EVENTS:** Folklore is very much alive and there is always some form of folk festival occurring. It is almost impossible for a visitor to be anywhere in the country for more than a fortnight without something taking place. The Ministry of Tourism produces a booklet listing and describing Spain's many national, regional and international feasts and festivals, of which there are over 3000 each year. Fiestas, Saints' Days, *Romerías* (picnics to religious shrines) and *Verbenas* (night festivals on the eve of religious holidays) are all celebrated with great spirit and energy. 'Holy Week' is probably the best time of year to visit for celebrations and it is then that the individuality of each region's style of pageantry is best revealed. For further information contact the Spanish National Tourist Office. The following is a list of some of the more notable *fiestas* and other events of interest to the visitor: **Apr 1-Jul 15 '95** *El Legado Andalusí (exhibitions on the Arab influence on Spanish civilisation)*, Grenada, Seville and other main cities of Andalucia. **Apr 9-16** *Holy Week*, Seville and throughout Spain. **Apr 25-30** *April Fair*, Seville. **Apr 22-24** *Moors and Christians* (processions, displays and dancing), Alcoy, Alicante. **May 7-14** *Horse Fair*, Jerez. **Jun 3-5** *Virgin of El Rocío Fiesta*, El Rocío. **Jul 6-14** *Running of the Bulls*, Pamplona. **Jul 25** *St James Festival*, La Coruña, Santiago de Compostela. **Aug** *International Festival* (month-long celebrations), Santander. **Sep 24** *La Merced Festival*, Barcelona. **Oct 27-29** *The Saffron Festival*, Consuegra, Toledo. **Feb/Mar '96** *Carnival*, throughout Spain. **Mar 12-19** *Fallas Festival*, Valencia.

Note: See also the list of individual town festivals for 1995/96 given in the *Public Holidays* section above.

SOCIAL CONVENTIONS: Spanish life has undergone rapid change in recent years and many of the stricter religious customs are giving way to more modern ways, particularly in the cities and among women. Nonetheless, many old customs, manners and traditions have not faded and hospitality, chivalry and courtesy remain important. Handshaking is the customary form of greeting. Normal social courtesies should be observed when visiting someone's home. If invited to a private home, a small gift is appreciated. Flowers are only sent for special celebrations. Conservative casual wear is widely acceptable. Some hotels and restaurants encourage men to wear jackets. Black tie is only necessary for very formal occasions and is usually specified if required. Outside resorts, scanty beachwear should be confined to beach or poolside. Smoking is widely accepted. **Tipping:** Service charges and taxes are usually included in hotel bills, however in addition, a tip should be left for the chambermaid and porters should be tipped per bag. It is also customary to leave a tip for the waiter. Restaurants include service in the bill and a tip is discretionary. In cafés and bars it is usual to leave loose change. Tip taxis 2-3% when metered.

BUSINESS PROFILE

ECONOMY: Spain is a major industrialised European economy with a large agricultural sector. Until 1975, under the Franco regime, the Spanish economy developed almost in isolation, protected from foreign competition by tight import controls and high tariffs, and evolved from an essentially agrarian economy to an industrial one. Spain joined the European Community in 1986, and the transition, which was widely expected to be very difficult, has actually passed off exceptionally well. Despite the decline of many of its industries, such as shipbuilding, steel and textiles – all of which were badly hit during the world recession – Spain achieved the highest average growth rate in the Community during the 1980s. Inflation, which threatened at one point to veer out of control, has been tamed especially since the Peseta was tied to the European Monetary System. Unemployment, however, has remained stubbornly high. Spain's economy ranks eighth in the world according to its GNP. The agricultural sector produces cereals, vegetables, citrus fruit, olive oil and wine: EU investment and modernisation have fostered a vast improvement in efficiency. The processed foods industry has expanded rapidly. The fishing fleet, once among the world's largest, has shrunk although it remains important. Energy requirements are met by indigenous coal and natural gas, imported oil (mostly from Algeria) and a sizeable nuclear power programme. In the manufacturing sector, the decline of older industries has been offset by rapid expansion in chemicals, electronics, information technology and industrial design. Tourism also contributes substantially to the economy. The EU countries, the USA and Japan are the country's main trading partners.

BUSINESS: Business people are generally expected to dress smartly. Although English is widely spoken, an interest in Spanish and an effort on the part of the visitor to speak even a few words will be appreciated. Business cards are exchanged frequently as a matter of courtesy and appointments should be made. **Office hours:** Tend to vary considerably. Business people are advised to check before making calls.

COMMERCIAL INFORMATION: The following organisations can offer advice: Consejo Superior de Cámaras Oficiales de Comercio, Industria y Navegación de Espana, Calle Claudio Coello 19, 1°, 28001 Madrid. Tel: (1) 575 3400. Fax: (1) 435 2392. Telex: 23227; *or* Cámara de Comercio Internacional, Avenida Diagonal 452, 3°, 08006 Barcelona. Tel: (3) 416 9300. Fax: (3) 416 9301.

CONFERENCES/CONVENTIONS: In 1982 the Spanish Convention Bureau was founded as a non-profitmaking organisation, by a confederation of 14 towns for the purpose of helping conference organisers select locations for their events with suitable facilities and back-up services. Most of these towns have dedicated convention centres in addition to the facilities provided by hotels. Seating capacity ranges from 540 in Jaca to 4200 in Palma de Mallorca; Madrid can seat up to 2650 persons. Full details can be obtained from the Spain Convention Bureau, Paseo de la Castellana 99, 28046 Madrid. Tel: (1) 337 8100. Fax: (1) 597 1094.

CLIMATE

Spain's climate varies from temperate in the north to dry and hot in the south. The best months are from April to October, although mid-summer (July to August) can be excessively hot throughout the country except the coastal regions. Madrid is best in late spring or autumn. The central plateau can be bitterly cold in winter.

Required clothing: Light- to medium-weights and rainwear, according to the season.

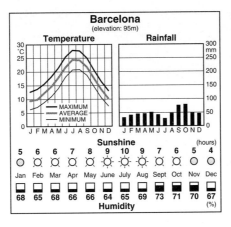

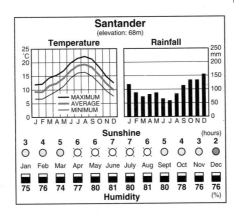

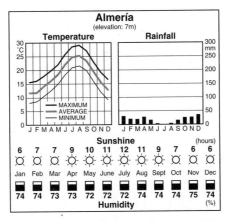

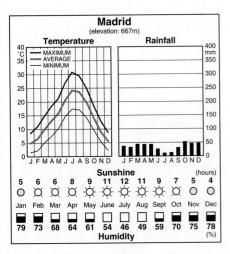

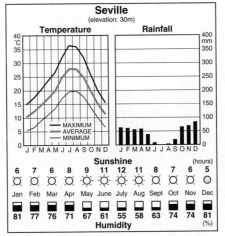

Balearic Islands

Ibiza, Mallorca, Menorca & Formentera

Location: Mediterranean, 240km (150 miles) due east of Valencia on the Spanish coast.

Note: The *Passport/Visa* and *Health* requirements for visiting the Balearic Islands are exactly the same as for visiting mainland Spain, and information may be found by consulting the respective sections above. Likewise, Spanish currency is used, and all the details given in the *Money* section apply.

AREA: Mallorca: 3640 sq km (1405 sq miles). **Menorca:** 700 sq km (270 sq miles). **Ibiza:** 572 sq km (220 sq miles). **Formentera:** 100 sq km (38 sq miles). **Total:** 5014 sq km (1935 sq miles).
POPULATION: 709,138 (1991 estimate).
POPULATION DENSITY: 141.4 per sq km.
CAPITAL: Palma de Mallorca. **Population:** 296,754 (1991).
GEOGRAPHY: Mallorca, Menorca and Ibiza are the main islands in this group, which is situated 193km (120 miles) south of Barcelona off the east coast of Spain. The landscape of these islands is characterised by woodlands, almond trees, fertile plains and magnificent coastlines with numerous sandy coves separated by craggy cliffs. The largest island, **Mallorca** (also known as the 'Isle of Dreams'), has a varied landscape, mountains and valleys, rocky coves and sandy beaches. The main geographical feature is the Sierra del Norte, a mountain range running along the northern coast. The island is covered with fresh green pines, ancient olive and almond trees, which blanket the countryside with blossoms in springtime. **Menorca** has evidence of ancient history and a strong feeling of connection with Britain, due to Admiral Nelson's stay on the island. Both the capital Mahón and the old town of Ciudadela at the north end of the island are set at the apex of deep inlets forming natural harbours. There are many bays and lovely beaches on this unspoilt and relatively quiet island. **Ibiza**, the third-largest island, has a rugged coastline with many fruit orchards and woods. The main town of the same name is situated above a busy harbour. A narrow channel separates Ibiza from **Formentera**, the smallest inhabited island in the group.

TRAVEL

AIR: Approximate flight times: From London to *Palma de Mallorca* is 2 hours 15 minutes, to *Menorca* is 2 hours 20 minutes and to *Ibiza* is 2 hours 20 minutes.
International airports: *Palma de Mallorca (PMI)* (Son San Juan), 9km (5.5 miles) southeast of the city. The airport has a duty-free shop. Coach to the city leaves every 30 minutes 0630-2400. Return is from Iberia Office, Archiduque, Luis Salvador 2. Taxis to the city are also available.
Mahón (MAH), 6km (4 miles) from Mahón. Coach or taxis are available to the town.
Ibiza (IBZ), 8km (5 miles) from the town of Ibiza. Bus to the city leaves hourly from 0730-2230. Taxis are available to the city.
SEA: The following shipping lines run services to the Balearic Islands: *Compañia Transmediterránea* (car ferry) from Alicante, Barcelona, Valencia and inter-

island; *Isnasa-Islena de Navegación; CNAN – Compagnie Nationale Algérienne de Navigation* (car ferry) from Algiers; *DFDS* (car ferry) from Italy. There is also a ferry service from Sète (France) to Palma.
Local: There are regular ferries from Ibiza to Formentera.
RAIL: On Mallorca, narrow-gauge trains run from Palma to Soller five times daily, and to Inca every hour. Inter-Rail passes are not valid. There are no railways on any of the other islands.
ROAD: There are generally good bus services on the islands connecting resorts with main towns. Car and scooter hire is generally available. The steep, narrow inland roads make it difficult for coaches and cars to pass each other (although there are special passing points). It is best to check coach timetables before commencing your journey to avoid difficulties; hotels can often provide this information.

ACCOMMODATION

Establishments of all categories exist in the Balearics, including hotels catering for over 227,000 visitors, chalets, apartments and bungalows. It is possible to rent furnished or unfurnished chalets for the season, although visitors must book in advance due to demand. Rates vary according to season and the standard of accommodation. Numerous 'packages' are available.

RESORTS & EXCURSIONS

Mallorca: Of all the Balearic Islands, Mallorca probably has the most to see and explore, lending itself to a number of half- and full-day excursions (especially to the north of the island), all of which can be made from Palma, and include Mallorca's highlights. The trip from Palma to *Puerto Soller* by special train is highly recommended, as is a trip to the *Formentor Peninsula* at the island's northeastern tip. This area is famous for its pinewoods and secluded coves and for the more inquisitive visitor, there are plenty of half-hidden bays and mountain villages to be discovered.
The island's coastline is 300km (186 miles) long and although some tourist centres have suffered from overdevelopment, there are still numerous beautiful bays and the interior offers scope for many interesting excursions. Apart from the area around Palma, most of the resorts are on the eastern coast. The north is the least developed region; the mountainous terrain ensures that the road is close to the coast in only a few places, and after Puerto Soller it stays well inland until reaching Formentor. Only one side-road manages to fight its way through to *La Colobra* on the coast, and elsewhere, the only access to the sea is by path. The inland plain is noted for its almond trees, of which there are estimated to be over six million. **Palma,** the capital, clearly demonstrates its long association with maritime commerce and its history as a major Mediterranean port. The old city is beautifully situated in the middle of the broad sweep of *Palma Bay*, with modern developments to the east and west. Palma is overlooked by the 14th-century *Castle of Belver*, and other notable buildings include the golden sandstone cathedral *(La Seo)*, the *Archbishop's Palace*, the *Monastery and Church of San Francisco* and the *Montesion Church*. Apart from these major buildings, there are many beautiful palaces and churches in the city, many of which were built from the profits of commerce.
Menorca: The second-largest island lies some 40km (25 miles) northeast of Mallorca. The capital of **Mahón** (on the east coast) is a compact town, with many of the buildings dating back to the period of British occupation, and is best explored on foot. The main attractions include the Town Hall *(Casa Consistorial)*, the *Church of Santa Maria* and the *Church of San Francisco*. Trips are available around the harbour. A good highway links Mahón with the older town of **Ciudadela** (the former capital) on the opposite side of the island. It has a cathedral which dates back, in part, to the 14th century, and also boasts several elegant palacios and medieval churches. Despite the lack of coastal roads, it is nevertheless possible to make a wide variety of excursions from these two main centres, both of which also have several good beaches within easy reach. All over the island the visitor will come across prehistoric dolmens, taulas or talayouts. At **Talah** there is a construction resembling Stonehenge, believed to have been erected 4000 years ago. Menorca has preserved its stock-farming and leather-working traditions, making its economy less dependent on the revenue earned through tourism.
Ibiza: The third-largest in the group and a very popular tourist destination, the island still retains some of its traditional atmosphere. The north and south in particular are still densely wooded with pine, and elsewhere there are many orchards. Large sandy beaches are found south of the capital. **Ibiza Town**, dominated by a medieval fortress, and the *Dalt Vila* (Upper Town), are well worth exploring. To the southwest of the town centre is the *Puig des Molins,* a Punic cemetery. The two other major tourist centres are the coastal towns of *San Antonio Abad* and *Santa Eulalia del Río*.
Formentera: Separated from Ibiza by a 4km (2-mile) channel (hourly boat services operate during the summer), the main settlement is the large village of *San Francisco Javier.* Like the other islands in the group, Formentera has no shortage of pinewoods and sandy beaches, and the pace of life is generally even more relaxed than on neighbouring Ibiza.

SOCIAL PROFILE

FOOD & DRINK: The varied local cuisine includes rabbit, a wide selection of seafood and pork dishes and numerous locally grown fruits and vegetables. Dishes include Mallorcan *ensaimada* (light, sweet pastry roll), Ibizan *flao, graixonere de peix, tumbet, escaldums* of chicken, *sobresada,* Mallorcan soups, and mayonnaise, the famous culinary invention from Menorca. **Drink:** The islands have plenty of good wines and aromatic liqueurs, such as *palo,* which is made from locally grown *St John's bread* (carob beans) and *frigola.* Imported alcoholic and soft drinks are also widely available.
NIGHTLIFE: There are numerous nightclubs and discotheques, some with open-air dancefloors overlooking the sea, floorshows, live bands and orchestras. There are also many cinemas, theatres, concerts and art exhibitions. 18km (11 miles) west of Palma, in Magaluf, there is an elegant casino with a large restaurant. For the latest news on the local nightlife, and details of current events, artistic and cultural, consult the local English-language newspaper *The Bulletin.*
SHOPPING: On the Balearic Islands there is a strong tradition of craftsmanship. Purchases include furniture, hand embroideries, handpainted ceramics, carved olive-wood panels, wrought ironwork, glassware, items made from raffia and palm leaves, handmade shoes, the famous pearls made in Mallorca and other costume jewellery from Menorca.
SPORT: Swimming: It is possible to swim in the sea virtually all year round. Innumerable heated swimming pools are also available. **Sailing:** There are facilities for different forms of sailing in the many sheltered bays. The Balearic Islands are also an arrival point for all Mediterranean yacht cruises. Mooring fees in any of the yacht clubs (Palma de Mallorca, Mahón, Ciudadela, Andraitx and Ibiza) are reasonable. **Watersports:** Facilities for most other water activities are available including water-skiing, windsurfing, parasailing and subaqua. Underwater fishing is especially popular and there are plentiful sea bass, sole, dentex, dorado and sea bream. **Tennis** can be played in the Real Club of Palma and in Ibiza, as well as on the private courts of the major hotels of the different towns. **Golf:** There are golf courses attached to the big hotels, and numerous mini-golf courses on all the islands. **Bowling:** American bowling rinks are available on all the islands.

CLIMATE

The islands enjoy a temperate, Mediterranean climate. The maximum temperatures are not excessive, even in high summer, due to the cooling influence of the sea. The climate during the winter is mild and dry and temperatures below zero are practically unknown.

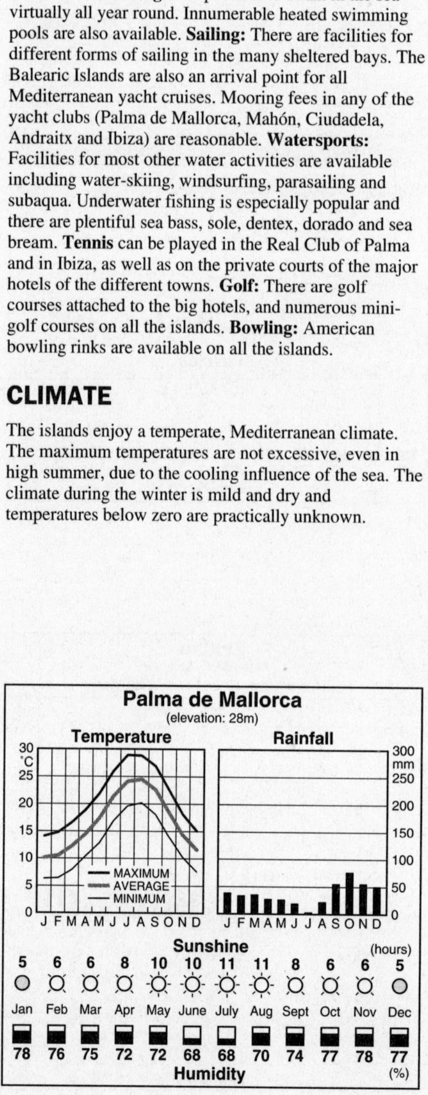
Palma de Mallorca
(elevation: 28m)
Temperature
Rainfall
°C
mm
MAXIMUM
AVERAGE
MINIMUM
J F M A M J J A S O N D
Sunshine
(hours)
5 6 6 8 10 10 11 11 8 6 6 5
Jan Feb Mar Apr May June July Aug Sept Oct Nov Dec
78 76 75 72 72 68 68 70 74 77 78 77
Humidity
(%)

The Canary Islands

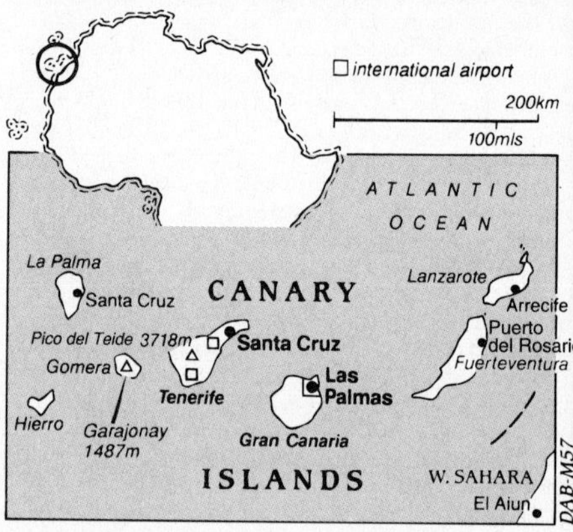
international airport
200km
100mls
ATLANTIC
OCEAN
La Palma
Santa Cruz
CANARY
Lanzarote
Arrecife
Puerto del Rosario
Fuerteventura
Pico del Teide 3718m
Santa Cruz
Gomera
Tenerife
Las Palmas
Hierro
Garajonay 1487m
Gran Canaria
ISLANDS
W. SAHARA
El Aiun
DAB-M57

Location: North Atlantic, west of the African coast.

Note: The *Passport/Visa* and *Health* requirements for visiting the Canary Islands are exactly the same as for visiting mainland Spain, and information may be found by consulting the respective sections above. Likewise, Spanish currency is used, and all the details given in the *Money* section apply.

AREA: 7242 sq km (2796 sq miles).
POPULATION: 1,601,812 (1991).
POPULATION DENSITY: 221.2 per sq km.
CAPITAL: Santa Cruz de Tenerife (Tenerife). **Population:** 200,172 (1991). Las Palmas de Gran Canaria. **Population:** 354,877 (1991 estimate).
GEOGRAPHY: The Canary Islands are situated off the northwest coast of Africa and consist of seven islands which are divided into two provinces. **Las Palmas** comprises the islands of Gran Canaria, Fuerteventura and Lanzarote. **Santa Cruz de Tenerife** is made up of Tenerife, La Palma, Gomera and Hierro. All the islands are of volcanic origin and the climate is subtropical, dry and warm throughout the year. The landscape is varied, and includes imposing peaks and mountain ranges, hidden valleys, volcanic deserts, abrupt rocky cliffs, geometrically perfect craters and attractive forests.
TIME: GMT (GMT + 1 April to September).
BBC World Service and Voice of America frequencies: From time to time these change. See the section *How to Use this Book* for more information.

BBC:				
MHz	**17.70**	**15.07**	**12.09**	**9.410**
Voice of America:				
MHz	**15.20**	**9.670**	**6.040**	**5.995**

TRAVEL

AIR: Approximate flight times: From London to *Las Palmas* is 6 hours 10 minutes (including stopover in Madrid) and to *Tenerife* is 6 hours 10 minutes (including stopover in Madrid). Direct flights from London to either destination take 4 hours 15 minutes.
International airports: *Las Palmas (LPA)*, 22km (14 miles) south of the city on Gran Canaria. Hotel coaches to the city leave every 30 minutes from 0610-0110. Return journey is from Iberia terminal (Hotel Iberia), Avenida Maritima from 0530-2330. Public bus service to the city leaves every 15 minutes, operating a 24-hour service. Return is from the bus station, Parque de San Telmo. Taxis to the city are available, with a surcharge after 2200.
Tenerife-Norte Los Rodeos (TCI), in the north of the island, is 13km (8 miles) from Santa Cruz. Bus service runs every 30 minutes from 0600-2300.
Tenerife-Sur Reina Sofia (TFS), in the south of the island, is used for resorts such as Playa de las Americas. Bus service is scheduled according to flight arrivals.
Local flights run by *Iberia (IB)* link all the islands with the exception of Gomera.
SEA: The majority of cruises stop in the Canaries. Further details are available from the Spanish National Tourist Office, or from Southern Ferries, agents for *Transmediterránea*, 4th Floor, 179 Piccadilly, London W1V 9DB. Tel: (0171) 491 4968. Fax: (0171) 491 3502.

Local: All the islands are linked by regular car and passenger ferries. Day trips to the smaller islands are quickly and easily arranged.
ROAD: There are bus services available. Cars may be hired.

RESORTS & EXCURSIONS

Tenerife is the largest of the islands, and is dominated by a central mountain range and several spectacular valleys. It has a national park, a gigantic natural crater some 19km (12 miles) in diameter and, to the north, the *Pico del Teide,* the highest mountain in Spain. The capital, **Santa Cruz,** is a city rich in architecture (including the *Church of San Francisco)* and museums housing art treasures and historical momentoes of the Canaries. **Puerto de la Cruz** is the most important resort, and also has several buildings which date back to the 17th century. Elsewhere on the island, places to visit include the second city of **La Laguna, La Orotava** (centre of a lush valley), **Güimar, Garachico** (the 'Pearl by the Sea') and **Los Cristianos.**
La Palma has the greatest altitudes in the world in relation to its perimeter, and in its centre is one of the largest craters in the world, the *Caldera de Taburiente,* best viewed from the *La Cumbrecita* look-out point. The island's capital of **Santa Cruz** (not to be confused with Santa Cruz de Tenerife) is also worth exploring with its examples of 16th-century architecture and the *Natural History Museum.* Other places of interest on the island include **Los Llanos de Aridane, Tazacorte, Mazo,** the *Belmaco Cave* and *Cueva Bonita,* a beautiful natural grotto.
Gomera (capital **San Sebastián**) is rich in vegetation and has several white sand beaches. The landscape is rugged, although not as mountainous as other islands in the group, and the most practical method of transportation around the island is often by sea. San Sebastián is interesting for its connections with the explorer Christopher Columbus, who is commemorated by the *Torre del Conde,* an old fortress, now an historic national monument. Gomera is also famous for its *whistling* language, which is used by the islanders to call from mountain to mountain. Other interesting places on the island include **Hermigüa, El Bosque del Cedro,** the uniquely beautiful **Vallehermoso** and the fishing ports of **Playa de Santiago** and **La Rajita.**
Hierro is the most westerly island with **Valverde** as its capital. The island has hardly any beaches, as most of the coastline consists of sheer cliffs; this explains why, of all the islands in the Canaries, Hierro is the only one with an inland capital. The highest point, *Malpaso,* is over 1300m (4265ft). It is an island of unspoilt, rugged, pine-clad countryside, dotted with small villages; **La Restinga** (the most southern point of the Canaries, and hence Spain, and hence – politically if not strictly geographically – of Europe as well), **Taibique, Frontera** and **El Barrio** (the 'suburb'), a collection of settlements close to the main town. Most of the western part of the island is wholly uninhabited.
Gran Canaria is the third-largest island in the archipelago, and has as its capital the city of **Las Palmas** (not to be confused with the smaller island of La Palma). It has been called a 'miniature continent', as plants usually associated with Europe, Africa and America all flourish here. There are splendid beaches, including the *Playa del Inglés* and *Maspalomas* which is nearly 6km (4 miles) long. The capital is a major city with many sites of historical and architectural interest. These include the *Museo de Nestor,* the *Old Town* and the Gothic *Cathedral of Santa Ana.* Columbus lived here for a time before setting out on his voyage of discovery. Other places worth a visit include **Telde, Tejeda, Ingenio** (famous for its crafts), **San Bartolomé de Tirajana** (situated in the crater of a volcano), **Agüimes, Arinaga, San Agustín, Playa del Inglés,** the historic cities of **Galdar** and **Agaete,** the *Tara Caves* and the maritime town of **Sardina del Norte.**
Fuerteventura is the second largest of the Canary Islands and has a large number of fine beaches. The island's capital, **Puerto del Rosario,** is home of about one-third of the island's population, and was built in the late 18th century. Attractions on the island include **Corralejo** in the far north (where straw hats are woven in the traditional manner); the many prehistoric sites; and, to the west, the Norman castle of *Rico Roque,* near **Cotillo. Betancuria,** the ancient capital of the island, houses its most important monument, the *Church of Santa María,* noted for its painted ceiling and murals. One of the most attractive areas is *Jandía* in the south, particularly notable for its beaches. Camels are a common method of transport on this sandy island.
Lanzarote is the most easterly of the Canaries, a dry and fairly flat island which owes its eerie landscape to the activity of volcanoes long since dormant. The volcanic ash and craters have now been turned to the islanders'

advantage in a novel method of vine cultivation. The capital, the port of **Arrecife,** is to be found on the southeast coast and in the area of flattest land on the island, so communications with nearby towns are good. The highest areas are in the north and east. Places of interest include **Teguise** (the old capital), with the *Guanapay Castle* set on a volcanic cone; the oasis-like **Haría; Malpaís de la Corona,** where an immense volcanic cave called *Los Verdes,* 6km (3.5 miles) long, is located; and the nearby *Jameo del Agua* lagoon. The *National Park of Timanfaya* is a spectacular stretch of lava which covers nearly one-third of the island and is awe-inspiring in its majesty and barrenness. The most popular excursion is to the volcanoes on camels.

SOCIAL PROFILE

FOOD & DRINK: The cuisine of the Canaries offers many dishes based on fish, which are usually served with wrinkled potatoes and a special sauce called *mojo picón.* The traditional dishes are watercress soup and the popular *sancocho canario,* a dish based on a fish salad with a hot sauce. Locally grown bananas, tomatoes, avocados and papayas also play an important part in the Canaries cuisine. Corn meal, wheat flour, corn or barley, previously roasted, are eaten instead of bread with certain local dishes. In pastry are found the excellent *tirijalas, bienmesabes, frangollo, bizcochos lustrados,* meat pies, nougats of corn meal and molasses. In the main resorts restaurants offer the full range of international cuisine, as well as local delicacies. Often restaurants cater for the tastes of particular nationalities. **Drink:** Full range of wines, spirits and liqueurs from throughout the world. Spanish wines and spirits are particularly good value and spirits are slightly cheaper than in the UK. Local beers are pilsner-type lagers and, on the whole, rather weak. Local wines are also produced; typical of the island of Hierro are the *quesadillas* as well as the *rapaduras y marquesotes* of La Palma. Other drinks originating from the islands are rum, honey-rum and malmsey wine.
SHOPPING: Besides the excellent duty-free shopping there are numerous local items to tempt the visitor. Craftsmanship is represented mainly by skilled open-

work and embroidery. Pottery, basket-work based on palm leaves, cane and reed and delicate woodcarvings are also popular. Tobacco produced here is excellent and world-famous. Cigars from the Canary Islands are outstanding in quality.
SPORT: The islands provide an ideal setting for all kinds of sport. The warm, clear sea is excellent for underwater **fishing, diving, snorkelling** and **swimming.** Facilities for **water-skiing** and **windsurfing** are also available from beaches or from hotels. There are numerous **tennis** courts (often owned by the hotel or attached to one's apartment), **golf** courses and **riding** stables. **Spectator sports** include *jai-alai,* the stick game (a sort of fencing with long poles), Canaries wrestling and the *garrocha* which is especially practised on the island of La Palma.

CLIMATE

The climate in the northern islands of the Canaries is subtropical; the south of the islands tend to be hotter and drier, although rainfall is generally low throughout the islands.
Required clothing: Lightweight cottons and linens, with light- to medium-weight clothes for winter.

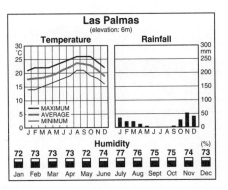

Sri Lanka

150km
100mls

INDIA

Palk Strait

Jaffna
Rameswaram
Palk Bay
Adam's Bridge
Mannar I.
Mullaittivu
INDIAN OCEAN

DAB-M211
INDIA

Aruvi
Anuradhapura
Trincomalee

Puttalam
Sigiriya
Polonnaruwa
Mahaweli
Batticaloa

Gulf of Mannar
SRI LANKA
Kurunegala
Kandy

Negombo
Pidurutalagala 2524m△
Badulla

Colombo SRI-JAYAWARDENAPURA
Nuwara Eliya
Adam's Peak 2243m△
Pottuvil

Kalutara

Galle
Matara Dondra Head
Wajawe
Hambantota

□ international airport

Location: Indian sub-continent.

Note: There is a long-standing armed conflict between the Sri Lankan government and a Tamil extremist group, the Liberation Tigers of Tamil Ealam (LTTE). Fighting between government security forces and the LTTE continues in the north and parts of the east and travellers are advised not to visit these areas. Sri Lankan defence regulations restrict travel to much of the island's northern area. Areas such as Wilpattu and Galoya National Parks are considered especially unsafe. A state of emergency exists in Colombo itself and terrorist bombings have occurred in or near the capital where there is a general risk of getting caught up in random acts of violence. The rest of the island is calm and there is no indiciation of any direct threat outide these areas.
Sources: FCO Travel Advice Unit – November 17, 1994 and US State Department – April 22, 1994.

Sri Lanka Tourist Board
PO Box 1504, 78 Stewart Place, Colombo 3, Sri Lanka
Tel: (1) 437 059. Fax: (1) 437 953. Telex: 21867.
High Commission for the Democratic Socialist Republic of Sri Lanka
13 Hyde Park Gardens, London W2 2LU
Tel: (0171) 262 1841/7. Fax: (0171) 262 7970. Opening hours: 0915-1700 Monday to Friday. *Visa section:* 0930-1300 Monday to Friday.
Sri Lanka Tourist Board
Address as for High Commission
Tel: (0171) 262 5009 *or* 262 1841. Fax: (0171) 262 7970. Telex: 25844 (a/b LETCON G).
British Embassy
PO Box 1433, 190 Galle Road, Kollupitiya, Colombo 3, Sri Lanka
Tel: (1) 437 336. Fax: (1) 430 308. Telex: 21101 (a/b UKREP CE).

Embassy of the Democratic Socialist Republic of Sri Lanka
2148 Wyoming Avenue, NW, Washington, DC 20008
Tel: (202) 483 4025/8. Fax: (202) 232 7181.
Embassy of the United States of America
PO Box 106, 210 Galle Road, Colombo 3, Sri Lanka
Tel: (1) 448 007. Fax: (1) 437 345. Telex: 21305.
High Commission for the Democratic Socialist Republic of Sri Lanka
Suites 102-4, 85 Range Road, Ottawa, Ontario K1N 8J6
Tel: (613) 233 8440/9. Fax: (613) 238 8448.
Consulate in: Vancouver.
Canadian High Commission
PO Box 1006, 6 Gregory's Road, Cinnamon Gardens, Colombo 7, Sri Lanka
Tel: (1) 695 841/3. Fax: (1) 687 049. Telex: 21106 (a/b DOMCAN CE).

AREA: 64,454 sq km (24,886 sq miles).
POPULATION: 17,240,000 (1991 estimate).
POPULATION DENSITY: 267.5 per sq km.
CAPITAL: Colombo. **Population:** 615,000 (1990 estimate).
GEOGRAPHY: Sri Lanka is an island off the southeast coast of the Indian state of Tamil Nadu. It is separated from India by the Indian Ocean, in which lie the chain of islands called Adam's Bridge. Sri Lanka has an irregular surface with low-lying coastal plains running inland from the northern and eastern shores. The central and southern areas slope into hills and mountains. The highest peak is Pidurutalagala (2524m/8281ft).
LANGUAGE: Sinhala, Tamil and English.
RELIGION: Buddhist, with Hindu, Christian and Muslim minorities.
TIME: GMT + 5.30.
ELECTRICITY: 230/240 volts AC, 50Hz. Round 3-pin plugs are usual, with bayonet lamp fittings.
COMMUNICATIONS: Telephone: IDD facilities are available to the principal cities. Country code: 94. Outgoing international code: 00. **Fax:** The General Post Office in Colombo (address below) provides a service. Many hotels also have facilities. **Telex/telegram:** Telex facilities are available at the Overseas Telephone Service Counter, Duke Street Post Office, Colombo. Telegrams can be sent from all post offices. **Post:** Airmail to Europe takes up to a week. **Press:** Daily newspapers published in English include the *Daily News, The Island* and the *Observer.*
BBC World Service and Voice of America frequencies: From time to time these change. See the section *How to Use this Book* for more information.
BBC:

MHz	17.79	15.31	11.95	9.740

A service is also available on 1413kHz.
Voice of America:

MHz	21.49	15.60	9.525	6.035

PASSPORT/VISA

Regulations and requirements may be subject to change at short notice, and you are advised to contact the appropriate diplomatic or consular authority before finalising travel arrangements. Details of these may be found at the head of this country's entry. Any numbers in the chart refer to the footnotes below.

	Passport Required?	Visa Required?	Return Ticket Required?
Full British	Yes	No/1	Yes
BVP	Not valid	-	-
Australian	Yes	No/1	Yes
Canadian	Yes	No/1	Yes
USA	Yes	No/1	Yes
Other EU (As of 31/12/94)	Yes	No/1	Yes
Japanese	Yes	No/1	Yes

PASSPORTS: Passport valid for at least 3 months required by all.
British Visitors Passport: Not accepted.
VISAS: Required by all except:
(a) nationals of EU countries entering as tourists for a maximum stay of 30 days;
(b) nationals of Australia, Bangladesh, Finland, Malaysia, New Zealand, Philippines, Sweden and the USA who are bona fide tourists will be issued a 90-day Entry visa free of charge at point of entry;
(c) nationals of Albania, Austria, Bahrain, Bosnia-Hercegovina, Bulgaria, Canada, CIS, Croatia, Cyprus, Czech Republic, Estonia, Hungary, Indonesia, Israel, Japan, Kuwait, Latvia, Lithuania, Maldives, Norway, Nepal, Oman, Pakistan, Poland, Qatar, Romania, Saudi Arabia, Singapore, Slovak Republic, Slovenia, South Korea, Switzerland, Thailand, Turkey and United Arab Emirates entering as tourists for a

maximum stay of 30 days.
Note [1]: All business visitors require a visa.
Types of visa: Tourist and Business. Prices vary according to nationality.
Validity: 30 days. Visitors can request to extend their stay by applying to the Department of Immigration & Emigration, Chaitya Road, Colombo 1. Tel: (1) 436 353/6 *or* 436 367/8. Fax: (1) 437 040. Telex: 23264. This is issued at the discretion of the authorities who must be satisfied that the applicant has at least US$15 per day for the stay and holds an onward or return ticket for travel.
Application to: Consulate (or Consular section at Embassy or High Commission). For addresses, see top of entry.
Application requirements: (a) Valid passport. (b) Completed application form. (c) 1 passport-size photo signed on the back by applicant. (d) Fee with self-addressed envelope, stamped for £3.50, for return of passport. (e) Proof of sufficient funds for duration of stay. (f) For Business visa, a letter from sponsor in the national's own country.
Working days required: At least 4.
Temporary residence: Enquire at Embassy or High Commission.

MONEY

Currency: Sri Lanka Rupee (SL Re, singular; SL Rs, plural) = 100 cents. Notes are in denominations of SL Rs1000, 500, 100, 50, 20 and 10. Coins are in denominations of SL Rs10, 5, 2 and 1, and 50, 25, 10, 5, 2 and 1 cents. There are also a large number of commemorative coins in circulation.
Currency exchange: Foreign currency must be changed only at authorised exchanges, banks and hotels, and these establishments must endorse such exchanges on the visitor's Exchange Control D form which is issued on arrival and must usually be returned at time of departure.
Credit cards: American Express, Visa and Access/Mastercard are widely accepted. Diners Club has more limited acceptance. Check with your credit card company for details of merchant acceptability and other services which may be available.
Travellers cheques: The rate of exchange for travellers cheques is better than the rate of exchange for cash.
Exchange rate indicators: The following figures are included as a guide to the movements of the Sri Lanka Rupee against Sterling and the US Dollar:

Date:	Oct '92	Sep '93	Jan '94	Jan '95
£1.00=	67.00	74.64	72.81	77.70
$1.00=	42.22	48.88	49.21	49.66

Currency restrictions: The import and export of local currency is limited to SL Rs1000. The import of notes from India and Pakistan is not allowed, otherwise the import of foreign currency is not restricted but subject to declaration. Export of foreign currency is limited to the amount declared on import.
Banking hours: 0900-1300 Monday and Saturday; 0900-1500 Tuesday to Friday. Colombo airport's banking facilities serve all incoming and outgoing flights.

DUTY FREE

The following items may be imported into Sri Lanka without incurring customs duty:
200 cigarettes or 50 cigars or 375g of tobacco or a combination of these not exceeding 340g; 2 bottles of wine and 1.5 litres of spirits; a small quantity of perfume or 250ml of eau de toilette.
Note: (a) Precious metals, including gold, platinum and silver (and including jewellery), must be declared on arrival in Sri Lanka. (b) There is no gift allowance.

PUBLIC HOLIDAYS

Jan 1 '95 New Year's Day. **Feb 4** Independence Commemoration Day. **Mar 2** Eid al-Fitr (End of Ramadan). **Apr 14** Good Friday. **Apr 17** Easter Monday. **May 1** May Day. **May 10** Eid al-Adha (Feast of the Sacrifice). **May 22** National Heroes' Day. **Jun 30** Special Bank Holiday. **Aug 9** Milad un-Nabi (Prophet's Birthday). **Dec 25** Christmas Day. **Dec 26** Boxing Day. **Dec 31** Special Bank Holiday. **Jan 1 '96** New Year's Day. **Feb 4** Independence Commemoration Day. **Feb 22** Eid al-Fitr (End of Ramadan). **Apr 5** Good Friday. **Apr 8** Easter Monday.
Note: (a) In addition to the above there is a *poya* holiday on the day of each full moon. In general, Hindu and Buddhist festivals are declared according to local astronomical observations and it is often only possible to forecast the approximate time of their occurrence. (b)

Muslim festivals are timed according to local sightings of various phases of the Moon and the dates given above are approximations. During the lunar month of Ramadan that precedes Eid al-Fitr, Muslims fast during the day and feast at night and normal business patterns may be interrupted; however, since Sri Lanka is not a predominantly Muslim country restrictions (which travellers may experience elsewhere) are unlikely to cause problems.

HEALTH

Regulations and requirements may be subject to change at short notice, and you are advised to contact your doctor well in advance of your intended date of departure. Any numbers in the chart refer to the footnotes below.

	Special Precautions?	Certificate Required?
Yellow Fever	No	1
Cholera	Yes	2
Typhoid & Polio	Yes	-
Malaria	3	-
Food & Drink	4	-

[1]: A yellow fever vaccination certificate is required from travellers over one year of age arriving from infected areas.
[2]: Following WHO guidelines issued in 1973, a cholera vaccination certificate is not a condition of entry to Sri Lanka. However, cholera is a serious risk in this country and precautions are essential. Up-to-date advice should be sought before deciding whether these precautions should include vaccination as medical opinion is divided over its effectiveness. See the *Health* section at the back of the book.
[3]: Malaria risk, predominantly in the benign *vivax* form, exists throughout the year in the Districts of Amparai, Anuradhapura, Batticaloa, Badulla, Hambantota, Jaffna, Kandy, Kegalle, Kurunegala, Mannar, Matale, Matara, Moneragala, Polonnaruwa, Puttalam, Ratnapura, Trincomalee and Vavuniya. The malignant *falciparum* strain is also present and is reported to be 'highly resistant' to chloroquine.
[4]: All water should be regarded as being potentially contaminated. Water used for drinking, brushing teeth or making ice should have first been boiled or otherwise sterilised. Bottled water and a variety of mineral waters are available at most hotels. Unpasteurised milk should be boiled. Powdered or tinned milk is available and is advised, but make sure that it is reconstituted with pure water. Pasteurised and sterilised milk is available in some hotels and shops. Avoid all dairy products made with unboiled milk. Only eat well-cooked meat and fish, preferably served hot. Pork, salad and mayonnaise may carry increased risk. Vegetables should be cooked and fruit peeled.
Rabies is present. For those at high risk, vaccination before arrival should be considered. If you are bitten abroad seek medical advice without delay. For more information, consult the *Health* section at the back of the book.
Health care: Treatment is free at government hospitals and dispensaries; 24-hour treatment is available at Colombo General Hospital. Some hotels also have doctors.

TRAVEL - International

AIR: Sri Lanka's national airline is *Air Lanka (UL).*
Approximate flight times: From Colombo to *Hong Kong* is 5 hours 10 minutes, to *London* is 13 hours 45 minutes, to the *Seychelles* is 3 hours 55 minutes and to *Tokyo* is 12 hours.
International airport: *Colombo (CMB)* (Katunayake) is 32km (21 miles) from the city. There are full duty-free facilities at Colombo airport, as well as a restaurant, bar, snack bar, bank, post office and car hire. Bus no. 240 goes to the city every 30 minutes 0600-2100. It returns from Pettah bus station, Olcott Mawatha Street. Bus no. 187 goes to the city hourly 0600-2100. It returns from Fort bus station, Olcott Mawatha Street. Taxis to the city are available. There is a train to Maradana station (one mile from the city centre) at 0756, 0830, 1632 and 1720 (travel time – 1 hour 25 minutes). Return is from Fort railway station, Olcott Mawatha Street at 0510, 0526, 1340 and 1520.
Departure tax: SL Rs500 is levied on all international departures. Transit passengers and children under two years are exempt.
SEA: International ports include Colombo, Talaimannar, Trincomalee and Galle. Passenger services to Sri Lanka are operated by *Flagship Cruises, Holland America, Nauru Line, Norwegian American, P&O, Royal Viking, CIT* and *Cunard.* Cargo/passenger lines running services to Sri Lanka include *Bank, Hauraise, Lloyd, Triestine* and *Swedish American.*

TRAVEL - Internal

AIR: The major domestic airport is *Ratmalana* at Colombo. There are daily flights to smaller airports at Batticaloa, Gal Oya, Palali and Trincomalee. The airport at Jaffna is currently closed.
Helicopter tours: *Helitours of Ceylon,* with pilots from the Sri Lanka Air Force, offers charter tours of major tourist areas.
RAIL: Trains connect Colombo with all tourist towns, but first-class carriages, air-conditioning and dining cars are available on only a few. New fast services operate on the principal routes, otherwise journeys are fairly leisurely. The total network covers 1500km (900 miles).
Note: Rail services to Jaffna have recently been much reduced due to the violent political disruptions in the northern area.
ROAD: Traffic drives on the left. Most roads are tarred, with a 56kmph (35mph) speed limit in built-up areas and 75kmph (45mph) outside towns. **Bus:** An extensive network of services of reasonable quality is provided by the *Sri Lanka Central Transport Board.* **Taxi:** These are available in most towns. **Car hire:** This is available from several international agencies. Air-conditioned minibuses are also available. Chauffeur-driven cars are less expensive and well recommended. Avoid remote areas and travelling at night.
Documentation: In order to avoid bureaucratic formalities in Sri Lanka, an International Driving Permit should be obtained before departure. If not, a temporary licence to drive is obtainable on presentation of a valid national driving licence. This must be endorsed at the AA office in Colombo. The minimum age for driving a car is 18.
URBAN: Bus: The Central Transport Board provides intensive urban bus operations in Colombo, where there are also private buses and minibuses. Fares are generally collected by conductors. Services are often crowded. **Taxi:** These are metered with yellow tops and red and white plates. Drivers expect a 5% tip.
JOURNEY TIMES: The following chart gives approximate journey times (in hours and minutes) from Colombo to other major cities/towns in Sri Lanka.

	Air	Road	Rail
Kandy	-	2.30	3.00
Galle	-	3.00	3.00
Bentota	-	1.45	1.45
Matara	-	4.00	4.30
Badulla	-	9.30	9.00
Negombo	-	0.45	0.45
Nuwara Eliya	-	3.30	5.00
Anuradhapura	0.45	5.30	6.00
Pollonnaruwa	1.00	6.00	7.00
Trincomalee	1.00	6.00	7.00
Kataragama	-	6.30	-

ACCOMMODATION

HOTELS: Sri Lanka offers a wide choice of accommodation. There are seven international-class 5-star hotels with every modern facility. **Grading:** Hotels are classified from **1** to **5 stars.**
GUEST-HOUSES: Inns, guest-houses and rest houses offer comfortable but informal accommodation.
PRIVATE HOMES: For visitors who would like to get to know the Sri Lankans and see how they live, arrangements can be made to stay in private homes or on a tea or rubber plantation.
PARK BUNGALOWS: There are also many park bungalows run by the Department of Wild Life Conservation which are furnished and equipped for comfort rather than sophistication.
YOUTH HOSTELS: Information about youth hostels can be obtained from the YHA.

RESORTS & EXCURSIONS

Ancient sites include Anuradhapura, Polonnaruwa, Sigiriya, Dambulla, Panduwasnuwara and Yapahuwa. All these places contain the remains of a great civilisation which grew through the centuries under the influence of Buddhism, a gentle faith still preserved in Sri Lanka in its purest form. Vast man-made lakes, large parks, shrines, temples and monasteries speak eloquently of the grandeur of the past and bear testimony to a cultured and imaginative people. The regions in the following guide are used for convenience only and have no administrative significance.

Colombo

Sri Lanka's capital is a fascinating city, blending its older culture with modern Western influences. A palm-fringed drive of 34km (21 miles) leads from the Katunayake (Colombo) International Airport to Colombo city.
Fort: So called as it was a military garrison during the Portuguese and Dutch occupation from the 16th to the 18th century, today it is the commercial capital of Sri Lanka.
Pettah: 2km (1 mile) from Fort is the busy bazaar area known as the Pettah.
Buddhist temples: *Kelani Rajamaha Viharaya,* 10km (6 miles) from Fort; the *Vajiraramaya* at Bambalapitiya, 6km (4 miles) from Fort; *Dipaduttaramaya* at Kotahena, 5km (3 miles) from Fort; and *Gotami Vihare* at Borella, 7km (4.5 miles) from Fort. Also worth visiting are *Gangaramaya Bhikkhu Training Centre* and *Sima Malaka* at 61, Sri Jinaratana Road, Colombo, 3km (2 miles) from Fort; the *Purana Viharaya* at Metharamaya, Lauries Road, Colombo 4; and the *Purana Viharaya* at Hendala, half a mile on the Colombo–Negombo road, en route to the *Pegasus Reef Hotel.*
Hindu temples: At Kochikade Kotahena, the *Pettah and Bambalapitiya,* Colombo 4; *Sri Siva Subramania Swami Kovil,* Gintupitiya – within walking distance of Sea Street, Colombo 11 (Pettah).
Mosques: *Davatagaha* mosque at Union Place, Colombo 2; *Afar Jumma* mosque in the Pettah.
Parliament Building is at Sri Jayawardenepura, Kotte.
Parks: The *Vihara Maha Devi Park,* named after the mother of one of Sri Lanka's greatest kings, is noteworthy for its collection of beautiful flowering trees, a blossoming spectacle in March, April and early May. The park is open until 2100 daily and is well illuminated.
Other attractions: *The Planetarium, The National Zoological Gardens* and several museums and art galleries.

Kandy & the Hill Country

Kandy, a picturesque, naturally fortified town 115km (72 miles) from Colombo, was the last stronghold of the Kandyan Kings. It withheld foreign conquest until 1815 when it was ceded by treaty to the British. It is now a cultural sanctuary where age-old customs, arts, crafts, rituals and ways of life are well-preserved.
Good sightseeing trips should include: the Temple of the Sacred Tooth Relic (Dalada Maligawa); Embekke Devale; Lankatillaka; Gadaladeniya; Degaldoruwa temples; museums; Royal Botanic Gardens; Peradeniya; Elephants' Bath at Katugastota; the Kandyan Arts Association; Kalapura (Craftsmen's Village) at Nattarampotha (6.5km/4 miles from Kandy); and Henawela Village – famous for its 'Dumbara Mats' (16km/10 miles from Kandy).

Beaches

Sri Lanka has approximately 1600km (1000 miles) of beautiful palm-shaded beaches as well as warm, pure seas and colourful coral reefs.
Southwest Coast: The best time to visit is from November to April.
Mt Lavinia, 11km (7 miles) from Colombo, is a good beach resort close to Colombo and the domestic airport.
Beruwela, 58km (36 miles) from Colombo, has good bathing in the bay all year round.
Bentota, 61km (38 miles) from Colombo, is a pleasant self-contained resort destination, between the sea and the river.
Hikkaduwa, 99km (62 miles) from Colombo, is a beautiful coral reef and beach.
Galle, 115km (72 miles) from Colombo, is famous for its old Dutch fort, and is also a centre for lace-making, ebony-carving and gem-polishing.
Tangale, 195km (122 miles) from Colombo, is a beautiful bay and there is safe swimming all year round.
Negombo, 37km (32 miles) from Colombo near Katunayake International Airport, is Sri Lanka's oldest and best-known fishing village. It stands on a strand separating the sea from a lagoon. The seafood here, particularly the shellfish, is a speciality.
East Coast & Jaffna: *Visitors are advised to check with the Tourist Board regarding the situation in these areas prior to departure.*
The best time to visit is from April to September.
Trincomalee, 265km (160 miles) from Colombo, is the ideal refuge for the beach addict. It boasts one of the finest natural harbours in the world and excellent beaches. All watersports, including fishing, are available here.
Batticaloa, 312km (195 miles) from Colombo, is famous for its 'singing fish' and the old Dutch fort.
Kalkudah, 32km (20 miles) from Batticaloa, is ideal for bathing as the sea is clear, calm and reef-protected.

Passekudah, close to Kaludah, has a fine bay, clear waters and safe swimming.
Nilaveli, 18km (11 miles) from Trincomalee, is very much a resort centre, all beach and watersports.
Arugam Bay, 314km (196 miles) from Colombo, 3km (2 miles) from Potuvil, has a beautiful bay and good surfing.
Jaffna is 396km (240 miles) from Colombo. It is the unofficial capital of the Tamil separatists and different from the rest of Sri Lanka in its topography, history, people and way of life. The city was devastated during the prolonged siege by Indian forces in 1987, but was once noted for its Hindu temples, Dutch forts, the *Keerimalai Baths*, the tidal well and the *Chundikulam Sanctuary*. Jaffna has many scenic beaches, the best known of which is *Casuarina Beach*. Check with the Tourist Board, Embassy or High Commission whether the area is off-limits to foreign visitors.

SOCIAL PROFILE

FOOD & DRINK: Standard foods are spicy and it is advised to approach curries with caution. There are many vegetables, fruits, meats and seafoods. Continental, Chinese, Indian and Japanese menus are available in Colombo. A speciality is basic curry, made with coconut juice, sliced onion, green chilli, aromatic spices such as cloves, nutmeg, cinnamon and saffron and aromatic leaves. *Hoppers* is a cross between a muffin and a crumpet with a wafer-crisp edge, served with a fresh egg soft-baked on top. *Stringhoppers* are steamed circlets of rice flour, a little more delicate than noodles or spaghetti. *Jaggery* is a fudge made from the crystallised sap of the kitul palm. The *durian* fruit is considered a high delicacy. **Drink:** Tea is the national drink and considered to be amongst the best in the world. *Toddy*, the sap of the palm tree, is a popular local drink; fermented, it becomes *arrack* which, it should be noted, comes in varying degrees of strength. Alcohol cannot be sold on *poya* holidays (which occur each lunar month on the day of the full moon).
NIGHTLIFE: Some Colombo hotels have supper clubs with music for dancing. There are theatres in Colombo, cinemas showing films from the USA, ballet, concerts and theatre productions.
SHOPPING: Special purchases include handicrafts and curios of silver, brass, bone, ceramics, wood and terracotta. Also cane baskets, straw hats, reed mats and tea. Some of the masks, which are used in dance-dramas, in processions and on festival days, can be bought by tourists. The '18-disease' mask shows a demon in possession of a victim; he is surrounded by 18 faces – each of which cures a specific ailment. Versions produced for the tourist market are often of a high standard. Sri Lanka is also rich in gems. Fabrics include batiks, cottons, rayons, silks and fine lace.
Shopping hours: 0800/0900-1700 Monday to Friday. Many stores also open Saturday morning.
SPORT: Golf: Offered on a temporary membership basis at several courses. **Fishing:** Sport fishing is popular in Sri Lanka and several clubs offer membership to visitors. **Skindiving:** Underwater Safaris, 25 Barnes Place, Colombo 7, conducts skindiving expeditions and supplies equipment.
Swimming: With over 1600km (1000 miles) of fine beaches and several swimming clubs, there is plenty of scope for swimmers. **Water-skiing:** Available with Sun Stream Boat Services (National Holiday Resort, Bentota). **Windsurfing** is a sport that is gaining popularity and facilities are located in Kalutara, Bentota, Beruwela and Negombo. **Other sports:** **Rugby, hockey, cricket, football, squash** and other indoor games are also available. Apply to a local Travel Information Centre.
SPECIAL EVENTS: The following list is a selection of the events taking place in Sri Lanka annually. For further information and exact dates, contact the Tourist Board (for addresses, see top of entry).
Jan *Duruthu Perahera Festival* (commemorating a visit of the Buddha to Sri Lanka), Kelaniya; *Thai Pongal* (traditional Hindu festival where thanksgiving prayers are offered to the deities, and milk rice is boiled at dawn in the direction of the rising sun). **Feb** *Navam Perahera Festival* (colourful street procession with about 100 elephants and 'low country' dancers), Colombo. **Feb 4** *Independence Commemoration Day.* **Apr** *Sinhala* and *Tamil New Year.* **May** *Vesak Festival* (commemorates the Birth, Enlightenment and Death of the Buddha). **Jul/Aug** *Kataragama Festival,* Tissamaharama; *Esala Perahera Festival,* Kandy. **Dec** *Sanghamitta Day.*
SOCIAL CONVENTIONS: Shaking hands is the normal form of greeting. It is customary to be offered tea when visiting and it is considered impolite to refuse. Punctuality is appreciated. A small token of appreciation, such as a souvenir from home or

company, is always welcomed. Informal, Western dress is suitable. Visitors should be decently clothed when visiting any place of worship. Beachwear is not suitable for temples and shrines, and shoes and hats must be removed. Jackets and ties are not required by men in the evenings except for formal functions when lightweight suits should be worn. **Tipping:** Most hotels include a service charge of 10%. Extra tipping is optional.

BUSINESS PROFILE

ECONOMY: The economy is predominantly agricultural. The main cash crops are tea, rubber and coconuts, which provide over 75% of export earnings. Rice is grown mainly for domestic consumption, and Sri Lanka is almost self-sufficient in rice. The main industrial sectors are mining and manufacturing, which are currently doing most to support the growth of the Sri Lankan economy. Graphite is the most important mineral, but recent growth is largely a result of increasing export of gemstones. Iron ore, limestone, clay and uranium are present in commercially exploitable quantities. Oil exploration has so far failed to yield significant deposits, but a number of major oil companies have signed long-term contracts to continue test drilling. Several key manufacturing industries are under government control, including cement and textiles – the latter being an important export industry – which are typical of the Government's strategy of promoting export-oriented industries within the country. Forestry and fishing are also important. Hydroelectricity is the main source of power. The biggest problem facing the economy at present is the dislocation caused by the internal security situation, although it has picked up in the early 1990s with a sharp fall in the trade and current account deficits and a recovery of the tourism industry which was hit particularly badly. The Government has introduced a number of economic reforms in an attempt to lure foreign investors. There has been a limited privatisation programme and a liberalisation of exchange controls. These measures seem to be having the desired effect. Sri Lanka's principal imports are foodstuffs, oil and machinery; the market for consumer goods is comparatively underdeveloped and offers promising future opportunities for exporters. The UK is the third largest exporter to Sri Lanka after Japan and the USA and also the third-largest overseas market for Sri Lankan goods. Sri Lanka has run a sizeable trade deficit for years, which is met through overseas aid and loans.
BUSINESS: Business attire is casual. English is widely spoken in business circles. Appointments are necessary and it is considered polite to arrive punctually. It is usual to exchange visiting cards on first introduction. **Office hours:** 0830/0900-1615/1700.
COMMERCIAL INFORMATION: The following organisation can offer advice: Federation of Chambers of Commerce and Industry of Sri Lanka, 29 Gregory's Road, Colombo 7. Tel: (1) 698 225. Fax: (1) 699 530.

CLIMATE

Tropical climate. Upland areas are cooler and more temperate and coastal areas are cooled by sea breezes. There are two monsoons, which occur May to July and December to January.
Required clothing: Lightweights and rainwear.

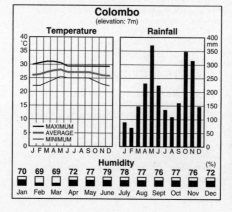

Colombo
(elevation: 7m)

Temperature | Rainfall

	Jan	Feb	Mar	Apr	May	June	July	Aug	Sept	Oct	Nov	Dec
Humidity (%)	70	69	69	72	77	79	78	77	76	77	76	72

DAB-M212

international airport

Location: Northeast Africa.

Note: Travel in all parts of Sudan is considered potentially hazardous. Western interests in Khartoum have been the target of terrorist acts several times in recent years. Civil war persists in southern Sudan in the three provinces of Upper Nile, Bahr El Ghazal and Equatoria. Banditry and incursions by southern Sudanese rebels are common in western Sudan, particularly in Darfur Province along the Chadian and Libyan borders and in southern Kordofan Province. Visitors should seek advise from their Embassy before travelling to these areas. The ferry route between Egypt and Sudan at Wadi Halfa has been suspended. There is no alternative overland route between Egypt and Sudan. Travellers attempting to cross the Egyptian–Sudanese border elsewhere have been subjected to heavy penalties, including imprisonment.
Sources: US State Department – March 3, 1994 and FCO Travel Advice Unit – December 2, 1994.

Public Corporation of Tourism and Hotels
PO Box 7104, Khartoum, Sudan
Tel: (11) 81764. Telex: 22346.
Embassy of the Democratic Republic of Sudan
3 Cleveland Row, St James Street, London SW1A 1DD
Tel: (0171) 839 8080. Opening hours: 0900-1600
Monday to Friday; 0930-1200 Monday to Friday (Visa section).
British Embassy
PO Box 801, Street 10, Off Sharia Al Baladiya, Khartoum East, Sudan
Tel: (11) 70760/6/9. Telex: 22189 (a/b PRDM SD).
Embassy of the Democratic Republic of Sudan
2210 Massachusetts Avenue, NW, Washington, DC 20008
Tel: (202) 338 8565/6/7. Fax: (202) 667 2406.
Embassy of the United States of America
PO Box 699, Sharia Ali Abdul Latif, Khartoum, Sudan
Tel: (11) 74700 *or* 74611. Telex: 22619 (a/b AMEM SD).
Embassy of the Democratic Republic of Sudan
Suite 507, 85 Range Road, Ottawa, Ontario K1N 8J6
Tel: (613) 235 4000. Fax: (613) 235 6880.

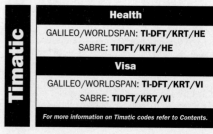

Timatic

Health	
GALILEO/WORLDSPAN:	**TI-DFT/KRT/HE**
SABRE:	**TIDFT/KRT/HE**

Visa	
GALILEO/WORLDSPAN:	**TI-DFT/KRT/VI**
SABRE:	**TIDFT/KRT/VI**

For more information on Timatic codes refer to Contents.

The Canadian Embassy in Addis Ababa deals with enquiries relating to Sudan (see *Ethiopia* earlier in the book).

AREA: 2,505,813 sq km (967,500 sq miles).
POPULATION: 23,797,000 (1988 estimate).
POPULATION DENSITY: 9.5 per sq km.
CAPITAL: Khartoum. **Population:** 473,597 (1983).
GEOGRAPHY: Sudan is bordered by Egypt to the north, the Red Sea to the northeast, Ethiopia and Eritrea to the east, Kenya, Uganda and Zaïre to the south, the Central African Republic and Chad to the west and Libya to the northwest. There is a marked difference between the climate, culture and geography of northern and southern Sudan. The far north consists of the contiguous Libyan and Nubian Deserts which extend as far south as the capital, Khartoum, and are barren except for small areas beside the Nile River and a few scattered oases. This gives way to the central steppes which cover the country between 15°N and 10°N, a region of short, coarse grass and bushes, turning to open savannah towards the south, largely flat to the east but rising to two large plateaux in the west and south, the Janub Darfur (3088m/10,131ft) and Janub Kordofan (500m/1640ft) respectively. Most of Sudan's agriculture occurs in these latitudes in a fertile pocket between the Blue and White Niles which meet at Khartoum. South of the steppes is a vast shallow basin traversed by the White Nile and its tributaries, with the Sudd, a 120,000 sq km (46,332 sq miles) marshland, in the centre. This gives way to equatorial forest towards the south, rising to jungle-clad mountains on the Ugandan border, the highest being Mount Kinyeti, at 3187m (10,456ft).
LANGUAGE: Arabic is the official language. English and many local dialects are widely spoken.
RELIGION: Muslim in the north; Christian and traditional Animist religions in the south.
TIME: GMT + 2.
ELECTRICITY: 240 volts AC, 50Hz.
COMMUNICATIONS: Telephone: IDD is available. Country code: 249. Outgoing international calls must go through the operator. **Telex/telegram:** The Central Telegraph Office is open at Khartoum (Gamma Avenue) 24 hours a day including holidays. Telex facilities exist at main post offices. All previous 3-digit numbers are now preceeded by 22. **Post:** Post offices are open 0830-1200 and 1730-1830 Saturday to Thursday. Airmail to Europe takes up to a week. **Press:** The main dailies are *El Sudan*, *El Watini* and *El Muslaha*. There is an English-language magazine entitled *Sudan Now*.
BBC World Service and Voice of America frequencies: From time to time these change. See the section *How to Use this Book* for more information.
BBC:

MHz	21.47	17.64	15.07	9.410

Voice of America:

MHz	21.49	15.60	9.525	6.035

PASSPORT/VISA

Regulations and requirements may be subject to change at short notice, and you are advised to contact the appropriate diplomatic or consular authority before finalising travel arrangements. Details of these may be found at the head of this country's entry. Any numbers in the chart refer to the footnotes below.

	Passport Required?	Visa Required?	Return Ticket Required?
Full British	Yes	Yes	Yes
BVP	Not valid	-	-
Australian	Yes	Yes	Yes
Canadian	Yes	Yes	Yes
USA	Yes	Yes	Yes
Other EU (As of 31/12/94)	Yes	Yes	Yes
Japanese	Yes	Yes	Yes

Restricted entry: The Sudanese authorities refuse entry and transit to nationals of Israel and holders of passports that contain visas for Israel (either valid or expired).
PASSPORTS: Valid passport required by all. Passport must have been valid for at least 6 months.
British Visitors Passport: Not accepted.
VISAS: Required by all except nationals of Algeria, Bahrain, Egypt, Iraq, Jordan, Kuwait, Lebanon, Libya, Morocco, Oman, Qatar, Saudi Arabia, Somalia, Syria, Tunisia, United Arab Emirates and Yemen.
Types of visa: Tourist or Business; cost: £53.25 (postal order, company cheque or cash).
Validity: 3 months from the date of issue. Enquire at Embassy.
Transit visa: Required by all passengers who

continue their journey to a third country within 24 hours by the same or first connecting aircraft. Visitors must remain in the airport and must hold confirmed reservations and the necessary documents for their onward journey. There is no hotel accommodation at the airport.
Application to: Consular section at Embassy. For addresses, see top of entry.
Application requirements: (a) 2 completed application forms. (b) 2 passport-size photographs. (c) Fee. (d) Company letter or invitation from Sudan for Business visas. (e) Return/onward ticket. (f) Travellers cheques for Tourist visas.
Working days required: 7 days to 3 weeks.
Temporary residence: Enquire at Embassy.
Note: Special permits are required for travel to all parts of Sudan, apart from the capital. These are obtainable from the Passport and Immigration office in Khartoum. 2 days should be allowed for the issue of a permit.

MONEY

Currency: Sudanese Pound (Sud£) = 100 piastres. Notes are in denominations of Sud£100, 50, 20, 10, 5 and 1, and 50 and 25 piastres. Coins are in denominations of 50, 10, 5, 2 and 1 piastres. There are also a number of commemorative coins in circulation.
Credit cards: American Express is widely accepted, Access/Mastercard and Diners Club have more limited use. Check with your credit card company for merchant acceptability and other services which may be available.
Travellers cheques: These have limited acceptance and should be in a major currency.
Exchange rate indicators: The following figures are included as a guide to the movements of the Sudanese Pound against Sterling and the US Dollar:

Date:	Oct '92	Sep '93	Jan '94	Jan '95
£1.00=	15.82	19.89	19.20	48.62
$1.00=	9.97	13.03	12.98	31.08

Currency restrictions: There is no limit on the import and export of foreign currency, subject to declaration. The import and export of local currency is prohibited.
Banking hours: 0830-1200 Saturday to Thursday.

DUTY FREE

The following items may be imported into Sudan by visitors over 10 years of age without incurring customs duty:
200 cigarettes or 50 cigars or 225g of tobacco; perfume and eau de toilette for personal use.
Prohibited items: The import of goods from South Africa and Israel is prohibited. Sudan also adheres to the list of prohibited goods drawn up by the Arab League and these include alcoholic beverages.

PUBLIC HOLIDAYS

Jan 1 '95 Independence Day. **Mar 3** Eid al-Fitr (End of Ramadan) and Unity Day. **Apr 6** Uprising Day. **Apr 24** Sham an-Nassim (Coptic Easter Monday). **May 10** Eid al-Adha (Feast of the Sacrifice). **May 31** Islamic New Year. **Jul 1** Decentralisation Day. **Aug 9** Mouloud (Prophet's Birthday). **Dec 25** Christmas. **Jan 1 '96** Independence Day. **Feb 22** Eid al-Fitr (End of Ramadan). **Mar 3** Unity Day. **Apr 6** Uprising Day.
Note: Muslim festivals are timed according to local sightings of various phases of the Moon and the dates given above are approximations. During the lunar month of Ramadan that precedes Eid al-Fitr, Muslims fast during the day and feast at night and normal business patterns may be interrupted. Many restaurants are closed during the day and there may be restrictions on smoking and drinking. Some disruption may continue into Eid al-Fitr itself. Eid al-Fitr and Eid al-Adha may last anything from two to ten days, depending on the region. For more information see the section *World of Islam* at the back of the book.

HEALTH

Regulations and requirements may be subject to change at short notice, and you are advised to contact your doctor well in advance of your intended date of departure. Any numbers in the chart refer to the footnotes below.

	Special Precautions?	Certificate Required?
Yellow Fever	Yes	1
Cholera	Yes	2
Typhoid & Polio	Yes	-
Malaria	3	-
Food & Drink	4	-

[1]: The risk of yellow fever is primarily in the equatorial south. A yellow fever vaccination certificate is required from travellers over one year of age arriving from infected areas, and may be required from travellers leaving Sudan. Those countries and areas formerly classified as endemic zones are considered by the Sudanese authorities to be infected areas. Travellers arriving from non-endemic zones should note that vaccination is strongly recommended for travel outside the urban areas, even if an outbreak of the disease has not been reported and they would normally not require a vaccination certificate to enter the country.
[2]: Following WHO guidelines issued in 1973, a cholera vaccination certificate is no longer a condition of entry to Sudan. However, cholera is a serious risk in the country and precautions are essential. Up-to-date advice should be sought before deciding whether these precautions should include vaccination as medical opinion is divided over its effectiveness. See the *Health* section at the back of the book.
[3]: Malaria risk, predominantly in the malignant *falciparum* form, exists throughout the year throughout the country. High resistance to chloroquine and resistance to sulfadoxine-pyrimethamine has been reported.
[4]: All water should be regarded as being a potential health risk. Water used for drinking, brushing teeth or making ice should have first been boiled or otherwise sterilised. Milk is unpasteurised and should be boiled. Powdered or tinned milk is available and is advised but make sure that it is reconstituted with pure water. Avoid dairy products which are likely to have been made from unboiled milk. Only eat well-cooked meat and fish, preferably served hot. Pork, salad and mayonnaise may carry increased risk. Vegetables should be cooked and fruit peeled.
Rabies is present. For those at high risk vaccination before arrival should be considered. If you are bitten abroad seek medical advice without delay. For more information consult the *Health* section at the back of the book.
Bilharzia (schistosomiasis) is present. Avoid swimming and paddling in fresh water. Swimming pools which are well-chlorinated and maintained are safe.
Visceral leishmaniasis is currently highly endemic in the country. Vaccination is strongly recommended. The disease is transferred through sandflies which mainly occur on river banks and in wooded areas.
Health care: Medical treatment may be free at certain establishments but health insurance is essential and should include cover for emergency repatriation. Medical facilities are limited outside Khartoum.

TRAVEL - International

AIR: The national airline is *Sudan Airways (SD)*.
Approximate flight time: From London to Khartoum is 8 hours, including stopover.
International airport: *Khartoum (KRT)* (Civil), 4km (2.5 miles) southeast of the city (travel time – 20 minutes). There are full duty-free facilities at the airport. Taxi services are available with a surcharge after 2200.
Departure tax: Sud£500 is levied on international departures. Transit passengers and children under two years are exempt.
SEA: The only sea port is Port Sudan on the Red Sea, served by passenger lines from Europe *(Polish Ocean Lines)*, the USA *(Hellenic Lines)* and several African countries. *Sudan River Transport Corporation* operates regular Nile cruises from Aswan and Abu Simbel in Egypt, calling at Wadi Halfa. There are services from Saudi Arabia and Yemen *(Fayez Trading Company* and *Mohammed Sadaka Establishment Company)*.
RAIL: Rail links run from Cairo (Egypt) to Aswan High Dam and then by riverboat to Wadi Halfa.
ROAD: Sudan can be reached by road from Egypt, Libya, Chad, Uganda and the Central African Republic. Entry via Ethiopia is at present not possible. Motorists must apply for permission to drive through Sudan well in advance. Applications must be made to government representatives abroad or in Khartoum, listing vehicle and passenger details, with documents from a recognised automobile club or guarantee from a bank or business firm.

TRAVEL - Internal

Note: Travel to the southern provinces is restricted; see end of *Passport/Visa* section.
AIR: *Sudan Airways (SD)* run services to 20 airports, including Dongola, Juba, Port Sudan and El Obeid. The most reliable route is Port Sudan to Khartoum. There is also an air-taxi service operating twice-weekly to Nyala, available from Khartoum.
Departure tax: Sud£200 on domestic flights.

SEA: River steamers serve all towns on the Nile but conditions are mostly unsuitable for tourist travel. Services depend on fluctuating water levels. It is wise to take food and water. Destinations include Dongola, Karima, Kosti and Juba. A 320km (200-mile) navigable canal, the *Jonglei*, is under construction in the south.
RAIL: Sudan has an extensive rail network but the service is extremely slow and uncomfortable. There are three normal classes of travel plus *mumtaza* (deluxe). Sleeping cars are available on main routes from Khartoum to Wau/Nyala, Khartoum to Kassala/Wadi Halfa and Port Sudan to Khartoum. There are a few air-conditioned carriages, for which a supplement is charged.
ROAD: Only a small proportion of roads are asphalted; road conditions are poor outside towns and roads to the north are often closed during the rainy season (July to September). Due to the bad conditions, a full set of spare parts should be carried for long journeys. Vehicles must be in good working condition. Traffic drives on the right.
Bus: Services run between the main towns and depart from the market places. *Souk* (market) lorries are a cheap but uncomfortable method of transport. **Taxi:** These can be found at ranks or hailed in the street. Taxis are not metered, fares must be agreed in advance. **Car hire:** Available in the main towns and at major hotels but charges are high. **Documentation:** *Carnet de Passage,* adequate finance and roadworthiness certificate (from the Embassy) are all needed. An International Driving Permit is recommended, although not legally required. A temporary driving licence is available from local authorities on presentation of a valid British or Northern Ireland driving licence. Trailers and cars of less than 1500cc are refused entry.
URBAN: Publicly-operated bus services in Khartoum have of late become unreliable and irregular which has led to the proliferation of private *bakassi* minibuses, nicknamed *boks.* They pick up and set down with no fixed stops. These operations are on the fringes of legality and should be used with care.

ACCOMMODATION

HOTELS: Accommodation is scarce outside Khartoum and Port Sudan. Khartoum has 11 medium-sized hotels, including some of international standard, and Port Sudan has three. There are a few smaller hotels in the main towns and several hostels.
YOUTH HOSTELS: Contact the Youth Hostel Association, PO Box 1705, Khartoum. Tel: (11) 81464 *or* 22087.

RESORTS & EXCURSIONS

Sudan has only recently been developed as a tourist destination and communications and facilities are still limited outside Khartoum. Travel restrictions are also in force in much of the country (see *Passport/Visa* section above) due to the presence of separatist insurgents.
KHARTOUM: The capital is situated at the confluence of the Blue and White Niles. With **Omdurman**, the old national capital, and **Khartoum North**, it forms one unit called the 'three-towns capital'. Among the tourist attractions are the Omdurman camel market and the Arab *souk.* A good selection of Sudanese handicrafts is sold in several shops in the centre and in the reception halls of bigger hotels.
Particularly noteworthy from an historic and artistic point of view is a visit to the well-organised *National Museum* which contains archaeological treasures dating back to 4000BC and earlier. A visit to the *Khalifa's House Museum* will reward those who are interested in Sudan's more recent history, especially the reign of the Mahdi (1881-1899).
Excursions: A visit to the Gezira model farm or a trip along the Nile to the dam at *Jebel Aulia,* where the Nile is especially rich in fish, are recommended. Sunset on the river is spectacular.
THE NORTH & EAST: The main areas of archaeological interest in Sudan are to be found beside the Nile north of Khartoum. They include **Bajrawiya, Naga, Musawarat, El Kurru, Nuri** and **Meroe.**
The Dinder National Park, covering 6475 sq km (2500 sq miles) southeast of Khartoum on the Ethiopian border, is one of the largest in the world. There are many species of wild animals, including lion, giraffe, leopard, kudu, bushbuck and antelope, and birds such as guinea fowl, vulture, pelican, stork, kingfisher and the beautiful crown crane. Special 3-day trips from Khartoum are organised in the high season (December to April).
The Red Sea, with the transparency of its water, the variety of its fish and the charm of its marine gardens and coral reefs, is one of Sudan's main tourist attractions. The busy **Port Sudan, Suakin,** famous

during the Ottoman era, and the **Arous Tourist Village,** 50km (30 miles) north of Port Sudan, are just three centres from which to explore the coast. Erkowit, 1200m (3930ft) above sea level, is a beautiful resort in the coastal mountains and is famed for its evergreen vegetation.
THE WEST: Jebel Marra, at more than 3088m (10,100ft), is the highest peak in the Darfur region of western Sudan. It is a region of outstanding scenic beauty, with waterfalls and volcanic lakes and a pleasant climate, and consequently a favoured resort.
THE SOUTH: The Southern Provinces are characterised by green forests, open parkland, waterfalls and treeless swamps abounding with birds and wild animals such as elephant, black and white rhino, common eland, Nile lechwe, lesser kudu, bisa oryx, zebra, crocodile, hippo, hyena, buffalo and the almost extinct shoebill. The **Gemmeiza Tourist Village,** situated in the heart of East Equatoria, is considered of special interest, owing to the abundance of game in that area.
Note: The people of the south are largely Christian and this has led to friction with the ruling Muslim factions in the north. Civil war is a constant threat. Check with the Embassy before travelling if a visit to this region is intended (see also *Passport/Visa* section above).

SOCIAL PROFILE

FOOD & DRINK: The staple diet is *fool,* a type of bean, and *dura,* cooked maize or millet, which are eaten with various vegetables. The hotel restaurants in Khartoum and Port Sudan serve international cuisine and there are a few Greek and Middle Eastern restaurants. If invited to a Sudanese home more exotic food will usually be served. Alcohol is banned by the Islamic *Sharia* code.
NIGHTLIFE: The best entertainment is found in Khartoum and Omdurman, with a national theatre, music hall, cinemas, open-air and hotel entertainment.
SHOPPING: The *souk* has stalls selling food, local crafts, spices, cheap jewellery and silver. Special purchases include basketwork, ebony, gold and silver and assorted handicrafts. Visitors must not buy cheetah skins: the killing of cheetahs is prohibited and they are a protected species under the World Wildlife Act.
Shopping hours: 0800-1330 and 1730-2000 Saturday to Thursday.
SPORT: There is great scope for **watersports** on the Red Sea coast, including **swimming, skindiving** on coral reefs and **fishing** for barracuda, sharks and grey cod.
SOCIAL CONVENTIONS: In the north, Arab culture predominates while the people in the more fertile south belong to many diverse tribes, each with their own lifestyle and beliefs. Because Sudan is largely Muslim, women should not wear revealing clothing. Official and social functions as well as some restaurants will expect formal clothes to be worn. The Sudanese have a great reputation for hospitality. **Tipping:** Not customary.

BUSINESS PROFILE

ECONOMY: Once described as the bread basket of the Arab world, Sudan is a country of high, though largely unrealised, economic potential which is presently crippled by repeated droughts, civil war and a massive foreign debt. Agriculture employs most of the workforce producing cotton – the major export – wheat, groundnuts, sorghum and sugar cane. *Gum Arabic,* once important, has declined through the introduction of synthetic substitutes and increasing competition, particularly from West Africa. Livestock breeding has suffered due mainly to the drought. The small manufacturing sector concentrates on processing the country's agricultural output – sugar-refining, for example – and the production of consumer goods such as textiles, cigarettes and batteries. There are commercially significant, though not vast oil deposits. Earnings from these, however, have been depressed by the low world oil price. Other mineral deposits have been located but have yet to be fully exploited. Sudan's trade has fallen sharply since the early 1980s, due to a chronic shortage of foreign exchange. Saudi Arabia is the largest exporter to Sudan, followed by the UK, Italy, the USA and Germany. Sudan finds markets for its exports in Egypt, Saudi Arabia, Italy and Japan. Foreign aid is vital to stave off total economic collapse especially as the war against secessionists in the Christian south is estimated to cost up to US$2 million a day. Sudan is saddled with an enormous foreign debt. It was US$17 billion in arrears to the IMF in 1994. Despite introducing sweeping economic reforms in 1992 the World Bank stopped funds going to Sudan because of the shortfall in repayments and the IMF is now rumoured to have started the process of getting Sudan

removed from membership of the fund. This spells absolute disaster for the Sudanese economy.
BUSINESS: Businessmen should wear a lightweight suit. Muslim customs should be respected by visiting business people. English is widely spoken in business circles although knowledge of a few words of Arabic will be well received. Punctuality is less important than patience and politeness. Personal introductions are an advantage; business cards should have an Arabic translation on the reverse. **Office hours:** 0830-1300 Saturday to Thursday.
COMMERCIAL INFORMATION: The following organisations can offer advice: Sudan Development Corporation, PO Box 710, 21 al-Amarat, Khartoum. Tel: (11) 42425. Fax: (11) 40473. Telex: 24078 (a/b SDC SD); *or*
Sudan Chamber of Commerce, PO Box 81, Khartoum. Tel: (11) 72346.

CLIMATE

Extremely hot (less so November to March). Sandstorms blow across the Sahara from April to September. In the extreme north there is little rain but the central region has some rainfall from July to August. The southern region has much higher rainfall, the wet season lasting May to October. Summers are very hot throughout the country, whilst winters are cooler in the north.
Required clothing: Tropical clothes all year, warmer clothes for cool mornings and evenings (especially in the desert).

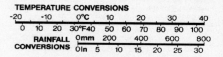

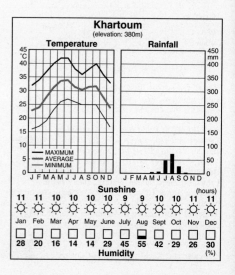

Suriname

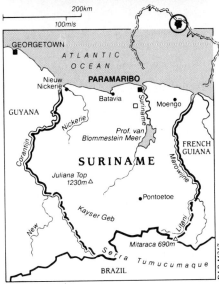

□ *international airport*

Location: North coast of South America.

Note: While the situation in the countryside is at present stable, there is insufficient police authority over much of the interior of Suriname to offer assistance in an emergency. Unaccompanied travel to the interior, particularly the East-West Highway between Paramaribo and Albina, is considered risky due to the high incidence of robberies and assaults along this route. The rate of violent crime has increased. Burglary and armed robbery are increasingly common in the capital city of Paramaribo, as well as in the outlying areas. Banditry occurs along routes in the interior of the country where police protection is inadequate.
Source: US State Department – October 18, 1994.

Suriname Tourism Department
Cornelis Jongbauwstraat 2, Paramaribo, Suriname
Tel: 410 357.
Suriname Tourism Company
METS Ltd, Rudielaan 5, Paramaribo, Suriname
Tel: 492 892 *or* 497 180. Fax: 497 062.
Embassy of the Republic of Suriname
Alexander Gogelweg 2, 2517 JH The Hague, The Netherlands
Tel: (70) 365 0844. Fax: (70) 361 7445. Telex: 32220.
Consulaat-Generaal van de Republiek Suriname
De Cuserstraat 11, 1081 CK Amsterdam, The Netherlands
Tel: (20) 642 6137 *or* 642 6717.
Suriname Tourism Company
c/o Trips Worldwide, 9 Byron Place, Clifton, Bristol, BS8 1JT
Tel: (0117) 929 2199. Fax: (0117) 929 2545.
British Honorary Consulate
c/o VSH United Buildings, PO Box 1300, Van't Hogerhuysstraat, Paramaribo, Suriname
Tel: 472 870. Fax: 475 515. Telex: 144 (a/b UNITED SN).
Embassy of the Republic of Suriname
Suite 108, Van Ness Centre, 4301 Connecticut Avenue, NW, Washington, DC 20008
Tel: (202) 244 7488 *or* 244 7490/1/2. Fax: (202) 244 5878. Telex: 892656.
Consulate General in: Miami.

Also deals with enquiries from Canada.
Embassy of the United States of America
PO Box 1821, Dr Sophie Redmondstraat 129, Paramaribo, Suriname
Tel: 472 900. Fax: 410 025. Telex: 383 (a/b AMEMSU SN).
The Canadian High Commission in Georgetown deals with enquiries relating to Suriname (see *Guyana* earlier in the book).

AREA: 163,265 sq km (63,037 sq miles).
POPULATION: 404,310 (1991 estimate).
POPULATION DENSITY: 2.5 per sq km.
CAPITAL: Paramaribo. **Population:** 150,000 (1988 estimate).
GEOGRAPHY: Suriname is bordered to the north by the Atlantic Ocean, to the east by the Marowijne River which forms the border with French Guiana, to the west by the Corantijn River dividing it from Guyana, and to the south by forests, savannahs and mountains which separate it from Brazil. In the northern part of the country are coastal lowlands covered with mangrove swamps. Further inland runs a narrow strip of savannah land. To the south the land becomes hilly and then mountainous, covered with dense tropical forest, and cut by numerous rivers and streams.
LANGUAGE: Dutch is the official language. *Sranan Tongo,* originating in Creole, is the popular language. The other main languages are Hindi and Javanese. English, Chinese, French and Spanish are also spoken.
RELIGION: 45% Christian, 27% Hindu, 18% Muslim.
TIME: GMT - 3.
ELECTRICITY: 127/220 volts AC, 60Hz. European round 2-pin plugs and screw-type lamp fittings are in use.
COMMUNICATIONS: Telephone: IDD is available. Country code: 597. There are no area codes. Outgoing international code: 001. **Telex/telegram:** Telegrams can only be sent from offices of *Telesur* (Telecommunicatie Beoryf Suriname) in both Paramaribo and the districts. International telex services available. **Post:** Airmail to and from Europe usually takes about a week to arrive. **Press:** Dailies include *De West* and *De Ware Tijd*.
BBC World Service and Voice of America frequencies: From time to time these change. See the section *How to Use this Book* for more information.
BBC:

MHz	17.84	15.22	9.915	5.975

Voice of America:

MHz	15.21	11.74	9.815	6.030

PASSPORT/VISA

Regulations and requirements may be subject to change at short notice, and you are advised to contact the appropriate diplomatic or consular authority before finalising travel arrangements. Details of these may be found at the head of this country's entry. Any numbers in the chart refer to the footnotes below.

	Passport Required?	Visa Required?	Return Ticket Required?
Full British	Yes	No	Yes
BVP	Not valid	-	-
Australian	Yes	Yes	Yes
Canadian	Yes	Yes	Yes
USA	Yes	Yes	Yes
Other EU (As of 31/12/94)	Yes	1	Yes
Japanese	Yes	No	Yes

PASSPORTS: Valid passport required by all.
British Visitors Passport: Not accepted.
VISAS: Required by all except:
(a) **[1]** nationals of Denmark and the UK (all other EU nationals *do* require visas);
(b) nationals of Antigua & Barbuda, Brazil, Chile, Dominica, Ecuador, Finland, Gambia, Grenada, Guyana, Israel, Japan, South Korea, Netherlands Antilles, Norway, St Lucia, Sweden, Switzerland and Trinidad & Tobago.
Those exempted above do, however, require 60-day Tourist Cards, which are issued on arrival for a fee of S Gld25 to those able to present a valid passport, 1 passport-size photograph and onward or return tickets. For stays of over 60 days, enquire at a Suriname mission (see below).
Transit visas: Not required by those continuing their journey to a third country by the same or the first connecting aircraft.
Cost: Enquire at the appropriate office.
Application to: Those requiring visas should apply to:
(a) Suriname missions in Belgium or The Netherlands if holding a West European passport;
(b) Suriname missions in Belgium, Guyana or The Netherlands if holding an East European passport;
(c) any Suriname mission if holding an Asian or African passport;
(d) the Suriname mission in Washington, DC or Miami if

holding a North, Central or South American passport;
(e) the office of *Suriname Airways* in Curaçao, NA, if holding a Caribbean passport (other offices of *Suriname Airways* may in some circumstances be able to issue visas to would-be visitors from the Caribbean and elsewhere, but check well in advance of the intended departure date).
Application requirements: (a) 1 completed application form. (b) 1 passport-size photo. (c) Passport valid for at least 3 months. (d) Valid ticket.
Working days required: 1-6 weeks, although applications can be processed in approximately 1 week if this is necessary.

MONEY

Currency: Suriname Guilder (S Gld) = 100 cents. Notes are in denominations of S Gld500, 250, 100, 25, 10 and 5. Coins are in denominations of S Gld2.50 and 1, and 25, 10, 5 and 1 cents.
Currency exchange: Suriname Guilders and cents are the only legal tender. Banks and some hotels are authorised to exchange money.
Credit cards: American Express is the most widely accepted credit card; Diners Club has limited acceptance. Check with your credit card company for merchant acceptability and other facilities which may be available.
Travellers cheques: Must be changed at banks.
Exchange rate indicators: The following figures are included as a guide to the movements of the Suriname Guilder against Sterling and the US Dollar:

Date:	Oct '92	Sep '93	Jan '94	Jan '95
£1.00=	2.82	2.73	2.64	516.74
$1.00=	1.78	1.79	1.78	330.29

Currency restrictions: The import and export of local currency is limited to S Gld100. Foreign currency must be declared if it exceeds the equivalent of S Gld5000. On departure, the imported currency can be exported again, providing an exchange permit is produced.
Note: Foreign visitors to Suriname are required to exchange US$175 or N Gld300 on arrival. Children aged 2-12 are expected to exchange half this amount
Banking hours: 0730-1400 Monday to Friday.

DUTY FREE

The following items may be imported into Suriname without incurring customs duty:
400 cigarettes or 100 cigars or 200 cigarillos or 500g of tobacco; 2 litres of spirits; 4 litres of wine; 50g of perfume; 1 litre of eau de toilette; 8 rolls of unexposed film; 60m of unexposed ciné film; 100m of unrecorded tape.
Prohibited items: Fruit (except that of reasonable quality from The Netherlands), meat and meat products, unless a valid health certificate is shown.

PUBLIC HOLIDAYS

Jan 1 '95 New Year's Day. **Mar** *Phagwa. **Mar 3** Eid al-Fitr (End of Ramadan). **Apr 14-17** Easter. **May 1** Labour Day. **Jun 5** Whitsun. **Jul 1** Unity Day. **Nov 25** Independence Day. **Dec 25-26** Christmas. **Jan 1 '96** New Year's Day. **Feb 22** Eid al-Fitr (End of Ramadan). **Mar** *Phagwa. **Apr 5-8** Easter.
Note: (a) In addition, Chinese, Jewish and Indian businesses will be closed for their own religious holidays. (b) Muslim festivals are timed according to local sightings of various phases of the Moon and the dates given above are approximations. During the lunar month of Ramadan that precedes Eid al-Fitr, Muslims fast during the day and feast at night and normal business patterns may be interrupted. Many restaurants are closed during the day and there may be restrictions on smoking and drinking. Some disruption may continue into Eid al-Fitr itself, which may last anything from two to ten days, depending on the region. For more information, see the section *World of Islam* at the back of the book. (c) [*] Hindu festivals are declared according to local astronomical observations and it is only possible to forecast the approximate time of their occurrence.

HEALTH

Regulations and requirements may be subject to change at short notice, and you are advised to contact your doctor well in advance of your intended date of departure. Any numbers in the chart refer to the footnotes below.

	Special Precautions?	Certificate Required?
Yellow Fever	Yes	1
Cholera	No	No
Typhoid & Polio	Yes	-
Malaria	2	-
Food & Drink	3	-

[1]: A yellow fever vaccination certificate is required from travellers arriving from infected areas. Travellers arriving from non-endemic zones should note that vaccination is strongly recommended for travel outside the urban areas, even if an outbreak of the disease has not been reported and they would normally not require a vaccination certificate to enter the country.
[2]: Malaria risk throughout the year in the whole country excluding Paramaribo District and coastal areas north of 5°N. The predominant *falciparum* strain is reported to be 'highly resistant' to chloroquine and 'resistant' to sulfadoxine/pyrimethamine.
[3]: Mains water is normally chlorinated, and whilst relatively safe may cause mild abdominal upsets. Bottled water is available and is advised for the first few weeks of the stay. Drinking water outside main cities and towns is likely to be contaminated and sterilisation is considered essential. The *Melk Centrale* (Government Dairy Company) sells pasteurised milk but otherwise milk is unpasteurised and should be boiled. Powdered or tinned milk is available and is advised, but make sure that it is reconstituted with pure water. Avoid dairy products which are likely to have been made from unboiled milk. Only eat well-cooked meat and fish, preferably served hot. Pork, salad and mayonnaise may carry increased risk. Vegetables should be cooked and fruit peeled.
Rabies is present. For those at high risk, vaccination before arrival should be considered. If you are bitten abroad, seek medical advice without delay. For more information, consult the *Health* section at the back of the book.
Bilharzia (schistosomiasis) is present. Avoid swimming and paddling in fresh water. Swimming pools which are well-chlorinated and maintained are safe.
Health care: Health insurance is strongly recommended. There are five well-equipped hospitals in Paramaribo and a few in outlying areas.

TRAVEL - International

AIR: The national airline is *Suriname Airways (SLM). KLM, Antillean Airlines (ALM,* and *Air France* also operate to Suriname.
Approximate flight time: From London to Paramaribo is 10 hours, excluding stopover time in Amsterdam or Miami, either of which may involve an overnight stay, due to a lack of connecting flights.
International airport: *Paramaribo (PBM)* (Johan Adolf Pengel) is 45km (28 miles) south of the city. A coach meets all arrivals. There are also buses or taxis to the city.
Departure tax: US$5 (£3).
SEA: The main international port is Paramaribo. *Suriname Navigation Company* sails from New Orleans and Mexico monthly. There are coastal services between ports and services to The Netherlands and Germany. The *Royal Netherlands Steamship Company* provides a service from Amsterdam to Suriname with limited passenger accommodation. There are regular ferry services across the Suriname River and Marowijne River to French Guiana and across the Corantijn River to Guyana.
ROAD: The coastal road from Paramaribo serves the borders of Guyana and French Guiana.

TRAVEL - Internal

AIR: Domestic flights to towns in the interior are operated from Paramaribo (Zorg en Hoop airfield) by *Suriname Airways (SLM)*. They also provide services from Paramaribo to the Nieuw Nickerie district, and maintain a charter service.
Note: It is advisable to check the weather conditions before setting out for the interior, as heavy rains can cause delays.
RAIL: There are currently no services in operation.
ROAD: Traffic drives on the left. There is a reasonable, if patchy, road network. Drivers using their own cars should make sure they carry a full set of spares. **Bus:** There are services from the capital to most villages, with fixed routes at low prices. **Taxi:** These are not metered, prices should be agreed before departure and tipping is unnecessary. **Car hire:** Available at the airport and in Paramaribo through main hotels. **Documentation:** International Driving Permit is not required, but recommended.

ACCOMMODATION

HOTELS: Paramaribo has a number of modern hotels with air-conditioning, but advance booking is essential due to the limited number of beds. A 10% service charge is added. There are several small guest-houses and pensions in the city and elsewhere but it is advisable to check with the tourist office for further information. Hotels and restaurants are rare outside the capital, and travellers are advised to bring their own hammock and food. For further information contact SHATA (Suriname Hotel and Tourism Association), PO Box 1514, Hotel Torarica Arcade, Paramaribo. Tel: 471 500 *or* 477 432. Fax: 411 682. Telex: 167.
CAMPING: Cola Kreek, Blaka Watra, Zandery 1 and Republiek are inland resorts with picnic grounds and camping/bathing facilities.
YOUTH HOSTELS: There is a YWCA in Paramaribo (Heerenstraat).

RESORTS & EXCURSIONS

PARAMARIBO: The 17th-century capital is graced with attractive Dutch, French, Spanish and British colonial architecture. The nearby restored Fort Zeelandia houses the *Suriname Museum*. Other attractions include the 19th-century Roman-Catholic cathedral (made entirely of wood – as is the 17th-century synagogue which lies in stark contrast to the biggest mosque in the Caribbean), *Independence Square*, the *Presidential Palace* (with an attractive palm garden) and the lively waterfront and market districts. *Palmentuin* is a pleasant park, as is the *Cultuurtuin*, but the latter is a fair distance from the town and there are no buses.
ELSEWHERE: The countryside is sparsely populated, and the scenery and the tropical vegetation and wildlife provide the main attractions: mangrove swamps, rivers and rapids of all sizes, Amazonian rainforest and mountains, and jaguars, tapirs, snakes, tropical birds and giant sea turtles from the Matapica and Galibi beach reserves, as well as highly endangered species such as the Cock of the Rock, the Harpy Eagle, the Giant Otter and the Mantee. There are no beaches. There are a number of nature reserves, including the *Raleighvallen/Voltzberg Nature Park* and *Brownsberg Nature Park*. Some offer accommodation in lodges.

SOCIAL PROFILE

FOOD & DRINK: Due to the diverse ethnic mixture of the population, Suriname offers a good variety of dishes including Indonesian, Creole, Chinese, Indian, European and American. Indonesian dishes are recommended, usually *rijsttafel* with rice (boiled or fried) and a number of spicy meat and vegetable side dishes, *nasi goreng* (Indonesian fried rice) and *bami goreng* (Indonesian fried noodles). Creole dishes include *pom* (ground tayer roots and poultry), *pastei* (chicken pie with various vegetables) and peanut soup. Indian dishes such as *roti* (dough pancake) served with curried chicken and potatoes and Chinese dishes such as *chow-mein* and *chop suey* are excellent. *Moksi meti* (various meats served on rice) is a local favourite. Local drinks include the Indonesian *Dawet* (a coconut drink), *Gemberbier* (Creole ginger drink) and *Pilsener Parbo Bier*. There are some restaurants in Paramaribo and Niew-Nickerie, but they tend to be scarce outside the capital.
NIGHTLIFE: There are several nightclubs in Paramaribo, often attached to a hotel, with live music and dancing. There are also a number of discotheques and several cinemas including a drive-in. In general it is best to stick to the hotels unless accompanied by locals who know the reputations of other nightspots, in particular those out of the town centre. The *Local Events Bulletin* lists all current activities and is usually available in hotels.
SHOPPING: Popular items include Maroon tribal woodcarvings, hand-carved and hand-painted trays and gourds, Amerindian bows and arrows, cotton hammocks, wicker and ceramic objects, gold and silver jewellery, Javanese bamboo and batik, as well as tobacco and liquor products. Chinese shops sell imported jade, silks, glass, dolls, needlework and wall decorations. **Shopping hours:** 0800-1630 Monday to Friday; 0800-1300 Saturday.
SPORT: Swimming: Besides the beaches (which are not of the highest standard), there are hotel pools and, in Paramaribo, Niew-Nickerie, Moengo and Groningen, there are public pools. Visitors can also swim in the city's private clubs if introduced. **Tennis:** Some private clubs and hotels have courts and games can be arranged through an introduction. Hotels provide further information. **Golf:** An 18-hole golf course is located 5km (3 miles) from Paramaribo on the airport road. **Sailing:** There are facilities at *Jachthaven Ornamibo*. **Fishing:** Tarpon and piranha offer excellent sport. **Spectator sports: Football** can be seen regularly at the Andre Kamperveen Stadium and **basketball, volleyball, badminton** and **indoor soccer** matches are held at the Ismay Van Wilgen Sports Hall (both in Paramaribo). Other venues are Amos Sports Hall and Anthony Esty Sports Hall.
SOCIAL CONVENTIONS: Informal dress is suitable for most occasions. *Guayabera* or safari outfits are increasingly worn in place of jackets and ties. Women should wear long trousers on trips to the interior. Beachwear should be confined to the beach or poolside. **Photography:** It is inadvisable to photograph public places, particularly of a political or military nature (including police stations). There is a general sensitivity about the taking of photographs – it is advisable to seek prior permission. **Tipping:** Hotels include 10-15% service charge and restaurants may also add 10% to the bill.

BUSINESS PROFILE

ECONOMY: Until the civil war, aluminium and related industries provided over 75% of the country's foreign exchange earnings. Other raw materials include iron ore, copper, nickel, gold and platinum. The vast resources held within Suriname's extensive jungles remain largely untapped, although the timber industry is developing rapidly. There is great agricultural potential; rice, citrus fruits, vegetables and bananas are the main crops. Shrimp fishing is both important and lucrative. There is a small manufacturing sector producing goods ranging from soap to telephone exchanges for the domestic market. Economic relations with The Netherlands, once crucial to the economy, suffered following the military takeover, and The Netherlands suspended its aid programme. By early 1987, the civil war had brought the aluminium industry to a standstill and destroyed crucial sectors of the country's infrastructure. The establishment of a transitional government restored some of the mother country's goodwill and aid resumed in February 1988. It was, however, suspended once again after a further military coup in December 1990 – and resumed again following the 1991 elections. The economy has since shown signs of improvement, generating a trade surplus, although there seems to be some danger of overheating as inflation has risen sharply from single-figure levels in the late 1980s. Suriname signed a loan agreement with Brazil in January 1988. The leading importers into Suriname are the USA, The Netherlands, Trinidad & Tobago and Brazil. Suriname has observer status within the Carribean trade bloc CARICOM.
BUSINESS: A suit is expected for business. **Office hours:** 0700-1500 Monday to Friday. **Government office hours:** 0700-1500 Monday to Friday.
COMMERCIAL INFORMATION: The following organisation can offer advice: Suriname Chamber of Commerce and Industry, PO Box 149, Dr J C de Mirandastraat 10, Paramaribo. Tel: 473 527. Fax: 474 779. Telex: 375.

CLIMATE

Tropical climate cooled by the northeast tradewinds. The best time to visit is December to April. The hot season runs from May to October and has the highest rainfall.
Required clothing: Lightweights and rainwear.

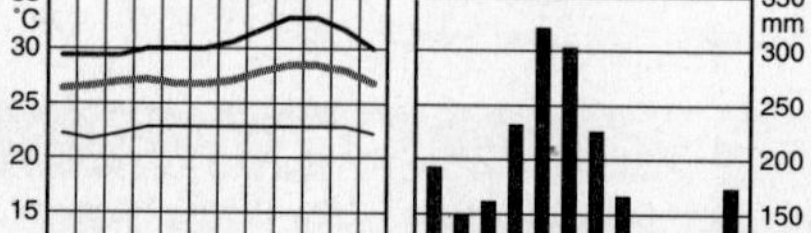

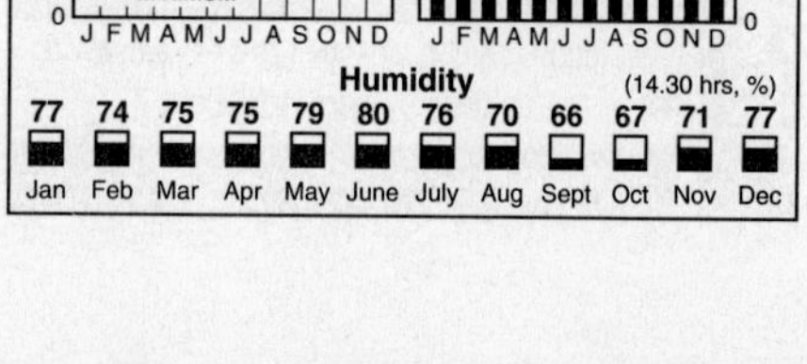

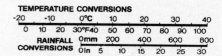

SURINAM AIRWAYS

Surinam Airways with Paramaribo as its home base ... is to be considered the first hop to the entire Caribbean and the rest of South America.

Amsterdam

New York

- Passengers Handling
- Catering Services
- Charter Services
- Cargo Handling
- Technical Services

Miami

Surinam Airways has as subsidiary:

METS

Movement for Eco-Tourism in Suriname

Barbados

Curaçao

Trinidad

Georgetown

Paramaribo

Cayenne

Belém

The METS caters to a special type of traveller who understands the delicate social and environmental balance and likes to visit unspoiled land and friendly people.

With three resorts in the interior, METS offers personal service to meet the needs of individuals and small groups seeking extraordinary travel experiences.
In addition to one-of-a-kind rainforest interior excursions, tours are also available throughout the rest of the country and in combination with the Guyanas, Curaçao, Trinidad & Tobago, Barbados and Brazil.

Together we will make your rainforest fantasy become reality

" *Fly Surinam Airways and be sure !* "

SURINAM AIRWAYS: HEAD-OFFICE PARAMARIBO
136 COPPENAMESTRAAT
TEL.: (597) 46 57 00 FAX.: (597) 49 00 30

SURINAM AIRWAYS   AMSTERDAM, HOLLAND
165 WETERINGSCHANS
TEL.: (020) 626 2060/(020) 648 0333 FAX.: (020) 626 4549

METS n.v. HEAD-OFFICE PARAMARIBO
05 RUDIELAAN SURINAME SOUTH-AMERICA
TEL.: (597) 49 28 92 FAX.: (597) 49 70 62

☐ international airport

Location: Southern Africa.

Ministry of Broadcasting, Information and Tourism
PO Box 338, Mbabane, Swaziland
Tel: 42761. Fax: 42774.
Kingdom of Swaziland High Commission
58 Pont Street, London SW1X 0AE
Tel: (0171) 581 4976/7/8. Fax: (0171) 589 5332. Telex:
28853 (a/b SWAZI G). Opening hours: 0900-1630
Monday to Thursday; 0900-1600 Friday.
British High Commission
Allister Miller Street, Mbabane, Swaziland
Tel: 42581. Fax: 42585. Telex: 2079 (a/b WD).
Embassy of the Kingdom of Swaziland
3400 International Drive, NW, Washington, DC 20008
Tel: (202) 362 6683/5. Fax: (202) 244 8059.
Embassy of the United States of America
PO Box 199, Central Bank Building, Warner Street,
Mbabane, Swaziland
Tel: 46441/5. Fax: 45959. Telex: 2016 (a/b WD).
High Commission for the Kingdom of Swaziland
Suite 1204, 130 Albert Street, Ottawa, Ontario K1P 5G4
Tel: (613) 567 1480. Fax: (613) 567 1058.
**The Canadian Embassy in Pretoria deals with
enquiries relating to Swaziland (see** *South Africa*
earlier in the book).

AREA: 17,363 sq km (6704 sq miles).
POPULATION: 768,000 (1990 estimate).
POPULATION DENSITY: 44.2 per sq km.
CAPITAL: Mbabane. **Population:** 38,290 (1986).
GEOGRAPHY: Swaziland is surrounded to the north,
west and south by the Transvaal of South Africa and to
the east by Mozambique. There are four main
topographical regions: the Highveld Inkangala, a wide
ribbon of partly reforested, rugged country including the
Usutu pine forest; the Peak Timbers in the northwest; the
Middleveld, which rolls down from the Highveld through
hills and fertile valleys; and the Lowveld, or bush
country, with hills rising from 170-360m (560-1180ft).
The Lubombo plateau is an escarpment along the eastern
fringe of the lowveld, comprising mainly cattle country
and mixed farmland. One of the best-watered areas in
southern Africa, Swaziland's four major rivers are the

Komati, Usutu, Mbuluzi and Ngwavuma, flowing
west–east to the Indian Ocean.
LANGUAGE: English and Siswati.
RELIGION: Christian with Animist minority.
TIME: GMT + 2.
ELECTRICITY: 220 volts AC, 50Hz. 15-amp round
pin plugs are in use.
COMMUNICATIONS: Telephone: IDD is available.
Country code: 268. Outgoing international calls must go
through the international operator. Public telephones are
available. **Fax:** Some hotels have facilities.
Telex/telegram: Facilities are available in the capital.
Post: Post offices are in all main centres. Airmail to
Europe takes up to two weeks. Post office hours: 0800-
1300 and 1400-1700 Monday to Friday, 0800-1100
Saturday. **Press:** The two English-language newspapers
in Swaziland are *The Times of Swaziland* (Monday to
Friday) and the *Swazi Observer* (Sunday).
**BBC World Service and Voice of America
frequencies:** From time to time these change. See the
section *How to Use this Book* for more information.
BBC:

MHz	21.66	11.94	6.190	3.255
Voice of America:				
MHz	21.49	15.60	9.525	6.035

PASSPORT/VISA

*Regulations and requirements may be subject to change at short notice, and you
are advised to contact the appropriate diplomatic or consular authority before
finalising travel arrangements. Details of these may be found at the head of this
country's entry. Any numbers in the chart refer to the footnotes below.*

	Passport Required?	Visa Required?	Return Ticket Required?
Full British	Yes	No	2
BVP	Not Valid	-	-
Australian	Yes	No	2
Canadian	Yes	No	2
USA	Yes	No	2
Other EU (As of 31/12/94)	Yes	1	2
Japanese	Yes	Yes	2

PASSPORTS: Valid passport required by all.
British Visitors Passport: Not accepted.
VISAS: Required by all except:
(a) nationals of countries as shown in the chart above;
(b) [1] nationals of EU countries (nationals of France,
Germany and Spain *do* require a visa);
(c) nationals of Bahamas, Barbados, Botswana, Cyprus,
Finland, Gambia, Ghana, Grenada, Guyana, Iceland,
Israel, Jamaica, Kenya, Lesotho, Liechtenstein, Malawi,
Malaysia, Malta, Nauru, New Zealand, Norway, Papua
New Guinea, San Marino, Seychelles, Sierra Leone,
Singapore, Solomon Islands, South Africa, Sweden,
Tanzania, Tonga, Trinidad & Tobago, Uganda, Uruguay,
Western Samoa, Zambia and Zimbabwe (including
holders of an unexpired Rhodesian passport).
Note [2]: A return ticket is recommended, although not
essential.
Types of visa: Single entry – £8; Multiple entry (3
months) – £16; Multiple entry (6 months)– £24; Multiple
entry (9 months) – £38; Multiple entry (12 months) – £52.
Available free of charge to those EU citizens requiring
visas (see above) upon arrival at the port of entry.
Validity: Entry visa is valid for 3, 6 or 12 months. Any
visitor wishing to extend stay should apply for a
temporary residence permit from the Chief Immigration
Officer in Swaziland.
Application to: Consulate (or Consular section at
Embassy or High Commission). For addresses, see top of
entry.
Application requirements: (a) Application form. (b) 2
passport-size photographs. (c) Fee. (d) Valid passport. (e)
Proof of means of support during stay.
Working days required: Postal – 48 hours; in person –
24 hours.
Temporary residence: Apply to Chief Immigration
Officer.

MONEY

Currency: Lilangeni (E) = 100 cents. The plural of
Lilangeni is Emalangeni. Notes are in denominations of
E50, 20, 10, 5 and 2. Coins are in denominations of E1,
and 50, 20, 10, 5, 2 and 1 cents. The South African Rand
is also accepted as legal tender (E1 = 1 Rand) although
coins are not accepted.
Currency exchange: Visitors are advised to exchange
Emalangeni back to their own currency before leaving
Swaziland.
Credit cards: American Express and Access/Mastercard
are widely accepted, whilst Visa has more limited use.
Check with your credit card company for details of

merchant acceptability and other facilities which may be
available.
Travellers cheques: Widely accepted.
Exchange rate indicators: The following figures are
included as a guide to the movements of the Lilangeni
against Sterling and the US Dollar:

Date:	Oct '92	Sep '93	Jan '94	Jan '95
£1.00=	4.68	5.15	5.03	5.54
$1.00=	2.95	3.38	3.39	3.54

Currency restrictions: The import and export of foreign
and local currency is unrestricted.
Banking hours: 0830-1300 Monday to Friday, 0830-
1100 Saturday.

DUTY FREE

The following items may be imported into Swaziland
without incurring customs duty:
*400 cigarettes and 50 cigars and 250g of tobacco; 1 litre
of spirits and 2 litres of wine; 50ml of perfume and 250ml
eau de toilette per person; gifts up to a value of E200 per
person.*

PUBLIC HOLIDAYS

Jan 1 '95 New Year's Day. **Mar 13** Commonwealth
Day. **Apr 14-17** Easter. **Apr 19** Birthday of King
Mswati. **Apr 25** National Flag Day. **May 25** Ascension
Day. **Jul 22** Birthday of the late King Sobhuza. **Aug 24**
Umhlanga-Reed Dance Day. **Sep 6** Somhlolo
Independence Day. **Oct 24** United Nations Day. **Dec 25-
26** Christmas. **Jan 1 '96** New Year's Day. **Mar 14**
Commonwealth Day. **Apr 5-8** Easter. **Apr 19** Birthday
of King Mswati. **Apr 25** National Flag Day.

HEALTH

*Regulations and requirements may be subject to change at short notice, and
you are advised to contact your doctor well in advance of your intended date of
departure. Any numbers in the chart refer to the footnotes below.*

	Special Precautions?	Certificate Required?
Yellow Fever	No	1
Cholera	Yes	-
Typhoid & Polio	Yes	-
Malaria	2	-
Food & Drink	3	-

[1]: A yellow fever vaccination certificate is required of
travellers arriving from infected areas.
[2]: Malaria risk exists throughout the year in all
Lowveld areas. The predominant *falciparum* strain is
reported to be 'highly resistant' to chloroquine.
[3]: Tap water is considered safe to drink. Drinking water
outside main cities and towns may be contaminated and
sterilisation is advisable. Milk is pasteurised and dairy
products are safe for consumption. Local meat, poultry,
seafood, fruit and vegetables are generally considered
safe to eat.
Rabies is present. For those at high risk vaccination
before arrival should be considered. If you are bitten
abroad seek medical advice without delay. For more
information, consult the *Health* section at the back of the
book.
Bilharzia (schistosomiasis) is present. Avoid swimming
and paddling in fresh water. Swimming pools which are
well-chlorinated and maintained are safe.
Health care: Health insurance is recommended.

TRAVEL - International

AIR: Swaziland's national airline is *Royal Swazi
National Airways Corporation (ZC).*
Approximate flight time: From London to Manzini is
16 hours including stopover.
International airport: *Manzini (MTS)* (Matsapha), 8km
(5 miles) from the city. Airport facilities include
banks/bureaux de change (0700-1730), restaurants and
snack bar. Coach and taxi service is available at all
arrivals.
Departure tax: E10.
ROAD: There are good roads from Johannesburg,
Durban and northern Zululand, as well as tourist buses
running from Natal and the Transvaal. **Bus:** There is a
weekly service from Mbabane and Manzini to
Johannesburg, and a twice-weekly connection from
Mbabane to Maputo.

TRAVEL - Internal

ROAD: The road system is largely well developed,
although some roads are often winding depending on the
topography of the different areas. The maximum speed
limit on all roads is 80kmph (50mph). Traffic drives on

the left. **Bus:** There are numerous buses connecting the different parts of the country, including nonstop buses. **Car hire:** There are a number of car hire companies in Swaziland such as *Hertz, Imperial, Avis,* etc. **Documentation:** National driving licences are valid for up to six months provided they are printed in English or accompanied by a certified translation. International Driving Permits are also recognised.
JOURNEY TIMES: The following chart gives approximate journey times (in hours and minutes) from Mbabane to other major towns in Swaziland.

	Road
Manzini	0.45
Nhlangano	2.00
Piggs Peak	1.00
Siteki	1.30

ACCOMMODATION

There are some good hotels in Swaziland, some of international standard, but it is necessary to book well in advance. There are also smaller motels and inns, campsites and caravan parks outside the city. For further information, contact the Hotel and Tourism Association of Swaziland, PO Box 462, Sokhamlilo Building, Johnson/Walker Streets, Mbabane. Tel: 42218. Fax: 44516. **Grading:** The star-grading system is in use.

RESORTS & EXCURSIONS

The lush **Ezulwini Valley** is a miracle of nature and the seat of Swaziland's major tourist attractions. Though Swaziland has long been regarded as one of the most beautiful countries in Africa, it was not until an Italian and South African syndicate built southern Africa's first casino hotel on a prime valley site some 12 years ago that Swaziland geared itself towards tourism.
In the valley is the magnificent Royal Swazi golf course, the casino, the hot mineral spring – one of eight in the country – known affectionately by locals and guests as the 'Cuddle Puddle', a health studio and a cluster of fine hotels forming the *Holiday Valley* complex.
Swaziland's industrial centre of **Manzini** lies east across the valley, a good half-hour's drive. On the way visitors pass signposts to Swaziland's most famous waterfall, *Mantenga Falls*, the thriving *Mantenga Arts & Crafts Centre*, *Mlilwane Game Sanctuary*, **Lobamba**, the spiritual and legislative capital of the kingdom, Matsapha Airport and the industrial area of **Matsapha**, which produces everything from beer to television sets.
Mlilwane, the oldest established game sanctuary in Swaziland, was once privately owned but was offered to the nation as a sanctuary for wild animals. A strong effort has been made to bring back wildlife to the country. Following the establishment of Mlilwane, two other game sanctuaries have been proclaimed: **Malolotsha**, in the north near Piggs Peak, and **Hlane**, in the shadow of the escarpment in the northeast. Hlane has wide open spaces supporting big herds of game where the visitor can see the old traditional scenes of Africa. Malolotsha, situated on top of a mountain range and surrounded by steep canyons and waterfalls, is breathtaking in its beauty. Both are easily reached by road.
Although southern Swaziland is currently being developed for tourism, there are at present no plans for a game sanctuary in this area. The first project in the development of the southern region has been the construction of another casino hotel at **Nhlangano**, about 120km (75 miles) south of Mbabane. The sports facilities, which include a golf course and swimming pool, are excellent. The nearby **Mkondo River** twists its way through gorges and valleys, past waterfalls, pools and rapids and, in the distance, the mountain ranges gleam brown, mauve and blue. Some of Swaziland's finest Bushmen paintings are found in this area. Other Bushmen paintings are located in the mountains north of Mbabane.

SOCIAL PROFILE

FOOD & DRINK: Restaurants are found mainly in the larger centres and at hotels. Most serve international cuisine; Greek, Hungarian and Indian food is available. Food stalls in the local markets sell traditional Swazi meat stew and maize meal or stamped mealies and roasted corn on the cob (in season). **Drink:** There is a good selection of spirits, beers and wines. Traditional Swazi beer can be tasted in rural areas. There are no formal licensing hours.
NIGHTLIFE: In the main centres of Mbabane and Ezulwini Valley there are nightclubs and discotheques, some with live music and cabaret. The main attraction in Ezulwini Valley is the casino at the Royal Swazi Hotel. There is also a cinema here.
SHOPPING: There is a modern shopping complex in Mbabane but local markets are always interesting places

to shop. Purchases from craft centres include beadwork, basketry, grass and sisal mats, copperware, wooden bowls, local gemstone jewellery, wooden and soapstone carvings, calabashes, knobkerries, battleaxes, walking sticks, *karosses* (animal skin mats), drums, woven cloth and batik and tie-dye, which are often incorporated into traditional Swazi garments. **Shopping hours:** 0800-1700 Monday to Friday, 0800-1300 Saturday.
SPORT: Golf: There is an 18-hole golf course in the Ezulwini Valley attached to the Royal Swazi Sun Hotel and Spa and the Havelock Golf Course. **Tennis:** Courts are available at numerous major hotels, notably the Royal Swazi. **Swimming:** Several hotels have pools and non-residents are generally able to use the facilities. **Hiking:** A popular hike is up Sheba's Breasts. Others include the ascent to Malolotsha Falls at Piggs Peak and the climb up Emlembe, Swaziland's highest peak.
SPECIAL EVENTS: Every December or January at a time carefully chosen by astrologers the *Incwala* ('Fruit Ceremony') takes place. It is a 4-day ceremony encompassing the entire nation and culminates in a ritual during which the king eats the first fruit of the new season. The ceremony confers the blessing of their ancestors on the nation's consumption of these fruits. In August or September the *Umhlanga* ('Reed Dance') is an event in which young women pay homage to the Queen Mother.
SOCIAL CONVENTIONS: Traditional ways of life are still strong and Swazi culture in the form of religious music, dance, poetry and craftsmanship play an important part in daily life. Casual wear is normal although more formal wear is customary at the casino and sophisticated hotels. Visitors wishing to camp near villages should first inform the headman. He can normally help with customs. **Photography:** Permission to photograph individuals should always be sought. In some cases a gratuity may be asked for (especially if the subject has gone to some effort to make a show – for example, by wearing traditional regalia). It is prohibited to photograph the Royal Palace, the Royal Family, uniformed police, army personnel, army vehicles or aircraft and bank buildings. Visitors wishing to photograph traditional ceremonies should first contact the Government Information Service, PO Box 338, Mbabane. Tel: 42761. **Tipping:** 10% of the bill is customary in restaurants and hotels.

BUSINESS PROFILE

ECONOMY: The economy is dominated by and closely linked with that of South Africa and the country is a member of the Southern African Customs Union and part of the Rand Monetary Area. Agriculture is by far the largest part of the economy, employing over 75% of the working population. Sugar, citrus fruits and pineapples are the main cash crops. Important industries include sugar refining, forestry, asbestos and coal. Tourism, mostly from South Africa, is increasing. In recent years the country has suffered from a reduction in world demand for its main exports and a shortage of foreign capital. Government policy is currently concerned with trying to encourage investment in the agricultural and mining sectors. This effort was hampered by the frequent suspicion that much of its apparent trade comprised

goods in transit to and from South Africa evading international embargoes. This practice, proven by a US congressional inquiry in 1987, declined temporarily but soon resumed its previous level. The end of international sanctions against South Africa will ease pressure on the Swazi economy in the long term, although there may be some short-term loss of revenue. Expansion of the mining sector is the most promising avenue for economic growth which has been at best sluggish in recent years. Apart from South Africa, which dominates Swazi trade, the most important trading partners are the UK and France.
BUSINESS: Lightweight suits are generally expected for business. Appointments are necessary and business cards are exchanged. English is widely spoken in business circles. **Office hours:** 0800-1300 and 1400-1700 Monday to Friday, 0800-1300 Saturday.
COMMERCIAL INFORMATION: The following organisations can offer advice: Swaziland Industrial Development Co (SIDC), PO Box 866, Dhlan'Ubeka House, Tin/Walker Streets, Mbabane. Tel: 43391. Fax: 45619. Telex: 2052; *or*
Swaziland Chamber of Commerce and Industry, PO Box 72, Mbabane. Tel/Fax: 44408. Fax: 45442.
CONFERENCES/CONVENTIONS: The principal facilities are at the Royal Swazi Convention Centre in the Ezulwini Valley, which has seating for up to 600 persons. Several hotels also have facilities for smaller numbers, with back-up services. The Ministry of Broadcasting, Information and Tourism (address at beginning of entry) can supply information.

CLIMATE

Due to the variations in altitude the weather is changeable. Except in the lowland it is rarely uncomfortably hot and nowhere very cold, although frosts occasionally occur in the Highveld which has a wetter, temperate climate. The Middleveld and Lubombo are drier and subtropical with most rain from October to March.

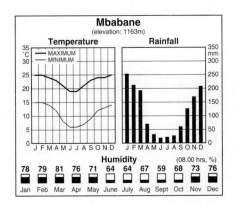

Mbabane
(elevation: 1163m)

Humidity												(08.00 hrs, %)
78	79	81	76	71	64	64	67	59	68	73	76	
Jan	Feb	Mar	Apr	May	June	July	Aug	Sept	Oct	Nov	Dec	

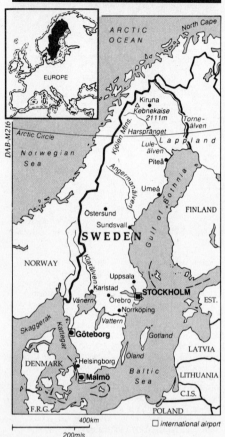

Location: Northeast Europe, Scandinavia.

Swedish Travel & Tourism Council
PO Box 3030, 103 61 Stockholm, Sweden
Tel: (8) 725 5500. Fax: (8) 725 5531.
Svenska Turistföreningen (Swedish Touring Club)
PO Box 25, Drottninggatan 31-33, 101 20 Stockholm, Sweden
Tel: (8) 790 3100. Fax: (8) 201 332.
Royal Swedish Embassy
11 Montagu Place, London W1H 2AL
Tel: (0171) 917 6400. Fax: (0171) 724 4174. Telex: 28249. Tel: (0171) 917 6413 or 917 6413 (Visa section). Opening hours: 0900-1230 Monday to Friday. Telephone enquiries: 0900-1230 and 1400-1600 Monday to Friday.
Swedish Travel & Tourism Council
73 Welbeck Street, London W1M 8AN
Tel: (0171) 485 3135/6. Fax: (0171) 935 5853. Opening hours: 0930-1600 Monday to Friday.
British Embassy
PO Box 27819, Skarpögatan 6-8, 115 93 Stockholm, Sweden
Tel: (8) 671 9000. Fax: (8) 662 9989. Telex: 19340 (a/b BRITEMB S).
Consulates in: Gothenburg (Göteborg), Malmö, Luleå and Sundsvall.
Royal Swedish Embassy
Suites 1200 & 715, 600 New Hampshire Avenue, NW, Washington, DC 20037
Tel: (202) 944 5600. Fax: (202) 342 1319.
Consulates in: Los Angeles and New York (tel: (212) 751 5900).

Timatic	Health	
	GALILEO/WORLDSPAN: **TI-DFT/STO/HE**	
	SABRE: **TIDFT/STO/HE**	
	Visa	
	GALILEO/WORLDSPAN: **TI-DFT/STO/VI**	
	SABRE: **TIDFT/STO/VI**	
	For more information on Timatic codes refer to Contents.	

Swedish Travel & Tourism Council
18th Floor, 655 Third Avenue, New York, NY 10017
Tel: (212) 949 2274. Fax: (212) 697 0835.
Scandinavian Tourist Boards in: Chicago and Beverly Hills.
Embassy of the United States of America
Strandvägen 101, 115 89 Stockholm, Sweden
Tel: (8) 783 5300. Fax: (8) 661 1964.
Royal Swedish Embassy
Mercury Court, 377 Dalhousie Street, Ottawa, Ontario K1P 9N8
Tel: (613) 241 8553. Fax: (613) 236 5720. Telex: 0533331 (a/b SVENSK OTT).
Consulates in: Calgary, Edmonton, Fredericton, Halifax, Montréal, Québec, Regina, St John's, Toronto, Vancouver and Winnipeg.
Canadian Embassy
PO Box 16129, 7th Floor, Tegelbacken 4, 103 23 Stockholm, Sweden
Tel: (8) 613 9900. Fax: (8) 242 491.

AREA: 440,945 sq km (170,250 sq miles).
POPULATION: 8,692,013 (1992 estimate).
POPULATION DENSITY: 19.3 per sq km.
CAPITAL: Stockholm. **Population**: 684,576 (1992).
GEOGRAPHY: Sweden is bordered by Norway to the west and Finland to the northeast, with a long Baltic coast to the east and south. Approximately half the country is forested and most of the many thousands of lakes are situated in the southern central area. The largest lake is Vänern, with an area of 5540 sq km (2140 sq miles). Swedish Lappland to the north is mountainous and extends into the Arctic Circle.
LANGUAGE: Swedish. Lapp is spoken by the Sami population in the north. English is taught as the first foreign language from the age of nine.
RELIGION: Swedish State Church (Evangelical Lutheran); other Protestant minorities.
TIME: GMT + 1 (GMT + 2 from last Sunday in March to Saturday before last Sunday in September).
ELECTRICITY: 220 volts, 3-phase AC, 50Hz. 2-pin continental plugs are used.
COMMUNICATIONS: **Telephone**: Full IDD is available. Country code: 46. Outgoing international code: 009. Unlike other European countries, telephones are not found in post offices but in special 'Telegraph Offices'. **Fax**: Widely available throughout the country. **Telex/telegram**: Facilities are available in every main town. **Post**: Post offices are open during normal shopping hours (0900-1800 Monday to Friday; 1000-1300 Saturday). Some branches may be closed Saturday during July. Post boxes are yellow. Stamps and aerograms are on sale at post offices and also at most bookstalls and stationers. Airmail within Europe takes three to four days. *Poste Restante* facilities are widely available in post offices. **Press**: The provinces have their own newspapers which are widely read in their respective regions; the major dailies are confined largely to the capital. Many papers are financed by political parties but independence and freedom of the press is firmly maintained. All papers are in Swedish.
BBC World Service and Voice of America frequencies: From time to time these change. See the section How to Use this Book for more information.
BBC:

MHz	15.07	12.09	9.410	6.195

Voice of America:

MHz	11.97	9.670	6.040	5.995

PASSPORT/VISA

Regulations and requirements may be subject to change at short notice, and you are advised to contact the appropriate diplomatic or consular authority before finalising travel arrangements. Details of these may be found at the head of this country's entry. Any numbers in the chart refer to the footnotes below.

	Passport Required?	Visa Required?	Return Ticket Required?
Full British	1	No/2	No
BVP	Valid	-	-
Australian	Yes	No	No
Canadian	Yes	No	No
USA	Yes	No	No
Other EU (As of 31/12/94)	1	No	No
Japanese	Yes	No	No

PASSPORTS: Valid passport required by all except:
(a) [1] nationals of Belgium, France, Germany, Italy, Luxembourg and The Netherlands, provided they hold a valid national ID card (for a stay of up to 3 months) or, for UK citizens, a BVP;
(b) nationals of Austria, Switzerland and Liechtenstein provided they hold valid national ID cards (for a stay of up to 3 months).
British Visitors Passport: BVPs are valid for holidays or unpaid business trips of up to 3 months. Visits to Denmark, Sweden, Norway and Iceland as a group must not exceed 3 months in any 9-month period.
VISAS: Required by all except:
(a) nationals of the countries referred to in the chart above ([2] but note that UK passport holders who are subject to British Immigration controls may need visas);
(b) nationals of Andorra, Argentina, Austria, Bahamas, Barbados, Belize, Bolivia, Botswana, Brazil, Brunei, Chile, Colombia, Costa Rica, Croatia, Cuba, Cyprus, Czech Republic, Dominica, Dominican Republic, Ecuador, El Salvador, Fiji, Finland, Gambia, Grenada, Guatemala, Honduras, Hong Kong (UK passport holders), Hungary, Iceland, Israel, Jamaica, Kenya, Kiribati, South Korea, Lesotho, Liechtenstein, Malaysia, Malta, Malawi, Mauritius, Mexico, Monaco, Namibia, New Zealand, Nicaragua, Norway, Panama, Paraguay, Peru, Poland, St Lucia, St Vincent & the Grenadines, San Marino, Seychelles, Singapore, Slovenia, Solomon Islands, Suriname, Swaziland, Switzerland, Tanzania, Thailand, Trinidad & Tobago, Tuvalu, Uganda, Uruguay, Venezuela, Zambia and Zimbabwe.
Types of visa: Ordinary (tourist/business) and Transit. Cost: £13.50. Visa fees are waived for the following:
(a) applicants under 16 years of age;
(b) British Protected Persons travelling on UK passports;
(c) nationals of Algeria, Antigua & Barbuda, Bangladesh, Benin, Bosnia-Hercegovina, Bulgaria, Burkina Faso, China, Côte d'Ivoire, Estonia, Guyana, India, Indonesia, Iraq, North Korea, Kuwait, Latvia, Lithuania, Maldives, Morocco, Niger, Pakistan, Papua New Guinea, Philippines, St Kitts & Nevis, Sri Lanka, Syria, Togo, Tunisia and Turkey.
Validity: 90 days.
Application to: Consulate (or Consular section at Embassy). For addresses, see top of entry.
Application requirements: (a) Valid passport. (b) 2 passport-size photographs. (c) Fee (cheque or postal order only if sent by post). (d) Completed application form. (e) Stamped, self-addressed envelope for return of passport.
Working days required: 2-8 weeks.
Temporary residence: Enquire at Embassy.

MONEY

Currency: Swedish Krona (SKr) = 100 öre. Notes are in denominations of SKr1000, 500, 100, 50, 20 and 10. Coins are in denominations of SKr10, 5 and 1, and 50 öre.
Currency exchange: Personal cheques can be cashed in Swedish banks under the Eurocheque system.
Credit cards: Diners Club, American Express, Visa and Access/Mastercard are all widely accepted. Check with your credit card company for details of merchant acceptability and other facilities which may be available.
Travellers cheques: Widely accepted.
Exchange rate indicators: The following figures are included as a guide to the movements of the Swedish Krona against Sterling and the US Dollar.

Date:	Oct '92	Sep '93	Jan '94	Jan '95
£1.00=	9.17	12.08	12.33	11.63
$1.00=	5.78	7.91	8.34	7.43

Currency restrictions: There are no restrictions on the import or export of local or foreign currencies.
Banking hours: Generally 0930-1500 Monday to Friday, but in many large cities banks close at 1800. All banks are closed Saturday.

DUTY FREE

The following items may be imported into Sweden without incurring customs duty by:
(a) European residents:
200 cigarettes or 100 cigarillos or 50 cigars or 250g of tobacco; 1 litre wine (2 litres if no spirits are imported); 1 litre spirits (over 20 years of age); 2 litres of beer (over 20 years of age); a reasonable quantity of perfume; gifts up to the value of SKr1000.
(b) Non-European residents:
400 cigarettes or 100 cigars or 500g of tobacco or 500g tobacco products; the same quantity of other duty-free items as European residents.
Note: Drink regulations are strictly enforced.

PUBLIC HOLIDAYS

Jan 1 '95 New Year's Day. **Jan 6** Epiphany. **Apr 14** Good Friday. **Apr 17** Easter Monday. **May 1** May Day. **May 25** Ascension Day. **Jun 5** Whit Monday. **Jun 24** Midsummer Holiday. **Nov 4** For All Saints' Day. **Dec 25** Christmas Day. **Dec 26** St Stephen's Day. **Jan 1 '96** New Year's Day. **Jan 6** Epiphany. **Apr 5** Good Friday. **Apr 8** Easter Monday.

HEALTH

Regulations and requirements may be subject to change at short notice, and you are advised to contact your doctor well in advance of your intended date of departure. Any numbers in the chart refer to the footnotes below.

	Special Precautions?	Certificate Required?
Yellow Fever	No	No
Cholera	No	No
Typhoid & Polio	No	-
Malaria	No	-
Food & Drink	No	-

Health care: There are full Reciprocal Health Agreements with most other European countries including the UK. The UK Agreement allows free hospital in-patient treatment (including medicines) to those presenting a UK passport; children are also allowed free dental treatment. Out-patient treatment at hospitals, all treatment at clinics and general surgeries, most prescribed medicines and ambulance travel must be paid for. Travelling expenses to and from hospital may be partially refunded.

TRAVEL - International

AIR: The national airline is *SAS Scandinavian Airlines (SK).*
For free advice on air travel, call the Air Travel Advisory Bureau on (0171) 636 5000 (London) *or* (0161) 832 2000 (Manchester).
Approximate flight times: From *London* to Stockholm is 2 hours 30 minutes and to Gothenburg is 1 hour 45 minutes.
From *Los Angeles* to Stockholm is 14 hours 10 minutes.
From *New York* to Stockholm is 7 hours 45 minutes.
International airports: *Stockholm (STO)* (Arlanda) is 41km (25 miles) north of the city. Airport facilities: full outgoing duty-free shop; car hire (several major firms); bank/bureau de change (0700-2200); restaurant/bar (1130-2130); and coffee shop (0630-2130 Monday to Friday, 0630-0030 weekends). There is a frequent coach service between the airport and the city (travel time – 40 minutes). Limousine and taxi services are available.
Gothenburg (GOT) (Landvetter) is 25km (15 miles) east of the city (travel time – 25 minutes). Airport facilities: full outgoing duty-free shop; car hire; bank/bureau de change (0800-2000 Monday to Friday, 0800-1200 and 1300-1700 Saturday, 1230-1700 and 1800-2000 Sunday); restaurant/bar (1145-1930 Monday to Friday, 1200-1730 Saturday, 1200-1900 Sunday); and coffee shop (0600-2145). Coach services are frequent between the airport and the Central Station. Limousine and taxi services are available.
Malmö (MMA) (Sturup) is 31km (20 miles) southeast of the city (travel time – 40 minutes). Bus and taxi services go to the city.
Malmö Harbour Hoverport (HMA), 200m (650ft) from the Central Station, is now the city's main terminal for international air passengers using the hovercraft service operated by *SAS* which connects with flights at *Copenhagen Airport.* The terminal has its own duty-free facilities. Taxi services are available.
SEA: *Scandinavian Seaways* ferries sail all year round from Harwich to Gothenburg and in summer from Newcastle to Gothenburg. There are also ferry connections with Copenhagen and Helsingør.
RAIL: The UK–Sweden route is from London (Victoria and Liverpool Street) to either Hook of Holland or Ostend, and onwards via Copenhagen; travel time – approximately 22-25 hours. There are connections by ferry from Denmark and through rail routes from Norway (Oslo, Narvik and Trondheim).

IMPORTANT NOTE

As of 1 January 1995, Austria, Finland and Sweden are due to join the EU.

However, for the purposes of the passport and visa information, these three countries have been treated as separate from the EU; it will take some time for other countries to decide how they want to change their regulations towards nationals of these countries.

For up-to-the-minute information on nationals of Austria, Finland and Sweden, please contact the relevant embassies before travelling.

ROAD: From the UK visitors can either drive to Sweden through Europe via Denmark or Germany, or catch a car ferry from Harwich (all year) to Gothenburg on the southwest coast (sailing time – 24 hours). **Coach:** There are services from London (Victoria) to a number of Swedish cities throughout the year (restricted service in winter). Contact the Swedish Travel & Tourism Council for a list of operators.
See below for information on **documentation** and **traffic regulations.**

TRAVEL - Internal

AIR: *SAS* and *Linjeflyg (LF)* serve over 30 local airports. Travel by air is relatively cheap and there are a number of reduced fares offered by *Linjeflyg* and *SAS.* Contact airlines for further details.
SEA/LAKE: Frequent coastal sailings to all ports and on the hundreds of lakes throughout the country, especially in the north. For details contact local authorities.
RAIL: The excellent and extensive rail system is run by *Swedish State Railways (SJ),* 105 50 Stockholm. Tel: (8) 762 2000. Fax: (8) 762 3757. The network is more concentrated in the populated south where hourly services run between the main cities, but routes extend to the forested and sparsely populated lake area of the north, which is a scenic and popular holiday destination. Restaurant cars and sleepers are provided on many trains. Reservations are essential for most express services. Motorail car-sleeper services are operated during the summer on the long-distance routes from Malmö, Gothenburg and Västerås to Kiruna and Luleå.
Cheap fares: There are reductions for families and regular passengers, as well as a link-up with other Scandinavian countries via the *Nord-Turist Railpass* (also known as the *Scanrail Card),* which provides unlimited travel in Denmark, Norway, Finland and Sweden for 21 days. It also gives free travel on the ferries between Helsingør and Helsingborg. Children under 16 travel at half the fare or reduced fare, two children under 12 accompanied by an adult travel free. Half-price fares are available for second-class travel on specified off-peak trains within Sweden throughout the week. The discount applies on trains shown in the timetable as 'low price' or 'red departures'.
ROAD: Traffic drives on the right. Sweden's roads are well-maintained and relatively uncrowded, but watch out for game crossing the road in remote areas. Credit cards are becoming more acceptable as a means of payment at filling stations. Most filling stations have 24-hour automatic petrol pumps; they accept SKr100, 50 and 10 notes. **Bus:** Express coach services and local buses are run by *GDG* and *Swebus,* and also the *Swedish Post Office* in the north. Cheap and efficient links are available to all towns. Many coach operators do special offers on tickets at the weekends (Friday to Sunday). Information is available in Sweden from local tourist offices. **Taxi:** Available in all towns and airports. Intercity taxis are also available. **Car hire:** Available in most towns and cities. All international agencies are represented. **Regulations:** Speed limits outside built-up areas are 110, 90 or 70kmph (68, 56 or 43mph) depending on road width and traffic density. In built-up areas the limit is 50kmph (31mph) or 30kmph (19mph) in school areas. Severe fines and sometimes prison sentences are imposed on drivers over the alcohol limit. There are on-the-spot fines for traffic offences. The use of dipped headlights is compulsory in the daytime for cars and motorcycles. Crash helmets are compulsory for motorcyclists. Children under seven may not travel in a car if it is not equipped with a special child restraint or a normal seat belt adapted for the child's use. Emergency warning triangles are strongly advised. Spiked tyres are only permitted from October 1 to April 30.
Documentation: National driving licence is sufficient. The minimum age for car drivers is 18; for motorcyclists it is 17. The car's log book and written permission must be carried if driving someone else's car. A Green Card is not required by Swedish authorities, but it tops up the cover provided by a domestic policy. It is advisable to check the validity of insurance policies prior to departure.
URBAN: Public transport is efficient, comprehensive and well-integrated. Stockholm has bus, trams, metro *(T-banan)* and local rail services. Pre-purchase multi-tickets and passes are sold, though single tickets can also be obtained on the bus. There are trams in Gothenburg and Norrköping. Taxis are widely available and several of the main cities, particularly Stockholm, have boat excursions and services. See *Resorts & Excursions* below.
JOURNEY TIMES: The following chart gives approximate journey times (in hours and minutes) from Stockholm to other major cities/towns in Sweden.

	Air	Road	Rail
Gothenburg	0.50	6.00	4.30
Malmö	1.05	8.00	6.45
Östersund	0.55	8.00	6.30
Karlstad	0.40	5.00	3.30
Luleå	1.15	20.00	15.00
Mora	1.00	6.00	4.30

ACCOMMODATION

HOTELS: Hotels are usually of a high standard. Most have a restaurant and/or cafeteria and a TV lounge. Good first- and medium-class hotels are found in every Swedish town. They are mostly private but are, in many cases, operated by hotel groups and offer special reduced rates for the summer and weekends. Special packages are available throughout the year in Stockholm, Malmö and Gothenburg. There is no formal grading structure, but most first-class hotels display the *SHR* sign indicating that they belong to the *Swedish Hotel & Restaurant Association (SHR),* Sveriges Hotell & Restaurang Förbund, PO Box 1158, Kammarkargatan 39, 111 81 Stockholm. Tel: (8) 231 290. Fax: (8) 215 861.
Tourist hotels: Scattered all over Sweden are country hotels, characterised by good food and attractive settings. Some are renovated and modernised manor houses or centuries-old farmhouses which have frequently been in the same family for generations. They are mostly independently owned and are often located in picturesque surroundings. Others are traditional old inns. During the summer many hotels offer facilities for swimming, fishing, boating, golf and flower-spotting or bird-watching excursions.
Mountain hotels: There are also a number of mountain hotels which are ideal for those who want a peaceful holiday. They provide a good base for expeditions in the mountains and guided walks are often arranged, as well as other activities like keep-fit classes, fishing and canoeing. Many are also popular skiing hotels in the winter.
Hotel discount schemes: Many Swedish hotels offer discounted rates throughout the summer and at weekends during the winter and some of the leading chains have special deals which can be booked in advance, including the *SARA Hotels Scandinavian Bonus Pass,* the *Scandic Hotel Cheque scheme* and the *Sweden Hotel Pass.* Details of these offers and other discount schemes are contained in the annual guide *Hotels in Sweden,* obtainable from the Swedish Travel & Tourism Council.
MOTELS: Sweden has a large number of motels, most of which are new, usually situated on the outskirts of towns or in the countryside. Parking is free. They may have swimming pools, a gymnasium and saunas, restaurants and self-service cafeterias.
FARM HOUSE ACCOMMODATION: A limited number of farms throughout Sweden offer accommodation, either in the main farm house or in an adjoining cottage. Accommodation is normally on a bed & breakfast basis, with self-catering facilities. Some farms offer full board. Accommodation can be booked through local tourist offices.
SELF-CATERING: Forest cabins and chalets are available throughout the country, generally set in beautiful surroundings, near lakes, in quiet forest glades or on an island in some remote archipelago. Purpose-built chalets generally consist of a living room, two or three bedrooms, a well-equipped kitchen and a toilet. They can generally accommodate up to six people, and cooking utensils, cutlery, blankets and pillows are provided. Visitors will have to supply only sheets and towels. Log cabins offer a slightly more simple type of accommodation. Renovated cottages and farm buildings are also available, usually in remote spots.
Chalet villages: Sweden's 250 chalet villages offer the advantage of amenities such as a grocery, general shops, leisure facilities, restaurants, swimming pools, saunas, launderette, playgrounds, mini-golf, tennis, badminton or volleyball. Some have programmes of special activities such as music, dancing, barbecues, riding, fishing and

Swedish Railways

Swedish Railways (SJ) operate a punctual and efficient network of frequent services throughout the whole of Sweden (hourly service between Stockholm and Gothenburg). Virtually all our long-distance trains include a restaurant car or buffet, with sleeping cars and couchettes (both 1st- and 2nd-class) available on all longer overnight routes. Our new high-speed X2000 supertrains on the Stockholm – Gothenburg, Stockholm – Karlstad, Stockholm – Falun and Stockholm – Malmo routes provide comfort-conscious passengers with a convenient and viable alternative to air-travel

BUDGET TRAIN TRAVEL IN SWEDEN

Don't miss out on Swedish Railways' wide range of special fares for budget-conscious travellers.

SCANRAIL TICKET

The Scanrail Ticket is a 1-month ticket which entitles you to unlimited travel in Sweden, Norway, Denmark and Finland. Prices for adults start at £245 (1st-class £306), children between 4-11 £123 and young travellers between 12-25 £184.

FOR EUROPEAN SENIOR CITIZENS

Passengers holding the 'European senior citizens' railcard qualify for a 30% reduction on Swedish rail fares.

FOR YOUNG TRAVELLERS
FOR YOUNG TRAVELLERS

Young people under the age of 18 travel for half the full or reduced fare. A supplementary fare is payable on X2000 high-speed services and on certain trains designated as a 'City Express'.

BUDGET TRAVEL CARD

A 25% discount is available for second-class travellers with the Discount Card Tuesday to Thursday and on Saturdays. The discount applies to trains shown in the timetable as 'low price' or 'red departures'. The discount card can be bought at any local station for SEK 150 and is valid during 1995.

SEAT RESERVATIONS

Required in trains designated 'R', Red Departure, or 'IC', Inter-City, in timetable. Reservations can be made at any time up to departure. Charge: SEK 30*

*Supplementary charge for X2000 high-speed services and certain City Express services.

---

walking trails. It is often possible to rent boats or bicycles. Information on rental of holiday cottages or flats can be obtained from specialist agencies, local tourist offices in Sweden or the Swedish Travel & Tourism Council.
CAMPING/CARAVANNING: Family camping holidays are extremely popular in Sweden and there is a tremendous variety of attractive sites. Most are located in picturesque surroundings, often on a lakeside or by the sea with free bathing facilities close at hand. There are about 750 campsites, all officially approved and classified by the Swedish Travel & Tourism Council. Many offer facilities such as boat or bicycle rental, mini-golf, tennis, riding or saunas. Many campsites have facilities for the handicapped. Most authorised sites are open with full service Jun 1-Aug 15. Many sites are also open in April or May but the full range of ancillary facilities, such as the post office, may not be open. About 200 sites remain open in the winter, particularly in the winter sports areas in central and northern Sweden. All sites open during the winter have electric sockets for caravans.
The price for one night for the whole family plus tent or caravan and use of services is one of the lowest rates in Europe, although at some sites there are small charges for the use of services like showers or launderette. A camping *carnet* is needed at most sites. It is issued at the first site that is visited and is then valid for the whole season. The *carnet* is not required by holders of the 'Camping International' card. Standards of facilities and cleanliness at Swedish campsites are probably the highest in Europe. Approved sites are inspected annually by the Swedish Travel & Tourism Council and are awarded a 1-, 2- or 3-star rating according to the facilities provided, as follows:
3-star: Supervision 24 hours a day, postal service, car wash, cafeteria, cooking facilities, play and recreational activities and assembly room.
2-star: Supervision throughout the day, illuminated and fenced-in area, drains for caravans, shaving points, kiosk, grocery shop, telephone and electric sockets for caravans.
1-star: Daily inspection, a barrier at the entrance, dustbin, drinking water, toilets, washing facilities and hot water for dish-washing, laundering and showers.
Camping Cheques, valid at more than 350 sites, can be purchased before the holiday but only as part of a package including a return car-ferry journey. Each cheque is valid for one night's stay for a family with car plus tent or caravan. Detailed information about camping in Sweden is contained in a pamphlet which is available free of charge

from the Swedish Travel & Tourism Council; an abbreviated list of campsites is also available. Motor homes and caravans can be rented.
Fuel: *Camping Gaz* is not normally available in Sweden and visitors are recommended to take their own supplies. Only propane gas (eg Primus) is obtainable. This is widely available at more than 2000 Primus dealers along with the necessary equipment at reasonable prices. It is important to ensure that equipment designed to burn butane is not refilled with propane; this is both illegal and highly dangerous.
CAMPING CABINS: A useful alternative to tent or caravan camping is to rent one of 4400 camping cabins which are available at 350 sites.
YOUTH HOSTELS: The 280 hostels range from mansions to a renovated sailing ship, the *Af Chapman,* in the centre of Stockholm, and there are also many purpose-built hostels. There are no restrictions on who may use Sweden's hostels. Hostels have 2-4 beds per room, or family rooms and self-catering facilities. The hostels are run by the *Swedish Touring Club (STF)* but members of the UK *Youth Hostels Association* or *Scottish Youth Hostels Association* qualify for a cheaper rate, on production of a membership card. All youth hostels are open during the summer and some for the whole year. They are closed during the day but are open to check in new guests 0800-0930 and 1700-2200. During the summer it is advisable to book in advance. A list of Swedish youth hostels can be ordered direct from *STF*; address at beginning of entry. The hostels are also listed in the 'International Youth Hostel Handbook', available through the *YHA* in the UK.
SWEDISH TOURING CLUB: The *Swedish Touring Club (STF)* runs Sweden's youth hostels and several mountain stations in the north of the country and looks after the many mountain huts along the long-distance hiking trails. *STF* also publishes a list of guest harbours and issues guidance to hikers and canoeing enthusiasts.

RESORTS & EXCURSIONS

For the purpose of clarity, information on resorts and excursions has been divided into nine main sections: Stockholm and the islands; Gothenburg; Skåne; The Glass Country; The West Coast; The Golden Coast; Gotland and Öland; Swedish Lakeland; The Midnight Sun Coast; and Lappland. The natural environment is protected by a

law called *Allemanrätten*, allowing visitors to stay in places of natural beauty provided they do not destroy the environment. For further information, contact the Swedish Travel & Tourism Council, the Swedish Touring Club or a local tourist information centre.

Stockholm and the islands

Built on a string of islands, **Stockholm** was founded 700 years ago by King Birger Jarl at the strategic point where the fresh water of Lake Mälaren meets the salt water of the Baltic. A good starting point for an exploration of the city is the 'Old Town' *(Gamla Stan),* a cluster of old buildings and narrow cobbled streets which formed the original Stockholm. The old buildings are beautifully preserved and the main streets, *Österlånggatan* and *Västerlånggatan,* are pedestrian precincts with a host of boutiques, handicrafts and antique shops. The Old Town has three churches of historic interest, *Storkyrkan* and *Riddarholm Church,* both dating from the 13th century and the *German Church* with its magnificent Baroque interior. Overlooking the harbour is the *Royal Palace,* which contains the State Apartments, the Crown Jewels, the Hall of State and Chapel Royal, Royal Armoury and Palace Museum. Within easy reach of the Old Town, in a magnificent setting on the edge of Lake Mälaren, is Stockholm's elegant City Hall *(Stadshuset),* inaugurated about 60 years ago. There is a spectacular view of the capital from the top of the 100m (350ft) tower. Another spot for a magnificent view is the observation platform on the *Kaknäs* communications tower which, at 155m (508ft), is the highest building in Scandinavia.
The island of **Djurgården,** can be reached either by bus from the city centre or by ferry across the busy harbour. The best-known attraction here is the purpose-built *Vasa Museum* housing the restored 360-year-old wooden warship which was recovered from the depths of Stockholm's harbour in 1961. Also in Djurgården is *Skansen,* an open-air folk museum which celebrated its centenary in 1991. It has about 150 traditional buildings from different regions of Sweden, as well as an open-air zoo and an aquarium. Across the road is *Gröna Lund,* a lively amusement park.
The city boasts over 50 museums. No less than eight can be visited in the Djurgården area, including the Nordic Museum *(Nordiska Museet), Waldemarsudde House,* which was the home of the artist Prince Eugen until

SWEDEN BY ANDERS ZORN (1860-1920)

"SPETSSÖMNAD" ZORN MUSEUM MORA

EVA-MARIE RUNDQVIST/LINK

SWEDEN BY SCANRAIL

Travelling by rail in Sweden gives you a front-row seat to a pageant of scenic landscapes and unspoiled nature. Nature that has inspired famous artists like Anders Zorn, Ingmar Bergman and Carl Larsson.

When you travel on a ScanRail ticket you'll find the fare is easy on your pocket and the scenery easy on your eye.

ScanRail is a new railway ticket that offers you inexpensive vacation adventure in Scandinavia.

In Sweden you travel on modern Inter City trains that resemble mobile hotels. They have attractive compartments with comfortable seats. The restaurants serve traditional Swedish cuisine and exclusive delicacies.

You may also travel on the X 2000, a high speed train that gets you where you're going fast, with a high level of service and comfort. The X 2000 runs from city centre to city centre between the most interesting towns in Sweden. For example, the royal capital Stockholm and Gothenburg – the pearl of the west coast.

Your ScanRail ticket can also take you to North Cape and the wide open spaces of Europe's last wilderness. You travel there in comfort on a modern, highly efficient railway network.

In Sweden, the trains wind their way through scenic landscapes against a backdrop of tall mountains, valleys, lakes, rolling plains and shimmering seas. They carry you north to rushing rapids, meandering rivers and Lapp culture in the land of the Midnight Sun and Northern Lights.

Sweden welcomes you with beautiful countryside and long, light summer nights. Go there by rail this summer.

ScanRail. Valid for one month, for unlimited rail travel in Sweden, Norway, Denmark and Finland. Fare: adults 1 month 2nd class £245 .

ScanRail Flexi. Valid 5/15 days, 10 days/ 1 month. Periods of validity of 15 days and 1 month respectively, with unlimited travel on any 5 or 10 days respectively within the period. Fare: adults Flexi 5/15 days 2nd class £125, adults Flexi 10 days/1 month 2nd class £170.

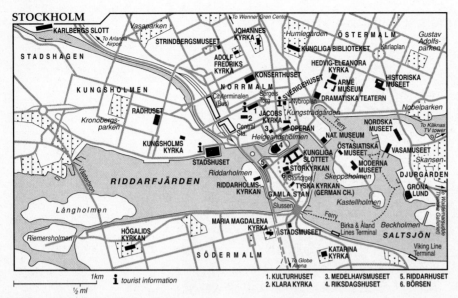

STOCKHOLM

1. KULTURHUSET   3. MEDELHAVSMUSEET   5. RIDDARHUSET
2. KLARA KYRKA   4. RIKSDAGSHUSET   6. BÖRSEN

ℹ *tourist information*

1947, and *Liljevalchs Konsthall*. The Historical Museum (*Historiska Museet*) has some priceless treasures and implements from prehistoric Sweden, as well as examples of medieval art. The *National Museum* is Sweden's central museum for the national collections of painting, sculpture, applied arts, printing and drawings. Every visitor to Stockholm should invest in a special discount card, the 'Stockholm Card' (*Stockholmskortet*) which cuts sightseeing and entertainment costs. Cards of longer validity are available at an extra charge, available in Stockholm from the Stockholm Tourist Centre.
EXCURSIONS: There is a whole armada of boat excursions on offer. 'Under the Bridges of Stockholm' takes a circular tour through part of the harbour as well as *Lake Mälaren*. A longer trip can be taken out into the archipelago to resorts like **Sandhamn, Saltsjöbaden** or **Vaxholm**. Visitors can also take a boat from the City Hall to *Drottningholm Palace*. The *Royal Theatre* has been preserved in its original 18th-century form and plays are still performed there in period costume. There is also a museum depicting the development of the theatre since the Renaissance period.

Gothenburg

The history of Sweden's second city **Gothenburg** (Göteborg) is closely tied to the sea, and is still the arrival point for hundreds of thousands of visitors from abroad each year. The basic pattern of the city owes much to the Dutch architects who designed it; the spacious streets are laid out at right angles and there is a network of canals. The *Nordstaden Kronhuset* area houses the oldest building of the city, built in 1643 and now the *City Museum*. Nearby is *Kronhusbodarna*, an arts and craft workshop centre dating from the 18th century. A visit to the Botanical Gardens (*Botaniska Trädgården*) is a must; the rock garden there is regarded as one of the most impressive in the world, with about 3000 species of Alpine plants. In the city centre is the beautiful *Garden of Trädgårdsföreningen* with its restored *Palm House*, built in the style of what was London's Crystal Palace. Another must during the summer is the *Liseberg Amusement Park*, an ideal spot for children. There are also many museums, such as the Maritime Museum (*Sjöfartsmuseet*) which illustrates Sweden's maritime history and the development of its shipbuilding industry. The 'Gothenburg Discount Card' can be purchased for free admission to many tourist attractions.
EXCURSIONS: One of the best ways of sightseeing in Gothenburg is on one of the famous *Paddan* boats. Departure is from the terminal at Kungsportsplatsen for an hour-long tour under 20 bridges and out into the busy harbour. Another popular boat trip is to the 17th-century *Nya Elfsborg Fortress* built on an island at the harbour mouth. There are also sightseeing tours of varying duration by bus with an English-speaking guide. A cheap way of travelling around the city is to buy a 24-hour ticket on the tram network. Gothenburg is the starting point for the classic 3-day trip to Stockholm through Sweden's great lakes and the historic *Göta Canal*.
RESORTS: See *The Golden Coast* below.

Skåne

At the southernmost tip of Sweden is the province of **Skåne**, an area of fertile fields and meadows which was ruled by the Danes until 1658. To this day the Skånians have maintained their own distinctive dialect. As a reminder of the days of Danish rule there are more than 200 castles and manors scattered over the province, often forming part of a farm. This region is famous for its food, and the landscape is characterised by rolling fields and pastures and forests but only a few lakes. The best spots for swimming and fishing are along the east, south and west coasts. Inland there are countless small lanes ideal for cycling tours. For golfers, Skåne has some of the finest and most beautifully located courses in Sweden. Especially recommended is the 'Malmö Card' which can be purchased at the Malmö Tourist Board and entitles visitors to free travel on local buses, free admission to museums and discounts on a wide variety of purchases.
EXCURSIONS: The medieval town of **Lund** has a 12th-century cathedral and 14th-century astrological clock.
RESORTS: Malmö, Lund, Helsingborg, Ystad, Falsterbo, Mölle and Båstad.

The Glass Country

In the middle of the 18th century, German immigrants established the province of **Småland**, north of Skåne, as the home of the Swedish glass-making industry. Småland is a very large province and the 'glass country' forms only a small part of it. It is also good holiday country with vast forests, pleasant lakes and winding lanes along which red cottages are dotted. In the province of **Blekinge** there are large oak forests and softer landscapes. This region has many coastal towns that stretch along the Baltic. The *Mörrumsån River* is noted for salmon and sea trout and *Lake Vättern* for char fishing. Three quarters of the Swedish glassworks are found in the counties of **Kronoberg** and **Kalmar.** They are located off the beaten track surrounded by vast tracts of forest and attract many visitors each year.
EXCURSIONS: Visitors can watch the craftsmen in most of the glassworks 0800-1500 Monday to Friday. Most of the works have their own shops. Boat trips are available to the island of **Visingsö** on Lake Vättern. *High Chaparral* is a reconstructed wild west town. There is a fortress on the Baltic island of **Öland** (see below).
RESORTS: Sölvesborg, Karlshamn, Ronneby, Karlskrona, Ljungby, Värnamo, Gislaved, Gnosjö, Jönköping, Växjö and Kalmar.

The West Coast

Halland is a long, narrow province strung out along the picturesque west coast. Unlike its northern neighbour, Bohuslän (see below), its landscape is gentle, with mile after mile of long sandy beaches, often fringed with pinewoods. Inland, the scenery changes as it meets the tableland of Småland and the landscape is characterised by a series of ridges and valleys. There are also vast forests and heather-covered moors.
Areas of note are **Kungsbacka**, a northern market town and the nearby Onsala peninsula, ideal for bathing, sailing and fishing, and **Fjärås Bräcka**, an unusual gravel ridge formed during the Ice Age. Further south is **Varberg**, one of Halland's main coastal resorts, dominated by the 13th-century *Varberg Fortress*. Other resorts are the port of **Falkenberg** and **Tylösand**, with its long sandy beach sheltered by dunes and pine trees. Halland's capital is the important seaport and industrial town of **Halmstad**. Warmed by the waters of the Gulf Stream, the west coast is a natural choice for seaside holidays. The long narrow province of **Bohuslän** has

countless spots where visitors can enjoy an idyllic holiday in the sun. The coastline is deeply indented and there are hundreds of rocky islands. All along the coast are picturesque villages with their typical red-painted huts where the nets are hung out to dry. The province is also one of the most important centres of ancient Swedish civilisation and there are many archaeological relics dating back to the Bronze Age and Viking times.

The Golden Coast

This area is situated in the southwest of Sweden and has vast stretches of beaches, warm sea and holiday resorts reaching for 400km (250 miles) from **Laholm** in the south to **Strömstad** in the north. Here there are flat, sandy beaches, bare rocks and fjord-like inlets with meadows stretching down to the seashore and tiny fishing villages.
RESORTS: Gothenburg (see above), Halmstad, Lysekil, Tylösand, Falkenberg, Varberg, Bovallstrand, Hunnebostrand, Kungshamn, Smögen and the islands of Orust and Tjörn.

Gotland and Öland

These are Sweden's largest islands, situated off the southeast coast in the Baltic Sea. There is more sunshine here than elsewhere, making it a favourite summer holiday spot with the Swedes, as a result the beaches are rather crowded. The islands are of particular interest to ornithologists and botanists and there is a wealth of historic sites. Several ferries serve both islands and daily coach trips are available to Öland over Europe's longest bridge, starting just outside Kalmar on the mainland. Cycles can be hired on the islands.
EXCURSIONS: There are Stone, Bronze and Iron Age sites on both islands. On **Gotland** the *Lummelunda Caves* with their spectacular stalactites and stalagmites and a preserved medieval town at **Kattlundsgård.** On **Öland** are the royal summer residence at **Solliden**; *Borgholm Castle;* a restored medieval church at **Gärdslösa**; a recently excavated fortified village at **Eketorp**; and many Viking stones and the local windmills.
RESORTS: Visby and Borgholm.

Swedish Lakeland

This region comprises the nine provinces of **Västergötland, Dalsland** and **Värmland** in the west, **Närke, Västmanland** and **Dalarna** in the north, and **Östergötland, Södermanland** and **Uppland** to the east. These form a large part of Sweden with a mixture of open water, vast lakes, plains and meadows – an area of wild natural scenery. The provinces in the west are dominated by Vänern, Sweden's largest lake, while in the north and east are the lakes of Vättern, Mälaren, Hjälmaren and Siljan as well as the Baltic Sea. The whole region is considered the cradle of Swedish culture, and it is here that the majority of Swedes live. For visitors there is a wide variety of hotels, campsites and country inns.
EXCURSIONS: **Västergötland** has the castle of *Läckö*, the Trollhättan hydro-electric waterfalls, canoe trips and fishing. **Närke** contains the *Stjerhov Manor* and a 17th-century inn at **Grythyttan** in Västmanland. In **Dalarna** visitors can meet Father Christmas at the *Santaworld* theme park. On the island of **Sollerön** there are Viking graves and in **Kolmården** there is a zoo and safari park. *Gripsholm Castle* is in **Södermanland**, with the university city of **Uppsala** and the Baroque *Castle of Skokloster*, with a vintage car museum in Uppland.
RESORTS: Skara, Karlstad, Lidköping, Örebro, Askersund, Grythyttan, Rättvik, Leksand, Vadstena, Linköping, Tällberg, Sunne, Mariefred, Uppsala, Sigtuna and Björkön.

The Midnight Sun Coast

The midnight sun coast is a 1500km (900-mile) stretch of Baltic coastline which runs all the way to the Finnish border. In the south are the spruce forests of the province of **Gästrikland**; immediately to the north of this region is **Hälsingland** with its spectacular views, extensive lakes and typical wood-built mansions. Forestry has traditionally been the dominant industry of **Medelpad**, today one of Sweden's most industrialised areas, although there are plenty of opportunities for visitors who want to fish in unspoilt outback country or rent a cottage in the middle of a countryside rich in prehistoric monuments and relics of ancient cultures.
In the province of **Ångermanland** is some of Sweden's most breathtaking scenery, consisting of forests, lakes, islands, fjords and mountains plunging dramatically to the sea. This magnificent district is called the High Coast. **Västerbotten** offers unspoilt wilderness and the

Norrland Riviera coastline is ideal for a relaxed holiday. There are also countless clear lakes and rivers teeming with fish, and excellent roads lead inland to the southern part of Lappland. Further north along the coast at **Lövånger** there are hundreds of renovated timber cottages which are rented out to holidaymakers. Nearer the Arctic Circle the air and water temperatures in the summer are much the same as in the Mediterranean and this area has an excellent sunshine record. **Norrbotten** is a fisherman's paradise with plenty of mountain streams and sea fishing.
RESORTS: Furuvik, Gävle, Söderhamn, Hudiksvall, Bollnäs, Ljusdal, Arbrå, Järvsö, Sundsvall, Härnösand, Örnsköldsvik, Ramsele, Umeå, Piteå, Luleå and Boden.

Lappland

The enormous expanse of **Lappland**, one of Europe's last wildernesses, covers a quarter of the area of Sweden but has only 5% of the population. It is both inviting and inhospitable at the same time. Fell-walkers who leave the marked routes do so at their own risk. The best-known route is *Kungsleden,* which also gives experienced mountaineers the chance to climb Sweden's highest peak, *Kebnekaise*. Other favourite areas for walking are the national parks of **Sarek** and **Padjelanta**. In the west the mountains soar up towards the Norwegian border and the region experiences rapid changes in the weather. **Jämtland**, bordering southern Lappland, has plenty of good hiking and fast-flowing rivers for fishermen. It is known for its skiing. Wildlife is abundant in **Härjedalen,** with reindeer, buzzard, beaver, lynx and Sweden's only herd of musk ox.
EXCURSIONS: Lapps celebrate their annual church festivals in **Gällivare**. In **Jokkmokk** there are collections of Lapp art and culture, and a *Lapp Staden,* an old village of 70 cone-shaped Lapp huts. **Arjeplog** has an interesting Lapp museum. Iron Age burial grounds and a medieval church are on the island of **Frösö**. The cable-car trip from **Åre** leads up to the summit of Åreskutan.
RESORTS: Kiruna, Gällivare, Jokkmokk, Arvidsjaur, Ammarnäs, Tärnaby, Åre, Storlien, Storuman, Sylarna, Blåhammaren and Östersund. *Ski resorts* include Åre and Storlien.

SOCIAL PROFILE

FOOD & DRINK: Swedes like straightforward meals, simply prepared from the freshest ingredients. As a seafaring country with many freshwater lakes, fish dishes are prominent on hotel or restaurant menus. The Scandinavian cold table, called *smörgåsbord,* is traditional. First pickled herring with boiled potatoes, then perhaps a couple more fish courses, smoked salmon or anchovies followed by cold meat, pâté, sliced beef, stuffed veal or smoked reindeer. The hot dishes come next, for instance, another herring dish, small meatballs (*köttbullar*) or an omelette. A fruit salad and cheese with crispbreads round off the meal. Other dishes to look out for are smoked reindeer from Lappland; *gravlax,* salmon that has been specially prepared and marinaded; wild strawberries; and the cloudberries that are unique to Scandinavia. Once on the open road the traveller is well catered for with picnic sites on the way, often with wooden tables and seats. **Restaurants:** Top-class restaurants in Sweden are usually fairly expensive, but even the smallest towns have reasonably priced self-service restaurants and grill bars. Many restaurants all over Sweden offer a special dish of the day at a reduced price which includes main course, salad, soft drink and coffee. Waiter service is common although there are many self-service snack bars. **Drink:** *Snapps,* the collective name for *aquavit* or *brännvin,* is a Swedish liqueur which is traditionally drunk chilled with *smörgåsbord.* It is made under a variety of brand names with flavours varying from practically tasteless to sweetly spiced. Swedish beers are lager- and pilsner-type brews and come in four strengths. The minimum age for buying alcoholic beverages is 20. Wine, spirits and beer are sold through the state-owned monopoly, *Systembolaget,* open during normal shopping hours. Before 1300 Sunday alcohol cannot be bought in bars, cafés or restaurants. After midnight alcohol can only be bought in nightclubs that stay open until 0200 or 0300. In a restaurant or a nightclub, the minimum age for buying alcoholic beverages is 18. Stiff penalties are enforced for drinking and driving.
NIGHTLIFE: Stockholm has pubs, cafés, discos, restaurants, cinemas and theatres. In the more rural areas evenings tend to be tranquil. From August to June the Royal Ballet performs in Stockholm. Music and theatre productions take place in many cities during the summer at open air venues. Outside Stockholm in the 18th-century Court Theatre of the Palace of Drottningholm there are performances of 18th-century opera.
SHOPPING: VAT *(Moms)* is refundable to tourists or visitors who are resident outside the Nordic countries on goods bought at shops participating in the Tax-Free Shopping scheme. The refund is payable to the customer when departing from Sweden at either airports or customs offices at ports. Special purchases include glassware and crystal, stainless steel and silver, *hemslöjd* (cottage industry artefacts) and wood carvings. Women's and children's clothes are good buys, especially handknitted Nordic sweaters. **Shopping hours:** 0900-1800 Monday to Friday, 1000-1300 Saturday. In larger towns, certain department stores open some evenings until 2000/2200 and some are also open 1200-1600 Sundays. In rural areas, shops and petrol stations close by 1700/1800.
SPORT: Hiking routes are on well laid-out paths in almost every part of the country. **Cycling** is a popular holiday recreation, particularly in the south. The Swedish Cycling Promotion Institute, in cooperation with regional tourist offices, has scheduled cycling tours in almost every region. **Golf:** There are excellent golf courses and facilities provided for members and visitors. Sweden has about 150 courses. One situated north of the Arctic Circle enjoys 24-hour daylight during the summer months and many midsummer championships take place at midnight. Clubs and golf carts can usually be rented. **Winter sports:** There are excellent facilities for **skiing, skating, tobogganing** and **dog-sledging.** Most skiing takes place in the north, particularly in Jämtland, Dalarna and Härjedalen. **Watersports:** Sweden has hundreds of miles of beaches, particularly on the west coast, and 96,000 lakes. There are numerous **water-skiing** and **windsurfing** centres on the coast and more accessible lakes. **Skindiving** is mostly confined to the rocky coasts and islets on the west coast both north and south of Gothenburg. Courses are held from June to August. **Boating:** There are about 50 centres where canoes are for hire. Many campsites offer a hire service. Sailing boats and motor-cruisers can be hired in more than 25 places in Sweden or visitors can bring their own. Many of Sweden's canals run through beautiful countryside and are well maintained to provide an ideal boating holiday. Short sightseeing trips are available on several canals but the classic journey is by steamer along the Göta Canal. All meals and accommodation are included in the price. Many cruises, some in vintage steamers, are operated from Stockholm out into the archipelago with its 30,000 islands. **Fishing:** Sweden has more than 96,000 lakes and visitors can enjoy fishing in most of them. There are also thousands of miles of rivers, streams and brooks and a coastline of 6760km (4200 miles). The salmon season at Mörrum near Karlshamn opens at the beginning of spring. Sea-trout can be caught throughout the year, except in high summer, which is the best time for char and grayling (typical fish from the northern part of the country). Fishing is generally free all along the coastline and in the larger lakes, including Mälaren, Vättern and Vänern, but a special permit is required to fish in other lakes and rivers. Information is available from local tourist offices. Sea-fishing tours of varying lengths are arranged on the west coast and in the south. Guest harbours are available all round the coast and on lakes Mälaren, Vänern and Vättern. The Swedish Touring Club (STF) publishes a list of 330 with some information in English.
SPECIAL EVENTS: The following is a selection of major festivals and other special events celebrated in Sweden during 1995/96. For a complete list, contact the the Swedish Travel & Tourism Council.
Mar 15-Jun 15 '95 *Uppsala University 400-year anniversary celebrations.* **Apr 1** *Salmon Fishing Premiere,* Mörrum River. **Apr 23-May 7** *1995 World Championship in Ice Hockey,* Stockholm. **May 19-28** *Festival of Humour,* Örebro. **May 27-Sep 4** *Opera Season,* Drottningholm Court Theatre, Stockholm. **Jun 23-25** *Midsummer Celebrations,* all over Sweden. **Jul 2-9** *Music at Lake Siljan,* Dalarna. **Jul 8** *Hälsingehambon 30 years* (traditional dancing), Järvsö. **Aug** *Cray Fish Premiere.* **Aug 4-13** *World Athletics Championships,* Gothenburg. **Aug 6-13** *Medieval Week,* Gotland. **Aug 10-12** *Gothenburg Trad Jazz Festival.* **Aug 11-20** *Stockholm Water Festival.* **Sep 8-29** *Swedish Design 150 years.* **Dec 10** *Nobel Prize Day,* Stockholm.
SOCIAL CONVENTIONS: Normal courtesies should be observed. It is customary for the guest to refrain from drinking until the host makes a toast. He should also thank him for the meal with 'Tack för maten'. Casual dress is acceptable for everyday occasions; smarter wear for social occasions, exclusive restaurants and clubs. Evening wear (black tie) will usually be specified when required. Smoking is prohibited on public transport and in most public buildings. **Tipping:** Hotel prices include a service charge. Service in restaurants is included in the bill. Late at night the service charge is higher. Taxi drivers are always tipped at least 10% of the fare on the meter.

BUSINESS PROFILE

ECONOMY: Sweden boasts one of Europe's most advanced industrial economies and one of the highest standards of social welfare in the world. A prolonged period of peace, which included a policy of neutrality during both World Wars, has contributed much to its economic development. Over half of the country is covered by forests, supplying raw material for the wood-based industries – paper, wood pulp and finished products such as furniture – which account for 20% of Swedish exports. Other major exports are vehicles, office and telecommunications equipment and chemicals. Many industries are state-owned. The country is rich in mineral resources, which include 15% of the world's identified uranium deposits and large deposits of iron ore, although production has declined sharply since the 1970s. Parts of the south and central regions are given over to agriculture. Lacking indigenous fossil fuels, which must be imported, Sweden has a large nuclear power programme meeting around 40% of total energy requirements. Domestic political considerations mean that this proportion is unlikely to be increased. Oil and coal are the largest items on Sweden's import bill; manufactured goods make up most of the rest. Sweden was a member of the European Free Trade Association (EFTA) which links the economies of those Western European nations outside the European Union. This trade was boosted by the creation in 1991 of the European Economic Area, a free-trade zone encompassing the EU and EFTA. Nonetheless, full membership of the European Union remained a key aspiration, and the following year, Stockholm lodged a formal application to assume membership. This was accepted, along with Austria and Finland, and on January 1, 1995 the three became the newest members of the Union. Sweden's major bilateral trading partners are Germany, the UK and the USA.
BUSINESS: Business people are expected to dress smartly. English is widely spoken in business circles. Punctuality is important for business and social occasions. Business cards are commonly used. **Office hours:** Flexible working hours are a widespread practice, with lunch between 1200-1300.
COMMERCIAL INFORMATION: The following organisation can offer advice: Federation of Swedish Commerce and Trade, PO Box 5512, Grevgatan 34, 114 85 Stockholm. Tel: (8) 666 1100. Fax: (8) 662 7457. Telex: 19673.
There are also chambers of commerce for other major towns and regions in Sweden.
CONFERENCES/CONVENTIONS: The main venues are in Stockholm, Gothenburg and Malmö; the Swedish Travel & Tourism Council also lists two in Lappland. The Globe Arena in Stockholm can seat up to 5000 persons and there are other venues in the city catering for up to 3000 persons. Elsewhere in Sweden most venues have facilities for 200-500 persons (although Malmö and Gothenburg have capacity for 1500). The Swedish Travel & Tourism Council's *Meetings and Incentive Planner* gives information on over 30 venues; it also supplies addresses for the main regional organisers.

CLIMATE

In spite of its northern position, Sweden has a relatively mild climate which varies due to its great length. The summers can be very hot but get shorter further north. The midnight sun can be seen between mid-May and mid-June above the Arctic Circle. Winters can be bitterly cold, especially in the north.
Required clothing: Lightweight for summer, heavyweights for winter and all year.

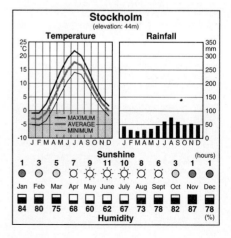

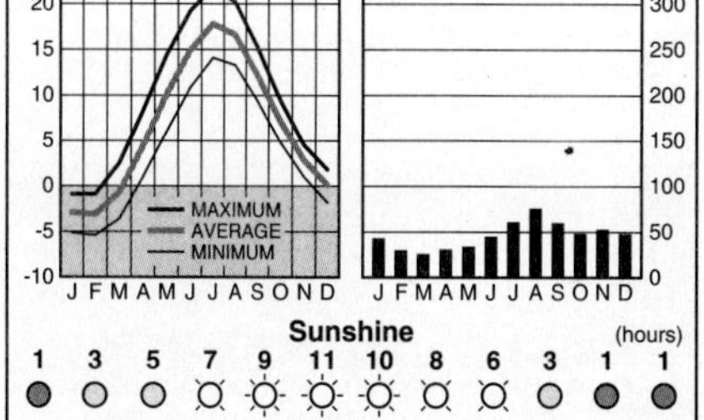
Stockholm
(elevation: 44m)
Temperature
Rainfall
25 °C 20 15 10 5 0 -5 -10
350 mm 300 250 200 150 100 50 0
MAXIMUM
AVERAGE
MINIMUM
J F M A M J J A S O N D
J F M A M J J A S O N D
Sunshine (hours)
1 3 5 7 9 11 10 8 6 3 1 1
Jan Feb Mar Apr May June July Aug Sept Oct Nov Dec
84 80 75 68 60 62 67 73 78 82 87 78
Humidity (%)

Location: Western Europe.

Swiss National Tourist Office
Bellariastrasse 38, CH-8027 Zurich, Switzerland
Tel: (1) 288 1111. Fax: (1) 288 1205.
Embassy of the Swiss Confederation
16-18 Montagu Place, London W1H 2BQ
Tel: (0171) 723 0701 *or* (0891) 331 313 (recorded visa information; calls are charged at the higher rate of 39/49p per minute). Fax: (0171) 724 7001. Telex: 28212 (a/b AMSWIS G). Opening hours: 0930-1230 Monday to Friday.
Swiss Consulate General
24th Floor, Sunley Tower, Piccadilly Plaza, Manchester M1 4BT
Tel: (0161) 236 2933. Fax: (0161) 236 4689. Telex: 665918 (a/b CONSUI G). Opening hours: 0900-1230 Monday to Friday (personal callers); 0800-1630 Monday to Thursday; 0800-1530 Friday (telephone enquiries).
Swiss National Tourist Office
Swiss Centre, Swiss Court, London W1V 8EE
Tel: (0171) 734 1921. Fax: (0171) 437 4577. Opening hours: 0900-1700 Monday to Friday.
British Embassy
Thunstrasse 50, CH-3005 Bern 15, Switzerland
Tel: (31) 352 5021/6. Fax: (31) 352 0583.
Consulates in: Geneva, Montreux, Zurich, Lugano and Valais.
Embassy of the Swiss Confederation
2900 Cathedral Avenue, NW, Washington, DC 20008
Tel: (202) 745 7900. Fax: (202) 387 2564. Telex: 440055 (a/b AMWN UI) *or* 64180 (a/b AMSWIS).
General Consulates in: Atlanta, Chicago, Houston, Los Angeles, New York (tel: (212) 758 2560) and San Francisco.
Swiss National Tourist Office
608 Fifth Avenue, New York, NY 10020
Tel: (212) 757 5944. Fax: (212) 262 6116.
Also in: Los Angeles and Chicago.
Embassy of the United States of America
Jubiläumsstrasse 93, CH-3005 Bern, Switzerland
Tel: (31) 357 7011. Fax: (31) 357 7344.
Consulates in: Geneva and Zurich.
Embassy of the Swiss Confederation
5 Marlborough Avenue, Ottawa, Ontario K1N 8E6
Tel: (613) 235 1837. Fax: (613) 563 1394.

Consulates in: Calgary, Edmonton, Montréal, Québec, Toronto and Vancouver.
Swiss National Tourist Office
926 The East Mall, Etobicoke, Ontario M9B 6K1
Tel: (416) 695 2090. Fax: (416) 695 2774.
Canadian Embassy
PO Box 3000, Kirchenfeldstrasse 88, CH-3005 Bern 6, Switzerland
Tel: (31) 352 6381-5. Fax: (31) 352 7315.
Consulate in: Geneva.

AREA: 41,293 sq km (15,943 sq miles).
POPULATION: 6,907,959 (1992 estimate).
POPULATION DENSITY: 167.3 per sq km.
CAPITAL: Bern. **Population:** 130,390 (1992 estimate).
GEOGRAPHY: Switzerland is bordered by France to the west, Germany to the north, Austria to the east and Italy to the south. It has the highest mountains in Europe, waterfalls and lakes set amid green pastures and the spring Alpine flowers covering the valleys and lower mountain slopes. The highest peaks are Monte Rosa, 4634m (15,217ft), on the Italian border; the Dom, 4548m (14,917ft); the Matterhorn, 4477m (14,698ft); and the Jungfrau, 4166m (13,669ft). The most popular areas are: the Engadine, the Berner Oberland, the Valais and the Ticino.
LANGUAGE: 73% German in central and eastern areas, 20% French in the west and 4% Italian in the south. Raeto-Romansch is spoken in the southeast by 1%. English is spoken by many. Overlapping cultural influences characterise the country.
RELIGION: Roman Catholic and Protestant.
TIME: GMT + 1 (GMT + 2 from last Sunday in March to Saturday before last Sunday in September).
ELECTRICITY: 220 volts AC, 50Hz.
COMMUNICATIONS: Telephone: Full IDD is available. Country code: 41. Outgoing international code: 00. **Fax:** Facilities are available in all telegraph offices, most major hotels and post offices. **Telex/telegram:** Many hotels have telex facilities, and telegrams and telex messages can be sent from post offices. Telegrams can also be arranged by dialling 110 on the telephone. **Post:** Airmail within Europe takes three days. *Poste Restante* is available at all post offices. Post office hours: 0730-1200 and 1345-1830 Monday to Friday. Saturday closing is at 1100 except in major cities. **Press:** The high level of interest in local politics throughout Switzerland has led to a large number of regional newspapers. However, the most popular dailies are *Blick* and *Tages-Anzeiger Zürich*. European newspapers are widely available. There are no local English-language newspapers printed in Switzerland.
BBC World Service and Voice of America frequencies: From time to time these change. See the section *How to Use this Book* for more information.
BBC:

| MHz | 15.07 | 12.09 | 9.750 | 6.195 |

A service is also available on 648kHz and 198kHz (0100-0500 GMT).
Voice of America:

| MHz | 15.20 | 11.85 | 9.760 | 6.040 |

PASSPORT/VISA

Regulations and requirements may be subject to change at short notice, and you are advised to contact the appropriate diplomatic or consular authority before finalising travel arrangements. Details of these may be found at the head of this country's entry. Any numbers in the chart refer to the footnotes below.

	Passport Required?	Visa Required?	Return Ticket Required?
Full British	1	No	Yes
BVP	Valid	-	-
Australian	Yes	No	Yes
Canadian	Yes	No	Yes
USA	Yes	No	Yes
Other EU (As of 31/12/94)	1	No	Yes
Japanese	Yes	No	Yes

PASSPORTS: Valid passport required by all except:
(a) **[1]** nationals of EU countries holding a valid national ID card or, in the case of UK nationals, a BVP;
(b) nationals of Austria, Cyprus, Finland, Liechtenstein, Malta, Monaco and San Marino holding valid national ID cards.
British Visitors Passport: Acceptable.
VISAS: Required by all except:
(a) nationals of countries referred to in the chart above;
(b) nationals of countries in South and Central America (except nationals of Belize and Peru who *do* need a visa);
(c) nationals of Caribbean island states (except nationals of the Dominican Republic and Haiti who *do* need a visa);

(d) nationals of Andorra, Austria, Brunei, Cyprus, Czech Republic, Fiji, Finland, Hungary, Iceland, Israel, Kiribati, South Korea, Liechtenstein, Malaysia, Malta, Monaco, New Zealand, Norway, Poland, San Marino, São Tomé e Príncipe, Singapore, Slovak Republic, Slovenia, Solomon Islands, South Africa, Sweden, Tuvalu and Vatican City;
(e) nationals of Bosnia-Hercegovina, Croatia, Turkey and Yugoslavia (Serbia and Montenegro) *provided they are resident in Canada, USA, EU or EFTA countries.*
The exemptions listed under (a)-(e) are for stays of up to 3 months provided that the visitor does not engage in employment or other gainful activity. If staying longer than 6 months within a 12-month period, a 'Residence Permit' is required which has to be applied for within 8 days of entry to Switzerland.
Types of visa: Single-entry, Multiple-entry and Transit visas (maximum 24 hours in country). Cost: £12 for passengers over 18 years of age (a married couple *or* one parent and one child over 16 travelling on a joint passport need only pay for one visa); £6 for unmarried passengers under 18.
Validity: 3 months.
Application to: Consulate (or Consular section at Embassy). For addresses, see top of entry. UK applicants should note that residents of Northern Ireland, Scotland, Cheshire, Cleveland, Cumbria, Derbyshire, Durham, Greater Manchester, Humberside, Isle of Man, Lancashire, Leicestershire, Lincolnshire, Merseyside, Northumberland, Nottinghamshire, Tyne & Wear and Yorkshire must obtain their visas from the Swiss Consulate General in Manchester (for address, see top of entry).
Application requirements: (a) 1 completed application form. (b) 1 passport-size photo. (c) Passport or travel document valid for at least 6 months after intended visit. (d) Return/onward ticket and visa for next country of destination if required. (e) Proof of sufficient funds, ie SFr100 (£50) for each day of stay, or SFr30 (£15) per day for students presenting a valid student ID card and letter from their university. (f) For visitors staying with Swiss residents, an invitation from the host stating that the visitor's expenses would be met by the host, which must then be approved, stamped and signed by the Aliens Police of the resident's canton. (g) For a Business visa, proof of existing business connections or invitation from Swiss company or business partner.
Working days required: Generally within 24 hours.
Temporary residence: Nationals of most European and some overseas countries do not require a visa if they intend to take up employment or residence in Switzerland; however, before entry they must obtain an *Assurance of a Residence Permit* from their employer in Switzerland. Students who wish to attend school, college or university for more than 3 months may apply to the local Aliens Police for a residence permit after entry, but as many Swiss educational establishments are overcrowded, they are advised to apply for the *Assurance of a Residence Permit* well in advance through their local Embassy or Consulate.

MONEY

Currency: Swiss Franc (SFr) = 100 rappen or centimes. Notes are in denominations of SFr1000, 500, 100, 50, 20 and 10. Coins are in denominations of SFr5, 2 and 1, and 50, 20, 10 and 5 centimes.
Currency exchange: Personal cheques within the Eurocheque system are accepted.
Credit cards: Access/Mastercard, American Express, Diners Club and Visa are widely accepted. Check with your credit card company for details of merchant acceptability and other facilities which may be available.
Travellers cheques: Sterling, US Dollar or Swiss Franc cheques are accepted at airports, railway stations and banks.
Exchange rate indicators: The following figures are included as a guide to the movements of the Swiss Franc against Sterling and the US Dollar:

Date:	Oct '92	Sep '93	Jan '94	Jan '95
£1.00=	2.17	2.17	2.20	2.05
$1.00=	1.37	1.42	1.48	1.31

Currency restrictions: There are no restrictions on the import or export of local or foreign currencies.
Banking hours: 0830-1630 Monday to Friday.

DUTY FREE

The following items may be imported into Switzerland by persons over 17 years of age without incurring customs duty by:
(a) Visitors from European countries:
200 cigarettes or 50 cigars or 250g of tobacco; 2 litres of alcohol (up to 15° proof); 1 litre of alcohol (over 15° proof); gifts up to a value of SFr100 (SFr50 for passengers under 17 years of age).
(b) Visitors from non-European countries:

LE RICHEMOND

Presque un Club privé

Hôtel Le Richemond   Jardin Brunswick   Genève   Tél. (022) 731 14 00 - Télex 412 560 - Téléfax (022) 731 67 09

400 cigarettes or 100 cigars or 500g of tobacco; 2 litres of alcohol (up to 15° proof); l litre of alcohol (over 15° proof); gifts up to a value of SFr100 (SFr50 for passengers under 17 years of age).
Prohibited items: All meat and processed meat, absinth and narcotics are prohibited. There are strict regulations on importing animals and firearms.

PUBLIC HOLIDAYS

Jan 1 '95 New Year's Day. **Apr 14** Good Friday. **Apr 17** Easter Monday. **May 25** Ascension Day. **Jun 5** Whit Monday. **Dec 25-26** Christmas. **Jan 1 '96** New Year's Day. **Apr 5** Good Friday. **Apr 8** Easter Monday.
Note: There are additional regional holidays which are observed in certain cantons only. For 1995/96 they are:
Jan 2 '95 For New Year. **May 1** Labour Day. **Jun 15** Corpus Christi. **Aug 1** National Day. **Jan 2 '96** For New Year.

HEALTH

Regulations and requirements may be subject to change at short notice, and you are advised to contact your doctor well in advance of your intended date of departure. Any numbers in the chart refer to the footnotes below.

	Special Precautions?	Certificate Required?
Yellow Fever	No	No
Cholera	No	No
Typhoid & Polio	No	-
Malaria	No	-
Food & Drink	No	-

Health care: Health insurance is essential. Medical facilities in Switzerland are among the best in Europe, but treatment is expensive. Various leaflets giving information on health spas and clinics are available from the SNTO.

TRAVEL - International

AIR: Switzerland's national airline is *Swissair (SR)*. For free advice on air travel, call the Air Travel Advisory Bureau on (0171) 636 5000 (London) *or* (0161) 832 2000 (Manchester).
Approximate flight times: From *London* to Basel, Bern, Geneva or Zurich is 1 hour 30 minutes.
From *Los Angeles* to Geneva is 17 hours and to Zurich is 14 hours 35 minutes.
From *New York* to Geneva is 9 hours 45 minutes and to Zurich is 7 hours 20 minutes.
International airports: *Zurich (ZRH)* (Kloten), 13km (8 miles) from the city (travel time – 10 minutes). Trains run every 20 minutes from 0600-2400, from under Terminal B. Passengers arriving in Switzerland by air via Zurich, Geneva or Basel airports can check in their baggage from the airport abroad through to their Swiss destination. Home-going air travellers whose flights are booked from Basel, Zurich or Geneva airports can check their luggage through to their final destination from many Swiss towns and resorts. Return is from Hauptbahnhof (main railway station). Taxis to the city are available. *Geneva (GVA)* (Gen), 5km (3 miles) northwest of the city. Taxis to the city are available. There is a regular train service to Geneva Cornavin, Station (travel time – 7 minutes).
Bern (BRN) (Belp), 9km (5.5 miles) from the city (travel time – 20 minutes). Bus services are available to Bern Bahnhof. A rail service runs from Bern to Zurich Airport 0455-2147. Taxis are also available.
Basel (BSL) (Basel-Mulhouse), 12km (7 miles) from the city. Bus runs to Basel SBB Luftreisebüro. Taxis are also available.
Departure tax: Basel: SFr15. Bern: SFr12. Geneva: SFr13. Lugano: SFr10. Zurich: SFr12.50.
Note: Portable computers may not be carried as hand luggage on international flights departing from Swiss airports. This ban was introduced as a security measure and may be lifted at any time; check with the respective airline before travelling.
RAIL: Connections from London via the main channel crossings are available (minimum travel time of about 14-15 hours to Basel and Lausanne, the main points of entry). There are also through trains from many other European cities.
ROAD: Switzerland can be reached by road from Italy, Germany, France and Austria. Some approximate driving times to Geneva and Zurich by the most direct routes are:
Calais–Geneva: 12/13 hours (747km/464 miles);
Dunkirk–Geneva: 12/13 hours (732km/454 miles);
Calais–Zurich: 13/14 hours (790km/490 miles);
Dunkirk–Zurich: 14/15 hours (880km/546 miles).
Coach: There are coach services to Switzerland, such as *Europabus*, as well as scheduled coach tour operators.

TRAVEL - Internal

AIR: All services are operated by *Swissair* and *Crossair*. Domestic air travel is fast but expensive, and with the exception of the Geneva to Zurich flight (flight time – 45 minutes), many business people prefer to travel by rail or road.

RAIL: Rail transport is particularly well-developed in Switzerland, with excellent services provided by *Schweizerischen Bundesbahnen (SBB)* and many other operators. Use of the 'Swiss Pass' (see below) is a superb way to view the scenery, although mainline services are geared to the needs of the hurried business traveller. Trains run at least hourly from the major centres and there is a country-wide timetable of regular services. There are dining cars on many trains, and snacks and refreshments are widely available. Independent railways, such as the *Rhätische Bahn* in the Grisons and the *Berner-Oberland-Bahn*, provide services in certain parts of the country. There are also a large number of mountain railways which are sometimes the only means of access to winter resorts. The SBB has introduced specialised cars for disabled people using wheelchairs. Facilities include a lift for wheelchairs, a specially adapted WC and radios adapted for people with hearing difficulties.

Cheap fares are available from SNTO. The 'Swiss Pass' gives unlimited travel on rail services, those of other main regional operators, lake steamers and the extensive network of postal buses, as well as reduced price travel on other mountain railways not included in the full scheme. If travelling with parents on a family ticket, children up to 15 years of age travel free and those aged 16-25 pay half price. Senior citizen cards are available and provide a significant discount. There are also regional tickets for unlimited travel in different parts of Switzerland at various rates. There is a leaflet describing all the schemes which is available from the SNTO. A comprehensive timetable for all Swiss public transport can also be purchased. Inter-Rail cards are valid.

ROAD: Traffic drives on the right. Road quality is generally good. Many mountain roads are winding and narrow, and often closed in heavy winter conditions; otherwise chains and snow tyres may be necessary. Rail is often more efficient than driving. **Bus:** Postal motor coaches provide a service to even the remotest villages, but under the integrated national transport policy few long-distance coaches are allowed to operate. **Taxi:** All taxis have meters for short and long trips, although it is advisable to agree the fare for longer distances out of town. **Car hire:** Available in all towns from hotels and airports and at all manned rail stations. All major European companies are represented. **Regulations:** Seatbelts are obligatory and children under 12 years must travel in the back of the car. Dipped headlights are compulsory in bad light. Drink-driving fines are heavy. **Speed limits:** 80kmph (50mph) on country lanes; 120kmph (75mph) on motorways; and 50kmph (31mph) in towns. **Organisations:** The *AA* and *RAC* in the UK are linked with *TCS (Touring Club Suisse)* and *ACS (Automobil Club der Schweiz)*. Contact the *Automobil Club der Schweiz (ACS)*, Wasserwerkgasse 39, CH-3000 Bern 13. Tel: (31) 311 7722. Fax: (31) 311 0310. In emergencies there is a breakdown service, for assistance tel: 140 throughout Switzerland. **Motorway tax (vignette):** Since January 1, 1985, an annual road tax of SFr40 has been levied on all cars using Swiss motorways. An additional fee of SFr30 applies to trailers and caravans. The *vignette* (sticker) is valid between December 1 of the year preceding and January 31 of the one following the year printed on the vignette. These permits, which are available at border crossings, are valid for multiple re-entry into Switzerland within the duration of the licensed period. To avoid hold-ups at the frontier, however, it is advisable to purchase the vignette in advance from the nearest SNTO. **Documentation:** A national driving licence is sufficient. Green Card insurance is advised – ordinary domestic insurance policies are valid but do not provide full cover. The Green Card tops the cover up to the level provided by the visitor's domestic policy.

URBAN: Highly efficient and integrated urban public transport systems serve as a model for other countries. There are tramways and light rail services in Basel, Bern, Geneva, Neuchâtel and Zurich. These and a further dozen cities also have trolleybuses. Fares systems are generally automated with machines issuing single or multiple tickets at the roadside. Tickets are also available at enquiry offices. Fares are generally zonal. There is a day ticket for travel in one or more Swiss cities on any given day at a standard fare. Taxis are widely available and drivers expect a 15% tip.

JOURNEY TIMES: The following chart gives approximate journey times (in hours and minutes) from Zurich to other major cities/towns in Switzerland.

	Air	Road	Rail
Basel	0.30	1.10	1.05
Bern	-	1.15	1.10
Geneva	0.40	2.45	2.55
Lugano	0.45	3.00	3.00

ACCOMMODATION

HOTELS: Hotels are of high quality and in high demand. Advance booking is advised. Bookings cannot be made through the SNTO. All standards from luxury to family hotels and pensions are available. 40% of hotels in Switzerland are affiliated to the *Schweizer Hotelier Verein* (Swiss Hotels Association) (SHV), PO Box 2657, Monbijoustrasse 130, CH-3001 Bern. Tel: (31) 370 4111. Fax: (31) 370 4444. 75% of all overnight stays in the country are at SHV member hotels.

Grading: The SHV classifies all its hotels according to a 5-star rating system, which stipulates a range of facilities as follows:

5-star (Luxury): Very high standard of comfort and facilities including all rooms with private bath, colour television and 16/24-hour room service. Minimum size of hotel: 35 rooms. There are 87 SHV-classified 5-star hotels in Switzerland.

4-star (First class): High standard of comfort and facilities including all rooms with private bath and 16/24-hour room service. 60% of rooms with colour television. Minimum size of hotel: 25 rooms. There are 438 SHV-classified 4-star hotels in Switzerland.

3-star (Good middle-class): Very good standard of comfort and facilities including 75% of rooms with private bath. Minimum size of hotel: 10 rooms. There are 1037 SHV-classified 3-star hotels in Switzerland.

2-star (Comfortable): Good standard of comfort and facilities including 30% of rooms with private bath. There are 565 SHV-classified 2-star hotels in Switzerland.

1-star (Simple): Simple, clean accommodation offering basic amenities. There are 295 SHV-classified 1-star hotels in Switzerland.

Note: Membership of the SHV is voluntary, and there may be some first-class hotels which do not have a star rating.

Prices vary slightly according to the popularity of the resort. The SHV (see above for address) issues an annual guide of 2700 member hotels and pensions. This shows the

rates, addresses, telephone/telex numbers, opening dates and amenities of the various hotels. Also included are lists of spas, resorts, sports facilities and climate. A list of hotels and restaurants catering for Jewish visitors is available from the SHV, as well as a hotel guide for the disabled and a list of hotels especially suitable for families. All lists are available from the SNTO.
CHALETS & APARTMENTS: Information regarding the rental of chalets, houses, flats and furnished apartments is available from local tourist offices and estate agents in Switzerland. A list of contacts is available from the SNTO.
SPAS: Switzerland has about 22 different mineral springs for the treatment of various health conditions. A guide to Swiss spas, including hotels, is available from the SNTO. Information can also be obtained from the Swiss Spa Association (SSA), PO Box 1456, CH-5400 Baden. Tel: (56) 225 318. Fax: (56) 225 320.
PRIVATE CLINICS: Details of accommodation in private sanatoria and clinics is included in the publication *Private Clinics in Switzerland,* available from the SNTO.
CAMPING: There are approximately 450 campsites in Switzerland. Camping on farmland is not advisable. Local area laws and fees vary. Camping guides published by the *Swiss Camping Federation* and the *Swiss Camping Association* can be purchased from the SNTO. The *Swiss Camping and Caravanning Association (SCA)* can be contacted at Habsburgerstrasse 35, CH-6000 Lucerne (tel: (41) 234 822).
YOUTH HOSTELS: Youth hostel accommodation is available for tourists up to the age of 25 years. Hostellers over 25 are admitted if there is room. Visitors from abroad must hold a membership card of a national organisation affiliated to the *International Youth Hostels Federation.* To avoid disappointment, wardens of youth hostels should be given prior notice (at least five days) of arrival. An *International Reply Paid Postcard (Youth Hostel Edition)* should be used if confirmation is required. For further information, contact the Swiss Youth Hostel Federation (SYHF), Schaffhauserstrasse 14, CH-8042 Zurich. Tel: (1) 360 1414.
A list of Swiss youth hostels is obtainable from the SNTO.

RESORTS & EXCURSIONS

For the purpose of this guide Switzerland has been divided into six resort sections: Western, Northern, Central, Eastern and Southern Switzerland; and Ski Resorts.

Western Switzerland

Jura, Neuchâtel & Fribourg: The lakes of Biel, Murten and Neuchâtel are strung along the foot of the Jura. Although not one of the most popular regions for

GENEVA

To United Nations (Palace des Nations), GATT & Red Cross
Parc Mon Repos
LAC LÉMAN
PALAIS WILSON
LES PÂQUIS
To Genève-Cointrin Airport
Gare de Cornavin
Place de Cornavin
Place des Alpes
CASINO DE GENEVE
Jetée des Paquis
QUAI DU MONT-BLANC
Square du Mont-Blanc
EGLISE DE NOTRE-DAME
MONUMENT BRUNSWICK
Jetée des Eaux-Vives
Jet d'Eau
Place St-Gervaise
RHONE
Île Rousseau
Jardin Anglais
QUAI G. ADOR
SECTION CITÉ
To Gare des Eaux-Vives
GRAND THÉATRE
MUSÉE RATH
CATHÉDRALE ST-PIERRE
Rond-Point de Rive
CONSERVATOIRE
Place Neuve
COLLÈGE CALVIN
Plaine de Plainpalais
Promenade des Bastions
MUSEUM D'HISTOIRE NATURELLE
Rond-Point de Plainpalais
COLLECTIONS BAUR
MUSÉE D'ETHNOGRAPHIE
1km
½ ml
tourist information

1. AUDITOIRE
2. HÔTEL DE VILLE
3. MONUMENT DE LA RÉFORMATION
4. PALAIS EYNARD
5. UNIVERSITÉ
6. Place du Bourg de Four
7. Prom. de St-Antione
8. MUSÉE D'ART & D'HISTOIRE
9. MUSÉE D'INSTRUMENTS
10. MUSÉE D'HORLOGERIE

tourists, the rolling hills, the *Franches Montagnes* in the Neuchâtel region and the foothills of the Alps of the canton of Fribourg on the other side of the lakes are excellent for hiking, camping and fishing. The waterfalls of the *Doubs* and the gorges of the *Areuse* are very impressive. Well worth a visit is the *Lac Talliers*, the medieval town of **Romont**, south of **Morat** and the *Folk Art Museum* at **Tafers**. **Fribourg,** where a Romanesque-Germanic atmosphere prevails, is one of the most interesting historical cities in Switzerland. In the south of the canton Fribourg is the Gruyère region, in the foothills of the Alps. It is famous for its dairy farming which produces one of the best Swiss cheeses: Gruyère. The town of **Gruyères** is still completely surrounded by its old city walls. Swiss precision watches are produced in Western Switzerland; do not miss the *Horological Museum* at **La-Chaux-de-Fonds**. Visitors can try to solve the mystery of the precision watch at the watch-making factories at La-Chaux-de-Fonds and **Le Locle**. The area is also famous for its food and wines.
Resorts: St-Blaise, La-Chaux-de-Fonds, Le Locle, Neuchâtel, Auvernier, Colombier, La Neuveville, Boudry, Fribourg, Gruyères, Les Bioux, Murten, Le Brassus and St Ursanne.
Geneva & Lake Geneva (Lac Léman in French; **Genfer See** in German): **Geneva** is a university town set at the Rhône-outlet of the lake at the foot of the Jura. It owes its cosmopolitan nature to the presence of the United Nations, the International Red Cross and many other international organisations. The *Palais des Nations* should be part of every itinerary. Its popularity is, however, not only due to its excellent surroundings. Elegant shops, nightclubs, restaurants, fine museums and art galleries and an extensive calendar of cultural activities make it a favourite with many visitors. The old city centre should be explored on foot. One of the finest examples of Romanesque architecture is the *Cathedral St Pierre Genève*. There is also an original flower clock in the *Jardin Anglais*. Do not miss a boat-trip on the lake. The lake, which is dominated by the *Jet d'Eau*, a 145m-high (476ft) water fountain, is generally covered with sailing boats. A crisp breeze known as the *bise* blows across the lake and there are facilities for all kinds of watersports, as well as golf and riding.
Mountaineering is popular at *Mont Salève*, south of the city, where there is an excellent school. In winter there is skiing and skating. Vineyards cover the slopes of *Monts du Lavaux;* the villages of **Riez** and **Epesse** produce delicious wines. *Chateau d'Oex*, in the canton of Vaud, is the gateway to the *Pays d'Enhaut* ('upper land').
Lausanne, the capital of the canton, is situated on the northern shore of Lake Geneva. The symbol of the city is the *Cathedral Notre Dame* in the *Cité*, the old centre, and the *Château St Maire* (1397-1431). A walk along the promenade of the old *Port d'Ouchy* reverts to a slower pace of life; or a funicular can be taken from Ouchy to the inner city of Lausanne. Several rivulets and rolling hills dominate the canton Vaud, a famous wine-producing region. In the midst of vineyards is the *Château d'Aigle*, the former residence of the Bernse Landvogts. Also in this area is one of the most important historical buildings of Switzerland: the Benedictine monastery *Church of St Pierre* (11th century) in the small town of **Romainmotier**. There is summer skiing on the glacier at **Les Diablerets** (noteworthy for its panoramic views of *Mont Blanc* and the icy peaks and green valleys of the Alps), and rafting or hydrospeeding precariously down the *Sarine*, from **Chateau d'Oex**, is the area's newest sport. Each summer there is a rock festival at **Leysin**. **Montreux** is renowned for its mild climate and the *International Jazz Festival*. At **Villars** there is an 18-hole golf course. The region's more traditional activities include wood sculpture, cheese-making and paper cut-out artistry.
Summer resorts: Lausanne, Montreux, Yverdon, Nyon-Coppet, Morges, Lausanne Chexbres, Vevey, Villeneuve, Château d'Oex, Les Diablerets, Leysin, Villars, Gryon, Payerne, Sainte Croix, Orbe and Vallée de Joux.
Winter resorts: Rochers-de-Naye, Les Avants, Château d'Oex, Rougemont, Les Diablerets, Leysin, Villars, Gryon, Saint Cergue, Sainte Croix and Vallée de Joux.

Northern Switzerland

Zurich: Switzerland's largest city is set on its own lake on the banks of the *Limmat River*, and is a German-speaking business and banking centre. The old part of the town is picturesque, and the town has a full cultural season. Plays are performed in the *Zürcher Schauspielhaus,* which is counted among the most prestigious German-speaking theatres. On a walk through the old centre do not miss the *Basilica Fraumünster* (11th-13th century) with its three naves and the stained glass windows by Marc Chagall. The skyline is dominated by the *Grossmünster* with its twin towers. Other sights include the impressive *Town Hall*, a fine example for the late Renaissance (17th century), the *Swiss Country Museum* and the porcelain collection at the Baroque *Zunfthaus zur Meise*. Local trains and buses leave for the hills, woods and parks that surround Zurich; during the summer, steamer cruises on the lake are also popular. Zurich is set in the Mittelland ('middle country'), a very lush and picturesque region dotted with small historic towns, spotless villages and vineyards. **Regensberg** is one of the most appealing medieval cities in the country; the medieval castle at **Rapperswil** is well worth a visit. A day-trip to the *Uetliberg* is recommended. On clear days the panorama from the platform includes the Valais and Berner Alps to the west and in the east the Black Forest.
Schaffhausen is set above the *Rhine Falls* on the northern bank.
Northwest Switzerland: Not one of the more important tourist areas, but there are a few well-known holiday resorts. **Basel,** the ancient university and trading city, straddles the Rhine between the Jura and the Alsace, and is a centre of art and research. During the three days of the *Basler Fasnacht* (carnival), no serious sightseeing should or can be done, as visitors are required to take part. The townspeople even built a *Fasnacht Fountain* in front of the *City Theatre*. The collection in the *Art Museum* ranges from Cranach and Holbein via Rembrandt to Monet, Picasso and Max Ernst. The old city centre houses the *Münster* (parts date from the 9th-13th century) with its two towers. Other sights include the *Spulentor* (1370) and the *Church of St Peter* (15th century). Away from the town, mountain paths zigzag up to the heights of the Jura. The prevalent architectural styles of **Solothurn** are Renaissance and Baroque. Day trips to **Aarau** and **Baden** are also recommended. Do not miss the 13th-century moated castle at **Binningen,** the *Waldenburg* and the spa resort of *Rheinfelden.*

Central Switzerland

The **Berner Oberland** with Interlaken and the Jungfraujoch is one of the main tourist areas of Switzerland with a spectacular scenery of famous peaks, mountain lakes, alpine streams and wild flowers. **Adelboden, Grindelwald** and **Lenk** were already famous with the European noblesse and artists of the 19th century. **Interlaken,** situated between the lakes of Thun and Brienz, is a renowned climatic health resort and the gateway to the Berner Oberland. From here a network of roads and mountain railways auch as the narrow-gauge *Berner-Oberland-Bahn* (BOB) serve the resorts in the Jungfrau region. Jungfrau (4158m/13,642ft), Mönch (4099m/13,448ft) and Eiger (3970m/13,024ft), whose dangerous, nearly perpendicular northern ascent was climbed in 1938 for the first time, are the *Finsteraarhorn Group*. Finsteraarhorn (4275m/14,026ft), the highest peak of the *Berner Alps,* is dominated by glaciers which reach from the upper Aare and the Rhône valley to Lake Geneva. Excursions to the *Schilthorn* and the *Allmendhubel* with funiculars, the waterfalls at **Giessbach** and the open-air museum at **Ballenberg** are recommended. **Adelboden** and **Zweisimmen** are reached from Spiez on *Lake Thun. Thun's Castle* should not be missed.
Bern, the ancient capital, provides opportunities for sightseeing and shopping in the 11th-century arcaded streets. The backdrop is provided by the Jura in the west and the south is dominated by the Alps and their foothills. On the *Aare Peninsula* is the medieval city centre between the *Zeitglockenturm* and the *Nydeggchurch*. Vegetable and flower stalls are scattered over the pretty *Bear Market* Tuesday and Saturday mornings.
Summer resorts: Interlaken, Mürren, Wengen, Lenk, Grindelwald, Brienz, Meiringen, Thun and Spiez.
Winter resorts: Interlaken, Mürren, Wengen, Grindelwald, Gstaad, Lauterbrunnen, Scheidegg, Zweisimmen and Meiringen.
Lucerne area: This region of mountains, lakes, pine forests and meadows is traditionally a very popular tourist area. The lakes of *Zug, Ageri* and *Lauerz* surround the Rigi massif. **Lucerne** is on the *Vierwaldstätter See*. Its medieval old town remains intact; important buildings include the *Hofkirche*, the old *Town Hall* (1602-1606) and the famous *Lion Memorial*. Spanning the Reuss is the 170m-long (558ft), covered wooden *Chapel Bridge*, the oldest in Switzerland (1333). Lucerne also houses the *Richard Wagner Museum* and the transport museum. An international music festival is held here every year. Cablecars, passenger lifts and cogwheel railways provide transport to the *Sonnenberg,* the *Gütsch,* the *Pilatus* and other mountains.
Summer resorts: Lucerne, Engelberg, Weggis, Vitznau,

Schwyz, Sarnen, Küssnacht, Hergiswil, Gersau, Einsiedel and Brunnen.
Winter resorts: Engelberg, Andermatt, Melchsee-Frutt, Rigi Kaltbad and Sorenberg.

Eastern Switzerland

Graubünden: There are 150 valleys in the rugged mountainous country of the Grisons. The climatic health resorts of St Moritz, Davos, Klosters and Arosa are renowned the world over, not only for their winter sports facilities. Typical Engadine stone houses characterise the cities of **St Moritz, Pontresina** and **Zuoz.** The highest peak in the canton is the Bernina (4049m/13,284ft) on the border to Italy and Austria. **Chur**, the oldest Swiss city, is the hub for *St Moritz, Davos, Klosters, Arosa* and countless other ski resorts. Sights of the city include the *St Lucius Church*, the *Cathedral* (12th-13th century) and the *Rhaetic Museum.* A bus ride from Chur to **Bellinzona** goes over the *San Bernardino Pass.* In the Engadine valley, small villages beyond **Zernez** and the *Swiss National Park* have cross-country skiing or summer walking areas. This mountain republic has probably the longest history of any region of Switzerland and has castles, fortresses and countless churches and chapels. The 168-sq-km (65-sq-mile) Swiss National Park is covered to a third with dense forest and is home to several wildlife species, among them roe and deer, eagles, marmot and lizards.
All-year resorts: Flims, St Moritz, Arosa, Davos, Bad Scuol, Bad Tarasp-Vulpera, Bad Vals, Bergun, Chur, Disentis, Grusch, Klosters, Laax, Lenzerheide, Mustair, Obersaxen, Pontresina, Poschiavo, San Bernardino, Samedan, Savognin, Sedrun, Sils, Silvaplana and Zernez.
East & North of Lake Constance: This area of eastern Switzerland rises slowly over the rugged range of the Churfirsten near St Gallen to the Glarner Alps.
Appenzell, in the northeastern part of Switzerland, with its highest peak Säntis (2504m/8215ft), is ideal for hiking tours. The Rhine, which springs from Lake Toma in the *St Gotthard*, runs through Lake Constance and cascades into the fall at Schaffhausen. **Stein am Rhein** is a picturesque small town with a medieval atmosphere. **St Gallen's** old city centre is dominated by burgher houses from the 17th and 18th century. Not to be missed is the Baroque *Cathedral,* the famous *Abbey Library* in the courtyard of the old Benedictine monastery (incunabula and illuminated manuscripts) and the city library, *Vadiana* (1551). Old traditions remain very much alive in Appenzell and national costumes are still worn for village and folk festivals. The wild valley of the Linth, lakeboat trips on Lake Constance to Friedrichshafen in Germany, excursions to the Berner Oberland and to the Valais and the Duchy of Liechtenstein can easily be arranged.
Summer resorts: Schaffhausen, Toggenburg, Stein am Rhein, Lake Constance, Wildhaus and Unterwasser.
Winter resorts: Toggenburg Valley, Wildhaus and Unterwasser.

Southern Switzerland

Valais: The valley stretches all the way from the Rhône Glacier past **Brig**, **Sion** and **Martigny** down to **Lake Geneva**. Nestling between the northern and the southern side of the Alps is a diverse landscape which will entice every visitor. Glaciers can be found on all peaks of the *Valais Alps* which are also the highest in Switzerland: Monte Rosa (4635m/15,207ft), Dom (4551m/14,931ft), Weisshorn (4509m/14,793ft) and the Matterhorn (4479m/14,695ft). Small villages of weathered wooden-beamed houses, with flowers pouring out of the windowboxes in summer, perch in clearings high on the slopes. High transverse valleys give access to their resorts at the foot of the alpine giants such as **Saas Fee** in the Saas Valley and **Zermatt** in the Nikolai Valley; the Matterhorn provides a magnificent backdrop for the latter. In the internationally well-known resort of Zermatt, cars are not allowed and transport is either on foot or horse and cart. There are well-posted walks and cablecars, with lifts and tows to the tops of the slopes for more ambitious climbing. The historic town of **Brig** boasts the most important Baroque castle in Switzerland, the *Stockalperschloss*. **Sion**, an episcopal town, and **Martigny**, with a castle ruin, are worth a visit and are also ideal starting points for excursions to the surrounding area. Castle enthusiasts should visit **Leuk**, **Sierre** and **Monthey**. Europe's highest aerial cable goes up to the *Little Matterhorn* at **Zermatt**. Any visit to the area should include the *Rhône Glacier* and grotto at **Gletsch** and the subterranean lake at **Saint Leonard**.
All-year resorts: Zermatt, Saas Fee, Crans Montana, Leukerbad, Champex, Champéry, Riederalp, Bettmeralp and Verbier.
Winter resorts: Bellwald, Fiesch, Grachen, Les Marecottes, Champéry-Planachaux, Morgins, Salvan and Finhaut.
Ticino: The Italian-speaking, southernmost tip of Switzerland is the Ticino. The climate is subtropical and the atmosphere Mediterranean. From the Alpine valleys the road runs down to the narrow streets, pavement cafés and lakeside lido of **Locarno,** on the shores of Lago di Maggiore. The largest Tessinian city **Lugano** is a health and holiday resort and lies on the Lago di Lugano between the peaks of *San Salvatore* and *Monte Bré.* It is a favourite holiday destination for the Swiss. Piazzas, palazzos, palms, the *Cathedral San Lorenzo* and the promenade along the lakeshore give the city a special flair. During spring the area is in full bloom with fig and olive trees, pomegranates and myrtle. Local buses visit the picturesque villages of the area and funiculars run to the top of *Mount San Salvatore.* Coach excursions to the great passes of *Furka, Oberalp* and *Lukmanier,* and to Milan and Venice, can be arranged locally. The islands of **Brissago** are worth a visit; on the larger is an interesting botanical garden with Mediterranean flora. The unspoiled wilderness of **Bolle di Magadino** is a must for nature enthusiasts and the *Paleological Museum* at **Meride** is also interesting.
Resorts: Locarno, Ascona, Brissago, Lugano, Morcote and Gandria.

Ski Resorts

ADELBODEN AREA: Adelboden: Christmas to beginning of April. Quiet town and nightlife, mainly for serious skiers. **Lenk:** Season is mid-December to end-March. Superb skiing, but very quiet. Excellent for families. Little nightlife. **Kandersteg:** All types of skiing but not extensive. Does not share lift pass.
CRANS/MONTANA AREA: Crans sur Sierre: Mid-December to mid-April. Very chic, with plenty of choice of nightlife. **Montana:** More rustic and down-to-earth. Nightlife varied, but restrained. **Anzère:** Mid-December to mid-March. A young people's place. Close-knit English community. **Grimentz:** Small attractive village. Limited nightlife, but all standards of skiing. **Zinal:** Beginners and intermediates. Good nightlife.
DAVOS/KLOSTERS AREA: Davos: Beginning of December to mid-April. Fewer facilities for younger people. Lots of varied après-ski. **Klosters:** December to mid-April. Quiet and expensive après-ski. More a resort for the middle-aged. **Arosa:** Beginning of December to end-April. Good for skiers and non-skiers. Horse-drawn sleighs.
ENGADINE AREA: St Moritz: Early December to end of April. Large expensive resort. All types and ages. Varied nightlife. **Pontresina:** Near St Moritz. Early December to mid-April. **Celerina:** Attractive, traditional village. For nightlife, St Moritz is up the road. **Samnaun (Grisons):** Many Germans. Good cross-country skiing. Duty-free area. **Zuoz:** Limited downhill skiing. Charming village.
FLIMS AREA: Laax: Ancient farming village. Excellent skiing sites of all types. **Flims:** Mid-December to mid-April. Quiet. Ski school. Excellent standard. Good facilities for non-skiers.
GSTAAD (WEISSES HOCHLAND) AREA: Gstaad: Christmas to beginning of April. Very glamorous resort. Trendy and expensive. Much après-ski. **Château d'Oex:** Mostly beginners. Traditional town. Most accommodation in chalets. **Rougemont:** Unspoiled village. Good cross-country. Quiet nightlife.
Saanenmoser, Schonried and Saanen: Also has summer skiing on glacier. Attractive chalets. Runs to suit all standards. **Zweisimmen:** Small town. Ski school. All standards. Quiet nightlife. **Les Diablerets:** Mid-December to mid-April. Quiet. Ideal for families. Good nursery slopes. Non-skiing activities. Summer skiing on glacier. **Leysin:** Mid-December to mid-March. Nightlife gentle. Lots of schoolchildren. **Villars sur Ollon:** Mid-December to end of March. Quiet. Typically Swiss. Restricted nightlife. **Les Mosses:** Intermediates and beginners. Nightlife quiet.
JUNGFRAU AREA: Grindelwald: Mid-December to end-March. Rather old-fashioned. Quiet in the evening. **Wengen:** December to April. A lot of English spoken. Plenty of non-skiing activity. **Mürren:** Early December to mid-April. Rustic village with chalet accommodation.
LENZERHEIDE AREA: Valbella: Varied skiing. One difficult run. Suitable for families. Very beautiful area. **Lenzerheide:** Mid-December to mid-April. Good food. Nightlife moderate.
OBERTOGGENBURG AREA: Alt St Johann: Picturesque. Popular but not too crowded. Intermediate with some advanced runs. **Wildhaus:** Not too crowded. Runs for all standards. Good for non-skiers. Nightlife mostly in hotels.
PORTES DU SOLEIL AREA: Champéry: Mid-December to beginning of April. Quiet. Family resort. **Champoussin:** Lots of English-speaking instructors. Excellent skiing for all standards. **Morgins:** Pretty resort. Skiing relatively easy. Good resort for families.
RIEDERALP AREA: Bettmeralp: Two beginner runs, two advanced, the rest intermediate. Good restaurants. Prices reasonable. **Riederalp:** Early December to end-March. Minimal nightlife. Beautiful surroundings. Peaceful.
SARGANS AREA: Wangs-Pizol: Some exhilarating skiing. Good ski school for children and beginners. Nightlife minimal. **Braunwald:** Does not share lift pass. Beginners and intermediate. **Flumserberge:** Suitable for cross-country skiing. Good for families. Few non-skiing activities. **Malbun:** Intermediates and beginners. One advanced run. Nightlife is noisy and lively.
VERBIER/LES QUATRE VALLÉES AREA: Verbier: Mid-December to end-April. Serious skiers and lots of facilities for young people. **Bruson:** Quieter. Main slopes suitable for beginners and intermediates. **Super St Bernard:** More a ski station. No accommodation. Good day's outing. All standards. **Thyon 2000:** Modern resort. One long run, the rest suitable for beginners and intermediate. Not lively but suitable for groups and families.
ANDERMATT AREA: Andermatt: Mid-December to mid-April. Nightlife quite lively. Plenty of non-skiing activities. **Engelberg:** Mid-December to mid-April. Historic town. Some runs very difficult. Some nightlife. Casino. Some intermediate.
Hoch-Ybrig (Central Switzerland): Good place for families. Nightlife moderate. Beautiful area.
ZERMATT AREA: Zermatt: Early December to mid-April. Much variety of skiing and nightlife. Plenty of non-skiing activities. **Saas Fee:** Early December to mid-April. Après-ski quiet, but fun. No cars. **Grachen:** Beginners and intermediates. Good non-ski facilities.

SOCIAL PROFILE

FOOD & DRINK: Swiss cuisine is varied. The great speciality is *fondue,* the delicious concoction of *Gruyère* and *Emmental* cheese, melted and mixed with white wine, flour, *Kirsch* and a little garlic. Other cheese specialities are *Emmental* and *Tête de Moine.* Regional specialities include *viande sechée* (dried beef or pork) from Valais and the Grisons where it is called *bündnerfleisch.* The meat is cut wafer thin, with pickled spring onions and gherkins. *Papet vaudoir* is a delicious dish made from leeks and potatoes. Geneva's great speciality is *pieds de porc* (pigs feet). Pork sausages or salami come in a variety of local recipes including *landjäger, beinwurst, engadinerwurst, leberwurst* (pâté), *kalbsleberwurst* (calf's liver pâté), and *knackerli.* Try *rösti* (shredded fried potatoes) and *fondue Bourguignonne* (cubed meat with various sauces). Cakes and pastries are also varied: *leckerli* are Basel specialities (spiced honey cakes topped with icing sugar); in Bern they are decorated with a white sugar bear; *gugelhopf* (a type of sponge cake with a hollow centre), *fasnachtküchli* (sugar-dusted pastries eaten during Carnival) and *schaffhausen* (cream-filled cakes) are also popular. Although there are many self-service snack bars, table service is normal.
Drink: A great variety of Swiss wines are available throughout the country. There are also spirits made from fruit, the most popular being *Kirsch, Marc, Pflümli* and *Williams.* Swiss beer of a lager type is also available. Bottled mineral water is an accepted beverage, local brands including *Henniez* and *Passuger.* Bars/cocktail lounges have table and/or counter service.
NIGHTLIFE: Most major towns and resorts have nightclubs or discotheques with music and dancing, sometimes serving food. There are also cinemas and theatres, and some bars and restaurants have local folk entertainment.
SHOPPING: Special purchases include embroidery and linen, Bernse woodcarving, chocolate, cheese, Swiss army knives and luxury handmade clocks and watches.
Shopping hours: 0830-1200 and 1330-1830 Monday to Friday; 0800-1200 and 1330-1600 Saturday.
SPORT: Mountaineering/hiking: Switzerland's topography is ideal for climbers of every class from the highly experienced to the casual hill walker. However, whatever their standard, all participants must be aware of basic safety, well informed on the weather forecasts and suitably equipped. **Golf:** A list of courses is available at the SNTO. **Tennis:** Many hotels have courts. **Cycling:** Bicycle hire is available. **Watersports:** Lakes such as Lake Geneva, Lugano and Neuchâtel offer sailing, water-skiing and canoeing. **Winter sports:** Switzerland's winter resorts are a principal international tourist attraction and Swiss teams participate in all international skiing events. Skiing and winter sport facilities are innumerable. For more details, contact the SNTO.
SPECIAL EVENTS: The following is a selection of special events celebrated in Switzerland during 1995. For further details, contact the SNTO.
Mar 6-8 '95 *Fasnacht,* Basel. **Mar 15** *Spring Market,*

Amriswil. **Apr 22-May 1** *Spring Snow Festival*, Samnaun. **Apr 23-24** *Sechseläuten*, Zurich. **Apr 30-May 6** *Golden Rose of Montreux* (TV awards). **May 3-7** *International Jazz Festival*, Bern. **May 5** *Jodling Sunday*, Winterthur. **May 13** *Flower Festival*, Montreux. **May 20** *Fête de Mai* (wine festival), La Chaux-de-Fonds. **May 22-28** *Ladies European Open* (tennis), Lucerne. **Jun 3-10** *Alpine Horn Week*, Mürren. **Jun 14-19** *Art 26 '95* (international art fair), Basel. **Jun 20-21** *Swiss Bonsai Tree Exhibition*, Lucerne. **Jun 30-Jul 2** *Jodlerfest*, Brunnen. **Jul 7-22** *Festival International de Jazz*, Montreux. **Jul 29** *Village and Lake Festival*, Oberägeri. **Aug 1** *Fireworks at the Rhine Falls*, Schaffhausen; *National Day*, throughout the country. **Aug 3-13** *International Film Festival*, Locarno. **Aug 5-6** *Wine Festival*, Anzère. **Aug 5-6** *Rock-Open-Air*, Chur. **Aug 10-13** *Fêtes de Genève* (folk festival), Geneva. **Aug 15** *Midsummer Festival*, Anzère. **Aug 16** *International Athletics Meeting*, Zurich. **Aug 16-Sep 9** *International Music Week* (classical), Lucerne. **Aug 31-Sep 3** *European Masters* (golf), Crans-Montana. **Sep 1-10** *Folklore Festival*, St Stephan. **Oct 7** *Cheese Festival*, Piotta. **Oct 28-Nov 12** *Autumn Fair*, Basel. **Nov 27** *Zibelmärit* (folk festival), Bern. **Dec 8-10** *Fête de l'escalde* (historical procession), Geneva. **Dec 10-17** *European Championships* (curling), Grächen. **Dec 26-31** *International Spengler-Cup* (icehockey), Davos.

SOCIAL CONVENTIONS: It is customary to give unwrapped flowers to the hostess when invited for a meal. Avoid red roses; never give chrysanthemums or white asters as they are considered funeral flowers. Informal wear is widely acceptable. First-class restaurants, hotel dining rooms and important social occasions may warrant jackets and ties. Black tie is usually specified when required. **Tipping:** A service charge of 15% is included in all hotel, restaurant, café, bar, taxi and hairdressing services by law.

BUSINESS PROFILE

ECONOMY: Switzerland has a typical West European mixed economy with a bias towards light and craft-based industries: Swiss watch-making is renowned throughout the world. The country is highly industrialised and heavily dependent on exports of finished goods. In manufacturing, the machinery and equipment industry specialises in precision and advanced technology products: machine tools, printing and photographic equipment, electronic control and medical equipment. There is also a substantial chemical industry, employing 10% of the workforce, which continues to experience steady growth. Although half the country's food is imported, the agricultural sector is strong and a major employer. The processed foods industry has a high international profile, particularly in chocolate, cheese and baby foods. The service sector is dominated by banking. Uninterrupted peace since 1815 initially made Switzerland an attractive location for depositors concerned about political stability. More recently, the particular reputation of the Swiss banking community for discretion has attracted large deposits. Inevitably, some of this money has been illegally procured and the Swiss authorities have come under heavy pressure, especially from Washington, to relax the country's strict banking secrecy laws to assist international criminal investigation. For the time being, Switzerland remains one of Europe's major financial centres. Among other service industries, tourism is of growing importance. Switzerland is not a member of the EU, although nearly two-thirds of its exports are sold to EU countries. It may apply to join before the end of the 1990s depending on the political situation. As a member of the European Free Trade Association (EFTA), however, Switzerland does belong to the European Economic Area, the combined EU/EFTA trading bloc established in 1991. In May 1992, Switzerland gained admission to the IMF and World Bank. Switzerland's main export markets are: Germany (22%), France (10%), Italy (9%) and the UK (6%).

BUSINESS: Business people are expected to wear suits. Although English is widely spoken, it is always appreciated if a visitor attempts to say a few words in the language of the host. When visiting a firm a visiting card is essential. **Office hours:** 0800-1200 and 1400-1700 Monday to Friday.

COMMERCIAL INFORMATION: The following organisations can offer advice: Schweizerische Zentrale für Handelsförderung – Office Suisse d'Expansion Commerciale (OSEC), Stampfenbachstrasse 85, CH-8035 Zurich. Tel: (1) 365 5151. Fax: (1) 365 5221. Telex: 817272; *or* Schweizerischer Handels- und Industrie-Verein (Swiss National Association of Trade and Industry), PO Box 690, Mainaustrasse 49, CH-8034 Zurich. Tel: (1) 382 2323. Fax: (1) 382 2332. Information can also be obtained from the regional chambers of commerce in each canton.

CONFERENCES/CONVENTIONS: The neutrality, stability and conveniently central location of Switzerland make the country a favourite meeting place for conventions and international organisations. It has an extensive and highly developed network of conference destinations with all the major cities and many of the smaller alpine and lake resorts offering hotels and convention centres which are fully equipped with a complete range of facilities including interpretation and audio-visual services. Each of Switzerland's main cities has its own Convention Bureau, whilst the Association of Swiss Convention Centres, *Swiss Congress*, oversees meetings activity throughout the country. The organisation is made up of the 19 leading congress locations in Switzerland and can help with the organisation of a meeting in any region of the country. Contact Swiss Congress and Incentives (SCI), 23 avenue de Belmont, CH-1820 Montreux. Tel: (21) 963 1759. Fax: (21) 963 1837.

CLIMATE

The Alps cause many climatic variations throughout Switzerland. In the higher Alpine regions temperatures tend to be low, while the lower land of the northern area has higher temperatures and warm summers.
Required clothing: Warm clothes and rainwear; lightweights for summer.

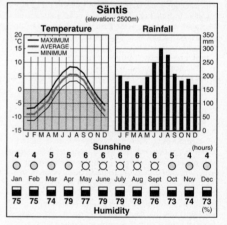

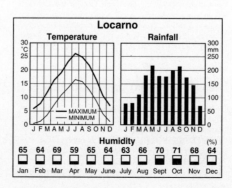

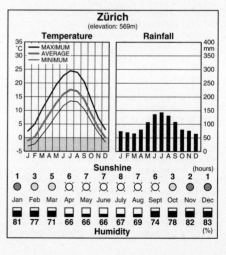

Syrian Arab Republic

section *How to Use this Book* for more information.

BBC:

MHz	21.47	15.57	11.76	9.410
Voice of America				
MHz	9.670	6.040	5.995	1.260

PASSPORTS

Regulations and requirements may be subject to change at short notice, and you are advised to contact the appropriate diplomatic or consular authority before finalising travel arrangements. Details of these may be found at the head of this country's entry. Any numbers in the chart refer to the footnotes below.

	Passport Required?	Visa Required?	Return Ticket Required?
Full British	Yes	Yes	Yes
BVP	Not valid	-	-
Australian	Yes	Yes	Yes
Canadian	Yes	Yes	Yes
USA	Yes	Yes	Yes
Other EU (As of 31/12/94)	Yes	Yes	Yes
Japanese	Yes	Yes	Yes

Restricted entry and transit: Holders of Israeli passports will be refused admission; so will any passenger holding a passport containing a visa (valid or expired) for Israel and those holding a stamp indicating an Israel-Jordan border crossing. All holders of South Korean passports and female nationals of Afghanistan, Bangladesh, The Philippines, Sri Lanka and Thailand must obtain prior approval from the Passports and Immigration Department in Syria before entering the country.

* De facto part of Turkey but claimed by Syria

□ international airport

Location: Middle East.

Ministry of Tourism
rue Victoria, Damascus, Syria
Tel: (11) 221 5916. Fax: (11) 242 636. Telex: 411672.
Embassy of the Syrian Arab Republic
8 Belgrave Square, London SW1X 8PH
Tel: (0171) 245 9012. Fax: (0171) 235 4621. Opening hours: 0930-1500 Monday to Friday; 1000-1200 Monday to Friday (Visa section).
British Embassy
BP 37, Quarter Malki, 11 rue Mohammad Kurd Ali, Immeuble Kotob, Damascus, Syria
Tel: (11) 712 561/2/3 *or* 711 179. Fax: (11) 713 592.
Telex: 411049 (a/b BRITEM SY).
Consulate in: Aleppo.
Embassy of the Syrian Arab Republic
2215 Wyoming Avenue, NW, Washington, DC 20008
Tel: (202) 232 6313. Fax: (202) 234 9548.
Honorary Consulate in: Houston.
Also deals with enquiries from Canada.
Embassy of the United States of America
BP 29, Abu Roumaneh, rue al-Mansur 2, Damascus, Syria
Tel: (11) 333 0788 *or* 332 814. Fax: (11) 224 7938.
Telex: 411919 (a/b USDAMA SY).
Canadian Embassy
BP 3394, Lot 12, Mezzeh Autostrade, Damascus, Syria
Tel: (11) 223 6851 *or* 223 6892. Fax: (11) 222 8034.
Telex: 412422 (a/b CANADA SY).

AREA: 185,180 sq km (71,498 sq miles).
POPULATION: 15,276,806 (1993 estimate).
POPULATION DENSITY: 82.5 per sq km.
CAPITAL: Damascus. **Population:** 2,000,000 (1990 estimate).
GEOGRAPHY: The country can be divided geographically into four main areas: the fertile plain in the northeast, the plateau, coastal and mountain areas in the west, the central plains, and the desert and steppe region in the central and southeastern areas. The Euphrates flows from Turkey in the north, through Syria, down to Iraq in the southeast. It is the longest river in Syria, the total length being 2330km (1450 miles), of which 600km (370 miles) pass through Syria. The

Khabur River supports the al-Khabur Basin in the northeast.
LANGUAGE: Arabic, French and English.
RELIGION: 80% Muslim, 15% Christians (mostly Orthodox and Greek Catholic) and other minority groups including Jews.
TIME: GMT + 2 (GMT + 3 from April 1 to September 30).
ELECTRICITY: 220 volts AC, 50Hz. European-style 2-pin plugs.
COMMUNICATIONS: Telephone: IDD is available. Country code: 963. International outgoing calls are direct. **Telex/telegram:** Public telex service available from main hotels and the main telegraph office in Damascus. **Post:** Airmail to Western Europe takes up to one week. Parcels sent from Syria should be packed at the post office. There are post offices in virtually all towns. Post office hours: 0800-1400; larger branches will be open all day. **Press:** Most newspapers will have political or governmental affiliations. The English-language daily newspaper is the government-controlled *Syria Times,* whilst the most important Arab publications are *al-Baath, Tishrin* and *al-Thawrah.*
BBC World Service and Voice of America frequencies: From time to time these change. See the

St Simeon Cathedral

Timatic	
Health	
GALILEO/WORLDSPAN:	**TI-DFT/DAM/HE**
SABRE:	**TIDFT/DAM/HE**
Visa	
GALILEO/WORLDSPAN:	**TI-DFT/DAM/VI**
SABRE:	**TIDFT/DAM/VI**
For more information on Timatic codes refer to Contents.	

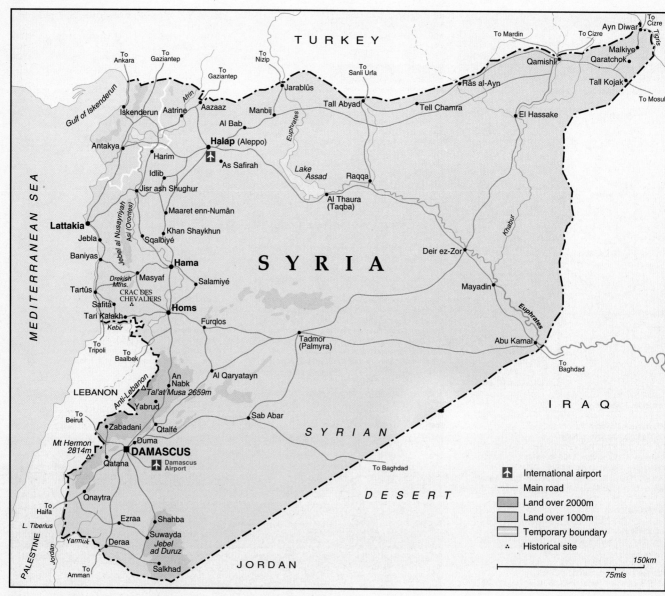

Map supplied by **Ministry of Tourism, Syrian Arab Republic, Damascus**

PASSPORTS: Valid passport required by all except nationals of Lebanon holding valid national ID cards.
VISAS: Required by all except nationals of Algeria, Bahrain, Egypt, Jordan, Kuwait, Lebanon, Libya, Mauritania, Morocco, Oman, Qatar, Saudi Arabia, Somalia, Sudan, Tunisia, United Arab Emirates and Yemen. In countries where Syria does not have an Embassy, citizens can get their visa at the borders.
Cost: *Single-entry* – £35. *Double-entry* – £70. These fees apply to nationals of the UK, Ireland, New Zealand and Australia. The cost of visas for other nationalities varies; consult the Embassy for further information.
Note: Travel regulations are liable to change at short notice and prospective visitors are advised to consult the Embassy for up-to-date information.
Types of visa: Tourist and Business (Single-, Double- and Multiple-entry); Transit. Transit visas are not required by those who continue their journey to a third country within 24 hours by the same or first connecting aircraft without leaving the transit area. Documents for the next destination, including visas (where applicable) and tickets with confirmed onward reservations, must be held.
Validity: *Tourist:* 3 months; *Transit:* 3 months; *Business:* 6 months. All visitors who stay more than 15 days should contact the Immigration and Passport Department.
Application to: Consulate (or Consular section at Embassy). For addresses, see top of entry.
Application requirements: (a) 1 completed application form. (b) Passport. (c) 1 passport-size photograph. (d) For Business visa, company letter stating nature of business. (e) For Tourist visa, letter indicating the itinerary in the Middle East and stating the number of journeys into Syria. (f) Fee. (g) A stamped, self-addressed envelope. (h) Groups of more than 10 can get visas from the airport.

Working days required: 3-4 days.
Temporary residence: Applications to the Syrian Immigration Department, Damascus.

MONEY

Currency: Syrian Pound (S£) = 100 piastres. Notes are in denominations of S£500, 100, 50, 25, 10 and 5. Coins are in denominations of S£1, and 100, 50, 25, 10 and 5 Piastres.
Currency exchange: Since 1986, stringent restrictions on illegal currency transactions have forced the black market to all but disappear. Syrian currency cannot generally be reconverted to hard currency. The country's banking system is state-owned, and there is at least one branch of the Commercial Bank of Syria in every main town. Hard currency can be exchanged for local currency in these branches.
Credit cards: American Express and Diners Club are most readily accepted; some hotels will accept Access/Mastercard. Tickets may be bought with credit cards. Check with your credit card company for merchant acceptability and for other services which may be available.
Travellers cheques: Not always exchangeable at Damascus airport.
Exchange rate indicators: The following figures are included as a guide to the movements of the Syrian Pound against Sterling and the US Dollar:

Date:	Jan '94	Jan '95
£1.00=	62.10	35.54
$1.00=	42.00	22.72

Currency restrictions: The import of local currency is unlimited; its export is prohibited. Import of foreign currency is unlimited, although amounts over US$5000 must be declared upon arrival. The export of foreign currency is limited to US$5000, or up to the amount

declared on arrival.
Banking hours: 0800-1400 Saturday to Thursday (banks tend to close early on Thursday).

DUTY FREE

The following items may be imported into Syria without incurring customs duty:
200 cigarettes or 50 cigars or 250g of tobacco; 1 litre of spirits and 1 bottle of wine; a reasonable quantity of perfume and eau de toilette.
Note: All gold jewellery must be declared on arrival.

PUBLIC HOLIDAYS

Jan 1 '95 New Year's Day. **Mar 3** Eid al-Fitr (End of Ramadan). **Mar 8** Revolution Day. **Mar 21** Mother's Day. **Apr 16** Easter (Greek Catholic). **Apr 17** Independence Day. **Apr 23** Easter (Greek Orthodox). **May 1** Labour Day. **May 6** Martyrs' Day. **May 10** Eid al-Adha (Feast of the Sacrifice). **May 31** Islamic New Year. **Aug 9** Mouloud (Prophet's Birthday). **Oct 6** October Liberation War. **Dec 25** Christmas Day. **Jan 1 '96** New Year's Day. **Feb 18** Eid al-Fitr (End of Ramadan). **Mar 8** Revolution Day. **Mar 21** Mother's Day. **Apr 7** Easter (Greek Catholic). **Apr 14** Easter (Greek Orthodox). **Apr 17** Independence Day. **Apr 28** Eid al-Adha (Feast of the Sacrifice). **May 1** Labour Day. **May 6** Martyrs' Day. **May 19** Islamic New Year. **Jul 28** Mouloud (Prophet's Birthday). **Oct 6** October Liberation War. **Dec 25** Christmas Day.
Note: Muslim festivals are timed according to local sightings of various phases of the Moon and the dates given above are approximations. During the lunar month of Ramadan that precedes Eid al-Fitr, Muslims fast during the day and feast at night and working hours are 0900-1400. Many restaurants are closed during the day

A VISIT TO SYRIA IS A PLEASURE TO THE HEART AND THE MIND

Syria is a fabulous country with a dazzling charm; deserts, mountains covered with snow, beautiful valleys inviting you to dream, sunny beaches overlooking the Mediterranean, huge fortresses dating back to the Middle Ages and old mosques.

Syria lies on the eastern coast of the Mediterranean Sea. Here civilization flourished 6 millenia ago, at the dawn of civilization. It is a meeting place and a crossroads where different people, cultures and empires converge. A country which is progressively modern while at the same time conveying its heritage in every way. It is a country of civilization but bound to its original Arab traditions of generosity and hospitality.

FOR MORE INFORMATION CONTACT: Syrian Arab Republic, Ministry of Tourism. Tel: 963 1124 2636. Fax: 963 1124 2636.

and there may be restrictions on smoking and drinking. For more information, see the section *World of Islam* at the back of the book.

HEALTH

Regulations and requirements may be subject to change at short notice, and you are advised to contact your doctor well in advance of your intended date of departure. Any numbers in the chart refer to the footnotes below.

	Special Precautions?	Certificate Required?
Yellow Fever	No	1
Cholera	No	2
Typhoid & Polio	No	-
Malaria	3	-
Food & Drink	4	-

[1]: A yellow fever vaccination certificate is required from travellers coming from infected areas.
[2]: Following WHO guidelines issued in 1973, a cholera vaccination certificate is not a condition of entry to Syria. Up-to-date advice should be sought before deciding whether precautions should include vaccination, as medical opinion is divided over its effectiveness. See the *Health* section at the back of the book.
[3]: Malaria risk exists (in the benign *vivax* form only) between May and October in some tiny pockets of the northern border areas.
[4]: Mains water is normally chlorinated, and whilst relatively safe may cause mild abdominal upsets. Bottled water is available and is advised for the first few weeks of the stay. Drinking water outside main cities and towns is likely to be contaminated and sterilisation is considered essential. Milk is unpasteurised and should be boiled. Powdered or tinned milk is available and is advised but make sure that it is reconstituted with pure water. Avoid dairy products which are likely to have been made from unboiled milk. Only eat well-cooked meat and fish, preferably served hot. Vegetables should be cooked and fruit peeled.
Health care: Health insurance is recommended. There is no Reciprocal Health Agreement with the UK. There are about 200 hospitals (12,000 beds) and 16,000 doctors. Medical care is provided free of charge to those who cannot afford to pay.
For more information, see the *Health* section at back of book.

TRAVEL - International

AIR: Syria's national airline is *Syrian Arab Airlines (RB)*.
Approximate flight times: From London to *Damascus* is 7 hours 30 minutes and to *Aleppo* is 4 hours 20 minutes.
International airports: *Damascus (DAM)*, 30km (18 miles) southeast of the city (travel time – 30 minutes). Facilities include banking, restaurants/snack bars, duty-free shop and tourist information. A bus service runs every 20 minutes. Return is from the city centre. Taxis are available, but it is advisable to negotiate fares beforehand if there is no taxi meter in the cab.
Aleppo (ALP) (Nejrab), 10km (6.5 miles) from the city (travel time – 20 minutes). Facilities include banking, restaurants/snack bars and tourist information. Bus and taxi services go to the city.
Lattakia Airport is situated 25km (16 miles) from the city. Although there are no scheduled flights serving this airport, some chartered flights run here.
Departure tax: S£200. Transit passengers are exempt.
SEA: The principal ports are Lattakia, Tartus and Banyas. The nearest car ferry sails to Badrum in western Turkey. There are no passenger lines.
RAIL: Links go via Istanbul and Ankara (Turkey). Change at Ankara for the *Taurus Express* to Aleppo. The connection from Damascus to Amman (Jordan) has been suspended since 1983.
ROAD: The road network comprises 30,208km (18,880 miles), of which about 22,500km (14,063 miles) are tarred, including 783km (489 miles) of rapid highways connecting Syria with other contries and the rest of the world. The principal international routes are from Istanbul, the E5 road to Ankara, Adana and Iskeuderun in Turkey. Enter at Bab-al-Hawa for Aleppo, or at Kassab for Lattakia. From the south, the best routes are from Aqaba on the Red Sea in Jordan. **Bus:** Services are available across the desert on routes from Baghdad via Damascus, and Amman to Damascus.

TRAVEL - Internal

AIR: *Syrian Arab Airlines (RB)* fly to Aleppo, Palmyra, Deir ez Zor, Qamishly and Lattakia. Fares in general are exceedingly cheap.

Above left: Omayyad Mosque, Damascus. Above right: Princess from Ugarit. Right: St Marie's Convent, Seydnaya

RAIL: The railway extends 3735km (2321 miles), of which 1785km (1054 miles) are of standard gauge, the rest narrow gauge. Services are provided to the north of the country from Damascus, but these are irregular and there are no sleeping or restaurant cars except in the through train to Turkey. Some air-conditioned accommodation is available. There is also a connection from Haleb to the Lebanese border.
ROAD: The road network comprises 30,208km (18,880 miles), of which about 22,500km (14,063 miles) are tarred. Second-class roads are unreliable during the wet season. The principal route is Aleppo to Damascus and Dar'a (north–south axis). Traffic drives on the right. **Bus:** Services run from Damascus and Aleppo to most towns and are cheap and efficient. There are orange-and-white air-conditioned *Karnak* (government-operated) buses. Reservations should be made well in advance. Karnak bus routes serve their own terminals, which are usually in or near the city centres. There are also privately-run bus and microbus services which started recently all over Syria. **Taxi:** Shared taxis are available to all parts of the country. Service taxis (old limousines) run on major routes and cost 50-70% more than Karnak buses.
Regulations: Speed limits: 20kmph (12mph) in the city; 80kmph (50mph) on highways. **Documentation:** International Driving Permit required. Green Cards are

bookings. Tariffs are the same throughout the year. All rates are subject to a 15% service charge. **Grading:** Hotels range from fairly low grade to luxurious 5-star accommodation. The best-quality hotels are found in Damascus, where there are three 5-star hotels, and several other hotels with the lowest grade being 3-star. Aleppo has several hotels, ranging from 2- to 5-star. In addition there are hotels in Homs (with a range of 2- to 4-star), Hama (with one 5-star hotel), Lattakia (with a good range, from 1- to 5-star), the Lattakia suburbs in the mountains (1- to 3-star hotels) and Tartus (1- to 4-star). There is one hotel in Edleb (2-star), a 5-star hotel in Palmyra and there are 3-star hotels in Swaida and 1- to 3-star hotels in Al Hasakah, 1- to 2-star hotels in Qamishly, 2-star hotels and one 5-star hotel in Deir ez Zor and Dar'a, one 5-star hotel in Bosra and 1- to 4-star hotels in Raqqa.

GUEST-HOUSES: Available in Damascus, Zabadani, Aleppo, Idlib, Dar'a and Bosra. *Cités Universitaires* offer summer accommodation.

CAMPING/CARAVANNING: There are two official campsites near Damascus, one in Aleppo, one in Lattakia and one in Tartus. Otherwise, camping is permitted near resorts.

RESORTS & EXCURSIONS

For the purposes of covering the main areas of interest to the visitor, Syria is divided laterally into four regions: South, Central and North and East.

The South

Damascus: The capital of Syria is the world's oldest inhabited city. A central feature of this cluttered and clamorous city is the *Ummayyad Mosque,* entered by passing through the *Al-Hamidiyah Bazaar.* The history of the mosque in many ways traces the history of Damascus; built on the site of a temple to the ancient Aramean god Haddad, the original temple was adapted and enlarged by the Romans and used as a temple to Jupiter. It was later knocked down by the Byzantines, who replaced the pagan temple with the Cathedral of John the Baptist, and it was subsequently converted into a mosque to accommodate the Islamic teachings brought by the Arabs in AD636. The mosque houses the *Tomb of St John the Baptist.* The *Tikiyeh* mosque, built in the mid-16th century, stands out by its two elegant minarets and great dome. The 18th-century *Al-Azem* palace is now a national museum, where there are, amongst other examples of Islamic art, beautifully illuminated copies of the Quran. Situated in old Damascus, a little way off the famous *Via Recta,* or 'Straight Street', is the *House of Hanania,* where St Paul hid, using the underground chapel for worship. The church in the Damascus Wall from where St Paul escaped in a basket is also still preserved. Also worth seeing is the *Long Souk.* Other attractions include the *Sayyida Zainab Shrine* (the granddaughter of the Prophet Muhammed), the *Tomb of Saladin* at the backyard of the Ummayyad Mosque, and the outskirts of Damascus, especially **Dummar,** with seasonal entertainment and restaurants. **Ghota,** the fruit orchards surrounding Damascus, is at its best during the blooming of apricot, plums, cherries and other trees in early spring.

Bosra: A Roman city with a well-preserved amphitheatre in which the musical festival is held every two years.

Central Region

Palmyra: This town is set in a desert oasis. The city was ruled by the legendary Queen Zenobia, who stood against the two great empires of the Romans and the Persians. Zenobia was taken captive to Rome when the Emperor Aurelian conquered and destroyed the city in 272. The ruins of the *Valley of Tombs,* the *Hypogeum of the Three Brothers,* the *Temple of Baal* and the *Monumental Arch* are some of the fine remains found over a wide radius of the city, prized as some of the most famous monuments to the Classical period in the Middle East.

Homs: The third-largest city in Syria, Homs is known for its industry, and is the site of Syria's first oil refinery. Of historical interest is the mausoleum of *Khalid Ibn al-Walid.*

Crac des Chevaliers: 65km (40 miles) outside Homs, Crac des Chevaliers is the most famous crusader castle in the world. A stronghold of the Hospitallers during the days of the Latin Kingdom of Jerusalem (1100-1290), it maintained a garrison of a couple of thousand soldiers in peacetime. The castle, rising from an altitude of 670m (2200ft), was protected by watch-towers and supplied with food from the surrounding fertile countryside. The crusader castles of *Salaheddin,* near Lattakia and *Markab,* near Banyas also merit a visit.

Hama: 45km (28 miles) from Homs. Situated on the

not yet accepted in Syria. Insurance is required by law and a customs certificate is needed. These are available from touring and automobile clubs.

URBAN: Publicly-owned bus services operate in all major towns and cities. Most buses outside the capital, however, have no signs in a European script to indicate destination or stops, which can make travelling rather difficult. Taxis are widely available. Fares should be agreed in advance and according to the meter in the cities.

JOURNEY TIMES: The following chart gives approximate journey times (in hours and minutes) from Damascus to other major cities/towns in the Syrian Arab Republic.

	Air	Road
Aleppo	1.00	5.30
Lattakia	1.00	5.00
Deir ez Zor	1.00	8.00
Qamishly	1.00	8.00
Palmyra	1.25	3.00
Dar'a	-	5.00
Al Hasakah	-	8.00
Homs	-	1.30
Hama	-	2.00
Tartus	-	3.00

ACCOMMODATION

HOTELS: Accommodation can be difficult to obtain in the high season and care should be taken to confirm

Azem Palace, Damascus

River Orontes, Hama dates back to beyond 5000BC. The *Norias,* gigantic wooden waterwheels, are a unique feature, still used to provide water for the city and to irrigate the many public gardens. The orchards, the *Great Mosque* and the *Al Azem Palace's Museum* are also of interest.

The North

Aleppo: Older possibly even than Damascus, Aleppo's massive *Citadel* stands on the site of a Hittite acropolis. This is one of the most magnificent examples of Islamic Arab military architecture in Syria. There is an impressive number of mosques in the city. For the tourist, the *souk,* made up of 16km (10 miles) of meandering low corridors lined with shops and bustling with activity, is probably the greatest attraction. The well preserved *hammams,* or public baths, are of interest, as are the ancient *khans* (rest houses). Some fine artefacts and historic reminders of Syria's rich cultural past are housed in the archaeological museum. Aleppo is also the commercial and industrial centre of Syria.
Lattakia: Syria's principal port and the metropolitan city of the country. Set on the Mediterranean coast, Lattakia is a major holiday resort. The city stands at the foot of the forested chain of mountains overlooking the coastal strip on one side and the edge of the *Fertile Plains* (the 'Cradle of Civilisation') on the other. There are a number of antiquities, including the ruined *Temple of Bacchus* and a triumphal arch.
Resorts/excursions: *Tartus,* beaches and mountains, Lattakia mountain resorts of *Kassab* and *Slounfeh.* 10km (6 miles) inland, near Tartus, are the *Drekish Mountains,* famous for the purity of their water.

The East

The sites and cities included in this regional account are described in order of appearance as the Euphrates river flows southwestward.
Ja'bar Citadel is one of the Seleucid fortresses. Situated to the west of Raqqa, it stands on a spit of land and is reflected in the blue waters of the Euphrates.
Situated on the left bank of the river, the ancient city of **Raqqa** was built by Alexander the Great in the 4th century BC. Since the construction of the Euphrates Dam, it has played an important economic role in the life of modern Syria.
Halabiyé and **Zalabiya** are situated 40km (25 miles) from Deir ez Zor. Their ruins bear witness to their important military role during the reign of Queen Zenobia.
Deir ez Zor, considered to be the 'pearl of the Euphrates', is located on the right bank of the river. The garden and orchards along the banks of the Euphrates harmonise beautifully with the golden desert hues and the silver thread of the river.

Rahba Citadel, near **Mayadin,** was built to ensure the protection of the Euphrates route and to withstand Tatar and Mongol invasions.
The ancient city of **Doura Europos** (Salhieh) played an important economic and military role during the time of the ancient Greeks, Romans, Persians and the Palmyrans.
Mari was built at a strategic point on the trade routes from Syria to Mesopotamia. The town's oldest ruins date back 5000 years. Mari's most impressive sight is the extraordinary *Royal Palace.* Built by Zimrilim, ruler of this important city-state 2000 years ago, this enormous palace boasts 300 rooms and halls. It was rediscovered in the course of excavations during the 1930s and is now protected by a modern roof.

SOCIAL PROFILE

FOOD & DRINK: There are numerous restaurants in Damascus and Aleppo serving a variety of Oriental and European dishes. National dishes are *kubbeh* (minced semolina and meat formed in balls and stuffed with minced meat, onion and nuts), *yabrak* (vine leaves stuffed with rice and minced meat), *ouzi* (pastry stuffed with rice and minced meat) and a variety of vegetables cooked with meat and tomato sauce, usually presented on separate plates and eaten by mixing it with cooked rice. Among these vegetables are *okra*, French beans and *malukhiyya*. Table service is the norm and a meal is paid for afterwards. **Drink:** There are bars serving a wide range of alcoholic drinks. Alcohol is permitted but restrictions are imposed during Ramadan when it is illegal to drink in public from dawn to dusk, even for non-Muslims.
SHOPPING: *Souks* (markets) are the best places, notably those in Aleppo. Local handicrafts in Syria are numerous and precious, including mother-of-pearl items (such as backgammon boards), olive-wood carvings, weaving and embroidery, leather goods and gold and silver jewellery. **Shopping hours:** 0930-1400 and 1630-2100 Saturday to Thursday (summer); 0930-1400 and 1600-2000 Saturday to Thursday (winter).
SPORT: The Mediterranean resorts offer **canoeing**, **scuba diving** and other **watersports**. Inland, there are numerous hotel **swimming** pools and public baths, particularly in Aleppo and Damascus.
SPECIAL EVENTS: The following is a selection of the major festivals and other special events celebrated annually in Syria.
Apr *Flower Show*, Lattakia. **Apr 28-May 1** *Desert Festival*, Palmyra. **May** *International Flower Exhibition*, Damascus. **Jul** *Vine Festival*, Sweida; *Cotton Festival*, Aleppo. **Aug-Sep** *International Fair*, Damascus. **Oct** *Festival of Folklore and Music*, Bosra. **Nov** *Film and Theatre Festival*, Damascus.
SOCIAL CONVENTIONS: The Syrians take as much

pride in their modern amenities as in their unique heritage and in the tradition of exquisite craftsmanship, and both should be appreciated. Visitors will enjoy the hospitality that is a deep-rooted Arab tradition and sharing the pleasures of an attractive Oriental way of life. It is customary to shake hands on meeting and on departure. A visitor will be treated with great courtesy and will frequently be offered refreshment, usually coffee. As a guest in someone's home or, more usually, in a restaurant, visitors should respect Arab customs and traditions. A souvenir from the visitor's home or company is well received. Conservative casual wear is suitable. Beachwear or shorts should not be worn away from the beach or poolside. Smoking follows Western habits and in most cases it is obvious where not to smoke. Smoking is prohibited in public from dawn to dusk during Ramadan. **Photography:** No attempt should be made to photograph anything remotely connected with the armed forces or in the vicinity of defence installations, which even includes radio transmission aerials. It is wise to take a good look at what will be appearing in the background of holiday snaps before pointing the camera. **Tipping:** Not necessary, but 10% is acceptable for most services.

BUSINESS PROFILE

BUSINESS PROTOCOL: Formal suits are necessary for business. Business people generally speak English and French. Appointments are necessary and visiting cards are widely used. Arabs often discuss business with more than one person at a time. A list of notarised translators is available from the British Embassy. **Office hours:** 0800-1430 Saturday to Thursday. All government offices, banks and Muslim firms close Friday and remain open Sunday; Christian firms are generally open Friday and closed Sunday. During the month of Ramadan, Government offices start work one hour later than usual.
COMMERCIAL INFORMATION: The following organisations can offer advice: Damascus Chamber of Commerce, BP 1040, rue Mou'awiah, Damascus. Tel: (11) 221 1339. Telex: 411326; or Federation of Syrian Chambers of Commerce, BP 5909, rue Mousa Ben Nousair, Damascus. Tel: (11) 333 7344. Fax: (11) 335 920. Telex: 411194.

CLIMATE

Syria's climate is characterised by hot, dry summers and fairly cold winters. Nights are often cool.
Required clothing: Lightweights are essential in summer with protective headwear. Heavy winter clothing is advisable from November to March.

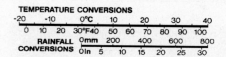

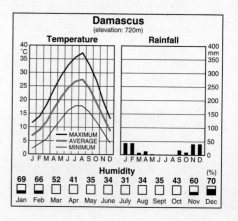

Tahiti and Her Islands

For location please see 'Pacific' section at the front of the book

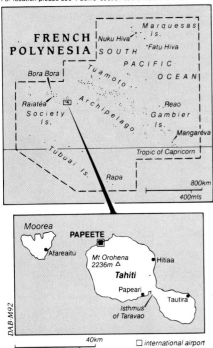

FRENCH POLYNESIA

SOUTH PACIFIC OCEAN

Marquesas Is.
Nuku Hiva
Fatu Hiva
Bora Bora
Tuamoto Archipelago
Raiatea
Society Is.
Reao
Gambier Is.
Mangaréva
Tubuai Is.
Tropic of Capricorn
Rapa

800km
400mls

Moorea
PAPEETE
Afareaitu
Mt Orohena 2236m △
Hitiaa
Tahiti
Papeari
Tautira
Isthmus of Taravao

40km
20mls
□ international airport

DAB·M92

Location: South Pacific.

Diplomatic representation: Tahiti and her Islands are officially known as 'French Polynesia' and constitute a French Overseas Territory; addresses of French Embassies, Consulates and Tourist Offices may be found in the *France* section above.

GIE Tahiti Tourisme
BP 65, Fare Manihini, boulevard Pomare, Papeete, Tahiti
Tel: 505 700 *or* 505 703. Fax: 436 619.
Tahiti Tourist Promotion Board
c/o Maison de la France, 178 Piccadilly, London W1V 0AL
Tel: (0891) 244 123 (Information Line; calls are charged at the higher rate of 39/49p per minute). Fax: (0171) 493 6594. Telex: 21902. Opening hours: 0900-1700 Monday to Friday.
Tahiti Tourism (Representation for Europe)
Haingasse 22, D-61348 Bad Homburg, Federal Republic of Germany
Tel: (6172) 21021. Fax: (6172) 25570.
Also deals with enquiries from English-speaking countries.
Office du Tourisme de Tahiti et ses Iles
28 boulevard Saint Germain, 75005 Paris, France
Tel: (1) 46 34 50 59. Fax: (1) 43 25 41 65.
Deals with enquiries from French-speaking countries.

British Consulate
BP 1064, Avis Rent-A-Car, rue Charles Vienot, Papeete, Tahiti
Tel: 428 457 *or* 424 355. Fax: 410 847. Telex: 537 (a/b FP PTE).
Tahiti Tourist Promotion Board
Suite 180, 300 N Continental Boulevard, El Segundo, CA 90245
Tel: (310) 414 8484. Fax: (310) 414 8490.

AREA: 4167 sq km (1609 sq miles).
POPULATION: 199,031 (1991 estimate).
POPULATION DENSITY: 47.8 per sq km.
CAPITAL: Papeete (Tahiti Island). **Population:** 23,555 (1988).
GEOGRAPHY: French Polynesia comprises 130 islands divided into five archipelagos. The Windward and Leeward Islands, collectively called the Society Archipelago, are mountainous with coastal plains. Tahiti, the largest of the Windward group, is dominated by Mount Orohena at 2236m (7337ft) and Mount Aorai at 2068m (6786ft). Moorea lies next to Tahiti, a picturesque volcanic island with white sand beaches. The Leeward Islands to the west are generally lower in altitude. The largest islands are Raiatea and Bora Bora. Tuamotu Archipelago comprises 80 coral atolls, located 298km (185 miles) east of Tahiti. The Marquesas Islands lie 1497km (930 miles) northeast of Tahiti and are made up of two clusters of volcanic islands divided into a southern and northern group. The grass-covered Austral Islands south of Tahiti are scattered in a chain from east to west over a distance of 499km (310 miles).
LANGUAGE: The official languages are Tahitian and French. Other Polynesian languages are spoken by the indigenous population. English is widely understood, mainly by islanders accustomed to dealing with foreign visitors.
RELIGION: Protestant 55%; Catholic 24%.
TIME: GMT - 9 Gambier Islands; GMT - 9.5 Marquesas Islands; GMT - 10 Society Archipelago, Tubuai Islands, Tuamotu Archipelago (except Gambier Islands), Tahiti.
ELECTRICITY: 110/220 volts AC, 60Hz.

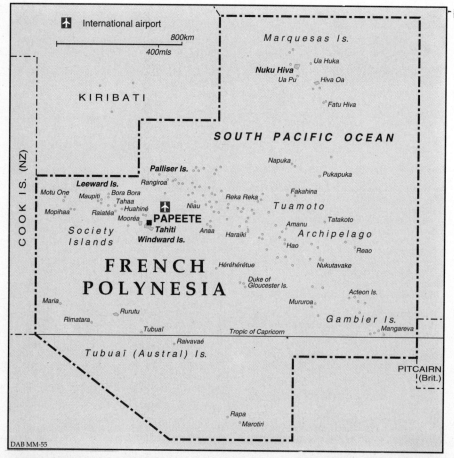

COMMUNICATIONS: Telephone: IDD is available. Country code: 689. Outgoing international code: 00. Operator assistance may be required for international calls. **Fax:** Post offices and some hotels have facilities. **Telex/telegram:** Facilities are limited to Papeete and Uturoa (Raiatea). Telex and telegrams can be sent from the post office on boulevard Pomare, Papeete. **Post:** Airmail to Western Europe takes up to two weeks. Post office hours: 0700-1800 Monday to Friday (restricted service in the afternoon); 0800-1000 at weekends. **Press:** There is an English-language weekly, the *Tahiti Beach Press*.
BBC World Service and Voice of America frequencies: From time to time these change. See the section *How to Use this Book* for more information.
BBC:

MHz	17.83	15.34	11.95	9.640

Voice of America:

MHz	18.82	15.18	9.525	1.735

PASSPORT/VISA

The regulations for Tourist and Business visas are the same as for France (see the *Passport/Visa* section for France above). Visitors should specify that they wish to visit Tahiti when they make their application.

MONEY

Currency: French Pacific Franc (CFP Fr) = 100 centimes. Notes are in denominations of CFP Fr10,000, 5000, 1000 and 500. Coins are in denominations of CFP Fr100, 50, 20, 10, 5, 2 and 1. Tahiti and Her Islands are part of the French Monetary Area, CFP Fr18.18 = FFr = 1.
Currency exchange: Exchange facilities are available at the airport, major banks and at authorised hotels and shops in Papeete.
Credit cards: American Express is the most widely accepted, while Visa, Diners Club and Access/Mastercard have more limited use. Check with your credit card company for details of merchant acceptability and other services which may be available.
Travellers cheques: The recommended means of importing foreign currency.
Exchange rate indicators: The following figures are included as a guide to the movements of the French Pacific Franc against Sterling and the US Dollar:

Date:	Oct '92	Sep '93	Jan '94	Jan '95
£1.00=	150.00	156.25	158.00	152.40
$1.00=	94.52	102.32	106.79	97.41

Currency restrictions: As for France.
Banking hours: 0800-1530 Monday to Friday.

DUTY FREE

The following items may be imported into Tahiti without incurring customs duty:
200 cigarettes or 100 cigarillos or 50 cigars or 250g of tobacco; 2 litres of spirits over 22% and 2 litres of still wine (for passengers over 18 years of age); 50g of perfume and 250ml of eau de toilette; goods up to a value of CFP Fr5000 (CFP Fr2500 for passengers up to 15 years of age).
Note: (a) Plants, fruit, cats, dogs, dangerous goods and drugs may not be imported. (b) All baggage coming from Brazil, Samoa and Fiji is collected for compulsory fumigation on arrival in Papeete; allow two hours.

PUBLIC HOLIDAYS

Jan 2 '95 For New Year's Day. **Apr 17** Easter Monday. **May 1** Labour Day. **May 9** Liberation Day. **May 25** Ascension. **Jun 5** Whit Monday. **Jul 14** *Fall of the Bastille. **Nov 11** Armistice Day. **Dec 25** Christmas Day. **Jan 1 '96** New Year's Day.
Note [*]: Celebrations continue for up to ten days.

Health		
GALILEO/WORLDSPAN: **TI-DFT/PPT/HE**		
SABRE: **TIDFT/PPT/HE**		
Visa		
GALILEO/WORLDSPAN: **TI-DFT/PPT/VI**		
SABRE: **TIDFT/PPT/VI**		

For more information on Timatic codes refer to Contents.

THE AWAKENING OF THE SENSES

Paradise is far, but not out of reach. Call +49 6172 2 1021

Tahiti
TOURISME

HEALTH

	Special Precautions?	Certificate Required?
Regulations and requirements may be subject to change at short notice, and you are advised to contact your doctor well in advance of your intended date of departure. Any numbers in the chart refer to the footnotes below.		
Yellow Fever	No	1
Cholera	No	No
Typhoid & Polio	Yes	-
Malaria	No	-
Food & Drink	2	-

[1]: A yellow fever vaccination certificate is required from travellers over one year of age coming from infected areas.
[2]: Mains water is normally chlorinated, and whilst relatively safe may cause mild abdominal upsets. Bottled water is available and is advised for the first few weeks of the stay. Drinking water outside main cities and towns may be contaminated and sterilisation is advisable. Milk is pasteurised and dairy products are safe for consumption. Local meat, poultry, seafood, fruit and vegetables are generally considered safe to eat.
Health care: Private medical insurance is recommended. There are about 30 hospitals and 140 doctors throughout the islands.

TRAVEL - International

AIR: Tahiti is served by *A.O.M. French Airlines (AOM), Corsair Nouvelles Frontières, Air Calédonie International (SB), Air France (AF), Qantas (QF), Air New Zealand (NZ), LAN Chile (LA)* and *Hawaiian Airlines (HA)* for long-haul international flights.
Approximate flight times: From Papeete to *Auckland* is 5 hours 35 minutes, to *Honolulu* is 7 hours, to *London* is 20 hours, to *Los Angeles* is 8 hours 15 minutes, to *New York* is 16 hours and to *Sydney* is 9 hours 35 minutes.
International airport: *Papeete (PPT)* (Faaa), on Tahiti, is 6.5km (4 miles) from the city (travel time – 15 minutes). Airport facilities include bank/bureau de change, post office (0500-1200 and 1800-2230), duty-free shop, bar (0200-2200), restaurant (0800-1500), tourist information (24 hours) and car hire. Taxis are available.
SEA: International port is Papeete on Tahiti, served by *Sitmar, Cunard, Holland America, Norwegian America* and *Chandris.* Cruise ships include *Swedish America* and *Royal Viking.*

TRAVEL - Internal

AIR: Domestic flights run by *Air Tahiti (VT)* connect Tahiti with neighbouring islands (Moorea, Huahine, Raiatea, Bora Bora, Maupiti) and remote archipelagos (Tuamotu East and North with Rangiroa, Tikehau, Manihi, Takapoto; Austral Islands of Rurutu and Tubuai; Marquesas Islands of Hiva oa, Nuku Hiva and Ua Pou).
SEA: There are inter-island connections on the many copra boats and schooners that make regular trips throughout the islands. Daily connections between Papeete, Moorea, Huahine, Raiatea and Bora Bora.
ROAD: Traffic drives on the right. **Bus:** Basic buses, known as *trucks,* offer an inexpensive method of travel. They leave from the central market in Papeete town centre travelling to all destinations. No schedule is operated. **Taxi:** Available in Tahiti, Moorea, Bora Bora, Huahine and Raiatea. *Roll's Tahiti* offers a chauffeur-driven Silver Shadow Rolls Royce or a Daimler Double-Six for city shopping tours, sunset cruise with champagne, airport transfers, etc. **Car hire:** Major and local agencies including *Hertz, Budget, Rent-a-car* and *Avis* rent cars in main islands.
Documentation: National driving licence will be sufficient.

ACCOMMODATION

Accommodation varies from air-conditioned, carpeted, deluxe rooms with telephones and room service, to thatched-roofed bungalows (Tahitian *pensions* where the bathroom is shared and may be outdoors with cold showers). In the outer islands, resort hotels normally have individual gardens and over-water bungalows and rooms, many built of bamboo, with shows and dance bands. There is a youth hostel in Papeete with 14 rooms; a youth hostel or student card is required. It is possible to rent a room in a family home through the Tourist Board (GIE) for a more genuine experience. For address, see top of entry.

Main picture: Island of Huahine. Above left: Basket making. Above right: Typical house.

RESORTS & EXCURSIONS

Papeete, the capital of **Tahiti,** has in recent years been transformed into a bustling city, very much at variance with the traditional 'haere maru' (take it easy) attitude of the rest of the country. It is, however, still an attractive and colourful port set in magnificent scenery. To the west of the capital is *Venus Point,* where the first Europeans set foot on the island in 1767. It is overlooked by *Mount Orohena,* the highest point on the island. The Papeete public market, *Le Marché,* is open from 0500-1800 all week, but really comes to life on Sunday mornings. Flowers, spices, fabrics and fresh produce are on offer. The surrounding area is characterised by its spectacular tropical scenery, banana groves, plantations and flowers. Places to see include the *Blowhole of Arahoho,* which throws water skywards; the *Faarumai* and *Vaipahi waterfalls;* the *Paul Gauguin Museum* and *Botanical Gardens* in **Papeari**; the 'marae' (open-air temple) of *Mahaiatea, Papara Marae Grotto* and *Arahurahu.* The *Lagoonarium de Tahiti* offers four fish parks (including a shark pen) and an amazing underwater display (0900-1800 daily); admission is free.

Moorea, 17km (11 miles) from Tahiti, and connected to it by a 45-minute ferry service or 7-minute flight, is an island with a simpler and more rustic lifestyle and yet offers plenty of entertainment for the tourist, including traditional-style nightlife. Dominated by volcanic peaks, it also has dazzling white sand beaches and clear lagoons ideal for swimming, diving and snorkelling. Excursions include a visit to the beautiful *Opunohu Valley,* an ancient dwelling place, uninhabited for a century and a half, with 500 ancient structures including temples or *marae,* some of which have been restored. *Le Belvédère* is a lookout spot from where the best view of the island may be had.

Tetiaroa, recently opened to the public and accessible only by air, is an important seabird sanctuary.

The **Leeward Islands,** Huahine, Raiatea and Tahaa, are ancient and unspoilt islands, all less than an hour from Tahiti by plane or ferry. **Huahine,** to the northwest of Tahiti, comprises Huahine-Nui (big Huahine) and Huahine-Iti (little Huahine) which are linked by a narrow isthmus. Sheltered by the surrounding coral reef, the coastal waters and lagoons are good for encountering the local aquatic life. The archaeological site near *Maeva Village* is well worth a visit. **Raiatea** is the second largest island of French Polynesia, 193km (120 miles) from Tahiti, and is the administrative centre for the Leeward Islands. In former times, the island was known as Havai'i, the royal and cultural centre of the region. The ideal conditions make the island a year-round destination for sailing and fishing enthusiasts. The 'Vanilla Island' of **Tahaa** is surrounded by the same reef as Raiatea, and offers a tranquil and relaxed lifestyle as tourism is only starting here. The breeze constantly carries the aroma of vanilla, from the island's numerous vanilla plantations.

Bora Bora is 45 minutes from Tahiti by plane. Excursions include visits to the small villages outside the main town of **Vaitape** and climbs up the two mountains of *Otemanu* and *Pahia.* There are many opportunities for watersports such as deep-sea fishing, trips by glass-bottomed boat around the lagoons, scuba diving, snorkelling and swimming on a nearby 'motu' (small sandy atoll within the reef of Bora Bora). In common with so many other Polynesian islands, Bora Bora has many ancient temples. There are good hotels on the island.

The **Tuamotu** group of islands are largely uninhabited. There are air and ferry links between Tahiti and several of the more popular islands, including **Rangiroa,** which has facilities for all forms of watersports, mostly organised through the *Kia Ora* hotel.

The **Marquesas Islands** are less well-known among tourists, and as yet they have no first-class hotels. Paul Gauguin is buried on **Hiva Oa,** and on **Ua Huka** it is possible to go horseriding between the numerous valleys. The islands are four hours from Tahiti by plane.

The **Austral Islands** have a generally cooler climate than the rest of French Polynesia. The mutineers of the 'Bounty' attempted to make a settlement on *Tubuai* in 1789. Accommodation is plentiful in the form of bungalows on or near the beach.

Note: Most excursions, sightseeing trips and other leisure activities can be organised by hotels on the islands.

SOCIAL PROFILE

FOOD & DRINK: All the classified hotels have good restaurants. French, Italian, Chinese and Vietnamese food is served, as well as the Polynesian specialities; Papeete is noted for French and Chinese cuisine. Tahitian food can be found in some hotels. Popular dishes include smoked breadfruit, mountain bananas, *fafa* (spinach) served with young suckling pig, *poisson cru* (marinated

Over-water bungalows, Hotel Bora Bora

fish), or *poe* (starchy pudding made of papaya, mango and banana). *Trucks* or lunch wagons parked on the waterfront sell steak, chips, chicken, *poisson cru brochettes* and *shish kebabs* (barbecued veal hearts).
Drink: A full range of alcoholic drinks is widely available.
NIGHTLIFE: Papeete is full of life in the evenings with restaurants and nightclubs. Most hotels feature Tahitian dance shows, bands and other traditional entertainment.
SHOPPING: Facilities are concentrated in Papeete. Special purchases include Marquesan woodcarvings, dancing costumes, shell jewellery, Tahitian perfumes, *Monoi Tiare Tahiti* (coconut oil scented with Tahiti's national flower), vanilla beans and brightly patterned *pareu* fabrics that make the traditional Tahitian *pareo*.
Shopping hours: 0730-1700 Monday to Friday; 0730-1100 Saturday. Tourist shops are open until late. Lunch breaks vary.
SPORT: Fishing: Fully equipped deep-sea fishing boats are available for charter at *Tahiti Actinautic*. The *Haura (Marlin) Club* is a member of the International Game Fishing Association. Other holiday villages and hotels can arrange trips. **Golf:** There is an 18-hole golf course at Atimanono. Hourly and day-long **horseriding** tours can be arranged through *Club Equestre de Tahiti* and *Centre de Tourisme Equestre de Tahiti,* both at the Hippodrome, Pirae, Tahiti. **Watersports:** Equipment for **skindiving** can be hired, as can charter boats to take divers to the best areas. Further details are available from the Tourist Office. To supplement the numerous sandy beaches and clear lagoons, there is an Olympic-size swimming pool at boulevard Pomare, Papeete, as well as pools at many hotels. **Tennis:** Courts are available at *Fautaua Tennis Club,* which offers temporary membership to visitors. Many of the island hotels have courts and some are available to non-residents. **Sailing:** The largest yachting organisation is the *Yacht Club de Tahiti*. Waters around the islands are ideal for small craft and several clubs and hotels hire out craft. *Club Alpin* in Arue provides information and assistance for **climbing** Mount Aorai, with a shelter at 1798m (5900ft), Mount Orohena and Mount Diademe. **Spectator sports: Football** is popular throughout the islands and can be seen almost anywhere. Fautaua stadium near Papeete is a major venue on

Sunday afternoons. Tahitian-style **horseracing** can be seen at the Hippodrome in Pirae. Races are held 12-15 times a year. Other scheduled spectator sports include **archery, cycling, boxing, canoeing, sailing** and **track events**.
SPECIAL EVENTS: The biggest festival is *Heiva I Tahiti* (akin to Bastille Day), starting around Jul 14 and continuing for about ten days. There are many feasting, dancing and sporting events for which enthusiastic crowds of local inhabitants and tourists gather. The *Annual Tree Festival* takes place in October, each year with a different theme. Of great importance is also the *Festival of Tiare*, when the white Gardenia Taitensis is woven into frangrant tiare (emblem of Tahiti). Other festivals of note include *New Year's Day* celebrations (including *Chinese New Year*), and various *Flower and Handicraft Festivals* and *Island Beauty Contests*.
SOCIAL CONVENTIONS: The basic lifestyle of the islands is represented by the simple Tahitian *fares* built of bamboo with *pandanus* roofs. Local women dress in bright *pareos* and men in the male equivalent, but casual dress is expected of the visitor. Traditional dances are still performed mostly in hotels, with Western dance styles mainly in tourist centres. Normal social courtesies are important. **Tipping:** In general not practised but tolerated, since it is contrary to the Tahitian idea of hospitality.

BUSINESS PROFILE

ECONOMY: The traditional Polynesian economy was agricultural (coconuts and vanilla) with, more recently, black pearls and shark meat joining the main products. Tourism has grown quickly to the point where it is vital for economic survival, especially that of Tahiti, which is the largest of the island group. Nonetheless, imports exceed exports by a factor of ten, so that considerable aid is needed from the French to balance the country's finances. France dominates the islands' trade; the USA is the other important trade partner.
BUSINESS: Informal in atmosphere. Literature will be in French, but English is understood in some business circles, particularly those connected with tourism. **Office**

hours: 0730-1200 and 1330-1730 Monday to Friday.
COMMERCIAL INFORMATION: The following organisation can offer advice: Chambre de Commerce et d'Industrie de Polynésie Française, BP 118, rue Docteur Cassiau, Papeete. Tel: 420 344. Fax: 435 184.

CLIMATE

Temperate, but cooled by sea breezes. Two main seasons: humid (hot and wet) from November to February, cool and dry from March to October.
Required clothing: Lightweight cottons and linens are worn, with a warm wrap for cooler evenings. Rainwear is advisable.

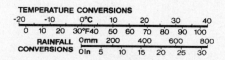

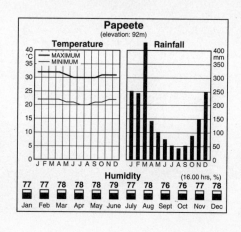

Taiwan, China

international airport

Location: Between the South and East China Seas, off the southeast coast of the People's Republic of China.

Taiwan Visitors Association
5th Floor, 9 Minchuan East Road, Section 2, Taipei, Taiwan, China
Tel: (2) 594 3261. Fax: (2) 594 3265. Telex: 20335.
Tourism Bureau, Ministry of Transportation and Communications
9th Floor, 290 Chung Hsiao East Road, Section 4, Taipei, Taiwan, China
Tel: (2) 721 8541 or 349 1635. Fax: (2) 773 5487. Telex: 26408.
Taipei Representative Office in the UK
50 Grosvenor Gardens, London SW1 0EB
Tel: (0171) 396 9152 or 396 9148 (press information). Fax: (0171) 396 9151.
Opening hours: 0930-1730 Monday to Friday. *Visa section:* Tel: (0171) 396 9143. Fax: (0171) 396 9144. Opening hours: 0930-1300 and 1400-1730 Monday to Friday.
Republic of China Co-ordination Council *and* **Information Division (CCNAA Office)**
4201 Wisconsin Avenue, NW, Washington, DC 20016
Tel: (202) 895 1850. Fax: (202) 364 0416 or 362 6144.
Also in: Atlanta, Boston, Chicago (tel: (312) 346 1038), Guam, Honolulu, Houston, Kansas City, Los Angeles, Miami, New York (see below), San Francisco (tel: (312) 346 1038) and Seattle.
Taiwan Visitors Bureau
Suite 7953, 1 World Trade Center, New York, NY 10048
Tel: (212) 466 0691/2. Fax: (212) 432 6436.
Also in: Chicago and San Francisco.
American Institute in Taiwan
Suite 7, Lane 134, Hsin Yi Road, Section 3, Taipei, Taiwan, China
Tel: (2) 709 2000. Fax: (2) 702 7675.
Taiwan Visitors Association
Suite 820, 222 Spadina Avenue, Toronto, Ontario, M5T 3A2

Timatic	
Health	
GALILEO/WORLDSPAN:	**TI-DFT/TPE/HE**
SABRE:	**TIDFT/TPE/HE**
Visa	
GALILEO/WORLDSPAN:	**TI-DFT/TPE/VI**
SABRE:	**TIDFT/TPE/VI**
For more information on Timatic codes refer to Contents.	

Tel: (416) 971 6912. Fax: (416) 490 0083. *Visa Information:* Tel: (416) 369 9030. Fax: (416) 369 1473.

AREA: 36,000 sq km (13,900 sq miles).
POPULATION: 20,556,842 (1991).
POPULATION DENSITY: 571 per sq km.
CAPITAL: Taipei. **Population:** 2,717,992 (1991 estimate).
GEOGRAPHY: Taiwan (China) is the main island of a group of 78 islands. It is dominated by the Central Mountain Range covering 75% of its land area and running its full length north to south on the eastern seaboard. Over 60 peaks exceed 3000m (9850ft), the highest being *Yu Shan* (Jade Mountain) at 3950m (12,959ft), and most are heavily forested. About 25% of the country is alluvial plain, most of it on the coastal strip. The Pescadores (Fisherman's Isles), which the Chinese call Penghu, comprise 64 islands west of Taiwan (China) with a total area of 127 sq km (49 sq miles). The offshore island fortress of Quemoy (Kinmen) and Matsu, form part of the mainland province of Fukien.
LANGUAGE: The official language is Northern Chinese (Mandarin). English and Japanese are widely spoken.
RELIGION: Buddhism; also Taoism, Christianity (Roman Catholic and Protestant) and Muslim.
TIME: GMT + 8.
ELECTRICITY: 110 volts AC, 60Hz.
COMMUNICATIONS: Telephone: Full IDD is available. Country code: 886. Outgoing international code: 002. There is an extensive internal telephone system. **Fax:** Facilities are available at the ITA Main Office, 28 Hangchow South Road, Section 1, Taipei. Good hotels also have facilities. **Telex/telegram:** Telegrams may be sent from the ITA office (address above), or one of four branch offices. Telex equipment is available at major hotels or at the ITA Main Office. **Post:** Airmail to Western Europe takes up to ten days. *Poste Restante* facilities are available in main cities. **Press:** English-language dailies include *China News, China Post* and *Free China Journal.*
BBC World Service and Voice of America frequencies: From time to time these change. See the section *How to Use this Book* for more information.
BBC:

MHz	15.36	11.95	9.740	9.570
Voice of America:				
MHz	17.74	11.76	7.275	1.575

PASSPORT/VISA

Regulations and requirements may be subject to change at short notice, and you are advised to contact the appropriate diplomatic or consular authority before finalising travel arrangements. Details of these may be found at the head of this country's entry. Any numbers in the chart refer to the footnotes below.

	Passport Required?	Visa Required?	Return Ticket Required?
Full British	Yes	2/3	1
BVP	Not valid	-	-
Australian	Yes	2/3	1
Canadian	Yes	2/3	1
USA	Yes	2/3	1
Other EU (As of 31/12/94)	Yes	2/3	1
Japanese	Yes	2/3	1

Restricted entry and transit: Passengers holding passports issued by the People's Republic of China will be refused entry.
Return tickets: [1] Open-ended tickets *may* be accepted in the case of business visitors or in other special circumstances.
PASSPORTS: Passport valid for at least 6 months required by all.
British Visitors Passport: Not acceptable.
VISAS: Required by all except:
(a) [2] nationals of Belgium, France, Germany, Luxembourg, The Netherlands and the UK provided their stay does not exceed 14 days (which period *cannot* be extended), they are holding a passport valid for at least 6 months and are of previous good record. Nationals of these countries staying for more than 14 days and other EU nationals *do* need a visa;
(b) [2] nationals of Australia, Austria, Canada, Japan, Luxembourg, The Netherlands, New Zealand and USA provided their stay does not exceed 14 days (which period *cannot* be extended), they are holding a passport valid for at least 6 months and are of previous good record. Nationals of these countries staying for more than 14 days *do* need a visa.
Note [3]: Nationals of Australia, Austria, Belgium, Canada, France, Germany, Japan, Luxembourg, The

Netherlands, New Zealand, Sweden, UK and USA are eligible to apply for a Landing visa on arrival on condition that they are holding tickets for an onward destination. The Landing visa is valid for 30 days and cannot be extended. Return ticket holders are not eligible to apply. Applicants should have previous good records and their passports should be valid for at least 6 months. Passengers need to be accompanied by a member of the airline company's staff when going to the Consular Affairs office in the airport to make their application. They must provide a passport-size photograph of themselves and pay the fee of NT$500. Landing visas can only be issued at Chiang Kai-shek Airport.
Types of visa: Single Visitor, Multiple-entry and Landing. Cost: *Single Visitor visa:* £25; *Multiple-entry visa:* £50; *Landing visa:* NT$1500. A visa is not required by travellers continuing their journey by the same or connecting aircraft on the same day of arrival, provided they have confirmed onward tickets, the necessary travel documentation and do not depart from the transit lounge.
Validity: *Single Visitor:* 60 days (valid for 3 months from date of issue). *Business Multiple-entry:* valid over a period of 6 months. *Landing:* 30 days.
Application to: Taipei Representative Office in the UK (address at beginning of entry) who will issue a letter of introduction for a visa to be issued on arrival.
Application requirements: (a) Application form. (b) 2 passport-size photos. (c) Passport (valid for at least 6 months). (d) Tickets and letter from company for business visit. (e) Certificates declaring immunity against cholera and yellow fever if having arrived or passed through an infected area.
Working days required: 24 hours.
Temporary residence: Those wishing to stay more than 6 months must apply for a Resident visa. Contact the Taipei Representative Office in the UK for further information (see address above).

MONEY

Currency: New Taiwan Dollar (NT$) = 100 cents. Notes are in denominations of NT$1000, 500, 100 and 50. Coins are in denominations of NT$50, 10, 5 and 1, and 50 cents.
Credit cards: Accepted in most hotels, restaurants and shops.
Travellers cheques: Accepted in most hotels, restaurants and shops.
Exchange rate indicators: The following figures are included as a guide to the movements of the New Taiwan Dollar against Sterling and the US Dollar:

Date:	Oct '92	Sep '93	Jan '94	Jan '95
£1.00=	40.23	41.22	39.39	41.13
$1.00=	25.35	27.00	26.62	26.29

Currency restrictions: The import and export of local currency is limited to NT$40,000. Free import of foreign currency is allowed, subject to declaration. The export of foreign currency is limited to the equivalent of US$5000 for passengers leaving within six months of arrival, or up to the amount imported and declared. All exchange receipts must be retained.
Banking hours: 0900-1530 Monday to Friday; 0900-1230 Saturday.

DUTY FREE

The following items may be imported by persons over 20 years of age without incurring customs duty:
200 cigarettes or 25 cigars or 454g of tobacco; 1 litre of alcoholic beverage; other goods for personal use up to the value of NT$20,000 (NT$10,000 for passengers under 20 years of age).
Note: Prohibited items include narcotics, gambling articles, non-canned meat products and toy pistols. All baggage must be itemised and declared in writing.

PUBLIC HOLIDAYS

Jan 1-2 '95 New Year's Day and Founding Day. **Jan 31-Feb 2** Chinese New Year. **Mar 29** Youth Day. **Apr 4** Women and Children's Day. **Apr 5** Tomb-Sweeping Day and Death of President Chiang Kai-shek. **May 1** Labour Day. **Jun 2** Dragon Boat Festival. **Sep 3** Armed Forces Day. **Sep 9** Mid-Autumn Moon Festival. **Sep 28** Birthday of Confucius (Teachers' Day). **Oct 10** Double Tenth National Day. **Oct 25** Retrocession Day. **Oct 31** Birthday of Chiang Kai-shek (Veterans' Day). **Nov 12** Dr Sun Yat Sen's Birthday. **Dec 25** Constitution Day. **Jan 1-2 '96** New Year's Day and Founding Day. **Feb 19-21** Chinese New Year. **Mar 29** Youth Day. **Apr 4** Women and Children's Day. **Apr 5** Tomb-Sweeping Day and Death of President Chiang Kai-shek.

HEALTH

Regulations and requirements may be subject to change at short notice, and you are advised to contact your doctor well in advance of your intended date of departure. Any numbers in the chart refer to the footnotes below.

	Special Precautions?	Certificate Required?
Yellow Fever	No	1
Cholera	Yes	2
Typhoid & Polio	Yes	-
Malaria	No	-
Food & Drink	3	-

[1]: A yellow fever vaccination certificate is required of travellers arriving from infected areas.
[2]: A cholera vaccination certificate is a condition of entry if arriving or having passed through an infected area. Cholera is a risk in this country and precautions are essential. Up-to-date advice should be sought before deciding whether these precautions should include vaccination, as medical opinion is divided over its effectiveness. See the *Health* section at the back of the book.
[3]: All water should be regarded as being potentially contaminated. Water used for drinking, brushing teeth or making ice should have first been boiled or otherwise sterilised. Milk is unpasteurised and should be boiled. Powdered or tinned milk is available and is advised, but make sure that it is reconstituted with pure water. Avoid dairy products which are likely to have been made from unboiled milk. Only eat well-cooked meat and fish, preferably served hot. Pork, salad and mayonnaise may carry increased risk. Vegetables should be cooked and fruit peeled.
Rabies is present. For those at high risk, vaccination before arrival should be considered. If you are bitten abroad seek medical advice without delay. For more information consult the *Health* section at the back of the book.
Health care: Emergency health care is available at the Mackey Memorial Hospital in Taipei. Imported medicines are expensive, but locally produced and manufactured medicines are plentiful. Health insurance is recommended.

TRAVEL - International

AIR: The national airline is *China Airlines (CI)*. As of March 1993, *EVA Air*, privately-owned, offers a London–Vienna–Bangkok–Taipei route.
Approximate flight time: From London to Taipei is 20 hours, including connection in Amsterdam and subsequent stopovers.
International airports: *Taipei (TPE)* (Chiang Kai-shek) is 40km (25 miles) southwest of the city (travel time – 40 minutes). Airport facilities include an outgoing duty-free shop (0800-1900), post office, car hire (0900-1900), bank/bureau de change (0900-1900), bar/restaurant (0900-1900) and a tourism bureau. The coach to the city returns from the railway station (Chung Hsiao East Road). Bus no. 1 goes every 15 minutes from 0640-2300. Return is from *Sung Shan* (domestic) airport bus terminal at Tun-Hwa North Road. Taxi service is available to the city. A bus service goes every 15 minutes from 0630-2230 (travel time – 45 minutes) to *Sung Shan,* which is located in the city itself.
Kaohsiung International (KHH) is 9km (4 miles) from the town centre. Airport facilities include an outgoing duty-free shop (0800-1900), car hire (0900-1900), bank/bureau de change (0900-1900) and bar/restaurant (0900-1900). A free hotel bus service is available (travel time – 30 minutes). There is a taxi service to the town.
Departure tax: NT$300 is levied on international departures. Transit passengers and children under two years are exempt.
SEA: There are sea links with Macau, Hong Kong and Japan.

TRAVEL - Internal

AIR: *China Airlines (CI)* and *Far Eastern Air Transport* run services to major cities from *Sung Shan* airport, Taipei. See above for information on shuttle bus to *Chiang Kai-shek* international airport.
SEA: There are reasonable connections from local ports. For details contact port authorities.
RAIL: Services are provided by the *Taiwan Railway Administration* along west and east coast routes, with the main tourist routes being Taipei–Taichung–Chiayi–Tainan–Kaohsiung (a top-class service), Taipei–Taichung–Sun Moon Lake (with the last leg of the journey by bus), Chiayi–Alishan (with spectacular mountain scenery) and Taipei–New Hualian–Taitung (scenic coastal route). Air-conditioned electric trains run at least hourly from Taipei to Kaohsiung; some trains have restaurant and sleeping cars. Children under three travel free; children aged 3-13 pay half fare. Train tickets are purchasable at many major hotels in Taipei, as well as at the main railway station.
ROAD: Traffic drives on the right. There is an adequate road system joining all major cities. Some main streets have English signs. **Bus:** There are both local and long-distance bus and coach services. **Taxi:** These are plentiful and inexpensive (metered). The destination must be written in Chinese for the driver. **Car hire:** This is available in major towns. **Documentation:** An International Driving Permit is required.
URBAN: A number of private bus companies provide extensive services in Taipei. Metered taxis are available in Taipei and tipping is not expected, but is starting to come into practice.
JOURNEY TIMES: The following chart gives approximate journey times (in hours and minutes) from Taipei to other major cities/towns.

	Air	Road	Rail
Kaohsiung	0.40	5.30	6.00
Tainan	0.40	4.30	5.00
Taichung	-	2.30	3.00
Hualien	0.30	7.00	3.00
Taitung	0.50	10.00	5.30
Sun Moon L.	-	4.30	-
Alishan	-	6.00	-
Kenting	-	6.30	-
Makung	0.40	-	-

ACCOMMODATION

HOTELS: There are over 100 tourist hotels in the country offering a broad range of accommodation and services. Prices range from US$30-50 a day for smaller hotels with US$90-150 a day being average. For details, contact the Press Division of the Taipei Representative Office in the UK or the Taiwan Visitors Bureau. Many hotels belong to the National Association of Hotelkeepers of the Republic of China, 26-1 Wenchang Street, Hsinying City, Tainan Hsien. Tel: (6) 632 4090.
Grading: Hotels are rated on a scale of **1** to **5 'Plum Blossoms'** using a system equivalent to the more familiar 5-star system, with three Plum Blossoms being about average:
4 to 5 Plum Blossoms: 50 hotels (half of which are in Taipei) are in these categories. The hotels are luxury class with a range of services and facilities, eg tennis courts, swimming pools and beauty salons.
2 and 3 Plum Blossoms: The 80 hotels in these categories are clean, comfortable and functional.
CAMPING/CARAVANNING: Campsites are available.
YOUTH HOSTELS: Dormitory and non-dormitory rooms are available in major cities and in scenic areas.

RESORTS & EXCURSIONS

For the purposes of this section, the country has been divided into four regions: Taipei; North; Central; and South.

Taipei

The principal city in the north, Taipei was designated a 'special municipality' in July 1967, thus acquiring the same status as a province and its mayor the same rank as a provincial governor. The area of the city has expanded to four times its original size, making it the fastest-growing city in Asia.
Sightseeing: The city centre contains the *National Museum of History*, the *Taipei Fine Arts Museum,* the *Taiwan Provincial Museum* and *Chung Cheng (Chiang Kai-shek) Memorial Hall*, which is a fine example of classical Chinese architecture. The magnificent main entrance is more than 30m (100ft) high. One of Taipei's new attractions is a tour of the *Fu Hsing Dramatic Arts Academy* where traditional Chinese opera and acrobatic performers are trained and stage shows. Also new to Taipei is the *City of Cathay,* a replica of an ancient Chinese town with cultural performances, handicraft demonstrations and regional food, which is located within the *Chinese Culture and Movie Centre.*
The *Lungshan (Dragon Mountain) Temple* is dedicated to Kuan Yin, the Goddess of Mercy, and was built in 1740. The temple, one of more than 5000 temples and shrines in the country, is regarded as the island's finest example of temple architecture.
Among other outstanding buildings of classical Chinese architecture in Taipei are the *Martyrs' Shrine*, the *Sun Yat-sen Memorial Hall* and the *Chungsham Building* in the Yangmingshan district of the metropolis, 40 minutes drive from the centre of Taipei, where the *National Palace Museum* can also be found; it houses the world's largest and most priceless collection of Chinese art treasures. *Yangmingshan Park* is famous for its cherry and azalea trees and attracts thousands of visitors at blossom time.

North

Keelung has an imposing hilltop statue of *Kuan Yin,* the Goddess of Mercy. The northeast coastal road offers a spectacular drive, passing the foothills of the Central Mountain Range and overlooking the East China Sea and the Pacific Ocean. The traveller will pass through many small villages whose lifestyles have changed little with the advent of high technology. Other outstanding attractions of the area include **Yehliu**, noted for its fantastic rock formations (Queen's Head); *Green Bay* and *Chinshan* beaches, with full beach resort facilities; *Shihmen Dam;* and **Wulai**, a mountain resort south of Taipei. Wulai is the site of a hilltop park and of a village inhabited by aboriginals who, besides making and selling artefacts, give lively song and dance performances for tourists. The **Northeast Coast National Scenic Area**, also with unusual rock formations, is not only good for swimming, diving, surfing, water-skiing and camping, but also the best place for seashore fishing and rock climbing. *Window on China* at **Lungtan**, 53km (33 miles) southwest of Taipei, contains reproductions on a scale of 1:25 of historical and other notable Chinese sites.

Central

The centre of the island has the most varied landscape. The east–west cross-island highway passes through spectacular mountain passes, most notably the *Taroko Gorge,* a ravine with towering cliffs shot through with extensive marble deposits. **Lishan**, located 1945m (6381ft) up on *Pear Mountain,* is a popular mountain resort. Other popular sights in the mountains include the *Sun Moon Lake*, the *Chitou Forest* recreation area, *Yu Shan* (Jade Mountain), and the alpine railway to **Alishan**. Throughout the central area there are numerous temples. The region's main towns are **Taichung**, one of the largest ports on the island, and **Hualien** in the east.

South

Kenting National Park is a popular forest recreation area boasting fine beaches, coral lakes, a bird sanctuary and, more recently, facilities for watersports and golf, all set amidst tropical coastal forest. **Kaohsiung** is the main industrial centre and has the island's only other main airport, besides Taipei's Chiang Kai-shek. **Tainan**, the oldest city on the island, is known as the 'City of 100 Temples'; there are in fact 220, amongst them some of the best examples of Confucian temple architecture on the island. **Lanyu** (Orchid Island), one of the smaller islands off the east coast, is the home of the aboriginal Yami, one of the world's last surviving hunter-gatherer tribes. *Lotus Lake* is the site of the Spring and Autumn pavilions and of the Dragon and Tiger pagodas.

SOCIAL PROFILE

FOOD & DRINK: The Chinese, never at a loss for vivid description, describe their cuisine as an 'ancient art of ultimate harmony: pleasing to the eye; mouth-watering; and a delight to the palate'. Culinary styles are from all over China including Canton, Peking, Szechuan, Shanghai, Hunan, Mongolia and Taiwan. Cantonese food is more colourful and sweeter than that of other regions. Dishes include fried shrimp with cashews, onion-marinated chicken, beef with oyster sauce and sweet-and-sour pork. Pastries include steamed dumplings stuffed with meat, sweet paste or preserves, buns, deep-fried spring rolls and tarts. Pekinese cooking is mild, combining roast or barbecued meat (often cooked at the table), vegetables and flat pancake wrappers. Dishes include *Peking duck*, carp cooked three ways, steamed prawns, chicken-in-paper, diced chicken in heavy sauce, eels with pepper sauce and ham marrow sauce. Szechuan cooking is hot and spicy, based on red chilli pepper and garlic. Dishes include *Mother Ma's bean curd*, aubergine with garlic sauce, *Gungbao chicken*, fried prawns with pepper sauce, minced chicken with *Gingko* nuts. Fried breads make a pleasant change from rice.
Shanghai cooking is mostly seafood with rich salty sauces. Dishes include shark's fin in chicken, mushroom with crab meat, *ningpo* (fried eel), shark's fin soup and West Lake fish. Hunan has both spicy and steamed dishes including steamed ham and honey sauce, diced chicken with peanuts, steamed silver thread rolls and smoked duck. Mongolian comprises two basic dishes of *Huoguo*

('firepot' – meat dipped in a sauce based on sesame paste, shrimp oil, ginger juice and bean paste) and barbecue (various slices of meat and vegetables cooked on an iron grill and eaten in a sesame bun). Taiwanese cooking is mostly seafood with thick sauces. It relies on garlic in the north and soy sauce in the south. Dishes include spring rolls with peanut butter, sweet-and-sour spare ribs, bean curd in red sauce, oyster omelette and numerous excellent seafoods. More information on Chinese cuisine can be found by consulting the corresponding sections in the entries for The People's Republic of China and Hong Kong; see the *Contents* pages for details.

Restaurants/bars: Restaurants almost always have table service although some hotels have buffet/barbecue lunches. Most hotels have restaurants offering both Western and Chinese cuisine and some of the larger hotels offer several styles of Chinese cooking (the Chinese word for hotel, *fan-dien*, means 'eating place'). Most bars have counter service. **Drink:** There are no set licensing hours and alcohol is widely available.

NIGHTLIFE: Most top hotels have nightclubs with dinner, dancing and a show. Smaller bars often present 'entertainments'. Taiwanese opera is performed on the streets, in open spaces, outside temples and anywhere a stage can be erected. Ballet, opera and drama can be seen at the National Theatre and the City Hall in Taipei. Performances with puppets are offered in villages and temples during festivals. There are also cinemas which show Chinese and foreign films.

SHOPPING: One of the best ways to shop is to visit the night-markets. Purchases include Formosan sea-grass mats, hats, handbags and slippers, bamboo items, Chinese musical instruments, various dolls in costume, handpainted palace lanterns made from silk, lacquerware, ceramics, teak furniture, coral, veinstone and jade items, *ramie* fibre rugs, brassware, handmade shoes, fabrics and chopsticks (decorated, personalised sticks of wood or marble).

SPORT: Fishing: Lakes, rivers, fish farms and the sea offer mainly unrestricted fishing. Near Taipei there is good fishing at the Tamsui and Hsintien rivers, Green Lake and Shihmen Reservoir. **Golf:** There are several year-round golf courses. Sponsorship, if needed, can be arranged through travel agencies. For further information, contact the *Chinese Taipei Golf Association,* 75 Lane 187, Tunhua South Road, Taipei. **Mountaineering:** Slopes range from beginner to bare rock faces. **Skating:** There are several roller-skating rinks in major cities and two ice rinks in Taipei. **Skindiving:** The coral reefs of the south and the Pescadores Islands are considered good skindiving areas. Contact the *Chinese Diving Federation,* 123 Chui Chuan Street, Taipei. **Swimming:** Rivers, lakes and the sea are ideal for swimming. Best time for swimming on the north coast is May to September while on the south coast the water is warm all year. **Tennis:** There are tennis courts at most universities, colleges and many hotels. Every major city has bowling alleys. **Hot springs** abound throughout the country. Some of the sites are easily accessible and provide baths, hot tubs and hotel facilities.

SPECIAL EVENTS: There are numerous festivals throughout the year, all with variable dates. For an up-to-date list, contact the Taipei Representative Office in the UK or the Taiwan Visitors Bureau, but a selection is included here:
Mar '95 *Birthday of Kuan Yin* (Goddess of Mercy). **Apr** *Festival of the Birth of Matsu, Goddess of the Sea,* Matsu temples around the island with major celebration at Peikang's Chaotien Temple. **Apr** *Flying Fish Festival of the Yami people,* Lanyu. **Jun** *Dragon Boat Festival; Lukang Folk Arts Festival,* Lukang. **Jun/Jul** *Birthday of Cheng Huang.* **Aug** *Harvest Festival of the Ami people,* Hualien and Taitung counties; *Harvest Festival of the Rukai people,* Kaohsiung, Pingtung and Taitung counties. **Sep** *Mid-Autumn Moon Festival.* **Feb 19-21 '96** *Chinese Lunar New Year* (Lantern Festival). **Mar** *Festival of the Birth of Kuan Yin* (Goddess of Mercy).

SOCIAL CONVENTIONS: Handshaking is common. Casual wear is widely acceptable. Ancient festivals and customs are celebrated enthusiastically and traditional holidays are important. Entertainment is usually offered in restaurants, not at home. Visitors are not expected to entertain. Chinese culture in the form of drama, opera and art is very strong. Despite rapid industrialisation and development, the way of life is very much Chinese, steeped in tradition and old values. **Tipping:** Tipping is not an established custom, although it is on the increase. Taipei hotels and restaurants add 10% service charge and extra tipping is not expected. It is not customary to tip taxi-drivers.

BUSINESS PROFILE

ECONOMY: After phenomenal economic growth from the 1950s onwards, Taiwan (China) had by 1980

emerged among the top 20 trading nations in the world. The island's success has been on a policy of rapid industrialisation, coupled with low overheads and labour costs which have allowed Taiwanese products to compete successfully in world markets. Textiles, shipbuilding, metals, plywood, furniture and petrochemicals are the principal industries; the Government is now seeking to promote financial services, electronics and information technology to sustain economic growth. Agriculture and fisheries, despite declining in relative terms, are large enough to afford a considerable measure of self-sufficiency in food. The island leads the 'Tiger economies' of the Pacific basin, boasting the highest standard of living in East Asia outside Japan and the largest reserves of foreign currency (US$87 billion in 1991) of any country in the world. Exports in 1988 totalled US$53.5 billion. Apart from the USA, the major trading partners are Japan, Germany, Australia, Saudi Arabia and The People's Republic of China, with whom both-way trade now exceeds US$5 billion. Taiwanese investors, both private and government-sponsored, have also been active in Europe in recent years. The domestic boom is showing definite signs of deflating: growth is sluggish and investment tailing off. However, reduced trade barriers and the relaxation of foreign exchange controls have made exporting easier. The Gulf crisis and the consequent oil price hike have sharply increased the island's import bill.

BUSINESS PROTOCOL: Although many business people speak English, interpreters may be needed. Appointments should be made and punctuality is expected. Visiting cards are widely used. **Office hours:** 0830-1730 Monday to Friday; 0830-1230 Saturday.

COMMERCIAL INFORMATION: The following organisations can offer advice: General Chamber of Commerce, 6th Floor, 390 Fu Hsing South Road, Section 1, Taipei. Tel: (2) 701 2671. Fax: (2) 754 2107. Telex: 11396; *or* China External Trade Development Council, 4th-8th Floors, 333 Keelung Road, Section 1, 10548 Taipei. Tel: (2) 725 5200. Fax: (2) 757 6653. Telex: 21676.

CONFERENCES/CONVENTIONS: The Tourism Bureau's brochure *Convention Facilities in Taiwan* lists 27 venues of which the largest is Sun Yat-sen Memorial Hall, with seating for up to 2653 persons; several other venues can seat over 2000. Hotels offer a comprehensive range of facilities and there are some with seating for 1000 and over. For further information, contact Taipei International Convention Center (TICC), 1 Hsin Yi Road, Section 5, Taipei. Tel: (2) 723 2535. Fax: (2) 723 2590.

CLIMATE

A subtropical climate with moderate temperatures in the north, where there is a winter season. The southern areas enjoy sunshine every day and temperatures are slightly higher and there is no winter season. The typhoon season is from June to October.

Required clothing: Light- to medium-weights, with rainwear advised.

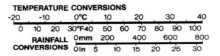

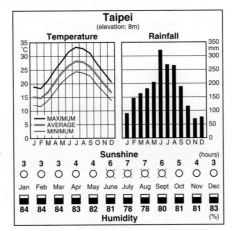

Tajikistan

□ *international airport*

Location: Central Asia.

Note: Travellers are advised against visiting Tajikistan. Although a ceasefire is in effect between warring factions and peaceful elections were held at the end of 1994, sporadic fighting continues along the Tajikistan-Afghanistan border and travel within 15 minutes of the border is tightly controlled and potentially very dangerous. In addition, unsettled conditions exist in some areas of the countryside, particularly in parts of the Gharm Valley and Gorno-Badakhshan. There is a potential for terrorist actions in the capital Dushanbe, primarily targeted against Russians. However, Khojard (formerlyLeninabad) province and the Zeravshan valley west of Highway N34 are peaceful.
Sources: US State Department – December 12, 1994 and FCO Travel Advice Unit – August 17, 1994.

Intourist Tajikistan
c/o Hotel Tajikistan, ulitsa Shotemur 22, Dushanbe 734001, Tajikistan
Tel: (3772) 274 373. Fax: (3772) 275 155.
Council of Ministers
80 Rudaki Pr, Dushanbe,Tajikistan
Tel: (3772) 228 247 *or* 232 793. Fax: (3772) 271 987 *or* 275 155.
Ministry of Foreign Affairs
Prospekt Rudaki 42, Dushanbe 734051, Tajikistan
Tel: (3772) 232 971. Fax: (3772) 232 964. Telex: 116277.
Intourist
Intourist House, 219 Marsh Wall, Isle of Dogs, London E14 9PD
Tel: (0171) 538 8600 *or* 0891 516 951 (Russian Tourist Information Service – calls charged at the higher rate of 39/49p per minute). Fax: (0171) 538 5967.
Tajikistan Mission to the United Nations
136 East 67th Street, New York, NY 10026
Tel: (212) 472 7645. Fax: (212) 628 0252.
Intourist USA Inc
Suite 603, Rockefeller Center, 610 Fifth Avenue, New York, NY 10020
Tel: (212) 757 3884/5. Fax: (212) 459 0031.
Embassy of the United States of America
Residence:
4th Floor, Hotel Independence, Prospekt Rudaki 105a, Dushanbe 734001, Tajikistan
Tel: (3772) 210 356 *or* 210 270 *or* 211 280.
Interim Chancery:
ul. Ainii 39, Dushanbe, Tajikistan
Tel: (3772) 248 233.
Intourist (Russian Travel Information Office)
Suite 630, 1801 McGill College Avenue, Montréal, Québec H3A 2N4
Tel: (514) 849 6394. Fax: (514) 849 6743.
The Canadian Embassies in Almaty and Moscow deal with enquiries relating to Tajikistan (see *Kazakhstan* and the *Russian Federation* earlier in this book).

AREA: 143,100 sq km (55,250 sq miles).
POPULATION: 5,556,000 (1993 estimate).
POPULATION DENSITY: 38.8 per sq km.
CAPITAL: Dushanbe. **Population:** 602,000 (1990 estimate).
GEOGRAPHY: Tajikistan is bordered by Kyrgyzstan and Uzbekistan to the north, Afghanistan to the south and China to the east. 93% of the republic is occupied by mountains, most notably by the sparsely populated Pamir Mountains, which include Pik Kommunizma (7495m/24,590ft), the highest point of the former Soviet Union. The mountainous terrain means that in winter it is impossible to reach the east or the north of the country by road without taking a detour through Uzbekistan and Kyrgyzstan. In the fertile plains of the southwest, cotton dominates the agriculture. In the north, the Khojand (formerly Leninabad) region, cotton and silk are the main crops.
LANGUAGE: Tajik is the official language, an ancient Persian language similar to the languages of Iran and Afghanistan. In the Pamir Mountains, there are at least five different languages, all related to an even more ancient form of Iranian. Russian is widely used (35% of the population speak Russian fluently), and discrimination against Russian speakers is prohibited by law. English is frequently spoken by those involved in tourism.
RELIGION: Predominantly Sunni Muslim with a large Ishmaeli minority in the Pamirs and a smaller and shrinking Russian Orthodox minority.
TIME: GMT + 5.
ELECTRICITY: 220 volts AC, 50Hz. Round 2-pin continental plugs are standard.
COMMUNICATIONS: Telephone: IDD to Tajikistan is available. Country code: 7 (3772 for Dushanbe). International telephone calls can be made from telephone offices which will usually be found attached to a post office (in Dushanbe in Maidoni Dusti, formerly Ploshchad Lenina). International calls can also be ordered from some hotels such as the Hotel Tajikistan and the Hotel Independence. International calls have to go through the operator. Direct-dial calls within the CIS are obtained by dialling 8 and waiting for another dial tone and then dialling the city code. Calls within the city limits are free of charge. **Fax:** Services are available from major hotels for residents only. **Telex/telegram:** Telegram and telex services (the latter with dual Cyrillic and Roman keyboards, impractical except in emergencies) are available from post offices in large towns. Telex services are available for residents in major hotels. **Post:** Mail to Western Europe and the USA can take between two weeks and two months. Stamped envelopes can be bought from post offices. Addresses should be laid out in the following order: country, postcode, city, street, house number and lastly the person's name. Postal services available include registered mail, restricted delivery, special delivery and Express mail (in Dunshanbe only). Both surface or air mail is available for parcels. Post office hours: 0800-1800 Monday to Friday. Visitors can also use the post offices located within the major Intourist hotels. **Press:** The press in Tajikistan is still censored. All the main newspapers are printed in Dushanbe and include *Colas Tajikistana*, *Narodnaya Gazeta* and *Vicherny Dushanbe* (all published in Russian), *Sardoyi Mardum, Jumhuriat* and *Nidoyi Ranjibar* (all in Tajik) and *Halk Ovozy* (Uzbek). *Marifaki Shugnan* is published in Khorog.
BBC World Service and Voice of America frequencies and wavelengths: From time to time these change. See the section *How to Use this Book* for more information.

BBC:				
MHz	**17.64**	**15.57**	**11.76**	**7.160**
Voice of America:				
MHz	**9.670**	**6.040**	**5.995**	**1.260**

PASSPORT/VISA

Regulations and requirements may be subject to change at short notice, and you are advised to contact the appropriate diplomatic or consular authority before finalising travel arrangements. Details of these may be found at the head of this country's entry. Any numbers in the chart refer to the footnotes below.

	Passport Required?	Visa Required?	Return Ticket Required?
Full British	Yes*	Yes*	No*
BVP	Not valid	-	-
Australian	Yes*	Yes*	No*
Canadian	Yes*	Yes*	No*
USA	Yes*	Yes*	No*
Other EU (As of 31/12/94)	Yes*	Yes*	No*
Japanese	Yes*	Yes*	No*

Note [*]: Visa regulations within the CIS are currently liable to change. Prospective travellers are advised to contact *Intourist Travel Ltd* who offer a comprehensive visa service for all of the republics within the CIS. Tel: (0171) 538 5902 in the UK; (212) 757 3884 in the USA.
PASSPORTS: 10-year passport valid for at least six months after date of departure required by all.
British Visitors Passport: Not acceptable.
VISAS: Required by all. At present, visas cannot be obtained on arrival at the airport, but may be obtained on arrival at the border. Visas must list towns to be visited, but it is possible to have these added on arrival. Permission from the Ministry of Foreign Affairs in Tajikistan or Intourist Tajikistan is required for all visas. This can be done by the individual directly or the applicant's tour company in a fax/telex to the Foreign Ministry and should include the applicant's name, passport details and the planned itinerary. The Tajik authorities then send a faxed authorisation to the Russian Embassy in the applicant's home country with a confirmation to the applicant. It is also possible to apply direct to the Russian Embassy, but this may take longer. Special visas must also be obtained by those wishing to visit the Gorno-Babakhshan region (the Pamir Mountains).
Types of visa: Tourist, Business, Multiple-entry and Transit.
Cost: A Business visa for up to 3 months costs £10 or US$25, with an additional £10/US$25 (£5/US$10 for Transit visas) charged if the visa is needed urgently. Tourist visas cost £10 in the UK or US$30 in the USA. A one-year Multiple-entry visa costs £100 or US$250. Prices for certain nationals may be more expensive and nationals of countries other than the USA or UK should check with the Russian Embassy for relevant visa fees.
Validity: Tourist, Business and Multiple-entry visas are individually specified for each visitor. Transit visas are valid for a maximum of 3 days.
Application to: Russian Embassy. It is also possible to get Tajik visas at either the Tajik Embassy in Moscow, or Intourist in Moscow; the latter has the right to issue Tajik visas without consultation with Dushanbe. Visas may also be available at the Tajikistan border.
Application requirements: (a) Application form. (b) Valid 10-year passport or photocopies of pages from the passport with personal information and passport validity. (c) 3 recent passport-size photos with applicant's name clearly written on the opposite side. (d) Fee by cheque or postal order. (e) For Business visa, letter of invitation from a Tajik company or organisation, itinerary and companies to be visited. (f) For Tourist visa, copy of voucher from travel company. (g) For Transit visa, confirmation of flight details. (h) Strong, stamped, self-addressed return envelope for postal applications.
Working days required: 10 days if the application is addressed directly to Tajikistan; a minimum of 14 days if applying in person to a Russian Embassy; 3 weeks if applying by post.
Temporary residence: Applications should be addressed to the Consular Affairs section of the Foreign Ministry.

MONEY

Currency: Tajikistan is one of the only two states of the former Soviet Union to remain in the Rouble Zone, the other being Belarus. Having been forced to continue using the old pre-1993 money long after the rest of the Rouble Zone abandoned it, Tajikistan finally received its allocation of 120 billion new post-1992 Roubles in January 1994. Notes are in denominations of Rub50,000, 10,000, 5000, 1000, 500, 200 and 100. There are few coins currently in circulation, although they are expected to be introduced on a larger scale soon. It is hoped that the introduction of the Russian Rouble will cut the hyperinflation that had raged with the old, pre-1993 Rouble. The initial effect was to drive prices up. The black market rate can be as much as 30% higher than the official rate, but this varies. Tajikistan is considering the introduction of a national currency, the Somon.
Currency exchange: The preferred hard currency is the US Dollar, although other hard currencies are in theory also acceptable. All bills are normally settled in cash, and tourists must pay in hard currency for accommodation in hotels, although these are normally included in the price of organised tours. Owing to a shortage of change, a supply of small notes should be carried. International banking services are not available. All money should be changed at the official bureaux de change found in hotels or banks and the receipts should be kept. However, this law is not rigidly enforced.
Credit cards: Visa, Diners Club and Eurocard are accepted in some hotels in the capital, but should not be relied upon anywhere else. Check with your credit card company for details of merchant acceptability and other services which may be available.
Travellers cheques: Not accepted.
Exchange rate indicators: The following figures are included as a guide to the movements of the Rouble against Sterling and the US Dollar:

Date:	**Oct '92**	**Sep '93**	**Jan '94**	**Jan '95**
£1.00=	***0.95**	***0.86**	***0.86**	**1.04**
$1.00=	***0.60**	***0.56**	***0.58**	**0.67**

Note [*]: Official rate. The true market rate differs immensely (£1 = Rub5613, US$1 = Rub3587 according to the *Financial Times*; Jan 1995). A single exchange rate is established for the Rouble by the Central Bank of Russia twice-weekly.
Currency restrictions: The import of local currency is prohibited for foreigners; residents of Tajikistan are allowed up to the amount they declared on departure. It is possible for foreigners to take Roubles out of the country if a receipt for their exchange can be shown, although some border guards seem unaware of this. Therefore, visitors are advised to convert all remaining local currency at the point of departure. Residents of Tajikistan are allowed to export up to Rub500,000. The import of foreign currency is unlimited, subject to declaration on arrival. The export of foreign currency for foreigners is limited to the amount declared on arrival. Residents of Tajikistan are allowed to export up to the equivalent of US$500 provided they obtain permission from an authorised bank or submit a custom declaration form TC-28 proving the amount had originally been imported.
Banking hours: 0900-1300 Monday to Friday (closed Saturday).

Timatic	
	Health
	GALILEO/WORLDSPAN: **TI-DFT/DYU/HE**
	SABRE: **TIDFT/DYU/HE**
	Visa
	GALILEO/WORLDSPAN: **TI-DFT/DYU/VI**
	SABRE: **TIDFT/DYU/VI**
	For more information on Timatic codes refer to Contents.

DUTY FREE

The following goods may be imported into Tajikistan by persons of 18 years of age or older without incurring customs duty:
400 cigarettes or 100 cigars or 500g of tobacco products; 2 litres of alcholic beverage; a reasonable quantity of perfume for personal use; other goods to the value of US$5000 for personal use only.
Note: All foreign currency and valuable items such as jewellery, cameras, computers, etc must be declared on arrival.

PUBLIC HOLIDAYS

Jan 1 '95 New Year's Day. **Mar 3** Ramazon (End of Ramadan). **Mar 8** International Women's Day. **Mar 21** Navrus. **May 9** Victory Day. **Sep 9** Independence Day. **Oct 14** Day of Formation of the Tajik Republic. **Jan 1 '96** New Year's Day. **Feb 22** Ramazon (End of Ramadan).

HEALTH

Regulations and requirements may be subject to change at short notice, and you are advised to contact your doctor well in advance of your intended date of departure. Any numbers in the chart refer to the footnotes below.

	Special Precautions?	Certificate Required?
Yellow Fever	No	No
Cholera	1	No
Typhoid & Polio	Yes	-
Malaria	Yes/2	-
Food & Drink	3	-

[1]: There was a cholera outbreak in 1993 which led to five deaths. Visitors are advised to take extra precautions.
[2]: There have reportedly been cases of malaria, predominantly in the benign *vivax* form, on Tajikistan's southern border. Those wishing to visit the area should bring suitable medication with them.
[3]: All water should be regarded as being a potential health risk. Water used for drinking, brushing teeth or making ice should have first been boiled or otherwise sterilised. Milk is pasteurised and dairy products are safe for consumption. Only eat well-cooked meat and fish, preferably served hot. Pork, salad and mayonnaise may carry increased risk. Vegetables should be cooked and fruit peeled.

Rabies is present. For those at high risk, vaccination before arrival should be considered. If you are bitten abroad, seek medical advice without delay. For more information, consult the *Health* section at the back of the book.
Health care: Medical insurance is strongly recommended. As the domestic health service is plagued by shortages of medicines and drugs, travellers are advised to take a first-aid kit containing basic medicines with them.

TRAVEL - International

AIR: The new international airline, *Tajikistan International Airlines (TIA)*, began operation in 1994 and flies regularly to London and Delhi. Negotiations are underway to add Karachi, Frankfurt/M and Bangkok to the itinerary by mid-1995 and a destinations in Iran and the USA thereafter. There are also flights to Moscow, St Petersburg and Sharja (UAE) which leave at irregular intervals. For further information, contact *Tajikistan International Airlines,* 154 Horn Lane, Acton, London W3 6PG. Tel: (0181) 993 8885. Fax: (0181) 896 3887.
Approximate flight times: From Dushanbe to *London* is 6 hours, to *Moscow* is 4 hours, to *Karachi* is 2 hours and to *Delhi* is 1 hour 30 minutes.
International airport: *Dushanbe Airport (DYU)* is south of the city. It is served by trolleybuses and taxis.
RAIL: Trains are the most reliable way of reaching Dushanbe for those not arriving by air, ie not coming from London, Moscow or the sub-continent. Dushanbe is connected to a spur of the Trans-Caspian Railway which winds down to the Afghan border in Uzbekistan before heading north towards Dushanbe. Travellers are advised to sit with their back to the engine, as throwing rocks at the windows of passing trains seems to be a popular pastime among local children. The journey from Tashkent to Dushanbe takes approximately 22 hours; from Moscow it takes approximately 4 days. Khojand in the north of the country can be reached directly from Samarkand in Uzbekistan.
ROAD: Tajikistan can be approached by road from Uzbekistan and Kyrgyzstan, subject to occasional unannounced border closures and snow. **Bus:** Services have been severely disrupted by border closures and should not be relied upon. The service between Dushanbe and Samarkand was resumed in January 1994. The border between Tajikistan and Afghanistan is officially closed.

TRAVEL - Internal

AIR: The domestic airline is *Tajik Air,* offering internal flights to Khorog in Gorno-Badakhshan (one of the most technically demanding regularly scheduled flights in the world), Khojand and Kulyab, subject to weather and the endemic fuel shortages of the region. Flights from Dushanbe to Khorog take 1 hour, to Khojand 1 hour and to Kulyab 30 minutes. It is also possible to fly to Moscow, Tashkent and Almaty when services have not been suspended due to fuel shortages (flights to Tashkent have been suspended since 1992). Internal services are subject to cancellations, long delays and overloading of passengers. Ashgabat (Turkmenistan) and Chelyabinsk (Siberia) are discussed as additional destinations.
RAIL: There are only three rail lines in Tajikistan: one leading south from Dushanbe through Kurgan-Tyube and Shaartuz to the Uzbek/Afghan border at Termez; one that leads due south from Dushanbe, through Kurgan-Tyube to Tugul on the Afghan border; and one in the northern region which runs from Samarkand, through Khojand to the Fergana Valley. The railway south from Dushanbe was briefly closed when the track was dynamited in the autumn of 1993, but it has been repaired. A spur from Kulyab to Kurgan-Tyube is currently under construction.
Note: Travellers are advised to store their valuables in the compartment under the bed/seats, to ensure the door is securely shut from the inside by tying it close with wire or strong chord and not to leave the compartment unattended.
ROAD: There is a reasonable road network in Tajikistan, though some parts may be seasonally impassable. During the winter (October to March), three of the four main roads from the capital and the southwest of the country (east to Khorog via Khalaikum, northeast to Osh via the Garm valley, and north to Khojand via the Anzob Pass and Ayni) are all closed by snow. The only way of reaching these areas is through Uzbekistan. The direct road between Dushanbe and Khorog was also closed during the summer of 1993 due to fighting north of the town of Khalaikum, and the bridge at Ayni was blown up in August 1993, but has since been repaired. The road between Osh (in Kyrgyzstan) and Khorog is kept open all year round and traverses one of the most beautiful and unspoilt regions in the world, the Pamir Mountains. Recent political and economic troubles have meant that road maintenance has been widely neglected. Foreigners are, in theory, allowed to go anywhere except border zones – it is worth noting that the road from Dushanbe to Khorog is in a border zone for much of its length – without having to get special permission (other than an endorsement on their visas). Those travelling on Intourist invitations should inform Intourist of their plans. If travelling independently, it is worth getting as many official-looking documents as possible in order to negotiate the many checkpoints. Traffic drives on the right. **Bus:** There are services between the major towns when the roads are open. **Taxi:** These and chauffeur-driven cars for hire can be found in all major towns. Many are unlicensed and travellers are advised to agree a fare in advance. Officially marked taxis are safe, but sharing with strangers should be avoided. As many of the street names have changed since independence, it is also advisable to ascertain both the old and the new street names when asking directions. **Car hire:** Self-drive car hire is not available. **Documentation:** It is in theory possible to bring, or buy, one's own transport: drivers should have an International Driving Licence and have arranged insurance before departure.

ACCOMMODATION

HOTELS: Tajikistan is not well supplied with hotels outside the capital. Although there are no restrictions on where visitors may stay, hotels other than the main Intourist hotels, the Hotel Tajikistan (tel: (3772) 274 373; fax: (3772) 275 155) and the Hotel Independence (tel: (3772) 211 280), are unused to accommodating foreigners and all but the most insistent visitors may find it difficult to obtain a room in them. The main hotels are clean and friendly, although it is difficult to get a room in the Oktyabrskaya, which houses both the US and Russian embassies. At the time of writing, guests in the Hotel Tajikistan have to order dinner at least five hours in advance as the restaurant does not formally operate in the evening. Meals can be obtained in the Hotel Oktyabrskaya, but the restaurant stops serving at 1900. Outside the capital, accommodation can be hard to find. The Hotel Leninabad in Khojand is clean and relatively used to foreigners. Chikalovsk, a short drive south of Khojand, boasts the modern Hotel Khojand, but Chikalovsk is a closed town and anyone wishing to stay in the hotel *must* get permission from the local military authorities.
DACHAS: It is possible to stay in the government dachas in Khorog, but do not expect Western standards of comfort, amenities or cleanliness.

RESORTS & EXCURSIONS

Tajikistan was never well-equipped with a comprehensive infrastructure for tourists, and some sites were destroyed in the civil war at the end of 1992. However, there is still much to see and the following are recommended.
Situated only three hours from the border with Afghanistan is the Tajik capital **Dushanbe**, lying in the Hissar valley in the southwest of the country. Known primarily for its Monday market (the name Dushanbe is derived from the Tajik word for Monday), it was no more than a village until the Trans-Caspian Railway reached it in 1929. Soviet power had only been established in the region for six years and, somewhat unoriginally, the city was renamed *Stalinabad* and proclaimed capital of the new Soviet Socialist Republic of Tajikistan. It was from here that Brezhnev launched his invasion of Afghanistan in 1979. The main points of interest all lie on, or close to, Prospekt Rudaki which runs from the railway station in the south to the bus station in the north. As well as the principal mosque, this area boasts a synagogue that dates back to the late 19th century, a Russian church and a columned opera house. Other features in the city include the *Tajikistan Unified Museum*, situated just north of the railway station in Ploshchad Aym, which has stuffed snow leopards and Marco Polo sheep amongst its exhibits. The ethnographic museum on ul. Somoni, not far from the Hotel Tajikistan, is currently closed.
16km (10 miles) west of Dushanbe lies the **Hissar Port**, a site built between the 16th and 19th centuries which contains, among other things, a ruined citadel, two *madrassahs* (Islamic seminaries), a *caravanserai* and a mausoleum.
Further west still, at **Penjikent** on the Uzbek border, lie the remains of a Sogdian fort that are only now being excavated. The frescoes in Penjikent are reputed to be extremely fine.
South of Penjikent lie the **Muragazor Lakes;** a system of seven lakes of differing colours that change as the light changes.
There are remains of Buddhist temples near **Kurgan-Tyube** in the south, from which the biggest Buddha in Central Asia was recovered and is now stored, ignominiously carved up in 60 pieces, in Dushanbe.
The **Pamirs** are at the hub of Asia – often described as the *Roof of the World*, these mountains form one of the most unexplored regions on earth. High, cold and remote, they have attracted climbers and hunters from the former Soviet Union for years, but only now are they opening up for the rest of the world. The bulk of the Pamirs lies in the semi-autonomous region of Gorno-Badakhshan and visitors should be aware that some elements have been conducting an armed campaign to gain even more autonomy. However, the campaign has been confined to a number of well-defined theatres, most of which are well away from areas likely to interest visitors; the road between Dushanbe and Khorog is the exception.
The only town of any significance on the *Pamir Highway*, which stretches from Dushanbe into Kyrgyzstan, is **Khorog**. The capital of the eastern Tajik region of *Gorno-Badakhshan*, Khorog is a small one-street town with a museum containing stuffed animals and a display of photographs of Lenin. The flight into Khorog from the Tajik capital is said to be the most difficult in the world. **Lake Sareskoye,** in the heart of the Pamirs, was formed in 1911 when the side of a mountain was dislodged by an earthquake and fell into the path of a mountain river. In the north of the Pamirs, **Lake Kara-Kul**, formed by a meteor 10 million years ago, is 3915m (12,844ft) above sealevel and hence too high for any aquatic life. **Pik Lenina** and **Pik Kommunizma** are to the northwest and west respectively of Lake Kara-Kul. At well over 7000m (22,966ft) these two peaks tower over Tajikistan and the neighbouring republic of Kyrgyzstan to the north. *Intourist Tajikistan* offers helicopter flights for those wishing to climb them. Many people are convinced that *Yetis* are alive and thriving in this remote wilderness.
Climbing trips can be arranged by *Intourist Tajikistan* and *Alp-Navruz* (tel/fax: (3772) 245 373). Hunting trips for the rare Marco Polo sheep can be arranged by *Pamir-Balchuk* (tel: (3772) 275 852), however, prospective hunters should be aware that a single Marco Polo costs US$29,000 to shoot and some countries, including the USA, have banned the import of Marco Polo trophies, as it is regarded as an endangered species. The border guards in Murghab district in the east of Badakhshan are reported to be shooting two or three a day for food. *Alp-Navruz* and *Pamir-Balchuk* will organise itineraries to suit individual tastes. *Intourist Tajikistan* offers a number of set itineraries, mostly in the southwest of the country and its immediate surrounding mountains and generally during the summer months. The trips generally start in Moscow and include a 14-day trekking trip around the ancient Sogdian lakes such as *Iskander-kul*, north of Dushanbe and the Muragazor Lakes, finishing in Samarkand in Uzbekistan; and a trip to the mountain passes of the *Kara-Tak*, north of Dushanbe, walking 8-10km (5-6 miles) per day, with the baggage being carried by donkeys, and staying in mountain villages.

SOCIAL PROFILE

FOOD & DRINK: Traditional Tajik meals start with sweet dishes such as *halwa* and tea and then progress to soups and meat before finishing with *plov. Plov* is made up of scraps of mutton, shredded yellow turnip and rice, fried in a large wok, and is a staple dish in all the Central Asian republics. *Shashlyk* (skewered chunks of mutton grilled over charcoal, served with raw sliced onions) and *lipioshka* (round unleavened bread) are often sold on street corners and served in restaurants and make an appetizing meal: the Vastoychny bar restaurant in Dushanbe (on Prospekt Rudaki near the Hotel Tajikistan) serves particularly good *shashlyk. Manty* (large noodle sacks of meat), *samsa* (samosas) and *chiburekki* (deep-fried dough cakes) are all popular as snacks. *Shorpur* is a meat and vegetable soup; *laghman* is similar to *shorpur*, but comes with noodles. In the summer Tajikistan is awash with fruit: its grapes and melons were famous throughout the former Soviet Union. The bazaars also sell pomegranates, apricots, plums, figs and persimmons. Little of the food served in hotels indicates its Tajik heritage: *borcht* is cabbage soup, *entrecote* are well-done steaks, *cutlet* are grilled meatballs, and *strogan* is the local equivalent of beef Stroganoff. *Pirmeni*, originated in Ukraine, are small boiled noodle sacks of meat and vegetables similar to ravioli, sometimes in a vegetable soup, sometimes not.
Drink: Tea or *chai* is the most widespread drink on offer and can be obtained almost anywhere. Beer, wine, vodka, brandy and sparkling wine *(shampanski)* are intermittently available in many restaurants. If the restaurant is unable to supply it, it is acceptable to bring your own. *Kefir,* a thick drinking yoghurt, is often served with breakfast.
NIGHTLIFE: There are no restaurants operating in the evenings except for the one in the Hotel Oktyabrskaya which shuts at 1900 (a hangover from the curfew that

was raised in January 1994). There is a dollar bar in the basement of the Hotel Tajikistan which is open some evenings. The opera and ballet theatre on Prospekt Rudaki is still operating, albeit with a reduced programme of matinees. The streets of Dushanbe are deserted after 2000.

SHOPPING: Shortages are the norm in Tajikistan; there is a bazaar and street market behind the Hotel Tajikistan where it is possible to buy food and sometimes handicrafts. Shokhmansur (also known as Zilyoni) Bazaar near Ploshchad Ayni also sells food. There is a souvenir shop on the corner of Prospekt Rudaki and ul. Ismail Somoni, under an art gallery which exhibits and sells the work of local artists. **Shopping hours:** Food shops open 0800-1700, all others open 0900-1800.

SPORT: The national sport is **wrestling**, called *Gushtin Geri*. *Bushkashi* is a team game in which the two mounted teams attempt to deliver a headless and legless goat's carcass weighing 30-40kg over the opposition's goal line. Players are allowed to wrestle the goat from an opponent, but physical assault is frowned upon. The mountains make Tajikistan a popular destination for **climbing** and **trekking**, and there is **skiing** and **hunting** in the hills behind Dushanbe.

SPECIAL EVENTS: There is a carnival at Navrus, when a special dish called *Sumalak* is prepared from germinating wheat.

SOCIAL CONVENTIONS: *Lipioshka* (bread) should never be laid upside down, and it is normal to remove shoes, but not socks, when entering someone's house. Shorts are rarely seen in Tajikistan and, worn by females, are likely to provoke unwelcome attention from the local male population.

BUSINESS PROFILE

ECONOMY: Tajikistan was one of the poorest of the states of the Soviet Union and the civil war in 1992/93 destroyed much of what it did have. The budget deficit in 1993 ran at over 50% of GDP and the country is currently surviving on aid from the Russian Federation. Economic production is concentrated in two main areas: the Khojand region in the north and the Hissar valley in the southwest, which includes Dushanbe. The main products are cotton (the most dominant industry), silk, aluminium (which provides over 50% of the country's hard-currency income), uranium, silver (Tajikistan claims to have the largest silver reserves in the world), gold, iron, mercury, lead and tin. The exploitation of minerals is considered the most promising avenue for the country's future economic development. There are also large reserves of decorative building materials and semi-precious stones such as lapis lazuli. In the wake of civil war much of the Russian minority, which provided the bulk of the technicians, fled, leading to the rapid decay of infrastructure such as the telephone and banking systems. The civil war also caused grave disruption to the agricultural infrastructure. 93% of the land is occupied by mountains, making expansion of the agricultural sector difficult (although grain and fruit are still produced in somewhat sizeable quantities). Other areas of interest are livestock breeding and the chemical industry. Neighbouring Uzbekistan's habit of cutting fuel supplies is not making the rebuilding of the economy any easier. Hopes are pinned on the exploitation of the gold and silver reserves and the development of cotton-processing facilities to maximise the value added of the raw material. The country's energy requirements are largely met by harnessing the mountain rivers for hydroelectric projects. Oil and gas imports from elsewhere in the former Soviet Union were an essential supplement to these but were disrupted along with much of the rest of Tajikistan's trade by the collapse of the internal Soviet trading system. Russia remains the the principal destination for Tajik exports, chiefly aluminium, textiles, cotton, silk, marble and fruit and vegetables. However, persistent hyperinflation forced the government to cede partial control of economic policy to the Russian central bank in exchange for currency support and US$100 million of financial credits. In total, Russia now accounts for 60% of Tajik trade; the other republics, principally Kazakhstan, Uzbekistan and Ukraine, account for a further 20-30% in trade. Outside the former Soviet Union, Sweden and Austria are important trading partners. The Government has embarked upon a programme of privatisation, starting with the service sector, to try to breathe life into the economy. Tajikistan became a member of the Economic Cooperation Organisation of Central Asian Republics in 1992, and joined the International Monetary Fund and the World Bank in the following year. It is also a member of the European Bank for Reconstruction and Development.

BUSINESS: Tajikistan is looking for foreign investment in a number of sectors, particularly in

aluminium-processing which needs extensive modernisation. Foreign businesses are not barred from any economic sphere: although land, livestock and mineral resources are owned by the Government, it is possible to lease them. Foreign concerns are allowed to participate in the privatisation programme. Foreign investments in certain priority areas, which are as yet undefined, are eligible for tax holidays – including import and export duties – although, in effect, each foreign investor negotiates his or her own terms and many are better than the standard laid down in law. All foreign investors must be registered with the Ministry of External Economic Affairs. **Office hours:** 0900-1900 Monday to Friday.

COMMERCIAL INFORMATION: The following organisations can offer advice: Chamber of Commerce and Industry, ul. Mazayeva 21, 734012 Dushanbe. Tel: (3772) 279 519; *or*
Somonion – Tajikvneshtorg Industrial Association, PO Box 48, Prospekt Rudaki 25, 734025 Dushanbe. Tel: (3772) 232 903. Fax: (3772) 228 120. Telex: 201104 (a/b SAVDO SU).
The Ministry of External Economic Affairs is in the process of moving office, but can be reached by telex on 201141 (a/b NUKRA SU).
Information can also be obtained from the US Department of Commerce Business Information Service for the Newly Independent States, Room 7413, US Department of Commerce, Washington, DC 20230. Tel: (202) 482 4655. Fax: (202) 482 2293.

CLIMATE

In Dushanbe the temperatures vary between a minimum -12°C in December/January to a maximum 45°C in July/August. Humidity is generally low. In the mountains it can reach -50°C when the wind chill factor is taken into consideration, and rises to 20°C in summer.
Required clothing: Warm clothing should be taken by anyone intending to visit the mountains. Those intending to visit the southwest in summer should bring light, loose clothing.

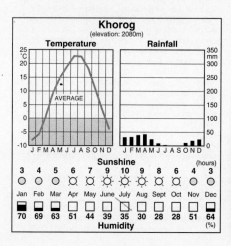

TEMPERATURE CONVERSIONS

Khorog
(elevation: 2080m)

	Jan	Feb	Mar	Apr	May	June	July	Aug	Sept	Oct	Nov	Dec
Sunshine (hours)	3	4	5	6	7	9	10	9	8	6	4	3
Humidity (%)	70	69	63	51	44	39	35	30	28	28	51	64

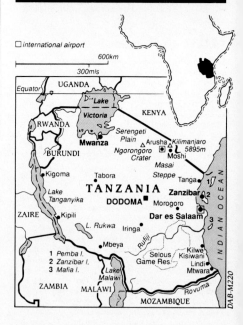

Tanzania

☐ *international airport*

Location: East Africa.

Tanzania Tourist Board
PO Box 2485, Dar es Salaam, Tanzania
Tel: (51) 27671. Fax: (51) 46780. Telex: 41061.
Tanzania Wildlife Corporation
PO Box 1144, Arusha, Tanzania
Tel: (57) 8830. Fax: (57) 8239. Telex: 42080.
High Commission for the United Republic of Tanzania
43 Hertford Street, London W1Y 8DB
Tel: (0171) 499 8951/4. Fax: (0171) 491 9321. Telex: 262504. Opening hours: 1000-1230 Monday to Friday.
Tanzanian Trade Centre
78-80 Borough High Street, London SE1 1LL
Tel: (0171) 407 0566. Fax: (0171) 403 2003. Opening hours: 0900-1700 Monday to Friday.
British High Commission
PO Box 9200, Hifadhi House, Samora Avenue, Dar es Salaam, Tanzania
Tel: (51) 29601/5 *or* 46300/4. Fax: (51) 46301. Telex: 41004 (a/b UKREP).
Embassy of the United Republic of Tanzania
2139 R Street, NW, Washington, DC 20008
Tel: (202) 939 6125. Fax: (202) 797 7408. Telex: 64213.
Embassy of the United States of America
PO Box 9123, 36 Laibon Road, Dar es Salaam, Tanzania
Tel: (51) 66010/5. Fax: (51) 66701. Telex: 41250 (a/b USA TZ).
High Commission for the United Republic of Tanzania
50 Range Road, Ottawa, Ontario K1N 8J4
Tel: (613) 232 1500/9. Fax: (613) 232 5184.
Canadian High Commission
PO Box 1022, 38 Mirambo Street, Dar es Salaam, Tanzania
Tel: (51) 46000/11. Fax: (51) 46005. Telex: 41015 (a/b DOMCAN TZ).

AREA: 945,087 sq km (364,900 sq miles).
POPULATION: 25,635,000 (1990 estimate).
POPULATION DENSITY: 27.1 per sq km.

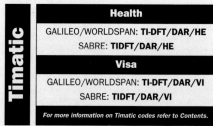

Health	
GALILEO/WORLDSPAN:	**TI-DFT/DAR/HE**
SABRE:	**TIDFT/DAR/HE**
Visa	
GALILEO/WORLDSPAN:	**TI-DFT/DAR/VI**
SABRE:	**TIDFT/DAR/VI**

For more information on Timatic codes refer to Contents.

Timatic

CAPITAL: Dodoma (administrative capital).
Population: 85,000 (1985 estimate). Dar es Salaam remains the commercial capital for the time being.
Population: 1,096,000 (1985 estimate).
GEOGRAPHY: The United Republic of Tanzania lies on the Indian Ocean and is bordered by Kenya and Uganda to the north, by Burundi, Rwanda and Zaïre to the west, and by Zambia, Malawi and Mozambique to the south. The Tanzanian mainland is divided into several clearly defined regions: the coastal plains, which vary in width from 16-64km (10-39 miles) and have lush, tropical vegetation; the Masai Steppe in the north, 213-1067m (698-3500ft) above sea level; and a high plateau in the southern area towards Zambia and Lake Nyasa (Lake Malawi). Savannah and bush cover over half the country, and semi-desert accounts for the remaining land area, with the exception of the coastal plains. Over 53,000 sq km (20,463 sq miles) is inland water, mostly lakes formed in the Rift Valley. The United Republic of Tanzania includes the islands of Zanzibar and Pemba, about 45km (28 miles) off the coast to the northeast of the country.
LANGUAGE: Swahili and English are the official languages. Other African languages such as Bantu and those of Nilo-Hamitic and Khoisan origin are also spoken.
RELIGION: Muslim, Christian, Hindu and traditional beliefs.
TIME: GMT + 3.
ELECTRICITY: 230 volts AC, 50Hz. Plugs may be round or square 3-pin, fused or unfused.
COMMUNICATIONS: Telephone: IDD is available. Country code: 255. Outgoing international calls must go through the operator. There are many public call boxes in post offices and main towns. **Telex/telegram:** Telex facilities are available at the Kilimanjaro Hotel, Dar es Salaam, Mount Meru Hotel in Arusha and at the post office in Dar es Salaam. Telegrams can be sent from the post office. **Post:** Airmail to Europe takes five days. **Press:** The English-language newspaper is the *Daily News,* a government publication, printed in Dar es Salaam.
BBC World Service and Voice of America frequencies: From time to time these change. See the section *How to Use this Book* for more information.

BBC:				
MHz	**21.47**	**17.88**	**15.42**	**9.630**
Voice of America:				
MHz	**21.49**	**15.60**	**9.525**	**6.035**

PASSPORT/VISA

Regulations and requirements may be subject to change at short notice, and you are advised to contact the appropriate diplomatic or consular authority before finalising travel arrangements. Details of these may be found at the head of this country's entry. Any numbers in the chart refer to the footnotes below.

	Passport Required?	Visa Required?	Return Ticket Required?
Full British	Yes	No/2	Yes
BVP	Not valid	-	-
Australian	Yes	No/2	Yes
Canadian	Yes	No/2	Yes
USA	Yes	Yes	Yes
Other EU (As of 31/12/94)	Yes	1/2	Yes
Japanese	Yes	Yes	Yes

Note: Visa requirements are liable to change at short notice. For up-to-date information contact the nearest embassy or consulate.
PASSPORTS: Valid passport required by all.
British Visitors Passport: Not accepted.
VISAS: Required by all except:
(a) **[1]** nationals of Denmark, Ireland and the UK. All other EU nationals *do* require a visa;
(b) nationals of Antigua & Barbuda, Bahamas, Bangladesh, Barbados, Belize, Botswana, Brunei, Cyprus, Dominica, Fiji, Finland, Gambia, Ghana, Grenada, Guyana, Iceland, Jamaica, Kenya, Kiribati, Lesotho, Malawi, Malaysia, Maldives, Malta, Mauritius, Nauru, New Zealand, Norway, Papua New Guinea, Rwanda, St Kitts & Nevis, St Lucia, St Vincent & the Grenadines, Seychelles, Sierra Leone, Singapore, Solomon Islands, Sri Lanka, Swaziland, Sweden, Tonga, Trinidad & Tobago, Tuvalu, Uganda, Vanuatu, Western Samoa, Zambia and Zimbabwe;
(c) holders of a Tanzanian re-entry pass.
Note [2]: However, *all* temporary visitors must hold a *Visitor's Pass.* Visitors are advised to obtain such a Pass from Tanzanian representations before the commencement of their journey.
Cost: Dependent on nationality. Visitor's Pass is issued free of charge.
Application requirements: (a) 1 completed application form (different for visa and Visitor's Pass). (b) For business visitors, a letter of invitation. (c) 2 passport-size photos. (d) Passport. (e) Fee (visas only).
Application to: Consulate (or Consular section at High Commission or Embassy). For addresses, see top of entry.
Working days required: 5 days.
Temporary residence: Enquire at High Commission or Embassy.

MONEY

Currency: Tanzanian Shilling (TSh) = 100 cents. Notes are in denominations of TSh1000, 500, 200, 100, 50, 20 and 10. Coins are in denominations of TSh20, 10, 5 and 1, and 50, 20, 10 and 5 cents.
Currency exchange: Money may be changed at authorised dealers or bureaux de change.
Credit cards: Access/Mastercard and Diners Club both have limited acceptance. Check with your credit card company for details of merchant acceptability and other facilities which may be available.
Travellers cheques: May be cashed with authorised dealers or bureaux de change.
Exchange rate indicators: The following figures are included as a guide to the movements of the Tanzanian Shilling against Sterling and the US Dollar:

Date:	**Oct '92**	**Sep '93**	**Jan '94**	**Jan '95**
£1.00=	**506.08**	**673.40**	**703.05**	**819.27**
$1.00=	**318.90**	**440.99**	**475.19**	**523.67**

Currency restrictions: The import and export of local currency is prohibited. The import of foreign currency is unlimited, subject to declaration. The export of foreign currency is limited to TSh4000 or the amount declared on arrival.
Banking hours: 0830-1230 Monday to Friday, 0830-1130 Saturday; 0900-1130 Sunday.

DUTY FREE

The following items may be imported into Tanzania without incurring customs duty:
200 cigarettes or 50 cigars or 250g of tobacco; 1 litre of wine or 1 litre of spirits; 250ml of perfume.

PUBLIC HOLIDAYS

Jan 12 '95 Zanzibar Revolution Day. **Feb 5** Chama Cha Mapinduzi Day. **Mar 2** Eid al-Fitr (End of Ramadan). **Apr 14-17** Easter. **Apr 26** Union Day. **May 1** International Labour Day. **May 10** Eid al-Haji (Feast of the Sacrifice). **Jul 7** Saba Saba (Peasants' Day). **Aug 9** Maulidi (Prophet's Birthday). **Dec 9** Independence Day. **Dec 25** Christmas. **Jan 12 '96** Zanzibar Revolution Day. **Feb 5** Chama Cha Mapinduzi Day. **Feb 22** Eid al-Fitr (End of Ramadan). **Apr 5-8** Easter. **Apr 26** Union Day.
Note: Muslim festivals are timed according to local sightings of various phases of the Moon and the dates given above are approximations. During the lunar month of Ramadan that precedes Eid al-Fitr, Muslims fast during the day and feast at night and normal business patterns may be interrupted. Many restaurants are closed during the day and there may be restrictions on smoking and drinking. Some disruption may continue into Eid al-Fitr itself. Eid al-Fitr and Eid al-Haji (Eid al-Adha) may last anything from two to ten days, depending on the region. For more information, see the section *World of Islam* at the back of the book.

HEALTH

Regulations and requirements may be subject to change at short notice, and you are advised to contact your doctor well in advance of your intended date of departure. Any numbers in the chart refer to the footnotes below.

	Special Precautions?	Certificate Required?
Yellow Fever	Yes	1
Cholera	Yes	2
Typhoid & Polio	Yes	-
Malaria	3	-
Food & Drink	4	-

[1]: A yellow fever vaccination certificate is required of all travellers over one year of age.
[2]: A vaccination certificate is an essential requirement for entry into Zanzibar. Following WHO guidelines issued in 1973, a cholera vaccination certificate is no longer a condition of entry to Tanzania. However, cholera is a risk in this country and precautions are essential. Up-to-date advice should be sought before deciding whether these precautions should include vaccination as medical opinion is divided over its effectivenss. See the *Health* section at the back of the book.
[3]: Malaria risk, predominantly in the malignant *falciparum* form, exists all year throughout the country below 1800m. The strain is reported to be 'highly resistant' to chloroquine and 'resistant' to sulfadoxine/pyrimethamine.
[4]: All water should be regarded as being potentially contaminated. Water used for drinking, brushing teeth or making ice should have first been boiled or otherwise sterilised. Milk is unpasteurised and should be boiled. Powdered or tinned milk is available and is advised, but make sure that it is reconstituted with pure water. Avoid dairy products which are likely to have been made from unboiled milk. Only eat well-cooked meat and fish, preferably served hot. Pork, salad and mayonnaise may carry increased risk. Vegetables should be cooked and fruit peeled.
Rabies is present. For those at high risk, vaccination before arrival should be considered. If you are bitten abroad seek medical advice without delay. For more information, consult the *Health* section at the back of the book.
Bilharzia (schistosomiasis) is present. Avoid swimming and paddling in fresh water. Swimming pools which are well-chlorinated and maintained are safe.
Health care: Private health insurance is recommended. There are 2000-3000 hospitals and clinics; some Christian missions also provide medical treatment.

TRAVEL - International

AIR: Tanzania's national airline is *Air Tanzania Corporation.*
Approximate flight times: From London to *Dar es Salaam* is 12 hours 45 minutes and to *Kilimanjaro* is 14 hours.
International airports: *Dar es Salaam International (DAR),* 15km (9 miles) southwest of the city (travel time – 25 minutes). Airport facilities include outgoing duty-free shop, car hire, post office, banking and currency exchange facilities, a bar and restaurant. A shuttle bus service and taxi services to the city are available.
Kilimanjaro International Airport (JRO). Airport facilities include shops, post office, bar and restaurant. Shuttle bus services and taxis are available to the nearest town of Arusha.
Departure tax: *Residents:* TSh1000; *non-residents:* US$20. The latter has to be paid in US Dollars. Transit passengers and children under two years are exempt.
SEA: Dar es Salaam is served by ocean freighters and passenger liners. Contact the *National Shipping Agencies Co Ltd (NASACO),* PO Box 9082, Dar es Salaam (telex: 41235); *or* the *Tanzanian Harbours Authority (THA),* PO Box 9184, Dar es Salaam. Tel: (51) 21212. Fax: (51) 32066. Telex: 41346.
RAIL: There is a twice-weekly restaurant car service by *Tanzania – Zambia Railway Authority (Tazara)* from Dar es Salaam to Kapiri Mposhi (Zambia), with a change of train at the border. Lake steamer connections operate from railheads at Kigoma and Mwanza to Burundi, Rwanda and Uganda. Trains may get very crowded but officials can be readily persuaded to find seats for tourists. Travellers should take special care of their baggage. It is unwise to forward luggage. Rail connections between Tanzania and Kenya have been suspended for many years, following a dispute over ownership of locomotives and rolling stock.
ROAD: The tarmac road connecting Tanzania with Zambia is in good condition, as is the road north to Kenya. From Lusaka in Zambia the Great North Road is paved all the way to Dar es Salaam. Road links from Rwanda and Mozambique are poor.

TRAVEL - Internal

AIR: *Air Tanzania* runs regular services to all main towns. These are reliable and efficiently run, but check with the town airline office before leaving for the airport. All national parks have airstrips and there are two charter companies operating single- and twin-engined aircraft to any town or bush strip in the country. In addition there are numerous bush airfields and airstrips in many towns which can be used by the charter companies.
SEA/LAKE: There is a daily speed-boat service between Dar es Salaam and Zanzibar which takes 2-3 hours in each direction. There is also a sailing from Zanzibar to Pemba Island. Both Lake Tanganyika and Lake Victoria have a steamer service. First-, second- and third-class seating is available on both services, though first class has more comfortable seats and is likely to be less crowded. The service on Lake Victoria calls at the ports of Bukoba, Mwanza and Musoma, but the timetable for the service is unlikely to be reliable. For further details, contact the *Tanzania Railways Corporation* or *NASACO.*
RAIL: *Tanzania Railways Corporation (TRC)* provides the principal services, while those on the route to Zambia are run by *Tazara. TRC* runs a daily service from Dar es

Salaam to Mwanza on Lake Victoria and Kigoma on Lake Tanganyika with a restaurant car. There are also daily trains from Dar es Salaam to Moshi and Arusha. *Tazara* runs daily trains to the Zambian border.
ROAD: Traffic drives on the right. Tanzania has a good network of tarmac and all-weather roads connecting all major towns. Most minor roads are in bad condition becoming impassable to all except 4-wheel-drive vehicles during the long rains in April and May. It is not advisable to drive at night because of wild animals, cattle and goats on the road. There are often petrol shortages and spare parts for vehicles are hard to find. **Bus:** Inexpensive buses connecting most places are operated by the *State Travel Service,* but services are often unreliable or break down. The worst times to travel by bus are at the end of the month and during the April/May rains. **Car hire:** Self-drive car hire is extremely expensive and is discouraged by most companies. Vehicles with drivers are offered, and this is often more reliable. **Documentation:** An International Driving Licence is recommended, although it is not legally required; it must be endorsed by the police on arrival. A temporary licence to drive is available from the police on presentation of a valid national driving licence.
URBAN: Buses and minibuses operate in Dar es Salaam on a flat-fare basis. Services are usually crowded and inefficient. In Dar es Salaam, taxis at hotels have fixed rates for journeys within the city. In other towns, taxi fares should be negotiated in advance. Drivers expect a tip of 10%.

ACCOMMODATION

HOTELS: Tanzania has a range of accommodation from very good, expensive hotels to cheaper hotels which, although adequate, lack comfort. Although accommodation is on the expensive side, it is often possible for two people to share a single room except in top hotels. The less expensive hotels are often fully booked.
WILDLIFE LODGES: There are wildlife lodges in all national parks. Reservations can be booked through the *Tanzania Tourist Corporation (TTC)* in Dar es Salaam or the *Tanzania Wildlife Corporation* in Arusha (see top of entry for addresses and telephone numbers).
GUEST-HOUSES: These are often offshoots of local

bars and provide cheap accommodation, but there may be problems with drunken behaviour and theft. Sharing a room is advisable and special attention to possessions should be paid while staying there. These are not bookable in advance. Prices are higher in the larger towns, but in general the quality can be assessed from the tariffs.
CAMPING/CARAVANNING: There are campsites in Arusha, Arusha National Park (four), Tarangire National Park (two), Lake Manyara National Park (two), Ngorongoro Conservation Area Authority (two), Serengeti National Park (seven), Kilimanjaro National Park (one), Mikumi National Park (two) and Ruaha National Park (two). Some have standard facilities, including taps, toilets, bivouac huts and firewood; others are more basic. Permits for entry to each park and also for photography and filming must be obtained before arrival. It is advisable to check the prices and site procedure before arrival. All bookings can be made through the Office of the Director, Tanzania National Parks, PO Box 3134, Arusha. Tel: (57) 3471. Alternatively, write directly to the Park Warden in charge of the individual parks.
YOUTH HOSTELS: There are youth hostels in Lake Manyara National Park (primarily educational groups) and Serengeti National Park, YMCA hostels in Moshi and Dar es Salaam, and a YWCA hostel, which takes couples as well as women, in Dar es Salaam.

RESORTS & EXCURSIONS

For convenience and ease of reference, this section has been divided into five regions: Dar es Salaam; The Coast; Zanzibar & Mafia Island; Mount Kilimanjaro; and The National Parks.

Dar es Salaam

The capital city (though this function is gradually being moved to Dodoma) and a major port, **Dar es Salaam** is the natural starting point for trips in Tanzania. It is near Mount Kilimanjaro, Dodoma and the nearby island of Zanzibar. Parts of Dar es Salaam have a tranquil air that belies industrial and commercial growth.
Places to visit: The *National Museum,* housing the skull of Nutcracker Man; *Observation Hill* with the campus

and facilities of the University of Dar es Salaam; and the *Village Museum* with exhibits of traditional housing and crafts.

The Coast

The fishing village of **Msasani**, 8km (5 miles) from the capital, contains tombs dating back to the 17th century. Further south, at **Kilwa Klsiwani**, there are ruins of Portuguese and Arab architecture.
Many beautiful beaches are within easy reach of Dar es Salaam, such as those at **Kunduchi, Mjimwena** and **Mbwa Maji. Kunduchi,** 24km (15 miles) north of the city, is a fishing village with nearby ruins of Persian tombs and mosques. The *Bahari* and *Kunduchi Beach Hotels* are within 3km (2 miles) of offshore **Mbudya Island**. This uninhabited island forms part of the protective coral reef which is a good place for diving, snorkelling and fishing. **Sinda Island**, some 14km (9 miles) off Dar es Salaam, also offers facilities for snorkelling and shell fishing.
A 72km (45-mile) drive north of Dar es Salaam is **Bagamoyo**, a one-time slave port and terminus for the caravans. This tiny township is the nearest mainland point to Zanzibar and possesses sandy beaches set in a beautiful bay. Livingstone's body rested in the tiny chapel of the convent here on its way back to London. The town mosque and Arab tombs date from the 18th and 19th centuries. 5km (3 miles) to the south is the village of **Kaole,** near which are the ruins of a mosque and pillars believed to be 800 years old. To the north of Bagamoyo is the country's second port, **Tanga.** From here the visitor can drive to the beautiful *Usambara Mountains* and **Moshi** on the slopes of Mount Kilimanjaro.

Zanzibar & Mafia Island

The beautiful island of **Zanzibar** is only 20 minutes flight from Dar es Salaam. The visitor can still see the house where Dr Livingstone lived, as well as that used by Burton and Speke. The *Anglican Cathedral Church of Christ* stands on the site of the old slave market, while on the seafront are the palace of the former sultan and the towering *Beit-el-Ajaib* ('The House of Wonders'). Zanzibar is the 'Island of Spices' where cloves, nutmeg and cinnamon are grown. It is a fascinating place with its palaces, forts, stone aqueducts and baths. Its history as a

30km

15mls

cosmopolitan centre of trade gives it a unique atmosphere. **Note:** Visitors to Zanzibar should observe the strict Muslim rules regarding dress. For more information, see the section *World of Islam* at the back of the book.

Only 40 minutes flight south of Dar es Salaam, **Mafia Island** is one of the most exciting big-game fishing locations in the world and also a unique marine park. Power boats and tackle are available for hire.

Mount Kilimanjaro

At 5895m (19,341ft), Africa's highest mountain is a major attraction for mountaineers. Expeditions must be accompanied by a guide, and very warm clothes are required for the last section of the climb. The ascent takes about three days, allowing for rests at the three huts and a day or so at the final hut to acclimatise before tackling the final stage to the summit. See also the *Sport* section below.

The National Parks

Tanzania has 11 national parks, extending over some 33,660 sq km (13,000 sq miles). In addition there is the unique *Ngorongoro Conservation Unit,* in which wildlife is protected and where the Masai tribesmen also live and herd their cattle. There are also some ten game reserves where government-approved hunting safaris operate under licence and about 40 controlled areas where the hunting of game is controlled by a quota system.
Serengeti National Park: This is a plain-dwellers' stronghold of 13,000 sq km (5000 sq miles), claimed to be the finest in Africa. Here are 35 species of plain-dwelling animals, including wildebeest and zebra, which feature in the spectacular Serengeti migration, and also an extensive selection of birdlife. Probably the best time to see them is from December to May.
Ngorongo Crater: Rising high above the plains of the Serengeti is the rim of the Ngorongo Crater, the location of another animal world. The 260 sq km (100 sq miles) of a collapsed volcano is the home of zebra, wildebeest, gazelles, elephant, rhino, leopard and buffalo.
Lake Manyara National Park: Famous for its tree-climbing lions. The wall of the *Great Rift Valley* forms a backdrop to the park, before which lies forest, open grassland, swamp and the soda lake. Wildlife includes lions, herds of buffalo, baboons, elephant, rhino, impala, giraffe, leopard, zebra, bushbuck, reedbuck, waterbuck and blue and vervet monkeys. Manyara is also noted for its birdlife, particularly the flamingos.
Arusha National Park: This park lies within the *Ngurdoto Crater,* a volcano that has probably been extinct for a quarter of a million years. Visitors are able to see buffalo, rhino, elephant, giraffe and warthog.
Mikumi National Park: This park, 1300 sq km (500 sq miles) in area, offers a chance to see lion, zebra, hippo, leopard, cheetah, giraffe, impala, wildebeest and warthog. A popular spot for visitors is the *Kikaboga Hippo Pool.* Although December to March is the ideal time for viewing at Mikumi, there are animals throughout the year.
Ruaha National Park: The largest elephant sanctuary in the country, lying 118km (73 miles) from Iringa in the Southern Highlands along an all-weather road. The

park affords views of unparalleled scenery along the *Ruaha Gorge,* with many sightings of antelope. **Iringa** is also connected with Dar es Salaam and other centres by air and bus service. The best time to visit is from July to November.
Tarangire National Park: Only 130km (80 miles) from Arusha and 8km (5 miles) off the Great Cape to Cairo road, it is nonetheless an area which compares favourably with the Serengeti in terms of wildlife density.
Gombe National Park: This park is near **Kigoma** on the shores of *Lake Tanganyika* and is the home of about 200 chimpanzees, more easily seen here in their natural habitat than anywhere else in the world. This is the place where Jane Goodall has devoted her life to recording chimpanzee ethology in a 30 year study; this has yielded many surprises and will almost certainly yield more, providing human interference doesn't exterminate the chimp.
Selous Game Reserve in southern Tanzania is one of the biggest in the world and has one of the world's largest elephant populations. There is also a high concentration of stalking lions and other game.

SOCIAL PROFILE

FOOD & DRINK: Most hotels serve local Tanzanian food of maize and beans or maizemeal with fish or meat, while the major hotels offer Western food. There is a variety of good seafood such as tuna and shark and an abundance of tropical fruit such as coconuts, pawpaws, mangoes, pineapples and bananas. Table service is normal in restaurants. **Drink:** Coffee and tea are of high quality. Tanzania is a non-secular state and alcohol is not prohibited. A good lager beer is produced locally, as is a popular gin called *Konyagi,* a chocolate and coconut liqueur called *Afrikoko* and a wine called *Dodoma,* which comes in red or rosé. Bars generally have counter service.
NIGHTLIFE: In Dar es Salaam there are four nightclubs and a cabaret. There are seven cinemas, all air-conditioned, and one drive-in cinema. There is also a *Little Theatre* at Oyster Bay. Generally the nightlife centres are in the top tourist hotels.
SHOPPING: The city and town centres usually have markets which sell curios such as African drums, old brass and copper, carved chess sets, jewellery, and one speciality, large wooden salad bowls carved from one piece of teak, *mninga* or ebony. **Shopping hours:** 0800-1200 and 1400-1800 Monday to Saturday.
SPORT: Temporary membership can be obtained for hotels and private clubs' sports facilities. Sports facilities offered in resorts include **tennis** and **basketball**.
Mountaineering: It is possible to climb mountains such as Mount Kilimanjaro, but it is essential to have the right equipment (such as warm clothing, boots, gloves and a hat) and some experience. All climbers should be aware that guides and porters are essential even to the lower peaks. Organised climbs with food and staff can be arranged at some cost through selected hotels. It is advisable to book well in advance. Alternatively, climbers can bring their own supplies and hire staff and equipment (Arctic sleeping bags and extra trousers) at the park gate. **Watersports: Sailing, swimming** and **fishing** in the coastal resorts. The main fishing season is from September to March.
SPECIAL EVENTS: The *Sukuma* (or *Bujora*) *Museum,* 15km (9 miles) east of Mwanza, gives approximately weekly performances of traditional dances of the Wasukuma tribe, including the *Bugobobobo* (Sukuma Snake Dance). During the Muslim festival of *Eid al-Fitr,* there is an event at Makunduchi in Zanzibar in which men from the north and south flail each other with banana branches, followed by the townswomen singing traditional songs and a night of feasting and dancing.
SOCIAL CONVENTIONS: When meeting and parting, hands are always shaken; this applies throughout the country in both rural and urban areas. The standard greeting when addressing an individual is *Jambo* to which the reply is also *Jambo.* The greeting for a group is *Hamjambo* to which the reply is *Hatujambo.* People are delighted if visitors can greet them in Kiswahili. There is no fixed protocol to do with hospitality, but when invited for a meal the food is traditionally eaten with hands. A token of appreciation is welcome when invited for a meal. Dress is smart and a good appearance is highly regarded. Suits and ties or safari suits are worn by men and suits or dresses by women. Ashtrays are usually an indication of permission for a visitor to smoke. Smoking is prohibited in cinemas and on public transport. **Photography:** In some places a charge will be levied on visitors wishing to take photographs; elsewhere a permit may be required.
Tipping: Discouraged except in 'Western situations', when waiters, porters and others may be tipped.

BUSINESS PROFILE

ECONOMY: Agriculture employs 90% of the working population, much of it subsistence, but cash crops, including cotton, coffee, tea, sisal, tobacco and cashew nuts, are the country's main export earners. Depressed prices have kept Tanzanian revenues at a static level despite increases in production. There is a small minerals sector: diamonds are mined commercially along with, on a smaller scale, gold and other gemstones. The Government has granted exploration licences in the hope of locating offshore deposits of oil and gas. The industrial sector is small: sugar processing, brewing, textiles and cigarette manufacture are the most important industries. Many of Tanzania's imported goods come through Kenya. This is due in part to the superior port facilities of Mombasa compared to those of Dar es Salaam, along with the more acceptable trading conditions in Kenya. Nevertheless, there are many port agents available at Dar es Salaam. The UK is Tanzania's largest supplier; currently there exists a 6-year backlog of commercial debt (value of £70m) with UK commercial suppliers. Aid organisations (principally World Bank and EU aid) are an important source of finance for Tanzanian imports. The Government has also been forced to adopt austerity measures, including currency devaluation and strict budgetary controls, by the IMF in exchange for financial support.
BUSINESS: Normal courtesies should be shown when visiting local business people. Almost all executives speak English. **Office hours:** 0730-1430 Monday to Friday; 0730-1200 Saturday.
COMMERCIAL INFORMATION: The following organisation can offer advice: Dar es Salaam Chamber of Commerce, PO Box 41, Kelvin House, Samora Machel Avenue, Dar es Salaam. Tel: (51) 21893. Telex: 41628.

CLIMATE

The climate is tropical, and coastal areas are hot and humid. The rainy season lasts from March to May. The central plateau is dry and arid. The northwestern highlands are cool and temperate and the rainy season here lasts from November to December and February to May.
Required clothing: Tropical clothing is worn throughout the year, but in the cooler season from June to September jackets and sweaters may be needed, especially in the evenings.

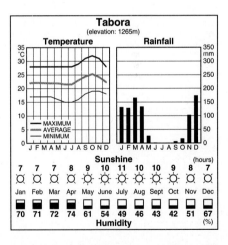

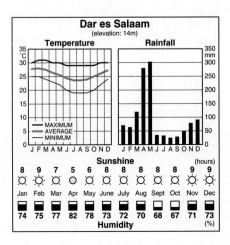

Thailand

□ *major international airport*

Location: South-East Asia.

Tourism Authority of Thailand
372 Bamrung Muang Road, Bangkok 10100, Thailand
Tel: (2) 226 0060 *or* 226 0072 *or* 226 0085. Fax: (2) 224 6221.
Royal Thai Embassy
29-30 Queen's Gate, London SW7 5JB
Tel: (0171) 589 2944 (main switchboard) *or* (0891) 600 150 (recorded visa information; calls are charged at the higher rate of 39/49p per minute) *or* 584 5421 (information bureau). Fax: (0171) 823 9695. Consular section opening hours: 0930-1300 Monday to Friday.
Consulates in: Birmingham, Cardiff, Glasgow, Hull and Liverpool.
Tourism Authority of Thailand
49 Albemarle Street, London W1X 3FE
Tel: (0171) 499 7679. Fax: (0171) 629 5519. Opening hours: 0900-1700 Monday to Friday.
British Embassy
Wireless Road, Bangkok 10330, Thailand
Tel: (2) 253 0191. Fax: (2) 255 8619 *or* 255 6051.
Consulate in: Chiang Mai.
Royal Thai Embassy
2300 Kalorama Road, NW, Washington, DC 20008
Tel: (202) 483 7200. Fax: (202) 234 4498.
Consulates in: Atlanta, Boston, Chicago, Coral Gables, Dallas, Denver, El Paso, Honolulu, Kansas City, Los Angeles, Montgomery, New Orleans, New York (tel: (212) 754 1770), Portland and Tulsa.

Tourism Authority of Thailand
Suite 3443, 5 World Trade Center, New York, NY 10048
Tel: (212) 432 0433/5. Fax: (212) 912 0920.
Offices in: Chicago and Los Angeles.
Embassy of the United States of America
95 Wireless Road, Bangkok 10330, Thailand
Tel: (2) 252 5040. Fax: (2) 254 2990.
Consulates in: Chiang Mai and Udon.
Royal Thai Embassy
180 Island Park Drive, Ottawa, Ontario, K1Y 0A2
Tel: (613) 722 4444. Fax: (613) 722 6624.
Consulates in: Edmonton, Montréal, Toronto and Vancouver.
Canadian Embassy
PO Box 2090, 11th Floor, Boonmitr Building, 138 Silom Road, Bangkok 10500, Thailand
Tel: (2) 237 4125 *or* 238 4452. Fax: (2) 236 6463 *or* 236 7467.

AREA: 513,115 sq km (198,115 sq miles).
POPULATION: 58,995,000 (1995).
POPULATION DENSITY: 115 per sq km.
CAPITAL: Bangkok. **Population:** 7,753,000, including Thon Buri (1995).
GEOGRAPHY: Thailand is bounded to the west by Myanmar and the Indian Ocean, to the south and east by Malaysia and the Gulf of Thailand, to the east by Cambodia, and to the north and east by Laos. Central Thailand is dominated by the Chao Phraya River. In the northeast the Korat Plateau rises about 305m (1000ft) above the central plain. This largely arid region covers one-third of the country. In the north, another one-third consists of forested hills.
LANGUAGE: Thai is the official language. English, Malay and a dialect of Chinese (Tachew) are also spoken.
RELIGION: The vast majority adhere to Buddhism (Theravada), with Muslim and Christian minorities.
TIME: GMT + 7.
ELECTRICITY: 220 volts AC, 50Hz. American- and European-style 2-pin plugs are in use.
COMMUNICATIONS: Telephone: IDD is available. Country code: 66. Outgoing international code: 001. Public international telephone facilities are available at the Central General Post Office, New Road, Bangkok. **Fax:** Facilities are widely available. **Telex/telegram:** Telegrams can be sent from the GPO Building or from any telegraph office. Public telex facilities are available at the GPO Building and hotels (at extra cost). **Post:** Airmail to Europe takes up to one week. The Central Post Office in Bangkok is open 0800-1800 Monday to Friday and 0900-1300 weekends and holidays. Post offices up-country are open 0800-1630. **Press:** English-language dailies are the *Bangkok Post* and *The Nation*.
BBC World Service and Voice of America frequencies: From time to time these change. See the section *How to Use this Book* for more information.
BBC:

| MHz | 17.79 | 11.75 | 9.740 | 3.915 |

Voice of America:

| MHz | 17.73 | 15.43 | 15.16 | 6.110 |

PASSPORT/VISA

Regulations and requirements may be subject to change at short notice, and you are advised to contact the appropriate diplomatic or consular authority before finalising travel arrangements. Details of these may be found at the head of this country's entry. Any numbers in the chart refer to the footnotes below.

	Passport Required?	Visa Required?	Return Ticket Required?
Full British	Yes	No	Yes
BVP	Not valid	-	-
Australian	Yes	No	Yes
Canadian	Yes	No	Yes
USA	Yes	No	Yes
Other EU (As of 31/12/94)	Yes/1	No/2	Yes
Japanese	Yes	No	Yes

Restricted entry: The Government of Thailand may refuse entry to persons whose general appearance and clothing does not comply with government requirements.
[1] The Government of Thailand does not recognise identity cards issued for children by Germany (*Kinderausweis*).
PASSPORTS: A valid passport is required by all except holders of a Hong Kong certificate of identity bearing a Thai visa issued in Hong Kong. Passports must be valid for 6 months beyond length of stay.
British Visitors Passport: Not accepted.
VISAS: The following are permitted to stay in Thailand *for a maximum of 15 days* without a visa provided they are bona fide tourists with valid passports and hold a confirmed date return ticket:
(a) nationals of countries exempted in the chart above

Umbrella painting, Bo Sang, Chiang Mai

ประเทศไทย
T H A I L A N D

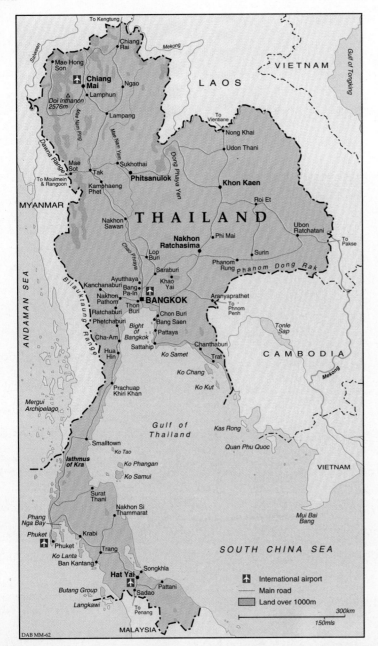

MONEY

Currency: Baht (Bt) = 100 satang. Notes are in denominations of Bt1000, 500, 100, 50, 20, 10, 5 and 1. The three smallest of these denominations are no longer issued, but are still legal tender. Coins are in denominations of Bt10, 5, 2 and 1, and 50 and 25 satangs. In addition, there are a vast number of commemorative coins which are also legal tender.
Credit cards: American Express, Access/Mastercard and Visa are widely accepted, while Diners Club has more limited use. Check with your credit card company for details of merchant acceptability and other facilities which may be available.
Eurocheques: These are acceptable.
Travellers cheques: Accepted by all banks and large hotels and shops.
Exchange rate indicators: The following figures are included as a guide to the movements of the Baht against Sterling and the US Dollar:

Date:	Oct '92	Sep '93	Jan '94	Jan '95
£1.00=	40.13	38.40	37.79	39.28
$1.00=	25.28	25.15	25.54	25.10

Currency restrictions: There are no restrictions on the import of local and foreign currency but it should be declared. Export of local currency is restricted to Bt50,000. The export of foreign currency is unlimited.
Banking hours: 0830-1530 Monday to Friday.

DUTY FREE

The following goods may be imported into Thailand without incurring customs duty:
200 cigarettes or 250g of tobacco or equal weight of cigars; 1 litre of wine or spirits; goods up to a value of Bt3000.
Note: There are restrictions on the export of items of archaeological interest or historical value without a certificate of authorisation from the Department of Fine Arts in Thailand. The export of images of Buddha and other religious artefacts is also subject to this ruling.

PUBLIC HOLIDAYS

Jan 1 '95 New Year's Day. **Feb 14** Magha Puja. **Apr 6** Chakri Day. **Apr 12-14** Songkran. **May 5** Coronation Day. **May 10** Royal Ploughing Ceremony. **May 13** Viskha Puja. **Jul 11** Asalha Puja. **Jul 12** Khao Phansa. **Aug 12** Queen's Birthday. **Oct 23** Chulalongkorn Day. **Dec 5** King's Birthday. **Dec 10** Constitution Day. **Dec 31** New Year's Eve. **Jan 1 '96** New Year's Day. **Feb** Magha Puja. **Apr 6** Chakri Day. **Apr 12-14** Songkran.

HEALTH

Regulations and requirements may be subject to change at short notice, and you are advised to contact your doctor well in advance of your intended date of departure. Any numbers in the chart refer to the footnotes below.		
	Special Precautions?	**Certificate Required?**
Yellow Fever	No	1
Cholera	Yes	2
Typhoid & Polio	Yes	-
Malaria	3	-
Food & Drink	4	-

[1]: A yellow fever vaccination certificate is required from travellers over one year of age arriving from infected areas. Countries and areas included in endemic zones are considered to be infected areas.
[2]: Following WHO guidelines issued in 1973, a cholera vaccination certificate is not a condition of entry to Thailand. However, cholera is a serious risk in this country and precautions are essential. Up-to-date advice should be sought before deciding whether these precautions should include vaccination, as medical opinion is divided over its effectiveness. See the *Health* section at the back of the book.
[3]: Malaria risk exists throughout the year in rural areas throughout the country, and especially in forested and hilly areas. There is no risk in cities and the main tourist resorts, eg Bangkok, Chiang Mai, Pattaya and Phuket. The malignant *falciparum* form is present and is reported to be 'highly resistant' to chloroquine and 'resistant' to sulfadoxine/pyrimethamine. Resistance to mefloquine and to quinine has been reported from areas near the borders to Myanmar and Cambodia.
[4]: All water should be regarded as being potentially contaminated. Water used for drinking, brushing teeth or making ice should have first been boiled or otherwise sterilised. Hotels provide free drinking water in flasks or bottles. Unpasteurised milk should be boiled, although there are a number of good dairies in Thailand (as a result

(but see note above concerning German identity cards); (b) nationals of Argentina, Austria, Brazil, Brunei, Fiji, Finland, Hong Kong (holders of British passports), Iceland, Indonesia, Kenya, Malaysia, Mexico, Myanmar, Papua New Guinea, Philippines, Senegal, Singapore, Switzerland, Turkey, Vanuatu and Western Samoa.
The following nationals are permitted to enter Thailand for tourist purposes without a visa provided a valid passport, 2 passport-size photos and a confirmed return or onward ticket is held and a visa is obtained (for a period of 15 days maximum) on arrival at the immigration checkpoints at Don Muang airport (Bangkok), Chiang Mai airport, Phuket airport and Hat Yai airport: Albania, Andorra, Antigua & Barbuda, Bahamas, Barbados, Belize, Bhutan, Bolivia, Botswana, Bulgaria, Burkina Faso, Burundi, Cameroon, Cape Verde, Central African Republic, Chad, Chile, Colombia, Comoro Islands, Costa Rica, Côte d'Ivoire, Cyprus, Djibouti, Dominica, Dominican Republic, Ecuador, Equatorial Guinea, Ethiopia, Gabon, Gambia, Grenada, Guatemala, Guinea-Bissau, Guinea Republic, Haiti, Honduras, India, Jamaica, Kiribati, Lesotho,

Liberia, Liechtenstein, Malawi, Maldives, Mali, Malta, Mauritania, Mauritius, Monaco, Morocco, Nauru, Niger, Panama, Paraguay, Peru, Rwanda, St Kitts & Nevis, St Lucia, St Vincent & the Grenadines, San Marino, São Tomé e Príncipe, Seychelles, Sierra Leone, Solomon Islands, Somalia, Suriname, Swaziland, Tanzania, Togo, Tonga, Trinidad & Tobago, Tuvalu, Uganda, Uruguay, Vatican City, Venezuela, Zaïre, Zambia and Zimbabwe.
The fee for this service is US$15 which has to be paid in US Dollars or the Thai Baht equivalent.
The following nationals are permitted to stay in Thailand for a maximum of 90 days without a visa: South Korea, New Zealand, **[2]** Denmark, Finland, Sweden and Norway.
Types of visa: *Transit:* for visits of up to 30 days; cost: £5. *Tourist:* for visits of up to 60 days; cost: £8. *Non-immigrant* (including business visits): for visits of up to 90 days; cost: £15. All visas are valid for 90 days from date of issue. It is possible to get a multiple-entry visa. When applying it is necessary to specify the number of entries required. Each entry costs an extra £8 in addition to the standard fee. The visa is only valid for six months from the date of issue.
Application to: Consulate (or Consular section at Embassy). For addresses, see top of entry.
Application requirements: (a) Passport (valid for at least 6 months after intended stay). (b) 1 completed application form. (c) 2 recent passport-size photographs. (d) Fee (cash or postal order only). (e) If requesting non-immigrant visa for business visit, letter from sponsor in country of origin guaranteeing financial status and repatriation costs. (f) Registered stamped, self-addressed envelope for postal enquiries.
Working days required: At least 48 hours.

of joint ventures with various Western governments), where pasteurised or homogenised milk may be bought. Powdered or tinned milk is available and is advised, but make sure that it is reconstituted with pure water. Avoid dairy products which are likely to have been made from unboiled milk. Only eat well-cooked meat and fish, preferably served hot. Pork, salad and mayonnaise may carry increased risk. Vegetables should be cooked and fruit peeled.

Japanese encephalitis exists particularly in rural areas between June and October. A vaccine is available, and travellers are advised to consult their doctor prior to departure. Precautions should be taken to guard against mosquito bites due to the risk of *Japanese encephalitis* and *Dengue fever*.

Rabies is present. For those at high risk, vaccination before arrival should be considered. If you are bitten abroad, seek medical advice without delay. For more information, consult the *Health* section at the back of the book.

Health care: Health insurance is recommended. Medical facilities are good in main centres. All major hotels have doctors on call.

TRAVEL - International

AIR: Thailand's national airline is *Thai Airways International (TG)*.

For free advice on air travel, call the Air Travel Advisory Bureau in the UK on (0171) 636 5000 (London) *or* (0161) 832 2000 (Manchester).

Approximate flight times: From *London* to Bangkok is 11 hours 45 minutes; from *Manila* is 3 hours 10 minutes; from *Singapore* is 2 hours 15 minutes and from *Sydney* is 11 hours.

International airports: *Bangkok International (BKK)* (Don Muang) is 30km (19 miles) north of the city (travel time – 30/45 minutes). Airport facilities include a duty-free shop, car hire *(Avis, Hertz, Sintat* and *Rent-a-Car),* 24-hour banks/bureaux de change, 24-hour restaurant and bar inside the departure lounge (0630-2315), 24-hour post office situated inside the departure lounge, accommodation and insurance bureaux (0700-2200). There is a direct coach service to Pattaya at 0900, 1200 and 1900, returning at 0600 and 1600. Limousines are available at all hours: service is every 20 minutes depending on flights.

Chiang Mai International Airport (CNX), 15km (9 miles) from the city (travel time – 20 minutes). Airport facilities include car hire *(Avis, Hertz, Sintat* and *Rent-a-Car),* banks/bureaux de change (0830-1530), restaurant (0800-2200) and bar (2100-0200). Taxi service is available to the city centre.

Phuket International Airport (HKT) is 35km (22 miles) from Phuket. Airport facilities include car hire *(Avis, Hertz, Sintat* and *Rent-a-Car),* restaurant (0800-2200) and bar (2100-0200).

Hat Yai International has recently been opened; so far it is only used for flights to Asian destinations and domestic flights. Nearest town – Songkhla (approximately 20km/12.5 miles). Taxis, bus and train services are available.

Departure tax: Bt200 for all international departures. Transit passengers and children under two years of age are exempt.

SEA: The main international port is Bangkok. Limited passenger services are available. Cargo/passenger lines: *Ben Shipping, Glen, Hansa, Polish Ocean, Royal Inter-Ocean* and *States Steamship.*

RAIL: Through trains operate to Kuala Lumpur, with daily connections to Singapore and to the borders with Cambodia (at Aranyaprathet) and Laos. The journey to Singapore takes 48 hours.

ROAD: There are international roads from Malaysia, Myanmar and Laos. Roads into Cambodia are not officially open to tourist traffic.

TRAVEL - Internal

AIR: *Thai Airways International (TG)* and *Bangkok Airways* run services to all major towns. Discounts are available in off-peak seasons and during special promotional periods.

Departure tax: Bt30 for all domestic flights. Children under two years are exempt.

RIVER: Thailand has, depending on the season, up to 1600km (1000 miles) of navigable inland waterway. Services operate between Thanon Tok and Nonthaburi, and luxury cruises are available on the *Oriental Queen.* Long-tailed motorboats and taxi-boat ferries also operate.

RAIL: The railway network extends over 4450km (2781 miles) linking all major towns with the exception of Phuket. It has recently been extended to serve centres on

the east coast. There are four main trunk routes to the northern, eastern, southern and northeastern regions, and also a line serving Thon Buri, River Kwai Bridge and Nam Tok. There are several daily services on each route, with air-conditioned, sleeping and restaurant cars on the principal trains. The journeys are leisurely but comfortable, and travelling by train is certainly one of the best ways to get around the country. The *Southern Line Express* stops at Surat Thani for those who wish then to take the bus and ferry to the offshore island of Ko Samui. Some railway timetables are published in English.

ROAD: There is a reasonable road network comprising many highways and 44,400km (27,750 miles) of national and provincial roads. All major roads are paved. Traffic drives on the left. **Bus:** There are inter-urban routes to all provinces. Fares are very cheap, and the buses very crowded. Privately owned air-conditioned buses (seats bookable) are comfortable and moderately priced. **Taxi:** There are plenty of taxis, which operate day and night. There are three types: *taxi-meter, taxis* which are unmetered and 3-wheeled *tuk-tuks.* Where there is no meter, fares should be agreed before

departure. It is sometimes possible to agree fares for longer trips even in taxi-meters. Tipping is not expected. It is also possible to take a *motorbike taxi.* These are especially useful in Bangkok's horrendous rush-hour traffic. **Car hire:** Available in all main cities. **Motorcycle** hire is also available. **Documentation:** International Driving Permit required.

URBAN: Conventional bus services in Bangkok are operated by the *Government Mass Transit Authority,* but there are also extensive private minibus operations and passenger-carrying trucks. Premium fares are charged for air-conditioned and express buses. Fares are generally low and are collected by conductors. Ferries and long-tailed motorboats operate on the Chao Phraya River which are a quick and cheap way to get about. Bus maps of the city are available, on arrival, from the tourist office at Don Muang Airport.

JOURNEY TIMES: The following chart gives approximate journey times (in hours and minutes) from Bangkok to other major cities/towns in Thailand.

	Air	Road	Rail
Chiang Rai	1.15	12.00	-
Chiang Mai	1.00	10.00	14.00

RESORTS & EXCURSIONS
Bangkok

The capital, although increasingly westernised in appearance, is underpinned by a strong sense of tradition. Thais refer to the capital as 'Krung Thep'. This is the shortened Thai name of the city which actually consists of 32 words. Bangkok is the cultural, political and financial centre of the country. The rapid pace of change and the increasing prosperity that gives the city much of its vibrancy have also caused some problems. There is too much traffic and the city is often in a state of virtual gridlock. The canals (*khlongs*) which wind their way through the city are untouched by this fast and loud streetlife. Through the city flows the *Chao Phraya River* on whose banks can be found some of the best hotels in Bangkok. It is also where visitors will also find the *Grand Palace*. Covering a huge area, this is one of the major sites. Here, also, is *Wat Phra Kaeo*, a temple-complex which houses the Emerald Buddha. This Buddha-statue is not covered in emeralds, as the name might suggest, but is made of translucent green jade. It is important to dress repectfully when visiting holy sites. Clothes should not be revealing or entry will be refused. Up river from the Grand Palace are the *Royal Barges*. These richly ornamented barges are still used today for special processions on the Chao Phraya. Within the city limits is a wealth of over 300 Buddhist temples and shrines. Most famous are *Wat Benchamabophit* (Marble Temple), *Wat Arun* (Temple of Dawn) and *Wat Trimit* (Temple of the Golden Buddha). One of the largest temple-complexes in the country is *Wat Pho*. Altogether, there are over 30 individual temples scattered here, of which the *Temple of the Reclining Buddha* is the largest. The Buddha's statue is enormous, an amazing 47.5m long and 15m high. The gardens surrounding the temples offer an escape from the hectic pace of the big city. The temple also houses the national school for traditional Thai massage. The *Floating Market* is an interesting place to visit although it has become more and more of a tourist attraction rather than a genuine market for Thais. Other sights include *Lak Muang* (the city stone), the *Erawan Shrine* where local offerings are made daily, and the *National Museum*. Housed in the Suan Pakkard Palace is a collection of precious antiques. Also interesting is the former home of the American silk-dealer *Jim Thompson* who vanished without a trace in 1967. Today the house is a craft museum with a shop selling high-quality silks at reasonable prices. The *Bangkok Zoo* and the *Snake Farm* at the Red Cross Centre where antiserums are produced also make an interesting visit.
Excursions: Up-river is the old capital of **Ayutthaya** and the old summer palace at **Bang Pa-In**. Within its confines are striking structures such as a classic Thai pavilion, a neoclassical palace, a Chinese-style pagoda and a Buddhist temple that resembles a Gothic church. East of Bangkok lies the *Ancient City*, a vast private park with models, some full-sized, some reduced, of most of Thailand's historic monuments, and the temple ruins of the Khmer Empire, situated near the Cambodian border; also just outside the city is the *Rose Garden Country Resort* with daily performances of Thai music, dance, games and ceremonies.

The Centre

The **Central Plains** north of Bangkok form the prosperous heart of the country, a rich environment that has seen the rise and fall of great cities and kingdoms. **Phitsanulok** makes a convenient base for excursions into the area. The town is also the site of the *Wat Phra Si Rattana Mahathat*. This important monastery houses the well-known Phra Buddha Chinnarat, reputedly one of the most beautiful Buddha images of Thailand. From Phitsanulok one can visit the ancient city kingdoms of **Sukhothai** and **Kamphaeng Phet**. UNESCO included Sukhothai and its environs on its list of World Heritage Sites. It covers a huge area and includes palaces, temples and pavilions as well as lakes, ponds and canals.
The province of **Kanchanaburi** now has modern hotels from which trips around this beautiful part of Thailand can be made. Kanchanaburi is the site of the famous *Bridge Over The River Kwai*; a place where thousands of Thai forced labourers and Allied prisoners of war died at the hands of the Japanese. It is an area that also boasts several beautiful waterfalls and limestone caves.
In the **northeast**, about three hours by road from Bangkok, is the **Khao Yai National Park & Wildlife Reserve**. The most popular of the country's national parks, it has been developed into a modest resort. As well as the attractions of the wildlife and jungle, the park can be used as a base to visit the many ancient and historical sites in the northeast of Thailand. The northeast also houses some excellent Khmer sites. Among these are

Hat Yai	1.15	15.00	17.00
Hua Hin	0.40	2.45	4.00
Pattaya	-	1.45	-
Phitsanulok	0.45	5.30	6.00
Phuket	1.10	10.45	-
Samui	1.10	10.45	12.00
Surat Thani	1.00	9.00	13.00
U-R*	1.45	8.00	8.30
Udon Thani	1.35	8.00	10.15

Note [*]: Ubon Ratchathani.

ACCOMMODATION

HOTELS: Bangkok has some of Asia's finest hotels, with over 12,000 rooms meeting international standards. All luxury hotels have swimming pools, 24-hour room service, air-conditioning and a high staff-to-guest ratio. Accommodation styles cover every range, however, and the budget traveller is also well catered for. Baglampho is the main area for cheap accommodation. Hotels outside the capital and developed tourist areas are less lavish but are extremely economical. Member hotels of the Thai

Hotels Association can be booked on arrival at the counter of Bangkok's Don Muang airport, and at similar counters in some provincial airports. For information, contact the Thai Hotels Association (THA), 1 Soi Pra Jane, Wireless Road, Patumwan, Bangkok 10330. Tel: (2) 251 3017. Fax: (2) 252 5582. **Grading:** There is no official system of grading hotels but prices generally give a good indication of standards. The Tourism Authority of Thailand publishes regional accommodation guides which give comprehensive details on pricing and facilities.
SELF-CATERING: Holiday villas and flats can be rented. For details, look in the English newspapers' advertisements columns.
CAMPING/CARAVANNING: Most of Thailand's campsites are in the area of the National Parks which are under the management of the Department of Forestry; there are also some private tourist resorts which provide camping facilities. In general, camping in Thailand is not popular, as other accommodation is available at such reasonable prices.
YOUTH HOSTELS: YMCA, YWCA and small, cheap hotels are available all over the country.

Bottom left: Chiang Rai. Right: Fruit market.

Pimai, **Lopburi** and **Phanom Rung**. The northeast also provides its own special festival celebrations, the most exciting being the elephant round-up at **Surin** each November.

Chiang Mai

In the far north is Thailand's second-largest city and a centre for excursions to the region's ancient and beautiful temples, the teak forests and their working elephants, caves and waterfalls, and journeys to visit the northern hill tribes. The Doi Suthep temple here is one of the most famous temples in northern Thailand. Perched high on a hilltop, it offers fine views over the city on clear days. The trip up can either be made via a funicular (price per person Bt5) or via a grand staircase with 400 steps. The banisters alone are worth a visit: a giant green-and-red glazed serpent winds its way down to end in a magnificent dragon's head. There are many small villages in the area surrounding the city where local handicrafts are produced. In the **Mae Sa Valley** there is an elephant training school and, nearby, an orchid farm; longer trips can be made to the **Doi Inthanon National Park** and to **Chiang Rai**, from which the **Mekong River** and the **Golden Triangle** can be reached. Another interesting route to take is the road to **Mae-Hon-Song** near the border with Myanmar. It is a good base from which to go trekking or motorcycle touring. On the way round the Mae-Hon-Song loop, it is possible to stop at the small town of **Pai**, a relaxed and friendly place.

Beaches

In the Eastern Gulf is **Pattaya**, South-East Asia's most renowned beach resort, and the much quieter resort of **Bang Saen**. A little further away is **Ko Samet,** an idyllic island about half an hour's boat ride from **Rayong**. Two hours south of Bangkok are **Cha'am** and **Hua Hin**. The latter was a royal watering place and is currently enjoying a renaissance.

The island of **Phuket** (attached by a causeway to the mainland) in the southwest corner of the country is one of several resorts on the Indian Ocean. In the last couple of years many new hotels have opened in Phuket, which now challenges Pattaya as the number one beach resort in South-East Asia.

Phang Nga Bay, which is readily reached from Phuket, boasts one of the world's most stunning seascapes; the area was featured in a James Bond film. Approximately 3500 islands (*hongs*) are scattered in this Bay. Though forbidding and seemingly impenetrable from the outside, they harbour a wealth of untouched fauna and flora in their hollow interior. Until recently they were believed inaccessible from the surrounding sea. There are now canoe trips through tunnels and cracks in the rock, although this is dependent on the prevailing tide. Group numbers are limited and advanced booking is recommended. It is important to treat the hongs with respect, talking should be avoided and 'souvenirs' should not be removed.

On the other side of the isthmus in the Gulf of Thailand are the islands of **Ko Samui**, a popular resort, and **Ko Panghan** which is still much less developed. **Songkhla**, on the eastern side of the Gulf, is 1300km (800 miles) from Bangkok. It is a pleasant, relaxed resort with a Chinese ambience. On the route from Bangkok to the southern islands is **Surat Thani**. This is near a national park where one can see a tract of particularly unspoiled rainforest.

POPULAR ITINERARIES: 5-day: (a) Bangkok–Pattaya–Ko Samet–Bangkok. (b) Bangkok–Ayutthaya–Phitsanulok–Sukhothai–Bangkok. **7-day:** (a) Bangkok–Chiang Mai–Chiang Rai–Golden Triangle–Bangkok. (b) Bangkok–Surat Thani–Ko Phangan–Ko Samui–Bangkok. (c) Bangkok–Mae-Hon-Song–Pai–Chiang Mai–Bangkok.

SOCIAL PROFILE

FOOD & DRINK: There are many European and Asian restaurants. Thai food is hot and spicy, but most tourist restaurants tone down the food. *Pri-kee-noo,* a tiny red or green pepper, is one of the hot ingredients that might best avoided. These are generally served on a sideplate in a vinaigrette with the main course. Thai dishes include *tom yam* (a coconut-milk soup prepared with *makroot* leaves, ginger, lemon grass, prawns or chicken); *gang pet* (hot 'red' curry with coconut milk, herbs, garlic, chillies, shrimp paste, coriander and seasoning) served with rice; *kaeng khiaw* ('green' curry with baby aubergines, beef or chicken) served with rice and *gai yang* (barbecued chicken); and *kao pat* (fried rice with pieces of crab meat, chicken, pork, onion, egg and saffron) served with onions, cucumber, soy sauce and chillies. Desserts include *salim* (sweet noodles in coconut milk) and *songkaya* (pudding of coconut milk, eggs and sugar often served in a coconut shell). Well worth trying is sticky rice and mangoes (rice cooked in coconut milk served with slices of mango), a favourite breakfast dish in the mango harvest season (March-May). Other popular fruits are *papaya, jackfruit, mangosteens, rambutans, pomelos* (similar to grapefruits) and, above all, *durians* which *farangs* (foreigners) either love or hate. Due to the strong smell of the latter, the majority of hotels do not allow them onto the premises. **Drink:** Local whisky, either *Mekhong* or *Sangthip* is worth sampling. The local beer comes in varying strengths. Fruit juices are also worh trying. Coconut milk straight from the shell is available during the harvest season. Bars have counter or table service. There are no licensing laws.

NIGHTLIFE: Bangkok's nightlife is famous the world over; there are nightclubs, open-air restaurants, classical dancing and films. Nightclubs are air-conditioned and many of the sleazier variety provide hostesses.

SHOPPING: Good buys include Thai silks and cottons, silver, pottery with *celadon* green glaze, precious and semi-precious stones, dolls, masks, lacquerware, bamboo artefacts and bronzeware. The weekend market at *Chatuchak Park* in Bangkok is a regular cornucopia with items ranging from genuine antiques to fighting fish. Tailor-made clothes are also good value and can be made in a matter of days. **Shopping hours:** 1000-1900 (department stores), 0800-2100 (others) Monday to Sunday.

SPORT: Golf courses are available in most major tourist areas. **Skindiving** is popular at Pattaya and Phuket seaside resorts, and **water-skiing** at Pattaya, inland on the Chao Phraya at Nonthaburi and at Pakred outside Bangkok. **Spectator sports: Thai kick-boxing** can be seen at the Lumpini Stadium on Tuesday, Friday and Saturday afternoon. Ratchadamnoen Stadium has bouts Monday, Wednesday, Thursday and Sunday. **Horseraces** are held at the Royal Bangkok Sports Club on Saturday and at the Royal Turf Club on Sunday.

SPECIAL EVENTS: The following is a list of major events and festivals celebrated in various parts of Thailand during 1995/6. For further details and exact dates, contact the Tourism Authority of Thailand.

Jan 1, 1995-Dec 31, 1996: *50th Anniversary Celebrations of His Majesty's Accession to the Throne.* A highlight will be the celebrations on Jun 6 which marks the actual anniversary.

Throughout 1996: *700th Anniversary of the city of Chiang Mai.*

Jan 20-22 '95 *Bo Sang Umbrella Fair.* **Jan 28-Feb 3** *Dragon and Lion Parade,* Nakhon Sawan. **Feb-Apr** *Traditional Thai Games & Sports Festival*, Bangkok. **Feb 3-5** *Flower Festival*, Chiang Mai. **Mar 23-Apr 3** *Thao Suranari Fair*, Nakhon Ratchasima. **Apr 14** *Phanom Rung Fair*, Buri Ram. **Apr 17-19** *Pattaya Festival*, Pattaya. **Apr 12-14** *Songkran Festival.* **May 10** *Royal Ploughing Ceremony*, Bangkok. **Jun** *Phi Ta Khon Festival*, Loei. **Jul 11-12** *Candle Festival*, Ubon Ratchathani. **Aug 2-8** *Rambutan Fair,* Surat Thani. **Sep** *Phichit Boat Races*, Phichit. **Sep 20** *Chinese Lunar Festival*, Songkhla. **Oct 3-9** *Illuminated Boat Procession*, Nakhon Phanom. **Oct 9** *Tak Bat Devo*, Uthai Thani. **Nov-Dec** *Mexican Sunflower Blooming Season*, Mae-Hong-Son. **Nov 4-6** *Festival of Lights*, Ayutthaya; *Loi Krathong and Candle Festival,* Sukhothai. **Nov 18-19** *Surin Elephant Round-up*, Surin. **Nov 26** *Chinese Banquet for Monkeys*, Lopburi. **Dec 10-11** *I-San Kite Festival*, Buri Ram.

SOCIAL CONVENTIONS: Present-day Thai society is the result of centuries of cultural interchange, particularly with China and India but more recently with the West. Western visitors will generally receive a handshake on meeting someone. A Thai will be greeted with the traditional closed hands and a slight bow of the head, the *wai*. Buddhist monks are always greeted in this way. The Thai Royal Family are regarded with an almost religious reverance. Visitors should respect this. It is very bad manners to make public displays of anger. Thais regard such behaviour as boorish and a loss of 'face'. Shoes should be removed before entering someone's home or a temple. Informal dress is widely acceptable and men are seldom, if ever, expected to wear suits. A traditional Thai shirt is the most suitable attire for men at any official function. Beachwear should be confined to the beach and topless sunbathing is frowned upon. Smoking is widely acceptable. **Tipping:** Most hotels will add 10% service charge and 11% government tax to the bill. Taxi drivers are not tipped.

BUSINESS PROFILE

ECONOMY: Thailand is relatively prosperous by Asian standards. Nevertheless, certain aspects of the economic performance have in recent years given cause for concern, notably the foreign debt and the shortcomings of the taxation system. Agriculture is the main economic activity, but continues to decline in relative importance as the industrial base expands and develops. The main crops are rice – of which Thailand is a leading exporter – sugar, cassava, maize, rubber, cotton and tobacco. Fishing is substantial. Timber has suffered from excessive logging, although the Government has plans to replant the now treeless areas. Thailand's other important natural resource is tin, although earnings from this too have suffered following the collapse in the mid-1980s of the London-based International Tin Council which controlled most of the world trade in the metal. The most promising discovery of late has been offshore deposits of natural gas. Industrialisation got under way in the early 1960s and Thailand now has a strong base in cement manufacturing, electronics, jewellery, sugar and oil refining. In the service sector, tourism has grown steadily during the last two decades, although it has recently been hit by political upheaval: a quick recovery is hoped for provided political stability can be maintained. Trade has been boosted by a sharp increase in industrial investment and consequent demand for machinery and equipment. Thailand's rapid and consistent growth suggests that these conditions will prevail for some time.

BUSINESS: Most people in senior management speak English but in very small companies, or those situated outside the industrial belt of Bangkok, English is less well-known. Most businesses of substantial size prefer visitors to make appointments. Visiting cards are essential. **Office hours:** 0800-1700 Monday to Friday. **Government office hours:** 0830-1200 and 1300-1630 Monday to Friday.

COMMERCIAL INFORMATION: The following organisation can offer advice: Thai Chamber of Commerce, 150 Thanon Rajbopit, Bangkok 10200. Tel: (2) 225 0086. Fax: (2) 225 3372. Telex: 72093.

CONFERENCES/CONVENTIONS: The Thailand Incentive and Convention Association has 191 members representing all sectors of business interested in conventions and incentives. Members include hotels, airlines, publishing houses, advertising agencies, cruise operators, travel agents, lawyers, equipment suppliers and banks. The aim of the association is to provide help with every possible query that an organiser may have as well as providing practical assistance. It publishes a quarterly newsletter, an annual guide, a gift-ideas catalogue and a social programme. The Bangkok Convention Centre is the largest venue in the country, but there are many other venues (including hotels) in Bangkok and elsewhere. The largest markets for delegates in 1988 were Malaysia, Japan, the USA, Taiwan and Australia, though interest from Canada and Germany showed a considerable increase. In October 1991, Thailand hosted the annual meeting of the World Bank and International Monetary Fund attended by 15,000 delegates. Further information can be obtained from the Thailand Incentive and Convention Association (TICA), Room 1509/2, 15th Floor, Bangkok Bank Building, Bangkok. Tel: (2) 235 0731. Fax: (2) 235 0730.

CLIMATE

Generally hot, particularly between mid-February and June. The monsoon season runs from May to October, when the climate is still hot with torrential rains. The best time for travelling is November to February (cool season).

Required clothing: Lightweights and rainwear are advised.

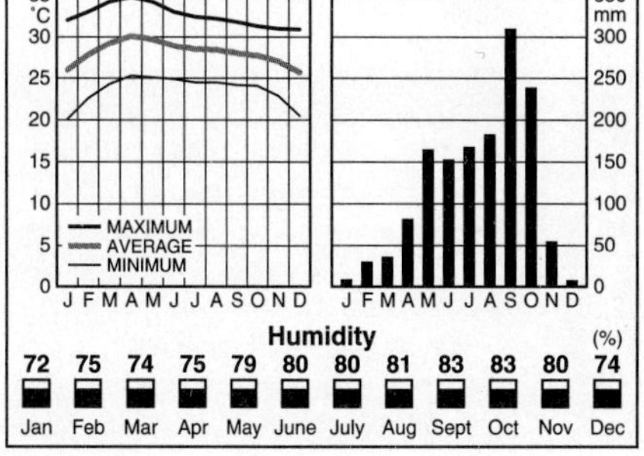

Bangkok
(elevation: 2m)
Temperature
Rainfall
35 °C 30 25 20 15 10 5 0
350 mm 300 250 200 150 100 50 0
MAXIMUM
AVERAGE
MINIMUM
J F M A M J J A S O N D
J F M A M J J A S O N D
Humidity
(%)
72 75 74 75 79 80 80 81 83 83 80 74
Jan Feb Mar Apr May June July Aug Sept Oct Nov Dec

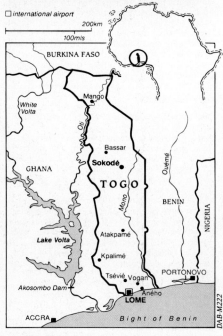

□ international airport

Location: West Africa.

Direction des Professions Touristiques
BP 1289, Lomé, Togo
Tel: 215 662. Telex: 5007.
Embassy of the Republic of Togo
8 rue Alfred Roll, 75017 Paris, France
Tel: (1) 43 80 12 13. Fax: (1) 43 80 90 71. Telex: 290497.
British Honorary Consulate
BP 20050, British School of Lomé, Lomé, Togo
Tel: 214 606. Fax: 214 989.
Embassy of the Republic of Togo and **Togo Tourist
Information Office**
2208 Massachusetts Avenue, NW, Washington, DC 20008
Tel: (202) 234 4212/3. Fax: (202) 232 3190.
Embassy of the United States of America
BP 852, angle rue Pelletier Caventou et rue Vauban,
Lomé, Togo
Tel: 217 717 or 212 991/2/3/4. Fax: 217 952.
Embassy of the Republic of Togo
12 Range Road, Ottawa, Ontario, K1N 8J3
Tel: (613) 238 5916/7. Fax: (613) 235 6425.
Consulates in: Calgary, Montréal and Toronto.
**The Canadian Embassy in Accra deals with enquiries
relating to Togo (see** *Ghana* **earlier in the book).**

AREA: 56,785 sq km (21,925 sq miles).
POPULATION: 3,643,000 (1991 estimate).
POPULATION DENSITY: 64.2 per sq km.
CAPITAL: Lomé. **Population:** 500,000 (1987).
GEOGRAPHY: Togo shares borders with Burkina Faso
to the north, Benin to the east and Ghana to the west with
a short coast on the Atlantic in the south. The country is a
narrow strip, rising behind coastal lagoons and swampy
plains to an undulating plateau. Northwards, the plateau
descends to a wide plain irrigated by the River Oti. The
central area is covered by deciduous forest while
savannah stretches to the north and south. In the east, the
River Mono runs to the sea; long sandy beaches shaded
by palms characterise the coastline between Lomé and
Cotonou in Benin.

Timatic		
Health		
GALILEO/WORLDSPAN: **TI-DFT/LFW/HE**		
SABRE: **TIDFT/LFW/HE**		
Visa		
GALILEO/WORLDSPAN: **TI-DFT/LFW/VI**		
SABRE: **TIDFT/LFW/VI**		
For more information on Timatic codes refer to Contents.		

LANGUAGE: French is the official language, while
Ewe, Watchi and Kabiyé are the most widely spoken
African languages. Very little English is spoken.
RELIGION: 50% traditional or animist, 35% Christian
and 15% Muslim.
TIME: GMT.
ELECTRICITY: 220 volts AC, 50Hz single phase.
Plugs are square or round 2-pin.
COMMUNICATIONS: Telephone: IDD is available to
main cities. Country code: 228. There are no area codes.
Outgoing international code: 00. **Telex/telegram:** Slow,
limited and expensive services are available only in the
capital (the facilities at the main post office are the least
expensive). The telegram service is dependable; calls to
France and West Africa are less expensive. **Post:** Postal
facilities are limited to main towns. *Post Restante*
facilities are available and are very reliable. Airmail to
Western Europe takes up to two weeks. **Press:**
Newspapers are exclusively in French. The main
newspaper is the government-owned *La Nouvelle
Marche.*
**BBC World Service and Voice of America
frequencies:** From time to time these change. See the
section *How to Use this Book* for more information.
BBC:

MHz:	17.79	15.40	15.07	9.600
Voice of America:				
MHz	21.49	15.60	9.525	6.035

PASSPORT/VISA

Regulations and requirements may be subject to change at short notice, and you are advised to contact the appropriate diplomatic or consular authority before finalising travel arrangements. Details of these may be found at the head of this country's entry. Any numbers in the chart refer to the footnotes below.

	Passport Required?	Visa Required?	Return Ticket Required?
Full British	Yes	No	Yes
BVP	Not valid	-	-
Australian	Yes	Yes	Yes
Canadian	Yes	No	Yes
USA	Yes	No	Yes
Other EU (As of 31/12/94)	Yes	1	Yes
Japanese	Yes	Yes	Yes

PASSPORTS: Valid passport required by all except:
(a) nationals of Ghana, Mauritania and Nigeria bearing a
'Carnet de Voyage';
(b) nationals of Benin, Burkina Faso, Central African
Republic, Chad, Côte d'Ivoire, Guinea Republic, Mali,
Niger and Senegal bearing a 'Carnet de Voyage' *or* a
valid national ID card.
Note: Joint passports are not accepted.
British Visitors Passport: Not accepted.
VISAS: Required by all except:
(a) nationals of those countries listed in the chart above;
(b) **[1]** nationals of Belgium, Denmark, France, Germany,
Greece, Ireland, Italy, Luxembourg, The Netherlands and
the UK (nationals of Portugal and Spain *do* require visas);
(c) naitonals of Andorra, Benin, Burkina Faso, Cape
Verde, Central African Republic, Chad, Côte d'Ivoire,
Gabon, Gambia, Ghana, Guinea Republic, Guinea-Bissau,
Liberia, Madagascar, Mali, Mauritania, Monaco, Niger,
Nigeria, Norway, Senegal, Sierra Leone and Sweden;
(d) nationals of Cameroon for a period of 10 days only.
Types of visa: Tourist and Business. Group visas can
also be obtained. Check with Embassy for visa fees.
Validity: 30 days. Business and Tourist visas can be
extended on arrival in Lomé at the Sûreté Nationale for
visits not exceeding 6 months.
Application to: Consulate (or Consular section at
Embassy). For address, see top of entry.
Application requirements: (a) 2 completed application
forms. (b) 3 passport-size photos. (c) Company letter for
Business visa. (d) Yellow fever vaccination certificate.
Working days required: 2 days.
Temporary residence: Apply in Togo.

MONEY

Currency: CFA Franc (CFA Fr) = 100 centimes. Notes
are in denominations of CFA Fr10,000, 5000, 1000 and
500. Coins are in denominations of CFA Fr500, 100, 50,
10, 5, 2 and 1.
Note: At the beginning of 1994, the CFA Franc was
devalued against the French Franc.
Currency exchange: Togo currency is legal tender in the
countries which formerly comprised French West Africa
(Benin, Burkina Faso, Côte d'Ivoire, Niger, Senegal and
Togo). Togo belongs to the French Franc Zone and is a
member of the West African Monetary Union. The CFA
Franc is pegged to the French Franc at a fixed rate.
Credit cards: American Express is widely accepted,

with more limited use of Diners Club, Visa and
Access/Mastercard. Check with your credit card
company for details of merchant acceptability and other
facilities which may be available.
Travellers cheques: International travellers cheques are
accepted in Lomé.
Exchange rate indicators: The following figures are
included as a guide to the movements of the CFA Franc
against Sterling and the US Dollar:

Date:	Oct '92	Sep '93	Jan '94	Jan '95
£1.00=	431.75	433.87	436.80	834 94
$1.00=	260.71	284.13	295.22	533.68

Currency restrictions: The import of local currency is
limited to CFA Fr1 million, the export to CFA Fr25,000.
There are no restrictions on the import of foreign
currency, subject to declaration. The export of foreign
currency is limited to the amount declared on entry.
Banking hours: 0800-1600 Monday to Friday.

DUTY FREE

The following goods may be imported into Togo without
incurring customs duty:
*100 cigarettes or 50 cigars or 1kg of tobacco; 1 bottle of
spirits and 1 bottle of wine; a reasonable quantity of
perfume for personal use.*
Note: Visitors may also import for the duration of their
stay clothes (not new) and personal effects, two cameras
with film, one pair of binoculars, one musical instrument,
one typewriter and small items of camping and sporting
equipment.

PUBLIC HOLIDAYS

Jan 1 '95 New Year's Day. **Jan 13** Liberation Day. **Jan
24** Day of Victory (anniversary of the failed attack at
Sarakawa). **Mar 3** Eid al-Fitr (End of Ramadan). **Apr 17**
Easter Monday. **Apr 24** Day of Victory. **Apr 27**
Independence Day. **May 1** Labour Day. **May 10** Tabaski
(Feast of the Sacrifice). **May 25** Ascension Day. **Jun 5**
Whit Monday. **Aug 15** Assumption. **Sep 24** Anniversary
of the failed attack on Lomé. **Nov 1** All Saints' Day. **Dec
25** Christmas Day. **Jan 1** '96 New Year's Day. **Jan 13**
Liberation Day. **Jan 24** Day of Victory (anniversary of
the failed attack at Sarakawa). **Feb 22** Eid al-Fitr (End of
Ramadan). **8** Easter Monday. **Apr 24** Day of Victory.
Note: Muslim festivals are timed according to local
sightings of various phases of the Moon and the dates
given above are approximations. During the lunar month
of Ramadan that precedes Eid al-Fitr, Muslims fast
during the day and feast at night and normal business
patterns may be interrupted. Many restaurants are closed
during the day and there may be restrictions on smoking
and drinking. Some disruption may continue into Eid al-
Fitr itself. Eid al-Fitr and Tabaski (Eid al-Adha) may last
anything from two to ten days, depending on the region.
For more information, see the *World of Islam* section at
the back of the book.

HEALTH

*Regulations and requirements may be subject to change at short notice, and
you are advised to contact your doctor well in advance of your intended date of
departure. Any numbers in the chart refer to the footnotes below.*

	Special Precautions?	Certificate Required?
Yellow Fever	Yes	1
Cholera	Yes	2
Typhoid & Polio	Yes	-
Malaria	3	-
Food & Drink	4	-

[1]: A yellow fever vaccination certificate is required
from travellers over one year of age arriving from all
countries.
[2]: Following WHO guidelines issued in 1973, a cholera
vaccination certificate is not a condition of entry to Togo.
However, cholera is a serious risk in this country and
precautions are essential. Up-to-date advice should be
sought before deciding whether these precautions should
include vaccination, as medical opinion is divided over its
effectiveness. See the *Health* section at the back of the book.
[3]: Malaria risk exists throughout the year in the whole
country. The predominant malignant *falciparum* form is
reported to be resistant to chloroquine.
[4]: All water should be regarded as being a potential
health risk. Water used for drinking, brushing teeth or
making ice should have first been boiled or otherwise
sterilised. Milk is unpasteurised and should be boiled.
Powdered or tinned milk is available and is advised but
make sure that it is reconstituted with pure water. Avoid
dairy products which are likely to have been made from
unboiled milk. Only eat well-cooked meat and fish,
preferably served hot. Pork, salad and mayonnaise may

carry increased risk. Vegetables should be cooked and fruit peeled.
Rabies is present. For those at high risk, vaccination before arrival should be considered. If you are bitten abroad seek medical advice without delay. For more information, consult the *Health* section at the back of the book.
Bilharzia (schistosomiasis) is present. Avoid swimming and paddling in fresh water. Swimming pools which are well-chlorinated and maintained are safe.
Health care: Health insurance and a good supply of personal medical provisions are advised.

TRAVEL - International

AIR: The main airline running services to Togo is *Air Afrique (RK)*, in which Togo is a shareholder. Togo has become an important transit point for air travel in Africa. There are frequent flights to major African destinations.
Approximate flight time: From London to Lomé is 7 hours.
International airport: *Lomé (LFW)* is 4km (2.5 miles) northeast of the city. Airport facilities include bar, restaurant, snack bar, shops, bank, post office, duty-free shop and car hire. Taxi and bus services are available to the city centre.
SEA: Ferries from Benin and Ghana call at Lomé and coastal ports. For details, contact the port authorities.
ROAD: There are routes from Benin, Ghana and Burkina Faso but conditions are unreliable.
Note: The border with Ghana is officially closed; however the situation is likely to keep changing. If the border is closed, it may be possible to obtain a pass (laissez-passer) from the Togolese Government

TRAVEL - Internal

AIR: *Air Togo* runs services to Sokodé, Mango, Dapango, Lama-Kara, Niamtougou and Lomé.
SEA: Ferries run along the coast. For details, contact the port authorities.
RAIL: There are services between Lomé, Atakpamé and Blitta; Lomé and Kpalimé; and Lomé and Aného. Trains run at least daily on each route.
ROAD: Traffic drives on the right. Tarred roads run to the border countries and the major northern route is called 'The Highway of Unity'. There are roads linking most settlements, but these are largely impassable during the rainy season. **Bus/taxi:** National bus and taxi systems are reasonably efficient and cheap. Taxis are widely available in Lomé and shared taxis are available between towns. Drivers do not expect a tip. **Car hire:** This is available in Lomé. **Documentation:** An International Driving Permit is required.

ACCOMMODATION

HOTELS: Only Lomé and Lama-Kara have international-class accommodation but there are hotels in all the main towns. There is a severe shortage of accommodation, so it is advisable to book in advance.
CAMPING: This is available free of charge though not recommended.

RESORTS & EXCURSIONS

Lomé: Togo boasts the only capital in the world which is situated right next to a border. The city itself is a mixture of the traditional, especially around the *Grand Marché*, and the modern. The fetish market, with its intriguing voodoo charms, lotions and potions, is an interesting place to wander. The coast is rather disappointing and visitors have to leave the city well behind to find a nice spot. Other towns of interest include **Togoville**, where the colonial treaty between the Germans and the ruler Mlapa III was signed. The chief still shows copies of the treaty to visitors. In the village itself, there are numerous voodoo shrines and the *Roman Catholic Cathedral*, built by the Germans. **Aného** has the most colonial atmosphere of any town in Togo, which is reflected in such attractions as the 19th-century *Peter and Paul Church*, the *Protestant Church* and the *German Cemetery*. The short coastline is home to several small fishing villages, sometimes with examples of colonial architecture.
Togo's wildlife parks include the *Fazao National Park* outside **Sokodé**, the *Kéran National Park* near **Kara** and the *Fosse aux Lions* (Lions' Den) southwest of **Dapaong**.

SOCIAL PROFILE

FOOD & DRINK: Most restaurants catering for visitors tend to be French orientated, although some do serve African dishes. In Lomé in particular, there are many small cafés serving local food. Dishes include soups based on palm nut, groundnut and maize. Meat, poultry and seafoods are plentiful and well prepared, as are the local fruit and vegetables. **Drink:** A good selection of alcoholic drinks is available – some produced locally.

NIGHTLIFE: There are numerous nightclubs, particularly in Lomé. Most serve food and are open until the early hours for dancing to a mixture of West African and Western popular music. There are also cinemas showing French and English-language films.
SHOPPING: Market purchases include wax prints, indigo cloth, Kente and dye-stamped Adinkira cloth from Ghana, embroideries, batik and lace from The Netherlands, locally-made heavy marble ashtrays, gold and silver jewellery, traditional masks, wood sculpture and religious statuettes. Voodoo stalls display an extraordinary range of items used in magic, among them, cowrie shells. **Shopping hours:** 0800-1730 Monday to Friday; 0730-1230 Saturday.
SPORT: Beaches are unsafe for all but the best swimmers, but there are several pools along the beach at Lomé. Hotel pools and the lakeside resort of Porto Seguro (a short drive from Lomé) offer safe **swimming**. There are also **water-skiing** and **sailing** facilities at Porto Seguro. Some hotels have **tennis** courts.
SPECIAL EVENTS: The following is a selection of festivals and special events celebrated annually in Togo:
Mid-Jul *Evala* (initiation ceremonies, a custom which involves traditional wrestling), Kabiyé region; *Akpema* (girls' initiation ceremonies), Kabiyé region. **Aug** *Kpessosso* (a harvest festival of the Guens); *Ayize* (Bean Harvest Festival celebrated by the Ewe). **First Thursday in Sep** *Agbogbozan* (Ewe Diaspora Festival). **First Week of Sep** *Dipontre* (Yam Festival), Bassar region. **Dec** *Kamou* (Harvest Festival), Kabiyé region.
SOCIAL CONVENTIONS: Music and dance are the most popular forms of culture. The Togolese have had a varied colonial heritage which has resulted in the variety of Christian denominations and European languages; the voodoo religion is a strong influence in the country and many young girls, after fulfilling an initiation period, will devote their lives to serving the religion and the voodoo village priest. Practical, casual clothes are suitable. Beachwear should not be worn away from the beach or poolside. **Tipping:** When not included, a tip of about 10% is customary. Taxi drivers do not usually expect a tip.

BUSINESS PROFILE

ECONOMY: Although most of the population is employed in agriculture, Togo's principal export earners are the ores from the country's phosphate mines. A wide range of tropical crops is produced: cocoa, coffee, palm kernels, cotton, copra, groundnuts and maize. New projects include the growing of tomatoes, herbs and sugar. Most of the country's industry is based on the processing of these products, apart from a handful of factories engaged in textiles, marble and consumer goods for domestic consumption. There is little other industrial output apart from the very high-quality phosphate which is one of the country's main sources of foreign exchange. The mining industry is under government control. France is Togo's leading trading partner followed by The Netherlands. In the region, Côte d'Ivoire and Senegal have significant trade links, much of it based on re-export from Togo of imported consumer goods. IMF-imposed austerity measures, in force throughout the 1980s, have continued into the next decade. The economy remains weak, suffering from low commodity prices and a lack of investment arising from continuing political unrest.
BUSINESS: It is acceptable for visiting business people to wear a safari suit except on very formal business and social occasions. Business is conducted in French, only a few executives speak English. Appointments should be made and business cards should be carried. **Office hours:** 0700-1730 Monday to Friday.
COMMERCIAL INFORMATION: The following can offer advice: Chambre de Commerce, d'Agriculture et d'Industrie du Togo (CCAIT), BP 360, angle avenue de la Présidence, Lomé. Tel: 217 065. Fax: 214 730. Telex: 5023.

CLIMATE

From December to January the *Harmattan* wind blows from the north. The rainy season lasts from April to July. Short rains occur from October to November. The driest and hottest months are February and March.

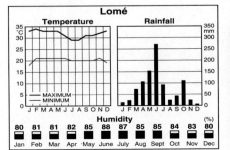
Lomé

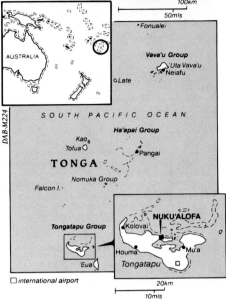
□ *international airport*

Location: South Pacific.

Tonga Visitors' Bureau
PO Box 37, Vuna Road, Nuku'alofa, Tonga
Tel: 23366. Fax: 22129. Telex: 66269 (a/b PRIMO TS).
High Commission for the Kingdom of Tonga
36 Molyneux Street, London W1H 6AB
Tel: (0171) 724 5828. Fax: (0171) 723 9074.
Opening hours: 0900-1700 Monday to Friday.
British High Commission
PO Box 56, Vuna Road, Nuku'alofa, Tonga
Tel: 21020/1. Fax: 24109. Telex: 66226 (a/b UKREP TS).
Tonga General Consulate
Suite 604, 360 Post Street, San Francisco, CA 94108
Tel: (415) 781 0365. Fax: (415) 781 3964.
The Canadian High Commission in Wellington deals with enquiries relating to Tonga (*see New Zealand earlier in the book*).

AREA: 748 sq km (289 sq miles).
POPULATION: 94,485 (1989 estimate).
POPULATION DENSITY: 121 per sq km.
CAPITAL: Nuku'alofa. **Population:** 21,383 (1986).
GEOGRAPHY: Tonga is an archipelago of 172 islands in the South Pacific, most of which are uninhabited, covering an area of 7700 sq km (3000 sq miles). The major island groups are Tongatapu and 'Eua, Ha'apai and Vava'u. Tonga's high volcanic and low coral forms give the islands a unique character. Some volcanoes are still active and Falcon Island in the Vava'u group is a submerged volcano that erupts periodically, its lava and ash rising above sea level forming a visible island which disappears when the eruption is over. Nuku'alofa, on Tongatapu Island, has a reef-protected harbour lined with palms. The island is flat with a large lagoon, but no running streams, and many surrounding smaller islands. 'Eua Island is hilly and forested with high cliffs and beautiful beaches. The Ha'apai Islands, a curving archipelago 160km (100 miles) north of Tongatapu, have excellent beaches. Tofua, the largest island in the group, is an active volcano with a hot steaming lake in its crater. The Vava'u Islands, 90km (50 miles) north of Ha'apai, are hilly, densely wooded and interspersed with a maze of narrow channels. They are known for their stalagmite-filled caves.

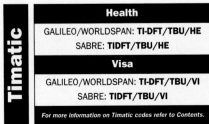

Health	
GALILEO/WORLDSPAN: **TI-DFT/TBU/HE**	
SABRE: **TIDFT/TBU/HE**	
Visa	
GALILEO/WORLDSPAN: **TI-DFT/TBU/VI**	
SABRE: **TIDFT/TBU/VI**	

For more information on Timatic codes refer to Contents.

Timatic

LANGUAGE: Tongan and English.
RELIGION: Wesleyan Church, Roman Catholic, Anglicans.
TIME: GMT + 13.
ELECTRICITY: 240 volts AC, 50Hz.
COMMUNICATIONS: Telephone: IDD is available. Country code: 676. There are no area codes. Outgoing international code: 0. **Fax:** *Cable & Wireless* provide fax services. **Telex/telegram:** Telegrams and cables can be booked through *Cable & Wireless Limited,* Tonga. **Post:** The main post office is located in the centre of Nuku'alofa and open 0830-1600 Monday to Friday. All mail must be collected from the post office. Airmail to Europe takes approximately ten days. There are branch offices on Ha'apai and Vava'u. **Press:** The *Tonga Chronicle* and *The Times of Tonga* are the weekly newspapers.
BBC World Service and Voice of America frequencies: From time to time these change. See the section *How to Use this Book* for more information.
BBC:

MHz	17.83	15.34	11.95	9.740

Voice of America:

MHz	18.82	15.18	9.525	1.735

PASSPORT/VISA

Regulations and requirements may be subject to change at short notice, and you are advised to contact the appropriate diplomatic or consular authority before finalising travel arrangements. Details of these may be found at the head of this country's entry. Any numbers in the chart refer to the footnotes below.

	Passport Required?	Visa Required?	Return Ticket Required?
Full British	Yes	No/1	Yes
BVP	Not valid	-	-
Australian	Yes	No/1	Yes
Canadian	Yes	No/1	Yes
USA	Yes	No/1	Yes
Other EU (As of 31/12/94)	Yes	No/1	Yes
Japanese	Yes	No/1	Yes

Note: All passengers must be in possession of valid onward or return tickets and have proof of adequate funds for their stay. If visitors wish to extend their stay beyond 30 days, they must request permission from the Principal Immigration Officer, who may grant permission for up to 6 months.
PASSPORTS: Valid passport required by all.
British Visitors Passport: Not accepted.
VISAS: [1] Visas are issued on arrival to nationals of all countries.
Types of visa: Tourist and Business. Cost: free.
Validity: 30 days.
Application to: Consular section at Embassy or High Commission. For addresses, see top of entry.
Working days: 2-7 days.

MONEY

Currency: Pa'anga (T$) = 100 seniti. Notes are in denominations of T$50, 20, 10, 5, 2 and 1, and 50 seniti. Coins are in denominations of T$2 and 1, and 50, 20, 10, 5, 2 and 1 seniti.
Credit cards: Limited use of both Diners Club and Visa.
Travellers cheques: Accepted at banks and at some hotels and tourist shops.
Exchange rate indicators: The following figures are included as a guide to the movements of the Pa'anga against Sterling and the US Dollar:

Date:	Oct '92	Sep '93	Jan '94	Jan '95
£1.00=	2.22	2.36	2.18	2.02
$1.00=	1.40	1.55	1.47	1.29

Currency restrictions: There are no restrictions on the import or export of foreign or local currencies.
Banking hours: 0930-1530 Monday to Friday; 0900-1200 Saturday.

DUTY FREE

The following goods may be imported into Tonga by persons over 18 years of age without incurring customs duty:
400 cigarettes; 2 litres of spirits or wine.
Note: (a) The import of arms, ammunition and pornography is prohibited. (b) Birds, animals, fruit and plants are subject to quarantine regulations. (c) There are several duty-free shops in Tonga. (d) The export of valuable artefacts and certain flora and fauna is restricted.

PUBLIC HOLIDAYS

Jan 1 '95 New Year's Day. **Apr 14-17** Easter. **Apr 14-17** Easter. **Apr 25** ANZAC Day. **May 4** HRH The Crown Prince's Birthday. **Jun 4** Independence Day. **Jul**

4 HM The King's Birthday. **Nov 4** Constitution Day. **Dec 4** Tupou I Day. **Dec 25-26** Christmas. **Jan 1 '96** New Year's Day. **Apr 5-8** Easter. **Apr 25** ANZAC Day.

HEALTH

Regulations and requirements may be subject to change at short notice, and you are advised to contact your doctor well in advance of your intended date of departure. Any numbers in the chart refer to the footnotes below.

	Special Precautions?	Certificate Required?
Yellow Fever	No	1
Cholera	No	No
Typhoid & Polio	Yes	-
Malaria	No	-
Food & Drink	2	-

[1]: A yellow fever vaccination certificate is required from travellers over one year of age arriving from infected areas.
[2]: Mains water in Nuku'alofa is normally chlorinated, and whilst relatively safe may cause mild abdominal upsets. Drinking water outside the capital should be considered a potential health risk and sterilisation is advisable. Bottled water is available and is advised for the first few weeks of the stay. Milk is pasteurised and dairy products are safe for consumption. Local meat, poultry, seafood, fruit and vegetables are generally considered safe to eat.
Health care: Health insurance is recommended. There are medical facilities in all major centres. For emergency services, dial 911.

TRAVEL - International

AIR: The main airline serving Tonga is *Air Pacific (FJ)*. *Air New Zealand* and *Polynesian Airways* also serve the country. *Polynesian Airways* offer a 'Polypass' which allows the holder to fly anywhere on the airline's network: Sydney (Australia), Auckland (New Zealand), Western Samoa, American Samoa, the Cook Islands, Vanuatu, New Caledonia, Fiji and, on payment of a supplement, Tahiti. The pass is valid for 30 days.
Approximate flight time: From London to Nuku'alofa is 20 hours.
International airport: *Tongatapu (TBU)* is 21km (13 miles) from Nuku'alofa. Transport by taxi and bus is available. There are car hire services and a duty-free shop.
Departure tax: T$15. There are no exemptions.
SEA: Ports of entry are Nuku'alofa, Pangai, Neiafu, Niuatoputapu. There are no regular passenger services, but berths may be available on cruise ships.

TRAVEL - Internal

AIR: *Royal Tongan Airlines* provide regular services between Vava'u, Ha'apai, 'Eua, Niuatoputapu and Tongatapu. Bookings and information are available from *Royal Tongan Airlines,* Nuku'alofa.
SEA: Local ferries sail between all the island groups. There are regular sailings from Faua Wharf in Nuku'alofa to Ha'apai and Vava'u. Ferry schedules are subject to change according to demand or the weather.
ROAD: Traffic drives on the left. There is a good network of sealed roads. Horses are often used. **Bus:** Minibus services are available throughout Tongatapu.
Taxi: Saloon-car taxis, minimokes, mini-buses and *ve'etolus* (3-wheeler open-air taxis) are available. There are no fixed rates, therefore it is advisable to negotiate the cost beforehand. **Car hire:** May be arranged through various agencies. Self-drive or chauffeur-driven cars are available. **Documentation:** A current local driving licence is required, available from the Police Traffic Department in Nuku'alofa on production of a valid national or international licence, the fee and a passport. The minimum driving age is 18.
JOURNEY TIMES: The following chart gives approximate journey times (in hours and minutes) from Nuku'alofa to other major centres on Tonga.

	Air	Sea
Neiafu (Vava'u)	1.00	24.00
Pangai (Ha'apai)	0.30	18.00
'Eua	0.10	3.00

ACCOMMODATION

HOTELS: There are excellent hotels, motels and resort villages of Tongan-style houses. Traditional boarding houses are also very popular with tourists. There is a growing selection of accommodation and capacity is expected to increase to 900 rooms. Contact the Tonga Visitors Bureau for a complete list of available accommodation. For address, see top of entry.
CAMPING: Niu-akalo Hotel offers camping grounds.

RESORTS & EXCURSIONS
Tongatapu Group

Sightseeing on Tongatapu should include the *Royal Palace* on the waterfront in **Nuku'alofa,** just beyond Vuna Wharf. The Palace was completed in 1867. The grounds are decorated with tropical shrubs and flowers. While visitors are not allowed to enter the palace or gardens, there are good views from the low surrounding walls. The *Mala'ekula* (Royal Tombs) are situated in the southern part of the business district along Taufa'ahau Road. The tombs have been a burial place for Tongan royalty since 1893. One of the most impressive sights in Tonga are the *Blow Holes,* found along the coastline at **Houma,** 14.5km (9 miles) from Nuku'alofa. Waves send sea water spurting some 18m (60ft) into the air through holes in the coral reef. This stretch of coastline is known as the **Mapu 'a Vaea** (the Chief's Whistle) by Tongans because of the whistling sound made by the geyser-like spouts.
At **Kolovai,** 18km (11 miles) west of Nuku'alofa, one can find the rare *flying foxes,* dark brown fruit bats, some with wingspans of up to 1m (3ft). The *Ha'atafu* and *Monotapu* beaches are also situated at the western end of the island; they are easily accessible and well protected.
On the eastern end of the island are the *Langi* (Terraced Tombs), 9.5km (6 miles) from the Ha'amonga Trilithon (see below) towards Nuku'alofa. The tombs form quadrilateral mounds faced with huge blocks of stone rising in terraces to heights of 4m (13ft), built for the old *Tu'i tonga* (Spiritual Kings). The stones are of coral, built around AD1200, possibly carried from Wallis Island on large canoes known as *lomipeau*.
Ha'amonga Trilithon is a massive stone arch possibly used as a seasonal calendar, erected at the same time as the Terraced Tombs and again made from coral. Each stone is thought to weigh in the region of 40,000kg (about 40 tons).
Other sights include: The *Anahulu Cave,* an underground cavern of stalactites and stalagmites near the beach of the same name, about 24km (15 miles) from the capital; and *Oholei Beach,* with good bathing and excellent barbecues organised by the *International Dateline Hotel.*
The island of **'Eua,** a 10-minute flight away from Tongatapu, has recently been promoted as a tourist destination. It has a blend of modern comfort (the island has one hotel and a motel) and the traditional South Sea island lifestyle. Many species of exotic birds live on the island.

Vava'u Group

Lying 240km (150 miles) north of Tongatapu, this cluster of 50 or so thickly wooded islands has one hotel, one motel, one beach resort and four guest-houses. There is a daily 1-hour flight from the capital and a weekly ferry service; private cruisers and ferries also operate from the harbour at **Neiafu,** the main town. There is excellent diving, with visibility often as much as 30m (100ft). Other attractions include the *Fangatongo Royal Residence,* the view from *Mount Talau* and *Sailoame Market* in Neiafu.

SOCIAL PROFILE

FOOD & DRINK: Restaurants have table service, and are found mainly in hotels. Apart from hotel and boarding-house dining rooms, there are restaurants featuring Tongan, French, Taiwanese and Japanese cuisine. Local staples are *'ufi* (a large white yam) and *taro*. Other dishes include *lu pullu* (meat and onions, marinaded in coconut milk, baked in *taro* leaves in an underground oven), *feke* (grilled octopus or squid in coconut sauce), devilled clams, *'ota* (raw fish marinaded in lemon juice) and lobster. Tropical fruits and salads are excellent. Feasts play a major role in the Tongan lifestyle. Up to 30 different dishes may be served on a *pola* (a long tray of plaited coconut fronds), and will typically include suckling pig, crayfish, chicken, octopus, pork and vegetables steamed in an *umu* (underground oven), served with a variety of tropical fruits.
NIGHTLIFE: Nightlife is sedate, limited to music and dancing in the hotels, clubs and occasionally at the *Yacht Club*. Floorshows are held on some nights in the main hotels and the Tongan National Centre. Tongan feasts and entertainment are also organised.
SHOPPING: Special purchases are hand-decorated and woven *tapa* cloth, woven floor coverings, *To'avala pandanus* mats, woven *pandanus* baskets, 'Ali Baba' laundry baskets, polished coconut-shell goblets and ashtrays, model outrigger canoes, tortoiseshell ornaments, brooches, earrings, rings and silver-inlaid knives. Tongan stamps and coins are collectors' items; complete sets are on sale at the philatelic section of the Tongan Treasury. There are duty-free shops on Tongatapu and Vava'u. A government tax of 5% is added to all bills for goods and services. **Shopping hours:** 0800-1700 Monday to Friday; 0800-1200 Saturday.
SPORT: There are sandy beaches and excellent

swimming throughout the islands, with pools at some hotels. **Surfing:** There is a world-standard surfing beach on the island of 'Eua, 11km (7 miles) from Tongatapu. Niutoua Beach, on the main island, and Ha'apai and Vava'u islands are also good for surfing. **Horseriding:** Horses are available on 'Eua, Vava'u and Tongatapu Islands. **Fishing:** There are plentiful game fish including barracuda, tuna, marlin and sailfish. Charter boats are available. **Water-skiing:** Available in Tongatapu. **Diving:** Tongan coral reefs provide great beauty and variety for **scuba diving** and **snorkelling;** fully equipped boats, scuba diving and snorkelling equipment can be hired. Contact the Tonga Visitors Bureau for information. **SPECIAL EVENTS: May '95** *Vava'u Festival.* **Jul** *Heilala Festival.*

SOCIAL CONVENTIONS: Shaking hands is a suitable form of greeting. Although by Western standards Tongan people are by no means rich, meals served to visitors will always be memorable. A token of appreciation, while not expected, is always welcome, especially gifts from the visitor's homeland. Casual wear is acceptable, but beachwear should be confined to the beach. *It is illegal not to wear a shirt in public.* Sunday is regarded as a sacred day, an aspect of Tongan life thrown into sharp relief by the controversy surrounding the so-called 'Tongan loop'. The International Date Line forms a loop around the islands, thereby making them a day ahead of Samoa, even though Samoa is almost due north of Tonga. Members of the Seventh Day Adventist Church therefore maintain that a Tongan Sunday is really a Saturday, and are unwilling to attend church on a day which is only a Sunday because of an apparently arbitrary manifestation of international law. This complex and almost insoluable problem may cause visitors a certain amount of confusion, but travellers to Tonga are advised to respect the religious beliefs of the islanders. **Tipping:** Not encouraged, but no offence is caused if services are rewarded in this way.

BUSINESS PROFILE

ECONOMY: Tonga's economy produces mostly agricultural items, such as copra, bananas, squash pumpkins and dessicated coconut meal. Manufacturing activities are scarce other than handicrafts to supply the slowly growing tourist trade, although small manufacturing enterprises and food-processing are potential growth areas. The search for oil continues offshore despite repeated failures to find deposits. The island's main imports are flour, meat, oil products, machinery and transport equipment, as well as manufactured goods. Australia and New Zealand are the main suppliers and the largest markets for Tongan goods. Some UK exports appear in Tonga as re-exported products from Australia and New Zealand. In a recent development, Tonga has exploited its geographical position to lay claim to six geostationary satellite positions to be used for trans-Pacific communications. With the approval of the relevant international governing body (*Intelsat*), the *Tongasat* company earns valuable revenue for the country by leasing these facilities to foreign telecommunications operators.
BUSINESS: Shirts and ties will suffice for business visits. English and French are widely spoken. **Office hours:** 0830-1630 Monday to Friday; 0800-1200 Saturday.
COMMERCIAL INFORMATION: The following organisation can offer advice: Office of the Minister of Labour, Commerce and Industries, PO Box 110, Nuku'alofa, Tonga. Tel: 23688. Fax: 23887. Telex: 66235.

CLIMATE

Tonga's climate is marginally cooler than most tropical areas. The best time is from May to November. Heavy rains occur from December to March.

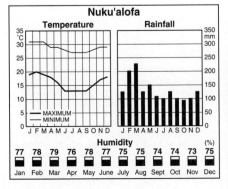

Trinidad & Tobago

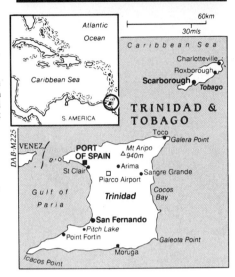

Location: Southern Caribbean, off Venezuelan coast.

Tourism and Industry Development Corporation of Trinidad and Tobago (TIDCO)
Albion Court, 61 Dundonald Street, Port of Spain, Trinidad
Tel: 624 2953. Fax: 625 4755.
Trinidad & Tobago Hotel and Tourism Association
Uptown Mall, 44-58 Edward Street, Port of Spain, Trinidad
Tel: 624 3928. Fax: 624 3928.
High Commission for the Republic of Trinidad & Tobago
42 Belgrave Square, London SW1X 8NT
Tel: (0171) 245 9351. Fax: (0171) 823 1065. Opening hours: 0900-1700 Monday to Friday; 1000-1400 Monday to Friday (for visa applications).
Trinidad & Tobago Tourism Office
The Tourist Office is in the process of moving offices. Tel: (0181) 367 5449. (Temporary contact number).
British High Commission
PO Box 778, 3rd & 4th Floors, Furness House, 90 Independence Square, Port of Spain, Trinidad
Tel: 625 2861/2/3/4/5/6. Fax: 623 0621.
Embassy of the Republic of Trinidad & Tobago
1708 Massachusetts Avenue, NW, Washington, DC 20036
Tel: (202) 467 6490. Fax: (202) 785 3130.
Consulate in: New York (tel: (212) 682 7272 *or* 682 7399).
Trinidad & Tobago Tourism Development Authority
Suite 1508, 25 West 43rd Street, New York, NY 10036
Tel: (212) 719 0540. Fax: (212) 719 0988.
Also deals with enquiries from Canada.
Embassy of the United States of America
PO Box 752, 15 Queen's Park West, Port of Spain, Trinidad
Tel: 622 6372/6 *or* 622 6176. Fax: 628 5462.
High Commission for the Republic of Trinidad & Tobago
Suite 508, 75 Albert Street, Ottawa, Ontario K1P 5E7
Tel: (613) 232 2418/9. Fax: (613) 232 4349.
Consulates in: Willowdale and Winnipeg.
Canadian High Commission
PO Box 1246, Huggins Building, 72 South Quay, Port of Spain, Trinidad
Tel: 623 7254. Fax: 624 4016. Telex: 22429 (a/b DOMCAN WG).

Timatic	Health	
	GALILEO/WORLDSPAN: **TI-DFT/POS/HE**	
	SABRE: **TIDFT/POS/HE**	
	Visa	
	GALILEO/WORLDSPAN: **TI-DFT/POS/VI**	
	SABRE: **TIDFT/POS/VI**	
	For more information on Timatic codes refer to Contents.	

AREA: 5128 sq km (1980 sq miles).
POPULATION: 1,253,000 (1991 estimate).
POPULATION DENSITY: 244.3 per sq km.
CAPITAL: Port of Spain. **Population:** 59,200 (1988 estimate).
GEOGRAPHY: Trinidad and her tiny sister island of Tobago lie off the Venezuelan coast. Along the north of Trinidad runs the Northern Range of mountains, looming over the country's capital, Port of Spain. South of Port of Spain on the west coast the terrain is low, and the Caroni Swamps contain a magnificent bird sanctuary largely inhabited by the scarlet ibis. On the north and east coast lie beautiful beaches. Central Trinidad is flat and largely given over to agriculture.
LANGUAGE: The official language is English. French, Spanish, Hindi and Chinese are also spoken.
RELIGION: 36% Roman Catholic, 23% Hindu, 21% Anglican, 14% other Christian denominations and 6% Muslim.
TIME: GMT - 4.
ELECTRICITY: 115 volts AC, 60Hz. Continental 2-pin plugs are standard, though variations may be found.
COMMUNICATIONS: Telephone: IDD is available. Country code: 1 809. There are no area codes. Outgoing international code: 01. **Fax:** Some hotels have facilities.
Telex/telegram: Port of Spain has good facilities in Independence Square and Edward Street; *Textel* is open 24 hours a day. Cables can also be sent from hotels and the airport. Telex facilities are also available in Scarborough, Tobago, run by *Cable & Wireless (WI) Ltd.*
Post: The main post office is on Wrightson Road, Port of Spain. Airmail to Western Europe takes up to two weeks.
Press: English-language dailies include *The Sun, The Trinidad Guardian, The Trinidad & Tobago Express* and *USA Today.*
BBC World Service and Voice of America frequencies: From time to time these change. See the section *How to Use this Book* for more information.
BBC:

MHz	17.84	15.22	9.915	5.975
Voice of America:				
MHz	15.21	11.70	6.130	0.930

PASSPORT/VISA

Regulations and requirements may be subject to change at short notice, and you are advised to contact the appropriate diplomatic or consular authority before finalising travel arrangements. Details of these may be found at the head of this country's entry. Any numbers in the chart refer to the footnotes below.

	Passport Required?	Visa Required?	Return Ticket Required?
Full British	Yes	No	Yes
BVP	Not valid	-	-
Australian	Yes	Yes	Yes
Canadian	Yes	No	Yes
USA	Yes	No	Yes
Other EU (As of 31/12/94)	Yes	No	Yes
Japanese	Yes	Yes	Yes

PASSPORTS: Valid passport required by all persons 16 years and over. Passports must be valid at least for the duration of stay and visitors must be in possession of a valid return ticket to their country of residence or citizenship and sufficient funds to maintain themselves whilst in Trinidad & Tobago.
British Visitors Passport: Not accepted.
VISAS: Required by all except:
(a) nationals of EU countries;
(b) nationals of the USA arriving as tourists for stays not exceeding 2 months;
(c) nationals of Antigua & Barbuda, Austria, Bahamas, Bangladesh, Barbados, Belize, Botswana, Brazil, Canada, Colombia, Cyprus, Dominica, Finland, French Guiana, Gambia, Ghana, Grenada, Guadeloupe, Guyana, Iceland, Israel, Jamaica, Kenya, Kiribati, Lesotho, Liechtenstein, Malawi, Malaysia, Malta, Martinique, Mauritius, Nauru, Netherlands Antilles, Norway, Pakistan, St Kitts & Nevis, St Lucia, St Vincent & the Grenadines, Seychelles, Sierra Leone, Singapore, Solomon Islands, Suriname, Sweden, Swaziland, Switzerland, Tonga, Turkey, Tuvalu, Vanuatu, Western Samoa, Zambia and Zimbabwe for stays not exceeding 3 months;
(d) nationals of Venezuela arriving from Venezuela for stays not exceeding 14 days.
Types of visa: Tourist. Cost: £8.50.
Validity: 3 months.
Application to: Consulate (or Consular section at Embassy or High Commission). For addresses, see top of entry.
Working days required: Tourist visas will normally be issued within 48 hours. Applications from the following nationals must be made at least 3-4 weeks prior to the

Nuku'alofa

Temperature / Rainfall / Humidity

	Jan	Feb	Mar	Apr	May	June	July	Aug	Sept	Oct	Nov	Dec
Humidity (%)	77	78	79	76	78	77	75	75	74	74	73	75

proposed date of departure as they have to be referred to the authorities in Port of Spain: Albania, Bosnia-Hercegovina, Bulgaria, China, Croatia, CIS, Cuba, Czech Republic, Dominican Republic, Estonia, Haiti, Hungary, Iraq, Jordan, North Korea, Kuwait, Former Yugoslav Republic of Macedonia, Latvia, Lebanon, Lithuania, Libya, Nigeria, Papua New Guinea, Poland, Romania, Saudi Arabia, Slovak Republic, Slovenia, Sri Lanka, Syria, Taiwan (China), Tanzania, Uganda, Vietnam and Yugoslavia (Serbia and Montenegro).
Temporary residence: Enquire at Embassy or High Commission.

MONEY

Currency: Trinidad & Tobago Dollar (TT$) = 100 cents. Notes are in denominations of TT$100, 20, 10, 5 and 1. Coins are in denominations of TT$1, and 50, 25, 10, 5 and 1 cents.
Currency exchange: Foreign currency can only be exchanged at authorised banks and some hotels. Delays may be experienced in obtaining foreign exchange, though banks are authorised to sell up to £50 in Sterling notes for legitimate travelling requirements.
Credit cards: Access/Mastercard, Diners Club, American Express and Visa are accepted by selected banks, shops and tourist facilities. Check with your credit card company for details of merchant acceptability and other services which may be available.
Travellers cheques: These are very widely accepted and will often prove the most convenient means of transaction. Banks charge a fee for exchanging travellers cheques. Check for the best rates.
Exchange rate indicators: The following figures are included as a guide to the movements of the Trinidad & Tobago Dollar against Sterling and the US Dollar:

Date:	Oct '92	Sep '93	Jan '94	Jan '95
£1.00=	7.20	8.47	8.15	8.87
$1.00=	4.53	5.55	5.51	5.67

Currency restrictions: Residents can import up to TT$200 in local currency, for non-residents the import of local currency is unlimited. The export of local currency is limited to TT$200. There is free import of foreign currency, subject to declaration. The export of foreign currency is limited to the amount declared on entry. Residents can export up to TT$2500 in foreign currency per year, all other amounts have to be authorised by the Exchange Control Department.
Banking hours: 0900-1400 Monday to Thursday; 0900-1200 and 1500-1700 Friday.

DUTY FREE

The following goods may be imported into Trinidad & Tobago by persons over 17 years of age without incurring customs duty:
200 cigarettes or 50 cigars or 225g of tobacco; 1.136 litres of wine or spirits; gifts up to the value of US$50.

PUBLIC HOLIDAYS

Jan 1 '95 New Year's Day. **Feb 27-28** Carnival. **Mar 3** Eid al-Fitr. **Apr 14-17** Easter. **Jun 5** Whit Monday. **Jun 15** Corpus Christi. **Jun 19** Labour Day. **Aug 1** Emancipation Day. **Aug 31** Independence Day. **Sep 24** Republic Day. **Oct** Divali. **Dec 25-26** Christmas. **Jan 1 '96** New Year's Day. **Feb** Carnival. **Feb 22** Eid al-Fitr. **Apr 5-8** Easter.
Note: (a) Muslim festivals are timed according to local sightings of various phases of the Moon and the dates given above are approximations. During the lunar month of Ramadan that precedes Eid al-Fitr, Muslims fast during the day and feast at night and normal business patterns may be interrupted. However, since Trinidad & Tobago is not a predominantly Muslim country, restrictions (which travellers may experience elsewhere) are unlikely to cause problems. (b) Hindu festivals are declared according to local astronomical observations and it is only possible to forecast the month of their occurrence.

HEALTH

Regulations and requirements may be subject to change at short notice, and you are advised to contact your doctor well in advance of your intended date of departure. Any numbers in the chart refer to the footnotes below.		
	Special Precautions?	**Certificate Required?**
Yellow Fever	No	1
Cholera	No	No
Typhoid & Polio	Yes	-
Malaria	No	-
Food & Drink	2	-

[1]: A yellow fever vaccination certificate is required of travellers over one year of age arriving from infected areas.
[2]: Mains water is normally chlorinated, and whilst relatively safe may cause mild abdominal upsets. Bottled water is available and is advised for the first few weeks of the stay. Drinking water outside main cities and towns may be contaminated and sterilisation is advisable. Milk is pasteurised and dairy products are safe for consumption. Local meat, poultry, seafood, fruit and vegetables are generally considered safe to eat.
Rabies is present. For those at high risk, vaccination before arrival should be considered. If you are bitten abroad seek medical advice without delay. Bats are a problem as far as the transmission of rabies is concerned. For more information, consult the *Health* section at the back of the book.
Health care: Health insurance is recommended. There is one doctor for every 1500 inhabitants.

TRAVEL - International

AIR: Trinidad & Tobago's national airline is *BWIA (BW)*. *BWIA* fly to other Caribbean islands and to several towns on the South American coast. *LIAT (LI)* also offer inter-Caribbean flights.
Approximate flight times: From *Barbados* to Port of Spain is 45 minutes. From *London* is 10 hours 30 minutes (with a further 30-minute flight to Scarborough, Tobago), from *New York* is 10 hours 20 minutes and from *St Lucia* is 50 minutes.
International airport: *Port of Spain (POS)* is 25.5km (16 miles) southeast of the city. There are taxis to the city for hotels throughout the island with set fares posted in taxis. Fares increase after midnight. Sharing taxis is an accepted practice. Buses operate to Port of Spain. Airport facilities include a duty-free shop.
Departure tax: TT$75 is levied on international departures. Transit passengers and children under five years of age are exempt.
SEA: The main ports are Port of Spain, Point-à-Pierre and Point Lisas.

TRAVEL - Internal

AIR: There are regular flights run by *BWIA* to Scarborough *(Crown Point Airport)* on Tobago, 13km (8 miles) south of the town. Flights are usually every hour, with some night services. During peak seasons these are often heavily booked.
SEA: There is a regular car ferry/passenger service from Port of Spain to Tobago (Scarborough) (travel time – 5 hours). The day journey gives a good view of the two islands but the night journey can be uncomfortable. Return by plane is recommended; fares are quite low.
ROAD: The road network in Trinidad between major towns is good. Two major highways run north–south and east–west. Roads which run off major routes are very unpredictable, and are susceptible to poor weather conditions. Traffic drives on the left. **Bus:** Services are operated by the state *Public Service Corporation (PTSC)*. In the absence of a railway, the main towns are served by bus but although these are cheap, they are crowded and unreliable. The use of shared taxis has increased due to the shortcomings of the bus network; these are available both outside and within Port of Spain. **Taxi:** All taxis have registration 'H'. *Route* taxis serve standard routes within Trinidad & Tobago. These have fixed rates. **Car hire:** Cars and motorcycles are available in Port of Spain or Scarborough, and can be arranged via hotels.
Documentation: Visitors in possession of a valid driving permit issued in any of the countries listed below may drive in Trinidad & Tobago for a period of up to three months. They are, however, entitled to drive only a motor vehicle of the class specified on their permit. Drivers must at all times have in their possession: (a) their National Driver's Permit; and (b) any travel document on which is certified their date of arrival in Trinidad & Tobago. Visitors whose stay exceeds the 3-month period are requested to apply to the Licensing Department, Wrightson Road, Port of Spain, for a local Driving Permit. The above information applies to all signatories to the Convention on International Driver's Permits including: the USA, Canada, France, the UK, Germany and the Bahamas. *Excluded*: China and Vietnam.
URBAN: Due to the deterioration of bus services, most public transport journeys in Port of Spain are now made by shared taxis, which may take the form of either cars or minibuses. They serve specific zones, and are coloured accordingly. Zone fares are standardised. Basic operations are on fixed routes, with pick-ups at central points, but they can also be hailed anywhere along the route; drivers will often sound their horns to indicate that there is room in the vehicles. Taxis will generally not

start the journey until full. Most route taxis terminate at points around Independence Square, Port of Spain. Other roaming taxis are much more expensive, and rates should be agreed in advance. The Tourism and Industry Development Corporation publishes a list of fares for standard routes. For address, see top of entry.

ACCOMMODATION

HOTELS: There are major international chain hotels in Port of Spain, and a number of smaller hotels in the surrounding areas. Resort hotels are recommended, especially in Tobago. There is a wide range of prices. For further information, contact the Trinidad & Tobago Hotel and Tourism Association (for address, see top of entry). There is a 10% government room tax and VAT levied.
GUEST-HOUSES: The Tourism and Industry Development Corporation publishes a list of guest-houses found throughout Trinidad & Tobago.
Note: All types of accommodation must be booked well in advance for the Carnival (see below under *Social Profile*).

RESORTS & EXCURSIONS

The home of carnival, steel bands, calypso and limbo dancing, Trinidad & Tobago's blend of different cultures give them an air of cosmopolitan excitement.

Trinidad

Port of Spain, surrounded by lush green hills, is the capital and business hub of oil-rich Trinidad. The city captures the variety of Trinidadian life, with bazaars thronging beneath modern skyscrapers and mosques rubbing shoulders with cathedrals. The architecture of the city incorporates a mixture of styles: these include Victorian houses with gingerbread fretwork; the *German Renaissance Queen's Royal College; Stollmeyer's Castle*, an imitation of a Rhine fortress; the President of the Republic's residence and the Prime Minister's office at **Whitehall** (both built in Moorish style); and the 19th-century Gothic *Holy Trinity Cathedral*. Places of interest include the shopping district centred on Frederick Street; the *Royal Botanic Gardens;* the *Red House* (a stately colonial building now the seat of government); and the *National Museum* and *Art Gallery*.
Queen's Park Savannah, a magnificent park just to the north of the capital and well within walking distance, is spread out at the foot of the Northern Range. A mixture of natural and man-made beauty, with attractive trees and shrubs (including the African Tulip, or 'Flame of the Forest'), it forms a backdrop to a race-course and playing fields and the elaborate mansions, now mostly government offices.
On the outskirts of the city is **Fort George**. Built in 1804, it offers an excellent view of Port of Spain and the mountains of northern Venezuela.
Maracas Bay, Las Cuevas and *Chaguaramas* are the nearest beaches to the Port of Spain.
13km (8 miles) to the south of the capital by road and boat is the *Caroni Bird Sanctuary*, home of the Scarlet Ibis (see also below under *Wildlife*). The *Diego Mountain Valley*, 16km (10 miles) from Port of Spain, contains one of the island's most beautiful water wheels. In the village of **Chaguanas** it is possible to sample the most exotic of West Indian culinary specialities. **Arima**, the third largest town on the island, has an *Amerindian Museum* at the *Cleaver Woods Recreation Centre* on the west of town. About 13km (8 miles) north is the *Asa Wright Nature Centre* at **Blanchisseuse**, containing a collection of rare specimens such as the Oilbird or *Guacharo*. The *Aripo Caves* are noted for their stalactites and stalagmites. On the east coast is **Valencia**, a lush tropical forest near the *Hollis Reservoir*. **Cocal** and **Mayaro** are also worth visiting.
San Fernando is the island's second town. Close by is the fascinating natural phenomenon of the *Pitch Lake,* a 90-acre lake of asphalt which constantly replenishes itself.

Tobago

Tobago is very different from its larger neighbour 32km (20 miles) away. It is a tranquil island with calm waters and vast stretches of white sand beaches. The capital, **Scarborough**, has many quaint houses which spill down from the hilltop to the waterside, as well as interesting *Botanic Gardens*. It is overshadowed by the *King George Fort*, built in 1779 during the many struggles between the French and the English, an excellent point from which to view the sunset. Nearby is the small town of **Plymouth** with its tombstone inscriptions dating from 1700. There are a number of fine beaches. They include *Pigeon

Point on the southwest coast (admission is charged); *Store Bay,* where brown pelicans can be seen diving into the waters to catch fish; *Man O'War Bay,* at the opposite end of the island, and *Mount Irvine* and *Bacolet Bays.* *Buccoo Reef* is an extensive coral reef lying a mile offshore from Pigeon Point. Excursions can be made in glass-bottomed boats and it is an excellent place for snorkelling.

At *Fort James* there is a well-maintained red brick building, and at *Whim,* a large plantation house. *Arnos Vale Hotel* is a former sugar plantation, now a hotel; a disused sugar mill fitted out with formidable crushing wheels, made in 1857, is still on the grounds. There is bird-watching is a favourite pastime here.

Charlotteville is a fishing town commanding precipitous views of the headlands. Looming above the town is *Pigeon Peak,* the highest point on the island. There are good swimming beaches in the region. *Tobago Forest Reserve* has many trails which provide excellent long hikes for the more active visitor.

On the Atlantic side of the island are the tiny villages of **Mesopotamia**, **Goldsborough** and **Roxborough** and several beautiful bays. **Speyside** is a colourful beach settlement, from which can be seen tiny **Goat Island** and **Little Tobago,** a 450-acre bird sanctuary.

Wildlife

These islands have a unique wealth of wild birds and flowers, butterflies and fish, mostly undisturbed, yet accessible. The island boasts no less than 622 species of **butterfly** and over 700 species of **orchid**. The latter are perhaps best seen in Trinidad's *Botanic Gardens* in Port of Spain (along with a wide selection of indigenous trees, shrubs, ferns and cacti). The *Emperor Valley Zoo* has a similarly representative selection of local wildlife – reptile as well as mammal. Birdwatchers on Trinidad should head for the *Nariva Swamp,* the *Aripo Savannah* and the *Asa Wright Nature Centre* and look out in particular for the national bird, the **Scarlet Ibis**, conserved in the *Caroni Bird Sanctuary.* The sight of these scarlet birds flying in formation to roost before sundown is a stunning and colourful spectacle. While on Tobago a visit to *Little Tobago Island* is recommended. **Hummingbirds** are ubiquitous on Tobago; there are 19 recorded species, seven of which are unique to the island. Beneath the waters of the Caribbean is a spectacular treasure trove of tropical fish and coral gardens lying easily visible just below the water's surface, the *Buccoo Reef.*

SOCIAL PROFILE

FOOD & DRINK: Bars and restaurants open until late, with a very wide choice of local and Western food and drink. Chinese, Indian and West Indian cooking is available in Trinidad. British, American and Creole cooking is available in Tobago, as well as some notable seafood specialities such as lobster, conch and jackfish. Local dishes include pilau rice and Creole soups, the best being *sans coche, calaloo* and peppery pigeon pea soup. *Tatoo, manicou,* pork souse, green salad, *tum-tum* (mashed green plantains), roast venison, *lappe* (island rabbit), *quenk* (wild pig), wild duck and *pastelles* (meat folded into cornmeal and wrapped in a banana leaf) are also available. Seafood including bean-sized oysters, *chip-chip* (tiny shellfish similar in taste to clams) and crab *malete* is excellent, as is the freshwater fish *cascadou.* Indian dishes include *roti* (dough stuffed with chicken, fish or meat) and hot curries. **Drink:** Excellent rums and Angostura bitters are used to make rum punch. The local beers are *Carib* and *Stag,* which are best drunk very cold.

NIGHTLIFE: Trinidad has a wide and varied nightlife including hotel entertainment and nightclubs with *calypso,* limbo dancers and steel bands.

SHOPPING: Goods from all over the world can be found in Port of Spain, but local goods are always available. Special purchases include Calypso records, steel drums, leather bags and sandals, ceramics and woodcarvings. Gold and silver jewellery can be good value, as can Indian silks and fabrics. Rum should also be considered. Bright, printed fabrics and other summer garments are available in Trinidad & Tobago. **Shopping hours:** 0800-1600 Monday to Friday; 0800-1200 Saturday. Some shops stay open later in Port of Spain. Shops close on public holidays, especially during Carnival.

SPORT: Tennis: There are facilities at most large hotels for tennis. **Golf:** This can be enjoyed just outside Port of Spain or in Tobago at the marvellous Mount Irvine Golf Course. **Fishing:** Fishing of all kinds from deep-sea to inland is widely available and usually rewarding on and off both islands. Kingfish, Spanish mackerel, wahoo, bonito, dolphin and yellow tuna are the usual catches,

with grouper, salmon and snapper also to be found off the west and north coasts of Trinidad. **Cricket:** This is the major spectator sport and the season runs from February to June. The best national and international matches can be seen at the Queen's Park Oval, in Port of Spain. **Racing:** Trinidadians are keen sportsmen and the Queen's Park Savannah hosts a number of major meetings, particularly around New Year and Easter. The meetings are well organised. **Watersports:** There are good facilities for all types of watersports, especially at the beaches along the north and east coasts of Trinidad, and all around Tobago. Buccoo Reef, just off the southwest coast of Tobago, offers exciting **scuba diving** with its magnificent coral formations and abundant marine life. Trips in glass-bottomed boats are very popular.

SPECIAL EVENTS: A vast mixture of races has led to a varied cultural life, the diversity of which is reflected in costume, religion, architecture, music, dance and place names.

The major event in Trinidad is the *Carnival,* renowned throughout the Caribbean and the rest of the world. The festivities climax at the beginning of Lent, on the two days immediately preceding Ash Wednesday, although the run-up to Carnival starts immediately after Christmas when the Calypso tents open and the Calypsonians perform their latest compositions and arrangements. During Carnival normal life grinds to a halt and the whole of Trinidad & Tobago is absorbed in the festivities.

A week before the Carnival proper, *Panorama* is staged. This is the Grand Steel Drum (pan) tournament; all the big steel bands parade their skills around the Savannah, the large park in the north of Port of Spain. *Hosay,* coinciding with the Muslim New Year, sees the Muslim population of Port of Spain, San Fernando and Tunapuna take to the streets in a festival of their own. Contact the Tourism Development Authority for dates of all of the above. The following is a selection of festivals and other special events celebrated annually in Trinidad & Tobago:

Mar '95 *Tobago Jazz Festival,* Palm Tree Village, Tobago; *National Flower Show,* Port of Spain. **Apr** *Fun Run,* Port of Spain. **May-Jun** *National Best Village Programme.* **May** *La Divina Pastora Festival,* Siparia; *Trinidad & Tobago Song Festival,* St Ann's. **Jun** *Tobago Harvest Festival,* Tobago; *Trinidad & Tobago Marathon,* Port of Spain. **Jun-Jul** *Fishermans' Festival*; *St Peter's Day,* Carenage. **Jul-Aug** *Tobago Heritage Festival,* Tobago; *Hosay; Sand Sculpture Competition; Santa Rosa Festival,* Arima. **Sep** *Caribbean Cup Volleyball Championships,* Port of Spain. **Oct** *Ramleela Hindu Festival; National Flower Show; Orchid Show; School Steelband Music Festival; National Indoor Hockey Championships,* Port of Spain; *Amerindian Heritage Festival,* Arima. **Nov** *Trinidad & Tobago Pan Jazz Festival.* **Dec** *International Drag Racing,* Wallerfield.

Feb '96 *Carnival.*

Note: It is no exaggeration to say that the Trinidadians, like most of the people living in the Caribbean, are warm and friendly with an exuberant love of life. Nevertheless, visitors are well-advised to exercise care with their personal belongings during Carnival.

SOCIAL CONVENTIONS: *Liming,* or talking for talking's sake, is a popular pastime, as is talking about, watching and playing cricket. Many local attitudes are often reflected in the lyrics of the *calypso,* the accepted medium for political and social satire. Hospitality is important and entertaining is commonly done at home. Casual wear is usual with shirt sleeves generally accepted for business and social gatherings. Beachwear is not worn in towns. **Tipping:** Most hotels and guest-houses add 10% service charge to the bill, otherwise a 10-15% tip is usual in hotels and restaurants.

BUSINESS PROFILE

ECONOMY: The economy has steadily contracted since the early 1980s when the country's oil production, begun ten years earlier, started to decline. By way of compensation, however, large reserves of natural gas have been located and these have provided the raw material for the islands' burgeoning petrochemical industry in which the Government has rested many of its hopes for future economic development. The revenues have also been used to establish indigenous plastics and electronics industries. A major expansion of this sector was launched in 1991. Apart from oil and gas, Trinidad has the world's largest deposits of asphalt. The other important foreign exchange earner is tourism, although this has not reached its full potential as the Government has been reluctant to make extensive investments. The agricultural sector is small with sugar as the main commodity. Once a net exporter of foodstuffs, Trinidad now imports the bulk of its requirements. Trinidad & Tobago is a member of the Caribbean economic union, CARICOM. The three largest exporters to Trinidad and Tobago are the USA, Japan and the UK. Machinery and transport equipment are the islands' main imports other than foodstuffs. In 1992, the Government announced a limited programme of privatisation.

BUSINESS: Lightweight suits or 'shirt jacks' should be worn. The best time to visit is from December to April, avoiding the Christmas festivities. **Office hours:** 0800-1600 Monday to Friday.

COMMERCIAL INFORMATION: The following organisation can offer advice: Trinidad and Tobago Chamber of Industry and Commerce (Inc), PO Box 499, Room 950-952, Hilton Hotel, Port of Spain. Tel: 627 4461 *or* 624 6082. Fax: 627 4376.

CLIMATE

The tropical climate is tempered by northeast trade winds. The dry season is from November to May, but it is hottest between June and October.

Required clothing: Tropical lightweights are required. Rainwear is advisable, especially for the wet season.

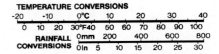

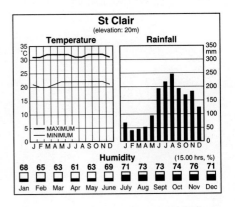

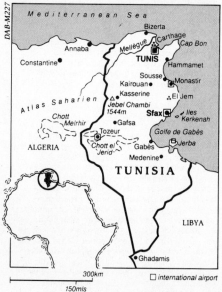

300km
150mls

□ *international airport*

Location: North Africa.

Office National du Tourisme Tunisien
1 avenue Mohamed V, 1002 Tunis, Tunisia
Tel: (1) 341 077. Fax: (1) 350 997. Telex: 14381.

Embassy of the Republic of Tunisia
29 Prince's Gate, London SW7 1QG
Tel: (0171) 584 8117. Fax: (0171) 225 2884. Telex:
23736. Opening hours: 0930-1630 Monday to Friday;
0930-1300 Monday to Friday (visa enquiries).

Tunisian National Tourist Office
77a Wigmore Street, London W1H 9LJ
Tel: (0171) 224 5561 (enquiries) *or* 224 5598
(administration). Fax: (0171) 224 4053. Telex: 261368
(a/b TTOLDN). Opening hours: 0930-1730 Monday to
Friday.

British Embassy
5 place de la Victoire, Tunis, Tunisia
Tel: (1) 341 444 *or* 341 689 *or* 340 239. Fax: (1) 354
877. Telex: 14007 (a/b PRDROM TN).

Consular and Visa Section
141-143 avenue de la Liberté, Tunis, Tunisia
Tel: (1) 773 322 *or* 794 810. Fax: (1) 792 644. Telex:
17128 (a/b BRICON TN).
Consulate in: Sfax.

Embassy of the Republic of Tunisia
1515 Massachusetts Avenue, NW, Washington, DC
20005
Tel: (202) 862 1850. Fax: (202) 862 1858.

Consulate in: Miami and San Francisco.

Embassy of the United States of America
144 avenue de la Liberté, Belvédère, 1002 Tunis, Tunisia
Tel: (1) 782 566. Fax: (1) 789 719. Telex: 18379 (a/b
AMTUN TN).

Embassy of the Republic of Tunisia
515 O'Connor Street, Ottawa, Ontario K1S 3P8
Tel: (613) 237 0330 *or* 237 0332. Fax: (613) 237 7939.
Telex: 0534161.
Consulate in: Montréal.

Canadian Embassy
PO Box 31, 3 rue du Sénégal, place d'Afrique,
Belvédère, 1002 Tunis, Tunisia
Tel: (1) 798 004 *or* 796 577. Fax: (1) 792 371. Telex:
15324 (a/b DOMCAN TN).

AREA: 164,000 sq km (63,320 sq miles).
POPULATION: 8,735,885 (1994 estimate).
POPULATION DENSITY: 53.3 per sq km.
CAPITAL: Tunis. **Population:** 1,500,000.
GEOGRAPHY: The Republic of Tunisia lies on the
Mediterranean coast of Africa, 130km (80 miles)
southwest of Sicily and 160km (100 miles) due south of
Sardinia. The landscape varies from the cliffs of the north
coast to the woodlands of the interior, from deep valleys
of rich arable land to desert, and from towering
mountains to salt pans lower than sea level. South of
Gafsa and Gabès is the Sahara desert. The 1100km (700
miles) of coastline is dotted with small islands, notably
Jerba in the south and Kerkenah in the east, and from the
northwest to the southeast the coastline is backed
successively by pine-clad hills, lush pasture, orchards,
vineyards and olive groves.
LANGUAGE: The official language is Arabic. French
and English are spoken in major cities and resorts.
RELIGION: The principal religion is Islam; there are
Roman Catholic and Protestant minorities.
TIME: GMT + 1.
ELECTRICITY: 220 volts AC, 50Hz. A 2-pin
continental plug/adaptor is needed.
COMMUNICATIONS: Telephone: Full IDD is
available. Country code: 216. Outgoing international
code: 00. Automatic dialling extends to almost every part
of the country and covers direct international calls. Area
codes for major cities and towns: Tunis 1, Bizerta and
Menzel Bourguiba 2, Sousse 3, Gabès 5, Kairouan 7.
Fax: Facilities are available in main towns.
Telex/telegram: The Telecommunications Centre in
Tunis (29 Jamal Abdelnasser) is equipped with a public
telex system. Telegraph facilities are available at the
Central Post Office at rue Charles de Gaulle, Tunis. **Post:**
Airmail to Europe takes three to five days. *Poste
Restante* facilities are available in main cities. Post office
hours: 0800-1300 Monday to Saturday (summer,
approximately June 15-September 15); 0800-1200 and
1400-1800 Monday to Friday, 0800-1200 Saturday
(winter, approximately September 16-June 16); 0800-
1500 Monday to Saturday (during Ramadan). **Press:**
Daily newspapers are printed in Arabic or French, the
most popular being *As-Sabah, Al Horia* and *La Presse.*
The weekly *Tunisia News* is published in English.
**BBC World Service and Voice of America
frequencies:** From time to time these change. See the
section *How to Use this Book* for more information.

BBC:

MHz	17.70	15.07	12.09	9.410

Voice of America:

MHz	21.49	15.60	9.525	6.035

PASSPORT/VISA

*Regulations and requirements may be subject to change at short notice, and you
are advised to contact the appropriate diplomatic or consular authority before
finalising travel arrangements. Details of these may be found at the head of this
country's entry. Any numbers in the chart refer to the footnotes below.*

	Passport Required?	Visa Required?	Return Ticket Required?
Full British	1	No	Yes
BVP	Valid	-	-
Australian	Yes	Yes	Yes
Canadian	Yes	No	Yes
USA	Yes	No	Yes
Other EU (As of 31/12/94)	Yes	No	Yes
Japanese	Yes	No	Yes

PASSPORTS: Valid passport required by all **[1]** except
UK nationals in possession of a British Visitors Passport.
British Visitors Passport: Acceptable. BVPs may be
used for holidays or unpaid business trips of up to 3
months.
VISAS: Required by all except:
(a) nationals of countries referred to in the chart above;
(b) nationals of Algeria, Antigua & Barbuda, Austria,

Monastir, the Old City

WHY JUST HAVE ONE HOLIDAY WHEN YOU CAN GO TO TUNISIA

Just two and a half hours away

Uncrowded beaches

Modern Hotels

European food

Golf, tennis, and watersports

History galore

Sunshine all year round

Big T.V. campaigns backed by 197 press ads will get the bookings to your door.

Tunisian National Tourist Office at 77A Wigmore Street London W1H 9LJ.
Tel: 071 224 5561.
Telex: 261 368 TTO LDN.
Fax: 071 224 4053.
Prestel: 460 439.

TUNISIA

Bahrain, Barbados, Belize, Bermuda, Bosnia-Hercegovina, Brunei, Bulgaria, Chile, Côte d'Ivoire, Croatia, Dominica, Fiji, Finland, Gambia, Gibraltar, Gilbert Islands, Ghana, Grenadines, Guernsey, Guinea Republic, Hong Kong, Hungary, Iceland, Kiribati, South Korea, Kuwait, Libya, Liechtenstein, Former Yugoslav Republic of Macedonia, Malaysia, Mali, Malta, Mauritania, Mauritius, Monaco, Montserrat, Morocco, Niger, Norway, Oman, Qatar, Romania, St Helena, St Kitts & Nevis, St Lucia, St Vincent & Grenadines, San Marino, Saudi Arabia, Senegal, Seychelles, Slovenia, Solomon Islands, Sweden, Switzerland, Turkey, United Arab Emirates, Vatican City and Yugoslavia (Serbia and Montenegro).

Check with the Embassy for details of length of stay.
Types of visa: Tourist and Transit. Cost: £4.37.
Transit: Transit visas are not required for passengers holding confirmed onward tickets and travel documents valid for departure within 48 hours (24 hours for nationals of People's Republic of China, Lebanon and Syria) by the same or first connecting flight provided they do not leave the airport.
Validity: *Tourist:* up to 4 months, depending on nationality; *Transit:* 7 days.
Application to: Consulate (or Consular section at Embassy). For addresses, see top of entry.
Application requirements: (a) Valid passport. (b) Photocopy of first three pages of passport. (c) 2 completed application forms. (d) 2 passport-size photos. (e) Fee, payable by postal order. (f) Registered, stamped, self-addressed envelope.
Working days required: 2-3 weeks, for both postal and personal applications.
Temporary residence: Apply to the Ministry of Interior, avenue Habib Bourquiba, Tunis, Tunisia.

MONEY

Currency: Tunisian Dinar (TD) = 1000 millimes. Notes are in denominations of TD20, 10 and 5. Coins are in denominations of TD5 and 1, and 500, 100, 50, 20, 10 and 5 millimes.
Currency exchange: All banks change money, as do most hotels of three stars and above.
Credit cards: Access/Mastercard, American Express, Diners Club and Visa are widely accepted. Check with

your credit card company for details of merchant acceptability and other services which may be available.
Travellers cheques: Readily cashed in banks and the usual authorised establishments.
Exchange rate indicators: The following figures are included as a guide to the movements of the Tunisian Dinar against Sterling and the US Dollar:

Date:	Oct '92	Sep '93	Jan '94	Jan '95
£1.00=	1.41	1.54	1.54	1.54
$1.00=	0.89	1.01	1.04	0.99

Currency restrictions: The import and export of local currency is strictly prohibited. The import of foreign currency is unlimited, although amounts over the value of TD500 must be declared. The export of foreign currency is limited to the amount imported. All currency documentation must be retained. Reconversion of local into foreign currency is possible for up to 30% of total foreign currency exchanged up to a maximum of TD100 per person.
Banking hours: 0730-1100 Monday to Friday (summer); 0800-1100 and 1400-1600 Monday to Thursday, 0800-1130 and 1300-1515 Friday (winter).

DUTY FREE

The following goods may be imported into Tunisia without incurring customs duty:
400 cigarettes or 100 cigars or 500g of tobacco; 1 litre of spirits of more than 25% alcohol; 2 litres of alcoholic beverages of up to 25% alcohol; 250ml of perfume; 1 litre of eau de toilette; gifts up to a value of TD100; 2 cameras (not identical); 20 rolls of film; 1 video camera; 1 radio cassette player.
Restricted items: The export of antiques is subject to a permit from the Ministry of Cultural Affairs.
Prohibited items: Firearms (unless for hunting), explosives, drugs, Tunisian Dinars, obscene publications, forged books, walkie-talkies, any other produce which may be regarded as dangerous to public security, health, morality, etc.

PUBLIC HOLIDAYS

Jan 1 '95 New Year's Day. **Mar 3** Aid el-Seghir (End of Ramadan). **Mar 20** Independence Day. **Mar 21** Youth Day. **Apr 9** Martyrs' Day. **May 1** Labour Day. **May 10**

Aid el-Kebir (Feast of the Sacrifice). **Jul 25** Republic Day. **Aug 13** Women's Day. **Oct 15** Evacuation of Bizerta. **Nov 7** Accession of President Ben Ali. **Jan 1 '96** New Year's Day. **Feb 18** Aid el-Seghir (End of Ramadan). **Mar 20** Independence Day. **Mar 21** Youth Day. **Apr 9** Martyrs' Day. **Apr 29** Aid el-Kebir (Feast of the Sacrifice).
Note: Muslim festivals are timed according to local sightings of various phases of the Moon and the dates given above are approximations. During the lunar month of Ramadan that precedes Aid el-Seghir (Eid al-Fitr), Muslims fast during the day and feast at night and normal business patterns may be interrupted. Many restaurants are closed during the day and there may be restrictions on smoking and drinking. Some disruption may continue into Aid el-Seghir itself. Aid el-Seghir and Aid el-Kebir (Eid al-Adha) may last for two days. For more information, see the section *World of Islam* at the back of the book.

HEALTH

Regulations and requirements may be subject to change at short notice, and you are advised to contact your doctor well in advance of your intended date of departure. Any numbers in the chart refer to the footnotes below.

	Special Precautions?	Certificate Required?
Yellow Fever	Yes	1
Cholera	Yes	2
Typhoid & Polio	Yes	-
Malaria	No	-
Food & Drink	3	-

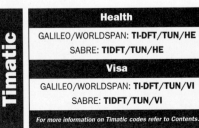

Timatic

Health	
GALILEO/WORLDSPAN:	**TI-DFT/TUN/HE**
SABRE:	**TIDFT/TUN/HE**
Visa	
GALILEO/WORLDSPAN:	**TI-DFT/TUN/VI**
SABRE:	**TIDFT/TUN/VI**

For more information on Timatic codes refer to Contents.

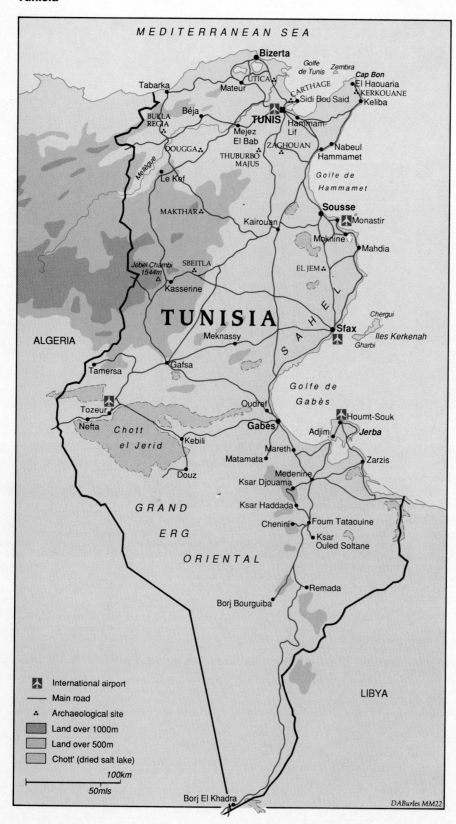

MEDITERRANEAN SEA

Bizerta
Golfe
de Tunis
Zembra
Cap Bon
Tabarka
Mateur
UTICA
CARTHAGE
El Haouaria
KERKOUANE
Béja
Sidi Bou Said
Keliba
BULLA
REGIA
TUNIS
Hammam-
Lif
Mejez
El Bab
ZAGHOUAN
Nabeul
DOUGGA
THUBURBO
MAJUS
Hammamet
Le Kef
Golfe de
Hammamet
MAKTHAR
Kairouan
Sousse
Moknine
Monastir
Mahdia
Jebel Chambi
1544m
SBEITLA
EL JEM
Kasserine
Chergui
TUNISIA
Sfax
Iles Kerkenah
Meknassy
Gharbi
ALGERIA
Gafsa
Tamersa
Golfe de
Gabès
Tozeur
Oudref
Nefta
Kebili
Gabès
Houmt-Souk
Chott
Adjim
Jerba
el Jerid
Mareth
Douz
Matamata
Zarzis
Medenine
Ksar Djouama
GRAND
Ksar Haddada
ERG
Chenini
Foum Tataouine
Ksar
Ouled Soltane
ORIENTAL
Remada
Borj Bourguiba
LIBYA

✈ International airport
— Main road
∴ Archaeological site
Land over 1000m
Land over 500m
Chott' (dried salt lake)

100km
50mls

Borj El Khadra

DABurles MM22

[1]: A yellow fever certificate is required from travellers over one year of age arriving from infected areas.
[2]: Following WHO guidelines issued in 1973, a cholera vaccination certificate is not a condition of entry to Tunisia. However, precautions are advised. Up-to-date advice should be sought before deciding whether these precautions should include vaccination, as medical opinion is divided over its effectiveness. See the *Health* section at the back of the book.
[3]: Mains water is normally chlorinated, and whilst safe may cause mild abdominal upsets. Bottled water is available and is advised for the first few weeks of the stay. Drinking water outside main cities and towns may be contaminated. Milk should be boiled when unpasteurised (ie if not commercially processed and packed). Powdered or tinned milk is available and is advised but make sure that it is reconstituted with pure water. Avoid dairy products which are likely to have

been made from unboiled milk. Only eat well-cooked meat and fish, preferably served hot. Salad and mayonnaise may carry increased risk. Vegetables should be cooked and fruit peeled.
Rabies is present. For those at high risk, vaccination before arrival should be considered. If you are bitten abroad, seek medical advice without delay. For more information, consult the *Health* section at the back of the book.
Health care: Health insurance is recommended. Tunisia has a comparatively well-developed public health service and 70% of the population qualify for free medical treatment. There is one doctor for every 7000 inhabitants.

TRAVEL - International

AIR: The national airline is *Tunis Air (TU)*.
Approximate flight times: From London to *Tunis* is 2

hours 30 minutes, to *Jerba* is 3 hours, to *Monastir* is 2 hours 45 minutes and to *Sfax* is 3 hours.
International airports: *Tunis (TUN)* (Carthage International) is 8km (5 miles) northeast of the city (travel time – 10 minutes). There is a duty-free shop open both to incoming and outgoing passengers. Five banks are open all day for currency exchange, and at least one remains open for night flights. An airport-city coach service operates every 15 minutes, and buses depart every 30 minutes. Return is from Hotel Africa Meridien (city air terminal). Taxis are available; a surcharge is levied at night.
Monastir (MIR) (Skanes) is 8km (5 miles) from the city. Buses are available to the city centre.
Jerba (DJE) (Melita) is 8km (5 miles) from the city.
Sfax (SFA) is 15km (9 miles) from the city.
Tozeur (TOE) (Nefta) is 10km (6 miles) from the city. All the above airports have bars, restaurants and both incoming and outgoing duty-free shops. Taxis are available at all the airports.
Note: Tunisian currency is *not* valid in duty-free shops.
Departure tax: None for visitors, but TD45 is levied for Tunisians. Children under 2 years of age are exempt.
SEA: There are regular shipping services from France and Italy to Tunisia. All the shipping lines have representatives in European cities. For details, contact the National Tourist Office. The following are major routes and journey times:
Marseilles–Tunis: 21-24 hours.
Genoa–Tunis: 21-24 hours.
Naples–Tunis: 21-24 hours.
Palermo–Tunis: 10 hours.
Sicily (Trapani)–Kelibia: *3 hours.
Note [*]: Hydrofoil May-September.
RAIL: There is a rail link from Tunis to Algiers (subject to closures due to the political situation in Algeria; check before departure).
ROAD: There are several points of entry by road from Algeria, normally served by buses and long-distance taxis: Annaba (in Algeria) to Tabarka (following the coast road); Souk Ahras (in Algeria) to Ghardimaou; and El Oued (Algeria) to Gafsa. Entry by road from Libya is via the coast road at Gabès, via Ben Gardane and Ras Ajdir.

TRAVEL - Internal

AIR: *Tuninter* runs regular services six times a day between Tunis and Jerba airports (flight time – 1 hour 5 minutes). There is a daily flight to Sfax from Tunis and two on Wednesday and Thursday, and a weekly flight to Monastir. Tozeur is served from Tunis by two flights on Monday and one on Thursday, Friday, Saturday and Sunday. A new set of flights will run from Tunis to the newly-opened airport at Tabarka. *Tuninter* is represented internationally by *Tunis Air*. Prices are reasonable and services are normally heavily subscribed, so it is advisable to book ahead. For details, contact *Tunis Avia*, 19 avenue Habib Bourguiba, Tunis. Tel: (1) 254 239 *or* 518 017.
SEA: Ferries operate between Sfax and the Kerkenah Islands twice-daily, and between Jorf and Jerba Island regularly during the day.
RAIL: Regular trains (run by *SNCFT*) connect Tunis, Hammamet, Nabeul, Sousse, Sfax, Sbeitla, Kasserine, Mateur, Bizerta, Tabarka, Beja, Ghardimaou and Gabès. It is essential to purchase a ticket before boarding the train, or the traveller will have to pay double the fare. Several daily trains run on each route, many with air-conditioned accommodation and a buffet. It is highly advisable to book in advance, if possible, especially for the more popular air-conditioned routes.
Cheap fares: A reduction is made on round-trip tickets and children (4-9 years) travel at three-quarters of the standard fare. Children under 4 years of age travel free.
ROAD: Tunisia has a widespread road network. In case of breakdown, the *Garde Nationale* (National Guard) will assist free of charge (they usually contact the nearest garage). Traffic drives on the right. **Bus:** *Société Nationale des Transports* and other buses connect all the main cities and towns. Intercity bus services are cheap and reasonably comfortable. Passengers are allowed 10kg of luggage without additional charge. Each piece of luggage must, however, be registered. The major (but far from insurmountable) difficulty for most tourists will be determining the destination of the numerous buses. **Taxi:** Long-distance taxis (usually large Mercedes or similar), called *louages*, are authorised to carry five passengers. They have no fixed schedule and leave their respective departure points when full. They serve the whole of Tunisia. This is the quickest form of public road transport. There are many *louage* stations and prices are similar to those of buses and trains. **Car hire:** This can be very expensive. To rent a self-drive car the driver must be over 21 years of age. A full driving licence, which has been valid for at least one year, is acceptable.

Speed limits: 50kmph (30mph) in towns; 100kmph (60mph) on major highways. **Documentation:** Log books, valid national driving licences and Green Card insurance are essential. Both the *RAC* and *AA* are affiliated to the *National Automobile Club (NACT)* based in Tunis. Insurance valid for up to 21 days can be purchased at the border.

Note: For safety reasons, it is forbidden to drive a car in the Sahara without first contacting the National Guard post at the nearest town, giving the planned itinerary and the expected point of exit from the area. Full provisions, a suitable vehicle and an experienced guide are necessary for any travel in the Sahara.

URBAN: Publicly owned transport services *(SNT)* operate in all major towns, and are extensive but crowded. There is a rail link from Tunis to the suburbs of La Goulette and La Marsa. **Taxi:** Within Tunis and other cities, city taxis are numbered and have meters. The price on the meter is what you should pay. There is a 50% surcharge on night fares.

JOURNEY TIMES: The following chart gives approximate journey times (in hours and minutes) from Tunis to other major cities/towns in Tunisia.

	Air	Road	Rail
Hammamet	-	0.45	1.00
Nabeul	-	0.45	1.00
Sousse	-	2.00	2.30
Port el Kantaoui	-	2.00	2.30
Monastir	0.35	3.00	3.00
Sfax	0.50	4.00	4.00
Gabès	-	5.00	6.00
Jerba	0.60	7.00	-
Tozeur	1.10	6.00	-

Note: Travellers to Port el Kantaoui are advised to take the train to Sousse, and travel the remaining 7km (4 miles) by taxi. For Monastir they should change in Sousse for the Metro Leger. For Jerba they should take the train to Gabès and then the shuttle-bus.

ACCOMMODATION

HOTELS: Tunisia has approximately 150,000 hotel beds. There are also several vacation villages within each area. There is a new luxury resort in Tabarka which hosts the International Underwater Photography Exhibition. **Grading:** Hotel accommodation is classified by a star system ranging from deluxe (**5-star**) to clean but simple (**1-star**).

MARHALAS: *Marhalas* are converted caravanserais and often consist of several connected underground houses (in *Matmata* and *ksars* – ancient granaries), where sleeping quarters and communal bathing and toilet facilities have been installed. They also have their own simple, but clean and adequate, restaurants. There are *Marhalas* at Houmt Souk, Nefta and Kairouan.

CAMPING/CARAVANNING: Tents can be pitched or trailers parked on beaches and in parks with permission from the property owner or from the nearest police or National Guard station. The major campsites are *Le Moulin Bleu* (Blue Mill) at Hammam-Plage, 20km (12 miles) from Tunis; *L'Auberge des Jasmins* (Jasmin Inn) at Nabeul, 65km (40 miles) from Tunis, equipped with showers, wash-basins, toilets, hot and cold running water, shop, restaurant and outdoor theatre in an extensive orange grove; *L'Idéal Camping* at Hammamet, 60km (35 miles) from Tunis, with restaurant facilities; *Sonia Camping & Caravan Site* at Zarzis, 505km (313 miles) from Tunis; and *The Youth Centre of Gabès,* 404km (251 miles) from Tunis (summer only).

YOUTH HOSTELS: Youth Hostels are open to all young people who are members of the *International Youth Hostel Association.* It is recommended to make reservations well in advance, especially for groups. For details, contact the National Tourist Office.

RESORTS & EXCURSIONS

For the purposes of this section, Tunisia has been divided into six main regions. There is also information on the major historic sites in the country.

Tunis & the Suburbs

Tunis is a modern international metropolis with sophisticated hotels, shops, entertainment and flower-lined avenues, but within it is the *medina*, one of the best-preserved medieval cities in the Islamic world. The main entrance to this area – by the Porte de France and the British Embassy – leads straight into the rue Djamaa Ez-Zitouna. This is the main street of the *souk* markets. From here many other individual *souks* branch off, often specialising in particular types of product. If you get lost, your landmark is the Grand Mosque, *Djamaa Ez-Zitouna*, in the street of the same name.

The *Bardo Museum,* housed in what was once the Bey's palace, contains important Carthaginian, Roman,

Ksar Haddada, wheat storage

Byzantine and Arab treasures. The *Carthage Museum* holds prehistoric, Punic, Roman and Byzantine exhibits and stands over the remains of the *Baths of Antoninus*, which are open to the public.

The city is overlooked by the cool, wooded *Belvedere Park* which has a delightful Muslim pavilion, and a zoo. There is a golf course and a riding stable in the suburbs of **La Soukra.**

RESORTS: To the northeast of Tunis is the beach resort and port of **La Goulette**, where on hot summer nights the outdoor restaurants and cafés offer fresh fish specialities, as well as typical Tunisian cuisine. Further along the coast are the remains of **Carthage**, once the equal of ancient Rome (described more fully in *Historic Sites* below), then **Sidi-Bou Said** and **La Marsa**. All these towns are linked by rail with Tunis. Sidi-Bou Said is on a headland bedecked with bougainvillaea, carnations, geraniums and the bright blue doors and shutters of white

Andalusian-style villas. The town is a centre for the production of domed wire-filigree birdcages and is also famous for its cafés. Amid greenery sweeping down to superb sandy beaches, La Marsa, Gammarth and Raouad have fine hotels, cosmopolitan restaurants and nightlife. In the southern suburbs lies **Hammam-Lif**, a small resort village on the beach, dominated by *Jebel Bou Kornine* ('two-horned mountain').

The Coral Coast

Often known as 'Green Tunisia', this is a delightful part of the country, a region of hills, mountains and fertile plains. Temperature variations can be great, and occasional snow covers the peaks of Khroumiria. The weather is cooler in the summer season than in the south. First-rate hotels are situated on this coast.

Bizerta, formerly the Roman city of Hippo Diarrytus, was a key port during World War II. It retains its old fishing harbour, a kasbah and medina, the Andalusian quarter, wide avenues and a palm-fringed promenade. Modern hotels in landscaped gardens and a splendid *Congress Hall* are spread along the Corniche above sand dunes. Scenic drives can be enjoyed around *Cap Bizerta* and *Cap Blanc* or around *Lake Bizerta* and *Lake Ichkeul.* The latter provides the habitat for numerous varieties of wildfowl, and the wooded mountain of *Jebel Ichkeul* is the home of buffalo sent as a royal gift to the Bey of Tunis.

Utica, 32km (20 miles) from both Bizerta and Tunis, is an old Phoenician settlement; see the *Historic Sites* section below. Nearby **Raf Raf** is a charming hilltop town.

Tabarka, a picturesque port and resort about 140km (90 miles) west of Bizerta, can be reached by an undulating country route through **Teskraia** and **Jebel Abiod,** a horse-breeding centre. Tabarka is now a more peaceful place than its formidable Genoese fortress would suggest; today, it is given over largely to coral fishing, with spectacular scope for skindivers on the coral reefs, and for the netting of red mullet and hake. Tabarka's importance in the expanding tourist trade is exemplified by the construction of a 10,000-bed complex based around a marina, its golf course, as well as the building of a new international airport.

The wooded and flower-decked foothills of *Khroumiria,* behind The Coral Coast, have more than a hint of unspoiled Provence, although the forests are of cork trees rather than olive. Deer, lynx, civets and jackals may be glimpsed by naturalists throughout the year. Southwards, past **Bulla Regia** (see *Historic Sites*) stands lofty **Le Kef** which has thermal springs. The region also has historical associations stretching from Roman, Punic and early Christian days up to the time of the Second World War.

Cap Bon

Hammamet, where no hotel may be built higher than the tallest of the adjacent trees, is situated on the southern corner of fertile Cap Bon, about 65km (40 miles) from Tunis. It is Tunisia's major and most mature seaside playground. The numerous hotels are built in various modern Moorish styles, which sometimes mirror the white domes of the picturesque *medina* (old town) nearby. The sea-girt *medina* is walled, and guarded by a tawny-coloured *kasbah* whose towers offer a hawk's-eye view of the neat warren of narrow streets below, with their workshops, souvenir arcades and boutiques selling leather and woollen goods, sponges and embroidery. Like the *kasbah* and mosque, the Turkish baths *(hammam)* date from the 15th century. Foreigners are welcome to use them.

A wide sandy beach leads from the old town to the resort area; just behind this, quite near the medina, is a complex of shops, restaurants, nightclubs, bars and cafés. The resort boasts two golf courses. The holiday hotels themselves tend to have plenty of in-house entertainment, including discos and folklore evenings, while beach activities can include horse or camel rides.

One of the most beautiful gardens in Tunisia is that of the *International Cultural Centre,* originally a villa created by Georges Sebastien, friend and host to many French artists and writers. Churchill stayed here and, during the Tunisian campaign, Rommel requisitioned the villa for his personal use. Now the centre is the setting for open-air concerts and plays of international interest, as well as for Tunisian folklore performances.

Nabeul is a relatively modern town, about 10km (6 miles) north of Hammamet. It stands on an ancient Punic and Roman site and maintains a centuries-old tradition in its manufacture of pottery and fine ceramics, perfumes (from local orange and jasmine blossom), lace and leatherwork. There is a camel market here every Friday. The holiday hotels, sometimes containing traditional-style bungalows for self-caterers, look onto a sand beach as fine as that in Hammamet, and have facilities and entertainments similar to those of the bigger resorts. The line of hotels eventually merges into the orchards and fields of Cap Bon, with their hedges of prickly pear and cactus. For further information, see the *Accommodation* section above.

Cap Bon has a maritime climate (mild throughout the year), varied landscapes and an easily accessible coast, a combination of features which made this a popular holiday region amongst the Punic and Roman aristocrats. Jutting out between the Gulf of Tunis and the Gulf of Hammamet, Cap Bon encompasses important wine-growing areas and produces fine figs, olives, oranges, lemons and cereals. At **Korbous,** a former palace of the Bey of Tunis has been converted into a centre for the treatment of arthritis and skin ailments with therapeutic spa waters. Nearby **Sidi Daoud** is a fishing centre, and from here the islets of **Zembra** and **Zembretta** can be reached.

El Haouraria, a village in a wooded region near the end of the cape, is the site of a falconry festival every spring – it is on the migratory path of several bird species.

Main picture: Port of Sfax. Above left: Tunis. Right: Golf Citrus, Hammamet.

Nearby cliffs soar to 400m (1300ft). **Kerkouane** has an important Punic archaeological site. **Kelibia** has a romantic castle ruin and a thriving fishing port. Some local inhabitants, many of whom have blue eyes and red hair, are known as 'Lengleez', and are believed to be descended from British sailors shipwrecked years ago. Inland from Cap Bon are **Zaghouan** and **Thuburbo Majus**.

The Sahel

This central coastal area is a region of hills and plains, with gardens and groves of olive, pomegranate and almond trees. The hills slope down towards a coastline of white sandy beaches or occasional rocky cliffs and underwater reefs.

The Sahel today is the most densely populated region of Tunisia. A common feature of the sun-bleached villages which dot the stony landscape is the cultivation of olive and fruit trees. In the small country museums there are collections of gold jewellery dating back many centuries and this is still a speciality of town artisans today. The region is traditionally known for its weaving. The visitor will especially appreciate the cottons of **Ksar Hellal** and the wool embroidery of **Mahdia** and **El Jem** (see *Historic Sites* below). Some of the smallest villages offer the most original handicrafts; the inhabitants of **Hergla**, for example, make the alfalfa filters that are used all over the country in olive presses.

Many of the towns and villages in the Sahel stand on the remains of Roman or Punic urban centres. The museums of Sousse and El Jem have collections of unusually rich mosaics which show the extraordinary wealth of the area during the Roman era. It was for this reason that the Arabs founded their most important capitals, Kairouan, an important spiritual centre, and Mahdia, today an important holiday centre, in this region.

Sousse, a major port and Tunisia's third-largest city, is set in a convenient central position on the eastern coast. The sand beaches, with horse and camel riding, reach beyond Port el Kantaoui, 7km (4 miles) to the north (see below). Most of Sousse's beach hotels are outside the modern town, whose cafés, bars, discos and excellent restaurants are alternative attractions to the hotels' in-house activities and folklore evenings. Impressive ancient ramparts surround the old town. The 8th-century *Ribat* is one of a chain of fortified monasteries built to defend North Africa from Christian attacks. The men and women who inhabited its spartan quarters had vowed to die if necessary to preserve the Muslim faith. Its watchtower gives a splendid view over the *medina*, as does the garden terrace of Sousse's museum – whose intriguing 'cartoon strip' mosaics should be seen, especially by those who have not visited the Bardo Museum in Tunis.

Port el Kantaoui is a garden village which has an 18-hole championship golf course and a marina. Several of the hotels have spacious lawns facing the soft sand beach. There are good opportunities for sea fishing from here. **Monastir** is 24km (15 miles) further south, an intimate and fashionable small resort which is famous for its 10th-century *mosque*. The town is served by Skanes – Monastir's airport. Monastir is a mixture of ancient and modern. The 20th century has given Monastir other attractions, such as the elegant yacht marina which nestles between small sandy coves.

There are many festivals throughout the high season, horseracing to watch and a museum of Islamic arts to visit. A new rail link to Sousse has recently opened; this helps to attract business people to its well-equipped International Convention Centre. There is now a second golf course near the town.

21km (13 miles) to the south is the market town of **Moknine**. Part of its population is Jewish and the traditional jewellery items they make are among the exhibits in the town's fascinating little folk museum. **Mahdia**, 25km (17 miles) further along the coast, is a fishing port and beach resort, a town with an important place in Arab Muslim history. The all-powerful Obaid Allah, known as the Mahdi, developed it in the 10th century as a stronghold and capital of the Fatimite Dynasty.

The Isles of Jerba & Kerkenah

The island of **Jerba**, 614 sq km (240 sq miles), is joined to the mainland by a 6km-long (4 mile) causeway. There is also a ferry-boat service and an air link. The main centre, **Houmt Souk,** is a small market town serving outlying farms and villages, most of which have fine examples of the distinctive local architecture. The island has about 40 beach hotels and a golf course.

The inhabitants of two Jerban villages are Jews, descendants of refugees who fled from Jerusalem after the Roman conquest of the city in AD70. Their influence is seen in the design of the jewellery sold locally. Jerban villages often specialise in one product. At **Guellala**, for instance, it is pottery; whilst at **Adjim,** it is sponges. **Kerkenah's** two inhabited islands, **Gharbi** and **Chergui**, can be reached by car ferry from the pleasant city of **Sfax**. A holiday village and a few hotels and bars indicate that tourism has (however unobtrusively) arrived to supplement the islands' staple industry of fishing. Kerkenah is also notable for its traditional and colourful wedding ceremonies, which visitors are welcome to watch.

Central Tunisia

The oases and the *chotts* (vast dried salt lakes) provide a strange, unearthly atmosphere. The *chotts,* white-crusted in summer (when roads across them are most negotiable), give an impression of infinite open space; even more so than the sand-duned desert further south. A ground haze shimmers in the sun, and a far-distant camel train seems to be floating on air. Mirages of palm trees can sometimes be seen in the afternoon, as in the Sahara.
The main oases, which must have seemed visions of paradise to early travellers, nourish countless date palms. Pomegranates, bananas and other fruit are cultivated by their limpid streams. Palm sap is made into a wine called *lagmi,* for whose potency there are prodigious claims.
The easily accessible **Gabès**, site of a southerly seaside oasis which can be toured in a horse-drawn *caleche,* is also a port and a good base for excursions through the *chotts* to the inland oases of **Gafsa, Tozeur, Nefta** and **Douz,** or southwards to the Sahara and the *Matmata Mountains* (see *The Deep South* section).
Gafsa, about 160km (100 miles) inland, is a city of rose-pink walls, whose 30°C thermal water spring bubbles up into three large Roman cisterns. Just out of town is a zoo displaying indigenous animals and birds, as well as the oasis, which can be toured by horse-drawn carriage.
Tozeur has perhaps the most luxuriant oasis of all. Its 200 springs feed thousands of the best date-palms – each towering tree is said to need 100 cubic metres (3500 cubic ft) of water a day. It can be toured by donkey or camel, and contains a 'Paradise Garden' profuse with exotic flowers and fruits. Tozeur's town buildings are built with unfired yellow bricks picked out in geometric patterns similar to those found on Arab rugs. There is an international airport and Tozeur and Nefta are sometimes featured as destinations in package deals, 'twin-centring' them with a coastal resort.
Nefta's oasis resembles a bowl, and is known locally as a basket or 'horn of plenty'. The town, made up of sand-coloured houses, is on a plateau above it. Guides are available for the trek on donkey back to the oasis. Nefta has the feeling of being a rather remote frontier post (but less so than Douz), although it has a 4-star-deluxe hotel.
North of Tozeur and Nefta are the mainly mud-walled villages of **Chebika**, **Tamerza** and **Mides**.
To the southeast, via Kebili, lies **Douz**, on the *Grand Erg Oriental,* the great sand-sea of the eastern Sahara. Its Thursday camel market is a camera-worthy event, as is the *marhoul* ceremony celebrating the start of the seasonal desert migration. Such rituals – as well as camel-wrestling, poetry 'jousts' and folk dance and music – are incorporated into a Sahara Festival which takes place near Douz every January.
Around this region live veiled people of pure Berber stock. You may also find a 'desert rose' of crystalline minerals baked by the sun into petal-like formations.
Note: Any trip into the desert region must be planned carefully, using suitable transport, adequate provisions and a guide (see *Travel-Internal* above). Overnight lodging and restaurants can be found throughout southern Tunisia. Hard-topped roads and dirt tracks make it possible to drive to all points of interest, even across the crusted beds of the *chotts.*

The Deep South

A hole-in-the-ground hotel in a lunar landscape; civilised cave dwellings tunnelled into a mountainside; homes like giant honeycomb cells in ancient stone granaries; these are just some of the intriguing sights to be investigated on trips southwards from Gabès, Jerba or Zarzis.
Matmata (a location used during the filming of 'Star Wars') consists (as do other Berber villages) largely of sizeable holes burrowed into the ground, a useful defence against the fierce summer heat and cold winter winds. Their homes are built on two levels, the upper one containing storage rooms. In some cases, several of these underground dwellings have been connected together to make hotels and restaurants. 'Mod cons' are generally available, although the furnishings are normally traditional. The mosque there is underground, as is the communal bakery. There are even subterranean oil factories where olives are pressed by a camel-driven mill with a huge olive trunk. Domes that rise above ground level usually mark *marabouts,* the shrines of holy men.
The Matmata landscape is typified by deeply-eroded, conical hillocks separated by narrow ravines, where olive and fig trees sometimes grow. The region is speckled with flat plots of land where goats are pastured among the gardens and clumps of olive trees.
The road southeast from Gabès leads through **Mareth**, scene of a battle in 1943, to **Medenine**. This market town has a *ksar,* a fortified citadel surrounded by former grain stores *(ghorfas),* some two or three storeys high, sometimes used as homes. Some *ghorfas* have been converted into tourist accommodation and others are now little shops selling Bedouin silver jewellery.
On a circular route from Medenine to Foum Tataouine are several more *ksars,* including **Ksar Djouama,** probably 14th century in origin; **Beni Kheddache,** on a mountain-top; **Ksar Haddada,** with a small hotel; and **Ghoumrassen,** in a valley. All have cave dwellings. The road is rough and is best negotiated by jeep.
Two of the most beautiful mountain *ksars* are **Ouled Soltane,** south of Tataouine, and **Chenini,** to the west. The road to Chenini is a memorable one, zigzagging through a cinnamon-coloured mountainscape.
The fringes of the Sahara lie to the south of **Tataouine, Remada** and **Borj Bourguiba.** Some internal tour operators arrange Land-Rover treks into the desert. Independent travellers wishing to visit it should note that, as a precaution against their becoming stranded or lost, it is a strict requirement that they should first contact the National Guard Post in Medenine or the nearest town. Vehicles should be suitable for this kind of travel, and be equipped with ample water, provisions, repair kits and a tent. An experienced accompanying guide is advisable, as is a preliminary check of the meteorological conditions – particularly before a trip of any length. Drivers (preferably in convoy) should stop at every guard post on the way and tell the officer in charge where they are going.
Zarzis, on the coast facing Jerba, is a beach resort in a coastal oasis of about 500,000 palm trees and 100,000 olive trees.

Historic Sites

Tunisia has a wide variety of historical settlements, Punic, Roman, Byzantine and Islamic, many of which are in excellent condition.
Tunisia's most famous historic site is probably **Carthage,** in the suburbs of Tunis. It was the city of the legendary Queen Dido, and once the great rival of Rome in the struggle for domination of the Mediterranean. When the Romans, furious at humiliations inflicted by Hannibal and the Carthaginians, conquered it in 146BC, they razed and ploughed it into the ground, which they symbolically sterilised with salt. Later they rebuilt the city, making it their provincial capital of North Africa. Then the city suffered at the hands of the Vandals who conquered the region at the end of the 5th century. They lived up to their name, vandalising many of the Roman statues by chipping off their proud noses. Then again, in AD698, it was razed to the ground – this time by Arab invaders.
The small whitewashed town of **El Jem** (about 40km/25 miles inland from Mahdia) is dominated by the well-preserved *Colosseum.* Its lion-coloured outer walls are 35m (120ft) high and there was seating for 30,000.
Kairouan (50km/30 miles inland from Sousse) is the fourth most holy city in the Islamic world – after Mecca, Medina and Jerusalem. It was founded in AD670 by a disciple of the Prophet Mohammed and is situated on the spot where a new spring of water and other miraculous revelations were manifested to him during a journey. According to legend, seven visits to Kairouan equal one to Mecca. The courtyard in front of its *Great Mosque* (which can be visited by non-Muslims) is said to be able to hold 200,000 pilgrims on holy days. There are many other mosques and shrines, but the Great Mosque is the most sanctified place. Its prayer room is supported by a variegated 'forest of pillars' of Roman, Byzantine and Arab periods, made of stone, marble or porphyry. The 5m-high (18ft), gloriously carved wooden pulpit dates from the 9th century – as does its minaret with 128 steps.
Utica, reached from Tunis or Bizerta, was a Phoenician colony founded around 1100BC – earlier than Carthage, its rival in later centuries. After entering by a great arched gateway, one can see marble flooring of a mansion set in a garden fragrant with rosemary. Mosaics depicting sea fish decorate a waterbasin and the pool of a former fountain. The remains of several other houses reveal decorated flooring of the Punic, Roman and Byzantine periods, and the Punic tombs contain interesting remains.
Dougga is a major Roman site in a lofty setting 100km (60 miles) southwest of Tunis. The theatre, built in AD168 to seat 3500, resounds again when Greek-based classical plays and other performances are staged, sometimes by the *Comédie Française.* Visitors with a more down-to-earth humour may be amused by the neighbourly arrangement of 12 seats over latrines in the *Bath of Cyclops*. However, decorum is restored with a view of the city's capitol, claimed by some to be the grandest in North Africa.
Bulla Regia, south of Tabarka, is a site with at least 23 special features from the Roman, early-Christian and Byzantine periods. Some of its best mosaics have been removed to the Bardo Museum in Tunis, but its 'Hunting Palace' has vivid mosaics of wild animals and the chase, and recognisable remnants of a dining room, kitchen and bedrooms.
Sbeitla, 160km (100 miles) inland from Sousse and Sfax, is one of the country's largest archaeological sites. Its numerous attractions include Roman temples and baths, early-Christian churches and Byzantine fortresses.
It is possible in most resorts to arrange excursions to important historical sites.
POPULAR ITINERARIES: 5-day: Kairouan–El Jem–Sfax–Gabès–Matmata–Douz–Tozeur–Gafsa–Sbeitla. **7-day:** Tunis–Carthage–Bulla Regia–Dougga–Thuburbo Majus–Zaghouan–Kairouan–Sbeitla–Tozeur–Nefta–Douz–Matmata–Gabès–Sfax–El Jem–Mahdia–Sousse–Hammamet–Kerkouane–Korbous.

SOCIAL PROFILE

FOOD & DRINK: Tunisian food is well prepared and delicious, particularly the authentic lamb or *dorado* (bream) *cous-cous,* the fish dishes, *tajine* and *brik* or *brik à l'oeuf* (egg and a tasty filling fried in an envelope of pastry). Tunisian dishes are cooked with olive oil, spiced with aniseed, coriander, cumin, caraway, cinnamon or saffron and flavoured with mint, orange blossom or rose water. Restaurants catering for tourists tend to serve rather bland dishes and 'international' cuisine, and visitors are advised to try the smaller restaurants. Prices vary enormously, and higher prices do not necessarily mean better meals. Tunis and the main cities also have French, Italian and other international restaurants. Self-service may sometimes be found but table service is more common. **Drink:** Moorish cafés, with their traditional decor, serve excellent Turkish coffee or mint tea with pine nuts. Although Tunisia is an Islamic country, alcohol is not prohibited. Tunisia produces a range of excellent table wines, sparkling wines, beers, aperitifs and local liqueurs, notably *Boukha* (distilled from figs) and *Thibarine*.
NIGHTLIFE: In Tunisia the theatre season lasts from October to June when local and foreign (especially French) companies put on productions and concerts. International groups appear at Tunis Theatre and in the towns of Hammamet and Sousse. There are numerous cinemas in the larger cities. There are nightclubs in most of the beach hotels as well as in the big city hotels. Belly dancing is a common cabaret feature and lively local bands often play traditional music.
SHOPPING: Special purchases include copperware (engraved trays, ashtrays and other utensils); articles sculpted in olive wood; leather goods (wallets, purses, handbags); clothing (kaftans, jelabas, burnuses); pottery and ceramics; dolls in traditional dress; beautiful embroidery; fine silverware and enamelled jewellery. Among the most valuable of Tunisia's products are carpets. The two major types are woven (non-pile) and knotted (pile). The quality of all carpets is strictly controlled by the National Handicrafts Office, so be sure to check the ONA seal before buying. **Shopping hours:** 0800-1200 and 1600-1900 (summer), 0830-1200 and 1500-1800 (winter). **Weekly markets:** A source of good purchases are the markets which are set up on certain days in many Tunisian towns and villages. All the products of the region are displayed, including handicrafts, farm produce and secondhand goods. There are ONA workshops and stores throughout the country where visitors can buy items at fixed prices (payment can be made by Eurocheque with a bankers card). ONA stores make a reduction of 10% on the price of goods purchased in foreign currency. No duty is payable on articles up to £900 in value which are shipped to EU countries, only if accompanied by an EUR1 form. Visitors who make a purchase of more than TD5, anywhere in Tunisia, should ask for a sales slip and keep all sales slips, along with bank receipts for any currency exchanged, for Customs inspection.
SPORT: Gliding: The best-known venue for gliding enthusiasts is the Federal Gliding Centre at Jebel Rassas, 25km (15 miles) from Tunis, where gliders and qualified instruction in the sport are available to visitors. **Golf:** The Tunisian Open Golf Tournament 1982-85 became one of the major tournaments on the PGA European tour. There are excellent courses at Port el Kantaoui near Sousse, Monastir, Tabarka, Tunis, Hammamet and Jerba. Players of all abilities will find very high-quality facilities. The Open Golf Championships there have already attracted many leading competitors from all over the world. Created by eminent golf-course architects, the courses

are dotted with palm, olive and pomegranate trees, and are next to the sea. Each of the 18 holes is on a different kind of terrain, and treated turf has been imported from California. The courses are well-suited to all players. There are luxurious clubhouses, equipment to rent and training/practice grounds with putting green. In Tunis, the golf course at the Country Club at La Soukra has recently undergone extension and re-landscaping. More courses are planned for every major resort. **Fishing:** The abundance and great variety of fish makes fishing a popular sport. Underwater fishing is also good. The range includes mullet, ray, dogfish, groupers, red rock mullet, crayfish and shrimp. A wetsuit is necessary only between November and April. You can watch coral fishing at Tabarka, octopus fishing off the Kerkenah Islands, sponge fishing at Sfax, on the island of Jerba and in the Gulf of Gabès, and tuna fishing by the experts at Sidi Daoud. These 'fishing spectacles' take place in May and June. **Scuba diving:** Fully-equipped scuba diving centres are located in Tabarka, Monastir and Port el Kantaoui. For underwater fishing, it is necessary to bring your own equipment, and obtain details of conservationist underwater fishing restrictions from the National Tourist Office. Visitors who have brought their own equipment can refill their air bottles at the offices of the *Société d'Air Liquide* at Mégrine, 7km (4 miles) from Tunis, and at Sfax. In case of accident, there are decompression chambers at the Naval Station at Bizerta. **Swimming:** Tunis has three public swimming pools open to visitors. Most hotels on the coast have a heated pool as well as a private beach. **Birdwatching:** Tunisia has many species of birds, many of which are protected in national parks. The cork-oak forests of Ain Draham, the lake and marshes of Ichkeul near Bizerta, the coastal lagoons round Tunis and Sousse, the rocky hills and steps from Kef to Kasserine, and the oases and deserts of the south all have their characteristic birds. Birdlife also varies with the seasons; in winter, spoonbills, geese, ducks, robins and wagtails seek refuge from the cold further north, while in spring and autumn migrant swallows and warblers and birds of prey at Cap Bon pass through on their journeys between Africa and Europe. In summer, Mediterranean species like storks, bee-eaters and rollers stay to nest. **Health spas:** There are about 100 hot-spring stations throughout Tunisia – mostly in the north of the country. Many of the spas have been used for this purpose since Roman and Punic times. The most important stations are run by personnel specialised in the medical and paramedical fields and treatments are available for rheumatism, arthritis, a variety of lung and skin complaints, circulatory troubles, gynaecology and paediatrics. More information is available at the National Tourist Office. **Sailing:** Port el Kantaoui is a port of international standard offering mooring for 340 boats, harbour-master's office, deep-sea navigation school, sailing school, ship-chandler, boat-rental and a dry docking area with maintenance shops. Prices are competitive, especially for winter careening services. There is a newly-opened marina at Cap Monastir with similar facilities. Among other sailing (and water-skiing) centres is *Le Club Nautique de Sidi-Bou Said,* which has a marina complex. A new marina has recently been completed at Tabarka.

SPECIAL EVENTS: The following information gives some idea of Tunisian festivals in 1995. A complete list is available from the National Tourist Office.
Jun '95 *Festival of the Sparrow Hawk,* El Haouaria, near Nabeul. **Jun** *Festival of Malouf* (Andalusian folklore), Testour; *Ulysses Festival* (traditional songs and dances of the island of Jerba), Houmt Souk; *Festival of Dougga* (classical plays in Roman theatre), Beja. **Jul** *El Jem Festival,* Roman colosseum. **Jul-Aug** *Festival of Carthage* (music, theatre, dance and folklore), Roman theatre; *Monastir Festival* (international music, dance and theatre). **Aug** *Festival of Hammamet* (music, theatre, dance, folklore), International Cultural Centre. **Sep** *Festival of Cavalry* (traditional Arab horse festival with racing and dancing), Kairouan. **Dec** *Festival of the Tozeur Oasis* (parades of decorated floats, folklore, camel fights); *Douz Festival* (folklore, camel-racing, cavalry and music), Sahara.
SOCIAL CONVENTIONS: Arabic in culture and tradition, Tunisia is nevertheless one of the more liberal and tolerant Muslim countries. The nomadic Bedouin still follow their traditional way of life in the southern desert. The Tunisians' varied origins are shown in the architecture, crafts, music and regional folk dances. Tunisia has also developed an international reputation as an intellectual and cultural centre. Shaking hands is the usual form of greeting. Hospitality is very important and a small gift in appreciation of hospitality or as a token of friendship is always appropriate. Dress can be informal but should respect the conventions of Islam when visiting religious monuments, ie shoulders and knees must be covered. Outside tourist resorts, scanty beachwear should not be worn. **Tipping:** 10-15% for all services.

Bedouin

BUSINESS PROFILE

ECONOMY: Tunisia lacks the vast natural resources of its immediate neighbours, but careful and successful economic management has brought the country reasonable prosperity. Agriculture and mining are the foundations of the economy. The main agricultural products are wheat, barley, olive oil, wine and fruit, but large quantities of other foodstuffs have to be imported. Large quantities of phosphate ores are mined, along with iron, lead and zinc. Tunisia is also a modest oil exporter, although this sector has recently been in decline. There is a small manufacturing sector which is involved in processing organic chemicals derived from petroleum and purifying the phosphate ore. The economy has suffered from recent falls in oil and phosphate prices, which has forced the Government to relax price controls on basic commodities. France and Italy are Tunisia's principal trading partners. The Government is trying to broaden the base of the economy by introducing more liberal economic policies, backed by the IMF which has offered soft loans in exchange for a brake on public expenditure and an export drive.
BUSINESS: Arabic and French are the most widely used languages in business circles and a knowledge of either is useful. Interpreter services are available. Appointments are required. **Office hours:** 0800-1230 and 1430-1800 Monday to Friday, 0800-1200 Saturday (winter); 0700-1300 Monday to Saturday (summer).
COMMERCIAL INFORMATION: The following organisations can offer advice: Agence de Promotion de l'Industrie (API), 63 rue de Syrie, 1002 Tunis. Tel: (1) 792 144. Fax: (1) 792 144. Telex: 14166; *or* Chambre de Commerce et d'Industrie de Tunis, 1 rue des Entrepreneurs, 1000 Tunis. Tel: (1) 242 872. Fax: (1) 241 202. Telex: 14718.
CONFERENCES/CONVENTIONS: The following

organisation can supply information: Direction du Marketing, Office National du Tourisme Tunisien, 1 avenue Mohamed V, 1002 Tunis. Tel: (1) 341 077. Fax: (1) 350 997. Telex: 14381.

CLIMATE

Tunisia has a warm climate all year. Best periods are spring and autumn. Temperatures can be extremely high inland. Winter is mild and has the highest rainfall.
Required clothing: Lightweights in summer, mediumweights and rainwear in winter. Sunglasses are advised.

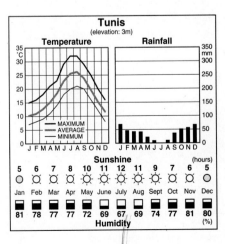

800km
400mls

UKRAINE
MOLDOVA
ROMANIA
Danube
BULGARIA
Black Sea
GEORGIA
Edirne
Sinop
Istanbul
Samsun
Trabzon
Kars
ARM.
Bursa
ANKARA
Kizil Irmak
Erzurum
Izmir
Sivas
L.Van
Ephesus
Konya
TURKEY
Dalaman
Antalya
Adana
Gaziantep
Mt Ararat
5165m
Alanya
Euphrates
CYPRUS
Tigris
Med. Sea
SYRIA
IRAQ
GREECE
IRAN
DAB-M228
SAUDI ARABIA
AFRICA

□ international airport

Location: Southeastern Europe/Asia Minor.

Ministry of Tourism
Ismet Inönü Bul. 5, Bahçelievler, Ankara, Turkey
Tel: (312) 212 8300. Fax: (312) 212 8391. Telex: 42448.

Embassy of the Republic of Turkey
43 Belgrave Square, London SW1X 8PA
Tel: (0171) 393 0202 *or* 235 6968 (press office). Fax:
(0171) 393 0066 *or* 245 9547 (press office). Telex:
884236 (a/b TURKE LG).

Turkish Consulate General
Rutland Lodge, Rutland Gardens, London SW7 1BW
Tel: (0171) 589 0360 *or* 589 0949 *or* (0891) 600 130
(recorded visa information; calls are charged at the
higher rate 39/49p per minute). Fax: (0171) 584 6235.
Opening hours: 0930-1200 (for visas) and 0930-1600
(other enquiries) Monday to Friday.

Turkish Tourist Office
First Floor, 171-173 Piccadilly, London W1V 9DD
Tel: (0171) 355 4207. Fax: (0171) 491 0773.

British Embassy
Sehit Ersan Caddesi 46/A, Cankaya, Ankara, Turkey
Tel: (312) 42 74 31 01. Fax: (312) 468 3214. Telex:
42320 (a/b PROD TR).

Consulates in: Antalya, Bodrum, Iskenderun, Istanbul,
Izmir, Marmaris and Mersin.

Embassy of the Republic of Turkey
1714 Massachusetts Avenue, NW, Washington, DC
20036
Tel: (202) 659 8200 *or* 659 0742 (Consular section). Fax:
(202) 659 0744.
Consulates in: Chicago, Houston, Los Angeles and New
York.

Turkish Tourist Office
4th Floor, 821 UN Plaza, New York, NY 10017
Tel: (212) 687 2194. Fax: (212) 599 7568.
Also in: Washington, DC.

Embassy of the United States of America
PO Box 5000, Atatürk Bulvar 110, Ankara, Turkey
Tel: (312) 468 6110. Fax: (312) 467 0019 *or* 468 6131
(Consular section).
Consulates in: Istanbul, Izmir and Adana.

Embassy of the Republic of Turkey
197 Wurtemburg Street, Ottawa, Ontario K1N 8L9
Tel: (613) 789 4044 *or* 789 3440. Fax: (613) 789 3442.

Canadian Embassy
Nenehatun Caddesi 75, Gaziosmanpasa 06700, Ankara,
Turkey
Tel: (312) 436 1275. Fax: (312) 446 4437. Telex: 42369
(a/b DCAN TR).
Consulate in: Istanbul.

AREA: 774,815 sq km (299,156 sq miles).
POPULATION: 57,326,000 (1991 estimate).
POPULATION DENSITY: 73.5 per sq km.
CAPITAL: Ankara. **Population:** 3,200,000 (1991).
GEOGRAPHY: Turkey borders the Black Sea and
Georgia and Armenia to the northeast, Iran to the east,
Iraq to the southeast, Syria and the Mediterranean to the
south, the Aegean Sea to the west and Greece and
Bulgaria to the northwest. Asia Minor (or Anatolia)
accounts for 97% of the country and forms a long, wide
peninsula 1650km (1025 miles) from east to west and
650km (400 miles) from north to south. Two east–west
mountain ranges, the Black Sea Mountains in the north
and the Taurus in the south, enclose the central Anatolian
plateau, but converge in a vast mountainous region in the
far east of the country. It is here that the ancient Tigris
and Euphrates rivers rise.
LANGUAGE: Turkish. French, German and English are
widely spoken in cities.
RELIGION: Muslim with a small Christian minority.
Turkey is a secular state which guarantees complete
freedom of worship to non-Muslims.
TIME: GMT + 2 (GMT + 3 from last Sunday in March
to Saturday before last Sunday in September).
ELECTRICITY: 220 volts AC, 50Hz.
COMMUNICATIONS: Telephone: IDD is available.
Country code: 90. Outgoing international code: 00. There
is an extensive internal telephone network, but often an
interpreter will be needed for more remote areas. **Fax:**
All hotels and PTT offices have facilities.
Telex/telegram: Telex and telegrams may be sent from
all post offices. It is also possible to use the 'Valuables
Despatch Service' for valuable belongings or important
documents. **Post:** Airmail to Europe takes three days.
Turkish post offices are recognisable by their yellow *PTT*
signs. Major post offices are open 0800-2400 Monday to
Saturday and 0900-1900 Sunday. Small post offices have
the same opening hours as government offices. **Press:**
The main newspapers are *Hurriyet, Cumhuriyet, Sabah*
and *Milliyet.* English-language daily newspapers include
The Turkish Daily News.
**BBC World Service and Voice of America
frequencies:** From time to time these change. See the
section *How to Use this Book* for more information.

BBC:

MHz	17.64	12.09	9.410	1.323

Voice of America:

MHz	11.90	9.700	9.530	6.060

PASSPORT/VISA

*Regulations and requirements may be subject to change at short notice, and you
are advised to contact the appropriate diplomatic or consular authority before
finalising travel arrangements. Details of these may be found at the head of this
country's entry. Any numbers in the chart refer to the footnotes below.*

	Passport Required?	Visa Required?	Return Ticket Required?
Full British	Yes	Yes/3	Yes
BVP	Valid	-	-
Australian	Yes	No	Yes
Canadian	Yes	No	Yes
USA	Yes	Yes/4	Yes
Other EU (As of 31/12/94)	Yes	2/3	Yes
Japanese	Yes	No	Yes

Denizli, Pamukkale-lime terraces

THE • ART • OF • GREAT • HOLIDAY • SNAPS

LIES • IN • THE • VIEW • FINDER

HOLIDAY IN TURKEY AND DISCOVER BEAUTY TO FILL AN ARCHIVE

TURKEY

P A R A D I S E   P R E S E R V E D

FOR A BROCHURE CALL **0990 212 212** OR FOR HOLIDAY DETAILS VISIT YOUR **ABTA** TRAVEL AGENT

SEE C4 TELETEXT PAGE 353 FOR MORE INFORMATION. TURKISH TOURIST OFFICE, 1st FLOOR, 170/173 PICCADILLY, LONDON W1V 9DD. TEL 0171 734 8681

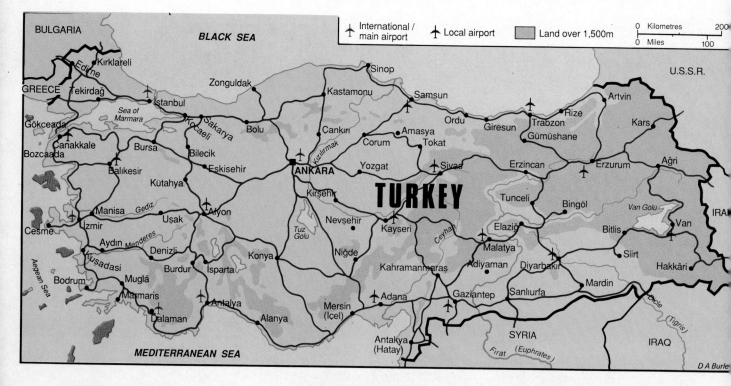

PASSPORTS: Required by all.

British Visitors Passport: Accepted for tourist visits of up to 3 months.

VISAS: Required by all except:

(a) nationals of countries referred to in the chart above for stays of up to 3 months;

(b) **[2]** nationals of EU countries for stays of up to 3 months (except Ireland, Italy, Portugal, Spain and the UK who *do* need visas, but see **[3]** below);

(c) nationals of Argentina, Bahamas, Bahrain, Barbados, Belize, Chile, Ecuador, Fiji, Finland, Grenada, Iceland, Iran, Israel, Jamaica, Kenya, South Korea, Kuwait, Liechtenstein, Malaysia, Malta, Mauritius, Monaco, Morocco, New Zealand, Northern Cyprus, Norway, Oman, Qatar, St Lucia, San Marino, Saudi Arabia, Seychelles, Singapore, Sweden, Switzerland, Trinidad & Tobago, Tunisia, United Arab Emirates and Vatican City for stays of up to 3 months;

(d) nationals of Bosnia-Hercegovina, Croatia, Indonesia, Former Yugoslav Republic of Macedonia, Romania, Slovenia and passport-holders of the former Yugoslavia if they reside in the Former Yugoslav Republic of Macedonia for stays of up to 2 months;

(e) nationals of Bolivia, Kazakhstan, Kyrgyzstan and South Africa for stays of up to 1 month.

Tourists and business visitors from the following countries can obtain their visas at the point of entry for a fee:

(a) **[3]** Ireland, Italy, Portugal, Spain and UK for visits not exceeding 3 months;

(b) Austria, Hong Kong and **[4]** USA for visits not exceeding 3 months;

(c) *CIS, Czech Republic, Estonia, Hungary, Jordan, Latvia, Lithuania, Poland and Slovak Republic for visits not exceeding 1 month;

(d) Guatemala for visits not exceeding 15 days.

Notes: (a) **[*]** Visas are only available for CIS nationals at Istanbul-Atatürk and Ankara-Esenboga airports; Sarp and Kapikule land borders; and Istanbul, Trabzon, Samsun, Giresun, Hopa and Rize ports. (b) Nationals of the UK and Ireland must pay their visa fees in UK£ and nationals of Austria must pay in Austrian currency. All other nationals eligible for visas on arrival must pay for their visas in US Dollars. All nationals listed above are advised to check with the Turkish Consulate regarding visa fees before travelling. (c) Those staying longer or travelling for the purposes of employment, education,

research or residence *must* obtain their visas in advance from the nearest Turkish consular mission.

Visas issued to nationals of the following countries will be stamped on a removable insert in the passport: Greek Cyprus, North Korea and Taiwan (China).

Types of visa: Tourist/Business Single-entry visa; Tourist/Business Multiple-entry visa; Employment, Education, Residence or Research visa; and Transit visa. Prices vary according to nationality.

Transit visas: These are *not* required by:

(a) those exempted from Tourist/Business visas;

(b) those continuing their journey by the same or first connecting aircraft, if in possession of confirmed onward tickets (and visas when appropriate) and who do not leave the airport.

Transit visas are required by all others continuing their journey within 72 hours; full visas are required for longer transit periods. Transit visas are only issued to those with valid passports and confirmed onward documentation. The cost varies according to the nationality of the applicant: contact the nearest Turkish Consulate. All nationals must obtain Transit visas before travelling to Turkey.

Validity: Dependent on nationality of applicant.

Application to: Consulate General. For addresses, see top of entry.

Application requirements: (a) Valid passport. (b) Application form. (c) Fee (varies for different nationals).

Working days required: 1-5 days.

MONEY

Currency: Turkish Lira (TL). Notes are in denominations of TL1,000,000, 500,000, 250,000, 100,000, 50,000, 20,000, 10,000 and 5000. Coins are in denominations of TL5000, 2500, 1000, 500, 100 and 50.

Currency exchange: All exchange certificates and purchase receipts must be retained to prove that legally exchanged currency was used. Money and travellers cheques can be exchanged at all PTT branches. Many UK banks offer differing rates of exchange depending on what denominations of Turkish currency are being bought or sold. Check with banks for details and current rates.

Credit cards: Access/Mastercard, American Express, Diners Club and Visa are accepted. Check with your credit card company for details of merchant acceptability and other services which may be available.

Travellers cheques & Eurocheques: Can be cashed immediately upon proof of identity. However, it may take several days to cash cheques from private accounts.

Exchange rate indicators: The following figures are included as a guide to the movements of the Turkish Lira against Sterling and the US Dollar:

Date:	Oct '92	Sep '93	Jan '94	Jan '95
£1.00=	12,567	17,582	22,076	60,546.3
$1.00=	7919	11,514	14,921	38,700.1

Currency restrictions: There are no restrictions on the import of local or foreign currency, though visitors bringing in a large amount of foreign currency should

obtain a written declaration from the Turkish authoritie. No more than the equivalent of US$5000 in local currency may be exported. Foreign currency may be exported up to US$5000, but no more than the amount imported and declared.

Banking hours: 0830-1200 and 1300-1700 Monday to Friday.

DUTY FREE

The following goods may be imported into Turkey without incurring customs duty:

5 litre bottles or 7 bottles of spirits (70cc); 200 cigarettes or 50 cigars or 200g of tobacco; 1.5kg of coffee; 1.5kg of instant coffee; 500g of tea; 1kg of chocolate; 1kg of sweets; 5 bottles of eau de cologne (120ml), eau de toilette, perfume or lavender water or lotion; gifts up to a value of DM500.

Note: (a) **[*]** A further 400 cigarettes or 100 cigars or 500g of tobacco may be imported if purchased on arrival at a duty-free shop. (b) Very specific amounts and categories of personal belongings may be imported duty free, according to a list available from the Consulate General. Most tourists are unlikely to find themselves exceeding these allowances, but should note that the limits imposed on personal belongings include: one camera and five rolls of film; one pocket calculator; one table clock; one manual typewriter (duty must be paid on electric and electronic models); one video camera and five blank cassettes; one 8mm cine-camera and ten blank cassettes; one portable radio or radio/cassette (speakers should not be detachable); five LPs or compact discs (no two the same); and one portable computer with no more than 4K bytes of memory.

Prohibited imports: More than two sets of playing cards, narcotics, sharp implements and weapons.

Restricted exports: (a) The export of souvenirs such as carpets is subject to customs regulations regarding age and value. (b) The export of antiques is forbidden. (c) Minerals may only be exported under licence from the General Directorate of Mining Exploration & Research.

PUBLIC HOLIDAYS

Jan 1 '95 New Year's Day. **Mar 3** Seker Bayrami/Ramazan Bayrami (End of Ramazan). **Apr 23** National Independence and Childrens' Day. **May 1** Spring Day. **May 10** Kurban Bayrami (Feast of the Sacrifice). **May 19** Youth and Sports Day. **Aug 30** Victory Day. **Oct 29** Republic Day. **Jan 1 '96** New Year's Day. **Mar** Seker Bayrami (End of Ramazan). **Apr 23** National Independence and Childrens' Day.

Note: Muslim festivals are timed according to local sightings of various phases of the Moon and the dates given above are approximations. During the lunar month of Ramazan that precedes Seker Bayrami/Ramazan Bayrami (Eid al-Fitr), Muslims fast during the day and feast at night and normal business patterns may be interrupted. Some restaurants are closed during the day and there may be restrictions on smoking and drinking.

Some disruption may continue into Seker Bayrami itself. Seker Bayrami and Kurban Bayrami (Eid al-Adha) may last anything from two to ten days, depending on the region. For more information see the section *World of Islam* at the back of the book.

HEALTH

Regulations and requirements may be subject to change at short notice, and you are advised to contact your doctor well in advance of your intended date of departure. Any numbers in the chart refer to the footnotes below.

	Special Precautions?	Certificate Required?
Yellow Fever	No	No
Cholera	1	No
Typhoid & Polio	Yes	-
Malaria	2	-
Food & Drink	3	-

[1]: The Turkish Health Authorities have reported no cases of cholera in recent years. A vaccination is recommended to give improved protection against the disease. It is, however, wise to follow simple precautions when eating and drinking – see **[3]** below.
[2]: Potential malaria risk (exclusively in the benign *vivax* form) exists from March to the end of November in the Çukorova/Amikova area and from mid-May to mid-October in southeast Anatolia.
[3]: Tap water is usually chlorinated in larger towns and cities, but should not be assumed to have been so treated: if used for drinking or making ice it should have first been boiled or otherwise sterilised. If a water source bears the words *içilmez*, it means that it is not for drinking; sources labelled *içilir, içme suyu* or *içilebilir* are safe to drink. Bottled spring water is widely available. Milk is pasteurised. Only eat well-cooked meat and fish, preferably served hot.
Rabies is present. For those at high risk, vaccination before arrival should be considered. If you are bitten abroad, seek medical advice without delay. For more information, consult the *Health* section at the back of the book.
Health care: Turkey has a large health sector: one doctor and one hospital bed for, respectively, every 1700 and 470 inhabitants. A great number of Turkish doctors and

dentists speak a foreign language, particularly at major hospitals. Private health insurance is recommended.

TRAVEL - International

AIR: Turkey's national airline is *THY Turkish Airlines (TK)*.
For free advice on air travel, call the Air Travel Advisory Bureau in the UK on (0171) 636 5000 (London) *or* (0161) 832 2000 (Manchester).
Approximate flight times: From *Frankfurt/M* to Istanbul is 2 hours 45 minutes, from *London* is 3 hours 45 minutes and from *New York* is 11 hours.
International airports: *Ankara (ANK)* (Esenboga) is 28km (17.5 miles) northeast of the city. Airport facilities include incoming and outgoing duty-free shops; bank/bureau de change; restaurant and bar. *THY* buses go from the city 90 minutes before domestic flights and 135 minutes before international flights. There is a taxi service available into the city.
Istanbul (IST) (Atatürk, formerly Yesikoy) is 24km (15 miles) west of the city (travel time – 30 minutes). Airport facilities include incoming and outgoing 24-hour duty-free shop; bank/exchange services; restaurant; bar and car hire *(Avis* and *Europcar)*. A coach (*THY* bus) goes every 15 minutes to the *THY* terminal. There are taxi services to the city.
Izmir (IZM) (Adnan Menderes). Airport facilities include bank/exchange services; restaurant and bar. A *THY* bus leaves from the city 75 minutes before departure.
There are other international airports at Adana, Trabzon, Dalaman and Antalya.
SEA: Major ports are Istanbul, Izmir, Mersin, Antalya and Bodrum. The following cruise lines run services to Turkey: *TUI Cruises, Epirotiki, BI, Lauro, Costa, CTC, Norwegian American, Turkish Maritime, 'K' Lines* and *Sun Line. Turkish Maritime Lines* operate car-ferry services from Izmir to Venice.
RAIL: There are connections from London (Liverpool Street) via Hook of Holland and Cologne to Istanbul on the *Istanbul Express,* which also carries cars from several other European cities. There is a weekly sleeper from Moscow. *Inter-Rail* tickets are available in the European part of Turkey as far as Istanbul. Other international rail routes go to Germany, Greece, Bulgaria, Serbia and Georgia.
ROAD: There are roads from the CIS, Greece, Bulgaria

and Iran. **Coach:** There are regular services between Turkey and Austria, France, Germany and Switzerland, also Jordan, Iran, Saudi Arabia and Syria.

TRAVEL - Internal

Note: There is considerable unrest in the east of the country. Advice should be sought before travel to or through this region. Contact the FCO Travel Advice Unit. Tel: (0171) 270 4129.
AIR: *Turkish Airlines* provides an important network of internal flights from Istanbul, Ankara and Izmir to all of the major Turkish cities. *Turkish Airlines* offer reductions of 60% on international flights (with the exception of Middle Eastern destinations) and 10% on domestic flights to holders of International Student Travel Conference (ISTC) cards.
SEA: *Turkish Maritime Lines* offer several coastal services with their *Adriatic Line* subsidiary, providing excellent opportunities for sightseeing; they also operate a car ferry between Mersin and Magosa (via Latakia). The *Mersin Tourist Line* operates from Mersin to Izmir and Istanbul via Antalya, Bodrum and Kusadasi. There are also services between Istanbul and Izmir, with overnight accommodation and ferry routes along Turkey's northern Black Sea coast. A frequent car ferry crosses the Dardanelles at Gallipoli, from Canakkale to Eceabat and Gelibolu to Lapseki.
Turkish Maritime Lines offer discounts of 15% on single and 25% on return passages for international routes and 50% for domestic routes to holders of ISTC cards.
RAIL: Rail fares are comparatively cheap. Many trains of the *Turkish State Railways (TCDD)* have sleeping cars, couchettes and restaurant cars. The following are non-air-conditioned accommodation. Fares are more expensive for express and mail trains, even though express trains are relatively slow, and some routes are indirect. Steam engines, such as the *Anatolia Express* which traverses eastern Turkey, are retained for tourist trains on some routes. Tickets can be purchased at *TCDD* offices at railway stations and *TCDD*-appointed agents. *TCDD* offer discounts of 20% to holders of ISTC cards. Children under seven travel free; children aged 7-11 pay half fare. Discount fares are available for Students (10% off), Groups (30% off for groups of 24 or more), Roundtrips (20% off) and Sport Teams (50% off for groups of five or more)

ROAD: There is an extensive road maintenance and building programme; 1400km (900 miles) of motorway are under construction. Traffic drives on the right. In case of an accident, contact the Turkish Touring & Automobile Association (*Turkiye Turing ve Otomobil Kurumu*). Tel: (312) 213 9761. **Coach:** Many private companies provide frequent day and night services between all Turkish cities. Services are often faster than trains and recent competition between operators has led to lower fares. Tickets are sold at the bus or coach companies' branch offices either at stations or in town centres. One should shop around the ticket offices for the best prices. Coaches depart from the bus stations (*otogar*) in large towns and from the town centre in small towns. **Car hire:** Both chauffeur and self-drive cars are available in all large towns. All international companies are represented. **Documentation:** For stays longer than three months it is necessary to apply to the Turkish Touring & Automobile Club for a customs *triptique*. An International Driving Permit is required for vehicles hired in Turkey, but a valid national driving licence is sufficient for those bringing in their own car. Insurance requirements are a Green Card (or similar international cover) endorsed for Turkish territory.
URBAN: Bus and trolleybus: Extensive conventional bus (and some trolleybus) services operate in Istanbul, Ankara and Izmir. There are buses in all other large towns. These are generally reliable, modern and easy to use, although publicity is non-existent. Tickets are

bought in advance from kiosks and dropped into a box by the driver. **Taxi:** There are many types of taxi, shared taxi and minibus in operation. Taxis are numerous in all Turkish cities and are recognisable by their chequered black and yellow bands. Metered taxis are now available in Ankara, Istanbul and other big cities. Where no metered taxis are available, the fare should be agreed beforehand.
A *dolmus* is a collective taxi which follows specific routes and is recognisable by its yellow band. Each passenger pays according to the distance travelled to specific stops. The fares are fixed by the municipality. The *dolmus* provides services within large cities to suburbs, airports and often to neighbouring towns. This is a very practical means of transport and much cheaper than a taxi. Taxis may turn into a *dolmus* and vice versa according to demand. **Ferries:** There are extensive cross-Bosphorus and short-hop ferries between the parts of Istanbul. In 1988 a second bridge over the river was opened. **Metro:** There are plans to construct a metro system in Ankara.
JOURNEY TIMES: The following chart gives approximate journey times (in hours and minutes) from Ankara to other major cities/towns in Turkey.

	Air	Road	Rail
Istanbul	0.45	6.00	7.00
Izmir	0.50	7.00	10.00
Antalya	1.00	8.00	-
Adana	0.55	6.00	13.00
Erzurum	1.15	11.00	18.00
Van	1.15	15.00	23.00
Trabzon	1.40	13.00	-
Mugla	1.25	10.00	-

ACCOMMODATION

HOTELS: In recent years Turkey has made a considerable effort to develop its hotel facilities. A certain number of hotels throughout the country are registered with the Ministry of Tourism offering satisfactory facilities. They abide by certain regulations and standards of facilities, and these are given the name 'Touristic'. There are other establishments registered with local authorities, and these, too, correspond to a certain standard as regards facilities and services. It is compulsory for establishments to have a book in which guests can register remarks, suggestions and complaints. Complaints can also be made direct to the Ministry of Tourism (address above), or to the Ministry of Tourism Directorate of the city concerned. **Grading:** Hotels are graded from **1 star** (tek yildizli) to **5 stars** (5 yildizli). Classification is based on the standard of service and facilities. Motels and holiday villas are first class (1 sinif) or second class (2 sinif).
GUEST-HOUSES: Guest-houses (pensions) can be found in holiday resorts and major towns.
SELF-CATERING: Villas and apartments can be rented. Contact the Information Counsellor's Office.

CAMPING/CARAVANNING: There are numerous sites, but facilities are generally limited.

YOUTH HOSTELS: Holders of ISTC cards, International Youth Hostel Federation cards and those registered as 'student' or 'teacher' on their passports can benefit from the youth holiday opportunities available in Turkey. There are youth hostels in Istanbul, Kumla and Canakkale.

Some Turkish organisations, such as *Turkish Airlines*, recognise the ISTC card and accordingly grant reductions to holders.

RESORTS & EXCURSIONS

For the purpose of this section the country has been divided into several regions; in addition, there is also a section on ski resorts. See also the map of Turkey for the location of the main towns, resorts and communication routes.

Istanbul

Spanning the continents of Europe and Asia, Istanbul is situated on the Golden Horn peninsula. Istanbul is a bustling, cosmopolitan city, and its history as the former capital of the Byzantine and Ottoman empires has left a rich legacy of mosques, churches, museums and magnificent palaces, coupled with bustling bazaars and a vibrant street life.

Istanbul is made up of three distinct cities. The old city of **Istanbul** is decorated with parks and gardens. The main attractions include *Topkapi*, the residential palace of the Ottoman sultans overlooking the *Sea of Marmara* and the *Bosphorus*; the *Blue Mosque*, the only mosque in the world with six minarets; *St Sophia*, once a Byzantine cathedral, later a mosque and now a museum; and, underground, the Byzantine cistern supported by 336 Corinthian columns. (St Sophia is the largest free-standing building in the world and has survived several earthquakes which have destroyed the foundations of smaller structures.)

Across the Golden Horn, in stark contrast, is modern Istanbul, **Pera**, where the larger hotels arer situated.

On the third shore lies **Uskudar** (Scutari), the Asian part of Istanbul, where Florence Nightingale nursed the sick during the Crimean War. Two suspension bridges (the longest in Europe) now span the Bosphorus and afford a panoramic view of Istanbul.

Istanbul is convenient in that many seaside resorts on the Bosphorus, including *Tarabya* and *Machka,* are only a short drive away. Other attractions are the ancient fortifications at *Rumeli Hisarti,* the *National Park* of *Mount Olympus*, the ruins of *Troy* and the boat trips on the Bosphorus to the *Princes Islands.*

Thrace & Marmara

The Dardanelles, the Sea of Marmara and the Bosphorus separate European Thrace from Turkey's heartland in Asia. **Edirne**, the provincial capital, is rich in history. Three of the finest Turkish mosques, the *Eski Cami, Uc Serefeli Cami* and the famed *Selimiye* are among the attractions. The landscape is made up of forests, mountains and sandy beaches. It is an important leisure area; there are coastal resorts at *Yalova, Erdek* and *Gemlik. Mount Uludag,* the ancient *Mount Olympus of Mysia,* is now Turkey's most popular ski resort. Lying at the foot of *Mount Uludag,* the thermal resort and historic city of **Bursa** is famous for elegant Ottoman buildings, including the *Green Mausoleum* and the *Great Mosque.* **Iznik** is the site of Roman, Byzantine, Seljuk and Ottoman remains. It is also famous for the tiles used to decorate mosques and palaces throughout Turkey. The city of **Izmit**, now sadly polluted, has ancient walls and a Roman aqueduct.

The Aegean Coast

The magnificent coast of ancient Ionia, a crucible of western civilisation, boasts many important historical sites. It is thought that the remains of Troy lie along this coast. Of the nine levels of the excavated settlement mound, the sixth is supposed to be the Troy depicted in Homer's Iliad. The ruins of the great city of *Pergamum* (modern *Bergama*) lie to the south of Troy. The city was famous in antiquity for its splendid library. It is here that you will find the *Sanctuary of Asclepieion* and two fine temples, the Acropolis and the red-brick Basilica.

Izmir, the birthplace of Homer, is Turkey's third city and an important port. It is a modern metropolis set in a curving bay surrounded by terraced hillsides. As a result of earthquakes and a great fire, there are only a few reminders of old *Smyrna – Kadifekale*, the 4th-century fortress situated on top of *Mount Pagos*. The fortress affords a superb view of the city and the *Gulf of Izmir*, the Roman agora with some well-preserved porticos and

Main picture: Kaunos, rock tombs. Above left: Ishak-Pasa Palace. Above right: Side holiday resort.

Statues of Poseidon and Artemis. **Çesme** is one of the many popular resorts in the Izmir region. It has excellent beaches, thermal springs and a 15th-century fortress. The port of *Sigacik,* the ruins of the ancient Ionian city of **Teos** and the sandy beach at a *Akkum* are all between Izmir and Çesme. The remains of the Hellenistic and Roman city of Ephesus (modern **Seljuk**) founded in the 13th century BC, lie at the foot of Mount Pion. The *Grand Theatre* has been restored and there is a 2nd-century *Temple to Serapis* and the elegant façade to the temple of Hadrian. The site of *Meryemana,* reputed to be the house of the Virgin Mary, lies very close to **Ephesus** in the small vale of *Mount Bulbul Dagi* (Nightingale Mountain). It has become a world-famous shrine, attracting thousands of pilgrims each year. The ruins of *Priene, Miletus* and *Didyma* are also of great interest and, like Ephesus, are within easy reach of **Kusadasi**, an attractive resort, surrounded by sandy bays.

The attractions of the southwest Aegean include the popular seaside town of **Bodrum**, dominated by the magnificent 15th-century *Castle of St Peter*; *Marmaris,* set in a deep fjord-like inlet; the fishing village of **Datca**; and the Lycian rock tombs in **Fethiye**. Not far from Fethiye is the newly discovered *Ölü Deniz*, a stunning crystal-clear lagoon surrounded by pine-covered mountains and protected from rampant commercial development by its status as a national park. **Pamukkale**, near Denizli, is famous for its spectacular calcified waterfall and thermal waters, used since Roman times for their therapeutic powers. Pamukkale also contains the ruins of the Roman city of *Hierapolis.*

The Western Mediterranean Coast

With sunshine for most of the year and a magnificent coastline, the Mediterranean (or Turquoise) Coast is a popular holiday area. It is also a region steeped in history and legend, dotted with important sites and great Crusader castles.

Situated on a cliff promontory, **Antalya** is a popular resort and, with its modern hotels, is the ideal starting point for tours to the outlying Roman cities of *Perge, Aspendos* and *Side.* Antalya itself boasts the monumental *Hadrian's Gate, Kesik Minare* and *Yivli Minare* mosques and *Hidirlik Kulesi,* the round Roman tower. One of the largest and best-preserved Roman stadiums lies outside the Hellenistic wall which surrounds the ruins of Perge. In addition to the *Victory Portal,* thermal bath and agora, the marks of chariot wheels can still be detected. The remarkable 2nd-century theatre at **Aspendos** is a fine surviving example of the ancient world and is still used for performances of classical plays. Turkey's finest Roman aqueduct lies to the north of the city. In **Side**, now a thriving seaside resort, the Greek enclosure walls are still virtually undamaged. The town also boasts an exquisite fountain, a theatre, two agoras and Roman baths. Nestling at the foot of a rocky promontory and crowned by a Seljuk fortress, **Alanya** is a town with a lot of history in addition to some fine beaches.

The Eastern Mediterranean Coast

A spectacularly scenic road connects **Anamur**, striking for the Byzantine castle built on a towering cliff, and **Silifke**. The museum in ancient Silifke contains finds from the many archaeological sites in the vicinity. **Mersin**, built on a site dating back to Paleolithic times, is a major port. The prosperous city of **Adana**, in the middle of the flat Cukurova plain, is the centre of Turkey's cotton industry. The massive *Taskopru Bridge,* built by Hadrian in the 2nd century, the ancient covered bazaar and nearby Crusader castles and Hittite settlements are all interesting sites. The road from **Iskenderun** leads through the Belen Pass to **Antakya**, the Biblical Antioch, where St Peter founded the first Christian community. The grotto where he preached can be seen just outside the town.

The Black Sea Coast

This rugged, mountainous region of Turkey has a wild beauty, but lacks the historical and climatic attractions of the rest of the country. Despite the variable weather, there are several coastal resorts with good, sandy beaches. These include, from east to west, *Kilyos, Sile, Akcakoca, Sinop Unye, Ordu* and *Giresun.* Accommodation is, however, often very basic. A good and scenic coastal road connects **Samsun** and **Trabzon**, the two regional centres. Although little remains to testify to its ancient origins, Samsun's important place in modern history is reflected by one of the finest monuments in Turkey; the War of Independence began here in 1919. The ruins of a Byzantine fortress can still be seen in Trabzon, together with many fine buildings including the *Church of St Sophia* which was built during the Comnene's 200-year rule. 54km (34 miles) from

Pigeon houses, Uçhisar

Trabzon is the 14th-century convent dedicated to the Virgin Mary. Set into the face of a sheer cliff, 300m (1000ft) above the valley floor, it contains some magnificent frescoes.

Central Anatolia

The hub of this vast, central plateau – the cradle of the ancient Hittite and Phrygian civilisations – is the modern metropolis of **Ankara**. Kemal Atatürk supervised the construction of Ankara, a capital to replace Istanbul, in this hitherto underpopulated region during the 1920s and 1930s. Atatürk's mausoleum dominates the new city. Ankara was, however, built on the site of more ancient settlements and it is fitting that the *Museum of Anatolian Civilisations*, built under the ramparts of the Citadel, should house a magnificent collection of Neolithic and Hittite artefacts. There are also reminders of the area's more recent past as part of the Roman and Seljuk empires. The Hittite state archives were found in **Bogazkale** (Hattusas) in 1906, and contained within the Bogazkale–Alacahoyuk–Yazilikaya triangle are the most important sites of the Hittite Empire. **Sungurlu** is a good base for visitors to this fascinating but underdeveloped region. **Amasya**, one of the most attractive towns in Anatolia, was the capital of the Pontic Kingdom. The rock tombs of the Pontic kings and the ruins of a citadel, perched on a rock face and containing the remains of an Ottoman palace, can still be seen. The nearby towns of **Tokat** and **Sivas** are noted for their Seljuk architecture. **Cappadocia** is a spectacular, almost surreal landscape of rock and cones, capped pinnacles and fretted ravines. Dwellings have been hewn from the soft, volcanic rock since 400BC, and the elaborate cave systems have sheltered generations of persecuted settlers. Some villages, notably **Soganli**, are still inhabited but most have been evacuated due to the persistent threat of rock falls. At **Goreme** there are magnificent rock churches with Byzantine frescoes and at **Zelve** a somewhat eerie monastic complex. The villages of **Ortahisar** and **Uchisar**, clustered around rock pinnacles and crowned by citadels, offer good views. The canyon of *Ihlara* and the underground cities of **Kaymakli** and **Derinkuyu** should not be missed. Small, friendly hostels and campsites are dotted around Cappadocia, but the best hotels are to be found in the main towns of **Nevsehir** and **Urgup**. The ancient settlements of *Kanes, Karum* and *Fraktin* (now a ski resort), near the old city of **Kayseri**, are worth seeing.

Konya, the old Seljuk capital and Turkey's fourth-largest city, is one of the world's oldest settlements, dating back to the 7th millenium BC. Konya was also the home of the Mevlana, one of Islam's most celebrated mystics and founder of the Order of Whirling Dervishes. The mausoleum of Mevlana became a museum in 1927 under Atatürk's secularisation policy, but remains a place of worship. Other places of interest include Alaeddin's 13th-century mosque, the *Ince Minare Medrese* and the *Iplikci Mosque*, Konya's oldest structure. The ancient sites of *Beysehir, Catalhoyuk* and *Binbir Kilise* are all close to Konya.

The Eastern Provinces

The vast, empty expanse of eastern Anatolia differs profoundly from the rest of the country. The landscape has a desolate beauty, with ochre red plains and fertile valleys, lakes, waterfalls and snow-capped peaks. There are fine mosques, palaces and monuments. **Erzurum**, the largest town in the region, was one of the eastern bastions of Byzantium for many centuries, and has mosques and mausolea from the Seljuk and Mongol eras, Byzantine walls and two Quranic colleges characterised by minarets and finely carved portals. The frontier town of **Kars**, to the north of Erzurum, is dominated by a formidable 12th-century Georgian fortress. The ruins of the 10th-century *Ani* lie east of Kars. Overshadowed by *Agri Dagri*, the biblical Mount Ararat where, according to legend, Noah's Ark came to rest, is the palace and mosque of *Ishak Pasha* at **Dogubayazit.** The site is remote and fascinating. The walled town of **Van**, on the eastern shore of the immense *Lake Van*, was an important Urartu fortress from 800-600BC. The citadel dominates the ruins of Seljuk and Ottoman mosques and many rock tombs. On the island of **Akdamar**, in Lake Van, is the enchanting 10th-century *Church of the Holy Cross*. Other places of interest include **Diyarbakir**, built in the 4th century and surrounded by forbidding triple walls of black basalt; the white-coloured medieval architecture and Roman citadel of **Mardin**; **Urfa**, site of the ancient pools of Abraham and **Nemrut Dagi**, the home of the colossal stone statues erected by King Antiochus I in the 1st century BC. Accommodation in this area is very basic and often hard to find.

Ski Resorts

Winter sports resorts in Turkey are generally located in forested mountains of average height. The following ski centres are easily accessible by road or *Turkish Airlines* domestic flights.

Bursa – Uludag: 36km (22 miles) south of Bursa, this resort is accessible by a good asphalt road or by cable car. The season runs from January to April. There are beginners' slopes, slalom and giant slalom courses, three ski lifts, three chair lifts and après-ski facilities. A wide range of accommodation is available – hotels and chalets with a capacity for 3100 – and the resort also has a small hospital.

Antalya – Saklikent: 48km (30 miles) north of Antalya, in the Bakirli Dagi mountain range, reaches 2546m (8353ft) high. Accommodation consists of pensions and chalets, with a capacity of 2500. The special attraction of this centre is that in March and April one can ski in the morning, then drive down to the coast and swim in the warm waters of the Mediterranean in the afternoon.
Bolu – Koroglu: This resort is situated on the Istanbul–Ankara highway, 50km (30 miles) from Bolu and surrounded by pine forests; the ski area is 1900-2350m (6235-7710ft) high. The second-class Kartal hotel with 400-bed capacity has a swimming pool, ski lift, equipment for hire, and ski instructors.
Erzurum – Palandoken: This centre, 5km (4 miles) from Erzurum, lies at an altitude of 2200-3100m (7200-10,000ft) with some of the longest and most difficult courses in Turkey. Accommodation is available at a 140-bed, centrally-heated ski lodge, with a chair lift, ski instructors and equipment for hire. The newly opened, 274-bed hotel Dedeman offers 4-star accommodation and facilities. There are also a number of hotels in Erzurum. December to April is the most popular season.
Kars – Sarikamis: Situated near Kars at 2250m (7400ft), this centre has good runs and ideal snow conditions. The best season is January to March. There is accommodation in Kars and at the 60-bed, centrally-heated ski lodge with a chair lift and ski instructors.
Kayseri – Erciyes: 25km (15 miles) from Kayseri, this centre lies at 2150m (7050ft) on the eastern face of Erciyes Dagi. The season runs from November to May and there is a 140-bed ski lodge, equipment-hire facilities and instructors.
POPULAR ITINERARIES: 5-day: Istanbul–Troy–Izmir–Ephesus–Bodrum. **7-day:** (a) Ankara–Konya–Cappadocia–Goreme–Alanya–Pamukkale–Izmir. (b) Istanbul–Bursa–Pamukkale–Izmir–Bodrum.

SOCIAL PROFILE

FOOD & DRINK: Turkish food combines culinary traditions of a pastoral people originating from Central Asia and the influences of the Mediterranean regions. Lamb is a basic meat featured on all menus, often as *shish kebab* (pieces of meat threaded on a skewer and grilled) or *doner kebab* (pieces of lamb packed tightly round a revolving spit). Fish and shellfish are very fresh and *barbunya* (red mullet) and *kiliç baligi* (swordfish) are delicious. *Dolma* (vine leaves stuffed with nuts and currants) and *karniyarik* (aubergine stuffed with minced meat) are other popular dishes. Guests are always able to go into a kitchen and choose from the pots if they cannot understand the names of the dishes. Table service is common. **Drink:** *Ayran* (a refreshing yoghurt drink) and strong black Turkish coffee are widely available. Turkey is a secular state and alcohol is not prohibited, although

Süleymaniye Mosque, Istanbul

during Ramadan it is considered polite for the visitor to avoid drinking alcohol. Turkish beer, red and white wines are reasonable. The national drink is *raki* (anisette) which clouds when water is added, known as 'lion's milk'. Drinking *raki* is a ritual and is traditionally accompanied by a variety of *meze* (hors d'oeuvres).

NIGHTLIFE: There are nightclubs in most main centres, either Western or Oriental, with music and dancing. There are theatres with concerts in Izmir, Istanbul and Ankara and most towns have cinemas. Restaurants and hotels sometimes offer floorshows. Turkish baths are popular.

SHOPPING: Istanbul's *Kapali Carsi Bazaar* has jewellery, carpets and antiques for sale. Turkish handicrafts include a rich variety of textiles and embroideries, articles of copper, onyx and tile, mother-of-pearl, inlaid articles, leather and suede products, jewellery and, above all, carpets and *kilims*. **Shopping hours:** 0900-1300 and 1400-1900 Monday to Saturday (closed Sunday). Summer: In the Aegean and Mediterranean regions of Turkey, government offices and many other establishments are closed during the afternoon in the summer months. The summer hours are fixed each year by the provincial governors.

SPORT: Mountaineering: Turkey has a number of mountain ranges with peaks ranging from heights of 3250m (10,660ft) to the 5165m (16,945ft) of Mount Agri (Ararat), the highest mountain in Anatolia, which provide excellent climbing possibilities for both the amateur and more expert climber. Permission is required from the Turkish Mountaineering Club. **Skiing:** Winter sports resorts in Turkey are generally located in forested mountains. Ski centres are often easily accessible by road or by *Turkish Airlines* domestic flights. Most resorts are in the north (near Ankara) and the western interior. **Watersports:** The Mediterranean coast, particularly Izmir, has very warm waters and watersports are widely available.

SPECIAL EVENTS: The following festivals are held annually:
Jan *Camel Wrestling Festival,* Selçuk. **Mar** *Istanbul International Film Festival; 1915 Sea Victory Celebration,* Çanakkale. **Apr** *Traditional 'Mesir' Festival,* Manisa. **Apr 23** *International Children's Day,* Ankara. **Apr-May** *Ephesus International Festival of Culture & Tourism,* Selçuk; *Ankara International Arts Festival.* **May** *International Nysa Culture & Art Festival,* Sultanhisar; *Yunus Emre Culture & Art Week,* Eskisehir; *Aksu Culture & Art Festival,* Giresun; *International Music and Folklore Festival,* Silifke; *International Yachting Festival,* Marmaris. **May-Jun** *International Asia-Europe Biennial,* Ankara. **Jun** *Alanya Tourism Festival; Barlin Strawberry Festival; International Tea Festival,* Rize; *International Offshore Races Istanbul–Izmir; Foça Music, Folklore and Watersports*

Festival; Marmaris Festival; Bergama Festival; Atatürk Culture Festival, Amasya; *Kalkasöl Culture & Art Festival,* Artvin; *Bursa International Festival; International Kus Cenneti Culture & Tourism Festival,* Bandirma; *Safranboly Architectural Treasures and Folklore Week.* **Jun-Jul** *Çesme Sea and Music Festival; Istanbul International Art & Culture Festival; Traditional Kirkpinar Wrestling,* Edirne; *Ihlara Tourism and Art Week,* Aksaray. **Jul** *Erzurum International Congress; Tourism & Culture Festival,* Iskenderun; *International Folk Dance Festival,* Samsun; *Ceramic Festival,* Kütahya; *Nasreddin Hoca Festival,* Aksehir; *Hittite Festival,* Çorum; *Troy Festival,* Çanakkale. **Aug** *Insuyu Festival,* Burdur; *Hacibektas Veli Commemoration Ceremony; Mengen Chefs Festival,* Izmir. **Aug-Sep** *Izmir International Fair.* **Sep** *Erfugrul Gazi Commemoration Ceremony,* Söğüt; *Seyh Edibali'l Commemoration and Culture Festival,* Bilecik; *GAP Culture & Art Festival,* Gazlantep; *Javelin Games,* Konya; *Kemer Festival; International Meerschaum (White Gold) Festival,* Eskisehir; *Folklore Week,* Safranbolu; *Sivas Congress Culture & Art Week; International Grape Harvest Festival,* Ürgüp; *International Fair,* Mersin; *Allin Portakal Film Festival; Yagci Bedir Carpet Festival,* Sindirgi Balikesir. **Sep-Oct** *International Plastic Arts Biennial,* Istanbul; *International Akdeniz Song Contest,* Antalya; *Culture & Art Festival,* Diyarbakir; *Mersin Art & Culture Festival.* **Oct** *Ahl-Brotherhood Cultural Week,* Kirsehir; *International Bodrum Cup; International Gullei Festival,* Bozburun. **Nov** *International Yacht Race,* Marmaris. **Dec** *International St Nicolas Symposium,* Kale, Antalya; *Meviana Commemoration Ceremony,* Konya.

SOCIAL CONVENTIONS: Shaking hands is the normal form of greeting. Hospitality is very important and visitors should respect Islamic customs. Informal wear is acceptable, but beachwear should be confined to the beach or poolside. Smoking is widely acceptable but prohibited in cinemas, theatres, city buses and *dolmuses* (collective taxis). **Tipping:** A service charge is included in hotel and restaurant bills.

BUSINESS PROFILE

ECONOMY: Agriculture which accounts for only 18% of GNP and approximately 15% of exports has its traditional importance, in this vast land of variations. Export crops are hazelnuts, cotton, tobacco, raisins and figs. Other products include wheat, olives and citrus fruit. In mining, Turkey is an important producer of copper, borax, chromium and to a lesser extent, bauxite and coal. A competitive industry, ie textiles in the manufacturing sector, heads the list of exports. Iron and steel as well as food processing industries are also important. Tourism is in a phase of rapid expansion and is now a key source of

foreign exchange. Turkish trade patterns have shifted from the Middle East in favour of Europe and the EU in particular. Turkey is an associate member, and due to join a customs union with the EU in 1996. The country is also a member of ECO which was formed by Turkey, Iran and Pakistan and was later joined by Azerbaijan, Kyrgyzstan, Tajikistan, Turkmenistan and Uzbekistan. Net foreign direct investments reached US$779 million in 1992. On the other hand, exports have increased at an average of 80% of industrial goods. The Government attaches great importance and is in the process of privatising state economic enterprises. Germany (which employs many Turkish immigrant workers), the USA, Italy, France and the UK are Turkey's main trading partners.

BUSINESS: A formal suit or jacket and tie should always be worn for business. English is widely spoken in business circles, although an effort by the visitor to speak a little Turkish is appreciated. The majority of people in business value punctuality and visiting cards are widely used. **Office hours:** 0830-1200 and 1300-1730 Monday to Friday.

COMMERCIAL INFORMATION: The following organisation can offer advice: Union of Chambers of Commerce, Industry, Maritime Commerce and Commodity Exchanges of Turkey (UCCET), Atatürk Bul. 149, Bakanhliklar, Ankara. Tel: (312) 417 7700. Telex: 42343.

CLIMATE

Marmara and the Aegean and Mediterranean coasts have a typical Mediterranean climate with hot summers and mild winters.
Required clothing: Light- to medium-weights and rainwear.

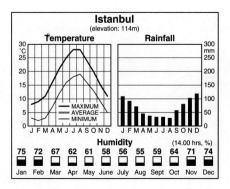

□ international airport

Location: Central Asia.

Turkmenintour
Ulitsa Makhtumkhuli 74, Ashgabat, Turkmenistan
Tel: (3632) 256 932 *or* 255 191. Fax: (3632) 293 169.
Telex: 228192 (a/b CONSUL SU).
Ministry of Culture and Tourism
Ul. Pushkin 14, Ashgabat 744000, Turkmenistan
Tel: (3632) 253 560. Fax: (3632) 511 991. Telex: 116175
(a/b TINTO SU).
Ministry of Foreign Affairs
Ulitsa Makhtumkhuli 83, Ashgabat, Turkmenistan
Tel: (3632) 294 709 (general enquiries) *or* 251 666
(visas). Fax: (3632) 251 463 (general enquiries) *or* 253
583 (visas). Telex: 116338 (a/b ULKE SU).
Intourist
219 Marsh Wall, Isle of Dogs, London E14 9FJ
Tel: (0171) 538 8600. Fax: (0171) 538 5967.
Embassy of Turkmenistan
Suite 412, 1511 K Street, NW Washington , DC 20005
Tel: (202) 737 4800. Fax: (202) 737 1152.
Fairwinds Trading Company
Suite 1610, 5151 E Broadway, Tucson, AZ 85711
Tel: (520) 748 1288. Fax: (520) 748 1347. Telex:
6507151271 (a/b MCI UW)
Embassy of the United States of America
c/o Hotel Jubilienaya, ul. Teheran 6 (formerly
ul.Temiryasev, formerly ul. Ostrovskaya), Ashgabat
744012, Turkmenistan
Tel: (3632) 244 925 *or* 244 922
**The Canadian Embassy in Almaty deals with
enquiries relating to Turkmenistan (see *Kazakhstan*
earlier in this book).**

AREA: 488,100 sq km (188,456 sq miles).
POPULATION: 4,254,000 (1993 estimate).
POPULATION DENSITY: 8.7 per sq km.
CAPITAL: Ashgabat. **Population:** 517,200 (1990 estimate).
GEOGRAPHY: Turkmenistan shares borders with
Kazakhstan to the north, Uzbekistan to the east,
Afghanistan to the southeast and Iran to the south. To the
west is the Caspian Sea. Nearly 80% of the country is
taken up by the Kara-Kum (Black Sand) desert, the
largest in the CIS. The longest irrigation canal in the
world stretches 1100km (687 miles), from the Amu-
Darya River in the east, through Ashgabat, before being
piped the rest of the way to the Caspian Sea.

LANGUAGE: Turkmen is the official state language,
and is closer to Turkish, Azeri and Crimean Tartar than
those of its neighbours Uzbekistan and Kazakhstan. The
Turkmen was changed from Latin to Cyrillic in 1940, but
the process of changing back to the Turkish version of
the Latin script is underway.
RELIGION: Predominantly Sunni Muslim with a small
Russian Orthodox minority. Turkmenistan shares the
Central Asian Sufi tradition.
TIME: GMT + 5.
ELECTRICITY: 220 volts AC, 50Hz. Round 2-pin
continental plugs are standard.
COMMUNICATIONS: Telephone: Country code: 7
(3632 for Ashgabat). IDD from Ashgabat is not yet
available, but calls can be booked through the
international operator, who speaks English, or made at
the Main Post Office on ul. Karl Libnicht. Direct-dial
calls within the former USSR are obtained by dialling 8
and waiting for another dial tone and then dialling the
city code. Calls within the city limits are free of charge.
Fax: Services are available in the main hotels for
residents only. **Telex/telegram:** Telegram and telex
services (the latter with dual Cyrillic and Latin keyboards
– impractical except in emergencies) are available from
post offices in large towns. Telex facilities are also
available to residents in the main hotels. **Post:** Letters to
Western Europe and the USA can take between two
weeks and two months. Stamped envelopes can be
bought from post offices. Mail addresses should be laid
out in the following order: country, postcode, city, street,
house number and lastly the person's name. Post office
hours: 0900-1800 Monday to Friday. The Main Post
Office in Ashgabat is open until 1900 (for address, see
above). Visitors can also use the post offices situated in
the major Intourist hotels. **Press:** The press in
Turkmenistan is still censored. The main newspapers in
Ashgabat are *Turkmenistan* and *Watan* (both in
Turkmen) and *Turkmenskaya Iskra* (Russian).
**BBC World Service and Voice of America
frequencies:** From time to time these change. See the
section *How to Use this Book* for more information.
BBC:

MHz	17.64	15.57	11.76	7.160

Voice of America:

MHz	9.670	6.040	5.995	1.260

PASSPORT/VISA

Regulations and requirements may be subject to change at short notice, and you are advised to contact the appropriate diplomatic or consular authority before finalising travel arrangements. Details of these may be found at the head of this country's entry. Any numbers in the chart refer to the footnotes below.

	Passport Required?	Visa Required?	Return Ticket Required?
Full British	Yes*	Yes*	No*
BVP	Not valid*	-	-
Australian	Yes*	Yes*	No*
Canadian	Yes*	Yes*	No*
USA	Yes*	Yes*	No*
Other EU (As of 31/12/94)	Yes*	Yes*	No*
Japanese	Yes*	Yes*	No*

Note [*]: Visa regulations within the CIS are currently
liable to change. Prospective travellers are advised to
contact *Intourist Travel Ltd* well in advance of intended
date of departure. They offer a comprehensive visa
service for all of the republics within the CIS. Tel: (0171)
538 5902 in the UK; (212) 757 3884 in the USA.
Passports: Valid passports required by all.
British Visitors Passport: Not acceptable.
VISAS: Issued on arrival in Turkmenistan. Special
permission must be sought by those wishing to visit
border zones.
Types of visa:
(a) Ordinary: 10 days (US$10), 20 days (US$20), 1
month (US$30), 3 months (US$30 per month), 1 year
(US$20 per month);
(b) Multiple entry: 1 month (US$50), 3 to 12 months
(US$30 per month);
Visa extensions are available for up to 30 days
(US$10 for 10 days).
Validity: Subject to the nature of the visit and the
discretion of the authorities in Turkmenistan.
Temporary residence: Applications for temporary
residence to carry out business are handled by the
Interior Ministry; those wishing to obtain temporary
residence for other reasons should apply to the
Consular Affairs Office at the Foreign Ministry.

MONEY

Currency: 1 Manat = 100 tenge. Notes are in
denominations of 1000, 500, 100, 50, 10, 5 and 1 Manats.

Coins are in denominations of 50, 20, 10, 5 and 1 tenge.
The Manat was introduced in November 1993, after the
Russian Federation decided on a radical reform of the
Rouble.
Currency exchange: The preferred hard currency is US
Dollars and visitors carrying other currencies may find it
hard to change them. Foreign currency can be changed at
banks and major hotels. Foreigners are expected to pay
all travel and hotel bills in hard currency, and prices bear
little relation to what locals are expected to pay.
Turkmenintour packages are all-inclusive and extra
payment of accommodation and meals is unnecessary.
Credit cards: Credit cards are not accepted.
Travellers cheques: Only travellers cheques drawn on
banks with reciprocal arrangements with the Turkmen
National Bank are accepted.
Eurocheques are not accepted.
Exchange rate indicators: Exchange rates for the Manat
were £1.00 = 3.40*, US$1.00 = 2.30* in February 1994.
The Manat is not convertible on the international market.
Note [*]: The official exchange rate was set in December
1993. The black-market rate in Ashgabat was 40 Manats
to the US Dollar and falling (Feb 1994).
Currency restrictions: The export of local currency is
prohibited. Foreign currency should be declared on
arrival.

DUTY FREE

The following goods may be imported into Turkmenistan
without incurring customs duty:
*400 cigarettes, 100 cigars or 500g of tobacco products; 2
litres of alcoholic beverage; a reasonable quantity of
perfume for personal use; other goods up to the value of
US$5000.*
Note: On entering the country, tourists must complete a
customs declaration form which must be retained until
departure. This allows the import of articles intended for
personal use, including currency and valuables which
must be registered on the declaration form. Customs
inspection can be long and detailed. It is advisable when
shopping to ask for a certificate from the shop which
states that goods have been paid for in hard currency.
Presentation of such certificates should speed up customs
formalities.
Prohibited imports: Military weapons and ammunition,
narcotics and drug paraphernalia, pornography, loose
pearls and anything owned by a third party that is to be
carried in for that third party. If you have any query
regarding items that may be imported, an information
sheet is available on request from Intourist.
Prohibited exports: As prohibited imports, as well as
annulled securities, state loan certificates, lottery tickets,
works of art and antiques (unless permission has been
granted by the Ministry of Culture), saiga horns, Siberian
stag, punctuate and red deer antlers (unless on organised
hunting trip) and punctuate deer skins.

PUBLIC HOLIDAYS

Jan 1 '95 New Year's Day. **Jan 12** Remembrance Day
(Anniversary of the battle of Geok-Tepe). **Feb 19**
Birthday of Turkmen President Sapurmurat
Turkmenbashi. **Mar 21** Navrus Bayram. **Mar 8**
International Women's Day. **May 9** Victory Day. **May
18** Day of Revival and Unity. **May 10** Gurban Bayram.
Oct 27-28 Independence Day. **Jan 1 '96** New Year's
Day. **Jan 12** Remembrance Day (Anniversary of the
battle of Geok-Tepe). **Feb 19** Birthday of Turkmen
President Sapurmurat Turkmenbashi. **Feb 22** Navrus
Bayram. **Mar 8** International Women's Day. **Apr 29**
Gurban Bayram.

HEALTH

Regulations and requirements may be subject to change at short notice, and you are advised to contact your doctor well in advance of your intended date of departure. Any numbers in the chart refer to the footnotes below.

	Special Precautions?	Certificate Required?
Yellow Fever	No	No
Cholera	No	No
Typhoid & Polio	No	No
Malaria	1	-
Food & Drink	2	-

[1]: There have been reports of malaria cases among
visitors to the Amu-Darya River in the east of
Turkmenistan. Precautions are advised.
[2]: All water should be regarded as a potential health risk.
Water used for drinking, brushing teeth or making ice
should be boiled or otherwise sterilised. Milk is
pasteurised and dairy products are safe for consumption.
Only eat well-cooked meat and fish, preferably served hot.

Pork, salad and mayonnaise may carry increased risk. Vegetables should be cooked and fruit peeled.
Rabies is present. For those at high risk, vaccination should be considered. If you are bitten abroad, seek medical advice without delay. For more information, consult the *Health* section at the back of the book.
Health care: Medical insurance is highly recommended. Emergency health care is available free of charge for visitors. Travellers are advised to take a well-equipped first-aid kit with them containing basic medicines and any prescriptions that they may need.

TRAVEL - International

AIR: The domestic airline is *Turkmenistan Airlines*. There are international connections to Istanbul (Turkey), Abu Dhabi (UAE) and Karachi (Pakistan). Ashgabat is also served by *Iranian Airlines* from Tehran and by *Turkish Airlines* from Istanbul. There are connections within the CIS to Moscow and St Petersburg (Russian Federation), Tashkent (Uzbekistan), Almaty (Kazakhstan) and Kiev (Ukraine). All flight tickets bought by foreigners within Turkmenistan must be paid for in hard currency. The prices tend to be ten times as much as what locals pay.
Approximate flight times: From *Istanbul* to Ashgabat is 2 hours 30 minutes, from *Abu Dhabi* is 2 hours, from *Karachi* is 4 hours 30 minutes, from *Tehran* is 1 hour, from *Moscow* is 3 hours 30 minutes, from *Tashkent* is 2 hours, from *Almaty* is 2 hours 30 minutes and from *Kiev* is 2 hours.
International airport: *Ashgabat Airport (ASB)* is about 4km (2.5 miles) north of the city centre. There is a new international airport 6km (4 miles) from the city centre. The airport is served by buses and taxis.
SEA: There are ferries to Turkmenbashi (formerly Krasnovodsk) from Baku (Azerbaijan) and an irregular service to Astrakhan (Russian Federation). It is theoretically possible to travel from Moscow to Turkmenbashi via the Volga River and the Caspian Sea without setting foot on dry land.
RAIL: The *Trans-Caspian Railway* connects Turkmenistan with the rest of the Central Asian republics and thence to Moscow and the rest of the CIS. The terminus is in Turkmenbashi (formerly Krasnovodsk) on the Caspian Sea from where it runs through Ashgabat before it crosses into Uzbekistan near the city of Chardzhou. A rail connection to Mashad in Iran is under construction (expected to start operation in 1996) and another to Bandar Shahi (Iran) is planned. The possiblity of a spur running north to western Uzbekistan is being discussed. Approximate rail times from Turkmenbashi to Tashkent is 24 hours, to Dushanbe is 36 hours and to Moscow is 3 days.
ROAD: Turkmenistan is connected by road to Kazakhstan, Uzbekistan and to Mashad and Tehran in Iran. The crossing into Iran is only open to nationals of the CIS and Iran. It is possible to obtain a special permission to cross the border from the Iranian and Turkmen authorities, but this should be done before departure. There is also a road to Herat in Afghanistan from Mary. **Bus:** Services are available to the capitals of the neighbouring republics, and north across the Kara-Kum desert to Kunya-Urgench with connections to Urgench and Khiva in Uzbekistan.

TRAVEL - Internal

AIR: *Turkmenistan Airways* runs regular flights between Ashgabat, Mary, Chardzhou and Turkmenbashi. All flight tickets have to be paid for in hard currency.
Approximate flight times: From Ashgabat to *Mary* is 1 hour and to *Chardzhou* is 1 hour 30 minutes.
RAIL: The *Trans-Caspian Railway* runs from Turkmenbashi (formerly Krasnovodsk) in the west, through Ashgabat and Mary to Chardzhou in the east before continuing to Bukhara in Uzbekistan.
ROAD: Traffic drives on the right. The main road in Turkmenistan runs along the route of the *Trans-Caspian Railway* (see above). There is also a road that runs north from Ashgabat to Tashauz and Kunya-Urgench before crossing into Uzbekistan. This road crosses 500km (311 miles) of the Kara-Kum desert. **Bus:** Services are available to all the major towns, including Kunya-Urgench. **Taxi:** Taxis and chauffeur-driven cars for hire can be found in all major towns. Many are unlicensed and travellers are advised to agree the fare in advance. As many of the street names have changed since independence, it is also advisable to ascertain both the old and the new street names when asking directions.
Car hire: Self-drive hire is not yet available, but there are plans to introduce it in the near future.
Documentation: When car hire is available, an International Driver's Licence will be required.

ACCOMMODATION

HOTELS: There are no restrictions on where foreigners can stay in Turkmenistan. When Turkmenistan gained independence, there was an acute shortage of hotel accommodation, a situation which the Turkmen are working hard to rectify. Feverish hotel construction is underway in Ashgabat. A row of luxury hotels have recently been built on the edge of town along a road known locally as the 'Miracle Mile'. These are small hotels with between 15-40 rooms that are owned and run by various ministries and governmental organisations. Architectural motifs are mosques, palaces and fortresses. They are in the upper price bracket with singles running at about US$200 per night. The Ak Altin Plaza Hotel should be open by spring 1995 and will offer Western-style amenities. Room rates are US$180-215 per night. The Kolkhozchy Hotel in central Ashgabat is a basic, clean property that cooperates with Fair Winds Trading Company, an American hotel firm that can arrange bookings in the US (see top of entry for address). The Kolkhozchy's room rates are between US$60-$160 per night. The main hotels in Ashgabat are the Hotel Ashgabat (the main tourist hotel), the Hotel Oktyabrskaya and the Hotel Turist. The Hotel Jubilienaya houses both the US and German embassies and reservations are difficult to obtain. Every provincial centre has at least one hotel, but visitors should not expect Western standards of comfort and amenities. The exception is a new hotel which recently opened in Turkmenbashi; however, as it only has 40 rooms, it is advisable to contact *Turkmenintour* for a reservation. Accommodation and services in hotels are payable in hard currency, usually US Dollars.
REST HOUSES: *Dom Otdykha* (literally 'rest houses') were built on the shores of the Caspian Sea by cooperatives and other concerns for fatigued workers. It is sometimes possible for travellers to obtain accommodation in them.
CAMPING: There are campsites on the shores of the Caspian Sea and *Turkmenintour* is in the process of improving the facilities.

RESORTS & EXCURSIONS

Turkmenistan is a hot and dry country – the most southerly of the former Soviet republics – and almost all the attractions lie around the fringes of the desert and in oases such as Merv.
The capital, **Ashgabat,** on the southern rim of the *Kara-Kum* desert, is a modern city. It replaced the one founded in 1881, which was destroyed in an earthquake in 1948 which measured 10.5 on the Richter scale, killed 30% of the population and razed the city to the ground. There are a number of museums, including an art museum and a geographical museum in the same building on ul. Makhtumkhuli, although these are currently being renovated (February 1994). There is a small carpet museum attached to the carpet factory on ul. Kuragli (formerly Piervomaiskaya). The Sunday market in Ashgabat is the best place anywhere to buy Turkmen carpets, misleadingly called Bukhara carpets in the west. The new *Tekke* bazaar is built almost entirely of marble. In spring and autumn horseraces are held at the *Hippodrome,* and 10km (6 miles) south of Ashgabat is the *Turkmenbashi Stud Farm* where the famous Akilteken horses are bred. Also close to Ashgabat are the remains of *Old Nisa,* the capital of the Parthian kings who ruled from the 3rd century BC to the 3rd century AD over an empire which included Iraq and stretched as far as Syria. The *Firyusa Gorge* in the mountains south of Ashgabat is a popular escape for Ashgabatis during the hot summer months.
40km (25 miles) west of Ashgabat are the remains of *Geok-Tepe,* the fort where as many as 20,000 Tekke Turkmen were killed by the Russian General Skobileff in 1881. A pleasant day trip is to *Kov Ata*, 90km (56 miles) west of Ashgabat. The underground mineral lake is fed by hot springs and has a constant temperature of 37°C. Accommodation is not available.
Mary, due east of Ashgabat, is Turkmenistan's second city. It lies near the remains of the city of *Merv,* which was once the second city of Islam and known as the 'Queen of Cities' until an earlier tourist, Ghengis Khan's son Toloi, reduced it to rubble and reportedly killed as many as a million of its inhabitants in 1221. The remains of that Merv and of the many that both preceded it and succeeded it are spread over a large area. Most of what remains are the brick-built mausolea of rulers and holy men – including the impressive *Mausoleum of Sultan Sanjar,* completed in 1140. Time, weather and invasions have taken their toll on the mud-built cities of the Turkmen.
Turkmenbashi was known as Krasnovodsk, but it was renamed in honour of President Saparmurat Niyazov, who has been given the title 'Turkmenbashi' or 'leader of all the Turkmen'. Situated on the shores of the Caspian Sea, it is a Russian creation, built as a bridgehead for the campaign to subdue Central Asia, and later to become the terminal for the *Trans-Caspian Railway*. The *Museum of History and Natural History* makes an interesting visit. 500km (311 miles) north of Ashgabat, across the Kara-Kum desert, lies **Kunya-Urgench,** the former *Gurganj,* boasting the tallest remaining minaret in Central Asia, the 62m-high (203ft) *Kutluk Timur Minaret,* built in the 14th century.
POPULAR ITINERARIES: *Turkmenintour* are in the process of developing set itineraries, but at present visitors are invited to either design their own or list their interests and Turkmenintour will tailor-make them accordingly.

SOCIAL PROFILE

FOOD & DRINK: Turkmen food is similar to that of the rest of Central Asia. There are a number of good Western-standard restaurants in Ashgabat, although they rarely have an extensive menu. *Plov* – pronounced 'plof' in Turkmenistan – is the staple food for everyday and celebrations and consists of chunks of mutton, shredded yellow turnip and rice fried in a large wok. *Shashlyk* (skewered chunks of mutton grilled over charcoal – kebabs – which come with raw sliced onions) and *lipioshka* (rounds of unleavened bread) are served in restaurants and are often sold in the street, but the quality can be variable. *Manty* are larger noodle sacks filled with meat. *Shorpa* is a meat and vegetable soup.
There are, however, a number of dishes that are particularly characteristic of Turkmenistan: *ka'urma* is mutton deep-fried in its own fat and *churban churpa* is mutton fat dissolved in green tea. *Ishkiykli* are dough balls filled with meat and onion which are traditionally cooked in sand which has been heated by a fire. On the shores of the Caspian Sea, seafood is often substituted for mutton in traditional dishes such as *plov*. In the west of Turkmenistan there is a speciality in which mutton is roasted in a clay oven fired with aromatic woods.
In general, hotel food shows strong Russian influence: *borcht* is cabbage soup, *entrecote* is a well-done steak, *cutlet* are grilled meat balls, and *strogan* is the local equivalent of beef Stroganoff. *Pirmeni*, originated in Ukraine, are small boiled noodle sacks of meat and vegetables similar to ravioli, sometimes in a vegetable soup, sometimes not.
Drink: Green tea is very popular and can be obtained almost anywhere. Beer, wine, vodka, brandy and sparkling wine *(shampanski)* are all widely available in restaurants. *Kefir,* a thick drinking yoghurt, is often served with breakfast.
NIGHTLIFE: Ashgabat has an opera and ballet theatre, which shows both Russian and European works and a drama theatre. There are also a few restaurants offering dancing.
SHOPPING: The Sunday market is the best place in the world to buy the misleadingly named Bukhara rugs, which are actually made in Turkmenistan. There is a shop in the Art Gallery which sells traditional Turkmen handicrafts, silver and costumes including the distinctive Turkmen sheepskin hats. The central bazaar in Ashgabat is a good place to buy food and curiosities. **Shopping hours:** Food shops open 0800-1700, all others open 0900-1800. Bazaars open at dawn.
SPECIAL EVENTS: There are a number of festivals which provide an interesting spectacle for visitors. The following are a selection of events celebrated annually:
Apr (last Sunday) *Akilteken Day* – Celebration of the Akilteken horse with parades and races.
May (last Sunday) *Day of the Turkmen Carpet.*
Sep (second Sunday) *Bakshi Day* – Celebration of Turkmen folk singers.
Nov (last Sunday) *Harvest Festival.*
SOCIAL CONVENTIONS: *Lipioshka* (bread) should never be laid upside down, and it is normal to remove shoes, but not socks, when entering someone's house. Shorts are rarely seen in Turkmenistan and, worn by females, are likely to provoke unwelcome attention from the local male population.

BUSINESS PROFILE

ECONOMY: During the Soviet era, Turkmenistan was an impoverished and exploited outpost of the empire, and the legacy of this is still visible. However, the outlook for the future holds strong hope. Since independence in 1991, Turkmenistan has grown to become the world's fourth-largest producer of natural gas, and has also begun to exploit its vast oil reserves. Turkmenistan hopes to increase its oil and gas production five-fold before the turn of the century. The main limitation on this growth is Turkmenistan's ability to export the oil and gas. There is currently only one pipeline out of the republic which has limited capacity and does not lead directly towards the more lucrative markets of Europe and the Far East. In the short term, this means that the main customers for Turkmen oil and gas will remain the other former states of the Soviet Union, many of whom are unable to pay world prices, or in some cases, to pay at all. There are several plans to build pipelines, and there has been much foreign investment in the Turkmen oil and gas industry in anticipation of their eventual construction, but as yet there are no concrete decisions on routing. There are other mineral reserves including sulphur, salt, iodine and ferrous bromide. The agricultural sector still employs over 50% of the population. However, the agricultural potential of the republic is limited by an acute lack of water: the main supply comes from the Amu-Darya River by the Kara-Kum canal, and any further drainage of the Amu-Darya would exacerbate the ecological disaster area that is the Aral Sea, into which the Amu-Darya drains. Currently Turkmenistan grows cotton, wheat – the Government has implemented a programme to try to make the republic self-sufficient in grain as soon as possible – silk, fruit and vegetables, and wool, including Karakul sheepskins. Turkmenistan's industrial base is small and the Government is trying to encourage growth in this sector. Much of what there is is concentrated in the petrochemical industry. The main drive for industrialisation is in the upgrading of existing plants and the creation of a new secondary production sector to refine the agricultural raw materials that are produced domestically. Economic growth has been hampered by hyper-inflation of the new currency and the breakdown of the ex-USSR trading bloc. However, barter trade for mineral resources has ensured a minimum of shortages in the republic. The Government provides limited amounts of free energy to the population and they have high expectations of future prosperity.

BUSINESS: The Government is particularly interested in encouraging foreign investment in a number of areas, including oil and gas production and refining; agricultural production and processing (particularly in cotton); consumer goods; export-orientated products; research and development; environmental protection and infrastructure. The Turkmen government has put a number of measures in place to encourage foreign investment. Eight Free Enterprise Economic Zones – one in each of the *velayat* (regions) – have been created with special incentives for companies that invest in them. These include: no import duties, a 3-year tax holiday from the start of production, with a further 13 years of reduced taxes; full-profit repatriation; and a swifter licensing procedure. 100% foreign-owned concerns must be sited in Free Enterprise Economic Zones, but joint ventures are allowed to set up anywhere. All foreign investments are protected by government guarantee from expropriation. All foreign companies and individuals wishing to invest in Turkmenistan must go through the Commission for International Economic Affairs of the Office of the President of Turkmenistan.

COMMERCIAL INFORMATION: The following organisations can offer advice: Commission for International Economic Affairs of the Office of the President of Turkmenistan, ul. Kemine 92, Ashgabat 744000. Tel: (3632) 298 770. Fax: (3632) 297 524. Information can also be obtained from the US Department of Commerce Business Information Service for the Newly Independent States, Room 7413, US Department of Commerce, Washington, DC 20230. Tel: (202) 482 4655. Fax: (202) 482 2293.

CLIMATE

Turkmenistan has an extreme continental climate: temperatures in Ashgabat vary between 46°C in summer and -5°C in winter, although it has been known to reach -22°C in extremity. Temperatures in the desert in summer can reach 50°C during the day before falling rapidly at night. During the winter it can reach -10/-15°C.
Required clothing: For those intending to visit the desert in summer, lightweights are vital for the day with warmer clothing for those intending to spend the night in the open. Heavyweights should be taken for winter visits.

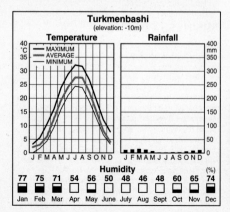

Turkmenbashi
(elevation: -10m)

| Temperature | Rainfall |

MAXIMUM / AVERAGE / MINIMUM

Humidity

| 77 | 75 | 71 | 54 | 56 | 50 | 48 | 46 | 48 | 60 | 65 | 74 | (%) |
| Jan | Feb | Mar | Apr | May | June | July | Aug | Sept | Oct | Nov | Dec |

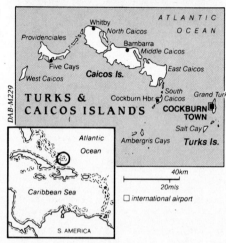

Turks & Caicos Islands

DAB-M229

Location: Caribbean, southeast of the Bahamas.

Diplomatic representation: The Turks & Caicos Islands are a British Dependent Territory and are formally represented abroad by British diplomatic missions. However, information and advice may be obtained at the addresses below:

Turks & Caicos Islands Tourist Board
PO Box 128, Pond Street, Grand Turk, Turks & Caicos Islands
Tel: 946 2321. Fax: 946 2733.
Turks & Caicos Tourist Information Office
International House, 47 Chase Side, Enfield, Middlesex EN2 6NB
Tel: (0181) 364 5188. Fax: (0181) 367 9949. Telex: 24457. Opening hours: 0930-1730 Monday to Friday.
Commonwealth Information Centre
Commonwealth Institute, Kensington High Street, London W8 6NQ
Tel: (0171) 603 4535, ext 210 (information). Fax: (0171) 602 7374.
Turks & Caicos Travel Bureau
4197 Braganza Street, Coconut Grove, Miami, FL 33133
Tel: (305) 667 0966. Fax: (305) 667 2494.
Turks & Caicos Islands Tourist Board
US and Canadian Representatives, Trombone Associates Inc, 420 Madison Avenue, New York, NY 10017
Tel: (212) 223 2323 *or* (800) 241 0824 (tollfree; USA and Canada only). Fax: (212) 223 0260.

AREA: 500 sq km (193 sq miles).
POPULATION: 12,350 (1990).
POPULATION DENSITY: 24.7 per sq km.
CAPITAL: Cockburn Town (Grand Turk). **Population:** 3761 (1990).
GEOGRAPHY: The Turks & Caicos are an archipelago of more than 40 islands forming the southeastern end of the Bahamas chain. There are two principal groups, each surrounded by a continuous coral reef. Caicos is the larger group and includes Providenciales, Middle (or Grand) Caicos, and the islands of North, South, East and West Caicos, plus numerous small cays, some of which are inhabited. The Turks group, separated by a 35km-wide (22-mile) channel of water, consists of Grand Turk, Salt Cay and a number of small uninhabited cays.
LANGUAGE: English.

| Health |
| GALILEO/WORLDSPAN: **TI-DFT/GDT/HE** |
| SABRE: **TIDFT/GDT/HE** |

| Visa |
| GALILEO/WORLDSPAN: **TI-DFT/GDT/VI** |
| SABRE: **TIDFT/GDT/VI** |

For more information on Timatic codes refer to Contents.

RELIGION: Roman Catholic, Anglican, Methodist, Baptist, Seventh Day Adventist and Pentecostal.
TIME: GMT - 5 (GMT - 4 from first Sunday in April to Saturday before last Sunday in October).
ELECTRICITY: 110 volts AC.
COMMUNICATIONS: Telephone: IDD is available. Country code: 809. Outgoing international code: 01. Good communications network run by *Cable & Wireless (WI) Ltd*, with automatic exchange on all the islands. USA 800 calls are charged at the normal rate. The local telephone directory lists charges for international calls. There is a 10% tax on all calls. Public card-phones are in operation on all the islands; phonecards are available from *Cable & Wireless* and outlets near phone booths, in denominations of US$20, 10 and 5, plus 10% tax. Cheap rates are in operation 1900-0600 weekdays and all day Saturday and Sunday. **Fax:** All the islands have facsimile services. **Telex/telegram:** International services are available from the capital and main hotels from 0800-1800 Monday to Saturday. **Post:** The General Post Office is on Grand Turk, with sub-offices in South Caicos, Salt Cay and Providenciales. Airmail to Western Europe takes five days. Post office hours: 0800-1600 Monday to Thursday; 0800-1530 Friday. **Press:** *The Turks & Caicos Free Press* is published bi-weekly, *The Turks and Caicos News* weekly, *The Times of the Islands Magazine* quarterly, with *The Turks and Caicos Pocket Guide* appearing seasonally.
BBC World Service and Voice of America frequencies: From time to time these change. See the section *How to Use this Book* for more information.

BBC:
| MHz | 17.84 | 15.22 | 9.915 | 6.195 |

Voice of America:
| MHz | 15.21 | 11.70 | 6.130 | 0.930 |

PASSPORT/VISA

Regulations and requirements may be subject to change at short notice, and you are advised to contact the appropriate diplomatic or consular authority before finalising travel arrangements. Details of these may be found at the head of this country's entry. Any numbers in the chart refer to the footnotes below.

	Passport Required?	Visa Required?	Return Ticket Required?
Full British	Yes	No	Yes
BVP	Not valid	-	-
Australian	Yes	No	Yes
Canadian	1	No	Yes
USA	1	No	Yes
Other EU (As of 31/12/94)	Yes	No	Yes
Japanese	Yes	No	Yes

PASSPORTS: Valid passport required by all except [1] nationals of Canada and the USA if holding proof of identity (ie Birth Certificate & Photo ID).
British Visitors Passport: Not acceptable.
VISAS: Required by former Eastern bloc countries and some non-Commonwealth countries. Since visa regulations are subject to frequent change, it is strongly advised to check with the visa department of the British Passport Office prior to departure (see below).
Types of visa: Entry visa. Cost: £20 (£28 if the application has to be referred to Grand Turk).
Validity: Variable; each application is judged on individual merit.
Application to: British Passport Office, Clive House, Petty France, London SW1. Tel: (0171) 279 4000 *or* 271 8552 (visa department). Opening hours: 0900-1600 Monday to Friday.
Application requirements: (a) Passport. (b) Passport-size photo. (c) Return or onward ticket.
Temporary residence: Work and residence permits are required; apply to the Chief Immigration Officer, Government Buildings, Grand Turk.

MONEY

Currency: US Dollar (US$) = 100 cents. Notes are in denominations of US$100, 50, 20, 10, 5, 2 and 1. Coins are in denominations of US$1, and 50, 25, 10, 5 and 1 cents.
Credit cards: Access/Mastercard and Visa are widely accepted. Check with your credit card company for details of merchant acceptability and other services which may be available.
Travellers cheques: Accepted in most hotels, shops and banks.
Exchange rate indicators: The following figures are included as a guide to the movements of the US Dollar against Sterling:

Date:	Oct '92	Sep '93	Jan '94	Jan '95
£1.00=	1.58	1.52	1.48	1.56

Currency restrictions: None.
Banking hours: 0830-1430 Monday to Thursday, 0830-1230 and 1430-1630 Friday (Barclays Bank); 0830-1430 Monday to Thursday and 0830-1630 Friday (Scotia Bank).

DUTY FREE

The following items may be imported into the Turks & Caicos Islands without incurring customs duty:
200 cigarettes or 50 cigars or 225g of tobacco; 1.136 litres of spirits or wine.
Note: (a) The above applies to UK residents over 17 years of age. Allowances for other nationals vary, and it is advisable to consult the Tourist Board for details. (b) There are no restrictions on the import of cameras, films or sports equipment except spear guns. Firearms are prohibited without a permit.

PUBLIC HOLIDAYS

Jan 1 '95 New Year's Day. **Mar 6** Commonwealth Day. **Apr 14-17** Easter. **May 15** National Heroes' Day. **Jun 10** HM The Queen's Birthday. **Aug 1** Emancipation Day. **Sep 22** National Youth Day. **Oct 9** For Columbus Day. **Oct 24** International Human Rights Day. **Dec 25-26** Christmas. **Jan 1 '96** New Year's Day. **Mar 5** Commonwealth Day. **Apr 5-8** Easter.

HEALTH

Regulations and requirements may be subject to change at short notice, and you are advised to contact your doctor well in advance of your intended date of departure. Any numbers in the chart refer to the footnotes below.

	Special Precautions?	Certificate Required?
Yellow Fever	No	No
Cholera	No	No
Typhoid & Polio	Yes	-
Malaria	No	-
Food & Drink	1	-

[1]: All water should be regarded as being potentially contaminated. Water used for drinking, brushing teeth or making ice should have first been boiled or otherwise sterilised. Powdered or tinned milk is available and is advised, but make sure that it is reconstituted with pure water. Only eat well-cooked meat and fish, preferably served hot. Pork, salad and mayonnaise may carry increased risk. Vegetables should be cooked and fruit peeled.
Health care: There is a Reciprocal Health Agreement with the UK. On presentation of proof of residence in the UK (NHS card, driving licence, etc), those under 16 or over 65 receive all medical and dental treatment free of charge. Other UK residents are entitled to free treatment as follows: on *Grand Turk,* dental treatment, prescribed medicines and ambulance travel; on the *outer islands*, medical treatment at government clinics and prescribed medicines. There is a hospital on Grand Turk, and clinics on South Caicos, Middle Caicos, North Caicos, Providenciales and Salt Cay.

TRAVEL - International

AIR: The main airline is *Turks & Caicos Airways (QW).* Other airlines are *American Airlines (AAL)* and *Carnival Airlines (KW).*
Approximate flight times: From *London* to Grand Turk is 13 hours 30 minutes, including a stopover of 1 hour in Nassau; the route via Miami no longer requires an overnight stop.
From *Miami* to Grand Turk is 1 hour 30 minutes and to Providenciales is 1 hour 20 minutes.
From *New York* to Grand Turk is 4 hours (via Miami) and to Providenciales is 5 hours 50 minutes.
International airports: *Grand Turk (GDT).* There is a taxi service from Grand Turk to hotels; prices vary. Airport facilities include incoming duty-free shop; car hire and bank/bureau de change (0800-1300 and 1400-1630 Monday to Friday; 0800-1200 Saturday).
There are international airstrips on *South Caicos* and *Providenciales.*
Departure tax: US$15.
SEA: The archipelago is off the beaten track for most major cruise lines. Boats can be chartered to sail to islands in the Bahamas or Haiti. The main ports are Cockburn Harbour (South Caicos) and Salt Cay, Grand Turk and Providenciales. Harbour facilities on South Caicos are currently being improved. There are plans to build a new port on North Caicos.

TRAVEL - Internal

AIR: In addition to the international airports on Grand Turk, South Caicos and Providenciales (see above), there are landing strips on Middle Caicos, Pine Cay, Parrot Cay, North Caicos and Salt Cay. *Turks & Caicos Airways* run a twice-daily air-taxi service to all the inhabited islands as well as flights to Puerto Plata, Cape Haïtien and Nassau. Charter flights at competitive rates are also available.
SEA: Limited coast-hopping and inter-island services. Boats may be chartered at most of the inhabited islands.
ROAD: There are over 120km (75 miles) of roads in the islands, of which about one-fifth are sealed. Traffic drives on the left. **Taxi:** Available at most airports, but the supply may be limited and sharing is often necessary.
Car hire: Limited selection available from some local firms on Grand Turk, Providenciales and North and South Caicos. **Documentation:** Local licence available for a fee if holding a national driving licence or an International Driving Permit.
JOURNEY TIMES: The following chart gives approximate journey times (in hours and minutes) from Grand Turk to other major cities/towns on the islands.

	Air
Salt Cay	0.05
South Caicos	0.15
Middle Caicos	0.20
North Caicos	0.25
Pine Cay	0.30
Providenciales	0.30

ACCOMMODATION

HOTELS: There is accommodation on Grand Turk, North, Middle and South Caicos, Salt Cay, Providenciales and Pine Cay, including hotels, inns, a guest-house and self-catering apartment complexes. The standard is high, and many have beach frontage, private gardens, swimming pool and extensive watersports facilities. On Providenciales there is a Club Med Village and a Ramada Resort Hotel. All rooms are subject to 7% tax and 10% service charge. Advance reservation is necessary. The Tourist Board can supply further details and make reservations. Information is also available from the Turks & Caicos Hotel Association, Third

Turtle Inn, Providenciales (tel: 946 4230) *or* the Turks & Caicos Islands Resort Association, c/o the Ramada Turquoise Reef Resort and Casino, Providenciales. Tel: 946 5555. Fax: 946 5522. The Association provides advice on conferences and conventions. **Grading:** There are a number of standard hotels as well as two luxury and two deluxe hotels.

RESORTS & EXCURSIONS

The Turks & Caicos Islands are a perfect destination for those who wish to get away from it all. There are numerous national parks, nature preserves, sanctuaries and historical sites. The islands remain uncommercialised and unspoilt with small, personal places to stay and a heavy emphasis on eco-tourism.

The Caicos Group

There are six principal islands and numerous small cays, most of which are uninhabited.
Providenciales is the centre of the islands' major tourist development, with a *Ramada Hotel* and *Club Mediterranée* centre. It is a beautiful island. The main tourist centre lies around Turtle Cove, with its peaceful yacht basin, and the Grace Bay.
The abrupt coastline and deep water make **West Caicos** a fine fishing ground and provide opportunities for some excellent scuba diving. Uninhabited, it is presently only visited by the occasional adventurous yachtsman and fishermen, and by many thousands of sea birds.
North Caicos is known as the 'Garden Island' of the Caicos, its better-quality soils and water providing good farmland. Along its miles of deserted white sand beaches lie the *Prospect of Whitby, Pelican Beach* and *Ocean Beach* hotels. Here you can walk or relax in absolute peace and seclusion.
Pine Cay has one of the most beautiful beaches in the Caicos Islands, if not the Caribbean. It is also the home of *The Meridian Club,* one of the islands' select tourist developments, and is part of the *Caicos Cays National Underwater Park.* Be sure not to miss the reefs of the Caicos bank, with their rich variety of corals and vividly coloured fish.
Parrot Cay lies between Providenciales and North Caicos. Although hardly inhabited at present, a sophisticated holiday development is being built.
Middle Caicos, or Grand Caicos, is undeveloped. Blessed with a lovely coastline, to the west of Conch Bar the shoreline dips in and out with bluffs and small coves. Visitors should try not to miss the island's spectacular caves.
East Caicos is uninhabited but when flying to South Caicos, look down for the salmon in the translucent green water. Some of the most beautiful beaches in the Caribbean are to be found here.
The town of **Cockburn Harbour** is situated on a small ridge at the extreme southwest of the island of **South Caicos**. It was once the chief port for the shipment of salt from the islands. The town is a quiet and pleasant place to potter around in the evening. During the day there are numerous beaches to explore, and, as everywhere in the Turks & Caicos group, there is superb diving, yachting and big-game fishing.

The Turks Group

These are smaller, separated from the Caicos' by the 35km (22-mile) deep-water channel the Columbus Passage (formerly the 'Turks Island Passage'), and consist of two main islands and a number of small, uninhabited cays.
Grand Turk, a few minutes from South Caicos by air, with the small metropolis **Cockburn Town**, is the islands' seat of government and commerce, as well as its historic and cultural centre. The *Turks & Caicos National Museum* situated on the waterfront, tells the story of the oldest shipwreck discovered in the Americas and exhibits rare prints and manuscripts from all of the islands. Front Street has a number of colonial-style buildings, dating from the early 19th century. They have imposing entrances in the high, whitewashed walls which surround their gardens. There are many delightful bays on the eastern shores of Grand Turk. The island is also a fine base for diving and fishing.
Salt Cay is the most charming and atmospheric of all the Salt Islands. There are fine beaches and also still-productive salt ponds. The island is dominated by a great white house, built in the 1830s in solid Bermudian style.

SOCIAL PROFILE

FOOD & DRINK: With rare exceptions, dining takes place in hotels. Island specialities include whelk soup, conch chowder, lobster and special types of fresh fish. Continental dishes are also available as are American/European snacks such as hot dogs and hamburgers.

Although some establishments have buffet-style serveries, table service is common. **Drink:** Alcohol is freely available. Rum-based punch and cocktails are delicious and a wide selection of imported beer, wines and spirits can be found in most bars.
NIGHTLIFE: There are nightclubs and discotheques and hotels arrange beach parties and other entertainments. Events are broadcast in advance on local radio.
SHOPPING: The islands' small shops sell locally made baskets, shells, sponges, hand-screened cloth, souvenir T-shirts and rare conch pearls.
SPORT: Swimming: With more than 370km (230 miles) of beaches, there is plenty of opportunity for safe bathing supplemented by hotel pools. **Scuba diving:** The spectacular reefs and underwater life surrounding the islands attract divers from all over the world. Most clubs and centres have qualified instructors, equipment can be hired and diving trips arranged. **Fishing:** There is good fishing off all the islands; boats can be hired from most hotels and individual island fishermen can be hired as guides. **Golf:** A new 18-hole championship course has recently been opened in Providenciales. **Tennis:** Courts are available at most hotels throughout the islands. **Cricket** is a popular pastime during the annual cricket season. **Birdwatching:** There are many bird and butterfly sanctuaries. **Whalewatching:** During February, March and April a large number of the North Atlantic Humpback Whale population passes very close to the western shores of Grand Turk and Salt Cay en route to their breeding grounds nearby.
SPECIAL EVENTS: The following is a list of special events taking place in 1995 on the islands:
Apr '95 *Spring Garden Festival,* Grand Turk. **May** *South Caicos Regatta.* **Jun** *Annual Turks & Caicos Billfish Tournament,* Providenciales. **Jun 10** *Queen's Official Birthday Celebration.* **Jul** *Festarama,* North Caicos; *Provo Summer Festival.* **Aug** *MC Expo,* Middle Caicos; *Cactusfest,* Grand Turk. **Dec 31** *Dandamist,* Grand Turk.
SOCIAL CONVENTIONS: Shaking hands is the normal form of greeting. Hospitality is important and, when visiting someone's home, normal social courtesies should be observed – if possible a return invitation should be made. A souvenir from home is well received. Informal dress is accepted for most events, but beachwear should be confined to the beach. **Tipping:** There is no tipping in hotels on any of the islands, 10-15% is added to every bill. In restaurants, tip 10-15%.

BUSINESS PROFILE

ECONOMY: Since salt mining ceased in the mid-1960s, the Turks & Caicos Islands have relied on tourism and offshore financial services for most of their income. The expansion of tourism, recommended in a recent official report, is now seen as essential to the islands' future economic health. Fishing is the other main industry and the sole contributor to the islands' food requirements, the remainder of which must be imported; it is also a valuable export earner, particularly from the USA which buys much of the catch. Aid from Britain is needed to balance the budget and fund capital projects. The UK is the largest single trading partner.
BUSINESS: The informal relaxed atmosphere prevails even in business circles. A lightweight tropical suit will be the most needed. Best months to visit are from April to October. **Office hours:** 0800-1300 and 1400-1630 Monday to Friday, 0800-1200 Saturday.
COMMERCIAL INFORMATION: The following organisation can offer advice: Chamber of Commerce, c/o Turks and Caicos Banking Co Ltd, PO Box 148, Harbour House, Grand Turk. Tel: 946 2368. Fax: 946 2365. Telex: 2365.

CLIMATE

Tropical; tempered by trade winds, generally pleasant. Cool nights. Rain in winter.
Required clothing: Tropical lightweights. Light sweaters are advised for evenings.

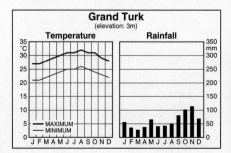

Grand Turk
(elevation: 3m)

Temperature — Rainfall

Tuvalu

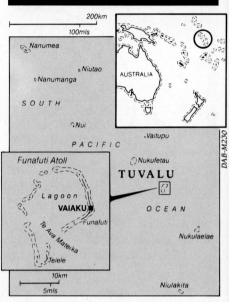

Location: West Pacific.

Ministry of Finance, Commerce and Public Corporation (Tourist Information)
PO Box 33, Funafuti, Tuvalu
Tel/Fax: 829.
Honorary Consulate General of Tuvalu
Klövensteenweg 115A, 22559 Hamburg, Germany
Tel: (40) 810 580. Fax: (40) 811 016.
The British Embassy in Suva deals with inquiries relating to Tuvalu (see *Fiji* earlier in the book). The Canadian High Commission in Wellington deals with enquiries relating to Tuvalu (see *New Zealand* earlier in this book).

AREA: 26 sq km (10 sq miles).
POPULATION: 9045 (1991).
POPULATION DENSITY: 365.4 per sq km.
CAPITAL: Funafuti. **Population:** 2810 (1985).
GEOGRAPHY: Tuvalu (formerly the Ellice Islands) is a scattered group of nine small atolls in the western Pacific Ocean extending about 560km (350 miles) from north to south. Nearest neighbours are Fiji (to the south), Kiribati (north) and the Solomon Islands (west). The main island, Funafuti, is also the capital and lies 1920km (1200 miles) north of Suva, Fiji.
LANGUAGE: Tuvaluan and English are the main languages.
RELIGION: Approximately 98% Protestant.
TIME: GMT + 12.
ELECTRICITY: 240 volts AC, 60Hz (Funafuti only).
COMMUNICATIONS: Telephone: IDD service is available. Country code: 688. There are no area codes. Outgoing international calls must go through the international operator. However, demand is high and the capacity as yet limited. Operator-controlled calls are available at the following times: 1930-0830 Monday to Thursday; 1930-0300 Friday; 0400-0800 and 2200-2400 weekends and public holidays. **Fax:** Available at the Telecommunication Centre in Funafuti.
Telex/telegrams: A public telex facility is available at

Timatic	**Health**		
	GALILEO/WORLDSPAN: **TI-DFT/FUN/HE**		
	SABRE: **TIDFT/FUN/HE**		
	Visa		
	GALILEO/WORLDSPAN: **TI-DFT/FUN/VI**		
	SABRE: **TIDFT/FUN/VI**		

For more information on Timatic codes refer to Contents.

the Telecommunication Centre in Funafuti (Telex: TV COMM 4800). Overseas telegrams may be sent via the Post Office in Funafuti. **Post:** Airmail services to Europe take between five and ten days to arrive, but can be erratic. Tuvalu stamps are among the most sought-after in the world. **Press:** The Government Broadcasting and Information Division publishes *Sikuleo o Tuvalu* (in Tuvaluan) and *Tuvalu Echoes* (in English, on a fortnightly basis).
BBC World Service and Voice of America frequencies: From time to time these change. See the section *How to Use this Book* for more information.

BBC:
| MHz | 17.83 | 15.34 | 11.95 | 9.640 |
Voice of America:
| MHz | 18.82 | 15.18 | 9.525 | 1.735 |

PASSPORT/VISA

Regulations and requirements may be subject to change at short notice, and you are advised to contact the appropriate diplomatic or consular authority before finalising travel arrangements. Details of these may be found at the head of this country's entry. Any numbers in the chart refer to the footnotes below.

	Passport Required?	Visa Required?	Return Ticket Required?
Full British	Yes	1	Yes
BVP	Not valid	-	-
Australian	Yes	No	Yes
Canadian	Yes	No	Yes
USA	Yes	Yes	Yes
Other EU (As of 31/12/94)	Yes	1	Yes
Japanese	Yes	Yes	Yes

PASSPORTS: Valid passports required by all.
British Visitors Passport: Not accepted.
VISAS: Not required by:
(a) nationals referrred to in the chart above;
(b) **[1]** nationals of Belgium, Denmark, Germany, Greece, Italy, Luxembourg, The Netherlands, Spain and the UK, provided that they have proof of onward travel and sufficient funds for stays of up to 1 month (other EU nationals *do* need a visa);
(c) nationals of Antigua & Barbuda, Bahamas, Bangladesh, Barbados, Belize, Botswana, Cyprus, Dominica, Fiji, Finland, Gambia, Ghana, Grenada, Guyana, Iceland, India, Jamaica, Kenya, Kiribati, Lesotho, Liechtenstein, Malawi, Malaysia, Maldives, Malta, Mauritius, Nauru, New Zealand, Nigeria, Norway, Papua New Guinea, St Lucia, St Vincent & the Grenadines, San Marino, Seychelles, Sierra Leone, Singapore, Solomon Islands, Sri Lanka, Swaziland, Sweden, Switzerland, Tanzania, Tonga, Trinidad & Tobago, Tunisia, Turkey, Uganda, Uruguay, Vanuatu, Western Samoa, Zambia and Zimbabwe.
Types of visa: Entry and Transit. Transit visas are not required by those holding confirmed onward tickets and continuing their journey to another country.
Validity: Visitors are normally permitted to remain in Tuvalu for up to 1 month, after meeting visa requirements; their visit may then be extended for a maximum of 3 months.
Application requirements: Visas may be obtained on arrival by passengers with onward tickets, valid passports and sufficient funds for their length of stay.

MONEY

Currency: Australian and Tuvaluan currency are both in use, but transactions over one dollar are always conducted in Australian Dollars.
Australian Dollar (A$) = 100 cents. Notes are in denominations of A$100, 50, 20, 10, 5 and 2. Coins are in denominations of A$1, and 50, 20, 10, 5, 2 and 1 cents. Tuvaluan Dollar (TV$) = 100 cents. Coins are in denominations of TV$1, and 50, 20, 10, 5, 2 and 1 cents.
Credit cards: Credit cards are not accepted, but Mastercard may be used at the National Bank of Tuvalu for cash advances.
Exchange rate indicators: The following figures are included as a guide to movements of the Australian Dollar against Sterling and the US Dollar:

Date:	Oct '92	Sep '93	Jan '94	Jan '95
£1.00=	2.22	2.36	2.18	2.01
$1.00=	1.40	1.54	1.47	1.29

Currency restrictions: There are no restrictions on the import and export of foreign or local currency.
Banking hours: 0930-1300 Monday to Thursday; 0830-1200 Friday.

DUTY FREE

The following items may be imported into Tuvalu without incurring customs duty:

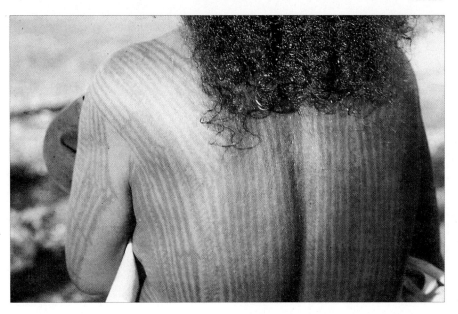

200 cigarettes or 225g tobacco or cigars; 1 litre of spirits and 1 litre of wine (if over 18); goods up to the value of A$25.
Prohibited items: Pornography, pure alcohol, narcotics, arms and ammunition. All plant and animal material must be declared and quarantined.

PUBLIC HOLIDAYS

Jan 1 '95 New Year's Day. **Mar 6** Commonwealth Day. **Apr 14-17** Easter. **Jun 10** Queen's Official Birthday. **Aug 2** National Children's Day. **Oct 1-2** Tuvalu Day (Anniversary of Independence). **Nov 14** Prince of Wales' Birthday. **Dec 25-26** Christmas. **Jan 1 '96** New Year's Day. **Mar 7** Commonwealth Day. **Apr 5-8** Easter.

HEALTH

Regulations and requirements may be subject to change at short notice, and you are advised to contact your doctor well in advance of your intended date of departure. Any numbers in the chart refer to the footnotes below.

	Special Precautions?	Certificate Required?
Yellow Fever	No	1
Cholera	No	-
Typhoid & Polio	Yes	-
Malaria	No	-
Food & Drink	2	-

[1]: A yellow fever vaccination certificate is required of travellers over one year of age arriving from an infected or endemic area.
[2]: All water is stored in tanks and supply is limited so visitors are advised to use water sparingly and take local advice.
Health care: Visitors are advised to bring antiseptic cream as cuts are inclined to turn septic, but apart from this precaution there are no serious health risks. The mosquitos are non-malarial, but the visitor may nevertheless wish to take protective measures. There is a well-equipped 31-bed hospital on Funafuti's main island.

TRAVEL - International

AIR: There are plans to implement a national airline in the near future. Presently *Air Marshall*, the airline of the Marshall Islands, offers return flights twice a week from Majuro (Marshall Islands) via Tarawa (Kiribati) to Funafuti and three times a week from *Nadi* and *Suva* in Fiji. It is advisable to book in advance.
International airport: *Funafuti International (FUN).* There is a pick-up service to the only hotel.
Departure tax: A$10 is levied on international departures.
SEA: Shipping services operate from Fiji, Australia and New Zealand, calling at the main port of Funafuti. Adventure cruises organised by *Society Expeditions of Seattle* (USA) also call from time to time.

TRAVEL - Internal

AIR: The only airstrip is at Funafuti. There is no internal air service in Tuvalu.

SEA: The islands are served by a passenger and cargo vessel, the *Nivaga II,* based at Funafuti, which occasionally calls at Suva (Fiji).
ROAD: There are a few roads, constructed from impacted coral, and several dirt tracks that span the islands. There are **taxis,** but limited transport service is also provided by privately operated **minibuses.** The usual form of transport on the islands are small **pick-up trucks, motorcycles** and **pushbikes,** which can be hired at the hotel. For more information, contact The Tuvalu Government Travel Office, Funafuti. Tel: 737.

ACCOMMODATION

The only hotel in Tuvalu is the Vaiaku Lagi Hotel in Funafuti. As there are only seven rooms at present, visitors are advised to book early and may be asked to share rooms. There are plans to upgrade existing facilities to a 16-room hotel with amenities for meetings. In addition there are a few private guest-houses available. The Travel Office can supply details (for telephone number, see under *Travel – Internal* above).

RESORTS & EXCURSIONS

Tuvalu is said to fulfil the classic image of a South Sea paradise and visitors come to the islands to enjoy the unspoilt peaceful atmosphere. Pandanus, papaya, banana, breadfruit and most commonly coconut palms are typical. The greatest attraction is the beautiful (and enormous) *Funafuti Lagoon,* which is 14km (9 miles) wide and about 18km (11 miles) long. In the Funafuti area, tourists will find many palm-fringed islands of scenic beauty. Boats for sightseeing and excursions can be hired from the Government or from private operators. Adjacent to the Government offices in Vaiaku is the open-sided national Parliament *(maneapa).* The *Women's Handicraft Centre* is well worth visiting and the *Philatelic Bureau* is visited by stamp collectors from all over the world. Traditional buildings with thatched roofs can be seen virtually everywhere on the islands.

SOCIAL PROFILE

FOOD & DRINK: The emphasis is on fish and local tropical foods. The Vaiaku Lagi Hotel serves meals daily and has a barbecue in the courtyard once a fortnight. There are also a number of privately-owned snackfood shops and two restaurants on Funafuti's main island with licensed bars and a good variety of food. **Drink:** Beer is imported.
NIGHTLIFE: There is a fortnightly disco at the Vaiaku Lagi Hotel.
SHOPPING: Near the hotel there is a handicraft centre selling handmade articles from all the islands ranging from hats, mats and shell necklaces to traditional lidded wooden boxes *(tulumas)* used by fishermen. There are also a number of souvenir and clothing shops. Visitors should be aware that general shopping facilities are limited and many things that visitors take for granted elsewhere may be unobtainable, eg developing of photographs.
Shopping hours: 0630-1730 Monday to Saturday.
SPORT: Visitors interested in **watersports** should bring their own equipment as there is none for hire. **Swimmers** should wear sandshoes as stonefish are an occasional hazard. Due to the strong tide,

swimming in the ocean is very dangerous. Swimming in the lagoon is considered fairly safe. Visitors who wish to use the hotel's **tennis** court should bring their own rackets and balls. **Volleyball** and **basketball** are also available here. **Football** is very popular, as is *kilikiti,* a local version of cricket. *Te ano* is a much-loved traditional ballgame reminiscent of volleyball.

SOCIAL CONVENTIONS: Traditional values continue to dominate Tuvaluan culture. Footwear should be removed when entering a church, a village meeting house *(manepa),* or private house. Sunday is a day of rest and church-going for the locals and visitors are advised to choose activities which do not cause too much disruption. The consumption of alcohol outside licensed premises is not permitted. Whilst dress is usually casual, it is customary for women to keep their thighs covered and beachwear should be confined to the beach or poolside. There are procedures which should be followed by those invited to a feast and visitors should take local advice about this and other matters. It is customary not to speak a foreign language in the presence of a person who does not know it, so apparent indications of a desire to hold a private or confidential conversation should be interpreted as simple courtesy to fellow-islanders. Visitors are welcome to join in the numerous local festivals and celebrations with feasting and traditional entertainment. **Tipping:** Optional, but not expected.

BUSINESS PROFILE

ECONOMY: The main source of income for the islands is remittances from abroad. Stamp sales are the principal foreign currency earner. The indigenous economy is dominated by fishing, and Tuvalu also receives valuable revenue from licences granted to American and Japanese fleets to fish in Tuvalu waters. On land, copra is the only significant export since the soil is of unsuitable quality for agriculture. Australia, New Zealand and Fiji are the main trading partners, while the UK provides an aid package mainly to assist the development of the island's infrastructure. A Trust Fund has been established to generate income for development projects from foreign investment.
BUSINESS: A high standard of business ethics is to be expected, given that the overwhelming majority of the population are congregationalists.
Government office hours: 0730-1615 Monday to Thursday and 0730-1245 Friday.
COMMERCIAL INFORMATION: The following organisations can offer advice: Tuvalu Cooperative Society Ltd, PO Box 17, Funafuti. Tel: 724. Fax: 800. Telex: 4800; *or* Development Bank of Tuvalu, PO Box 9, Funafuti. Tel: 850. Telex: 4800.

CLIMATE

The climate is humid and hot with a mean annual temperature of 28°C and comparatively little seasonal variation. March to October tends to be cooler and more pleasant, whilst some discomfort may be experienced during the wet season from November to February. The average rainfall is about 300mm annually.
Required clothing: Lightweight for summer, rainwear for the wet season.

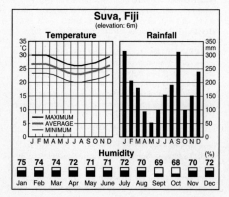

Suva, Fiji (elevation: 6m) — Temperature and Rainfall chart with Humidity

Uganda

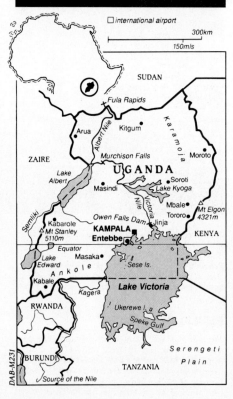

□ *international airport*
300km
150mls

Location: Central/East Africa.

Note: Because of a resurgence of rebel and bandit activity and renewed fighting in the area along the Sudanese border, travel in the northern part of Uganda is extremely dangerous. There have been at least two instances of land mine explosions in the roads north of Gulu. Additionally, random acts of violence involving American and other tourists have occurred in northern Uganda, such as a grenade attack at a tourist hotel in Arua. The area affected encompasses the entire northern part of Uganda (Apac, Arua, Gulu, Kitgum, Kotido, Lira, Moroto, Moyo, Nebbi and Soroti districts). Travel in this area, whether by private vehicle, in convoys or by official vehicle (UN programme vehicle etc) is unsafe. Vehicles have been stopped and destroyed, and passengers have been robbed and/or killed. The inability of the Ugandan government to ensure the safety of visitors to these areas makes travel dangerous and unwise.
Source: US State Department – December 14, 1994.

Uganda Tourist Development Corporation
PO Box 7211, Plot 6, 2nd Street, Kampala, Uganda Tel: (41) 245 261. Telex: 61150.
Ministry of Tourism, Wildlife and Antiquities
PO Box 4241, Parliament Avenue, Kampala, Uganda Tel: (41) 232 971. Telex: 62218.
High Commission for the Republic of Uganda
Uganda House, 58-59 Trafalgar Square, London WC2N 5DX
Tel: (0171) 839 5783. Fax: (0171) 839 8925. Telex: 915141. Opening hours: 0930-1300 and 1400-1730 Monday to Friday.
British High Commission
PO Box 7070, 101-12 Parliament Avenue, Kampala, Uganda

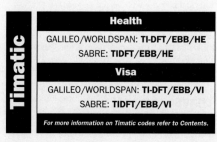

Health	
GALILEO/WORLDSPAN: **TI-DFT/EBB/HE**	
SABRE: **TIDFT/EBB/HE**	
Visa	
GALILEO/WORLDSPAN: **TI-DFT/EBB/VI**	
SABRE: **TIDFT/EBB/VI**	

For more information on Timatic codes refer to Contents.

Tel: (41) 257 301/4 *or* 257 054/9. Telex: 61202 (a/b UKREP KAMPALA).
Embassy of the Republic of Uganda
5909 16th Street, NW, Washington, DC 20011 Tel: (202) 726 7100. Fax: (202) 726 1727. *Consulate in:* New York (tel: (212) 949 0110).
Embassy of the United States of America
PO Box 7007, Kampala, Uganda Tel: (41) 259 792/3/5. Fax: (41) 241 863.
High Commission for the Republic of Uganda
231 Cobourg Street, Ottawa, Ontario K1N 8J2 Tel: (613) 789 7797/8. Fax: (613) 789 8909. Telex: 0534469.
Canadian Consulate
c/o Uganda Bata, PO Box 422, Fifth Street, Industrial Area, Kampala, Uganda Tel: (41) 258 141. Fax: (41) 241 380. Telex: 61049 (a/b BATA UGA).

AREA: 241,139 sq km (93,104 sq miles).
POPULATION: 16,582,674 (1991 estimate).
POPULATION DENSITY: 68.8 per sq km.
CAPITAL: Kampala. **Population:** 773,550 (1991).
GEOGRAPHY: Uganda shares borders with Sudan to the north, Kenya to the east, Lake Victoria to the southeast, Tanzania and Rwanda to the south and Zaïre to the west. Kampala is on the shores of Lake Victoria, and the White Nile flowing out of the lake traverses much of the country. The varied scenery includes tropical forest and tea plantations on the slopes of the snow-capped Ruwenzori Mountains, the arid plains of the Karamoja, the lush, heavily populated Buganda, the rolling savannah of Acholi, Bunyoro, Tororo and Ankole, and the fertile cotton area of Teso.
LANGUAGE: English is the official language, with Luganda and Kiswahili also widely spoken.
RELIGION: 60% Christian, 32% Animist and 8% Muslim.
TIME: GMT + 3
ELECTRICITY: 240 volts AC, 50Hz.
COMMUNICATIONS: Telephone: IDD is available to and from principal towns in Uganda. Country code: 256. Outgoing international calls must go through the operator. Service for local calls can be unreliable.
Fax/telex: Telex and fax service is available at the *Postal & Telecommunications Office,* 35 Kampala Road, Kampala, central post offices in Jinja and Mbale between 0800-1600, and in some hotels. **Post:** Airmail to Europe can take from three days to several weeks. Post office hours: 0830-1230 and 1400-1630 Monday to Friday.
Press: The English-language daily papers are *The Monitor, The People, New Vision, The Star* and the weekly *Topic.*
BBC World Service and Voice of America frequencies: From time to time these change. See the section *How to Use this Book* for more information.
BBC:

MHz	21.47	17.88	15.42	9.630

Voice of America:

MHz	21.49	15.60	9.525	6.035

PASSPORT/VISA

Regulations and requirements may be subject to change at short notice, and you are advised to contact the appropriate diplomatic or consular authority before finalising travel arrangements. Details of these may be found at the head of this country's entry. Any numbers in the chart refer to the footnotes below.

	Passport Required?	Visa Required?	Return Ticket Required?
Full British	Yes	No	Yes
BVP	Not valid	-	-
Australian	Yes	No	Yes
Canadian	Yes	No	Yes
USA	Yes	No	Yes
Other EU (As of 31/12/94)	Yes	No	Yes
Japanese	Yes	No	Yes

Restricted entry: Entry may be refused to passengers not holding sufficient funds, return or onward tickets and other necessary travel documents.
PASSPORTS: Valid passport required by all.
British Visitors Passport: Not valid.
VISAS: Required by all except:
(a) nationals referred to in the chart above;
(b) nationals of Antigua & Barbuda, Angola, Austria, Bahamas, Bahrain, Barbados, Belize, Botswana, Burundi, Comoros, Cyprus, Djibouti, Eritrea, Ethiopia, Fiji, Finland, Gambia, Ghana, Grenada, Hong Kong, Israel, Jamaica, Kenya, South Korea, Kuwait, Lesotho, Libya, Malawi, Malaysia, Malta, Madagascar, Mauritius, Mozambique, Namibia, New Zealand, Norway, Oman, Rwanda, Saudi Arabia, Seychelles, Sierra Leone, Singapore, Solomon Islands, St Lucia, St Vincent & the

Grenadines, Sudan, Swaziland, Sweden, Switzerland, Taiwan, Tanzania, Tonga, Turkey, UAE, Vanuatu, Zambia and Zimbabwe.

Types of visa: Tourist and Business; Single- and Multiple-entry.

Cost: *Single-entry:* £10; *Multiple-entry:* £20.

Validity: *Single-entry*: 3 months from date of issue; *Multiple-entry:* 6 months from date of issue.

Application to: Consulate (or Consular section at High Commission or Embassy). For addresses, see top of entry.

Application requirements: (a) Valid passport. (b) 1 completed application form. (c) 2 passport-size photos. (d) Fee (cash or postal orders only). (e) Letter of invitation/introduction if travelling on business. (f) Registered SAE if applying by post.

Working days required: 1 day.

Temporary residence: Enquire at High Commission.

MONEY

Currency: Uganda Shilling (USh) = 100 cents. Notes are in denominations of USh200, 100, 50, 20 and 10. Coins are in denominations of USh5, 2 and 1, and 50, 20, 10 and 5 cents. The Shilling is not a stable currency and has been substantially devalued several times in recent years.

Currency exchange: Money should be changed at the tourist exchange rate (known as 'Window 2') which is more advantageous than the official bank rate. Foreign currency may be exchanged at the Central Bank, commercial banks and foreign exchange bureaux. Tourists should not be tempted to use unofficial alternatives, which are numerous and widespread, as heavy fines and even prison sentences are imposed on offenders.

Credit cards: Visa is widely accepted with less widespread use of Access/Mastercard. Check with your credit card company for details of merchant acceptability and other services which may be available.

Exchange rate indicators: The following figures are included as a guide to the movements of the Uganda Shilling against Sterling and the US Dollar:

Date:	Oct '92	Sep '93	Jan '94	Jan '95
£1.00=	1856.25	1819.25	1674.40	1435.29
$1.00=	1169.66	1191.39	1131.73	917.41

Currency restrictions: The import and export of local currency is prohibited. Free import of foreign currency if declared on arrival. It is imperative to obtain a currency declaration form on arrival in Uganda. The export of foreign currency is limited to the amount imported and declared. Unspent shillings can be reconverted to foreign currency.

Banking hours: 0830-1400 Monday to Friday.

DUTY FREE

The following items may be imported into Uganda without incurring customs duty:
200 cigarettes or 225g of tobacco; 1 bottle of spirits or wine; 568ml of perfume.

PUBLIC HOLIDAYS

Jan 1 '95 New Year's Day. **Mar 3** Eid al-Fitr (End of Ramadan). **Apr 14-17** Easter. **May 1** Labour Day. **May 10** Eid al-Adha (Feast of the Sacrifice). **Jun 3** Martyrs' Day. **Jun 9** Heroes' Day. **Oct 9** Independence Day. **Dec 25** Christmas Day. **Jan 1 '96** New Year's Day. **Feb 22** Eid al-Fitr (End of Ramadan). **Apr 5-8** Easter.

Note: Muslim festivals are timed according to local sightings of various phases of the Moon and the dates given above are approximations. During the lunar month of Ramadan that precedes Eid al-Fitr, Muslims fast during the day and feast at night and normal business patterns may be interrupted. Many restaurants are closed during the day and there may be restrictions on smoking and drinking. Some disruption may continue into Eid al-Fitr itself. Eid al-Fitr and Eid al-Adha may last anything from two to ten days, depending on the region. For more information, see the section *World of Islam* at the back of the book.

HEALTH

Regulations and requirements may be subject to change at short notice, and you are advised to contact your doctor well in advance of your intended date of departure. Any numbers in the chart refer to the footnotes below.

	Special Precautions?	Certificate Required?
Yellow Fever	Yes	1
Cholera	Yes	2
Typhoid & Polio	Yes	-
Malaria	3	-
Food & Drink	4	-

[1]: A yellow fever vaccination certificate is required from travellers over one year of age arriving from infected areas. Travellers arriving from non-endemic zones should note that vaccination is strongly recommended for travel outside the urban areas, even if an outbreak of the disease has not been reported and they would normally not require a vaccination certificate to enter the country.

[2]: Following WHO guidelines issued in 1973, a cholera vaccination certificate is not a condition of entry to Uganda. However, cholera is a serious risk in this country and precautions are essential. Up-to-date advice should be sought before deciding whether these precautions should include vaccination, as medical opinion is divided over its effectiveness. See the *Health* section at the back of the book.

[3]: Malaria risk, predominantly in the malignant *falciparum* form, all year throughout the country, including urban areas. Resistance to chloroquine has been reported.

[4]: All water should be regarded as being a potential health risk. Water used for drinking, brushing teeth or making ice should have first been boiled or otherwise sterilised. Milk is unpasteurised and should be boiled. Powdered or tinned milk is available and is advised, but make sure that it is reconstituted with pure water. Avoid dairy products which are likely to have been made from unboiled milk. Only eat well-cooked meat and fish, preferably served hot. Pork, salad and mayonnaise may carry increased risk. Vegetables should be cooked and fruit peeled.

Rabies is present. For those at high risk, vaccination before arrival should be considered. If you are bitten abroad, seek medical advice without delay. For more information, consult the *Health* section at the back of the book.

Bilharzia (schistosomiasis) is present. Avoid swimming and paddling in fresh water. Swimming pools which are well-chlorinated and maintained are safe.

Meningitis risk exists, depending on area visited and time of year.

Health care: Bring personal supplies of medicines that are likely to be needed, but enquire first at Embassy or High Commission whether such supplies may be freely imported. Comprehensive health insurance is essential and should include cover for emergency air repatriation in case of serious accident or illness. The Ugandan health service has still not recovered from the mass departure of foreign personnel in 1972 and there are medical facilities of a reasonable standard only in large towns and cities.

TRAVEL - International

AIR: Uganda's main airline is *Uganda Airlines Corporation (QU)*.

Approximate flight time: From London to Kampala is 8 hours.

International airport: *Entebbe (EBB)* is 35.5km (22 miles) south of Kampala (travel time – 30 minutes). Coach services to Kampala go every three hours 0800-1800. Bus services go every two hours 0800-1600. Taxis are also available. Airport facilities include a duty-free shop, restaurant, bank, post office, car hire and hotel reservations.

Departure tax: US$23 is levied on international departures. Transit passengers and children under two years of age are exempt.

Note: All airline tickets purchased in Uganda must be paid for in hard currency.

RAIL: The line from Nairobi (Kenya) crosses the border at Tororo. It may be necessary to change trains to travel further into Uganda. Rail travel can be slow and uncomfortable.

ROAD: There are connections with all neighbouring countries. Road access from Kenya is good, roads to Rwanda are currently being improved. The Uganda/Rwanda border is closed at weekends. **Bus:** The road from Kenya is used by buses and tour company coaches from Nairobi. There is a twice-weekly service from Kampala to Kigali (Rwanda).

TRAVEL - Internal

AIR: *Uganda Airlines* offer flights from Entebbe to all main towns including Arua and Kasese. Charter flights are also available.

RAIL: There are more than 1000km (625 miles) of track, running in a single arc from Pakwach on Lake Albert (Lake Mobutu) near the border with Zaïre, through several northern towns to Tororo on the Kenyan border, then on to Lake Victoria and Kampala and finally to Kasese, near Lake George. Trains run twice-daily from Tororo to Kampala, and once-daily elsewhere. Passenger facilities are limited, but the rolling stock is new and reasonably comfortable. Timetables are somewhat erratic.

ROAD: Traffic drives on the right. The road network extends over 27,540km (17,113 miles). The roads are of variable quality and radiate from Kampala, although the network is sparse in the north. There are still some army and police check points on roads and railways. **Bus:** Services run between most parts of Uganda but are unreliable and often very crowded. Scheduled services operate between Entebbe and Kampala (travel time – 1 hour) and to and from the airport (see above).

Documentation: A national driving licence or International Driving Permit is required.

ACCOMMODATION

In Kampala there are a number of large international hotels. In smaller towns hotels are generally of a more limited quality. Information can be obtained from Uganda Hotel Limited, PO Box 7173, Kampala, Uganda. Tel: 234 296. Some of the major National Parks offer accommodation (see below).

RESORTS & EXCURSIONS

Kampala: The capital is set among hills with fine modern architecture, tree-lined avenues, cathedrals, mosques and palaces of the old Kingdom of Buganda and the Uganda Museum. The *Kabaka Tombs* are on *Kasubi Hill.* Shoes must be removed before entering the buildings.

Jinja: The second-largest town in Uganda lies on the shores of Lake Victoria. Though somewhat underpopulated there is a very lively Saturday market. The nearby *Owen Falls Dam* is the source of the Nile.

Entebbe: The major gateway to Uganda for air travellers, it has fine botanical gardens and a lakeside beach, although bathing is not advisable because of the dangers of bilharzia.

Fort Portal: A good base for exploring the *Ruwenzori Mountains,* the hot springs at **Bundibugyo** and the *Toro Game Reserve.*

Kisoro: The starting point for climbing expeditions to *Mounts Muhavura* and *Mgahinga.* There are seven lakes in the vicinity which offer fishing and possible duck shooting and the *Bwindi forest* where one can see mountain gorillas.

Mbale: Set in fertile and lush country near *Mount Elgon,* which is popular with hikers and inexperienced mountaineers.

National Parks: There are a number of good national parks and game reserves, some acclaimed as being among Africa's best. The major parks are *Kabalega, Ruwenzori* and *Kidepo. Kabalega* and *Ruwenzori* have good accommodation facilities; *Ruwenzori National Park* (also known as Queen Elizabeth National Park) is regarded as one of the most spectacular in Africa. The *East National Park* near Kampala has good lodges, *banda* (cabins) and campsites.

SOCIAL PROFILE

FOOD & DRINK: There are restaurants in and around Kampala. All state-owned hotels serve local food. Popular dishes include *matoke* (a staple made from bananas), millet bread, *cassava,* sweet potatoes, chicken and beef stews and freshwater fish. **Drink:** The national drink is *waragi,* a banana gin, popular among visitors as a cocktail base.

SHOPPING: Purchases include bangles, necklaces and bracelets, wood carvings, basketry, tea, coffee and ceramics. **Shopping hours:** 0830-1700 Monday to Friday and 0830-1900 Saturday.

SPORT: Climbing expeditions to Mount Muhavura and Mount Mgahinga, starting from Kisoro, are popular with climbers, while the ascent of Mount Elgon from Mbale is popular with hikers. There is excellent **fishing** in numerous inland waters, notably the seven lakes in the vicinity of Kisoro. It is unwise to **swim** in most of the lakes, with the exception of Lake Nagubo in the Kigezi hills, due to bilharzia.

SPECIAL EVENTS: The following is a selection of events taking place in 1995. For full details contact the Uganda Tourism Development Corporation.
Jan '95 *National Resistance Movement Victory Celebrations.* **Mar 8** *Women's Day.* **Jun 9** *Heroes' Day.*

SOCIAL CONVENTIONS: Shaking hands is the normal form of greeting. Casual dress is usual for most occasions in the daytime or evening. **Photography:** Since June 1992, photography has been allowed in all areas with the exception of military installations. However, some areas are still sensitive and it is advisable to take local advice. **Tipping:** It is customary to give waiters and taxi drivers a 10% tip.

BUSINESS PROFILE

ECONOMY: Uganda's thriving agricultural economy has been damaged by the oil crisis, local mismanagement and the military campaigns of 1979 which saw the overthrow of General Amin and the civil war that followed. Coffee is the main export commodity, while tea is developing well from a low base. Copper mining, once important, is being re-established. Manufacturing is also recovering: tobacco, brewing and sugar refining have been successfully rehabilitated. The Government has also sponsored a large amount of barter trade. Despite these successes, excessive military expenditure and the uncertain security situation ensured that at the end of the 1980s the economy's long-term prospects looked bleak. But during the last three years there has been a remarkable improvement. The Government has made full use of a better security situation to support economic development and (under pressure from foreign aid donors) cut military spending. GDP growth of 6% in 1990 exceeded all expectations and it now seems that Uganda may at last be on the road to fulfilling at least some of its immense potential. The UK is the largest exporter to Uganda with, according to 1986 figures, about 8% of the US$330-million market.

BUSINESS: A suit and tie are best worn by men for business meetings. English is used for all business discussions. Appointments should always be made.
Office hours: 0800-1230 and 1400-1630 Monday to Friday.
COMMERCIAL INFORMATION: The following organisations can offer advice: Uganda National Chamber of Commerce and Industry, PO Box 3809, Plot 17-19, Jinja Road, Kampala. Tel: (41) 258 791. Fax: (41) 285 793. Telex: 61272; *or*
Uganda Investment Authority, PO Box 7418, Crest House, Nkruman Road, Kampala. Tel: (41) 234 105. Fax: (41) 242 903.
CONFERENCES/CONVENTIONS: The Uganda International Conference Centre with its main auditorium and its three committee rooms has seating for up to 2000 persons. It is adjacent to the 4-star Nile Hotel and is 3km (2 miles) from the centre of Kampala. For further information contact the Uganda International Conference Centre, PO Box 3496, Kampala. Tel: (41) 258 619 *or* 258 0181/9. Fax: (41) 259 130 *or* 257 824. Telex: 61092 (a/b INTLCONF).

CLIMATE

Temperatures in some parts of the country can be quite cool owing to the country's high altitude, despite its position on the Equator. The mountain areas become much cooler and the top of Mount Elgon is often snow-covered. Other parts of the country are much warmer. There is heavy rain between March and May and October and November.
Required clothing: Lightweights and rainwear, with warm wraps for the evenings are advised.

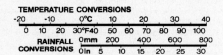

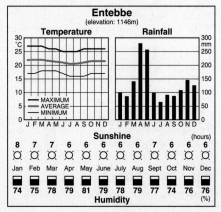

Ukraine

☐ *international airport*

Location: Central Eastern Europe.

Association of Foreign Tourism
Yaroslaviv Val 36, Kiev, Ukraine
Tel: (044) 212 5570.
Ukrainian Foreign Ministry
Mikhailovska Square 1, Kiev, Ukraine
Tel: (044) 293 1535. Fax: (044) 212 8618.
Embassy of Ukraine
78 Kensington Park Road, London W11 2PL
Tel: (0171) 727 6312 *or* (0891) 515 919 (recorded visa information; calls are charged at the higher rate of 39/49p per minute). Fax: (0171) 792 1708. Opening hours: 0900-1800 Monday to Friday; *Visa section:* 0930-1230 Monday to Friday.
Intourist
219 Marsh Wall, Isle of Dogs, London E14 9FJ
Tel: (0171) 538 8600 (general enquiries) *or* 538 5902 (visas). Fax: (0171) 538 5967.
British Embassy
vul. Desyatinna 9, 252025 Kiev, Ukraine
Tel: (044) 228 0504 *or* 229 1287. Fax: (044) 228 3972. Telex: 131429 (a/b PRODRS U).
Embassy of Ukraine
3350 M Street, NW, Washington, DC 20007
Tel: (202) 333 0606. Fax: (202) 333 01817.
Consulates in: Chicago and New York (tel: 212) 371 5690).
Intourist USA Inc
Suite 603, 610 Fifth Avenue, New York, NY 10020
Tel: (212) 757 3884. Fax: (212) 459 0031.
Embassy of the United States of America
vul. Yuri Kotsyubinsky 10, 252053 Kiev 53, Ukraine
Tel: (044) 244 7349 *or* 244 3745. Fax: (044) 244 7350. Telex: 131142.
Embassy of Ukraine
331 Metcalfe Street, Ottawa, Ontario K2P 1S3
Tel: (613) 230 2961 *or* 230 8015 (Consular section). Fax: (613) 230 2400 *or* 230 2655 (Consular section).
Consulate in: Toronto.
Canadian Embassy
Yaroslaviv Val 31, Kiev 252034, Ukraine
Tel: (044) 212 2112 *or* 212 0212 *or* 212 2263. Fax: (044) 225 1305 (immigration) *or* 212 2339 (trade). Telex: 131479 (a/b UYUT SU).

AREA: 603,700 sq km (241,200 sq miles).
POPULATION: 52,057,000 (1992).
POPULATION DENSITY: 86.2 per sq km.
CAPITAL: Kiev. **Population:** 2,616,000 (1990 estimate).
GEOGRAPHY: Ukraine is bordered by the Russian Federation to the north and east; Belarus to the north;

Poland, the Slovak Republic and Hungary to the west; and Romania and Moldova to the southwest. It is a varied country with mountains in the west, plains in the centre and breathtaking Black Sea views in the south. The north of the state is dominated by forests. Its other two main features are wooded steppe with beech and oak forests and the treeless steppe. The River Dnieper, part of which it shares with Romania, divides Ukraine roughly in half, and flows into the Black Sea.
LANGUAGE: Ukrainian is the sole official state language. A member of the eastern Slav languages and similar to Russian, it was discouraged for centuries by tsarist and Soviet authorities. It is still widely spoken in western and central Ukraine, although Russian is spoken by virtually everyone. Russian is the main language spoken in Kiev, eastern Ukraine and Crimea. The present Government uses every opportunity to promote the revival of Ukrainian, particularly in schools. There are 12 million ethnic Russians in Ukraine, 500,000 Jews and more than 250,000 Crimean Tatars.
RELIGION: There are about 35 million Ukrainian Orthodox faithful, although the church is divided into a traditional pro-Moscow and a breakaway pro-Kiev faction. Five million Eastern-rite (Uniate) Catholics, subservient to Rome, are concentrated in western Ukraine and it is now three years since a Stalin-era ban on their church was lifted. There are also Protestant and Muslim minorities. Mass emigration has reduced the numbers of Jews, concentrated in Kiev, Lviv and Odessa.
TIME: GMT + 2 (GMT + 3 from last Sunday in March to Saturday before last Sunday in September).
ELECTRICITY: 220 volts AC, 50Hz.
COMMUNICATIONS: Telephone: Ukraine now has reliable communications with the West, and most major cities provide IDD facilities and can be dialled from abroad. Country code: 7. Outgoing international code: 810. Telephone counters in the central post offices of city centres are usually open 24 hours. **Fax:** Facilities are good and are available in most offices and hotels.
Telex/telegram: These can be sent from central post offices in large cities 24 hours a day. **Post:** Services are erratic. Letters to Western Europe can take two weeks or more. The Main Post Office in Kiev is located at Khreshchatik 22 and it is open 24 hours. Post office hours: Generally 0800-1700. **Press:** Ukrainian newspapers are uncensored, but generally dull. The most popular and lively daily is the Russian-language *Kievskiye Vedomosti*. Also widely read are the liberal *Nezavisimost* and the parliamentary daily *Holos Ukrainy*. The Russian press is also widely available. *News from Ukraine* is published in English and available in 70 other countries. Western newspapers are now available in Kiev, but not in other parts of the country. **Media:** *Ukrinform* is the national news agency at vul. Bohdan Khmelnitsky 8/16. Tel: (044) 226 3230. Fax: (044) 229 2439 *or* 229 8665. **Radio/TV:** Stations are located at Khreshchatik 26, Kiev. Tel: (044) 226 3144. Fax: (044) 229 1170. National television broadcasts are in Ukrainian. Radio broadcasts are in Ukrainian and Russian.
BBC World Service frequencies: From time to time these change. See the section *How to Use this Book* for more information.
BBC:

MHz	12.09	9.410	6.180	1.764

PASSPORT/VISA

	Passport Required?	Visa Required?	Return Ticket Required?
Full British	Yes*	Yes*	Yes*
BVP	Not valid	-	-
Australian	Yes*	Yes*	Yes*
Canadian	Yes*	Yes*	Yes*
USA	Yes*	Yes*	Yes*
Other EU (As of 31/12/94)	Yes*	Yes*	Yes*
Japanese	Yes*	Yes*	Yes*

Note [*]: Visa regulations are liable to change. Prospective travellers are advised to contact *Intourist Travel Ltd* who offer a comprehensive visa service for all of the republics within the CIS. Tel: (0171) 538 5902 in the UK; (212) 757 3884 in the USA. If transiting between Ukraine and other member states of the CIS, several visas must be held. Travellers who enter the Russian Federation from Ukraine without a Russian Federation visa are charged a penalty of US$250 for illegal entry. Ukrainian visas are *not* valid in the Russian Federation,

TEMPERATURE CONVERSIONS

| -20 | -10 | 0°C | 10 | 20 | 30 | 40 |

| 0 | 10 | 20 | 30°F | 40 | 50 | 60 | 70 | 80 | 90 | 100 |

RAINFALL CONVERSIONS

| 0mm | 200 | 400 | 600 | 800 |
| 0In | 5 | 10 | 15 | 20 | 25 | 30 |

Entebbe
(elevation: 1146m)

Temperature / **Rainfall**

Sunshine (hours)

	Jan	Feb	Mar	Apr	May	June	July	Aug	Sept	Oct	Nov	Dec
Sunshine	8	7	7	6	6	6	6	6	7	6	6	6
Humidity (%)	74	75	78	79	81	79	78	79	77	74	76	76

Humidity

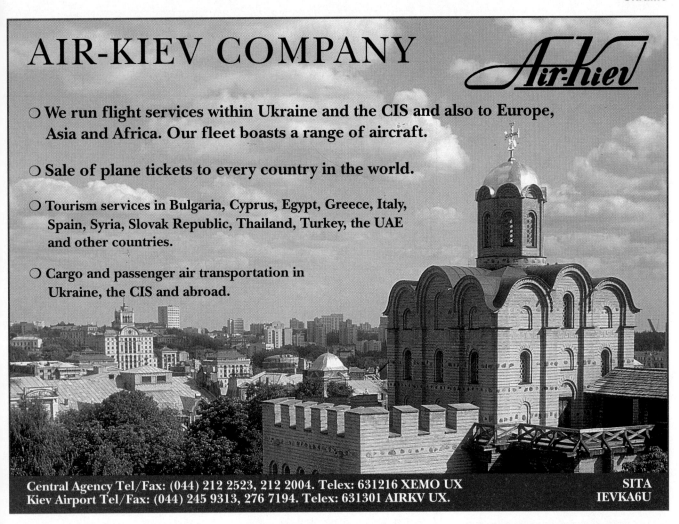
as Russian Federation visas are *not* valid in Ukraine. As a general rule, visitors should apply for a visa before travelling.
PASSPORTS: Valid passports required by all.
British Visitors Passport: Not accepted.
VISAS: Required by all
Note: According to previous agreements between the Soviet Union and the former Communist Block countries nationals of former COMECON countries may not need a visa if resident in their country of origin. However, Ukrainian consular authorities advise nationals of *all* countries to contact the nearest Ukrainian consular representative well in advance of travel.
Types of visa: Business; Private; Individual Tourist; Group Tourist (minimum 7 participants); Long-term; Multiple-entry and Transit. There are also special visas issued for the purpose of visiting relatives.
Validity: 90 days. *Long-term and Multiple-entry:* 6 months. Visas must be stamped inside the passport.
Cost: *Single-entry* – £20; *Double-entry* – £40; *Multiple-entry* – £80; *Transit (single-entry)* – £10; *Transit (double-entry)* – £20. No fee is charged for children under 16 years and for applicants delivering humanitarian aid or providing technical assistance to Ukraine. Urgent and Express visa services cost between two and three times as much as standard visa applications (see *Working days required* below).
Application to: Consulate (or Consular section at Embassy). For addresses, see top of entry. Short-stay visas (72 hours) can sometimes be obtained at Immigration Offices at border crossings, at Kiev airport and at the ports of Simferopol, Yalta and Odessa. If entering by air into Kiev, applications for visas are often

handed out on the plane. The following fees apply if travelling from a country where a Ukrainian embassy or consulate exists: *Single-entry visa:* US$150. *Single-entry transit visa:* US$50. These fees are halved if entering from a country where there is no Ukrainian embassy or consulate.
Application requirements: (a) Valid passport. (b) 1 completed application form. (c) 1 passport-size photo. (d) Company letter of invitation for Business visa. (e) Hotel voucher for Tourist visa. (f) Letter of invitation from a private individual in Ukraine for private visa. (g) Fee (cheque or postal order made payable to the 'Embassy of Ukraine'). Cheques should be endorsed 'A/C payee only, not negotiable' and must have a cheque guarantee card number written on the back. (h) Stamped, self-addressed envelope for postal applications.
For *Group visas*, individual passports, photos and application forms are not necessary. It is sufficient if the tour operator supplies photocopies of the passports and a list in triplicate with the following details for every participant: Name, first names, date of birth, nationality and passport number. Included should also be a copy of the planned itinerary.
Working days required: For *Business, Tourist, Private, Single-* and *Multiple-entry visa* – 7 working days; for *Group Tourist visa* and *Transit visa* – 5 working days. Allow extra time for postal applications. Applications requesting Urgent service take 3 working days. The Express service ensures that applications are processed on the same or next day (not available for Multiple-entry visas).

MONEY

Currency: Ukraine's interim currency, in circulation since January 1992, is called the Karbovanets. Plans to introduce a permanent new currency, the Hryvnya, have been shelved indefinitely. Introduced on a par with the Rouble, the value of the Karbovanets plunged throughout 1993 and was worth about 20 to the Rouble and 36,000 to the US Dollar in February 1994.
Currency exchange: Money should only be changed at currency booths on the street or in banks. Changing money with black-market traders is not recommended and can be dangerous.

Credit cards: Not readily accepted. Only a few restaurants and hotels will accept them.
Exchange rate indicators: The following figures are included as a guide to the movements of the Karbovanets Sterling and the US Dollar;

Date:	Feb '95
£1.00=	162,916
$1.00=	104,133

DUTY FREE

There are no fixed rules for duty-free allowances in the chaos of post-Soviet regulations. Visitors should not attempt to take caviar or artwork out of the country without appropriate permits.

PUBLIC HOLIDAYS

Jan 1 '95 New Year's Day. **Jan 7** Orthodox Christmas. **Mar 8** International Women's Day. **Jan 1 '96** New Year's Day. **Jan 7** Orthodox Christmas. **Mar 8** International Women's Day.

HEALTH

Regulations and requirements may be subject to change at short notice, and you are advised to contact your doctor well in advance of your intended date of departure. Any numbers in the chart refer to the footnotes below.

	Special Precautions?	Certificate Required?
Yellow Fever	No	No
Cholera	No	No
Typhoid & Polio	No	-
Malaria	No	-
Food & Drink	1	-

[1]: All water should be regarded as being a potential health risk. Water used for drinking, brushing teeth or making ice should have first been boiled or otherwise sterilised. Milk is pasteurised and dairy products are safe for consumption. Only eat well-cooked meat and fish, preferably served hot. Pork, salad and mayonnaise may

carry increased risk. Vegetables should be cooked and fruit peeled.
Widespread outbreaks of *cholera* and *diphtheria* have been reported. Visitors are advised to seek medical advice about immunisation and precautionary measures. Good personal hygiene and care with water and food supplies are essential.
Rabies is present. For those at high risk, vaccination before arrival should be considered. If you are bitten abroad, seek medical advice without delay. For more information, consult the *Health* section at the back of the book.
Health care: The health service does, in theory, provide free medical treatment for all citizens and travellers who become ill. However, as in most parts of the former Soviet Union, health care is a serious problem. For minor difficulties, visitors are advised to ask the management at their hotels for help. For major problems, visitors are well advised to seek help outside the country. Travel insurance is therefore recommended for all travellers. It is advisable to take a supply of those medicines that are likely to be required (but check first that they may be legally imported) as medicines can prove difficult to get hold of.

TRAVEL - International

AIR: *Air Ukraine International*, an Irish-Ukrainian joint venture, links Kiev and many European destinations by Boeing aircraft and is up to Western standards. *Air Ukraine* serves some European points and North America. It also flies to Moscow and other Russian cities aboard aircraft reclaimed from the former Soviet airline *Aeroflot*. Flights are also available from Lviv to Warsaw, from Simferopol to Turkey and from Ivano-Frankivsk to the UK (summer only).
Approximate flight times: From Kiev to *London* is 3 hours 30 minutes, to *Moscow* is 1 hour 15 minutes and to *Vienna* is 2 hours.
International airport: *Borispol Airport (KBT)* is about 40km (25 miles) from central Kiev. Though chaotic and dirty, it is undergoing extensive renovation. Transport to the airport is unreliable. A taxi is the best means, costing about US$20.
SEA/RIVER: The main ports are Izmail on the River Danube and Odessa. Services are available to the Russian Federation ports of Novorossiysk and Sochi, as well as to Batumi and Sukhumi in Georgia. The republic's most important internal waterway is the River Dnieper. Black Sea cruises around the Crimean peninsula are available and well-recommended. Most cruises leave from Turkey, Bulgaria or Romania and stopover in Yalta, but there are also cruises which leave from Yalta.
RAIL: The 22,730km (14,207 miles) of railway track link most towns and cities within the republic and further links extend from Kiev to all other CIS member states. There are direct lines to Warsaw in Poland, Budapest in Hungary and Bucharest in Romania. Ukrainian trains are slow. Journeys can range from pleasant to terribly uncomfortable if, for instance, the heating is not switched on. Security can also be a problem, as many muggings have been reported. If travelling by overnight train, do not leave the compartment unattended. Buying tickets is extremely difficult and can be done almost exclusively through the black market. From Kiev to Moscow takes 16 hours and to St Petersburg is about 36 hours. Further information is available from the State Railway Transport Administration. Tel: (044) 223 4213.
ROAD: Of the 247,300km (154,563 miles) of road network, 201,900km (126,188 miles) are paved. Ukrainian roads tend to be in reasonable condition. Border points are at Mostiska, Uzhgorod and Chop. Private car repair garages have recently become available, along with state-owned ones; however, spare parts are still scarce. The biggest problem is availability of suitable petrol (for instance, unleaded petrol is not available). Never set out on a journey without large numbers of petrol cans.
See below for information on **traffic regulations** and **documentation**.

TRAVEL - Internal

AIR: Fuel shortages have resulted in sharp reductions in flights within Ukraine and timetables are erratic. *Air Ukraine's* repainted *Aeroflot* aircraft are far from comfortable and buying tickets is extremely difficult and almost guaranteed to involve complicated negotiations with the Intourist office. Winter weather frequently grounds aircraft. The most reliable flights are from Kiev to Lviv, Dnipropetrovsk, Donetsk and Odessa.
RAIL: Again, buying tickets is a difficult undertaking. Journeys are slow, though trains are more reliable than air travel in winter.
ROAD: Bus: Buses between cities exist, but are not recommended. **Taxi:** Hiring a driver for a long-distance destination is a realistic option, costing about US$200 from Kiev to Odessa or a similar journey. **Car hire:** Self-drive hire cars are, so far, extremely rare.
Traffic regulations: Speed limits are 60kmph (37mph) in built-up areas, 90kmph (55mph) in outside areas and 110kmph (69mph) on the motorways. Traffic drives on the right; righthand-drive cars are forbidden.
Documentation: An International Driving Licence is necessary.
URBAN: Kiev's metro is clean, cheap and efficient, though it runs less frequently than it once did. Buses and trolleybuses are packed beyond description and are best avoided. Taxis are available. State-owned taxis have yellow-and-black signs on the roof and are metered. Some shared taxis and minibuses exist on fixed routes. Hitchhiking is very common – travellers can indicate the need for a lift and the driver will take them to their destination cheaply by Western standards (US$3-5), but prices should be agreed in advance. There are no public transport services from 0100-0500/0600.

ACCOMMODATION

HOTELS: There are only a few hotels that approach Western standards. The plush Grand Hotel in Lviv is of Western standard, as is the Hotel Dnister (tel: (0322) 720 783). In Kiev, the Hotel Complex Kievskaya Rus (tel: (044) 220 1934) is also of Western standard, although it is very expensive. Some of the cheaper hotels in Kiev include Hotel Dnipro on vul. Khreshchatik 1/2 (tel: (044) 229 8287) and Hotel Lybid (tel: (044) 274 0063). The restored London Hotel in Odessa is elegant and more or less of Western standard. In Yalta, the Hotel Yalta is only a few metres from the sea and of a good standard.
PRIVATE ROOMS: A room in a private home is an excellent accommodation option in Ukraine as the people are friendly and hospitable and prices tend to be far more reasonable. However, there is no organisation as such that arranges rooms in private homes. Visitors can, however, ask around, as the financial savings and greater comfort may be well worth the effort (as long as due caution is observed).
CAMPING/CARAVANNING: Campsites are available on the outskirts of cities.

RESORTS & EXCURSIONS

Kiev is the capital of Ukraine and the third-largest city in the CIS. It is also the cradle of Russian civilisation, the origin of the Kiev Rus State founded in the 8th and 9th centuries and the city from which the Orthodox faith spread throughout Eastern Europe.
Even though many of its buildings were destroyed in the Second World War, Kiev still has much to offer. The *Caves Monastery* in the city centre is the focal point of the early Orthodox church. Visitors have to carry candles to see the church relics which are set in a maze of catacombs. It is the headquarters of the pro-Russian Orthodox church. The 11th-century *St Sofia Cathedral* contains splendid icons and frescoes and is situated in lovely grounds. The *Golden Gate of Kiev* is the last remnant of the 10th-century walls built to defend the city. Other attractions include the *Cathedral of St Vladimir* (the headquarters of the rival pro-Ukrainian church), the *Opera House*, the *Museum of Ukrainian Art* (with its collection of the work of regional artists from the 16th century to the present), and the *Historical Museum of Ukraine*. *Andreyev Hill* is a restored cobbled street in central Kiev now used by artists to sell their wares. There are a lot of cafés and restaurants in this area.
Khreshchatik Street and *Independence Square* are Kiev's main thoroughfares. The square is particularly elegant with its chestnut trees and fountains. *Martinsky Palace and Parliament* is the official residence of Ukraine's President. The nearby *Park of Glory* is a war memorial, with a vast and controversial monument of a woman with a sword and shield overlooking the river. Locals go swimming in summer in the *Dnieper River* and climb onto its thin ice in winter to fish. It is possible to take boat trips on the river. There is a park and a beach on *Trukhaniv Island*.
Lviv (Russian name: Lvov) is a city of striking Baroque and Renaissance architecture and is the focal point of Ukrainian national culture. It was the centre of Ukrainian nationalist ambition at the beginning of the Soviet era. The *City Castle* was the first building to fly Ukraine's blue-and-yellow national flag. Lviv is also the headquarters of Ukraine's Greek Orthodox church.
Odessa is the site of the famous 192 steps of the *Potemkin stairway* from Sergei Eisenstein's film 'Battleship Potemkin'. In addition Odessa is also a centre of renewal of Jewish culture, with a community of 45,000. There is a vast *Opera House* – one of the world's largest. The ceiling is decorated with scenes from the plays of Shakespeare. Also worth visiting is the *Statue of the Duke of Richelieu*, the *Vorontsov Palace* on the waterfront, and the *Archaeological Museum* with exhibits from the Black Sea area and Egypt.
THE CRIMEA: This was once a summer playground for Kremlin leaders. Hotels and services are relatively cheap for Westerners, and the place is a favourite with German tourists. The region's dusty capital of **Simferopol** has few tourist sights. It is **Yalta,** the 'Pearl of the Crimea', which draws visitors. Former Communist Party spas have now been turned into resort centres. The region's vineyards produce good quality wine which can be tasted locally quite cheaply. The *Wine Tasting Hall* in Yalta is as good aplace as any. The *Vorontsov Palace* was designed by Edward Blore, one of the architects of Buckingham Palace. *Nikitsky Gardens*, just outside of Yalta, is a good afternoon's excursion. Industry is centred on **Massandra,** above Yalta. **Livada** is where Roosevelt, Churchill and Stalin met in the *Livada Palace* in 1945. **Foros** is where Gorbachev was held for three days during the 1991 coup.

SOCIAL PROFILE

FOOD & DRINK: Specialities include *borshch* (different kinds of beetroot soup), *varenniki* (dough containing cheese, meat or fruit) and *holubtsi* (cabbage rolls). Chicken Kiev exists but is better known in the West. Finding a good, reasonably-priced restaurant in Ukraine can be a problem. **Drink:** Crimean wines are excellent, especially dessert wines such as *Krasny Kamen* ('Red Stone'). For those who prefer dry wine, *Abrau* and *Miskhako* are excellent brands of cabernet. Also outstanding are *Artyomov* champagne (bottled in eastern Ukraine) and fortified wines from Massandra, particularly one named 'Black Doctor'.
NIGHTLIFE: Opera is performed in the ornate theatres of Kiev, Lviv and Odessa. Ukrainians, particularly women, have a deep-rooted tradition for singing at every occasion, particularly family gatherings. Most cities also have a good musical comedy, puppet-theatre and troupes performing theatrical works in Ukrainian and Russian. Tickets are very cheap by Western standards and readily available on the day of performance at the box offices. Post-Soviet economics unfortunately means that many performances are badly attended. Prominent visiting artists most often perform in Kiev's vast Ukraine Theatre, where prices are higher.
SHOPPING: Artwork is the best buy for tourists. Top-quality paintings, ceramics and jewellery may be purchased quite cheaply at galleries or direct from artists on the street. Avoid the state shops which have dull fare.
Shopping hours: Large state or department stores tend to be open from 0800-1900, whereas small boutiques are generally open 0900-1800. Some shops stay open as late as 2000.
SPORT: Ukrainians go **skiing** in the Carpathian Mountains in the west, where top resorts are in Yeremcha and Vorokhta near the Romanian border and Slavsko, close to the Slovak Republic. The most popular spectator sport is **football**, although successes in the international arena for Oksana Baiul, Andrei Medvedev and Sergei Bubka have attracted many to figure skating, tennis and athletics.
SPECIAL EVENTS: Odessa hosts an extravagant *April Fool's Day* celebration with costumes and street dancing. The *Sarochin Market* in central Ukraine takes place in August and draws people from far and wide. The *Independence Day* celebrations on August 24 are good fun, as are the celebrations for Orthodox Christmas on January 7.
SOCIAL CONVENTIONS: Ukrainian people are warm and particularly friendly to visitors. It is not at all uncommon for a Ukrainian to invite a stranger into his own home. People on the street are friendly despite the rigours of post-Soviet life. Formal attire is rarely required, though people dress smartly for the theatre. Visitors should avoid ostentatious displays of wealth in public places. **Tipping:** Small gifts or a tip are always appreciated and will help visitors to get things they might want from what could otherwise be a recalcitrant official. Service is sometimes included in first-class restaurants and hotel bills.

BUSINESS PROFILE

ECONOMY: The second most important of 15 former Soviet republics and a major industrial and agricultural power in Eastern Europe, Ukraine has for centuries been in the shadow of Russia. Market reforms in Ukraine now lie far behind those in neighbouring Russia and the drop in living standards has been more marked. Privatisation is moving more slowly here than in the Russian Federation, bogged down by bureaucracy and unwieldy legislation. Post-Soviet Ukraine hopes to restore to its turn-of-the-century status of bread basket of Europe. Although it has few natural resources of its own and is largely dependent on Russia for energy, it is a major steel and coal producer and also refines large quantities of oil. Industry is centred on eastern Ukraine's Donbass coalfield and steel mills, as well as sectors such as mechanical engineering, metalworking, transport and chemicals. Ukraine's leadership is pinning its hopes on agriculture and hopes even to develop exports after last year's bumper harvest. Ukraine remains one of Europe's key sugar producers. The republic enjoys large areas of exceptionally fertile land – the famous 'black earth' – but rural areas remain undeveloped, often lacking amenities such as running water. The defence industry played a huge role in Soviet Ukraine's industrial make-up and the country hopes to convert these factories to civilian use. Another impediment is the aftermath of the 1986 disaster at the Chernobyl nuclear power plant which left huge chunks of territory contaminated and still soaks up 11% of the national budget. Over 95% of industry remains in state hands. With monthly inflation running at over 50%, urgent action is needed. The Government had hoped that the introduction of a coupon-based currency, the Karbovanets – as a transitional stage before Ukraine was planning to introduce its own currency the Hryvnya – would ease inflationary pressure, but this seems not to have happened. Foreign investment has been slow in coming, largely because of the perceived slow pace of reform. Soaring inflation of 10,000% in 1993 and a 20% drop in production have bought the country close to economic collapse. This has not been aided by the Government's failure to control the money supply while trying to finance its own budget deficit. Nonetheless, Ukraine does have great economic potential provided it can survive this difficult transitional period.

BUSINESS: Suits, and ties for men, are required for official business. Exchange of business cards is extremely common and visitors are advised to bring company calling cards. **Office hours:** 0900-1300 and 1430-1700/1800. Lunch hours tend to be at least 1 hour 30 minutes.

COMMERCIAL INFORMATION: The following organisations can offer advice: Chamber of Commerce and Industry, vul. Velyka Zhytomyrska 33, 252055 Kiev. Tel: (044) 212 2911 or 212 3290 or 212 2840. Fax: (044) 212 3353. Telex: 131379; or Ministry of Foreign Affairs, vul. Chekistiv 1, 252024 Kiev. Tel: (044) 226 3379. Fax: (044) 293 6950; or Ministry of Foreign Economic Relations, Lvivska pl. 8, 252053 Kiev. Tel: (044) 226 2733.

CLIMATE

Temperate with warm summers; crisp, sunny autumns; and cold, snowy winters.
Required clothing: Lightweight clothes needed in summer, light- to medium-weight in the spring and autumn and heavyweight in the winter.

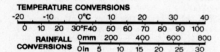

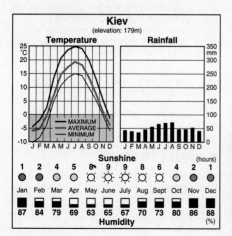

Kiev
(elevation: 179m)

United Arab Emirates

☐ international airport

200km

100mis

1 Umm al Qaiwain
2 Ras al-Khaimah
3 Khor Fakkan

Location: Middle East.

Federal Ministry of Information & Culture
PO Box 17, Abu Dhabi, UAE
Tel: (2) 453 000. Fax: (2) 451 155.
Embassy of the United Arab Emirates
30 Prince's Gate, London SW7 1PT
Tel: (0171) 581 1281. Fax: (0171) 581 9616. Telex: 918459 (a/b EMARAT). Opening hours: 0930-1500 Monday to Friday.
Consulate of the United Arab Emirates
48 Prince's Gate, London SW7 1PT
Tel: (0171) 589 3434. Opening hours: 0930-1300 Monday to Friday (outside Ramadan); 0930-1200 Monday to Friday (during Ramadan).
Dubai Commerce and Tourism Promotion Board
34 Buckingham Palace Road, London SW1W 0RE
Tel: (0171) 828 3153. Fax: (0171) 828 4891. Opening hours: 0900-1730 Monday to Friday.
British Embassy
PO Box 248, Abu Dhabi, UAE
Tel: (2) 326 600 (7 lines) or 321 364. Fax: (2) 341 744 or 318 138. Telex: 22234 (a/b PRODRO EM);
and
PO Box 65, Dubai, UAE
Tel: (4) 521 070 or 521 893 (Commercial section). Fax: (4) 525 750. Telex: 45426 (a/b PRODR EM).
Embassy of the United Arab Emirates
Suite 600, 3000 K Street, NW, Washington, DC 20007
Tel: (202) 338 6500.
Embassy of the United States of America
PO Box 4009, Al-Sudan Street, Abu Dhabi, UAE
Tel: (2) 436 691/2. Fax: (2) 434 771. Telex: 22229 (a/b AMEMBY EM).
Consulate in: Dubai.
Consulate General of the United Arab Emirates
c/o Permanent Mission of the United Arab Emirates to the United Nations
747 Third Avenue, New York, NY 10017
Tel: (212) 371 0480. Fax: (212) 371 4923.
Also deals with enquiries from Canada.
The Canadian Embassy in Kuwait City deals with enquiries relating to the United Arab Emirates (see Kuwait earlier in this book).

	Health
GALILEO/WORLDSPAN: **TI-DFT/AUH/HE**	
SABRE: **TIDFT/AUH/HE**	
	Visa
GALILEO/WORLDSPAN: **TI-DFT/AUH/VI**	
SABRE: **TIDFT/AUH/VI**	

For more information on Timatic codes refer to Contents.

AREA: 77,700 sq km (30,000 sq miles).
POPULATION: 2,083,100 (1993).
POPULATION DENSITY: 26.8 per sq km.
CAPITAL: Abu Dhabi. **Population:** 798,000 (1991).
GEOGRAPHY: The Emirates are bordered to the north by the Gulf and the Musandam Peninsula, to the east by Oman, to the south and west by Saudi Arabia and to the northwest by Qatar. They comprise a federation of seven small former sheikhdoms. Abu Dhabi is the largest Emirate, and the remainder (Dubai, Sharjah, Ajman, Fujairah, Umm al Qaiwain and Ras al-Khaimah) are known collectively as the Northern States. The land is mountainous and mostly desert. **Abu Dhabi** is flat and sandy, and within its boundaries is the Buraimi Oasis. **Dubai** has a 16km (10-mile) deep-water creek, giving it the popular name of 'Pearl of the Gulf'. **Sharjah** has a deep-water port on the Batinah coast at Khor Fakkan, facing the Indian Ocean. **Ras al-Khaimah** is the fourth emirate in size. **Fujairah,** one of the three smaller sheikhdoms located on the Batinah coast, has agricultural potential, while **Ajman** and **Umm al Qaiwain** were once small coastal fishing villages.
LANGUAGE: Arabic is the official language. English is widely spoken.
RELIGION: 96% Sunni Muslim.
TIME: GMT + 4.
ELECTRICITY: Abu Dhabi: 220/240 volts AC, 50Hz. **Northern States:** 220 volts AC, 50Hz. Square 3-pin plugs are widespread.
COMMUNICATIONS: Telephone: IDD is available both to and from all states. Country code: 971. Outgoing international codes (Abu Dhabi): 00. Main area codes: Abu Dhabi 2; Ajman, Sharjah and Umm al Qaiwain 6; Al Ain 3; Dubai 4; Fujairah 9; Jebel Ali 84 and Ras al-Khaimah 7. There is a good local telephone network. Telephone calls *within* each state are free. **Fax:** *ETISALAT* offices at main centres provide a service. All hotels have facilities. **Telex/telegram:** Services are run by *ETISALAT*, which has offices throughout the Emirates and are also available through main post offices. **Post:** Airmail letters and parcels take about five days to reach Europe. **Press:** English-language daily newspapers include *Gulf News, Khaleej Times* and *Emirates News.*
BBC World Service and Voice of America frequencies: From time to time these change. See the section *How to Use this Book* for more information.
BBC:

MHz	21.47	15.57	11.76	7.160

A service is also available on 1413kHz and 702kHz (0100-0500 GMT).
Voice of America:

MHz	21.57	11.90	9.705	6.060

PASSPORT/VISA

Regulations and requirements may be subject to change at short notice, and you are advised to contact the appropriate diplomatic or consular authority before finalising travel arrangements. Details of these may be found at the head of this country's entry. Any numbers in the chart refer to the footnotes below.

	Passport Required?	Visa Required?	Return Ticket Required?
Full British	Yes	1	Yes
BVP	Not valid	-	-
Australian	Yes	Yes	Yes
Canadian	Yes	Yes	Yes
USA	Yes	Yes	Yes
Other EU (As of 31/12/94)	Yes	Yes	Yes
Japanese	Yes	Yes	Yes

Restricted entry: The United Arab Emirates refuse admission and transit to nationals of Israel and to holders of passports containing a visa (valid or expired) for Israel. Travel documents and certificates of identity issued under the Convention of 1951 are not accepted.
PASSPORTS: Valid passport required by all. Often a sponsor will hold a visitor's passport. In these cases a receipt will be issued. This will generally be accepted in place of a passport where a transaction may require one.
British Visitors Passport: Not accepted.
VISAS: Required by all except:
(a) nationals of Bahrain, Kuwait, Oman, Qatar and Saudi Arabia;
(b) **[1]** nationals of the UK with the endorsement 'British Subject Citizen of the United Kingdom and Colonies' or 'British Citizen' for a maximum of 30 days.
Note: As a general rule, visas for tourists and travellers (intending to visit family) must be arranged via the hotel/package tour operator or UAE resident concerned. To obtain approval the sponsor will require the visitor's proposed flight and passport details in advance.

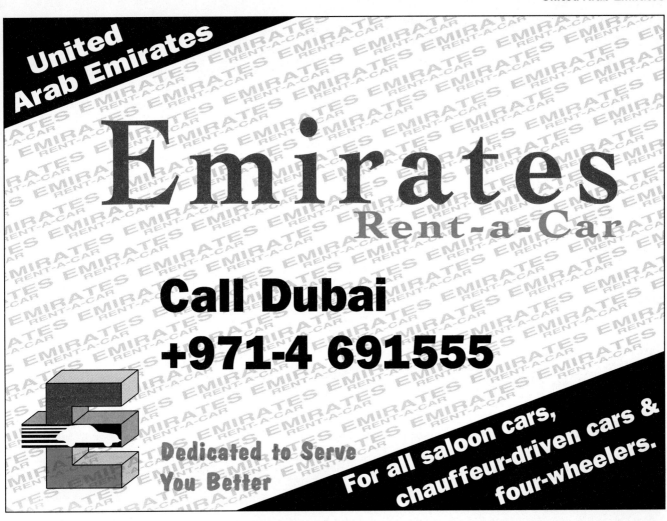

Business visits are made by invitation only.
Flights between airports in the UAE are regarded as international and visitors intending to visit more than one state should have a Multiple-entry visa.
Types of visa: 30-day Visitors' visa and 14-day Transit visa available by prior arrangement through a UAE sponsor. Transit visas are not required by travellers continuing their journey by the same or first connecting flight, provided they do not leave the confines of the airport.
Application to: Consulate (or Consular section at Embassy). For addresses, see top of entry.
Application requirements: (a) Valid passport. (b) 2 completed application forms. (c) 2 passport-size photos. (d) Fee. (e) For Business visas, a letter in duplicate from sponsor in country of origin. (f) Fax of invitation from sponsor in UAE, which must be sent direct to Embassy.
Note: Applications *must* be made in person.

MONEY

Currency: UAE Dirham (UAE Dh) = 100 fils. Notes are in denominations of UAE Dh1000, 500, 100, 50, 10, 5 and 1. Coins are in denominations of UAE Dh1, and 50, 25, 10, 5 and 1 fils.
Currency exchange: Most hotels will handle the exchange of foreign currency.
Credit cards: American Express, Diners Club, Visa and Access/Mastercard are widely accepted. Check with your credit card company for details of merchant acceptability and other services which may be available.
Travellers cheques: These are widely accepted.
Exchange rate indicators: The following figures are included as a guide to the movements of the UAE Dirham against Sterling and the US Dollar:

Date:	Oct '92	Sep '93	Jan '94	Jan '95
£1.00=	5.92	5.62	5.43	5.75
$1.00=	3.73	3.68	3.67	3.67

Currency restrictions: The import and export of both local and foreign currency are unrestricted. The Israeli Shekel are prohibited.
Banking hours: 0800-1200 Saturday to Wednesday; and 0800-1100 Thursday in Abu Dhabi and 0800-1200 Thursday in the Northern States. Some also open 1600-1730.

DUTY FREE

The following items may be imported into the United Arab Emirates without incurring customs duty:
2000 cigarettes or 400 cigars or 2kg of tobacco; 2 litres of spirits and 2 litres of wine (non-Muslims only); a reasonable amount of perfume for personal use (opened).
Prohibited items: Drugs, firearms and ammunition.

PUBLIC HOLIDAYS

Jan 1 '95 New Year's Day. **Feb 1** Beginning of Ramadan. **Mar 3** Eid al-Fitr (End of Ramadan). **May 10** Eid al-Adha (Feast of the Sacrifice). **May 31** Muharram (Islamic New Year). **Aug 6** Accession of HH Sheikh Zayed (Abu Dhabi only). **Aug 9** Mouloud (Prophet's Birthday). **Dec 2** National Day. **Dec 20** Leilat al-Miraj. **Jan 1 '96** New Year's Day. **Jan 22** Beginning of Ramadan. **Feb 22** Eid al-Fitr (End of Ramadan). **Apr 29** Eid al-Adha (Feast of the Sacrifice).
Note: Muslim festivals are timed according to local sightings of various phases of the Moon and the dates given above are approximations. During the lunar month of Ramadan that precedes Eid al-Fitr, Muslims fast during the day and feast at night and normal business patterns may be interrupted. Many restaurants are closed during the day and there may be restrictions on smoking and drinking. Some disruption may continue into Eid al-Fitr itself. Eid al-Fitr and Eid al-Adha may last anything from two to ten days, depending on the region. For more information see the section *World of Islam* at the back of the book.

HEALTH

Regulations and requirements may be subject to change at short notice, and you are advised to contact your doctor well in advance of your intended date of departure. Any numbers in the chart refer to the footnotes below.

	Special Precautions?	Certificate Required?
Yellow Fever	No	No
Cholera	Yes	1
Typhoid & Polio	Yes	-
Malaria	2	-
Food & Drink	3	-

[1]: Following WHO guidelines issued in 1973, a cholera vaccination certificate is not a condition of entry to the United Arab Emirates. However, cholera is a risk in this country and precautions are essential. Up-to-date advice should be sought before deciding whether these precautions should include vaccination, as medical opinion is divided over its effectiveness. See the *Health* section at the back of the book.
[2]: Malaria is not present in the Emirate of Abu Dhabi nor in the cities of Dubai, Sharjah, Ajman or Umm al Qaiwain. There is, however, a risk of contracting the disease (predominantly the benign *vivax* form) in the valleys and on the lower slopes of mountainous areas of the Northern States.
[3]: Tap water in major cities is safe to drink, but in small villages it should be filtered, or bottled water should be used. Water used for drinking, brushing teeth or making ice should have first been boiled or otherwise sterilised. Milk is unpasteurised and should be boiled. Powdered or tinned milk is available and is advised, but make sure that it is reconstituted with pure water. Avoid dairy products which are likely to have been made from unboiled milk. Only eat well-cooked meat and fish, preferably served hot. Salad and mayonnaise may carry increased risk. Vegetables should be cooked and fruit peeled.
Rabies is present. For those at high risk, vaccination before arrival should be considered. If you are bitten abroad seek medical advice without delay. For more information, consult the *Health* section at the back of the book.
Health care: Medical facilities are of a very high quality, but are extremely expensive. Private health insurance is essential.

TRAVEL - International

AIR: The national airlines are *Emirates (EK)* and *Gulf Air (GF)*. *Emirates* operates international flights to and from Dubai; *Gulf Air* serves all UAE airports. *Emirates* is expanding services to the Far East.
Approximate flight times: From *London* to Abu Dhabi is 6 hours 35 minutes and to Dubai is 7 hours; from *Frankfurt/M* to Dubai is 6 hours; from *Hong Kong* to Dubai is 8 hours and from *Nairobi* to Dubai is 4 hours.
International airports: *Abu Dhabi (AUH)* (Nadia) is

37km (23 miles) southwest of the city (travel time – 25 minutes). Airport facilities include duty-free shop, 24-hour bank, bar, snack bar and car hire. Bus and taxis are available at the airport.

Dubai (DBX) is 4km (2.5 miles) from the city (travel time – 10 minutes). Airport facilities include duty-free shop, bank, post office, shops, car hire, restaurant, snack bar and bar. Taxis are available at the airport.

Ras al-Khaimah (RKT) is 15km (9 miles) from the city. Airport facilities include a duty-free shop and restaurant/snack bar. Taxis are available at the airport.

Sharjah (SHJ) is 10km (6 miles) from the city. Airport facilities include duty-free shop, car hire, bar, restaurant, snack bar and bank (only open restricted hours). Taxis are available at the airport.

There is also an airport at *Fujairah* with duty-free facilities, and one is being constructed at *Al Ain*.

SEA: The main international ports are Jebel Ali, Rashid and Zayed (Abu Dhabi), Khalid (Sharjah), Saqr (Ras al-Khaimah) and Fujairah. Cruises call at Abu Dhabi, and there are passenger/cargo services to the USA, the Far East, Australia and Europe.

ROAD: There is a good road into Oman and a fair one into Qatar which connects with the Trans-Arabian Highway on the overland route to Europe.

TRAVEL - Internal

AIR: A daily flight now links Abu Dhabi and Dubai. Flights can also be chartered and there are small landing fields throughout the United Arab Emirates.
SEA: Commercial and passenger services serve all coastal ports. A water taxi travels between Dubai and Deira across the creek.
ROAD: There are good tarmac roads running along the west coast between Abu Dhabi and Dubai, Sharjah and Ras al-Khaimah; between Sharjah and Dhaid; and linking Dubai with other Northern States and the interior. Traffic drives on the right and the speed limit in built-up areas is 60kmph (38mph) and 80-100kmph (50-63mph) elsewhere. **Bus:** Limited services link most towns. However, most hotels run their own scheduled bus services to the airport, city centre and beach resorts. **Taxi:** Available in all towns. In Abu Dhabi, urban journey fares are metered, whilst fares for longer journeys should be agreed in advance. There is a surcharge for air-conditioned taxis. Many travellers find taxis to be the quickest and most convenient method of travel from Abu Dhabi to Dubai. **Car hire:** Most international car hire companies have offices at airports or hotels. **Documentation:** An International Driving Permit is recommended, although it is not legally required. A local driving licence can be issued on presentation of a valid national driving licence. A letter from the visitor's sponsor is also required.

ACCOMMODATION

Accommodation is plentiful and some very reasonable prices can be found, with rates remaining constant all year round. Most of the major international hotel chains are represented, ie Hyatt, Forte, Sheraton, Hilton, Inter-Continental, Marriott and Ramada. There are also top-class beach resort hotels at Jebel Ali and Chicago Beach and a mountain resort hotel at Hatta Fort. Confirmation of reservation by fax or telex is necessary.

RESORTS & EXCURSIONS

For the purposes of this survey, the United Arab Emirates have been divided into the following areas: Abu Dhabi; Dubai; The Desert; The East Coast; and The Northern Emirates.

Abu Dhabi

A predominantly modern city, Abu Dhabi nevertheless retains some of its ancient past. The *Diwan Amiri* (White Fort) was built in 1793 and still survives. There are many mosques, from the massive blue mosque on the corner of the *Corniche* to the tiny one in the centre of *Khalifa Street Roundabout*, surrounded by trees. There is also a museum. The oldest part of the town is the *Batin* area, served daily by the fishing dhows bringing their catch of Gulf prawns and other fish to the small harbours. The old building yards demonstrate craftsmen's skills which have remained unchanged for centuries. The city has ancient burial mounds at *Um al Nar*.
Excursions: Al Ain, 100km (60 miles) from Abu Dhabi, is an oasis and former caravan stop, built on a

huge fertile plain. There is spectacular scenery along the journey from Abu Dhabi. The resort includes a camel market, zoo and museum containing old and new artefacts and Mesopotamian pottery. There is also a water spring at *Ain Faidha*, 14km (9 miles) from Al Ain. There are important archaeological digs at *Hili*, 10km (6 miles) from Al Ain. The stone tombs, including the famous *Great Sepulchre*, date back 5000 years. South of Al Ain is the *Hafit Mountain*, containing ancient tombs, pottery and swords. There are more ancient sites worth visiting at **Um Al Nar** and **Badi'i Bent Saud.** A fun park is situated at **Al-Hir** and majestic sand seas are to be seen at **Liwa.** Other areas of great scenic beauty include **Qarn Island, Belghilam Island** (famous for its gazelle breeding), near to **Sadiyat Island,** and **Abul-Abyadh Island.**

Dubai

The 'Pearl of the Arabian Gulf' is concentrated mainly on its exquisite creek, the finest natural shelter in 1600km (1000 miles) of coastline. **Bur Dubai,** the original town, has substantial areas of old buildings, atmospheric alleyways and *souks* (markets). There is also the *Sikket-El-Kheil souk* and a museum. The modern city is on the Deira-side of the creek and is cosmopolitan and lively, with many attractive gardens and first-class shopping facilities, ranging from Western-style shops to the ancient *souks* where spices, perfume, clothing, antiques, handicrafts and jewels are available. One-fifth of the world's gold passes through Dubai by air or sea. There are outstanding sporting facilities in Dubai, including powerboat racing, water-skiing, snorkelling and ice-skating. The recreation and sporting complex en route to **Jebel Ali** includes a golf course, with an all-grass cricket pitch under construction. Freshwater lakes can also be seen here, full of Japanese carp. There is an all-grass 18-hole golf course at the *Emirates Golf Club,* 20km (12.5 miles) west of Dubai City, which also offers a swimming pool, tennis courts, squash courts and a snooker room. Another all-grass 18-hole golf course was recently landscaped in Dubai at the new *Dubai Creek Golf Club* on the creek. The site features a miniature golf course, tennis courts, picnic and barbecue sites, children's play areas, cycling and jogging tracks and acres of beautiful gardens. The three main parks in Dubai are the *Mushrif Park, Jumeira Beach Park* and the *Safa Park* (currently under renovation).
Excursions: The ancient fortressed village of **Hatta** and *Wadi Hatta,* a lush and attractive valley in the foothills of the *Hajar Mountains* with superb desert scenery on the journey from Dubai.

The Desert

A spectacular and varied wilderness of magnificent red dunes and stark mountains with pockets of green oases. It is possible to meet the nomadic *Bedu* folk, whose hospitality is famous, and to watch camel races at dawn.
Excursions: Include visits to Bedu villages and to the stunning white sand dunes at *Awir,* where there is a national park. There is a selection of 'safari' holidays available.

The East Coast

This impressive stretch of lush coastline makes a dramatic change after the desert, with steep mountains, unspoilt sandy bays and beaches, ancient fortresses and date palm groves sloping down to the edge of the Indian Ocean with its host of marine life. Scuba diving and snorkelling are very popular here and many forms of watersports are available at the hotels.
Excursions: Include visits to the resorts of *Dibba* and *Fujairah,* where there is a museum, a Necropolis, an old fort and, nearby, many small mountain villages.

The Northern Emirates

This region has undergone a dramatic transformation since the discovery of natural gas in 1980 and there has been a considerable amount of expansion in the commercial sector. **Sharjah** is an excellent shopping centre, with its new *souk* containing hundreds of shops. There is also an ancient fort.
Excursions: Include visits to **Ras al-Khaimah,** where there is an old seaport with spectacular views over the coast and the *Hajar Mountains;* and also visits to the *Dhaid* and *Khatt* oases, the latter with mineral water springs. There are also trips available to the natural harbour at *Dibba* and the beautiful *Khor Kalba,* one of

the most famous shell beaches in the world. The archaeological site at *Mileiha* (in **Sharjah** itself) dates back to the 4th century BC; 80-million-year-old fossils are to be seen here. Other archaeological sites include *Dur* at **Umm al Qaiwain** where Hellenistic ruins can be seen (210-100BC), the *Drabhaniya* ruins in **Ras al-Khaimah** and the *Zaura* ruins in **Ajman.** Important resort areas are *Khor Fakkan*, which has excellent beaches and watersports facilities and *Khalid Lagoon* (an aquatic park with several islands and a miniature Disneyland).

SOCIAL PROFILE

FOOD & DRINK: Specialities of Arab cuisine include *hoummus* (chickpea and sesame paste), *tabbouleh* (bulghur wheat with mint and parsley), *ghuzi* (roast lamb with rice and nuts), *warak enab* (stuffed vine leaves) and *koussa mashi* (stuffed courgettes). In the Emirates *makbous* (spicy lamb with rice) and seafood with spicy rice are also popular. Local fruit and vegetables are increasingly available and there is excellent local fish. Hotels serve both European and Arab food and there are also a number of Chinese, Indian and other restaurants. Frozen foods from all over the world are available in supermarkets.
Drink: All the Emirates, with the exception of Sharjah, permit the consumption of alcohol by non-Muslims. It is illegal to drink alcohol in the street or to buy it for a UAE citizen. *Ayran* (a refreshing yoghurt drink) or strong black coffee are served on many occasions.
NIGHTLIFE: There are several nightclubs located in major centres and entertainment ranges from Arabic singers and dancers to international pop stars. Bars are found in all top hotels and range from sophisticated cocktail lounges to English-style pubs. Some hotels also have discos. Traditional dances are performed on public holidays. Most large towns have cinemas showing English-language films.
SHOPPING: Customs duties are low and therefore luxury goods are cheaper than in most countries. The Dubai duty-free shop is one of the cheapest in the world. *Souks* sell traditional Emirate leather goods, gold, brass and silverware.
SPORT: Golf: The Emirates Golf Club, Dubai, which opened in 1988, was the first grass golf course in the Gulf. In addition, there is also the recently completed Dubai Creek Golf Club. **Fishing:** There is an abundance of game fish in the Gulf. Fully-equipped boats with crew can be hired from the Jebel Ali Hotel marina for deep-sea fishing trips. **Water-skiing:** Boats and water-skiing equipment are available for hire. **Sailing** and **windsurfing** are popular around Dubai and boats are available for hire from the Dubai Offshore Sailing Club. **Swimming:** Bathing is possible in the many hotel pools or beaches. **Ice-skating:** Dubai has two year-round ice rinks and skates and instruction are available. **Horseriding:** Available at several riding centres, and rides through the desert are organised regularly. **Tennis/squash:** Many hotels and clubs have tennis courts and there are squash courts in main centres. **Bowling** alleys can be found in hotels and clubs. **Scuba diving:** The waters off Dubai are considered among the best areas in the world for diving. There are sub-aqua clubs in main centres and an extensive range of equipment is available for hire. **Spectator sports: Boat races** for about 30 rowers are a traditional sport that is becoming increasingly popular. **Camel-** and **horse-races** are also held at various race tracks. **Football** has become more popular and can be seen in most large towns and there are three thriving **rugby** clubs in Dubai. **Falconry** is very popular among Arabs.
SPECIAL EVENTS: The following is a selection of major festivals and other special events celebrated in the United Arab Emirates during 1995:
Apr 25-28 '95 *Britain in the Gulf Exhibition.* **May 16-20** *Middle East International Boat Show.* **May 28-31** *Germany in the Gulf* (trade fair). **Sep 27-Oct 1** *INDEX '95* (interior design exhibition). **Oct 9-13** *Arab Water Technology Exhibition.* **Oct 18-22** *Arab Horse '95.* **Oct 28-31** *GITEX* (computer exhibition). **Nov 12-16** *Dubai '95 Airshow.* **Nov 21-25** *Middle East International Motor Show.*
SOCIAL CONVENTIONS: Muslim religious laws should be observed. Women are expected to dress modestly and men should dress formally for most occasions. Smoking is the same as in Europe and in most cases it is obvious where not to smoke, except during Ramadan when it is illegal to eat, drink or smoke in public. **Tipping:** Most hotels, restaurants and clubs add fairly high service charges to the bill, therefore tipping is not necessary. Taxi drivers are not tipped.

BUSINESS PROFILE

ECONOMY: Oil and gas are the Emirates' main industry and underpin the country's considerable prosperity. Although revenues declined in real terms during the 1980s, due to low world oil prices and OPEC-imposed production ceilings, the Emirates have had sufficient money to invest in major industrial and infrastructural projects: a large foreign workforce (estimated at two-thirds of the total population) has been recruited for these. Outside the oil and gas sector, most economic activity is government-sponsored and designed to diversify the economy and reduce dependence on oil. There are major construction projects, including a new international airport, and several industrial zones have been established to produce materials for domestic consumption. Imports into the UAE are dominated by the Japanese, who have about two-thirds of the US$7-billion market, followed by the USA and Turkey.
BUSINESS: Business entertaining will often be lavish. Suits should be worn and prior appointments are essential. English is widely spoken in business circles, but translation services are likely to be available. **Office hours:** 0800-1300 and 1600-1900 Saturday to Wednesday and 0700-1200 Thursday. **Government office hours:** 0730-1330 Saturday to Wednesday and 0730-1200 Thursday (winter); 0700-1300 Saturday to Thursday (summer). All offices are closed every afternoon during the month of Ramadan.
COMMERCIAL INFORMATION: The following organisations can offer advice: Federation of UAE Chambers of Commerce and Industry, PO Box 3014, Abu Dhabi. Tel: (2) 214 144. Fax: (2) 339 210. Telex: 23883; *or*
Dubai Chamber of Commerce and Industry, PO Box 1457, Diera, Dubai. Tel: (4) 221 181. Fax: (4) 211 646. Telex: 45997.
In addition, each of the Emirates has its own Chamber of Commerce.
CONFERENCES/CONVENTIONS: Though the Emirates are not primary convention locations, there are many first-class hotels with meeting facilities. The Dubai World Trade Centre hosts a multitude of events (including car rallies and tennis exhibitions). For further information on conference and convention facilities, contact the Dubai World Trade Centre, PO Box 9292, Dubai. Tel: (4) 314 200 *or* 306 4025. Fax: (4) 306 4033 *or* 306 4086.

CLIMATE

The best time to visit is between October and May. The hottest time is from June to September with little rainfall.
Required clothing: Lightweights with mediumweights from November to March, warmer clothes for evening.

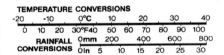

TEMPERATURE CONVERSIONS

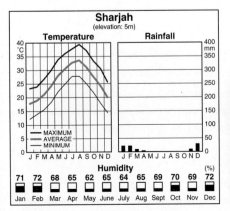

Sharjah
(elevation: 5m)

United Kingdom

400km
200mls

major international airport

Location: Northwest Europe.

British Tourist Authority and English Tourist Board
Thames Tower, Black's Road, Hammersmith, London W6 9EL
Tel: (0181) 846 9000 *or* 563 3329 (Business Services Unit). Fax: (0181) 563 0302. Opening hours: 0900-1800 Monday to Friday.
British Travel Centre
12 Lower Regent Street, Piccadilly Circus, London SW1
Opening hours: 0900-1830 Monday to Friday; 1000-1600 Saturday and Sunday.
Personal visits only.
Scottish Tourist Board
23 Ravelston Terrace, Edinburgh EH4 3EU
Tel: (0131) 332 2433. Fax: (0131) 343 1513. Telex: 72272.
Wales Tourist Board
Brunel House, 2 Fitzalan Road, Cardiff CF2 1UY
Tel: (01222) 499 909. Fax: (01222) 485 031.
Northern Ireland Tourist Board
St Anne's Court, 59 North Street, Belfast BT1 1NB
Tel: (01232) 231 221. Fax: (01232) 240 960.
Embassy of the United Kingdom of Great Britain and Northern Ireland
3100 Massachusetts Avenue, NW, Washington, DC 20008
Tel: (202) 462 1340. Fax: (202) 898 4255. Telex: 892370 (a/b PRODROM B WSH).
Consulate Generals in: Atlanta, Boston, Chicago, Cleveland, Dallas, Houston, Los Angeles, New York (tel: (212) 745 0200) and San Francisco.
British Tourist Authority
7th Floor, 551 Fifth Avenue, New York, NY 10176-0799

Timatic	Health
	GALILEO/WORLDSPAN: **TI-DFT/LHR/HE**
	SABRE: **TIDFT/LHR/HE**
	Visa
	GALILEO/WORLDSPAN: **TI-DFT/LHR/VI**
	SABRE: **TIDFT/LHR/VI**

For more information on Timatic codes refer to Contents.

Tel: (212) 986 2200 *or* (1 800) 654 3001.
Also in: Atlanta, Chicago and Los Angeles.
Embassy of the United States of America
24-31 Grosvenor Square, London W1A 1AE
Tel: (0171) 499 9000. Fax: (0171) 409 1637.
British High Commission
80 Elgin Street, Ottawa, Ontario K1P 5K7
Tel: (613) 237 1530. Fax: (613) 237 7980.
Consulates in: Halifax, Montréal, St John's, Toronto, Vancouver and Winnipeg.
British Tourist Authority
Suite 450, 111 Avenue Road, Toronto, Ontario M5R 3J8
Tel: (416) 925 6326. Fax: (416) 961 2175.
Canadian High Commission
Macdonald House, 1 Grosvenor Square, London W1X 0AB
Tel: (0171) 258 6600 *or* 258 6316 (Consular section). Fax: (0171) 445 3333 *or* 258 6533 (Consular section). Telex: 261592 (a/b CDALDN G).

INTRODUCTION

The United Kingdom of Great Britain and Northern Ireland consists of *England, Scotland, Wales* and *Northern Ireland*. Although they form one administrative unit (with regional exceptions) they have had separate cultures, languages and political histories. Within this entry are also the *Channel Islands* (excluding *Guernsey* and *Jersey* which have their own separate entries earlier in this book) and the *Isle of Man* which, although only dependencies of the British Crown, are included for convenience of reference. The *United Kingdom* entry has been arranged as follows. First, a general introduction, covering the aspects which the four countries have in common. Then following, sections devoted to the four constituent countries and, finally, sections dealing respectively with the Channel Islands and the Isle of Man.

AREA: 242,429 sq km (93,602 sq miles).
POPULATION: 57,649,200 (1991 estimate).
POPULATION DENSITY: 237.8 per sq km.
CAPITAL: London. **Population:** 6,803,1000 (Greater London, 1991 estimate).
GEOGRAPHY: The British landscape can be divided roughly into two kinds of terrain – highland and lowland. The highlands area comprises the mountainous regions of Scotland, Northern Ireland, northern England and north Wales. The English Lake District in the northwest contains lakes and fells. The lowland area is broken up by sandstone and limestone hills, long valleys and basins such as the Wash on the east coast. In the southeast, the North and South Downs culminate in the White Cliffs of Dover. The coastline includes fjord-like inlets in the northwest of Scotland, spectacular cliffs and wild sandy beaches on the east coast and, further south, beaches of rocks, shale and sand sometimes backed by dunes, and large areas of fenland in East Anglia.
Note: More detailed geographical descriptions of the various countries may be found under the respective entries.
LANGUAGE: English. Some Welsh is spoken in parts of Wales, Gaelic in parts of Scotland and Northern Ireland, and French and Norman French in the Channel Islands. The many ethnic minorities within the UK also speak their own dialects and languages (eg Hindi, Urdu, Turkish, Greek, Cantonese, Mandarin, etc).
RELIGION: Predominantly Protestant (Church of England), but many other Christian denominations also: Roman Catholic, Church of Scotland, Evangelical, Nonconformist and Baptist. There are sizeable Jewish, Muslim and Hindu minorities.
TIME: GMT (GMT + 1 from last Sunday in March to Saturday before last Sunday in September).
ELECTRICITY: 240 volts AC, 50Hz. Square 3-pin plugs are standard and the visitor is unlikely to come across the older round 3-pin type.
COMMUNICATIONS: Telephone: IDD is available. Country code: 44. Outgoing international code: 00. There are numerous public call boxes. Some boxes take coins, others phonecards only. There are two suppliers of telecommunication networks, British Telecom and Mercury. **Fax:** There are many high-street bureaux in major cities. Most hotels and offices have facilities.
Telex/telemessage: There are telex bureaux in all the main cities. Telemessages may be sent from a post office or from a private telephone. **Post:** Stamps are available from post offices and many shops and stores. There are stamp machines outside some post offices. Post boxes are red. First-class internal mail normally reaches its destination the day after posting (except in remote areas of Scotland), and most second-class mail the day after that. International postal connections are good. Post office opening hours are 0900-1730 Monday to Friday and 0900-1230 Saturday. **Press:** Dominated by about ten

major newspapers, UK circulation figures are amongst the highest in the world. The most influential newspapers are *The Times, The Guardian, The Daily Telegraph, The Financial Times, The Observer* and *The Independent.* The more popular 'tabloid' newspapers are *The Sun, The Daily Mirror, The Daily Express, The Daily Mail* and *Today.* Most papers have an associated Sunday newspaper, though there are some independents. There are also daily regional newspapers, particularly in Scotland and the north. The London *Evening Standard* is produced in several editions daily, the first being in the early afternoon.

PASSPORT/VISA

Regulations and requirements may be subject to change at short notice, and you are advised to contact the appropriate diplomatic or consular authority before finalising travel arrangements. Details of these may be found at the head of this country's entry. Any numbers in the chart refer to the footnotes below.

	Passport Required?	Visa Required?	Return Ticket Required?
Full British	1	-	-
BVP	Valid	No	No
Australian	Yes	No	No
Canadian	Yes	No	No
USA	Yes	No	No
Other EU (As of 31/12/94)	2	No	No
Japanese	Yes	No	No

PASSPORTS: Valid passport required by all except:
(a) **[1]** nationals of the United Kingdom and colonies holding a BVP;
(b) **[2]** nationals of EU countries with a valid national ID card for tourist visits not exceeding 3 months;
(c) nationals of Austria, Liechtenstein, Monaco and Switzerland holding a valid national ID card for touristic/social visits of less than 6 months and in possession of a British Visitor's Card available from travel agencies.
Note: (a) A passport is not required for travel between Great Britain and Ireland, Northern Ireland, the Channel Islands or the Isle of Man. (b) Passports should be valid for at least 6 months beyond the period of intended stay. (c) Passengers transiting the UK destined for the Republic of Ireland are advised to hold return tickets to avoid delay and interrogation. (d) Passports issued by Taiwan (China), and the former South African 'homelands' of Bophuthatswana, Ciskei, Transkei and Venda are not recognised.
British Visitors Passport: Accepted.
VISAS: Not required by EU nationals and citizens of countries listed in the chart above.
Citizens of the following countries *do* require visas:
Afghanistan, Albania, Algeria, Angola, Armenia, Azerbaijan, Bangladesh, Belarus, Benin, Bhutan, Bosnia-Hercegovina, Bulgaria, Burkina Faso, Burundi, Cambodia, Cameroon, Cape Verde, Central African Republic, Chad, China, Comoros, Congo, Côte d'Ivoire, Cuba, Djibouti, Egypt, Equatorial Guinea, Eritrea, Ethiopia, Gabon, Georgia, Ghana, Guinea, Guinea-Bissau, Haiti, India, Indonesia, Iran, Iraq, Jordan, Kazakhstan, Kyrgyzstan, North Korea, Laos, Lebanon, Liberia, Libya, Former Yugoslav Republic of Macedonia, Madagascar, Mali, Mauritania, Moldova, Mongolia, Morocco, Mozambique, Nepal, Nigeria, Oman, Pakistan, Philippines, Romania, Russia, Rwanda, São Tomé e Príncipe, Saudi Arabia, Senegal, Sierra Leone, Somalia, Sri Lanka, Sudan, Syria, Taiwan (China), Tajikistan, Thailand, Togo, Tunisia, Turkey, Turkmenistan, Uganda, Ukraine, Uzbekistan, Vietnam, Yemen, and Yugoslavia (Serbia and Montenegro), Zaïre. All other nationals do *not* require visas.
Note: Commonwealth citizens except nationals of Bangladesh, Ghana, India, Nigeria, Pakistan, Sri Lanka and Uganda do not require visas. Citizens of these countries must generally have their passport or identity document endorsed with a valid United Kingdom visa, issued for the purpose for which they seek entry. Those who have settled in the UK may be exempt: enquire at the UK Passport Office if in the UK, otherwise at a British Embassy or High Commission.
Types of visa: Temporary visitor's and Business. Cost: US$56.10; US$28.05 for travellers under 25. A 6-month

Multiple-entry visa costs US$76.50 and a 2-year visa costs US$110. Visa prices are standard. *Transit visas* are not required if continuing the journey to a third country by the first connecting aircraft within 24 hours, and possessing confirmed onward travel documentation. Travellers who do not qualify for this exemption must possess a Transit visa, which is valid for 7 days.
Application to: The nearest visa-issuing post in the country in question, ie British Consulate (or Consular section at Embassy or High Commission).
Application requirements: Depends on nationality of applicant.
Working days required: Depends on nationality of applicant. Applications that are referred to the Home Office may take 6 weeks or more.
Temporary residence: Enquire at nearest British Consulate, Embassy or High Commission.

MONEY

Note: For information on currency specific to Jersey and Guernsey, see their separate entries earlier in the book; for the Isle of Man and Northern Ireland, see the subsections that follow this general UK entry.
Currency: Pound (£) = 100 pence. Notes are in denominations of £50, 20, 10 and 5. There are in addition bank notes issued by Scottish banks which are legal tender in all parts of the UK. Coins are in denominations of £1, and 50, 20, 10, 5, 2 and 1 pence. In 1990 a new, smaller 5-pence piece came into circulation. Similarly, a new smaller 10-pence piece was introduced in 1992. The old 5- and 10-pence pieces are no longer legal tender.
Currency exchange: Money can be exchanged in banks, exchange bureaux and many hotels. The exchange bureaux are often open outside banking hours but charge higher commission rates.
Credit cards: Access/Mastercard, American Express, Diners Club and Visa are all widely accepted. Check with your credit card company for details of merchant acceptability and other services which may be available.
Travellers cheques: Widely accepted.
Exchange rate indicators: The following figures are included as a guide to the movements of Sterling against the US Dollar:

Date:	Oct '92	Sep '93	Jan '94	Jan '95
$1.00=	0.63	0.65	0.67	0.64

Currency restrictions: There are no restrictions on the import or export of either local or foreign currency.
Banking hours: 0930-1530/1630 Monday to Friday (there may be some further variation in closing times). Some branches of certain banks are open Saturday morning. Some branches of the Co-operative Bank stay open until 1730.

DUTY FREE

Note: The Channel Islands are treated as being outside of the EU for the *Duty Free* section.
The following items may be imported into the UK without incurring customs duty by:
(a) Travellers from non-EU European countries or bought duty free within the EU:
200 cigarettes or 50 cigars or 100 cigarillos or 250g of tobacco; *1 litre of alcoholic beverages stronger than 22° proof or 2 litres less than 22° proof or 2 litres of fortified wine; *2 litres of wine; *8 litres of non-sparkling Luxembourg wine; *50g of perfume and 250ml of toilet water; *other goods to the value of £32.
(b) Travellers originating from outside Europe:
400 cigarettes or 100 cigars or 500g tobacco; *wine, spirits and perfume same as for non-EU European countries; *other goods to the value of £136.
(c) Travellers aged 17 years and above arriving from EU countries with duty-paid goods:
800 cigarettes and 400 cigarillos and 200 cigars and 1kg tobacco; 90 litres of wine including up to 60 litres of sparkling wine; 10 litres of spirits; 20 litres of fortified wine; 110 litres of beer.
Note: [*] (a) Only for travellers aged 17 years and above.
Note: (b) Although there are now no legal limits imposed on importing duty-paid tobacco and alcoholic products from one EU country to another, travellers may be questioned at customs if they exceed the above amounts and may be asked to prove that the goods are for personal use only. (c) Enquiries concerning current import

regulations should be made to the UK Embassy in the country of departure. (d) The UK is one of the few regions of the world completely free of rabies, and all cats and dogs imported into the country must spend six months in quarantine. To bring animals and birds into the UK, an import licence must be obtained, at least six months in advance. *Severe penalties are imposed on persons attempting to smuggle domestic animals into the country. An illegally imported animal is liable to be destroyed.* For further information contact the Ministry of Agriculture, Fisheries & Food, Government Buildings, Hook Rise South, Kingston Bypass, Tolworth, Surbiton, Surrey KT6 7NF. Tel: (0181) 330 4411. Fax: (0181) 337 3640; *or* the nearest British mission abroad.

PUBLIC HOLIDAYS

Jan 2 '95 For New Year. **Jan 3** Bank Holiday (Scotland only). **Apr 14** Good Friday. **Apr 17** Easter Monday. **May 1** May Day (Scotland only). **May 8** For May Day Bank Holiday. **May 29** Spring Bank Holiday. **Aug 7** Summer Bank Holiday (Scotland only). **Aug 28** Late Summer Bank Holiday (excluding Scotland). **Dec 25** Christmas Day. **Dec 26** Boxing Day. **Jan 1 '96** New Year's Day. **Jan 2** Bank Holiday (Scotland only). **Apr 5** Good Friday. **Apr 8** Easter Monday.
Note: Public holidays are often referred to as 'bank holidays' in the UK.

HEALTH

Regulations and requirements may be subject to change at short notice, and you are advised to contact your doctor well in advance of your intended date of departure. Any numbers in the chart refer to the footnotes below.

	Special Precautions?	Certificate Required?
Yellow Fever	No	No
Cholera	No	No
Typhoid & Polio	No	-
Malaria	No	-
Food & Drink	No	-

Health care: The National Health Service provides free medical treatment (at hospitals and general surgeries) to all who are ordinarily resident in the UK but requires payment for dental treatment, prescriptions and spectacles. Immediate first aid/emergency treatment is free for all visitors, after which charges are made unless the visitor's country has a Reciprocal Health Agreement with the UK. The following have signed such Agreements: all EU countries (but Danish residents of the Faroe Islands are not covered), Anguilla, Australia, Austria, British Virgin Islands, Bulgaria, Channel Islands (applies only if visitor is staying less than three months), Falkland Islands, Finland, Hong Kong, Hungary, Iceland, Isle of Man, Malta (for visits up to 30 days), Montserrat, New Zealand, Norway, Poland, Romania, St Helena, Sweden and the Turks & Caicos Islands. The Agreements provide differing degrees of exemption for different nationalities; full details of individual Agreements are available from the Department of Health. See also the *Health* section at the back of this book.

TRAVEL - International

AIR: The principal national airline is *British Airways (BA).*
Approximate flight times: From *Birmingham* to Amsterdam is 1 hour; to Dublin is 50 minutes; to Düsseldorf is 1 hour 15 minutes; to Frankfurt/M is 1 hour

30 minutes; and to Paris is 1 hour 5 minutes.
From *Glasgow* to Paris is 1 hour 35 minutes.
From *Manchester* to Amsterdam is 1 hour 5 minutes; to Brussels is 30 minutes; to Copenhagen is 1 hour 45 minutes; to Dublin is 45 minutes; to Düsseldorf is 1 hour 20 minutes; to Frankfurt/M is 1 hour 45 minutes; to Milan is 2 hours 5 minutes; to Nice is 2 hours 5 minutes; to Paris is 1 hour 15 minutes; to Rome is 2 hours 40 minutes; and to Zurich is 2 hours 50 minutes.
For approximate durations of international flights from London, see *Travel – International* sections in entries of the destination country.
International airports: See relevant country sections below for information on UK airports. For free advice on air travel, call the Air Travel Advisory Bureau on (0171) 636 5000 (London) *or* (0161) 832 2000 (Manchester).
THE CHANNEL TUNNEL
Road vehicles: All road vehicles are carried through the tunnel in *Le Shuttle* running between the two terminals, one near Folkestone in Kent, with direct access from the M20, and one just outside Calais with links to the A16/A26 motorway (Exit 13). Each shuttle is made up of

12 single- and 12 double-deck carriages, and vehicles are directed to single-deck or double-deck shuttles depending on their height. The first phase of commercial operation of the tourist shuttle is for cars and motorcycles. Facilities for coaches, minibuses, caravans, campervans and other vehicles over 1.85m (6.07ft) as well as bicycles are due to become operational in summer 1995. Passengers generally travel with their vehicles. Heavy goods vehicles are carried on special shuttles with a separate passenger coach for their drivers. Terminals and shuttles are well-equipped for disabled passengers and Passenger Terminal buildings contain duty-free shops, restaurants, bureaux de change and other amenities. The journey takes about 35 minutes from platform to platform and about one hour from motorway to motorway. In January 1995, shuttles ran hourly 24 hours per day with a projected increase to twice-hourly in March and four times (in peak hours) by summer 1995. Services run every day of the year. The reservation system was due to be replaced by a turn-up-and-go service in April 1995. By contacting Eurotunnel Customer Services in Coquelle (tel: 21 00 61 00; fax: 21 00 63 61) as they approach the

French terminal, motorists can find out when the next shuttle leaves and how busy the service is. Motorists pass through customs and immigration before they board the shuttle without further checks on arrival. Fares are charged according to length of stay and time of year. The price remains constant throughout the day and applies to the car, regardless of the number of passengers or size of the car. The fare may be paid by cash, cheque or credit card. Introductory fares valid until March 30, 1995 were: Day Return: £49 (FFr390); 5-Day Return: £75 (FFr620); Standard Return: £136 (FFr1140). Lower rates apply to motorcycles. Tickets may be purchased in advance from travel agents, or from Eurotunnel Customer Services in France or the UK with a credit card. For further information, contact Eurotunnel Customer Services in the UK on (0990) 353 535. Fax: (01303) 272 690.
Direct Rail links: The direct *Eurostar* train link through the Channel Tunnel between London and Lille, Brussels or Paris started operating on November 14, 1994. *Eurostar* is a service provided by the railways of Belgium, the United Kingdom and France, operating direct high-speed trains from Paris *(Gare du Nord)* to

London *(Waterloo International)* and to Brussels *(Midi)*. It takes 3 hours from Paris to London. When the high-speed rail link from London through Kent to the tunnel is operational (expected to be in the year 2002), the travel time between the two capitals will be reduced to two and a half hours. It takes 3 hours 15 minutes from London to Brussels (2 hours 40 minutes with the completion of the high-speed Belgian link in 1997/98). As of January 23, 1995, trains depart four times daily (five on Friday) from Waterloo to Paris and three times daily from Waterloo to Brussels. A direct service to Lille (travel time – 2 hours 10 minutes) runs once daily from Waterloo. Services, including overnight sleeper trains, will also run from major regional centres. Access to the entire British railway network will be provided, bringing many British business centres within a comfortable day's journey. Plans also envisage the use of London's St Pancras station by Eurostar travelling north of London, and also as a second London terminus. The Eurostar trains are equipped with standard-class and first-class seating, buffet, bar and telephones, and will be staffed by multi-lingual, highly trained personnel. Pricing is competitive with the airlines, and range from *Discovery Gold* (first class) to *Discovery Special* (standard class). Whilst the latter offer the best value, tickets must be booked at least 14 days before travel, cannot be exchanged or refunded and are subject to availability. *Discovery* tickets, also standard class, can be exchanged or refunded, but prices are higher. Children aged between 4-11 years benefit from a special fare in first class as well as in standard class. Children under 4 years old travel free but cannot be guaranteed a seat. Wheelchair users and blind passengers together with one companion get a special fare. For more information, contact Eurostar Enquiries, EPS House, Waterloo Station, London SE1 8SE (tel: (0181) 784 1333; fax: (01233) 617 998). Telephone reservations may be made by travel agents on (01233) 617 599 and by members of the public on (01233) 617 575. For information on special fares for groups of at least ten people, telephone (0171) 922 6049. All enquiries in France should be made to SNCF in Paris. Tel: (1) 45 82 50 50.

SEA: There are many ports offering ferry connections between the UK and mainland Europe, Ireland, the Channel Islands, the Isle of Wight, the Scilly Isles and the Isle of Man.

RAIL: *British Rail* trains meet connecting ferries at Dover, Newhaven, Portsmouth, Weymouth and Folkestone sailing for France, Germany and Belgium (board at Victoria Station in London); and at Harwich sailing for The Netherlands, Germany and Scandinavia (board at Liverpool Street).

ROAD: Few formalities are encountered when driving between Northern Ireland and the Republic of Ireland.

TRAVEL - Internal

Note: This section is a general introduction to transport within the UK. Further information is given in the *Travel* sections for England, Scotland, Wales, Northern Ireland, the Channel Islands and the Isle of Man below.

AIR: *British Airways* operates a shuttle service to Belfast, Edinburgh, Glasgow and Manchester. Other internal operators include: *Aer Lingus, Air UK, British Midland Airways, Inter City Airlines, Jersey European Airways, Logan Air, London City Airlines* and *Ryanair*.

Approximate flight times: From *London* to Aberdeen is 1 hour 25 minutes; to Belfast is 1 hour 10 minutes; to Edinburgh is 1 hour 10 minutes; to Glasgow is 1 hour 10 minutes; to Jersey is 50 minutes; to Manchester is 50 minutes; and to Newcastle is 1 hour.

From *Aberdeen* to Birmingham is 1 hour 40 minutes; to Glasgow is 50 minutes; to London is 1 hour 25 minutes; to Manchester is 1 hour 35 minutes; to Orkney is 45 minutes; and to Shetland is 1 hour 5 minutes.

From *Belfast* to Birmingham is 50 minutes; to Glasgow is 45 minutes; to London is 1 hour 5 minutes; and to Manchester is 45 minutes.

From *Birmingham* to Aberdeen is 1 hour 40 minutes; to Belfast is 55 minutes; to Edinburgh is 55 minutes; to Glasgow is 1 hour; and to Manchester is 30 minutes.

From *Edinburgh* to Birmingham is 55 minutes and to London is 50 minutes.

From *Glasgow* to Aberdeen is 50 minutes; to Belfast is 50 minutes; to Birmingham is 55 minutes; to Inverness is 50 minutes; to London is 1 hour 10 minutes; to Manchester is 50 minutes; and to Stornoway is 1 hour 5 minutes.

From *Manchester* to Aberdeen is 1 hour; to Belfast is 45 minutes; to Birmingham is 30 minutes; to Glasgow is 50 minutes; to Jersey is 1 hour 5 minutes; and to London is 50 minutes.

SEA: Information on travel to the Scottish islands is given below under *Scotland*, on travel to Ireland below under *Northern Ireland*.

RAIL: The UK is served by an excellent network of

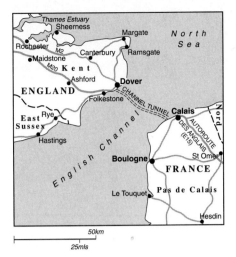

railways (16,000km/10,000 miles – in total). *Intercity* lines provide fast services between London and major cities, and there are services to the southeast and to major cities in the Midlands and the north, south Wales and between Edinburgh and Glasgow. Some rural areas are less well served (eg the north coast of the west country, parts of East Anglia, North Yorkshire and Northumberland, parts of inland Wales, Northern Ireland and southern and northern Scotland), although local rail services are generally fairly comprehensive. There is a Motor Rail service across the country; this enables travellers to travel quickly by train while still having the facility of their car at the other end.

There are many **discretionary fares,** and visitors using trains may like to consider an all-line *British Rail* pass giving unlimited travel. Contact *British Rail* for details. Disabled travellers are also entitled to discounted train fares; see the relevant section at the back of the book. *Inter-Rail* cards are valid; holders may be entitled to discounts on ferry fares.

ROAD: There are trunk roads ('A' roads) linking all major towns and cities in the UK. Roads in rural areas ('B' roads) can be slow and winding, and in upland areas may become impassable in winter. Motorways radiate from London and there is also a good east–west and north–south network in the north and the Midlands. The M25 motorway circles London and connects at various junctions with the M1, M4, M3, M40, M10 and M11. The only motorway that leaves England is the M4 from London to south Wales. Access to Scotland is by the A1/A1(M) or the A68 to Edinburgh, or the M6 to Carlisle followed by the A74 to Glasgow. Within Scotland, motorways link Edinburgh, Glasgow and Perth. In Northern Ireland, motorways run from Belfast to Dungannon and from Belfast to Antrim. For further information on roads within each country, see the respective sections below. **Coach:** Every major city has a coach terminus, in London it is Victoria Coach station, about 1km (0.7 miles) from the train station. There are rapid coach services to all parts of the country. Many coaches have on-board toilets, refreshments and video. Private coaches may be hired by groups wishing to tour the UK; these can be booked in advance and will visit most major tourist attractions. Many of these destinations now have coach parks nearby. The main carrier is *National Express*. **Traffic regulations:** Traffic drives on the left. Speed limits are 30mph (48kmph) in urban areas, 70mph (113kmph) on motorways and dual carriageways, elsewhere 50mph (80kmph) or 60mph (97kmph) as marked. Petrol is graded in a star system: 2-star (90 octane) and 4-star (97 octane). Unleaded petrol is also available at all petrol stations and is sold at a lower price than leaded petrol. Seatbelts must be worn by driver and front seat passenger. Where rear seat belts have been fitted they must also be worn. **Documentation:** National driving licences are valid for one year. Drivers must have Third Party insurance and vehicle registration documents. **Automobile associations:** The *RAC* and *AA* are able to provide a full range of services to UK members touring the UK, they can also assist people who are travelling from abroad with maps, tourist information and specially marked routes to major events or places of interest.

URBAN: All cities and towns have bus services of varying efficiency and cost. London, Newcastle, Liverpool and Glasgow have metros, London and Glasgow's being very old and Newcastle's very new. The urban areas of Glasgow, Cardiff, Manchester, Liverpool and Birmingham are also well served by local

railway trains. Manchester has recently introduced a modern tram service. Licensed taxi operators are generally metered; small supplements may be charged for weekends, 'bank holidays', excess baggage and late-night travel. In the larger cities, unlicensed operators offer a cheaper (but less efficient and knowledgeable) unmetered service with fares based loosely on elapsed clock mileage; these taxis are known as mini-cabs and must be summoned by telephone.

ACCOMMODATION

Accommodation in all parts of the UK is plentiful. **HOTELS:** These tend to be much more expensive in large cities, especially London. Different classification schemes are used by the various countries. See the relevant country sections below. More information is also available from the British Hospitality Association, 40 Duke Street, London W1M 6HR. Tel: (0171) 499 6641. Fax: (0171) 355 4596.
GUEST-HOUSES: There are guest-houses and bed & breakfast facilities throughout the country.
SELF-CATERING: Cottages can be rented in many areas. For information contact the RTB or consult the relevant section in local and national papers.
CAMPING/CARAVANNING: There are camping and caravan sites throughout the UK, for short and long stays. Some sites hire out tents or a caravan to those without their own equipment. Most sites offer basic facilities, while some have playgrounds, clubs, shops, phones and sports areas.
HOLIDAY CAMPS: These offer accommodation, food and a full range of leisure activities generally at an all-inclusive price. They provide good holidays for families, and some run baby-sitting and children's clubs.
YOUTH HOSTELS: Standards vary greatly, from very basic night-time accommodation for hikers and cyclists, to modern hostels and motels which are often used by families and groups. Prices are very reasonable. For information contact the Youth Hostel Association, 8 St Stephen's Hill, St Albans, Herts AL1 2DY. Tel: (01727) 855 215. Fax: (01727) 844 126.

RESORTS & EXCURSIONS

Details of resorts and places of interest throughout the four countries of the UK may be found by consulting the respective entries below.

SOCIAL PROFILE

Each of the countries of the United Kingdom has its own particular national dishes and drinks, festivals and other events of interest, its own attractions for shoppers and its own nightlife and other entertainments. Details may be found by consulting the respective entries below.
SOCIAL CONVENTIONS: The monarchy, though now only symbolic, is a powerful and often subconscious unifying force, and members of the Royal family are the subject of unceasing fascination, with their every move avidly followed and reported by the popular press, both in Britain and abroad. Handshaking is the customary form of greeting. Normal social courtesies should be observed when visiting someone's home and a small present such as flowers or chocolates is appreciated. It is not customary to start eating until everyone is served.
Clothing: A tie, trousers and shoes (as opposed to jeans and trainers) are necessary for entry to some nightclubs and restaurants, otherwise casual wear is widely acceptable. **Use of Public Places:** Topless sunbathing is allowed on certain beaches and tolerated in some parks.

Smoking or non-smoking areas will usually be clearly marked. Cigarettes should not legally be sold to children under 16. **Tipping:** In hotels, a service charge of 10-15% is usual, which may be added to the bill. 10% is usual for restaurants and it too is often added to the bill, in which case a further tip is not required. 10% is also usual for taxi drivers and hairdressers but this is *not* included in the bill. There is no legal requirement to pay service charges that have been added to bills and if the service has been unsatisfactory, it may be deducted by the customer. Remember, however, that in the UK wage levels for catering staff are set at a deliberately low level in the expectation that tips will make up the difference.

BUSINESS PROFILE

ECONOMY: The UK is one of the world's leading industrial nations. North Sea oil is one of the mainstays of the economy, together with heavy engineering, chemicals, electronics, textiles and service industries including tourism, financial services and media. Agriculture and fishing are also important but employ only 3% of the population. Recent government policy under the Conservative governments has been dominated by principles of non-intervention, privatisation and tight controls on public spending. Many former state-owned industries, including oil, telecommunications, gas and electricity, have been sold to private shareholders. The 1980s saw a significant shift from manufacturing – which suffered badly from the recession of the early 1980s – to service industries. The beginning of the 1990s, however, brought further recession which hit those sectors, principally building and retail, which had largely escaped the slump of the previous decade. The bulk of the UK's trade is conducted with the European Union and the USA.
Note: The economies of mainland UK countries are closely linked and are therefore dealt with together in this section. For information about *Jersey* and *Guernsey*, see their separate entries earlier in the book; for the *Isle of Man, Northern Ireland* and the other *Channel Islands*, see the subsections that follow this general UK entry.
BUSINESS: Business people are generally expected to dress smartly (suits are the norm). Appointments should be made and the exchange of business cards is customary. A knowledge of English is essential. **Office hours:** 0900-1700 *or* 0930-1730 Monday to Friday.
COMMERCIAL INFORMATION: The following organisation can offer advice: Association of British Chambers of Commerce, 9 Tufton Street, London SW1P 3QB. Tel: (0171) 222 1555. Fax: (0171) 799 2202.
CONFERENCES/CONVENTIONS: The UK conference scene is well-organised with several publications comprehensively listing every possible kind of venue (including dedicated centres, hotels, universities, football grounds, race courses, manor houses, castles and theatres). In addition regional and local tourist boards promote their own areas vigorously. London and Birmingham have an international reputation; there are several excellent conference venues. There are other towns with facilities of near comparable size, and comprehensive back-up services are available everywhere. Glasgow, Manchester, Newcastle and Bristol are among the great cities offering a variety of venues, whilst smaller towns such as Chester, Salisbury, York, Llandudno and Inverness offer uniquely attractive environments without sacrificing efficiency. The large political parties of the UK traditionally hold their conferences in seaside towns during the winter; locations include Blackpool (the famous Winter Gardens), Bournemouth and Brighton. Those looking for conventional venues will find the maximum seating capacity (19,000 persons) in London; however, if an organiser wished to book the Wembley Stadium he could probably do it, so, effectively, there is no upper limit. All parts of the UK are easily accessible by rail and air from London. *The British Conference Destinations Directory* gives brief regional details and is published by the British Association of Conference Towns (BACT), First Floor, Elizabeth House, 22 Suffolk Street, Queensway, Birmingham B1 1LS. Tel: (0121) 616 1400. Fax: (0121) 616 1364. Enquiries can also be made to the International Congress and Convention Association (ICCA), UK-1 Secretariat, 137 Sheen Road, Richmond, Surrey TW9 1YJ. Tel: (0181) 940 3431. Fax: (0181) 332 1920.

CLIMATE

Owing to its being an island, the UK is subject to very changeable weather. Extremes of temperature are rare but snow, hail, torrential rain and heatwaves can occur almost without warning. Detailed descriptions follow in the respective sections below.
Required clothing: Waterproofing throughout the year. Warm clothing is advisable at all times, and is essential for any visits to upland areas.

England

Location: Great Britain.

English Tourist Board
Thames Tower, Black's Road, London W6 9EL
Tel: (0181) 846 9000. Fax: (0181) 563 0302.

AREA: 130,423 sq km (50,356.37 sq miles).
POPULATION: 48,068,400 (1991 estimate).
POPULATION DENSITY: 368.6 per sq km.
CAPITAL: London. **Population:** 6,803,100 (Greater London, 1991 estimate).
GEOGRAPHY: Much of the countryside is relatively flat, consisting of fertile plains and gentle hills. Mountains, moors and steeper hills are found mainly in the north and the west; the Lake District (Cumbria) and the northwest are divided from the Dales of Yorkshire, and the northeast, by the (relatively) high-rising Pennines, 'the backbone of England'. The eastern part of the country, particularly East Anglia, is the most low-lying. The coastline is varied, and ranges from long stretches of sandy beaches to steep cliffs and isolated rocky coves.
LANGUAGE: English. The multiplicity of local dialects throughout the country, overlaid with class, and town and country accents make English a language of astonishing diversity – words and forms of syntax which are obsolete in the southeast may often be found elsewhere. Cornish is still spoken by a few people in Cornwall. In the larger cities, particularly London, there are many communities who do not speak English as a first language (or who have a *patois* – originating outside of this country – which adds yet more variety to the English language).
Note: *For information on time, electricity, communications, passport/visa, money, public holidays and business see the general UK section above.*

TRAVEL

AIR: England's principal international airports are:
Heathrow (LHR): Located 24km (15 miles) west of central London. Airport information: (0181) 745 7702. The airport has three passenger terminals grouped together in the airport's central area. The fourth terminal, a short distance from the main complex, handled 7,787,900 passengers in 1989. **Facilities:** Banks (7 days a week) and currency exchange in all terminals (T1/T2: 0700-2300; T3: 24 hours for arrivals, 0630-2130 for departures; T4: 24 hours for arrivals with a mobile bureau de change in departure lounge 0700-2100 daily); left luggage in all terminals; post office in T2 (0830-1800 Monday to Saturday, 0900-1800 Friday, 0900-1300 Sunday and public holidays); T1, T3 and T4 have pillar boxes and coin-operated stamp machines; T4 also has a sub-post office in the bureau de change in the departures area; buffet in all terminals (24-hour); quick grill and restaurant facilities in all terminals (24-hour); airside bars (0700-2230); full restaurant service at the 'Petit Four' (T4) and 'Runway Restaurant' (T2); babycare rooms in all terminals (0700-2200); St George's Chapel, opposite entrance to T2 car park (tel: (0181) 745 4261); duty free in all terminals; gift/general shops in all terminals; Travel Care Unit in Queen's Building (tel: (0181) 745 7495, open 0900-1800 Monday to Friday, 0930-1630 Saturday and Sunday); Heathrow Business Centre, next to T2 (tel: (0181) 759 2434); 24-hour emergency medical service; hotel reservation service in all terminals; facilities for the disabled: wheelchairs, telephones, toilets, special parking bays in short-term car park and coach link to long-term car park. There is also an induction loop link system for the hard of hearing.
Underground: The airport is linked to the entire Greater London area by the underground railway network. Stations for Heathrow Terminals 1, 2, 3 and 4 are on the Piccadilly Line, with direct trains to Hammersmith (change for Victoria), Earl's Court, South Kensington (change for Paddington, Blackfriars, Cannon Street and Tower Hill), Knightsbridge, Green Park (change for Charing Cross and Baker Street), Piccadilly Circus (change for Waterloo and Marylebone), Leicester Square (change for Euston), Holborn (change for Bank and Liverpool Street), Kings Cross (change for Moorgate and London Bridge) and Finsbury Park. The travel time to the West End takes 47 minutes, and to the British Rail stations Kings Cross and St Pancras 55 minutes. All other mainline stations can be reached with only one change of train in central London (see above for suggested connections). Services run 0508-0018 Monday to Saturday, and 0601-2352 Sunday. More information on the *London Regional Transport* network may be obtained by dialling (0171) 222 1234 day or night. **Train:** *British Rail* operates a Rail Air Link, with frequent express coaches connecting Heathrow with trains at Reading and Woking stations. The Reading Link takes 55 minutes and runs 0700-2300. The Woking Link operates 0820-2120 and takes 45 minutes. Details are available from British Rail desks in each terminal. Tel: (0181) 745 7582. **Coach:** *London Transport* operates *Airbuses* with two express services operating between Heathrow and London. Airbuses call at all terminals and have ample space for passengers and baggage. There are also wheelchair facilities for the disabled. The A1 service to Victoria Station runs every 20 minutes, from Heathrow 0620-2210, and from Victoria 0640-2110. The A2 service to Woburn Place, W1, and other central and west London stops runs every 30 minutes from Heathrow 0610-2130 and from Woburn Place 0630-2030 (travel time – 1 hour 10 minutes).
London Country/Green Line's Jetlink 777 operates every 30 minutes (0630-2300) to Gatwick. The journey takes 1 hour 10 minutes. The service has now been extended to Luton airport, running approximately every 90 minutes from 0700-2330. Further *London Country/Green Line* services include: *701/724*: Maidenhead, Windsor, Hammersmith and Victoria; *724:* Windsor, Egham, Staines, Watford, Hatfield, Welwyn Garden City, Hertford and Harlow; *726:* Windsor, Slough, Ashford, Kingston, Sutton, Croydon, Bromley and Dartford; and *727:* Crawley, Gatwick, Reigate, Epsom, Kingston, Uxbridge, Watford and Luton. Tel: (0171) 730 0202 for information on all services.
National Express runs direct Rapide coach services from Heathrow to most parts of the UK including Manchester six times a day (travel time – 6 hours); Bristol 14 times a day (travel time –1 hour 55 minutes); Birmingham eight times a day (travel time – 3 hours 15 minutes); and Liverpool five times a day (travel time – 6 hours 20 minutes). Tel: (0171) 730 0202 (information and bookings). Speedlink coaches connect Heathrow with Gatwick and Stansted (travel time – 1 hour 20 minutes). Many private companies have long-distance coach services linking Heathrow with the rest of the country. Oxford and West Midlands area: *Flights Coaches,* tel: (0121) 322 2222. East Anglia: *Cambridge Coaches,* tel: (01223) 236 333. Southend and Basildon: *Southend Transport,* tel: (01702) 434 444. Birmingham: *Aziz Coach Services,* tel: (0121) 440 2015. **Local bus:** *London Transport's* services A1, A2, 105, 111, 140, 223, 285 and its night bus N97 operate from Heathrow Central bus station to various parts of London (tel: (0171) 222 1234). Oxford/South Midland's 390 operates to Henley, Wallingford, Abingdon and Oxford; and 790 to Uxbridge, High Wycombe, Wheatley and Oxford. The X70 service runs directly between Heathrow and Oxford at hourly and half-hourly intervals, depending on the time of day. Tel: (01865) 774 611. *London Country/Green Line* also operate local services (see above for coach operations). **Note:** London Travelcheck (tel: (0171) 222 1200) gives up-to-the-minute information on how London services are running. **Taxi:** Available for hire outside each airport terminal. Each

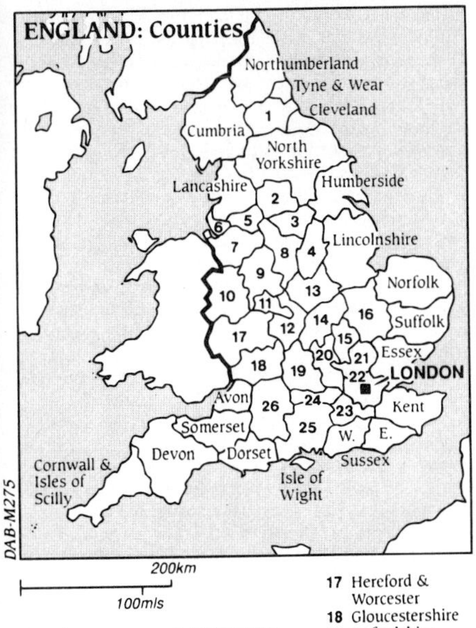
ENGLAND: Counties
Northumberland
Tyne & Wear
Cleveland
Cumbria
North Yorkshire
Lancashire
Humberside
Lincolnshire
Norfolk
Suffolk
Essex
LONDON
Kent
Avon
Somerset
Devon
Dorset
Sussex
W.
E.
Cornwall & Isles of Scilly
Isle of Wight
DAB-M275
200km
100mls
1
2
3
4
5
6
7
8
9
10
11
12
13
14
15
16
17
18
19
20
21
22
23
24
25
26

1 Durham
2 West Yorkshire
3 South Yorkshire
4 Nottinghamshire
5 Gtr. Manchester
6 Merseyside
7 Cheshire
8 Derbyshire
9 Staffordshire
10 Shropshire
11 West Midlands
12 Warwickshire
13 Leicestershire
14 Northamptonshire
15 Bedfordshire
16 Cambridgeshire
17 Hereford & Worcester
18 Gloucestershire
19 Oxfordshire
20 Buckinghamshire
21 Hertfordshire
22 Greater London
23 Surrey
24 Berkshire
25 Hampshire
26 Wiltshire

terminal has its own taxi rank and the information desk can give an indication of fares. **Car hire:** *Avis, Budget, Hertz* and *Europcar* self-drive and chauffeur-driven cars can be hired from desks in each airport terminal. To central London takes 30 minutes to 1 hour. **Private car:** Heathrow, 38km (24 miles) from central London, is reached either through the tunnel of the M4 motorway spur or from the A4 (Bath) road. It is also close to the M25 orbital motorway, making journeys to virtually all parts of the country relatively simple. It is advisable to avoid the area during peak times (0700-1300 Friday to Sunday), especially in summer. Unloading but no waiting is allowed outside terminals. Short- and long-term car parking is available; coach connection from long-term car park to all terminals.

Gatwick (LGW): Located 45km (27 miles) south of central London. Airport information: (01293) 535 353. **Facilities:** Banks/currency exchange, shops, restaurants, left luggage, duty-free shops, chapel, babycare rooms, medical room and facilities for the disabled. All facilities are available 24 hours. **Train:** *British Rail's* London to Brighton line runs underneath the Gatwick terminal and there are non-stop trains from Victoria Station (travel time – 30 minutes) at 15-minute intervals during the day and hourly throughout the night for 24 hours' seven days a week. Tel: (0181) 668 7261. Passengers travelling with *British Airways* or scheduled airlines handled by them can check in their luggage at the air terminal at Victoria Station. There are also services to Gatwick from London Bridge Station every half hour (travel time – 35 minutes). There are fast and frequent trains from Gatwick which connect with mainline stations throughout southeast England. There are three direct trains daily between Gatwick and Manchester, Birmingham, Coventry, Edinburgh, Glasgow, Luton, Oxford, Stoke-on-Trent and Wolverhampton, with stops en route. Tel: (0171) 928 5100 for services in the south of England; tel: (0171) 278 2477 for services to the northeast of England. **Coach**: *Speedlink* luxury non-stop service links Gatwick with all four terminals at Heathrow. Services depart every 15 minutes to 1300, every 30 minutes in the afternoon and the evening until 2200 (travel time – 1 hour). Tel: (01293) 507 178. *Flightline 777* to Victoria Coach Station runs every hour 0515-2200 (travel time – 1 hour 10 minutes). *Jetlink 747* to Heathrow runs every 30 minutes 0705-1605 and hourly thereafter (travel time – 1 hour), with an extension to Luton airport every hour. The service to Heathrow continues every hour until 0005 with additional journeys at 0600 and 2200. There is a surcharge for services operating 0000-0659. Tel: (0181) 668 7261 *or* (01293) 507 178. *National Express* have direct coach services to most parts of the UK including Birmingham, eight times a day (travel time – 5 hours 5 minutes); Leicester, seven times a day (travel time – 3 hours 25 minutes); Manchester, six times a day (travel time – 6 hours 45 minutes). Tel: (0171) 730 0202 (information and bookings). *Flightlink* goes from Manchester and Birmingham. *Other services* calling at the terminal include Oxford Citylink, National Express 015 (from Bournemouth and Poole), 225 (from Manchester and Birmingham) and National Express (from Glasgow). Certain charter tour operators also provide coaches from Gatwick for arriving passengers. Check with relevant tour operator. **Local bus:** There are local buses to Crawley and Horley on routes C1, C2, 405, 455 and 773. Tel: (01293) 502 116. **Taxi:** Available outside the terminal. Travel time to central London – 1 hour. Tel: (01293) 502 808. **Car hire:** *Avis, Europcar, Budget* and *Hertz* self-drive and chauffeur-driven cars can be hired from desks in the arrivals hall. **Private car:** Gatwick can be reached from London on the A23 or M23 motorway. It is also close to the M25 orbital motorway, linking all main routes from London. There are ample parking facilities for short and long stays. Fee enquiries: tel: (01293) 502 737 *or* 502 748.

London City Airport (LCY): Located 10km (6 miles) east of the City of London. This airport, situated in the Royal Docks in the London Borough of Newham, opened in autumn 1987 and provides frequent scheduled air services linking the City of London with Paris, Amsterdam, Rotterdam, Lille, Strasbourg and Brussels. The airport works on the STOL-port concept, for aircraft capable of Short Take Off and Landing. Scheduled Airlines include *Air France, City Jet, Cross Air, Lufthansa, Sabena, Virgin* and *VLM.* All scheduled services are business class. Check-in time is usually about ten minutes. **Facilities:** Duty-free shops (0600-2200), car hire, bank and bureau de change, restaurant and bars, newsagent and bookstore, and business centre with meeting rooms for up to 40 persons. **Train/Underground:** Silvertown Station on the North London Link is 300 yards from the airport terminal, connecting with the Underground at West Ham (District and Hammersmith and City Lines), Stratford (Central and Docklands Light Railway), Highbury and Islington (Victoria Line), West Hampstead (Jubilee Line) and Willesden Junction (Bakerloo Line). Plaistow (District Line) is approximately 3km (2 miles) from the airport; it has its own taxi rank. **Coach/bus:** A courtesy shuttle bus operates between the terminal and Canary Wharf to connect with the Docklands Light Railway (0700-2030 Monday to Friday). **Taxi:** Widely available; may be booked in-flight. **Car hire:** *Europcar* and *Hertz* both offer hire cars. Tel: (0171) 474 5555 (City Airport), ext 2530 and 2525 respectively. **Private car:** The airport is reached from the City via Commercial Road/East India Dock Road (A13) over the Canning Town Flyover, turning right into Prince Regent Lane; from the M25 via the M11 and North Circular (A406) or the A13. Access from the City of London will usually present no problems provided the morning and evening rush hours are avoided. London City Airport has ample car parking space located just two minutes walk from the terminal building.

Stansted (STN): Located 55km (34 miles) northeast of central London. Airport information: (01279) 662 379. **Facilities:** Information desk, executive lounge, lost property, bureau de change, landside buffet and bar plus self-service restaurant, airside buffet and 24-hour bar, nursing mothers' room, 24-hour emergency medical service, duty-free shop, wheelchairs and toilets for the disabled as well as induction loop system in the international departures lounge. **Train:** Services run throughout the day from London Liverpool Street to Stansted, every 30 minutes (travel time – 44 minutes) 0530-2300. Further information is available from *British Rail* (tel: (0171) 928 5100). There are also services from Stansted to Cambridge and the North. Tel: (01223) 311 999. **Coach:** *Cambridge Coach Services* operate services between Stansted and Cambridgefour times daily (travel time – 2 hours). Services also run from Cambridge to Norfolk and the Midlands. Tel: (01223) 236 333. *Eastern National* run services to Braintree, Chelmsford, Colchester and Harlow. *Rail Air Link* services 33, 333 and X70 operate between Bishop's Stortford station and the airport to connect with all scheduled services (travel time – 15 minutes). Service is hourly on Sunday. Tel: (01245) 353 104. *Jetlink 747* and *Speedlink* operate between Stansted and Gatwick or Heathrow. Tel: (0181) 668 7261. **Taxi:** To central London takes 90 minutes. **Car hire:** Cars can be hired from desks in the terminal building. For details contact: *Budget Rent-a-Car* (tel: (01279) 681 194); *Hertz* (tel: (01279) 680 154/5). For air taxis/business aviation services contact *Artac Air Chartering Service* on (01279) 871 871. **Private car:** Situated 54km (34 miles) northeast of London, the airport is easily accessible by road on M25/M11 from London. The Midlands and the North are reached via the A1, A604 and M11. Long- and short-term car parking space is available.

Birmingham (BHX): Located 14km (9 miles) southeast of the city centre. Airport information: (0121) 767 7145. **Facilities** include bank and foreign exchange services, buffet, bar, duty-free shop, facilities for the disabled, nursing mothers' room, shops, spectators' viewing gallery and left-luggage office. **Train:** The terminal is linked to Birmingham International Station by the Maglev shuttle which takes 90 seconds and is free of charge. Birmingham International is connected to the Intercity network and regional lines and has a fast service to London Euston (1 hour 20 minutes). Train information: (0121) 643 2711. Birmingham New Street Station, in the city centre, is ten minutes away by Intercity or local services and provides interchange for services throughout the rest of the country. **Coach/bus:** *West Midlands Travel* operates local services into the suburbs. *National Express* service 825 offers a daily service, every two hours, to central Birmingham, Coventry, Lancashire and the London airports. Service 305 runs to Birmingham, Coventry, Northampton, Cambridge and Clacton/Lowestoft. Tel: (0121) 622 4373. *Flightlink* operate connections to Gatwick and Heathrow with various collection points along the rout. Tel: (0121) 322 2222. Frequent coaches run to and from Birmingham from London Victoria and most major cities and towns throughout the country. **Local bus:** Service 900 runs to the city centre Monday to Friday (travel time – 40 minutes). **Taxi:** Travel time to city centre – 25 minutes. Taxis are available outside the airport. **Car hire:** *Avis, Hertz* and *Europcar* have offices at the airport. **Private car:** M1, M5, M6, M42 and M40 are the main routes to Birmingham. The airport is well signposted from the city. There is multi-storey and open-air parking (over 8000 spaces) at the airport.

Note: The 'Eurohub' terminal opened in July 1991. The aim is to facilitate flight-transfer in anticipation of a change in intra- and extra-European air travel organisation towards a more American system, in which major airports serve as hubs from which flights radiate out to other airports in an integrated fashion, making more use of connecting flights.

Luton (LTN): Located 48km (35 miles) northwest of London. Airport information: (01582) 405 100. Scheduled flights: *Britannia Airways, British Airways, British Midland, Manx Airlines, Netherlines* and *Ryanair.* **Facilities:** Landside bank (with extended opening hours), general shops, grill restaurant (0700-2300), bar, 24-hour buffet/ bar, nursing mothers' room, free play area (2-8 years) in departure lounge, duty-free shop, medical services and facilities for the disabled – wheelchairs, toilets and ambulift. **Train:** There is a service from London St Pancras to Luton railway station from 0518 to late in the evening, except Sunday. Frequent buses connect with the airport. The present hourly service from 2400-0600 continues. There are also frequent trains from Luton to Bedford, Leicester, Nottingham, Derby and Sheffield. Tel: (01582) 27612. **Coach:** *National Express* service 325 runs every two hours to Birmingham, Manchester, Heathrow and Gatwick. Services also run to most other parts of the UK (tel: (01733) 237 141 or, for information, (0171) 730 0202). *Speedlink* 750/751 operates at two-hourly intervals from the airport to Hemel Hempstead, Hertford, Hitchin, Rickmansworth, Stevenage, Uxbridge and Ware (tel: (01923) 257 405). *Jetlink 747* is a direct (limited stop) service from Stevenage, calling at Luton and continuing to Heathrow and Gatwick, which operates hourly from Luton and twice-hourly from Stevenage. It runs via Hemel Hempstead and Watford. *London Link 757 Express* runs a daily service from the airport to Luton and on to central London. *United Counties* operate directly to Bedford (with connection to Cambridge), Huntingdon, Northampton, Peterborough and St Neots. Services are twice-hourly. Tel: (01234) 262 151 for details. *Flightlink Ltd* operates direct between the airport and Birmingham, Coventry and Wolverhampton (all seven times daily), and Stafford, Stoke (Newcastle) and Manchester (all five times daily). **Local bus:** Buses no. 12 and 38 run from the airport to Luton bus and rail stations, with frequent services during the day, and hourly evening and Sunday services. Summer-only services run to Bournemouth and Southampton. Tel: (01582) 404 074. **Taxi:** Can be hired from the rank immediately outside the terminal building. **Car hire:** *Avis, Swan National* and local operators *Intercity Cars* and *Woodside Private Hire* have desks at the airport. **Private car:** The airport can be reached on the M1 exiting at Junction 10. Access to the airport from the east is via the A505 dual carriageway from Hitchin. The M25 connects all motorways and the airport can therefore be accessed from the East, South and West via M25, M4, M11 and M23. Travelling from the west also provides several routes from the Dunstable area through Luton. Airport signs should be followed throughout. Long- and short-term car-parking is available within the airport boundary.

Manchester (MAN): Located 16km (10 miles) south of the city centre. Airport information: (0161) 489 3000.

Facilities: Restaurant (0700-2230), buffet, bar, ice-cream parlour, duty-free shop, nursery, chemist, gift shop, newsagent, banking service and three service tills, bureau de change, post office, full facilities for the disabled and range of other shops. **Train:** There is a station linking the airport to Manchester city centre, departing every 15 minutes Monday to Friday, every 20 minutes Sunday (travel time – 23 minutes). Frequent train services to Manchester (Piccadilly) and Crewe via Wilmslow are available for connections with main Intercity services. Services to the north of England are from Manchester Piccadilly station. Tel: (0161) 228 2141. **Coach/bus:** *National Express* runs daily services to most parts of the UK including Scotland, tel: (0161) 228 3881. Express coach service 100 runs throughout the week to Victoria and Piccadilly rail stations and the city centre. Service 44 runs every 20 minutes throughout the week to Manchester Piccadilly via Gatley, Northenden and Withington. Service 500 runs to Bolton via Stockport and various other stops. The 757 airport shuttle (Monday to Saturday) provides a regular service to the city centre every 45 minutes 0600-2300. For more detailed information on times and frequency of these services, contact *Greater Manchester Buses,* tel: (0161) 228 7811. **Taxi:** Travel time to the city centre – 25 minutes. A taxi rank is situated at ground level adjacent to the arrival hall in Terminals A and B. **Car hire:** *Hertz* (tel: (0161) 437 8208), *Avis* (tel: (0161) 436 2020), *EuroDollar* (tel: (0161) 834 3020 *or* 499 3320) have booking offices in both the arrivals halls. **Private car:** The airport is at the heart of the country's motorway network and a specially constructed spur from the M56 runs directly into the terminal building. Road connections serve Greater Manchester, Merseyside, Lancashire, Cheshire, the Midlands and West and South Yorkshire. There is car parking space within the airport boundary.

Newcastle (NCL): Located 10km (6 miles) northwest of the city centre. Airport information: (0191) 286 0966. **Facilities:** Bureau de change (0600-2145 Sunday to Friday, 0600-1830 Saturday), restaurant/bars (1200-2000), shops (0600-2030), duty-free shop, emergency medical services and facilities for the disabled. **Metro:** The Tyneside Metro Rapid Transport system extends to Kenton Bank Foot, 3km (2 miles) south of the airport and bus services 76 and 77 link the airport with the city. *Busways* provide a linkup with the Metro at Kenton Bank Foot every ten minutes and takes 15-20 minutes. The Metro runs to Newcastle city centre, across the River Tyne to Gateshead and South Shields and to Tynemouth and the coast. Traveline (Public Transport Information): (0191) 232 5325. **Train:** Nearest railway station is Newcastle Central, 11km (7 miles) from the airport, linked by express buses operated by *Busways,* which run every 30 minutes Monday to Saturday, and every hour on Sunday. Tel: (0191) 232 6262. **Bus:** The X77 ('Airport Express') provides a direct link to Newcastle city centre, operating 16 hours a day (half-hourly 1035-1735); the travel time is 25 minutes. Services 75, 76, 76E, 77, 77E, 78, 78E and 79 run from Eldon Square bus concourse, in the centre of Newcastle. These stop on the main road at the airport entrance (travel time – 20 minutes). *Blue Bus Services,* tel: (0191) 276 5657. **Coach:** *National Express* and *Scottish Citylink* operate services to the airport from most major cities in Scotland and the North and Midlands of England. **Car hire:** *Hertz* (tel: (0191) 286 0966), *Avis* (tel: (0191) 286 0815) and *EuroDollar* (tel: (0191) 286 0966) self-drive agents are located at the airport. **Taxi:** Travel time to city centre – 15-20 minutes. A taxi rank is situated outside the railway station, and at the Haymarket near the Eldon Square bus concourse in Newcastle city centre. Only licensed taxi cabs are allowed to pick up at the airport. **Private car:** The airport can be reached from the south by the A1(M) north, then the A696 Jedburgh trunk road, and from the north by the A1 south, then the A696 Jedburgh trunk road. Open-air long- and short-term parking facilities are available (no advanced booking required).

SEA: UK ferry operators: *Sealink* (tel: (01233) 647 047); *P&OEuropean Ferries* (tel: (01304) 240 077); *Hoverspeed* (tel: (01304) 240 241); *Sally Line* (tel: (01843) 595 522); *Sealink Dieppe Ferries* (tel: (01233) 647 047); *Norse Irish Ferries* (tel: (01232) 779 090); *Condor Ferries* (tel: (01305) 761 551); *Brittany Ferries* (tel: (01705) 827 701 *or* (01202) 666 466); *Isle of Scilly Steamship Co.* (tel: (01736) 62009); *Red Funnel* (tel: (01703) 330 333); *Scandinavian Seaways* (tel: (01255) 240 240); *North Sea Ferries* (tel: (01482) 377 177); *Colour Line* (tel: (0191) 296 1313); *Smyril Line* (tel: (01224) 572 615); *Swansea–Cork Ferries* (tel: (01792) 456 116); *B&I Line* (tel: (0171) 734 4681); *Isle of Man Steam Packet Co.* (tel: (01624) 661 661); *United Baltic* (tel: (0151) 227 3131); *Caledonian Macbrayne* (tel: (01475) 650 100); and *Wightlink* (tel: (01705) 827 744).

RAIL: The *Intercity* network serves all main cities in the UK mainland. All routes radiate from London.

For general travel enquiries, weekdays only, tel: (0171) 928 5100. Alternatively, and at weekends, ring the number of the appropriate terminus station for information. Terminus stations in London serve the following regions:

Southern England and South London: *Charing Cross, Victoria* and *Waterloo.* Tel: (0171) 928 5100.

East Anglia, Essex, North East and East London: *Liverpool Street.* Tel: (0171) 928 5100.

South Midlands, West of England, South Wales and West London: *Paddington.* Tel: (0171) 262 6767.

East and West Midlands, North Wales, North East England, West Coast of Scotland and West London: *Euston, St Pancras* and *Marylebone.* Tel: (0171) 387 7070.

East and North East England, East Coast of Scotland and North London: *Kings Cross.* Tel: (0171) 278 2477.

There are also many smaller lines which operate less frequently. There are services to the Republic of Ireland via Holyhead, and to Northern Ireland. Tel: (0171) 387 7070. Services to the Republic of Ireland via Fishguard are also available. Tel: (0171) 262 6767.

ROAD: England is served by a good network of motorways and trunk roads which connect all the main cities and towns.

The main motorways are: **M1:** London, Luton, Leicester, Sheffield, Leeds. **M2/A2:** London to Dover. **M3:** London to Winchester. **M4:** London, Reading, Bristol, Newport, Cardiff, Swansea. **M5:** Birmingham, Gloucester, Bristol, Exeter. **M6:** Coventry, Birmingham, Stoke, Warrington (connecting with the M62 for Liverpool and Manchester), Preston (connecting with the M55 for Blackpool), Morecambe, Carlisle. **M11:** London to Cambridge. **M20/A20:** London to Folkestone. **M40:** London to Birmingham. **M62:** Liverpool, Warrington, Manchester, Huddersfield, Leeds, Hull. **M25:** London orbital.

The main trunk roads are: **A1/A1(M)** (motorway in parts): London, Peterborough, Doncaster, Darlington, Newcastle, Edinburgh. **A2:** London to Dover. **A3:** London, Guildford, Portsmouth. **A5:** London, St Albans, Nuneaton, Birmingham area, Shrewsbury, across inland north Wales to Holyhead. **A6:** London, Bedford, Leicester, Manchester. **A11:** London to Norwich. **A12:** London, Ipswich, Great Yarmouth. **A23:** London to Brighton. **A30:** London, Basingstoke, Yeovil, Exeter, Penzance. **A40:** London, Oxford (M40), Gloucester, Cheltenham, across inland south Wales to Fishguard.

Distances from London (by road): To Birmingham 169km (105 miles), Manchester 299km (186 miles), Liverpool 325km (202 miles), Exeter 278km (173 miles), Penzance 452km (281 miles), Bristol 185km (115 miles), Carlisle 484km (301 miles), Newcastle 441km (274 miles), Sheffield 257km (160 miles), York 311km (193 miles), Cambridge 89km (55 miles), Southampton 124km (77 miles), Dover 114km (71 miles), Oxford 92km (57 miles), Norwich 182km (113 miles), Portsmouth 113km (70 miles) and Harwich 122km (76 miles).

Coach: Many coach companies offer express and stopping services throughout England and the rest of the UK. The *National Express* enquiry office provides nationwide coach information. Tel: (0171) 730 0202. The head office is at 4 Vicarage Road, Edgbaston, Birmingham B15 3ES. Tel: (0121) 456 1122. Fax: (0121) 456 1397.

URBAN: All towns and cities have bus services. In addition, the areas of Birmingham, Liverpool, Manchester and the cities in South Yorkshire and Newcastle have suburban rail services. Newcastle also has a metro, which consists of a circular line with three branches. It connects with Newcastle Central, Manors and Heworth *British Rail* stations and terminates at South Shields (ferry connection to North Shields, also on the metro), St James and Bank Foot. All cities have taxi services, many using London-type black cabs. Taxi ranks are usually placed near bus stations, railway stations and town centres. Local telephone directories give the numbers of mini-cabs and hire cars.

LONDON: Travel enquiries: For bus and underground enquiries, tel: (0171) 222 1234 (24-hour service). For *British Rail* enquiries, phone the number of the *British Rail* terminus for the respective region. Maps and leaflets are widely available.

The Underground: The 'tube' is the oldest and one of the most extensive underground railway networks in the world. There are 11 lines, including the recently opened *Docklands Light Railway*, and some such as the *Central* and the *Metropolitan* extend well into the surrounding suburbs. Each line has its own colour on the network map, copies of which are widely available. Some lines operate certain sections during peak hours and some stations close altogether in the evenings or at weekends. There is also an extensive network of *British Rail* services in the London area, particularly in the southeast, many of which connect with *Underground* services. All the *British Rail* terminus stations connect with at least one *Underground* line, with the exception of Fenchurch Street (which is however virtually adjacent to Tower Hill). Various travel discounts are available. The one-day *Travelcard* offers unlimited travel on bus, *Underground* and *British Rail* in one or more zones; it is is one of the best methods for visitors to travel throughout London. Weekly and monthly Travelcards require a passport-size photograph. **Note:** The maps of the *Underground* and *British Rail* networks are diagrammatic, and do not indicate the relative distances between stations.

Bus: London is served by an excellent network of buses (about 300 routes), although recent policy has been to cut some of the lesser-used services. Some operate only partial routes at specific times or may discontinue service in the evenings or at weekends. During rush hours, bus travel in central London can become agonisingly slow, although the introduction of bus lanes and 'red routes' on some roads has partly improved this situation. There is a good timetabled network of night bus services, and all routes passing through central London call at Trafalgar Square.

Taxi/car hire: Black cabs can be hailed in the street or ordered by phone. Fares are metered but surcharges are levied for extra passengers, large amounts of luggage, travel at night, and on Sundays or public holidays. Over 3000 new black cabs have facilities for wheelchair-bound passengers. Mini-cabs and cars for hire are also available; numbers are listed in the telephone directory yellow pages.

ACCOMMODATION

Accommodation is available at hotels, motels and posthouses, guest-houses, farm houses, inns and self-catering establishments and on campsites.

HOTELS: It is rare to find a town in England, however small, which does not have at least one hotel, in villages very often doubling as the local pub. Some London hotels, for example the Savoy, are famous the world over but there are many newer first-class hotels. In addition, there are many smaller hotels throughout the larger cities; in London, Earl's Court and the area around Kings Cross are famous for their many streets of small hotels bearing such names as the Apollo, Victoria or Albany. For further information, contact the British Hospitality Association, 40 Duke Street, London W1M 6HR. Tel: (0171) 499 6641. Fax: (0171) 355 4596; *or* the British Federation of Hotel, Guest-Houses & Self-Catering Associations, 5 Sandicroft Road, Blackpool FY1 2RY. Tel: (01253) 352 683.

Grading: The English Tourist Board has a 'crown' classification system which is used throughout their publications; RTB brochures also use this system. There are 11,000 places to stay that have a national crown rating; 13,000 holiday homes have a key rating and 900 holiday Q rating. (The AA and RAC use a star system which is similar to the ETB crowns.) The main hotel, guest-house, inn or farm house classifications are as follows:

'Listed': Clean and comfortable accommodation, although the facilities and services may be limited.

1-crown: Better equipped accommodation with a wider range of facilities including washbasins in all rooms, a lounge area and use of a telephone.

2-crown: Accommodation offering more extensive facilities (such as bedside lights, colour TV in lounge or bedroom, and at least 20% of bedrooms with private WC, bath or shower), as well as services including early morning tea/coffee and calls.

3-crown: The range of facilities increases, with at least one-half of bedrooms having bath or shower and WC en suite, plus easy chair and full-length mirror in all bedrooms. Shoe-cleaning facilities, hairdryers and hot evening meals are also available.

4-crown: An even wider range of facilities and services, with at least 90% of bedrooms having bath or shower and WC en suite, colour TV, radio and telephone. Lounge service is available until midnight and there is 24-hour access to the establishment.

5-crown: The highest classification, with an extensive range of facilities and services, including room service, 24-hour night porter, laundry service, all-night lounge service and restaurant open for breakfast, lunch and dinner. All rooms have bath, shower and WC en suite.

Brochures, booklets and leaflets giving full information on accommodation are available from the English Tourist Board or any of the regional tourist boards.

GUEST-HOUSES: There are guest-houses and bed & breakfast facilities throughout the country. The crown grading system applies. For listings contact the RTB for regional information.

SELF-CATERING: Cottages and bungalows can be rented in many areas. For information contact the RTB or look in the relevant section in local and national papers. Standards may vary. **Grading:** The English Tourist Board has a 'key' classification system:

1-key: Clean and comfortable, adequate heating, lighting and seating, TV, cooker, fridge and crockery.

2-key: Colour TV, easy chairs or sofas for all occupants,

fridge with icemaker, bedside units or shelves, plus heating in all rooms.
3-key: Dressing tables, bedside lights, linen and towels available, vacuum cleaner, iron/ironing board.
4-key: All sleeping in beds or bunks, supplementry lighting in living areas, more kitchen equipment, use of an automatic washing machine and tumble dryer.
5-key: Automatically controlled heating, own washing machine and tumble dryer, bath and shower, telephone, dishwasher, microwave and fridge freezer.
CAMPING/CARAVANNING: There are camping and caravan sites throughout the UK, for short and long stays. Some sites hire out tents or caravans. Most sites offer basic facilities, while some have playgrounds, clubs, shops, phones and sporting areas.
HOLIDAY CAMPS: Offer accommodation, food and a full range of leisure activities generally at an all-inclusive price.
YOUTH HOSTELS: Standards vary greatly, from very basic night-time accommodation for hikers and cyclists, to modern hostels and motels which are often used by families and groups. Prices are very reasonable. For information contact the *Youth Hostel Association,* 8 St Stephen's Hill, St Albans AL1 2DY. Tel: (01727) 855 215. Fax: (01727) 844 126.

RESORTS & EXCURSIONS

This section has been divided into 11 regions, following the divisions employed by the English Tourist Board. Except in the case of Dorset (which is split between the South West and Southern England) and the Peak District of Derbyshire (which comes under the North West), all these divisions follow county boundaries. At the head of each sub-section is the address and telephone number of the local tourist board which can supply further information.
For further information on *National Trust* properties in England, Wales and Northern Ireland, 36 Queen Anne's Gate, London SW1H 9AS. Tel: (0171) 222 9251. Fax: (0171) 222 5097.

London

The London Tourist Board & Convention Bureau, 26 Grosvenor Gardens, London SW1W 0DU. Tel: (0171) 730 3450 (group bookings). Fax:

(0171) 730 9367.
London is a city without an easily recognisable centre, a result of the fact that it grew out of two distinct cities: the *City of London,* the site of the original Roman settlement and, further west, the *City of Westminster.* Before long, these two settlements had grown together

and were engulfing surrounding villages and hamlets. It was not until the Green Belt legislation of the 1950s that this expansion was halted. Today, the 32 London boroughs and the City of London cover an area of nearly 385 sq km, but the way in which the city has grown has left it with a comparatively low population

LONDON

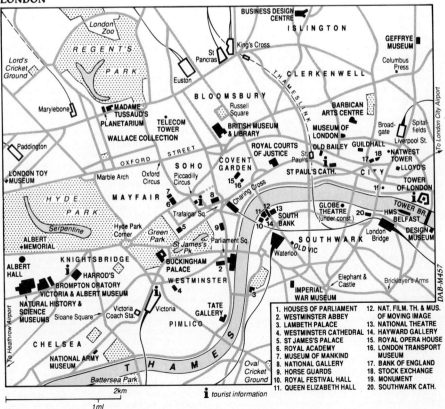

1. HOUSES OF PARLIAMENT
2. WESTMINSTER ABBEY
3. LAMBETH PALACE
4. WESTMINSTER CATHEDRAL
5. ST JAMES'S PALACE
6. ROYAL ACADEMY
7. MUSEUM OF MANKIND
8. NATIONAL GALLERY
9. HORSE GUARDS
10. ROYAL FESTIVAL HALL
11. QUEEN ELIZABETH HALL
12. NAT. FILM. TH. & MUS. OF MOVING IMAGE
13. NATIONAL THEATRE
14. HAYWARD GALLERY
15. ROYAL OPERA HOUSE
16. LONDON TRANSPORT MUSEUM
17. BANK OF ENGLAND
18. STOCK EXCHANGE
19. MONUMENT
20. SOUTHWARK CATH.

i tourist information

density as well as a great deal of open parkland, commons and even woods.

The **Central Area** of London, roughly bounded by the Circle Line of the Underground, includes the West End, Westminster and the City of London. The West End contains many of the principal theatres, cinemas, restaurants, hotels and nightclubs, as well as some of the best-known shopping areas, such as Oxford Street, Covent Garden, Regent Street and Bond Street. The main places of interest in this area are *Westminster Abbey, Big Ben and the Houses of Parliament, The National Gallery* in *Trafalgar Square,* the *British Museum, Buckingham Palace,* the buildings of the *Horse Guards* in **Whitehall** and the *Tate Gallery* in Pimlico. At the *Rock Circus,* created by the Tussaud's Group, the story of rock and pop music is brought to life. The Courtauld Institute paintings are on display at *Somerset House* (which formerly housed records of births, marriages and deaths). Further west, in **Kensington** and **Chelsea,** are several other famous shopping streets (King's Road, Knightsbridge and Portobello Road), as well as three of London's largest museums *(The Victoria & Albert, Science* and *Natural History),* and the *Albert Hall,* home of the Promenade Concerts during the summer. The central area of London also contains four parks: Hyde Park (by far the largest), St James's Park, Green Park and, slightly further north, Regent's Park.

The **City of London,** with a population of less than 5000, is, during the day, the workplace of over half a million people. Its best-known building is *St Paul's Cathedral,* completed in 1711. Clearly visible from the City, although in fact just beyond its boundaries and in the neighbouring borough of Tower Hamlets, is *The Tower of London,* built by William the Conqueror in the 11th century. The *Tower Hill Pageant,* a history of the River Thames, has recently opened. *The Bank of England, The Stock Exchange, Lloyd's of London* (the world's leading insurance market), *Mansion House* (the official residence of the Lord Mayor), *The Central Criminal Court* ('The Old Bailey'), *Dr Johnson's House* behind Fleet Street, *The Monument* and *The Royal Exchange* are other famous landmarks; a more recent addition to the City skyline is the *Barbican* centre which contains an arts complex which is home to both the Royal Shakespeare Company and the London Symphony Orchestra. *Tower Bridge* is one of the most famous bridges in the world, and it is possible to visit the control room containing the machinery for raising and lowering the central section and to walk along the overhead walkway. *HMS Belfast,* which can be viewed from the bridge, is moored at Symons Wharf near Tooley Street and is open to visitors. The City is best explored during evenings, weekends or public holidays. Its narrow alleyways and passages contain impressive but often half-hidden 17th- and 18th-century buildings. Contact the London Tourist Board for details of organised walks.

South London is in general less often visited by tourists. *The South Bank Arts Centre,* near Waterloo Station, is among the most famous and accessible attractions south of the river; it contains the *Royal National Theatre* and the *Royal Festival Hall.* In this complex, too, can be found *MOMI* (The Museum of the Moving Image) which traces the story of moving images from the earliest cinematic experiments to the latest TV technology. Nearby is *The Old Vic,* recently refurbished and one of London's best-known theatres. *Southwark Cathedral,* near London Bridge, is one of the finest Gothic churches in the city. Also in Southwark, is a reconstruction of the famous *Globe Theatre,* and nearby the site of the similar *Swan Theatre* was discovered. Other attractions near the river include *The Imperial War Museum* in **Lambeth,** *Lambeth Palace,* the *Florence Nightingale Museum,* based at St Thomas' Hospital, *Battersea Park* and, further west, *The Botanical Gardens* (and palace) at **Kew,** and *Richmond Park,* where thousands of deer are free to graze. 15 minutes' journey by train from Charing Cross is **Greenwich,** home of *The National Maritime Museum,* the clipper *Cutty Sark* (one of the fastest ships before, and at times even after, the Age of Steam), *The Royal Naval College* and *The Royal Observatory,* through which runs the Greenwich Meridian, zero degrees longitude. In Greenwich you can also find the *Queen's House* which has recently been restored to its 17th-century glory. Over 2000 fans are displayed at the relatively new *Fan Museum* in Greenwich. Other attractions in south London include *The National Sports Centre* at **Crystal Palace,** *The All England Tennis Club* at **Wimbledon,** the attractive 'village' of **Dulwich,** which has the oldest art gallery in England, and *Brunel's Engine House* in **Rotherhithe,** the site of the world's first underwater tunnel.

West London: London's two major exhibition centres, **Earl's Court** and **Olympia,** are situated slightly to the west of the central London area. The Boat Show and the Ideal Home Exhibition are among their principal events. Not far away, *Whiteleys* of **Bayswater** is a luxury

Edwardian shopping centre comprising over 80 shops, also restaurants and a multi-screen cinema. *Chiswick House* in **Chiswick** is a superb Italian-style villa. Further west is *Syon Park* in **Brentford** (which includes a beautiful 16th-century house), the *London Butterfly House;* nearby is the *Musical Museum,* the *Living Steam Museum* and the *Waterman's Arts Centre.* South of Brentford and Chiswick are several elegant riverside houses which are open to the public, the greatest of these being *Hampton Court Palace,* built by Cardinal Wolsey in the early 16th century and added to by Henry VIII, Charles I, Charles II and William III; others include the *Orleans House Gallery, Ham House* and *Marble Hill House.* In northwest London is *Wembley Stadium* (England's premier football ground) and *Wembley Arena and Conference Centre.* The August Bank Holiday weekend is celebrated in the **Notting Hill** area with the famous West Indian Carnival.

North London contains the fashionable residential area of **Hampstead,** set on a steep hill to the north of central London. *Hampstead Heath* is one of the largest expanses of parkland to be found in any big city anywhere in the world. Hampstead itself has many narrow twisting streets and alleyways and numerous cafés, restaurants, wine bars and shops. Places to visit include *Burgh House, The Kenwood Bequest* (a Georgian country house, which contains a fine collection of paintings, and set in beautiful parkland) and *Keats' House* in Wentworth Place. Slightly to the east, and also on a hill, is **Highgate,** another attractive former village, best known for its cemetery which includes the graves of Karl Marx and George Eliot. In **St John's Wood** visitors can find the Gestetner Tours of *Lords' Cricket Ground.*

East London and in particular the East End (Whitechapel, Bethnal Green, Mile End and Bow) is in many ways the 'real London', although the architecture of this part of the capital suffered badly both during the Second World War and at the hands of the urban planners in the 1960s. Today the City is encroaching on the traditional East End areas of **Whitechapel** and **Aldgate.** The *Whitechapel Art Gallery* is, however, a source of local pride. One major area of recreational redevelopment is the *Lea Valley Park,* which stretches from Hertfordshire to Bromley-by-Bow in the East End and has extensive leisure and recreational facilities. Attractions include the 16th-century *Queen Elizabeth's Hunting Lodge* in **Chingford** and the 11th-century *Waltham Abbey.* Of more recent construction is the remarkable *Thames Flood Barrier,* situated down-river from Greenwich. The renovated *St Katharine's Dock* is now a yacht harbour and at **Wapping** there are many old warehouses, the majority of which have been converted into homes and amenities – a process which is under way throughout East London. Here can be found *Tobacco Dock,* a leisure complex with restaurants and entertainment. Two replica 18th-century pirate ships are moored at the quayside. The whole docklands area, on both banks of the river, is undergoing much redevelopment and a new light railway opened in July 1987, giving greater access to the area of the **Isle of Dogs.** A separate development, *Canary Wharf,* with its 245m-high (800ft) tower was completed in 1992. Walks along the river and in the dockland areas are often very rewarding, offering unexpected glimpses of 18th- and 19th-century London.

London in literature: The Tower of London and the royal palaces have probably had more written about them in works of historical romance than anywhere else. But, these aside, it is the works of Charles Dickens, in particular, that have coloured visitors' (and even Londoners') perceptions of the city, though it is probably true to say that, apart from the Inns of Court, very little remains of the London he depicted – not even the famous *pea-souper* (London fog) famously depicted in *Bleak House.* The site of the debtors' prison in Marshalsea Road (into which Mr Pickwick was cast) retains squalid associations even now. It is perhaps worth bearing in mind that many of the changes (though certainly not all) would have been welcomed by Dickens; the London we have now is, to some extent, his handiwork. The most famous fictional citizen of London is undoubtedly Conan Doyle's Sherlock Holmes (who, as a fictional recipient of fan mail, probably comes second only to Santa Claus). The *Sherlock Holmes Museum* has recently opened at 221B Baker Street, with a representation of his apartment. Of the diarists who have strong associations with London, Pepys occupies the first place; his account of the plague in 1665 and of the Fire of London in 1666 resonates through places that have long since changed their character. There are many tours based on London's literary associations. In 1994 a reconstruction of the *Globe Theatre* in **Southwark** will give visitors the chance to see Shakespeare's plays in their original setting.

Tours: Addresses of companies which offer guided tours of London and the surrounding area (either by car or on

foot) may be obtained from the London Tourist Board or Tourist Information Centres. The London Tourist Board and the individual borough councils also produce a range of booklets and pamphlets giving information on events and attractions in the capital; these range from street markets, sports centres, guided walks, fringe theatre to festivals and flower shows. There is a great variety of entertainment in the capital, not all restricted to the centre.

South East

East Sussex, Kent, Surrey, West Sussex.
South East England Tourist Board, The Old Brew House, Warwick Park, Tunbridge Wells, Kent TN2 5TU. Tel: (01892) 540 766. Fax: (01892) 511 008.

The sparkling array of seaside resorts, such as Brighton, Eastbourne, Margate and Worthing, are as popular now as they were with 18th-century patrons. With safe beaches, seafront gardens, piers (except Margate) and promenades, they all are strongly associated with the great British seaside holiday.

Brighton is perhaps the most popular and lively of the southeast resorts, made famous by the Prince of Wales (later George IV) who had the remarkable *Pavilion* constructed here. There are splendid 19th-century terraces and crescents, two piers, the 'Lanes' area of antique shops, a museum and an art gallery.

Other resorts include **Dover,** famous for the *White Cliffs,* the remains of the *Pharos,* a Phoenician lighthouse, and the Norman *Dover Castle* with the new *White Cliffs Experience.* The one-time Cinque Port of **Hythe** still contains three *Martello Towers.* There are Roman remains at *Saltwood Castle* and *Lympne Castle.* The former port of **Rye** has a medieval atmosphere and retains its 14th-century walls, albeit crumbling.

Behind the resorts spread the *South Downs:* an expanse of farmland, hills and woods, with the South Downs Way (a long-distance footpath) stretching some 130km (80 miles) from Eastbourne to the Hampshire border. Nestling at the foot of the Downs is the historic county town of **Lewes,** with its famous castle and picturesque High Street, while nearby the world-renowned opera house of *Glyndebourne* sits in its own grounds and welcomes the greatest singers from all over the world each year for its summer season. There are many villages of interest in the area including half-timbered **Biddenden** and **Chiddingstone** and the old smuggling centres of **Rye, Dymchurch, Hawkhurst** and **Alfriston,** all of which are on the boundaries of the Romney marshes. There remain, to this day, smuggling tunnels under the town of Rye and there are ancient escape routes across the marshes that only the smugglers would dare to use. Other places of interest include **Runnymede,** the riverside fields where the Magna Carta was signed; the historic town of **Guildford** in Surrey; and *Hever Castle* in Kent, the childhood home of Anne Boleyn.

The *North Downs* stretch from Surrey into Kent. Curving across the hills from Farnham to Dover is another long-distance footpath, the North Downs Way. This merges in places with the traditional Pilgrims' Way leading to the archiepiscopal city of **Canterbury,** which retains its medieval charms. Thomas a' Becket was murdered in Canterbury Cathedral in 1170. It is also the centre of the Anglican Church. *St Martin's Church* is one of the oldest churches in use in the country and services were held as far back as AD500.

The Kent countryside has been dubbed the 'Garden of England' for its copious quantities of fruit, hops and garden produce. The best time to visit is in April or May when the orchards and woodlands are clouded with blossom. **Rochester** in Kent is a charming old town and has strong connections with Dickens, including *Restoration House,* which is thought to be the prototype for Miss Haversham's house in *Great Expectations.* The South East offers an excellent choice of bases for longer stays or weekends away: the elegant spa of **Tunbridge Wells; Maidstone,** in the centre of the hop-growing country; **Chichester,** in West Sussex, with its lively harbour and 12th-century cathedral.

The South East has many historic houses and gardens, such as *Penshurst Place, Leeds Castle,* the *Martello Towers* at Dymchurch, Seaford and Eastbourne and numerous castles and battlefields which bear witness to the area's position as the invader's gateway to England.

Central Southern England

Berkshire, Buckinghamshire, Eastern Dorset, Hampshire, the Isle of Wight, Oxfordshire.
Southern Tourist Board, 40 Chamberlayne Road, Eastleigh, Hants SO5 5JH. Tel: (01703) 620 006. Fax: (01703) 620 010.

The area comprising Hampshire, Dorset, the Isle of Wight and South Wiltshire, embraces some of the best-known beauty spots, spectacular coastline and historic

The National Trust

The National Trust will be 100 years old in 1995. It was founded in 1895 by three imaginative people who foresaw the increasing threat to the countryside posed by industrialisation and growth of the urban population.

Today, the National Trust has grown to become Britain's largest conservation charity. It permanently protects 590,000 acres of countryside, 550 miles of coastline and over 200 historic houses and gardens in England, Wales and Northern Ireland. 2.2 million people are members of the National Trust, and there are over 10 million recorded visitors to Trust properties every year. Members gain free admission to most National Trust properties open to the public which include world-famous gardens and landscaped parks, magnificent stately homes, castles, monastic and Roman remains and a wide variety of working mills.

For a free comprehensive map guide to National Trust properties or details on National Trust membership, contact:

The Travel Trade Office,
The National Trust,
36 Queen Anne's Gate,
London SW1H 9AS.

Tel: (0171) 227 4810.
Fax: (0171) 222 5097.

towns and cities in the country.

The **New Forest** was decreed as a Royal Hunting Preserve in 1079, its 376 sq km (145 sq miles) of undulating heaths and woodlands are dotted with picturesque cottages and grazing animals. To the west of the Forest lie the seaside resorts of **Bournemouth**, **Poole** and **Swanage**. In the east, Southern England can lay claim to two of the greatest maritime centres, **Southampton** and **Portsmouth**, each with a host of naval heritage and attractions to see.

Also in the area are the picturesque *Hamble* and *Test* valleys with their famous chalk streams. To the north lies the Hampshire Borders' with its wealth of pretty villages and rolling countryside.

Isle of Wight: Less than two hours by train from London (and a short car ferry or passenger ride from Southampton, Portsmouth or Lymington), the Isle of Wight, with its beautiful countryside, rugged downland, unspoilt coastline and mile after mile of sandy beaches, is blessed with one of the best sunshine records in the country. Quiet and relaxing or sporting and energetic, it has all the ingredients to make the visitor's stay unforgettable. Craft centres, country parks, historic buildings, sporting and leisure facilities, the island with its stunning contrasts in scenery and entertainment is often described as 'England in Miniature'.

Cowes, world famous for yachting, also plays host to many national and international events, from sailing to power boating. Traditional English and foreign restaurants, cafés, pubs and wine bars provide a wide ranging choice of cuisine which can be complemented with a local wine from one of the island's five vineyards.

Dorset is a delightful county that has plenty for everyone, including historic towns, pretty villages nestling in idyllic English countryside, scenic coastline and lively resorts.

Called the 'Garden City by the sea', the Dorset resort of **Bournemouth**, just two hours from London, is foremost among British holiday locations for its sense of style. It has fine sandy beaches, excellent shopping, top-class entertainment and comfortable hotels and flats making the town an ever-popular holiday resort.

Nearby **Poole** has the second-largest natural harbour in the world and the lovely island nature reserve of *Brownsea* lies in its midst. Pleasure boats wait at the quayside and regularly make the short trip over. The new *Tower Park* leisure complex offers a host of up-to-the-

minute entertainments. The town's old Quay retains its 18th-century atmosphere and has become an ideal location for displaying maritime influences on the area. The new waterfront museum can be visited here.

Just to the west of Poole is an area known as the **Isle of Purbeck**. The coastline is full of variety and is known for its dramatic coastal scenery and the popular holiday resort of **Swanage**.

A little further westwards is the holiday town of **Weymouth**, with its top, clean 'Blue Flag' award beach, panoramic Georgian Bay and picturesque harbour. There is entertainment and activities for all the family plus many top attractions and events including the new *Brewer's Quay* leisure and shopping development.

Portland, joined to Weymouth by the *Chesil Beach* and causeway, is a fascinating island. Famous for its stone, the Island also has several castles, a lighthouse and small, sheltered coves.

Lying inland, northeast of Weymouth, is **Shaftesbury**, Dorset's most ancient hilltop town, characterised by steep cobbled streets. Slightly to the south is the handsome 18th-century town of **Blandford Forum**. A little further south east is **Wimborne Minster**, a small market town, with the distinction of having one of the most unusual churches in Dorset.

Hampshire: Lovers of the sea and open spaces will delight in this county. The region is one of great natural beauty but also enjoys the benefits of up-to-the-minute shopping, leisure facilities and nightlife. The county is justly famous for the **New Forest**, 376km (145 sq miles) of open heathland, where ponies, deer and cattle roam freely. The New Forest is a paradise for riders and walkers; there are lots of lovely places to stay and campsites are plentiful. *Beaulieu Motor Museum* and *Bucklers Hard* are well worth a visit.

Southampton is one of the most rapidly expanding cities on the South Coast with exciting new marinas, leisure facilities and shopping malls including the *Waterfront*, *Ocean Village* and the new *Bargate* shopping centre. There is a wealth of maritime history in the neighbouring city of **Portsmouth** – *HMS Victory*, *HMS Warrior*, the *Mary Rose* and the *Royal Naval Museum*. The *D-Day Museum* at **Southsea** tells the story of the 1944 allied Normandy landings.

Winchester, in central Hampshire, and Romsey to the south are worth including in any itinerary. Winchester has a magnificent 11th-century *Cathedral* and is

surrounded by the most lovely rolling countryside.

Romsey is an attractive old market town proud to be associated with *Broadlands*, the 18th-century home of Lord Mountbatten.

Yachtsmen are well catered for in Hampshire.

Lymington is a very attractive small town lying on the edge of the New Forest, with its own pretty harbour.

Hamble to the east is a mecca for yachtsmen, the *Hamble River* providing good sheltered moorings, making it an ideal place to start a cruise around its waters or over to the Isle of Wight.

The **Hampshire Borders**, in the north of the county, have some lovely countryside and the area is home to a past winner of the Best Kept Village competition, **Hartley Wintney**. There are a number of historic houses in the region and lots of military museums. A wide variety of accommodation can be found in and around **Basingstoke**, making it a good base from which to explore and the area is well connected by road and rail to London.

The Thames, with its many riverside pubs and hotels, winds its way through attractive and colourful towns and villages such as **Abingdon** and **Wallingford** and the regatta towns of **Marlow** and **Henley**. The ancient university city of **Oxford** also lies on the Thames. The college buildings, gardens, squares, cathedral and gracious streets that make up this historic city are probably best appreciated on foot or on an open-top bus tour. Northwest of Oxford, on the fringes of the Cotswolds, is impressive *Blenheim Palace*, birthplace of Sir Winston Churchill. The *Cotswold Wildlife Park* and *Broughton Castle* are situated in Oxfordshire.

Almost on the outskirts of London but still on the Thames, is **Windsor**, dominated by its famous castle. For the 900 years since William the Conqueror, Windsor has been the home of the monarch and is today the home of Her Majesty the Queen. The fire of 1992 destroyed the *St George's Chapel* and larger parts of the *State Apartments*. Renovation and repair works are currently underway and access to the castle during this time is restricted. Guided tours of the town are available, as well as bus tours and river cruises. At Windsor's Central Station a recreation of Queen Victoria's Jubilee in 1897 brings famous Victorian figures to life using the latest computerised techniques. Across a footbridge lies **Eton**, home of the famous college founded by Henry VI.

Nearby are the 4800 acres of *Windsor Great Park*, with

its glorious gardens.
The Berkshire Downs are criss-crossed with ancient byways and dotted with interesting towns and villages. There is **Wantage**, birthplace of King Alfred the Great, and **Newbury**, home of the famous racecourse and annual Spring Festival. In the beautiful Kennet Valley lies **Hungerford**, known for the unusual antiques arcade. Astride the *River Lambourn* at **Bagnor,** near Newbury, stands the jewel-box *Watermill Theatre*, renowned for its varied and entertaining plays.
Buckinghamshire has been called the Queen of the Home Counties. It boasts many picturesque villages and fine old towns such as **Olney** and **Buckingham**, as well as the new city of **Milton Keynes** in the north, with its extensive covered shopping centre. The Ouse and the *Grand Union Canal* flow through the north of the county, and the Thames through the south, with the magnificent beechwoods of the Chilterns running along its eastern edge. The county's historic houses include *Cliveden* and *Hughendon Manor.*

The West Country

Cornwall, Devon, Somerset, Wiltshire, Avon, Western Dorset, Isles of Scilly.
The West Country Tourist Board, 60 St David's Hill, Exeter EX4 4SY. Tel: (01392) 76351. Fax: (01392) 420 891.
The superb West Country resorts, together with 1000km (650 miles) of varied and spectacular coastline, have always been a great attraction for holidaymakers.
The coastline of **Cornwall**, which has both the southernmost and westernmost points on the English mainland, is characterised by tiny harbours, rocky headlands and magnificent cliffs. The north coast, washed by Atlantic breakers, has particularly good stretches of fine golden sandy beaches. **Bude**, the picturesque harbour at **Boscastle** and the clifftop castle at **Tintagel** are worth visiting. **Newquay** is the region's main resort, and has excellent beaches, modern hotels and good shops. **St Ives** is an old fishing port and a delightful holiday centre.
The south coast is in complete contrast, generally less dramatic, with many wooded estuaries, sheltered coves, picturesque fishing ports and several popular resorts. There are excellent facilities for sailing and deep-sea fishing at **Penzance** and **Fowey**. **Falmouth**, a town of many beaches and several beautiful gardens, is the main resort. **Mevagissey** and **Looe** are fine examples of traditional Cornish fishing ports. The coastline is also notable for its old smuggling villages, such as **Coverack.** Inland Cornwall consists mainly of flower-bordered lanes, gentle valleys and granite-capped moors. The three main towns inland are **Bodmin, Launceston** (the county town of Cornwall) and the cathedral city of **Truro**. *Bodmin Moor* is an area of stark natural beauty, and the setting for Daphne du Maurier's famous novel *Jamaica Inn*.
Devon: The area known as the *English Riviera* comprises **Torquay, Brixham** and **Paignton.** The major city in this region is **Plymouth**, a principal English seaport for over 500 years and the place where the West countryman Sir Francis Drake finished his game of bowls before setting sail to defeat the Spanish Armada. In 1620 the Pilgrim Fathers set out for the New World from Plymouth on the *Mayflower,* and parts of the town dating from this period still survive. Seaside trips in this region can also be combined with holidays inland into the peaceful wilderness of the **Dartmoor National Park** where native wild ponies roam freely across a beautiful landscape dotted with prehistoric remains. The county town, **Exeter**, has a long history and there are remains of Roman walls, underground passages, a beautiful cathedral and the oldest Guildhall in the Kingdom.
Western Dorset: Virtually all of the coast and much of the inland regions of the county has been designated an 'Area of Outstanding Natural Beauty'. Along the coast from **Christchurch** to **Lyme Regis** there is a fascinating variety of sandy beaches, towering cliffs and shingle banks, whilst inland is a rich mixture of lonely heaths, fertile valleys, historic houses and beautiful villages of thatch and mellow sandstone buildings. **Weymouth** is the main resort in this part of the country. Inland, the hills of Dorset abound with ancient trackways and early British hill forts; the county town of Dorchester was itself founded by the Romans.
The north of the county is a region of farms, woods and river valleys. The three main towns are **Sherborne, Sturminster Newton** and **Shaftesbury**.
Somerset, another attractive rural county, has three fine coastal resorts, **Weston-super-Mare, Burnham-on-Sea** and **Minehead**. Much of west Somerset lies within the **Exmoor National Park**. Attractions in this region include the tiny *Culbone Church,* the clapper bridge at *Tarr Steps,* the idyllic villages of *Selworthy, Dunster* or a climb to the top of *Dunkery Beacon.* The county town of **Taunton** is to the west of the county, near the southern end of the wooded *Quantock Hills*. The county's northern boundary is emphasised by the limestone range of the *Mendip Hills*. Along the southern edge are the attractions of the *Cheddar Gorge, Wookey Hole* and the great cathedral at **Wells**. The southeastern corner of the county around **Yeovil** has many historic houses open to the public.
Even in prehistoric times the inland county of **Wiltshire** proved attractive to early settlers, and the evidence of long occupation – at places such as *Stonehenge, Avebury, Old Sarum* and others – make Wiltshire the best county for exploring prehistoric remains. In addition, some of England's greatest Stately Homes are in Wiltshire, including *Longleat, Wilton, Lacock Abbey, Corsham* and *Stourhead*. Longleat is a very grand Elizabethan mansion, famous for its safari park, and Stourhead, built in 1722, has particularly fine gardens leading down to its own lake and *Wilton House.*
The city of **Salisbury** is dominated by the 123m (404ft) cathedral spire, the tallest in England. The grounds of *Salisbury Cathedral* contain many notable houses that are open to the public. *Mompesson House* is a perfectly preserved 18th-century home and *Malmesbury House* was once sanctuary for King Charles II, who was fleeing after the Battle of Worcester in the 17th century. The city has a harmonious blend of gabled houses, historic inns and 18th-century architecture and offers a great choice of hotels, restaurants and shopping. Guided tours can be taken around the city by open-top bus or horse-drawn omnibus. The *Barchester Chronicles* of Anthony Trollope, which provide an entertaining account of life in a 19th-century cathedral town, are a fictional evocation of Salisbury. The remains of *Old Sarum*, an ancient city and Norman fortress, can be seen but the most important site is *Stonehenge,* 3km (2 miles) away on Salisbury Plain. The enormous stones are arranged in an inner and an outer circle, and the site is believed to have been first used as long ago as 1500BC.
The new county of **Avon** has two cities of note: **Bristol**, which is one of the largest ports in the country (the *Cathedral* and *St Mary Redcliffe Church* are worth seeing, as is Brunel's impressive *Clifton Suspension Bridge*, which spans the Avon Gorge) and **Bath**, which is usually regarded as the most elegant Georgian city in the country, and has been immortalised in countless photographs, paintings and novels. The city also has Roman remains and an abbey.
Historical and literary associations can be found in many places throughout the West Country; King Alfred reputedly burnt his cakes at Athelney, while Cadbury may have been *Camelot*. RD Blackmore's novel *Lorna Doone* was set in Exmoor (now a national park), while many of Daphne du Maurier's were set in Cornwall. Lyme Regis, in Dorset, was one of Jane Austen's favourite towns, and, along with Bath, was one of the settings for her novel *Persuasion*. **Dorchester** is the birthplace of Thomas Hardy, the West Country's most famous literary figure, who immortalised both this town and much of the surrounding countryside – referred to in his books as 'Wessex', the name of the old Saxon kingdom in that area. Hardy's cottage lies 5km (3 miles) out of town. The museum in Dorchester contains many pre-Roman exhibits and a Thomas Hardy memorial room. *Maiden Castle,* 3km (2 miles) from Dorchester, is one of the most impressive prehistoric sites in the country.
The **Isles of Scilly** lie 50km (30 miles) off Land's End. Though there are about a hundred of them, only five are inhabited. They are a popular holiday destination, as the climate is warmer and more temperate than on the mainland. The tourism industry was undoubtedly boosted when, during his prime ministership, it became known that Harold Wilson had a holiday home there. Horticulture is now the islands' second-largest industry. Boat trips to visit the smaller islands are popular, particularly from *St Mary's*, the largest of the islands. The Isles of Scilly can be reached by ferry or helicopter.

Heart of England

Gloucestershire, Herefordshire & Worcestershire, Shropshire, Staffordshire, Warwickshire, The West Midlands Boroughs.
Heart of England Tourist Board, Larkhill Road, Worcester, Worcestershire WR5 2EF. Tel: (01905) 763 436. Fax: (01905) 763 450.
Some of the country's most famous landscapes lie in the Heart of England. Little has changed over the centuries in the **Cotswolds**, where gentle uplands are studded with beautiful old villages and towns, many of which are frequently built from the locality's yellow limestone and graced by magnificent churches erected chiefly from the wealth of the medieval wool trade.
Two important rivers cross this heartland. The Severn winds through the ancient city of **Worcester**, skirting the *Malvern Hills* to meet the Avon at Tewkesbury. The Avon flows past the fertile *Vale of Evesham* and passes **Stratford**, home town of William Shakespeare.
The dark mountains of Wales give way to the border area called *The Marches* and the English hills of *Long Mynd, Wenlock Edge* and *Clun Forest.* This area was once less tranquil than it is today and its turbulent past is indicated by ancient barrows, pre-Roman camps and the entrenchment of *Offa's Dyke* (now a long-distance footpath). In turn, the Normans and Plantagenets left remains of splendid castles at **Shrewsbury**, **Goodrich** and **Ludlow**, built to protect England from invasion.
The first sparks of the Industrial Revolution ignited at **Ironbridge**, now a showplace of industrial archaeology, while in neighbouring Staffordshire, where the scenery rises to peaks and moorland, that same era bequeathed a legacy of canals (now popular for pleasure-craft) and the Potteries with their famous china factories.
Gloucestershire & The Cotswolds: This region comprises a range of low limestone hills stretching in a curve from Bath to the vicinity of Stratford-upon-Avon. The charming and well-preserved towns and villages of the Cotswolds are built in a honey-coloured stone, and are set in one of the finest areas of unspoilt countryside in England. Historically, the area's wealth was based on sheep farming and the wool industry, and sheep are still very much in evidence today. The area is accessible by road from London, and many of the towns by rail from Paddington. **Gloucester** is an ancient cathedral city on the River Severn. Many of the streets and parts of the old city wall date back to the Middle Ages. The revitalised docks now have massive warehouses which are gradually being filled. The *National Waterways Museum* (opened in 1988), the *Marina and Tall Ships*, plus the fascinating *Opie Collection of Packaging*, are open to the public. **Cheltenham**, an elegant Regency spa town, is famous for its *National Hunt Racecourse* and annual music and literature festival. The flowers and gardens of the suburbs are also worth seeing. **Malmesbury** contains a fine example of Norman building in its abbey, the ruins of a 12th-century castle, a market square and several attractive 17th- and 18th-century houses. **Cirencester** contains extensive Roman remains, and is a good centre for exploring the Cotswolds. To the east of the Wye Valley is the *Forest of Dean*, 130 sq km (50 sq miles) of ancient hunting forest, once the property of the medieval kings but now given over to trails and picnic sites.
Herefordshire & Worcestershire: The stretch of country between Worcester and the Welsh border is one of the richest farming areas in Great Britain, with fields and meadows full of cider apples, hops and white-faced red cattle. Characteristic black and white half-timbered buildings decorate the villages and market towns such as **Ledbury.** The Wye Valley, the Malvern Hills and the *Teme Valley* all add to the area's beauty.
The **Wye Valley** is an exceedingly beautiful region, with the river flowing at first through water meadows and gentle countryside but later winding its way through spectacular gorges in the region of *Symonds Yat*. The town of **Ross-on-Wye** provides a good base for exploring this area. Northwest of Ross is **Hereford**, also on the *River Wye,* an attractive cathedral city and a thriving market centre. There is a city museum and art gallery as well as a cider museum. Nell Gwynne was said to have been born here. To the west of Hereford is the *Golden Valley*, a remote region containing many attractive villages. At the northern tip of the valley on the Welsh border is the town of **Hay-on-Wye**, famous for having one of the largest second-hand bookshops in the world. The ancient city of **Worcester** on the bank of the *River Severn* has a cathedral, the museum and factory of the famous Royal Worcester Porcelain Company, a magnificent Guildhall with a Queen Anne façade and a number of streets with overhanging half-timbered houses from the Tudor period. Worcester is also the ancient Commandey, once the battle headquarters of Charles II, and now housing a Civil War audio-visual display. South of Worcester are the *Malvern Hills*, a very steep range topped with open moorland which offer superb views across the rich agricultural landscape. The spa town of **Great Malvern** was built as a fashionable spa resort in the 19th century; Malvern spring water can still be tasted at *St Anne's Well.* 32km (20 miles) north of Worcester is the *Wyre Forest*, ideal for walking and riding. The main towns in this region are **Stourport**, **Bewdley** and **Kidderminster**, terminus for the Severn Valley Railway, the longest full-gauge steam railway in England.
Warwickshire & The West Midlands: The industrial heart of Britain on the edge of some lovely countryside, particularly in Warwickshire. **Birmingham**, Britain's second-largest city, is a centre both of industry and culture. It has a magnificent library, and the *Central Museum & Art Gallery* is one of the finest in the country. Birmingham is the home of the *National Exhibition Centre,* site of many of the major exhibitions and fairs for which Britain is renowned. Birmingham also lies at the

centre of a vast network of canals, most of which are still navigable. Canal holidays represent one of the best ways of seeing not only the countryside of the area but also some unusual views of the gaunt architecture of the industrial revolution in the cities. There are also many museums which trace the region's industrial past.
Coventry is famous for its new cathedral, designed by Sir Basil Spence after the original one was destroyed in the Second World War. **Warwick** contains many 17th- and 18th-century houses and the castle, one of the most imposing medieval strongholds in the country, is open to visitors even though it is still inhabited. The *Church of St Mary*, the *Lord Leycester Hospital* and the *Doll Museum* are all worth visiting.
Stratford-upon-Avon, in the county of Warwickshire, is one of the most famous towns in the country. It was the birth and burial place of *William Shakespeare*, and the life and works of the great playwright are commemorated throughout the year in almost every aspect of the town's public life, chiefly through the productions of his works at the Royal Shakespeare Theatre. Other buildings in the town associated with Shakespeare include his birthplace in Henley Street, the 15th-century grammar school which he attended, the early home of his wife Anne Hathaway, the *Shakespeare Centre*, *Holy Trinity Church,* where Shakespeare and his family are buried and *Halls Croft*, once the home of Shakespeare's daughter. Other buildings of note include the *Motor Museum*; the RSC's other venues, the 'Other Place' and the 'Swan Theatre'; and *Harvard House*, built in the late 16th century and owned by the family who founded the American University of the same name. The whole of Stratford is a beautifully preserved town, with many excellent examples of Elizabethan, Jacobean, Restoration and Georgian buildings. It makes an ideal centre for exploring the surrounding towns and countryside. Places of interest close to Stratford include *Ragley Hall* and *Coughton Court* near Alcester, *Charlecote Park* and *Upton House*, Edge Hill.
Staffordshire is both an industrial and an agricultural county. Part of it lies within the *Peak District National Park* and contains some of the most spectacular countryside in England, such as *Thor's Cave* and the limestone gorge at **Dovedale**. East of the industrial region of the Potteries lie the scenic *Churnet Valley* and the *Vale of Trent*, the latter containing *Cannock Chase,* an attractive area of heath and woodland. One of the most famous sights in the county is *Lichfield Cathedral,* which has three spires. Nearby **Tamworth** has a fine castle.
Shropshire is a county with a varied landscape, including moorlands, forests, gentle hills and open pastures. Despite this appearance of rural tranquillity, Shropshire is also the county where the industrial revolution began, evidence of which may be seen in the area of *Ironbridge Gorge*, which includes the towns of **Coalbrookdale**, **Coalport** and **Ironbridge**. The *Ironbridge Gorge Museum* is spread out over a large number of sites but the area's most famous landmark is probably the Ironbridge itself, built in 1779. On the eastern boundary of this district is the magnificent Restoration house and parkland known as *Weston Park*. Nearby is **Boscobel** where the future Charles II hid in the now famous Royal Oak after the Battle of Worcester. To the west is the area of *The Wrekin*, a conical-shaped hill that figures in many local tales and legends. The county's capital of **Shrewsbury** is one of the finest Tudor towns in England, celebrated for the flower market held every summer. South and southwest of Shrewsbury are the *Shropshire Hills,* designated as an area of outstanding natural beauty. **Ludlow** (dominated by the ruins of its castle), *Church Stretton, Bishop's Castle, Much Wenlock* and *Bridgenorth* are also worth visiting. The north of the county is dominated by a large plain with many quiet roads, making it ideally suited to a cycling or walking holiday. **Market Drayton, Wem** (famous for its beer), **Whitchurch** and **Oswestry** are the major market towns in this region.

East Anglia

Bedfordshire, Cambridgeshire, Essex, Hertfordshire, Norfolk, Suffolk.
East Anglia Tourist Board, Toppesfield Hall, Hadleigh, Ipswich, Suffolk IP7 5DN. Tel: (01473) 822 922. Fax: (01473) 823 063.
The county of Essex has some lovely remote and unspoilt villages including Finchingfield, Thaxted (with its medieval church and windmill), Saffron Walden and Dunmow. Also in Essex are the well-known seaside resorts of Southend, Clacton-on-Sea and Maldon, a maritime town on the estuary of the River Blackwater. Colchester the oldest continuously occupied town in the country with the Roman Walls still remaining. The town is a good base for exploring the neighbouring Constable Country.
A relatively under-exploited part of East Anglia is the marshland called the **Fens**, drained in the 17th and 18th centuries by Dutch engineers to create a system of canals. The main centres in the Fens are the cathedral cities of **Peterborough** and **Ely**, site of *Cromwell House*, home of Oliver Cromwell, which is open to the public. Not as famous is the heath area known as **Breckland**, now overgrown with pine forests. Many archaeological discoveries have been made here. **Thetford** is a good base from which to visit this area.
The towns in East Anglia show many examples of the wealthy past of the region. The late 14th, 15th and 16th centuries were a period of great prosperity, largely as a result of the wool trade; the architecture of towns such as **Lavenham** being superb testimony to the wealth of the Tudor wool merchants. Many of Cambridge's colleges were founded at this time and elsewhere in the region solid stone guildhalls, manor houses and thatched inns were built, as well as a wealth of churches. Because the towns largely escaped the influence of the Industrial Revolution, Norman castles, medieval churches, Tudor half-timbered houses and 18th-century mansions are still numerous.
Cambridge is famous for its university (the second oldest in the country) and gracious buildings, including *Henry VI's Chapel* at King's College, the *Great Court* at Trinity College, the *Bridge of Sighs* at St John's College and the *Cloister Court* at Queens' College. A river trip along the *Cam* affords the best view of the colleges whose lawns sweep down to the river, a view known as 'the Backs'. Bear in mind that most of the colleges are closed to visitors during the exam periods in the early summer.
Ipswich, county town of Suffolk, retains much of its medieval street pattern and several of the buildings from this period remain. **Kings Lynn** is a medieval town, once one of the country's major ports. **Aldeburgh** is a pleasant and peaceful old fishing town. **Norwich** is an attractive city with a Norman cathedral, a castle with a museum and art gallery, and medieval houses set in narrow streets. The *Maddermarket Theatre* is an Elizabethan theatre with an apron stage. Over 160km (100 miles) of navigable waterways make up *The Broads,* an area of reed-fringed lagoons and rivers, teeming with wildlife and waterfowl, and ideal for a boating holiday. In between many of the coastal resorts are secluded marshes and estuaries, popular among birdwatchers and yachtsmen.
The *Great Ouse* winds gently through the county of **Bedfordshire**, a region of great natural beauty, with a number of country parks and riverside walks. It has many historic connections, including the 4000-year-old *Icknield Way* and the *Roman Watling Street*, both crossing the county. John Bunyan is a famous son of Bedfordshire and many associations with him can be found in and around **Bedford.** The county's historic houses include *Luton Hoo* and *Woburn Abbey,* famous for its *Safari Park*. Animal lovers should also visit *Whipsnade Wild Animal Park,* southeast of Dunstable.
Hertfordshire is a region of gently undulating countryside. The historic town of **St Albans** contains many reminders of the town's great past when, as Verulamium, it was one of the great cities of the Roman Empire. The *Verulamium Museum* reveals these Roman connections through a nationally important collection of Iron Age and Roman artefacts. Other museums of note in the county include the *Tring Zoological Museum*, a branch of the British Museum; *St Albans Organ Museum* with its magnificent collection of fairground and dance-hall organs and the innovative *Stevenage Museum* which tells the town's history from prehistory to the present through displays of everyday objects.
The region has many **historic houses**, including Audley End, Sandringham, Ickworth, Wimpole Hall, Hatfield House, Knebworth House, Woburn Abbey and Luton Hoo.
Seaside resorts: *Essex:* Southend, Clacton, Walton, Frinton and Harwich. *Norfolk:* Cromer, Wells-next-the-Sea, Sheringham, where a steam railway operates daily in the summer, and Great Yarmouth, one of Britain's largest and most popular resorts. *Suffolk:* Lowestoft, as well as being a major resort, is also the home of England's main fishing fleet. To the south is Oulton Broad and the resort of Southwold. Beyond Southwold is Aldeburgh, home of a summer music festival. Hunstanton gives a magnificent view of the Wash, and is also notable for its red-and-white striped cliffs.

East Midlands

Derbyshire, Leicestershire, Lincolnshire, Northamptonshire, Nottinghamshire.
East Midlands Tourist Board, Exchequergate, Lincoln, Lincolnshire LN2 1PZ. Tel: (01522) 531 521. Fax: (01522) 532 501.
Solid, historic houses make their presence felt throughout the area: *Chatsworth*; medieval *Haddon Hall*; *Althorp*, family home of the Princess of Wales; *Sudbury Hall* with its Museum of Childhood; the gardens at *Melbourne Hall*; and Elizabethan *Doddington Hall*. A strong sense of history can be felt throughout the region – in the cathedrals of Lincoln and Southwell, in Leicester's Guildhall, Nottingham's Castle and at Derby's Industrial Museum, and also in the wealth of churches, particularly in Lincolnshire and Northamptonshire.
The traditional dining-table of this area reflects the presence of the English landed gentry over the centuries. Sporting specialities include game soup, flavoured with port wine; Melton Mowbray pork pies; and Melton Hunt Cake, made to a 120-year-old recipe. Red Leicester and Stilton cheeses and Bakewell Pudding are other local favourites.
The spa town of **Buxton** in **Derbyshire**, makes a good base from which to explore the Peak District, now a 1300-sq-km (500-sq-mile) National Park with limestone dales and open moors. Other places of interest in Derbyshire include **Matlock Bath,** with its cable car ride across the *Derwent Gorge* and show-caves to visit; **Bolsover**, a small market town with a 17th-century castle set in rich farmland; **Creswell Crags,** with the Visitor Centre at the site of archaeological finds such as Creswellian Man; **Chesterfield**, another convenient base for exploring the Peak District and famous for its crooked-spire church; Chatsworth House, Baslow; Kedleston Hall, near Derby; and Sudbury Hall, Sudbury. The county town of **Derby** is the home of Royal Crown Derby porcelain and the city's cathedral, museums and *Assembly Rooms* are all worth visiting.
Nottinghamshire was the home of Robin Hood, and parts of his Sherwood Forest still survive in the Country Park. The city of **Nottingham** has a beautiful neo-Classical *Council House*, a castle which overlooks the city, and *Wollaton Hall,* an Elizabethan mansion now housing a natural history museum. North Nottinghamshire is a rural area with many old villages, and the home of several of the Pilgrim Fathers. **Newark-on-Trent** in the heart of the county has a 12th-century castle. *Rufford County Park* at **Ollerton** is also worth visiting.
Lincolnshire, the largest county in the East Midlands and the only one with a coastline, has several seaside resorts, notably **Skegness** and **Mablethorpe**, both of which are towns with good sunshine records. Inland are the gently rolling hills of the *Lincolnshire Wolds,* where Tennyson spent much of his early life. The area around **Spalding** is the richest farmland in the country, and is famous for growing bulbs. During the 12th century, **Boston** was one of the three most important ports in England, and from here many of the Pilgrim Fathers planned to set sail for The Netherlands to find religious freedom, but were betrayed and imprisoned in cells still in *Boston Guildhall.* The county town of **Lincoln** is a well-preserved medieval city and the *Cathedral*, set on a limestone hill, has three towers, a fine Norman west front and a particularly beautiful 13th-century presbytery. The aptly named *Steep Hill* has some interesting shops and the *Jew's House*, halfway up its incline, is worth a visit.
Stamford, situated at the border of four counties, is another medieval town, with several fine churches and buildings of mellow stone. Nearby is *Burghley House*, built by one of Elizabeth I's most powerful ministers. The medieval *Old Hall* at **Gainsborough** in north Lincolnshire is also worth a visit.
The county of **Leicestershire** has many castles, manor houses and market towns. **Leicester** has Roman remains and a great deal of medieval architecture, but is nowadays more important as a major shopping centre. Other towns of interest in the county include **Market Harborough, Oakham, Lutterworth** (the home of John Wycliffe) and **Melton Mowbray,** the home of Stilton cheese and pork pies. Near Leicester is **Market Bosworth**, the site of one of the most famous battles in English history, when Henry Tudor defeated Richard III, the last Plantagenet king. Also worth visiting are *Belvoir Castle* near Melton Mowbray and *Oakham Castle,* with its collection of decorative horseshoes.
Northamptonshire is traversed by major road and rail links but most of the countryside remains unspoilt. One of the most attractive regions is the *Rockingham Forest* area, which contains several historic houses. Of *Fotheringhay Castle* (where Mary Queen of Scots was executed in 1587) only the mound remains, but most of the other houses are in much better condition, and many are still occupied. Of these, *Althorp* and *Rockingham Castle,* north of **Corby,** are particularly worth visiting. Other places of interest include the *Nene Valley Steam Railway* and the *Central Museum* in Northampton with its fine shoe collection.

The North West

Cheshire, Greater Manchester, Lancashire, Merseyside, the High Peak District of Derbyshire.
North West Tourist Board, Swan House, Swan

Meadow Road, Wigan Pier, Wigan WN3 5BB. Tel: (01942) 821 222. Fax: (01942) 820 002.

The North West's 250km (150-mile) coastline is characterised by dune-backed sandy beaches. The seven large resorts, the most popular of which is **Blackpool,** attract millions of holiday-makers each year. Other resorts include **Lytham St Annes**, **Ainsdale**, **Fleetwood**, **Morecambe** and **Southport**. All have extensive facilities and a wide choice of accommodation and entertainment.

Further north, **Blackburn, Bolton, Nelson** and **Burnley** offer varied accommodation as bases for trips round the western slopes of the *Pennines*, while long stretches of footpaths and bridleways wind through the landscape of heather and wild bilberries. Throughout the area there are fine examples of the stately homes of England: 16th-century *Speke Hall* near Liverpool; *Gawsworth Hall* near Macclesfield; timbered *Bramall Hall* near Stockport; and *Tatton Park* near Knutsford, whose interior is familiar to viewers of the BBC television adaptation of Evelyn Waugh's *Brideshead Revisited*.

The countryside includes the gentle *Cheshire Plain* dotted with small natural lakes, old water-wheels and distinctive villages with black and white houses. In the **Peak District National Park**, the limestone valleys and vast caverns of the White Peak give way to the dramatic moorlands of the Dark Peak.

In the south is the *Mersey Estuary* and the port of **Liverpool**, home town of the Beatles. It also contains the *Walker Art Gallery* with Dutch, French, Italian and English paintings, the *New Tate Gallery* and two cathedrals, one Anglican and one Roman Catholic. Attractions in and around the city include the *Merseyside County Museum*, *St George's Hall* and the 16th-century *Speke Hall*. From Liverpool there are regular ferry sailings to the Isle of Man.

Across the river is the *Wirral Peninsula* with the resort of **New Brighton** and a large country park. From here there are views across the Dee estuary to the Welsh Hills. On the *River Dee* near the Welsh border is the historic walled city of **Chester,** well-known for its concentration of Cheshire's black and white 'magpie' houses. To the east of the city is the 4000-acre *Delamere Forest* and the rich pastures of the Cheshire Plain, a region which has a network of canals several hundred kilometres long.

Northeast of Cheshire is the city of **Manchester**, in many ways the 'capital' of the north of England. Attractions here include the *Opera House*, the *Palace Theatre*, the *Royal Exchange Theatre* (in the building that, 100 years ago, was at the very centre of the world's cotton industry), the *Free Trade Hall* and the mock-Gothic *John Rylands Library.* The city's cathedral was built in the 15th century, although most of the more immediately noticeable buildings date from the city's period of greatest prosperity in the 19th century.

Further north is the *Forest of Bowland*, a vast and lonely area of high moor-backed hills which also contains the beautiful wooded valley of the River *Ribble*. The historic county town of **Lancaster** is to the northwest, a short distance inland from the resorts of **Morecambe** and **Heysham**.

Cumbria

Cumbria Tourist Board, Ashleigh, Holly Road, Windermere, Cumbria LA23 2AQ. Tel: (015394) 44444. Fax: (015394) 44041.

Cumbria is proud to boast England's largest national park, containing the highest English peak (*Scafell Pike*) and *Windermere,* the largest lake. Cumbria is climbing country, with easy fell walks, and sailing, fishing, canoeing and pony-trekking facilities in a stunningly beautiful setting of mountains and lakes. The ancient sport of Cumberland and Westmorland wrestling takes place at the annual sports meetings in Grasmere, Ambleside and Coniston. Traditional fell-racing (to the top of the nearest hill and back) can also be seen at some of the Cumbrian sports meetings.

Many of the towns and villages, hidden among moorland, perched on mountainsides or tucked away along the coast, hold fairs, shows and sheepdog trials throughout the year. Local crafts are practised and workshops, smithies and potteries welcome visitors. It is possible to watch weaving in Grasmere, pencils made at Keswick and clogs fashioned in **Whitehaven**. Sweaters sold in **Ambleside** are made from the wool of local Herdwick sheep.

Grasmere is where Wordsworth lived for several years and his home, *Dove Cottage*, is open to the public. He also lived at the nearby *Rydal Mount*. **Keswick**, on the shores of *Derwent Water*, is an attractive market town with a museum in *Fitz Park*, which contains many manuscripts and letters of Shelley, Southey, Wordsworth and Coleridge. The region also has several coastal resorts such as *Maryport, Silloth, St Bees* and *Grange-over-Sands.*

To the north of the county is the 2000-year-old cathedral

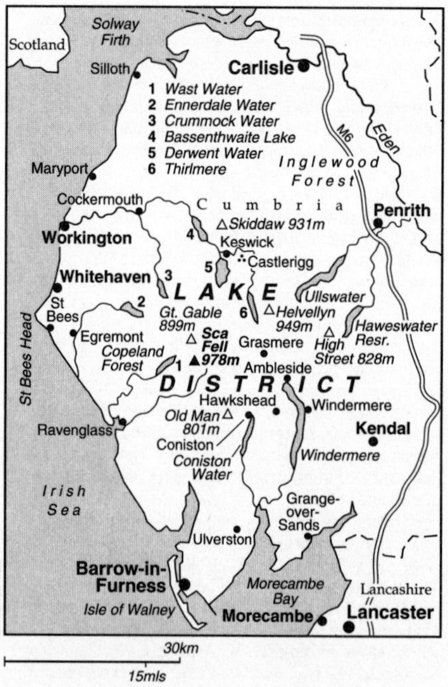

city of **Carlisle,** close to Hadrian's Wall and once a Roman camp. Likewise, the once important 18th-century trading port of Whitehaven today preserves an echo of former glories in its Georgian buildings. Another historic town, **Penrith,** makes a good base for touring the rich and peaceful *Eden Valley* and the wide-open spaces of the *Cumbrian Pennines.*

Yorkshire & Humberside

Humberside, North Yorkshire, South Yorkshire, West Yorkshire.

Yorkshire & Humberside Tourist Board, 312 Tadcaster Road, York YO2 2HF. Tel: (01904) 707 961. Fax: (01904) 701 414.

Yorkshire & Humberside is a region of scenic softness, rugged castles, stately homes and ancient churches all packed tightly into a compact area with good transport communications.

For many people, the scenic grandeur of the *Yorkshire Dales National Park* – 1761 sq km (680 sq miles) of unspoilt countryside, rivers, caves and unforgettable views – is a major attraction all year round. This is the landscape made famous by JMW Turner and, most recently, by the worldwide success of the books and TV series featuring Dales vet, James Herriot. The surgery and locations used in the filming can be seen in **Askrigg**, in Wensleydale. Walking is a very popular pastime in the area, with everything from gentle strolls to hearty climbs such as the ascent of the *Three Peaks* of Ingleborough, Whernside and Pen-y-ghent. An even bigger challenge is the *Pennine Way*, the toughest of many long-distance footpaths to be found in Yorkshire & Humberside.

Historic castles abound in the region, such as the great fortresses of *Richmond* and *Middleham,* the latter associated with Richard III. *Bolton Castle* in **Wensleydale** once served as a prison for the ill-fated Mary Queen of Scots, whilst an even more tragic scenario was played out at *Pontefract Castle* in **West Yorkshire**, where Richard II was murdered.

A more stable period for the aristocracy is reflected in the great houses to be found dotted throughout the region, notably *Castle Howard*, near **Malton**, world famous as the setting for Evelyn Waugh's *Brideshead Revisited*. Other fine houses open to the public include *Harewood House, Duncombe Park, Nostell Priory, Sledmere House* and *Burton Constable Hall.*

The great city of **York,** with its unparalleled wealth of historic sites, continues to be a strong magnet for visitors; more than two million people visit the *Minster* – northern Europe's largest Gothic cathedral – every year. Other top attractions are the *National Railway Museum*, the *Castle Museum* and the *Jorvik Viking Centre*, whilst many people come to see the medieval ring of walls or to shop in the *Shambles*. **Humberside** is a maritime county with powerful links with Britain's proud seafaring tradition. The city of **Hull** is an important working port, and has recently been transformed by the new waterfront marina development, whilst the majestic *Humber Bridge* is an attraction in its own right. Beyond Hull is the gentle lowland area of **Holderness**, which ends in the bird sanctuary at lonely *Spurn Point*. To the north lies the ancient market town of **Beverley**, with its Georgian houses in the shadow of the minster. Close by is the racecourse and the fascinating *Museum of Army Transport.*

The **North York Moors** National Park has miles of open moorland with picturesque villages nestling in hollows. *The North Yorkshire Moors Railway*, starting at **Pickering**, is one of the most scenic in Britain, and is one of the many steam railways in the region – others include the *Embsay Steam Railway* at **Skipton** and the *Keighley and Worth Valley Railway*.

On the coast, traditional family resorts include: **Scarborough**, **Bridlington** and **Cleethorpes** which have added many new attractions in recent times, such as Bridlington's popular *Leisure World Complex.* There are also many smaller resorts, each with their own special character, such as **Whitby** with its busy harbour and clifftop abbey, linked to Bram Stoker's *Dracula*.

Between the coast and the Vale of York lie *The Wolds*, a gentle range of rolling hills with timeless villages and quiet lanes, ideal for walking or cycling. On the edge of *The Wolds* is **Malton**, one of the many interesting towns to be found dotted throughout the region – others worth a visit include **Thirsk, Skipton, Selby, Ilkley** and **Harrogate.**

The cities of South and West Yorkshire make interesting destinations, their potent industrial heritage combined with a new spirit of renovation and renewal. **Bradford** has led the way, with the award-winning *National Museum of Photography, Film and Television.* **Wakefield** boasts *Caphouse Colliery,* home of the *Yorkshire Mining Museum*. Close by are the Wild Moors of the Pennines including the Brontë Village of **Haworth**.

Northumbria

Cleveland, Durham, Tyne & Wear, Northumberland.

Northumbria Tourist Board, Aykley Heads, Durham, Co Durham DH1 5UX. Tel: (0191) 384 6905. Fax: (0191) 386 0899.

A region of contrasts, Northumbria offers miles of coastline, city lights, quiet countryside, castles and cathedrals, industrial tourism, Hadrian's Wall and much more.

Northumberland, lying between the Scottish Border and Tyne & Wear, is a rural county with numerous attractive villages and market towns. On its northern boundary it has **Hadrian's Wall** as its most famous landmark. The wall was built to protect Roman Britain from the incursions of the Picts and Scots from north of the border; much of the surviving architecture tells of centuries of border warfare, such as the chain of castles built to defend the countryside and the long Northumberland coastline. These include dramatic **Bamburgh**, gaunt craggy **Dunstanburgh** and impressive **Alnwick**. In contrast, the simple cross at **Chollerford, Lindisfarne** (Holy Island) and *St Wilfred's* at **Hexham** reflect the important role Northumberland played in the spread of Christianity. Hexham makes a good base from which to explore the whole Northumbrian region. Much of the county is a National Park, with rolling moorlands stretching from the North Sea to the *Cheviot Hills* on the Scottish border. England's most northerly town, **Berwick-upon-Tweed**, was a regular casualty in the border battles, and changed hands between Scotland and England at least 13 times. Its medieval town walls, reconstructed in Elizabethan times, are among the best-preserved in Europe. Today the town makes a convenient base for touring northern Northumberland and the Borderlands.

Tyne & Wear spans the mouths of the two major rivers in its name. **Newcastle-upon-Tyne** (originally no more than a fort on Hadrian's Wall) has city centre shopping, museums, theatres, hotels, restaurants and all the services expected in a major city. There is also a cathedral and a castle. Across the river are **Gateshead** with the *Metro Centre* indoor shopping and **South Shields**, home of popular author Catherine Cookson. **Sunderland** stands at the mouth of the *River Wear* and nearby is **Washington**, famous as the original home of US President George Washington's family. Christian heritage comes to the fore at *Tynemouth Priory* and **Jarrow**, home of The Venerable Bede.

Transport in the Newcastle area is particularly good owing to its excellent *Metro.*

County Durham, where Prince Bishops ruled for 600 years, surrounds **Durham City** with its spectacular castle and Norman Cathedral built overlooking a gorge on the River Wear. The surrounding countryside is pleasant and studded with small market towns such as **Bishop Auckland** and *Barnard Castle. The Bowes Museum, Raby Castle, High Force Waterfall* and *Beamish Open Air Museum* attract thousands of visitors to the county each year. There are several castles, in varying stages of dilapidation. Bishop Auckland is an ancient market town; nearby is an 800-acre deer park. Also within this county is the wild region of the *North Pennines, Weardale* and

Teesdale. **Darlington,** which made its name in the 19th century with the world's first passenger railway to nearby Stockton, has a famous railway museum. There are many other attractive towns and villages throughout County Durham, and many opportunities for walks in the hills and moors.

Cleveland, in the south of the region close to the Yorkshire border, is an industrial county dominated by **Middlesbrough.** It boasts Australia's discoverer Captain Cook as its most famous son. The *Captain Cook Birthplace Museum* in Middlesbrough tells his story. Coastal towns include **Redcar, Saltburn** and **Hartlepool,** with its maritime museum, restored ships and marina (under construction). Cleveland's long industrial history dates from the early 19th century (the world's first passenger train steamed into Stockton-on-Tees in 1825). Towns of interest include **Marske, Guisborough** and **Upleatham,** with reputedly the smallest church in England.

POPULAR ITINERARIES: 5-day: (a) London–Oxford–Cheltenham–Gloucester–Stratford-Upon-Avon–London. (b) London–Colchester–Aldeburgh–Kings Lynn–Ely–Cambridge–London. (c) London–Canterbury–Tunbridge Wells–Lewes–Alfriston–Brighton–London. **7-day:** (a) London–Oxford–Bath–Bristol–Salisbury–Lyme Regis–Dartmoor–St Ives–London. (b) Manchester–Bradford–York–Harrogate–Durham–Penrith–Lancaster–Manchester.

SOCIAL PROFILE

FOOD & DRINK: Good English cooking is superb and there are restaurants specialising in old English dishes. In general, the north of the country tends to offer more substantial and traditional food, at more reasonable prices than the south. Every region, however, will have its own speciality; these will include roast beef and Yorkshire pudding, game or venison pies, rack of lamb and many fish dishes. Britain is still the home of puddings: *spotted dick* (suet pudding with currants and raisins); *plum duff* (suet roll stuffed with plums); and *syllabub* (a medieval dish consisting of double cream, white wine and lemon juice). The English cream tea is still served in tea rooms, particularly in south coast seaside resorts. It generally consists of scones, jam, butter, clotted or double cream and, of course, tea. There are many regional varieties in baking: the flat pancake-type scones of the North of England and Scotland; Scottish black bun, a fruit cake on a pastry base; Bakewell tart, a pastry base covered with jam, almond filling and topped with icing; and breads of all description. For those who want variety, London offers every type of ethnic food imaginable, Indian and Chinese being particularly popular and good value for money. *Cheddar* and *Stilton* are the most famous British cheeses. Tipping is not compulsory and it is up to the individual to pay the 10% service charge often added automatically to bills. Table service is usual but there are self-service snack bars. Set price lunches, especially on Sundays, with a choice of about three dishes, are particularly good value, as is pub food. **Drink:** The British pub is nothing short of a national institution and even the smallest village in the remotest corner of the country will usually have at least one. There are about as many beers in England as there are cheeses in France and the recent revival of real ale has greatly improved the range and qualities of brews available. Look out for the sign 'Free House' outside a pub, meaning that beer from more than one brewery will be sold there. Bitter and lager are the most popular beers, but Guinness, pale ale, brown ale and cider are also widely drunk. Wine bars and cocktail bars are now common in the larger cities and towns, and the latter will often have a 'happy hour' (when prices are reduced) in the early evening. Under 18's may not be served with alcohol and children under 16 are not generally allowed into pubs, although they may sit in the garden. Licensing hours vary from Monday to Saturday but many pubs, especially in main centres, are open typically 1100-2300; the visitor should not be surprised however if he finds a pub closing for a period in the afternoon. On Sundays, hours are 1200-1500 and 1900-2230. Private clubs often have an extension to these hours.

NIGHTLIFE: The main cities, London in particular, have a vast range to choose from: theatre (including open-air in the summer), opera, ballet, concerts, films, restaurants, nightclubs and discotheques, as well as, of course, pubs. In the provinces the choice is not as great. The weekly magazine *Time Out* publishes a comprehensive guide to the events in the capital.

SHOPPING: Woollen and woven goods such as *Harris Tweeds* are famous. Printed cottons and silks are to be found, as well as fashionable ready-made clothes. China and porcelain *Wedgwood, Crown Derby, Royal Worcester* and *Royal Doulton* are good buys, as are luxury food and chocolates. Antiques are to be found all over the country. In London, Charing Cross Road is

famous for bookshops, and there are the street markets: Petticoat Lane for clothes and Bermondsey for antiques, to name just two. **Tax Free Shopping:** Many shops throughout the country now operate a tax-free shopping scheme for overseas visitors. The store will provide a form which should be completed at the time of purchase. Upon arrival at Customs, present the goods and the forms (within three months) to the Customs Officer, who will stamp the vouchers certifying that the goods are being exported, and that you will be entitled to a refund of Value Added Tax. For further information contact the British Tourist Office which will be able to supply details. **Shopping hours:** In major cities 0900-1730 Monday to Saturday; in London's West End and other large shopping centres, shops stay open to 2000. Many local shops stay open to 1900 or 2000 and some even later; many of these are open on Sunday mornings or all day. Some towns and areas of cities may have early closing one day a week, usually Wednesday or Thursday.

SPORTS: Golf, tennis, squash, riding, sailing and **swimming** are all possible. Swimmers should be warned that the sea is invigorating rather than warm. In Cornwall there are some opportunities for **surfing.** Spectator sports include **horseracing** (both flat and steeplechasing, according to the season); **rugby; football** from mid-August to April (there are 92 first-class clubs in England and Wales); **tennis** (particularly at Wimbledon); and **cricket,** 17 counties have first-class cricket teams playing from April to September. The most famous ground is Lords' in north London, the home of cricket.

SPECIAL EVENTS: The following is a selection of the major festivals and other special events celebrated annually in England. For a complete list contact the English Tourist Board.

Throughout 1995: *Purcell Tercentenary Festival,* countrywide. **Mar 16-19 '95** *Crufts Dog Show,* London. **Mar 16-Apr 9** *Daily Mail Ideal Home Exhibition,* London. **Apr 1** *Oxford and Cambridge University Boat Race,* London. **Apr 2** *London Marathon.* **May 1-Jan '96** *Shakespeare Festival Season,* Stratford-upon-Avon. **May 5-28** *Brighton International Festival.* **May 20** *FA Challenge Cup Final,* Wembley, London. **May 23-26** *Chelsea Flower Show,* London. **May 27-28** *Air Fête '95,* Bury St Edmunds, Suffolk. **Jun 8-14** *Appleby Horse Fair,* Cumbria. **Jun 17** *Trooping the Colour (The Queen's Official Birthday Parade),* London. **Jun 20-Jul 7** *City of London Festival.* **Jun 26-Jul 9** *Lawn Tennis Championships,* Wimbledon, London. **Jun 28-Jul 2** *Henley Royal Regatta,* Henley-on-Thames. **Jul 21-Sep 16** *Henry Wood Promenade Concerts,* Royal Albert Hall, London. **Aug 27-28** *Notting Hill Carnival,* London. **Sep 9-11** *International Sheepdog Trials,* Armathwaite, Cumbria. **Sep 16-24** *Southampton International Boat Show.* **Oct 5-7** *Nottingham Goose Fair.* **Nov 5** *London to Brighton Veteran Car Run.* **Nov 11** *Lord Mayor's Procession and Show,* London. **Feb '96** *Jorvik Festival,* York. **Mar** *Crufts Dog Show,* London; *Ideal Home Exhibition,* London; *Oxford and Cambridge University Boat Race,* London; *Leeds International Concert Season.* **Apr** *Harrogate International Youth Music Festival.*

CLIMATE

The climate is temperate with warm wet summers and cool wet winters. It is variable from day to day and throughout the country as a whole. The west coast and mountainous areas receive the most rain; the east coast, particularly in the north, is colder and windier. The southeast is sunnier than the north with less rain and a climate approaching the continental. The southwest has overall the mildest climate.

Required clothing: European according to season, plus rainwear.

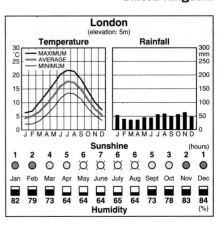

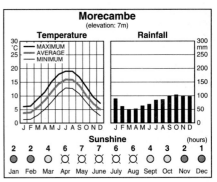

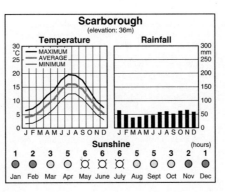

Location: Northern part of Great Britain.

Scottish Tourist Board
23 Ravelston Terrace, Edinburgh EH4 3EU
Tel: (0131) 332 2433. Fax: (0131) 315 2906. Telex: 72272.

AREA: 77,772 sq km (30,414 sq miles).
POPULATION: 5,111,200 (1992 estimate).
POPULATION DENSITY: 66.2 per sq km.
CAPITAL: Edinburgh. **Population:** 439,000 (1992 estimate).
GEOGRAPHY: The country consists of the southern Lowland area, a region of moorland and pastoral scenery – where most of the population is concentrated – and the

Northern Highlands, dominated by the Grampian Mountains and Ben Nevis, the highest peak in the British Isles. The whole of the exceedingly beautiful coastline is indented with lochs (particularly in the north and west). Off the west coast there are many islands, the largest of which are Skye and Lewis, the latter being part of the Outer Hebrides. The Orkney and Shetland Islands lie to the northeast of the Scottish mainland, across the Pentland Firth from John O'Groats.
LANGUAGE: English. Gaelic is still spoken by some, mostly in the West and Highlands.
Note: *For information on time, electricity, communications, passport/visa, duty free, money and health, see general UK entry above.*

PUBLIC HOLIDAYS

Public holidays observed in Scotland are similar to those observed in the rest of the UK (*see the general entry above*), with the addition of:
Jan 3 '95 Bank Holiday. **May 1** May Day. **Aug 7** Bank Holiday. **Dec 31** *Hogmanay* (New Year's Eve, celebrated with particular fervour in Scotland). **Jan 1-2 '96** Bank Holiday.

TRAVEL

AIR: Scotland's main international airports are *Edinburgh* and *Glasgow*.
Edinburgh (EDI): Located 11km (7 miles) west of the city centre. Airport information: (0131) 333 1000.
Facilities include duty free; general and specialist shops; tourist information; hotel reservations service; bureau de change, emergency first-aid facilities, parent and baby room; *Gingham's* restaurant, *Costa* coffee boutique, *Uppercrust* and *Café* select bars; conference facilities for 30; facilities for the disabled – toilets, wheelchairs, induction loops, telephones, swivel seats in some taxis.
Train/bus: *Airlink* bus 100 operates from the airport to Waverley Bridge 0745-2230 Monday to Friday, half hourly at peak times. Weekend services are less frequent, and operate 1020-2230. Further details are available from *Lothian Region Transport* on (0131) 220 4411. *Guide Friday Airbus* operates from the airport to Waverley Bridge 0825-2040 Monday to Friday, half hourly at peak times. Weekend services operate 0835-1935 (2035 on Sunday). Further details are available from *Guide Friday* on (0131) 556 2244. **Taxi:** Available from the rank outside the airport (travel time to city centre – 25 minutes). **Car hire:** *Avis, Hertz, Europcar* and *Alamo* self-drive and chauffeur-driven cars can be hired from desks within the terminal. **Private car:** The A8 runs direct to the airport from the city centre. If coming from the west or north follow the signs on the M9, M8 and A90.
Glasgow (GLA): Located 14kms (9 miles) west of the city centre. Airport information: (0141) 887 1111.
Facilities include 24-hour emergency medical services, left luggage (0600-2200), general shops, pharmacy (24-hour), post office (0900-1300 and 1400-1730 Monday to Friday, 0900-1300 Saturday), buffet (24-hour), *Garfunkels* (second floor – snack bar/restaurant), *The Tap and Spile* (first floor – Scottish beers, real ales and snacks), *Costa* coffee boutiques (first floor and International Arrivals area), *The Granary* (second floor – open 24 hours – snacks, salads, soup, hot-plate selection), duty-free shop, hotel reservation service, conference facilities for 40 (tel: (0141) 887 1111) and facilities for the disabled – wheelchairs, toilets and telephones. **Train:** Paisley's Gilmour Street station is 3km (2 miles) from the airport. Services run every 15 minutes from 0630-2346 Monday to Saturday, every 30 minutes 0925-2348 Sunday (travel time – 10 minutes). Main-line connections are available to most parts of the country. *British Rail:* (0141) 204 2844. **Coach:** *Airlink* services 160 and 180 (Clydeside) coach link from the airport to Paisley's Gilmore Street runs every 10 minutes in the day and every 30 minutes in the evening 0605-2315 (travel time – 10 minutes). *Scottish Citylink* service 500 runs from the airport to Glasgow and Edinburgh via the M8. Travel time to Edinburgh is 1 hour 50 minutes (20 minutes to Glasgow city centre). **Bus:** Services 500 and 502 *Scottish City Link* to city centre Monday to Saturday every 30 minutes, every hour in the evening 0625-2355 and every hour 0755-2255 Sunday. Bus information: (0141) 332 9191. **Local bus:** Regular service to Renfrew and Paisley. **Taxi:** To the city centre is 20 minutes; to Paisley BR station is 5 minutes. Taxis are available from the rank on the terminal forecourt. **Car hire:** *Alamo, Avis, Europcar* and *Hertz* have desks outside International Arrivals. **Private car:** The M8 runs direct to the airport from the city centre. Car parking space is available for 2000 cars.
Other airports: *Inverness (INV)* is the major airport serving the Highlands, with transfer connections available to airports in the north of Scotland.
There are several smaller airports in the north of Scotland which are served by flights from Glasgow and, in some cases, from Aberdeen, Inverness and Edinburgh as well. These include *Kirkwall* (Orkney), *Lerwick* (Shetland), *Tiree, Stornoway, Benbecula* and *Barra.* For further information, contact Glasgow Airport. Tel: (0141) 887 1111.
SEA: Ferry services operate between the mainland and all the Scottish islands but some of these will be infrequent. *Caledonian MacBrayne* operates the largest network of ferries on the river Clyde and west coast, serving 23 islands including the Inner and Outer Hebrides. During the summer, services often operate hourly or half-hourly but in the winter they are less frequent. For details of fares, routes and timetables contact *Gourock.* Tel: (01475) 650 100. Fax: (01475) 650 000. *P&O Ferries* operate services to the Orkneys and Shetlands; from Aberdeen to Lerwick up to three times a week (travel time – 14 hours); and from Scrabster to Stromness up to 11 times a week (travel time – 2 hours). Tel: (01224) 572 615. Fax: (01224) 574 411.
Other routes include *P&O's* service between Cairnryan and Larne up to five times a day (travel time – 2 hours 20 minutes); and *Sealink's* service between Stranraer and Larne eight times a day (travel time – 2 hours 15 minutes). *Seacat* have opened a new route between Stranraer and Belfast Harbour five times a day and four crossings daily during the low season (travel time – 1 hour 30 minutes). Tel: (0345) 523 523. Fax: (01776) 702 355.
RAIL: There are two main-line routes into Scotland from England: from London, Euston up the west coast to Glasgow Central and beyond to Perth and Inverness; and from London, King's Cross up the east coast to Edinburgh, Waverley and beyond to Dundee and Aberdeen. Tel: (0171) 387 7070 (Euston) *or* 278 2477 (King's Cross). Particularly in the Edinburgh-Glasgow area, there are good services connecting all the main towns. Many of the routes which pass through the Highlands (such as the Perth to Inverness, Inverness to Kyle of Lochalsh and the Glasgow to Mallaig via Fort William) are very spectacular. The network extends right up to Thurso and Wick in the extreme north of the country. Sleeper services are available on Intercity routes from England.
ROAD: Scotland is connected to the main UK road network by good trunk roads, and has several internal motorways. Main access from England is via the A74 (Carlisle to Glasgow), the A696/A68 (Newcastle to Edinburgh via the Cheviots) and the A1 (Newcastle to Edinburgh via the coast). The main motorways within Scotland connect Edinburgh with Glasgow (M8), Edinburgh with Stirling (M9), and the Forth Bridge, near Edinburgh, with Perth (M90). In general, the internal trunk road network is better and more direct on the east coast, and roads north of Inverness tend to be slower and often single track. Driving in winter in the Highland areas can be dangerous and motorists are advised to follow local advice concerning weather conditions. The main cross-country road, the A9, connects Perth with Inverness and Thurso.
Car hire: Self-drive cars are widely available in the major centres. The Scottish Tourist Board will be able to supply a list of companies in each area.
Distances: *From London:* Edinburgh 610km (378 miles), Glasgow 640km (397 miles), Aberdeen 810km (503 miles), Inverness 860km (536 miles), Fort William 640km (398 miles), Perth 670km (415 miles) and Thurso 1945km (651 miles).
From Edinburgh: Glasgow 65km (42 miles), Aberdeen 200km (125 miles), Inverness 255km (158 miles), Fort William 235km (146 miles), Perth 70km (44 miles) and Thurso 450km (278 miles).
URBAN: All the major towns and cities have bus services. Glasgow also has an underground and a suburban train network.

ACCOMMODATION

The Scottish Tourist Board publishes a series of *Where to Stay* guides covering hotels and guest-houses, bed & breakfast, self-catering and camping and caravanning, for which there is a charge plus postage and packing.
There is a wide range of accommodation available in Scotland, with many hotels having been built, modernised or refurbished during the last few years. There are many guest-houses and bed & breakfast premises throughout Scotland.
Since 1985 the Scottish Tourist Board has operated the official scheme for accommodation assessment in Scotland, annually inspecting nearly 6000 hotels, guest-houses, bed & breakfast and self-catering holiday homes. Establishments have their facilities and services measured using the Crown Classification criteria and their quality and conditions are reflected in the Quality Grade. Classification ranges from the minimum *(Listed),*

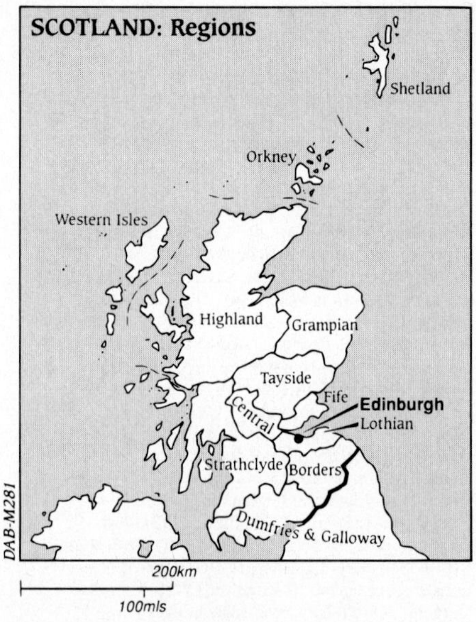
SCOTLAND: Regions
Shetland
Orkney
Western Isles
Highland
Grampian
Tayside
Fife
Edinburgh
Lothian
Central
Strathclyde
Borders
Dumfries & Galloway
DAB-M281
200km
100mls

and thereafter from *1* to *5 Crowns;* the Quality Grades are: *Approved, Commended, Highly Commended* and *Deluxe.* In addition there are three categories of Disability Access also awarded by the Scottish Tourist Board. They are: Unassisted Wheelchair Access for Residents, Assisted Wheelchair Access for Residents and Access for Residents with mobility difficulties. The Scottish Tourist Board also operates the annual British Graded Holiday Parks Scheme and Thistle Awards Scheme. The former denotes the overall quality standard of a park through use of *1* to 5 *Tick* symbols and the Thistle Award reflects the highest quality standard of the individual units on a 4- or 5-Tick park.

RESORTS & EXCURSIONS

Scotland is a beautiful and sparsely populated country with rolling lowland, dramatic mountains, lochs and many offshore islands.
For further information on the many historical properties in Scotland, please contact either of the following organisations:
The National Trust for Scotland, 5 Charlotte Square, Edinburgh EH2 4DU. Tel: (0131) 226 5922. Fax: (0131) 243 9501; *or*
Historic Scotland, Longmore House, Salisbury Place, Edinburgh EH9 1SH. Tel: (0131) 668 8600. Fax: (0131) 668 8888.

Edinburgh

One of the most beautiful cities in Great Britain, Edinburgh is the social and cultural centre of Scotland. *Edinburgh Castle,* Scotland's number one tourist attraction and home to the Scottish Crown Jewels, sits at the head of the Royal Mile which stretches down to the *Palace of Holyroodhouse,* the Queen's official residence in Scotland. Attractions such at *St Giles Cathedral, John Knox House,* the *Scotch Whisky Heritage Centre* and the *Camera Obscura* pepper the **Old Town** along with galleries and museums.
In contrast to the narrow streets of Old Town, Edinburgh's **New Town** is an elegant series of wide streets, crescents and squares offering the best examples of Georgian architecture in Britain.
Edinburgh is also the home of Scotland's National Galleries and Royal Museums, including the *National Gallery of Scotland,* the *Scottish National Portrait Gallery,* the *Scottish National Gallery of Modern Art* and the *National Museum of Antiquities.*
Edinburgh's cultural life continues after dark with a programme of theatre, music and dance unrivalled outside London.
The city boasts Britain's largest stage and largest theatre in the new *Festival Theatre* and the *Edinburgh Playhouse* respectively. These and other venues are used to the full during the three weeks of August's festival, bringing the best of every conceivable art form to Edinburgh to create the world's largest arts festival. The season starts off with the spectacular *Military Tattoo,* taking up residence on the Castle Esplanade in early August delighting thousands during its 3-week run.
Attractions close to Edinburgh include the resort of **Aberdour; Dunfermline,** whose abbey is the burial

EDINBURGH

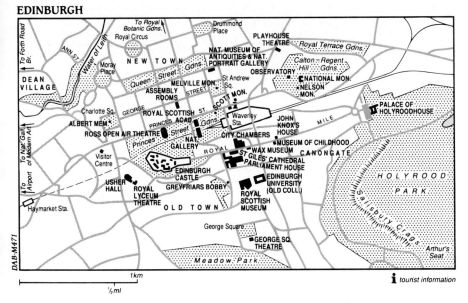

1km

½ml

i *tourist information*

ABERDEEN

1. TOWN HOUSE & TOLBOOTH
2. PROVOST ROSS'S HOUSE
3. PROVOST SKENE'S HOUSE
4. JAMES DUN'S HOUSE
5. ST NICHOLAS'S KIRK

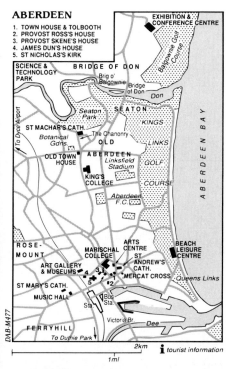

2km

1ml

i *tourist information*

GLASGOW

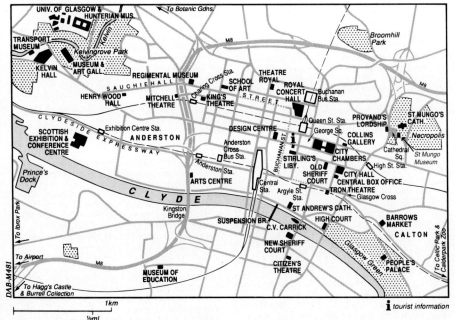

1km

½ml

i *tourist information*

14th-century bridge, the *Brig O'Balgownie*. Nearby **Braemar** is the site of the most famous of the highland gatherings. There are several National Trust properties within easy reach of Aberdeen, including *Fyvie Castle* and *Castle Fraser*. Continuing north to **Peterhead** and **Fraserburgh**, the coastal trail goes through charming fishing villages, then further northwards along the Moray Firth to the Georgian town of **Banff** and magnificent *Duff House* where part of the reserve collection of the National Galleries can be seen. Further along this coastline is **Elgin** which has a ruined cathedral and a well-restored abbey church. **Inverness** is the northernmost large town in the country; many of the buildings date back to the 17th century. Inverness is also famous for being situated at the head of *Loch Ness*, the deep-water home of the elusive monster. Nearby is the site of the *Battle of Culloden* where the forces of Bonnie Prince Charlie were crushed in 1746. There are many highland gatherings and games in this region. Beyond Inverness, the countryside consists mainly of moorlands, glens and forests and is the last remaining home of some of Britain's once common indigenous animals, including red deer, wildcats and golden eagles. Most of the towns in this area are little more than villages, and include *Golspie, Ullapool* and *Lybster, near* which are several neolithic tombs. The towns of **Thurso** and **Wick** mark the end of the railway line. **John O'Groats**, due north of Wick, is the northern-most village on the British mainland.

Glasgow

Glasgow is Scotland's largest and liveliest city. It enjoys a well earned reputation as one of Europe's most dynamic cultural centres with a variety of exciting events taking place year-round – and of course the world-famous *Burrell Collection* and the recently opened *Glasgow Royal Concert Hall*. Glasgow was the 1990 Cultural Capital of Europe. It has some fine parks and the only complete medieval cathedral in Scotland (containg the tomb of St Mungo). A short ride away from George Square is *Kelvingrove Park;* the art gallery there has paintings by some of the most famous Renaissance and modern painters. The city is home to Scottish Opera, Scottish Ballet, the Royal Scottish National Orchestra and many theatre companies.

Attractions near Glasgow include *Ayr*, on the coast, and **Alloway**, the birthplace of Robert Burns and, on a cliff overlooking the Firth of Clyde, *Culzean Castle,* once the home of the American Kennedy family. Another lowland place of interest is *Loch Lomond*. On the way north from Glasgow is the ancient town of **Stirling** which boasts a fine castle in a very dramatic location. Nearby is the site of the Battle of Bannockburn where Robert the Bruce inflicted humiliating defeat on the English. A little further north is the castle of **Doon**. The hills of of the **Trossachs** can be reached via the town of **Callendar**.

Dumfries, Galloway & the Borders

These regions are the southernmost in Scotland. Much of their area is lowland, rising in the north towards the Southern Uplands. The **Borders** area was the setting for many of the battles which were regularly fought between Scotland and England through the centuries. It is a region of lush green hills and moorlands, occasionally pitted with valleys, gorges and roaring waterfalls. The area's wealth allowed the construction of several outstanding ecclesiastical buildings, notably the abbeys at *Jedburgh, Dryburgh* and *Melrose*. The ancient border towns of **Selkirk**, **Galashiels**, **Peebles** and **Hawick** are still the centre of a thriving wool, tweed and knitwear industry. **Abbotsford** in this area was the home of Sir Walter Scott.

The region of **Dumfries** and **Galloway** consists of open, undulating countryside, lakes and pine forests. Towns such as **Dumfries**, home of Robert Burns; **Kirkcudbright**, a former artist's colony; and the charming market town of **Gatehouse of Fleet** are all popular centres. Country houses, castles, gardens and special interest museums can be found wherever one goes. Quiet country roads, quality accommodation to suit any cost, and local crafts and craftsmen at work all add to the enjoyment of a visit.

The Highlands & the West Coast

The **Scottish Highlands** contain probably the most breathtaking scenery in the British Isles. Railway and road traverse the countryside between the capital and Inverness, passing through the *Grampian Mountains* and the *Forest of Atholl*. The lochs of the central highlands feed the *River Tay*, one of the best fishing rivers in the British Isles. Also in the Highlands are the *Pass of Killiecrankie*, *Blair Atholl*, *Kingussie* and *Aviemore*, the winter skiing resort.

---

place of several Scottish kings; *Blackness, Dunbar* and *Tantallon* castles; and the old village of **Dalmeny.**

The East Coast

St Andrews, north of Edinburgh in Fife, is the home of golf. In addition, the town has a university, castle and cathedral. The *Lammas Fair* takes place in August. Across the Firth of Tay is the city of **Dundee**. Dundee, City of Discovery and Scotland's fastest growing tourist attraction, is home to Scotland's premier *Visitor Centre Discovery Point* based around Captain Scott's exploration ship, *Royal Research Discovery*, which lies alongside. Some 25km (15 miles) to the north is **Glamis**, whose castle was featured in Shakespeare's Macbeth and was the birthplace of Princess Margaret. West of Dundee is **Perth**. King James I, one of Scotland's most able rulers, was murdered here, and John Knox preached one of his earliest sermons in the town. **Scone**, where all of Scotland's kings were crowned, is a few kilometres away and was the centre of the Pictish Kingdom. This area was also the northernmost to be occupied by the Romans in an earlier era. Up the coast from Dundee is **Carnoustie**, world-known in golfing circles. Next is **Arbroath**, which has a famous ruined *Abbey* and a remarkable fishing heritage. To the north, the town of **Montrose** is noted for its fine broad streets and sandy beaches. 56km (35 miles) north of Montrose is **Aberdeen**, Scotland's third city, built largely of granite. Aberdeen is the centre of Britain's North Sea Oil industry. The city itself has a 16th-century cathedral, a 15th-century university and a

The West Coast has some pretty coastal resorts and also some exceedingly beautiful scenery, particularly the mainland opposite Skye.

Fort William is one of the best-known towns on this coast, as well as one of the largest. Nearby is **Glencoe** where the Campbells deviously and treacherously massacred the Macdonald clan in their sleep; when shrouded in mist, Glencoe still has an ominous air about it. At the mouth of *Loch Linnhe* is **Oban**, the gateway to many of the islands and the beautiful region of *Kintyre*. To the east of Kintyre is the island of **Arran**, while to the west are **Islay** and **Jura**. **Iona**, the burial place of many Scottish kings and chiefs, **Mull** and the **Western Isles** can be visited from Oban. Further north is the town of **Mallaig** which, like Oban, is situated at the end of a railway line from Glasgow. Separated from the mainland by the *Sound of Sleat* and the *Inner Sound* is the **Isle of Skye**, which can be reached from Mallaig or **Kyle of Lochalsh** (also on the railway). The town of **Ullapool** is still an important fishing port, and is also the departure point for car ferries to the **Isle of Lewis** in the Outer Hebrides. North of Ullapool, the road passes through the beautiful **Inverpolly Nature Reserve** into Sutherland, and the landscape becomes even wilder with isolated mountains rising starkly out of a rocky plateau. The rugged west and north coastlines are studded with fishing villages and crofting townships – **Lochinver, Scourie, Kinlochbervie, Durness, Tongue** and **Melvich** are all worth visiting – as are the many clean beaches that are sandwiched between cliffs and headlands. Inland is one of Europe's last great wildernesses, an area of mountains, moorland, lochs and rivers, rich in wildlife. Travelling along the coast, the road skirts around several lochs passing towns such as Durness and Melvich, before reaching **Thurso**, embarkation point for ferries to the Orkney Islands.

The Orkney & Shetland Islands

These two island groups lie northeast of the Scottish mainland, and can be reached by air or sea. See the *Travel* section above.

Orkney: 67 islands, 20 of which are inhabited, the Orkneys are separated from the mainland by the Pentland Firth. The islands are fertile although with very few trees, and enjoy a predominantly mild, variable climate. The main town, situated on the island known as Mainland, is **Kirkwall**, boasting an impressive 12th-century cathedral and many other places of interest. The islands are rich in archaeological remains, including the Stone Age village of **Skara Brae**, the *Maes Howe* burial mound, and the standing stones at the *Ring of Brogar*. On the other side of Scapa Flow is the island of **Hoy**, whose sheer cliffs and windswept sandstone landscape make it one of the most dramatic islands of the Orkney group. Other islands of interest include **Westray** and **South Ronaldsay**. The islands are of particular interest to birdwatchers and sea anglers.

Birds are also the main attraction on **Fair Isle,** between the Orkneys and the Shetlands. It is owned by the National Trust for Scotland, who should be contacted by anyone planning a visit (tel: (0131) 226 5922). It is served by air and sea from both the Orkneys and Shetlands.

Shetland: This group of 100 rugged, hilly and heather-rich islands is located at the most northerly point of Britain. Their climate is surprisingly mild considering their northerly latitude (the same as St Petersburg, Hudson Bay and Southern Alaska). The largest island (also called Mainland) is indented by fjords and inlets. The chief town of **Lerwick** relied in former days almost solely on fishing but now, like most parts of the Shetlands and Orkneys, has benefited from the North Sea oil boom. Other places of interest include the Bronze Age settlement at **Jarlshof**, the island of **Foula**, the nature reserve on the island of **Noss**, **Mousa Broch** on the uninhabited island of **Mousa**, and, reputedly, the most northern castle in the world on the island of **Unst**. All the islands in the group can be reached from Lerwick and, like the Orkneys, their main attraction is their unique Scandinavian heritage, their birdlife and outstanding loch and sea fishing. Weather conditions can change suddenly and local advice should be sought and heeded.

POPULAR ITINERARIES: 5-day: Glasgow–Stirling–Doon–Callendar–Trossachs–Edinburgh. **7-day:** Glasgow–Oban–Mull–Skye–Glencoe–Loch Ness.

SOCIAL PROFILE

FOOD & DRINK: In the main cities and towns, a wide variety of British and continental food is available. Local dishes include *haggis* (chopped oatmeal and offal cooked in the stomach of a sheep), *cullen skink* (fish soup), smoked haddock and salmon and *partan bree* (crab with rice and cream). Baked food such as cakes and biscuits are exceedingly popular and some of the more famous

are flat pancake-type scones, oatcakes and *black bun,* a fruit cake on a pastry base. **Drink:** Scotch whisky is the national drink, and is famous the world over. There are also many local beers, known as *light* and *heavy,* as well as lager. Licensing hours are subject to greater variation than in England; some pubs may be open from 1030-2400, others only 1130-1430 and 1830-2300.

NIGHTLIFE: In major cities there are many bars, restaurants, nightclubs, theatres and cinemas. Nightlife may be more limited in the smaller villages and islands.

SPORT: Golf is one of the most popular national sports and St Andrew's has arguably the finest course in the world. Gleneagles and Troon are also excellent. **Fishing** is popular throughout the country and the salmon fishing in particular is widely regarded as being among the best in the world. **Spectator sports** include **rugby** and **football**. The Scottish countryside is also ideal for **birdwatching, walking** and **pony trekking**. There are also several **winter sports** centres, notably at Glencoe, the Nevis Range, Glenshee, The Lecht and Aviemore, in the Cairngorms.

SPECIAL EVENTS: The highlight of the cultural year in Scotland is the *Edinburgh Festival*, which runs during the last two weeks of August and the first week of September. Almost every room in the city large enough to hold an audience is in use during this time, and it is possible to see as many as ten shows in one day; these might range from a short open-air concert to a full-scale production by the RSC or the LSO. Accommodation in Edinburgh is booked up months in advance at this time. There are also many Highland Games during the summer, which include caber-tossing and hammer-throwing competitions. The following is a selection of other events in Scotland (for a complete list contact the Scottish Tourist Board):

Mar 31-Apr 17 '95 *Edinburgh International Science Festival.* **Apr 19-24** *Kirkcaldy Links Market.* **Apr 28-30** *Girvan Folk Festival.* **Apr 28-May 20** *Mayfest,* Glasgow. **May 27-28** *Scottish Beer Festival,* Innerleithen. **May 28** *Blair Atholl International Highland Games.* **Jun 22-25** *Royal Highland Show,* Edinburgh. **Jun 30-Jul 9** *Glasgow International Jazz Festival.* **Jul 15-18** *Cutty Sark Tall Ships Race,* Leith, Edinburgh. **Aug 4-26** *Military Tattoo,* Edinburgh. **Aug 5-12** *Edinburgh International Jazz Festival.* **Aug 12** *World Pipe Band Championships,* Glasgow. **Aug 13-Sep 2** *Edinburgh International Festival.* **Aug 24** *Argyllshire Gathering,* Oban. **Aug 25-26** *Cowal Highland Gathering,* Dunoon. **Sep 2** *Braemar Highland Gathering.* **Oct 5-Nov 5** *Fotofeis '95,* countrywide. **Oct 13-20** *Royal National MOD,* Golspie, Sutherland. **Dec 30 '95-Jan 1 '96** *Edinburgh's Hogmanay.*
Note: Some of the above dates are provisional.

BUSINESS PROFILE

BUSINESS: See main UK entry above.
CONFERENCES/CONVENTIONS: In 1988 the Greater Glasgow Tourist Board and Convention Bureau was voted the UK's Best Convention Bureau by organisers. The Scottish Tourist Board has a number of publications for conference organisers. For information contact the Scottish Convention Bureau, c/o Scottish Tourist Board, 23 Ravelston Terrace, Edinburgh EH4 3EU. Tel: (0131) 343 1608. Fax: (0131) 343 1844.
Note: See the general UK section for other business information.

CLIMATE

Scotland is rarely much colder than England, despite its more northerly latitude. The west tends to be wetter and warmer than the cool dry east. On upland areas snow is common in winter, and fog and mist may occur at any time of year.
Required clothing: Similar to the rest of the UK, according to season. Waterproofing advised throughout the year and warm clothing for the Highlands.

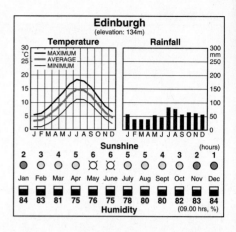

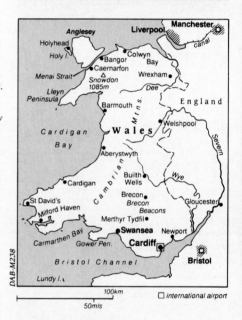

Location: Western Great Britain.

Wales Tourist Board
Brunel House, 2 Fitzalan Road, Cardiff CF2 1UY
Tel: (01222) 499 909. Fax: (01222) 485 031.
Wales Tourist Board
c/o British Tourist Authority, 7th Floor, 551 Fifth Avenue, New York, NY 10176
Tel: (212) 986 2200 *or* 986 2266. Fax: (212) 986 1188.
Wales Tourist Board
c/o British Tourist Authority, Suite 450, 111 Avenue Road, Toronto, Ontario M5R 3J8
Tel: (416) 925 6326. Fax: (416) 961 2175.

AREA: 20,766 sq km (8017 sq miles).
POPULATION: 2,886,400 (1991 estimate).
POPULATION DENSITY: 139 per sq km.
CAPITAL: Cardiff. **Population:** 290,000 (1991 estimate).
GEOGRAPHY: Wales is a country of great geographical variation with many long stretches of attractive and often rugged coastline. South Wales is mainly known for its industrial heritage but the western part of the coast between Carmarthen Bay and St David's is similar to that of the more pastoral west country of England, and backed by some equally beautiful countryside. The scenery of mid-Wales includes rich farming valleys, the broad sandy sweep of Cardigan Bay and rolling hill country. North Wales is one of the most popular tourist areas in the British Isles, with many lively coastal resorts. Inland, the region of Snowdonia has long been popular with walkers and climbers. Much of the central inland area of the country is mountainous, with some breathtaking scenery.
LANGUAGE: English, but at least a fifth of the

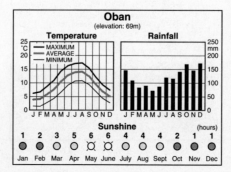

population also speak Welsh.
Note: *For information on time, electricity, communications, passport/visa, money and business see the general UK section above.*

PUBLIC HOLIDAYS

Public holidays observed in Wales are the same as in England.

TRAVEL

AIR: Wales' international airport is ***Cardiff Wales Airport (CWL).*** **Facilities** include free-flow buffet and bar, bureau de change, duty-free, news and gift shop, restaurant, medical room and first aid, and facilities for the disabled. Airport Information: (01446) 711 111, ext 2201. **Train:** Local buses link the airport with Cardiff Central station, which is 19km (12 miles) away. The station is served by the Intercity network and regional lines, including a fast service to London Paddington. Tel: (01222) 228 000. **Coach:** Regular coach services operate to Cardiff Central Bus Station from London Victoria and other major destinations with connections to the rest of the country. **Local bus:** A local bus no. X51 runs from Cardiff bus station to the airport on an hourly basis. **Taxi:** Available through local operator *Cardiff Airport Taxis*. Tel: (01446) 710 693. **Car hire:** *Europcar Interrent* has an office at the airport. Tel: (01222) 497 111. **Private car:** Cardiff is reached on the M4 from London, exiting at Junction 33 and following the signs. Car-parking facilities are available at the airport for short- and long-term stays.
SEA: The main ports are Pembroke Dock and Fishguard (Dyfed) and Holyhead (Anglesey), all of which have ferry connections to the Republic of Ireland.
RAIL: There are two main-line routes into Wales. One runs from London Paddington to Fishguard along the south Wales coast (branching at Whitland to serve Haverfordwest and Milford Haven), while the other links Holyhead with Chester and northeast England. In addition, the line from Cardiff to Chester (via Newport, Hereford and Shrewsbury) links the south Wales cities with Abergavenny in Gwent to Wrexham in Clwyd. There are also two smaller cross-country lines: these run from Shrewsbury to Welshpool, Aberystwyth, Barmouth, Harlech, Porthmadog and Pwllheli; and from Craven Arms (on the Shrewsbury to Ludlow line) through Llandrindod Wells and Llandovery down to the south coast to Swansea.
There are also a large number of local steam railways, rescued by railway enthusiasts during the Beeching era, known collectively as *The Great Little Trains of Wales.* The most famous of these is the one at Ffestiniog at Porthmadog in Snowdonia, which has lovingly restored locomotives and carriages from the last century. Others include the Welshpool and Llanfair Railway (in north Powys), the Fairbourne and Talyllyn Railways (both near Barmouth in Cardigan Bay) and the Bala Lake Railway. Wanderers' Tickets are available, giving access to all the railways for a specific period. For further information, contact The Great Little Trains of Wales, c/o Welshpool and Llanfair Railway, Llanfair, Caereinion Station, Welshpool, Powys SY21 0SF. Tel: (01938) 810 441.
ROAD: The best road approach to Wales from southern England is via the M4 motorway, which runs from west London to Newport, Cardiff and Swansea, almost to Carmarthen. The A5 links London and the Midlands with the ferry port of Holyhead, and the A55 links Holyhead with Chester. The best cross-country road is probably the A44/A470 from Oxford to Aberystwyth. Many of the smaller roads are slow, and in upland areas may become impassable during bad weather.
Distances: From London to *Cardiff* is 250km (157 miles), to *Fishguard* is 420km (260 miles), to *Holyhead* is 430km (268 miles) and to *Aberystwyth* is 340km (210 miles).
URBAN: All the main cities have local bus services. There is a good network of local train services radiating from Cardiff.

ACCOMMODATION

HOTELS: All hotels are inspected by Wales Tourist Board agents. **Grading:** Hotels in Wales are subject to the Wales Tourist Board's 'crown' classification scheme – which is part of the UK-wide classification scheme. The higher the crown rating, the greater the range of equipment, facilities and services on offer. The system is not intended as a guide to quality but only to show the level of facilities provided at each hotel. All hotels participating in this scheme are inspected annually. Further information may be obtained from the brochures produced by the Wales Tourist Board (tel: (01222) 499 909). In addition, the Board's north, mid- and south Wales regional offices have lists of accommodation available in their areas. For north Wales, tel: (01492) 531 731; mid-Wales, tel: (01654) 702 653; and south Wales, tel: (01792) 781 212.
SELF-CATERING: There is a very wide range of self-catering accommodation, ranging from holiday villages in or near popular coastal resorts to remote cottages in the mountains of Snowdonia. Contact the regional offices referred to above for an up-to-date list. **Grading:** Accommodation is graded on a scale of 1 to 5 as follows: **1** – Standard. **2** – Approved. **3** – Good. **4** – Very good. **5** – Excellent.
CAMPING/CARAVANNING: There are over 300 caravan parks in the country, both permanent and touring parks, and all sites referred to in accommodation lists or brochures supplied by tourist offices will meet certain minimum requirements. There are many campsites throughout the country. **Grading:** Sites are graded with from 1 to 5 'Q's reflecting quality, neatness and cleanliness but not necessarily facilities.

RESORTS & EXCURSIONS

Wales may be divided into three areas: South Wales, containing the capital Cardiff, the cities of Swansea and Newport, Carmarthen Bay and the Brecon Beacons; Mid-Wales, with the Cambrian Mountains and the attractive coastal resorts of Cardigan Bay; and North Wales, with the popular resorts of Llandudno and Rhyl, the island of Anglesey and the Snowdonia National Park, containing *Mount Snowdon,* the highest mountain in Wales. Cardiff is connected to London by road, rail and air and is a convenient starting point for a journey through Wales from south to north.

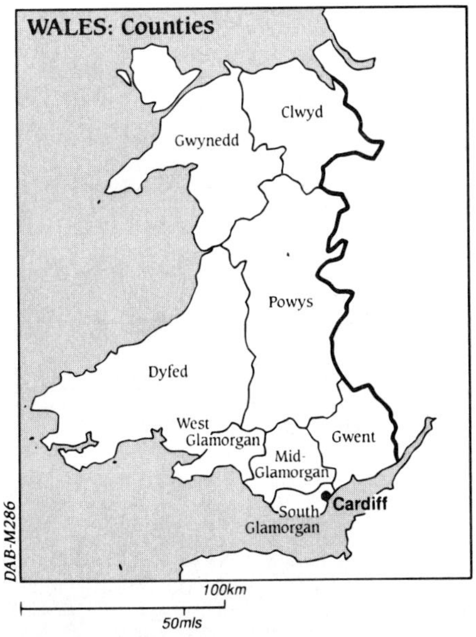
WALES: Counties
Clwyd
Gwynedd
Powys
Dyfed
West Glamorgan
Gwent
Mid Glamorgan
South Glamorgan
Cardiff
DAB-M286
100km
50mls

South Wales

Cardiff is the principality's capital and principal seaport. The castle, much of which dates back to the Middle Ages, was extensively added to during the 19th century, thus creating a strongly Victorian Gothic result. Cardiff also houses the *National Museum of Wales*, with Welsh archaeology, arts and crafts as well as European paintings. 8km (5 miles) west of Cardiff is **St Fagans** with its open-air *Welsh Folk Museum.*
Travelling towards England, the town of **Chepstow** straddles the border. The castle dates from the reign of King Edward I and the narrow streets are still in part enclosed by the medieval town walls. Nearby **Caerwent** is rich in Roman remains. Between Cardiff and the English border is *Newport,* the country's third-largest town which has a 15th-century cathedral.
There are several resorts on the coast between Cardiff and Swansea with sandy beaches; these include *Barry, Porthcawl* and *Aberavon,* near Port Talbot.
Swansea is Wales' second city and a major cultural, industrial and shipping centre. Swansea has over 45 parks, a fact which only partly compensates for the grim industrial aspect of much of the city and the surrounding towns, but it is also a popular seaside resort, as well as being conveniently situated close to the *Gower Peninsula. The Mumbles,* almost a suburb of Swansea, is the main resort in this region. In the Penclawdd region, cockle-gathering is still carried on in the traditional way, on donkey-back. Other resorts on the Gower Peninsula include *Oxwich* and *Port Eynon.*
The most popular inland destination in South Wales is the area of the *Brecon Beacons,* a national park stretching from the Vale of Towy to the Usk Valley. **Brecon** and **Abergavenny** are the major centres for touring the Brecon Beacons. There is a narrow-gauge railway, the *Brecon Mountain Railway*, which runs for a few kilometres through the hills, giving superb views across the countryside. For more information, see under 'The Great Little Trains of Wales' in the *Travel* section above.
West of Brecon, across the other side of the Black Mountains, is **Carmarthen**, a quiet country town set in gentle undulating countryside which comes alive on market days. Across Carmarthen Bay is the resort town of **Tenby**, beyond which lies the former county of Pembroke. This part of the country was colonised by Normans, and from the 11th century onwards by weavers from Flanders. Henry Tudor, later to become Henry VII after the Battle of Bosworth, was born in *Pembroke Castle*, the remains of which still survive in the former county town of **Pembroke.** The whole region has many castles, as well as several monasteries, abbeys and priories. The most famous religious building in the area, however, is undoubtedly the cathedral at **St David's,** founded in the late 12th century. St David's was for many centuries a place of pilgrimage. Nearby are the larger towns of **Haverfordwest** and the deep-water port of **Milford Haven,** near which there are several island bird sanctuaries. To the north is the ferry port of **Fishguard**.

Mid-Wales

The town of **Cardigan** on Cardigan Bay is a pleasant market town which makes a good starting point for exploring Mid-Wales. Between Cardigan and Aberystwyth there are many small towns and villages, most of which are unpronounceable to non-Welsh speakers, with small rocky coves and sandy beaches. The university town of **Aberystwyth**, about midway round the bay, is a popular resort and base for visits to *Devil's Bridge,* one of the most notable beauty spots in the British Isles which is linked to the town by a narrow-gauge steam railway. There are two other narrow-gauge steam railways close by; the *Talyllyn Railway*, which runs for about 10km (16 miles) through beautiful countryside in the hills behind the town of Tywyn where it terminates; and the Fairbourne Railway linking Fairbourne with the Barmouth Ferry. **Barmouth** was once one of the most popular resorts in the British Isles and was frequented by, amongst others, Charles Darwin and Lord Tennyson. There are good beaches, both in the town and also near *Dyffryn Ardudwy,* a few kilometres to the north. Inland from Barmouth is **Dolgellau**, at the foot of *Cader Idris*, a small and attractive market town. Other towns of interest inland from Aberystwyth or Barmouth include **Builth Wells,** an important cattle-trading town; **Strata Florida Abbey;** the towns of **Lampeter** and **Tregaron** on the *River Teifi,* and **Llandrindod Wells,** one of many towns with therapeutic waters and Wales' leading spa in the late 18th and early 19th centuries, leaving a legacy of elegant architecture to be enjoyed by its latter-day inhabitants and visitors. Beyond Barmouth, on the northern tip of Cardigan Bay, is **Harlech**, famous both for its castle which overlooks the peaks of Snowdonia and for the song 'Men of Harlech', referring to the defence of the castle in the 15th century. South of Harlech is **Llanbedr**, a popular yachting centre.

North Wales

This region is one of the oldest-established tourist areas in the British Isles, and resorts such as **Llandudno** and **Rhyl** are still exceedingly popular.
North of the *Mawddoch Estuary* is the town of **Porthmadog**, a holiday resort with excellent facilities. It has the oldest independent narrow-gauge railway in the world, now known as the *Ffestiniog Railway,* which carries thousands of visitors each year. West from Porthmadog is the *Lleyn peninsula,* where there are many good beaches, particularly on the south coast, at towns such as **Criccieth** (Lloyd George's birthplace), **Pwllheli** (the end of the railway line), **Abersoch, Aberdaron,** and, on the northern coast, **Nefyn** and **Clynnog-Fawr.**
Further north, facing the Isle of Anglesey across the *Menai Strait*, is **Caernarfon**, a town still surrounded by 13th-century walls and dominated by the 13th-century castle. It was here that Prince Charles was invested as Prince of Wales in 1969. The **Isle of Anglesey,** known as *Ynys Môn* in Welsh, is notable for a remarkable bridge, the ferry port of **Holyhead** and the town of **Llanfair PG,** the abbreviation for its real name, whose 58 letters make it the longest place name in the world (the sign on the platform of the the local railway station is worth photographing). The main town on the island, **Beaumaris**, has excellent leisure facilities and a castle

built by Edward I. Back on the mainland on the other side of the Strait is the university and cathedral city of **Bangor**; its attractions include a huge doll collection housed in *Penrhyn Castle*.

The **Snowdonia National Park** is 2200 sq km (840 sq miles) of some of the most beautiful countryside in the British Isles, with 14 peaks over 915m (3000ft), the highest of which is *Mount Snowdon*. The Snowdon Mountain Railway, running from Llanberis, is certainly the least exacting way of reaching the summit of the mountain. Other attractions in the region include *Betws-y-Coed,* in the Gwydyr Forest; *Bethesda,* southeast of Bangor; *Bala Lake,* which also has a narrow-gauge railway; and *Beddgelert* in the Nant Gwynant valley.

On the north coast, continuing east from Bangor, is the historic town of **Conwy**, with a mighty medieval castle and complete medieval town walls. Nearby is the superb *Bodnant Gardens.* At the other side of Great Ormes Head is **Llandudno,** one of the country's most popular tourist resorts. It has almost every possible facility and amenity as well as being within striking distance of the beautiful hinterland which includes the Snowdonia National Park. The chain of resorts continues almost unbroken for several miles; *Rhos-on-Sea, Colwyn Bay, Abergele* and *Prestatyn* all have good beaches, and in particular **Rhyl**, a town with a 5km-long (3-mile) promenade and extensive leisure and recreation facilities. It is also a good base for excursions to **St Asaph**, a city with the smallest medieval cathedral in Britain. Further east lies **Bagillt** and **Flint,** once the capital of the tiny county of the same name.

To the southeast of Flint is **Wrexham**, a kilometre south of which is *Erdigg,* a 17th-century squire's house containing much of the traditional furniture and with many of the outbuildings still in their original condition and in working order. Further south is *Chirk Castle,* a 14th-century Marcher fortress built to guard the frontier between England and Wales which it straddles. To the west and the south is an area of great natural beauty, including the forests of *Dyfnant, Ceiriog* and *Penllyn.* Southwest of Wrexham is **Llangollen,** set in forested landscape overlooking the salmon-rich River Dee and containing a bridge that is a masterpiece of medieval engineering. It is also the setting for the International Musical Eisteddfod – for further information, see the *Social Profile* section below. Nearby is the 13th-century *Vale Crucis Abbey* and the beautiful *Horseshoe Pass.* Due south of Llangollen is **Welshpool**, an attractive town with many Georgian buildings and a narrow-gauge railway. South of the town is *Powys Castle,* built in the 13th century and modernised during the 16th century.

POPULAR ITINERARIES: 5-day: (a) Chester (England)–Rhyl–Llandudno–Conwy–Bangor–Caernarfon–Pwllheli–Criccieth–Porthmadog–Ffestiniog–Snowdonia National Park. (b) Ross-on-Wye (England)–Symond's Yat (England)–Abergavenny–Brecon–Hay-on-Wye–Builth Wells–Llandridnod Wells. **7-day:** Chepstow–Cardiff–Gower Peninsula–Carmarthen–Tenby–Pembroke–St David's–Aberystwyth–Dolgellau–Barmouth.

SOCIAL PROFILE

FOOD & DRINK: In most major centres, British and continental food is available. Welsh cooking is, in general simple, with abundant fresh local produce, particularly meat and fish. Near the coast, seafood is also widely available. Local dishes include *Welsh rarebit, leek soup* and *laver bread,* which is made with seaweed. **Drink:** There is only one small part of Wales which is still 'dry' on Sunday, ie alcohol may not be bought: the Dwyfor area of the county of Gwynedd (mainly the Lleyn peninsula, northwest Wales). Nevertheless, hotels in the locality may serve drink to their guests.

NIGHTLIFE: In general similar to that in an English town of comparable size, with bars, restaurants and cinemas being common in the cities and large towns.

SPORT: Rugby is the national sport, and is played to the very highest level of skill. There are a huge number of local clubs and the international team plays matches at the national stadium *Cardiff Arms Park.* **Cricket** (Glamorgan CCC) and, to a lesser extent, **football** are also popular spectator sports. There are many **golf** courses, **tennis** courts and sports centres throughout the country. **Sea fishing** is good off all coasts and there are also many opportunities for **coarse** and **game fishing** inland; the areas of Snowdonia, Brecon and the River Teifi (Cardigan) are among the most popular.

SPECIAL EVENTS: *St David's Day* (March 1) is dedicated to the patron saint of Wales. Although it is not a public holiday, schoolchildren celebrate and learn about their culture through music, poetry and cookery on this day. Many Welsh villages hold an *Eisteddfod* once a year – a contest for local poets, singers and musicians. All but the largest ones are generally only advertised inside the town itself but visitors are welcome to attend. Other special events celebrated during 1995/96 include: **Jan 1-Dec 31 '95** *UK Year of Literature and Writing,* Swansea and throughout Wales. **May 12-14** *Mid-Wales May Festival,* Newton, Powys. **May 26-Jun 4** *Hay Festival,* Hay-on-Wye. **May 27-Jun 3** *St David's Cathedral Festival* (classical music and art), St David's. **May 27-Jun 4** *Beaumaris Festival.* **May 29-Jun 3** *Welsh League of Youths National Eisteddfod,* Boncath, Dyfed. **Jun 10-11** *Chepstow Horse Trials.* **Jun 11-17** *Cardiff Singer of the World Competition.* **Jun 17-26** *Criccieth Festival.* **Jun 30-Jul 2** *Welsh International Festival of Storytelling,* St Donats. **Jul 4-9** *Llangollen International Musical Eisteddfod.* **Jul 8-9** *Mid-Wales Festival of Transport,* Powys Castle. **Jul 13-22** *Welsh Proms '95,* Cardiff. **Jul 24-27** *Royal Welsh Show,* Builth Wells. **Aug 5-12** *National Eisteddfod,* Abergele. **Aug 11-13** *Brecon Jazz Festival.* **Aug 19-27** *Llandrindod Wells Victorian Festival.* **Sep 9-Oct 7** *Cardiff Festival of Music.* **Sep 14-16** *International Sheepdog Trial 1995,* Holywell, Clwyd. **Sep 16-23** *North Wales Music Festival,* various venues. **Sep 17** *Vintage Car Rally,* Newport. **Sep 25-Nov 5** *Swansea Festival of Music and the Arts.* **Oct 14-22** *Llandudno October Festival.* **Nov 10-19** *Welsh International Film Festival,* Aberystwyth. **Dec 5** *Royal Welsh Agricultural Winter Fair,* Builth Wells.

Note: For further details on events contact the Wales Tourist Board. Accommodation at festival times should be booked well in advance.

BUSINESS PROFILE

BUSINESS: See main UK entry above.

CONFERENCES/CONVENTIONS: The Wales Tourist Board publishes a booklet entitled *Wales: The Business Travel Planner.* For information contact the Business Travel Department, Wales Tourist Board, Brunel House, 2 Fitzalan Road, Cardiff, South Glamorgan CF2 1UY. Tel: (01222) 475 202. Fax: (01222) 498 076.

CLIMATE

Wales tends to be wetter than England, and has slightly less sunshine. The coastal areas, however, can be very warm in summer. Conditions in upland areas can be dangerous and changeable at all times of the year.

Required clothing: Similar to the rest of the UK, according to season. Waterproofing advised throughout the year, and warm clothes are required for upland areas.

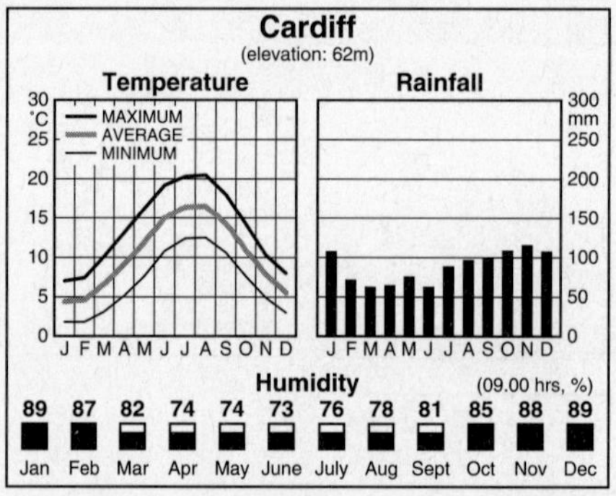
Cardiff
(elevation: 62m)
Temperature
Rainfall
°C
MAXIMUM
AVERAGE
MINIMUM
mm
30 25 20 15 10 5 0
300 250 200 150 100 50 0
J F M A M J J A S O N D
J F M A M J J A S O N D
Humidity
(09.00 hrs, %)
89 87 82 74 74 73 76 78 81 85 88 89
Jan Feb Mar Apr May June July Aug Sept Oct Nov Dec

Northern Ireland

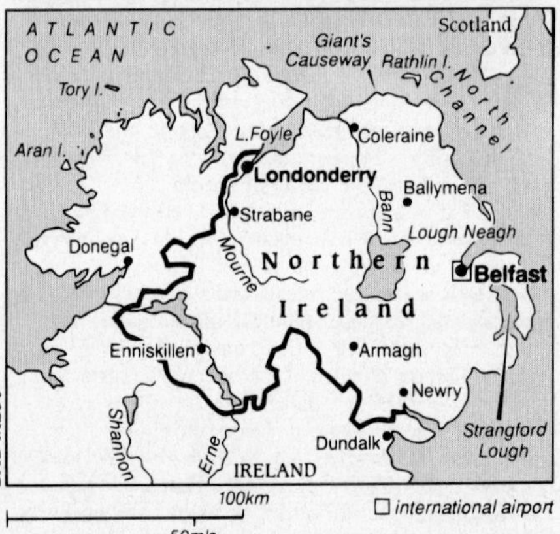
ATLANTIC
OCEAN
Scotland
Giant's Causeway
Rathlin I.
North Channel
Tory I.
L.Foyle
Coleraine
Aran I.
Londonderry
Ballymena
Bann
Strabane
Lough Neagh
Donegal
Northern
Belfast
Mourne
Ireland
Enniskillen
Armagh
Newry
Shannon
Erne
Dundalk
Strangford Lough
IRELAND
DAB-M236
100km
50mls
international airport

Location: Northern Ireland.

Northern Ireland Tourist Board
11 Berkeley Street, London W1X 5AD
Tel: (0171) 355 5040 *or* (0800) 282 662 (information). Fax: (0171) 409 0487. Opening hours: 0900-1700 Monday to Friday; *or*
St Anne's Court, 59 North Street, Belfast BT1 1NB
Tel: (01232) 231 221. Fax: (01232) 240 960.

Tourist Information Centre
Ireland Desk, British Travel Centre, 4-12 Lower Regent Street, London SW1Y 4PQ
Tel: (0171) 839 8416/7. Fax: (0171) 839 6179. Opening hours: 0900-1830 Monday to Friday; 1000-1600 Saturday and Sunday.

Northern Ireland Tourist Board
Suite 701, 551 Fifth Avenue, New York, NY 10176
Tel: (212) 922 0101. Fax: (212) 922 0099.

Northern Ireland Tourist Board
Suite 450, 111 Avenue Road, Toronto, Ontario M5R 3J8
Tel: (416) 925 6368. Fax: (416) 961 2175.

AREA: 13,483 sq km (5206 sq miles).
POPULATION: 1,610,300 (1992 estimate).
POPULATION DENSITY: 119.4 per sq km.
CAPITAL: Belfast. **Population:** 288,700 (1992).
GEOGRAPHY: Northern Ireland contains some beautiful scenery, from the rugged coastline in the north and northeast to the gentle fruit-growing regions of Armagh. To the west are the Sperrin Mountains and the lake of Fermanagh, where the winding River Erne provides excellent fishing. The high moorland plateau of Antrim in the northeast gives way to the glens further south and to the Drumlin country of County Down; further south still the Mountains of Mourne stretch down to the sea.
LANGUAGE: English.
Note: *For information on time, electricity, communications, public holidays and passport/visa see the general UK entry above. No passports are needed for travel between Northern Ireland and the mainland.*

MONEY

Note: For travelling around and staying at small hotels, cash is needed. Elsewhere, as in England, cheques backed by a banker's card are widely accepted.
For **currency, credit cards,** etc, see the general UK entry above.
Banking hours: In very small villages, the bank may open two or three days a week only, so aim to get cash in the bigger centres.
Changing money outside banking hours: *Thomas Cook,* 11 Donegall Place, Belfast BT1, is open 0900-1730 Monday to Saturday. Some hotels will also change money, but *Thomas Cook* and the banks give the best rate of exchange.

PUBLIC HOLIDAYS

Public holidays observed in Northern Ireland are the same as those observed in the rest of the UK *(see the general entry above)* with the addition of:
Mar 17 '95 St Patrick's Day. **Jul 12** Orangemen's Day.

TRAVEL

AIR: Northern Ireland's international airport is ***Belfast International Airport (BFS),*** 29km (18 miles) northwest of the city centre. Airport information: (018494) 22888. **Facilities** include bureau de change, duty-free shop, restaurant/buffet, bar, general shops, emergency medical services, nursing mothers' room, wheelchairs for the disabled, free-port facilities and business centre. Belfast International Airport has been designated a freeport for Northern Ireland. The 70-acre freeport site is located in the northwestern corner of the airport complex and has first-class access by road as well as internal access from the aircraft movements area and freight village. Freeport Northern Ireland operates on a 24-hour, 7-days-a-week basis. A modern, well-appointed business and conference centre operates five days per week and on request at weekends. Full state-of-the-art office equipment, secretarial services and translation facilities are available – for parties/groups of up to 100. **Train:** There is at present no direct rail link to Belfast International Airport, but trains run from Londonderry, Coleraine, Portrush, Ballymoney, Ballymena and Belfast to Antrim (8km/5 miles away) from where a taxi may be hired to the airport. There are also train connections from Lurgan, Portadown, Dundalk, Drogheda and Dublin. **Bus:** *Airbus* (Ulsterbus) runs to the city centre Monday to Saturday half-hourly (0645-2215) and Sunday hourly (0715-2215). **Taxi:** Travel time to city centre – 35 minutes. Taxis are available for hire outside the main airport building. **Car**

hire: *CC Economy Car Hire, Cosmo-EuroDollar, Dan Dooley, Avis, Hertz* and *McCausland Car Hire* are represented at the airport. **Private car:** The M1 provides the main link with Fermanagh and the west of the Province whilst forming part of the journey to and from Dublin and the east coast of Ireland. The M2 is the airport's main link with the centre of Belfast and to Londonderry, 116km (72 miles) to the northwest. There is nearby car parking for short and long stays. Access is from the M1 and M2 (parking is available) or train to Antrim and then taxi. Regular bus services run to the city centre. Car hire and taxi services are available.
The small airport at *Belfast Harbour* is handy for flights to some provincial British cities, such as Liverpool and Manchester and also the Isle of Man. Regular train and bus services run to the city centre. Tel: (01232) 457 745.
Note: For approximate durations of a selection of domestic flights from Belfast, see the *Travel* section in the general UK entry above.
SEA: Two ferry companies operate direct services between mainland Europe and Ireland. *Irish Ferries* operate between Le Havre and Rosslare with three departures per week in each direction (approximate travel time – 22 hours). Their ships also ply between Cherbourg and Rosslare and there is a peak summer-only Cork–Lettaire service. *Brittany Ferries* operate the Roscoff–Cork route with one departure per week in each direction during the summer season only (travel time – 16 hours).
When travelling via Great Britain to Northern Ireland there is a choice of four services across the Irish Sea: Stranraer (southern Scotland) to Larne, frequent daily services by *Sealink Scotland* (travel time – 2 hours 15 minutes); and Cairnryan (southern Scotland) to Larne, frequent daily services (travel time – 2 hours) by *P&O European Ferries.* In addition there are daily crossings between Stranraer and Belfast Harbour (travel time – 1 hour 30 minutes) by *Seacat.* An overnight service is offered on the Liverpool to Belfast route by *Norse Irish Ferries* (travel time – 9 hours).
Northern Ireland's only inhabited island is Rathlin, a few kilometres off the north coast. There are frequent passenger boats between Ballycastle and the island.
At peak holiday times a sailing/regulation ticket is required as well as a travel ticket. Check when booking. It is always advisable to book your journey both ways before leaving home.
RAIL: There are three main rail routes from Belfast Central Station north to Londonderry City via Ballymena and Coleraine, east to Bangor along the shores of Belfast Lough, and south to Dublin, in the Irish Republic, via Lisburn and Newry. The Belfast–Dublin non-stop express takes two hours. There are six trains daily in both directions (only three on Sunday). The busiest times are holiday weekends and the first and last trains Friday and Sunday, when it is best to reserve seats. Rail runabout tickets (seven days unlimited travel on scheduled rail services from April to October) are available from main Northern Ireland railway stations.
A special rail-link bus runs between York Road and the Central Station regularly from 0730-2030 Monday to Saturday. Outside those hours other buses will connect with Oxford Street bus station or City Hall.
For information on timetables for *all* rail services, contact Northern Ireland Railways Information Centre, Central Station, East Bridge Street, Belfast BT1 3PB. Tel: (01232) 899 411. Opening hours: 0630-2300.
ROAD: Bus: Northern Ireland has an excellent bus network and there are particularly good bus links between those towns which are not served by rail. Belfast has two main bus stations: Great Victoria Street, near Europa Hotel, and Oxford Street, near the main railway station. Express buses run from Belfast to Antrim, Armagh, Ballymena, Banbridge, Coleraine, Cookstown, Dungannon, Enniskillin, Hillsborough, Larne (port), Londonderry, Lurgan, Magherafelt, Newry, Omagh, Portadown, Portrush (near Giant's Causeway) and Strabane. In July and August *Ulsterbus* run day and half-day tours to the glens of Antrim, Antrim Coast and Giant's Causeway, Fermanagh Lakeland, the Mountains of Mourne, Ards Peninsula and Armagh. Tours leave Belfast (Great Victoria Street Bus Station) seven days a week. Excursions include Lammas Fair and Ulster Grand Prix. Cheap day-returns include Causeway, Newcastle and Cushendun (Oxford Street Bus Station) and unlimited travel bus tickets. Contact *Ulsterbus:* tel: (01232) 333 000 (timetable) *or* 337 002/3 (Cross Channel) *or* 337 004 (tours). *Citybus* enquiries (Belfast area only): (01232) 246 485.
Traffic regulations: Traffic drives on the left. The speed limit is 30mph (48kmph) in towns and cities unless signs show 40mph (64kmph) or 50mph (80kmph). On country roads the limit is 60mph (96kmph); on dual carriageways, trunk roads and motorways 70mph (112kmph) unless signs show otherwise.
Breakdowns: If the car is rented, contact the rental company. Members of the continental equivalent of the *Automobile Association (AA)* can contact their 24-hour breakdown service. Tel: (0800) 887 766. The *Royal Automobile Club (RAC)* provides a similar service. Tel: (0800) 828 282. They can be contacted from their roadside phones or from any call box. Non-members should consult the Yellow Pages for breakdown services.

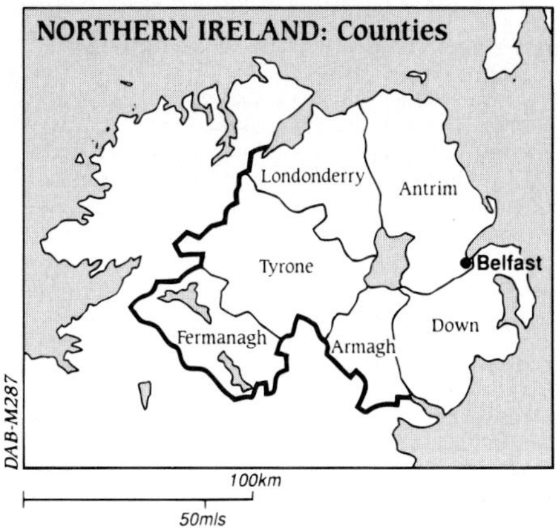

Parking: Permitted where there is a blue 'P' sign, which indicates a car park in towns or a lay-by at the roadside outside towns. Drivers can park elsewhere on the street except when there is a single yellow line, when parking is permitted only at the times shown on the yellow signs nearby; or when there is a double yellow line which prohibits all parking. Control Zones, which are usually in town centres, are indicated by yellow signs 'Control Zone. No Unattended Parking'. An unattended car in a Control Zone is treated as a security risk. Never park on zigzag markings near pedestrian crossings. In some towns the centre may be sealed off at certain times, particularly overnight. Alternative routes will be signposted.
Taxi: Available at main stations, ports and Belfast Airport and are also bookable by telephone in larger towns and cities.
Car hire: The main firms – *Avis, Hertz* and *Europcar* – all operate in Northern Ireland and have desks at Aldergrove Airport with cars available on the spot. There is also a host of smaller firms.

ACCOMMODATION

A wide range of accommodation is available in Northern Ireland. Contact the Northern Ireland Tourist Board for brochures and booklets giving full lists of available accommodation.
HOTELS: Brochures from the Northern Ireland Tourist Board give full details of services. Most establishments belong to the Hospitality Association of Northern Ireland. For further information, contact the The Hospitality Association of Northern Ireland, 108-110 Midland Buildings, Whitla Street, Belfast BT15 1JP. Tel: (01232) 351 110. Fax: (01232) 351 509.
Grading: The Northern Irish Tourist Board operates a 'star' classification system which is used throughout their publications. The main hotel classifications are as follows:
4-star: High standard of comfort and service, including room service and well-equipped premises. Food and beverages are obliged to meet the most exacting standards.
3-star: Good facilities and a wide range of services in comfortable surroundings, including en suite bathroom. Refreshments are available during the day.
2-star: Good facilities, offering satisfactory standards of accommodation and food, with en suite bathroom.
1-star: Acceptable standards of accommodation and food. Some bedrooms offer en suite bathroom.
FARM & COUNTRY HOUSE HOLIDAYS: This is currently one of the most popular forms of holidaying in Northern Ireland. The *Northern Ireland Farm & Country Holidays Association* produces an accommodation voucher, valid for bed and breakfast for one night. The brochure *Farm & Country Holidays* can be obtained from the Northern Ireland Tourist Board. The *Northern Ireland Town & Seaside House Association* has houses in some of Northern Ireland's most beautiful areas, from the Mourne Mountains to the Causeway Coast, from the Fermanagh Lakes to the Ards Peninsula, each house offering good home-cooking and a traditional Ulster welcome. The Association offers a Tour Operator rate and is happy to arrange 'go as you please' itineraries. A brochure, *Town and Seaside House Holidays,* is obtainable from the Northern Ireland Tourist Board. For further information contact the Northern Ireland Farm and Country Holidays Association, Whincrest, Ballymartin, Kilkeel, Co Down BT34 4NU. Tel/Fax: (016937) 63012.
SELF-CATERING: There are self-catering establishments in all of Northern Ireland's six counties. For further information contact Charlton Cottages who distribute brochures on behalf of the Northern Ireland Self-Catering Association. Tel: (01365) 658 181.
CAMPING/CARAVANNING: There are over 100 caravan and camp sites throughout the six counties of Northern Ireland. Details of the prices and facilities are contained in an information bulletin *Camping & Caravan Parks,* available from the Northern Ireland Tourist Board. The Northern Ireland Forest Service issues permits for camping in forest areas. Contact Forest Services, Department of Agriculture, Dundonald House, Newtownards Road, Belfast BT4 3SB. Tel: (01232) 520 100.
YOUTH HOSTELS: For further information contact the Youth Hostel Association of Northern Ireland, 22 Donegal Road, Belfast BT12 5JN. Tel: (01232) 324 733. Fax: (01232) 439 699.

RESORTS & EXCURSIONS

Northern Ireland, often referred to as the 'six counties', is described county by county in this guide, with an additional section on *Farm Study Tours.*

Antrim

To the southeast of the county, **Belfast** provides 6-day shopping and city entertainment in the shape of theatres, cinema, a wide range of restaurants, the *Grand Opera House* and all the other attractions of any capital city. To the northwest lies the *Causeway Coast,* with its holiday resorts and the *Giant's Causeway* as the dominant feature. There are many sleepy villages between the nine glens of Antrim and the spectacular coast road, and inland are towns like Antrim with its ancient round tower and splendid park. There is a lakeside steam railway at *Shane's Castle,* golf at **Portrush** and elsewhere throughout the county, as well as bathing, boating and fishing along its 160km (100 miles) of coast.

Down

Attractions include the *Folk and Transport Museum* at **Cultra** and the ancient shrines of St Patrick's country around the cathedral hill of *Downpatrick*; the flat sandy beaches of the *Ards Peninsula* and the beautiful *Mountains of Mourne;* lively **Newcastle** with its seaside festival; and stately homes like *Mount Stewart* and *Castle Ward* open to visitors. At **Rostrevor,** a small sheltered resort on *Carlingford Lough,* orchids and palm trees flourish in the balmy climate. Horseriding, sailing, angling and golf are within easy reach, also motor racing at **Kirkistown** and sea angling in Strangford Lough.

Armagh

Northern Ireland's smallest county rises gently from *Lough Neagh's* banks, southwards through apple orchards, farmland and hill forest to the rocky summit of *Slieve Gullion,* mountain of Cuchulain. The crown of **Armagh** is the city itself, a religious capital older than Canterbury, with two cathedrals, the *Georgian Mall* and the *Planetarium/Space Centre.* **Craigavon** has a leisure centre and ski-slope, with lakes for watersports; and there is sailing on Lough Neagh and angling and canoeing on the *Blackwater River.*

Fermanagh

Ulster's lakeland spreads its web of waterways, islands, forest and glen, castles and abbey ruins right across the county. **Enniskillen,** county town and shopping centre, strides the narrows between Upper and Lower Lough Erne. From there pleasure boats run daily cruises in summer. Golf, sailing, water-skiing and even pleasure flying are available nearby. Fishermen need no reminder that these are the waters where record catches are made. Two of Ireland's finest houses, *Florence Court* and *Castle Coole,* are open to the public. The nearby *Marble Arch Caves* were opened to the public for the first time in May 1985 and the tour begins with an underground boat trip through the caves (opening times: 0900-1800 September to May, 0900-2200 June to August). Visitors to the old pottery at **Belleek** can watch craftsmen at work on fine porcelain.

Londonderry

This is a fertile agricultural county, with small farms scattered across the broad sweeping land, and long Atlantic beaches. The city of **Derry** is best known for its massive ring of fortified walls and 'singing pubs'. In the county's northeast corner is **Coleraine** (with one of the main campuses of the University of Ulster), conveniently close to the seaside resorts of **Portstewart** and **Castlerock** for sea angling, golf and children's amusements. For rewarding scenic drives the *Sperrin Mountains* are best approached from Limavady and the beautiful Roe Valley Country Park. The *Bann River* is noted for trout and salmon.

Tyrone

Between the *Sperrins* in the north and the green *Clogher Valley* with its village cathedral in the south lies a region of great historical interest. The county's associations with the USA are recalled in the *Ulster-American Folk Park* near **Omagh**. Gray's old printing shop at **Strabane** still contains its 19th-century presses. A mysterious ceremonial site of stone circles and cairns near *Davagh Forest* has recently been uncovered and there are other Stone Age and Bronze Age remains in the area. There are forest parks, *Gortin Glen* and *Drum Manor*, for driving or rambling, excellent trout and salmon waters near **Newtonstewart**, market towns for shopping and recreation. **Dungannon** is notable for its fine glassware, Tyrone Crystal.

Farm Study Tours

Northern Ireland is primarily an agricultural country and is world-famous for its farming techniques. Study tours can be arranged for specialised or general visits with guides and experts on hand. Options for study tours: Greenmount, Loughry and Enniskillen Colleges of Agriculture offer research facilities on residential courses or visit the research establishment at Loughgall, County Armagh, Hillsborough, County Down, Cross-na-Creevy, Castlereagh, the Northern Ireland Pig Testing Station, Antrim and the Veterinary Research Laboratories at Stormont, Belfast. Major horticulture centres include Greenmount, Grovelands, Balmoral or Loughgall. Fane Valley, Fair Country Fruit Growers and Killyman Cooperatives are also well worth a visit, as is the Ulster Folk and Transport Museum.
POPULAR ITINERARIES: 5-day: (a) Belfast–Glens of Antrim–Causeway Coast–Londonderry–Sperrin Mountains–Belfast. (b) Belfast–Armagh–Enniskillen–Omagh–Strabane–Sperrin Mountains–Belfast.

SOCIAL PROFILE

FOOD & DRINK: The best value for money meals in Ulster are to be had at lunchtime (midday), when many restaurants and pubs offer special menus. Most Ulster families have high tea at about 1800 and many hotels and restaurants offer the same. High tea usually consists of a lightly cooked meal (an Ulster fry – perhaps eggs, sausages, ham or fish with chips) and a wide variety of bread, scones and cakes. Dinner is served from about 1900. Typical Northern Ireland foods include shellfish, home-made vegetable soups, potato dishes, dried seaweed, locally grown fruit and home-baked cakes and pastries. A useful booklet is *Where to Eat in Northern Ireland*, available from newsagents and Tourist Information centres, which lists all the places where food is served, a price indication and brief description of the sort of food. It is advisable to book ahead for the more popular restaurants, especially towards the weekend. **Drink:** The pubs are open all day 1130-2300 Monday to Saturday and 1230-1430/1900-2200 Sunday with half an hour 'drinking-up' time. Popular drinks are, of course, *Guinness* – a dark heavy stout with a creamy head – and *whiskey* (Northern Ireland also boasts the world's oldest whiskey distillery at Bushmills). Irish whiskey is often drunk along with a bottle of stout. Real ale fans can try *Hilden* produced at Lisburn and obtainable locally.
NIGHTLIFE: There are summer theatres in Newcastle and Portrush, plus the Riverside Theatre at Coleraine. The Belfast Festival at Queen's (three weeks in November each year) is Europe's biggest arts festival after Edinburgh. There is an Autumn festival in Armagh and Londonderry and towns like Newry, Omagh and Enniskillen have first-rate theatre and music. Traditional Irish music in 'singing pubs' provides a good evening's entertainment in many places, particularly Belfast and Londonderry.
SHOPPING: Shops in Belfast city centre are open 0900-1730 six days a week (late-night shopping on Thursday). Other cities and towns close half day one day a week (it differs from town to town) and some small shops close at lunchtime. Modern shopping centres on the outskirts of towns have late night shopping to 2100 Thursday and Friday. Shopping bags and contents may be examined at the door of big stores. Ulster is well known for its pure Irish linen; cut-glass goblets, decanters, bowls; creamy Belleek pottery; handwoven tweed; pure wool jumpers

and cardigans hand-knitted in traditional patterns; hand-embroidered wall hangings; Carrickmacross lace and silver jewellery.
SPORT: Fishing: Sea fishing is popular all along the coast and skippered boats of all sizes can be hired at most resorts. Strangford Lough is famous for its skate and tope. Carlingford Lough is nearly as good and the coast of Belfast Lough is dotted with sea angling clubs. There are superb waters for river and lake fishing, particularly in the Mournes area of Down, the Glens of Antrim and the River Bann. In most areas a rod licence and a coarse fishing permit are necessary. Day permits are available. Check at the nearest tackle shop. **Golf:** Some of the best golf courses are situated on the coast – at Whitehead, Bangor, Royal Portrush, Ballycastle, Royal County Down at Newcastle and the Chairndhu Club near Larne. Weekly and daily rates for playing on the courses are available from the club itself or the nearest tourist information centre. **Walking:** There is a multitude of walks around Northern Ireland – from the Mourne Mountains and forest parks in County Down to the nine Glens in County Antrim. The Ulster Way is an 800km (500-mile) walking route around Northern Ireland and various walking holidays are arranged throughout the summer. **Sub-aqua:** Northern Ireland can offer the experienced diving enthusiast several areas to explore; these include Strangford Lough, some 29km (18 miles) long and averaging 6km (3.5 miles) wide, a fascinating underwater world with many contrasting diving sites. The long history of sea traffic has left a legacy of wrecks in and around the Lough such as the 'Lees' wreck, an old liberty ship now lying at 12m (39ft), or the remains of the largest vessel wrecked on the Co Down coast, the American troopship 'Georgetown Victory'. Also of interest to experienced divers is the rugged, towering coast of Rathlin Island and Northern Ireland's famous north coast. **Cruising:** Loch Erne has in recent years become very popular for cruising holidays and several tour operators and local companies can arrange holidays. Contact the Tourist Board for further details. **Other sports:** Leisure centres have been springing up in most Ulster towns over the past few years. They have facilities for squash, badminton, tennis, gymnastics and other sports. There is also hang-gliding, gliding and rock climbing in the Mournes, Co Down; gliding, hang-gliding and parascending at Magilligan, Bellarena and Aghadowey, Co Londonderry; water-skiing on the River Bann at Coleraine; archery at Groomsport; canoeing at Bangor and Newcastle; pony trekking in the mountains and forests around Newcastle and Castlewellan, North Down coast and the Causeway Coast.
SPECIAL EVENTS: The following is a selection of the major festivals and other special events celebrated annually in Northern Ireland. For a complete list, contact the Northern Ireland Tourist Board:
Mar 4-11 '95 *Opera Northern Ireland*, Belfast. **Mar 17** *St Patrick's Day celebrations.* **May 6-Jun 3** *The Lord Mayor's Show*, Belfast. **May 9** *Ireland v Kent International Cricket*, Comber. **May 25-29** *International Jazz and Blues Festival*, Londonderry. **Jun 2-4** *Classic Carrickfergus*, Carrickfergus. **Jun 6-18** *Fleadh Amhrán agus Rince*, Ballycastle. **Jun 17-24** *Belfast Folk Festival.* **Jul 12** *Battle of the Boyne Commemorations.* **Jul 19-21** *International Cricket*, Belfast, Comber, Downpatrick. **Jul 20-Aug 5** *O'Doherty Clan Rally*, Londonderry and Donegal. **Aug 6-13** *Féile An Phobail*, Belfast. **Aug 28-29** *Oul'Lammas Fair*, Ballycastle.
SOCIAL CONVENTIONS: Due to the political situation in Northern Ireland, visitors should take care when visiting certain parts of the main cities and the border area. No problems should arise providing the visitor follows local advice and avoids expressing dogmatic opinions on political or religious topics.

BUSINESS PROFILE

ECONOMY: The Northern Ireland economy has traditionally been divided between manufacturing, concentrated in shipbuilding and aerospace in the east of the province, and agriculture, which is prevalent throughout. The province is one of the poorest regions of the UK and suffered disproportionately under the recession of the early 1980s. Central government and European support have produced some improvement in Northern Ireland's economic fortunes, but the hoped-for boom in advanced technological industries (parallel to that in the Irish Republic) has not happened. It is more than likely that if the 1994 peace initiatives bear fruit, the economy will see an upturn with an increase in investment and tourism.
COMMERCIAL INFORMATION: The following organisation can offer advice: Northern Ireland Chamber of Commerce and Industry, Chamber of Commerce House, 22 Great Victoria Street, Belfast BT2 7BJ. Tel: (01232) 244 113. Fax: (01232) 247 024.

CLIMATE

In general, the weather is similar to the rest of the United Kingdom, but Northern Ireland tends to have less sunshine and more rain. Extremes of temperature are rare but conditions can be changeable.
Required clothing: Similar to the rest of the UK, according to season. Waterproofs are advisable throughout the year.

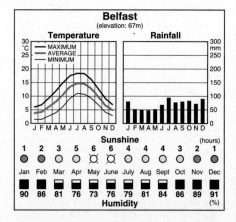

Isle of Man

Location: Irish Sea.

Isle of Man Department of Tourism, Leisure and Transport
Sea Terminal Buildings, Douglas, Isle of Man IM1 2RG
Tel: (01624) 686 801. Fax: (01624) 686 800.

AREA: 572 sq km (221 sq miles).
POPULATION: 69,788 (1991).
POPULATION DENSITY: 122 per sq km.
CAPITAL: Douglas. **Population:** 22,214 (1991).
GEOGRAPHY: The Isle of Man is situated in the Irish Sea, 114km (71 miles) from Liverpool and 133km (83 miles) from Dublin. The island has a mountain range down the middle, the highest peak being Snaefell at 620m (2036ft) and a flat northern plain to the Point of Ayre, the most northerly point. The Calf of Man, an islet off the southwest coast, is administered as a nature reserve and bird sanctuary by the Manx Museum and National Trust.
LANGUAGE: Manx Gaelic, the indigenous language, is an offshoot of Scots and Irish Gaelic. At one time spoken by all the Manx, the tongue was replaced by English during the last century, and now only 600 or so people

speak it to some degree. On Tynwald Day, summaries of the new laws are read out in Manx and English. Manx Gaelic evening classes are regularly held, and a weekly radio programme and newspaper column appear in the language.
TIME: GMT (GMT + 1 from March 29 to October 31).
ELECTRICITY: 220 volts AC, 50Hz.
COMMUNICATIONS: Telephone: To telephone the Isle of Man from the UK, the STD (area) code is 01624. **Fax:** Services are available. **Post:** Services are administered by the Isle of Man Post Office Authority which issues its own postage stamps, recognised internationally under the auspices of the Universal Postal Union. Only Isle of Man Post Office Authority stamps are valid for postal purposes in the island. **Press:** There are several local papers published on the island and English papers are widely available.

PASSPORT/VISA

No passports are required for travel between the UK and the Isle of Man. See the *Passport/Visa* section of the general UK entry above.

MONEY

Currency: The Isle of Man Government issues its own decimal coinage, and currency notes of £50, 20, 10 and 1, all of which are on a par with the UK's equivalents. The coins and notes of England, Scotland and Northern Ireland circulate freely in the island. The coins and notes of Eire are not equivalent to Manx or UK currency, although they may be accepted at the appropriate exchange rate at some establishments.
Banking hours: 0930-1530 Monday to Friday. Some are open 1000-1200 Saturday.

DUTY FREE

There are no duty-free allowances between the UK and the Isle of Man. Duty-free allowances are available between the Isle of Man and the Republic of Ireland.

PUBLIC HOLIDAYS

Public holidays observed in the Isle of Man are the same as those observed in the rest of the UK *(see the general entry above)* with the addition of:
Jul 5 '95 Tynwald Fair Day.
Note: The Friday of the *Isle of Man TT* (motorcycle race) week is also a holiday.

HEALTH

No vaccination certificates are required to enter the Isle of Man. There is a Reciprocal Health Agreement with the UK, allowing all visitors from the mainland free medical treatment; dental treatment and prescribed medicines must be paid for. No proof of UK residence is required to benefit from the Agreement. The island has two first-class hospitals and many dental practices.

TRAVEL

AIR: *Manx Airlines (JE)* operate year-round services between the Isle of Man and London Heathrow, Manchester, Liverpool, Birmingham, Luton, Glasgow, Blackpool, Belfast and Dublin.
The island's airport is *Ronaldsway (IOM),* 11km (7 miles) from Douglas. Airport information: (01624) 823 311. **Facilities** include restaurant, buffet, bar (normal licensing hours), general shop and newsagents, fruit and flower shop, duty-free shop, and facilities for the disabled. Airport opening times: 0615-2045 Monday to Saturday; 0700-2045 Sunday. Airport opening times may change in summer. There are regular coach services to and from the airport in summer. A local **bus** operates approximately half hourly in summer, and hourly in winter. **Taxis** and **car hire** are also available. Those wishing to hire cars can contact *Athol Garage Car Hire* (tel: (01624) 822 481) or *Mylchreests Car Hire* (tel: (01624) 823 533). It is 16km (10 miles) to Douglas by private car. There is one contract and one public car park.
SEA: Daily sailings are run by *The Isle of Man Steam Packet Company* from Heysham. In addition, the *Company* operates summer sailings from Belfast, Dublin and Liverpool.
RAIL: Horse trams run along the 3km (2 miles) of the Douglas Promenade during the summer. *The Steam Railway* operates from Douglas to Port Erin and *The Manx Electric Railway* runs from Douglas to Ramsey and the top of Snaefell in the summer months.
ROAD: The island is served by *Isle of Man National Transport* **buses** throughout the year. There are also a number of coach operators who operate full- and half-day excursions. Private **taxis** operate all year round and there

are a number of **car hire** firms. **Bicycles** are available for hire in the summer months. **Regulations:** Traffic drives on the left. There is no maximum speed limit except in built-up areas. **Documentation:** Full UK driving licence is acceptable.

ACCOMMODATION

Hotel, guest-house and self-catering accommodation is available, but pre-booking is necessary in the summer months. Camping is only permitted on the official campsite. The importation of caravans is prohibited.

RESORTS & EXCURSIONS

For information on National Trust properties in the Isle of Man, contact Manx National Heritage. Tel: (01624) 675 522. Fax: (01624) 661 899.
Douglas is set in a bay at the confluence of the *Dhoo* and *Glass* rivers, and has a promenade 3km (2 miles) long. *The Manx Museum* in Finch Road has exhibits illustrating the island's history, works by local artists and items dating to Celtic and Viking periods. At *Ballasalla* are the ruins of *Rushen Abbey,* which was founded in 1134, and dissolved at a later date than those of the British Isles. *Creigneish* is the most southerly point of the island and includes such sights as the *Mull* or *Meayll Circles,* a group of six chamber tombs, and *The Manx Open Air Folk Museum* which has a group of thatched cottages restored to their original furnishing. The scenery in this part of the island is fairly wild and rugged and cliffs fall away steeply to the sea. Across the Calf Sound lies the *Calf of Man,* a bird reserve with a large population of rare sea-birds, as well as seals. The sanctuary can be visited outside the nesting season by boat from Port Erin. **Peel** is a picturesque fishing port on the west coast of the island at the mouth of the *River Neb,* and it is claimed produces some of the best kippers. Linked to the town by a causeway is *St Patrick's Isle* which houses a tiny cathedral, and *Peel Castle,* a red sandstone structure enclosed by walls. From Laxey it is possible to take an electric mountain train up **Snaefell,** the island's highest point, from which the four countries of England, Wales, Scotland and Northern Ireland can be seen on a clear day.
Museums: The Manx Museum, off Crellin's Hill, Douglas. Open weekdays, entrance free. The Folk Museum, Manx Cottages, Creigneish. The Nautical Museum, Bridge Street, Castletown. The Grove Rural Life Museum, Andreas Road, Ramsey. The Railway Museum, Port Erin. Motorcycle Museum, Snaefell. 'Odin's Raven', Viking Longboat House, Mill Road East, Peel.

SOCIAL PROFILE

FOOD & DRINK: Cuisine is English and Manx. Local specialities include *queenies* (small scallops) and world-famous Manx kippers. A wide variety of alcoholic beverages are available, including Real Manx Ale from the wood and Manx whiskey, gin and vodka. All drinks are relatively cheaper than in the UK. **Licensing hours:** From Maundy Thursday to September 30 (inclusive) public houses are open 1030-2245 Monday to Saturday. On Sunday public houses are open 1200-1330 and 2000-2200. Special opening hours apply to the Christmas/New Year period.
SHOPPING: VAT is at the same rate as the UK and prices are in general similar to those in the UK. Special purchases include Manx tartan, crafts and pottery.
Shopping hours: 0900-1800 Monday to Saturday. Early closing Thursday during the winter months.
SPORT: There are seven **golf** courses on the island and green fees are much cheaper than in the UK. The resorts have facilities for squash, badminton, tennis, bowls, putting and miniature golf. There are boating lakes in Onchan and Ramsey. There is a sailboard and water-skiing centre in the south of the island. The waters around the island are ideal for yachting.
Note: *For information on people, religion, social conventions, business, tipping and eating and drinking, see the general UK entry above.*
SPECIAL EVENTS: The following is a selection of the major motoring events held throughout the year. For a complete list, contact the Isle of Man Department of Tourism.
May 13 '95 *Manx National Car Rally.* **May 29-Jun 9** *Isle of Man TT* (motorcycle racing). **Jun 18-23** *International Cycle Week.* **Jun 24-Jul 9** *Mananan International Festival of Music and the Arts.* **Jul 10-13** *Southern 100 Motorcycle Races.* **Jul 11-15** *Shakespeare Festival.* **Sep 21-24** *Classic Car Racing.*

BUSINESS PROFILE

ECONOMY: The Island's economy has taken off in the financial and business sector and is now a leading

financial services base. Exports include Manx tweeds, foodstuffs, herring and shellfish; the principal imports are fertilisers and timber.
BUSINESS: See the main UK entry above.
COMMERCIAL INFORMATION: The following organisation can offer advice: Isle of Man Chamber of Commerce, 17 Drinkwater Street, Douglas IM1 1PP. Tel: (01624) 674 941. Fax: (01624) 663 367.
CONFERENCES/CONVENTIONS: Seating is available for up to 1700 persons, though facilities on the island lend themselves very well to meetings of 100 persons or less. Conferences hosted include those of the National Federation of Young Farmers' Clubs and the Union of Communication Workers. All conference hotels have superb back-up services. For further information contact the Department of Tourism.

CLIMATE

The climate of the Isle of Man is temperate. There is a considerable variation in rainfall over the island, the driest parts being in the extreme south and over the northern plain; the wettest being the hilly interior. Frost and snow occur much less frequently than in other parts of the British Isles.

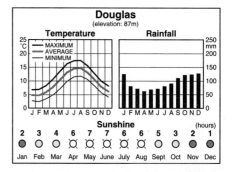

Channel Islands

Alderney, Guernsey, Jersey, Sark & Herm.
There are other, very small islands in the group, but these are not normally open to visitors. Guernsey and Jersey have their own sections elsewhere in this book.

Location: English Channel, the northernmost Channel Island; off the north coast of France.

States of Alderney Tourism Office
Alderney, QE II Street, Channel Islands, 2GY9 3AA
Tel: 822 994.

AREA: 7.9 sq km (3.1 sq miles).
POPULATION: 2000 (1985).
POPULATION DENSITY: 253.2 per sq km.
CAPITAL: St Anne's.
GEOGRAPHY: The most northerly of the Channel
Islands, Alderney lies 12km (8 miles) off the coast of
Normandy in France and some 32km (20 miles) from
Guernsey. The central part of the island is a plateau
varying in height from 76-90m (250-296ft). The land is
flat to the edge of the southern and southwestern cliffs
where it falls abruptly to the sea. On the northern, eastern
and southeastern sides it slopes gradually towards rocky
and sandy bays and quiet beaches.
LANGUAGE: English.
TIME: GMT.
ELECTRICITY: 240 volts AC, 50Hz.
COMMUNICATIONS: Telephone: Alderney is linked
to the British STD service; the area code is 01481. **Post:**
Only Guernsey and Alderney stamps will be accepted on
outgoing mail. **Press:** Jersey, Guernsey and British
papers are available on the island.

PASSPORT/VISA

No passports are required for travel between the UK, the
other Channel Islands and Alderney. See the
Passport/Visa section of the general UK entry above.

MONEY

The currency is Sterling. UK notes and coins are legal
tender and circulate together with Channel Islands issue,
which are in the same denominations. Channel Islands
notes can be reconverted at parity in UK banks, although
they are not accepted as legal tender in the UK.
Banking hours: 0930-1300 and 1430-1530 Monday to
Friday.

DUTY FREE

The following items can be imported into Alderney
without incurring customs duty on arrival in the UK:
*200 cigarettes or 50 cigars or 100 cigarillos or 250g of
tobacco; 1 litre of alcoholic beverages if over 38.8%
proof or 2 litres if under 38.8% proof or 4 litres of wine
(2 sparkling and 2 still); 50g perfume and 250ml of eau
de toilette.*

PUBLIC HOLIDAYS

Public holidays observed in Alderney are the same as
those in the rest of the UK (see general entry above).

HEALTH

No vaccination certificates are required to enter
Alderney. There is a Reciprocal Health Agreement with
the UK, allowing all short-stay visitors (three months
maximum) from the mainland free medical treatment and
free emergency dental treatment; prescribed medicines
must be paid for. Proof of UK residence (driving licence,
NHS card, etc) is required to benefit from the Agreement.
The island has a small hospital and two medical and
dental practices.

TRAVEL

AIR: *Aurigny Air Services* offer flights to Guernsey
(flight time – 15 minutes), Jersey, Southampton (flight
time – 45 minutes) and Bournemouth in the UK, and to
Dinard and Cherbourg in France. For further information,
contact Aurigny Air Services, Alderney. Tel: 822 804
(administration) *or* 822 886 (reservations). Fax: 3344.
International airport: The island's airport is *The Blaye
(ACI),* with flights to Southampton, Bournemouth,
Guernsey, Jersey and Cherbourg. Airport facilities: buffet
and shop (0800-1830 winter, 0800-1930 summer); taxis
(rank adjacent to terminal building).
SEA: During the summer months *Torbay Seaways* have
direct sailings from Torquay to Alderney. *Condor of
Guernsey* have twice-weekly hydrofoil services during
the summer between Guernsey and Alderney.
RAIL: For information on rail travel, contact *Alderney
Railway,* PO Box 75, Alderney.
ROAD: Caravans may not be imported to Alderney.
Bus: During the summer months an internal bus service
operates on the island running from St Anne's to the five
main beaches. **Taxi:** Private taxi companies operate on
the island. **Car hire:** There is a car hire company on the
island and a number of garages have rental cars. **Bicycle
hire:** There are several bike hire firms that rent out
bicycles at daily or weekly rates. **Regulations:** Traffic

drives on the left. Maximum speed limit is 30mph
(48kmph). **Documentation:** Full UK driving licence is
accepted.

ACCOMMODATION

Hotel, guest-house and self-catering accommodation is
available, but pre-booking is necessary in the summer
months. Camping is only permitted on the one official
campsite. The import of caravans is prohibited.

RESORTS & EXCURSIONS

The island is almost treeless and has a heavily indented
shoreline which has created many sandy bays and rugged
crags. The principal town, **St Anne's,** dates back to the
15th century and has many shops and inns lining its
cobbled streets.

SOCIAL PROFILE

FOOD & DRINK: Cuisine is largely French influenced.
The local speciality is shellfish. A wide variety of
alcoholic beverages is available. Spirits, beers and wines
are relatively cheaper than on the mainland.
SHOPPING: There is no VAT, but a Guernsey
Bailiwick tax is imposed on certain goods such as spirits,
wines, beers and tobacco. Prices on luxury goods are
relatively cheaper than in the UK, although the overall
cost of foodstuffs is higher. Special purchases include
Alderney pullovers, local pottery and crafts. **Shopping
hours:** These vary, but the majority of shops are open
0930-1230 and 1430-1730. Shops generally close earlier
Wednesday.
SPORT: Golf: There is a well-maintained 9-hole golf
course with a bowling green. **Windsurfing/surfing:**
Surf/sail boards are available for hire on the island; ask at
the tourist office for further information. **Sailing:** The
sailing club facilities are open to visiting yachtsmen from
established clubs. Various open events are held during
the summer. **Tennis/squash:** Facilities are available on
the island for both squash and tennis.
SPECIAL EVENTS: *Alderney Week* takes place in late
July/early August and the first Saturday in August sees a
cavalcade and torchlight procession.
Note: *For information relating to Alderney on people,
religion, social conventions, business, tipping, as well as
information on the government, economy and history, see
the separate entry on Guernsey.*

CLIMATE

The island enjoys a temperate climate with warm
summers and milder winter temperatures than those
experienced in the UK.

Guernsey

For information on Guernsey, see the separate entry
earlier in the *World Travel Guide.*

Jersey

For information on Jersey, see the separate entry earlier
in the *World Travel Guide.*

Sark & Herm

Location: English Channel.

Sark Tourism Information Centre
Tel: 832 345. Fax: 832 483.
Herm Island Administration Office
Tel: 722 377. Fax: 700 334.

AREA: Sark: 5.5 sq km (2.1 sq miles). **Herm:** 2 sq km
(0.8 sq miles).
POPULATION: Sark: 420 (1984). **Herm:** 107 (1971),
including Jethou.
POPULATION DENSITY: Sark: 76.4 per sq km.
Herm: 53.5 per sq km.

GEOGRAPHY: Sark is an hour's boat journey east of
Guernsey. It is almost two islands, the two parts being
joined by a narrow isthmus known as *La Coupée*. Most
of the people live on La Collinette on a steep hill
overlooking the harbour of La Maseline. The coastline is
rugged, with many cliffs and caves. **Herm** lies between
Guernsey and Sark. It has lush and varied scenery, with
meadows, unusual wild flowers and steep cliffs
overlooking secluded coves and pounding surf. Herm
attracts up to 3000 visitors a day during the summer.
LANGUAGE: Local *patois*, a mixture of Norman
French and Old English. English is widely spoken.
Note: *For information on time, electricity, passport/visa
and climate, and for further information on
communications and money, see the separate entry on
Guernsey earlier in this book.*
COMMUNICATIONS: Telephone: Sark and Herm are
connected to the UK STD telephone network. Area code:
01481. **Post:** There is a post office on Sark.

MONEY

Both Sark and Herm use Sterling as currency and UK
mainland banks such as *Midland Bank Plc* and *National
Westminster Bank Plc* can be found on the islands.

TRAVEL

SEA: Sark and Herm can be reached by sea from either
Jersey or Guernsey. **Sark:** The *Isle of Sark Shipping
Company* runs daily services (travel time – 35/45
minutes) between Guernsey and Sark in summer, with a
more limited service in winter, as well as services
between Sark and Herm (summer only). For further
information, contact Isle of Sark Shipping Company Ltd,
The White Rock, St Peter Port, Guernsey. Tel: 724 059.
Herm: There is a ferry service daily between Guernsey
and Herm (travel time – 20 minutes). Ferries leave every
half hour from Guernsey to Herm and faster catamarans
can be chartered. Carriers include: *Herm Seaways –
Picquet House, St Peter Port, Guernsey; tel: 724 161;
Herm Express Ferry – tel: 721 342; Munson Herm Ferry
– tel: 722 613; and Trident Charter Company –
Weighbridge, St Peter Port, Guernsey; tel: 721 379.*
ROAD: No cars are allowed on either island, but there
are 58 tractors on Sark – indeed, even the ambulance on
Sark is drawn by a tractor. The Sark 'taxi' is a horse-
drawn carriage which takes visitors around the island.
Bicycles can also be hired on Sark. Herm has only a few
essential tractors and an emergency Land-Rover.

ACCOMMODATION

There are a few hotels, guest-houses and self-catering
units on Sark. Herm has one country inn, surrounded by
flower gardens, and a few self-catering cottages. For
further information, contact the Guernsey Tourist Office.
Tel: 726 611. Fax: 721 246.

RESORTS & EXCURSIONS

Sark: A feudal state ruled over by a single man – the
grandson of the famous Dame of Sark. There is a
medieval parliament called the Chief Pleas. The *Island
Hall* is a wooden building used for dances, film shows,
card games and many other forms of entertainment.
There are several excellent beaches, including the *Venus
Pool, Adonis Pool* and *Creux Derrible*; most of these
beaches can only be reached at low tide. Most of the
island's accommodation is to be found at *Dixcart Bay*.
Herm: Privately leased, and run as a resort island.
Attractions include a 'Tom Thumb' village restored from
derelict houses, a restored chapel, woods, caves, the shell
beach, covered by countless shells deposited by the Gulf
Stream, some from as far away as Mexico, swimming in
rock pools. There are quite a few pubs on the island
which devise their own opening hours on a rota system;
one will almost always be open.

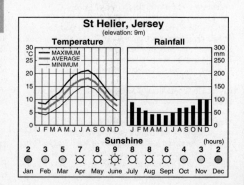

St Helier, Jersey
(elevation: 9m)

898

➊	EDINBURGH	➒	ARRAN
➋	GLASGOW	➓	SKYE
➌	DUMFRIES	⑪	ORKNEY
➍	RENFREWSHIRE	⑫	ABERDEEN
➎	SPEYSIDE	⑬	KINCRAIG
➏	OBAN	⑭	KINGUSSIE
➐	INVERNESS	⑮	ABERFELDY
➑	MULL		

SCOTLAND – Advertiser Key

904

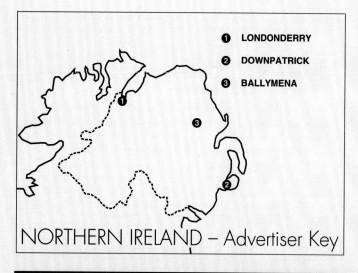
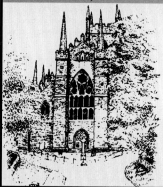

Enjoy yourself in Donegal at Inniskeel House

Comfortable Hostel catering for 40 people facing the sea, a mile-long beach and tidal island with monastic ruins.

- Ideal for school/youth/study groups.
- Beautiful scenery with interesting local geology and monuments.
- Off-road biking/canoeing/body boarding/camping/team building available.
- Self-catering or catering.

To find out more:
Tel/fax: 075 45103
Outside Republic of Ireland:
Tel/fax: 010 353 75 45103

LOGANS
executive travel

LOGANS OFFERS THE CLIENT A CHOICE ...

- We cater for all size groups from chauffeur driven cars to full-size executive coaches.
- We cover all destinations in Ireland and mainland U.K.
- We are ground handling agents

Style • Comfort • Flexibility

The company has earned a reputation for style and quality by maintaining a high standard of service and attention to detail.

Logans Executive Travel,
58 Galdanagh Road, Dunloy,
Ballymena, Co. Antrim BT44 9DB
Tel: (012656) 57203/57431
Fax: (012656) 57559

VISIT THE IRISH NATIONAL HERITAGE PARK
FERRYCARRIG, WEXFORD

20 minutes from Rosslare, 5 minutes from Wexford town.

'Where Ireland's Heritage Trail starts'

- 14 carefully reconstructed sites laid out in a beautiful 35-acre park with many streams, ponds and lakes.
- The Park describes Ireland's heritage from the Stone Age to the arrival of the Normans.
  - Hands-on exhibits, craft demonstrations.
  - Beautiful views of the River Slansy.
- Audio-visual • Guided tours • Café • Souvenir shop

Open March 31st – early November.
Tel: +353 53 20733. Fax: +353 53 20911.

Visit the colourful, turbulent world of Gaelic Ireland

The larger-than-life story of Granuaile, or Grace O'Malley (1530-1600), is imaginatively recounted at the **Granuaile Centre.** Audio visual displays, depict the *Pirate Queen's* legendary exploits at sea, during this turbulent and eventful epoch in Irish history.

**Granuaile Centre, Louisburgh, Co. Mayo
Tel: 098 66195. Fax: 098 66485. Open May-Oct.**

THE UNIVERSITY OF DUBLIN
TRINITY COLLEGE

When visiting Ireland why not stay in one of Europe's oldest Colleges. Founded in 1592 the College is located downtown in the city centre on a 35-acre campus. Facilities include:

- 1000 rooms fully-serviced (self-catering facilities and ensuite facilities)
- Restaurants
- Bars
- Launderette
- Banks
- Car Parking
- Crèche
- Shopping
- Credit Cards

Available June 1 to October 1. Tel: +353 1 608 1177. Fax: +353 1 671 1267.

Inishowen – Look at it This Way ...

Inishowen – nestling on the northern coast of Donegal and rightly known as 'Ireland's best kept secret'.
Natural wonders, from the magnificent Malin Head to countless beaches and sparkling streams.
In short, it's a place for relaxation, for the gentle contemplation of our stunning countryside: but if you're feeling a bit more energetic ...
Sports and activities are widely available: golf, angling, horseriding, cycling – a wealth of choice to suit every taste.
History is also something we are rich in, a history stretching far back to antiquity. After all, this is one of the cradles of Western civilization.
Opportunities exist, in short, for doing whatever you want to do – even if that's just letting the whole wonderful atmosphere gently wash over you.
Write to us at the address below, or call (0)77 74933, for more information.
Everything you've ever dreamed about Ireland is waiting for you –
Now!

Inishowen Tourism, Chapel Street, Carndonagh, Inishowen, Co. Donegal.
Tel: (0) 77 74933/74934. Fax: (0) 77 74935.

Situated 10km from Waterford City (off the N25), Celtworld, through the use of stunning audio-visual effects technology, brings to life the myths and legends of Irish Celtic Folklore.

Housed in a purpose-built modern building, which contains Europe's largest moving theatre, Celtworld offers you an opportunity to explore Ireland's Celtic mythological past in an exciting and unique way.

In no other part of Ireland will you apperceive such a unique and dramatic presentation of Irish Celtic mythology in comparison to what you will experience at this unrivalled visitor attraction.

Celtworld – Where Legend Lives...

OPEN APRIL TO SEPTEMBER
Tramore, Co. Waterford, Ireland.
Tel: +353 (051) 386166. Fax: +353 (051) 390146.

KILVAHAN HORSE DRAWN CARAVANS

is based in the beautiful midland county of Laois on a working farm with restored Georgian country house and courtyard, offering full facilities – toilets, showers, reception lounge with open turf-fire, picnic area, barbecue, etc.

Visitors spend first and last night on the base and then spend six days travelling quiet country roads, stopping at night in small country pubs or farmhouses.

All caravans are new, authentic and very comfortable. They sleep 4 adults or 2 adults and 3 children (gas stove, lights, linen, crockery, etc. included). Our horses are gentle and docile.

This family-run business is committed to excellence in all areas and time is given to fulfil the needs and expectations of all our clients.

No experience needed. Full instuctions provided. All details of routes and maps provided.

- Irish Tourist Board approval • Included in World's best 101 holidays (*UK Times*)
- Irish Farm Enterprise Awards – National Winner 1994

**Kilvahan Horse Drawn Caravans, Kilvahan, Portlaoise, Co. Laois, Ireland.
Tel: 353 502 27048. Fax: 353 502 27225.**

United States of America

□ *major international airport*

Location: North America.

United States Travel & Tourism Administration
Fourth and Constitution Avenue, NW, Washington, DC
20230
Tel: (202) 482 3811. Fax: (202) 482 2887.
Embassy of the United States of America
24 Grosvenor Square, London W1A 1AE
Tel: (0171) 499 9000. Fax: (0171) 629 9124.
United States Consulate General (Visa Branch)
5 Upper Grosvenor Street, London W1A 2JB
Tel: (0171) 499 6846 (visa information) *or* (0891) 200
290 (recorded visa information; calls are charged at the
higher rate of 39/49p per minute). Fax: (0171) 495 5012.
Opening hours: 0830-1130 Monday to Friday.
Consulate in: Edinburgh (tel: (0131) 556 8315).
United States Immigration Department
5 Upper Grosvenor Street, London W1A 2JB
Tel: (0171) 499 9000 *or* (0891) 200 290 (recorded visa
information; calls are charged at the higher rate of 39/49p
per minute). Fax: (0171) 495 4330. Opening hours: 0900-
1200 Monday to Friday.
**United States Travel & Tourism Administration
(USTTA)**
PO Box 1EN, London W1A 1EN
Tel: (0171) 495 4466. Fax: (0171) 409 0566. Information
can be obtained by phone, fax or post only. Opening
hours: 0900-1600 Monday to Friday.
British Embassy
3100 Massachusetts Avenue, NW, Washington, DC
20008
Tel: (202) 462 1340. Fax: (202) 898 4255. Telex: 216760
(a/b BRITEM).
Consulates in: Anchorage, Atlanta, Boston, Chicago,
Cleveland, Dallas, Houston, Kansas City, Los Angeles
(tel: (310) 477 3322), Miami, New Orleans, New York
(tel: (212) 745 0200), Miami, Norfolk, Philadelphia,
Portland (Oregon), San Francisco and Seattle.
Embassy of the United States of America
PO Box 866, 100 Wellington Street, Station B, Ottawa,
Ontario K1P 5T1
Tel: (613) 238 5335 *or* 238 4470. Fax: (613) 238 5720.
Consulates in: Ottawa, Calgary, Halifax, Montréal,
Québec, Toronto and Vancouver.
**United States Travel & Tourism Administration
(USTTA)**
Suite 602, 480 University Avenue, Toronto, Ontario
M5G 1V2
Tel: (416) 595 5082 (trade enquiries) *or* (905) 890 5662
(consumer enquiries). Fax: (416) 595 5211.
Also in: Montréal and Vancouver.
Canadian Embassy
501 Pennsylvania Avenue, NW, Washington, DC 20001
Tel: (202) 682 1740. Fax: (202) 682 7726. Telex: 89664
(a/b DOMCAN A WSH).
Consulates in: Atlanta, Boston, Buffalo, Chicago, Dallas,
Detroit, Los Angeles (tel: (213) 687 7432), Miami,
Minneapolis, New York (tel: (212) 596 1600) and
Seattle.

INTRODUCTION

Information on the United States of America is provided
in three sections: the general factfinder (immediately
below); the *States A-Z* section, which briefly covers all
States not included under *US Gateways* and gives sources
of further information; and the *US Gateways* section,
providing detailed information on the major tourist
destinations – details of travel, excursions, leisure
activities and special events in the States of Arizona,
California, Colorado, Florida, Georgia, Hawaii, Illinois,
Louisiana, Maryland, Massachusetts, Michigan,
Minnesota, Missouri, New Jersey, New York, Ohio,
Pennsylvania, Texas, Washington State and Washington
DC (all of these States have gateway airports).

AREA: 9,372,614 sq km (3,618,770 sq miles).
POPULATION: 255,082,000 (1992).
POPULATION DENSITY: 27.2 per sq km.
CAPITAL: Washington DC. **Population:** 606,900
(1990). Sixteen other cities have a population larger than
that of Washington DC. New York is the largest city,
with a population of over seven million. Los Angeles,
Chicago, Houston, Philadelphia, San Diego, Detroit and
Dallas had populations of over one million in 1990.
GEOGRAPHY: Covering a large part of the North
American continent, the United States of America shares

borders with Canada to the north and Mexico to the south
and has coasts on the Atlantic, Pacific and Arctic Oceans,
the Caribbean and the Gulf of Mexico. The State of
Alaska, in the northwest corner of the continent, is
separated from the rest of the country by Canada, and
Hawaii lies in the central Pacific Ocean. One of the
largest countries in the world, the USA has an enormous
diversity of geographical features. The climate ranges
from subtropical to Arctic, with a corresponding breadth
of flora and fauna. For a more detailed description of
each region's geographical characteristics, see below
under the *States A-Z*.
LANGUAGE: English. Many other languages are
widely spoken in certain areas of the cities, in
communities and in States bordering Mexico where
Spanish has, in some areas, completely supplanted
English.
RELIGION: Protestant with Roman Catholic, Jewish
and many ethnic minorities. In large cities people of the
same ethnic background often live within defined
communities.
TIME: The USA is divided into six time zones:
Eastern Standard Time: GMT - 5.
Central Standard Time: GMT - 6.
Mountain Standard Time: GMT - 7.
Pacific Standard Time: GMT - 8.
Alaska: GMT - 9.
Hawaii: GMT - 10.
Note: When calculating travel times, bear in mind the
adoption of *Daylight Saving Time (DST)* by most States
in summer. From the first Sunday in April to the last
Sunday in October clocks are put forward one hour,
changing at 0200 hours local time. Regions not observing
DST include most of Indiana, all of Arizona and Hawaii.
The USA adopts *DST* one week later than the UK, so for
a week the time difference changes.
ELECTRICITY: 110/120 volts AC, 60Hz. Plugs are of
the flat 2-pin type. European electrical appliances not
fitted with dual-voltage capabilities will require a plug
adaptor, which is best purchased *before* arrival in the
USA.
COMMUNICATIONS: Telephone: Full IDD is
available. Country code: 1. Outgoing international code:
011. For emergency police, fire or medical services in
major cities, dial 911. **Fax:** There are bureaux in all main
centres, and major hotels also have facilities. Fax
services are very widely available. **Telex/telegram:**
Western Union telex facilities are available throughout
the USA. Telegrams can be sent through all telegraph
and post offices. **Post:** There are only a limited number
of post offices, so it is advisable to buy stamps in bulk.
There are, however, stamp machines in hotels and shops,
but these have a 25% price mark-up. Airmail to Europe
takes up to a week. Post office hours: 0900-1700 (24
hours at main offices in larger cities). If sending gifts
valued at less than US$50 to the USA, the recipient will
not have to pay tax if the package is marked 'Unsolicited
Gift'. **Press:** The most influential papers are *The New
York Times, Washington Post, Los Angeles Times,
International Herald Tribune* and the *Wall Street
Journal*. Owing to the high degree of self-government of
each State, newspapers tend to be regionalised, although
recent economic pressures have resulted in large-scale
mergers. Even so, the USA publishes more newspapers
than any other country, and has perhaps the heaviest

Sunday newspapers in the world, particularly the Sunday
edition of *The New York Times*.
BBC World Service frequencies: From time to time
these change. See the section *How to Use this Book* for
more information.
BBC:

MHz	17.84	15.26	9.590	5.975

PASSPORT/VISA

*Regulations and requirements may be subject to change at short notice, and you
are advised to contact the appropriate diplomatic or consular authority before
finalising travel arrangements. Details of these may be found at the head of this
country's entry. Any numbers in the chart refer to the footnotes below.*

	Passport Required?	Visa Required?	Return Ticket Required?
Full British	1	2/3	Yes
BVP	Not valid	-	-
Australian	Yes	Yes	Yes
Canadian	1	No	No
USA	-	-	-
Other EU (As of 31/12/94)	Yes/1	2	Yes
Japanese	Yes	4	Yes

Entry restrictions: The following will be refused entry
to the United States of America unless a 'waiver of
ineligibility' has first been obtained:
(a) people afflicted with certain serious communicable
diseases;
(b) anyone with a criminal record;
(c) narcotics addicts or abusers and drug traffickers;
(d) anyone who has been deported from or denied
admission to the USA within the previous 5 years.
PASSPORTS: [1] A valid passport is required on entry
by all except: (a) Canadian nationals arriving from
anywhere in the Western hemisphere with at least one
proof of identity; (b) residents of Canada or Bermuda
who have a common nationality with nationals of Canada
or with British subjects in Bermuda (eg are citizens of a
Commonwealth country or Ireland) who are arriving
from North, Central or South America (except Cuba).
British Visitors Passport: Not valid.
VISAS: Required by all except:
(a) nationals exempted under *Passports* above;
(b) **[2]** nationals of Belgium, Denmark, France,
Germany, Italy, Luxembourg, The Netherlands, Spain
and the UK who are travelling on an unexpired passport
for holiday, transit or business purposes for a stay not

Timatic	Health
	GALILEO/WORLDSPAN: **TI-DFT/JFK/HE**
	SABRE: **TIDFT/JFK/HE**
	Visa
	GALILEO/WORLDSPAN: **TI-DFT/JFK/VI**
	SABRE: **TIDFT/JFK/VI**
	For more information on Timatic codes refer to Contents.

exceeding 90 days and, if entering by air or sea, hold a return or onward ticket and completed form I-94-W and enter aboard an air or sea carrier participating in the Visa Waiver Pilot Program (lists of participating air or sea carriers are available from most travel agents). Nationals of Ireland, Greece and Portugal *do* require visas;
(c) **[3]** British subjects resident in the Cayman Islands or the Turks & Caicos Islands who arrive directly from those islands for non-immigration purposes;
(d) **[4]** nationals of Japan who are travelling on an unexpired passport for holiday, transit or business purposes for a stay not exceeding 90 days and, if entering by air or sea, hold a return or onward ticket and completed form I-94-W and enter aboard an air or sea carrier participating in the Visa Waiver Pilot Program (lists of participating air or sea carriers are available from most travel agents);
(e) nationals of Andorra, Austria, Brunei, Finland, Iceland, Liechtenstein, Monaco, New Zealand, Norway, San Marino, Sweden and Switzerland who are travelling on an unexpired passport for holiday, transit or business purposes for a stay not exceeding 90 days and, if entering by air or sea, hold a return or onward ticket and completed form I-94-W and enter aboard an air or sea carrier participating in the Visa Waiver Pilot Progam (lists of participating air or sea carriers are available from most travel agents).
Note: (a) Nationals of countries exempted above may also enter the USA overland from Canada or Mexico without a visa provided they are in possession of a completed form I-94-W issued by the immigration authorities at the port of entry. (b) UK passports with the endorsement British subject or British Dependent Territories Citizen, British Overseas Citizen or British National (Overseas) Citizen do *not* qualify for visa exemption. Persons unsure about visa requirements (including those defined in 'Entry restrictions' above) should write to the US Consulate General or the Visa Department of the US Embassy (addresses and telephone numbers above).
Types of visa: *Non-immigrant* (business and pleasure), *Student* (participating in academic or exchange programmes), *Journalist, Temporary worker* and *Transit*. There are further classifications of non-immigrant visas; enquire at the Embassy for more information. *Transit:* Certain airlines are authorised to carry foreign nationals in transit without a visa, provided

they continue their journey from the same airport within 8 hours and hold confirmed documentation for onward travel and valid entry requirements for the onward destination. In other cases, a Transit visa will be required; contact the nearest visa branch (see below) for further information.
Cost: £13.75 regardless of whether the visa is denied or issued and regardless of the duration of the visa or entries required. Nationals of Mexico will not be charged the application fee. The visa application fee must be paid in cash at a bank prior to submitting an application to the US Embassy. In the UK, Barclays Bank does not charge a handling fee for this service. One part of the two-part stamped receipt must be stapled to the visa application form. Some nationals may also have to pay a reciprocal visa issuance fee.
Validity: 10 years. Some visas are valid for multiple entry (see above). The length of stay in the USA is determined by US immigration officials at the time of entry, but is generally 6 months. For extensions and further information, apply to the US Immigration & Naturalisation Service.
Note: A visa no longer expires with the expiry of the holder's passport. An unexpired visa in an expired passport may be presented for entry into the USA as long as the visa itself has not been cancelled, is less than ten years old and is presented with a valid non-expired passport, provided that both passports are for the same nationality.
Application to: Visa branches at Consulate Generals. Those residing in England, Scotland or Wales should apply to the Consulate General in London. Nationals of Northern Ireland should apply to the Consulate General in Belfast. The Consulate General in Scotland no longer deals with visa applications. For addresses, see top of entry.
Application requirements: (a) Valid passport. (b) Sufficient funds for duration of stay. (c) 1 passport-size colour photo. (d) Completed application form. (e) Fee receipt (see *Cost* above). (f) Stamped, self-addressed envelope.
Further documentation may be required to substantiate details and the purpose of visit plus proof of intention to return to country of residence.
Working days required: Postal applications – at least 3 weeks. Applications submitted by authorised agents or courier service – 72 hours.

Residence: The law in the USA is complex for those wishing to take up residence. More information may be obtained from the Immigration Department (for address, see top of entry).

MONEY

Currency: US Dollar (US$) = 100 cents. Notes are in denominations of US$500, 100, 50, 20, 10, 5, 2 and 1. Coins are in denominations of US$1, and 50, 25, 10, 5 and 1 cents.
Currency exchange: Hotels do not, as a rule, exchange currency and only a few major banks will exchange foreign currency, so it is advisable to arrive with dollars.
Credit cards: Most major credit cards are accepted throughout the USA, including Diners Club, American Express, Access/Mastercard and Visa. Check with your credit card company for details of merchant acceptability and other services which may be available. Visitors are advised to carry at least one major credit card, as it is common to request pre-payment for hotel rooms and car hire when payment is *not* by credit card.
Travellers cheques: Widely accepted in hotels, stores and restaurants, providing they are US Dollar cheques; Sterling travellers cheques are not acceptable. American Express travellers cheques are often accepted as cash, preferably in denominations of US$10 or US$20. It should be noted that many banks do not have the facility to encash travellers cheques (the US banking system differs greatly from that of the UK) and those that do are likely to charge a high commission. One or in some cases two items of identification (passport, credit card, driving licence) may also be required.
Exchange rate indicators: The following figures are included as a guide to the movements of the US Dollar against Sterling:

Date:	Oct '92	Sep '93	Jan '94	Jan '95
£1.00=	1.59	1.53	1.48	1.56

Currency restrictions: There are no limits on the import or export of either foreign or local currency. However, movements of more than US$10,000 or the equivalent (including 'bearer bonds') must be registered with US Customs on Form 4790. All gold coins and any quantity of gold must be declared before export.
Banking hours: Variable, but generally 0900-1500 Monday to Friday.

New Orleans' Newest Hotel!

THE HOLIDAY INN DOWNTOWN-SUPERDOME

All new features include:

- 300 newly renovated rooms
- 3 de luxe suites
- Concierge Floor
- Holiday Streetcar Restaurant
- Mardi Gras Lounge
- Roof-top pool
- Complimentary morning coffee & donuts
- Executive meeting planner program
- 5 meeting and banquet rooms
- 2 blocks from the Superdome
- 3 blocks from the French Quarter

Call and mention Acct. #1076 to qualify for upgrades to our Concierge Floor and 12% commission.

**Downtown-Superdome
New Orleans**

330 Loyola Avenue
New Orleans, LA 70112
Tel: 504-581-1600
Toll Free: 1-800-535-7830
Fax: 504-586-0833

DUTY FREE

The following goods may be imported by visitors over 21 years of age into the USA without incurring customs duty:

200 cigarettes or 50 cigars or 2kg of tobacco or proportionate amounts of each; l litre of alcoholic beverage; *gifts or articles up to a value of US$100 (including 100 cigars in addition to the tobacco allowance above).

Note: [*] Up to US$300 for Hawaii. (a) Items should not be gift-wrapped as they must be available for customs inspection. (b) The alcoholic beverage allowance above is the national maximum; certain States allow less and if arriving in those States, the excess will be taxed or withheld. (c) The gift allowance may only be claimed once in every six months and is only available to non-residents who intend to stay in the USA for more than 72 hours. (d) For information about the importation of pets, refer to the brochure *Pets, Wildlife – US Customs*, available at US Embassies and Consulates.

Prohibited items: The following are either banned or may only be imported under licence: (a) Narcotics and dangerous drugs, unless for medical purposes (doctor's certificate required). (b) Absinthe, biological materials, some seeds, fruits and plants (including endangered species of plants and vegetables and their products). (c) Firearms and ammunition (with some exceptions – consult Customs). (d) Hazardous articles (fireworks, toxic materials). (e) Meat and poultry products. (f) Pornographic material. (g) Switchblade knives.

PUBLIC HOLIDAYS

Jan 1 '95 New Year's Day. **Jan 16** Martin Luther King Day. **Feb 20** President's Day. **May 29** Memorial Day. **Jul 4** Independence Day. **Sep 4** Labor Day. **Oct 9** Columbus Day. **Nov 11** Veterans' Day. **Nov 23** Thanksgiving Day. **Dec 25** Christmas Day. **Jan 1 '96** New Year's Day. **Jan 15** Martin Luther King Day. **Feb 19** President's Day.
Note: Other holidays may be observed on different dates from State to State.

HEALTH

Regulations and requirements may be subject to change at short notice, and you are advised to contact your doctor well in advance of your intended date of departure. Any numbers in the chart refer to the footnotes below.

	Special Precautions?	Certificate Required?
Yellow Fever	No	No
Cholera	No	No
Typhoid & Polio	No	-
Malaria	No	-
Food & Drink	1	-

[1]: Tap water is considered safe to drink. Milk is pasteurised and dairy products are safe for consumption. Local meat, poultry, seafood, fruit and vegetables are generally considered safe to eat.
Rabies is present. For those at high risk, vaccination before arrival should be considered. If you are bitten abroad seek medical advice without delay. For more information, consult the *Health* section.
Health care: Medical insurance providing cover up to at least US$500,000 is strongly advised. Only emergency cases are treated without prior payment and treatment will often be refused without evidence of insurance or a

deposit. Medical facilities are generally of an extremely high standard. Those visiting the USA for long periods with school-age children should be aware that school entry requirements include proof of immunisation against diphtheria, measles, poliomyelitis and rubella throughout the USA, and schools in many States also require immunisation against tetanus, pertussis and mumps.

TRAVEL - International

Note: The vast majority of arrivals are by air and consequently a special *US Gateways* section is included after the *States A-Z* below. The information to be found immediately below is of a more general nature.
AIR: The principal US airlines operating international services are: *American Airlines, Continental Airlines, Delta Air, Northwest Airlines, Trans World Airlines (TWA)* and *United Airlines*. Many other airlines operate services from all over the world to the USA.
For free advice on air travel, call the Air Travel Advisory Bureau on (0171) 636 5000 (London) *or* (0161) 832 2000 (Manchester).
Approximate flight times: From *London* to Anchorage is 8 hours 55 minutes, to Detroit is 8 hours 30 minutes, to Los Angeles is 11 hours, to Miami is 9 hours 35 minutes, to New York is 7 hours 30 minutes (3 hours 50 minutes by Concorde), to San Francisco is 10 hours 45 minutes, to Seattle is 9 hours 40 minutes and to Washington DC is 8 hours 5 minutes (all times are by non-stop flight).
From *Singapore* to Los Angeles is 18 hours 45 minutes and to New York is 21 hours 25 minutes.
From *Sydney* to Los Angeles is 17 hours 55 minutes and to New York is 21 hours 5 minutes.
More international flight times may be found in the *US Gateways* section below.
Note: Flights from Europe to the USA take longer than those coming back; ie flying east to west takes longer than west to east. Flights to Europe from the east coast of the USA take approximately 30-40 minutes less and from the west coast of the USA approximately one hour less.
International airports: See below under *US Gateways*.
SEA: Numerous cruise lines sail from ports worldwide to both the east and west coasts. Contact a travel agent for fares and details.
RAIL: The US and Mexican rail networks connect at Tecate (Tijuana), Yuma, Nogales, Douglas, El Paso, Del Rio and Laredo, but there are few scheduled passenger services. There are several connections with the Canadian network. The major routes are: New York to Montréal and New York to Toronto. Milwaukee, Chicago, Detroit and Buffalo are all connected via terminals in Toronto, Hamilton and Ottawa.
ROAD: There are many crossing points from Canada to the USA. The major road routes are: New York to Montréal/Ottawa, Detroit to Toronto/Hamilton, Minneapolis to Winnipeg and Seattle to Vancouver/Edmonton/Calgary.

TRAVEL - Internal

Note: More detailed information may be found in the *US Gateways* section below.
AIR: The USA may be crossed within 5 hours from east to west and within 2 hours from north to south. Strong competition between airlines has resulted in a wide difference between fares. Categories of fares include first-class, economy, excursion and discount. Night flights are generally cheaper. **Cheap fares:** Money-saving schemes for the visitor include discounts on all internal flights offered by *TWA, Delta* and other principal airlines. The traveller should buy tickets 21 days in

advance. *Delta, British Airways* and *Virgin Atlantic* offer a *Discover America Pass* which includes a minimum of three and a maximum of 12 coupons entitling the passenger to that number of flights within the USA at a discounted fare. The cost of the pass is according to the number of coupons requested. The coupons must be purchased outside the USA.
Agents are advised to contact the offices of individual airlines once a basic itinerary has been organised.
Note: Baggage allowance is often determined by number and size rather than weight.
Approximate flight times: Consult the *US Gateways* section below.
SEA & RIVER: There are extensive water communications both along the coastline and along the great rivers and lakes.
Great Lakes: The Ohio River carries more water traffic than any other inland waterway in the world. Tour ships and passenger and freight lines crisscross all the Great Lakes from Duluth, Sault Sainte Marie, Milwaukee, Chicago, Detroit, Toronto, Rochester, Cleveland and Buffalo.
RAIL: Although the US rail network has more than 300,000km (186,410 miles) of track, passenger trains run over only a small part of the system. Outside the densely populated northeast, trains run once-daily over a handful of long-distance routes. Nearly all the long-distance trains are operated by the *National Railroad Passenger Corporation (Amtrak)*, but suburban and some medium-distance services are run by local agencies. Amtrak's main route is the Boston–New York–Washington DC northeast corridor; other routes run south to Florida and New Orleans, and between Boston, New York and Washington DC to Chicago. From Chicago, daily services radiate to Seattle, Portland, Oakland (San Francisco), Los Angeles (via Omaha–Denver–Salt Lake City–Las Vegas or via Kansas City–Albuquerque–Flagstaff), New Orleans and San Antonio (via St Louis and Dallas/Fort Worth). A connection exists also exists between San Antonio and Los Angeles via El Paso, Tucson and Phoenix. There is a thrice-weekly train from Los Angeles to New Orleans.
Amtrak **tour packages:** There are over 74 different tours in 34 States throughout the USA. Full details are provided in the *Amtrak* brochure, which is widely available. Nearly all trains have one-class seating and air-conditioning, with a variety of sleeping accommodation available on payment of a supplementary fare. All long-distance trains have dining facilities. The railroads often pass through fine scenery, particularly on east–west routes. While most Americans drive or take the bus, the passenger trains continue to attract a discerning and ever-increasing clientele. Indeed, rail travel in the USA – as in many other countries – has undergone a considerable revival in recent years, and the signs are that this trend will continue. For further *Amtrak* information, tel: (212) 582 6875 (New York) *or* (213) 683 6987 (Los Angeles) *or* (0171) 978 5212 (London).
Cheap fares: There are regional and nationwide *USA Rail Passes;* nationwide passes give 15 or 30 days unlimited travel on the whole *Amtrak* network up to Montréal. Overnight sleepers, auto trains and the 'Metroliner' between New York and Washington are not included in the pass. The *National Rail Pass* is valid for rail travel anywhere in the USA for 15 or 30 days. The 15-day pass costs US$340 per person in the peak season (from May 28-August 29) and US$229 per person (off-peak); the 30-day pass costs US$425 per person (US$339 off-peak). Regional passes are broken down into the following: *East Region Pass* is valid for unlimited travel in the region east of Chicago and New Orleans up to

Montréal for 15 or 30 days – the 15-day pass costs US$200 per person (US$179 off-peak) and the 30-day pass costs US$255 per person (US$229 off-peak); *West Region Pass* is valid for unlimited travel in the region west of Chicago to New Orleans for 15 or 30 days – the 15-day pass costs US$255 per person (US$209 off-peak) and the 30-day pass costs US$320 per person (US$279 off-peak); *Far West Pass* is valid for unlimited travel in the region from Seattle to San Diego and to Salt Lake City and Flagstaff for 15 or 30 days – the 15-day pass costs US$200 per person (US$179 off-peak) and the 30-day pass costs US$255 per person (US$229 off-peak); and *Coastal Region Pass* is valid for unlimited travel from Montréal to Miami on the east coast and from Seattle to San Diego on the west coast for 30 days only and costs US$225 per person (US$199 off-peak). These passes *cannot* be purchased in the USA. Passports must be presented at the time of purchase and passes must be used within 90 days of purchase. The passes cover coach-class travel tickets and seat reservations on *Amtrak* passenger services. *However, rail passes act as a form of payment for seats only – to guarantee a seat on any specific Amtrak train, a reservation must be made.* Travellers should contact the nearest *Amtrak* station to find out whether reservations are required on specific journeys they wish to make. For journeys where reservations are required, train times should be reconfirmed 24 hours prior to departure. Travellers aiming to travel during peak times should make reservations well in advance. Higher class and other accommodation is available on payment of the usual supplements. Children aged 2-15 pay half the adult fare and children under two years of age travel free. Group, family, weekend and tour packages are all available, although fares may still exceed combined bus and air fares.

In many cases, point-to-point tickets bought outside the USA will be considerably cheaper. UK nationals can check with *Destination Marketing* (tel: (0171) 978 5212; fax: (0171) 924 3171) for further details.

Approximate journey times: See below under *US Gateways* for approximate times for train connections between a selection of major US cities.

ROAD: Driving is a marvellous way to see the USA, although the distances between cities can be enormous. A realistic evaluation of travel times should be made to avoid over-strenuous itineraries. Driving conditions are excellent and the road system reaches every town. Petrol is cheaper than in Europe. The *American Automobile Association (AAA)* offers touring services, maps, advice and insurance policies, which are compulsory in most States, even for hiring. Tel: (407) 253 9100. Membership of a visitor's own national automobile association (eg *AA* or *RAC* membership for the UK) entitles the traveller to *AAA* benefits.

Coach: There is one major coach carrier covering the whole of the USA: *Greyhound World Travel.* This main national service is supplemented by over 11,000 other tour lines, covering the country with reasonably priced and regular services. Air-conditioning, toilets and reclining seats are available on intercity routes. *Greyhound* covers the Southern States, the Southern-Central States, the South Rockies area and also extends into Mexico and Canada. Facilities for left luggage and food are available, usually 24 hours a day. Once disembarked at a bus terminal, passengers are not permitted to wait there overnight for an onward bus (ie no sleeping in the terminal). **Cheap fares:** *Greyhound Lines* offer the *Ameripass*, which gives 4, 7, 15 or 30 days unlimited travel throughout the USA. Extensions are available, payable by the day. The pass must be bought outside the USA through *Greyhound World Travel. Ameripass* offers half-price fares for children 2-11 years old. Unlimited stopovers are allowed on ordinary tickets. *Greyhound Lines* also offer excursion fares for point-to-point travel. *Intra* and *Intercity Tours (Greyhire)* are run throughout the USA. Contact *Greyhound Lines* at their international offices in New York (tel: (212) 971 6300) *or* Los Angeles (tel: (213) 629 8400).

Car hire: Major international companies have offices at all gateway airports and in most cities. There are excellent discounts available for foreign visitors. Credit card deposits and inclusive rates are generally required. As a guide to car sizes an 'Economy' or 'Compact' refers to a car the size of a standard European car, while a 'Standard' refers to a car the size of a limousine. Minimum ages for hirers vary according to the rental company, pick-up point and method of payment. Agents are advised to contact the individual companies for information on drivers under 25 years of age. *Columbus Press* publishes a handy booklet, *Driving In the USA,* dealing with most aspects of car hire in the USA.

Drive away: The *AAA* and *Auto Driveaway* provide a service enabling the traveller to drive cars to and from a given point, only paying the price of petrol. A deposit is often required and time and mileage limits are set for delivery, which leaves very little time for sightseeing (there are heavy financial penalties for those who exceed the limits). Details are published under *Automobile & Truck Transporting* in the US Yellow Pages. Some companies allow the driver to finish the journey in Canada. For further information, phone *Auto Driveaway.* Tel: (312) 341 1900.

Campers/motorhomes: The hire of self-drive campers or motorhomes, which are called 'recreational vehicles' in the USA, are a good means of getting around. Contact the USTTA Travel Information Centre for more information. For addresses, see top of entry.

Documentation: An International Driving Permit is recommended, although it is not legally required (it is often very useful as an additional proof of identity). A full national driving licence is accepted for up to one year. *Insurance:* All travellers intending to rent or drive cars or motorhomes in the USA are strongly advised to ensure that the insurance policy covers their total requirements, covering all drivers and passengers against injury or accidental death. A yellow 'non-resident, interstate liability insurance card' which acts as evidence of financial responsibility is available through motor insurance agents.

Traffic regulations: Traffic drives on the right. Speed limit: usually 55mph (89kmph) on motorways, but varies from State to State. Speed limits are clearly indicated along highways and are strictly enforced, with heavy fines imposed. Note that it is illegal to pass a school bus that has stopped to unload its passengers (using indicators and warning lights) and all vehicles must stop until the bus has moved back into the traffic stream. It is illegal for drivers not to have their licences immediately to hand. If stopped, do not attempt to pay a driving fine on the spot (unless it is demanded) as it may be interpreted as an attempt to bribe. **Note:** There are extremely tough laws against drinking and driving throughout the USA. These laws are strictly enforced.

Approximate journey times: Approximate self-drive and *Greyhound* journey times between a selection of US cities may be found below under *US Gateways.*

URBAN: Some US cities now have good public transport services following a 'transit renaissance' after the energy crises of the 1970s. There are a number of underground train systems in operation in major cities including New York (subway), Washington DC (metro), Boston ('T'), Chicago (train) and San Francisco (BART – Bay Area Rapid Transit); others are being planned or built, for instance a long-overdue network in Los Angeles. There are also several tramway and trolleybus systems, including the much-loved antique trams found in San Francisco.

Note: Many of the underground train systems are dangerous during off-peak hours (the New York subway, in particular, has acquired an almost gothic reputation for violence, although this has been much exaggerated), but they offer cheap, quick and efficient travel during the working day, particularly in New York, Boston and Chicago. Travel by any other means during the day is likely to be slow and arduous.

ACCOMMODATION

HOTELS: There are many good traditional hotels. However, the majority are modern and part of national and international chains, often with standard prices. In general the quality of accommodation is high, with facilities such as televisions and telephones in each room. For further information, contact the American Hotel & Motel Association, Suite 600, 1201 New York Avenue, NW, Washington, DC 20005-3931. Tel: (202) 289 3100. Fax: (202) 289 3199. **Grading:** Basic categories fall into 'Super', 'Deluxe', 'Standard', 'Moderate' and 'Inexpensive'. Prices vary according to standards.

Pre-paid voucher schemes: Several companies offer a pre-paid voucher scheme for use at various hotel and motel chains throughout the USA. Further details are available from the USTTA Travel Information Centres.

GUEST-HOUSES: There is a network of guest-houses (boarding houses) throughout the USA. For details, contact The Director, Tourist House Association of America, PO Box 355-AA, Greentown, PA 18426. Tel: (717) 676 3222.

BED & BREAKFAST: This long-established tradition in the UK is now spreading across the USA. B&B signs are not generally displayed by individual homes, but most homes offering this service are listed in directories, which may be purchased by interested travellers.

RANCH HOLIDAYS: There are ranches all over the southern and western States offering riding, participation in cattle drives, and activity holidays in mountain and lakeland settings.

CAMPING/CARAVANNING: This is extremely popular, especially in the Rocky Mountains and New England. The camping season in the north lasts from mid-May to mid-September. Camping along the side of highways and in undesignated areas is prohibited. For information on campsites, contact KOA (Kampgrounds of America). Tel: (406) 248 7444. The 24,000-plus campsites fall into two general categories:

Public sites – Usually linked with National or State Parks and Forests, offering modest but comfortable facilities. Most of them will have toilet blocks, electricity hook-ups and picnic areas. Campsites are usually operated on a first-come, first-served basis and will often restrict the length of stay. Advance reservations are possible at some national parks.

Privately-run sites – These range from basic to resort luxury. Most have laundry and drying facilities, entertainment and information services. Reservations can be made through a central reservation office in the USA.

YMCA/YOUTH HOSTELS: There are 74 *YMCA* centres in 68 cities throughout the USA. Membership is not necessary, but reservations should be made two days prior to arrival via the Head Offices. The *YMCA* offers centrally-located accommodation at attractive rates coast to coast throughout the USA. Most centres offer single and double accommodation for both men and women and many also have sports facilities. Youth hostels offer their members simple, inexpensive overnight accommodation usually located in scenic, historical or cultural places. *Youth Hostel Association* membership is open to everyone with no age limit and there are individual, family and organisation memberships. British visitors should take out membership in the UK before travelling.

SELF-CATERING: Self-catering facilities, known in the USA as 'apartments', 'condominiums' (or 'condos'), 'efficiencies' or 'villas', are also available. Further details are available from the USTTA Travel Information Centre (for addresses, see top of entry).

HOME EXCHANGE: There are several agents who offer home exchange programmes between the USA and the UK. Further information is available from the USTTA Travel Information Centres.

RESORTS & EXCURSIONS

Major tourist attractions are given in the section *States A-Z* and in the *Resorts & Excursions* sub-sections of *US Gateways* below.

POPULAR ITINERARIES: 7-day: (a) New York–Providence–Newport–Martha's Vineyard–Cape Cod–Boston. (b) New Orleans–Baton Rouge–Memphis–St Louis. **10-day:** (a) Miami–Fort Lauderdale–Palm Beach–Tampa–Orlando–Jacksonville–Tallahassee–Pensacola. (b) Houston–San Antonio–El Paso–Tucson–Grand Canyon–Phoenix. (c) San Diego–Los Angeles–Santa Barbara–Monterey–Redwood–San Francisco.

SOCIAL PROFILE

FOOD & DRINK: In large cities, restaurants are mostly modern and very clean, offering a vast range of cuisines, prices and facilities. American breakfasts are especially notable for such specialities as pancakes or waffles with maple syrup, home fries and *grits* (a Southern dish). Foreigners are often perplexed by the common question of how they would like their eggs fried, ie 'over easy' (flipped over briefly) or 'sunny side up' (fried on one side only). Fast food chains serving hot dogs ('weenies'), hamburgers and pizzas are everywhere. Regional specialities range from Spanish flavours in the southwest to Creole or French in the Deep South. Restaurants come in all shapes and sizes, ranging from fast-food, self-service and counter service to drive-in and table service. The 'diner' is an integral part of the American way of life; consisting of a driveway, neon lights and simple food served from the counter; it is generally located in or just outside smaller towns. Discounts on eating out include *Early Bird Dinners,* where discounts are offered for meals served prior to 1800; *Children's Platters,* selections from a low-cost children's menu; and *Restaurant Specials,* when a different specific meal is offered each day at a discount price or there is an all-you-can-eat menu. **Drink:** There are also many types of bars, ranging from the smart cocktail lounge, café-style, high 'saloon' style bars and imitations of English pubs to the 'regular' bar. In cities many have 'happy hours' with cheaper drinks and free snacks on the counter. Generally speaking, waiter/waitress service costs more. Drinking laws are set by States, counties, municipalities and towns, although traditionally closing time in bars is between 2400 and 0300. The legal age for drinking also varies from 18 to 21 from State to State and the laws on the availability of alcohol run from Nevada's policy of anytime, anywhere and to anyone, to localities where drinking is strictly prohibited. Where the laws are severe, there are often private clubs or a town only a few kilometres away from the 'dry town' where alcohol sales

are legal. It is important to be aware of these laws when visiting an area and it is worth remembering that where alcohol is available, visitors may be asked to produce some form of identity that will prove their age. It should also be noted that it is illegal to have an open container of alcohol in a vehicle or on the street. Beer is the most popular and widespread drink and is served ice cold. Californian wines are gaining popularity.

See also the *Food & Drink* section under the individual States in *US Gateways* below.

NIGHTLIFE: Clubs generally stay open until the early hours in cities, where one can find music and theatre of all descriptions. Theatre tickets for Broadway, New York's equivalent of London's West End 'Theatreland', can be booked for groups of over 20 through *Group Sales Box Office,* 3rd Floor, 226 West 47th Street, New York, NY 10036. Tel: (212) 398 8383. Fax: (212) 398 8389. Tickets must be paid for in advance and will be kept at the theatre box office for collection on the night of the performance. Gambling is only allowed in licensed casinos and the legal age for gamblers is 21 years of age or over.

SHOPPING: Variety, late opening hours, competitive prices and an abundance of modern goods typify American shopping. Many small stores, specialist food shops and hypermarkets are open 24 hours a day. Clothes and electronic goods can be bought direct from factories. Retail outlets range from flea markets and bargain stores to large chain department stores. Malls are a popular way of shopping in the USA and consist of a cluster of different kinds of shops in one building, often a few storeys high, connected by an indoor plaza. Note that a sales tax is levied on all items in most States and the addition is not included on the price label; 3-15% is normal. A guide to the customs and laws of American shopping is available from PO Box 95-M, Oradell, NJ 07649. **Shopping hours:** 0900/0930-1730/1800 Monday to Saturday. There may be late-night shopping one or two evenings a week. Some States permit Sunday trading.

SPORT: American football, baseball and **basketball** are the national sports. The baseball season lasts from April to September, the football season from September to January, the basketball season from November to April and the hockey season from October to March. **Ice-hockey** is also very popular, as is **tennis**. The visitor can buy temporary membership at over 200 clubs. **Golf:**

A few clubs and courses are open to visitors. For information, contact the Taconic Golf Club, PO Box 183, Williamstown, MA 01267. Tel: (413) 458 9669. **Outward Bound:** America's vast expanses of wild country and mountains lend themselves to outdoor pursuits. The national office is Outward Bound, Route 9DR2, Box 280, Garrison, New York, NY 10524. Tel: (914) 424 4000. Fax: (914) 424 4280. **Horseracing:** The heart of racing in the USA is the 'bluegrass country', focused around the State of Kentucky. The most important races of the year, the *Bluegrass Stakes* and the *Kentucky Derby*, are run at the Churchill Downs racecourse in Louisville, Kentucky. There are also major tracks in New England. **Rodeos:** Held in Colorado, Oklahoma, Texas and throughout the western States, rodeos are a legacy of the historical development that resulted from the spread of cattle ranching. **Downhill skiing:** The principal areas are: *Eastern States* – Maine, New Hampshire, Vermont; *California* – Lake Tahoe, Squaw Valley, Mammoth Mountain; and *Colorado* – Aspen, Summit County. Skiing is also possible in Idaho, Montana, New Mexico and Utah. **Cross-country skiing:** New England, California, Minnesota, Wisconsin, Colorado and Wyoming. A *Ski Touring Guide* is published by the *Ski Touring Council,* based in New York.

SPECIAL EVENTS: The holidays which are closest to the people's hearts are Thanksgiving and Christmas. **Christmas:** The Americans celebrate Christmas in a big way, both religiously and as consumers. Northern regions have the added bonus of wintery weather and snowfall, and a 'White Christmas' (a fairly common event in the New England area and other northern States) always adds to the atmosphere. **Thanksgiving:** Thanksgiving takes place on November 4. It is a festival celebrated with close family and friends. Blessings are shared and prayers of thanks are said over a meal of roast turkey, bread stuffing, roast potatoes and yams. This holiday originated in the first year after the Pilgrim Fathers arrived in the New World as a feast to thank the American Indians for their aid and advice in helping the immigrants come to grips with a new land. **The 4th of July:** In honour of America's victory against the British in the Revolutionary War, this holiday is celebrated throughout the country with spectacular fireworks displays. American fireworks are among the best in the world and some of the most dazzling shows

take place over lakes, rivers or on the coast, where the sky is lit up without any architectural obstacles and the light is reflected from the water. **Halloween:** Another holiday celebrated in the USA is Halloween (October 31). Children dress up in, often, ghoulish costumes, as witches, devils and ghosts and tour the neighbourhood, usually in groups, knocking on the doors of nearby houses and saying 'trick or treat'. The owner of the house is then obliged to give the children some sort of 'treat', usually food or sweets. Failure to comply can result in the 'trick'. The night before Halloween is known as *Mischief Night,* when children roam their neighbourhoods making a nuisance of themselves with pranks such as ringing doorbells and running away or spreading toilet paper along fences and telephone poles. Both of these nights are somewhat unpopular with adults, but children have a great time and the tradition is probably too engrained in American tradition to be discontinued. **Mardi Gras:** Every year New Orleans celebrates Mardi Gras, attracting visitors from all over the USA and abroad. There are parades, dancing in the streets and revellers in masks and costumes all in a spirit of wild abandon. The celebrations will next take place between February 6-20, 1996.

In addition to the above, details of special events are listed for many States under their individual headings in the *US Gateways* section.

SOCIAL CONVENTIONS: The wide variety of national origins and America's relatively short history has resulted in numerous cultural and traditional customs living alongside each other. In large cities people of the

same ethnic background often live within defined communities. Shaking hands is the usual form of greeting. A relaxed and informal atmosphere is usually the norm. As long as the fundamental rules of courtesy are observed there need be no fear of offending anyone of any background. Americans are renowned for their openness and friendliness to visitors. Gifts are appreciated if one is invited to a private home. As a rule dress is casual. Smart restaurants, hotels and clubs insist on suits and ties or long dresses. Smoking is often restricted in public buildings and on city transport. There will usually be a notice where no smoking is requested and many restaurants have smoking and non-smoking sections. **Tipping:** Widely practised, and service charges are not usually included in the bill. Waiters generally expect 15%, as do taxi drivers and hairdressers. It should be noted that a cover charge is for admission to an establishment, not a tip for service. Porters generally expect US$1 per bag.

BUSINESS PROFILE

ECONOMY: The US economy is the world's most powerful and diverse. The physical expansion and development of the country during the 19th century, mass immigration, technological and marketing innovations, exploitation of natural resources and the expansion of international trade – all developments which have taken place within a political and economic system well able to exploit them – has made the USA a country of unprecedented wealth. With her large foreign investments, US interests dominate world markets in almost every sector, thus giving the dollar a crucial role. The USA has large areas under cultivation producing a wide range of commodities: the most important of these are cotton, cereals and tobacco, all of which are exported on a large scale. Mining operations produce oil and gas, coal, copper, iron, uranium and silver. The manufacturing industry is a world leader in many fields, including steel, vehicles, aerospace, telecommunications, chemicals, electronics and consumer goods. Since the late 1970s, however, the biggest employer has been the service sector, particularly finance (including banking, insurance and equities), leisure and tourism. Despite the wealth and range of its economy, there is a growing feeling in many quarters that the US economy now faces inevitable decline. Imports of many products have risen sharply during the last ten years (crucially, faster than exports) and previously dominant industries have found themselves under fierce competition from Japan, the European Community and the NICs – the newly-industrialised countries of the Pacific Rim. Oil, chemicals, vehicles and even advanced technology industries such as computing are threatened. There is a worrying trade deficit and a vast overspend on the Federal budget, which escalated to an astonishing US$4 trillion following the Reagan presidency. The protectionist lobby in the USA has grown quickly in the last few years and has now started to exert a significant influence on the Government. There have been a series of bilateral disputes between the USA and, successively, Japan and the European Community over a variety of products and services (semiconductors, transport and financial services). The crunch is likely to come over agriculture where both EU and Japanese farmers enjoy well-protected internal markets. The creation of the Single European Market in 1992 has triggered several potentially explosive arguments. Agriculture and services featured prominently in the latest round of GATT talks, which were resolved in January 1994. On the American continent, however, free trade has scored a major success with the 3-way agreement between the USA, Canada and Mexico to establish the North American Free Trade Agreement (NAFTA). This establishes a trading bloc of remarkably similar proportions to the EU. With a total population of 345 million, the EU has an economic output of US$6.1 trillion. NAFTA has a total population of 365 million and an economic output of US$6.2 trillion. **BUSINESS:** Business people are generally expected to dress smartly, although a man may wear a short-sleeved shirt under his suit in hot weather. Normal business courtesies should be observed, although Americans tend to be less formal than Europeans. Appointments and punctuality are normal procedure and business cards are widely used. Dates in America are written month-day-year: 4 July 1994 would thus be abbreviated as 7/4/94. Write out the month in full to avoid confusion. **Office hours:** 0900-1730 Monday to Friday. **COMMERCIAL INFORMATION:** The following organisations can offer advice: New York Chamber of Commerce and Industry, 1 Battery Park Plaza, New York, NY 10004. Tel: (212) 493 7400. Fax: (212) 344 3344; *or* Chamber of Commerce of the USA, 1615 H Street, NW, Washington, DC 20062-0001. Tel: (202) 659 6000. Fax: (202) 463 5836; *or*

United States Department of Commerce, International Trade Administration, Room 3718, Federal Office Building, 26 Federal Plaza, Foley Square, New York, NY 10278. Tel: (212) 264 0600. Fax: (212) 264 1356; *or* National Foreign Trade Council Inc, 1270 Avenue of the Americas, New York, NY 10020. Tel: (212) 399 7128. **CONFERENCES/CONVENTIONS:** In the last 20 years ABTA (the Association of British Travel Agents) has held its annual convention in US cities four times; its 1991 convention was in Orlando, Florida. The convention has previously been held in Miami, Los Angeles and Phoenix. That no other country has been revisited so often clearly indicates the importance of the USA as a conference destination; there are State, city and regional travel and convention organisations in every part of the country, each actively promoting its own assets. With so much information available the real problem for the organiser is to find some way of getting through it all and there are several magazines devoted to this end; they include *Meeting & Conventions Magazine, Successful Meetings Magazine* and *Corporate Meetings and Incentive Magazine.* Of statistical interest is Chicago's status as host to more trade shows than any other city in the world. Organisers interested in US venues should contact the USTTA or the travel organisations listed in the State sections of the *States A-Z* entry below. In addition to the State organisations, addresses of travel and convention organisations for cities and counties are also included.

CLIMATE

See *Climate* sections in *US Gateways* below.

States A-Z

The following section gives information on all the States in the USA, arranged alphabetically. More detailed information on States which have a gateway city may be found in *US Gateways* below. See also the *Introduction* above.

ALABAMA

POPULATION: 4,136,000.
CAPITAL: Montgomery.
TIME: GMT - 6. *Daylight Saving Time* is observed.
THE STATE: Alabama offers mountains, lakes, caverns, woodland and beaches. Birmingham is its largest city and cultural centre. Attractions include the new civic sports and arts centre and the Birmingham Museum of Art. Other tourist destinations include the Huntsville Space & Rocket Center; the Russell Cave National Monument; historic Montgomery; and Mobile, a major seaport and resort area on the Gulf Coast.
Further information from: Alabama Bureau of Tourism & Travel, Suite 126, 401 Adams Avenue, Montgomery, AL 36103. Tel: (205) 242 4169 *or* (1 800) 252 2262 (toll

free). Fax: (205) 242 4554.
City and council information: Greater Birmingham Convention & Visitors Bureau, 2200 Ninth Avenue North, Birmingham, AL 35203-1100. Tel: (205) 252 9825. Fax: (205) 458 8086; *or*
Huntsville and Madison County Convention & Visitors Bureau, 700 Monroe Street, Huntsville, AL 35801. Tel: (205) 551 2230. Fax: (205) 551 2324; *or*
Mobile Convention & Visitors Corporation, 1 South Water Street, Mobile, AL 36602. Tel: (205) 415 2000. Fax: (205) 415 2060.

ALASKA

POPULATION: 587,000.
CAPITAL: Juneau.
TIME: GMT - 9, east of W169° 30'; GMT - 10, west of W169° 30' (the Aleutian Islands). *Daylight Saving Time* is observed.
THE STATE: The largest State in the USA, Alaska is a land of glaciers, rivers, waterfalls, fjords, forests, tundra and meadows. Anchorage is the largest city. Alaskan attractions include Denali National Park, Kenai Peninsula, Alyeska ski area, Chugach National Forest, Portage Glacier, Pribilof Islands and Juneau, the State capital and historic gold-mining city. Mount McKinley, at 6194m (20,320ft), is the highest mountain in North America.
Further information from: Alaska Division of Tourism, PO Box 110801, Juneau, AK 99811-0901. Tel: (907) 465 2012. Fax: (907) 586 8399.
City and council information: Anchorage Convention & Visitors Bureau, Suite 200, 1600 A Street, Anchorage, AK 99501-5162. Tel: (907) 276 4118. Fax: (907) 278 5559.

ARIZONA

POPULATION: 3,832,000.
CAPITAL: Phoenix.
GATEWAY: Phoenix. For further information, see under *US Gateways* below.

ARKANSAS

POPULATION: 2,399,000.
CAPITAL: Little Rock.
TIME: GMT - 6. *Daylight Saving Time* is observed.
THE STATE: A varied landscape of plains, mountains, forests, rivers, cattle farms, industrial centres and oil wells. Its many lakes are among the chief tourist attractions. Others include the Hot Springs National Park; Blanchard Spring Caverns; Buffalo River; Crater of Diamonds State Park; Eureka Springs, a town built into the mountainside; and Mountain View, the Ozark Mountain folk centre. Little Rock, one of the State's earliest settlements, contains parks, museums and arts centres. Bill Clinton was the Governor of Little Rock, Arkansas before becoming President.
Further information from: Arkansas Division of Parks & Tourism, 1 Capitol Mall, Little Rock, AR 72201. Tel: (501) 682 7777 *or* (1 800) NATURAL (toll free). Fax: (501) 682 1364.
City and council information: Little Rock Convention &

USA: States

[Map of the United States showing state names: Washington, Oregon, Idaho, Nevada, California, Montana, Wyoming, Utah, Arizona, North Dakota, South Dakota, Nebraska, Colorado, New Mexico, Minnesota, Iowa, Kansas, Oklahoma, Texas, Wisconsin, Illinois, Missouri, Arkansas, Louisiana, Michigan, Indiana, Ohio, Kentucky, Tennessee, Mississippi, Alabama, Georgia, Florida, Maine, New York, Pennsyl., Virginia, North Carolina, South Carolina, WASHINGTON Dist. of Columbia]

1 New Hampshire
2 Vermont
3 Massachusetts
4 Rhode Island
5 Connecticut
6 New Jersey
7 Delaware
8 Maryland
9 West Virginia

Alaska
Hawaii

2000km
1000mls

DAB-M284

Visitors Bureau, PO Box 3232, Little Rock, AR 72203.
Tel: (501) 376 4781. Fax: (501) 374 2255; *or*
Hot Springs Convention & Visitors Bureau, PO Box K,
134 Convention Boulevard, Hot Springs National Park,
AR 71902. Tel: (501) 321 2277. Fax: (501) 321 2136.

CALIFORNIA

POPULATION: 30,867,000.
CAPITAL: Sacramento.
GATEWAYS: Los Angeles and San Francisco. For
further information, see under *US Gateways* below.

COLORADO

POPULATION: 3,470,000.
CAPITAL: Denver.
GATEWAY: Denver. For further information, see under
US Gateways below.

CONNECTICUT

POPULATION: 3,281,000.
CAPITAL: Hartford.
TIME: GMT - 5. *Daylight Saving Time* is observed.
THE STATE: Connecticut offers quiet colonial villages,
upmarket 'commuter towns' for New York executives,
lakes, mountains, forests and broad sandy beaches.
Hartford is the insurance capital of the USA. State
attractions include Mark Twain House, Hartford; New
Haven, home of Yale University and the well-known
Peabody Museum of Natural History; Mystic Seaport, a
living museum of whaling; Long Island Sound, with its
chain of resort towns and fishing ports; and the Gillette
Castle Park in Hadlyme.
Further information from: Connecticut Office of
Tourism, 865 Brook Street, Rocky Hill, CT 06067. Tel:
(203) 258 4300 *or* (1 800) 262 6863 (toll free). Fax:
(203) 258 4275.
City and council information: New Haven Visitors
Bureau, 1 Longwharf Drive, New Haven, CT 06511. Tel:
(203) 777 8550. Fax: (203) 495 6949; *or*
Greater Stamford Visitors Bureau, 1 Landmark Square,
Stamford, CT 06901. Tel: (203) 359 4761. Fax: (203)
363 5069; *or*
Greater Hartford Visitors Bureau, 1 Civic Center Plaza,
Hartford, CT 06103. Tel: (203) 728 6789. Fax: (203) 293
2365; *or*
Mystic Information Center, Building 1D, Olde Mystic
Village, Mystic, CT 06355. Tel: (203) 536 1641.

DELAWARE

POPULATION: 689,000.
CAPITAL: Dover.
TIME: GMT - 5. *Daylight Saving Time* is observed.
THE STATE: Wilmington is this small State's
administrative and commercial centre. Founded in 1638,
the city includes museums, galleries and a port. Its Fort
Christina Historic Park is the site of Delaware's first
permanent settlement. The rest of the State is mostly
rural. Attractions include the small capital city of Dover;
historic New Castle; the fishing town of Lewes;
Rehoboth Beach and Delaware Seashore State Park.
Further information from: Delaware Tourism Office, PO
Box 1401, 99 Kings Highway, Dover, DE 19903. Tel:
(302) 739 4271 *or* (1 800) 441 8846 (toll free). Fax:
(302) 739 5749.
City and council information: Greater Wilmington
Convention & Visitors Bureau, Suite 504, 1300 Market
Street, Wilmington, DE 19801. Tel: (302) 652 4088. Fax:
(302) 652 4726.

FLORIDA

POPULATION: 13,488,000.
CAPITAL: Tallahassee.
GATEWAYS: Miami, Orlando and Tampa. For further
information, see under *US Gateways* below. See also the
special sections on Northwest Florida, Orlando and
Naples in the *Florida* section of *US Gateways*.

GEORGIA

POPULATION: 6,751,000.
CAPITAL: Atlanta.
GATEWAY: Atlanta. For further information, see under
US Gateways below.

HAWAII

POPULATION: 1,160,000.
CAPITAL: Honolulu.
GATEWAY: Honolulu. For further information, see
under *US Gateways* below.

IDAHO

POPULATION: 1,067,000.
CAPITAL: Boise.
TIME: GMT - 7. *Daylight Saving Time* is observed in
the greater part of the State.
THE STATE: Idaho includes Hell's Canyon, the deepest
in North America; the largest stand of white pine in the
world at Clearwater National Forest; and two of the
finest big-game hunting areas in the USA – Chamberlain
Basin and Selway. Boise hosts a summer festival and the
August Idaho State Fair. The well-known Sun Valley
resort area offers skiing and winter sports and a range of
summer activities. Other attractions include the massive
Shoshone Falls; the Shoshone Indian Ice Caves; historic
Fort Hall; the Craters of the Moon National Monument
area; the Coeur d'Alene mining district; and the Nez
Perce National Historical Park.
Further information from: Idaho Department of
Commerce, 700 West State Street, Boise, ID 83720. Tel:
(208) 334 2470. Fax: (208) 334 2631.
City and council information: Boise Convention &
Visitors Bureau, PO Box 2106, Suite 200, 168 North 9th
Street, Boise, ID 83701. Tel: (208) 344 7777. Fax: (208)
344 6236.

ILLINOIS

POPULATION: 11,631,000.
CAPITAL: Springfield.
GATEWAY: Chicago. For further information, see
under *US Gateways* below.

INDIANA

POPULATION: 5,662,000.
CAPITAL: Indianapolis.
TIME: GMT - 5 (in the greater part of the State).
Daylight Saving Time is not observed.
THE STATE: Indiana, bordered by Lake Michigan to
the north, features lakes, deep valleys, plains, foothills,
industrial areas and vast farmlands. Indianapolis is a
national centre for industry, commerce and culture. Its
international airport is 8km (5 miles) from the city centre.
State attractions include the Indiana Dunes National
Lakeshore and park; Amish Acres, a restored 19th-
century Amish community at Nappanee; the Conner
Prairie Pioneer Settlement; the Squire Boone Caves; and
Fort Wayne, scene of many bloody battles.
Further information from: Indiana Tourism Division,
Department of Commerce, Suite 700, Indiana Commerce
Center, 1 North Capitol, Indianapolis, IN 46204-2288.
Tel: (317) 232 8860 *or* (1 800) 323 4639 (toll free). Fax:
(317) 233 6887.
City and council information: Indianapolis Convention &
Visitors Bureau, Suite 100, 1 RCA Dome, Indianapolis,
IN 46225. Tel: (317) 639 4282. Fax: (317) 639 5273; *or*
Greater Lafayette Convention & Visitors Bureau, PO
Box 5547, 301 Frontage Road, Lafayette, IN 47903. Tel:
(317) 447 9999. Fax: (317) 447 5062; *or*
Bloomington/Monroe County Convention & Visitors
Bureau, 2855 North Walnut Street, Bloomington, IN
47404. Tel: (812) 334 8900. Fax: (812) 334 2344; *or*
Grant County Convention & Visitors Bureau, 215 South
Adams Street, Marion, IN 46952. Tel: (317) 668 5435.
Fax: (317) 668 5443.

IOWA

POPULATION: 2,812,000.
CAPITAL: Des Moines.
TIME: GMT - 6. *Daylight Saving Time* is observed.
THE STATE: Almost 95% of Iowa's gently undulating
land is given over to agriculture, but it also offers cities,
scenic parks and many lakes and recreation areas, such as
East and West Okoboji, Spirit Lake and Clear Lake. Its
rich cultural heritage is shown in the German, Swiss and
Alsatian Amana colonies, with their many historic sites
and museums. Pella reflects its Dutch past in its tulip
fields, customs and architecture. Other attractions include
the Boone and Scenic Valley Railroad; Effigy Mounds
Park, with its relics of ancient Indian culture; and Fort
Dodge, now restored as a museum.
Further information from: Iowa Division of Tourism,
200 East Grand Avenue, Des Moines, IA 50309. Tel:
(515) 242 4705 *or* (1 800) 345 4692 (toll free). Fax:
(515) 242 4749.
City and council information: Des Moines Convention &
Visitors Bureau, Ruan Two Building, 601 Locust, Des
Moines, IA 50309. Tel: (515) 286 4960. Fax: (515) 244
9757; *or*
Iowa City Convention & Visitors Bureau, 408 First
Avenue, Coralville, IA 52241. Tel: (319) 337 6592. Fax:
(319) 337 9953.

KANSAS

POPULATION: 2,523,000.
CAPITAL: Topeka.
TIME: GMT - 6. *Daylight Saving Time* is observed.
THE STATE: At the geographic centre of North
America, Kansas is largely agricultural, with vast fields
of wheat. It boasts many monuments to its Old West past,
as well as numerous recreation centres, reservoirs and
rivers offering all kinds of outdoor pursuits. Attractions
include the restored cattle town of Dodge City; the
Kansas Cosmosphere and Discovery Center in
Hutchinson; and the Swedish settlers' town of Lindsborg.
Wichita, its largest city, includes museums, parks, and
centres for art, music, theatre and sport.
Further information from: Kansas Travel & Tourism,
Suite 1300, 700 SW Harrison Street, Topeka, KS 66603-
3712. Tel: (913) 296 2009 *or* (1 800) 252 6727 (toll
free). Fax: (913) 296 6988.
City and council information: Wichita Convention &
Visitors Bureau, Suite 100, 100 South Main, Wichita, KS
67202. Tel: (316) 265 2800. Fax: (316) 265 0162.

KENTUCKY

POPULATION: 3,755,000.
CAPITAL: Frankfort.
TIME: GMT - 5 (eastern part); GMT - 6 (western part).
Daylight Saving Time is observed.
THE STATE: Kentucky is best known for horses, caves,
bourbon and bluegrass music. Lexington is the horse-
breeding centre and many of its surrounding farms
welcome visitors on free tours. Louisville boasts the
famous Kentucky Derby, along with historic buildings,
top arts venues, a space museum and steamboat trips.
Other attractions include the Fort Knox gold bullion
store; the pioneer town at Kentucky Lake, one of the
largest man-made lakes in the world; the Daniel Boone
National Forest; and Bardstown, the 'bourbon capital of
the world'.
Further information from: Kentucky Department of
Tourism, Suite 2200, 500 Mero Street, Frankfort, KY
40601. Tel: (502) 564 4930 *or* (1 800) 225 4787 (toll
free). Fax: (502) 564 5695.
City and council information: Louisville Bureau of
Tourism, 400 South First Street, Louisville, KY 40202.
Tel: (502) 584 2121. Fax: (502) 584 6697; *or*
Greater Lexington Convention & Visitors Bureau, 301
West Vine Street, Lexington, KY 40507. Tel: (606) 233
1221. Fax: (606) 254 4555; *or*
Northern Kentucky Convention & Visitors Bureau, 605
Philadelphia Street, Covington, KY 41011. Tel: (606)
261 4677. Fax: (606) 261 5135.

LOUISIANA

POPULATION: 4,287,000.
CAPITAL: Baton Rouge.
GATEWAY: New Orleans. For further information, see
under *US Gateways* below.

MAINE

POPULATION: 1,235,000.
CAPITAL: Augusta.
TIME: GMT - 5. *Daylight Saving Time* is observed.
THE STATE: Maine offers some of the most beautiful
scenery in the north. About four-fifths of its area is
forested, but it also includes more than 2200 lakes,
together with mountains, valleys and seashore. Bangor is
a major commercial, financial and cultural centre.
Portland, Maine's largest city, features a renovated old
port section. Other State attractions include the Acadia
National Park on the Atlantic Ocean, one of the most
beautiful in the USA; Kittery, the State's oldest town;
and Kennebunkport, one of the prime beauty spots on the
north coast.
Further information from: Maine Publicity Bureau, PO
Box 2300, Hallowell, ME 04347. Tel: (207) 623 0363.
Fax: (207) 623 0388.
City and council information: Portland Convention &
Visitors Bureau, 305 Commercial Street, Portland, ME
04101. Tel: (207) 772 4994. Fax: (207) 874 9043; *or*
Kennebunk-Kennebunkport Tourism Board, PO Box
740, Kennebunk, ME 04043. Tel: (207) 967 0858.

MARYLAND

POPULATION: 4,908,000.
CAPITAL: Annapolis.
GATEWAY: Baltimore. For further information, see
under *US Gateways* below.

MASSACHUSETTS

POPULATION: 5,998,000.
CAPITAL: Boston.
GATEWAY: Boston. For further information, see under *US Gateways* below.

MICHIGAN

POPULATION: 9,437,000.
CAPITAL: Lansing.
GATEWAY: Detroit. For further information, see under *US Gateways* below.

MINNESOTA

POPULATION: 4,480,000,
CAPITAL: St Paul.
GATEWAY: Minneapolis/St Paul. For further information, see under *US Gateways* below.

MISSISSIPPI

POPULATION: 2,614,000.
CAPITAL: Jackson.
TIME: GMT - 6. *Daylight Saving Time* is observed.
THE STATE: Mississippi is noted for its pre-Civil War mansions, fine beaches and scenery. More than 16,000 acres have been set aside for camping and recreation, including the Clarbco and Percy Quinn State parks. National forests include Bienville, DeSoto, Delta and Holly Springs, famed for its restored country houses. Natchez, with its fine 18th- and 19th-century architecture, is near the start of the restored Natchez Trace Trail to Nashville. The route passes the ancient Indian Emerald Mound and the ghost town of Rocky Springs. Other attractions include Vicksburg, with its national military park; and Biloxi, on the state's beach-lined border with the Gulf of Mexico.
Further information from: Mississippi Division of Tourism, PO Box 1705, Oceanspring, MS 39566-1705. Tel: (601) 359 3297 *or* (1 800) WARMST (toll free). Fax: (1 800) 873 4780 (toll free).
City and council information: Meridian-Lauderdale County Partnership, PO Box 790, Suite 800, 721 Front Street, Meridian, MS 39302. Tel: (1 800) 748 9970 (toll free). Fax: (601) 693 5638; *or*
Natchez-Adams County Convention & Visitors Bureau, PO Box 1485, 422 Main, Natchez, MS 39121. Tel: (601) 446 6345. Fax: (601) 442 0814.

MISSOURI

POPULATION: 5,193,000.
CAPITAL: Jefferson City.
GATEWAY: St Louis. For further information, see under *US Gateways* below. See also the special sections on Kansas City, Missouri Division of Tourism and Springfield in the *Missouri* section of *US Gateways*.

MONTANA

POPULATION: 824,000.
CAPITAL: Helena.
TIME: GMT - 7. *Daylight Saving Time* is observed.
THE STATE: Montana boasts vast areas of national forest and wilderness, together with glaciers, mountain lakes, rivers, trails, waterfalls and ski resorts. Its major tourist destinations include the spectacular Yellowstone (shared with Wyoming, see below) and Glacier national parks. Its numerous recreation areas include the Bob Marshall Wilderness Area and the huge Charlie Russell Wildlife Refuge. Helena offers fine 19th-century architecture, museums and the Gothic-style St Helena Cathedral. Other attractions include the Custer Battlefield, site of Custer's Last Stand; the restored Old West towns of Virginia City and Nevada City; and the National Bison Range.
Further information from: Montana Travel Promotion Division, PO Box 200533, Helena, MT 59620. Tel: (406) 444 2654 *or* (1 800) VISITMT (toll free). Fax: (406) 444 1800.
City and council information: Missoula Convention & Visitors Bureau, PO Box 7577, 825 East Front, Missoula, MT 59807-7577. Tel: (406) 543 6623. Fax: (406) 543 6625.

NEBRASKA

POPULATION: 1,606,000.
CAPITAL: Lincoln.
TIME: GMT - 6. *Daylight Saving Time* is observed in the greater part of the State.
THE STATE: Nebraska rises from the Missouri prairie lands to the Great Plains and foothills of the Rocky Mountains. Omaha, its largest city, is one of the State's major tourist destinations. Boys Town, the famous homeless boys' community, is nearby. Lincoln boasts the State Capitol, the University of Nebraska Museum and the well-known Sheldon Art Gallery. Other State attractions include the Homestead National Monument; the pioneer landmarks of Scotts Bluff and Chimney Rock; Fort Robinson, where Chief Crazy Horse surrendered; and the Buffalo Bill Historical Park.
Further information from: Nebraska Division of Travel & Tourism, PO Box 94666, Lincoln, NE 68509. Tel: (402) 471 3794 *or* (1 800) 228 4307 (toll free). Fax: (402) 471 3026.
City and council information: Greater Omaha Convention & Visitors Bureau, Suite 202, 6800 Mercy Street, Omaha, NE 68106-2627. Tel: (402) 444 4660. Fax: (402) 444 4511.

NEVADA

POPULATION: 1,327,000.
CAPITAL: Carson City.
GATEWAY: Las Vegas.
TIME: GMT - 8. *Daylight Saving Time* is observed.
THE STATE: Nevada includes everything from pine forests, desert, mountains and ghost towns to neon-lit cities. Las.Vegas is its largest city and one of the major gambling and entertainment centres of the world. Luxury hotels, casinos and show venues line 'The Strip', a section of Las Vegas Boulevard South. A lower-priced, smaller version is found at the Downtown Casino Center. Outdoor sports, top restaurants and nightclubs are also on offer. Reno, another entertainment and casino city, is also known for its quiet residential areas and surrounding historic and natural attractions. Lake Tahoe spans the California-Nevada border. It is the largest mountain lake in the USA and one of America's most famous mountain resort areas, with year-round sports and activities. Other State attractions include the Lake Mead National Recreation Area; the Valley of Fire State Park; Pyramid Lake; Mount Charles; and the spectacular Lehman Caves and Death Valley.
Further information from: Nevada Commission on Tourism, 5151 South Carson Street, Carson City, NV 89710. Tel: (702) 687 4322. Fax: (702) 687 6779.
City and council information: Las Vegas Convention & Visitors Bureau, 3150 Paradise Road, Las Vegas, NV 89109. Tel: (702) 892 0711. Fax: (702) 892 2824; *or* Reno-Sparks Convention & Visitors Authority, PO Box 837, 4590 South Virginia Street, Reno, NV 89502. Tel: (702) 827 7600. Fax: (702) 827 7646.

NEW HAMPSHIRE

POPULATION: 1,111,000.
CAPITAL: Concord.
TIME: GMT - 5. *Daylight Saving Time* is observed.
THE STATE: New Hampshire is noted for its scenic beauty, from Mount Washington in the northern White Mountains and the centre-State lakes to the ocean beaches near Hampton. The Cog Railway ride to the top of Mount Washington affords panoramic views of Canada and the surrounding States. Franconia Notch, a dramatic 13km (8-mile) gorge nearby, is one of New England's most acclaimed beauty spots. Major ski resorts include Cannon Mountain, Loon Mountain and Waterville Valley. The town of Laconia, between lakes Winnipesaukee and Winnisquam, is another popular tourist destination.
Further information from: New Hampshire Office of Tourism, PO Box 1856, 172 Pembroke Road, Concord, NH 03302-0856. Tel: (603) 271 2666 *or* (1 800) 386 4664, ext. 145 (toll free). Fax: (603) 271 2629; *or* New Hampshire Lodging & Restaurant Association, PO Box 1175, 4 Park Street, Concord, NH 03302-1175. Tel: (603) 228 9585. Fax: (603) 226 1829.
City and council information: Mount Washington Valley Tourism Office, PO Box 2300, North Conway, NH 03860. Tel: (603) 356 5701. Fax: (603) 356 7069.

NEW JERSEY

POPULATION: 7,789,000.
CAPITAL: Trenton.
GATEWAY: Newark. For further information, see under *US Gateways* below.

NEW MEXICO

POPULATION: 1,581,000.
CAPITAL: Santa Fe.
TIME: GMT - 7. *Daylight Saving Time* is observed.
THE STATE: New Mexico has deserts, forests, cities, lakes and mountains. Its Pueblo Indian and Spanish cultures are still very much alive. Albuquerque, the largest city, has an international airport and its Old Town, museums and cultural centres help make it an important tourist destination and a good base for travelling through the State. Santa Fe, with its *adobe* architecture, is the USA's oldest State capital. Other attractions include the Sandia Peak area and ski runs; the Carlsbad Caverns; the mountain resort of Ruidoso; the Spanish colonial village of La Mesilla; prehistoric Indian sites; and the Navajo Indian Reservation near Farmington.
Further information from: New Mexico Tourism & Travel Division, Lamy Building, 491 Old Santa Fe Trail, Santa Fe, NM 87503. Tel: (505) 827 7400 *or* (1 800) 545 2040 (toll free). Fax: (505) 827 7402.
City and council information: Albuquerque Convention & Visitors Bureau, PO Box 26866, Albuquerque, NM 87125. Tel: (505) 842 9918. Fax: (505) 247 9101; *or* Santa Fe Convention & Visitors Bureau, PO Box 909, Santa Fe, NM 87504-0909. Tel: (505) 984 6760. Fax: (505) 984 6679.

NEW YORK

POPULATION: 18,119,000.
CAPITAL: Albany.
GATEWAY: New York City. For further information, see under *US Gateways* below.

NORTH CAROLINA

POPULATION: 6,843,000.
CAPITAL: Raleigh.
TIME: GMT - 5. *Daylight Saving Time* is observed.
THE STATE: Natural attractions in North Carolina range from sandy beaches in the east to high mountain ranges in the west. Charlotte, the largest city, is a thriving convention and entertainment centre. The Outer Banks barrier islands along the coast include resorts, fishing villages and stretches of national seashore. Cape Hatteras National Seashore also boasts areas of undeveloped beach. Other attractions include Raleigh, with its fine architecture and cultural centres, Great Smoky Mountains National Park and the Qualla Boundary Cherokee Indian Reservation.
Further information from: North Carolina Tourism Office, 430 North Salisbury Street, Raleigh, NC 27611. Tel: (919) 733 4171. Fax: (919) 733 8582.
City and council information: Raleigh Convention & Visitors Bureau, PO Box 1879, Raleigh, NC 27602. Tel: (919) 834 5900. Fax: (919) 831 2887; *or* Asheville Area Convention & Visitors Bureau, 151 Haywood Street, Asheville, NC 28801. Tel: (704) 258 6111. Fax: (704) 254 6054; *or* Charlotte Convention & Visitors Bureau, 122 East Stonewall Street, Charlotte, NC 28202-1838. Tel: (704) 334 2282. Fax: (704) 342 3972.

NORTH DAKOTA

POPULATION: 636,000.
CAPITAL: Bismarck.
TIME: GMT - 6. *Daylight Saving Time* is observed in the greater part of the State.
THE STATE: North Dakota, one of the most rural States in the USA, is famous for its scenery and Old West heritage. The 70,000-acre Theodore Roosevelt

National Park in the Badlands offers spectacular views and includes the restored cow-town of Medora. Fort Lincoln, south of Mandan, was HQ for Colonel Custer and the 7th Cavalry. The Slant Indian Village nearby traces the area's history from the first Indian settlements. Fargo is the State's largest city. Other attractions include the beaches of Lake Metigoshe; Sully's Hill Game Preserve and the recreation areas around Lake Sakakawea and the Little Missouri River.
Further information from: North Dakota Office of Tourism, 2nd Floor, Liberty Memorial Building, 604 East Boulevard, Bismarck, ND 58505. Tel: (701) 328 2525 *or* (1 800) 435 5663 (toll free). Fax: (701) 328 4878.
City and council information: Greater Grand Forks Convention & Visitors Bureau, Suite 200, 202 North 3rd Street, Grand Forks, ND 58203. Tel: (701) 746 0444. Fax: (701) 746 0775.

OHIO

POPULATION: 11,016,000.
CAPITAL: Columbus.
GATEWAYS: Cincinnati and Cleveland. For further information, see under *US Gateways* below.

OKLAHOMA

POPULATION: 3,212,000.
CAPITAL: Oklahoma City.
TIME: GMT - 6. *Daylight Saving Time* is observed.
THE STATE: Oklahoma comprises mountains, forests and lakes to the east, plains and farmland in the centre, and wide-open ranching country to the west. It is the home of more Indian tribes than any other State in the USA. Oklahoma City offers many tourist attractions, including the Western Heritage Center and operating oil wells. Tulsa also has an international airport and boasts some of the West's major art centres and galleries. State park resorts and recreation areas include Eufaula Lake; Lake Texom; Arrowhead; Quartz Mountain and Western Hill. Indian City USA and the Cherokee Heritage Center recreate the Indian life of centuries ago.
Further information from: Oklahoma Tourism & Recreation, 505 Will Rogers Building, 2401 Lincoln Boulevard, Oklahoma City, OK 73105. Tel: (405) 521 3981. Fax: (405) 521 3992.

City and council information: Tulsa Convention & Visitors Bureau, Metropolitan Chamber of Commerce, Suite 100, 616 South Boston Avenue, Tulsa, OK 74119-1298. Tel: (918) 585 1201. Fax: (918) 592 6244; *or* Oklahoma City Convention & Visitors Bureau, 123 Park Avenue, Oklahoma City, OK 73102. Tel: (405) 297 8912. Fax: (405) 297 8916.

OREGON

POPULATION: 2,977,000.
CAPITAL: Salem.
TIME: GMT - 8. *Daylight Saving Time* is observed.
THE STATE: Oregon has many areas of great natural beauty and boasts more than 230 State parks and hundreds of camping areas in 13 national forests. Portland, the 'City of Roses', boasts fine gardens, restaurants, shops, concerts, jazz festivals and theatres. Its international airport is 14km (9 miles) east of downtown Salem. State tourist destinations include the spectacular coast north of the California border; historic Astoria on the Columbia River; the Sea Lion Caves; Mount Hood Forest; Crater Lake Park; 19th-century Jacksonville; the Oregon Cave; and Hells Canyon.
Further information from: Oregon Tourism Division, 775 Summer Street NE, Salem, OR 97310. Tel: (503) 986 0000. Fax: (503) 986 0001.
City and council information: Portland/Oregon Convention & Visitors Bureau, 26 South West Salmon, Portland, OR 97204-3299. Tel: (503) 275 9750. Fax: (503) 275 9774; *or* Lane County Convention & Visitors Association, Suite 190, 115 West 8th Street, Eugene, OR 97441. Tel: (503) 484 5307. Fax: (503) 343 6335.

PENNSYLVANIA

POPULATION: 12,009,000.
CAPITAL: Harrisburg.
GATEWAY: Philadelphia. For further information, see under *US Gateways* below.

RHODE ISLAND

POPULATION: 1,005,000.
CAPITAL: Providence.
TIME: GMT - 5. *Daylight Saving Time* is observed.

THE STATE: Rhode Island, the smallest of the 50 States, offers broad sandy beaches, parks, cities and a wealth of historic buildings. Providence is the second-largest city in New England. Its East Side contains many fine restored homes. Newport, one of the chief resorts, has beautiful 17th- and 18th-century wooden buildings, good beaches, famous yachting events, and music and art festivals. Many of its magnificent mansions (including those built by the Vanderbilts and the Astors) are open to the public. Block Island, a summer island resort, is reached by ferry from Newport and Galilee. The State's scenic centrepiece, Narragansett Bay, is home to yachting regattas and a thriving fishing industry.
Further information from: Rhode Island Tourism Division, 7 Jackson Walkway, Providence, RI 02903. Tel: (401) 277 2601 *or* (1 800) 556 2484 (toll free). Fax: (401) 277 2102.
City and council information: Providence Convention & Visitors Bureau, 30 Exchange Terrace, Providence, RI 02903. Tel: (401) 274 1636. Fax: (401) 351 2090.

SOUTH CAROLINA

POPULATION: 3,603,000.
CAPITAL: Columbia.
TIME: GMT - 5. *Daylight Saving Time* is observed.
THE STATE: South Carolina boasts a rich history and scenery ranging from lakes and mountains to some of the best beaches in the USA, as well as beautiful 'Gone With The Wind' plantations and the northwestern foothills where fierce battles were fought during the Civil War. Charleston, situated on the coast, is one of its chief tourist destinations, being the site of the first permanent English settlement. The historic downtown district of this port city has cobbled streets and hundreds of pastel-painted pre-Civil War buildings with lovely wrought-iron work and lush gardens. Carriages are available. Attractions in and around the city include the many museums, antique shops and restaurants as well as the marina, Charles Towne Landing State Park and Middleton Place Gardens, among the oldest in the USA. The nearby Magnolia Gardens, Cypress Gardens and Middelton Place Plantation have attractive landscaping and seasonal blooms and shrubs. Columbia's Riverbanks Zoo is one of the top ten in the USA. Other State attractions include Myrtle Beach, a popular resort city famous among other things for its golf, centred on the

Business Network Communications

Business Network Communications
2770 Ridgway
Walled Llake 48390
USA
Tel: (810) 669 5300 Fax: (810) 669 9068

sun-drenched 95km (60-mile) stretch of coastline on the northern border; peaceful island resorts such as Kiawah, Seabrook and Hilton Head which has 20km (12 miles) of beautiful beaches, unspoilt forest and golf courses; and the Oconee State Park in the lush northern Upcountry.
Further information from: South Carolina Division of Tourism, Suite 522, 1205 Pendleton Street, Columbia, SC 29201. Tel: (803) 734 0129. Fax: (803) 734 1163.
City and council information: Columbia Convention & Visitors Bureau, PO Box 15, 301 Gervais Street, Columbia, SC 29202. Tel: (803) 254 0479. Fax: (803) 799 6529; *or*
Charleston Trident Visitors Bureau, PO Box 975, 81 Mary Street, Charleston, SC 29402. Tel: (803) 577 2510. Fax: (803) 723 4853.

SOUTH DAKOTA

POPULATION: 711,000.
CAPITAL: Pierre.
TIME: GMT - 6 (eastern part); GMT - 7 (western part). *Daylight Saving Time* is observed.
THE STATE: South Dakota includes the dramatic Badlands, fertile prairies, early pioneer towns and the Black Hills, with forests, lakes and caves. By far its biggest tourist attraction is the Mount Rushmore Memorial, where the faces of four US presidents have been blasted and carved out of the mountain. Sioux Falls and Rapid City are gateways to the area and have good air connections. State attractions include the Black Hills National Forest; Badlands National Park; and the Wind Cave National Park. All offer a host of outdoor pursuits.
Further information from: South Dakota Division of Tourism, 711 East Wells Avenue, Pierre, SD 57501-3369. Tel: (605) 773 3301. Fax: (605) 773 3256.
City and council information: Rapid City Area Convention & Visitors Bureau, PO Box 747, 444 Mount Rushmore Road North, Rapid City, SD 57709. Tel: (605) 343 1744. Fax: (605) 348 9217; *or*
Sioux Falls Convention & Visitors Bureau, PO Box 1425, Suite 102, 200 North Philips Avenue, Sioux Falls, SD 57101-1425. Tel: (605) 336 1620. Fax: (605) 336 6499.

TENNESSEE

POPULATION: 5,024,000.
CAPITAL: Nashville.
TIME: GMT - 6. *Daylight Saving Time* is observed in the greater part of the State.
THE STATE: More than half of Tennessee is forested and great tracts have been set aside as State and national parks, forests, wilderness areas and game preserves. Nashville is a major music performance and recording centre. It also boasts a host of fine colleges and churches, a full-size replica of the Parthenon, the Country Music Hall of Fame and the Opryland USA music entertainment complex. Memphis, the State's largest city, is a major trading centre. Its major tourist attraction is Graceland, the home of Elvis Presley, and famous Beale Street is featured in many blues songs. At Chattanooga, take a ride up Lookout Mountain, with its Rock City Gardens and Ruby Falls. Gatlinburg is the starting point for trips into the Great Smoky Mountain National Park.
Further information from: Tennessee Tourism Office, PO Box 23170, Nashville, TN 37202-3170. Tel: (615) 741 2158 *or* (1 800) 836 6200 (toll free). Fax: (615) 741 7225.
City and council information: Nashville Convention & Visitors Bureau, 161 4th Avenue North, Nashville, TN 37219. Tel: (615) 259 4760. Fax: (615) 244 6278; *or*
Memphis Convention & Visitors Bureau, 47 Union

Avenue, Memphis, TN 38103. Tel: (901) 543 5300. Fax: (901) 543 5350; *or*
Knoxville Convention & Visitors Bureau, PO Box 15012, 810 Clinch Avenue, Knoxville, TN 37901. Tel: (615) 523 7263. Fax: (615) 673 4400.

TEXAS

POPULATION: 17,656,000.
CAPITAL: Austin.
GATEWAYS: Dallas/Fort Worth and Houston. For further information, see under *US Gateways* below.

UTAH

POPULATION: 1,813,000.
CAPITAL: Salt Lake City.
TIME: GMT - 7. *Daylight Saving Time* is observed.
THE STATE: Utah's attractions include canyons, colourful towns and breathtaking national parks. Salt Lake City, with its international airport 11km (7 miles) west of downtown, is the world centre of the Mormon Church. Utah, surrounded by the Wasatch Mountains, boasts historic buildings, churches, museums, science exhibitions and arts festivals. Other State attractions include Zion National Park around the Virgin River Canyon, with its temple-like rock formations; Canyonlands, Arches and Capitol Reef national parks; and Timpanogos Cave and the Dinosaur National Monument near Vernal.
Further information from: Utah Travel Council, Council Hall, Capitol Hill, Salt Lake City, UT 84114. Tel: (801) 538 1030 *or* (1 800) 200 1160 (toll free). Fax: (801) 538 1399.
City and council information: Salt Lake City Convention & Visitors Bureau, 180 South West Temple, Salt Lake City, UT 84101. Tel: (801) 521 2822. Fax: (801) 355 9323.

VERMONT

POPULATION: 570,000.
CAPITAL: Montpelier.
TIME: GMT - 5. *Daylight Saving Time* is observed.
THE STATE: Vermont is the only New England State without a seashore, but its border with Lake Champlain more than compensates. Its largest city, Burlington, affords magnificent views of the water, with its many sporting and recreation areas. The State's attractions include Stowe, the famous ski resort on the slopes of Mount Mansfield; Heritage Park, with its early New England buildings; and Green Mountain National Forest, with its historical trails and drives. Other major ski areas include Killington, Sugarbush, Mount Snow, Jay Peak, Smuggler's Notch and Haystack.
Further information from: Vermont Travel Division, 134 State Street, Montpelier, VT 05602. Tel: (802) 828 3236/7. Fax: (802) 828 3233.
City and council information: Burlington Visitors Bureau, 60 Main Street, Burlington, VT 05401. Tel: (802) 863 3489. Fax: (802) 863 1538.

VIRGINIA

POPULATION: 6,377,000.
CAPITAL: Richmond.
TIME: GMT - 5. *Daylight Saving Time* is observed.
THE STATE: Virginia is one of the country's most historic and scenic States. Some of its leading attractions are located along the Potomac River – Arlington National Cemetery, with the grave of John F Kennedy; Old Town Alexandria; and Mount Vernon, George Washington's country estate. Richmond, the capital of the Confederacy in the Civil War, has many fine old buildings. Williamsburg, Yorktown and Jamestown, the birthplace of the USA and three of its most historic sites, are situated further east. Shenandoah Valley, with its caverns, waterfalls and popular resorts, is to the west. Other attractions include Virginia Beach resort; Cumberland Gap; and the Great Falls Park. Norfolk is an important Atlantic seaport.
Further information from: Virginia Division of Tourism, 901 Byrd Street, Richmond, VA 23219. Tel: (804) 786 2051. Fax: (804) 786 1919.
City and council information: Norfolk Convention & Visitors Bureau, 236 East Plume Street, Norfolk, VA 23510. Tel: (804) 441 5266. Fax: (804) 622 3663; *or*
Alexandria Convention & Visitors Bureau, 221 King Street, Alexandria, VA 22314. Tel: (703) 838 4200. Fax: (703) 838 4683; *or*
Virginia Beach Convention & Visitors Development, Suite 500, 2101 Parks Avenue, Virginia Beach, VA 23451. Tel: (804) 437 4700. Fax: (804) 437 4747.

WASHINGTON STATE

POPULATION: 5,136,000.
CAPITAL: Olympia.
GATEWAY: Seattle. For further information, see under *US Gateways* below.

WEST VIRGINIA

POPULATION: 1,812,000.
CAPITAL: Charleston.
TIME: GMT - 5. *Daylight Saving Time* is observed.
THE STATE: Monongahela National Forest occupies a vast area in the eastern part of this mountain State and includes the Spruce Knob-Seneca Rocks National Recreation Area. West Virginia also boasts some of the nation's best State parks, with good sports and recreation facilities. These include Bluestone and Pipestem. Other attractions include the Greenbrier luxury resort; Smoke Hole Scenic Gorge; Mammoth Mound, one of the world's tallest prehistoric Indian burial grounds; and the State Capitol in Charleston, one of the best Italian Renaissance buildings in the USA.
Further information from: West Virginia Division of Tourism, PO Box 1469, Room B564, Building 6, State Capitol Complex, 1900 Kanawha Boulevard, East Charleston, WV 25305-0317. Tel: (304) 558 2766 *or* (1 800) 225 5982 (toll free). Fax: (304) 558 0108.
City and council information: Charleston Convention & Visitors Bureau, Room 002, 200 Civic Center Drive, Charleston, WV 25301. Tel: (304) 344 5075. Fax: (304) 344 1241; *or*
Northern West Virginia Convention & Visitors Bureau, 709 Beechurst Avenue, Morgantown, WV 26505. Tel: (304) 292 5081. Fax: (304) 291 1354.

WISCONSIN

POPULATION: 5,007,000.
CAPITAL: Madison.
TIME: GMT - 6. *Daylight Saving Time* is observed.
THE STATE: Wisconsin has more than 15,000 lakes and thousands of kilometres of rivers and streams. Its varied countryside also includes sandstone cliffs, sandy beaches, northern forests and rich, southern farmland. Milwaukee is the State's largest city, on the shores of Lake Michigan. It is well known for its German heritage, top performing arts companies and fine restaurants. Its parks and museums are among the best in the USA. Other State attractions include the sculptured cliffs of the Wisconsin Dells; Lake Geneva, a favourite recreation spot; and Green Bay, the State's oldest settlement.
Further information from: Wisconsin Division of Tourism, 123 West Washington Avenue, Madison, WI 53703. Tel: (608) 266 2345. Fax: (608) 266 3403.
City and council information: Greater Milwaukee Convention & Visitors Bureau, 110 West Kilburn Avenue, Milwaukee, WI 53203. Tel: (414) 273 3950. Fax: (414) 273 5596; *or*
Greater Madison Convention & Visitors Bureau, 615 East Washington Avenue, Madison, WI 53703. Tel: (608) 255 2537. Fax: (608) 258 4950; *or*
Fond Du Lac Tourism & Visitors Bureau, 19 West Scott Street, Fond Du Lac, WI 54935. Tel: (414) 923 3010. Fax: (414) 929 6846.

WYOMING

POPULATION: 466,000.
CAPITAL: Cheyenne.
TIME: GMT - 7. *Daylight Saving Time* is observed.
THE STATE: Wyoming, the 'Cowboy State', boasts 11 major mountain ranges, prairies, grasslands, parks, forests, lakes and rivers. The huge Yellowstone National Park includes geysers, hot springs, canyons, mountain lakes, waterfalls and a huge variety of wildlife. Old Faithful Geyser, the park's most famous attraction, erupts almost hourly. Other State attractions include Grand Teton National Park; Devil's Tower, the core of a now extinct volcano; the Buffalo Bill Historical Center in Cody; Fort Laramie pioneer post; Bighorn Canyon; and Prior Mountain Wild Horse Range, with more than 200 free-roaming wild horses.
Further information from: Wyoming Division of Tourism, I-25 At College Drive, Cheyenne, WY 82002. Tel: (307) 777 7777. Fax: (307) 777 6904.
City and council information: Green River Convention & Visitors Bureau, 1450 Uinta Drive, Green River, WY 82935. Tel: (307) 875 5711. Fax: (307) 875 1646; *or*
Cheyenne Area Convention & Visitors Bureau, PO Box 765, 309 West Lincolnway, Cheyenne, WY 82003. Tel: (307) 778 3133. Fax: (307) 778 3190; *or*
Jackson Hole Visitors Council, PO Box E, Jackson, WY 83001. Tel: (307) 733 7606. Fax: (307) 733 5585.

US Gateways

Arizona

Including **Phoenix**, gateway to the southwestern States of Arizona, New Mexico, Colorado, Utah and Nevada and the western Pacific State of California.

Arizona Office of Tourism
1100 West Washington Street, Phoenix, AZ 85007
Tel: (602) 542 8687 *or* (1 800) 842 8257 (toll free). Fax: (602) 542 4068.

Phoenix and Valley of the Sun Convention & Visitors Bureau
Suite 600, 1 Arizona Center, 400 East Van Buren, Phoenix, AZ 85004
Tel: (602) 254 6500. Fax: (602) 253 4415.

Scottsdale Chamber of Commerce
7343 Scottsdale Mall, Scottsdale, AZ 85251-4498
Tel: (602) 945 8481. Fax: (602) 947 4523.

Tucson Convention & Visitors Bureau
130 South Scott Avenue, Tucson, AZ 85701
Tel: (602) 624 1817. Fax: (602) 884 7804.

TIME: GMT - 7. *Daylight Saving Time* is not observed.
THE STATE: Arizona has spectacular scenery, including arid plateaux, mountains and broad desert plains. It contains the famous Grand Canyon, Painted Desert and Petrified Forest National Parks. Phoenix, the largest city in the State, shares borders with Scottsdale, the primary resort destination in Arizona. Both cities have a variety of accommodation and attractions, unique shopping, fine art galleries and many cultural events. Other State attractions include Tucson, the second-largest city; Saguaro National Monument; Arizona-Sonora Desert Museum; Kaibab Forest; Monument Valley Navajo Tribal Park; Hoover Dam; Montezuma Castle; and Tombstone, site of the infamous shoot-out at the OK Corral.

TRAVEL

AIR: Approximate flight times: From Phoenix to *Atlanta* is 3 hours 30 minutes, to *Chicago* is 3 hours 30 minutes, to *Los Angeles* is 2 hours, to *Miami* is 4 hours and to *New York* is 4 hours.
International airport: *Phoenix Sky Harbor International Airport (PHX)* is 6km (4 miles) from the city centre (tel: (602) 273 3300). Bus service to the city centre runs every 25 minutes 0600-1830; travel time – 22 minutes. (Tel: (602) 253 5000 for more detailed bus information.) 24-hour limousine service provides door-to-door service. Taxis are also available 24 hours a day. A 24-hour super-shuttle service leaves every 15 minutes 0900-2100 and less frequently 2100-0900 (tel: (602) 244 9000 for further information). The newly-built Terminal Four opened in 1991 to accommodate more international flights.
RAIL: *Amtrak* offers services from Phoenix to many major cities. International trains run direct to El Paso and Los Angeles. Domestic services run frequently on two *Amtrak* lines, the Sunset Limited line (Benson–Tucson–Phoenix–Yuma) and the Southwest Limited line (Winslow–Flagstaff–Seligman–Kingman). The *West Region Pass* is available for 30 days unlimited travel from the Midwest as far east as Chicago, from as far southeast as New Orleans and as far west as the Pacific coast. The *Far West Region Pass* is also available for 15 or 30 days of travel in the west, from the Pacific coast to as far east as Denver. First-class sleeping cars can be reserved for an additional fee.
ROAD: Most major routes run east–west. **Bus:** *Greyhound* and *Continental Trailways* buses are available to many northern, central and southern city destinations. *Gray Line,* with offices in Phoenix, Tucson and Flagstaff, offers 2-hour to 2-day local sightseeing tours.
Approximate driving times: From Phoenix to *Tucson* is 2 hours, to *Las Vegas* is 7 hours, to *San Diego* is 6 hours, to *Los Angeles* is 6 hours 30 minutes, to *El Paso* is 8 hours 30 minutes and to *Albuquerque* is 9 hours.
Approximate *Greyhound* journey times: From Phoenix (tel: (1 800) 231 2222; toll free) to *Tucson* is 2 hours, to *Las Vegas* is 7 hours 30 minutes, to *San Diego* is 8 hours, to *Los Angeles* is 8 hours 30 minutes, to *El Paso* is 9 hours and to *Albuquerque* is 10 hours.
URBAN: Bus: Phoenix buses run every 30 minutes from every bus stop throughout the day and every 10-20 minutes during peak traffic hours. Tickets are sold in books of ten and and there is a local and an express fare. An all-day local pass is available, as well as a local monthly pass. Tickets for express services are more expensive. Discount fares are available for children under 18, pensioners (over 65) and disabled persons. Special dial-a-ride services are available in Phoenix and Scottsdale 0630-1000 Monday to Friday. An excellent bus service is available between Phoenix and Scottsdale.

Car hire: Easily available in Phoenix with many car hire firms offering special weekend or weekly rates.

RESORTS & EXCURSIONS

PHOENIX: The eighth-largest city in the USA and capital of Arizona, Phoenix has recently grown in importance, due to its improved airport facilities and recent large investment in extensive urban redevelopment. It claims to have more 5-star hotels than any other US city. Just some of the new development projects in the downtown area include: *Renaissance Square,* a 26-storey office tower with a newly completed 28-storey twin tower; the US$20-million, 225-suite *Hilton Hotel,* located in the downtown business district; the *Arizona Center* (an 8-block complex with a 600-room hotel, offices, restaurants, shops and entertainment); and *Patriots Square Park,* in the centre of Phoenix, with a sophisticated and spectacular laser light system that is visible for miles around.
Sightseeing: *Encanto Park; Pueblo Grande; Papago Park,* including the Phoenix Zoo and Desert Botanical Garden; *South Mountain Park;* and the *Heard Museum,* devoted to the art, anthropology, history and Indian culture of Arizona.
Excursions: The Grand Canyon is accessible by airplane from the centre of Phoenix on *Arizona Air,* by helicopter on *Grand Canyon Helicopters* or by the *Grand Canyon Railroad* (tel: (602) 635 4000).
LAKE HAVASU CITY: This desert city has recently become known as the new home of *London Bridge,* where it now spans the Colorado River and is the focal point for an array of English-style shops, pubs and lodgings. Further information is available from Lake Havasu Convention & Visitors Bureau on (602) 453 3444.
SCOTTSDALE: 'The Valley of the Sun'. Founded in 1888 and known as 'The West's most Western town', Scottsdale has matured into a mecca for lovers of relaxed lifestyles. Year-round sunshine makes the outdoors a way of life in Scottsdale, with its 125 golf courses, scores of tennis courts, and pools and spas at almost every resort.
Sightseeing: *Taliesin West,* the home and workshop of the famous designer, Frank Lloyd Wright, is open for viewing daily. A new 2-storey aquarium has been built in the *Scottsdale Galleria* with over 100 species of fish and marine life.
Excursions: Many river-rafting expeditions on the Salt and Verde rivers are organised by *Desert Voyagers* (tel: (602) 998 7238), as well as combination river rafting and desert jeep tours which take in the *Sonoran Desert* and its rivers. There are also special Barnstormer Bi-planes (replicas of the post-World War I open cockpit 2-winged Waco). Rides, complete with 1930s goggles and helmets, are available, with aerobatics displays for the brave. Other outdoor fun includes gliders, hot-air balloons and horseriding.
SEDONA/OAK CREEK CANYON: An attractive town nestled in the extraordinary red-rock formations and cliffs at the foot of Oak Creek.
Sightseeing: The beautiful *Verde River Canyon* provides lush scenery and there are prehistoric Indian ruins to be seen.
Excursions: Trips into the canyon are available, sometimes including Western-style barbecues by the river and live entertainment.
TUCSON: This popular winter resort is one of the fastest-growing areas in the USA. Surrounded by a ring of mountain ranges in the Sonoran Desert, it is known for its constant sunshine, and its location only 160km (100 miles) from the Mexican border is apparent in its architecture, cuisine and lively fiestas and cultural festivals.
Sightseeing: *Tucson Children's Museum,* with many hands-on exhibitions, is a favourite with children and adults; *Tubac,* an artist's colony with shops and galleries, is also the site of a walled fort and archaeological dig; and *Tohono Chul Park,* a desert sanctuary where visitors can learn about and experience the desert with the added benefit of cool refreshments available at the park's Tea Room.
APACHE TRAIL: An extraordinary scenic drive passing through arid deserts, winding canyons, looming buttes, glistening lakes and the ominous volcanic dome known as Superstition Mountain.
Sightseeing: *Goldfield Ghost Town and Mine Tours; Superstition Mountain Museum; Tortilla Flat,* an old stagecoach stop offering 'killer' chilli and prickly-pear cactus ice cream; *Roosevelt Bridge,* the world's largest single-span bridge; and *Tonto National Monument,* well-preserved cliff dwellings occupied 500 years ago by the Salado Indians and featuring examples of their weavings, jewellery, weapons and tools.
GRAND CANYON: This is perhaps the most famous natural tourist site in America and its impact is awe-inspiring. This massive rend in the earth can be reached

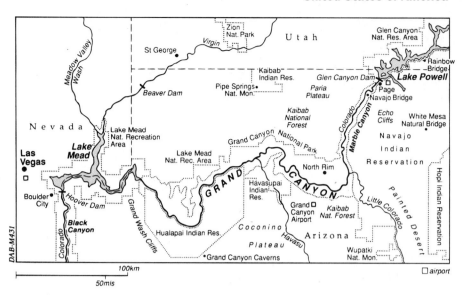

in a variety of different ways: by airplane, helicopter, railroad, 1901 period steam train from Williams to the South Rim or by a Lake Powell tour boat from Wahweap Lodge to Rainbow Bridge (the world's biggest natural stone arch). There are some hotels in the Canyon but advanced booking is usually essential. As the Canyon is far from any city, those wanting to save time and see it all can take a 'flightseeing' trip over the Grand Canyon, the Havasupai Canyon (a remote side canyon of the Grand), Canyon de Chelly and the spectacular Monument Valley.
INDIAN RESERVATIONS: There are 64,750 sq km (25,000 sq miles) of *Navajo Indian Reservation* – home to 200,000 Navajos. Once a semi-nomadic and warlike people, they are known for their adaptability and have incorporated many skills into their culture from the Spanish and early settlers. They live in hogans (dome-shaped houses of log and adobe) in small, scattered settlements. In the middle of the Navajo Reservation sits the *Hopi Indian Reservation,* comprising 6475 sq km (2500 sq miles) and 7000 Hopis. They have lived in the region for 1500 years and are known for their amazing agricultural talents in farming dry and difficult land. The Hopis live in snug pueblo-style villages on top of mesas. This area is treasured for its outstanding natural beauty. Further information is available from Native American Travel Center, Suite 114, 4130 N Goldwater Boulevard, Scottsdale, AZ 85251 (tel: (602) 945 0771).
LAKE POWELL: A scenic wonderland of red rocks and blue waters.
Excursions: Many tour boats ply the waters of this large and beautiful lake. Information on lake cruises is available from Wahweap Lodge and Marina. Tel: (602) 645 2433.
Note: For information on attractions in neighbouring States, see above under *States A-Z.*

SOCIAL PROFILE

FOOD & DRINK: Most restaurants serve American or American/Continental food but Mexican, Chinese and Italian cuisine are also available. **Drink:** Drinking is legal in any licensed bar, restaurant, hotel or inn 0600-0100 weekdays and 1200-0100 Sunday. Minimum legal drinking age is 19. Many supermarkets and drug stores sell alcoholic beverages. Most liquor stores close at 2300.
THEATRE & CONCERTS: *Herberger Theater Center* in Phoenix is a new US$19-million development and is now home to the *Arizona Theater Company, Arizona Opera, Ballet Arizona* and *Actors Theater of Phoenix.*
NIGHTLIFE: Phoenix, Scottsdale and Tucson have various nightclubs and there is evening entertainment at many resorts in the area.
SHOPPING: Phoenix has excellent shopping facilities. The new Arizona Center in downtown Phoenix has good shopping opportunities and Mercado, also in the downtown area, is a new US$14-million shops and restaurant complex with a Mexican atmosphere. Civic Plaza, in the centre of Phoenix, is also a big and comprehensive shopping area. Special buys in Arizona include Navajo silver and turquoise jewellery, sand paintings, rug weaving and paintings; and Hopi silver jewellery, kachina carvings, pottery, basketry and paintings.
SPORT: American football games are held weekly during the football season at Sun Devil Stadium between

the Phoenix Cardinals and other visiting teams. Arizona is the training ground for some excellent major-league **baseball** teams, including the Cleveland Indians (Tucson), the San Francisco Giants (Phoenix), Chicago Cubs (Mesa), Milwaukee Brewers (Sun City), Seattle Mariners (Tempe) and San Diego Padres (Yuma). **Basketball** games take place between the Phoenix Suns and other visiting teams in Phoenix where construction is now underway on the new US$89-million America West Arena. **Boxing** matches take place in Phoenix and Tucson. **Horseracing** can be seen at Turf Paradise in Phoenix and Rillito Downs in Tucson. **Car-racing** can be viewed in Tucson at Corona Speedway and Tucson Dragway and in Phoenix at Beeline Dragway, Manzanita Park, Phoenix Dragway and Phoenix International Raceway. **Rodeos** are popular in Arizona and there are over 25 major rodeo sites throughout the state. **Skiing** is available in the winter at The Arizona Snow Bowl near Flagstaff, Mount Lemmon (an hour outside of Tucson) and Sunrise Ski Area outside Springerville. Other sports available include **archery, horseriding, bowling, fishing, golf, hiking, hunting, swimming, river tubing, hang-gliding, ballooning** and **tennis.**
SPECIAL EVENTS: The annual *Navajo Nation Fair* is the largest Indian fair in the world. It takes place in Window Rock, capital of the Navajo Nation, for five days in September. It includes lasso competitions, rodeos, horseracing, arts and crafts exhibitions, country & western dances, song and dance competitions, livestock and agricultural exhibits, food and a big parade. *The Festival in the Sun* takes place in Tucson in February/March and is a large celebration of visual and performing arts.

CLIMATE

Warm and comfortable all year round, ranging from refreshing breezes in the mountains to hot temperatures in the desert.
Required clothing: Lightweight cotton clothing for all seasons, with a wrap for cool nights. Warmer clothing is needed in the mountains, especially in the ski areas.

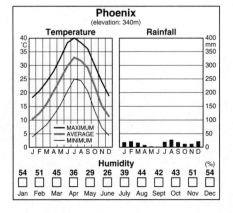

Perfection.

Par For The Course.

Experience a resort where the extraordinary is expected. Luxury a
necessity. Perfection found in every detail. Our 6500-yard, par 71 championship golf course is
an incomparable blend of beauty and challenge. From tee to green, each hole is an adventure
you won't soon forget. The course is just one of the impeccable amenities you'll enjoy as our guest.
Come discover the beauty of perfection. Discover The Phoenician.

THE PHOENICIAN
S C O T T S D A L E

ITT SHERATON LUXURY COLLECTION

Call The Phoenician or your travel professional today. Reservation Office: 0800 353535 (Toll-Free) • 602-941-8200 (U.S.A.)
6000 East Camelback Road • Scottsdale, Arizona 85251 U.S.A.• FAX 602-947-4311

Settle For More.

The promise is simple. The best. And nothing less.
Here you'll find guest rooms sheathed in Italian marble, Berber carpet and rattan. Four
uncompromising restaurants. More than an acre of tiered pools and waterfalls. Spectacular golf
and tennis amidst 130 acres of desert, garden and mountain.
And of course, nightly turn down service.

THE PHOENICIAN

S C O T T S D A L E

ITT Sheraton Luxury Collection

Call The Phoenician or your travel professional today. Reservation Office: 0800 353535 (Toll-Free) • 602-941-8200 (U.S.A.)
6000 East Camelback Road • Scottsdale, Arizona 85251 U.S.A.• FAX 602-947-4311

California

Including **Los Angeles** and **San Francisco,** gateways to the West (Pacific) Coast, Nevada, Oregon and Arizona.

California Division of Tourism
PO Box 1499, Suite 1600, 801 K Street, Sacramento, CA 95812
Tel: (916) 322 2881 *or* 322 1396 (recorded message) *or* (1 800) 862 2543 (toll free). Fax: (916) 322 3402.
Los Angeles Convention & Visitors Bureau
Suite 6000, 633 West 5th Street, Los Angeles, CA 900171
Tel: (213) 624 7300. Fax: (213) 624 9746.
San Diego Convention & Visitors Bureau
Suite 1400, 401 B Street, San Diego, CA 92101
Tel: (619) 232 3101 *or* 236 1212 (visitor information).
Fax: (619) 696 9371
San Francisco Convention & Visitors Bureau
Suite 900, 201 3rd Street, San Francisco, CA 94103-3185
Tel: (415) 974 6900 *or* 391 2000 (visitor information).
Fax: (415) 227 2602.
California Tourism Information Office
Suite 433, High Holborn House, 52 High Holborn, London WC1V 6RB
Tel: (0171) 405 4746 *or* 242 3131. Fax: (0171) 242 2838.
Opening hours: 1000-1700 Monday to Friday.
Trade enquiries only.

TIME: GMT - 8. *Daylight Saving Time* is observed.
THE STATE: Known as 'the Golden State' because of its sunny climate and the discovery of gold in pioneering days, California is a mixture of beaches, mountains, rugged coastline, Hollywood glamour, desert, woodland and orchards. The most populous State in the USA, its major tourist destinations include Los Angeles, San Francisco and San Diego, the lush resorts of Santa Barbara and Palm Springs and the artists' communities of Laguna Beach and Mendocino.

TRAVEL

AIR: Approximate flight times: From **Los Angeles** to *Anchorage* is 6 hours 40 minutes, to *Chicago* is 4 hours 15 minutes, to *Guatemala City* is 4 hours 35 minutes, to *Honolulu* is 5 hours 30 minutes, to *London* is 10 hours 15 minutes, to *Mexico City* is 4 hours 55 minutes, to *Miami* is 4 hours 55 minutes, to *New York* is 5 hours 20 minutes, to *Orange County* is 30 minutes, to *Papeete* (Tahiti) is 8 hours 10 minutes, to *San Diego* is 45 minutes, to *San Francisco* is 1 hour 20 minutes, to *Singapore* is 20 hours 25 minutes, to *Sydney* is 19 hours 30 minutes and to *Washington DC* is 4 hours 30 minutes.
From **San Francisco** to *Anchorage* is 5 hours 35

minutes, to *Chicago* is 4 hours 15 minutes, to *Honolulu* is 5 hours 40 minutes, to *London* is 12 hours 10 minutes, to *Los Angeles* is 1 hour 20 minutes, to *Mexico City* is 5 hours 10 minutes, to *Miami* is 6 hours 20 minutes, to *New York* is 5 hours 40 minutes, to *Papeete* (Tahiti) is 10 hours 40 minutes, to *Seattle* is 1 hour 50 minutes, to *Singapore* is 21 hours 25 minutes, to *Sydney* is 16 hours 40 minutes, to *Vancouver* is 2 hours 35 minutes and to *Washington DC* is 6 hours.
International airports: *Los Angeles International (LAX)* is located on Santa Monica Bay, 24km (15 miles) from the city centre. A train service is available and coaches provide reasonably priced services to all major downtown locations as well as many surrounding areas such as Hollywood.
San Francisco (SFO) is 25km (15 miles) southeast of the city; travel time – 30 minutes. *Airporter* buses leave every 20 minutes 0500-2300. Limousine, taxi and public bus services are also available.
Oakland (OAK), located across the Bay 32km (20 miles) from downtown San Francisco, receives international charter flights and US domestic flights. *Airporter* buses link Oakland with downtown Oakland and *San Francisco International Airport. Air-BART* buses connect with the BART rapid transit (underground) system, which gives access to downtown San Francisco.
Domestic airports: *Burbank (BUR)* airport is 34km (21 miles) from downtown Los Angeles, and receives US domestic services only.
San Diego International (SAN), 5km (3 miles) west of San Diego city centre, is primarily a gateway to southern California for domestic traffic.
SEA: A ferry service links San Francisco with the Bay communities of Sausalito, Larkspur in scenic Marin County, Tiburon, Vellejo, Oakland and Alameda. San Francisco departure is from Pier 1, adjoining the Ferry Building at the foot of Market Street.
RAIL: The *Amtrak* terminal in **Los Angeles** is Union Station at 800 North Alameda Street on the edge of the business district. It is at the western end of several major routes across the southern Rockies and is also the southern terminus of the West Coast line to Seattle (although there are frequent shuttle services heading further south to San Diego).
In **San Francisco,** the *Transbay Terminal* at 425 Mission Street is used only for limited suburban services; the *Amtrak Terminal* at Oakland, across the Bay, is far larger, being the central node on the West Coast line and also the western terminus of a line running across the high Rockies to Salt Lake City and beyond.
Amtrak provides coach shuttles between their Oakland and San Francisco terminals.
Approximate *Amtrak* journey times: From *Los Angeles* on the 'Texas Eagle' to Phoenix is 8 hours, to El Paso is 18 hours, to San Antonio is 29 hours, to Austin is 32 hours, to Fort Worth is 37 hours, to Dallas is 39 hours, to St Louis is 54 hours and to Chicago is 61 hours; on the 'Southwest Chief' to Flagstaff is 9 hours, to Albuquerque is 16 hours, to Kansas City is 32 hours and to Chicago is 38 hours; on the 'Sunset Limited' to Houston is 34 hours and to New Orleans is 43 hours; on the 'Coast Starflight' to San Jose is 9 hours, to Oakland is 11 hours, to Sacramento is 13 hours, to Portland (Oregon) is 29 hours and to Seattle is 33 hours.
From *Oakland* on the 'California Zephyr' to Reno is 6 hours, to Salt Lake City is 16 hours, to Denver is 31 hours and to Chicago is 50 hours.
ROAD: Approximate driving times: From *Los Angeles* to San Diego is 2 hours, to Las Vegas is 6 hours, to San Francisco is 8 hours, to Phoenix is 8 hours, to Reno is 10 hours, to Albuquerque is 16 hours, to Seattle is 24 hours, to Dallas is 29 hours, to Chicago is 44 hours, to Miami is 58 hours and to New York is 58 hours.
From *San Francisco* to Reno is 4 hours, to Portland (Oregon) is 13 hours, to Albuquerque is 12 hours, to Seattle is 16 hours, to Dallas is 36 hours, to Chicago is 45 hours, to New York is 61 hours and to Miami is 65 hours.
All times are based on non-stop driving at or below the applicable speed limits.
Approximate *Greyhound* journey times: From *Los Angeles* (tel: (1 800) 231 2222; toll free) to San Diego is 2 hours 30 minutes, to Las Vegas is 5 hours 30 minutes, to San Francisco is 7 hours 30 minutes, to Phoenix is 8 hours 30 minutes, to Yosemite is 10 hours 15 minutes, to Sacramento is 12 hours 30 minutes, to Albuquerque is 17 hours 30 minutes and to Portland (Oregon) is 22 hours.
From *San Francisco* (tel: (1 800) 231 2222; toll free) to Sacramento is 2 hours, to Lake Tahoe is 5 hours, to Reno is 5 hours 30 minutes, to Los Angeles is 7 hours 30 minutes, to Yosemite is 7 hours 30 minutes and to Portland (Oregon) is 16 hours.
URBAN: Los Angeles: The distances between Los Angeles' various attractions can be intimidating at first but it is a relatively easy city to get around quickly, provided the visitor has a car. The freeways are well-marked, though congested during rush hours. Leading car

hire and motor camper rental agencies have offices at the airport and downtown LA. Within Los Angeles County, the *Southern California Rapid Transit District (RTD)* provides a good bus service. For trips beyond Los Angeles, the *Orange County Transit District* accepts transfers from *RTD* for services throughout suburban Orange County. Buses are reasonably priced but travellers may have to wait some time to catch one. Though taxis are readily available, the geographic size of Los Angeles makes them expensive and impractical.
San Diego: Buses give good service at moderate prices. Taxis are expensive. Car rentals are readily available, with *Avis, Budget, Dollar-A-Day, Hertz* and *National* all providing services.
San Francisco: Public transport is excellent. The network of buses, streetcars and cable cars is the most economical way to get to destinations beyond walking distance. The basic fare includes transfers between the different forms of transport. Passengers must have exact change when they board, drivers carry no change. Taxis are readily available in most of the downtown area and other major streets. Because San Francisco is comparatively small in area, taxi fares tend to be less than in most other major cities. All major national car hire agencies are represented in San Francisco; motor campers may also be rented. For information on local companies, look in the San Francisco *Classified Telephone Directory.* Buses and streetcars also provide services from downtown to more distant points in the city, including Golden Gate Park, Twin Peaks, Seal Rocks, Mission Dolores, the Presidio and Golden Gate Bridge. The futuristic *Bay Area Rapid Transit (BART)* subway and surface-rail system links San Francisco with communities on the east side of sprawling San Francisco Bay, including Oakland, Alameda, Fremont, Richmond and Berkeley, site of the huge University of California campus.

RESORTS & EXCURSIONS

LOS ANGELES: The 'City of Angels' is the primary gateway to Southern California and the Far West. Founded in 1781, it now has the second-highest population of any US city and covers 1930 sq km (746 sq miles) between mountains and sea. Greater LA is actually a collection of many communities, each with their own distinct character. Snowcapped mountains, vast deserts, sandy beaches and canyons are all within driving distance of the city.

Sightseeing: Beverly Hills is one of the most elegant communities in southern California; many of the luxurious homes are owned by film and TV stars. *Chinatown,* in the heart of LA, has the aromas, sounds and architecture of mainland China. Footprints of the stars are cast in cement outside *Mann's Chinese Theater* on *Hollywood Boulevard.* Many of the celebrities are featured in *Movieland Wax Museum* in *Buena Park.*

Griffith Park, one of the world's largest city parks, features the *Los Angeles Zoo,* an observatory, a miniature railroad, golf courses and tennis courts. *El Pueblo de Los Angeles State Historical Park* is the original site of the city, dating back 200 years, where much of LA's Spanish heritage has been restored and preserved. Museums and galleries include *Los Angeles County Museum of Art, The Armand Hammer Museum of Art & Cultural Center, California Afro-American Museum, Japanese-American National Museum* and the *Museum of Contemporary Art.* Historical museums in Los Angeles include *Gene Autry Western Heritage Museum, George C Page Museum, Grier-Musser Museum, Hollywood Bowl Museum, Hollywood Entertainment Museum, Wells Fargo History Museum, Los Angeles Maritime Museum, Southwest Museum, Martyrs Memorial* and *Museum of the Holocaust* and the *Natural History Museum of Los Angeles County.* Located between Beverly Hills and Hollywood, **West Hollywood's** world-famous *Sunset Strip* has been a star-studded nightlife mecca since the 1920s and still sparkles with the sounds of jazz, R&B, rock, cabaret and comedy. Other West Hollywood attractions include *Melrose Avenue,* the Cesar Pelli-designed *Pacific Design Center,* the *Avenue of Design* (with its more than 200 speciality shops, antique shops and interior design showrooms) and *Sunset Plaza,* an oasis of tree-lined sidewalks punctuated by outdoor cafés and trendy fashion and jewellery boutiques.
Excursions: Picturesque **Santa Barbara** overlooks the Pacific from the Santa Ynez foothills; *Mission Santa Barbara* is perhaps the most beautiful of all old Spanish churches in California. Other popular local tourist attractions include **Pasadena, Burbank** and **Anaheim,** home of *Knott's Berry Farm* Old West theme park.
Disneyland: The original theme park created by Walt Disney is 43km (27 miles) southeast of the Los Angeles Civic Center. Over 80 acres of land have been used to create seven theme lands. *Adventureland* explores the exotic regions of Asia, Africa and the South Pacific. *Critter Country* is a down-home backwoods setting for the 'Country Bear Playhouse' and 'Splash Mountain', which is based on the adventures of Brer Rabbit, Brer Bear and Brer Fox from the Walt Disney film 'Song of the South'. Visitors travel in hollowed-out logs through twisting backwoods waterways before descending the world's longest flume drop, which reaches a top speed of 64kmph (40mph). *Fantasyland* is a kingdom of storybook enchantment. *Frontierland* is an exciting realm of pioneers and a return to the heritage of the Old West; *Main Street USA* is a composite of small-town America around 1900. *New Orleans Square* is the home of ghosts, pirates and quaint shops. Finally, *Tomorrowland* shows the world of the future, a panorama on the move.

SAN DIEGO: This, the second-largest and oldest city in California, has a distinctly Spanish flavour. A major gateway city for southern California, it is 215km (134 miles) south of Los Angeles.
Sightseeing: The easiest and cheapest way to get around San Diego is on *The Bus That Goes in Circles,* a private service connecting the major hotels and tourist attractions. *Balboa Park* is a huge leisure area containing *San Diego Zoo* (home to 3400 creatures), *San Diego Wild Animal Park, Anza Borrego Desert State Park* and *Sea World,* as well as museums, art galleries, theatres and sports facilities. *Old Town* was the first European settlement in California. There are old missions at San Diego and *Seaport Village.* There is a resort area at *La Jolla* and there are miles of sandy beaches to the north and south of the city.
Excursions: Tourist destinations within easy reach of San Diego include *Marineland of the Pacific* in **Rancho Palos Verdes;** the *Queen Mary* ocean liner, docked in **Long Beach** harbour; **Palm Springs,** 160km (100 miles) from Los Angeles – a wintertime destination favoured by the jet set, famed for its health resorts, spas, golf and tennis clubs, and an aerial tramway; *Six Flags Magic Mountain* entertainment complex in **Valencia;** the *J. Paul Getty Museum* near **Malibu,** the wealthiest museum in the world; **Pasadena,** home of the New Year's Day *Tournament of Roses Parade* and *Rose Bowl* football game, and of the *Norton Simon Museum of Art;* and **Death Valley National Monument,** 5790 sq km (2235 sq miles) of rugged desert, sand dunes, salt flats and canyons, with extreme heat in summer (best visiting times: early November to late April).
SAN FRANCISCO: Gateway to the scenic region of the Far West, northern California, northern Nevada and Oregon. This cosmopolitan port by the Golden Gate Bridge was first settled by Spanish missionaries but its real development began with the California Gold Rush. Cable cars, a San Franciscan trademark, travel up and down its steep hills and are an exciting way to explore this beautiful city's well-known restaurants, shopping areas and many tourist attractions.
Sightseeing: *Chinatown* is the largest Chinese community outside Asia; enjoy Chinese theatres, museums, restaurants and cultural centres. *The Japan Center* is a 2-hectare complex of Japanese restaurants, shops, fountains, tea rooms and baths. *Golden Gate Bridge,* the city's most famous landmark, affords spectacular views of the city. *Alcatraz Island* in San Francisco Bay has been transformed from the USA's most infamous prison to one of the city's leading tourist attractions. *Lombard Street,* known as the 'Crookedest Street in the World', is lined with handsome homes and flower gardens. *Golden Gate Park,* one of the great city

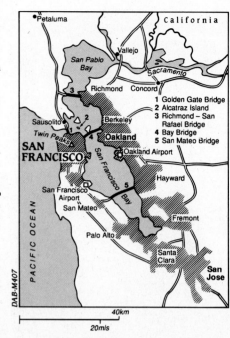

parks of the USA, has museums, beautiful lakes, botanical gardens and many miles of scenic drives, bridle paths and foot trails. The *Twin Peaks* afford one of the finest panoramic views of the city. Among San Francisco's main museums and galleries are the *San Francisco Museum of Modern Art,* the *M H de Young Memorial Museum* in Golden Gate Park, the *Asian Art Museum,* the *Cartoon Art Museum,* the *California Academy of Sciences* with its planetarium and new anthropology hall, the *Museum of the City of San Francisco,* the *California Palace of the Legion of Honour,* the *Old Mint* and *Octagon House.* Cable cars, a famous San Francisco attraction, are also a fun way to get around parts of the downtown area. The *Cable Car Museum, Powerhouse & Car Barn* shows how the system works. *North Beach* is home to many of the city's Italian-Americans, boasting art galleries, sidewalk cafés, bookshops and coffee houses.
Excursions: The artists' colony of **Sausalito,** with its colourful yachts and houseboats, restaurants, galleries and antique shops, lies just across the bay. **Mendocino** is another attractive artists' colony on the coast further north. **St Helena** is a small town at the centre of many well-known wineries. *Muir Woods National Monument* features centuries-old coastal redwoods, about 24km (15 miles) from San Francisco. *Great America* theme park is to be found in **Vallejo.** *Marine World/Africa USA* is on San Francisco Bay. **Redwood National Park** between Eureka and Crescent City has 23,472 hectares of redwood forest and dramatic coastline. **Lassen Volcanic National Park,** dominated by a massive plug volcano, is to be found at *Mount Lassen.* The *Monterey Peninsula,* where sea otters and sea lions feed in the kelp just offshore, is famous for historic **Monterey** city and its September jazz festival. The city is also known for its association with Nobel Prize-winning author, John Steinbeck; it provides the setting for several of his novels including 'Cannery Row', 'Sweet Thursday' and 'Tortilla Flat'. There is yet another artists' colony at **Carmel. Sequoia** and **Kings Canyon National Parks** have magnificent and ancient forests bordering *Mount Whitney,* the highest point in California. **Yosemite National Park,** centred around a spectacular glacial valley, is famous for its mountains, meadows, pine forests, sequoia groves, waterfalls, sports and activities. **Sacramento,** state capital and former gold-rush town, has California's first pioneer outpost, *Sutter's Fort. Lake Tahoe,* beneath the peaks of the Sierra Nevada and spanning the California-Nevada border, has ski areas, beaches, watersports and other activities.
Note: For information on attractions in neighbouring States, see above under *States A-Z.*

SOCIAL PROFILE

FOOD & DRINK: Los Angeles: Cosmopolitan cuisine; seafood and grilled meats are specialities of the region. **San Francisco:** A limitless variety of ethnic, American, health food and international cuisine. Sample fresh crab and shrimp at the seafood houses that line the famous

Hollywood and Vine

Fisherman's Wharf. There are numerous 'fast food' places. **Drink:** Excellent California wines rival many of the renowned vintages of Europe.

THEATRES & CONCERTS: Los Angeles: Broadway hits can be seen at theatres in the US$34.5-million *Music Center* complex, 135 N Grand Avenue. The *Dorothy Chandler Pavilion* is home of the film industry's annual *Academy Awards* and of the *Los Angeles Philharmonic* and the *Civic Light Opera*. The world-famous *Hollywood Bowl*, 2301 N Highland Avenue, stages summer concerts. The *Universal Amphitheater* in the grounds of *Universal Studios* presents major pop and rock concerts. Other top venues include the *Mark Taper Forum*, the *Ahmanson Theater*, the *Shubert Theater* and the outdoor *Greek Theater* in Griffith Park.
San Francisco: The *Orpheum Theater* offers light opera. *Geary Theater* is the home of the *American Conservatory Theater*, which also stages special performances at *Marines Memorial Theater*. *Curran* and *Golden Gate Theaters* show major Broadway productions. The *San Francisco Symphony* performs in the magnificent new *Louise M Davies Symphony Hall*; while popular music concerts are given in the *Civic Auditorium* in July. The *San Francisco Ballet* also performs in the *Opera House* during the December holiday season. The San Francisco opera season, one of the most outstanding in the country, runs from mid-September to November.
NIGHTLIFE: Los Angeles: Nightclubs offer top-rate acts and a chance to rub shoulders with the stars. Most clubs are concentrated around Sunset Boulevard, Hollywood and the San Fernando Valley. Many hotels present star entertainment.
San Francisco: Everything from strip joints through *chic* piano bars to elegant supper clubs.
SHOPPING: Los Angeles: Smart shops, boutiques and department stores are found in downtown Los Angeles and Beverly Hills. Good value gifts, jewellery and handicrafts are sold in Little Tokyo and Olvera Street.
San Francisco: Art, jewellery and handcrafted items are especially notable. The principal shopping district surrounds Union Square in the city centre. Others include Ghirardelli Square and the Cannery (trendy clothes, foods, art, kitchen imports); Union Street (boutiques, antiques, arts and handicrafts in restored Victorian settings); Pier 39, a shopping/restaurant complex on a long pier; Chinatown and Japantown.
SPORT: Los Angeles: Horseracing is held at Santa

Anita Park, Arcadia (October and December to April); and thoroughbred-racing (mid-April to late July) and night harness-racing (August to early December) at Hollywood Park, Inglewood. The area also has professional baseball (August to December), professional basketball and hockey. **San Francisco:** The city offers major-league baseball (April to September) and professional football US-style (September to December). There is thoroughbred-, quarterhorse- and harness-racing at Bay Meadows Race Track and San Mateo (September to June) and thoroughbred-racing at Golden Fields, Albany (winter and spring).
SPECIAL EVENTS: Los Angeles: *National Orange Show* is held for 11 days each spring in San Bernadino. **April** sees the *Conejo Valley Days Chili Cook-Off* at the Oaks Rotary Club, attended by over 15,000 visitors. *Cinco de Mayo* in **May** is a traditional Mexican festival, held in El Pueblo de Los Angeles Historic Park. *Long Beach Indy Grand Prix* also takes place in May. The *Los Angeles County Fair* is held each **September** in Pomona. **November's** *Doo Dah Parade* in Pasadena has no theme, no judging, no prizes and no order of marching, and is well worth a visit. The *Annual Gourmet Food and Wine Festival* takes place every **February** at Thousand Oaks. It is also the month of the *Golden Dragon Parade* in Chinatown, ushering in the new year with floats, dancers and other traditional activities. *The City of Los Angeles Marathon,* with over 20,000 competitors, is in **March**.
San Francisco: The *Midsummer Music Festival* offers ten free Sunday afternoon programmes in the Sigmund Stern Grove, 19th Avenue and Sloat Boulevard. Performances include ballet, symphony, opera, jazz, ethnic dance programmes and musicals. From **September** to the end of **May** there is a wide range of productions from which to choose. *Fleet Week Celebration* is in **October**, an annual celebration of seamanship as the US Navy sails into Fisherman's Wharf. The *Great Halloween & Pumpkin Festival* at the end of October is paradise for children, featuring costume parades and festivities in the Richmond District. The *International Accordian Festival* at Fisherman's Wharf, and the *San Francisco Fall Antiques Show* are also at the end of October. The *Film Arts Festival* is a showcase of Bay Area Independent Film and Video, and takes place at the Roxie Cinema (Mission District) at the beginning of **November**.

CLIMATE

Summers are hot, while the winter months are mild with wetter weather.
Required clothing: Lightweight during the summer with warmer wear for the cooler winter period.

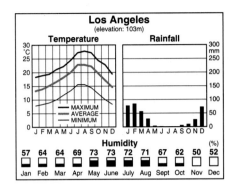

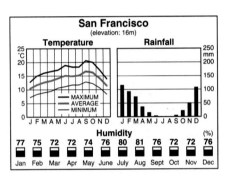

Colorado

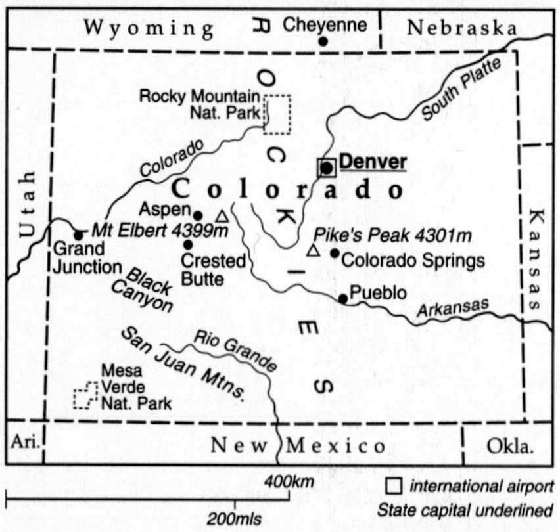

Including **Denver** and **Colorado Springs**, gateways to the **ski resorts** of the Rocky Mountains and to the neighbouring States of Kansas, Oklahoma, Nebraska and Wyoming.

Colorado Tourism Board
Suite 1700, 1625 Broadway, Denver, CO 80202
Tel: (303) 592 5510. Fax: (303) 592 5406.
Colorado Springs Convention & Visitors Bureau
Suite 104, 104 South Cascade Avenue, Colorado Springs, CO 80903
Tel: (719) 635 7506. Fax: (719) 635 4968.
Denver Metro Convention & Visitors Bureau
225 West Colfax, Denver, CO 80202
Tel: (303) 892 1112. Fax: (303) 892 1636.
Colorado Ski Country USA
Suite 1440, 1560 Broadway, Denver, CO 80202
Tel: (303) 837 0793. Fax: (303) 837 1627.

TIME: GMT - 7. *Daylight Saving Time* is observed.
THE STATE: Much of Colorado is high up in the famous Rocky Mountains. The State offers spectacular national parks, forests, gold-rush ghost towns, ancient Indian temples and fine ski resorts. The capital, Denver, contains many museums, parks, gardens and a restored Victorian square. State attractions include Colorado Springs; Pikes Peak; the Rocky Mountain and Mesa Verde National Parks; Black Canyon and the sandstone formations of the Garden of the Gods.

TRAVEL

AIR: Approximate flight times: From Denver to *Atlanta* is 3 hours 5 minutes, to *Boston* is 4 hours, to *Chicago* is 2 hours 30 minutes, to *Dallas* is 2 hours, to *Houston* is 2 hours, to *London* is 9 hours 50 minutes, to *Los Angeles* is 2 hours, to *Miami* is 3 hours 50 minutes, to *New York* is 3 hours 45 minutes, to *San Francisco* is 2 hours 20 minutes, to *Seattle* is 2 hours 25 minutes and to *Washington DC* is 3 hours 30 minutes.
International airport: The new *Denver International Airport* (*DIA*) was opened on March 9, 1994 and is the largest airport in the world. It covers 137 sq km (53 sq miles), which is twice the size of Manhattan Island. The airport is located 38km (24 miles) northeast of Denver (travel time – 30 minutes).
Domestic airports: The major ski resorts are all served by their own airports with domestic flights from many major centres in the USA. Airports include *Aspen, Colorado Springs, Vail/Eagle County, Gunnison Airport, Grand Junction, Duranga/La Plata Airport* and *Yampa Valley* (for Steamboat).
RAIL: Denver's growth is historically linked to its importance as a rail centre. It is a hub on the major *Amtrak* east–west route, with three arrivals and three departures daily, serving Los Angeles, San Francisco, Seattle and Chicago. Westbound trains pass through Glenwood Canyon, which is one of the most beautiful railway routes in the USA. The *Ski Train* makes a scenic 2-hour journey through the Rockies throughout the skiing season.
ROAD: Approximate driving times: From Denver to *Albuquerque* is 9 hours, to *Atlanta* is 30 hours 30 minutes, to *Boston* is 40 hours 10 minutes, to *Chicago* is 20 hours 20 minutes, to *Cleveland* is 27 hours 30 minutes, to *Dallas* is 16 hours, to *Detroit* is 26 hours, to *Los Angeles* is 23 hours 50 minutes, to *Miami* is 42 hours 30 minutes, to *Minneapolis* is 17 hours 30 minutes, to *New Orleans* is 25 hours 50 minutes, to *New York* is 37 hours, to *St Louis* is 17 hours 10 minutes, to *Salt Lake City* is 10 hours, to *San Francisco* is 25 hours 20 minutes, to *Seattle* is 28 hours 30 minutes and to *Washington DC* is 34 hours.
Approximate *Greyhound* journey times: From Denver to *Cheyenne* is 2 hours 30 minutes, to *Las Vegas* is 16 hours, to *Albuquerque* is 9 hours 30 minutes, to *Amarillo* is 10 hours 30 minutes and to *Kansas City* is 13 hours.
URBAN: Denver is well served with buses, a light rail system *(MAC)* and taxis. The *16th Street Mall Shuttle* provides free transportation every 90 seconds along the mile-long pedestrian mall in the downtown area. Car rentals are readily available with *Alamo, Avis, Budget, Dollar* and *Hertz* all providing services.

RESORTS & EXCURSIONS

DENVER: Located on high rolling plains at the foot of the *Rocky Mountains*, Denver has a population of 1.9 million people and is the largest city within a 1000km (625-mile) radius. Founded as a gold-mining camp in 1859, Denver was the centre of the Old West, filled with wagon trains, cowboys, Indians, gamblers and gunfighters. Today the city is known for its wonderful museums, architecture, cultural facilities and parks. Denver has an invigorating and sunny climate with four distinct seasons and is compact enough to be enjoyed on foot. The *Colorado State Capitol*, with its spectacular genuine gold roof, enjoys sweeping views over the city and the Rockies. Standing on the 15th step of the Capitol building one is exactly 2km (1 mile) above sea-level, hence Denver's self-styled title of the *Mile High City*. Nearby are the *US Mint* with the second-largest storehouse of gold bullion in the USA, and the *Denver Art Museum* which houses a fine Native American collection as well as many other exhibits. Other museums in Denver include the *Museum of Western Art* with the third-largest collection of Western art in the USA, and the *Colorado History Museum* which documents the colourful stories of the Indians, cowboys, miners and explorers who have called Colorado home. *Larimer Square*, a Victorian block of shops and cafés, is the gateway to the *Lower Downtown District* of Denver. Also known as *LoDo*, this area comprises 20 blocks of century-old warehouses and buildings which have been converted to antique shops, galleries, clubs, restaurants and offices. The *16th Street Mall* is a mile-long tree-lined promenade in the heart of the city, which is alive with pedestrians, cafés, street performers and fountains. Those seeking a refuge from the downtown bustle can head for one of Denver's 205 parks. The *City Park* is home to *Denver Zoo, City Park Golf Course* and the *Denver Museum of Natural History,* whilst the *Denver Botanic Gardens* comprise water gardens, a Japanese garden, a rock alpine garden and an award-winning conservatory housing a collection of orchids and bromeliads.
COLORADO SPRINGS: 2000m (6562ft) above sea-level and an hour south of Denver, Colorado Springs is dominated by the red sandstone pinnacles of the *Garden of the Gods*. Other attractions in or near the city include *Manitou & Pikes Peak Cog Railway* with views of the Continental Divide; *Manitou Springs*; *Old Colorado City*; *Pikes Peak Ghost Town*; *Royal Gorge Bridge*; *US Air Force Training Center* and the *US Olympic Training Centre.*
SKI RESORTS: With their champagne powder snow and sparkling blue skies the Rocky Mountains of Colorado, and the ritzy resort of Aspen in particular, are renowned the world over for perfect skiing. In recent years the region has gained considerable popularity with European ski enthusiasts as well as visitors from within the USA and the range of facilities and accommodation is unrivalled. **Aspen**, located 256km (160 miles) west of Denver, attracts the rich and famous from all over the world and is perhaps America's most sophisticated ski resort, offering a full range of winter and summer activities and countless restaurants and shops. **Vail**, two hours west of Denver, is among the top ski destinations in the nation and is built in a Tyrolean style, while **Summit County** is home to the popular ski resorts of *Keystone, Arapahoe Basin, Copper Mountain* and *Breckenridge*. Other ski resorts in the state include *Tiehack/Buttermilk* (popular with beginners), *Beaver Creek Resort* (especially popular with families), *Ski Cooper* (near to the historic city of Leadville), *Copper Mountain Resort, Crested Butte Mountain Resort, Cuchara Valley Ski Resort, Eldora Mountain Resort, Howelsen Ski Area* (the oldest ski area in Colorado and home to the most complete ski jumping complex), *Keystone Resort* (with the longest ski season in the State), *Loveland Ski Areas, Monarch, Powderhorn, Purgatory-Durango* (an uncrowded ski area in the southwest of the state with the famous *Durango–Silverton* narrow-gauge steam railway), *Silver Creek* (affordable family skiing), *Snowmass Ski Area, Steamboat* (with its nickname *Ski Town USA* and its distinctly Western heritage), *Ski Sunlight* (with the world's largest hot springs pool at *Glenwood Springs*), *Telluride* and *Winter Park* (which is also home to the National Sports Center for the Disabled). All the resorts offer reliable amounts of snow and an extensive range of accommodation and other facilities.
NATIONAL PARKS AND MONUMENTS: The Colorado Rocky Mountains are home to two spectacular national parks. Located in the high plateau country of southwestern Colorado, the 52000-acre **Mesa Verde National Park** is designated as a World Heritage Site and contains some of the largest and most impressive examples of the dramatic *Anasazi* culture cliff dwellings. Built over 700 years ago, these amazing structures have as many as 200 rooms. The park has paved roads offering views over the major ruins. There is a museum which attempts to explain the riddle of why the Indians built their villages in caves, and why, by the year 1300, they had completely abandoned the Mesa Verde plateau. The **Rocky Mountain National Park** is located 104km (65 miles) northwest of Denver and is Colorado's most popular attraction. Reaching heights of 3736m (12,183ft), *Trail Ridge Road* crosses the park and forms one of the highest continuous highways in North America. Massive peaks, rugged canyons, flower-strewn meadows, peaceful lakes and thundering waterfalls combine to offer the visitor over 640km (400 miles) of spectacular wilderness. With its majestic mountain backdrop and picturesque main street the resort village of **Estes Park,** on the edge of the Rocky Mountain National Park, is very popular with visitors. National Monuments in Colorado include the **Black Canyon of the Gunnison National Monument** which preserves the most spectacular 19km (12-mile) stretch of the 85km (53-mile) gorge carved by the Gunnison River. A paved road circles the rim of the canyon, which at some points is nearly half a mile deep. The **Colorado National Monument** is an area of fantastic red rock canyons, monoliths, pillars and cliffs, while the **Dinosaur National Monument** is a plateau cut by two rivers and is home to one of the world's richest deposits of dinosaur and reptile fossils. At the eastern edge of the San Luis Valley lies the **Great Sand Dunes National Monument** with some of the highest inland sand dunes in North America. The **Hovenweep National Monument** features the ruins of an ancient civilisation, with prehistoric towers, pueblos and cliff dwellings dating back almost 900 years.
Note: For information on attractions in neighbouring States, see above under *States A-Z*.

SOCIAL PROFILE

FOOD & DRINK: Local specialities include fresh rainbow trout, buffalo and elk steaks and Mexican dishes. There are also restaurants offering South-East Asian cuisine, innovative *New Southwestern* cuisine and international cuisines in every price range. For a distinctly Colorado-style meal, visitors can visit one of the many small breweries and *brewpubs* in Denver, Boulder and many mountain towns, which offer freshly-brewed local beer and delicious food. **Drink:** Colorado brews more beer than any other State in the USA. Many of the 30 locally-brewed beers on tap in Denver are not available in any other city, while the internationally-known *Coors* beer offers free tours around its brewery, which is the largest-single brewing facility in the world. Minimum legal drinking age is 21 and ID may be requested in order to purchase or consume alcohol. Bars stop serving alcohol at 0200.
NIGHTLIFE: The *Denver Performing Arts Complex* is the fifth-largest performing arts centre in the USA and houses seven theatres and the *Boettcher Concert Hall.* Among the other varied entertainments in the city there are smaller venues staging theatre, popular music, jazz, dance, comedy and country & western music. For detailed information on scheduled events, visitors can consult *The Denver Post* or the *Rocky Mountain News.* Many of the ski resorts, especially Aspen, have countless restaurants, bars and other *après-ski* diversions.
SHOPPING: Denver offers extensive shopping facilities. Cherry Creek Shopping Center, the Tabor Center (located at the one end of the 16th Street Mall), Tivoli Denver (a 19th-century brewery transformed into a shopping mall) and Larimer Square (see *Resorts & Excursions* above) all offer a pleasant shopping environment. Aspen in the Rocky Mountains has an unsurpassed range of shops and up-market boutiques. All the famous designer names are represented here. Special buys in Colorado include gold earrings and necklaces, Indian jewellery, Navajo rugs, and handicrafts such as pottery, windchimes and wildlife sculptures.
SPORT: Colorado is truly a paradise for the sports enthusiast. The Rocky Mountains offer perfect **skiing** in winter (see *Resorts & Excursions* above) as well as every other form of winter sport, while in the summer the

mountain landscape offers **white-water rafting, hiking, mountain biking, horseriding, fishing, golf** and **tennis.** Popular spectator sports include **football, basketball** and **baseball** (the *Colorado Rockies* are the only Major League Baseball franchise in the *Mountain Time Zone*). In late August the streets of Downtown Denver are transformed into a **motor-racing** course when the 3-day *Texaco Havoline Grand Prix* takes place.

SPECIAL EVENTS: Mar '95 *Denver March Pow Wow* (over 700 dancers and musicians representing nearly 70 tribes from 22 States gather for this annual event), Denver; *St Patrick's Day Parade*, Denver. **Apr** *Easter Sunrise Service*, Red Rocks. **May** *US West Theatre Fest* (the world premiers of four new American works), Denver; *Cinco de Mayo* (Denver celebrates its Hispanic heritage and culture), Denver; *Kinetic Conveyance Challenge* (people-powered crafts race over land and water), Boulder; *Mother's Day Spring Fair*, Denver; *Indian Nations Rendezvous* (Native Americans from around the nation meet to celebrate their heritage with art, entertainment and food), Denver; *Bolder Boulder* (gruelling 10km (6-mile) race with world-class runners and over 23,000 other participants), Boulder. **Jun** *Capitol Hill People's Fair*, Denver; *Cherry Blossom Festival* (Sakura Square comes alive with the art, sounds, tastes and dances of Denver's Japanese community), Denver; *Bathesda Dutch Festival* (featuring authentic Dutch foods, imports from The Netherlands and entertainment), Denver; *Juneteenth* (annual celebration commemorating the end of slavery in Texas), Denver; *Greek Marketplace* (authentic Greek foods, music and dancing), Denver. **Jun/Jul** *Colorado Music Festival* (performances in magnificent foothills setting), Chautauqua Auditorium; *Colorado Renaissance Festival* (outdoor theme fair that seeks to recreate medieval England), Larkspur. **Jul** *Cherry Creek Arts Festival*, Cherry Creek North; *Denver Black Arts Festival*, Denver; *Festival of Asian Arts & Culture*, Denver. **Aug** *Rocky Mountain Scottish Festival and Highland Games*, Highland Heritage Park; *Western Welcome Week* (arts and crafts market), Littleton; *The International* (golf tournament), Castle Pines Golf Club. **Sep** *Festival of Mountain and Plain*, Denver; *Oktoberfest*, Denver. **Oct** *Colorado Performing Arts Festival*, Denver; *Great American Beer Festival*, Denver; *Denver International Film Festival*, Denver; *Halloween* (celebrations include *Trick or Treat Street* at the *Children's Museum of Denver*, *Boo at the Zoo* and *Downtown Goes Ghoulish*), Denver. **Nov** *ArtReach Festival of Trees*, Denver. **Nov/Dec** *Holiday in the City* (16th Street Mall gears up for Christmas), Denver. **Dec** *Blossoms of Light* (the Botanic Gardens become a wonderland filled with giant flowers made from lights), Denver; *Parade of Lights* (a 2-mile holiday parade). **Jan '96** *National Western Stock Show and Rodeo*, Denver. **Feb** *Buffalo Bill's Birthday Celebration*, Denver.

Note: The ski resorts all hold their own individual festivals during the winter season including season opening and closing celebrations, Christmas markets, competition events, carnivals and torchlight parades.

CLIMATE

The capital, Denver, has a mild, dry climate with an average of 300 sunny days a year. Spring is mild with warm days and cool evenings; summer has very warm days with low humidity and cool evening breezes. Denver often enjoys an Indian Summer right into November, while winter is cold, sunny and crisp with some snow falls. The mountains enjoy warm summer days with cool evenings. Autumn arrives early in the high ground with abundant snow falls from December to April and temperatures around freezing point.

Required clothing: Warm clothing, especially in the mountains, from November to March/April. Cottons and linens during the summer months.

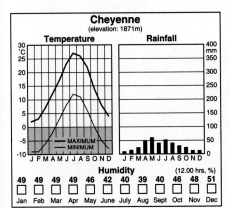

Cheyenne
(elevation: 1871m)

Temperature / Rainfall

Humidity (12.00 hrs, %)

	Jan	Feb	Mar	Apr	May	June	July	Aug	Sept	Oct	Nov	Dec
	49	49	49	49	46	42	40	39	40	46	48	51

Florida

300km / 150mls

□ international airport
State capital underlined

Including **Miami, Tampa** and **Orlando,** gateways to the southern States of Georgia and Alabama, as well as Central and South America and the Caribbean.

Florida Division of Tourism
Department of Commerce, Suite 511, Collins Building, 107 West Gaines Street, Tallahassee, FL 32399-2000
Tel: (904) 488 5607 or 488 9187. Fax: (904) 921 9158.
Visitor enquiries direct mail service:
126 West Van Buren Street, Tallahassee, FL 32301
Tel: (904) 487 1462.

Greater Fort Lauderdale Tourism Center
Suite 1500, 200 East Las Olas Boulevard, Fort Lauderdale, FL 33301
Tel: (305) 765 4466. Fax: (305) 765 4467.

Greater Miami Convention & Visitors Bureau
Suite 2700, 701 Brickell Avenue, Miami, FL 33131
Tel: (305) 539 3092. Fax: (305) 539 3113.

Tallahassee Area Convention & Visitors Bureau
PO Box 1369, 200 West College Avenue (32301), Tallahassee, FL 32302
Tel: (904) 413 9200. Fax: (904) 487 4621.

Pensacola Visitors Center
1401 E. Gregory Street, Pensacola, FL32501
Tel: (904) 434 1234 or (1 800) 874 1234 (toll free). Fax:(904) 432 8211.

Panama City Beach Convention & Visitors Bureau
PO Box 9473, Panama City Beach, FL 32417
Tel: (904) 233 6503 or (1 800) 553 1330 (toll free). Fax: (904) 233 5072.

Beaches of South Walton
South Walton Tourist Development Council
PO Box 1248, Santa Rosa Beach, FL 32459
Tel: (904) 267 1216 or (1 800) 822 6877 (toll free). Fax: (904) 267 3943.

Gulf Breeze & Navarre Beaches
South Santa Rosa County Tourist Development Council
PO Box 5337, Navarre, FL 32566
Tel: (904) 939 2691. Fax: (904) 539 0085.

Emerald Coast Convention & Visitors Bureau
PO Box 609, Fort Walton Beach, FL 32549-0609
Tel: (904) 651 7131 or (1 800) 322 3319 (toll free). Fax: (904) 651 7149.

Orlando/Orange County Convention & Visitors Bureau
Suite 300, 7208 Sand Lake Road, Orlando, FL 32819-5273
Tel: (407) 363 5849 or 363 5800. Fax: (407) 363 5899.

Naples Area Tourism Bureau
Suite 351, 853 Vanderbilt Beach Road, Naples, FL 33963
Tel: (813) 598 3202. Fax: (813) 275 6501.

Central Florida Convention & Visitors Bureau
PO Box 1839, Suite 300, 600 North Broadway Avenue, Bartow, FL 33830
Tel: (813) 534 4372 or 534 4375. Fax: (813) 533 1247.

Tampa/Hillsborough Convention & Visitors Association
Suite 1010, 111 Madison Street, Tampa, FL 33602
Tel: (813) 223 1111. Fax: (813) 229 6616.

St Petersburg/Clearwater Area Convention & Visitors Bureau
Suite A, Florida Suncoast Dome, One Stadium Drive, St Petersburg, FL 33705
Tel: (813) 582 7892 or (1 800) 345 6710 (toll free). Fax: (813) 582 7949.

Lee County Visitor & Convention Bureau

PO Box 2445, Fort Myers, FL 33902-2445
Tel: (813) 338 3500 or (1 800) 237 6444 (toll free). Fax: (813) 334 1106.

Jacksonville & The Beaches Convention and Visitors Bureau
3 Independent Drive, Jacksonville, FL 32202
Tel: (904) 798 9148. Fax: (904) 798 9103.

St Augustine/St Johns County Chamber of Commerce
1 Ribiera Street, St Augustine, FL 32084
Tel: (904) 829 5681. Fax: (904) 829 6477.

Daytona Beach Area Convention & Visitors Bureau
126 E Orange Avenue, Daytona Beach, FL 32114
Tel: (904) 255 0415. Fax: (904) 255 5478.

Florida Division of Tourism
ABC Florida, PO Box 35, Abingdon, Oxon, OX14 4SF
Tel: (0171) 727 1661 (recorded message) or (0891) 600 555 (Florida Information Service); calls are charged at the higher rate of 39/49p per minute). Fax: (0171) 792 8633.
The office is closed to the public.

Greater Fort Lauderdale Convention & Visitors Bureau
1/2 Castle Lane, London SW1E 6DN
Tel: (0171) 630 5995. Fax: (0171) 828 8877.
The office is closed to the public.

Orlando/Orange County Visitors & Convention Bureau
18-24 Westbourne Grove, London W2 5RH
Tel: (0171) 243 8072. Fax: (0171) 792 8633.
The office is closed to the public.

Palm Beach County Tourism Office
20 Barclay Road, Croydon, Surrey CR0 1JN
Tel: (0181) 688 1640. Fax: (0181) 666 0365.
The office is closed to the public.

Tampa/Hillsborough Convention & Visitors Association
The Eliot Group, Suite 7, Museum House, Museum Street, London WC1A 1JT
Tel: (0171) 323 1587 or 439 1216. Fax: (0171) 631 0029 or 439 1206.
The office is closed to the public.

St Petersburg/Clearwater Area Convention & Visitors Bureau
First Floor, 182/184 Addington Road, Selsdon, Surrey CR2 8LB
Tel: (0181) 651 4742. Fax: (0181) 651 5702.
The office is closed to the public.

TIME: GMT - 5. *Daylight Saving Time* is observed in the greater part of the State.
THE STATE: Once an ancient Indian homeland, the Florida peninsula now offers everything from serene and simple seclusion in the sun to luxurious high-life. The State is one of the country's leading tourist regions, with winding waterways, freshwater lakes, hills, forests, swamps, cities, 13,560km (8426 miles) of coast, countless bays, inlets and islands and a legendary climate. On its southeastern tip are Miami and Miami Beach, famous and glamorous resorts where the sun shines all year long. Florida's greatest expanse of beach, the 'Emerald Coast', stretching from Apalachicola to Pensacola on the northwest coast, offers more than 160km (100 miles) of pure white and often deserted sand. Then there are the 45km (28 miles) of soft, sandy beaches along the coast near Tampa in the St Petersburg/Clearwater area, fantasy fun at Walt Disney World, the Kennedy Space Center and much, much more.

TRAVEL

AIR: Approximate flight times: From Miami to *Atlanta* is 1 hour 50 minutes, to *Barbados* is 3 hours 25 minutes, to *Caracas* is 3 hours 10 minutes, to *Charlotte* is 2 hours, to *Chicago* is 3 hours 10 minutes, to *Dallas/Fort Worth* is 3 hours 20 minutes, to *Freeport* is 40 minutes, to *Grand Turk* is 1 hour 45 minutes, to *Guatemala City* is 2 hours 40 minutes, to *Honolulu* is 12 hours 15 minutes, to *Houston* is 3 hours, to *London* is 8 hours 10 minutes, to *Los Angeles* is 7 hours, to *Mexico City* is 3 hours 15 minutes, to *New York* is 2 hours 40 minutes, to *Orlando* is 55 minutes, to *Panama City* is 3 hours, to *Port-au-Prince* is 45 minutes, to *Providenciales* is 1 hour 35 minutes, to *St Croix* is 2 hours 40 minutes, to *San Francisco* is 7 hours 25 minutes, to *San Juan* is 2 hours 25 minutes, to *Santo Domingo* is 2 hours 10 minutes, to *Tampa* is 55 minutes and to *Washington DC* is 2 hours 20 minutes.
From **Tampa** to *London* is 11 hours 35 minutes (including stopover), to *Miami* is 55 minutes and to *New York* is 2 hours 40 minutes.
From **Orlando** to *London* is 12 hours (including stopover), to *Miami* is 55 minutes, to *New York* is 2 hours 30 minutes and to *Washington DC* is 2 hours 5 minutes.
International airports: *Miami* (MIA) is 8km (5 miles) northwest of the city (travel time – 25 minutes). Tel: (305) 876 7000. There is a 24-hour coach service to the downtown bus station and hotels on request. Bus no. 20 departs every 30 minutes 0600-0100. Taxi and limousine services are also available. *Greyhound* run services to

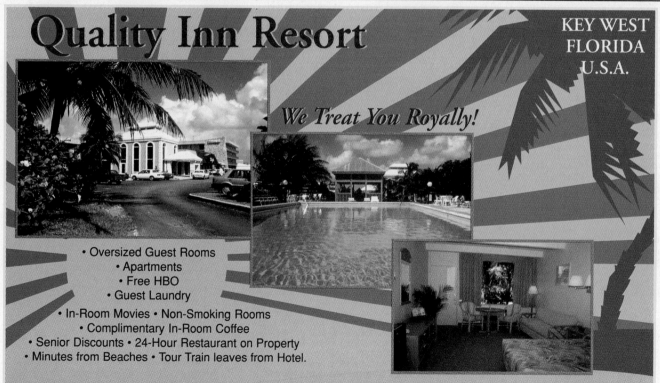

Homestead, Islamorada, Key Largo, Key West and Marathon.
Tampa (TPA) is 8km (5 miles) west of the city (travel time – 15 minutes). Tel: (813) 870 8700. A bus service runs into the city; limousine and taxi services are also available.
Orlando (ORL) is 12km (7 miles) south of the city (travel time – 15 minutes). Tel: (407) 825 2001. Rental cars, coach, bus, taxi and limousine services are available.
SEA: The port of Miami has been called 'the Cruise Capital of the World' and offers ocean liners for everything from business meetings and weekend getaways to luxurious extended cruises. The port of Fort Lauderdale, Port Everglades, is the second most important cruise port in Florida. Other cruise ports on the east coast include Port Canaveral and Port of Palm Beach. The main west coast cruise ports include St Petersburg and Tampa. Major cruise lines in Florida include *Admiral, Carnival, Chandris Fantasy-Celebrity Cruises, Commodore, Costa, Crown, Cunard, Dolphin, Holland America, Norwegian, Premier, Princess, Regency, Royal Caribbean, Royal Viking, Seabourn, SeaEscape, Sitmar* and *Sun Line.*
RAIL: *Amtrak's* Miami Station is 11km (7 miles) north of the downtown area. It is the southernmost point on the network, marking the southern end of the main East Coast line from New York (and ultimately Boston; see *New York* section below for approximate journey times on this line). A branch line terminates at Sarasota, a few miles south of Tampa on the Gulf of Mexico. There are no direct services between the two.
ROAD: The best major routes through Florida are: Daytona Beach to St Petersburg (I-4), Jacksonville to the Alabama border (I-10), St Petersburg to Tampa (I-275), the lower west coast to Fort Lauderdale (I-75), the north–south highway (I-95) and the east–west cross-State highway from Clearwater to Vero Beach (State 60). Most roads are excellent throughout the State.
Approximate driving times: From *Miami* to Orlando is 4 hours, to Tampa is 5 hours, to Daytona Beach is 5 hours, to New York is 27 hours, to Chicago is 27 hours, to Dallas is 28 hours, to Los Angeles is 57 hours and to Seattle is 69 hours.
From *Tampa* to Orlando is 1 hour 30 minutes.
All times are based on non-stop driving at or below the applicable speed limits.

Approximate *Greyhound* journey times: From Miami (tel: (305) 374 6160) to *Fort Lauderdale* is 1 hour 55 minutes, to *Palm Beach* is 3 hours, to *Orlando* is 7 hours 15 minutes, to *St Petersburg* is 8 hours 30 minutes, to *Jacksonville* is 9 hours 30 minutes, to *Tampa* is 10 hours, to *Tallahassee* is 13 hours and to *Atlanta* is 18 hours.
URBAN: Miami/Miami Beach: A new, improved public transport system has been launched for the downtown Miami area, with plans to expand it still further. It includes an elevated *Metrorail* system and an expanded bus system. The *Downtowner People Mover* combines the fun of a theme park with the convenience of above street-level travel. Buses operate frequently through most areas of Greater Miami. Fares are moderate and transfers are available. Taxis can be expensive in the Miami area; one can usually hail them but delays may be encountered at rush hours. Taxis can also be booked by telephone. Most major car hire and motor camper rental firms have offices at the airport or downtown Miami. Many provide a drop-off service in other parts of the State. Major hotels can often arrange immediate car rentals.

RESORTS & EXCURSIONS

MIAMI/MIAMI BEACH: Twin gateways to the Florida peninsula, Miami and Miami Beach also serve as the southernmost gateway to Central and South America and the Caribbean and constitute the world's largest cruise port, able to dock 14 cruise ships at one time. Once strictly a winter resort, the area is now a year-round haven for tourists. Temperatures range from about 20°C in December to around 27°C in August. Hotel and apartment rates drop in April and remain low until mid-December. Miami Beach is an island connected to the mainland by causeways and bridges. Consisting of 80 blocks and 800 buildings surrounding Flamingo Park, the area boasts the world's largest concentration of 1930s Art Deco architecture.
Sightseeing: Miami has experienced a major renovation renaissance in recent years, including the US$93-million *Bayside Marketplace,* an impressive complex of shops, restaurants and pavilions surrounding Miami Marina, which opened in 1988. The 28-acre *Bayfront Park* winds along the Bayfront connecting Riverwalk to Bayside.

Greater Miami, or Metropolitan Dade County, is made up of many municipalities, including the city of Miami itself, Miami Beach, Coral Gables, South Miami, Haileah, Key Biscayne, Coconut Grove, Little Havana (with its Cuban restaurants and cafés) and others. The northeast area contains the popular *Sunny Isles Motel Row.* The southwest section embraces the 'Miracle Mile' shopping section in Coral Gables (with its *Venetian Municipal Pool)* and the modern university campus. To the north, *Greynolds Park* has picnic facilities, boat rentals and a 9-hole golf course, as well as the 12th-century *Cloisters of the Monastery of St Bernard de Clairvaux,* bought by newspaper magnate William Randolf Hearst and moved stone by stone from Spain. Greater Miami's 'palaces of culture' include the *Miami Wax Museum,* the *Metropolitan Museum Art Center,* the *Lowe Art Museum* (which has large collections of primitive art and of Oriental and European painting) and the *Bass Museum of Art. American Sightseeing Tours* offer daily tours by bus, ranging from half- to full-day trips through the Greater Miami area. Several tour companies offer boat trips. Helicopters take off regularly from **Watson Island** to give tourists a bird's-eye view of the Miami and Miami Beach area; the round trip lasts 14 minutes.
Excursions: The *Fairchild Tropical Garden,* on Old Cutler Road in South Miami, is the largest botanical garden in the USA, with 83 acres of palms, cycads and colourful tropical plants from around the world, as well as a rainforest, a sunken garden, a palm glade and a rare plant house. *Miami Metrozoo,* off the Florida turnpike exit, 152nd Street West, represents state-of-the-art zoo design, with exotic animals in habitats very similar to their original homes in the wild. *Miccosukee Indian Village,* west of Miami, shows how this Indian tribe existed (and still exists) in the heart of the Florida Everglades. The *Monkey Jungle,* south on Florida Turnpike exit 216 Street West, 'where humans are caged and monkeys run wild', gives visitors the chance to see North America's first colony of wild monkeys in lush tropical jungle surroundings; other attractions there are 'Wild Monkey Swimming Pool', the 'Amazonian Rainforest' and the 'Ape Encounter'. *Vizcaya,* south of downtown Miami on Biscayne Bay, is a beautiful 70-room Italian Renaissance-style palace set in ten acres of picturesque formal gardens and housing an outstanding collection of furnishings and art objects. The *Miami Museum of Science & Space Transit Planetarium,* near Vizcaya on South Miami Avenue, has many attractions, including laser shows. The *Parrot Jungle,* 18km (11 miles) south of Miami, has 1100 birds on display, including colourful macaws. The enormous *Everglades National Park,* west of Miami, is the largest subtropical wilderness in North America and at 1.4 million hectares runs into three counties and covers most of Florida's southern tip; it is the home of 600 varieties of fish, 300 species of birds, countless mammals, and plant species not found anywhere else in the world. There are hiking trails, swimming areas, campsites, guided tours, horseriding trails, as well as canoeing and boating. North of the Everglades is a stretch of road linking Miami and Tampa, known as the *Tamiami Trail.* From here the only access to the 5439 sq km (2100 sq miles) of subtropical wilderness is by water.
THE KEYS: The world-famous Florida Keys stretch for 290km (180 miles) over 42 bridges from Miami's Biscayne Bay to a mere 145km (90 miles) from Havana at the Dry Tortugas, known to many as the 'end of the world'. The Keys are divided into the Upper, Middle and Lower Keys (the latter including Key West). **Key Largo** is known as a diver's dream and features the only living coral reef within the continental USA. **Islamorada Key,** in the Upper Keys, is known for its sport-fishing opportunities and hosts many fishing tournaments throughout the year. Sailing, scuba diving, jet skiing and windsurfing are also popular here. Also in the Upper Keys is **Key Marathon,** with a large manatee population. The largest of the Lower Keys is **Big Pine Key,** a wildlife haven. But the most famous and popular key is **Key West,** a 13-sq-km (5-sq-mile) island of charming gingerbread houses, Bahamian architecture and fascinating history (Ernest Hemingway wrote many of his major works here in the 1930s).
Sightseeing: The *Miami Seaquarium,* on **Virginia Key** and fronting on Biscayne Bay, is a tropical island paradise where visitors can see killer whales, dolphins and sea lions. *Planet Ocean,* also on Virginia Key, via Rickenbacker Causeway, explores and explains the mysteries of the world's oceans. Visitors can see and feel a hurricane, walk through an indoor cloud and rainstorm, climb inside a submarine, listen to ships at sea, and watch the birth of the oceans. Starting at **Key Largo,** visitors can see North America's only living coral reef at the *John Pennekamp Coral Reef State Park,* with 21,000 hectares of undersea coral reef which can be viewed in glass-bottom boats and the adjacent *Key Largo National Marine Sanctuary.* **Key Biscayne,** 10.4km (6.5 miles) from downtown Miami across Rickenbacker Causeway, has fine

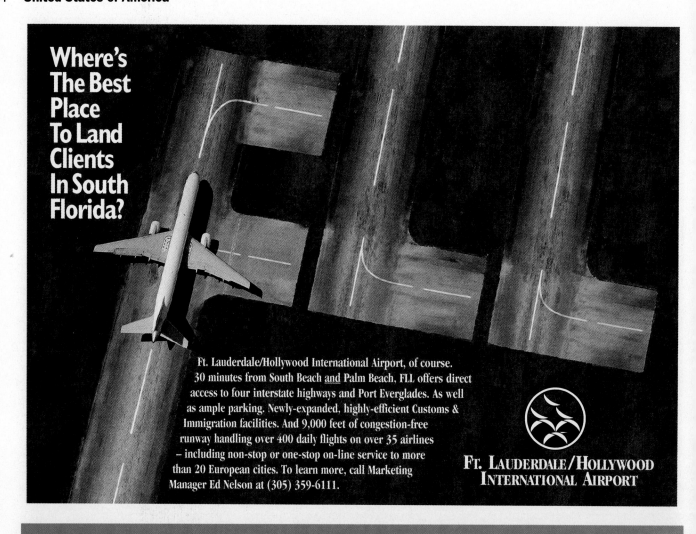

beaches, a zoo, picnic grove, cabanas, bath-houses, a miniature train ride and *Bill Baggs Cape Florida State Park*, with picnicking, fishing, boating and swimming. The *Theater of the Sea*, on **Islamorada Key,** is one of the oldest marine parks in the country and a favourite tourist attraction. **Big Pine Key** has the *National Key Deer Refuge* and drivers are advised to pay extra attention when driving through to avoid disturbing the deer. *Crane Point Hammock*, a 63.5-acre wilderness sanctuary, and the *Dolphin Research Center* are special attractions on **Key Marathon**. **Key West** has a variety of attractions, including *Audubon House and Gardens,* the 19th-century home of the famous ornithologist; *East Martello Museum and Art Gallery*; *Ernest Hemingway Home and Museum; Key West Aquarium; Key West Lighthouse Museum;* and *Turtle Kraals,* home to loggerhead turtles weighing as much as 400lbs, with a touch tank and bird aviary.

FORT LAUDERDALE: North of Miami, Fort Lauderdale has been compared to Venice, because of its elegant stretches of lagoons, rivers and over 300km (188 miles) of canals. Watersports activities are therefore popular and include deep-sea fishing and boating. Airboat rides and day cruises are also widely available. There are 37km (23 miles) of wide sandy beach; more than 50 golf courses; 288 parks offering horseriding, nature trails, picnicking and camping; and excellent shopping along the renowned Las Olas Boulevard. Extensive accommodation is available in elegant resorts or small properties along the beach.

Sightseeing: Boats can be hired from Bahia Mar Marina, or visitors can try the *Jungle Queen* (an Everglades cruiser). The town is home port for some 30,000 boats. *Ocean World*, in downtown Fort Lauderdale, includes dolphin and sea lion shows and demonstrations featuring sharks, alligators, sea and land turtles and tropical birds. *Bonnet House,* the winter residence of artist Fredric Bartlett, is a 35-acre subtropical estate just south of Sunrise Boulevard offering tours of the grounds. The *Discovery Center,* a hands-on science, art and history museum, is a perfect family outing and includes a planetarium and insect zoo. Interesting museums include the *International Swimming Hall of Fame Aquatic Complex, Museum and Pool;* the *Museum of Art,* with an excellent ethnic art collection; and the *Museum of Archaeology. Trolley Tours Inc.* offers guided historical tours of the entire city area. Day passes are available for US$8 per person. For children under 10 they are free.

Excursions: *Atlantis, the Water Kingdom,* located just outside of Fort Lauderdale in **Hollywood,** is south Florida's largest water theme park with 65 acres of slides, rides and attractions.

PALM BEACH COUNTY: The beautiful beach resort of **Palm Beach** hosts the *Henry Morrison Flagler Museum,* a tribute to the railroad mogul who established the area as a famous resort by laying out glamorous, palm-lined boulevards. Other attractions in the Palm Beach area include *Dreher Park Zoo, Morikami Museum and Japanese Gardens, Norton Gallery of Art, South Florida Science Museum* and *Lion Country Safari Park,* with more than 1000 wild animals, free boat cruises, miniature golf and a dinosaur and reptile park. West of West Palm Beach is *Lake Okeechobee,* the second-largest lake in the USA, popular for large-mouth bass fishing.

TAMPA: Situated on Florida's west coast, Tampa is the State's third-largest city. Long considered the preserve of the 'seriously rich', it has managed to retain the Latin colour and flavour of its Spanish origins and now has a thriving tourist industry.

Sightseeing: *Ybor City,* within the metropolitan boundary, is a thoroughly Spanish community named after Vincent Martinez Ybor who was the first Cuban cigar-maker to set up business in Tampa in 1866. Ybor City has wrought-iron balconies, plazas, arcades and sidewalk coffee shops.

Excursions: The world-famous **St Petersburg/ Clearwater Area,** half an hour from Tampa on the interstate highway, is a year-round resort area with an average of 361 days of sunshine a year. Its 45km (28 miles) of sandy beaches and 205km (128 miles) of shoreline string together the Gulf Coast resorts of Clearwater Beach, Dinedin, Holiday Isles, Madeira Beach, St Peter's Beach (with its *London Wax Museum),* Tarpon Springs (with its *Sponge Docks),* Treasure Island and **St Petersburg,** one of the most popular retirement and resort cities in the USA. The *Salvador Dali Museum* in St Petersburg has the largest collection of the artist's work anywhere in the world. Further down the coastline is **Fort Myers,** with its famous palm-lined boulevards and beautifully restored turn-of-the-century downtown area. The lovely islands of **Sanibel, Captiva, Estero** and **Pine** can be visited from here. At the *Edison Winter Home,* on Fort Myers' MacGregor Boulevard, visitors can see the estate of the great inventor, with his botanical gardens, laboratory and home just as he left them. Spectacular water, light and music shows, both indoors and outdoors, can be seen at *Waltzing Waters,* south of Fort Myers. The

Homosassa Springs Nature World, near Crystal River, allows visitors to walk underwater with 10,000 fish and friendly manatees (aquatic mammals). *Busch Gardens* ('The Dark Continent') is a 300-acre turn-of-the-century African theme park with wild animals, and is one of Tampa's most famous attractions. There are rides of every description (including monorail, skyride, steam train, the *Kumba* roller coaster and water rides to *Adventure Island),* shows, zoos and the *Moroccan Palace Theater.* The *Ringling Museum of Art,* set in the 68-acre estate of the late John Ringling in downtown **Sarasota,** is the official State Museum of Florida. Also in downtown Sarasota can be found *Bellm's Cars & Music of Yesteryear,* which has over 170 antique cars (the earliest built in l897), over 1200 music machines, a country store, a livery stable, a blacksmith's shop and a 250-piece antique arcade. The *Everglades Wonder Gardens* in **Bonita Springs** give a glimpse of Florida's past and of the Everglades' wildlife, including bears, otters, panthers, deer, birds of prey, alligators, snakes and the endangered Everglades crocodile. The *African Safari* at the Caribbean Gardens in **Naples,** on the edge of Big Cypress Swamp, comprises 52 acres of tropical beauty with wild animals. *Fort de Soto Park* is an historic fort providing an ideal point from which to watch the ocean-going ships leaving Tampa Bay. Other parks include *Adventure Island Theme Park, Hillsborough River Park, Lowry Park* and the *Waterfront Park.*
ORLANDO: In the heart of Florida, Orlando is the centre of the State's fun attractions. It has 47 parks and 54 lakes within the city limits.
Sightseeing: *Eola Park,* the 50-acre *Le Gardens, Orange Country Historical Museum, Orlando International Toy Train Museum* and the *Cartoon Museum. Celebrity,* central Florida's only dinner theatre, has a 5-play season.
Excursions: Orlando is the closest city to **Walt Disney World,** one of the top USA tourist attractions (see section below). *Citrus Tower* on Highway 27 at **Clermont** offers visitors a wonderful view over the citrus-producing regions of central Florida. *Sea World* is the world's largest marine theme park and includes killer whales, dolphins, penguins, sharks, seals and sea lions. *Medieval Times,* west of **Kissimmee,** offers an 11th-century castle, banquetting, jousting and sword-fighting. The *NASA Kennedy Space Center's Spaceport USA,* an hour-and-a-half's drive from Orlando on the east coast in **Titusville,** has photographic and art exhibitions and

audio-visual demonstrations with an 'IMAX Theater' showing space shuttle launches and space activity on a huge screen. *Gatorland Zoo,* north of Kissimmee, is the world's largest alligator farm, with Florida wildlife, birds, a 'primeval swampwalk' and thousands of alligators and crocodiles. The lovely *Florida Cypress Gardens,* started in the 1930s in **Winter Haven,** is an expanse of immaculately landscaped grounds, moss-draped cyprus, flowers, pools and grottos; it includes a zoological park and hosts the 'Southern Ice' skating review, the 'Aquacade' high-diving and synchronised swimming show and a famous water-ski show. At *Silver Springs,* visitors can cruise in glass-bottom boats through the jungle atmosphere. Nearby, the *Wild Waters* theme park has flume rides, a wave pool and a miniature golf course. Finally, for energetic walkers only, is the *Florida Hiking Trail,* which winds for 2100km (1300 miles) through the centre of the State. Orlando's latest attraction is *Universal Studios,* a 444-acre motion picture studio and entertainment attraction featuring shows and models from many hit movies, such as 'ET', 'Jaws' and 'Back to the Future'. A tour around the studio offers a behind-the-scenes look at how films and TV shows are made.
Walt Disney World: This immensely popular theme park is located 32km (20 miles) southwest of Orlando at *Lake Buena Vista.* Opened in 1971, it now attracts 20 million visitors a year. The park covers 28,000 acres, including 7200 designated as a wilderness preserve and transportation between the various attractions is by monorail train, ferry and launch. Walt Disney World is open throughout the year.
The *EPCOT Center* (standing for 'Experimental Prototype Community of Tomorrow') opened in 1982 and covers 260 acres. Themed areas focus on discovery and scientific achievements. Major attractions include *Spaceship Earth, The Universe of Energy, The World of Motion, Journey into Imagination, The Land, Computer Central, Horizons, The Living Seas* and *The Wonders of Life.* The *World Showcase* (also in the *EPCOT Center*) features exhibits celebrating 11 nations around a *World Showcase Lagoon* – Canada, the United Kingdom, France, Japan, the 'American Adventure', Italy, Germany, China, Morocco, Mexico and Norway.
Vacation Kingdom is a collection of themed resort hotels set in 2500 acres. Visitors can choose between the *Polynesian Village,* the *Disney Inn, Fort Wilderness Campground,* the *Grand Floridian Beach Resort* and the

Caribbean Beach Resort. There are convention rooms, restaurants, shops, nightclubs, entertainment lounges, championship golf courses, tennis courts, horseriding, pools and lakes for swimming, boating and water-skiing, as well as *River Country* water thrills, *Discovery Islands* tropical gardens and wildlife sanctuary and *Typhoon Lagoon Water Park.*
Within Vacation Kingdom, the *Magic Kingdom* includes 45 major adventures on a 100-acre site. There are seven 'lands', each with entertainments, restaurants and shops based on favourite Disney themes of yesterday and tomorrow: *Adventureland, Liberty Square, Frontierland, Main Street, Fantasyland, Tomorrowland* and *Mickey's Birthday Land.*
Disney MGM Studios are a working TV and film studio, and there are production, tour and entertainment facilities.
The *Walt Disney World Village* contains the *Disney Village Market Place* (which has 30 shops, ten restaurants, the 'Empress Lilly' riverboat and a *Village Lounge),* the *Disney Village Clubhouse & Village Resort,* Hotel Plaza, the *Village Office Plaza,* the *Conference Center* and *Pleasure Island* – a 6-acre night-time dining and entertainment complex.
JACKSONVILLE: Situated a few miles upstream from the Atlantic on the banks of the St Johns River in northern Florida, Jacksonville is a large and picturesque port. It was named after President Andrew Jackson. Jacksonville Beach has excellent shopping, dining and fishing facilities on its beach pier and boardwalk.
Sightseeing: *Fort Caroline National Memorial,* the *Cummer Gallery of Art and Gardens,* the *Jacksonville Art Museum* and the *Jacksonville Zoological Gardens.*
Excursions: St Augustine, the USA's oldest town, has winding streets and a restored Spanish Quarter. *Zorayda Castle,* in downtown St Augustine, is a reproduction of the Alhambra, with fabulous treasures from all over the world and exhibitions on how the Moorish kings lived, entertained and ruled Spain. *Ripley's Believe-it-or-not Museum,* a short walk from St George Street in the historic area, houses a large collection of oddities, curiosities and art objects collected by Robert Ripley from around the world. **Daytona Beach** is famous for its wide beach and the *Daytona International Speedway* which features NASCAR's season opening race, the Daytona 500.
TALLAHASSEE: The capital of Florida is a city full of

southern charm and history, located just 32km (20 miles) north of the Gulf of Mexico and 22km (14 miles) south of Georgia.

Sightseeing: The *Governor's Mansion* was modeled after the Tennessee plantation home of one of America's military heros, Andrew Jackson. The nearby modern *Capitol Building* towers high above the city, with a 22nd-floor observatory and gallery open to visitors. Beside it stands the original capitol building, restored to its 1902 grandeur, offering an exhibit of Florida's political evolution. Other historic attractions include *Black Archives Research Center and Museum* (with one of the most extensive collections of African-American artifacts), *Union Bank* (Florida's oldest surviving bank building), *Bellevue* (plantation home of Princess Catherine Murat, the great-grandniece of George Washington), *Knott House Museum* (a 19th-century historic house museum), the 19th-century *Meginnis-Munroe House* (housing an art collection) and the *Vietnam Veterans' Memorial* (a massive 12m (40ft) American flag suspended between twin granite towers to honour soldiers killed in Vietnam). There are also a number of historical walking tours around the city, such as *Adams Street Commons* (a brick-paved downtown block with 18th-century storefronts and speciality shops), *Calhoun Street Historic District* (with a number of historic homes) and *Park Avenue Historic District* (including *The Columns*, Tallahassee's oldest remaining residence; *Old City* and *St John's cemeteries;* and *Walker Library*). Many of these historical sites can also be viewed on the *Downtown Trolley Tour*, an excellent way to see the city. Other special Tallahassee attractions include *Maclay State Gardens*, offering swimming, nature trails, canoeing, fishing and boating; the *Museum of Florida History; Tallahassee Museum of History and*

Natural Science, featuring red wolves, Florida panthers, alligators and other native wildlife in a 52-acre natural habitat zoo with nature trails; and *Wakulla Springs State Park*, the site of several 1930s Tarzan movies with glass-bottom boat cruises, swimming, restaurants, nature trails and Florida wildlife.

Excursions: 19km (12 miles) north of Tallahassee in **Havana** is the *Civil War Museum* with native American and cowboy exhibits. *Birdsong Nature Center*, 32km (20 miles) north of Tallahassee, is a haven for wildlife in its 565 acres of lush fields, wooded forests and swamp. There are also two State Parks in the area: *Florida Caverns State Park*, 105km (65 miles) west of Tallahasee, offering stalactite and stalagmite caverns, horse and nature trails, camping, fishing, swimming and canoeing; and *Torreya State Park*, 80km (50 miles) west of Tallahassee, featuring 46m (150ft) bluffs along the Apalachicola River, rare trees, camping and a 11km (7-mile) hiking course.

PENSACOLA: One of the chief resorts along the lovely northwest Florida coast, Pensacola has been under Spanish, British and French rule since the first Spanish settlers arrived in 1559. There is much here to interest the visitor, from historic districts and museums to 64km (40 miles) of soft sandy beaches from Pensacola Beach to Perdido Key.

Sightseeing: *Seville Square* (with its oak-shaded park, restaurants and speciality shops), *Plaza Ferdinand, The National Museum of Naval Aviation* (one of the largest air & space museums in the world with over 100 aircraft), the Spanish forts and the historic downtown area are all worthwhile attractions. The *Pensacola Historic District* has been designated a National Historic Landmark and museums in this district include *Pensacola Museum of Art, T. T. Wentworth Museum,*

Museum of Industry, Museum of Commerce (featuring a reproduction of a 19th-century streetscape), *Pensacola Historical Museum* and *Julee Cottage Museum of Black History*. The *Pensacola Zoo* has over 700 animals in 50 acres of natural landscapes and botanical gardens and features a petting zoo and the *Safari Line Limited* train through 30 acres of free-roaming animals in their natural habitat.

Excursions: Cedar Keys is a string of about 100 islands off the coast of northwest Florida. Three of the islands have been designated as the *Cedar Keys National Wildlife Refuge*. The many beautiful beaches in the area include **Panama City, Gulf Breeze Beach, Navarre Beach, Pensacola Beach, Destin Beach, Perdido Key, Fort Walton Beach** and **South Walton Beach** and there are a number of well-known fishing areas, such as *Bob Sikes Bridge Fishing Pier, Pensacola Bay Bridge Fishing Pier, Pensacola Beach Fishing Pier* (at *Casino Beach), Fort Pickens Fishing Pier* and *Navarre Beach Pier.*

Note: For information on attractions in neighbouring States, see above under *States A-Z.*

SOCIAL PROFILE

FOOD & DRINK: Miami/Miami Beach: There are more than 300 fine restaurants and most hotels maintain excellent dining rooms. Some gourmet places are rather expensive but many popular restaurants have economy prices. Cuban and Mexican food is very popular in Miami. Because Florida is surrounded almost entirely by water, seafood is a State speciality. Fresh stone crabs are available nowhere else in the USA. **Tampa:** There is a clear emphasis on Latin cuisine in Tampa but all tastes are catered for, with

Florida Vacation Rental Managers Association

This year, for the first time ever, travel agents can book their clients into privately owned vacation condominiums and vacation homes throughout Florida with confidence, and earn a commission of 10-20% for their service. Thanks to the efforts of the Florida Vacation Rental Managers Association (FVRMA), state legislative changes were passed making it legal for vacation rental managers of privately owned homes and condominiums to pay travel agency commissions for referring guests. "Even though vacation rental houses and condominiums have been in high demand among the traveling public for many years in Florida, travel agents and tour operators have been reluctant to recommend privately owned homes and condominiums to their guests seeking this highly sought after, affordable accommodation alternative to a hotel room", says Gail Palmer, President of the Florida Vacation Rental Managers Association. "It is easy to understand why. Until mid-year of 1994, Florida managers dealing exclusively in vacation rental properties could not legally pay travel agency commissions; therefore, they did not take advantage of advertising resources and publications that cater to the travel trade. Travel agents had a difficult time locating quality condominium and vacation homes for their guests without doing a significant amount of independent research. Such efforts, while appreciated by their clients, hardly seemed worthwhile considering they would not be compensated by the property for the booking."

The general public was the focus of most vacation rental manager's advertising and marketing dollars. A survey of most companies confirmed that the majority of their business was derived from retail traffic through direct advertising. Most vacationers and business travelers discovered the convenience of this type of accommodation through word of mouth, referrals and area newspapers and publications. The return visits statistics often exceed 50% of the average reservation source. Even though retail bookings were generated, it was increasingly obvious that travel agents were still unaware of our industry, or avoided these accommodations because of the inability to be compensated for their efforts. The public has become accustomed to the benefits of the professional and convenient services derived by utilizing a travel agency when planning vacation and business itineraries. It seemed more important than ever to introduce ourselves to this valuable resource.

FVRMA has changed all that. Well over 350,000 private accommodations are available in Florida's most desirable vacation destinations. The managers of these properties formed a State-wide trade association to work toward aggressively marketing this type of alternative lodging. We want to tell the public, as well as the travel and tourism trade, there is a better, more affordable way to vacation. We are an alternative to the hotel room, and vacation rental managers offer variety, quality service, convenience and affordability. We pulled together the vast experience of professionals in the property management, real estate and vacation rental industry and united to form a comprehensive plan of achievement. Education, ethics and marketing strategies are greatly improved by our affiliation.

If your client's budget demands economy or extravagance; if they desire a luxury penthouse, romantic bungalow or rustic cabin; if their idea of a dream come true is the splendor of the seaside, a golfing extravaganza, a private swimming pool or even Disney til they drop, virtually every imaginable combination is available in a private house or condominium through vacation rental management companies.

Matching your client with the right property may require a little checking. Many companies are very happy to offer complimentary or discounted accommodations to travel agents on familiarization trips. If you cannot visit the property and do not know anyone who has prior experience with the vacation rental company, start by reviewing the information in the property advertisement. FVRMA recommends you ask a few questions before you book the first time. Find out how long the vacation rental management company has been in business and if they are a member of FVRMA. Membership will give the added confidence of professionalism. Have them mail you brochures and any travel agency agreements they may have. Be sure to ask about the availability of daily, weekly or departure cleaning and if it is included in the quoted price. Inquire about minimum stay requirements. Many homes provide linens, private telephones, cable television and fully equipped kitchens. If the home has a swimming pool, ask if it is heated. Is the home equipped with central air-conditioning? When was it built or last renovated? Is the home within driving or walking distance to major shopping, restaurants, attractions, waterfronts, etc? Will your client need a rental car or is other transportation available? Does the property offer 24-hour emergency services or security? Find out what the check-in procedure is and if damage deposits are required. Many properties require payment to be made in full and in advance of arrival. Be sure you understand cancellation and refund policies and if major credit cards or personal checks are accepted.

FVRMA hopes you will take advantage of this exciting alternative the next time you plan a vacation for your client. We know you will discover what millions of Florida visitors already know. The benefits of privacy, spaciousness and convenience combined with the freedom to cook your own meals whenever you choose, the peace of mind knowing the children are in the next room, while you relax or enjoy a ball game, visit with the locals, walk on the beach, or take in the attractions or a round of golf. It is like being on vacation with all the comforts of home.

TRAVEL AGENTS ARE INVITED TO CONTACT FVRMA FOR MORE INFORMATION ON VACATION RENTAL PROPERTIES IN FLORIDA BY WRITING GAIL G. PALMER, PRESIDENT, FVRMA, PO BOX 720684, ORLANDO, FL 32872, OR CALLING (407) 658 9504.

everything from international restaurants to fast-food shops.

THEATRE & CONCERTS: Miami/Miami Beach: There are many theatres and auditoria in the metropolis. Best known are the *Theaters of Performing Arts* at *Miami Beach Convention Center Complex*, and *Coconut Grove Playhouse*, 3500 Main Highway, which plays major Broadway hits. The *Opera Guild of Greater Miami* books major stars; their shows are usually staged at *Dade Country* or *Miami Beach Auditoria*. **Fort Lauderdale:** *Parker Playhouse* was created by Zev Buffman, owner of the Coconut Grove Playhouse, and shows usually move on from there to the Parker. *Sunrise Music Theater* features big-name performers such as Frank Sinatra and Pat Boone.

NIGHTLIFE: Miami/Miami Beach: Nightclubs exist in most hotels and resorts, and the *Coconut Grove* area, with its trendy nightclubs and cocktail bars, offers a swinging nightlife both inside the clubs and out on the streets, where many come just for a stroll and to be where the action is. The most lavish and lively clubs are Cuban supper clubs and *Les Violins* and *Les Folies*, both on Biscayne Boulevard, are highly recommended, featuring spectacular shows and excellent food.

SHOPPING: Miami: The city's main shopping streets are Flagler Street, between Biscayne Bay and Miami Avenue; and Biscayne Boulevard, between Flagler Street and north to 16th Street – site of the ultra-modern Omni Shopping Complex. A flea market operates every Saturday and Sunday on the grounds of Tropicaire Drive-In Theater, 7751 Bird Road, Miami. **Miami Beach:** The principal shopping street is Lincoln Road Mall. Just north of Miami Beach is the Bal Harbour shopping district. **Tampa:** The main shopping area is around Franklin Street Mall.

SPORT: Florida's sports opportunities are endless. **Greyhound-racing** is held in Pensacola, Jacksonville, Daytona Beach, Orange Lake, St Petersburg, Tampa, Bonita Springs, Palm Beach, Miami, Fort Lauderdale and the Keys; **Jai Alai** in Chattahoochee, Daytona Beach, Tampa, Palm Beach, Fort Lauderdale and Miami; **harness-racing** in Pompano; and **thoroughbred horseracing** in Tampa, Miami and Fort Lauderdale. Other spectator sports include **professional basketball**, played in Miami at the Miami Arena; **professional football**, with the *Miami Dolphins* team playing at the Joe Robbie Stadium in Miami, the

Orlando Thunder team in Orlando and the *Tampa Bay Buccaneers* team in Tampa; and **polo**, played in Palm Beach at the Palm Beach Polo and Country Club. Other sports on offer include **golf, fishing, boat-racing, motorcar-racing, rodeo, baseball, tennis, sailing, diving** and **cycling.** Hunting and Fishing Licenses are sometimes required by persons over 16 years of age – check with the Florida Game and Freshwater Fish Commission. Tel: (904) 488 1960. For further information and brochures on any of the above-named sports, contact the Florida Sports Foundation, Suite 466, 107 West Gaines Street, Collins Building, Tallahassee, FL 32399-2000. Tel: (904) 488 8347. Fax: (904) 922 0482.

SPECIAL EVENTS: Mar '95 *Chasco Fiesta*, New Port Richey; *Florida Strawberry Festival* (11-day event), Plant City; *Manatee Heritage Week*, Bradenton; *Sarasota Medieval Fair*, Sarasota; *Kissimmee Bluegrass Festival*, Kissimmee; *Lipton Championships* (international tennis tournament), Miami; *Carnival Miami/Calle Ocho* (Hispanic celebration), Miami. **Apr** *Fort Walton Beach Seafood Festival; Springtime Tallahassee; Bausch and Lomb Tennis Championship* (women's), Amelia Island; *Pensacola Jazz Festival; St Augustine Easter Parade; Sarasota Jazz Festival; Florida Heritage Festival*, Bradenton; *Fort Lauderdale Seafood Festival; Sunfest '95*, West Palm Beach. **May** *Destin Mayfest*, Destin/Fort Walton Beach; *Gulf Coast Triathlon*, Panama City Beach; *Hog's Breath Hobie Regatta*, Fort Walton Beach; *Annual Flagler County Bluegrass Jamboree*, Bunnell; *Heritage Days*, Jacksonville; *Mug Race*, Palatka; *Naples Tropicool Fest; Greater Daytona Beach Striking Fish Tournament*. **Jun** *Billy Bowlegs Festival*, Destin/Fort Walton Beach; *Fiesta of Five Flags*, Pensacola; *Spanish Night Watch 1740*, St Augustine; *Southwest Florida Wine Fair*, Captiva Island. **Jul** *Suncoast Offshore Grand Prix*, Sarasota; *Hemingway Days*, Key West. **Jul 4** *Fourth of July Celebrations*, Tallahassee, Flagier Beach and Daytona Beach. **Aug** *Panama City Beach Fishing Classic; Caribbean Calypso Festival*, St Petersburg. **Sep** *Pensacola Seafood Festival; Sunsational Museums Month*, St Petersburg. **Oct** *Indian Summer Seafood Festival*, Panama City Beach; *Destin Fish Rodeo*, Destin; *16th Annual International Festival*, Palm Coast; *Jacksonville Jazz Festival; Florida Horse and Agricultural Fair*, Ocala; *Florida*

State Art Fair, Kissimmee; *15th Annual John's Pass Seafood Festival*, Madeira Beach; *Fall Cycle Scene*, Daytona Beach; *Fifth Avenue Oktoberfest*, Naples; *Columbus Day Regatta*, Miami; *Fantasy Fest*, Key West. **Nov** *Blue Angels Homecoming Airshow*, Pensacola; *Greater Gulfcoast Arts Festival*, Pensacola; *South Walton Sportsfest*, Santa Rosa Beach; *Amelia Heritage Festival*, Amelia Island/Fernandino Beach; *Sarasota French Film Festival; St Petersburg Boat Show; Annual Chrysanthemum Festival*, Winter Haven; *Festival of Lights*, Naples; *Fort Myers Beach Sandsculpting Contest; Greater Fort Lauderdale Film Festival; Miami Book Fair International.* **Dec** *Southern Accents of Winter*, Tallahassee; *Grand Illumination and Christmas Parade*, St Augustine; *Victorian Seaside Christmas*, Fernandina Beach; *Florida Citrus Sailfest*, Sanford; *Edison/Ford Homes Holiday House*, Fort Myers; *King Orange Jamboree Parade*, Miami; *Winterfest Boat Parade*, Fort Lauderdale.

CLIMATE

The climate is influenced by the adjacent Atlantic Ocean, which has the effect of slightly lowering temperatures in summer. It has more thunderstorms than any other State in the USA. The region is also affected by hurricanes or less severe tropical storms, which account for the heavy rainfall during the months of July to October. Winters are mild.

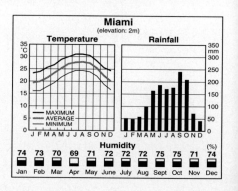

Miami (elevation: 2m)

	Jan	Feb	Mar	Apr	May	June	July	Aug	Sept	Oct	Nov	Dec
Humidity (%)	74	73	70	69	71	72	72	72	75	75	71	74

CVB *Focus*

Northwest Florida

THE BEACHES OF SOUTH WALTON

PAST TO PRESENT

Named after Colonel George Walton in 1824, South Walton was inhabited by Choctaw & Euchee Indians until the late 18th century. Evidence of their history can still be seen today, mostly around the Sandestin resort area. Grayton Beach developed as the first seaside resort between Apalachicola and Pensacola, coinciding with the return of Coco Chanel from southern Europe who made tanning fashionable amongst the rich and well-travelled. Willis Herbert Butler was the major innovator of the style of the wooden houses and wide sandy tree-lined streets leading to the beach, that has become characteristic of the area.

Vacation homes along the shore increased in popularity and between 1970 and 1985 larger, more expensive resorts such as Sandestin Beach Resort, Seascape and later Seaside began to emerge. The South Walton Tourist Development Council was formed in 1986 to promote and protect the pristine beaches.

MEETING THE BEACHES

The South Walton Grayton Beach community was voted the best beach in continental USA by the University of Maryland. The beaches of South Walton are a collection of 18 separate communities, each a distinct and unique destination, and are among the least developed and most pristine of Florida's beaches. In keeping with this character, there are no fast-food restaurants on the beaches – only locally-owned sandwich bars and cafés for a quick bite to eat.

WHERE TO STAY

Whether you have a taste for the adventurous, luxurious or simply a bed and breakfast you'll find it all along the Beaches of South Walton with a choice from over 3000 penthouse suites, hotels, beach houses, condominiums, cottages and camp grounds. South Walton is home to an incomparable array of conference, meeting and resort facilities designed to meet all your needs whether on business or on vacation. Wherever you stay is always guaranteed to be the best . . . right down to the last detail.

SPORTS AND RESORTS

Enjoy sensational sailing, water-skiing or windsurfing. Plan snorkeling and scuba diving expeditions beneath the crystal-clear waters of the South Walton coast. Or just relax on a beach under the warm Florida sun. Test your game at one of the many tennis clubs or choose between one of the five 18-hole golf courses. The Sportfest, one of the nation's most exciting sport festivals, spans three weekends in November, with athletes competing in a series of 15 competitions and tournaments.

Whatever your choice you'll enjoy the Beaches of South Walton!

PANAMA CITY BEACH

PANAMA CITY BEACH FLORIDA

'The World's Most Beautiful Beaches' . . . 'emerald green water' . . . 'snow white sand' . . . all these phrases have been used to describe Panama City Beach. In 1992 America's top travel editors named Panama City Beach as the top domestic beach for value, awarding it the Golden Compass Award established by News Travel Network to recognise 'outstanding value among leisure travel destinations'. Having been discovered as one of the most reasonably priced destinations in Florida, Panama City Beach is attracting new visitors from all over America and Canada.

TOP THE LIST

With over 43km (27 miles) of snow-white beaches on the Gulf of Mexico, water activities are always at the top of the list. For those interested in fishing there is no better place than here. The waters are alive with Red Snapper, Black Grouper, King Mackerel and Amberjack. If entertainment's on your mind then check out the Wave pool for exciting water rides or relax on the Lazy River at the Shipwreck Island Water Park with activities for all the family. If the Gulf's on your mind then consider snorkeling, parasailing, jet-skiing or dolphin-feeding. Explore the mysteries and look for treasures at the Museum of Man in the Sea, experience a walk through a shark tank or pet a sting ray at the Gulf World Marine Park.

EVENING ATTRACTIONS

When the sun goes down, Panama City Beach comes alive with night-time activities for visitors of all ages . . . and there's so much to choose from. Perhaps an exciting evening at an amusement park might be what you have in mind, or some challenging rounds of mini-golf, or a heated go-cart race. The Ocean Opry Music Show highlights tunes from Broadway to country to rock and roll, and features impersonations of some of the best musical entertainers throughout American music history. It's a full evening of music and comedy featuring the talents of three generations of the Rader family. All types of atmospheres imaginable are offered at Panama City beach clubs and, after a night of fun, why not take a leisurely stroll along the shore, the silence of the warm night broken only by the soft sound of the waves breaking on the beach.

DINING IN PANAMA CITY BEACH

Local restaurants capitalise on the bountiful catch from the Gulf offering the best, freshest seafood all year round. Whatever your taste you'll never find it difficult to stay within your budget and experience the best delicacies the Gulf of Mexico has to offer. The cuisine here is as memorable as watching the sun set from the beach.

A DESTINATION FOR ALL SEASONS

With average water temperatures in the 70s and an air temperature of 23°C (74°F), Panama City Beach is extremely pleasant all year-round. The height of the tourist season begins as early as February and continues through early October. During the winter months, visitors form the colder climates find a lovely refuge in Panama

City Beach's moderate temperatures. Special events are held each year for snowbirds (as they are affectionately known by the locals), including welcome parties, bridge and golf tournaments.

Even in winter, cold snaps seldom occur in temperate Panama City Beach and rarely last for more than 48 hours due to Gulf Stream breezes. Spring comes early. By Gebruary, warm temperatures are attracting sun worshippers to the beaches and by March even the most timid are outdoors, enjoying the tropical climate. Amusement parks and attractions are at their peak between Memorial Day and Labor Day. For familites with children, summer at Panama City Beach is the best time of the year.

In the fall, September and October, you'll find the water warm and beaches less crowded. Seafood is at its best and the water is crystal clear. If you choose to visit at this time, you'll find accommodation in Panama City Beach offer excellent off-season packages.

One of the secrets of our sea-side community's far-reaching popularity is the diversity of its accommodations – there's literally something for every budget and style – from beach-front RV resorts and campgrounds to luxury resorts and condominiums, family-owned and operated motels to private, beachside cottages.

More than 16,000 motel, hotel and condominium units include tennis and golf resorts, motels that cater to sports fishermen and divers, beach properties that specialize in family-style vacation homes, church retreats, and budget-conscious vacation packages. Other unusual options in the area are RV resorts, excellent campgounds, overnight dock facilities (perfect for seafares traveling the Intracoastal Waterway), and bed and breakfast inns.

Reservations are recomm-ended. Call the Panama City Beache's Chamber of Commerce Referral Service at 1 (904) 234 3193.

MEETINGS & CONVENTIONS

Panama City Beach is uniquely equipped to host meetings, groups, incentives and conventions – anything from a social club gathering to a nation-wide corporate convention.

Sun-and-sand destinations are always favorites for large gatherings as long as they are easily accessible, have an adequate number of quality hotel rooms, offer good food and spacious meeting facilities, and provide entertainment activities and shopping for accompanying family members. Panama City Beach qualifies on all counts.

Panama City Beach has many large hotels and resorts particularly suited for group business. These sizable lodgings have a variety of meeting rooms, ballrooms and banquet facilities. Several of the larger resorts have conference centers with a complete selection of meeting rooms and audio-visual equipment, as well as golf, tennis, fishing and other amusements.

Within the past year, the City of Panama City Beach has purchased 28 acres of property for a proposed multi-purpose Convention Center which will accommodate conventions, trade shows and meetings.

EASY ACCESS

Adding to Panama City Beach's appeal is its accessibility. Our lovely beachfront community is less that 480km (300 miles) from Atlanta, 800km (500 miles) from Memphis and 1120km (700 miles) from St Louis, Cincinnati and Houston. Interstate 10 runs east and west, just 48km (30 miles) to the north. U.S. 231 drops down almost to the beach. U.S. 231 and State Road 79 run directly north and south from Interstate 10 if you drive. Daily flights to and from Panama City/Bay County International Airport include airlines such as Delta, Atlantic Southeast, Northwest Air Link, and US Air Express.

The airport has taxi and limousine service as well as major car rentals. Two fixed-base operations for general aviation offer a full range of services. From Atlanta, less than an hour away by air, you can make connections to anywhere in the country and the world.

PENSACOLA –
FLORIDA'S FIRST PLACE CITY

HISTORICAL PENSACOLA

Originally Pensacola, a natural deep-water port, was founded by the Spanish in 1519. Today the Spanish, French and English have all left their traces in the rich and exotic heritage. Stroll down many of the magnolia-shaded avenues and experience living examples of periods spanning from colonial to the present.

YOU'RE NEVER RAINED OUT IN PENSACOLA

The temperature is one of Pensacola's biggest advantages. Mild winters and an average temperature of 24°C (75°F) means that the outdoors is never out of reach. Not far from Pensacola you'll find the 'Canoe capital of Florida', an extensive waterway for kayaking, paddle boats and canoes. Combined with the soft white-sand beaches at Perdido Key and Pensacola Beach, nature trails, national and state parks and sporting facilities, there's always plenty to do outdoors in and around Pensacola, Florida's First Place City.

ARTS AND CULTURE

Four hundred years and five flags mean a diverse yet distinct southern style reflected through the museums as well as through day-to-day life. The Pensacola Museum of Art and the University of West Florida draw large crowds as do the many music and art festivals every year. The T. T. Wentworth

Museum arranges a hands-on interactive display for children as part of its extensive range of local exhibits.

ATTRACTIONS AND ENTERTAINMENT

The 'Cradle of Naval Aviation' has for long described the close ties with the Navy at the Pensacola Naval Air Station. The station's 'Blue Angels' regularly put on displays in the area. Take a trip to the nearby National Museum of Naval Aviation, one of the largest of its type anywhere in the world. Much of Pensacola's extraordinary history is best revealed by a visit to Historic Pensacola Village, Seville and Palafox Historic Districts downtown, and the North Hill Preservation District. Visit the Civic Center for family shows or to arrange a conference or convention.

HOW TO GET HERE

No matter where you're travelling from in the USA, Pensacola is closer than any other city resort in Florida and well serviced throughout the county by the Pensacola Regional Airport and major interstate highways. On arrival car rentals are available at the airport and many other locations and bus transportation covers all the major attractions. The only problem with accommodation is what to choose. With over 7200 available rooms of all types, there is definitely a place for you in Pensacola.

TALLAHASSEE

FLORIDA WITH A SOUTHERN ACCENT!

Originally an Indian ceremonial centre, Tallahassee has been recognised as the capital of Florida since 1823. Florida's capital city remains firmly linked with the past, as evidenced by the unearthed 1539 winter encampment of Spanish explorer Hernando de Soto: this was the site of America's first Christmas celebration.

THE BEST-KEPT SECRET

Tallahassee is closer to New Orleans than to Miami; known as 'the other Florida', it is the best-kept secret in the Southern States. America's largest concentration of original plantation homes, charming canopy roads and lush rolling hills await the international traveller. Both Atlanta and Orlando are just five hours' drive away, making this the perfect fly-drive option to your touring holiday.

NATURAL AND HISTORICAL ATTRACTIONS

'Big ones' are often pulled from the waters at Lake Jackson and Talquin which are renowned for bass fishing the world over. The Florida National Scenic Trail, St Mark's National Wildlife Refuge and Apalachicola National Forest are just a few of the local wildlife areas in which you can enjoy camping, picnicking or just exploring at your own pace. At nearby Wakulla Springs – one of the world's deepest freshwater springs and the set for many of the Tarzan movies – a safari boat will whisk you through a wildlife paradise of native birds, alligators and jumping fish. Red wolves, Florida Panthers and other fascinating wildlife roam the 52-acre natural habitat at the Tallahassee Museum of History and Natural Science.

NO BONES ABOUT IT

Visit Herman the mastadon, who is between 12 and 18 thousand years old and who in his prime weighed five tons, now living at the Museum of Florida History. The Black Archives Museum takes you back to the days of slavery and the cotton-growing plantations. The Knott House is filled with eccentric rhymes written by the matron of this park-front mansion which are attached to furnishings reflecting the social, economic and political history of Tallahassee. Roam the halls of the Old Capitol, restored to its 1902 American Renaissance appearance, and view Tallahassee's rich natural resources from the 22nd-floor observatory of the New Capitol. These are just some of the many museums and heritage sites on offer when you visit 'Florida with a Southern Accent'.

A PREFERRED MEETING PLACE

Even before the 'white man's discovery', Tallahassee had been a 'preferred meeting place' – serving as an Indian tribal center for centuries.

Since those first historic meetings, Tallahassee has remained the perfect location to meet for its gracious beauty, Southern hospitality, abundant and affordable accommodation, impressive convention facilities, accessibility by air and ground, and tremendous resources of state government and two major universities. The variety of meeting diversions range from bass fishing, hunting for wild game and jungle safaris to leisurely historic tours and body bronzing on nearby beaches.

From luxury to economy, Tallahassee offers more than 5000 rooms hotels and motels. It spans a wide specturm; a quaint inn of governors, restored plantation bed and breakfast, rustic 'gentlemen' lodges, country-club golf course suites, beachside historic escapes, and familiar chain and corporate hotels. Average guest room rates begin modestly at $45. Tallahassee features traditional and unique meeting and convention options totaling 167,225 sq metres (180,000 sq ft) of space with 57,599 sq metres (62,000 sq ft) in 29 hotels.

The Old and New Capitols, Thallahassee.

DESTIN/FORT WALTON BEACH
NW FLORIDA'S EMERALD COAST

SIMPLY IRRESISTIBLE

Unpretentious, uncomplicated and breathtakingly beautiful, the Emerald Coast is simply irresistible. Famous for 38km (24 miles) of dazzling sugar-white sands and brilliant green waters, the Southern sea towns of Destin and Fort Walton Beach present simple pleasures – the 'World's Luckiest Fishing Village', spirited seaside celebrations, great golf courses and the freshest seafood in Florida are all embraced with an unassuming charm.

THERE'S A TIME AND A SEASON

This relaxed slice of Florida's Northern Gulf Coast is actually closer in distance – and demeanour – to Dixie than to the rest of Florida. Not surprisingly, the perceived time warp is reality as the Emerald Coast is in the Central Time Zone while the rest of the State follows Eastern Standard time. Likewise, its seasons are pure Deep South – sensational springs, sultry summer days and coolish winter evenings – for tempting temperatures year-round.

MIRACLES OF NATURE

The 100-fathom curve draws closer to Destin than to any other spot in Florida – creating the speediest deep-water access in the Gulf and making the Emerald Coast one of the top five shelling destinations in the world. Exceptional snorkeling and diving are possible directly from the beach. Undoubtedly the most mesmerizing distraction on the Emerald Coast is the combination of sun-bleached shore and emerald-green waters, complemented by perfect, picture-postcard sunrises *and* sunsets. The 208-acre Henderson Beach State Park, James Lee Park and Wayside Park are three of the five parks and five beach overwalks being created or renovated along the Emerald Coast.

OUTDOOR PURSUITS

Hailed as the 'World's Luckiest Fishing Village', Destin's East Pass is only 16km (10 miles) from 100-foot depths. Harboring the largest and most elaborately-equipped charter boat fleet in Florida, more billfish are caught each year on the Emerald Coast than all other Gulf ports combined. For more earth-bound pleasures, the Emerald Coast boasts 225 holes of great golf escapes, 104 tennis courts, while the pristine wilderness of Blackwater State Park and Eglin Reservation offer tubing and canoeing down crystal-clear rivers, and camping and hiking amid acres of pine, hickory and maple.

DELECTABLE DINING

Emerald Coast eateries are out to impress one thing . . . the taste buds. From oyster bars to cafés and restaurants, local seafood is celebrated with simple zest, straight from the harbour to your table.

GULF BREEZE AND NAVARRE BEACHES

THE PERFECT VACATION

Gulf Breeze and Navarre Beaches are truly a vacationer's delight, offering golfing, fishing, sailing, snorkeling, camping, hiking and miles of glistening white beaches and crystal-clear waters.

SHOPPING AND SEAFOOD BY THE BEACH

The Gulf Breeze and Navarre Beaches area combines the best of two worlds – a relaxed atmosphere featuring modern shopping centres and fresh seafood markets offering the freshest catch of the day and restaurants ranging from casual to elegant waterfront dining, with direct access to glorious beaches.

GOLF BY THE GULF

For those with a passion for golf this vacation spot will definitely be a hit. Within minutes of Gulf Breeze and Navarre are four challenging golf courses. Tiger Point is a 36-hole championship course overlooking beautiful Santa Rosa Sound and the Gulf of Mexico. The Club at Hidden Creek offers an 18-hole championship course which was voted 'Outstanding Course in Northwest Florida', while the Moors offers 18 holes of golf with a Scottish flavor of gently rolling terrain.

FISHING AND DIVING

Aspiring fishermen can try their luck in local waters, which are teeming with white and speckled trout, red fish, flounder, sheepshead, black drum and mackerel. South Santa Rosa County offers superb fishing from beaches, public piers, small boats or deep-sea charter boats. A breathtaking underwater world exists for snorkelers and divers alike. Divers can explore underwater wrecks such as a sunken Russian freighter, coal barges and the USS Massachusetts. For a change of scenery, canoe rental agencies offer leisurely trips on a number of freshwater rivers. These sleepy rivers gently wind through secluded wooded areas giving you a relaxing change of pace. Camping enthusiasts will find many area campgrounds from which to choose.

GO WILD AT THE ZOO

One of the county's most popular attractions is The Zoo, located on Highway 98 between Gulf Breeze and Navarre. Colossus, one of the largest Lowland gorillas in captivity, is The Zoo's most famous resident along with 700 other animals, including many endangered species. Visitors can catch the Safari Line train through 30 acres of natural wildlife habitat, ride Ellie the African Elephant, or enjoy The Zoo's gorgeous Tea House of the Yellow Camellia, the only authentic Japanese Garden in Northwest Florida.

GETTING THERE

South Santa Rosa County is located in Florida's Northwest Panhandle and is convenient whether arriving by car or plane. The county is served by the Pensacola Regional Airport and Okaloosa Airport, while interstate connections are available from I-10 by traveling I-110 south through Pensacola, then taking the Three Mile Bridge directly to Gulf Breeze on Highway 98. Travelers can reach the Navarre area directly by taking Highway 87 south.

CVB *Focus*

Orlando

THE LOCATION

Orlando is located just north of the centre of the State of Florida, 380km (236 miles) north of Miami, 137km (85 miles) northeast of Tampa and 225km (140 miles) south of Jacksonville. Florida is the most southeastern state on the Atlantic seaboard of the USA mainland. It is a peninsula surrounded on three sides by water, with the Atlantic Ocean to the east and the Gulf of Mexico to the west. To the northeast it is bordered by the State of Georgia and to the northwest by the State of Alabama.

THE CULTURE AND HISTORY

The city of Orlando is thought to have been named after a US soldier called Orlando Reeves. The story goes that he was on sentinel duty for a scouting party and, while his companions slept, an Indian approached disguised as a rolling log. Orlando saw him for what he was and fired his gun, waking the other campers and saving their lives, but was killed by the Indian's swift arrow. Before then, the community had been known as Jernigan after Aaron Jernigan who had come from Georgia and settled in the Orlando area in 1842. The first post office opened in 1850 and the city's name was changed to Orlando in 1857. It then developed a reputation as a centre for citrus production until 1971 when it became even better known as the location of Walt Disney World. Orlando is the county seat of Orange County which, until 1845, was known as Mosquito County.

WHAT MAKES ORLANDO SPECIAL

Orland Has All The Sports

Professional and spectator sports bring big names and big leagues to Central Florida all year round. The NBA's Orlando Magic, for example, sold out its first three seasons of professional basketball at the 15,000-seat Orlando Arena. Ice hockey, concerts and other events also take place at this stadium. Orlando also hosts the Florida Citrus Bowl, a New Year's Day college football classic. Major League baseball teams from Houston and Kansas City hold spring training in and around Orlando. Two PGA-sanctioned golf tournaments are played here – the Nestlé Invitational and the Walt Disney World Classic.

There's a wealth of less structured recreation too. The Central Florida area has 44 golf courses, elaborate mini-golf, 21 tennis centres with more than 800 courts, plus hot-air ballooning, parachuting, horseriding, houseboating, canoeing, powerboating, sailing, water-skiing, fishing and swimming, all offering a relaxing change of pace.

Wonderful Weather

Florida has rightly earned its nickname of 'The Sunshine State'. Abundant sunshine and warm, pleasant temperatures are the norm in Central Florida. Summer weather (temperatures from 18-33°C; 65-92°F) arrives in Orlando in late May and lasts through to the end of September. The humidity is often interrupted in the late afternoon by thunderstorms. Fortunately, the rain usually lasts only half an hour – just long enough to cool things off.

The region's subtropical climate lends itself to a generally informal dress code. Lightweight, casual attire is suggested when visiting the theme parks or attending matches. Sneakers or other comfortable walking shoes are a must.

Florida's summer heat and humidity can feel especially intense

When Your Clients Visit Orlando, They Expect The World... And We Give It To Them!

Just one mile from the WALT DISNEY WORLD® Resort Area.

Discover Lake Buena Vista's only all-suite hotel that offers so much for your clients' vacation dollar! A host of amenities, children's activities and a luxurious two-room suite, with a spacious living room and separate bedroom complement a location second to none. Embassy Suites® Resort Lake Buena Vista is only three miles from Sea World® and just seven miles from Universal Studios Florida® We're a Free scheduled shuttle ride and just a mile from the entrance to the MAGIC KINGDOM® Park, EPCOT® Center and Disney-MGM Studios Theme Park. Plus, we're close to golf, night life and just a short drive to either coast. From recreation to relaxation, Embassy Suites Resort Lake Buena Vista has something for everyone!

TWICE THE VALUE

A typical family of 4 will **save $89 per day** by staying at Embassy Suites Resort Lake Buena Vista:

	Other Orlando Resorts	Embassy Suites Resort
Breakfast	$33.64	FREE!
Cocktails*/Soft Drinks	21.36	FREE!
Transportation to and from Disney	34.00	FREE!
Total Savings Per Day	**$89.00**	**FREE!**

EMBASSY SUITES ℠

——— RESORT LAKE BUENA VISTA ———

8100 LAKE AVE., ORLANDO, FL 32836

For information and reservations, call: 0-992-441517 FAX: 0-992-467731 Request Suite **MCOWD**.
Discover America Marketing, Priest House, 90 High Road, Broxbourne, Herts, EN107DZ England
Near WALT DISNEY WORLD® Resort Area. Subject to state and local laws. ©1994 EMBASSY SUITES Inc.

to visitors from cooler, northern climates. Clothing should be of lightweight fabric such as cotton that lets skin breathe. Avoid over-exposure to the sun; apply sunblock before going outdoors and reapply every few hours. The sun can burn unprotected skin, even on overcast days.

Gorgeous Gardens

Oranges aren't the only thing that grow in Florida's sunshine. Florida's gardens are in bloom all year round with colourful and exotic plants. In nearby Polk County, less than an hour's drive from Orlando, can be found two grand gardens – Bok Tower Gardens and Cypress Gardens.

Bok Tower Gardens is a beautiful and serene sanctuary in the scenic highlands of Polk County that has been visited by over 20 million visitors since 1928. Thousands of azaleas, camellias and magnolias provide seasonal vistas of colour. Squirrels, quail and wood ducks roam the grounds. In the middle of the garden, amidst the reflecting pools and winding paths, is the 'Singing Tower', a 69m (225ft) stone and marble structure with 57 bronze bells. It features music from one of the world's great carillons every half hour and a 45-minute recital is presented at 1500 daily. Open 0800-1700 daily, admission is $4 for adults, children aged 5-12 pay $1 and under 5s are free. For further information, telephone (813) 676 1408.

Cypress Gardens, just 15 minutes north of Bok Tower Gardens, is known for its botanical displays, water-skiing shows, high-diving shows, synchronised swimmers and ice-skating shows. It also features 'Plantation Gardens' and 'Wings of Wonder', a butterfly aviary featuring free-flying butterflies from around the world, fountains with sculptured butterflies and two chrysalis – cocoons

that contain future butterflies. 'Totally Mardi Gras – A Water Spectacular' recently opened on February 28, 1995. This water-ski show is Cypress Gardens' most elaborate water-ski production ever, featuring a host of aquatic parade floats, giant walk-around characters and an all-new element – made-for-speed stunt kites. 'Kodak's Island in the Sky' provides a panoramic view of the gardens and Lake Eloise. Cypress Gardens is open 0930-1730 daily. For further information, telephone (813) 324 2111 *or* (1 800) 282 2123 (US & Canada only; toll free) *or* (1 800) 237 4826 (all others; toll free).

Beautiful Beaches

With hundreds of miles of coastline, Florida is home to some of the world's most famous beaches, and many are just a short drive from Orlando.

On the Atlantic coast, Daytona, New Smyrna and Cocoa beaches are just an hour's drive east of Orlando. Cars can cruise right along the water's edge on the hard-packed sands of Daytona Beach, noted for its carnival-like atmosphere and oceanfront boardwalk. Beach enthusiasts in search of a more serene setting may opt for New Smyrna Beach, Daytona's neighbour to the south, while surfers flock to Cocoa Beach.

Less than two hours west of Orlando, the Gulf Coast beaches of Clearwater and St Petersburg are noted for their sugary-white sands which border the tranquil blue-green waters of the Gulf of Mexico. Visitors should make sure they pack their bathing suits, sunglasses and sunscreen for a few hours of blissful sunbathing and swimming and, as the sun goes down, visitors should experience Florida's exquisite beach sunsets, as they rarely fail to give an extraordinary performance.

With 788 guest rooms & suites and all the

extras to make your vacation really special,

Sheraton World Resort in Orlando has a

fresh new sparkle as bright as the Florida

ORLANDO'S WORLD OF VACATION VALUE!

sun! Orlando's perfectly-located meetings

and vacations hotel is the place to enjoy 3

outdoor pools, miniature golf, 5 lighted

tennis courts, the Tarpon Bar & Grill

Restaurant, Max's Deli/Mini Mart and a

wonderfully central location, all at value

prices. For information, call (407) 352-

1100 or for reservations call (800)

327-0363, in Florida (800) 341-4292.

Fax (407) 352-3679.

Sheraton World
R E S O R T
ORLANDO

OUR WORLD REVOLVES AROUND YOU

10100 International Drive, Orlando, FL 32821-8095

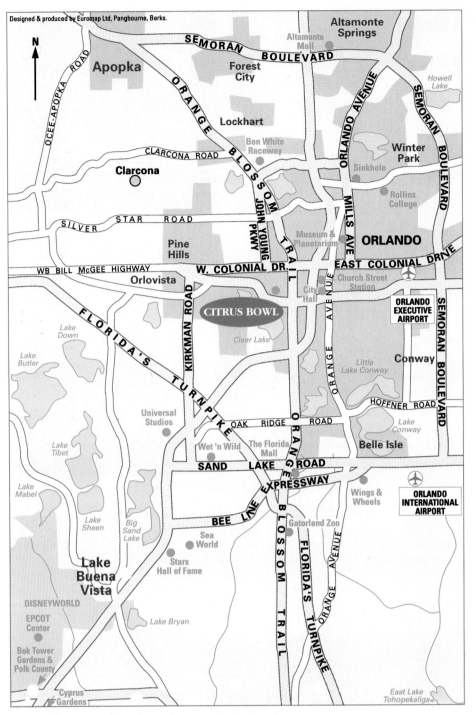

Designed & produced by Euromap Ltd, Pangbourne, Berks.

major rides (Back to the Future, Kongfrontation, ET, Earthquake and The Funtastic World of Hanna Barbera) early in the morning or in late afternoon.

• Just a few minutes of planning ensure a smoother, more memorable visit. Many of the theme parks and other attractions – including Sea World, Church Street Station, Walt Disney World and Universal Studios – offer special packages. For more information, contact Orlando/Orange County Convention and Visitors Bureau, Inc, Suite 300, 7208 Sand Lake Road, Orlando, Florida 32819. Tel: (407) 363 5800. Fax: (407) 363 5899.

DISNEY WORLD'S NEW ATTRACTIONS

No mention of Orlando would be complete without *Walt Disney World*. Attracting visitors from all over the world, its appeal is endless and, despite being around for 20 years, new things are still happening at Disney World.

Disney's MGM Studios Theme Park's newest attraction features a 13-storey free-fall aboard a runaway elevator in the *Twilight Zone Tower of Terror*. The Tower is part of a storm-scarred hotel at the end of the new Sunset Boulevard district that includes shops, a ranch market and expanded *Theater of the Stars*, which opened in July. The MGM Studios also pay tribute to Walt Disney's hit movie 'Aladdin' with a daily parade called 'Aladdin's Royal Caravan'. The caravan depicts Aladdin's entrance into the city of Agrabah after discovering the magic lamp and becoming Prince Ali. A brass band leads the procession down Hollywood Boulevard followed by Aladdin's 10m (32ft) genie. Music, dance and humour combine with acrobats, camels, rope climbers and snake charmers. The studios also feature the 'Voyage of the Little Mermaid'. Through the creative use of puppetry, audio-animatronics figures and film clips, this musical production takes the audience deep into the ocean with Ariel, the little mermaid. The highly acclaimed movie 'Beauty and the Beast' is the basis for a 30-minute song-and-dance stage production. One-day tickets to the theme park and tour are $38.16 for adults and $30.74 for children aged three to nine.

Disney's Epcot Center received an updated mission in 1994 as an ever-changing showplace for invention and technology. *Innoventions*, a 100,000-sq-ft exhibition of the newest products for home, work and play, is the feature pavilion of the new Epcot. But the park also will regularly add exhibits throughout World Showcase to portray important examples of progress in many nations.

The Magic Kingdom features the opening of the new *Tomorrowland* early this year with the new *ExtraTERRORestrial*

TIPS FOR VISITING THE ATTRACTIONS

Travellers can save time by following these tips on visiting major attractions:

• Guests may leave parks in the afternoon after having their hands stamped, then return in the evening when crowds are smaller.

• Shopping at the end of the day keeps guests from toting parcels through the parks.

• Walt Disney World suggests that guests arrive early and also make dining reservations early in the day.

• Sea World's simultaneous seating for shows and continuous viewing of exhibits make for a relaxing day, but it's still wise to pick up a show schedule when entering any park, then use it to plan the day.

• Universal Studios suggests that guests plan to see the

Alien Encounter and the *Transportarium* attractions. *Alien Encounter* features a futuristic Convention Center where a demonstration of a new teleportation system goes horribly wrong. An attempt to transport results in a close encounter with a frightening alien. The Transportarium, which opened in late 1994, features a journey through time in a theater-in-the-round. Another popular attraction is *Splash Mountain,* promising guests a 64kmph (40mph) descent. Disney's fastest ride is based on animated sequences in Walt Disney's 1946 film 'Song of the South' and boasts the world's longest flume drop. Four- and 5-day passes are available which include admission to all three Disney parks. Four-day passes are $102.82 for adults and $131.44 for children. Five-day passes are $189.74 for adults and $151.58 for children.

Construction began last year on *Celebration*, Disney's $2.5-billion residential, shopping and cultural centre. Completion of the project could span two decades and will eventually include a city of 20,000 residents and 25,000 workers sitting on 4400 acres off Interstate 4 and US 192. Besides four residential communities, a shopping mall, office space and the cultural centre, Disney plans an environmental centre, three championship golf courses, schools,

parks, a transportation hub and a 150-bed hospital and medical centre. Disney officials are aiming for 1995 for the opening of the residential portion of the city and the hospital.

For more information on Walt Disney World, call (407) 934 7500 or 934 7383 (international publicity).

WATER WORLDS

As Florida is almost entirely surrounded by water, it should come as no surprise that many of its most fascinating sites should be water-orientated. From the amazing creatures that live underneath the surface to the outrageous fun that can be had on the surface, Florida has it all.

Gatorland is home to one of Florida's most famous residents – the alligator. Visitors may view 5000 alligators doing what they do naturally. Recent additions to the park include an 800-seat gator-wrestling stadium and a 10-acre breeding marsh and observation platform. The park has also added an educational and entertainment show called 'Snakes of Florida'. Future plans include a 'Crocodiles of the World' exhibit and a 'Cracker' village modelled after early 20th-century Florida settlements. For further information, telephone (407) 855 5496.

If alligators are not to one's taste, visit *Sea World of Florida,* where various species of underwater mammals, such as dolphins, sea lions, killer whales and otters, make their mark. Orlando's world-renowned marine-life park will open 'Wild Arctic' in late May 1995. 'Wild Arctic' is the largest undertaking in Anheuser-Busch theme park history and features a simulated flight over the frozen North and real-life encounters with animals, including polar bears, that live there. Sea World recently opened a package of new shows including the 'Shamu – World Focus' killer whale show, 'The Big Splash Bash' in the new Nautilus Theatre, 'Mermaids, Myths and Monsters' night-time extravangza and the 'Shamu: Close Up' killer whale breeding and research habitat. 'Shamu: World Focus' combines rare video footage with live action featuring the Shamu family. Sea World also added two behind-the-scenes Sea Safari Guided Tours. The tours allow guests to interact with animals and learn about animal ecosystems and Sea World's Animal Rescue, Rehabilitation and Release program. There is also a water-ski and speedboat show, botanical gardens, a Hawaiian village, Penguin and Shark Encounters, Cap'n Kids World, World of the Sea Aquarium and Sky Tower ride. For further information, telephone (407) 351 3600.

Silver Springs is famous for its glass-bottom boat jungle cruises and was the filming site for six original Tarzan films. 'Lost River Voyage' is a 30-minute boat excursion along the river on a newly designed open-air, glass-bottom boat. The boat enables visitors to observe the beauty of the river above and below the surface, while stopping at the wildlife outpost for an informative presentation. For further information, telephone (904) 236 2121.

But for visitors who want to really get their feet wet, Water Mania and Wet 'n Wild are the places to go. *Water Mania* has a new slide called the 'Abyss', an enclosed tube that sends guests through 91m (300ft) of blue darkness dropping into a splashing pool. A 12m (40ft) pirate ship with water cannons, tunnels and slides has recently been added to the Rain Forest children's water playground; and the 'Aqua Express', a giant train with tunnels and slides, has been added to the Squirt Pond playground. And if that's not enough, Water Mania also has the 1992 International Association of Amusement Parks and Attractions Ride of the Year – 'Wipe Out', which is a simulated surfing ride. *Wet 'n Wild* has some of the same kind of fun. Their newest slide is the 'Bomb Bay', which plunges thrill-seekers into a nearly vertical free-fall down a 24m (76ft) slide. In 1992, Wet 'n Wild opened the $1-million Bubba Tub, a giant inner-tube ride which sends up to five riders splashing, turning and dipping down a river of water the length of a football field. Both parks are open year-round and feature heated pools. For information on Water Mania, telephone (407) 396 2626 and for Wet 'n Wild, telephone (407) 351 1800.

NIGHTS ON THE TOWN

A night in Orlando can mean dancing until dawn, strolling in the moonlight along a quiet lakefront or laughing it up at a local comedy club. Orlando Centroplex features events at the Orlando Arena and Florida Citrus Bowl, as well as theatrical productions at *Bob Carr Performing Arts Centre.* This 2534-seat performing arts facility hosts the Southern Ballet, visiting operas and theatrical performances. Serious music enthusiasts will also find an impressive selection of rock, jazz, country & western, blues, cajun or disco. Entertainment complexes like *Disney's Pleasure Island* or downtown Orlando's *Church Street Station* offer some of each, with a variety of nightclubs and restaurants in a themed setting. Or visitors can join the locals at popular neighbourhood spots such as a jazz & blues club in downtown Orlando or a country & western lounge with live music and dancing. Visitors should remember wherever they go to be sure to carry identification – driver's licence

ORLANDO WELCOMES YOU

Welcome to Orlando, where the magic begins the moment you arrive! Like no other city in the world, Orlando makes any visit magical. Thrills, adventure, beauty and wonder awaits visitors to this exciting one-of-a-kind destination.

ORLANDO'S MAGIC began when nature blessed the area with resplendent beauty, abundant sunshine and year-round warm weather. The opening of Walt Disney World's Magic Kingdom in 1971 paved the way for the transformation of this quiet, agricultural community into one of the world's most popular holiday destinations. Today, Central Florida is home not only to the Magic Kingdom and the Epcot Center but also to Universal Studios Florida, Sea World, Cypress Gardens, Busch Gardens, Wet 'n Wild, Spaceport USA and 50 other theme attractions.

LODGING IN ORLANDO With more than 80,000 hotel rooms, suites and villas, Orlando offers something for every taste and budget. Accommodation ranges from campsites and moderately priced lodging to suite hotels and high-class resorts.

DINING IN ORLANDO Grab a sandwich on-the-run between matches or dine in elegance on epicurean delights prepared by some of the world's most talented chefs. Sample international cuisine or chow down on barbecued gator ribs. Orlando has enough variety to satisfy any taste buds.

SAFETY TIPS Unfortunately, crime never takes a holiday. Secure valuables such as jewellery and excess cash in the hotel safe. Take only necessary valuables with you when travelling. Travellers cheques are generally regarded as the best way to meet cash needs on holiday. Determine who's there before opening hotel doors. Use peepholes, windows or phone the hotel desk. Place your room key in a safe place in a purse or on your person when at the pool, bar or dining room. Always lock your car. Lock valuables in the boot, glove box or luggage compartment. **Note:** Heat sensitive items such as film or electronic equipment may be damaged by the extreme temperatures of a parked vehicle.

CURRENCY EXCHANGE Currency exchange facilities can be found in major national and state banks, at many Central Florida hotels and at major attractions.

INTERPRETERS Orlando's Language Bank provides volunteer multilingual interpreter services. The bank provides information by phone. Arrangements for a paid interpreter or guide may also be obtained.
Welcome! You're a treasured guest in our hometown of Orlando, where dreams still come true.

From Wit Tuttle, Public Relations Representative of Orlando/Orange County Convention & Visitors Bureau.

ORLANDO INTERNATIONAL
THE WORLD CLASS GATEWAY TO THE BEST OF FLORIDA!

Welcome to Central Florida – a world business and vacation destination - with more natural and man-made attractions than anywhere else under the sun! And welcome to Orlando International Airport – the only gateway to the heart of Florida!

In Orlando, at the crossroads of the State, Orlando International Airport is easily accessible to all major Florida cities, business centers, attractions, deep-water ports, the space coast, and world-famous beaches. For business or pleasure, you can get anywhere quickly and effortlessly from Orlando International Airport.

From the moment you arrive, you will notice that Orlando International Airport is one of the most beautiful, sophisticated and environmentally concerned airports in the nation. It's practically an attraction in itself! Inside and out, the airport has incorporated the celebrated Florida sunshine and atmosphere into its ultra-modern design. An enclosed elevated passenger shuttle system links your gate to the tri-level main terminal, giving you a preview of the incredible Florida environment. The newest 24-gate airside view of the many lakes, landscaped islands and lush Florida vegetation surrounding the airport, creates a unique visual experience for travelers.

The terminal itself is a showcase of modern technology and convenience. It's bright, attractive and easy to navigate. A myriad of restaurants, stores and services caters to your needs. The new 450-room Hyatt Regency Hotel on top of the main terminal with an eight-story atrium featuring royal palms and a 'city park' atmosphere add an open feeling to the airport.

Most major airlines serve over 100 of the most requested destinations in the United States from Orlando International Airport. There is more convenient direct domestic passenger service from Orlando International Airport than from any other airport in Florida. At the nation's sixth busiest port of entry, direct scheduled service is available from the United Kingdom, Iceland, Germany, The Netherlands, Central and South America, Mexico, Japan and the Caribbean. Charter airlines fly direct routes from the United Kingdom and other parts of Europe, South America and Canada.

Currently, the airport serves over 22 million passengers annually. As the fastest growing major metropolitan airport in the nation, Orlando International Airport is your gateway to Central Florida, eager to serve your business or pleasure travel needs.

WELCOME TO OUR WORLD CLASS CITY!

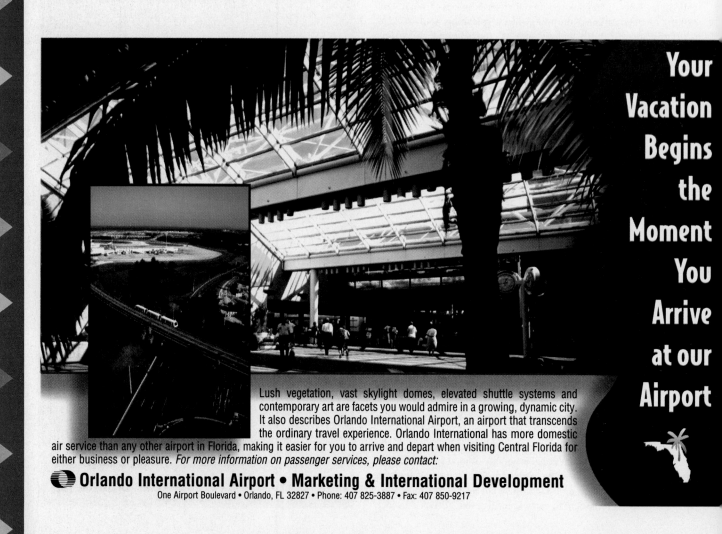

Your Vacation Begins the Moment You Arrive at our Airport

Lush vegetation, vast skylight domes, elevated shuttle systems and contemporary art are facets you would admire in a growing, dynamic city. It also describes Orlando International Airport, an airport that transcends the ordinary travel experience. Orlando International has more domestic air service than any other airport in Florida, making it easier for you to arrive and depart when visiting Central Florida for either business or pleasure. *For more information on passenger services, please contact:*

Orlando International Airport • Marketing & International Development

One Airport Boulevard • Orlando, FL 32827 • Phone: 407 825-3887 • Fax: 407 850-9217

or passport – as most clubs that serve alcoholic beverages require patrons to be at least 21 years of age. Casual dress is appropriate for most nightclubs, although some do not allow shorts or tank tops.

THE AIRPORT

Orlando International Airport is located 8km (5 miles) northwest of the city. *United, Delta* and *USAir* are Orlando's major airlines. Passengers and baggage arriving in Orlando on direct international flights must pass through US Customs and Immigration & Naturalization Services. Visitors' baggage will be transported to the main terminal baggage claim. When getting off the shuttle, visitors should check the baggage claim locations posted above the shuttle. The baggage claim areas are down the escalator on Level 2 of the main terminal. Foreign currency may be exchanged at the Main Terminal from 0800-2100 on the B-side second-level Bag Claim; on the second-level Bag Claim A or at international gates based on international arrival and departure times. Car rental agencies are available at the airport and include *Dollar* and *Hertz*. Airport Information Centers, offering a multilingual service, are located in front of the security checkpoint for Gates 1-59 in the Great Hall and in front of security checkpoint for Gates 60-99 in the Hotel Atrium. These are open every day 0700-2300. For more information, telephone (407) 825 2352 *or* 825 2118 for TDD (Tele-type Deaf Unit).

GETTING TO ORLANDO

Buses/Shuttle Vans/Limousines

Bus or van passage is available from the airport to International Drive or downtown Orlando. The fare is $10 one-way and $17 round-trip for adults; $7 one-way, $11 round-trip for children. Transportation to Lake Buena Vista is $12 one-way and $21 round-trip for adults; $7 one-way, $11 round-trip for children. Limousines are available from the airport to International Drive, Lake Buena Vista or downtown Orlando. Costs range from $10-$25 for adults and $5-$15 for children.

Mears Transportation Group: A full-service, 24-hour ground transportation service. Taxis and shuttles are available to all area hotels and attractions from the baggage claim level of Orlando Airport. For further information, telephone (407) 423 5566.

Alpha Shuttle Inc: Offers minibuses and luxury sedans for airport transfers and tours anywhere in Florida. For further information, telephone (407) 856 7139.

Bethany Limousines Inc: Complete transportation service offers luxury sedans, limousines, vans and buses for airport transfers and tours. Meet-and-greet service available. For further information, telephone (407) 839 3777.

Transtar Limousine Service: Transportation to and from Orlando Airport and all Orlando area hotels 24 hours a day. Sedans and limousines available. For further information, telephone (407) 856 7777.

Taxi

Visitors should use a metered cab and confirm the cost of the trip with the driver at the beginning. Rates for taxi service average $2.50 for the first mile and $1.50 for each additional mile travelled.

Rail

Amtrak serves Orlando with four daily trains originating in New York, Tampa and Miami, with stops in Winter Park and Sanford.

Chaffeured Transportation

Shuttles, taxis and even stretch limousines are available for travel from airport to hotels, attractions and throughout the city. Tour operators offer group and individual services ranging from airport meet-and-greet and translation to handicapped transportation.

Self-Drive

Car rental firms in Orlando include *Alamo, Avis, Budget, Dollar, General, Major, National, Payless, Phoenix, Superior* and *Thrifty*. Vehicles range from minibuses to sleek convertibles. Recreational vehicles are available at *Holiday RV* and *Cruise America RV*. To hire a car visitors must have a valid driver's licence from their own country, a major credit card and be at least 25 years of age. Some car rental companies require an International Driver's Licence.

Orlando may be reached from the Midwest by major highway networks including Interstate 75 connecting with the Florida Turnpike, whose southern terminal is Miami; from the Atlantic coastal states via Interstate 95; and from Daytona and Tampa on Interstate 4 running east–west. Visitors should be aware that unmanned toll booths require exact change, so they should have plenty of US coins (especially quarters) to hand when driving. Also fuel tends to be 3-6 cents cheaper at self-service petrol stations.

CVB *Focus*

Naples

NAPLES
IT'S SIMPLY CHARMING

WHEREVER YOU ARE IN NAPLES, THERE'S ALWAYS A BEACH NEARBY

It's nice to know that no matter where you unpack your bags in the Naples area, you're simply never far from the white sandy shores. All along the 'platinum coast', the city provides plenty of boardwalks for convenient access and public parking. Along these beaches you can sink your toes in the soft white sand, stoop for sea shells, cast your fishing line into the surf or dive into the gentle waves for a refreshing swim. Pack your lunch, park your chair under a swaying palm tree and stay all day, or just jog for a while. And of course, don't miss the infamous Southwest Florida sunsets — they're sure to become a favorite ritual of your stay.

Here are a few of the Naples Area Tourism Bureau's best bets for a memorable day in the sun and sand:

• Off Vanderbilt Drive in North Naples, *Delnor-Wiggins State Recreation Area* offers miles of pristine shoreline, protected sea oats and mangroves, and every amenity from lifeguards to an observation tower, barbecue grills, showers and wheelchair access. Hours are 7am to sundown.

• Just north of Wiggins Pass is *Barefoot Beach State Recreation Area*. A purist's beach, this practically untouched stretch of sand has no facilities or lifeguards, and no entrance fee. Hours are 8am until sundown.

• Also in North Naples is *Cocohatchee River Park* off Vanderbilt Beach Drive. This new county park has a boat launch, picnic shelters, restrooms, a recreation pavilion and children's play area. Parking is free from 7am until dusk every day.

• In Naples proper, you can enjoy a stroll or a tram ride through a mangrove forest via an elevated boardwalk at *Clam Pass Park*. After winding through the watery wilderness, the boardwalk ends in the sugary sand of the Gulf beach. Clam Pass has concessions, restrooms and plenty of public parking.

• *Lowdermilk Park* is in the heart of Old Naples on Gulf Shore Boulevard. This expansive city park offers 305m (774ft) of prime beach, perfect for the many community activities that take place here throughout the year. There are also restrooms and showers, a pavilion, vending machines and plenty of picnic tables and playground equipment, too. Parking is metered, and the area is open from dawn until dusk every day.

• Another city landmark is the *Naples Fishing Pier* extending 305m (774ft) into the Gulf of Mexico at 12th Avenue South. A favorite spot for sunset strolls, the pier also hosts serious fishermen in pursuit of snook, grouper, red snapper and several other local species. Parking is metered; admission to the pier is free. There's also a bait shack, snack bar, restrooms and

Naples Florida

... it's simply charming

Less than two hours away from Miami and a little more than three from Orlando is one of Florida's best kept secrets: Naples, on Southwest Florida's Gulf coast.

Bordered by the Gulf of Mexico and the Everglades, Naples is a pristine reserve of sugar-soft beaches, verdant green golf courses, spectacular shopping and full of friendly people who call this paradise "home".

Two words quickly spring to mind when visiting Naples – simply charming. From the spectacular sunsets on the Gulf to the natural beauty of the mangrove forests, Naples is redefining a traditional "Florida vacation".

For the traveller who enjoys a casual stroll along avenues of quaint shops or bycycling along manicured streets; for the sporting enthusiast who fishes in the Gulf or is at the tee until sunset; for the family seeking time together to marvel at exotic animals or tour the majestic Everglades; Naples is quite simply charming.

Fast becoming a must-see destination for travellers, Naples and its neighbouring communities of Golden Gate and Immokalee are growing in popularity not only in the spring-like winter months, but also during the spring and summer, too. This is the time of year when wise visitors are attracted by the lure of lower rates, seasonal celebrations and uncrowded beaches and highways.

For a complete guide to Naples' attractions, museums, beaches, golf courses, accommodations and rentals, call the Naples Area Tourism Bureau toll-free in the United Kingdom at 0800-96-2122; from Germany call 0130-81-1954; other international calls dial (813) 262-2712 or fax (813) 262-2113.

Naples Area Tourism Bureau

Naples, Florida. One visit and you'll agree... It's Simply Charming.

Please note: On May 28, 1995, the "813" area code changes to "914".

NAPLES, FLORIDA...IT'S SIMPLY CHARMING.

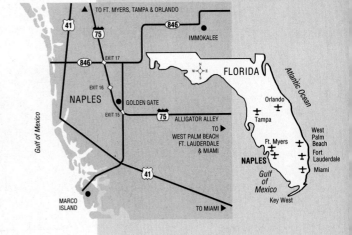

showers. The pier itself is open 24 hours; concessions operate from 7am to 6pm every day.

MOTHER NATURE KNOCKS AT NAPLES' BACK DOOR

Nestled between the Florida Everglades and the Gulf of Mexico, it's obvious why Mother Nature holds many more surprises for Naples area visitors who want to explore the backwoods and backwaters of this diverse natural environment. Through public and private preserves, man has access to cypress swamps, alligator haunts, mangrove forest where birds abound and watery trails where otters might meet manatees.

• *The Conservancy's Naples Nature Center* – An educational center featuring a natural science museum, exhibits, a wildlife clinic complete with pelican/ shorebird pool, aviary, loggerhead sea turtle tank, a 'Snakes Alive' serpentarium and free guided trail tours and mini-boat tours along a tidal lagoon and the Gordon River. The center is on 14th Avenue North, off Goodlette-Frank Road in Naples. Call (813) 262 0304.

• *The Conservancy's Briggs Nature Center* – This center just north of Marco Island has marine aquariums, butterfly gardens, a nature store and a half-mile boardwalk through the pinelands and mangroves of Rookery Bay National Estuarine Research Reserve. Briggs Nature Center is on Shell Island Road off State Road 951, just a few minutes east of Naples. Call (813) 775 8569.

• *The National Audubon Society's Corkscrew Swamp Sanctuary* – This 11,000-acre wilderness preserve is home to alligators, bobcats, otters and the winter nesting site of the North American wood stork. A boardwalk loops through a natural cathedral formed by giant bald cypress trees that are hundreds of years old. The entrance to the Corkscrew Swamp Sanctuary is off Immokalee Road, about 22km (14 miles) north of Naples and 16km (10 miles) west of Immokalee. Call (813) 657 3771.

• *Everglades National Park*, the country's third largest national park – a haven for birdwatchers, nature photographers and salt-water sport fishermen, this huge expanse of grassy river is home to 14 endangered species, including the Florida panther, and more than 24 different kinds of orchids. Tram, boat tours and boat rentals are all available. The entrance is 27km (17 miles) southeast of Naples; call the park headquarters toll-free at (1 800) 445 7724 for further information.

FUN THINGS TO SEE AND DO

The area's attractions offer distractions when another day on the beach won't do . . . shopping, golf and tennis – there's still much more to do and see in and around Naples. Consider these popular attractions where residents and visitors of all ages and interests find entertainment and education throughout the year:

• A variety of indoor entertainment is featured at the *Seminole Gaming Palace*, including bingo, low-stakes poker, video-gaming machines and a continental dining room. Located at 506 South First Street in Immokalee on land from the Seminole Indian Tribe reservation trust. Call (813) 658 1313.

• A 'beary' special wonderland awaits youngsters and the young at heart when they visit the *Teddy Bear Museum* of Naples. The only one of its kind in the country, the 8000-sq-foot museum is home to more than 2400 teddy bears. You'll find it nestled in the woods at 2511 Pine Ridge Road. Call (813) 598 2711.

• A visit to the *Caribbean Gardens* is a day's adventure through 52

Exit 15 off I-75; call (813) 352 0508. The new *Golden Gate Aquatic Center* makes a big splash with a competitive swimming pool, a water slide with separate landing pool and an activity pool for toddlers. This state-of-the-art swim center is part of the Golden Gate Community Park, which offers everything a family could want: concessions, restrooms and a picnic area with playground and courts for tennis, racquetball and basketball. Located at 330 Santa Barbara Boulevard; admission is $2. Call (813) 353 7128 for information.

Known as 'My Home' by the Seminole Indians, *Immokalee* is a major center of Florida's agricultural and citrus business with the state's third largest Farmer's Market. Immokalee is located 17km (11 miles) from the Corkscrew Swamp Sanctuary and recreational facilities include two county parks with picnic tables and playgrounds. Fresh-water fishing and boating are favorites at the 1,800-acre Lake Trafford, which also features guided tours, rest rooms and RV facilities. The area is home to some of the best hunting in Florida with deer, bear, turkey, quail and other game.

Immokalee is a short trip from Naples, 48km (30 miles) northeast in Collier County. For additional information, contact the Immokalee Chamber of Commerce at (813) 657 3237 or stop by the Chamber at 907 Roberts Avenue.

NAPLES AREA TOURISM BUREAU

For more information about these and other attractions in the Naples area, call the Naples Area Tourism Bureau toll free from the UK on (0800) 962 122 or toll free from Germany on (0130) 811 954, or call direct on (813) 262 2712 or fax (813) 262 2113 for a free packet of information.

GETTING HERE

The Naples area is easily accessible from several international airports and Interstate 75. Travel times will vary depending on the time of year and the amount of traffic; it's always a good idea to allow a little extra time. Three exits from I-75 lead to the Naples area; if your destination is specific, choose Exit 17 for Immokalee; Exit 16 for Naples and Exit 15 for Golden Gate and Marco Island. Naples Airport offers connecting commuter flights from Tampa, Orlando, Key West and Miami.

From Southwest Florida International Airport: Drive south on I-75 for 48km (30 miles) or about a 30-minute drive.

From Orlando International Airport: Follow the Beeline Expressway to connect with I-4 West/South. From I-4, connect with I-75 South and drive 402km (251 miles) to Naples, approximately 3 hours 30 minutes.

The Miami International Airport, Fort Lauderdale International Airport and the Palm Beach International Airport are all around a 2- to 3-hour drive across 'Alligator Alley', or I-75.

From Miami: Head north on I-95 to connect with I-75 across the Alley to Naples for approximately 177km (111 miles), or 1 hour 30 minutes.

From Fort Lauderdale: Connect with I-75 straight across Alligator Alley for 169km (106 miles), or 1 hour 30 minutes.

From Palm Beach: Take I-95 South to Sawgrass Parkway and head west until the intersection of I-75. Follow I-75 South to Naples; approximately 225km (141 miles) or 2 hours 30 minutes.

From Tampa International Airport: I-75 is a straight shot south for 262km (164 miles), or 3 hours.

acres of botanical and zoological gardens complete with safari cruises, wildlife encounters, elephant rides, a petting farm and playground, educational lectures and exciting interactions between leopards, tigers, lions and primates and their expert handlers. The Caribbean Gardens are at 1590 Goodlette-Frank Road in Naples. Call (813) 262-5409 for details about shows, tours, hours and prices.

If you're up for an easy day-trip from Naples, the surrounding area presents even more options for your enlightenment about the history, flora and fauna of Florida.

Among them are:

• *The Thomas Edison and Henry Ford Estates* in Fort Myers give visitors a glimpse into the lives of these two geniuses who revolutionized the world. Both are near downtown Fort Myers, almost 45 minutes north of Naples; call (813) 334 3614.

• *Big Cypress National Preserve* – these scenic marshlands are the sites of herons, bald eagles, deer and the endangered Florida panther. The entrance is on US 41 in Ochopee, about 32km (20 miles) south of Naples; call (813) 695 4111.

NAPLES NEIGHBORS OFFER FUN ALTERNATIVES

For families and travellers seeking extra value for their vacation dollar, Naples offers two charming alternatives: Golden Gate and Immokalee. These neighboring communities offer distinctive amenities with convenient access to beaches, parks, dining and shopping.

Golden Gate is home to several world-wide hotel chain properties, plus the site of the annual Swampbuggy Races at the Florida Sports Park in October and the Naples 'Hammer' Senior PBA Open bowling tournament in September. The area recently introduced a new Visitor's Center at 8801 Davis Boulevard, 2km (1 mile) from

Georgia

Including **Atlanta,** gateway to the southern Atlantic States of Georgia, North Carolina and South Carolina, and the southern States of Alabama, Tennessee and Kentucky.

Department of Industry, Trade & Tourism
Tourist Division, PO Box 1776, Suite 1000, Marriott Marquis Two Tower, 285 Peachtree Center Avenue, NE (30301-1232), Atlanta, GA 30303
Tel: (404) 656 3590 *or* (1 800) VISITGA (toll free). Fax: (404) 651 9063.
Georgia Hospitality & Travel Bureau
Suite 1500, 600 West Peachtree Street, Atlanta, GA 30308
Tel: (404) 873 4482. Fax: (404) 874 5742.
Atlanta Convention & Visitors Bureau
Suite 2000, Harris Tower, 233 Peachtree Street NE, Atlanta, GA 30303
Tel: (404) 521 6625 *or* 521 6642 *or* 521 6600. Fax: (404) 584 6331.
Athens Convention & Visitors Bureau
PO Box 948, 7th Floor, Harris Tower, 220 College Avenue (30601), Athens, GA 30603
Tel: (706) 546 1805. Fax: (706) 549 5636.
Savannah Area Convention & Visitors Bureau
Savannah Chamber of Commerce, PO Box 1628, Suite 100, 222 West Oglethorpe Avenue (31402), Savannah, GA 31401
Tel: (912) 944 0456. Fax: (912) 944 0468.

TIME: GMT - 5. *Daylight Saving Time* is observed.
THE STATE: Georgia, founded in 1732, is the youngest of the 13 original colonies. It is a mixture of the Old and New South, and is geographically diverse, with landscapes ranging from mountains in the northeast to the mysterious, low-lying Okefenokee Swamp in the south, called the land of the 'trembling earth' by the region's Indian tribes. Its varied climate ranges from the low humidity of the Blue Ridge Mountains to the subtropical southern coastal region.

TRAVEL

AIR: Approximate flight times: From Atlanta to *London* is 9 hours 15 minutes, to *Miami* is 1 hour 40 minutes, to *New York* is 2 hours 20 minutes and to *Washington DC* is 1 hour 30 minutes.
International airport: Hartsfield Atlanta International Airport (ATL) is 14.5km (9 miles) south of the city (travel time – 20 minutes). A 24-hour coach service runs every 15 minutes. Bus no. 72 runs every 30 minutes 0500-2300. Taxi and limousine services are available.
RAIL: The *Amtrak* service linking New York with New Orleans stops at Brookwood Station, Peachtree Street; see the *New York* section below for approximate journey times on this line.
ROAD: *Greyhound* and *Southern Stage* both use the Greyhound terminal at International Boulevard.
Approximate driving times: From Atlanta to *Birmingham* is 3 hours, to *Charlotte* is 5 hours, to *Nashville* is 5 hours, to *Tallahassee* is 5 hours, to *Salt Lake City* is 6 hours, to *Jacksonville* is 7 hours, to *Charleston* (South Carolina) is 7 hours, to *Memphis* is 8 hours, to *New Orleans* is 10 hours, to *Cincinnati* is 10 hours, to *Charleston* (West Virginia) is 11 hours, to *Miami* is 13 hours, to *Chicago* is 14 hours, to *New York*

is 17 hours, to *Dallas* is 17 hours, to *Los Angeles* is 45 hours and to *Seattle* is 59 hours.
All times are based on non-stop driving at or below the applicable speed limits.
Approximate *Greyhound* journey times: From Atlanta (tel: (404) 584 1728) to *Chattanooga* is 2 hours 30 minutes, to *Birmingham* is 3 hours, to *Charlotte* is 5 hours 30 minutes, to *Mobile* is 8 hours 30 minutes, to *Jacksonville* is 8 hours, to *St Petersburg* is 14 hours and to *Miami* is 18 hours.
URBAN: The public transport system is excellent. The most economical transport is the *Metropolitan Atlanta Rapid Transport Authority (MARTA)*, which consists of 89km (60 miles) of rapid rail or bus lines. **Car hire:** Cars and motorcampers can be hired for touring the Atlanta area. Contact local companies through the Atlanta classified telephone directory.

RESORTS & EXCURSIONS

ATLANTA: Now a booming manufacturing centre with a population of more than two million, Atlanta is the city that most dramatically expresses the transition from Old South to New. Along its residential streets, magnolia and dogwood trees surround handsome Georgian-style homes, yet only blocks away, some of the country's most dazzling contemporary buildings are rising at record speed to add new beauty to Atlanta's ever-growing skyline.
Sightseeing: The *Georgia State Capitol* in Washington Street on Capitol Square, which also houses the *Georgia Hall of Fame* and the *Hall of Flags*. The *Zero Mile Post* under Central Avenue Bridge marks the city's birthplace. The *Tomb of Martin Luther King* is located at the Ebenezer Baptist Church. The 14-storey *Omni Megastructure* houses offices, a hotel, international boutiques, six cinemas, an ice-skating rink and sports area. *Underground Atlanta*, a restored 4-square block area, is located near the business centre of downtown Atlanta. *Grant Park* contains the *Atlanta Zoo*, the restored Confederate *Fort Walker*, and the *Cyclorama*, a world-famous 123m (406ft) circumference painting of the Battle of Atlanta. *Piedmont Park* has facilities for swimming, tennis and golf.
Excursions: 24km (16 miles) east of downtown Atlanta is *Stone Mountain*, where gigantic representations of three confederate heroes – Robert E Lee, Jefferson Davis and Stonewall Jackson – have been carved into a cliff-face. Within easy travelling distance of Atlanta are: **Augusta,** home of the *Masters Golf Tournament* every April; **Dahlonega,** an old mining town where visitors can still pan for gold; and **Madison,** an antique town that was spared from ruin during Sherman's March. The nearby *Pine Mountains* area is noted for its *Callaway Gardens* and for President Franklin D Roosevelt's *Little White House* at **Warm Springs.**
SAVANNAH: On the Atlantic coast, 400km (240 miles) southeast of Atlanta, Savannah was the USA's first planned city. It has become the greatest urban historic preservation site in the USA.
Sightseeing: Much of Savannah's original beauty remains, and more than a thousand of its buildings are historically important, including the Regency-style *Owens-Thomas House* designed by William Jay, and *Davenport House,* one of the best examples of Georgian architecture in the New World. *Fort Pulaski,* one of Savannah's five forts open to the public, is named after the Polish hero of the American Revolution. *Savannah Beach* features sands, a boardwalk, fishing piers and an amusement park.
Excursions: The **Golden Isles,** south of the city, are known for their leisurely resorts, with sandy white beaches, fine golfing, tennis and fishing. *St Simons* is the largest of the islands, with vast woodlands and stretches of unspoilt marshes and coastline. **Waycross** is one of three gateways to the *Okefenokee Swamp*, one of the country's most beautiful wilderness areas. The swamp is a refuge of exotic plant and animal life including alligators.
Note: For information on attractions in neighbouring States, see above under *States A-Z*.

SOCIAL PROFILE

FOOD & DRINK: Atlanta offers a wide variety of food. Its boarding houses may offer as many as 14 or 15 main course dishes. Creole and Cajun food is well represented throughout Georgia.
THEATRES & CONCERTS: *Academy Theater* features new and experimental plays. *Alliance Theater Company,* housed in the *Memorial Arts Center,* presents an 18-week main stage season from January to May; the *Atlanta Children's Theater* performs at various locations throughout the city. *Atlanta University Center Summer*

Theater presents drama for and by black people, as does *New Cosmos Cultural Theater,* a black professional resident company. The *Atlanta Ballet* performs during autumn, winter and spring.
NIGHTLIFE: Nightlife varies from intimate piano bars and dinner theatres to the underground music clubs of Atlanta and Athens.
SHOPPING: Both Peachtree Center and Omni Center shelter a collection of chic boutiques. Lenox Square Mall and Phipps Plaza, both suburban shopping centres, can be reached by *MARTA* bus.
SPECIAL EVENTS: Mar 17-26 '95 *International Cherry Blossom Festival,* Macon. **Apr 7-9** *Atlanta Dogwood Festival.* **Apr 22-23** *Mossy Creek Barnyard Festival,* Perry. **May 6-9** *Cotton Pickin' Fair,* Gay. **May 13-14** *Prater's Mill Country Fair,* Dalton. **May 27** *Howard Finster Art Festival,* Summerville. **Jun 17-18** *Stone Mountain Village Arts & Crafts Festival,* Stone Mountain. **Jun 24** *Georgia Blueberry Festival,* Alma. **Jul 2-4** *Fantastic Fourth Celebration,* Stone Mountain. **First two weeks of Jul** *Watermelon Days Festival,* Cordele. **Mid-Aug** *Georgia Mountain Fair,* Hiawassee. **End Aug** *Beach Music Festival,* Jekyll Island. **Early Sep** *Powers' Crossroads Country Fair & Art Festival,* Newman. **Mid-Sep** *Savannah Jazz Festival; Arts Festival of Atlanta.* **Sep-Oct** *Oktoberfest,* Helen. **Early Oct** *Oliver Hardy Festival,* Harlem; *Georgia Marble Festival,* Jasper. **Mid-Oct** *Big Pig Jig,* Vienna; *Scottish Festival Tattoo and Highland Games,* Stone Mountain. **Nov** *Mule Day,* Calvary; *Toccoa Fall Harvest Festival.* **Nov-Dec** *Fantasy In Lights,* Pine Mountain. **Dec** *Christmas on the River,* Savannah; *Victorian Candlelight Christmas,* Tifton.

CLIMATE

Humid/hot in summer. Frequent rain. Mild winter. Cooler in the northern mountains. Temperature generally ranges from 30°F (-1°C) to 90°F (33°C).
Required clothing: Lightweight cotton clothes and rainwear. Warmer clothing for evenings, the winter season and mountain areas.

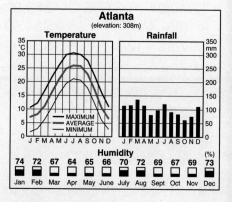

Hawaii

Including **Honolulu,** gateway to the Pacific Islands.

Hawaii State Office of Tourism
PO Box 2359, Suite 1100, 220 South King Street, Honolulu, HI 96804
Tel: (808) 586 2550. Fax: (808) 586 2549 *or* 922 8991.

Hawaii Visitors Bureau
Suite 801, Waikiki Business Plaza, 2270 Kalakaua Avenue, Honolulu, HI 96815
Tel: (808) 923 1811 *or* 924 0266. Fax: (808) 922 8991 *or* 924 2120 *or* 923 0678 (conferences/conventions information).

Hawaii Visitors Bureau
56-60 Great Cumberland Place, Marble Arch, London W1H 8DD
Tel: (0171) 723 7011. Fax: (0171) 724 2808. Opening hours: 0900-1700 Monday to Friday.

Hawaii Visitors Bureau
Suite 205, 1624 56th Street, Delta, British Columbia V4L 2B1
Tel: (604) 943 8555. Fax: (604) 943 1642.

Hawaii Hotel Association
Room 1103, 11th Floor, 2270 Kalakaua Avenue, Honolulu, HI 96815
Tel: (808) 923 0407. Fax: (808) 924 3843.

Chamber of Commerce of Hawaii
Suite 200, 1132 Bishop Street, Honolulu, HI 96813
Tel: (808) 522 8800. Fax: (808) 545 4309.

TIME: GMT - 10. *Daylight Saving Time* is not observed.
THE STATE: The island group of Hawaii comprises over 200 islands and atolls of which seven are inhabited and make up the State itself. Oahu contains the capital, Honolulu, and is the most commercialised, while Hawaii is the biggest island. 3862km (2400 miles) from the American Pacific coast, the islands are a less wild version of Polynesia. Oahu has two diagonal mountain ranges (the Waianae and Koolau), with many beautiful waterfalls. Hawaii is cloaked in orchards and bordered by sheer cliffs. The many volcanoes on Hawaii are almost without vegetation. The islands support rainforest and green flatlands.

PUBLIC HOLIDAYS

Hawaii observes all the public holidays observed in mainland US States (see *USA* above), plus the following: **Mar 26 '95** Prince Kuhio Day. **May 1** Lei Day. **Jun 11** King Kamehameha Day. **Aug 18** Admission Day. **Oct 9** Discoverer's Day.

TRAVEL

AIR: *Hawaiian Airlines, Aloha Airlines* and two inter-island carriers offer frequent inter-island services.
Approximate flight times: From Honolulu to *Anchorage* is 5 hours 40 minutes, to *Chicago* is 9 hours 55 minutes, to *London* is 17-19 hours (including stopover, and depending on route taken), to *Los Angeles* is 5 hours 20 minutes, to *Miami* is 10 hours 35 minutes, to *New York* is 11 hours 40 minutes, to *San Francisco* is 5 hours 5 minutes, to *Singapore* is 18 hours 15 minutes, to *Sydney* is 12 hours 30 minutes and to *Washington DC* is 11 hours.
International airport: *Honolulu International Airport (HNL)* is about 6km (4 miles) west of the city and 10km (6 miles) west of Waikiki. Coaches to Waikiki hotels meet all flight arrivals during the day (travel time – 25 minutes). Bus no. 8 runs every 30 minutes from 0618-0118 (travel time – 30 minutes). Taxis are available.
Local airports: *Kauai:* Princeville (private), Lihue. *Molokai:* Kaunakakai. *Maui:* West Maui, Kahului, Kaanapali. *Lanai:* Lanai City. *Hawaii:* Kamuela, Kona, Hilo.
SEA: Hawaii's main ports are Honolulu, Lahaina and Hilo. The following cruise lines run services to Hawaii: *P&O (Honolulu), Nauru Pacific, American Hawaii, Royal Viking, Cunard, Union Lloyd* and *Princess.* There is no scheduled ferry service.
RAIL: The Hawaiian Railway Society on Oahu offers 1-hour journeys on a historical diesel-electric locomotive formerly used to haul sugar cane. For further information, telephone (808) 681 5461.
ROAD: Driving is on the right. Right-hand turns are permitted in the right lane at a stop light unless signposted otherwise. Pedestrians are given the right of way most of the time. **Bus:** Deluxe modern buses operate on all islands. **Taxi:** Metered and available throughout the main islands. **Car hire:** Available through local and international agencies. Drivers must be over 21 years of age for car rentals. **Documentation:** Foreign driving licence is required.
URBAN: Good local bus services are provided on Oahu. An exact flat-fare system operates. For further information, telephone *The Bus* Information Line on (808) 848 5555. On other islands only taxi or car hire is possible.
JOURNEY TIMES: The following chart gives approximate average journey times (in hours and minutes) from Honolulu to other major islands.

	Air
Kauai Island	0.20
Maui Island	0.20
Hawaii Island	0.25

RESORTS & EXCURSIONS

OAHU: Honolulu, the capital, is the starting point for most holidays in Hawaii. *Waikiki Beach* is a particularly popular resort region of the city. Other attractions include *Kalakaua Avenue, Kilohana Square,* the *Ala Moana Center* and the *Kahala Mall* (all noted for their shopping); the zoo in *Kapiolani Park* (where the Honolulu Marathon is held annually); the *Punchbowl,* a grassy crater with graves of American war casualties; downtown Honolulu, including *Chinatown;* the *Academy of Arts; Bishop Museum; Iolani Palace* and the spectacular *Nuuanu Pali.* There are also many other parks, plus aquaria, museums and theatres in the city and its environs.
A variety of excursions are available. At least a day should be allowed for the *Grand Island Tour,* which takes in the whole of Oahu. Attractions en route include *Waimea Valley* and *Waimea Falls Park; Pearl Harbor;* the *Polynesian Cultural Centre; Sea Life Park;* the *Waialua Plantation;* the *Sacred Birthstones; Kaena Point;* and *Sunset Beach.*
HAWAII: This is the largest island in the group. Attractions include the city of **Hilo;** beach resorts such as *Kailua-Kona* and the 'Gold Coast' of *Kawaihae;* the *National Historic Park of Honaunau;* the tropical highlands; *Waipio Valley; Akaka Falls; Parker Ranch;* and the two famous mountains – *Mauna Kea* and *Mauna Loa.*
MAUI: Attractions include the town of **Wailuku;** the more bustling town of **Kahului;** the *Iao Valley;* the historic whaling town of **Lahaina;** *Mount Haleakala,* which translates as the House of the Sun, a massive volcanic crater; the tranquil beauty of the *Eastern Shore;* the beautiful *Hana Valley;* and the waterfalls at *Wailua Cove.*
LANAI: Attractions include **Kaunolo Village;** the *Munro Trail,* leading to the spectacular *Hauola Gulch;* and the petroglyph rock carving on *Shipwreck Beach.*
MOLOKAI: Attractions include the harbour town of **Kaunakakai;** *Mount Kamakou;* the *Moaulu Falls;* the beautiful *Halowa Valley; Molokai Ranch Wildlife Park;* and *Father Damien's Community* at **Kalaupapa.**
KAUAI: Attractions include *Mount Waialeale;* the capital town of **Lihue;** *Waimea Canyon;* the tropical rainforest in the centre of the island; the *Wailua River;* the *Fern Grotto;* the *Na Pali Coast* and the nearby temple of *Heiau-Holo-Holo-Ku.*

SOCIAL PROFILE

FOOD & DRINK: The food is basically American with oriental influences brought in by the assortment of nationals that make up the population. The classic Hawaiian feast is the *luau* based around a *puaa kalua* (whole pig) that has been skinned and rubbed with rock salt and buried in the ground. It is then placed on chicken wire, filled with hot stones from the *imu* fire, and cooked in the *imu* along with sweet potatoes, plantains and sometimes *laulaus* (pork, butterfish and spinach-like *taro* shoots wrapped in leaves and steamed). The steam is prevented from escaping by encircling the pig with corn husks and taro leaves. The *kalua* pig is eaten with fingers and is accompanied by the traditional Hawaiian *poi* (thick paste made from ground *taro*), *opihi* (a salty, black, clam-like mollusk) and *lomi lomi* salmon (salmon rubbed with an onion and tomato marinade). *Chicken luau* comprises tender chicken pieces cooked with *taro* tops and coconut cream. Garnishes include *limu* (dried seaweed), *paakai* rock salt and chopped roasted *kukui* nuts. Local seafoods include *moi* (mullet) *ulua, opakapaka* (pink snapper), lobster and yellowfin tuna. Hawaiian breakfast specialities are macadamia nuts and banana and coconut pancakes with coconut syrup. Fresh fruit and nut ice-creams or sorbets make excellent desserts. **Drink:** The minimum legal drinking age is 21 years. It is illegal to consume alcohol in parks and on beaches.
NIGHTLIFE: There are many bars and nightclubs. Top international stars are booked whilst *luau* shows are, in themselves, a great attraction. Jazz, big band music, tea dances, hula groups, disco and Elvis (and others) impersonations are all available.
SHOPPING: The International Marketplace, Royal Hawaiian Shopping Center and the Ala Moana Shopping Center in Waikiki Beach, Honolulu, are popular shopping areas. **Opening hours:** 0900-2200 Monday to Saturday. Some shops may open 0830-1800 Sunday.
SPORT: Golf: Courses are numerous and scenic. **Hunting:** Facilities are available. **Fishing:** Deep-sea fishing is very popular off the island of Hawaii. **Watersports:** The Hawaiian islands are particularly good for watersports. **Yachting:** One-week charters are available, with or without crews. All boats are equipped with Coast Guard-approved safety equipment and are under Coast Guard supervision. **Surfing** is, of course, a very popular sport – for both participants and spectators. **Snorkelling** is best near the Molokini Crater off Maui. In addition, there are some exciting international events such as the *Canoe Race,* in which outrigger canoes race against each other across Waikiki Harbor.
SPECIAL EVENTS: The following is a list of events celebrated in Hawaii during 1995/96:
Apr 14-16 '95 *3rd Annual Ritz-Carlton Kapalua Celebration of the Arts,* Kapalua. **Apr 16-22** *Merrie Monarch Festival,* Hilo. **Apr 22** *Whale Day,* Kihei (Maui). **May 1** *Lei Day Celebrations,* Honolulu, Waikiki, Lihue and Kauai. **May 6-7** *Pineapple Festival,* Lanai City. **May 12** *Asian and Pacific Islander Day,* Kona. **May 20** *Molokai Ka Hula Piko* (celebration of the birth of hula), Molokai. **May 25-28** *4th Annual Big Bounty Festival* (Hawaiian food festival), Mauna Lani. **Jun 5-18** *Town & Country Surf Pro-Am Surfing Contest,* Honolulu. **Jun 10** *King Kamehameha Celebrations,* State-wide. **Jun 17-18** *Waiki'i Music Festival,* Kona. **Jun 30-Jul 9** *Hawaii State Farm Fair,* Honolulu. **Jul 4** *Fourth of July Celebrations,* State-wide; *11th Annual Maui Inter-Continental Wailea Resort Tennis Open Championship,* Wailea, Maui. **Jul 17-23** *34th Annual International Festival of the Pacific,* Hilo. **Jul 23** *Kakaako Seafood Fest,* Oahu. **Jul 27-30** *2nd Hawaii International Jazz Festival,* Wakiki. **Jul 29** *13th Annual Kilauea Volcano Marathon and Rim Runs,* Hawaii Volcano National Park. **Aug 5-6** *Hawaii State Championships,* Maui. **Aug 15** *Toro Nagashi* (Buddhist Floating Lantern Ceremony), Waikiki. **Aug 22-30** *37th Annual Hawaiian International Billfish Tournament,* Kailua-Kona. **Sep 2-3** *24th Annual Queen Liliuokalani World Championship Long Distance Canoe Races,* Kailua-Kona. **Sep 15-Oct 29** *Aloha Festivals,* State-wide. **Sep 30-Oct 1** *Annual Waimea Falls Park Makahiki Festival,* Waimea Falls Park. **Oct 21** *11th Annual Kahala Country Fair,* North Kahala. **Nov 2-5** *Lincoln Mercury Kapalua International Golf Tournament,* Kapalua. **Dec 7** *Bishop Square's Annual Christmas Lighting,* Honolulu. **Mar 17 '96** *St Patrick's Day Parade.* **Mar 26** *Prince Kuhio Festival.*

CLIMATE

Warm throughout the year. Heavy rainfall can occur in some mountainous areas from December to February, although most areas only receive short showers, while others remain totally arid.
Required clothing: Lightweights are advised throughout the year, with warmer clothes for winter. Beachwear is popular and protection from the midday sun, such as sunglasses and sun hats, is advisable.

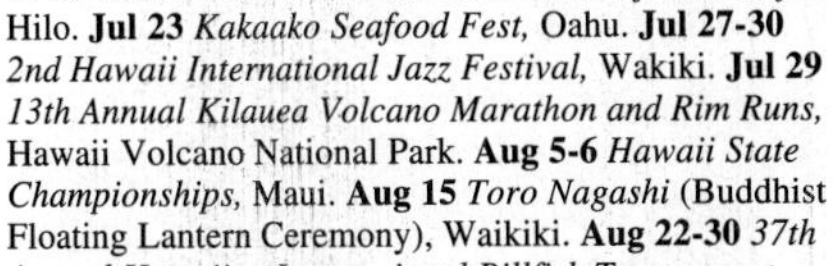

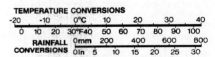

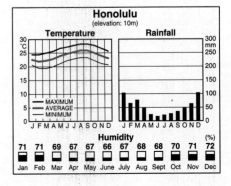

Illinois

Including **Chicago,** gateway to the Great Lakes, the great plains and the northern Midwest States of Wisconsin, Iowa, Missouri, Kentucky and Indiana.

Illinois Bureau of Tourism
Suite 3-400, State of Illinois Center, 100 West Randolph Street, Chicago, IL 60601
Tel: (312) 814 4732 *or* (1 800) 223 0121 (toll free). Fax: (312) 814 6175 *or* 814 6581.
Chicago Convention & Tourism Bureau
2301 South Lake Shore Drive, Chicago, IL 60616-1497
Tel: (312) 567 8500. Fax: (312) 567 8533.
Chicago Southland Convention & Visitors Bureau
Suite 202, 20200 Governor's Drive, Olympia Fields, IL 60461
Tel: (708) 503 1800. Fax: (708) 503 1298.
Springfield Convention & Visitors Bureau
109 North Seventh Street, Springfield, IL 62701
Tel: (217) 789 2360. Fax: (217) 544 8711.

TIME: GMT - 6. *Daylight Saving Time* is observed.
THE STATE: Illinois, stretching from Lake Michigan to the Mississippi River, embraces vast, rich farmlands, the giant city of Chicago, rolling glacial plains and, to the south, the hills and valleys of the Illinois Ozarks. Abraham Lincoln, the 16th US President, spent most of his professional (he was a lawyer) and political life here.

TRAVEL

AIR: Approximate flight times: From Chicago to *Anchorage* is 7 hours 30 minutes, to *Honolulu* is 10 hours 20 minutes, to *London* is 7 hours 35 minutes, to *Los Angeles* is 4 hours 45 minutes, to *Miami* is 3 hours 20 minutes, to *Montréal* is 2 hours 15 minutes, to *New York* is 2 hours 5 minutes, to *Toronto* is 1 hour 40 minutes, to *Vancouver* is 6 hours 10 minutes and to *Washington DC* is 2 hours.
International airport: *Chicago (CHI)* (O'Hare International), 35km (21 miles) northwest of the city, is the world's busiest airport. Buses, taxis and commuter trains ply to and from the city almost 24 hours a day. Most major car hire firms have offices at the airport.
Domestic airport: *Midway Airport (MDW),* on

Chicago's southwest side, handles some regional and local flights.
RAIL: Downtown Chicago's Union Station is the focal point of the rail passenger network: three of the four trans-continental lines converge here and it is also the northern terminus of north–south lines to San Antonio and New Orleans. A sixth line runs northeast to Toronto and Montréal. Services to neighbouring cities are limited.
Approximate *Amtrak* journey times: From Chicago on the 'Broadway Limited' to *Pittsburgh* is 9 hours, to *Philadelphia* is 17 hours and to *New York* is 19 hours; on the 'Lake Shore Limited' to *Toledo* is 4 hours, to *Cleveland* is 7 hours, to *Buffalo* is 10 hours and to *New York* is 18 hours; on the 'Cardinal' to *Indianapolis* is 3 hours, to *Washington DC* is 23 hours, to *Baltimore* is 24 hours and to *New York* is 27 hours; on the 'City of New Orleans' to *Memphis* is 10 hours and to *New Orleans* is 18 hours; on the 'International' to *Kalamazoo* is 2 hours, to *Port Huron* is 6 hours and to *Toronto* is 10 hours; on the 'Ann Rutledge' to *St Louis* is 6 hours and to *Kansas City* is 12 hours; on the 'Empire Builder' to *Minneapolis/St Paul* is 9 hours and to *Spokane* (connections to Portland and Seattle) is 25 hours; and on the 'Pioneer' to *Omaha* is 8 hours, to *Denver* is 18 hours, to *Salt Lake City* is 33 hours, to *Portland* is 52 hours and to *Seattle* is 56 hours.
Approximate times for Chicago–Los Angeles and Chicago–Oakland services may be found in the *California* section above.
ROAD: Approximate driving times: From Chicago to *Milwaukee* is 2 hours, to *Madison* is 3 hours, to *Indianapolis* is 4 hours, to *Detroit* is 5 hours, to *St Louis* is 6 hours, to *Des Moines* is 7 hours, to *Cleveland* is 7 hours, to *Nashville* is 9 hours, to *Kansas City* is 10 hours, to *New York* is 16 hours, to *Dallas* is 19 hours, to *Miami* is 27 hours, to *Seattle* is 44 hours and to *Los Angeles* is 44 hours.
All times are based on non-stop driving at or below the applicable speed limits.
Approximate *Greyhound* journey times: From Chicago (tel: (1 800) 231 2222; toll free) to *Milwaukee* is 2 hours, to *Indianapolis* is 4 hours, to *Detroit* is 6 hours, to *St Louis* is 7 hours, to *Cleveland* is 7 hours 30 minutes, to *Omaha* is 10 hours 30 minutes and to *Memphis* is 11 hours 30 minutes.
URBAN: Bus: A wide network of bus routes run by the *Chicago Transit Authority (CTA)* covers the city on the major north–south and east–west streets. **Car hire:** Cars and motor campers are available.

RESORTS & EXCURSIONS

CHICAGO: Nicknamed 'Windy City', Chicago is one of the world's giant trade, industry and transportation centres and the birthplace of the skyscraper; whilst, in contrast, its Lake Michigan shoreline is dotted with sandy beaches, hundreds of parks, harbours, zoos and vast expanses of forest preserve. It is one of the USA's largest cities and the hub of the Midwest, with a population of about three million and more than 43,000 hotel rooms in the downtown and airport districts alone. For visitors to the USA, it is the gateway to the farmlands and cities of Illinois and Indiana and the recreation areas of Wisconsin.
Sightseeing: The *Museum of Science* has more than 2000 exhibits. The *Field Museum of Natural History* spans the development of the universe from 4.5 billion years ago to the present day. Other attractions include the *Art Institute of Chicago, Brookfield Zoo, Tropic World, Seven Seas Panorama* and *Six Flags Great America Amusement Park.* Many of Chicago's soaring skyscrapers have observation towers, such as the *Sears Tower* and the *John Hancock Center.* The *Old Water Tower,* a landmark that survived the Great Chicago Fire of 1871, houses a tourist information centre, open daily.
Excursions: Springfield is the capital of Illinois. It was here that Abraham Lincoln married and began his legal career. Attractions include *Lincoln's Tomb* (a State Historical Site) and the *Illinois State Museum. New Salem State Park* nearby is a re-creation of the pioneer community as it was in Lincoln's day. Southern Illinois was one of the first regions of North America to be settled by the French. This colourful heritage is reflected in towns such as **Prairie du Rocher** and **Kaskaskia.** The *Shawnee National Forest,* with its huge areas of wilderness and many tourist sites, stretches across the lower part of Illinois. To the west, *Fort Crevecoeur* is a replica of a French outpost. The *Dickson Mounds* were raised by Mississippian Indians many centuries ago. To the north is **Galena,** a Victorian city, with many historic sites and tourist activities. The *Starved Rock State Park & Lodge* has hiking trails, picnic areas and excursion boats from May to September.
Note: For information on attractions in neighbouring States, see above under *States A-Z.*

SOCIAL PROFILE

FOOD & DRINK: Chicago is known for its prime rib steaks and thick-crusted Chicago pizza. It is packed with restaurants of all types, serving food from around the world.
THEATRES & CONCERTS: Major theatres include the *Goodman, Shubert, Blackstone* and *Arie Crown.* The *Auditorium Theater* stages ballet and musical events. The *Civic Center for the Performing Arts* stages performances by the *Lyric Opera Company.* The *Chicago Symphony Orchestra* performs at *Orchestra Hall.*
NIGHTLIFE: Chicago boasts everything from nightclubs, jazz spots, cinemas and discotheques to belly dancing, rock bands and folk music. It is the home of 'urban blues', a form developed by such greats as Muddy Waters and Elmore James, continued today in Chicago and around the world by performers such as Buddy Guy and Robert Cray.
SHOPPING: The main shopping areas in Chicago include State Street Mall, North Michigan Avenue's Magnificent Mile, Woodfield Mall and the quaint speciality stores in Old Town, Lincoln Avenue and New Town.
SPECIAL EVENTS: Jun 2-4 '95 *Chicago Blues Festival.* **Jun 6-Aug 29** *114th Infantry Civil War Regiment Retreat Ceremony,* Springfield. **Jun 16-17** *Chicago Highland Games and Scottish Festival.* **Jun 23-25** *Long Grove Strawberry Festival.* **Jul 3** *Third of July Concert and Fireworks,* Chicago. **Jul 21-22** *Fiesta de Hemingway,* Oak Park. **Jul 22-Nov 26** *Claude Monet: 1840-1926,* The Art Institute of Chicago. **Sep 8-10** *Cascade of Colors Balloon Festival,* Carbondale. **Oct 14-15** *Union County Fall Colorfest.* **Nov 3 '95-Jan 14 '96** *Lake Shelbyville Festival of Lights,* Findlay. **Nov 4-Dec 31** *Country Christmas,* Galena. **Dec 8-9** *Lucia Lights,* Bishop Hill.

CLIMATE

Wide variation between hot summers and freezing winters, especially in the north of the State. The highest humidity is in the summer near the Great Lakes.
Required clothing: Warm winter clothes are needed in the coldest months. Light- to medium-weights are advised for the summer. Rainwear may be useful.

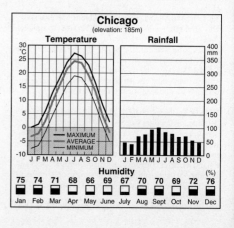

Chicago's O'Hare International Airport

We offer more connections to more cities, more often than any other airport in the world.

The new International Terminal features:

- **156 ticketing positions for instant check-in**

- **21 gates to accommodate arrivals and departures**

- **68 FIS inspection booths designed for the most efficient customs clearance network**

- **11 moving walkways to speed you through the terminal**

- **State-of-the-art Airport Transit System for quick and easy transfer to all domestic connecting flights**

- **Easy accessibility to and from the City and suburbs**

O'Hare is dedicated to providing better service to more than 180,000 passengers every day. Our multi-lingual staff has been trained by the professionals at Walt Disney to insure the best customer service offered by any international gateway.

While in Chicago, why not head for the Magnificent Mile to experience world-class shopping and international amenities. Visit the lakefront and enjoy the finest hotels, museums, theaters, dining and night life in the world. It will come as no surprise that Chicago recently received the "Most Livable City" award by the U.S. Conference of Mayors. With one of the fastest growing economies in the nation, Chicago welcomes new companies from around the globe every day.

WELCOME TO CHICAGO!

Louisiana

150km
75mls
☐ *international airport*

Including **New Orleans,** gateway to the southern States of Mississippi and Arkansas.

Louisiana Office of Tourism
Department of Culture, Recreation & Tourism, PO Box 94291, Capitol Station, Baton Rouge, LA 70804-9291
Tel: (504) 342 8100 *or* (1 800) 334 8626 (toll free). Fax: (504) 342 8390.
New Orleans Metropolitan Convention & Visitors Bureau
1520 Sugar Bowl Drive, New Orleans, LA 70112
Tel: (504) 566 5011. Fax: (504) 566 5046.
Southwest Louisiana Convention & Visitors Bureau
PO Box 1912, 1211 North Lakeshore Drive, Lake Charles, LA 70602
Tel: (318) 436 9588. Fax: (318) 494 7952.
Shreveport-Bossier Convention & Visitors Bureau
PO Box 1761, 629 Spring Street (71101), Shreveport, LA 71166
Tel: (318) 222 9391. Fax: (318) 222 0056.

TIME: GMT - 6. *Daylight Saving Time* is observed.
THE STATE: Louisiana's marshy Mississippi valley is one of the most attractive areas of the USA. New Orleans, its largest city, is one of the country's major tourist destinations. It is famed for Dixieland jazz, its architecture, superb cuisine and its unique French Quarter. The city also boasts a wide choice of museums and galleries. Other places to see in the State include Lafayette, a city of magnificent gardens and the start of the 40km (25-mile) Azalea Trail; the Atchafalaya Basin, the largest and most remote swamp in the USA; the huge salt domes of Avery and Jefferson Islands; Alexandria, surrounded by forests and parks; and the Hot Wells resort and spa. The 138m-high (452ft) marble Capitol Building is situated in Baton Rouge.

TRAVEL

AIR: Approximate flight times: From New Orleans to *Atlanta* is 1 hour 19 minutes, to *Chicago* is 2 hours 22 minutes, to *Los Angeles* is 4 hours, to *Miami* is 1 hour 53 minutes and to *New York* is 3 hours.
International airport: *New Orleans International Airport (MSY)*, 23km (14 miles) from the city centre, is America's ninth-largest airport (travel time – 20/30 minutes). A US$200-million airport expansion programme is presently underway. *Jefferson Transit* provides a bus service to the city centre every 15-20 minutes (weekdays) and every 30 minutes (weekends). *Greyhound* also has buses from the airport to many destinations. *Rhodes Transportation* (tel: (504) 522 6010) offers a limousine service to the city centre. *Mississippi Coast Limousine Service (Coastliner)* provides a shuttle service to the Gulf coast and many other places along the route, making nine trips 0800-2330 daily. Taxis are available 24 hours to the city centre. Airport facilities

include two banks, shops, snack bars, restaurant/bar, post office and car hire (*Avis, Hertz, Budget, Dollar* and *National*).
RAIL: *Amtrak* and *Southern Railways* both serve New Orleans. *Amtrak* offers a special *Eastern Region Rail Pass* which allows 45 days of unlimited travel to as far north as Burlington and as far west as Chicago. Passengers leave from Union Station, located at 1001 Loyola Avenue.
ROAD: Bus: Bus and coach services are provided to nearby major cities on *Greyhound* and *Trailways*.
Approximate driving times: From New Orleans to *Mobile* is 3 hours, to *Houston* is 6 hours, to *Birmingham* is 7 hours and to *Memphis* is 8 hours.
All times are based on non-stop driving at or below the applicable speed limits.
Approximate *Greyhound* journey times: From New Orleans (tel: (504) 525 6075) to *Mobile* is 4 hours, to *Houston* is 8 hours, to *Birmingham* is 9 hours and to *Memphis* is 10 hours.
URBAN: Bus: The famous 'Streetcar named Desire' in New Orleans has been replaced by a bus. Extensive bus services are available throughout the city. **Car hire:** *Avis, Hertz, Budget, Dollar, Econocar, Thrifty, National* and *American International* all have offices in or near the airport. A national driving licence and a major credit card are needed to hire a car. **Streetcar:** These still run on St Charles Avenue and Carrollton in New Orleans, starting from Canal Street. **Horsecab:** Horse-drawn carriages offer a scenic means of transport through the French Quarter.

RESORTS & EXCURSIONS

NEW ORLEANS: Famous the world over for its unique charms, New Orleans offers a melting pot of influences, including French, Spanish, African, Caribbean, German and Cajun, which is apparent in its blend of architecture, cuisine and culture. It is the birthplace of jazz and the cocktail, and these perfectly describe the sort of lifestyle that New Orleans represents. The *French Quarter* is a favourite tourist haunt, full of colonial architecture, intimate courtyards, exquisite iron grillwork and the uplifting sounds of New Orleans jazz wafting through the lively streets. *Jackson Square*, the heart of the French Quarter, is a street entertainment nexus for mimes, musicians, tap dancers and sidewalk artists. There are many excellent restaurants, bars and nightclubs. Its location at the crux of the Mississippi River and the Gulf of Mexico makes it a perfect place for a walk by the river or a stroll down the esplanade overlooking the sea.
Sightseeing: *Cabildo*, former seat of Spanish rulers and the setting for the Louisiana State Purchase; *Casa Hove*, a perfect example of Creole architecture; the *International Trade Mart*; *Duelling Oaks*, where affairs of honour were settled in the 18th century; *Conti Wax Museum*; *Audubon's House*, where the famous wildlife draftsman lived and worked; *Audubon Zoo and Zoological Garden* (0930-1630 Monday to Friday, 0930-1730 weekends), ranked among the top three zoos in the USA; *Aquarium of the Americas*, where four different environment simulations depict the wildlife and marine life within; *Vieux Carré*; *Orleans Ballroom*; *St Louis Cathedral*; the *French Market*, located on the waterfront, with excellent coffee bars serving french pastries; *Pontalba House*, a State museum with period furnishings and decor; *Preservation Hall*, where authentic New Orleans jazz is played nightly and *The Garden District*, featuring white-columned mansions, draping oak trees and beautiful gardens surrounded by elegant wrought-iron fences.
Excursions: There are many ferries that provide transport across or up and down the *Mississippi River*, departing from the levee at the foot of Canal Street. One- to 11-day cruises are also available: *Steamboat NATCHEZ* has harbour and dinner cruises, *Bayou Jean Lafitte* offers a 72km (45-mile) Louisiana Bayou adventure, *Cotton Blossom* has a zoo cruise between the Aquarium and Riverfront Park to the Audubon Zoo and *Bayou Segnette Swamp Boat Tours* offer special cruises through the Louisiana swamps. For further information on boat cruises, contact New Orleans Steamboat Company, Suite 1300, 2 Canal Street, New Orleans, LA 70130. Tel: (504) 586 8777.
BATON ROUGE: The capital of Louisiana and heart of the Southern plantation region. The 'blues' are a large part of the Baton Rouge heritage, sung by slaves as they picked plantation cotton, and it was the original home of many of America's most well-known blues musicians. Many clubs, concerts and festivals in the area pay homage to this seminal music.
Sightseeing: *Capitol Building*, a 34-storey building with a viewing platform overlooking 27 acres of formal gardens in the Capitol grounds; the *Old Capitol*, with its

Norman, Gothic and Moorish blend of architecture; the Louisiana *Governor's Mansion*, with exhibits of art, natural history and anthropology; *Baton Rouge Zoo*, 140 acres of walk-through areas and forest settings for over 400 animals; the *Louisiana Arts and Science Center Riverside*, located in a remodelled railroad station; and *The Rural Life Museum*, an outdoor museum located on the grounds of a former plantation, showing the type of work done in a 19th-century plantation community.
Excursions: Many magnificent old plantation mansions are available for viewing in this area, some offering bed & breakfast facilities as well as tours. The most spectacular plantation home in the region is called *Le Petit Versailles* and was owned by a 19th-century planter called Valcourt Aimé who was also known as 'Louis XIV of Louisiana'.
LAFAYETTE: The industrial and cultural hub of 'Cajun' country and home to 100,000 people, many of whom are French-speaking Canadians from Nova Scotia who settled in the region after 1764 when they were deported by the British for refusing to give up the Catholic faith or pledge allegiance to the British crown. These people were originally known as 'Acadians' but the name was eventually shortened to 'Cajuns'. The land is full of swamps and bayous.
Sightseeing: *Acadian Village* and *Vermilionville* have faithful replicas of early Cajun communities.
Excursions: **Houma,** a bayou town known for its many swamp tours, where alligators, wading birds and myriad other swamplife thrive; **New Iberia,** home of world-famous *Tabasco* sauce, offering tours of subtropical gardens, stately antebellum homes, rice mills and the hot sauce and pepper plant farms; **St Martinville** is a quiet and elegant town once known as 'Le Petit Paris' for its luxurious balls, operas and highlife, and its Cajun museum and church are well worth visiting; and the *Creole Nature Trail* near **Lake George,** where ducks, geese, alligators, nutria and muskrats run rampant.
NATCHITOCHES: The oldest town in Louisiana, perched on the Cane River, it was first established as a fort and trading post in 1714 to prevent the Spanish from encroaching on French territory and is now a charming river town and farm centre. It has numerous historic homes, many offering bed & breakfast, and is surrounded by pecan orchards, cotton farms and 18th-century plantation homes. The region around Natchitoches is known as the 'Crossroads' region because it is where the French and Spanish heritage of the south meets the pioneer spirit of the north. It is also a haven for country music, spawning such luminaries as Jerry Lee Lewis and Mickey Gilley, and the annual Fiddle Championship takes place in this region in Marthaville.
Excursions: Nearby **Monroe,** another river town, also has many historical homes and a museum; *The Louisiana Purchase Gardens and Zoo* in Monroe is a 100-acre park with moss-laden oaks, formal gardens and winding waterways. *Dogwood Trail Drive* is a 29km (18-mile) journey over the State's highest hills, among blossoming dogwood trees, revealing the region's particular beauty.
SHREVEPORT: A leading oil and gas centre located close to the Texan border with a distinctly American West flavour. It is also renowned as a trade and entertainment area and hosts three major annual events, attracting visitors from far and wide (see *Special Events* below). Shreve Square has an attractive cluster of nightclubs, restaurants and shops.
Sightseeing: *Louisiana State Exhibit Museum* with dioramas, an art gallery, historical murals and

archaeological relics; *RW Norton Museum*, featuring Old West artists; *Pioneer Heritage Center;* and the *American Rose Center*, a famous showplace.

Excursions: This region is known as 'Sportman's Paradise' for its many forests and lakes offering opportunities for fishing, hunting, canoeing and hiking, and excursions can be arranged for these activities. An annual *Fishing Tournament* takes place at **Toledo Bend**. *Louisiana Downs Thoroughbred Racetrack*, across the Red River in **Bossier City**, is open for racing from late spring until the autumn. *Poverty Point State Commemorative Area* is an ancient Indian civilisation dating from 1700BC and one of the most important archaeological finds in the USA.

Note: For information on attractions in neighbouring States, see above under *States A-Z*.

SOCIAL PROFILE

FOOD & DRINK: Creole cuisine is a speciality in Louisiana and should be experienced. The Louisiana mix of cultures has resulted in an innovative cuisine using the best elements of each nationality. The state's location makes it a prime spot for seafood and fresh fish, shrimp, crabs, oysters and crayfish abound. Game meat is also popular in Louisiana cuisine, including rabbit and wild turkey. Exotic fruits, such as bananas and pineapples, are used often in Creole cuisine, along with spices such as hot peppers and *filé* (the ground powder for making gumbo). The Crescent City district in New Orleans is known for its superb restaurants offering such Creole specialities as oysters Rockefeller, bananas Foster and *pompano en papillote*. Oyster bars are prevalent, especially along the seaside or riverfront. Creole cafés serve traditional favourites such as gumbo and red beans and rice. Other Cajun specialities include *étouffée, sauce piquante* and *jambalaya*. A meat pie, shaped like a half-moon and filled with a spicy mixture of ground beef and pork, is a speciality of Natchitoches. The town of Henderson, on the edge of Atchafalaya Swamp, is famous for its Cajun cuisine and its many restaurants, specialising in seafood, attract visitors from miles away. *Southern Cookin'*, found in the Crossroads region in northern Louisiana, is savoured for its delicious fried chicken, barbecued meat, cornbread and peach pie. **Drink:** Given its southern climate, cold drinks are much relished in this state. Iced tea is a favourite. Alcohol can only be purchased by those over 18 years of age and is available at supermarkets and liquor stores. Some parts of northern Louisiana do not sell alcohol.

THEATRES & CONCERTS: *Le Petit Théâtre du Vieux Carré* in New Orleans is one of the oldest theatre groups in the country and is highly recommended. Shreveport also houses one of the best-known US community theatre groups in its *Little Theater*. Louisiana has engendered a rich black music scene derived from the rythmic chants of riverboat men and the soulful gospel tunes of field hands through to such jazz greats as Jelly Roll Morton and Louis Armstrong, both natives of New Orleans. Therefore, jazz, blues, gospel, rythmn 'n' blues, *zydeco* (played by the French-speaking blacks of the region), Cajun and country music can all be heard in concerts throughout Louisiana. Many music concerts are held on riverboats on the Mississippi.

NIGHTLIFE: Nightlife is especially lively in New Orleans. The burlesque shows and cabarets of Bourbon Street are notorious – every third door on this famous street is a nightclub. Also, just minutes from downtown New Orleans there is a district known as *Fat City* which houses many nightclubs and 24-hour cafés.

SHOPPING: The French Quarter of New Orleans has many excellent shopping opportunities. Souvenirs are plentiful, and other good buys include Creole pecan pralines, Mardi Gras masks, beautifully bottled and handmixed perfumes, and various antiques on sale in shops on Royal Street. Other excellent shopping areas in New Orleans include Canal Place, The Esplanade, the French Market, Riverwalk and Uptown Square Shopping Center. Northgate Mall in Lafayette and Lakeside Shopping Center in Metairie are also excellent. Louisiana offers tax-free shopping to international visitors for items sold by a participating merchant. Request a tax refund voucher from any *Louisiana Tax Free Shopping (LTFS)* participator and it can be refunded at the airport on presentation of voucher, receipt and travel ticket. Refunds can also be obtained by mail if sent with voucher, receipts, travel ticket and a notarised statement stating why vouchers were not redeemed at the airport and the present whereabouts of the merchandise.

SPORT: Fishing, both freshwater and saltwater, is popular all year round. King mackerel, jewfish, marlin, bluefish, cobia, channel bass, *pompano*, red snapper

and jack are found in coastal areas and the Gulf of Mexico, whereas crayfish is an inland speciality. It is one of the best States for bass fishing. Tarpon fishing is available near Houma. A freshwater fishing licence is necessary for non-residents but no licence is necessary for saltwater fishing. **Hunting** is available during the winter months with a licence and popular game includes duck, squirrel, deer, turkey and wildfowl. Bear, deer and turkey require a special licence (further information available from the *Wildlife and Fish Commission* in New Orleans). **Swimming** is available in recreation areas throughout Louisiana. 18-hole **golf** courses are available in Lafayette (City Park Golf Course), Shreveport (Andrew Querbes Park), Lakeside and New Orleans (Lakewood Country Club, which also sponsors the Greater New Orleans Open every spring).

SPECIAL EVENTS: The New Orleans Carnival, or *Mardi Gras,* comes to a climax on Shrove Tuesday (47 days before Easter). Costumes, dazzling floats, street dancing and general wild abandon are the order of the day. Mardi Gras country-style celebrations also take place in the Cajun towns of Church Point and Mamou with music, dancing and enough gumbo to feed the whole town. The *Spring Fiesta* begins on the first Friday after Easter with jazz parades, street dancing, riverboat concerts and outdoor art shows. The *New Orleans Jazz and Heritage Festival* is held for two weeks each spring in late April and early May and is a celebration of food, music and crafts, with jazz, ragtime, gospel, blues and country music concerts, as well as parades and river cruises. The *Festival International de Louisiane*, held each April in Lafayette, is a tribute to southern Louisiana's music and food, with live bands playing Carribean music. *Festival of Lights* in Natchitoches is a Christmas celebration when elaborate scenes of multicoloured electric lights depicting camels, the Magi and other yuletide themes are turned on all at once, their reflection in the Cane River increasing their radiance; a firework display is then launched over the river. Shreveport celebrates three major annual events: the 10-day *Holiday in Dixie* in April, with flower shows, sports competitions, an air show, pet show, treasure hunt, carnival, two fancy-dress balls and a grand finale parade; the *State Fair* in the autumn, also lasting ten days, attracting half a million visitors for auto races,

rodeo exhibitions, carnival rides, arts and crafts displays, band concerts and fireworks; and the *Red River Revel*, a celebration of the arts which takes place on the riverfront.

CLIMATE

Humid and subtropical. Hot temperatures in summer, mild temperatures in spring and autumn and colder temperatures in winter.

Required clothing: Lightweight cotton clothing for summer, with sweaters and jackets for winter. Rainwear or umbrella is advised for all seasons.

HOUMAS HOUSE PLANTATION AND GARDENS

Located on the banks of the mighty Mississippi, colorful gardens and 200-year-old oaks form a romantic background for the magnificent Greek Revival mansion (1840). Before the Civil War, Houmas was Louisiana's largest sugar plantation. Fully restored in 1940, it is authentically furnished with period antiques. Tours are led by guides in antebellum dress. "Hush, Hush Sweet Charlotte" starring Bette Davis was filmed here. Group rates are available for 20 or more people. Easily accessible from New Orleans (one hour) or Baton Rouge (one-half hour) via Interstate 10.

40136 Highway 942, Burnside, Darrow, LA 70725-2302. USA
Telephone: (504) 473-7841   Fax: (504) 474-0480

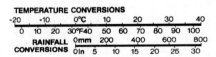

TEMPERATURE CONVERSIONS

-20	-10	0°C	10	20	30	40
0	10	20	30°F 40	50	60	70	80	90	100

RAINFALL 0mm 200 400 600 800
CONVERSIONS 0In 5 10 15 20 25 30

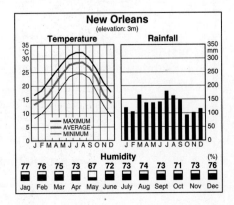

New Orleans
(elevation: 3m)

	Jan	Feb	Mar	Apr	May	June	July	Aug	Sept	Oct	Nov	Dec
Humidity (%)	77	76	75	73	67	72	73	74	73	71	73	76

Maryland

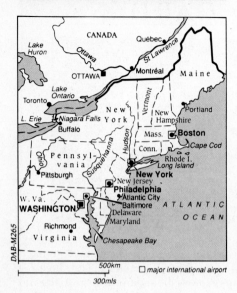

Including **Baltimore,** gateway to the northeast Atlantic coast States of Delaware and Virginia and the inland States of West Virginia and Pennsylvania.

Maryland Division of Tourism & Promotion
9th Floor, 217 East Redwood Street, Baltimore, MD 21202
Tel: (410) 333 6611. Fax: (410) 333 6643.

Annapolis Information & Tourism Office
26 West Street, Annapolis, MD 21401
Tel: (410) 268 8687 *or* 280 0445. Fax: (410) 263 9591.
Baltimore Area Convention & Visitors Association
12th Floor, 100 Light Street, Baltimore, MD 21202
Tel: (410) 659 7300. Fax: (410) 659 7313.
Tri-County Council for Western Maryland
111 South George Street, Cumberland, MD 21502
Tel: (301) 777 2158. Fax: (301) 777 2495.

TIME: GMT - 5. *Daylight Saving Time* is observed.
THE STATE: Maryland was one of the original 13 States of the USA, founded by Lord Baltimore in 1634. Its Atlantic Plain, divided by Chesapeake Bay, rises through the rolling hills and scenic farmland of the State's heartland to the Allegheny Mountains of the northwest. Its tourist destinations range from the 16km (10 miles) of white, sandy beaches at Ocean City to Baltimore's bustling Inner Harbor, located on Chesapeake Bay; its 6437km (4000 miles) of shoreline, including its tributaries, separate the eastern shore area of Maryland from the rest of the State. The twin-spanned Chesapeake Bay Bridge, 12km (7 miles) across, is the major link between the two sections. Maryland is also the 'bridge' linking Baltimore and Washington DC. The distance between the two is only about 60km (40 miles).

TRAVEL

AIR: Approximate flight times: From Baltimore to *London* is 7 hours 40 minutes (direct) and to *New York* is 1 hour 15 minutes.
International airport: *Baltimore/Washington International (BWI)* is 16km (10 miles) south of Baltimore and 55km (34 miles) northeast of Washington DC. This airport has been expanding its international services rapidly over the past year, resulting in immense profits and a greatly increased number of carriers, passengers and cargo. Airport buses are available to downtown Washington and there are frequent rail and shuttle-bus connections to Baltimore. Taxis ply to and from Baltimore but distance makes fares to Washington DC prohibitive.
RAIL: Baltimore is on the main East Coast *Amtrak* line and consequently receives direct services from as far

afield as New Orleans and Miami. There are also frequent shuttles to Washington DC and New York. For approximate journey times on this line, see the *New York* section below.
ROAD: Approximate driving times: From Baltimore to *Washington DC* is 50 minutes, to *Philadelphia* is 2 hours, to *New York* is 4 hours, to *Chicago* is 15 hours, to *Miami* is 23 hours, to *Dallas* is 29 hours, to *Los Angeles* is 56 hours and to *Seattle* is 59 hours.
All times are based on non-stop driving at or below the applicable speed limits.
Approximate *Greyhound* journey times: From Baltimore (tel: (410) 752 0919) to *Washington DC* is 1 hour, to *Philadelphia* is 2 hours 15 minutes and to *New York* is 3 hours 40 minutes.
URBAN: Redevelopment in Baltimore during the last decade has provided a subway system and new expressways. The entire metropolitan area is covered by the *Mass Transit Administration.* Taxis can be hailed easily on the street or ordered by phone. Cars and motorcampers can be rented.

RESORTS & EXCURSIONS

BALTIMORE: Maryland's major city is one of the USA's busiest ports. Restoration of the city's Inner Harbor area has created one of the major tourist destinations in the mid-Atlantic region. Baltimore has a cosmopolitan population of more than two million and an attractive village-like atmosphere.
Sightseeing: Docked in the Inner Harbor at Pier 1 is the frigate *Constellation,* first ship of the US Navy (1797) and the oldest ship in the world still afloat. The 3-acre Inner Harbor also contains the *World Trade Center,* the *National Aquarium,* the *Maryland Science Center* and two pavilions on the water's edge filled with shops and restaurants. An open-air amphitheatre is the site of the annual summer-long street performer's festival. Nearby is the *Charles' Center* with 22 acres of offices, tower blocks, overhead walkways, fountains and plazas; it includes the *Morris Mechanic Theater.* Also nearby is the *Baltimore Arena and Festival Hall,* site for ice hockey, music concerts and other special attractions. City museums include the *Baltimore Museum of Art,* which houses many post-impressionist works; *Walters Art Gallery;* and the *City Life Museum,* a city-block of

buildings demonstrating life in Baltimore during the 19th century. *Mount Vernon Place* contains 19th-century houses and squares and various cultural institutions, such as the *Maryland Historical Society* and the *Peabody Conservatory of Music.* It also includes the *Washington Monument*, which can be climbed for a panoramic view.

Excursions: A short water-taxi ride away from the Inner Harbor is the star-shaped brick-built *Fort McHenry National Monument*, whose bombardment in 1814 inspired the writing of the 'Star Spangled Banner' and where special drills and military ceremonies are performed in the summer.

ANNAPOLIS: The State capital has an attractive harbour, the impressive campus of the US Naval Academy and beautiful period architecture.

Excursions: The *Chesapeake & Ohio Canal National Historic Park*, stretching 295km (184 miles) from Washington DC to Cumberland in western Maryland, is where the young Lieutenant-Colonel George Washington began his military career. His headquarters can still be seen. The canal was once a major avenue of commerce. The towpath for mule-drawn barges now serves as a popular hiking and biking trail. **Ocean City,** one of the State's main resort areas, boasts an expansive white sand beach, a 5km (3-mile) boardwalk, amusements, tram rides, boating and deep-sea fishing. *Muddy Creek Falls* is located near Deep Creek Lake, Garrett County. *Carroll Country Farm Museum* is a working 19th-century farm near **Westminster.** *Old Trinity Church,* at **Church Creek,** is the oldest Protestant church actively used in the USA.

FREDERICK: A town of quaint brick buildings and parks.

Excursions: In and around Frederick, there are a number of sights. *Gambrill State Park*, just west of town, offers outstanding panoramic views from the Catoctin peaks. *Camp David Presidential Retreat* near **Thurmont** is the traditional holiday resort for US Presidents. The public is not allowed inside but visitors can experience the same lovely landscape in *Catoctin Mountain Park*, which surrounds it. *Cunningham Falls State Park* is also nearby.

Other attractions in Maryland include **Smith Island** and *Tangier Sound*, the home of Chesapeake Bay fishermen who earn their living from oysters, crabs and clams.

Note: For information on attractions in neighbouring States, see above under *States A-Z.*

SOCIAL PROFILE

FOOD & DRINK: Baltimore is well known for its many outstanding restaurants offering fresh seafood caught in Chesapeake Bay. Establishments range from the very expensive to the cheap fast-food counters.

THEATRES & CONCERTS: The *Baltimore Symphony Orchestra* gives concerts in the *Myerhoff Symphony Hall* and the *Lyric Theater* in Baltimore. Dinner theatres are popular in Baltimore and good performances can be experienced in the lounges of hotels and supper clubs. *The Left Bank Jazz Society* gives concerts on Sunday afternoons at the *Famous Ballroom. Hopkins Plaza* has many music concerts and *Center Plaza* hosts various rock concerts.

NIGHTLIFE: Baltimore has many late-night clubs. Baltimore Street is a famous area for burlesque shows and there are some raunchy nightclubs in an area of Baltimore known as The Block.

SHOPPING: The main department stores are in the Howard Street area and in Harbor Place and Antique Row. Charles Street has elegant fashion and furniture. Mount Vernon Place is an attractive area with many shops and boutiques among grand 19th-century architecture.

SPECIAL EVENTS: Mar 25-26 '95 *Maryland Days Weekend* (celebrating the founding of Maryland with 17th-century entertainment, craft demonstrations, exhibitions, military drills and food), St Mary's City. **May 6** *Chesapeake Bay Bridge Walk*, Annapolis. **May 12-21** *Maryland Preakness Celebration & Race* (horserace celebrations with street festival, balloon races and regattas), Baltimore. **Jun 24-25** *Tangier Sound Country Music Festival,* Crisfield. **Jul 21-23** *Artscape* (literary, performing and visual arts festival), Baltimore. **Aug 4-6** *Rocky Gap Country/Bluegrass Music Festival*, Cumberland. **Aug 7-11** *22nd Annual White Marlin Open.* **Aug 26-Sep 4** *Maryland State Fair*, Timonium. **Aug 26-Oct 15** *Annual Renaissance Festival*, Anne Arundel County. **Sep 2-3** *Southern Maryland Wildlife Festival*, Indian Head. **Sep 21-24** *Sunfest*, Ocean City. **Oct 5-15** *US Sailboat Show and US Powerboat Show*, Annapolis. **Oct 13-15** *National Craft Fair*, Gaithersburg. **Nov 10-12** *Waterfowl Festival*, Easton. **Dec 31** *First Night Annapolis*, Annapolis.

CLIMATE

Hot, damp summers and mild, damp winters.

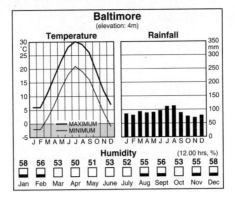

Baltimore
(elevation: 4m)

Temperature — Rainfall

Humidity												(12.00 hrs, %)
58	56	53	50	51	53	52	55	56	53	55	58	
Jan	Feb	Mar	Apr	May	June	July	Aug	Sept	Oct	Nov	Dec	

Massachusetts

Including **Boston**, gateway to New England (which comprises the States of Massachusetts, Maine, Vermont, New Hampshire, Connecticut and Rhode Island).

Massachusetts Office of Travel & Tourism
13th Floor, 100 Cambridge Street, Boston, MA 02202
Tel: (617) 727 3201. Fax: (617) 727 6525.
Greater Boston Convention & Visitors Bureau
PO Box 990468, Suite 400, Prudential Tower, Boston, MA 02199-0468
Tel: (617) 536 4100. Fax: (617) 424 7664 *or* 424 0073.
Greater Springfield Convention & Visitors Bureau
34 Boland Way, Springfield, MA 01103
Tel: (413) 787 1548. Fax: (413) 781 4607.
Cape Cod Chamber of Commerce
PO Box 16, Junction Routes 6 & 132, Hyannis, MA 02601
Tel: (508) 362 3225. Fax: (508) 362 3698.
Representatives of the Massachusetts Office of Tourism
c/o First Public Relations, 2 Cinnamon Row, Plantation Wharf, York Place, London SW11 3TW
Tel: (0171) 978 5233. Fax: (0171) 924 3134. Opening hours: 0930-1730 Monday to Friday.

TIME: GMT - 5. *Daylight Saving Time* is observed.
THE STATE: Massachusetts was the destination of the *Mayflower* in 1620 and is one of the original 13 States. It is now a major manufacturing State, offering everything from cobblestoned streets and village greens to space-age technology centres. The Berkshire Hills cut across its western corner. To the east the land rolls down to the sea,

embracing the State capital, Boston, and the beaches of the Cape Cod National Seashore. The two regions are divided by the Connecticut River Valley.

TRAVEL

AIR: Approximate flight times: From Boston to *London* is 7 hours 15 minutes, to *New York* is 1 hour and to *Providence* is 25 minutes.
International airport: *Boston Logan International (BOS)*, 6km (4 miles) from the city centre, is the largest airport in New England. Airport services include a free shuttle-bus (marked *MASSPORT*) stopping at each airline terminal and the *MBTA* subway station which has a service every 8-12 minutes (travel time to downtown Boston – 15 minutes). Taxis and limousine service, car rentals, and buses are also available. *MASSPORT Water Shuttle*, serviced by a separate bus, offers a 7-minute boat ride from the airport to Rowes Wharf in downtown Boston.
RAIL: *Amtrak* links Boston with Washington DC, New York City, Chicago and Montréal in Canada, and offers summer service from New York City to Cape Cod.
Approximate journey time: From Boston to New York is 4 hours 30 minutes.
ROAD: Approximate driving times: From Boston to *Hartford* is 2 hours, to *Portland* (Maine) is 2 hours, to *Albany* is 3 hours, to *New York* is 4 hours, to *Montréal* is 6 hours, to *Chicago* is 20 hours, to *Miami* is 31 hours, to *Dallas* is 37 hours, to *Los Angeles* is 63 hours and to *Seattle* is 63 hours.
All times are based on non-stop driving at or below the applicable speed limits.
Approximate *Greyhound* journey times: From Boston (tel: (617) 526 1801) to *Albany* is 3 hours 30 minutes, to *New York* is 4 hours 30 minutes, to *Montréal* is 8 hours 30 minutes and to *St John* is 10 hours 30 minutes.
URBAN: *Massachusetts Bay Transport Authority (MBTA* or the 'T') operates Boston's subway system, as well as bus and train services throughout the city and surrounding towns. Fares are moderate and passengers can transfer easily between surface and underground transportation. Suburban buses extend travel beyond the immediate city. Taxis can be hailed throughout the city, but delays can be experienced during rush hours; they can also be called by telephone. Car hire is available. Commuter trains operate to points north, northwest, south and west of Boston.

RESORTS & EXCURSIONS

BOSTON: Boston is a city of contrasts, a gentle blend of the old and the new. The city has a very 'English' feel about it, with hilly, crooked cobblestoned streets, a thickly-lawned common and cosy Victorian townhouses with polished brass door-knockers. It also played a vital role in the opposition to colonial rule that led to the American War of Independence.
Sightseeing: The *Freedom Trail* is a walk that passes 16 points of historical interest. Some of these are in the *Boston National Historical Park;* which is marked by signs and a red pavement line. The highest observation point in New England, the 60-floor *John Hancock Observatory*, offers a bird's-eye view of the city. Other attractions include harbour cruises, some of which enable the visitor to see the Boston skyline, the airport and the 1822 *USS Constitution* at Charlestown Navy Shipyard; the *Museum of Fine Arts*; the famous *Museum of Science*; the *John F Kennedy Library and Museum*; the *New England Aquarium;* the *Old North Church*; the *Boston Tea Party Ship & Museum; Faneuil Hall;* the *Prudential Building* viewing platform on the 52nd floor, open office hours; and the *Cheers Bar*, where the popular TV series is made.
Excursions: Cambridge lies across the Charles River from Boston. Here stands *Harvard University*, the USA's oldest university (1636). South of Boston is **Quincy,** the birthplace of Presidents John Adams and John Quincy Adams. **Salem,** north of Boston, is famous for its 1692 witch trials. Just west of Boston, **Concord** is one of the most historic and beautiful towns in the USA. *Plimoth Plantation*, in **Plymouth** is an open-air museum recreating a 1627 Pilgrim village. Nearby, the *Edaville*

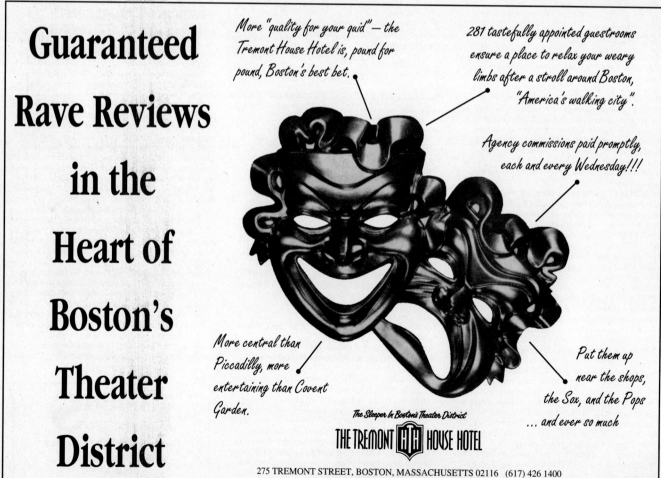

Railroad offers rides on an antique steam train. *Battleship Cove,* in **Fall River,** harbours 20th-century US Navy vessels and is the largest complex of its kind in the country. **New Bedford,** a restored whaling community, has the *Seamen's Bethel,* which inspired Herman Melville's description in 'Moby Dick'. **Cape Cod** has some 400km (250 miles) of beautiful beaches, and 21 seaside towns and fishing villages, making it one of the USA's prime resort areas. **Provincetown,** at the tip of the Cape, is where the Pilgrims first landed. **Martha's Vineyard,** a picture-postcard island, lies off the coast of Cape Cod. Its airport in **Edgartown** receives flights from Boston and New York. **Nantucket Island,** once a great whaling port, is now a popular sun resort. *Old Sturbridge Village,* in central Massachusetts, is a living history museum recreating an 1830s New England town. Just two hours from Boston are the *Berkshire Hills* and the *Mohawk Trail.* The legendary Indian trail winds through 500,000 acres of State parks, forests and reservations. It is very popular for foliage viewing in the autumn. The *New England Science Center* in **Worcester** has a zoo, various exhibits and a range of lectures which provide an ideal learning opportunity for all members of the family. **Note:** For information on attractions in neighbouring States, see above under *States A-Z.*

SOCIAL PROFILE

FOOD & DRINK: There is a wide variety of very good restaurants. Boston has many ethnic communities, and culinary opportunities range from Greek and Portuguese to Chinese and Syrian. Seafood is a speciality throughout Massachusetts, including local lobster, scallops, scrod and delicious clam chowder.
THEATRES & CONCERTS: Boston is the traditional review town for Broadway shows. The theatrical season is mainly in the autumn and winter. The *Boston Symphony Orchestra,* one of the greatest of all international ensembles, has a full schedule of autumn and winter concerts and makes its summer home at *Tanglewood* in the Berkshires. 'Boston Pops' concerts are staged in the spring and summer.
NIGHTLIFE: Boston offers a variety of jazz clubs, dance clubs and intimate piano bar lounges.
SHOPPING: The high-fashion district in Boston is Newbury Street in Back Bay. Department stores and Filene's Bargain Basement are in the downtown area. Faneuil Hall Marketplace, rather along the lines of London's Covent Garden, contains shops and restaurants.
SPECIAL EVENTS: The following events are celebrated in Boston in 1995/96:
Apr 17 '95 *Boston Marathon.* **Jul 5-10** *Harborfest,* Boston. **Jul-Aug** *Tanglewood Music Festival,* Lenox. **Sep 15-Oct 2** *The Eastern States Exhibition,* Springfield. **Oct 15-31** *Haunted Happenings,* Salem. **Oct 21** *Head of the Charles Regatta,* Boston. **Dec 31** *First Night Celebration,* State-wide. **Apr 15 '96** *Boston Marathon.*

CLIMATE

Warm and sunny from May to October; cold winters.

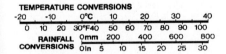

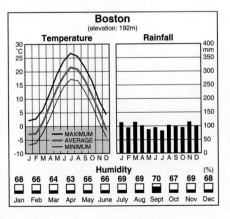

Boston
(elevation: 192m)

Michigan

Including **Detroit,** gateway to the Great Lakes and the Midwest.

Michigan Travel Bureau
Department of Commerce, PO Box 30226, Suite F, 333 South Capitol (48933), Lansing, MI 48909
Tel: (517) 373 0670 *or* (1 800) 543 2937 (toll free). Fax: (517) 373 0059.
Metropolitan Detroit Convention & Visitors Bureau
Suite 1900, 100 Renaissance Center, Detroit, MI 48243-1056
Tel: (313) 259 4333. Fax: (313) 259 7583.
Jackson Convention & Tourist Bureau
6007 Ann Arbor Road, Jackson, MI 49201
Tel: (517) 764 4440. Fax: (517) 764 4480 *or* 764 4440.
Michigan Information Centre
110 St Martin's Lane, London WC2N 4DY
Tel: (0171) 240 1422. Fax: (0171) 240 4270.

TIME: GMT - 5. *Daylight Saving Time* is observed in the greater part of the State.
THE STATE: Michigan comprises two peninsulas. These are divided by Lake Michigan, and linked by one of the world's longest suspension bridges across the Straits of Mackinac. Lakes Superior, Huron and Erie also form the State's shorelines. The Lower Peninsula, mainly agricultural and industrial, contains inland lakes, meadows and sandy beaches as well as the 'Motor City' of Detroit. The Upper Peninsula is more rugged, and boasts forests, white beaches, trout streams and winter ski resorts.

TRAVEL

AIR: Approximate flight times: From Detroit to *London* is 7 hours 10 minutes and to *New York* is 1 hour 40 minutes.
International airport: *Detroit Metropolitan Airport* is 32km (20 miles) west of the city centre. Buses and taxis are available to downtown areas; car hire is also available.
RAIL: Detroit is on *Amtrak's* Chicago–Toronto line; see the *Illinois* section above for approximate journey times.
ROAD: Approximate driving times: From Detroit to *Cleveland* is 3 hours, to *Indianapolis* is 5 hours, to *Cincinnati* is 5 hours, to *Toronto* is 5 hours, to *Chicago* is 5 hours, to *Buffalo* is 6 hours, to *New York* is 13 hours, to *Dallas* is 24 hours, to *Miami* is 27 hours, to *Los Angeles* is 49 hours and to *Seattle* is 49 hours.
All times are based on non-stop driving at or below the applicable speed limits.
Approximate *Greyhound* journey times: From Detroit (tel: (313) 961 8562) to *Cleveland* is 4 hours, to *Cincinnati* is 6 hours, to *Chicago* is 6 hours, to *Toronto* is 6 hours, to *Indianapolis* is 7 hours and to *Duluth* is 19 hours.
URBAN: Most larger communities have bus and taxi services. Detroit also has a downtown rapid rail system, the *People Mover.*

RESORTS & EXCURSIONS

DETROIT: Industrial Detroit is the nation's car manufacturing centre. The oldest city in the Midwest, founded in 1701, it is now the ninth-largest city in the USA, with a population of around one million. Its link with the St Lawrence Seaway, giving access to the Atlantic Ocean, means Detroit is also a major port.
Sightseeing: There are many museums, art galleries, zoos and amusement parks, and cultural events and major league sports are frequent crowd-pullers. The *Renaissance Center* houses dozens of restaurants, a 1400-room hotel and a variety of shops. *Belle Isle,* the nation's largest urban island park, offers biking, canoeing, an aquarium and a Great Lakes museum. The *Cultural Center* features the *Detroit Historical Museum,* the *Detroit Science Center* and the *Detroit Institute of Arts,* one of the largest art museums in the USA. The *Detroit Zoological Park* contains more than 5000 animals in natural settings (the grounds can be toured by tractor-train). *Greektown,* along Monroe Avenue, offers Greek food, entertainment and speciality shops. *Fort Wayne Military Museum* is one of the nation's best-preserved Civil War forts.
Excursions: Special tour books guide visitors around *Lake Michigan, Lake Superior* and *Lake Huron.* *Greenfield Village* and the *Henry Ford Museum* can be found at **Dearborn,** a Detroit suburb: the 12-acre indoor museum focuses on America's industrial development and the 240-acre village comprises more than 80 buildings, a train and a riverboat. *Cranbrook Educational Community* and *Cranbrook House and Gardens* are located in **Bloomfield Hills,** just north of Birmingham and 40km (25 miles) north of downtown Detroit. The grounds contain a beautiful country estate and landscaped gardens with an art museum, nature centre, planetarium, observatory and various educational institutions. **Ann Arbor** is the home of the *University of Michigan.* Michigan's *Great Lakes,* 60,000km (36,000 miles) of rivers and 11,000 inland lakes, offer boating, canoeing, fishing and watersports. **Traverse City,** on the west side of the State, is the heart of a recreational haven featuring sand dunes, resorts, golf and skiing. **Mackinac Island** is a well-known summer resort; cars are not allowed and visitors must walk, cycle or use horse-drawn carriages. Attractions include the impressive *Grand Hotel* and *Fort Mackinac,* a restored 18th-century military outpost. *Isle Royale National Park* is a beautiful wilderness island in Lake Superior.
Note: For information on attractions in neighbouring States, see above under *States A-Z.*

SOCIAL PROFILE

FOOD & DRINK: The state has a wide variety of American and ethnic restaurants. Steak and seafood are especially popular.
THEATRES & CONCERTS: In Detroit, the *Fisher Theater* presents Broadway shows, and the *Detroit Symphony Orchestra* performs in *Orchestra Hall* (September to April) and at the *Meadow Bank Music Festival,* Oakland University (June to mid-August). The *Michigan Opera Theater* presents its spring season at the *Masonic Temple* and its autumn season at the *Fisher Theater.* Opera, ballet and drama are also performed at the *Music Hall Center* (October to December). Summer theatre is found throughout the state. *Cobo Arena* stages rock and soul concerts.
NIGHTLIFE: Includes supper clubs with star entertainment. Clubs offer a variety of music, ranging from 'Motown' soul music (which originated in Detroit), blues (this is the hometown of John Lee Hooker) to classical music.
SHOPPING: Detroit's main shopping areas include the Renaissance Center, Greektown and suburban malls. Resorts have speciality shops and gallery districts.
SPORT: Detroit offers professional **basketball, hockey, football** and **horseracing.** The state has more public-access **golf** courses than any other.
SPECIAL EVENTS: Apr 30-May 7 '95 *Blossomtime Festival,* Benton Harbor and St Joseph. **May 10-20** *Holland Tuliptime Festival,* Holland (MI). **Jun** *Spirit of Detroit Thunderfest (*hydroplane races and an airshow), Downtown on the Detroit River; *13th Annual Valvoline Detroit Grand Prix* (Indy cars zoom around the Belle Isle Circuit), Belle Isle. **Jun 9-11** *Cereal Festival* (celebration in the town that gave the world cornflakes and inspired the novel *The Road to Wellville),* Battle Creek. **Jun 13-18** *Frankenmuth Bavarian Festival,* Frankenmuth. **Jun 21-Jul 4** *International Freedom Festival* (celebrates the friendship between Canada and the USA), Detroit. **Jul 8-15** *National Cherry Festival,* Traverse City. **Jul 19-22** *Ann Arbor Arts Fair,* Ann Arbor. **Sep 1-4** *Montreux-Detroit Jazz Festival,* Detroit.
Detroit's *Riverfront Festivals* take place from **May to September,** including ethnic festivals and other special

events featuring music, dancing and cuisine from various cultures held on weekends.

CLIMATE

Summers are warm with cool nights. Winters are cold, especially around the Great Lakes where conditions can be severe (however, there are good conditions for winter sports).

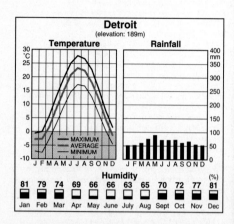

Minnesota

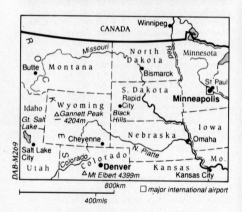

Including **Minneapolis/St Paul,** gateway to the Great Lakes, the prairielands of Minnesota, Wisconsin and Iowa, and the great plains and Badlands of Nebraska, North Dakota and South Dakota.

Minnesota Office of Tourism
121 7th Place East, 100 Metro Square, St Paul, MN 55101-2112
Tel: (612) 296 5029 *or* (1 800) 657 3700 (toll free). Fax: (612) 296 7095.
Greater Minneapolis Convention & Visitors Association
4000 Multifoods Tower, 33 South 6th Street, Minneapolis, MN 55402
Tel: (612) 661 4700. Fax: (612) 348 9396.
St Paul Convention & Visitors Association
102 Norwest Center, 55 East 5th Street, St Paul, MN 55101-1713
Tel: (612) 297 6985. Fax: (612) 297 6879.

TIME: GMT - 6. *Daylight Saving Time* is observed.
THE STATE: Minnesota, the second northernmost State in the USA (after Alaska), is one of the nation's leading tourist destinations, with 64 State parks, 55 State forests and more than 11,000 lakes. The State borders Canada, the upper Midwest States and Lake Superior, the largest freshwater lake in the world. The southern two-thirds are prairieland, while to the north lie reafforested hills, the basis of the State's timber industry.

TRAVEL

AIR: Approximate flight times: From Minneapolis/St Paul to *London* is 12 hours 45 minutes (including stopover), to *New York* is 2 hours 50 minutes and to *Salt Lake City* is 2 hours 40 minutes.
International airport: *Minneapolis-St Paul International (MSP)* is 16km (10 miles) from the cities (which are contiguous). An airport limousine service and taxis are available.
RAIL: Minneapolis/St Paul is on *Amtrak's* Chicago–Seattle line; for approximate journey times see the *Illinois* section above.
ROAD: Approximate driving times: From Minneapolis/St Paul to *Duluth* is 3 hours, to *Madison* is 5 hours, to *Fargo* is 5 hours, to *Sioux Falls* is 5 hours, to *Omaha* is 7 hours, to *Chicago* is 8 hours, to *Winnipeg* is 8 hours, to *St Louis* is 11 hours, to *Rapid City* is 11 hours, to *Denver* is 17 hours, to *Dallas* is 19 hours, to *New York* is 25 hours, to *Seattle* is 34 hours, to *Miami* is 35 hours

and to *Los Angeles* is 41 hours.
All times are based on non-stop driving at or below the applicable speed limits.
Approximate *Greyhound* journey times: From Minneapolis (tel: (612) 371 3323) to *Duluth* is 3 hours, to *Fargo* is 5 hours 30 minutes and to *Milwaukee* is 8 hours.

RESORTS & EXCURSIONS

MINNEAPOLIS: Minneapolis and St Paul adjoin each other on either side of the Mississippi River and have a metropolitan area population of more than two million. They began as frontier towns, with German, Irish and Scandinavian immigrants. Minneapolis is modern with fine theatres, nightclubs, stores, a year-round sports programme and a distinguished symphony orchestra. The city is also the site of one of the world's largest universities, the University of Minnesota.
Sightseeing: *Nicollet Mall* is a world-famous downtown shopping promenade and includes the 57-storey *IDS (Investors Diversified Services) Center*, which towers over the downtown area and has an observation deck offering panoramic views of the 'Twin City'. The *Science Museum & Planetarium* is also at Nicollet Mall. The *Minneapolis Institute of Arts* exhibits major art masterpieces from Europe, the Orient and the Americas. *The Walker Art Center* stages contemporary art exhibits, concerts and lectures. Other attractions include the *Minnesota Transportation Museum; Valleyfair* amusement park; and *Minnesota Zoo*, with more than

OVERVIEW OF MINNESOTA

Centuries ago the Dakota Indians called the land that sparkled with thousands of lakes, 'Minnesota', meaning 'sky-tinted waters'. Now called Minnesota, 'land of 10,000 lakes', it is really the land of more than 12,000 lakes. Located in the heart of North America, sharing a border with Canada, Minnesota is home to cities, prairies, forests and farms. Half of Minnesota's four million people live in the Minneapolis-St. Paul metropolitan area.

These 'Twin Cities' are served by Minneapolis/St. Paul International Airport, which welcomes visitors from all parts of the world. Northwest Airlines, headquartered in Eagan, flies non-stop to London and has direct flights to Japan. International connecting flights are available through New York, Chicago and Los Angeles.

MINNESOTA'S INDIAN HERITAGE AND PEOPLE

Minnesota's woodlands were home to American Indians long before the white man arrived. Minnesota's Indians are members of two tribes: the Dakota or Sioux, and the Ojibwe or Chippewa.

Two national monuments celebrate the State's Indian history. Grand Portage National Monument is located at the northeast tip of Minnesota near Canada. In southwestern Minnesota, Pipestone National Monument preserves the quarries of the soft red stone used by the Indians in making peace pipes.

Indian pow-wows are exciting and colorful celebrations of Indian spiritual life and culture; many welcome visitors. A variety of Indian-made crafts and arts are available in shops around the State.

EXPLORING MINNESOTA

Each part of Minnesota offers unique holiday experiences – from the shores of Lake Superior to Bluff Country on the southeastern border.

The north shore of Lake Superior is one of the most scenic drives in America with a rugged, beautiful shore on one side of the highway and the Superior National Forest on the other. Travel the Gunflint Trail from Grand Marais into the wilderness; canoe in the Boundary Water Canoe Area, 1.1 million acres of pristine lakes; visit Duluth, a popular port city or explore the Iron Range, a region that once produced nearly two-thirds of the nation's iron ore. Ironworld USA celebrates the history of the range with entertainment, a theme park and history center.

The Mississippi River begins as a trickle, easily crossed by foot, in Itasca State Park in northern Minnesota, before flowing 2500 miles to the Gulf of Mexico.

In nearby Bemidji, visit the statue of Paul Bunyan, legendary giant lumberjack. Travel to 'lake country' near Brainerd, where hundreds of lakes provide year-round recreation. Choose accommodations at a large resort with all the amenities or enjoy the intimacy of a smaller self-catering resort. Just a short drive away in Little Falls, the home of Charles A. Lindbergh, aviation hero, is open to visitors.

From Little Falls, the Mississippi River flows south to the Twin Cities of Minneapolis-St. Paul. The 'twins' are very different in personality: Minneapolis is modern and trendy, while the capitol city of St. Paul is proud of the city's culture and traditions. Both offer a wealth of attractions, sports, entertainment and dining. The Mall of America, the largest shopping-entertainment complex in the USA, is just a few minutes from the airport in Bloomington.

In southeastern Minnesota, over centuries the Mighty Mississippi has carved its way through limestone bluffs that now tower as high as 300 feet over the charming river towns. Visitors come to enjoy festivals, biking, hiking, boating, birdwatching and sightseeing.

Travel the trail of pioneers through southern Minnesota, land of the Dakota Indian. Discover Walnut Grove, Laura Ingalls Wilder's *Little House on the Prairie,* New Ulm's German heritage and Jesse James, infamous bandit, who 'robs' the Northfield bank each summer during Jesse James Days. Join the Grand Island Rendezvous celebration which re-enacts the encampment of fur traders and American Indians. The American Frontier comes alive in Minnesota's festivals!

Minnesota's Voyageur's National Park, our national forests, 65 State parks, festivals, wildlife and cities are waiting to be explored. Contact the Minnesota Office of Tourism, 100 Metro Square, 121 7th Place East, St. Paul, MN 55101-2112, USA, or fax (612) 296 7095 for travel information.

2000 plant varieties and 375 species of animal. *Minnehaha Park Falls* were made famous in Longfellow's poem, *The Song of Hiawatha*.

ST PAUL: Older and perhaps more dignified than Minneapolis, as befits a state capital, the city has abundant parks and lakes.

Sightseeing: The *St Paul Art Center for the Performing Arts* offers drama, concerts and art galleries. The *Science Center* is just across the street. The *Landmark Center* now houses galleries, displays relating to the city's history and a restaurant. The old *Federal Courts* date back to 1892.

Excursion: *Fort Snelling State Park,* 10km (6 miles) southwest of the city, is a restored 1819 military post.

DULUTH: This scenic port at the western tip of Lake Superior receives ships from all over the world (via the St Lawrence Seaway).

Sightseeing: Attractions include harbour and lake cruises; the *Canal Park Museum;* the *Depot*, a restored village at the *St Louis Country's Heritage & Arts Center;* the *Aerial Life Bridge;* and the *Skyline Parkway* drive high above the city.

Excursions: *Spirit Mountain* is a year-round holiday and outdoor recreation centre 11km (7 miles) south of Duluth. The spectacular *North Shore Drive* (US Highway 61) follows the north shore of Lake Superior for 240km (150 miles) from Duluth to the Canadian border. The 'North Woods' region embraces vast wilderness and lakes. Major resort areas include *Brainerd, Bemidji, Detroit Lakes, Lake Mille Lacs* and *Grand Rapids. Split Rock Lighthouse State Park* preserves one of the most scenically-situated lighthouses in the USA, about 43km (27 miles) north of **Two Harbors.** *Gooseberry Falls*, 23km (14 miles) north of Two Harbors along the North Shore Drive, plunge 30m (100ft) into Lake Superior.

Note: For information on attractions in neighbouring States, see above under *States A-Z.*

SOCIAL PROFILE

FOOD & DRINK: The cities have many excellent restaurants. Regional seafood is a speciality. There are many excellent steak restaurants in the 'Twin City', as well as many exotic restaurants from Greek to Japanese.

THEATRES & CONCERTS: The cities offer more

theatres than any other US metropolitan area outside New York City, with more than 90 theatre companies. The *Guthrie Theater* in Minneapolis is dedicated to the innovative presentation of classical drama. The *University of Minnesota Theater* features summer theatre aboard the 'Showboat', moored on the Mississippi near the campus (June to August). The renowned *Minnesota Orchestra* performs regularly at *Orchestra Hall* in Minneapolis. The *St Paul Chamber Orchestra's* home is the *Ordway Music Theater.*

NIGHTLIFE: The 'Twin City' nightclubs offer rock groups, jazz combos and musical comedy. Popular gathering places are the *Loon* and the *Monte Carlo* in Minneapolis and *Gallivan's* in St Paul.

SPORT: Due to its many lakes, Minnesota has plenty of **fishing** opportunities, as well as every kind of **watersport.** It is excellent for **camping** and **hiking,** as well as **hunting,** with white-tailed and caribou deer, moose, elk and many smaller game in abundance. **Canoeing** is available in the Quetico Reserve in the Superior Natural Forest. There are also good **horseriding, tennis** and **golf** facilities. Winter sports are also well provided for, abetted by the State's strategic northern location, and **skiing, ice-skating, bobsledding, ice fishing, dog sledding** and **snowmobiling** are all available.

SPECIAL EVENTS: Apr 1-2 '95 *Minnesota Festival of Music,* New Ulm. **May 14** *Family Festival,* St Paul. **May 5** *Cinco de Mayo* (Hispanic celebration featuring music, costumes, food and a parade), St Paul. **May 17** *Syttende Mai* (Norwegian Independence celebration), Benson. **May 19-21** *Waterfront City Festival,* Duluth. **May 20** *Front Porch Festival,* Hastings. **Jun 16-17** *Great Midwestern Think-Off* (philosophy debates, parade, street dance, food), New York Mills. **Jun 17** *Bayport Arts & Crafts Fair,* Bayport. **Jul 1-3** *Red Lake* (traditional American Pow Wow), Red Lake. **Jul 2** *Arts in the Park,* Brainerd. **Jul 7-8** *Korn & Klover Karnival,* Hinckley. **Jul 14-15** *Range Polka Fest,* Chisholm. **Jul 14-16** *Heritagefest* (a celebration of Germanic heritage), New Ulm. **Jul 14-16** *Folk Festival,* Two Harbors. **Jul 14-23** *Mines & Pines Jubilee,* Hibbing. **Jul 14-23** *Aquatenniel* (a 10-day festival of sports events, art fairs, boat races and parades), Minneapolis. **Aug 5-6** *Berne Swissfest,* West Concord. **Aug 6** *Taste of Dorset,* Dorset. **Aug 11-13** *Bayfront Blues Festival,* Duluth. **Aug 13** *Craftsman's Fair,* Crosslake. **Aug 4-Sep 4**

Minnesota State Fair, St Paul. **Mar '96** *St Urho's Day* (celebrated by the Finns of Menahga and Finland, Minnesota).

CLIMATE

Winters are cold, with severe conditions along the Great Lakes. Summers are warm and there are frequent heat waves and droughts.

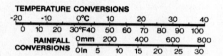

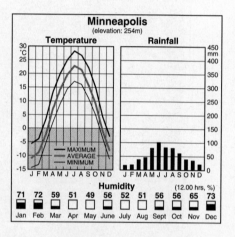

MSP America's North Coast Gateway

Minneapolis/St. Paul International Airport (MSP) is nearly as old as aviation. Established in 1920, it is one of the world's pioneer airports, and has grown to be a key hub in the center of North America.

Located midway across the continent near the Twin Cities of Minneapolis and St. Paul, MSP served as the jumping off point for air routes expanding to America's West Coast and to the Orient. Learning from the 1931 "North to the Orient" flight made by Charles and Anne Morrow Lindbergh, Northwest Airlines initiated the "Great Circle Route" in 1947 over the Arctic to Japan, China, Korea and the Philippines. This route bought cities along the northern boundaries of the United States 2000 miles closer to the Orient than over traditional transpacific routes.

In the 1970s hundreds of miles were shaved off travel to Europe as well by flying across the top of the world from MSP to London and northern Europe.

One of the world's busiest and safest airports, MSP's landings and takeoffs totalled 460,000 in 1994.

Last year more than 340,000 metric tons of cargo and 23.4 million passengers from all over the world passed through MSP's facilities. In total passengers, it ranked as the 11th busiest airport in the US., and 17th busiest in the world.

The airport is served by eight major airlines, two international airlines, seven regional and 18 charter airlines and 16 cargo carriers.

Home to Northwest Airlines and one of its major hubs, MSP is served by nonstop or one-stop same-plane flights to more than 160 destinations, 16 of them international. With nonstop service to London and Amsterdam and direct flights to Frankfurt and Tokyo, plus access to many additional destinations in Europe and Asia through Northwest/KLM hubs at Amsterdam and Tokyo, cargo and passengers move quickly to their final destination. MSP also has nonstop service to Montreal, Vancouver and major Canadian cities in between.

MSP's direct access to major cities around the world is a vital factor in attracting and keeping large, high-profile corporate headquarters in the Twin Cities. Forty three of the Fortune 500 industrial and service corporations and the Forbes 400 privately held corporations are headquarted here... names like 3M, Honeywell, General Mills, Medtronic, Cargill, Pillsbury and Land 'O Lakes, to name only a few.

Many of these companies are either multi-national businesses or export their products to international markets around the world.

Minneapolis/St. Paul International Airport
"America's North Coast Gateway"

Missouri

400km
200mls
□ *major international airport*

Including **St Louis** and **Kansas City**, gateways to south/central USA – Missouri, Kansas, Oklahoma and Arkansas.

Missouri Division of Tourism
PO Box 1055, Jefferson City, MO 65102
Tel: (314) 751 1910 *or* 751 4133 *or* (1 800) 877 1234 (toll free). Fax: (314) 751 5160.
Cape Girardeau Convention & Visitors Bureau
PO Box 617, Cape Girardeau, MO 63702-0617
Tel: (314) 335 1631. Fax: (314) 334 6702.
Greater Kansas City Convention & Visitors Bureau
Suite 2550, 1100 Main Street, Kansas City, MO 64105
Tel: (816) 691 3828/9. Fax: (816) 691 3805 *or* 221 5242.
St Louis Convention & Visitors Commission
Suite 1000, 10 South Broadway, St Louis, MO 63102
Tel: (314) 421 1023. Fax: (314) 421 0039.
Springfield Convention & Visitors Bureau
3315 East Battlefield Road, Springfield, MO 65804-4048
Tel: (417) 881 5300. Fax: (417) 881 7201.

TIME: GMT - 6. *Daylight Saving Time* is observed.
THE STATE: Missouri, in the heart of the USA, is a blend of frontier West, gracious South, the sophisticated East and industrial North. The Missouri Valley was a major pioneer route, with St Louis known as the 'Gateway to the West'. It is bounded by the Mississippi River in the east. Prairies lie north of the Missouri, the longest river in the USA, with great plains to the west, rolling hills in the south and the Mississippi cotton lands to the southeast. Its riverboat culture was immortalised by Mark Twain in 'Life on the Mississippi' and his tales of Tom Sawyer and Huckleberry Finn.

TRAVEL

AIR: Approximate flight times: From London to *St Louis* is 9 hours 10 minutes (including stopover) and to *Kansas City* is 13 hours 20 minutes (including stopover). *TWA* operate direct flights from London to St Louis.
International airports: *Lambert International Airport* is 21km (13 miles) northwest of downtown St Louis (travel time – 30 minutes). Buses, taxis, airport limousines and hire cars are available.
Kansas City International Airport (KCI) is 15km (9 miles) from the city centre (travel time – 30 minutes). Airport buses, limousines, taxis, hotel shuttle buses and hire cars are available.
RAIL: St Louis is a stopping point on *Amtrak's* Chicago–San Antonio line. Kansas City is on the Chicago–Los Angeles line. For approximate journey times on the former line, see the *Illinois* section above; for the latter see *California*. There is also a daily direct service from Kansas City (departing 1545) via St Louis (2105) and Memphis (0505 the following day) to New Orleans (arriving 1250).
ROAD: Long-distance coach companies operating in the State include *Greyhound, Gulf Transport, Great Southern* and *Vandalia*.
Approximate driving times: From *St Louis* to Kansas City is 5 hours, to Indianapolis is 5 hours, to Louisville is 5 hours, to Chicago is 6 hours, to Nashville is 6 hours, to

Memphis is 6 hours, to Cincinnati is 7 hours, to Little Rock is 7 hours, to Des Moines is 7 hours, to Oklahoma City is 10 hours, to Minneapolis/St Paul is 11 hours, to Dallas is 13 hours, to New York is 19 hours, to Miami is 25 hours, to Los Angeles is 39 hours and to Seattle is 45 hours.
From *Kansas City* to Topeka is 2 hours, to Omaha is 4 hours, to Des Moines is 4 hours, to Oklahoma City is 7 hours, to Little Rock is 7 hours, to Memphis is 9 hours, to Chicago is 10 hours, to Dallas is 12 hours, to New York is 25 hours, to Miami is 30 hours, to Los Angeles is 34 hours and to Seattle is 40 hours.
All times are based on non-stop driving at or below the applicable speed limits.
Approximate *Greyhound* journey times: From *St Louis* (tel: (314) 231 4485) to Indianapolis is 5 hours, to Kansas City is 5 hours, to Louisville is 6 hours, to Chicago is 7 hours, to Memphis is 7 hours, to Tulsa is 9 hours and to Nashville is 9 hours.
From *Kansas City* (tel: (1 800) 231 2222; toll free) to Omaha is 5 hours, to St Louis is 5 hours, to Oklahoma City is 9 hours and to Denver is 13 hours.
URBAN: St Louis: Tour bus companies operating in the city and surrounding areas include *Gray Line, St Louis Sightseers* and *St Louis Tram Tours*. Hire cars and taxis are available.
Kansas City: There are public bus services around the city and surrounding suburbs. Several tour bus companies provide sightseeing trips in and around Kansas City. Hire cars and taxis are available.

RESORTS & EXCURSIONS

ST LOUIS: The largest city in Missouri and the country's largest inland port, St Louis was once a booming centre for fur traders and explorers opening up 'The West'. It is now a modern communications, commercial, industrial and cultural centre. It still retains its 'love affair' with the Mississippi River, on whose banks can be heard ragtime and Dixieland jazz. The influence of the many ethnic groups that created the city can still be seen in the German burgher houses and elegant French mansions (on its southside), and in the Italian and Serb neighbourhoods.
Sightseeing: The *Gateway Arch* on the riverfront is, at 192m (630ft), the nation's tallest memorial. It marked the starting point for settlers beginning their trek west and contains an observation deck and exhibits on the American West. Other attractions include the *Six Flags Over Mid-America* theme park; the *National Museum of Transport*; the *Missouri Botanical Garden National Historical Landmark*; and the *St Louis Zoological Park*.
Excursions: Hannibal in northeast Missouri was Mark Twain's hometown. Many museums and shows celebrate the author's life and works.
KANSAS CITY: Once the eastern terminus for some of the West's most famous trails, such as the Oregon, California and Santa Fe, Kansas City is now a major commercial and agricultural centre for the Midwest. Kansas City is situated on the State line between Missouri to the east and Kansas to the west.
Sightseeing: The *Worlds of Fun* entertainment complex has more than 120 rides, roller coasters and riverboat cruises. The *Country Club Plaza*, the nation's oldest shopping centre, was established in 1922. Other attractions include *Oceans of Fun*, a water theme park, and the *Nelson-Atkins Museum of Art*.
Excursions: Independence, 16km (10 miles) east of Kansas City, celebrates its association with Harry S Truman (he once lived there) at the *Truman Library & Museum*. Sightseeing and dinner-dance riverboat cruises are available. **St Joseph,** north of Kansas City, boasts the *Pony Express Stables Museum* and the *Patee House Museum*. The *Lake of the Ozarks* in central Missouri has more than 1600km (1000 miles) of forested shoreline and offers watersports, canoeing, golfing, tennis, caves, shows and museums. It is home to three outstanding State parks – *Bennett Springs*, the *Lake of the Ozarks* and *Ha Ha Tonka*.
Note: For information on attractions in neighbouring States, see above under *States A-Z*.

SOCIAL PROFILE

FOOD & DRINK: St Louis: Everything from elegant downtown restaurants to more casual eateries serving traditional ethnic fare. **Kansas City:** Famous for its steaks.
THEATRES & CONCERTS: St Louis: There are performances at the *Powell Symphony Hall*, the *Fox Theater* and the *Muny Theater*. **Kansas City:** The *Kansas City Philharmonic* play at the *Music Hall*. The *Missouri Repertory Theater* performs on the University of Missouri's campus. Other venues include the *Lyric*

Theater and *Starlight Theater*.
NIGHTLIFE: There are many clubs and restaurants on the riverfront in St Louis, some actually on the river in permanently-berthed riverboats, where jazz and ragtime music is performed nightly. Discotheques exist in most modern hotels in St Louis.
SHOPPING: The most elegant shopping area in St Louis is Plaza Frontenac in west county, with fashionable boutiques, speciality shops, gourmet delicatessens and antique stores. The Soulard Market in south St Louis is a colourful and amusing place to shop on the weekends. Begun as a farmer's market in 1847, outside stalls around the main building offer fresh country goods, such as meat and home-baked items, as soon as they arrive in the city.
SPECIAL EVENTS: The following is a selection of major events celebrated in Missouri in 1995. For the complete list contact the Missouri Division of Tourism.
Apr 21-22 '95 *Lake of the Ozarks Dogwood Music Festival*, Camdenton. **May 3-6** *St Louis Storytelling Festival*, Gateway Arch. **May 20-21** *Lewis and Clark Rendezvous*, St Charles. **Jun 9-10** *Riverfest*, Cape Girardeau. **Jul 1** *Firefall '95*, Springfield. **Jul 1-4** *Fair St Louis*. **Jul 16** *Blessing of the Fleet*, Portage des Sioux. **Jul 20-22** *Bluegrass Festival*, Patterson. **Jul 28-Aug 6** *Ozark Empire Fair*, Springfield. **Aug 9-12** *Kahoka Festival of Bluegrass Music*, Kahoka. **Aug 9-12** *Jaycee Bootheel Rodeo*, Skeston. **Aug 17-27** *Missouri State Fair*, Sedalia. **Aug 18-20** *Festival of the Little Hills*, St Charles; *Trails West!*, St Joseph. **Aug 18-27** *US National Hot Air Balloon Championships*, Columbia. **Sep 25-30** *Cotton Carnival*, Sikeston. **Oct 7-8** *Oktoberfest*, Hermann. **Oct 20-22** *Missouri Day Festival*, Trenton.

CLIMATE

The region has the most continental climate of any area in the USA. Winters are cold and summers warm, with frequent heat waves.

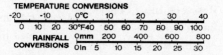

TEMPERATURE CONVERSIONS

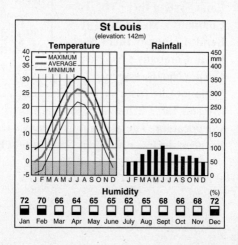

St Louis
(elevation: 142m)
Temperature | Rainfall
— MAXIMUM
— AVERAGE
— MINIMUM
Humidity
72 70 66 64 65 65 62 65 68 66 68 72 (%)
Jan Feb Mar Apr May June July Aug Sept Oct Nov Dec

The unique appeal of Missouri

MISSOURI DIVISION OF TOURISM

MISSOURI WELCOMES INTERNATIONAL VISITORS

Visitors from other nations are beginning to discover an exciting vacation land right in the heart of the United States. It's a place where travelers can enjoy history, rolling hills and valleys, water fun, big cities and spectacular scenery – all in a fairly compact area. It's the State of Missouri and it's growing in popularity with international visitors.

Located at the center of the US – and convenient for visitors flying from overseas – Missouri is easily accessible for travelers from around the world. Missouri and the other States of mid-America are ideal as an 'alternate' destination for international visitors, many of whom already have explored the traditional holiday sites on the United States' east and west coasts.

THE MISSOURI 'TRIANGLE'

For visitors unfamiliar with Missouri, a basic 'triangle' route offers a quick look at the State's appeal. The triangle tour covers St Louis/eastern Missouri – the lakes and Ozark hills of southern Missouri – and Kansas City/western Missouri. Travelers on the triangle tour (with a few strategic detours) can enjoy much of Missouri's beauty, history and excitement.

Begin, for example, in St Louis, the State's eastern metropolis. St Louis, along with Kansas City on the western side of the State, is a primary gateway for travelers flying to Missouri from overseas. Both cities have major airports, providing easy access for visitors from many nations.

Historically the 'gateway to the West', St Louis is one of Missouri's finest holiday sites. This bustling city sits on the west bank of the mighty Mississippi River and offers many reminders of the days when the river was America's western frontier.

Capsule elevators carry visitors to the top of the Gateway Arch on the riverfront. As the keystone of the Jefferson National Expansion Memorial, the Arch is America's tallest man-made national monument (248m/630ft high) and celebrates St Louis' role as a gateway city for pioneers headed west in the 19th century. Underground, beneath the Arch, the Museum of Westward Expansion explains the chronology of America's westward movement.

Nearby, visitors can sample the city's history – the Old Courthouse, the Old Cathedral, the home of children's poet Eugene Field – or cheer St Louis Cardinals baseball at Busch Stadium. Riverboats, offering excursions, restaurants and casino gambling, line the Mississippi. Just north of the Arch, Laclede's Landing has become one of the city's premier shopping and entertainment districts in an historic area of cobblestone streets, cast-iron lamps and warehouse-like buildings.

West of downtown is 1,300-acre Forest Park, still fondly remembered as the site of the 1904 World's Fair. Today, the huge urban park is the home of major attractions including one of the world's best zoos, the St Louis Art Museum, the Science Center, the Muny outdoor summer theatre and much more.

Among other 'must-see' St Louis attractions are the beautifully renovated Union Station, an architectural masterpiece now housing shops, restaurants and nightspots – the green and growing appeal of the Missouri Botanical Garden, including America's largest traditional Japanese Garden – and the excitement of Six Flags Over Mid-America, a themed fun park with rides and shows for the whole family.

Just minutes to the west, St Charles preserves Missouri's first State capitol. Here, where explorers Lewis and Clark set out their 1804 voyage to the Pacific Northwest, visitors enjoy a charming historic district surrounding the first capitol building. Antique and crafts stores, boutiques and restaurants add to the appeal of riverboat gaming, dinner theater on the historic Goldenrod Showboat and other fun.

MARK TWAIN'S HOMETOWN

Two hours' drive north along the Mississippi River is Hannibal, Mark Twain's hometown. No visit to the heartland would be complete without a visit to the boyhood home of one of America's (and the world's) greatest writers. Travelers in Hannibal can relive the adventures of Tom Sawyer – peer into the white-frame home where Twain grew up, cruise his beloved Mississippi on an old-time riverboat, explore Mark Twain Cave where Twain played as a youth – or see an outdoor drama recreating scenes from his best-known novels.

TOURING INTO THE OZARKS

South and west from St Louis, the Ozarks are at the second point of the Missouri triangle. Water is one of the major ingredients of this region's recipe for luring travelers. With over 900,000 acres of water (including 80,000km (50,000 miles) of rivers and streams), Missouri is ideal for water fun of all kinds.

Much of the Ozarks' water is impounded in large lakes, famous for fishing, boating, swimming and other aquatic activities. Of course, not all the water is impounded. Much of it bubbles, gurgles, flows and ripples, singing a liquid refrain as it crosses the State. From the major rivers – the Mississippi and the Missouri – to smaller Ozarks streams, Missouri's rivers delight travelers.

LAKE OF THE OZARKS

From St Louis, the first stop for travelers on the Ozarks leg of the triangle could be the Lake of the Ozarks in central Missouri. The State's largest lake is one of mid-America's favorite vacation destinations, with over 2200km (1,375 miles) of winding, twisting shoreline. And it's all trimmed in green, set amid a multi-hued tapestry of Ozark hills.

Besides swimming and other on-the-water fun, travelers here can tour area caves, challenge championship golf courses and sample several music shows. Numerous malls, factory outlets and specialty stores make the lake area a year-round mecca for shoppers, especially during the Christmas season. Resort communities on and near the lake offer a wide range of dining and lodging choices, from elegant to family-style.

Continuing south on the triangle route, visitors come to Springfield, Missouri's third largest city and a perfect headquarters for an Ozarks tour. America's only ride-through cave (Fantastic Caverns) is here, as is Bass Pro Shops Outdoor World, the largest mall complex for the sports-minded in the world. Missouri's Civil War heritage comes to life at the Wilson's Creek National Battlefield. And Springfield is the gateway to the border lakes and the Branson area, just south.

BRANSON'S MUSIC AND HILL COUNTRY FUN

Reminders of the hill country lifestyle and a chain of large lakes – Table Rock, Bull Shoals, Taneycomo and Norfork – have drawn travelers to Ozark Mountain Country for nearly a century. In recent years, however, Branson has been singing a different tune. Music shows, many featuring famous country and pop music stars, have turned the little Ozarks town into America's live music capital where more than six million visitors come each year.

All this and more make the Ozarks the southern star of the Missouri triangle. Throughout the area (the Ozarks cover almost the entire southern half of Missouri), there are caves to explore and homes of famous Missourians to

WAKE UP TO MISSOURI

For a better picture of the real America take a closer look at Missouri.

From Jesse James' hideout to Mark Twain's hometown, from sprawling cities like St. Louis and Kansas City to the entertainment hub of Branson, no other state exemplifies America like Missouri. It's something you'll discover in "Visions," the 22-minute movie designed to help improve your tour business.

For your copy of this incredible selling tool, call Kris Lokemoen at 1-800-535-3210 and ask for the Missouri video, "Visions." You can also fax your request to (314) 751-5160. Or write us at P.O. Box 1055, Jefferson City, MO 65102.

So order "Visions" today. It's more than a marketing tool. It's a work of art.

WAKE UP TO
MISSOURI

Top picture: The Missouri State Flag. Above: Mark Twain's boyhood home, on historic Hill Street in Hannibal, is a reminder of one of Missouri's (and the world's most beloved authors.

visit (such as former President Harry Truman, scientist and educator George Washington Carver, and Laura Ingalls Wilder, author of the "Little House" children's books). To the west is the Joplin/Carthage area, on historic Route 66. To the east is the most 'natural' part of Missouri, including the pristine rivers of the Ozark National Scenic Riverways and America's largest single-outlet spring, Big Spring at Van Buren.

NEXT STOP: KANSAS CITY

From the Ozarks, the triangle route leads north to the Kansas City area. This modern city lures travelers with its museums, fine dining, parks, boulevards, fountains and other attractions. From pro sports at the twin-stadium Truman Sports Complex or Kemper Arena, to riverboat gambling, to performances of the State Ballet and Lyric Opera, Kansas City has it all.

Visitors enjoy historic Westport, in the oldest section of the city, with shops and restaurants in buildings once frequented by 19th-century settlers. The elegant Country Club Plaza, developed in the 1920s as America's first shopping center, features fountains and Moorish architecture. For contrast, travelers can head to ultra-modern Crown Center, home of Hallmark Cards, for shopping and dining – or lodging in a world-class hotel with a waterfall splashing through the lobby. There's beautiful Swope Park, with its zoo and outdoor Starlight Theatre, or a look into the past amid the recovered, preserved cargo from the sunken 1858 steamboat *Arabia* at the Arabia Steamboat Museum.

Just minutes from downtown is Independence, once a major stop for pioneers heading west. Independence showcases its heritage today at the national Frontier Trails Center. Diaries, artefacts and a film tell the story of the hardy settlers who passed through this area. North of Kansas City, St Joseph remembers its days as the starting point of the Pony Express. The old stables are now part of the Pony Express National Memorial. Nearby is the four-

storey Patee House, once the headquarters of the Express and now a museum of Americana. On the grounds of the Patee House, visitors can tour the frame home where infamous outlaw Jesse James was killed in 1882. Varied museums – and a riverboat casino on the Missouri River – are among St Joseph's other appeals for travelers. Also in the area is a national wildlife refuge at Squaw Creek. And the largest tobacco market west of the Mississippi is at Weston, a town where history comes to life in more than 100 buildings pre-dating the Civil War.

COMPLETING THE TRIANGLE

The third leg of the triangle takes travelers back across the heart of Missouri, east toward St Louis. Stops along the way focus on history and reminders of famous Missourians.

Paralleling the route of the Missouri River across central Missouri, travelers may stop at Lexington to see reminders of the 1861 Civil War 'battle of the hemp bales'. At Arrow Rock, virtually the entire town is preserved as a State historic site, focusing on its role at the start of the frontier Santa Fe Trail.

Further east is Columbia, home of the University of Missouri's main campus. Mid-Missouri's largest city is a popular lodging, dining and shopping stop, mid-way between Kansas City and St Louis. Just south, a stop at the State Capitol Building in Jefferson City is well worthwhile. Murals, statuary and a State museum are highlights of the building, on a bluff overlooking the Missouri River. The Capitol, Governor's Mansion and Jefferson Landing State Historic Site all offer perspectives on the evolution of Missouri's State government.

EVEN MORE FAMOUS MISSOURIANS

Well north of the river, memorable Missourians are remembered at Marceline (Walt Disney's boyhood home), Laclede (home of World War I leader General John J Pershing) and Kirksville (where Dr Andrew Taylor Still founded the world's first College of Osteopathic Medicine).

Continuing toward St Louis, visitors may choose to stop by Fulton, where Sir Winston Churchill delivered his memorable "Iron Curtain" speech in 1946. The centuries-old Church of St Mary Aldermanbury, shipped in pieces from London and reassembled in Fulton, is the heart of the Winston Churchill Memorial. With a section of the Berlin Wall standing nearby, the memorial now symbolizes both the start and the end of the Cold War.

THE VARIETY OF ATTRACTIONS

Once back in St Louis, the Missouri triangle tour is complete.

And, of course, there's more . . . every part of the State has its unique appeal. And when you list Missouri's attractions, you can be sure the list will never be complete.

There's a whole year full of fairs, festivals and other fun times, for example. There's an extensive system of State parks and historic sites. Parks with intriguing names like Elephant Rocks, Johnson's Shut-Ins and Trail of Tears. Historic sites that include rustic covered bridges and old grist mills.

There's hunting and fishing that ranks among America's best. Plus hiking, biking and backpacking on public lands, State forests and the Mark Twain National Forest. There's even 'hiking' underground in 24 beautiful caves open for tours. There's scenery that runs the gamut from plains to forests to mountains to bayou-like lowlands. There are wineries, museums, bed-and-breakfast inns, golf courses and so much more.

With all its appeals, Missouri has enough to fill several trips. But a quick tour along the Missouri triangle provides a good look at the State's diversity and a smiling introduction to Missouri's friendly people. For a traveler from another State – or nation – the Missouri triangle is a three-pointed invitation to fun in mid-America.

WAKE UP TO MISSOURI

DISCOVER THE SECRETS OF KANSAS CITY

KANSAS CITY CVB

KANSAS CITY HAS IT ALL

When some think of Kansas City, images of cowboys and pioneers, dusty trails and a land called Oz may instantly come to mind. But those who have visited this jazzy city in America's heartland know that a more realistic picture is that of an entertaining metropolis brimming with surprises; a city with a great future forged by its rich historical past. Kansas City truly is one of the nation's finest treasures.

Part of Kansas City's charm lies in its beauty. The city, known as the 'City of Fountains' is built around an impressive network of boulevards and parks. And Kansas City's entertainment opportunities are endless. From dining to shopping; museums to amusement parks; performing arts to sports – Kansas City has it all.

THE HEART OF AMERICA

Kansas City truly is the 'Heart of America', centrally located at the junction of the Missouri and Kansas (Kaw) Rivers. Kansas City is a bi-State metropolitan area which straddles the Missouri-Kansas State line, and is the only major city located within 400km (250 miles) of both the geographic and population centers of the nation. The maximum distance from Kansas City to anywhere in the contiguous United States is approximately 3040km (1,900 miles), or half the distance from coast to coast. Approximately 1.6 million people live in the Kansas City metro area, which has approximately the same land area as the State of Connecticut.

GOIN' TO KANSAS CITY

Located 25 minutes northwest of downtown, Kansas City International Airport eliminates much of the hassle of air travel. Three C-shaped terminals offer aircraft loading around the perimeters with passenger parking in the center. Distance from aircraft to curb is less than 30m (75ft), which is one of the reasons the airport is consistently rated one of the most user-friendly in the United States. A variety of transportation options are available from the airport including the KCI Shuttle, which runs over 100 daily departures between the airport and selected hotels in the Crown Center, Plaza, Westport and other suburban areas. Other transportation options include taxis, buses and rental cars. And once you arrive in Kansas City, there are nearly 17,000 hotel and motel rooms throughout the area that provide a wide range of accommodations to suit any taste and budget.

KANSAS CITY'S CLIMATE

Kansas City enjoys four distinct seasons. Early spring brings a period of frequent and rapid fluctuations in weather, with the last frost generally occurring in early April. The summer season is characterized by warm days and mild nights. The fall season is normally mild, characterized by mild, sunny day, cool nights and a brilliant color spectacular as the leaves change colours in preparation for winter. The first freeze usually occurs in early October. Winters are not severely cold, and snowfalls of ten inches or more are comparatively rare.

KC CUISINE

Though famous for steaks and barbeque, the city really offers an incredible variety of cuisine. Recognized by many as a major culinary center, visitors are delighted by the abundance of excellent restaurants of every ethnic origin. And with over 60 barbeque restaurants to its credit, the city truly is the nation's barbeque headquarters. Kansas City barbeque is always slow smoked over wood, which is usually hickory, for up to 18 hours to obtain that one-of-a-kind flavor. Each restaurant has developed its own recipe

for sauce, too, which is put on just before serving. Every October over 200 teams flock to Kansas City to compete in the largest barbeque competition in the world, the American Royal Barbeque Contest.

UNIQUE SHOPPING & ENTERTAINMENT DISTRICTS

The Country Club Plaza, built in 1922, has become one of Kansas City's favorite attractions. Modeled after Seville, Spain (one of Kansas City's sister cities), the Plaza's red-tiled roofs, ornate ironwork, pastel-colored buildings and majestic towers recreate the flavor of Europe. With exquisite mosaics, statues and sparkling fountains, the Plaza is more than just a shopping district, it is an outdoor museum. The Plaza contains more than 150 of the finest stores in the country, as well as dozens of restaurants. Visitors can ride a horse-drawn carriage through the streets or take a self-guided walking art tour to discover the full majestic beauty of the Plaza. During the holidays, over 200,000 colorful lights outline its 75 miles of rooftops, archways and towers. Summer is a time for sampling savory delights in a patio or courtyard café, listening to an outdoor concert, or relaxing by a splashing fountain.

Another creative shopping development in Kansas City can be found at the southern edge of the downtown area. Crown Center, a privately financed project of Hallmark Cards, Inc, surrounds the international headquarters of the world's largest greeting card company. The enclosed shopping and entertainment center features more than 80 shops and restaurants, live theatres, cinemas and two hotels. The free tour of the Hallmark Visitors Center features multimedia exhibits, a timeline depicting the history of greeting cards, interactive displays and craftsmen at work. Crown Center's central square features fountains, an outdoor café in summer, ice skating in winter and is home to one of the nation's tallest Christmas trees (over 37m/95ft) during the holidays.

For a quick step back into Kansas City's history, take a trip to Westport. More than a century ago, this famous spot was the jumping-off point for the Santa Fe, California and Oregon Trails. Westport became a bustling trade town with immigrants, freight wagons and businessmen. One of Kansas City's most popular 'watering holes' is found in the heart of Westport. Kelly's Westport Inn, housed in Kansas City's oldest building, was once a store operated by Albert Gallatin Boone, grandson of Daniel Boone. Today, you can jump off to an afternoon of unique shopping in the district's one-of-a-kind boutiques or spend an evening sampling the nightlife found in the dozens of Westport clubs.

ART IN THE HEARTLAND

Kansas City is home to a number of outstanding history and art museums. The Nelson-Atkins Museum of Art is one of America's most comprehensive general art museums, and features 30,000 items dating from 3000BC to the present. Among the richest of the Nelson's wonders is one of the finest collections of Asian art in the Western World. The museum also displays works by some of the world's greatest masters and contemporary artists. The museum is home to the largest collection of monumental bronzes by the renowned British artist Henry Moore outside his native England.

The most recent addition to the Kansas City art scene is the Kemper Museum of Contemporary Art and Design of the Kansas City Art Institute. The first museum in Kansas City devoted entirely to contemporary art and design, the museum provides direct access to important works created by international contemporary artists.

WILD ABOUT HARRY

A trip to Independence, Missouri, located about 20 minutes from downtown Kansas City, is a

The story of the American west is told in a thousand little places. But we were in Kansas City, where it all began.

The west was born at the confluence two of America's greatest rivers – the Kaw and the Missouri. Arteries commerce, fingers into the frontier, hundreds of steamboats plied these treacherous waterways, reaching west from Kansas City.

So we kicked things off at the Steamboat Arabia Museum. In 1856, the Arabia sank in the Missouri River, loaded with supplies destined for pioneers out west. Over 200 tons of cargo are on display – the most complete collection of its kind in the country. Clothes, tools, cookware, china, jewelry, food – all the necessities and some of the luxuries for life on the plains.

In fact, Kansas City was the jumping-off point for virtually every pioneer heading west across the Great American Desert. So a visit to the National Frontier Trails Center in Independence, Missouri was at the top of our list.

The stories and artifacts from those journeys are incredible! Draught, sickness, scorching heat, bone-chilling cold. But also incredible, unspoiled beauty. Imagine buffalo herd so vast it took three days to pass!

Besides launching the Old West, Kansas City is best known for helping launch those uniquely American forms of music – jazz and blues! It claims more live music clubs than any city in the midwest except Chicago. So we visited the Grand Emporium, voted "Best Blues Club In America" two years running! With this kind of heritage, where else would you put the International Jazz Hall of Fame? 18th and Vine in K.C., of course.

We ended our day aboard one of the city's riverboat casinos. With plenty of action inside and a beautiful starry night outside, it was a perfect ending to a wonderful day.

The history of America's west and the history of America's music aren't really secrets. After all, you can read a lot about them. Or you can come to Kansas City and discover the secrets that make them real!

·GAMING·
float away, on the river of play,

·VOYAGERS·
from the river to the mountains and beyond.

JAZZ
where the beat goes on

DISCOVER KANSAS THE CITY SECRETS

For more information about discovering the secrets of Kansas City write or call the Convention & Visitors Bureau at the address and telephone below:

Convention and Visitors Bureau of Greater Kansas City
1100 Main Street, Suite 2550 • Kansas City, MO, USA • 64105 • (816) 691-3828

trip back in time. Known as the 'Queen City of the Trails' for the wagon trains that once headed westward from the town, Independence has played an important role in the history of America and the world.

Most people will associate Independence as the home of Harry S. Truman, the 33rd President of the United States, and there are several sites of interest which revolve around this famous man and his family. The Harry S. Truman Library, located in Independence, Missouri, is one of nine US presidential libraries. The museum contains exhibits relating to Mr Truman's presidency, including a re-creation of his White House Oval Office. Visitors can also visit the Truman Home for a glance into the Truman's private lives away from the White House. The house and contents have been left unchanged including the calendar on the kitchen wall and Harry's hat and cane hanging in the side entry.

A CITY WITH A HISTORY

A unique collection of museums is located throughout the metropolitan area. Science, technology and history come alive with hands-on activities and exhibits at the Kansas City Museum. The museum features re-creations of a trading post, log cabin, covered wagon, Indian lodge and a blacksmith's shop. Permanent exhibits in the Natural History Hall are spacious dioramas of North American animals in their natural habitats.

The Toy and Miniature Museum of Kansas City is a treasure house of antique toys and fine miniatures that delight young and old alike. The museum features a vast collection of over 500,000 miniatures, antique toys, doll houses and furnishings dating from the mid-1800s to the present.

Fort Osage, a restored 19th-century fort, overlooks the Missouri River and was the first US outpost in the Louisiana Purchase, a site chosen by explorers Lewis and Clark. This living history museum allows visitors to view artefacts in the blockhouse and trading house, as well as the officers' quarters and soldiers' barracks.

The Negro Leagues Baseball Museum, located in the heart of the historic 18th and Vine district, is dedicated to preserving and recounting the history of black baseball in America.

Several historic attractions recounting the life and legend of famed outlaw Jesse James are also found in the Kansas City area. The Jesse James Bank Museum in Liberty, Missouri is the site of the world's first daylight peacetime bank robbery – executed by the infamous James Gang. Jesse James' home and original gravesite are on the James Farm near Kearney, Missouri. Tours are offered of this restored homestead where Frank and Jesse James grew up. A museum near the home tells the story of Jesse James and his gang. . .

Those interested in history will want to tour the Worpall House Museum, an authentically restored pre-Civil War home of one of Kansas City's earliest settlers. The home was used as a hospital during the Civil War's Battle of Westport.

AMUSING ATTRACTIONS

Step aboard the Kansas City Trolley to get a good overview of the city. The bright-red trolleys circle Kansas City's central corridor, providing a narrated and entertaining look at the downtown River Market, Westport, Crown Center and Country Club Plaza areas . . .

Added excitement comes to Kansas City each spring and summer with the opening of Worlds of Fun amusement park and Oceans of Fun aquatic park. Worlds of Fun, an internationally themed park, presents more than 140 rides, shows and attractions including one of the top roller coasters in the world. Oceans of Fun, the Midwest's largest water park, features sun, sand and water sports including a million-gallon wave pool and giant water slides.

Or try your hand at one of Kansas City's newest entertainment options – casino gaming. The area is home to several riverboat gaming facilities, offering slot machines, blackjack and other games aboard glittering riverboat casinos. And in Kansas City, Kansas, the Woodlands offers the fast pace of greyhound- and

thoroughbred- racing and wagering.

THAT'S ENTERTAINMENT!

Kansas City sparkles in its offering of performing arts. The State Ballet of Missouri delights audiences in both classical and contemporary productions. The Lyric Opera, one of the few opera companies to offer performances in English, and the Kansas City Symphony, a stunning national orchestra, are tremendous success stories among the Kansas City arts scene. The Midland Center for the Performing Arts, housed in a former 1928 movie palace, provides an elegant atmosphere while hosting Broadway touring shows and concerts. The oldest and one of the most colorful theatres in Kansas City is the Folly Theatre. Once a thriving burlesque house, the theatre has been completely refurbished, and offers a wide mix of performances. Each July, the Heart of America Shakespeare Festival celebrates the works, spirit and time of William Shakespeare with free, outdoor classical performances.

GOIN' TO KANSAS CITY

Kansas City's role in the history and development of jazz is legendary throughout the world. Kansas City's jazz tradition was born in the 1920s and was nurtured by such legends as Charlie Parker, Count Basie and Joe Turner. The Kansas City Blues and Jazz Festival, one of the top concert series in the nation, presents concerts by national and local performers each July. Additionally, numerous clubs feature year-round jazz entertainment.

THE SPORTING LIFE

Kansas City is a major league city in every respect, and its fame as a sports city is well deserved. Boasting five professional sports franchises, Kansas City offers a wide variety of sports action. For the sports enthusiast who prefers to participate rather than to be a spectator, Kansas City has many fine golf courses, tennis courts and other sports facilities throughout the city. The metropolitan area includes 600 public parks and 24 public lakes which offer boating, fishing, sailing and swimming.

ON THE HORIZON

Kansas City is on the move with many major, new attractions and many more due to open in the near future. A beautiful new enhancement is underway to Brush Creak, which winds through the Country Club Plaza. The project is creating a 10km (6-mile) linear park, which will include a tennis center, fountains, water cascades, landscaped walkways and a 30-acre lake. A $71-million renovation and expansion of the Kansas City Zoological Gardens will be completed in 1995. Sections of the new zoo are already open. The new naturalistic exhibits are re-creating the wilds of Africa and Australia, replacing traditional zoo cages.

IF YOU GO

The Convention and Visitors Bureau of Greater Kansas City

provides free information regarding things to see and do, as well as places to stay in Kansas City. Contact the Bureau on (816) 691 3829 *or* (1 800) 767 7700 (toll free; US and Canada only). Or write to: Convention and Visitors Bureau of Greater Kansas City, 1100 Main, Suite 2550, Kansas City, MO 64105.

IN SEARCH OF THE AMERICAN SPIRIT – THE OZARKS

THE AMERICA OF YESTERYEAR

Perhaps no region of the United States better represents America's feisty pioneer spirit and rugged individualism than the Ozarks of Southwest Missouri. Here among the remotest hills and hollows, where some settlers eked out a living without electricity as late as the 1950s, the traditions of craft making, music making, and the love of outdoors life are still alive and well. From modern Springfield, the region's Queen City, to booming Branson, the music show capital of America, the charm of a younger, more innocent America is here for you to enjoy.

WHERE TO START

The best introduction to the region – and the only way to arrive by major airline – is its population and retailing center, Springfield. Accessible by direct flights from Chicago, Dallas, Denver, Kansas City, Memphis, Nashville, and St Louis, Springfield is served by seven airlines.

If you are arriving by car, you'll find Springfield at the intersection of I-44 and US-65. Springfield once was a major stop along old Route 66, and parts of America's famous 'Mother Road' are still visible in some areas of town.

However you arrive, you'll find over 4,600 guest rooms to choose from in Springfield and over 400 restaurants. Incidentally, at least 50 of those restaurants serve a local classic called Cashew Chicken. An unlikely blend of Oriental chicken and Ozarks gravy, Cashew Chicken is found in only a few other locations around the country, where it often is identified as Springfield Cashew Chicken.

MISSOURI'S NUMBER ONE ATTRACTION

Springfield is home to Missouri's largest tourist attraction, which surprisingly is a retail store. What makes Bass Pro Shops Outdoor World so special it attracts four million visitors every year from all over the world? It represents the kind of entrepreneurial mayhem that is America at its best. And it's so typically Ozarkian!

Immodestly billed as the 'World's Greatest Sporting Goods Store', Bass Pro lives up to its reputation, offering 150,000 sq ft (and counting!) filled with everything sportsmen and outdoors lovers could want. Wander amid an array of fully loaded sports and pleasure boats, casual clothing (from unabashedly utilitarian to country chic), camping equipment, and fishing and hunting gear, including some 7,000 different kinds of fishing lures!

As every good sportsman knows, Bass Pro Shops is the mail order house for sporting goods. But visiting Outdoor World is more than an out-of-catalog experience! After all, you can't mail order the fun you'll have putting on the indoor green, testing your skill at the indoor firing range, and swapping fish tales at Bass Pro's own barber shop.

If you're serious about exploring the real Ozarks wilderness, fortify your outdoors acumen with some special-interest seminars in the auditorium. Watch a pro tie a fly and consult an expert marksman. Or just hike upstairs for a fresh fish dinner at atmospheric Hemingway's Blue Water Cafe. Time your meal right, and you'll be there when aquatic curator Blayk Michaels hand-feeds the lemon shark, who circles daily in the cafe's 30,000-gallon saltwater aquarium.

MORE SHOPPING

For travelers who gravitate toward a slightly more civilized shopping experience, headquarters is the Battlefield Mall (named for the nearby Civil War battleground, not the scrappy bargain-hunters). Here you'll find some of America's trendiest boutiques and most popular department stores.

Stock up on everything you need to look like a local dude when you visit PFI, Missouri's largest authentic Western store. Put on a fancy bolo, belt buckle, fringed jacket, and some pointy lizard-skin boots from PFI and head for the nearest dance floor. Another remarkable mail order success, PFI has a brand new retail store, easily accessible from US-65.

Or go on a treasure hunt in old Springfield, where historic Commercial Street is chock-full of antique furniture, clothes, and bric-a-brac of all vintages. More antiques await you 15 minutes south of Springfield in and around Ozark, the little town boasting over 100 antique shops!

AMERICA'S HISTORICAL CROSSROADS

Famous people are always passing through Springfield – always have. After one of his famous pony express runs, Wild Bill Hickok stopped off in Springfield in the summer of 1865 and shot a man dead in public square. To Wild Bill's credit, it was the other guy that shot first! This incident was the first recorded shoot-out in American history.

Just a few years before, the Springfield area was the site of several clashes between the Union and the Confederacy. Visit the site of Missouri's bloody entrance into the Civil War at Wilson's Creek National Battlefield, some 16km (10 miles) southwest of Springfield. Operated by the National Park Service, the battlefield provides self-guided auto and walking tours. A film and displays provide more information at the visitor's center.

When Route 66 was completed through town in 1931, Springfield saw more traffic than ever, famous and otherwise. Vaudevillians and Broadway troupes frequently stopped to play the ornate Landers theater, recently restored to its former 1909 grandeur. It hosts the local performing arts companies and their guests.

The even fancier Gilloiz theater, featuring exotic painted and gilded plaster moldings with Egyptian influences, is under restoration. The great old 1920s movie house was the site of two world premieres, including Ronald Reagan's Winning Team in 1952. On hand for the festivities was an interesting trio: President Harry S. Truman with Reagan and his soon-to-be wife Nancy Davis.

ENTERTAINMENT TODAY

Today, the nation's best touring companies play Springfield's modern-day classic theater, the visually and acoustically stunning Juanita K. Hammons Hall for the Performing Arts. Since it opened in the fall of 1992, the Hall has hosted Broadway touring companies, major dance troupes, top musical artists, as well as the Springfield Symphony, Springfield Little Theatre, Springfield Ballet, and Springfield Regional Opera productions. Even those who've been seated in the rafters swear there

WAKE UP TO
MISSOURI

isn't a bad seat in the house!

For the flavor of Branson without leaving Springfield, get your tickets for the 'Sounds of Branson' at the Gateway Theater. It's packed with country music, comedy, and Ozarks-style family fun – just the kind of fast-moving music show that has made Branson famous.

If your idea of enjoying the music includes some country boot-scootin', there are plenty of local clubs where you can get in line for some Cotton-eyed Joe. No experience necessary.

ATTRACTIONS AND EXCURSIONS

Players and armchair quarterbacks alike will enjoy the new John Q. Hammons Missouri Sports Hall of Fame. Here you can actually try your favorite sport, experience a 160kmh (100-mph) pitch from a catcher's point of view, and become a pro coach using interactive computer displays.

Reflect on nature at the Japanese Stroll Garden near the Gray/Campbell Farmstead, Springfield's oldest residence, at Nathanael Greene Park. Wander amid ponds and islands, over the moon bridge, and through the tea hut, and enjoy all its unique and expressive environments. The 7.5-acre garden was developed with assistance from the people of Isesaki, Japan, Springfield's sister city. Springfield Conservation Nature Center, an 80-acre preserve on Lake Springfield, offers scenic hiking trails and plenty of hands-on activities and educational exhibits. Youngsters especially love flushing the simulated toilet in the groundwater display! Kids also enjoy visiting Dickerson Park Zoo, famous nationwide for its elephant breeding program; and Buena Vista Exotic Animal Paradise, where you can take a drive-through safari. And everyone's a spelunker at Fantastic Caverns, where all the underground sightseeing is by Jeep-drawn tram.

BRANSON!

No tour of the Ozarks would be complete without a visit to some Branson shows, where there's always a large serving of music, seasoned with a sprinkle of comedy, and topped with some rousing Gospel. With more theater seats than Broadway, Branson offers a variety of entertainers, including Kenny Rogers, Jim Stafford, the Osmonds, Mel Tillis, Charlie Pride, Roy Clark, Moe Brandy and many others.

Although its galaxy of stars has increased significantly since 1989, Branson's music show industry didn't exactly spring up overnight. The first shows, the Presleys' and the Baldknobbers, opened their doors some 30 years ago. The Baldknobbers are named for the vigilantes that once burned the town where Silver Dollar City theme park now stands.

Perhaps it's just as well the old town went down in flames, because Silver Dollar City theme park is a lot more fun. With all its sights, sounds and smells, the City transports you to the America of the 1890s. Here old-time craftsmen still ply their trades, pioneer cooks whip up delicious temptations, music shows set toes a-tapping, and themed rides offer thrills for all.

Other Branson attractions include the Shepherd of the Hills outdoor pageant (located beneath 90m/230ft Inspiration Tower). The new *Branson Belle,* America's largest ship on a landlocked body of water, offers dining and entertainment aboard themed cruises.

Of course, behind all the shows, parks, and attractions is the natural beauty of the Ozarks. Swim, ride a jet ski, para-sail, camp out in a rented houseboat, cast a line for bass, or picnic on the shores of lovely Table Rock Lake. Visitors centers at sites throughout the lakes area offer natural history displays, hiking trails, and fun activities for the kids, too.

THE SPIRIT OF AMERICA'S PAST

Few destinations in America offer the sense of time and place that permeates Ozark Mountain Country. Its unassuming, friendly people take few things seriously beyond their belief in a higher being and weekends on the lake. Spend some time in these old hills and hollows, and experience the lively spirit and country charm of America's past.

For more information please contact fax no: (417) 881 7201.

WAKE UP TO MISSOURI

ENTERTAINMENT GALORE

ENTERTAINMENT GALORE

In the lefthand corner of Missouri, in the centre of the Ozark Mountain area, lies the State's best-known little town – Branson. Branson offers more family fun than anywhere else, highlighted by more than 40 music and variety shows. Some shows, such as Presleys' and the Baldknobbers, have been delighting audiences for decades. Recent years have brought many new names, and spacious new theatres, presenting musical styles that range from traditional country music and pop 'classics' to today's sounds.

NEW ATTRACTIONS

Music shows aren't the only form of entertainment Branson has to offer. There's no end of things to do in Branson and visitors will find the variety of activities particularly refreshing. And brand new attractions are constantly being added to the wealth of activities already available. Some of Branson's newest highlights include:

Ozarks Discovery IMAX Theatre

3562 Shepherd of the Hills Expressway, Branson
A giant, 6-storey IMAX screen features exciting theme films. For further information, telephone 1-800 419 4832 (toll free) or (417) 335 4832.

Branson Scenic Railway, Inc

206 E. Main, Branson
A 64km (40-mile) round trip scenic train ride traverses bridges, high trestles and tunnels in the Ozark Mountains in luxury rail cars from the 40s and 50s available from March to December. For further information, telephone (417) 334 6110.

Dixie Stampede

1527 West Highway 76, Branson
This dinner attraction with 4-course meal and equestrian entertainment is themed on friendly North/South rivalry. For further information, telephone 1-800 520 5544 (toll free) or (615) 453 9473.

Polynesian Princess

South on Hwy. 65 to 86 W, turn at Gage's Marina, Branson
This 115-passenger dinner yacht sails on Table Rock Lake from April to Oct. For further information, telephone (417) 334 5186.

Ripley's Believe It Or Not! Museum

3326 W. Hwy. 76, blk W of Hwy. 165 & Gretna Road, Branson
A showcase of hundreds of fascinating oddities and unusual artefacts from around the world has interactive exhibits, illusions and more and is open all year round. For further information, telephone 1-800 998 4418 (toll free).

Showboat Branson Belle

Hwy. 265 between Table Rock Dam & State Park, Branson
An authentic paddlewheel showboat cruise and show, available from April to December. For further information, telephone (417) 336 7400.

STEEPED IN HISTORY

Despite being full of modern entertainment, Branson has its foundations firmly rooted in the past. At Shepherd of the Hills Homestead and Outdoor Theatre you can take a tram tour of this literary historic site, enjoy crafts and games, then watch the fast-paced drama re-creating the Shepherd's tale of life on the Ozarks frontier. The Branson Civil War Museum on 3069 Shepherd of the Hills Expressway features large exhibits of original Civil War objects and artefacts, from both North and South. Films are

Mountain Folk Music Festival, Silver Dollar City

shown continuously. The Museum is open from March to November, open 6-7 days per week (for further information, telephone (417) 334 1861). The Harold Bell Wright Theater & Museum at West Highway 76 and Mutton Hollow features a 30-minute film on the life of author Harold Bell Wright. There are also manuscripts, antiques and paintings. The museum is open from April to October (for further information, telephone (417) 334 0065).

Nearby Silver Dollar City will also transport you back to the turn of the century. Here you'll see crafts being practised, and thrill to exciting rides and music shows, all in the setting of an 1890s Ozarks town.

THE DOORSTEP TO SURROUNDING DELIGHTS

On Branson's doorstep is river-like Lake Taneycomo, with sprawling Table Rock just west and Bull Shoals and Norfork to the east. Fishing, boating, swimming, and just relaxing are favorite pastimes on these sparkling lakes. Towns around all four lakes have plenty to offer. In Eagle Rock, Forsyth, Kimberling City, Pontiac, Rockaway Beach, Shell Knob, and Theodosia, among others, you'll find Ozark crafts, art and antique shops, plus museums, resorts and more.

Another group of towns that warmly welcomes visitors are along the *Ozark Mountain Parkway* (Hwy. 265), a scenic shortcut to Branson from the north. There's Marionville with its rare white squirrels, 'The City of Art' at Reeds Spring, and crafts galore at Lakeview (Branson West).

NATURE'S PLAYGROUND

Outdoor enthusiasts receive a warm welcome in the Branson area. Places to fish, hike and otherwise enjoy nature are waiting for you here. Hiking trails from a few hundred yards to dozens of miles wind through spectacular scenery. The following are some of the outdoors areas available to visitors in the Branson area:

Table Rock Lake and State Park

Five miles (8km) west of Branson from MO 76 on MO 165, visitors to 'Shepherd of the Hills' country can make their headquarters in Table Rock State Park, located on the 53,300-acre (21,570-hectare) Table Rock Lake. This popular southwest Missouri lake is surrounded by both natural beauty and manmade attractions and is especially good for boating, water-skiing, swimming and fishing. Also, the clear deep water draws more scuba divers than any other Missouri lake. Campsites are plentiful, with 17 public-use areas, and much national forest lands. Boaters have 19 marinas, and there are 125 motels and resorts with direct access to the water. A visitor centre with displays and a nature trail is open during

WAKE UP TO MISSOURI

the summer at the dam. Tours of the dam and power-house are available. Camping and picnicking are also available here (for further information, telephone (417) 334 4704).

Shepherd of the Hills Trout Hatchery & Visitor Center

The State's largest trout hatchery is located 10km (6 miles) southwest of Branson on Hwy. 165. The Visitor Centre has exhibits, aquariums and slide shows describing hatchery operation. There are also hiking trails and fishing and boating access to Lake Taneycomo all year round (for further information, telephone (417) 334 4865).

Vineyards

Missouri produces some of America's best wines. Before Prohibition, Missouri was the nation's second-largest producer of wines. Today, Missouri's wine industry is enjoying sustained growth. Several historic wineries have been joined in recent years by a number of other dedicated vintners. Stone Hill Winery in Branson, two blocks south of W. Hwy. 76 on Hwy. 165, is nestled in the Ozark countryside. Visitors can experience an enjoyable hour's discovery tour and get a fascinating and historical view of how still and sparkling wines are made, as well as a chance to sample them afterwards. The Stone Hill Winery is open Monday to Saturday. For further information, telephone (417) 334 1897.

Colossal Caves

There are over 5,000 caves in Missouri, which is how Missouri earned the nickname, 'The Cave State'. Caves honeycomb many hills and valleys. Some caves offer guided tours, which are safe, easy and fun, and most are conducted along specially lighted pathways. Inside you'll discover scenic wonders which eons of time have combined with the elements to create delicate beauty unlike anything else on earth. In addition to incredible stalactites and stalagmites are such unique formations as 'soda straws', 'popcorn', flowstone and more. *Marvel Cave,* in Branson/Silver Dollar City, is America's third-largest cavern and its main chambers are 20 storeys high. There is also a huge waterfall. The cave can be visited from mid-April to late October (telephone (417) 336 7100 for further information). *Talking Rocks Cavern,* half a mile south on Highway 13, Branson West, has varied formations and a sight-and-sound show. This cave is open all year round (tel: (417) 272 3366 for further information).

GOLF

When you come to Branson, be sure to bring your golf clubs. There are a number of courses available within Branson alone, and many others only a short drive away. The following are a few of Branson's own 18-hole Golf Courses: Pointe Royale Village & Country Club (tel: (417) 334 4477), Holiday Hills Golf Course (tel: (417) 334 4838) and Thousand Hills Golf Club (tel: (417) 334 4553).

SHOW TIME

Branson is probably best known for its variety of musical entertainment. The following is a list of some of the many music shows available to visitors:

Andy Williams Moon River Theatre

2500 W. Highway 76, Branson
Superstar Andy Williams performs two special shows daily from April to December. For further information, telephone (417) 334 4500.

Baldknobbers Jamboree Show

Highway 76, Country Boulevard, Branson
The first show in Branson – country music and comedy. This is what Branson is all about. The season runs from March to December. For further information, telephone (417) 334 4528.

Our Tradition in the Ozarks

Holiday Hills is the ideal location for the visitor who desires to be close to the musical magic of Branson while still experiencing the finest in area accommodations and amenities. Visitors here enjoy a host of amenities, including tennis, swimming, miniature golf and 18 holes of golf on the most established course in the Ozarks.

- Luxury Condominiums
- Swimming Pools
- 18 Hole Golf Course & Pro Shop
- Sand Volleyball/ Tennis Courts
- Horse Stables/ Trail Rides
- Miniature Golf Course
- Marina facilities available

Perched on a mountaintop overlooking Table Rock Lake, Ozark Mountain Resort Swim & Tennis Club is just brimming with a wide selection of vacation activities to suit everyone's needs. Guests enjoy all types of boating activities as well as fishing, horseback riding, miniature golf, plus tennis and swimming. It's the perfect place for both action and relaxation.

- Luxury Condominiums
- Lake/Boat Dock
- Canoe/Paddle Boats
- Horse Stables/Trail Rides
- Swimming Pool, Tennis
- Miniature Golf
- Set on 150 rolling wooded acres

Call for reservations: 1/800/225/2422

<u>**Travel Agents:**</u> *We Gladly Pay You Commissions!*

Blackwood Family

Thunderbird Theatre, West Highway 76, Branson

Features country music, gospel, variety and comedy of the Blackwood Family, who have won nine Grammy Awards and sold 40 million albums. Shows run from April to December. For further information, telephone (417) 336 2542.

Bobby Vinton Blue Velvet Theatre

2701 West Highway 76, Branson

Bobby Vinton and the Glenn Miller Orchestra perform their chart-topping hits from April to mid-December. For further information, telephone (417) 334 2500 *or* 1-800 872 6229 (toll free).

The Boxcar Willie Theater

3454 West Highway 76, Branson

Boxcar Willie & the Texas Trainmen perform a family-oriented variety show, featuring traditional country music from April to December. A museum highlights the star's railroad and airplane collection. There is a motel behind the theater where visitors may stay. For further information, telephone (417) 334 8696.

Braschler Music Show

Off Hwy. 76, Branson

This complete variety show features country, comedy, instrumentals and gospel from April to December. For further information, telephone (417) 334 4363.

Buck Trent Breakfast Show

Hwy. 165, Branson

Features banjo picker and comedian Buck Trent with fiddlin' Moore Brothers and Cindi Barr. Season runs from March to December. For further information, telephone (417) 334 5428.

Champagne Theatre

1984 Highway 165, 5km (3 miles) south of Highway 76, Branson

Legendary Lawrence Welk's Champagne sounds and bubbles continue on in Branson, featuring the Lennon Sisters, Jo Ann Castle and famous 20-piece orchestra, plus a rotating cast of original Welk stars. Shows run from April to December. For further information, telephone 1-800 505 WELK (9355; toll free) *or* (417) 337 7469.

Charley Pride Theatre

755 Gretna Road, Branson

This 2000-seat theatre features country music legends Charley Pride and Don Williams from April to December. For further information, telephone (417) 336 2292.

Cristy Lane Theatre

West Highway 76, Branson

Featuring a variety of entertainment, including country favourites, old-time classics and inspirational music, the season runs from February to December. For further information, telephone (417) 335 5111.

The Dino Christmas Extravaganza

Branson

Starring Dino Kartsonakis in an elaborate musical spectacular, 'Magical Journey of Christmas.' Shows run from November to December. There is also a Piano Spectacular from September to November, two shows a day, Monday to Saturday. For further information, telephone (417) 335 6866.

Echo Hollow Theater

Branson/Silver Dollar City

Outstanding presentation of traditional and modern music and comedy. For further information, telephone (417) 338 2611.

Glen Campbell Goodtime Theatre

Highways 65 & 248, Branson

The good times roll in the legendary musician's all-new variety show. Enjoy Glen's hits and new production featuring Debby Campbell, ventriloquist Jim Barber and more. Show time is April to October. For further information, telephone (417) 336 1220 *or* 337 5900.

The Grand Palace

2700 76 Country Boulevard, Branson

Branson's largest (4000-seat) and most elaborate theatre features superstars such as Barbara Mandrell and co-owner Kenny Rogers from March to the end of December. For further information, telephone 1-800 5PALACE (toll free) *or* (417) 336 7001.

The Jim Owen Morning Show

Highway 165, Branson

Start your morning with music, comedy and fun! Jim was twice 'Entertainer of the Year' in Las Vegas, wrote 'Louisiana Woman, Mississippi Man', and portrayed Hank Williams Sr. in two movies. Shows run from April to December. For further information, telephone 1-800 844 1687 (toll free) *or* (417) 335 2764.

Jim Stafford Theatre

W. Highway, Branson

See comic genius behind 'Spiders and Snakes', 'Swamp Witch', 'Cow Patti' and more. For reservations, telephone (417) 335 8080 *or* 335 2639.

Moe Bandy's Americana Theatre

West Highway 76, Branson

Moe reaches into the soul of country music in a show that pleases the whole family from Monday to Saturday, two shows daily, April to December. Mornings feature Bob Eubanks $25,000 TV Game Show Spectacular from April to November. For further information, telephone (417) 335 8176.

Osmond Family Theater

Hwy. 76 & Rt. 165, Branson

This 1277-seat theater is the setting for fast-paced, high-energy family entertainment featuring the Osmond Brothers, from March 3 to December 17. For further information, telephone (417) 336 6100.

Ozark Jubilee Theatre

3115 West Highway 76, Branson

An award-winning Jubilee Show with some of Branson's top talent. Country, pop, gospel, 40s & 50s and patriotic music combine with a dazzling light show. For further information, telephone (417) 334 6400.

Presleys' Jubilee

3115 W Hwy. 76, Branson

The original live country music and comedy stage show on 76 Country Boulevard runs from February to December. For further information, telephone (417) 334 4874.

Pump Boys and Dinettes

Highways 165 & 76, Branson

Branson's only full-service dinner theatre stars four gas-station jockeys and two big-hearted waitresses serving up delightful tunes and good times. Shows run year round, with lunch-time shows from Wednesday to Saturday, April to December. For further information, telephone 1-800 743 2386 (toll free) *or* (417) 336 4319.

The Shoji Tabuchi Show

Shepherd of the Hills Expressway, Branson

Country and a variety of music for all ages, featuring the violin

artistry of Shoji Tabuchi. For further information, telephone (417) 334 7469 *or* 334 3734.

The Thunderbird Theatre

2215 West Highway 76, Branson
The Thunderbird Band plays 50s and 60s rock & roll, six nights a week, from April to December. For further information, telephone (417) 336 2542.

Will Rogers Follies

Hwys. 65 & 248, Branson
Show celebrating the life story of Will Rogers with an extravangza of dance, song, laughter and romance. For further information, telephone (417) 336 1333 *or* 335 8512.

OTHER EXCITING ATTRACTIONS

For those seeking excitement outside the music venues, Branson has a number of different types of attractions on offer. Here are just some of the pastimes to be enjoyed by adults and children alike:

Mutton Hollow Entertainment Park and Craft Village

W. Hwy. 76, Branson
Old-time music shows, working craftsmen, beautiful landscapes, and delicious dining can be found at turn-of-the-century Ozark Mountain theme park from April to December. For further information, telephone (417) 334 4947.

Shepherd of the Hills Outdoor Theatre

West Highway 76
This theme park and night-time drama in the amphitheater runs from April to late October. Christmas activities exist from November to December. For further information, telephone (417) 334 4191.

Waltzing Waters

West Highway 76, Branson
An indoor water spectacular and country music show. For further information, telephone (417) 334 4144.

UNUSUAL WAYS TO TRAVEL AROUND BRANSON

There are a variety of ways to view the Branson area, from coasting along its limpid lakes to soaring above its skylines. Here are some of the angles visitors have to choose from:

Lake Queen

On Lake Taneycomo, downtown Branson
The lake's largest ship and only sternwheeler cruises from April to mid-December. For further information, telephone (417) 334 3015.

Sailing Charters of the Americas

Table Rock State Park, Marina Road, Branson
The only sailboat charters and rentals available in the State also offers certified instruction. Facilities are available from mid-April to mid-October. For further information, telephone (417) 337 8399.

Sammy Lane Pirate Cruise Water Pageant

Foot of Main Street Branson
A scenic 24km (15-mile) folklore cruise featuring a live pirate attack; available from late-April to October. For further information, telephone (417) 334 3015.

Table Rock Helicopters Inc

3309 West Highway 76, Branson
Helicopter tours of Table Rock Lake and Dam areas are available from March to December. For further information, telephone (417) 334 6102.

WAKE UP TO MISSOURI

THIS IS THE LAST PAGE

New Jersey

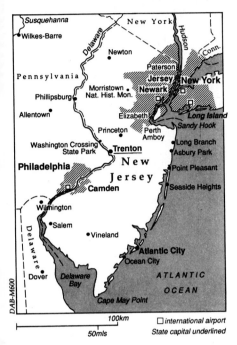

Including **Newark,** gateway to the North Atlantic States of New Jersey, New York and Maryland and the northeastern State of Pennsylvania.

New Jersey Division of Travel & Tourism
CN 826, 20 West State Street, Trenton, NJ 08625-0826
Tel: (609) 292 2470 or (1 800) JERSEY7 (toll free). Fax: (609) 633 7418.
Atlantic City Convention & Visitors Bureau
2314 Pacific Avenue, Atlantic City, NJ 08401
Tel: (609) 348 7100. Fax: (609) 345 2200.
Greater Wildwood Division of Tourist Information
Scheloenger Avenue, On the Boardwalk, Wildwood, NJ 08260
Tel: (609) 522 1408. Fax: (609) 729 2234.

TIME: GMT - 5. *Daylight Saving Time* is observed.
THE STATE: New Jersey, one of the Mid-Atlantic States, is bordered by the Atlantic Ocean to the east and the Delaware River to the west. Small in size, the State features hundreds of miles of beautiful beaches, rolling countryside and natural parkland set amidst mountains, lakes and forests. Atlantic City, one of the nation's oldest resorts, boasts luxury casino hotels and world-class entertainment by the sea. The famous Meadowlands Sports Complex is home to professional sports teams and championship horseracing. Historic towns, amusement parks and bargain shopping outlets are also scattered throughout New Jersey.

TRAVEL

AIR: Approximate flight times: See flight times from New York, as they are almost exactly the same.
International airports: *Newark International Airport (EWR)* is 27km (16 miles) southwest of midtown Manhattan. The airport has extensive facilities, including banks, a barber, shops and duty-free shops, restaurants, bars and coffee shops, a nursery and car hire (*Avis, Budget, Hertz* and *National*). There is a free 24-hour bus service to other terminals and a parking lot. Bus service is available to Newark city centre and nearby New Jersey destinations.
Transportation to New York City: *New Jersey Transit* airlink bus no. 302 departs every 20-30 minutes 0605-0140 weekdays and Sunday, and every 30 minutes 0625-0155 Saturday, and connects at Newark's Penn Station to the PATH Rapid Transit system, stopping at the World Trade Center, Christopher Street, 9th Street, 14th Street, 23rd Street and 33rd Street in Manhattan (travel time to World Trade Center – 45 minutes; to 33rd Street – 1 hour). The cost is US$4 for the bus, and US$1 for the PATH fare per person. *New Jersey Transit* express bus

no. 300 runs from the airport to the Port Authority Bus terminal at 42nd Street and 8th Avenue every 15-30 minutes 24 hours a day (travel time – 30 minutes). The cost is US$7 per person. For further information, contact *New Jersey Transit Information Center* on (201) 762 5100. *Olympia Trails* airport express bus service runs from Newark Airport to One World Trade Center in downtown Manhattan (NYC) every 30 minutes 0645-2045 weekdays and 0715-2045 weekends (travel time – 20/40 minutes). It also runs another airport express bus stopping at Grand Central Station (41st Street and Park Avenue) and Penn Station (34th Street and 8th Avenue) every 20-30 minutes between 0615 and 2400 daily (travel time – 30/60 minutes). Fares on both *Olympia Trails* buses are US$7 per person. For further information, contact *Olympia Trails* on (212) 964 6233. *Gray Line Air Shuttle* (tel: (212) 315 3006) offers a shared minibus from the airport to anywhere from 23rd-63rd Street according to passenger demand 0800-2300 at US$17 per person (travel time – 55 minutes). A 24-hour taxi service is available to downtown and mid-Manhattan (the west side between Battery Park and 72nd Street) and fares range from US$30-31, plus tolls. For destinations on the east side of Manhattan above 14th Street, taxi drivers charge an additional US$2. There is a charge of US$1 for each piece of luggage over 24 inches in length. Limousine service is on a per person flat rate.
Transportation to New Jersey destinations: Ground Transportation Centers are located on the lower levels of Terminals A, B and C. Information on buses, minibuses, sedans, limousines and private cars is available here, including schedules and fares. *New Jersey Transit* airlink bus no. 302 departs regularly to Newark's Penn Station, the downtown business district and Broad Street Station. The fare is US$4. *New Jersey Transit* also provides a scheduled service to other New Jersey destinations stopping at Fort Dix, McGuire Air Force Base and destinations in Elizabeth, Essex, Union, Somerset and Hunterdon counties. Fares range from US$1.15-5.30. *Princeton Airporter* runs a scheduled bus service to Middlesex and Mercer counties. Fares are from US$14-18. For further information, contact *Princeton Airporter* on (609) 587 6600. *Trans-Bridge Lines* operate a scheduled coach service to Hunterdon County. Fares range from US$9.20-11.30. For further information, contact *Trans-Bridge Lines* on (215) 868 6001. Scheduled limousines are available to Fort Monmouth, Middlesex, Morris, Monmouth and Union counties. Fares range from US$13-20. For further information, contact *Airport Limousine Express* on (201) 621 7300. A 24-hour taxi service is available at taxi stands which are located on the lower (arrivals) level at Terminals A, B and C. Flat rates apply to all destinations and typical fares are posted at the taxi stands. During peak hours, stands are attended by taxi dispatchers to assist passengers. Fares to the city of Newark are determined by zone. From Terminals A, B and C to points in Newark, the taxi fare will range from US$10-14. Special 'share-and-save' group rates are available 0800-2400. Travelling to the airport from the city of Newark, the fare is the amount shown on the meter.
Transportation to other destinations: Limousine, bus and rail services (via *Airlink* connection) are also available to Pennsylvania, Connecticut and upstate New York.
Inter-Airport transfers: *Princeton Airporter* runs a scheduled bus service from Newark Airport to JFK Airport. Fare is US$19. There is also an inter-airport helicopter service to JFK. From Port Authority Bus Terminal, connections are available to LaGuardia and JFK airports every 30 minutes from 0715-2215 via *Carey Transportation Coaches*. Fares are US$8.50 to LaGuardia and US$11 to JFK. For further information, contact *Carey Transportation Coaches* on (718) 632 0500. Limousine services are also available from Newark to JFK and LaGuardia. A flat taxi fare from Newark to JFK is US$53.50 plus tolls and to LaGuardia, the fare is US$44.50 plus tolls.
SEA: *Circle Line Tours* operates a year-round ferry service to the Statue of Liberty and Ellis Island from Liberty State Park in Jersey City. *Hoboken Ferry Service, TNT Hydrolines* and *Port Imperial Ferry* operate services to and from New York City. *Cape May-Lewes Ferry* operates a service to and from Cape May to the State of Delaware.
RAIL: Penn Station in Newark serves both *Amtrak* (nationwide) and *New Jersey Transit.*
ROAD: Travel from New Jersey to New York City is across the George Washington Bridge or through the Lincoln and Holland Tunnels. Bridges connecting to Philadelphia, Pennsylvania are the Walt Whitman Bridge and the Benjamin Franklin Bridge. The Delaware Memorial Bridge connects New Jersey with Delaware. The New Jersey Turnpike runs north and south through the State, while the Garden State Parkway takes travellers to the shore points. **Bus:** Penn Station

(McCarter Highway/Market Street, Newark) handles long-distance and regional buses.
Approximate driving times: From Newark to *Philadelphia* is 1 hour 30 minutes, to *Hartford* is 2 hours 30 minutes, to *Albany* is 3 hours 30 minutes, to *Boston* is 4 hours 30 minutes, to *Baltimore* is 3 hours 30 minutes, to *Washington DC* is 4 hours 30 minutes, to *Portland* (Maine) is 6 hours 30 minutes, to *Montréal* is 7 hours 30 minutes, to *Buffalo* is 7 hours, to *Pittsburgh* is 6 hours, to *Toronto* is 8 hours, to *Cleveland* is 9 hours, to *Indianapolis* is 14 hours, to *Chicago* is 15 hours, to *Miami* is 26 hours 30 minutes, to *Dallas* is 32 hours 30 minutes, to *Los Angeles* is 57 hours, to *San Francisco* is 60 hours and to *Seattle* is 60 hours.
All times are based on non-stop driving at or below the applicable speed limits.
Approximate *Greyhound* journey times: From New Jersey (tel: (1 800) 231 2222; toll free) to *Philadelphia* is 1 hour 40 minutes, to *Albany* is 3 hours, to *Washington DC* is 4 hours 40 minutes, to *Boston* is 4 hours 45 minutes, to *Montréal* is 8 hours 30 minutes, to *Buffalo* is 9 hours, to *Pittsburgh* is 9 hours and to *Cleveland* is 9 hours 30 minutes.

RESORTS & EXCURSIONS

NEWARK: Newark is the third oldest of the major US cities and the largest in New Jersey. It is a hubbub of transportation connections, arts and culture, and fast city life.
Sightseeing: The *'New' Newark Museum* is considered one of the nation's most comprehensive fine arts museums, with 66 galleries of ancient and modern art, a planetarium and a mini-zoo. *Branch Brook Park* is famous for having more cherry blossoms than Washington DC in the springtime, and plays host to an annual cherry blossom festival.
Excursions: Just east of Newark lies the *Statue of Liberty* and *Ellis Island.* The *Circle Line* ferry operates services to these important historic sites from *Liberty State Park* in **Jersey City.** North of Newark is *Palisades Interstate Park,* comprising 2500 acres of scenic roads, stunning views, picnic areas, an historic museum and nature sanctuary, and hiking and skiing trails, plus an enormous funpark that is a terrific treat for kids. For sports enthusiasts, the *Meadowlands Sports Complex,* in **East Rutherford,** northwest of Newark, is home to professional football, basketball and ice hockey teams, as well as a world-class racetrack.
ATLANTIC CITY: Known as the 'Queen of Resorts', it features 12 casino hotels, world-class entertainment, championship sporting events, gourmet restaurants, shops, beautiful beaches and the world's first boardwalk – it is one of the top tourist destinations in the USA.
Sightseeing: The *Atlantic City Boardwalk* is an attraction in itself, lined with dazzling casinos, amusement rides, games and shops on one side and by 10km (6 miles) of sand beach and surf on the other. The notorious *Trump Plaza Hotel and Trump Taj Mahal Casino* (one of the largest in the world) is to be found here (the luxurious folly of millionaire Donald Trump) and *Convention Hall,* an Art Deco architectural extravaganza which houses the world's largest pipe organ. The *Atlantic City Art Center and Historic Museum* traces the city's history as a 150-year-old seaside resort and entertainment centre, including photos and memorabilia from the Miss America Pageant which takes place here every year. *The Shoppes* on Ocean One is a modern shopping mall situated on a boardwalk pier shaped like an ocean liner.
Excursions: The Greater Atlantic City region also has a quieter side. The *Towne of Historic Smithville* is an authentic 18th-century shopping village well worth a visit, while nearby, coastal wildlife is preserved at the *Edwin B Forsythe National Wildlife Refuge,* due north of Atlantic City in **Brigantine** where the *Sea Life Museum* can also be found, open 1200-1600 Saturday and Sunday, free of charge. The region is also home to the *Renault Winery and Glass Museum* in **Egg Harbor,** one of the oldest vineyards in the USA.
TRENTON: Capital of New Jersey (and once the capital of the USA in 1794), it is also the heart of the Delaware River region. Located in the eastern heart of New Jersey, the region is steeped in history and natural beauty. Visitors to Trenton, Princeton (the home of Princeton University) and **Washington Crossing State Park** will learn about New Jersey's important role in the birth of the USA. Arts and culture can be experienced at the many museums and theatres in the region.
Sightseeing: *Old Barracks Museum* on Barracks Street is the site of the famous day-after-Christmas battle during the Revolutionary War and has restored soldiers' quarters, 18th-century period rooms and antiques. *William Trent House; State House,* the second-oldest State hall in the USA; and *New Jersey State Planetarium and Museum,* which examines New Jersey history back to 500BC, are also well worth visiting.

Excursions: Princeton, 18km (11 miles) north of Trenton, is the home of the world-renowned *Princeton University,* an old and prestigious US university which sits proudly in this charming educational and historic town. The town offers excellent art exhibitions and music, as well as dance and theatre performances. Other attractions include *Einstein's House* (when he was a Princeton University lecturer), *Princeton University Art Museum, Bainbridge House, Clarke House* on the *Princeton Battlefield,* and *Drumthwacket,* a stately Greek Revival Southern-style mansion which is now the Governor's official residence. **Camden,** a town 43km (27 miles) south of Trenton in the Delaware River region, has *Walt Whitman's House,* the *Campbell Soup Museum* and the *New Jersey Aquarium.* Historic **Salem,** 53km (33 miles) south of Camden on Route 45, has 60 18th-century buildings along *Market Street,* museums, exhibits and 500-year-old *Salem Oak* near the court house. Camping, canoeing, swimming, fishing, horseriding and hiking can be enjoyed in a venture out to the *Pine Barrens,* a national preserve that ranks as the largest wilderness area east of the Mississippi River.

SHORE REGION: Encompassing a portion of New Jersey's 203km (127 miles) of coastline, the Shore Region is ideal for vacations and excursions, boasting white sandy beaches, rolling farmland and historic sites.

Sightseeing: Dotting the shore are exciting towns like **Seaside Heights** and **Point Pleasant,** which are home to boardwalk amusement rides and games. Quieter towns like **Spring Lake** and **Ocean Grove** offer quaint bed & breakfast inns. **Asbury Park,** home of rock star Bruce Springsteen, is a somewhat dilapidated seaside boardwalk amusement town, but with a vibrant nightlife that will appeal to certain thrill-seeking nightowls. Exciting amusement rides and the world's largest safari park are located at *Six Flags Great Adventure* in **Jackson Township,** where a full day should be set aside for fun and games. *Allaire State Park* in **Farmingdale** is an 18th-century restored bog-iron mining village offering period shops, bakeries, churches, a blacksmith, a ride on the *Pinecreek Railroad train,* a nature centre, museum and picnic area, along with craft/antique shows and square-dancing on weekends.

Excursions: Cruises can be taken aboard the *River Belle* or *River Queen,* large stern-wheelers that ply the waters off *Point Pleasant Beach,* where deep-sea fishing boats are also available. Party cruises can be taken aboard the *Sandy Rock Lady,* an authentic paddle-wheel steamer which runs from the Atlantic highlands harbour and offers a scenic ride along the historic Shrewsbury River. Fishing is also good in the *Manasquan Inlet.*

SKYLANDS REGION: Some of the most beautiful and unspoiled land in the northeastern USA is found in the Skylands Region of northwestern New Jersey. It is a perfect vacation area for all seasons: during the winter, ski resorts such as Vernon Valley/Great Gorge provide challenging skiing for all skill levels; and during the summer, camping, hiking and watersports can be enjoyed at *Action Park,* one of the largest self-participating theme parks in the world. Numerous State and National Parks offer camping and hiking opportunities; these include the *Delaware Water Gap National Recreation Area.* Revolutionary War historic sites, wineries, museums, antique stores and bed & breakfast inns, scattered throughout the region, are available in all seasons.

Sightseeing: The *Clinton Historical Museum* and *Spruce Run Reservoir* in **Clinton** have quaint shops and charming restaurants in an idyllic setting. *Waterloo Village* in **Stanhope** is a restored 18th-century village of colonial craftshops and homes, and hosts a summer concert series of jazz and bluegrass festivals. *Morristown National Historic Park* in **Morristown** was the site of George Washington's army winter encampments and the *Ford Mansion,* now a museum. Battle re-enactments take place throughout the year. Special treats for the children include *Land of Make Believe* in **Hope,** 30 acres of childhood fantasies – the largest childrens' amusement park in New Jersey, and *Fairy Tale Forest* in **Oak Ridge,** an enchanted forest with life-size animated characters depicting famous fairytales.

Excursions: Hiking, canoeing, fishing and river rafting on the *Delaware River* can be organised during the summer and ice-skating, tobogganing, snowmobiling, skiing and ice fishing are available during the winter. State Parks ideal for winter sports include *Jenny Jump, Swartswood, Wawayanda, Worthington, Allmuchy, Spruce Run* and *Voorhees.*

SOUTHERN SHORE REGION: Located along the southeastern tip of New Jersey on the Atlantic Ocean is a region for those who enjoy seaside culture and heritage, boardwalk amusements, fishing and birdwatching.

Sightseeing: The **Wildwoods** and **Ocean City** boardwalks buzz with excitement while **Stone Harbor** and **Avalon** are quieter retreats. **Cape May,** a National Historic Landmark, is a popular Victorian seaside town which is famous for its many bed & breakfast inns, trolley tours and the superb *Cape May County Zoo,* one of the top zoos in the world. *Wheaton Village* in **Millville** is the world's largest museum of American glass with a 7000-item collection ranging from paperweights to Tiffany masterpieces. *Cold Spring Village* in **Cold Spring** is a recreation of an old farm village, with period shops and restaurants, that displays the life and crafts of yore. Stroll through 25 different gardens, teeming with greenery and fishponds, at *Leaming's Run Gardens and Colonial Farm* in **Swainton.**

Note: For information on attractions in neighbouring States, see above under *States A-Z.*

SOCIAL PROFILE

FOOD & DRINK: New Jersey offers everything from gourmet cuisine to 'home-cooking' country food, from restaurants to diners. In addition to the staple US fare of steaks, seafood and hamburgers, cuisines from around the world can be found throughout New Jersey.

THEATRES & CONCERTS: There are numerous theatres scattered throughout New Jersey that offer productions ranging from Shakespeare to contemporary works. Concerts and special performances by the renowned *New Jersey Symphony Orchestra* and famous entertainers are held throughout the year at a variety of venues including the *Brendan Byrne Arena* at the *Meadowlands Sports Complex, Atlantic City Casino Showrooms* and the *Garden State Arts Center* in Holmdel. The *Paper Mill Playhouse,* the official State theatre of New Jersey, shows musicals and plays year round, as does the *George Street Playhouse* in New Brunswick.

NIGHTLIFE: The nightclubs and casinos of Atlantic City are open until the small hours and afford a perfect haven for gamblers. Ocean City and some of the other oceanfront towns have many clubs and entertainment centres that are open late hours and the general atmosphere along the boardwalks is lively far into the evenings.

SHOPPING: Shopping in New Jersey appeals to all tastes and budgets. Upscale malls feature the famous department stores of Macy's, Bloomingdales and Saks Fifth Avenue. Terrific bargains on brand-name merchandise can be found at the Secaucus Outlet Center in Secaucus. Similarly Liberty Village and Turntable Junction outlet centres in Flemington offer equally attractive deals. Antique stores fill New Jersey's small towns while outdoor flea markets offer an eclectic array of jewellery, clothing, housewares, furniture and more. There is no sales tax on clothing in New Jersey.

SPECIAL EVENTS: There are literally dozens of festivals and events that are celebrated throughout the State each year. The following is a list of some of the major events in New Jersey in 1995.

Apr 21-23 '95 *14th Annual Tulip Festial,* Cape May. **May 14-Jun 24** *Cape May Music Festival,* Cape May. **May 27-29** *Annual Spring Juried,* Wastampton Township; *American Indian Arts Festival,* Rankokus Indian Reservation. **Jun 3-4** *Heritage Days,* Trenton Downtown. **Jun 10-11** *New Jersey Seafood Festival,* Beimar. **Jun 22-Jul 9** *Meadowlands Fair,* East Rutherford. **Jul 14-16** *Return to Beaver Creek Pow Wow,* Belvidere. **Jul 20-26** *St Anne's Italian Street Festival,* Hoboken. **Aug 5-6** *Harborfest '95 Music and Arts Festival,* Atlantic City; *World Championship Ocean Marathon Swim,* Historic Gardner's Basin. **Sep 16-17** *Garden State WIne Growers Fall Wine Festival,* Belvidere. **Oct 8** *Chowderfest,* Beach Haven.

CLIMATE

See the *New York* gateway section immediately following for information on the climate in the New Jersey region.

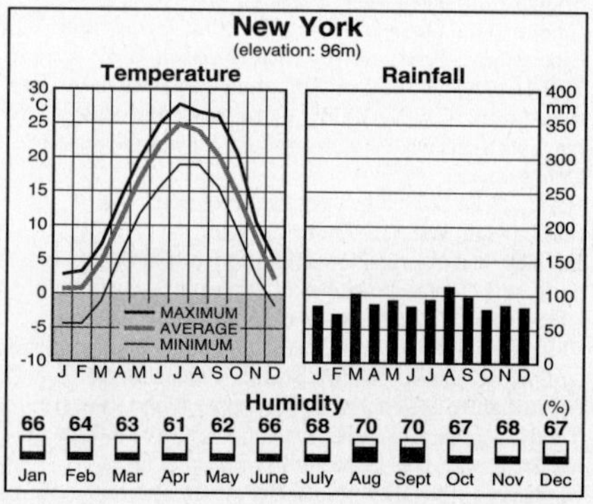
New York
(elevation: 96m)
Temperature
Rainfall
°C
mm
MAXIMUM
AVERAGE
MINIMUM
J F M A M J J A S O N D
Humidity
(%)
66 64 63 61 62 66 68 70 70 67 68 67
Jan Feb Mar Apr May June July Aug Sept Oct Nov Dec

New York

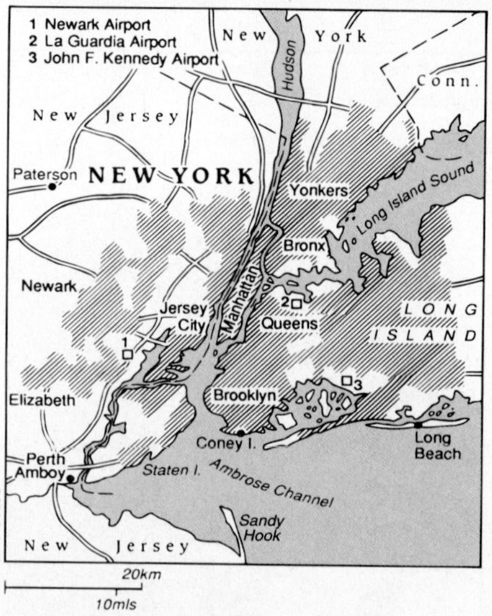
1 Newark Airport
2 La Guardia Airport
3 John F. Kennedy Airport
New York
Conn.
New Jersey
Hudson
Paterson
NEW YORK
Yonkers
Long Island Sound
Bronx
Newark
Jersey City
Manhattan
Queens
LONG ISLAND
Elizabeth
Brooklyn
Coney I.
Long Beach
Perth Amboy
Staten I.
Ambrose Channel
Sandy Hook
New Jersey
DAB-M405
20km
10mls

Including **New York City,** gateway to the States of the Eastern (Atlantic) Seaboard, George Washington Country and the Great Lakes.

New York State Division of Tourism
51st Floor, 1515 Broadway, New York, NY 10036
Tel: (212) 827 6251 or (1 800) CALLNYS (toll free). Fax: (212) 827 6237.

New York Convention & Visitors Bureau
Visitors Center, Two Columbus Circle, New York, NY 10019
Tel: (212) 397 8222. Fax: (212) 245 5943.

Hotel Association of New York City
36th Floor, 437 Madison Avenue, New York, NY 10022-7398
Tel: (212) 754 6700. Fax: (212) 754 0243.

Travellers Aid Society
2nd Floor, North Wing, Port Authority Bus Terminal, 625 8th Avenue, New York, NY 10018
Tel: (212) 944 0013. Fax: (212) 502 2579.
(Multilingual staff offer help to travellers and foreign visitors, including help with legal, medical or other problems; facilities also at JFK airport.)

Albany County Convention & Visitors Bureau
52 South Pearl Street, Albany, NY 12207
Tel: (518) 434 1217. Fax: (518) 434 0887.

Niagara Falls Convention & Visitors Bureau
310 Fourth Street, Niagara Falls, NY 14303
Tel: (716) 285 2400. Fax: (716) 285 0809.

New York State Division of Tourism
9 Gower Street, London WC1E 6HA
Tel: (0171) 916 4112. Fax: (0171) 916 4114. Opening hours: 0900-1730 Monday to Friday.

TIME: GMT - 5. *Daylight Saving Time* is observed.

THE STATE: New York State is a vast expanse of land that stretches from the Atlantic coast to Canada and the Great Lakes. Its capital, Albany, offers everything from stately homes to the US$2-billion Rockefeller Empire State Plaza, as well as access to scenic villages, underground waterfalls and national parkland in the surrounding mountains. Long Island, a 241km (150-mile) glacial moraine, extends into the Atlantic, a mixture of suburbia and woodland. The Hudson Valley makes a deep north–south trench on the east. To the west, the Finger Lakes, rolling hills and parklands lead towards Niagara Falls. The Catskill Mountains to the northeast and, upstate, the Adirondack Mountains offer large areas of rivers, lakes and wooded slopes. The 1000 Islands, a myriad of outcrops in Lake Ontario, are also within easy reach. The extraordinary metropolis of New York City has the largest population of any city in the USA.

TRAVEL

AIR: Approximate flight times: From New York to *Anchorage* is 8 hours 30 minutes, to *Atlanta* is 2 hours 40 minutes, to *Baltimore* is 1 hour 20 minutes, to *Barbados* is 4 hours 40 minutes, to *Bermuda* is 2 hours, to *Boston* is 1 hour 10 minutes, to *Buenos Aires* is 10 hours 15 minutes, to *Buffalo* is 1 hour 50 minutes, to *Caracas* is 4 hours 55 minutes, to *Chicago* is 2 hours 50 minutes, to *Cincinnati* is

2 hours 10 minutes, to *Cleveland* is 1 hour 45 minutes, to *Dallas/Fort Worth* is 4 hours, to *Detroit* is 2 hours, to *Frankfurt/M* is 7 hours 30 minutes, to *Hartford* is 1 hour, to *Honolulu* is 12 hours, to *Houston* is 4 hours, to *London* is 6 hours 50 minutes (3 hours 50 minutes by Concorde), to *Los Angeles* is 6 hours, to *Mexico City* is 5 hours 10 minutes, to *Miami* is 3 hours 10 minutes, to *Minneapolis/St Paul* is 3 hours 10 minutes, to *Montréal* is 1 hour 25 minutes, to *Moscow* is 8 hours 50 minutes, to *Nassau* is 3 hours, to *New Orleans* is 3 hours 25 minutes, to *Norfolk* is 1 hour 30 minutes, to *Orlando* is 2 hours 50 minutes, to *Philadelphia* is 50 minutes, to *Pittsburgh* is 1 hour 30 minutes, to *Providence* is 1 hour, to *Rio de Janeiro* is 9 hours 15 minutes, to *Rome* is 8 hours 10 minutes, to *St Croix* is 4 hours, to *St Maarten* is 3 hours 50 minutes, to *St Thomas* is 3 hours 50 minutes, to *Santo Domingo* is 3 hours 50 minutes, to *San Francisco* is 6 hours 10 minutes, to *San Juan* is 3 hours 50 minutes, to *Shannon* is 6 hours 5 minutes, to *Singapore* is 21 hours 55 minutes, to *Sydney* is 26 hours, to *Tampa* is 3 hours, to *Tel Aviv* is 12 hours 30 minutes, to *Toronto* is 1 hour 30 minutes and to *Washington DC* is 1 hour 10 minutes.

International airports: *John F Kennedy (JFK)* and *LaGuardia (LGA).* Both airports handle domestic and international flights, but most international flights into New York arrive at *JFK.* Flights from or via London *Heathrow (LHR)* to New York land at *JKF,* and flights from London *Gatwick (LGW)* land at *JFK* and *EWR* in Newark. Some transfer connections via continental Europe land at *LGA,* but the airport's primary function is to handle internal USA flights.

Travellers from Europe arriving at *JFK* will generally make their onward connection from there. Connections to smaller locations, and connections for travellers arriving at *EWR, may* have to be made by transferring to *LGA.* For transfer details, see below under *Inter-Airport transfers.*

John F Kennedy International (JFK): 24km (15 miles) southeast of central Manhattan. For transportation into the city, *JFK Express,* an efficient 24-hour bus/underground route runs every 10 minutes 0500-2400 and every 30 minutes at other times; the bus connects to the NYC subway at Howard Beach Station on the 'A' train from where there are links to all areas of the city; return is from midtown or downtown Manhattan (travel time – 60/75 minutes). The cost of the bus is free and the subway fare is US$1.25. The Q3 bus/underground route connects to the NYC subway 'F' or 'R' trains with links to Manhattan and Brooklyn. The cost of the bus is US$1.25 (exact fare) and then another US$1.25 for the subway. For further information on either *JFK Express* or *Q3* bus/subway routes, telephone (718) 330 1234. The *Q10* bus/underground route connects to subway stations at Lefferts Boulevard (for 'A' subway to Brooklyn, Lower and West Side Manhattan) and at Kew Gardens-Union Turnpike (for 'E' and 'F' subways to Queens and mid-Manhattan). Bus fare is US$1.25 (exact fare) and then US$1.25 for the subway. For further information, contact *Green Bus Lines* on (718) 995 4700. Bus services from JFK are provided by *Carey Transportation Coaches.* Departures are every 30 minutes 0600-2400, to six midtown Manhattan stops: 125 Park Avenue (opposite Grand Central Station at 41st-42nd Streets), Port Authority Bus Terminal (42nd Street between 8th-9th Avenues), New York Hilton Hotel (53rd Street and 6th Avenue), Sheraton Manhattan Hotel (7th Avenue between 51st-52nd Streets), Marriott Marquis Hotel (Broadway between 45th-46th Streets) and the Holiday Inn Crowne Plaza (48th Street at Broadway). There are also buses from Grand Central Station to *JFK* 0500-0100 as well as from Port Authority Bus Terminal to *JFK* 0715-2215 and from the hotels 0545-2200. The cost is US$11-12.50 per person

one-way (travel time – 40/60 minutes). For further information, contact *Carey Transportation Coaches* on (718) 632 0500. *Gray Line Air Shuttle* (tel: (212) 315 3006) has a service available on demand 0700-2300 for a shared minibus to anywhere from 23rd-63rd Street in Manhattan at US$16 per person (travel time – 40/60 minutes). *New York Helicopters* offers a service throughout the day from Gate 32 Terminal to East 34th Street in midtown Manhattan for US$65 per person (travel time – 10 minutes). Call *New York Helicopters* on (1 800) 645 3494 (toll free) for complete schedule information and reservations. Taxis are expensive (approximately US$28 into Manhattan, plus tolls) and travellers are advised not to travel with a taxi driver who approaches them first. Always find out the standard rate since unscrupulous drivers may overcharge. A 50-cent surcharge is in effect 2000-0600 in all yellow taxis.

Transportation to other destinations: Limousine services are available to some cities in Connecticut, Long Island and upstate New York. Coach services are available to New Jersey and Pennsylvania.

LaGuardia (LGA): 13km (8 miles) east of Manhattan, in the borough of Queens. For transportation into the city, bus services are provided by *Carey Transportation Coaches.* These depart every 30 minutes 0645-2400, to six midtown Manhattan stops: Grand Central Station, Port Authority Bus Terminal, New York Hilton Hotel, Marriott Manhattan Hotel and the Holiday Inn Crowne Plaza. There are also buses from Grand Central Station to LaGuardia 0600-2400 as well as from Port Authority Bus Terminal to LaGuardia 0715-2315 and from the hotels 0545-2200. The cost is US$8.50-10 per person one-way (travel time – 30 minutes). *Gray Line Air Shuttle* offers a service on demand 0700-2300 from the airport to anywhere between 23rd-63rd Streets for US$12 per person (travel time – 30/45 minutes). There is also a ferry service, the *Delta Water Shuttle,* which departs from the Marine Air Terminal to 34th Street on the East River or to Pier 11 on Wall Street in downtown Manhattan for US$25 per person one-way or US$45 return (travel time – 30/45 minutes). For ferry schedules, telephone (1 800) 221 1212 (toll free). Yellow taxis are readily available from designated taxi stands. Fares to midtown Manhattan average at US$23 from LaGuardia.

Transportation to other destinations: Limousine, bus and rail services (via *Airlink* connection) are also available to Pennsylvania, Connecticut and upstate New York.
Inter-Airport transfers: Regular helicopter transfers are available on *New York Helicopter (HD)* between New York airports and to Newark Airport Terminal C. *Carey Transportation Coaches* offer links between *JFK* and *LaGuardia,* as well as Newark. Coaches to *LGA* airport depart every 30 minutes 0730-2130. A limousine service is available to Newark Airport. Taxis are also available.
SEA: The *Staten Island Ferry* operates from Battery Park (downtown) past the Statue of Liberty and Ellis Island to Staten Island. *Circle Line Tours* operate a 3-hour guided tour around Manhattan Island (departing from Pier 83, West 43rd Street), plus tours to the Statue of Liberty. Longer river tours run from New York City to Poughkeepsie. New York is a major international port.
RAIL: Pennsylvania Station (34th Street/6th Avenue) serves both the *Long Island Railroad* (Long Island and New Jersey) and *Amtrak* (nationwide). Grand Central Station (42nd Street/Park Avenue) is the terminus for services to upstate New York *(Metro North)* and Connecticut. There are two daily trains to Montréal and one to Toronto.
Approximate *Amtrak* journey times: From New York on the 'Adirondack' to *Montréal* is 14 hours 30 minutes; on the 'Pennsylvanian' to *Philadelphia* is 1 hour 30 minutes and to *Harrisburg* is 16 hours; on the 'Maple Leaf' to

Buffalo is 8 hours, to *Niagara Falls* is 9 hours and to *Toronto* is 12 hours; on the 'Silver Meteor' to *Baltimore* is 3 hours, to *Washington DC* is 4 hours, to *Jacksonville* is 18 hours, to *Orlando* (Disney World) is 21 hours and to *Miami* is 26 hours; on the 'Silver Meteor' to *Tampa* is 23 hours; and on the 'Crescent' to *Charlotte* is 10 hours, to *Atlanta* is 16 hours, to *Birmingham* is 19 hours and to *New Orleans* is 27 hours. There are frequent shuttles to *Washington DC* and *Boston,* taking 3 hours 15 minutes and 4 hours 30 minutes respectively.
For journey times on lines connecting New York with Chicago, see the *Illinois* section above.
ROAD: Travel from Manhattan to New Jersey is across George Washington Bridge or through the Lincoln or Holland Tunnels. The Verrazano-Narrows Bridge connects Brooklyn with Staten Island. Queensborough Bridge links Manhattan and Queens. Take Triborough Bridge for upstate New York and the New England Thruway and Bruckner Expressway to New England. **Bus:** The Port Authority Bus Terminal (40th Street/8th Avenue) handles long-distance and regional buses.
Approximate driving times: New York to *Philadelphia* is 2 hours, to *Hartford* is 2 hours, to *Albany* is 3 hours, to *Boston* is 4 hours, to *Baltimore* is 4 hours, to *Washington DC* is 5 hours, to *Portland* (Maine) is 6 hours, to *Montréal* is 7 hours, to *Buffalo* is 8 hours, to *Pittsburgh* is 8 hours, to *Toronto* is 9 hours, to *Cleveland* is 10 hours, to *Indianapolis* is 15 hours, to *Chicago* is 16 hours, to *Miami* is 27 hours, to *Dallas* is 33 hours, to *Los Angeles* is 58 hours, to *San Francisco* is 61 hours and to *Seattle* is 61 hours.
All times are based on non-stop driving at or below the applicable speed limits.
Approximate *Greyhound* journey times: New York (tel: (1 800) 231 2222; toll free) to *Philadelphia* is 2 hours 20 minutes, to *Albany* is 3 hours, to *Washington DC* is 4 hours 40 minutes, to *Boston* is 4 hours 45 minutes, to *Montréal* is 8 hours 30 minutes, to *Buffalo* is 9 hours, to *Pittsburgh* is 9 hours and to *Cleveland* is 9 hours 30 minutes.
URBAN: Subway: Despite its notorious reputation, the New York subway is fast, air-conditioned, cheap and runs 24 hours a day, 7 days a week. Express trains run between major stops and local trains stop at every station. Subway maps are posted in each subway car and pocket maps are available from token booths. Tokens cost US$1.25, regardless of destination. These can be purchased from subway booths or newsagents and can be used on buses. There are half-fares for senior citizens and the disabled. For further information, contact the *Department of Transit* on (212) 788 4636. Streets are laid out in a grid pattern and are frequently congested. The streets and avenues mostly follow a pattern of alternate one-way flow. Broadway is an old Indian trail; it cuts right through New York State from downtown Manhattan to Albany. **Bus:** Services are extensive and are run mostly by the *New York City Transit Authority.* Tokens are available, or one may pay the driver, in which case the exact fare (cost – US$1.25, regardless of destination) is needed. Three-quarters of the city's buses are equipped with wheelchair lifts at the rear door. It is advisable to get hold of a map. *Gray Line Bus Tours:* Located at 900, 8th Avenue between West 53rd and West 54th Streets, *Gray Line* offers bus tours around the city. Open 0800-2000 daily. There are four bus tours available: Lower Manhattan; Harlem and Upper Manhattan; the Grand Tour (most of the city); and 'Number 5' (including the Statue of Liberty and Upper and Lower Manhattan). **Taxi:** The standard yellow cab is metered and reasonably cheap. An average fare costs between US$5 and US$7 for a 4.5km (3-mile) ride. There is no charge for extra passengers, but there is a 50-cent surcharge 2000-0600. **Hansom cabs:** Horse-drawn carriages line up at 59th Street and Fifth Avenue, just

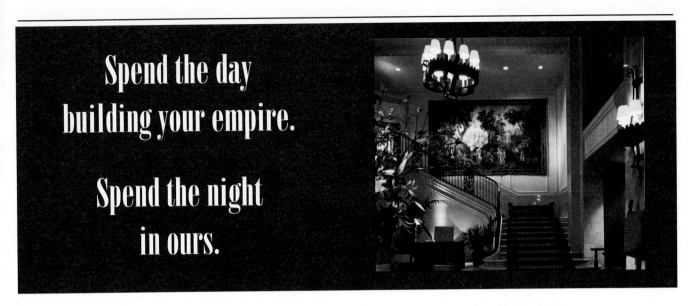
outside the *Plaza Hotel*. **Car hire:** All the major national car rental companies are represented in New York City and many have offices at the city's airports.

RESORTS & EXCURSIONS

NEW YORK CITY: The 'Big Apple' has no equal. It was first settled by Dutch colonists more than 350 years ago, when the scent of flowers from Manhattan Island reached sailors on ships approaching the harbour. Nowadays, a dramatic skyline of soaring skyscrapers signals the approach to the city. New York is the third-largest city in the world and the largest and most cosmopolitan in the USA. Its population of more than seven million includes Germans, Poles, Puerto Ricans, West Indians, Greeks, Scots, Hungarians, Chinese, Koreans, Irish, Italians, Africans and Romanians. New York City is made up of five boroughs and is laid out on a grid of avenues and streets. Most tourist sites are found on Manhattan Island, the business and entertainment centre of the metropolis. Its streets, running east–west, are numbered 1st-240th. Avenues, stretching north–south, run from 1-12 and A-D. South of Canal Street, the grid scatters and street names are used. The remaining four boroughs are primarily residential – the Bronx to the north, Queens to the east, Brooklyn to the southeast and Staten Island to the southwest. Each has wealthy and salubrious districts alongside slum zones – demonstrating as ever New York's uniquely varied social mix.

Sightseeing: The Manhattan skyline is one of the world's few instantly recognisable sights. Many of the skyscrapers are architecturally memorable and offer superb views of the city. The *World Trade Center* is one of several with facilities for tourists; visitors may go onto the roof of one of its two tower blocks during the day or sit in one of its restaurants or bars to see the city at night (smart dress is required in the bars and restaurants). The *Empire State Building*, one of the world's most famous skyscrapers, is on 34th Street at 5th Avenue; take a lift to the top floor for a spectacular view of the city by day or night. The *Statue of Liberty* may be reached by boat from *Battery Park* on the tip of Manhattan Island. An elevator and stairway inside the Statue takes visitors up to an observation platform. The *Staten Island Ferry* is one of the best transportation and touring bargains in the USA. The voyage is very cheap, lasts approximately 25 minutes and affords a magnificent view of Manhattan

and New York harbour. *Brooklyn Bridge*, the remarkable suspension bridge across the East River, provides spectacular views of the city. The *Rockefeller Center*, between 5th and 6th Avenues, houses *Radio City Music*

NEW YORK: Lower Manhattan

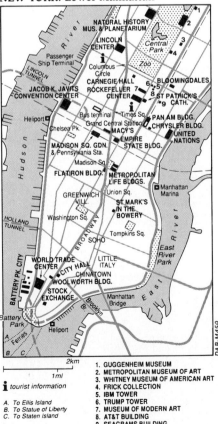

1. GUGGENHEIM MUSEUM
2. METROPOLITAN MUSEUM OF ART
3. WHITNEY MUSEUM OF AMERICAN ART
4. FRICK COLLECTION
5. IBM TOWER
6. TRUMP TOWER
7. MUSEUM OF MODERN ART
8. AT&T BUILDING
9. SEAGRAMS BUILDING

i *tourist information*

A. To Ellis Island
B. To Statue of Liberty
C. To Staten Island

Hall and the *Lower Plaza*, where the café area is converted into a popular skating rink in winter. Nearby is *Broadway* and the heart of the theatre district. Other attractions include the *Lincoln Center for the Performing Arts*, the *United Nations Building* (the organisation's world headquarters), *Coney Island*, the *Bronx Zoo* and *Roosevelt Island Tramway*. The city is famous for its ethnic quarters, such as *Chinatown* and *Little Italy* in Lower Manhattan and *Germantown* along 86th Street. *Greenwich Village*, once the 'Bohemian' quarter, now has coffee and craft shops, theatres and nightclubs.

Museums & galleries: There are many dozens – the most famous is probably the *Metropolitan Museum of Art* on 5th Avenue at 82nd Street. It is the largest art museum in the Western hemisphere and its outstanding collections cover all periods. A donation is requested in lieu of admission. The *Museum of Modern Art* on 11 West 53rd Street has the most important modern art collection in the USA. There is also an outdoor sculpture garden. The *Guggenheim Museum* on 5th Avenue at 88th Street is a 7-storey conical building worth visiting for its design alone (by Frank Lloyd Wright). It features 19th- and 20th-century paintings. Visitors ride an elevator to the top, then walk down a gently spiralling ramp. The *Whitney Museum of American Art* on Madison Avenue at 75th Street is a futuristic structure with exhibits of all types of American art. The *Frick Collection* on 5th Avenue at 70th Street is a neo-Classical palazzo containing its original furnishings and paintings by many European masters.

Parks & gardens: The best-known parks include *Central Park* (extending from Fifth Avenue to Central Park West and 59th Street to 110th Street) with its skating rink, boating lake and zoo; *Riverside Park*, running along the Hudson; *Fort Tryon Park* at the northern tip of Manhattan; *Battery* and *Washington Square* parks in lower Manhattan; *Prospect* and *Marine* parks in Brooklyn; and *Flushing Meadows/Corona*, *Cunningham, Kissina* and *Jacob Riis* parks in Queens. *Clove Lake Park* and *Fort Wadsworth* on Staten Island, a quiet area beneath the Verrezano-Narrows Bridge, have impressive views of New York harbour. The Bronx has a famous *Botanical Garden* and *Pelham Bay* and *Van Cortlandt* parks. Visitors should be aware that it is dangerous to walk alone after dark in the parks.

Beaches: There are several fine beaches to the east of New York City. Nearest to Manhattan are *Coney Island*, *Brighton Beach* and *Manhattan Beach*. Beaches also run

along the north and south shore of Long Island. *Jacob Riis Park* and *Rockaway Beach* are accessible from Queens and Brooklyn. Other beaches include *Orchard Beach* in Pelham Bay Park, *South Beach* and *Wolfe's Pond Park* on Staten Island. The most popular beach with New Yorkers is *Jones Beach State Park*. This 20km (12-mile) strand has all the amenities of a thriving resort. An hour's drive from the city, there are road/rail excursions available from Pennsylvania Station, and daily coach trips from the Port Authority Bus Terminal.
ALBANY: The capital of New York State, Albany stands beside the Hudson River north of New York City. It is a good base from which to explore 'upstate New York'. Cars and campers may be rented. The city is dominated by the US$2-billion *Rockefeller Empire State Plaza*.
Excursions: The quickest access to gigantic *Adirondack Park* is by plane; the *Adirondack Railway* is also fairly fast *(Amtrak* can provide more information). The park's mountainous region, which includes *Lake Placid*, site of the 1932 and 1980 Winter Olympics, offers the widest variety of winter sports in the USA. Hiking, fishing, camping and boating are also on offer. Canoeists will enjoy the *Fulton Chain of Lakes*. *Lake George* is the most popular resort region in the southeastern corner of the park. The *Saratoga Spa State Park* in the Hudson Valley just south of Lake George has mineral baths and a *Performing Arts Center*, summer home of the *Philadelphia Orchestra* and the *New York City Ballet*. *Saratoga Race Track* and *Saratoga Harness Park* are major venues for racing enthusiasts. The *Thousand Island* region along the border with Canada has in fact almost 2000 islands, ranging from the tiny to the substantial, dotted around the St Lawrence River's entrance to Lake Ontario. Boat tours are available. *Alexandria Bay* is the central resort. The *Catskill Mountains,* southwest of Albany, are another popular wilderness area.
BUFFALO: Standing at the eastern extremity of Lake Erie on the border with Canada, Buffalo is a large industrial city. It is the gateway to Niagara Falls, one of the most outstanding spectacles on the North American continent and to the Finger Lakes region. It is also within easy reach of Lake Ontario and Toronto. Watkins Glen at the head of Lake Seneca has a famous motor-racing circuit.
NIAGARA FALLS: There are limousine services from *Greater Buffalo Airport (BUF)* to the city, 14.5km (9 miles) away, or direct to Niagara Falls. Taxis are also available. *Amtrak* offer rail links from Buffalo to Niagara and there are frequent local buses. *Greyhound* provide a direct service from New York to Niagara. There are in fact three main waterfalls, American, Canadian (Horseshoe) and Bridal Veil Falls, each in a different stream of the Niagara River. The drop is about 55m (180ft). Boat trips are available above and below Niagara Falls. Observation platforms set in the cliffs beside (and even behind) the Falls are reached via tunnels. Niagara is a popular honeymoon destination.
Note: For information on attractions in neighbouring States, see above under *States A-Z*.

SOCIAL PROFILE

FOOD & DRINK: New York runs the whole gamut, from *haute cuisine* to *pretzel* stalls. The staple US fare of steaks, seafood and hamburgers is sold all over the city. Excellent French food is available in the East 50s and 60s, in particular between 5th and 3rd Avenues. Authentic Spanish, Indian, Thai, Turkish, Jewish and Cuban restaurants can be found in Broadway along the Upper West Side. German, Czech and Hungarian restaurants are found in Yorkville, Italian and Chinese restaurants in Little Italy and Chinatown, and Greek and Armenian food near 5th Avenue. Greenwich Village offers predominantly Mexican, Italian and Spanish food. Uptown and midtown Manhattan offer everything from cheap, unexciting diners to coffee shops, milk bars and luxury restaurants. Late-night eateries are everywhere. Portions are large and many establishments offer good value meals.
Information on dining out: The Convention & Visitors Bureau publishes a free guide, while *New Yorker Magazine* provides weekly listings of city and suburban restaurants.
Drink: 'Singles bars' are mainly located on the Upper East Side between 59th and 86th Streets, on 3rd, 2nd and 1st Avenues. Moderate prices are charged for food and drink. Bars and lounges often stay open until 0400. They range from smart pre-theatre cocktail bars to seedy establishments for seasoned drinkers. The choice of drinks is extremely wide in most medium- to better-class establishments. 'Happy hour' is generally between 1730 and 1900 and many bars offer free hot and cold food to entice further custom.
THEATRES & CONCERTS: There are numerous theatres both 'on-' and 'off-' Broadway and many smaller, less expensive establishments are located all over the city. Concerts, revues and special performances are held at *Radio City Music Hall* throughout the year. The *Lincoln Center* complex includes the *Metropolitan Opera House,* the *New York City Opera & Ballet* and the *American Ballet Theater.* There are symphony concerts and recitals in *Carnegie Hall* during the autumn, winter and spring seasons. Greenwich Village and SoHo offer the best selection of jazz and rock clubs, cinemas and off-Broadway fringe shows in the world. (Midtown offers more commercial cinema and Broadway plays or musicals.) Cheap tickets for same-day performances can be obtained at the *TKTS* booth at 47th Street and Broadway. Free tickets for recordings of television shows are also available.
NIGHTLIFE: Few would argue that New York's nightlife is the most vibrant and diverse in the world. Entertainment magazines such as *Where*, *Promenade*, the *Village Voice* and the *New Yorker* can keep you in touch with what's going on in and around the 'Big Apple'.
Nightclubs: 'Supper clubs' are plush places for dinner or late supper, with two shows nightly by a famous entertainer. Generally the cover charge per person is quite high; 'cover charges' do not cover either food or drink. Other nightclubs have a minimum amount customers are obliged to spend. There are numerous underground clubs and discos throughout the city.
SHOPPING: There is an incomparable variety of goods and services in New York City – both in the elegant stores along 5th Avenue and in Herald Square, and in the smart uptown boutiques. The most famous department stores are Bloomingdales, Macy's (the largest), Gimbels, Alexander's and Saks Fifth Avenue. Ethnic goods may be purchased in Chinatown, Little Italy and Yorkville; bargains on Orchard Street; and an array of antiques, jewellery, leather and 'trendy' fashions catering to every imaginable taste in Greenwich Village. There are many popular galleries, bookstores, art shows and flea markets.
Bargains: These can be found on the Lower East Side, generally away from midtown. Each street has a speciality – fashion, jewellery, music, flowers or gourmet foods. Discount shops often offer better value than 'special sales' at the big-name stores.
SPECIAL EVENTS: The following are a selection of the events taking place in New York State in 1995/96. For full details, contact the New York State Visitors Bureau.
Throughout 1995: *100th Anniversary of the New York City Library; 100th Anniversary Year of the Wildlife Conservation Society.*
Apr 23 & May 14 & Sep 10 '95 *Nyack Street Fairs,* Hudson Valley region. **Apr 29-30** *32nd Annual Western New York Maple Festival* (arts, crafts and antique show with pancake breakfast), Chauatuqua-Allegheny region. **May 12-14** *Tulip Festival,* Albany. **May 19-21** *The Great Hudson Valley Balloon Race,* Hudson Valley region; *Orange County Delaware River Festival,* Hudson Valley region. **Jun** *24th Annual Lesbian/Gay Pride March,* Fifth Avenue. **Jun 19-25** *Jazzfest* (the largest free jazz festival in the northeast), Syracuse. **Jul 4** *Macy's Fireworks Celebrations,* Lower Hudson River. **Jul 15-16** *Keeper of the Western Door Pow-Wow* (annual American Native dance competition), Chauatuqua-Allegheny region. **Jul 27-30** *Harborfest '95,* Thousand Islands region. **Aug 5-6** *Park Avenue Festival,* Rochester. **Aug 26** *City Slickers Stampede and Hoedown* (featuring cowboy skills), Adirondack region. **Aug 26-27** *Finger Lakes Wine Festival.* **Aug-Sep** *US Open Tennis Championships,* Flushing Meadow. **Sep** *Labor Day Parade,* Fifth Avenue. **Sep 1-2** *Barbershop Quartet and Chorus Singing Festival,* Adirondack region. **Sep 11-15** *BC Open PGA Golf Tournament,* Central Leatherstocking Region. **Oct 6-16** *Long Island Fair.* **Oct 9** *Columbus Day Parade,* Fifth Avenue, 44th to 86th Streets. **Oct 14-15** *Oyster Festival,* Long Island region. **Nov** *The Fall Flower Show,* New York Botanical Garden, Bronx. **Nov 18-Dec 31** *15th Annual Festival of Lights,* Niagra Falls. **Feb '96** *Chinese New Year Celebrations,* Chinatown, New York City.

CLIMATE

The climate is changeable with moderate rainfall throughout the year. During the summer heatwaves are common, with temperatures staying at over 37°C for several days.

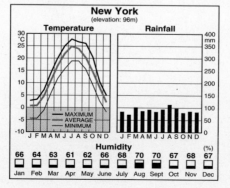

New York
(elevation: 96m)
Temperature
Rainfall
°C
mm
MAXIMUM
AVERAGE
MINIMUM
J F M A M J J A S O N D
Humidity
(%)
66 64 63 61 62 66 68 70 70 67 68 67
Jan Feb Mar Apr May June July Aug Sept Oct Nov Dec

Ohio

Detroit
CANADA
Michigan
Lake Erie
Erie
Pennsylvania
Toledo
Cedar Point
Sandusky
Cleveland
Aurora
Fort Wayne
Akron
Youngstown
Canton
Lima
Indiana
Ohio
Pittsburgh
Springfield
Columbus
Zanesville
Dayton
Hocking Hills
Muskingum
Scioto
Hamilton
Cincinnati
Parkersburg
Monogahela
Ohio
Portsmouth
West Virginia
Kentucky
Charleston
Huntingdon
Lexington
200km
100mls
international airport
State capital underlined

Including **Cincinnati** and **Cleveland**, gateways to the midwestern States of Kentucky, Indiana, West Virginia and Pennsylvania.

Ohio Division of Travel & Tourism
PO Box 1001, Action Response Center, 29th Floor, 77 High Street South, Columbus, OH 43266-0101
Tel: (614) 466 8844 *or* (1 800) 282 5393 (toll free). Fax: (614) 466 6744.
Greater Columbus Convention & Visitors Bureau
Suite 1300, 10 Broad Street W, Columbus, OH 43215
Tel: (614) 221 2489. Fax: (614) 221 5618.
Greater Cincinnati Convention & Visitors Bureau
300 Sixth Street W, Cincinnati, OH 45202-2361
Tel: (513) 621 7862 *or* (1 800) 344 3445 (toll free; USA and Canada only). Fax: (513) 621 5020.
Convention & Visitors Bureau of Greater Cleveland
3100 Terminal Tower, Tower City Center, Cleveland, OH 44113
Tel: (1 800) 321 1004 (tourist information; toll free) *or* (216) 621 4110 (Convention Bureau). Fax: (216) 621 5967.

TIME: GMT - 5. *Daylight Saving Time* is observed.
THE STATE: Ohio, birthplace of seven US presidents, is located in the heart of the Midwest and is the 35th-largest State in the USA. The sandy shores of Lake Erie mark the State's northern border and the long and winding Ohio River marks its eastern border with West Virginia. It is mainly an expanse of fertile farmland dotted with industrial centres, but its 107,040 sq km (41,328 sq miles) also embrace the rolling hills overlooking the Scioto River Valley in the north, which become wilder and steeper as they reach the foothills of the Appalachian mountain chain, and the thick forest lands full of waterfalls and sandstone cliffs in the south, which includes Hockings Hills State Park and the vast Wayne National Forest stretching across 11 counties. The Cuyahoga Valley National Recreation area in the northeast near Cleveland has rugged terrain with river valleys and steep, forested hills. The State also boasts 40,869km (25,543 miles) of waterway, including the inland rivers of the Mohican and Tuscarawas rivers. Columbus is Ohio's capital and is the largest city in both area and population – it is the 16th-largest city in the USA.

TRAVEL

AIR: Approximate flight times: From *Cincinnati* to London is 9 hours, to New York is 1 hour 30 minutes, to Los Angeles is 4 hours 15 minutes, to Miami is 2 hours 15 minutes and to Washington DC is 1 hour.
From *Cleveland* to London is 11 hours 30 minutes (including 1-hour-30-minute stopover in Atlanta) or 10 hours (including 1-hour stopover in Cincinnati); to Paris is 11 hours (including 1-hour stopover in Atlanta) or 12 hours (including 3-hour stopover in New York City); to Los Angeles is 12 hours (including 1-hour stopover in Cincinnati); to Miami is 6 hours (including 1-hour stopover in Orlando) or 5 hours (including 1-hour stop-

over in Atlanta); to Washington DC is 3 hours 30 minutes (including 45-minute stopover in Cincinnati); to Orlando is 4 hours; to Atlanta is 2 hours; to New York is 1 hour 40 minutes and to Cincinnati is 1 hour 15 minutes.
International airports: *Cincinnati/Northern Kentucky (CVG)* is 19km (12 miles) southwest of the city centre (travel time – 15 minutes). *American Airlines, Continental Airlines, USAir, Northwest Airlines* and *Delta Airlines* all offer regular international flights to and from Cincinnati. *Comair* is a Cincinnati-based regional airline offering frequent flights to 30 cities in the Ohio Valley, Great Lakes, the mid-south and Toronto, Canada. Airport facilities include four restaurants (0600-2100), four snack bars, five bars, three nurseries, three post offices (0800-1700 Monday to Friday), banks/bureaux de change (0900-1700 Monday to Friday), duty-free shop, shops, barber shop, business centre, 24-hour medical centre and car hire *(Avis, Budget, Dollar, Hertz* and *National* – located in the baggage claim areas in each of the three terminals). Coaches depart for the city centre every 15 minutes, costing approximately US$11 (travel time – 30 minutes). Taxis are also available and cost approximately US$20 to the city centre. There are also limousine services to various destinations in the area.
Cleveland Hopkins International (CLE) is 18km (10 miles) southwest of the city centre (travel time – 20 minutes). *Air Canada, American Airlines, Continental Airlines, Delta Airlines, Northwest Airlines, Southwest Airlines, TWA, United Airlines* and *USAir* offer regular international flights to and from Cleveland. *Chart Air* also offers charter flights to and from Cleveland. Airport facilities include 24-hour bank teller machines, bureau de change (0530-1830), 24-hour restaurants, snack bars (0600-2359), bars, 24-hour limited-service post office, shops (0600-2359), left luggage (0600-0100), disabled facilities (telephones, parking, ramps and toilets), hotel and travel information centres (0700-1900) and car hire, including *Avis, Dollar Rent-a-Car, Hertz* and *Thrifty Car Rental,* available from the baggage claim level (there are also car rental facilities available for the disabled). The Greater Cleveland Regional Transit Authority (RTA) offers a rapid transit system from the airport to Tower City Center in the downtown city square and back (travel time – 20 minutes one-way). Trains depart from the airport's lower level daily from 0430-0100 every 15 minutes during peak time and every 20 minutes off-peak. Fare is US$1.50 one-way. There is also a Downtown Loop bus system to and from the airport for 50 cents. Limousine services are located at Exit 6 at the south end of the baggage claim level. There is also a limousine information desk at Exit 3 on the baggage claim level and Red Courtesy phones for limousine information at every exit vestibule. Taxis are available 24 hours and will go to any location within Cuyahoga County. Americab and Yellow Cab operate at Exit 2 of the baggage claim level and taxi phones are at each end of the exit vestibule. The journey costs approximately US$22 to the city centre.
RIVER: There are over 1600km (1000 miles) of canals in Ohio and there are many canalboat excursions available. These include the Roscoe Village excursion on the Ohio River and Erie Canal near Coshocton, which operates from May to October; Canal Fulton, carrying passengers from the downtown area of Fulton to Lock 4 on the Ohio and Erie Canal; and the Piqua Historical Area, a 2km-long (1-mile) section of the Miami and Erie Canal carrying passengers through beautiful scenery on a mule-drawn canal boat.
RAIL: *Amtrak* offers daily services from Akron, Alliance, Cincinnati, Cleveland, Fostoria, Hamilton, Toledo and Youngstown to many major cities throughout the USA. For Amtrak travel information, telephone (216) 696 5115.
Ohio has a number of scenic railway excursions including: the *Bluebird Special,* a diesel locomotive running from both Waterville and Grand Rapids for 32km (20 miles) and over the 274m (900ft) bridge overlooking the Maumee River; the *Indiana & Ohio Scenic Railway,* a 29km (18-mile) trip through the hills of southwest Ohio from Mason to Lebanon; the *Ohio Central Railroad,* running 10km (6 miles) and back from Sugarcreek to Baltic through Amish country; *Buckeye Central Scenic Railroad,* offering weekend excursions through Licking County countryside; the *Cuyahoga Valley Line Railroad,* a first-generation diesel train running parallel to the Erie Canal through the Cuyahoga Valley National Recreation Area; and the *Hocking Valley Scenic Railway,* a 1916 coal-burning locomotive which travels through historic country, stopping at Robbins Crossing, a 19th-century town inhabited by costumed guides (weekends only).
ROAD: Ohio has 181,462km (113,414 miles) of roads. Visitors needing road information and conditions are advised to telephone the Department of Highway Safety on (614) 466 2660. To report car breakdowns and accidents, telephone (1 800) 525 5555 (toll free). The *AAA* is available in emergencies by telephoning (513) 762 3222. **Bus:** *Greyhound Bus Line* offers services throughout the State. **Regulations:** Speed limits are 55mph (88kmph) on urban interstate and rural State highways and 65mph (104kmph) on rural interstates outside urban areas. Posted speed limits must be followed on all stretches of highway, especially in construction zones. Safety belts are required according to Ohio State law by the driver and all front seat passengers. Children under 40 pounds or less than four years of age must be restrained with a certified child-safety restraint (violation of this law carries a US$10 fine). In Cincinnati and northern Kentucky it is legal to turn right on a red light after fully stopping (unless a sign forbids it).
Approximate *Greyhound* journey times: From *Cincinnati* (tel: (1 800) 231 2222; toll free) to Louisville is 2 hours, to Columbus is 2 hours, to Indianapolis is 2 hours 30 minutes, to Cleveland is 5 hours, to Detroit is 6 hours, to Pittsburgh is 6 hours, to Knoxville is 6 hours 30 minutes, to Chicago is 7 hours, to St Louis is 8 hours, to Chattanooga is 9 hours, to Atlanta is 12 hours, to Washington DC is 12 hours, to Philadelphia is 13 hours and to New York is 15 hours.
From *Cleveland* (tel: (1 800) 231 2222; toll free) to Pittsburgh is 3 hours, to Detroit is 4 hours, Buffalo is 4 hours, to Toronto is 7 hours, to Chicago is 7 hours 30 minutes, to Washington DC is 9 hours, to New York is 9 hours 30 minutes, to Philadelphia is 10 hours and to Albany is 11 hours,
From *Columbus* (tel: (1 800) 231 2222; toll free) to Cleveland is 3 hours, to Pittsburgh is 4 hours, to Indianapolis is 4 hours, to St Louis is 9 hours, to Washington DC is 10 hours, to Philadelphia is 11 hours and to New York is 13 hours.
URBAN: Bus: The Cincinnati bus system offers services throughout Hamilton County and portions of Clermont County every day of the year. Most bus fares are 50 cents and maximum fare is 95 cents (exact change is required). For further information, telephone Metrocenter at (513) 621 4455 weekdays from 0630-1830 and weekends from 0800-1730. Cleveland has three rapid-transit lines and 100 separate bus routes. **Metro:** Tower City Center Station in Cleveland's downtown Public Square is the central terminal and all rapid transit lines are served from this station. For further information, telephone the Regional Transit Authority on (216) 621 9500. **Taxis** are available in the major cities.

RESORTS & EXCURSIONS

CINCINNATI: Cincinnati is both a friendly and sophisticated city, offering a variety of museums and galleries, fine dining, festivals and events, attractions and sports, parks, recreational activities and excellent shopping. Its museums include the *Behringer-Crawford Museum* (archaeology, paleontology, wildlife, history and art); *Cincinnati Art Museum* (newly renovated with exhibitions of masterpieces and Asian art, offering free admission Wednesday evening); *Contemporary Arts Center* (painting, sculpture, photography, multi-media installations, conceptual and video art); *Harriet Beecher Stowe House* (home of the author of *Uncle Tom's Cabin); Skirball Museum* (Jewish history, artefacts, ceremonial objects and paintings); *The Museum Center at Cincinnati Union Terminal* (the Cincinnati Historical Museum; Cincinnati Museum of Natural History and the OMNIMAX Theater are housed here in a 1930s Art Deco train station); *Taft Museum* (former home of Charles Taft) and the *Warren County Historical Society Museum.* Other attractions of interest to the visitor include riverboat and steamboat cruises on the Ohio River; the *Basilica of the Assumption,* with gargoyles, flying buttresses and the largest stained-glass window in the world; the *Kentucky Horse Center,* an escorted tour of a working thoroughbred-training facility; *Kentucky Horse Park,* a museum celebrating the horse (where horseriding is also available); and the *William Howard Taft National Historic Site,* the birthplace of the former US President and Chief Justice.
CLEVELAND: Cleveland is a city of turn-of-the-century architecture, grand public monuments, lush gardens and parks, miles of lakefront park and beaches, museums and performing arts institutions, and a multitude of diverse neighbourhoods which celebrate over 100 festivals every year. Its many and varied museums include the *African American Museum; Crawford Auto-Aviation Museum* (with over 200 vintage cars and aircraft); *Hower House* (a 28-room Victorian mansion); *Kent State University Museum* (a fashion museum); the *Temple Tifereth-Israel Museum;* and *Trolleyville* (a streetcar and locomotive museum). Cleveland also abounds in special historical areas. *The Flats,* located where the Cuyahoga River meets Lake Erie just west of Public Square, was once the centre of heavy industry and has now become the primary entertainment district. Its converted warehouses, full of restaurants and nightclubs, offer outdoor dining and superb riverfront views. The *Historic Warehouse District,* located between West 3rd and West 10th streets just northwest of Public Square, is on the National Register of Historic Places and has some of Cleveland's finest turn-of-the century architecture, as well as art galleries, restaurants and shops. The *North Coast Harbor,* located on Lake Erie at the East 9th Street Pier, is a new development complex. The *Steamship William G Mather,* a floating steamship museum, is docked here, and a Rock and Roll Hall of Fame Museum, Great Waters Aquarium and the Great Lakes Museum of Science, Environment and Technology are among new developments due to open.
University Circle, located 8km (5 miles) east of the city centre, is the cultural centre of Cleveland. *Cleveland Museum of Art,* specialising in Asian and medieval European art, *Cleveland Museum of Natural History* and *Cleveland Children's Museum,* with hands-on exhibitions, are all situated here within walking distance of one another in a pleasant park-like setting.
Cleveland also has a number of wildlife and recreational attractions. The *African Safari Wildlife Park* is the Midwest's only drive-through safari and offers elephant and camel rides, bird shows and, for children, the turtle taxi and Jungle Junction Playground. *Cleveland Metroparks Zoo and The Rainforest,* 8km (5 miles) south of downtown, is one of the oldest zoos in the country, with more than 3300 animals occupying 165 acres of wooded and rolling land. The Rainforest features more than 600 animals and insects from seven continents in realistic habitats with a 2-storey atrium, simulated tropical thunderstorms and a 8m (25ft) waterfall.
For nature-lovers, there are a number of parks and gardens, including *Cleveland Cultural Gardens; Holden Arboretum* (the largest in the USA); *Garden Center of Greater Cleveland* and *Rockefeller Park Greenhouse.* Other attractions include numerous art galleries and the *Lake Erie Circle Tour,* a boat tour making a scenic loop around Lake Erie from the US to Canadian shores.
COLUMBUS: Columbus is the largest city in Ohio. Its museums include the excellent *Ohio Historical Center* (exploring the history, archaeology and natural history of the Ohio region along with exhibitions of glassware, ceramics, furniture and decorative arts); *Ohio Village* (a re-created community where visitors can experience daily life in a pre-Civil War town); the *Wexner Center for the Arts,* on the Ohio State University campus (renowned for its innovative architecture as well as its fine arts programme); *Columbus Museum of Art* (specialising in European Impressionist, post-Impressionist and German Expressionist masterpieces); *Ohio's Center of Science and Industry,* also known as COSI (four floors of interactive permanent and temporary science exhibits); and *Thurber House* (the restored boyhood home of the writer/cartoonist James Thurber). Two of the most interesting neighbourhoods are the *German Village,* lavishly restored with superb architecture, fine restaurants and taverns, German bakeries and bookstores, and *The Brewery District,* 27 acres of vintage buildings with old beer-making factories containing restaurants, speciality shops and fine beer taverns. Other attractions include *Columbus Zoo,* housing a large reptile collection and the first gorilla born in captivity; *Wyandot Lake Amusement and Water Park,* with 13 water slides and a wave pool; the *Santa Maria,* a replica of the famous ship moored on the Scioto River in the downtown area; *Franklin Park Conservatory,* a crystal palace with two sections, one full of tropical plants in a formal Victorian setting and the other including seven of the world's ecosystems ranging from tropical rainforest to sun-parched desert; and the *Short North Gallery District,* between the Ohio State University campus and downtown, with a plethora of contemporary galleries among shops selling everything from exquisite glass sculpture to second-hand clothing.
THE SOUTHEAST: This near-mountainous region is known as Ohio's outback with its high hills, steep ravines and beautiful waterfalls. This natural scenery can be observed in *Wayne National Forest* and *Archer's Fork Loop,* a 15km (9.5-mile) trail highly recommended to hikers. **Hocking Hills State Park** is open year-round and has a number of natural wonders to interest visitors: *Ash Cave* (Ohio's largest cave, where a misty waterfall plunges 27m/90ft to a pool below), *Old Man's Cave* (with three waterfalls and a natural sandstone statuary including the 'Sphinx Head' and the 'Devil's Bathtub'), *Cedar Falls* (nestling in a valley of towering hemlock trees), *Rock House* (a series of large rooms mysteriously carved into the side of a cliff), *Conkle's Hollow* (a huge canyon encircling a deep gorge), the 46m (150ft) *Cantwell Cliffs,* and *Hocking Forest* (where rock climbing is permitted).
Chillicothe, Ohio's first capital, is surrounded by an area of historical sites, such as the **Hopewell Culture National Historical Park,** one of the greatest concentrations of Hopewell Indian burial sites. The town

also offers the *Adena State Memorial,* built in 1807, and *Ross County Historical Society Museum.* Another historic town is **Marietta,** the first organised American settlement in the Northwest Territories. Historical sites include *Campus Martius Museum* (the site of the first government and the fortification that protected the settlers during the Ohio Indian Wars in 1790-94), the *Ohio River Museum* and *Showboat Becky Thatcher* (where theatre is performed as it was on the riverboats 100 years ago). In September the town celebrates *The Ohio River Sternwheel Festival* when visitors can board America's most famous steamboat, the *Delta Queen.* There are also local tours of the *Rossi Pasta* factory and the *Lee Middleton Original Doll Factory.*

Zanesville offers a narrated ride on a sternwheeler and the *National Road/Zane Grey Museum,* with information about the building of America's first highway and Zanesville's famous Western writer. 24km (15 miles) south of Zanesville is **The Wilds,** a 9000-acre nature preserve with a 16km (10-mile) 'exploration road' providing scenic views and educational materials about endangered species. **Athens** has a college-town atmosphere with a 4-block area of narrow brick streets, historic buildings and interesting shops. *The Bob Evans Farm* in **Bidwell,** the former home of a famous Ohioan sausage-maker, includes a 19th-century statecoach stop, an authentic log-cabin village, a farm museum, horseriding and canoeing excursions.

The *Ohio River* is a perfect location for a scenic drive, especially the route along the river from Pomeroy to Gallipolis. The town of **Pomeroy** is perched on the edge of a sandstone cliff high above the river and the 1848 *Meigs County Courthouse* is one of the most picturesque buildings in southern Ohio. **Gallipolis** was orginally settled by the French and has an interesting historic district and French art-colony galleries at *Riverby,* a historic Federal-style home.

THE NORTHEAST: From the skyscraper city of **Cleveland** to the sparse beauty of the Amish towns, the northeast has a wide variety of sights. The world's largest Amish population resides in the northeast's **Holmes, Wayne, Tuscarawas** and **Stark** counties. The Amish seldom venture more than a few miles from home and therefore need to have their stores close by. The result is a haven of country shops selling everything from handwoven baskets, handmade quilts and antiques to homemade cornmeal. The *Livestock Auction* in **Farmerstown,** where exotic animals such as llamas and emus are sold, and *Kidron Auction,* selling animals and Amish food specialties, are interesting to visit. For a glimpse into the Amish lifestyle, the *Yoder's Amish Home* offers two reproduction Amish farmhouses and buggy rides for children.

The town of **Canton** has a museum complex including the *McKinley National Memorial* (with memorabilia on the assassinated president), *Discover World* (with three distinct time-zone exhibits from the prehistoric to the futuristic) and the *Museum of History, Science and Industry* (with hands-on exhibits). *The Pro Football Hall of Fame* is also located here. In **Mansfield,** there is the *Richland Carrousel Park* and *Kingwood Center,* a mansion and flower park with English gardens, landscaped ponds and strutting peacocks. **Youngstown** features the *Butler Institute of American Art* and *Youngstown Historical Center of Industry and Labour,* which highlights the steel industry that made the city famous. Other sites in the region include the Tudor-style *Stan Hywet Hall* in **Akron,** a 65-room manor house, the largest private residence in Ohio, with formal English and Japanese gardens and a greenhouse; *Sea World of Ohio,* with a superb Shark Encounter exhibit; and *Geauga Lake Amusement Park,* a 240-acre lakeside park with over 100 rides and attractions, in **Aurora.**

The *Cuyahoga Valley National Recreation Area* comprises 33,000 acres between Akron and Cleveland and encompasses a 35km-long (22-mile) river surrounded by steep, forested hills, sandstone gorges and hidden waterfalls. The park also offers programmes on local history, archaeology and geology; bird-watching expeditions; and narrated hikes on restored sections of the old Ohio & Erie Canal towpath. Within this area is also the *Hale Farm and Village,* a living-history museum depicting life in the mid-1800s along with artisans demonstrating 19th-century crafts.

THE CENTRAL AREA: This is an area which ranges from the energetic bustle of **Columbus** to tranquil farm country. Surrounding the capital are a circle of historic small towns, such as Granville, Lancaster and **Mount Vernon.** In **Granville** there are 19th-century shops, homes, churches, a hilltop college campus, two landmark inns, three museums and many fine restaurants. **Lancaster** has *Square 13* (one of America's most beautiful and well-preserved residential blocks), *The Sherman House Museum* (with memorabilia on this famous political family) and *The Georgian Museum* (a restored mansion with period furniture). **Circleville,** site

of the annual *Pumpkin Show* in October, has outstanding architecture and numerous antique shops. There are two castles east of **West Liberty,** built by one of Ohio's first families, the Piatts, who served with Washington in the Revolutionary War and helped found the town of Cincinnati. The oldest, *Mac-A-Cheek* (1863), contains antique furniture and 300 years of family weapons, war relics and Indian artifacts. The newer castle, *Mac-O-Chee* (1879) is lavishly decorated and frescoed by French artist Oliver Frey and contains an impressive collection of tapestries, art objects and furniture from the 12th-19th centuries. Near the castles are the *Ohio Caverns,* the State's largest caves. The *Zane Caverns,* 8km (5 miles) east of **Bellefontaine,** contain amazing pearl-like deposits. 10km (6 miles) east of Bellefontaine is *Mad River Mountain Resort,* a ski resort.

Sites which give an insight into the Native American culture in the region are *Flint Ridge State Memorial and Museum* in **Brownsville,** built over a flint pit used by the Hopewell, with exhibits of how the Indians used to make their weapons; and *Moundbuilders State Memorial* in **Newark,** great circular earthworks, 366m (1200ft) in diameter with 2-4m (8-14ft) walls, created over 2000 years ago by Hopewell Indians; the adjacent *Moundbuilders Museum* is the first museum in the USA exclusively devoted to prehistoric Native American art.

THE NORTHWEST: Lake Erie is the main attraction in this area, being a centre for recreation: boating, fishing and touring the islands. The largest islands are South Bass Island, Middle Bass Island and Kelleys Island. On **South Bass Island,** the Victorian-style village of **Put-in-Bay** offers plenty of gift shops, vintage saloons and fine restaurants. For a view of the island and lake, visitors may take the elevator to the 97m-high (317ft) observation deck of *Perry's Victory and International Peace Memorial,* commemorating Commodore Perry's victory over the British in 1812 and the subsequent peace between the USA and Canada. **Middle Bass Island** is dominated by the Gothic castle of the *Lonz Winery,* which began in 1860 and is still making wine – winery tours and wine-tasting are available to visitors. **Kelleys Island** is on the National Register of Historic Places. Along with old, picturesque homes, it offers historical sights such as *Inscription Rock,* an exceptionally large Native American pictograph, and *Glacial Grooves,* a site with evidence of glacial movement. Ferries run regularly between the islands and the mainland. For detailed timetables, contact *Miller Boat Line* on (419) 285 2421 (services running March to November) and *Jet Express* on (1 800) 245 1JET (toll free) for South Bass Island (services running May to September) and *Kelleys Island Ferry Boat Lines* on (419) 798 9763 for Kelleys Island (both services running April to November).

Another popular area in the northwest is **Sandusky Bay.** Four waterfront towns, arranged around the three sides of the bay, are ideal for fun and recreation. **Lakeside** is known for its Victorian architecture and summertime concerts, **Marblehead** for its lighthouse and lakefront shops and artists' studios and **Port Clinton** for its fine restaurants and fishing. **Sandusky** is the largest town, full of gardens, historic homes and excellent museums. The *Merry-Go-Round Museum* has a working carousel inside it and the *Follett House Museum* has a stone mansion built in 1834, exhibits of Lake Erie memorabilia and a widow's walk with a magnificent view. But the town is most famous for *Cedar Point Amusement Park,* the nation's largest theme park. Located on a narrow spit of land on the bay, surrounded by water, it has ten roller-coasters, four vintage carousels and one of the best swimming beaches on Lake Erie.

Toledo is the northwest's largest city and has its own appeal, with its glass towers reflecting the lights along the Maumee River. Famous for its glass-making, visitors may view or buy some of the city's speciality at *Libbey Glass Factory Outlet Store.* Toledo is also famous for the *Toledo Museum of Art* and the *University Arts Center* in Toledo's West End. The new *Arts Center* opened recently, adjacent to the Museum of Art, which has just undergone a US$8-million renovation and expansion and is considered to be among the top ten art museums in the USA. Further up the Maumee River are the restored riverfront towns of **Grand Rapids** and **Waterville,** which feature train and riverboat excursions. The *Shawnee Princess,* a steam-powered paddlewheeler, plies the river and the *Bluebird Special* runs alongside it.

Other attractions in the northwest include the *Neil Armstrong Air & Space Museum* in **Wapakoneta** (the first men to fly, the Wright brothers, and the first man on the moon, Neil Armstrong, were all Ohioans); *Saunder Farm and Craft Village* in **Archbold** (a pioneer village with a museum, quilt shops and craft-making displays); and the *Edison Birthplace Museum* and *Historical*

Museum in **Milan.**

THE SOUTHWEST: A region full of friendly, southern hospitality, from the skyscrapers of **Cincinnati** to the charm of old river towns. The **Kings Island** area, just north of Cincinnati, is a popular entertainment and recreational centre. *Kings Island Theme Park* offers Broadway-style shows and big-name stars, as well as a 15-acre water park and thrill rides; *Beach Waterpark* offers 1m (4ft) waves, plenty of sand, volleyball and speed slides; and the *Jack Nicklaus Sports Center* has two excellent golf courses designed by Nicklaus himself. Once a large spa resort, **Yellow Springs** is still one of Ohio's most scenic towns, with an interesting historic district and *Glen Helen Nature Preserve,* adjacent to the *Antioch College* campus. Just 3km (2 miles) east of the town, on the Little Miami River, is the spectacular 31m (100ft) waterfall at **Clifton Gorge,** and *Clifton Mill,* one of America's largest operating gristmills.

The *Carillon Historical Park* in the city of **Dayton** is an 18-building complex with authentic re-creations of 19th-century homes, businesses and industries; one of the planes flown by the Wright brothers; and one of the largest carillons in Ohio. Near here is the *Aviation Trail,* with many historical sites relating to the Wright brothers. The *Paul Laurence Dunbar State Memorial* was the house of the famous African-American author and is now a museum. *SunWatch Archaeological Park* is a prehistoric Indian village offering visitors close-up looks at ongoing digs, reconstruction daub-and-thatch lodges and scheduled lectures on this Indian society. 10km (6 miles) northeast of Dayton is the *US Air Force Museum,* the world's largest and oldest military aviation museum, open free of charge. The exhibition ranges from the Wright brothers' first military airplane in 1909 to today's experimental aircraft and there is an IMAX Theater with the latest in film and sound technology. Other sites in the southwest include the *National Afro-American Museum and Cultural Center* (an audio-visual exhibition from slavery to the Civil Rights movement) in **Wilberforce;** *Rankin House* (the house where the abolitionist Reverend John Rankin hid more than 2000 slaves from 1825-1865) in **Ripley;** *Serpent Mound State Memorial* (a giant snake, a quarter of a mile long and 6m/20ft wide, created by the Adena Indians over 2000 years ago) near **Locust Grove;** *Fort Ancient State Memorial* (an archaeological site displaying evidence of the Hopewell and Fort Ancient Indian tribes), 11km (7 miles) southeast of **Lebanon;** and the **Piqua Historical Area,** offering restored 19th-century architecture and rides on a canalboat down a stretch of the Miami & Erie Canal.

Note: For information on attractions in neighbouring States, see above under *States A-Z.*

SOCIAL PROFILE

FOOD & DRINK: As Ohio is farm country, the local produce is fresh and of high quality. The Ohioans love big wholesome meals. Pork and beef are more common than lamb, and fried chicken features on many menus in the State, especially in the south. Corn (maize) is one of the staple ingredients of Ohioan cooking and is used in many local specialitities, such as *cornmeal mush* (a delicious breakfast dish made with cracked corn, eggs and milk, then fried) and *hominy* (made from the kernels of white corn). Corn-on-the-cob is another favourite. Desserts usually centre around homemade fruit pies and apple pie is particularly popular, almost always served à la mode (with ice cream). Berries, particularly blackberries, are another favourite dessert. The Amish people in the northcentral area offer some regional specialities such as hand-cranked ice cream, homemade granola and maple-cinnamon rolls. **Drink:** The local milk is excellent and is served with most home-cooked meals. Soft drinks are served everywhere, which the locals call 'pop'. Tomato juice is the Ohio State beverage and Ohio is second only to California in tomato-growing. Kentucky bourbon is a popular alcoholic drink. Liquor is sold only at State stores from Monday to Saturday, opening at 1000 and with variable closing times. Hard liquor can only be purchased with cash. Beer and wine are available in grocery stores and drug stores. Wine can only be bought from 1300-2400 Sunday. Wine, liquor and beer can only be sold to people over 21 years of age. Drinking hours in restaurants and bars are determined by the type of liquor license held by the establishment.

THEATRES & CONCERTS: Cincinnati: The *Cincinnati Opera* (the second-oldest opera company in the USA) and *The Cincinnati Pops Orchestra* perform at *Music Hall* (the Pops Orchestra has a summer season at *Riverbend Music Center*). Theatres include *Cincinnati Playhouse in the Park* and the *Ensemble Theater of Cincinnati.* Dinner theatre can be sampled at *The New La Comedia Dinner Theater.* **Cleveland:** A series of

more than 100 concerts is presented annually at the *Cleveland Institute of Music* by the Institute's *Symphony and Chamber Orchestras, Opera Department* and *Contemporary Music Ensemble*. Many are free and open to the public. There is also *The Cleveland Opera* and *Lyric Opera Cleveland*. The *Cleveland Ballet* performs at *Playhouse Square*, the *Ohio Chamber Orchestra* in the *Little Theater* at the Cleveland Convention Center and the *Cleveland Orchestra* at *Severance Hall* from September to May and at *Blossom Music Center* during the summer. Theatre can be seen at the *Cleveland Public Theater, The Cleveland Play House, Playhouse Square Center* and *Karamu House* (a multiracial arts centre). Dinner theatres include *Another Door Theater Company* and *Carrousel Dinner Theater. Cain Park* has dance, theatre and music concerts (ranging from jazz to classical) in the summer. Tickets for many of the above performances are available through Advantix, a Cleveland-based computerised ticket company. Tel: (216) 241 6444 *or* (1 800) 766 6048 (toll free).
Columbus: The *Wexner Center for the Arts* in the Short North district has an excellent performing arts programme including classical music, dance and jazz. The *Martin Luther King Jr Performing and Cultural Arts Complex* has performances by a variety of black artists. The *Jazz Arts Group* of Columbus has an excellent programme. The *Ohio Light Opera Company* in *Wooster, Center for the Arts* in *Canton* and the *Ariel Theater* in *Gallipolis* are also highly recommended.
NIGHTLIFE: The Flats in Cleveland is a popular nightlife entertainment area. The Short North District, German Village and the Brewery District in Columbus have excellent nightlife. Nightlife areas in Cincinnati include The Wharf at Covington Landing and the Oldenberg Brewery Complex. Dayton is known for its jazz clubs.
SHOPPING: Major outlet shopping centres include Ohio Factory shops, 58km (36 miles) south of Columbus and 54km (34 miles) east of Dayton; Jefferson Outlet Center in Jefferson, 56km (35 miles) south of Columbus; Aurora Farms Factory outlets, 5km (3 miles) south of Sea World of Ohio; Lake Erie Factory Outlet Center in Milan, and JC Penney Outlet Store and Brice Outlet Mall in Columbus. The towns of Lebanon and Waynesville are known as the Antiques Capital of the Midwest – Lebanon claims 20 antique shops in its historic business district alone and Waynesville has 35 shops, five malls and over 100 additional dealers and galleries all within an area of five blocks. For speciality Amish buys, the best areas for shopping are the 8km (5-mile) radius around Fredericksburg in Wayne County and the area between Charm and Farmerstown in Holmes County.
SPORT: The State's **baseball** teams are the *Cincinnati Red Socks* and the *Cleveland Indians*; the **football** team is the *Cleveland Browns*, with **basketball** being played by the *Cleveland Cavaliers*. Basketball can be seen at The Coliseum in Richfield and the Columbus Convention Center; **hockey** at The Coliseum in Richfield, Cincinnati Gardens, Hara Complex in Dayton, the Ohio State Fairgrounds in Columbus and the Toledo Sports Arena; and **soccer** at Canton Civic Center in Canton and Dayton Convention Center. **Skiing** is also available and the major ski resorts are Alpine Valley Ski Area in Chesterland (29km/18 miles east of Cleveland), Boston Mills/Brandywine Ski Resort (40km/25 miles south of Cleveland), Clear Fork Ski Area in Butler (24km/15 miles southeast of Mansfield), Mad River Mountain Ski Resort (8km/5 miles east of Bellefontaine) and Snow Trails Ski Resort (8km/5 miles south of Mansfield). Cleveland Metroparks has 19,000 acres of walking and **hiking** trails, nature centres and **golf** courses (boat, canoe and cross-country skis are available for rent in appropriate seasons). **Fishing, swimming, watersports** and **boating** can be enjoyed on Lake Erie; **canoeing** on the Mohican and Tuscarawas rivers; fishing and **sailing** on the Muskingum Watershed Conservancy District lakes; hiking and **rock climbing** in Hocking Hills State Park and Wayne National Forest; hiking, boating, golf, fishing, swimming and **horseriding** in Deer Creek State Park; hiking, boating, fishing and swimming at Burr Oak State Park; boating, hiking, fishing and swimming at Salt Fork State Park; and hiking, boating, fishing, swimming and horseriding at Shawnee State Park.
SPECIAL EVENTS: Jun 3-4 '95 *Strawberry Festival,* Troy. **Jul 7-9 & Sep 15-17** *Great Mohican Indian Pow Wow & Rendezvous,* Loudonville. **Jul 21-23** *River Expo,* Cleveland. **Jul 21-29** *Pro Football Hall of Fame Festival,* Canton. **Jul 22-23** *Dayton Air Show.* **Aug 5-6** *Twin Days* (the world's largest gathering of twins and others of multiple birth), Twinsburg. **Aug 26-Oct 15** *Ohio Renaissance Festival,* near Waynesville. **Oct 11-15** *Tall Stacks '95* (18 padddlewheelers will sail into the port of Cincinnati), Cincinnati. **Oct 18-21** *Pumpkin Show,* Circleville.

CLIMATE

Cold winters and hot summers.
Required clothing: Lightweights for the summer and heavyweights for the winter.

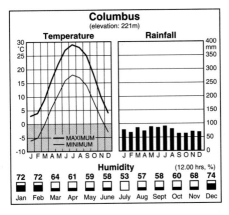

Including **Philadelphia**, gateway to George Washington Country – the States of Pennsylvania, Delaware, Maryland, West Virginia and Virginia.

Pennsylvania Bureau of Travel Development
Department of Commerce, Office of Travel Marketing, Room 453, Forum Building, Harrisburg, PA 17120
Tel: (717) 787 5453 *or* (1 800) 847 4872 (toll free). Fax: (717) 234 4560.
Philadelphia Convention & Visitors Bureau
Suite 2020, 1515 Market Street, Philadelphia, PA 19102
Tel: (215) 636 3300. Fax: (215) 636 3327.
Pittsburgh Convention & Visitors Bureau
Suite 514, 4 Gateway Center, Pittsburgh, PA 15222
Tel: (412) 281 7711. Fax: (412) 644 5512.
Gettysburg Travel Council
35 Carlisle Street, Gettysburg, PA 717
Tel: (717) 334 6274. Fax: (717) 334 1166.

TIME: GMT - 5. *Daylight Saving Time* is observed.
THE STATE: Pennsylvania is the State in which the USA was born. The country's Founding Fathers signed the Declaration of Independence and the Constitution at Independence Hall in Philadelphia – now one of the largest cities in the USA. Pennsylvanians represent a rich mix of cultural and ethnic backgrounds, while its boundaries embrace farmland, mountain ranges, forests,

scenic rivers and waterways. Its northwestern edge borders on one of North America's Great Lakes, Lake Erie.

TRAVEL

AIR: Approximate flight times: From Philadelphia to *London* is 9 hours 25 minutes (including stopover) and to *New York* is 50 minutes.
International airports: *Philadelphia International (PHL)* is 13km (8 miles) southwest of the city (travel time – 25 minutes). The cheapest way to reach the city centre is *Southeastern Pennsylvania Transit Authority's (SEPTA) Airport Express Train,* running every 30 minutes to all three city centre stations, 0600-2400 daily. Taxis, hire cars and limousine services are also available. *Greater Pittsburgh Airport* receives international, USA long-distance and regional flights. It is 22.5km (14 miles) west of Pittsburgh city centre. Limousine services, taxis, *Greyhound* buses and *Amtrak* rail services are available. *SEPTA* has interconnecting buses, streetcars and elevated railways. The *Cultural Bus Loop* tours the city's major attractions.
RAIL: Philadelphia is served by *Amtrak's* shuttle service between Washington DC and New York (travel time – 1 hour 30 minutes to both cities) and also receives trains from New Orleans, Miami and Chicago. See *Illinois* and *New York* sections above for examples of journey times on several services passing through the city.
ROAD: Road travel in Pennsylvania is excellent, with good roads to Philadelphia, Scranton, Harrisburg, Pittsburgh and to outside destinations such as Binghamton in New York and Morgantown in West Virginia. The Pennsylvania Turnpike is a toll road providing swift and efficient travel across the State from New Jersey to Ohio.
Approximate driving times: From Philadelphia to *New York* is 2 hours, to *Baltimore* is 2 hours, to *Washington DC* is 3 hours, to *Pittsburgh* is 6 hours, to *Chicago* is 15 hours, to *Miami* is 25 hours, to *Dallas* is 31 hours, to *Los Angeles* is 56 hours and to *Seattle* is 59 hours.
All times are based on non-stop driving at or below the applicable speed limits.
Approximate *Greyhound* journey times: From Philadelphia (tel: (1 800) 231 2222; toll free) to *New York* is 2 hours, to *Washington DC* is 3 hours, to *Pittsburgh* is 7 hours, to *Chicago* is 18 hours, to *Miami* is 30 hours, to *Dallas* is 37 hours, to *Los Angeles* is 65 hours and to *Seattle* is 74 hours.

RESORTS & EXCURSIONS

PHILADELPHIA: Situated on the Delaware River, Philadelphia is the gateway for those travelling west into Pennsylvania Dutch Country, north into the ski resorts of the Pocono Mountains and southeast to the Delaware Peninsula and Atlantic Seaboard beaches. Now the fifth-largest city in the USA, it is a vibrant national centre of commerce, industry, medical education, research and the arts, while preserving quiet pockets of some of the nation's most historic territory.
Sightseeing: In 1776, the Declaration of Independence and the Constitution were signed in *Independence Hall,* which stands in the centre of *Independence National Historical Park.* The glass *Liberty Bell Pavilion* houses the bell that was sounded at the first public reading of the Independence Declaration. *Franklin Court,* where Franklin's home once stood, houses an underground museum. Other places of interest include the *Old City Hall,* early home of the US Supreme Court; *Christ Church,* where Franklin and George Washington once worshipped; *Fairmount Park* by the Schuylkill River, one of the USA's largest city parks; the *Philadelphia Museum of Art & Rodin Museum; Penn's Landing,* where State founder William Penn first arrived in 1682; and *Valley Forge National Historical Park,* just west of the city, one of the most revered shrines of the American Revolution.
PITTSBURGH: The second-largest city in the State, Pittsburgh is an energetic metropolis of towering skyscrapers and landscaped parks. It was once known primarily as the USA's pre-eminent centre of steel production, but the steel mills are today in decline.
Sightseeing: The *Point State Park Fountain* symbolises the meeting of the Monongahela, Allegheny and Ohio rivers; it may be found in the breathtaking downtown area known as the *Golden Triangle.* Other attractions include the *Buhl Science Center;* the *University of Pittsburgh,* a 42-storey cathedral of learning; the *Museum of Natural History* at the *Carnegie Institute;* and the *Fort Pitt Museum,* which celebrates west Pennsylvanian history.
Excursions: *Pennsylvania Dutch Country* (actually settled by Germans in the 18th century) is in the southeast of the State. Many of the people belong to the

Amish sect and retain the beliefs and customs of their forefathers. Amish men wear beards, black hats and coats. The women wear bonnets and simple, full-length dresses. Towns to visit include **Lancaster, Lititz, Strasburg, Bird-in-Hand** and **Ephrata. Harrisburg** has a magnificent 650-room State Capitol building. **Gettysburg**, the famous American Civil War battle site, features the *Gettysburg National Military Park* and the *Eisenhower National Historic Site*. The *Pocono Mountains* offer fishing, hunting, hiking, riding and camping, with skiing in the winter. Their resorts rival Niagara Falls as popular honeymoon destinations.
Note: For information on attractions in neighbouring States, see above under *States A-Z*.

SOCIAL PROFILE

FOOD & DRINK: Various regions in Pennsylvania have their own specialities. In the Pocono Mountains area, superb local mountain trout is featured in many restaurants. Pennsylvania Dutch food is a unique variation of German cuisine, including pickles, relishes, apple butter, dumplings, pretzels, molasses and shoo-fly pie. Seven sweet and seven sour dishes are served in a type of smorgasbord. There are some sausages and cold cuts that originate from this region, such as the delicious Lebanon baloney and dried beef. The best restaurants for this unique cuisine can be found around Lancaster.
Drink: The legal age for drinking is 21 in Pennsylvania and bottled liquor is only sold in State stores.
THEATRES & CONCERTS: Summer performances in the round are staged at the *John B Kelly Playhouse*. The city's opera house and concert hall is at the *Academy of Music*, the home of the *Philadelphia Orchestra*. The huge *Mann Music Center* in Fairmount Park stages summer concerts.
NIGHTLIFE: There are numerous supper clubs, nightclubs, jazz clubs and ethnic entertainments.
SHOPPING: Philadelphia has always been famous for antiques and handicrafts. The main shopping areas include New Market, Head House Square and the Bourse. John Wanamaker is an elegant department store in Philadelphia well worth a visit.
SPECIAL EVENTS: The following is a selection of some of the major events taking place during 1995. For full details contact the Philadelphia Convention & Visitors Bureau.
Mar 5-12 '95 *Philadelphia Flower Show.* **May 19-21** *National Pike Festival.* **May 25-29** *Mayfair,* Allentown. **May 27-29** *The 9th Annual Jambalaya Jam,* Philadelphia. **Late May-late Sep** *Longwood Gardens Festival of Fountains,* Philadelphia. **Jun 2-18** *Three Rivers Arts Festival,* Pittsburgh. **Late Jun-early Jul** *Gettysburg Civil War Heritage Days,* Adams County. **Jul 1-9** *46th Annual Kutztown Folk Festival,* Berks County. **Jul 29-30** *River Blues Festival,* Philadelphia. **Early Aug-early Oct** *Pennsylvania Renaissance Faire,* various venues, weekends. **Mid-Aug** *Musikfest,* Philadelphia. **Late Aug** *Little League World Series,* Williamsport. **Aug 17-20** *We Love Erie Days,* Lake Erie. **Aug 25-27** *Philadelphia Folk Festival.* **Sep 23-30** *The Bloomsburg Fair.* **Mid-Oct** *Shawnee Autumn Hot Air Balloon Festival.* **Nov 24 '95-Jan 7 '96** *Brandywine Christmas,* Brandywine. **Dec 25** *Re-enactment of Washington Crossing the Delaware,* Philadelphia.

CLIMATE

The weather can be changeable, with moderate amounts of rain throughout the year. Summers are warm with occasional heatwaves.
Required clothing: Lightweights during the summer, heavyweights for the winter months.

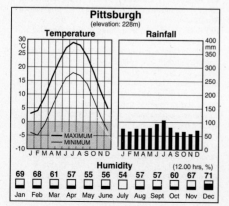

Texas

800km
400mls   □ *major international airport*

Including **Dallas/Fort Worth** and **Houston,** gateways to the southwest States of New Mexico, Oklahoma, Arkansas and Louisiana.

Texas Department of Tourism & Commerce
PO Box 128, Suite 1190, 816 Congress, Austin, TX 78711
Tel: (512) 936 0213 *or* (1 800) 888 8TEX (toll free). Fax: (512) 3936 0089.
Austin Convention & Visitors Bureau
201 East 2nd Street, Austin, TX 78701
Tel: (512) 474 5171. Fax: (512) 474 5182/3.
Arlington Convention & Visitors Bureau
PO Box A, Suite 650, 1250 East Copeland Road, Arlington, TX 76011
Tel: (817) 265 7721. Fax: (817) 265 5640.
Dallas Convention & Visitors Bureau
Suite 2000, 1201 Elm Street, Dallas, TX 75270
Tel: (214) 746 6646 *or* 746 6677. Fax: (214) 746 6688.
Fort Worth Convention & Visitors Bureau
415 Throckmorton Street, Fort Worth, TX 76102
Tel: (817) 336 8791. Fax: (817) 336 3282.
Greater Houston Convention & Visitors Bureau
3rd Floor, 801 Congress Avenue, Houston, TX 77002
Tel: (713) 227 3100. Fax: (713) 227 6336.
San Antonio Convention & Visitors Bureau
PO Box 2277, 121 Alamo Plaza, San Antonio, TX 78298
Tel: (210) 270 8700. Fax: (210) 270 8782.
El Paso Convention & Visitors Bureau
1 Civic Center Plaza, El Paso, TX 79901
Tel: (915) 534 0696 (convention information) *or* 534 0600 (tourist information). Fax: (915) 532 2963.

TIME: GMT - 6. *Daylight Saving Time* is observed in the greater part of the State.
THE STATE: Big, bold and colourful, the 'Lone Star State' is the second-largest in the USA, covering more than 431,000 sq km (262,017 sq miles). Spain was the first European power to lay claim to Texas; it also flew the flags of France and Mexico before gaining its independence in 1836. It was granted US statehood in 1846. Texas borders Mexico along the Rio Grande and embraces vast mountain ranges and canyons to the west; lakes, plantations and pine forests to the east; broad plains to the north; citrus groves, Gulf of Mexico beaches and low-lying alluvial plains to the south; and emerald hill country and clear natural springs at its heart. Its great wealth stems from its vast oil reserves. It has several booming cities: Houston, Dallas, Fort Worth, San Antonio, El Paso and its capital city, Austin.

TRAVEL

AIR: Approximate flight times: From *Dallas/Fort Worth* to Austin is 50 minutes, to London is 11 hours (including stopover), to Miami is 2 hours 40 minutes and to New York is 3 hours 30 minutes.
From *Houston* to London is 10 hours 15 minutes, to Miami is 2 hours 25 minutes and to New York is 3 hours 30 minutes.

International airports: *Dallas/Fort Worth International (DFW)* is 27km (17 miles) from both cities; travel time – 35 minutes. Complimentary coach is available to most major hotels. There are bus services to downtown areas of both cities three times daily. Taxis are also available. *Houston (IAH)* (Intercontinental) is 32km (20 miles) north of the city; travel time – 30 minutes. Complimentary coaches depart for most major hotels every 30 minutes, 24 hours a day. There are buses to downtown and surrounding areas at reasonable prices. Taxis are also available, but expensive. *San Antonio International Airport* is 14km (8.5 miles) from downtown, with flights from Latin America and major US cities. Express bus to the city centre costs 40 cents and there is a shuttle to the city centre for US$6. Taxis are available to the city centre for an approximate cost of US$12. Some hotels provide complimentary coaches from the airport to the hotel.
Domestic airports: *Love Field* is 9.5km (6 miles) from Dallas city centre.
El Paso International Airport is 13km (8 miles) east of downtown; it serves as a gateway to the mountain and canyon country.
RAIL: *Amtrak* journeys between main cities are difficult and can only be made on the daily long-distance trains. Dallas/Fort Worth is on the Los Angeles–San Antonio–Chicago line and Houston on the Los Angeles–New Orleans line. See *California* section above for approximate journey times. There are no local rail services.
ROAD: *Greyhound* runs frequent services connecting Dallas, Fort Worth, Houston, San Antonio and other major towns and cities in Texas and further afield. Local bus services off the main routes are not highly developed.
Approximate driving times: From *Dallas/Fort Worth* to Oklahoma City is 4 hours 30 minutes, to Houston is 4 hours 30 minutes, to San Antonio is 6 hours, to Little Rock is 7 hours, to Amarillo is 7 hours, to Kansas City is 7 hours, to Jackson is 8 hours, to New Orleans is 10 hours, to El Paso is 12 hours, to St Louis is 13 hours, to Denver is 16 hours, to Chicago is 19 hours, to Mexico City is 24 hours, to Miami is 28 hours, to Los Angeles is 29 hours, to New York is 33 hours and to Seattle is 44 hours.
From *Houston* to San Antonio is 4 hours, to Brownsville is 7 hours, to New Orleans is 7 hours, to El Paso is 15 hours, to Chicago is 24 hours, to Miami is 25 hours, to Los Angeles is 31 hours, to New York is 36 hours and to Seattle is 49 hours.
All times are based on non-stop driving at or below the applicable speed limits.
Approximate *Greyhound* **journey times:** From *Dallas/Fort Worth* (tel: (1 800) 231 2222; toll free) to Oklahoma City is 4 hours 30 minutes, to Houston is 4 hours 30 minutes, to San Antonio is 6 hours, to Tulsa is 7 hours, to Amarillo is 8 hours, to Memphis is 13 hours 30 minutes, to New Orleans is 13 hours and to El Paso is 13 hours.
From *Houston* (tel: (713) 759 6581) to San Antonio is 4 hours, to Dallas is 4 hours 30 minutes and to New Orleans is 8 hours 30 minutes.
URBAN: Dallas/Fort Worth: The various bus networks are well-run and reasonably priced. Buses between Dallas and Fort Worth are operated by *Greyhound*. Most major car-hire companies have offices in both cities. Local firms with cars and motor campers for rent are listed in the Dallas/Fort Worth classified telephone directory.
Houston: The *Metropolitan Transport Authority (METRO)* provides reasonably priced bus services. Taxis are readily available, but this type of travel can be impractical and expensive for short distances. Rental cars are the best way to get around, but visitors are advised to make advance reservations as the demand is high. For local firms see the Houston classified telephone directory under 'Car Rentals'.

RESORTS & EXCURSIONS

DALLAS: Originally a trading post, Dallas has grown into a centre for commerce and fashion of worldwide importance. It has a glittering high-rise skyline, elegant stores, fine restaurants and a rich cultural life. Located in the heart of the north Texas prairie, Dallas is a modern sophisticated city, yet still possessing the much-renowned Texan hospitality and southwestern charm. It is increasingly recognised for its cosmopolitan spirit and entrepreneurial flair.
Sightseeing: Dallas is a city rich in historical sites and futuristic sights. The downtown area features shimmering glass towers and angled spires, whereas down below in the *West End Historic District* there are 100-year-old buildings now occupied by lively shops, restaurants and museums. The *McKinney Avenue Trolley* rolls down red-brick streets. *Old City Park* is a pioneer community

featuring homes, a church, a schoolhouse and Main Street as it was in the days of the original settlers. The 50-storey *Reunion Tower* has a glass-elevator ride to observation terraces and a revolving restaurant with night-time dancing. *Dealey Plaza* is the site where President John F Kennedy was assassinated and there is a dramatic exhibit on the event located on the sixth floor. The *John F Kennedy Memorial* at Main and Market Streets is open all year round. Popular attractions are the *DeGolyer Estate*, built by a rich oil baron and *Southfork Ranch*, the home of famous TV series' Ewing clan. Amongst its many other attractions are the *Age of Steam Museum*, *Dallas Health & Science Museum*, with many hands-on exhibitions, the *Planetarium*, *Dallas Museum of Art*, *Dallas Museum of Natural History*, with a superb dinosaur exhibition, and the *Texas Hall of State*. Favourite family activities include *Penny Whistle Park*, the *Dallas Aquarium*, the *Farmer's Market* and the *Dallas Zoo*, featuring 'the Wilds of Africa'. Outdoor activities include the *Dallas Arboretum* and the Dallas *Civic Garden Center*. The major recreational centre is *State Fair Park*. Recreational facilities available in Dallas include paddleboating among the ducks on *Bachman Lake* and horseriding through the backwoods of a real Texan ranch.

FORT WORTH: Much more 'Western' in spirit, Fort Worth started as a military outpost and then became a cow town where cattlemen brought their herds to be shipped. Much of the Old West is preserved in Fort Worth today and it continues to be a centre for the cattle industry.
Sightseeing: The historic stockyards on Northside retain the flavour of the Old West. There is also a log-cabin village, a zoological park and a Japanese garden. Museums include the *Amon Carter Museum of Western Art*, the *Sid Richardson Collection of Western Art*, the *Fort Worth Art Museum* and the *Kimbell Art Museum*.
Excursions: The *Six Flags Over Texas* theme park, between Dallas and Fort Worth, offers more than 200 rides and attractions. **Abilene,** 242km (151 miles) west of Fort Worth, has a reconstructed frontier settlement. *Palo Duro Canyon State Park* near **Amarillo** in the far north of the State has startling scenery and facilities for hiking, picnicking, camping and horseriding. The *Panhandle-Plains Museum* in the nearby city of **Canyon** charts the region's development from early Indian life to modern farming and ranching.

HOUSTON: The fourth-largest city in the USA and the largest in Texas, with a population of more than 2.7 million, Houston has been the centre of the US oil industry ever since 'black gold' was discovered at nearby Beaumont in 1901. The city is named after Texas hero General Sam Houston, the first President of the Republic of Texas. It is also the space headquarters of the USA (NASA's Lyndon B Johnson Space Center is nearby) and a thriving international port, being connected to the Gulf of Mexico by the 80km (50-mile) Houston Ship Canal. Houston's towering skyscrapers reflect its booming economy.
Sightseeing: Downtown attractions include the modern *Civic Center*, *Sam Houston Historical Park, Tranquility Park* and the *Old Market Square*. The *Houston Zoological Gardens' Discovery Hall* exhibit is popular with children for its collection of friendly and pettable animals. Admission is free. The veteran pre-World War I battleship 'Texas' is moored on the San Jacinto River near the *Battleground Monument,* which marks the 1836 battle for Texan independence. The *Lyndon B Johnson Space Center* has exhibitions of space technology and stages regular film shows explaining the US space programme.
Excursions: The spectacular *Astrodome* sports stadium is 10km (6 miles) from Houston city centre. Nearby *Astroworld* is a family entertainment park with live shows, restaurants and rides; whilst next door is *Waterworld,* a water recreation park. **Galveston Island,** southeast of Houston on the Gulf of Mexico, is rich in history and pirate lore and noted for its sandy beaches, fishing and watersports.

SAN ANTONIO: This modern, prosperous city retains much of its Spanish heritage with its fiestas, buildings and lifestyle and is the Number 1 visitor city in Texas. The city's Paseo del Rio shopping and entertainments area is unique.
Sightseeing: In 1836, the *Alamo* was the site of a furious battle between a handful of independence-seeking Texans (led by Davy Crockett) and a large Mexican army. Today it is a shrine to Texan courage and patriotism. The 6-storey-high *IMAX Theater* tells the whole story of the Alamo in a gripping film. *Brackenridge Park,* nearby, embraces the headwaters of the San Antonio River and groves of ancient oaks. San Antonio is also home to two major theme parks – the world's largest marine-life park, *Sea World of Texas;*

and *Fiesta Texas,* which features continuous live stage shows and the world's highest and fastest wooden roller-coaster.
Excursions: Pack-trips and working ranch holidays are widely available in the hill country to the west of San Antonio. **New Braunfels,** between Austin and San Antonio, was founded by German immigrants in the 1840s. Today their descendants celebrate their heritage with traditional German festivals. **Corpus Christi** on the Gulf of Mexico, an ideal pirates' hideaway in the 1800s, is now a major seaport and resort, famous for its fishing and surfboarding competitions. Just off the coast is **Padre Island,** a narrow 170km (95-mile) barrier island with watersports, fishing centres and an impressive expanse of protected National Seashore, wildlife refuges and birdlife sites; it is connected to Corpus Christi by a causeway.

AUSTIN: The State capital, 128km (80 miles) northeast of San Antonio, is the gateway to the Texas Hill Country and the chain of Highland lakes. It is one of the most beautiful cities in the USA and the golf paradise of Texas.
Sightseeing: The *Capitol Building*, nine historical districts, the *Austin Steam Train* and *Celis Brewery*. The 300-acre *University of Texas* campus offers the *Lyndon B Johnson Presidential Library,* the *Texas Confederate Museum* and the 1856 *Governor's Mansion*.
Excursions: The 240km (150-mile) chain of *Highland Lakes,* to the northwest of the city, are excellent for fishing, boating and swimming. A day trip into the scenic hill country where several award-winning wineries are located is well worthwhile.

EL PASO: The State's westernmost city stands beside the Rio Grande in the dramatic *Franklin Mountains*. The largest US city on the Mexican border, it is actually closer to metropolitan areas of New Mexico, Arizona and southern California than it is to any major Texan cities. The city's aerial tramway gives breathtaking views across Texas and Mexico. El Paso offers a wide variety of cultural and sports activities, including symphony concerts, theatre, museums, libraries, horse-and hound-racing and many other sports. The *University of Texas,* known for its Bhutanese-style architecture, and *Sun Bowl* stadium are located here.
Excursions: *Big Bend National Park,* south of El Paso, boasts spectacular views of stark desert, forests, mountains and canyons carved by the *Rio Grande*.

Discover Dallas'
Fair Park

LOCATION

Fair Park, located 2 miles from downtown Dallas, Texas, is the site each year for more than 100 special events including concerts, rodeos and festivals.

ART DECO STYLE

Fair Park has the largest collection of 1930's style art deco exposition style architecture in the United States.

HISTORY

In 1886, Fair Park originated with the acquisition of 80 acres of land in East Dallas for an exposition site. From this genesis, the park has been developed into 277 acres which has earned the park's designation as a National Historic Landmark.

MUSEUMS

African American Museum
(214) 565-9026

Age of Steam Railroad Museum
(214) 428-0101

Dallas Aquarium
(214) 670-8443

Dallas Civic Garden Center
(214) 428-7476

Hall of State - Dallas Historical Society
(214) 421-4500

Dallas Museum of Natural History
(214) 421-DINO

The Science Place & The Science Place Planetarium
(214) 428-7200

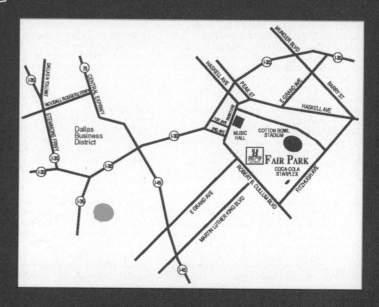

Call (214) 670-8400 for information about this Texas Treasure

A Special Event & Entertainment Venue

FAIR PARK
DALLAS

ATTRACTIONS

Fair Park —

— has eight museums, the largest collection of cultural facilities in Dallas.

— is the site each year for more than 100 special events including concerts, rodeos and festivals.

— has six performance facilities including the Cotton Bowl Stadium, the Music Hall at Fair Park and the Coca-Cola Starplex Amphitheatre, that will accommodate a total of 109,000 people.

— is the home to the State Fair of Texas, which has a midway with 67 different rides including the "Texas Star," the tallest Ferris wheel in North America.

— features the lushly landscaped Leonhardt Lagoon, the Esplanade with its central reflecting pool, the Texas Vietnam Veterans Memorial, the Smith Memorial Fountain, the commemorative brick-paved Texas Promenade Walkway, the Magnolia Lounge historical building housing the Friends of Fair Park, the oldest radio station in Texas-WRR FM Radio, and the Daughters of the American Revolution House.

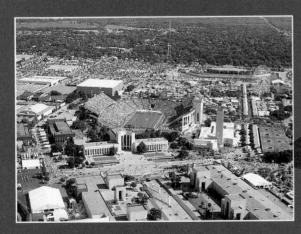

With a central North American location that puts travelers within 4 hours of any major city in the U.S., Mexico and Canada, it should come as no surprise that DFW International Airport is the world's second busiest and fastest growing. With more than 2,200 flights daily to nearly 200 world-wide destinations, we're one of the most convenient airports you'll find anywhere. And we offer many unique benefits:

• User-friendly facilities designed with multi-lingual, easy-to-understand signage.

• Passenger Services Agents fluent in 21 languages.

• Quick, efficient customs clearance in four terminals. (We're talking minutes, not hours.)

• Convenient, affordable, one-stop shopping with new food, beverage and retail outlets.

And as if all this were not extraordinary enough — DFW is located in the heart of the Dallas/Fort Worth metroplex. One of the most exciting places on earth with everything from a world-class symphony to a world-renown rodeo. So try DFW next time you're shopping for an airport. Because we're the one airport in the world that has everything in the world, when and where you want it.

DFW

WE'RE CLOSE TO EVERYTHING.

INTERNATIONAL AIRPORT

*D*allas/Fort Worth International Airport is your gateway to Texas and North America. With more than 2,200 flights daily to nearly 200 world-wide destinations, DFW Airport offers convenience. Dallas/Fort Worth International Airport has more than 100 boarding gates and a sophisticated ground operations system that expedites travelers to their final destination. And unlike destinations on the East or West Coast, Dallas/Fort Worth International Airport is only three and-a-half hours away from every

AND FAR FROM ORDINARY.

major city in the United States and Mexico, and just four hours away from all major cities in Canada.

What may be most important to international travelers is quick and efficient customs clearance. With customs facilities provided in three separate terminals, clearance is measured in minutes, not hours. Currency exchange booths also are available upon arrival and departure.

On the ground, travelers can expect a Texas-size welcome and friendly service. Whatever your appetite, you will appreciate the variety, quality and convenience of dining at any of DFW's 109 food and beverage locations. DFW travelers receive courteous attention from the Airport Assistance Center's 40 volunteers who staff the central information center and seven information booths in the baggage claim areas at the Airport. The information booths are located in Sections A and B of Terminal 2W, Sections A and C of Terminal 2E, Sections A and B of Terminal 3E and Sections B and C of Terminal 4E. The Airport Assistance Center operates 24 hours a day.

DFW Airport's passenger service agents meet international flights, providing a courteous, friendly welcome in one's own language. Passenger service agents speak 21 different languages and dialects. Ground transportation options include taxis, shuttle buses and rental cars. Auto rental telephone counters are located near baggage claim areas, providing direct telephone service to the four rental car companies servicing DFW. Rental car facilities are located on airport property and are available to visitors by a short ride on the Airport Train or rental car courtesy buses, which depart every 10 minutes from the lower level of each terminal.

Ground transportation information to Dallas, Fort Worth and area hotels is available at the information booths located in the baggage claim areas. Taxi service is available along all upper-level curbside exits. Fares to downtown Dallas are about US $28 and fares to downtown Fort Worth are about US $32.

Dallas and Fort Worth's main attractions are easily accessible from the airport by an excellent freeway system. In addition, Dallas Area Rapid Transit crisscrosses the city with convenient, scheduled bus services with special routes through the downtown area and to special events. Taxis are also readily available within the city.

The Dallas/Fort Worth area has almost 60,000 hotel rooms, beginning with the Hyatt Regency DFW located in the center of the Airport itself. The Hyatt Regency DFW, one of the world's largest airport hotels, has 1,400 rooms.

By using DFW Airport as their gateway, travelers can experience both the Wild West culture of Fort Worth or the urban, East Coast culture of Dallas. The airport is just 18 miles (29 km) from the central business districts of Dallas and Fort Worth, and the two cities themselves are only 30 minutes apart.

Dallas, the eighth-largest city in the United States, is remarkable for both its down-home

Dallas/Fort Worth International Airport
P.O. Drawer 619428
DFW Airport, TX 75261-9428
phone (214) 574-6701
fax (214) 574-3780

charm and cosmopolitan glamour. The glittering skyline, the renowned Morton H. Meyerson Symphony Center and Dallas Museum of Art are but a few of the attractions that offer a wide variety of entertainment options for visitors.

Dallas offers excellent shopping, with more retail space than any other U.S. city, more restaurants per person than New York City, and more four-diamond AAA-rated hotels than any other city in the world. Visitors will find every type of cuisine imaginable, from Continental and Southwest to Mexican and some of the best barbecue in the world.

Fair Park is at the edge of downtown Dallas, just minutes away from numerous hotels and restaurants, the Arts District, Deep Ellum, and the West End Historic District. Located within Fair Park itself is the Dallas Museum of Natural History, the Science Place, the Museum of African-American Life & Culture, the Dallas Historical Society, the Dallas Civic Garden Center, the Dallas Aquarium, the Age of Steam Railroad Museum, as well as the Music Hall and Starplex Amphitheater, which features a variety of classical and popular entertainment.

Fort Worth offers a more traditional Texas flavor, beginning with the Old West atmosphere of the historic Stockyards District and Billy Bob's Texas, the world's largest saloon and a variety of restaurants, from continental cuisine to simple home cooking fare.

For art lovers, Fort Worth has some of the finest museums in the country. The collection at the Kimbell Art Museum includes works by Fra Angelico, Caravaggio, Rembrandt, Picasso and Mondrian, as well as pre-Columbian and African works. Most recently, Kimball hosted impressionist masterpieces from the Barnes Collection highlighting works of Cézanne to Matisse. The Amon Carter Museum features 19th and early-20th century art, with works by Thomas Eakins, Frederic Remington and Georgia O'Keefe. The Modern Art Museum of Fort Worth includes 20th century European and American art by such artists as Pollock, Louis, Motherwell and Ruscha.

Between Dallas and Fort Worth, just 15 minutes from Dallas/Fort Worth International Airport, is a major entertainment corridor that includes Six Flags Over Texas amusement park, The Ball Park in Arlington, The Palace of Wax, Ripley's Believe It Or Not, and numerous shopping malls.

Note: For information on attractions in neighbouring States, see above under *States A-Z.*

SOCIAL PROFILE

FOOD & DRINK: Dallas/Fort Worth: Beef features widely, this being cattle country, but there is also a great variety of international cuisine including French, Italian, Chinese, Spanish and Mexican. Dallas has three AAA Five Diamond-rated restaurants – more than any other US city; they include The French Room at the Adolphus Hotel, The Mansion on Turtle Creek and Routh Street Café. In all, Dallas boasts more than 5000 restaurants. Country cooking is popular and includes such local specialities as chicken-fried steak and catfish fried in cornmeal batter. There are several dinner theatres where visitors can eat and see a show. There are also many cafeterias and coffee shops. **Houston:** A great variety of restaurants serving many different types of food. Specialities include Mexican and Spanish cuisine and Gulf seafood. The Convention & Visitors Council publishes a restaurant directory. **Austin:** Approximately 1500 restaurants offer a variety of cuisine including Texan-style steaks and barbecues, Mexican, Mediterranean, Italian, typical American and many more. **San Antonio:** Tex-Mex was practically invented here and this native cuisine can be found throughout the city, along with everything from down-home barbeque specialities to 4-star French cuisine.
THEATRES & CONCERTS: Dallas: The *Dallas Music Hall* in State Fair Park stages concerts, musicals and operas. The *Dallas Theater* presents a wide range of drama. The downtown arts district houses the *Morton H Meyerson Symphony Center, Dallas Museum of Art* and the *Arts District Theater.* Avant-garde theatres can be found in Deep Ellum. **Fort Worth:** The *William Edrington Scott Theater* presents plays, musicals and films. *Casa Manana* stages Broadway musicals during the summer. **Houston:** The *Jesse H Jones Hall for the Performing Arts* is the home of the *Houston Symphony Orchestra,* the *Houston Ballet* and the *Grand Opera.* Other venues include the renowned *Alley Theater,* the open-air *Miller Theater* in Herman Park and the *Music Hall.* **Austin:** The *Paramount Theater* presents top name entertainers in musicals, comedies, concerts and dramas. The *Zachary Scott Theater* presents musicals and plays,

and the *Zilker Hillside Theater* has outdoor musicals and plays. The *Frank Erwin Center* is known for its major recording artist concerts. **San Antonio:** The *Majestic Theater* hosts the *San Antonio Symphony,* as well as travelling Broadway shows and concerts. The unique *Arneson Theater* is an outdoor theatre on the banks of the Paseo del Rio.
NIGHTLIFE: Dallas has clubs, cabarets, discos, singles bars and corner pubs, with music ranging from classical to jazz and from country to contemporary rock. Some clubs are listed as 'private' – ie they are located in a 'dry' area and require membership if you are to be served alcohol. Membership is usually available for a nominal fee. There are also some comedy clubs sprinkled throughout the city and others offer comedy and drama while customers dine. **Fort Worth** also has a number of nightclubs, but the musical emphasis here is on country & western music. **Houston's** many night spots range from big-name entertainment to supper club revues, pavement cafés, discos and singles bars. **Austin** is noted worldwide for its nightly live music venues. Historic 6th Street takes on a lively atmosphere in the evenings as people go pub-crawling between venues catering for country & western, soul, R&B, rock 'n' roll and jazz music. **San Antonio** offers all sorts of musical entertainment, including traditional 'Tejano' sounds, Dixieland jazz, symphony concerts, country & western and college music. The Paseo del Rio is the centre for much of the city's nightlife.
SPORT: The *Dallas Cowboys* (**American football**) and the *Dallas Sidekicks* (**soccer**) play at Texas Stadium (State Highway 183 at Loop 12). The Houston football team is the *Houston Oilers.* The *Texas Rangers* play **baseball** at Arlington Stadium on the Dallas-Fort Worth Turnpike and the *Houston Astros* play baseball at the famous Astrodome. The *Dallas Blackhawks* play **hockey** in Fair Park. Professional **basketball** is played by the *Dallas Mavericks* at Reunion Arena in Dallas, by the *Houston Rockets* in Houston and by the *San Antonio Spurs* at the new 65,000-seat Alamodome. **Golf** courses are available in and around Austin and Dallas, and San Antonio has 11 courses. Dallas also has many facilities for tennis, softball, running, bicycling and polo.
SHOPPING: Dallas/Fort Worth: The elegant and original Neiman Marcus department store should be on any tourist's itinerary. Dallas Market Center is the largest wholesale trade shopping centre in the world and also

offers fine restaurants. Dallas has more shopping centres per capita than any other US city and some of the largest shopping malls in the southwest. Both cities have fine speciality shops. **Houston:** World-class shopping is available in more than 300 stores at the famous Galleria shopping centre. The best buys are Western-style clothes, hats, boots, saddles and riding equipment. A printed guide to stores is available from the Convention & Visitors Council. **San Antonio:** Authentic Mexican folk art can be found throughout the city and there are nine major shopping malls.
SPECIAL EVENTS: The following is list of some of the major events taking place in 1995. Contact the Texas Department of Commerce, Tourism Division for details. **Arp 21-30 '95** *Fiesta San Antonio,* San Antonio. **Jun/Jul** *Peach Jamboree,* Stonewall; *Watermelon Thump,* Luling; *Peach & Melon Festival,* De Leon. **Jun 7-Aug 19** *Texas* (musical), Palo Duro Canyon State Park. **Jul** *Great Texas Mosquito Festival,* Clute. **Sep 15-24** *Four States Fair & Rodeo,* Texarkana. **Sep 29-Oct 22** *State Fair of Texas,* Dallas. **Oct** *Texas Rose Festival,* Tyler; *East Texas Fire Ant Festival,* Marshall. **Nov** *World Championship Chili Cook-Off,* Terlingua; *Pecan Festival,* Seguin. **Nov 3-12** *Wurstfest,* New Braunfels. **Apr 19-28 '96** *Fiesta San Antonio,* San Antonio.

CLIMATE

Dry and warm to very hot throughout the year. Occasional freak rainstorms.
Required clothing: Lightweights throughout most of the year and warmer during winter.

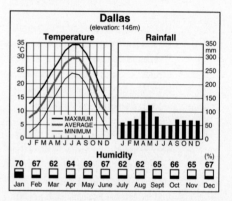

Washington State

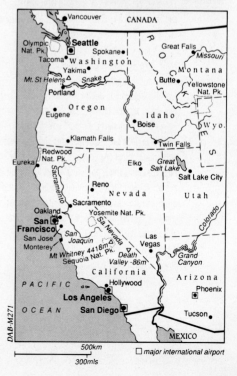

major international airport

Including **Seattle,** gateway to the Pacific northwest States of Washington, Oregon, Idaho and Alaska.

Washington State Tourism Division
PO Box 42500, Olympia, WA 98504-2500
Tel: (206) 753 5601 *or* (1 800) 544 1800 (toll free). Fax: (206) 753 4470.
Seattle/King County Convention & Visitors Bureau
Suite 1300, 520 Pike Street, Seattle, WA 98101
Tel: (206) 461 5800. Fax: (206) 461 5855.
Washington State Convention & Trade Center
Visitor Information, Galleria Level, 800 Convention Place, Seattle, WA 98101
Tel: (206) 461 5840. Fax: (206) 447 5000.
Spokane Regional Convention & Visitors Bureau
Suite 180, West 926 Sprague Avenue, Spokane, WA 99204
Tel: (509) 624 1341. Fax: (509) 623 1297.
Port of Seattle Information Office
First Public Relations, 2 Cinnamon Row, Plantation Wharf, York Place, London SW11 3TW
Tel: (0171) 978 5233. Fax: (0171) 924 3134. Opening hours: 0900-1730 Monday to Friday.

TIME: GMT - 8. *Daylight Saving Time* is observed.
THE STATE: Washington State, bordering Canada and the Pacific Ocean, offers some of the nation's finest scenery for outdoor recreation. It has the second-highest population of any western State, yet visitors can travel from any city centre to peaceful countryside within minutes. The Snake and Columbia rivers flow through eastern Washington State before joining to cut a passage through the Cascades, the north–south mountain range that dominates the centre of the State, rising to 4392m (14,408ft) at Mount Rainer. There are many fine beaches and small resorts on the Pacific coast. Much of the State is covered by coniferous forest. Holiday highlights include yachting on Puget Sound, hiking along the Pacific Crest National Scenic Trail and mountain climbing in the Cascades and Olympics. Excellent accommodation is available, ranging from bed & breakfast establishments to 5-star luxury hotels.

TRAVEL

AIR: Both *British Airways* and *United Airlines* offer nonstop flights to Seattle. Other airlines provide a one-stop service.
Approximate flight times: From Seattle to *London* is 9 hours 5 minutes (direct) and to *San Francisco* is 1 hour 50 minutes.
International airport: *Seattle-Tacoma International (SEA)* is 22km (14 miles) south of the city; travel time – 20 minutes. Buses link the airport to points throughout the city. Taxis are available.
SEA: *Washington State Ferries* link Seattle with the Olympic Peninsula, Bainbridge Island and other points in the region. The Victoria Clipper links Victoria and British Columbia in Canada to Seattle via high-speed catamarans.
RAIL: Seattle is on the main *Amtrak* network, which provides rail links eastwards to Chicago via Salt Lake City or Spokane and southwards to Oakland and Los Angeles (see *Illinois* and *California* sections above for approximate journey times).
ROAD: Approximate driving times: From Seattle to *Vancouver* is 2 hours, to *Portland* is 3 hours, to *Spokane* is 6 hours, to *Boise* is 10 hours, to *Calgary* is 15 hours, to *Los Angeles* is 24 hours, to *Chicago* is 44 hours, to *Dallas* is 45 hours, to *New York* is 61 hours and to *Miami* is 69 hours.
All times are based on non-stop driving at or below the applicable speed limits.
Approximate *Greyhound* journey times: From Seattle (tel: (1 800) 231 2222; toll free) to *Vancouver* is 4 hours, to *Portland* is 4 hours and to *Spokane* is 7 hours.
URBAN: Seattle has an excellent bus system. An underground bus tunnel operates through downtown Seattle from the International District to the Convention Center, with stops at Pioneer Square, the financial district and Westlake Center. A high-speed monorail links the downtown area with the *Seattle Center.* Public transport is free in the downtown area. Taxis and hire cars are also available.

RESORTS & EXCURSIONS

SEATTLE: The 'Emerald City' is the primary international and domestic gateway to Washington State and the Pacific northwest. The State's largest city, Seattle is surrounded by the waters of Lake Washington and Puget Sound and enjoys spectacular views of the

Cascades and Olympic Mountains. The waterfront area is known for its seafood restaurants, shops and water excursions.
Sightseeing: The *Seattle Center,* built for the 1962 World Fair, is the city's cultural heart, the home of opera, symphony, ballet and repertory theatre companies. It also contains the *Space Needle,* 185m (610ft) tall with an observation deck, restaurant and cocktail bar. *Pioneer Square* is a 17-sq-block national historic district showcasing Seattle's early history with shops, art galleries, restaurants and the one-of-a-kind underground tour. The *Kingdome* stadium is also situated here, home to the Seattle Mariners baseball team and the Seattle Seahawks football team. *Chinatown,* location of the Oriental community, offers arts, crafts and cuisine from China and Japan. *Pike Place Public Market,* situated just above the waterfront, is the oldest continually operating farmer's market in the USA featuring abundant seafood and produce, as well as handcrafted items from the Pacific northwest. Harbour tours and fishing excursions are easily available and the excursion to *Tillicum Village* is highly recommended. Other major attractions include *Woodland Park Zoo, Seattle Aquarium* and the *Japanese Garden.*
Excursions: Tacoma, south of Seattle, is the State's third-largest city. Its *Point Defiance Park* is one of the finest urban parks in the Pacific northwest. **Olympic National Park,** west of Seattle, has glacier-studded mountains, rainforests, lakes, streams and miles of unspoiled coastline. **Spokane,** near the border with Idaho in eastern Washington, is the State's second-largest city; it boasts the outstanding *Riverfront Park.* The famous *Ellensburg Rodeo* is held every Labor Day weekend at Ellensburg. **Kennewick, Pasco** and **Richland** are at the heart of the region's wine country. **Mount Rainier National Park,** southwest of Tacoma, offers breathtaking views and skiing and other winter sports. *Mount St Helens* in the **Gifford Pinchot National Park** in southwest Washington is the site of the infamous volcanic eruption of 1980, which left a gigantic crater in the mountain's north flank. It is possible to take short trips by light airplane over the summit.
Note: For information on attractions in neighbouring States, see above under *States A-Z.*

SOCIAL PROFILE

FOOD & DRINK: Seattle is noted for its seafood and has more than 2000 restaurants serving many different types of cuisine. Restaurant/bars can stay open until 0200 all week. Beer and wine are available in grocery stores and hard liquor in State stores, usually 1000-2000 every day, except Sunday. Stores in big cities have later closing hours. Minimum drinking age is 21.
THEATRES & CONCERTS: The *Seattle Opera's* season runs from September to May. The *Seattle Symphony Orchestra* plays from November to April. The *Pacific Northwest Ballet* is also recommended and both the *Pacific Northwest Ballet* and the *Seattle Repertory* seasons are from October to May.
NIGHTLIFE: Jazz spots, nightclubs and discotheques are scattered throughout the city.
SHOPPING: Westlake Center, Nordstrom and Le Bon Marché are the major mall and department store respectively, located in the heart of the retail district. Other interesting shopping areas include Pioneer Square, the Waterfront Gold Rush Strip and Pike Place Market.
SPECIAL EVENTS: The following is a list of some of the major events taking place in 1995.
Mar-end of May '95 *Whale Fest,* Westport. **Mar 4-5** *Beachcomber's Fun Fair,* Ocean Shores. **Mar 11-12** *Speelyi-Mi Arts & Crafts Trade Fair,* Toppenish. **Mar 17** *Northwest Microfest,* Lacey. **Late Apr-early May** *Washington State Apple Blossom Festival,* Wenatchee. **Apr 22** *Daffodil Parade,* Tacoma. **May 12-14** *Walla Walla Balloon Stampede,* Walla Walla. **May 12-21** *Spokane Lilac Festival.* **May 17-21** *Viking Fest,* Poulsbo. **May 27-28** *Ski-to-Sea Race,* Bellingham; *Laser Light Festival,* Grand Coulee. **Early Jun** *Spring Barrel Tasting,* Tri-Cities; *Tinowit International Pow Wow,* Yakima. **Mid-Jun** *Northwest Microbrewery Festival,* Fall City. **Jun 1-4** *Mason County Forest Festival,* Shelton. **Jul 21-23** *Columbia Gorge Bluegrass Festival,* Stevenson. **Jul 7-9** *Chewelah Chataqua,* Chewelah. **Aug 4-6** *Vintiques Northwest,* Yakima. **Aug 11-12** *Omak Stampede and Suicide Race.* **Aug 21-27** *Washington State International Kite Festival,* Long Beach. **Sep 1-4** *Ellensburg Rodeo; Bumbershoot,* Seattle. **Oct 7-8** *Oysterfest,* Shelton; *Issaquah Salmon Days.* **Oct 20-21** *Harvest Festival,* Lynden; *Cranberry Festival,* Ilwaco. **Nov 24-26** *Thanksgiving in the Wine Country,* Yakima Valley. **Dec 2-16** *Dickens Family Christmas,* Cosmopolis.

CLIMATE

Washington has two distinct climate zones. Summer days west of the Cascades rarely rise above 26°C, and winter days seldom drop below 8°C, while the east of the State has warm summers and cool winters.

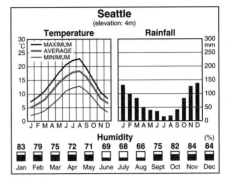

Gateway to George Washington Country, including Pennsylvania, Maryland, Delaware, Virginia and West Virginia.

Washington DC Convention & Visitors Association
Suite 600, 1212 New York Avenue, NW, Washington, DC 20005
Tel: (202) 789 7000. Fax: (202) 789 7037.
Destination Washington DC
375 Upper Richmond Road West, London SW14 7NX
Tel: (0181) 392 9187. Fax: (0181) 392 1318. Opening hours: 0930-1800 Monday to Friday.

TRAVEL

AIR: Approximate flight times: From Washington DC to *Anchorage* is 10 hours 25 minutes, to *Atlanta* is 1 hour 40 minutes, to *Chicago* is 2 hours 10 minutes, to *Frankfurt/M* is 7 hours 40 minutes, to *Honolulu* is 13 hours 40 minutes, to *London* is 6 hours 50 minutes, to *Los Angeles* is 5 hours 40 minutes, to *Miami* is 2 hours 30 minutes, to *Montréal* is 2 hours 5 minutes, to *New York* is 1 hour, to *Orlando* is 2 hours 10 minutes, to *Paris* is 8 hours 20 minutes, to *San Francisco* is 7 hours 10 minutes, to *Singapore* is 25 hours 45 minutes and to *Toronto* is 2 hours 20 minutes.
International airports: *Washington-Dulles International (WAS)* is 43km (27 miles) from the city (in Virginia); travel time – 50 minutes. Coach runs every hour from 0630-2400. Taxis are also available.
The capital is also served by *Baltimore-Washington*

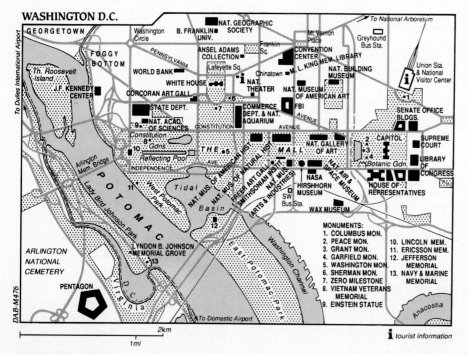

WASHINGTON D.C.

MONUMENTS:
1. COLUMBUS MON.
2. PEACE MON.
3. GRANT MON.
4. GARFIELD MON.
5. WASHINGTON MON.
6. SHERMAN MON.
7. ZERO MILESTONE
8. VIETNAM VETERANS MEMORIAL
9. EINSTEIN STATUE
10. LINCOLN MEM.
11. ERICSSON MEM.
12. JEFFERSON MEMORIAL
13. NAVY & MARINE MEMORIAL

ℹ tourist information

International Airport (BWI), west of Baltimore; see above in entry for Maryland.

Domestic airport: Washington National (DCA) receives transfer connections from other USA gateways. It is 5km (3 miles) southwest of the city. Coach runs every 30 minutes 0700-2200. Metro rail service runs every 5 minutes 0600-2400 to Metro Center. Taxi service is also available. There is a frequent airport bus service between Washington National and Dulles International airports.
RAIL: The principal corridor is the New York–Philadelphia–Baltimore–Washington DC route, with frequent fast trains. There are also routes from Philadelphia and Washington DC to Pittsburgh. Florida-bound trains run from Washington DC to Richmond. There are also local trains to the Philadelphia area. The journey time to New York is 3 hours 15 minutes. See New York section above for further East Coast journey times.
ROAD: Approximate driving times: From Washington DC to Baltimore is 1 hour, to Richmond is 2 hours, to Norfolk is 4 hours, to New York is 5 hours, to Pittsburgh is 5 hours, to Charleston (West Virginia) is 7 hours, to Charlotte is 8 hours, to Cincinnati is 10 hours, to Chicago is 14 hours, to Miami is 22 hours, to Dallas is 28 hours, to Los Angeles is 55 hours and to Seattle is 58 hours.
All times are based on non-stop driving at or below the applicable speed limits.
Approximate Greyhound **journey times:** From Washington DC (tel: (1 800) 231 2222; toll free) to Richmond is 2 hours, to Philadelphia is 3 hours 30 minutes, to New York is 4 hours 30 minutes, to Pittsburgh is 5 hours 30 minutes and to Knoxville is 12 hours 30 minutes.

URBAN: The Metro (subway) system offers quick and comfortable transport within the downtown area; fares are zonal. Lines are being extended into the suburban areas of Maryland and northern Virginia. There are also suburban and downtown bus services. It is possible to transfer from Metro to bus without additional charge (except during rush hour), but not from bus to Metro. Taxis are available within the city area; fares are again zonal (and comparatively cheap by big-city standards). Most major car hire and motor camper rental agencies have offices in Washington DC.

RESORTS & EXCURSIONS

WASHINGTON DC: 'DC' stands for 'District of Columbia', not a State but an administrative district created specifically to avoid having the capital city in any one State. Washington DC is a city of green parks, wide tree-lined streets, white marble buildings and, surprisingly for a US city, very few skyscrapers, which gives it a European air. It is the centre for visiting diplomats and has the fourth-largest concentration of hotel and motel rooms. Tourism is the leading private industry and business interests are increasingly attracted by the many light industrial and research companies that are now moving into the vicinity.
Sightseeing: The streets are a rectangular grid cut by long diagonals radiating from important sites such as the Capitol and the White House; the diagonals are named after States. Aligned with this grid is a grand formal vista, the Green Mall, which extends from Capitol Hill to Potomac Park on the river of the same name. A second rectangular garden runs northwards at right angles as far as the White House, which has been the home of every US President since 1800 and is visited by more than one million people every year. The Tidal Basin, a beautiful lake famous for its Japanese cherry trees, lies just to the southwest. The Green Mall contains many of Washington DC's most important monuments and institutions, including the Lincoln and Jefferson Memorials; the Washington Monument (at 169m/555ft, the tallest masonry structure in the world); the Smithsonian Institute; the old Museum of Natural History; the modern National Gallery of Art, with its stunning East Building designed by the world-famous architect I M Pei; and, of course, the Capitol, where Senators and Representatives meet under a magnificent 55m (180ft) dome to shape US legislative policy. It also offers many recreational activities, including boat trips on the Potomac (the jetty is to the south of the Lincoln Memorial). Arlington National Cemetery, on the other side of the river, contains the graves of 175,000 US soldiers who fought in wars from the Revolution onwards. Other sights include Chinatown, where many of the city's oriental shops and restaurants are centred; Constitution Gardens, with more than 50 acres of trees and lawns; the J Edgar Hoover Building (the FBI's headquarters) at 9th Street and Pennsylvania Avenue; the Pentagon; and the US Supreme Court, the highest

court in the country.
Note: For information on attractions in neighbouring States, see above under States A-Z.

SOCIAL PROFILE

FOOD & DRINK: Washington has a renowned selection of good restaurants, and almost any national cuisine can be found.
THEATRES & CONCERTS: Pennsylvania Avenue houses the National and Ford Theaters. The John F Kennedy Center for the Performing Arts stands at the foot of New Hampshire Avenue overlooking the Potomac River. Here there are four theatres for live performances of opera, concerts, musical plays, drama and festival occasions. A fifth theatre houses the American Film Institute. Open-air concerts are held at the Jefferson Memorial in the summer and the National Gallery of Art has Sunday evening concerts in the East Court Garden, September to June.
NIGHTLIFE: Washington has few bona fide nightclubs with live entertainment. However, there are numerous bars and discotheques in downtown Washington, Georgetown and the suburbs.
SHOPPING: There are several shopping areas in Washington DC. The F Street Mall (between 15th and 11th streets) is the most traditional; Connecticut Avenue between K Street and Dupont Circle has many speciality shops; and Georgetown, in the area of Wisconsin and M streets, offers a wide range of boutiques, antique dealers, arts and crafts shops, and pavement stalls selling jewellery and leather goods. Visit some of the government buildings for unique souvenirs and gifts.
SPECIAL EVENTS: Mar 1-5 '95 Washington Flower & Garden Show. **Mar 12** St Patrick's Day Parade. **Mar 17** St Patrick's Day Celebrations, Arlington. **Mar 25** Smithsonian Kite Festival. **Mar 25-Apr 8** National Cherry Blossom Festival. **Apr 17** White House Easter Egg Roll. **Apr 19-30** Filmfest DC. **Apr 26-30** Smithsonian's Craft Show. **May 7** Takoma Park House & Garden Tour, Takoma Park. **May 7-13** 12th Annual National Tourism Week. **May 29** Memorial Day Jazz Festival, Old Town Alexandria. **Jun 5-11** Dance Africa DC; Kemper Open Pro-Ams Golf Tournament. **Jun 17-18** Northern Virginia Antiques Show, Arlington. **Jul 1-4** DC World Jazz Festival. **Jul 4** National Independence Day (firework display over the Washington Monument). **Sep 2** National Frisbee Festival; African Cultural Festival. **Sep 10** DC Blues Festival, Rock Creek Park. **Sep 23-24** International Children's Festival, Vienna, VA. **Oct 7** Annual Fall Farm Festival, Oxon Hill Farm Park. **Oct 7-9** Taste of DC (food festival). **Oct 22-29** Washington International Horse Show, Landover. **Nov 17-19** Sugarloaf's Autumn Crafts Festival, Gaithersburg. **Dec 1 '95-Jan 2 '96** Annual Winter Festival of Lights, Watkins Regional Park.

CLIMATE

Summers are very warm while winter temperatures can be extremely low.

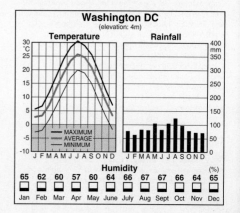

TEMPERATURE CONVERSIONS

-20	-10	0°C	10	20	30	40

0	10	20	30°F 40	50	60	70	80	90	100

RAINFALL CONVERSIONS

0mm	200	400	600	800

0in	5	10	15	20	25	30

Washington DC
(elevation: 4m)

Temperature   Rainfall

— MAXIMUM
— AVERAGE
— MINIMUM

J F M A M J J A S O N D   J F M A M J J A S O N D

Humidity

65	62	60	57	60	64	66	67	66	67	64	65	(%)
Jan	Feb	Mar	Apr	May	June	July	Aug	Sept	Oct	Nov	Dec	

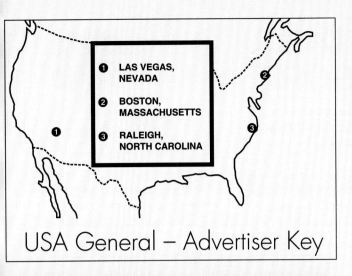

USA General – Advertiser Key

❶ LAS VEGAS, NEVADA

❷ BOSTON, MASSACHUSETTS

❸ RALEIGH, NORTH CAROLINA

THE DURHAM BULLS

AMERICA'S FAVORITE FARM TEAM!

The Durham Bulls, the Class A affiliate of the Atlanta Braves, were immortalized in the 1988 film, "Bull Durham," starring Kevin Costner and Susan Sarandon. The Bulls play a 70-game home season running from April-September, and will christen their brand-new 7,500-seat ballpark in 1995. To experience minor league baseball in all its charm, be sure to include a Bulls' game when you visit the Raleigh-Durham region of North Carolina!

CALL (919) 956-BULL (2855)
FOR TICKET INFORMATION

❶ SARASOTA
❷ DAYTONA BEACH
❸ ORLANDO
❹ NAPLES
❺ BRADENTON
❻ KISSIMMEE
❼ NAVARRE
❽ BONITA SPRINGS
❾ SEAGROVE BEACH

USA Florida – Advertiser Key

1022

US External Territories

The following is a list of the US External Territories; some US External Territories have their own entries in this book, but basic facts are included here for the others. For more information on these islands, contact the US Embassies. *American Samoa, Guam, Palau* (under the Pacific Islands of Micronesia) and the *US Virgin Islands* are dealt with separately in this book.

Baker & Howland Islands and Jarvis Islands

Location: Central Pacific Ocean.

US Fish & Wildlife Service
PO Box 50167, Refuge Complex Office, Honolulu, HI 96850
Tel: (808) 541 1201.

Population: Presently uninhabited. **Geography:** Baker & Howland Islands are two low-lying coral atolls located about 2575km (1600 miles) southwest of Honolulu, Hawaii. There are no lagoons on the islands. Jarvis Island is a low-lying coral island about 2090km (1300 miles) south of Hawaii. **Time:** GMT - 12. **History:** The islands were originally settled by the Americans in 1935, but were subsequently evacuated during the Second World War. In 1974, the islands were registered as national wildlife refuges to be administered by the US Fish & Wildlife Service and visitors wishing to land on the islands must seek permission from this organisation (for address, see above). In 1990, Congress passed legislation for the islands to be included within the boundaries of the State of Hawaii.

Johnston Atoll

Location: Central Pacific Ocean.

FCDNA
Commander, Johnston Atoll, APO San Francisco, CA 96035.

Area: 2.6 sq km (1 sq mile). **Population:** 327, all on Johnston Island (1980). **Geography:** Located 1319km (820 miles) west–southwest of Honolulu, Johnston Atoll consists of Johnston Island, Sand Island and two man-made islands, East (Hikina) and North (Akua). **Time:** GMT - 10. **History:** The USA began a chemical disposal facility on Johnston Atoll in 1983, but it was not until 1989 that it gained the world's attention when the USA agreed to destroy 400 tons of nerve gas here after transporting it from the Federal Republic of Germany. Complaints were lodged by the South Pacific Forum nations and various environmental groups which resulted in the USA sending a group of scientists to monitor the safety of the disposal facility's activities. The Atoll is closed to the public and has been designated a Naval Defense Sea Area and Airspace Reservation administered by the FCDNA Commander (for address, see above).

Kingman Reef

Location: Pacific Ocean.

US Department of Defense
Department of the Navy, The Pentagon, Washington, DC 20350
Tel: (202) 695 0965.

Geography: Located 1500km (925 miles) southwest of Hawaii, Kingman Reef consists of a reef and shoal

measuring 8km (5 miles) by 15km (9.5 miles). **History:** The reef is closed to public access and has been designated a Naval Defense Sea Area and Airspace Reservation administered by the US Department of Defense (for address, see above). In 1990, Congress passed legislation for the reef to be included within the boundaries of the State of Hawaii.

Midway Islands

Location: Northern Pacific Ocean.

US Department of Defense
Department of the Navy, The Pentagon, Washington, DC 20350
Tel: (202) 695 0965.

Area: 5 sq km (2 sq miles). **Population:** 2200 (1983). **Geography:** Located 1850km (1150 miles) northwest of Hawaii, the Midway Islands consist of Sand and Eastern islands. **Time:** GMT - 11. **History:** Like Baker & Howland Islands and Jarvis Island, the Midway Islands became included as part of the State of Hawaii in 1990. Designated a Naval Defense Sea Area, public access to the Midway Islands is authorised by the US Department of Defense (for address, see above).

Palmyra

Location: Pacific Ocean.

Area: 100 hectares. **Population:** Uninhabited. **Geography:** Palmyra is made up of 50 low-lying islets about 1600km (1000 miles) south of Honolulu. **Time:** GMT - 11. **History:** Administered by the US Department of the Interior since 1961, Palmyra was included within the boundaries of the State of Hawaii after legislation in 1990. The area is privately owned by Leslie, Dudley and Ainlie Fullard-Leo of Hawaii and permission must be granted by the owners to land on the island.

Wake Island

Location: Western Pacific, Micronesia.

US Department of Defense
Department of the Air Force, The Pentagon, Washington, DC 20380
Tel: (202) 694 8010.

Area: 8 sq km (3 sq miles). **Population:** 1600 (1983). **Geography:** Wake Island lies in the Pacific Ocean, along with its neighbours Wilkes and Peale Islands, approximately 2060km (1290 miles) east of Guam and 500km (310 miles) north of the Marshall Islands. The location (not the size) of this island makes it of major importance to the US government. **Time:** GMT + 12. **History:** A protectorate island of the USA, the US flag having been formally raised over the island in 1898, its strategic location has led in the past to its use as a trans-Pacific telegraph relay station and a stopover for flights in the days before jet flight became universal. From 1941-44 it was occupied by the Japanese. In 1990, Congress passed legislation for the islands to be included within the boundaries of Guam. The island has been a military air force base since 1972, and is administered by the USAF (for address, see above).

US Virgin Islands

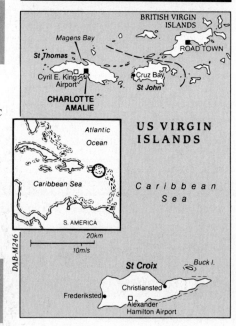

Location: Caribbean.

Diplomatic representation: The US Virgin Islands are represented abroad by US Embassies. For addresses, see the *USA* entry earlier in the book. Information and advice may also be obtained at the addresses below.

US Virgin Islands Division of Tourism
PO Box 6400, Charlotte Amalie, St Thomas, VI 00804-6400
Tel: 774 8784. Fax: 774 4390.
US Virgin Islands Division of Tourism
PO Box 200, Cruz Bay, St John, VI 00830
Tel: 776 6450.
US Virgin Islands Division of Tourism
PO Box 4538, Christiansted, St Croix, VI 00822
Tel: 773 0495. Fax: 778 9259; *or*
Custom House Building, Strand Street, Frederiksted, St Croix, VI 00840
Tel: 772 0357.
US Virgin Islands Division of Tourism (European Office)
2 Cinnamon Row, Plantation Wharf, York Place, London SW11 3TW
Tel: (0171) 978 5262. Fax: (0171) 924 3171. Opening hours: 0930-1730 Monday to Friday.
The office is closed to the public.
US Virgin Islands Division of Tourism
Suite 2108, 1270 Avenue of the Americas, New York, NY 10020
Tel: (212) 332 2222. Fax: (212) 332 2223.
Offices also in: Atlanta, Chicago, Los Angeles, Miami and Washington, DC.
US Virgin Islands Division of Tourism
Suite 3120, Center Tower, 3300 Bloor Street, Toronto, Ontario MX8 2X3
Tel: (416) 233 1414 *or* (1 800) 465 8784 (toll free). Fax: (416) 233 9367.

AREA: 354.8 sq km (137 sq miles).
POPULATION: 101,809 (1990 estimate).

Health	
GALILEO/WORLDSPAN: **TI-DFT/JFK/HE**	
SABRE: **TIDFT/JFK/HE**	

Visa	
GALILEO/WORLDSPAN: **TI-DFT/JFK/VI**	
SABRE: **TIDFT/JFK/VI**	

For more information on Timatic codes refer to Contents.

POPULATION DENSITY: 286.9 per sq km.
CAPITAL: Charlotte Amalie (St Thomas). **Population:** 11,842 (1980).
GEOGRAPHY: The islands are situated 50km (30 miles) east of Puerto Rico and comprise some 50 islands covered with lush tropical vegetation and fringed by iridescent shores. St Thomas is long and thin, rising abruptly to a ridge with an excellent deep-water harbour. St John is covered partly in bay forests. St Croix consists of 218 sq km (84 sq miles) of rolling ex-plantation land.
LANGUAGE: English is the official language. Spanish and Creole are also widely spoken.
RELIGION: Christian, mainly Protestant.
TIME: GMT - 4.
ELECTRICITY: 120 volts AC, 60Hz.
COMMUNICATIONS: Telephone: IDD is available. Country code: 1 809. There are no area codes. Outgoing international code: 011. **Fax:** Services are available. **Telex:** Facilities are available. **Post:** Airmail to Europe takes up to a week. Post office hours: 0900-1700 Monday to Friday, 0900-1200 Saturday. **Press:** The daily newspapers are *Virgin Islands Daily News* and *St Croix Avis.*
BBC World Service and Voice of America frequencies: From time to time these change. See the section *How to Use this Book* for more information.

BBC:				
MHz	**17.84**	**15.22**	**9.915**	**5.975**
Voice of America:				
MHz	**15.21**	**11.70**	**6.130**	**0.930**

PASSPORT/VISA

Immigration requirements for the US Virgin Islands are the same as for the USA. See the general *USA* entry earlier in the book.

MONEY

Currency: US Dollar (US$) = 100 cents.
Currency restrictions: Import and export of amounts in excess of US$10,000 must be declared.
See the *USA* section above for information on currency exchange, exchange rates, credit cards, etc.
Banking hours: 0900-1430 Monday to Thursday; 0900-1400 and 1530-1700 Friday.

DUTY FREE

Duty must be paid on all gifts and alcohol brought in from abroad. Other customs regulations, duty-free exemptions and prohibitions are as for the USA. See the *Duty Free* section in the *USA* entry above.

PUBLIC HOLIDAYS

Jan 1 '95 New Year's Day. **Jan 6** Three Kings' Day. **Jan 16** Martin Luther King Day. **Feb 20** Presidents' Day. **Mar 31** Transfer Day. **Apr 13** Holy Thursday. **Apr 14** Good Friday. **Apr 17** Easter Monday. **May 29** Memorial Day. **Jun 19** Organic Act Day. **Jul 4** Independence Day. **Jul 24** *Supplication Day. **Sep 4** Labor Day. **Oct 9** Columbus Day. **Oct 16** Local Thanksgiving Day. **Nov 1** D Hamilton Jackson Day. **Nov 11** Veterans' Day. **Nov 23** Thanksgiving Day. **Dec 25-26** Christmas. **Jan 1 '96** New Year's Day. **Jan 6** Three Kings' Day. **Jan 15** Martin Luther King Day. **Feb 19** Presidents' Day. **Mar 31** Transfer Day. **Apr 4** Holy Thursday. **Apr 5** Good Friday. **Apr 8** Easter Monday.
Note [*]: Not celebrated as a full public holiday but some offices and shops may be closed.

HEALTH

Regulations and requirements may be subject to change at short notice, and you are advised to contact your doctor well in advance of your intended date of departure. Any numbers in the chart refer to the footnotes below.

	Special Precautions?	Certificate Required?
Yellow Fever	No	No
Cholera	No	No
Typhoid & Polio	Yes	-
Malaria	No	-
Food & Drink	1	-

[1]: Water precautions are advised outside the main centres. Tap water is considered safe to drink. Milk is pasteurised and dairy products are safe for consumption. Local meat, poultry, seafood, fruit and vegetables are generally considered safe to eat.
Health care: Medical costs are very high and health insurance is essential. Medical facilities are of a similar standard to those in the USA.

TRAVEL

AIR: *Continental Airlines* flies daily from New York (Newark) to St Thomas and St Croix. *American Airlines* offers daily services from New York (JFK) and Miami to St Thomas and St Croix. *Delta* flies daily from Atlanta and New York to St Thomas. *British Airways* offers a same-day connection via Puerto Rico to St Thomas or St Croix as of April 1995. Commuter service from San Juan is available through *Sunaire Express, American Eagle* and *Sea Air Shuttle*. For schedules of these and other operator's routes to the US Virgin Islands, contact the airlines direct.
Approximate flight times: From St Croix to *London* is 14 hours (including stopover), to *New York* is 3 hours 45 minutes, to *Miami* is 2 hours 30 minutes, to *St Maarten* is 45 minutes, to *St Thomas* is 30 minutes and to *San Juan* is 30 minutes.
International airports: *St Thomas (STT)* (Cyril E King) is 3km (2 miles) from Charlotte Amalie, and *St Croix (STX)* (Alexander Hamilton) is about 14.5km (9 miles) from Christiansted.
SEA: The main passenger ports are Charlotte Amalie (St Thomas) and Frederiksted on St Croix. A number of cruise lines operating out of Miami and San Juan include the US Virgin Islands in their itineraries around the Caribbean. Regular ferries sail between St Thomas and St John and the British Virgin Islands. Ferries leave from downtown Charlotte Amalie and Red Hook Dock on St Thomas, and Cruz Bay on St John. For more information on cruise ships to the US Virgin Islands, contact the Cruise Ship Activities Office, c/o West Indian Company Dock, St Thomas. Tel: 774 8784. Fax: 774 4390.
ROAD: Well-maintained roads connect all main towns, but not much else. Driving is on the left. **Bus:** Public services operate on St Thomas from Charlotte Amalie to Red Hook and Bordeaux, and St Croix has a taxi-van service between Christiansted and Frederiksted. St John has no bus services. **Taxi:** Available on all the islands. These follow standard routes between various points, and the fares for these are published. Sharing taxis is a common practice. **Car hire:** There are international car hire agencies at the airports and in the main towns on St Thomas and St Croix. St John has four rental agencies. Jeeps or mini-mokes are popular modes of travel and these too can be hired. **Documentation:** National licences are accepted; an International Driving Permit is not required.
JOURNEY TIMES: The following chart gives approximate journey times (in hours and minutes) from Charlotte Amalie to other major cities/towns in the US Virgin Islands.

	Air	Road	Sea
Chris'sted, SC*	0.25	-	-
Cruz Bay, SJ*	-	-	0.45
Magens Bay	-	0.20	-
Coral World	-	0.40	-

Note [*]: SC = St Croix; SJ = St John.

ACCOMMODATION

HOTELS: The islands have more hotels per sq mile than anywhere in the Caribbean. Costs vary according to standard, but are generally quite high compared to other Caribbean islands. The islands' hotel association has a counter at the airport to assist with reservations. The following organisations can give further information: St Thomas & St John Hotel Association, PO Box 2300, St Thomas, VI 00803. Tel: 774 6835. Fax: 774 4993; *or* St Croix Hotel Association, PO Box 24238, Gallows Bay, St Croix, VI 00824. Tel: 773 7117. Fax: 773 5883.
CAMPING: There are two main campsites, both on the more rural island of St John. The first is Cinnamon Bay Camp, located inside the 7028-acre St John National Park. Inexpensive bare plots and one-room beach units are both available for a maximum stay of two weeks. The site is very popular, so reservations should be booked well in advance by contacting Cinnamon Bay Camp, Box 720, St John, VI 00830. Tel: 776 6330. The other campsite is at Maho Bay near a beautiful beach and offers 99 units. Contact Maho Bay Camp, Cruz Bay, St John, VI 00830. Tel: 776 6240. Fax: 776 6504.

RESORTS & EXCURSIONS

St Croix is the largest of the US Virgin Islands. **Christiansted** is one of the two major towns showing early-Danish influence. *Fort Christiansværn* (dating from 1774), *Government House*, the *Old Custom House and Art Gallery* and the wharf area are among its historic sites. Outside of Christiansted, on West Airport Road, is the *Cruz Rum Distillery* where visitors can taste the islands' rum and and watch it being made. On the way to **Frederiksted** is *Whim Greathouse,* portraying plantation life in the 1700s. Frederiksted is also of Danish origin and has a 15-acre tropical rainforest nearby.
Buck Island can easily be reached by sailing the 10km (6-mile) channel which separates it from Christiansted. Offshore is one of the world's most impressive marine gardens, maintained by the National Park Service as an underwater protected reef.
St Thomas is the second-largest and the most interesting of this chain of islands. Like St Croix, it has many associations with the Danes and retains much Danish influence. The main town, **Charlotte Amalie,** is the group's capital. Imported goods from all over the world make it a marvellous shopping centre and stores tucked into remodelled Danish warehouses line each side of the picturesque Main Street. Cobblestone alleys with numerous boutiques lead down to the waterfront. *Blackbeard's Castle* is the earliest fortification in the US Virgin Islands. Other attractions include *Fort Christian,* built in 1672; the *Coral World Observatory;* the *Frederick Lutheran Church* of 1850; *Government House* on Government Hill, 1866; *Venus Pillar* on Magnolia Hill; *Bluebeard's Tower,* the 19th-century pirate's one-time abode; and the Synagogue on *Crystal Gade*, one of the oldest in the USA. On the northern coast is *Magens Bay,* claimed to be one of the world's top ten beaches.
St John is the most 'unspoilt' of the islands. It has no airport, and two-thirds of the island's deep valleys and most of its shoreline have been set aside as a National Park. *Cruz Bay* is a small town offering excellent gift shops and dive centres. *Trunk Bay* is a beautiful beach, and the diving is very good. Accommodation on the island is limited. *Caneel Bay Plantation* is a luxurious cottage colony. *Cinnamon Bay* and *Maho Bay* have campsites. Cottages can also be rented.

SOCIAL PROFILE

FOOD & DRINK: High-quality restaurants serve everything from French and Italian to Chinese cuisine. Island specialities include fresh fish and lobster. Dining out is casual and there are an increasing number of eateries on the main islands offering seafoods, burgers, steaks and native fare. **Drink:** *St John's Bay* rum is strong and distinctive.
NIGHTLIFE: Steel bands, folk singing, calypso and limbo dancing are popular. Discos are also available. St Thomas has several nightclubs; many hotels also offer entertainment. Cinemas on St Croix and St Thomas show English-language films.
SHOPPING: All luxury items up to US$200 are cheap as they are duty free. Charlotte Amalie on St Thomas is the best shopping centre. Best buys include watches, cameras, fine jewellery, china, leather goods, perfume, liquor and designer clothing. **Shopping hours:** 0900-1700/1730 Monday to Saturday.
SPORT: Golf: There are two 18-hole courses on St Croix, at Carambola Resort and at Buccaneer Hotel. A 9-hole course is located at the Reef. St Thomas has an excellent 18-hole course at Mahogany Run. **Tennis:** There are many tennis courts available on St Croix and St Thomas and a few on St John. **Horseriding** is available in Frederiksted and Christiansted on St Croix, and at Bordeaux Mountain on St John. **Watersports:** Deep-sea **fishing, scuba diving, surfing** and other watersports facilities are available on all three islands. **Parasailing** is available on St Croix and St Thomas. **Spectator sports: Horseracing** is popular.
SPECIAL EVENTS: The following is a list of special events celebrated during 1995 in the US Virgin Islands. **Mar 4 '95** *Calypso Competition,* St Thomas. **Mar 11** *Preservation Hall Jazz Band Performance,* St Croix. **Mar 29** *Classics in the Gardens,* St Thomas. **Apr 18-22** *Virgin Islands Carnival Events,* St Thomas. **Apr 21-23** *22nd Annual International Rolex Cup Regatta,* St Thomas. **Apr 28** *Virgin Islands Carnival Children's Parade,* St Thomas. **Apr 29** *Virgin Islands Carnival Adults' Parade,* St Thomas. **May 7** *St Croix International Triathlon.* **May 13** *STARfest 1995,* St Thomas. **Jun 18-Jul 4** *St John Carnival.* **Jul 4** *St John Carnival Parade.* **Jul 13-16** *8th Annual American Yacht Harbor Billfish Tournament,* St Thomas. **Oct 5-9** *30th Annual Virgin Islands–Puerto Rico Friendship Day Activities,* St Croix. **Oct 7-9** *Mumm's Cup Regatta 4th Annual International Regatta,* St Croix. **Oct 12-21** *Jazz & Caribbean Music & Art Festival,* St Croix. **Nov 18-19** *St Thomas/St John Agriculture Food Fair.*

BUSINESS PROFILE

ECONOMY: When Denmark sold the islands to the US government in 1917, they insisted that the existing privileges of the inhabitants be respected; a result of this is that the Virgin Islands are not part of the Federal Customs Area, a right which the islanders are reluctant to relinquish. This fact has helped the growth of tourism as a mainstay of the economy, but the islands also have the world's largest oil refinery and a thriving trade in rum. The current rapid population growth is causing some concern, as is the high level of immigration caused by the high quality of life and the low prices.

COMMERCIAL INFORMATION: The following organisations can offer advice: St Croix Chamber of Commerce, PO Box 4369, Kingshill, St Croix, VI 00851. Tel: 773 1435; *or*
St Thomas-St John Chamber of Commerce, PO Box 324, 6-7 Main Street, St Thomas, VI 00804. Tel: 776 0010.

CONFERENCES/CONVENTIONS: The US Virgin Islands are an idyllic place to hold a conference or convention. In St Croix, facilities are available in four major hotels for up to 200 people and in two beach resorts for up to 125. In St John, facilities are available at the Hyatt Regency for up to 350 persons and in the National Park for 50 persons. St Thomas has meeting facilities in two hotels for up to 300 persons and in seven beach resorts for up to 850 persons. For further information on conference/convention facilities in the US Virgin Islands, contact the US Virgin Islands Division of Tourism (for addresses, see above).

CLIMATE

Hot throughout the year, cooled by the eastern trade winds. Lowland areas have fairly evenly distributed rainfall, with August to October being the wettest time. Further details on the climate of the region may be found by consulting the climate charts for Dominica and Montserrat; both of these islands enjoy a similar climate to that of the US Virgin Islands.
Required clothing: Lightweight clothes throughout the year. Umbrella or light waterproof clothing is useful.

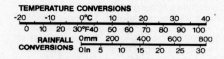

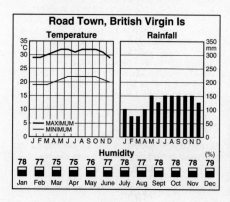

Uruguay

□ *international airport*

Location: South America.

Dirección Nacional de Turismo
Agraciada 1409, 4°, 5° y 6°, Montevideo, Uruguay
Tel: (2) 904 148.
Embassy of the Oriental Republic of Uruguay
2nd Floor, 140 Brompton Road, London SW3 1HY
Tel: (0171) 584 8192 or 589 8735 (Visa section). Fax: (0171) 581 9585. Opening hours: 0900-1700 Monday to Friday. *Visa section:* Tel: (0171) 589 8735. Opening hours: 1000-1600 Monday to Friday.
British Embassy
PO Box 16024, Calle Marco Bruto 1073, 11300 Montevideo, Uruguay
Tel: (2) 623 630 *or* 623 650. Fax: (2) 627 815. Telex: 22249 (a/b PRODROM UY).
Embassy of the Oriental Republic of Uruguay
1918 F Street, NW, Washington, DC 20006
Tel: (202) 331 1313/6 *or* 331 8142 (Visa section). Fax: (202) 331 8142.
Consulates in: Chicago, Miami, New Orleans, New York and San Juan (Puerto Rico).
Embassy of the United States of America
Lauro Muller 1776, Montevideo, Uruguay
Tel: (2) 236 061 *or* 487 777. Fax: (2) 488 611.
Embassy of Uruguay
Suite 1905, 130 Albert Street, Ottawa, Ontario K1P 5G4
Tel: (613) 234 2727. Fax: (613) 233 4670.
Consulate in: Vancouver.
The Canadian Embassy in Buenos Aires deals with enquiries relating to Uruguay (see *Argentina* earlier in this book).

AREA: 176,215 sq km (68,037 sq miles).
POPULATION: 3,112,000 (1991 estimate).
POPULATION DENSITY: 17.7 per sq km.
CAPITAL: Montevideo. **Population:** 1,251,647 (1985).
GEOGRAPHY: Uruguay is one of the smallest of the South American republics. It is bounded to the north by Brazil, to the southeast by the Atlantic, and is separated from Argentina in the west and south by the River Uruguay, which widens out into the Rio de la Plata estuary. The landscape is made up of hilly meadows broken by streams and rivers. There is a string of beaches along the coast. Most of the country is grazing land for sheep and cattle. Montevideo, the most southern point of the nation, accommodates more than half of the

population. About 90% of the land is suitable for agriculture, although only 12% is used in this way. Uruguay is known as the 'Oriental Republic' because it stands on the eastern bank of the Rio de la Plata.
LANGUAGE: Spanish. Some English is spoken in tourist resorts.
RELIGION: Roman Catholic.
TIME: GMT - 3.
ELECTRICITY: 220 volts AC, 50Hz. Plugs are continental flat 3-pin or round 2-pin.
COMMUNICATIONS: Telephone: IDD is available *to* Uruguay, but callers *from* Uruguay may experience difficulty, though direct dialling is possible. Country code: 598. Outgoing international code: 00. The local telephone service, which is operated by the Government, is generally adequate but long-distance calls may take a considerable time to be put through. **Fax:** Some hotels have facilities. **Telex/telegram:** Telex services are available from *Antel* and at major hotels. Telegrams can be sent worldwide through *ITT Comunicaciones, Mundiales SA, Italcable* and *Western Telegraph Co Ltd.* **Post:** Post offices are open 0800-1800 (main post office in the old city, Montevideo: 0800-2200). Airmail to Europe takes three to five days. **Press:** All newspapers are in Spanish.
BBC World Service and Voice of America frequencies: From time to time these change. See the section *How to Use this Book* for more information.
BBC:

| MHz | 17.79 | 15.19 | 11.75 | 9.915 |

Voice of America:

| MHz | 15.12 | 11.58 | 9.590 | 5.995 |

PASSPORT/VISA

Regulations and requirements may be subject to change at short notice, and you are advised to contact the appropriate diplomatic or consular authority before finalising travel arrangements. Details of these may be found at the head of this country's entry. Any numbers in the chart refer to the footnotes below.

	Passport Required?	Visa Required?	Return Ticket Required?
Full British	Yes	No	Yes
BVP	Not valid	-	-
Australian	Yes	Yes	Yes
Canadian	Yes	Yes	Yes
USA	Yes	No	Yes
Other EU (As of 31/12/94)	Yes	1	Yes
Japanese	Yes	No	Yes

PASSPORTS: Valid passport required by all except:
(a) nationals of Uruguay who arrive from Argentina, Brazil, Chile or Paraguay with an identity card, and foreign residents of Uruguay arriving from Argentina with an identity card or residence permit valid for 3 years;
(b) nationals of Argentina, Bolivia, Brazil, Chile and Paraguay with appropriate identification, for stays of up to 90 days.
British Visitors Passport: Not accepted.
VISAS: Required by all except the following, for stays not exceeding 3 months:
(a) nationals of countries referred to in the chart above;
(b) **[1]** nationals of EU countries (except nationals of France who *do* need a visa);
(c) nationals of Argentina, Austria, Belize, Bolivia, Brazil, Chile, Colombia, Costa Rica, Dominican Republic, Ecuador, Finland, Guatemala, Honduras, Hungary, Iceland, Israel, Liechtenstein, Malta, Mexico, Nicaragua, Norway, Panama, Paraguay, Peru, Poland, Seychelles, Sweden and Switzerland;
(d) holders of re-entry permits.
Types of visa: Transit, Business and Tourist; cost: £22. Transit visas are not required by those who continue their journey to a third country from the same airport within 8 hours after arrival. The traveller must hold onward tickets with confirmed seats.
Application to: Consulate (or Consular section at Embassy). For address, see top of entry.
Application requirements: (a) Valid passport. (b) 1 passport-size photo. (c) Travel documentation. (d) Letter from sponsor in country of origin if requesting Business visa. (e) Return ticket. (f) Postal applications should be accompanied by a stamped, self-addressed envelope.
Working days required: Normally 4 days.
Temporary residence: Enquire at Embassy.

MONEY

Currency: Uruguayan Peso = 100 centésimos. Notes are in the denominations of 200,000, 100,000, 50,000, 20,000, 10,000, 5000, 1000, 500, 200, 100 and 50 pesos. Coins are in denominations of 500, 200, 100, 50, 10, 5 and 1 pesos.

Note: On March 1, 1993, a new currency, the Uruguayan Peso (equivalent to 1000 former pesos), was introduced.
Currency exchange: Visitors are advised to buy local currency at banks and exchange shops, as hotels tend to give unfavourable rates. Inflation in Uruguay, though less severe than in other Latin American countries, leads to frequent changes in the exchange rate.
Credit cards: Access/Mastercard, American Express, Diners Club and Visa are the most commonly used. Check with your credit card company for details of merchant acceptability and other services which may be available.
Travellers cheques: Sterling travellers cheques can only be changed at *The Bank of London & South America;* visitors are therefore advised to carry US Dollar travellers cheques.
Exchange rate indicators: The following figures are included as a guide to the movements of the Uruguayan Peso against Sterling and the US Dollar:

Date:	Oct '92	Sep '93	Jan '94	Jan '95
£1.00=	5531.44	6.23	6.59	8.82
$1.00=	2979.50	4.08	4.45	5.64

Currency restrictions: There are no restrictions on the import or export of either local or foreign currency. It is advisable not to change more than needed in order to avoid delays and losses when changing local currency back into foreign currency.
Banking hours: 1330-1730 Monday to Friday (summer); 1300-1700 Monday to Friday (winter).

DUTY FREE

The following items may be imported into Uruguay without incurring customs duty by: (a) Residents of Uruguay arriving from Argentina, Bolivia, Brazil, Chile or Paraguay (maximum four times a year) **[1]**:
200 cigarettes or 25 cigars or 250g of tobacco; 1 litre of alcohol; 2kg of foodstuffs.
(b) All other nationals **[2]**:
400 cigarettes or 50 cigars or 500g of tobacco; 2 litres of alcohol; 5kg of foodstuffs.
Notes: Persons under 18 years of age are entitled to 50% of the above allowances. **[1]:** Total value of exempted imports not to exceed US$30. **[2]:** Total value of exempted imports not to exceed US$150.

PUBLIC HOLIDAYS

Jan 1 '95 New Year's Day. **Jan 6** Epiphany. **Apr 19** Landing of the 33 Patriots. **May 1** Labour Day. **May 18** Battle of Las Piedras. **Jun 19** Birth of General Artigas. **Jul 18** Constitution Day. **Aug 25** National Independence Day. **Oct 12** Discovery of America. **Nov 2** All Souls' Day. **Dec 8** Blessing of the Waters. **Dec 25** Christmas Day. **Jan 1 '96** New Year's Day. **Jan 6** Epiphany. **Apr 19** Landing of the 33 Patriots.
Note: During Carnival Week which covers Ash Wednesday week (February), many businesses are closed.

HEALTH

Regulations and requirements may be subject to change at short notice, and you are advised to contact your doctor well in advance of your intended date of departure. Any numbers in the chart refer to the footnotes below.

	Special Precautions?	Certificate Required?
Yellow Fever	No	No
Cholera	No	No
Typhoid & Polio	1	-
Malaria	No	-
Food & Drink	2	-

[1]: There is a risk of typhoid fever but no cases of polio have been reported in Uruguay in recent years.
[2]: Tap water is considered safe to drink. Drinking water outside main cities and towns may be contaminated and sterilisation is advisable. Milk is pasteurised and dairy products are safe for consumption. Local meat, poultry, seafood, fruit and vegetables are generally considered safe to eat.
Rabies is present. For those at high risk, vaccination before arrival should be considered. If you are bitten abroad, seek medical advice without delay. For more information, consult the *Health* section at the back of the book.
Health care: Uruguay has an excellent medical service. Private health insurance is recommended.

TRAVEL - International

AIR: Uruguay's national airline is *Primeras Líneas Uruguayas de Navegación Aérea (PLUNA) (PU).*
Approximate flight times: From *London* to Montevideo is 15 hours 15 minutes (including 1 hour 30 minutes stopover in Madrid) and from *New York* is 14 hours.
International airport: *Montevideo (MVD)* (Carrasco) is 21km (13 miles) from the city (travel time – 35 minutes). A coach leaves every two hours 0700-2100. It returns from the *IBAT* terminus, Yaguarón 1318, 0730-1930. Buses leave every 15 minutes 0500-2400, and return from the bus terminal, Arenal Grande, 0500-2300. Taxis are available. There is a duty-free shop.
Departure tax: US$12 is levied on international departures (US$6 to Buenos Aires). Children under two years of age are exempt.
SEA: Montevideo, the main international port, is served by cargo lines from the USA and Europe. There is a night-ferry service from Buenos Aires to Montevideo (the crossing takes ten hours). There are also services from Colonia (160km/100 miles west of Montevideo) to Buenos Aires by steamer and a thrice-daily hydrofoil service.
RAIL: There are services from Brazil and Argentina.
ROAD: Coaches and ONDA and TTL buses travel regularly between Brazil and Uruguay – these are modern coaches with bar, TV, WC and radio. The travel time between Montevideo and Porto Alegre (Brazil) is 14 hours; to Rio de Janeiro (Brazil) is 59 hours. Buses run by COIT depart weekly for Asunción and Iguazú Falls in Paraguay, while another service, also weekly, links Montevideo and Santiago in Brazil.

TRAVEL - Internal

AIR: *PLUNA (PU)* runs daily flights to all major points within the country but flying is very costly in comparison with other means of internal travel. *TAMU,* a branch of the Uruguayan Air Force, also operates services to the main towns of Paysandú, Salto, Rivera, Artigas and Melo.
Note: There is a 3.5% surcharge on all air tickets issued and paid for in Uruguay.
SEA/RIVER: There are no scheduled boat services along the principal rivers but the River Uruguay is navigable from Colonia to Salto, and the Rio Negro (flowing across the country from northeast to northwest) is navigable as far as the port of Mercedes.
RAIL: Four main trunk lines and branches connect Montevideo with all major cities. There are no air-conditioned coaches but a buffet service is available on some trains.
ROAD: Traffic drives on the right. There are 45,000km (28,000 miles) of roads in Uruguay, 80% of which are paved or otherwise improved for all-weather use. **Bus:** Three main bus lines *(CITA, COT* and *ONDA)* provide services throughout the country, connecting all towns and the Brazilian border points. **Car hire:** Available in Montevideo. **Documentation:** An International Driving Permit is not legally required but recommended. A temporary licence to drive in Uruguay, valid for 90 days, must be obtained from the Town Hall *(Municipio).*
URBAN: Extensive bus and some trolleybus services operate in Montevideo and the suburbs. There are flat fares for the central area and suburban services. Metered taxis are available in all cities and from the airport. Drivers carry a list of fares. A surcharge is made for each item of baggage and between 2400-0600. Within city limits taxis may be hired by the hour at an agreed rate.

ACCOMMODATION

HOTELS: There are numerous first-class hotels in Montevideo and along Uruguay's coastal resorts, where rates are usually a little more expensive. It is essential to book during the summer and during carnival week in Montevideo. There are several lower-priced hotels in the city for more basic accommodation. **Grading:** Three categories according to price and standard. Prices tend to be higher during the tourist season. There is an 18% value added tax in Montevideo. At the beaches, many hotels offer only American-plan terms (full board).
CAMPING: Allowed at numerous designated sites throughout the country; elsewhere it is necessary to get police permission.
YOUTH HOSTELS: There are several youth hostels throughout Uruguay offering cheap accommodation.

RESORTS & EXCURSIONS

Uruguay draws more visitors than any other South American state. The country enjoys 500km (300 miles) of fine sandy beaches on the Atlantic and the Rio de la Plata, woods, mountains, hot springs, hotels, casinos, art festivals and numerous opportunities for sport and entertainment.
Montevideo: The capital contains more than half of Uruguay's population and is the country's natural trading centre. There are nine major bathing beaches, the best of which are *Playas, Ramírez, Malvin, Pocitos, Carrasco* and *Miramar.* The suburbs have restaurants, nightclubs and hotels.
Punta del Este: The Atlantic coast resorts are popular from December to April, and have fine beaches. Most fashionable of these is Punta del Este, 145km (90 miles) from Montevideo. It has two main beaches and offers water-skiing, fishing, surfing and yachting; there is also a golf course. Villas and chalets can be rented in the wooded area on the edge of town. Two nearby islands, **Gorniti** and **Lobos,** are worth a visit.
Other attractions: To the west of Montevideo is **Colonia Suiza** ('The Swiss colony'), reached by hydrofoil from the capital. It has an excellent old quarter. Other beach resorts along the Uruguayan coast include *Atlántida, Piriápolis* and the fishing port of *Paloma. Carmelo* on the River Uruguay and Mercedes on the Rio Negro (a tributary) are amongst the many picturesque river ports; further up the Uruguay is **Salto,** one of the country's largest cities. **Fray Bentos**, near **Mercedes,** gave its name to the famous processed meat company. The journey north through **Florida** and **Durazno** to **Tacuarembó** on the Brazilian border takes one through the heart of the country's agricultural lands. The beautiful mountains surrounding the town of **Minas** are well worth a visit, as is **Colonia del Sacramento**, which has been rebuilt in its original 18th-century style.

SOCIAL PROFILE

FOOD & DRINK: The majority of restaurants are parrilladas (grillrooms) and beef is a part of most meals. Dishes include *asado* (barbecued beef), *asado de tira* (ribs), *pulpa* (boneless beef), *lomo* (fillet steak) and *bife de chorrizo* (rump steak). *Costillas* (chops) and *milanesa* (a veal cutlet) are also popular, usually eaten with mixed salad or chips. *Chivito* is a sandwich filled with slices of meat, lettuce and egg. Other local dishes are *puchero* (beef with vegetables, bacon, beans and sausages), pizza, pies, barbecued pork, grilled chicken in wine, *cazuela* (stew), usually served with *mondongo* (tripe), seafoods, *morcilla dulce* (sweet black sausage made from blood, orange peel and walnuts) and *morcilla salada* (salty sausage). Desserts include *chaja* (ball-shaped sponge cake filled with cream and jam), *mossini* (cream sponge), lemon pie and *yemas* (crystallized egg yolk). Table service is usual in restaurants. Cafés or bars have either table and/or counter service. **Drink:** Local wines are mixed (*medio-medio,* red and white) in Montevideo and range from acceptable to undrinkable. Beers are very good. Imported beverages are widely available. Local spirits are *caña, grappa* and locally distilled whisky and gin. There are no set licensing hours.
NIGHTLIFE: Theatre, ballet and symphonic concerts are staged in Montevideo from March to January. Nightlife, however, is minimal. There are discotheques in the Carrasco area, some with good floorshows. There are several dinner-dance places in Montevideo. Large Montevideo hotels have good bars. When there is music for dancing, the prices of drinks increase quite considerably. There are also several casinos.
SHOPPING: Special purchases include suede jackets, amethyst jewellery, antiques and paintings. **Shopping hours:** 0900-1200 and 1400-1900 Monday to Friday; 0900-1230 Saturday.
SPORT: Golf: There is a municipal course in Montevideo, plus clubs at the Victoria Plaza Hotel and Punta del Este Country Club. **Fishing:** There are three fishing areas: along the Rio de la Plata from Colonia to Piriápolis for surf-casting; from Piriápolis to Punta del Este (considered one of the best fishing areas in the world); and along the Atlantic Coast towards the Brazilian border. Boats and tackle can be rented in fishing clubs in Salto, Paysandú, Fray Bentos, Punta del Este, Montevideo and Mercedes. **Swimming:** There are plenty of places to swim when the weather permits. The 'metropolitan' beaches (from Ramírez and including Pocitos) tend to be dirty and unsuitable for bathing. Those along the Atlantic coast are, however, clean and are suitable for swimming. Many of the resort areas in the interior have swimming pools. The mineral baths at Minas are worth a visit. **Windsurfing** and **water-skiing** are popular along the coast. **Boating:** A favourite Uruguayan pastime. Santiago Vazquez on the St Lucia River is one of several popular centres. Arrangements can be made for rental of motor or sailing boats in Montevideo and elsewhere. **Horseracing:** There are two main tracks: Hipodromo de Maronas (Saturday and Sunday afternoon); and Las Piedras (Thursday, Saturday and Sunday). **Football:** The most popular spectator sport; matches are played regularly throughout the country.
SPECIAL EVENTS: The principal festival is the national Carnival Week. Although this 'fiesta' is officially only for the Monday and Tuesday preceding Ash Wednesday (mid-February), Uruguay closes down most of its shops and businesses for the entire week. Houses and streets are appropriately decorated and humorous shows are staged at open-air theatres.
SOCIAL CONVENTIONS: Shaking hands is the normal form of greeting. Uruguayans are very hospitable and like to entertain both at home and in restaurants. Normal courtesies should be observed. Smoking is not

allowed in cinemas or theatres or on public transport.
Tipping: 10% when no service charge is added. Taxi
drivers expect a tip.

BUSINESS PROFILE

ECONOMY: Uruguay is one of the more prosperous
Latin American countries. The economy is predominantly
agricultural, with beef and wool being the most important
products (cows and sheep outnumber people by about 9:1).
There are also substantial dairy exports to other Latin
American countries. Crop farming is widespread,
producing mostly cereals, rice, fruit and vegetables, but
production levels fluctuate. Uruguay relies on imported oil
– exploration has proved repeatedly unsuccessful –
although two recently-constructed hydroelectric power
plants are sufficient to meet almost all the country's
energy requirements. Development of light industry, the
most productive sector of the economy, is a prime
Government objective: existing manufacturing capacity is
concentrated in food-processing, textiles, metal industries
and rubber. There is no heavy industry and there are no
plans to establish any. Of all the Latin American republics,
Uruguay has the smallest area, one of the smallest rates of
population growth, the highest literacy rate and one of the
most even distributions of wealth. An efficient system of
social welfare is in operation, although the Government
has come under recent pressure to reduce its scope to
relieve budgetary pressure. Like the rest of South America,
Uruguay suffers from the continent's perennial bane,
overseas debt: however, at US$6 billion, this problem is
less severe (both per capita and in absolute terms) than in
most other states. Uruguay is a member of the Asociación
Latinoamericana de Integración (ALADI), the South
American trade organisation, but also a founder member of
a more influential economic body known as the Southern
Common Market, Mercosur, which was set up in March
1991. Uruguay should benefit from Mercosur by allowing
the country to develop its potential which has, despite a
well-educated population and modern infrastructure, been
hampered by the small size of its internal market.
Economic fashion has also persuaded the Lacalle
government to privatise some state-owned industries
starting with the PTT, airline and electricity utility,
although this has stalled in the face of public opposition.
The country's main trading partners are Brazil, Argentina,
the USA and Germany. Lacalle sees Uruguay's economic
future as the region's principal provider of financial and
other services.
BUSINESS: Businessmen should wear conservative suits
and ties. As far as communication is concerned, some
knowledge of Spanish will prove invaluable, although
English may be spoken by many in business and tourist
circles. Appointments are necessary and punctuality is
expected. Visiting cards are essential and it would be an
advantage to have the reverse printed in Spanish. Avoid
visits during 'Carnival & Tourist Week' (mid-February).
Office hours: 0830-1200 and 1430-1830/1900 Monday to
Friday. **Government office hours:** *Mid-March to mid-
November:* 1200-1900 Monday to Friday; *mid-November
to mid-March:* 0730-1330 Monday to Friday.
COMMERCIAL INFORMATION: The following
organisation can offer advice: Cámara Nacional de
Comercio, Edificio de la Bolsa de Comercio, Misiones
1400, Casilla 1000, 11000 Montevideo. Tel: (2) 961 277.
Fax: (2) 961 243.

CLIMATE

Uruguay has an exceptionally fine temperate climate,
with mild summers and winters. Summer is from
December to March and is the most pleasant time; the
climate during other seasons offers bright, sunny days
and cool nights.

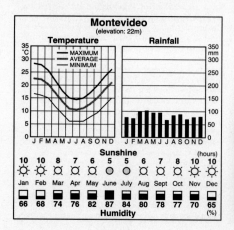

Montevideo
(elevation: 22m)

Fergana Basin:
1 Namangan   3 Fergana
2 Andizhan   4 Kokand

☐ *international airport*

Uzbekistan

Location: Central Asia.

National Company Uzbektourism
47 Khorezmakaya Street, Tashkent 700047, Uzbekistan
Tel: (3712) 335 414. Fax: (3712) 327 948. Telex: 116180
(a/b UZTUR RU).
Ministry of Tourism
47 Khorezmakaya Street, Tashkent 700047, Uzbekistan
Tel: (3712) 338 431. Fax: (3712) 327 948.
Ministry of Foreign Affairs
Ploschad Mustakilik 5, Tashkent, Uzbekistan
Tel: (3712) 336 475. Fax: (3712) 394 348. Telex:
116116.
Embassy of the United Kingdom
6 Murtazaev Street, Tashkent 700000, Uzbekistan
Tel: (3712) 347 658. Fax: (873) 340 465 *or* 891 549.
Embassy of Uzbekistan
Suite 619/623, 1511 K Street, NW, Washington, DC
20005
Tel: (202) 638 4266/7. Fax: (202) 638 4268.
Embassy of the United States of America
Ulitsa Chilanzar 82, Tashkent, Uzbekistan
Tel: (3712) 771 407 *or* 772 231. Fax: (3712) 776 953.
**The Canadian Embassy in Almaty deals with
enquiries relating to Uzbekistan (see *Kazakhstan*
earlier in this book).**
Tour Operators recognised by Uzbektourism:
HY Travel (also General Sales Agent for *Uzbekistan
Airways*)
69 Wigmore Street, London W1H 9LG
Tel: (0171) 935 4775 *or* 935 4778 (reservations). Fax:
(0171) 935 5531.
United States of America United Tours Corporation
Suite 42C, Ritz Plaza, 235 West 48th Street, New York
NY 10036
Tel: (212) 245 1100. Fax: (212) 245 0292.

AREA: 447,400 sq km (172,740 sq miles).
POPULATION: 21,207,000 (1992).
POPULATION DENSITY: 47.4 per sq km.
CAPITAL: Tashkent. **Population:** 2,094,000 (1990
estimate).
GEOGRAPHY: Uzbekistan is bordered by Afghanistan
to the south, Turkmenistan to the west, Kazakhstan to the
north, Kyrgyzstan to the northeast and Tajikistan to the

	Health
GALILEO/WORLDSPAN:	**TI-DFT/TAS/HE**
SABRE:	**TIDFT/TAS/HE**
	Visa
GALILEO/WORLDSPAN:	**TI-DFT/TAS/VI**
SABRE:	**TIDFT/TAS/VI**

Timatic

For more information on Timatic codes refer to Contents.

---

east and has a colourful and varied countryside. The
south and east are dominated by the Tien-Shan and
Pamir-Alai mountain ranges and the Kyzyl Kum desert
lies to the northeast. The northwestern autonomous
region of Karakalpakstan is bounded by the Aral Sea and
the sparsely populated Ustyurt Plateau with its vast
cotton fields.
LANGUAGE: The official language is Uzbek, a Turkic
tongue closely related to Kazakh and Kyrgyz. There is a
small Russian-speaking minority. Many people involved
with tourism speak English. The Government has stated
its intention to change the Cyrillic script to the Latin.
RELIGION: Predominantly Sunni Muslim, with Shia
(15%), Russian Orthodox and Jewish minorities.
TIME: GMT + 5.
ELECTRICITY: 220 volts AC, 50Hz. Round 2-pin
continental plugs are standard.
COMMUNICATIONS: Telephone: Country code: 7
(3712 for Tashkent). IDD is available, but calls from
hotel rooms still need to be booked either from reception
or from the floor attendant. International calls can also be
made from main post offices (in Tashkent this is on
Prospekt Navoi). Direct-dial calls within the CIS are
obtained by dialling 8 and waiting for another dial tone
and then dialling the city code. Calls within the city
limits are free of charge. **Fax:** Services are available
from major hotels for residents only. **Telex/telegram:**
Telegram and telex services (the latter with dual Cyrillic
and Latin keyboards, impractical except in emergencies)
are available from post offices in large towns. Telex
facilities are also available to residents in main hotels.
Post: Letters to Western Europe and the USA can take
between two weeks and two months. Stamped envelopes
can be bought from post offices. Addresses should be
laid out in the following order: country, postcode, city,
street, house number and lastly the person's name. Post
office hours: 0900-1800 Monday to Friday. The Main
Post Office in Tashkent (see above) is open until 1900.
Visitors can also use the post offices situated in the major
Intourist hotels. There are a number of international
courier services based in Tashkent, these include: DHL
(tel: (3712) 781 436) and UPS (tel: (3712) 768 625).
Press: There are no independent daily newspapers in
Uzbekistan. The main editions are published in Tashkent
and include *Narodnoye Slova, Vescherny Tashkent,
Pravda Vostoka* and *Molodiozh Uzbekistana* (all
published in Russian); and *Halk Suza* and *Tashkent
Okshomy* (in Uzbek). **Radio/TV:** There are two Uzbek
TV channels. The BBC is planning to set up an Uzbek
service.
**BBC World Service and Voice of America frequencies
and wavelengths:** From time to time these change. See
the section *How to Use this Book* for more information.
BBC:

MHz	17.64	15.57	11.76	7.160

Voice of America:

MHz	9.670	6.040	5.995	1.260

PASSPORT/VISA

*Regulations and requirements may be subject to change at short notice, and you
are advised to contact the appropriate diplomatic or consular authority before
finalising travel arrangements. Details of these may be found at the head of this
country's entry. Any numbers in the chart refer to the footnotes below.*

	Passport Required?	Visa Required?	Return Ticket Required?
Full British	Yes*	Yes*	No*
BVP	Not valid	-	-
Australian	Yes*	Yes*	No*
Canadian	Yes*	Yes*	No*
USA	Yes*	Yes*	No*
Other EU (As of 31/12/94)	Yes*	Yes*	No*
Japanese	Yes*	Yes*	No*

Note [*]: Visa regulations within the CIS are currently
liable to change. Prospective travellers are advised to
contact *Intourist Travel Ltd* who offer a comprehensive
visa service for all of the republics within the CIS. Tel:
(0171) 538 5902 in the UK; (212) 757 5902 in the USA.
PASSPORTS: Valid passport required by all.
British Visitors Passport: Not accepted.
VISAS: Required by all except nationals of the CIS and
some former Eastern bloc countries.
Types of visa: Tourist, Business and Transit.
Validity: Tourist visas are normally Single-entry/exit
and are valid for the duration of the tour. Business visas
are Multiple-entry, valid for 6 months in the first instance
and extendable. Transit visas are valid for 3 days and,
although they are not extendable in themselves, can be
changed once within the country. Towns to be visited
still have to be listed on the visa for all nationalities
except for the UK. However, changes now in progress
may eliminate this requirement.

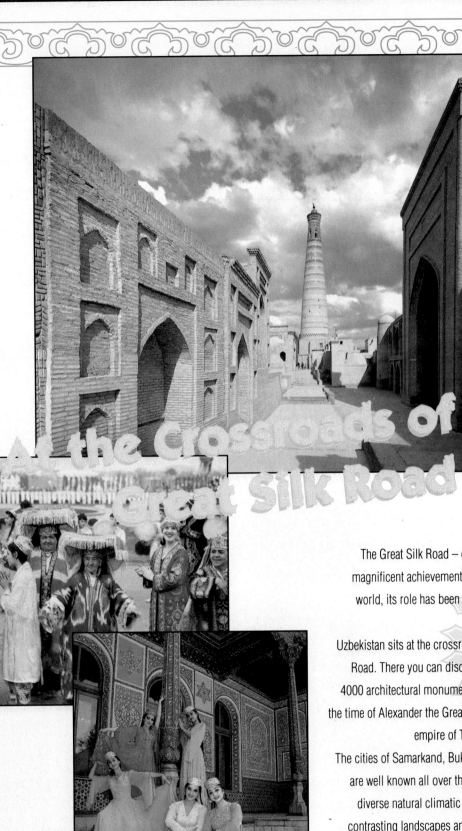

At the Crossroads of the Great Silk Road

The Great Silk Road – one of the most magnificent achievements of the ancient world, its role has been both broad and diverse.

Uzbekistan sits at the crossroads of the Silk Road. There you can discover more than 4000 architectural monuments dating from the time of Alexander the Great through to the empire of Timur the Great.

The cities of Samarkand, Bukhara and Khiva are well known all over the world and the diverse natural climatic conditions with contrasting landscapes and warm climate mean that tourists can be received the whole year round.

Uzbektourism is the first step on your way to discovering this ancient land.

UZBEKTOURISM
NATIONAL COMPANY

National Company "Uzbektourism", 47 Khorezmskaya Str, Tashkent 700047, Republic of Uzbekistan.
Tel: (3712) 335414. Fax: (3712) 327948. Telex: 116180 UZTUR RU

Cost: *Transit* – US$20; *Entry/Exit* – US$40 (7 days), US$50 (15 days); *Multiple-entry* – US$150 (6 months). There are preferential rates for students and various other categories of long-stay visitors.
Application to: Uzbek embassies where they exist (in the USA, France, Germany and Italy), although at the time of writing (February 1995), the Uzbek Embassy in the USA had temporarily suspended its visa service. An Uzbek Embassy is due to open in London during 1995; contact *Uzbekistan Airways* for further information (tel: (0171) 935 1899). A recent decree promises that the visa-issuing system will be streamlined in the near future. It is possible to arrange to pick up a pre-arranged visa at the international arrivals lounge at Tashkent airport. *Uzbekistan Airways* require proof that a visa has been granted. Joining a group or package tour is the easiest way of obtaining a visa, although *Intourist Travel Ltd* can arrange a visa for independent travellers provided they have a hotel voucher and letter of invitation.
Application requirements: For Business visas, an invitation from an Uzbek company is still required. Tourists must have booked a tour with a recognised tour company who arranges visas through *Uzbektourism*. For address, see top of entry.
Working days required: 20 days should be allowed for a Tourist visa. Business visas can be obtained more quickly but this should not be relied upon. A new procedure for visa applications is under discussion.
Temporary residence: It is possible to apply for temporary residence. The government of Uzbekistan officially requires visitors to carry a medical certificate proving they are free of HIV infection, but this is only sporadically enforced.

MONEY

Currency: In June 1994 Uzbekistan introduced the Som.
Currency exchange: Tourists and business persons without special status have to pay for hotels, hotel services and transport in hard currency; US Dollars are the most widely acceptable form. All bills are normally settled in cash. It is illegal to change money on the black market, and penalties can be harsh. Banks and the currency exchange bureaux in major hotels will change at the official rates.
Credit cards: Acceptable in some of the major hotels in tourist centres. Uzbekistan has said that it intends to introduce its own Visa card in the near future.
Eurocheques: These are not accepted.
Travellers cheques: These are not accepted.
Exchange rate indicators: The Som is not exchangeable on the international market. It can only be exchanged within Uzbekistan.
Currency restrictions: The import of foreign currency is unlimited, but should be declared on arrival. The export of foreign currency is permitted up to the amount declared on arrival. The import and export of local currency is prohibited.
Banking hours: 0900-1700 Monday to Friday.

DUTY FREE

The following goods may be imported into Uzbekistan by passengers aged 18 and older without incurring customs duty:
400 cigarettes or 100 cigars or 500g of tobacco products; 2 litres of alcoholic beverages; a reasonable quantity of perfume for personal use; other goods for personal use whose value does not exceed US$5000.
All valuable items such as jewellery, cameras and computers should be declared on arrival.
Prohibited items: Firearms, ammunition and drugs.
Prohibited exports: Items more than 100 years old and those of special cultural importance require special permissions for export. When buying items that may be more than 100 years old, ask for a certificate stating the age of the item(s).

PUBLIC HOLIDAYS

Jan 1-2 '95 New Year. **Mar 8** International Women's Day. **Mar 21** Navrus. **Sep 1** Independence Day. **Dec 8** Constitution Day. **Jan 1-2 '96** New Year. **Mar 8** International Women's Day. **Mar 21** Navrus.

HEALTH

Regulations and requirements may be subject to change at short notice, and you are advised to contact your doctor well in advance of your intended date of departure. Any numbers in the chart refer to the footnotes below.

	Special Precautions?	Certificate Required?
Yellow Fever	No	No
Cholera	1	No
Typhoid & Polio	Yes	-
Malaria	Yes/2	-
Food & Drink	3	

[1]: There was a minor outbreak of cholera in Tashkent in the summer of 1993, but it was probably imported from Tajikistan.
[2]: There have been reports of Malaria cases on the Uzbek/Afghan border. Visitors to this area should take appropriate precautions.
[3]: All water, particularly outside main centres, should be regarded as being a potential health risk. Water used for drinking, brushing teeth or making ice should have first been boiled or otherwise sterilised. Milk is pasteurised and dairy products are safe for consumption. Only eat well-cooked meat and fish, preferably served hot. Pork, salad and mayonnaise may carry increased risk. Vegetables should be cooked and fruit peeled.
Rabies is present. For those at high risk, vaccination before arrival should be considered. If you are bitten abroad seek medical advice without delay. For more information, consult the *Health* section at the back of the book.
Vaccinations against *hepatitis* and *typhoid* are advised.

Health care: Medical insurance is highly recommended. Emergency health care is available free of charge for visitors, although medical care in Uzbekistan is limited. Doctors and hospitals often expect cash payment for health services. There is a severe shortage of basic medical supplies, including disposable needles, anaesthetics, antibiotics and vaccines. Travellers are therefore advised to take a well-equipped first-aid kit with them containing basic medicines and any prescriptions that they may need.

TRAVEL - International

AIR: The national airline is *Uzbekistan Airways National Air Company (Havo Yullari)*. Since independence the airline has expanded its routes and started to renew some of its fleet. In 1993 it purchased two Airbuses for its international routes. It now flies to London, Frankfurt/M, Beijing, Bangkok, Delhi, Istanbul, Tel Aviv, Jeddah, Karachi, Sharjah and Kuala Lumpur. Within the CIS, it also flies to Moscow, Almaty (Kazakhstan), Ashgabat (Turkmenistan) and Kiev (Ukraine). Tashkent is also served by a number of other international carriers: *Lufthansa* (Frankfurt/M and Almaty), *Pakistan International Airways* (Islamabad), *Air India* (Delhi), *Turkish Airlines* (Istanbul), *Shinjiang Airways* (Urumchi in China) and *Arianna* (Kabul). Flights to Tajikistan have been suspended since the Tajik civil war at the end of 1992. For further information, contact *Uzbekistan Airways* in Tashkent, tel: (3712) 337 036. *HY Travel* in London are agents for *Uzbekistan Airways* (see address at top of entry).
Approximate flight times: From Tashkent to *London* is 7 hours (direct), to *Moscow* is 3 hours 30 minutes, to *Frankfurt/M* is 6 hours, to *Tel Aviv* is 4 hours 30 minutes, to *Istanbul* is 3 hours 30 minutes, to *Delhi* is 3 hours 30 minutes, to *Bangkok* is 6 hours 30 minutes and to *Beijing* is 5 hours 30 minutes.
International airport: *Tashkent International Airport (TAS)* is in the south of the town, about 6km (4 miles) from the centre. It is served by buses and taxis.
RAIL: Tashkent is the nodal point for rail services from Central Asia. Lines lead west to Ashgabat (Turkmenistan), south to Samarkand and on to Dushanbe (Tajikistan), east to Bishkek (Kyrgyzstan) and Almaty (Kazakhstan) and north to Moscow (Russian Federation). From Tashkent along the *Saratov-Syr Darya Line* the journey to Moscow takes two and a half days. There is also a spur line to the Fergana Valley in the east of the country which leads to Osh in Kyrgyzstan. It is possible to connect to China through Almaty, and an extension of the line to Iran, in order to connect with the Near and Middle East, has recently been agreed. Foreigners have to pay for rail tickets in hard currency, preferably US Dollars, but it is still a cheap option by Western standards.
ROAD: Uzbekistan has road connections to all its neighbours. The border between Afghanistan and Uzbekistan is closed to all except Uzbek and Afghan nationals. **Bus:** There are services to all the neighbouring countries although the occasional border closures between Uzbekistan and Tajikistan make this route unreliable. Long-distance buses leave the Tashkent bus station (Tashkent Avtovokshal) near the Hippodrome (as opposed to the Samarkand bus station). Foreigners have to pay for tickets in hard currency. **Car hire:** It is possible to hire cars with drivers for long journeys; they will normally ask to be paid in US Dollars. The best place to look for these are at the long-distance bus and train stations.
Approximate travel times: From Tashkent to *Bishkek* is 10 hours, to *Almaty* is 15 hours, to *Ashgabat* is 24 hours and to *Khojand* is 3 hours 30 minutes.

TRAVEL - Internal

AIR: *Uzbekistan Airways* flies to all the major towns and cities in Uzbekistan on a regular basis. Destinations include Tashkent, Samarkand, Navoi (which is 45 minutes by bus from Bukhara), Nukus, Karshi, Termez, Andijan and Namangan. Flights within Uzbekistan and to other CIS countries are subject to delays owing to fuel shortages and overbooking. It is necessary to register with Ovir (the police emigration department) at the airport to have one's ticket endorsed before flying. Foreigners must pay for flights in US Dollars. Tickets can be bought at the *Uzbekistan Airways* ticket agency opposite the Hotel Russia on Shota Rustaveli in Tashkent.
Approximate flight times: From Tashkent to *Termez* is 1 hour 20 minutes, to *Nukus* is 2 hours, to *Samarkand* is 40 minutes, to *Navoi* is 1 hour and to *Namangan* is 1 hour 40 minutes.
RAIL: There are 3400km (2113 miles) of railways linking Termez, Samarkand, Bukhara, the Fergana Valley and Nukus. There are two train stations in Tashkent – North and South. The *Trans-Caspian Railway* traverses

the country from Chardzhou in Turkmenistan via Kagan (near Bukhara), Samarkand and Dzhizak, where the railway branches off to serve the capital Tashkent. Passengers should store valuables under the bed or seat, and should not leave the compartment unattended.
ROAD: The republic of Uzbekistan is served by a reasonable road network. Traffic drives on the right. **Bus:** Services connect all the major towns within Uzbekistan. **Taxi:** Taxis and cars for hire can be found in all major towns. It is safer to use officially marked taxis, although many taxis are unlicensed. Travellers are advised to agree a fare in advance, and not to share taxis with strangers. As many of the street names have changed since independence, it is also advisable to ascertain both the old and the new street names when asking directions. Cars can be hired by the trip, by the hour or by the day or week. **Documentation:** An International Driving Licence will be required when car hire facilities have been introduced.
URBAN: Tashkent is served by taxis, buses, trolleybuses, trams and the only metro in Central Asia. The metro network was expanded in 1991, making it 31km (19 miles) long, which includes 23 stations. Public transport is very cheap and is generally reliable. Valuables should not be flaunted. There are regular bus services to all major towns in Uzbekistan.

ACCOMMODATION

HOTELS: Tourists are still required to stay in hotels that are licensed by Uzbektourism and most hotels are run by them. However, a number of independent hotels are now being licensed. It is necessary for visitors to have a slip of paper stamped by the hotel to prove that they have stayed there. Services and facilities are not up to Western standards, but there is an effort being made to improve them. Most tourist hotel rooms have a shower and WC en suite, although supplies of soap and toilet paper can be unreliable. The main hotels in Tashkent are the Hotel Uzbekistan (tel: (3712) 333 959), the Hotel Tashkent (tel: (3712) 335 491) and the Hotel Russia (tel: (3712) 562 874). In Bukhara, there is the Hotel Bukhara (tel: (36522) 30124) and the Hotel Zerafshan (tel: (36522) 34067). In Samarkand, the Hotel Samarkand (tel: (3662) 358 812) and the Hotel Zerafshan (tel: (3662) 333 372). All other regional capitals have at least one Uzbektourism hotel that will accept foreigners. Many tourists will have booked tours which include accommodation, others will have to pay in US Dollars, unless they have special exemptions.
BED & BREAKFAST: There are a number of bed & breakfast hotels springing up, but they are small and can be difficult to get into.
CAMPING: Uzbektourism runs a number of temporary campsites in the mountains.

RESORTS & EXCURSIONS

Uzbekistan lies astride the *Silk Road*, the ancient trading route between China and the West. Trade brought riches and riches brought architects and scholars in its wake. The country has the best-preserved relics of the time when Central Asia was a centre of empire and a centre of learning. The cities of Samarkand, Bukhara, Khiva and Tashkent live on in the imagination of the West as symbols of oriental beauty and mystery.
The capital, **Tashkent**, lies in the valley of the River Chirchik and is the fourth-largest city of the CIS. Tashkent has been in the past, and continues to be, an important international transport junction. Unfortunately, it preserves only a small proportion of its architectural past. A massive earthquake in 1966 flattened much of the old city and it was rebuilt with broad, tree-lined streets and the new buildings are of little architectural interest. The earlier buildings lie in the old town to the west of the centre. A myriad of narrow winding alleys, it stands in stark contrast to the more modern Tashkent. Among the interesting older buildings are the 16th-century *Kukeldash Madrasa*, which is being restored as a museum, and *Kaffali-Shash Mausoleum*. Many of the Islamic sites in Tashkent are not open to non-Muslims, and visitors should always ask permission before entering a mosque or other religious building.
Tashkent houses many museums of Uzbek and pre-Uzbek culture. Among the more important are the *State Art Museum*, which houses a collection of paintings, ceramics and the Bukharan royal robes. The *Museum of Decorative and Applied Arts* exhibits embroidered wall hangings and reproduction antique jewellery. As the Soviet version of Uzbek history is being re-written to reinstate some of the important historical figures of Uzbekistan, such as Amir Timur – better known as Tamerlane in the West – the exhibits and perspective of the museums is also changing.
Samarkand is the site of Alexander the Great's slaying of his friend Cleitos, the pivot of the Silk Road and the city transformed by Tamerlane in the 14th century into one of the world's greatest capitals. Founded over 5000 years ago, the city flourished until the 16th century before the sea routes to China and the rest of the East diminished its importance as a trading centre. Much of its past glory survives or has been restored. The centre of the historical town is the *Registan Square* where three huge *madrasas* (Islamic seminaries) – including *Shir-Dor* and *Tillya-Kari* – built between the 15th and 17th centuries, dominate the area. Decorated with blue tiles and intricate mosaics, they give some idea of the grandeur that marked Samarkand its heyday.
The *Bibi Khanym Mosque*, not far from the Registan, is testimony to Timur's love for his wife. Now it is a pale shadow of its former self and permanently under repair, but it is still possible to see the breadth of vision of the man who conquered so much of central and south Asia Timur himself is buried in the *Gur Emir*. On the ground floor, under the massive cupola, lie the ceremonial graves of Timur and his descendants. The stone that commemorates Timur is reputed to be the largest chunk of Nephrite (jade) in the world. The actual bodies are situated in the basement, which unfortunately is not open to the public.
The *Shah-i-Zinda* is a collection of the graves of some of Samarkand's dignitaries, and the oldest date from the 14th century as Samarkand was starting to recover from the depredations of the Mongol hordes of the 13th century. Other sites of interest in Samarkand include the *Observatory of Ulug Beg*, Timur's grandson, which was the most advanced astronomical observatory of its day and, it seems, of several succeeding centuries. There is also the *Afrasiab Museum*, not far from the observatory, containing a frieze dating from the 6th century which shows a train of gifts for the Sogdian ruler of the day.
Bukhara lies west of Samarkand and was once a centre of learning renowned throughout the Islamic world. It was here that the great Sheikh Bahautdin Nakshbandi lived. He was a central figure in the development of the mystical Sufic approach to philosophy, religion and Islam. In Bukhara there are more than 350 mosques and 100 religious colleges. Its fortunes waxed and waned through succeeding empires until it became one of the great Central Asian Khanates in the 17th century.
The centre of historical Bukhara is the *Shakristan*, which contains the *Ark*, or palace complex of the Emirs. Much of this was destroyed by fire in the 1920s, but the surviving gatehouse gives an impression of what the whole must have been like. Near the gatehouse is the *Zindan* or jail of the Emirs, which has a display of some of the torture methods employed by the Emirs against their enemies.
Not far from the Ark, the 47m-high (154ft) *Kalyan Minaret*, or tower of death, was built in 1127 and, with the *Ishmael Samani Mausoleum*, is almost the only structure to have survived the Mongols. It was from here that convicted criminals were thrown to their death. Other sites of interest in Bukhara include the *Kalyan Mosque*, which is open to non-Muslims, the *Ulug Beg Madrasa* – the oldest in Central Asia – and, opposite, the *Abdul Aziz Madrasa*. Bukhara, with the narrow, twisting alleyways of its old quarter, is full of architectural gems.
Khiva, northeast of Bukhara, is near the modern and uninteresting city of **Urgench** – not to be confused with Kunya-Urgench over the border in Turkmenistan. Khiva is younger and better preserved than either Samarkand or Bukhara. The city still lies within the original city walls, and has changed little since the 18th century. Part of its attraction is its completeness; although it has been turned into a museum town and is hardly inhabited; it is possible to imagine what it was like in its prime when it was a market for captured Russian and Persian slaves.
The *Art Gallery* in **Nukus**, the capital of Karakalpakstan, in the west of the country, has the best collection of Russian avant-garde art outside St Petersburg.
The **Chatkalsky reserve** in the western Tien-Shan is a narrow unspoilt gorge and contains snow tigers, the rare Tien-Shan grey bear and the Berkut eagle.
POPULAR ITINERARIES: Uzbektourism will arrange tours to suit taste and budget. An increasing number of Western tour companies, such as *Voyages Jules Verne*, offer packages that take travellers to Tashkent, Bukhara and Samarkand, with all accommodation and travel paid before leaving. Owing to the difficulties of doing a tour independently, travellers with limited time are advised to buy a package and make use of the services of a recognised tour company.

SOCIAL PROFILE

FOOD & DRINK: Uzbek food is similar to that of the rest of Central Asia. *Plov* is the staple food for everyday and celebrations and consists of chunks of mutton, shredded yellow turnip and rice fried in a large wok. *Shashlyk* (skewered chunks of mutton barbecued over charcoal – kebabs – served with sliced raw onions) and *lipioshka* (rounds of unleavened bread) are served in restaurants and are often sold on street corners and make an appetizing meal. Uzbeks pride themselves on the quality and variety of their bread. *Samsa* (samosas) are also sold in the street, but the quality is variable. *Manty* are large boiled noodle sacks of meat and *shorpa* is a meat and vegetable soup. During the summer and autumn there is a wide variety of fruit: grapes, pomegranates, apricots – which are also dried and sold at other times of the year – and dwarfing them all, mountains of honeydew and water melons.
In general, hotel food shows a strong Russian influence: *borcht* is a beetroot soup, *entrecote* is well-done steak, *cutlet* are grilled meat balls and *strogan* is the local equivalent of Beef Stroganoff. *Pirmeni* originated in Ukraine and are small boiled noodle sacks of meat and vegetables, similar to ravioli, sometimes served in a vegetable soup. There are a number of restaurants that serve both European and Korean food (Stalin transported many Koreans from their home in the east of the former Soviet Union, believing them to be a security threat). There is a hard-currency restaurant at the top of the Hotel Uzbekistan that serves Korean and Chinese food.
Drink: Tea is the staple drink of Central Asia, and *chai-khanas* (tea houses) can be found almost everywhere in Uzbekistan, full of old men chatting the afternoon away with a pot of tea in the shade. Beer, wine, vodka, brandy and sparkling wine (*shampanski*) are all widely available in restaurants. *Kefir*, a thick drinking yoghurt, is often served with breakfast.
NIGHTLIFE: Tashkent has a variety of theatres which show everything from European operas to traditional Uzbek dancing and music. The Navoi theatre, opposite the Tashkent Hotel, shows opera and ballet. The prices are very low by Western standards; shows start at 1800. The entertainment in restaurants is normally provided by live bands of varying skill who may play too loud for Western tastes.
SHOPPING: The best place to experience Central Asia is in the bazaars. The bazaars of Tashkent and Samarkand offer goods ranging from herbs and spices to Central Asian carpets. A variety of fresh, and not so fresh, produce is sold. In the Alaiski Bazaar in Tashkent it is possible to buy decorated Uzbek knives. Visitors are advised to take a local who can steer them clear of the dross. Many museums have small shops which sell a variety of modern reproductions and some original items. It is possible to buy carpets and embroidered wall hangings. Bukhara is famous for its gold embroidery, and visitors can buy elaborately embroidered traditional Uzbek hats. Visitors should be aware that it is illegal to export anything more than 100 years old or items which have a cultural significance. **Shopping hours:** Food shops open 0800-1700, all others open 0900-1800.
SPORT: The national sport *bushkashi* is a team game in which the two mounted teams attempt to deliver a headless and legless goat's carcass weighing 30-40kg over the opposition's goal line. Players are allowed to wrestle the goat from an opponent, but physical assault is frowned upon. There is **skiing** in the mountains above Tashkent. The **martial arts**, particularly *Taekwon-Do*, are also popular.
SOCIAL CONVENTIONS: *Lipioshka* (bread) should never be laid upside down and should never be put on the ground, even if it is in a bag. It is normal to remove shoes but not socks when entering someone's house or sitting down in a *chai-khana*. Shorts are rarely seen in Uzbekistan and, worn by females, are likely to provoke unwelcome attention from the local male population. Avoid ostentatious displays of wealth (eg jewellery) in public places.

BUSINESS PROFILE

ECONOMY: Uzbekistan's economy has fared better than many in the period since independence. The maintenance of strict controls, which are only now beginning to be relaxed, has meant that the endemic shortages of the other republics have generally been avoided in Uzbekistan. During the Soviet era Uzbekistan's economy was almost entirely devoted to producing cotton, and building machinery to grow more cotton, and this is still true today, despite the Government's attempts to diversify. 60% of Uzbekistan's population live in the countryside and the country is the world's fourth-largest producer of cotton – cotton accounted for 70% of Uzbekistan's exports in 1992 – but gaining this position has not been without its costs in both financial and ecological terms. The monoculture has exhausted the land, with the result that more and more fertilisers are required to maintain the crop. Highly toxic pesticides have resulted in irreparable damage to the environment. The salinity of the soil has risen rapidly through inefficient irrigation, further reducing the land's productivity. The massive amounts of irrigation water required to make the arid steppes viable as cotton-growing areas has been drawn from the Amu-Darya and

Syr-Darya rivers with the result that the Aral Sea into which they drain has shrunk drastically. The desire to diversify into other agricultural products has been hampered by a need for the hard currency that the cotton crops produce, and the absence of the infrastructure to sow and harvest other crops. The level of self-subsistence is therefore relatively low and Uzbekistan has to rely heavily on imports of foodstuffs from other CIS members. To counteract this, plans have been drawn up to expand the cultivation of wheat and fruit. Other agricultural products include silk, fruit and vegetables, grapes and melons. The other mainstay of the economy are natural resources including oil and gas, gold, uranium, silver, copper, zinc and coal. The republic hopes to become self-sufficient in energy resources in the near future. Gold production is estimated to be approximately 70 tons per annum by Western analysts and Uzbekistan is one of the world's major suppliers. There is little secondary or tertiary refining of the products of Uzbekistan's economy. There is some cotton ginning, but the bulk of the industrial base relies on imported raw and semi-finished materials. When Uzbekistan was forced to leave the Rouble Zone in November 1993, it had a severely disruptive effect on industry, with many factories being unable to buy from their Russian suppliers. In January 1994 President Karimov signed a decree that could mark the beginning of a new economic era for Uzbekistan. The decree relaxed many of the controls over the economy that had previously been in the hands of the Government, lifted import and export duties for all products, and speeded-up and increased the scope of the privatisation process that had previously been stumbling in the face of bureaucratic inertia. The republic is a member of the Central Asian economic zone ECO.

BUSINESS: Uzbekistan's government is actively encouraging foreign investment particularly in the processing industries for its raw material output. The January 1994 decree puts into law a number of tax incentives for foreign investors, formally lays out guarantees for property protection, and promises a faster and less bureaucratic method of registration for foreign concerns. Other areas in which the Uzbeks would like to encourage foreign investment include the financial sector, energy production, extraction and processing of mineral raw materials, textiles, telecommunications, tourism and ecology. All foreign companies currently have to be registered with the Ministry of Foreign Economic Relations. **Business hours:** 0900-1700.

COMMERCIAL INFORMATION: The following organisations can offer advice: Ministry of Foreign Economic Relations, ul. Buyak Ipak Yulli 75, Tashkent. Tel: (3712) 689 256. Fax: (3712) 687 231. Telex: 116294; *or* Tashkent International Business Centre, ul. Pushkina 17, Tashkent. Tel: (3712) 323 231 *or* 560 915. Fax: (3712) 334 414. Telex: 116530 (a/b IBC SU). Information can also be obtained from the US Department of Commerce Business Information Service for the Newly Independent States, Room 7413, US Department of Commerce, Washington, DC 20230. Tel: (202) 482 4655. Fax: (202) 482 2293.

CLIMATE

Uzbekistan has an extreme continental climate. It is generally warmest in the south and coldest in the north. Temperatures in December average -8°C in the north and 0°C in the south. However, extreme fluctuations can take temperatures as low as -35°C. During the summer months temperatures can climb to 45°C and above. Humidity is low. The best time to visit is during the spring and autumn.

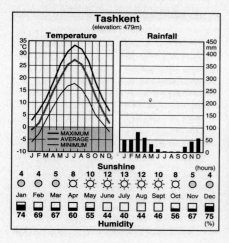

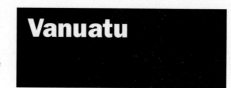

Vanuatu

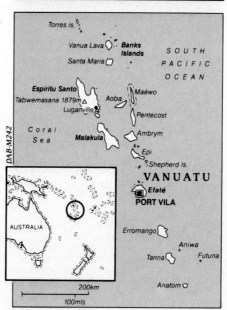

□ *international airport*

Location: Southwest Pacific.

National Tourism Office of Vanuatu
PO Box 209, Kumul Highway, Port Vila, Vanuatu
Tel: 22515 *or* 22685 *or* 22813. Fax: 23889.
Tourism Council of the South Pacific
375 Upper Richmond Road West, London SW14 7NX
Tel: (0181) 392 1589 *or* 392 1838. Fax: (0181) 878 0998.
British High Commission
PO Box 567, KPMG House, rue Pasteur, Port Vila, Vanuatu
Tel: 23100. Fax: 23651. Telex: 1027 (a/b UKREP NH).
The Canadian High Commission in Canberra deals with enquiries relating to Vanuatu (see *Australia* earlier in this book).

AREA: 12,190 sq km (4707 sq miles).
POPULATION: 147,000 (1990).
POPULATION DENSITY: 12.1 per sq km.
CAPITAL: Port Vila (Island of Efaté). **Population:** 19,311 (1989).
GEOGRAPHY: Vanuatu, formerly called the New Hebrides, forms an incomplete double chain of islands stretching north to southeast for some 900km (560 miles). Together with the Banks and Torres islands, the chains comprise about 40 mountainous islands and 40 islets and rocks. The islands are volcanic in origin and there are five active volcanoes. Most of the islands are densely forested and mountainous with narrow bands of cultivated land along the coasts.
LANGUAGE: Bislama (Pidgin English). This most widely used day-to-day language is a Melanesian mixture of French and English. French and English are widely spoken and both English and French names exist for all towns. There are many other local dialects (totalling over 100).

Timatic	
Health	
GALILEO/WORLDSPAN: **TI-DFT/VLI/HE**	
SABRE: **TIDFT/VLI/HE**	
Visa	
GALILEO/WORLDSPAN: **TI-DFT/VLI/VI**	
SABRE: **TIDFT/VLI/VI**	

For more information on Timatic codes refer to Contents.

RELIGION: Presbyterian, Anglican, Roman Catholic, Seventh Day Adventist, Apostolic Church and Church of Christ.
TIME: GMT + 11.
ELECTRICITY: 220-240 volts AC, 50Hz. Australian 3-pin plugs are in use.
COMMUNICATIONS: Telephone: IDD is available. Country code: 678. There are no area codes. Outgoing international calls must go through the international operator. There are public telephones at airports and post offices. **Fax:** Some hotels have facilities. **Telex/telegram:** Available at the Central Post Office in Port Vila and at main hotels. **Post:** Post offices are located on the main streets in Port Vila and Luganville, on Espiritu Santo. Airmail to Europe takes about seven days. Post office hours: 0715-1130 and 1330-1600. **Press:** *Vanuatu Weekly* is published in three languages. The English-language monthly is *Pacific Island Profile*. For tourist information see the publication *What's doing in Vanuatu?*
BBC World Service and Voice of America frequencies: From time to time these change. See the section *How to Use this Book* for more information.
BBC:

MHz	17.83	15.34	11.95	9.740
Voice of America:				
MHz	18.82	15.18	9.525	1.735

PASSPORT/VISA

Regulations and requirements may be subject to change at short notice, and you are advised to contact the appropriate diplomatic or consular authority before finalising travel arrangements. Details of these may be found at the head of this country's entry. Any numbers in the chart refer to the footnotes below.

	Passport Required?	Visa Required?	Return Ticket Required?
Full British	Yes	No	Yes
BVP	Not valid	-	-
Australian	Yes	No	Yes
Canadian	Yes	No	Yes
USA	Yes	No	Yes
Other EU (As of 31/12/94)	Yes	No	Yes
Japanese	Yes	No	Yes

Restricted entry: The Government authorities of Vanuatu refuse admission to persons of dubious morality and persons who may become a public charge.
PASSPORTS: Valid passport (valid for at least 4 months beyond period of stay) required by all.
British Visitors Passport: Not accepted.
VISAS: Required by all except the following, for visits of up to 30 days, provided they are bona fide tourists in possession of confirmed onward travel documents:
(a) nationals of countries listed in the chart above;
(b) nationals of all Commonwealth countries;
(c) nationals of French Overseas Departments and Territories;
(d) nationals of Austria, Cameroon, China, Cuba, Fiji, Finland, South Korea, Federated States of Micronesia, Norway, Pakistan, Philippines, Sweden, Switzerland, Taiwan (China) and Thailand.
Types of visa: Transit and Visitors (for tourist and business purposes). Cost: V2500. Transit visas are not required for those continuing their journey to a third country by the same aircraft and not leaving the airport.
Validity: Valid for 1 month, for use within 3 months of issue. Visas may be extended once in Vanuatu.
Application to: Principal Immigration Officer, Private Mail Bag 014, Port Vila, Vanuatu. Tel: 22354. Fax: 25492. British Consulates in EU countries also issue visas for Vanuatu.
Application requirements: (a) 1 Valid passport. (b) 1 passport-size photo. (c) Proof of sufficient funds and/or accompanying business letter.

MONEY

Currency: Vatu (V) = 100 centimes. Notes are in denominations of V5000, 1000, 500 and 100. Coins are in denominations of V100, 50, 20, 10, 5, 2 and 1. Australian Dollars are also accepted.
Currency exchange: Exchange facilities are available at the airport and trade banks.
Credit cards: Access/Mastercard, American Express, Diners Club, Visa and other major credit cards are accepted. Check with your credit card company for details of merchant acceptability and other services which may be available.
Travellers cheques: These are widely accepted.
Exchange rate indicators: The following figures are included as a guide to the movements of the Vatu against

Sterling and the US Dollar:

Date:	Oct '92	Sep '93	Jan '94	Jan '95
£1.00=	181.50	186.80	180.20	172.88
$1.00=	114.37	122.33	121.80	110.50

Currency restrictions: There are no restrictions on the import or export of either local or foreign currency.
Banking hours: Generally 0830-1500 Monday to Friday, with some closing for lunch at midday.

DUTY FREE

The following items may be imported into Vanuatu by passengers aged 15 and over without incurring customs duty:
200 cigarettes or 100 cigarillos or 250g of tobacco or 50 cigars; 1.5 litres of spirits and 2 litres of wine; 250ml of eau de toilette and 100ml of perfume; other articles up to a value of V20,000.

PUBLIC HOLIDAYS

Jan 1 '95 New Year's Day. **Apr 14-17** Easter. **May 1** Labour Day. **May 25** Ascension Day. **Jul 30** Independence Day. **Aug 15** Assumption. **Oct 5** Constitution Day. **Nov 29** Unity Day. **Dec 25** Christmas Day. **Jan 1 '96** New Year's Day. **Apr 5-8** Easter.

HEALTH

Regulations and requirements may be subject to change at short notice, and you are advised to contact your doctor well in advance of your intended date of departure. Any numbers in the chart refer to the footnotes below.		
	Special Precautions?	Certificate Required?
Yellow Fever	No	No
Cholera	No	No
Typhoid & Polio	Yes	-
Malaria	1	-
Food & Drink	2	-

[1]: Malaria risk, predominantly in the malignant *falciparum* form, exists throughout the year everywhere except Futuna Island. The strain is reported to be 'highly resistant' to chloroquine and 'resistant' to sulfadoxine-pyrimethamine.
[2]: Mains water is normally chlorinated, and whilst relatively safe may cause mild abdominal upsets. Bottled water is available and is advised for the first few weeks of the stay. Milk is pasteurised and dairy products are safe for consumption. Local meat, poultry, seafood, fruit and vegetables are generally considered safe to eat.
Health care: There are hospitals in Port Vila, Espiritu Santo, Tanna, Malakula, Epi and Aoba and smaller clinics and medical dispensaries on the smaller islands. Health insurance is advised.

TRAVEL - International

AIR: The national airline is *Air Vanuatu,* which offers weekly services between Port Vila and Sydney, Brisbane and Melbourne in Australia, and Auckland (New Zealand). The airline has one Boeing 727-200. Another international airline serving the islands is *Polynesian Airways,* which offers a 'Polypass' allowing the holder to fly anywhere on the airline's network: Sydney (Australia), Auckland (New Zealand), Western Samoa,

American Samoa, Cook Islands, Vanuatu, New Caledonia and Fiji.
The pass is valid for 30 days.
Approximate flight time: From London to Vanuatu is 30 hours.
International airport: *Port Vila (VLI)* (Baver Field) is 10.3km (6 miles) from Port Vila (travel time – 15 minutes). Coaches and taxis are available. Facilities are being upgraded.
Departure tax: V2000 is levied on all international departures and V200 on domestic flights.

TRAVEL - Internal

AIR: Domestic services are provided by the Government-owned *Vanair.* It offers scheduled services to destinations throughout the archipelago. The airline has three Britten Norman Islanders and one Trislander.
SEA: Inter-island ferries operate from Port Vila and Espiritu Santo to the northern and southern islands. *Coral* and *Hibiscus Tours* operate boats to various islands.
ROAD: Traffic drives on the right. Of the 1000km (600 miles) of road, 35km (22 miles) are paved. **Bus:** There are limited buses serving the town centre and the airport in Port Vila. **Taxi:** Available near *The Cultural Centre* in Port Vila. **Car hire:** Major car hire operators have offices in Port Vila. **Documentation:** A national driving licence is acceptable.

ACCOMMODATION

Accommodation is available throughout Vanuatu; it is advisable to make prior reservations. Port Vila offers a variety of accommodation, most reasonably priced. Outside Port Vila there is bungalow-style accommodation at Mele Island and Takara, and on the south coast. Accommodation is also to be found on the islands of Espiritu Santo and Tanna. There is no hotel tax or service charge. Full details are available from the National Tourism Office of Vanuatu (for address, see top of entry).

RESORTS & EXCURSIONS

There are a number of tours available in Vanuatu, including trips to see volcanoes (by air), harbour cruises, sailing trips, cultural tours and visits to World War II relics. The capital, **Port Vila,** is on **Efaté Island;** its *Cultural Centre* has one of the most extensive Pacific artefact collections in the world. There are also plenty of opportunities for active holidaymakers, especially those interested in watersports. On **Tanna Island** the village of the *John Frum* cargo cult can be visited; it began with the arrival of an American soldier in World War II and believers wait for him to return with great riches. **Espiritu Santo Island** inspired James A Michener to write 'South Pacific'. Here, scuba divers can see where the liner *President Coolidge* and the destroyer *USS Tucker* rest on the sea-bed. On **Pentecost Island** during April and May visitors can, for a fee, see men performing the ritual leap *(Naghol)* to ensure a bountiful yam harvest; they tie vines to their ankles and leap from a 30m (100ft) tower, falling head first. Only the vine saves them from death. This ceremony was only recently opened to the public and the fee goes towards local projects. Visitors who are interested should contact the National Tourism Office of Vanuatu well in advance.

SOCIAL PROFILE

FOOD & DRINK: There are many restaurants in the main tourist areas. Seafood features strongly on hotel and restaurant menus in Port Vila and the main towns. The numerous ethnic backgrounds of the inhabitants of Vanuatu are reflected in the numerous styles of cooking. Chinese and French influences are the strongest. Food is generally excellent everywhere. French cheese, pâtés, bread, cognac and wine are available in Port Vila's two major shops. Local fruit is excellent.
NIGHTLIFE: Port Vila has several nightclubs with music and dancing. There are two cinemas and a drive-in in Port Vila. Evening cruises are also organised with wine, snacks and island music. Traditional music and dancing takes place at various island festivities to which visitors are welcome, and some hotels put on evening entertainment and dancing. Details are available from the National Tourism Office of Vanuatu.
SHOPPING: Special purchases include grass skirts from Futuna and Tanna, baskets and mats from Futuna and Pentecost, carved forms and masks from Ambrym and Malekula, woodwork from Tongoa and Santo, and pig tusks and necklaces made of shells or colourful seeds

from villages near Port Vila. Duty-free shops sell a selection of luxury items. **Shopping hours:** 0730-1130 and 1330-1700 Monday to Friday. Chinese stores are open Sunday mornings from 0800 and in the evenings.
SPORT: Ornithology: Birdlife is prolific and varied, particularly in the southern islands during the breeding season (September to January). **Tennis:** There is a tennis club at Port Vila and at the hotel at Erakor Lagoon. **Golf:** There are several 9-hole golf courses; visitors can arrange games through hotels or the Vanuatu National Tourism Office. **Watersports:** There are many excellent beaches and several hotels have swimming pools. Some hotels can provide scuba equipment – the coastal waters offer excellent diving. There are several independent divers in Port Vila who provide instruction and boat charters, listed at the National Tourism Office of Vanuatu. Ask at hotels or the National Tourism Office of Vanuatu for their locations.
SPECIAL EVENTS: The ritual of *Naghol* on Pentecost Island, which takes place during April and May, is described in *Resorts & Excursions* above. Visitors are also welcome at the traditional ceremonies on Tanna Island, where the foot-pounding *Toka* dance is performed.
SOCIAL CONVENTIONS: Informal wear is suitable for most occasions. Some of the more up-market establishments appreciate men wearing long trousers in the evenings. Life goes at its own pace and while modern influences can be seen in the main centres, in the hill villages and outlying islands age-old customs continue.
Tipping: Contrary to Melanesian customs.

BUSINESS PROFILE

ECONOMY: Agriculture and fishing are the mainstays of the Vanuatu economy and occupy most of the working population. Fruit and vegetables are grown for domestic consumption, while copra, beef and fish are the main export commodities. Copra is particularly valuable, and responsible for around three-quarters of export earnings. There is considerable room for development, both of agriculture and associated industries such as food-processing; manufacturing, which is almost entirely based on agriculture, accounts for around 5% of GDP. Tourism is growing steadily, assisted by the establishment of a national airline, *Air Vanuatu.* Vanuatu has also sought to promote offshore financial services and has created a shipping register which offers a flag of convenience. These have served to boost 'invisible' trade earnings and offset recent declines in the visible trade surplus. France, Australia and Japan are the main trading partners.
BUSINESS: A casual approach to business prevails. Shirts and smart trousers will suffice – ties are only necessary for the most formal occasions. Business is conducted in Pidgin English or French. **Office hours:** 0730-1130 and 1330-1630 Monday to Friday.
COMMERCIAL INFORMATION: The following organisation can offer advice: Vanuatu Chamber of Commerce, PO Box 189, Port Vila. Tel/Fax: 23255.

CLIMATE

Subtropical. Trade winds occur from May to October. Warm, humid and wet between November and April. Rain is moderate. Cyclones are possible between December and April.

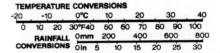

TEMPERATURE CONVERSIONS

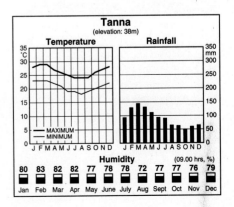

Tanna
(elevation: 38m)
Temperature   Rainfall

Vatican City

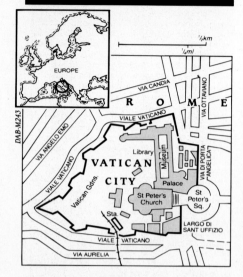

Location: Europe, Italy (Rome).

Note: Italian State Tourist Offices can provide information and advice on visiting the Vatican City. For addresses, see the top of the *Italy* section earlier in the book.

Apostolic Nunciature
54 Parkside, London SW19 5NE
Tel: (0181) 946 1410. Fax: (0181) 947 2494. Opening hours: 0900-1700 Monday to Friday.
British Embassy
Via Condotti 91, 00187 Rome, Italy
Tel: (6) 678 9462 *or* 679 7479. Fax: (6) 684 0684. Telex: 626119 (a/b BREM BI).
Apostolic Nunciature
3339 Massachusetts Avenue, NW, Washington, DC 20008
Tel: (202) 333 7121. Fax: (202) 337 4036. Telex: 440117.
Embassy of the United States of America
Villino Pacelli, Via Aurelia 294, 00165 Rome, Italy
Tel: (6) 46741. Fax: (6) 638 0159. Telex: 622322 (a/b AMBRMC).
Apostolic Nunciature
724 Manor Avenue, Rockliffe Park, Ottawa, Ontario K1M 0E3
Tel: (613) 746 4914. Fax: (613) 746 4786.
Canadian Embassy
Via della Conciliazione 4/D, 00193 Rome, Italy
Tel: (6) 68 30 73 16 *or* 68 30 73 86 *or* 68 30 73 98. Fax: (6) 68 80 62 83.

AREA: 0.44 sq km (0.17 sq mile).
POPULATION: 752 (1988 estimate).
POPULATION DENSITY: 1709 per sq km.
GEOGRAPHY: The Vatican City is situated entirely within the city of Rome, sprawling over a hill west of the River Tiber, and separated from the rest of the city by a wall. The Vatican City comprises St Peter's Church, St Peter's Square, the Vatican and the Vatican Gardens.
LANGUAGE: Italian.
TIME: GMT + 1 (GMT + 2 in summer).
ELECTRICITY: 220 volts, 50Hz.
COMMUNICATIONS: Telephone: IDD is available. The international dialling code to the Vatican switchboard is 39 66982. Outgoing international code: 00. The Vatican has its own telephone network.
Telex/telegram: The Vatican City has its own telex and telegraph services. The telex country code is 504 VA.
Post: Stamps issued in the Vatican City are valid throughout Rome. **Press:** The daily newspaper published in the Vatican City is *L'Osservatore Romano*, with weekly editions in English.

PASSPORT/VISA

There are no formalities required to enter the Vatican City, but entry will always be via Rome and Italian regulations must therefore be complied with. See the *Passport/Visa* section under *Italy* earlier in the book.
There is free access only to certain areas of the Vatican City; these include St Peter's Church, St Peter's Square, the Vatican Museum and the Vatican Gardens. Special permission is required to visit areas other than those mentioned.

MONEY

Currency: Vatican coins are similar in value, size and denomination to those of Italy, although the monetary system is separate from that of Italy; Italian notes and coins are, however, legal tender in the Vatican City. Refer to the *Money* section under the entry for *Italy*. Vatican coins are the Gold Lire 100 (nominal); Silver Lire 500; 'Acmonital' Lire 100 and 50; 'Italma' Lire 10, 5 and 1; and 'Bronzital' Lire 20.

DUTY FREE

There are no taxes and no customs/excise in the Vatican City. For Italian duty-free allowances refer to the *Duty Free* section under the entry for *Italy*.

PUBLIC HOLIDAYS

See the *Public Holidays* section under the entry for *Italy*.

HEALTH

See the *Health* section under the entry for *Italy*.

TRAVEL

The Vatican City has its own railway station and a helicopter pad. For travel in Rome, see the entry for *Italy*. There is a speed limit of 30kmph (20mph) in the Vatican City.

ACCOMMODATION

Board and lodging is not available to members of the general public in the Vatican City itself; for information on accommodation in Rome, see the entry for *Italy* above.

RESORTS & EXCURSIONS

The Vatican City is best known to tourists and students of architecture for the magnificent **St Peter's Basilica.** Visitors are normally admitted to the dome 1615-1800. *The Museum & Treasure House* is open 0900-1200 and 1500-1700. Leading up to it is the 17th-century **St Peter's Square,** a superb creation by Bernini. On either side are semi-circular colonnades, and in the centre of the square is an Egyptian obelisk hewn in the reign of Caligula. It is also possible to visit the *Necropoli Precostantiniana,* the excavations under St Peter's, although permission has to be obtained in advance and is usually granted only to students and teachers with a professional interest in the work being carried out. Contact the Tourist Information Office in St Peter's Square. The **Vatican Gardens** can be visited only by those on guided tours or bus tours. Tickets are available from the Tourist Information Office in St Peter's Square; it is advisable to apply two days in advance. To the right of St Peter's stands the **Vatican Palace,** the Pope's residence. Among the principal features of the Palace are the Stanze, the **Sistine chapel,** the Garden House or Belvedere, the Vatican Library and the Vatican Collections, containing major works of art and valuable pictures. The Museum & Treasure House includes the Collection of Antiquities, Museo Pio-Clementino, the Egyptian Museum, the Etruscan Museum and the Museum of Modern Religious Art. There is a restaurant in the museum and a bar and cafeteria on the roof of St Peter's.

BUSINESS PROFILE

ECONOMIC: The Vatican has three main sources of income: the *Istituto per le Opere di Religione* (IOR, Institute of Religious Works); voluntary contributions known as 'Peter's Pence' and the interest on the Vatican's investments. The IOR – the Vatican Bank – has attracted some controversy in recent years through its association with the Banco Ambrosiano, which collapsed with debts running into hundreds of millions of pounds. Despite these heavy losses and poor recent returns on its investments which have left it running a current account deficit, the Vatican continues to wield immense financial influence. The Vatican does not produce goods for export and virtually all of its material requirements are met by the Italians.
COMMERCIAL INFORMATION: The following organisations can offer advice: Prefecture of the Economic Affairs of the Holy See, Palazzo delle Congregazioni, Largo del Colonnato 3, 00193 Rome. Tel: (6) 69 88 42 63. Fax: (6) 69 88 50 11; *or* Istituto per le Opere di Religione (IOR), 00120 Città del Vaticano, Rome. Tel: (6) 69 88 33 54. Fax: (6) 69 88 38 09. Telex: 610030.

CLIMATE

See the *Climate* section under the entry for *Italy*.

Venezuela

Location: South America.

Corpoturismo
Corporación de Turismo de Venezuela, Apartado 50200, Centro Capriles, 7°, Plaza Venezuela, Caracas, Venezuela
Tel: (2) 781 8370. Telex: 27328.
Embassy of the Republic of Venezuela
1 Cromwell Road, London SW7 2HW
Tel: (0171) 584 4206/7. Fax: (0171) 589 8887. Telex: 264186 (a/b EMVEN G). Opening hours: 0900-1600 Monday to Friday.
Venezuelan Consulate
56 Grafton Way, London W1P 5LB
Tel: (0171) 387 6727. Fax: (0171) 383 3253. Opening hours: 0930-1500 Monday to Friday.
British Embassy
Apartado 1246, Edificio Torre Las Mercedes, 3°, Avenida la Estancia, Chuao, Caracas 1060, Venezuela
Tel: (2) 993 4111. Fax: (2) 920 314. Telex: 23468 (a/b PROCA VE).
Consulates in: Maracaibo and Mérida.
Embassy of the Republic of Venezuela
1099 30th Street, NW, Washington, DC 20007
Tel: (202) 342 2214.
Venezuelan Consulate General
7 East 51st Street, New York, NY 10022
Tel: (212) 826 1660.
Also in: Baltimore, Boston, Chicago, Houston, Coral Gables, New Orleans, Philadelphia, San Francisco and Santurce (Puerto Rico).
Embassy of the United States of America
PO Box 62291, Avenida Francisco de Miranda and Avenida Principal de la Floresta, Caracas 1060A, Venezuela
Tel: (2) 285 2222 *or* 285 3111. Fax: (2) 285 0336. Telex: 25501 (a/b AMEMB VE).
Consulate in: Maracaibo.
Embassy of the Republic of Venezuela
32 Range Road, Ottawa, Ontario K1N 8J4
Tel: (613) 235 5151. Fax: (613) 235 3205.
Consulates in: Calgary, Montréal and Toronto.
Canadian Embassy
Apartado 62302, 7th Floor, Edificio Torre Europa,

Health	
GALILEO/WORLDSPAN: **TI-DFT/CCS/HE**	
SABRE: **TIDFT/CCS/HE**	
Visa	
GALILEO/WORLDSPAN: **TI-DFT/CCS/VI**	
SABRE: **TIDFT/CCS/VI**	

For more information on Timatic codes refer to Contents.

Timatic

Avenida Francisco de Miranda, Campo Alegre, Caracas 1060A, Venezuela
Tel: (2) 951 6166. Fax: (2) 951 4950. Telex: 23377 (a/b DOMCA VE).

AREA: 912,050 sq km (352,144 sq miles).
POPULATION: 20,226,227 (1991 estimate).
POPULATION DENSITY: 22.2 per sq km.
CAPITAL: Caracas. **Population:** 3,435,795 (metropolitan area, 1990 estimate).
GEOGRAPHY: Venezuela is bounded to the north by the Caribbean, to the east by Guyana and the Atlantic Ocean, to the south by Brazil, and to the west and southwest by Colombia. The country consists of four distinctive regions: the Venezuelan Highlands in the west; the Maracaibo Lowlands in the north; the vast central plain of the Llanos around the Orinoco; and the Guyana Highlands, which take up about half of the country.
LANGUAGE: Spanish is the official language. English, French, German and Portuguese are also spoken by some sections of the community.
RELIGION: Roman Catholic.
TIME: GMT - 4.
ELECTRICITY: 110 volts AC, 60Hz. American-type 2-pin plugs are the most commonly used fittings.
COMMUNICATIONS: Telephone: IDD is available. Country code: 58. Outgoing international code: 00. **Fax:** Available at the larger hotels. **Telex/telegram:** Public telex facilities are available. Telegram services are available from public telegraph offices. **Post:** There is an efficient mail service from Venezuela to the USA and Europe. Airmail to Europe takes three to seven days. Internal mail can sometimes take longer. Surface mail to Europe takes at least a month. **Press:** The English-language daily newspaper is *The Daily Journal*, published in Caracas.
BBC World Service and Voice of America frequencies: From time to time these change. See the section *How to Use this Book* for more information.
BBC:

| MHz | 17.84 | 15.22 | 9.915 | 5.975 |

Voice of America:

| MHz | 15.21 | 11.58 | 9.775 | 5.995 |

PASSPORT/VISA

Regulations and requirements may be subject to change at short notice, and you are advised to contact the appropriate diplomatic or consular authority before finalising travel arrangements. Details of these may be found at the head of this country's entry. Any numbers in the chart refer to the footnotes below.

	Passport Required?	Visa Required?	Return Ticket Required?
Full British	Yes	No/1	Yes
BVP	Not valid	-	-
Australian	Yes	No/1	Yes
Canadian	Yes	No/1	Yes
USA	Yes	No/1	Yes
Other EU (As of 31/12/94)	Yes	1/2	Yes
Japanese	Yes	Yes	Yes

PASSPORTS: Valid passport required by all. Passports must be valid for at least 6 months.
British Visitors Passport: Not accepted.
VISAS: Required by all except [1] nationals of the following countries, who do, however, require a 60-day Tourist Card issued from an authorised air or sea carrier:
(a) [2] EU countries (except nationals of Greece and Portugal who *do* require visas);
(b) Australia, Canada and the USA;
(c) Andorra, Antigua & Barbuda, Austria, Barbados, Belize, Brazil, Costa Rica, Dominica, Finland, Iceland, Liechtenstein, Mexico, Monaco, Netherlands Antilles, New Zealand, Norway, San Marino, St Kitts & Nevis, St Vincent & the Grenadines, Sweden, Switzerland, Taiwan (China) and Trinidad & Tobago.
Note: Special authorisation is required from the Ministry of Internal Affairs to grant entry to certain nationalities; enquire at the Embassy for details.
Types of visa: Tourist, Business and Transit.
Cost: Business; £42. Tourist; £22. Transit; £22.
Validity: *Tourist* and *Business:* up to 1 year; *Transit:* 3 days.
Application to: Consulate (or Consular section at Embassy). For addresses, see top of entry.
Application requirements: (a) Completed application forms. (b) Letter of introduction from company or bank for Business visa. (c) Stamped, self-addressed envelope.
Working days required: 2.
Temporary residence: Special authorisation is required from the Ministry of Internal Affairs in Caracas.

MONEY

Currency: Bolívar (B) = 100 céntimos. Notes are in denominations of B500, 100, 50, 20, 10 and 5. Coins are in denominations of B5, 2 and 1, and 50, 25, 10 and 5 céntimos.
Currency exchange: Banks and *cambios* will change money in Venezuela; so too will hotels, although often at a less favourable rate.
Credit cards: Visa, American Express and Access/Mastercard are widely accepted; Diners Club has more limited acceptance. Check with your credit card company for details of merchant acceptability and for other facilities which may be available.
Travellers cheques: Widely accepted, although one may be asked to produce a receipt of purchase when changing them in Venezuela. Exchange is more difficult in some places than others. Some kinds of travellers cheques are not accepted; seek advice before travelling.
Exchange rate indicators: The following figures are included as a guide to the movements of the Bolívar against Sterling and the US Dollar:

Date:	Oct '92	Sep '93	Jan '94	Jan '95
£1.00=	120.75	146.23	157.12	265.76
$1.00=	76.09	95.76	106.20	169.87

Note: The above rates are for non-commercial transactions. 'Essential Import' and 'Preferential' rates are also used.
Currency restrictions: The import and export of either foreign or local currency is unlimited.
Banking hours: 0830-1130 and 1400-1630 Monday to Friday.

DUTY FREE

The following items may be imported into Venezuela without incurring customs duty:
200 cigarettes and 25 cigars; 2 litres of alcoholic beverages; 4 small bottles of perfume.

PUBLIC HOLIDAYS

Jan 1 '95 New Year's Day. **Feb 27-28** Carnival. **Mar 10** Holiday (La Guaira only). **Apr 14-17** Easter. **Apr 19** Declaration of Independence. **May 1** Labour Day. **Jun 24** Battle of Carabobo. **Jul 5** Independence Day. **Jul 24** Birth of Simón Bolívar and Battle of Lago de Maracaibo. **Sep 4** Civil Servants' Day. **Oct 12** Columbus Day. **Oct 24** Holiday (Maracaibo only). **Dec 24-25** Christmas. **Dec 31** New Year's Eve. **Jan 1 '96** New Year's Day. **Feb** Carnival. **Mar 10** Holiday (La Guaira only). **Apr 5-8** Easter. **Apr 19** Declaration of Independence.

HEALTH

Regulations and requirements may be subject to change at short notice, and you are advised to contact your doctor well in advance of your intended date of departure. Any numbers in the chart refer to the footnotes below.

	Special Precautions?	Certificate Required?
Yellow Fever	Yes	1
Cholera	No	No
Typhoid & Polio	Yes	-
Malaria	2	-
Food & Drink	3	-

[1]: A yellow fever vaccination certificate is not required as a condition of entry but vaccination is advised for all travellers over one year of age who intend to travel outside urban areas.
[2]: Malaria risk exists throughout the year in rural areas in parts of Anzoátegui, Apure, Barinas, Bolívar, Mérida, Monagas, Portuguesa, Sucre, Táchira and Zulia States and the Federal Territory of Amazonas and Delta Amacuro. The malignant *falciparum* form is present and is reported to be 'highly resistant' to chloroquine.
[3]: Mains water is normally chlorinated, and whilst relatively safe may cause mild abdominal upsets. Bottled water is available and is advised for the first few weeks of the stay. Drinking water outside main cities and towns may be contaminated and sterilisation is advisable. Milk is pasteurised and dairy products are safe for consumption. Local meat, poultry, seafood, fruit and vegetables are generally considered safe to eat.
Rabies is present. For those at high risk, vaccination before arrival should be considered. If you are bitten abroad seek medical advice without delay. For more information, consult the *Health* section at the back of the book.
Bilharzia (schistosomiasis) is present in north-central Venezuela. Avoid swimming and paddling in fresh water. Swimming pools which are well-chlorinated and

maintained are safe.
Health care: The cost of medical and dental treatment in Venezuela is high. Facilities are good in major centres. There is one doctor for every 1270 inhabitants. Health insurance is recommended.

TRAVEL - International

AIR: Venezuela's national airline is *Viasa (VA)*.
Approximate flight times: From Caracas to *London* is 12 hours (including stopover); to *Los Angeles* is 9 hours and to *New York* is 5 hours.
International airport: *Caracas (CCS)* (Simon Bolívar) is 22km (14 miles) from the city (travel time – 30 minutes). Airport facilities include duty-free shop, bank/bureau de change (0800-1830), bar/restaurant, 24-hour tourist information and car hire *(Avis, Budget* and *National)*. There is a 24-hour coach service to the city every 10 minutes. Return is from the Parque Central terminus, Avenida Lecuna, and pick-ups are at the Hilton, Macuto, Sheraton and Inter-Continental hotels. Buses *(littoral)* are available to the city every 45 minutes from 0600-2200. Return is from Nuevo Circo bus station. Taxis to the city are available on ranks.
Departure tax: B505 is levied on all international departures regardless of nationality; tourists pay an extra charge of B530 for an exit form and stamp tax. Transit passengers and children under two years are exempt.
SEA: The principal Venezuelan ports are La Guaira, Puerto Cabello, Maracaibo, Guanta, Porlamar and Ciudad Bolívar (on the Orinoco River). The principal shipping lines operating to Venezuela are, from the USA: *Venezuelan Line, Delta Line Cruises* and *Royal Netherlands SS Company;* from Amsterdam, Le Havre or Bilbao: *Royal Netherlands SS Company;* from Mediterranean ports: *French Line* and the Spanish ships 'Cabo San Juan' and 'Cabo San Roque'; and from other European ports: *Polish Ocean Lines* and *Lauro*. The Cunard *'Countess'* and *'Princess'* offer Caribbean cruises from San Juan that include a stop in Caracas. Other cruise lines are *Costa, Princess Cruises* and *Delta Cruises*. There are ferry connections between Falcon State, Curaçao and Aruba on the Swedish *Almirante Luis Brion*, which carries 1200 passengers and 40 cars. The distance of 160km (100 miles) is covered in 3 hours 30 minutes. The ferry leaves the Muaco dock near Falcon's capital.
Departure tax: There is a tax on all sea departures regardless of nationality; enquire locally for current rate.
RAIL: There are no international rail links with neighbouring countries.
ROAD: Road access is from Colombia (Barranquilla and Medellin) to Maracaibo and the Amazon territory of Brazil (Manaus) to Caracas.

TRAVEL - Internal

AIR: Almost all large towns are connected with scheduled services operated by two domestic airlines: *Aeropostal (LV)* and *Avensa (VE)*. The *Avensa Air Pass* gives tourists 4, 7 or 21 days unlimited air travel within the country. Air travel is the best means of internal transport but services are often over-booked and even confirmation does not always ensure a seat. Travellers are advised to arrive at the airport well before the minimum check-in time in order to obtain confirmed seats. Schedule changes and flight cancellations with no advance warning are also likely hazards.
Departure tax: B40 for domestic departures.
SEA: Ferries link Puerto La Cruz with Margarita Island (2 hours 45 minutes).
RAIL: The only railway link runs between Barquisimeto and Puerto Cabello, with four trains daily but no air-conditioning. There are plans for a considerable extension to the rail network. There are ambitious plans for a 2000km (1200-mile) national network by the year 2000.
ROAD: Traffic drives on the right. Internal roads between principal cities are of a high standard, with 17,050km (10,595 miles) of paved motorways, 13,500km (8400 miles) of macadam highways and 5850km (3635 miles) of other roads. **Bus:** There are a few inter-urban bus services. **Car hire:** Self-drive cars are available at the airport and in major city centres but are expensive.
Documentation: International Driving Permit is required.
URBAN: Caracas has a 35-station metro, which is comfortable and inexpensive. Conventional **bus** services have badly deteriorated in recent years and there has been a rapid growth in the use of *por puestos* (shared taxis). These are operated by minibus companies and tend to serve as the main form of public transport in Caracas and major cities. Fares charged are in general similar to those on the buses, although they are higher during the evenings and at weekends. **Taxis** in Caracas are metered but the fare can nonetheless be negotiated

CORPORACION DE TURISMO
Venezuela
Un país para querer

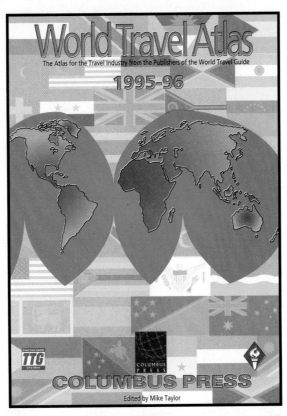

At Last – a Travel Atlas for the Travel Trade!

Have you ever picked up your atlas to discover that important resort you are looking for is not on the map? This is a common problem in the travel industry, as non-specialist atlases often do not recognise the particular needs of the busy travel agent. All too often they fail to show important travel resorts or destinations and are very poor on back-up tourist information. Such atlases are an embarrassment to our industry! But you don't have to put up with this any longer ...

At last – a travel atlas for the travel trade. We've taken a conventional atlas, then augmented it with over 100 plates – featuring over 6,000 resorts and attractions – all designed specifically for the travel industry. From cruises to climate, flight times to French resorts, cultural wonders to national parks, this is a publication that truly covers the world of travel. Armed with this easy-to-use atlas you will be able to give your clients the kind of advice they will return for, time after time!

New country frontiers. The world has changed much in recent years: is *your* atlas up to date? Eastern Europe, the CIS, South Africa – for your clients' business or leisure requirements, for staff training or general reference, this now the only atlas you'll need.

An atlas which has got its priorities right. Accuracy, relevance and ease of use make this a publication that will save you time and earn you money. Exhaustively indexed, meticulously researched and fully up to date, this is *the* atlas the travel industry has been waiting for. 'Excellent,' says one user, 'brilliant,' says another. What more can we say? Don't delay, order yours today!

Price: **£19.50.** (Bulk discounts available.)

For further information including details of hardback copies embossed with your company logo please contact Stephen Collins at the address above.

Columbus Press Limited
Columbus House, 28 Charles Square London N1 6HT, United Kingdom
Tel: +44 (0)171 417 0700. Fax: +44 (0)171 417 0710.

with the driver. It is customary not to use meters after midnight; the fare should be agreed before setting out. Taxi fares double after 2000. Taxi rates are posted at the airport. Motorcycles may not be used in Caracas after 2200.
JOURNEY TIMES: The following chart gives approximate journey times (in hours and minutes) from Caracas to other major cities/towns in Venezuela.

	Air
Porlamar	0.45
Los Roques	0.50
Mérida	1.00
Canaima	1.15
Cumana	0.45
Maracaibo	1.00
Ciudad Bolívar	0.50

ACCOMMODATION

HOTELS: There are many excellent hotels in Caracas. Numerous smaller hotels are open throughout the country but it is essential to make reservations at both these and the larger international hotels well in advance. **Grading:** Hotels in Venezuela have been graded into three categories; 3-star (65 hotels), 4-star (22) and 5-star (15). It normally follows that the more expensive the hotel, the better the facilities. Hotels do not add a service charge, and generally there is no variation in seasonal rates. Hotels outside the capital tend to be cheaper and the standard may not be as high. A useful guide is the *Guía Turistica de Caracas Littoral y Venezuela*, published by the Corporación de Turismo de Venezuela, available at local tourist offices. The Venezuelan Consulate holds a reference copy (address at top of entry).
CAMPING/CARAVANNING: Camping in Venezuela can involve spending a weekend at the beach, on the islands, in the Llanos or in the mountains. Camping can also be arranged with companies who run jungle expeditions. As in much of South America, however, good facilities are not widespread and camping is not used by travellers as a substitute for hotels on the main highways. No special campsites are yet provided for this purpose.

RESORTS & EXCURSIONS

Venezuela offers the tourist a great variety of landscape – tropical beaches, immense plains, enormous rivers, forests, jungle, waterfalls and great mountains. The country has, for the purposes of this survey, been divided into four major areas: Caracas, The North Coast, The Llanos and Eastern Venezuela.

Caracas

Nestling in a long narrow valley in the coastal mountain range 16km (10 miles) from the north coast, Caracas is typical of the 'new Venezuela', despite being one of the oldest established cities in the country (founded 1567). The city is constantly growing and changing but, among the new developments, there are still areas of the old towns intact – **San José** and **Las Pastora**, for example. Other periods of the country's history have left substantial monuments; these include the *Plaza Bolívar,* flanked by the old cathedral and the Archbishop's residence, the *Casa Amarilla* and the *Capitol* (the National Congress) building, erected in 1873 in only 114 days, which has a fine mural depicting Venezuelan military exploits. Other places worth visiting include the *Panteon Nacional* (which contains the body of Simon Bolívar), the *Jardín Botánico*, the *Parque Nacional del Este*, and, for recreation, the Country Club. **Museums** in the capital include the *Museo de Bellas Artes*, the *Museo del Arte Colonial*, the *Museo del Arte Contemporáneo*, the *Museo de Transporte* and the *Casa Natal del Libertadora* (a reconstruction of the house where Bolívar was born; the first was destroyed in an earthquake). Next door is a museum containing the Liberator's war relics. There are also a large number of art galleries, as well as daily concerts, theatrical productions, films and lectures. The city also has a wide range of nightclubs, bars and coffee shops, especially along the *Boulevarde Sabana Grande*.
Excursions: *Mount Avila* gives a superb view across the city and along the coast. There are several beaches within 30km (20 miles) of the capital, with excellent 'taverns' and restaurants. For further information on these and other coastal resorts, see the following section.

The North Coast

The 4000km (2800 miles) of Caribbean coastline represents the major tourist destination in the country. The area has numerous excellent beaches and resorts ranging from the comparatively luxurious to the unashamedly opulent which stretch along the coastline. **Maiquetia** is one of the best and most popular, offering wide beaches, an extensive range of watersports and some of the best fishing (including an international competition for the giant blue sailfish). There are daily air-shuttles from Maiquetia to **Porlamar**, on **Margarita Island**, a popular tourist resort with beautiful beaches, good hotels and extensive shopping centres. Also to the west of Caracas are **Macuto, Marbella, Naiguta, Carabelleda, Leguna** and **Oriaco** which all have excellent beaches. To the north of Maiquetia is the idyllic island of **Los Roques**.
La Guaira is the main port for Caracas. Although now heavily industrialised, the winding hilltop route from the city and the old town are worth visiting. Further west along the Inter-American highway is **Maracay** with its opera house, bullring and *Gomez Mausoleum*. Excursions run to **Lake Valencia** and Gomez's country house, the *Rancho Grande*.
The coastal resorts of **Ocumare de la Costa** and **Cata** can be reached by way of the 1130m (3710ft) *Portachuelo Pass* through the central highlands. The coastline is dotted with fine beaches and islands, many inhabited only by flamingoes and scarlet ibis. Most can be reached by hired boat. **Morrocoy**, off the coast from Tucacas, is the most spectacular of these – hundreds of coral reefs with palm beaches ideal for scuba diving and fishing. **Palma Sola** and **Chichiriviche** are also popular. Ferries run from La Vela de Coro and Punto Fijo to the islands of Aruba and Curaçao. Journeys take about four hours and delays are to be expected.
Puerto la Cruz is a popular coastal resort with bars and restaurants and good beaches. It is also a good centre for travelling to remoter beaches. There is the Morro marina development in the Lecherías area adjacent to Puerto la Cruz, and the attractive town of **Pueblo Viejo** with 'old' Caribbean architecture and a Venetian lagoon layout – boats are the only means of transport. The attractiveness of the Puerto la Cruz area means that there has been an increase of foreign investment here in recent years.
South of Coro is **Barquisimeto**, one of the oldest settlements in Venezuela, now the country's fourth-largest city and capital of the *Llanos*, the great Venezuelan plateau and cattle range (see below for further information on this region). Its cathedral is one of the most famous modern buildings in the country.
Along the Colombian border is the Cordillera de Mérida and, to the east of this range, the **Cordillera Oriental**. Set in the area between these two ranges are the city of **Maracaibo** and *Lake Maracaibo.* Windless and excessively humid, the city and its environs are dominated by the machinery of oil production from the largest oilfields in the world, discovered in 1917. Sightseeing tours are available from here to the peninsula of **Guajira,** where the Motilone and Guajiro Indians live.
To the north of Maracaibo live the Goaro Indians whose lifestyle has changed little since the days of the first Spanish settlers. Their houses are raised above the lake on stilts and are in fact the original inspiration for naming the country Venezuela, or 'Little Venice'.
The **Cordillera de Mérida** are the only peaks in the country with a permanent snowline. Frosty plateaux and lofty summits characterise the landscape and many cities have grown up at the foot of the mountains, combining tradition with modern ways of life as well as diversified rural and urban scenery. The scenery in this area is extremely varied – lagoons, mountains, rivers, beaches, ancient villages, historical cities, oil camps, sand dunes and Indian lake dwellings on stilts. The **Sierra Nevada National Park** offers opportunities to ski between November and June but, at an altitude of 4270m (14,000ft), this is recommended only for the hardiest and most dedicated.
Mérida, to the south, is today a city of wide modern avenues linking mainly large-scale 20th-century developments, although, wherever possible, relics of the colonial past have been allowed to stand. A university town and tourist centre, it nestles in the *Sierra Nevada*, overshadowed by *Bolívar Peak* (5007m/15,260ft) and *Mirror Peak* (where the world's highest cable car climbs to an altitude of 4675m/14,250ft). Mérida has modern and colonial art museums and much more worth seeing, including the *Valle Grande*, the *Flower Clock*, *Los Chorros de Milla,* the lagoons of *Mucubaji*, *Los Anteojos*, *Tabay, Pogal, Los Patos, San-say* and the famous *Black Lagoon*. A mountain railway runs from the town to **Pico Espejo**. The view from the summit looks over the highest peaks of the Cordillera and the Llanos. *The Andean Club* in Mérida arranges trips to **Los Nervados**, the highest village in the mountains. Again, this is only recommended for the hardy. Other excursions from Mérida include **San Javier del Valle**, a relaxing mountain retreat, and **Jaji**, which has some fine examples of colonial architecture.

The Llanos

This is an expansive, sparsely populated area of grassland east of the Cordillera de Mérida and north of the Orinoco, reaching up to the north coast. The area is the heart of the Venezuelan cattle country and the landscape is flat and only varied here and there by slight outcrops of land. It is veined by numerous slow-running rivers, forested along their banks. The swamps are the home of egrets, parrots, alligators and monkeys. The equestrian skills of the plainsmen can be seen at many rodeos throughout the Llanos, as well as exhibitions of cattle roping and the *Joropo*, Venezuela's national dance.

Eastern Venezuela

The coastal regions to the north of the Guyana Highlands have some fine tourist beaches and resorts. These include *Higuerote*, *La Sabana* and also *Lecheria* where the San Juan Drum Festival is held during late June.
The **Guyana Highlands** lie to the south of the Orinoco River and constitute half the land area of the country. Their main value is as a source of gold and diamonds. The *Orinoco* and its delta have been developed as major trade centres. **Ciudad Bolívar**, formerly known as Angostura, and the home of Angostura bitters, is an old city on the south bank of the Orinoco and still bears traces of its colonial past, although it is currently the centre of modern developments. The **Gran Sabana National Reserve** is the largest of the Venezuelan plateaux and has an extraordinary array of wildlife. **Santa Elena,** *Guri Dam* and *Danto Falls* are all worth a visit. **Santa Elena de Uairén** is a rugged frontier town which holds a Fiesta in August. **Mount Roraima,** suggested as the site of Conan Doyle's 'Lost World', can be climbed on foot. A fortnight's supplies and full camping equipment should be taken as the trip can take up to two weeks. The nearest village to the mountain is **Peraitepin**. *Tepuy Peak* is also worth a visit. Trips can be arranged to the diamond mines at **Los Caribes**. In **Icaban** after a heavy rainfall it is common to see children searching the slopes for gold nuggets washed down from the slopes.
It is possible to arrange trips by boat up the Orinoco River delta to **La Tucupita**. **Canaima** (one of the world's largest national parks, comprising three million hectares) is the setting for the spectacular *Angel Falls,* which carry the waters of the *Churum River* into an abyss. At 979m (3212ft) they are the highest in the world, a sight no visitor should miss. Trips can be arranged which take in the waterfalls and other nearby attractions, including many rare plants – Canaima has over 500 species of orchid alone. Overnight accommodation is available on the shores of the lagoon. Other national parks in Venezuela are to be found in Bolívar State and the Amazonas Federal Territory, for example, **El Cocuy** and **Autana.**

SOCIAL PROFILE

FOOD & DRINK: Cumin and saffron are used in many dishes but the distinctive and delicate flavour of most of the popular dishes comes from the use of local roots and vegetables. Some local specialities are *tequenos,* a popular hors d'oeuvres (thin dough wrapped around a finger of local white cheese and fried crisp); *arepas* (the native bread), made from primitive ground corn, water and salt; and *tostadas,* which are used for sandwiches (the mealy centre is removed and the crisp shell is filled with anything from ham and cheese to spiced meat, chicken salad or cream cheese). *Guasacaca* is a semi-hot relish used mostly with grilled meats. *Pabellón criollo* is a hash made with shredded meat and served with fried plantains and black beans on rice. *Hallaca* is a local delicacy, eaten at Christmas and New Year; cornmeal is combined with beef, pork, ham and green peppers, wrapped in individual pieces of banana leaves and cooked in boiling water. *Parrilla criolla* is beef marinated and cooked over a charcoal grill. *Hervido* is soup made with chunks of beef, chicken or fish and native vegetables or roots. *Purée de apio* is one of the more exotic local roots (boiled and puréed, with salt and butter added, it tastes like chestnuts). *Empanadas* (meat turnovers), *roast lapa* (a succulent, large rodent) and *chipi chipi* soup (made from tiny clams) are excellent. Table service is the norm and opening hours are 2100-2300. **Drink:** There is no good local wine, although foreign wines are bottled locally. There are several good local beers, mineral waters, gin and excellent rum. Coffee is very good and a *merengada* (fruit pulp, ice, milk and sugar) is recommended. *Batido* is similar but with water and no milk. *Pousse-café* is an after-dinner liqueur. Bars have either table or counter service. A *lisa* is a glass of draught beer and a *tercio* a bottled beer. Most bars are open very late and there are no licensing laws.

NIGHTLIFE: There are many nightclubs and discotheques in the major cities of Venezuela. The National and Municipal Theatres offer a variety of concerts, ballet, plays, operas and operettas. There are other theatres, some of which are open-air, in Caracas, as well as several cinemas.

SHOPPING: There are many handicrafts unique to Venezuela which are made by local Indian tribes. Good purchases are gems and jewellery, *cacique* coins, gold, pearls, pompom slippers, seed necklaces, shoes and handbags, Indian bows, arrows, mats, pipes and baskets, *alpargatas* (traditional local footwear of the Campesinos), *chinchorros* (local hammocks) and many other Indian goods. **Shopping hours:** 0900-1300 and 1500-1900 Monday to Saturday.

SPORT: Jungle trips: Various companies offer 'off-the-beaten-track' expeditions. **Golf:** There are various clubs at which temporary membership can be arranged.
Hunting: All hunting in Venezuela has been prohibited for the past six years. **Watersports:** Available less than an hour from Caracas on the Caribbean, where there are several excellent beaches with full facilities. Sailing and yachting regattas are held every year at Macuto. There are skindiving and water-skiing facilities at Chichiriviche, Cata Bay and Macuto. The snorkelling off Margarita Island is very enjoyable. **Winter sports:** The season is from May to October. **Horseracing:** Caracas has South America's largest and most modern race track – La Rinconada – open Saturday and Sunday. **Boxing, baseball & football:** These are the most popular spectator sports in Venezuela and can be seen all year round. The winter baseball leagues feature many young US baseball stars. **Wrestling:** The indigenous *lucha libre* wrestling is a weekly event.

SPECIAL EVENTS: Every village and town in Venezuela celebrates the feast of its patron saint. It is during these provincial festivals that the tourist can enjoy the colourful folklore that is a mixture of the cultures of pre-Columbian Indians, African slaves and Spanish colonialists.

SOCIAL CONVENTIONS: Shaking hands or using the local *abrazo,* a cross between a hug and a handshake, are the normal forms of greeting. In Caracas conservative casual wear is the norm. Men are expected to wear suits for business, and jackets and ties are usual for dining out and social functions. Dress on the coast is less formal but beachwear and shorts should not be worn away from the beach or pool. Smoking follows European habits and in most cases it is obvious where not to smoke. Some public buildings are also non-smoking areas. **Tipping:** Tips are discretionary but in the majority of bars and restaurants 10% is added to the bill and it is customary to leave another 10% on the table. Bellboys and chambermaids should be tipped, and in Caracas tips are higher than elsewhere. Taxi drivers are not tipped unless they carry suitcases. Petrol pump attendants expect a tip.

BUSINESS PROFILE

ECONOMY: Venezuela was a primarily agricultural country until the discovery and extraction of oil began in the 1920s. Oil now dominates the economy and has made Venezuela the wealthiest country in South America. With the second-largest known reserves in the world (after Saudi Arabia), little change in the structure of the economy may be expected for the foreseeable future. Agriculture's share of the workforce has now fallen below 25%, but the sector remains important with dairy and beef farming being major export earners. Most of the rest of farming activity is devoted to staple crops for domestic consumption, although some crops – mostly rice, sugar and coffee – are grown as cash crops. The Venezuelan economy stabilised in the late 1980s after a difficult period following the collapse of the oil price which slashed revenues and brought numerous industrial and social programmes to a halt. Firm fiscal management was responsible on that occasion, despite persistent problems with debt servicing and low currency reserves, and laid the foundations for a strong economic performance in the late 1980s and early 1990s when annual growth reached 9%. However, the political uncertainty following the February 1992 coup attempt had a knock-on effect on the economy: growth has slowed to around 5% while inflation has climbed to 30%. The Government is hoping to develop other sectors of the economy, particularly minerals including aluminium and gold, but this depends on substantial investment. Meanwhile oil revenues continue to be depressed due to low world prices. A labour shortage in key sectors of the economy has induced the Government to launch an immigration drive aimed at Eastern Europe. It is planned that 50,000 people will join the existing population of 19 million by 1997. Venezuela is a member of both OPEC and the Asociación Latinoamericana de Integración, which seeks to promote a common market for Latin

America. Most kinds of industrial and consumer goods are in demand in Venezuela from foreign exporters. The USA is the dominant trade partner, followed by Germany, Japan and Brazil.

BUSINESS: English is becoming more widely spoken in business circles, particularly at executive level. Nevertheless, Spanish is essential for most business discussions. Appointments are necessary and a business visitor should be punctual. It is common to exchange visiting cards. **Office hours:** 0800-1800 Monday to Friday with a long mid-day break.

COMMERCIAL INFORMATION: The following organisation can offer advice: Federación Venezolana de Cámaras y Asociaciones de Comercio y Producción (FEDECAMARAS) (Federation of Chambers of Commerce and Industry), Apartado 2568, Edificio Fedecámaras, 5°, Avenida El Empalme, Urb El Bosque, Caracas. Tel: (2) 731 1711. Fax: (2) 731 0220. Telex: 29890.

CONFERENCES/CONVENTIONS: Larger hotels have facilities.

CLIMATE

The climate varies according to altitude. Lowland areas have a tropical climate. The dry season is from December to April and the rainy season from May to December. The best time to visit is between January and April.

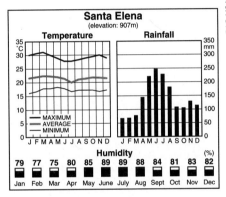

Santa Elena
(elevation: 907m)

	Jan	Feb	Mar	Apr	May	June	July	Aug	Sept	Oct	Nov	Dec
Humidity (%)	79	77	75	80	85	89	89	88	84	81	83	82

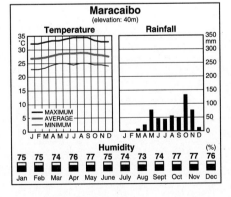

Maracaibo
(elevation: 40m)

	Jan	Feb	Mar	Apr	May	June	July	Aug	Sept	Oct	Nov	Dec
Humidity (%)	75	75	74	76	77	75	74	73	74	77	77	76

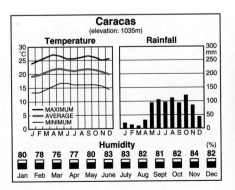

Caracas
(elevation: 1035m)

	Jan	Feb	Mar	Apr	May	June	July	Aug	Sept	Oct	Nov	Dec
Humidity (%)	80	78	76	77	80	83	83	82	81	82	84	82

Vietnam

☐ international airport

Location: South-East Asia.

Vietnam Tourism
30A Ly Thuong Kiet, Hanoi, Vietnam
Tel: (4) 264 154. Fax: (4) 257 583. Telex: 411272.
Embassy of the Socialist Republic of Vietnam
12-14 Victoria Road, London W8 5RD
Tel: (0171) 937 1912. Fax: (0171) 937 6108. Telex: 887361 (a/b VIETEMG). Opening hours: 0900-1200 and 1400-1800 Monday to Friday.
West East Travel (UK handling agent for Vietnam Tourism)
39B Nicoll Road, London NW10 9EX
Tel: (0181) 961 0117. Fax: (0181) 965 2558.
Vietnam Travel & Trade Europe (EurAsia Ltd)
PO Box 693, 2501 CR The Hague, The Netherlands
Tel: (70) 363 2558. Fax: (70) 310 6009.
British Embassy
16 Pho Ly Thuong Kiet, Hanoi, Vietnam
Tel: (4) 252 349. Fax: (4) 265 762. Telex: 411405.
Embassy of the Socialist Republic of Vietnam
25B Davidson Drive, Gloucester, Ontario K1J 6L7
Tel: (613) 744 4963 *or* 745 9735 (Consular section). Fax: (613) 744 1709 *or* 744 5072 (Consular section). Telex: 0533205.
Canadian Embassy
39 Nguyen Dinh Chieu Street, Hanoi, Vietnam
Tel: (4) 265 840 *or* 265 845. Fax: (4) 265 837.

AREA: 330,341 sq km (127,545 sq miles).
POPULATION: 66,200,000 (1990 estimate).
POPULATION DENSITY: 200.4 per sq km.
CAPITAL: Hanoi. **Population:** 3,056,146 (1989).
GEOGRAPHY: Vietnam shares borders to the north with the People's Republic of China and to the west with Laos and Cambodia. The South China Sea lies to the east and south. The land is principally agricultural with a central tropical rainforest.

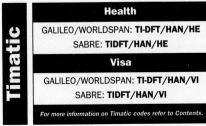

Health	
GALILEO/WORLDSPAN:	**TI-DFT/HAN/HE**
SABRE:	**TIDFT/HAN/HE**
Visa	
GALILEO/WORLDSPAN:	**TI-DFT/HAN/VI**
SABRE:	**TIDFT/HAN/VI**
For more information on Timatic codes refer to Contents.	

Timatic

LANGUAGE: Vietnamese is the official language. English, French and occasionally Russian and German are known.

RELIGION: Buddhist majority. There are Taoist, Confucian, Hoa Hao, Caodaist and Christian (predominantly Roman Catholic) minorities.

TIME: GMT + 7.

ELECTRICITY: 110/220 volts AC, 50Hz.

COMMUNICATIONS: Telephone: IDD is available only to Hanoi and Ho Chi Minh City. Country code: 84. International calls must be made through the operator. **Fax:** Available in most major offices. **Telex/telegram:** Telex facilities limited to main cities only. Telegram facilities are available in most towns. **Post:** Postal services can be slow. Airmail to Europe can take up to three weeks. **Press:** Daily and weekly newspapers in Vietnam include *Hanoi Moi* and *Nhan Dan* ('The People'). The *Vietnam Economic Times, Vietnam Investment Review, Saigon Times* and *Business Vietnam* are published in English. The *Bangkok Post, The Nation* and *The South China Morning Post* are often available in Ho Chi Minh City and Hanoi.

BBC World Service and Voice of America frequencies: From time to time these change. See the section *How to Use this Book* for more information.

BBC:

MHz	11.955	11.75	9.74	6.195

Voice of America:

MHz	15.43	11.72	5.985	1.143

PASSPORT/VISA

Regulations and requirements may be subject to change at short notice, and you are advised to contact the appropriate diplomatic or consular authority before finalising travel arrangements. Details of these may be found at the head of this country's entry. Any numbers in the chart refer to the footnotes below.

	Passport Required?	Visa Required?	Return Ticket Required?
Full British	Yes	Yes	Yes
BVP	Not valid	-	-
Australian	Yes	Yes	Yes
Canadian	Yes	Yes	Yes
USA	Yes	Yes	Yes
Other EU (As of 31/12/94)	Yes	Yes	Yes
Japanese	Yes	Yes	Yes

PASSPORTS: Valid passport required by all.

British Visitors Passport: Not acceptable.

VISAS: Required by all. At the present time visas can be issued for either groups or individuals.

Types of visa: Single-entry. Costs and conditions are liable to change.

Validity: 1 month. Visas can usually be extended for another month, at extra cost, in the larger towns.

Application to: Consulate (or Consular section at Embassy).

Application requirements: (a) 3 completed application forms. (b) 3 passport-size photos. (c) Valid passport. (d) Fee (once application has been approved). (e) For postal applications, a registered, stamped self-addressed envelope.

Working days required: 10 days.

Note: Since March 1993 a travel permit is no longer required. It might, however, still be necessary to check with city authorities when planning to visit remote outlying villages.

MONEY

Currency: New Dông (D). Notes are in denominations of D50,000, 10,000, 5000, 2000, 1000, 500, 200 and 100. Coins are not used.

Currency exchange: The US Dollar is the most favoured foreign currency. British, Australian, Japanese, French, German, Belgian, Dutch, Singapore and Thai currency can usually be changed in the larger cities; great difficulty may be encountered in trying to exchange any other currencies.

Credit cards: An increasing number of outlets accept Visa and Mastercard. Check with your credit card company for details for merchant acceptability and other services which may be available.

Travellers cheques: American Express and Thomas Cook travellers cheques are widely accepted in hotels and banks.

Exchange rate indicators: The following figures are included as a guide to the movements of the New Dông against Sterling and the US Dollar:

Date:	Oct '92	Sep '93	Jan '94	Jan '95
£1.00=	17,198.81	16,384.0	16,010.5	17,323.6
$1.00=	10,837.30	10,729.5	10,821.6	11,072.9

Currency restrictions: Import and export of local currency is prohibited. Import and export of foreign currency over US$3000 is subject to declaration.

DUTY FREE

Duty-free regulations are subject to frequent amendment; check with the Embassy prior to departure. At the time of going to press, the following could be freely imported to Vietnam by foreign visitors:

200 cigarettes and 50 cigars or 250g of loose tobacco; 1 bottle of spirits; a reasonable quantity of perfume.

Prohibited items: The importation of non-prescribed drugs, firearms and pornography is prohibited.

PUBLIC HOLIDAYS

Jan 1 '95 New Year's Day. **Jan/Feb** *Têt, Lunar New Year (three days). **Apr 7** Emperor-Founder Hung Vuong. **Apr 30** Liberation of Saigon. **May 1** May Day. **Sep 1-2** National Day. **Jan 1 '96** New Year's Day. **Jan/Feb** *Têt, Lunar New Year (three days). **Apr 7** Emperor-Founder Hung Vuong. **Apr 30** Liberation of Saigon.

Notes [*]: Check with the Embassy for the exact date. Visitors may experience difficulties during this period as shops, restaurants and public services close and prices tend to go up in the few shops that remain open.

HEALTH

Regulations and requirements may be subject to change at short notice, and you are advised to contact your doctor well in advance of your intended date of departure. Any numbers in the chart refer to the footnotes below.

	Special Precautions?	Certificate Required?
Yellow Fever	No	1
Cholera	Yes	2
Typhoid & Polio	Yes	-
Malaria	3	-
Food & Drink	4	-

[1]: A yellow fever vaccination certificate is required from travellers over one year of age arriving from infected areas.

[2]: Following WHO guidelines issued in 1973, a cholera vaccination certificate is not an official condition of entry to Vietnam. However, cholera is a serious risk in this country and precautions are essential. Up-to-date advice should be sought before deciding whether these precautions should include vaccination, as medical opinion is divided over its effectiveness. See the *Health* section at the back of the book.

[3]: Malaria risk exists throughout the year everywhere except urban areas and the river deltas. The benign *vivax* form is predominant in the northern provinces. The malignant *falciparum* form is reported to be 'highly resistant' to chloroquine and 'resistant' to sulfadoxine-pyrimethamine. Larium is usually the prescribed prophylactic.

[4]: All water should be regarded as being potentially contaminated. Water used for drinking, brushing teeth or making ice should have first been boiled or otherwise sterilised. Milk is unpasteurised and should be boiled. Powdered or tinned milk is available and is advised, but make sure that it is reconstituted with pure water. Avoid dairy products which are likely to have been made from unboiled milk. Only eat well-cooked meat and fish, preferably served hot. Pork, salad and mayonnaise may carry increased risk. Vegetables should be cooked and fruit peeled.

Rabies is present. For those at high risk, vaccination before arrival should be considered. If you are bitten abroad, seek medical advice without delay. For more information, consult the *Health* section at the back of the book.

Bilharzia (schistosomiasis) is present in the delta of the Mekong River. Avoid swimming and paddling in fresh water. Swimming pools which are chlorinated and well-maintained are safe.

Japanese encephalitis is a risk between June and October, particularly in rural areas. A vaccine is available and travellers are advised to consult their doctors prior to departure.

Plague is present in natural foci. Further information should be sought from the Department of Health or from any of the hospitals specialising in tropical diseases listed in the *Health* section at the back of this book.

Tuberculosis is present all over Vietnam. Vaccination is recommended.

Health care: There are hospitals in major towns and cities and health care centres in all provinces but everywhere facilities are limited. Health insurance is essential and should include cover for emergency repatriation by air.

TRAVEL - International

AIR: Vietnam's national airline is *Vietnam Airlines (VN)*. The most usual routes to Vietnam are from Bangkok, Kuala Lumpur, Hong Kong, Taipei, Manila and Singapore.

Approximate flight time: From London to Hanoi is 17 hours, including 2 hours stopover in Bangkok.

International airports: *Noi Bai International Airport (HAN)* at Noi Bai is 45km (28 miles) from Hanoi. Buses and a few taxis are available.

Tan Son Nhat International Airport (SGN) is 7km (4.5 miles) from Ho Chi Minh City. Buses and a few taxis are available.

Departure tax: US$8.

SEA: The major ports are Ho Chi Minh City, Vung Tau, Haiphong, Da Nang and Ben Thuy. International cruise facilities are available.

RAIL: It is now possible to cross into China by rail from Lao Cai to Kunming in the Yunnan province of China or through Lang Son to Nanning.

ROAD: There are routes to China through Lang Son, Cambodia through Moc Bai and also to Laos.

Note: It is important to remember that all Vietnamese visas are issued with a specified exit point. If this exit point needs to be altered, it must be done so at an immigration office or through a travel agent in Hanoi or Ho Chi Minh City.

TRAVEL - Internal

AIR: *Vietnam Airlines* operates regular services between Hanoi, Ho Chi Minh City and Da Nang. Frequent services are provided between Hanoi or Ho Chi Minh City and and other major towns.

SEA: A local network operates between ports. Cruise facilities are available. Contact the Embassy before departure.

RAIL: Visitors may use the rail transport system independently or as part of a rail tour. Long-distance trains are more expensive but are faster, more reliable and more comfortable.

ROAD: There is a reasonable road network. Traffic drives on the right. Roads, especially in the north, are often in a bad state of repair and may be impassable during the rainy season. Driving in Vietnam can be a hair-raising experience as the normal rules of highway discipline are rarely followed by the majority of drivers. **Bus:** Services are poor and overcrowded. Minibuses often run between tourist hotels in the major towns. **Car hire:** It is possible to hire chauffeur-driven cars. **Documentation:** An International Driving Permit is not officially required, but is advised. **URBAN:** There are local bus services in Ho Chi Minh City and in Hanoi, which also has a tramway. It is also possible to travel by cycle rickshaw (cyclo) taxi or motorbike.

ACCOMMODATION

Tourist facilities have vastly improved in the last few years and most towns have small hotels and guest-houses. In the major towns there is a full range of accommodation to suit all budgets.

RESORTS & EXCURSIONS

The capital, **Hanoi**, sprawls on the banks of the Red River. It is a beautiful city which retains an air of French colonial elegance with pretty yellow stucco buildings lining leafy streets. Hanoi is also a city of lakes which adds to its air of sleepy grace. At present there are few cars – most people travel by bicycle or moped. Although the streets are busy there is little serious congestion and pollution is not yet a problem. It is a city that, at present, appears lodged in a bygone age. In the middle of the city lies the peaceful *Hoan Kiem Lake* (Lake of the Restored Sword) with the 18th-century *Ngoc Son (Jade Mountain) Temple* sitting on an island in its centre. The temple can be reached by *The Huc (Rising Sun) Bridge*. To the north of Hoan Kiem Lake is the *Old Quarter*, a fascinating maze of small antiquated streets lined with markets and pavement restaurants and cafés. West of the Old Quarter and south of the *West Lake* is the former *Ville Française*. This is the old French administrative centre and is characterised by enormous colonial-era châteaux and wide spacious boulevards. It also houses Hanoi's most popular attraction, the *Ho Chi Minh Mausoleum*. When visiting the Mausoleum, it is important to be respectful both in dress and attitude. Ho Chi Minh was the father of the modern state and is still held in reverential regard. His house, built in 1958, is also on public view. Other museums in Hanoi include the *History Museum (Bao Tang Lich Su)*, the *Army Museum (Bao Tang Quan Doi)*, *Ho Chi Minh Museum, Fine Arts Museum (Bao Tang My Thuat), Revolutionary Museum (Bao Tang Cach Manh)*

Promise Them The World.

We'll Deliver.

Travellers expect the world from Asian airlines these days.
New aircraft, generous service, convenient schedules,
exotic destinations, and a wide international route network.

It may surprise you to know that Vietnam Airlines has it all.
Our fleet is one of the youngest in the world; our service
reflects a tradition of grace and hospitality; our routes span
four continents, and best of all we offer *Vietnam* – a world
of our own – the most enchanting and exciting Asian
destination for 1995 and beyond.

Next time you're booking a client to Asia, recommend Vietnam
Airlines. We'll give them a lift, and won't let you down.
Vietnam Airlines. A world of difference.

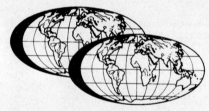

and *Independence Museum.* There are a number of interesting pagodas in Hanoi. The *One Pillar Pagoda*, first constructed in 1049 (subsequently destroyed by the French just before they were ejected from the city and then rebuilt by the new government), was built to resemble a lotus flower – the symbol of purity rising out of a sea of sorrow. The *Temple of Literature* built in 1076 was the first university in Vietnam. It is a graceful complex of small intricate buildings and peaceful courtyards. To the northwest of the *Citadel* is the West Lake which is about 13km (9 miles) in circumference. The shores of the lake are popular amongst the Hanoians for picnics and there are a number of cafés. The lake also contains the wreckage of a crashed American B52 bomber.

About 160km (100 miles) from Hanoi, near the port of **Haiphong**, is **Halong Bay**. This is an amazing complex of 3000 chalk islands risng out of the South China Sea. The area is strange, eerie and very beautiful. Many of the islands contain bizarre cave formations and grottoes.

Near Halong Bay is **Catba Island** which is a designated National Park and a rich repository of plants and wildlife.

About 250km (155 miles) north of Hanoi, high in the Hoang Lien mountains, is the old hill station of **Sapa**. This area is inhabited by the Hmong and Zhao hill tribes. Every weekend there is a market when the local tribes people come into town to trade. In the evening they celebrate with huge amounts of potent rice alcohol. It is absolutely vital that when visiting this area tourists are sensitive to local culture and traditions. If one follows the road from Sapa 200km (125 miles) further into the mountains (this can only realistically be attempted by jeep) one reaches *Dien Bien Phu*, scene of the humiliating defeat of the French by the Viet Minh that finally put paid to French colonial occupation in Indochina. This is a wild, beautiful and remote region.

Far to the south of Hanoi lies the city of **Hué**. The former capital of the emperors of Vietnam, it is known for its beautiful imperial architecture, although a great deal of this was destroyed during the Tet offensive in 1968. The *Perfume River* forms the border between the city itself and the former 'Forbidden Purple City', the mighty *Citadel*. This 'city within a city' with its tombs, pagodas and lakes covered in lotus flowers was largely destroyed during the Vietnam War, but one can still see evidence of its former magnificence. Within easy reach of the city are the tombs of several of Vietnam's emperors. Most interesting, perhaps, are the *Tomb of Minh Mang* and the *Tomb of Tu Duc*. The city also houses fine examples of Buddhist pagodas and other temples, such as the *Thien Mu Pagoda*.

Near Hué is **Da Nang**, city of *China Beach*, the *Marble Mountains* and the *Cham Museum,* which houses magnificant examples of the art of the Indianised Cham civilisation. 20km (12 miles) from Da Nang is **Hoi An.** This is a delightful small riverine town replete with temple and pagodas.

A day's drive from Hoi An, through some of Vietnam's most breathtaking scenery, is **Nha Trang**. This is a pleasant resort with a good beach. From here it is easy to reach the town of **Dalat** in the Central Highlands which is popular among domestic tourists for its cool climate and alpine scenery. It is very French.

Set back from the delta formed by the Mekong River, **Ho Chi Minh City** (formerly Saigon) is the main commercial centre of the southern part of Vietnam, receiving its name in honour of the leader who successfully led the nation against both the French and the Americans. Locals still like to refer to it as Saigon. More modern than other Vietnamese cities, Ho Chi Minh City has also retained its French colonial influences. Its vibrancy is maintained by the ever-entrepreneurial Saigonese who have taken the Government reforms to heart and re-embraced the capitalist ethic with unrestrained enthusiasm. The streets are jam-packed with mopeds and scooters, often carrying whole families. The markets are chaotically busy. There is a lot to see in Ho Chi Minh City. The colourful *Emperor of Jade Pagoda* is an excellent example of a Chinese temple. Inside, there are elaborate woodcarvings decorated with gilded characters and sculptures depicting local deities. The hustle and bustle of trading is best observed in the markets of **Cholon**, the ancient Chinese quarter. The *Hôtel de Ville* is a wonderful example of French colonial architecture. *The War Crimes Museum* bears witness to the suffering inflicted on the Vietnamese people during the Vietnam War in the 1960s and 1970s. Other sites relevant to that era are *Re-Unification Hall* and the former US Embassy. Interesting excursions from Saigon are visits to the *Cu Chi Tunnels* in which the South Vietnamese Communists concealed themselves and from which they launched attacks on the Americans. **Tay Ninh,** northwest of Ho Chi Minh City, is interesting as it is the home of the Caodai religion. This is a purely Vietnamese sect formed in this century that takes teachings and precepts from most of the world's major religions. Tay Ninh is the site of the largest Caodaist temple in Vietnam. This structure is colourful and unique.

South of Ho Chi Minh city are the flat, verdant planes of the **Mekong Delta** where much of Vietnam's rice crop is grown. There a number of towns in this region from which the visitor can take boat trips on the many tributaries of the Mekong.

SOCIAL PROFILE

FOOD: Vietnamese cooking is varied and usually very good. It is a mixture of Vietnamese, Chinese and French traditions with a plethora of regional specilities. As in all countries of the region, rice or noodles usually provide the basis of a meal. Not surprisingly, fish is plentiful. Breakfast is generally noodle soup locally known as *pho* (pronounced 'fur'). French-style baguettes are available throughout Vietnam. Local specialities include *nem* (pork mixed with noodles, eggs and mushrooms wrapped in rice paper, fried and served hot) and *banh chung* (glutinous rice, pork and onions wrapped in large leaves and cooked for up to 48 hours, to be eaten cold at any time). Vietnamese dishes are not complete without *nuoc mam* (a fish sauce) or *mam tom* (a shrimp sauce). Western-style cooking is on offer wherever tourists or business people are to be found in any numbers.

DRINK: Green tea is refreshing and available everywhere. Apart from baguette the French culinary legacy also embraces rich, fresh, filter coffee, usually brewed on the table in front of the customer. Vietnamese often have a fondness for beer. It is possible to get both local and imported brands. When in Hanoi it is worth trying the local draught beer available at street stalls. It is called *Bia Hoi* and is not only cheap, but free of additives. *Rice wine* is also a favourite throughout the country. It is generally extremely potent.

SHOPPING: Local specialities include lacquer painting, reed mats, embroidery, tailor-made *ao dais* (female national costume) and mother-of-pearl inlay on ornaments and furniture, not to mention the ubiquitous conical hat. **Shopping hours:** 0800-1900 Monday to Sunday.

SPECIAL EVENTS: Most regions, particularly where the minority groups live, have their own traditional festivals incorporating music, opera and dance. *Têt* (Lunar New Year) and important Buddhist festivals are celebrated during February and March each year. (Although celebrated, Buddhist and Christian festivals are not considered national holidays.)

SOCIAL CONVENTIONS: Handshaking and a vocal greeting is normal. Clothing should be kept simple, informal and discreet. Avoid shorts if possible as they are usually only worn by children. Footwear should be removed when entering Buddhist pagodas. Vietnamese people should not be touched on the head. **Photography:** There are restrictions at ports, airports and harbours, and in similar areas elsewhere. It is courteous to ask permission first before taking photographs of people. **Tipping:** Officially prohibited but widely practised, especially in the south. Discretion is advised.

BUSINESS PROFILE

ECONOMY: The economy of Vietnam was devastated by 30 years of war up to 1975, after which mismanagement and the US boycott combined stifled development. After the Communist victory in 1975, Vietnam operated a Soviet-style command economy. However, in the wake of the political and economic upheaval in the former Soviet Union and Vietnam's other former allies in COMECON, Vietnam acted quickly to implement its own form of *perestroika*, known as *doi moi,* with market reforms and privatisation. These reforms have been implemented on the Chinese model, involving liberalisation of the economy while the state has maintained a tight grip on central power. How long the Government can keep this up under the inevitably strong influences engendered by individual wealth and extensive contact with the outside world remains to be seen. Agriculture employs about 70% of the population, rice being the most important crop. Recent improvements in harvests and the implementation of reforms in land ownership have ended Vietnam's occasional reliance on UN food aid earlier in the 1980s, and the country is now one of the world's leading rice exporters. The north holds most of the country's natural resources, particularly coal. The exception to this pattern is oil, which is believed to be present in some quantity off Vietnam's southern coast. Much of Vietnam's industry was destroyed during the war but the principal industries – food-processing, cement, metallurgy, chemicals, textiles and paper – have all recovered to a greater or lesser extent. Tourism is also a rapid growth area. According to official statistics, 650,000 foreign tourists visited Vietnam in 1993 as opposed to 250,000 in 1990. The continuation of the US embargo until February 1994 severely impeded Vietnam's economic development, not so much because of low bilateral economic links but because of US influence in blocking Vietnamese access to funds from international institutions such as the World Bank and IMF (the USA officially dropped their objections in 1993 as a precursor to ending the boycott). President Clinton's decision to lift the embargo was virtually inevitable in the light of the desires of US business interests to gain access to the quickly-developing Vietnamese markets and compete against their already-established European and Asian rivals. Full diplomatic relations have yet to be established. Although they should not be long in coming, they remain a prerequisite if Vietnam is to exploit fully its potential and join the other Asian 'tiger' economies. Foreign countries are now falling over themselves to invest in Vietnam. The full cultural and political consequences of this scramble for foreign investment are not yet clear.

BUSINESS: Smart lightweight casuals would usually be worn for meetings as suits are needed for only the most formal occasions. English is not spoken by all officials and a knowledge of French will be useful. Business cards should have a Vietnamese translation on the back. **Office hours:** 0730-1200 and 1300-1630 Monday to Saturday.

COMMERCIAL INFORMATION: The following organisation can offer advice: Vietcochamber (Chamber of Industry and Commerce of Vietnam), 33 Ba Trieu, Hanoi. Tel: (4) 252 961. Fax: (4) 256 446. Telex: 411257.

CLIMATE

Because of its geography the climate in Vietnam varies greatly from north to south. Tropical monsoons occur from May to October. It is almost totally dry throughout the rest of the year.

Required clothing: Tropicals and washable cottons are worn all year. Rainwear is essential during the rainy season.

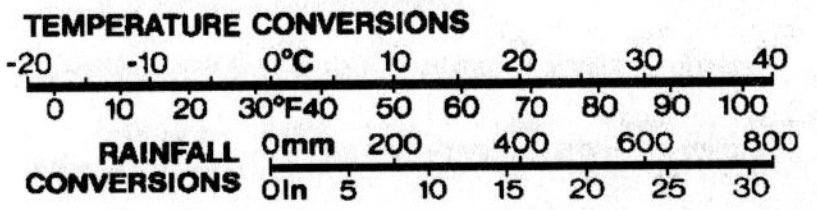

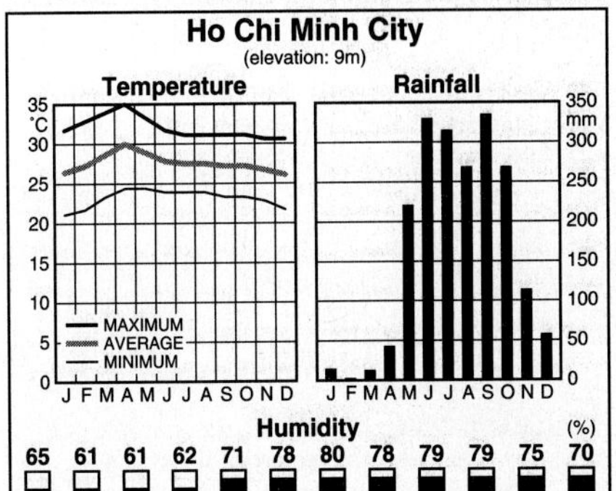

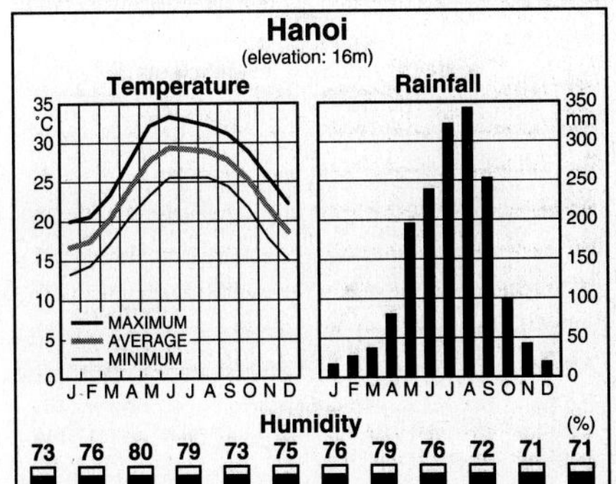

Western Samoa

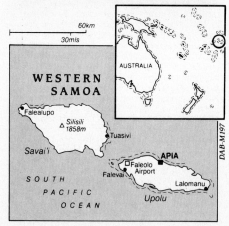

60km
30mls

AUSTRALIA

WESTERN SAMOA

Faleaiupo
Silisili △ 1858m
Tuasivi

Savai'i

APIA
Faleolo Airport
Falevai
Laiomanu

SOUTH PACIFIC OCEAN

Upolu

DAB-M197

Location: South Pacific.

Western Samoan Visitors' Bureau
PO Box 862, Apia, Western Samoa
Tel: 20878. Fax: 22848. Telex: 220 (a/b A PTRGRMS SX).

Embassy of Western Samoa
avenue Franklin D Roosevelt 123, B-1050 Brussels, Belgium
Tel: (2) 660 8454. Fax: (2) 675 0336. Telex: 2567.

Tourism Council of the South Pacific
375 Upper Richmond Road West, London SW14 7NX
Tel: (0181) 392 1589 or (0181) 878 0998.

Office of the Honorary British Representative
c/o Kruse Va'ai and Barlow, PO Box 2029, Apia, Western Samoa
Tel: 21895. Fax: 21407.

Western Samoan Embassy and **Mission to the United Nations**
Suite 800D, 820 Second Avenue, New York, NY 10017
Tel: (212) 599 6196/7. Fax: (212) 599 0797.
Also deals with enquiries from Canada.

Embassy of the United States of America
PO Box 3430, 5th Floor, Beach Road, Apia, Western Samoa
Tel: 21631. Fax: 22030. Telex: 275 (a/b AMEMB SX).
The Canadian High Commission in Wellington deals with enquiries relating to Western Samoa (see *New Zealand* **earlier in this book).**

AREA: 2831 sq km (1093 sq miles).
POPULATION: 159,862 (1991).
POPULATION DENSITY: 56.5 per sq km.
CAPITAL: Apia (Upolu Island). **Population:** 36,000 (1984).
GEOGRAPHY: Western Samoa consists of nine islands. The largest of these is Savai'i, which covers 1610 sq km (622 sq miles); fertile Upolu, the second-largest (1120 sq km/433 sq miles), lies 13km (8 miles) to the southeast across the Apolima Strait. The islands are quiescent volcanoes and reach heights of up to 1858m (6097ft) on Savai'i and 1100m (3608ft) on Upolu. Volcanic activity has not occurred since 1911. The main city, Apia, is located in the north of Upolu.
LANGUAGE: Samoan is the national language. In business and commerce English is customary.
RELIGION: Congregational Church, Roman Catholic, Methodist and Latter Day Saints.
TIME: GMT - 11.

Timatic

Health	
GALILEO/WORLDSPAN: **TI-DFT/APW/HE**	
SABRE: **TIDFT/APW/HE**	
Visa	
GALILEO/WORLDSPAN: **TI-DFT/APW/VI**	
SABRE: **TIDFT/APW/VI**	

For more information on Timatic codes refer to Contents.

ELECTRICITY: 110 volts AC, 60Hz.
COMMUNICATIONS: Telephone: Ingoing IDD is available. Country code: 685. There are no area codes. Outgoing international calls must be made through the operator. **Fax:** Services are available from the telegraph office above the post office. There are hotels with facilities. **Telex/telegram:** Available from the telegraph office above the post office. Also in main towns and at major hotels. **Post:** The main post office is open from 0900-1200 and 1300-1630 Monday to Friday. Airmail to Europe takes about three weeks. **Press:** The main newspapers are *The Observer* and *The Samoa Times*.
BBC World Service and Voice of America frequencies: From time to time these change. See the section *How to Use this Book* for more information.
BBC:

MHz	17.10	15.34	11.95	9.740

Voice of America:

MHz	18.82	15.18	9.525	1.735

PASSPORT/VISA

Regulations and requirements may be subject to change at short notice, and you are advised to contact the appropriate diplomatic or consular authority before finalising travel arrangements. Details of these may be found at the head of this country's entry. Any numbers in the chart refer to the footnotes below.

	Passport Required?	Visa Required?	Return Ticket Required?
Full British	Yes	1	Yes
BVP	Not valid	-	-
Australian	Yes	1	Yes
Canadian	Yes	1	Yes
USA	Yes	1	Yes
Other EU (As of 31/12/94)	Yes	1	Yes
Japanese	Yes	1	Yes

PASSPORTS: Required by all. Passports must be valid 6 months beyond the intended stay in Western Samoa.
British Visitors Passport: Not accepted.
VISAS: [1] Not required by tourists for visits up to a maximum of 30 days provided they hold confirmed onward travel documentation and a valid passport. For longer stays, visas should be obtained before arrival. Visitors staying longer than 90 days require an exit permit.
Types of visa: *Tourist* – no charge; *Business* – £25.
Application to: The Immigration Division of the Ministry of Foreign Affairs in Apia (PO Box L1861), or any Western Samoan, New Zealand or British Consulate, Embassy or High Commission.
Working days required: Apply at least 2 months in advance.
Temporary residence: Not considered.

MONEY

Currency: Western Samoa Dollar or Tala (S$) = 100 sene. Notes are in denominations of S$100, 50, 20, 10, 5 and 2. Coins are in denominations of S$1, and 50, 20, 10, 5, 2 and 1 sene.
Currency exchange: Available at the airport or through trade banks.
Credit cards: Access/Mastercard is accepted on a limited basis. Check with your credit card company for details of merchant acceptability and other services which may be available.
Travellers cheques: Accepted in major hotels, banks and tourist shops.
Exchange rate indicators: The following figures are included as a guide to the movements of the Western Samoa Dollar against Sterling and the US Dollar:

Date:	Oct '92	Sep '93	Jan '94	Jan '95
£1.00=	3.88	3.94	3.86	3.91
$1.00=	2.45	2.58	2.60	2.50

Currency restrictions: There are no restrictions on the import and export of either local or foreign currency.
Banking hours: 0830/0900-1500 Monday to Friday; some banks open 0830-1230 Saturday.

DUTY FREE

The following items may be imported into Western Samoa without incurring customs duty:
200 cigarettes or 50 cigars or 680g of tobacco; 750ml of spirits.
Prohibited items: Firearms, ammunition, explosives, non-prescribed drugs and indecent publications. Live animals and plants (including seeds, fruit, soil, etc) may not be imported without prior permission from the Director of Agriculture, Apia (PO Box 206).

PUBLIC HOLIDAYS

Jan 1 '95 Independence Day. **Jan 2** For New Year. **Apr 14-17** Easter. **Apr 25** Anzac Day. **Jun 1-3** Independence Holiday. **Jun 5** Whit Monday. **Nov 23** National Women's Day. **Dec 25** Christmas Day. **Dec 26** Boxing Day. **Jan 1 '96** Independence Day/New Year's Day. **Apr 5-8** Easter. **Apr 25** Anzac Day.

HEALTH

Regulations and requirements may be subject to change at short notice, and you are advised to contact your doctor well in advance of your intended date of departure. Any numbers in the chart refer to the footnotes below.

	Special Precautions?	Certificate Required?
Yellow Fever	No	1
Cholera	No	No
Typhoid & Polio	Yes	-
Malaria	No	-
Food & Drink	2	-

[1]: A yellow fever vaccination certificate is required from travellers over one year of age arriving within six days of leaving or transiting an infected area.
[2]: Mains water is normally chlorinated, and whilst relatively safe may cause mild abdominal upsets. Bottled water is available and is advised for the first few weeks of the stay. Drinking water outside main cities and towns may be contaminated and sterilisation is advisable. Milk is pasteurised and dairy products are safe for consumption. Local meat, poultry, seafood, fruit and vegetables are generally considered safe to eat.
Health care: Health insurance is recommended. Emergency medical facilities are available at Apia General Hospital. Private medical and dental treatment is also available. There are over 30 district hospitals and medical centres.

TRAVEL - International

AIR: Western Samoa's national airline is *Polynesian Airways (PH)*. Others operating to the islands are *Air Pacific, Air New Zealand, Air Nauru* and *Hawaiian Airlines. Polynesian Airways* offer a 'Polypass' which allows the holder to fly anywhere on the airline's network: Sydney (Australia), Auckland (New Zealand), Western Samoa, American Samoa, Cook Islands, Vanuatu, New Caledonia and Fiji. The pass is valid for 30 days.
Approximate flight time: From London to Apia is 26 hours 30 minutes, excluding stopover time in Honolulu but including stopover in Pago Pago (American Samoa). There are two direct flights a week from Honolulu, four from Auckland, one from Sydney, two from Tonga, two from Suva and six from Pago Pago.
International airport: *Apia (APW)* (Faleolo) is 34km (21 miles) from the capital (travel time – 40 minutes). Airport facilities include banks/bureaux de change, post office (0800-1630 Monday to Friday), duty-free shop and car rental (*Budget* and national firms). Buses and taxis operate to the city.
Departure tax: S$20 for adults, S$10 for children aged 5-9. Transit passengers and children under five years are exempt.
SEA: The international port is Apia, on Upolu. It is served by both cargo and passenger ships from New Zealand, Australia, Japan, Europe and the USA. There is also a thrice-weekly ferry service from Pago Pago on American Samoa.

TRAVEL - Internal

AIR: *Polynesian Airways (PH)* operates daily flights from Apia or Faleolo on Upolu to Asau and Maota on Savai'i. Charter and sightseeing flights are available. Bookings for aerial sightseeing tours and charter flights can be arranged through *Polynesian Airlines* (tel: 21261).
SEA: There are passenger/vehicle ferries between Upolu (Apia) and Savai'i (travel time – 90 minutes).
ROAD: Traffic drives on the right. **Bus:** Public transport covers most of the islands. There are no timetables; policemen at the New Market Bus Stand in Apia have information on bus departures. **Taxi:** Cheap and readily available in Apia. They are not metered and prices should be negotiated in advance. **Car hire:** Available from several agencies. Deposit and insurance are usually required. **Bicycles** and **motor scooters** are also available.
Documentation: An International Driving Licence for drivers over 21 years; or a valid national licence. The Transport Ministry issues a local licence for a small fee.

ACCOMMODATION

There is a government-backed programme to improve and extend facilities for visitors. In recent years new hotels and resorts have opened.
HOTELS: There are a number of distinctive hotels in Western Samoa; they are of a high standard and reasonably priced. At some, prices are inclusive of meals. There are also hotels located in rural areas, including Upolu's south coast and Savai'i.
SELF-CATERING: A village resort offers the opportunity for self-catering though, if visitors prefer, a restaurant is also provided. There are many sporting and other facilities for guests. Beach cottages are less expensive and offer fewer facilities, though many of them can be found nearby.

RESORTS & EXCURSIONS

UPOLU: The most populous island. **Apia,** the capital and main commercial centre, lies on the beautiful north coast. Nearby at **Vailima** is the house built by the Scottish poet and novelist Robert Louis Stevenson, who lived there from 1888 until his death (the local name for him was *Tusitala,* meaning 'teller of tales'). From the lawn, one can see his tomb on top of *Mount Vaea.* The house is now the official home of Western Samoa's Head of State.
Aleipata district: A 65km (40-mile) drive along the east coast from Apia are the *Falefa Falls, Mafa Pass* and *Fuipisia Falls.* This area is the most beautiful part of Samoa and has a 55m (180ft) waterfall, white sand beaches, an old village and four offshore islets.
Lefaga Village: On the southwest coast, an attractive village can be reached by a cross-island road. 'Return to Paradise' was filmed here in 1952.
Manono Island: Just off the coast of Upolu, this island was the inspiration for the legendary 'Bali Hai' in Rodgers and Hammerstein's musical, 'South Pacific'.
SAVAI'I: The largest island in the Samoan archipelago, this has been described as 'Polynesia at its truest'. There are scheduled flights and a regular car ferry from Apia on Upolu.
EXCURSIONS: A drive anywhere on the two larger islands will inevitably pass through regions of remarkable beauty. Ferries sail regularly between Upolu and Savai'i. The smaller islands are more difficult to reach.

SOCIAL PROFILE

FOOD & DRINK: There are hotel dining rooms but no elaborate restaurants. A variety of Chinese food is available in a few places and there are several snack and light meal restaurants in Apia serving fast food and other Western food. At Samoan feasts the traditional fare includes fresh seafood, roast suckling pig, chicken, breadfruit and fruit. **Drink:** *Kava* is the national drink (see also the entry on *American Samoa* earlier in the book). Liquor may not be purchased on Sundays except by hotel residents and their guests.
NIGHTLIFE: Several nightclubs offer dancing and other entertainment. Several cinemas show English-language films and Chinese films with subtitles.
SHOPPING: Local items include *siapo* (tapa) cloth, made from mulberry bark and painted with native dyes; mats and baskets; *kava* drinking bowls, made of hardwood and polished to a high gloss; shell jewellery; and Samoan stamps, available from the Philatelic Bureau. **Shopping hours:** 0800-1200 and 1330-1630 Monday to Friday; 0800-1230 Saturday. Some shops remain open during the lunch hour.
SPORT: Boating: Boats can be hired for net, spear, deep-sea and snorkel fishing. **Golf:** The 18-hole course belonging to the Royal Samoa Golf Club at Fagali'i is open to non-members. **Bowling:** The bowling club at Apia is open to visitors. **Diving:** Western Samoa is a diver's paradise but diving equipment is difficult to obtain. Contact: *Samoa Marine Ltd,* PO Box 4700, Apia. Tel: 22721. **Swimming:** There are many beautiful beaches and there is excellent freshwater swimming at Falefa Falls, Puila Cave Pool, Fogaafu Falls and Papase'ea Sliding Rock. **Tennis:** Played all year on grass, concrete and asphalt courts. Games can be arranged through hotels. **Spectator sports: Boxing** matches are held weekly from July to October. A type of **cricket** is played locally and is very popular. British-rules cricket matches are played from November to March. The Apia Rugby Union **rugby** season is from March to June and schools also play at this time. Popular matches can be seen on Saturday afternoons at Apia Park.
SPECIAL EVENTS: The following festivals are celebrated annually in Western Samoa. For a complete list contact the Tourist Board.
Jun '95 *Independence Day with the Fautasi* (long-boat

races). **Oct** *White Sunday.* **Dec** *Christmas and New Year.*
SOCIAL CONVENTIONS: Even more than their American Samoan neighbours, Western Samoans adhere to traditional moral and religious codes of behaviour. According to the Government, the Samoan is the purest surviving Polynesian type, with a reputation for being upright and dignified in character. Life in each village is still regulated by a council of chiefs with considerable financial and territorial power; this 'extended family' social system is intricately and unusually linked with the overall political system. Within certain limits, dress is relatively informal; men do not need to wear ties, though in outside resorts and hotels it is preferable for women to wear dresses. Beachwear should not be worn in the street or when shopping but shorts are acceptable for men.
Tipping: Not customary.

BUSINESS PROFILE

ECONOMY: The majority of Samoans are involved in subsistence agriculture but some cash crops are also grown for export, the most important of which are coconut, cocoa and bananas. A newly built coconut-oil mill has recently come into operation to allow the islands to move into the world copra market, and there are also plans to develop a large-scale timber industry. Timber is currently exported in small quantities but volumes are declining due to the poor quality of the wood. This setback has been typical of Western Samoa's recent economic fortunes: coconut production has fallen sharply and banana exports are scarcely more than zero. There is some small-scale manufacturing industry, mostly concerned with food-processing, textiles, woodworking and light engineering. There are also a number of small factories producing consumer goods for the domestic market. The Government is trying to promote tourism and export-oriented manufacturing to develop the economy. Overseas aid and remittances from Western Samoans working overseas (mostly New Zealand and, to a lesser extent, Australia) keep the economy afloat while it recovers from the damage wrought by Cyclone Ofa (which struck during 1990 and resulted in a fall in GDP of around 3% for that year) and Cyclone Val in December 1991 which repeated the damage. Food, oil, machinery and transport equipment are the main imports. New Zealand, Australia, Singapore, Fiji, Japan and the USA are the major trading partners. Western Samoa is a member of the South Pacific Forum.
BUSINESS: Shirt and smart trousers will suffice for business visits. Ties need only be worn for formal occasions. Best time to visit is from May to October.
Office hours: 0800-1200 and 1300-1630 Monday to Friday.
COMMERCIAL INFORMATION: The following organisations can offer advice: Chamber of Commerce, c/o Pacific Forum Line, Matautu-tai, PO Box 655, Apia. Tel: 20345; *or* Department of Trade, Commerce and Industry, PO Box 862, Apia. Tel: 20471. Fax: 21646.

CLIMATE

A warm tropical climate tempered by trade winds between May and September. Temperatures remain relatively constant throughout the year, becoming cooler at night. There are more than 2500 hours of sunshine annually. Rainfall is heaviest between December and April. Sea temperatures rarely fall below 24°C.
Required clothing: Lightweight cottons and linens with warmer clothes for evenings. Rainwear is advisable.

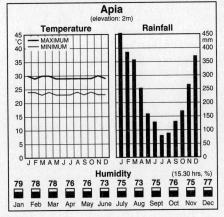

Apia (elevation: 2m)

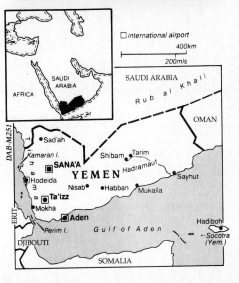

Republic of Yemen

international airport

400km
200mls

Location: Middle East, Arabian Peninsula.

Note: On May 22, 1990 the merger of the Yemen Arab Republic and the Yemen People's Democratic Republic took place. Complete integration of currency and other regulations has not yet been achieved, so where necessary there are different entries. Following the civil war, Sana'a has remained calm and is now relatively safe for returning residents, their dependents and those with business commitments. The security situation in Yemen is continuing to improve, but in Aden and other parts of the country there remains potential for instability. Following the recent reports of incidents along the Yemeni/Saudi border, travellers are strongly advised to avoid any travel to this area. Armed theft of vehicles, particularly of the 4-wheel-drive models, is not uncommon. There remains some danger from mines laid during the civil war in the southern and eastern governorates. Off-road travel is not recommended. All travellers to Yemen should register with their embassy upon arrival.
Source: FCO Travel Advice Unit – October 18, 1994.

Yemen Tourist Company
PO Box 1526, Sana'a, Republic of Yemen.
Embassy of the Republic of Yemen
57 Cromwell Road, London SW7 2ED
Tel: (0171) 584 6607 (Consular section). Fax: (0171) 589 3350. Telex: 262733. Opening hours: 0900-1530 Monday to Friday; 0900-1400 Monday to Friday (Visa section).
British Embassy
PO Box 1287, 129 Haddah Road, Sana'a, Republic of Yemen
Tel: (1) 215 630/3. Fax: (1) 263 059. Telex: 2251 (a/b BRITEM YE).
British Consulate General
PO Box 6304, 28 Shara Ho Chi Minh, Khormaksar, Aden, Republic of Yemen
Tel: (2) 32712/34.
Embassy of the Republic of Yemen
Suite 705, 2600 Virginia Avenue, NW, Washington, DC 20037
Tel: (202) 965 4760/1. Fax: (202) 337 2017. Telex: 897027 (a/b GHAMDAN WASH).
Embassy of the United States of America
PO Box 22347, Dhahr Himyar Zone, Sheraton Hotel

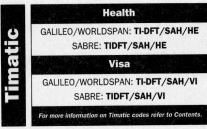

Health	
GALILEO/WORLDSPAN:	TI-DFT/SAH/HE
SABRE:	**TIDFT/SAH/HE**
Visa	
GALILEO/WORLDSPAN:	TI-DFT/SAH/VI
SABRE:	**TIDFT/SAH/VI**

For more information on Timatic codes refer to Contents.

Timatic

District, Sana'a, Republic of Yemen
Tel: (2) 238 843 *or* 238 852. Fax: (2) 251 563. Telex: 2697 (a/b EMBSAN YE).
Embassy of the Republic of Yemen
Suite 1100, 350 Sparks Street, Ottawa, Ontario K1R 7S8
Tel: (613) 232 8525 *or* 232 8582. Fax: (613) 232 8276.
Canadian Consulate
c/o Yemen Computer Co Ltd, PO Box 340, Building 4, Street 11, off Haddah Street, Sana'a, Republic of Yemen
Tel: (1) 208 814. Fax: (1) 209 523. Telex: 2406 (a/b YCC YE).

AREA: 527,969 sq km (203,850 sq miles).
POPULATION: 12,500,000 (1990 estimate).
POPULATION DENSITY: 23.3 per sq km.
CAPITAL: Sana'a. **Population:** 427,150 (1986).
Economic & Commercial Capital: Aden. **Population:** 407,000 (1986).
GEOGRAPHY: The Republic of Yemen is bordered in the northwest, north and northeast by Saudi Arabia, in the east by Oman and in the south by the Gulf of Aden. To the west lies the Red Sea. The islands of Perim and Karam in the southern Red Sea are also part of the Republic. Yemen is predominantly mountainous, supporting terraced agriculture. The Hadramaut is a range of high mountains in the centre of the country. Highlands rise steeply in central Yemen, ranging in height from approximately 200m (656ft) to the 4000m (13,123ft) peak of Jabal Nabi Shoveb. In contrast is *Tihama*, a flat semi-desert coastal plain to the west, 50-100km (30-60 miles) wide. Surface water flows down from the mountains through the valleys during the rainy season and the area is cultivated for cotton and grain. In the east the mountains drop away to the *Rub al-Khali* or 'Empty Quarter' of the Arabian Peninsula, a vast sea of sand. The arid coastal plains are fringed with sandy beaches.
LANGUAGE: Arabic. English is spoken in some urban areas.
RELIGION: Sunni Muslim (especially in the north) and Shia Muslim, small Christian and Hindu communities.
TIME: GMT + 3.
ELECTRICITY: 220/230 volts AC, 50Hz.
COMMUNICATIONS: Telephone: IDD is available in parts of the country. Country code: 967. Outgoing international code: 00. **Fax:** Some hotels have facilities.
Telex/telegram: Telex messages may be sent through *Cable & Wireless Ltd* in Sana'a (Gamal Abdul Nasser Street), Hodeida (Alamnie Building, 26 September Street) and Ta'izz (Hayel Saeed Building, Agaba Street). The better hotels, business houses, banks, etc have telex facilities. Telegram facilities are available. *Yemen Telecommunications Co.* have offices at Steamer Point (24 hours) and at Crater. Telexes can be sent from the Aden Frantel Hotel and from public offices at Steamer Point and Khormaksar. **Post:** Airmail to Western Europe from Sana'a takes about four days; mail to and from other towns may take longer. Post office hours: 0800-1400 and 1600-2000 Saturday to Thursday. **Press:** No English-language newspapers are published in the Republic of Yemen. Dailies include *Al-Jumhuriya* and *Al-Thaura*.
BBC World Service and Voice of America frequencies: From time to time these change. See the section *How to Use this Book* for more information.
BBC:

| MHz | 21.47 | 15.57 | 12.09 | 1.413 |

A service is also available on 1413kHz (0100-0500 GMT).
Voice of America:

| MHz | 11.97 | 9.670 | 6.040 | 5.995 |

PASSPORT/VISA

Regulations and requirements may be subject to change at short notice, and you are advised to contact the appropriate diplomatic or consular authority before finalising travel arrangements. Details of these may be found at the head of this country's entry. Any numbers in the chart refer to the footnotes below.

	Passport Required?	Visa Required?	Return Ticket Required?
Full British	Yes	Yes	Yes
BVP	Not valid	-	-
Australian	Yes	Yes	Yes
Canadian	Yes	Yes	Yes
USA	Yes	Yes	Yes
Other EU (As of 31/12/94)	Yes	Yes	Yes
Japanese	Yes	Yes	Yes

Entry restrictions: The Government of the Republic of Yemen refuses entry and transit facilities to: (a) holders of Israeli passports; (b) holders of passports containing visas valid or expired for Israel or any indication, such as entry or exit stamps, that the holder has visited Israel.
PASSPORTS: Required by all.
British Visitors Passport: Not accepted.
VISAS: Required by all except nationals of Egypt, Iraq, Jordan, Oman, Qatar, Saudi Arabia, Syria, UAE and holders of re-entry permits.
Types of visa: Tourist and Business. Cost: £20 for British passport holders; £25 for other nationalities. Transit visas may also be required.
Validity: 1 month during a 3-month period.
Application to: Consulate (or Consular section at Embassy). For address, see top of entry.
Application requirements: (a) Completed application form. (b) 2 passport-size photos. (c) Return ticket. (d) Valid passport.

MONEY

Note: The currency of the former Yemen Arab Republic and the currency of the Yemen People's Democratic Republic are both in circulation (1 Dinar = 26 Riyals). No date has yet been fixed for the adoption of a single currency. Some details of the two currencies are therefore listed separately below.
Currency exchange: It is inadvisable to change too much money as local currency is not easily reconverted.
Credit cards: Diners Club and American Express are the most widely accepted cards. Check with your credit card company for details of merchant acceptability and other services which may be available.
Travellers cheques: Can be exchanged at some banks and hotels.
Banking hours: 0800-1200 Saturday to Wednesday, and 0800-1130 Thursday.
YEMENI RIYAL (FORMER YAR CURRENCY)
Currency: Yemen Riyal (YR) = 100 fils. Notes are in denominations of YR100, 50, 20, 10, 5 and 1. Coins are in denominations of 50, 25, 10, 5 and 1 fils.
Exchange rate indicators: The following figures are included as a guide to the movements of the Yemeni Riyal against Sterling and the US Dollar:

Date:	Oct '92	Sep '93	Jan '94	Jan '95
£1.00=	26.09	25.25	24.37	88.30
$1.00=	16.44	16.53	16.47	56.44

YEMANI DINAR (FORMER YPDR CURRENCY)
Currency: Yemeni Dinar (YD) = 1000 fils. Notes are in denominations of YD10, 5 and 1, and 500 and 250 fils. Coins are in denominations of 50, 25, 5, 2.5 and 1 fils.
Exchange rate indicators: The following figures are included as a guide to the movements of the Yemeni Dinar against Sterling and the US Dollar:

Date:	Oct '92	Sep '93	Jan '94	Jan '95
£1.00=	0.74	0.70	0.68	0.69
$1.00=	0.46	0.46	0.46	0.44

Currency restrictions: There are no restrictions on the import of foreign currency, subject to declaration; export is limited to the amount declared (not exceeding US$3000). The limit on the import and export of local currency is YAR2000 (or equivalent).

DUTY FREE

The following items may be imported into the Republic of Yemen without incurring customs duty:
200 cigarettes or 50 cigars or 250g of tobacco; 2 quarts of alcoholic beverages (non-Muslims only); 568ml of perfume or eau de toilette.

PUBLIC HOLIDAYS

Jan 1 '95 New Year's Day. **Feb 1** Start of Ramadan. **Mar 3** Eid al-Fitr (End of Ramadan). **Mar 8** International Women's Day. **May 1** Labour Day. **May 10** Eid al-Adha (Feast of the Sacrifice). **May 31** Muharram (Islamic New Year). **Jun 13** Corrective Movement Anniversary. **Jun 9** Ashoura. **Aug 9** Mouloud (Prophet's Birthday). **Oct 14** National Day. **Dec 20** Leilat al-Meiraj (Ascension of the Prophet). **Jan 1 '96** New Year's Day. **Jan 22** Start of Ramadan. **Feb 22** Eid al-Fitr (End of Ramadan). **Mar 8** International Women's Day. **Apr 29** Eid al-Adha (Feast of the Sacrifice).
Note: Muslim festivals are timed according to local sightings of various phases of the Moon and the dates given above are approximations. During the lunar month of Ramadan that precedes Eid al-Fitr, Muslims fast during the day and feast at night and normal business patterns may be interrupted. Many restaurants are closed during the day and there may be restrictions on smoking and drinking. Some disruption may continue into Eid al-Fitr itself. Eid al-Fitr and Eid al-Adha may last anything from two to ten days, depending on the region. For more information see the section *World of Islam* at the back of the book.

HEALTH

Regulations and requirements may be subject to change at short notice, and you are advised to contact your doctor well in advance of your intended date of departure. Any numbers in the chart refer to the footnotes below.

	Special Precautions?	Certificate Required?
Yellow Fever	No	1
Cholera	Yes	2
Typhoid & Polio	Yes	-
Malaria	3	-
Food & Drink	4	-

[1]: A yellow fever vaccination certificate is required from travellers over one year of age arriving from infected areas.
[2]: Following WHO guidelines issued in 1973, a cholera vaccination certificate is not an official condition of entry to the Republic of Yemen. However, cholera is a risk in this country and precautions are essential. Up-to-date advice should be sought before deciding whether these precautions should include vaccination, as medical opinion is divided over its effectiveness. See the *Health* section at the back of the book.
[3]: Malaria risk, almost exclusively in the malignant *falciparum* form, exists throughout the year, but mainly from September through February, in the whole country excluding Aden and the immediate surrounding areas. Resistance to chloroquine has been reported.
[4]: Whilst relatively safe, where mains water is chlorinated it may cause mild abdominal upsets; supplies in Sana'a are said to be safe. Bottled water is available and is advised for the first few weeks of the stay. Drinking water outside main cities and towns is likely to be contaminated and sterilisation is considered essential. Water used for drinking, brushing teeth or making ice should have first been boiled or otherwise sterilised. Milk is unpasteurised and should be boiled. Powdered or tinned milk is available and is advised, but make sure that it is reconstituted with pure water. Avoid dairy products which are likely to have been made from unboiled milk. Only eat well-cooked meat and fish, preferably served hot. Salad and mayonnaise may carry increased risk. Vegetables should be cooked and fruit peeled.
Rabies is present. For those at high risk, vaccination before arrival should be considered. If you are bitten abroad, seek medical advice without delay. For more information, consult the *Health* section at the back of the book.
Bilharzia (schistosomiasis) is present. Avoid swimming and paddling in fresh water. Swimming pools which are well-chlorinated and maintained are safe.
Health care: Medical facilities are limited. Acclimatisation may be necessary for high altitude. Medical insurance is essential.

TRAVEL - International

AIR: The Republic of Yemen's national airline is *Yemen Airways (Yemenia) (IY)*.
Approximate flight times: From London to *Sana'a* is 10 hours (direct) and to *Aden* is 9 hours, excluding stopover time.
International airports: *Sana'a (SAH)* (El-Rahaba) is 3km (2 miles) north of the city (travel time – 20 minutes). Taxis and buses are available. Airport facilities include a bank (0600-2200) and car hire.
Ta'izz (TAI) (al-Janad) is 4km (2.5 miles) from the city (travel time – 10 minutes). Taxis, buses and hire cars are available.
Hodeida (HOD) is 8km (5 miles) from the city. Taxis, buses and hire cars are available.
Aden (ADE) (Khormaksar) is 9.5km (6 miles) from the city (travel time – 20 minutes). Limited bus and taxi services available.
Departure tax: US$10 on international flights.
SEA: The main international ports are Aden, Hodeida, Mokha, Sulif and Lohenja. Cargo vessels with passenger berths call at Hodeida. *Norwegian American* operate a shipping service to Aden.
ROAD: Driving to Yemen is not recommended but there are routes from Riyadh, Mecca and Jeddah (in Saudi Arabia) to Sana'a.

TRAVEL - Internal

AIR: *Yemen Airways (IY)* operate services between Sana'a, Ta'izz and Hodeida. There are also flights from Aden. Flight reservations and times should be double-checked.
Departure tax: US$3 on domestic flights.
SEA: Local ferries connect local ports. For details

contact port authorities.
ROAD: Within Sana'a and from Ta'izz to Mokha, the roads are reliable. From Aden to Ta'izz is three to five hours driving time. A road links Aden and Sana'a, otherwise the road network is mainly limited to desert tracks. Use of 4-wheel-drive vehicles and a guide is recommended. There is a road from Aden to Mukalla of 500km (310 miles). Traffice drives on the right. **Bus:** Regular intercity bus services. The *Yemen Tourist Company* runs landcruisers and tourist coaches to all towns. **Taxi:** Recognisable by yellow licence plates. Taxi sharing is the cheapest transport between cities. There are minimum charges within main cities but fares should be negotiated beforehand for intercity journeys. **Car hire:** Available in main towns. **Documentation:** An International Driving Permit is required.
JOURNEY TIMES: The following chart gives approximate journey times (in hours and minutes) from Sana'a to other major cities/towns in the Yemen Republic.

	Air	Road
Ta'izz	0.45	3.30
Hodeida	0.40	3.00
Aden	0.45	4.30

ACCOMMODATION

HOTELS: In Sana'a, there are two 5-star hotels, one 4-star hotel and five 3-star hotels; there are also a number of 3-star hotels in Ta'izz and Hodeida, and a 3-star hotel in Mareb. In Aden, the hotels for foreign visitors (including two of 'international' standard) are located in Tawahi. There are also hotels at Mukalla (al-Shaab), Seiyyum (al-Salaam), Shihr (al-Sharq), Mukheiras and Jaar. Outside the main centres, facilities are limited. Accommodation varies from ancient palace hotels and modern luxury hotels to *funduks* and tribal huts. It is necessary to book in advance and to receive a written confirmation. Winter and summer rates are the same. All bills are subject to a 15% service charge.
CAMPING: Khokha and Mokha have campsites; details may be obtained from local travel agents in Sana'a.

RESORTS & EXCURSIONS

The Republic of Yemen is the least known, and in many ways the most spectacular, region of all Arabia. As much of the Central Highlands rise over 3000m (10,000ft), travellers should be prepared for the high altitudes. The attraction of the Republic of Yemen for the visitor is largely its striking scenery, spectacular Islamic and pre-Islamic architecture and the deep sense of the past. Tours are available within and around the major cities; enquire at local travel agents for details.

The Central Region

This area has been intensely cultivated for centuries and is the site of many of the major towns.
Sana'a, the modern capital and long an important citadel along the trade route between Aden and Mecca, dates back to the first century and, according to popular legend, to early biblical days. The citadel, *Qasr al-Silah,* was rebuilt after the arrival of Islam in the 7th century and is still intact. The old centre is surrounded by the remains of the city walls, which can be seen in the south along Zuberi Street before Bab al-Yemen, in the east along *Mount Nugum* starting from the walls of the citadel, and in the north on the road from Bab Sha'oob to Taherir Square. The 1000-year-old *Bab al-Yemen Market* is divided into 40 different crafts and trades. The spice market is one of the best to visit, standing out from the rest by the rich aroma of incense and famed Arabian spices. Other markets include the *Souk al-Nahaas*, once the copper market, now selling embroidered head-dresses, belts and *jambias* (curved daggers). The *Great Mosque of Sana'a* is the oldest and largest of the mosques in Sana'a and one of the oldest in the Muslim world, constructed in the lifetime of the prophet and enlarged in AD705. The layout is typical of early Islamic architecture, with an open square courtyard, surrounded by roofed galleries. The *National Museum* is located in Taherir Square in **Dar al-Shukr** (or the 'Palace of Gratefulness'); it contains engravings of pre-Islamic times, bronze statues, a beautiful *mashrabia* (cooling place for water) and several examples of folk art. It offers a good view of Taherir Square and the *Muttawakelite Estate* from the roof.
Rawdha, 8km (5 miles) north of Sana'a, is a garden city, famous for its sweet grapes, the mosque built by Ahmed ibn al-Qasim and the *Rawdha Palace,* now used as a hotel.
Amran, north of Rawdha, lies on the edge of the fertile basin of *al-Bawn.* The city is surrounded by the old clay city walls of pre-Islamic, Sabean origin.
Hajja is a day's journey to the northwest of Sana'a. The countryside is made up of high mountains and large valleys, including the *Wadi Sherez,* 1000m (3280 ft), and *Kohlan,* 2400m (7875ft). Hajja itself is a citadel, situated on the central hill of Hajja, famous for underground prison cells used by the Imams.
Hadda Mountain, south of Sana'a, is dotted with villages and orchards growing apricots, peaches, walnuts and almonds. The village of Hadda has two old Turkish mills.
Wadi Dhar, 10km (6 miles) from Sana'a, is an idyllic valley filled with grapes, pomegranates and citrus fruits, surrounded by a barren plateau.
Shibam, 36km (22 miles) from Sana'a, is a pre-Islamic settlement, protected by the great fortification of *Koukaban.*

The West & Southwest

The **Tihama** in the west has a negligible rainfall and is predominantly hot, humid and sparsely populated. The road south from Sana'a runs through extremely mountainous countryside and passes the towns of **Dhofar**, the ancient capital of the Himyarites (115BC-AD525), and **Ibb**, a once-important stopping point on the Sana'a to Ta'izz road. Remains of the city walls and an aqueduct can still be seen. The **Sumara Pass,** at an altitude of 2700m (8860ft), gives a spectacular panoramic view over the Yarim and Dhamar basins.
Ta'izz lies in the south at an altitude of 1400m (4590ft). The old city has been all but swallowed up by the fast-growing modern city around it but beautiful old houses and mosques remain within the line of the 13th-century city wall, which is still intact along the southern side. To the north only the gates of *Bab Musa* and *al-Bab al-Kabir* remain. The southern wall offers a splendid view of Ta'izz. *Al-Qahera,* within the city walls, is the fortress and the oldest part of the city. *Al-Ashrafiya* and *al-Mudhaffar* are two of the most beautiful mosques in Yemen. The museum in the *Palace of Imam Ahmed* contains the personal effects of the last Imam, and has preserved the spirit of Yemen from before the beginning of the Republic. The *Salah Palace,* to the east just outside the city, is another museum of the royal family. The *Souk Ta'izz* sells a variety of goods, including silverware and carpets.
Mount Saber is 18km (11 miles) from Ta'izz and offers a breathtaking view of the city and the Ta'izz basin. A heavy-duty vehicle is needed to drive to the top. The mountain rises to an altitude of 3000m (9840ft) and the weather can be very cold.
Mokha is an old Himyarite port on the Red Sea. In the 17th and 18th centuries Mokha enjoyed a boom period exporting coffee, which was becoming fashionable in Europe (particularly Venice and Amsterdam, where the first coffee houses were opened). Coffee was later cultivated elsewhere and Mokha fell into decline. In recent years, the Government has improved the harbour and communications within Mokha in an attempt to resurrect this once-prosperous city.
Hodeida is reached via the mountains of *Manakha.* A modern city port on the Red Sea, the harbour itself was completed in 1961. There is little here of historical interest apart from the fish market, where fishing boats are traditionally built from wood in the same way they have been for hundreds of years.
Beit al-Faqih, 60km (37 miles) from Hodeida, has a good craft market. **Manakha**, once a road station for the Ottoman Turks, is situated on a saddle of the *Haraz Mountains*. Traditional Ismaeli villages lie to the east. This area is exceptionally good for hiking.

The Northern Region

Between Sana'a and Sad'ah in the north lies the **Wadi Wa'aar.** The climate here is subtropical, and mangoes, papayas and bananas grow freely. Out of this rises the **Shahara,** a huge mountain massif, the highest point being nearly 3000m (9840ft) above sea level. This can be climbed by foot or by 4-wheel-drive car; Shahara City offers overnight accommodation. *Shahara Bridge*, built in the 17th century, connects two mountains and can still be crossed by foot.
Sad'ah, a walled city, was once an iron mining and tanning centre and an important station along the Himyarite Sana'a–Mecca trade route. Later Sad'ah was chosen as the capital of the Zaydi state and became the centre of Zaydi learning. The *al-Hadi Mosque* is still an important institution for education in Zaydism. It is possible to walk along the top of the city walls, which afford good views of the city. The *Najran Gate* in the north is the most interesting of the gates, protected by an alleyway leading to the doors. The *Great Mosque* is the central building in the city. The market sells traditional stone necklaces and some fine silverware. The *Sad'ah Fortress* is the seat of the provincial government, thickly walled, and once the Imam's residence. Outside the city is the *Zaydi Graveyard,* filled with some of the most beautiful gravestones in Yemen. The *Sad'ah Basin* is strikingly fertile, providing Yemen's early crops of grapes, and is excellent for walking and hiking.

The Eastern Region

The **Eastern Mountains** (al-Mashrik) slope down from an altitude of 3000-1100m (9840-3610ft). The landscape gradually turns to sand dunes where the population decreases; agriculture is concentrated around wadies.
Mareb was once the capital of the kingdom of Sheba but the city is now largely in a state of disrepair. Blocks of stone with Sabean writing bear testament to the history of the city. Southwest of Mareb is the ancient *Mareb Dam,* used thousands of years ago to irrigate the surrounding land. The dam fell into disuse around AD570, after which large numbers of people emigrated northwards. The stonework is impressive, measuring 600m (1968ft) wide and 18m (60ft) deep.

Aden

The history of **Aden** as a port goes back a long way; it is mentioned in the Biblical *Book of Ezekiel* (circa 6th century BC). There is a collection of pre-Islamic artefacts in the *National Museum of Antiquities* near Tawahi Harbour. *Crater*, the oldest part of the city, lies in the crater of an extinct volcano and is where the most ancient constructions in Aden may be seen. These are the *Aden Tanks*, man-made reservoirs, partly cut out of the rock, with a storage capacity of 50,000,000 litres. When it rains, the upper basins fill up first and then overflow into the lower basins. Also in Crater may be found the *Ethnographical Museum* and *Military Museum.* The 14th-century *Mosque of Sayyid Abdullah al-Aidrus* commemorates the patron saint of Aden. In *Ma'allah* the visitor can see traditional Arab boats. To the south of Aden is *Little Aden*, also in the crater of an extinct volcano; this is an area of small fishing villages in sheltered bays, with several superb beaches fringing the Indian Ocean.

SOCIAL PROFILE

FOOD & DRINK: Hotel restaurants serve both Western and Oriental dishes, particularly Indian and Chinese. There are a few independent restaurants serving international and Arab cuisine. Seafood is particularly recommended, as is *haradha* (a mincemeat and pepper dish). **Drink:** Alcohol is not generally available but may be served in hotels. It is illegal to buy alcohol for a Yemeni citizen.
SHOPPING: *Souks* (markets) are interesting places to shop and buy handicrafts. Purchases include *foutah* (national costume), leather goods, *jambia* (daggers), candlesticks, scarves (woven with gold thread), amber beads, brightly coloured cushions and ceramics. Other items include gold- and silver-work, spice, perfume, *bukhur* incense with charcoal and pottery containers in which to burn it, coloured mats and sharks' teeth.
Shopping hours: 0800-1200/1300 and 1600-2100 Sunday to Thursday.
NIGHTLIFE: This is generally centred on the major hotels; see above under *Accommodation.*
SPORTS: Most major hotels have squash and tennis courts, swimming pools and saunas. Many beaches along the coast offer safe swimming. There are swimming clubs offering temporary membership for visitors.
SOCIAL CONVENTIONS: Traditional values are still very much part of everyday life and visitors will be treated with traditional courtesies and hospitality. Many of the population work in agriculture, with several thousand dependent on fishing. The rest live and work in towns and there is a small nomadic minority living along the northern edges of the desert. Guns become more noticeable further north, slung over the shoulder and carried in addition to the traditional *jambia*. In towns, women are veiled with black or coloured cloth, while in the villages such customs are not observed. Yemenis commonly chew *qat,* a locally-grown shrub bearing shoots that have a narcotic effect, chewed in markets and cafés but more stylishly sitting on cushions in a guestroom or *mafrai* at the top of a multi-storeyed Yemeni house. For the visitor, conservative casual clothes are suitable; visiting businessmen are expected to wear suits. Men need to wear a jacket and tie for formal occasions and in smart dining rooms. Women are expected to dress modestly and beachwear and shorts should be confined to the beach or poolside. Smoking is forbidden during Ramadan. **Tipping:** The practice of tipping is becoming more common. Waiters and taxi drivers should be tipped 10-15%.

BUSINESS PROFILE

ECONOMY: The northwestern part of the country, formerly the Yemen Arab Republic, is the most fertile region on the Arabian peninsula and thus agriculture employs most of the population. The principal crops are cereals, cotton, coffee, fruit, vegetables and qat (a narcotic leaf). Livestock is also important. Fishing is underdeveloped and has prospects for growth. Industry is a small but growing sector. Goods are produced mostly for domestic consumption. Salt mining has been in progress for some years and continues to expand steadily. By contrast, the southern part of the the country (formerly the People's Democratic Republic) is almost entirely arid; agriculture is mostly subsistence and although the country can, for the most part, meet its own requirements for vegetables, most of its grain has to be imported. Only 1% of the Aden hinterland is cultivable. Fishing is a more promising industry, particularly given the rich waters of the Arabian Sea, and much recent investment in the economy has been directed to this sector. At the moment it is hampered by poor equipment and an inadequate marketing and distribution system. The main Yemeni export earners are oil and gas which, although not large by regional standards, have done much to improve the state of the economy. In Aden, formerly the capital of the south, oil refining is now the major economic activity: the city never recovered from the decline of its port after independence, before which its earnings as a freeport and the key staging post on the sea route via Suez to India and the Far East was a great national asset. There was much foreign interest in oil exploration in Yemen after several onshore discoveries during 1983, but exploitation has been stalled by oil companies' reluctance to offend the Saudis. Yemen continues to suffer considerable economic problems as a result of the Gulf War, both from the collapse of regional trade and the Government's policy of supporting Iraq. Total losses are estimated at around US$2 billion a year for 1991 and 1992. Almost one million workers were expelled from Saudi Arabia and their arrival back in Yemen has put severe strains upon the economic and social fabric. Western aid provisions have also been drastically reduced, mainly due to Saudi diplomatic pressure on donors. The United Arab Emirates, the UK and Japan are the largest importers into Yemen.
BUSINESS: Business people are expected to dress smartly for meetings and formal social occasions. English is commonly used in business circles. Appointments are needed and visitors should be punctual. Visiting cards are often exchanged. Do not be surprised during a meeting if Yemeni businessmen chew qat. **Office hours:** 0800-1230 and 1600-1900 Monday to Wednesday; 0800-1100 Thursday. **Government office hours:** 0800-1400 Sunday to Thursday.
COMMERCIAL INFORMATION: The following organisations can offer advice: General Corporation for Foreign Trade, PO Box 710, Sana'a. Tel: (1) 207 571. Telex: 2349; or
Federation of Chambers of Commerce, PO Box 16992, Sana'a. Tel: (1) 224 262. Telex: 2229.

CLIMATE

The climate varies according to altitude. The coastal plain is hot and dusty throughout most of the year. The highlands are warm in summer and during winter, from October to March, nights can be very cold in the mountains. Annual rainfall is extremely low and temperatures, particularly in summer, are very high. The most pleasant time is from October to April.
Required clothing: Lightweight clothes are worn in the coastal plain all year. Warmer clothes are needed from November to April in the highlands.

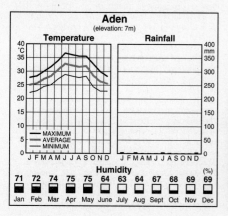

Aden
(elevation: 7m)

Yugoslavia

□ *international airport*

Location: Southern Central Europe.

Note: In 1992 the republics of Serbia and Montenegro agreed to uphold the Yugoslav state, thereby limiting the borders to the boundaries of these two republics. Due to the extreme political instability in the region at the time of writing, travel is not advised. Prospective travellers are advised to contact the Foreign Office (or exterior affairs department of their respective country) before considering travel. At the time of writing, UN sanctions were still in force against the newly-styled Federal Republic of Yugoslavia for an indefinite period, including a ban on all commercial transactions. Civilian air links have been resumed on a limited basis. There have been cases of robberies and muggings on the erratic international train services. Avoid the border area with Bosnia-Hercegovina due to the ongoing conflict as well as the border with Croatia, the Sandzak Region and Kosovo. There are checkpoints throughout the country which are manned generally by policemen/militia but occasionally by undisciplined, untrained reserve militia groups. Travellers are expected to provide identification and cooperate fully at these checkpoints. The following information reflects the situation before the present conflict and is included in the hope that it will be useful again in the future. For further information contact the Foreign Office Travel Advice Unit (tel: (0171) 270 4129).
Source: Foreign Office Travel Advice Unit – December 7, 1994 and US Department of State – November 2, 1994.

Turisticki savez Jugoslavije (Tourist Association of Yugoslavia)
Postanski fah 595, Mose Pijade 8/IV, 11001 Belgrade, Yugoslavia
Tel: (11) 339 041. Fax: (11) 634 677. Telex: 11863.

AREA: Now comprising only Serbia with 88,361 sq km (34,116 sq miles) and Montenegro with 13,812 sq km (5331 sq miles), respectively the largest and smallest of the former republics, Yugoslavia officially covers 102,173 sq km (39,449 sq miles), or 40% of the territory of the former federation (255,804 sq km/98,766 sq miles). Unofficially it is around 50% larger, given that various Serbian politico-military entities loyal to Belgrade control 65% of the disputed territory of Bosnia-Hercegovina and 30% of the disputed territory of Croatia, thereby giving the Federal Republic of Yugoslavia or 'Greater Serbia' around 60% of the former territory of the former Yugoslav federation.
POPULATION: Together, Serbia (9,791,475; 1991) and Montenegro (615,267; 1991), respectively the most- and least-populous of the ex-Yugoslav republics, have a total population of 10,406,742 or around 45% of the population of the former Yugoslav federation.
POPULATION DENSITY: 101.8 per sq km (Serbia and Montenegro only; 83.3 per sq km if including Serb-controlled territories in Croatia and Bosnia-Hercegovina).
CAPITAL: Belgrade (Beograd). **Population:** 1,087,915 (1991).
GEOGRAPHY: Roughly rectangular in shape and on a major European communications axis north–west and south–east, the Federal Republic of Yugoslavia borders Hungary to the north, Romania to the northeast, Bulgaria to the southeast, the Former Yugoslav Republic of Macedonia and Albania to the south, Bosnia-Hercegovina to the west and Croatia to the northwest. The southern half of Serbia is mountainous and thickly forested, whilst the north is dominated by the flat, fertile farmland of the Danube and Tisza valleys. The scenery varies from rich Alpine valleys, vast fertile plains and rolling green hills to bare, rocky gorges as much as 1140m (3800ft) deep, thick forests and gaunt limestone mountain regions. Belgrade, the capital of the new Federal Republic, lies on the Danube. Montenegro is a small mountainous region on the Adriatic coast north of Albania, bordering on Bosnia-Hercegovina to the west. Its small Adriatic coastline comprises the main ports of Bar and those in the Gulf of Kotor.
LANGUAGE: Serbo-Croat which uses the Cyrillic alphabet. Albanian and Hungarian are also spoken in the autonomous regions of Kosovo and Vojvodina respectively.
RELIGION: 70% Eastern Orthodox Serbs, with a large Muslim ethnic Albanian minority (especially in the province of Kosovo) and a small Roman Catholic ethnic Hungarian minority (mainly located in the province of Vojvodina).
TIME: GMT + 1 (GMT + 2 from last Sunday in March to Saturday before last Sunday in September).
ELECTRICITY: 220 volts AC, 50Hz.
COMMUNICATIONS: Telephone: IDD is still available as part of the former Yugoslav federation. Country code: 38. Outgoing international code: 99. Telephone links with Zagreb, Ljubljana and Sarajevo have been completely cut, whereas Skopje can still be

reached intermittently. **Fax** and **telex** transmissions are available to and from Western Europe. **Post:** All postal services between the former Yugoslav republics have been suspended indefinitely. Postal services within Serbia are reasonable. Due to the UN sanctions imposed against Serbia and Montenegro in June 1992, international postal services take twice as long as before, ie one week to ten days for airmail via third parties to the UK. **Press:** The main local newspapers and magazines, in decreasing order of circulation, are *Vecernje Novosti* (Belgrade), *Politika Ekspres* (Belgrade), *Politika* (Belgrade), *NIN* (Belgrade) and *Pobjeda* (Podgorica). The state news agency, *TANJUG* (PO Box 439, Obilicév Venac 2, 11000 Belgrade; tel: (11) 332 230; telex: 11220), produces material in English for international distribution, plus *Newsday*, a daily newspaper, and *Yugoslav Life*, a quarterly magazine, both published in English. *TANJUG* also provides a CITI service for business subscribers worldwide. **Radio/TV:** The state TV/radio station, *RTV Serbia* (formerly *RTV Belgrade*), also produces a daily (1700-2300) unscrambled programme, including news in English, for a worldwide audience via *Eutelsat 1F4*.
BBC World Service and Voice of America frequencies: From time to time these change. See the section *How to Use this Book* for more information.
BBC:

MHz	**17.64**	**15.07**	**9.410**	**6.180**

Voice of America:

MHz	**9.670**	**6.040**	**5.995**	**1.260**

Note: *CNN* is also available via satellite (*Astra*) in a number of Belgrade and Montenegrin (Adriatic coast) hotels.

PASSPORT/VISA

Regulations and requirements may be subject to change at short notice, and you are advised to contact the appropriate diplomatic or consular authority before finalising travel arrangements. Details of these may be found at the head of this country's entry. Any numbers in the chart refer to the footnotes below.

	Passport Required?	Visa Required?	Return Ticket Required?
Full British	Yes	Yes	Yes
BVP	Not valid	-	-
Australian	Yes	Yes/2	Yes
Canadian	Yes	Yes/2	Yes
USA	Yes	Yes/2	Yes
Other EU (As of 31/12/94)	Yes	1/2	Yes
Japanese	Yes	No	Yes

Note: Due to the current political situation in Yugoslavia, entry requirements are liable to change at short notice. The suspension of commercial transactions in accordance with UN sanctions against the Federal Republic of Yugoslavia have made legal border crossings difficult. It is advisable to contact the Embassy or the Foreign & Commonwealth Office for up-to-date information (see telephone numbers at top of entry).
Restricted entry: Nationals of Malaysia are refused entry.
PASSPORTS: Valid passport required by all.
British Visitors Passport: Not accepted.
VISAS: Required by all except:
(a) **[1]** nationals of Italy (all other EU nationals *do* require a visa);
(b) nationals of Japan;
(c) nationals of Algeria, Argentina, Botswana, Bolivia, Bulgaria, Chile, Cyprus, Costa Rica, Cuba, Hungary, Iraq, Mexico, Monaco, Niger, Romania, San Marino, Seychelles, Tunisia, Zambia and Zimbabwe.
All visa exemptions are granted for a maximum stay of 3 months.
Types of visas: Fee varies according to nationality of applicant and type of visa. For nationals of the UK, a Single-entry/Single-exit costs £10; Double-entry/Double-exit: £21; Multiple-entry: £30. Transit visas, valid for 7 days (to be used within 6 months of issue), cost £10 for Single-transit, £21 for Double-transit and £30 for Multiple-transit. Children under 14 years of age pay half.
Note [2]: Nationals of Australia, Canada, Denmark and the USA are issued visas free of charge.
Validity: Where they are required, visas must be used within 6 months from date of issue and cannot be postdated.
Application to: Consular section at Embassy. For addresses, see top of entry. Visas may be issued at frontier posts only in special circumstances.
Application requirements: (a) Completed application form. (b) Valid passport. (c) Stamped, self-addressed, registered envelope for return of passport and documents. (d) Fee payable to Embassy in cash or by postal order

(cheques will only be accepted from travel agencies, firms and companies). (e) Return ticket.
Note: Those who require visas must have a letter of invitation sponsored by the Yugoslav authorities and may be expected to state on entry that they have at least US$150 per person per day for their intended stay in Yugoslavia, and may be asked to produce a return ticket.
Working days required: Immediate issue to personal callers. Postal applications: 7 days.
Temporary residence: Enquire at Embassy. Visas can be extended if local authorities are contacted within 7 days of arrival.

MONEY

Currency: New Yugoslav Dinar (Yu D) = 100 paras. Notes are in denominations of Yu D50,000, 20,000, 500, 200, 100 and 50. Coins are in denominations of Yu D50, 20, 10, 5, 2 and 1. The second New Yugoslav Dinar was issued in December 1991. The currency was initially pegged to the German DM at an official parity of DM1 = Yu D13; in September 1992 it stood at DM1 = Yu D136, following repeated devaluations earlier in the year. Due to hyper-inflation and further devaluations another new Dinar was re-issued on October 1, 1993, valued at 1 million of the former units. However, on December 30, 1993 the currency was again devalued by a factor of 1000 million. In January 1994 the Government introduced a new currency at a parity of Yu D1 = DM1.
Currency exchange: On January 1, 1990, Yugoslavia launched the New Yugoslav Dinar, which has been re-issued a number of times since. As elsewhere in the ex-Yugoslav republics, the only true repositories of value and frequently exchanged currencies are the German DM and the US Dollar (the Pound Sterling is rarely used in the republic). Local hyper-inflation is the basic cause of the collapse of the Yu D. Certain Serbian commercial banks even offer rates of 300-450% above the entirely nominal exchange rates against the DM and the US Dollar. The thriving black market only started trading after the economic sanctions came into force, and is fuelled by high war-related government expenditure.
Credit cards/Travellers cheques: Eurocheques, travellers cheques and credit card payments are prohibited under the terms of the UN trade embargo. The only means of payment in Yugoslavia is by direct cash settlement.
Exchange rate indicators: The following figures are included as a guide to the movement of the New Yugoslav Dinar against Sterling and the US Dollar:

Date:	Oct '92	Sep '93	Jan '94	Jan '95
£1.00=	325.00	160.70	*	*
$1.00=	204.79	105.24	*	*

Note [*]: Not available.
Banking hours: 0700-1500 Monday to Friday; some branches are open Saturday for payments and withdrawals.

DUTY FREE

The following items may be imported into Yugoslavia by persons over 16 years of age without incurring customs duty:
200 cigarettes or 50 cigars or 250g of tobacco; 750ml of spirits or 1 litre of wine; 250ml of eau de toilette; a reasonable quantity of perfume.

PUBLIC HOLIDAYS

Jan 1-2 '95 New Year. **May 1-2** Labour Days. **Jul 4** Fighters' Day. **Jul 7** Public Holiday (Serbia only). **Jul 13** Public Holiday (Montenegro only). **Nov 29-30** Republic Days. **Jan 1-2 '96** New Year.
Note: Orthodox Christian holidays may also be celebrated throughout much of the region.

HEALTH

Regulations and requirements may be subject to change at short notice, and you are advised to contact your doctor well in advance of your intended date of departure. Any numbers in the chart refer to the footnotes below.

	Special Precautions?	Certificate Required?
Yellow Fever	No	No
Cholera	No	No
Typhoid & Polio	No	-
Malaria	No	-
Food & Drink	1	-

[1]: Mains water is normally chlorinated, and whilst relatively safe may cause mild abdominal upsets. Bottled water is available and is advised for the first few weeks of the stay. Milk is pasteurised and dairy products are safe for consumption. Local meat, poultry, seafood, fruit

and vegetables are generally considered safe to eat. *Rabies* is present. For those at high risk, vaccination before arrival should be considered. If you are bitten abroad seek medical advice without delay. For more information, consult the *Health* section at the back of the book.
Health care: Medical facilities are limited. Many medicines and basic medical supplies are often unavailable. Hospitals usually require payment in hard currency. Prescribed medicines must be paid for. Health insurance with emergency repatriation is strongly recommended. Visitors may be asked to pay first and seek reimbursement later.

TRAVEL - International

Note: Present Foreign Office advice is to avoid the Federal Republic of Yugoslavia until further notice. This is due to both the security situation and the fact that the country is under UN sanctions.
AIR: The national airline is *JAT Yugoslav Airlines*. Foreign carriers have been slow to re-introduce connections to Belgrade since the suspension of air links has been lifted for civilian flights.
International airports: *Belgrade (BEG)* (Surcin) is 20km (12 miles) west of the city. Minor airports exist elsewhere, such as *Podgorica* (formerly Titograd) in Montenegro.
SEA: The principal passenger ports are Bar and Kotor. *BI* serves Kotor. Ferries link the Yugoslav Adriatic coast with Italian and Greek ports. The principal ferry routes are: Bari–Bar–Bari (ferry 'Sveti Stefan' of the *Prekooceanska Plovidba Company*, from Bar); and Rijeka–Rab–Zadar–Split–Hvar–Korcula–Dubrovnik–Bar –Corfu–Igoumenitsa (*Jadrolinija* ferry).
RAIL: Connections and through coaches were once available from principal East and West European cities. It is still possible to travel to Belgrade via the Hungarian border crossing. For up-to-date information, contact British Rail international enquiries. Tel: (0171) 834 2345. International trains have couchette coaches as well as bar and dining cars. On some lines transport for cars is provided.
Note: Train travel should be avoided as assaults and robberies have been reported.
ROAD: On account of the conflict with Croatia, the main road/rail route to and from Western Europe is now closed, with extensive detours via Hungary for international traffic going south–north to and from Greece. Due to the Greek and Serbian economic blockade of Former Republic of Macedonia (which is itself attempting to comply with UN economic sanctions against its northern neighbour), rail services between Serbia and Greece are uncertain and intermittent. Delays should be expected when crossing the border from Hungary, Macedonia (Greece) and Bulgaria by car. The same is true in relation to connections between Bulgaria and Serbia. The following frontier posts are open for road traffic:
From **Hungary:** Redics–Dolga Vas; Letenye–Gorican; Barcs–Terezino Polje; Dravaszabolcs–Donji Miholjac; Udvar–Knezevo; Hercegszanto–Backi Breg (Bezdan); Tompa–Kelebija; and Roszke–Horgos.
From **Romania:** Jimbolia–Srpska Crnja; Stamora Moravita–Vatin; Naidas–Kaludaerova (Bela Crkva); and Portile de Fier–(Turnu Severin)–Daerdap (Kladovo).
From **Bulgaria:** Bregovo–Mokranje (Negotin); Kula–Vrska Cuka (Zajecar); Kalotina–Gradina; Otomanci–Ribarci; Kjustendil–Deve Bair (Kriva Palanka); Blagoevgrad–Delcevo; and Petric–Novo Selo.
From **Albania:** Podgradec–Cafa San (Struga); Kukes–Vrbnica; and Han i Hotit–Bozaj.
Nearly all the passes mentioned above are open 24 hours a day.
See below for information regarding **documentation** and **traffic regulations**.

TRAVEL - Internal

AIR: *JAT Yugoslav Airlines* offer connections between Belgrade and Podgorica.
RAIL/ROAD: Internal rail services are generally poor. Services are often overbooked, unreliable and unsafe. Drivers should not rely on local petrol stations for fuel, due to continually-worsening shortages of oil caused by the UN trade embargo, although hard currency might make otherwise rationed and scarce petrol available. Spare parts are very difficult to obtain. **Coach:** Efficient and cheap coaches used to connect all towns. The fuel shortages have restricted the services severely. **Taxi:** Main cities have metered taxis. **Car hire:** Available from airports and main towns. **Traffic regulations:** Traffic drives on the right. Speed limits are 120kmph (75mph) on motorways and 100kmph (62mph) on other roads. Road signs may be poorly marked and new signs are

likely to be in Cyrillic script in some areas of the country. **Documentation:** Full national driving licence is accepted. No customs documents are required but car log books and Third Party Green Card insurance are necessary.
URBAN: There are good bus services in the main towns, with tramways and trolleybuses in Belgrade. Multi-journey tickets are available and are sold in advance through tobacconists. The passenger punches the ticket in a machine on board. Fares paid to the driver are at double the pre-purchase prices.
JOURNEY TIMES: The following chart gives approximate journey times (in hours and minutes) from Belgrade to other major cities/towns in Yugoslavia.

	Air	Road	Rail
Bar	-	7.00	6.00
Podgorica	0.30	6.00	5.30

ACCOMMODATION

Note: The availability of accommodation is severely affected by the current economic and political situation in Yugoslavia. All information is subject to rapid change. **HOTELS:** Deluxe/A-class hotels are confined to Belgrade and a number of Montenegrin Adriatic resorts, most notably the exclusive island of Sveti Stefan. Further down the scale, and particularly in the smaller towns, services are poor. The best hotels are always heavily booked, so advanced booking is essential. Prices are very high, and payable in hard currency for visiting foreign nationals. Also, the Montenegrin resorts are now extremely overcrowded, following the closure of the Croatian coastline to all Yugoslav nationals. **Grading:** Classification is from deluxe to A, B, C and D class. **Pensions:** First-, second- and third-class pensions are available throughout the country. **Inns:** Motels are found on most main roads. Prices are set independently according to region, tourist season and the quality of service.
GUEST-HOUSES: Many people offer rooms, often with meals, to visitors in villages without hotels. Discounts are available off-season. Contact tourist offices or travel agencies for details.
SELF-CATERING: Holiday villages are available in many resorts as well as a selection of apartments and villas. Travel agencies and tourist offices have further information.
CAMPING/CARAVANNING: Only available on official sites. A permit from the local tourist office is required for off-site camping. A list is available from the National Tourist Office. *Alpine Club* mountain huts are available in all mountain areas. Camping and caravan holidays are offered by a number of tour operators (*Yugotours* etc). **Note:** Caravans are allowed in duty free for up to one year.
YOUTH HOSTELS: The *Youth Hostel Authority* is at Farijalni Savez Jugoslavije, Mose Pijade 12/1, 11000 Belgrade. Tel: (11) 339 666 *or* 339 802. Student and youth travel is arranged by *Naromtravel*, Mose Pijade 12, 11000 Belgrade. Tel: (11) 331 610.

RESORTS & EXCURSIONS

Serbia

The largest of the republics, Serbia was under Turkish rule and many traces of Muslim influence remain, particularly in the Kosovo-Metohija region. **Belgrade** is the capital of Serbia and the national capital. Its strategic location on the edge of the Carpathian Basin near the joining of the Sava River and the Danube and also its position on the Stambul Road from Turkey into Central Europe made it a centre of commerce and communications. Many of the buildings were built after the Second World War. The *Kalemegdan Citadel* straddles a hilltop overlooking the junction of the Sava and the Danube. The *National Museum* is interesting, and there is also the *Museum of Modern Art* and the *Ethnographical Museum*. Well worth a visit is the *Palace of Princess Ljubica* (1831) with a good collection of period funiture. *Skadarlija* is the 19th-century Bohemian quarter with cafés, street dancers, singers and open-air theatres. **Pristina**, the capital of Kosovo, contains the *Imperial Mosque* built in the 15th century and also several 19th-century Turkish buildings. Near **Kraljevo** is the restored *Monastery of Zica*, now painted bright red as it was in medieval times. It was there that the Kings of Serbia were crowned. The *Kalenic Monastery* is a fine example of the Serbian style.

Montenegro

Montenegro (given as the birthplace of Rex Stout's fictional American detective, Nero Wolfe) is at the southern end of Yugoslavia's coast, an area of spectacular mountain ranges with villages perched like eagles' nests on high peaks. This stands in direct contrast to the republic's coastal region, which extends from the *Gulf of Kotor* to the Albanian border. **Kotor** itself is a bustling port with a picturesque old city quarter. The general architecture is mainly of Venetian origin, as this power dominated the region until 1797. Entering the city through the town gate brings the visitor to the square with the 17th-century *Clock Tower*, overshadowed by the twin towers of the *Cathedral of St Tryphon* (12th century). A visit to the *Naval Museum* and the *Church of St Lucas* (1195) should not be missed.

SOCIAL PROFILE

FOOD & DRINK: Cuisine varies greatly from one region to another. On the whole the meat specialities are better than the fish dishes. National favourites include *pihtije* (jellied pork or duck), *prsut* (smoked ham), *cevapcici* (charcoal-grilled minced meat), *raznjici* (skewered meat), *sarma* or *japrak* (vine or cabbage leaves stuffed with meat and rice). Desserts are heavy and sweet including *strukli* (nuts and plums stuffed into cheese balls and then boiled), *lokum* (Turkish delight) and *alva* (nuts crushed in honey). Table service is usual in hotel restaurants. **Drink:** Wine is widely available and cheap. Ljutomer, Traminer and Riesling wines from Montenegro are the best known. Varieties include *Dingac, Postup, Krstac* and *Vranac*. The white *Vugava* produced in Vis is excellent. Popular national spirits are *slivovica* (a potent plum brandy), *loza* and *maraskino* (made of morello cherries). Bars and cafés have counter and table service. Most places serving alcohol close by 2200.
NIGHTLIFE: There is a wide range of nightlife in all the main cities and resorts, including bars, nightclubs, cinemas and theatres. Cinemas stay open until 2300, nightclubs to 0300 and restaurants to 2400.
SHOPPING: Special purchases include embroidery, lace, leatherwork, *Pec* filigree work, metalwork and Turkish coffee sets. **Shopping hours:** 0800-1200 and 1700-2000 Monday to Friday, 0800-1500 Saturday.
SPORT: Skiing and **spa resorts** exist in all regions, but particularly in Kopaonik and Brezovica (Serbia). **Fishing** permits are available from hotels or local authorities. Local information is necessary. Fishing on the Adriatic coast is unrestricted, but freshwater angling and fishing with equipment needs a permit. 'Fish-linking' with a local small-craft owner is popular. **Sailing** is popular along the coast. Berths and boats can be hired at all ports. Permits are needed for boats brought into the country. **Spectator sports:** Football is one of the more popular.
SPECIAL EVENTS: The following is a selection of the major festivals and other special events that may be celebrated annually in Yugoslavia.
Belgrade: *Summer Festival* (mid-July to mid-September).
Kotor: *Boka Night* (July).
Nationwide: Many major cities hold theatre festivals in October.
SOCIAL CONVENTIONS: Hitherto a relatively open, informal and secure society, Yugoslavia is now changing for the worse under the impact of war. Once virtually non-existent, violent crime is now common in the big cities, while xenophobia is growing. A veneer of normality belies underlying social tensions, often exploding into violence. Foreign nationality is no longer a guarantee of safety.

BUSINESS PROFILE

Note: All business and commercial transactions are indefinitely suspended in accordance with UN sanctions effective from June 1992.
ECONOMY: The new Yugoslav federation of Serbia and Montenegro is estimated to possess about 50% of the natural resources of the former Yugoslavia, 40% of its GDP, 50% of its agricultural and electrical output, 35% of its industrial output and 30% of industrial employment. With the collapse of the internal Yugoslav market and the violent conflicts that followed, unemployment levels reached 20% even before the UN imposed sanctions and the displacement of about 500,000 people. Despite widespread sanction-busting, the socio-economic consequences have been catastrophic. Industrial output and GDP fell to approximately 20-30% in the period 1991-92, while unemployment rose to 30-40%. Only the relatively high degree of self-sufficiency in foodstuffs and electricity generation prevented a complete collapse. Yugoslavia's economic output is divided roughly equally between agriculture, industry and services. Maize, wheat, sugar and potatoes are the main crops. Mining (of coal copper ore and bauxite) and manufacture of machinery, textiles, transport equipment iron and steel are the principal industrial operations. Coal and hydroelectric resources have been just about sufficient to met the country's energy needs. In the service sector, tourism and transit trade have been devastated.
The historically poor export performance, especially to Western markets, has further deteriorated; on the other hand, previously large trade deficits have been cut by reducing imports. The loss of these important markets means that the Government cannot hope to service its share of the foreign debt of the former federation. Including unallocated federal debts, Serbia is liable for US$8 billion and Montenegro for a further US$1 billion. Under the present conditions, a formal debt rescheduling is unlikely to be granted by creditors, as the majority of the National Bank of Yugoslavia's hard-currency reserves (US$2 billion in 1992) were frozen by various governments. The country is likely to default on its debts and risks international bankruptcy.
Prior to June 1992, and based upon DTI data for 1990-91, Serbia's share of bilateral UK trade with the former federation was 65%, with a surplus on the UK side. At that time the UK was the fourth most important EU trading partner of the former Yugoslavia. Yugoslavia's international isolation has extended to membership of international economic organisations, from which it has been barred until the political situation is satisfactorily resolved. The disastrous consequences to the Yugoslavian economy of international isolation have had some effect on the will of President Milosevic to implement an effective settlement in neighbouring Bosnia. In this he has largely failed, apparently due to the intransigence of the Bosnian Serb leadership. Recovery remains dependent on a wider settlement of the conflicts in the Balkans as a whole. At the beginning of 1995 the UN lifted the suspension of passenger flights to Belgrade. Commercial links remained suspended under the terms of the international embargo.
BUSINESS: As with Croatia, but unlike Slovenia, things go very slowly or not at all on account of the cumbersome bureaucracy and general socio-economic collapse. Communication, however, is not a major problem, as English is popular as a second language. **Office hours:** 0700-1430 Monday to Friday. **Government office hours:** 0700-1500 Monday to Friday.
COMMERCIAL INFORMATION: Because of UN sanctions, commercial transactions with Yugoslavia are illegal. If, however, the sanctions are lifted the following organisations should be able to offer advice:
Privredna Komora Jugoslavije (Yugoslav Chamber of Economy), PO Box 1003, Terazije 23, 11000 Belgrade, Yugoslavia. Tel: (11) 339 461. Fax: (11) 631 928. Telex: 11638; *or*
Chamber of Economy of Serbia, Ulica Generala Zdanova 13-15, 11000 Belgrade. Tel: (11) 340 611. Fax: (11) 330 949; *or*
Chamber of Economy of Montenegro, Novaka Miloseva 29/II, 81000 Podgorica. Tel: (81) 31071. Fax: (81) 34926.

CLIMATE

Serbia has a continental climate with cold winters and warm summers. Montenegro is largely the same, but with alpine conditions in the mountains and a Mediterranean climate on the Adriatic coast.
Required clothing: *Winter:* mediumweight clothing and heavy overcoat. *Summer:* lightweight clothing and raincoat required.

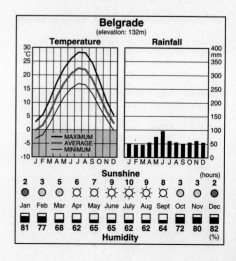

DAB-M253

CENTRAL AFRICAN REPUBLIC
SUDAN
CAMEROON
Bondo
Libenge
Ubangi
Yangambi
Kisangani
Mbandaka
UGANDA
Equator
GABON
Salonga
Nat. Park
Kasai
Bukavu
R.
B.
CONGO
Z A Ï R E
Mitumba Mtns.
TANZ.
KINSHASA
Kananga
Lake
Tangan.
Matadi
Kikwit
Mbuji-
Mayi
Sankuru
ANGOLA
Likasi
Lubumbashi
Zambezi
ZAMBIA
800km
400mls
☐ international airport

Location: Central Africa.

Note: It is strongly advised not to visit or transit Zaïre.
The areas bordering Rwanda should be avoided at all
costs. Large numbers of refugees including former
Rwandan military remain in the Kivu area to the east of
the country. Transportation out of dangerous areas may
prove extremely difficult. There are considerable
shortages of money, food, water and medical supplies
and the security situation is volatile. There is little control
of firearms, and crime is rife. The situation could
deteriorate very quickly. Foreign nationals should
register with their embassy in Kinshasa.
*Sources: FCO Travel Advice Unit – September 13, 1994
and US State Department – September 2, 1994.*

Office National du Tourisme
BP 9502, 2a/2b avenue des Orangers, Kinshasa-Gombe,
Zaïre
Tel: (12) 30070.
Embassy of the Republic of Zaïre
26 Chesham Place, London SW1X 8HH
Tel: (0171) 235 6137. Fax: (0171) 235 9048. Telex:
25651 (a/b ZAIRE G). Opening hours (for visa
enquiries): 0930-1300 Monday to Friday.
British Embassy
BP 8049, avenue de Trois Z, Kinshasa-Gombe, Zaïre
Tel: (12) 34775/8.
Consulates in: Lubumbashi, Goma and Kisangani.
Embassy of the Republic of Zaïre
1800 New Hampshire Avenue, NW, Washington, DC
20009
Tel: (202) 234 7690/1.
Embassy of the United States of America
Unit 31550, 310 avenue des Aviateurs, Kinshasa, Zaïre
Tel: (12) 21532 *or* 21628. Fax: (12) 21534. Telex: 21405
(a/b US EMB ZR).
Embassy of the Republic of Zaïre
18 Range Road, Ottawa, Ontario K1N 8A2
Tel: (613) 236 7103 *or* 236 4815. Fax: (613) 236 9166.
Telex: 0534314.
Consulate in: Montréal.
Canadian Representative Office
c/o Embassy of the United States of America, Unit

31550, 310 avenue des Aviateurs, Kinshasa, Zaïre
Tel: (12) 21532 ext. 2314. Fax: (12) 43805.

AREA: 2,344,885 sq km (905,365 sq miles).
POPULATION: 36,672,000 (1991 estimate).
POPULATION DENSITY: 15.6 per sq km.
CAPITAL: Kinshasa. **Population:** 2,778,281 (1985,
including Maluku).
GEOGRAPHY: Zaïre is the third-largest country in
Africa and is bordered to the north by the Central African
Republic and Sudan, to the east by Uganda, Rwanda,
Burundi and Tanzania, to the south by Zambia and
Angola and to the west by the Congo. Zaïre has a
coastline of only 27km (17 miles), at the outlet of the
Zaïre River, which flows into the Atlantic. The country
straddles the Equator and has widely differing
geographical features, including mountain ranges in the
north and west, a vast central plain through which the
Zaïre River flows, and the volcanoes and lakes of the
Kivu region. The Zaïre River has given rise to extensive
tropical rainforests on the western border with the
Congo.
LANGUAGE: The official language is French. There
are many local dialects, the most widely spoken being
Lingala, Swahili, Tshiluba and Kikongo.
RELIGION: Predominantly Roman Catholic, with a
minority of Protestant and traditional beliefs.
TIME: Kinshasa and Mbandaka: GMT + 1.
Haut-Zaïre, Kasai, Kivu and Shaba: GMT + 2.
ELECTRICITY: 220 volts AC, 50Hz.
COMMUNICATIONS: Telephone: IDD is available.
Country code: 243. Outgoing international code: 00.
Internal telephone service is often unreliable. **Fax:** A few
hotels have facilities. **Telex/telegram:** Telex facilities
are only available at Kinshasa and Lubumbashi post
offices and at the Intercontinental Hotel. Telegrams can
be sent from chief telegraph offices, but are unreliable
and sometimes subject to delays – particularly internal.
Post: Post office opening hours: 0800-1800 Monday to
Saturday. Zaïre is included in the Universal Postal Union
and the African Postal Union. Airmail to Europe takes 4-
18 days. **Press:** The daily newspapers are in various
African languages. The two main newspapers are *Elima*
and *Salongo*, both government-owned.
**BBC World Service and Voice of America
frequencies:** From time to time these change. See the
section *How to Use this Book* for more information.
BBC:

MHz	21.66	21.47	17.79	15.40

Voice of America:

MHz	21.49	15.60	9.525	6.035

PASSPORT/VISA

*Regulations and requirements may be subject to change at short notice, and you
are advised to contact the appropriate diplomatic or consular authority before
finalising travel arrangements. Details of these may be found at the head of this
country's entry. Any numbers in the chart refer to the footnotes below.*

	Passport Required?	Visa Required?	Return Ticket Required?
Full British	Yes	Yes	Yes
BVP	Not valid	-	-
Australian	Yes	Yes	Yes
Canadian	Yes	Yes	Yes
USA	Yes	Yes/1	Yes
Other EU (As of 31/12/94)	Yes	Yes	Yes
Japanese	Yes	Yes	Yes

PASSPORTS: Required by all.
British Visitors Passport: Not acceptable.
VISAS: Required by all except holders of an exit/re-
entry permit.
Types of visa: Tourist, Transit and Business; valid for
Single- or Multiple-entry for 1, 2 or 3 months. Transit
visas are required by all except those persons continuing
their journey within 48 hours provided they hold
confirmed onward tickets.
Application to: Consulate (or Consular section at
Embassy). For addresses, see top of entry.
Note [1]: The US State Department has advised US
nationals to apply for a visa to the Zaïreian Embassy in
Washington well in advance of any planned trip.
Application requirements: (a) Valid passport. (b) 3
application forms. (c) 3 passport-size photos. (d) Yellow
fever vaccination certificate. (e) Return or onward travel
documentation. (f) Stamped, addressed envelope (or cost
of return postage) with postal application.
Further documentation may be required depending on the
purpose of travel, eg for visits to relatives or family, a
letter of invitation from them approved by the Zaïrean
authorities; for tourist visits, letters from
employer/university and from bank to prove sufficient
funds are held to cover duration of stay; for business

visits, letters from sponsors in both country of origin and
Zaïre. Fees are payable on collection of visa, in cash or
certified banker's drafts/postal orders only.
Working days required: 48 hours minimum, in person
or by post.
Temporary residence: Apply to Embassy.

MONEY

Currency: Zaïre (Z) = 100 makuta. Due to the
precarious nature of the Zaïrean economy the exact
denomination of the Zaïre is subject to rapid change.
Currency exchange: Because of the parlous state of the
economy the only true repository of value is the US
Dollar. There is a thriving black market for foreign
currency, but it is illegal to exchange money through any
but official bureaux de change. Note that purchase of
airline tickets within Zaïre can be made only with
officially exchanged money.
Credit cards: The use of Access/Mastercard and Visa
are limited to main towns only. Check with your credit
card company for details of merchant acceptability and
other services which may be available.
Exchange rate indicators: The following figures are
included as a guide to the movements of the Zaïre against
Sterling and the US Dollar:

Date:	Oct '92	Sep '93	Jan '94	Jan '95
£1.00=	2,391,600	8,952,500	*8.94	4975.00
$1.00=	1,506,994	5,862,803	*6.04	3179.93

Note [*]: In October 1993 Zaïre devalued its currency by
3 million. This measure has fast been offset by an
inflation rate of 8000%.
Currency restrictions: Import and export of local
currency is prohibited. Import of foreign currency is
unlimited subject to declaration. Export of foreign
currency is limited to the amount declared on import.
Banking hours: 0800-1130 Monday to Friday.

DUTY FREE

The following items may be imported into Zaïre without
incurring customs duty:
*100 cigarettes or 50 cigars or equivalent in tobacco; 1
bottle of alcoholic beverage (opened); a reasonable
amount of perfume for personal use.*
Note: An import licence is required for arms and
ammunition.

PUBLIC HOLIDAYS

Jan 1 '95 New Year's Day. **Jan 4** Day of the Martyrs of
Independence. **May 1** Labour Day. **May 20** Anniversary
of the Mouvement Populaire de la Révolution. **Jun 24**
Anniversary of Zaïre currency, Promulgation of the 1967
Constitution and Day of the Fishermen. **Jun 30**
Independence Day. **Aug 1** Parents' Day. **Oct 14** Youth
Day and Birthday of President Mobutu. **Oct 27**
Anniversary of naming the country Zaïre. **Nov 17** Army
Day. **Nov 24** Anniversary of the Second Republic. **Dec
25** Christmas Day. **Jan 1 '96** New Year's Day. **Jan 4**
Day of the Martyrs of Independence.

HEALTH

*Regulations and requirements may be subject to change at short notice, and
you are advised to contact your doctor well in advance of your intended date of
departure. Any numbers in the chart refer to the footnotes below.*

	Special Precautions?	Certificate Required?
Yellow Fever	Yes	1
Cholera	Yes	2
Typhoid & Polio	Yes/3	-
Malaria	4	-
Food & Drink	5	-

[1]: A yellow fever vaccination certificate is required of
travellers over one year of age.
[2]: Following WHO guidelines issued in 1973, a cholera
vaccination certificate is not an official condition of entry
to Zaïre. However, cholera is a serious risk in this
country and precautions are essential. Up-to-date advice
should be sought before deciding whether these
precautions should include vaccination as medical
opinion is divided over its effectiveness. See the *Health*
section at the back of the book.
[3]: The WHO recommends a vaccination against
typhoid.
[4]: Malaria risk, predominantly in the malignant
falciparum form, exists throughout the year in the whole
country. The malignant form is reported to be 'highly

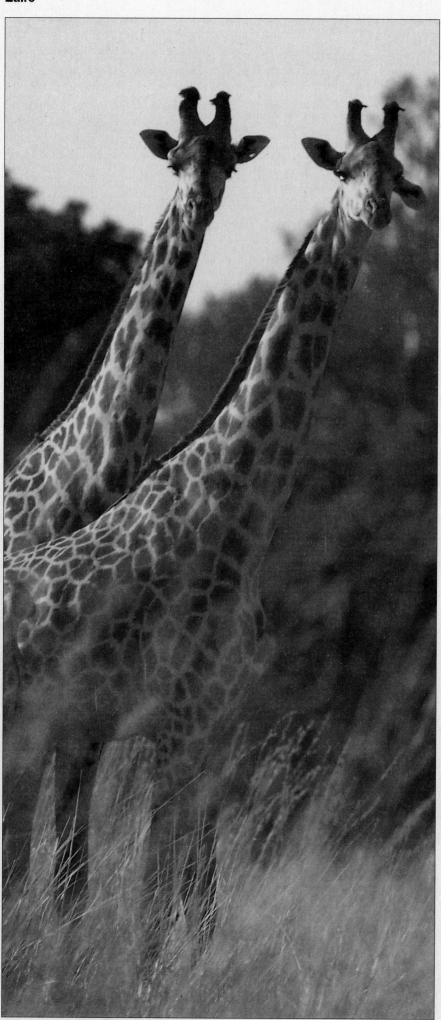

resistant' to chloroquine.

[5]: All water should be regarded as being a potential health risk. Water used for drinking, brushing teeth or making ice should have first been boiled or otherwise sterilised. Milk is unpasteurised and should be boiled. Powdered or tinned milk is available and is advised, but make sure that it is reconstituted with pure water. Avoid dairy products which are likely to have been made from unboiled milk. Only eat well-cooked meat and fish, preferably served hot. Pork, salad and mayonnaise may carry increased risk. Vegetables should be cooked and fruit peeled.

Rabies is present. For those at high risk, vaccination before arrival should be considered. If you are bitten abroad, seek medical advice without delay. For more information, consult the *Health* section at the back of the book.

Bilharzia (schistosomiasis) is present. Avoid swimming and paddling in fresh water. Swimming pools which are well-chlorinated and maintained are safe.

Plague is present in natural foci. Further information should be sought from the Department of Health or from any of the hospitals specialising in tropical diseases listed in the *Health* section at the back of this book.

Health care: Government expenditure on health is low, even by African standards. It is advisable to take specific personal medicines as medical facilities are available only in larger centres. Doctors and hospitals expect cash payment in full for health services. Health insurance is *essential* and it is advisable to include cover for emergency air evacuation.

TRAVEL - International

Note: There are indefinite restrictions for entry into the Republic of Zaïre. Travellers wishing to either enter or cross the country should note that (a) entry by air is only permitted at the capital, Kinshasa, and (b) entry from Rwanda is only permitted at Goma and only for visits to the Kahuzi-Biega National Park in Bukavu (return must be by the same route).

AIR: Zaïre's national airline is *Air Zaïre (QC)*.

Approximate flight time: From London to Kinshasa is 7-9 hours.

International airport: *Kinshasa (FIH)* (N'djili) is 25km (15 miles) east of the city (travel time – 45 minutes). Coaches run to and from city with return from Hotel Memling, 50 avenue du Tchad. Taxis are available. Airport facilities include 24-hour bank/bureau de change, post office, restaurant and car hire (*Avis, Budget, Europcar, InterRent* and *Hertz*).

Departure tax: US$20 for all international departures.

SEA: The international port is Matadi on the Zaïre River. There are services to Antwerp, run by *Compagnie Maritime Belge* and the *Compagnie Maritime du Zaïre*, and to the UK by *Elder Dempster Lines* and *Palm Line*.

RAIL: There are rail connections to Dar es Salaam in Tanzania and to Zambia, Zimbabwe, Mozambique and South Africa. The rail link to Lobito in Angola is unreliable due to the unstable political situation.

ROAD: The majority of Zaïre has connecting roads to surrounding countries, the major routes being through the Sudan, Uganda and Zambia. At the time of going to press, it is not advisable to travel from Zaïre to Kenya via Uganda because of the uncertain political situation in the latter country. All areas bordering Rwanda are very dangerous due to the conflict and the refugee situation. Ferries from the western border with the Congo and the northern border with the Central African Republic run across the Zaïre and Oubangui rivers.

TRAVEL - Internal

Note: There are indefinite restrictions for tourist travel within or across Zaïre. Overland journeys by local public transport, hitch-hiking, or by foreign vehicle or motorcycle (with a foreign registration number) are forbidden.

AIR: *Air Zaïre* (QC) connects *N'djili Airport* (Kinshasa) to over 40 internal airports and 150 landing strips. Small planes are available for charter.

Departure tax: US$8 for adults and US$6 for children on all domestic departures.

RIVER: Over 1600km (1000 miles) of the Zaïre River are navigable and there are services from Kinshasa to the upriver ports of Kisangani and Ilebo. This is one of the best ways to travel, but services can be unreliable due to fuel shortages.

RAIL: The main internal railway runs from Lubumbashi to Ilebo, with a branch to Kalemie and Kindu, and from Kinshasa to the port of Matadi. Rail services are generally basic, although deluxe and first-class cars are comparable to those in Europe. There is no air-conditioning, but there are couchettes and dining cars on the principal trains.

ROAD: Traffic drives on the right. Due to poor maintenance, the roads are among the worst in Africa and only achieve a fair standard around the main towns. It is wise to check that bridges are safe before crossing. Vehicle thefts, including hijackings at gunpoint, are on the increase. **Bus:** Services run between the main towns but are crowded and unreliable. **Taxi:** Available in Kinshasa but unreliable. **Car hire:** Available on a limited basis at the airport. **Documentation:** International Driving Permit required.
URBAN: Conventional bus services in Kinshasa can be severely overcrowded. Minibuses and converted truck-buses also offer public transport, and are known as *fula fulas*. Pick-up trucks are known as 'taxibuses'. A better standard of transport is provided by shared taxis, which are widely available. There is little or no public transport in most other large centres.

ACCOMMODATION

Zaïre is not the easiest country for the visitor as it is crippled by transport problems, while the difficult terrain has resulted in relatively few settlements except along river banks. Accommodation is therefore largely restricted to the main cities, and is scarce in the interior. For further details contact the Embassy.
HOTELS: The few hotels that cater for European visitors are expensive and generally booked-up well in advance. The majority of hotels are in Kinshasa, with others in Muanda, Boma, Matadi, Mbanzangunu, Mbandaka, Lubumbashi, Bukavu, Kolwezi, Kananga and Kisangani. Information can be obtained from the Société Zaïroise de l'Hôtellerie, BP 1076, Immeuble Memling, Kinshasa. Tel: (12) 23260.

RESORTS & EXCURSIONS

Zaïre is a vast country, made even larger by inadequate transport infrastructure. It has not been developed for tourism.

Kinshasa

The capital does not have many sights of historic interest, but the visitor interested in the past should not miss the prehistoric and ethnological museums at the *Kinshasa University*, an ensemble of light, rectangular, well laid-out buildings standing on a hillside. A brightly-coloured chapel crowns the top of the hill. Nearby is a corner of the equatorial forest surrounding a beautiful lake called 'Ma Valée' with a charming tavern on its banks. Other attractions include the fishing port of **Kinkole**, the *Gardens of the Presidential Farm of Nsele* made of pagodas, and the extensive pools where angling and swimming may be enjoyed. In both the markets and the suburbs of Kinshasa there are craftsmen who produce wood and metal items. Visit the *National Museum* which includes some unique pieces of genuine Zaïrean art.

Southwest Zaïre & Bandundu

The *Insiki Falls* (60m/197ft high) at **Zongo** and the caves in the region of **Mbanza-Ngungu** may be visited in one day, but it is preferable to stay for two or three days, for Mbanza-Ngungu is a pleasant resort with a good climate. While in the Mbanza-Ngungu area the visitor should not fail to stop at Kisantu to visit the *'Frère Gillet' Botanic Gardens* with their world-famous rare orchids.
Further west are the wild slopes and gorges of the *River Kwilu*, 120km (75 miles) from Mataoi; on the right bank of the river is a spot of rugged beauty called *Inga*. The woods, caves and waterfalls of *Boma* and equatorial **Mayumbe** and the *Tombs of Tshela*, can be visited on the way to the ocean beach of *Moanda*.
Less easily accessible is the upper valley of the *Kwango* in the southwest. A long journey through a region of unspoiled natural beauty leads to the *Tembo* (formerly Guillaume) *Falls*.

Kasai & Shaba

In the south, the **Upemba National Park** straddles the *Lualaba River*, northeast of Bugama, and includes several lakes inhabited by hippos, crocodiles and numerous aquatic birds. Here too are numerous fishermen, cattle farmers and peasants, as well as a number of mining communities. Kananga and **Mbuji-Mayi** are typical tropical towns; **Kalemie** and the banks of *Lake Tanganyika* are reminiscent of the French Riviera.
The whole of the south of Zaïre is dotted with freshwater lakes such as *Munkamba*, *Fwa* and *Kasai*; there are also numerous impressive waterfalls, such as *Kiobo*, on the Lufira, and *Lofol* 384m (1259ft) high, north of Lubumbashi.

Upper Zaïre & the Kivu

The high plateaux of Zaïre extend across the eastern part of the country, around lakes Tanganyika, Kivu, Idi Amin Dada, Mobutu Sese Seko and Bukavu. **Goma** and **Bunia** are small, pretty towns featuring villas, restaurants and hotels.
In the north is the **Garamba National Park**, covering 400,000 hectares and featuring lions, leopards, elephants, rhinos and giraffes.
Lake Mobutu Sese Seko, which contains more fish than any other lake in Africa, lies at an altitude of over 618m (2027ft). It can be reached from Bunia, which is also the point of departure for numerous excursions into the forests and mountains, the Pygmy villages, the *Caves of Mount Hoyo* and the *'Escaliers de Venus' Falls*. *Lake Idi Amin Dada* is the home of birds of all sizes and colours. The highest peak in the Ruwenzori range is the *Pic Marguerite*, at an altitude of 5119m (15,795ft). The snowline is at 450m (1776ft). This region is also inhabited by gorillas and by the extremely rare okapi. The mountain scenery between Goma and Beni is regarded as some of the most spectacular in Africa, although the road is not always in good condition.

Virunga National Park

Covering an area of 12,000 sq km (4633 sq miles), this comprises an immense plain bounded by two jagged mountain ranges that serve as a natural enclosure for the animals which roam at liberty in this huge natural reserve. Game includes numerous lions, elephants, buffaloes, warthogs, antelopes, hippos and colourful aquatic birds. In this park, near Goma, you can also climb the still-active volcanoes of *Nyamuragira*, 3055m (10,022ft), and *Nyiragongo*, 3470m (11,385ft).

SOCIAL PROFILE

FOOD & DRINK: There are a number of good restaurants in Kinshasa and Lubumbashi, but prices are high. Hotels and restaurants which cater for Europeans are generally expensive and serve international and Zaïrean dishes. A typical speciality is *moambe* chicken, cooked in fresh palm oil with rice and spinach. The capital Kinshasa offers French, Belgian and Zaïrean cuisine, but again restaurants are expensive and cater largely for businessmen. Small restaurants and snack bars offer Chinese, Tunisian and Greek food.
NIGHTLIFE: Kinshasa is the best place for nightlife, especially in the sprawling township of the 'Cité', where most of the population live. There are four main casinos and several large nightclubs. Local bands offer an exciting evening and have a keen local following.
SHOPPING: Local craftware includes bracelets, ebony carvings and local paintings. The large towns all have markets and shopping centres, selling everything from fresh ginger to baskets and African carvings. **Shopping hours:** 0800-1800 Monday to Saturday.
SPORT: Mountaineering is a growing sport, especially in the Ruwenzori mountain range. There are eight **safari** reserves, and touring is popular. Most of the rivers and lakes yield excellent **fishing**. Facilities for **sailing** available at the country's only seaport of Matadi. **Tennis** and **golf** are also popular.
SOCIAL CONVENTIONS: Casual clothes are widely suitable although scanty beachwear should be confined to the beach or poolside. **Photography:** A permit is required. Even then, local authorities are likely to be sensitive. Avoid official areas. **Tipping:** 10% service charge is added to hotel and restaurant bills. Extra tipping is unnecessary.

BUSINESS PROFILE

ECONOMY: With rich agricultural land and extensive mineral and energy deposits, Zaïre is potentially one of Africa's richest countries. The country has rich natural resources and, by regional standards, a highly industrialised base manufacturing for the domestic market. However, two-thirds of the population are still involved in subsistence farming and industry runs well below capacity due to a lack of spare parts and foreign exchange with which to acquire them. The mining sector, which enjoys investment priority and is equipped with some of the latest available technology, also produces cobalt, manganese, zinc, uranium and tin. There are also large offshore oil deposits. Compared to mining, the rest of Zaïre's industry is comparatively underdeveloped. Most enterprises turn out consumer goods – textiles, cement, food and beverages, wood products and plastics – for domestic consumption. Agriculture remains the largest employer, however, and an important source of foreign exchange. Zaïrean farmers produce palm oil,

coffee, tea, cocoa, rubber, cotton, tropical woods, fruit, vegetables and rice. Any economic improvement depends – in the short-term at any rate – on increases in commodity prices on world markets. Long-term development will need considerable improvement to the country's poor infrastructure and external financial assistance. This may not be forthcoming since the IMF, with which Zaïre has had a difficult relationship, declared it a 'non-cooperative' nation in April 1992. Bilateral assistance has been cut as a result of the political upheaval, which has also deterred foreign investors. China, the USA, Belgium and other EU countries are Zaïre's main trading partners. As a result of political instability the economy is now in a state of freefall. In 1994 the World Bank closed its office in Kinshasa declaring the country to be insolvent. There is an 8000% rate of hyper-inflation and despite a 3,000,000% devaluation of the currency, the Zaïre is now virtually worthless.
BUSINESS: Business people should wear lightweight suits. Interpreter and translation services are available as business is mainly conducted in French. The best time to visit is in the cool season (which varies from one part of the country to another). *Citoyen* is the term used to address men and *Citoyenne* is used to address women. **Office hours:** 0730-1700 Monday to Friday, 0730-1200 Saturday.
COMMERCIAL INFORMATION: The following organisation might be able to offer advice: Chambre de Commerce, d'Industrie et d'Agriculture du Zaïre, BP 7247, 10 avenue des Aviateurs, Kinshasa. Tel: (12) 22286. Telex: 21071.

CLIMATE

Varies according to distance from the Equator, which lies across the north of the country. The dry season in the north is from December to March, and in the south May to October. The annual temperatures are warm and humidity is high.
Required clothing: Lightweight clothes are recommended all year, with rainwear during the rainy season.

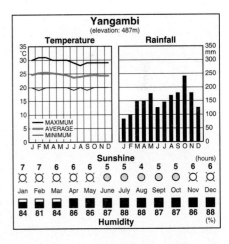

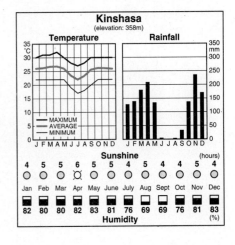

Location: Central southern Africa.

Zambia National Tourist Board
PO Box 30017, Century House, Cairo Road, Lusaka, Zambia
Tel: (1) 229 087/90. Fax: (1) 225 174. Telex: 41780.
Tour Operators Association of Zambia
PO Box 35211, Lusaka, Zambia
Tel: (1) 223 113 *or* 224 464 *or* 223 110. Fax: (1) 223 048 *or* 226 348.
Travel Agents Association of Zambia
c/o Lubi Travel, PO Box 37782, Lusaka, Zambia
Tel: (1) 225 650 *or* 223 216.
High Commission for the Republic of Zambia
2 Palace Gate, London W8 5NG
Tel: (0171) 589 6655. Fax: (0171) 581 1353. Opening hours: 0930-1300 and 1400-1700 Monday to Friday; *Visa section:* 1000-1300 Monday to Friday.
Zambia National Tourist Board
Address as High Commission
Tel: (0171) 589 6343/4. Fax: (0171) 225 3221. Opening

hours: 0930-1300 and 1400-1700 Monday to Friday.
British High Commission
PO Box 50050, Independence Avenue, 15101 Ridgeway, Lusaka, Zambia
Tel: (1) 228 955 *or* 251 956 (after hours). Fax: (1) 262 215. Telex: 41150 (a/b UKREP ZA).
Embassy of the Republic of Zambia
2419 Massachusetts Avenue, NW, Washington, DC 20008
Tel: (202) 265 9717/8/9. Fax: (202) 332 0826.
Zambia National Tourist Board
237 East 52nd Street, New York, NY 10022
Tel: (212) 308 2155.
Embassy of the United States of America
PO Box 31617, corner of Independence and United Nations Avenues, Lusaka, Zambia
Tel: (1) 228 595 *or* 228 601/2/3. Fax: (1) 261 538. Telex: 41970 (a/b AMEMB ZA).
High Commission of the Republic of Zambia
Suite 1610, 130 Albert Street, Ottawa, Ontario K1P 5G4
Tel: (613) 563 0712. Fax: (613) 235 0430.
Canadian High Commission
PO Box 31313, 5199 United Nations Avenue, Lusaka, Zambia
Tel: (1) 261 007. Fax: (1) 261 172. Telex: 42480 (a/b DOMCAN ZA).
Zambia National Tourist Board
Postal address: PO Box 591232, Kengray 2100, South Africa
Street address: First Floor, Finance House, Ernest Oppenheinzer Road, Bruma Lake Office Park, Bruma 2198, South Africa
Tel: 622 9206/7. Fax: 622 7424.
Zambia National Tourist Board
c/o Alessandra Callegari, Relazioni Turishche, Via Mauro Macchi 42, 20124 Milan, Italy
Tel: (2) 669 0341 *or* 66 98 27 87 *or* 66 98 32 53. Fax: (2) 66 98 73 81.
Zambia National Tourist Board
c/o Obitair International Pty Ltd, Level 10, 36 Clarence Street, Sydney NSW 2000, Australia
Tel: (2) 299 5300. Fax: (2) 290 2665.

AREA: 752,614 sq km (290,586 sq miles).
POPULATION: 8,700,000 (1992 estimate).
POPULATION DENSITY: 11.5 per sq km.
CAPITAL: Lusaka. **Population:** 995,315 (1992 estimate).
GEOGRAPHY: Zambia is a vast plateau bordered by Angola to the west, Zaïre to the north, Tanzania to the northeast, Malawi to the east, Mozambique to the southeast, Zimbabwe and Botswana to the south and the Caprivi Strip of Namibia to the southwest. The Zambezi River together with Lake Kariba forms the frontier with Zimbabwe. Victoria Falls, at the southern end of the man-made Lake Kariba, is one of the most spectacular sights in Africa (if not the world). In the east and northeast the country rises to a plateau 1200m (3937ft) high, covered by deciduous savannah, small trees, grassy plains or marshland. The magnificent Luangwa and Kafue National Parks have some of the most prolific animal populations in Africa.
LANGUAGE: English is the official language, but there are over 73 tribal dialects. The main languages are Nyanja, Tonga, Bemba, Lozi, Kaonde, Luvale and Lunda.
RELIGION: Recently declared a Christian nation, with a minority of traditional beliefs and some Muslims and Hindus.
TIME: GMT + 2.
ELECTRICITY: 220 volts AC, 50Hz.
COMMUNICATIONS: Telephone: IDD is available. Country code: 260. Outgoing international code: 00. There are public telephones and most calls are made through a post office. **Fax/telex/telegram:** There are public telex and fax facilities at the Central Post Office in Lusaka and at principal hotels. Telegrams may be sent from telegraph offices in main centres, open 0800-1630 Monday to Friday, 0800-1230 Saturday (closed on Sundays and public holidays). The Central Telegraph Office in Lusaka accepts telegrams up to 1600 Monday to Saturday. **Post:** Airmail to Western Europe takes 7-14 days. **Press:** *The Times of Zambia, Zambia Daily Mail, The Sun, Crime News, Financial Review, The National Mirror, The Weekly Express* and *The Post* are published in English.
BBC World Service and Voice of America frequencies: From time to time these change. See the section *How to Use this Book* for more information.
BBC:

MHz	21.66	11.94	6.005	3.255

Voice of America:

MHz	21.49	15.60	9.525	6.035

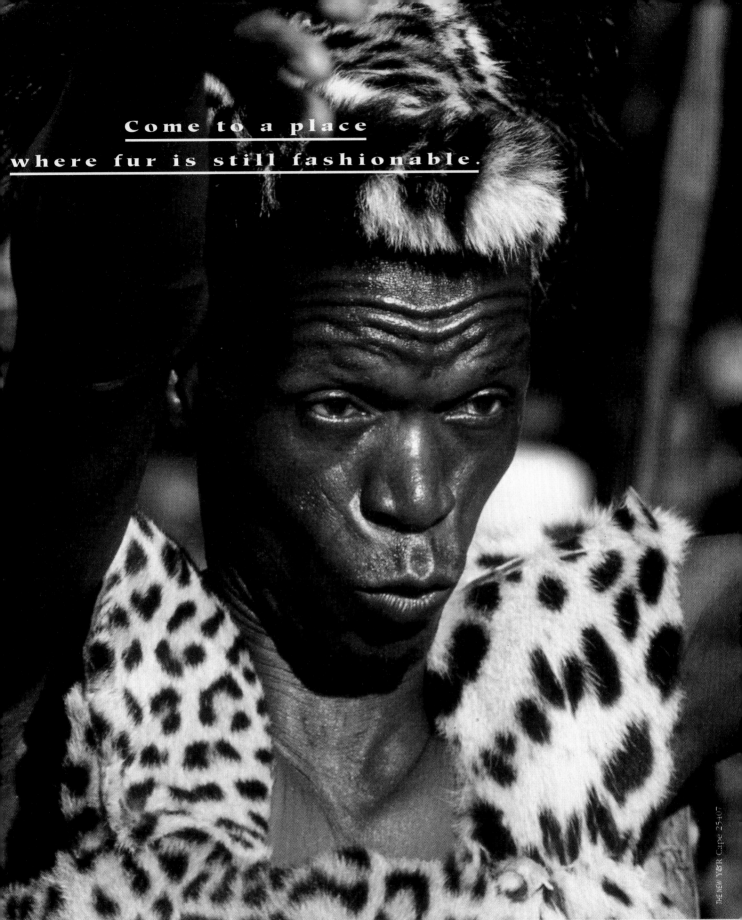

Come to a place
where fur is still fashionable.

*N*ot that we don't care about our furry friends. After all, we've given them sixty thousand square kilometres to roam in. Nineteen national parks. Thousands of elephants, hippo, buffalo, giraffe, crocodile, antelope and the almost extinct black rhino to play with. Point is, wildlife is not the only wild thing about Zambia. The Zambezi offers the best white-water rafting in the world. An exciting melting-pot of African tribes and traditions. And Musi-oa-Tunya, less romantically known as Victoria Falls, is one of the seven natural wonders of the world. Get in touch with the soul of Africa, and feel yours soar. **ZAMBIA. THE VERY SOUL OF AFRICA**

Zambia
NATIONAL TOURIST
BOARD

THE NEW Y&R Cape 2547

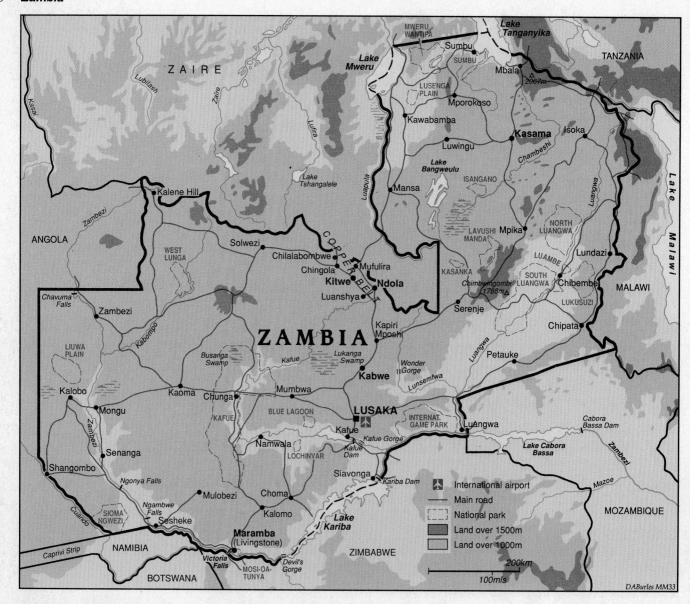

PASSPORT/VISA

Regulations and requirements may be subject to change at short notice, and you are advised to contact the appropriate diplomatic or consular authority before finalising travel arrangements. Details of these may be found at the head of this country's entry. Any numbers in the chart refer to the footnotes below.

	Passport Required?	Visa Required?	Return Ticket Required?
Full British	Yes	No	Yes
BVP	Not valid	-	-
Australian	Yes	No	Yes
Canadian	Yes	No	Yes
USA	Yes	Yes	Yes
Other EU (As of 31/12/94)	Yes	1	Yes
Japanese	Yes	Yes	Yes

PASSPORTS: Valid passport required by all.
British Visitors Passport: Not accepted.
VISAS: Required by all except:
(a) **[1]** nationals of the UK and Ireland (nationals of other EU countries *do* require visas);
(b) nationals of Commonwealth, Dependent and Associated states (with the exception of Cyprus, Ghana, India, Nigeria and Pakistan who *do* need visas);
(c) nationals of Fiji, Finland, Norway, Romania, Sweden and Yugoslavia (Serbia and Montenegro).
Types of visa: Tourist, Business and Transit; cost – £6. Transit visas are not required by those exempted from full visas or by those continuing their journeys by the same or next connecting flight within 24 hours and not leaving the airport.
Validity: Visas may be used up to 3 months from date of issue, for a maximum stay of 90 days.
Application to: Consulate (or Consular section at High Commission). For addresses, see top of entry.
Application requirements: (a) 2 completed application forms. (b) 2 passport-size photos. (c) Valid passport. (d)

Sufficient funds to cover stay. (e) Business applications must be covered by an explanatory letter.
Working days required: At least 3 days.
Temporary residence: For visits in excess of 90 days, apply to Chief Immigration Officer (CIO), PO Box 50300, Lusaka.

MONEY

Currency: Kwacha (K) = 100 ngwee. Notes are in denominations of K500, 100, 50 and 20. Coins are in denominations of K10, 5 and 1.
Currency exchange: Exchange of foreign currency is carried out at authorised banks and bureaux de change.
Credit cards: American Express is widely accepted, with more limited use of Access/Mastercard, Diners Club and Visa. Check with your credit card company for details of merchant acceptability and other services which may be available.
Exchange rate indicators: The following figures are included as a guide to the movements of the Kwacha against Sterling and the US Dollar:

Date:	Oct '92	Sep '93	Jan '94	Jan '95
£1.00=	317.88	627.50	965.65	1066.63
$1.00=	200.30	410.94	652.69	694.55

Currency restrictions: The import and export of local currency is limited to K1000. Free import of foreign currency subject to declaration on arrival. The export of foreign currency is limited to the amount declared on import.
Note: Currency declaration forms and exchange receipts must be shown if purchasing airline tickets in Zambia.
Banking hours: 0815-1430 Monday to Friday.

DUTY FREE

The following items may be imported into Zambia without incurring customs duty:
400 cigarettes or 500g of tobacco; 1 bottle of spirits and

wine and 2.5 litres of beer (opened); 1oz bottle of perfume.
Note: Souvenirs may be exported without restriction but game trophies such as tooth, bone, horn, shell, claw, skin, hair, feather or other durable items are subject to export permits.

PUBLIC HOLIDAYS

Jan 1 '95 New Year's Day. **Mar 11** Youth Day. **Apr 14-17** Easter. **May 1** Labour Day. **May 25** African Freedom Day (Anniversary of the OAU's Foundation). **Jul 3** Heroes' Day. **Jul 4** Unity Day. **Aug 7** Farmers' Day. **Oct 24** Independence Day. **Dec 25** Christmas Day. **Jan 1 '96** New Year's Day. **Mar 11** Youth Day. **Apr 5-8** Easter.
Note: It is advisable to check dates in advance.

HEALTH

Regulations and requirements may be subject to change at short notice, and you are advised to contact your doctor well in advance of your intended date of departure. Any numbers in the chart refer to the footnotes below.

	Special Precautions?	Certificate Required?
Yellow Fever	Yes	1
Cholera	Yes	2
Typhoid & Polio	Yes	-
Malaria	3	-
Food & Drink	4	-

[1]: A yellow fever vaccination certificate is required from travellers over one year of age arriving from infected areas. All passengers must hold an 'International Certificate of Vaccination' booklet even if no vaccination is required. Travellers arriving from non-endemic zones should note that vaccination is strongly recommended for travel outside the urban areas, even if an outbreak of the

disease has not been reported and they would normally not require a vaccination certificate to enter the country.
[2]: Following WHO guidelines issued in 1973, a cholera vaccination certificate is not a condition of entry to Zambia. However, cholera is a risk in this country and precautions are essential. Up-to-date advice should be sought before deciding whether these precautions should include vaccination, as medical opinion is divided over its effectiveness. See the *Health* section at the back of the book.
[3]: Malaria risk exists, predominantly in the malignant *falciparum* form, in the whole country throughout the year. The malignant form is reported to be 'highly resistant' to chloroquine.
[4]: Water used for drinking, brushing teeth or making ice should have first been boiled or otherwise sterilised. Milk is pasteurised and dairy products are generally safe for consumption. Only eat well-cooked meat and fish, preferably served hot. Pork, salad and mayonnaise may carry increased risk. Vegetables should be cooked and fruit peeled.
Rabies is present. For those at high risk, vaccination before arrival should be considered. If you are bitten abroad, seek medical advice without delay. For more information, consult the *Health* section at the back of the book.

Timatic		
Health		
GALILEO/WORLDSPAN:	**TI-DFT/LUN/HE**	
SABRE:	**TIDFT/LUN/HE**	
Visa		
GALILEO/WORLDSPAN:	**TI-DFT/LUN/VI**	
SABRE:	**TIDFT/LUN/VI**	
For more information on Timatic codes refer to Contents.		

Bilharzia (schistosomiasis) is present. Avoid swimming and paddling in fresh water. Swimming pools which are well-chlorinated and maintained are safe.
Health care: Health service is not free and health insurance is advisable. Adequate health care cannot be assured outside main towns. It is advisable to carry basic medical supplies.

TRAVEL - International

AIR: Zambia's national airline is *Aero Zamiba* (Room 114, Pamodzi Hotel; tel: (1) 254 455; fax: (1) 254 005). Other airlines that fly to Zambia are *British Airways, Air France, South Africa Airways, Aeroflot, Air Malawi, Kenya Airways, Air Tanzania, Air Zimbabwe, Air India, Air Namibia, Air Botswana* and *Royal Swazi Airways*.
Approximate flight time: From London to Lusaka is 10 hours.
International airport: *Lusaka (LUN)* is 26km (16 miles) east of the city (travel time – 30 minutes). Airport and city bus services are available. Taxi service is also available to the city. Return is by prior arrangement with taxis from Pamodzi, Ridgeway, International and Lusaka hotels (taxi fares are negotiable). Airport facilities include outgoing duty-free shop (0600 until last flight); car hire, bank/bureau de change (0600 until last flight), restaurant (0400 until last flight) and post office (0600-1430 Monday to Friday; 0600-1100 Saturday).
Departure tax: US$20. Transit passengers are exempt.
RIVER/LAKE: Zambia has no coastline but there are crossings from Mpulungu across Lake Tanganyika to Kigoma in Tanzania to Bujumbura in Burundi, and a service across the Zambezi from Kazungula to Botswana.
RAIL: There are two major rail routes linking Zambia with Zimbabwe and Tanzania. *Zambia Railways* serves Livingstone and has a connection across the Victoria Falls to Bulawayo and Harare in Zimbabwe. There are two trains daily in either direction, the journey taking 9-12 hours depending on whether the ordinary or express

service is used. *Tanzania–Zambia Railways Authority (TAZARA)* operates trains Mondays, Tuesdays and Fridays from Kapiri Mposhi to Dar es Salaam in Tanzania. A further line from Kapiri Mposhi connects with Lubumbashi (Zaïre) via Ndola. Services are often suspended and it is advisable to check at the tourist office in Lusaka for details.
ROAD: The main routes are from Zimbabwe via Chirundu, Kariba and Livingstone; from Botswana via Kansane and Kazungula; from Mozambique via Villa Gambito and Zumbo; from Tanzania via Nakonde and Mbala; from Malawi via Chipata and Lundazi; and from Zaïre via Kashiba, Mwenda, Sakania, Mokamba, Kasumbalesa and Kapushi.

TRAVEL - Internal

AIR: *Roan Air* and local tour operators operate domestic services. There are over 127 airports, aerodromes and airstrips in the country.
Departure tax: K3500 for domestic services.
RIVER/LAKE: Local ferries operate on all waterways. Contact local authorities for details.
RAIL: Routes serve Lusaka, Ndola, Kitwe and Mulobezi. Local services, centred on Lusaka, are very limited. Children under 3 years of age travel free, children between 3-15 years pay half price. There is first- and second-class accommodation and light refreshments are available on some services.
ROAD: Traffic drives on the left. There is a fairly good network of roads although these are not in very good condition in some places. **Bus:** The network of intercity bus services is run by private operators and *Zambia Telecommunications (Zamtel)*. The service can be unreliable and the buses often crowded. *Zamtel's* coach service, linking Lusaka with the Copperbelt and Livingstone on alternate days, should be booked well in advance. **Car hire:** Several firms operate in main

centres. Information is available from the Zambia National Tourist Board (address at top of entry) or the *Lusaka Bus Terminus* on Dedan Kimathi Road, Lusaka. *Zungulila*, *Big Five Travel & Tours Ltd* and other car hire firms can provide chauffeur-driven cars.

Documentation: An International Driving Permit is legally required and is valid for six months. Thereafter, a Zambian driving licence is required, granted after passing a local driving test.

URBAN: Bus services in Lusaka are provided by private minibuses and shared taxis. The buses are somewhat basic, and can become very crowded. Taxis are not metered and fares should be agreed in advance.

JOURNEY TIMES: The following chart gives approximate journey times (in hours and minutes) from Lusaka to other major cities/towns in Zambia.

	Air	Road	Rail
Livingstone	1.20	6.30	11.00
Ndola	1.00	4.00	6.30
Kitwe	1.00	4.30	7.00
Mfuwe	1.30	-	-

ACCOMMODATION

Accommodation in Zambia may be divided into four main categories: hotels, motels, lodges and camps; and two minor categories: GRZ-resthouses and camping/caravan sites. Zambia is a large, wild and, as yet, largely undeveloped country. Only the major tourist sites are fully prepared to cater for the needs of the visitor.

HOTELS & MOTELS: Hotels are concentrated around Lusaka, Livingstone and the Copperbelt region. Others are widely dispersed around the country along principal roads or near towns. It is advisable to book in advance and to obtain confirmation in writing. All bills are subject to a 10% service charge in lieu of tips and 23% sales tax. Tipping in hotels is not permitted by law. **Grading:** Hotels are graded according to a 5-star system and range from an ungraded class to one 5-star hotel. For further information contact the Hotel and Caterers Association of Zambia, c/o Ndeke Hotel, PO Box 30815, Lusaka. Tel: (1) 252 779 *or* 252 422.

NATIONAL PARKS: All lodges and many camps in the parks are offered on a fully catered basis. As the quality of accommodation and associated facilities varies

enormously from one place to another, visitors intending to stay should contact the relevant tour operator/tourist office for detailed information.

Lodges: These are generally stone buildings with thatched roofs designed to complement the natural environment, housing a maximum of 40 beds.

Camps: The most common and most widely used type of accommodation for safaris. In general, standard facilities include hot and cold running water, electricity and waterborne sanitation plus the basic accoutrements for comfortable living. For instance, Luangwa's camps have beds, clean linen, refrigerator, crockery, cutlery, mosquito nets, lamps, toilets and showers. At non-catering camps visitors must bring their own food and drink. Some are open all year round while others open from June to October or November.

GRZ-HOSTELS: These are available throughout the provinces. They have a small capacity, rising in exceptional cases to 24 rooms. Government resthouses are available in many centres but they are very basic.

CAMPING/CARAVANNING: Sites are available at most of the tourist centres, including several national parks. It is best to make reservations well in advance. If booking is more than four weeks in advance some operators will charge a 15% deposit. The peak seasons are June 1 to October 15, December 15 to January 4, and Easter. Prices may increase by 20-30% during these periods. For further information, contact the Zambia National Tourist Board, who can supply a list of Zambian tour operators.

RESORTS & EXCURSIONS

Note: Most tourist organisations are controlled by tour operators and prices of tours need to be fixed well in advance.

NATIONAL PARKS: The Zambian government has long recognised the economic importance of its wildernesses and is acutely aware of enviromental concerns: almost 9% of the country is given over to national parks and game reserves. Most tourism is concentrated in five of the 19 parks – Sumbu, Kafue, Lochinvar, Luangwa and Mosi-oa-Tunya – the remainder, as yet, having fewer facilities. In general, safaris are limited to six to eight persons per vehicle (always accompanied by experienced guides),

permitting the animal/bird lover to appreciate, in uninterrupted peace, the African wildlife roaming through an unspoilt natural environment. Herds of buffalo, elephant and antelope are easily spotted and there are plenty of lions and zebra. There are also rhinos, monkeys, baboons, wild pigs, hippopotami and crocodiles. The region is good for bird enthusiasts; 400 different species of bird have been recorded in Lochinvar alone. The flood plains and river banks teem with water birds, especially in the Lochinvar and Luangwa National Parks. Fishing is also popular and international fishing competitions are often held on Zambian lakes and rivers.

The usual method of animal watching is from an open-topped Land-Rover, but walking tours are available for the more adventurous. As a precaution, no more than six may make up a walking party and the guide will be armed. Nocturnal safaris are also possible in open four-wheel-drive vehicles equipped with searchlights.

All the main national parks are accessible by car and plane. National parks require an entry permit bought from the main gate during opening hours (0600-1800 seven days a week).

For further and more detailed information about safaris, contact the Zambia National Tourist Board.

Kafue National Park: Situated in the centre of the southern half of the country, Kafue encompasses a huge area (22,500 sq km/8687 sq miles) and is one of the biggest game sanctuaries in Africa. Noted for its beauty, the park is bisected by the Kafue River, which attracts hundreds of species of birds and offers good game fishing. 8-day walking and driving tours are available. The principal attraction is the prolific wildlife. Accommodation is provided throughout the year at *Mukambi Lodge* (no guided safaris during the rainy season, November to April), and the *Musungwa Lodges,* and at *New Kalala Camp* (full catering) and others. There are also several seasonal non-catered camps.

Luangwa Valley National Park: Regarded as one of the most exciting game reserves in the world, the Luangwa Valley is home for a huge variety of animals: among many others, elephants, hippopotami, lions, zebras, giraffes, antelopes, buffaloes, monkeys and wild dogs. Blossoming trees and exotic flowers set the scene. The main rainy season runs from November/December to May. There are lodges at *Chichele*, *Mfuwe* and *Kapani* (all year), *Luamfwa* and *Tundwe* (dry season), and

catered camps at *Chibembe, Tena Tena, Kaingo Camp*
(dry season) and *Chinzombo* (all year). There are also
several seasonal non-catered camps. Facilities in the park
include luxury double rooms in chalets, private baths and
toilets, full 3-course meals, bar facilities and swimming
pools.

Lochinvar National Park: Exceptional diversity of
birdlife. One lodge, open throughout the year.

Sumbu National Park: The sandy shorelines of *Lake
Tanganyika* provide the setting for three all-year beach
resorts: at *Kasaba, Ndole* and *Nkamba* bays. There is also
a small non-catered camp at Ndole Bay. Activities
include swimming, sunbathing, boat rides and freshwater
big-game fishing for the Goliath tigerfish (up to 35kg),
giant catfish and the Nile perch (both up to 50kg and
more). It is possible to arrange visits into the surrounding
bush to watch game. *Kasaba Lodge* boasts an afternoon
tea service, a bar and beach barbecues. *Nkamba Bay
Lodge* offers exactly the same facilities as Kasaba but
facilities are housed in rondavels. The park's spectacular
sunsets are not to be missed. Book with Inter Continental
Travel, PO Box 37209, 1st Floor, Mukuba Pension
House, Dedan Kimathi Road, Lusaka. Tel: (1) 223
839/42/43. Fax: (1) 222 904.

Victoria Falls/Mosi-oa-Tunya National Park: Located
on the southernmost edge of Zambia bordering
Zimbabwe, the astonishing Victoria Falls are the
mightiest cataracts in the world – the 2.5km-wide (1.5-
mile) Zambezi River drops 100m (330ft) into a narrow
chasm at the rate of 550 million litres every minute. The
spray can be seen 30km (20 miles) away. The Mosi-oa-
Tunya National Park nearby is small by Zambian
standards but is home to most of Zambia's more common
wild animals. Also nearby is **Livingstone**, 'Tourist
Capital of Zambia', with several luxury hotels, a casino,
and the *National Museum*, housing Livingstone
memorabilia and anthropological exhibits. The *Railway
Museum* is also situated in Livingstone.

Adventure holidays: White-water rafting adventure
holidays are becoming very popular and 1- to 7-day
navigations of the Zambezi from the base of the Victoria
Falls to Lake Kariba and shorter white-water raft safaris
are also available. Canoeing safaris are also available.

LUSAKA: Attractions in the capital include nightclubs,
restaurants, cinemas, the *Kabwata Cultural Village*
(devoted to the preservation of indigenous arts and crafts
and displays of native dancing), the *Cathedral of the
Holy Cross* and the *Munda Wanga Botanical Gardens
and Zoo*.

SOCIAL PROFILE

FOOD & DRINK: Due to the liberalisation of the
economy there is now plenty of food in the shops. Local
specialities include bream from the Zambezi, Kafue and
Luapula rivers, and Nile perch, lake salmon and other
freshwater fish. **Drink:** *Mosi* and imported beers and
assorted soft drinks are available. Spirits are also
available.

NIGHTLIFE: Lusaka has dancing and floorshows in the
main hotels, cinemas and theatres. The Copperbelt and
Livingstone areas offer a variety of entertainments
including casinos and nightclubs.

SHOPPING: Lusaka has modern shops, supermarkets
and open-air markets. Special purchases include African
carvings, pottery and copperware, beadwork and local
gemstones. **Shopping hours:** 0800-1700 Monday to
Friday and 0800-1300 Saturday.

SPORT: Tennis, bowls and **golf** are all available. Sports
facilities are available through private clubs, many of
which offer temporary membership to visitors if
introduced by a member. **Horseriding** is available in
Lusaka and Kitwe. **Swimming, speedboating** and other
watersports are available at Mindola Dam in the
Copperbelt. At Kariba houseboats can be used. Many
private clubs have **swimming** pools and clubs in Lusaka
offer facilities for **sailing**.

SPECIAL EVENTS: Events likely to be of interest to
the visitor include *Ncwala* on February 24 when the chief
of the Ngoni people tastes the first fresh fruit of the year,
the *Ku-omboka* (early Feb/Mar), when the Lozi chief
(*Litunga*) together with his entire household is paddled
up a natural canal flood plain from Leaului to Limulunga,
his residence in the rainy season. The *Livingstone Annual
Festival* takes place in March/April. In July, the *Likumbi
Lya Mize* is celebrated. On July 29, *Umutomoboko* is
celebrated by the Lunda people of Luapala Province, and
in September/October on the weekend of the full moon
Shimunenga is a ceremony of the Ba-Ila people at Maala
on the Kafue Flats.

SOCIAL CONVENTIONS: African culture and
traditions remain prominent and there are various
customs, folklore and traditional crafts in the different
regions. Traditional dancing is popular and there are
many colourful annual ceremonies that take place

throughout the country. Visitors to the outlying areas should expect to be met with curiosity. Shaking hands is the normal form of greeting. **Photography:** Visitors are able to take photographs in most places but are advised to avoid military installations. **Tipping:** A 10% sales tax is added to all bills. Tipping in hotels has been abolished by law but a 10% may be expected or included in bills elsewhere.

BUSINESS PROFILE

ECONOMY: The geographical isolation imposed by southern Rhodesia's Unilateral Declaration of Independence (UDI) in 1965, together with its landlocked position, crippled Zambia's economy during the first decade after independence (forcing it into heavy expenditure on transport to maintain its trade links) and the country has since had to struggle to achieve economic self-sufficiency, nationalising the copper mines and (with Chinese help) building a long rail link to Dar es Salaam in Tanzania. Copper has been the mainstay of the economy. The world depression of the 1970s hit copper prices badly, and the mining industry suffered from low world prices throughout the 1980s; real income per head halved between 1974 and 1980. Meanwhile, agriculture (in which 65% of the population is engaged) has been afflicted by a series of droughts, of which the 1992 one was the most serious, causing further damage to an already inefficient and poorly equipped industry. Maize and cattle are the main cash producers in this sector; the bulk of other products are earmarked for domestic consumption but are supplemented by large-scale grain imports during drought periods. Despite a slight recovery in both agriculture and world copper prices in the late 1980s, the economy has remained weak, with aid and debt rescheduling essential to sustain it. Aid is in the hands of the 'Paris Club' of Western donors who are, at least for the time being, better disposed towards the new government of Frederick Chiluba than its predecessor, to whom aid was cut off because of Kaunda's failure to adhere to previous terms agreed with the IMF. President Chiluba's administration has adopted the standard set of market-orientated reforms (subsidy cuts, trade liberalisation, privatisation) and resumed debt

repayments, as a result of which financial and development aid have been resumed. The Government has now agreed a 3-year Structural Adjustment Programme with the IMF and World Bank as a main plank of its economic programme. Zambia is a member of the Southern African Development Community (SADC). Leading trading partners are Japan, the UK and China (for exports), and Japan, South Africa, the UK and the USA (for imports).

BUSINESS: Formal dress (suit and tie) is acceptable for men at business meetings. English is widely used in business circles. **Office hours:** 0800-1300 and 1400-1700 Monday to Friday.

COMMERCIAL INFORMATION: The following organisations can offer advice: Ministry of Commerce, Trade and Industry, PO Box 31968, Kwacha Annex, Cairo Road, Lusaka. Tel: (1) 228 301 *or* 221 184. Telex: 45630; *or*
Lusaka Chamber of Commerce and Industry, PO Box 30844, Lusaka. Tel: (1) 252 369. Telex: 40124; *or*

Investment Centre, PO Box 34580, Ndeke House, Haile Selassie Avenue, Lusaka. Tel: (1) 252 130/3 *or* 252 152. Fax: (1) 252 150.
CONFERENCES/CONVENTIONS: For further information contact the Mulungushi International Conference Centre, Lusaka. Tel: (1) 292 693/4. Fax: (1) 292 696.

CLIMATE

Although Zambia lies in the tropics, the height of the plateau ensures that the climate is seldom unpleasantly hot, except in the valleys. There are three seasons: the cool, dry winter season from May to September; the hot, dry season in October and November; and the rainy season, which is even hotter, from December to April. **Required clothing:** Lightweights or tropical with rainwear.

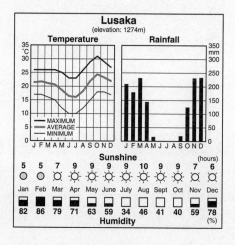

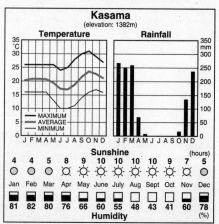

Zimbabwe

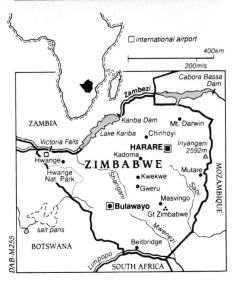

□ international airport

400km

200mls

DAB-M255

Location: Southern Africa.

Zimbabwe Tourist Development Corporation (ZTDC)
PO Box 8052, Tourism House, Jason Moo Avenue and
4th Street, Harare, Zimbabwe
Tel: (4) 793 666 *or* 706 571. Fax: (4) 793 669. Telex:
26082 (a/b ZIMTOR ZW).
High Commission for the Republic of Zimbabwe
Zimbabwe House, 429 Strand, London WC2R 0SA
Tel: (0171) 836 7755. Fax: (0171) 379 1167. Telex:
262114 *or* 262115. Opening hours: 0900-1700 Monday
to Friday; 0900-1300 Monday to Friday (Visa section).
Zimbabwe Tourist Board
Zimbabwe House, 429 Strand, London WC2R 0QE
Tel: (0171) 836 7755. Fax: (0171) 379 1167. Opening
hours: 0930-1630 Monday to Friday.
British High Commission
PO Box 4490, Stanley House, Jason Moyo Avenue,
Harare, Zimbabwe
Tel: (4) 793 781. Fax: (4) 728 380. Telex: 24607 (a/b
UKREP ZW).
Embassy of the Republic of Zimbabwe
1608 New Hampshire Avenue, NW, Washington, DC
20009
Tel: (202) 332 7100. Fax: (202) 483 9326.
Zimbabwe Tourist Office
Suite 412, 1270 Avenue of the Americas, New York, NY
10020
Tel: (212) 332 1090. Fax: (212) 332 1093.
Also deals with enquiries from Canada.
Embassy of the United States of America
PO Box 3340, 172 Herbert Chitepo Avenue, Harare,
Zimbabwe
Tel: (4) 794 521. Fax: (4) 796 488. Telex: 24591 (a/b
USUFCS ZW).
High Commission for the Republic of Zimbabwe
332 Somerset Street West, Ottawa, Ontario K2P 0J9
Tel: (613) 237 4388/9 *or* 237 4484. Fax: (613) 563 8269.
Canadian High Commission
PO Box 1430, 45 Baines Avenue, Harare, Zimbabwe
Tel: (4) 733 881-5. Fax: (4) 732 917. Telex: 24465 (a/b
CANADA ZW).

AREA: 390,759 sq km (150,873 sq miles).
POPULATION: 10,401,767 (1992 estimate).

POPULATION DENSITY: 26.6 per sq km.
CAPITAL: Harare. **Population:** 681,000 (1983
estimate).
GEOGRAPHY: Zimbabwe is bordered by Zambia to
the northwest, Mozambique to the northeast, South
Africa to the south and Botswana to the southwest. The
central zone of hills gives rise to many rivers, which
drain into the man-made Lake Kariba to the north, the
marshes of Botswana to the west or into the Zambezi
River to the northeast. The *highveld* landscape is dotted
with *kopjes* (massive granite outcrops). Along the eastern
border for some 350km (220 miles) is a high
mountainous region of great scenic beauty, rising to
2592m (8504ft) at Mount Inyangani, the country's
highest point. Zimbabwe offers some of the best wildlife
parks in southern Africa, notably Hwange (southwest),
Matapos (south) and Nyanga (northeast) national parks.
These, together with the Victoria Falls and Great
Zimbabwe, are the principal attractions for visitors.
LANGUAGE: The official languages are English and
the Shona and Ndebele dialects.
RELIGION: Christianity with traditional beliefs in rural
areas, and some Hindu and Muslim minorities.
TIME: GMT + 2.
ELECTRICITY: 220/240 volts AC, 50Hz.
COMMUNICATIONS: Telephone: Full IDD is
available. Country code: 263. Outgoing international
code: 110. **Fax:** Widely available. **Telex/telegram:**
Available at post offices and major hotels. **Post:** Airmail
to Europe takes up to a week. **Press:** The two dailies,
both in English, are *The Herald* and *The Chronicle*.
**BBC World Service and Voice of America
frequencies:** From time to time these change. See the
section *How to Use this Book* for more information.
BBC:

MHz	21.66	11.94	6.190	3.255

Voice of America:

MHz	11.97	9.670	6.040	5.995

PASSPORT/VISA

Regulations and requirements may be subject to change at short notice, and you are advised to contact the appropriate diplomatic or consular authority before finalising travel arrangements. Details of these may be found at the head of this country's entry. Any numbers in the chart refer to the footnotes below.

	Passport Required?	Visa Required?	Return Ticket Required?
Full British	Yes	No	Yes
BVP	1	-	-
Australian	Yes	No	Yes
Canadian	Yes	No	Yes
USA	Yes	No	Yes
Other EU (As of 31/12/94)	Yes	2/3	Yes
Japanese	Yes	No	Yes

PASSPORTS: Valid passport required by all.
British Visitors Passport: [1] Although the immigration
authorities of this country may in certain circumstances
accept British Visitors Passports for persons arriving for
holidays or unpaid business trips of up to 3 months,
travellers are reminded that no formal agreement exists
and the situation may, therefore, change at short notice.
In addition, UK nationals using a BVP and returning to
the UK from a country with which no such formal
agreement exists may be subject to delays and
interrogation by UK immigration officials.
VISAS: Required by all except:
(a) nationals of countries referred to in the chart above;
(b) **[2]** nationals of EU countries (except nationals of
Portugal who *do* need a visa);
(c) **[3]** nationals of all French overseas territories;
(d) nationals of Antigua & Barbuda, Bahamas, Barbados,
Belize, Botswana, Brunei, Cyprus, Dominica, Dominican
Republic, Fiji, Gambia, Ghana, Grenada, Guyana,
Iceland, Jamaica, Kenya, Kiribati, Lesotho,
Liechtenstein, Madagascar, Malawi, Malaysia, Maldives,
Malta, Mauritius, Monaco, Namibia, Nauru, Nepal, New
Caledonia, New Zealand, Norway, Papua New Guinea,
San Marino, Seychelles, Sierra Leone, Singapore,
Solomon Islands, St Lucia, Swaziland, Sweden,
Switzerland, Tanzania, Tonga, Trinidad & Tobago,
Tuvalu, Uganda, Vanuatu, Western Samoa and Zambia.
Nationals of other countries may obtain visas on arrival
in Zimbabwe, *apart from those specified below:*
Afghanistan, Albania, Algeria, Angola, Bangladesh,
Bhutan, Bulgaria, Cambodia, Cape Verde, China, CIS,
Cuba, Czech Republic, Ethiopia, Guinea-Bissau,
Hungary, India, Iran, Iraq, Israel, Laos, Lebanon, Libya,
Mali, Mongolia, Mozambique, Myanmar, Nigeria, North
Korea, Pakistan, Philippines, Portugal, Poland, Romania,
Senegal, Slovak Republic, Somalia, Sri Lanka, Sudan,
Syria, Vietnam, Yemen, Yugoslavia (Serbia and
Montenegro) and Zaïre.

Note: Visa requirements for citizens of Bosnia-
Hercegovina, Croatia, Former Yugoslav Republic of
Macedonia and Slovenia should contact the nearest
Zimbabwean diplomatic representation in order to obtain
up-to-date information on visa requirements.
Types of visa: Single-, Double- and Multiple-entry.
Cost: *Single:* US$25; *Double:* US$40; *Multiple:* US$50.
Validity: 3 months from date of issue.
Application to: Consular section at Embassy or High
Commission. For addresses, see top of entry.
Application requirements: (a) Completed application
form(s). (b) Return or onward ticket. (c) Evidence of
sufficient funds to cover the stay in Zimbabwe.
Working days required: Up to 1 week on receipt of fee
payment.
Temporary residence: Apply to Chief Immigration
Officer, Private Bag 7717, Causeway, Harare,
Zimbabwe.

MONEY

Currency: Zimbabwe Dollar (Z$) = 100 cents. Notes are
in denominations of Z$50, 20, 10, 5 and 2. Coins are in
denominations of Z$1, and 50, 20, 10, 5 and 1 cents.
Currency exchange: Major foreign currencies can be
exchanged at banks and major hotels at the official
exchange rate.
Credit cards: American Express, Diners Club and Visa
are widely accepted, whilst Access/Mastercard has more
limited use. Check with your credit card company for
details of merchant acceptability and other services
which may be available.
Travellers cheques: Banks and major hotels will
exchange these.
Exchange rate indicators: The following figures are
included as a guide to the movements of the Zimbabwe
Dollar against Sterling and the US Dollar:

Date:	Oct '92	Sep '93	Jan '94	Jan '95
£1.00=	8.25	9.92	10.22	13.08
$1.00=	5.20	6.50	6.91	8.36

Currency restrictions: The import and export of local
currency is limited to Z$250. Unrestricted import of
foreign currency, subject to declaration. The export of
foreign currency is limited to the amount declared on
import, supported by the visitor's currency declaration
form.
Banking hours: 0800-1500 Monday, Tuesday, Thursday
and Friday; 0800-1300 Wednesday and 0800-1130
Saturday.

DUTY FREE

The following items may be imported into Zimbabwe
without incurring customs duty:
*Goods up to a value of Z$2000 inclusive of tobacco,
perfume and gifts; 5 litres of alcoholic beverages (up to 2
litres of which may be spirits).*
Prohibited items: (a) The import of agricultural
products including bulbs, cuttings, cycads, eggs, fresh
meat, fruit, honey, plants, seeds and vegetables; animals,
birds and used bee-keeping equipment are prohibited. (b)
Permission for the import of non-prescribed drugs,
firearms and replicas, flick knives, lockable knives,
ammunition and explosives, indecent films and
publications, and telecommunications equipment has to
be obtained on arrival.

PUBLIC HOLIDAYS

Jan 2 '95 For New Year's Day. **Apr 14-17** Easter. **Apr
18** Independence Day. **May 1** Workers' Day. **May 25**
Africa Day. **Aug 11** Heroes' Day. **Aug 12** Armed
Forces' Day. **Dec 25-26** Christmas. **Jan 1 '96** New
Year's Day. **Apr 5-8** Easter. **Apr 18** Independence Day.

HEALTH

Regulations and requirements may be subject to change at short notice, and you are advised to contact your doctor well in advance of your intended date of departure. Any numbers in the chart refer to the footnotes below.

	Special Precautions?	Certificate Required?
Yellow Fever	No	1
Cholera	Yes	2
Typhoid & Polio	Yes	-
Malaria	3	-
Food & Drink	4	-

[1]: A yellow fever vaccination certificate is required
from travellers arriving from infected areas.
[2]: Following WHO guidelines issued in 1973, a cholera
vaccination certificate is not a condition of entry to
Zimbabwe. However, cholera is a risk in this country and

precautions are essential. Up-to-date advice should be sought before deciding whether these precautions should include vaccination, as medical opinion is divided over its effectiveness. See the *Health* section at the back of the book.

[3]: Malaria risk, predominantly in the malignant *falciparum* form, exists from November to June in all areas below 1200m and throughout the year in the Zambezi Valley. Resistance to chloroquine has been reported.

[4]: All water should be regarded as being a potential health risk. Water used for drinking, brushing teeth or making ice should have first been boiled or otherwise sterilised.

Rabies is present. For those at high risk, vaccination before arrival should be considered. If you are bitten abroad, seek medical advice without delay. For more information, consult the *Health* section at the back of the book.

Bilharzia (schistosomiasis) is present. Avoid swimming and paddling in fresh water. Swimming pools which are well-chlorinated and maintained are safe.

Health care: Medical facilities are good in the major towns and there are well-equipped clinics in most outlying areas. Health insurance is essential.

TRAVEL - International

AIR: Zimbabwe's national airline is *Air Zimbabwe (UM).*

Approximate flight time: From London to Harare is 9 hours 50 minutes (there are no direct flights connecting London with Bulawayo or Victoria Falls; connections from the capital to either take approximately 1 hour).

International airports: *Harare* (HRE) is 12km (7.5 miles) southeast of the city. Coaches run every hour 0600-2000 (travel time – 30 minutes). Taxis and full duty-free facilities are available. Airport facilities include post office (0830-1600 Monday to Friday; 0830-1130 Saturday), restaurant (1200-1430 and 1800-2230) and bank/bureau de change.

Bulawayo (BUQ) is 24km (15 miles) from the city. Limited bus and taxi services are available.

Victoria Falls (VFA) is 22km (13 miles) from the town. Limited bus and taxi services are available.

Departure tax: US$20 (non-residents) or Z$20 (residents) for all international departures. Children under 12 years are exempt.

RAIL: There are train connections from South Africa through Botswana to Bulawayo. There is a link to Zambia via Victoria Falls. Trains to Mozambique are currently suspended because of the political situation.

ROAD: There are roads from Tanzania, Malawi, South Africa, Mozambique, Botswana and Zambia. Off the main routes (Beitbridge and Victoria Falls) travel conditions are often primitive and difficult during heavy rains. For details contact the Embassy or High Commission; addresses at top of entry.

TRAVEL - Internal

AIR: Connections to Kariba, Hwange, Victoria Falls, Bulawayo, Gweru, Masvingo and Buffalo Range are run by *Air Zimbabwe (UM).*

RAIL: There are daily trains between Plumtree, Bulawayo, Victoria Falls, Harare, Mutare and Triangle, run by *National Railways of Zimbabwe.*

ROAD: There is an excellent road network, with paved roads connecting all major towns and many rural areas. Traffic drives on the left. **Bus/coach:** The *Zimbabwe United Passenger Company* provides bus services in most parts of the country. Routes via Great Zimbabwe, Masvingo, Nyanga, Rusape and Harare are run by *Express Motorways Africa (Central) Limited.* For more details contact the Tourist Board. **Car hire:** Available at airports and main hotels. **Documentation:** Zimbabwe law requires that vehicles carry identification at all times. **URBAN:** A reasonable bus service is provided in Harare by a subsidiary of the *Zimbabwe Omnibus Company.* Tickets are bought in advance from booths. There is also a local bus network in Bulawayo.

ACCOMMODATION

HOTELS: There are hotels and lodges (which are similar to guest-houses and provide bed and breakfast). A list of registered hotels is available from the Tourist Board. Non-residents must pay hotel bills in hard currency. Local currency is not acceptable even on presentation of exchange certificates. **Grading:** All hotels are graded on a 5-star system, with those classified 1-star or above being registered with the Tourist Board. Over 70 hotels are registered. Further information can be obtained from the Hotel and Restaurants Association of Zimbabwe, 9th Floor, Travel Centre, Jason Moyo

Avenue, Harare. Tel: (4) 733 211. Fax: (4) 26698.
CAMPING/CARAVANNING: Most centres and tourist areas have caravan parks and campsites.

RESORTS & EXCURSIONS

Nowhere else on the continent is there such a balance between wilderness and civilisation as exists in Zimbabwe. The best months to visit are from July to October. For details contact the Tourist Board.

The Highveld

Running from northeast to southwest down the centre of the country, and connecting its two largest cities, this chain of low mountains is Zimbabwe's most populous area.

Harare: Formerly Salisbury, the capital is Zimbabwe's commercial and industrial centre and also the usual starting point for any visit. It is a clean and sophisticated city, characterised by flowering trees, colourful parks and contemporary architecture. Local sightseeing includes the modern museum and art gallery, the *Robert McIlwaine Recreational Park*, which has a lake and game reserve, the *Lion & Cheetah Park*, the *Larvon Bird Gardens* and the landscaped gardens of aloes and cycads at *Ewanrigg Botanical Gardens*. Because of its sunny climate, Harare is known as the 'Sunshine City'.

Bulawayo: Zimbabwe's second city is a major commercial, industrial and tourist centre. The city is rich in historical associations and is the home of the *National Museum* and headquarters of the National Railways of Zimbabwe. Nearby are the ancient *Khami ruins*, while to the south is the **Rhodes Matopos National Park**, notable for its exotic formations of huge granite boulders. Dams with excellent fishing, caves with rock paintings, Cecil Rhodes' grave and a well-stocked game park make this area popular with visitors.

Parks & Wildlife

From the forested mountains of the Eastern highlands to the sun-washed grasslands of Hwange National Park, from the hot Mopani Forest to the shores of Lake Kariba, more than 11% of Zimbabwe's land – 44,688 sq km (17,254 sq miles) – has been set aside as parks and wildlife estates. There are ten national parks and ten recreational parks around the country, plus several botanical gardens, sanctuaries and 14 national safari areas for hunting (which helps to finance the conservation programme and is strictly controlled).

Hwange (formerly Wankie) **National Park** is Zimbabwe's largest national park, both in size, 14,620 sq km (5,644 sq miles), and in the variety of animals and birds that may be seen. From the three camps, networks of game-viewing roads guide visitors to areas with good animal concentrations and to waterholes where, in the evenings, great numbers of wild animals congregate. At some waterholes platforms are erected where one can observe game closely and in safety. Hwange is one of the last of the great elephant sanctuaries in Africa and herds of up to 100 elephants may be seen drinking and bathing at the waterholes, particularly at the end of the dry season in September.

120km (75 miles) from the Hwange National Park are the **Victoria Falls**, the largest waterfalls in the world – 2.5km (1.5 miles) wide, 550 million litres of water plunge every minute 100m (330ft) into a narrow chasm; the spray can be seen 30km (20 miles) away. To gain an overall impression of the Falls, the 'Flight of the Angels' light plane trip is a must, as is a cruise up the mighty Zambezi River. It is possible to walk across to Zambia (with the minimum of formalities) to view from the other side; this is also highly recommended, for the Falls are without a doubt one of the world's grandest natural spectacles and every viewpoint reveals something new. Nearby is the **Zambezi National Park,** where sable antelopes and other exotic animals graze in a parkland setting.

Mana Pools National Park is one of Zimbabwe's most beautiful national parks, occupying 2196 sq km (848 sq miles) of forest along the shores of the Zambezi River. The animal population includes hippo, elephant, rhino, buffalo and many types of antelope. Game-viewing on foot is allowed. The birdlife along the river and in the bush is particularly prolific. It is possible to fish for tigerfish, bream and the giant vundu.

Lake Kariba, in the northwest of the country on the Zambian border, covers 7770 sq km (3000 sq miles) and holds a million gallons of water. Game can be viewed from the luxury of the *Bumi Hills Safari Lodge*, the comfort of various safari camps, or from well-appointed cruise vessels and self-contained safari-crafts.

A holiday in Zimbabwe would be incomplete without a visit to the **Great Zimbabwe National Monument.** This

forms the largest complex of ruins in Africa south of the pyramids in Egypt. The *Main Enclosure*, or *Temple*, has walls over 9m (30ft) tall, 4m (14ft) thick and over 228m (250 yards) in circumference, giving approximately 485,521 cubic metres (635,000 cubic ft) of hand-trimmed mortarless stonework. The remains are what is left of a city-state that flourished between the 13th and 15th centuries, trading in gold. **Lake Kyle National Park** is not far away; there is a well-organised campsite close to the lake.

Note: For safety reasons, visitors may not enter any national park by motorcycle.

The Eastern Highlands

The *Inyanga, Vumba* and *Chimanimani* mountain ranges are one of the country's principal holiday areas for both Zimbabweans and tourists and are ideal for those who want to relax and enjoy crisp mountain air. The country's highest mountain, *Inyangani* (2592m/8504ft), is in this area. The scenery is striking in its variety, with deep valleys, gorges, bare granite peaks, pine-forested slopes and bubbling trout streams rolling down to steep cliffs. There are challenging hilly golf courses and pony rides through the heather, as well as the opportunity for mountain climbing, squash, tennis, bowls, fishing, snooker and gambling in the casino. Because of the mountainous and forested terrain, game-viewing in this region is more a matter of chance but for the lucky there are leopards and rare forest antelopes.

SOCIAL PROFILE

FOOD & DRINK: Zimbabwe is a cosmopolitan society and enjoys both local and international cuisine. Eating out is popular and comparatively cheap. Meat dishes are usually excellent. A traditional dish is *sadza* (a stiff maize meal) eaten with meat and/or gravy and a relish. Table service is the norm in restaurants. **Drink:** Beer is the most widely drunk alcoholic beverage. Imported wines, spirits and liqueurs are available in hotels. Traditional maize beer, *whawha*, is made in large quantities on special occasions. Public bars are almost always part of a hotel. Licensing hours in Zimbabwe are 1030-1500 and 1630-2300. Major hotels have 24-hour bars and room service.

NIGHTLIFE: Rather limited outside the cities with the emphasis on eating and discos, but larger cities have nightclubs, cinemas and repertory theatres. The three main tourist areas have casinos.

SHOPPING: A sales tax of 10-22% is added to all purchases, the higher rate being on luxury items, except those which are to be exported. Special purchases are copper, wooden and soapstone carvings, gameskin and leather products, pottery and basketwork. **Shopping hours:** 0800-1700 Monday to Friday and 0800-1300 Saturday.

SPORT: Football and **cricket** are the national sports, while **tennis, squash, riding, rugby** and **hockey** are also very popular. For the more adventurous there are clubs for **hang-gliding, water-skiing, windsurfing** and **parachuting.**

SPECIAL EVENTS: Apr/May '95 *Zimbabwe Trade Fair*, Bulawayo. **Early Aug** *International Book Fair*.

SOCIAL CONVENTIONS: Urban culture in Zimbabwe is greatly influenced by Western culture and education but in rural areas traditional values and crafts continue. Shaking hands is the customary form of greeting. European courtesies and codes of practice should be observed when visiting someone's home. Return invitations are appreciated. Giving a token of

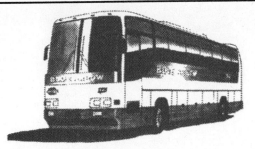

FRONTIERS

r a f t i n g

Cecil House
95 Jason Moyo Avenue
P.O. Box 4876
Harare, Zimbabwe
Tel: (+263)-4-732911/732948
Tel/Fax: 704759
Telex: 26022 Mosi ZW

Frontiers Rafting aims to maintain our high standards of professionalism and promises to provide the adventure tourist with a white water rafting experience which rates as one of Zimbabwe's premier attractions.

Various packages can also be put together that offer the adventure tourist a wide range of safari activities throughout Zimbabwe. The following are some of the activities which can be booked:

RIVER CRUISES (Upper Zambezi)
CANOEING SAFARIS (Upper Zambezi)
BUNGI JUMPING (Victoria Falls Bridge)

Detailed information on all of the above will be forwarded upon request.
Frontiers are also the organisers of the world-famous Zambezi River Festival held in Victoria Falls every year.

appreciation is optional. Casual wear is suitable for daytime and men are only expected to wear suits and ties for business meetings. Smart restaurants or hotel bars require male guests to wear a jacket and tie. Smoking is common, although it is prohibited on public transport and in some public buildings. **Tipping:** A 10-15% tip is usual.

BUSINESS PROFILE

ECONOMY: Zimbabwe is fortunate in its strong agricultural base, which did not suffer so badly from the drought problems which afflicted much of the rest of the continent. Tobacco and other cash crops, including sugar, coffee, cotton, tea and groundnuts, are key export earners. In addition, Zimbabwe exports high-quality beef to the EU under the terms of the Lomé Convention (which governs trade between the EU and the ACP – African, Caribbean and Pacific – countries). The mining industry is also important with chromium, copper, tungsten and asbestos produced for export. Large coal deposits supply the country's power stations. Other minerals are processed before being exported: ferro-chrome and refined gold are examples. The manufacturing industry is well-developed by regional standards, significantly as the result of import substitution projects set up while international trade sanctions were applied against Rhodesia during UDI. The Government has identified the manufacturing sector as the key for guaranteeing sustained economic growth in the future: this offers one of the best opportunities for British exporters, since much of Zimbabwean industry relies on very old equipment which needs replacing. Zimbabwe remains somewhat dependent on South Africa economically, both for imports of manufactured goods and for seaports (Zimbabwe is landlocked) to transport exports, and the Government has taken Zimbabwe into the Southern African Development Co-ordination Conference which aims to reduce South African economic domination of the region. Nonetheless, the economy is fairly strong – GDP growth is around 4% per annum – and its prospects are reasonably bright if the country can survive the present crisis caused by drought and a

chronic shortage of foreign exchange which hinders the importation of goods needed for expansion and development. A 5-year programme agreed with the IMF commits Zimbabwe to reducing government controls throughout the economy in exchange for financial assistance. Economic issues currently dominate the domestic political arena: trade liberalisation, which is being introduced after three years of debate, and land reform are the most important of these. Import quotas are being replaced by a general license system. Main export markets: Germany, Japan, the UK and the USA. Main import sources: South Africa, the UK, the USA and Germany.
BUSINESS: Normal courtesies should be observed and men should wear a suit and tie. The atmosphere will generally be less formal than in many European countries. **Office hours:** 0800-1630 Monday to Friday.
COMMERCIAL INFORMATION: The following organisations can offer advice: Ministry of Industry & Commerce, Private Bag 7708, 12-14th Floor, Mukwati

Building, 4th Street, Causeway, Harare. Tel: (4) 702 731. Telex: 24472; *or*
Zimbabwe National Chambers of Commerce, PO Box 1934, Equity House, Rezende Street, Harare. Tel: (4) 753 444. Fax: (4) 753 450. Telex: 22531.
CONFERENCES/CONVENTIONS: Contact the Zimbabwe Tourist Development Corporation. For address, see top of entry.

CLIMATE

Although located in the tropics, temperate conditions prevail all year, moderated by altitude and the inland position of the country. The hot and dry season is from September to October, and the rainy season from November to March. The best months to visit are April to May and August to September.
Required clothing: Tropical lightweights and rainwear for the wet season.

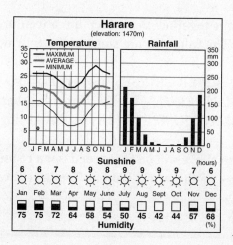

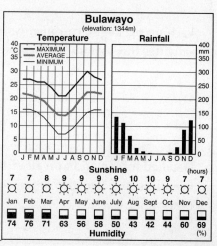

Diving

DIVE TRAVEL AND THE TRAVEL AGENT

Dive travel is a very lucrative, yet specialised field. Recreational scuba divers travel all over the world experiencing a variety of popular, and not so popular, diving destinations.

However, there are many aspects to dive travel that the typical travel agent may not be aware of. For instance, did you know that dive travellers must wait at least 24 hours after their last dive before flying home?

Much of this information can be obtained by visiting a local PADI dive centre. PADI International encourages travel agents to visit these local dive operations to develop on-going business relationships. There are many aspects to dive travel that PADI professionals can share with travel agents. Likewise, there are aspects to travel that agents can share with dive operations. Working together, the customer receives a quality dive vacation at an affordable price. Everyone wins.

A PRIMER ON A TRAVEL SEGMENT THAT SELLS

by W. Lynn Seldon Jr.

Scuba diving and dive travel sell. Smart travel agents throughout the world are exploring the dive travel market and earning big commissions from this exploding travel trend. It is just a matter of learning the basics of scuba diving, dive travel and the specific marketing methods needed to sell trips.

Scuba diving is one of the fastest-growing outdoor sports and travel trends in the world. Last year, more than 560,000 people became new certified divers through the Professional Association of Diving Instructors (PADI), the largest certifying agency in the world. That makes more than 5 million divers worldwide and many more to follow.

These numbers mean certified divers and those who want to learn to dive can be a big market to travel agents. The sport of scuba diving recently celebrated its 50th anniversary and it is an ideal time for travel agents to be selling dive travel.

"The increase in the number of divers and those getting certified means a large increase in dive travel," says Professional Association of Diving Instructors (PADI) communications specialist Scott Jones. "It's a great market for travel agents. Travel is one of the primary reasons that people are attracted to scuba diving."

DIVE BASICS

The basics of scuba (Self-Contained Underwater Breathing Apparatus) are surprisingly simple. Divers use specialised modern equipment that adapts to the aquatic environment. Scuba equipment provides a portable air supply that allows divers to spend an extended time underwater (from a few minutes to several hours, depending on factors like depth and breathing efficiency).

The tank is a high-pressure cylinder that stores plain old compressed air – never oxygen – that is released with a valve. This passes through a regulator to deliver a controlled amount of air when you inhale. A gauge lets you monitor the air supply.

The tank and regulator are typically held in place by a buoyancy control device (BCD), an expandable bladder that can be inflated or deflated to control a diver's buoyancy. The mask is the window to the underwater world, creating an air space which allows divers to see.

Fins allow you to move through the water with far less effort and far greater efficiency. A weight belt is also worn to allow you to sink.

A snorkel is attached to the mask and allows divers to breathe at the surface without having to lift their heads. Snorkelling offers an introduction to the wonders of the underwater world and often leads to a desire to try scuba diving.

Divers must complete a certification process to take advantage of dive travel opportunities around the world. There are three general ways of getting certified. Everything can be completed locally through a dive store or independent instructor. Another popular

method is to complete the classroom and pool sessions locally and then finish the open water part on a warm-weather (commissionable) vacation. The entire certification process can also be completed at some exotic (and fully-commissionable) dive destination.

The certification process is interesting and easy. It is divided into three parts, stretched over approximately thirty hours: classroom (using a book and visual aids), pool (confined water), and open-water instruction.

The classroom and pool sessions generally take place at the same time, while the open-water dives (at least four of them) serve as a test of all skills. The classroom time demystifies much of the matter that tends to scare people about diving. New divers learn that diving is far less risky than skiing and that sunburn, and not a shark, is usually the greatest danger facing divers.

By the end of the first class, most people are ready to hit the pool. The pool time is often filled with a bunch of awkward underwater virgins banging into each other. By the second time in the pool, however, everyone looks like the Cousteau family exploring the pool for underwater treasure. During the pool sessions, people practise breathing efficiently, removing and replacing masks, buddy breathing (using another

diver's breathing apparatus), removing and replacing tanks, and much more.

The only thing needed to jump right in is good health, desire, and reasonable comfort level with water. The pool sessions even turn out to be fun, as divers learn new skills and develop confidence in their ability to have fun while getting wet.

The open-water dives are usually completed at a popular local dive site, where all scuba skills are reviewed and tested. After completing a final written exam, anyone can become an underwater god (and a dive travel client). Most instructors recommend that clients buy the following for the certification course: booties ($25-60); fins ($40-125); mask ($40-90); snorkel ($15-45); and weight belt ($10-60). Renting tanks of air usually runs from $5-20. The cost of getting certified can range from $150-400.

The largest certifying organisation in the world is the Professional Association of Diving Instructors (PADI). A certification card from PADI means clients can rent or buy scuba equipment, obtain air for tanks, and participate in other exciting diving activities throughout the world. Your client should never leave home without it.

DEFINING DIVE TRAVEL

Dive travel is big business. Continued interest in active travel and the environment has caused a boom in the dive travel business. Dive travel is now a billion-dollar business and growing rapidly, according to the Diving Equipment and Marketing Association (DEMA).

Dive travel is loosely defined as a vacation with scuba diving as a small or large part of the overall travel plan. The quantity and quality of resorts and dive travel opportunities have grown astronomically in the last decade, giving agents many possibilities when it comes to booking trips for clients.

The resulting packages can result in big commissions. "Travel agents who pursue dive travel bookings quickly learn that their commission virtually doubles when they sell a dive-package vacation," says Ron Kipp, owner of *Bob Soto's Diving* on Grand Cayman.

This means smart agents are learning about diving, dive travel, and how to market it. It is just a matter of taking the time to understand the basics and going after the business.

THE DEMOGRAPHICS OF DIVING AND DIVE TRAVEL

By Lynn Seldon

A little research makes it easy for travel agents to find potential clients in the dive travel segment. Many prospects are already existing clients, while others are easy to locate through a variety of national and local resources.

"People who enjoy walking, running, tennis, cycling, golf, hunting, hiking, snow and water skiing, fishing and even bridge gravitate to diving," says Sean Combs, editor of *Dive Training,* a leading US magazine for new divers covering dive education and dive travel.

DIVER DEMOGRAPHICS

The most recent study performed by the Professional Association of Diving Instructors (PADI) reveals much about divers and dive travel. Their statistics can be used by travel agents to find divers, in that they typically certify nearly 70% of all divers in the USA.

PADI's study revealed today's divers are young, educated and affluent. Women comprise about one-third

of those recently certified and represent an ideal market for agents. There are also large numbers of diving couples, making for efficient contacts by agents. More than 70% of new divers are between the ages of 18 and 34. While there are obviously many older and more veteran divers, the sport and resulting travel seem to draw a younger audience.

Divers are definitely interested in other sports and active travel opportunities. Only 10% say that diving is their 'top' activity, but one-third say they enjoy diving along with one or two other activities. This means agents can contact active clients and prospects to see if they dive or want to learn during their next vacation.

Divers are equally divided in marital status. Married divers may be more interested in dive travel that accommodates the entire family. Singles may have more disposable income and interest in more exotic dive travel. In terms of income, divers are generally in an elite group. More than half report annual household income of greater than $50,000 and more than 15% report income in excess of $100,000. That means divers have the money to spend on dive travel.

Divers typically learn about diving and dive travel through other divers. More than 75% try snorkelling before diving. Once they see the potential of diving, most people want to get a certification and take dive vacations. PADI found that the 'quality of diving' is the greatest influence on the selection of diving destinations, while price is less of a concern. Dive travellers tend to be serious about good diving and are willing to pay for it. While dive instructors and retail shop personnel greatly influence equipment purchases, they are not the prime resource for dive travel recommendations. This leads to a great opportunity for travel agents who combine their destination experience, industry insight, and dive travel demographics to get the business.

DIVING IN

These demographic figures make it easy for agents to understand dive travel prospects. Many existing clients may already be divers or may be very interested in getting certified locally or during a vacation. They are ideal targets for dive vacation packages.

With this demographic knowledge, agents can locate and market packages to new divers, existing divers, and those who are interested in trying diving and dive travel. Dive industry leaders all agree that it is a virtually untapped

resource for travel agencies.

Diving can turn prospects into clients. Local and national adventure travel organisations, ski clubs, dive shops, diving publications, and many other entities can provide lists of many prospects. It is just a matter of diving in.

Professional Association of Diving Instructors

BACKGROUND

The Professional Association of Diving Instructors (PADI) was founded in 1967. Since that time, the organisation has issued more than 5 million scuba certifications.

With its headquarters in Santa Ana, California, PADI International's primary mission is to promote and educate the public about recreational scuba diving in a safe and enjoyable fashion.

PADI International services 110 countries and territories from its Santa Ana facility. Eight Local Area Offices service remaining areas around the globe. PADI services are currently available in more than 175 countries worldwide.

In 1993, PADI International issued more than 560,000 scuba certifications. Domestically, seven out of every ten divers enrolling in a scuba course enrol in a PADI course, taught by a PADI Instructor.

DIVER EDUCATION

PADI promotes and educates the public about scuba diving through PADI-affiliated dive centres and professional members (instructors, divemasters and assistant instructors). Each member has met strict standards for training and professionalism.

There are currently more than 2500 PADI dive centres worldwide. These dive stores are part of the dive industry's largest trade association, the PADI Retail Association. In 1993, there were more than 55,000 PADI professional dive educators.

PADI's Open Water Diver Course was the first performance-based, modular scuba diving course offered to new divers. The course has become the standard for diver education throughout the world. PADI courses have been recommended for college credit by the American Council on Education. No other diver training programme has received this recognition. The strength of PADI's educational system is its consistency. Students taking PADI courses anywhere in the world must meet the same performance standards and demonstrate the same techniques and diving knowledge. This consistency allows divers to build on skills and diving knowledge with each PADI course they take, regardless of who their PADI instructor may be.

SERVING THE DIVE INDUSTRY

PADI maintains an extensive staff of specialists in various fields, all working in tandem to provide the latest in high-quality diver education and instructional products.

PADI has developed several organisations designed to concentrate on providing service to various facets of the diving industry. These include:

PADI Retail Association – more than 2300 dive stores that meet all areas of dive consumers' needs. These include education, equipment and dive travel.

PADI International Resort Association – provides dive resorts, operators, hotels and other travel-related organisations a support system within the industry.

PADI Industry Resource Network – provides data for the dive industry through surveys of certified divers, manufacturers travellers and dive travel wholesalers.

FOR MORE INFORMATION:

PADI's Marketing department can provide additional information or answer any other questions. Please contact Scott D. Jones, Communications Specialist, PADI International, 1251 E. Dyer Road, #100, Santa Ana, California 92705-5605. Tel: (714) 540 7234 ext. 236. Fax: (714) 540 2609.

DIVE CANOUAN

Dive Canouan, located at the Tamarind Beach Hotel, offers snorkel and dive tours, boat trips, SCUBA certificaton courses and watersport activities. A complete selection of equipment is available for purchase or rental on a daily or weekly basis. Rendezvous service and boat trips to Tobago Cays, Mayreau and Palm Island are also on offer. Dive packages available.

Dive Canouan, Tamarind Beach Hotel, PO Box 530, Canouan, St. Vincent, West Indies. Tony Alongi – Owner/Operator. Tel: (809) 458 8648. Fax: (809) 458 8851.

GRENADINES DIVE

Grenadines Dive at Sunny Grenadines Hotel on Union Island offers a full range of dive and snorkel tours, day trips, full resort certification, and advanced SCUBA diving courses. Equipment rental by the day or week is available, or you can purchase your own new equipment. Also offered are rendezvous service and boat trips to Tobago Cays, Mayreau, Palm Island, Petit St. Vincent and Canouan. Dive packages available.

Grenadines Dive, Sunny Grenadines Hotel, Union Island, St. Vincent, West Indies. Glenroy Adams – Owner/Operator. Tel: (809) 458 8138 Work. Tel: (809) 458 8122 Home. Fax: (809) 458 8122.

DIVE ST. VINCENT

Dive St. Vincent offers one-and two-tank dives from 3 dive boats. Night dives, day trips to Bequia and the Falls of Baleine, resort certification and full certification courses are offered in NAUI, PADI and CMAS. Underwater camera rental is also available. Dive packages available.

Dive St. Vincent Young Island Dock St. Vincent, West Indies. Bill Tewes – Owner/Operator. Tel: (809) 457 4928. (809) 457 4714 Fax: (809) 457 4948.

DIVE PACKAGES CAN BE MIXED BETWEEN ALL 3 SHOPS, PARTICULARLY GOOD WHEN SAILING.

Travel Agents! Your Clients Won't Dive in at the Deep End!

.....They'll simply thank you for sending them to **South Africa's** Best for Beginners

"South Africa is set to become the holiday capital of the World" Independent TV's "Holiday Programme" 13th September 1994 (UK)

•What we do.........
provide some of the best diving in the world, in a **PADI-5 Star** centre with underwater scenic adventures rated amongst the top ten in the world by Signature Magazine. Suitable for beginners and experienced divers alike.

•Why the Whaler?.........
everything we do is guaranteed to provide safety coupled with enjoyment. Your clients will thank you for sending them here and will return to you again and again for their South African holiday.

•Where we are.........
in Umkomaas, five hours from Johannesburg and fifteen minutes from Paradise.

•What we'll give you.........
very generous commissions for substantial business you provide us!

To find out more call:
Mickey Louw **Tel: (27) 323 31562/3**
After hours: (27) 323 732253
Fax: (27) 323 31564

Now.........
as bookings are limited for the coming year

PADI Resort Association Member

The Whaler Dive Centre, Roland Norris Drive, Umkomaas P.O. Box 1327, Umkomaas 4170, South Africa.

NAUI

National Association of Underwater Instructors

BACKGROUND

Formed over 30 years ago, NAUI is an international training giant supporting the teaching of thousands of courses and the leading of millions of diving experiences in countries around the globe.

Growing from a small group of industrial experts, NAUI today is the largest democratic diving instructor membership organisation in the world.

Dedicated to its motto, 'Safety Through Education', NAUI has led more than 2 million students through fun and challenging dive courses.

DIVER EDUCATION

Planning your annual vacation getaway? Then plan on getting wet with the NAUI Passport Diver Programme. In just a few hours, you can be scuba diving among the coral gardens of an exotic isle under the caring guidance of a NAUI instructor. You will still have plenty of relaxing time for all your other favourite vacation activities. Moreover, once you have taken your initial Passport Diver Training, you may continue to dive for up to 12 months at any one of the many NAUI resorts around the world. As an added bonus, you can apply your passport diving experiences toward a full NAUI Scuba Diver Certificate (minimum age 12).

FOR MORE INFORMATION

NAUI's Marketing Department can provide information or answer any other questions. Please contact Kathleen Moon, National Association of Underwater Instructors (NAUI), PO Box 14650, Montclair, California 91763, USA. Tel: (909) 621 5801. Fax: (909) 621 6405.

British Sub Aqua Club

The British Sub Aqua Club (BSAC) is the governing body for Sub Aqua Diving in Britain with over 40 years' experience in diver training. It is the largest diving club in the world with over 50,000 members and 1400 branches worldwide. The BSAC diver training programme has evolved with the changing developments in equipment and diving knowledge, and is recognised as the leading sports diver training agency.

Whether abroad or in the UK, learning to dive with the BSAC could not be simpler; the worldwide network of schools and branches both provide the same high standard of diver training, starting with the Novice Diver course which can be completed over a weekend.

BSAC have schools at all the major diving locations, offering both novice and more advanced diver training courses. For further information on BSAC schools and branches, telephone BSAC Headquarters on (0151) 357 1951 and ask for an information pack on learning to dive.

DIVING ORGANISATIONS

The following resorts and dive operators all offer education and vacations for both the professional and first-time diver. For more information on any resort, please contact the organisation directly.

National Association of Underwater Instructors (NAUI)
PO Box 14650, Montclair, California 91763
Tel: (909) 621 5801. Fax: (909) 621 6405.

PADI International
1251 E. Dyer Road, #100, Santa Ana, California 92705-5605
Tel: (714) 540 7234 ext. 236. Fax: (714) 540 2609.

PADI International Resort Association
Unit 6, Unicorn Park, Whitby Road, Bristol BS4 4EX, UK
Tel: (0117) 971 1717. Fax: (0117) 971. 0400.

The British Sub Aqua Club
Telford's Quay, Ellesmere Port, South Wirral, Cheshire

L65 4FY. Tel: (0151) 357 1951. Fax: (0151) 357 1250.

Deep Sea Divers Den
319 Draper Street, Cairns, Queensland 4870, Australia
Tel: (70) 312223. Fax: (70) 311210.

Out Island Divers
Tel: (303) 586 6020. Fax: (303) 586 6124.

Aquanauts Ltd.
PO Box 30147, Grand Cayman, BWI
Tel: 945 1990. Fax: 945 1991.

Brac Aquatics
PO Box 273781, Tampa, FL 33688-3781, USA
Tel: (813) 962 2236. Fax: (813) 264 2742.

Cydive
1 Poseidon Avenue, Kato Paphos, Cyprus
Tel: (6) 234 271. Fax: (6) 235 307.

St Andrew's Divers Cove
St Simon Street, Xlendi Bay, Island of Gozo, Malta
Tel: 55 13 01. Fax: 56 15 48.

Strand Diving Services
PO Box 20, Church Street, St Paul's Bay, SPBOI, Malta
Tel: 574 502. Fax: 577 480.

Siam Diving Centre
121/9 Patak Road, Mu 4 Karon, 83100 Phukat, Thailand
Tel: (76) 330 936. Fax: (76) 330 608.

Samui International Diving School
PO Box 40, Koh Samui, 84140 Surat Thani, Thailand
Tel: (77) 421 465 or 421 056. Fax: (77) 421 465.

Sam's Dive Tours
PO Box 428, Koror 96940, Republic of Palau
Tel: 488 1720. Fax: 488 1471.

Turtle Inn Divers
PO Box 152, Providenciales, Turks & Caicos Islands, BWI
Tel: 941 5389.

Dive Center Corralejo
PO Box 29, 35660 Corralejo, Fuerteventura, Canary Islands, Spain
Tel/Fax: (28) 866 243.

Granada Sub (Centro de Buceo)
Paseo Andrés Segovia 6, 18697 La Herradura, Granada, Spain
Tel: (58) 827 944. Fax: (58) 827 945.

Bud n' Mary's Dive Center
PO Box 1126, Islamorada, Florida Keys 33036
Tel: (1 800) 344 7352 (toll free).

Note: Refer to the respective country sections for further publicity information on the above.

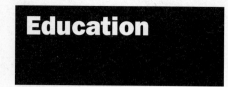

Education

TRAINING IN TOURISM

by Mike Taylor, Principal Lecturer, University of Brighton

Many writers may lead you to believe that travel and tourism is one of the 'new' industries of the 20th century. Although true in one sense, man has always travelled for both work and pleasure. The thing that has changed is that travel and tourism is now widely available and is not a luxury restricted to the rich and elite. In response to this socio-economic development, education and training have evolved quite rapidly in nearly all sectors.

Technology, especially in the area of transport, has had a major effect on the distances customers are able to travel. This has had a significant impact on the cost of transport and the subsequent price charged to the customer. During the last three decades the world has shrunk. In terms of accessibility, destinations previously too far away are now within reach.

This increase in accessibility to new destinations, plus the increase in disposable income that allows people to make economic choices has led to a massive growth not only on the demand side, but also on the supply end of the economic equation. Employment in the tourism industry has seen growth in both the developing countries and in the traditional manufacturing countries of the northern hemisphere. By the 1970s the UK had 1.4 million people, out of a working population of 24 million, working within the industry. This is still forecast to grow as the industry continues to expand. Education and training was a low priority in nearly every sector of the industry up to and including the 1970s. In sectors with little or no regulations, travel agency especially, training was almost non-existent. The only area that provided any formal training was the hotel and catering industry where there has been a long tradition, particularly in the kitchen craft area, of both 'on the job' and 'off the job' training.

In the regulated sector, specifically the transport areas, where safety is a high priority, education and training have been requirements. Airports, airlines and railways particularly, have invested large amounts of funds in technical training. Most of these sectors require qualifications either in GCE Advanced level subjects or a vocational degree.

From the 1970s the public sector, through the further education colleges and the three training boards, ie Road Transport Industry Training Board, Air Transport & Travel Industry Training Board and Hotel & Catering Industry Training Board started to respond to the growth in both employment and the demands of the industry. Most of the training introduced was at a low technical operative level, with some element of transferable skill.

The Further Education sector continued to develop the vocational Hotel & Catering courses they had provided for many years. Seven colleges offered 2-year business studies courses with a travel and tourism context. These centres were the embryonics for the mass course provision that occurred during the 1980s. At the higher level there was some provision for hotel and catering and transport, but very little in travel or tourism.

Trade courses came on stream rapidly. Notable introductions were the national syllabus for tourist guides known as the 'blue badge'. This was adopted across the 13 English regions and has a version in Wales and Scotland. The other major introduction was the ATTIB course and examination called COTAC, the Certificate of Travel Agency Competence. This highly successful format of COTAC became the blueprint for professional competency examinations in tourist offices, tour operating and travel management.

Full-time provision grew very rapidly during the 1980s. Hotel and catering courses went through a number of reviews. The focus moved from craft skills to business skills. The popular BTEC National qualification in Travel & Tourism, equivalent to three GCE A-levels, was offered at over 100 further education colleges. The

qualification became widely accepted by the travel trade. It was the first really academic qualification of an approved national standard to have both trade and higher education acceptance.

Simultaneously the Government supported trade and industry with grants for training courses. Nearly all sectors of the industry took up the opportunity and developed the Youth Training Service programmes. Some areas were more successful than others. The Association of British Travel Agents' National Training Board launched a very successful and nationally-approved 2-year YTS course. These continue to date, revised and reformed, providing basic skill training in various sectors of the industry. It was not until the 1980s that the polytechnics started to develop degree courses outside the hotel and catering provision which had been in operation for some time. The travel and tourism degree course was rooted in the BTEC/HND Business Studies programmes which had a 'travel' option. By the mid 1980s some 28 polytechnics offered not only degrees in hotel catering and tourism, but also in areas like museum, exhibition and leisure centre management.

The move into the 1990s has seen that all areas of the tourism industry have well-established training and educational programmes. The whole area has now gained academic credence which has been hard fought for in a world where it can take centuries to establish a discipline with rigour. Recognition of tourism as an area of study has finally been established with the development of post-graduate courses. Although a number have existed for quite a few years they have been a minority. With a range of MSc, MA and MBA now on offer to the market from those universities having focused on Hospitality Management and on Tourism, the industry in education training terms has 'come of age'.

In an industry that is dynamic, one could not imagine that training and education would stand still for long. Review and re-thinking about how and what we do in training and education is now taking place. The Government focus on vocational education in the 1990s has re-enforced the importance of the hospitality and tourism industries. The introduction by the Government of the new National Vocational Qualifications (NVQ) has been taken up, to varying degrees by the industry. The aim is to establish industry lead standards of competencies at designated levels. These levels start at one, the basic, extending through to five, the highest level of competency.

The NVQ comes in two forms, largely dependent on whether it is undertaken 'on the job' or at college full-time. The college version is called the General National Vocational Qualification (GNVQ) and has the added value of transferable skill development and some level of academic outcome. Although both GNVQ and NVQ have had mixed reactions from both the public and private sectors of the hospitality and tourism industries their evolution and recognition are set for the future.

The trade has not become complacent with regard to the issue of employers being economic resources. 'Welcome Host', a training course in customer care, taken on first by the Wales Tourist Board a few years ago, is now in its second year with the English Tourist Board. This significant initiative is aimed at developing the awareness of all staff in all sectors of the importance of customer care and is a national programme aimed at providing a nationally recognised standard of training that can be identified by employees, employers and customers alike. Some 19,000 employees have already been exposed to the one-day course.

The respective professional bodies and trade associations continue to use a combination of public sector full/part certificated courses and their own specific technically orientated courses. The diverse, fragmented nature of the hospitality, travel and tourism industry makes this inevitable. It is indeed a maze for both employee and employer. The one redeeming feature is that the industry at all levels is now beginning to take training and education seriously and there appears to be a wide range of courses and qualifications to meet the need.

What has always been considered the 'Cinderella' of the hospitality and tourism industry is the language training. Right across British industry language training has been an issue that has provoked discussion. Initiatives have come and gone, but as yet the language base of the commercial sector of industry has not, in real terms, been taken seriously.

This is reflected in the Government's changing policies towards language education and training in our schools and colleges. Not only does controversy rage about how it should be taught, but which languages should dominate the schools timetables. Traditionalists still hang on to French, German and Italian, and economists might suggest that this is the right path. Re-actionists refer to the economics of the world rather than the continent, identifying national growth rates and economic development. Chinese and Japanese are often sited as the languages to learn for the future. More visionary people suggest Spanish or Portuguese as the languages to learn, because of the latent economic potential of South America.

The British colonial past has not helped to develop a national motivation to learn foreign languages. A quarter of the world population came under the influence of the English language during this colonial period. The second invasion through pop music and fast food has re-enforced English as a cross-frontier language. The travel trade, especially in the maritime and air sectors, have long used English as their formal means of communication. This continues to underpin English as both the formal and informal language of world tourism. The motivation of the British to learn foreign languages is still acutely impaired by the widespread use of English in the rest of the world.

However, that cannot be said for the 'English as a Foreign Language' provision. Here we have seen large-scale growth both in the demand for courses and in the range of courses offered by the public and private sectors. Global markets, international distribution systems and worldwide satellite, radio and television are all dominated by English language companies which has enhanced the importance of the need to read and speak English.

Many south coastal towns like Brighton, Bournemouth and Hastings become international language teaching centres during the late spring and summer months. In Eastbourne it is estimated that on any one night in the summer the town hosts up to 14,000 overseas students learning English. The British Council recognises formally 200 public and private institutions as providers of 'English as a Foreign Language'. These schools are rigorously inspected yearly against five established criteria. The quality of English language residential education has now been assured to some extent. However, like the tourism and hospitality industry it suffers from a maze of examining boards, levels and examinations.

It is doubtful whether any industry during or since the industrial revolution has grown so quickly. The education and training function has supported and promoted the industry increasing the quality of the labour element of the business. Tourism has now gained a wider function and has become an accepted learning vehicle for those not intending to enter the industry. With the introduction of the GCSE in Tourism it can be used to teach economics, sociology, mathematics and law. We should be pleased that it has now become a recognized industry and an academic discipline.

For further information contact:

The Travel Training Company
The Corner Stone, The Broadway, Woking, Surrey, TU21 5AR
Tel: (01483) 727 321. Fax: (01483) 756 698.

SCHILLER
INTERNATIONAL UNIVERSITY

INTERNATIONAL SCHOOL OF TOURISM
& HOSPITALITY MANAGEMENT

*Florida, USA; London, England; Strasbourg, France;
Paris, France; and Engelberg, Switzerland*

Diploma, Associate, Bachelor and Master
degree programs in Hotel Management and
International Hotel & Tourism Management

•

English is the language of instruction

•

Study opportunities in other disciplines

•

Term Abroad programs

•

Courses begin January, June and September

Schiller International University
DEPT 11WTGHT , Royal Waterloo House,
51-55 Waterloo Road London SE1 8TX
Tel: 44 0171 928 1372
Fax: 44 0171 620 1226

Accredited member ACICS, Washington DC, USA

COLLEGIUM PALATINUM

DEUTSCH, FRANÇAIS,
ENGLISH, ESPAÑOL, ITALIANO

■ Standard courses at all levels,
throughout the year

■ Summer courses of 3 to 4 weeks

■ Combination courses

■ Individual and group courses

■ Cultural and leisure programme

■ Accommodation: Residential, host
family or private arrangements

HEIDELBERG, MADRID, LONDON,
FLORIDA, LEYSIN (SWITZERLAND),
ROME, FLORENCE, SIENA

Collegium Palatinum
Dept SA/CP, Adenauerplatz 8
69115 Heidelberg, Germany.
Tel: (+49 6221) 46289. Fax: (+49 6221) 182023.

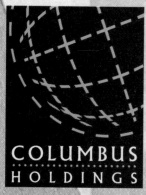

Publication	**Media Information**	**Additional Information**

AGENT CANADA

Travel Trade Magazine

#300, 1534 West Second Avenue
Vancouver
British Columbia V6J 1H2
Canada

Tel: (604) 731 0481.
Fax: (604) 731 2589.

Circulation:	11,201.
Frequency:	Weekly.
Distribution:	Courier and postal system.
Trim Size (depth x width):	274mm x 209mm. 10⅞ ins. x 8⅛ ins.
Language:	English.
Published in:	Canada.
Publisher:	Douglas W Keough.
Year Est:	1978.

Agent Canada is published weekly with a circulation of over 11,000 magazines reaching all travel agencies in Canada. Three regional distributions – *Agent West*, *Agent America* and *Agent Ontario* – are published twice a month, as well as the ACTA *Annual Directory* distributed every August for the Canadian Travel Industry.
Agent Canada now also publish *SKAL Canada Magazine* six times a year. It is technically a supplement of *Agent Canada*.

AL DIA – TRAVEL AGENT UPDATE

Editorial: *Pepperdine Enterprises Inc.*
1367 Tadsworth Ter.
Heathrow, FL
32746
USA
Advertising USA: *The Gilhuly Co.*
Advertising Europe: *The Media Partnership*

Tel (Editorial): (407) 333 3393.
Fax (Advertising): (407) 333 3533.
Tel (Advertising USA): (305) 444 2460.
Fax (Advertising USA): (305) 444 2650.
Tel (Advertising Europe): (01494) 791 179.
Fax (Advertising Europe): (01494) 775 220.

Circulation:	5000.
Frequency:	Monthly from Mar-Nov.
Distribution:	ABC audited circulation.
Trim Size (depth x width):	273mm x 204mm. 10¾ ins. x 8⅛ ins.
Language:	Spanish and English.
Published in:	USA.
Publisher:	Noemi Pepperdine.
Year Est:	1991.

AL DIA – Travel Agent Update is the most comprehensive and effective trade publication reaching the Latin American travel market, with a mailing list that includes over 90% of endorsed IATA Latin American travel agents and is the only trade publication that is targeted to the decision makers of those travel agencies. Over 70% of our readers are owners, general managers or directors of marketing of travel agencies who have requested *AL DIA*. *AL DIA* publishes technical, educational and informative articles that assist agencies professionally, features destinations and keeps the travel agent abreast of the latest travel industry news. *AL DIA* writers are some of the most qualified and experienced in the travel industry.

AL-HAYAT AL-SIYAHIYAT UPDATE

1A Kings Avenue
London SW4 8DK
UK

Tel: (0171) 274 9381.
Fax: (0171) 326 1783.

Circulation:	38,000.
Frequency:	Monthly.
Distribution:	Newsagent or subscription.
Trim Size (depth x width):	280mm x 210mm. 11 ins. x 8¼ ins.
Language:	Arabic.
Published in:	UK.
Publisher:	Dahabi Idrissi.
Year Est.:	1983.

Al-Hayat Al-Siyahiyat is a leading international tourist and travel magazine distributed throughout the Arab world and in Europe. It provides the latest travel news and information and is meant for everyone who takes an interest in tourism, especially the top executive professionals working in the travel and tourist field. It has also opened travel horizons by providing advice to millions of Arab tourists on the best way to spend their holidays.

AMBASSADOR (SAFEER)

66 Clifton Court
Northwick Terrace
London NW8 8HU
UK

Tel: (0171) 289 5903.
Fax: (0171) 289 2664.

Circulation:	40,000.
Frequency:	Quarterly.
Distribution:	Airmail.
Trim Size (depth x width):	197mm x 210mm. 7⅝ ins. x 8¼ ins.
Language:	English and Urdu.
Published in:	Pakistan.
Year Est:	1992.

This is Pakistan's first ever travel, leisure and business quarterly. *Ambassador* is set to be the highest circulated and widest read publication of Pakistan. The magazine will be distributed in the new Jinnah Terminal in Karachi and it is estimated that 7 million national and international passengers will be embarking, disembarking and passing through its gateways in transit.

ASTA AGENCY MANAGEMENT

Pace Communications
1301 Carolina Street
Greensboro, NC
27401
USA

Tel: (910) 378 6065.
Fax: (910) 378 6828.

Circulation:	25,000.
Frequency:	Monthly.
Distribution:	ASTA members worldwide.
Trim Size (depth x width):	276mm x 207mm. 10¾ ins. x 8⅛ ins.
Language:	English.
Published in:	USA.
Publisher:	William A Lawrence.
Year Est:	1987 ('75 as ASTA Travel News).

ASTA Agency Management is an upscale business publication targeted to the owner/manager of America's travel agencies. It delivers the information needed to make well-informed and profitable business decisions and provides in-depth coverage in two main areas: industry trends (with reports that ask and answer the tough business questions that have an effect on agencies) and travel agency management (including articles that provide readers with ideas, suggestions, facts, figures and instructions on how to be a more profitable and professional agency).

Publication	Media Information		Additional Information

BUSINESS TRAVEL NEWS

33rd Floor
1515 Broadway
New York, NY
10036
USA

Tel: (212) 869 1300.
Fax: (212) 302 6273.

Circulation:	63,000.
Frequency:	27 per year.
Distribution:	Controlled circulation (post).
Trim Size (depth x width):	365mm x 273mm. 14⅜ ins. x 10¾ins.
Language:	English.
Published in:	USA.
Publisher:	Bill Besch.
Year Est:	1984.

Edited for corporate executives and travel agents who plan, purchase and manage business travel and small meetings. Every issue includes news and analysis of travel management trends, supplier activities (airline, hotel, car rental, etc), international business travel and major business travel and meetings destinations worldwide. Pull-out supplements include *Business Travel Decisions*, emphasising how to implement travel management strategies, and *Meetings Under 100*, which covers the information needs of subscribers booking short-term corporate meetings.

BUSINESS TRAVEL WORLD

67 Clerkenwell Road
London EC1R 5BH
UK

Tel: (0171) 404 2763.
Fax: (0171) 405 5868.

Circulation:	N/A.
Frequency:	Monthly.
Distribution:	Subscription.
Trim Size (depth x width):	330mm x 240mm. 13 ins. x 9⅝ ins.
Language:	English.
Published in:	UK.
Publisher:	Richard Caisley.
Year Est:	1993.

Each month *Business Travel World* provides news, information and comment specifically designed to fulfil the needs of travel professionals, to aid planning of travel itineraries and improve the management of travel budgets.

CANADIAN TRAVEL PRESS

310 Dupont Street
Toronto
Ontario M5R 1V9
Canada

Tel: (416) 968 7252.
Fax: (416) 968 2377.

Circulation:	12,800.
Frequency:	Weekly.
Distribution:	First-class mail/private delivery.
Trim Size (depth x width):	337mm x 251mm. 13¼ ins. x 9⅞ ins.
Language:	English.
Published in:	Canada.
Publisher:	David McClung.
Year Est:	1968.

Canadian Travel Press is a high-quality, glossy, tabloid-size magazine published 46 times a year. It deals with timely coverage of events of concern to the travel industry and carries in-depth reports on such destinations as Canada, the United States, the Caribbean, the Pacific and Africa, to name but a few. Periodically, issues such as automation, business travel, tax and legal matters affecting the industry and forecasting will be dealt with. The magazine is distributed to subscribers in every province within Canada, as well as in key border cities in the United States.

CANADIAN TRAVELLER

Altrac's Publishing
Suite #902, 469 Granville Street
Vancouver
British Columbia V6C 1T2
Canada

Tel (Editorial):   (604) 276 0818.
Fax: (604) 276 0843.

Circulation:	14,500.
Frequency:	Monthly.
Distribution:	Controlled circulation.
Trim Size (depth x width):	206mm x 276mm. 8⅛ ins. x 10⅞ ins.
Language:	English.
Published in:	Canada.
Publisher:	Altracs Publishing.
Year Est:	1983.

Canadian Traveller provides in-depth information about the travel destinations of the world, and is written for and distributed to Canadian travel agents. The editorial style is colourful and concise, and is designed to aid agents in selling destinations to their clients. It also supplies practical, reliable destination information of benefit to both leisure and corporate travellers, as well as frequent special issues, such as their Railways of the World issues. Their readership includes tour operators, government tourism bureaus, carriers, hotels and resorts.

DELEGATES

Blenheim Business Publications Ltd.,
Blenheim House
630 Chiswick High Road
London W4 5BG
Tel (Editorial):   (01636) 74807.
Tel (Advertising):   (0181) 742 2828.
Fax (Editorial):   (01636) 611 965.
Fax: (Advertising): (0181) 742 6387.

Circulation:	18,363.
Frequency:	Bi-monthly.
Distribution:	Controlled circulation.
Trim Size (depth x width):	297mm x 210mm. 11¾ ins. x 8¼ ins.
Language:	English.
Published in:	UK.
Publisher:	Georgina Faux.
Year Est:	1985.

Delegates magazine is a publication for the buyers of incentive and conference facilities worldwide with regard to how the buyers view the marketplace. It is the magazine for the buyers about the buyers in the industry and is totally international in its editorial coverage, its circulation and its advertising.

Publication	Media Information		Additional Information

EDITUR

Gran Via Carlos III, 86, 7°
08028 Barcelona
Spain

Tel: (3) 330 7052.
Fax: (3) 330 7496 or 330 2401.

Circulation:	O.J.D. 7023 per week.
Frequency:	Weekly.
Distribution:	Subscription.
Trim Size (depth x width):	340mm x 240mm. 13⅜ ins. x 9½ ins.
Language:	Spanish.
Published in:	Spain.
Publisher:	Luisa Vila Regard.
Year Est:	1960.

Editur is Spain's only weekly publication devoted to the professional world of tourism in its many facets. It is circulated entirely by subscription among travel agencies, tour operators, hotels, apartments, airlines, railway and overland carriers, property developers, holiday industry suppliers, etc. Eight other travel magazines are published regularly by the company, and all represent an important aid for the professional in Spain and for those in other countries who work with them.

FVW INTERNATIONAL

PO Box 323462
20119 Hamburg
Editorial:
Jungfrauenthal 47
20149 Hamburg
Federal Republic of Germany

Tel (Editorial): (40) 44 18 73 83.
Tel (Advertising): (40) 44 18 73 82.
Tel (Subscription): (40) 44 18 73 81.
Fax: (40) 44 18 73 29.

Circulation:	25,155.
Frequency:	Bi-weekly.
Distribution:	Mail subscription.
Trim Size (depth x width):	340mm x 240mm.
Language:	German; some in English.
Published in:	Federal Republic of Germany.
Publisher:	Ines Niedecken.
Year Est:	1967.

FVW International is the leading German travel market magazine in terms of editorial pages, paid and distributed circulation and total advertisement volume. It is an informative and critical working tool for travel agencies, company travel departments and tour operators and has a very loyal readership.

GIT (GUIA INT. DE TRAFICO)

3rd Floor, Suipacha 207
Oficina 316
1088 Buenos Aires
CP 1008
Argentina

Tel: (1) 394 9008 or 394 9040.
Fax: (1) 394 9034.
Telex: 25955 ARVIL AR.

Circulation:	10,200.
Frequency:	Monthly.
Distribution:	Mail.
Trim Size (depth x width):	260mm x 180mm. 10¼ ins. x 7⅛ ins.
Language:	Spanish.
Published in:	Argentina, Paraguay and Uruguay.
Publisher:	A Rodrigué/S Rodrigué.
Year Est:	1963.

GIT is a leading airline guide and travel trade magazine reaching Argentina, Paraguay, Uruguay and Miami in the USA. There are more than 450 pages of travel industry news, features and information offering public relations and marketing services, as well as promotional activities (such as organising workshops). The magazine serves as an invaluable source of reference for anyone whose job involves planning in the travel business.

GREEK TRAVEL PAGES
MONTHLY

International Publications Ltd
6 Psylla and Filellinon Streets
10557 Athens
Greece

Tel: (1) 324 7511.
Fax: (1) 325 4775 or 324 996.

Circulation:	6000.
Frequency:	Monthly.
Distribution:	Airmail.
Trim Size (depth x width):	220mm x 150mm. 8⅝ ins. x 5⅞ ins.
Language:	English.
Published in:	Greece.
Publisher:	Eleftherios Theofanopoulos.
Year Est:	1975.

Greek Travel Pages is a publication used by tourist professionals worldwide and gives comprehensive travel information.

GROUP TRAVEL ORGANISER

4th Floor, Quadrant House
250 Kennington Lane
London SE11 5RD
UK

Tel (Editorial): (0171) 735 5240.
Tel (Advertising): (0171) 735 5058.
Fax: (0171) 735 1299.

Circulation:	8500.
Frequency:	10 per year.
Distribution:	Controlled mailing.
Trim Size (depth x width):	297mm x 210mm. 11¾ ins. x 8¼ ins.
Language:	English.
Published in:	UK.
Publisher:	Peter Stonham.
Year Est:	1988.

Group Travel Organiser is the only magazine specifically dedicated to the arena of group travel. It reaches more than 8000 named individuals known to be active group travel organisers for sports and social clubs affiliated to companies, women's institutes, retirement associations and various other special interest groups. It also has a trade readership exceeding 1000 and covers news and features on group travel opportunities throughout the UK and abroad.

Publication	Media Information		Additional Information
GSA TRAVEL MARKETING *PO Box 3239* *6th Floor, JHI House* *5, Heerengracht* *Cape Town 8000* *South Africa* Tel: (21) 419 1671. Fax: (21) 419 4851.	Circulation: Frequency: Distribution: Trim Size (depth x width): Language: Published in: Publisher: Year Est:	4200. Monthly. Subscription. 297mm x 210mm. 11¾ ins. x 8¼ ins. English. South Africa. Jeff Hawthorne. 1980.	Since its inception in February 1980, GSA *Travel Marketing* has grown to become the most comprehensive reference source available to the Southern African Travel Industry. Published monthly, it contains updated information on tour operators, hotels, general sales agents, airlines, car rental companies, cruise operators, other travel-related services and visa requirements. More than 800 agencies from Southern Africa and beyond subscribe to over 4200 copies a month and it is used constantly every day by travel personnel actively selling to their clients.
GUIDA VIAGGI *Via Larga 2* *20122 Milano* *Italy* Tel: (2) 876 936 *or* 866 562. Fax: (2) 866 561.	Circulation: Frequency: Distribution: Trim Size (depth x width): Language: Published in: Publisher: Year Est:	7500. Weekly. Free. 420mm x 305mm. 16½ ins. x 12 ins. Italian. Italy. Givi Srl. 1971.	*Guida Viaggi* is a publication providing articles, news and information concerning the travel market. It is addressed to travel agents, airlines, shipping lines, touristic agents, local tourist organisations for workers' free-time activities and magazines and newspapers with tourist columns.
HOLIDAY MARKETING *Prestige Publications (UK) Ltd.* *Lindsay House* *19 Lindsay Road* *New Haw* *Addlestone* *Surrey KT15 3BD* *UK* Tel/Fax (Editorial): (01932) 353 687. Tel/Fax (Advertising): (01932) 347 658.	Circulation: Frequency: Distribution: Trim Size (depth x width): Language: Published in: Publisher: Year Est:	14,030. 6 per year. ATD. 297mm x 210mm. 11¾ ins. x 8¼ ins. English. UK. Nick Barbasiewicz. 1986.	*Holiday Marketing* is the only travel trade magazine to concentrate on marketing and selling. Like its predecessor, *Holiday Shop Magazine* (which it now incorporates) it is dedicated to covering tour operators' programmes, plus features, legal advice, reader feedback and brochure reviews.
IATA REVIEW *PO Box 672* *33 route de l'Aéroport* *1215 Geneva 15* *Switzerland* Tel (Editorial): (22) 799 2967 (Geneva). Tel (Advertising): (514) 844 6311 (Montréal). Fax: (22) 799 2685 (Geneva).	Circulation: Frequency: Distribution: Trim Size (depth x width): Language: Published in: Publisher: Year Est:	12,000. 6 per year. Direct mail. 280mm x 210mm. 11 ins. x 8¼ ins. English. Switzerland. IATA Public Relations. 1966.	*IATA Review* is the news magazine of the International Air Transport Association. It contains news, commentary and background information relating both to IATA activities and to the civil aviation industry in general. Its editorial content, written by IATA specialists and external industry experts, covers a wide range of technical, regulatory, commercial and financial issues affecting air transport. Readership includes airline chief executives, directors of civil aviation, ministers of transport, airport authorities, aircraft manufacturers, financiers, tourist boards, travel agents, consumer organisations, academic institutions and the media.
INTERLINE & TRAVEL NEWS ITALIA *Via Bissolati 54* *00187 Roma* *Italy* Tel: (6) 482 7632. Fax: (6) 474 1095.	Circulation: Frequency: Distribution: Trim Size (depth x width): Language: Published in: Publisher: Year Est:	10,000. Bi-monthly/monthly (Jul & Aug). Post. 300mm x 211mm. 11⅞ ins. x 8¼ ins. Italian; some in English. Italy. Alberto Marani. 1970.	*Interline & Travel News* has been the official mouthpiece for airline and tourism personnel for over 20 years. Each issue, of which 8000 copies are distributed in Italy and 2000 worldwide, is the official publication of the Interline Italia Club, which promotes the many special offers available to the staff of international airlines, travel agencies, airports and civil aviation boards who are club members. It lists countless travel opportunities at amazing prices and is an ideal vehicle for operators, airlines and other tourism-related organisations to present, promote and sell their products through both advertising and editorial support.

Publication	Media Information		Additional Information
JAX FAX MARKETING *PO Box 4013* *397 Post Road* *Darien, CT* *06820-1413* *USA* Tel (Editorial): (203) 655 8746. Fax: (203) 655 6257.	Circulation: Frequency: Distribution: Trim Size (depth x width): Language: Published in: Publisher: Year Est:	30,000. Monthly. Mail. 277mm x 206mm. 10⅞ ins. x 8⅛ ins. English. USA. Clifton N Cooke. 1973.	*Jax Fax Marketing* is for reservations, sales and management personnel of retail travel agencies, tour wholesalers, group and incentive organisers and all those engaged in the sale and marketing of air transportation and inclusive tours on both scheduled and charter flights. It has over 3000 listings of low-cost high-value flights and/or tours for international and domestic destinations (including departure date, return date, number of days, price range, type of flight or tour and name of the airline), and 100 pages on new travel products, destinations and companies.
L'AGENZIA DI VIAGGI *Via Rasella 155* *00187 Roma* *Italy* Tel: (6) 482 1539. Fax: (6) 482 6721.	Circulation: Frequency: Distribution: Trim Size (depth x width): Language: Published in: Publisher: Year Est:	12,450. Daily. 72.5% to paying subscribers. 280mm x 400mm. 10⅞ ins. x 15¾ ins. Italian. Italy. Marco Valerio Ambrosini. 1965.	*L'Agenzia di Viaggi* is a daily travel magazine offering impartial travel news and in-depth reporting on tourism in Italy and throughout the world. Articles include reports on trends and styles in where to go, how to get there and where to stay. The Saturday edition is 4-colour and features special destinations and resorts. It is practically the only Italian travel trade market magazine in Italy.
L'ECHO TOURISTIQUE *6 rue Marius Aufan* *92300 Levallois-Perret* *France* Tel: (1) 47 58 20 00. Fax: (1) 47 58 72 00.	Circulation: Frequency: Distribution: Trim Size (depth x width): Language: Published in: Publisher: Year Est:	9000. Weekly. Subscription. 280mm x 395mm. 11 ins. x 15½ ins. French. France. Claude Barou. 1930.	*L'Echo Touristique* is a trade-only magazine devoted to the travel industry. It provides information on tour operators, travel agencies, hotels, transportation and international markets, as well as features every week on tourism destinations or on tourism companies and leaders. Several times during the year there are special features, such as articles on wages in tourism, results of the French tourism companies, training in tourism, etc. It has a reputation for reliability, accuracy and objectivity.
MATILDA TRAVEL *Zvole 96* *252 45 Prague - západ* *Czech Republic* Tel: (2) 275 424. Fax: (2) 272 745.	Circulation: Frequency: Distribution: Trim Size (depth x width): Language: Published in: Publisher: Year Est:	3500. Bi-monthly. Paid subscription/free. 297mm x 210mm. 11¾ ins. x 8¼ ins. Czech. Czech Republic. Slavomír Horsky. 1992.	*Matilda Travel* is a Czech travel trade magazine with special issues devoted to the the GO travel fair in Brno and the *Holiday World* travel fair in Prague. Published on every first and third Wednesday in the month, it is distributed to Czech, Slovak and some Polish travel agents, tour operators, transport companies, hotels, municipal authorities and other travel industry professionals.
MIDDLE EAST TRAVEL *PO Box 6655* *Dubai* *UAE* Tel: (4) 206 5709. Fax: (4) 274 906.		6000. 6 per year. Controlled/subscription. 270mm x 210mm. 10⅝ ins. x 8¼ ins. English. Cyprus. Alan Le Coyte. 1977.	*Middle East Travel* is the leading travel news magazine for this region, providing up-to-date and authoritative comment on developments affecting the airline, hotel and travel industries. Circulated to the major tour operators, travel agents, hotels and airlines, as well as the Ministries of Tourism throughout the Arab world, it is recognised as the main source of information in this growing market.

Publication	Media Information	Additional Information

NEW FOCUS TÜRKIÏE TOURISM MAGAZINE

S-M Publications Ltd
Muratreis
Muradiye Mektep sk. 13/1
Baglarbasi 81140
Istanbul
Turkey

Tel (Editorial): (216) 391 3795.
Tel (Advertising): (216) 341 9290.
Fax: (216) 391 3796.

Circulation:	5000.
Frequency:	Bi-monthly.
Distribution:	Subscription and free copies.
Trim Size (depth x width):	275mm x 200mm. 10⅞ ins. x 7⅞ ins.
Language:	English and Turkish.
Published in:	Turkey.
Publisher:	Suat Töre.
Year Est:	1991.

New Focus Türkiÿe Tourism Magazine is the leading travel trade magazine in Turkey. Its readers are all travel professionals and include travel agents, tour operators and hotel and airline personnel. *New Focus Türkiÿe Tourism Magazine* is distributed by the Ministry of Tourism to all tourist offices within Turkey and 16 countries overseas, as well as at every major international tourism exhibition worldwide. Its mission is to attract tourists to Turkey and to promote Turkish tourism enterprises.

PANROTAS GUIDE

Av. Jabaquara 1761
04045-901 São Paulo
Brazil

Tel: (11) 584 0211.
Fax: (11) 276 1602.

Circulation:	11,488.
Frequency:	Monthly.
Distribution:	Annual subscriptions.
Trim Size (depth x width):	280mm x 210mm. 11 ins. x 8¼ ins.
Language:	Portuguese.
Published in:	Brazil.
Publisher:	M V M Condomi Alcorta.
Year Est:	1974.

Panrotas Guide is ordered by qualified travel retailers, wholesalers, transportation and promotion departments, and others who sell or influence the sale of travel to the public. Besides the domestic and international schedules and tariffs, airline ticket offices and embassies' addresses, and a wide range of technical and useful information for those who work in the travel industry, each issue also contains destination features, specialised articles to support the marketing of the travel industry, details of new packages, tours, airlines, hotels, tour operators and interviews with key industry personnel.

PTN ASIA/PACIFIC

100 Beach Road
#2600 Shaw Towers
Singapore 0718

Tel (Editorial): 833 5022 (Hong Kong); 294 3366 (Singapore); (3) 255 7314/12 (Malaysia); (21) 337 379 (Indonesia).
Tel (Advertising): 833 5022 (Hong Kong); 294 3366 (Singapore); (3) 255 7314/24 (Malaysia); (212) 382 3960 (USA).
Tel (Production): 294 3366 (Singapore).
Tel (Circulation): 294 3366 (Singapore).
Fax: 834 5132 (Hong Kong).

Circulation:	13,291.
Frequency:	Monthly.
Distribution:	Free if within terms of control.
Trim Size (depth x width):	285mm x 210mm. 11¼ ins. x 8¼ ins.
Language:	English.
Published in:	Singapore.
Publisher:	Chris Sweeting.
Year Est:	1987.

PTN Asia/Pacific is the official monthly magazine for the *Pacific Asia Travel Association (PATA)* in the Asia/Pacific region. The publication's editorial is pertinent, authoritative and well-recognised by key professionals and decision-makers in the travel industry. Its carefully controlled circulation to travel management and PATA members provides an efficient and cost-effective way to reach the people who buy travel.

PTN EUROPE

Morgan Grampian House
London SE18 6QH
UK

Tel (Editorial): (0181) 855 7777.
Tel (Advertising): (0181) 316 3314.
Fax: (0181) 316 3119.

Circulation:	12,904.
Frequency:	4 per year.
Distribution:	Controlled postal circulation.
Trim Size (depth x width):	285mm x 210mm. 11¼ ins. x 8¼ ins.
Language:	English.
Published in:	UK.
Publisher:	Stuart Baker.
Year Est:	1988.

PTN Europe is the official PATA publication for Europe, bringing the Asia/Pacific travel market closer to the people of Europe who buy travel. It offers cost-effective rates to advertisers, everything needed to plan a promotional campaign anywhere in Europe and covers all the important news, events and people in the far-reaching business of travel.

PUBLITURIS TRAVEL TRADE JOURNAL

Rua Marechal Saldanha 4-1
1200 Lisbon
Portugal

Tel (Editorial): (1) 346 0045.
Tel (Advertising): (1) 347 5201.
Fax: (1) 342 7718.

Circulation:	7500.
Frequency:	Fortnightly; 1st and 15th.
Distribution:	Subscription.
Trim Size (depth x width):	280mm x 190mm. 11 ins. x 7½ ins.
Language:	Portuguese.
Published in:	Portugal.
Publisher:	Publiotel Ltd.
Year Est:	1968.

Publituris is a travel publication for travel agencies, airlines, hotels, car hire companies, real estate companies, meetings and congress organisers, tourist offices, hotel and restaurant schools and other travel trade organisations.

Publication	Media Information		Additional Information

REISELIV

Editorial address:
Fred. Olsensgt 1
0152 Oslo 1
Norway
Publisher's address:
Northra Produksjon AS
PO Box 591 Sentrum
0106 Oslo, Norway

Tel (Editorial):   (2) 414 660.
Tel (Advertising): (2) 419 305.
Fax (Editorial):   (2) 337 277.
Fax (Publishers):   (2) 336 672.

Circulation:	5000.
Frequency:	10 issues annually.
Distribution:	Post.
Trim Size (depth x width):	297mm x 210mm. 11¾ ins. x 8¼ ins.
Language:	Norwegian.
Published in:	Norway.
Publisher:	Annar Lille-Maehlum.
Year Est: •	1921.

Reiseliv (which means 'travel business/trade') is aimed especially at key persons within the travel business and among public servants and politicians dealing with the travel industry. The articles are concerned with travel politics and the development of incoming trade and traffic, describing market conditions, activities, what other countries have to offer, as well as surveys and reports of product developments within the travel trade.

REISREVUE

Postbus 1110
3600 BC Maarssen
The Netherlands

Tel: (3465) 50611.
Fax: (3465) 50282.

Circulation:	15,000.
Frequency:	Weekly.
Distribution:	Subscription & free copies basis.
Trim Size (depth x width):	260mm x 194mm. 10¼ ins. x 7⅝ ins.
Language:	Dutch.
Published in:	The Netherlands.
Publisher:	Uitgeversmÿ Misset BV.
Year Est:	1982.

Reisrevue provides a news summary of the Dutch travel market for travel agencies, airline/cruise/ferry companies and hotels. It includes compact information about the travel products of tour operators, airlines and others in the travel business, as well as developments in the Dutch and European market, with background information and comments when necessary. The style is short, powerful and to the point.

REISVAKMAGAZINE DIT

Postbus 122
3100 AC Schiedam
The Netherlands

Tel: (10) 427 4100.
Fax: (10) 473 9911.

Circulation:	5000.
Frequency:	Fortnightly.
Distribution:	Subscription by mail.
Trim Size (depth x width):	272mm x 185mm. 10¾ ins. x 7¼ ins.
Language:	Dutch.
Published in:	The Netherlands.
Publisher:	Bert van Loon.
Year Est:	1958.

Reisvakmagazine DIT is a travel trade magazine and professional trade journal for the entire travel market in The Netherlands and includes an independent editorial content of key issues of concern, such as information on market and industry developments and practical information for the day-to-day running of business operations. Its fortnightly circulation guarantees up-to-date information and makes it a good medium for flexible and intensive advertising strategies.

resFLEX

PinfoR ab
PO Box 11063
720 11 Västerås
Sweden

Tel: (21) 354 800.
Fax: (21) 354 320.

Circulation:	10,000.
Frequency:	Monthly (except July).
Distribution:	Subscription by mail.
Trim Size (depth x width):	370mm x 245mm. 14⅝ ins. x 9⅝ ins.
Language:	Swedish.
Published in:	Sweden.
Publisher:	PinfoR ab.
Year Est:	1986.

resFLEX is a Swedish travel trade monthly magazine which specialises in keeping the companies in the travel trade in Scandinavia informed about news concerning travel, hotels, transport companies, actual problems, etc of interest to the travel market. *resFLEX* is read by people employed in all areas of the travel trade such as travel agents, airline companies, tour operators and transport companies and will also be found in the biggest companies in Sweden.

SCOTTISH TRAVEL AGENTS NEWS

71 Henderson Street
Bridge of Allan
Scotland FK9 4HG
UK

Tel: (01786) 834 238.
Fax: (01786) 834 295.

Circulation:	900 (trade only).
Frequency:	Weekly.
Distribution:	Mail.
Trim Size (depth x width):	300mm x 210mm. 11⁹⁄₁₀ ins. x 8³⁄₁₀ ins.
Language:	English.
Published in:	Scotland.
Publisher:	S&G Publishing (Scotland) Ltd.
Year Est:	1990.

Scottish Travel Agents News contains news, editorial and advertising of interest to all Scottish Travel Agents.

Publication	Media Information		Additional Information

SELLING LONG-HAUL

BMI Publications Ltd
Suffolk House
George Street
Croydon
Surrey CR9 1SR
UK

Tel: (0181) 649 7233.
Fax: (0181) 649 7234.

Circulation:	17,000.	
Frequency:	10 issues annually.	
Distribution:	UK agents/long-haul principals.	
Trim Size (depth x width):	297mm x 210mm. 11¾ ins. x 8¼ ins.	
Language:	English.	
Published in:	UK.	
Publisher:	Alan Orbell.	
Year Est:	1990.	

Selling Long-Haul tells travel agents and incentive travel organisers how to sell long-haul products and services. Every editorial item and advertisement carries a unique Fast Facts number to request further information about the products and services that interest them. All of these sale leads (more than 250,000 to date) are processed and mailed directly to the companies concerned to be converted into firm business. During 1992 *Selling Long-Haul* was nominated the UK's number one travel trade publication for long-haul travel.

STAND BY TRAVEL TRADE JOURNAL

1 Vester Farimagsgade
DK-1606 Copenhagen V
Denmark

Tel: 33 93 87 00.
Fax: 33 93 87 01.

Circulation:	25,000.	
Frequency:	Monthly, except Jan, Jul, Aug.	
Distribution:	First-class mail.	
Trim Size (depth x width):	360mm x 266mm. 14¼ ins. x 10½ ins.	
Language:	Danish, Swedish and English.	
Published in:	Denmark.	
Publisher:	Preben Jack Petersen.	
Year Est:	1982.	

Stand By Travel Trade Journal is distributed as paid subscription in Denmark, Norway, Sweden and Finland, as well as the Faroe Islands, Iceland and Greenland. Its readership includes on-line and off-line tour operators, airlines, hotels, restaurants, car rental companies, travel agents, tourist bus companies, tourist offices, foreign tourist representatives, top companies in Scandinavia and all members of Dansk Rejse-Klub (the Scandinavian equivalent of IAPA).

TAKE OFF

Frederiksberg Allé 3
DK-1621 Copenhagen V
Denmark

Tel: 31 23 80 99.
Fax: 31 23 70 42.

Circulation:	6000.	
Frequency:	15th of every month.	
Distribution:	Subscription.	
Trim Size (depth x width):	270mm x 187mm. 10⅝ ins. x 7⅜ ins.	
Language:	Dan/Swed/Norweg/Eng.	
Published in:	Scandinavia.	
Publisher:	Skandinavisk Bladforlag A/S.	
Year Est:	1955.	

Take Off is a major high-quality Scandinavian travel trade magazine. It is an active and serious publication written by experts for experts with a modern layout. Written by journalists with an excellent knowledge of the travel and tourist trade in Scandinavia and other parts of the world, it keeps abreast of new developments in travel wherever the news breaks – in air travel, ferry travel, hotels, travel agencies, tour operators, or any other area of the travel trade.

THE MEETING MANAGER

Meeting Planners International
1950 Stemmons Freeway
Dallas, TX
75207-3109
USA

Tel (Editorial):   (214) 712 7733.
Tel (Advertising):   (214) 712 7739.
Fax: (214) 712 7770.

Circulation:	12,416.	
Frequency:	Monthly.	
Distribution:	2nd Class Mail.	
Trim Size (depth x width):	280mm x 210mm. 11 ins. x 8¼ ins.	
Language:	English.	
Published in:	USA.	
Publisher:	Edwin L Griffin Jr., CAE.	
Year Est:	1980.	

The Meeting Manager is designed exclusively for the meetings professional and contains information and instruction on a range of meeting management topics, plus news on industry people and trends, and the issues that are making an impact on the travel trade. It is packed with vital information on sales and marketing, international meetings, computers, personal management, taxes and legal topics, as well as other relevant in-depth features. A classified advertising section, listing positions wanted and available, also provides a useful resource for travel professionals.

TOUR & TRAVEL NEWS

600 Community Drive
Manhasset, NY
11030
USA

Tel (Editorial):   (516) 562 5649.
Tel (Advertising):   (516) 562 5708.
Fax: (516) 562 5465.

Circulation:	54,507.	
Frequency:	Weekly.	
Distribution:	ABC and BFA audited circ.	
Trim Size (depth x width):	347.5mm x 266.7mm. 13¹¹⁄₁₆ ins. 10½ ins.	
Language:	English.	
Published in:	USA.	
Publisher:	Bob Sullivan.	
Year Est:	1985.	

Tour & Travel News, the weekly paper for the retail travel industry, is written for retail travel agencies, travel consortium headquarters and travel consulting/management companies, tour operators, incentive travel companies, meeting planning and trade show producers and other travel businesses. It covers the news in a timely manner and includes special departments and destinations sections. *Tour & Travel* publishes *Travel Counselor*, the magazine for CTCs and career travel agents, six times per year; *Tour & Travel Marketplace*; and special magazines and supplements.

Publication	Media Information		Additional Information

TOURIST GUIDE OF GREECE

137 Patission Street
112 51 Athens
Greece

Tel: (1) 864 1688/9 *or* (1) 864 9000.
Fax: (1) 864 1693.

Circulation:	26,000.
Frequency:	Annual.
Distribution:	Subscription and free copies.
Trim Size (depth x width):	280mm x 210mm. 11 ins. x 8¼ ins.
Language:	English.
Published in:	Greece.
Publisher:	Sophocles Papaioannou.
Year Est:	1972.

The *Tourist Guide of Greece* is an annual publication containing all tourist enterprises in Greece as follows: airlines, shipping companies, cruise lines, yacht brokers, hotel groups and representatives, travel agencies, car rental companies, camping sites, convention centres and organisers, licensed air taxi operators, special interest holidays, museums and archaeological sites, international travel agencies co-operating with Greece, and the GNTO offices abroad. The purpose is to promote tourist enterprises and to attract tourists to Greece. The *Tourist Guide* organises Greek stands at international tourism exhibitions such as WTM and ITB.

TOURISTIK AKTUELL

Jaeger Verlag Gmbh
Postfach 10463
64204 Darmstadt
Federal Republic of Germany

Tel (Editorial):   (6154) 6995-311.
Tel (Advertising):   (6154) 6995-320.
Fax: (6154) 6995-325.

Circulation:	14,485.
Frequency:	Weekly.
Distribution:	Subscription and free copies.
Trim Size (depth x width):	310mm x 220mm. 12½ ins. x 8⅝ ins.
Language:	German.
Published in:	Federal Republic of Germany.
Publisher:	Günter M Hulwa.
Year Est:	1969.

Touristik Aktuell's reports centre on the product seen from two angles: 'Product Philosophy' from the point of view of travel organisers, carriers and hotels, supplemented by reports on actual experiences behind the counter, enhanced by brief information about trends within the branch and economic developments of significance to daily work. Monthly reports give information on the German and the Asian Pacific market. Case studies provide first-hand information on problem solving, helping readers to keep track of things in this increasingly complicated day-to-day business.

TOURISTIK MANAGEMENT

Reichenhaller Strasse 46
81547 München
Federal Republic of Germany

Tel: (89) 692 2522.
Fax: (89) 695 771.

Circulation:	19,000.
Frequency:	10 per year.
Distribution:	Subscription controlled circ.
Trim Size (depth x width):	252mm x 184mm. 10 ins. x 7¼ ins.
Language:	German.
Published in:	Federal Republic of Germany.
Publisher:	Axel Thunig.
Year Est:	1983.

Touristik Management is a professional trade magazine for travel agencies, counter staff, tour operators and company travel departments. It is the only German-speaking trade publication with a 'Counter trainer' for counter staff. The magazine deals with both tourism and business travel and informs its readers of all the specific problems and developments in this field and gives them practical help in their daily work.

TOURISTIK R.E.P.O.R.T.

WDV Wirtschaftsdienst
Gesellschaft für Medien & Kommunikation mbH &
Co. OHG
Dieselstrasse 36
63071 Offenbach
Federal Republic of Germany

Tel: (69) 29907-442.
Fax: (69) 29907-479.

Circulation:	19,320.
Frequency:	Fortnightly.
Distribution:	Mail.
Trim Size (depth x width):	297mm x 210mm. 11¾ ins. x 8¼ ins.
Language:	German.
Published in:	Federal Republic of Germany.
Publisher:	Heiner Berninger.
Year Est:	1980.

Touristik R.E.P.O.R.T. is the authoritative trade magazine for the travel and tourist industry. Articles in *Touristik R.E.P.O.R.T.* are researched in-house and statements and information are carefully checked while analysis is supported by facts and data. It cultivates specialist, critical journalism, takes on burning issues and is free and independent in its reporting. *Touristik R.E.P.O.R.T.* reports on and for all areas of the travel trade including travel agents, tour operators, hotels, airlines, tourist offices and health resorts.

TRAVEL AGENCY

Maclean Hunter House
Chalk Lane
Cockfosters Road
Barnet
Herts EN4 0BU
UK

Tel: (0181) 242 3000.
Fax: (0181) 242 3098.

Circulation:	10,284.
Frequency:	Monthly.
Distribution:	Free circulation control.
Trim Size (depth x width):	260mm x 184mm. 10¼ ins. x 7¼ ins.
Language:	English.
Published in:	UK.
Publisher:	Ann Hughes.
Year Est:	1963 (From 1925 as *Travel Topics*).

Travel Agency is a publication that offers all the information required by ABTA travel agents to help them buy and sell business and leisure travel.

Publication	Media Information		Additional Information
TRAVEL AGENT *801 Second Avenue* *New York, NY* *10017* *USA* Tel: (212) 370 5050. Fax: (212) 370 4491.	Circulation:	53,000.	*Travel Agent* is the only national news weekly for the travel industry and contains in-depth editorial coverage and analysis of vital industry news. *Travel Agent* gathers, interprets and analyses the week's important events for today's busy travel agents. It provides a comfort level for readers by offering a greater understanding of complex issues and their impact upon the travel industry.
	Frequency:	Weekly.	
	Distribution:	2nd Class Mail.	
	Trim Size (depth x width):	277mm x 213mm. 10⅞ ins. x 8⅜ ins.	
	Language:	English.	
	Published in:	USA.	
	Publisher:	Richard P Friese.	
	Year Est:	1930.	
TRAVEL AGENTS TRAVEL CLUB MAGAZINE *Glebe House* *83 Glebe Street* *London W4 2BE* *UK* Tel: (0181) 742 3456. Fax: (0181) 742 3016.	Circulation:	25,200.	*Travel Agents Travel Club Magazine* replaced the UK Travel Agent Magazine in March 1994, with a brand-new look, more to read and increased publishing frequency. The monthly magazine features absorbing articles on travel, from far-flung exotic places to country hotels in the Lake District; travel news, features on places, people and jobs, trip reports (with prizes), humour, league tables, roadshow reports and education trips on offer.
	Frequency:	Monthly.	
	Distribution:	TATC members.	
	Trim Size (depth x width):	348mm x 265mm. 14 ins. x 10 ins.	
	Language:	English.	
	Published in:	UK.	
	Publisher:	John Warren.	
	Year Est:	1994.	
TRAVEL AUSTRALIA *The Australian Tourism Magazine Pty Ltd* *GPO Box 7039* *Sydney NSW 2001* *Australia* Tel: (2) 233 6789. Fax: (2) 231 5559.	Circulation:	6703.	*Travel Australia* is the only Australian trade paper dedicated entirely to the domestic and inbound markets. Its policy is to provide accurate, balanced and concise news and features coverage on developments in Australian tourism. It provides a vital communication link between the principals of the travel trade – airlines, hotels, tour operators, retail and wholesale travel agents – in Australia and worldwide.
	Frequency:	Monthly.	
	Distribution:	Subscription.	
	Trim Size (depth x width):	295mm x 210mm. 11⅜ ins. x 8¼ ins.	
	Language:	English.	
	Published in:	Australia.	
	Publisher:	Shamoli Dutt.	
	Year Est:	1987.	
TRAVEL BRITAIN *3rd Floor, Foundation House* *Perseverance Works* *38 Kingsland Road* *London E2 8DD* *UK* Tel (Editorial): (0171) 729 5171. Tel (Advertising): (0171) 729 4337. Fax: (0171) 729 1716.	Circulation:	25,000 (US travel trade only).	*Travel Britain* is the only travel trade paper promoting tour packages, car hire, air travel, hotels, conference centres/venues, coach and rail travel, etc to and throughout the UK, to the US travel trade. The USA is the UK's biggest tourism revenue earner and *Travel Britain* has established itself – being published as it is in the UK – as the mouthpiece of all tourism in Britain.
	Frequency:	Bi-monthly.	
	Distribution:	Express Surface Post/airmail.	
	Trim Size (depth x width):	400mm x 290mm. 15¾ ins. x 11¼ ins.	
	Language:	English.	
	Published in:	UK.	
	Publisher:	Bob MacBeth-Seath.	
	Year Est:	1989.	
TRAVEL DAYS *Judd House* *65 Judd Street* *London WC1* *UK* Tel: (0171) 833 0820. Fax: (0171) 833 3386.	Circulation:	20,530.	*Travel Days* was established in 1991 as the European independent voice of the travel trade covering segments of the travel and tourism market often overlooked by existing publications. For this reason, it is the product of an independent mind and is privately funded. It has been warmly accepted since its first issue by the world of tourism, and its independent voice is becoming stronger and stronger whilst following a new concept in strategy and growth.
	Frequency:	Fortnightly.	
	Distribution:	Direct mailing.	
	Trim Size (depth x width):	430mm x 305mm. 17 ins. x 12 ins.	
	Language:	English.	
	Published in:	UK.	
	Publisher:	Tommaso Bruccoleri.	
	Year Est:	1991.	

Publication	**Media Information**	**Additional Information**
TRAVEL GBI *3rd Floor, Foundation House* *Perseverance Works* *38 Kingsland Road* *London E2 8DD* *UK* Tel (Editorial): (0171) 729 5171. Tel (Advertising): (0171) 729 4337. Tel (Administration): (0171) 729 4337. Tel (Ad Production): (0171) 729 4337. Fax: (0171) 729 1716.	Circulation: 18,385 (ABC). Frequency: Monthly. Distribution: Mailed controlled circulation. Trim Size 402mm x 290mm. (depth x width): 15³/₄ ins. x 11³/₈ ins. Language: English. Published in: UK. Publisher: Robert MacBeth-Seath. Year Est: 1978.	*Travel GBI* is the UK's only domestic travel trade newspaper for any marketing plans involving the UK business or leisure travel industry. It plays a cost-effective advertising role in the domestic marketplace and reflects modern developments and thinking within the travel trade. Insight features offer a complete update on various subjects, companies and destinations in an easy-to-read format. The new look – created in November 1990 – afforded more colour, a cleaner page layout, a strong new logo and improved comprehensive editorial coverage of all sectors of the market.
TRAVEL NEWS ASIA *Blk C, 10/F Seaview Estate* *2-8 Watson Road* *North Point* *Hong Kong* Tel (Editorial): 566 8381 (Hong Kong); (0171) 706 1513 (London). Tel (Advertising): 566 8381 (Hong Kong); (0171) 636 3961 (London). Fax: 508 0255 (Hong Kong).	Circulation: 19,478. Frequency: Fortnightly. Distribution: Controlled to Asia travel trade. Trim Size 414mm x 287mm. (depth x width): 16¹/₄ ins. x 11¹/₄ ins. Language: English. Published in: Hong Kong. Publisher: Martin Savery. Year Est: 1974.	*Travel News Asia* is the most widely read travel trade publication in Asia. 65% of its readers are travel agents and tour operators, giving it the widest agents/operators reach of any travel trade publication in the region. The magazine reports on issues that affect the day-to-day travel business in Asia, as well as new projects, services and trends. It provides distinct sections on airlines, hotels, agents/operators, tourism, technology and a comprehensive section which helps the industry come to grips with the latest technological changes going on in the business. Its reputation as an educational resource for travel agents makes it Asia's first choice.
TRAVELSCOPE *3rd Floor, Foundation House* *Perseverance Works* *38 Kingsland Road* *London E2 8DD* *UK* Tel: (0171) 729 4337. Fax: (0171) 729 1716.	Circulation: 400,000-500,000 per quarter. Frequency: Dec, Mar, Jun and Sep. Distribution: Personalised, paid for and circulated by travel agents. Trim Size 421mm x 315mm. (depth x width): 16½ ins. x 12⅜ ins. Language: English. Published in: UK. Publisher: Robert MacBeth-Seath. Year Est: 1974.	*Travelscope* publishes the world's largest grouping of consumer travel newspapers, with personalised newspapers for leading ABTA/IATA travel agency outlets to be distributed by them to their established clients and relevant households in their areas. They are designed specifically for retail companies. Advertisers appear in all the newspapers, affording a complete approach to consumer travel marketing and generating sales and consumer demand for those advertisers appearing within, thus creating closer ties and increased sales for the participating advertisers.
TRAVELTRADE MAGAZINE *308 Great South Road* *Greenlane* *PO Box 9596 (or 9901 for subscriptions)* *Newmarket* *Auckland* *New Zealand* Tel: (9) 529 3000. Fax: (9) 529 3001.	Circulation: 1700. Frequency: 2nd & 4th Fri. of each month. Distribution: Paid subscription. Trim Size 420mm x 290mm. (depth x width): 16¹/₂ ins. x 11³/₈ ins. Language: English. Published in: New Zealand. Publisher: Chauncy Stark. Year Est: 1972.	*Traveltrade Magazine* is a fortnightly tabloid publication produced for the travel trade in New Zealand. It is directed towards the frontline consultant and the person whose job it is to sell travel. The magazine is very informative and has regular destination and educational features. Produced on high-quality glossy paper, it contains the latest up-to-date news and events and is by far the leading trade publication in New Zealand.
TRAVEL RETAIL, DUTY & TAX FREE MARKETS, MIDDLE EAST AND AFRICA *B.I.A Enterprises, S.A.* *66 Clifton Court* *London NW8 8HU* *UK* Tel: (0171) 289 5903. Fax: (0171) 289 2664.	Circulation: 7000. Frequency: Bi-monthly (6 issues annually). Distribution: Controlled circulation. Trim Size 297mm x 210mm. (depth x width): 11¾ ins. x 8¼ ins. Language: Arabic, English and Russian. Published in: UK. Publisher: BIA Enterprises. Year Est: 1990.	*Travel Retail, Duty & Tax Free Markets, Middle East and Africa* is a bi-monthly trade publication which reflects the purchasing attitudes and economic trends as they affect the duty- and tax-free trade in the Middle East and Africa. The magazine's aim is to encourage and stimulate the developing countries' operators, markets and products to seek international opportunities offered by the trade. While providing a regular update of new developments in these regions, it serves as a contact forum for both purchasers and suppliers.

Publication	Media Information		Additional Information

TRAVEL TRADER'S NEWS

Case Postale 2244
13 rue Chantepoulet
1211 Genève 1
Switzerland

Tel: (22) 738 5858.
Fax: (22) 738 5888.

Circulation:	6000.
Frequency:	Weekly.
Distribution:	Subscription.
Trim Size (depth x width):	290mm x 210mm. 11³/₈ ins. x 8¹/₄ ins.
Language:	French.
Published in:	Switzerland.
Publisher:	Trinidad Nanzer.
Year Est:	1988.

Travel Trader's News (TTN) is the leading Swiss magazine for the professional world of tourism. It is distributed all over Switzerland and neighbouring France (Lyon, Grenoble, Besançon and Colmar) as well as some other countries. The editorial staff is composed of journalists and photographers who are specialists in tourism and the magazine's main goals are to inform professionals in the travel field and to help them communicate with each other.

TRAVEL WEEK

Peter Isaacson Publications Pty Ltd.
46 Porter Street
Prahran
VIC 3181
Australia

Tel: (3) 245 7777.
Fax: (3) 245 7750.

Circulation:	8913 (CAB).
Frequency:	Fortnightly.
Distribution:	Post and hand delivery.
Trim Size (depth x width):	360mm x 260mm. 14¼ ins. x 10¼ ins.
Language:	English.
Published in:	Australia.
Publisher:	Peter Isaacson Publications P/L.
Year Est:	1961.

Travel Week is Australia's leading travel industry newspaper with the most experienced editorial and advertising team, the highest ABC and CAB audited circulation and the greater market share of any Australian travel industry publication (MMS Research). It has a strong commitment to editorial excellence, production quality, readership relevance and advertising cost-effectiveness. As part of an international family of top travel industry publications (*TTG Asia*, *TTG Europa* and *TTG UK & Ireland*), it offers unbeatable advertising opportunities for the travel industry.

TRAVELWEEK BULLETIN

553 Church Street
Toronto
Ontario M4Y 2E2
Canada

Tel: (416) 924 0963.
Fax: (416) 924 5721.

Circulation:	7200.
Frequency:	Mon & Thur (Sep-Apr), then Thur only.
Distribution:	Distribution by Alltours/post.
Trim Size (depth x width):	210mm x 273mm. 8¹/₄ ins. x 10³/₄ ins.
Language:	English.
Published in:	Canada.
Publisher:	Wayne Lahtinen.
Year Est:	1974.

Travelweek Bulletin is a travel trade publication serving the Canadian market. It is circulated to every travel agency in Canada, twice per week in the peak winter season and once a week in summer. The magazine is a 'hard news' vehicle specialising in keeping the travel agent informed of fast-breaking events in an industry known for its rapid changes. It publishes over 30 'Spotlight Reports' every year, featuring major destinations, trade shows and other areas of interest to the trade.

TRAVEL WEEKLY

Quadrant House
The Quadrant
Sutton
Surrey SM2 5AS

Tel: (0181) 652 3500.

Circulation:	24,000.
Frequency:	Weekly.
Distribution:	Controlled circulation (ABC) and subscription.
Trim Size (depth x width):	403mm x 298mm. 15⁷/₈ ins. x 11³/₄ ins.
Language:	English.
Published in:	UK.
Publisher:	Mike Orlov.
Year Est:	1969.

Travel Weekly is a trade newspaper for the travel industry. Its content includes news stories and features drawing from the world market for outbound business and leisure travel. The magazine caters to key decision-makers from the top downwards in airlines, tour operators' offices, hotels, travel agencies, transport companies and other associated industries. It is part of the HTM International Division of *Reed Travel Group*.

TRAVEL WEEKLY

500 Plaza Drive
Secaucus, NJ
07096
USA

Tel: (201) 902 2000.
Fax: (201) 319 1755.

Circulation:	51,000 (ABC audited).
Frequency:	Bi-weekly/Focus Issues monthly.
Distribution:	Drop ship, polybag with label.
Trim Size (depth x width):	347mm x 267mm. 13¹¹/₁₆ ins. x 10¹/₂ ins.
Language:	English.
Published in:	USA.
Publisher:	Steven F. Bailey.
Year Est:	1958.

The *Travel Weekly* group of publications – newspapers, focus issues, special sections and reference guides – provide the latest news, industry feature articles and destination stories for US travel agents, tour operators, corporate travel executives and travel industry suppliers. It also publishes the biennial *US Travel Agency Survey* and a number of travel agent polls on pertinent topics as a special service to the industry. Reaching over 187,000 US travel agents per issue, it is the only 100% paid publication in the field.

Publication	Media Information	Additional Information

TRAVEL WORLD NEWS

50 Washington Street
Norwalk, CT
06854
USA

Tel (Editorial): (203) 853 4955.
Tel (Advertising): (203) 838 4594.
Fax: (203) 866 1153.

Circulation:	35,000.
Frequency:	Monthly.
Distribution:	Mailed controlled circulation.
Trim Size (depth x width):	276mm x 206mm. 10^7/$_8$ ins. x 8^1/$_8$ ins.
Language:	English.
Published in:	USA.
Publisher:	Charlie Gatt.
Year Est:	1988.

Travel World News is a monthly review trade magazine for travel agents, supplying them with all the important industry news and product information of the month in a concise, easy-to-read format. Regular sections include industry news, an events calendar, cruises, flights, agents' familiarisation trips, special interest articles and destination features on North America, the Caribbean, Latin America, Africa, the Middle East, Eastern and Western Europe.

TTG ASIA

100 Beach Road
#26-00 Shaw Tours
Singapore 0718

Tel (Editorial): 805 5661 (Hong Kong); 294 3366 (Singapore); (3) 255 7314/24 (Malaysia); (21) 337 379 (Indonesia).
Tel (Advertising): 805 5661 (Hong Kong); 294 3366 (Singapore); (3) 255 7314/24 (Malaysia); (201) 850 8339 (USA).
Tel (Production): 294 3366 (Singapore).
Tel (Circulation): 294 3366 (Singapore).
Fax: 960 0977 (Hong Kong); 298 5534 (Singapore).

Circulation:	16,325 (ABC).
Frequency:	Weekly.
Distribution:	Free if within terms of control.
Trim Size (depth x width):	420mm x 282mm. 16^1/$_2$ ins. x 11^1/$_8$ ins.
Language:	English.
Published in:	Singapore.
Publisher:	Darren Ng.
Year Est:	1974.

TTG Asia is the region's only weekly travel newspaper and is widely read and held in high esteem by the area's travel professionals. With its comprehensive network of correspondents, it provides readers with the latest news and information required to keep abreast of the fast-paced and constantly changing travel industry. It has a wide network of news correspondents with three full-time bureaux, a high level of advertising support and reciprocal news agreements with its associate travel trade publications. With the impact of its high-quality reproduction and glossy paper, it keeps readers in touch with events both regionwide and throughout the world.

TTG CHINESE

Asian Business Press Ltd
100 Beach Road
#26-00 Shaw Towers
Singapore 0718
Tel (Editorial): 805 5661 (HK); 294 3366 (Singapore); (3) 255 7314/24 (Malaysia); 255 1480 (Thailand); (21) 337 379 (Indonesia).
Tel (Advertising): 805 5661 (HK); 294 3366 (Singapore); (3) 255 7314/24 (Malaysia); (212) 382 3960 (USA).
Tel (Production): 294 3366 (Singapore).
Tel (Circulation): 294 3366 (Singapore).
Fax: 298 5534 (Singapore).
Fax: 960 0977 (Hong Kong).

Circulation:	7720.
Frequency:	Monthly.
Distribution:	Free controlled circulation.
Trim Size (depth x width):	285mm x 210mm. 11^1/$_4$ ins x 8^1/$_4$ ins.
Language:	Chinese.
Published in:	Singapore.
Publisher:	Darren Ng.
Year Est:	1992.

TTG Chinese is a Chinese-language travel trade publication for travel agents and corporate travel planners in Taiwan (China), Hong Kong, China (People's Republic of) and other Chinese-speaking communities in Asia. It is the only monthly travel trade publication with a region-wide appeal to Chinese-speaking professionals in the travel trade.

TTG CZECH REPUBLIC

Wenzigova 14
120 00 Prague 2
Czech Republic

Tel: (2) 269 8625.
Fax: (2) 269 8625.

Circulation:	5000
Frequency:	Fortnightly.
Distribution:	Controlled circulation by mail.
Trim Size (depth x width):	386mm x 269mm. 12^3/$_8$ ins. x 8^3/$_4$ ins.
Language:	Czech.
Published in:	Czech Republic.
Publisher:	Renzo Druetto.
Year Est:	1991.

TTG Czech Republic was launched in reply to the growing demand for professional information in the wake of the rapid developments within Eastern Europe. *TTG Czech Republic* is published and controlled by *TTG Italia* and produced by a highly skilled editorial team in Prague. In keeping with TTG's successful formula, *TTG Czech Republic* keeps local travel trade professionals up-to-date on international news and events in their own language. The newspaper is also actively involved in the organisation of professional workshops and other travel and tourism events.

TTG EUROPA

Travel Trade Gazette Ltd.
Morgan Grampian House
London SE18 6PH
UK

Tel (Editorial): (0181) 855 7777.
Tel (Advertising): (0181) 316 3314.
Fax: (0181) 316 3119.

Circulation:	18,925.
Frequency:	26 times a year.
Distribution:	Controlled postal circulation to all IATA travel agents across Europe.
Trim Size (depth x width):	400mm x 292mm. 15^5/$_8$ ins. x 11^1/$_2$ ins.
Language:	English.
Published in:	UK.
Publisher:	Stuart Baker.
Year Est:	1974.

TTG Europa is the only pan-European travel trade publication. It reaches all IATA agents in 18 countries across Europe and Scandinavia. For advertisers it is the ideal cost-effective opportunity to nestle between up-to-the-minute editorial, gathered by TTG's network of reporters, that spans the globe.

Publication	Media Information	Additional Information

TTG HUNGARY

Liszt F. ter 10
H-1061 Budapest
Hungary

Tel: (1) 121 4607.
Fax: (1) 121 4607.

Circulation: 3000.
Frequency: Monthly.
Distribution: Controlled circulation by mail.
Trim Size (depth x width): 386mm x 269mm. 12⅝ ins. x 8⅞ ins.
Language: Hungarian.
Published in: Hungary.
Publisher: Renzo Druetto.
Year Est: 1990.

TTG Hungary was launched in reply to the growing demand for professional information in the wake of the rapid developments within Eastern Europe. *TTG Hungary* is published and controlled by *TTG Italia* and produced by a highly skilled editorial team in Budapest. In keeping with TTG's successful formula, *TTG Hungary* keeps local travel trade professionals up-to-date on international news and events in their own language. The newspaper is also actively involved in the organisation of professional workshops and other travel and tourism events.

TTG ITALIA

Via Nota 6
10122 Torino
Italy

Tel: (11) 436 6300.
Fax: (11) 436 6500.

Circulation: 9500.
Frequency: Twice a week.
Distribution: Audited circulation by mail.
Trim Size (depth x width): 264mm x 396mm. 11⅜ ins. x 16⅞ ins.
Language: Italian.
Published in: Italy.
Publisher: Renzo Druetto.
Year Est: 1973.

TTG Italia is an authoritative Italian travel newspaper seeking to keep travel professionals reliably informed. Twice a week *TTG Italia* reaches professionals and decision makers in the Italian travel trade providing them with up-to-date and objective international news in their own language. In the overcrowded world of Italian travel trade publications, *TTG Italia* is number one in terms of reliability, authoritativeness and readership. From 1994 *TTG Italia* is the only Italian travel trade newspaper to have its circulation audited. *TTG Italia* is member of CSST (Consorzio Stampa Specilaizzata Tecnica) which has recently been acknowledged by the International Federation of Audit Bureaux of circulations.

TTG JAPAN

100 Beach Road
#26-00 Shaw Towers
Singapore 0718

Tel (Editorial): 805 5661 (Hong Kong); 294 3366 (Singapore); (3) 255 7314/24 (Malaysia); (21) 570 4444 (Indonesia).
Tel (Advertising): 805 5661 (Hong Kong); 294 3366 (Singapore); (3) 255 7314/24 (Malaysia); (808) 735 9188 (USA).
Tel (Production): 294 3366 (Singapore).
Tel (Circulation): 294 3366 (Singapore).
Fax: 298 5534 (Singapore).
Fax: 960 0977 (Hong Kong).

Circulation: 5120.
Frequency: Monthly.
Distribution: Free if within terms of control.
Trim Size (depth x width): 285mm x 210mm. 8¼ ins. x 11¼ ins.
Language: Japanese.
Published in: Singapore.
Publisher: Darren Ng.
Year Est: 1990.

Launched in October 1990, *TTG Japan* provides Japanese producers and buyers with an update on the latest products and developments in the Asian market in an easy-to-read format and in their own language, and is the only Japanese-language publication that supplies Japanese outbound travel agents with travel product information about the Asia-Pacific.

TTG POLAND

Nowogrodzko 14
00511 Warsaw
Poland

Tel: (2) 621 1801.
Tel: (2) 621 1801.

Circulation: 3000.
Frequency: Monthly.
Distribution: Controlled circulation by mail.
Trim Size (depth x width): 269mm x 386mm. 8⅞ ins. x 12⅝ ins.
Language: Polish.
Published in: Poland.
Publisher: Renzo Druetto.
Year Est: 1992.

TTG Poland was launched in reply to the growing demand for professional information in the wake of the rapid developments within Eastern Europe. *TTG Poland* is published and controlled by *TTG Italia* and produced by a highly skilled editorial team in Warsaw. In keeping with TTG's successful formula, *TTG Poland* keeps local travel trade professionals up-to-date on international news and events in their own language. The newspaper is also actively involved in the organisation of professional workshops and other travel and tourism events.

TTG UK & IRELAND

Travel Trade Gazette Ltd
Morgan Grampian House
Woolwich
London SE18 6QH
UK

Tel (Editorial): (0181) 316 3536.
Tel (Advertising): (0181) 316 3460.
Fax (Editorial): (0181) 316 7783.
Fax (Advertising): (0181) 316 3119.

Circulation: 27,000.
Frequency: Weekly.
Distribution: Controlled circulation.
Trim Size (depth x width): 402mm x 292mm. 15¾ ins. x 11½ ins.
Language: English.
Published in: UK.
Publisher: Kevin Rolfe.
Year Est: 1953.

TTG UK & Ireland has led the way in reporting travel industry news for 40 years. It gives the reader a full picture of the travel business, offers a wide range of comment and informative writing and seeks to be the first to break big news stories. Added to this are quality features on business travel and leisure destinations, such as the Far East, Australia and the USA, and is an invaluable tool in the day-to-day work within the travel industry. Its award-winning journalists have made it a newspaper enjoyed by advertisers and readers alike.

Publication	Media Information		Additional Information

TURINFO

Cherniakhovskogo 9
125319 Moscow
Russia

Tel (Editorial):	*(7-095) 152 63 31*
Tel (Advertising):	*(7-095) 152 67 11.*
Tel (Circulation):	*(7-095) 152 43 61.*
Fax:	*(7-095) 152 67 11.*

Circulation:	50,000
Frequency:	Fortnightly, 1st and 15th.
Distribution:	Subscription and free copies.
Trim Size **(depth x width):**	290mm x 238mm. 11.5 ins x 9.5ins.
Language:	Russian.
Published in:	Russia.
Publisher:	Turinfo Ltd.
Year Est:	1993.

Turinfo is a specialist newspaper for travel agents and tour operators. About 6000 companies involved in tourism in Russia and the rest of the CIS subscribe to the newspaper. Its distribution base is being widened to include large industrial enterprises, banks, joint ventures, in other words, the main customers for tourism.

The newspaper publishes news about international and Russian tourism exhibitions, interpreters, hotels, passport, visa and customs regulation, and information about incoming travel. Listings of Russian tour operators are published in each issue.

TURIZMUS

Muzeum u. 11
H-1088 Budapest
Hungary

Tel:	(1) 138 4638 *or* 138 4098.
Fax:	(1) 138 4293.

Circulation:	10,000.
Frequency:	Bi-weekly.
Distribution:	Subscription.
Trim Size **(depth x width):**	420mm x 296mm. 16½ ins. x 11¾ ins.
Language:	Hungarian.
Published in:	Hungary.
Publisher:	Kurir Rt.
Year Est:	1962.

Turizmus is the leading travel trade paper in Hungary and is subscribed to by all the country's travel agencies, tour operators, hotels, guest-houses, catering companies, major restaurants, airlines and coach operators. *Turizmus* also reaches the travel consultants of the most prominent industrial and trade companies of Hungary. The paper is published by a private publishing company, but was founded by the Hungarian Tourist Board which still considers *Turizmus* to be the official paper of this governmental body.

Health

The health of any traveller abroad may not be protected by services and legislation well-established at home. Changes in food and water may bring unexpected problems, as may insects and insect-borne diseases, especially in hot countries. Few have at their fingertips the current detailed knowledge needed to advise the traveller going to a particular country and personal reminiscences may not always reflect current or common problems. A danger of generalising is that it may be forgotten, for example, that malaria is a risk in Turkey, poliomyelitis occurs in Europe, and *hepatitis A* virus occurs worldwide and is not destroyed by many methods of purifying drinking water. Specific advice on which diseases are present in countries to be visited is likely to be complicated. A practical starting point for the traveller seeking advice is to consider which diseases can be prevented by immunisation, prophylactic tablets, or other measures, and decide whether it is appropriate to do so for each individual.

An unpredictable environment is especially a problem for the overland traveller who plans his own journey, and he needs greater knowledge of disease prevention and management than the traveller in an airplane or on a sea cruise, whose environment, food and drink are largely in the hands of the operator. Unforeseen changes in timetables may lead to stays in accommodation not of the expected standard. Delays at airports can take place in overcrowded and unhygienic conditions where the facilities have not kept pace with increased demand, and also insect-borne diseases may be contracted. Jet-lag and exhaustion may prompt a traveller to take risks with food and drink. More experienced travellers tend to have fewer health problems. Better planning, immunisations and experience in prevention may all play a part, as well as salutary lessons learnt on previous occasions.

A questionnaire survey of returning travellers (most of whom had been to Europe, especially the Mediterranean countries) showed that half had had diarrhoea or respiratory symptoms while abroad. Excessive alcohol, sun and late nights can add to the problems. About one in 100 package holidaymakers who take out a health insurance policy make a claim. Diarrhoea and sunburn are principal reasons, but accidents are also common. Injuries occur especially in and around swimming pools, to pedestrians forgetting that traffic drives on the right, and from unfamiliar equipment such as gates on lifts. Sexually transmitted diseases may be contracted and may require urgent treatment.

Long-stay travellers may adapt to these initial problems, but then find themselves suffering from diseases endemic in their chosen country, such as malaria, hepatitis, diarrhoea and skin problems. Two per cent of British Voluntary Service Overseas personnel contract *hepatitis A* within eight months if they are not protected. Poliomyelitis would be common if most travellers were not effectively immunised. Car accidents occur while driving on unmetalled roads, and some emotional problems may be resolved only by an early return home.

The traveller should be insured against medical expenses and most policies include the cost of emergency repatriation when appropriate. Such insurance, however, rarely covers a service overseas similar to that available at home. Language and administrative differences are likely to present problems. Leaflet *T5* issued yearly by the Department of Health describes the free or reduced-cost medical treatments available in other countries and the documents (passport, NHS medical card, form *E111*) which the traveller has to have with him or her. Reciprocal arrangements between countries differ and money may have to be paid and then reclaimed in the visited country itself, which can be time consuming. Extra provision should be made for such emergencies. Any reciprocal arrangement between the UK and a country is mentioned in each country's entry.

Form *E111*, obtainable from post offices, is needed in some countries of the European Union. Only a 'small' supply of medicines for personal use may be taken out of Britain, unless Home Office permission is obtained. Medicines and immunisations which are used

ADVICE CENTRES

Note: Members of the public should be aware that personal medical advice cannot necessarily be obtained from organisations listed in this section. In many cases their own medical practitioner will be in the best position to take account of relevant personal factors. Where specialist advice is supplied to members of the public (very often for a fee) this has been noted. Some addresses, however, are provided particularly to assist professionals in the travel trade who wish to keep abreast of developments in the rapidly changing medical world.

UK

MASTA (Medical Advisory Service for Travellers Abroad) of the London School of Hygiene and Tropical Medicine offers a print-out of the necessary immunisation and definitive malaria advice from £10-32.50. Tel: (0171) 631 4408.

BA TRAVEL CLINICS Tel: (0171) 831 5333 for nearest location. 38 clinics nationwide.

TRAVELLERS HEALTHLINE Tel: (0891) 224 100 (49p per minute peak, 39p per minute cheap).
This is a regularly updated advice line (with inter-active technology) for travellers seeking information about vaccinations etc in most countries and regions.

SCOTTISH CENTRE FOR INFECTION AND ENVIRONMENTAL HEALTH Ruchill Hospital, Glasgow G20 9NB. Tel: (0141) 946 7120. Fax: (0141) 946 4359.

DEPARTMENT OF COMMUNICABLE AND TROPICAL DISEASES Immunisation Section, Birmingham Heartland Hospital, Yardley Green Road, Birmingham B9 5PX. Tel: (0121) 766 6611.

DEPARTMENT OF HEALTH Public Enquiries Office, Richmond House, 79 Whitehall, London SWIA 2NS. Tel: (0171) 210 4850. Fax: (0171) 210 5523.

LIVERPOOL SCHOOL OF TROPICAL MEDICINE Pembroke Place, Liverpool L3 5QA,. Tel: (0151) 708 9393. Fax: (0151) 708 8733.

DEPARTMENT OF INFECTIOUS DISEASES & TROPICAL MEDICINE North Manchester General Hospital, Delaunays Road, Manchester M8 6RB. Tel: (0161) 795 4567.

ROSS INSTITUTE MALARIA ADVISORY SERVICE London School of Hygiene and Tropical Medicine, Keppel Street, London WCIE 7HT. Tel: (0171) 636 7921 (24-hour tape).

BRITISH DIABETIC ASSOCIATION 10 Queen Anne Street, London W1M 0BD. Tel: (0171) 323 1531. Fax: (0171) 637 3644.
Issues leaflets and travel guides to the more popular countries with advice pertinent to the diabetic.

RADAR 12 City Forum, 250 City Road, London ECIC 8AF. Tel: (0171) 250 3222. Fax: (0171) 250 0212.
A wide range of leaflets and services are available to help the handicapped arrange, insure and enjoy their travels. (See separate section on *The Disabled Traveller*.)

SWITZERLAND

INTERNATIONAL ASSOCIATION FOR MEDICAL ASSISTANCE TO TRAVELLERS Gotthardstrasse 17, CH-6300 Zug, Switzerland.
Membership is free, but voluntary contributions are welcome. The association issues a directory of English-speaking doctors and leaflets on climate, acclimatisation, immunisation, etc.

USA

CENTERS FOR DISEASE CONTROL TRAVELERS' HEALTH SECTION Tel: (404) 332 4559.
In Atlanta. Run a 24-hour automated telephone system giving advice by region and on special problems such as malaria, food and water precautions and for pregnant travellers.

CONVENIENCE CARE CENTERS Suite 100, 10301 East Darvey, Armani, CA 91733.
Undertakes all the necessary vaccinations for overseas travel.

INTERNATIONAL ASSOCIATION FOR MEDICAL ASSISTANCE TO TRAVELERS 417 Center Street, Lewiston, NY 14092.
A non-profit organisation dedicated to the gathering and dissemination of health and sanitary information worldwide.

US DEPARTMENT OF HEALTH AND HUMAN SERVICES Public Health Service, Centers for Disease Control, Center for Prevention Services, Division of Quarantine, Atlanta, GA 30333. Tel: (404) 331 2316.

INTERMEDIC 777 Third Avenue, New York, NY 10017.
A list of recommended English-speaking doctors in many countries is available to members (subscription US$6).

CENTRE HOSPITALIER DE LUXEMBOURG
4, rue Barblé   L-1210 Luxembourg
Tel: (352) 44 11-1   Fax: (352) 45 87 62

Our institution, founded in 1975, is an academic medical centre of diagnostic, care, treatment, hospitalisation, research and teaching.
It is the biggest and best-equipped hospital in the Grand-Duchy of Luxembourg.
To face the continuous development in medicine and in order to keep its well-known reputation, the hospital is engaged in a programme of permanent structural extension.
Located in the capital of the Grand-Duchy of Luxembourg, Luxembourg City, it offers essentially the following medical specialities:

Anaesthesia-surgical intensive care
Allergology-Immunology
Cardiology
Child and adolescent psychiatry
Dermatology
Diagnostic and interventional radiology
Diagnostic and interventional neuroradiology
Endocrinology
ENT
Gastroenterology
Gynaecology-Obstetrics
Haematology-Oncology
Infectious diseases
Medical intensive care
Medical polyclinic

Nephrology and Dialysis
Neurology and Neuropaediatrics
Neurosurgery
Nuclear medicine
Ophthalmology
Orthopaedic surgery
Paediatrics
Paediatric surgery
Plastic, reconstructive and aesthetic surgery
Pneumology
Psychiatry
Rheumatology
Urology
Visceral, vascular and thoracic surgery

Now foreign citizens can receive medical care in Stockholm

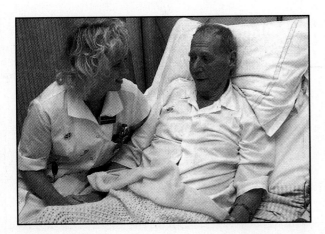

The world-famous Swedish Health Care System with well-known university hospitals such as Karolinska and Huddinge, is now also available to foreign citizens.

The procedure is simple and safe, thanks to Stockholm Care, a service organisation within the Stockholm County Council.

Just call us for further information or mail/fax your present demands for specific medical care and your medical report (in English).

Stockholm Care AB
Box 12134, S-102 24 Stockholm, Sweden
Telephone: +46 8 672 24 00
Fax: +46 8 656 12 99

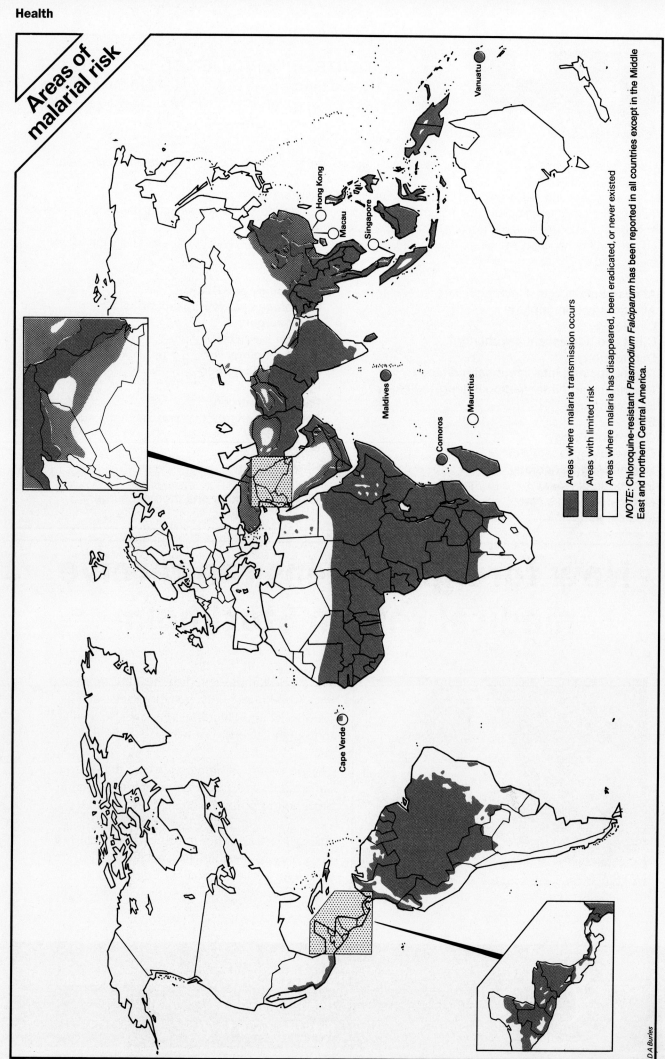

Areas of malarial risk

Hong Kong

Macau

Singapore

Vanuatu

Maldives

Mauritius

Comoros

Cape Verde

Areas where malaria transmission occurs

Areas with limited risk

Areas where malaria has disappeared, been eradicated, or never existed

NOTE: Chloroquine-resistant *Plasmodium Falciparum* has been reported in all countries except in the Middle East and northern Central America.

D A Burles

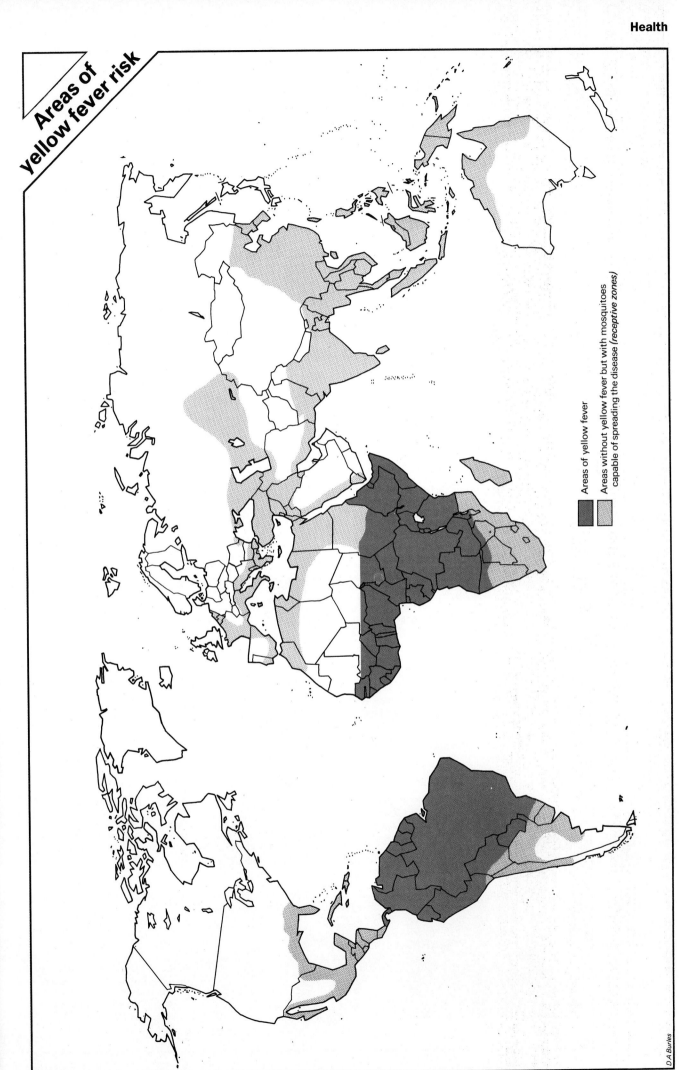

Areas of yellow fever risk

Areas of yellow fever

Areas without yellow fever but with mosquitoes capable of spreading the disease (*receptive zones*)

D A Burles

to prevent diseases contracted abroad should not be prescribed on form *FP10*.

IMMUNISATION

Yellow Fever

This disease is caused by a virus that circulates in animals indigenous to certain tropical forested areas. It mainly infects monkeys, but if man enters these areas the virus may be transmitted to him by mosquitoes whose normal hosts are monkeys. This is *jungle yellow fever*. It occurs haphazardly and is clearly related to man's habits. If, from an animal source, the virus begins to circulate between man and his own mosquitoes, primarily *Aedes aegypti*, epidemics of *urban yellow fever* result. Immunisation protects the individual and is effective in preventing the spread of the virus to countries where *Aedes aegypti* is prevalent. It is therefore reasonable for such countries to request a certificate of vaccination of all travellers from areas where human cases are occurring. Many national administrations, however, require immunisation of all travellers over one year of age from all countries, or else all travellers over one year from countries where enzootic *foci* occur. A map of zones where yellow fever is endemic (enzootic) can be found on page 1091. Immunisation is clearly not indicated when travelling outside the enzootic zones. Within the zones, if it is not compulsory, it is not always necessary. For instance, in the absence of an epidemic of yellow fever, a business trip within the confines of Nairobi would be perfectly safe. Nevertheless, local and current knowledge of cases is required for such decisions to be made, so in practice immunisation is recommended to all travellers within enzootic zones. Immunisation in Great Britain is undertaken only at recognised yellow fever vaccination centres.
Once immunised (a single vaccination is used), the vaccination certificate is valid after ten days for ten years. It is not recommended for pregnant women and children under nine months.

Cholera

In 1973 the WHO, recognising that immunisation cannot stop the spread of cholera among countries, deleted from the International Health Regulations the requirement of

cholera immunisation as a condition of admission to any country. In 1990 the WHO stated that immunisation against cholera was not effective and they do not recommend it. In 1991 the WHO confirmed that certification was no longer required by any country or territory.
Nevertheless, some countries do still require certification from travellers entering from an infected area. When immunisation is for certification one dose will suffice and the certificate is valid after six days for six months. It is not to be given to children under six months of age.

Typhoid Fever

Typhoid fever is endemic worldwide and is usually spread faecal-orally. The risk of infection is increased in areas of high carriage rates and poor hygiene. The risk is not significantly increased for the traveller to areas with public health standards similar to those of Britain – namely, northern Europe, USA, Canada, Australia, New Zealand and Japan – and immunisation for these areas is not necessary. Outside these areas the risks reflect not

only local hygiene and carriage rates but also lifestyle. Travelling or living rough, living in rural areas, or 'eating out' make transmission more likely. The risks are therefore small for the air traveller with full board at a reputable hotel, and immunisation is unnecessary. On the other hand, overland travel to Australia would be a clear indication for immunisation. Between these extremes there are many circumstances for which risks cannot be precisely defined. Typhoid vaccine is now no longer routinely recommended for the millions of tourists to southern Europe each year, although it may still be advisable not only for those whose lifestyle or occupation increase the risk of such exposure, but also during local outbreaks.

Hepatitis A

The *hepatitis A* virus is endemic worldwide and spread by the faecal-oral route; protection from symptomatic infection can be provided by active immunisation or passively acquired immunoglobulin. The virus circulates freely in our own population however, and many

travellers will be immune already. Protection should be offered to the same groups as are offered typhoid immunisation, as exposure to one infection would imply the risk of exposure to the other. The recurrent tropical traveller may have his antibodies against *hepatitis A* checked. If antibodies are present, that person is immune. If antibodies are absent, immunoglobulin or inactivated *hepatitis A* vaccine should be given. Immunoglobulin requires to be given at least every six months while the risk continues. *Hepatitis A* in children is usually mild and more often asymptomatic, so immunisation is not essential. Immunoglobulin can, however, be given in reduced doses. *Hepatitis A* vaccine is also available for use in children over the age of 12 months.

Poliomyelitis

A survey undertaken in Scotland in 1989 showed that 20% of the tested population did not have antibodies to all three serotypes of poliovirus. Hence a consultation about travel abroad is a vital opportunity to complete primary courses or boost immunisations which are nationally recommended. Oral poliomyelitis vaccine is given, but supplies of inactivated polio vaccine are available if oral vaccine is contra-indicated.

Tetanus

As with poliomyelitis, all individuals should gain or maintain immunity to tetanus. It is as firmly recommended for life in Britain as for travel abroad. A preparation combined with low dose diphtheria toxoid is now widely available and is recommended for travellers when immunity requires boosting.

SPECIAL/RARE DISEASES

Rabies

Most doctors do not think it is necessary to immunise the ordinary traveller going to areas where rabies is endemic, although it may be advisable for those in remote areas who would be many days' travel away from a source of vaccine and rabies immunoglobulin. However, all travellers should avoid contact with animals, especially cats and dogs. If they do get bitten,

wounds should be promptly washed with copious soap and water followed by the application of alcohol (spirits like gin and whisky can be used). If the animal's owner is available, it should be checked whether the animal has been vaccinated against rabies (check certification). A forwarding address or telephone number should be left to enable contact to be made should the animal become unwell over the next two weeks. Seek local medical advice promptly and give details of the incident to the local police. On return, the traveller's medical practitioner should be informed.

Diphtheria

Diphtheria is endemic worldwide, but there are current resurgences in Eastern Europe following decreased immunisation rates. From 1983 to 1987, only seven cases were notified in Great Britain, mostly from an imported source. Most morbidity and mortality are in children and they should be immunised as nationally recommended (initial primary course and booster on school entry and school leaving). Adult travellers with a high risk of infection are those in contact with children in poorer areas – for example, health workers and teachers. Such travellers may have their immunity boosted, without Schick testing, by a low dose preparation of diphtheria toxoid. A preparation combined with tetanus toxoid is now available.

Meningococcal meningitis

Although the bacteria responsible for this illness circulate widely throughout the world, certain areas, like the dry areas bordering the southern Sahara, are renowned for recurrent epidemics and many areas suffer occasional epidemics, as in India, Nepal and Brazil, and during the Mecca pilgrimages in recent years. Immunisation is available for the types of meningococci usually responsible for these outbreaks, and should be considered for travellers to such areas with current outbreaks, particularly those staying long-term.

Tick-borne encephalitis

Tick-borne encephalitis is caused by an arbovirus, transmitted by the bite of an infected tick. Its distribution is confined to warm and low-forested

areas in parts of Central Europe and Scandinavia, particularly Austria, Czech Republic, Slovak Republic, Germany and throughout all the republics of the former Yugoslavia. The forests are usually deciduous with heavy undergrowth. Those normally at risk are foresters and those clearing such areas, but increasing contact will occur with increased recreational use, such as camping and walking. Most human illness occurs in late spring and early summer. Tick bites are best avoided by limiting contact with such areas, wearing clothing to cover most of the skin surface and using insect repellents on outer clothes and socks. Where prolonged contact is necessary, a killed vaccine is available from Immuno Ltd on a named patient basis. Tel: (01732) 458 101. Fax: (01732) 455 175.

Japanese B encephalitis

This virus infection is transmitted by mosquitoes in certain rural areas of eastern Asia, the Indian subcontinent and a few Pacific islands. Occasional larger outbreaks develop and this infection tends to have a higher mortality than the many other similar viruses that can cause encephalitis. If planning to sleep in rural areas with a high risk or an active outbreak, immunisation should be considered; this is available from Cambridge Self Care Diagnostics. Tel: (0191) 261 5950. Fax: (0191) 261 5915. Considerable protection is offered by avoiding mosquito bites (see below in the *Malaria Prophylaxis* section) and staying indoors at night in rural areas where known cases are occurring.

Plague

Plague is an infection of wild rodents transmitted by fleas. It exists in many rural areas of Africa, Asia and the Americas. The risk to the traveller from the bite of an infected flea is *low*. Routine immunisation is not recommended. In enzootic areas, usually rural and hilly, contact with rodents should be discouraged by preventing their access to food and waste, avoiding dead rodents and rodent burrows. Fleas can be discouraged by insect repellents. During the plague outbreak in small areas of India in 1994, travellers were advised to avoid infected areas. Immunisation was not part of the general advice given.

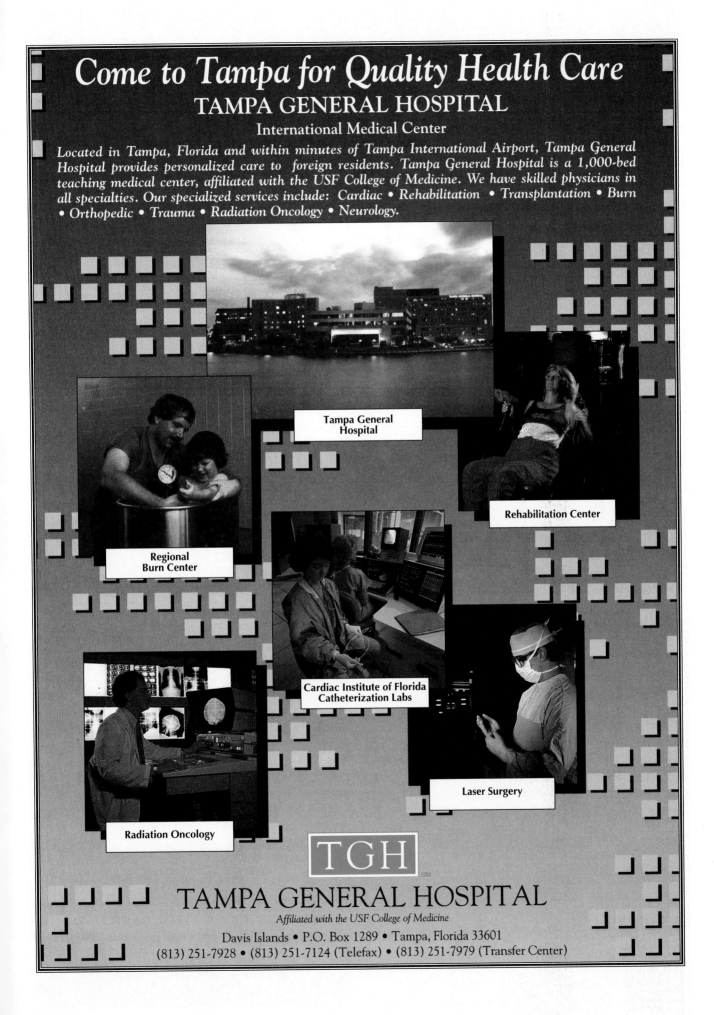

QUICK GUIDE TO VACCINATION/PROPHYLAXIS REQUIREMENTS & PROGRAMMES

When time permits, immunisation should be started well in advance so that adequate intervals between doses can be maintained. If notice to travel is short, a rapid course or single dose may be given, but the immunity provided will not be as good.
Children should be up-to-date with routine UK vaccination schedule. Extra consideration should be given to the need for vaccinating pregnant women. If it is known that a full initial (primary) course of any of these vaccines has been given, then only single booster doses are necessary.

Against	No. of injections in primary course (inc. period of protection)	Validity of certificate	Revaccination	Other details
Yellow Fever	One injection gives protection for 10 years.	10 days after inoculation for 10 years.	Every 10 years validity taking immediate effect.*	Reactions to vaccination are rare, though some discomfort might be experienced. Not for infants under 9 months or pregnant women.
Cholera **	2 injections given 4-6 weeks apart give some protection for 6 months. See note below.	6 days after inoculation for 6 months.	A single booster every six months.	Local tenderness, swelling and redness with slight general upset may occur. Not for infants under 1 year.
Typhoid Fever (a) Inactivated	Two injections separated by 4-6 weeks.	Not applicable.	Single booster every 3 years.	Local tenderness, swelling and redness with slight general upset may occur. Not for infants under 1 year.
(b) Vi vaccine	One injection.	Not applicable.	Single booster every 3 years.	Local and systematic reactions less than above. More expensive. Not for children under 18 months of age.
(c) Oral	One capsule on alternate days for 3 doses.	Not applicable.	3-dose booster annually for recurrent travellers.	Only mild reactions expected. To be kept refrigerated. Do not use with antibiotics, within 12 hours of mefloquine, in pregnant or immuno-compromised or concurrent oral polio vaccine. Not for children under 6 years of age. Most expensive.
Tetanus	Three injections given at four weekly intervals.	Not applicable.	Single booster every 10 years.	Local tenderness, swelling and redness may occur.
Poliomyelitis	Three oral doses given at four weekly intervals.	Not applicable.	Single booster every 10 years. Use combined with low dose diptheria toxoid to boost both.	Different (inactivated) vaccine available for pregnant women.
Hepatitis A (c) Immunoglobulin	500mg gammaglobulin taken just prior to departure gives reasonable protection for up to 6 months. 250mg gammaglobulin will protect for up to 2 months.	Not applicable.	Further gammaglobulin should be given every 6 months if risk persists.	Immediately protective for travel at short notice.
(b) Vaccine	One injection will provide protection for 6 months to 1 year.	Not applicable.	Single booster at 6 months to 1 year can be expected to provide 10 years' protection.	Equally protective as immunogloulin. Useful for recurrent travellers. Half-dose preparation now available for ages 1-15 years.
Malaria	Tablets should be taken a few days prior to departure and continued regularly while in malarial zone. It is essential to continue taking tablets for 4 weeks after leaving zone (see *Malaria Prophylaxis*).	Not applicable.	Not applicable.	Pregnant women and newborn infants require special consideration.

* If vaccination is recorded on a new certificate, travellers are advised to retain thier old certificate until their new certificate is valid.
** The World Health Organisation state that vaccination against cholera cannot prevent the introduction of the infection into a country. The WHO therefore amended the International Health Regulations in 1973 so that cholera vaccination should no longer be required of any traveller, although some countries still request a certificate as a condition of entry or the granting of a visa.

P U B L I C A T I O N S

The following list is selective, but includes sources that are readily available and frequently updated.

HEALTH ADVICE FOR TRAVELLERS (T5) – DEPARTMENT OF HEALTH

These are available free by dialling (0800) 555 777. If more than ten copies are required, they can be ordered from Health Publications Unit, No 2 Site, Heywood Stores, Manchester Road, Heywood, Lancs OL10 2PZ. This is a yearly publication containing advice on how to reduce health risks, with a list, by country, of compulsory and recommended immunisations. It advises about travel insurance and entitlement to reduced cost medical treatment in other countries.

INTERNATIONAL TRAVEL AND HEALTH World Health Organisaiton, Geneva, yearly

This lists, by country, compulsory immunisations and the risk of malaria and gives the distribution by geographical area of other health risks and appropriate advice. It is aimed particularly at national health administrations and is not recommended for the individual traveller without medical knowledge.

TRAVELLERS' HEALTH (3RD EDITION) ed. R. Dawood, Oxford University Press, 1992.

A multi-author book by mostly tropical disease specialists. some medical knowledge is necessary to understand the extensive coverage of many conditions met by the traveller. Most suitable for those residing long-term in tropical climates and highly motivatded to understand their health needs.

ABC OF HEALTHY TRAVEL (4TH EDITION) E. Walker, G. Williams, F. Raeside, British Medical

Journal, 1993
An easy-to-read guide to the health problems of travel intended for the general practioner and informed lay person.

PRESERVATION OF PERSONAL HEALTH IN WARM CLIMATES

Ross Institute of Tropical Hygiene, 1992.
Aimed at the traveller, particularly those becoming resident abroad, A concise and detailed account of health problems, how they arise and how they may be modified.

BRITISH MEDICAL JOURNAL 1988 – WELL AWAY E. Walker, G. Williams.

Less detailed than the above, but more understandable for the average traveller without medical knowledge.

TRAVEL AND HEALTH IN THE ELDERLY I.B. McIntosh, Quay Publishing, 1992

A comprehensive guide that also has helpful advice for younger people.

STAY HEALTHY WHILE YOU TRAVEL Tim Symonds and Lesley Abdela, Columbus Press, 1988

An invaluable travel-size guide which gives the traveller basic information needed for safe travel in hot countries.

CARE IN THE AIR Air Transport Users Council, 5th Floor, Kingsway House, 103 Kingsway, London WC2B

6QX. Tel: (0171) 242 3882.
Advice for handicappped travellers and a useful planning guide.

YOUR PATIENT AND AIR TRAVEL British Airways Health Centre, Passenger Clearance Department,

Queens Building, Ground Floor (N121) Heathrow Airport, Hounslow, Middlesex TW6 2JA. Tel: (0181) 562 7070.
Useful booklet for medical practitioners with advice on fitness to travel and specific contra-indications.

THE CARE OF BABIES AND YOUNG CHILDREN IN THE TROPICS D. Morley, National

Association for Maternal and Child Welfare, 1st Floor, 40-42 Osnaburgh Street, London NW1 3ND. Tel: (0171) 383 4115.

HEALTH INFORMATION FOR INTERNATIONAL TRAVEL, available from Superintendent of

Documents, US Govt Printing Office, Washington, DC 20402.

Hepatitis B

Vaccination should be considered for groups such as medical, nursing and laboratory staff planning to work among populations with high HBsAg carriage rates. The recommended regimen consists of three doses, the boosters being given one month and six months after the initial dose. Immunity is predicted to last about five years but those who remain at risk should have antibodies checked three months after completion of course.

Aids

This disease develops in people who have been infected with the human immunodeficiency virus (HIV). People infected with HIV, and who may appear perfectly well, pass on the infection by sexual intercourse or if their blood is inoculated into other people, as in the sharing of needles by drug users, the transfusion of untested blood, or the re-use of injection needles without sterilisation between patients. Certain areas of the world, such as parts of tropical Africa, South America and Asia have a higher number of carriers of HIV. However, the potential for infection exists worldwide and precautions should always be taken whether at home or abroad. The use of condoms and spermicidal cream during sexual intercourse should reduce the level of risk. Thought must also be given to the need for blood transfusions, where blood is not tested for HIV antibodies, and the need for injections where there is doubt about the sterility of the needles (these may be sterilised by placing in boiling water for 20 minutes). Kits containing appropriate needles and syringes are available. Travellers should know their blood group. The World Health Organisation is vigorously opposed to any country requiring travellers to present a certificate stating that they are free from HIV infection. Besides being against International Health Regulations, it is both clinically unsound and epidemiologically unjustifiable as a means of limiting infection. However, at least 40 countries have introduced restrictions, such as compulsory HIV testing or refusal of entry of 'suspicious' visitors, though mostly those planning to stay, work or study long-term.

MALARIA PROPHYLAXIS

Malaria is widespread in tropical and subtropical areas of the world and is spread by the bite of a female anopheline mosquito that has been infected by the malaria parasite.

The increasing mobility of the population, especially through air travel, brings a further hazard since travellers may be bitten by mosquitoes at airports en route as well as in the countries where they stay. The speed of travel means that first symptoms may occur in a country and in a context where the disease will not be immediately considered. Mosquitoes may even be brought in airplanes to non-endemic areas and infect, for example, airport staff or travellers' relatives. Infection also occurs through blood transfusion (cold storage does not destroy the parasites) and the sharing of needles by drug users.

The life-threatening form of malaria is caused by *Plasmodium falciparum*. Because of the travelling habits of those living in Britain, this form of malaria is usually imported from Africa but also from Asia. Prevention is primarily aimed at this parasite. Nevertheless, the same advice is given to those likely to be exposed to the less dangerous *P vivax*, *P malariae*, and *P ovale*, partly to prevent an unpleasant illness but also because *P falciparum* infection can never be presumed to be absent in any malarious area. There is no immediate prospect of an effective vaccine, so regular ingestion of prophylactic tablets is necessary. This requires habits which some find difficult or even distasteful, and because of increasing resistance to these tablets, they can no longer guarantee protection from illness. Bites must be avoided or reduced (see below) and any flu-like illness with fever and shivers lasting more than two days should be promptly diagnosed. If such symptoms develop after return, even months afterwards, the attending doctor should be reminded of the date and place of travel.

Note: A map showing areas of malarial risk and areas where chloroquine resistance has been reported is printed on page . Source: WHO, Geneva.

Personal precautions

(1) Avoid mosquito bites, especially after sunset, when the anopheline mosquitoes responsible for transmitting malaria are most active. Long trousers, sleeves and dresses, netting on windows, and mosquito nets over beds help to prevent mosquito bites.

(2) Insect repellents may be used on exposed skin and insecticides inside buildings or on breeding sites. Repellent-impregnated wrist and ankle bands, and electrical insecticide vaporisers may also be used.

(3) Mosquitoes should not be encouraged to breed by leaving stagnant water – for example, in blocked drains or around plant pots.

(4) Prophylactic tablets are necessary because the above measures, although valuable, are unlikely to be fully effective.

Precautions before travel

(a) Start tablets one week before departure to confirm tolerance and obtain adequate blood concentrations before exposure.

(b) Take the tablets *with absolute regularity*. Prophylactic doses of drugs are not normally curative once the infection is established.

(c) Continue prophylaxis for at least four weeks after leaving an endemic area: all forms of the parasite develop first in the liver and only later re-enter the blood, where most prophylactic drugs take effect.

(d) Seek advice on which type of tablet to take from an advice centre (see beginning of entry).

CHILDREN

As children begin to crawl and walk they become more vulnerable to faecal-oral infections and hazards such as bites, accidents and burns. Open wounds should be kept clean and covered with dressings until healed. Deaths from scorpion bites are unusual but mostly occur in children aged under two years. Allowing toddlers to play outside unattended can be particularly hazardous. Taking adequate malarial prophylaxis should not encourage the traveller to ignore the risks from other mosquito-borne diseases such as dengue, which can be more severe in children. Protection from mosquito bites is also important in those children who are strongly allergic to them. Appropriate clothes and bed or window netting at night are usually more valuable in the long term than insect repellents.

PREGNANCY

Live vaccinations are best not given during pregnancy, although if someone unprotected against yellow fever is going to live in a high risk area, the theoretical risk of vaccination is outweighed by the serious nature of the illness. If the vaccine is not given, a doctor's letter endorsed with a health board or authority stamp to say the inoculation is contra-indicated is usually accepted. Inactivated poliomyelitis vaccine may be used instead of oral live vaccine.

A mother immunised against tetanus passes on protection to her baby over the neonatal period and a booster can be given during pregnancy if necessary. *Hepatitis A* in pregnancy may be more severe and also result in premature labour. Prevention with normal immunoglobulin is generally encouraged for those at risk. Malarial prophylaxis should be maintained throughout pregnancy but the risks of some drugs have to be balanced against the type of malaria and likelihood of its transmission in different areas and specialist advice should be sought.

CONTRACEPTION

Those using oral contraceptives should be aware that absorption may be affected during gastrointestinal illnesses, that some brands may not be available locally, and that they may be continued over the usual break in the cycle if menstruation is going to occur at an inconvenient time such as during a long journey. They may contribute to the fluid retention that some people experience in hot climates. Reliable condoms are not available in all localities abroad.

> FOR AREAS OF MALARIA RISK AND AREAS OF YELLOW FEVER RISK SEE MAPS ON PAGES 1090 AND 1091.

The Disabled Traveller

INTRODUCTION

Disability – whether short term or permanent – does not stop people *wanting* to travel for pleasure, or *needing* to travel for business. Arranging travel for someone who has impaired vision or hearing, or who may be a wheelchair user, can be an alarming prospect, but does not have to be an impossible problem. Careful and sometimes painstaking planning is needed, but provided you and your client are frank with one another over what you can and cannot do, there is no reason why both of you should not be happy with the outcome.

What disablement means

Disability can take many forms: to be disabled means having an impairment which takes away abilities which someone would otherwise be able to enjoy.

When a person uses a wheelchair, or can only move about on sticks and crutches, their disability is only too evident. Although they are likely to have the greatest difficulties in travelling, there are many more people who may not be obviously disabled, but have some problem which can make it difficult to move about easily and to enjoy a holiday without problems or worries. People who have had strokes or are arthritic, blind or epileptic are likely to be among these.

There are also many people whose mobility is impaired temporarily, such as those who may have broken limbs, or women who are in the late stages of pregnancy.

Travel opportunities and choice for disabled people have grown dramatically over the past few years, and travel agents can play an important role in ensuring the success of what may, in many cases, be a first trip away from home.

HELPING THE TRAVELLER

In order to help a disabled traveller to plan a holiday or business trip, the most important thing is to obtain as much information as possible. Find out when, where and for how long the person has travelled on previous occasions, and what problems, if any, were encountered. It is also necessary to know whether he or she will be travelling alone and, if so, whether he or she is able to be completely independent – in a different environment, possibly in an unfamiliar climate that could cause discomfort, and where language may be a problem. Help will usually be at hand at terminals and in hotels, but should not be expected nor relied upon unless confirmed in writing beforehand. If complete independence is impossible, he or she *must* be accompanied by someone who can give the extra help needed. If this is out of the question, there are some organisations specialising in holidays for severely disabled unaccompanied people, both in this country and abroad. For details, contact the *Holiday Care Service* at the address below.

The name of the person's disability and its effects are also vital information. There are many kinds of disability, both temporary and permanent. Not all necessitate permanent wheelchair use or limit mobility; a broken leg creates different problems from a heart condition or respiratory complaint. The following checklist covers the kind of information that needs to be communicated to tour operators, carriers and hoteliers:

• The name of the disability;
• The limitations to mobility – for example, ability to walk unaided, the use of a stick or crutches, the need to hold someone's arm to help over long distances;
• Whether the use of a wheelchair is permanent, most of the time, or for distance only;
• Whether transfer from a wheelchair into a coach, air or train seat is easy or difficult;
• Whether one or both legs need to be fully extended whilst travelling;
• The overall dimensions of the wheelchair, whether it is collapsable and if it is battery operated;
• Any other effects of the disability;
• Whether the person is being accompanied by someone who can provide all the personal assistance needed whilst on holiday and, if not, whether help will be required with feeding, washing, bathing, toileting, dressing or simply pushing the wheelchair. If this kind of help is needed, and the traveller will not be accompanied by a friend or relative, it will probably be necessary to join a special holiday for disabled people where such assistance is available: *Holiday Care Service* has details;

• Any special requirements for the holiday or the journey, such as a special diet, oxygen or other aids;
• Any other information which may be helpful to the travel agent or tour operator in ensuring the most comfortable trip;
• If travelling as a group, apart from the usual questions about budget, it is useful to know the proportion of able-bodied to disabled people; the nature of the disabilities; the number of wheelchair users; whether or not there is a doctor or nurse in the party; and the age groups involved.

ARRANGING THE TOUR

Booking an inclusive tour

The *Holiday Care Service* provides a list of operators whose programmes can be considered by a disabled traveller (some mention this in their brochures and give a contact name and telephone number). If a particular country or resort has been asked for, the Service can tell you which operators serve that destination, and in some cases will be able to give detailed information about facilities for disabled people in hotels there.
Communication is essential when booking a disabled client on a package tour. It is the travel agent's task to provide all the information a tour operator might need to ensure the success of the trip for the client. Misunderstandings will be minimised if the enquiry and booking are backed up with a letter clearly stating the client's needs, and requesting written confirmation that these can be met. The points to be covered will include transport to, from and at the destination; accommodation; and facilities at the resort and during excursions. The paragraphs which follow on transport and accommodation will also help to ask the tour operator the right questions.

THE INDEPENDENT TRAVELLER

As long as the necessary information is available, it should not be difficult to meet the requirements for a business trip or holiday – but every detail must be double-checked, particularly on a complicated journey where the risk of a problem is greater.

Air

Where there is a choice of airlines, check on their policy and attitude towards carrying disabled people; the facilities they have for them (both on the ground and in the air); the type of aircraft (some are more comfortable than others); the availability of special diets; the method of boarding and disembarking people; and so on.
The time of day for travelling can be important to someone with a disability, as can the difference between a non-stop flight or one which involves stopovers.
The most comprehensive advice on air travel for disabled people is found in 'Care in the Air', available free from the Air Transport Users Council, 5th Floor, Kingsway House, 103 Kingsway, London WC2B 6QX. Tel: (0171) 242 3882. Fax: (0171) 831 4132.
Each UK airport gives details of the services that they can offer to disabled travellers. For information contact the relevant airport. The 'Welcome to Gatwick' publication covers provision for disabled people at Gatwick Airport. This is available from Gatwick Airport Ltd, Gatwick, West Sussex RH6 0HZ.
The Heathrow Airport 'Special Needs Guide' provides information for disabled travellers who wish to fly to and from the airport. This is available from Heathrow Airport Ltd, Hounslow, Middlesex TW6 1JH. Tel: (0181) 745 6156. Brochure Line: (0123) 321 1207.
British Airways publishes a leaflet intended as a general guide to doctors entitled 'Your Patient and Air Travel'. Details of facilities and services for disabled people at over 280 airports in 40 countries are contained in 'Access Travel; Airports', published by the US Department of Transportation, and available from Access America, Washington, DC 20202, USA. *Publications such as these should only provide preliminary guidance; checking is still important.*
Check to make certain the arrangements for checking in and boarding and remember that equal care is needed at the end of the journey; ensure any airport transfer arrangements are appropriate, and provide the traveller with the telephone numbers needed to confirm arrangements for the homeward journey; if there is a change in the time, airline or airport, the new arrangements will have to be checked for their suitability.

Sea

An increasing number of ferries have incorporated special facilities for disabled people and, where there is a choice of routes and/or companies, you can check which offers the best facilities. Not all the vessels in a fleet will

have the same facilities.
The *Holiday Care Service* keeps details of what is currently available; whether or not a ferry or hovercraft offers special facilities, it is still vitally important that the company is informed in advance that someone is disabled.
When booking a crossing for a disabled passenger, ensure the company knows the nature of the disability and the sort of help needed during the journey.
Cruises can be especially attractive to older and disabled people, and most shipping lines offering cruises or fly/cruises are used to carrying disabled passengers. However, the following problems should be borne in mind:
• A cruise is almost certainly out of the question for someone who cannot walk at all and is unaccompanied;
• Shore excursions may not be possible, especially if tendering is involved and passengers have to board launches;
• Coaches on shore excursions are unlikely to have any special facility for a disabled person;
• Bad weather can be distressing for everyone, but especially so for someone not too steady on their feet or a wheelchair user.
When booking a disabled client on a cruise, and they are a wheelchair user, obtain the following information before making definite reservations:
• Width of lift floors, and whether they offer access to all parts of the ship;
• Width of cabin and toilet/bathroom doors; whether the doors open outwards, and if not, whether they block the plumbing; whether any existing steps at the doorways can be ramped temporarily;
• Whether any cabins have an extra basin in the room to save some trips to the bathroom; where they are located; how much they cost, and their location in relation to lifts etc;
• Whether a wheelchair user is excluded from any part of the ship because of stairs, narrow doorways or other obstacles;
• Which excursions ashore require a launch to be used, and whether help would be available if the stairs down to the launch cannot be used; whether the gangplank used by passengers is too steep for a wheelchair user, and whether the one used by the crew is any lower and could be used instead;
• What special arrangements might be needed at the start and finish of the cruise;
• What special diets are available;
• Any restrictions on the type of wheelchair used;
• Availability of laundry and/or launderette facilities.

Road and Rail

The provision of facilities for disabled travellers in coaches, taxis, hire cars and trains varies considerably from country to country. Even where there are specially adapted vehicles, as in the United Kingdom, these may not be available on all routes or at more than a few locations. Check with the relevant carrier for further information.
British Rail in the UK has done much recently to improve the service offered to disabled passengers. This includes *Motor Rail* services; all terminals now have wheelchairs available to assist disabled people. For full details ask for the 'Motor Rail' brochure, available from stations, travel centres and BR-appointed travel agents.
'Disabled Person's Railcard' gives discounts to holders and is available to people with a variety of disabilities. For information ask for the leaflet 'Disabled Person's Railcard' at stations, travel centres and post offices, which gives details and includes an application form. Blind or partially-sighted travellers who do not have a 'Disabled Person's Railcard' are entitled to discounts on standard and season tickets. Guide dogs accompanying blind people are always conveyed free of charge.
British Rail can give assistance to disabled travellers from the moment they leave their door, through to the time they reach their destination. For full details ask for the 'British Rail and Disabled Travellers' leaflet available free from all stations and travel centres. The leaflet also gives the name and addresses of the Area Manager who should be contacted in advance of travel. This gives the opportunity for all the relevant information to be compiled so that a comprehensive service can be offered at the time of travel.
Note: Since November 1989 all new *licensed London cabs* have been equipped to carry wheelchairs. There are now approximately 3900 cabs that are capable of this, and it is hoped that by 1999 all cabs in service will be able to take wheelchairs on board. These cabs are available from cab ranks at stations, airports, hotels across London and can be hailed in the normal way. Where there are no special facilities, it may still be possible for a disabled person to travel by road or rail, always ensuring that prior notification is given to the operator, giving precise details of route and timing. Where appropriate, help may then be provided.

Car rental

Some international car rental firms have cars equipped with hand controls for drivers with lower-limb disability. For further details, contact car hire companies.

ACCOMMODATION

The nature and degree of the disability will dictate the type of accommodation required. The points below will be important, and are particularly relevant to wheelchair users; however, when booking, ask what facilities will be needed for minimum and maximum comfort, request these facilities, back up your request with a letter, and ask for confirmation in writing that they are available.

Access

For wheelchair access, entrance or side doors need to be ramped or level, with a minimum width of 75cm (2.5ft). Interior doors also need to be at least this width, with no steps leading into public rooms (restaurant, lounge, bar, toilets, etc).
There are many disabled people who do not use wheelchairs, but are unable to use steps or stairs. A number of accommodation guides, details of which can be obtained from the *Holiday Care Service,* show where there are ground-floor bedrooms. Most of these also show where there is a lift available, so even if there are no ground-floor bedrooms, access may be just as feasible because there is a lift. If making enquiries about a hotel or guest-house with a lift, do make sure that the bedroom is as near to the lift as possible, and do ask whether there are any steps in the corridor between the lift doors and the bedroom.

General facilities

If ground-floor bedrooms are not available, there should be a lift large enough to take a wheelchair, ie at least 120cm (4ft) deep by 80cm (2.6ft) wide.

Bedroom

The door should be at least 75cm (2.5ft) wide; there should be sufficient turning space for a wheelchair, ie 120cm (4ft) by 120cm (4ft), and free width of at least 80cm (2.5ft) to one side of the bed.

Bathroom

The door should be at least 75cm (2.5ft) wide; enough room is needed to enter in a wheelchair and close the door, with space beside the WC for a wheelchair to enable sideways transfer; support rails near the bath and WC are also needed.

Outside

There should be a route without steps and with a firm smooth surface which wheelchairs can use; this would ideally facilitate access to the swimming pool or beach without needing to negotiate steps; the availability or otherwise of a swimming-pool hoist should be indicated; the accommodation should be in a central position with shopping and entertainment facilities within easy reach, otherwise specially-arranged transport would be needed to enable disabled holidaymakers to go on trips or excursions.

The Accessible Symbol

The Hotel and Holiday Consortium, made up of 21 organisations including ABTA, the BTA and the British Hospitality Association, has drawn up a range of minimum standards which must be met by an establishment before the Accessible Symbol can be awarded. Requirements for the new symbol are as follows:
• A public entrance to the building must be accessible to disabled people from a setting-down or car-parking point;
• Where an establishment has a car park, a parking space must be reserved for a disabled guest on request;
• Disabled people must have access to the following areas (if provided): reception, restaurant or dining room, lounge, TV lounge (unless TV is provided in the bedroom) and bar;
• A minimum of one guest room with bath or shower and WC facilities en suite, which is suitable for a wheelchair user, should be provided. Where these facilities are not en suite, a unisex WC compartment and a bath or shower room suitable for a wheelchair user must be provided on the same floor level.

O R G A N I S A T I O N S

HOLIDAY CARE SERVICE

2 Old Bank Chambers, Station Road, Horley, Surrey RH6 9HW. Tel: (01293) 774 535. Fax: (01293) 784 647. Minicom: (01293) 776 943.

The *Holiday Care Service*, which was established as a registered charity in 1981, is the UK's central source of holiday information for people whose age, disability, or other personal or family circumstances make it difficult for them to find a holiday. An entirely non-commercial organisation, it provides details of accommodation, transport, facilities or publications which are most appropriate to the person's needs, although it does not make reservations direct.

At present the following areas of information are covered by the service; new topics are being added continuously.

Overseas holidays for disabled people: Planning and booking the holiday; information on insurance; specialised group holidays; commercial packages; cruises; handling agents; self-catering; camping and caravanning; car hire; pilgrimages; serviced accommodation; transport advice; resort information and hotel descriptions for the major European tourist destinations.

UK holidays for disabled people: Specialist commercial and voluntary operators; access, accommodation and catering guides; self-catering accommodation; hotels and guest-houses; special interest and activity holidays; farm holidays; specially adapted accommodation; group facilities; university and college accommodation; holiday camps and centres; accommodation where personal or nursing care is provided; boating holidays; coach, rail, taxi and ambulance information; car hire; non-smoking accommodation; holidays suitable for those with epilepsy; holidays for people with learning difficulties; opportunities for those with mental health needs; escorts; financial assistance; information for deaf and/or blind people; various holidays for physically, mentally and/or sensorily handicapped children; use of oxygen on holiday; holiday facilities for kidney dialysis.

It is vital that adequate insurance cover is arranged. One of the most difficult problems disabled people have faced in the past has been the inclusion in policies of a 'pre-existing medical condition' exclusion clause. These still appear in the policies offered by quite a number of tour operators. Do check very carefully that the policy offered does not have this clause. Even those who exclude nothing often require that a 'fitness to travel' certificate is obtained from a doctor beforehand. The *Holiday Care Service* offers information on insurance for disabled travellers. Details are contained in the organisation's 'Holiday Insurance' leaflet.

As a travel agent, it would be useful to find out how your client got on, if anything went wrong or if the client has any handy hints to pass on. Any feedback, whether good or bad, is helpful to you and to disabled people.

RADAR

(Royal Association for Disability and Rehabilitation), 12 City Forum, 250 City Road, London EC1V 8AF. Tel: (0171) 250 3222. Fax: (0171) 250 0212. Minicom: (0171) 250 4119. RADAR is a national organisation working with and for physically disabled people. It acts as a pressure group to improve the environment for disabled people, campaigning for their rights and needs, and challenging negative attitudes and stereotypes. *RADAR* is particularly involved with education, health, social services, employment, housing, mobility and holidays. The organisation publishes several books, including 'Holidays and Travel Abroad. A Guide for Disabled People' and 'Holidays in the British Isles. A Guide For Disabled People', as well as a number of fact sheets covering all aspects of travel.

ACROSS TRUST

Bridge House, 70/72 Bridge Road, East Molesey, Surrey KT8 9HF. Tel: (0181) 783 1355. Fax: (0181) 783 1622. *Across Trust* arranges holidays for severely disabled people through *Jumbulance Holidays Across Europe*.

BREAK

20 Hooks Hill Road, Sherringham, Norfolk NR26 8NL. Tel: (01263) 823 170. Fax: (01263) 825 560. *Break* caters mainly for physically and mentally handicapped children and adults. *Break* can supply an information pack which also includes an application form. Write to the address above.

BRITISH RED CROSS SOCIETY

9 Grosvenor Crescent, London SW1X 7EJ. Tel: (0171) 235 5454. Fax: (0171) 245 6315. An information pack can be supplied on request. The *Red Cross* will provide regional contact addresses and telephone numbers, so that local help can be found.

TRIPSCOPE

The Courtyard, Evelyn Road, London W4 5JX. Tel: (0181) 994 9294. Fax: (0181) 994 3618. or Pamwell House, 160 Pennywell Road, Bristol B53 0TX. Tel: (0117) 941 4094. Fax: (0117) 941 4024. *Tripscope* is a free travel and transport information service for disabled and elderly people, and can advise on planning local, long-distance and international journeys.

Much of the information contained above is based on material supplied by *Holiday Care Service*; the publishers wish to thank them for their help in preparing this section of the 'World Travel Guide'.

COUNTRY CURRENCY CODES

COUNTRY	CURRENCY	CODE	COUNTRY	CURRENCY	CODE
Afghanistan	Afghani	AFA	Czech Republic	Koruna	CZK
Albania	Lek	ALL	Denmark	Danish Krone	DKK
Algeria	Algerian Dinar	DZD	Djibouti	Djibouti Franc	DJF
Andorra	Spanish Peseta	ESP	Dominica	East Caribbean Dollar	XCD
	French Franc	FRF	Dominican Republic	Dominican Peso	DOP
Angola	New Kwanza	AOK	Ecuador	Sucre	ESC
Anguilla	East Caribbean Dollar	XCD	Egypt	Egyptian Pound	EGP
Antarctica	No universal currency	-	El Salvador	El Salvador Colón	SVC
Antigua & Barbuda	East Caribbean Dollar	XCD	Equatorial Guinea	CFA Franc	XAF
Argentina	Argentine Peso	ARS	Estonia	Kroon	EEK
Aruba	Aruban Guilder	AWG	Ethiopia	Ethiopian Birr	ETB
Australia	Australian Dollar	AUD	Falkland Islands	Falkland Island Pound	FKP
Austria	Schilling	ATS	Fiji	Fiji Dollar	FJD
Bahamas	Bahamian Dollar	BSD	Finland	Markka	FIM
Bahrain	Bahraini Dinar	BHD	France	French Franc	FRF
Bangladesh	Taka	BDT	French Guiana	French Franc	FRF
Barbados	Barbados Dollar	BBD	French Overseas Possessions	French Franc	FRF
Belgium	Belgian Franc	BEF	French Polynesia	CFP Franc	XPF
Belize	Belize Dollar	BZD	Gabon	CFA Franc	XAF
Benin	CFA Franc	XOF	Gambia, The	Dalasi	GMD
Bermuda	Bermudian Dollar	BMD	Georgia	Rouble	RUR
Bhutan	Indian Rupee	INR	Germany	Deutsche Mark	DEM
	Ngultrum	BTN	Ghana	Cedi	GHC
Bolivia	Boliviano	BOB	Gibraltar	Gibraltar Pound	GIP
Bonaire	Netherlands Antilles Guilder	ANG	Greece	Drachma	GRD
Bosnia-Hercegovina	New Yugoslav Dinar	BAD	Greenland	Danish Krone	DKK
Botswana	Pula	BWP	Grenada	East Caribbean Dollar	XCD
Brazil	Brazil Cruzeiro	BRC	Guadeloupe	French Franc	FRF
British Dep. Territories	Ocean Territory US Dollar	USD	Guatemala	Quetzal	GTQ
Brunei	Brunei Dollar	BND	Guinea Republic	Guinea Franc	GNF
Bulgaria	Lev	BGL	Guinea-Bissau	Guinea-Bissau Peso	GWP
Burkina Faso	CFA Franc	XOF	Guyana	Guyana Dollar	GYD
Burundi	Burundi Franc	BIF	Haiti	Gourde	HTG
Cambodia	Riel	KHR		US Dollar	USD
Cameroon	CFA Franc	XAF	Honduras	Lempira	HNL
Canada	Canadian Dollar	CAD	Hong Kong	Hong Kong Dollar	HKD
Cape Verde Islands	Cape Verde Escudo	CVE	Hungary	Forint	HUF
Cayman Islands	Cayman Island Dollar	KYD	Iceland	Iceland Krona	ISK
Central African Republic	CFA Franc	XAF	India	Indian Rupee	INR
Chad	CFA Franc	XAF	Indonesia	Rupiah	IDR
Chile	New Chilean Peso	CLP	Iran	Iranian Rial	IRR
China, People's Republic of	Yuan Renminbi	CNY	Iraq	Iraqi Dinar	IQD
Colombia	Colombian Peso	COP	Ireland, Republic of	Irish Punt	IEP
CIS	Rouble	RUR	Israel	Shekel	ILS
Comoro Islands	Comoro Franc	KMF	Italy	Italian Lira	ITL
Congo	CFA Franc	XAF	Jamaica	Jamaican Dollar	JMD
Cook Islands	New Zealand Dollar	NZD	Japan	Yen	JPY
Costa Rica	Costa Rican Colon	CRC	Jordan	Jordanian Dollar	JOD
Côte d'Ivoire	CFA Franc	XOF	Kenya	Kenyan Shilling	KES
Croatia	Croatian Dinar	HRD	Kiribati	Australian Dollar	AUD
Cuba	Cuban Peso	CUP	Korea (North)	North Korean Won	KPW
Curaçao	Netherlands Antilles Guilder	ANG	Korea (South)	Won	KRW
Cyprus	Cyprus Pound	CYP	Kuwait	Kuwait Dinar	KWD

Three-letter codes assigned to each of the world's currencies by the International Standards Organisation.

COUNTRY	CURRENCY	CODE	COUNTRY	CURRENCY	CODE
Laos	Laotian New Kip	LAK	St Eustatius	Netherlands Antilles Guilder	ANG
Latvia	Latvian Lat	LVL	St Kitts & Nevis	East Caribbean Dollar	XCD
Lebanon	Lebanese Pound	LBP	St Lucia	East Caribbean Dollar	XCD
Lesotho	Rand	ZAR	St Maarten	Netherlands Antilles Guilder	ANG
	Loti	LSL	St Vincent & the Grenadines	East Caribbean Dollar	XCD
Liberia	Liberian Dollar	LRD	San Marino	Italian Lira	ITL
Libya	Libyan Dinar	LYD	São Tomé e Príncipe	Dobra	STD
Liechtenstein	Swiss Franc	CHF	Saudi Arabia	Saudi Riyal	SAR
Lithuania	Litas	LTL	Senegal	CFA Franc	XOF
Luxembourg	Luxembourg Franc	LUF	Seychelles	Seychelles Rupee	SCR
Macau	Pataca	MOP	Sierra Leone	Leone	SLL
Macedonia	Denar	MKD	Singapore	Singapore Dollar	SGD
Madagascar	Malagasy Franc	MGF	Slovak Republic	Koruna	SKK
Malawi	Kwacha	MWK	Slovenia	Slovene Tolar	SIT
Malaysia	Malaysian Ringgit	MYR	Solomon Islands	Solomon Islands Dollar	SBD
Maldives Republic	Rufiyaa	MVR	Somalia	Somali Shilling	SOS
Mali	CFA Franc	XOF	South Africa	Rand	ZAR
Malta	Maltese Lira	MTL	Spain	Spanish Peseta	ESP
Martinique	French Franc	FRF	Sri Lanka	Sri Lanka Rupee	LKR
Mauritania	Ouguiya	MRO	Sudan	Sudanese Pound	SDD
Mauritius	Mauritius Rupee	MUR	Suriname	Suriname Guilder	SRG
Mexico	Mexican Peso	MXN	Swaziland	Lilangeni	SZL
Monaco	French Franc	FRF	Sweden	Swedish Krona	SEK
Mongolia	Tugrik	MNT	Switzerland	Swiss Franc	CHF
Montserrat	East Caribbean Dollar	XCD	Syria	Syrian Pound	SYP
Morocco	Moroccan Dirham	MAD	Taiwan	New Taiwan Dollar	TWD
Mozambique	Metical	MZM	Tanzania	Tanzanian Shilling	TZS
Myanmar	Kyat	MMK	Thailand	Baht	THB
Namibia	Namibian Dollar	NAD	Togo	CFA Franc	XOF
Nauru	Australian Dollar	AUD	Tonga	Pa'anga	TOP
Nepal	Nepalese Rupee	NPR	Trinidad & Tobago	Trinidad & Tobago Dollar	TTD
Netherlands, The	Netherland Guilder	NLG	Tunisia	Tunisian Dinar	TND
New Caledonia	CFP Franc	XPF	Turkey	Turkish Lira	TRL
New Zealand	New Zealand Dollar	NZD	Turks & Caicos Islands	US Dollar	USD
Nicaragua	Córdoba	NIC	Tuvalu	Australian Dollar	AUD
Niger	CFA Franc	XOF	Uganda	Uganda Shilling	UGX
Nigeria	Naira	NGN	United Arab Emirates	UAE Dirham	AED
Norway	Norwegian Krone	NOK	United Kingdom	Pound Sterling	GBP
Oman	Rial Omani	OMR	United States of America	US Dollar	USD
Pacific Islands of Micronesia	US Dollar	USD	US Islands Am. Samoa/Guam/ US Virgin Islands	US Dollar	USD
Pakistan	Pakistani Rupee	PKR			
Panama	Balboa	PAB	Uruguay	Uruguayan Peso	UYU
	US Dollar	USD	Vanuatu	Vatu	VUV
Papua New Guinea	Kina	PGK	Vatican City	Italian Lira	ITL
Paraguay	Guaraní	PYG	Venezuela	Bolívar	VEB
Peru	Nuevo Sol	PES	Vietnam	Dong	VND
Philippines	Philippine Peso	PHP	Virgin Islands, British	US Dollar	USD
Poland	Zloty	PLZ	Western Samoa	Tala	WST
Portugal	Portuguese Escudo	PTE	Yemen, Republic of	Yemeni Rial	YER
Puerto Rico	US Dollar	USD		Yemeni Dinar	YER
Qatar	Qatari Rial	QAR	Yugoslavia	New Yugoslav Dinar	YUX
Réunion	French Franc	FRF	Zaïre	New Zaïre	ZRN
Romania	Leu	ROL	Zambia	Kwacha	ZMK
Rwanda	Rwanda Franc	RWF	Zimbabwe	Zimbabwe Dollar	ZWD
Saba	Netherlands Antilles Guilder	ANG			

Weather

The following gives an indication of the way in which weather conditions affect people. The comfort or discomfort felt in different conditions depends on temperature, humidity and wind. For information on weather conditions in each country, see the relevant country entry.

HUMIDITY

Humidity is the amount of moisture in the air. Expressed as a percentage, a relative humidity of 100% is the maximum possible moisture content held at any given temperature. As air can hold more moisture at greater heat, so 100% humidity at 26°C (79°F) holds more moisture than 100% humidity at 10°C (50°F). Low humidity results in rapid evaporation; perspiration evaporates easily and wet clothes dry quickly. Such conditions prevail in hot and dry climates, where one experiences far less discomfort and can endure relatively high temperatures. In a hot climate with high humidity conditions, perspiration cannot evaporate easily and clothes dry slowly. One feels hot and uncomfortable as heat loss through perspiration is minimised. A breeze can sometimes relieve the discomfort associated with high humidity. Below freezing point the air can hold very little moisture and humidity has little effect. Although damp (raw) cold is less pleasant than dry cold in temperatures above freezing point, wind is a more important factor.

WIND

One feels cooler in wind because air movement around the body has the effect of carrying body heat away. In hot weather the body temperature is regulated chiefly by the evaporation of perspiration. When the air temperature exceeds normal skin temperature (about 34°C; 93°F), in a dry climate the cooling power of wind becomes critical. In low temperatures the wind speed is equally critical. A temperature of 0°C (32°F) with a wind speed of 50kmph (30mph) feels colder than the lower temperature of -20°C (4°F) in calm conditions. High wind speeds can increase the risk of frostbite.
Many regions have particular winds which occur at certain times of the day or seasons of the year, and there are general rules – for instance, winds generally drop at night and increase by day (especially on the coast). Wind speed almost always increases with altitude. However, average wind statistics are almost impossible to supply although forecasts are given in some countries, such as the USA, on television and radio or in newspapers.

WIND-CHILL FACTOR

The wind-chill factor indicates outdoor conditions and how a suitably dressed person would feel, and can be deduced from wind speeds and average temperatures. In less extreme conditions a sunny day will produce extra warmth. The rate of heat loss from the body can be measured in kilogram calories per square metre of body surface per hour. The wind-chill factor is often given in weather bulletins.

TEMPERATURE RANGE

This can be estimated by measuring the difference between the maximum and minimum temperatures, which usually occur just after midday and just before dawn. In cloudy, rainy areas the range may be quite small but in very sunny, dry climates such as deserts or mountainous regions there may be a large range with surprisingly cold nights. As a general rule the greatest range is inland and the lowest on the coast.

PRECIPITATION

Precipitation includes all forms of moisture falling on the ground as rain, snow, sleet, hail or fog drip. Generally this is rain but on high mountains, or in countries with very cold winters such as Canada, the Russian Federation parts of the USA, China or Scandinavia, it may well fall as snow. All forms are measured as the melted equivalent of rain, one foot of snow being roughly equivalent to one inch of rain. Generally, below 2°C (36°F) snow or sleet are as likely as rain. At freezing point or below, snow is most likely. Rain falling below freezing point, although rare, is very dangerous especially on roads.

PRECAUTIONS

Height above sea level

The general fall in temperature is at the rate of 0.6°C for every 100m (1°F for every 300ft), especially in cloud. Higher altitudes can also mean a wide range of day and night-time temperatures. Atmosphere becomes thinner over 1800m (6000ft), the sun's rays are more powerful and breathing and exertion become more difficult. Adequate clothing should always be taken when walking or climbing.

Heat

In high temperatures the body keeps cool by sweating. However, if the humidity is too low or evaporation is increased by wind, the body may not sweat fast enough to match the rate of evaporation. In such conditions the risk of heat exhaustion or heatstroke increases.
Heat Exhaustion: Symptoms are loss of appetite, lassitude and general discomfort, with possible hallucinations and vomiting. The sufferer should be moved to a cool place and drink salty water to replace moisture and salt lost in perspiration.
Heatstroke: When the body's cooling mechanism stops, the body becomes dry and temperature rises. The symptoms are burning sensations and dry skin followed by feverishness, sometimes developing into headache and confusion. Immediate medical attention is essential as heatstroke may be fatal. The patient should be cooled as fast as possible, preferably put in a cool place, splashed with cold or iced water, wrapped in a wet sheet with a fan directed on the body. Vigorous massage can also help.
Prevention: In a very hot country do not over-exert until after about a week's acclimatisation, especially after air travel. (Air-conditioning delays the process of acclimatisation.) Drink plenty of liquids, not too much alcohol and take salt. Avoid sunburn and wear comfortable, light clothing.

Cold

Body heat can be generated by physical activity and maintained by wearing suitable clothing. The danger occurs if one stops moving, becomes tired or if one remains in a strong wind below freezing point.
Hypothermia: Otherwise known as 'exposure'. The body temperature falls and this can be fatal. Risks of hypothermia usually occur through lack of adequate clothing in mountainous regions or at sea, especially at night and if clothes become wet (evaporation from wet clothing causes the body to lose heat more rapidly). Rain and snow with a strong wind increase the danger. Old people are particularly susceptible. Hypothermia becomes critical at a very low level of body temperature, around 25°-28°C (77°-82°F). The body should be rewarmed rapidly, preferably in a bath of 40°-45°C (104°-113°F). Artificial respiration and cardiac massage are required if breathing has stopped.
Frostbite: Affects flesh exposed to extreme cold, usually the face, hands and feet. The flesh freezes and this can result in the loss of limbs. The affected parts should be rewarmed slowly though as soon as possible, preferably in water no hotter than 40°-44°C (104°-111°F). Do not bandage, massage or rub frostbitten skin.

CLIMATE GRAPH CONVERSIONS

Easy to use and informative climate charts are provided at the end of each country's entry. Very occasionally a climate chart from a nearby country will be used.

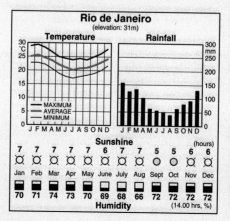

Rio de Janeiro
(elevation: 31m)

| | Temperature | | Rainfall | |

Sunshine (hours)

Jan	Feb	Mar	Apr	May	June	July	Aug	Sept	Oct	Nov	Dec
7	7	7	7	7	6	7	7	5	5	6	6

| 70 | 71 | 74 | 73 | 70 | 69 | 68 | 66 | 72 | 72 | 72 | 72 |

Humidity (14.00 hrs, %)

World of Buddhism

INTRODUCTION

Buddhism was born as a result of the works and teachings of Siddhartha, a member of the Shakyan clan who lived in and around the Ganges Plain during the 5th and 6th centuries BC. He is believed to have been born in 563BC, and was for many years a follower of the Vedic religion, a very diffuse set of spiritual and philosophical beliefs, one aspect of which was Brahmanism. Siddhartha's religion, achieved as a result of an 'Enlightenment', was in many ways a critique of Vedic doctrines. In particular, he was highly critical of its caste system and the use of sacrifices. In its place he developed a spiritualism which would enable man to escape from the pain and suffering of the world and achieve *Nirvana*. The word 'Buddha' means 'enlightened', and the achieving of this is the ultimate goal. Siddhartha was very keen to stress that he was neither God, nor the son of God, nor even a prophet but merely an ordinary man who had, through his own spiritualism, achieved enlightenment. The religion was non-theistic, having at its centre not a God but man in a fully-enlightened state. Full enlightenment is striven for through meditation and personal religious experience, combined with a strict morality and altruism. It is not regarded as being a static state but one which constantly changes; Siddhartha himself modified his teachings throughout his life in the light of circumstances and his own personal experiences.
Having established itself in northern India during the 5th century BC, Buddhism was contained within the subcontinent for about a hundred years. The teaching spread to Nepal by the 4th century BC, and reached Kashmir, Sri Lanka and Central Asia by the 2nd century BC. The later spread of the religion occurred partly through trade and partly through the work of missionaries. By the time of the birth of Christ, Buddhism was established in China, reaching Korea by the end of the 3rd century. The increased trade in the Far East at this time gave greater impetus to the spread of the religion, and by the 7th century Buddhists were to be found in Java, Sumatra, Japan, Tibet, Thailand and Myanmar. Further westward expansion was halted by Islamic conquests but conversion still persisted; Bhutan, for instance, was not reached until the 9th century but today is one of the most strongly Buddhist countries in the world.
The spread of Buddhism over a period of over 1500 years led to the development of three different strands:

Theravada Buddhism

Found in Thailand, Sri Lanka, Myanmar, Laos and Cambodia. The monks are distinguished by orange or yellow robes.

Mahayana Buddhism

Found in China, Japan and Korea. The priests wear brown, grey or black robes.

Vajrayana Buddhism

Found in Tibet, Nepal, Sikkim, Bhutan and Mongolia. The monks wear maroon robes.

Buddhism is not a centralised religion with centralised institutions, although it does have a hierarchical form of organisation within each of the three main groups (see above). In countries such as Thailand, Sri Lanka, Myanmar and Bhutan, where the Government and a large part of the population are Buddhist, the state is very closely associated with the religion and its organisation and institutions tend to be more formalised. In other countries, such as Japan, the religion exists within a looser framework.

FESTIVALS

Visitors are welcome to attend the many festivals which are an integral part of Buddhist life. The major obstacle is finding out the date, as these are scheduled by the lunar calendar and often take place on the full moon, and therefore change annually. Each country also has its own special festivals, so it is advisable to check well in advance. This can be done either by consulting the relevant country entries in this book under *Public Holidays,* or by contacting the embassies or tourist boards (addresses are at the beginning of each entry). The main festivals are as follows:
Wesak (Buddha Day) – Commemorating the Buddha's Enlightenment (as well as his Birthday and Death). It is celebrated in the Theravada countries around the full moon in May. Houses and streets are decorated and roads are packed with processions. Long lines of monks and worshippers throng the temples either meditating or listening to religious discourses.
Tooth Ceremony – takes place annually in Kandy, Sri Lanka, lasting for about a week in July or August. Up to 100 elephants take part.
Songkran – Celebrated in Thailand during April, this 3-day festival involves water-splashing, the freeing of fish, fighting kites, dancing, etc.
Hana Matsuri (the flower festival in April), **Jodo-e** (December) and **Nehan-e** (February) are celebrated in Japan to commemorate respectively the Birth, Enlightenment and Death of Buddha.
Chinese New Year – The main festival celebrated in China, the Vajrayana countries and by the Chinese populations in Malaysia, Taiwan (China), Hong Kong and Hawaii. This is actually a pre-Buddhist festival to mark the beginning of spring. It usually falls in February or late January and lasts for up to a week. The third day is the *Feast of Lanterns* when the long painted dragons dance in the streets. Vajrayana countries also have very colourful festivals and ceremonies, with demon-dancing and the blowing of enormous long horns by brightly-hatted monks. The dates for these festivals are variable, so it is best to enquire nearer the time when more information will be available.

Further information

Friends of the Western Buddhist Order (FWBO)
Madhya Maloka
30 Chantry Road
Birmingham B13 8DH
Tel: (0121) 449 3700.
Alternatively, contact the *London Buddhist Centre* on (0181) 981 1225.

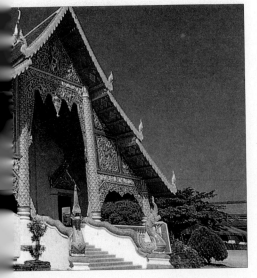

World of Christianity

CHRISTIAN BELIEF

The Bible consists of the Old Testament inherited from Judaism and the New Testament which tells the story of Jesus and his apostles, and also contains letters written to Christian communities, especially those by St Paul. Discussion of the Old Testament and St Paul's letters is omitted in the following for reasons of space.

THE NEW TESTAMENT STORY

The Christian belief is based on the life and teachings of Jesus who, as recorded in the gospels of Matthew, Mark, Luke and John, travelled through Palestine for three years declaring his message and performing miracles until he was arrested, accused of being a rebel against the occupying Roman authorities and crucified. The Jewish authorities were particularly upset by his claim to be the son of God, and therefore the long-awaited Messiah. According to believers, three days after his crucifixion Jesus rose from the dead and for the next few weeks appeared several times to his followers. He then 'ascended' to heaven.
Subsequent to his death, resurrection and Ascension his apostles (see below) and other disciples travelled through the Roman Empire preaching and gaining converts. Of these converts St Paul, who was in the first place fanatically anti-Christian, is perhaps the most important; many Christian doctrines are based on his letters to the various Christian communities.

THE MIRACLES

In the gospels, Jesus is often portrayed as reluctant to perform miracles, performing them only out of compassion, with a reminder that people should not believe in him for his miracles. The miracles most often mentioned involve making the lame walk and the blind see, from others he 'casts out devils' (a phrase now given a psychological slant by many). A few seem to have a mystical or symbolic significance: turning the water to wine at the wedding in Cana, the feeding of the five thousand (with two loaves and three fishes) and calming the storm on Lake Galilee seem to fall into this category.

THE PARABLES

The miracles are often a prelude to a discussion in which a parable, or maybe several, are told. Jesus is not primarily someone who lays down moral laws; it is the attitude and approach to life of his listeners that he targets. Taken collectively the parables form a set of yardsticks against which the Christian can measure himself. As they are stories, rather than codes of behaviour, their origin many years ago in a largely pastoral and Roman-occupied Middle East does not confine and date them. Phrases from the parables occur naturally in conversations of those who live in societies moulded by Christianity (no matter how secular they have become). A 'Good Samaritan' is a person who helps a stranger in need; a 'Prodigal Son' is one who is wayward; 'to sort out the sheep from the goats' is to separate the good from the bad; 'to turn the other cheek' is to withhold retaliation. There are many other examples. The parables emphasise ethical precepts central to Christianity: returning good for evil, forgiveness, welcoming the sinner and valuing a person for *what* he is, not for *who* he is. The most direct statements of Christian ethics in the Bible are perhaps to be found in the Beatitudes, the most famous being 'Blessed are the meek for they shall inherit the Earth'.

THE APOSTLES

The 12 apostles were disciples who were particularly close to Jesus; several were fishermen. Notable among the apostles was Peter (meaning 'stone'), who through force of character, or perhaps conviction, was able to overcome his weaknesses. Another apostle, Matthew, symbolises the universal nature of the Christian appeal; he had been a tax-collector (a universally corrupt and despised profession in the Roman Empire). Most notorious was Judas Iscariot, who betrayed Jesus to the authorities; down the centuries his actions, and those of the priests he assisted, have been used as a justification for persecution of the Jewish people throughout the centuries.

THE GOSPELS & APOSTLES

John's Gospel is accepted as being the closest eye-witness account. The visionary nature of his work, however, inclines many interpreters against being over-literal. The other Gospels are called collectively the 'synoptic' Gospels; though there are differences between them, they draw on the same source material. Mark's, the earliest, is a bald 'no frills' narrative; the aim is clearly to bring the material together and put it in writing. Matthew's is written from a Jewish perspective and has a clear emphasis on putting the story into the context of Jewish tradition. Luke, on the other hand, as a gentile convert, emphasises the universal elements of the story. From Luke also comes the Acts of the Apostles, an account of the early days of Christianity, which significantly gives us a picture of the second major progenitor of Christianity: St Paul.

PRACTICES

Whilst Christian denominations vary radically in their practices, virtually all perform the Act of Holy Communion (see below) and hold services on Sunday (the day of the Resurrection, traditionally the Christian day of rest), though such activities are not necessarily confined to Sunday. A prayer ('grace') is often said at table before meals, especially the evening meal. It may be read or memorised and may also give mention to preoccupations or current events. It is customary for persons in attendance to lower their eyes, bow their head and clasp their hands in front of them or hold the hand of the persons sitting next to them. The prayer always finishes with the word 'Amen' (meaning 'So be it'), at which time those attending can resume their normal posture and begin their meal. It is a breach of manners to begin eating before the prayer is completed.
In general, practising Christians are definably members of a community centred on their church; originally the act of baptism symbolised the acceptance of a Christian as a full member, but it is now performed at so young an age (in most denominations) that there is usually some other recognised form of acceptance, which occurs when a person is old enough to take responsibility for his actions. The nature of this form of acceptance varies greatly, but what is centrally important, and sets Christianity apart, is that individuals are offered the choice of whether or not to accept it.

COMMUNION

At the Last Supper, when Jesus celebrated the Jewish Passover immediately before being taken prisoner and crucified, he broke bread and drank wine with his apostles, saying: "Do this in remembrance of me". This has become the Christian sacrament of Communion when by re-enacting this event Christians renew their ties with God. There is no particular time or place for this sacrament, though over the centuries many rites and practices have grown around it, mostly perhaps in the Roman Catholic Mass.

THE CHRISTIAN CALENDAR

The most important event in the Christian calendar is Easter, which celebrates the death and resurrection of Jesus: Good Friday, the day when hope was lost; Easter Sunday, the day it was restored. Very much second in importance is Christmas, which celebrates the Birth of Jesus. The Christmas tradition of exchanging gifts and family celebration is very much a secular affair and not rooted in any Christian doctrine. The older European tradition is to celebrate on St Nicholas' Day (December 6) whilst other churches prefer to commemorate the arrival of the Magi with their gifts. Many other events in the life of Jesus are celebrated in the Christian calendar. The most important dates are as follows:
Christmas (generally: December 25; Orthodox: variable) – Celebrates the Birth of Jesus. See above.
Epiphany (January 6, 12 days after Christmas) – The coming of the wise men with their gifts.
Ash Wednesday (40 days before Easter) – Commencement of Lent, traditionally a period of fasting and self-denial leading up to Easter.
Palm Sunday (a week before Easter) – Celebrates the arrival into Jerusalem of Jesus riding on a mule.
Good Friday (two days before Easter) – Traditionally referred to as three days before Easter Sunday, this commemorates the crucifixion.
Easter Sunday (*) – The day of the Resurrection. See above.
Note [*]: This is a moveable Feast which usually occurs in March or April. Western and Orthodox churches determine its date according to different calendars.
Ascension Day (40 days after Easter) – The day Jesus ascended to heaven on a cloud following his resurrection

and last appearances on Earth.

Whit Sunday (six weeks after Easter) – Marking the day the Holy Spirit entered the disciples left behind and the beginning of their ministry.

The above dates are marked by virtually all Christian churches; Orthodox and Catholic churches, in particular, mark other occasions such as Noah's Flood (Orthodox) and the Immaculate Conception (Roman Catholic).

DOCTRINES

Only the foolhardy could set out a list of Christian doctrines; the following beliefs are held, with differing degrees of literalness, by most Christians:

(1) There is only one God.

(2) Jesus is his son.

(3) He was born of the Virgin Mary.

(4) He lived, was crucified, resurrected from the dead and ascended to heaven (the meaning of this is explained separately, see below).

(5) Through the working of the Holy Spirit his apostles were moved to preach in the name of Jesus, and establish the church as we know it.

(6) God, Jesus and the Holy Spirit are not three entities but one and the same (the complex doctrine of the Trinity).

(7) The Bible, including the Jewish Old Testament seen in the light of the New Testament, represents the word of God to his people.

(8) God remains today in commune with his church and its members.

There is a broad range of attitudes to these beliefs, from the Roman Catholics' insistence on orthodoxy to the Quakers' belief in the 'still, small voice'.

THE SIGNIFICANCE OF THE RESURRECTION

To Christians, the significance of the Resurrection is essentially about personal and collective redemption through the self sacrifice of one man. According to the New Testament, the story of Jesus is the story of a man who preached an emphasis on the importance of spiritual guiding values as opposed to the primacy of tradition or law defined by man. According to the Gospels he was angered by hypocrisy, relished debate, spoke of forgiveness and returning love for hate and, having spoken of these things, was betrayed and abandoned by those closest to him. In the Resurrection Jesus joins humanity again, but this time with his divinity in the ascendant. For a Christian, the belief in the resurrection of Christ is the belief in the potential redemption of both the individual and the redemption of mankind as a whole.

DENOMINATIONS

The following is a list of some of the main Christian denominations worldwide, together with a brief description of their particular customs.

Roman Catholic

(Worldwide, especially in Latin countries & Europe): Roman Catholics believe that the Pope inherits supreme authority within the church directly from St Peter. Elaborate rituals are performed and the role of the priest is central; it is his responsibility to listen to *Confession,* assign penances and give absolution (forgiveness). Many saints are venerated and countries with the Roman Catholic denomination are often noted for their fiestas on Saints' Days; spectacular carnivals before or after Easter also occur. Modesty in dress when visiting churches is required (eg covering the head for women).

Orthodox

(Russia, Middle East & Central Europe): Orthodox churches are similar to Catholic ones in the elaborate style of their liturgies and rituals (called 'Greek Rite'). Services are long with the congregation standing throughout; stress is laid on the importance of the Ascension and saints are highly regarded. In some places, icons (usually miniature religious paintings on small pieces of wood) are used as an aid to contemplation. Each *province* has its own Patriarch and, whilst there is no overriding central control, the Patriarch of Istanbul is recognised as the most senior. Modesty in dress when visiting churches is required (eg covering the head for women).

Anglican & Episcopalian

(English-speaking countries): The Church of England parted from the Roman Catholic church in the 16th century. Many of its rites are similar to those of the Catholic church, although over the centuries the influences of Puritanism and non-conformity have, for the most part, tended to concentrate worship on the main doctrines and away from the veneration of saints etc. The priest is also less of an intermediary between his congregation and God. Anglican and Episcopalian churches throughout the world have forms of service derived from that of the Church of England. The church is broad and 'high' churches tend to be similar in character to Roman Catholicism, whilst 'low' churches look more to non-conformist influences. Requirements on dress are not as strict as those of Catholic and Orthodox churches, but respect is always appreciated.

Methodist, Presbyterian & Congregationalist

(English-speaking countries & the Pacific): Industriousness, temperance (meaning more than just sobriety), straightforwardness and honesty are the values of these churches; qualities which the New Testament sums up in the concept of 'stewardship'. In form of service, some are similar to the 'low' church of the Church of England whilst others are more austere and Calvinistic (putting emphasis on the relationship man–God, strongly opposing the role of priest as mediator).

Baptist

(CIS, USA & parts of the Far East): Most churches practise baptism within a few weeks of birth. For Baptists the consent of the baptised is essential if the rite is to be significant and adult, or 'believer's baptism', is practised. Congregations are autonomous and independent of each other though each belongs to a national union. Other beliefs are similar to those described above under *Methodist etc.*

Pentecostal

(Caribbean & USA): These are the most exuberant churches of all, with much community singing and uninhibited celebration; 'speaking in tongues' and dancing often enter into church services. Beliefs are usually Fundamentalist.

Seventh Day Adventist

(USA & the Pacific): This Fundamentalist church celebrates the Sabbath on Saturday (the 'seventh day'). Church members look forward to the 'Second Coming' when Jesus will return to Earth and there is a heavy emphasis on the Old Testament.

Evangelical

Many churches have evangelical congregations and this is an area in which the Pentecostal church has been influential. The importance of proclaiming God's word is emphasised.

THE GROWTH OF CHRISTIANITY

The history of Christianity is central to the history of the modern world and pervades every aspect of philosophy, politics and culture, certainly in Europe. Space here does not permit more than a brief survey and it should be remembered that although originally a Middle Eastern religion, it was in Europe that Christianity most firmly took root and survived. The following survey has been written largely from a Western European viewpoint; this is not to belittle the achievements of the many founding fathers of the Church, many of whom lived in Syria and north Africa.

The early church, initially small groups converted by the remaining apostles and St Paul, grew rapidly in the Roman Empire but suffered considerable persecution and also many heresies and schisms. The remarkable spread of the religion culminated in the reign of the Emperor Constantine (306-337), who became a Christian himself and summoned the first Ecumenical council of the Church (325) in an attempt to settle the matter of the Arian heresy, the first sign of a split between the eastern and western churches which was never subsequently healed. The church was at this time organised under the leadership of several patriachs (at Alexandria, Antioch, Jerusalem, Constantinople and Rome), with the latter accorded a somewhat vague primacy. Christianity spread rapidly throughout Europe during the so-called Dark Ages (although parts of Eastern and northeastern Europe were not converted until the 11th/12th centuries), a growth mirroring the breakdown of secular power. The propensity of Christianity to produce schismatic groups in no way abated during this period and led to the establishment of many diverse Christian groups, such as the Coptics and Maronites, which still survive to this day. The rapid and dramatic spread of Islam in the 7th century resulted in many Christian lands (such as Spain and almost all of the Middle East) being over-run; the conquest of Jerusalem was particularly keenly felt, the city being revered by Christians, as well as by Muslims and Jews. The career of Charlemagne (771-814) produced a revival both of Christianity and of secular power, and his coronation as Holy Roman Emperor in Rome on Christmas Day 800 – thus recreating the Roman Empire in the West and formalising the concept of Christendom – was an event of enormous significance, not least because it brought into sharp focus the conflicting aspirations of Church and State. It was widely believed that Constantine had granted the Church ultimate supremacy in earthly affairs (the so-called 'Donation of Constantine', later proved to be a forgery), and this dispute rumbled on throughout the Middle Ages, often flaring into armed conflict. The launching of the Crusades in 1096 was motivated not only by a desire to reinforce ecclesiastical supremacy in the West, but also to come to the aid of the Byzantine Empire which had come consistently under attack. There existed also the fainter hope of producing a reconciliation between Rome and Constantinople. The astounding success of the First Crusade, which led to the establishment of Christian states in the Middle East for almost 200 years, brought Christianity, Judaism and Islam into sharp and violent conflict. The triumph of Islam in the East was assured after the conquest of Constantinople in 1453; the Eastern (Orthodox) church retained its hold in Greece and Russia, and also in many isolated (and often heretical) communities in the Middle East. Shortly afterwards the 'seamless robe of Christ' was split still further by the Reformation and the teachings of Luther, Calvin and Zwingli. By the end of the 16th century, despite the work of the Counter-Reformation and the Council of Trent, much of northern Europe had turned to Protestantism. Increasingly, the religious split in Europe manifested itself in many of the wars of the period – the French Wars of Religion, the Dutch War of Independence and the English Civil War and Revolution, for instance – culminating in the gruesome politico-religious violence of the Thirty Years' War (1618-1648). By this time most of the major European powers had started to establish overseas empires, exporting religion at the same time, and by the 18th century Christianity had established itself as the most widely spread faith in the world. Methodism was the last of the major Christian denominations to take root, and by that time most of the established churches in Europe had achieved a more tranquil *modus vivendi* with their secular counterparts by the rationalism of the Enlightenment. From this time on the most zealous Christians, from the Jesuits to Evangelicals, were finding that the most fertile ground for their teaching lay in the colonies: during the 19th century the work of conversion in all parts of the world proceeded apace. The 20th century has seen the Christian Church in Europe holding an increasingly small constituency and relying more on moral and ethical, rather than theological, influence on the life of its adherents. Certainly the increasing power and sophistication of the state has, in our century, resolved the ancient Church and State dispute very firmly in favour of the secular arm. The foundation of the ecumenical World Council of Churches in 1948 can be seen partly as an attempt to bury old differences between the denominations. Despite the increasing drift away from religion in the West, revivals, often of a dramatic nature, have taken place throughout the century, and one should in particular cite the recent rise of fundamentalist preachers in the USA. Two other events are worthy of particular mention. Firstly, the work of the Second Vatican Council in the 1960s, an attempt to bring the Catholic Church in line with the needs of the modern world: it has been said that, convened 500 years earlier, it would certainly have prevented the Reformation. Secondly, the spread of the so-called 'Liberation theology' in the Third World and Eastern Europe, born of an attempt to use the moral authority and teachings of the Church to aid the struggle against political and social oppression. Although in many ways a return to the fundamental teaching of Christ, the development is viewed with alarm by the Vatican and, to a lesser extent, by other Church leaders. The legacy of Christianity to the world is incalculable: almost every work of literature, art and music before about 1600 – and many after this date – were inspired by the faith, while the soaring cathedrals of both Western and Eastern Europe rank among the greatest achievements of mankind. Certainly the religion will continue to guide, comfort and inspire countless millions across the globe, although it seems unlikely to spawn any further major global changes.

For more information

Contact a local church or the Council of Churches for Britain & Ireland, Inter-Church House, 35-41 Lower Marsh, London SE1 7RL. Tel: (0171) 620 4444. Fax: (0171) 928 0010.

World of Islam

INTRODUCTION

Mohammed, the Prophet of Islam, was born in AD570, the posthumous son of a Hashemite from Mecca. His mother died when he was about six and he was brought up by his grandfather, who had him set up as a merchant by the time he was 25. His teachings began around 612, but despite gaining some followers he was rejected by the townsmen and was forced to leave for Medina in 622. For the next decade he organised the Commonwealth of Islam, creating a community based on the will of God. A considerable amount of conflict was caused by his activities, mainly with the Meccans, but by his death in 632 many of the Arabian tribes had been subdued. Within a year of the Prophet's death, the Muslims had advanced into Iraq, and by the early years of the following century had reached the River Indus and the Pyrenees. In the context of this remarkable expansion, the victory of Charles Martel at Tours (732) must rank as one of the most decisive in history. Most of the countries which were conquered during this period still remain Islamic or else have large Muslim populations.
The history of Islam and its influence on Christian Europe, with which it coexisted uneasily for centuries, repays careful study. Certain European countries, notably Spain, Portugal and Sicily, have fascinating reminders of both cultures; it is also worth remembering that during the Middle Ages the Islamic world was far advanced compared with those of the West in the fields of philosophy, medicine, science, geography, poetry and music. Many classical works only survived because they were translated into Arabic during the so-called 'Dark Ages' before being brought to Western Europe in the 12th century; the rediscovery of the works of Aristotle in this way was of fundamental importance to the development of Western philosophy. During the Crusades (1100-1290), armies of Christian Europe and Islam came into violent conflict, and there is little doubt that it was the Muslims who in general displayed greater tolerance and humanity. In recent years an understanding of Islam has often been obscured by political complexities, and the following section is an attempt to explain some of the important tenets of the faith. Anyone planning to visit a Muslim country should familiarise themselves with at least a little of the history, culture and beliefs of this increasingly influential religion. Many books cover the subject in considerably more depth than is possible here.

ISLAM

The Islamic religion is based on the 'submission to the will of God (Allah)'. Islam has teachings for the mind, body and spirit; also laws on education, economy, politics, science, crimes and punishment, human behaviour and all aspects of morality in daily life for individuals (men and women of any race), families, governments and whole societies anywhere in the world. The **Quran/Koran** and **Sunnah** are the two basic sources of Islamic teachings, law and order. The *Quran* is the main religious book for Muslims; it is the spoken word of **Allah** (God) and has 30 volumes which contain 114 chapters (or *Sura*) in Arabic. The *Sunnah* is complementary to the *Quran* and contains the sayings of the **Prophet Mohammed** and his way of life.
The Prophet received the spoken word of Allah containing the foundation of the faith (the *Quran/Koran*) while in **Mecca** in the 7th century AD. The city is now Islam's principal holy city. Medina, also in Saudi Arabia, a little over 300km (200 miles) due north of Mecca, is second only to Mecca in importance. It was to Medina that Mohammed and his followers moved after his monotheistic beliefs were given a hostile reception by some Meccans. The journey from Mecca to Medina (*Hijra*) is celebrated each year, the event being taken as the starting point of the Islamic calendar (Ah 1). Prior to their return to Mecca the Prophet and his followers made a pilgrimage (*Hajj*) to the Holy City during the month of *Ramadan*. After Mohammed's death in AD632 temporal authority was assumed by a series of Khalifahs, with various sects developing. Today the strongest sects within Islam (that is those with the most followers) are the *Sunni* (in Indonesia, India, Malaysia, Pakistan, Bangladesh, Syria, parts of Lebanon, Egypt, north Africa, Saudi Arabia, the Gulf States and large parts of Turkey) and the *Shia* (in Iran, southern Lebanon, parts of India, Afghanistan and Pakistan and the greater part of Iraq).

THE FIVE PILLARS OF ISLAM

There are five basic religious tenets, generally called the *Five Pillars of Islam:*
Shahada – The profession of faith: 'I testify there is no God but Allah and Mohammed is the Messenger of Allah.'
Salah – The faithful must turn towards Mecca and recite a prescribed prayer five times daily at dawn, noon, *asr* (between noon and sunset), sunset and before sleeping. In some Muslim countries the activities of the day stop at the time of prayer. The *muezzin* calls to prayer, chanting from the minaret of each mosque. For obvious practical

reasons, not all Muslims go to a mosque for prayer. Shopkeepers and businessmen will offer prayers on their premises, usually on a mat set to one side. Non-Muslims should not be embarrassed if they happen to witness this. The most important prayer is the Friday prayer, delivered from a pulpit of the mosque by a prayer leader. In many Muslim countries, Friday is a holiday, with banks and shops closed all day.

Zakat – A form of almsgiving which was originally an obligatory act of charity, and is now a property tax for the benefit of widows, the poor and children within the community. It is a religious duty to give alms to the needy, especially during Ramadan.

Ramadan – All Muslims are required to fast during the Holy Month of Ramadan (a lunar month of four weeks, which falls 11 days earlier each year, depending on sightings of the moon). All Muslims abstain totally from food, drink, sex and tobacco from dawn to dusk. Non-Muslims should respect this practice and wherever possible avoid infringing these laws in front of Muslims, since this would be considered an insult. Practically speaking, when Ramadan falls during the summer months, the abstentions become a test of endurance. Often shops and restaurants will open much earlier and close during the afternoons and in smaller towns some will close altogether, but some businesses do open at night. At sunset most, if not all, Muslims will break their fast, and little business or travel will be practical for the visitor at this time.

Originally the festival celebrated the month during which the *Quran* was first revealed and later when Mohammed's followers won a great victory over opponents to his faith in Mecca. *Eid al-Fitr,* an official holiday in some Muslim countries of three or more days, takes place at the end of Ramadan. It is a celebratory feast when those luxuries which have been denied are enjoyed with relish.

The Hajj – The pilgrimage to Mecca. Every Muslim who can afford it and is fit enough must make the journey. Some Muslims, especially those in Saudi Arabia, make the pilgrimage more than once. At the time of the pilgrimage, the pilgrim *(Hajji/Hajja)* enters the holy precincts of Mecca wearing a white, seamless garment *(ihram)* and performs the sevenfold circumambulation of the *Kaabah* (the black stone housed in the centre of the Holy Mosque) and the sevenfold course between the little hills of Safa and Marwah near Mecca. Muslims perform this in memory of Haggar who is mentioned in the Old Testament, who ran seven times between Safa and Marwah seeking a spring for her thirsty son. The *Hajj* lasts from the seventh to the eighth of *Dhu-al-Hijja.* On the ninth day pilgrims stand praying on the mountain **Arafat** – an essential part of the ritual of the *Hajj.* The pilgrimage formally ends with *Eid al-Adha* (Feast of the Sacrifice), which is an official holiday of four or more days, in which a camel, sheep or horned domestic animal is sacrificed on the tenth of *Dhu-al-Hijja.* After shaving the head the *ihram* is discarded and normal dress *(ihlal)* resumed. As long as the *hajji/hajja* is in a *muhrim* (sanctified place) he/she must refrain from sexual intercourse, the shedding of blood, hunting and the uprooting of plants. All of the different activities of the *Hajj* are symbolic and have stories associated with them.

SOCIAL CUSTOMS

Muslims regard Islam as an integral part of daily life, resulting in an ordered society in which a man's social, spiritual and economic status is clearly defined. This way of life is for the most part drawn from the *Quran.* Greetings and replies in particular are formal and stylised. Manners and courtesy reflect a deeply-held convention of hospitality and mutual respect. It is customary for Muslim households to extend hospitality to people whom Western society would disregard socially. For instance, tradition dictates that anyone who appears at meal times must be invited to share the meal, and this would apply as much to strangers or tradesmen, whatever the reason for their call, as it would to friends or relatives. Hospitality was a part of Arab culture before Islam and the laws and teaching of Islam reinforced it. Subjects such as illness or death are not surrounded by taboo as they are in many Western societies, and are discussed with frankness by all. Muslims are encouraged to have close relationships and keep an open heart, an understanding of others and to try and help with their problems.

The label of a family can cover any number of individuals rather than just those related by blood ties. Arab families are close-knit, and the importance of family unity cannot be stressed too strongly. Inter-family disputes are a cause for public shame and require immediate attention.

WOMEN AND ISLAM

Probably the aspect of Islam which non-Muslims find most difficult to accept is the treatment of women, and it is the aspect most deeply criticised. The demand that women should dress and behave modestly is seen by Muslims as symbolic of the importance and value placed on women as mothers and guardians of the family. The Prophet encouraged monogamy although polygamy was allowed, provided that the husband was in a position to provide for all wives and treated them equally. Polygamy may also occur in special circumstances, such as when the number of women in society is larger than the number of men, or when the wife is chronically ill or sterile. Today monogamy is more common, polygamy being allowed but not encouraged. Many, but not all, royal families have employed polygamy to ensure succession, and for practical reasons such as providing ministers and administrators, but otherwise it is not the norm.

The theory behind modest dress and veil for women is to preserve respect, dignity and virginity and safeguard them from interference or abuse by men, although for some time this tradition has been slowly relaxed in many countries through contact with non-Islamic cultures. Other traditions, however, such as arranged marriages or the seating of females upstairs or at a separate table in a restaurant, are still rigidly observed. Many of the public traditions serve to distinguish male dominance in society. Women are allowed to work in some cases, especially when the need arises, but the Islamic code of dress and modesty must always be observed. In some jobs it is obligatory to have female teachers or doctors, for example when dealing with Muslim girls or women. Today in the Arab and Muslim world, many Muslim women are working because of financial need and because of the liberalising of religious practice or observance. Women invariably rule the household and the family. Given the importance of the family, this affords the older women considerable influence. Younger women, however, hold no such position and although many Islamic countries have relaxed restrictions and women have begun to play an active part in many spheres of activity (particularly in medicine, education, public services and the media), a number of countries still follow traditional practices.

The difference between the measure of adherence to Quranic practices of one country and another is most easily judged by the degree of freedom afforded to women. Fundamentalism, enjoying a resurgence in many Islamic countries, is as much as anything else an articulation of the resentment felt at the interference of stronger foreign economies in their internal affairs. However, this can often manifest itself in a retreat back to almost medieval traditions as a positive form of disapproval of the decadence of the West. Thus, in many countries the position of women can be protected and their role in society appreciated, whilst at the same time their ability to control their own lives is largely denied.

Note: The above account of women and Islam, which describes widely-held beliefs and customs, should not be taken as authoritative. *Women in Islam,* published by the Islamic Foundation, gives an account of one of the sessions of the International Islamic Conference held in London in 1976. The session was addressed by two Islamic women with a Western background and followed by a discussion. *Women in Islam* looks at issues more deeply and is a useful starting point for those who wish to learn about issues alive in Islam today.

SOCIAL CONVENTIONS

Forms of address: The Arabic equivalent of 'Mr' is *Sayyid* (for Muslims) and *Khawaja* (for Christians), while married women should be addressed as *Sayyida* or *Sitt,* and girls as *Anissa.* In Islam it is also encouraged to call a Muslim man 'my brother' and a Muslim woman 'my sister'. Islam regards men as equal, but social conventions, hospitality and politeness of Islamic societies prevent overfamiliarity.

Greeting: There follows a short list of Arabic greetings and phrases. The transliterations are phonetic and intended to assist pronunciation.
Marharba - Hello;
Markhabtain - Hello (reply);
Ma'a Salama - Goodbye;
Ahlan wa sahlan - Welcome;
Ahlan feekum - Welcome (reply);
Sabah al-khir - Good morning;
Sabah innoor - Good morning (reply).
These were all originally purely Arabic greetings. In Islam the common greeting still widely used is *Assalmu Alaykum* ('Peace be with you').

Note: Throughout the Arab world English is widely spoken in business, and it is not essential for English-speakers to learn Arabic. However, attempts to say even a few words and phrases in Arabic are generally very much appreciated.

Business: This must *always* be conducted on a personal introduction or invitation basis only. Without invitations or introductions a business visit, while being courteously received, will ultimately amount to nothing. Honesty is the basis of all business dealings in Islamic countries and a word is a bond. Arguing and haggling over prices is the norm and an Arabic tradition of buying and selling. Once a bargain has been struck the deal cannot be renegotiated or cancelled unless either party cannot raise the money.

Clothing conventions: These are derived in part from religious beliefs and in part from climatic necessity. Western business suits are only practical during the summer if they are lightweight. Businessmen will be accepted if they wear open-necked shirts, as long as they are well turned out. Women are advised not to wear revealing clothes as this will attract unwelcome attention or ridicule at best, and resentment and hostility at worst. Women should also cover their heads when entering a Mosque. Muslim women are generally advised to show face and hands only.

Do not sit in a position which places the soles of the feet towards anyone, as this is considered a deliberate insult. Shoes should be removed upon entering a Mosque or a house.

Sexual politics: Remember the position that women hold in Islam (see above), and that some gestures considered normal by westerners can be interpreted as serious insults. Divorce and marriage are considered civil matters and while divorce is not a common practice it is relatively easy. Adultery is considered an insult to Allah and society and severely punished, often by flogging, but sometimes by stoning to death.

Giving and receiving: Always use the right hand. To offer gifts with the left hand is considered an insult.

Drug use: Although many countries cultivate hashish or marijuana, it is not culturally acceptable and in the majority of countries the possession, use or trading of drugs is severely punished. Drug abuse is not permitted in Islam, particularly hard drugs such as heroin, morphine or cocaine, but also any drug which interferes with the consciousness, reasoning or judgement, affecting work, study or family life.

Alcohol: The consumption of alcohol is forbidden by law. Many non-practising Muslims will, however, drink alcohol and will offer drinks to guests when outside their own country. Most Islamic countries (with the exception of Libya, Saudi Arabia and Kuwait) permit the sale and consumption of alcohol by non-Muslims. Generally the sale of alcohol will be confined to international hotels, but visitors may in some cases buy alcohol from wholesalers with a permit from their company or local Embassy. Bars are usually closed during Ramadan. Never drink alcohol while eating. Drunkenness is considered disgraceful, and the visitor is advised to *never* consume more than he or she can gracefully manage.

Gambling: This is considered by most Islamic countries to be an evil, and is strictly outlawed.

Smoking: This is also discouraged in Islam because of the health hazards associated with it. However, do not refuse a cigarette unless you are an ardent non-smoker, as an offer of a cigarette is often a compliment, especially from one's host. If invited to smoke a *narghileh* (hookah) do not refuse and follow the ritual behaviour exhibited. This essentially social activity is popular in some, but by no means all, Arab countries.

Food: Pork is forbidden by Islamic law and all meat is killed by cutting the animal's throat and draining the blood. This is called *halal* meat. It is customary for the host/hostess to cut up whole items of food (especially with *mezzeh,* the Arabic equivalent of hors d'oeuvres) and distribute them. It is also customary to offer guests the most succulent parts of the meal, often the entrails or eyes. To refuse these is considered an insult. In restaurants the person who makes the invitation pays the bill and it is considered an insult to contravene.

Note: Etiquette in all Islamic countries is complicated and highly evolved, and all those wishing to learn more are advised to read books on the subject.

THE ISLAMIC CALENDAR

Based on lunar months, ie the first of each month coincides with the date of the actual New Moon. In 'Common' years of 354 days, the months are alternately 30 and 29 days long; in the 'Kabishah' year of 355 days the last month has 30 days. During a 30-year period there are 19 Common and 11 Kabishah years. The ninth month is Ramadan. The Islamic months are as follows:
Muharram, Safar, Rarabia (1), Rarabia (2), Jumada (1), Jumada (2), Rajab, Shaaban, Ramadan, Shawwal, Dhul-al-Qa'da, Dhu-al-Hijja.
These months are used especially in Saudi Arabia.

For further information contact:
Muslim Information Services
233 Seven Sisters Road
London N4 2DA
Tel: (0171) 272 5170. Fax: (0171) 272 3214.

Travel Contacts

Travel Contacts Limited
45 Idmiston Road
London SE27 9HL
Tel: +44 (0181) 766 7868. Fax:+44 (0181) 766 6123.

ALBANIA

A S TOUR
R.Durresi 65, TIRANA
Tel & Fax: +355 42 23700

Contact: Mr Ilir Mati
Special Interest: trekking, canoeing, sub-aqua, bicycling, moutaineering, ski-touring.

ANTIGUA

ANTOURS
BWIA Sunjet House, P O Box 508, Long & Thames Streets, ST JOHN'S
Tel: +1 (809) 462 4788/9 Fax: 462 4799 Tlx: 2168

ANTOURS AK
Contact: Mrs Alwyn Fletcher
Established: 1982
Languages: Eng, Fr, Ger, It, Sp.
Associations: Caribbean Hotels Assn, Caribbean Tourist Assn.

ARGENTINA

Viamonte 524 - 3rd, 1053 BUENOS AIRES
Tel: +54 (1) 311-1553/ 1489/ 1105; 313-0173 Fax: 313-0177/ 313-7267 Tlx: (33) 18364 TURY AR & 24261 CLARI AR

Contacts: Mr Harry Uryson, Ms Maria Virginia del Rio, Ms Mabel Taranto
Established: 1980; 15 employees.
Languages: Eng, Fr, Ger, It, Polish, Port, Sp.
Associations: ASTA, IATA, DMC, SITE, WATA, Internet, Intralink.
Special Interest: agriculture, gourmet eating, wildlife (1-12); hunting (3-7); whale-watching (6-11); fishing (8-9); horse breeding (8-12); dairy farming (9-12); diving, trekking, (11-3); animal breeding (12-5).

ARUBA

ECO DESTINATION MANAGEMENT SERVICES OF ARUBA
Ponton 36 F, ORANJESTAD
Tel: +297 (8) 26034 Fax: 31078

Contact: Mrs Wichita M Every
Established: 1989; 20 employees.
Languages: Eng, Dutch, Fr, Ger, It, Sp.
Associations: SITE.
Special Interest: caves, coral reefs, deep-sea fishing, diving, fishing, gambling, golf, sailing, tennis, water-skiing, windsurfing (1-12); carnivals (2-3); jazz festival (6).

LANDMARK (SOUTH PACIFIC) PTY LTD
53 Cross Street, P O Box 207, DOUBLE BAY, NSW 2028
Tel: +61 (2) 327 8433 Fax: 327 6704 Tlx: AA 171728

Contact: Judy Ashton
European Marketing Offices:
P O Box 9 bis, B-1390 GREZ-DOICEAU, Belgium
Tel: +32 (1) 084 2619 Fax: 084 2920
Sales & Promotion Services, Duisbergerstr.125, 40479

DUSSELDORF, Germany
Tel: +49 (211) 491 1638 Fax: 491 1676-7

Special Interest: agriculture, botany, cattle breeding,

coral reefs, cruises, gemstones, golf, horse-breeding, ornithology, all sports, wildlife, wines & vineyards.

AUSTRIA

AUSTROBUS WELCOME TOURISTIC
Lueger-Ring 8, 1014 VIENNA
Tel: +43 (1) 53411-0 Fax: 53411-203 Tlx: 114239 AUBU A

Established: 1932; 15 employees (Inbound Dept).
Languages: Eng, Fr, It, Sp.
Associations: ASTA, NETWORLD, UFTAA, ORV, IATA, WATA, SITE.
Special Interest: architecture, art, castles, cathedrals, history, medicine, museums (1-12); bicycle touring, walking (spring/autumn); opera (9-7); wines & vineyards (autumn); skiing (11-3).

BAHAMAS - GRAND BAHAMA

SUN ISLAND TOURS LTD
P O Box F-2585, FREEPORT
Tel: +1 (809) 352 4811/2/3/4 Fax: 352 3493 Tlx: (297) 30051 FPO 51

Contact: Mrs Lydia Guglielmo-Saunders

BAHAMAS - NEW PROVIDENCE ISLAND

MAJESTIC TOURS LTD
Hillside Manor, Cumberland Street, P O Box 1401, NASSAU
Tel: +1 (809) 322 2606/7 Fax: 328 2712/ 326 5785 Tlx: 20176 REGAL

Contact: William A. Saunders
Special Interest: coral reefs, deep-sea fishing, diving, gambling, game fishing, golf, sailing, sub-aqua sport (1-12); carnivals (6-9,12).

BARBADOS

SUNLINC BARBADOS
Bulkeley Great House, Bulkeley, ST GEORGE
Tel: +1 (809) 436 1710 Fax: 436 1715

Contact: Helen Schur-Parris, Vice President, Sales & Marketing
Established: 1983; 26 employees.
Languages: Eng, Fr, Ger, Sp, Swiss-Ger.
Associations: SITE Intl, SITE Caribbean.
Special Interest: caves, flowers/horticulture, sub-aqua sport, history, zoos, underwater marine park, museums, house tours, watersports, yachting, driving tours, shopping, deep sea fishing (1-12).

BELGIUM

BRUSSELS INTERNATIONAL TRAVEL SERVICE
rue Arthur Diderich 30, 1060 BRUSSELS
Contacts: Mr Marc Dans, Mr Igor Korn, Mr Ives Dubus
Established: 1988; 4 employees.
Languages: Dutch, Eng, Fr, Ger, Pol, Russ, Sp.
Associations: CMT, API, Euromic
Special Interest: architecture, art, breweries, food, gourmet eating, museums, pharmaceuticals (1-12); flowers (4-6); history (4-10); caves (5-9); educational visits (9-6); universities (10-5).

BERMUDA

PENBOSS-MEYER DESTINATION MANAGEMENT
35 Church Street, P O Box 510, HAMILTON HM, CX
Tel: +1 (809) 295 9733 Fax: 292 8251/ 4823

Contact: Ms Carla Fountain, CDS, CEP.
Established: 1948; 50 employees.
Languages: Eng, Ger, Port, Sp.
Associations: ASTA, IATA, SITE, IFWTO, HSMAI.
Special Interest: deep-sea fishing, gourmet eating (1-12); golf, tennis (10-6); sailing (4-11); coral reefs (5-11).

BOLIVIA

Avenida 16 de Julio 1650, P O Box 5889, LA PAZ
Tel: +591 (2) 357 817/ 354 049 Fax: 391 310 Tlx: 2358

BALTOUR

Contact: Mr Jean-Jacques Valloton
Associations: IATA, COTAL, ASTA, UFTAA.
Special Interest: agriculture, anthropology, architecture, carnivals, golf, photography, steamboats, pilgrimages (1-12); mountaineering (4-9).

BONAIRE

BONAIRE SIGHTSEEING TOURS N.V.
Kaya Lodewijk D. Gerharts 22, P O Box 115, KRALENDIJK
Tel: +599 (7) 8778 Fax: 8118/ 8865

Contact: Anne Thomson

BRAZIL

G B INTERNACIONAL
Rua Capitao Salomao 40, 22271 RIO DE JANEIRO
Tel: +55 (21) 537 8001 Fax: 286 9484/ 537 4515 Tlx: 21-31575 GBIT BR or 21-21113

Established: 1972; 22 employees.
Languages: Eng, Fr, Ger, Jap, Port, Sp.
Associations: ABAV, IATA, SITE, ASTA.
Special Interest: agriculture, architecture, art gemstones, golf, hydro-electrics, textiles (1-12); cattle breeding, fishing (3-11); deep sea fishing, diving (12-3).

BULGARIA

LYUB TRADE & TOURISM
11 Milin kamak Str., 1421 SOFIA,
Tel: +359 (2) 66 74 13/ Tel/Fax: 66 25 23

Contacts: Mrs Lyuboslava Terzieva-Boyanina & Mr Bruce Wightman
Established: 1990
Special Interest: archaeology, art & icon study, mountain trekking, photography, ethnic culture & folklore, history from Thrace to today, wine tasting, food & gourmet eating.

CAMBODIA

DIETHELM TRAVEL (CAMBODIA) LTD
Tel: +855 (23) 26648/24930 Fax: 26676

CANADA - EAST

GROUP SPECIALISTS CANADA
980 Yonge Street, Suite 200, TORONTO M4W 2J5
Tel: +1 (416) 323 9090 Fax: 323 3980 Tlx: 06-218776 CISS
Contact: Joan Cooper, Director

CANADA - FRENCH (QUEBEC)

GROUPE VOYAGES QUEBEC, INC.
174 Grande-Allee Ouest, QUEBEC, QC, G1R 2G9
Tel: +1 (418) 525 4585 Fax: 522 4398

Contacts: Paul Plourde, Rene Poitras
European Office:
46, rue Victor Hugo, 93500 PANTIN, France
Tel: +33 (1) 4866 7482 Fax: 4844 2348
Languages: Eng, Fr, Sp.
Associations: IATA, ACTA, SITE.
Special Interest: snowmobiling (12-4), Winter Carnival (2), maple harvest (3-4), Montreal Grand Prix (6), Montreal International Jazz Festival (7-8), World Film Festival (8-9), fall foliage (9-10), fishing, white water rafting, whale-watching, hunting.

CANADA - WEST

CONTACTS PACIFIC SERVICES INC
Suite 600, 1090 W Georgia St, VANCOUVER, BC, Canada V6E 3V7
Tel: +1 (604) 683 2174 Fax: 688 6972 Tlx: 04-55434

Contact: Mr George Bartel

Established: 1973; 15 employees.
Languages: Eng, Fr, Ger, It, Jap, Sp.
Special Interest: anthropology, aquaculture, sports, (1-12); whale watching (3-4); forestry, hydro-electrics, ranching (4-10); skiing (12-4).

CAYMAN ISLANDS

MAJESTIC TOURS
P O Box 298, GRAND CAYMAN
Tel: +1 (809) 949 7773 Fax: 949 8647 Tlx: 4304
MAJESTIC

Associations: American Sightseeing Intl.
Special Interest: coral reefs, deep sea fishing, diving, game fishing, golf, museums, sailing, sub-aqua sport (1-12).

CHANNEL ISLANDS

STAR TRAVEL LTD
1st Floor, Freight Terminal, l'avenue de la Commune,
ST PETER
Tel: +44 (1534) 499599 Fax: 499588

Contacts: Iain MacFirbhisigh, Director, & Ms Sue Gillen, Manager
Established: 1990; 6 employees
Languages: Eng, Fr, Ger, Norw, Swed.
Associations: ABTA, IATA, CITOG, Avis
Special Interest: bicycling, boating & boat races, bowls, castles, deep-sea fishing, finance, flowers & horticulture, food & gourmet eating, golf, military history, insect life, museums, ornithology, sailing, walking, yachting, zoo.

CHILE

TURISMO COCHA
Av. El Bosque Norte 0430, PO Box 191, Correo 35,
SANTIAGO DE CHILE
Tel: +56 (2) 230 1000 Fax: 203 5110 Tlx: 441228
COCHA

Associations: IATA, COTAL, ASTA, USTOA, WOODSIDE
Special Interest: canal cruising (3-11); fishing, geology (4-8); hot springs (4-10); flowers, horse breeding (9-1); botany, diving (9-3); ornithology (9-4); wildlife (10-3); forestry (9-3); wines & vineyards (11-4).

COMORES, FED. ISLAMIC REPUBLIC

TOURISM SERVICES COMORES
P O Box 1226, MORONI
Tel: +269 733 044 Fax: 733 054

Contact: Mr Veera Govindan
U.K. Office:
29 Elmfield Mansions, Elmfield Rd, LONDON SW17 8AA
Tel: +44 (181) 675 4498 Fax: 673 8358

Contact: Ms Dendy Barker
U.S. Office:
620 Longview, Longboat Key, FL 34228 USA
Contact: Ms Jean Walden
Special Interest: botany, coral reefs, deep sea fishing, diving, watersports.

COSTA RICA

DESTINATION COSTA RICA, DMC
P O Box 590-1151, SAN JOSE
Tel: +506 223 0744 Fax: 222 9747
Contact: Thomas Niebuhr, General Manager

American Office: 2801 Blue Ridge Road, Ste.110,
RALEIGH, NC 27607 Tel: +1 (919) 782 9417 (US toll free: (800) 835 1223) Fax: 782 8766

Contact: Hertha Lasky
Established: 1991.
Special Interest: tropical forest, Pacific & Caribbean beaches, volcanoes, hiking, white water rafting, photo safaris, bird watching, museums.

CROATIA

Pile 1, 5000 DUBROVNIK
Tel: +385 (50) 44 2222 Fax: 411 100/ 28342

Tlx: 27515/ 27583 ATLAS

Contact: Mr Tonko Kolendic
Established: 1923; 1200 employees
Languages: Dutch, Eng, Fr, Ger, It, Sp, Swed.
Associations: UFTAA, IATA, JATA, DRV, USTOA, ICCA, COTAL, ACTA, ASTA, ABTA, API, Internet, FUAVV, WTT, ORV.

Special Interest: archaeology, art, history, tennis, pilgrimages, ornithology, naturism, rafting, canoeing, sailing, wines & vineyards, skiing.

CURAÇAO

TABER TOURS INC
P O Box 3304, CURAÇAO, Netherlands Antilles
Tel: +599 (9) 376 637 Fax: 379 539

Contact: Mr Marcial Garcia

CYPRUS

CYDEM TOURS LTD
20 Stassicrates Street, P O Box 4134, NICOSIA

Contacts: Aristos Demetriou, Panikos Apeyitos
Associations: IATA, ACTA, SITE, ITA UK.
Special Interest: archaeology, botany, bicycle touring, diving (5-10); geology, horticulture, ornithology, pilgrimages, trekking, walking, wines & vineyards (8-11); skiing (2).

CZECH REPUBLIC

WELCOME TOURISTIC PRAHA
Incoming Dept, Klimentska 52, P O Box 1, 110 15
PRAGUE 015
Tel: +42 (2) 2481 0585/ 231 7598 Fax: 231 4426

Contact: Mrs Ingrid Kent
Registered Office: Na Porici 10, 110 00 PRAGUE 1, P O Box 726 Tel: +42 (2) 2481 2505/ 2481 2435 Fax: 2481 2419
Contact: Mr Vaclav Dvorak
Established: 1990; 25 employees
Languages: Cz, Eng, Fr, Ger.
Associations: SITE, ASTA, DFR, MPI

DENMARK

HAYES & HANDS & RITZAU
Skovshovedvej 10c, DK-2920 CHARLOTTENLUND
(Copenhagen)
Tel: +45 3164 5600/ 3164 2839 Fax: 3163 4143

Contacts: Mrs Mari Hayes & Mrs Majken Ritzau
Established: 1990; 5 employees
Languages: Dan, Eng, Fr, Ger.
Associations: SITE, MPI
Special Interest: architecture, art, agriculture, castles, cattle/dairy, gourmet cooking & eating, textile design (1-12); medicine (1-6,9-12); antiques/appraisers, ballet, opera (4-5,9-11); ornithology (4-8); horticulture & gardens (4-10); sailing & cruising (5-9); theatre (10-4).

DOMINICA

KEN'S HINTERLAND ADVENTURE TOURS
62 Hillsborough Street, Box 447, ROSEAU
Tel: +1 (809) 44 84850 Fax: 44 88486

Contact: Mr Ken George Dill, Managing Director

DOMINICAN REPUBLIC

Leopoldo Navarro 4, SANTO DOMINGO
Tel: +1 (809) 686 4020/ 685 4020 Fax: 688 3890/ 221 5135 Tlx: (326) 0554/ 4536 TURITER

Contact: Felix A. Jimenez
Branch Offices:
Plaza Jose Augusto Puig, PUERTO PLATA
Tel: +1 (809) 586 3911/ 586 2315 Fax: 586 4755 Tlx: (346) 2034
Jose El Julian no 2, Higuey, PUNTA CANA
Tel: +1 (809) 554 5565
Established: 1976; 130 employees
Languages: Eng, Fr, It, Sp.

Special Interest: baseball, caves, driving tours, gambling, golf, real estate, underwater marine parks, watersports, yachting, handicraft, cable cars, whale watching.

DUBAI - SEE UNITED ARAB EMIRATES

ECUADOR/GALAPAGOS ARCHIPELAGO

KLEINTOURS/KLEINGALAPAGOS
Av. Shirys 1000 y Holanda, QUITO
Contacts: Maria A Klein, Gen Mgr, & Francisco Jarrin, Incoming Mgr

Established: 1983.
Languages: Eng, Fr, Ger, Sp.
Special Interest: Galapagos cruises, arts/culture, ecotourism, adventure, mountain climbing, Amazon safaris, ornithology, deep sea fishing, diving.

EGYPT

MENATOURS TRAVEL & TOURIST AGENCY
El Nasr Building, El Nil Street, P O Box 46, GIZA
Tel: +20 (2) 349 0168/ 348 2387/ 348 2231 Fax: 348 4016 Tlx: 93889/ 21176 MENAT UN

Contacts: Mr Badran Kamel, Managing Director & Mr Samy Khalil, Marketing Manager.

Luxor Office:
Salah el Din Square, LUXOR
Tel: +20 (95) 385 660 Fax: 374 724

Contact: Mr Sarwat Agamy
Languages: Eng, Fr, Ger, It.
Associations: ASTA, ACTA, IATA, UFTAA, COTAL, DRV, PATA.
Special Interest: diving, gambling, sub-aqua sport, surfing, waterskiing, windsurfing (1-12); horse-breeding (2); archaeology (10-2); Nile cruises (10-5).

ESTONIA

VIRONE TRAVEL BUREAU
Pronksi 11, EE-0007 TALLINN
Tel: +372 (2) 443992/ 425398 Fax: +372 631 2213 Tlx: 64-173824 VIRON

Contacts: Mrs Ene Truusa, Incoming Manager & Mr Enn Vilgo, Managing Director.
Established: 1989; 7 employees
Languages: Eng, Estonian, Fin, Fr, Ger, It, Russ, Swed.
Asociations: EATA
Special Interest: agriculture & farming, architecture, ballet, ethnic culture, folk dancing, forestry, history, hunting, museums, opera, ornithology, religion (1-12); sailing, yachting, golf (4-11).

FIJI

ROSIES THE TRAVEL SERVICE
Tel: +679 722 755 Fax: 722 607 Tlx: 5143 FJ

Contact: Tony Whitton
Special Interest: agriculture, coral reefs, deep-sea fishing, scuba-diving, game-fishing, golf, horticulture, squash, tennis (1-12); cricket (10-5); rugby (5-10); charter yachting (5-11).

FINLAND

FINLAND TRAVEL BUREAU LTD: INCOMING & INCENTIVE DEPT
Kaivokatu 10A, P O Box 319, 00100 HELSINKI
Tel: +358 (0) 18261 Fax: 612 1547 Tlx: 124626 FTBHK SF

Contact: Ms Sari Viljamaa, Manager
Established: 1909; 15 employees (Incoming Dept).
Languages: Eng, Fin, Fr, Ger, It.
Associations: ASTA, AFTA, Hickory Europe, Network, SITE, UFTAA.
Special Interest: architecture (1-12); hospitals (1-6, 8-12); safaris (2-10); ornithology (5-7); music festivals/ jazz/ opera (5-8); forestry, paper, trekking (5-10); agriculture, canoeing, fishing (6-9).

FRANCE - PARIS & NORTH

HOLT PARIS WELCOME SERVICE SA
Tel: +33 (1) 4523 0814 Fax: 4247 1989 Tlx: 660195
HOLT F

Contacts: Mr Alan Holt, Mrs Susan Holt & Mr Jean
Pierre Chiama.
Associations: SITE.
Special Interest: art, architecture, food, horse-racing,
medicine, museums, railways, religion, wines (1-12);
cookery, theatre (1-6, 9-12).

FRANCE - THE RIVIERA & MONACO

VIP RIVIERA SERVICE
205 Promenade des Anglais, P O Box 152, 06203 NICE
Cedex 3
Tel: +33 9344 2233 Fax: 9337 4993 Tlx: 660195

Contact: Mr Ralph Holt
Established: 1979; 6 employees
Languages: Eng, Fr, Ger, It.
Associations: Welcome People, SITE, SKAL, UFTAA,
FUAVV.
Special Interest: cruises, golf, museums, opera, railways,
tennis (1-12); carnivals (2-3); flowers, gardens (4-8);
yachting (4-10); Grand Prix (5); jazz (7); horse-racing.

GAMBIA

P O Box 101, BANJUL
Tel: +220 392259/ 392505 Fax: 391013 Tlx: 2215 GV

Contact: Mr Samba Fye
Associations: ATA (African Travel Assoc)
Special Interest: cattle breeding, fishing, gambling, golf,
hunting, pottery (1-12); butterflies (5-9); insect life (7-9);
safaris (10-5); deep-sea fishing, river cruises (11-5);
ornithology (11-12).

GEORGIA

CAUCASIAN TRAVEL LTD.
Office Address: 7 N. Nikoladze Str., 380008 TBILISI
Postal Address: P O Box 160, 380008, TBILISI
Tel: +7 (8832) 987400/ 987399 Fax: 987399/ 931824
(att: S Kiknadze) Tlx: 212 912 GGS

Contacts: Mr Saba Kiknadze, General Manager, Mr
David Rakviashvili, Managing Director
Languages: Eng, Fr, Ger, Russ, Georgian.
Special Interest: agriculture, archaeology, architecture,
caves, ethnic culture, food & gourmet eating, geology,
helicoptering, hunting, moutaineering, rafting, skiing,
trekking, walking, wines & vineyards.

GERMANY - BERLIN

Kaiserdamm 30, P O Box 1207, D-14057 BERLIN
Tel: +49 (30) 301 7027 Fax: 301 9625 Tlx: 182 834

Contact: Peter Antoni
Established: 1981; 9 employees
Languages: Eng, Fr, Ger, Russ, Sp.
Associations: SITE, UFTAA, BTC
Special Interest: museums & galleries, architecture,
WWII & Cold War relics, fashion shows, opera &
cabaret, ballooning, history.

GERMANY - DRESDEN

CLASSIC TOURS
Dresdenerstrasse 95, D-01689 WEINBOHLA
Tel: +49 (35243) 32389 Fax: 32389

Contact: Kathrin Mueller
Established: 1990; 4 employees
Languages: Eng, Fr, Ger, Russ.
Special Interest: architecture, art, museums, river cruises.

GERMANY - DÜSSELDORF

FIRST CONVENTIONS & INCENTIVES,
HARTMANN & JONEN GmbH
Conrad-Adenauer Platz 11, D-40210 DUSSELFDORF
Tel: +49 (211) 1606-400 Fax: 389197
Contact: Ms Vicky Gebhardt
Associations: DRV, American Ch of Commerce
Special Interest: funfairs (7); carnivals (2); breweries,

museums, castles, monorail, cathedrals (1-12).

GERMANY - FRANKFURT

GTS - GRIMM TRAVEL SERVICE
Max-Planck-Str.21, D-61381 FRIEDRICHSDORF
Tel: +49 (6172) 7 50 11 Fax: 7 73 72

Contact: Mr Walter Dierks
Established: 1990; 4 employees
Languages: Eng, Ger.
Traffic: all types.
Special Interest: cattle breeding, dolls, museums, wines
(4-10); castles, river cruises, disabled, military history,
railways (5-9); pottery (1-12).

GERMANY - HAMBURG

COLUMBUS TOURS
Ost-West-Str.59, D-20457 HAMBURG
Tel: +49 (40) 3705 2580 Fax: 3705 2233 Tlx:
21321629 HS D

Contact: Mr Klaus Schneider
Established: 1978; 8 employees
Languages: Eng, Fr, Ger, Sp.
Associations: SITE, DRV, IATA.
Special Interest: architecture, gourmet eating, history,
public transport, universities, zoo (1-12); sailing (4-9);
agriculture, horticulture, cattle breeding/dairy farming
(4-10);tennis (5-6); butterflies (5-9); horse-racing (6-
7).

GERMANY - MUNICH

WELCOME DESTINATION TRAVEL
MANAGEMENT, GmbH
Mauerkircherstrasse 4, D-81679 MUNICH
Tel: +49 (89) 988 835 Fax: 980 208

Contact: Mrs Renate Freyberger
Established: 1985; 6 employees
Languages: Eng, Fr, Ger.
Special Interest: architecture, art, beer festivals, castles,
museums, music festivals, universities (1-12); skiing (1-
4).

GHANA

BLACK BEAUTY TOURS LIMITED
The Loom Building, Samlotte House, Kwame Nkrumah
Ave, Adabraka, P O Box 2189, ACCRA
Tel: +233 (21) 227078/ 220384 Fax: 220062
Tlx: 3033 GH BLACK BEAUTY

Contacts: Joseph K Ankumah, MBA (Managing
Director) & Mrs Elizabeth E Ankumah (Tour Manager)
Established: 1969; 10 employees.
Languages: Eng.
Associations: IATA, ASTA, American Sightseeing Intl.
Special Interest: cruises, golf, pilgrimages, pottery (1-
12); safari (4-9); gardens, history, museums, religion,
universities (6-9); castles, music festivals (6,7,9).

GREECE

ARVANITIS TOURIST AND TRAVEL BUREAU
Tel: +30 (1) 3232 375/ 3220 383 Fax: 3232 340 Tlx:
215781 ARDI GR

Contact: Mr Yannis Lagios
Established: 1950; 15 employees.
Languages: Eng, Fr, Ger, Greek, Jap, Port.
Associations: HATA, COTAL, CMT, FIYTO, FIAV,
IATA, EUROMIC, ASTA, SITE, MPI, AIR, ASATA
(Assoc), AFTA (non-res), TAANZ (allied).
Special Interest: history, religion, spas (1-12); botany
(4-6); insect life (4-7); agriculture (5-6) cruises, sea
sports (summer); ornithology, yachting (spring/autumn);
wines & vineyards (9); archaeology (winter).

HOLLAND - SEE NETHERLANDS

HONG KONG

ABERCROMBIE & KENT (Hong Kong) Ltd
27th Floor, Tai Sang Commercial Bldg, 24 Hennessy
Road, WANCHAI
Tel: +852 865 7818 Fax: 866 0556

Contact: Patrick MacLeod, Managing Director

London Office:
A & K Overseas, Sloane Square House, Holbein Pl,
LONDON SW1W 8NS
Tel: +44 (171) 730 9600 Fax: 973 0478

Languages: Chin, Eng, Fr.
Special Interest: arts/cultural festivals, China tours,
cruises, food/groumet eating, history, golf, Rugby 7,
shopping (1-12); water sports (5-11); Macau Grand Prix
(9).

HUNGARY

CONCORDE TRAVEL LTD
Andrassy ut 56, H-1062 BUDAPEST
Tel: +36 (1) 153 0935/ 269 5447-8 Fax: 153 0417

Contact: Ms Judit Varkonyi
Established: 1991; 5 employees
Languages: Fr, Ger, It, Russ.
Special Interest: agriculture, architecture, art, food and
gourmet eating, history, horse riding, hot springs,
hunting, Jewish heritage, music festivals, ornithology,
wines & vineyards.

ICELAND

URVAL/UTSYN TRAVEL
Lagmuli 4, 108 REYKJAVIK
Tel: +354 (1) 699300 Fax: 685033 Tlx: 2036 UTSYN
IS

Contact: Ms Johanna Larusdottir
Associations: IATA, UFTAA, TIA, MPI
Established: 1970; 55 employees
Languages: Chin, Dan, Dutch, Eng, Fin, Fr, Ger, Ice,
Jap, Norw, Sp, Swed.
Special Interest: geology, photography, ornithology,
fishing, horse-riding, golf, rafting, volcano visits,
gourmet eating, hunting, agriculture, hot springs, hiking,
hydro-electricity, jeep safaris, glacier trips, waterfalls,
whale-watching.

INDIA

TRADE-WINGS TOURS LTD
30K Dubash Marg, Fort, BOMBAY 400 023
Tel: +91 (22) 244334 Fax: 2044223 Tlx: 11 85470/
82494 TWBB IN
Contacts: Mr Vinoo Ubhayakar & Ms Beena Patkar
European Office:
171 rue St Honore, F-75001 PARIS, France
Tel: +33 (1) 4297 4674 Fax: 4286 0490

Contact: Mr Ashok Kohli
Languages: Eng, Fr, Ger.
Associations: USTOA, IATA, UFTAA, ASTA, TAAI,
PATA, AFTA, JATA.
Special Interest: agriculture, archaeology, cricket,
fishing, gourmet eating, houseboats, jungle
expeditions, pilgrimages, railways, textiles, trekking,
wildlife (10-3).

INDONESIA

SANTA BALI TOURS & TRAVEL
Jln. By Pass Ngurah Rai 70 D, Sanur, DENPASAR
Tel: +62 (361) 286826/7/8 Fax: 286825/ 236508
or c/o The Grand Bali Beach Hotel, Jln. Hang
Tuah, Sanur, DENPASAR
Tel: +62 (361) 288057/ 287628 Tlx: 35133, HBB IA
(Attention: Santa Bali)

Contact: Mr Ketut Sedanartha
Representatives in: Medan, Padang, Yogyakarta,
Surabaya, Ujung Pandang and Lombok.

IRAN

PASARGAD TOUR
Tel: +98 (21) 2270274 Fax: 655517 TLx: 212300

Contact: Mr Sudabeh Hassani

IRELAND

THE O'MARA TRAVEL COMPANY LIMITED
37 Main Street, Donnybrook, DUBLIN 4

Tel: +353 (1) 2696033 Fax: 2696705 Tlx: 91342

Contacts: Ms Lise Whelan, Miss Susanne Monks
Established: 1978; 11 employees
Languages: Dan, Eng, Fr, Sp.
Associations: ITAA, ITOA, ASTA, IATA
Special Interest: heritage, golf, country pursuits, festivals, castles & gardens, theatre and music.

ISRAEL

PALEX TOURS LTD
59 Ha'atzmaut Road, 33033 HAIFA
Tel: +972 (4) 524254-9 Fax: 522491 Tlx: 46745 PALEX IL

Established: 1937
Associations: DRV, ASTA.
Special Interest: hot springs, medicine, pilgrimages, universities (1-12); agriculture, dairy farming, irrigation (spring); disabled tours (spring/autumn); wines & vineyards (8); health and fitness (11).

ITALY - SICILY

DIMSI S.P.A.
Via Vampolieri 8/A, 95020 ACI S.FILIPPO (Catania)
Tel: +39 (95) 896192/ 879855/ 896183 Fax: 879899
Tlx: 970401 DIMSI I

Contact: Mr Salvo Zappala
Established: 1985; 18 employees
Languages: Eng, Fr, Ger, It, Sp.
Associations: FIAVET, ECB
Special Interest: history, archaeology, vulcanology, ethnic culture, gastronomy, religious itineraries, opera, sports, events, carnivals and festivals.

ITALY - VENICE & MAINLAND

CLEMENTSON TRAVEL OFFICE
Tel: +39 (41) 5200466 Fax: 5231203

Contact: Mr Corrado Spalazzi
Established: 1946; 8 employees
Languages: Eng, Fr, Ger, It.
Associations: FIAVET, SITE, UFTAA, MPI.
Special Interest (Venice itself): architecture, art, gourmet eating, museums, opera, painting, theatre.
Special Interest (Italy): archaeology, botany, car racing, cruises, film festivals, gardens, golf, rowing, skiing, tennis, volcanos, wines & vineyards.

JAMAICA

XAYMACA TOURS
P O Box 1381, MONTEGO BAY
Tel: +1 (809) 952 3274-6 Fax: 952 9270 Tlx: 2001 MOBAY JA

Contact: Linda Leslie, General Manager
Special Interest: caves, deep sea fishing, diving, golf, rafting, sailing, tennis (1-12).

JAPAN

Toppan Yaesu Building, 2-2-7, Yaesu, Chuo-ku,
TOKYO 104
Central P O Box 1948
Tel: +81 (3) 3276 8113 Fax: 3271 7670 Tlx: 2228464 TOPTRV J

Contacts: Mr Ken Kato, Mr R Wittwer
Associations: IATA, JATA, PATA, ASTA.
Special Interest: architecture, railways, religion (1-12); spas/hot springs (5-10); botany, flowers, gardens, horticulture, pottery (5 & 10); mountaineering (5-9); skiing (12-3); music festival (11).

JERSEY - SEE CHANNEL IS.

JORDAN

BISHARAT TOURS CORPORATION
P O Box 35010, AMMAN
Tel: +962 (6) 41350 Fax: 659330 Tlx: 21363 BTC JO
Contact: Dr Faik Bisharat
Established: 1966; 6 employees
Languages: Arab, Eng, Fr, Ger, It, Sp.

Associations: IATA, UFTAA, ASTA, ISTA, COTAL, American Sightseeing Intl., WTA, PATA.

KENYA

ABERCROMBIE & KENT LTD
Bruce House, Standard St, P O Box 59749, NAIROBI
Tel: +254 (2) 334 955/ 334 919/ 334 355 Fax: 215 752
Tlx: 22853/ 25574 KENTOURS

Contact: Julian Hutton
London Office:
A & K Overseas, Sloane Square House, Holbein Pl,
LONDON SW1W 8NS
Tel: +44 (171) 730 9600 Fax: 973 0478
Contact: George Morgan-Grenville
Established: 1962; 75 employees
Languages: Eng, Fr, Ger, Jap, Sp.
Associations: KATO
Special Interest: anthropology, botany, film sets, golf, mountaineering, safaris, sub-aqua sport, trekking, wildlife, deep sea fishing, migration.

LAOS

DIETHELM TRAVEL LAOS
Tel (direct dialling not possible): 4442/ 5911 Fax: 5911
Tlx: 4491/ 4492 TE VTE LS (ATTN DIETHELM LAOS)

LATVIA

PAVADONIS TRAVEL COMPANY LTD
Elizabetes Street 45, LV-1010 RIGA
Tel: +371 (2) 332 402 Fax: 221 733 Tlx: 161178 OAZIS SU

Contact: Mr Alexander Gulpe & Mrs Ludmila Martynova
Established: 1990; 10 employees
Associations: ALTA, PATA
Special Interest: art, architecture, folk dance and song, horse-riding, cycling, boating, bob-sleighing, ballooning, fishing, hunting, religion, theatre, museums, opera.

LUXEMBOURG

WEZENBERG INCENTIVE TRAVEL SERVICES
B.P.2479, L-1024 LUXEMBOURG
Tel: +352 402332 Fax: 481801

Contact: Mr Han Wezenberg
Languages: Dan, Dutch, Eng, Fr, Ger, Lux.
Associations: Hickory, MPI.
Special Interest: art & painting, ballooning, castles, cycling, fishing, gambling, golf, gourmet eating, music festivals, squash, tennis, wines & vineyards, walking, war history; European City of Culture 1995.

MALAYSIA

WORLD EXPRESS
2-14 Angkasa Raya, KUALA LUMPUR 50450
Tel: +60 (3) 248 5412 Fax: 242 1129 Tlx: 31132

Contact: Mr Henry Ong

Penang Office:
126 Jalan Burmah, Unit 227, PENANG 10050
Tel: +60 (4) 361 910 Fax: 369 654 Tlx: 40793

Contact: Ms P.Y. Lim
Established: 1970; 12 employees
Special Interest: agriculture/botany, festivals, gourmet eating, golf, horse-racing, jungle expeditions, museums, pottery, railways, religion, shopping, zoos.

MALDIVES REPUBLIC

SUNLAND TRAVEL (PVT) LTD
Asrafee Building, 3F, 1/44 Chandhanee Magu,
P O Box 20145, MALE
Tel: +960 324658/ 324758 Fax: 325543 Tlx: (896) 77064

Contact: Mr Mohamed Nazeer

MALTA

SPECIAL INTEREST TRAVEL LTD
103, Archbishop Street, VALLETTA
Tel: +356 233121 Fax: 235145/ 242851 Tlx: 1278

OJAMED MW
Contacts: Mr Michael C Kamsky, Mr Jose Calleja
Established: 1977; 12 employees
Associations: Conference & Incentive Travel Bureau, Malta
Special Interest: archaeology, architecture, fortresses, cathedrals, history, museums, religion, coral reefs, military history (1-12); diving, windsurfing (4-11); carnival (pre-Lent).

MAURITIUS

MAUTOURCO
MAURITIUS TOURING CO LTD/TRANSMAURICE LTD
Gustave Colin Street, Forest Side
Tel: +230 674 3695-6 Fax: 674 3720 Tlx: 4435
HERMCO IW

Contact: Mr Jacques de Speville
Established: 1955; 100 employees
Languages: Eng, Fr.
Associations: Hertz franchise.
Special Interest: coral reefs, folk-dancing, gardens, golf, history, religion, scuba-diving, water-skiing, wildlife (1-12); horse racing (5-11); yacht cruises, deep-sea fishing, hunting (summer).

MEXICO

DESTINATION MEXICO
Tel: +52 (5) 264 5179/264 3234 Fax: 264 3547

Contact: Peter Crossley

Branch Office:
Plaza Centro Local 217, Av. Nader 8 S.M.5, CANCUN,
Quintana Roo.
Tel: +51 (96) 84 7458/84 2750 Fax: 84 7055

Contact: Ms Jan Revell

UK Office:
8 Gleneagles, Amington, TAMWORTH, B77 4NS
Tel: +44 (1827) 67498 Fax: 67498

Contact: Keith Fortune

MONACO: SEE FRANCE - SOUTH

MOROCCO

TRAVEL LINK
19 rue Mauritania, App.8, MARRAKECH GUELIZ
Tel: +212 (4) 448797/ 448765 Fax: 448839

Contact: Mr Ahmed Nait

NEPAL

YETI TRAVELS PVT LTD
Tel: +977 (1) 22 1234/ 22 1739/ 22 1754/ 22 2285 Fax: 22 6153
Tlx: 2204 YETI NP/ 2303 AMXREP NP/ 2648 YETI NP

Contact: Mr J L Khanna
Established: 1966; 350 employees
Languages: Eng, Fr, Ger, It, Jap, Sp.
Associations: IATA, WATA, PATA, AFTA, ASTA, UFTAA, USTOA, ISTA, COTAL, JATA, NATA, TAAI (non-res), IATO, ICCA.
Special Interest: folk dancing, gambling, hospitals, museums, photography, pottery, rafting, safaris, wildlife (1-12); golf (9-6); mountaineering (2-4 & 8-9); trekking (10-6).

NETHERLANDS

BEUK TRAVEL CONSULTANTS
Strawinskylaan 911, 1077 XX AMSTERDAM
Tel: +31 (20) 662 6277/ 662 6322 Fax: 662 9826

Contacts: Mr John Brandenburg, Consultant, Mr Han Kuipers, Operations Manager, Mr Marc Beuk, Managing Director, Mr L Balm, Incentive Organiser
Established: 1974; 7 employees (incoming dept)
Languages: Dutch, Eng, Fr, Ger, It, Sp.
Associations: ANVR, ASTA, UFTAA, PATA, VNC (Congress Organisers)
Special Interest: agriculture, architecture, cattle breeding,

flowers, food, hospitals, medicine, museums, public transport (1-12); dairy farming (3-10); gardens, horticulture (4-9); Holland & Belgium tours, German tours.

NEW ZEALAND

LANDMARK TRAVEL (SOUTH PACIFIC LTD)
125 Vincent St, P O Box 6786, Wellesley St, AUCKLAND 1
Tel: +64 (9) 309 3350 Fax: 309 3741

Contact: Alberto Ubeda, MD; Derek Green, Inbound Tours Mgr; Anne Wilks, Mgr, C.Europe

European Marketing Offices:
P O Box 9-bis, B-1390 GREZ-DOICEAU, Belgium
Tel: +32 (1) 084 2619 Fax: 084 2920
Sales & Promotion Services, Duisburgerstr.125, 40479 DUSSELDORF, Germany
Tel: +49 (211) 491 1638 Fax: 491 1676-7

Languages: Dutch, Eng, Fr, Ger, It, Sp.
Associations: SITE, IATA, ITOC, PATA, COTAL, USTOA (Allied).
Special Interest: agriculture, golf, hydro-electrics (1-12); wines & vineyards (1-4); rugby (5-9); skiing (8-9); dairy farming, cattle & horse-breeding (10-4); deep sea fishing, yachting (11-4); trekking (12-1).

NIGERIA

JEMI-ALADE TOURS
P O Box 3794, Ikeja, LAGOS
Tel: 234 960297 Fax: 963301

Contact: Mr Ladi Jemi-Alade

NORWAY

PERFECTION DESTINATION BERGEN
Engelgarden, Bryggen, N-5003 BERGEN
Tel: +47 55 31 88 99 Fax: 55 32 70 32

Contact: Ms Eli Lilleheim Aamodt
Established: 1987; 3 employees.
Languages: Eng, Fr, Ger, Norw.
Associations: SITE
Special Interest: fjord cruises, seaplane flights (4-10); midnight sun (5-8); arctic winter (12-4); fishing (5-10); rafting (7-8); mediaeval wood architecture, Viking & Hanseatic heritage, music of Grieg, industrial themes (1-12).

OMAN

GRAY MACKENZIE TRAVEL - GULF VENTURES
P O Box 3985 MUSCAT

Contact: Mr Pradip Hazaldar
Special Interest: archaeology, coral reefs, bird watching, sailing, deep sea fishing, desert & mountain safaris.

PAKISTAN

SITARA TRAVEL CONSULTANTS (PVT) LTD
Sitara House, 232 Khadim Hussain Road, P O Box 63, RAWALPINDI
Tel: +92 (51) 564 750-1/ 566 272 Fax: 584 958 Tlx: 5751 STARA PK

Contact: Mr Shiraz M Poonja

International Sales Office:
3526 West 41st Avenue, VANCOUVER, B.C., Canada V6N 3E6
Tel: +1 (604) 264 8747 Fax: 264 7774 Tlx: 0455768

Established: 1974; 52 employees
Languages: Eng.
Associations: ASTA, TAAP, PATA, USTOA, JATA, KATA.

PAPUA NEW GUINEA

TRANS NIUGINI TOURS
P O Box 371, MT HAGEN
Tel: +675 521 438 Fax: 522 470
Contact: Bob Bates
Established: 1976; 50 employees

Languages: Eng.
Associations: PATA, ASTA, AFTA, TAPNG, USTOA.
Special Interest: anthropology, botany, butterflies, canoeing, cultural, diving, flowers, jungle expeditions, ornithology, rafting, safaris (adventure), trekking, war relics (1-12).

PARAGUAY

INTER-EXPRESS
Yegros 690, ASUNCION
Tel: +595 (21) 490-111/5 Fax: 449156 Tlx: 264 IE PY

Contact: Mr Ronald Birks, Partner/Manager, Incoming Dept
Special Interest: agriculture, cattle breeding, fishing, gambling, history, hydro-electricity, wild orchids, old trains (1-12).

PERU

DASATOUR S.A.
Jose Llana Zapata 331 - Suite 901/3 Miraflores, LIMA 18; P O Box 649, LIMA 100
Tel: +51 (14) 415 045/ 401 750 Fax: 422 970 Tlx: 21002 PE PB HCSAR FOR DASATOUR & 20053 PE PB LIMT FOR DASATOUR

Contact: Mr Jose Lemor
Associations: IATA, ASTA, COTAL, ICCA, SATA, PATA, USTOA.
Special Interest: anthropology, archaeology, museums, railways, canoeing, jungle expeditions, pottery, golf, rafting, wildlife (1-12); trekking (5-11); mountaineering (5-8).

PHILIPPINES

INTAS TRAVEL AND TOURS, INC.
Room 205, Diplomat Condominium, Roxas Blvd. Cnr. Russel St, Barclaran Paranaque, METRO MANILA
Tel: +63 (2) 883 0392 Fax: 831 0021 Tlx: 45255 INTAS PN/ 63683 INTAS PN

Contact: Ms Sonia Teresita Henderson
Shangri-La's EDSA Plaza Hotel, 1 Garden Way, Ortigas Center, Mandaluyong, METRO MANILA.
Tel: +63 (2) 633 6550/ 634 3595 Fax: 634 5565/ 817 3565
Shangri-La's Mactan Island Resort, Punta Engano, Mactan, CEBU.
Tel: +63 (32) 310 288 Fax: 311 688
Special Interest: agriculture, coral reefs, diving, jungle expeditions, mountaineering, air safaris, volcano visits, ethnic culture, trekking, golf.

POLAND

AIR TOURS POLAND GROUP CO LTD
9 Warynskiego Street
00-655 WARSAW
Tel: +48 (22) 299054 Fax: 293757 Tlx: 816569

Contact: Ms Alina Markiewicz, Vice-President, Incoming.
Established: 1992; 50 employees.
Languages: Eng, Fr, Ger, Pol, Sp.
Associations: IATA, JATA
Special Interest: arts & culture, castles, religion, Jewish heritage, opera, ballet, sports events, horse riding, hunting.

PORTUGAL

MILTOURS
Rua Verissimo de Almeida 14, P-8000 FARO
Tel: +351 (89) 80 20 30 Fax: 80 60 79/ 80 20 37 Tlx: 56336 MTOUR P

Contact: Ms Anja Julian
Established: 1980; 72 employees.
Languages: Eng, Fr, Ger, Norw, Port, Sp, Swed.
Associations: IATA, ASTA, ACTA
Special Interest: gold, tennis, football, shotting, horse riding, deep sea fishing, bird-watching, jeep safaris, history.

PORTUGAL - LISBON

MILTOURS

Rua Conde Redondo 21, P-1100 LISBON
Tel: +351 (1) 352 41 66 Fax: 54 29 88 Tlx: 60428 MILTUR P
Contact: Mrs Laura Antunes Silva
Established: 1989; 16 employees.
Languages: Eng, Fr, Ger, It, Port, Sp.
Special Interest: art, castles, gardens, golf, history museums, wines & vineyards, religion/pilgrimages, sports events, car rallies, jeep safaris.

PORTUGAL - OPORTO

MILTOURS
Rua Simon Bolivar 209, Saia 4 S/L, P-4470 MAIA
Tel: +351 (2) 941 4671 Fax: 941 4674 Tlx: 20753 MTOUR P

Contact: Mrs Rosa Maria Koehler
Established: 1992; 4 employees.
Languages: Eng, Dutch, Fr, Ger, Port, Sp.
Associations: IATA, ASTA, ACTA
Special Interest: art, castles, gardens, golf, history, museums, wines & vineyards, religion/pilgrimages, sports events.

PORTUGAL - MADEIRA

MILTOURS
Avenida do Infante, Centro Commercial Avenida, Loja 1, P O Box 2780, P-9000 FUNCHAL

Contact: Mr Duarte Correia
Established: 1991; 14 employees
Languages: Eng, Fr, Port, Sp.
Associations: IATA, APAVT
Special Interest: nature, gardens, walking (levadas), golf, wines, sports events.

ROMANIA

EAST COAST TRAVEL
10 Unirii Blvd, Block 7b, Entrance 2, 6th floor, Suite 45, BUCHAREST
Tel & Fax: +40 1312 5463

RUSSIA

Bolshaya Naberezhnaya Ul. 5-233, 123362 MOSCOW
Tel: +7 (095) 490 5195 Fax: 490 5195

Contact: Sergey Kholdenko, General Manager
Sub-office:
Ul Suslova 9-5-9, 198255 ST PETERSBURG
Tel & Fax: +7 (812) 152 9682
London Coordinating Office:
Research House, Fraser Road, PERIVALE, UB6 7AQ
Tel: +44 (181) 566 9424 Fax: 566 8845 Tlx: 918439 RPTLON G

Other offices in: LVOV, MINSK, IRKUTSK, ULANUDE, NOVGOROD, PSKOV, SAMARKAND, BOKHARA & ABAKHAN: please contact Moscow or London.

Special Interest: trans-Siberian express itineraries, opera, ballet, music, trekking, bicycling, rafting, kayaking, religious groups, central Asia cities routes, private home stays, camel trekking, horse-riding.

SAINT LUCIA

CONFERENCE & INCENTIVE SERVICES LTD
Tel: +1 (809) 45 27058/ 31652 Fax: 45 31780 Tlx: 6201 CISLC

Contacts: David Coathup
Associations: St Lucia Hotel & Tourism Assn.
Special Interest: natural beauty, watersports (windsurfing, waterskiing, diving), yachting, ethnic culture, golf, tennis, walking, carnivals & festivals.

SAINT MARTIN (SINT MAARTEN)

ST-MARTIN EVASION
B P 1144 Galisbay Road, MARIGOT 97150, St Martin FWI.
Tel: +590 871 360 Fax: 871 359 Tlx: 919161 GL

Contact: Isabelle Patry
Languages: Eng, Fr, Ger, It, Sp.
Special Interest: deep sea fishing, helicopter rides, horse

riding, sailing, SCUBA diving.

SAINT VINCENT & THE GRENADINES

BAREFOOT HOLIDAYS
Tel: +1 (809) 456 9334 Fax: 456 9238 Tlx: 7506

Contacts: Martin and Mary Barnard
Special Interest: aircraft charters, yachting, volcanoes, nature trails, botanical gardens, museums, waterfall, forts, handicrafts, cathedrals.

SEYCHELLES

TRAVEL SERVICES (SEYCHELLES) LTD
Victoria House, P O Box 356, Victoria, MAHE
Tel: +248 322 414 Fax: 321 366 Tlx: 2234 LINWES SZ

Contact: Mr Christian Lenferna

U.K. Office:
29 Elmfield Mansions, Elmfield Rd, LONDON SW17 8AA
Tel: +44 (181) 675 4498 Fax: 673 8538

Contact: Ms Dendy Barker

U.S. Office:

Contact: Ms Jean Walden
Special Interest: botany, conservation, coral reefs, deep sea fishing, diving, ornithology, painting, photography, sailing, walking, wildlife, windsurfing.

SICILY: SEE ITALY - SICILY

SINGAPORE

WORLD EXPRESS GROUP
114 Middle Road, 05-01, SINGAPORE 0718
Tel: +65 336 3877 Fax: 339 8625 Tlx: 33372 WXPSIN

Contact: Mr Tan Chee Chye
Established: 1969; 50 employees
Languages: Chin, Eng, Fr, Ger, It.
Associations: ASTA, SITE, ICCA, PATA, AFTA, TAANZ.
Special Interest: architecture, art/painting, gardens, golf, gourmet eating, horse racing, hospitals, museums, religion, wet market & other shopping, windsurfing, zoos (1-12).

SLOVENIA

ATLAS AMBASSADOR
Tel: +386 (61) 222 741 Fax: 222 711
Contact: Mrs Nada Miklus

SOUTH AFRICA

WALTHERS TOURS (PTY) LTD
P O Box 3247, RANDBURG 2125 (Johannesburg)
Tel: +27 (11) 789 3624 Fax: 789 5255

Contact: Mr Klaus Walther
Established: 1981; 11 employees
Languages: Afrikaans, Eng, Fr, Ger, It, Sp.
Associations: SITE, SATSA, ASATA, WATA.
Special Interest: agriculture, cattle breeding, dairy farming, ethnic cultures, flowers/horticulture, fishing, gemstones, golf, mining, photography, wildlife, wines & vineyards.

SPAIN - BALEARIC ISLANDS

C I C (CONVENTIONS, INCENTIVES & CONGRESSES) SA
San Miguel 30-4 D-bis, 07002 PALMA DE MALLORCA
Tel: +34 (71) 724 934 Fax: 713 545 Tlx: 69127 CICP E

Established: 1977
Associations: ITP, MTB
Special Interest: art festivals, bird-watching, cycling, photography, walking (1-12); cruises, sailing, yachting (4-10); golf (9-5).

SPAIN - BARCELONA & COSTA BRAVA

LATITUD 4 DESTINATION MANAGEMENT
Diputacion 279, 08007 BARCELONA
Tel: +34 (3) 488 2220 Fax: 488 2361 Tlx: 98934

Contact: Mr Eduardo Subirats, Managing Director
Established: 1982; 24 employees
Languages: Eng, Fr, Ger, Port, Sp.
Associations: ACAV
Special Interest: archaeology, architecture, art, cathedrals, gourmet eating, museums, pharmaceuticals, pottery, wines & vineyards (1-12); fashions (4-5, 10-11); opera (10-5).

SPAIN - BILBAO

LATITUD 4 DESTINATION MANAGEMENT
Tel: +34 (4) 423 60 93 Fax: 463 26 66

Contact: Patricio Arana
Established: 1982; 24 employees
Associations: ACAV
Special Interest: art, climbing, gourmet-eating, history, museums, music, opera, theatre, walking.

SPAIN - MARBELLA, SEVILLA, GRANADA & JEREZ

CITITRAVEL, S.A.
Plaza de Ole 5, 29630 BENALMADENA COSTA, Malaga
Tel: +34 (5) 244 5645 Fax: 244 5647/ 244 1358

Contacts: Carlos Charters, Karen Jessen
Established: 1985; 20 employees
Languages: Dutch, Eng, Fr, Ger, Sp.
Associations: ITMA
Special Interest: art, history, wines, gourmet eating, beaches, golf, sports.

SPAIN - GRAND CANARY

Edf. Mercurio, Torre I, 3/A, Avenida de Tirajana, s/n, E-35100 PLAYA DEL INGLES
Tel: +34 (28) 769 604 Fax: 761 410 Tlx: 96724 VIANE

Contact: Mr Damian Ribas
Established: 1987; 40 employees
Languages: Dutch, Eng, Fr, Ger, Sp.
Associations: FEAAV

SPAIN - LANZAROTE

VIAJES NECAN, S.A.
Avenida de Las Playas, C.C. Matagorda, Local 44, E-35510 PUERTO DEL CARMEN
Tel: +34 (28) 511 924 Fax: 511 925 Tlx: 96481

Contact: Mrs Helga Benitez
Established: 1987; 40 employees
Languages: Dutch, Eng, Fr, Ger, Sp.
Associations: FEAAV

SPAIN - MADRID

Po. de la Castellana, 121, 28046 MADRID
Tel +34 (1) 597 08 22 Fax: 556 23 26 Tlx: 49008 LTD E

Contact: Ma. Eugenia Gomez, Manager
Special Interest: art, gourmet eating, history, museums, opera.

SPAIN - TENERIFE

VIAJES LIDER CANARIAS SA
Calle La Hoya 58, 38400 PUERTO DE LA CRUZ, Tenerife
Tel: +34 (22) 382 100 Fax: 380 768/ 371 832 Tlx: 92398/ 92772 LIDE E

Contacts: Mr Jose Alonso & Mr Nick Padilla
Branch Office:
Edificio Veronica II, 38660 PLAYA DE LAS AMERICAS
Tel: +34 (22) 790 813-4 Fax: 796 520 Tlx: 92394 LIDE E
Established: 1987; 29 employees

SRI LANKA

QUICKSHAWS LTD
P O Box 1830, 3 Kalinga Place, COLOMBO 05
Tel: +94 (1) 583133-5 Fax: 587613 Tlx: 21267 QUIKTUR CE

Contacts: Ms Nirmala de Mel & Mr Jayanthan Innasithamby
Associations: ASTA, IATA, PATA, JATA, UFTA.
Special Interest: environmental & nature programmes, alternative & tropical medicine, oriental religions, archaeology; festivals & processions; gems, cricket, golf, sailing, diving, walking, handicrafts, agriculture.

SURINAME

METS - SURINAME TOURISM COMPANY LTD
5 Rudielaan, PARAMARIBO
Tel: +597 492 892/ 497 180 Fax: 497 062

Contact: Mr Jerry R. A-Kum
Special Interest: fishing, river cruises, wildlife, rainforest tours, trekking, climbing, ornithology, white-water rafting, ethnic culture.

SWEDEN

Drottninggatan 71A, 4th Floor, P O Box 5128, S-102 43 STOCKHOLM
Tel: +46 (8) 21 47 07/ 21 48 73 Fax: 24 03 80

Contact: Tom Risbecker
Established: 1977; 5 employees
Associations: SITE, MPI, HSMA, ASTA, DRV.
Special Interest: agriculture, canal cruising, folk-dancing, forestry, golf, gourmet eating, hospitals, hunting, museums, rafting.

SWITZERLAND

WELCOME SWISS
C.P. 141, avenue Tribunal Federal 34, 1000 LAUSANNE 5
Tel: +41 (21) 320 6821 Fax: 323 1366 Tlx: 454803 WST CH
Contacts: Andrew Done, Marc Tassera
Associations: SITE, ITMA, ACE.

TAIWAN, CHINA

INTER-ASIA HOLIDAYS
Tel: +886 (2) 511 6341 Fax: 563 0028/ 511 9204 Tlx: 13385/ 20450 CHRISLAW

Contact: Christopher Law
Established: 1970
Languages: Chin, Eng.
Associations: UFTAA, USTOA, PATA, ASTA, SITE

TANZANIA

ABERCROMBIE & KENT LTD
Arusha International Conference Centre, P O Box 427, ARUSHA
Tel: +255 (57) 8347 Fax: 8273 Tlx: 42005 TZ

Contact: Mr Sandy Evans

London Office:
A & K Overseas, Sloane Square House, Holbein Pl, LONDON SW1W 8NS
Tel: +44 (171) 730 9600 Fax: 973 0478

Contact: George Morgan-Grenville
Languages: Eng, Fr, Ger, It.
Special Interest: agriculture, anthropology, botany, gemstones, hospitals, ornithology, photography, safaris, wildlife (1-12); mountaineering, walking (1-3, 6-12).

THAILAND

DIETHELM TRAVEL
Kian Gwan II Building, 140/1 Wireless Road, BANGKOK 10330
Tel: +66 (2) 255-9150/ 9160/ 9170 Fax: 256 0248-9 Tlx: 81183/ 21763/ 227001 DIETRAV TH

Contact: Mr Chaladol Ussamarn

Associations: ASTA, ICCA, PATA, USTOA, TICA, TTI, Networld.
Special Interest: archaeology, cruises, gemstones, jungle expeditions, ornithology, rafting, trekking, walking, diving, bicycling, canoeing, golfing, sailing, watersports, yachting, Myanmar (Burma) tours.

TRINIDAD & TOBAGO

THE TRAVEL CENTRE, LTD
Level 2, Uptown Mall, Edward Street, PORT OF SPAIN

Contact: Catherine de Gannes-Martin, Managing Director
Established: 1988; 8 employees
Languages: Eng.
Associations: IATA, ASTA, ISMP.
Special Interest: carnivals, coral reefs, scuba-diving, sailing, golf, nature, sports, squash, food, flowers, ornithology.

TURKEY - ISTANBUL & ANTALYA

VIP TOURISM DESTINATION MANAGEMENT COMPANY
Cumhuriyet Caddesi 269/2, Harbiye, 80230
ISTANBUL
Tel: +90 (212) 241 6514/ 230 1331 Fax: 241 1995 Tlx: 27089 VIP TR

Contact: Mr Ceylan Pirinccioglu
Established: 1968
Languages: Eng, Fr, Ger, Greek, Jap, Russ, Sp, Turk.

Branch Offices:
Halici Sokak No. 8/3 Gaziosmanpasa, ANKARA
Tel: +90 (312) 467 65 05/ 467 02 10; Fax: 467 01 04
Tel: +90 (242) 474 376/7 Fax: 412 144
Associations: ASTA, IATA, ICCA, Internet, JATA, SITE, DRV, UFTAA, USTOA.
Special Interest: food, gourmet eating, museums (1-12); archaeology, spas, religion (4-6,9-10); ornithology (4/5, 10/11); yachting (5-10); music festivals, agriculture (6-9); art (9-6); universities (10-6).

TURKEY - IZMIR & AEGEAN COAST

TURCEM TOURISM AND TRAVEL LTD
858 Sokak No.2, Cakiroglu is Hani 301, 35250
KONAK, IZMIR
Tel: +90 (232) 425 7657 Fax: 484 4511 Tlx: 53775 TCMT TR

Contacts: Mr Nazmi Buldanlioglu & Mr Cuneyr Ustuntunalioglou
Established: 1988; 5 employees
Languages: Eng, Ger, Turk.
Associations: UFTAA, ASTA, TURSAB, SKAL
Special Interest: folk dancing, food, walking (1-12); flowers, religion (4-5); steam trains (4-5,9-10); cruises, sailing, spas/hot springs, yachting (4-10); agriculture, diving (5-9).

UGANDA

ABERCROMBIE & KENT (Uganda) Ltd
Tel: +256 (41) 242 495-6 Fax: 242 490

Contact: David Woods
London Office:
A & K Overseas, Sloane Square House, Holbein Pl, LONDON SW1W 8NS
Tel: +44 (171) 730 9600 Fax: 973 0478
Contact: George Morgan-Grenville

UKRAINE

EUGENIA TRAVEL ODESSA
12 Suvorov Str., ODESSA 270004
Tel: +7 (0482) 224047 Fax: 220554 Tlx: 232141

Contact: Mrs Janna Belousova
USA Sales Office:
415 S. Orange Ave, BREA, CA 92621
Tel: +1 (714) 990 4305 Fax: 990 0729

UNITED ARAB EMIRATES - DUBAI

MMI - GULF VENTURES
P O Box 70, DUBAI

Tel: +971 (4) 346 838 Fax: 345 029 Tlx: 45425
GRAY EM

Contact: Mr Gamal Fathy
Special Interest: archaeology, coral reefs, deep-sea fishing, sailing, (1-12); camel races (10-2); cricket, diving, golf, safaris (10-5).

UNITED KINGDOM

Being based in Britain ourselves, it was impossible to choose one operator exclusively and we have therefore asked our many friends in the industry to apply for inclusion and to write a brief profile of their companies.

ANGLO AMERICAN TRAVEL LTD
35 Spencer Road, Wimbledon, LONDON SW20 0QN
Tel: +44 (181) 947 3416 Fax: 947 1175

Contact: Roger Stevens
Associations: BITOA.

COLCHESTER, CO6 1EB
Tel: +44 (1206) 213 456 Fax: 213 457

Contacts: Michael Wheeler & Jacqueline Bonner
Languages: Eng, Fr, Ger.

EVENTS INTERNATIONAL LTD
53 St Owen Street, HEREFORD, HR1 2JQ
Tel: +44 (1432) 263 263 Fax: 342 323

Contact: Paul Terry, Managing Director & Angela Rosier
Established: 1985; 8 employees
Languages: Eng, Fr, Ger, Sp.
Special Interest: corporate market, activity events, tickets.

JOURNEYS (Journeys Abroad Ltd)
Bro Dyffryn, Llwynmawr, LLANGOLLEN, Clwyd
LL20 7BH, Wales
Tel & Fax: +44 (1691) 718 919 Fax: 718 285

Contact: Hugh Jordan, Managing Director
Languages: Eng, Fr, Ger, Pol, Russ, Welsh.
Special Interest: schools/colleges, railway enthusiasts, country sports.

LEISURE EXECUTIVE UK
125 Welbeck Crescent, TROON, Scotland, KA10 6AR
Tel: +44 (1292) 316846 Fax: 316846

Contact: John Carruthers
Languages: Arabic, Chinese (Mand), Eng, Gaelic, Pol, Russ.
Special Interest: castles, lochs, cruises, mediaeval banquets, sailing, historic tours, golf, soccer, rugby, ornithology, steam trains, wildlife.

MARKETING SERVICES & PROMOTIONS (MSP) LTD
12 Penn Place, RICKMANSWORTH, WD3 1RE
Tel: +44 (1923) 772 828 Fax: 896 109

Contact: Annabella Senior, Managing Director
OPTIMUM LTD
P O Box 68, COVENTRY CV5 9YZ
Tel: +44 (1676) 522491 Fax: 522497
Contact: Ms Trish Twigger, Director

SPENCER SCOTT TRAVEL LTD
3 Cromwell Place, LONDON, SW7 2JE
Tel: +44 (171) 225 2988 Fax: 581 9109

Contact: Elizabeth Drake, Managing Director
Special Interest: opera & music festivals, viticulture, archaeology and architecture, photography and painting, ornithology and wildlife, gardens and horticulture, walking and climbing, mountain biking and equestrian; Wimbledon, FA Cup Final and last night of the Proms.

SPORTSWORLD GROUP PLC
New Abbey Court, Stert Street, ABINGDON OX14 3JZ
Tel: +44 (1235) 555 844 Fax: 550 428

Contacts: Jonathan Callow or Sarah FurnessThe
Languages: Fr, Ger, It, Pol, Port, Sp.
TRAVEL MANAGEMENT TEAM LIMITED
44 The Grove, Ilkley, Yorkshire LS29 9EE
Tel: +44 (1943) 816 656 Fax: 816 473
Contact: Carol Patton, Managing Director

USA - ALASKA

ALASKA VACATIONS
3107 Cottonwood Street, ANCHORAGE, AK 99508
Tel: +1 (907) 258 2746 Fax: 278 8832
Contacts: Ms Irene Greene, Mr Stanley May
Established: 1989; 7 employees
Languages: Dutch, Eng, Fr, Ger, It, Jap, Sp
Special Interest: fishing, hunting, arctic winter tours.

USA - ARIZONA & SOUTHWEST

SOUTHWEST ARRANGERS LTD
4520 East Grant Road, TUCSON, AZ 85712
Tel: +1 (602) 881 4474 Fax: 881 8165

Contact: Mr Garet Kanter
Special Interest: cowboy experience, river rafting the Grand Canyon.

USA - CALIFORNIA

PATTI ROSCOE & ASSOCIATES, INC
2456 Broadway, SAN DIEGO, CA 92102
Tel: +1 (619) 234 9440 Fax: 232 5869

Contact: Ms Patti Roscoe

Branch Offices:
11925 Wilshire Blvd, Ste 332, LOS ANGELES, CA 90025
42-900 Bob Hope Dr, Ste 104, RANCHO MIRAGE (Palm Springs), CA 922790
Tel: +1 (619) 776 4377 Fax: 779 0018
150 Paularino Ave, Ste 155, COSTA MESA, CA 95626
Tel: +1 (714) 755 1500 Fax: 755 1511

USA - COLORADO

ORGANIZERS, ETC
7373 South Alton Way, Suite B100, ENGLEWOOD, CO 80112
Tel: +1 (303) 771 1178 Fax: 771 1157

Contact: Craig Cook
Established: 1981; 12 employees
Languages: Fr, Ger, It, Sp.
Special Interest: cattle drives, city tours, fishing, golf, guest ranches, rafting, skiing, tennis.

USA - FLORIDA

SUNCOAST DESTINATION MGT SCES
6149 Chancellor Drive, Suite 700, ORLANDO, FL 32809

Contact: Graydon Hall
Branch offices:
150, 153rd Ave, Suite 301, MADEIRA BEACH, FL 33708
13899 Briscayne Blvd, Suite 142, MIAMI, FL 33181

London Office:
6 Baron's Gate, LONDON W4 5HT
Tel: +44 (181) 995 7458 Fax: 994 7388

Contact: Maggi Smit
Established: 1980; 350 employees
Languages: Dutch, Eng, Fr, Ger, It, Jap, Sp.
Associations: SITE, MPI, CFCSA.
Special Interest: car racing, cruising, farms, food/gourmet eating, golf, horse breeding, yachting.

USA - GEORGIA

2964 Peachtree Road NW, Suite 652, ATLANTA, GA 30305
Tel: +1 (404) 262 7660 Fax: 233 2426

Contacts: Susan Henderson & Judy Kluttz
Languages: Eng, Fr, Ger, It, Sp.
Associations: MPI, NTA, ASAE, NAEM, PCMA, HCEA, ISES, SITE.
Special Interest: private homes, historic locales, architecture, gardens, museums, gourmet-eating, Afro-American heritage, gospel music, sports events, golf, tennis; rafting.

USA - HAWAII

MARY CHARLES & ASSOCIATES, INC.

2334 South King Street, Suite 205, HONOLULU 96826
Tel: +1 (808) 942 9655 Fax 949 1273 Tlx: (743) 1705
MCAHI

Contact: Mary Charles
Associations: SITE, MPI, HSMAI.
Special Interest: rugby (6-8); history, surfing, volcano
visits, windsurfing, yachting (1-12).

USA - ILLINOIS

100, North LaSalle Street, Suite 2010, CHICAGO, IL
60602
Tel: +1 (312) 641 6633 Fax: 641 6641 Tlx: 4955963

Contact: Mr Rex Fritschi
Established: 1969; 8 employees
Languages: Eng, Fr, Ger.
Associations: ASTA, SITE, IATAN
Special Interest: architecture (world centre for modern
architecture), financial, jazz and blues (1-12); railways
(4-10); agriculture (4-11); music (6-8, 10-3); opera (11-
3).

USA - LOUISIANA

CUSTOM CONVENTIONS OF NEW ORLEANS
P O Box 50958, NEW ORLEANS, LA 70150
Tel: +1 (504) 944 0814 Fax: 944 0815

Contact: Carling Dinkler III
Established: 1976; 7 employees.
Languages: Eng.
Associations: MPI.
Special Interest: architecture, beaches, Cajun culture,
river & swampland cruises, cuisine, southern
plantations.

USA - MISSOURI

ST LOUIS SCENE, INC
711 North 11th Street, ST LOUIS, MO 631012
Tel: +1 (314) 569 0226 Fax: 569 1204

Contact: Peggy Schweig
Established: 1974; 20 employees.
Associations: MPI, HSAE, HSMA, PCMA, ISES, SITE,
The Network, IAEM.
Special Interest: Gateway Arch, Mississippi cruises, river
boat gambling, zoo, botanical gardens, museums, art &
sculpture.

USA - NEVADA (LAS VEGAS)

SUNCOAST DESTINATION MGT SCES
3750-60 S Jones Blvd, LAS VEGAS, NV 89103
Tel: +1 (702) 221 8812 Fax: 228 0559

Contacts: Joanne Ballard
London Office:
6 Baron's Gate, LONDON W4 5HT
Contact: Ms Maggi Smit
Languages: Eng
Special Interest: snow skiing, water skiing, boating,
canyons, river rafting, fishing, cruising, ghost towns,
golf, mountain climbing, houseboating, gambling.

USA - NEW YORK

MANHATTAN PASSPORT
151 East 80th Street, Suite 5a, NEW YORK, NY 10021
Tel: +1 (212) 861 2746 Fax: 861 2426 Tlx: 6972498

Contact: Ms Ina Lee Selden, President
Associations: SITE, NYCVB.
Special Interest: gourmet eating, jazz, museums, theatre
(1-12); ballet (2-5); gardens (4-8); baseball (4-9); tennis
(9); opera (9-4); autumn foliage (10-11); football (10-1);
basketball (10-4).

USA - N CAROLINA

CAROLINA MEETING & INCENTIVE GROUP, INC.
2801 Blue Ridge Road, Suite 110, RALEIGH, NC 27607

Contacts: Jacqueline Wells & Robin Long
Associations: IATA, ARTA, CLTA, ARC, SITE, MPI,
ASAE, PCMA
Special Interest: golf, history, medicine, snow skiing,
water skiing, mountain adventures, hiking, river rafting,

arts & crafts, fishing, sailing, beaches, hunting, car
racing, musical events, museums.

USA - PUERTO RICO

TRAVEL SERVICES, INC
1052 Ashford Ave, Condado, P O Box 4606, SAN
JUAN, PR 00905
Tel: +1 (809) 724 6281 Fax: 725 6245

Contact: Mr Paul Ferguson, President
Established: 1955; 60 employees
Languages: Eng, Fr, Sp.
Associations: ASTA, American Sightseeing, PR Hotel
Assn, PRCB, SITE, CHA, IATAN, CAREY
Special Interest: art, caves, deep-sea fishing, food,
gambling, golf, horse-riding, museums, sailing, tennis,
water-skiing, windsurfing (1-12).

USA - TENNESSEE

HELEN L MOSKOVITZ & ASSOCIATES
Tel: +1 (615) 352 6900 Fax: 356 9285

Contacts: Helen L Moskovitz
Established: 1979; 12 employees.
Associations: MPI, ASAE, HSMA, PCMA, HCEA,
ISES, SITE, The Network.
Special Interest: antebellum mansions, country music,
country food, barbecues, country dancing, historic homes
(e.g. President Andrew Jackson), private homes, river boats,
sports - golf, tennis etc.

USA - TEXAS

WILD WEST TOURS OF TEXAS
16903 Lilly Crest, SAN ANTONIO, TX 78232
Tel: +1 (210) 494 6133 Fax: 490 7490

Contact: Mr Bob Marsh
Established: 1970; 5 employees
Languages: Eng, Fr, Ger, It, Sp.
Special Interest: wilderness & wildlife, cattle & ranches,
horseback riding, cowboys & Indians, cookouts &
country music, festivals & fiestas, river rafting, beaches,
water theme parks, agriculture, Mexican culture.

USA - VIRGINIA (FOR WASHINGTON DC)

8249 Honeysuckle Road, MANASSAS, VA 22111
Tel: +1 (703) 791 5930 Fax: 791 3513

Contact: Mr Ingo Blondal, Managing Director
Established: 1989; 6 employees.
Languages: Dan, Eng, Fr, Ger, Swed.
Special Interest: autumn foliage, civil war, gardens, golf,
gourmet-eating, history, horse-breeding, museums,
performing arts, photography, quilting, sailing & boating,
shopping, wines & vineyards.

USA - VIRGIN ISLANDS: ST THOMAS

TROPIC TOURS
The Guardian Building, Havensight, P O Box 1855, ST
THOMAS, US Virgin Is, 00803-1855
Tel: +1 (809) 774 1855 Fax: 776 9597 Tlx: 49573862

Contact: Ms Brooks Reid Brown, Manager
Special Interest: coral reefs, deep-sea fishing, diving,
golf, shopping, sailing, sightseeing, submarine
helicopters, underwater marine parks, tennis, (1-12);
carnival (April).

USA - WASHINGTON (STATE) & PACIFIC NW

PACIFIC NORTHWEST TRAVEL (A division of World
Travelers Inc)
Tel: +1 (206) 441 8682 Fax: 441 8862

Contact: Mr Malte Klutz
Associations: SKCCVB
Special Interest: art & architecture (1-12); wine &
vineyards, adventure tours, whale-watching, river rafting,
volcano tours, water sports (6-8); skiing (1-4); deep sea
fishing (5-9); river fishing (4-10); golf, hiking, bicycling,
bird-watching (6-10); Alaska cruise add-ons (5-9).

VENEZUELA

CANDES TURISMO C.A.
Edificio Roraima, Av. Francisco de Miranda,
CARACAS; P O Box 61142 CARACAS 1060
Tel: +58 (2) 953 2059/ 953 4710/ 953 3821/ 953 1632
Fax: 953 3176/ 953 6755 Tlx: 23 330 CANDE VC
Contact: Mr Richard Falsone
Established: 1950; 30 employees
Languages: Eng, Fr, Ger. It.
Special Interest: cable car, coral reefs, diving, driving
tours, game fishing, hydro-electrics, jungle expeditions,
ornithology, sailing, yachting, waterfalls, wildlife (1-12).

VIETNAM

DIETHELM TRAVEL (VIETNAM) LTD
Tel: +84 (8) 443370/ 440508 Fax: 443376

YEMEN REPUBLIC

UNIVERSAL TRAVEL & TOURISM
Saif Bin Dhi Yezen Street, P O Box 10473, SANA'A
Tel: +967 (1) 275 028-30/ 275 129-30 Fax: 274 150/ 275
134 Tlx: 2688/ 2369 ALAMIA YE

Contacts: Marco Livadiotti & Mahmood Al Shaibani
Special Interest: archaeology, architecture, photography,
trekking, camping.

ZIMBABWE

WILD AFRICA SAFARIS
P O Box 1737, HARARE
Tel: +263 (4) 738 329-0 Fax: 737 956 Tlx: 26641 ZW

Contact: David Ballantyne
Worldwide Sales Offices:
Contact: Peter Boot
Tel: +44 (1372) 362 288 Fax: 360 147
Associations: ABTA, ATOL, ITMA

Canada:
Ste 1119 - 409 Granville St, VANCOUVER BC, V6C
1T2
Tel: +1 (604) 682 1610 Fax: 682 1615

Contact: Mr Chris Bradshaw

France:
Horizons Sauvages, La Boursidiere, Boite 101, Rte
Nationale 186, 92357 LE PLESSIS ROBINSON, France
Tel: +33 (1) 3975 4907 Fax: 3975 6414

Germany:
c/o Sonnenhol Promotions, Briennerstr.48, 80333
MUNICH
Tel: +49 (89) 525 479 Fax: 523 6244

Contact: Ms Astrid Sonnenhol
SOUTH AFRICA
P O Box 822, Ferndale 2194, JOHANNESBURG
Tel: +27 (11) 886 0422 Fax: 886 2643

Contact: Mrs Anne Jones
Special Interest: adventure tours, wildlife, canoeing,
white-water rafting, photography, fishing, ornithology,
botany, sports tours.